Ancestry & Ethnicity in America:
A Comparative Guide to over 200 Ethnic Backgrounds

2012

Second Edition

Ancestry & Ethnicity in America:

A Comparative Guide to over 200 Ethnic Backgrounds

Where We Come From • How We Identify Ourselves • Where We Live Now

Volume I

National Population Profiles & Maps

State Population Profiles: Alabama–New York

A Universal Reference Book

Grey House Publishing

PUBLISHER: Leslie Mackenzie
EDITORIAL DIRECTOR: Laura Mars
SENIOR EDITOR: David Garoogian
MARKETING DIRECTOR: Jessica Moody

Grey House Publishing, Inc.
4919 Route 22
Amenia, NY 12501
518.789.8700
FAX 845.373.6390
www.greyhouse.com
e-mail: books @greyhouse.com

First edition published 2003
Printed in Canada

Publisher's Cataloging-In-Publication Data
(Prepared by The Donohue Group, Inc.)

Ancestry & ethnicity in America : a comparative guide to over 200 ethnic backgrounds / Grey House Publishing.— 2nd ed.

2 v. : ill. ; cm.

"A universal reference book."
"Where we come from, how we identify ourselves, where we live now."
1st ed.: Ancestry in America: a comparative guide to over 200 ethnic backgrounds. 2003.
ISBN: 978-1-59237-997-2

1. Ethnology—United States—Statistics. 2. Population research—United States.
3. United States—Population—Statistics. I. Grey House Publishing, Inc. II. Title: Ancestry and ethnicity in America III. Title: Ancestry in America.

E184.A1 .A53 2012
305.8/00973/021

Table of Contents

NOTE: Based on US Census categories, data in all sections of *Ancestry & Ethnicity in America* is displayed in the following sequence:

- Ancestry: 106 groups and subgroups from Afghan to Zimbabwean
- Hispanic Origin: 25 groups and subgroups by country and region
- Race: 5 major groups—African American/Black; American Indian/Alaska Native; Asian; Hawaii Native/Pacific Islander; White—and 82 subgroups by country, tribe and Hispanic identification

VOLUME I

SECTION ONE:
National Population Profile

SECTION TWO:
State Population Profiles

Each state chapter contains a state summary and population profiles for places with population of 7,500 or more. Each profile contains population size & percent of the total population for all 218 groups & subgroups.

VOLUME II

SECTION TWO: State Population Profiles

Each state chapter contains a state summary and population profiles for places with population of 7,500 or more. Each profile contains population size & percent of the total population for all 218 groups & subgroups.

SECTION THREE: Statistical Rankings

Introduction

The first edition of *Ancestry in America: A Comparative City-by-City Guide to over 200 Ethnic Backgrounds—with Rankings* was published in 2003. It was compiled from 2000 Census data, and included all places with populations over 10,000.

This second edition, nearly ten years in the making, is new and improved in many significant ways. Now divided between two volumes, the updated title—*Ancestry & Ethnicity in America: A Comparative Guide to over 200 Ethnic Backgrounds*—indicates not only a look back but also shows *Where We Come From • How We Identify Ourselves • Where We Live Now.* It is the most detailed look at the ethnic make-up of America in 2012 on the market today.

Praise for the first edition:

> *"...finding information in this voluminous source is easy compared with [other sources]...this work is of use to researchers in demography, marketing, sociology and political science."*
>
> —Library Journal

> *"This compilation will serve a wide range of research requests for population characteristics. Since it reports data on more than 200 different ethnic and racial categories, it offers much more detail than other sources..."*
>
> —Booklist

> *"...compilation and synthesis of disparate data files...along with the comparative rankings, make this a value-added, easy-to-use publication. Recommended for academic, public and special libraries."*
>
> —Reference & User Services Quarterly

> *"...a unique statistical compilation [whose] real value is in the ethnic breakdowns.* Ancestry in America *should also prove a statistical bonanza for those doing in-depth research on ethnic populations in the U.S."*
>
> —Against the Grain

NEW CONTENT

- This second edition includes 1,765 more places, now based on population of 7,500 instead of 10,000.
- *Ethnicity & Ancestry in America* starts off with a New Section of National Profiles, both alphabetical and ranked by group.
- The National Section also includes State-by-State charts and colorful National Maps that show population concentrations of Americans in the top 20 ancestries, those with Hispanic origin, and those in census designated racial groups.
- Each of the specific ranking sections—Ancestry, Hispanic Origin, Race—begins with an Introduction and Cross Reference Guide specific to those ethnic groups.

ARRANGEMENT

The basis for this massive two-volume work is the U.S. Census. Census 2010 collected and arranged data in specific groups, and we have maintained that arrangement throughout this work. The data in all sections of *Ancestry & Ethnicity in America* are arranged in the following groups:

- Ancestry: 106 groups and subgroups from Afghan to Zimbabwean
- Hispanic Origin: 25 groups and subgroups by country and region
- Race: 5 major groups—African American/Black, American Indian/Alaska Native, Asian, Hawaii Native/Pacific Islander, White—and 82 subgroups by country, tribe and Hispanic identification

Section One: National Population Profile

This section includes two national tables—one alphabetical by group and one ranked by size of group. Both of these tables show the population of each group, plus the percent of the U.S. population.

Following the national tables are state tables that show how many people in each state are in the top 20 ancestry groups, how many are of Hispanic origin, and how many are in each racial group. You'll be able to quickly see, for example, which state has the most Panamanians, or people of African, sub-Saharan descent.

Plus, this section includes 26 colorful maps that show where, in the country, each group is concentrated.

Section Two: State Population Profiles

This section is arranged by state. Each state chapter begins with a state overview: population numbers and percentages of U.S. population for all ancestries, for people of Hispanic origin, and for all racial groups.

The state summary is followed by profiles, in alphabetical order, of places within that state that have populations of 7,500 or more. Each place profile shows the county is resides in, the type of place it is (city, town, village, etc.) and both the number of people in each of 218 groups, as well as that group's percentage of U.S. population.

You can see at a glance, for example, how many people living in Speedway, Indiana consider themselves to be of Ethiopian descent, or what percentage of Hobbs, New Mexico's total population reported Canadian ancestry.

Section Three: Statistical Rankings

This section is comprised of three subsections: Ancestry Group Rankings; Hispanic Origin Rankings; and Racial Group Rankings. Each subsection starts with an Introduction, that gives more detail about the source and presentation of data. Following the Introduction is a Cross Reference Guide for that subsection, that makes easy work of finding those ethnicities that are part of a larger category (i.e. Pakistani, *see* Race—Asian: Pakistani or Armenian, *see* Ancestry—Armenian). Then, each group and subgroup is ranked three ways:

- Top 150 places with the largest number of persons reporting that particular group, regardless of total population
- Top 150 places with the highest percentage of persons reporting that particular group, regardless of total population
- Top 150 places, with 7,500 population or more, with the highest percentage of persons reporting that particular group

Master Place Name Index

This Master Index is an alphabetical list of every place included in this second edition of *Ancestry & Ethnicity in America.* This index includes the place name, type, county, state and the page on which their profile appears.

Ancestry & Ethnicity in America is also available as an e-book. In addition, e-states are available on CD-ROM, which include profiles of all places in that state regardless of population.

Explanation of Data

Places Covered

Section One of this book covers all 5,971 places in the U.S. with populations of 7,500 or more. It also includes profiles for the United States, all 50 states, and the District of Columbia. The ranking tables in Section Two are based on 37,950 places in the U.S. Places covered fall into one of the following categories:

Incorporated Places. Depending on the state, places are incorporated as either cities, towns, villages, boroughs, municipalities, independent cities, or corporations. A few municipalities have a form of government combined with another entity (e.g. county) and are listed as special cities or consolidated, unified, or metropolitan governments.

Census Designated Places (CDP). The U.S. Bureau of the Census defines a CDP as "a statistical entity," defined for each decennial census according to Census Bureau guidelines, comprising a densely settled concentration of population that is not within an incorporated place, but is locally identified by a name. CDPs are delineated cooperatively by state and local officials and the Census Bureau, following Census Bureau guidelines.

Minor Civil Divisions (called charter townships, districts, gores, grants, locations, plantations, purchases, reservations, towns, townships, and unorganized territories) for the states where the Census Bureau has determined that they serve as general-purpose governments. Those states are Connecticut, Maine, Massachusetts, Michigan, Minnesota, New Hampshire, New Jersey, New York, Pennsylvania, Rhode Island, Vermont, and Wisconsin. In some states incorporated municipalities are part of minor civil divisions and in some states they are independent of them.

Note: Several states have incorporated municipalities and minor civil divisions in the same county with the same name. Those communities are given separate entries (e.g. Burlington, New Jersey, in Burlington County will be listed under both the city and township of Burlington). A few states have Census Designated Places and minor civil divisions in the same county with the same name. Those communities are given separate entries (e.g. Bridgewater, Massachusetts, in Plymouth County will be listed under both the CDP and town of Bridgewater).

Source of Data

The ethnicities shown in this book were compiled from two different sources. Data for Race and Hispanic Origin was taken from Census 2010 Summary File 1 (SF1) while Ancestry data was taken from the American Community Survey (ACS) 2006-2010 Five-Year Estimate. The distinction is important because SF1 contains 100-percent data, which is the information compiled from the questions asked of all people and about every housing unit. ACS estimates are compiled from a sampling of households. The 2006-2010 Five-Year Estimate is based on data collected from January 1, 2006 to December 31, 2010.

The American Community Survey (ACS) is a relatively new survey conducted by the U.S. Census Bureau. It uses a series of monthly samples to produce annually updated data for the same small areas (census tracts and block groups) formerly surveyed via the decennial census long-form sample. While some version of this survey has been in the field since 1999, it was not fully implemented in terms of coverage until 2006. In 2005 it was expanded to cover all counties in the country and the 1-in-40 households sampling rate was first applied. The full implementation of the (household) sampling strategy for ACS entails having the survey mailed to about 250,000 households nationwide every month of every year and was begun in January 2005. In January 2006 sampling of group quarters was added to complete the sample as planned. In any given year about 2.5% (1 in 40) of U.S. households will receive the survey. Over any 5-year period about 1 in 8 households should receive the survey (as compared to about 1 in 6 that received the census long form in the 2000 census). Unfortunately, receiving the survey is not the same as responding to it, since the Bureau has adopted a strategy of sampling for non-response. This has resulted in something closer to 1 in 11 households actually participating in the survey over any 5-year period. For more information about the American Community Survey visit http://www.census.gov/acs/www.

Ancestry

Ancestry refers to a person's ethnic origin, heritage, descent, or "roots," which may reflect their place of birth or that of previous generations of their family. Some ethnic identities, such as "Egyptian" or "Polish" can be traced to geographic areas outside the United States, while other ethnicities such as "Pennsylvania German" or "Cajun" evolved in the United States.

The intent of the ancestry question was not to measure the degree of attachment the respondent had to a particular ethnicity, but simply to establish that the respondent had a connection to and self-identified with a particular ethnic group. For example, a response of "Irish" might reflect total involvement in an Irish community or only a memory of ancestors several generations removed from the individual. The question was based on self-identification; the data on ancestry represent self-classification by people according to the ancestry group(s) with which they most closely identify.

The Census Bureau coded the responses into a numeric representation of over 1,000 categories. Responses initially were processed through an automated coding system; then, those that were not automatically assigned a code were coded by individuals trained in coding ancestry responses. The code list reflects the results of the Census Bureau's own research and consultations with many ethnic experts. Many decisions were made to determine the classification of responses. These decisions affected the grouping of the tabulated data. For example, the "Indonesian" category includes the responses of "Indonesian," "Celebesian," "Moluccan," and a number of other responses.

Ancestry

Afghan
African, Sub-Saharan
- African
- Cape Verdean
- Ethiopian
- Ghanaian
- Kenyan
- Liberian
- Nigerian
- Senegalese
- Sierra Leonean
- Somalian
- South African
- Sudanese
- Ugandan
- Zimbabwean
- Other Sub-Saharan African

Albanian
Alsatian
American
Arab
- Arab
- Egyptian
- Iraqi
- Jordanian
- Lebanese
- Moroccan
- Palestinian
- Syrian
- Other Arab

Armenian
Assyrian/Chaldean/Syriac
Australian
Austrian
Basque
Belgian
Brazilian
British
Bulgarian
Cajun
Canadian
Carpatho Rusyn
Celtic
Croatian
Cypriot
Czech
Czechoslovakian
Danish
Dutch
Eastern European
English
Estonian
European
Finnish
French, ex. Basque
French Canadian
German
German Russian
Greek
Guyanese
Hungarian
Icelander
Iranian
Irish
Israeli
Italian
Latvian
Lithuanian
Luxemburger
Macedonian
Maltese
New Zealander
Northern European
Norwegian
Pennsylvania German
Polish
Portuguese
Romanian
Russian
Scandinavian
Scotch-Irish
Scottish
Serbian
Slavic
Slovak
Slovene
Soviet Union
Swedish
Swiss
Turkish
Ukrainian
Welsh
West Indian, ex. Hispanic
- Bahamian
- Barbadian
- Belizean
- Bermudan
- British West Indian
- Dutch West Indian
- Haitian
- Jamaican
- Trinidadian/Tobagonian
- U.S. Virgin Islander
- West Indian
- Other West Indian

Yugoslavian

The ancestry question allowed respondents to report one or more ancestry groups. Generally, only the first two responses reported were coded. If a response was in terms of a dual ancestry, for example, "Irish English," the person was assigned two codes, in this case one for Irish and another for English. However, in certain cases, multiple responses such as "French Canadian," "Scotch-Irish," "Greek Cypriot," and "Black Dutch" were assigned a single code reflecting their status as unique groups. If a person reported one of these unique groups in addition to another group, for example, "Scotch-Irish English," resulting in three terms, that person received one code for the unique group (Scotch-Irish) and another one for the remaining group (English). If a person reported "English Irish French," only English and Irish were coded. If there were more than two ancestries listed and one of the ancestries was a part of another, such as "German Bavarian Hawaiian," the responses were coded using the more detailed groups (Bavarian and Hawaiian).

The Census Bureau accepted "American" as a unique ethnicity if it was given alone or with one other ancestry. There were some groups such as "American Indian," "Mexican American," and "African American" that were coded and identified separately.

The ancestry question is asked for every person in the American Community Survey, regardless of age, place of birth, Hispanic origin, or race.

Although some people consider religious affiliation a component of ethnic identity, the ancestry question was not designed to collect any information concerning religion. Thus, if a religion was given as an answer to the ancestry question, it was listed in the "Other groups" category which is not shown in this book.

Ancestry should not be confused with a person's place of birth, although a person's place of birth and ancestry may be the same.

Hispanic Origin

The data on the Hispanic or Latino population were derived from answers to a question that was asked of all people. The terms "Spanish," "Hispanic origin," and "Latino" are used interchangeably. Some respondents identify with all three terms while others may identify with only one of these three specific terms. Hispanics or Latinos who identify with the terms "Spanish," "Hispanic," or "Latino" are those who classify themselves in one of the specific Spanish, Hispanic, or Latino categories listed on the questionnaire ("Mexican," "Puerto Rican," or "Cuban") as well as those who indicate that they are "other Spanish/Hispanic/Latino." People who do not identify with one of the specific origins listed on the questionnaire but indicate that they are "other Spanish/Hispanic/Latino" are those whose origins are from Spain, the Spanish-speaking countries of Central or South America, the Dominican Republic, or people identifying themselves generally as Spanish, Spanish-American, Hispanic, Hispano, Latino, and so on. All write-in responses to the "other Spanish/Hispanic/Latino" category were coded.

Hispanic Origin

Hispanic or Latino
- Central American, ex. Mexican
  - Costa Rican
  - Guatemalan
  - Honduran
  - Nicaraguan
  - Panamanian
  - Salvadoran
  - Other Central American
- Cuban
- Dominican Republic
- Mexican
- Puerto Rican
- South American
  - Argentinean
  - Bolivian
  - Chilean
  - Colombian
  - Ecuadorian
  - Paraguayan
  - Peruvian
  - Uruguayan
  - Venezuelan
  - Other South American
- Other Hispanic or Latino

Race

African-American/Black	Crow	Spanish American Indian	Korean
Not Hispanic	Delaware	Tlingit-Haida *(Alaska Native)*	Laotian
Hispanic	Hopi	Tohono O'Odham	Malaysian
American Indian/Alaska Native	Houma	Tsimshian *(Alaska Native)*	Nepalese
Not Hispanic	Inupiat *(Alaska Native)*	Ute	Pakistani
Hispanic	Iroquois	Yakama	Sri Lankan
Alaska Athabascan *(Ala. Nat.)*	Kiowa	Yaqui	Taiwanese
Aleut *(Alaska Native)*	Lumbee	Yuman	Thai
Apache	Menominee	Yup'ik *(Alaska Native)*	Vietnamese
Arapaho	Mexican American Indian	**Asian**	**Hawaii Native/Pacific Islander**
Blackfeet	Navajo	*Not Hispanic*	*Not Hispanic*
Canadian/French Am. Indian	Osage	*Hispanic*	*Hispanic*
Central American Indian	Ottawa	Bangladeshi	Fijian
Cherokee	Paiute	Bhutanese	Guamanian/Chamorro
Cheyenne	Pima	Burmese	Marshallese
Chickasaw	Potawatomi	Cambodian	Native Hawaiian
Chippewa	Pueblo	Chinese, ex. Taiwanese	Samoan
Choctaw	Puget Sound Salish	Filipino	Tongan
Colville	Seminole	Hmong	**White**
Comanche	Shoshone	Indian	*Not Hispanic*
Cree	Sioux	Indonesian	*Hispanic*
Creek	South American Indian	Japanese	

Origin can be viewed as the heritage, nationality group, lineage, or country of birth of the person or the person's parents or ancestors before their arrival in the United States. People who identify their origin as Spanish, Hispanic, or Latino may be of any race.

Ethnicities Based on Race

The data on race were derived from answers to the question on race that was asked of individuals in the United States. The Census Bureau collects racial data in accordance with guidelines provided by the U.S. Office of Management and Budget (OMB), and these data are based on self-identification.

The racial categories included in the census questionnaire generally reflect a social definition of race recognized in this country and not an attempt to define race biologically, anthropologically, or genetically. In addition, it is recognized that the categories of the race item include racial and national origin or sociocultural groups. People may choose to report more than one race to indicate their racial mixture, such as "American Indian" and "White." People who identify their origin as Hispanic, Latino, or Spanish may be of any race.

African American or Black: A person having origins in any of the Black racial groups of Africa. It includes people who indicated their race(s) as "Black, African Am., or Negro" or reported entries such as African American, Kenyan, Nigerian, or Haitian.

American Indian or Alaska Native: A person having origins in any of the original peoples of North and South America (including Central America) and who maintains tribal affiliation or community attachment. This category includes people who indicated their race(s) as "American Indian or Alaska Native" or reported their enrolled or principal tribe, such as Navajo, Blackfeet, Inupiat, Yup'ik, or Central American Indian groups or South American Indian groups.

Asian: A person having origins in any of the original peoples of the Far East, Southeast Asia, or the Indian subcontinent, including, for example, Cambodia, China, India, Japan, Korea, Malaysia, Pakistan, the Philippine Islands, Thailand, and Vietnam. It includes people who indicated their race(s) as "Asian" or reported entries such as "Asian Indian," "Chinese," "Filipino," "Korean," "Japanese," "Vietnamese," and "Other Asian" or provided other detailed Asian responses.

Native Hawaiian or Other Pacific Islander: A person having origins in any of the original peoples of Hawaii, Guam, Samoa, or other Pacific Islands. It includes people who indicated their race(s) as "Pacific Islander" or reported entries such as "Native Hawaiian," "Guamanian or Chamorro," "Samoan," and "Other Pacific Islander" or provided other detailed Pacific Islander responses.

White: A person having origins in any of the original peoples of Europe, the Middle East, or North Africa. It includes people who indicated their race(s) as "White" or reported entries such as Irish, German, Italian, Lebanese, Arab, Moroccan, or Caucasian.

Section One: National Population Profile

The first table in this section, *National Profiles: Alphabetical by Major Category & Ethnic Group,* shows the population and percentages for all 218 ethnicities alphabetically by major category (ancestry, Hispanic origin, and race) and then by ethnic group. Column one displays the ancestry/Hispanic origin/race name, column two displays the number of people reporting each ancestry/Hispanic origin/race, and column three is the percent of the total population reporting each ancestry/Hispanic origin/race. The 2010 population (based on 100-percent data from Census 2010 Summary File 1), shown in the footnote, is used to calculate the value in the "%" column for ethnicities based on race and Hispanic origin. The 2006-2010 estimated population figure from the American Community Survey, also shown in the footnote, is used to calculate the value in the "%" column for all other ancestries.

For ethnicities in the ancestries group, the value in the "Number" column includes multiple ancestries reported. For example, if a person reported a multiple ancestry such as "French Danish," that response was counted twice in the tabulations, once in the French category and again in the Danish category. Thus, the sum of the counts is not the total population but the total of all responses. Numbers in parentheses indicate the number of people reporting a single ancestry. People reporting a single ancestry includes all people who reported only one ethnic group such as "German." Also included in this category are people with only a multiple-term response such as "Scotch-Irish" who are assigned a single code because they represent one distinct group. For example, the count for German would be interpreted as "The number of people who reported that German was their only ancestry."

For ethnicities based on Hispanic origin, the value in the "Number" column represents the number of people who reported being Mexican, Puerto Rican, Cuban or other Spanish/Hispanic/Latino (all written-in responses were coded). All ethnicities based on Hispanic origin can be of any race.

For ethnicities based on race data the value in the "Number" column represents the total number of people who reported each category alone or in combination with one or more other race categories. This number represents the maximum number of people reporting and therefore the individual race categories may add to more than the total population because people may be included in more than one category. The figures in parentheses show the number of people that reported that particular ethnicity alone, not in combination with any other race. For example, the entry for Samoan shows 109,637 in parentheses and 184,440 in the "Number" column. This means that 109,637 people reported being Samoan alone and 184,440 people reported being Samoan alone or in combination with one or more other races.

The second table, *National Profiles: By Major Category, Population Size & Percent of U.S. Population,* shows the exact same information as the first table, except the data is sorted in descending order by population size, within each major category (ancestry, Hispanic origin, and race).

The third table, *Top 20 Ancestries by State,* shows the largest 20 ancestries by population in the United States, broken down by state. The figures show the percentage of the total population reporting each ancestry. For example, 46.9% of the population of North Dakota report German as an ancestry (includes persons of mixed ancestry). The 20 national maps which follow this table, give a visual representation of the same data. Please note that Alaska and Hawaii are not shown on the maps.

The last table, *Hispanic Origin & Race by State,* shows Hispanic origin and race data, broken down by state. Column two shows the percentage of the total population reporting any Hispanic origin. Columns three through seven show the percentage of the total population reporting each of the five major racial groups: White; African-American/Black; Asian; American Indian/Alaska Native; and Hawaii Native/Other Pacific Islander. For example, 14.92% of the population of California report being Asian (includes persons reporting Asian alone or in combination with any other race). The six national maps which follow this table, give a visual representation of the same data. Please note that Alaska and Hawaii are not shown on the maps.

Section Two: State Population Profiles

Each Section Two profile shows the name of the place, the county (if a place spans more than one county, the county that holds the majority of the population is shown), and the 2010 population (based on 100-percent data from Census 2010 Summary File 1). The rest of each profile is comprised of all 218 ethnicities grouped into three sections: ancestry; Hispanic origin; and race.

Column one displays the ancestry/Hispanic origin/race name, column two displays the number of people reporting each ancestry/Hispanic origin/race, and column three is the percent of the total population reporting each ancestry/Hispanic origin/race. The population figure shown is used to calculate the value in the "%" column for ethnicities based on race and Hispanic origin. The 2006-2010 estimated population figure from the American Community Survey (not shown) is used to calculate the value in the "%" column for all other ancestries.

For ethnicities in the ancestries group, the value in the "Number" column includes multiple ancestries reported. For example, if a person reported a multiple ancestry such as "French Danish," that response was counted twice in the tabulations, once in the French category and again in the Danish category. Thus, the sum of the counts is not the total population but the total of all responses. Numbers in parentheses indicate the number of people reporting a single ancestry. People reporting a single ancestry includes all people who reported only one ethnic group such as "German." Also included in this category are people with only a multiple-term response such as "Scotch-Irish" who are assigned a single code because they represent one distinct group. For example, the count for German would be interpreted as "The number of people who reported that German was their only ancestry."

For ethnicities based on Hispanic origin, the value in the "Number" column represents the number of people who reported being Mexican, Puerto Rican, Cuban or other Spanish/Hispanic/Latino (all written-in responses were coded). All ethnicities based on Hispanic origin can be of any race.

For ethnicities based on race data the value in the "Number" column represents the total number of people who reported each category alone or in combination with one or more other race categories. This number represents the maximum number of people reporting and therefore the individual race categories may add to more than the total population because people may be included in more than one category. The figures in parentheses show the number of people that reported that particular ethnicity alone, not in combination with any other race. For example, in Alabama, the entry for Korean shows 8,320 in parentheses and 10,624 in the "Number" column. This means that 8,320 people reported being Korean alone and 10,624 people reported being Korean alone or in combination with one or more other races.

Section Three: Statistical Rankings

In Section Three, each ethnicity has four ranking tables. The first table is split into two parts. Part one ranks the U.S. and all 50 states plus the District of Columbia by ethnic population. Part two ranks the same areas by percent of the total population. The second table shows the top 150 places sorted by ethnic population (based on all places, regardless of total population), the third table shows the top 150 places sorted by percent of the total population (based on all places, regardless of total population), the fourth table shows the top 150 places sorted by percent of the total population (based on places with total population of 7,500 or more).

Within each table, column one displays the place name, the state, and the county (if a place spans more than one county, the county that holds the majority of the population is shown). Column one in the first table displays the state only. Column two displays the number of people reporting each ancestry (includes people reporting multiple ancestries), Hispanic origin, or race (alone or in combination with any other race). Column three is the percent of the total population reporting each ancestry, Hispanic origin or race. For tables representing ethnicities based on race or Hispanic origin, the 100-percent population figure from SF1 is used to calculate the value in the "%" column. For all other ancestries the 2006-2010 five-year estimated population figure from the American Community Survey is used to calculate the value in the "%" column.

Alphabetical Ethnicity Cross-Reference Guide

Afghan *see* Ancestry–Afghan
African *see* Ancestry–African, Sub-Saharan: African
African-American *see* Race–African-American/Black
African-American: Hispanic *see* Race–African-American/Black: Hispanic
African-American: Not Hispanic *see* Race–African-American/Black: Not Hispanic
Alaska Athabascan *see* Race–Alaska Native: Alaska Athabascan
Alaska Native *see* Race–American Indian/Alaska Native
Alaska Native: Hispanic *see* Race–American Indian/Alaska Native: Hispanic
Alaska Native: Not Hispanic *see* Race–American Indian/Alaska Native: Not Hispanic
Albanian *see* Ancestry–Albanian
Aleut *see* Race–Alaska Native: Aleut
Alsatian *see* Ancestry–Alsatian
American *see* Ancestry–American
American Indian *see* Race–American Indian/Alaska Native
American Indian: Hispanic *see* Race–American Indian/Alaska Native: Hispanic
American Indian: Not Hispanic *see* Race–American Indian/Alaska Native: Not Hispanic
Apache *see* Race–American Indian: Apache
Arab *see* Ancestry–Arab: Arab
Arab: Other *see* Ancestry–Arab: Other
Arapaho *see* Race–American Indian: Arapaho
Argentinean *see* Hispanic Origin–South American: Argentinean
Armenian *see* Ancestry–Armenian
Asian *see* Race–Asian
Asian Indian *see* Race–Asian: Indian
Asian: Hispanic *see* Race–Asian: Hispanic
Asian: Not Hispanic *see* Race–Asian: Not Hispanic
Assyrian *see* Ancestry–Assyrian/Chaldean/Syriac
Australian *see* Ancestry–Australian
Austrian *see* Ancestry–Austrian
Bahamian *see* Ancestry–West Indian: Bahamian, except Hispanic
Bangladeshi *see* Race–Asian: Bangladeshi
Barbadian *see* Ancestry–West Indian: Barbadian, except Hispanic
Basque *see* Ancestry–Basque
Belgian *see* Ancestry–Belgian
Belizean *see* Ancestry–West Indian: Belizean, except Hispanic
Bermudan *see* Ancestry–West Indian: Bermudan, except Hispanic
Bhutanese *see* Race–Asian: Bhutanese
Black *see* Race–African-American/Black
Black: Hispanic *see* Race–African-American/Black: Hispanic
Black: Not Hispanic *see* Race–African-American/Black: Not Hispanic
Blackfeet *see* Race–American Indian: Blackfeet
Bolivian *see* Hispanic Origin–South American: Bolivian
Brazilian *see* Ancestry–Brazilian
British *see* Ancestry–British
British West Indian *see* Ancestry–West Indian: British West Indian, except Hispanic
Bulgarian *see* Ancestry–Bulgarian
Burmese *see* Race–Asian: Burmese
Cajun *see* Ancestry–Cajun
Cambodian *see* Race–Asian: Cambodian
Canadian *see* Ancestry–Canadian
Canadian/French American Indian *see* Race–American Indian: Canadian/French American Indian
Cape Verdean *see* Ancestry–African, Sub-Saharan: Cape Verdean
Carpatho Rusyn *see* Ancestry–Carpatho Rusyn
Celtic *see* Ancestry–Celtic
Central American *see* Hispanic Origin–Central American, except Mexican
Central American Indian *see* Race–American Indian: Central American Indian
Central American: Other *see* Hispanic Origin–Central American: Other Central American
Chaldean *see* Ancestry–Assyrian/Chaldean/Syriac
Chamorro *see* Race–Hawaii Native/Pacific Islander: Guamanian or Chamorro
Cherokee *see* Race–American Indian: Cherokee
Cheyenne *see* Race–American Indian: Cheyenne
Chickasaw *see* Race–American Indian: Chickasaw
Chilean *see* Hispanic Origin–South American: Chilean
Chinese (except Taiwanese) *see* Race–Asian: Chinese, except Taiwanese
Chippewa *see* Race–American Indian: Chippewa
Choctaw *see* Race–American Indian: Choctaw
Colombian *see* Hispanic Origin–South American: Colombian
Colville *see* Race–American Indian: Colville
Comanche *see* Race–American Indian: Comanche
Costa Rican *see* Hispanic Origin–Central American: Costa Rican
Cree *see* Race–American Indian: Cree
Creek *see* Race–American Indian: Creek

Croatian *see* Ancestry–Croatian
Crow *see* Race–American Indian: Crow
Cuban *see* Hispanic Origin–Cuban
Cypriot *see* Ancestry–Cypriot
Czech *see* Ancestry–Czech
Czechoslovakian *see* Ancestry–Czechoslovakian
Danish *see* Ancestry–Danish
Delaware *see* Race–American Indian: Delaware
Dominican Republic *see* Hispanic Origin–Dominican Republic
Dutch *see* Ancestry–Dutch
Dutch West Indian *see* Ancestry–West Indian: Dutch West Indian, except Hispanic
Eastern European *see* Ancestry–Eastern European
Ecuadorian *see* Hispanic Origin–South American: Ecuadorian
Egyptian *see* Ancestry–Arab: Egyptian
English *see* Ancestry–English
Eskimo *see* Race–Alaska Native: Inupiat
Estonian *see* Ancestry–Estonian
Ethiopian *see* Ancestry–African, Sub-Saharan: Ethiopian
European *see* Ancestry–European
Fijian *see* Race–Hawaii Native/Pacific Islander: Fijian
Filipino *see* Race–Asian: Filipino
Finnish *see* Ancestry–Finnish
French (except Basque) *see* Ancestry–French, except Basque
French Canadian *see* Ancestry–French Canadian
German *see* Ancestry–German
German Russian *see* Ancestry–German Russian
Ghanaian *see* Ancestry–African, Sub-Saharan: Ghanaian
Greek *see* Ancestry–Greek
Guamanian *see* Race–Hawaii Native/Pacific Islander: Guamanian or Chamorro
Guatemalan *see* Hispanic Origin–Central American: Guatemalan
Guyanese *see* Ancestry–Guyanese
Haitian *see* Ancestry–West Indian: Haitian, except Hispanic
Hawaii Native *see* Race–Hawaii Native/Pacific Islander
Hawaii Native: Hispanic *see* Race–Hawaii Native/Pacific Islander: Hispanic
Hawaii Native: Not Hispanic *see* Race–Hawaii Native/Pacific Islander: Not Hispanic
Hispanic or Latino: *see* Hispanic Origin–Hispanic or Latino (of any race)
Hispanic or Latino: Other *see* Hispanic Origin–Other Hispanic or Latino
Hmong *see* Race–Asian: Hmong
Honduran *see* Hispanic Origin–Central American: Honduran
Hopi *see* Race–American Indian: Hopi
Houma *see* Race–American Indian: Houma
Hungarian *see* Ancestry–Hungarian
Icelander *see* Ancestry–Icelander
Indonesian *see* Race–Asian: Indonesian
Inupiat *see* Race–Alaska Native: Inupiat
Iranian *see* Ancestry–Iranian
Iraqi *see* Ancestry–Arab: Iraqi
Irish *see* Ancestry–Irish
Iroquois *see* Race–American Indian: Iroquois
Israeli *see* Ancestry–Israeli
Italian *see* Ancestry–Italian
Jamaican *see* Ancestry–West Indian: Jamaican, except Hispanic
Japanese *see* Race–Asian: Japanese
Jordanian *see* Ancestry–Arab: Jordanian
Kenyan *see* Ancestry–African, Sub-Saharan: Kenyan
Kiowa *see* Race–American Indian: Kiowa
Korean *see* Race–Asian: Korean
Laotian *see* Race–Asian: Laotian
Latvian *see* Ancestry–Latvian
Lebanese *see* Ancestry–Arab: Lebanese
Liberian *see* Ancestry–African, Sub-Saharan: Liberian
Lithuanian *see* Ancestry–Lithuanian
Lumbee *see* Race–American Indian: Lumbee
Luxemburger *see* Ancestry–Luxemburger
Macedonian *see* Ancestry–Macedonian
Malaysian *see* Race–Asian: Malaysian
Maltese *see* Ancestry–Maltese
Marshallese *see* Race–Hawaii Native/Pacific Islander: Marshallese
Menominee *see* Race–American Indian: Menominee
Mexican *see* Hispanic Origin–Mexican
Mexican American Indian *see* Race–American Indian: Mexican American Indian
Moroccan *see* Ancestry–Arab: Moroccan
Native Hawaiian *see* Race–Hawaii Native/Pacific Islander: Native Hawaiian
Navajo *see* Race–American Indian: Navajo
Nepalese *see* Race–Asian: Nepalese
New Zealander *see* Ancestry–New Zealander
Nicaraguan *see* Hispanic Origin–Central American: Nicaraguan
Nigerian *see* Ancestry–African, Sub-Saharan: Nigerian
Northern European *see* Ancestry–Northern European
Norwegian *see* Ancestry–Norwegian
Osage *see* Race–American Indian: Osage
Ottawa *see* Race–American Indian: Ottawa
Pacific Islander *see* Race–Hawaii Native/Pacific Islander
Pacific Islander: Hispanic *see* Race–Hawaii Native/Pacific Islander: Hispanic
Pacific Islander: Not Hispanic *see* Race–Hawaii Native/Pacific Islander: Not Hispanic
Paiute *see* Race–American Indian: Paiute
Pakistani *see* Race–Asian: Pakistani
Palestinian *see* Ancestry–Arab: Palestinian
Panamanian *see* Hispanic Origin–Central American: Panamanian
Paraguayan *see* Hispanic Origin–South American: Paraguayan
Pennsylvania German *see* Ancestry–Pennsylvania German
Peruvian *see* Hispanic Origin–South American: Peruvian
Pima *see* Race–American Indian: Pima
Polish *see* Ancestry–Polish
Portuguese *see* Ancestry–Portuguese
Potawatomi *see* Race–American Indian: Potawatomi
Pueblo *see* Race–American Indian: Pueblo
Puerto Rican *see* Hispanic Origin–Puerto Rican
Puget Sound Salish *see* Race–American Indian: Puget Sound Salish
Romanian *see* Ancestry–Romanian
Russian *see* Ancestry–Russian
Salvadoran *see* Hispanic Origin–Central American: Salvadoran
Samoan *see* Race–Hawaii Native/Pacific Islander: Samoan
Scandinavian *see* Ancestry–Scandinavian
Scotch-Irish *see* Ancestry–Scotch-Irish
Scottish *see* Ancestry–Scottish
Seminole *see* Race–American Indian: Seminole

Senegalese *see* Ancestry–African, Sub-Saharan: Senegalese
Serbian *see* Ancestry–Serbian
Shoshone *see* Race–American Indian: Shoshone
Sierra Leonean *see* Ancestry–African, Sub-Saharan: Sierra Leonean
Sioux *see* Race–American Indian: Sioux
Slavic *see* Ancestry–Slavic
Slovak *see* Ancestry–Slovak
Slovene *see* Ancestry–Slovene
Somalian *see* Ancestry–African, Sub-Saharan: Somalian
South African *see* Ancestry–African, Sub-Saharan: South African
South American *see* Hispanic Origin–South American
South American Indian *see* Race–American Indian: South American Indian
South American: Other *see* Hispanic Origin–South American: Other South American
Soviet Union *see* Ancestry–Soviet Union
Spanish American Indian *see* Race–American Indian: Spanish American Indian
Sri Lankan *see* Race–Asian: Sri Lankan
Sub-Saharan African *see* Ancestry–African, Sub-Saharan
Sub-Saharan African: Other *see* Ancestry–African, Sub-Saharan: Other
Sudanese *see* Ancestry–African, Sub-Saharan: Sudanese
Swedish *see* Ancestry–Swedish
Swiss *see* Ancestry–Swiss
Syriac *see* Ancestry–Assyrian/Chaldean/Syriac
Syrian *see* Ancestry–Arab: Syrian
Taiwanese *see* Race–Asian: Taiwanese
Thai *see* Race–Asian: Thai
Tlingit-Haida *see* Race–Alaska Native: Tlingit-Haida
Tohono O'Odham *see* Race–American Indian: Tohono O'Odham
Tongan *see* Race–Hawaii Native/Pacific Islander: Tongan
Trinidadian and Tobagonian *see* Ancestry–West Indian: Trinidadian and Tobagonian, except Hispanic
Tsimshian *see* Race–Alaska Native: Tsimshian
Turkish *see* Ancestry–Turkish
U.S. Virgin Islander *see* Ancestry–West Indian: U.S. Virgin Islander, except Hispanic
Ugandan *see* Ancestry–African, Sub-Saharan: Ugandan
Ukrainian *see* Ancestry–Ukrainian
Uruguayan *see* Hispanic Origin–South American: Uruguayan
Ute *see* Race–American Indian: Ute
Venezuelan *see* Hispanic Origin–South American: Venezuelan
Vietnamese *see* Race–Asian: Vietnamese
Welsh *see* Ancestry–Welsh
West Indian *see* Ancestry–West Indian: West Indian, except Hispanic
West Indian (except Hispanic) *see* Ancestry–West Indian, except Hispanic
West Indian: Other *see* Ancestry–West Indian: Other, except Hispanic
White *see* Race–White
White: Hispanic *see* Race–White: Hispanic
White: Not Hispanic *see* Race–White: Not Hispanic
Yakama *see* Race–American Indian: Yakama
Yaqui *see* Race–American Indian: Yaqui
Yugoslavian *see* Ancestry–Yugoslavian
Yuman *see* Race–American Indian: Yuman
Yup'ik *see* Race–Alaska Native: Yup'ik
Zimbabwean *see* Ancestry–African, Sub-Saharan: Zimbabwean

SECTION ONE:
National Population Profile

National Profile

Alphabetical by Major Category & Ethnic Group

Ancestry‡	Population	%
Afghan (71,406)	77,029	0.03
African, Sub-Saharan (2,326,027)	2,783,033	0.92
African (1,393,403)	1,731,621	0.57
Cape Verdean (68,034)	92,936	0.03
Ethiopian (161,188)	172,984	0.06
Ghanaian (79,074)	83,718	0.03
Kenyan (40,326)	45,177	0.01
Liberian (47,649)	52,299	0.02
Nigerian (225,650)	250,819	0.08
Senegalese (8,463)	10,055	<0.01
Sierra Leonean (14,560)	16,343	0.01
Somalian (96,162)	100,011	0.03
South African (37,567)	53,088	0.02
Sudanese (35,880)	38,432	0.01
Ugandan (7,753)	8,565	<0.01
Zimbabwean (5,474)	6,098	<0.01
Other Sub-Saharan African (104,844)	120,887	0.04
Albanian (142,965)	172,149	0.06
Alsatian (3,591)	12,104	<0.01
American (19,094,109)	19,094,109	6.28
Arab (1,052,350)	1,547,365	0.51
Arab (202,189)	259,644	0.09
Egyptian (150,064)	179,853	0.06
Iraqi (59,384)	73,896	0.02
Jordanian (50,459)	60,056	0.02
Lebanese (252,187)	485,917	0.16
Moroccan (56,413)	74,908	0.02
Palestinian (65,940)	83,241	0.03
Syrian (72,443)	147,426	0.05
Other Arab (143,271)	182,424	0.06
Armenian (314,013)	447,580	0.15
Assyrian/Chaldean/Syriac (70,920)	89,410	0.03
Australian (44,636)	94,368	0.03
Austrian (191,714)	766,033	0.25
Basque (26,957)	59,586	0.02
Belgian (116,510)	386,694	0.13
Brazilian (273,724)	347,346	0.11
British (638,061)	1,223,541	0.40
Bulgarian (65,816)	89,808	0.03
Cajun (67,601)	108,696	0.04
Canadian (361,182)	716,067	0.24
Carpatho Rusyn (3,354)	7,501	<0.01
Celtic (26,449)	52,937	0.02
Croatian (162,219)	417,130	0.14
Cypriot (4,631)	5,843	<0.01
Czech (471,510)	1,597,950	0.53
Czechoslovakian (144,153)	320,161	0.11
Danish (374,442)	1,453,897	0.48
Dutch (1,226,388)	4,950,629	1.63
Eastern European (371,065)	419,221	0.14
English (9,605,188)	27,404,243	9.02
Estonian (13,785)	28,312	0.01
European (2,680,293)	3,074,695	1.01
Finnish (228,585)	677,272	0.22
French, ex. Basque (2,023,095)	9,326,380	3.07
French Canadian (983,474)	2,138,601	0.70
German (16,912,041)	49,840,035	16.40
German Russian (8,076)	16,037	0.01
Greek (654,228)	1,337,576	0.44
Guyanese (168,490)	202,258	0.07
Hungarian (495,861)	1,537,238	0.51
Icelander (19,198)	51,234	0.02
Iranian (356,928)	425,587	0.14
Irish (10,112,947)	35,751,251	11.76
Israeli (97,763)	136,351	0.04
Italian (7,183,882)	17,571,808	5.78
Latvian (41,851)	91,096	0.03
Lithuanian (238,647)	708,860	0.23
Luxemburger (12,943)	45,597	0.02
Macedonian (36,419)	52,386	0.02
Maltese (18,593)	43,082	0.01
New Zealander (11,059)	19,197	0.01
Northern European (207,253)	230,027	0.08
Norwegian (1,495,440)	4,602,337	1.51
Pennsylvania German (221,667)	346,187	0.11
Polish (3,426,104)	9,835,471	3.24
Portuguese (684,301)	1,426,867	0.47
Romanian (254,082)	468,281	0.15
Russian (1,308,378)	3,072,756	1.01
Scandinavian (280,751)	582,549	0.19
Scotch-Irish (2,182,988)	5,227,887	1.72
Scottish (1,774,629)	5,821,321	1.92
Serbian (89,070)	175,165	0.06
Slavic (48,290)	136,830	0.05
Slovak (287,511)	805,282	0.26
Slovene (62,962)	174,808	0.06
Soviet Union (1,721)	2,123	<0.01
Swedish (1,041,503)	4,293,208	1.41
Swiss (236,264)	1,003,505	0.33
Turkish (125,598)	177,841	0.06
Ukrainian (487,008)	956,909	0.31
Welsh (385,061)	1,922,914	0.63
West Indian, ex. Hispanic (2,061,121)	2,548,218	0.84
Bahamian (28,484)	41,029	0.01
Barbadian (43,480)	57,742	0.02
Belizean (37,389)	49,872	0.02
Bermudan (4,310)	6,728	<0.01
British West Indian (73,326)	91,048	0.03
Dutch West Indian (15,733)	61,278	0.02
Haitian (744,768)	813,186	0.27
Jamaican (772,443)	941,339	0.31
Trinidadian/Tobagonian (149,522)	189,059	0.06
U.S. Virgin Islander (10,871)	14,760	<0.01
West Indian (177,634)	276,827	0.09
Other West Indian (3,161)	5,350	<0.01
Yugoslavian (207,105)	330,705	0.11

Hispanic Origin	Population	%
Hispanic or Latino (of any race)	50,477,594	16.35
Central American, ex. Mexican	3,998,280	1.30
Costa Rican	126,418	0.04
Guatemalan	1,044,209	0.34
Honduran	633,401	0.21
Nicaraguan	348,202	0.11
Panamanian	165,456	0.05
Salvadoran	1,648,968	0.53
Other Central American	31,626	0.01
Cuban	1,785,547	0.58
Dominican Republic	1,414,703	0.46
Mexican	31,798,258	10.30
Puerto Rican	4,623,716	1.50
South American	2,769,434	0.90
Argentinean	224,952	0.07
Bolivian	99,210	0.03
Chilean	126,810	0.04
Colombian	908,734	0.29
Ecuadorian	564,631	0.18
Paraguayan	20,023	0.01
Peruvian	531,358	0.17
Uruguayan	56,884	0.02
Venezuelan	215,023	0.07
Other South American	21,809	0.01
Other Hispanic or Latino	4,087,656	1.32

Race*	Population	%
African-Am./Black (38,929,319)	42,020,743	13.61
Not Hispanic (37,685,848)	40,123,525	13.00
Hispanic (1,243,471)	1,897,218	0.61
Am. Indian/Alaska Native (2,932,248)	5,220,579	1.69
Not Hispanic (2,247,098)	4,029,675	1.31
Hispanic (685,150)	1,190,904	0.39
Alaska Athabascan *(Ala. Nat.)* (15,623)	22,484	0.01
Aleut *(Alaska Native)* (11,920)	19,282	0.01
Apache (63,193)	111,810	0.04
Arapaho (8,014)	10,861	<0.01
Blackfeet (27,279)	105,304	0.03
Canadian/French Am. Ind. (6,433)	14,822	<0.01
Central American Ind. (15,882)	27,844	0.01
Cherokee (284,247)	819,105	0.27
Cheyenne (11,375)	19,051	0.01
Chickasaw (27,973)	52,278	0.02
Chippewa (112,757)	170,742	0.06
Choctaw (103,910)	195,764	0.06
Colville (8,114)	10,549	<0.01
Comanche (12,284)	23,330	0.01
Cree (2,211)	7,983	<0.01
Creek (48,352)	88,332	0.03
Crow (10,332)	15,203	<0.01
Delaware (7,843)	18,264	0.01
Hopi (12,580)	18,327	0.01
Houma (8,169)	10,768	<0.01
Inupiat *(Alaska Native)* (24,859)	33,360	0.01
Iroquois (40,570)	81,002	0.03
Kiowa (9,437)	13,787	<0.01
Lumbee (62,306)	73,691	0.02
Menominee (8,374)	11,133	<0.01
Mexican American Ind. (121,221)	175,494	0.06
Navajo (286,731)	332,129	0.11
Osage (8,938)	18,576	0.01
Ottawa (7,272)	13,033	<0.01
Paiute (9,340)	13,767	<0.01
Pima (22,040)	26,655	0.01
Potawatomi (20,412)	33,771	0.01
Pueblo (49,695)	62,540	0.02
Puget Sound Salish (14,320)	20,260	0.01
Seminole (14,080)	31,971	0.01
Shoshone (7,852)	13,002	<0.01
Sioux (112,176)	170,110	0.06
South American Ind. (20,901)	47,233	0.02
Spanish American Ind. (13,460)	19,951	0.01
Tlingit-Haida *(Alaska Native)* (15,256)	26,080	0.01
Tohono O'Odham (19,522)	23,478	0.01
Tsimshian *(Alaska Native)* (2,307)	3,755	<0.01
Ute (7,435)	11,491	<0.01
Yakama (8,786)	11,527	<0.01
Yaqui (21,679)	32,595	0.01
Yuman (7,727)	10,089	<0.01
Yup'ik *(Alaska Native)* (28,927)	33,889	0.01
Asian (14,674,252)	17,320,856	5.61
Not Hispanic (14,465,124)	16,722,710	5.42
Hispanic (209,128)	598,146	0.19
Bangladeshi (128,792)	147,300	0.05
Bhutanese (15,290)	19,439	0.01
Burmese (91,085)	100,200	0.03
Cambodian (231,616)	276,667	0.09
Chinese, ex. Taiwanese (3,137,061)	3,794,673	1.23
Filipino (2,555,923)	3,416,840	1.11
Hmong (247,595)	260,073	0.08
Indian (2,843,391)	3,183,063	1.03
Indonesian (63,383)	95,270	0.03
Japanese (763,325)	1,304,286	0.42
Korean (1,423,784)	1,706,822	0.55
Laotian (191,200)	232,130	0.08
Malaysian (16,138)	26,179	0.01
Nepalese (51,907)	59,490	0.02
Pakistani (363,699)	409,163	0.13
Sri Lankan (38,596)	45,381	0.01
Taiwanese (196,691)	230,382	0.07
Thai (166,620)	237,583	0.08
Vietnamese (1,548,449)	1,737,433	0.56
Hawaii Native/Pacific Isl. (540,013)	1,225,195	0.40
Not Hispanic (481,576)	1,014,888	0.33
Hispanic (58,437)	210,307	0.07
Fijian (24,629)	32,304	0.01
Guamanian/Chamorro (88,310)	147,798	0.05
Marshallese (19,841)	22,434	0.01
Native Hawaiian (156,146)	527,077	0.17
Samoan (109,637)	184,440	0.06
Tongan (41,219)	57,183	0.02
White (223,553,265)	231,040,398	74.83
Not Hispanic (196,817,552)	201,856,108	65.38
Hispanic (26,735,713)	29,184,290	9.45

*Notes: Hispanic Origin and Race percentages are based on the Census 2010 population (308,745,538); Ancestry percentages are based on the American Community Survey 2006-2010 Five-Year Estimated population (303,965,272); ‡ Numbers in parentheses indicate the number of people reporting a single ancestry; * Numbers in parentheses indicate the number of persons reporting this race alone, not in combination with any other race; Please refer to the Explanation of Data in the front of the book for more detailed information.*

National Profile

By Major Category, Population Size & Percent of U.S. Population

Ancestry‡	Population	%
German (16,912,041)	49,840,035	16.40
Irish (10,112,947)	35,751,251	11.76
English (9,605,188)	27,404,243	9.02
American (19,094,109)	19,094,109	6.28
Italian (7,183,882)	17,571,808	5.78
Polish (3,426,104)	9,835,471	3.24
French, ex. Basque (2,023,095)	9,326,380	3.07
Scottish (1,774,629)	5,821,321	1.92
Scotch-Irish (2,182,988)	5,227,887	1.72
Dutch (1,226,388)	4,950,629	1.63
Norwegian (1,495,440)	4,602,337	1.51
Swedish (1,041,503)	4,293,208	1.41
European (2,680,293)	3,074,695	1.01
Russian (1,308,378)	3,072,756	1.01
African, Sub-Saharan (2,326,027)	2,783,033	0.92
West Indian, ex. Hispanic (2,061,121)	2,548,218	0.84
French Canadian (983,474)	2,138,601	0.70
Welsh (385,061)	1,922,914	0.63
African (1,393,403)	1,731,621	0.57
Czech (471,510)	1,597,950	0.53
Arab (1,052,350)	1,547,365	0.51
Hungarian (495,861)	1,537,238	0.51
Danish (374,442)	1,453,897	0.48
Portuguese (684,301)	1,426,867	0.47
Greek (654,228)	1,337,576	0.44
British (638,061)	1,223,541	0.40
Swiss (236,264)	1,003,505	0.33
Ukrainian (487,008)	956,909	0.31
Jamaican (772,443)	941,339	0.31
Haitian (744,768)	813,186	0.27
Slovak (287,511)	805,282	0.26
Austrian (191,714)	766,033	0.25
Canadian (361,182)	716,067	0.24
Lithuanian (238,647)	708,860	0.23
Finnish (228,585)	677,272	0.22
Scandinavian (280,751)	582,549	0.19
Lebanese (252,187)	485,917	0.16
Romanian (254,082)	468,281	0.15
Armenian (314,013)	447,580	0.15
Iranian (356,928)	425,587	0.14
Eastern European (371,065)	419,221	0.14
Croatian (162,219)	417,130	0.14
Belgian (116,510)	386,694	0.13
Brazilian (273,724)	347,346	0.11
Pennsylvania German (221,667)	346,187	0.11
Yugoslavian (207,105)	330,705	0.11
Czechoslovakian (144,153)	320,161	0.11
West Indian (177,634)	276,827	0.09
Arab (202,189)	259,644	0.09
Nigerian (225,650)	250,819	0.08
Northern European (207,253)	230,027	0.08
Guyanese (168,490)	202,258	0.07
Trinidadian/Tobagonian (149,522)	189,059	0.06
Other Arab (143,271)	182,424	0.06
Egyptian (150,064)	179,853	0.06
Turkish (125,598)	177,841	0.06
Serbian (89,070)	175,165	0.06
Slovene (62,962)	174,808	0.06
Ethiopian (161,188)	172,984	0.06
Albanian (142,965)	172,149	0.06
Syrian (72,443)	147,426	0.05
Slavic (48,290)	136,830	0.05
Israeli (97,763)	136,351	0.04
Other Sub-Saharan African (104,844)	120,887	0.04
Cajun (67,601)	108,696	0.04
Somalian (96,162)	100,011	0.03
Australian (44,636)	94,368	0.03
Cape Verdean (68,034)	92,936	0.03
Latvian (41,851)	91,096	0.03
British West Indian (73,326)	91,048	0.03
Bulgarian (65,816)	89,808	0.03
Assyrian/Chaldean/Syriac (70,920)	89,410	0.03
Ghanaian (79,074)	83,718	0.03
Palestinian (65,940)	83,241	0.03
Afghan (71,406)	77,029	0.03
Moroccan (56,413)	74,908	0.02
Iraqi (59,384)	73,896	0.02
Dutch West Indian (15,733)	61,278	0.02
Jordanian (50,459)	60,056	0.02
Basque (26,957)	59,586	0.02
Barbadian (43,480)	57,742	0.02
South African (37,567)	53,088	0.02
Celtic (26,449)	52,937	0.02
Macedonian (36,419)	52,386	0.02
Liberian (47,649)	52,299	0.02
Icelander (19,198)	51,234	0.02
Belizean (37,389)	49,872	0.02
Luxemburger (12,943)	45,597	0.02
Kenyan (40,326)	45,177	0.01
Maltese (18,593)	43,082	0.01
Bahamian (28,484)	41,029	0.01
Sudanese (35,880)	38,432	0.01
Estonian (13,785)	28,312	0.01
New Zealander (11,059)	19,197	0.01
Sierra Leonean (14,560)	16,343	0.01
German Russian (8,076)	16,037	0.01
U.S. Virgin Islander (10,871)	14,760	<0.01
Alsatian (3,591)	12,104	<0.01
Senegalese (8,463)	10,055	<0.01
Ugandan (7,753)	8,565	<0.01
Carpatho Rusyn (3,354)	7,501	<0.01
Bermudan (4,310)	6,728	<0.01
Zimbabwean (5,474)	6,098	<0.01
Cypriot (4,631)	5,843	<0.01
Other West Indian (3,161)	5,350	<0.01
Soviet Union (1,721)	2,123	<0.01

Hispanic Origin	Population	%
Hispanic or Latino (of any race)	50,477,594	16.35
Mexican	31,798,258	10.30
Puerto Rican	4,623,716	1.50
Other Hispanic or Latino	4,087,656	1.32
Central American, ex. Mexican	3,998,280	1.30
South American	2,769,434	0.90
Cuban	1,785,547	0.58
Salvadoran	1,648,968	0.53
Dominican Republic	1,414,703	0.46
Guatemalan	1,044,209	0.34
Colombian	908,734	0.29
Honduran	633,401	0.21
Ecuadorian	564,631	0.18
Peruvian	531,358	0.17
Nicaraguan	348,202	0.11
Argentinean	224,952	0.07
Venezuelan	215,023	0.07
Panamanian	165,456	0.05
Chilean	126,810	0.04
Costa Rican	126,418	0.04
Bolivian	99,210	0.03
Uruguayan	56,884	0.02
Other Central American	31,626	0.01
Other South American	21,809	0.01
Paraguayan	20,023	0.01

Race*	Population	%
White (223,553,265)	231,040,398	74.83
White: Not Hispanic (196,817,552)	201,856,108	65.38
AAB (38,929,319)	42,020,743	13.61
AAB: Not Hispanic. (37,685,848)	40,123,525	13.00
White: Hispanic (26,735,713)	29,184,290	9.45
Asian (14,674,252)	17,320,856	5.61
Asian: Not Hispanic (14,465,124)	16,722,710	5.42
AIAN (2,932,248)	5,220,579	1.69
AIAN: Not Hispanic (2,247,098)	4,029,675	1.31
Chinese, ex. Taiwanese (3,137,061)	3,794,673	1.23
Filipino (2,555,923)	3,416,840	1.11
Indian (2,843,391)	3,183,063	1.03
AAB: Hispanic. (1,243,471)	1,897,218	0.61
Vietnamese (1,548,449)	1,737,433	0.56
Korean (1,423,784)	1,706,822	0.55
Japanese (763,325)	1,304,286	0.42
HNOPI (540,013)	1,225,195	0.40
AIAN: Hispanic (685,150)	1,190,904	0.39
HNOPI: Not Hispanic (481,576)	1,014,888	0.33
Cherokee (284,247)	819,105	0.27
Asian: Hispanic (209,128)	598,146	0.19
Native Hawaiian (156,146)	527,077	0.17
Pakistani (363,699)	409,163	0.13
Navajo (286,731)	332,129	0.11
Cambodian (231,616)	276,667	0.09
Hmong (247,595)	260,073	0.08
Thai (166,620)	237,583	0.08
Laotian (191,200)	232,130	0.08
Taiwanese (196,691)	230,382	0.07
HNOPI: Hispanic (58,437)	210,307	0.07
Choctaw (103,910)	195,764	0.06
Samoan (109,637)	184,440	0.06
Mexican American Indian. (121,221)	175,494	0.06
Chippewa (112,757)	170,742	0.06
Sioux (112,176)	170,110	0.06
Guamanian/Chamorro (88,310)	147,798	0.05
Bangladeshi (128,792)	147,300	0.05
Apache (63,193)	111,810	0.04
Blackfeet (27,279)	105,304	0.03
Burmese (91,085)	100,200	0.03
Indonesian (63,383)	95,270	0.03
Creek (48,352)	88,332	0.03
Iroquois (40,570)	81,002	0.03
Lumbee (62,306)	73,691	0.02
Pueblo (49,695)	62,540	0.02
Nepalese (51,907)	59,490	0.02
Tongan (41,219)	57,183	0.02
Chickasaw (27,973)	52,278	0.02
South American Indian (20,901)	47,233	0.02
Sri Lankan (38,596)	45,381	0.01
Yup'ik *(Alaska Native)* (28,927)	33,889	0.01
Potawatomi (20,412)	33,771	0.01
Inupiat *(Alaska Native)* (24,859)	33,360	0.01
Yaqui (21,679)	32,595	0.01
Fijian (24,629)	32,304	0.01
Seminole (14,080)	31,971	0.01
Central American Indian (15,882)	27,844	0.01
Pima (22,040)	26,655	0.01
Malaysian (16,138)	26,179	0.01
Tlingit-Haida *(Alaska Native)* (15,256)	26,080	0.01
Tohono O'Odham (19,522)	23,478	0.01
Comanche (12,284)	23,330	0.01
Alaska Athabascan *(Ala. Nat.)* (15,623)	22,484	0.01
Marshallese (19,841)	22,434	0.01
Puget Sound Salish (14,320)	20,260	0.01
Spanish American Ind. (13,460)	19,951	0.01
Bhutanese (15,290)	19,439	0.01
Aleut *(Alaska Native)* (11,920)	19,282	0.01
Cheyenne (11,375)	19,051	0.01
Osage (8,938)	18,576	0.01
Hopi (12,580)	18,327	0.01
Delaware (7,843)	18,264	0.01
Crow (10,332)	15,203	<0.01
Canadian/French Am. Indian (6,433)	14,822	<0.01
Kiowa (9,437)	13,787	<0.01
Paiute (9,340)	13,767	<0.01
Ottawa (7,272)	13,033	<0.01
Shoshone (7,852)	13,002	<0.01
Yakama (8,786)	11,527	<0.01
Ute (7,435)	11,491	<0.01
Menominee (8,374)	11,133	<0.01
Arapaho (8,014)	10,861	<0.01
Houma (8,169)	10,768	<0.01
Colville (8,114)	10,549	<0.01
Yuman (7,727)	10,089	<0.01
Cree (2,211)	7,983	<0.01
Tsimshian *(Alaska Native)* (2,307)	3,755	<0.01

*Notes: Hispanic Origin and Race percentages are based on the Census 2010 population (308,745,538); Ancestry percentages are based on the American Community Survey 2006-2010 Five-Year Estimated population (303,965,272); ‡ Numbers in parentheses indicate the number of people reporting a single ancestry; * Numbers in parentheses indicate the number of persons reporting this race alone, not in combination with any other race; AIAN–American Indian/Alaska Native; HNOPI–Hawaii Native/Other Pacific Islander; AAB–African-American/Black; Please refer to the Explanation of Data in the front of the book for more detailed information.*

Top 20 Ancestries by State

State	Ancestry (%)									
	German	Irish	Mexican	English	American	Italian	Polish	French, ex. Basque	Scottish	Scotch-Irish
Alabama	7.73	10.42	2.57	9.59	13.35	1.78	0.70	1.91	2.11	2.40
Alaska	19.45	12.34	3.05	10.04	3.54	3.64	2.51	3.51	3.20	2.38
Arizona	16.19	10.69	25.93	10.10	4.37	4.65	2.59	2.87	2.08	1.66
Arkansas	12.20	13.27	4.74	10.27	10.77	1.70	0.86	2.30	1.85	2.04
California	9.57	7.50	30.66	6.78	2.43	4.21	1.41	2.12	1.54	1.19
Colorado	22.93	12.87	15.06	11.91	4.46	5.18	2.54	3.37	2.86	2.21
Connecticut	10.19	17.34	1.42	10.26	2.67	19.05	8.39	6.35	2.05	1.38
Delaware	16.02	18.20	3.37	12.31	4.25	9.87	5.17	2.19	1.93	1.75
District of Columbia	6.64	6.78	1.41	5.19	1.42	3.05	2.01	1.64	1.36	1.01
Florida	11.95	10.69	3.35	8.80	6.86	6.57	2.76	2.73	1.81	1.56
Georgia	8.02	9.10	5.36	9.06	10.69	2.31	1.09	1.62	1.95	1.94
Hawaii	6.73	4.97	2.60	4.48	0.78	2.11	1.04	1.72	1.14	0.93
Idaho	20.25	10.82	9.50	17.66	9.77	3.04	1.35	3.08	3.43	2.01
Illinois	20.67	12.94	12.49	6.56	4.61	6.36	7.69	2.13	1.26	1.12
Indiana	26.37	12.90	4.56	9.71	10.04	2.88	3.28	2.61	1.93	1.49
Iowa	39.64	15.41	3.84	9.85	5.61	2.22	1.35	2.71	1.68	1.53
Kansas	30.74	13.80	8.67	11.13	6.77	2.32	1.43	3.34	2.18	2.06
Kentucky	15.93	13.68	1.89	11.53	19.75	2.07	0.95	1.86	2.00	2.10
Louisiana	8.68	8.09	1.73	6.68	9.17	5.07	0.50	15.08	1.02	1.29
Maine	8.37	17.92	0.39	23.17	6.96	5.71	2.29	17.50	5.60	3.72
Maryland	16.23	12.18	1.52	8.85	4.87	5.47	3.51	1.90	1.76	1.44
Massachusetts	6.73	23.41	0.59	11.54	3.27	13.94	5.23	8.40	2.66	1.90
Michigan	22.65	11.92	3.22	10.39	4.76	4.81	9.05	5.12	2.47	1.58
Minnesota	37.38	11.44	3.32	6.27	2.72	2.45	4.91	4.08	1.32	1.01
Mississipp	6.10	9.69	1.77	8.54	11.87	1.80	0.52	2.92	1.61	2.27
Missouri	27.11	14.80	2.46	10.36	9.34	3.63	1.84	3.81	1.88	1.94
Montana	29.08	16.13	2.03	13.01	6.09	3.62	2.11	4.09	3.33	2.61
Nebraska	41.50	14.68	7.01	9.54	3.66	2.78	3.77	2.73	1.52	1.58
Nevada	13.42	10.33	20.03	9.29	3.77	6.43	2.31	2.63	1.93	1.40
New Hampshire	9.48	22.29	0.59	18.81	4.33	10.45	4.42	16.54	4.80	2.61
New Jersey	12.26	15.72	2.48	5.80	3.22	17.45	6.48	1.38	1.20	0.95
New Mexico	10.41	7.55	28.70	7.96	3.37	2.52	1.17	2.15	1.72	1.59
New York	11.64	13.34	2.36	6.14	3.58	14.20	5.24	2.63	1.18	0.86
North Caroline	11.63	9.49	5.11	10.59	11.50	3.07	1.42	1.84	2.66	3.67
North Dakota	46.90	8.09	1.37	4.76	2.46	1.08	2.65	4.15	1.33	1.19
Ohio	27.97	14.48	1.49	9.66	7.91	6.50	4.02	2.47	1.99	1.65
Oklahoma	15.45	13.01	7.12	8.82	9.56	1.70	0.90	2.43	1.93	1.85
Oregon	21.91	12.96	9.65	13.51	4.88	3.79	1.78	3.68	3.45	2.57
Pennsylvania	28.02	17.85	1.02	8.35	4.36	12.51	6.98	1.86	1.67	1.99
Rhode Island	6.20	20.06	0.86	12.79	2.17	19.13	4.17	12.44	2.22	1.45
South Carolina	10.30	9.66	2.99	9.39	12.49	2.67	1.29	1.98	2.15	3.36
South Dakota	43.66	11.13	1.70	7.17	3.48	1.26	1.61	2.86	1.29	1.18
Tennessee	10.52	11.30	2.94	10.51	17.25	2.07	1.04	1.83	2.26	3.20
Texas	10.99	7.86	31.62	7.30	5.62	1.92	1.15	2.38	1.60	1.66
Utah	12.16	6.17	9.37	27.08	6.46	2.89	0.90	2.15	4.65	1.34
Vermont	10.38	17.90	0.40	18.15	6.78	7.51	3.94	15.48	4.92	2.69
Virginia	12.90	10.78	1.94	11.75	10.65	4.05	1.98	2.13	2.41	2.57
Washington	20.29	12.30	8.95	12.11	4.09	3.63	1.91	3.79	3.24	2.47
West Virginia	19.78	15.14	0.52	12.28	13.40	4.66	1.90	1.72	2.14	2.85
Wisconsin	44.34	11.72	4.29	6.60	2.98	3.57	9.55	3.81	1.14	0.85
Wyoming	28.65	14.62	6.69	15.67	6.89	3.47	2.18	3.44	3.82	3.02

Note: Figures include multiple ancestries reported. A visual representation of each ethnicity appears on pages 14 through 33 (Alaska and Hawaii are not included on the maps).

Source: U.S. Census Bureau, American Community Survey, 2006-2010 Five-Year Estimates

Ancestry (%)										
Dutch	Puerto Rican	Norwegian	Swedish	Chinese, ex. Taiwan.	Filipino	Asian Indian	Russian	French Canadian	Welsh	State
1.19	0.26	0.33	0.39	0.22	0.17	0.31	0.18	0.22	0.38	Alabama
2.23	0.63	4.14	2.73	0.51	3.58	0.27	1.45	1.02	0.94	Alaska
1.65	0.54	1.88	1.75	0.63	0.83	0.63	0.94	0.55	0.72	Arizona
1.89	0.16	0.48	0.65	0.20	0.22	0.31	0.18	0.22	0.46	Arkansas
1.15	0.51	1.10	1.25	3.62	3.96	1.58	1.22	0.32	0.49	California
1.98	0.46	2.34	2.81	0.63	0.52	0.48	1.23	0.60	0.96	Colorado
0.85	7.08	0.56	1.88	0.99	0.46	1.42	2.01	2.95	0.42	Connecticut
1.61	2.51	0.53	0.83	0.75	0.52	1.37	0.85	0.37	1.07	Delaware
0.63	0.52	0.65	0.69	1.03	0.61	1.07	1.64	0.33	0.46	District of Columbia
1.26	4.51	0.64	0.89	0.48	0.65	0.81	1.29	0.65	0.55	Florida
0.92	0.74	0.38	0.47	0.52	0.29	1.09	0.47	0.26	0.44	Georgia
0.76	3.24	0.77	0.78	14.61	25.15	0.35	0.42	0.24	0.39	Hawaii
2.39	0.19	3.48	3.40	0.33	0.40	0.18	0.61	0.57	1.47	Idaho
1.58	1.43	1.36	2.37	0.88	1.08	1.59	1.07	0.29	0.41	Illinois
2.25	0.47	0.57	1.02	0.38	0.26	0.48	0.40	0.27	0.61	Indiana
4.91	0.16	5.63	3.26	0.36	0.20	0.41	0.36	0.34	0.76	Iowa
2.36	0.32	1.13	2.46	0.44	0.33	0.55	0.84	0.37	0.81	Kansas
1.37	0.26	0.32	0.42	0.23	0.19	0.33	0.24	0.20	0.53	Kentucky
0.61	0.26	0.27	0.29	0.25	0.23	0.29	0.18	2.54	0.24	Louisiana
1.05	0.33	0.76	1.89	0.32	0.22	0.18	0.73	7.54	0.87	Maine
1.04	0.74	0.51	0.65	1.29	0.99	1.54	1.46	0.36	0.74	Maryland
0.73	4.06	0.52	1.90	2.01	0.29	1.30	1.86	4.14	0.41	Massachusetts
5.18	0.38	0.87	1.73	0.49	0.33	0.86	0.79	1.79	0.52	Michigan
2.03	0.20	16.54	9.47	0.54	0.30	0.72	0.85	1.04	0.48	Minnesota
0.79	0.20	0.24	0.29	0.17	0.19	0.22	0.12	0.23	0.31	Mississipp
1.96	0.20	0.77	1.10	0.41	0.30	0.44	0.54	0.27	0.69	Missouri
2.72	0.15	9.86	3.43	0.19	0.29	0.09	1.02	0.99	1.05	Montana
2.16	0.18	2.11	4.95	0.30	0.27	0.37	0.72	0.33	0.65	Nebraska
1.33	0.77	1.59	1.48	1.41	4.59	0.53	1.04	0.48	0.69	Nevada
0.96	0.89	0.91	2.03	0.56	0.26	0.69	1.01	8.64	0.66	New Hampshire
1.27	4.94	0.49	0.62	1.59	1.44	3.54	2.26	0.28	0.44	New Jersey
1.16	0.39	0.95	0.93	0.36	0.41	0.28	0.48	0.31	0.55	New Mexico
1.44	5.52	0.45	0.69	3.09	0.65	1.90	2.47	0.70	0.46	New York
1.29	0.75	0.47	0.57	0.41	0.31	0.67	0.45	0.35	0.58	North Caroline
1.39	0.15	30.04	4.78	0.25	0.25	0.26	3.82	1.83	0.28	North Dakota
1.80	0.82	0.37	0.68	0.41	0.24	0.62	0.70	0.28	1.18	Ohio
2.20	0.33	0.65	0.76	0.30	0.29	0.38	0.30	0.25	0.52	Oklahoma
2.55	0.23	4.03	3.12	1.03	0.76	0.53	1.37	0.74	1.13	Oregon
2.13	2.88	0.34	0.91	0.73	0.26	0.89	1.60	0.24	1.49	Pennsylvania
0.53	3.32	0.43	1.80	0.75	0.39	0.54	1.09	4.96	0.30	Rhode Island
1.00	0.57	0.38	0.51	0.24	0.33	0.39	0.34	0.34	0.50	South Carolina
4.78	0.18	14.93	3.82	0.19	0.23	0.18	1.63	0.56	0.49	South Dakota
1.35	0.33	0.44	0.56	0.27	0.23	0.42	0.29	0.26	0.55	Tennessee
1.00	0.52	0.55	0.65	0.66	0.55	1.07	0.34	0.30	0.42	Texas
2.41	0.26	2.48	4.09	0.56	0.39	0.27	0.40	0.24	2.19	Utah
1.57	0.36	0.85	1.83	0.44	0.17	0.28	1.36	8.28	1.24	Vermont
1.16	0.92	0.65	0.77	0.86	1.13	1.43	0.70	0.41	0.74	Virginia
2.47	0.38	6.04	3.73	1.68	2.04	1.03	1.31	0.84	1.08	Washington
2.50	0.20	0.22	0.41	0.16	0.17	0.21	0.37	0.18	0.78	West Virginia
2.72	0.81	8.27	2.81	0.35	0.23	0.46	0.74	1.09	0.50	Wisconsin
2.41	0.18	3.56	3.44	0.23	0.29	0.13	0.89	0.50	1.20	Wyoming

German Ancestry

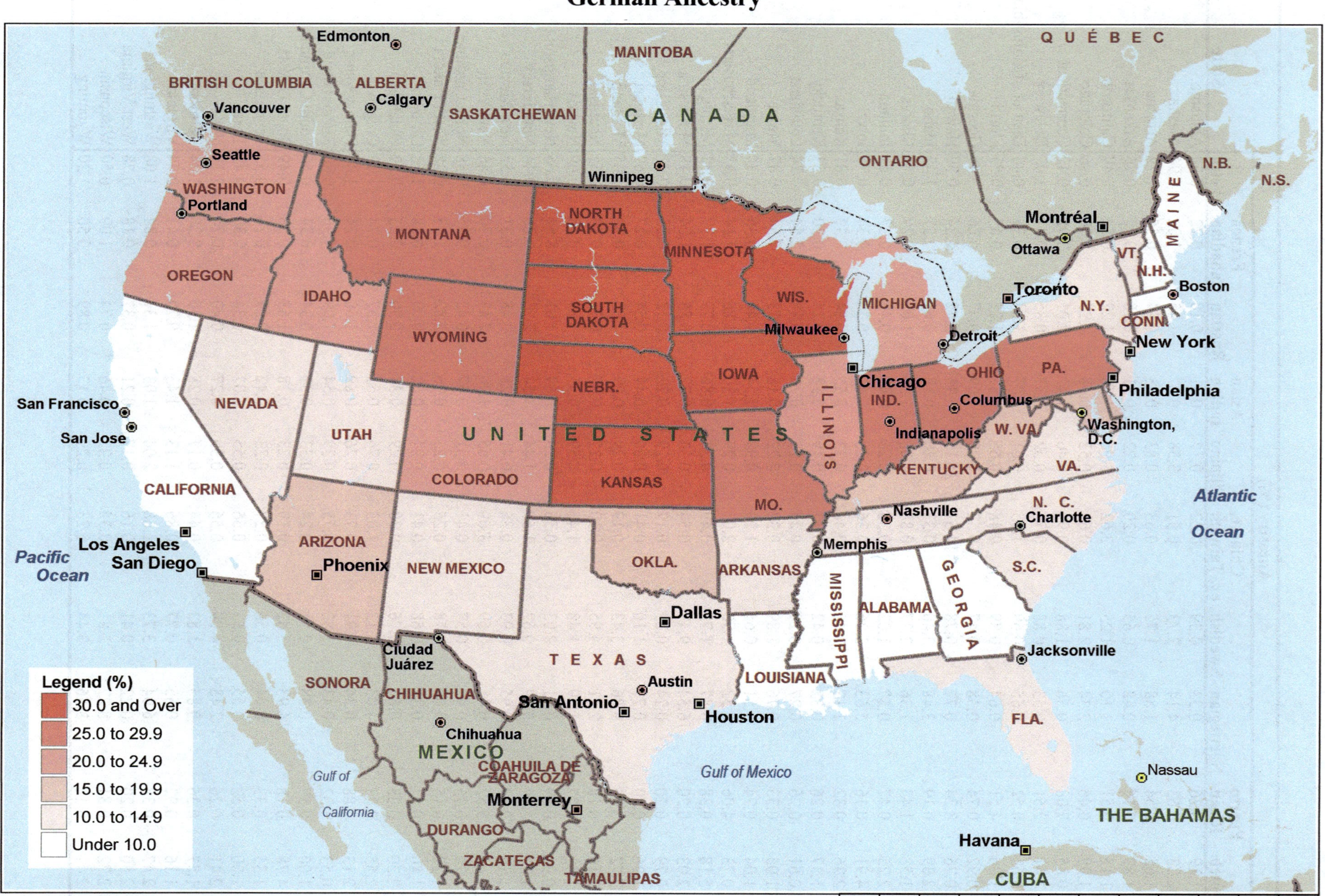

Note: Figures include multiple ancestries reported. Copyright © 1988-2003 Microsoft Corp. and/or its suppliers. All rights reserved.
Source: U.S. Census Bureau, American Community Survey, 2006–2010 Five-Year Estimates

Irish Ancestry

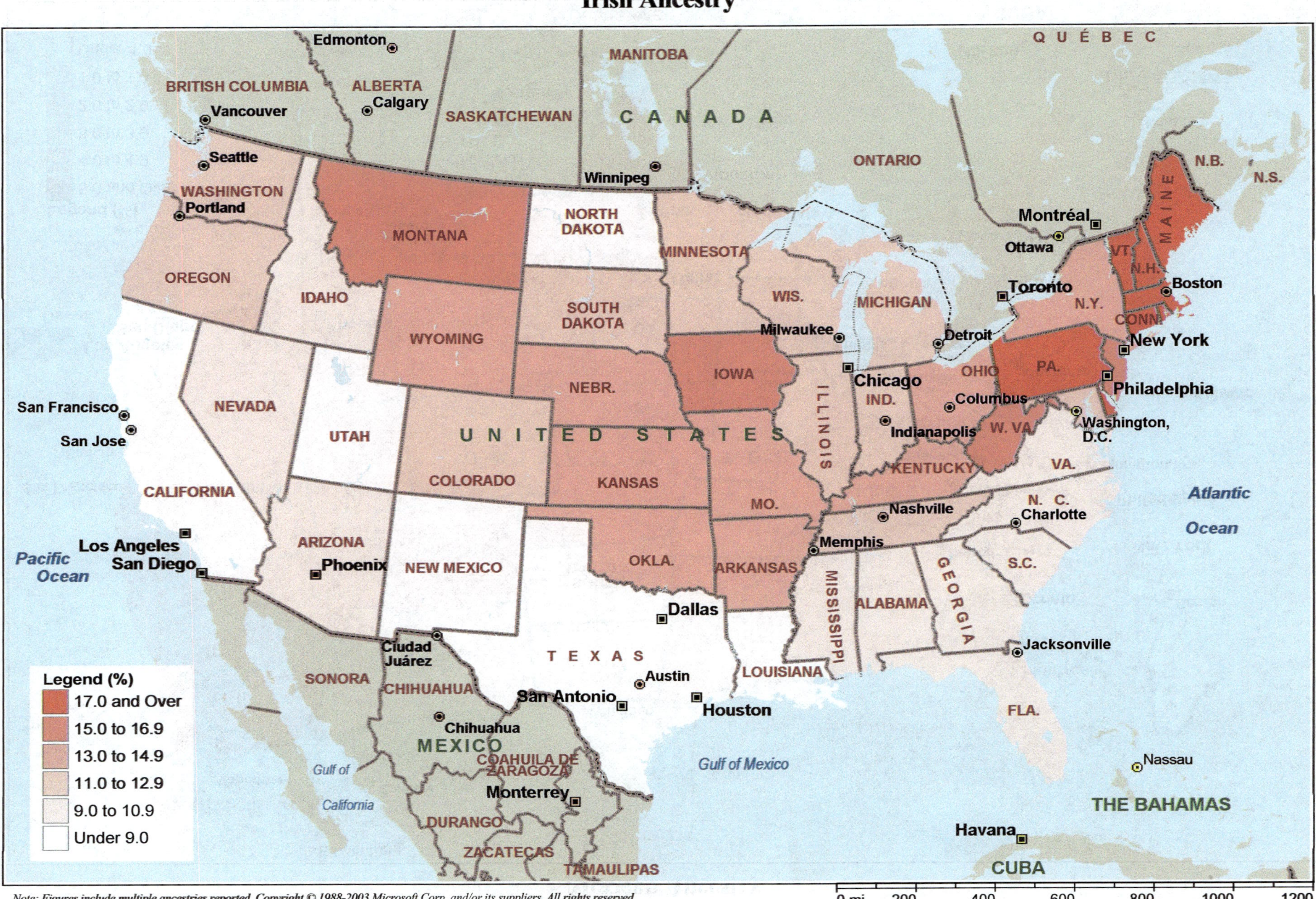

Note: Figures include multiple ancestries reported.

Source: U.S. Census Bureau, American Community Survey, 2006–2010 Five-Year Estimates

Mexican Ancestry

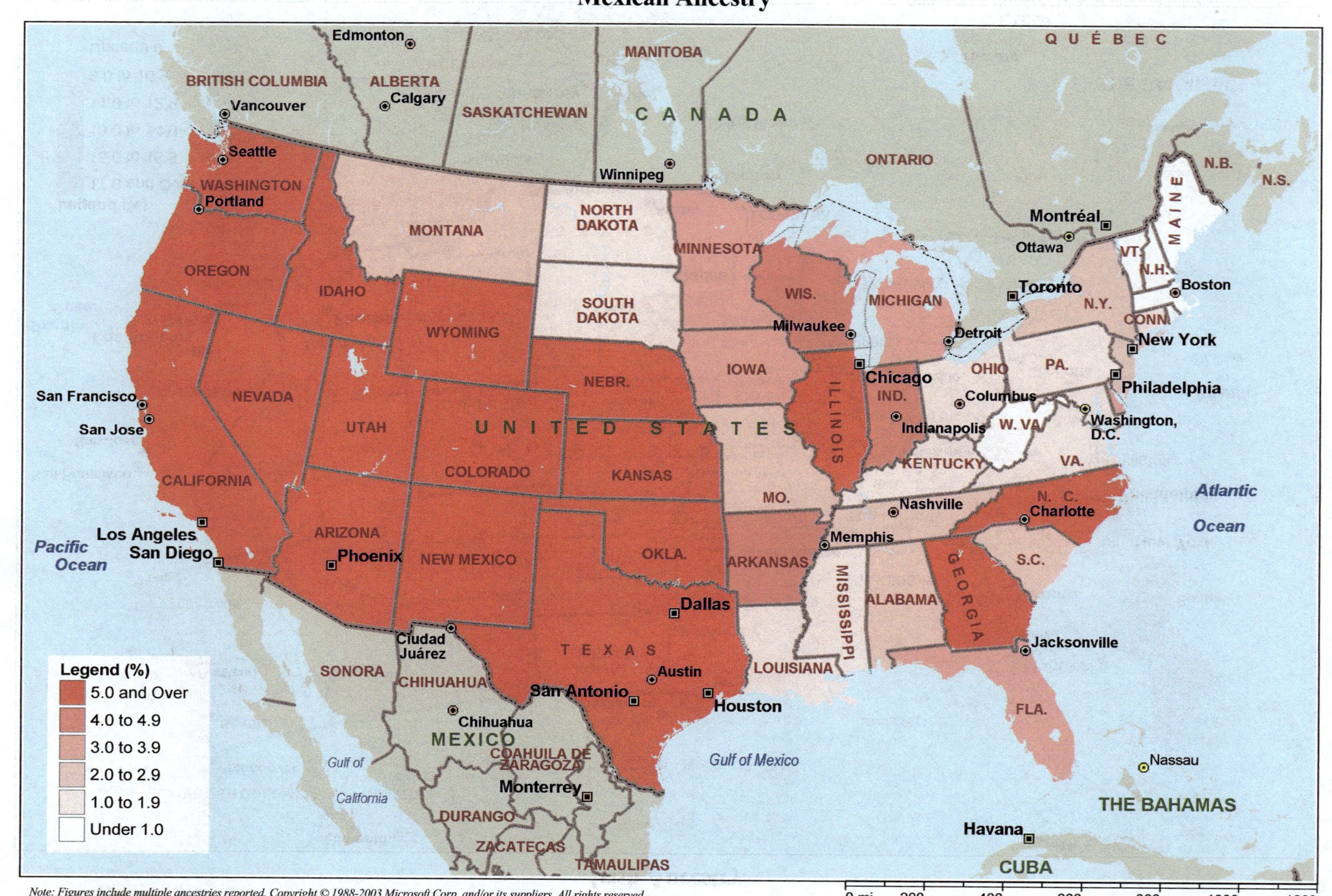

Note: Figures include multiple ancestries reported.
Source: U.S. Census Bureau, American Community Survey, 2006–2010 Five-Year Estimates

English Ancestry

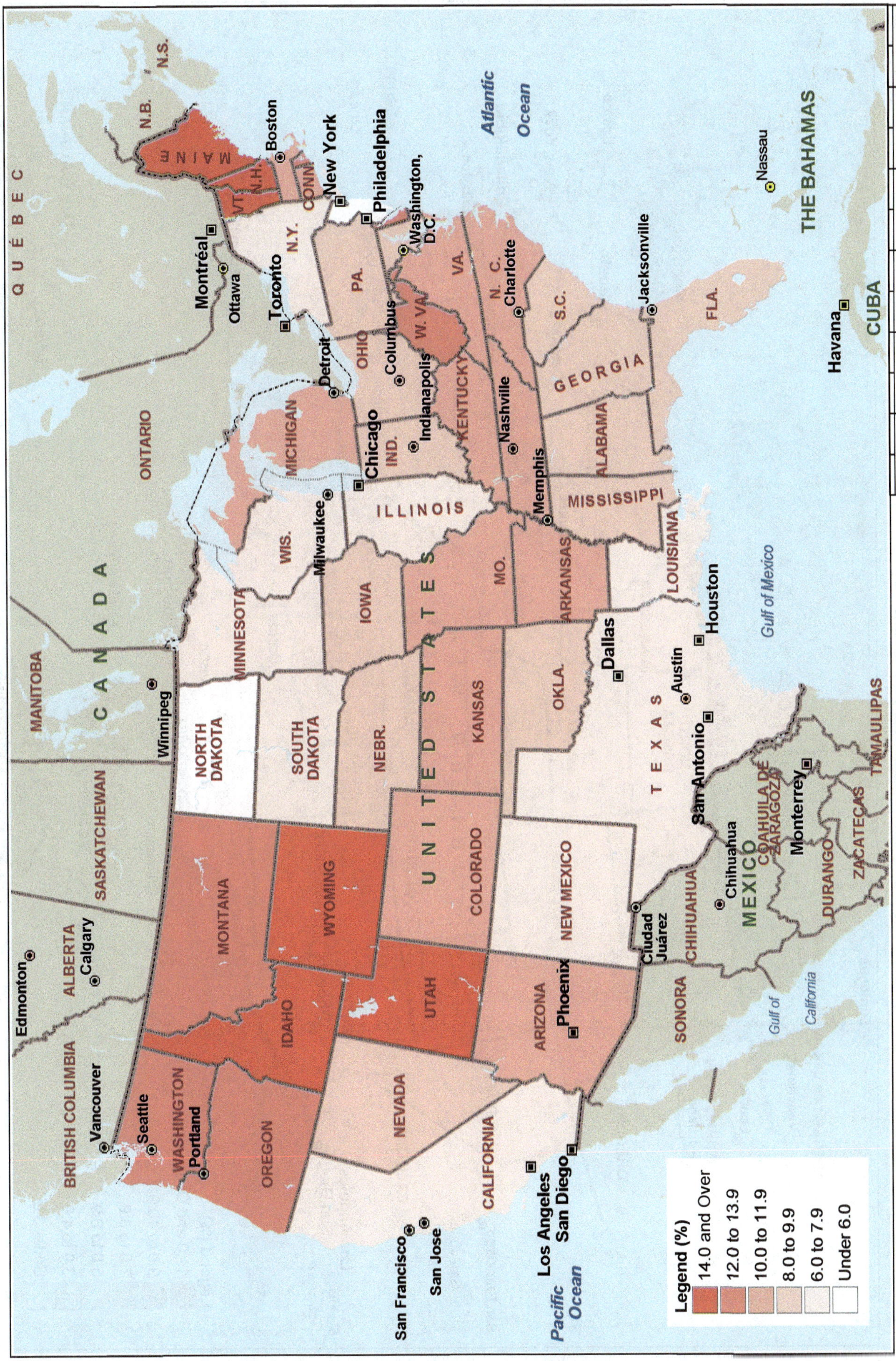

Legend (%)

- 14.0 and Over
- 12.0 to 13.9
- 10.0 to 11.9
- 8.0 to 9.9
- 6.0 to 7.9
- Under 6.0

Note: Figures include multiple ancestries reported.

Source: U.S. Census Bureau, American Community Survey, 2006–2010 Five-Year Estimates

American Ancestry

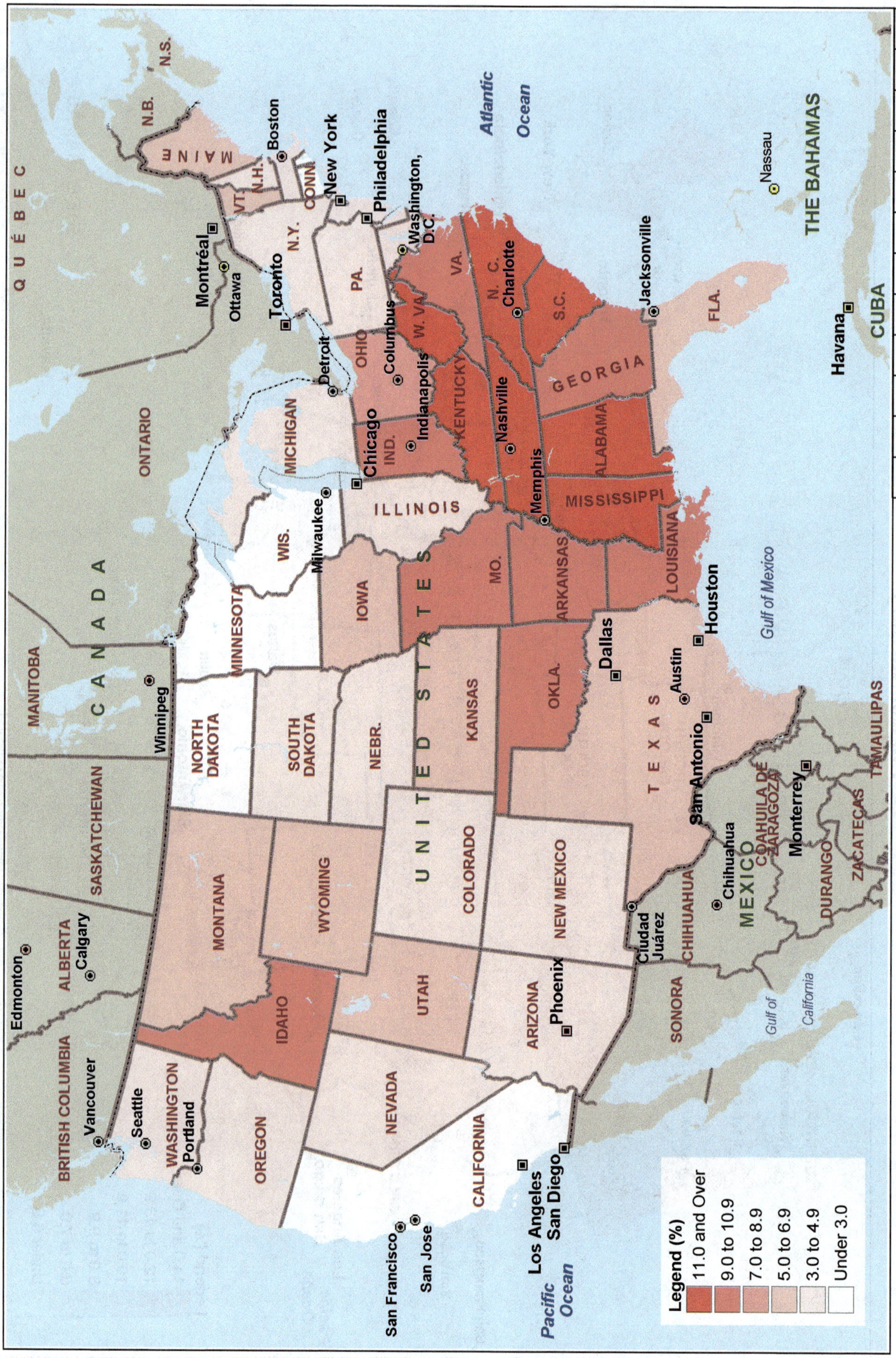

Legend (%)
- 11.0 and Over
- 9.0 to 10.9
- 7.0 to 8.9
- 5.0 to 6.9
- 3.0 to 4.9
- Under 3.0

Note: Figures include multiple ancestries reported.
Source: U.S. Census Bureau, American Community Survey, 2006–2010 Five-Year Estimates

Italian Ancestry

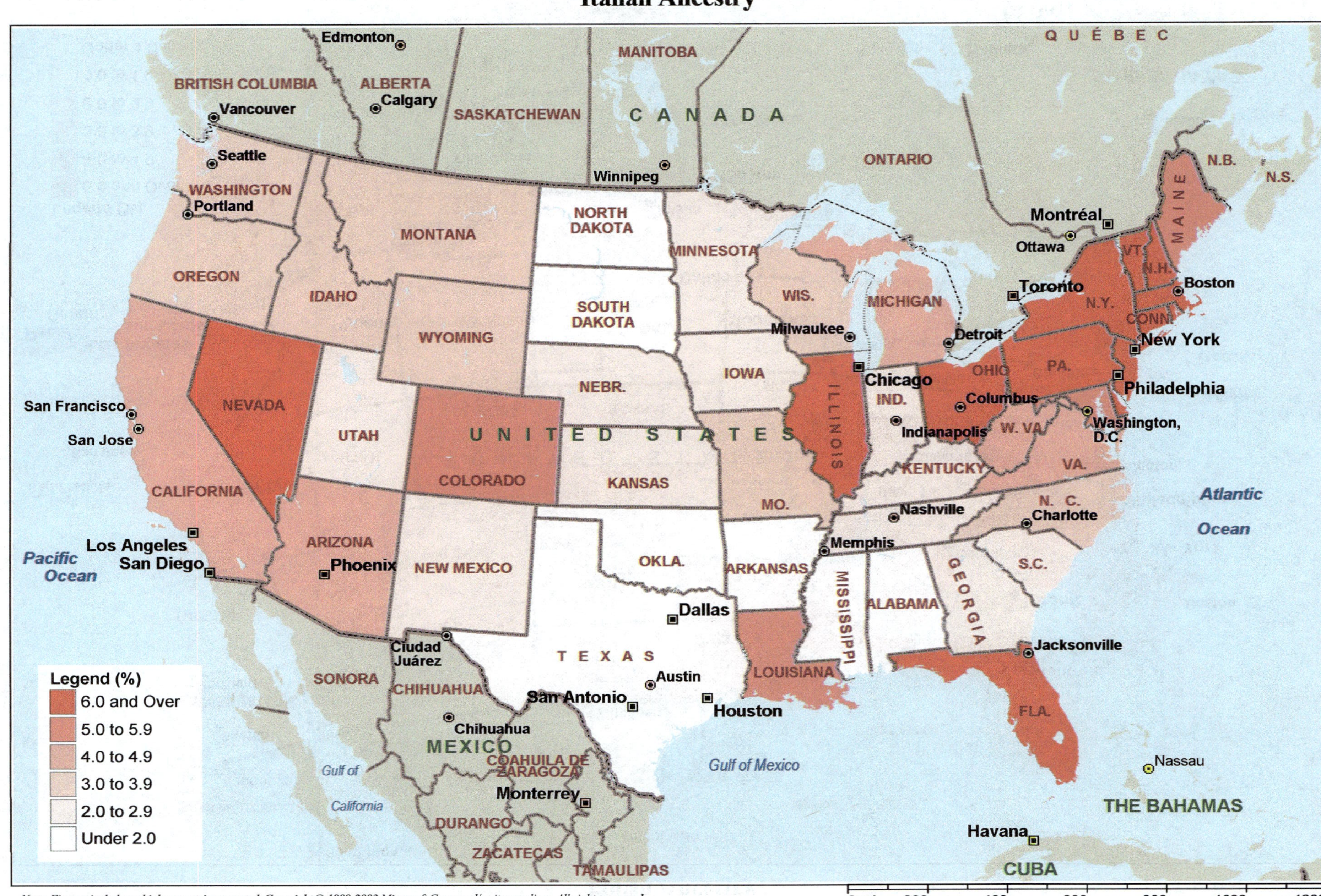

Note: Figures include multiple ancestries reported. Copyright © 1988-2003 Microsoft Corp. and/or its suppliers. All rights reserved.
Source: U.S. Census Bureau, American Community Survey, 2006–2010 Five-Year Estimates

Polish Ancestry

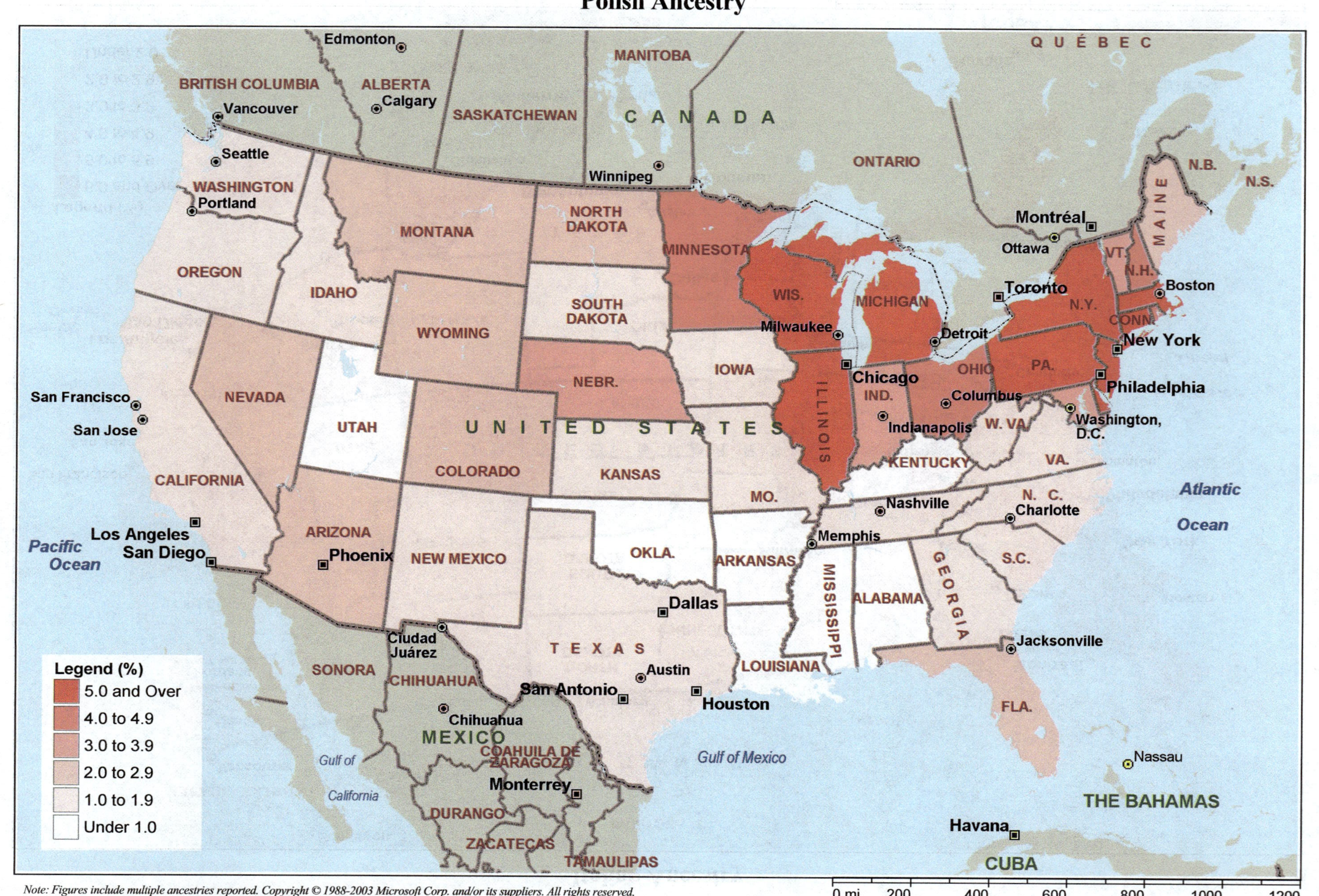

Note: Figures include multiple ancestries reported.
Source: U.S. Census Bureau, American Community Survey, 2006–2010 Five-Year Estimates

French (except Basque) Ancestry

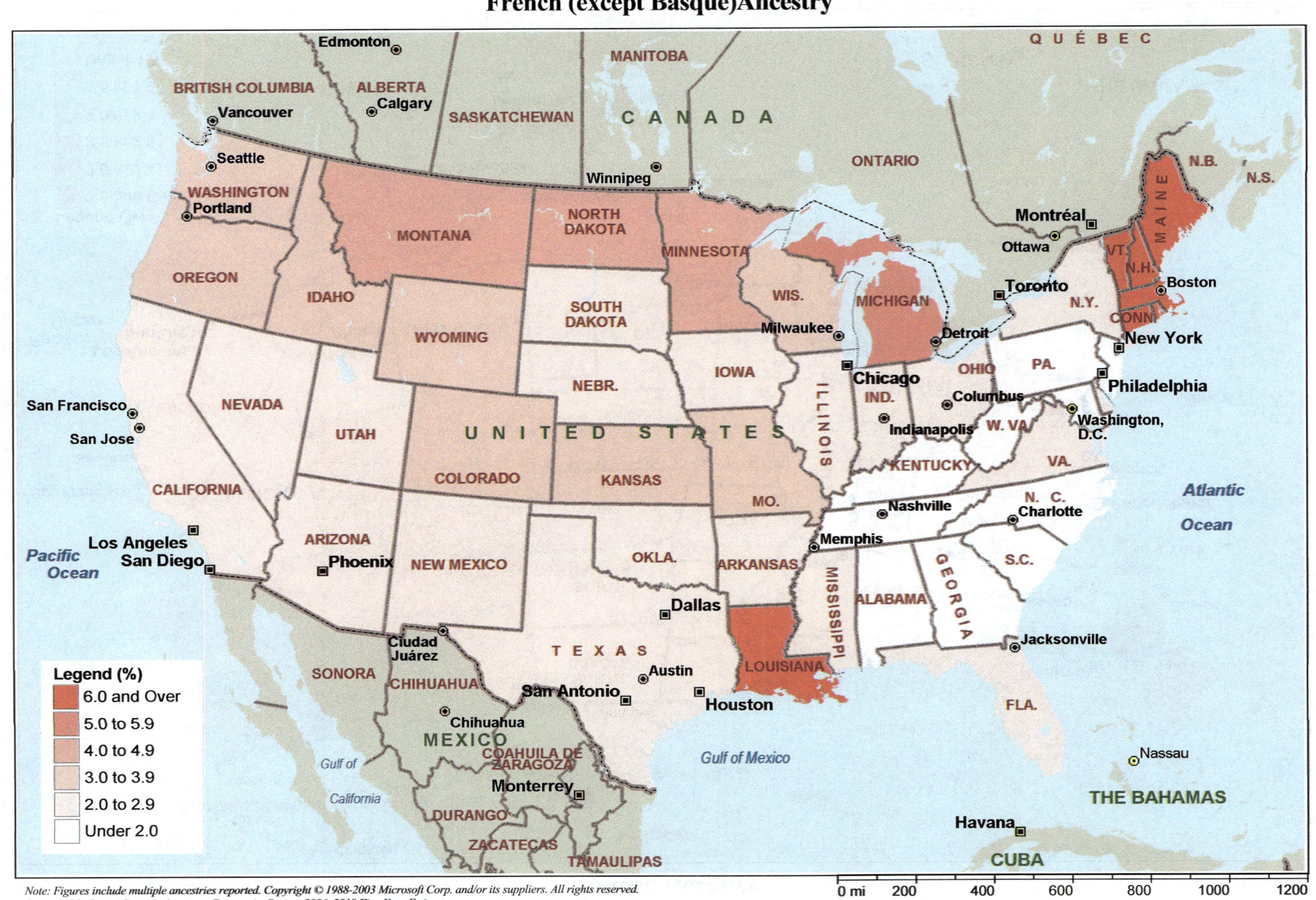

Note: Figures include multiple ancestries reported.
Source: U.S. Census Bureau, American Community Survey, 2006–2010 Five-Year Estimates

Scottish Ancestry

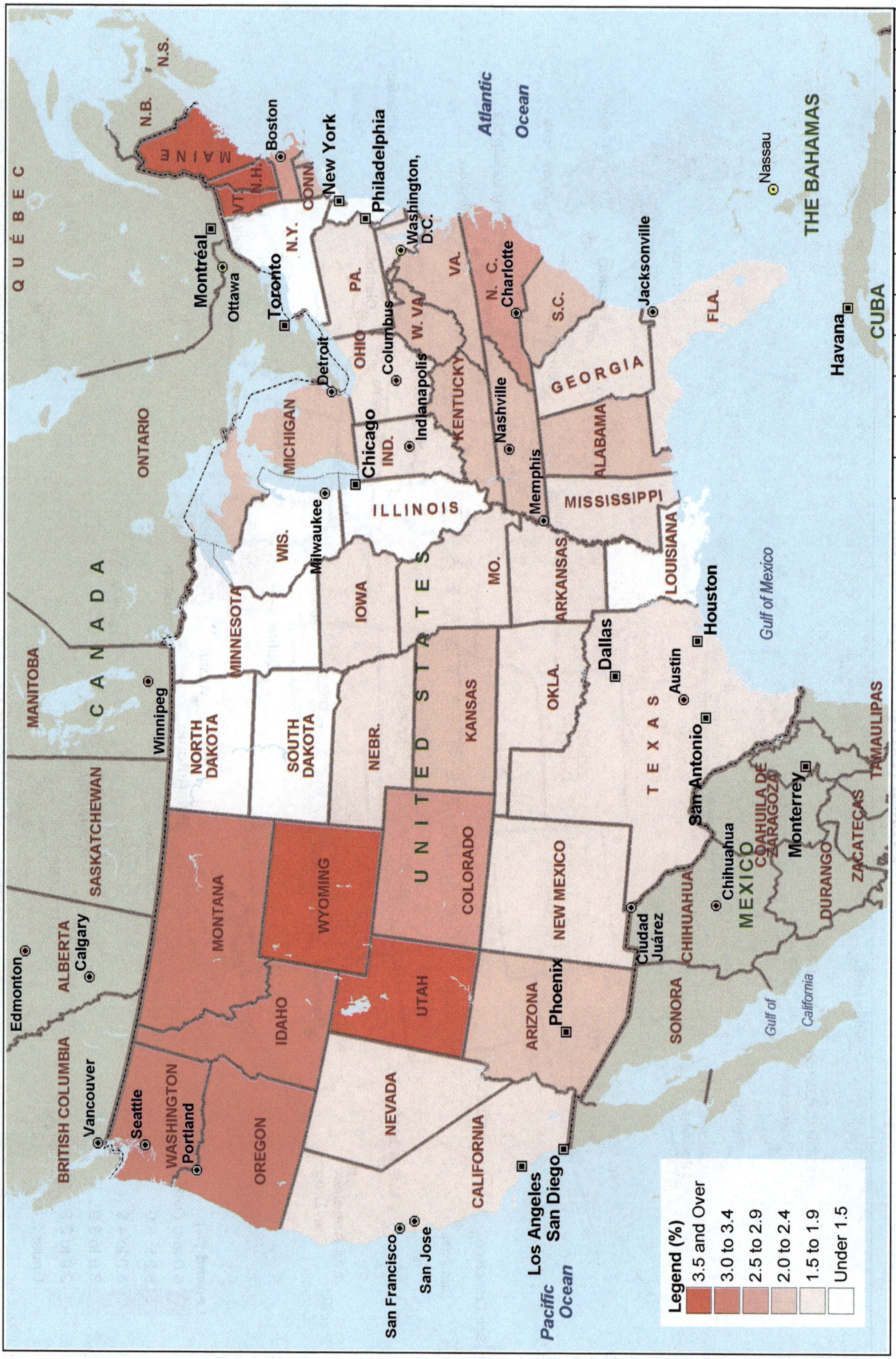

Legend (%)
- 3.5 and Over
- 3.0 to 3.4
- 2.5 to 2.9
- 2.0 to 2.4
- 1.5 to 1.9
- Under 1.5

Note: Figures include multiple ancestries reported.
Source: U.S. Census Bureau, American Community Survey, 2006–2010 Five-Year Estimates

Scotch-Irish Ancestry

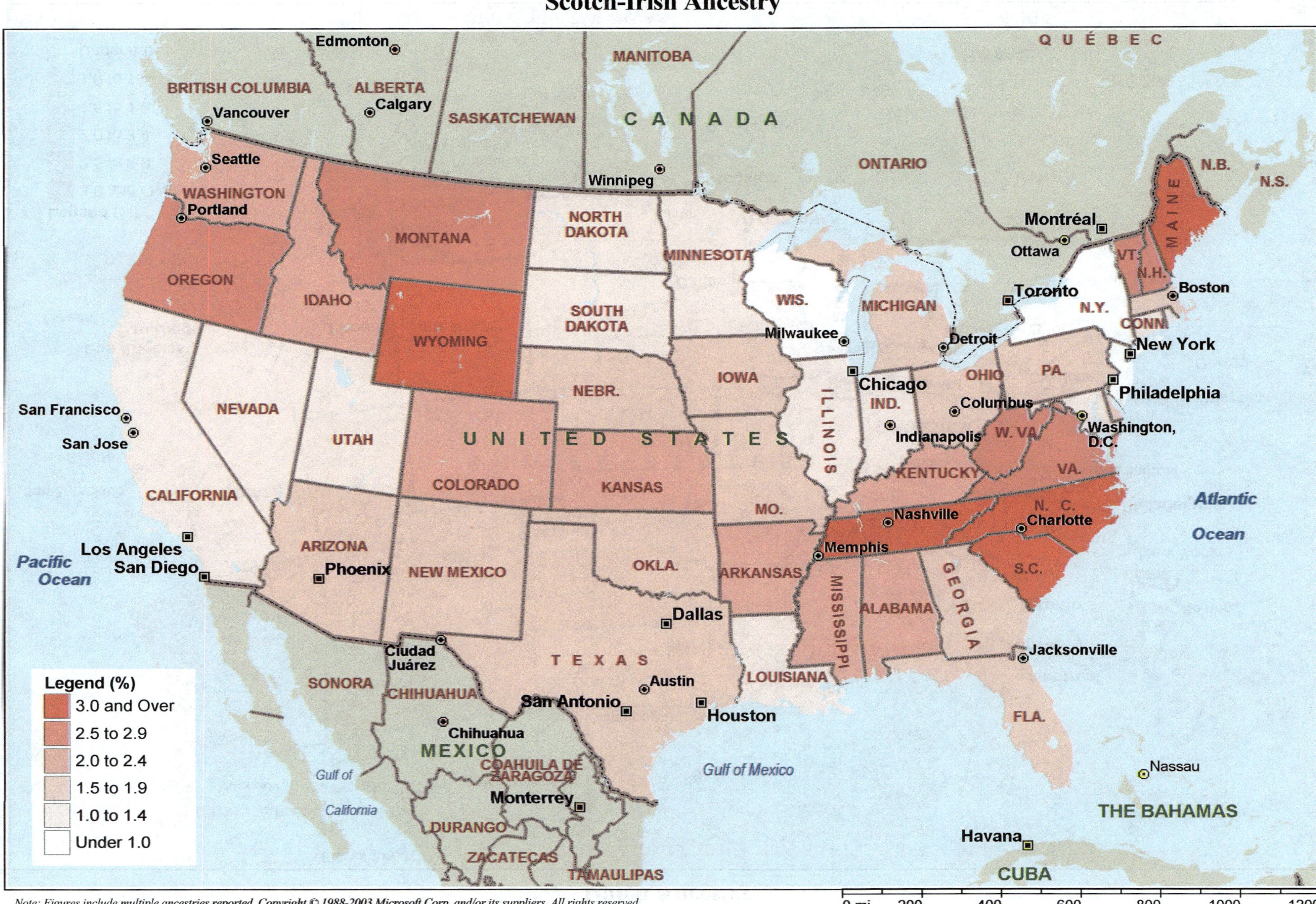

Note: Figures include multiple ancestries reported. Copyright © 1988-2003 Microsoft Corp. and/or its suppliers. All rights reserved.
Source: U.S. Census Bureau, American Community Survey, 2006–2010 Five-Year Estimates

Dutch Ancestry

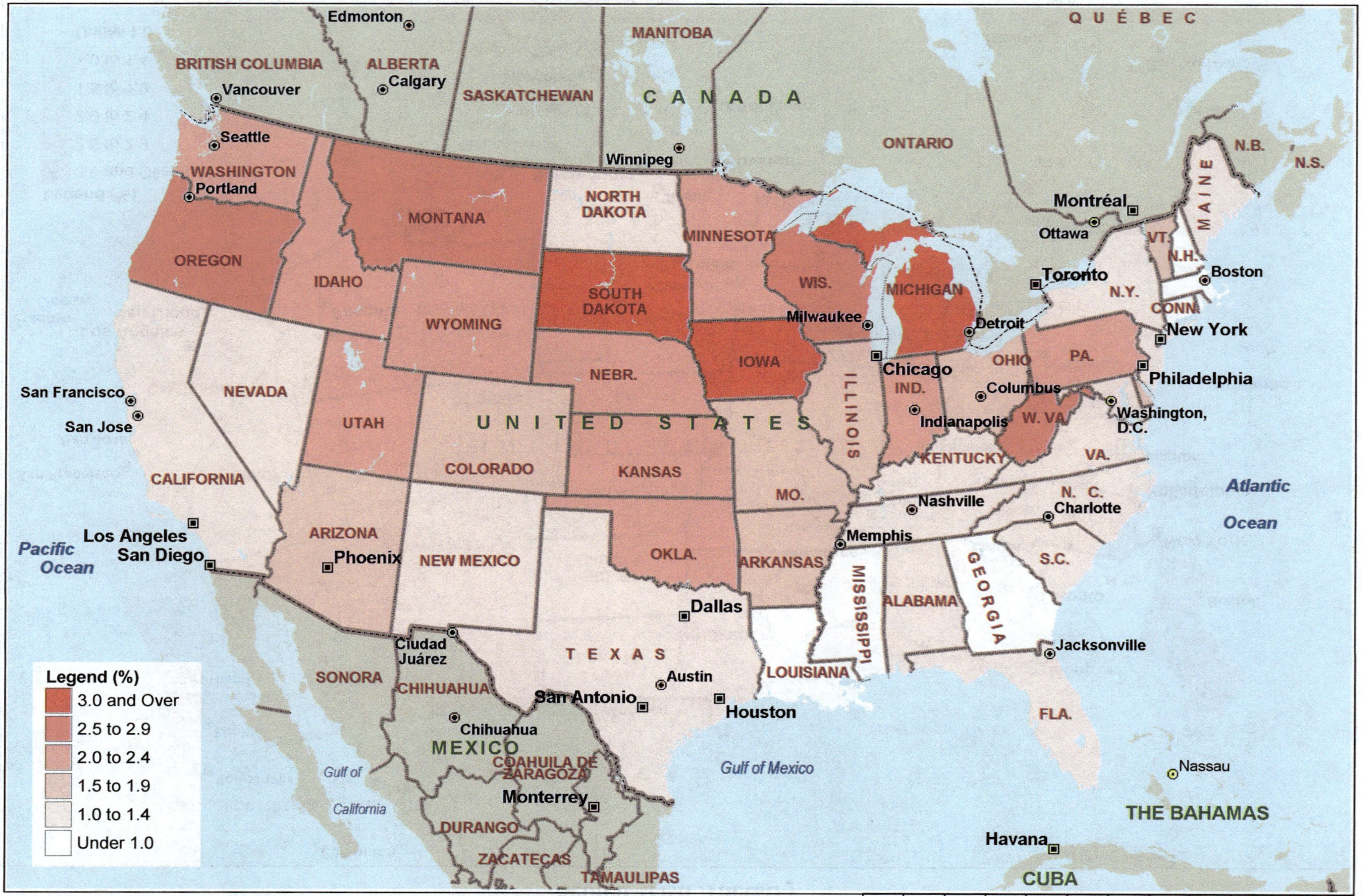

Legend (%)
- 3.0 and Over
- 2.5 to 2.9
- 2.0 to 2.4
- 1.5 to 1.9
- 1.0 to 1.4
- Under 1.0

Note: Figures include multiple ancestries reported.
Source: U.S. Census Bureau, American Community Survey, 2006–2010 Five-Year Estimates

Puerto Rican Ancestry

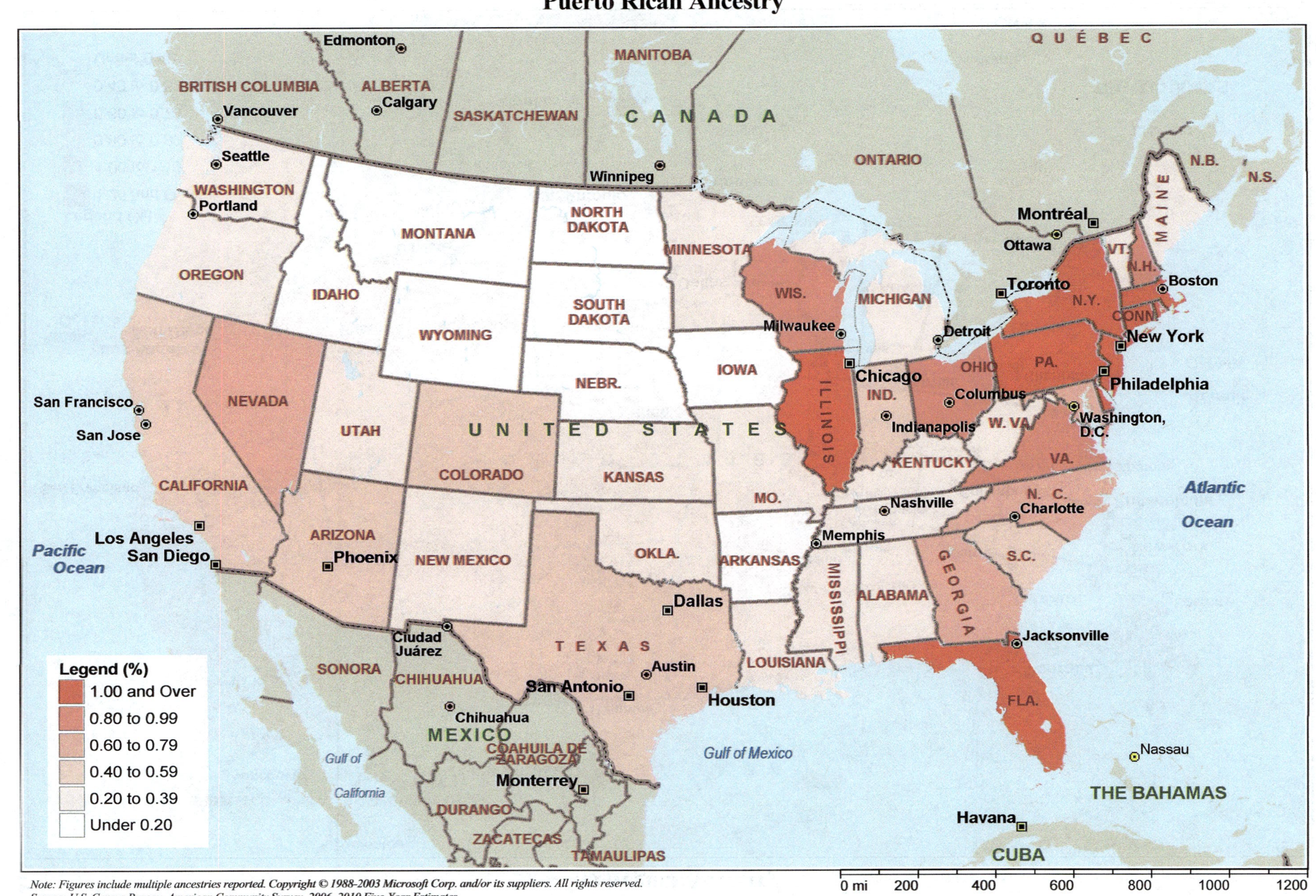

Note: Figures include multiple ancestries reported.
Source: U.S. Census Bureau, American Community Survey, 2006–2010 Five-Year Estimates

Norwegian Ancestry

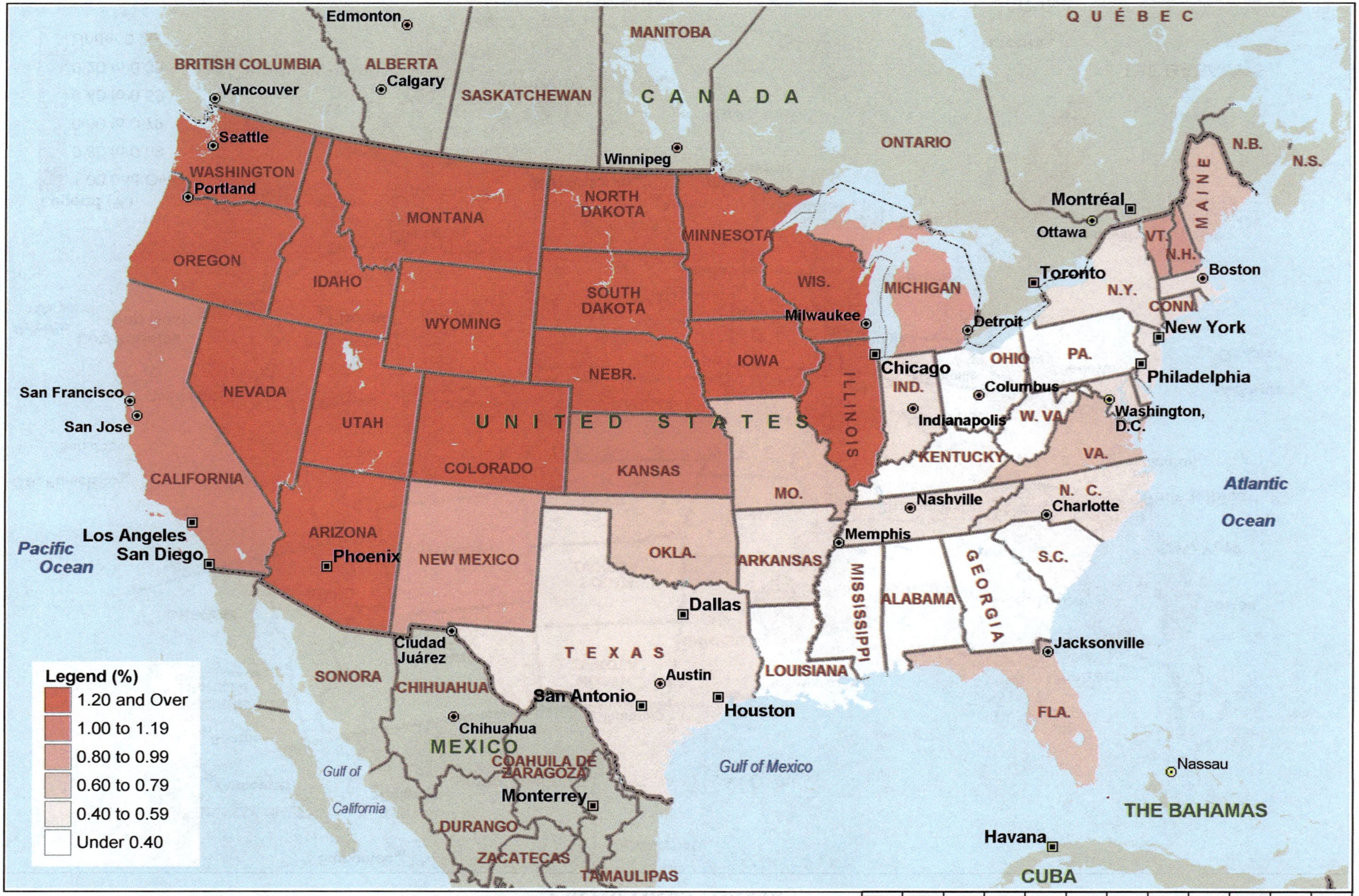

Note: Figures include multiple ancestries reported.
Source: U.S. Census Bureau, American Community Survey, 2006–2010 Five-Year Estimates

Swedish Ancestry

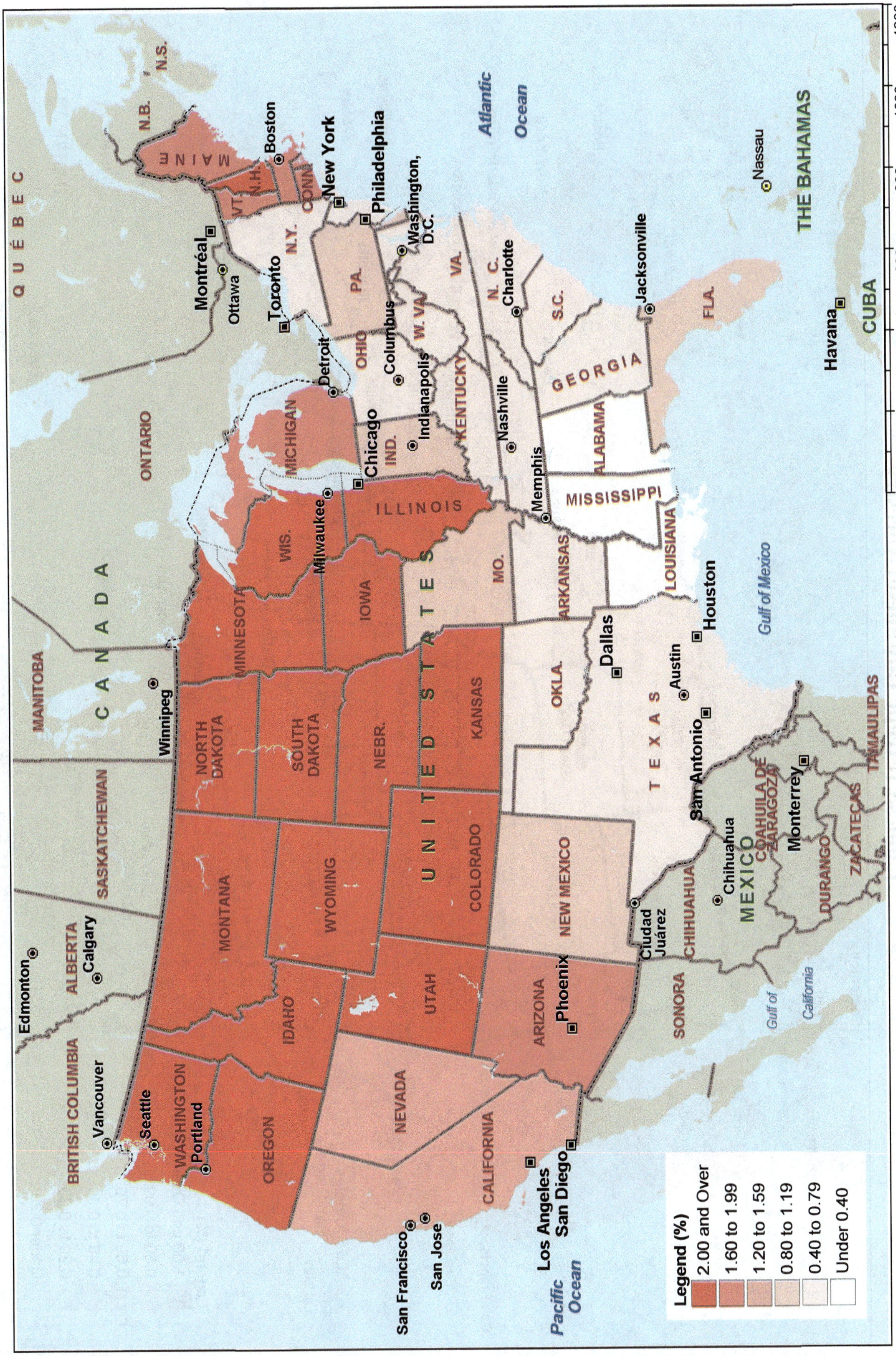

Legend (%)
- 2.00 and Over
- 1.60 to 1.99
- 1.20 to 1.59
- 0.80 to 1.19
- 0.40 to 0.79
- Under 0.40

Note: Figures include multiple ancestries reported.
Source: U.S. Census Bureau, American Community Survey, 2006–2010 Five-Year Estimates

Chinese, (except Taiwanese) Ancestry

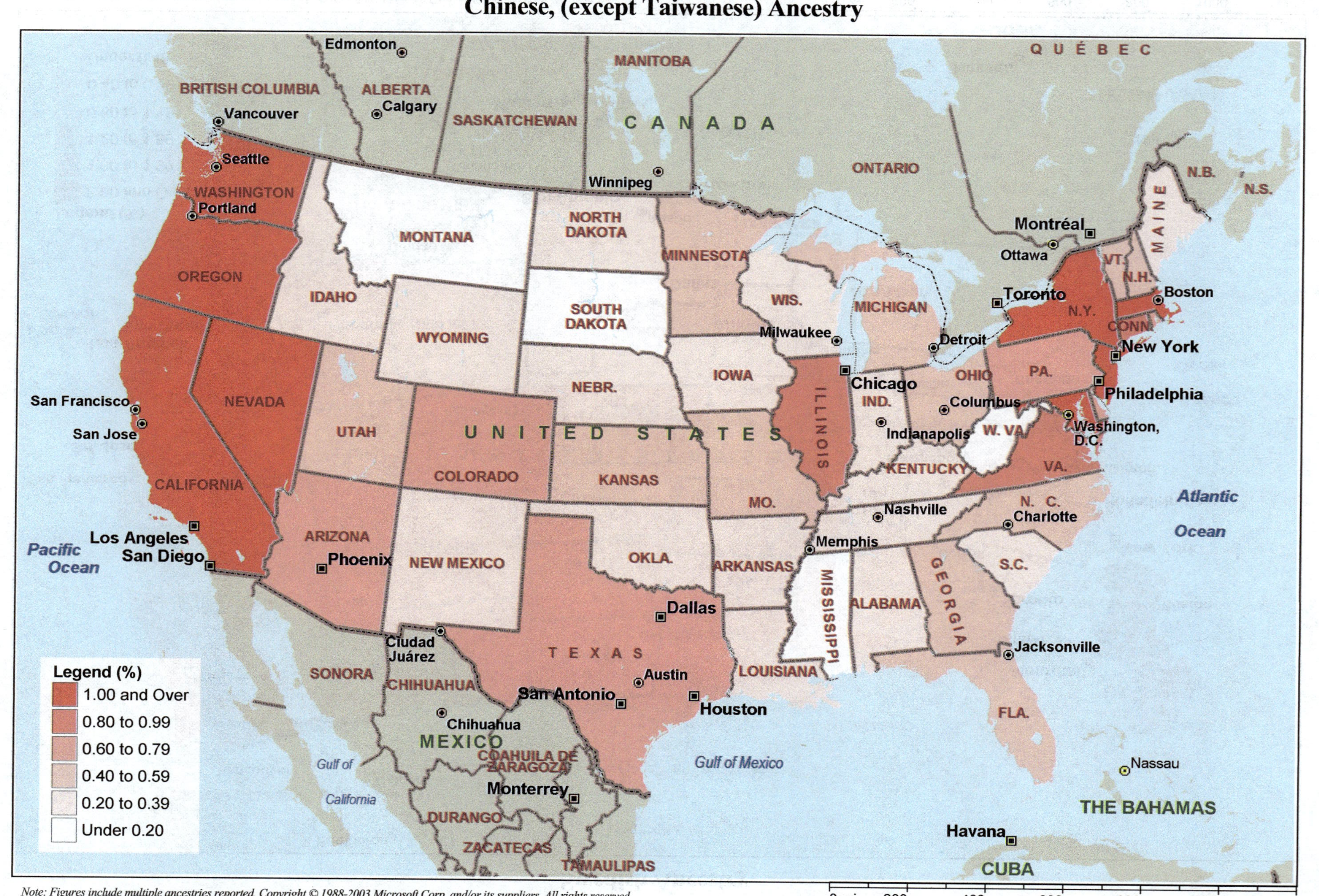

Note: Figures include multiple ancestries reported. Copyright © 1988-2003 Microsoft Corp. and/or its suppliers. All rights reserved.
Source: U.S. Census Bureau, American Community Survey, 2006–2010 Five-Year Estimates

Filipino Ancestry

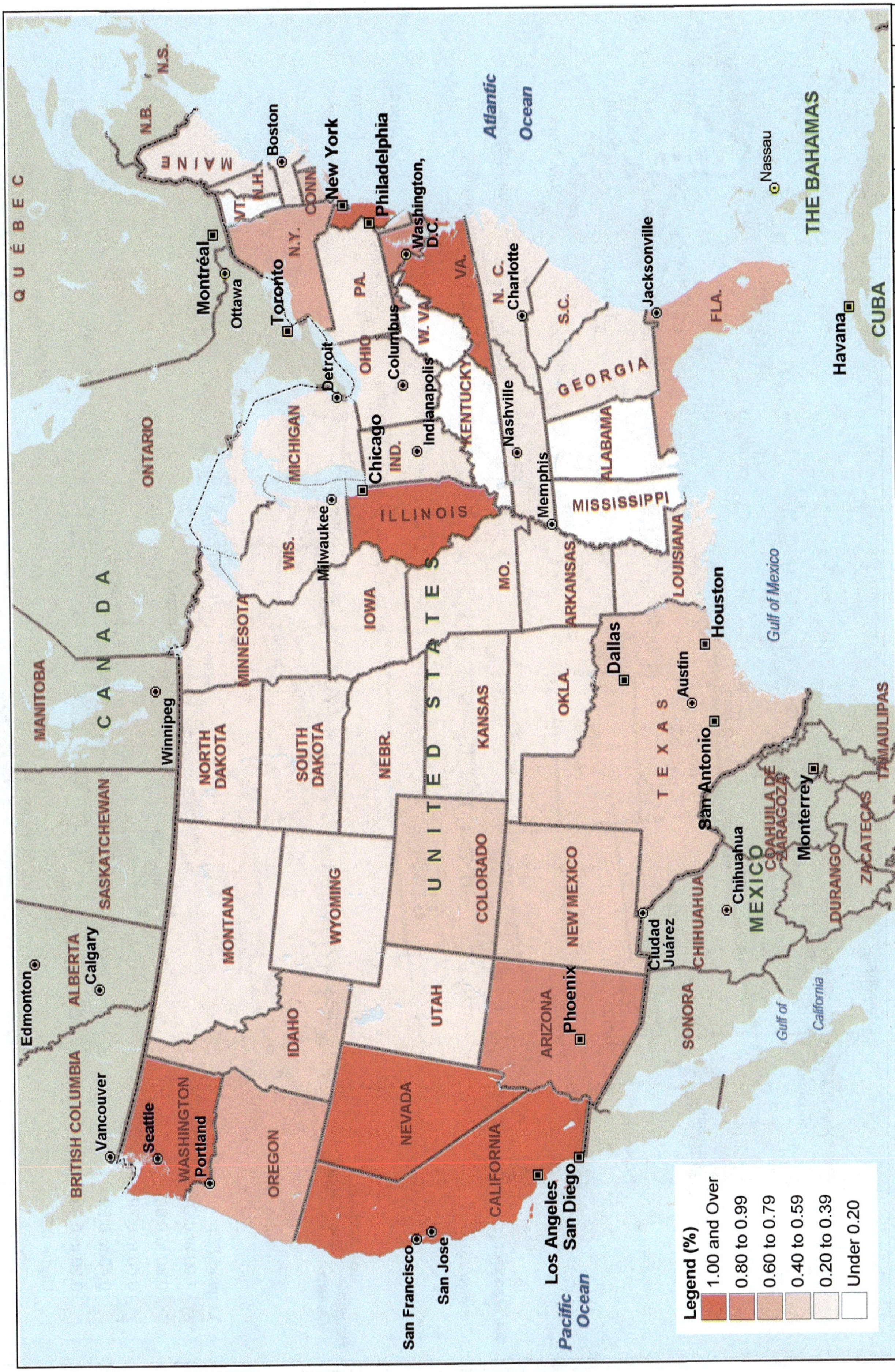

Legend (%)
- 1.00 and Over
- 0.80 to 0.99
- 0.60 to 0.79
- 0.40 to 0.59
- 0.20 to 0.39
- Under 0.20

Note: Figures include multiple ancestries reported.

Source: U.S. Census Bureau, American Community Survey, 2006–2010 Five-Year Estimates

Asian Indian Ancestry

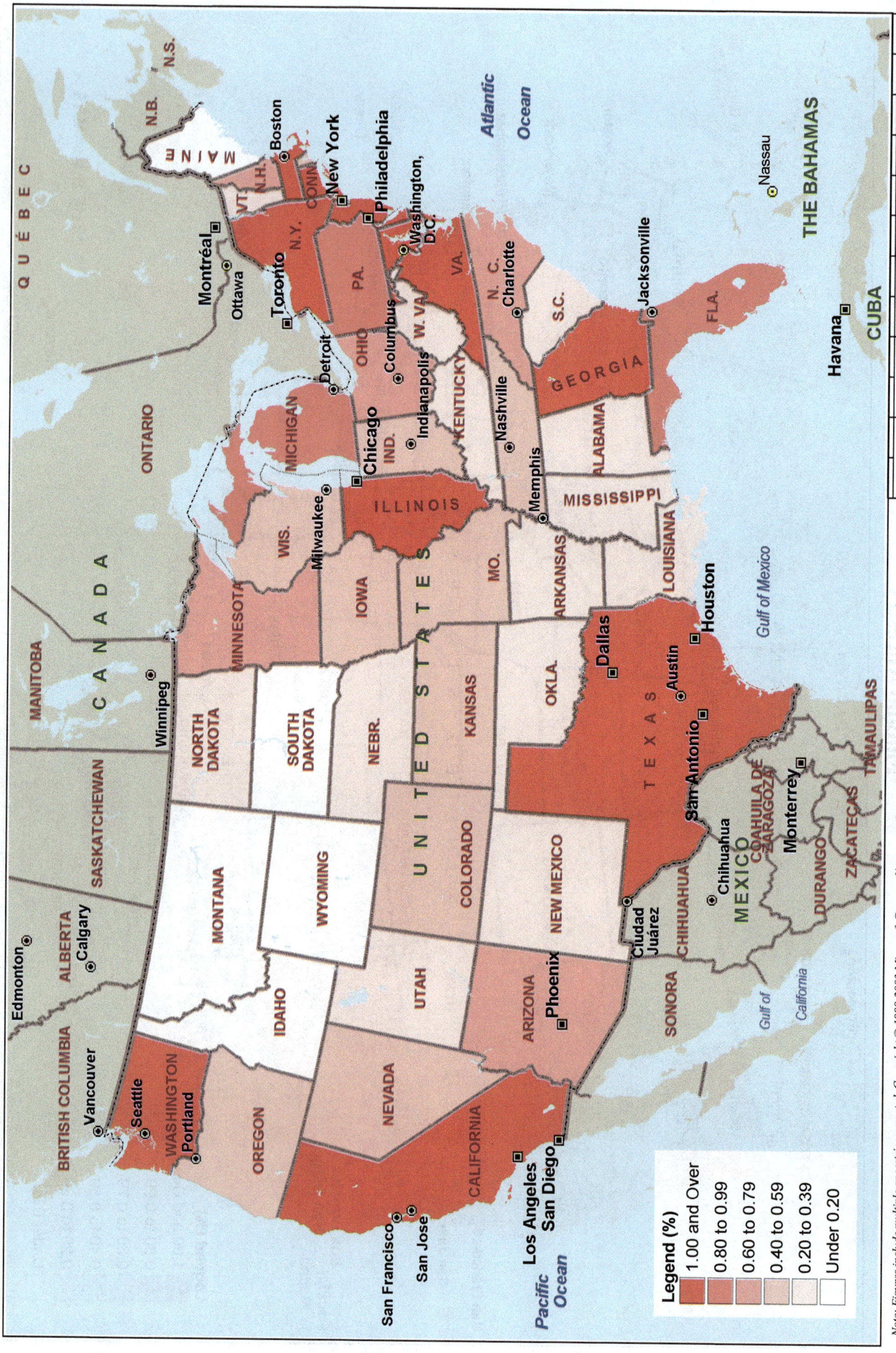

Legend (%)

- 1.00 and Over
- 0.80 to 0.99
- 0.60 to 0.79
- 0.40 to 0.59
- 0.20 to 0.39
- Under 0.20

Note: Figures include multiple ancestries reported.
Source: U.S. Census Bureau, American Community Survey, 2006–2010 Five-Year Estimates

Russian Ancestry

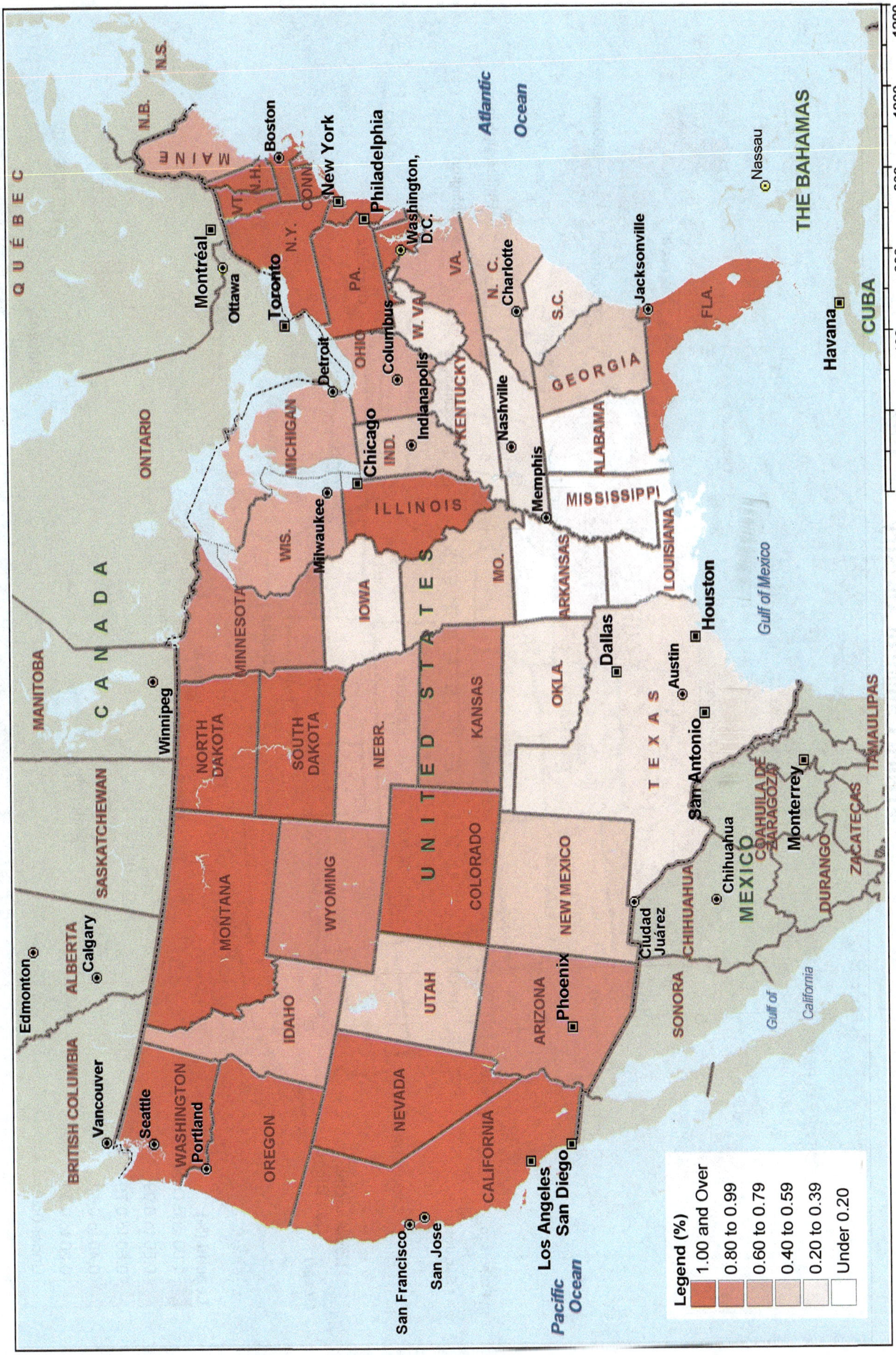

Note: Figures include multiple ancestries reported. Copyright © 1988-2003 Microsoft Corp. and/or its suppliers. All rights reserved.
Source: U.S. Census Bureau, American Community Survey, 2006–2010 Five-Year Estimates

French Canadian Ancestry

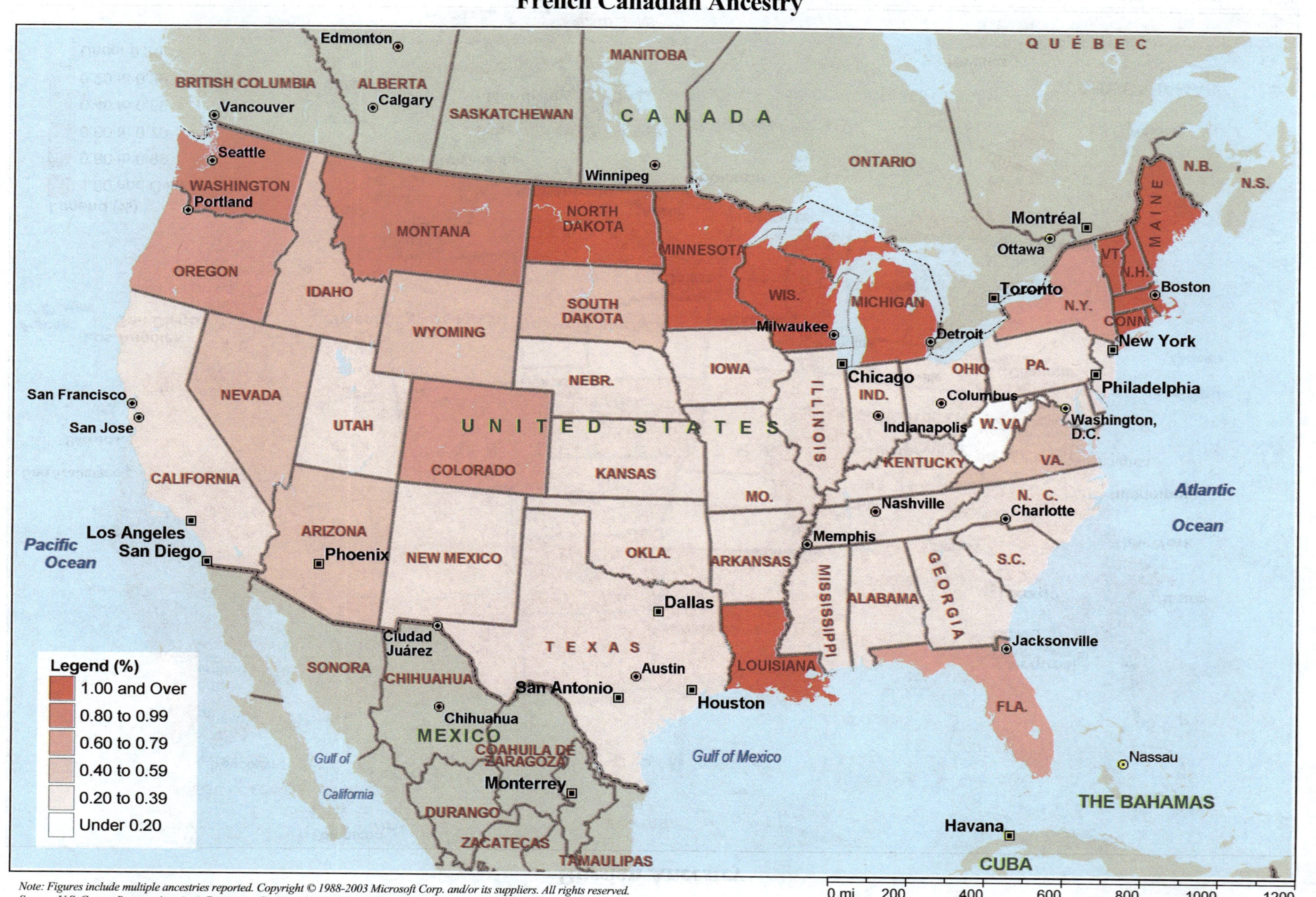

Note: Figures include multiple ancestries reported.

Source: U.S. Census Bureau, American Community Survey, 2006–2010 Five-Year Estimates

Welsh Ancestry

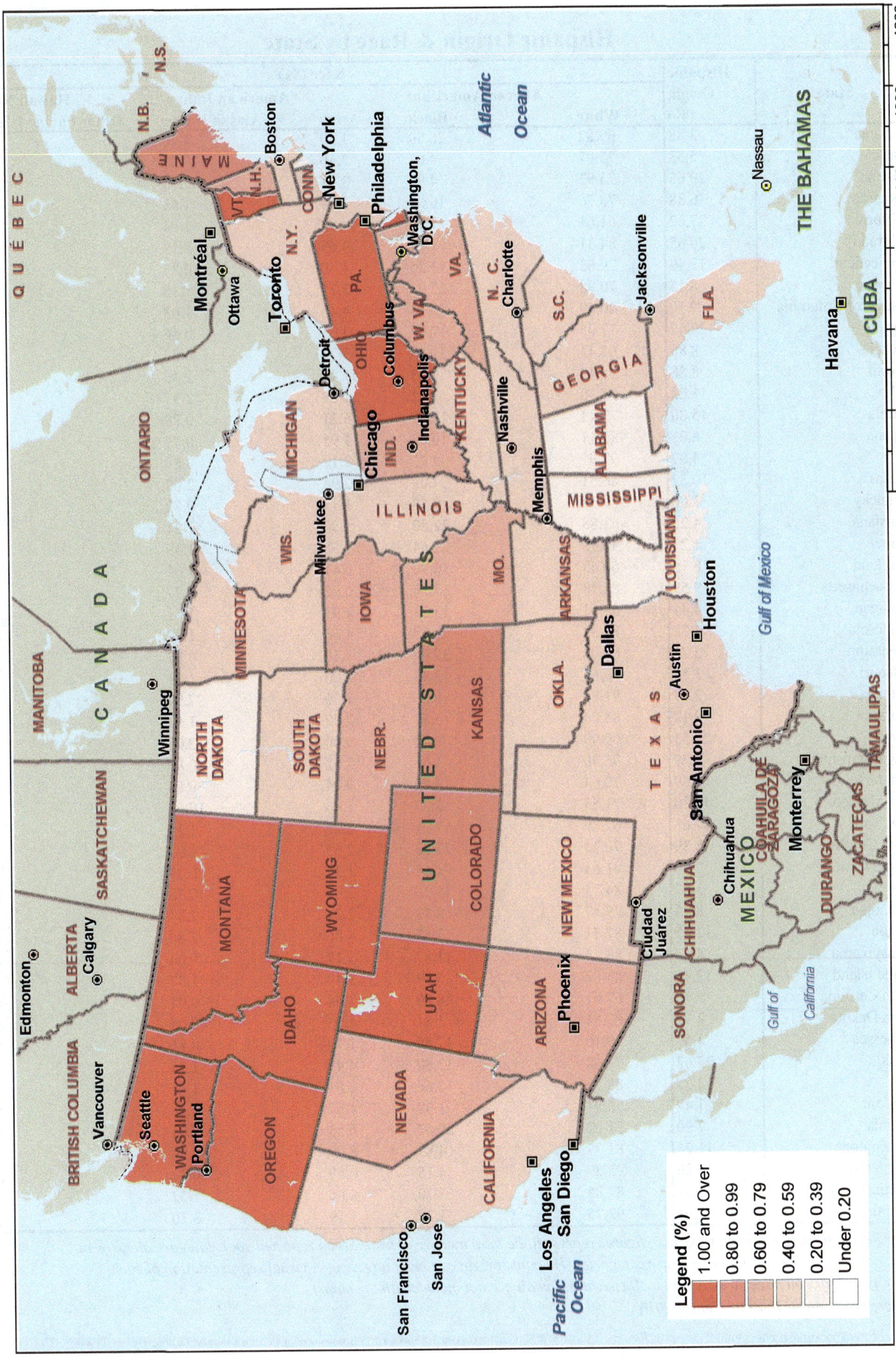

Legend (%)
- 1.00 and Over
- 0.80 to 0.99
- 0.60 to 0.79
- 0.40 to 0.59
- 0.20 to 0.39
- Under 0.20

Note: Figures include multiple ancestries reported.
Source: U.S. Census Bureau, American Community Survey, 2006–2010 Five-Year Estimates

Hispanic Origin & Race by State

State	Hispanic Origin (%)	Race (%)				
		White	African American/ Black	Asian	American Indian/ Alaska Native	Hawaii Native/ Other Pacific Islander
Alabama	3.88	69.82	26.80	1.40	1.20	0.12
Alaska	5.53	73.07	4.67	7.10	19.47	1.57
Arizona	29.65	75.92	4.99	3.61	5.53	0.39
Arkansas	6.38	78.76	16.07	1.54	1.63	0.27
California	37.62	61.61	7.20	14.92	1.94	0.77
Colorado	20.65	84.31	4.97	3.69	2.14	0.30
Connecticut	13.40	79.63	11.35	4.40	0.87	0.15
Delaware	8.15	70.98	22.93	3.75	1.10	0.14
District of Columbia	9.10	40.49	52.24	4.46	1.08	0.22
Florida	22.47	77.06	17.02	3.05	0.86	0.21
Georgia	8.81	61.43	31.53	3.77	0.87	0.16
Hawaii	8.88	41.49	2.85	57.41	2.46	26.16
Idaho	11.22	91.40	1.02	1.89	2.32	0.32
Illinois	15.80	73.44	15.39	5.21	0.79	0.11
Indiana	6.01	86.11	10.09	1.95	0.77	0.10
Iowa	4.97	92.91	3.72	2.12	0.80	0.13
Kansas	10.52	86.51	7.09	2.94	2.07	0.17
Kentucky	3.06	89.38	8.67	1.43	0.72	0.12
Louisiana	4.25	63.88	32.80	1.86	1.21	0.11
Maine	1.27	96.73	1.64	1.38	1.39	0.07
Maryland	8.15	60.43	30.90	6.41	1.02	0.17
Massachusetts	9.59	82.48	7.76	6.02	0.77	0.16
Michigan	4.41	81.01	15.23	2.93	1.41	0.09
Minnesota	4.72	87.39	6.18	4.66	1.92	0.12
Mississipp	2.75	60.08	37.60	1.10	0.87	0.09
Missouri	3.55	84.67	12.48	2.06	1.21	0.19
Montana	2.89	91.84	0.80	1.06	7.94	0.18
Nebraska	9.17	88.03	5.42	2.22	1.63	0.15
Nevada	26.53	69.99	9.42	9.00	2.07	1.22
New Hampshire	2.79	95.40	1.65	2.62	0.80	0.09
New Jersey	17.69	70.64	14.79	9.04	0.80	0.15
New Mexico	46.30	71.53	2.77	1.96	10.66	0.23
New York	17.63	67.89	17.21	8.15	1.14	0.19
North Caroline	8.39	70.24	22.56	2.65	1.93	0.15
North Dakota	2.00	91.64	1.65	1.37	6.39	0.12
Ohio	3.07	84.53	13.36	2.07	0.78	0.09
Oklahoma	8.85	77.47	8.73	2.24	12.87	0.22
Oregon	11.75	87.11	2.57	4.86	2.85	0.67
Pennsylvania	5.67	83.48	11.87	3.17	0.64	0.10
Rhode Island	12.41	83.82	7.39	3.49	1.37	0.21
South Carolina	5.10	67.61	28.80	1.64	0.91	0.13
South Dakota	2.72	87.84	1.81	1.25	10.08	0.11
Tennessee	4.57	79.10	17.45	1.79	0.86	0.12
Texas	37.62	72.68	12.60	4.42	1.25	0.19
Utah	12.97	88.56	1.56	2.81	1.81	1.33
Vermont	1.47	96.94	1.49	1.67	1.18	0.07
Virginia	7.90	71.02	20.67	6.53	1.01	0.19
Washington	11.24	81.37	4.83	8.99	2.96	1.05
West Virginia	1.20	95.29	4.15	0.89	0.72	0.07
Wisconsin	5.91	87.85	7.10	2.66	1.52	0.09
Wyoming	8.91	92.75	1.29	1.19	3.30	0.19

Note: For ethnicities based on race data, figures represent the total number of people who reported each category alone or in combination with one or more other race categories; Hispanic origin can be of any race; A visual representation of each ethnicity appears on pages 6 through 11 (Alaska and Hawaii are not included on the maps).

Source: U.S. Census Bureau, Census 2010

Hispanic Origin

Legend (%)
- 15.0 and Over
- 12.0 to 14.9
- 9.0 to 11.9
- 6.0 to 8.9
- 3.0 to 5.9
- Under 3.0

Note: Hispanic origin can be of any race. Copyright © 1988-2003 Microsoft Corp. and/or its suppliers. All rights reserved.
Source: U.S. Census Bureau, Census 2010

Race: White

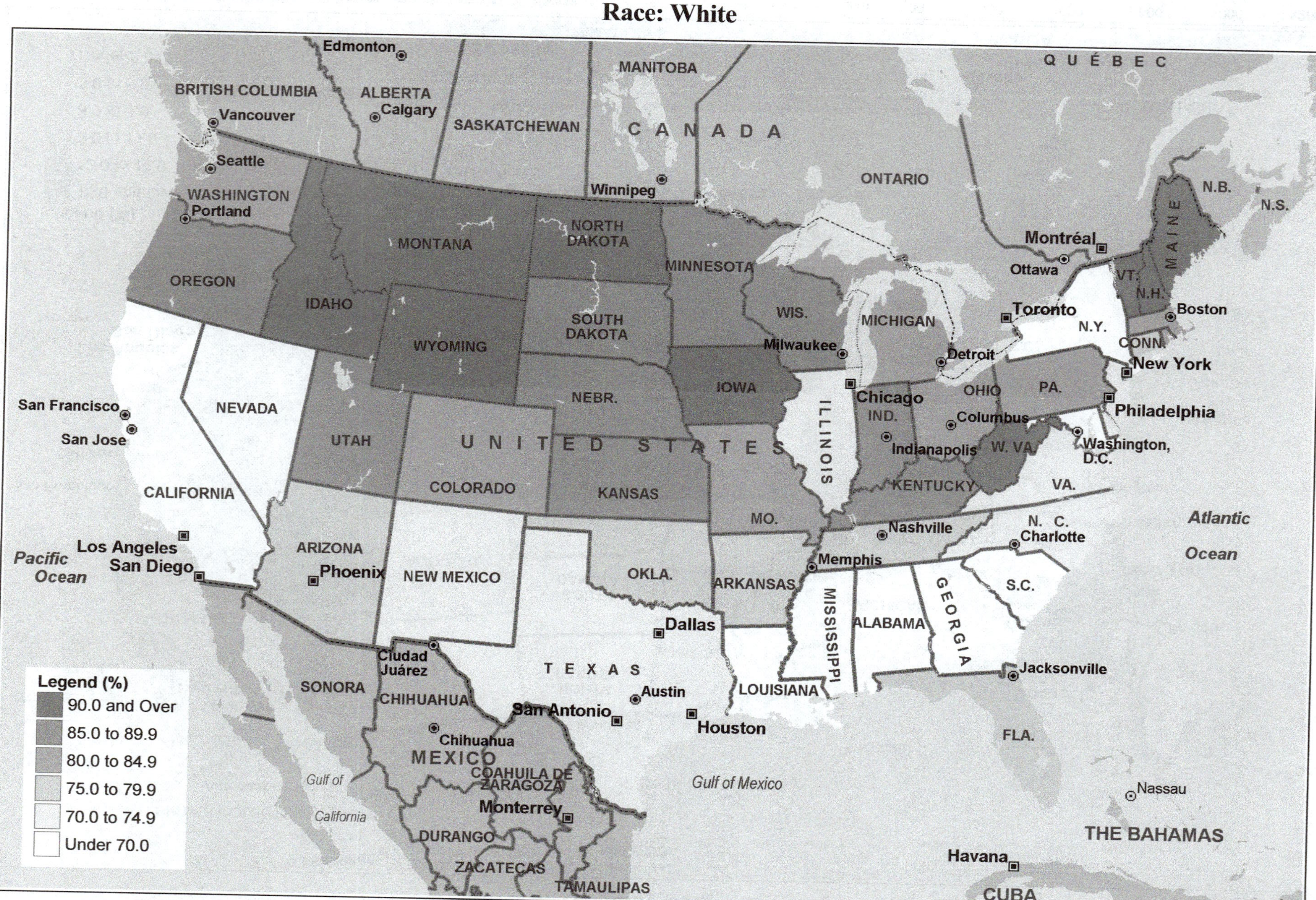

Note: Figures include race alone or in combination with any other race.
Source: U.S. Census Bureau, Census 2010

Legend (%)
- 15.0 and Over
- 12.0 to 14.9
- 9.0 to 11.9
- 6.0 to 8.9
- 3.0 to 5.9
- Under 3.0

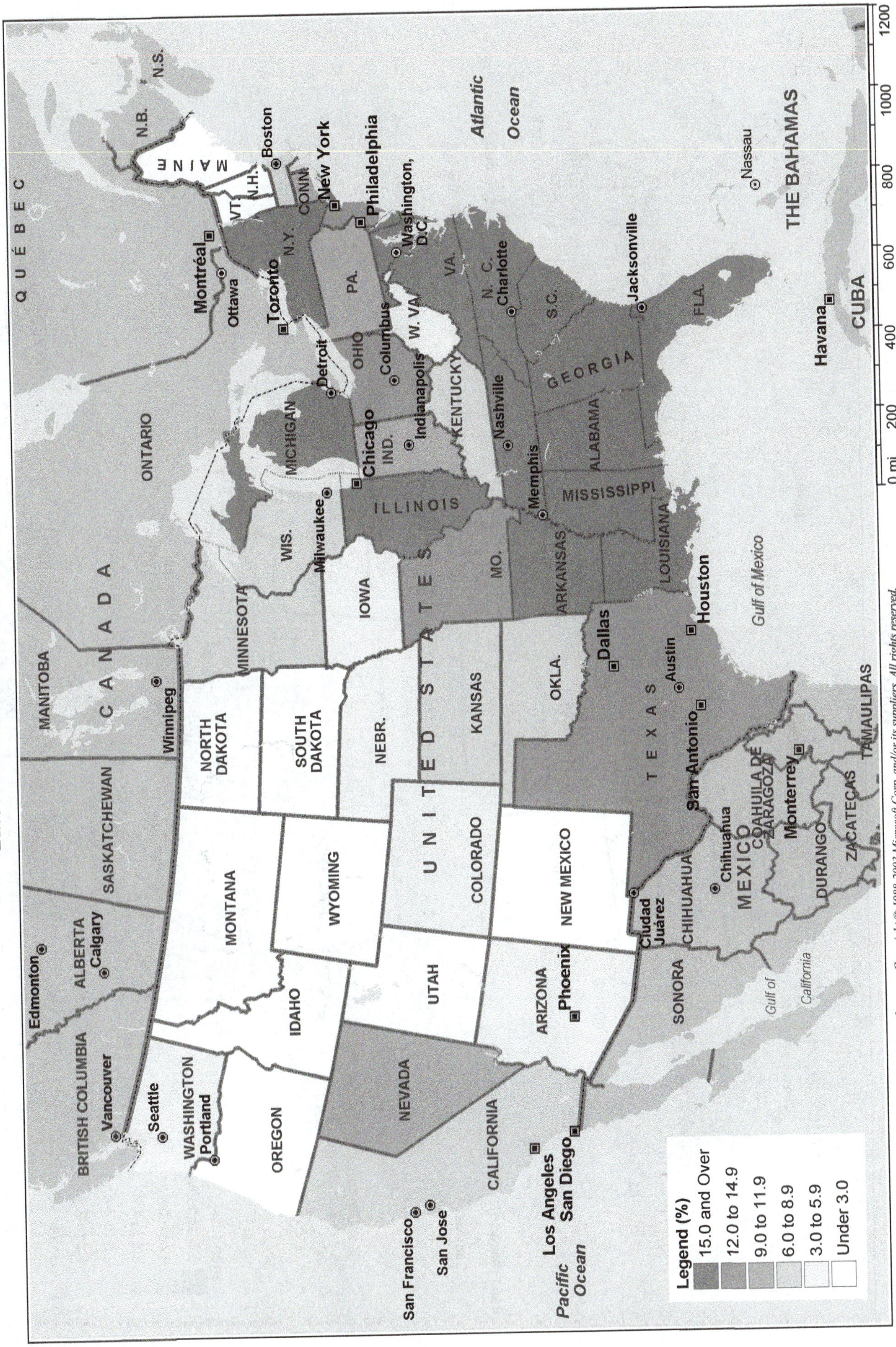

Note: Figures include race alone or in combination with any other race.
Source: U.S. Census Bureau, Census 2010

Race: Asian

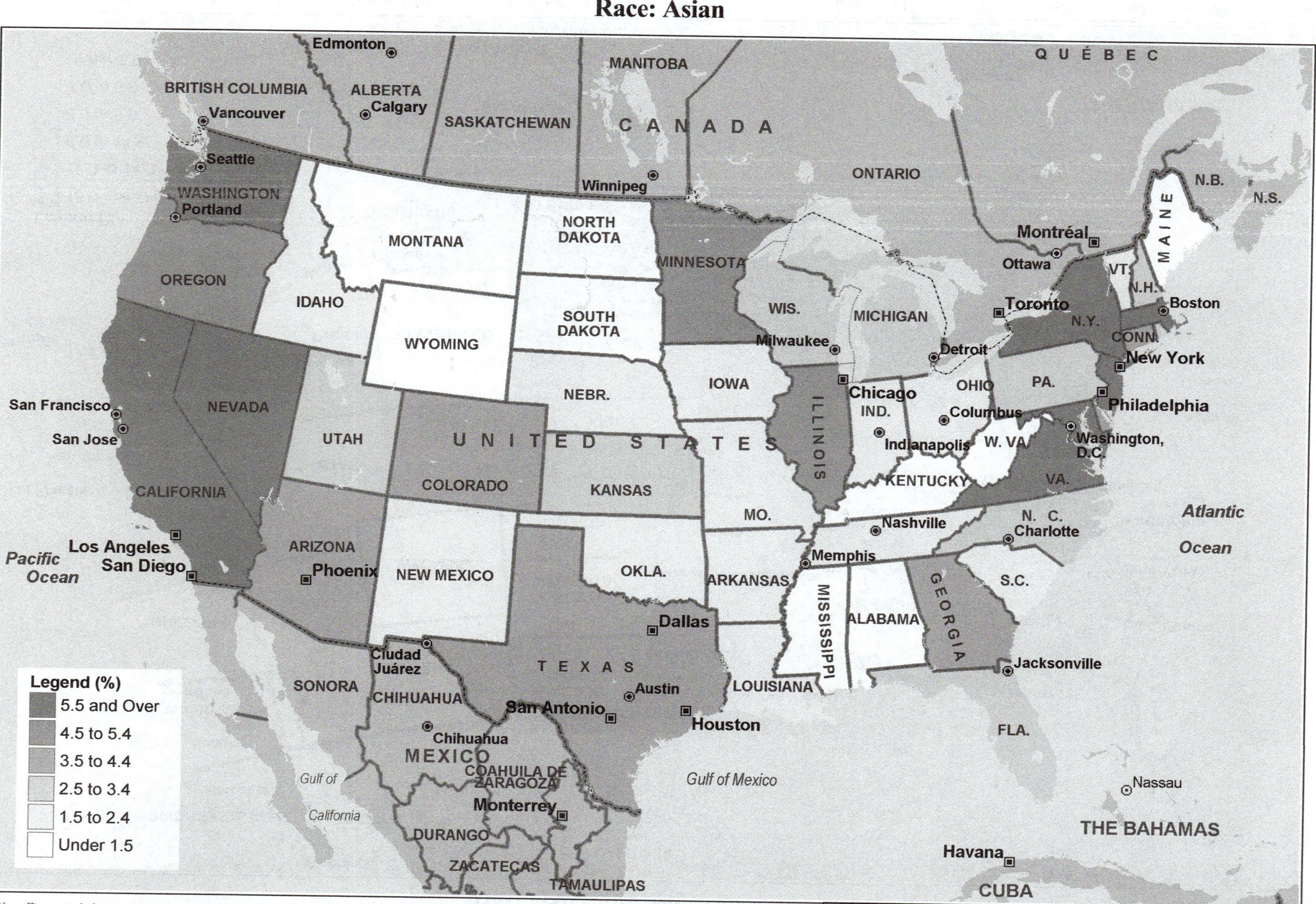

Note: Figures include race alone or in combination with any other race.
Source: U.S. Census Bureau, Census 2010

Race: American Indian/Alaska Native

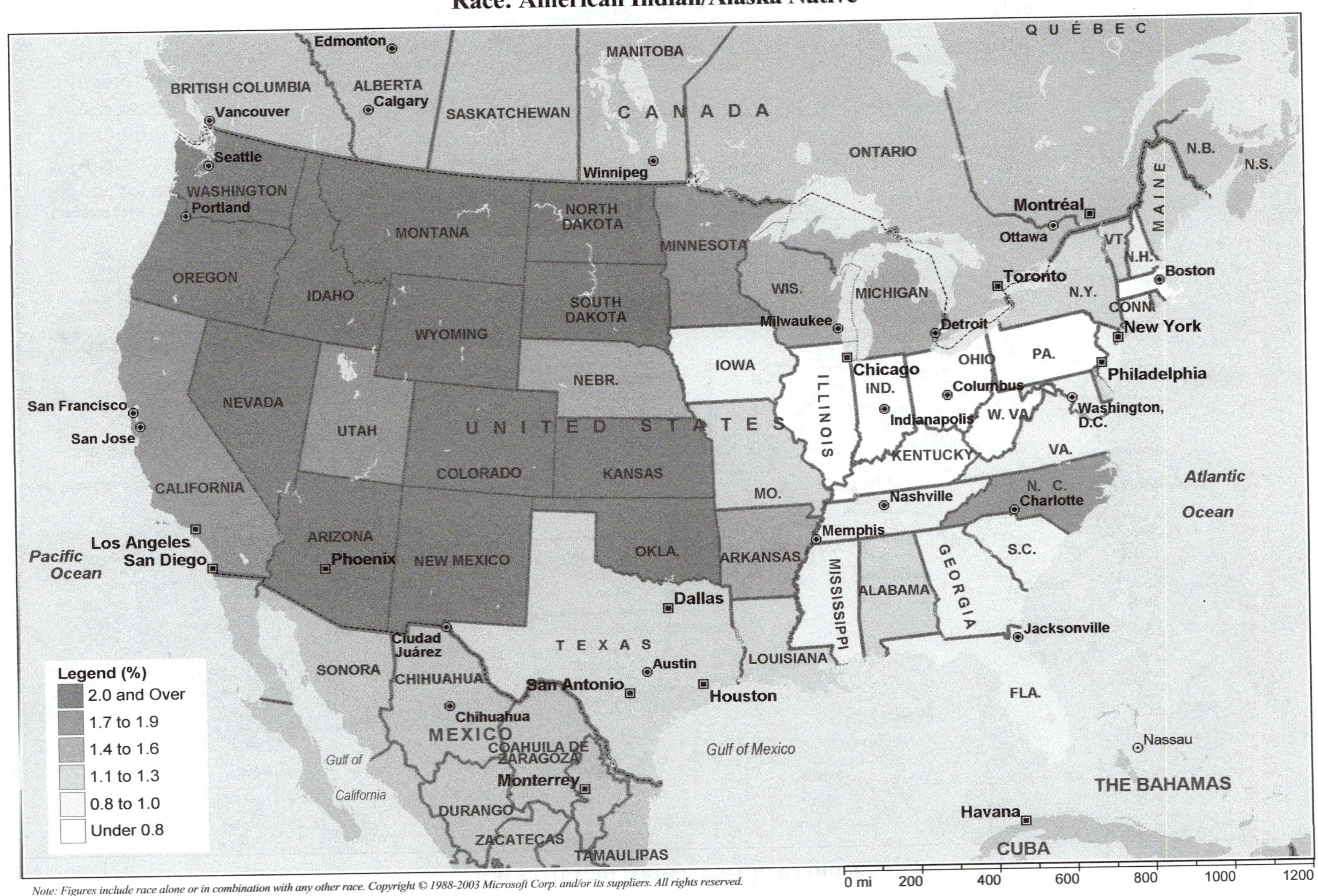

Note: Figures include race alone or in combination with any other race. Copyright © 1988-2003 Microsoft Corp. and/or its suppliers. All rights reserved.
Source: U.S. Census Bureau, Census 2010

Race: Hawaii Native/Pacific Islander

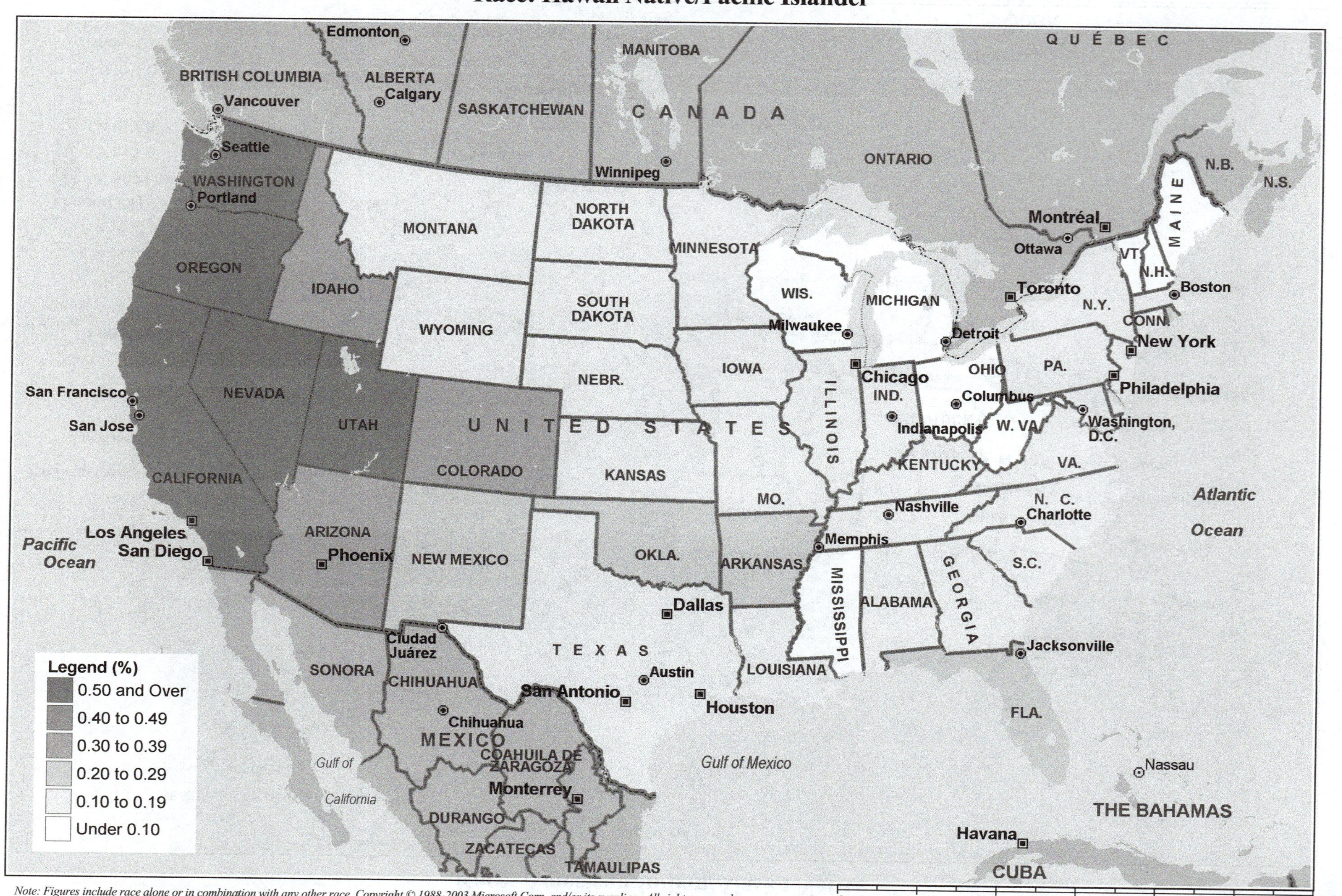

Note: Figures include race alone or in combination with any other race. Copyright © 1988-2003 Microsoft Corp. and/or its suppliers. All rights reserved.
Source: U.S. Census Bureau, Census 2010

SECTION TWO:
State & Place Population Profiles

ALABAMA

Place Type: State
Population: 4,779,736†

Ancestry‡	Population	%
Afghan (44)	59	<0.01
African, Sub-Saharan (31,086)	35,394	0.75
African (27,271)	30,949	0.66
Ethiopian (119)	217	<0.01
Ghanaian (93)	93	<0.01
Kenyan (881)	921	0.02
Liberian (85)	97	<0.01
Nigerian (1,322)	1,560	0.03
Sierra Leonean (0)	34	<0.01
Somalian (0)	11	<0.01
South African (301)	378	0.01
Sudanese (456)	456	0.01
Ugandan (35)	102	<0.01
Zimbabwean (53)	53	<0.01
Other Sub-Saharan African (470)	523	0.01
Albanian (106)	164	<0.01
Alsatian (9)	122	<0.01
American (629,152)	629,152	13.35
Arab (7,116)	10,369	0.22
Arab (1,062)	1,358	0.03
Egyptian (567)	757	0.02
Iraqi (214)	278	0.01
Jordanian (840)	924	0.02
Lebanese (2,398)	4,477	0.09
Moroccan (585)	603	0.01
Palestinian (515)	584	0.01
Syrian (134)	542	0.01
Other Arab (801)	846	0.02
Armenian (207)	522	0.01
Assyrian/Chaldean/Syriac (17)	32	<0.01
Australian (370)	984	0.02
Austrian (1,248)	4,068	0.09
Basque (36)	68	<0.01
Belgian (467)	1,332	0.03
Brazilian (501)	864	0.02
British (10,528)	17,673	0.38
Bulgarian (211)	346	0.01
Cajun (905)	1,592	0.03
Canadian (2,220)	3,696	0.08
Carpatho Rusyn (17)	26	<0.01
Celtic (372)	666	0.01
Croatian (627)	1,305	0.03
Czech (2,019)	5,484	0.12
Czechoslovakian (992)	1,883	0.04
Danish (1,176)	4,771	0.10
Dutch (11,550)	56,214	1.19
Eastern European (832)	887	0.02
English (244,490)	451,869	9.59
Estonian (21)	81	<0.01
European (33,246)	38,692	0.82
Finnish (717)	2,304	0.05
French, ex. Basque (23,147)	90,000	1.91
French Canadian (4,719)	10,509	0.22
German (125,153)	364,083	7.73
German Russian (115)	134	<0.01
Greek (4,388)	8,986	0.19
Guyanese (101)	149	<0.01
Hungarian (1,308)	4,869	0.10
Icelander (88)	173	<0.01
Iranian (1,526)	1,940	0.04
Irish (190,968)	491,029	10.42
Israeli (282)	353	0.01
Italian (36,011)	83,808	1.78
Latvian (179)	317	0.01
Lithuanian (602)	1,560	0.03
Luxemburger (91)	220	<0.01
Macedonian (75)	101	<0.01
Maltese (10)	122	<0.01
New Zealander (132)	215	<0.01
Northern European (1,233)	1,401	0.03
Norwegian (5,904)	15,596	0.33
Pennsylvania German (356)	595	0.01
Polish (11,776)	33,111	0.70
Portuguese (1,258)	4,011	0.09
Romanian (976)	1,435	0.03
Russian (2,974)	8,648	0.18
Scandinavian (1,490)	3,322	0.07
Scotch-Irish (63,857)	113,138	2.40
Scottish (43,950)	99,232	2.11
Serbian (138)	277	0.01
Slavic (180)	698	0.01
Slovak (518)	1,596	0.03
Slovene (170)	345	0.01
Swedish (5,603)	18,238	0.39
Swiss (1,388)	4,476	0.09
Turkish (1,215)	1,393	0.03
Ukrainian (1,219)	2,410	0.05
Welsh (4,625)	18,106	0.38
West Indian, ex. Hispanic (5,167)	7,971	0.17
Bahamian (144)	264	0.01
Barbadian (70)	105	<0.01
Belizean (56)	116	<0.01
Bermudan (80)	96	<0.01
British West Indian (98)	183	<0.01
Dutch West Indian (215)	774	0.02
Haitian (934)	1,121	0.02
Jamaican (2,298)	3,378	0.07
Trinidadian/Tobagonian (233)	504	0.01
U.S. Virgin Islander (141)	141	<0.01
West Indian (882)	1,178	0.02
Other West Indian (16)	111	<0.01
Yugoslavian (452)	1,097	0.02

Hispanic Origin	Population	%
Hispanic or Latino (of any race)	185,602	3.88
Central American, ex. Mexican	22,800	0.48
Costa Rican	504	0.01
Guatemalan	14,282	0.30
Honduran	3,280	0.07
Nicaraguan	739	0.02
Panamanian	1,450	0.03
Salvadoran	2,419	0.05
Other Central American	126	<0.01
Cuban	4,064	0.09
Dominican Republic	852	0.02
Mexican	122,911	2.57
Puerto Rican	12,225	0.26
South American	5,938	0.12
Argentinean	496	0.01
Bolivian	292	0.01
Chilean	451	0.01
Colombian	2,052	0.04
Ecuadorian	466	0.01
Paraguayan	121	<0.01
Peruvian	1,116	0.02
Uruguayan	129	<0.01
Venezuelan	757	0.02
Other South American	58	<0.01
Other Hispanic or Latino	16,812	0.35

Race*	Population	%
African-American/Black (1,251,311)	1,281,118	26.80
Not Hispanic (1,244,437)	1,271,554	26.60
Hispanic (6,874)	9,564	0.20
American Indian/Alaska Native (28,218)	57,118	1.20
Not Hispanic (25,907)	52,863	1.11
Hispanic (2,311)	4,255	0.09
Alaska Athabascan *(Ala. Nat.)* (25)	40	<0.01
Aleut *(Alaska Native)* (40)	61	<0.01
Apache (148)	440	0.01
Arapaho (11)	25	<0.01
Blackfeet (150)	738	0.02
Canadian/French Am. Ind. (34)	80	<0.01
Central American Ind. (147)	182	<0.01
Cherokee (9,438)	21,144	0.44
Cheyenne (15)	51	<0.01
Chickasaw (102)	276	0.01
Chippewa (194)	368	0.01
Choctaw (3,397)	4,513	0.09
Colville (17)	18	<0.01
Comanche (44)	101	<0.01
Cree (23)	65	<0.01
Creek (3,516)	5,905	0.12
Crow (17)	74	<0.01
Delaware (29)	66	<0.01
Hopi (9)	24	<0.01
Houma (71)	89	<0.01
Inupiat *(Alaska Native)* (28)	72	<0.01
Iroquois (123)	276	0.01
Kiowa (13)	21	<0.01
Lumbee (163)	239	0.01
Menominee (1)	5	<0.01
Mexican American Ind. (717)	970	0.02
Navajo (122)	251	0.01
Osage (13)	33	<0.01
Ottawa (24)	45	<0.01
Paiute (7)	12	<0.01
Pima (11)	16	<0.01
Potawatomi (57)	90	<0.01
Pueblo (44)	72	<0.01
Puget Sound Salish (10)	14	<0.01
Seminole (65)	196	<0.01
Shoshone (4)	19	<0.01
Sioux (242)	540	0.01
South American Ind. (63)	125	<0.01
Spanish American Ind. (45)	84	<0.01
Tlingit-Haida *(Alaska Native)* (29)	38	<0.01
Tohono O'Odham (14)	18	<0.01
Tsimshian *(Alaska Native)* (3)	4	<0.01
Ute (4)	13	<0.01
Yakama (7)	12	<0.01
Yaqui (20)	55	<0.01
Yuman (9)	13	<0.01
Yup'ik *(Alaska Native)* (15)	27	<0.01
Asian (53,595)	67,036	1.40
Not Hispanic (52,937)	65,311	1.37
Hispanic (658)	1,725	0.04
Bangladeshi (355)	395	0.01
Bhutanese (1)	1	<0.01
Burmese (127)	146	<0.01
Cambodian (700)	827	0.02
Chinese, ex. Taiwanese (8,965)	10,637	0.22
Filipino (4,952)	8,224	0.17
Hmong (108)	122	<0.01
Indian (13,036)	14,951	0.31
Indonesian (231)	362	0.01
Japanese (2,391)	4,336	0.09
Korean (8,320)	10,624	0.22
Laotian (1,306)	1,551	0.03
Malaysian (96)	151	<0.01
Nepalese (403)	430	0.01
Pakistani (1,323)	1,537	0.03
Sri Lankan (102)	122	<0.01
Taiwanese (462)	528	0.01
Thai (964)	1,481	0.03
Vietnamese (7,398)	8,488	0.18
Hawaii Native/Pacific Islander (3,057)	5,914	0.12
Not Hispanic (1,976)	4,112	0.09
Hispanic (1,081)	1,802	0.04
Fijian (15)	24	<0.01
Guamanian/Chamorro (1,774)	2,325	0.05
Marshallese (96)	117	<0.01
Native Hawaiian (522)	1,529	0.03
Samoan (213)	488	0.01
Tongan (10)	18	<0.01
White (3,275,394)	3,337,077	69.82
Not Hispanic (3,204,402)	3,257,662	68.16
Hispanic (70,992)	79,415	1.66

*Notes: † The Census 2010 population figure is used to calculate the percentages in the Hispanic Origin and Race categories. Ancestry percentages are based on the 2006-2010 American Community Survey population (not shown); ‡ Numbers in parentheses indicate the number of people reporting a single ancestry; * Numbers in parentheses indicate the number of persons reporting this race alone, not in combination with any other race; Please refer to the Explanation of Data for more information.*

Alabaster

Place Type: City
County: Shelby
Population: 30,352†

Ancestry‡	Population	%
African, Sub-Saharan (325)	325	1.10
African (159)	159	0.54
Kenyan (166)	166	0.56
American (3,305)	3,305	11.18
Arab (123)	139	0.47
Arab (5)	5	0.02
Lebanese (118)	134	0.45
Austrian (0)	44	0.15
Belgian (8)	8	0.03
British (75)	82	0.28
Bulgarian (15)	15	0.05
Canadian (25)	25	0.08
Czech (0)	54	0.18
Czechoslovakian (0)	53	0.18
Danish (0)	21	0.07
Dutch (94)	284	0.96
English (1,761)	3,615	12.23
European (616)	740	2.50
Finnish (0)	12	0.04
French, ex. Basque (253)	873	2.95
French Canadian (29)	107	0.36
German (957)	3,608	12.21
Greek (48)	91	0.31
Hungarian (0)	18	0.06
Irish (1,199)	3,825	12.94
Italian (487)	1,158	3.92
Latvian (0)	48	0.16
Lithuanian (0)	43	0.15
Norwegian (43)	149	0.50
Pennsylvania German (10)	10	0.03
Polish (173)	562	1.90
Portuguese (0)	7	0.02
Romanian (8)	8	0.03
Russian (73)	95	0.32
Scandinavian (12)	27	0.09
Scotch-Irish (565)	955	3.23
Scottish (558)	976	3.30
Slavic (0)	11	0.04
Swedish (23)	90	0.30
Swiss (23)	23	0.08
Ukrainian (7)	7	0.02
Welsh (107)	183	0.62
West Indian, ex. Hispanic (0)	32	0.11
Belizean (0)	11	0.04
Haitian (0)	21	0.07
Yugoslavian (15)	15	0.05

Hispanic Origin	Population	%
Hispanic or Latino (of any race)	2,723	8.97
Central American, ex. Mexican	330	1.09
Costa Rican	21	0.07
Guatemalan	15	0.05
Honduran	58	0.19
Nicaraguan	11	0.04
Panamanian	9	0.03
Salvadoran	214	0.71
Other Central American	2	0.01
Cuban	22	0.07
Dominican Republic	6	0.02
Mexican	2,080	6.85
Puerto Rican	83	0.27
South American	73	0.24
Argentinean	9	0.03
Bolivian	2	0.01
Chilean	5	0.02
Colombian	28	0.09
Ecuadorian	3	0.01
Paraguayan	1	<0.01
Peruvian	3	0.01
Uruguayan	6	0.02
Venezuelan	12	0.04
Other South American	4	0.01
Other Hispanic or Latino	129	0.43

Race*	Population	%
African-American/Black (4,105)	4,295	14.15
Not Hispanic (4,082)	4,250	14.00
Hispanic (23)	45	0.15
American Indian/Alaska Native (124)	253	0.83
Not Hispanic (88)	198	0.65
Hispanic (36)	55	0.18
Apache (1)	1	<0.01
Blackfeet (0)	2	0.01
Cherokee (35)	82	0.27
Chickasaw (1)	2	0.01
Chippewa (4)	4	0.01
Choctaw (8)	13	0.04
Comanche (0)	1	<0.01
Cree (1)	1	<0.01
Creek (8)	15	0.05
Hopi (0)	1	<0.01
Inupiat *(Alaska Native)* (1)	1	<0.01
Iroquois (1)	1	<0.01
Lumbee (1)	1	<0.01
Mexican American Ind. (15)	15	0.05
Navajo (2)	2	0.01
Shoshone (0)	1	<0.01
Sioux (2)	3	0.01
South American Ind. (4)	4	0.01
Asian (271)	374	1.23
Not Hispanic (269)	359	1.18
Hispanic (2)	15	0.05
Bangladeshi (4)	4	0.01
Cambodian (1)	4	0.01
Chinese, ex. Taiwanese (56)	74	0.24
Filipino (35)	74	0.24
Indian (58)	69	0.23
Indonesian (1)	1	<0.01
Japanese (13)	33	0.11
Korean (23)	34	0.11
Laotian (1)	1	<0.01
Pakistani (1)	1	<0.01
Taiwanese (4)	4	0.01
Thai (7)	8	0.03
Vietnamese (58)	65	0.21
Hawaii Native/Pacific Islander (10)	27	0.09
Not Hispanic (8)	22	0.07
Hispanic (2)	5	0.02
Guamanian/Chamorro (5)	5	0.02
Native Hawaiian (2)	16	0.05
Samoan (3)	3	0.01
White (24,103)	24,523	80.80
Not Hispanic (22,782)	23,093	76.08
Hispanic (1,321)	1,430	4.71

Albertville

Place Type: City
County: Marshall
Population: 21,160†

Ancestry‡	Population	%
American (2,909)	2,909	14.23
Arab (7)	7	0.03
Moroccan (7)	7	0.03
British (9)	19	0.09
Canadian (0)	13	0.06
Dutch (32)	305	1.49
English (2,227)	2,735	13.38
European (59)	59	0.29
French, ex. Basque (22)	204	1.00
French Canadian (17)	132	0.65
German (570)	1,315	6.43
Irish (758)	1,889	9.24
Italian (82)	229	1.12
Lithuanian (0)	38	0.19
Norwegian (33)	66	0.32
Polish (20)	28	0.14
Russian (0)	32	0.16
Scotch-Irish (494)	712	3.48
Scottish (126)	318	1.56
Swedish (16)	16	0.08
Welsh (0)	26	0.13
West Indian, ex. Hispanic (120)	120	0.59
Haitian (120)	120	0.59

Hispanic Origin	Population	%
Hispanic or Latino (of any race)	5,899	27.88
Central American, ex. Mexican	1,856	8.77
Guatemalan	1,740	8.22
Honduran	43	0.20
Nicaraguan	7	0.03
Panamanian	10	0.05
Salvadoran	50	0.24
Other Central American	6	0.03
Cuban	29	0.14
Dominican Republic	6	0.03
Mexican	3,457	16.34
Puerto Rican	79	0.37
South American	18	0.09
Argentinean	1	<0.01
Chilean	2	0.01
Colombian	6	0.03
Ecuadorian	4	0.02
Peruvian	1	<0.01
Venezuelan	4	0.02
Other Hispanic or Latino	454	2.15

Race*	Population	%
African-American/Black (405)	560	2.65
Not Hispanic (354)	465	2.20
Hispanic (51)	95	0.45
American Indian/Alaska Native (170)	306	1.45
Not Hispanic (105)	209	0.99
Hispanic (65)	97	0.46
Apache (0)	1	<0.01
Blackfeet (0)	1	<0.01
Central American Ind. (4)	4	0.02
Cherokee (49)	108	0.51
Chippewa (1)	1	<0.01
Choctaw (3)	10	0.05
Creek (6)	11	0.05
Mexican American Ind. (57)	66	0.31
Navajo (0)	2	0.01
Potawatomi (3)	3	0.01
Seminole (0)	1	<0.01
Shoshone (0)	1	<0.01
Sioux (1)	1	<0.01
Spanish American Ind. (1)	1	<0.01
Asian (97)	131	0.62
Not Hispanic (97)	105	0.50
Hispanic (0)	26	0.12
Burmese (17)	17	0.08
Chinese, ex. Taiwanese (10)	20	0.09
Filipino (17)	28	0.13
Indian (7)	19	0.09
Japanese (4)	10	0.05
Korean (4)	14	0.07
Taiwanese (0)	1	<0.01
Thai (3)	3	0.01
Vietnamese (22)	28	0.13
Hawaii Native/Pacific Islander (30)	64	0.30
Not Hispanic (23)	38	0.18
Hispanic (7)	26	0.12
Guamanian/Chamorro (18)	21	0.10
Native Hawaiian (1)	1	<0.01
White (16,062)	16,445	77.72
Not Hispanic (14,419)	14,645	69.21
Hispanic (1,643)	1,800	8.51

Alexander City

Place Type: City
County: Tallapoosa
Population: 14,875†

Ancestry‡	Population	%
African, Sub-Saharan (35)	35	0.24
Liberian (35)	35	0.24
American (2,162)	2,162	14.53
Dutch (51)	133	0.89
English (930)	1,529	10.28
European (167)	188	1.26

*Notes: † The Census 2010 population figure is used to calculate the percentages in the Hispanic Origin and Race categories. Ancestry percentages are based on the 2006-2010 American Community Survey population (not shown); ‡ Numbers in parentheses indicate the number of people reporting a single ancestry; * Numbers in parentheses indicate the number of persons reporting this race alone, not in combination with any other race; Please refer to the Explanation of Data for more information.*

French, ex. Basque (87)	186	1.25
French Canadian (21)	21	0.14
German (224)	725	4.87
Irish (353)	1,019	6.85
Italian (40)	64	0.43
Polish (24)	145	0.97
Portuguese (21)	94	0.63
Romanian (0)	12	0.08
Russian (0)	108	0.73
Scotch-Irish (243)	321	2.16
Scottish (345)	562	3.78
Swiss (10)	10	0.07
Welsh (0)	15	0.10
West Indian, ex. Hispanic (0)	16	0.11
Jamaican (0)	16	0.11

Hispanic Origin	Population	%
Hispanic or Latino (of any race)	708	4.76
Central American, ex. Mexican	29	0.19
Costa Rican	1	0.01
Guatemalan	7	0.05
Honduran	14	0.09
Nicaraguan	2	0.01
Panamanian	1	0.01
Salvadoran	4	0.03
Cuban	3	0.02
Mexican	624	4.19
Puerto Rican	6	0.04
South American	1	0.01
Colombian	1	0.01
Other Hispanic or Latino	45	0.30

Race*	Population	%
African-American/Black (4,757)	4,835	32.50
Not Hispanic (4,746)	4,814	32.36
Hispanic (11)	21	0.14
American Indian/Alaska Native (35)	82	0.55
Not Hispanic (35)	75	0.50
Hispanic (0)	7	0.05
Apache (1)	1	0.01
Cherokee (14)	33	0.22
Creek (4)	14	0.09
Tlingit-Haida *(Alaska Native)* (1)	1	0.01
Asian (139)	161	1.08
Not Hispanic (139)	161	1.08
Bangladeshi (1)	1	0.01
Chinese, ex. Taiwanese (23)	25	0.17
Filipino (3)	7	0.05
Indian (25)	29	0.19
Korean (68)	76	0.51
Taiwanese (3)	3	0.02
Thai (4)	6	0.04
Vietnamese (6)	6	0.04
Hawaii Native/Pacific Islander (2)	9	0.06
Not Hispanic (2)	9	0.06
Guamanian/Chamorro (0)	1	0.01
Native Hawaiian (0)	2	0.01
Samoan (1)	3	0.02
White (9,246)	9,361	62.93
Not Hispanic (9,131)	9,225	62.02
Hispanic (115)	136	0.91

Andalusia

Place Type: City
County: Covington
Population: 9,015†

Ancestry‡	Population	%
African, Sub-Saharan (37)	37	0.41
African (37)	37	0.41
American (2,593)	2,593	28.82
Arab (11)	11	0.12
Lebanese (11)	11	0.12
Australian (8)	16	0.18
British (0)	8	0.09
Cajun (0)	13	0.14
Dutch (0)	47	0.52
English (369)	689	7.66
European (11)	31	0.34
French, ex. Basque (22)	147	1.63
French Canadian (0)	31	0.34
German (120)	317	3.52
Irish (336)	653	7.26
Italian (81)	140	1.56
Norwegian (16)	30	0.33
Polish (0)	45	0.50
Scandinavian (0)	11	0.12
Scotch-Irish (220)	255	2.83
Scottish (93)	117	1.30
Welsh (30)	30	0.33

Hispanic Origin	Population	%
Hispanic or Latino (of any race)	167	1.85
Central American, ex. Mexican	7	0.08
Costa Rican	2	0.02
Honduran	1	0.01
Nicaraguan	1	0.01
Panamanian	3	0.03
Cuban	6	0.07
Dominican Republic	1	0.01
Mexican	83	0.92
Puerto Rican	25	0.28
South American	24	0.27
Argentinean	2	0.02
Chilean	2	0.02
Colombian	14	0.16
Peruvian	2	0.02
Venezuelan	4	0.04
Other Hispanic or Latino	21	0.23

Race*	Population	%
African-American/Black (2,337)	2,443	27.10
Not Hispanic (2,315)	2,417	26.81
Hispanic (22)	26	0.29
American Indian/Alaska Native (37)	83	0.92
Not Hispanic (34)	80	0.89
Hispanic (3)	3	0.03
Apache (0)	1	0.01
Cherokee (9)	22	0.24
Chippewa (1)	1	0.01
Choctaw (2)	2	0.02
Cree (0)	1	0.01
Creek (8)	15	0.17
Iroquois (1)	1	0.01
Mexican American Ind. (1)	1	0.01
Sioux (1)	1	0.01
Tlingit-Haida *(Alaska Native)* (1)	1	0.01
Ute (1)	1	0.01
Asian (91)	98	1.09
Not Hispanic (87)	93	1.03
Hispanic (4)	5	0.06
Chinese, ex. Taiwanese (14)	14	0.16
Filipino (3)	3	0.03
Indian (22)	24	0.27
Indonesian (1)	2	0.02
Japanese (2)	2	0.02
Korean (24)	31	0.34
Taiwanese (2)	2	0.02
Vietnamese (16)	17	0.19
Hawaii Native/Pacific Islander (0)	2	0.02
Not Hispanic (0)	1	0.01
Hispanic (0)	1	0.01
Samoan (0)	1	0.01
White (6,356)	6,504	72.15
Not Hispanic (6,262)	6,399	70.98
Hispanic (94)	105	1.16

Anniston

Place Type: City
County: Calhoun
Population: 23,106†

Ancestry‡	Population	%
African, Sub-Saharan (325)	362	1.55
African (325)	362	1.55
American (1,654)	1,654	7.10
Arab (12)	12	0.05
Lebanese (12)	12	0.05
Austrian (23)	23	0.10
British (12)	19	0.08
Croatian (27)	41	0.18
Dutch (42)	207	0.89
Eastern European (9)	9	0.04
English (895)	1,877	8.06
European (277)	300	1.29
Finnish (17)	17	0.07
French, ex. Basque (88)	422	1.81
French Canadian (0)	28	0.12
German (438)	1,318	5.66
Greek (0)	163	0.70
Hungarian (0)	13	0.06
Iranian (0)	38	0.16
Irish (560)	1,454	6.24
Italian (65)	194	0.83
Luxemburger (13)	37	0.16
Norwegian (11)	38	0.16
Pennsylvania German (53)	53	0.23
Polish (21)	91	0.39
Russian (12)	24	0.10
Scotch-Irish (270)	473	2.03
Scottish (109)	387	1.66
Slovene (0)	11	0.05
Swedish (2)	36	0.15
Swiss (0)	10	0.04
Welsh (27)	98	0.42
West Indian, ex. Hispanic (60)	74	0.32
Jamaican (60)	74	0.32

Hispanic Origin	Population	%
Hispanic or Latino (of any race)	613	2.65
Central American, ex. Mexican	46	0.20
Guatemalan	11	0.05
Honduran	10	0.04
Nicaraguan	3	0.01
Panamanian	16	0.07
Salvadoran	6	0.03
Cuban	33	0.14
Dominican Republic	7	0.03
Mexican	331	1.43
Puerto Rican	97	0.42
South American	34	0.15
Argentinean	1	<0.01
Chilean	4	0.02
Colombian	15	0.06
Ecuadorian	6	0.03
Peruvian	6	0.03
Venezuelan	2	0.01
Other Hispanic or Latino	65	0.28

Race*	Population	%
African-American/Black (11,903)	12,148	52.58
Not Hispanic (11,830)	12,045	52.13
Hispanic (73)	103	0.45
American Indian/Alaska Native (69)	182	0.79
Not Hispanic (64)	165	0.71
Hispanic (5)	17	0.07
Apache (0)	1	<0.01
Blackfeet (3)	12	0.05
Central American Ind. (0)	1	<0.01
Cherokee (15)	49	0.21
Chippewa (4)	4	0.02
Choctaw (2)	6	0.03
Creek (0)	1	<0.01
Delaware (1)	1	<0.01
Iroquois (0)	2	0.01
Lumbee (2)	2	0.01
Mexican American Ind. (0)	1	<0.01
Navajo (2)	2	0.01
Potawatomi (0)	4	0.02
Pueblo (2)	2	0.01
Sioux (0)	1	<0.01
South American Ind. (1)	1	<0.01
Asian (184)	266	1.15
Not Hispanic (183)	244	1.06
Hispanic (1)	22	0.10
Chinese, ex. Taiwanese (29)	35	0.15
Filipino (21)	42	0.18
Indian (46)	76	0.33

*Notes: † The Census 2010 population figure is used to calculate the percentages in the Hispanic Origin and Race categories. Ancestry percentages are based on the 2006-2010 American Community Survey population (not shown); ‡ Numbers in parentheses indicate the number of people reporting a single ancestry; * Numbers in parentheses indicate the number of persons reporting this race alone, not in combination with any other race; Please refer to the Explanation of Data for more information.*

Indonesian (0)	1	<0.01
Japanese (14)	20	0.09
Korean (19)	45	0.19
Pakistani (19)	24	0.10
Thai (1)	3	0.01
Vietnamese (18)	19	0.08
Hawaii Native/Pacific Islander (13)	33	0.14
Not Hispanic (11)	25	0.11
Hispanic (2)	8	0.03
Guamanian/Chamorro (3)	3	0.01
Native Hawaiian (4)	14	0.06
Samoan (6)	6	0.03
White (10,327)	10,618	45.95
Not Hispanic (10,065)	10,313	44.63
Hispanic (262)	305	1.32

Arab

Place Type: City
County: Marshall
Population: 8,050†

Ancestry‡	Population	%
African, Sub-Saharan (19)	19	0.24
African (19)	19	0.24
American (1,025)	1,025	12.93
Armenian (28)	28	0.35
British (9)	9	0.11
Dutch (39)	88	1.11
English (1,125)	1,364	17.20
European (54)	54	0.68
French, ex. Basque (12)	198	2.50
German (696)	1,377	17.37
Hungarian (15)	15	0.19
Irish (660)	1,339	16.89
Italian (0)	25	0.32
Polish (42)	42	0.53
Scandinavian (8)	8	0.10
Scotch-Irish (162)	283	3.57
Scottish (108)	185	2.33
Swedish (0)	16	0.20
Ukrainian (40)	75	0.95

Hispanic Origin	Population	%
Hispanic or Latino (of any race)	136	1.69
Cuban	1	0.01
Mexican	107	1.33
Puerto Rican	11	0.14
South American	7	0.09
Bolivian	1	0.01
Chilean	3	0.04
Venezuelan	3	0.04
Other Hispanic or Latino	10	0.12

Race*	Population	%
African-American/Black (8)	28	0.35
Not Hispanic (6)	26	0.32
Hispanic (2)	2	0.02
American Indian/Alaska Native (50)	106	1.32
Not Hispanic (45)	96	1.19
Hispanic (5)	10	0.12
Blackfeet (0)	2	0.02
Cherokee (30)	55	0.68
Creek (0)	1	0.01
Iroquois (0)	2	0.02
Lumbee (1)	1	0.01
Mexican American Ind. (2)	3	0.04
Navajo (1)	1	0.01
Pueblo (1)	1	0.01
Spanish American Ind. (1)	1	0.01
Yup'ik *(Alaska Native)* (0)	1	0.01
Asian (59)	73	0.91
Not Hispanic (59)	71	0.88
Hispanic (0)	2	0.02
Chinese, ex. Taiwanese (11)	13	0.16
Filipino (2)	5	0.06
Indian (20)	21	0.26
Japanese (1)	5	0.06
Korean (3)	7	0.09
Thai (0)	1	0.01
Vietnamese (21)	21	0.26
Hawaii Native/Pacific Islander (6)	13	0.16
Not Hispanic (6)	12	0.15
Hispanic (0)	1	0.01
Marshallese (0)	4	0.05
Native Hawaiian (1)	1	0.01
Samoan (1)	2	0.02
White (7,775)	7,859	97.63
Not Hispanic (7,714)	7,792	96.80
Hispanic (61)	67	0.83

Athens

Place Type: City
County: Limestone
Population: 21,897†

Ancestry‡	Population	%
African, Sub-Saharan (70)	107	0.51
African (70)	107	0.51
American (2,865)	2,865	13.60
Arab (0)	8	0.04
Iraqi (0)	8	0.04
Austrian (11)	21	0.10
British (8)	26	0.12
Canadian (8)	8	0.04
Dutch (54)	259	1.23
English (1,038)	2,477	11.76
European (169)	182	0.86
French, ex. Basque (120)	299	1.42
French Canadian (22)	56	0.27
German (736)	1,808	8.59
Greek (0)	164	0.78
Hungarian (23)	31	0.15
Irish (888)	2,360	11.21
Italian (128)	256	1.22
Latvian (10)	10	0.05
Lithuanian (0)	40	0.19
Norwegian (18)	25	0.12
Polish (79)	173	0.82
Romanian (0)	5	0.02
Russian (13)	67	0.32
Scandinavian (31)	31	0.15
Scotch-Irish (232)	519	2.46
Scottish (128)	399	1.89
Swedish (109)	374	1.78
Swiss (0)	6	0.03
Welsh (22)	50	0.24

Hispanic Origin	Population	%
Hispanic or Latino (of any race)	1,932	8.82
Central American, ex. Mexican	371	1.69
Costa Rican	1	<0.01
Guatemalan	340	1.55
Honduran	5	0.02
Nicaraguan	2	0.01
Salvadoran	19	0.09
Other Central American	4	0.02
Cuban	22	0.10
Dominican Republic	4	0.02
Mexican	1,358	6.20
Puerto Rican	63	0.29
South American	16	0.07
Argentinean	1	<0.01
Bolivian	3	0.01
Chilean	1	<0.01
Colombian	3	0.01
Ecuadorian	3	0.01
Paraguayan	1	<0.01
Peruvian	1	<0.01
Venezuelan	3	0.01
Other Hispanic or Latino	98	0.45

Race*	Population	%
African-American/Black (3,841)	4,054	18.51
Not Hispanic (3,805)	4,002	18.28
Hispanic (36)	52	0.24
American Indian/Alaska Native (139)	273	1.25
Not Hispanic (98)	208	0.95
Hispanic (41)	65	0.30
Apache (1)	2	0.01
Blackfeet (1)	4	0.02
Cherokee (54)	120	0.55
Chickasaw (0)	3	0.01
Chippewa (0)	3	0.01
Choctaw (1)	9	0.04
Comanche (2)	2	0.01
Creek (4)	8	0.04
Delaware (3)	4	0.02
Mexican American Ind. (2)	4	0.02
Navajo (2)	2	0.01
Osage (2)	2	0.01
Ottawa (0)	2	0.01
Potawatomi (4)	5	0.02
Seminole (0)	1	<0.01
Sioux (1)	2	0.01
Asian (200)	256	1.17
Not Hispanic (190)	244	1.11
Hispanic (10)	12	0.05
Chinese, ex. Taiwanese (26)	30	0.14
Filipino (26)	40	0.18
Indian (65)	75	0.34
Japanese (15)	24	0.11
Korean (20)	27	0.12
Laotian (7)	7	0.03
Nepalese (3)	3	0.01
Pakistani (4)	4	0.02
Thai (4)	8	0.04
Vietnamese (26)	26	0.12
Hawaii Native/Pacific Islander (22)	34	0.16
Not Hispanic (6)	12	0.05
Hispanic (16)	22	0.10
Guamanian/Chamorro (22)	27	0.12
Native Hawaiian (0)	1	<0.01
White (15,976)	16,357	74.70
Not Hispanic (15,498)	15,812	72.21
Hispanic (478)	545	2.49

Atmore

Place Type: City
County: Escambia
Population: 10,194†

Ancestry‡	Population	%
African, Sub-Saharan (114)	123	1.23
African (114)	123	1.23
American (794)	794	7.93
Arab (9)	9	0.09
Moroccan (9)	9	0.09
British (11)	22	0.22
Cajun (0)	20	0.20
Czechoslovakian (8)	8	0.08
Danish (0)	11	0.11
Dutch (54)	86	0.86
English (236)	445	4.45
Finnish (0)	8	0.08
French, ex. Basque (0)	40	0.40
German (79)	272	2.72
Irish (207)	602	6.02
Italian (13)	47	0.47
Pennsylvania German (40)	40	0.40
Polish (17)	17	0.17
Russian (0)	15	0.15
Scotch-Irish (115)	159	1.59
Scottish (52)	72	0.72
Welsh (11)	11	0.11
West Indian, ex. Hispanic (20)	30	0.30
Haitian (11)	21	0.21
Jamaican (9)	9	0.09

Hispanic Origin	Population	%
Hispanic or Latino (of any race)	185	1.81
Central American, ex. Mexican	2	0.02
Salvadoran	2	0.02
Cuban	2	0.02
Dominican Republic	2	0.02
Mexican	120	1.18
Puerto Rican	9	0.09
South American	2	0.02

*Notes: † The Census 2010 population figure is used to calculate the percentages in the Hispanic Origin and Race categories. Ancestry percentages are based on the 2006-2010 American Community Survey population (not shown); ‡ Numbers in parentheses indicate the number of people reporting a single ancestry; * Numbers in parentheses indicate the number of persons reporting this race alone, not in combination with any other race; Please refer to the Explanation of Data for more information.*

Chilean	2	0.02
Other Hispanic or Latino	48	0.47

Race*	Population	%
African-American/Black (5,672)	5,743	56.34
Not Hispanic (5,646)	5,714	56.05
Hispanic (26)	29	0.28
American Indian/Alaska Native (184)	269	2.64
Not Hispanic (182)	263	2.58
Hispanic (2)	6	0.06
Apache (0)	1	0.01
Blackfeet (1)	2	0.02
Canadian/French Am. Ind. (0)	1	0.01
Cherokee (9)	16	0.16
Chippewa (1)	1	0.01
Choctaw (2)	5	0.05
Cree (0)	2	0.02
Creek (129)	156	1.53
Iroquois (1)	1	0.01
Navajo (0)	1	0.01
Seminole (0)	3	0.03
Sioux (2)	3	0.03
Tlingit-Haida *(Alaska Native)* (0)	1	0.01
Asian (30)	43	0.42
Not Hispanic (26)	38	0.37
Hispanic (4)	5	0.05
Chinese, ex. Taiwanese (8)	12	0.12
Filipino (8)	11	0.11
Indian (8)	10	0.10
Japanese (0)	1	0.01
Korean (1)	2	0.02
Vietnamese (3)	4	0.04
Hawaii Native/Pacific Islander (6)	7	0.07
Not Hispanic (6)	6	0.06
Hispanic (0)	1	0.01
Native Hawaiian (3)	3	0.03
White (4,073)	4,189	41.09
Not Hispanic (4,007)	4,117	40.39
Hispanic (66)	72	0.71

Auburn

Place Type: City
County: Lee
Population: 53,380†

Ancestry‡	Population	%
African, Sub-Saharan (578)	642	1.26
African (169)	233	0.46
Ghanaian (4)	4	0.01
Kenyan (3)	3	0.01
Nigerian (119)	119	0.23
South African (10)	10	0.02
Sudanese (273)	273	0.53
American (3,291)	3,291	6.45
Arab (133)	178	0.35
Arab (19)	25	0.05
Egyptian (67)	67	0.13
Lebanese (31)	50	0.10
Syrian (6)	26	0.05
Other Arab (10)	10	0.02
Armenian (6)	8	0.02
Australian (84)	95	0.19
Austrian (29)	82	0.16
Basque (13)	13	0.03
Belgian (0)	40	0.08
Brazilian (46)	123	0.24
British (302)	474	0.93
Bulgarian (12)	12	0.02
Cajun (15)	31	0.06
Canadian (40)	93	0.18
Celtic (0)	3	0.01
Croatian (35)	57	0.11
Czech (14)	107	0.21
Czechoslovakian (61)	64	0.13
Danish (22)	53	0.10
Dutch (186)	474	0.93
Eastern European (17)	17	0.03
English (4,849)	10,045	19.67
European (620)	768	1.50
Finnish (10)	21	0.04
French, ex. Basque (474)	1,789	3.50
French Canadian (89)	164	0.32
German (2,223)	6,625	12.98
Greek (139)	257	0.50
Guyanese (0)	4	0.01
Hungarian (25)	87	0.17
Icelander (0)	6	0.01
Iranian (18)	18	0.04
Irish (2,120)	6,352	12.44
Italian (503)	1,589	3.11
Lithuanian (0)	21	0.04
Luxemburger (0)	3	0.01
Maltese (0)	42	0.08
Northern European (21)	21	0.04
Norwegian (115)	491	0.96
Polish (146)	775	1.52
Portuguese (19)	120	0.24
Romanian (42)	53	0.10
Russian (43)	222	0.43
Scandinavian (37)	71	0.14
Scotch-Irish (1,140)	2,078	4.07
Scottish (821)	2,224	4.36
Serbian (13)	16	0.03
Slavic (31)	38	0.07
Slovak (14)	51	0.10
Slovene (0)	49	0.10
Swedish (110)	520	1.02
Swiss (111)	328	0.64
Turkish (73)	84	0.16
Ukrainian (36)	86	0.17
Welsh (105)	516	1.01
West Indian, ex. Hispanic (29)	37	0.07
Bahamian (0)	4	0.01
Belizean (3)	3	0.01
Haitian (5)	5	0.01
Jamaican (14)	14	0.03
West Indian (7)	11	0.02
Yugoslavian (7)	42	0.08

Hispanic Origin	Population	%
Hispanic or Latino (of any race)	1,551	2.91
Central American, ex. Mexican	300	0.56
Costa Rican	13	0.02
Guatemalan	154	0.29
Honduran	53	0.10
Nicaraguan	34	0.06
Panamanian	28	0.05
Salvadoran	18	0.03
Cuban	134	0.25
Dominican Republic	18	0.03
Mexican	628	1.18
Puerto Rican	145	0.27
South American	154	0.29
Argentinean	16	0.03
Bolivian	4	0.01
Chilean	12	0.02
Colombian	48	0.09
Ecuadorian	4	0.01
Paraguayan	8	0.01
Peruvian	32	0.06
Uruguayan	2	<0.01
Venezuelan	27	0.05
Other South American	1	<0.01
Other Hispanic or Latino	172	0.32

Race*	Population	%
African-American/Black (8,834)	9,146	17.13
Not Hispanic (8,772)	9,035	16.93
Hispanic (62)	111	0.21
American Indian/Alaska Native (149)	391	0.73
Not Hispanic (143)	359	0.67
Hispanic (6)	32	0.06
Apache (0)	3	0.01
Arapaho (1)	1	<0.01
Blackfeet (0)	2	<0.01
Canadian/French Am. Ind. (0)	1	<0.01
Cherokee (35)	122	0.23
Chickasaw (1)	4	0.01
Chippewa (5)	6	0.01
Choctaw (11)	21	0.04
Comanche (1)	1	<0.01
Creek (10)	25	0.05
Crow (0)	1	<0.01
Delaware (1)	2	<0.01
Hopi (0)	2	<0.01
Iroquois (1)	1	<0.01
Kiowa (0)	1	<0.01
Lumbee (1)	1	<0.01
Mexican American Ind. (0)	2	<0.01
Navajo (1)	4	0.01
Osage (0)	2	<0.01
Pueblo (0)	1	<0.01
Seminole (0)	1	<0.01
Shoshone (0)	1	<0.01
Sioux (2)	7	0.01
South American Ind. (1)	1	<0.01
Tlingit-Haida *(Alaska Native)* (1)	3	0.01
Yakama (0)	1	<0.01
Yup'ik *(Alaska Native)* (1)	1	<0.01
Asian (2,825)	3,158	5.92
Not Hispanic (2,817)	3,141	5.88
Hispanic (8)	17	0.03
Bangladeshi (29)	29	0.05
Bhutanese (1)	1	<0.01
Cambodian (1)	5	0.01
Chinese, ex. Taiwanese (730)	793	1.49
Filipino (64)	119	0.22
Indian (602)	673	1.26
Indonesian (20)	22	0.04
Japanese (75)	112	0.21
Korean (948)	1,036	1.94
Laotian (11)	24	0.04
Malaysian (5)	7	0.01
Nepalese (16)	19	0.04
Pakistani (30)	33	0.06
Sri Lankan (19)	22	0.04
Taiwanese (54)	58	0.11
Thai (20)	35	0.07
Vietnamese (133)	157	0.29
Hawaii Native/Pacific Islander (16)	55	0.10
Not Hispanic (12)	47	0.09
Hispanic (4)	8	0.01
Guamanian/Chamorro (12)	18	0.03
Native Hawaiian (1)	8	0.01
Samoan (0)	3	0.01
Tongan (2)	2	<0.01
White (40,069)	40,811	76.45
Not Hispanic (39,255)	39,885	74.72
Hispanic (814)	926	1.73

Bay Minette

Place Type: City
County: Baldwin
Population: 8,044†

Ancestry‡	Population	%
African, Sub-Saharan (8)	15	0.19
African (8)	15	0.19
American (1,409)	1,409	17.50
Arab (8)	8	0.10
Lebanese (8)	8	0.10
Austrian (0)	10	0.12
English (262)	583	7.24
European (83)	93	1.15
French, ex. Basque (18)	66	0.82
French Canadian (8)	26	0.32
German (110)	313	3.89
Greek (0)	33	0.41
Irish (364)	827	10.27
Israeli (8)	8	0.10
Italian (61)	94	1.17
Lithuanian (9)	9	0.11
Norwegian (9)	32	0.40
Polish (9)	17	0.21
Scandinavian (0)	11	0.14
Scotch-Irish (43)	69	0.86
Scottish (42)	121	1.50
Swedish (9)	9	0.11

*Notes: † The Census 2010 population figure is used to calculate the percentages in the Hispanic Origin and Race categories. Ancestry percentages are based on the 2006-2010 American Community Survey population (not shown); ‡ Numbers in parentheses indicate the number of people reporting a single ancestry; * Numbers in parentheses indicate the number of persons reporting this race alone, not in combination with any other race; Please refer to the Explanation of Data for more information.*

SECTION TWO

West Indian, ex. Hispanic (10)	20	0.25
Jamaican (10)	20	0.25
Yugoslavian (9)	49	0.61

Hispanic Origin	Population	%
Hispanic or Latino (of any race)	142	1.77
Central American, ex. Mexican	4	0.05
Nicaraguan	3	0.04
Salvadoran	1	0.01
Cuban	1	0.01
Mexican	103	1.28
Puerto Rican	13	0.16
South American	9	0.11
Bolivian	1	0.01
Chilean	5	0.06
Colombian	1	0.01
Paraguayan	1	0.01
Peruvian	1	0.01
Other Hispanic or Latino	12	0.15

Race*	Population	%
African-American/Black (2,837)	2,903	36.09
Not Hispanic (2,826)	2,884	35.85
Hispanic (11)	19	0.24
American Indian/Alaska Native (77)	137	1.70
Not Hispanic (77)	137	1.70
Blackfeet (1)	2	0.02
Cherokee (11)	19	0.24
Choctaw (11)	12	0.15
Creek (39)	58	0.72
Iroquois (0)	4	0.05
Lumbee (1)	1	0.01
South American Ind. (1)	1	0.01
Asian (68)	85	1.06
Not Hispanic (68)	81	1.01
Hispanic (0)	4	0.05
Cambodian (5)	5	0.06
Chinese, ex. Taiwanese (12)	13	0.16
Filipino (19)	25	0.31
Indian (12)	15	0.19
Japanese (2)	3	0.04
Korean (2)	2	0.02
Thai (12)	14	0.17
Vietnamese (3)	3	0.04
Hawaii Native/Pacific Islander (1)	6	0.07
Not Hispanic (1)	3	0.04
Hispanic (0)	3	0.04
Guamanian/Chamorro (0)	2	0.02
Native Hawaiian (1)	1	0.01
White (4,861)	4,968	61.76
Not Hispanic (4,810)	4,907	61.00
Hispanic (51)	61	0.76

Bessemer

Place Type: City
County: Jefferson
Population: 27,456†

Ancestry‡	Population	%
African, Sub-Saharan (326)	343	1.23
African (326)	343	1.23
American (1,995)	1,995	7.17
Austrian (11)	11	0.04
British (46)	75	0.27
Cajun (11)	11	0.04
Czech (50)	116	0.42
Danish (0)	11	0.04
Dutch (0)	40	0.14
English (384)	563	2.02
European (124)	124	0.45
French, ex. Basque (203)	310	1.11
German (269)	564	2.03
Guyanese (21)	21	0.08
Irish (435)	699	2.51
Italian (89)	130	0.47
Lithuanian (5)	5	0.02
Norwegian (8)	8	0.03
Polish (0)	32	0.12
Scotch-Irish (101)	228	0.82
Scottish (65)	129	0.46
Serbian (0)	10	0.04
Swedish (36)	36	0.13
Welsh (0)	8	0.03
West Indian, ex. Hispanic (103)	116	0.42
Dutch West Indian (0)	13	0.05
Jamaican (103)	103	0.37

Hispanic Origin	Population	%
Hispanic or Latino (of any race)	1,113	4.05
Central American, ex. Mexican	66	0.24
Costa Rican	1	<0.01
Guatemalan	12	0.04
Honduran	6	0.02
Nicaraguan	2	0.01
Panamanian	5	0.02
Salvadoran	40	0.15
Cuban	8	0.03
Dominican Republic	1	<0.01
Mexican	922	3.36
Puerto Rican	12	0.04
South American	11	0.04
Argentinean	7	0.03
Colombian	1	<0.01
Uruguayan	3	0.01
Other Hispanic or Latino	93	0.34

Race*	Population	%
African-American/Black (19,546)	19,702	71.76
Not Hispanic (19,504)	19,649	71.57
Hispanic (42)	53	0.19
American Indian/Alaska Native (88)	177	0.64
Not Hispanic (77)	165	0.60
Hispanic (11)	12	0.04
Blackfeet (0)	2	0.01
Cherokee (19)	56	0.20
Choctaw (3)	4	0.01
Creek (3)	6	0.02
Delaware (1)	1	<0.01
Asian (53)	95	0.35
Not Hispanic (53)	90	0.33
Hispanic (0)	5	0.02
Bangladeshi (3)	3	0.01
Chinese, ex. Taiwanese (6)	15	0.05
Filipino (7)	18	0.07
Indian (22)	31	0.11
Indonesian (1)	2	0.01
Japanese (3)	7	0.03
Korean (3)	6	0.02
Thai (0)	1	<0.01
Vietnamese (8)	13	0.05
Hawaii Native/Pacific Islander (0)	16	0.06
Not Hispanic (0)	11	0.04
Hispanic (0)	5	0.02
Native Hawaiian (0)	6	0.02
Samoan (0)	1	<0.01
White (6,669)	6,841	24.92
Not Hispanic (6,482)	6,631	24.15
Hispanic (187)	210	0.76

Birmingham

Place Type: City
County: Jefferson
Population: 212,237†

Ancestry‡	Population	%
African, Sub-Saharan (2,729)	2,972	1.37
African (2,392)	2,600	1.20
Ethiopian (34)	34	0.02
Kenyan (65)	65	0.03
Liberian (11)	11	0.01
Nigerian (86)	86	0.04
South African (0)	35	0.02
Sudanese (27)	27	0.01
Ugandan (35)	35	0.02
Other Sub-Saharan African (79)	79	0.04
Albanian (41)	41	0.02
American (8,045)	8,045	3.72
Arab (656)	720	0.33
Arab (15)	18	0.01
Egyptian (55)	66	0.03
Iraqi (5)	5	<0.01
Lebanese (223)	255	0.12
Moroccan (178)	178	0.08
Palestinian (53)	71	0.03
Syrian (8)	8	<0.01
Other Arab (119)	119	0.05
Armenian (0)	9	<0.01
Australian (26)	26	0.01
Austrian (0)	45	0.02
Belgian (0)	87	0.04
Brazilian (10)	46	0.02
British (303)	531	0.25
Canadian (16)	63	0.03
Croatian (8)	8	<0.01
Czech (0)	110	0.05
Czechoslovakian (31)	48	0.02
Danish (39)	51	0.02
Dutch (366)	894	0.41
English (3,376)	8,030	3.71
European (932)	978	0.45
Finnish (0)	8	<0.01
French, ex. Basque (323)	1,928	0.89
French Canadian (67)	175	0.08
German (1,585)	5,998	2.77
Greek (166)	231	0.11
Guyanese (0)	25	0.01
Hungarian (13)	92	0.04
Iranian (101)	161	0.07
Irish (2,764)	7,890	3.65
Italian (1,004)	2,082	0.96
Lithuanian (0)	8	<0.01
Northern European (0)	8	<0.01
Norwegian (68)	336	0.16
Pennsylvania German (29)	29	0.01
Polish (316)	913	0.42
Portuguese (0)	52	0.02
Romanian (38)	38	0.02
Russian (182)	311	0.14
Scandinavian (18)	66	0.03
Scotch-Irish (1,771)	2,982	1.38
Scottish (1,288)	3,017	1.39
Serbian (19)	19	0.01
Slavic (0)	6	<0.01
Slovak (36)	118	0.05
Slovene (42)	63	0.03
Swedish (152)	322	0.15
Swiss (25)	120	0.06
Turkish (79)	79	0.04
Ukrainian (63)	63	0.03
Welsh (200)	627	0.29
West Indian, ex. Hispanic (230)	285	0.13
Bahamian (18)	18	0.01
Belizean (23)	23	0.01
Bermudan (30)	30	0.01
Dutch West Indian (0)	8	<0.01
Haitian (0)	22	0.01
Jamaican (103)	128	0.06
U.S. Virgin Islander (41)	41	0.02
West Indian (15)	15	0.01
Yugoslavian (0)	14	0.01

Hispanic Origin	Population	%
Hispanic or Latino (of any race)	7,704	3.63
Central American, ex. Mexican	841	0.40
Costa Rican	39	0.02
Guatemalan	331	0.16
Honduran	273	0.13
Nicaraguan	13	0.01
Panamanian	65	0.03
Salvadoran	106	0.05
Other Central American	14	0.01
Cuban	101	0.05
Dominican Republic	49	0.02
Mexican	5,237	2.47
Puerto Rican	338	0.16
South American	253	0.12
Argentinean	25	0.01
Bolivian	6	<0.01

*Notes: † The Census 2010 population figure is used to calculate the percentages in the Hispanic Origin and Race categories. Ancestry percentages are based on the 2006-2010 American Community Survey population (not shown); ‡ Numbers in parentheses indicate the number of people reporting a single ancestry; * Numbers in parentheses indicate the number of persons reporting this race alone, not in combination with any other race; Please refer to the Explanation of Data for more information.*

	Population	%
Chilean	20	0.01
Colombian	78	0.04
Ecuadorian	17	0.01
Paraguayan	5	<0.01
Peruvian	73	0.03
Uruguayan	8	<0.01
Venezuelan	21	0.01
Other Hispanic or Latino	885	0.42

Race*	Population	%
African-American/Black (155,791)	157,136	74.04
Not Hispanic (155,258)	156,470	73.72
Hispanic (533)	666	0.31
American Indian/Alaska Native (445)	1,141	0.54
Not Hispanic (361)	966	0.46
Hispanic (84)	175	0.08
Alaska Athabascan *(Ala. Nat.)* (1)	1	<0.01
Aleut *(Alaska Native)* (1)	1	<0.01
Apache (4)	6	<0.01
Arapaho (1)	1	<0.01
Blackfeet (5)	24	0.01
Central American Ind. (3)	4	<0.01
Cherokee (92)	281	0.13
Cheyenne (0)	1	<0.01
Chickasaw (3)	5	<0.01
Chippewa (0)	2	<0.01
Choctaw (9)	33	0.02
Comanche (1)	2	<0.01
Cree (0)	6	<0.01
Creek (19)	56	0.03
Crow (0)	2	<0.01
Iroquois (3)	9	<0.01
Lumbee (0)	1	<0.01
Mexican American Ind. (22)	58	0.03
Navajo (2)	6	<0.01
Pima (1)	1	<0.01
Potawatomi (1)	1	<0.01
Pueblo (0)	1	<0.01
Seminole (2)	3	<0.01
Sioux (5)	9	<0.01
South American Ind. (2)	3	<0.01
Tlingit-Haida *(Alaska Native)* (1)	1	<0.01
Ute (0)	1	<0.01
Yaqui (5)	5	<0.01
Yup'ik *(Alaska Native)* (1)	1	<0.01
Asian (2,152)	2,605	1.23
Not Hispanic (2,132)	2,552	1.20
Hispanic (20)	53	0.02
Bangladeshi (9)	10	<0.01
Burmese (1)	2	<0.01
Cambodian (18)	20	0.01
Chinese, ex. Taiwanese (437)	540	0.25
Filipino (175)	277	0.13
Hmong (1)	1	<0.01
Indian (783)	847	0.40
Indonesian (15)	16	0.01
Japanese (70)	135	0.06
Korean (164)	218	0.10
Laotian (1)	4	<0.01
Malaysian (16)	21	0.01
Nepalese (44)	47	0.02
Pakistani (60)	73	0.03
Sri Lankan (2)	4	<0.01
Taiwanese (37)	41	0.02
Thai (33)	41	0.02
Vietnamese (193)	234	0.11
Hawaii Native/Pacific Islander (86)	184	0.09
Not Hispanic (48)	119	0.06
Hispanic (38)	65	0.03
Fijian (2)	3	<0.01
Guamanian/Chamorro (38)	56	0.03
Marshallese (0)	2	<0.01
Native Hawaiian (10)	41	0.02
Samoan (8)	19	0.01
White (47,258)	48,829	23.01
Not Hispanic (44,819)	46,062	21.70
Hispanic (2,439)	2,767	1.30

Boaz

Place Type: City
County: Marshall
Population: 9,551†

Ancestry‡	Population	%
American (1,288)	1,288	14.08
Dutch (47)	236	2.58
English (1,134)	1,663	18.18
European (10)	10	0.11
French, ex. Basque (80)	119	1.30
French Canadian (9)	53	0.58
German (196)	593	6.48
Irish (619)	1,025	11.20
Italian (0)	11	0.12
Polish (35)	44	0.48
Portuguese (0)	29	0.32
Russian (0)	29	0.32
Scotch-Irish (196)	291	3.18
Scottish (42)	55	0.60
Swedish (26)	26	0.28
Welsh (0)	38	0.42

Hispanic Origin	Population	%
Hispanic or Latino (of any race)	1,356	14.20
Central American, ex. Mexican	556	5.82
Guatemalan	544	5.70
Honduran	2	0.02
Nicaraguan	3	0.03
Salvadoran	7	0.07
Cuban	17	0.18
Mexican	619	6.48
Puerto Rican	40	0.42
South American	12	0.13
Colombian	11	0.12
Venezuelan	1	0.01
Other Hispanic or Latino	112	1.17

Race*	Population	%
African-American/Black (169)	216	2.26
Not Hispanic (152)	198	2.07
Hispanic (17)	18	0.19
American Indian/Alaska Native (40)	92	0.96
Not Hispanic (21)	68	0.71
Hispanic (19)	24	0.25
Apache (1)	3	0.03
Blackfeet (0)	2	0.02
Cherokee (12)	40	0.42
Chippewa (1)	1	0.01
Creek (5)	6	0.06
Mexican American Ind. (5)	8	0.08
Seminole (0)	1	0.01
Sioux (2)	3	0.03
Spanish American Ind. (0)	1	0.01
Tohono O'Odham (0)	2	0.02
Asian (68)	93	0.97
Not Hispanic (68)	91	0.95
Hispanic (0)	2	0.02
Burmese (15)	16	0.17
Chinese, ex. Taiwanese (6)	9	0.09
Filipino (11)	16	0.17
Indian (27)	34	0.36
Japanese (5)	7	0.07
Korean (1)	4	0.04
Pakistani (0)	2	0.02
Thai (1)	1	0.01
Hawaii Native/Pacific Islander (30)	37	0.39
Not Hispanic (30)	35	0.37
Hispanic (0)	2	0.02
Native Hawaiian (0)	1	0.01
White (8,337)	8,477	88.76
Not Hispanic (7,813)	7,910	82.82
Hispanic (524)	567	5.94

Calera

Place Type: City
County: Shelby
Population: 11,620†

Ancestry‡	Population	%
African, Sub-Saharan (30)	30	0.29
African (5)	5	0.05
Kenyan (25)	25	0.24
American (1,201)	1,201	11.58
Armenian (4)	8	0.08
Austrian (0)	12	0.12
British (0)	24	0.23
Canadian (0)	9	0.09
Croatian (21)	21	0.20
Dutch (9)	154	1.48
English (533)	901	8.69
European (103)	103	0.99
French, ex. Basque (87)	333	3.21
French Canadian (0)	13	0.13
German (445)	1,204	11.61
Irish (430)	1,134	10.93
Italian (36)	95	0.92
Norwegian (21)	65	0.63
Polish (10)	17	0.16
Scandinavian (9)	17	0.16
Scotch-Irish (51)	157	1.51
Scottish (92)	250	2.41
Slovak (9)	9	0.09
Swedish (46)	76	0.73
Swiss (0)	12	0.12
Welsh (9)	55	0.53
West Indian, ex. Hispanic (12)	37	0.36
West Indian (12)	26	0.25
Other West Indian (0)	11	0.11

Hispanic Origin	Population	%
Hispanic or Latino (of any race)	578	4.97
Central American, ex. Mexican	65	0.56
Costa Rican	5	0.04
Guatemalan	1	0.01
Honduran	11	0.09
Nicaraguan	8	0.07
Panamanian	9	0.08
Salvadoran	31	0.27
Cuban	29	0.25
Dominican Republic	2	0.02
Mexican	383	3.30
Puerto Rican	25	0.22
South American	13	0.11
Chilean	1	0.01
Colombian	4	0.03
Ecuadorian	3	0.03
Peruvian	5	0.04
Other Hispanic or Latino	61	0.52

Race*	Population	%
African-American/Black (2,668)	2,783	23.95
Not Hispanic (2,651)	2,756	23.72
Hispanic (17)	27	0.23
American Indian/Alaska Native (23)	71	0.61
Not Hispanic (23)	68	0.59
Hispanic (0)	3	0.03
Blackfeet (0)	2	0.02
Cherokee (17)	47	0.40
Choctaw (0)	1	0.01
Cree (0)	1	0.01
Lumbee (1)	1	0.01
Mexican American Ind. (0)	1	0.01
Sioux (1)	3	0.03
Asian (75)	125	1.08
Not Hispanic (71)	118	1.02
Hispanic (4)	7	0.06
Chinese, ex. Taiwanese (9)	13	0.11
Filipino (10)	29	0.25
Indian (17)	18	0.15
Japanese (3)	9	0.08
Korean (14)	23	0.20
Pakistani (4)	6	0.05
Taiwanese (1)	1	0.01
Thai (1)	5	0.04
Vietnamese (14)	17	0.15
Hawaii Native/Pacific Islander (5)	11	0.09
Not Hispanic (3)	7	0.06
Hispanic (2)	4	0.03

*Notes: † The Census 2010 population figure is used to calculate the percentages in the Hispanic Origin and Race categories. Ancestry percentages are based on the 2006-2010 American Community Survey population (not shown); ‡ Numbers in parentheses indicate the number of people reporting a single ancestry; * Numbers in parentheses indicate the number of persons reporting this race alone, not in combination with any other race; Please refer to the Explanation of Data for more information.*

Fijian (0)	3	0.03
Guamanian/Chamorro (4)	4	0.03
Native Hawaiian (0)	2	0.02
Samoan (0)	2	0.02
White (8,273)	8,476	72.94
Not Hispanic (8,094)	8,260	71.08
Hispanic (179)	216	1.86

Center Point

Place Type: City
County: Jefferson
Population: 16,921†

Ancestry‡	Population	%
African, Sub-Saharan (171)	208	1.24
African (127)	164	0.98
Kenyan (27)	27	0.16
South African (17)	17	0.10
American (1,055)	1,055	6.28
British (36)	111	0.66
Bulgarian (8)	8	0.05
Celtic (13)	13	0.08
Czech (7)	19	0.11
Dutch (26)	35	0.21
English (392)	804	4.78
European (20)	20	0.12
Finnish (0)	10	0.06
French, ex. Basque (86)	237	1.41
French Canadian (6)	23	0.14
German (226)	768	4.57
Irish (190)	815	4.85
Italian (109)	239	1.42
Northern European (10)	10	0.06
Norwegian (0)	34	0.20
Polish (31)	90	0.54
Portuguese (26)	26	0.15
Russian (5)	48	0.29
Scotch-Irish (198)	331	1.97
Scottish (30)	208	1.24
Swedish (8)	18	0.11
West Indian, ex. Hispanic (146)	146	0.87
Dutch West Indian (27)	27	0.16
Jamaican (90)	90	0.54
West Indian (29)	29	0.17

Hispanic Origin	Population	%
Hispanic or Latino (of any race)	806	4.76
Central American, ex. Mexican	222	1.31
Guatemalan	73	0.43
Honduran	110	0.65
Nicaraguan	10	0.06
Panamanian	3	0.02
Salvadoran	21	0.12
Other Central American	5	0.03
Cuban	2	0.01
Dominican Republic	3	0.02
Mexican	465	2.75
Puerto Rican	30	0.18
South American	4	0.02
Colombian	2	0.01
Ecuadorian	1	0.01
Peruvian	1	0.01
Other Hispanic or Latino	80	0.47

Race*	Population	%
African-American/Black (10,635)	10,763	63.61
Not Hispanic (10,582)	10,695	63.21
Hispanic (53)	68	0.40
American Indian/Alaska Native (35)	81	0.48
Not Hispanic (31)	76	0.45
Hispanic (4)	5	0.03
Apache (1)	1	0.01
Blackfeet (0)	4	0.02
Central American Ind. (0)	1	0.01
Cherokee (10)	24	0.14
Choctaw (3)	4	0.02
Comanche (0)	1	0.01
Creek (0)	1	0.01
Inupiat *(Alaska Native)* (2)	2	0.01
Seminole (1)	1	0.01
Sioux (0)	1	0.01
Asian (65)	79	0.47
Not Hispanic (52)	65	0.38
Hispanic (13)	14	0.08
Chinese, ex. Taiwanese (11)	15	0.09
Filipino (17)	19	0.11
Indian (11)	11	0.07
Japanese (4)	8	0.05
Korean (1)	4	0.02
Pakistani (3)	3	0.02
Thai (0)	6	0.04
Vietnamese (12)	12	0.07
Hawaii Native/Pacific Islander (4)	10	0.06
Not Hispanic (4)	10	0.06
Native Hawaiian (1)	3	0.02
Samoan (2)	2	0.01
White (5,519)	5,672	33.52
Not Hispanic (5,268)	5,398	31.90
Hispanic (251)	274	1.62

Chelsea

Place Type: City
County: Shelby
Population: 10,183†

Ancestry‡	Population	%
African, Sub-Saharan (132)	141	1.53
African (132)	132	1.43
South African (0)	9	0.10
American (1,193)	1,193	12.96
Arab (66)	74	0.80
Lebanese (52)	60	0.65
Syrian (14)	14	0.15
Austrian (0)	14	0.15
British (14)	25	0.27
Canadian (0)	12	0.13
Croatian (0)	9	0.10
Czech (0)	22	0.24
Dutch (25)	149	1.62
Eastern European (0)	29	0.32
English (837)	1,403	15.25
European (156)	165	1.79
Finnish (24)	24	0.26
French, ex. Basque (61)	180	1.96
French Canadian (18)	18	0.20
German (318)	1,096	11.91
Greek (41)	68	0.74
Hungarian (9)	9	0.10
Iranian (21)	21	0.23
Irish (345)	1,101	11.96
Italian (278)	465	5.05
Norwegian (0)	98	1.06
Polish (55)	190	2.06
Russian (0)	9	0.10
Scotch-Irish (247)	349	3.79
Scottish (236)	403	4.38
Swedish (0)	49	0.53
Swiss (0)	11	0.12
Ukrainian (0)	14	0.15
Welsh (58)	117	1.27
West Indian, ex. Hispanic (17)	17	0.18
Dutch West Indian (17)	17	0.18

Hispanic Origin	Population	%
Hispanic or Latino (of any race)	325	3.19
Central American, ex. Mexican	20	0.20
Guatemalan	6	0.06
Honduran	10	0.10
Panamanian	3	0.03
Salvadoran	1	0.01
Cuban	20	0.20
Dominican Republic	10	0.10
Mexican	170	1.67
Puerto Rican	24	0.24
South American	39	0.38
Bolivian	2	0.02
Colombian	18	0.18
Ecuadorian	3	0.03
Peruvian	2	0.02
Venezuelan	14	0.14
Other Hispanic or Latino	42	0.41

Race*	Population	%
African-American/Black (582)	618	6.07
Not Hispanic (581)	608	5.97
Hispanic (1)	10	0.10
American Indian/Alaska Native (33)	67	0.66
Not Hispanic (33)	58	0.57
Hispanic (0)	9	0.09
Blackfeet (0)	1	0.01
Central American Ind. (1)	1	0.01
Cherokee (7)	27	0.27
Chippewa (0)	1	0.01
Cree (1)	1	0.01
Creek (2)	6	0.06
Iroquois (1)	1	0.01
Mexican American Ind. (0)	1	0.01
Sioux (0)	3	0.03
South American Ind. (1)	1	0.01
Yaqui (0)	1	0.01
Asian (208)	271	2.66
Not Hispanic (205)	252	2.47
Hispanic (3)	19	0.19
Chinese, ex. Taiwanese (39)	44	0.43
Filipino (28)	50	0.49
Indian (41)	49	0.48
Indonesian (1)	1	0.01
Japanese (4)	15	0.15
Korean (27)	31	0.30
Laotian (1)	3	0.03
Malaysian (2)	2	0.02
Nepalese (1)	2	0.02
Pakistani (4)	8	0.08
Thai (5)	11	0.11
Vietnamese (44)	45	0.44
Hawaii Native/Pacific Islander (13)	20	0.20
Not Hispanic (13)	20	0.20
Guamanian/Chamorro (10)	13	0.13
Native Hawaiian (0)	1	0.01
White (9,109)	9,215	90.49
Not Hispanic (8,919)	9,007	88.45
Hispanic (190)	208	2.04

Clanton

Place Type: City
County: Chilton
Population: 8,619†

Ancestry‡	Population	%
African, Sub-Saharan (0)	21	0.25
African (0)	21	0.25
American (1,615)	1,615	18.88
Danish (0)	22	0.26
Dutch (0)	29	0.34
English (414)	661	7.73
European (93)	163	1.91
French, ex. Basque (50)	99	1.16
French Canadian (0)	45	0.53
German (133)	488	5.70
Greek (9)	9	0.11
Irish (255)	586	6.85
Italian (45)	115	1.34
Scotch-Irish (69)	78	0.91
Scottish (240)	297	3.47
Swedish (0)	28	0.33
West Indian, ex. Hispanic (0)	11	0.13
Dutch West Indian (0)	11	0.13

Hispanic Origin	Population	%
Hispanic or Latino (of any race)	520	6.03
Central American, ex. Mexican	62	0.72
Guatemalan	48	0.56
Honduran	3	0.03
Nicaraguan	2	0.02
Salvadoran	9	0.10
Cuban	1	0.01
Mexican	361	4.19

*Notes: † The Census 2010 population figure is used to calculate the percentages in the Hispanic Origin and Race categories. Ancestry percentages are based on the 2006-2010 American Community Survey population (not shown); ‡ Numbers in parentheses indicate the number of people reporting a single ancestry; * Numbers in parentheses indicate the number of persons reporting this race alone, not in combination with any other race; Please refer to the Explanation of Data for more information.*

Puerto Rican	31	0.36
South American	5	0.06
Colombian	1	0.01
Paraguayan	1	0.01
Venezuelan	2	0.02
Other South American	1	0.01
Other Hispanic or Latino	60	0.70

Race*	Population	%
African-American/Black (1,642)	1,703	19.76
Not Hispanic (1,620)	1,673	19.41
Hispanic (22)	30	0.35
American Indian/Alaska Native (25)	53	0.61
Not Hispanic (24)	47	0.55
Hispanic (1)	6	0.07
Cherokee (6)	11	0.13
Creek (8)	8	0.09
Sioux (3)	5	0.06
Asian (53)	70	0.81
Not Hispanic (51)	63	0.73
Hispanic (2)	7	0.08
Chinese, ex. Taiwanese (9)	10	0.12
Filipino (15)	25	0.29
Indian (12)	12	0.14
Japanese (3)	7	0.08
Nepalese (2)	2	0.02
Thai (1)	2	0.02
Vietnamese (9)	12	0.14
Hawaii Native/Pacific Islander (6)	12	0.14
Not Hispanic (5)	6	0.07
Hispanic (1)	6	0.07
Guamanian/Chamorro (0)	1	0.01
Native Hawaiian (0)	3	0.03
Samoan (1)	4	0.05
White (6,454)	6,566	76.18
Not Hispanic (6,304)	6,382	74.05
Hispanic (150)	184	2.13

Clay

Place Type: City
County: Jefferson
Population: 9,708†

Ancestry‡	Population	%
American (1,440)	1,440	15.11
Arab (0)	41	0.43
Lebanese (0)	41	0.43
Australian (13)	13	0.14
Austrian (0)	10	0.10
Brazilian (26)	26	0.27
British (89)	89	0.93
Canadian (7)	7	0.07
Czech (10)	10	0.10
Czechoslovakian (7)	7	0.07
Dutch (26)	102	1.07
English (673)	1,416	14.86
European (40)	40	0.42
French, ex. Basque (35)	73	0.77
French Canadian (0)	14	0.15
German (339)	1,129	11.85
Greek (0)	27	0.28
Irish (861)	1,596	16.75
Italian (80)	164	1.72
Norwegian (39)	39	0.41
Polish (27)	69	0.72
Russian (0)	8	0.08
Scotch-Irish (357)	492	5.16
Scottish (178)	294	3.09
Welsh (7)	20	0.21

Hispanic Origin	Population	%
Hispanic or Latino (of any race)	127	1.31
Central American, ex. Mexican	11	0.11
Costa Rican	6	0.06
Guatemalan	2	0.02
Honduran	3	0.03
Mexican	86	0.89
Puerto Rican	5	0.05
South American	17	0.18
Bolivian	3	0.03
Peruvian	5	0.05
Uruguayan	9	0.09
Other Hispanic or Latino	8	0.08

Race*	Population	%
African-American/Black (1,292)	1,337	13.77
Not Hispanic (1,287)	1,331	13.71
Hispanic (5)	6	0.06
American Indian/Alaska Native (29)	69	0.71
Not Hispanic (28)	65	0.67
Hispanic (1)	4	0.04
Blackfeet (0)	1	0.01
Central American Ind. (1)	1	0.01
Cherokee (19)	23	0.24
Chippewa (0)	1	0.01
Iroquois (1)	1	0.01
Osage (0)	1	0.01
South American Ind. (0)	3	0.03
Asian (59)	88	0.91
Not Hispanic (59)	88	0.91
Chinese, ex. Taiwanese (8)	8	0.08
Filipino (12)	18	0.19
Indian (5)	10	0.10
Japanese (4)	6	0.06
Korean (5)	8	0.08
Pakistani (0)	1	0.01
Taiwanese (2)	2	0.02
Thai (1)	4	0.04
Vietnamese (18)	25	0.26
Hawaii Native/Pacific Islander (3)	5	0.05
Not Hispanic (3)	5	0.05
Guamanian/Chamorro (0)	1	0.01
White (8,168)	8,254	85.02
Not Hispanic (8,093)	8,177	84.23
Hispanic (75)	77	0.79

Cullman

Place Type: City
County: Cullman
Population: 14,775†

Ancestry‡	Population	%
American (1,870)	1,870	12.73
Austrian (9)	9	0.06
British (36)	47	0.32
Canadian (84)	100	0.68
Czech (0)	30	0.20
Czechoslovakian (9)	9	0.06
Danish (0)	14	0.10
Dutch (29)	197	1.34
Eastern European (19)	19	0.13
English (669)	1,693	11.53
European (27)	27	0.18
Finnish (0)	12	0.08
French, ex. Basque (144)	301	2.05
French Canadian (38)	79	0.54
German (1,080)	2,303	15.68
Hungarian (9)	9	0.06
Irish (1,523)	3,049	20.76
Italian (19)	147	1.00
Lithuanian (0)	23	0.16
Norwegian (15)	15	0.10
Polish (35)	98	0.67
Portuguese (0)	24	0.16
Romanian (11)	20	0.14
Russian (35)	79	0.54
Scandinavian (0)	84	0.57
Scotch-Irish (118)	467	3.18
Scottish (113)	386	2.63
Swedish (27)	27	0.18
Swiss (14)	46	0.31
Ukrainian (7)	7	0.05
Welsh (34)	68	0.46

Hispanic Origin	Population	%
Hispanic or Latino (of any race)	1,216	8.23
Central American, ex. Mexican	31	0.21
Guatemalan	14	0.09
Honduran	9	0.06
Nicaraguan	2	0.01
Panamanian	1	0.01
Salvadoran	5	0.03
Cuban	5	0.03
Mexican	1,090	7.38
Puerto Rican	32	0.22
South American	24	0.16
Chilean	1	0.01
Colombian	17	0.12
Ecuadorian	1	0.01
Paraguayan	2	0.01
Peruvian	2	0.01
Venezuelan	1	0.01
Other Hispanic or Latino	34	0.23

Race*	Population	%
African-American/Black (127)	175	1.18
Not Hispanic (113)	153	1.04
Hispanic (14)	22	0.15
American Indian/Alaska Native (49)	118	0.80
Not Hispanic (46)	104	0.70
Hispanic (3)	14	0.09
Blackfeet (0)	2	0.01
Cherokee (26)	45	0.30
Chickasaw (2)	2	0.01
Chippewa (1)	1	0.01
Creek (2)	3	0.02
Lumbee (0)	1	0.01
Mexican American Ind. (0)	3	0.02
Navajo (1)	1	0.01
Seminole (2)	2	0.01
Sioux (0)	1	0.01
South American Ind. (1)	3	0.02
Asian (139)	160	1.08
Not Hispanic (138)	158	1.07
Hispanic (1)	2	0.01
Cambodian (1)	1	0.01
Chinese, ex. Taiwanese (20)	21	0.14
Filipino (7)	17	0.12
Indian (33)	33	0.22
Indonesian (1)	3	0.02
Japanese (28)	33	0.22
Korean (10)	14	0.09
Taiwanese (4)	4	0.03
Thai (1)	1	0.01
Vietnamese (31)	32	0.22
Hawaii Native/Pacific Islander (3)	15	0.10
Not Hispanic (3)	9	0.06
Hispanic (0)	6	0.04
Guamanian/Chamorro (0)	3	0.02
Native Hawaiian (2)	7	0.05
Samoan (1)	2	0.01
White (13,797)	13,943	94.37
Not Hispanic (13,128)	13,245	89.64
Hispanic (669)	698	4.72

Daphne

Place Type: City
County: Baldwin
Population: 21,570†

Ancestry‡	Population	%
African, Sub-Saharan (147)	147	0.71
African (101)	101	0.49
South African (46)	46	0.22
American (3,422)	3,422	16.44
Arab (51)	119	0.57
Egyptian (51)	85	0.41
Other Arab (0)	34	0.16
Austrian (13)	27	0.13
British (80)	207	0.99
Cajun (32)	59	0.28
Canadian (12)	12	0.06
Czech (51)	74	0.36
Danish (0)	39	0.19
Dutch (49)	114	0.55
English (1,058)	2,578	12.38
European (249)	263	1.26

*Notes: † The Census 2010 population figure is used to calculate the percentages in the Hispanic Origin and Race categories. Ancestry percentages are based on the 2006-2010 American Community Survey population (not shown); ‡ Numbers in parentheses indicate the number of people reporting a single ancestry; * Numbers in parentheses indicate the number of persons reporting this race alone, not in combination with any other race; Please refer to the Explanation of Data for more information.*

French, ex. Basque (199)	822	3.95
French Canadian (75)	185	0.89
German (744)	2,255	10.83
Greek (89)	191	0.92
Hungarian (29)	89	0.43
Icelander (0)	14	0.07
Irish (1,031)	2,664	12.80
Italian (383)	1,107	5.32
Latvian (12)	12	0.06
Lithuanian (18)	18	0.09
Norwegian (30)	203	0.98
Polish (67)	332	1.59
Portuguese (10)	53	0.25
Romanian (35)	45	0.22
Russian (0)	66	0.32
Scandinavian (68)	91	0.44
Scotch-Irish (404)	680	3.27
Scottish (373)	890	4.28
Slovak (0)	15	0.07
Swedish (55)	222	1.07
Swiss (50)	61	0.29
Ukrainian (30)	43	0.21
Welsh (44)	205	0.98
West Indian, ex. Hispanic (91)	91	0.44
Jamaican (80)	80	0.38
West Indian (11)	11	0.05

Hispanic Origin	Population	%
Hispanic or Latino (of any race)	620	2.87
Central American, ex. Mexican	88	0.41
Costa Rican	11	0.05
Guatemalan	7	0.03
Honduran	11	0.05
Nicaraguan	10	0.05
Panamanian	24	0.11
Salvadoran	15	0.07
Other Central American	10	0.05
Cuban	52	0.24
Dominican Republic	2	0.01
Mexican	251	1.16
Puerto Rican	71	0.33
South American	77	0.36
Argentinean	2	0.01
Bolivian	3	0.01
Chilean	4	0.02
Colombian	22	0.10
Ecuadorian	10	0.05
Peruvian	18	0.08
Uruguayan	4	0.02
Venezuelan	14	0.06
Other Hispanic or Latino	79	0.37

Race*	Population	%
African-American/Black (2,536)	2,642	12.25
Not Hispanic (2,520)	2,622	12.16
Hispanic (16)	20	0.09
American Indian/Alaska Native (96)	198	0.92
Not Hispanic (90)	188	0.87
Hispanic (6)	10	0.05
Apache (0)	4	0.02
Blackfeet (0)	1	<0.01
Cherokee (14)	50	0.23
Chickasaw (2)	2	0.01
Chippewa (4)	5	0.02
Choctaw (1)	3	0.01
Comanche (1)	1	<0.01
Creek (26)	42	0.19
Houma (2)	2	0.01
Lumbee (7)	7	0.03
Mexican American Ind. (1)	1	<0.01
Seminole (0)	1	<0.01
Yaqui (3)	7	0.03
Asian (334)	404	1.87
Not Hispanic (334)	399	1.85
Hispanic (0)	5	0.02
Burmese (3)	3	0.01
Cambodian (8)	9	0.04
Chinese, ex. Taiwanese (106)	114	0.53
Filipino (35)	57	0.26
Indian (57)	66	0.31
Indonesian (4)	5	0.02
Japanese (14)	24	0.11
Korean (20)	28	0.13
Laotian (0)	4	0.02
Malaysian (1)	1	<0.01
Pakistani (1)	1	<0.01
Taiwanese (14)	14	0.06
Thai (34)	38	0.18
Vietnamese (16)	21	0.10
Hawaii Native/Pacific Islander (13)	23	0.11
Not Hispanic (10)	18	0.08
Hispanic (3)	5	0.02
Guamanian/Chamorro (4)	6	0.03
Native Hawaiian (2)	6	0.03
Samoan (3)	4	0.02
White (18,132)	18,376	85.19
Not Hispanic (17,715)	17,938	83.16
Hispanic (417)	438	2.03

Decatur

Place Type: City
County: Morgan
Population: 55,683†

Ancestry‡	Population	%
African, Sub-Saharan (49)	119	0.22
African (49)	97	0.18
Ethiopian (0)	22	0.04
American (6,240)	6,240	11.29
Arab (96)	131	0.24
Arab (68)	90	0.16
Lebanese (28)	41	0.07
Austrian (7)	28	0.05
Belgian (6)	53	0.10
Brazilian (28)	28	0.05
British (119)	266	0.48
Bulgarian (10)	10	0.02
Canadian (44)	81	0.15
Celtic (11)	11	0.02
Czech (11)	35	0.06
Czechoslovakian (8)	8	0.01
Danish (24)	75	0.14
Dutch (90)	493	0.89
Eastern European (10)	10	0.02
English (3,308)	5,710	10.33
European (350)	391	0.71
French, ex. Basque (324)	1,317	2.38
French Canadian (36)	139	0.25
German (1,782)	5,564	10.07
Greek (13)	51	0.09
Hungarian (58)	114	0.21
Irish (2,490)	6,724	12.17
Italian (299)	760	1.38
Lithuanian (20)	33	0.06
Northern European (7)	7	0.01
Norwegian (79)	150	0.27
Pennsylvania German (7)	7	0.01
Polish (46)	279	0.50
Portuguese (12)	31	0.06
Romanian (10)	10	0.02
Russian (41)	102	0.18
Scandinavian (18)	32	0.06
Scotch-Irish (898)	1,697	3.07
Scottish (492)	1,282	2.32
Slavic (11)	11	0.02
Slovak (0)	19	0.03
Swedish (27)	368	0.67
Swiss (11)	22	0.04
Turkish (87)	87	0.16
Ukrainian (82)	104	0.19
Welsh (16)	144	0.26
West Indian, ex. Hispanic (60)	103	0.19
Jamaican (33)	76	0.14
Trinidadian/Tobagonian (27)	27	0.05

Hispanic Origin	Population	%
Hispanic or Latino (of any race)	6,882	12.36
Central American, ex. Mexican	1,066	1.91
Costa Rican	8	0.01
Guatemalan	990	1.78
Honduran	19	0.03
Nicaraguan	12	0.02
Panamanian	17	0.03
Salvadoran	17	0.03
Other Central American	3	0.01
Cuban	68	0.12
Dominican Republic	9	0.02
Mexican	5,158	9.26
Puerto Rican	133	0.24
South American	62	0.11
Argentinean	1	<0.01
Bolivian	5	0.01
Chilean	3	0.01
Colombian	19	0.03
Ecuadorian	6	0.01
Paraguayan	5	0.01
Peruvian	14	0.03
Venezuelan	9	0.02
Other Hispanic or Latino	386	0.69

Race*	Population	%
African-American/Black (12,067)	12,637	22.69
Not Hispanic (11,971)	12,505	22.46
Hispanic (96)	132	0.24
American Indian/Alaska Native (391)	742	1.33
Not Hispanic (309)	623	1.12
Hispanic (82)	119	0.21
Apache (0)	7	0.01
Blackfeet (4)	5	0.01
Central American Ind. (3)	3	0.01
Cherokee (165)	345	0.62
Chickasaw (1)	4	0.01
Chippewa (2)	6	0.01
Choctaw (8)	23	0.04
Comanche (7)	8	0.01
Creek (13)	27	0.05
Crow (2)	4	0.01
Inupiat *(Alaska Native)* (0)	2	<0.01
Kiowa (0)	1	<0.01
Lumbee (7)	7	0.01
Mexican American Ind. (28)	43	0.08
Navajo (0)	1	<0.01
Pueblo (5)	5	0.01
Seminole (0)	2	<0.01
Sioux (4)	11	0.02
Spanish American Ind. (1)	1	<0.01
Asian (499)	642	1.15
Not Hispanic (480)	609	1.09
Hispanic (19)	33	0.06
Burmese (3)	3	0.01
Cambodian (0)	2	<0.01
Chinese, ex. Taiwanese (73)	101	0.18
Filipino (51)	80	0.14
Indian (196)	211	0.38
Indonesian (2)	8	0.01
Japanese (50)	67	0.12
Korean (17)	46	0.08
Laotian (5)	13	0.02
Nepalese (5)	5	0.01
Pakistani (1)	1	<0.01
Taiwanese (10)	10	0.02
Thai (10)	17	0.03
Vietnamese (56)	66	0.12
Hawaii Native/Pacific Islander (80)	108	0.19
Not Hispanic (43)	53	0.10
Hispanic (37)	55	0.10
Guamanian/Chamorro (64)	74	0.13
Native Hawaiian (11)	17	0.03
Samoan (0)	4	0.01
White (37,038)	38,145	68.50
Not Hispanic (35,037)	35,866	64.41
Hispanic (2,001)	2,279	4.09

Dothan

Place Type: City
County: Houston
Population: 65,496†

*Notes: † The Census 2010 population figure is used to calculate the percentages in the Hispanic Origin and Race categories. Ancestry percentages are based on the 2006-2010 American Community Survey population (not shown); ‡ Numbers in parentheses indicate the number of people reporting a single ancestry; * Numbers in parentheses indicate the number of persons reporting this race alone, not in combination with any other race; Please refer to the Explanation of Data for more information.*

Ancestry‡	Population	%
African, Sub-Saharan (393)	494	0.77
African (362)	431	0.67
Ethiopian (4)	21	0.03
Nigerian (14)	18	0.03
Somalian (0)	11	0.02
Sudanese (13)	13	0.02
American (9,085)	9,085	14.13
Arab (96)	153	0.24
Arab (34)	54	0.08
Egyptian (2)	2	<0.01
Lebanese (21)	52	0.08
Palestinian (31)	31	0.05
Syrian (0)	6	0.01
Other Arab (8)	8	0.01
Armenian (6)	6	0.01
Australian (3)	3	<0.01
Austrian (3)	22	0.03
Belgian (0)	14	0.02
Brazilian (22)	65	0.10
British (200)	309	0.48
Bulgarian (8)	10	0.02
Cajun (7)	33	0.05
Canadian (33)	70	0.11
Celtic (27)	34	0.05
Croatian (9)	15	0.02
Czech (14)	29	0.05
Czechoslovakian (0)	14	0.02
Danish (7)	42	0.07
Dutch (118)	681	1.06
Eastern European (8)	8	0.01
English (2,654)	5,487	8.53
Estonian (0)	4	0.01
European (368)	399	0.62
Finnish (14)	19	0.03
French, ex. Basque (205)	1,187	1.85
French Canadian (85)	151	0.23
German (1,833)	5,451	8.48
German Russian (22)	22	0.03
Greek (32)	64	0.10
Hungarian (62)	118	0.18
Iranian (4)	4	0.01
Irish (2,401)	6,579	10.23
Italian (355)	1,012	1.57
Latvian (12)	12	0.02
Lithuanian (7)	7	0.01
New Zealander (3)	3	<0.01
Northern European (5)	9	0.01
Norwegian (52)	156	0.24
Pennsylvania German (5)	14	0.02
Polish (133)	467	0.73
Portuguese (9)	16	0.02
Russian (34)	57	0.09
Scandinavian (29)	39	0.06
Scotch-Irish (931)	1,603	2.49
Scottish (584)	1,236	1.92
Slavic (2)	2	<0.01
Slovak (6)	24	0.04
Swedish (67)	275	0.43
Swiss (2)	41	0.06
Turkish (13)	16	0.02
Ukrainian (3)	6	0.01
Welsh (73)	293	0.46
West Indian, ex. Hispanic (70)	208	0.32
Jamaican (64)	192	0.30
West Indian (0)	10	0.02
Other West Indian (6)	6	0.01
Yugoslavian (11)	14	0.02

Hispanic Origin	Population	%
Hispanic or Latino (of any race)	1,889	2.88
Central American, ex. Mexican	244	0.37
Costa Rican	16	0.02
Guatemalan	108	0.16
Honduran	30	0.05
Nicaraguan	5	0.01
Panamanian	53	0.08
Salvadoran	27	0.04
Other Central American	5	0.01
Cuban	81	0.12
Dominican Republic	26	0.04
Mexican	945	1.44
Puerto Rican	284	0.43
South American	127	0.19
Argentinean	6	0.01
Bolivian	6	0.01
Colombian	51	0.08
Ecuadorian	10	0.02
Peruvian	26	0.04
Venezuelan	28	0.04
Other Hispanic or Latino	182	0.28

Race*	Population	%
African-American/Black (21,312)	21,962	33.53
Not Hispanic (21,207)	21,767	33.23
Hispanic (105)	195	0.30
American Indian/Alaska Native (236)	591	0.90
Not Hispanic (206)	530	0.81
Hispanic (30)	61	0.09
Apache (0)	1	<0.01
Blackfeet (1)	5	0.01
Canadian/French Am. Ind. (1)	1	<0.01
Central American Ind. (2)	2	<0.01
Cherokee (50)	159	0.24
Cheyenne (1)	2	<0.01
Chickasaw (0)	1	<0.01
Chippewa (1)	1	<0.01
Choctaw (3)	13	0.02
Comanche (1)	1	<0.01
Creek (43)	61	0.09
Iroquois (0)	6	0.01
Lumbee (3)	5	0.01
Mexican American Ind. (13)	15	0.02
Navajo (6)	11	0.02
Seminole (0)	6	0.01
Sioux (2)	4	0.01
South American Ind. (1)	2	<0.01
Spanish American Ind. (0)	1	<0.01
Yaqui (0)	4	0.01
Asian (724)	971	1.48
Not Hispanic (712)	935	1.43
Hispanic (12)	36	0.05
Bangladeshi (1)	1	<0.01
Chinese, ex. Taiwanese (79)	115	0.18
Filipino (72)	127	0.19
Indian (149)	182	0.28
Indonesian (5)	6	0.01
Japanese (82)	127	0.19
Korean (66)	95	0.15
Laotian (7)	7	0.01
Nepalese (2)	2	<0.01
Pakistani (27)	30	0.05
Sri Lankan (1)	1	<0.01
Taiwanese (9)	9	0.01
Thai (6)	10	0.02
Vietnamese (182)	213	0.33
Hawaii Native/Pacific Islander (46)	108	0.16
Not Hispanic (40)	83	0.13
Hispanic (6)	25	0.04
Fijian (1)	3	<0.01
Guamanian/Chamorro (16)	23	0.04
Marshallese (2)	2	<0.01
Native Hawaiian (11)	41	0.06
Samoan (14)	24	0.04
White (41,298)	42,242	64.50
Not Hispanic (40,412)	41,216	62.93
Hispanic (886)	1,026	1.57

Enterprise

Place Type: City
County: Coffee
Population: 26,562†

Ancestry‡	Population	%
African, Sub-Saharan (787)	787	3.11
African (787)	787	3.11
American (5,016)	5,016	19.84
Arab (124)	134	0.53
Arab (90)	90	0.36
Egyptian (0)	10	0.04
Lebanese (34)	34	0.13
Australian (33)	58	0.23
Austrian (0)	30	0.12
Brazilian (0)	9	0.04
British (47)	170	0.67
Czech (19)	39	0.15
Danish (17)	17	0.07
Dutch (58)	308	1.22
English (1,201)	2,313	9.15
European (187)	315	1.25
Finnish (24)	69	0.27
French, ex. Basque (31)	305	1.21
French Canadian (14)	65	0.26
German (1,195)	2,856	11.30
Hungarian (51)	51	0.20
Iranian (14)	68	0.27
Irish (652)	1,975	7.81
Italian (134)	599	2.37
Norwegian (31)	96	0.38
Polish (57)	412	1.63
Portuguese (13)	137	0.54
Romanian (9)	9	0.04
Russian (19)	75	0.30
Scandinavian (9)	40	0.16
Scotch-Irish (473)	866	3.42
Scottish (266)	544	2.15
Serbian (0)	15	0.06
Swedish (0)	97	0.38
Swiss (0)	15	0.06
Ukrainian (18)	78	0.31
Welsh (0)	85	0.34
West Indian, ex. Hispanic (27)	53	0.21
British West Indian (8)	8	0.03
Jamaican (19)	45	0.18

Hispanic Origin	Population	%
Hispanic or Latino (of any race)	2,328	8.76
Central American, ex. Mexican	540	2.03
Costa Rican	11	0.04
Guatemalan	333	1.25
Honduran	89	0.34
Nicaraguan	30	0.11
Panamanian	55	0.21
Salvadoran	11	0.04
Other Central American	11	0.04
Cuban	41	0.15
Dominican Republic	18	0.07
Mexican	1,022	3.85
Puerto Rican	489	1.84
South American	76	0.29
Argentinean	4	0.02
Bolivian	5	0.02
Chilean	12	0.05
Colombian	18	0.07
Ecuadorian	13	0.05
Peruvian	10	0.04
Venezuelan	14	0.05
Other Hispanic or Latino	142	0.53

Race*	Population	%
African-American/Black (5,508)	5,823	21.92
Not Hispanic (5,415)	5,691	21.43
Hispanic (93)	132	0.50
American Indian/Alaska Native (137)	351	1.32
Not Hispanic (125)	312	1.17
Hispanic (12)	39	0.15
Aleut *(Alaska Native)* (1)	3	0.01
Apache (7)	12	0.05
Arapaho (0)	1	<0.01
Blackfeet (0)	3	0.01
Cherokee (20)	75	0.28
Chickasaw (2)	2	0.01
Chippewa (5)	9	0.03
Choctaw (3)	18	0.07
Comanche (1)	1	<0.01
Creek (37)	57	0.21
Crow (0)	1	<0.01
Iroquois (7)	10	0.04
Lumbee (1)	1	<0.01

*Notes: † The Census 2010 population figure is used to calculate the percentages in the Hispanic Origin and Race categories. Ancestry percentages are based on the 2006-2010 American Community Survey population (not shown); ‡ Numbers in parentheses indicate the number of people reporting a single ancestry; * Numbers in parentheses indicate the number of persons reporting this race alone, not in combination with any other race; Please refer to the Explanation of Data for more information.*

Race*	Population	%
Mexican American Ind. (1)	3	0.01
Navajo (0)	5	0.02
Pima (3)	3	0.01
Potawatomi (0)	1	<0.01
Pueblo (0)	4	0.02
Seminole (0)	1	<0.01
Shoshone (1)	1	<0.01
Sioux (0)	2	0.01
Spanish American Ind. (0)	4	0.02
Yakama (2)	2	0.01
Asian (523)	776	2.92
Not Hispanic (510)	739	2.78
Hispanic (13)	37	0.14
Cambodian (2)	7	0.03
Chinese, ex. Taiwanese (44)	57	0.21
Filipino (106)	182	0.69
Indian (45)	49	0.18
Indonesian (2)	14	0.05
Japanese (37)	68	0.26
Korean (212)	300	1.13
Pakistani (3)	3	0.01
Taiwanese (2)	2	0.01
Thai (11)	21	0.08
Vietnamese (43)	59	0.22
Hawaii Native/Pacific Islander (84)	125	0.47
Not Hispanic (44)	79	0.30
Hispanic (40)	46	0.17
Guamanian/Chamorro (56)	60	0.23
Native Hawaiian (19)	32	0.12
Samoan (9)	13	0.05
White (18,442)	19,129	72.02
Not Hispanic (17,473)	18,040	67.92
Hispanic (969)	1,089	4.10

Eufaula

Place Type: City
County: Barbour
Population: 13,137†

Ancestry‡	Population	%
African, Sub-Saharan (127)	127	0.96
African (127)	127	0.96
American (1,365)	1,365	10.32
Austrian (15)	15	0.11
British (12)	36	0.27
Czechoslovakian (18)	18	0.14
Dutch (14)	72	0.54
Eastern European (8)	8	0.06
English (560)	984	7.44
European (109)	166	1.25
French, ex. Basque (4)	151	1.14
French Canadian (18)	18	0.14
German (264)	727	5.50
Greek (20)	20	0.15
Hungarian (0)	14	0.11
Icelander (0)	6	0.05
Irish (223)	788	5.96
Italian (28)	101	0.76
Norwegian (26)	26	0.20
Polish (46)	114	0.86
Scandinavian (0)	11	0.08
Scotch-Irish (196)	289	2.18
Scottish (163)	240	1.81
Swedish (22)	22	0.17
Welsh (0)	30	0.23
Yugoslavian (43)	91	0.69

Hispanic Origin	Population	%
Hispanic or Latino (of any race)	566	4.31
Central American, ex. Mexican	96	0.73
Guatemalan	88	0.67
Honduran	2	0.02
Nicaraguan	5	0.04
Salvadoran	1	0.01
Cuban	1	0.01
Dominican Republic	1	0.01
Mexican	400	3.04
Puerto Rican	25	0.19
South American	17	0.13
Argentinean	1	0.01
Chilean	3	0.02
Colombian	5	0.04
Paraguayan	2	0.02
Peruvian	1	0.01
Uruguayan	5	0.04
Other Hispanic or Latino	26	0.20

Race*	Population	%
African-American/Black (5,859)	5,915	45.03
Not Hispanic (5,838)	5,892	44.85
Hispanic (21)	23	0.18
American Indian/Alaska Native (71)	115	0.88
Not Hispanic (23)	65	0.49
Hispanic (48)	50	0.38
Blackfeet (0)	1	0.01
Central American Ind. (41)	41	0.31
Cherokee (1)	12	0.09
Chippewa (0)	4	0.03
Choctaw (3)	3	0.02
Cree (0)	3	0.02
Creek (4)	8	0.06
Lumbee (1)	3	0.02
Mexican American Ind. (6)	6	0.05
Navajo (0)	1	0.01
Potawatomi (2)	2	0.02
Asian (85)	95	0.72
Not Hispanic (85)	94	0.72
Hispanic (0)	1	0.01
Bangladeshi (0)	2	0.02
Chinese, ex. Taiwanese (10)	12	0.09
Filipino (1)	1	0.01
Indian (27)	30	0.23
Indonesian (0)	1	0.01
Japanese (1)	3	0.02
Korean (13)	14	0.11
Taiwanese (3)	3	0.02
Thai (1)	1	0.01
Vietnamese (23)	23	0.18
Hawaii Native/Pacific Islander (21)	23	0.18
Not Hispanic (19)	20	0.15
Hispanic (2)	3	0.02
Guamanian/Chamorro (17)	18	0.14
Native Hawaiian (4)	4	0.03
White (6,698)	6,786	51.66
Not Hispanic (6,509)	6,576	50.06
Hispanic (189)	210	1.60

Fairfield

Place Type: City
County: Jefferson
Population: 11,117†

Ancestry‡	Population	%
African, Sub-Saharan (253)	309	2.74
African (245)	259	2.30
Nigerian (8)	8	0.07
Other Sub-Saharan African (0)	42	0.37
American (340)	340	3.01
Arab (9)	9	0.08
Lebanese (9)	9	0.08
Dutch (0)	10	0.09
English (132)	141	1.25
French, ex. Basque (0)	12	0.11
German (248)	319	2.83
Irish (7)	23	0.20
Italian (35)	35	0.31
Portuguese (0)	21	0.19
Russian (0)	25	0.22
Scotch-Irish (16)	22	0.19
Welsh (0)	8	0.07
West Indian, ex. Hispanic (41)	41	0.36
Haitian (21)	21	0.19
Jamaican (20)	20	0.18

Hispanic Origin	Population	%
Hispanic or Latino (of any race)	127	1.14
Central American, ex. Mexican	7	0.06
Guatemalan	2	0.02
Honduran	4	0.04
Panamanian	1	0.01
Cuban	3	0.03
Mexican	90	0.81
Puerto Rican	7	0.06
Other Hispanic or Latino	20	0.18

Race*	Population	%
African-American/Black (10,518)	10,559	94.98
Not Hispanic (10,489)	10,528	94.70
Hispanic (29)	31	0.28
American Indian/Alaska Native (4)	20	0.18
Not Hispanic (3)	19	0.17
Hispanic (1)	1	0.01
Cherokee (2)	8	0.07
Chippewa (0)	1	0.01
Asian (1)	7	0.06
Not Hispanic (1)	7	0.06
Chinese, ex. Taiwanese (0)	2	0.02
Filipino (0)	1	0.01
Indian (0)	2	0.02
Korean (1)	2	0.02
Hawaii Native/Pacific Islander (3)	3	0.03
Not Hispanic (2)	2	0.02
Hispanic (1)	1	0.01
Guamanian/Chamorro (2)	2	0.02
White (462)	498	4.48
Not Hispanic (442)	477	4.29
Hispanic (20)	21	0.19

Fairhope

Place Type: City
County: Baldwin
Population: 15,326†

Ancestry‡	Population	%
American (2,237)	2,237	14.99
Arab (6)	57	0.38
Lebanese (6)	57	0.38
Austrian (0)	47	0.31
Belgian (0)	10	0.07
British (109)	145	0.97
Croatian (14)	25	0.17
Czech (26)	41	0.27
Czechoslovakian (0)	24	0.16
Danish (19)	59	0.40
Dutch (17)	218	1.46
English (1,368)	2,893	19.38
Estonian (13)	13	0.09
European (383)	531	3.56
Finnish (0)	28	0.19
French, ex. Basque (141)	775	5.19
French Canadian (82)	112	0.75
German (670)	1,850	12.39
Greek (19)	31	0.21
Hungarian (11)	18	0.12
Irish (786)	2,054	13.76
Italian (257)	723	4.84
Luxemburger (12)	26	0.17
Macedonian (16)	16	0.11
Norwegian (199)	240	1.61
Polish (30)	213	1.43
Portuguese (0)	18	0.12
Russian (20)	55	0.37
Scandinavian (9)	36	0.24
Scotch-Irish (436)	614	4.11
Scottish (294)	665	4.46
Serbian (22)	22	0.15
Slovak (60)	60	0.40
Slovene (0)	21	0.14
Swedish (70)	149	1.00
Swiss (13)	33	0.22
Turkish (184)	184	1.23
Ukrainian (16)	16	0.11
Welsh (21)	41	0.27
Yugoslavian (0)	17	0.11

Hispanic Origin	Population	%
Hispanic or Latino (of any race)	432	2.82

*Notes: † The Census 2010 population figure is used to calculate the percentages in the Hispanic Origin and Race categories. Ancestry percentages are based on the 2006-2010 American Community Survey population (not shown); ‡ Numbers in parentheses indicate the number of people reporting a single ancestry; * Numbers in parentheses indicate the number of persons reporting this race alone, not in combination with any other race; Please refer to the Explanation of Data for more information.*

Central American, ex. Mexican	58	0.38
Costa Rican	12	0.08
Guatemalan	15	0.10
Honduran	13	0.08
Nicaraguan	6	0.04
Panamanian	11	0.07
Salvadoran	1	0.01
Cuban	16	0.10
Dominican Republic	2	0.01
Mexican	212	1.38
Puerto Rican	57	0.37
South American	41	0.27
Argentinean	9	0.06
Chilean	4	0.03
Colombian	18	0.12
Ecuadorian	4	0.03
Paraguayan	1	0.01
Peruvian	2	0.01
Venezuelan	3	0.02
Other Hispanic or Latino	46	0.30

Race*	Population	%
African-American/Black (955)	1,011	6.60
Not Hispanic (952)	1,001	6.53
Hispanic (3)	10	0.07
American Indian/Alaska Native (28)	66	0.43
Not Hispanic (27)	64	0.42
Hispanic (1)	2	0.01
Apache (0)	1	0.01
Cherokee (3)	13	0.08
Chickasaw (0)	1	0.01
Chippewa (2)	2	0.01
Choctaw (3)	3	0.02
Creek (10)	19	0.12
Houma (1)	1	0.01
Iroquois (1)	1	0.01
Mexican American Ind. (1)	1	0.01
Asian (110)	138	0.90
Not Hispanic (106)	134	0.87
Hispanic (4)	4	0.03
Cambodian (5)	5	0.03
Chinese, ex. Taiwanese (45)	47	0.31
Filipino (6)	13	0.08
Indian (18)	23	0.15
Indonesian (1)	2	0.01
Japanese (6)	15	0.10
Korean (1)	6	0.04
Pakistani (3)	4	0.03
Thai (0)	5	0.03
Vietnamese (16)	23	0.15
Hawaii Native/Pacific Islander (7)	13	0.08
Not Hispanic (7)	13	0.08
Native Hawaiian (6)	7	0.05
Samoan (0)	1	0.01
White (13,961)	14,078	91.86
Not Hispanic (13,689)	13,791	89.98
Hispanic (272)	287	1.87

Florence

Place Type: City
County: Lauderdale
Population: 39,319†

Ancestry‡	Population	%
African, Sub-Saharan (165)	177	0.46
African (79)	91	0.23
Kenyan (6)	6	0.02
Nigerian (57)	57	0.15
South African (23)	23	0.06
American (4,894)	4,894	12.61
Arab (33)	33	0.09
Egyptian (18)	18	0.05
Lebanese (15)	15	0.04
Austrian (13)	87	0.22
Belgian (11)	11	0.03
Brazilian (10)	10	0.03
British (205)	225	0.58
Canadian (40)	40	0.10
Croatian (0)	20	0.05
Czech (26)	92	0.24
Czechoslovakian (0)	33	0.09
Danish (13)	76	0.20
Dutch (10)	482	1.24
English (2,353)	4,161	10.72
European (187)	232	0.60
Finnish (24)	24	0.06
French, ex. Basque (118)	509	1.31
French Canadian (54)	77	0.20
German (877)	3,269	8.42
Greek (12)	12	0.03
Hungarian (0)	78	0.20
Irish (1,960)	4,750	12.24
Italian (342)	767	1.98
Lithuanian (49)	49	0.13
Northern European (17)	17	0.04
Norwegian (88)	139	0.36
Polish (76)	186	0.48
Romanian (0)	8	0.02
Russian (0)	69	0.18
Scotch-Irish (937)	1,501	3.87
Scottish (385)	793	2.04
Swedish (11)	108	0.28
Swiss (0)	41	0.11
Turkish (78)	78	0.20
Welsh (38)	190	0.49

Hispanic Origin	Population	%
Hispanic or Latino (of any race)	1,407	3.58
Central American, ex. Mexican	155	0.39
Costa Rican	2	0.01
Guatemalan	125	0.32
Honduran	11	0.03
Nicaraguan	1	<0.01
Panamanian	12	0.03
Salvadoran	4	0.01
Cuban	29	0.07
Dominican Republic	16	0.04
Mexican	965	2.45
Puerto Rican	85	0.22
South American	56	0.14
Argentinean	3	0.01
Bolivian	2	0.01
Chilean	4	0.01
Colombian	21	0.05
Ecuadorian	1	<0.01
Peruvian	12	0.03
Uruguayan	6	0.02
Venezuelan	7	0.02
Other Hispanic or Latino	101	0.26

Race*	Population	%
African-American/Black (7,630)	8,041	20.45
Not Hispanic (7,573)	7,957	20.24
Hispanic (57)	84	0.21
American Indian/Alaska Native (157)	382	0.97
Not Hispanic (146)	355	0.90
Hispanic (11)	27	0.07
Alaska Athabascan *(Ala. Nat.)* (1)	2	0.01
Apache (1)	2	0.01
Blackfeet (0)	1	<0.01
Canadian/French Am. Ind. (1)	1	<0.01
Central American Ind. (0)	3	0.01
Cherokee (68)	170	0.43
Chickasaw (3)	6	0.02
Chippewa (1)	1	<0.01
Choctaw (3)	12	0.03
Comanche (1)	1	<0.01
Creek (8)	11	0.03
Delaware (1)	1	<0.01
Inupiat *(Alaska Native)* (2)	2	0.01
Iroquois (3)	4	0.01
Lumbee (0)	2	0.01
Mexican American Ind. (1)	5	0.01
Navajo (1)	7	0.02
Ottawa (1)	1	<0.01
Pueblo (0)	1	<0.01
Sioux (2)	3	0.01
South American Ind. (1)	1	<0.01
Asian (546)	640	1.63
Not Hispanic (537)	626	1.59
Hispanic (9)	14	0.04
Burmese (12)	12	0.03
Cambodian (6)	6	0.02
Chinese, ex. Taiwanese (187)	204	0.52
Filipino (28)	47	0.12
Hmong (1)	2	0.01
Indian (131)	141	0.36
Indonesian (1)	2	0.01
Japanese (66)	84	0.21
Korean (12)	23	0.06
Laotian (1)	1	<0.01
Malaysian (2)	2	0.01
Nepalese (17)	17	0.04
Pakistani (6)	6	0.02
Sri Lankan (0)	1	<0.01
Taiwanese (6)	6	0.02
Thai (1)	2	0.01
Vietnamese (53)	59	0.15
Hawaii Native/Pacific Islander (27)	39	0.10
Not Hispanic (16)	25	0.06
Hispanic (11)	14	0.04
Fijian (1)	1	<0.01
Guamanian/Chamorro (18)	18	0.05
Marshallese (1)	1	<0.01
Native Hawaiian (3)	8	0.02
Samoan (1)	4	0.01
White (29,505)	30,180	76.76
Not Hispanic (28,986)	29,558	75.17
Hispanic (519)	622	1.58

Foley

Place Type: City
County: Baldwin
Population: 14,618†

Ancestry‡	Population	%
African, Sub-Saharan (39)	39	0.29
African (39)	39	0.29
American (1,230)	1,230	9.06
Austrian (0)	126	0.93
Belgian (11)	22	0.16
British (12)	12	0.09
Bulgarian (11)	11	0.08
Cajun (12)	25	0.18
Celtic (11)	11	0.08
Croatian (12)	12	0.09
Czech (31)	110	0.81
Danish (18)	80	0.59
Dutch (148)	266	1.96
English (684)	1,730	12.75
European (106)	106	0.78
Finnish (7)	48	0.35
French, ex. Basque (267)	688	5.07
French Canadian (30)	65	0.48
German (483)	1,611	11.87
Hungarian (0)	64	0.47
Irish (534)	1,833	13.51
Italian (128)	381	2.81
Lithuanian (13)	13	0.10
Norwegian (23)	54	0.40
Polish (20)	93	0.69
Portuguese (0)	10	0.07
Russian (0)	14	0.10
Scandinavian (44)	44	0.32
Scotch-Irish (292)	409	3.01
Scottish (134)	331	2.44
Serbian (11)	11	0.08
Slovak (0)	8	0.06
Swedish (60)	172	1.27
Swiss (17)	60	0.44
Turkish (13)	13	0.10
Welsh (0)	60	0.44
West Indian, ex. Hispanic (75)	75	0.55
Jamaican (75)	75	0.55
Yugoslavian (0)	10	0.07

Hispanic Origin	Population	%
Hispanic or Latino (of any race)	1,390	9.51

*Notes: † The Census 2010 population figure is used to calculate the percentages in the Hispanic Origin and Race categories. Ancestry percentages are based on the 2006-2010 American Community Survey population (not shown); ‡ Numbers in parentheses indicate the number of people reporting a single ancestry; * Numbers in parentheses indicate the number of persons reporting this race alone, not in combination with any other race; Please refer to the Explanation of Data for more information.*

Central American, ex. Mexican	188	1.29
Guatemalan	33	0.23
Honduran	133	0.91
Nicaraguan	6	0.04
Panamanian	14	0.10
Salvadoran	2	0.01
Cuban	13	0.09
Dominican Republic	7	0.05
Mexican	1,026	7.02
Puerto Rican	66	0.45
South American	33	0.23
Argentinean	2	0.01
Bolivian	5	0.03
Colombian	17	0.12
Ecuadorian	1	0.01
Peruvian	7	0.05
Uruguayan	1	0.01
Other Hispanic or Latino	57	0.39

Race*	Population	%
African-American/Black (2,173)	2,288	15.65
Not Hispanic (2,148)	2,255	15.43
Hispanic (25)	33	0.23
American Indian/Alaska Native (87)	155	1.06
Not Hispanic (70)	135	0.92
Hispanic (17)	20	0.14
Blackfeet (1)	6	0.04
Canadian/French Am. Ind. (0)	1	0.01
Cherokee (18)	42	0.29
Chickasaw (3)	3	0.02
Chippewa (0)	1	0.01
Choctaw (4)	7	0.05
Creek (11)	16	0.11
Delaware (0)	3	0.02
Iroquois (3)	6	0.04
Kiowa (0)	1	0.01
Mexican American Ind. (2)	2	0.01
Navajo (1)	1	0.01
Seminole (5)	6	0.04
Asian (155)	198	1.35
Not Hispanic (155)	195	1.33
Hispanic (0)	3	0.02
Cambodian (4)	4	0.03
Chinese, ex. Taiwanese (14)	15	0.10
Filipino (22)	41	0.28
Indian (36)	38	0.26
Japanese (7)	12	0.08
Korean (9)	15	0.10
Laotian (2)	2	0.01
Pakistani (8)	8	0.05
Thai (6)	8	0.05
Vietnamese (40)	42	0.29
Hawaii Native/Pacific Islander (9)	17	0.12
Not Hispanic (7)	12	0.08
Hispanic (2)	5	0.03
Guamanian/Chamorro (3)	5	0.03
Native Hawaiian (6)	11	0.08
White (11,268)	11,483	78.55
Not Hispanic (10,626)	10,806	73.92
Hispanic (642)	677	4.63

Forestdale

Place Type: CDP
County: Jefferson
Population: 10,162†

Ancestry‡	Population	%
African, Sub-Saharan (56)	56	0.52
African (56)	56	0.52
American (581)	581	5.37
Arab (8)	8	0.07
Lebanese (8)	8	0.07
Celtic (0)	27	0.25
Czech (0)	7	0.06
Dutch (42)	102	0.94
English (102)	308	2.85
European (8)	8	0.07
French, ex. Basque (12)	103	0.95
French Canadian (4)	4	0.04
German (240)	434	4.01
Greek (20)	38	0.35
Irish (256)	380	3.51
Italian (141)	199	1.84
Norwegian (8)	8	0.07
Polish (0)	36	0.33
Scotch-Irish (81)	107	0.99
Scottish (79)	185	1.71
West Indian, ex. Hispanic (0)	9	0.08
Jamaican (0)	9	0.08

Hispanic Origin	Population	%
Hispanic or Latino (of any race)	142	1.40
Central American, ex. Mexican	27	0.27
Guatemalan	9	0.09
Honduran	14	0.14
Panamanian	3	0.03
Salvadoran	1	0.01
Mexican	86	0.85
Puerto Rican	14	0.14
South American	5	0.05
Colombian	3	0.03
Peruvian	2	0.02
Other Hispanic or Latino	10	0.10

Race*	Population	%
African-American/Black (7,260)	7,316	71.99
Not Hispanic (7,244)	7,299	71.83
Hispanic (16)	17	0.17
American Indian/Alaska Native (19)	71	0.70
Not Hispanic (19)	68	0.67
Hispanic (0)	3	0.03
Alaska Athabascan *(Ala. Nat.)* (0)	2	0.02
Blackfeet (0)	2	0.02
Cherokee (3)	21	0.21
Creek (2)	12	0.12
Lumbee (3)	5	0.05
Asian (22)	37	0.36
Not Hispanic (22)	37	0.36
Chinese, ex. Taiwanese (4)	8	0.08
Filipino (6)	10	0.10
Indian (2)	4	0.04
Japanese (1)	2	0.02
Korean (1)	3	0.03
Thai (1)	1	0.01
Vietnamese (6)	7	0.07
Hawaii Native/Pacific Islander (0)	1	0.01
Not Hispanic (0)	1	0.01
Native Hawaiian (0)	1	0.01
White (2,667)	2,745	27.01
Not Hispanic (2,632)	2,710	26.67
Hispanic (35)	35	0.34

Fort Payne

Place Type: City
County: DeKalb
Population: 14,012†

Ancestry‡	Population	%
American (1,895)	1,895	13.67
British (88)	137	0.99
Czech (0)	39	0.28
Czechoslovakian (0)	11	0.08
Danish (0)	40	0.29
Dutch (20)	373	2.69
English (1,040)	1,500	10.82
European (73)	73	0.53
French, ex. Basque (60)	230	1.66
French Canadian (0)	42	0.30
German (255)	983	7.09
Greek (56)	56	0.40
Guyanese (13)	13	0.09
Irish (784)	2,020	14.57
Italian (89)	217	1.57
Norwegian (103)	158	1.14
Polish (110)	184	1.33
Russian (10)	10	0.07
Scandinavian (0)	20	0.14
Scotch-Irish (146)	360	2.60
Scottish (244)	398	2.87
Swedish (20)	109	0.79
Swiss (0)	18	0.13
Welsh (33)	60	0.43
Yugoslavian (0)	27	0.19

Hispanic Origin	Population	%
Hispanic or Latino (of any race)	2,930	20.91
Central American, ex. Mexican	1,060	7.56
Guatemalan	980	6.99
Honduran	31	0.22
Salvadoran	46	0.33
Other Central American	3	0.02
Cuban	11	0.08
Dominican Republic	2	0.01
Mexican	1,566	11.18
Puerto Rican	24	0.17
South American	13	0.09
Colombian	9	0.06
Venezuelan	4	0.03
Other Hispanic or Latino	254	1.81

Race*	Population	%
African-American/Black (590)	700	5.00
Not Hispanic (569)	665	4.75
Hispanic (21)	35	0.25
American Indian/Alaska Native (123)	260	1.86
Not Hispanic (71)	193	1.38
Hispanic (52)	67	0.48
Apache (0)	1	0.01
Blackfeet (1)	7	0.05
Central American Ind. (3)	5	0.04
Cherokee (44)	115	0.82
Chippewa (0)	1	0.01
Choctaw (0)	1	0.01
Creek (10)	13	0.09
Iroquois (0)	1	0.01
Mexican American Ind. (23)	27	0.19
Seminole (0)	2	0.01
South American Ind. (0)	1	0.01
Spanish American Ind. (5)	5	0.04
Asian (115)	146	1.04
Not Hispanic (95)	118	0.84
Hispanic (20)	28	0.20
Cambodian (5)	6	0.04
Chinese, ex. Taiwanese (16)	21	0.15
Filipino (35)	40	0.29
Indian (31)	46	0.33
Japanese (3)	9	0.06
Korean (3)	6	0.04
Laotian (11)	12	0.09
Pakistani (0)	1	0.01
Thai (2)	2	0.01
Vietnamese (1)	7	0.05
Hawaii Native/Pacific Islander (25)	52	0.37
Not Hispanic (8)	19	0.14
Hispanic (17)	33	0.24
Guamanian/Chamorro (18)	25	0.18
Native Hawaiian (5)	15	0.11
Samoan (2)	3	0.02
White (10,867)	11,184	79.82
Not Hispanic (10,091)	10,326	73.69
Hispanic (776)	858	6.12

Fultondale

Place Type: City
County: Jefferson
Population: 8,380†

Ancestry‡	Population	%
American (2,178)	2,178	26.91
Belgian (12)	12	0.15
Canadian (0)	35	0.43
Dutch (54)	112	1.38
English (433)	748	9.24
European (27)	36	0.44
French, ex. Basque (15)	89	1.10
German (349)	681	8.41
Irish (431)	831	10.27

*Notes: † The Census 2010 population figure is used to calculate the percentages in the Hispanic Origin and Race categories. Ancestry percentages are based on the 2006-2010 American Community Survey population (not shown); ‡ Numbers in parentheses indicate the number of people reporting a single ancestry; * Numbers in parentheses indicate the number of persons reporting this race alone, not in combination with any other race; Please refer to the Explanation of Data for more information.*

Ancestry (cont.)	Population	%
Italian (0)	14	0.17
Polish (0)	11	0.14
Scandinavian (8)	8	0.10
Scotch-Irish (67)	192	2.37
Scottish (33)	83	1.03
Swedish (0)	8	0.10
Welsh (44)	91	1.12
West Indian, ex. Hispanic (0)	31	0.38
Jamaican (0)	16	0.20
Other West Indian (0)	15	0.19

Hispanic Origin	Population	%
Hispanic or Latino (of any race)	909	10.85
Central American, ex. Mexican	37	0.44
Costa Rican	1	0.01
Guatemalan	8	0.10
Honduran	6	0.07
Nicaraguan	2	0.02
Panamanian	3	0.04
Salvadoran	17	0.20
Cuban	1	0.01
Dominican Republic	9	0.11
Mexican	808	9.64
Puerto Rican	7	0.08
South American	5	0.06
Colombian	1	0.01
Ecuadorian	2	0.02
Venezuelan	2	0.02
Other Hispanic or Latino	42	0.50

Race*	Population	%
African-American/Black (1,391)	1,470	17.54
Not Hispanic (1,389)	1,456	17.37
Hispanic (2)	14	0.17
American Indian/Alaska Native (37)	102	1.22
Not Hispanic (33)	83	0.99
Hispanic (4)	19	0.23
Blackfeet (0)	1	0.01
Cherokee (21)	55	0.66
Choctaw (1)	1	0.01
Cree (0)	2	0.02
Creek (1)	10	0.12
Hopi (1)	2	0.02
Mexican American Ind. (0)	5	0.06
Pueblo (1)	1	0.01
South American Ind. (1)	1	0.01
Asian (83)	113	1.35
Not Hispanic (83)	103	1.23
Hispanic (0)	10	0.12
Cambodian (8)	8	0.10
Chinese, ex. Taiwanese (10)	14	0.17
Filipino (6)	13	0.16
Indian (19)	22	0.26
Indonesian (1)	1	0.01
Japanese (2)	4	0.05
Korean (7)	10	0.12
Pakistani (2)	2	0.02
Taiwanese (1)	1	0.01
Vietnamese (25)	25	0.30
Hawaii Native/Pacific Islander (12)	13	0.16
Not Hispanic (5)	6	0.07
Hispanic (7)	7	0.08
Guamanian/Chamorro (7)	7	0.08
Native Hawaiian (5)	6	0.07
White (6,297)	6,436	76.80
Not Hispanic (5,833)	5,940	70.88
Hispanic (464)	496	5.92

Gadsden

Place Type: City
County: Etowah
Population: 36,856†

Ancestry‡	Population	%
African, Sub-Saharan (147)	159	0.43
African (45)	57	0.15
Other Sub-Saharan African (102)	102	0.27
American (3,731)	3,731	10.04
Arab (0)	13	0.03
Syrian (0)	13	0.03
Austrian (0)	13	0.03
British (35)	42	0.11
Cajun (16)	16	0.04
Canadian (10)	10	0.03
Celtic (15)	15	0.04
Danish (0)	44	0.12
Dutch (353)	660	1.78
English (1,180)	2,663	7.17
European (165)	165	0.44
French, ex. Basque (88)	321	0.86
French Canadian (42)	42	0.11
German (749)	2,190	5.89
Greek (29)	39	0.10
Irish (1,675)	3,572	9.61
Italian (363)	530	1.43
Lithuanian (10)	10	0.03
Northern European (12)	12	0.03
Norwegian (31)	43	0.12
Polish (22)	78	0.21
Portuguese (11)	27	0.07
Scandinavian (0)	19	0.05
Scotch-Irish (534)	823	2.21
Scottish (218)	613	1.65
Swedish (97)	121	0.33
Swiss (0)	30	0.08
Welsh (27)	156	0.42
West Indian, ex. Hispanic (12)	22	0.06
Dutch West Indian (0)	10	0.03
Jamaican (12)	12	0.03

Hispanic Origin	Population	%
Hispanic or Latino (of any race)	1,986	5.39
Central American, ex. Mexican	663	1.80
Costa Rican	1	<0.01
Guatemalan	552	1.50
Honduran	26	0.07
Nicaraguan	8	0.02
Salvadoran	70	0.19
Other Central American	6	0.02
Cuban	38	0.10
Dominican Republic	13	0.04
Mexican	954	2.59
Puerto Rican	73	0.20
South American	48	0.13
Argentinean	1	<0.01
Chilean	3	0.01
Colombian	31	0.08
Ecuadorian	3	0.01
Peruvian	7	0.02
Venezuelan	3	0.01
Other Hispanic or Latino	197	0.53

Race*	Population	%
African-American/Black (13,361)	13,782	37.39
Not Hispanic (13,300)	13,695	37.16
Hispanic (61)	87	0.24
American Indian/Alaska Native (146)	336	0.91
Not Hispanic (94)	270	0.73
Hispanic (52)	66	0.18
Apache (0)	2	0.01
Blackfeet (0)	2	0.01
Canadian/French Am. Ind. (0)	2	0.01
Cherokee (48)	131	0.36
Chippewa (0)	4	0.01
Choctaw (5)	6	0.02
Comanche (0)	1	<0.01
Creek (7)	11	0.03
Hopi (0)	1	<0.01
Iroquois (2)	2	0.01
Mexican American Ind. (23)	24	0.07
Navajo (0)	1	<0.01
Pima (0)	1	<0.01
Asian (214)	272	0.74
Not Hispanic (200)	249	0.68
Hispanic (14)	23	0.06
Chinese, ex. Taiwanese (38)	45	0.12
Filipino (49)	65	0.18
Indian (56)	75	0.20
Japanese (15)	19	0.05
Korean (4)	8	0.02
Laotian (4)	4	0.01
Nepalese (2)	2	0.01
Pakistani (2)	4	0.01
Sri Lankan (1)	1	<0.01
Thai (3)	6	0.02
Vietnamese (21)	26	0.07
Hawaii Native/Pacific Islander (155)	173	0.47
Not Hispanic (26)	41	0.11
Hispanic (129)	132	0.36
Guamanian/Chamorro (153)	165	0.45
Native Hawaiian (1)	5	0.01
Samoan (1)	4	0.01
White (21,119)	21,724	58.94
Not Hispanic (20,631)	21,152	57.39
Hispanic (488)	572	1.55

Gardendale

Place Type: City
County: Jefferson
Population: 13,893†

Ancestry‡	Population	%
African, Sub-Saharan (37)	37	0.28
African (37)	37	0.28
American (1,933)	1,933	14.40
Arab (0)	14	0.10
Lebanese (0)	14	0.10
Austrian (9)	9	0.07
British (11)	31	0.23
Danish (43)	80	0.60
Dutch (110)	213	1.59
English (1,265)	1,999	14.90
European (181)	181	1.35
Finnish (0)	28	0.21
French, ex. Basque (71)	368	2.74
French Canadian (0)	8	0.06
German (409)	1,274	9.49
Greek (0)	39	0.29
Irish (924)	1,979	14.75
Italian (304)	574	4.28
Norwegian (17)	31	0.23
Polish (28)	91	0.68
Portuguese (0)	30	0.22
Scandinavian (0)	11	0.08
Scotch-Irish (355)	599	4.46
Scottish (70)	396	2.95
Swedish (9)	53	0.39
Swiss (8)	8	0.06
Welsh (18)	33	0.25

Hispanic Origin	Population	%
Hispanic or Latino (of any race)	207	1.49
Central American, ex. Mexican	17	0.12
Costa Rican	3	0.02
Guatemalan	5	0.04
Nicaraguan	7	0.05
Salvadoran	2	0.01
Cuban	9	0.06
Dominican Republic	8	0.06
Mexican	129	0.93
Puerto Rican	15	0.11
South American	7	0.05
Chilean	1	0.01
Colombian	4	0.03
Venezuelan	2	0.01
Other Hispanic or Latino	22	0.16

Race*	Population	%
African-American/Black (1,189)	1,252	9.01
Not Hispanic (1,184)	1,242	8.94
Hispanic (5)	10	0.07
American Indian/Alaska Native (41)	79	0.57
Not Hispanic (37)	74	0.53
Hispanic (4)	5	0.04
Canadian/French Am. Ind. (0)	1	0.01
Cherokee (21)	33	0.24
Chickasaw (0)	1	0.01
Chippewa (2)	2	0.01

*Notes: † The Census 2010 population figure is used to calculate the percentages in the Hispanic Origin and Race categories. Ancestry percentages are based on the 2006-2010 American Community Survey population (not shown); ‡ Numbers in parentheses indicate the number of people reporting a single ancestry; * Numbers in parentheses indicate the number of persons reporting this race alone, not in combination with any other race; Please refer to the Explanation of Data for more information.*

Choctaw (1)	4	0.03
Creek (5)	6	0.04
Lumbee (1)	1	0.01
Mexican American Ind. (1)	1	0.01
Asian (160)	194	1.40
Not Hispanic (158)	189	1.36
Hispanic (2)	5	0.04
Chinese, ex. Taiwanese (22)	26	0.19
Filipino (12)	21	0.15
Indian (26)	31	0.22
Japanese (1)	7	0.05
Korean (26)	32	0.23
Laotian (2)	2	0.01
Pakistani (1)	2	0.01
Taiwanese (4)	8	0.06
Vietnamese (64)	65	0.47
Hawaii Native/Pacific Islander (3)	12	0.09
Not Hispanic (3)	12	0.09
Native Hawaiian (0)	6	0.04
Samoan (2)	4	0.03
White (12,277)	12,407	89.30
Not Hispanic (12,180)	12,294	88.49
Hispanic (97)	113	0.81

Greenville

Place Type: City
County: Butler
Population: 8,135†

Ancestry‡	Population	%
African, Sub-Saharan (198)	198	2.50
African (198)	198	2.50
American (689)	689	8.70
Austrian (11)	11	0.14
Dutch (0)	18	0.23
English (259)	450	5.68
French, ex. Basque (0)	37	0.47
French Canadian (10)	10	0.13
German (99)	181	2.28
Irish (187)	399	5.04
Italian (60)	60	0.76
Norwegian (12)	12	0.15
Russian (6)	6	0.08
Scandinavian (10)	10	0.13
Scotch-Irish (16)	89	1.12
Scottish (10)	70	0.88
Welsh (0)	15	0.19

Hispanic Origin	Population	%
Hispanic or Latino (of any race)	102	1.25
Central American, ex. Mexican	2	0.02
Guatemalan	1	0.01
Salvadoran	1	0.01
Cuban	5	0.06
Mexican	64	0.79
Puerto Rican	5	0.06
South American	2	0.02
Colombian	2	0.02
Other Hispanic or Latino	24	0.30

Race*	Population	%
African-American/Black (4,511)	4,536	55.76
Not Hispanic (4,493)	4,516	55.51
Hispanic (18)	20	0.25
American Indian/Alaska Native (4)	19	0.23
Not Hispanic (4)	19	0.23
Cherokee (1)	6	0.07
Creek (0)	1	0.01
Potawatomi (1)	1	0.01
Sioux (1)	1	0.01
Asian (147)	156	1.92
Not Hispanic (144)	151	1.86
Hispanic (3)	5	0.06
Chinese, ex. Taiwanese (3)	4	0.05
Filipino (5)	7	0.09
Indian (38)	42	0.52
Korean (101)	102	1.25
Vietnamese (0)	2	0.02
Hawaii Native/Pacific Islander (4)	6	0.07
Not Hispanic (4)	6	0.07
Samoan (4)	4	0.05
White (3,390)	3,419	42.03
Not Hispanic (3,349)	3,375	41.49
Hispanic (41)	44	0.54

Gulf Shores

Place Type: City
County: Baldwin
Population: 9,741†

Ancestry‡	Population	%
American (1,225)	1,225	13.56
Belgian (0)	20	0.22
Brazilian (125)	125	1.38
British (28)	28	0.31
Cajun (13)	13	0.14
Czech (45)	102	1.13
Czechoslovakian (10)	10	0.11
Dutch (83)	461	5.10
English (351)	1,022	11.31
European (67)	67	0.74
Finnish (13)	25	0.28
French, ex. Basque (107)	437	4.84
French Canadian (14)	217	2.40
German (648)	1,623	17.96
Greek (11)	11	0.12
Hungarian (0)	14	0.15
Irish (337)	1,459	16.15
Italian (137)	297	3.29
Lithuanian (0)	6	0.07
Norwegian (32)	56	0.62
Polish (121)	197	2.18
Portuguese (0)	4	0.04
Romanian (15)	15	0.17
Russian (0)	55	0.61
Scotch-Irish (292)	457	5.06
Scottish (190)	398	4.41
Swedish (81)	190	2.10
Swiss (14)	52	0.58
Welsh (0)	83	0.92
West Indian, ex. Hispanic (29)	54	0.60
Jamaican (29)	54	0.60

Hispanic Origin	Population	%
Hispanic or Latino (of any race)	394	4.04
Central American, ex. Mexican	59	0.61
Costa Rican	4	0.04
Guatemalan	11	0.11
Honduran	36	0.37
Nicaraguan	1	0.01
Panamanian	3	0.03
Salvadoran	4	0.04
Cuban	7	0.07
Dominican Republic	5	0.05
Mexican	235	2.41
Puerto Rican	21	0.22
South American	20	0.21
Bolivian	2	0.02
Colombian	11	0.11
Ecuadorian	1	0.01
Paraguayan	3	0.03
Peruvian	3	0.03
Other Hispanic or Latino	47	0.48

Race*	Population	%
African-American/Black (148)	192	1.97
Not Hispanic (141)	185	1.90
Hispanic (7)	7	0.07
American Indian/Alaska Native (53)	160	1.64
Not Hispanic (51)	157	1.61
Hispanic (2)	3	0.03
Blackfeet (0)	10	0.10
Cherokee (11)	43	0.44
Chickasaw (0)	6	0.06
Chippewa (3)	4	0.04
Choctaw (2)	9	0.09
Creek (15)	31	0.32
Crow (0)	1	0.01
Iroquois (0)	2	0.02
Navajo (3)	4	0.04
Seminole (0)	3	0.03
Sioux (0)	1	0.01
South American Ind. (2)	2	0.02
Asian (92)	123	1.26
Not Hispanic (91)	117	1.20
Hispanic (1)	6	0.06
Chinese, ex. Taiwanese (21)	26	0.27
Filipino (12)	22	0.23
Indian (18)	21	0.22
Indonesian (2)	6	0.06
Japanese (2)	4	0.04
Korean (4)	10	0.10
Laotian (1)	1	0.01
Malaysian (0)	1	0.01
Thai (16)	19	0.20
Vietnamese (9)	10	0.10
Hawaii Native/Pacific Islander (11)	14	0.14
Not Hispanic (11)	12	0.12
Hispanic (0)	2	0.02
Guamanian/Chamorro (10)	10	0.10
Native Hawaiian (1)	3	0.03
White (9,095)	9,274	95.21
Not Hispanic (8,856)	9,023	92.63
Hispanic (239)	251	2.58

Guntersville

Place Type: City
County: Marshall
Population: 8,197†

Ancestry‡	Population	%
American (1,365)	1,365	16.90
Arab (16)	16	0.20
Syrian (16)	16	0.20
Australian (0)	14	0.17
British (33)	67	0.83
Czech (0)	26	0.32
Czechoslovakian (29)	29	0.36
Danish (0)	17	0.21
Dutch (39)	149	1.84
English (846)	1,238	15.33
European (50)	92	1.14
French, ex. Basque (48)	302	3.74
German (219)	668	8.27
Greek (27)	27	0.33
Hungarian (23)	23	0.28
Irish (453)	1,213	15.02
Italian (56)	170	2.10
Polish (0)	45	0.56
Russian (13)	28	0.35
Scandinavian (12)	22	0.27
Scotch-Irish (95)	203	2.51
Scottish (213)	358	4.43
Slovak (0)	42	0.52
Swedish (19)	37	0.46
Welsh (0)	9	0.11

Hispanic Origin	Population	%
Hispanic or Latino (of any race)	313	3.82
Central American, ex. Mexican	41	0.50
Costa Rican	1	0.01
Guatemalan	30	0.37
Honduran	2	0.02
Nicaraguan	2	0.02
Panamanian	2	0.02
Salvadoran	4	0.05
Cuban	3	0.04
Mexican	231	2.82
Puerto Rican	10	0.12
South American	6	0.07
Argentinean	1	0.01
Bolivian	1	0.01
Colombian	1	0.01
Uruguayan	1	0.01
Venezuelan	2	0.02
Other Hispanic or Latino	22	0.27

*Notes: † The Census 2010 population figure is used to calculate the percentages in the Hispanic Origin and Race categories. Ancestry percentages are based on the 2006-2010 American Community Survey population (not shown); ‡ Numbers in parentheses indicate the number of people reporting a single ancestry; * Numbers in parentheses indicate the number of persons reporting this race alone, not in combination with any other race; Please refer to the Explanation of Data for more information.*

Race*	Population	%
African-American/Black (640)	725	8.84
Not Hispanic (639)	723	8.82
Hispanic (1)	2	0.02
American Indian/Alaska Native (40)	89	1.09
Not Hispanic (34)	82	1.00
Hispanic (6)	7	0.09
Apache (0)	4	0.05
Cherokee (24)	37	0.45
Choctaw (0)	3	0.04
Creek (0)	1	0.01
Inupiat *(Alaska Native)* (0)	3	0.04
Lumbee (0)	1	0.01
Asian (127)	143	1.74
Not Hispanic (127)	143	1.74
Burmese (24)	27	0.33
Cambodian (0)	2	0.02
Chinese, ex. Taiwanese (22)	22	0.27
Filipino (12)	12	0.15
Indian (40)	49	0.60
Japanese (1)	4	0.05
Korean (1)	1	0.01
Thai (11)	17	0.21
Vietnamese (11)	13	0.16
Hawaii Native/Pacific Islander (1)	3	0.04
Not Hispanic (1)	2	0.02
Hispanic (0)	1	0.01
Guamanian/Chamorro (1)	2	0.02
White (7,032)	7,183	87.63
Not Hispanic (6,927)	7,068	86.23
Hispanic (105)	115	1.40

Hartselle

Place Type: City
County: Morgan
Population: 14,255†

Ancestry‡	Population	%
African, Sub-Saharan (171)	171	1.24
African (171)	171	1.24
American (1,607)	1,607	11.61
Arab (28)	28	0.20
Other Arab (28)	28	0.20
Austrian (0)	17	0.12
British (65)	76	0.55
Canadian (0)	12	0.09
Czech (0)	12	0.09
Danish (0)	8	0.06
Dutch (21)	190	1.37
English (833)	2,031	14.67
European (244)	254	1.84
French, ex. Basque (82)	236	1.71
German (610)	1,543	11.15
Greek (0)	14	0.10
Hungarian (13)	13	0.09
Irish (1,119)	2,857	20.64
Italian (95)	144	1.04
Norwegian (0)	11	0.08
Pennsylvania German (11)	11	0.08
Polish (42)	137	0.99
Romanian (0)	44	0.32
Russian (22)	32	0.23
Scotch-Irish (75)	380	2.75
Scottish (85)	273	1.97
Slavic (13)	13	0.09
Swedish (78)	118	0.85
Swiss (18)	18	0.13
Ukrainian (10)	10	0.07
Welsh (8)	55	0.40

Hispanic Origin	Population	%
Hispanic or Latino (of any race)	357	2.50
Central American, ex. Mexican	15	0.11
Guatemalan	6	0.04
Nicaraguan	3	0.02
Panamanian	5	0.04
Salvadoran	1	0.01
Cuban	5	0.04
Mexican	298	2.09
Puerto Rican	26	0.18
South American	1	0.01
Colombian	1	0.01
Other Hispanic or Latino	12	0.08

Race*	Population	%
African-American/Black (613)	705	4.95
Not Hispanic (600)	690	4.84
Hispanic (13)	15	0.11
American Indian/Alaska Native (109)	203	1.42
Not Hispanic (103)	196	1.37
Hispanic (6)	7	0.05
Blackfeet (0)	1	0.01
Cherokee (68)	123	0.86
Chickasaw (1)	1	0.01
Chippewa (2)	3	0.02
Choctaw (1)	3	0.02
Cree (0)	2	0.01
Creek (9)	11	0.08
Mexican American Ind. (1)	1	0.01
Osage (1)	1	0.01
Pueblo (1)	1	0.01
Seminole (0)	1	0.01
Sioux (0)	1	0.01
Asian (64)	86	0.60
Not Hispanic (61)	83	0.58
Hispanic (3)	3	0.02
Chinese, ex. Taiwanese (11)	14	0.10
Filipino (19)	20	0.14
Indian (16)	21	0.15
Indonesian (1)	2	0.01
Japanese (0)	1	0.01
Korean (4)	15	0.11
Nepalese (3)	3	0.02
Thai (2)	2	0.01
Vietnamese (5)	5	0.04
Hawaii Native/Pacific Islander (3)	13	0.09
Not Hispanic (3)	11	0.08
Hispanic (0)	2	0.01
Guamanian/Chamorro (1)	2	0.01
Native Hawaiian (2)	12	0.08
Samoan (0)	1	0.01
White (13,045)	13,273	93.11
Not Hispanic (12,915)	13,118	92.02
Hispanic (130)	155	1.09

Helena

Place Type: City
County: Shelby
Population: 16,793†

Ancestry‡	Population	%
African, Sub-Saharan (45)	45	0.29
African (37)	37	0.24
South African (8)	8	0.05
American (1,928)	1,928	12.47
Arab (112)	137	0.89
Jordanian (9)	9	0.06
Lebanese (8)	33	0.21
Moroccan (65)	65	0.42
Palestinian (30)	30	0.19
Armenian (18)	18	0.12
British (73)	141	0.91
Croatian (16)	34	0.22
Czech (0)	19	0.12
Czechoslovakian (0)	9	0.06
Danish (0)	12	0.08
Dutch (10)	204	1.32
Eastern European (57)	57	0.37
English (1,351)	2,985	19.30
European (132)	154	1.00
Finnish (17)	25	0.16
French, ex. Basque (87)	453	2.93
French Canadian (100)	131	0.85
German (686)	1,765	11.41
Greek (82)	90	0.58
Hungarian (10)	41	0.27
Irish (735)	2,435	15.75
Italian (488)	808	5.23
Lithuanian (7)	35	0.23
Luxemburger (13)	13	0.08
Norwegian (7)	46	0.30
Polish (49)	220	1.42
Portuguese (7)	7	0.05
Russian (0)	20	0.13
Scotch-Irish (282)	473	3.06
Scottish (363)	655	4.24
Swedish (24)	90	0.58
Swiss (0)	20	0.13
Ukrainian (6)	27	0.17
Welsh (32)	175	1.13
West Indian, ex. Hispanic (0)	23	0.15
Dutch West Indian (0)	23	0.15

Hispanic Origin	Population	%
Hispanic or Latino (of any race)	560	3.33
Central American, ex. Mexican	62	0.37
Costa Rican	3	0.02
Guatemalan	6	0.04
Honduran	12	0.07
Nicaraguan	8	0.05
Panamanian	8	0.05
Salvadoran	25	0.15
Cuban	7	0.04
Dominican Republic	8	0.05
Mexican	337	2.01
Puerto Rican	34	0.20
South American	66	0.39
Argentinean	17	0.10
Bolivian	1	0.01
Colombian	32	0.19
Peruvian	3	0.02
Uruguayan	1	0.01
Venezuelan	12	0.07
Other Hispanic or Latino	46	0.27

Race*	Population	%
African-American/Black (2,204)	2,293	13.65
Not Hispanic (2,193)	2,275	13.55
Hispanic (11)	18	0.11
American Indian/Alaska Native (35)	94	0.56
Not Hispanic (31)	85	0.51
Hispanic (4)	9	0.05
Aleut *(Alaska Native)* (0)	1	0.01
Apache (1)	1	0.01
Cherokee (6)	29	0.17
Chippewa (1)	1	0.01
Choctaw (1)	1	0.01
Creek (5)	6	0.04
Houma (2)	2	0.01
Iroquois (0)	1	0.01
Mexican American Ind. (0)	1	0.01
Shoshone (0)	2	0.01
Sioux (3)	3	0.02
Asian (250)	318	1.89
Not Hispanic (245)	311	1.85
Hispanic (5)	7	0.04
Bangladeshi (4)	4	0.02
Cambodian (1)	1	0.01
Chinese, ex. Taiwanese (47)	57	0.34
Filipino (19)	30	0.18
Hmong (2)	2	0.01
Indian (35)	44	0.26
Indonesian (1)	1	0.01
Japanese (9)	21	0.13
Korean (35)	55	0.33
Laotian (1)	2	0.01
Malaysian (0)	1	0.01
Pakistani (10)	11	0.07
Taiwanese (5)	7	0.04
Thai (2)	3	0.02
Vietnamese (69)	73	0.43
Hawaii Native/Pacific Islander (4)	15	0.09
Not Hispanic (4)	15	0.09
Guamanian/Chamorro (4)	4	0.02
Native Hawaiian (0)	10	0.06
White (13,851)	14,041	83.61
Not Hispanic (13,547)	13,720	81.70
Hispanic (304)	321	1.91

*Notes: † The Census 2010 population figure is used to calculate the percentages in the Hispanic Origin and Race categories. Ancestry percentages are based on the 2006-2010 American Community Survey population (not shown); ‡ Numbers in parentheses indicate the number of people reporting a single ancestry; * Numbers in parentheses indicate the number of persons reporting this race alone, not in combination with any other race; Please refer to the Explanation of Data for more information.*

Homewood

Place Type: City
County: Jefferson
Population: 25,167†

Ancestry‡	Population	%
African, Sub-Saharan (320)	344	1.37
African (69)	93	0.37
Kenyan (172)	172	0.69
Nigerian (65)	65	0.26
South African (14)	14	0.06
American (2,220)	2,220	8.85
Arab (177)	303	1.21
Arab (75)	75	0.30
Lebanese (71)	197	0.79
Syrian (29)	29	0.12
Other Arab (2)	2	0.01
Armenian (0)	17	0.07
Australian (10)	13	0.05
Austrian (10)	65	0.26
British (143)	224	0.89
Canadian (29)	44	0.18
Czech (58)	100	0.40
Czechoslovakian (35)	62	0.25
Danish (9)	23	0.09
Dutch (18)	279	1.11
English (1,823)	4,333	17.28
European (514)	548	2.19
Finnish (0)	50	0.20
French, ex. Basque (218)	674	2.69
French Canadian (17)	31	0.12
German (992)	2,513	10.02
Greek (115)	187	0.75
Hungarian (37)	91	0.36
Iranian (10)	10	0.04
Irish (782)	2,854	11.38
Israeli (23)	23	0.09
Italian (476)	936	3.73
Lithuanian (0)	10	0.04
Northern European (60)	68	0.27
Norwegian (29)	65	0.26
Polish (96)	208	0.83
Romanian (21)	21	0.08
Russian (53)	134	0.53
Scandinavian (2)	22	0.09
Scotch-Irish (727)	1,449	5.78
Scottish (413)	1,161	4.63
Slavic (3)	3	0.01
Slovak (0)	13	0.05
Swedish (10)	117	0.47
Swiss (56)	128	0.51
Turkish (8)	8	0.03
Ukrainian (21)	65	0.26
Welsh (63)	426	1.70
West Indian, ex. Hispanic (16)	16	0.06
Bahamian (16)	16	0.06
Yugoslavian (16)	16	0.06

Hispanic Origin	Population	%
Hispanic or Latino (of any race)	1,846	7.34
Central American, ex. Mexican	131	0.52
Costa Rican	7	0.03
Guatemalan	34	0.14
Honduran	56	0.22
Nicaraguan	11	0.04
Panamanian	11	0.04
Salvadoran	12	0.05
Cuban	27	0.11
Dominican Republic	14	0.06
Mexican	1,283	5.10
Puerto Rican	46	0.18
South American	158	0.63
Argentinean	25	0.10
Bolivian	1	<0.01
Chilean	7	0.03
Colombian	28	0.11
Ecuadorian	8	0.03
Peruvian	70	0.28
Uruguayan	4	0.02
Venezuelan	15	0.06
Other Hispanic or Latino	187	0.74

Race*	Population	%
African-American/Black (4,342)	4,475	17.78
Not Hispanic (4,306)	4,409	17.52
Hispanic (36)	66	0.26
American Indian/Alaska Native (50)	114	0.45
Not Hispanic (41)	97	0.39
Hispanic (9)	17	0.07
Alaska Athabascan *(Ala. Nat.)* (1)	1	<0.01
Cherokee (12)	34	0.14
Chickasaw (2)	2	0.01
Chippewa (1)	5	0.02
Choctaw (2)	4	0.02
Comanche (0)	2	0.01
Creek (2)	9	0.04
Mexican American Ind. (4)	4	0.02
Yaqui (0)	2	0.01
Asian (553)	688	2.73
Not Hispanic (548)	679	2.70
Hispanic (5)	9	0.04
Bangladeshi (10)	10	0.04
Burmese (5)	5	0.02
Chinese, ex. Taiwanese (106)	127	0.50
Filipino (76)	111	0.44
Indian (126)	151	0.60
Indonesian (3)	3	0.01
Japanese (16)	42	0.17
Korean (17)	29	0.12
Malaysian (1)	1	<0.01
Nepalese (25)	26	0.10
Pakistani (23)	23	0.09
Sri Lankan (7)	7	0.03
Taiwanese (13)	14	0.06
Thai (4)	7	0.03
Vietnamese (86)	100	0.40
Hawaii Native/Pacific Islander (8)	23	0.09
Not Hispanic (7)	15	0.06
Hispanic (1)	8	0.03
Guamanian/Chamorro (3)	4	0.02
Native Hawaiian (4)	10	0.04
White (18,774)	19,062	75.74
Not Hispanic (18,118)	18,346	72.90
Hispanic (656)	716	2.84

Hoover

Place Type: City
County: Jefferson
Population: 81,619†

Ancestry‡	Population	%
African, Sub-Saharan (420)	420	0.53
African (141)	141	0.18
Kenyan (134)	134	0.17
Nigerian (84)	84	0.11
South African (37)	37	0.05
Other Sub-Saharan African (24)	24	0.03
American (7,002)	7,002	8.91
Arab (725)	1,055	1.34
Arab (79)	79	0.10
Iraqi (0)	56	0.07
Jordanian (269)	269	0.34
Lebanese (223)	478	0.61
Moroccan (0)	10	0.01
Palestinian (95)	95	0.12
Syrian (0)	9	0.01
Other Arab (59)	59	0.08
Armenian (9)	60	0.08
Assyrian/Chaldean/Syriac (0)	12	0.02
Austrian (55)	223	0.28
Belgian (0)	42	0.05
British (461)	592	0.75
Cajun (11)	11	0.01
Canadian (31)	95	0.12
Celtic (0)	29	0.04
Croatian (0)	114	0.15
Czech (52)	281	0.36
Czechoslovakian (0)	52	0.07
Danish (20)	150	0.19
Dutch (62)	719	0.92
Eastern European (36)	50	0.06
English (5,543)	11,237	14.31
European (878)	978	1.25
Finnish (17)	129	0.16
French, ex. Basque (536)	2,329	2.97
French Canadian (25)	96	0.12
German (3,056)	9,357	11.91
Greek (146)	313	0.40
Hungarian (0)	68	0.09
Iranian (167)	180	0.23
Irish (3,723)	9,842	12.53
Israeli (22)	22	0.03
Italian (1,849)	3,996	5.09
Latvian (0)	14	0.02
Lithuanian (26)	85	0.11
Luxemburger (0)	33	0.04
Northern European (56)	56	0.07
Norwegian (163)	456	0.58
Polish (355)	1,258	1.60
Portuguese (145)	182	0.23
Russian (96)	190	0.24
Scandinavian (15)	137	0.17
Scotch-Irish (1,903)	3,272	4.17
Scottish (1,048)	2,694	3.43
Slavic (20)	20	0.03
Slovak (88)	187	0.24
Swedish (186)	702	0.89
Swiss (36)	109	0.14
Turkish (28)	46	0.06
Ukrainian (63)	158	0.20
Welsh (0)	481	0.61
West Indian, ex. Hispanic (159)	383	0.49
British West Indian (16)	16	0.02
Dutch West Indian (0)	45	0.06
Haitian (0)	18	0.02
Jamaican (11)	81	0.10
Trinidadian/Tobagonian (45)	136	0.17
U.S. Virgin Islander (87)	87	0.11
Yugoslavian (13)	13	0.02

Hispanic Origin	Population	%
Hispanic or Latino (of any race)	4,915	6.02
Central American, ex. Mexican	474	0.58
Costa Rican	32	0.04
Guatemalan	167	0.20
Honduran	60	0.07
Nicaraguan	20	0.02
Panamanian	20	0.02
Salvadoran	175	0.21
Cuban	152	0.19
Dominican Republic	40	0.05
Mexican	3,169	3.88
Puerto Rican	282	0.35
South American	362	0.44
Argentinean	30	0.04
Bolivian	3	<0.01
Chilean	26	0.03
Colombian	128	0.16
Ecuadorian	25	0.03
Paraguayan	4	<0.01
Peruvian	80	0.10
Uruguayan	4	<0.01
Venezuelan	59	0.07
Other South American	3	<0.01
Other Hispanic or Latino	436	0.53

Race*	Population	%
African-American/Black (12,114)	12,583	15.42
Not Hispanic (12,008)	12,419	15.22
Hispanic (106)	164	0.20
American Indian/Alaska Native (201)	450	0.55
Not Hispanic (143)	382	0.47
Hispanic (58)	68	0.08
Arapaho (1)	2	<0.01
Blackfeet (0)	1	<0.01
Cherokee (36)	108	0.13
Chickasaw (1)	4	<0.01
Chippewa (2)	6	0.01

*Notes: † The Census 2010 population figure is used to calculate the percentages in the Hispanic Origin and Race categories. Ancestry percentages are based on the 2006-2010 American Community Survey population (not shown); ‡ Numbers in parentheses indicate the number of people reporting a single ancestry; * Numbers in parentheses indicate the number of persons reporting this race alone, not in combination with any other race; Please refer to the Explanation of Data for more information.*

Choctaw (1)	11	0.01
Cree (0)	1	<0.01
Creek (10)	27	0.03
Houma (1)	1	<0.01
Mexican American Ind. (11)	14	0.02
Navajo (0)	1	<0.01
Potawatomi (2)	2	<0.01
Pueblo (1)	3	<0.01
Seminole (0)	3	<0.01
Sioux (1)	2	<0.01
South American Ind. (0)	1	<0.01
Yaqui (1)	1	<0.01
Asian (4,135)	4,686	5.74
Not Hispanic (4,120)	4,643	5.69
Hispanic (15)	43	0.05
Bangladeshi (23)	26	0.03
Burmese (11)	14	0.02
Cambodian (13)	13	0.02
Chinese, ex. Taiwanese (651)	722	0.88
Filipino (127)	196	0.24
Hmong (7)	7	0.01
Indian (1,788)	1,927	2.36
Indonesian (21)	42	0.05
Japanese (173)	214	0.26
Korean (344)	391	0.48
Laotian (2)	5	0.01
Malaysian (4)	7	0.01
Nepalese (15)	15	0.02
Pakistani (394)	436	0.53
Sri Lankan (1)	1	<0.01
Taiwanese (34)	36	0.04
Thai (27)	35	0.04
Vietnamese (337)	365	0.45
Hawaii Native/Pacific Islander (20)	68	0.08
Not Hispanic (16)	56	0.07
Hispanic (4)	12	0.01
Guamanian/Chamorro (9)	20	0.02
Native Hawaiian (5)	20	0.02
Samoan (3)	3	<0.01
White (61,302)	62,326	76.36
Not Hispanic (59,254)	60,100	73.63
Hispanic (2,048)	2,226	2.73

Hueytown

Place Type: City
County: Jefferson
Population: 16,105†

Ancestry‡	Population	%
African, Sub-Saharan (105)	149	0.93
African (105)	149	0.93
American (4,171)	4,171	26.02
Arab (11)	24	0.15
Lebanese (11)	24	0.15
Austrian (0)	11	0.07
British (13)	13	0.08
Canadian (14)	14	0.09
Celtic (9)	18	0.11
Dutch (32)	130	0.81
English (701)	1,198	7.47
European (137)	158	0.99
French, ex. Basque (103)	185	1.15
German (325)	788	4.92
Irish (660)	1,353	8.44
Italian (177)	310	1.93
Norwegian (43)	53	0.33
Polish (68)	231	1.44
Scotch-Irish (290)	431	2.69
Scottish (77)	195	1.22
Swedish (22)	33	0.21
Ukrainian (0)	11	0.07
Welsh (48)	115	0.72
West Indian, ex. Hispanic (22)	22	0.14
West Indian (22)	22	0.14
Yugoslavian (0)	10	0.06

Hispanic Origin	Population	%
Hispanic or Latino (of any race)	321	1.99
Central American, ex. Mexican	20	0.12
Costa Rican	1	0.01
Guatemalan	3	0.02
Honduran	4	0.02
Nicaraguan	5	0.03
Panamanian	1	0.01
Salvadoran	6	0.04
Cuban	1	0.01
Mexican	244	1.52
Puerto Rican	20	0.12
South American	9	0.06
Bolivian	1	0.01
Ecuadorian	1	0.01
Paraguayan	2	0.01
Peruvian	2	0.01
Venezuelan	3	0.02
Other Hispanic or Latino	27	0.17

Race*	Population	%
African-American/Black (4,388)	4,452	27.64
Not Hispanic (4,368)	4,427	27.49
Hispanic (20)	25	0.16
American Indian/Alaska Native (42)	114	0.71
Not Hispanic (41)	107	0.66
Hispanic (1)	7	0.04
Aleut *(Alaska Native)* (6)	6	0.04
Cherokee (5)	35	0.22
Choctaw (0)	1	0.01
Creek (4)	10	0.06
Crow (0)	4	0.02
Inupiat *(Alaska Native)* (3)	3	0.02
Mexican American Ind. (0)	3	0.02
Navajo (3)	3	0.02
Sioux (1)	1	0.01
Asian (75)	93	0.58
Not Hispanic (73)	91	0.57
Hispanic (2)	2	0.01
Chinese, ex. Taiwanese (38)	39	0.24
Filipino (5)	6	0.04
Indian (8)	13	0.08
Japanese (5)	5	0.03
Korean (4)	9	0.06
Pakistani (2)	2	0.01
Vietnamese (13)	14	0.09
Hawaii Native/Pacific Islander (0)	1	0.01
Not Hispanic (0)	1	0.01
Native Hawaiian (0)	1	0.01
White (11,270)	11,416	70.88
Not Hispanic (11,157)	11,280	70.04
Hispanic (113)	136	0.84

Huntsville

Place Type: City
County: Madison
Population: 180,105†

Ancestry‡	Population	%
African, Sub-Saharan (1,538)	1,837	1.05
African (1,134)	1,368	0.78
Ethiopian (20)	20	0.01
Ghanaian (15)	15	0.01
Kenyan (98)	98	0.06
Nigerian (202)	251	0.14
South African (0)	16	0.01
Zimbabwean (31)	31	0.02
Other Sub-Saharan African (38)	38	0.02
Albanian (10)	26	0.01
Alsatian (0)	14	0.01
American (18,369)	18,369	10.47
Arab (495)	799	0.46
Arab (92)	152	0.09
Egyptian (9)	53	0.03
Jordanian (27)	27	0.02
Lebanese (92)	228	0.13
Moroccan (32)	32	0.02
Syrian (10)	74	0.04
Other Arab (233)	233	0.13
Armenian (44)	60	0.03
Australian (0)	325	0.19
Austrian (50)	239	0.14
Belgian (66)	133	0.08
British (620)	1,159	0.66
Cajun (8)	130	0.07
Canadian (89)	110	0.06
Celtic (41)	83	0.05
Croatian (0)	30	0.02
Czech (105)	352	0.20
Czechoslovakian (41)	117	0.07
Danish (61)	239	0.14
Dutch (321)	1,848	1.05
Eastern European (37)	37	0.02
English (9,579)	19,637	11.19
European (1,968)	2,332	1.33
Finnish (22)	88	0.05
French, ex. Basque (1,008)	3,725	2.12
French Canadian (225)	474	0.27
German (5,763)	15,751	8.98
Greek (295)	458	0.26
Hungarian (13)	262	0.15
Iranian (399)	441	0.25
Irish (6,477)	17,337	9.88
Israeli (100)	100	0.06
Italian (2,192)	4,236	2.41
Latvian (26)	37	0.02
Lithuanian (77)	194	0.11
Macedonian (22)	22	0.01
New Zealander (21)	21	0.01
Northern European (132)	147	0.08
Norwegian (327)	844	0.48
Polish (713)	1,717	0.98
Portuguese (67)	261	0.15
Romanian (160)	172	0.10
Russian (169)	425	0.24
Scandinavian (137)	180	0.10
Scotch-Irish (2,851)	5,287	3.01
Scottish (1,710)	4,308	2.46
Serbian (15)	56	0.03
Slavic (11)	58	0.03
Slovak (21)	68	0.04
Swedish (242)	1,021	0.58
Swiss (63)	213	0.12
Turkish (19)	19	0.01
Ukrainian (26)	50	0.03
Welsh (182)	1,058	0.60
West Indian, ex. Hispanic (978)	1,205	0.69
Bahamian (28)	42	0.02
Barbadian (0)	11	0.01
Belizean (16)	16	0.01
Bermudan (39)	39	0.02
British West Indian (0)	15	0.01
Dutch West Indian (14)	23	0.01
Haitian (158)	179	0.10
Jamaican (442)	599	0.34
Trinidadian/Tobagonian (109)	109	0.06
West Indian (172)	172	0.10
Yugoslavian (8)	75	0.04

Hispanic Origin	Population	%
Hispanic or Latino (of any race)	10,512	5.84
Central American, ex. Mexican	886	0.49
Costa Rican	40	0.02
Guatemalan	445	0.25
Honduran	141	0.08
Nicaraguan	17	0.01
Panamanian	159	0.09
Salvadoran	83	0.05
Other Central American	1	<0.01
Cuban	257	0.14
Dominican Republic	104	0.06
Mexican	7,151	3.97
Puerto Rican	1,036	0.58
South American	350	0.19
Argentinean	40	0.02
Bolivian	21	0.01
Chilean	35	0.02
Colombian	111	0.06
Ecuadorian	23	0.01
Paraguayan	8	<0.01
Peruvian	63	0.03
Uruguayan	6	<0.01

*Notes: † The Census 2010 population figure is used to calculate the percentages in the Hispanic Origin and Race categories. Ancestry percentages are based on the 2006-2010 American Community Survey population (not shown); ‡ Numbers in parentheses indicate the number of people reporting a single ancestry; * Numbers in parentheses indicate the number of persons reporting this race alone, not in combination with any other race; Please refer to the Explanation of Data for more information.*

Venezuelan	41	0.02
Other South American	2	<0.01
Other Hispanic or Latino	728	0.40

Race*	Population	%
African-American/Black (56,229)	58,434	32.44
Not Hispanic (55,615)	57,523	31.94
Hispanic (614)	911	0.51
American Indian/Alaska Native (1,087)	2,566	1.42
Not Hispanic (940)	2,325	1.29
Hispanic (147)	241	0.13
Alaska Athabascan *(Ala. Nat.)* (3)	3	<0.01
Aleut *(Alaska Native)* (0)	3	<0.01
Apache (5)	11	0.01
Arapaho (1)	1	<0.01
Blackfeet (9)	58	0.03
Canadian/French Am. Ind. (2)	3	<0.01
Central American Ind. (6)	7	<0.01
Cherokee (438)	1,078	0.60
Cheyenne (0)	1	<0.01
Chickasaw (4)	12	0.01
Chippewa (5)	15	0.01
Choctaw (33)	80	0.04
Comanche (4)	5	<0.01
Cree (0)	4	<0.01
Creek (16)	54	0.03
Crow (4)	7	<0.01
Delaware (3)	8	<0.01
Hopi (1)	7	<0.01
Houma (2)	2	<0.01
Inupiat *(Alaska Native)* (3)	6	<0.01
Iroquois (3)	12	0.01
Kiowa (1)	1	<0.01
Lumbee (12)	26	0.01
Mexican American Ind. (60)	70	0.04
Navajo (5)	17	0.01
Osage (0)	2	<0.01
Paiute (1)	2	<0.01
Pima (1)	1	<0.01
Potawatomi (1)	3	<0.01
Pueblo (5)	6	<0.01
Puget Sound Salish (0)	1	<0.01
Seminole (8)	13	0.01
Sioux (26)	48	0.03
South American Ind. (4)	7	<0.01
Spanish American Ind. (1)	2	<0.01
Tlingit-Haida *(Alaska Native)* (6)	6	<0.01
Yakama (0)	1	<0.01
Yaqui (4)	5	<0.01
Yup'ik *(Alaska Native)* (0)	1	<0.01
Asian (4,349)	5,528	3.07
Not Hispanic (4,287)	5,414	3.01
Hispanic (62)	114	0.06
Bangladeshi (37)	37	0.02
Burmese (9)	10	0.01
Cambodian (18)	24	0.01
Chinese, ex. Taiwanese (738)	927	0.51
Filipino (312)	506	0.28
Indian (1,276)	1,425	0.79
Indonesian (29)	42	0.02
Japanese (236)	465	0.26
Korean (750)	1,017	0.56
Laotian (87)	104	0.06
Malaysian (6)	16	0.01
Nepalese (68)	71	0.04
Pakistani (78)	94	0.05
Sri Lankan (11)	13	0.01
Taiwanese (53)	56	0.03
Thai (83)	129	0.07
Vietnamese (400)	465	0.26
Hawaii Native/Pacific Islander (232)	431	0.24
Not Hispanic (194)	351	0.19
Hispanic (38)	80	0.04
Fijian (2)	2	<0.01
Guamanian/Chamorro (78)	106	0.06
Marshallese (51)	57	0.03
Native Hawaiian (35)	117	0.06
Samoan (16)	37	0.02
Tongan (0)	1	<0.01
White (108,618)	112,214	62.30
Not Hispanic (104,516)	107,686	59.79
Hispanic (4,102)	4,528	2.51

Irondale

Place Type: City
County: Jefferson
Population: 12,349†

Ancestry‡	Population	%
African, Sub-Saharan (175)	175	1.44
African (93)	93	0.76
Kenyan (82)	82	0.67
American (981)	981	8.05
Arab (10)	28	0.23
Lebanese (10)	28	0.23
Australian (9)	9	0.07
British (6)	19	0.16
Czech (0)	14	0.11
Czechoslovakian (8)	8	0.07
Dutch (23)	177	1.45
English (709)	1,268	10.41
European (107)	107	0.88
French, ex. Basque (11)	101	0.83
German (365)	830	6.81
Hungarian (11)	11	0.09
Irish (457)	988	8.11
Italian (282)	348	2.86
Lithuanian (12)	12	0.10
New Zealander (13)	13	0.11
Polish (113)	259	2.13
Russian (25)	58	0.48
Scandinavian (6)	19	0.16
Scotch-Irish (242)	416	3.42
Scottish (147)	364	2.99
Slovak (16)	16	0.13
Swedish (0)	12	0.10
Swiss (0)	12	0.10
Welsh (70)	91	0.75

Hispanic Origin	Population	%
Hispanic or Latino (of any race)	961	7.78
Central American, ex. Mexican	50	0.40
Costa Rican	12	0.10
Guatemalan	8	0.06
Honduran	17	0.14
Panamanian	6	0.05
Salvadoran	7	0.06
Cuban	14	0.11
Dominican Republic	1	0.01
Mexican	723	5.85
Puerto Rican	27	0.22
South American	48	0.39
Argentinean	6	0.05
Chilean	6	0.05
Colombian	13	0.11
Ecuadorian	4	0.03
Peruvian	11	0.09
Uruguayan	2	0.02
Venezuelan	6	0.05
Other Hispanic or Latino	98	0.79

Race*	Population	%
African-American/Black (4,369)	4,449	36.03
Not Hispanic (4,357)	4,423	35.82
Hispanic (12)	26	0.21
American Indian/Alaska Native (41)	97	0.79
Not Hispanic (26)	79	0.64
Hispanic (15)	18	0.15
Apache (1)	3	0.02
Blackfeet (1)	3	0.02
Cherokee (7)	30	0.24
Creek (2)	3	0.02
Mexican American Ind. (1)	1	0.01
Yuman (3)	4	0.03
Asian (177)	216	1.75
Not Hispanic (177)	216	1.75
Cambodian (3)	3	0.02
Chinese, ex. Taiwanese (20)	28	0.23
Filipino (25)	33	0.27
Indian (42)	50	0.40
Indonesian (6)	7	0.06
Japanese (16)	22	0.18
Korean (19)	24	0.19
Pakistani (3)	3	0.02
Sri Lankan (4)	5	0.04
Thai (2)	3	0.02
Vietnamese (32)	34	0.28
Hawaii Native/Pacific Islander (1)	3	0.02
Not Hispanic (1)	3	0.02
Samoan (1)	1	0.01
White (6,956)	7,106	57.54
Not Hispanic (6,670)	6,793	55.01
Hispanic (286)	313	2.53

Jacksonville

Place Type: City
County: Calhoun
Population: 12,548†

Ancestry‡	Population	%
African, Sub-Saharan (38)	49	0.42
African (38)	49	0.42
American (1,083)	1,083	9.18
Arab (16)	35	0.30
Lebanese (16)	35	0.30
Belgian (18)	18	0.15
British (90)	99	0.84
Canadian (0)	5	0.04
Croatian (0)	10	0.08
Czechoslovakian (0)	16	0.14
Dutch (19)	205	1.74
English (608)	1,081	9.17
European (107)	135	1.14
French, ex. Basque (85)	258	2.19
German (393)	1,123	9.52
Greek (17)	17	0.14
Guyanese (10)	21	0.18
Irish (364)	983	8.34
Italian (77)	221	1.87
Norwegian (0)	46	0.39
Polish (39)	98	0.83
Russian (0)	33	0.28
Scotch-Irish (172)	245	2.08
Scottish (35)	296	2.51
Slovene (14)	14	0.12
Swedish (31)	69	0.59
Ukrainian (0)	23	0.20
Welsh (0)	36	0.31
West Indian, ex. Hispanic (26)	26	0.22
Jamaican (26)	26	0.22

Hispanic Origin	Population	%
Hispanic or Latino (of any race)	284	2.26
Central American, ex. Mexican	26	0.21
Guatemalan	4	0.03
Honduran	9	0.07
Nicaraguan	3	0.02
Panamanian	5	0.04
Salvadoran	5	0.04
Cuban	1	0.01
Dominican Republic	6	0.05
Mexican	121	0.96
Puerto Rican	82	0.65
South American	19	0.15
Bolivian	1	0.01
Colombian	9	0.07
Ecuadorian	1	0.01
Paraguayan	2	0.02
Peruvian	1	0.01
Venezuelan	5	0.04
Other Hispanic or Latino	29	0.23

Race*	Population	%
African-American/Black (3,362)	3,499	27.88
Not Hispanic (3,333)	3,462	27.59
Hispanic (29)	37	0.29
American Indian/Alaska Native (65)	122	0.97
Not Hispanic (54)	107	0.85

*Notes: † The Census 2010 population figure is used to calculate the percentages in the Hispanic Origin and Race categories. Ancestry percentages are based on the 2006-2010 American Community Survey population (not shown); ‡ Numbers in parentheses indicate the number of people reporting a single ancestry; * Numbers in parentheses indicate the number of persons reporting this race alone, not in combination with any other race; Please refer to the Explanation of Data for more information.*

Hispanic (11)	15	0.12
Apache (2)	4	0.03
Blackfeet (1)	1	0.01
Cherokee (9)	28	0.22
Choctaw (2)	7	0.06
Creek (5)	13	0.10
Pueblo (1)	1	0.01
Sioux (1)	1	0.01
Yup'ik *(Alaska Native)* (1)	1	0.01
Asian (164)	230	1.83
Not Hispanic (161)	223	1.78
Hispanic (3)	7	0.06
Bangladeshi (3)	3	0.02
Chinese, ex. Taiwanese (22)	29	0.23
Filipino (19)	32	0.26
Indian (23)	29	0.23
Japanese (15)	20	0.16
Korean (31)	52	0.41
Malaysian (1)	2	0.02
Nepalese (2)	2	0.02
Pakistani (1)	2	0.02
Taiwanese (2)	2	0.02
Thai (3)	3	0.02
Vietnamese (33)	37	0.29
Hawaii Native/Pacific Islander (20)	36	0.29
Not Hispanic (20)	36	0.29
Guamanian/Chamorro (12)	12	0.10
Native Hawaiian (3)	17	0.14
Samoan (3)	5	0.04
White (8,618)	8,821	70.30
Not Hispanic (8,466)	8,651	68.94
Hispanic (152)	170	1.35

Jasper

Place Type: City
County: Walker
Population: 14,352†

Ancestry‡	Population	%
African, Sub-Saharan (24)	104	0.73
African (24)	104	0.73
American (1,952)	1,952	13.64
Belgian (16)	16	0.11
British (7)	7	0.05
Canadian (9)	9	0.06
Danish (0)	13	0.09
Dutch (126)	370	2.59
English (816)	1,486	10.39
European (18)	35	0.24
French, ex. Basque (22)	122	0.85
French Canadian (9)	9	0.06
German (430)	1,266	8.85
Greek (12)	20	0.14
Hungarian (0)	13	0.09
Irish (1,019)	2,479	17.33
Israeli (7)	7	0.05
Italian (64)	263	1.84
Norwegian (16)	16	0.11
Polish (35)	129	0.90
Scandinavian (0)	8	0.06
Scotch-Irish (185)	262	1.83
Scottish (277)	403	2.82
Swedish (12)	25	0.17
Welsh (31)	80	0.56
West Indian, ex. Hispanic (0)	17	0.12
Dutch West Indian (0)	17	0.12

Hispanic Origin	Population	%
Hispanic or Latino (of any race)	628	4.38
Central American, ex. Mexican	111	0.77
Guatemalan	98	0.68
Honduran	7	0.05
Salvadoran	6	0.04
Cuban	4	0.03
Mexican	404	2.81
Puerto Rican	24	0.17
South American	22	0.15
Argentinean	1	0.01
Chilean	3	0.02
Colombian	11	0.08
Ecuadorian	6	0.04
Peruvian	1	0.01
Other Hispanic or Latino	63	0.44

Race*	Population	%
African-American/Black (1,929)	2,032	14.16
Not Hispanic (1,913)	2,014	14.03
Hispanic (16)	18	0.13
American Indian/Alaska Native (43)	117	0.82
Not Hispanic (38)	108	0.75
Hispanic (5)	9	0.06
Apache (0)	2	0.01
Blackfeet (0)	2	0.01
Cherokee (14)	48	0.33
Choctaw (0)	2	0.01
Creek (7)	15	0.10
Houma (1)	1	0.01
Iroquois (1)	2	0.01
Ottawa (0)	1	0.01
Seminole (0)	1	0.01
Asian (107)	130	0.91
Not Hispanic (106)	126	0.88
Hispanic (1)	4	0.03
Cambodian (1)	1	0.01
Chinese, ex. Taiwanese (12)	16	0.11
Filipino (5)	6	0.04
Indian (30)	37	0.26
Japanese (1)	1	0.01
Korean (18)	26	0.18
Pakistani (5)	5	0.03
Thai (1)	2	0.01
Vietnamese (32)	34	0.24
Hawaii Native/Pacific Islander (27)	41	0.29
Not Hispanic (20)	25	0.17
Hispanic (7)	16	0.11
Guamanian/Chamorro (26)	32	0.22
Native Hawaiian (0)	8	0.06
Samoan (0)	3	0.02
White (11,670)	11,829	82.42
Not Hispanic (11,462)	11,598	80.81
Hispanic (208)	231	1.61

Leeds

Place Type: City
County: Jefferson
Population: 11,773†

Ancestry‡	Population	%
American (1,053)	1,053	9.31
Australian (10)	10	0.09
British (36)	36	0.32
Danish (0)	24	0.21
Dutch (0)	185	1.64
Eastern European (13)	13	0.11
English (749)	1,285	11.36
European (10)	27	0.24
Finnish (0)	74	0.65
French, ex. Basque (52)	160	1.41
French Canadian (15)	15	0.13
German (362)	1,057	9.34
Greek (31)	31	0.27
Hungarian (14)	37	0.33
Irish (654)	1,648	14.57
Italian (84)	153	1.35
Norwegian (0)	29	0.26
Polish (16)	56	0.49
Romanian (0)	47	0.42
Russian (22)	33	0.29
Scotch-Irish (193)	309	2.73
Scottish (222)	666	5.89
Slavic (0)	10	0.09
Slovene (17)	17	0.15
Swedish (39)	113	1.00
Swiss (0)	12	0.11
Welsh (51)	77	0.68

Hispanic Origin	Population	%
Hispanic or Latino (of any race)	774	6.57
Central American, ex. Mexican	46	0.39
Costa Rican	2	0.02
Guatemalan	21	0.18
Honduran	5	0.04
Panamanian	1	0.01
Salvadoran	17	0.14
Cuban	9	0.08
Mexican	656	5.57
Puerto Rican	9	0.08
South American	8	0.07
Colombian	4	0.03
Peruvian	3	0.03
Venezuelan	1	0.01
Other Hispanic or Latino	46	0.39

Race*	Population	%
African-American/Black (1,688)	1,787	15.18
Not Hispanic (1,683)	1,782	15.14
Hispanic (5)	5	0.04
American Indian/Alaska Native (42)	111	0.94
Not Hispanic (29)	93	0.79
Hispanic (13)	18	0.15
Apache (1)	2	0.02
Cherokee (10)	29	0.25
Cheyenne (1)	1	0.01
Chippewa (1)	5	0.04
Choctaw (0)	2	0.02
Cree (1)	1	0.01
Creek (0)	1	0.01
Seminole (1)	1	0.01
Asian (69)	101	0.86
Not Hispanic (67)	99	0.84
Hispanic (2)	2	0.02
Cambodian (1)	1	0.01
Chinese, ex. Taiwanese (9)	9	0.08
Filipino (6)	10	0.08
Indian (18)	23	0.20
Japanese (6)	16	0.14
Korean (0)	2	0.02
Pakistani (15)	15	0.13
Taiwanese (1)	2	0.02
Vietnamese (6)	13	0.11
Hawaii Native/Pacific Islander (11)	17	0.14
Not Hispanic (1)	4	0.03
Hispanic (10)	13	0.11
Guamanian/Chamorro (11)	14	0.12
Native Hawaiian (0)	1	0.01
White (9,270)	9,483	80.55
Not Hispanic (9,026)	9,195	78.10
Hispanic (244)	288	2.45

Madison

Place Type: City
County: Madison
Population: 42,938†

Ancestry‡	Population	%
African, Sub-Saharan (61)	72	0.18
African (19)	30	0.07
South African (42)	42	0.10
American (4,105)	4,105	10.19
Arab (157)	219	0.54
Arab (125)	172	0.43
Egyptian (19)	19	0.05
Lebanese (5)	20	0.05
Other Arab (8)	8	0.02
Armenian (0)	44	0.11
Australian (10)	10	0.02
Austrian (26)	118	0.29
Belgian (51)	80	0.20
Brazilian (38)	49	0.12
British (241)	376	0.93
Cajun (11)	11	0.03
Canadian (65)	86	0.21
Celtic (0)	14	0.03
Croatian (0)	45	0.11
Czech (40)	163	0.40
Czechoslovakian (19)	34	0.08
Danish (9)	223	0.55

SECTION TWO

*Notes: † The Census 2010 population figure is used to calculate the percentages in the Hispanic Origin and Race categories. Ancestry percentages are based on the 2006-2010 American Community Survey population (not shown); ‡ Numbers in parentheses indicate the number of people reporting a single ancestry; * Numbers in parentheses indicate the number of persons reporting this race alone, not in combination with any other race; Please refer to the Explanation of Data for more information.*

Dutch (72)	599	1.49
Eastern European (33)	33	0.08
English (2,161)	5,238	13.00
European (675)	815	2.02
Finnish (69)	110	0.27
French, ex. Basque (226)	1,177	2.92
French Canadian (37)	175	0.43
German (2,383)	6,165	15.30
Greek (55)	164	0.41
Hungarian (40)	127	0.32
Icelander (0)	47	0.12
Iranian (69)	69	0.17
Irish (1,980)	5,146	12.77
Italian (434)	1,238	3.07
Lithuanian (21)	21	0.05
New Zealander (16)	91	0.23
Northern European (37)	37	0.09
Norwegian (120)	483	1.20
Pennsylvania German (0)	20	0.05
Polish (234)	982	2.44
Portuguese (0)	32	0.08
Romanian (24)	33	0.08
Russian (84)	272	0.68
Scandinavian (18)	18	0.04
Scotch-Irish (569)	1,235	3.07
Scottish (342)	1,180	2.93
Slovak (12)	41	0.10
Slovene (19)	19	0.05
Swedish (169)	439	1.09
Swiss (15)	102	0.25
Ukrainian (57)	122	0.30
Welsh (134)	281	0.70
West Indian, ex. Hispanic (64)	229	0.57
Barbadian (15)	15	0.04
British West Indian (19)	19	0.05
Jamaican (22)	22	0.05
Trinidadian/Tobagonian (8)	173	0.43
Yugoslavian (27)	27	0.07

Hispanic Origin	Population	%
Hispanic or Latino (of any race)	1,834	4.27
Central American, ex. Mexican	128	0.30
Costa Rican	11	0.03
Guatemalan	31	0.07
Honduran	20	0.05
Nicaraguan	12	0.03
Panamanian	39	0.09
Salvadoran	15	0.03
Cuban	48	0.11
Dominican Republic	20	0.05
Mexican	994	2.31
Puerto Rican	334	0.78
South American	144	0.34
Argentinean	10	0.02
Bolivian	13	0.03
Chilean	6	0.01
Colombian	57	0.13
Ecuadorian	7	0.02
Paraguayan	3	0.01
Peruvian	30	0.07
Uruguayan	3	0.01
Venezuelan	14	0.03
Other South American	1	<0.01
Other Hispanic or Latino	166	0.39

Race*	Population	%
African-American/Black (6,249)	6,652	15.49
Not Hispanic (6,178)	6,537	15.22
Hispanic (71)	115	0.27
American Indian/Alaska Native (226)	519	1.21
Not Hispanic (208)	471	1.10
Hispanic (18)	48	0.11
Alaska Athabascan *(Ala. Nat.)* (1)	1	<0.01
Aleut *(Alaska Native)* (2)	2	<0.01
Apache (2)	8	0.02
Arapaho (1)	1	<0.01
Blackfeet (2)	4	0.01
Central American Ind. (0)	1	<0.01
Cherokee (123)	232	0.54
Chickasaw (2)	7	0.02
Chippewa (7)	10	0.02
Choctaw (7)	11	0.03
Comanche (1)	1	<0.01
Cree (0)	1	<0.01
Creek (4)	16	0.04
Crow (0)	3	0.01
Delaware (2)	4	0.01
Houma (2)	2	<0.01
Inupiat *(Alaska Native)* (0)	3	0.01
Iroquois (1)	4	0.01
Mexican American Ind. (7)	12	0.03
Navajo (11)	11	0.03
Osage (1)	1	<0.01
Ottawa (2)	3	0.01
Seminole (2)	3	0.01
Sioux (0)	1	<0.01
South American Ind. (1)	4	0.01
Spanish American Ind. (1)	1	<0.01
Asian (2,993)	3,495	8.14
Not Hispanic (2,974)	3,450	8.03
Hispanic (19)	45	0.10
Bangladeshi (38)	40	0.09
Burmese (0)	5	0.01
Cambodian (11)	15	0.03
Chinese, ex. Taiwanese (610)	686	1.60
Filipino (140)	258	0.60
Hmong (2)	2	<0.01
Indian (940)	998	2.32
Indonesian (10)	12	0.03
Japanese (106)	177	0.41
Korean (660)	745	1.74
Laotian (7)	7	0.02
Malaysian (0)	2	<0.01
Nepalese (35)	39	0.09
Pakistani (56)	61	0.14
Sri Lankan (9)	12	0.03
Taiwanese (35)	40	0.09
Thai (28)	50	0.12
Vietnamese (238)	279	0.65
Hawaii Native/Pacific Islander (42)	84	0.20
Not Hispanic (41)	80	0.19
Hispanic (1)	4	0.01
Fijian (0)	2	<0.01
Guamanian/Chamorro (7)	11	0.03
Marshallese (9)	9	0.02
Native Hawaiian (13)	34	0.08
Samoan (5)	11	0.03
White (31,757)	32,688	76.13
Not Hispanic (30,666)	31,478	73.31
Hispanic (1,091)	1,210	2.82

Meadowbrook

Place Type: CDP
County: Shelby
Population: 8,769†

Ancestry‡	Population	%
American (1,109)	1,109	12.64
Arab (50)	90	1.03
Lebanese (50)	90	1.03
Belgian (8)	14	0.16
British (40)	86	0.98
Czech (9)	42	0.48
Czechoslovakian (0)	9	0.10
Danish (13)	84	0.96
Dutch (9)	94	1.07
Eastern European (13)	13	0.15
English (825)	1,791	20.42
European (168)	211	2.41
French, ex. Basque (91)	435	4.96
French Canadian (13)	13	0.15
German (365)	1,140	13.00
Greek (34)	34	0.39
Hungarian (0)	54	0.62
Irish (386)	1,150	13.11
Italian (159)	429	4.89
Luxemburger (9)	9	0.10
Macedonian (0)	9	0.10
Norwegian (32)	75	0.85
Polish (45)	213	2.43
Portuguese (0)	11	0.13
Russian (8)	15	0.17
Scotch-Irish (506)	768	8.76
Scottish (155)	372	4.24
Slovak (13)	13	0.15
Swedish (8)	29	0.33
Swiss (9)	53	0.60
Welsh (0)	91	1.04

Hispanic Origin	Population	%
Hispanic or Latino (of any race)	138	1.57
Central American, ex. Mexican	18	0.21
Guatemalan	7	0.08
Honduran	1	0.01
Nicaraguan	4	0.05
Panamanian	3	0.03
Salvadoran	3	0.03
Cuban	21	0.24
Dominican Republic	3	0.03
Mexican	61	0.70
Puerto Rican	7	0.08
South American	19	0.22
Bolivian	1	0.01
Chilean	1	0.01
Colombian	4	0.05
Ecuadorian	2	0.02
Peruvian	1	0.01
Venezuelan	10	0.11
Other Hispanic or Latino	9	0.10

Race*	Population	%
African-American/Black (343)	362	4.13
Not Hispanic (342)	359	4.09
Hispanic (1)	3	0.03
American Indian/Alaska Native (8)	25	0.29
Not Hispanic (8)	24	0.27
Hispanic (0)	1	0.01
Central American Ind. (0)	1	0.01
Cherokee (4)	12	0.14
Creek (2)	5	0.06
Asian (185)	214	2.44
Not Hispanic (184)	213	2.43
Hispanic (1)	1	0.01
Chinese, ex. Taiwanese (41)	41	0.47
Filipino (14)	20	0.23
Indian (40)	49	0.56
Japanese (14)	26	0.30
Korean (33)	33	0.38
Malaysian (1)	1	0.01
Sri Lankan (1)	1	0.01
Thai (2)	3	0.03
Vietnamese (30)	31	0.35
Hawaii Native/Pacific Islander (2)	4	0.05
Not Hispanic (2)	4	0.05
Guamanian/Chamorro (2)	2	0.02
Native Hawaiian (0)	2	0.02
White (8,136)	8,198	93.49
Not Hispanic (8,029)	8,088	92.23
Hispanic (107)	110	1.25

Millbrook

Place Type: City
County: Elmore
Population: 14,640†

Ancestry‡	Population	%
Afghan (27)	27	0.19
African, Sub-Saharan (38)	38	0.27
African (38)	38	0.27
American (2,206)	2,206	15.72
British (20)	27	0.19
Canadian (0)	16	0.11
Czech (0)	34	0.24
Danish (0)	26	0.19
Dutch (0)	22	0.16
Eastern European (3)	3	0.02
English (705)	1,243	8.86
European (171)	189	1.35

*Notes: † The Census 2010 population figure is used to calculate the percentages in the Hispanic Origin and Race categories. Ancestry percentages are based on the 2006-2010 American Community Survey population (not shown); ‡ Numbers in parentheses indicate the number of people reporting a single ancestry; * Numbers in parentheses indicate the number of persons reporting this race alone, not in combination with any other race; Please refer to the Explanation of Data for more information.*

Finnish (9)	23	0.16
French, ex. Basque (45)	233	1.66
French Canadian (7)	29	0.21
German (352)	1,068	7.61
Greek (13)	16	0.11
Irish (853)	1,951	13.90
Italian (165)	371	2.64
Luxemburger (0)	16	0.11
Norwegian (57)	94	0.67
Polish (19)	54	0.38
Russian (15)	23	0.16
Scandinavian (10)	33	0.24
Scotch-Irish (357)	498	3.55
Scottish (117)	364	2.59
Slovak (0)	24	0.17
Swedish (0)	25	0.18
Welsh (31)	32	0.23
West Indian, ex. Hispanic (24)	24	0.17
Jamaican (24)	24	0.17

Hispanic Origin	Population	%
Hispanic or Latino (of any race)	410	2.80
Central American, ex. Mexican	39	0.27
Costa Rican	7	0.05
Guatemalan	6	0.04
Honduran	6	0.04
Nicaraguan	8	0.05
Panamanian	5	0.03
Salvadoran	7	0.05
Cuban	9	0.06
Dominican Republic	1	0.01
Mexican	222	1.52
Puerto Rican	79	0.54
South American	22	0.15
Bolivian	3	0.02
Chilean	1	0.01
Colombian	11	0.08
Ecuadorian	3	0.02
Peruvian	4	0.03
Other Hispanic or Latino	38	0.26

Race*	Population	%
African-American/Black (3,155)	3,282	22.42
Not Hispanic (3,142)	3,257	22.25
Hispanic (13)	25	0.17
American Indian/Alaska Native (52)	121	0.83
Not Hispanic (52)	117	0.80
Hispanic (0)	4	0.03
Apache (0)	1	0.01
Blackfeet (0)	1	0.01
Canadian/French Am. Ind. (0)	1	0.01
Cherokee (13)	35	0.24
Chippewa (5)	6	0.04
Choctaw (1)	4	0.03
Creek (11)	18	0.12
Inupiat *(Alaska Native)* (0)	1	0.01
Iroquois (0)	1	0.01
Lumbee (1)	1	0.01
Mexican American Ind. (0)	2	0.01
Navajo (1)	1	0.01
Seminole (2)	2	0.01
Sioux (0)	2	0.01
South American Ind. (0)	4	0.03
Yakama (4)	4	0.03
Asian (120)	196	1.34
Not Hispanic (118)	192	1.31
Hispanic (2)	4	0.03
Bangladeshi (0)	1	0.01
Cambodian (1)	3	0.02
Chinese, ex. Taiwanese (9)	17	0.12
Filipino (22)	38	0.26
Indian (25)	32	0.22
Japanese (5)	12	0.08
Korean (13)	26	0.18
Laotian (5)	5	0.03
Malaysian (1)	2	0.01
Thai (2)	5	0.03
Vietnamese (17)	20	0.14
Hawaii Native/Pacific Islander (7)	18	0.12
Not Hispanic (4)	13	0.09
Hispanic (3)	5	0.03
Guamanian/Chamorro (2)	5	0.03
Native Hawaiian (4)	8	0.05
Samoan (1)	3	0.02
White (10,863)	11,130	76.02
Not Hispanic (10,653)	10,880	74.32
Hispanic (210)	250	1.71

Mobile

Place Type: City
County: Mobile
Population: 195,111†

Ancestry‡	Population	%
African, Sub-Saharan (1,607)	1,912	0.98
African (1,498)	1,766	0.90
Ethiopian (9)	35	0.02
Ghanaian (59)	59	0.03
Nigerian (11)	11	0.01
South African (30)	41	0.02
Albanian (0)	15	0.01
Alsatian (9)	49	0.03
American (14,358)	14,358	7.34
Arab (886)	988	0.51
Arab (25)	37	0.02
Egyptian (176)	199	0.10
Iraqi (209)	209	0.11
Jordanian (41)	41	0.02
Lebanese (328)	395	0.20
Moroccan (50)	50	0.03
Other Arab (57)	57	0.03
Armenian (9)	9	<0.01
Australian (0)	18	0.01
Austrian (83)	212	0.11
Belgian (0)	31	0.02
Brazilian (19)	75	0.04
British (420)	734	0.38
Cajun (106)	186	0.10
Canadian (23)	74	0.04
Celtic (0)	18	0.01
Croatian (152)	197	0.10
Czech (79)	280	0.14
Czechoslovakian (47)	87	0.04
Danish (150)	357	0.18
Dutch (303)	1,703	0.87
Eastern European (50)	50	0.03
English (6,869)	14,542	7.43
European (1,224)	1,374	0.70
Finnish (46)	156	0.08
French, ex. Basque (1,169)	5,957	3.05
French Canadian (434)	747	0.38
German (4,840)	14,673	7.50
Greek (494)	777	0.40
Guyanese (10)	10	0.01
Hungarian (11)	124	0.06
Iranian (104)	104	0.05
Irish (5,583)	15,702	8.03
Italian (1,201)	3,490	1.78
Lithuanian (49)	95	0.05
Luxemburger (7)	7	<0.01
Maltese (10)	35	0.02
Northern European (31)	39	0.02
Norwegian (262)	812	0.42
Polish (316)	1,050	0.54
Portuguese (16)	112	0.06
Romanian (85)	111	0.06
Russian (290)	564	0.29
Scandinavian (71)	223	0.11
Scotch-Irish (2,834)	4,869	2.49
Scottish (1,609)	3,505	1.79
Serbian (13)	13	0.01
Slavic (10)	48	0.02
Slovak (17)	52	0.03
Slovene (11)	32	0.02
Swedish (248)	962	0.49
Swiss (71)	218	0.11
Turkish (233)	243	0.12
Ukrainian (65)	114	0.06
Welsh (151)	686	0.35
West Indian, ex. Hispanic (682)	823	0.42
Bahamian (26)	53	0.03
Barbadian (0)	8	<0.01
Belizean (8)	27	0.01
Bermudan (11)	11	0.01
British West Indian (29)	29	0.01
Haitian (290)	290	0.15
Jamaican (90)	99	0.05
West Indian (228)	252	0.13
Other West Indian (0)	54	0.03
Yugoslavian (85)	85	0.04

Hispanic Origin	Population	%
Hispanic or Latino (of any race)	4,600	2.36
Central American, ex. Mexican	570	0.29
Costa Rican	30	0.02
Guatemalan	159	0.08
Honduran	162	0.08
Nicaraguan	61	0.03
Panamanian	54	0.03
Salvadoran	101	0.05
Other Central American	3	<0.01
Cuban	380	0.19
Dominican Republic	71	0.04
Mexican	1,677	0.86
Puerto Rican	562	0.29
South American	555	0.28
Argentinean	32	0.02
Bolivian	51	0.03
Chilean	83	0.04
Colombian	111	0.06
Ecuadorian	26	0.01
Paraguayan	9	<0.01
Peruvian	148	0.08
Uruguayan	4	<0.01
Venezuelan	86	0.04
Other South American	5	<0.01
Other Hispanic or Latino	785	0.40

Race*	Population	%
African-American/Black (98,691)	100,265	51.39
Not Hispanic (98,202)	99,638	51.07
Hispanic (489)	627	0.32
American Indian/Alaska Native (623)	1,550	0.79
Not Hispanic (572)	1,440	0.74
Hispanic (51)	110	0.06
Alaska Athabascan *(Ala. Nat.)* (0)	1	<0.01
Aleut *(Alaska Native)* (1)	4	<0.01
Apache (1)	4	<0.01
Arapaho (2)	5	<0.01
Blackfeet (3)	22	0.01
Canadian/French Am. Ind. (2)	3	<0.01
Central American Ind. (4)	4	<0.01
Cherokee (82)	313	0.16
Cheyenne (1)	1	<0.01
Chickasaw (0)	10	0.01
Chippewa (5)	8	<0.01
Choctaw (66)	142	0.07
Colville (4)	4	<0.01
Comanche (0)	1	<0.01
Creek (69)	159	0.08
Crow (1)	2	<0.01
Delaware (0)	1	<0.01
Houma (8)	15	0.01
Inupiat *(Alaska Native)* (2)	2	<0.01
Iroquois (6)	11	0.01
Lumbee (3)	3	<0.01
Mexican American Ind. (5)	11	0.01
Navajo (2)	7	<0.01
Ottawa (1)	1	<0.01
Potawatomi (3)	7	<0.01
Pueblo (2)	3	<0.01
Seminole (4)	6	<0.01
Sioux (1)	24	0.01
South American Ind. (2)	4	<0.01
Spanish American Ind. (0)	2	<0.01
Tlingit-Haida *(Alaska Native)* (0)	1	<0.01
Tohono O'Odham (1)	1	<0.01
Asian (3,427)	4,100	2.10
Not Hispanic (3,409)	4,034	2.07

SECTION TWO

*Notes: † The Census 2010 population figure is used to calculate the percentages in the Hispanic Origin and Race categories. Ancestry percentages are based on the 2006-2010 American Community Survey population (not shown); ‡ Numbers in parentheses indicate the number of people reporting a single ancestry; * Numbers in parentheses indicate the number of persons reporting this race alone, not in combination with any other race; Please refer to the Explanation of Data for more information.*

Hispanic (18)	66	0.03
Bangladeshi (22)	25	0.01
Burmese (10)	10	0.01
Cambodian (37)	41	0.02
Chinese, ex. Taiwanese (411)	512	0.26
Filipino (395)	546	0.28
Indian (761)	848	0.43
Indonesian (22)	26	0.01
Japanese (124)	177	0.09
Korean (150)	208	0.11
Laotian (22)	30	0.02
Malaysian (14)	14	0.01
Nepalese (49)	58	0.03
Pakistani (84)	96	0.05
Sri Lankan (9)	10	0.01
Taiwanese (7)	7	<0.01
Thai (44)	57	0.03
Vietnamese (1,104)	1,194	0.61
Hawaii Native/Pacific Islander (77)	200	0.10
Not Hispanic (57)	156	0.08
Hispanic (20)	44	0.02
Fijian (1)	1	<0.01
Guamanian/Chamorro (21)	39	0.02
Native Hawaiian (24)	66	0.03
Samoan (8)	22	0.01
White (87,723)	89,828	46.04
Not Hispanic (85,613)	87,463	44.83
Hispanic (2,110)	2,365	1.21

Montgomery

Place Type: City
County: Montgomery
Population: 205,764†

Ancestry‡	Population	%
African, Sub-Saharan (1,625)	2,076	1.01
African (1,482)	1,891	0.92
Liberian (28)	40	0.02
Nigerian (82)	112	0.05
Other Sub-Saharan African (33)	33	0.02
American (18,629)	18,629	9.10
Arab (489)	663	0.32
Arab (45)	45	0.02
Lebanese (175)	277	0.14
Palestinian (84)	84	0.04
Syrian (26)	98	0.05
Other Arab (159)	159	0.08
Armenian (0)	32	0.02
Assyrian/Chaldean/Syriac (10)	10	<0.01
Austrian (0)	64	0.03
Belgian (134)	159	0.08
Brazilian (24)	39	0.02
British (482)	799	0.39
Cajun (130)	203	0.10
Canadian (186)	268	0.13
Celtic (12)	12	0.01
Croatian (33)	78	0.04
Czech (52)	95	0.05
Czechoslovakian (53)	62	0.03
Danish (17)	48	0.02
Dutch (243)	1,150	0.56
Eastern European (31)	40	0.02
English (6,282)	12,925	6.31
European (1,355)	1,515	0.74
Finnish (0)	5	<0.01
French, ex. Basque (622)	2,874	1.40
French Canadian (85)	258	0.13
German (3,060)	9,024	4.41
Greek (210)	409	0.20
Hungarian (85)	218	0.11
Icelander (43)	43	0.02
Iranian (69)	95	0.05
Irish (3,197)	8,741	4.27
Israeli (33)	33	0.02
Italian (1,219)	2,212	1.08
Lithuanian (14)	64	0.03
New Zealander (5)	5	<0.01
Northern European (180)	180	0.09
Norwegian (195)	512	0.25
Pennsylvania German (0)	24	0.01
Polish (348)	1,024	0.50
Portuguese (32)	53	0.03
Romanian (31)	70	0.03
Russian (77)	418	0.20
Scandinavian (40)	53	0.03
Scotch-Irish (2,121)	3,794	1.85
Scottish (1,354)	3,294	1.61
Serbian (45)	60	0.03
Slavic (0)	11	0.01
Slovak (33)	69	0.03
Swedish (197)	715	0.35
Swiss (24)	200	0.10
Turkish (16)	16	0.01
Ukrainian (0)	90	0.04
Welsh (141)	548	0.27
West Indian, ex. Hispanic (369)	685	0.33
Bahamian (15)	37	0.02
Haitian (16)	16	0.01
Jamaican (234)	371	0.18
Trinidadian/Tobagonian (9)	9	<0.01
U.S. Virgin Islander (13)	13	0.01
West Indian (82)	239	0.12
Yugoslavian (0)	9	<0.01

Hispanic Origin	Population	%
Hispanic or Latino (of any race)	7,998	3.89
Central American, ex. Mexican	821	0.40
Costa Rican	15	0.01
Guatemalan	343	0.17
Honduran	233	0.11
Nicaraguan	11	0.01
Panamanian	82	0.04
Salvadoran	136	0.07
Other Central American	1	<0.01
Cuban	160	0.08
Dominican Republic	40	0.02
Mexican	5,298	2.57
Puerto Rican	555	0.27
South American	225	0.11
Argentinean	15	0.01
Bolivian	12	0.01
Chilean	4	<0.01
Colombian	79	0.04
Ecuadorian	21	0.01
Paraguayan	3	<0.01
Peruvian	49	0.02
Uruguayan	6	<0.01
Venezuelan	31	0.02
Other South American	5	<0.01
Other Hispanic or Latino	899	0.44

Race*	Population	%
African-American/Black (116,524)	118,129	57.41
Not Hispanic (116,001)	117,426	57.07
Hispanic (523)	703	0.34
American Indian/Alaska Native (512)	1,272	0.62
Not Hispanic (449)	1,126	0.55
Hispanic (63)	146	0.07
Alaska Athabascan *(Ala. Nat.)* (2)	2	<0.01
Apache (3)	6	<0.01
Blackfeet (5)	14	0.01
Canadian/French Am. Ind. (1)	2	<0.01
Central American Ind. (9)	9	<0.01
Cherokee (69)	237	0.12
Chickasaw (0)	4	<0.01
Chippewa (7)	10	<0.01
Choctaw (21)	40	0.02
Comanche (0)	1	<0.01
Cree (1)	1	<0.01
Creek (75)	138	0.07
Delaware (0)	3	<0.01
Houma (0)	3	<0.01
Inupiat *(Alaska Native)* (0)	1	<0.01
Iroquois (1)	4	<0.01
Kiowa (2)	2	<0.01
Lumbee (1)	2	<0.01
Menominee (1)	2	<0.01
Mexican American Ind. (9)	10	<0.01
Navajo (2)	9	<0.01
Osage (3)	4	<0.01
Ottawa (6)	6	<0.01
Potawatomi (2)	2	<0.01
Pueblo (5)	7	<0.01
Seminole (0)	2	<0.01
Sioux (6)	15	0.01
South American Ind. (1)	2	<0.01
Tlingit-Haida *(Alaska Native)* (1)	1	<0.01
Tsimshian *(Alaska Native)* (0)	1	<0.01
Ute (3)	3	<0.01
Asian (4,609)	5,390	2.62
Not Hispanic (4,580)	5,288	2.57
Hispanic (29)	102	0.05
Bangladeshi (62)	71	0.03
Cambodian (6)	15	0.01
Chinese, ex. Taiwanese (416)	501	0.24
Filipino (300)	536	0.26
Hmong (4)	5	<0.01
Indian (981)	1,091	0.53
Indonesian (11)	20	0.01
Japanese (122)	224	0.11
Korean (1,740)	1,870	0.91
Laotian (234)	264	0.13
Malaysian (7)	11	0.01
Nepalese (4)	4	<0.01
Pakistani (66)	81	0.04
Sri Lankan (11)	13	0.01
Taiwanese (30)	30	0.01
Thai (96)	130	0.06
Vietnamese (300)	344	0.17
Hawaii Native/Pacific Islander (164)	324	0.16
Not Hispanic (79)	206	0.10
Hispanic (85)	118	0.06
Fijian (1)	1	<0.01
Guamanian/Chamorro (112)	140	0.07
Marshallese (1)	6	<0.01
Native Hawaiian (22)	81	0.04
Samoan (15)	31	0.02
Tongan (1)	1	<0.01
White (76,656)	78,597	38.20
Not Hispanic (74,227)	75,872	36.87
Hispanic (2,429)	2,725	1.32

Moody

Place Type: City
County: St. Clair
Population: 11,726†

Ancestry‡	Population	%
African, Sub-Saharan (65)	65	0.58
African (65)	65	0.58
American (2,562)	2,562	23.00
British (34)	69	0.62
Dutch (2)	190	1.71
English (568)	837	7.51
European (172)	172	1.54
Finnish (13)	13	0.12
French, ex. Basque (22)	136	1.22
French Canadian (47)	47	0.42
German (431)	1,154	10.36
Greek (0)	23	0.21
Iranian (0)	23	0.21
Irish (627)	1,590	14.28
Italian (93)	164	1.47
Lithuanian (18)	18	0.16
Norwegian (32)	32	0.29
Polish (17)	17	0.15
Scotch-Irish (25)	214	1.92
Scottish (35)	143	1.28
Swedish (0)	79	0.71
Swiss (0)	20	0.18
Welsh (29)	46	0.41

Hispanic Origin	Population	%
Hispanic or Latino (of any race)	247	2.11
Central American, ex. Mexican	15	0.13
Honduran	1	0.01
Nicaraguan	3	0.03
Panamanian	6	0.05

*Notes: † The Census 2010 population figure is used to calculate the percentages in the Hispanic Origin and Race categories. Ancestry percentages are based on the 2006-2010 American Community Survey population (not shown); ‡ Numbers in parentheses indicate the number of people reporting a single ancestry; * Numbers in parentheses indicate the number of persons reporting this race alone, not in combination with any other race; Please refer to the Explanation of Data for more information.*

Salvadoran	5	0.04
Cuban	7	0.06
Dominican Republic	1	0.01
Mexican	144	1.23
Puerto Rican	19	0.16
South American	24	0.20
Colombian	9	0.08
Ecuadorian	3	0.03
Peruvian	7	0.06
Venezuelan	5	0.04
Other Hispanic or Latino	37	0.32

Race*	Population	%
African-American/Black (912)	979	8.35
Not Hispanic (908)	973	8.30
Hispanic (4)	6	0.05
American Indian/Alaska Native (38)	94	0.80
Not Hispanic (27)	83	0.71
Hispanic (11)	11	0.09
Apache (1)	1	0.01
Cherokee (14)	47	0.40
Choctaw (1)	3	0.03
Creek (1)	10	0.09
Lumbee (2)	2	0.02
Spanish American Ind. (5)	5	0.04
Asian (166)	211	1.80
Not Hispanic (166)	208	1.77
Hispanic (0)	3	0.03
Chinese, ex. Taiwanese (17)	24	0.20
Filipino (6)	24	0.20
Indian (64)	70	0.60
Japanese (9)	17	0.14
Korean (10)	11	0.09
Laotian (2)	2	0.02
Pakistani (15)	15	0.13
Vietnamese (36)	46	0.39
Hawaii Native/Pacific Islander (0)	4	0.03
Not Hispanic (0)	4	0.03
Native Hawaiian (0)	2	0.02
White (10,348)	10,507	89.60
Not Hispanic (10,216)	10,359	88.34
Hispanic (132)	148	1.26

Mountain Brook

Place Type: City
County: Jefferson
Population: 20,413†

Ancestry‡	Population	%
American (2,433)	2,433	11.94
Arab (86)	121	0.59
Lebanese (64)	99	0.49
Other Arab (22)	22	0.11
Armenian (0)	12	0.06
Austrian (39)	139	0.68
Basque (0)	12	0.06
British (176)	304	1.49
Canadian (11)	11	0.05
Celtic (24)	36	0.18
Czech (7)	7	0.03
Danish (18)	18	0.09
Dutch (246)	450	2.21
Eastern European (244)	244	1.20
English (2,517)	4,865	23.87
European (655)	764	3.75
Finnish (0)	37	0.18
French, ex. Basque (214)	976	4.79
French Canadian (37)	82	0.40
German (731)	2,419	11.87
Greek (119)	179	0.88
Hungarian (10)	10	0.05
Irish (637)	2,060	10.11
Italian (214)	418	2.05
Latvian (14)	14	0.07
Lithuanian (2)	12	0.06
Northern European (115)	115	0.56
Norwegian (96)	124	0.61
Polish (192)	512	2.51
Romanian (34)	68	0.33
Russian (197)	436	2.14
Scandinavian (51)	112	0.55
Scotch-Irish (894)	1,474	7.23
Scottish (758)	1,550	7.61
Slovak (16)	16	0.08
Swedish (116)	198	0.97
Swiss (10)	67	0.33
Ukrainian (38)	54	0.26
Welsh (20)	124	0.61
West Indian, ex. Hispanic (0)	14	0.07
Jamaican (0)	14	0.07

Hispanic Origin	Population	%
Hispanic or Latino (of any race)	198	0.97
Central American, ex. Mexican	31	0.15
Costa Rican	1	<0.01
Guatemalan	10	0.05
Honduran	10	0.05
Nicaraguan	9	0.04
Other Central American	1	<0.01
Cuban	35	0.17
Dominican Republic	1	<0.01
Mexican	43	0.21
Puerto Rican	21	0.10
South American	38	0.19
Argentinean	1	<0.01
Bolivian	1	<0.01
Chilean	4	0.02
Colombian	18	0.09
Ecuadorian	5	0.02
Paraguayan	2	0.01
Peruvian	4	0.02
Uruguayan	1	<0.01
Venezuelan	2	0.01
Other Hispanic or Latino	29	0.14

Race*	Population	%
African-American/Black (210)	240	1.18
Not Hispanic (206)	235	1.15
Hispanic (4)	5	0.02
American Indian/Alaska Native (13)	47	0.23
Not Hispanic (13)	44	0.22
Hispanic (0)	3	0.01
Aleut *(Alaska Native)* (3)	3	0.01
Cherokee (2)	9	0.04
Creek (3)	5	0.02
Sioux (1)	1	<0.01
South American Ind. (0)	1	<0.01
Tohono O'Odham (0)	1	<0.01
Asian (190)	242	1.19
Not Hispanic (190)	238	1.17
Hispanic (0)	4	0.02
Burmese (0)	1	<0.01
Chinese, ex. Taiwanese (75)	87	0.43
Filipino (17)	22	0.11
Indian (39)	46	0.23
Indonesian (0)	1	<0.01
Japanese (8)	16	0.08
Korean (26)	33	0.16
Nepalese (1)	1	<0.01
Taiwanese (0)	1	<0.01
Thai (5)	7	0.03
Vietnamese (13)	15	0.07
Hawaii Native/Pacific Islander (0)	5	0.02
Not Hispanic (0)	4	0.02
Hispanic (0)	1	<0.01
White (19,848)	19,954	97.75
Not Hispanic (19,692)	19,792	96.96
Hispanic (156)	162	0.79

Muscle Shoals

Place Type: City
County: Colbert
Population: 13,146†

Ancestry‡	Population	%
African, Sub-Saharan (199)	199	1.53
African (56)	56	0.43
Sudanese (143)	143	1.10
American (2,198)	2,198	16.93
British (13)	77	0.59
Canadian (8)	8	0.06
Danish (0)	40	0.31
Dutch (0)	115	0.89
English (539)	1,258	9.69
European (49)	64	0.49
French, ex. Basque (54)	134	1.03
French Canadian (0)	10	0.08
German (283)	804	6.19
Greek (8)	8	0.06
Irish (868)	1,990	15.32
Italian (18)	34	0.26
Lithuanian (10)	10	0.08
New Zealander (13)	13	0.10
Polish (0)	24	0.18
Portuguese (0)	53	0.41
Russian (19)	19	0.15
Scandinavian (16)	46	0.35
Scotch-Irish (100)	196	1.51
Scottish (63)	158	1.22
Slovak (0)	11	0.08
Swedish (9)	50	0.39
Swiss (0)	14	0.11
Welsh (15)	184	1.42
West Indian, ex. Hispanic (33)	52	0.40
Haitian (33)	33	0.25
Jamaican (0)	19	0.15

Hispanic Origin	Population	%
Hispanic or Latino (of any race)	351	2.67
Central American, ex. Mexican	50	0.38
Guatemalan	29	0.22
Honduran	15	0.11
Nicaraguan	3	0.02
Panamanian	3	0.02
Cuban	15	0.11
Dominican Republic	1	0.01
Mexican	213	1.62
Puerto Rican	10	0.08
South American	6	0.05
Colombian	3	0.02
Ecuadorian	1	0.01
Peruvian	2	0.02
Other Hispanic or Latino	56	0.43

Race*	Population	%
African-American/Black (2,014)	2,114	16.08
Not Hispanic (2,000)	2,083	15.85
Hispanic (14)	31	0.24
American Indian/Alaska Native (36)	119	0.91
Not Hispanic (35)	117	0.89
Hispanic (1)	2	0.02
Cherokee (19)	66	0.50
Chickasaw (0)	4	0.03
Chippewa (1)	1	0.01
Choctaw (2)	7	0.05
Comanche (0)	1	0.01
Creek (1)	3	0.02
Iroquois (1)	5	0.04
Lumbee (2)	2	0.02
Mexican American Ind. (1)	1	0.01
Seminole (1)	1	0.01
Asian (117)	134	1.02
Not Hispanic (112)	129	0.98
Hispanic (5)	5	0.04
Chinese, ex. Taiwanese (27)	27	0.21
Filipino (19)	24	0.18
Indian (52)	53	0.40
Japanese (1)	8	0.06
Korean (8)	8	0.06
Thai (1)	2	0.02
Vietnamese (7)	10	0.08
Hawaii Native/Pacific Islander (6)	7	0.05
Not Hispanic (6)	7	0.05
Fijian (1)	1	0.01
Guamanian/Chamorro (0)	1	0.01
White (10,602)	10,788	82.06
Not Hispanic (10,454)	10,618	80.77
Hispanic (148)	170	1.29

*Notes: † The Census 2010 population figure is used to calculate the percentages in the Hispanic Origin and Race categories. Ancestry percentages are based on the 2006-2010 American Community Survey population (not shown); ‡ Numbers in parentheses indicate the number of people reporting a single ancestry; * Numbers in parentheses indicate the number of persons reporting this race alone, not in combination with any other race; Please refer to the Explanation of Data for more information.*

Northport

Place Type: City
County: Tuscaloosa
Population: 23,330†

Ancestry‡	Population	%
African, Sub-Saharan (14)	46	0.20
African (14)	14	0.06
Ugandan (0)	32	0.14
Alsatian (0)	8	0.04
American (2,903)	2,903	12.88
Austrian (19)	82	0.36
Brazilian (10)	10	0.04
British (49)	111	0.49
Cajun (12)	12	0.05
Canadian (13)	13	0.06
Croatian (12)	12	0.05
Czech (25)	42	0.19
Danish (10)	10	0.04
Dutch (68)	178	0.79
English (1,070)	1,818	8.07
European (144)	144	0.64
French, ex. Basque (75)	372	1.65
French Canadian (0)	34	0.15
German (452)	1,071	4.75
Greek (0)	63	0.28
Icelander (20)	20	0.09
Irish (1,278)	2,592	11.50
Italian (85)	362	1.61
Norwegian (11)	64	0.28
Polish (35)	54	0.24
Portuguese (12)	33	0.15
Romanian (22)	22	0.10
Russian (31)	69	0.31
Scotch-Irish (180)	320	1.42
Scottish (196)	301	1.34
Swedish (113)	184	0.82
Swiss (0)	9	0.04
Welsh (15)	98	0.43
Yugoslavian (0)	13	0.06

Hispanic Origin	Population	%
Hispanic or Latino (of any race)	957	4.10
Central American, ex. Mexican	326	1.40
Costa Rican	1	<0.01
Guatemalan	305	1.31
Honduran	11	0.05
Nicaraguan	3	0.01
Panamanian	2	0.01
Salvadoran	3	0.01
Other Central American	1	<0.01
Cuban	24	0.10
Mexican	484	2.07
Puerto Rican	32	0.14
South American	26	0.11
Argentinean	1	<0.01
Chilean	1	<0.01
Colombian	11	0.05
Ecuadorian	4	0.02
Peruvian	4	0.02
Venezuelan	4	0.02
Other South American	1	<0.01
Other Hispanic or Latino	65	0.28

Race*	Population	%
African-American/Black (6,278)	6,369	27.30
Not Hispanic (6,243)	6,321	27.09
Hispanic (35)	48	0.21
American Indian/Alaska Native (60)	146	0.63
Not Hispanic (46)	120	0.51
Hispanic (14)	26	0.11
Apache (0)	1	<0.01
Central American Ind. (0)	4	0.02
Cherokee (13)	31	0.13
Choctaw (3)	10	0.04
Comanche (1)	4	0.02
Creek (4)	8	0.03
Houma (0)	1	<0.01
Mexican American Ind. (14)	15	0.06
South American Ind. (0)	1	<0.01
Asian (247)	305	1.31
Not Hispanic (241)	295	1.26
Hispanic (6)	10	0.04
Bangladeshi (3)	3	0.01
Cambodian (2)	2	0.01
Chinese, ex. Taiwanese (59)	66	0.28
Filipino (34)	53	0.23
Indian (43)	51	0.22
Japanese (10)	19	0.08
Korean (32)	41	0.18
Malaysian (1)	4	0.02
Nepalese (2)	2	0.01
Pakistani (13)	13	0.06
Taiwanese (2)	2	0.01
Thai (5)	6	0.03
Vietnamese (36)	40	0.17
Hawaii Native/Pacific Islander (77)	94	0.40
Not Hispanic (42)	53	0.23
Hispanic (35)	41	0.18
Guamanian/Chamorro (74)	85	0.36
Native Hawaiian (1)	2	0.01
Samoan (0)	1	<0.01
Tongan (0)	1	<0.01
White (15,960)	16,178	69.34
Not Hispanic (15,586)	15,768	67.59
Hispanic (374)	410	1.76

Opelika

Place Type: City
County: Lee
Population: 26,477†

Ancestry‡	Population	%
African, Sub-Saharan (130)	190	0.73
African (81)	141	0.55
Nigerian (41)	41	0.16
South African (8)	8	0.03
American (1,802)	1,802	6.97
Arab (13)	13	0.05
Lebanese (13)	13	0.05
Austrian (0)	3	0.01
Belgian (5)	20	0.08
British (53)	99	0.38
Czech (16)	22	0.09
Czechoslovakian (4)	4	0.02
Danish (0)	4	0.02
Dutch (26)	172	0.66
Eastern European (8)	8	0.03
English (1,366)	2,692	10.41
European (122)	142	0.55
Finnish (14)	30	0.12
French, ex. Basque (132)	422	1.63
French Canadian (5)	72	0.28
German (661)	1,766	6.83
Greek (8)	26	0.10
Hungarian (3)	31	0.12
Irish (654)	2,173	8.40
Italian (131)	323	1.25
Northern European (7)	7	0.03
Norwegian (22)	34	0.13
Polish (60)	73	0.28
Romanian (0)	4	0.02
Russian (26)	56	0.22
Scandinavian (13)	13	0.05
Scotch-Irish (447)	784	3.03
Scottish (278)	557	2.15
Slovak (12)	15	0.06
Swedish (13)	113	0.44
Swiss (0)	17	0.07
Ukrainian (0)	16	0.06
Welsh (76)	144	0.56
West Indian, ex. Hispanic (0)	17	0.07
Haitian (0)	17	0.07

Hispanic Origin	Population	%
Hispanic or Latino (of any race)	1,166	4.40
Central American, ex. Mexican	167	0.63
Costa Rican	2	0.01
Guatemalan	107	0.40
Honduran	29	0.11
Nicaraguan	6	0.02
Panamanian	6	0.02
Salvadoran	17	0.06
Cuban	10	0.04
Dominican Republic	5	0.02
Mexican	728	2.75
Puerto Rican	85	0.32
South American	55	0.21
Argentinean	6	0.02
Bolivian	7	0.03
Colombian	9	0.03
Ecuadorian	2	0.01
Peruvian	3	0.01
Uruguayan	3	0.01
Venezuelan	25	0.09
Other Hispanic or Latino	116	0.44

Race*	Population	%
African-American/Black (11,513)	11,722	44.27
Not Hispanic (11,463)	11,650	44.00
Hispanic (50)	72	0.27
American Indian/Alaska Native (69)	153	0.58
Not Hispanic (55)	132	0.50
Hispanic (14)	21	0.08
Apache (1)	1	<0.01
Blackfeet (1)	2	0.01
Central American Ind. (1)	1	<0.01
Cherokee (7)	39	0.15
Chickasaw (5)	5	0.02
Chippewa (2)	2	0.01
Choctaw (0)	2	0.01
Creek (2)	10	0.04
Mexican American Ind. (3)	3	0.01
Navajo (6)	6	0.02
Seminole (1)	1	<0.01
Sioux (2)	2	0.01
South American Ind. (2)	3	0.01
Asian (456)	509	1.92
Not Hispanic (453)	498	1.88
Hispanic (3)	11	0.04
Bangladeshi (1)	2	0.01
Chinese, ex. Taiwanese (51)	59	0.22
Filipino (18)	36	0.14
Indian (76)	81	0.31
Indonesian (1)	2	0.01
Japanese (8)	14	0.05
Korean (142)	152	0.57
Laotian (110)	115	0.43
Malaysian (0)	1	<0.01
Nepalese (0)	1	<0.01
Pakistani (3)	3	0.01
Thai (8)	10	0.04
Vietnamese (19)	23	0.09
Hawaii Native/Pacific Islander (47)	57	0.22
Not Hispanic (18)	25	0.09
Hispanic (29)	32	0.12
Guamanian/Chamorro (41)	49	0.19
Native Hawaiian (2)	6	0.02
Samoan (2)	2	0.01
White (13,400)	13,681	51.67
Not Hispanic (13,033)	13,249	50.04
Hispanic (367)	432	1.63

Oxford

Place Type: City
County: Calhoun
Population: 21,348†

Ancestry‡	Population	%
African, Sub-Saharan (101)	101	0.48
African (101)	101	0.48
American (2,657)	2,657	12.67
Austrian (7)	7	0.03
British (273)	355	1.69
Czech (0)	28	0.13
Czechoslovakian (0)	23	0.11
Dutch (71)	555	2.65

*Notes: † The Census 2010 population figure is used to calculate the percentages in the Hispanic Origin and Race categories. Ancestry percentages are based on the 2006-2010 American Community Survey population (not shown); ‡ Numbers in parentheses indicate the number of people reporting a single ancestry; * Numbers in parentheses indicate the number of persons reporting this race alone, not in combination with any other race; Please refer to the Explanation of Data for more information.*

English (1,405)	2,549	12.16
European (128)	128	0.61
Finnish (0)	23	0.11
French, ex. Basque (110)	376	1.79
French Canadian (0)	51	0.24
German (932)	2,266	10.81
Greek (31)	75	0.36
Hungarian (0)	167	0.80
Irish (1,326)	3,260	15.55
Italian (172)	642	3.06
Norwegian (12)	42	0.20
Polish (0)	36	0.17
Romanian (22)	22	0.10
Russian (0)	13	0.06
Scandinavian (36)	36	0.17
Scotch-Irish (217)	482	2.30
Scottish (235)	358	1.71
Slovak (9)	9	0.04
Swedish (9)	178	0.85
Ukrainian (11)	48	0.23
Welsh (6)	20	0.10

Hispanic Origin	Population	%
Hispanic or Latino (of any race)	1,408	6.60
Central American, ex. Mexican	74	0.35
Costa Rican	1	<0.01
Guatemalan	35	0.16
Honduran	29	0.14
Panamanian	5	0.02
Salvadoran	4	0.02
Cuban	9	0.04
Dominican Republic	2	0.01
Mexican	1,156	5.42
Puerto Rican	67	0.31
South American	31	0.15
Argentinean	5	0.02
Bolivian	3	0.01
Chilean	1	<0.01
Colombian	5	0.02
Ecuadorian	3	0.01
Paraguayan	2	0.01
Peruvian	6	0.03
Venezuelan	6	0.03
Other Hispanic or Latino	69	0.32

Race*	Population	%
African-American/Black (2,682)	2,834	13.28
Not Hispanic (2,656)	2,789	13.06
Hispanic (26)	45	0.21
American Indian/Alaska Native (86)	181	0.85
Not Hispanic (70)	159	0.74
Hispanic (16)	22	0.10
Apache (2)	2	0.01
Blackfeet (0)	6	0.03
Cherokee (31)	69	0.32
Chickasaw (1)	1	<0.01
Choctaw (1)	4	0.02
Creek (2)	8	0.04
Iroquois (1)	3	0.01
Mexican American Ind. (6)	12	0.06
Navajo (0)	1	<0.01
Puget Sound Salish (1)	1	<0.01
Sioux (0)	1	<0.01
South American Ind. (0)	1	<0.01
Asian (237)	291	1.36
Not Hispanic (233)	281	1.32
Hispanic (4)	10	0.05
Chinese, ex. Taiwanese (38)	48	0.22
Filipino (26)	42	0.20
Indian (77)	81	0.38
Indonesian (4)	4	0.02
Japanese (2)	9	0.04
Korean (26)	37	0.17
Nepalese (3)	3	0.01
Pakistani (8)	9	0.04
Thai (9)	9	0.04
Vietnamese (34)	43	0.20
Hawaii Native/Pacific Islander (7)	28	0.13
Not Hispanic (7)	27	0.13
Hispanic (0)	1	<0.01
Guamanian/Chamorro (2)	7	0.03
Native Hawaiian (2)	11	0.05
Samoan (3)	9	0.04
Tongan (0)	1	<0.01
White (17,187)	17,462	81.80
Not Hispanic (16,695)	16,920	79.26
Hispanic (492)	542	2.54

Ozark

Place Type: City
County: Dale
Population: 14,907†

Ancestry‡	Population	%
African, Sub-Saharan (170)	221	1.48
African (170)	221	1.48
American (1,659)	1,659	11.13
Arab (0)	17	0.11
Lebanese (0)	17	0.11
Australian (11)	17	0.11
Austrian (39)	39	0.26
British (7)	30	0.20
Celtic (8)	8	0.05
Czech (0)	35	0.23
Danish (0)	75	0.50
Dutch (28)	207	1.39
English (658)	1,475	9.89
European (90)	119	0.80
French, ex. Basque (77)	472	3.17
French Canadian (29)	219	1.47
German (515)	1,787	11.99
Hungarian (22)	22	0.15
Irish (455)	1,778	11.93
Italian (91)	175	1.17
Lithuanian (0)	3	0.02
Norwegian (46)	46	0.31
Pennsylvania German (0)	3	0.02
Polish (25)	147	0.99
Portuguese (6)	67	0.45
Russian (0)	46	0.31
Scotch-Irish (83)	318	2.13
Scottish (91)	237	1.59
Swedish (25)	61	0.41
Swiss (16)	19	0.13
Turkish (3)	6	0.04
Ukrainian (0)	20	0.13
Welsh (0)	99	0.66
West Indian, ex. Hispanic (29)	31	0.21
Jamaican (0)	2	0.01
West Indian (29)	29	0.19

Hispanic Origin	Population	%
Hispanic or Latino (of any race)	472	3.17
Central American, ex. Mexican	61	0.41
Guatemalan	7	0.05
Honduran	5	0.03
Nicaraguan	4	0.03
Panamanian	45	0.30
Cuban	11	0.07
Dominican Republic	1	0.01
Mexican	175	1.17
Puerto Rican	144	0.97
South American	23	0.15
Bolivian	11	0.07
Chilean	1	0.01
Colombian	3	0.02
Ecuadorian	3	0.02
Peruvian	5	0.03
Other Hispanic or Latino	57	0.38

Race*	Population	%
African-American/Black (4,497)	4,703	31.55
Not Hispanic (4,461)	4,652	31.21
Hispanic (36)	51	0.34
American Indian/Alaska Native (97)	242	1.62
Not Hispanic (90)	221	1.48
Hispanic (7)	21	0.14
Alaska Athabascan *(Ala. Nat.)* (1)	4	0.03
Apache (4)	5	0.03
Blackfeet (0)	5	0.03
Cherokee (23)	61	0.41
Chickasaw (0)	2	0.01
Chippewa (1)	2	0.01
Choctaw (6)	14	0.09
Comanche (2)	3	0.02
Creek (17)	27	0.18
Mexican American Ind. (0)	1	0.01
Navajo (0)	2	0.01
Sioux (1)	2	0.01
South American Ind. (0)	1	0.01
Ute (0)	1	0.01
Asian (133)	196	1.31
Not Hispanic (130)	189	1.27
Hispanic (3)	7	0.05
Cambodian (1)	1	0.01
Chinese, ex. Taiwanese (11)	21	0.14
Filipino (16)	26	0.17
Indian (32)	38	0.25
Japanese (13)	33	0.22
Korean (24)	36	0.24
Pakistani (0)	1	0.01
Taiwanese (1)	1	0.01
Thai (7)	15	0.10
Vietnamese (20)	21	0.14
Hawaii Native/Pacific Islander (6)	30	0.20
Not Hispanic (6)	25	0.17
Hispanic (0)	5	0.03
Guamanian/Chamorro (0)	1	0.01
Native Hawaiian (5)	15	0.10
Samoan (1)	6	0.04
White (9,658)	9,989	67.01
Not Hispanic (9,417)	9,689	65.00
Hispanic (241)	300	2.01

Pelham

Place Type: City
County: Shelby
Population: 21,352†

Ancestry‡	Population	%
African, Sub-Saharan (142)	142	0.70
African (111)	111	0.55
Nigerian (22)	22	0.11
South African (9)	9	0.04
American (1,969)	1,969	9.68
Arab (8)	110	0.54
Lebanese (8)	70	0.34
Syrian (0)	40	0.20
British (94)	179	0.88
Cajun (11)	11	0.05
Croatian (0)	12	0.06
Czech (45)	81	0.40
Czechoslovakian (0)	27	0.13
Danish (33)	33	0.16
Dutch (48)	203	1.00
Eastern European (11)	11	0.05
English (1,723)	3,589	17.64
European (212)	222	1.09
Finnish (0)	16	0.08
French, ex. Basque (76)	375	1.84
French Canadian (0)	24	0.12
German (528)	2,018	9.92
Greek (23)	23	0.11
Iranian (40)	101	0.50
Irish (963)	2,962	14.56
Italian (592)	1,179	5.79
Northern European (7)	7	0.03
Norwegian (28)	46	0.23
Polish (204)	441	2.17
Romanian (19)	19	0.09
Russian (0)	25	0.12
Scandinavian (0)	57	0.28
Scotch-Irish (517)	862	4.24
Scottish (326)	659	3.24
Slavic (10)	59	0.29
Swedish (154)	332	1.63
Swiss (0)	52	0.26
Ukrainian (25)	25	0.12

*Notes: † The Census 2010 population figure is used to calculate the percentages in the Hispanic Origin and Race categories. Ancestry percentages are based on the 2006-2010 American Community Survey population (not shown); ‡ Numbers in parentheses indicate the number of people reporting a single ancestry; * Numbers in parentheses indicate the number of persons reporting this race alone, not in combination with any other race; Please refer to the Explanation of Data for more information.*

Welsh (87)	275	1.35
West Indian, ex. Hispanic (67)	74	0.36
Haitian (67)	67	0.33
Jamaican (0)	7	0.03

Hispanic Origin	Population	%
Hispanic or Latino (of any race)	3,174	14.87
Central American, ex. Mexican	216	1.01
Costa Rican	4	0.02
Guatemalan	39	0.18
Honduran	29	0.14
Nicaraguan	11	0.05
Panamanian	9	0.04
Salvadoran	123	0.58
Other Central American	1	<0.01
Cuban	35	0.16
Dominican Republic	8	0.04
Mexican	2,583	12.10
Puerto Rican	57	0.27
South American	143	0.67
Argentinean	24	0.11
Bolivian	1	<0.01
Chilean	13	0.06
Colombian	86	0.40
Ecuadorian	1	<0.01
Paraguayan	1	<0.01
Peruvian	5	0.02
Venezuelan	7	0.03
Other South American	5	0.02
Other Hispanic or Latino	132	0.62

Race*	Population	%
African-American/Black (1,598)	1,708	8.00
Not Hispanic (1,579)	1,666	7.80
Hispanic (19)	42	0.20
American Indian/Alaska Native (66)	161	0.75
Not Hispanic (49)	130	0.61
Hispanic (17)	31	0.15
Aleut *(Alaska Native)* (0)	1	<0.01
Apache (2)	2	0.01
Blackfeet (0)	4	0.02
Central American Ind. (0)	4	0.02
Cherokee (22)	55	0.26
Cheyenne (1)	3	0.01
Choctaw (0)	1	<0.01
Creek (1)	7	0.03
Crow (0)	3	0.01
Iroquois (1)	6	0.03
Kiowa (1)	1	<0.01
Lumbee (0)	1	<0.01
Mexican American Ind. (8)	8	0.04
Navajo (0)	2	0.01
Puget Sound Salish (1)	1	<0.01
Tlingit-Haida *(Alaska Native)* (2)	3	0.01
Yup'ik *(Alaska Native)* (0)	1	<0.01
Asian (516)	606	2.84
Not Hispanic (509)	590	2.76
Hispanic (7)	16	0.07
Bangladeshi (16)	16	0.07
Chinese, ex. Taiwanese (39)	42	0.20
Filipino (36)	60	0.28
Hmong (5)	5	0.02
Indian (144)	157	0.74
Indonesian (1)	2	0.01
Japanese (3)	22	0.10
Korean (49)	64	0.30
Laotian (2)	2	0.01
Malaysian (1)	1	<0.01
Nepalese (8)	9	0.04
Pakistani (39)	43	0.20
Taiwanese (4)	4	0.02
Thai (2)	4	0.02
Vietnamese (150)	157	0.74
Hawaii Native/Pacific Islander (14)	36	0.17
Not Hispanic (13)	27	0.13
Hispanic (1)	9	0.04
Guamanian/Chamorro (5)	8	0.04
Native Hawaiian (3)	5	0.02
Samoan (4)	7	0.03
White (17,344)	17,641	82.62
Not Hispanic (15,776)	15,971	74.80
Hispanic (1,568)	1,670	7.82

Pell City

Place Type: City
County: St. Clair
Population: 12,695†

Ancestry‡	Population	%
American (4,058)	4,058	33.17
Arab (20)	20	0.16
Lebanese (20)	20	0.16
Austrian (12)	12	0.10
British (20)	69	0.56
Canadian (36)	36	0.29
Dutch (15)	116	0.95
English (872)	1,429	11.68
European (221)	221	1.81
French, ex. Basque (133)	230	1.88
German (158)	794	6.49
Irish (486)	1,181	9.65
Italian (109)	218	1.78
Norwegian (0)	14	0.11
Pennsylvania German (17)	17	0.14
Polish (28)	53	0.43
Scandinavian (0)	18	0.15
Scotch-Irish (195)	238	1.95
Scottish (61)	79	0.65
Slavic (0)	70	0.57
Swedish (58)	233	1.90
Welsh (18)	18	0.15

Hispanic Origin	Population	%
Hispanic or Latino (of any race)	293	2.31
Central American, ex. Mexican	18	0.14
Costa Rican	8	0.06
Guatemalan	7	0.06
Panamanian	3	0.02
Cuban	8	0.06
Mexican	180	1.42
Puerto Rican	37	0.29
South American	14	0.11
Colombian	13	0.10
Ecuadorian	1	0.01
Other Hispanic or Latino	36	0.28

Race*	Population	%
African-American/Black (1,975)	2,061	16.23
Not Hispanic (1,963)	2,044	16.10
Hispanic (12)	17	0.13
American Indian/Alaska Native (36)	83	0.65
Not Hispanic (36)	82	0.65
Hispanic (0)	1	0.01
Apache (0)	2	0.02
Arapaho (0)	2	0.02
Blackfeet (0)	3	0.02
Cherokee (21)	39	0.31
Choctaw (1)	1	0.01
Creek (0)	3	0.02
Crow (0)	1	0.01
Iroquois (0)	1	0.01
Lumbee (2)	5	0.04
Potawatomi (1)	1	0.01
Sioux (0)	4	0.03
Asian (96)	122	0.96
Not Hispanic (96)	122	0.96
Chinese, ex. Taiwanese (13)	19	0.15
Filipino (12)	20	0.16
Indian (39)	41	0.32
Japanese (7)	8	0.06
Korean (1)	6	0.05
Pakistani (2)	2	0.02
Taiwanese (1)	1	0.01
Thai (2)	3	0.02
Vietnamese (13)	13	0.10
Hawaii Native/Pacific Islander (19)	24	0.19
Not Hispanic (15)	20	0.16
Hispanic (4)	4	0.03
Guamanian/Chamorro (9)	9	0.07
Samoan (0)	2	0.02
White (10,252)	10,425	82.12
Not Hispanic (10,117)	10,265	80.86
Hispanic (135)	160	1.26

Phenix City

Place Type: City
County: Russell
Population: 32,822†

Ancestry‡	Population	%
African, Sub-Saharan (336)	378	1.19
African (278)	320	1.01
Nigerian (58)	58	0.18
American (2,879)	2,879	9.08
Arab (44)	44	0.14
Lebanese (44)	44	0.14
Armenian (0)	9	0.03
Austrian (7)	7	0.02
Basque (0)	8	0.03
British (24)	50	0.16
Canadian (19)	31	0.10
Czechoslovakian (11)	57	0.18
Danish (0)	9	0.03
Dutch (82)	370	1.17
Eastern European (12)	12	0.04
English (664)	1,685	5.31
European (121)	155	0.49
French, ex. Basque (68)	373	1.18
French Canadian (24)	33	0.10
German (653)	2,248	7.09
Greek (0)	10	0.03
Guyanese (43)	43	0.14
Hungarian (31)	47	0.15
Iranian (19)	19	0.06
Irish (957)	2,587	8.16
Italian (132)	212	0.67
Latvian (14)	14	0.04
Lithuanian (9)	9	0.03
Norwegian (62)	225	0.71
Pennsylvania German (6)	6	0.02
Polish (49)	86	0.27
Portuguese (55)	75	0.24
Romanian (15)	15	0.05
Scotch-Irish (219)	433	1.37
Scottish (120)	475	1.50
Swedish (0)	61	0.19
Welsh (0)	82	0.26
West Indian, ex. Hispanic (171)	247	0.78
Haitian (14)	35	0.11
Jamaican (138)	193	0.61
West Indian (19)	19	0.06

Hispanic Origin	Population	%
Hispanic or Latino (of any race)	1,316	4.01
Central American, ex. Mexican	103	0.31
Guatemalan	23	0.07
Honduran	10	0.03
Nicaraguan	5	0.02
Panamanian	47	0.14
Salvadoran	18	0.05
Cuban	38	0.12
Dominican Republic	19	0.06
Mexican	552	1.68
Puerto Rican	366	1.12
South American	82	0.25
Argentinean	15	0.05
Bolivian	9	0.03
Chilean	5	0.02
Colombian	33	0.10
Ecuadorian	8	0.02
Peruvian	7	0.02
Uruguayan	2	0.01
Venezuelan	3	0.01
Other Hispanic or Latino	156	0.48

Race*	Population	%
African-American/Black (15,285)	15,672	47.75
Not Hispanic (15,162)	15,486	47.18

*Notes: † The Census 2010 population figure is used to calculate the percentages in the Hispanic Origin and Race categories. Ancestry percentages are based on the 2006-2010 American Community Survey population (not shown); ‡ Numbers in parentheses indicate the number of people reporting a single ancestry; * Numbers in parentheses indicate the number of persons reporting this race alone, not in combination with any other race; Please refer to the Explanation of Data for more information.*

Hispanic (123)	186	0.57
American Indian/Alaska Native (110)	290	0.88
Not Hispanic (94)	252	0.77
Hispanic (16)	38	0.12
Apache (1)	5	0.02
Blackfeet (2)	12	0.04
Cherokee (21)	67	0.20
Chickasaw (0)	7	0.02
Chippewa (0)	1	<0.01
Choctaw (8)	17	0.05
Creek (3)	20	0.06
Inupiat *(Alaska Native)* (0)	1	<0.01
Iroquois (0)	1	<0.01
Lumbee (1)	1	<0.01
Mexican American Ind. (9)	15	0.05
Navajo (0)	1	<0.01
Osage (2)	2	0.01
Potawatomi (1)	3	0.01
Pueblo (1)	1	<0.01
Seminole (0)	1	<0.01
Shoshone (1)	2	0.01
Sioux (1)	9	0.03
South American Ind. (1)	2	0.01
Tlingit-Haida *(Alaska Native)* (1)	1	<0.01
Yuman (1)	1	<0.01
Yup'ik *(Alaska Native)* (1)	3	0.01
Asian (220)	395	1.20
Not Hispanic (213)	371	1.13
Hispanic (7)	24	0.07
Burmese (1)	1	<0.01
Cambodian (1)	5	0.02
Chinese, ex. Taiwanese (25)	39	0.12
Filipino (66)	113	0.34
Hmong (1)	1	<0.01
Indian (28)	33	0.10
Indonesian (1)	2	0.01
Japanese (19)	40	0.12
Korean (32)	97	0.30
Malaysian (1)	1	<0.01
Pakistani (13)	14	0.04
Taiwanese (1)	1	<0.01
Thai (11)	21	0.06
Vietnamese (15)	18	0.05
Hawaii Native/Pacific Islander (56)	98	0.30
Not Hispanic (51)	85	0.26
Hispanic (5)	13	0.04
Guamanian/Chamorro (11)	29	0.09
Marshallese (2)	2	0.01
Native Hawaiian (22)	37	0.11
Samoan (7)	11	0.03
Tongan (2)	3	0.01
White (15,995)	16,572	50.49
Not Hispanic (15,391)	15,873	48.36
Hispanic (604)	699	2.13

Pleasant Grove

Place Type: City
County: Jefferson
Population: 10,110†

Ancestry‡	Population	%
African, Sub-Saharan (38)	38	0.38
African (38)	38	0.38
American (781)	781	7.77
Austrian (0)	20	0.20
British (58)	71	0.71
Dutch (32)	105	1.04
English (330)	709	7.06
European (35)	51	0.51
French, ex. Basque (12)	107	1.06
German (227)	764	7.60
Irish (552)	1,095	10.90
Italian (91)	169	1.68
Polish (18)	35	0.35
Portuguese (0)	16	0.16
Scandinavian (13)	13	0.13
Scotch-Irish (94)	207	2.06
Scottish (47)	130	1.29
Swedish (16)	16	0.16
Swiss (0)	8	0.08
Welsh (13)	41	0.41
Yugoslavian (0)	7	0.07

Hispanic Origin	Population	%
Hispanic or Latino (of any race)	57	0.56
Central American, ex. Mexican	8	0.08
Guatemalan	1	0.01
Nicaraguan	1	0.01
Salvadoran	6	0.06
Mexican	33	0.33
Puerto Rican	5	0.05
South American	3	0.03
Peruvian	1	0.01
Uruguayan	2	0.02
Other Hispanic or Latino	8	0.08

Race*	Population	%
African-American/Black (4,534)	4,566	45.16
Not Hispanic (4,524)	4,555	45.05
Hispanic (10)	11	0.11
American Indian/Alaska Native (35)	68	0.67
Not Hispanic (29)	62	0.61
Hispanic (6)	6	0.06
Aleut *(Alaska Native)* (3)	3	0.03
Blackfeet (3)	3	0.03
Cherokee (9)	17	0.17
Cheyenne (0)	2	0.02
Chickasaw (1)	1	0.01
Choctaw (0)	5	0.05
Cree (1)	1	0.01
Creek (0)	1	0.01
Iroquois (0)	1	0.01
Mexican American Ind. (6)	6	0.06
Navajo (4)	4	0.04
Sioux (0)	1	0.01
Asian (18)	28	0.28
Not Hispanic (18)	28	0.28
Chinese, ex. Taiwanese (0)	2	0.02
Filipino (0)	1	0.01
Indian (7)	8	0.08
Japanese (0)	3	0.03
Korean (1)	1	0.01
Pakistani (0)	1	0.01
Thai (4)	6	0.06
Vietnamese (6)	7	0.07
Hawaii Native/Pacific Islander (2)	3	0.03
Not Hispanic (1)	1	0.01
Hispanic (1)	2	0.02
Guamanian/Chamorro (1)	1	0.01
Native Hawaiian (1)	1	0.01
White (5,427)	5,492	54.32
Not Hispanic (5,406)	5,467	54.08
Hispanic (21)	25	0.25

Prattville

Place Type: City
County: Autauga
Population: 33,960†

Ancestry‡	Population	%
African, Sub-Saharan (8)	8	0.02
African (8)	8	0.02
American (4,656)	4,656	14.49
Arab (29)	54	0.17
Jordanian (29)	29	0.09
Lebanese (0)	25	0.08
Australian (10)	19	0.06
Austrian (49)	155	0.48
Belgian (0)	24	0.07
Brazilian (31)	31	0.10
British (91)	271	0.84
Cajun (13)	13	0.04
Canadian (87)	118	0.37
Celtic (0)	4	0.01
Croatian (3)	13	0.04
Czech (3)	3	0.01
Danish (10)	43	0.13
Dutch (121)	712	2.22
Eastern European (8)	8	0.02
English (1,709)	3,472	10.81
European (175)	215	0.67
Finnish (0)	28	0.09
French, ex. Basque (177)	764	2.38
French Canadian (119)	204	0.64
German (874)	2,986	9.30
Greek (5)	25	0.08
Hungarian (4)	104	0.32
Irish (1,351)	3,864	12.03
Italian (196)	598	1.86
Lithuanian (0)	3	0.01
Norwegian (68)	141	0.44
Pennsylvania German (13)	39	0.12
Polish (75)	315	0.98
Portuguese (0)	3	0.01
Romanian (5)	14	0.04
Russian (4)	58	0.18
Scandinavian (50)	50	0.16
Scotch-Irish (539)	878	2.73
Scottish (333)	926	2.88
Swedish (99)	178	0.55
Swiss (0)	16	0.05
Ukrainian (46)	96	0.30
Welsh (42)	100	0.31
West Indian, ex. Hispanic (0)	28	0.09
Dutch West Indian (0)	28	0.09
Yugoslavian (11)	11	0.03

Hispanic Origin	Population	%
Hispanic or Latino (of any race)	1,039	3.06
Central American, ex. Mexican	80	0.24
Costa Rican	11	0.03
Guatemalan	12	0.04
Honduran	17	0.05
Nicaraguan	4	0.01
Panamanian	25	0.07
Salvadoran	9	0.03
Other Central American	2	0.01
Cuban	26	0.08
Dominican Republic	20	0.06
Mexican	592	1.74
Puerto Rican	178	0.52
South American	42	0.12
Argentinean	9	0.03
Chilean	1	<0.01
Colombian	15	0.04
Ecuadorian	9	0.03
Peruvian	4	0.01
Venezuelan	4	0.01
Other Hispanic or Latino	101	0.30

Race*	Population	%
African-American/Black (5,659)	5,893	17.35
Not Hispanic (5,620)	5,833	17.18
Hispanic (39)	60	0.18
American Indian/Alaska Native (143)	326	0.96
Not Hispanic (129)	295	0.87
Hispanic (14)	31	0.09
Aleut *(Alaska Native)* (0)	1	<0.01
Apache (1)	7	0.02
Blackfeet (1)	4	0.01
Canadian/French Am. Ind. (1)	1	<0.01
Cherokee (40)	110	0.32
Chickasaw (0)	7	0.02
Chippewa (1)	1	<0.01
Choctaw (4)	8	0.02
Comanche (0)	1	<0.01
Cree (1)	1	<0.01
Creek (14)	25	0.07
Inupiat *(Alaska Native)* (1)	1	<0.01
Iroquois (3)	6	0.02
Lumbee (5)	9	0.03
Mexican American Ind. (2)	2	0.01
Navajo (2)	4	0.01
Pueblo (0)	1	<0.01
Seminole (0)	2	0.01
Sioux (3)	3	0.01
Yup'ik *(Alaska Native)* (4)	4	0.01
Asian (479)	677	1.99

*Notes: † The Census 2010 population figure is used to calculate the percentages in the Hispanic Origin and Race categories. Ancestry percentages are based on the 2006-2010 American Community Survey population (not shown); ‡ Numbers in parentheses indicate the number of people reporting a single ancestry; * Numbers in parentheses indicate the number of persons reporting this race alone, not in combination with any other race; Please refer to the Explanation of Data for more information.*

Not Hispanic (476)	666	1.96
Hispanic (3)	11	0.03
Bangladeshi (0)	3	0.01
Cambodian (2)	2	0.01
Chinese, ex. Taiwanese (68)	99	0.29
Filipino (74)	151	0.44
Indian (72)	89	0.26
Japanese (36)	68	0.20
Korean (141)	179	0.53
Laotian (6)	8	0.02
Nepalese (1)	2	0.01
Pakistani (6)	9	0.03
Taiwanese (2)	2	0.01
Thai (11)	18	0.05
Vietnamese (45)	54	0.16
Hawaii Native/Pacific Islander (30)	56	0.16
Not Hispanic (23)	45	0.13
Hispanic (7)	11	0.03
Guamanian/Chamorro (10)	15	0.04
Native Hawaiian (7)	22	0.06
Samoan (2)	7	0.02
White (26,665)	27,202	80.10
Not Hispanic (26,117)	26,590	78.30
Hispanic (548)	612	1.80

Prichard

Place Type: City
County: Mobile
Population: 22,659†

Ancestry‡	Population	%
African, Sub-Saharan (277)	455	1.93
African (277)	455	1.93
American (1,026)	1,026	4.35
Arab (0)	31	0.13
Arab (0)	31	0.13
Danish (16)	16	0.07
Dutch (38)	65	0.28
English (128)	351	1.49
European (50)	50	0.21
Finnish (0)	18	0.08
French, ex. Basque (0)	97	0.41
French Canadian (0)	11	0.05
German (102)	275	1.17
Greek (0)	52	0.22
Irish (307)	848	3.59
Italian (68)	84	0.36
Polish (49)	65	0.28
Scotch-Irish (135)	174	0.74
Scottish (94)	94	0.40
Welsh (0)	29	0.12
West Indian, ex. Hispanic (10)	21	0.09
Dutch West Indian (0)	11	0.05
Jamaican (10)	10	0.04

Hispanic Origin	Population	%
Hispanic or Latino (of any race)	170	0.75
Central American, ex. Mexican	8	0.04
Guatemalan	2	0.01
Honduran	2	0.01
Panamanian	1	<0.01
Salvadoran	2	0.01
Other Central American	1	<0.01
Cuban	12	0.05
Mexican	91	0.40
Puerto Rican	12	0.05
South American	1	<0.01
Chilean	1	<0.01
Other Hispanic or Latino	46	0.20

Race*	Population	%
African-American/Black (19,442)	19,603	86.51
Not Hispanic (19,380)	19,525	86.17
Hispanic (62)	78	0.34
American Indian/Alaska Native (86)	173	0.76
Not Hispanic (84)	163	0.72
Hispanic (2)	10	0.04
Blackfeet (0)	1	<0.01
Cherokee (8)	20	0.09
Chickasaw (1)	1	<0.01
Choctaw (22)	34	0.15
Creek (9)	20	0.09
Mexican American Ind. (1)	1	<0.01
Navajo (0)	1	<0.01
Ottawa (1)	1	<0.01
Asian (18)	51	0.23
Not Hispanic (16)	38	0.17
Hispanic (2)	13	0.06
Burmese (0)	1	<0.01
Chinese, ex. Taiwanese (0)	8	0.04
Filipino (2)	4	0.02
Indian (0)	14	0.06
Japanese (6)	9	0.04
Korean (0)	6	0.03
Vietnamese (6)	10	0.04
Hawaii Native/Pacific Islander (1)	21	0.09
Not Hispanic (0)	16	0.07
Hispanic (1)	5	0.02
Guamanian/Chamorro (0)	3	0.01
Native Hawaiian (0)	6	0.03
Samoan (0)	3	0.01
White (2,825)	2,942	12.98
Not Hispanic (2,803)	2,910	12.84
Hispanic (22)	32	0.14

Rainbow City

Place Type: City
County: Etowah
Population: 9,602†

Ancestry‡	Population	%
African, Sub-Saharan (66)	66	0.70
African (28)	28	0.30
Other Sub-Saharan African (38)	38	0.40
American (1,401)	1,401	14.91
Arab (166)	178	1.89
Jordanian (166)	166	1.77
Lebanese (0)	12	0.13
Armenian (19)	19	0.20
British (15)	15	0.16
Czech (20)	34	0.36
Dutch (9)	35	0.37
English (799)	1,431	15.23
European (91)	91	0.97
French, ex. Basque (12)	108	1.15
German (340)	862	9.17
Hungarian (0)	62	0.66
Iranian (85)	85	0.90
Irish (347)	852	9.07
Italian (84)	84	0.89
Norwegian (12)	72	0.77
Polish (59)	87	0.93
Portuguese (172)	172	1.83
Russian (8)	8	0.09
Scotch-Irish (85)	185	1.97
Scottish (86)	220	2.34
Slovak (15)	15	0.16
Swedish (0)	10	0.11
Welsh (16)	46	0.49
Yugoslavian (13)	13	0.14

Hispanic Origin	Population	%
Hispanic or Latino (of any race)	232	2.42
Central American, ex. Mexican	19	0.20
Costa Rican	1	0.01
Guatemalan	10	0.10
Honduran	2	0.02
Nicaraguan	4	0.04
Salvadoran	2	0.02
Cuban	2	0.02
Mexican	156	1.62
Puerto Rican	21	0.22
South American	20	0.21
Colombian	20	0.21
Other Hispanic or Latino	14	0.15

Race*	Population	%
African-American/Black (695)	752	7.83
Not Hispanic (685)	736	7.67
Hispanic (10)	16	0.17
American Indian/Alaska Native (42)	89	0.93
Not Hispanic (42)	87	0.91
Hispanic (0)	2	0.02
Cherokee (26)	55	0.57
Creek (5)	5	0.05
Iroquois (0)	1	0.01
Lumbee (1)	1	0.01
Asian (247)	266	2.77
Not Hispanic (247)	265	2.76
Hispanic (0)	1	0.01
Chinese, ex. Taiwanese (32)	33	0.34
Filipino (25)	33	0.34
Indian (105)	108	1.12
Indonesian (4)	4	0.04
Japanese (11)	11	0.11
Korean (12)	16	0.17
Nepalese (8)	8	0.08
Pakistani (12)	14	0.15
Sri Lankan (5)	5	0.05
Thai (0)	1	0.01
Vietnamese (24)	24	0.25
Hawaii Native/Pacific Islander (3)	3	0.03
Not Hispanic (3)	3	0.03
Native Hawaiian (3)	3	0.03
White (8,388)	8,512	88.65
Not Hispanic (8,265)	8,368	87.15
Hispanic (123)	144	1.50

Russellville

Place Type: City
County: Franklin
Population: 9,830†

Ancestry‡	Population	%
African, Sub-Saharan (8)	19	0.20
African (8)	19	0.20
American (1,071)	1,071	11.16
Austrian (0)	20	0.21
British (42)	110	1.15
Croatian (17)	17	0.18
Dutch (0)	24	0.25
English (571)	845	8.80
French, ex. Basque (0)	46	0.48
German (202)	443	4.62
Irish (497)	961	10.01
Italian (19)	40	0.42
Pennsylvania German (34)	34	0.35
Scandinavian (11)	11	0.11
Scotch-Irish (109)	133	1.39
Scottish (0)	64	0.67
Swedish (15)	15	0.16
Welsh (0)	12	0.13

Hispanic Origin	Population	%
Hispanic or Latino (of any race)	2,560	26.04
Central American, ex. Mexican	1,119	11.38
Costa Rican	2	0.02
Guatemalan	969	9.86
Honduran	17	0.17
Nicaraguan	18	0.18
Salvadoran	112	1.14
Other Central American	1	0.01
Cuban	35	0.36
Dominican Republic	15	0.15
Mexican	1,145	11.65
Puerto Rican	20	0.20
South American	17	0.17
Argentinean	1	0.01
Colombian	1	0.01
Ecuadorian	5	0.05
Peruvian	7	0.07
Uruguayan	2	0.02
Venezuelan	1	0.01
Other Hispanic or Latino	209	2.13

Race*	Population	%
African-American/Black (907)	986	10.03

*Notes: † The Census 2010 population figure is used to calculate the percentages in the Hispanic Origin and Race categories. Ancestry percentages are based on the 2006-2010 American Community Survey population (not shown); ‡ Numbers in parentheses indicate the number of people reporting a single ancestry; * Numbers in parentheses indicate the number of persons reporting this race alone, not in combination with any other race; Please refer to the Explanation of Data for more information.*

Not Hispanic (897)	965	9.82
Hispanic (10)	21	0.21
American Indian/Alaska Native (83)	122	1.24
Not Hispanic (29)	59	0.60
Hispanic (54)	63	0.64
Blackfeet (0)	2	0.02
Central American Ind. (8)	9	0.09
Cherokee (20)	37	0.38
Choctaw (0)	1	0.01
Comanche (0)	1	0.01
Creek (0)	2	0.02
Mexican American Ind. (35)	38	0.39
Asian (28)	33	0.34
Not Hispanic (19)	24	0.24
Hispanic (9)	9	0.09
Chinese, ex. Taiwanese (5)	5	0.05
Filipino (13)	14	0.14
Indian (0)	3	0.03
Vietnamese (10)	11	0.11
Hawaii Native/Pacific Islander (2)	4	0.04
Not Hispanic (1)	3	0.03
Hispanic (1)	1	0.01
Guamanian/Chamorro (2)	3	0.03
Native Hawaiian (0)	1	0.01
White (6,730)	6,892	70.11
Not Hispanic (6,200)	6,301	64.10
Hispanic (530)	591	6.01

Saks

Place Type: CDP
County: Calhoun
Population: 10,744†

Ancestry‡	Population	%
African, Sub-Saharan (21)	21	0.19
African (21)	21	0.19
American (1,638)	1,638	14.67
British (0)	39	0.35
Czechoslovakian (0)	15	0.13
Dutch (45)	238	2.13
English (710)	993	8.89
European (29)	29	0.26
French, ex. Basque (138)	394	3.53
French Canadian (26)	37	0.33
German (328)	955	8.55
Greek (9)	9	0.08
Irish (474)	1,292	11.57
Italian (198)	235	2.10
Lithuanian (0)	12	0.11
Norwegian (20)	88	0.79
Polish (0)	55	0.49
Scotch-Irish (126)	303	2.71
Scottish (38)	106	0.95
Swedish (12)	51	0.46
Welsh (13)	27	0.24
West Indian, ex. Hispanic (8)	35	0.31
Dutch West Indian (8)	35	0.31

Hispanic Origin	Population	%
Hispanic or Latino (of any race)	370	3.44
Central American, ex. Mexican	17	0.16
Guatemalan	1	0.01
Honduran	1	0.01
Panamanian	11	0.10
Salvadoran	4	0.04
Cuban	14	0.13
Dominican Republic	3	0.03
Mexican	248	2.31
Puerto Rican	48	0.45
South American	11	0.10
Colombian	10	0.09
Venezuelan	1	0.01
Other Hispanic or Latino	29	0.27

Race*	Population	%
African-American/Black (2,084)	2,189	20.37
Not Hispanic (2,050)	2,147	19.98
Hispanic (34)	42	0.39
American Indian/Alaska Native (47)	113	1.05
Not Hispanic (44)	107	1.00
Hispanic (3)	6	0.06
Apache (1)	4	0.04
Blackfeet (0)	10	0.09
Cherokee (11)	55	0.51
Chickasaw (1)	1	0.01
Chippewa (0)	1	0.01
Comanche (0)	3	0.03
Creek (3)	6	0.06
Pueblo (3)	3	0.03
Seminole (0)	1	0.01
Asian (82)	116	1.08
Not Hispanic (80)	110	1.02
Hispanic (2)	6	0.06
Chinese, ex. Taiwanese (4)	4	0.04
Filipino (31)	37	0.34
Indian (3)	4	0.04
Japanese (5)	7	0.07
Korean (30)	51	0.47
Laotian (1)	1	0.01
Thai (6)	9	0.08
Vietnamese (2)	2	0.02
Hawaii Native/Pacific Islander (3)	17	0.16
Not Hispanic (3)	17	0.16
Guamanian/Chamorro (3)	5	0.05
Native Hawaiian (0)	3	0.03
Samoan (0)	2	0.02
White (8,135)	8,332	77.55
Not Hispanic (7,996)	8,173	76.07
Hispanic (139)	159	1.48

Saraland

Place Type: City
County: Mobile
Population: 13,405†

Ancestry‡	Population	%
African, Sub-Saharan (43)	65	0.49
African (0)	22	0.17
Nigerian (43)	43	0.33
American (2,217)	2,217	16.83
British (16)	24	0.18
Cajun (0)	37	0.28
Canadian (0)	12	0.09
Croatian (44)	44	0.33
Czechoslovakian (18)	18	0.14
Dutch (7)	78	0.59
English (521)	1,070	8.12
European (11)	11	0.08
French, ex. Basque (101)	359	2.73
French Canadian (23)	34	0.26
German (409)	1,134	8.61
Greek (33)	41	0.31
Hungarian (0)	10	0.08
Irish (754)	2,293	17.41
Italian (108)	183	1.39
Polish (28)	48	0.36
Russian (25)	47	0.36
Scandinavian (0)	18	0.14
Scotch-Irish (165)	296	2.25
Scottish (83)	306	2.32
Swedish (6)	114	0.87
Welsh (0)	17	0.13

Hispanic Origin	Population	%
Hispanic or Latino (of any race)	336	2.51
Central American, ex. Mexican	27	0.20
Costa Rican	1	0.01
Guatemalan	12	0.09
Honduran	6	0.04
Panamanian	5	0.04
Salvadoran	1	0.01
Other Central American	2	0.01
Cuban	4	0.03
Mexican	212	1.58
Puerto Rican	21	0.16
South American	14	0.10
Colombian	4	0.03
Ecuadorian	1	0.01
Peruvian	3	0.02
Venezuelan	6	0.04
Other Hispanic or Latino	58	0.43

Race*	Population	%
African-American/Black (1,604)	1,652	12.32
Not Hispanic (1,601)	1,649	12.30
Hispanic (3)	3	0.02
American Indian/Alaska Native (104)	206	1.54
Not Hispanic (102)	204	1.52
Hispanic (2)	2	0.01
Apache (1)	2	0.01
Blackfeet (0)	2	0.01
Cherokee (10)	46	0.34
Choctaw (40)	70	0.52
Colville (2)	2	0.01
Creek (21)	38	0.28
Houma (1)	1	0.01
Navajo (3)	3	0.02
Sioux (1)	1	0.01
Asian (84)	126	0.94
Not Hispanic (83)	125	0.93
Hispanic (1)	1	0.01
Cambodian (1)	1	0.01
Chinese, ex. Taiwanese (22)	23	0.17
Filipino (12)	20	0.15
Indian (5)	8	0.06
Indonesian (0)	1	0.01
Japanese (1)	10	0.07
Korean (3)	10	0.07
Laotian (4)	8	0.06
Thai (1)	1	0.01
Vietnamese (27)	37	0.28
Hawaii Native/Pacific Islander (10)	15	0.11
Not Hispanic (0)	5	0.04
Hispanic (10)	10	0.07
Guamanian/Chamorro (10)	12	0.09
White (11,225)	11,389	84.96
Not Hispanic (11,094)	11,256	83.97
Hispanic (131)	133	0.99

Scottsboro

Place Type: City
County: Jackson
Population: 14,770†

Ancestry‡	Population	%
African, Sub-Saharan (35)	35	0.24
African (35)	35	0.24
American (3,458)	3,458	23.37
Arab (23)	23	0.16
Palestinian (11)	11	0.07
Syrian (12)	12	0.08
British (28)	60	0.41
Dutch (45)	279	1.89
English (1,326)	2,057	13.90
European (51)	51	0.34
Finnish (0)	44	0.30
French, ex. Basque (84)	330	2.23
French Canadian (39)	47	0.32
German (489)	1,190	8.04
Irish (494)	1,911	12.92
Italian (52)	156	1.05
Norwegian (14)	14	0.09
Polish (70)	106	0.72
Romanian (15)	15	0.10
Russian (0)	6	0.04
Scotch-Irish (205)	352	2.38
Scottish (74)	278	1.88
Swedish (20)	20	0.14
Swiss (0)	87	0.59
Welsh (21)	41	0.28

Hispanic Origin	Population	%
Hispanic or Latino (of any race)	522	3.53
Central American, ex. Mexican	121	0.82
Guatemalan	118	0.80
Honduran	2	0.01
Nicaraguan	1	0.01

*Notes: † The Census 2010 population figure is used to calculate the percentages in the Hispanic Origin and Race categories. Ancestry percentages are based on the 2006-2010 American Community Survey population (not shown); ‡ Numbers in parentheses indicate the number of people reporting a single ancestry; * Numbers in parentheses indicate the number of persons reporting this race alone, not in combination with any other race; Please refer to the Explanation of Data for more information.*

Cuban	8	0.05
Mexican	319	2.16
Puerto Rican	15	0.10
South American	6	0.04
Argentinean	1	0.01
Colombian	2	0.01
Ecuadorian	1	0.01
Paraguayan	1	0.01
Venezuelan	1	0.01
Other Hispanic or Latino	53	0.36

Race*	Population	%
African-American/Black (681)	765	5.18
Not Hispanic (672)	755	5.11
Hispanic (9)	10	0.07
American Indian/Alaska Native (112)	258	1.75
Not Hispanic (98)	233	1.58
Hispanic (14)	25	0.17
Blackfeet (0)	2	0.01
Cherokee (62)	143	0.97
Choctaw (1)	2	0.01
Creek (2)	8	0.05
Crow (1)	1	0.01
Delaware (0)	1	0.01
Houma (1)	1	0.01
Iroquois (0)	4	0.03
Mexican American Ind. (7)	7	0.05
Pueblo (0)	3	0.02
Sioux (1)	1	0.01
Spanish American Ind. (3)	3	0.02
Asian (117)	146	0.99
Not Hispanic (106)	133	0.90
Hispanic (11)	13	0.09
Chinese, ex. Taiwanese (22)	23	0.16
Filipino (16)	27	0.18
Hmong (1)	1	0.01
Indian (41)	47	0.32
Japanese (4)	8	0.05
Korean (2)	2	0.01
Laotian (3)	5	0.03
Pakistani (5)	5	0.03
Thai (0)	1	0.01
Vietnamese (16)	17	0.12
Hawaii Native/Pacific Islander (34)	39	0.26
Not Hispanic (27)	32	0.22
Hispanic (7)	7	0.05
Guamanian/Chamorro (29)	29	0.20
Native Hawaiian (0)	4	0.03
Tongan (1)	1	0.01
White (13,258)	13,512	91.48
Not Hispanic (13,093)	13,330	90.25
Hispanic (165)	182	1.23

Selma

Place Type: City
County: Dallas
Population: 20,756†

Ancestry‡	Population	%
African, Sub-Saharan (272)	325	1.58
African (272)	325	1.58
American (953)	953	4.63
British (8)	8	0.04
Dutch (18)	192	0.93
English (339)	684	3.32
European (19)	19	0.09
Finnish (6)	6	0.03
French, ex. Basque (16)	114	0.55
French Canadian (2)	10	0.05
German (325)	604	2.93
German Russian (93)	93	0.45
Hungarian (7)	7	0.03
Irish (249)	582	2.83
Italian (18)	18	0.09
Lithuanian (0)	24	0.12
Polish (15)	27	0.13
Romanian (28)	28	0.14
Russian (14)	14	0.07
Scotch-Irish (66)	206	1.00
Scottish (188)	263	1.28
Swedish (0)	12	0.06
Welsh (25)	67	0.33
West Indian, ex. Hispanic (17)	17	0.08
Jamaican (17)	17	0.08

Hispanic Origin	Population	%
Hispanic or Latino (of any race)	125	0.60
Central American, ex. Mexican	2	0.01
Panamanian	2	0.01
Cuban	7	0.03
Mexican	49	0.24
Puerto Rican	14	0.07
South American	1	<0.01
Venezuelan	1	<0.01
Other Hispanic or Latino	52	0.25

Race*	Population	%
African-American/Black (16,671)	16,799	80.94
Not Hispanic (16,599)	16,718	80.55
Hispanic (72)	81	0.39
American Indian/Alaska Native (34)	85	0.41
Not Hispanic (33)	83	0.40
Hispanic (1)	2	0.01
Apache (1)	4	0.02
Cherokee (5)	22	0.11
Chippewa (0)	1	<0.01
Choctaw (0)	1	<0.01
Creek (3)	4	0.02
Crow (0)	1	<0.01
Sioux (0)	1	<0.01
Asian (122)	141	0.68
Not Hispanic (121)	139	0.67
Hispanic (1)	2	0.01
Cambodian (7)	7	0.03
Chinese, ex. Taiwanese (11)	17	0.08
Filipino (12)	19	0.09
Indian (51)	52	0.25
Japanese (10)	12	0.06
Korean (4)	7	0.03
Pakistani (11)	11	0.05
Thai (1)	1	<0.01
Vietnamese (13)	15	0.07
Hawaii Native/Pacific Islander (5)	18	0.09
Not Hispanic (5)	15	0.07
Hispanic (0)	3	0.01
Guamanian/Chamorro (1)	1	<0.01
Native Hawaiian (2)	10	0.05
White (3,741)	3,844	18.52
Not Hispanic (3,716)	3,813	18.37
Hispanic (25)	31	0.15

Sheffield

Place Type: City
County: Colbert
Population: 9,039†

Ancestry‡	Population	%
African, Sub-Saharan (16)	16	0.18
African (16)	16	0.18
American (1,277)	1,277	13.97
Armenian (9)	9	0.10
British (18)	26	0.28
Canadian (12)	22	0.24
Czech (10)	10	0.11
Danish (0)	19	0.21
Dutch (0)	52	0.57
English (538)	881	9.64
European (29)	47	0.51
French, ex. Basque (7)	73	0.80
French Canadian (5)	15	0.16
German (170)	597	6.53
Greek (0)	85	0.93
Irish (512)	1,067	11.67
Italian (74)	158	1.73
Northern European (22)	22	0.24
Norwegian (21)	51	0.56
Polish (9)	23	0.25
Russian (0)	131	1.43
Scotch-Irish (101)	181	1.98
Scottish (44)	118	1.29
Slovak (0)	9	0.10
Welsh (0)	42	0.46
West Indian, ex. Hispanic (0)	44	0.48
Jamaican (0)	44	0.48

Hispanic Origin	Population	%
Hispanic or Latino (of any race)	211	2.33
Central American, ex. Mexican	20	0.22
Guatemalan	5	0.06
Honduran	4	0.04
Salvadoran	11	0.12
Cuban	2	0.02
Dominican Republic	4	0.04
Mexican	165	1.83
Puerto Rican	5	0.06
South American	3	0.03
Colombian	2	0.02
Ecuadorian	1	0.01
Other Hispanic or Latino	12	0.13

Race*	Population	%
African-American/Black (2,426)	2,507	27.74
Not Hispanic (2,409)	2,482	27.46
Hispanic (17)	25	0.28
American Indian/Alaska Native (25)	91	1.01
Not Hispanic (24)	86	0.95
Hispanic (1)	5	0.06
Cherokee (13)	48	0.53
Chippewa (0)	3	0.03
Choctaw (0)	3	0.03
Creek (1)	5	0.06
Iroquois (1)	1	0.01
Sioux (1)	1	0.01
Asian (31)	48	0.53
Not Hispanic (31)	48	0.53
Chinese, ex. Taiwanese (2)	4	0.04
Filipino (5)	10	0.11
Indian (22)	28	0.31
Japanese (1)	2	0.02
Korean (1)	4	0.04
Hawaii Native/Pacific Islander (6)	6	0.07
Not Hispanic (1)	1	0.01
Hispanic (5)	5	0.06
Guamanian/Chamorro (5)	5	0.06
Native Hawaiian (1)	1	0.01
White (6,298)	6,439	71.24
Not Hispanic (6,220)	6,351	70.26
Hispanic (78)	88	0.97

Southside

Place Type: City
County: Etowah
Population: 8,412†

Ancestry‡	Population	%
American (1,208)	1,208	14.48
British (47)	47	0.56
Czech (0)	12	0.14
Danish (0)	39	0.47
Dutch (13)	115	1.38
English (302)	770	9.23
European (113)	126	1.51
French, ex. Basque (27)	40	0.48
French Canadian (12)	40	0.48
German (223)	794	9.52
Irish (729)	1,358	16.28
Italian (82)	231	2.77
Norwegian (0)	10	0.12
Scandinavian (14)	14	0.17
Scotch-Irish (177)	428	5.13
Scottish (90)	101	1.21
Swedish (0)	24	0.29
Swiss (13)	33	0.40
Welsh (0)	13	0.16

Hispanic Origin	Population	%
Hispanic or Latino (of any race)	107	1.27

*Notes: † The Census 2010 population figure is used to calculate the percentages in the Hispanic Origin and Race categories. Ancestry percentages are based on the 2006-2010 American Community Survey population (not shown); ‡ Numbers in parentheses indicate the number of people reporting a single ancestry; * Numbers in parentheses indicate the number of persons reporting this race alone, not in combination with any other race; Please refer to the Explanation of Data for more information.*

Central American, ex. Mexican	7	0.08
Guatemalan	5	0.06
Honduran	2	0.02
Cuban	8	0.10
Mexican	52	0.62
Puerto Rican	15	0.18
South American	14	0.17
Argentinean	1	0.01
Bolivian	2	0.02
Chilean	1	0.01
Colombian	9	0.11
Venezuelan	1	0.01
Other Hispanic or Latino	11	0.13

Race*	Population	%
African-American/Black (123)	139	1.65
Not Hispanic (123)	138	1.64
Hispanic (0)	1	0.01
American Indian/Alaska Native (15)	35	0.42
Not Hispanic (15)	35	0.42
Cherokee (9)	14	0.17
Choctaw (0)	1	0.01
Creek (2)	6	0.07
Iroquois (0)	1	0.01
Seminole (0)	1	0.01
Asian (56)	71	0.84
Not Hispanic (56)	71	0.84
Chinese, ex. Taiwanese (20)	22	0.26
Filipino (5)	11	0.13
Indian (1)	3	0.04
Japanese (3)	6	0.07
Korean (4)	5	0.06
Pakistani (4)	4	0.05
Sri Lankan (1)	1	0.01
Thai (0)	2	0.02
Vietnamese (16)	19	0.23
Hawaii Native/Pacific Islander (3)	6	0.07
Not Hispanic (1)	2	0.02
Hispanic (2)	4	0.05
Guamanian/Chamorro (1)	1	0.01
Native Hawaiian (0)	1	0.01
White (8,121)	8,179	97.23
Not Hispanic (8,058)	8,110	96.41
Hispanic (63)	69	0.82

Sylacauga

Place Type: City
County: Talladega
Population: 12,749†

Ancestry‡	Population	%
African, Sub-Saharan (31)	31	0.24
African (31)	31	0.24
Albanian (32)	32	0.25
American (4,046)	4,046	31.64
Arab (41)	41	0.32
Arab (41)	41	0.32
Czech (24)	33	0.26
Dutch (19)	172	1.34
English (591)	808	6.32
European (12)	42	0.33
Finnish (5)	17	0.13
French, ex. Basque (54)	162	1.27
German (248)	618	4.83
Greek (14)	51	0.40
Iranian (13)	34	0.27
Irish (387)	780	6.10
Italian (36)	54	0.42
Latvian (0)	11	0.09
Polish (48)	48	0.38
Russian (9)	9	0.07
Scotch-Irish (40)	218	1.70
Scottish (67)	288	2.25
Swedish (0)	12	0.09
Welsh (23)	53	0.41

Hispanic Origin	Population	%
Hispanic or Latino (of any race)	289	2.27
Central American, ex. Mexican	28	0.22
Guatemalan	18	0.14
Honduran	2	0.02
Salvadoran	8	0.06
Cuban	3	0.02
Mexican	227	1.78
Puerto Rican	6	0.05
South American	2	0.02
Colombian	1	0.01
Venezuelan	1	0.01
Other Hispanic or Latino	23	0.18

Race*	Population	%
African-American/Black (3,846)	3,913	30.69
Not Hispanic (3,837)	3,904	30.62
Hispanic (9)	9	0.07
American Indian/Alaska Native (46)	89	0.70
Not Hispanic (39)	78	0.61
Hispanic (7)	11	0.09
Apache (4)	4	0.03
Cherokee (13)	28	0.22
Choctaw (0)	5	0.04
Creek (3)	12	0.09
Crow (1)	1	0.01
Mexican American Ind. (1)	1	0.01
Seminole (1)	1	0.01
Yaqui (0)	4	0.03
Asian (65)	86	0.67
Not Hispanic (63)	83	0.65
Hispanic (2)	3	0.02
Chinese, ex. Taiwanese (9)	10	0.08
Filipino (7)	9	0.07
Hmong (1)	2	0.02
Indian (24)	30	0.24
Indonesian (3)	3	0.02
Japanese (0)	1	0.01
Korean (4)	8	0.06
Vietnamese (16)	16	0.13
Hawaii Native/Pacific Islander (0)	9	0.07
Not Hispanic (0)	5	0.04
Hispanic (0)	4	0.03
Guamanian/Chamorro (0)	3	0.02
Native Hawaiian (0)	1	0.01
White (8,487)	8,607	67.51
Not Hispanic (8,397)	8,494	66.62
Hispanic (90)	113	0.89

Talladega

Place Type: City
County: Talladega
Population: 15,676†

Ancestry‡	Population	%
African, Sub-Saharan (156)	156	0.98
African (156)	156	0.98
American (2,130)	2,130	13.32
Arab (8)	8	0.05
Moroccan (8)	8	0.05
British (20)	74	0.46
Cajun (0)	10	0.06
Canadian (101)	101	0.63
Czech (0)	7	0.04
Dutch (8)	62	0.39
English (776)	1,050	6.57
European (122)	141	0.88
French, ex. Basque (81)	190	1.19
German (198)	382	2.39
Irish (429)	858	5.36
Italian (35)	68	0.43
Norwegian (13)	13	0.08
Polish (18)	26	0.16
Russian (0)	26	0.16
Scandinavian (0)	33	0.21
Scotch-Irish (68)	94	0.59
Scottish (69)	171	1.07
Swedish (0)	30	0.19
Swiss (0)	10	0.06
Ukrainian (7)	7	0.04
Welsh (10)	28	0.18
West Indian, ex. Hispanic (19)	57	0.36
Bahamian (9)	9	0.06
Dutch West Indian (0)	23	0.14
Haitian (0)	9	0.06
Jamaican (0)	6	0.04
West Indian (10)	10	0.06

Hispanic Origin	Population	%
Hispanic or Latino (of any race)	529	3.37
Central American, ex. Mexican	13	0.08
Guatemalan	1	0.01
Honduran	4	0.03
Salvadoran	8	0.05
Cuban	19	0.12
Dominican Republic	6	0.04
Mexican	404	2.58
Puerto Rican	36	0.23
South American	12	0.08
Colombian	11	0.07
Paraguayan	1	0.01
Other Hispanic or Latino	39	0.25

Race*	Population	%
African-American/Black (7,639)	7,754	49.46
Not Hispanic (7,588)	7,692	49.07
Hispanic (51)	62	0.40
American Indian/Alaska Native (45)	95	0.61
Not Hispanic (29)	76	0.48
Hispanic (16)	19	0.12
Blackfeet (0)	1	0.01
Cherokee (6)	19	0.12
Chippewa (0)	1	0.01
Choctaw (0)	2	0.01
Creek (2)	9	0.06
Mexican American Ind. (6)	6	0.04
Sioux (4)	4	0.03
Asian (75)	96	0.61
Not Hispanic (72)	86	0.55
Hispanic (3)	10	0.06
Chinese, ex. Taiwanese (23)	25	0.16
Filipino (13)	19	0.12
Indian (12)	14	0.09
Japanese (2)	4	0.03
Korean (6)	9	0.06
Laotian (0)	2	0.01
Pakistani (2)	3	0.02
Thai (2)	5	0.03
Vietnamese (12)	12	0.08
Hawaii Native/Pacific Islander (1)	11	0.07
Not Hispanic (1)	8	0.05
Hispanic (0)	3	0.02
Guamanian/Chamorro (0)	1	0.01
Native Hawaiian (0)	2	0.01
Samoan (0)	1	0.01
White (7,477)	7,634	48.70
Not Hispanic (7,287)	7,411	47.28
Hispanic (190)	223	1.42

Tillmans Corner

Place Type: CDP
County: Mobile
Population: 17,398†

Ancestry‡	Population	%
African, Sub-Saharan (8)	8	0.05
African (8)	8	0.05
American (2,946)	2,946	17.90
Arab (71)	71	0.43
Arab (24)	24	0.15
Lebanese (47)	47	0.29
Australian (0)	14	0.09
Austrian (15)	15	0.09
British (26)	39	0.24
Canadian (37)	45	0.27
Czech (30)	30	0.18
Czechoslovakian (0)	49	0.30
Danish (12)	36	0.22
Dutch (22)	188	1.14
English (542)	1,160	7.05
European (21)	49	0.30

*Notes: † The Census 2010 population figure is used to calculate the percentages in the Hispanic Origin and Race categories. Ancestry percentages are based on the 2006-2010 American Community Survey population (not shown); ‡ Numbers in parentheses indicate the number of people reporting a single ancestry; * Numbers in parentheses indicate the number of persons reporting this race alone, not in combination with any other race; Please refer to the Explanation of Data for more information.*

Finnish (13)	13	0.08
French, ex. Basque (266)	834	5.07
French Canadian (63)	125	0.76
German (697)	2,344	14.25
Greek (0)	37	0.22
Irish (799)	2,344	14.25
Italian (108)	370	2.25
Norwegian (0)	22	0.13
Polish (22)	254	1.54
Russian (0)	11	0.07
Scotch-Irish (188)	555	3.37
Scottish (209)	414	2.52
Swedish (42)	169	1.03
Welsh (42)	108	0.66

Hispanic Origin	Population	%
Hispanic or Latino (of any race)	662	3.81
Central American, ex. Mexican	115	0.66
Costa Rican	4	0.02
Guatemalan	32	0.18
Honduran	41	0.24
Nicaraguan	10	0.06
Panamanian	2	0.01
Salvadoran	26	0.15
Cuban	27	0.16
Dominican Republic	4	0.02
Mexican	331	1.90
Puerto Rican	49	0.28
South American	37	0.21
Argentinean	3	0.02
Bolivian	4	0.02
Chilean	12	0.07
Colombian	4	0.02
Peruvian	9	0.05
Venezuelan	5	0.03
Other Hispanic or Latino	99	0.57

Race*	Population	%
African-American/Black (1,989)	2,121	12.19
Not Hispanic (1,961)	2,088	12.00
Hispanic (28)	33	0.19
American Indian/Alaska Native (99)	229	1.32
Not Hispanic (93)	203	1.17
Hispanic (6)	26	0.15
Apache (0)	2	0.01
Blackfeet (1)	4	0.02
Cherokee (16)	58	0.33
Chickasaw (1)	1	0.01
Chippewa (0)	1	0.01
Choctaw (13)	26	0.15
Creek (17)	28	0.16
Inupiat *(Alaska Native)* (1)	2	0.01
Iroquois (0)	1	0.01
Lumbee (1)	3	0.02
Mexican American Ind. (1)	1	0.01
Shoshone (1)	1	0.01
Asian (367)	425	2.44
Not Hispanic (360)	416	2.39
Hispanic (7)	9	0.05
Bangladeshi (3)	3	0.02
Burmese (3)	3	0.02
Cambodian (8)	10	0.06
Chinese, ex. Taiwanese (25)	31	0.18
Filipino (29)	36	0.21
Indian (41)	48	0.28
Indonesian (2)	5	0.03
Japanese (5)	15	0.09
Korean (9)	15	0.09
Laotian (17)	25	0.14
Nepalese (1)	1	0.01
Thai (2)	4	0.02
Vietnamese (216)	229	1.32
Hawaii Native/Pacific Islander (25)	36	0.21
Not Hispanic (17)	28	0.16
Hispanic (8)	8	0.05
Guamanian/Chamorro (8)	8	0.05
Marshallese (6)	6	0.03
Native Hawaiian (3)	13	0.07
White (14,309)	14,617	84.02
Not Hispanic (13,996)	14,260	81.96
Hispanic (313)	357	2.05

Troy

Place Type: City
County: Pike
Population: 18,033†

Ancestry‡	Population	%
African, Sub-Saharan (3,290)	3,299	19.17
African (3,247)	3,256	18.92
Kenyan (43)	43	0.25
American (1,433)	1,433	8.33
Arab (1)	1	0.01
Lebanese (1)	1	0.01
Austrian (0)	13	0.08
British (56)	56	0.33
Canadian (29)	29	0.17
Czech (2)	19	0.11
Danish (8)	18	0.10
Dutch (2)	52	0.30
English (495)	715	4.16
European (180)	308	1.79
French, ex. Basque (19)	91	0.53
German (485)	870	5.06
Greek (102)	136	0.79
Hungarian (21)	55	0.32
Irish (592)	1,125	6.54
Italian (100)	262	1.52
Northern European (19)	19	0.11
Norwegian (34)	92	0.53
Polish (41)	103	0.60
Portuguese (0)	3	0.02
Romanian (19)	19	0.11
Scotch-Irish (437)	648	3.77
Scottish (176)	234	1.36
Swedish (16)	41	0.24
Swiss (15)	33	0.19
Turkish (132)	132	0.77
Ukrainian (13)	13	0.08
Welsh (2)	16	0.09
Yugoslavian (0)	34	0.20

Hispanic Origin	Population	%
Hispanic or Latino (of any race)	357	1.98
Central American, ex. Mexican	13	0.07
Costa Rican	2	0.01
Guatemalan	4	0.02
Honduran	6	0.03
Panamanian	1	0.01
Cuban	10	0.06
Dominican Republic	1	0.01
Mexican	203	1.13
Puerto Rican	63	0.35
South American	12	0.07
Ecuadorian	2	0.01
Peruvian	4	0.02
Venezuelan	2	0.01
Other South American	4	0.02
Other Hispanic or Latino	55	0.30

Race*	Population	%
African-American/Black (7,035)	7,164	39.73
Not Hispanic (6,980)	7,101	39.38
Hispanic (55)	63	0.35
American Indian/Alaska Native (73)	147	0.82
Not Hispanic (66)	134	0.74
Hispanic (7)	13	0.07
Alaska Athabascan *(Ala. Nat.)* (0)	1	0.01
Apache (0)	4	0.02
Blackfeet (1)	2	0.01
Cherokee (23)	55	0.30
Chickasaw (1)	1	0.01
Choctaw (1)	1	0.01
Comanche (4)	4	0.02
Creek (14)	29	0.16
Sioux (0)	1	0.01
South American Ind. (0)	1	0.01
Asian (606)	680	3.77
Not Hispanic (602)	672	3.73
Hispanic (4)	8	0.04
Cambodian (1)	1	0.01
Chinese, ex. Taiwanese (329)	337	1.87
Filipino (7)	26	0.14
Hmong (0)	1	0.01
Indian (110)	119	0.66
Indonesian (3)	3	0.02
Japanese (17)	25	0.14
Korean (55)	67	0.37
Laotian (0)	2	0.01
Malaysian (2)	2	0.01
Nepalese (19)	19	0.11
Pakistani (5)	5	0.03
Vietnamese (50)	56	0.31
Hawaii Native/Pacific Islander (8)	16	0.09
Not Hispanic (4)	12	0.07
Hispanic (4)	4	0.02
Guamanian/Chamorro (3)	8	0.04
Native Hawaiian (5)	6	0.03
White (9,919)	10,114	56.09
Not Hispanic (9,794)	9,965	55.26
Hispanic (125)	149	0.83

Trussville

Place Type: City
County: Jefferson
Population: 19,933†

Ancestry‡	Population	%
Alsatian (0)	14	0.08
American (2,541)	2,541	13.65
Arab (18)	18	0.10
Lebanese (18)	18	0.10
Armenian (0)	16	0.09
Austrian (11)	71	0.38
Belgian (0)	15	0.08
British (157)	218	1.17
Cajun (0)	8	0.04
Canadian (0)	11	0.06
Celtic (10)	53	0.28
Croatian (33)	42	0.23
Czech (21)	21	0.11
Czechoslovakian (0)	15	0.08
Danish (11)	23	0.12
Dutch (14)	273	1.47
English (1,740)	3,239	17.41
European (154)	181	0.97
French, ex. Basque (135)	441	2.37
French Canadian (0)	21	0.11
German (915)	2,956	15.88
Greek (12)	12	0.06
Icelander (0)	12	0.06
Iranian (14)	14	0.08
Irish (1,023)	2,846	15.29
Italian (291)	988	5.31
Lithuanian (15)	15	0.08
Polish (96)	213	1.14
Russian (92)	186	1.00
Scandinavian (17)	17	0.09
Scotch-Irish (470)	911	4.90
Scottish (203)	616	3.31
Slovene (3)	3	0.02
Swedish (10)	74	0.40
Swiss (56)	101	0.54
Ukrainian (0)	49	0.26
Welsh (23)	60	0.32
West Indian, ex. Hispanic (0)	20	0.11
Jamaican (0)	10	0.05
West Indian (0)	10	0.05

Hispanic Origin	Population	%
Hispanic or Latino (of any race)	250	1.25
Central American, ex. Mexican	31	0.16
Guatemalan	11	0.06
Honduran	7	0.04
Nicaraguan	1	0.01
Panamanian	3	0.02
Salvadoran	9	0.05
Cuban	5	0.03

*Notes: † The Census 2010 population figure is used to calculate the percentages in the Hispanic Origin and Race categories. Ancestry percentages are based on the 2006-2010 American Community Survey population (not shown); ‡ Numbers in parentheses indicate the number of people reporting a single ancestry; * Numbers in parentheses indicate the number of persons reporting this race alone, not in combination with any other race; Please refer to the Explanation of Data for more information.*

Mexican	110	0.55
Puerto Rican	33	0.17
South American	32	0.16
Argentinean	1	0.01
Bolivian	3	0.02
Chilean	3	0.02
Colombian	9	0.05
Ecuadorian	2	0.01
Peruvian	10	0.05
Venezuelan	4	0.02
Other Hispanic or Latino	39	0.20

Race*	Population	%
African-American/Black (1,313)	1,355	6.80
Not Hispanic (1,300)	1,341	6.73
Hispanic (13)	14	0.07
American Indian/Alaska Native (34)	85	0.43
Not Hispanic (33)	83	0.42
Hispanic (1)	2	0.01
Alaska Athabascan *(Ala. Nat.)* (1)	1	0.01
Aleut *(Alaska Native)* (1)	2	0.01
Apache (1)	3	0.02
Cherokee (17)	39	0.20
Choctaw (0)	1	0.01
Colville (2)	2	0.01
Creek (2)	2	0.01
Houma (3)	3	0.02
Inupiat *(Alaska Native)* (0)	2	0.01
Iroquois (0)	2	0.01
Lumbee (2)	2	0.01
Mexican American Ind. (1)	1	0.01
Navajo (0)	3	0.02
Asian (321)	378	1.90
Not Hispanic (317)	374	1.88
Hispanic (4)	4	0.02
Chinese, ex. Taiwanese (86)	89	0.45
Filipino (16)	29	0.15
Indian (44)	57	0.29
Japanese (16)	23	0.12
Korean (14)	18	0.09
Laotian (1)	1	0.01
Malaysian (3)	3	0.02
Nepalese (2)	2	0.01
Pakistani (26)	27	0.14
Taiwanese (5)	5	0.03
Thai (0)	1	0.01
Vietnamese (104)	116	0.58
Hawaii Native/Pacific Islander (18)	21	0.11
Not Hispanic (16)	19	0.10
Hispanic (2)	2	0.01
Guamanian/Chamorro (6)	6	0.03
Native Hawaiian (0)	1	0.01
White (17,997)	18,131	90.96
Not Hispanic (17,864)	17,988	90.24
Hispanic (133)	143	0.72

Tuscaloosa

Place Type: City
County: Tuscaloosa
Population: 90,468†

Ancestry‡	Population	%
African, Sub-Saharan (440)	617	0.70
African (284)	385	0.44
Nigerian (138)	145	0.17
Sierra Leonean (0)	34	0.04
Ugandan (0)	35	0.04
Other Sub-Saharan African (18)	18	0.02
American (4,519)	4,519	5.15
Arab (151)	268	0.31
Arab (55)	55	0.06
Egyptian (10)	10	0.01
Jordanian (0)	84	0.10
Lebanese (60)	93	0.11
Other Arab (26)	26	0.03
Austrian (26)	45	0.05
Belgian (25)	25	0.03
British (294)	538	0.61
Cajun (51)	51	0.06
Canadian (0)	28	0.03
Croatian (10)	29	0.03
Czech (100)	155	0.18
Czechoslovakian (28)	46	0.05
Danish (13)	56	0.06
Dutch (125)	591	0.67
English (3,463)	7,532	8.59
Estonian (0)	44	0.05
European (737)	823	0.94
Finnish (36)	53	0.06
French, ex. Basque (404)	1,533	1.75
French Canadian (41)	103	0.12
German (1,822)	5,417	6.18
German Russian (0)	19	0.02
Greek (182)	222	0.25
Hungarian (11)	38	0.04
Iranian (45)	85	0.10
Irish (2,365)	6,100	6.96
Italian (763)	1,524	1.74
Lithuanian (29)	39	0.04
Luxemburger (0)	14	0.02
Northern European (45)	52	0.06
Norwegian (98)	242	0.28
Pennsylvania German (9)	23	0.03
Polish (246)	400	0.46
Portuguese (45)	65	0.07
Romanian (109)	109	0.12
Russian (53)	188	0.21
Scandinavian (25)	61	0.07
Scotch-Irish (1,617)	2,705	3.09
Scottish (696)	1,845	2.10
Serbian (0)	15	0.02
Slavic (21)	21	0.02
Slovak (0)	35	0.04
Slovene (11)	29	0.03
Swedish (138)	418	0.48
Swiss (39)	39	0.04
Turkish (48)	57	0.07
Ukrainian (23)	46	0.05
Welsh (64)	294	0.34
West Indian, ex. Hispanic (70)	94	0.11
Barbadian (35)	35	0.04
Belizean (6)	6	0.01
Jamaican (29)	42	0.05
West Indian (0)	11	0.01
Yugoslavian (0)	44	0.05

Hispanic Origin	Population	%
Hispanic or Latino (of any race)	2,705	2.99
Central American, ex. Mexican	210	0.23
Costa Rican	7	0.01
Guatemalan	112	0.12
Honduran	23	0.03
Nicaraguan	30	0.03
Panamanian	21	0.02
Salvadoran	17	0.02
Cuban	110	0.12
Dominican Republic	5	0.01
Mexican	1,754	1.94
Puerto Rican	149	0.16
South American	187	0.21
Argentinean	19	0.02
Bolivian	7	0.01
Chilean	13	0.01
Colombian	64	0.07
Ecuadorian	13	0.01
Paraguayan	10	0.01
Peruvian	22	0.02
Uruguayan	6	0.01
Venezuelan	31	0.03
Other South American	2	<0.01
Other Hispanic or Latino	290	0.32

Race*	Population	%
African-American/Black (37,543)	38,029	42.04
Not Hispanic (37,417)	37,869	41.86
Hispanic (126)	160	0.18
American Indian/Alaska Native (220)	492	0.54
Not Hispanic (190)	436	0.48
Hispanic (30)	56	0.06
Alaska Athabascan *(Ala. Nat.)* (1)	1	<0.01
Apache (0)	1	<0.01
Blackfeet (0)	3	<0.01
Canadian/French Am. Ind. (0)	4	<0.01
Central American Ind. (1)	1	<0.01
Cherokee (55)	133	0.15
Cheyenne (0)	1	<0.01
Chickasaw (0)	6	0.01
Chippewa (0)	1	<0.01
Choctaw (8)	13	0.01
Comanche (0)	1	<0.01
Cree (0)	1	<0.01
Creek (5)	27	0.03
Delaware (0)	1	<0.01
Houma (1)	2	<0.01
Iroquois (3)	5	0.01
Lumbee (1)	1	<0.01
Mexican American Ind. (9)	12	0.01
Navajo (5)	6	0.01
Osage (0)	2	<0.01
Pueblo (1)	1	<0.01
Seminole (1)	4	<0.01
Sioux (2)	4	<0.01
Asian (1,666)	1,959	2.17
Not Hispanic (1,659)	1,935	2.14
Hispanic (7)	24	0.03
Bangladeshi (15)	16	0.02
Cambodian (5)	6	0.01
Chinese, ex. Taiwanese (520)	567	0.63
Filipino (102)	154	0.17
Hmong (2)	3	<0.01
Indian (438)	493	0.54
Indonesian (2)	3	<0.01
Japanese (60)	92	0.10
Korean (219)	263	0.29
Laotian (2)	3	<0.01
Malaysian (7)	7	0.01
Nepalese (15)	15	0.02
Pakistani (45)	57	0.06
Sri Lankan (5)	5	0.01
Taiwanese (16)	21	0.02
Thai (18)	27	0.03
Vietnamese (61)	83	0.09
Hawaii Native/Pacific Islander (22)	67	0.07
Not Hispanic (19)	60	0.07
Hispanic (3)	7	0.01
Fijian (1)	2	<0.01
Guamanian/Chamorro (7)	17	0.02
Marshallese (1)	1	<0.01
Native Hawaiian (6)	19	0.02
Samoan (4)	8	0.01
Tongan (1)	1	<0.01
White (48,684)	49,456	54.67
Not Hispanic (47,574)	48,228	53.31
Hispanic (1,110)	1,228	1.36

Tuscumbia

Place Type: City
County: Colbert
Population: 8,423†

Ancestry‡	Population	%
African, Sub-Saharan (9)	48	0.58
African (0)	39	0.47
Zimbabwean (9)	9	0.11
American (1,361)	1,361	16.37
Belgian (12)	12	0.14
Brazilian (10)	10	0.12
Canadian (14)	14	0.17
Dutch (9)	80	0.96
English (376)	610	7.34
European (40)	40	0.48
French, ex. Basque (0)	36	0.43
German (142)	554	6.66
Greek (19)	19	0.23
Irish (385)	961	11.56
Italian (22)	75	0.90
Norwegian (43)	43	0.52
Polish (0)	10	0.12

SECTION TWO

*Notes: † The Census 2010 population figure is used to calculate the percentages in the Hispanic Origin and Race categories. Ancestry percentages are based on the 2006-2010 American Community Survey population (not shown); ‡ Numbers in parentheses indicate the number of people reporting a single ancestry; * Numbers in parentheses indicate the number of persons reporting this race alone, not in combination with any other race; Please refer to the Explanation of Data for more information.*

Scotch-Irish (89)	176	2.12
Scottish (70)	92	1.11

Hispanic Origin	Population	%
Hispanic or Latino (of any race)	116	1.38
Central American, ex. Mexican	7	0.08
Guatemalan	1	0.01
Honduran	5	0.06
Salvadoran	1	0.01
Cuban	1	0.01
Mexican	76	0.90
Puerto Rican	5	0.06
South American	1	0.01
Colombian	1	0.01
Other Hispanic or Latino	26	0.31

Race*	Population	%
African-American/Black (1,783)	1,850	21.96
Not Hispanic (1,752)	1,819	21.60
Hispanic (31)	31	0.37
American Indian/Alaska Native (33)	96	1.14
Not Hispanic (33)	94	1.12
Hispanic (0)	2	0.02
Apache (0)	4	0.05
Cherokee (15)	43	0.51
Cheyenne (0)	3	0.04
Choctaw (0)	4	0.05
Creek (4)	5	0.06
Lumbee (3)	3	0.04
Sioux (0)	2	0.02
Asian (28)	43	0.51
Not Hispanic (28)	43	0.51
Chinese, ex. Taiwanese (1)	1	0.01
Filipino (2)	4	0.05
Indian (11)	13	0.15
Japanese (3)	8	0.09
Korean (2)	5	0.06
Thai (5)	5	0.06
Vietnamese (4)	7	0.08
Hawaii Native/Pacific Islander (0)	1	0.01
Not Hispanic (0)	1	0.01
Native Hawaiian (0)	1	0.01
White (6,394)	6,532	77.55
Not Hispanic (6,350)	6,482	76.96
Hispanic (44)	50	0.59

Tuskegee

Place Type: City
County: Macon
Population: 9,865†

Ancestry‡	Population	%
African, Sub-Saharan (122)	171	1.68
African (111)	152	1.49
Liberian (11)	11	0.11
Nigerian (0)	8	0.08
American (64)	64	0.63
Arab (2)	2	0.02
Lebanese (2)	2	0.02
Armenian (0)	10	0.10
Dutch (10)	10	0.10
English (21)	29	0.28
European (0)	14	0.14
German (15)	15	0.15
Scotch-Irish (0)	14	0.14
West Indian, ex. Hispanic (83)	185	1.82
Bahamian (0)	11	0.11
Barbadian (0)	16	0.16
Belizean (0)	25	0.25
Bermudan (0)	7	0.07
British West Indian (7)	7	0.07
Jamaican (76)	119	1.17

Hispanic Origin	Population	%
Hispanic or Latino (of any race)	126	1.28
Central American, ex. Mexican	7	0.07
Costa Rican	1	0.01
Honduran	2	0.02
Panamanian	3	0.03
Other Central American	1	0.01
Cuban	7	0.07
Dominican Republic	3	0.03
Mexican	55	0.56
Puerto Rican	26	0.26
South American	4	0.04
Bolivian	1	0.01
Chilean	1	0.01
Colombian	1	0.01
Ecuadorian	1	0.01
Other Hispanic or Latino	24	0.24

Race*	Population	%
African-American/Black (9,454)	9,567	96.98
Not Hispanic (9,395)	9,489	96.19
Hispanic (59)	78	0.79
American Indian/Alaska Native (8)	73	0.74
Not Hispanic (7)	67	0.68
Hispanic (1)	6	0.06
Arapaho (1)	1	0.01
Blackfeet (0)	7	0.07
Central American Ind. (0)	1	0.01
Cherokee (2)	28	0.28
Choctaw (0)	2	0.02
Creek (0)	2	0.02
Iroquois (0)	1	0.01
Mexican American Ind. (1)	1	0.01
Asian (50)	71	0.72
Not Hispanic (50)	64	0.65
Hispanic (0)	7	0.07
Bangladeshi (18)	18	0.18
Chinese, ex. Taiwanese (7)	8	0.08
Filipino (0)	5	0.05
Indian (21)	25	0.25
Japanese (0)	4	0.04
Korean (0)	2	0.02
Malaysian (1)	1	0.01
Nepalese (1)	1	0.01
Hawaii Native/Pacific Islander (0)	7	0.07
Not Hispanic (0)	4	0.04
Hispanic (0)	3	0.03
Guamanian/Chamorro (0)	3	0.03
Native Hawaiian (0)	1	0.01
Samoan (0)	1	0.01
White (191)	270	2.74
Not Hispanic (173)	245	2.48
Hispanic (18)	25	0.25

Valley

Place Type: City
County: Chambers
Population: 9,524†

Ancestry‡	Population	%
American (1,388)	1,388	14.57
Dutch (14)	88	0.92
English (787)	876	9.19
European (27)	46	0.48
French, ex. Basque (23)	130	1.36
French Canadian (0)	18	0.19
German (252)	490	5.14
Irish (503)	923	9.69
Italian (36)	36	0.38
Norwegian (2)	4	0.04
Polish (82)	88	0.92
Russian (9)	9	0.09
Scandinavian (8)	8	0.08
Scotch-Irish (32)	73	0.77
Scottish (70)	97	1.02
Swedish (0)	7	0.07

Hispanic Origin	Population	%
Hispanic or Latino (of any race)	162	1.70
Central American, ex. Mexican	11	0.12
Guatemalan	9	0.09
Honduran	1	0.01
Panamanian	1	0.01
Cuban	8	0.08
Mexican	103	1.08
Puerto Rican	19	0.20
Other Hispanic or Latino	21	0.22

Race*	Population	%
African-American/Black (3,143)	3,193	33.53
Not Hispanic (3,140)	3,188	33.47
Hispanic (3)	5	0.05
American Indian/Alaska Native (9)	33	0.35
Not Hispanic (7)	30	0.31
Hispanic (2)	3	0.03
Apache (0)	1	0.01
Cherokee (3)	17	0.18
Creek (0)	3	0.03
Houma (1)	1	0.01
Asian (111)	125	1.31
Not Hispanic (111)	125	1.31
Cambodian (1)	1	0.01
Chinese, ex. Taiwanese (0)	1	0.01
Filipino (8)	11	0.12
Indian (29)	30	0.31
Japanese (0)	1	0.01
Korean (64)	67	0.70
Pakistani (5)	5	0.05
Thai (0)	5	0.05
Vietnamese (2)	2	0.02
Hawaii Native/Pacific Islander (8)	10	0.10
Not Hispanic (6)	8	0.08
Hispanic (2)	2	0.02
Guamanian/Chamorro (2)	2	0.02
Native Hawaiian (6)	7	0.07
White (6,092)	6,187	64.96
Not Hispanic (6,010)	6,090	63.94
Hispanic (82)	97	1.02

Vestavia Hills

Place Type: City
County: Jefferson
Population: 34,033†

Ancestry‡	Population	%
African, Sub-Saharan (58)	70	0.21
African (0)	12	0.04
South African (7)	7	0.02
Other Sub-Saharan African (51)	51	0.15
American (3,441)	3,441	10.33
Arab (487)	601	1.80
Egyptian (92)	92	0.28
Lebanese (116)	204	0.61
Moroccan (163)	163	0.49
Palestinian (116)	131	0.39
Other Arab (0)	11	0.03
Australian (11)	11	0.03
Austrian (29)	64	0.19
British (285)	537	1.61
Cajun (28)	45	0.14
Canadian (11)	54	0.16
Croatian (11)	33	0.10
Czech (44)	68	0.20
Czechoslovakian (48)	48	0.14
Danish (57)	110	0.33
Dutch (124)	719	2.16
English (3,608)	7,214	21.66
European (595)	671	2.01
Finnish (13)	46	0.14
French, ex. Basque (267)	1,487	4.46
French Canadian (32)	54	0.16
German (1,373)	4,240	12.73
Greek (213)	354	1.06
Hungarian (41)	76	0.23
Iranian (93)	93	0.28
Irish (1,933)	4,403	13.22
Italian (688)	1,458	4.38
Latvian (16)	32	0.10
Lithuanian (0)	11	0.03
Norwegian (60)	209	0.63
Polish (200)	683	2.05
Portuguese (0)	19	0.06
Romanian (6)	6	0.02
Russian (22)	129	0.39

*Notes: † The Census 2010 population figure is used to calculate the percentages in the Hispanic Origin and Race categories. Ancestry percentages are based on the 2006-2010 American Community Survey population (not shown); ‡ Numbers in parentheses indicate the number of people reporting a single ancestry; * Numbers in parentheses indicate the number of persons reporting this race alone, not in combination with any other race; Please refer to the Explanation of Data for more information.*

Scandinavian (38)	38	0.11
Scotch-Irish (958)	1,994	5.99
Scottish (507)	1,870	5.61
Slavic (0)	10	0.03
Slovak (19)	19	0.06
Swedish (77)	232	0.70
Swiss (8)	83	0.25
Ukrainian (51)	77	0.23
Welsh (140)	446	1.34
Yugoslavian (0)	9	0.03

Hispanic Origin	Population	%
Hispanic or Latino (of any race)	835	2.45
Central American, ex. Mexican	68	0.20
Costa Rican	3	0.01
Guatemalan	21	0.06
Honduran	20	0.06
Nicaraguan	6	0.02
Panamanian	5	0.01
Salvadoran	13	0.04
Cuban	69	0.20
Dominican Republic	3	0.01
Mexican	412	1.21
Puerto Rican	53	0.16
South American	129	0.38
Argentinean	9	0.03
Bolivian	6	0.02
Chilean	3	0.01
Colombian	61	0.18
Ecuadorian	4	0.01
Paraguayan	5	0.01
Peruvian	26	0.08
Uruguayan	6	0.02
Venezuelan	9	0.03
Other Hispanic or Latino	101	0.30

Race*	Population	%
African-American/Black (1,279)	1,379	4.05
Not Hispanic (1,274)	1,365	4.01
Hispanic (5)	14	0.04
American Indian/Alaska Native (67)	177	0.52
Not Hispanic (60)	153	0.45
Hispanic (7)	24	0.07
Aleut *(Alaska Native)* (1)	2	0.01
Arapaho (0)	3	0.01
Canadian/French Am. Ind. (0)	1	<0.01
Cherokee (20)	51	0.15
Chickasaw (0)	3	0.01
Chippewa (3)	3	0.01
Choctaw (7)	9	0.03
Creek (6)	20	0.06
Iroquois (0)	3	0.01
Mexican American Ind. (1)	1	<0.01
Osage (2)	2	0.01
Potawatomi (2)	3	0.01
Sioux (1)	4	0.01
South American Ind. (0)	5	0.01
Spanish American Ind. (0)	1	<0.01
Asian (1,304)	1,432	4.21
Not Hispanic (1,300)	1,421	4.18
Hispanic (4)	11	0.03
Bangladeshi (7)	9	0.03
Cambodian (2)	4	0.01
Chinese, ex. Taiwanese (572)	588	1.73
Filipino (42)	54	0.16
Indian (403)	430	1.26
Indonesian (6)	13	0.04
Japanese (34)	53	0.16
Korean (103)	126	0.37
Malaysian (4)	7	0.02
Nepalese (4)	4	0.01
Pakistani (23)	23	0.07
Sri Lankan (1)	1	<0.01
Taiwanese (31)	32	0.09
Thai (13)	14	0.04
Vietnamese (23)	30	0.09
Hawaii Native/Pacific Islander (6)	10	0.03
Not Hispanic (6)	10	0.03
Guamanian/Chamorro (3)	3	0.01
Native Hawaiian (3)	5	0.01
White (30,758)	31,068	91.29
Not Hispanic (30,245)	30,509	89.65
Hispanic (513)	559	1.64

*Notes: † The Census 2010 population figure is used to calculate the percentages in the Hispanic Origin and Race categories. Ancestry percentages are based on the 2006-2010 American Community Survey population (not shown); ‡ Numbers in parentheses indicate the number of people reporting a single ancestry; * Numbers in parentheses indicate the number of persons reporting this race alone, not in combination with any other race; Please refer to the Explanation of Data for more information.*

ALASKA

Place Type: State
Population: 710,231†

Ancestry‡	Population	%
African, Sub-Saharan (2,620)	3,475	0.50
African (1,016)	1,717	0.25
Cape Verdean (4)	10	<0.01
Ethiopian (260)	260	0.04
Kenyan (82)	82	0.01
Liberian (32)	32	<0.01
Nigerian (131)	163	0.02
Senegalese (11)	11	<0.01
Sierra Leonean (6)	41	0.01
Somalian (408)	424	0.06
South African (17)	17	<0.01
Sudanese (544)	558	0.08
Ugandan (9)	9	<0.01
Other Sub-Saharan African (100)	151	0.02
Albanian (237)	471	0.07
Alsatian (3)	20	<0.01
American (24,459)	24,459	3.54
Arab (381)	1,207	0.17
Arab (49)	95	0.01
Egyptian (48)	81	0.01
Iraqi (34)	34	<0.01
Lebanese (144)	692	0.10
Moroccan (23)	41	0.01
Palestinian (18)	54	0.01
Syrian (13)	114	0.02
Other Arab (52)	96	0.01
Armenian (119)	271	0.04
Assyrian/Chaldean/Syriac (0)	14	<0.01
Australian (284)	593	0.09
Austrian (520)	2,075	0.30
Basque (142)	199	0.03
Belgian (113)	616	0.09
Brazilian (126)	432	0.06
British (1,943)	4,363	0.63
Bulgarian (175)	224	0.03
Cajun (74)	123	0.02
Canadian (1,071)	2,616	0.38
Carpatho Rusyn (32)	117	0.02
Celtic (287)	504	0.07
Croatian (267)	852	0.12
Czech (992)	3,516	0.51
Czechoslovakian (494)	1,237	0.18
Danish (1,453)	5,778	0.84
Dutch (3,279)	15,428	2.23
Eastern European (337)	460	0.07
English (18,951)	69,363	10.04
Estonian (124)	166	0.02
European (12,443)	14,134	2.04
Finnish (1,456)	4,418	0.64
French, ex. Basque (3,200)	24,258	3.51
French Canadian (2,172)	7,044	1.02
German (36,666)	134,424	19.45
German Russian (69)	99	0.01
Greek (652)	2,244	0.32
Guyanese (0)	45	0.01
Hungarian (780)	2,671	0.39
Icelander (62)	160	0.02
Iranian (79)	137	0.02
Irish (20,557)	85,326	12.34
Israeli (63)	109	0.02
Italian (7,440)	25,157	3.64
Latvian (137)	252	0.04
Lithuanian (261)	968	0.14
Luxemburger (87)	124	0.02
Macedonian (144)	215	0.03
Maltese (19)	169	0.02
New Zealander (79)	121	0.02
Northern European (1,483)	1,579	0.23
Norwegian (9,507)	28,598	4.14
Pennsylvania German (134)	496	0.07
Polish (5,068)	17,329	2.51
Portuguese (742)	2,567	0.37
Romanian (395)	804	0.12
Russian (4,265)	10,011	1.45
Scandinavian (1,695)	4,300	0.62
Scotch-Irish (5,413)	16,456	2.38
Scottish (5,673)	22,096	3.20
Serbian (106)	304	0.04
Slavic (159)	420	0.06
Slovak (334)	925	0.13
Slovene (63)	155	0.02
Swedish (4,246)	18,842	2.73
Swiss (784)	3,164	0.46
Turkish (106)	173	0.03
Ukrainian (774)	1,634	0.24
Welsh (948)	6,512	0.94
West Indian, ex. Hispanic (930)	1,523	0.22
Bahamian (43)	62	0.01
Belizean (0)	33	<0.01
British West Indian (205)	231	0.03
Dutch West Indian (189)	293	0.04
Haitian (103)	335	0.05
Jamaican (160)	245	0.04
Trinidadian/Tobagonian (65)	91	0.01
U.S. Virgin Islander (34)	37	0.01
West Indian (120)	185	0.03
Other West Indian (11)	11	<0.01
Yugoslavian (414)	895	0.13

Hispanic Origin	Population	%
Hispanic or Latino (of any race)	39,249	5.53
Central American, ex. Mexican	2,509	0.35
Costa Rican	140	0.02
Guatemalan	508	0.07
Honduran	272	0.04
Nicaraguan	176	0.02
Panamanian	446	0.06
Salvadoran	938	0.13
Other Central American	29	<0.01
Cuban	927	0.13
Dominican Republic	1,909	0.27
Mexican	21,642	3.05
Puerto Rican	4,502	0.63
South American	2,345	0.33
Argentinean	149	0.02
Bolivian	94	0.01
Chilean	223	0.03
Colombian	867	0.12
Ecuadorian	189	0.03
Paraguayan	18	<0.01
Peruvian	611	0.09
Uruguayan	24	<0.01
Venezuelan	140	0.02
Other South American	30	<0.01
Other Hispanic or Latino	5,415	0.76

Race*	Population	%
African-American/Black (23,263)	33,150	4.67
Not Hispanic (21,949)	30,367	4.28
Hispanic (1,314)	2,783	0.39
Am. Indian/Alaska Native (104,871)	138,312	19.47
Not Hispanic (102,556)	133,387	18.78
Hispanic (2,315)	4,925	0.69
Alaska Athabascan *(Ala. Nat.)* (12,318)	16,665	2.35
Aleut *(Alaska Native)* (7,696)	11,216	1.58
Apache (157)	367	0.05
Arapaho (38)	61	0.01
Blackfeet (173)	609	0.09
Canadian/French Am. Ind. (73)	173	0.02
Central American Ind. (10)	29	<0.01
Cherokee (920)	3,563	0.50
Cheyenne (26)	78	0.01
Chickasaw (58)	147	0.02
Chippewa (389)	872	0.12
Choctaw (295)	778	0.11
Colville (16)	50	0.01
Comanche (42)	98	0.01
Cree (31)	99	0.01
Creek (75)	185	0.03
Crow (35)	81	0.01
Delaware (19)	47	0.01
Hopi (14)	25	<0.01
Houma (4)	6	<0.01
Inupiat *(Alaska Native)* (20,941)	25,687	3.62
Iroquois (109)	309	0.04
Kiowa (10)	29	<0.01
Lumbee (46)	73	0.01
Menominee (30)	54	0.01
Mexican American Ind. (87)	155	0.02
Navajo (259)	475	0.07
Osage (19)	75	0.01
Ottawa (15)	39	0.01
Paiute (27)	45	0.01
Pima (24)	35	<0.01
Potawatomi (64)	131	0.02
Pueblo (77)	159	0.02
Puget Sound Salish (83)	158	0.02
Seminole (36)	112	0.02
Shoshone (36)	82	0.01
Sioux (290)	714	0.10
South American Ind. (43)	93	0.01
Spanish American Ind. (8)	16	<0.01
Tlingit-Haida *(Alaska Native)* (8,547)	13,186	1.86
Tohono O'Odham (19)	28	<0.01
Tsimshian *(Alaska Native)* (1,449)	1,939	0.27
Ute (19)	39	0.01
Yakama (25)	73	0.01
Yaqui (20)	42	0.01
Yuman (5)	21	<0.01
Yup'ik *(Alaska Native)* (27,329)	30,868	4.35
Asian (38,135)	50,402	7.10
Not Hispanic (37,459)	48,530	6.83
Hispanic (676)	1,872	0.26
Bangladeshi (33)	39	0.01
Bhutanese (35)	42	0.01
Burmese (24)	30	<0.01
Cambodian (228)	328	0.05
Chinese, ex. Taiwanese (1,998)	3,639	0.51
Filipino (19,394)	25,424	3.58
Hmong (3,427)	3,534	0.50
Indian (1,218)	1,911	0.27
Indonesian (77)	133	0.02
Japanese (1,476)	3,926	0.55
Korean (4,684)	6,542	0.92
Laotian (1,684)	2,121	0.30
Malaysian (16)	46	0.01
Nepalese (88)	114	0.02
Pakistani (139)	184	0.03
Sri Lankan (34)	49	0.01
Taiwanese (62)	88	0.01
Thai (951)	1,533	0.22
Vietnamese (960)	1,446	0.20
Hawaii Native/Pacific Islander (7,409)	11,154	1.57
Not Hispanic (7,219)	10,515	1.48
Hispanic (190)	639	0.09
Fijian (29)	42	0.01
Guamanian/Chamorro (380)	667	0.09
Marshallese (30)	49	0.01
Native Hawaiian (949)	3,006	0.42
Samoan (4,663)	5,953	0.84
Tongan (499)	762	0.11
White (473,576)	518,949	73.07
Not Hispanic (455,320)	495,498	69.77
Hispanic (18,256)	23,451	3.30

*Notes: † The Census 2010 population figure is used to calculate the percentages in the Hispanic Origin and Race categories. Ancestry percentages are based on the 2006-2010 American Community Survey population (not shown); ‡ Numbers in parentheses indicate the number of people reporting a single ancestry; * Numbers in parentheses indicate the number of persons reporting this race alone, not in combination with any other race; Please refer to the Explanation of Data for more information.*

Anchorage

Place Type: Municipality
County: Anchorage
Population: 291,826†

Ancestry‡	Population	%
African, Sub-Saharan (1,307)	1,845	0.65
African (554)	989	0.35
Cape Verdean (4)	10	<0.01
Ethiopian (127)	127	0.04
Kenyan (16)	16	0.01
Nigerian (127)	159	0.06
Somalian (15)	15	0.01
Sudanese (368)	382	0.13
Other Sub-Saharan African (96)	147	0.05
Albanian (221)	399	0.14
American (11,326)	11,326	3.98
Arab (251)	700	0.25
Arab (31)	73	0.03
Egyptian (48)	60	0.02
Iraqi (34)	34	0.01
Lebanese (72)	372	0.13
Palestinian (18)	54	0.02
Syrian (9)	68	0.02
Other Arab (39)	39	0.01
Armenian (35)	121	0.04
Assyrian/Chaldean/Syriac (0)	14	<0.01
Australian (113)	324	0.11
Austrian (308)	1,151	0.40
Basque (41)	62	0.02
Belgian (98)	220	0.08
Brazilian (113)	264	0.09
British (956)	1,984	0.70
Bulgarian (7)	7	<0.01
Cajun (15)	28	0.01
Canadian (438)	1,067	0.38
Carpatho Rusyn (28)	98	0.03
Celtic (195)	308	0.11
Croatian (94)	330	0.12
Czech (528)	1,771	0.62
Czechoslovakian (171)	505	0.18
Danish (591)	2,291	0.81
Dutch (1,174)	6,141	2.16
Eastern European (113)	137	0.05
English (6,823)	27,836	9.79
Estonian (124)	124	0.04
European (4,411)	5,161	1.82
Finnish (522)	1,830	0.64
French, ex. Basque (1,471)	10,635	3.74
French Canadian (981)	2,807	0.99
German (14,041)	54,988	19.34
German Russian (69)	99	0.03
Greek (312)	935	0.33
Guyanese (0)	39	0.01
Hungarian (287)	1,203	0.42
Icelander (28)	79	0.03
Iranian (64)	76	0.03
Irish (7,986)	35,919	12.64
Israeli (0)	46	0.02
Italian (3,186)	10,155	3.57
Latvian (50)	130	0.05
Lithuanian (154)	459	0.16
Luxemburger (84)	93	0.03
Macedonian (76)	90	0.03
Maltese (0)	68	0.02
New Zealander (18)	18	0.01
Northern European (477)	515	0.18
Norwegian (3,529)	11,185	3.93
Pennsylvania German (68)	306	0.11
Polish (2,118)	8,074	2.84
Portuguese (461)	1,168	0.41
Romanian (274)	422	0.15
Russian (1,514)	3,927	1.38
Scandinavian (628)	1,980	0.70
Scotch-Irish (1,942)	6,714	2.36
Scottish (1,989)	9,274	3.26
Serbian (76)	219	0.08
Slavic (106)	203	0.07
Slovak (179)	429	0.15
Slovene (0)	26	0.01
Swedish (1,221)	6,636	2.33
Swiss (264)	1,313	0.46
Turkish (29)	58	0.02
Ukrainian (104)	491	0.17
Welsh (354)	2,452	0.86
West Indian, ex. Hispanic (799)	1,233	0.43
Bahamian (40)	53	0.02
Belizean (0)	33	0.01
British West Indian (151)	177	0.06
Dutch West Indian (184)	249	0.09
Haitian (99)	256	0.09
Jamaican (122)	173	0.06
Trinidadian/Tobagonian (65)	91	0.03
U.S. Virgin Islander (34)	37	0.01
West Indian (93)	153	0.05
Other West Indian (11)	11	<0.01
Yugoslavian (137)	343	0.12

Hispanic Origin	Population	%
Hispanic or Latino (of any race)	22,061	7.56
Central American, ex. Mexican	1,475	0.51
Costa Rican	74	0.03
Guatemalan	354	0.12
Honduran	199	0.07
Nicaraguan	106	0.04
Panamanian	254	0.09
Salvadoran	474	0.16
Other Central American	14	<0.01
Cuban	521	0.18
Dominican Republic	1,626	0.56
Mexican	11,526	3.95
Puerto Rican	2,703	0.93
South American	1,500	0.51
Argentinean	86	0.03
Bolivian	45	0.02
Chilean	140	0.05
Colombian	557	0.19
Ecuadorian	110	0.04
Paraguayan	12	<0.01
Peruvian	447	0.15
Uruguayan	8	<0.01
Venezuelan	83	0.03
Other South American	12	<0.01
Other Hispanic or Latino	2,710	0.93

Race*	Population	%
African-American/Black (16,226)	22,494	7.71
Not Hispanic (15,308)	20,587	7.05
Hispanic (918)	1,907	0.65
American Indian/Alaska Native (23,130)	36,062	12.36
Not Hispanic (22,047)	33,633	11.53
Hispanic (1,083)	2,429	0.83
Alaska Athabascan *(Ala. Nat.)* (2,627)	4,333	1.48
Aleut *(Alaska Native)* (2,475)	3,982	1.36
Apache (70)	139	0.05
Arapaho (14)	28	0.01
Blackfeet (72)	278	0.10
Canadian/French Am. Ind. (10)	44	0.02
Central American Ind. (5)	17	0.01
Cherokee (331)	1,443	0.49
Cheyenne (6)	35	0.01
Chickasaw (26)	63	0.02
Chippewa (152)	334	0.11
Choctaw (130)	341	0.12
Colville (3)	17	0.01
Comanche (17)	28	0.01
Cree (5)	25	0.01
Creek (17)	70	0.02
Crow (15)	36	0.01
Delaware (7)	18	0.01
Hopi (9)	14	<0.01
Houma (0)	1	<0.01
Inupiat *(Alaska Native)* (4,018)	6,103	2.09
Iroquois (37)	109	0.04
Kiowa (5)	7	<0.01
Lumbee (14)	28	0.01
Menominee (23)	39	0.01
Mexican American Ind. (57)	105	0.04
Navajo (144)	261	0.09
Osage (10)	29	0.01
Ottawa (5)	19	0.01
Paiute (13)	17	0.01
Pima (10)	18	0.01
Potawatomi (31)	48	0.02
Pueblo (40)	80	0.03
Puget Sound Salish (24)	46	0.02
Seminole (4)	43	0.01
Shoshone (15)	36	0.01
Sioux (132)	276	0.09
South American Ind. (14)	42	0.01
Spanish American Ind. (5)	10	<0.01
Tlingit-Haida *(Alaska Native)* (1,291)	2,241	0.77
Tohono O'Odham (13)	19	0.01
Tsimshian *(Alaska Native)* (126)	221	0.08
Ute (2)	8	<0.01
Yakama (13)	23	0.01
Yaqui (12)	22	0.01
Yuman (5)	15	0.01
Yup'ik *(Alaska Native)* (3,243)	4,835	1.66
Asian (23,580)	30,047	10.30
Not Hispanic (23,208)	28,994	9.94
Hispanic (372)	1,053	0.36
Bangladeshi (30)	34	0.01
Bhutanese (35)	42	0.01
Burmese (17)	19	0.01
Cambodian (170)	239	0.08
Chinese, ex. Taiwanese (1,150)	2,104	0.72
Filipino (9,718)	12,768	4.38
Hmong (3,309)	3,408	1.17
Indian (739)	1,107	0.38
Indonesian (38)	73	0.03
Japanese (802)	2,067	0.71
Korean (3,570)	4,667	1.60
Laotian (1,529)	1,922	0.66
Malaysian (10)	21	0.01
Nepalese (79)	96	0.03
Pakistani (128)	160	0.05
Sri Lankan (14)	20	0.01
Taiwanese (40)	59	0.02
Thai (613)	969	0.33
Vietnamese (504)	780	0.27
Hawaii Native/Pacific Islander (5,901)	8,053	2.76
Not Hispanic (5,776)	7,652	2.62
Hispanic (125)	401	0.14
Fijian (23)	26	0.01
Guamanian/Chamorro (161)	312	0.11
Marshallese (11)	15	0.01
Native Hawaiian (557)	1,679	0.58
Samoan (4,195)	5,202	1.78
Tongan (328)	527	0.18
White (192,498)	212,398	72.78
Not Hispanic (182,814)	199,952	68.52
Hispanic (9,684)	12,446	4.26

Badger

Place Type: CDP
Borough: Fairbanks North Star
Population: 19,482†

Ancestry‡	Population	%
African, Sub-Saharan (0)	9	0.05
African (0)	9	0.05
American (753)	753	4.15
Austrian (0)	37	0.20
Belgian (0)	25	0.14
British (153)	374	2.06
Canadian (58)	106	0.58
Czech (14)	72	0.40
Czechoslovakian (14)	14	0.08
Danish (24)	150	0.83
Dutch (70)	672	3.70
English (682)	2,254	12.42
European (273)	273	1.50
Finnish (36)	171	0.94
French, ex. Basque (57)	1,137	6.27
French Canadian (78)	275	1.52
German (1,058)	4,921	27.12
Hungarian (15)	56	0.31

*Notes: † The Census 2010 population figure is used to calculate the percentages in the Hispanic Origin and Race categories. Ancestry percentages are based on the 2006-2010 American Community Survey population (not shown); ‡ Numbers in parentheses indicate the number of people reporting a single ancestry; * Numbers in parentheses indicate the number of persons reporting this race alone, not in combination with any other race; Please refer to the Explanation of Data for more information.*

Ancestry	Population	%
Irish (706)	3,500	19.29
Italian (257)	1,150	6.34
Lithuanian (0)	5	0.03
Northern European (58)	58	0.32
Norwegian (297)	633	3.49
Pennsylvania German (0)	6	0.03
Polish (62)	634	3.49
Romanian (0)	14	0.08
Russian (86)	129	0.71
Scandinavian (15)	38	0.21
Scotch-Irish (196)	464	2.56
Scottish (201)	482	2.66
Swedish (152)	902	4.97
Swiss (41)	106	0.58
Ukrainian (0)	10	0.06
Welsh (32)	144	0.79

Hispanic Origin	Population	%
Hispanic or Latino (of any race)	880	4.52
Central American, ex. Mexican	21	0.11
Costa Rican	1	0.01
Honduran	5	0.03
Nicaraguan	1	0.01
Panamanian	11	0.06
Salvadoran	3	0.02
Cuban	22	0.11
Dominican Republic	16	0.08
Mexican	547	2.81
Puerto Rican	127	0.65
South American	32	0.16
Argentinean	2	0.01
Chilean	2	0.01
Colombian	18	0.09
Ecuadorian	3	0.02
Peruvian	7	0.04
Other Hispanic or Latino	115	0.59

Race*	Population	%
African-American/Black (534)	703	3.61
Not Hispanic (500)	642	3.30
Hispanic (34)	61	0.31
American Indian/Alaska Native (950)	1,628	8.36
Not Hispanic (913)	1,543	7.92
Hispanic (37)	85	0.44
Alaska Athabascan *(Ala. Nat.)* (297)	426	2.19
Aleut *(Alaska Native)* (18)	31	0.16
Apache (1)	1	0.01
Arapaho (1)	5	0.03
Blackfeet (8)	18	0.09
Canadian/French Am. Ind. (9)	14	0.07
Cherokee (28)	84	0.43
Chickasaw (6)	7	0.04
Chippewa (21)	26	0.13
Choctaw (7)	14	0.07
Colville (5)	8	0.04
Comanche (2)	7	0.04
Cree (0)	4	0.02
Inupiat *(Alaska Native)* (125)	203	1.04
Iroquois (5)	14	0.07
Kiowa (1)	1	0.01
Navajo (5)	9	0.05
Osage (0)	2	0.01
Ottawa (4)	9	0.05
Paiute (0)	1	0.01
Pima (2)	2	0.01
Potawatomi (0)	3	0.02
Pueblo (3)	11	0.06
Puget Sound Salish (0)	4	0.02
Seminole (1)	1	0.01
Shoshone (2)	5	0.03
Sioux (6)	11	0.06
South American Ind. (1)	1	0.01
Spanish American Ind. (3)	5	0.03
Tlingit-Haida *(Alaska Native)* (26)	53	0.27
Tsimshian *(Alaska Native)* (0)	1	0.01
Yup'ik *(Alaska Native)* (52)	79	0.41
Asian (322)	618	3.17
Not Hispanic (317)	596	3.06
Hispanic (5)	22	0.11
Bangladeshi (0)	2	0.01
Chinese, ex. Taiwanese (38)	67	0.34
Filipino (154)	251	1.29
Hmong (8)	8	0.04
Indian (18)	32	0.16
Japanese (16)	81	0.42
Korean (50)	120	0.62
Malaysian (0)	1	0.01
Pakistani (0)	3	0.02
Taiwanese (1)	1	0.01
Thai (22)	39	0.20
Vietnamese (7)	18	0.09
Hawaii Native/Pacific Islander (33)	80	0.41
Not Hispanic (31)	75	0.38
Hispanic (2)	5	0.03
Guamanian/Chamorro (5)	17	0.09
Marshallese (0)	1	0.01
Native Hawaiian (17)	42	0.22
Samoan (6)	8	0.04
Tongan (1)	1	0.01
White (16,323)	17,388	89.25
Not Hispanic (15,807)	16,770	86.08
Hispanic (516)	618	3.17

College

Place Type: CDP
Borough: Fairbanks North Star
Population: 12,964†

Ancestry‡	Population	%
African, Sub-Saharan (40)	161	1.21
African (29)	150	1.13
Nigerian (4)	4	0.03
Sudanese (3)	3	0.02
Other Sub-Saharan African (4)	4	0.03
American (161)	161	1.21
Arab (0)	17	0.13
Other Arab (0)	17	0.13
Australian (7)	21	0.16
Austrian (18)	36	0.27
Basque (0)	4	0.03
Belgian (0)	9	0.07
Brazilian (0)	26	0.20
British (47)	106	0.80
Canadian (18)	26	0.20
Croatian (12)	18	0.14
Czech (36)	61	0.46
Danish (21)	82	0.62
Dutch (68)	320	2.41
Eastern European (18)	18	0.14
English (477)	1,461	11.01
European (124)	153	1.15
Finnish (0)	116	0.87
French, ex. Basque (44)	300	2.26
French Canadian (11)	120	0.90
German (672)	2,734	20.60
Hungarian (0)	22	0.17
Iranian (0)	6	0.05
Irish (564)	1,684	12.69
Israeli (1)	1	0.01
Italian (79)	580	4.37
Northern European (92)	92	0.69
Norwegian (323)	608	4.58
Polish (141)	371	2.80
Portuguese (0)	44	0.33
Romanian (0)	6	0.05
Russian (47)	143	1.08
Scandinavian (54)	141	1.06
Scotch-Irish (207)	536	4.04
Scottish (217)	465	3.50
Slavic (0)	3	0.02
Slovak (3)	43	0.32
Swedish (161)	667	5.03
Swiss (0)	159	1.20
Ukrainian (0)	4	0.03
Welsh (0)	254	1.91
West Indian, ex. Hispanic (13)	81	0.61
Haitian (0)	68	0.51
Jamaican (13)	13	0.10
Yugoslavian (0)	23	0.17

Hispanic Origin	Population	%
Hispanic or Latino (of any race)	687	5.30
Central American, ex. Mexican	29	0.22
Costa Rican	7	0.05
Guatemalan	8	0.06
Honduran	1	0.01
Nicaraguan	1	0.01
Panamanian	5	0.04
Salvadoran	7	0.05
Cuban	18	0.14
Dominican Republic	12	0.09
Mexican	388	2.99
Puerto Rican	80	0.62
South American	56	0.43
Argentinean	10	0.08
Bolivian	9	0.07
Chilean	1	0.01
Colombian	23	0.18
Ecuadorian	8	0.06
Peruvian	2	0.02
Venezuelan	3	0.02
Other Hispanic or Latino	104	0.80

Race*	Population	%
African-American/Black (419)	607	4.68
Not Hispanic (394)	556	4.29
Hispanic (25)	51	0.39
American Indian/Alaska Native (1,227)	1,838	14.18
Not Hispanic (1,188)	1,766	13.62
Hispanic (39)	72	0.56
Alaska Athabascan *(Ala. Nat.)* (510)	667	5.15
Aleut *(Alaska Native)* (18)	46	0.35
Apache (2)	2	0.02
Blackfeet (0)	5	0.04
Canadian/French Am. Ind. (0)	1	0.01
Cherokee (12)	54	0.42
Chippewa (12)	24	0.19
Choctaw (1)	4	0.03
Colville (0)	1	0.01
Comanche (1)	3	0.02
Creek (1)	3	0.02
Inupiat *(Alaska Native)* (173)	289	2.23
Iroquois (2)	3	0.02
Lumbee (1)	2	0.02
Mexican American Ind. (0)	1	0.01
Navajo (1)	4	0.03
Osage (2)	2	0.02
Paiute (0)	1	0.01
Potawatomi (3)	4	0.03
Pueblo (2)	2	0.02
Seminole (0)	3	0.02
Shoshone (0)	1	0.01
Sioux (3)	8	0.06
South American Ind. (1)	4	0.03
Tlingit-Haida *(Alaska Native)* (24)	35	0.27
Tsimshian *(Alaska Native)* (0)	2	0.02
Yakama (1)	1	0.01
Yaqui (0)	2	0.02
Yup'ik *(Alaska Native)* (119)	149	1.15
Asian (591)	879	6.78
Not Hispanic (573)	838	6.46
Hispanic (18)	41	0.32
Cambodian (2)	2	0.02
Chinese, ex. Taiwanese (141)	192	1.48
Filipino (104)	182	1.40
Hmong (1)	1	0.01
Indian (97)	122	0.94
Indonesian (4)	4	0.03
Japanese (68)	116	0.89
Korean (100)	169	1.30
Laotian (2)	4	0.03
Malaysian (3)	3	0.02
Pakistani (1)	2	0.02
Taiwanese (3)	4	0.03
Thai (30)	52	0.40
Vietnamese (4)	6	0.05
Hawaii Native/Pacific Islander (54)	128	0.99
Not Hispanic (54)	108	0.83
Hispanic (0)	20	0.15
Fijian (1)	1	0.01

*Notes: † The Census 2010 population figure is used to calculate the percentages in the Hispanic Origin and Race categories. Ancestry percentages are based on the 2006-2010 American Community Survey population (not shown); ‡ Numbers in parentheses indicate the number of people reporting a single ancestry; * Numbers in parentheses indicate the number of persons reporting this race alone, not in combination with any other race; Please refer to the Explanation of Data for more information.*

Guamanian/Chamorro (6)	13	0.10
Marshallese (1)	1	0.01
Native Hawaiian (17)	68	0.52
Samoan (24)	29	0.22
Tongan (1)	1	0.01
White (9,483)	10,429	80.45
Not Hispanic (9,139)	9,974	76.94
Hispanic (344)	455	3.51

Fairbanks

Place Type: City
Borough: Fairbanks North Star
Population: 31,535†

Ancestry‡	Population	%
African, Sub-Saharan (113)	113	0.36
African (47)	47	0.15
Kenyan (66)	66	0.21
Alsatian (0)	11	0.04
American (923)	923	2.96
Arab (0)	14	0.04
Moroccan (0)	14	0.04
Armenian (38)	38	0.12
Australian (11)	11	0.04
Austrian (30)	138	0.44
Basque (0)	15	0.05
Belgian (0)	12	0.04
British (140)	288	0.92
Cajun (10)	10	0.03
Canadian (19)	19	0.06
Celtic (21)	53	0.17
Czech (30)	179	0.57
Czechoslovakian (0)	17	0.05
Danish (33)	133	0.43
Dutch (207)	629	2.02
English (996)	2,650	8.50
European (263)	263	0.84
Finnish (26)	81	0.26
French, ex. Basque (156)	1,019	3.27
French Canadian (64)	160	0.51
German (2,550)	6,647	21.32
Greek (11)	21	0.07
Hungarian (31)	267	0.86
Iranian (0)	11	0.04
Irish (1,460)	4,011	12.86
Israeli (62)	62	0.20
Italian (654)	1,746	5.60
Lithuanian (3)	14	0.04
Northern European (28)	28	0.09
Norwegian (295)	939	3.01
Pennsylvania German (0)	25	0.08
Polish (242)	862	2.76
Portuguese (0)	141	0.45
Romanian (17)	17	0.05
Russian (169)	296	0.95
Scandinavian (40)	59	0.19
Scotch-Irish (320)	784	2.51
Scottish (286)	1,069	3.43
Serbian (12)	12	0.04
Slavic (11)	20	0.06
Slovene (19)	48	0.15
Swedish (194)	615	1.97
Swiss (17)	86	0.28
Ukrainian (24)	24	0.08
Welsh (19)	130	0.42
West Indian, ex. Hispanic (54)	80	0.26
British West Indian (54)	54	0.17
Dutch West Indian (0)	26	0.08
Yugoslavian (67)	67	0.21

Hispanic Origin	Population	%
Hispanic or Latino (of any race)	2,837	9.00
Central American, ex. Mexican	176	0.56
Costa Rican	24	0.08
Guatemalan	17	0.05
Honduran	15	0.05
Nicaraguan	15	0.05
Panamanian	75	0.24
Salvadoran	30	0.10
Cuban	84	0.27
Dominican Republic	71	0.23
Mexican	1,520	4.82
Puerto Rican	524	1.66
South American	159	0.50
Argentinean	5	0.02
Bolivian	17	0.05
Chilean	6	0.02
Colombian	94	0.30
Ecuadorian	10	0.03
Peruvian	20	0.06
Uruguayan	1	<0.01
Venezuelan	5	0.02
Other South American	1	<0.01
Other Hispanic or Latino	303	0.96

Race*	Population	%
African-American/Black (2,830)	3,682	11.68
Not Hispanic (2,653)	3,333	10.57
Hispanic (177)	349	1.11
American Indian/Alaska Native (3,148)	4,415	14.00
Not Hispanic (3,058)	4,228	13.41
Hispanic (90)	187	0.59
Alaska Athabascan *(Ala. Nat.)* (1,272)	1,631	5.17
Aleut *(Alaska Native)* (31)	57	0.18
Apache (8)	13	0.04
Blackfeet (8)	33	0.10
Canadian/French Am. Ind. (2)	8	0.03
Central American Ind. (1)	1	<0.01
Cherokee (35)	152	0.48
Cheyenne (1)	3	0.01
Chickasaw (3)	11	0.03
Chippewa (13)	23	0.07
Choctaw (16)	32	0.10
Colville (2)	6	0.02
Comanche (0)	1	<0.01
Cree (0)	1	<0.01
Creek (3)	9	0.03
Crow (2)	5	0.02
Delaware (0)	1	<0.01
Houma (3)	3	0.01
Inupiat *(Alaska Native)* (300)	447	1.42
Iroquois (9)	20	0.06
Lumbee (7)	10	0.03
Menominee (1)	3	0.01
Mexican American Ind. (2)	2	0.01
Navajo (23)	29	0.09
Osage (1)	2	0.01
Paiute (0)	3	0.01
Pima (2)	2	0.01
Potawatomi (1)	6	0.02
Pueblo (6)	12	0.04
Puget Sound Salish (2)	4	0.01
Seminole (4)	5	0.02
Sioux (11)	26	0.08
South American Ind. (1)	1	<0.01
Tlingit-Haida *(Alaska Native)* (36)	77	0.24
Tsimshian *(Alaska Native)* (2)	3	0.01
Ute (0)	1	<0.01
Yakama (2)	3	0.01
Yaqui (3)	6	0.02
Yup'ik *(Alaska Native)* (81)	132	0.42
Asian (1,124)	1,661	5.27
Not Hispanic (1,094)	1,578	5.00
Hispanic (30)	83	0.26
Bangladeshi (2)	2	0.01
Burmese (2)	2	0.01
Cambodian (8)	13	0.04
Chinese, ex. Taiwanese (147)	216	0.68
Filipino (367)	567	1.80
Hmong (6)	6	0.02
Indian (39)	70	0.22
Indonesian (10)	13	0.04
Japanese (76)	221	0.70
Korean (227)	350	1.11
Laotian (17)	26	0.08
Malaysian (1)	1	<0.01
Nepalese (1)	1	<0.01
Pakistani (0)	1	<0.01
Sri Lankan (4)	4	0.01
Taiwanese (7)	7	0.02
Thai (69)	99	0.31
Vietnamese (72)	95	0.30
Hawaii Native/Pacific Islander (262)	446	1.41
Not Hispanic (244)	390	1.24
Hispanic (18)	56	0.18
Fijian (0)	1	<0.01
Guamanian/Chamorro (98)	116	0.37
Marshallese (0)	1	<0.01
Native Hawaiian (31)	129	0.41
Samoan (60)	94	0.30
Tongan (5)	9	0.03
White (20,853)	23,016	72.99
Not Hispanic (19,496)	21,349	67.70
Hispanic (1,357)	1,667	5.29

Juneau

Place Type: Borough
Borough: Juneau
Population: 31,275†

Ancestry‡	Population	%
African, Sub-Saharan (87)	93	0.30
African (59)	65	0.21
Ethiopian (28)	28	0.09
Alsatian (3)	3	0.01
American (1,188)	1,188	3.84
Arab (0)	51	0.16
Lebanese (0)	45	0.15
Syrian (0)	6	0.02
Armenian (0)	1	<0.01
Australian (44)	44	0.14
Austrian (13)	54	0.17
Basque (64)	64	0.21
Belgian (0)	63	0.20
Brazilian (12)	39	0.13
British (101)	182	0.59
Cajun (0)	10	0.03
Canadian (81)	191	0.62
Croatian (3)	46	0.15
Czech (42)	116	0.37
Czechoslovakian (59)	94	0.30
Danish (96)	347	1.12
Dutch (185)	753	2.43
Eastern European (12)	19	0.06
English (953)	3,230	10.43
Estonian (0)	7	0.02
European (1,597)	1,675	5.41
Finnish (68)	243	0.78
French, ex. Basque (121)	1,072	3.46
French Canadian (31)	217	0.70
German (1,324)	5,707	18.42
Greek (7)	149	0.48
Hungarian (103)	166	0.54
Icelander (3)	35	0.11
Iranian (4)	9	0.03
Irish (896)	4,246	13.71
Italian (187)	888	2.87
Latvian (24)	27	0.09
Lithuanian (27)	77	0.25
Luxemburger (0)	14	0.05
Macedonian (6)	6	0.02
Northern European (142)	152	0.49
Norwegian (878)	2,080	6.72
Pennsylvania German (0)	15	0.05
Polish (330)	843	2.72
Portuguese (33)	102	0.33
Romanian (25)	85	0.27
Russian (68)	387	1.25
Scandinavian (145)	344	1.11
Scotch-Irish (187)	716	2.31
Scottish (334)	1,274	4.11
Serbian (6)	6	0.02
Slavic (0)	17	0.05
Slovak (49)	90	0.29
Slovene (14)	26	0.08
Swedish (341)	1,030	3.33
Swiss (15)	188	0.61
Turkish (0)	34	0.11

*Notes: † The Census 2010 population figure is used to calculate the percentages in the Hispanic Origin and Race categories. Ancestry percentages are based on the 2006-2010 American Community Survey population (not shown); ‡ Numbers in parentheses indicate the number of people reporting a single ancestry; * Numbers in parentheses indicate the number of persons reporting this race alone, not in combination with any other race; Please refer to the Explanation of Data for more information.*

Ukrainian (22)	99	0.32
Welsh (13)	346	1.12
Yugoslavian (39)	74	0.24

Hispanic Origin	Population	%
Hispanic or Latino (of any race)	1,588	5.08
Central American, ex. Mexican	68	0.22
Costa Rican	7	0.02
Guatemalan	12	0.04
Honduran	1	<0.01
Nicaraguan	16	0.05
Panamanian	9	0.03
Salvadoran	21	0.07
Other Central American	2	0.01
Cuban	23	0.07
Dominican Republic	25	0.08
Mexican	1,009	3.23
Puerto Rican	143	0.46
South American	95	0.30
Argentinean	6	0.02
Chilean	20	0.06
Colombian	20	0.06
Ecuadorian	18	0.06
Paraguayan	5	0.02
Peruvian	18	0.06
Uruguayan	4	0.01
Venezuelan	4	0.01
Other Hispanic or Latino	225	0.72

Race*	Population	%
African-American/Black (279)	593	1.90
Not Hispanic (259)	538	1.72
Hispanic (20)	55	0.18
American Indian/Alaska Native (3,692)	6,005	19.20
Not Hispanic (3,534)	5,656	18.08
Hispanic (158)	349	1.12
Alaska Athabascan *(Ala. Nat.)* (38)	119	0.38
Aleut *(Alaska Native)* (63)	186	0.59
Apache (3)	13	0.04
Arapaho (16)	16	0.05
Blackfeet (5)	19	0.06
Canadian/French Am. Ind. (7)	12	0.04
Central American Ind. (1)	2	0.01
Cherokee (32)	146	0.47
Chickasaw (3)	5	0.02
Chippewa (14)	44	0.14
Choctaw (6)	28	0.09
Colville (0)	3	0.01
Comanche (0)	1	<0.01
Cree (0)	6	0.02
Creek (1)	10	0.03
Crow (0)	2	0.01
Delaware (4)	5	0.02
Inupiat *(Alaska Native)* (65)	174	0.56
Iroquois (5)	15	0.05
Lumbee (2)	2	0.01
Menominee (1)	2	0.01
Mexican American Ind. (4)	6	0.02
Navajo (23)	44	0.14
Osage (0)	1	<0.01
Potawatomi (6)	13	0.04
Pueblo (5)	13	0.04
Puget Sound Salish (3)	9	0.03
Seminole (0)	3	0.01
Shoshone (2)	4	0.01
Sioux (8)	29	0.09
South American Ind. (0)	6	0.02
Tlingit-Haida *(Alaska Native)* (2,389)	3,825	12.23
Tsimshian *(Alaska Native)* (48)	114	0.36
Ute (0)	2	0.01
Yakama (0)	5	0.02
Yaqui (1)	1	<0.01
Yup'ik *(Alaska Native)* (65)	113	0.36
Asian (1,919)	2,850	9.11
Not Hispanic (1,879)	2,749	8.79
Hispanic (40)	101	0.32
Burmese (2)	6	0.02
Cambodian (11)	11	0.04
Chinese, ex. Taiwanese (103)	199	0.64
Filipino (1,423)	2,042	6.53
Indian (83)	120	0.38
Indonesian (1)	4	0.01
Japanese (64)	243	0.78
Korean (93)	147	0.47
Laotian (0)	5	0.02
Nepalese (3)	8	0.03
Pakistani (3)	6	0.02
Sri Lankan (8)	11	0.04
Thai (22)	34	0.11
Vietnamese (44)	71	0.23
Hawaii Native/Pacific Islander (218)	416	1.33
Not Hispanic (213)	401	1.28
Hispanic (5)	15	0.05
Fijian (5)	6	0.02
Guamanian/Chamorro (26)	38	0.12
Marshallese (6)	7	0.02
Native Hawaiian (22)	149	0.48
Samoan (61)	105	0.34
Tongan (85)	99	0.32
White (21,814)	24,334	77.81
Not Hispanic (21,065)	23,359	74.69
Hispanic (749)	975	3.12

Kalifornsky

Place Type: CDP
Borough: Kenai Peninsula
Population: 7,850[†]

Ancestry‡	Population	%
American (191)	191	2.55
Austrian (22)	22	0.29
British (0)	6	0.08
Canadian (18)	18	0.24
Croatian (27)	27	0.36
Czech (0)	7	0.09
Czechoslovakian (17)	17	0.23
Danish (8)	65	0.87
Dutch (7)	174	2.33
English (317)	897	12.00
European (433)	599	8.01
Finnish (14)	14	0.19
French, ex. Basque (18)	158	2.11
French Canadian (64)	218	2.92
German (479)	1,380	18.45
Greek (0)	47	0.63
Irish (265)	899	12.02
Italian (67)	82	1.10
Lithuanian (0)	6	0.08
Northern European (87)	87	1.16
Norwegian (179)	376	5.03
Polish (27)	79	1.06
Romanian (0)	9	0.12
Russian (7)	118	1.58
Scandinavian (17)	17	0.23
Scotch-Irish (73)	110	1.47
Scottish (37)	130	1.74
Slavic (11)	11	0.15
Swedish (45)	197	2.63
Swiss (11)	47	0.63
Welsh (17)	43	0.58

Hispanic Origin	Population	%
Hispanic or Latino (of any race)	272	3.46
Central American, ex. Mexican	19	0.24
Guatemalan	7	0.09
Honduran	3	0.04
Nicaraguan	1	0.01
Salvadoran	8	0.10
Cuban	2	0.03
Dominican Republic	1	0.01
Mexican	150	1.91
Puerto Rican	11	0.14
South American	12	0.15
Argentinean	1	0.01
Colombian	5	0.06
Ecuadorian	1	0.01
Peruvian	5	0.06
Other Hispanic or Latino	77	0.98

Race*	Population	%
African-American/Black (28)	53	0.68
Not Hispanic (26)	49	0.62
Hispanic (2)	4	0.05
American Indian/Alaska Native (392)	703	8.96
Not Hispanic (381)	684	8.71
Hispanic (11)	19	0.24
Alaska Athabascan *(Ala. Nat.)* (109)	168	2.14
Aleut *(Alaska Native)* (33)	54	0.69
Apache (1)	5	0.06
Blackfeet (2)	7	0.09
Canadian/French Am. Ind. (0)	1	0.01
Cherokee (14)	61	0.78
Cheyenne (1)	2	0.03
Chippewa (2)	7	0.09
Choctaw (10)	22	0.28
Comanche (0)	3	0.04
Cree (2)	2	0.03
Crow (1)	2	0.03
Hopi (1)	1	0.01
Inupiat *(Alaska Native)* (57)	94	1.20
Iroquois (0)	5	0.06
Mexican American Ind. (1)	1	0.01
Potawatomi (1)	2	0.03
Puget Sound Salish (1)	1	0.01
Sioux (0)	6	0.08
Tlingit-Haida *(Alaska Native)* (12)	20	0.25
Tsimshian *(Alaska Native)* (1)	2	0.03
Ute (1)	1	0.01
Yup'ik *(Alaska Native)* (35)	56	0.71
Asian (74)	167	2.13
Not Hispanic (74)	166	2.11
Hispanic (0)	1	0.01
Cambodian (1)	1	0.01
Chinese, ex. Taiwanese (4)	22	0.28
Filipino (29)	61	0.78
Indian (9)	18	0.23
Indonesian (1)	1	0.01
Japanese (8)	45	0.57
Korean (7)	22	0.28
Thai (6)	15	0.19
Vietnamese (1)	1	0.01
Hawaii Native/Pacific Islander (13)	62	0.79
Not Hispanic (13)	60	0.76
Hispanic (0)	2	0.03
Guamanian/Chamorro (2)	4	0.05
Native Hawaiian (8)	38	0.48
Samoan (2)	13	0.17
White (6,842)	7,254	92.41
Not Hispanic (6,658)	7,049	89.80
Hispanic (184)	205	2.61

Ketchikan

Place Type: City
Borough: Ketchikan Gateway
Population: 8,050[†]

Ancestry‡	Population	%
American (77)	77	0.96
Armenian (7)	35	0.44
Austrian (6)	23	0.29
British (6)	17	0.21
Celtic (0)	17	0.21
Czech (0)	10	0.13
Danish (59)	117	1.46
Dutch (43)	204	2.55
English (368)	729	9.12
European (169)	187	2.34
Finnish (5)	5	0.06
French, ex. Basque (10)	148	1.85
French Canadian (0)	67	0.84
German (347)	1,184	14.81
Hungarian (23)	27	0.34
Irish (152)	709	8.87
Italian (125)	375	4.69
Lithuanian (6)	6	0.08
Northern European (12)	12	0.15
Norwegian (265)	540	6.76

SECTION TWO

*Notes: † The Census 2010 population figure is used to calculate the percentages in the Hispanic Origin and Race categories. Ancestry percentages are based on the 2006-2010 American Community Survey population (not shown); ‡ Numbers in parentheses indicate the number of people reporting a single ancestry; * Numbers in parentheses indicate the number of persons reporting this race alone, not in combination with any other race; Please refer to the Explanation of Data for more information.*

Polish (53)	113	1.41
Portuguese (0)	23	0.29
Romanian (0)	4	0.05
Russian (26)	153	1.91
Scandinavian (9)	33	0.41
Scotch-Irish (61)	245	3.06
Scottish (93)	406	5.08
Swedish (84)	258	3.23
Swiss (16)	25	0.31
Ukrainian (4)	4	0.05
Welsh (19)	110	1.38
Yugoslavian (120)	120	1.50

Hispanic Origin	Population	%
Hispanic or Latino (of any race)	352	4.37
Central American, ex. Mexican	13	0.16
Costa Rican	1	0.01
Guatemalan	8	0.10
Nicaraguan	2	0.02
Panamanian	1	0.01
Salvadoran	1	0.01
Cuban	11	0.14
Dominican Republic	1	0.01
Mexican	206	2.56
Puerto Rican	34	0.42
South American	12	0.15
Argentinean	1	0.01
Chilean	1	0.01
Colombian	3	0.04
Peruvian	7	0.09
Other Hispanic or Latino	75	0.93

Race*	Population	%
African-American/Black (63)	127	1.58
Not Hispanic (61)	123	1.53
Hispanic (2)	4	0.05
American Indian/Alaska Native (1,345)	1,977	24.56
Not Hispanic (1,287)	1,872	23.25
Hispanic (58)	105	1.30
Alaska Athabascan *(Ala. Nat.)* (18)	49	0.61
Aleut *(Alaska Native)* (40)	85	1.06
Apache (5)	12	0.15
Blackfeet (5)	9	0.11
Canadian/French Am. Ind. (7)	11	0.14
Central American Ind. (1)	1	0.01
Cherokee (20)	49	0.61
Chippewa (5)	7	0.09
Choctaw (1)	6	0.07
Creek (1)	6	0.07
Crow (0)	1	0.01
Inupiat *(Alaska Native)* (16)	23	0.29
Iroquois (2)	5	0.06
Kiowa (0)	4	0.05
Mexican American Ind. (0)	1	0.01
Navajo (0)	1	0.01
Osage (0)	5	0.06
Ottawa (1)	1	0.01
Pima (0)	2	0.02
Potawatomi (1)	1	0.01
Pueblo (2)	3	0.04
Puget Sound Salish (1)	2	0.02
Sioux (1)	10	0.12
South American Ind. (0)	1	0.01
Tlingit-Haida *(Alaska Native)* (678)	988	12.27
Tsimshian *(Alaska Native)* (145)	254	3.16
Yakama (1)	3	0.04
Yup'ik *(Alaska Native)* (6)	18	0.22
Asian (868)	1,033	12.83
Not Hispanic (862)	1,015	12.61
Hispanic (6)	18	0.22
Cambodian (2)	6	0.07
Chinese, ex. Taiwanese (24)	49	0.61
Filipino (755)	891	11.07
Indian (22)	36	0.45
Indonesian (1)	1	0.01
Japanese (21)	41	0.51
Korean (11)	21	0.26
Taiwanese (1)	1	0.01
Thai (2)	7	0.09
Vietnamese (10)	12	0.15
Hawaii Native/Pacific Islander (23)	51	0.63
Not Hispanic (20)	47	0.58
Hispanic (3)	4	0.05
Guamanian/Chamorro (6)	11	0.14
Native Hawaiian (8)	18	0.22
Samoan (6)	12	0.15
White (4,887)	5,624	69.86
Not Hispanic (4,737)	5,399	67.07
Hispanic (150)	225	2.80

Knik-Fairview

Place Type: CDP
Borough: Matanuska-Susitna
Population: 14,923†

Ancestry‡	Population	%
African, Sub-Saharan (0)	11	0.09
African (0)	11	0.09
American (152)	152	1.24
Arab (0)	43	0.35
Lebanese (0)	43	0.35
Basque (13)	13	0.11
Belgian (0)	13	0.11
British (0)	33	0.27
Canadian (24)	313	2.56
Croatian (21)	43	0.35
Czech (52)	94	0.77
Czechoslovakian (19)	150	1.23
Danish (28)	39	0.32
Dutch (79)	417	3.41
Eastern European (12)	15	0.12
English (156)	1,179	9.64
European (486)	502	4.10
Finnish (46)	243	1.99
French, ex. Basque (13)	725	5.93
French Canadian (19)	227	1.86
German (662)	2,953	24.14
Greek (0)	74	0.60
Hungarian (14)	87	0.71
Irish (375)	1,882	15.38
Italian (134)	621	5.08
Latvian (0)	6	0.05
Lithuanian (0)	20	0.16
Northern European (18)	18	0.15
Norwegian (104)	564	4.61
Polish (189)	462	3.78
Romanian (41)	43	0.35
Russian (67)	309	2.53
Scandinavian (0)	37	0.30
Scotch-Irish (96)	461	3.77
Scottish (146)	416	3.40
Slovak (8)	17	0.14
Swedish (52)	342	2.80
Swiss (12)	185	1.51
Welsh (26)	154	1.26

Hispanic Origin	Population	%
Hispanic or Latino (of any race)	613	4.11
Central American, ex. Mexican	31	0.21
Costa Rican	1	0.01
Guatemalan	3	0.02
Honduran	2	0.01
Panamanian	9	0.06
Salvadoran	16	0.11
Cuban	16	0.11
Dominican Republic	10	0.07
Mexican	295	1.98
Puerto Rican	63	0.42
South American	25	0.17
Argentinean	1	0.01
Bolivian	3	0.02
Colombian	4	0.03
Peruvian	13	0.09
Venezuelan	1	0.01
Other South American	3	0.02
Other Hispanic or Latino	173	1.16

Race*	Population	%
African-American/Black (149)	297	1.99
Not Hispanic (141)	276	1.85
Hispanic (8)	21	0.14
American Indian/Alaska Native (787)	1,541	10.33
Not Hispanic (746)	1,441	9.66
Hispanic (41)	100	0.67
Alaska Athabascan *(Ala. Nat.)* (117)	200	1.34
Aleut *(Alaska Native)* (93)	162	1.09
Apache (3)	6	0.04
Blackfeet (1)	9	0.06
Canadian/French Am. Ind. (1)	1	0.01
Cherokee (38)	134	0.90
Chickasaw (1)	7	0.05
Chippewa (14)	35	0.23
Choctaw (21)	39	0.26
Cree (0)	1	0.01
Creek (0)	3	0.02
Crow (4)	4	0.03
Inupiat *(Alaska Native)* (128)	212	1.42
Iroquois (7)	13	0.09
Kiowa (0)	5	0.03
Lumbee (3)	3	0.02
Mexican American Ind. (2)	4	0.03
Navajo (2)	8	0.05
Paiute (3)	4	0.03
Potawatomi (1)	1	0.01
Pueblo (1)	1	0.01
Puget Sound Salish (3)	6	0.04
Seminole (0)	4	0.03
Shoshone (1)	3	0.02
Sioux (7)	20	0.13
Tlingit-Haida *(Alaska Native)* (39)	87	0.58
Tsimshian *(Alaska Native)* (1)	2	0.01
Yakama (0)	4	0.03
Yup'ik *(Alaska Native)* (57)	106	0.71
Asian (215)	423	2.83
Not Hispanic (212)	386	2.59
Hispanic (3)	37	0.25
Cambodian (10)	17	0.11
Chinese, ex. Taiwanese (11)	30	0.20
Filipino (72)	185	1.24
Hmong (22)	24	0.16
Indian (11)	18	0.12
Indonesian (1)	1	0.01
Japanese (13)	35	0.23
Korean (16)	58	0.39
Laotian (10)	10	0.07
Malaysian (0)	1	0.01
Taiwanese (1)	1	0.01
Thai (10)	19	0.13
Vietnamese (12)	20	0.13
Hawaii Native/Pacific Islander (55)	137	0.92
Not Hispanic (53)	114	0.76
Hispanic (2)	23	0.15
Guamanian/Chamorro (14)	20	0.13
Native Hawaiian (16)	71	0.48
Samoan (15)	18	0.12
Tongan (6)	6	0.04
White (12,579)	13,586	91.04
Not Hispanic (12,211)	13,101	87.79
Hispanic (368)	485	3.25

Lakes

Place Type: CDP
Borough: Matanuska-Susitna
Population: 8,364†

Ancestry‡	Population	%
African, Sub-Saharan (0)	8	0.09
African (0)	8	0.09
American (448)	448	4.91
Arab (0)	17	0.19
Egyptian (0)	17	0.19
Austrian (0)	33	0.36
British (21)	46	0.50
Canadian (76)	111	1.22
Croatian (7)	7	0.08
Czech (10)	84	0.92
Czechoslovakian (11)	37	0.41
Danish (20)	141	1.55

*Notes: † The Census 2010 population figure is used to calculate the percentages in the Hispanic Origin and Race categories. Ancestry percentages are based on the 2006-2010 American Community Survey population (not shown); ‡ Numbers in parentheses indicate the number of people reporting a single ancestry; * Numbers in parentheses indicate the number of persons reporting this race alone, not in combination with any other race; Please refer to the Explanation of Data for more information.*

Ancestry	Population	%
Dutch (116)	368	4.03
English (465)	1,519	16.65
European (165)	188	2.06
Finnish (43)	62	0.68
French, ex. Basque (12)	572	6.27
French Canadian (53)	192	2.10
German (474)	2,035	22.30
Hungarian (36)	64	0.70
Irish (312)	1,193	13.07
Italian (168)	322	3.53
Lithuanian (0)	18	0.20
Macedonian (12)	44	0.48
Northern European (18)	18	0.20
Norwegian (140)	282	3.09
Polish (138)	439	4.81
Portuguese (6)	71	0.78
Russian (80)	136	1.49
Scandinavian (35)	35	0.38
Scotch-Irish (182)	427	4.68
Scottish (134)	469	5.14
Slovak (11)	16	0.18
Swedish (111)	420	4.60
Swiss (72)	72	0.79
Welsh (0)	98	1.07
Yugoslavian (0)	7	0.08

Hispanic Origin	Population	%
Hispanic or Latino (of any race)	354	4.23
Central American, ex. Mexican	17	0.20
Guatemalan	1	0.01
Honduran	2	0.02
Panamanian	5	0.06
Salvadoran	5	0.06
Other Central American	4	0.05
Cuban	11	0.13
Dominican Republic	8	0.10
Mexican	199	2.38
Puerto Rican	37	0.44
South American	24	0.29
Argentinean	3	0.04
Bolivian	1	0.01
Colombian	10	0.12
Ecuadorian	3	0.04
Peruvian	2	0.02
Uruguayan	5	0.06
Other Hispanic or Latino	58	0.69

Race*	Population	%
African-American/Black (79)	144	1.72
Not Hispanic (78)	133	1.59
Hispanic (1)	11	0.13
American Indian/Alaska Native (439)	837	10.01
Not Hispanic (430)	804	9.61
Hispanic (9)	33	0.39
Alaska Athabascan *(Ala. Nat.)* (47)	80	0.96
Aleut *(Alaska Native)* (45)	92	1.10
Apache (4)	9	0.11
Blackfeet (10)	16	0.19
Canadian/French Am. Ind. (1)	1	0.01
Cherokee (21)	58	0.69
Cheyenne (1)	7	0.08
Chickasaw (2)	4	0.05
Chippewa (7)	16	0.19
Choctaw (3)	9	0.11
Colville (0)	1	0.01
Comanche (0)	1	0.01
Creek (1)	1	0.01
Crow (1)	1	0.01
Delaware (0)	1	0.01
Inupiat *(Alaska Native)* (67)	112	1.34
Iroquois (0)	3	0.04
Kiowa (0)	2	0.02
Menominee (0)	2	0.02
Navajo (1)	6	0.07
Osage (0)	5	0.06
Paiute (3)	4	0.05
Potawatomi (0)	8	0.10
Pueblo (0)	2	0.02
Puget Sound Salish (3)	3	0.04
Shoshone (0)	1	0.01
Sioux (1)	5	0.06
Tlingit-Haida *(Alaska Native)* (23)	45	0.54
Tohono O'Odham (2)	2	0.02
Tsimshian *(Alaska Native)* (4)	10	0.12
Ute (1)	1	0.01
Yup'ik *(Alaska Native)* (71)	115	1.37
Asian (75)	200	2.39
Not Hispanic (72)	179	2.14
Hispanic (3)	21	0.25
Chinese, ex. Taiwanese (5)	32	0.38
Filipino (44)	91	1.09
Indian (1)	4	0.05
Indonesian (1)	6	0.07
Japanese (5)	23	0.27
Korean (10)	32	0.38
Laotian (6)	6	0.07
Taiwanese (1)	3	0.04
Thai (0)	6	0.07
Vietnamese (1)	8	0.10
Hawaii Native/Pacific Islander (7)	40	0.48
Not Hispanic (7)	40	0.48
Guamanian/Chamorro (0)	9	0.11
Native Hawaiian (5)	29	0.35
Samoan (1)	2	0.02
White (7,111)	7,645	91.40
Not Hispanic (6,910)	7,385	88.30
Hispanic (201)	260	3.11

Meadow Lakes

Place Type: CDP
Borough: Matanuska-Susitna
Population: 7,570†

Ancestry‡	Population	%
Albanian (16)	16	0.24
American (413)	413	6.23
Austrian (15)	15	0.23
Belgian (3)	15	0.23
British (13)	79	1.19
Canadian (16)	16	0.24
Czech (0)	6	0.09
Danish (0)	21	0.32
Dutch (55)	122	1.84
English (130)	570	8.59
European (152)	194	2.92
Finnish (6)	12	0.18
French, ex. Basque (57)	260	3.92
French Canadian (73)	236	3.56
German (827)	2,222	33.49
Greek (0)	91	1.37
Hungarian (8)	50	0.75
Irish (152)	790	11.91
Italian (70)	141	2.13
Northern European (1)	1	0.02
Norwegian (164)	528	7.96
Polish (54)	101	1.52
Portuguese (79)	113	1.70
Romanian (8)	75	1.13
Russian (19)	61	0.92
Scandinavian (3)	3	0.05
Scotch-Irish (30)	158	2.38
Scottish (79)	181	2.73
Slavic (10)	10	0.15
Swedish (21)	229	3.45
Swiss (14)	26	0.39
Welsh (12)	115	1.73
Yugoslavian (0)	67	1.01

Hispanic Origin	Population	%
Hispanic or Latino (of any race)	258	3.41
Central American, ex. Mexican	17	0.22
Guatemalan	7	0.09
Panamanian	6	0.08
Other Central American	4	0.05
Cuban	5	0.07
Dominican Republic	1	0.01
Mexican	146	1.93
Puerto Rican	28	0.37
South American	10	0.13
Chilean	6	0.08
Colombian	4	0.05
Other Hispanic or Latino	51	0.67

Race*	Population	%
African-American/Black (51)	92	1.22
Not Hispanic (49)	82	1.08
Hispanic (2)	10	0.13
American Indian/Alaska Native (436)	777	10.26
Not Hispanic (426)	749	9.89
Hispanic (10)	28	0.37
Alaska Athabascan *(Ala. Nat.)* (70)	103	1.36
Aleut *(Alaska Native)* (54)	101	1.33
Apache (1)	5	0.07
Arapaho (0)	2	0.03
Blackfeet (4)	11	0.15
Canadian/French Am. Ind. (2)	10	0.13
Central American Ind. (1)	4	0.05
Cherokee (15)	61	0.81
Chickasaw (1)	1	0.01
Chippewa (3)	15	0.20
Choctaw (3)	12	0.16
Colville (1)	3	0.04
Comanche (1)	1	0.01
Cree (0)	1	0.01
Creek (7)	12	0.16
Crow (0)	1	0.01
Hopi (1)	1	0.01
Inupiat *(Alaska Native)* (53)	84	1.11
Iroquois (1)	3	0.04
Menominee (2)	3	0.04
Mexican American Ind. (2)	2	0.03
Navajo (1)	3	0.04
Potawatomi (1)	5	0.07
Seminole (1)	1	0.01
Sioux (2)	9	0.12
Tlingit-Haida *(Alaska Native)* (24)	35	0.46
Yup'ik *(Alaska Native)* (45)	76	1.00
Asian (78)	135	1.78
Not Hispanic (78)	128	1.69
Hispanic (0)	7	0.09
Chinese, ex. Taiwanese (5)	14	0.18
Filipino (27)	51	0.67
Hmong (8)	8	0.11
Indian (1)	2	0.03
Japanese (6)	23	0.30
Korean (9)	16	0.21
Laotian (15)	15	0.20
Malaysian (0)	2	0.03
Thai (3)	6	0.08
Hawaii Native/Pacific Islander (29)	60	0.79
Not Hispanic (28)	52	0.69
Hispanic (1)	8	0.11
Guamanian/Chamorro (4)	5	0.07
Native Hawaiian (9)	32	0.42
Samoan (1)	10	0.13
Tongan (2)	13	0.17
White (6,450)	6,896	91.10
Not Hispanic (6,305)	6,694	88.43
Hispanic (145)	202	2.67

Sitka

Place Type: Borough
Borough: Sitka
Population: 8,881†

Ancestry‡	Population	%
American (389)	389	4.37
Arab (0)	27	0.30
Other Arab (0)	27	0.30
Armenian (5)	5	0.06
Australian (102)	102	1.15
Austrian (0)	74	0.83
Belgian (0)	41	0.46
British (3)	36	0.40
Czech (25)	51	0.57
Danish (2)	30	0.34
Dutch (12)	57	0.64
Eastern European (78)	78	0.88

*Notes: † The Census 2010 population figure is used to calculate the percentages in the Hispanic Origin and Race categories. Ancestry percentages are based on the 2006-2010 American Community Survey population (not shown); ‡ Numbers in parentheses indicate the number of people reporting a single ancestry; * Numbers in parentheses indicate the number of persons reporting this race alone, not in combination with any other race; Please refer to the Explanation of Data for more information.*

Ancestry	Population	%
English (311)	1,107	12.45
European (68)	95	1.07
Finnish (31)	45	0.51
French, ex. Basque (63)	394	4.43
French Canadian (10)	151	1.70
German (508)	1,515	17.03
Greek (0)	67	0.75
Hungarian (3)	3	0.03
Irish (267)	1,023	11.50
Italian (131)	311	3.50
Macedonian (35)	35	0.39
New Zealander (0)	18	0.20
Norwegian (106)	459	5.16
Polish (39)	131	1.47
Portuguese (17)	106	1.19
Russian (25)	108	1.21
Scandinavian (0)	7	0.08
Scotch-Irish (18)	203	2.28
Scottish (42)	324	3.64
Serbian (6)	6	0.07
Slavic (0)	31	0.35
Slovak (0)	33	0.37
Swedish (27)	269	3.02
Swiss (3)	24	0.27
Turkish (11)	11	0.12
Ukrainian (0)	16	0.18
Welsh (59)	209	2.35

Hispanic Origin	Population	%
Hispanic or Latino (of any race)	437	4.92
Central American, ex. Mexican	10	0.11
Guatemalan	3	0.03
Honduran	2	0.02
Nicaraguan	1	0.01
Salvadoran	4	0.05
Cuban	15	0.17
Dominican Republic	1	0.01
Mexican	261	2.94
Puerto Rican	30	0.34
South American	27	0.30
Argentinean	3	0.03
Bolivian	1	0.01
Chilean	3	0.03
Colombian	3	0.03
Peruvian	7	0.08
Uruguayan	4	0.05
Venezuelan	2	0.02
Other South American	4	0.05
Other Hispanic or Latino	93	1.05

Race*	Population	%
African-American/Black (47)	88	0.99
Not Hispanic (43)	77	0.87
Hispanic (4)	11	0.12
American Indian/Alaska Native (1,493)	2,184	24.59
Not Hispanic (1,442)	2,070	23.31
Hispanic (51)	114	1.28
Alaska Athabascan *(Ala. Nat.)* (19)	45	0.51
Aleut *(Alaska Native)* (28)	77	0.87
Apache (3)	7	0.08
Blackfeet (2)	4	0.05
Canadian/French Am. Ind. (4)	5	0.06
Cherokee (26)	43	0.48
Chippewa (14)	32	0.36
Choctaw (1)	7	0.08
Colville (2)	3	0.03
Comanche (1)	1	0.01
Cree (0)	1	0.01
Creek (1)	2	0.02
Inupiat *(Alaska Native)* (44)	71	0.80
Iroquois (0)	1	0.01
Lumbee (1)	1	0.01
Navajo (1)	3	0.03
Osage (0)	2	0.02
Pueblo (0)	2	0.02
Puget Sound Salish (3)	4	0.05
Seminole (0)	1	0.01
Sioux (7)	22	0.25
South American Ind. (0)	5	0.06
Tlingit-Haida *(Alaska Native)* (907)	1,394	15.70
Tsimshian *(Alaska Native)* (40)	65	0.73
Yaqui (0)	2	0.02
Yup'ik *(Alaska Native)* (32)	60	0.68
Asian (529)	718	8.08
Not Hispanic (509)	675	7.60
Hispanic (20)	43	0.48
Chinese, ex. Taiwanese (14)	48	0.54
Filipino (414)	535	6.02
Indian (9)	20	0.23
Japanese (27)	70	0.79
Korean (20)	27	0.30
Malaysian (1)	8	0.09
Taiwanese (2)	4	0.05
Thai (5)	9	0.10
Vietnamese (12)	18	0.20
Hawaii Native/Pacific Islander (30)	78	0.88
Not Hispanic (29)	74	0.83
Hispanic (1)	4	0.05
Guamanian/Chamorro (1)	2	0.02
Marshallese (4)	7	0.08
Native Hawaiian (10)	30	0.34
Samoan (8)	16	0.18
Tongan (4)	13	0.15
White (5,798)	6,591	74.21
Not Hispanic (5,641)	6,345	71.44
Hispanic (157)	246	2.77

Tanaina

Place Type: CDP
Borough: Matanuska-Susitna
Population: 8,197†

Ancestry‡	Population	%
American (414)	414	4.79
British (7)	40	0.46
Bulgarian (22)	22	0.25
Cajun (7)	7	0.08
Canadian (0)	6	0.07
Carpatho Rusyn (0)	15	0.17
Czech (24)	24	0.28
Czechoslovakian (0)	31	0.36
Danish (0)	24	0.28
Dutch (62)	262	3.03
Eastern European (16)	16	0.19
English (225)	1,135	13.14
European (138)	170	1.97
Finnish (60)	78	0.90
French, ex. Basque (68)	525	6.08
French Canadian (33)	152	1.76
German (531)	2,155	24.95
Hungarian (0)	49	0.57
Irish (177)	1,223	14.16
Italian (161)	603	6.98
Norwegian (158)	754	8.73
Polish (60)	266	3.08
Russian (231)	357	4.13
Scandinavian (39)	85	0.98
Scotch-Irish (34)	204	2.36
Scottish (171)	352	4.08
Serbian (0)	6	0.07
Slovak (0)	7	0.08
Swedish (45)	435	5.04
Swiss (0)	33	0.38
Ukrainian (182)	215	2.49
Welsh (38)	117	1.35
Yugoslavian (5)	34	0.39

Hispanic Origin	Population	%
Hispanic or Latino (of any race)	371	4.53
Central American, ex. Mexican	16	0.20
Nicaraguan	1	0.01
Panamanian	7	0.09
Salvadoran	8	0.10
Cuban	9	0.11
Dominican Republic	7	0.09
Mexican	231	2.82
Puerto Rican	33	0.40
South American	9	0.11
Chilean	1	0.01
Colombian	5	0.06
Ecuadorian	1	0.01
Venezuelan	2	0.02
Other Hispanic or Latino	66	0.81

Race*	Population	%
African-American/Black (69)	150	1.83
Not Hispanic (64)	131	1.60
Hispanic (5)	19	0.23
American Indian/Alaska Native (368)	722	8.81
Not Hispanic (353)	680	8.30
Hispanic (15)	42	0.51
Alaska Athabascan *(Ala. Nat.)* (45)	93	1.13
Aleut *(Alaska Native)* (31)	105	1.28
Apache (3)	4	0.05
Arapaho (1)	1	0.01
Blackfeet (0)	1	0.01
Cherokee (11)	39	0.48
Chickasaw (1)	6	0.07
Chippewa (7)	12	0.15
Choctaw (2)	10	0.12
Colville (0)	2	0.02
Comanche (1)	1	0.01
Inupiat *(Alaska Native)* (62)	95	1.16
Iroquois (1)	8	0.10
Osage (0)	1	0.01
Potawatomi (2)	3	0.04
Puget Sound Salish (1)	1	0.01
Seminole (3)	5	0.06
Sioux (2)	5	0.06
Tlingit-Haida *(Alaska Native)* (26)	54	0.66
Tohono O'Odham (2)	2	0.02
Tsimshian *(Alaska Native)* (0)	3	0.04
Yup'ik *(Alaska Native)* (42)	76	0.93
Asian (101)	205	2.50
Not Hispanic (99)	189	2.31
Hispanic (2)	16	0.20
Chinese, ex. Taiwanese (5)	21	0.26
Filipino (56)	105	1.28
Hmong (1)	3	0.04
Indian (1)	4	0.05
Japanese (13)	29	0.35
Korean (15)	30	0.37
Laotian (4)	4	0.05
Taiwanese (1)	1	0.01
Thai (1)	3	0.04
Vietnamese (1)	3	0.04
Hawaii Native/Pacific Islander (11)	34	0.41
Not Hispanic (9)	26	0.32
Hispanic (2)	8	0.10
Native Hawaiian (6)	23	0.28
Samoan (3)	6	0.07
White (7,043)	7,536	91.94
Not Hispanic (6,833)	7,274	88.74
Hispanic (210)	262	3.20

Wasilla

Place Type: City
Borough: Matanuska-Susitna
Population: 7,831†

Ancestry‡	Population	%
American (324)	324	4.33
Austrian (37)	72	0.96
British (15)	83	1.11
Cajun (0)	16	0.21
Canadian (0)	12	0.16
Czech (6)	47	0.63
Czechoslovakian (3)	3	0.04
Danish (21)	32	0.43
Dutch (23)	215	2.87
Eastern European (0)	40	0.53
English (166)	793	10.59
European (94)	94	1.26
Finnish (8)	30	0.40
French, ex. Basque (25)	368	4.91
French Canadian (11)	130	1.74
German (574)	1,886	25.19
Greek (24)	85	1.14

*Notes: † The Census 2010 population figure is used to calculate the percentages in the Hispanic Origin and Race categories. Ancestry percentages are based on the 2006-2010 American Community Survey population (not shown); ‡ Numbers in parentheses indicate the number of people reporting a single ancestry; * Numbers in parentheses indicate the number of persons reporting this race alone, not in combination with any other race; Please refer to the Explanation of Data for more information.*

Hungarian (0)	21	0.28
Irish (326)	1,466	19.58
Italian (54)	299	3.99
Northern European (13)	13	0.17
Norwegian (172)	526	7.02
Polish (22)	128	1.71
Portuguese (0)	60	0.80
Romanian (0)	7	0.09
Russian (27)	129	1.72
Scandinavian (30)	54	0.72
Scotch-Irish (43)	144	1.92
Scottish (7)	150	2.00
Slovak (0)	11	0.15
Slovene (0)	23	0.31
Swedish (99)	506	6.76
Swiss (0)	3	0.04
Ukrainian (164)	202	2.70
Welsh (6)	86	1.15

Hispanic Origin	Population	%
Hispanic or Latino (of any race)	333	4.25
Central American, ex. Mexican	13	0.17
Costa Rican	2	0.03
Panamanian	9	0.11
Salvadoran	2	0.03
Cuban	21	0.27
Dominican Republic	3	0.04
Mexican	187	2.39
Puerto Rican	39	0.50
South American	27	0.34
Bolivian	1	0.01
Chilean	1	0.01
Colombian	13	0.17
Ecuadorian	4	0.05
Peruvian	7	0.09
Venezuelan	1	0.01
Other Hispanic or Latino	43	0.55

Race*	Population	%
African-American/Black (106)	188	2.40
Not Hispanic (98)	175	2.23
Hispanic (8)	13	0.17
American Indian/Alaska Native (406)	752	9.60
Not Hispanic (388)	702	8.96
Hispanic (18)	50	0.64
Alaska Athabascan *(Ala. Nat.)* (33)	76	0.97
Aleut *(Alaska Native)* (29)	65	0.83
Apache (2)	2	0.03
Blackfeet (6)	14	0.18
Cherokee (11)	74	0.94
Chickasaw (1)	1	0.01
Chippewa (7)	16	0.20
Choctaw (3)	4	0.05
Comanche (0)	3	0.04
Inupiat *(Alaska Native)* (48)	101	1.29
Iroquois (3)	5	0.06
Kiowa (0)	2	0.03
Mexican American Ind. (1)	1	0.01
Navajo (1)	2	0.03
Osage (1)	1	0.01
Potawatomi (1)	5	0.06
Puget Sound Salish (0)	2	0.03
Seminole (4)	5	0.06
Shoshone (1)	3	0.04
Sioux (5)	17	0.22
Tlingit-Haida *(Alaska Native)* (33)	49	0.63
Tsimshian *(Alaska Native)* (3)	3	0.04
Yakama (1)	3	0.04
Yaqui (0)	1	0.01
Yup'ik *(Alaska Native)* (67)	90	1.15
Asian (167)	252	3.22
Not Hispanic (164)	248	3.17
Hispanic (3)	4	0.05
Cambodian (2)	8	0.10
Chinese, ex. Taiwanese (7)	14	0.18
Filipino (62)	103	1.32
Indian (3)	4	0.05
Japanese (6)	25	0.32
Korean (51)	66	0.84
Laotian (8)	8	0.10
Thai (12)	19	0.24
Vietnamese (9)	15	0.19
Hawaii Native/Pacific Islander (19)	39	0.50
Not Hispanic (18)	35	0.45
Hispanic (1)	4	0.05
Guamanian/Chamorro (1)	6	0.08
Native Hawaiian (11)	17	0.22
Samoan (5)	8	0.10
Tongan (1)	2	0.03
White (6,529)	7,004	89.44
Not Hispanic (6,368)	6,784	86.63
Hispanic (161)	220	2.81

*Notes: † The Census 2010 population figure is used to calculate the percentages in the Hispanic Origin and Race categories. Ancestry percentages are based on the 2006-2010 American Community Survey population (not shown); ‡ Numbers in parentheses indicate the number of people reporting a single ancestry; * Numbers in parentheses indicate the number of persons reporting this race alone, not in combination with any other race; Please refer to the Explanation of Data for more information.*

ARIZONA

Place Type: State
Population: 6,392,017†

Ancestry‡	Population	%
Afghan (1,304)	1,386	0.02
African, Sub-Saharan (23,304)	28,150	0.45
African (10,387)	13,653	0.22
Cape Verdean (139)	263	<0.01
Ethiopian (1,255)	1,489	0.02
Ghanaian (614)	625	0.01
Kenyan (546)	616	0.01
Liberian (591)	690	0.01
Nigerian (1,925)	2,218	0.04
Senegalese (15)	15	<0.01
Sierra Leonean (29)	96	<0.01
Somalian (3,007)	3,028	0.05
South African (1,174)	1,570	0.03
Sudanese (1,571)	1,651	0.03
Ugandan (86)	86	<0.01
Zimbabwean (50)	59	<0.01
Other Sub-Saharan African (1,915)	2,091	0.03
Albanian (2,482)	2,656	0.04
Alsatian (61)	145	<0.01
American (272,761)	272,761	4.37
Arab (20,766)	29,862	0.48
Arab (3,555)	4,690	0.08
Egyptian (1,118)	1,788	0.03
Iraqi (4,613)	5,224	0.08
Jordanian (1,114)	1,279	0.02
Lebanese (5,406)	9,427	0.15
Moroccan (290)	490	0.01
Palestinian (653)	851	0.01
Syrian (1,599)	2,959	0.05
Other Arab (2,418)	3,154	0.05
Armenian (3,558)	5,863	0.09
Assyrian/Chaldean/Syriac (2,544)	2,956	0.05
Australian (921)	1,965	0.03
Austrian (4,051)	14,542	0.23
Basque (765)	1,969	0.03
Belgian (2,195)	6,568	0.11
Brazilian (1,123)	2,220	0.04
British (13,931)	25,456	0.41
Bulgarian (1,135)	1,750	0.03
Cajun (644)	1,101	0.02
Canadian (11,540)	20,054	0.32
Carpatho Rusyn (14)	85	<0.01
Celtic (517)	1,245	0.02
Croatian (3,286)	8,595	0.14
Cypriot (45)	54	<0.01
Czech (7,994)	29,168	0.47
Czechoslovakian (3,229)	6,850	0.11
Danish (12,935)	45,625	0.73
Dutch (25,649)	103,144	1.65
Eastern European (5,032)	5,805	0.09
English (209,593)	630,710	10.10
Estonian (207)	395	0.01
European (56,375)	63,900	1.02
Finnish (5,117)	13,597	0.22
French, ex. Basque (29,817)	179,366	2.87
French Canadian (15,135)	34,483	0.55
German (325,226)	1,011,650	16.19
German Russian (154)	406	0.01
Greek (9,728)	24,950	0.40
Guyanese (153)	299	<0.01
Hungarian (10,559)	30,350	0.49
Icelander (536)	1,449	0.02
Iranian (5,331)	7,024	0.11
Irish (177,374)	667,632	10.69
Israeli (879)	1,625	0.03
Italian (116,661)	290,274	4.65
Latvian (766)	1,588	0.03
Lithuanian (4,504)	13,206	0.21
Luxemburger (580)	1,492	0.02
Macedonian (297)	542	0.01
Maltese (507)	985	0.02
New Zealander (157)	495	0.01
Northern European (4,572)	5,102	0.08
Norwegian (44,561)	117,455	1.88
Pennsylvania German (1,911)	3,475	0.06
Polish (55,168)	161,575	2.59
Portuguese (6,744)	16,847	0.27
Romanian (8,179)	13,286	0.21
Russian (22,668)	58,691	0.94
Scandinavian (9,056)	18,210	0.29
Scotch-Irish (38,133)	103,566	1.66
Scottish (40,467)	130,243	2.08
Serbian (2,929)	4,909	0.08
Slavic (994)	2,540	0.04
Slovak (3,882)	10,327	0.17
Slovene (982)	2,595	0.04
Swedish (30,186)	109,020	1.75
Swiss (4,587)	20,063	0.32
Turkish (1,574)	2,477	0.04
Ukrainian (6,115)	14,120	0.23
Welsh (9,291)	44,751	0.72
West Indian, ex. Hispanic (4,478)	7,702	0.12
Bahamian (55)	118	<0.01
Barbadian (180)	193	<0.01
Belizean (290)	441	0.01
Bermudan (46)	78	<0.01
British West Indian (154)	276	<0.01
Dutch West Indian (132)	751	0.01
Haitian (489)	792	0.01
Jamaican (2,005)	3,184	0.05
Trinidadian/Tobagonian (413)	680	0.01
U.S. Virgin Islander (50)	88	<0.01
West Indian (560)	997	0.02
Other West Indian (104)	104	<0.01
Yugoslavian (7,918)	11,598	0.19

Hispanic Origin	Population	%
Hispanic or Latino (of any race)	1,895,149	29.65
Central American, ex. Mexican	36,642	0.57
Costa Rican	1,573	0.02
Guatemalan	13,426	0.21
Honduran	3,968	0.06
Nicaraguan	2,813	0.04
Panamanian	2,251	0.04
Salvadoran	12,225	0.19
Other Central American	386	0.01
Cuban	10,692	0.17
Dominican Republic	3,103	0.05
Mexican	1,657,668	25.93
Puerto Rican	34,787	0.54
South American	21,895	0.34
Argentinean	2,775	0.04
Bolivian	750	0.01
Chilean	1,955	0.03
Colombian	6,706	0.10
Ecuadorian	2,516	0.04
Paraguayan	175	<0.01
Peruvian	4,658	0.07
Uruguayan	422	0.01
Venezuelan	1,707	0.03
Other South American	231	<0.01
Other Hispanic or Latino	130,362	2.04

Race*	Population	%
African-American/Black (259,008)	318,665	4.99
Not Hispanic (239,101)	283,083	4.43
Hispanic (19,907)	35,582	0.56
Am. Indian/Alaska Native (296,529)	353,386	5.53
Not Hispanic (257,426)	294,027	4.60
Hispanic (39,103)	59,359	0.93
Alaska Athabascan *(Ala. Nat.)* (143)	222	<0.01
Aleut *(Alaska Native)* (128)	218	<0.01
Apache (24,987)	28,149	0.44
Arapaho (116)	185	<0.01
Blackfeet (351)	1,536	0.02
Canadian/French Am. Ind. (129)	298	<0.01
Central American Ind. (142)	233	<0.01
Cherokee (3,029)	11,178	0.17
Cheyenne (179)	328	0.01
Chickasaw (388)	848	0.01
Chippewa (955)	1,930	0.03
Choctaw (1,539)	3,516	0.06
Colville (72)	98	<0.01
Comanche (218)	469	0.01
Cree (79)	194	<0.01
Creek (416)	1,022	0.02
Crow (118)	235	<0.01
Delaware (83)	226	<0.01
Hopi (9,681)	11,612	0.18
Houma (12)	21	<0.01
Inupiat *(Alaska Native)* (232)	358	0.01
Iroquois (593)	1,275	0.02
Kiowa (199)	348	0.01
Lumbee (128)	215	<0.01
Menominee (61)	90	<0.01
Mexican American Ind. (3,939)	5,796	0.09
Navajo (131,367)	140,263	2.19
Osage (118)	312	<0.01
Ottawa (67)	164	<0.01
Paiute (466)	667	0.01
Pima (19,455)	22,119	0.35
Potawatomi (330)	574	0.01
Pueblo (1,468)	2,270	0.04
Puget Sound Salish (81)	161	<0.01
Seminole (124)	358	0.01
Shoshone (224)	378	0.01
Sioux (1,826)	3,478	0.05
South American Ind. (173)	411	0.01
Spanish American Ind. (332)	465	0.01
Tlingit-Haida *(Alaska Native)* (190)	325	0.01
Tohono O'Odham (16,829)	19,001	0.30
Tsimshian *(Alaska Native)* (17)	37	<0.01
Ute (195)	338	0.01
Yakama (53)	97	<0.01
Yaqui (14,215)	17,362	0.27
Yuman (4,509)	5,490	0.09
Yup'ik *(Alaska Native)* (69)	131	<0.01
Asian (176,695)	230,907	3.61
Not Hispanic (170,509)	212,889	3.33
Hispanic (6,186)	18,018	0.28
Bangladeshi (1,053)	1,161	0.02
Bhutanese (1,007)	1,210	0.02
Burmese (2,403)	2,675	0.04
Cambodian (2,079)	2,635	0.04
Chinese, ex. Taiwanese (30,688)	40,507	0.63
Filipino (35,013)	53,067	0.83
Hmong (181)	229	<0.01
Indian (36,047)	40,510	0.63
Indonesian (879)	1,602	0.03
Japanese (9,152)	19,611	0.31
Korean (15,022)	21,125	0.33
Laotian (1,893)	2,388	0.04
Malaysian (200)	365	0.01
Nepalese (638)	836	0.01
Pakistani (2,596)	3,008	0.05
Sri Lankan (479)	587	0.01
Taiwanese (1,582)	1,920	0.03
Thai (3,140)	4,977	0.08
Vietnamese (24,216)	27,872	0.44
Hawaii Native/Pacific Islander (12,648)	25,106	0.39
Not Hispanic (10,959)	20,167	0.32
Hispanic (1,689)	4,939	0.08
Fijian (146)	237	<0.01
Guamanian/Chamorro (2,646)	4,276	0.07
Marshallese (600)	666	0.01
Native Hawaiian (3,837)	9,549	0.15
Samoan (2,000)	3,547	0.06
Tongan (1,239)	1,792	0.03
White (4,667,121)	4,852,961	75.92
Not Hispanic (3,695,647)	3,795,629	59.38
Hispanic (971,474)	1,057,332	16.54

*Notes: † The Census 2010 population figure is used to calculate the percentages in the Hispanic Origin and Race categories. Ancestry percentages are based on the 2006-2010 American Community Survey population (not shown); ‡ Numbers in parentheses indicate the number of people reporting a single ancestry; * Numbers in parentheses indicate the number of persons reporting this race alone, not in combination with any other race; Please refer to the Explanation of Data for more information.*

Anthem

Place Type: CDP
County: Maricopa
Population: 21,700†

Ancestry‡	Population	%
African, Sub-Saharan (37)	73	0.37
African (0)	11	0.06
South African (25)	25	0.13
Other Sub-Saharan African (12)	37	0.19
American (731)	731	3.69
Arab (54)	54	0.27
Arab (29)	29	0.15
Lebanese (12)	12	0.06
Syrian (13)	13	0.07
Armenian (0)	34	0.17
Assyrian/Chaldean/Syriac (12)	12	0.06
Austrian (0)	43	0.22
Belgian (12)	12	0.06
British (48)	89	0.45
Canadian (107)	172	0.87
Croatian (0)	37	0.19
Czech (20)	181	0.91
Czechoslovakian (13)	13	0.07
Danish (122)	454	2.29
Dutch (50)	309	1.56
Eastern European (27)	27	0.14
English (396)	2,082	10.50
European (142)	233	1.18
Finnish (13)	143	0.72
French, ex. Basque (169)	1,064	5.37
French Canadian (54)	181	0.91
German (1,261)	5,068	25.56
Greek (75)	309	1.56
Guyanese (18)	18	0.09
Hungarian (45)	111	0.56
Icelander (59)	59	0.30
Iranian (15)	45	0.23
Irish (910)	3,303	16.66
Israeli (9)	28	0.14
Italian (1,007)	2,379	12.00
Lithuanian (43)	140	0.71
New Zealander (10)	10	0.05
Norwegian (146)	683	3.44
Polish (290)	834	4.21
Portuguese (9)	148	0.75
Romanian (80)	141	0.71
Russian (45)	201	1.01
Scandinavian (10)	55	0.28
Scotch-Irish (151)	283	1.43
Scottish (158)	664	3.35
Serbian (61)	77	0.39
Slovak (17)	28	0.14
Slovene (0)	8	0.04
Swedish (127)	703	3.55
Swiss (7)	90	0.45
Ukrainian (33)	159	0.80
Welsh (34)	219	1.10
Yugoslavian (41)	41	0.21

Hispanic Origin	Population	%
Hispanic or Latino (of any race)	1,997	9.20
Central American, ex. Mexican	77	0.35
Costa Rican	10	0.05
Guatemalan	18	0.08
Honduran	4	0.02
Nicaraguan	8	0.04
Panamanian	10	0.05
Salvadoran	27	0.12
Cuban	27	0.12
Dominican Republic	4	0.02
Mexican	1,433	6.60
Puerto Rican	152	0.70
South American	99	0.46
Argentinean	10	0.05
Chilean	10	0.05
Colombian	30	0.14
Ecuadorian	19	0.09
Paraguayan	2	0.01
Peruvian	13	0.06
Uruguayan	1	<0.01
Venezuelan	14	0.06
Other Hispanic or Latino	205	0.94

Race*	Population	%
African-American/Black (410)	571	2.63
Not Hispanic (382)	525	2.42
Hispanic (28)	46	0.21
American Indian/Alaska Native (141)	273	1.26
Not Hispanic (100)	199	0.92
Hispanic (41)	74	0.34
Alaska Athabascan *(Ala. Nat.)* (1)	1	<0.01
Aleut *(Alaska Native)* (2)	4	0.02
Apache (5)	14	0.06
Blackfeet (1)	1	<0.01
Cherokee (19)	50	0.23
Chickasaw (0)	2	0.01
Chippewa (4)	5	0.02
Choctaw (0)	3	0.01
Hopi (5)	7	0.03
Inupiat *(Alaska Native)* (3)	6	0.03
Iroquois (0)	1	<0.01
Kiowa (0)	1	<0.01
Mexican American Ind. (3)	7	0.03
Navajo (41)	46	0.21
Osage (0)	5	0.02
Ottawa (0)	1	<0.01
Pima (1)	2	0.01
Potawatomi (0)	5	0.02
Pueblo (4)	4	0.02
Seminole (0)	3	0.01
Shoshone (1)	1	<0.01
Sioux (5)	6	0.03
South American Ind. (2)	2	0.01
Yuman (1)	1	<0.01
Yup'ik *(Alaska Native)* (0)	1	<0.01
Asian (566)	820	3.78
Not Hispanic (548)	757	3.49
Hispanic (18)	63	0.29
Burmese (2)	3	0.01
Chinese, ex. Taiwanese (59)	107	0.49
Filipino (190)	293	1.35
Hmong (2)	2	0.01
Indian (103)	126	0.58
Indonesian (4)	7	0.03
Japanese (31)	56	0.26
Korean (65)	98	0.45
Laotian (4)	6	0.03
Malaysian (0)	1	<0.01
Pakistani (3)	4	0.02
Taiwanese (3)	10	0.05
Thai (8)	10	0.05
Vietnamese (74)	91	0.42
Hawaii Native/Pacific Islander (33)	79	0.36
Not Hispanic (23)	52	0.24
Hispanic (10)	27	0.12
Guamanian/Chamorro (22)	30	0.14
Native Hawaiian (4)	15	0.07
Samoan (6)	21	0.10
White (19,463)	20,055	92.42
Not Hispanic (18,176)	18,606	85.74
Hispanic (1,287)	1,449	6.68

Apache Junction

Place Type: City
County: Pinal
Population: 35,840†

Ancestry‡	Population	%
African, Sub-Saharan (19)	19	0.06
African (19)	19	0.06
American (1,334)	1,334	3.93
Arab (7)	116	0.34
Lebanese (7)	58	0.17
Moroccan (0)	19	0.06
Syrian (0)	39	0.11
Austrian (39)	123	0.36
Basque (0)	30	0.09
Belgian (74)	162	0.48
British (55)	150	0.44
Canadian (101)	182	0.54
Croatian (0)	25	0.07
Czech (25)	110	0.32
Czechoslovakian (0)	20	0.06
Danish (93)	245	0.72
Dutch (169)	694	2.04
Eastern European (9)	9	0.03
English (1,221)	3,863	11.38
European (126)	126	0.37
Finnish (33)	80	0.24
French, ex. Basque (161)	1,442	4.25
French Canadian (155)	233	0.69
German (3,232)	8,914	26.25
Greek (0)	70	0.21
Hungarian (48)	113	0.33
Irish (678)	4,140	12.19
Italian (379)	1,612	4.75
Latvian (12)	16	0.05
Lithuanian (53)	53	0.16
Northern European (22)	22	0.06
Norwegian (445)	1,199	3.53
Pennsylvania German (0)	31	0.09
Polish (245)	1,054	3.10
Portuguese (75)	166	0.49
Romanian (230)	252	0.74
Russian (73)	235	0.69
Scandinavian (50)	82	0.24
Scotch-Irish (176)	668	1.97
Scottish (335)	910	2.68
Serbian (14)	14	0.04
Slovak (58)	137	0.40
Swedish (361)	1,236	3.64
Swiss (13)	74	0.22
Ukrainian (15)	95	0.28
Welsh (38)	283	0.83
West Indian, ex. Hispanic (22)	22	0.06
Jamaican (12)	12	0.04
Other West Indian (10)	10	0.03
Yugoslavian (4)	13	0.04

Hispanic Origin	Population	%
Hispanic or Latino (of any race)	5,153	14.38
Central American, ex. Mexican	107	0.30
Costa Rican	1	<0.01
Guatemalan	44	0.12
Honduran	10	0.03
Nicaraguan	8	0.02
Panamanian	2	0.01
Salvadoran	40	0.11
Other Central American	2	0.01
Cuban	17	0.05
Dominican Republic	2	0.01
Mexican	4,410	12.30
Puerto Rican	130	0.36
South American	57	0.16
Argentinean	6	0.02
Bolivian	11	0.03
Chilean	1	<0.01
Colombian	23	0.06
Ecuadorian	1	<0.01
Peruvian	10	0.03
Uruguayan	4	0.01
Venezuelan	1	<0.01
Other Hispanic or Latino	430	1.20

Race*	Population	%
African-American/Black (431)	654	1.82
Not Hispanic (392)	574	1.60
Hispanic (39)	80	0.22
American Indian/Alaska Native (398)	678	1.89
Not Hispanic (320)	533	1.49
Hispanic (78)	145	0.40
Alaska Athabascan *(Ala. Nat.)* (1)	5	0.01
Aleut *(Alaska Native)* (2)	6	0.02
Apache (19)	33	0.09
Arapaho (5)	5	0.01
Blackfeet (6)	21	0.06
Canadian/French Am. Ind. (1)	1	<0.01

*Notes: † The Census 2010 population figure is used to calculate the percentages in the Hispanic Origin and Race categories. Ancestry percentages are based on the 2006-2010 American Community Survey population (not shown); ‡ Numbers in parentheses indicate the number of people reporting a single ancestry; * Numbers in parentheses indicate the number of persons reporting this race alone, not in combination with any other race; Please refer to the Explanation of Data for more information.*

Cherokee (18)	64	0.18
Cheyenne (5)	6	0.02
Chickasaw (0)	4	0.01
Chippewa (9)	13	0.04
Choctaw (17)	27	0.08
Colville (1)	1	<0.01
Cree (1)	2	0.01
Creek (1)	8	0.02
Delaware (1)	2	0.01
Hopi (8)	10	0.03
Iroquois (2)	11	0.03
Menominee (1)	1	<0.01
Mexican American Ind. (5)	14	0.04
Navajo (62)	84	0.23
Ottawa (0)	1	<0.01
Paiute (1)	4	0.01
Pima (8)	16	0.04
Potawatomi (0)	3	0.01
Pueblo (4)	5	0.01
Seminole (0)	2	0.01
Shoshone (3)	3	0.01
Sioux (5)	16	0.04
South American Ind. (3)	7	0.02
Tlingit-Haida *(Alaska Native)* (0)	2	0.01
Tohono O'Odham (11)	17	0.05
Ute (1)	1	<0.01
Yaqui (27)	41	0.11
Yuman (4)	5	0.01
Asian (279)	441	1.23
Not Hispanic (266)	410	1.14
Hispanic (13)	31	0.09
Burmese (0)	1	<0.01
Chinese, ex. Taiwanese (19)	41	0.11
Filipino (145)	219	0.61
Hmong (1)	2	0.01
Indian (7)	13	0.04
Indonesian (0)	2	0.01
Japanese (28)	58	0.16
Korean (22)	40	0.11
Pakistani (1)	1	<0.01
Sri Lankan (0)	1	<0.01
Thai (15)	21	0.06
Vietnamese (33)	40	0.11
Hawaii Native/Pacific Islander (26)	101	0.28
Not Hispanic (25)	81	0.23
Hispanic (1)	20	0.06
Guamanian/Chamorro (2)	13	0.04
Native Hawaiian (11)	57	0.16
Samoan (4)	18	0.05
Tongan (4)	10	0.03
White (32,092)	32,844	91.64
Not Hispanic (29,130)	29,621	82.65
Hispanic (2,962)	3,223	8.99

Arizona City

Place Type: CDP
County: Pinal
Population: 10,475†

Ancestry‡	Population	%
American (16)	16	0.30
Austrian (0)	18	0.33
Czech (0)	44	0.82
Danish (35)	35	0.65
Dutch (57)	329	6.10
English (141)	520	9.64
Finnish (47)	47	0.87
French, ex. Basque (0)	421	7.80
German (427)	1,196	22.16
Icelander (22)	22	0.41
Irish (52)	692	12.82
Italian (67)	155	2.87
Norwegian (30)	30	0.56
Polish (34)	186	3.45
Portuguese (0)	28	0.52
Romanian (29)	29	0.54
Scotch-Irish (58)	209	3.87
Scottish (37)	103	1.91
Swedish (103)	149	2.76
Welsh (0)	50	0.93

Hispanic Origin	Population	%
Hispanic or Latino (of any race)	3,583	34.21
Central American, ex. Mexican	39	0.37
Costa Rican	6	0.06
Guatemalan	16	0.15
Honduran	7	0.07
Panamanian	1	0.01
Salvadoran	9	0.09
Cuban	14	0.13
Mexican	3,223	30.77
Puerto Rican	55	0.53
South American	11	0.11
Chilean	2	0.02
Colombian	3	0.03
Ecuadorian	4	0.04
Paraguayan	1	0.01
Peruvian	1	0.01
Other Hispanic or Latino	241	2.30

Race*	Population	%
African-American/Black (436)	557	5.32
Not Hispanic (406)	482	4.60
Hispanic (30)	75	0.72
American Indian/Alaska Native (364)	510	4.87
Not Hispanic (228)	300	2.86
Hispanic (136)	210	2.00
Apache (7)	13	0.12
Blackfeet (0)	1	0.01
Cherokee (10)	27	0.26
Cheyenne (0)	1	0.01
Chippewa (4)	6	0.06
Choctaw (6)	13	0.12
Colville (1)	1	0.01
Creek (1)	3	0.03
Hopi (5)	5	0.05
Iroquois (1)	2	0.02
Kiowa (0)	1	0.01
Mexican American Ind. (7)	10	0.10
Navajo (19)	25	0.24
Ottawa (2)	2	0.02
Pima (39)	55	0.53
Potawatomi (1)	1	0.01
Pueblo (6)	8	0.08
Sioux (4)	7	0.07
Spanish American Ind. (0)	1	0.01
Tlingit-Haida *(Alaska Native)* (1)	1	0.01
Tohono O'Odham (92)	119	1.14
Ute (2)	2	0.02
Yaqui (17)	24	0.23
Asian (56)	102	0.97
Not Hispanic (47)	77	0.74
Hispanic (9)	25	0.24
Bangladeshi (4)	4	0.04
Cambodian (0)	1	0.01
Chinese, ex. Taiwanese (9)	18	0.17
Filipino (24)	43	0.41
Indian (6)	9	0.09
Japanese (1)	7	0.07
Korean (4)	10	0.10
Laotian (0)	1	0.01
Thai (3)	7	0.07
Vietnamese (1)	1	0.01
Hawaii Native/Pacific Islander (22)	30	0.29
Not Hispanic (15)	20	0.19
Hispanic (7)	10	0.10
Guamanian/Chamorro (3)	3	0.03
Native Hawaiian (10)	15	0.14
Samoan (9)	12	0.11
White (7,715)	8,156	77.86
Not Hispanic (6,016)	6,182	59.02
Hispanic (1,699)	1,974	18.84

Avondale

Place Type: City
County: Maricopa
Population: 76,238†

Ancestry‡	Population	%
African, Sub-Saharan (662)	865	1.23
African (351)	527	0.75
Cape Verdean (0)	27	0.04
Kenyan (84)	84	0.12
Liberian (105)	105	0.15
Nigerian (122)	122	0.17
American (2,386)	2,386	3.40
Arab (34)	34	0.05
Arab (13)	13	0.02
Lebanese (21)	21	0.03
Assyrian/Chaldean/Syriac (55)	55	0.08
Austrian (35)	79	0.11
Basque (10)	10	0.01
Belgian (0)	14	0.02
British (165)	265	0.38
Cajun (60)	76	0.11
Canadian (67)	116	0.17
Celtic (0)	21	0.03
Czech (42)	186	0.26
Czechoslovakian (25)	190	0.27
Danish (50)	212	0.30
Dutch (155)	496	0.71
English (1,071)	3,541	5.04
European (519)	618	0.88
Finnish (34)	214	0.30
French, ex. Basque (192)	1,182	1.68
French Canadian (91)	264	0.38
German (2,326)	7,899	11.24
Greek (16)	30	0.04
Hungarian (26)	79	0.11
Icelander (12)	12	0.02
Irish (1,053)	4,997	7.11
Italian (559)	2,031	2.89
Latvian (37)	74	0.11
Lithuanian (12)	79	0.11
Norwegian (186)	850	1.21
Polish (320)	830	1.18
Portuguese (135)	413	0.59
Romanian (60)	100	0.14
Russian (74)	256	0.36
Scandinavian (40)	82	0.12
Scotch-Irish (170)	601	0.86
Scottish (167)	886	1.26
Serbian (56)	93	0.13
Slovak (31)	190	0.27
Slovene (10)	10	0.01
Swedish (95)	677	0.96
Swiss (0)	29	0.04
Ukrainian (40)	94	0.13
Welsh (0)	184	0.26
West Indian, ex. Hispanic (56)	179	0.25
Jamaican (41)	41	0.06
West Indian (15)	138	0.20
Yugoslavian (12)	42	0.06

Hispanic Origin	Population	%
Hispanic or Latino (of any race)	38,340	50.29
Central American, ex. Mexican	854	1.12
Costa Rican	26	0.03
Guatemalan	249	0.33
Honduran	79	0.10
Nicaraguan	75	0.10
Panamanian	53	0.07
Salvadoran	371	0.49
Other Central American	1	<0.01
Cuban	90	0.12
Dominican Republic	75	0.10
Mexican	34,041	44.65
Puerto Rican	614	0.81
South American	330	0.43
Argentinean	25	0.03
Bolivian	6	0.01
Chilean	24	0.03
Colombian	128	0.17
Ecuadorian	60	0.08
Paraguayan	1	<0.01
Peruvian	59	0.08
Uruguayan	4	0.01
Venezuelan	17	0.02

*Notes: † The Census 2010 population figure is used to calculate the percentages in the Hispanic Origin and Race categories. Ancestry percentages are based on the 2006-2010 American Community Survey population (not shown); ‡ Numbers in parentheses indicate the number of people reporting a single ancestry; * Numbers in parentheses indicate the number of persons reporting this race alone, not in combination with any other race; Please refer to the Explanation of Data for more information.*

Other South American	6	0.01
Other Hispanic or Latino	2,336	3.06

Race*	Population	%
African-American/Black (7,102)	8,272	10.85
Not Hispanic (6,643)	7,468	9.80
Hispanic (459)	804	1.05
American Indian/Alaska Native (1,264)	1,910	2.51
Not Hispanic (746)	1,098	1.44
Hispanic (518)	812	1.07
Aleut *(Alaska Native)* (0)	1	<0.01
Apache (49)	78	0.10
Arapaho (0)	1	<0.01
Blackfeet (2)	19	0.02
Central American Ind. (1)	1	<0.01
Cherokee (22)	135	0.18
Cheyenne (0)	1	<0.01
Chickasaw (9)	14	0.02
Chippewa (3)	8	0.01
Choctaw (31)	55	0.07
Colville (2)	2	<0.01
Comanche (8)	8	0.01
Creek (3)	8	0.01
Crow (0)	1	<0.01
Delaware (0)	4	0.01
Hopi (13)	26	0.03
Houma (1)	1	<0.01
Inupiat *(Alaska Native)* (2)	2	<0.01
Iroquois (5)	9	0.01
Kiowa (2)	3	<0.01
Lumbee (2)	6	0.01
Mexican American Ind. (83)	110	0.14
Navajo (311)	385	0.50
Ottawa (1)	2	<0.01
Paiute (0)	9	0.01
Pima (45)	67	0.09
Potawatomi (0)	4	0.01
Pueblo (8)	15	0.02
Puget Sound Salish (2)	2	<0.01
Seminole (0)	3	<0.01
Shoshone (0)	2	<0.01
Sioux (22)	36	0.05
South American Ind. (2)	2	<0.01
Spanish American Ind. (8)	10	0.01
Tlingit-Haida *(Alaska Native)* (13)	13	0.02
Tohono O'Odham (58)	71	0.09
Ute (0)	2	<0.01
Yaqui (77)	100	0.13
Yuman (8)	22	0.03
Yup'ik *(Alaska Native)* (1)	1	<0.01
Asian (2,684)	3,550	4.66
Not Hispanic (2,532)	3,144	4.12
Hispanic (152)	406	0.53
Bangladeshi (1)	1	<0.01
Cambodian (39)	51	0.07
Chinese, ex. Taiwanese (258)	414	0.54
Filipino (864)	1,245	1.63
Hmong (3)	5	0.01
Indian (327)	400	0.52
Indonesian (4)	10	0.01
Japanese (93)	223	0.29
Korean (180)	292	0.38
Laotian (75)	84	0.11
Malaysian (1)	3	<0.01
Nepalese (3)	3	<0.01
Pakistani (32)	36	0.05
Sri Lankan (2)	2	<0.01
Taiwanese (10)	10	0.01
Thai (41)	63	0.08
Vietnamese (589)	676	0.89
Hawaii Native/Pacific Islander (274)	574	0.75
Not Hispanic (208)	434	0.57
Hispanic (66)	140	0.18
Fijian (4)	5	0.01
Guamanian/Chamorro (85)	134	0.18
Marshallese (18)	18	0.02
Native Hawaiian (61)	205	0.27
Samoan (61)	87	0.11
Tongan (10)	10	0.01
White (44,272)	47,017	61.67
Not Hispanic (25,958)	27,311	35.82
Hispanic (18,314)	19,706	25.85

Buckeye

Place Type: Town
County: Maricopa
Population: 50,876†

Ancestry‡	Population	%
African, Sub-Saharan (259)	322	0.73
African (40)	85	0.19
Ethiopian (27)	27	0.06
Nigerian (192)	200	0.46
Sudanese (0)	10	0.02
American (3,009)	3,009	6.85
Arab (85)	105	0.24
Egyptian (0)	10	0.02
Iraqi (35)	35	0.08
Syrian (12)	22	0.05
Other Arab (38)	38	0.09
Armenian (29)	61	0.14
Australian (0)	8	0.02
Austrian (17)	100	0.23
British (130)	163	0.37
Canadian (88)	138	0.31
Celtic (0)	15	0.03
Croatian (0)	41	0.09
Cypriot (11)	11	0.03
Czech (11)	119	0.27
Czechoslovakian (9)	9	0.02
Danish (135)	380	0.87
Dutch (112)	432	0.98
Eastern European (19)	19	0.04
English (606)	2,537	5.78
European (679)	794	1.81
Finnish (11)	56	0.13
French, ex. Basque (128)	699	1.59
French Canadian (97)	226	0.51
German (1,788)	5,254	11.96
Greek (40)	138	0.31
Guyanese (0)	42	0.10
Hungarian (25)	143	0.33
Iranian (20)	20	0.05
Irish (1,291)	4,602	10.48
Israeli (0)	29	0.07
Italian (601)	1,430	3.26
Lithuanian (0)	38	0.09
Norwegian (206)	563	1.28
Pennsylvania German (0)	11	0.03
Polish (319)	854	1.94
Portuguese (18)	76	0.17
Romanian (4)	62	0.14
Russian (63)	169	0.38
Scandinavian (24)	36	0.08
Scotch-Irish (297)	772	1.76
Scottish (253)	534	1.22
Slavic (12)	25	0.06
Slovak (9)	9	0.02
Slovene (18)	18	0.04
Swedish (152)	462	1.05
Swiss (12)	87	0.20
Ukrainian (10)	125	0.28
Welsh (41)	173	0.39
West Indian, ex. Hispanic (27)	89	0.20
Bahamian (11)	11	0.03
Jamaican (0)	41	0.09
West Indian (16)	37	0.08
Yugoslavian (4)	4	0.01

Hispanic Origin	Population	%
Hispanic or Latino (of any race)	19,489	38.31
Central American, ex. Mexican	569	1.12
Costa Rican	10	0.02
Guatemalan	132	0.26
Honduran	70	0.14
Nicaraguan	44	0.09
Panamanian	30	0.06
Salvadoran	279	0.55
Other Central American	4	0.01
Cuban	79	0.16
Dominican Republic	27	0.05
Mexican	17,133	33.68
Puerto Rican	452	0.89
South American	181	0.36
Argentinean	19	0.04
Bolivian	5	0.01
Chilean	15	0.03
Colombian	32	0.06
Ecuadorian	44	0.09
Peruvian	45	0.09
Uruguayan	6	0.01
Venezuelan	14	0.03
Other South American	1	<0.01
Other Hispanic or Latino	1,048	2.06

Race*	Population	%
African-American/Black (3,618)	4,272	8.40
Not Hispanic (3,412)	3,841	7.55
Hispanic (206)	431	0.85
American Indian/Alaska Native (909)	1,321	2.60
Not Hispanic (602)	872	1.71
Hispanic (307)	449	0.88
Alaska Athabascan *(Ala. Nat.)* (1)	1	<0.01
Aleut *(Alaska Native)* (1)	1	<0.01
Apache (19)	29	0.06
Arapaho (0)	4	0.01
Blackfeet (1)	14	0.03
Canadian/French Am. Ind. (1)	1	<0.01
Central American Ind. (3)	3	0.01
Cherokee (34)	85	0.17
Cheyenne (3)	5	0.01
Chickasaw (0)	5	0.01
Chippewa (5)	12	0.02
Choctaw (13)	30	0.06
Colville (0)	1	<0.01
Comanche (2)	3	0.01
Cree (4)	4	0.01
Creek (1)	3	0.01
Delaware (0)	9	0.02
Hopi (16)	22	0.04
Inupiat *(Alaska Native)* (2)	3	0.01
Iroquois (2)	7	0.01
Kiowa (0)	1	<0.01
Mexican American Ind. (40)	60	0.12
Navajo (144)	176	0.35
Ottawa (1)	3	0.01
Paiute (4)	4	0.01
Pima (32)	40	0.08
Pueblo (6)	15	0.03
Puget Sound Salish (0)	2	<0.01
Seminole (2)	4	0.01
Shoshone (0)	5	0.01
Sioux (12)	21	0.04
South American Ind. (1)	2	<0.01
Spanish American Ind. (2)	2	<0.01
Tlingit-Haida *(Alaska Native)* (3)	5	0.01
Tohono O'Odham (23)	35	0.07
Tsimshian *(Alaska Native)* (1)	1	<0.01
Ute (0)	1	<0.01
Yakama (0)	4	0.01
Yaqui (32)	39	0.08
Yuman (16)	18	0.04
Asian (913)	1,346	2.65
Not Hispanic (849)	1,172	2.30
Hispanic (64)	174	0.34
Cambodian (33)	43	0.08
Chinese, ex. Taiwanese (57)	100	0.20
Filipino (341)	550	1.08
Indian (75)	97	0.19
Indonesian (2)	4	0.01
Japanese (34)	84	0.17
Korean (100)	147	0.29
Laotian (24)	33	0.06
Malaysian (1)	2	<0.01
Pakistani (7)	7	0.01
Sri Lankan (17)	17	0.03
Taiwanese (1)	1	<0.01
Thai (41)	56	0.11
Vietnamese (116)	140	0.28

*Notes: † The Census 2010 population figure is used to calculate the percentages in the Hispanic Origin and Race categories. Ancestry percentages are based on the 2006-2010 American Community Survey population (not shown); ‡ Numbers in parentheses indicate the number of people reporting a single ancestry; * Numbers in parentheses indicate the number of persons reporting this race alone, not in combination with any other race; Please refer to the Explanation of Data for more information.*

Hawaii Native/Pacific Islander (100)	202	0.40
Not Hispanic (79)	151	0.30
Hispanic (21)	51	0.10
Guamanian/Chamorro (44)	71	0.14
Marshallese (1)	1	<0.01
Native Hawaiian (15)	61	0.12
Samoan (21)	36	0.07
White (33,424)	35,259	69.30
Not Hispanic (25,375)	26,238	51.57
Hispanic (8,049)	9,021	17.73

Bullhead City

Place Type: City
County: Mohave
Population: 39,540†

Ancestry‡	Population	%
African, Sub-Saharan (0)	95	0.24
South African (0)	95	0.24
American (2,167)	2,167	5.43
Arab (26)	95	0.24
Lebanese (26)	83	0.21
Syrian (0)	12	0.03
Armenian (68)	100	0.25
Assyrian/Chaldean/Syriac (20)	20	0.05
Austrian (13)	46	0.12
Belgian (12)	50	0.13
British (37)	37	0.09
Bulgarian (0)	29	0.07
Canadian (73)	99	0.25
Croatian (65)	65	0.16
Czech (9)	197	0.49
Czechoslovakian (17)	17	0.04
Danish (48)	208	0.52
Dutch (181)	960	2.40
English (1,629)	4,438	11.12
European (144)	144	0.36
Finnish (87)	197	0.49
French, ex. Basque (464)	1,761	4.41
French Canadian (213)	297	0.74
German (2,653)	8,344	20.90
Greek (0)	236	0.59
Hungarian (76)	139	0.35
Irish (1,517)	5,826	14.59
Italian (1,045)	2,490	6.24
Lithuanian (25)	119	0.30
Northern European (33)	33	0.08
Norwegian (500)	1,176	2.95
Pennsylvania German (0)	9	0.02
Polish (599)	1,330	3.33
Portuguese (69)	246	0.62
Romanian (31)	42	0.11
Russian (76)	459	1.15
Scandinavian (31)	120	0.30
Scotch-Irish (280)	709	1.78
Scottish (341)	990	2.48
Serbian (0)	28	0.07
Slovak (0)	19	0.05
Swedish (287)	958	2.40
Swiss (65)	500	1.25
Ukrainian (13)	37	0.09
Welsh (28)	144	0.36
West Indian, ex. Hispanic (0)	35	0.09
Belizean (0)	21	0.05
Dutch West Indian (0)	14	0.04
Yugoslavian (0)	12	0.03

Hispanic Origin	Population	%
Hispanic or Latino (of any race)	9,386	23.74
Central American, ex. Mexican	192	0.49
Costa Rican	7	0.02
Guatemalan	77	0.19
Honduran	10	0.03
Nicaraguan	3	0.01
Panamanian	8	0.02
Salvadoran	87	0.22
Cuban	43	0.11
Mexican	8,203	20.75
Puerto Rican	161	0.41
South American	95	0.24
Argentinean	19	0.05
Bolivian	1	<0.01
Chilean	5	0.01
Colombian	16	0.04
Ecuadorian	13	0.03
Peruvian	40	0.10
Venezuelan	1	<0.01
Other Hispanic or Latino	692	1.75

Race*	Population	%
African-American/Black (508)	725	1.83
Not Hispanic (466)	650	1.64
Hispanic (42)	75	0.19
American Indian/Alaska Native (450)	797	2.02
Not Hispanic (302)	568	1.44
Hispanic (148)	229	0.58
Alaska Athabascan *(Ala. Nat.)* (0)	2	0.01
Aleut *(Alaska Native)* (4)	4	0.01
Apache (22)	33	0.08
Arapaho (3)	5	0.01
Blackfeet (7)	21	0.05
Canadian/French Am. Ind. (1)	2	0.01
Cherokee (50)	127	0.32
Cheyenne (0)	1	<0.01
Chickasaw (4)	8	0.02
Chippewa (5)	8	0.02
Choctaw (12)	23	0.06
Colville (1)	1	<0.01
Comanche (0)	5	0.01
Cree (3)	3	0.01
Creek (9)	10	0.03
Delaware (1)	1	<0.01
Hopi (6)	8	0.02
Inupiat *(Alaska Native)* (4)	4	0.01
Iroquois (3)	5	0.01
Kiowa (1)	2	0.01
Lumbee (4)	4	0.01
Mexican American Ind. (26)	33	0.08
Navajo (46)	65	0.16
Osage (0)	1	<0.01
Paiute (5)	6	0.02
Pima (1)	1	<0.01
Pueblo (2)	6	0.02
Puget Sound Salish (1)	1	<0.01
Seminole (0)	1	<0.01
Sioux (12)	24	0.06
South American Ind. (0)	1	<0.01
Spanish American Ind. (1)	2	0.01
Tlingit-Haida *(Alaska Native)* (2)	2	0.01
Tohono O'Odham (0)	1	<0.01
Ute (2)	3	0.01
Yaqui (6)	12	0.03
Yuman (29)	42	0.11
Yup'ik *(Alaska Native)* (2)	4	0.01
Asian (556)	798	2.02
Not Hispanic (529)	719	1.82
Hispanic (27)	79	0.20
Burmese (2)	9	0.02
Cambodian (16)	22	0.06
Chinese, ex. Taiwanese (62)	93	0.24
Filipino (211)	300	0.76
Indian (35)	53	0.13
Indonesian (8)	16	0.04
Japanese (69)	122	0.31
Korean (41)	61	0.15
Pakistani (29)	31	0.08
Sri Lankan (2)	4	0.01
Taiwanese (1)	1	<0.01
Thai (21)	27	0.07
Vietnamese (28)	39	0.10
Hawaii Native/Pacific Islander (59)	154	0.39
Not Hispanic (55)	122	0.31
Hispanic (4)	32	0.08
Guamanian/Chamorro (9)	25	0.06
Native Hawaiian (23)	63	0.16
Samoan (17)	32	0.08
White (32,367)	33,431	84.55
Not Hispanic (28,127)	28,702	72.59
Hispanic (4,240)	4,729	11.96

Camp Verde

Place Type: Town
County: Yavapai
Population: 10,873†

Ancestry‡	Population	%
American (824)	824	7.54
Australian (0)	13	0.12
Belgian (0)	26	0.24
British (19)	27	0.25
Czech (12)	35	0.32
Czechoslovakian (0)	10	0.09
Danish (11)	171	1.57
Dutch (44)	207	1.90
English (332)	1,458	13.35
European (40)	53	0.49
Finnish (0)	12	0.11
French, ex. Basque (0)	532	4.87
French Canadian (45)	54	0.49
German (597)	2,181	19.97
Hungarian (0)	11	0.10
Irish (565)	2,040	18.68
Italian (91)	319	2.92
Northern European (8)	8	0.07
Norwegian (68)	169	1.55
Polish (164)	276	2.53
Portuguese (0)	10	0.09
Russian (9)	52	0.48
Scandinavian (0)	85	0.78
Scotch-Irish (75)	184	1.68
Scottish (69)	164	1.50
Swedish (95)	583	5.34
Welsh (0)	17	0.16
West Indian, ex. Hispanic (15)	15	0.14
Dutch West Indian (15)	15	0.14

Hispanic Origin	Population	%
Hispanic or Latino (of any race)	1,779	16.36
Central American, ex. Mexican	28	0.26
Guatemalan	4	0.04
Honduran	6	0.06
Panamanian	1	0.01
Salvadoran	17	0.16
Cuban	9	0.08
Dominican Republic	1	0.01
Mexican	1,445	13.29
Puerto Rican	21	0.19
South American	7	0.06
Argentinean	3	0.03
Bolivian	1	0.01
Colombian	1	0.01
Ecuadorian	1	0.01
Peruvian	1	0.01
Other Hispanic or Latino	268	2.46

Race*	Population	%
African-American/Black (50)	112	1.03
Not Hispanic (45)	99	0.91
Hispanic (5)	13	0.12
American Indian/Alaska Native (788)	1,059	9.74
Not Hispanic (645)	858	7.89
Hispanic (143)	201	1.85
Aleut *(Alaska Native)* (0)	1	0.01
Apache (37)	61	0.56
Blackfeet (0)	6	0.06
Canadian/French Am. Ind. (0)	1	0.01
Central American Ind. (1)	4	0.04
Cherokee (13)	56	0.52
Cheyenne (0)	1	0.01
Chickasaw (2)	4	0.04
Chippewa (2)	4	0.04
Choctaw (15)	27	0.25
Comanche (0)	1	0.01
Creek (1)	6	0.06
Crow (4)	6	0.06
Hopi (26)	56	0.52
Inupiat *(Alaska Native)* (0)	3	0.03
Iroquois (6)	12	0.11
Mexican American Ind. (5)	10	0.09

*Notes: † The Census 2010 population figure is used to calculate the percentages in the Hispanic Origin and Race categories. Ancestry percentages are based on the 2006-2010 American Community Survey population (not shown); ‡ Numbers in parentheses indicate the number of people reporting a single ancestry; * Numbers in parentheses indicate the number of persons reporting this race alone, not in combination with any other race; Please refer to the Explanation of Data for more information.*

Navajo (77)	97	0.89
Osage (1)	3	0.03
Pima (5)	13	0.12
Potawatomi (4)	5	0.05
Pueblo (2)	4	0.04
Shoshone (0)	4	0.04
Sioux (4)	5	0.05
Spanish American Ind. (1)	1	0.01
Tlingit-Haida *(Alaska Native)* (0)	1	0.01
Tohono O'Odham (2)	2	0.02
Yaqui (6)	6	0.06
Yuman (18)	37	0.34
Asian (46)	93	0.86
Not Hispanic (43)	82	0.75
Hispanic (3)	11	0.10
Chinese, ex. Taiwanese (18)	26	0.24
Filipino (12)	28	0.26
Indian (4)	5	0.05
Indonesian (1)	3	0.03
Japanese (2)	19	0.17
Korean (3)	5	0.05
Laotian (2)	2	0.02
Thai (1)	1	0.01
Vietnamese (0)	1	0.01
Hawaii Native/Pacific Islander (13)	47	0.43
Not Hispanic (12)	39	0.36
Hispanic (1)	8	0.07
Native Hawaiian (9)	40	0.37
Samoan (0)	2	0.02
Tongan (3)	4	0.04
White (8,885)	9,270	85.26
Not Hispanic (8,040)	8,306	76.39
Hispanic (845)	964	8.87

Casa Grande

Place Type: City
County: Pinal
Population: 48,571†

Ancestry‡	Population	%
Afghan (37)	37	0.09
African, Sub-Saharan (67)	74	0.17
African (67)	74	0.17
American (1,603)	1,603	3.72
Arab (32)	44	0.10
Arab (0)	12	0.03
Egyptian (15)	15	0.03
Syrian (17)	17	0.04
Armenian (0)	13	0.03
Austrian (24)	31	0.07
Basque (0)	15	0.03
Belgian (0)	36	0.08
British (155)	215	0.50
Canadian (94)	135	0.31
Croatian (7)	55	0.13
Czech (26)	37	0.09
Czechoslovakian (37)	64	0.15
Danish (111)	261	0.61
Dutch (181)	768	1.78
English (1,059)	3,399	7.90
European (268)	268	0.62
Finnish (46)	77	0.18
French, ex. Basque (122)	1,016	2.36
French Canadian (150)	279	0.65
German (2,744)	6,785	15.76
Greek (14)	27	0.06
Hungarian (41)	180	0.42
Icelander (9)	9	0.02
Iranian (35)	35	0.08
Irish (1,153)	4,180	9.71
Italian (251)	756	1.76
Lithuanian (36)	44	0.10
Norwegian (347)	938	2.18
Pennsylvania German (0)	37	0.09
Polish (343)	660	1.53
Portuguese (13)	102	0.24
Romanian (33)	33	0.08
Russian (32)	213	0.49
Scandinavian (0)	42	0.10
Scotch-Irish (200)	547	1.27
Scottish (271)	831	1.93
Serbian (0)	18	0.04
Slavic (0)	43	0.10
Slovene (13)	13	0.03
Swedish (157)	758	1.76
Swiss (17)	87	0.20
Turkish (15)	15	0.03
Ukrainian (56)	67	0.16
Welsh (15)	217	0.50
West Indian, ex. Hispanic (75)	175	0.41
British West Indian (14)	52	0.12
Jamaican (48)	65	0.15
U.S. Virgin Islander (13)	51	0.12
West Indian (0)	7	0.02

Hispanic Origin	Population	%
Hispanic or Latino (of any race)	18,932	38.98
Central American, ex. Mexican	225	0.46
Costa Rican	7	0.01
Guatemalan	28	0.06
Honduran	34	0.07
Nicaraguan	21	0.04
Panamanian	17	0.04
Salvadoran	117	0.24
Other Central American	1	<0.01
Cuban	60	0.12
Dominican Republic	33	0.07
Mexican	16,939	34.87
Puerto Rican	280	0.58
South American	156	0.32
Argentinean	5	0.01
Bolivian	9	0.02
Chilean	28	0.06
Colombian	48	0.10
Ecuadorian	23	0.05
Peruvian	33	0.07
Uruguayan	2	<0.01
Venezuelan	8	0.02
Other Hispanic or Latino	1,239	2.55

Race*	Population	%
African-American/Black (2,245)	2,858	5.88
Not Hispanic (1,998)	2,373	4.89
Hispanic (247)	485	1.00
American Indian/Alaska Native (2,232)	3,077	6.34
Not Hispanic (1,620)	2,004	4.13
Hispanic (612)	1,073	2.21
Alaska Athabascan *(Ala. Nat.)* (3)	3	0.01
Aleut *(Alaska Native)* (0)	1	<0.01
Apache (23)	45	0.09
Blackfeet (16)	24	0.05
Canadian/French Am. Ind. (1)	3	0.01
Central American Ind. (0)	1	<0.01
Cherokee (31)	93	0.19
Cheyenne (4)	10	0.02
Chickasaw (1)	7	0.01
Chippewa (20)	27	0.06
Choctaw (32)	58	0.12
Colville (1)	1	<0.01
Comanche (1)	2	<0.01
Cree (1)	2	<0.01
Creek (17)	26	0.05
Delaware (0)	2	<0.01
Hopi (21)	36	0.07
Iroquois (4)	7	0.01
Kiowa (2)	10	0.02
Lumbee (0)	2	<0.01
Menominee (2)	2	<0.01
Mexican American Ind. (48)	67	0.14
Navajo (135)	178	0.37
Osage (0)	2	<0.01
Ottawa (0)	1	<0.01
Paiute (1)	6	0.01
Pima (373)	475	0.98
Potawatomi (6)	8	0.02
Pueblo (6)	6	0.01
Puget Sound Salish (0)	1	<0.01
Seminole (1)	1	<0.01
Sioux (14)	24	0.05
South American Ind. (3)	6	0.01
Spanish American Ind. (3)	3	0.01
Tlingit-Haida *(Alaska Native)* (1)	2	<0.01
Tohono O'Odham (725)	873	1.80
Ute (3)	6	0.01
Yaqui (91)	140	0.29
Yuman (16)	34	0.07
Asian (875)	1,215	2.50
Not Hispanic (799)	1,030	2.12
Hispanic (76)	185	0.38
Bangladeshi (8)	9	0.02
Burmese (7)	7	0.01
Cambodian (4)	8	0.02
Chinese, ex. Taiwanese (66)	123	0.25
Filipino (426)	573	1.18
Hmong (4)	4	0.01
Indian (102)	114	0.23
Indonesian (2)	5	0.01
Japanese (27)	77	0.16
Korean (48)	93	0.19
Laotian (13)	16	0.03
Malaysian (2)	2	<0.01
Nepalese (2)	2	<0.01
Sri Lankan (0)	2	<0.01
Taiwanese (8)	8	0.02
Thai (9)	21	0.04
Vietnamese (117)	159	0.33
Hawaii Native/Pacific Islander (87)	198	0.41
Not Hispanic (74)	141	0.29
Hispanic (13)	57	0.12
Fijian (1)	1	<0.01
Guamanian/Chamorro (28)	44	0.09
Native Hawaiian (29)	84	0.17
Samoan (8)	13	0.03
Tongan (4)	7	0.01
White (32,687)	34,659	71.36
Not Hispanic (24,226)	24,884	51.23
Hispanic (8,461)	9,775	20.13

Casas Adobes

Place Type: CDP
County: Pima
Population: 66,795†

Ancestry‡	Population	%
African, Sub-Saharan (236)	244	0.36
African (157)	165	0.24
Kenyan (10)	10	0.01
Sudanese (20)	20	0.03
Other Sub-Saharan African (49)	49	0.07
Alsatian (0)	10	0.01
American (2,346)	2,346	3.47
Arab (255)	344	0.51
Arab (50)	50	0.07
Jordanian (6)	6	0.01
Lebanese (116)	138	0.20
Palestinian (17)	17	0.03
Syrian (21)	48	0.07
Other Arab (45)	85	0.13
Armenian (32)	86	0.13
Assyrian/Chaldean/Syriac (27)	27	0.04
Australian (45)	61	0.09
Austrian (30)	208	0.31
Belgian (59)	213	0.31
British (227)	382	0.56
Cajun (40)	40	0.06
Canadian (56)	193	0.29
Croatian (61)	110	0.16
Czech (112)	376	0.56
Czechoslovakian (33)	60	0.09
Danish (61)	634	0.94
Dutch (320)	1,554	2.30
Eastern European (31)	42	0.06
English (2,890)	8,394	12.40
Estonian (14)	14	0.02
European (615)	685	1.01
Finnish (54)	202	0.30
French, ex. Basque (322)	2,696	3.98
French Canadian (141)	372	0.55

*Notes: † The Census 2010 population figure is used to calculate the percentages in the Hispanic Origin and Race categories. Ancestry percentages are based on the 2006-2010 American Community Survey population (not shown); ‡ Numbers in parentheses indicate the number of people reporting a single ancestry; * Numbers in parentheses indicate the number of persons reporting this race alone, not in combination with any other race; Please refer to the Explanation of Data for more information.*

German (4,379)	13,838	20.44
Greek (153)	404	0.60
Hungarian (72)	273	0.40
Icelander (0)	16	0.02
Iranian (178)	221	0.33
Irish (2,138)	8,855	13.08
Israeli (0)	11	0.02
Italian (1,458)	4,048	5.98
Latvian (0)	11	0.02
Lithuanian (40)	169	0.25
Luxemburger (20)	35	0.05
New Zealander (0)	8	0.01
Northern European (139)	139	0.21
Norwegian (503)	1,493	2.21
Pennsylvania German (20)	37	0.05
Polish (603)	2,119	3.13
Portuguese (51)	216	0.32
Romanian (19)	122	0.18
Russian (352)	824	1.22
Scandinavian (31)	130	0.19
Scotch-Irish (504)	1,317	1.95
Scottish (670)	2,257	3.33
Serbian (28)	78	0.12
Slavic (0)	13	0.02
Slovak (80)	133	0.20
Slovene (10)	24	0.04
Swedish (603)	1,537	2.27
Swiss (240)	608	0.90
Turkish (0)	26	0.04
Ukrainian (68)	149	0.22
Welsh (156)	803	1.19
West Indian, ex. Hispanic (0)	51	0.08
Belizean (0)	9	0.01
Dutch West Indian (0)	42	0.06
Yugoslavian (22)	63	0.09

Hispanic Origin	Population	%
Hispanic or Latino (of any race)	13,956	20.89
Central American, ex. Mexican	197	0.29
Costa Rican	24	0.04
Guatemalan	62	0.09
Honduran	18	0.03
Nicaraguan	26	0.04
Panamanian	18	0.03
Salvadoran	48	0.07
Other Central American	1	<0.01
Cuban	104	0.16
Dominican Republic	36	0.05
Mexican	11,965	17.91
Puerto Rican	312	0.47
South American	286	0.43
Argentinean	38	0.06
Bolivian	13	0.02
Chilean	41	0.06
Colombian	63	0.09
Ecuadorian	28	0.04
Paraguayan	4	0.01
Peruvian	61	0.09
Uruguayan	7	0.01
Venezuelan	30	0.04
Other South American	1	<0.01
Other Hispanic or Latino	1,056	1.58

Race*	Population	%
African-American/Black (1,406)	1,970	2.95
Not Hispanic (1,275)	1,687	2.53
Hispanic (131)	283	0.42
American Indian/Alaska Native (637)	1,258	1.88
Not Hispanic (460)	818	1.22
Hispanic (177)	440	0.66
Alaska Athabascan *(Ala. Nat.)* (4)	4	0.01
Aleut *(Alaska Native)* (5)	5	0.01
Apache (29)	75	0.11
Blackfeet (2)	10	0.01
Canadian/French Am. Ind. (0)	2	<0.01
Central American Ind. (0)	1	<0.01
Cherokee (48)	186	0.28
Chickasaw (11)	16	0.02
Chippewa (12)	25	0.04
Choctaw (14)	34	0.05
Comanche (0)	1	<0.01
Cree (0)	1	<0.01
Creek (5)	10	0.01
Crow (1)	1	<0.01
Delaware (1)	3	<0.01
Hopi (7)	13	0.02
Houma (1)	1	<0.01
Iroquois (10)	19	0.03
Kiowa (0)	1	<0.01
Lumbee (4)	5	0.01
Menominee (0)	1	<0.01
Mexican American Ind. (16)	28	0.04
Navajo (134)	155	0.23
Osage (1)	1	<0.01
Ottawa (0)	1	<0.01
Paiute (1)	2	<0.01
Pima (3)	3	<0.01
Potawatomi (0)	1	<0.01
Pueblo (8)	16	0.02
Seminole (3)	9	0.01
Shoshone (4)	4	0.01
Sioux (15)	33	0.05
South American Ind. (5)	11	0.02
Spanish American Ind. (1)	3	<0.01
Tlingit-Haida *(Alaska Native)* (2)	2	<0.01
Tohono O'Odham (57)	80	0.12
Ute (1)	1	<0.01
Yakama (1)	1	<0.01
Yaqui (47)	86	0.13
Yuman (7)	7	0.01
Yup'ik *(Alaska Native)* (0)	1	<0.01
Asian (2,155)	2,842	4.25
Not Hispanic (2,087)	2,643	3.96
Hispanic (68)	199	0.30
Bangladeshi (6)	6	0.01
Burmese (59)	59	0.09
Cambodian (9)	15	0.02
Chinese, ex. Taiwanese (545)	694	1.04
Filipino (360)	555	0.83
Hmong (0)	2	<0.01
Indian (240)	293	0.44
Indonesian (8)	18	0.03
Japanese (166)	306	0.46
Korean (196)	265	0.40
Laotian (12)	14	0.02
Malaysian (10)	11	0.02
Nepalese (12)	12	0.02
Pakistani (37)	44	0.07
Sri Lankan (6)	9	0.01
Taiwanese (18)	24	0.04
Thai (31)	57	0.09
Vietnamese (314)	383	0.57
Hawaii Native/Pacific Islander (78)	209	0.31
Not Hispanic (65)	150	0.22
Hispanic (13)	59	0.09
Guamanian/Chamorro (25)	51	0.08
Marshallese (2)	2	<0.01
Native Hawaiian (26)	88	0.13
Samoan (13)	26	0.04
Tongan (2)	5	0.01
White (56,443)	58,570	87.69
Not Hispanic (47,575)	48,751	72.99
Hispanic (8,868)	9,819	14.70

Catalina

Place Type: CDP
County: Pima
Population: 7,569†

Ancestry‡	Population	%
African, Sub-Saharan (26)	26	0.32
African (9)	9	0.11
South African (17)	17	0.21
Albanian (16)	16	0.20
American (278)	278	3.39
Austrian (29)	29	0.35
British (43)	91	1.11
Czech (0)	16	0.20
Czechoslovakian (104)	104	1.27
Danish (24)	36	0.44
Dutch (181)	396	4.83
English (219)	963	11.74
European (26)	26	0.32
Finnish (25)	55	0.67
French, ex. Basque (76)	202	2.46
French Canadian (0)	29	0.35
German (538)	1,445	17.62
Greek (10)	10	0.12
Hungarian (51)	67	0.82
Irish (401)	1,309	15.96
Italian (224)	549	6.70
Northern European (16)	16	0.20
Norwegian (37)	48	0.59
Pennsylvania German (38)	72	0.88
Polish (62)	178	2.17
Russian (9)	23	0.28
Scandinavian (24)	41	0.50
Scotch-Irish (9)	97	1.18
Scottish (9)	248	3.02
Slavic (0)	13	0.16
Swedish (28)	76	0.93
Swiss (13)	28	0.34
Ukrainian (8)	8	0.10
Welsh (0)	29	0.35

Hispanic Origin	Population	%
Hispanic or Latino (of any race)	1,858	24.55
Central American, ex. Mexican	39	0.52
Guatemalan	9	0.12
Nicaraguan	9	0.12
Salvadoran	21	0.28
Cuban	7	0.09
Mexican	1,642	21.69
Puerto Rican	25	0.33
South American	16	0.21
Argentinean	3	0.04
Bolivian	2	0.03
Chilean	1	0.01
Colombian	4	0.05
Ecuadorian	2	0.03
Peruvian	2	0.03
Uruguayan	1	0.01
Venezuelan	1	0.01
Other Hispanic or Latino	129	1.70

Race*	Population	%
African-American/Black (71)	107	1.41
Not Hispanic (64)	92	1.22
Hispanic (7)	15	0.20
American Indian/Alaska Native (74)	154	2.03
Not Hispanic (46)	90	1.19
Hispanic (28)	64	0.85
Aleut *(Alaska Native)* (2)	2	0.03
Apache (5)	16	0.21
Blackfeet (1)	1	0.01
Cherokee (4)	22	0.29
Chickasaw (0)	1	0.01
Chippewa (2)	3	0.04
Choctaw (0)	1	0.01
Comanche (1)	3	0.04
Hopi (1)	6	0.08
Iroquois (2)	2	0.03
Mexican American Ind. (0)	11	0.15
Navajo (9)	11	0.15
Osage (0)	1	0.01
Pima (1)	1	0.01
Pueblo (0)	1	0.01
Puget Sound Salish (4)	4	0.05
Sioux (1)	3	0.04
South American Ind. (0)	1	0.01
Tohono O'Odham (2)	3	0.04
Ute (2)	2	0.03
Yaqui (6)	8	0.11
Yuman (1)	1	0.01
Asian (75)	132	1.74
Not Hispanic (64)	112	1.48
Hispanic (11)	20	0.26
Chinese, ex. Taiwanese (22)	34	0.45
Filipino (13)	27	0.36

*Notes: † The Census 2010 population figure is used to calculate the percentages in the Hispanic Origin and Race categories. Ancestry percentages are based on the 2006-2010 American Community Survey population (not shown); ‡ Numbers in parentheses indicate the number of people reporting a single ancestry; * Numbers in parentheses indicate the number of persons reporting this race alone, not in combination with any other race; Please refer to the Explanation of Data for more information.*

Indian (2)	5	0.07
Japanese (4)	13	0.17
Korean (8)	12	0.16
Laotian (1)	3	0.04
Taiwanese (3)	3	0.04
Thai (1)	1	0.01
Vietnamese (10)	15	0.20
Hawaii Native/Pacific Islander (6)	9	0.12
Not Hispanic (6)	9	0.12
Guamanian/Chamorro (5)	5	0.07
Native Hawaiian (0)	2	0.03
Samoan (1)	1	0.01
White (6,476)	6,696	88.47
Not Hispanic (5,398)	5,521	72.94
Hispanic (1,078)	1,175	15.52

Catalina Foothills

Place Type: CDP
County: Pima
Population: 50,796†

Ancestry‡	Population	%
African, Sub-Saharan (125)	158	0.30
African (0)	18	0.03
Nigerian (24)	24	0.05
South African (101)	116	0.22
Albanian (0)	12	0.02
Alsatian (8)	8	0.02
American (1,987)	1,987	3.78
Arab (314)	356	0.68
Arab (0)	16	0.03
Egyptian (26)	26	0.05
Iraqi (7)	7	0.01
Lebanese (103)	103	0.20
Moroccan (9)	9	0.02
Syrian (156)	182	0.35
Other Arab (13)	13	0.02
Armenian (115)	146	0.28
Australian (15)	27	0.05
Austrian (104)	309	0.59
Basque (25)	32	0.06
Belgian (83)	218	0.42
Brazilian (66)	83	0.16
British (461)	670	1.28
Canadian (223)	290	0.55
Croatian (7)	124	0.24
Czech (144)	429	0.82
Czechoslovakian (56)	56	0.11
Danish (200)	661	1.26
Dutch (181)	736	1.40
Eastern European (291)	300	0.57
English (2,177)	7,784	14.82
Estonian (0)	13	0.02
European (1,201)	1,273	2.42
Finnish (41)	59	0.11
French, ex. Basque (291)	1,667	3.17
French Canadian (174)	221	0.42
German (3,665)	11,056	21.05
German Russian (12)	12	0.02
Greek (223)	437	0.83
Hungarian (298)	601	1.14
Iranian (200)	216	0.41
Irish (1,891)	6,537	12.45
Israeli (12)	25	0.05
Italian (1,343)	2,987	5.69
Latvian (38)	46	0.09
Lithuanian (103)	286	0.54
Luxemburger (0)	14	0.03
New Zealander (13)	69	0.13
Northern European (249)	276	0.53
Norwegian (419)	1,316	2.51
Pennsylvania German (0)	24	0.05
Polish (759)	2,543	4.84
Portuguese (105)	175	0.33
Romanian (46)	135	0.26
Russian (1,067)	2,199	4.19
Scandinavian (173)	345	0.66
Scotch-Irish (434)	1,309	2.49
Scottish (518)	1,893	3.60
Serbian (0)	15	0.03
Slavic (46)	143	0.27
Slovak (25)	131	0.25
Slovene (0)	11	0.02
Swedish (390)	1,044	1.99
Swiss (39)	358	0.68
Turkish (17)	29	0.06
Ukrainian (113)	245	0.47
Welsh (107)	596	1.13
West Indian, ex. Hispanic (45)	54	0.10
Haitian (0)	9	0.02
Trinidadian/Tobagonian (45)	45	0.09
Yugoslavian (32)	59	0.11

Hispanic Origin	Population	%
Hispanic or Latino (of any race)	5,076	9.99
Central American, ex. Mexican	130	0.26
Costa Rican	11	0.02
Guatemalan	24	0.05
Honduran	24	0.05
Nicaraguan	9	0.02
Panamanian	21	0.04
Salvadoran	40	0.08
Other Central American	1	<0.01
Cuban	122	0.24
Dominican Republic	12	0.02
Mexican	3,924	7.73
Puerto Rican	162	0.32
South American	302	0.59
Argentinean	61	0.12
Bolivian	6	0.01
Chilean	46	0.09
Colombian	83	0.16
Ecuadorian	21	0.04
Paraguayan	2	<0.01
Peruvian	57	0.11
Uruguayan	5	0.01
Venezuelan	19	0.04
Other South American	2	<0.01
Other Hispanic or Latino	424	0.83

Race*	Population	%
African-American/Black (694)	918	1.81
Not Hispanic (655)	830	1.63
Hispanic (39)	88	0.17
American Indian/Alaska Native (213)	401	0.79
Not Hispanic (158)	280	0.55
Hispanic (55)	121	0.24
Alaska Athabascan *(Ala. Nat.)* (4)	4	0.01
Aleut *(Alaska Native)* (2)	2	<0.01
Apache (17)	26	0.05
Arapaho (0)	1	<0.01
Blackfeet (0)	3	0.01
Central American Ind. (1)	2	<0.01
Cherokee (16)	56	0.11
Chickasaw (2)	4	0.01
Chippewa (13)	14	0.03
Choctaw (5)	13	0.03
Creek (3)	6	0.01
Delaware (0)	2	<0.01
Hopi (3)	5	0.01
Inupiat *(Alaska Native)* (1)	1	<0.01
Iroquois (3)	5	0.01
Lumbee (2)	2	<0.01
Mexican American Ind. (10)	21	0.04
Navajo (24)	32	0.06
Osage (1)	3	0.01
Paiute (1)	1	<0.01
Pima (2)	2	<0.01
Potawatomi (0)	1	<0.01
Pueblo (1)	3	0.01
Puget Sound Salish (1)	1	<0.01
Seminole (1)	3	0.01
Sioux (2)	5	0.01
South American Ind. (7)	7	0.01
Tlingit-Haida *(Alaska Native)* (2)	3	0.01
Tohono O'Odham (13)	19	0.04
Yaqui (8)	17	0.03
Yup'ik *(Alaska Native)* (1)	1	<0.01
Asian (2,636)	3,191	6.28
Not Hispanic (2,601)	3,089	6.08
Hispanic (35)	102	0.20
Bangladeshi (33)	33	0.06
Cambodian (9)	9	0.02
Chinese, ex. Taiwanese (762)	914	1.80
Filipino (149)	251	0.49
Hmong (1)	1	<0.01
Indian (603)	676	1.33
Indonesian (2)	10	0.02
Japanese (195)	333	0.66
Korean (494)	576	1.13
Laotian (2)	2	<0.01
Malaysian (6)	12	0.02
Nepalese (4)	4	0.01
Pakistani (66)	66	0.13
Sri Lankan (21)	23	0.05
Taiwanese (46)	46	0.09
Thai (30)	40	0.08
Vietnamese (122)	147	0.29
Hawaii Native/Pacific Islander (31)	104	0.20
Not Hispanic (30)	96	0.19
Hispanic (1)	8	0.02
Fijian (4)	8	0.02
Guamanian/Chamorro (9)	18	0.04
Native Hawaiian (3)	26	0.05
Samoan (5)	5	0.01
Tongan (0)	4	0.01
White (45,147)	46,146	90.85
Not Hispanic (41,415)	42,125	82.93
Hispanic (3,732)	4,021	7.92

Chandler

Place Type: City
County: Maricopa
Population: 236,123†

Ancestry‡	Population	%
Afghan (33)	33	0.01
African, Sub-Saharan (1,443)	1,738	0.76
African (319)	595	0.26
Cape Verdean (22)	41	0.02
Ghanaian (140)	140	0.06
Nigerian (312)	312	0.14
Somalian (598)	598	0.26
Other Sub-Saharan African (52)	52	0.02
Alsatian (0)	10	<0.01
American (7,973)	7,973	3.47
Arab (928)	1,455	0.63
Arab (67)	109	0.05
Egyptian (18)	83	0.04
Iraqi (369)	403	0.18
Jordanian (112)	112	0.05
Lebanese (202)	405	0.18
Palestinian (9)	9	<0.01
Syrian (86)	153	0.07
Other Arab (65)	181	0.08
Armenian (373)	458	0.20
Assyrian/Chaldean/Syriac (83)	214	0.09
Australian (40)	126	0.05
Austrian (118)	486	0.21
Basque (17)	92	0.04
Belgian (123)	350	0.15
Brazilian (23)	105	0.05
British (607)	979	0.43
Bulgarian (0)	7	<0.01
Cajun (37)	37	0.02
Canadian (505)	834	0.36
Croatian (61)	314	0.14
Czech (307)	1,395	0.61
Czechoslovakian (98)	164	0.07
Danish (608)	2,230	0.97
Dutch (1,426)	4,546	1.98
Eastern European (178)	268	0.12
English (6,215)	22,635	9.86
Estonian (18)	18	0.01
European (2,562)	3,099	1.35
Finnish (114)	546	0.24
French, ex. Basque (1,063)	7,166	3.12
French Canadian (640)	1,529	0.67

*Notes: † The Census 2010 population figure is used to calculate the percentages in the Hispanic Origin and Race categories. Ancestry percentages are based on the 2006-2010 American Community Survey population (not shown); ‡ Numbers in parentheses indicate the number of people reporting a single ancestry; * Numbers in parentheses indicate the number of persons reporting this race alone, not in combination with any other race; Please refer to the Explanation of Data for more information.*

Ancestry	Population	%
German (12,829)	43,260	18.85
Greek (549)	1,441	0.63
Guyanese (24)	53	0.02
Hungarian (355)	1,451	0.63
Icelander (14)	143	0.06
Iranian (224)	412	0.18
Irish (7,491)	27,549	12.00
Israeli (101)	170	0.07
Italian (5,273)	13,856	6.04
Latvian (30)	162	0.07
Lithuanian (201)	455	0.20
Luxemburger (30)	64	0.03
Macedonian (36)	61	0.03
Maltese (58)	58	0.03
New Zealander (12)	37	0.02
Northern European (153)	153	0.07
Norwegian (1,733)	5,027	2.19
Pennsylvania German (144)	184	0.08
Polish (2,340)	7,404	3.23
Portuguese (203)	764	0.33
Romanian (266)	604	0.26
Russian (849)	2,273	0.99
Scandinavian (379)	824	0.36
Scotch-Irish (1,280)	3,742	1.63
Scottish (1,203)	4,917	2.14
Serbian (64)	126	0.05
Slavic (50)	116	0.05
Slovak (202)	721	0.31
Slovene (72)	97	0.04
Swedish (925)	4,164	1.81
Swiss (130)	735	0.32
Turkish (262)	282	0.12
Ukrainian (185)	597	0.26
Welsh (476)	1,641	0.71
West Indian, ex. Hispanic (241)	626	0.27
Bahamian (0)	40	0.02
Barbadian (40)	40	0.02
British West Indian (83)	158	0.07
Haitian (42)	103	0.04
Jamaican (76)	193	0.08
Trinidadian/Tobagonian (0)	77	0.03
West Indian (0)	15	0.01
Yugoslavian (240)	305	0.13

Hispanic Origin	Population	%
Hispanic or Latino (of any race)	51,808	21.94
Central American, ex. Mexican	1,418	0.60
Costa Rican	129	0.05
Guatemalan	479	0.20
Honduran	153	0.06
Nicaraguan	132	0.06
Panamanian	95	0.04
Salvadoran	428	0.18
Other Central American	2	<0.01
Cuban	371	0.16
Dominican Republic	221	0.09
Mexican	42,911	18.17
Puerto Rican	1,543	0.65
South American	1,265	0.54
Argentinean	130	0.06
Bolivian	45	0.02
Chilean	110	0.05
Colombian	434	0.18
Ecuadorian	112	0.05
Paraguayan	3	<0.01
Peruvian	281	0.12
Uruguayan	33	0.01
Venezuelan	103	0.04
Other South American	14	0.01
Other Hispanic or Latino	4,079	1.73

Race*	Population	%
African-American/Black (11,276)	13,924	5.90
Not Hispanic (10,580)	12,670	5.37
Hispanic (696)	1,254	0.53
American Indian/Alaska Native (3,589)	5,339	2.26
Not Hispanic (2,715)	3,806	1.61
Hispanic (874)	1,533	0.65
Alaska Athabascan *(Ala. Nat.)* (5)	7	<0.01
Aleut *(Alaska Native)* (7)	16	0.01
Apache (106)	184	0.08
Arapaho (0)	1	<0.01
Blackfeet (9)	37	0.02
Canadian/French Am. Ind. (16)	20	0.01
Central American Ind. (3)	5	<0.01
Cherokee (65)	291	0.12
Cheyenne (5)	10	<0.01
Chickasaw (4)	24	0.01
Chippewa (38)	70	0.03
Choctaw (41)	108	0.05
Colville (2)	2	<0.01
Comanche (3)	9	<0.01
Cree (0)	2	<0.01
Creek (13)	26	0.01
Crow (1)	7	<0.01
Delaware (0)	1	<0.01
Hopi (76)	108	0.05
Houma (0)	2	<0.01
Inupiat *(Alaska Native)* (2)	5	<0.01
Iroquois (40)	56	0.02
Kiowa (8)	15	0.01
Lumbee (5)	12	0.01
Menominee (0)	3	<0.01
Mexican American Ind. (111)	167	0.07
Navajo (985)	1,180	0.50
Osage (6)	11	<0.01
Ottawa (2)	8	<0.01
Paiute (18)	20	0.01
Pima (422)	529	0.22
Potawatomi (7)	13	0.01
Pueblo (46)	76	0.03
Puget Sound Salish (0)	1	<0.01
Seminole (3)	14	0.01
Shoshone (3)	5	<0.01
Sioux (59)	104	0.04
South American Ind. (4)	19	0.01
Spanish American Ind. (18)	20	0.01
Tlingit-Haida *(Alaska Native)* (1)	8	<0.01
Tohono O'Odham (100)	143	0.06
Ute (9)	10	<0.01
Yakama (2)	2	<0.01
Yaqui (277)	350	0.15
Yuman (30)	43	0.02
Yup'ik *(Alaska Native)* (3)	3	<0.01
Asian (19,401)	22,619	9.58
Not Hispanic (19,119)	21,753	9.21
Hispanic (282)	866	0.37
Bangladeshi (190)	210	0.09
Bhutanese (3)	4	<0.01
Burmese (31)	37	0.02
Cambodian (212)	282	0.12
Chinese, ex. Taiwanese (3,918)	4,702	1.99
Filipino (2,579)	3,615	1.53
Hmong (10)	12	0.01
Indian (5,592)	5,925	2.51
Indonesian (84)	139	0.06
Japanese (574)	1,212	0.51
Korean (1,757)	2,109	0.89
Laotian (106)	130	0.06
Malaysian (35)	51	0.02
Nepalese (33)	35	0.01
Pakistani (402)	455	0.19
Sri Lankan (40)	48	0.02
Taiwanese (274)	310	0.13
Thai (207)	334	0.14
Vietnamese (2,610)	2,943	1.25
Hawaii Native/Pacific Islander (405)	1,020	0.43
Not Hispanic (365)	844	0.36
Hispanic (40)	176	0.07
Fijian (4)	6	<0.01
Guamanian/Chamorro (96)	182	0.08
Marshallese (7)	10	<0.01
Native Hawaiian (102)	412	0.17
Samoan (77)	154	0.07
Tongan (39)	62	0.03
White (173,065)	180,690	76.52
Not Hispanic (145,724)	150,495	63.74
Hispanic (27,341)	30,195	12.79

Chino Valley

Place Type: Town
County: Yavapai
Population: 10,817†

Ancestry‡	Population	%
American (534)	534	5.01
Armenian (0)	12	0.11
Australian (10)	10	0.09
Belgian (0)	14	0.13
British (41)	80	0.75
Carpatho Rusyn (0)	19	0.18
Croatian (22)	37	0.35
Czech (0)	17	0.16
Danish (0)	34	0.32
Dutch (47)	292	2.74
English (551)	1,822	17.09
European (93)	105	0.98
Finnish (0)	11	0.10
French, ex. Basque (39)	404	3.79
French Canadian (80)	108	1.01
German (734)	2,606	24.44
Greek (42)	117	1.10
Hungarian (13)	102	0.96
Icelander (0)	28	0.26
Irish (516)	2,240	21.01
Italian (198)	579	5.43
Lithuanian (0)	45	0.42
Northern European (41)	41	0.38
Norwegian (115)	233	2.19
Polish (78)	304	2.85
Portuguese (47)	47	0.44
Russian (46)	58	0.54
Scandinavian (14)	14	0.13
Scotch-Irish (233)	354	3.32
Scottish (83)	327	3.07
Slavic (0)	17	0.16
Slovak (0)	45	0.42
Swedish (67)	321	3.01
Swiss (0)	33	0.31
Turkish (0)	3	0.03
Ukrainian (0)	38	0.36
Welsh (23)	183	1.72

Hispanic Origin	Population	%
Hispanic or Latino (of any race)	1,626	15.03
Central American, ex. Mexican	40	0.37
Guatemalan	13	0.12
Honduran	1	0.01
Panamanian	6	0.06
Salvadoran	18	0.17
Other Central American	2	0.02
Cuban	7	0.06
Mexican	1,370	12.67
Puerto Rican	32	0.30
South American	6	0.06
Argentinean	1	0.01
Chilean	2	0.02
Colombian	2	0.02
Peruvian	1	0.01
Other Hispanic or Latino	171	1.58

Race*	Population	%
African-American/Black (51)	85	0.79
Not Hispanic (46)	74	0.68
Hispanic (5)	11	0.10
American Indian/Alaska Native (100)	218	2.02
Not Hispanic (65)	147	1.36
Hispanic (35)	71	0.66
Apache (5)	9	0.08
Blackfeet (1)	4	0.04
Central American Ind. (3)	3	0.03
Cherokee (4)	43	0.40
Chippewa (2)	5	0.05
Choctaw (5)	12	0.11
Hopi (3)	4	0.04
Iroquois (0)	1	0.01
Mexican American Ind. (5)	10	0.09
Navajo (29)	42	0.39

*Notes: † The Census 2010 population figure is used to calculate the percentages in the Hispanic Origin and Race categories. Ancestry percentages are based on the 2006-2010 American Community Survey population (not shown); ‡ Numbers in parentheses indicate the number of people reporting a single ancestry; * Numbers in parentheses indicate the number of persons reporting this race alone, not in combination with any other race; Please refer to the Explanation of Data for more information.*

Pima (1)	3	0.03
Pueblo (1)	1	0.01
Seminole (0)	1	0.01
Sioux (0)	4	0.04
South American Ind. (0)	2	0.02
Tohono O'Odham (4)	4	0.04
Yaqui (10)	11	0.10
Asian (54)	102	0.94
Not Hispanic (48)	82	0.76
Hispanic (6)	20	0.18
Cambodian (1)	1	0.01
Chinese, ex. Taiwanese (14)	23	0.21
Filipino (16)	32	0.30
Indian (1)	6	0.06
Indonesian (0)	2	0.02
Japanese (9)	26	0.24
Korean (2)	7	0.06
Thai (1)	1	0.01
Vietnamese (4)	6	0.06
Hawaii Native/Pacific Islander (4)	16	0.15
Not Hispanic (4)	15	0.14
Hispanic (0)	1	0.01
Fijian (0)	1	0.01
Native Hawaiian (2)	7	0.06
Samoan (2)	7	0.06
White (9,589)	9,859	91.14
Not Hispanic (8,854)	9,000	83.20
Hispanic (735)	859	7.94

Coolidge

Place Type: City
County: Pinal
Population: 11,825†

Ancestry‡	Population	%
African, Sub-Saharan (14)	14	0.13
African (14)	14	0.13
American (387)	387	3.58
Canadian (26)	39	0.36
Czech (0)	37	0.34
Danish (31)	31	0.29
Dutch (25)	44	0.41
English (197)	593	5.48
European (34)	34	0.31
Finnish (9)	38	0.35
French, ex. Basque (24)	241	2.23
French Canadian (37)	37	0.34
German (510)	1,422	13.15
Greek (0)	6	0.06
Hungarian (9)	9	0.08
Irish (337)	1,090	10.08
Italian (74)	209	1.93
Macedonian (17)	17	0.16
Northern European (12)	12	0.11
Norwegian (27)	90	0.83
Pennsylvania German (30)	30	0.28
Polish (17)	124	1.15
Portuguese (0)	33	0.31
Romanian (0)	54	0.50
Scotch-Irish (100)	147	1.36
Scottish (88)	147	1.36
Swedish (60)	95	0.88
Swiss (32)	48	0.44
Welsh (16)	69	0.64

Hispanic Origin	Population	%
Hispanic or Latino (of any race)	4,962	41.96
Central American, ex. Mexican	30	0.25
Guatemalan	8	0.07
Honduran	1	0.01
Nicaraguan	4	0.03
Salvadoran	17	0.14
Cuban	10	0.08
Dominican Republic	3	0.03
Mexican	4,191	35.44
Puerto Rican	65	0.55
South American	10	0.08
Argentinean	1	0.01
Bolivian	1	0.01
Colombian	1	0.01
Ecuadorian	4	0.03
Peruvian	2	0.02
Venezuelan	1	0.01
Other Hispanic or Latino	653	5.52

Race*	Population	%
African-American/Black (928)	1,130	9.56
Not Hispanic (868)	1,007	8.52
Hispanic (60)	123	1.04
American Indian/Alaska Native (670)	887	7.50
Not Hispanic (445)	578	4.89
Hispanic (225)	309	2.61
Apache (10)	11	0.09
Blackfeet (2)	5	0.04
Cherokee (11)	50	0.42
Cheyenne (0)	1	0.01
Chickasaw (4)	11	0.09
Chippewa (8)	9	0.08
Choctaw (10)	17	0.14
Comanche (0)	6	0.05
Creek (4)	9	0.08
Hopi (1)	2	0.02
Kiowa (1)	1	0.01
Mexican American Ind. (21)	23	0.19
Navajo (28)	35	0.30
Osage (1)	1	0.01
Pima (103)	160	1.35
Potawatomi (1)	1	0.01
Pueblo (4)	4	0.03
Seminole (2)	2	0.02
Sioux (13)	14	0.12
Tohono O'Odham (100)	121	1.02
Yaqui (156)	188	1.59
Yuman (7)	11	0.09
Asian (115)	184	1.56
Not Hispanic (103)	140	1.18
Hispanic (12)	44	0.37
Chinese, ex. Taiwanese (19)	35	0.30
Filipino (47)	67	0.57
Indian (18)	20	0.17
Indonesian (1)	1	0.01
Japanese (3)	12	0.10
Korean (5)	11	0.09
Laotian (3)	3	0.03
Pakistani (1)	1	0.01
Sri Lankan (1)	1	0.01
Taiwanese (1)	3	0.03
Thai (1)	1	0.01
Vietnamese (4)	4	0.03
Hawaii Native/Pacific Islander (13)	43	0.36
Not Hispanic (9)	26	0.22
Hispanic (4)	17	0.14
Guamanian/Chamorro (0)	1	0.01
Native Hawaiian (4)	25	0.21
Samoan (1)	3	0.03
Tongan (2)	5	0.04
White (7,418)	7,866	66.52
Not Hispanic (5,153)	5,378	45.48
Hispanic (2,265)	2,488	21.04

Cottonwood

Place Type: City
County: Yavapai
Population: 11,265†

Ancestry‡	Population	%
African, Sub-Saharan (12)	12	0.11
South African (12)	12	0.11
American (528)	528	4.68
Arab (16)	16	0.14
Lebanese (16)	16	0.14
Austrian (0)	16	0.14
Belgian (16)	31	0.27
British (15)	87	0.77
Cajun (0)	19	0.17
Canadian (0)	42	0.37
Croatian (17)	17	0.15
Czech (0)	5	0.04
Czechoslovakian (15)	36	0.32
Danish (65)	125	1.11
Dutch (46)	353	3.13
English (406)	1,967	17.44
European (23)	36	0.32
French, ex. Basque (23)	313	2.77
French Canadian (32)	76	0.67
German (779)	1,889	16.75
Greek (16)	37	0.33
Hungarian (13)	34	0.30
Irish (274)	1,415	12.54
Italian (166)	426	3.78
Lithuanian (15)	65	0.58
Norwegian (16)	156	1.38
Pennsylvania German (0)	14	0.12
Polish (55)	163	1.45
Portuguese (14)	63	0.56
Romanian (0)	49	0.43
Russian (29)	172	1.52
Scotch-Irish (80)	312	2.77
Scottish (46)	538	4.77
Slovene (15)	15	0.13
Swedish (31)	219	1.94
Swiss (48)	133	1.18
Turkish (0)	49	0.43
Welsh (0)	161	1.43

Hispanic Origin	Population	%
Hispanic or Latino (of any race)	2,573	22.84
Central American, ex. Mexican	29	0.26
Costa Rican	3	0.03
Guatemalan	16	0.14
Honduran	3	0.03
Salvadoran	7	0.06
Cuban	5	0.04
Dominican Republic	4	0.04
Mexican	2,274	20.19
Puerto Rican	32	0.28
South American	24	0.21
Argentinean	6	0.05
Bolivian	3	0.03
Colombian	9	0.08
Ecuadorian	3	0.03
Peruvian	2	0.02
Venezuelan	1	0.01
Other Hispanic or Latino	205	1.82

Race*	Population	%
African-American/Black (88)	135	1.20
Not Hispanic (76)	112	0.99
Hispanic (12)	23	0.20
American Indian/Alaska Native (199)	343	3.04
Not Hispanic (157)	252	2.24
Hispanic (42)	91	0.81
Aleut *(Alaska Native)* (1)	1	0.01
Apache (5)	15	0.13
Blackfeet (0)	1	0.01
Canadian/French Am. Ind. (1)	1	0.01
Cherokee (7)	35	0.31
Cheyenne (0)	6	0.05
Chippewa (0)	1	0.01
Choctaw (5)	6	0.05
Comanche (0)	1	0.01
Creek (2)	2	0.02
Hopi (7)	12	0.11
Iroquois (2)	4	0.04
Mexican American Ind. (10)	16	0.14
Navajo (39)	45	0.40
Osage (1)	4	0.04
Ottawa (1)	1	0.01
Pima (2)	4	0.04
Potawatomi (0)	3	0.03
Pueblo (7)	8	0.07
Seminole (0)	1	0.01
Sioux (4)	5	0.04
South American Ind. (1)	2	0.02
Spanish American Ind. (1)	1	0.01
Tohono O'Odham (2)	2	0.02
Yaqui (6)	6	0.05
Yuman (3)	4	0.04

*Notes: † The Census 2010 population figure is used to calculate the percentages in the Hispanic Origin and Race categories. Ancestry percentages are based on the 2006-2010 American Community Survey population (not shown); ‡ Numbers in parentheses indicate the number of people reporting a single ancestry; * Numbers in parentheses indicate the number of persons reporting this race alone, not in combination with any other race; Please refer to the Explanation of Data for more information.*

Yup'ik *(Alaska Native)* (2)	2	0.02
Asian (106)	139	1.23
Not Hispanic (101)	128	1.14
Hispanic (5)	11	0.10
Chinese, ex. Taiwanese (19)	24	0.21
Filipino (21)	37	0.33
Indian (2)	5	0.04
Indonesian (1)	2	0.02
Japanese (15)	19	0.17
Korean (7)	9	0.08
Thai (5)	5	0.04
Vietnamese (32)	34	0.30
Hawaii Native/Pacific Islander (10)	24	0.21
Not Hispanic (9)	21	0.19
Hispanic (1)	3	0.03
Guamanian/Chamorro (1)	1	0.01
Native Hawaiian (4)	10	0.09
Samoan (1)	1	0.01
Tongan (0)	4	0.04
White (9,413)	9,687	85.99
Not Hispanic (8,195)	8,335	73.99
Hispanic (1,218)	1,352	12.00

Douglas

Place Type: City
County: Cochise
Population: 17,378†

Ancestry‡	Population	%
African, Sub-Saharan (77)	87	0.50
African (77)	87	0.50
American (241)	241	1.39
Austrian (27)	27	0.16
Basque (0)	12	0.07
British (48)	85	0.49
Cajun (9)	9	0.05
Czech (0)	28	0.16
Danish (32)	70	0.40
Dutch (31)	101	0.58
English (171)	576	3.33
European (9)	9	0.05
French, ex. Basque (13)	79	0.46
French Canadian (10)	42	0.24
German (155)	711	4.11
Greek (0)	13	0.08
Hungarian (0)	19	0.11
Irish (151)	550	3.18
Italian (102)	246	1.42
Norwegian (11)	27	0.16
Pennsylvania German (0)	10	0.06
Polish (30)	100	0.58
Portuguese (26)	26	0.15
Romanian (9)	9	0.05
Russian (0)	68	0.39
Scandinavian (10)	10	0.06
Scotch-Irish (93)	134	0.78
Scottish (0)	37	0.21
Swedish (18)	26	0.15
Swiss (0)	10	0.06
Welsh (0)	254	1.47

Hispanic Origin	Population	%
Hispanic or Latino (of any race)	14,353	82.59
Central American, ex. Mexican	15	0.09
Costa Rican	1	0.01
Guatemalan	4	0.02
Honduran	4	0.02
Panamanian	2	0.01
Salvadoran	4	0.02
Cuban	7	0.04
Dominican Republic	3	0.02
Mexican	13,363	76.90
Puerto Rican	62	0.36
South American	29	0.17
Argentinean	2	0.01
Chilean	3	0.02
Colombian	7	0.04
Ecuadorian	2	0.01
Peruvian	6	0.03
Uruguayan	2	0.01
Venezuelan	7	0.04
Other Hispanic or Latino	874	5.03

Race*	Population	%
African-American/Black (483)	518	2.98
Not Hispanic (409)	419	2.41
Hispanic (74)	99	0.57
American Indian/Alaska Native (296)	386	2.22
Not Hispanic (159)	176	1.01
Hispanic (137)	210	1.21
Apache (16)	23	0.13
Blackfeet (1)	3	0.02
Canadian/French Am. Ind. (1)	1	0.01
Central American Ind. (4)	4	0.02
Cherokee (2)	7	0.04
Chippewa (1)	1	0.01
Choctaw (4)	5	0.03
Hopi (2)	2	0.01
Inupiat *(Alaska Native)* (0)	2	0.01
Iroquois (0)	1	0.01
Mexican American Ind. (20)	43	0.25
Navajo (52)	56	0.32
Pima (20)	20	0.12
Pueblo (4)	4	0.02
South American Ind. (4)	4	0.02
Spanish American Ind. (2)	3	0.02
Tohono O'Odham (10)	10	0.06
Yaqui (23)	30	0.17
Yuman (7)	7	0.04
Asian (81)	155	0.89
Not Hispanic (61)	90	0.52
Hispanic (20)	65	0.37
Chinese, ex. Taiwanese (12)	32	0.18
Filipino (32)	54	0.31
Indian (12)	19	0.11
Japanese (6)	14	0.08
Korean (14)	15	0.09
Sri Lankan (1)	1	0.01
Taiwanese (1)	1	0.01
Vietnamese (1)	9	0.05
Hawaii Native/Pacific Islander (10)	33	0.19
Not Hispanic (4)	13	0.07
Hispanic (6)	20	0.12
Guamanian/Chamorro (1)	5	0.03
Marshallese (0)	3	0.02
Native Hawaiian (5)	12	0.07
Samoan (2)	10	0.06
Tongan (0)	6	0.03
White (11,848)	12,220	70.32
Not Hispanic (2,333)	2,382	13.71
Hispanic (9,515)	9,838	56.61

Drexel Heights

Place Type: CDP
County: Pima
Population: 27,749†

Ancestry‡	Population	%
African, Sub-Saharan (78)	136	0.47
African (78)	88	0.30
South African (0)	48	0.17
American (756)	756	2.62
Basque (0)	10	0.03
Belgian (9)	9	0.03
British (53)	92	0.32
Cajun (0)	10	0.03
Canadian (19)	29	0.10
Czech (7)	58	0.20
Czechoslovakian (11)	29	0.10
Danish (0)	10	0.03
Dutch (30)	70	0.24
English (535)	1,409	4.88
European (79)	111	0.38
Finnish (0)	7	0.02
French, ex. Basque (30)	263	0.91
French Canadian (7)	38	0.13
German (562)	2,089	7.23
Greek (37)	50	0.17
Hungarian (35)	45	0.16
Iranian (10)	10	0.03
Irish (403)	1,619	5.60
Israeli (0)	28	0.10
Italian (146)	441	1.53
Lithuanian (0)	41	0.14
Northern European (23)	23	0.08
Norwegian (46)	158	0.55
Pennsylvania German (34)	40	0.14
Polish (115)	363	1.26
Portuguese (0)	35	0.12
Romanian (22)	22	0.08
Russian (13)	147	0.51
Scandinavian (19)	41	0.14
Scotch-Irish (64)	233	0.81
Scottish (88)	240	0.83
Slavic (12)	12	0.04
Swedish (82)	176	0.61
Swiss (0)	20	0.07
Ukrainian (17)	17	0.06
Welsh (11)	65	0.23
Yugoslavian (6)	6	0.02

Hispanic Origin	Population	%
Hispanic or Latino (of any race)	19,586	70.58
Central American, ex. Mexican	108	0.39
Guatemalan	45	0.16
Honduran	13	0.05
Nicaraguan	11	0.04
Panamanian	10	0.04
Salvadoran	29	0.10
Cuban	27	0.10
Dominican Republic	9	0.03
Mexican	17,992	64.84
Puerto Rican	142	0.51
South American	47	0.17
Argentinean	7	0.03
Chilean	12	0.04
Colombian	20	0.07
Ecuadorian	3	0.01
Peruvian	2	0.01
Venezuelan	3	0.01
Other Hispanic or Latino	1,261	4.54

Race*	Population	%
African-American/Black (691)	898	3.24
Not Hispanic (549)	654	2.36
Hispanic (142)	244	0.88
American Indian/Alaska Native (1,470)	1,890	6.81
Not Hispanic (819)	957	3.45
Hispanic (651)	933	3.36
Apache (22)	56	0.20
Blackfeet (1)	4	0.01
Canadian/French Am. Ind. (0)	8	0.03
Cherokee (26)	68	0.25
Chickasaw (0)	1	<0.01
Chippewa (18)	21	0.08
Choctaw (5)	10	0.04
Comanche (0)	3	0.01
Creek (0)	3	0.01
Crow (1)	1	<0.01
Hopi (14)	27	0.10
Inupiat *(Alaska Native)* (0)	1	<0.01
Iroquois (1)	2	0.01
Kiowa (1)	1	<0.01
Mexican American Ind. (46)	65	0.23
Navajo (50)	66	0.24
Ottawa (2)	2	0.01
Paiute (1)	1	<0.01
Pima (7)	16	0.06
Pueblo (1)	4	0.01
Seminole (0)	2	0.01
Shoshone (0)	1	<0.01
Sioux (7)	19	0.07
South American Ind. (6)	7	0.03
Spanish American Ind. (0)	3	0.01
Tlingit-Haida *(Alaska Native)* (2)	2	0.01
Tohono O'Odham (346)	407	1.47
Ute (0)	2	0.01
Yakama (0)	1	<0.01

*Notes: † The Census 2010 population figure is used to calculate the percentages in the Hispanic Origin and Race categories. Ancestry percentages are based on the 2006-2010 American Community Survey population (not shown); ‡ Numbers in parentheses indicate the number of people reporting a single ancestry; * Numbers in parentheses indicate the number of persons reporting this race alone, not in combination with any other race; Please refer to the Explanation of Data for more information.*

SECTION TWO

Yaqui (593)	725	2.61
Yuman (7)	8	0.03
Asian (201)	391	1.41
Not Hispanic (174)	254	0.92
Hispanic (27)	137	0.49
Cambodian (5)	5	0.02
Chinese, ex. Taiwanese (26)	65	0.23
Filipino (72)	121	0.44
Indian (14)	31	0.11
Indonesian (1)	1	<0.01
Japanese (16)	36	0.13
Korean (16)	38	0.14
Laotian (25)	27	0.10
Nepalese (0)	1	<0.01
Pakistani (1)	4	0.01
Thai (8)	10	0.04
Vietnamese (13)	21	0.08
Hawaii Native/Pacific Islander (20)	63	0.23
Not Hispanic (11)	26	0.09
Hispanic (9)	37	0.13
Fijian (0)	2	0.01
Guamanian/Chamorro (4)	6	0.02
Native Hawaiian (11)	26	0.09
Samoan (3)	3	0.01
White (16,261)	17,185	61.93
Not Hispanic (6,271)	6,529	23.53
Hispanic (9,990)	10,656	38.40

El Mirage

Place Type: City
County: Maricopa
Population: 31,797†

Ancestry‡	Population	%
African, Sub-Saharan (409)	438	1.57
African (409)	438	1.57
Albanian (126)	126	0.45
American (5,912)	5,912	21.17
Arab (89)	99	0.35
Iraqi (10)	20	0.07
Syrian (79)	79	0.28
Belgian (0)	38	0.14
British (60)	72	0.26
Bulgarian (0)	11	0.04
Canadian (61)	85	0.30
Czech (65)	65	0.23
Danish (74)	181	0.65
Dutch (69)	245	0.88
Eastern European (19)	19	0.07
English (584)	1,160	4.15
European (81)	117	0.42
Finnish (30)	40	0.14
French, ex. Basque (74)	284	1.02
French Canadian (15)	68	0.24
German (881)	2,171	7.78
Greek (158)	169	0.61
Hungarian (62)	126	0.45
Irish (414)	1,413	5.06
Italian (599)	994	3.56
Norwegian (47)	199	0.71
Polish (32)	215	0.77
Portuguese (52)	62	0.22
Romanian (18)	30	0.11
Russian (0)	65	0.23
Scotch-Irish (30)	174	0.62
Scottish (32)	219	0.78
Swedish (45)	165	0.59
Swiss (0)	8	0.03
Ukrainian (14)	14	0.05
Welsh (13)	45	0.16
Yugoslavian (34)	34	0.12

Hispanic Origin	Population	%
Hispanic or Latino (of any race)	15,120	47.55
Central American, ex. Mexican	305	0.96
Costa Rican	8	0.03
Guatemalan	115	0.36
Honduran	14	0.04
Nicaraguan	33	0.10
Panamanian	12	0.04
Salvadoran	113	0.36
Other Central American	10	0.03
Cuban	45	0.14
Dominican Republic	18	0.06
Mexican	13,305	41.84
Puerto Rican	364	1.14
South American	97	0.31
Argentinean	4	0.01
Bolivian	3	0.01
Colombian	34	0.11
Ecuadorian	26	0.08
Peruvian	20	0.06
Uruguayan	8	0.03
Venezuelan	2	0.01
Other Hispanic or Latino	986	3.10

Race*	Population	%
African-American/Black (2,090)	2,589	8.14
Not Hispanic (1,926)	2,300	7.23
Hispanic (164)	289	0.91
American Indian/Alaska Native (451)	787	2.48
Not Hispanic (310)	499	1.57
Hispanic (141)	288	0.91
Alaska Athabascan *(Ala. Nat.)* (1)	1	<0.01
Aleut *(Alaska Native)* (1)	1	<0.01
Apache (23)	38	0.12
Blackfeet (2)	8	0.03
Central American Ind. (0)	1	<0.01
Cherokee (11)	54	0.17
Chickasaw (2)	2	0.01
Chippewa (3)	4	0.01
Choctaw (16)	27	0.08
Cree (0)	1	<0.01
Creek (0)	2	0.01
Hopi (2)	5	0.02
Iroquois (0)	4	0.01
Mexican American Ind. (31)	47	0.15
Navajo (135)	169	0.53
Osage (1)	1	<0.01
Paiute (1)	3	0.01
Pima (5)	8	0.03
Potawatomi (0)	1	<0.01
Pueblo (1)	6	0.02
Sioux (11)	23	0.07
South American Ind. (0)	3	0.01
Spanish American Ind. (10)	17	0.05
Tlingit-Haida *(Alaska Native)* (2)	3	0.01
Tohono O'Odham (2)	5	0.02
Yaqui (29)	36	0.11
Yuman (1)	5	0.02
Asian (517)	859	2.70
Not Hispanic (464)	704	2.21
Hispanic (53)	155	0.49
Burmese (0)	1	<0.01
Cambodian (15)	17	0.05
Chinese, ex. Taiwanese (48)	79	0.25
Filipino (226)	382	1.20
Indian (65)	99	0.31
Indonesian (6)	11	0.03
Japanese (15)	49	0.15
Korean (25)	56	0.18
Laotian (14)	17	0.05
Pakistani (5)	5	0.02
Sri Lankan (0)	1	<0.01
Taiwanese (1)	1	<0.01
Thai (19)	43	0.14
Vietnamese (47)	65	0.20
Hawaii Native/Pacific Islander (88)	172	0.54
Not Hispanic (74)	130	0.41
Hispanic (14)	42	0.13
Fijian (3)	3	0.01
Guamanian/Chamorro (21)	35	0.11
Native Hawaiian (22)	44	0.14
Samoan (36)	48	0.15
Tongan (1)	1	<0.01
White (19,350)	20,683	65.05
Not Hispanic (13,163)	13,772	43.31
Hispanic (6,187)	6,911	21.73

Eloy

Place Type: City
County: Pinal
Population: 16,631†

Ancestry‡	Population	%
African, Sub-Saharan (30)	30	0.20
African (30)	30	0.20
Albanian (3)	3	0.02
American (81)	81	0.54
Arab (19)	19	0.13
Arab (9)	9	0.06
Other Arab (10)	10	0.07
Armenian (17)	17	0.11
British (16)	31	0.20
Danish (0)	22	0.15
Dutch (20)	111	0.73
English (105)	332	2.20
European (9)	9	0.06
Finnish (0)	15	0.10
French, ex. Basque (17)	192	1.27
French Canadian (0)	28	0.19
German (144)	411	2.72
Greek (0)	9	0.06
Hungarian (0)	13	0.09
Irish (58)	341	2.25
Italian (213)	300	1.98
Lithuanian (0)	9	0.06
Norwegian (19)	27	0.18
Polish (41)	67	0.44
Portuguese (22)	56	0.37
Romanian (7)	10	0.07
Russian (18)	18	0.12
Scandinavian (16)	16	0.11
Scotch-Irish (3)	68	0.45
Scottish (32)	59	0.39
Slovak (14)	14	0.09
Swedish (0)	40	0.26
Swiss (0)	9	0.06
Welsh (0)	50	0.33
West Indian, ex. Hispanic (17)	17	0.11
Haitian (9)	9	0.06
Jamaican (8)	8	0.05

Hispanic Origin	Population	%
Hispanic or Latino (of any race)	9,648	58.01
Central American, ex. Mexican	58	0.35
Costa Rican	3	0.02
Guatemalan	17	0.10
Honduran	5	0.03
Nicaraguan	4	0.02
Panamanian	1	0.01
Salvadoran	25	0.15
Other Central American	3	0.02
Cuban	10	0.06
Dominican Republic	8	0.05
Mexican	8,531	51.30
Puerto Rican	125	0.75
South American	10	0.06
Argentinean	2	0.01
Colombian	3	0.02
Peruvian	5	0.03
Other Hispanic or Latino	906	5.45

Race*	Population	%
African-American/Black (1,685)	1,808	10.87
Not Hispanic (1,602)	1,677	10.08
Hispanic (83)	131	0.79
American Indian/Alaska Native (571)	698	4.20
Not Hispanic (378)	446	2.68
Hispanic (193)	252	1.52
Apache (13)	18	0.11
Blackfeet (1)	1	0.01
Central American Ind. (0)	1	0.01
Cherokee (9)	23	0.14
Chickasaw (3)	3	0.02
Chippewa (0)	2	0.01
Choctaw (4)	17	0.10
Creek (0)	8	0.05

*Notes: † The Census 2010 population figure is used to calculate the percentages in the Hispanic Origin and Race categories. Ancestry percentages are based on the 2006-2010 American Community Survey population (not shown); ‡ Numbers in parentheses indicate the number of people reporting a single ancestry; * Numbers in parentheses indicate the number of persons reporting this race alone, not in combination with any other race; Please refer to the Explanation of Data for more information.*

Hopi (10)	15	0.09
Inupiat *(Alaska Native)* (1)	1	0.01
Lumbee (0)	1	0.01
Mexican American Ind. (9)	11	0.07
Navajo (16)	25	0.15
Ottawa (1)	1	0.01
Pima (54)	68	0.41
Pueblo (1)	1	0.01
Sioux (6)	6	0.04
Tohono O'Odham (200)	221	1.33
Ute (1)	1	0.01
Yaqui (39)	45	0.27
Yuman (1)	1	0.01
Asian (755)	811	4.88
Not Hispanic (723)	756	4.55
Hispanic (32)	55	0.33
Cambodian (3)	3	0.02
Chinese, ex. Taiwanese (53)	57	0.34
Filipino (264)	281	1.69
Hmong (2)	2	0.01
Indian (22)	26	0.16
Japanese (95)	102	0.61
Korean (24)	26	0.16
Laotian (13)	13	0.08
Pakistani (1)	1	0.01
Thai (18)	19	0.11
Vietnamese (37)	38	0.23
Hawaii Native/Pacific Islander (958)	981	5.90
Not Hispanic (941)	958	5.76
Hispanic (17)	23	0.14
Fijian (2)	3	0.02
Guamanian/Chamorro (14)	17	0.10
Marshallese (1)	1	0.01
Native Hawaiian (772)	776	4.67
Samoan (122)	124	0.75
Tongan (16)	16	0.10
White (6,856)	7,250	43.59
Not Hispanic (3,144)	3,246	19.52
Hispanic (3,712)	4,004	24.08

Flagstaff

Place Type: City
County: Coconino
Population: 65,870†

Ancestry‡	Population	%
African, Sub-Saharan (41)	57	0.09
African (41)	57	0.09
American (1,635)	1,635	2.56
Arab (238)	252	0.39
Lebanese (43)	57	0.09
Syrian (12)	12	0.02
Other Arab (183)	183	0.29
Armenian (16)	44	0.07
Austrian (48)	303	0.47
Basque (49)	57	0.09
Belgian (18)	18	0.03
British (202)	456	0.71
Canadian (158)	216	0.34
Celtic (10)	10	0.02
Croatian (36)	36	0.06
Czech (46)	333	0.52
Czechoslovakian (46)	65	0.10
Danish (255)	708	1.11
Dutch (262)	793	1.24
Eastern European (47)	68	0.11
English (1,582)	6,391	10.00
Estonian (0)	8	0.01
European (1,708)	1,830	2.86
Finnish (40)	214	0.33
French, ex. Basque (325)	1,236	1.93
French Canadian (189)	580	0.91
German (3,367)	11,032	17.26
Greek (39)	135	0.21
Hungarian (56)	286	0.45
Iranian (30)	30	0.05
Irish (1,875)	7,779	12.17
Israeli (0)	33	0.05
Italian (948)	3,114	4.87
Lithuanian (20)	131	0.20
Luxemburger (10)	10	0.02
Northern European (127)	143	0.22
Norwegian (593)	1,436	2.25
Polish (347)	1,406	2.20
Portuguese (55)	115	0.18
Romanian (104)	136	0.21
Russian (129)	646	1.01
Scandinavian (119)	266	0.42
Scotch-Irish (528)	1,459	2.28
Scottish (394)	1,578	2.47
Serbian (40)	40	0.06
Slavic (7)	7	0.01
Slovak (11)	39	0.06
Slovene (32)	88	0.14
Swedish (421)	1,568	2.45
Swiss (85)	281	0.44
Turkish (29)	29	0.05
Ukrainian (82)	252	0.39
Welsh (169)	571	0.89
West Indian, ex. Hispanic (39)	48	0.08
Jamaican (22)	31	0.05
West Indian (17)	17	0.03
Yugoslavian (26)	113	0.18

Hispanic Origin	Population	%
Hispanic or Latino (of any race)	12,094	18.36
Central American, ex. Mexican	168	0.26
Costa Rican	17	0.03
Guatemalan	48	0.07
Honduran	11	0.02
Nicaraguan	13	0.02
Panamanian	14	0.02
Salvadoran	65	0.10
Cuban	61	0.09
Dominican Republic	13	0.02
Mexican	10,194	15.48
Puerto Rican	222	0.34
South American	210	0.32
Argentinean	27	0.04
Bolivian	5	0.01
Chilean	28	0.04
Colombian	49	0.07
Ecuadorian	18	0.03
Paraguayan	1	<0.01
Peruvian	67	0.10
Uruguayan	1	<0.01
Venezuelan	14	0.02
Other Hispanic or Latino	1,226	1.86

Race*	Population	%
African-American/Black (1,278)	1,749	2.66
Not Hispanic (1,173)	1,545	2.35
Hispanic (105)	204	0.31
American Indian/Alaska Native (7,704)	8,642	13.12
Not Hispanic (7,237)	7,922	12.03
Hispanic (467)	720	1.09
Alaska Athabascan *(Ala. Nat.)* (5)	7	0.01
Aleut *(Alaska Native)* (5)	11	0.02
Apache (90)	130	0.20
Arapaho (1)	4	0.01
Blackfeet (2)	14	0.02
Canadian/French Am. Ind. (0)	1	<0.01
Central American Ind. (1)	1	<0.01
Cherokee (32)	145	0.22
Cheyenne (4)	8	0.01
Chickasaw (2)	8	0.01
Chippewa (10)	34	0.05
Choctaw (7)	23	0.03
Comanche (11)	18	0.03
Cree (0)	3	<0.01
Creek (6)	17	0.03
Crow (4)	6	0.01
Delaware (1)	1	<0.01
Hopi (491)	625	0.95
Inupiat *(Alaska Native)* (9)	15	0.02
Iroquois (6)	15	0.02
Kiowa (10)	18	0.03
Lumbee (1)	3	<0.01
Menominee (0)	1	<0.01
Mexican American Ind. (34)	49	0.07
Navajo (4,978)	5,504	8.36
Osage (2)	3	<0.01
Ottawa (1)	4	0.01
Paiute (4)	4	0.01
Pima (18)	22	0.03
Potawatomi (3)	8	0.01
Pueblo (36)	67	0.10
Puget Sound Salish (12)	12	0.02
Seminole (3)	6	0.01
Shoshone (1)	3	<0.01
Sioux (30)	63	0.10
South American Ind. (1)	5	0.01
Spanish American Ind. (1)	1	<0.01
Tlingit-Haida *(Alaska Native)* (7)	16	0.02
Tohono O'Odham (17)	22	0.03
Ute (2)	9	0.01
Yakama (2)	3	<0.01
Yaqui (6)	17	0.03
Yuman (67)	77	0.12
Yup'ik *(Alaska Native)* (5)	6	0.01
Asian (1,227)	1,877	2.85
Not Hispanic (1,191)	1,747	2.65
Hispanic (36)	130	0.20
Bangladeshi (7)	9	0.01
Cambodian (1)	1	<0.01
Chinese, ex. Taiwanese (374)	498	0.76
Filipino (129)	320	0.49
Hmong (2)	2	<0.01
Indian (199)	247	0.37
Indonesian (5)	19	0.03
Japanese (137)	305	0.46
Korean (114)	188	0.29
Laotian (1)	2	<0.01
Malaysian (2)	5	0.01
Nepalese (9)	9	0.01
Pakistani (16)	27	0.04
Sri Lankan (4)	7	0.01
Taiwanese (25)	27	0.04
Thai (45)	54	0.08
Vietnamese (76)	100	0.15
Hawaii Native/Pacific Islander (115)	294	0.45
Not Hispanic (99)	248	0.38
Hispanic (16)	46	0.07
Fijian (3)	8	0.01
Guamanian/Chamorro (21)	41	0.06
Marshallese (4)	5	0.01
Native Hawaiian (42)	139	0.21
Samoan (15)	33	0.05
Tongan (4)	8	0.01
White (48,348)	50,379	76.48
Not Hispanic (42,446)	43,777	66.46
Hispanic (5,902)	6,602	10.02

Florence

Place Type: Town
County: Pinal
Population: 25,536†

Ancestry‡	Population	%
African, Sub-Saharan (21)	21	0.09
Ethiopian (10)	10	0.04
Nigerian (11)	11	0.05
American (307)	307	1.30
Arab (33)	43	0.18
Iraqi (19)	19	0.08
Other Arab (14)	24	0.10
Austrian (35)	77	0.33
Brazilian (0)	10	0.04
British (18)	18	0.08
Bulgarian (11)	11	0.05
Canadian (26)	98	0.41
Croatian (12)	12	0.05
Czech (0)	21	0.09
Czechoslovakian (9)	9	0.04
Danish (57)	162	0.69
Dutch (47)	364	1.54
English (399)	1,111	4.70
European (69)	80	0.34

*Notes: † The Census 2010 population figure is used to calculate the percentages in the Hispanic Origin and Race categories. Ancestry percentages are based on the 2006-2010 American Community Survey population (not shown); ‡ Numbers in parentheses indicate the number of people reporting a single ancestry; * Numbers in parentheses indicate the number of persons reporting this race alone, not in combination with any other race; Please refer to the Explanation of Data for more information.*

SECTION TWO

Finnish (12)	37	0.16
French, ex. Basque (58)	491	2.08
French Canadian (32)	53	0.22
German (682)	2,243	9.50
German Russian (9)	9	0.04
Greek (15)	40	0.17
Hungarian (0)	46	0.19
Icelander (0)	12	0.05
Irish (608)	2,121	8.98
Italian (285)	653	2.77
Latvian (0)	9	0.04
Lithuanian (11)	11	0.05
Northern European (11)	11	0.05
Norwegian (131)	306	1.30
Pennsylvania German (0)	13	0.06
Polish (89)	178	0.75
Portuguese (23)	62	0.26
Romanian (11)	36	0.15
Russian (29)	120	0.51
Scandinavian (79)	88	0.37
Scotch-Irish (180)	428	1.81
Scottish (71)	253	1.07
Slovak (23)	34	0.14
Swedish (54)	169	0.72
Swiss (0)	12	0.05
Turkish (11)	21	0.09
Ukrainian (13)	13	0.06
Welsh (44)	132	0.56
West Indian, ex. Hispanic (31)	31	0.13
Barbadian (13)	13	0.06
Jamaican (18)	18	0.08
Yugoslavian (9)	9	0.04

Hispanic Origin	Population	%
Hispanic or Latino (of any race)	7,978	31.24
Central American, ex. Mexican	122	0.48
Costa Rican	4	0.02
Guatemalan	27	0.11
Honduran	11	0.04
Nicaraguan	8	0.03
Panamanian	1	<0.01
Salvadoran	63	0.25
Other Central American	8	0.03
Cuban	26	0.10
Dominican Republic	19	0.07
Mexican	6,998	27.40
Puerto Rican	190	0.74
South American	32	0.13
Argentinean	6	0.02
Bolivian	1	<0.01
Chilean	1	<0.01
Colombian	12	0.05
Ecuadorian	1	<0.01
Peruvian	10	0.04
Venezuelan	1	<0.01
Other Hispanic or Latino	591	2.31

Race*	Population	%
African-American/Black (1,608)	1,795	7.03
Not Hispanic (1,545)	1,711	6.70
Hispanic (63)	84	0.33
American Indian/Alaska Native (3,681)	3,875	15.17
Not Hispanic (3,571)	3,717	14.56
Hispanic (110)	158	0.62
Apache (30)	40	0.16
Arapaho (0)	3	0.01
Blackfeet (0)	2	0.01
Canadian/French Am. Ind. (1)	1	<0.01
Cherokee (13)	27	0.11
Chippewa (1)	3	0.01
Choctaw (2)	6	0.02
Colville (0)	2	0.01
Creek (0)	2	0.01
Delaware (1)	1	<0.01
Hopi (12)	17	0.07
Inupiat *(Alaska Native)* (1)	1	<0.01
Iroquois (1)	1	<0.01
Kiowa (0)	2	0.01
Mexican American Ind. (11)	20	0.08
Navajo (123)	136	0.53
Paiute (2)	2	0.01
Pima (73)	79	0.31
Potawatomi (2)	2	0.01
Puget Sound Salish (1)	1	<0.01
Shoshone (2)	2	0.01
Sioux (1)	5	0.02
South American Ind. (1)	1	<0.01
Spanish American Ind. (1)	3	0.01
Tlingit-Haida *(Alaska Native)* (0)	1	<0.01
Tohono O'Odham (111)	117	0.46
Ute (2)	2	0.01
Yakama (0)	1	<0.01
Yaqui (28)	33	0.13
Yuman (12)	13	0.05
Asian (226)	288	1.13
Not Hispanic (218)	270	1.06
Hispanic (8)	18	0.07
Cambodian (7)	8	0.03
Chinese, ex. Taiwanese (27)	31	0.12
Filipino (64)	99	0.39
Hmong (1)	2	0.01
Indian (65)	67	0.26
Japanese (5)	11	0.04
Korean (6)	13	0.05
Laotian (2)	4	0.02
Nepalese (1)	1	<0.01
Pakistani (2)	2	0.01
Thai (2)	5	0.02
Vietnamese (20)	21	0.08
Hawaii Native/Pacific Islander (19)	34	0.13
Not Hispanic (19)	32	0.13
Hispanic (0)	2	0.01
Fijian (2)	3	0.01
Marshallese (1)	1	<0.01
Native Hawaiian (10)	17	0.07
Samoan (1)	3	0.01
Tongan (2)	2	0.01
White (16,190)	16,548	64.80
Not Hispanic (11,911)	12,069	47.26
Hispanic (4,279)	4,479	17.54

Flowing Wells

Place Type: CDP
County: Pima
Population: 16,419†

Ancestry‡	Population	%
American (629)	629	3.90
Austrian (0)	104	0.64
Belgian (0)	8	0.05
British (104)	118	0.73
Cajun (14)	14	0.09
Canadian (175)	184	1.14
Czech (0)	85	0.53
Danish (38)	155	0.96
Dutch (31)	149	0.92
English (539)	1,270	7.87
European (147)	160	0.99
Finnish (43)	43	0.27
French, ex. Basque (30)	286	1.77
French Canadian (12)	21	0.13
German (1,083)	2,601	16.11
Hungarian (0)	13	0.08
Icelander (15)	15	0.09
Irish (634)	1,751	10.85
Italian (307)	499	3.09
Lithuanian (0)	7	0.04
Norwegian (81)	186	1.15
Pennsylvania German (42)	52	0.32
Polish (88)	279	1.73
Portuguese (0)	23	0.14
Romanian (0)	21	0.13
Russian (31)	52	0.32
Scandinavian (49)	79	0.49
Scotch-Irish (167)	302	1.87
Scottish (526)	676	4.19
Slovak (22)	22	0.14
Swedish (93)	190	1.18
Swiss (0)	13	0.08
Ukrainian (42)	96	0.59
Welsh (220)	343	2.12
West Indian, ex. Hispanic (12)	28	0.17
Trinidadian/Tobagonian (12)	28	0.17

Hispanic Origin	Population	%
Hispanic or Latino (of any race)	5,953	36.26
Central American, ex. Mexican	50	0.30
Costa Rican	6	0.04
Guatemalan	17	0.10
Honduran	11	0.07
Nicaraguan	8	0.05
Panamanian	1	0.01
Salvadoran	5	0.03
Other Central American	2	0.01
Cuban	15	0.09
Dominican Republic	2	0.01
Mexican	5,306	32.32
Puerto Rican	61	0.37
South American	39	0.24
Argentinean	2	0.01
Bolivian	2	0.01
Chilean	8	0.05
Colombian	5	0.03
Ecuadorian	1	0.01
Paraguayan	1	0.01
Peruvian	14	0.09
Venezuelan	6	0.04
Other Hispanic or Latino	480	2.92

Race*	Population	%
African-American/Black (287)	425	2.59
Not Hispanic (245)	353	2.15
Hispanic (42)	72	0.44
American Indian/Alaska Native (335)	540	3.29
Not Hispanic (179)	312	1.90
Hispanic (156)	228	1.39
Apache (13)	21	0.13
Blackfeet (1)	10	0.06
Central American Ind. (2)	2	0.01
Cherokee (11)	45	0.27
Cheyenne (2)	2	0.01
Chickasaw (3)	3	0.02
Chippewa (1)	3	0.02
Choctaw (0)	6	0.04
Creek (7)	9	0.05
Crow (1)	1	0.01
Hopi (3)	3	0.02
Iroquois (2)	12	0.07
Lumbee (4)	4	0.02
Mexican American Ind. (19)	27	0.16
Navajo (39)	55	0.33
Osage (0)	5	0.03
Potawatomi (1)	1	0.01
Pueblo (1)	4	0.02
Seminole (4)	4	0.02
Shoshone (0)	1	0.01
Sioux (11)	15	0.09
South American Ind. (8)	9	0.05
Tlingit-Haida *(Alaska Native)* (2)	2	0.01
Tohono O'Odham (43)	57	0.35
Ute (0)	3	0.02
Yaqui (48)	59	0.36
Asian (200)	275	1.67
Not Hispanic (191)	236	1.44
Hispanic (9)	39	0.24
Cambodian (2)	2	0.01
Chinese, ex. Taiwanese (26)	43	0.26
Filipino (44)	72	0.44
Indian (6)	13	0.08
Indonesian (1)	1	0.01
Japanese (17)	29	0.18
Korean (7)	9	0.05
Laotian (1)	2	0.01
Pakistani (8)	8	0.05
Thai (3)	4	0.02
Vietnamese (78)	93	0.57
Hawaii Native/Pacific Islander (17)	35	0.21
Not Hispanic (10)	27	0.16
Hispanic (7)	8	0.05

*Notes: † The Census 2010 population figure is used to calculate the percentages in the Hispanic Origin and Race categories. Ancestry percentages are based on the 2006-2010 American Community Survey population (not shown); ‡ Numbers in parentheses indicate the number of people reporting a single ancestry; * Numbers in parentheses indicate the number of persons reporting this race alone, not in combination with any other race; Please refer to the Explanation of Data for more information.*

Guamanian/Chamorro (2)	2	0.01
Native Hawaiian (4)	16	0.10
Samoan (1)	1	0.01
Tongan (4)	4	0.02
White (12,754)	13,312	81.08
Not Hispanic (9,564)	9,800	59.69
Hispanic (3,190)	3,512	21.39

Fort Mohave

Place Type: CDP
County: Mohave
Population: 14,364†

Ancestry‡	Population	%
American (688)	688	4.77
Arab (383)	383	2.66
Iraqi (363)	363	2.52
Lebanese (20)	20	0.14
Armenian (0)	11	0.08
Austrian (0)	16	0.11
British (0)	47	0.33
Canadian (49)	60	0.42
Croatian (0)	40	0.28
Czech (0)	46	0.32
Danish (41)	204	1.41
Dutch (32)	208	1.44
English (610)	2,022	14.02
European (64)	64	0.44
Finnish (41)	84	0.58
French, ex. Basque (125)	960	6.66
French Canadian (33)	110	0.76
German (564)	2,674	18.54
Greek (0)	97	0.67
Hungarian (82)	106	0.73
Irish (721)	2,553	17.70
Italian (483)	1,061	7.36
Lithuanian (39)	55	0.38
Northern European (16)	16	0.11
Norwegian (125)	370	2.57
Pennsylvania German (26)	26	0.18
Polish (168)	612	4.24
Portuguese (12)	89	0.62
Romanian (0)	44	0.31
Russian (35)	112	0.78
Scandinavian (0)	31	0.21
Scotch-Irish (141)	318	2.20
Scottish (153)	339	2.35
Slavic (0)	17	0.12
Swedish (0)	385	2.67
Swiss (0)	11	0.08
Ukrainian (8)	8	0.06
Welsh (23)	110	0.76

Hispanic Origin	Population	%
Hispanic or Latino (of any race)	2,243	15.62
Central American, ex. Mexican	53	0.37
Costa Rican	2	0.01
Guatemalan	19	0.13
Honduran	3	0.02
Nicaraguan	4	0.03
Panamanian	12	0.08
Salvadoran	13	0.09
Cuban	23	0.16
Dominican Republic	2	0.01
Mexican	1,895	13.19
Puerto Rican	75	0.52
South American	12	0.08
Argentinean	1	0.01
Chilean	2	0.01
Colombian	4	0.03
Ecuadorian	2	0.01
Peruvian	3	0.02
Other Hispanic or Latino	183	1.27

Race*	Population	%
African-American/Black (128)	188	1.31
Not Hispanic (116)	164	1.14
Hispanic (12)	24	0.17
American Indian/Alaska Native (145)	294	2.05
Not Hispanic (116)	227	1.58
Hispanic (29)	67	0.47
Alaska Athabascan *(Ala. Nat.)* (2)	2	0.01
Apache (3)	5	0.03
Blackfeet (0)	2	0.01
Cherokee (13)	45	0.31
Chickasaw (5)	12	0.08
Chippewa (3)	7	0.05
Choctaw (3)	13	0.09
Comanche (0)	1	0.01
Creek (1)	1	0.01
Crow (0)	1	0.01
Delaware (0)	1	0.01
Hopi (0)	2	0.01
Houma (0)	5	0.03
Iroquois (3)	4	0.03
Mexican American Ind. (4)	4	0.03
Navajo (7)	11	0.08
Ottawa (1)	1	0.01
Paiute (1)	2	0.01
Pima (0)	1	0.01
Potawatomi (3)	3	0.02
Pueblo (5)	10	0.07
Sioux (8)	12	0.08
Tlingit-Haida *(Alaska Native)* (2)	2	0.01
Tohono O'Odham (2)	2	0.01
Yuman (23)	26	0.18
Asian (210)	301	2.10
Not Hispanic (201)	276	1.92
Hispanic (9)	25	0.17
Cambodian (2)	4	0.03
Chinese, ex. Taiwanese (7)	24	0.17
Filipino (92)	135	0.94
Indian (20)	23	0.16
Indonesian (2)	4	0.03
Japanese (18)	45	0.31
Korean (15)	25	0.17
Malaysian (0)	1	0.01
Pakistani (10)	11	0.08
Taiwanese (5)	7	0.05
Thai (8)	10	0.07
Vietnamese (12)	12	0.08
Hawaii Native/Pacific Islander (20)	50	0.35
Not Hispanic (19)	43	0.30
Hispanic (1)	7	0.05
Guamanian/Chamorro (3)	11	0.08
Native Hawaiian (10)	24	0.17
Samoan (7)	11	0.08
Tongan (0)	2	0.01
White (12,730)	13,103	91.22
Not Hispanic (11,429)	11,635	81.00
Hispanic (1,301)	1,468	10.22

Fortuna Foothills

Place Type: CDP
County: Yuma
Population: 26,265†

Ancestry‡	Population	%
African, Sub-Saharan (6)	11	0.04
African (6)	11	0.04
American (1,681)	1,681	6.13
Arab (19)	28	0.10
Egyptian (9)	9	0.03
Lebanese (10)	19	0.07
Australian (10)	10	0.04
Austrian (14)	51	0.19
Basque (9)	38	0.14
Belgian (0)	13	0.05
British (59)	79	0.29
Cajun (0)	15	0.05
Canadian (265)	298	1.09
Croatian (0)	18	0.07
Czech (28)	62	0.23
Czechoslovakian (0)	31	0.11
Danish (172)	344	1.25
Dutch (134)	647	2.36
Eastern European (11)	11	0.04
English (2,141)	4,872	17.76
European (252)	287	1.05
Finnish (118)	143	0.52
French, ex. Basque (133)	954	3.48
French Canadian (122)	212	0.77
German (2,246)	5,765	21.02
Greek (63)	195	0.71
Hungarian (28)	76	0.28
Iranian (0)	40	0.15
Irish (1,099)	3,207	11.69
Israeli (0)	15	0.05
Italian (171)	745	2.72
Latvian (0)	8	0.03
Lithuanian (12)	41	0.15
Norwegian (362)	1,113	4.06
Pennsylvania German (20)	31	0.11
Polish (157)	468	1.71
Portuguese (64)	109	0.40
Russian (119)	187	0.68
Scandinavian (58)	83	0.30
Scotch-Irish (269)	781	2.85
Scottish (240)	708	2.58
Slovak (0)	34	0.12
Swedish (214)	666	2.43
Swiss (60)	104	0.38
Ukrainian (42)	107	0.39
Welsh (57)	408	1.49
Yugoslavian (48)	56	0.20

Hispanic Origin	Population	%
Hispanic or Latino (of any race)	5,270	20.06
Central American, ex. Mexican	78	0.30
Costa Rican	6	0.02
Guatemalan	8	0.03
Honduran	11	0.04
Nicaraguan	8	0.03
Panamanian	17	0.06
Salvadoran	28	0.11
Cuban	23	0.09
Dominican Republic	18	0.07
Mexican	4,694	17.87
Puerto Rican	111	0.42
South American	28	0.11
Argentinean	6	0.02
Chilean	4	0.02
Colombian	9	0.03
Ecuadorian	3	0.01
Paraguayan	1	<0.01
Peruvian	3	0.01
Venezuelan	2	0.01
Other Hispanic or Latino	318	1.21

Race*	Population	%
African-American/Black (312)	440	1.68
Not Hispanic (255)	346	1.32
Hispanic (57)	94	0.36
American Indian/Alaska Native (245)	413	1.57
Not Hispanic (195)	339	1.29
Hispanic (50)	74	0.28
Alaska Athabascan *(Ala. Nat.)* (3)	4	0.02
Aleut *(Alaska Native)* (3)	3	0.01
Apache (2)	4	0.02
Blackfeet (3)	11	0.04
Canadian/French Am. Ind. (1)	2	0.01
Cherokee (27)	54	0.21
Cheyenne (0)	1	<0.01
Chickasaw (3)	6	0.02
Chippewa (7)	9	0.03
Choctaw (5)	14	0.05
Colville (3)	3	0.01
Creek (2)	2	0.01
Delaware (2)	2	0.01
Inupiat *(Alaska Native)* (2)	2	0.01
Iroquois (3)	6	0.02
Lumbee (1)	2	0.01
Mexican American Ind. (20)	25	0.10
Navajo (11)	14	0.05
Osage (2)	2	0.01
Paiute (2)	5	0.02
Pima (2)	6	0.02
Potawatomi (2)	5	0.02

*Notes: † The Census 2010 population figure is used to calculate the percentages in the Hispanic Origin and Race categories. Ancestry percentages are based on the 2006-2010 American Community Survey population (not shown); ‡ Numbers in parentheses indicate the number of people reporting a single ancestry; * Numbers in parentheses indicate the number of persons reporting this race alone, not in combination with any other race; Please refer to the Explanation of Data for more information.*

Pueblo (2)	2	0.01
Puget Sound Salish (4)	6	0.02
Seminole (0)	1	<0.01
Shoshone (6)	10	0.04
Sioux (8)	19	0.07
South American Ind. (1)	1	<0.01
Spanish American Ind. (1)	1	<0.01
Tlingit-Haida *(Alaska Native)* (3)	4	0.02
Tohono O'Odham (6)	8	0.03
Tsimshian *(Alaska Native)* (1)	1	<0.01
Yaqui (5)	8	0.03
Yuman (29)	34	0.13
Asian (261)	422	1.61
Not Hispanic (235)	348	1.32
Hispanic (26)	74	0.28
Cambodian (0)	1	<0.01
Chinese, ex. Taiwanese (38)	65	0.25
Filipino (86)	146	0.56
Hmong (3)	5	0.02
Indian (6)	21	0.08
Japanese (34)	66	0.25
Korean (45)	60	0.23
Laotian (5)	7	0.03
Malaysian (4)	4	0.02
Nepalese (2)	2	0.01
Pakistani (0)	1	<0.01
Taiwanese (1)	2	0.01
Thai (8)	12	0.05
Vietnamese (22)	27	0.10
Hawaii Native/Pacific Islander (25)	65	0.25
Not Hispanic (25)	56	0.21
Hispanic (0)	9	0.03
Guamanian/Chamorro (7)	10	0.04
Native Hawaiian (9)	37	0.14
Samoan (2)	5	0.02
White (22,995)	23,626	89.95
Not Hispanic (19,922)	20,253	77.11
Hispanic (3,073)	3,373	12.84

Fountain Hills

Place Type: Town
County: Maricopa
Population: 22,489†

Ancestry‡	Population	%
American (1,272)	1,272	5.65
Arab (107)	129	0.57
Arab (0)	13	0.06
Lebanese (107)	116	0.52
Armenian (45)	45	0.20
Australian (16)	16	0.07
Austrian (48)	120	0.53
Belgian (0)	12	0.05
British (44)	156	0.69
Canadian (56)	159	0.71
Celtic (18)	18	0.08
Croatian (28)	114	0.51
Czech (41)	87	0.39
Czechoslovakian (17)	17	0.08
Danish (24)	122	0.54
Dutch (308)	728	3.23
Eastern European (31)	31	0.14
English (1,188)	3,265	14.51
European (178)	178	0.79
Finnish (61)	206	0.92
French, ex. Basque (199)	940	4.18
French Canadian (81)	165	0.73
German (2,290)	6,005	26.68
Greek (168)	244	1.08
Hungarian (85)	177	0.79
Iranian (85)	101	0.45
Irish (959)	3,799	16.88
Israeli (0)	8	0.04
Italian (1,438)	2,999	13.33
Latvian (0)	38	0.17
Lithuanian (78)	205	0.91
Luxemburger (13)	13	0.06
Maltese (0)	43	0.19
Norwegian (292)	776	3.45
Pennsylvania German (0)	13	0.06
Polish (429)	1,023	4.55
Portuguese (78)	159	0.71
Romanian (0)	55	0.24
Russian (68)	273	1.21
Scandinavian (161)	199	0.88
Scotch-Irish (206)	492	2.19
Scottish (165)	485	2.15
Serbian (20)	25	0.11
Slavic (11)	23	0.10
Slovak (33)	75	0.33
Slovene (12)	23	0.10
Swedish (378)	898	3.99
Swiss (11)	85	0.38
Ukrainian (29)	59	0.26
Welsh (12)	148	0.66
West Indian, ex. Hispanic (0)	12	0.05
Jamaican (0)	12	0.05
Yugoslavian (56)	110	0.49

Hispanic Origin	Population	%
Hispanic or Latino (of any race)	925	4.11
Central American, ex. Mexican	34	0.15
Costa Rican	2	0.01
Guatemalan	10	0.04
Honduran	5	0.02
Nicaraguan	2	0.01
Panamanian	6	0.03
Salvadoran	9	0.04
Cuban	19	0.08
Dominican Republic	4	0.02
Mexican	569	2.53
Puerto Rican	91	0.40
South American	63	0.28
Argentinean	7	0.03
Chilean	9	0.04
Colombian	15	0.07
Ecuadorian	14	0.06
Paraguayan	1	<0.01
Peruvian	14	0.06
Uruguayan	2	0.01
Other South American	1	<0.01
Other Hispanic or Latino	145	0.64

Race*	Population	%
African-American/Black (219)	283	1.26
Not Hispanic (210)	263	1.17
Hispanic (9)	20	0.09
American Indian/Alaska Native (130)	199	0.88
Not Hispanic (107)	164	0.73
Hispanic (23)	35	0.16
Apache (6)	6	0.03
Blackfeet (0)	2	0.01
Cherokee (3)	16	0.07
Chippewa (2)	4	0.02
Choctaw (1)	3	0.01
Comanche (2)	3	0.01
Cree (1)	1	<0.01
Creek (2)	2	0.01
Delaware (0)	1	<0.01
Hopi (10)	13	0.06
Iroquois (5)	10	0.04
Menominee (0)	1	<0.01
Mexican American Ind. (3)	3	0.01
Navajo (16)	21	0.09
Ottawa (0)	3	0.01
Paiute (1)	1	<0.01
Pima (4)	5	0.02
Potawatomi (2)	3	0.01
Pueblo (1)	1	<0.01
Seminole (1)	1	<0.01
Shoshone (1)	1	<0.01
Sioux (2)	2	0.01
South American Ind. (1)	1	<0.01
Tlingit-Haida *(Alaska Native)* (2)	5	0.02
Tohono O'Odham (1)	1	<0.01
Yaqui (7)	7	0.03
Yuman (10)	13	0.06
Yup'ik *(Alaska Native)* (1)	1	<0.01
Asian (411)	535	2.38
Not Hispanic (403)	517	2.30
Hispanic (8)	18	0.08
Bangladeshi (2)	2	0.01
Cambodian (2)	2	0.01
Chinese, ex. Taiwanese (88)	106	0.47
Filipino (89)	121	0.54
Hmong (3)	3	0.01
Indian (63)	81	0.36
Indonesian (5)	8	0.04
Japanese (42)	69	0.31
Korean (32)	35	0.16
Laotian (1)	1	<0.01
Pakistani (14)	15	0.07
Taiwanese (4)	5	0.02
Thai (4)	5	0.02
Vietnamese (38)	48	0.21
Hawaii Native/Pacific Islander (22)	44	0.20
Not Hispanic (21)	40	0.18
Hispanic (1)	4	0.02
Guamanian/Chamorro (7)	10	0.04
Marshallese (1)	1	<0.01
Native Hawaiian (7)	20	0.09
Samoan (3)	3	0.01
White (21,162)	21,454	95.40
Not Hispanic (20,569)	20,779	92.40
Hispanic (593)	675	3.00

Gilbert

Place Type: Town
County: Maricopa
Population: 208,453†

Ancestry‡	Population	%
Afghan (14)	14	0.01
African, Sub-Saharan (661)	702	0.36
African (196)	228	0.12
Cape Verdean (55)	55	0.03
Ethiopian (149)	149	0.08
Ghanaian (86)	86	0.04
Kenyan (21)	21	0.01
Somalian (100)	100	0.05
Zimbabwean (0)	9	<0.01
Other Sub-Saharan African (54)	54	0.03
American (7,584)	7,584	3.89
Arab (1,285)	1,948	1.00
Arab (368)	469	0.24
Egyptian (80)	210	0.11
Iraqi (64)	76	0.04
Jordanian (45)	45	0.02
Lebanese (472)	718	0.37
Moroccan (20)	20	0.01
Syrian (80)	180	0.09
Other Arab (156)	230	0.12
Armenian (34)	127	0.07
Assyrian/Chaldean/Syriac (48)	58	0.03
Australian (52)	105	0.05
Austrian (27)	334	0.17
Basque (28)	244	0.13
Belgian (18)	150	0.08
Brazilian (62)	235	0.12
British (531)	838	0.43
Bulgarian (33)	115	0.06
Cajun (21)	21	0.01
Canadian (252)	614	0.31
Carpatho Rusyn (0)	9	<0.01
Celtic (9)	9	<0.01
Croatian (169)	510	0.26
Cypriot (11)	11	0.01
Czech (157)	829	0.43
Czechoslovakian (126)	398	0.20
Danish (850)	2,731	1.40
Dutch (866)	3,780	1.94
Eastern European (172)	180	0.09
English (9,100)	27,216	13.95
European (2,896)	3,197	1.64
Finnish (186)	669	0.34
French, ex. Basque (880)	6,475	3.32
French Canadian (397)	1,505	0.77
German (13,066)	42,680	21.88

*Notes: † The Census 2010 population figure is used to calculate the percentages in the Hispanic Origin and Race categories. Ancestry percentages are based on the 2006-2010 American Community Survey population (not shown); ‡ Numbers in parentheses indicate the number of people reporting a single ancestry; * Numbers in parentheses indicate the number of persons reporting this race alone, not in combination with any other race; Please refer to the Explanation of Data for more information.*

German Russian (0)	16	0.01
Greek (443)	1,217	0.62
Hungarian (258)	1,214	0.62
Icelander (18)	52	0.03
Iranian (140)	184	0.09
Irish (6,686)	26,594	13.63
Israeli (16)	116	0.06
Italian (4,374)	12,802	6.56
Latvian (21)	87	0.04
Lithuanian (11)	337	0.17
Luxemburger (9)	28	0.01
Macedonian (12)	30	0.02
Maltese (28)	32	0.02
Northern European (84)	84	0.04
Norwegian (1,664)	4,178	2.14
Pennsylvania German (12)	22	0.01
Polish (2,361)	7,033	3.61
Portuguese (172)	373	0.19
Romanian (144)	245	0.13
Russian (617)	1,805	0.93
Scandinavian (206)	772	0.40
Scotch-Irish (1,463)	3,608	1.85
Scottish (1,303)	4,530	2.32
Serbian (185)	219	0.11
Slavic (61)	161	0.08
Slovak (140)	455	0.23
Swedish (1,133)	4,884	2.50
Swiss (159)	711	0.36
Turkish (82)	156	0.08
Ukrainian (126)	323	0.17
Welsh (184)	1,169	0.60
West Indian, ex. Hispanic (201)	462	0.24
Haitian (11)	33	0.02
Jamaican (74)	276	0.14
Trinidadian/Tobagonian (7)	28	0.01
West Indian (109)	125	0.06
Yugoslavian (265)	390	0.20

Hispanic Origin	Population	%
Hispanic or Latino (of any race)	31,074	14.91
Central American, ex. Mexican	1,006	0.48
Costa Rican	92	0.04
Guatemalan	266	0.13
Honduran	130	0.06
Nicaraguan	124	0.06
Panamanian	75	0.04
Salvadoran	307	0.15
Other Central American	12	0.01
Cuban	353	0.17
Dominican Republic	190	0.09
Mexican	23,846	11.44
Puerto Rican	1,357	0.65
South American	1,276	0.61
Argentinean	180	0.09
Bolivian	44	0.02
Chilean	70	0.03
Colombian	396	0.19
Ecuadorian	113	0.05
Paraguayan	6	<0.01
Peruvian	305	0.15
Uruguayan	30	0.01
Venezuelan	115	0.06
Other South American	17	0.01
Other Hispanic or Latino	3,046	1.46

Race*	Population	%
African-American/Black (6,987)	9,138	4.38
Not Hispanic (6,606)	8,375	4.02
Hispanic (381)	763	0.37
American Indian/Alaska Native (1,736)	2,998	1.44
Not Hispanic (1,394)	2,309	1.11
Hispanic (342)	689	0.33
Alaska Athabascan *(Ala. Nat.)* (1)	5	<0.01
Aleut *(Alaska Native)* (6)	7	<0.01
Apache (75)	122	0.06
Arapaho (0)	1	<0.01
Blackfeet (10)	26	0.01
Canadian/French Am. Ind. (1)	4	<0.01
Central American Ind. (0)	3	<0.01
Cherokee (59)	231	0.11
Cheyenne (3)	5	<0.01
Chickasaw (7)	13	0.01
Chippewa (21)	44	0.02
Choctaw (53)	85	0.04
Colville (1)	2	<0.01
Comanche (2)	17	0.01
Cree (1)	1	<0.01
Creek (7)	19	0.01
Crow (0)	2	<0.01
Delaware (3)	7	<0.01
Hopi (26)	41	0.02
Inupiat *(Alaska Native)* (11)	15	0.01
Iroquois (11)	21	0.01
Kiowa (3)	3	<0.01
Lumbee (4)	6	<0.01
Menominee (2)	2	<0.01
Mexican American Ind. (27)	62	0.03
Navajo (570)	714	0.34
Osage (0)	1	<0.01
Ottawa (1)	5	<0.01
Paiute (1)	4	<0.01
Pima (96)	150	0.07
Potawatomi (4)	6	<0.01
Pueblo (25)	36	0.02
Puget Sound Salish (0)	14	0.01
Seminole (2)	8	<0.01
Shoshone (3)	3	<0.01
Sioux (38)	75	0.04
South American Ind. (8)	14	0.01
Spanish American Ind. (3)	4	<0.01
Tlingit-Haida *(Alaska Native)* (3)	6	<0.01
Tohono O'Odham (36)	50	0.02
Ute (4)	7	<0.01
Yakama (2)	2	<0.01
Yaqui (36)	67	0.03
Yuman (8)	32	0.02
Yup'ik *(Alaska Native)* (1)	1	<0.01
Asian (12,110)	14,950	7.17
Not Hispanic (11,877)	14,295	6.86
Hispanic (233)	655	0.31
Bangladeshi (177)	188	0.09
Burmese (14)	20	0.01
Cambodian (105)	148	0.07
Chinese, ex. Taiwanese (2,303)	2,966	1.42
Filipino (2,445)	3,345	1.60
Hmong (2)	2	<0.01
Indian (2,502)	2,745	1.32
Indonesian (41)	85	0.04
Japanese (416)	1,025	0.49
Korean (1,028)	1,414	0.68
Laotian (76)	96	0.05
Malaysian (6)	12	0.01
Nepalese (21)	27	0.01
Pakistani (195)	244	0.12
Sri Lankan (22)	28	0.01
Taiwanese (93)	119	0.06
Thai (148)	233	0.11
Vietnamese (2,025)	2,307	1.11
Hawaii Native/Pacific Islander (449)	987	0.47
Not Hispanic (406)	844	0.40
Hispanic (43)	143	0.07
Fijian (11)	18	0.01
Guamanian/Chamorro (70)	133	0.06
Marshallese (11)	11	0.01
Native Hawaiian (126)	368	0.18
Samoan (96)	181	0.09
Tongan (71)	111	0.05
White (170,483)	177,075	84.95
Not Hispanic (151,930)	156,360	75.01
Hispanic (18,553)	20,715	9.94

Glendale

Place Type: City
County: Maricopa
Population: 226,721†

Ancestry‡	Population	%
Afghan (183)	223	0.10
African, Sub-Saharan (950)	1,026	0.45
African (467)	534	0.23
Cape Verdean (12)	12	0.01
Nigerian (85)	94	0.04
Other Sub-Saharan African (386)	386	0.17
Albanian (131)	160	0.07
Alsatian (0)	9	<0.01
American (9,053)	9,053	3.94
Arab (1,094)	1,516	0.66
Arab (177)	242	0.11
Egyptian (12)	12	0.01
Iraqi (674)	703	0.31
Lebanese (97)	235	0.10
Palestinian (14)	14	0.01
Syrian (29)	205	0.09
Other Arab (91)	105	0.05
Armenian (110)	137	0.06
Assyrian/Chaldean/Syriac (221)	264	0.11
Australian (23)	102	0.04
Austrian (102)	455	0.20
Basque (0)	15	0.01
Belgian (93)	236	0.10
Brazilian (42)	71	0.03
British (444)	777	0.34
Bulgarian (14)	30	0.01
Canadian (234)	444	0.19
Celtic (42)	223	0.10
Croatian (65)	270	0.12
Czech (202)	857	0.37
Czechoslovakian (75)	166	0.07
Danish (350)	1,409	0.61
Dutch (930)	3,754	1.63
Eastern European (23)	23	0.01
English (6,528)	20,114	8.76
European (1,383)	1,479	0.64
Finnish (161)	464	0.20
French, ex. Basque (858)	5,863	2.55
French Canadian (356)	1,037	0.45
German (11,112)	35,213	15.33
German Russian (10)	10	<0.01
Greek (188)	608	0.26
Hungarian (512)	1,019	0.44
Icelander (0)	106	0.05
Iranian (111)	165	0.07
Irish (5,279)	22,705	9.89
Israeli (0)	10	<0.01
Italian (4,897)	11,053	4.81
Latvian (79)	87	0.04
Lithuanian (34)	317	0.14
Maltese (0)	18	0.01
Northern European (59)	117	0.05
Norwegian (818)	3,248	1.41
Pennsylvania German (60)	128	0.06
Polish (2,085)	6,360	2.77
Portuguese (178)	517	0.23
Romanian (672)	816	0.36
Russian (888)	1,551	0.68
Scandinavian (341)	461	0.20
Scotch-Irish (1,053)	2,882	1.25
Scottish (1,320)	3,774	1.64
Serbian (22)	185	0.08
Slavic (0)	25	0.01
Slovak (171)	381	0.17
Slovene (25)	100	0.04
Swedish (563)	3,079	1.34
Swiss (108)	463	0.20
Turkish (92)	92	0.04
Ukrainian (129)	413	0.18
Welsh (532)	1,672	0.73
West Indian, ex. Hispanic (118)	176	0.08
Bermudan (26)	26	0.01
Dutch West Indian (0)	58	0.03
Haitian (33)	33	0.01
Jamaican (31)	31	0.01
Trinidadian/Tobagonian (17)	17	0.01
West Indian (11)	11	<0.01
Yugoslavian (830)	901	0.39

Hispanic Origin	Population	%
Hispanic or Latino (of any race)	80,501	35.51
Central American, ex. Mexican	1,843	0.81

*Notes: † The Census 2010 population figure is used to calculate the percentages in the Hispanic Origin and Race categories. Ancestry percentages are based on the 2006-2010 American Community Survey population (not shown); ‡ Numbers in parentheses indicate the number of people reporting a single ancestry; * Numbers in parentheses indicate the number of persons reporting this race alone, not in combination with any other race; Please refer to the Explanation of Data for more information.*

Costa Rican	49	0.02
Guatemalan	662	0.29
Honduran	232	0.10
Nicaraguan	125	0.06
Panamanian	86	0.04
Salvadoran	663	0.29
Other Central American	26	0.01
Cuban	765	0.34
Dominican Republic	99	0.04
Mexican	69,929	30.84
Puerto Rican	1,346	0.59
South American	778	0.34
Argentinean	113	0.05
Bolivian	12	0.01
Chilean	67	0.03
Colombian	243	0.11
Ecuadorian	111	0.05
Paraguayan	1	<0.01
Peruvian	165	0.07
Uruguayan	15	0.01
Venezuelan	46	0.02
Other South American	5	<0.01
Other Hispanic or Latino	5,741	2.53

Race*	Population	%
African-American/Black (13,686)	16,561	7.30
Not Hispanic (12,766)	14,912	6.58
Hispanic (920)	1,649	0.73
American Indian/Alaska Native (3,784)	5,640	2.49
Not Hispanic (2,707)	3,928	1.73
Hispanic (1,077)	1,712	0.76
Alaska Athabascan *(Ala. Nat.)* (6)	11	<0.01
Apache (123)	267	0.12
Arapaho (2)	3	<0.01
Blackfeet (10)	57	0.03
Canadian/French Am. Ind. (2)	11	<0.01
Central American Ind. (3)	4	<0.01
Cherokee (111)	389	0.17
Cheyenne (7)	11	<0.01
Chickasaw (15)	28	0.01
Chippewa (35)	63	0.03
Choctaw (59)	146	0.06
Colville (4)	7	<0.01
Comanche (2)	3	<0.01
Cree (1)	6	<0.01
Creek (4)	23	0.01
Crow (1)	3	<0.01
Delaware (2)	8	<0.01
Hopi (137)	179	0.08
Houma (5)	5	<0.01
Inupiat *(Alaska Native)* (15)	24	0.01
Iroquois (28)	52	0.02
Kiowa (6)	6	<0.01
Lumbee (8)	11	<0.01
Menominee (1)	3	<0.01
Mexican American Ind. (148)	188	0.08
Navajo (1,347)	1,570	0.69
Osage (1)	3	<0.01
Paiute (17)	25	0.01
Pima (136)	199	0.09
Potawatomi (6)	15	0.01
Pueblo (48)	79	0.03
Puget Sound Salish (3)	6	<0.01
Seminole (2)	5	<0.01
Shoshone (6)	9	<0.01
Sioux (31)	81	0.04
South American Ind. (5)	12	0.01
Spanish American Ind. (19)	23	0.01
Tlingit-Haida *(Alaska Native)* (5)	17	0.01
Tohono O'Odham (117)	157	0.07
Tsimshian *(Alaska Native)* (0)	2	<0.01
Ute (7)	17	0.01
Yakama (1)	4	<0.01
Yaqui (88)	128	0.06
Yuman (26)	47	0.02
Yup'ik *(Alaska Native)* (10)	10	<0.01
Asian (8,855)	11,040	4.87
Not Hispanic (8,618)	10,239	4.52
Hispanic (237)	801	0.35
Bangladeshi (27)	32	0.01
Bhutanese (23)	25	0.01
Burmese (113)	115	0.05
Cambodian (147)	178	0.08
Chinese, ex. Taiwanese (1,280)	1,630	0.72
Filipino (1,598)	2,269	1.00
Hmong (7)	7	<0.01
Indian (1,565)	1,723	0.76
Indonesian (29)	51	0.02
Japanese (364)	772	0.34
Korean (677)	913	0.40
Laotian (85)	99	0.04
Malaysian (1)	7	<0.01
Nepalese (24)	28	0.01
Pakistani (92)	106	0.05
Sri Lankan (10)	10	<0.01
Taiwanese (59)	78	0.03
Thai (178)	267	0.12
Vietnamese (2,139)	2,326	1.03
Hawaii Native/Pacific Islander (430)	895	0.39
Not Hispanic (355)	690	0.30
Hispanic (75)	205	0.09
Fijian (6)	7	<0.01
Guamanian/Chamorro (91)	148	0.07
Marshallese (1)	7	<0.01
Native Hawaiian (114)	320	0.14
Samoan (105)	159	0.07
Tongan (12)	30	0.01
White (153,769)	161,331	71.16
Not Hispanic (116,866)	120,817	53.29
Hispanic (36,903)	40,514	17.87

Globe

Place Type: City
County: Gila
Population: 7,532†

Ancestry‡	Population	%
American (88)	88	1.16
Austrian (11)	54	0.71
Basque (10)	10	0.13
British (22)	53	0.70
Canadian (8)	8	0.11
Danish (6)	34	0.45
Dutch (14)	89	1.18
English (148)	589	7.79
European (87)	98	1.30
French, ex. Basque (93)	202	2.67
French Canadian (0)	9	0.12
German (319)	680	9.00
Hungarian (0)	20	0.26
Irish (165)	688	9.10
Italian (87)	353	4.67
Norwegian (36)	62	0.82
Pennsylvania German (0)	12	0.16
Polish (31)	79	1.05
Portuguese (0)	26	0.34
Russian (12)	28	0.37
Scandinavian (0)	13	0.17
Scotch-Irish (29)	167	2.21
Scottish (164)	224	2.96
Serbian (0)	11	0.15
Slovak (14)	14	0.19
Slovene (9)	9	0.12
Swedish (14)	58	0.77
Welsh (0)	18	0.24
Yugoslavian (4)	4	0.05

Hispanic Origin	Population	%
Hispanic or Latino (of any race)	2,775	36.84
Central American, ex. Mexican	3	0.04
Costa Rican	2	0.03
Nicaraguan	1	0.01
Cuban	1	0.01
Mexican	2,520	33.46
Puerto Rican	30	0.40
South American	14	0.19
Bolivian	9	0.12
Peruvian	5	0.07
Other Hispanic or Latino	207	2.75

Race*	Population	%
African-American/Black (69)	94	1.25
Not Hispanic (53)	62	0.82
Hispanic (16)	32	0.42
American Indian/Alaska Native (430)	519	6.89
Not Hispanic (377)	424	5.63
Hispanic (53)	95	1.26
Apache (184)	223	2.96
Arapaho (0)	2	0.03
Blackfeet (4)	9	0.12
Cherokee (6)	20	0.27
Chickasaw (1)	1	0.01
Choctaw (1)	4	0.05
Cree (1)	1	0.01
Hopi (3)	3	0.04
Inupiat *(Alaska Native)* (2)	4	0.05
Kiowa (0)	1	0.01
Mexican American Ind. (3)	3	0.04
Navajo (20)	28	0.37
Ottawa (1)	1	0.01
Pima (6)	6	0.08
Potawatomi (2)	2	0.03
Pueblo (0)	1	0.01
Shoshone (1)	1	0.01
Sioux (3)	6	0.08
Tohono O'Odham (4)	4	0.05
Ute (1)	1	0.01
Yaqui (0)	4	0.05
Yuman (8)	8	0.11
Asian (85)	115	1.53
Not Hispanic (78)	97	1.29
Hispanic (7)	18	0.24
Bangladeshi (1)	1	0.01
Chinese, ex. Taiwanese (14)	18	0.24
Filipino (29)	40	0.53
Indian (22)	25	0.33
Indonesian (0)	1	0.01
Japanese (2)	4	0.05
Korean (13)	23	0.31
Vietnamese (1)	1	0.01
Hawaii Native/Pacific Islander (9)	22	0.29
Not Hispanic (2)	10	0.13
Hispanic (7)	12	0.16
Native Hawaiian (1)	14	0.19
Samoan (6)	6	0.08
White (5,993)	6,192	82.21
Not Hispanic (4,163)	4,229	56.15
Hispanic (1,830)	1,963	26.06

Gold Canyon

Place Type: CDP
County: Pinal
Population: 10,159†

Ancestry‡	Population	%
American (357)	357	3.20
Arab (54)	84	0.75
Arab (0)	30	0.27
Egyptian (40)	40	0.36
Lebanese (14)	14	0.13
Armenian (0)	30	0.27
Australian (0)	10	0.09
Austrian (48)	119	1.07
Belgian (0)	15	0.13
British (14)	28	0.25
Canadian (47)	47	0.42
Croatian (25)	40	0.36
Czech (142)	337	3.02
Czechoslovakian (0)	47	0.42
Danish (29)	154	1.38
Dutch (167)	527	4.72
English (717)	2,177	19.51
European (107)	107	0.96
Finnish (18)	18	0.16
French, ex. Basque (49)	479	4.29
French Canadian (93)	169	1.51
German (1,426)	2,671	23.94
Greek (14)	45	0.40

*Notes: † The Census 2010 population figure is used to calculate the percentages in the Hispanic Origin and Race categories. Ancestry percentages are based on the 2006-2010 American Community Survey population (not shown); ‡ Numbers in parentheses indicate the number of people reporting a single ancestry; * Numbers in parentheses indicate the number of persons reporting this race alone, not in combination with any other race; Please refer to the Explanation of Data for more information.*

Ancestry	Population	%
Hungarian (45)	90	0.81
Icelander (15)	48	0.43
Irish (420)	1,747	15.66
Italian (339)	601	5.39
Lithuanian (88)	126	1.13
Luxemburger (13)	30	0.27
New Zealander (0)	10	0.09
Norwegian (155)	453	4.06
Pennsylvania German (14)	14	0.13
Polish (251)	501	4.49
Portuguese (36)	106	0.95
Romanian (0)	18	0.16
Russian (10)	67	0.60
Scandinavian (10)	10	0.09
Scotch-Irish (146)	288	2.58
Scottish (77)	299	2.68
Serbian (14)	29	0.26
Slovak (19)	34	0.30
Slovene (0)	16	0.14
Swedish (140)	360	3.23
Swiss (15)	73	0.65
Ukrainian (14)	14	0.13
Welsh (66)	127	1.14
West Indian, ex. Hispanic (0)	11	0.10
Dutch West Indian (0)	11	0.10

Hispanic Origin	Population	%
Hispanic or Latino (of any race)	560	5.51
Central American, ex. Mexican	7	0.07
Costa Rican	1	0.01
Guatemalan	3	0.03
Honduran	2	0.02
Salvadoran	1	0.01
Cuban	4	0.04
Dominican Republic	3	0.03
Mexican	420	4.13
Puerto Rican	33	0.32
South American	44	0.43
Argentinean	10	0.10
Chilean	7	0.07
Colombian	14	0.14
Ecuadorian	3	0.03
Peruvian	10	0.10
Other Hispanic or Latino	49	0.48

Race*	Population	%
African-American/Black (100)	128	1.26
Not Hispanic (94)	121	1.19
Hispanic (6)	7	0.07
American Indian/Alaska Native (41)	98	0.96
Not Hispanic (38)	76	0.75
Hispanic (3)	22	0.22
Aleut *(Alaska Native)* (0)	1	0.01
Apache (2)	5	0.05
Cherokee (7)	17	0.17
Choctaw (0)	3	0.03
Colville (0)	1	0.01
Cree (1)	1	0.01
Hopi (1)	3	0.03
Iroquois (2)	4	0.04
Navajo (14)	26	0.26
Pima (1)	3	0.03
Potawatomi (1)	2	0.02
Pueblo (0)	2	0.02
Puget Sound Salish (0)	2	0.02
Sioux (2)	7	0.07
South American Ind. (0)	1	0.01
Tohono O'Odham (2)	2	0.02
Asian (85)	141	1.39
Not Hispanic (82)	136	1.34
Hispanic (3)	5	0.05
Chinese, ex. Taiwanese (12)	21	0.21
Filipino (28)	44	0.43
Indian (8)	12	0.12
Indonesian (1)	3	0.03
Japanese (13)	27	0.27
Korean (14)	20	0.20
Thai (2)	2	0.02
Vietnamese (3)	8	0.08
Hawaii Native/Pacific Islander (12)	20	0.20
Not Hispanic (7)	15	0.15
Hispanic (5)	5	0.05
Guamanian/Chamorro (2)	2	0.02
Native Hawaiian (2)	3	0.03
Samoan (6)	7	0.07
White (9,612)	9,769	96.16
Not Hispanic (9,243)	9,369	92.22
Hispanic (369)	400	3.94

Golden Valley

Place Type: CDP
County: Mohave
Population: 8,370†

Ancestry‡	Population	%
American (164)	164	1.95
Armenian (18)	18	0.21
Austrian (0)	63	0.75
Basque (16)	16	0.19
British (0)	66	0.79
Czechoslovakian (0)	15	0.18
Danish (15)	15	0.18
Dutch (101)	256	3.05
English (354)	1,632	19.42
European (17)	17	0.20
Finnish (15)	15	0.18
French, ex. Basque (101)	755	8.98
French Canadian (150)	150	1.78
German (723)	2,449	29.14
Hungarian (37)	63	0.75
Irish (347)	1,727	20.55
Italian (99)	275	3.27
Lithuanian (0)	9	0.11
Norwegian (62)	230	2.74
Polish (49)	170	2.02
Portuguese (37)	37	0.44
Russian (66)	123	1.46
Scotch-Irish (66)	141	1.68
Scottish (41)	262	3.12
Slavic (0)	15	0.18
Slovak (0)	31	0.37
Swedish (62)	174	2.07
Swiss (0)	15	0.18

Hispanic Origin	Population	%
Hispanic or Latino (of any race)	882	10.54
Central American, ex. Mexican	11	0.13
Honduran	4	0.05
Nicaraguan	1	0.01
Panamanian	2	0.02
Salvadoran	4	0.05
Cuban	11	0.13
Mexican	752	8.98
Puerto Rican	26	0.31
South American	4	0.05
Chilean	3	0.04
Peruvian	1	0.01
Other Hispanic or Latino	78	0.93

Race*	Population	%
African-American/Black (39)	80	0.96
Not Hispanic (36)	68	0.81
Hispanic (3)	12	0.14
American Indian/Alaska Native (128)	252	3.01
Not Hispanic (97)	200	2.39
Hispanic (31)	52	0.62
Apache (1)	9	0.11
Arapaho (0)	1	0.01
Blackfeet (1)	3	0.04
Central American Ind. (2)	2	0.02
Cherokee (11)	39	0.47
Chickasaw (1)	1	0.01
Chippewa (2)	4	0.05
Choctaw (10)	13	0.16
Cree (0)	2	0.02
Creek (1)	2	0.02
Crow (1)	1	0.01
Delaware (0)	1	0.01
Hopi (1)	3	0.04
Iroquois (0)	4	0.05
Mexican American Ind. (1)	2	0.02
Navajo (12)	18	0.22
Osage (0)	1	0.01
Paiute (5)	5	0.06
Pima (3)	6	0.07
Potawatomi (0)	1	0.01
Pueblo (1)	1	0.01
Shoshone (1)	1	0.01
Sioux (5)	10	0.12
Spanish American Ind. (1)	1	0.01
Tohono O'Odham (1)	1	0.01
Ute (0)	1	0.01
Yaqui (3)	11	0.13
Yuman (3)	4	0.05
Asian (72)	113	1.35
Not Hispanic (66)	101	1.21
Hispanic (6)	12	0.14
Cambodian (2)	2	0.02
Chinese, ex. Taiwanese (4)	6	0.07
Filipino (38)	62	0.74
Indian (3)	5	0.06
Indonesian (0)	1	0.01
Japanese (8)	15	0.18
Korean (5)	7	0.08
Laotian (1)	2	0.02
Thai (4)	8	0.10
Vietnamese (4)	4	0.05
Hawaii Native/Pacific Islander (28)	49	0.59
Not Hispanic (28)	41	0.49
Hispanic (0)	8	0.10
Guamanian/Chamorro (0)	1	0.01
Native Hawaiian (8)	10	0.12
Samoan (19)	30	0.36
White (7,605)	7,818	93.41
Not Hispanic (7,093)	7,245	86.56
Hispanic (512)	573	6.85

Goodyear

Place Type: City
County: Maricopa
Population: 65,275†

Ancestry‡	Population	%
Afghan (5)	5	0.01
African, Sub-Saharan (236)	359	0.62
African (169)	292	0.50
South African (29)	29	0.05
Other Sub-Saharan African (38)	38	0.07
American (3,265)	3,265	5.64
Arab (26)	46	0.08
Jordanian (8)	8	0.01
Lebanese (18)	38	0.07
Australian (10)	67	0.12
Austrian (68)	137	0.24
Basque (32)	32	0.06
Belgian (0)	58	0.10
British (151)	216	0.37
Bulgarian (7)	7	0.01
Canadian (110)	264	0.46
Croatian (12)	160	0.28
Czech (22)	149	0.26
Czechoslovakian (25)	38	0.07
Danish (96)	553	0.96
Dutch (301)	677	1.17
Eastern European (61)	61	0.11
English (1,571)	4,009	6.93
Estonian (10)	10	0.02
European (976)	1,034	1.79
Finnish (44)	150	0.26
French, ex. Basque (253)	1,764	3.05
French Canadian (113)	251	0.43
German (2,959)	9,540	16.49
Greek (109)	183	0.32
Hungarian (138)	326	0.56
Icelander (14)	28	0.05
Iranian (12)	25	0.04
Irish (1,960)	6,349	10.97
Israeli (29)	29	0.05

SECTION TWO

*Notes: † The Census 2010 population figure is used to calculate the percentages in the Hispanic Origin and Race categories. Ancestry percentages are based on the 2006-2010 American Community Survey population (not shown); ‡ Numbers in parentheses indicate the number of people reporting a single ancestry; * Numbers in parentheses indicate the number of persons reporting this race alone, not in combination with any other race; Please refer to the Explanation of Data for more information.*

Italian (1,084)	3,040	5.25
Lithuanian (87)	215	0.37
Luxemburger (9)	22	0.04
Northern European (60)	60	0.10
Norwegian (549)	1,050	1.81
Polish (1,123)	1,983	3.43
Portuguese (78)	78	0.13
Romanian (308)	317	0.55
Russian (120)	579	1.00
Scandinavian (74)	113	0.20
Scotch-Irish (255)	627	1.08
Scottish (545)	1,223	2.11
Slavic (25)	25	0.04
Slovak (26)	55	0.10
Slovene (0)	23	0.04
Swedish (437)	1,528	2.64
Swiss (53)	91	0.16
Turkish (9)	9	0.02
Ukrainian (95)	116	0.20
Welsh (67)	397	0.69
West Indian, ex. Hispanic (12)	53	0.09
Belizean (0)	25	0.04
Dutch West Indian (0)	16	0.03
Jamaican (12)	12	0.02
Yugoslavian (76)	165	0.29

Hispanic Origin	Population	%
Hispanic or Latino (of any race)	18,136	27.78
Central American, ex. Mexican	484	0.74
Costa Rican	19	0.03
Guatemalan	143	0.22
Honduran	41	0.06
Nicaraguan	48	0.07
Panamanian	36	0.06
Salvadoran	191	0.29
Other Central American	6	0.01
Cuban	102	0.16
Dominican Republic	55	0.08
Mexican	15,412	23.61
Puerto Rican	491	0.75
South American	273	0.42
Argentinean	25	0.04
Bolivian	5	0.01
Chilean	19	0.03
Colombian	95	0.15
Ecuadorian	50	0.08
Paraguayan	3	<0.01
Peruvian	39	0.06
Uruguayan	6	0.01
Venezuelan	30	0.05
Other South American	1	<0.01
Other Hispanic or Latino	1,319	2.02

Race*	Population	%
African-American/Black (4,375)	5,218	7.99
Not Hispanic (4,132)	4,772	7.31
Hispanic (243)	446	0.68
American Indian/Alaska Native (848)	1,278	1.96
Not Hispanic (638)	927	1.42
Hispanic (210)	351	0.54
Aleut *(Alaska Native)* (2)	2	<0.01
Apache (25)	45	0.07
Arapaho (3)	3	<0.01
Blackfeet (1)	12	0.02
Canadian/French Am. Ind. (4)	6	0.01
Central American Ind. (0)	1	<0.01
Cherokee (23)	101	0.15
Cheyenne (1)	3	<0.01
Chickasaw (5)	11	0.02
Chippewa (19)	27	0.04
Choctaw (14)	27	0.04
Comanche (0)	3	<0.01
Cree (1)	1	<0.01
Creek (3)	8	0.01
Delaware (0)	3	<0.01
Hopi (15)	29	0.04
Houma (1)	1	<0.01
Inupiat *(Alaska Native)* (2)	10	0.02
Iroquois (0)	1	<0.01
Kiowa (1)	3	<0.01
Lumbee (1)	3	<0.01
Mexican American Ind. (31)	36	0.06
Navajo (135)	184	0.28
Osage (0)	5	0.01
Ottawa (3)	3	<0.01
Paiute (8)	12	0.02
Pima (9)	17	0.03
Potawatomi (1)	1	<0.01
Pueblo (5)	8	0.01
Puget Sound Salish (2)	2	<0.01
Seminole (2)	6	0.01
Shoshone (1)	2	<0.01
Sioux (8)	19	0.03
South American Ind. (1)	3	<0.01
Spanish American Ind. (6)	9	0.01
Tlingit-Haida *(Alaska Native)* (3)	4	0.01
Tohono O'Odham (14)	21	0.03
Ute (0)	1	<0.01
Yaqui (32)	38	0.06
Yuman (9)	9	0.01
Asian (2,830)	3,618	5.54
Not Hispanic (2,729)	3,342	5.12
Hispanic (101)	276	0.42
Bangladeshi (8)	8	0.01
Burmese (2)	3	<0.01
Cambodian (17)	25	0.04
Chinese, ex. Taiwanese (449)	603	0.92
Filipino (936)	1,280	1.96
Hmong (2)	3	<0.01
Indian (330)	382	0.59
Indonesian (6)	15	0.02
Japanese (114)	265	0.41
Korean (208)	296	0.45
Laotian (9)	16	0.02
Malaysian (5)	5	0.01
Nepalese (4)	4	0.01
Pakistani (29)	33	0.05
Sri Lankan (1)	1	<0.01
Taiwanese (5)	10	0.02
Thai (41)	67	0.10
Vietnamese (510)	571	0.87
Hawaii Native/Pacific Islander (110)	272	0.42
Not Hispanic (96)	220	0.34
Hispanic (14)	52	0.08
Guamanian/Chamorro (38)	68	0.10
Marshallese (1)	1	<0.01
Native Hawaiian (34)	107	0.16
Samoan (15)	27	0.04
Tongan (1)	1	<0.01
White (46,923)	49,127	75.26
Not Hispanic (38,064)	39,275	60.17
Hispanic (8,859)	9,852	15.09

Green Valley

Place Type: CDP
County: Pima
Population: 21,391†

Ancestry‡	Population	%
Albanian (9)	9	0.04
American (793)	793	3.71
Arab (15)	58	0.27
Lebanese (15)	58	0.27
Assyrian/Chaldean/Syriac (6)	6	0.03
Austrian (41)	117	0.55
Basque (8)	8	0.04
Belgian (32)	60	0.28
British (87)	95	0.44
Canadian (39)	106	0.50
Croatian (33)	49	0.23
Czech (111)	222	1.04
Czechoslovakian (40)	69	0.32
Danish (192)	390	1.82
Dutch (167)	583	2.72
Eastern European (11)	11	0.05
English (2,122)	5,447	25.45
Estonian (11)	11	0.05
European (167)	167	0.78
Finnish (61)	98	0.46
French, ex. Basque (209)	1,157	5.41
French Canadian (193)	282	1.32
German (2,623)	6,164	28.80
Greek (88)	147	0.69
Hungarian (43)	111	0.52
Irish (760)	2,526	11.80
Italian (612)	992	4.63
Latvian (29)	39	0.18
Lithuanian (22)	34	0.16
Maltese (8)	8	0.04
Northern European (27)	27	0.13
Norwegian (501)	1,092	5.10
Pennsylvania German (48)	80	0.37
Polish (468)	779	3.64
Portuguese (35)	82	0.38
Romanian (55)	68	0.32
Russian (50)	133	0.62
Scandinavian (43)	82	0.38
Scotch-Irish (326)	816	3.81
Scottish (282)	784	3.66
Slavic (10)	22	0.10
Slovak (23)	66	0.31
Slovene (0)	69	0.32
Swedish (336)	1,087	5.08
Swiss (79)	230	1.07
Ukrainian (125)	140	0.65
Welsh (84)	254	1.19
Yugoslavian (11)	26	0.12

Hispanic Origin	Population	%
Hispanic or Latino (of any race)	1,049	4.90
Central American, ex. Mexican	21	0.10
Costa Rican	1	<0.01
Guatemalan	2	0.01
Nicaraguan	4	0.02
Panamanian	5	0.02
Salvadoran	9	0.04
Cuban	9	0.04
Mexican	829	3.88
Puerto Rican	46	0.22
South American	30	0.14
Argentinean	6	0.03
Colombian	4	0.02
Ecuadorian	7	0.03
Paraguayan	1	<0.01
Peruvian	12	0.06
Other Hispanic or Latino	114	0.53

Race*	Population	%
African-American/Black (92)	114	0.53
Not Hispanic (88)	103	0.48
Hispanic (4)	11	0.05
American Indian/Alaska Native (66)	151	0.71
Not Hispanic (40)	109	0.51
Hispanic (26)	42	0.20
Alaska Athabascan *(Ala. Nat.)* (2)	2	0.01
Apache (2)	4	0.02
Blackfeet (0)	2	0.01
Central American Ind. (0)	1	<0.01
Cherokee (3)	36	0.17
Chickasaw (0)	1	<0.01
Chippewa (1)	2	0.01
Comanche (1)	3	0.01
Cree (1)	1	<0.01
Creek (1)	4	0.02
Inupiat *(Alaska Native)* (1)	1	<0.01
Iroquois (2)	3	0.01
Lumbee (1)	1	<0.01
Menominee (1)	1	<0.01
Mexican American Ind. (2)	3	0.01
Navajo (2)	3	0.01
Potawatomi (1)	2	0.01
Seminole (0)	1	<0.01
Sioux (0)	2	0.01
South American Ind. (2)	5	0.02
Tohono O'Odham (3)	3	0.01
Yaqui (4)	8	0.04
Asian (149)	171	0.80
Not Hispanic (146)	166	0.78
Hispanic (3)	5	0.02

*Notes: † The Census 2010 population figure is used to calculate the percentages in the Hispanic Origin and Race categories. Ancestry percentages are based on the 2006-2010 American Community Survey population (not shown); ‡ Numbers in parentheses indicate the number of people reporting a single ancestry; * Numbers in parentheses indicate the number of persons reporting this race alone, not in combination with any other race; Please refer to the Explanation of Data for more information.*

Burmese (1)	1	<0.01
Chinese, ex. Taiwanese (29)	34	0.16
Filipino (30)	38	0.18
Indian (10)	14	0.07
Japanese (33)	39	0.18
Korean (27)	29	0.14
Malaysian (1)	1	<0.01
Pakistani (3)	4	0.02
Thai (7)	7	0.03
Vietnamese (2)	2	0.01
Hawaii Native/Pacific Islander (9)	20	0.09
Not Hispanic (9)	20	0.09
Fijian (1)	3	0.01
Guamanian/Chamorro (2)	3	0.01
Native Hawaiian (2)	8	0.04
Samoan (2)	3	0.01
Tongan (1)	1	<0.01
White (20,710)	20,844	97.44
Not Hispanic (19,953)	20,046	93.71
Hispanic (757)	798	3.73

Kingman

Place Type: City
County: Mohave
Population: 28,068†

Ancestry‡	Population	%
African, Sub-Saharan (25)	29	0.10
African (25)	25	0.09
South African (0)	4	0.01
American (1,220)	1,220	4.39
Armenian (10)	10	0.04
Australian (22)	22	0.08
Austrian (0)	34	0.12
Belgian (26)	26	0.09
British (95)	154	0.55
Cajun (24)	24	0.09
Canadian (90)	90	0.32
Croatian (11)	26	0.09
Czech (11)	113	0.41
Czechoslovakian (0)	22	0.08
Danish (32)	91	0.33
Dutch (174)	804	2.89
English (1,083)	3,688	13.27
European (178)	203	0.73
French, ex. Basque (199)	1,529	5.50
French Canadian (112)	251	0.90
German (2,247)	7,094	25.53
Greek (51)	176	0.63
Hungarian (29)	115	0.41
Icelander (48)	65	0.23
Irish (1,545)	5,653	20.34
Italian (634)	1,455	5.24
Lithuanian (50)	80	0.29
Norwegian (308)	972	3.50
Pennsylvania German (0)	9	0.03
Polish (165)	717	2.58
Portuguese (0)	92	0.33
Romanian (0)	8	0.03
Russian (51)	120	0.43
Scandinavian (49)	204	0.73
Scotch-Irish (177)	612	2.20
Scottish (196)	976	3.51
Slovak (14)	14	0.05
Swedish (275)	863	3.11
Swiss (11)	31	0.11
Ukrainian (0)	51	0.18
Welsh (13)	291	1.05
West Indian, ex. Hispanic (72)	132	0.47
Belizean (29)	89	0.32
Jamaican (26)	26	0.09
West Indian (17)	17	0.06

Hispanic Origin	Population	%
Hispanic or Latino (of any race)	3,503	12.48
Central American, ex. Mexican	111	0.40
Costa Rican	12	0.04
Guatemalan	34	0.12
Honduran	10	0.04
Nicaraguan	5	0.02
Panamanian	1	<0.01
Salvadoran	49	0.17
Cuban	45	0.16
Dominican Republic	7	0.02
Mexican	2,677	9.54
Puerto Rican	114	0.41
South American	55	0.20
Argentinean	13	0.05
Colombian	18	0.06
Ecuadorian	5	0.02
Peruvian	13	0.05
Uruguayan	2	0.01
Venezuelan	3	0.01
Other South American	1	<0.01
Other Hispanic or Latino	494	1.76

Race*	Population	%
African-American/Black (289)	474	1.69
Not Hispanic (271)	422	1.50
Hispanic (18)	52	0.19
American Indian/Alaska Native (476)	824	2.94
Not Hispanic (402)	639	2.28
Hispanic (74)	185	0.66
Alaska Athabascan *(Ala. Nat.)* (0)	2	0.01
Apache (6)	27	0.10
Blackfeet (1)	15	0.05
Canadian/French Am. Ind. (0)	1	<0.01
Cherokee (29)	90	0.32
Cheyenne (0)	4	0.01
Chickasaw (3)	3	0.01
Chippewa (5)	13	0.05
Choctaw (16)	23	0.08
Colville (1)	1	<0.01
Comanche (0)	2	0.01
Creek (1)	2	0.01
Crow (0)	4	0.01
Delaware (2)	4	0.01
Hopi (15)	26	0.09
Inupiat *(Alaska Native)* (0)	1	<0.01
Iroquois (0)	5	0.02
Kiowa (4)	4	0.01
Mexican American Ind. (5)	11	0.04
Navajo (120)	156	0.56
Osage (1)	2	0.01
Paiute (1)	1	<0.01
Pima (3)	6	0.02
Potawatomi (6)	9	0.03
Pueblo (5)	7	0.02
Seminole (1)	3	0.01
Shoshone (3)	3	0.01
Sioux (14)	20	0.07
South American Ind. (0)	3	0.01
Spanish American Ind. (3)	7	0.02
Tlingit-Haida *(Alaska Native)* (2)	5	0.02
Tohono O'Odham (5)	5	0.02
Ute (1)	1	<0.01
Yaqui (6)	17	0.06
Yuman (71)	94	0.33
Yup'ik *(Alaska Native)* (0)	2	0.01
Asian (469)	651	2.32
Not Hispanic (452)	602	2.14
Hispanic (17)	49	0.17
Burmese (1)	1	<0.01
Chinese, ex. Taiwanese (35)	54	0.19
Filipino (166)	237	0.84
Indian (101)	118	0.42
Indonesian (5)	13	0.05
Japanese (28)	67	0.24
Korean (23)	41	0.15
Laotian (3)	4	0.01
Pakistani (42)	46	0.16
Taiwanese (0)	1	<0.01
Thai (18)	22	0.08
Vietnamese (27)	34	0.12
Hawaii Native/Pacific Islander (85)	144	0.51
Not Hispanic (85)	136	0.48
Hispanic (0)	8	0.03
Fijian (1)	1	<0.01
Guamanian/Chamorro (33)	40	0.14
Marshallese (1)	1	<0.01
Native Hawaiian (24)	58	0.21
Samoan (24)	32	0.11
White (24,711)	25,497	90.84
Not Hispanic (22,806)	23,312	83.06
Hispanic (1,905)	2,185	7.78

Lake Havasu City

Place Type: City
County: Mohave
Population: 52,527†

Ancestry‡	Population	%
African, Sub-Saharan (39)	39	0.07
African (39)	39	0.07
Albanian (61)	61	0.12
American (2,611)	2,611	4.98
Arab (26)	112	0.21
Iraqi (0)	12	0.02
Lebanese (0)	55	0.10
Syrian (0)	19	0.04
Other Arab (26)	26	0.05
Armenian (77)	77	0.15
Assyrian/Chaldean/Syriac (0)	12	0.02
Australian (17)	17	0.03
Austrian (100)	166	0.32
Belgian (65)	120	0.23
British (45)	113	0.22
Bulgarian (35)	35	0.07
Canadian (172)	236	0.45
Croatian (60)	82	0.16
Czech (153)	589	1.12
Czechoslovakian (35)	132	0.25
Danish (162)	398	0.76
Dutch (287)	1,160	2.21
Eastern European (28)	28	0.05
English (2,811)	7,283	13.88
European (256)	263	0.50
Finnish (52)	97	0.18
French, ex. Basque (299)	1,949	3.71
French Canadian (233)	405	0.77
German (4,661)	12,956	24.69
Greek (21)	59	0.11
Hungarian (190)	447	0.85
Iranian (50)	50	0.10
Irish (2,422)	7,175	13.67
Italian (1,648)	3,494	6.66
Latvian (0)	70	0.13
Lithuanian (33)	138	0.26
Luxemburger (13)	13	0.02
Maltese (0)	14	0.03
Northern European (49)	60	0.11
Norwegian (732)	1,629	3.10
Pennsylvania German (18)	37	0.07
Polish (463)	1,482	2.82
Portuguese (185)	316	0.60
Romanian (50)	61	0.12
Russian (153)	473	0.90
Scandinavian (29)	138	0.26
Scotch-Irish (506)	1,345	2.56
Scottish (508)	1,651	3.15
Serbian (10)	10	0.02
Slavic (18)	41	0.08
Slovak (45)	87	0.17
Slovene (0)	10	0.02
Swedish (236)	1,247	2.38
Swiss (196)	357	0.68
Ukrainian (45)	140	0.27
Welsh (132)	587	1.12
West Indian, ex. Hispanic (38)	38	0.07
Jamaican (38)	38	0.07
Yugoslavian (33)	122	0.23

Hispanic Origin	Population	%
Hispanic or Latino (of any race)	6,356	12.10
Central American, ex. Mexican	138	0.26
Costa Rican	8	0.02
Guatemalan	51	0.10
Honduran	12	0.02

*Notes: † The Census 2010 population figure is used to calculate the percentages in the Hispanic Origin and Race categories. Ancestry percentages are based on the 2006-2010 American Community Survey population (not shown); ‡ Numbers in parentheses indicate the number of people reporting a single ancestry; * Numbers in parentheses indicate the number of persons reporting this race alone, not in combination with any other race; Please refer to the Explanation of Data for more information.*

Nicaraguan	8	0.02
Panamanian	8	0.02
Salvadoran	51	0.10
Cuban	100	0.19
Dominican Republic	4	0.01
Mexican	5,221	9.94
Puerto Rican	173	0.33
South American	114	0.22
Argentinean	25	0.05
Bolivian	2	<0.01
Chilean	13	0.02
Colombian	31	0.06
Ecuadorian	11	0.02
Peruvian	24	0.05
Uruguayan	1	<0.01
Venezuelan	7	0.01
Other Hispanic or Latino	606	1.15

Race*	Population	%
African-American/Black (363)	551	1.05
Not Hispanic (329)	479	0.91
Hispanic (34)	72	0.14
American Indian/Alaska Native (544)	961	1.83
Not Hispanic (419)	720	1.37
Hispanic (125)	241	0.46
Alaska Athabascan *(Ala. Nat.)* (2)	3	0.01
Aleut *(Alaska Native)* (3)	6	0.01
Apache (5)	22	0.04
Blackfeet (6)	19	0.04
Canadian/French Am. Ind. (3)	7	0.01
Cherokee (53)	164	0.31
Cheyenne (1)	3	0.01
Chickasaw (1)	6	0.01
Chippewa (18)	29	0.06
Choctaw (16)	28	0.05
Comanche (4)	5	0.01
Cree (0)	2	<0.01
Creek (2)	7	0.01
Crow (3)	3	0.01
Delaware (0)	2	<0.01
Hopi (2)	2	<0.01
Inupiat *(Alaska Native)* (2)	8	0.02
Iroquois (7)	17	0.03
Kiowa (0)	2	<0.01
Lumbee (1)	1	<0.01
Mexican American Ind. (16)	19	0.04
Navajo (62)	77	0.15
Osage (1)	5	0.01
Ottawa (0)	3	0.01
Paiute (4)	7	0.01
Pima (7)	9	0.02
Potawatomi (5)	6	0.01
Pueblo (5)	9	0.02
Seminole (1)	2	<0.01
Shoshone (1)	5	0.01
Sioux (22)	44	0.08
Spanish American Ind. (1)	1	<0.01
Tlingit-Haida *(Alaska Native)* (0)	2	<0.01
Tohono O'Odham (2)	3	0.01
Tsimshian *(Alaska Native)* (0)	1	<0.01
Yakama (2)	6	0.01
Yaqui (4)	9	0.02
Yuman (20)	22	0.04
Yup'ik *(Alaska Native)* (1)	1	<0.01
Asian (504)	806	1.53
Not Hispanic (486)	742	1.41
Hispanic (18)	64	0.12
Chinese, ex. Taiwanese (85)	118	0.22
Filipino (170)	306	0.58
Indian (62)	81	0.15
Indonesian (9)	18	0.03
Japanese (52)	117	0.22
Korean (16)	36	0.07
Laotian (0)	1	<0.01
Malaysian (0)	1	<0.01
Pakistani (3)	6	0.01
Sri Lankan (2)	4	0.01
Taiwanese (4)	4	0.01
Thai (10)	12	0.02
Vietnamese (74)	87	0.17
Hawaii Native/Pacific Islander (67)	154	0.29
Not Hispanic (54)	115	0.22
Hispanic (13)	39	0.07
Fijian (0)	1	<0.01
Guamanian/Chamorro (17)	34	0.06
Native Hawaiian (23)	65	0.12
Samoan (18)	28	0.05
Tongan (0)	1	<0.01
White (47,335)	48,467	92.27
Not Hispanic (44,119)	44,813	85.31
Hispanic (3,216)	3,654	6.96

Marana

Place Type: Town
County: Pima
Population: 34,961†

Ancestry‡	Population	%
African, Sub-Saharan (227)	227	0.72
African (164)	164	0.52
Nigerian (63)	63	0.20
American (1,260)	1,260	4.01
Armenian (8)	17	0.05
Assyrian/Chaldean/Syriac (45)	45	0.14
Australian (23)	23	0.07
Austrian (33)	163	0.52
Basque (8)	17	0.05
Belgian (13)	27	0.09
British (61)	96	0.31
Bulgarian (0)	30	0.10
Canadian (81)	156	0.50
Croatian (15)	29	0.09
Czech (74)	165	0.52
Czechoslovakian (6)	19	0.06
Danish (67)	258	0.82
Dutch (85)	651	2.07
Eastern European (36)	36	0.11
English (1,324)	3,874	12.32
European (322)	322	1.02
Finnish (37)	89	0.28
French, ex. Basque (91)	661	2.10
French Canadian (78)	201	0.64
German (2,043)	6,133	19.51
Greek (77)	147	0.47
Hungarian (107)	204	0.65
Icelander (0)	54	0.17
Irish (1,289)	4,193	13.34
Italian (691)	1,848	5.88
Lithuanian (26)	77	0.24
Macedonian (0)	43	0.14
New Zealander (21)	21	0.07
Norwegian (265)	729	2.32
Pennsylvania German (11)	11	0.03
Polish (291)	1,176	3.74
Portuguese (66)	160	0.51
Romanian (33)	115	0.37
Russian (199)	478	1.52
Scandinavian (30)	30	0.10
Scotch-Irish (207)	551	1.75
Scottish (107)	536	1.70
Serbian (0)	5	0.02
Slavic (24)	54	0.17
Slovak (0)	32	0.10
Slovene (0)	58	0.18
Swedish (209)	740	2.35
Swiss (0)	137	0.44
Ukrainian (21)	51	0.16
Welsh (27)	347	1.10
West Indian, ex. Hispanic (14)	14	0.04
Jamaican (14)	14	0.04

Hispanic Origin	Population	%
Hispanic or Latino (of any race)	7,730	22.11
Central American, ex. Mexican	166	0.47
Costa Rican	5	0.01
Guatemalan	38	0.11
Honduran	21	0.06
Nicaraguan	20	0.06
Panamanian	29	0.08
Salvadoran	52	0.15
Other Central American	1	<0.01
Cuban	39	0.11
Dominican Republic	14	0.04
Mexican	6,478	18.53
Puerto Rican	251	0.72
South American	154	0.44
Argentinean	26	0.07
Bolivian	2	0.01
Chilean	7	0.02
Colombian	56	0.16
Ecuadorian	20	0.06
Paraguayan	4	0.01
Peruvian	30	0.09
Uruguayan	3	0.01
Venezuelan	5	0.01
Other South American	1	<0.01
Other Hispanic or Latino	628	1.80

Race*	Population	%
African-American/Black (874)	1,216	3.48
Not Hispanic (806)	1,031	2.95
Hispanic (68)	185	0.53
American Indian/Alaska Native (433)	744	2.13
Not Hispanic (282)	475	1.36
Hispanic (151)	269	0.77
Alaska Athabascan *(Ala. Nat.)* (0)	1	<0.01
Aleut *(Alaska Native)* (5)	5	0.01
Apache (21)	40	0.11
Blackfeet (3)	8	0.02
Canadian/French Am. Ind. (1)	1	<0.01
Central American Ind. (1)	1	<0.01
Cherokee (10)	58	0.17
Chickasaw (2)	5	0.01
Chippewa (7)	10	0.03
Choctaw (9)	25	0.07
Comanche (0)	1	<0.01
Creek (4)	6	0.02
Crow (0)	2	0.01
Hopi (7)	13	0.04
Iroquois (7)	10	0.03
Mexican American Ind. (10)	18	0.05
Navajo (42)	54	0.15
Osage (1)	1	<0.01
Pima (2)	5	0.01
Potawatomi (3)	4	0.01
Pueblo (2)	2	0.01
Seminole (0)	1	<0.01
Shoshone (0)	3	0.01
Sioux (8)	11	0.03
South American Ind. (1)	3	0.01
Spanish American Ind. (0)	2	0.01
Tohono O'Odham (47)	65	0.19
Ute (0)	1	<0.01
Yaqui (104)	134	0.38
Asian (1,322)	1,719	4.92
Not Hispanic (1,280)	1,578	4.51
Hispanic (42)	141	0.40
Burmese (4)	4	0.01
Cambodian (32)	37	0.11
Chinese, ex. Taiwanese (310)	395	1.13
Filipino (212)	334	0.96
Hmong (3)	4	0.01
Indian (161)	184	0.53
Indonesian (11)	14	0.04
Japanese (66)	171	0.49
Korean (113)	176	0.50
Laotian (8)	14	0.04
Malaysian (1)	3	0.01
Pakistani (5)	8	0.02
Sri Lankan (7)	11	0.03
Taiwanese (4)	8	0.02
Thai (23)	40	0.11
Vietnamese (263)	301	0.86
Hawaii Native/Pacific Islander (47)	161	0.46
Not Hispanic (34)	120	0.34
Hispanic (13)	41	0.12
Guamanian/Chamorro (14)	42	0.12
Native Hawaiian (19)	70	0.20
Samoan (3)	18	0.05

*Notes: † The Census 2010 population figure is used to calculate the percentages in the Hispanic Origin and Race categories. Ancestry percentages are based on the 2006-2010 American Community Survey population (not shown); ‡ Numbers in parentheses indicate the number of people reporting a single ancestry; * Numbers in parentheses indicate the number of persons reporting this race alone, not in combination with any other race; Please refer to the Explanation of Data for more information.*

Tongan (6)	8	0.02
White (28,654)	29,786	85.20
Not Hispanic (24,050)	24,674	70.58
Hispanic (4,604)	5,112	14.62

Maricopa

Place Type: City
County: Pinal
Population: 43,482†

Ancestry‡	Population	%
African, Sub-Saharan (116)	185	0.53
African (59)	111	0.32
Nigerian (26)	26	0.07
South African (14)	31	0.09
Ugandan (6)	6	0.02
Other Sub-Saharan African (11)	11	0.03
Albanian (17)	17	0.05
American (800)	800	2.30
Arab (48)	48	0.14
Arab (32)	32	0.09
Palestinian (16)	16	0.05
Armenian (0)	97	0.28
Austrian (24)	55	0.16
Basque (0)	22	0.06
Belgian (6)	65	0.19
British (60)	155	0.45
Canadian (0)	81	0.23
Czech (19)	86	0.25
Czechoslovakian (16)	16	0.05
Danish (87)	380	1.09
Dutch (343)	914	2.63
Eastern European (12)	12	0.03
English (853)	3,307	9.50
European (342)	393	1.13
Finnish (12)	67	0.19
French, ex. Basque (171)	1,368	3.93
French Canadian (149)	465	1.34
German (1,663)	6,178	17.75
Greek (46)	316	0.91
Hungarian (43)	110	0.32
Icelander (43)	43	0.12
Irish (795)	4,069	11.69
Italian (838)	2,594	7.45
Lithuanian (7)	105	0.30
Northern European (18)	27	0.08
Norwegian (245)	652	1.87
Polish (499)	1,308	3.76
Portuguese (12)	59	0.17
Romanian (0)	27	0.08
Russian (25)	228	0.66
Scandinavian (36)	52	0.15
Scotch-Irish (230)	898	2.58
Scottish (129)	510	1.47
Serbian (21)	21	0.06
Slovak (33)	33	0.09
Slovene (0)	53	0.15
Swedish (100)	599	1.72
Swiss (55)	84	0.24
Ukrainian (34)	70	0.20
Welsh (37)	244	0.70
West Indian, ex. Hispanic (87)	87	0.25
Barbadian (37)	37	0.11
British West Indian (11)	11	0.03
Dutch West Indian (17)	17	0.05
Jamaican (22)	22	0.06
Yugoslavian (0)	15	0.04

Hispanic Origin	Population	%
Hispanic or Latino (of any race)	10,617	24.42
Central American, ex. Mexican	371	0.85
Costa Rican	14	0.03
Guatemalan	81	0.19
Honduran	35	0.08
Nicaraguan	36	0.08
Panamanian	45	0.10
Salvadoran	159	0.37
Other Central American	1	<0.01
Cuban	139	0.32
Dominican Republic	20	0.05
Mexican	8,539	19.64
Puerto Rican	502	1.15
South American	271	0.62
Argentinean	29	0.07
Bolivian	14	0.03
Chilean	18	0.04
Colombian	93	0.21
Ecuadorian	26	0.06
Paraguayan	4	0.01
Peruvian	57	0.13
Uruguayan	3	0.01
Venezuelan	18	0.04
Other South American	9	0.02
Other Hispanic or Latino	775	1.78

Race*	Population	%
African-American/Black (4,206)	5,012	11.53
Not Hispanic (3,987)	4,596	10.57
Hispanic (219)	416	0.96
American Indian/Alaska Native (863)	1,314	3.02
Not Hispanic (638)	925	2.13
Hispanic (225)	389	0.89
Aleut *(Alaska Native)* (2)	3	0.01
Apache (27)	50	0.11
Blackfeet (1)	11	0.03
Canadian/French Am. Ind. (2)	4	0.01
Central American Ind. (1)	1	<0.01
Cherokee (16)	89	0.20
Cheyenne (3)	3	0.01
Chickasaw (1)	2	<0.01
Chippewa (4)	13	0.03
Choctaw (6)	21	0.05
Colville (0)	2	<0.01
Cree (0)	1	<0.01
Creek (1)	4	0.01
Crow (0)	5	0.01
Delaware (2)	2	<0.01
Hopi (12)	16	0.04
Inupiat *(Alaska Native)* (2)	2	<0.01
Iroquois (7)	12	0.03
Lumbee (0)	1	<0.01
Mexican American Ind. (20)	31	0.07
Navajo (217)	270	0.62
Osage (0)	4	0.01
Pima (116)	135	0.31
Potawatomi (1)	2	<0.01
Pueblo (9)	14	0.03
Seminole (1)	4	0.01
Shoshone (2)	2	<0.01
Sioux (16)	29	0.07
South American Ind. (0)	2	<0.01
Spanish American Ind. (6)	7	0.02
Tlingit-Haida *(Alaska Native)* (3)	3	0.01
Tohono O'Odham (30)	58	0.13
Yaqui (42)	51	0.12
Yuman (5)	9	0.02
Asian (1,800)	2,432	5.59
Not Hispanic (1,705)	2,173	5.00
Hispanic (95)	259	0.60
Bangladeshi (21)	21	0.05
Burmese (0)	1	<0.01
Cambodian (56)	67	0.15
Chinese, ex. Taiwanese (162)	259	0.60
Filipino (691)	975	2.24
Hmong (1)	2	<0.01
Indian (167)	207	0.48
Indonesian (6)	11	0.03
Japanese (65)	170	0.39
Korean (89)	165	0.38
Laotian (68)	87	0.20
Malaysian (2)	2	<0.01
Nepalese (0)	1	<0.01
Pakistani (7)	15	0.03
Sri Lankan (3)	4	0.01
Taiwanese (11)	19	0.04
Thai (29)	52	0.12
Vietnamese (341)	386	0.89
Hawaii Native/Pacific Islander (119)	264	0.61
Not Hispanic (114)	229	0.53
Hispanic (5)	35	0.08
Fijian (1)	2	<0.01
Guamanian/Chamorro (31)	42	0.10
Marshallese (5)	5	0.01
Native Hawaiian (26)	88	0.20
Samoan (16)	32	0.07
Tongan (19)	49	0.11
White (30,528)	32,460	74.65
Not Hispanic (25,084)	26,178	60.20
Hispanic (5,444)	6,282	14.45

Mesa

Place Type: City
County: Maricopa
Population: 439,041†

Ancestry‡	Population	%
Afghan (185)	185	0.04
African, Sub-Saharan (809)	984	0.22
African (659)	775	0.18
Ethiopian (26)	26	0.01
Ghanaian (3)	3	<0.01
Kenyan (27)	27	0.01
Nigerian (0)	17	<0.01
South African (27)	50	0.01
Sudanese (11)	11	<0.01
Ugandan (8)	8	<0.01
Other Sub-Saharan African (48)	67	0.02
American (22,368)	22,368	5.09
Arab (718)	1,231	0.28
Arab (99)	185	0.04
Egyptian (118)	118	0.03
Iraqi (130)	130	0.03
Jordanian (12)	31	0.01
Lebanese (217)	486	0.11
Moroccan (24)	24	0.01
Palestinian (16)	35	0.01
Syrian (20)	102	0.02
Other Arab (82)	120	0.03
Armenian (34)	177	0.04
Assyrian/Chaldean/Syriac (53)	76	0.02
Australian (11)	141	0.03
Austrian (207)	876	0.20
Basque (73)	92	0.02
Belgian (117)	231	0.05
Brazilian (89)	89	0.02
British (1,101)	2,465	0.56
Bulgarian (76)	76	0.02
Cajun (35)	84	0.02
Canadian (1,599)	2,400	0.55
Celtic (11)	33	0.01
Croatian (268)	687	0.16
Czech (542)	2,078	0.47
Czechoslovakian (250)	470	0.11
Danish (1,358)	5,214	1.19
Dutch (1,949)	7,556	1.72
Eastern European (321)	321	0.07
English (22,588)	59,240	13.47
Estonian (16)	16	<0.01
European (4,221)	4,591	1.04
Finnish (398)	1,047	0.24
French, ex. Basque (2,122)	12,261	2.79
French Canadian (1,318)	2,994	0.68
German (25,396)	77,211	17.56
German Russian (0)	19	<0.01
Greek (607)	1,412	0.32
Hungarian (787)	2,315	0.53
Icelander (39)	71	0.02
Iranian (155)	241	0.05
Irish (12,156)	46,956	10.68
Israeli (44)	126	0.03
Italian (7,816)	22,441	5.10
Latvian (11)	70	0.02
Lithuanian (261)	758	0.17
Luxemburger (37)	177	0.04
Macedonian (10)	31	0.01
Maltese (71)	156	0.04
New Zealander (8)	129	0.03
Northern European (374)	393	0.09

SECTION TWO

*Notes: † The Census 2010 population figure is used to calculate the percentages in the Hispanic Origin and Race categories. Ancestry percentages are based on the 2006-2010 American Community Survey population (not shown); ‡ Numbers in parentheses indicate the number of people reporting a single ancestry; * Numbers in parentheses indicate the number of persons reporting this race alone, not in combination with any other race; Please refer to the Explanation of Data for more information.*

Norwegian (5,354)	12,530	2.85
Pennsylvania German (158)	298	0.07
Polish (4,037)	11,558	2.63
Portuguese (625)	1,349	0.31
Romanian (263)	475	0.11
Russian (719)	2,582	0.59
Scandinavian (757)	1,725	0.39
Scotch-Irish (2,671)	8,003	1.82
Scottish (3,585)	10,547	2.40
Serbian (389)	536	0.12
Slavic (73)	222	0.05
Slovak (263)	760	0.17
Slovene (117)	259	0.06
Swedish (2,818)	9,428	2.14
Swiss (373)	1,916	0.44
Turkish (17)	87	0.02
Ukrainian (403)	913	0.21
Welsh (619)	3,484	0.79
West Indian, ex. Hispanic (226)	288	0.07
British West Indian (9)	9	<0.01
Dutch West Indian (0)	28	0.01
Haitian (34)	34	0.01
Jamaican (52)	62	0.01
Trinidadian/Tobagonian (17)	17	<0.01
West Indian (20)	44	0.01
Other West Indian (94)	94	0.02
Yugoslavian (243)	523	0.12

Hispanic Origin	Population	%
Hispanic or Latino (of any race)	115,753	26.36
Central American, ex. Mexican	3,147	0.72
Costa Rican	180	0.04
Guatemalan	1,446	0.33
Honduran	300	0.07
Nicaraguan	198	0.05
Panamanian	108	0.02
Salvadoran	885	0.20
Other Central American	30	0.01
Cuban	455	0.10
Dominican Republic	257	0.06
Mexican	99,666	22.70
Puerto Rican	2,441	0.56
South American	1,747	0.40
Argentinean	242	0.06
Bolivian	38	0.01
Chilean	141	0.03
Colombian	422	0.10
Ecuadorian	196	0.04
Paraguayan	9	<0.01
Peruvian	467	0.11
Uruguayan	29	0.01
Venezuelan	179	0.04
Other South American	24	0.01
Other Hispanic or Latino	8,040	1.83

Race*	Population	%
African-American/Black (15,289)	19,591	4.46
Not Hispanic (14,101)	17,431	3.97
Hispanic (1,188)	2,160	0.49
American Indian/Alaska Native (10,377)	14,041	3.20
Not Hispanic (8,359)	10,820	2.46
Hispanic (2,018)	3,221	0.73
Alaska Athabascan *(Ala. Nat.)* (18)	26	0.01
Aleut *(Alaska Native)* (7)	11	<0.01
Apache (517)	659	0.15
Arapaho (10)	14	<0.01
Blackfeet (22)	83	0.02
Canadian/French Am. Ind. (14)	27	0.01
Central American Ind. (10)	19	<0.01
Cherokee (163)	695	0.16
Cheyenne (16)	27	0.01
Chickasaw (13)	37	0.01
Chippewa (77)	160	0.04
Choctaw (70)	214	0.05
Colville (7)	9	<0.01
Comanche (14)	38	0.01
Cree (4)	13	<0.01
Creek (37)	95	0.02
Crow (6)	16	<0.01
Delaware (5)	16	<0.01
Hopi (267)	352	0.08
Houma (1)	2	<0.01
Inupiat *(Alaska Native)* (16)	26	0.01
Iroquois (47)	86	0.02
Kiowa (9)	17	<0.01
Lumbee (6)	7	<0.01
Menominee (4)	7	<0.01
Mexican American Ind. (295)	413	0.09
Navajo (3,737)	4,243	0.97
Osage (9)	23	0.01
Ottawa (8)	21	<0.01
Paiute (11)	30	0.01
Pima (1,115)	1,378	0.31
Potawatomi (18)	37	0.01
Pueblo (119)	174	0.04
Puget Sound Salish (1)	6	<0.01
Seminole (11)	28	0.01
Shoshone (9)	23	0.01
Sioux (109)	218	0.05
South American Ind. (14)	27	0.01
Spanish American Ind. (16)	25	0.01
Tlingit-Haida *(Alaska Native)* (12)	21	<0.01
Tohono O'Odham (200)	252	0.06
Tsimshian *(Alaska Native)* (4)	8	<0.01
Ute (26)	30	0.01
Yakama (3)	9	<0.01
Yaqui (408)	564	0.13
Yuman (97)	138	0.03
Yup'ik *(Alaska Native)* (3)	7	<0.01
Asian (8,493)	11,866	2.70
Not Hispanic (8,174)	10,900	2.48
Hispanic (319)	966	0.22
Bangladeshi (69)	74	0.02
Burmese (33)	35	0.01
Cambodian (152)	194	0.04
Chinese, ex. Taiwanese (1,310)	1,903	0.43
Filipino (2,156)	3,340	0.76
Hmong (7)	11	<0.01
Indian (1,104)	1,352	0.31
Indonesian (66)	110	0.03
Japanese (548)	1,295	0.29
Korean (643)	1,003	0.23
Laotian (77)	111	0.03
Malaysian (6)	21	<0.01
Nepalese (18)	19	<0.01
Pakistani (138)	169	0.04
Sri Lankan (21)	30	0.01
Taiwanese (69)	85	0.02
Thai (234)	328	0.07
Vietnamese (1,388)	1,648	0.38
Hawaii Native/Pacific Islander (1,672)	2,777	0.63
Not Hispanic (1,532)	2,391	0.54
Hispanic (140)	386	0.09
Fijian (15)	23	0.01
Guamanian/Chamorro (203)	293	0.07
Marshallese (103)	106	0.02
Native Hawaiian (269)	775	0.18
Samoan (212)	412	0.09
Tongan (521)	705	0.16
White (338,591)	351,626	80.09
Not Hispanic (282,505)	289,620	65.97
Hispanic (56,086)	62,006	14.12

New Kingman-Butler

Place Type: CDP
County: Mohave
Population: 12,134†

Ancestry‡	Population	%
African, Sub-Saharan (0)	21	0.14
African (0)	21	0.14
American (601)	601	4.14
Australian (0)	17	0.12
British (0)	13	0.09
Bulgarian (0)	53	0.37
Canadian (0)	31	0.21
Czech (0)	16	0.11
Czechoslovakian (0)	117	0.81
Danish (0)	15	0.10
Dutch (23)	466	3.21
English (477)	2,164	14.92
European (29)	43	0.30
Finnish (0)	34	0.23
French, ex. Basque (28)	586	4.04
French Canadian (50)	350	2.41
German (901)	3,137	21.63
Greek (13)	22	0.15
Hungarian (12)	46	0.32
Irish (746)	2,843	19.61
Italian (521)	1,212	8.36
Norwegian (119)	320	2.21
Polish (45)	260	1.79
Portuguese (0)	61	0.42
Romanian (0)	7	0.05
Russian (20)	39	0.27
Scotch-Irish (187)	364	2.51
Scottish (212)	456	3.14
Slovak (15)	15	0.10
Swedish (97)	487	3.36
Swiss (14)	14	0.10
Ukrainian (0)	16	0.11
Welsh (0)	93	0.64
West Indian, ex. Hispanic (0)	17	0.12
Dutch West Indian (0)	17	0.12
Yugoslavian (9)	9	0.06

Hispanic Origin	Population	%
Hispanic or Latino (of any race)	1,482	12.21
Central American, ex. Mexican	42	0.35
Costa Rican	5	0.04
Guatemalan	9	0.07
Honduran	3	0.02
Nicaraguan	5	0.04
Salvadoran	20	0.16
Cuban	11	0.09
Dominican Republic	2	0.02
Mexican	1,178	9.71
Puerto Rican	39	0.32
South American	7	0.06
Argentinean	1	0.01
Colombian	1	0.01
Ecuadorian	4	0.03
Peruvian	1	0.01
Other Hispanic or Latino	203	1.67

Race*	Population	%
African-American/Black (85)	163	1.34
Not Hispanic (80)	138	1.14
Hispanic (5)	25	0.21
American Indian/Alaska Native (180)	355	2.93
Not Hispanic (141)	275	2.27
Hispanic (39)	80	0.66
Alaska Athabascan *(Ala. Nat.)* (0)	1	0.01
Aleut *(Alaska Native)* (3)	3	0.02
Apache (5)	11	0.09
Blackfeet (4)	9	0.07
Canadian/French Am. Ind. (1)	1	0.01
Cherokee (10)	64	0.53
Cheyenne (1)	1	0.01
Chickasaw (0)	1	0.01
Chippewa (2)	2	0.02
Choctaw (7)	15	0.12
Cree (1)	2	0.02
Creek (6)	18	0.15
Crow (0)	1	0.01
Hopi (0)	1	0.01
Inupiat *(Alaska Native)* (1)	2	0.02
Iroquois (1)	3	0.02
Lumbee (4)	5	0.04
Mexican American Ind. (1)	1	0.01
Navajo (32)	45	0.37
Osage (0)	2	0.02
Paiute (1)	1	0.01
Pima (2)	11	0.09
Pueblo (1)	2	0.02
Seminole (0)	7	0.06
Shoshone (2)	7	0.06
Sioux (5)	10	0.08
South American Ind. (0)	2	0.02

*Notes: † The Census 2010 population figure is used to calculate the percentages in the Hispanic Origin and Race categories. Ancestry percentages are based on the 2006-2010 American Community Survey population (not shown); ‡ Numbers in parentheses indicate the number of people reporting a single ancestry; * Numbers in parentheses indicate the number of persons reporting this race alone, not in combination with any other race; Please refer to the Explanation of Data for more information.*

Spanish American Ind. (0)	4	0.03
Tlingit-Haida *(Alaska Native)* (1)	1	0.01
Tohono O'Odham (1)	1	0.01
Tsimshian *(Alaska Native)* (1)	1	0.01
Yaqui (3)	3	0.02
Yuman (22)	33	0.27
Asian (87)	180	1.48
Not Hispanic (81)	156	1.29
Hispanic (6)	24	0.20
Chinese, ex. Taiwanese (3)	12	0.10
Filipino (57)	122	1.01
Indian (5)	9	0.07
Indonesian (2)	3	0.02
Japanese (5)	14	0.12
Korean (3)	9	0.07
Laotian (1)	1	0.01
Taiwanese (0)	1	0.01
Thai (1)	1	0.01
Vietnamese (7)	8	0.07
Hawaii Native/Pacific Islander (23)	52	0.43
Not Hispanic (23)	48	0.40
Hispanic (0)	4	0.03
Guamanian/Chamorro (5)	5	0.04
Native Hawaiian (7)	26	0.21
Samoan (6)	9	0.07
Tongan (0)	2	0.02
White (10,859)	11,244	92.67
Not Hispanic (10,054)	10,316	85.02
Hispanic (805)	928	7.65

New River

Place Type: CDP
County: Maricopa
Population: 14,952†

Ancestry‡	Population	%
American (501)	501	4.28
Arab (149)	191	1.63
Lebanese (131)	173	1.48
Syrian (18)	18	0.15
Armenian (0)	35	0.30
Austrian (0)	11	0.09
Belgian (14)	26	0.22
British (30)	40	0.34
Canadian (7)	7	0.06
Croatian (0)	29	0.25
Czech (66)	101	0.86
Czechoslovakian (0)	73	0.62
Danish (28)	113	0.96
Dutch (13)	159	1.36
English (887)	1,713	14.63
European (119)	119	1.02
Finnish (117)	146	1.25
French, ex. Basque (79)	355	3.03
French Canadian (113)	113	0.96
German (1,592)	3,028	25.86
Hungarian (117)	169	1.44
Irish (641)	1,737	14.83
Italian (286)	663	5.66
Lithuanian (31)	220	1.88
Luxemburger (38)	38	0.32
Northern European (15)	15	0.13
Norwegian (57)	226	1.93
Polish (91)	290	2.48
Russian (13)	69	0.59
Scandinavian (17)	26	0.22
Scotch-Irish (91)	416	3.55
Scottish (67)	216	1.84
Serbian (0)	13	0.11
Slovene (0)	11	0.09
Swedish (67)	186	1.59
Swiss (0)	10	0.09
Ukrainian (0)	11	0.09
Welsh (31)	203	1.73
Yugoslavian (44)	44	0.38

Hispanic Origin	Population	%
Hispanic or Latino (of any race)	991	6.63
Central American, ex. Mexican	30	0.20
Costa Rican	3	0.02
Guatemalan	12	0.08
Honduran	6	0.04
Nicaraguan	5	0.03
Panamanian	3	0.02
Salvadoran	1	0.01
Cuban	5	0.03
Dominican Republic	2	0.01
Mexican	751	5.02
Puerto Rican	32	0.21
South American	28	0.19
Argentinean	5	0.03
Bolivian	3	0.02
Chilean	1	0.01
Colombian	7	0.05
Ecuadorian	2	0.01
Peruvian	9	0.06
Venezuelan	1	0.01
Other Hispanic or Latino	143	0.96

Race*	Population	%
African-American/Black (82)	130	0.87
Not Hispanic (73)	109	0.73
Hispanic (9)	21	0.14
American Indian/Alaska Native (84)	209	1.40
Not Hispanic (67)	158	1.06
Hispanic (17)	51	0.34
Alaska Athabascan *(Ala. Nat.)* (1)	2	0.01
Apache (0)	1	0.01
Blackfeet (1)	6	0.04
Cherokee (10)	40	0.27
Chickasaw (1)	2	0.01
Chippewa (1)	2	0.01
Choctaw (4)	8	0.05
Comanche (2)	5	0.03
Creek (1)	1	0.01
Delaware (0)	1	0.01
Hopi (1)	2	0.01
Iroquois (1)	1	0.01
Mexican American Ind. (2)	6	0.04
Navajo (16)	22	0.15
Osage (0)	3	0.02
Pima (1)	1	0.01
Potawatomi (1)	1	0.01
Pueblo (1)	1	0.01
Sioux (4)	6	0.04
South American Ind. (0)	1	0.01
Yaqui (3)	3	0.02
Yuman (1)	1	0.01
Asian (145)	210	1.40
Not Hispanic (140)	202	1.35
Hispanic (5)	8	0.05
Chinese, ex. Taiwanese (24)	46	0.31
Filipino (43)	59	0.39
Indian (5)	6	0.04
Indonesian (0)	10	0.07
Japanese (12)	27	0.18
Korean (12)	20	0.13
Laotian (1)	1	0.01
Taiwanese (4)	4	0.03
Thai (4)	7	0.05
Vietnamese (31)	33	0.22
Hawaii Native/Pacific Islander (8)	27	0.18
Not Hispanic (7)	25	0.17
Hispanic (1)	2	0.01
Guamanian/Chamorro (1)	2	0.01
Native Hawaiian (3)	9	0.06
White (14,081)	14,329	95.83
Not Hispanic (13,468)	13,647	91.27
Hispanic (613)	682	4.56

Nogales

Place Type: City
County: Santa Cruz
Population: 20,837†

Ancestry‡	Population	%
American (299)	299	1.43
Arab (142)	142	0.68
Lebanese (142)	142	0.68
Austrian (12)	24	0.11
British (18)	18	0.09
Dutch (48)	74	0.35
English (59)	113	0.54
Finnish (0)	37	0.18
French, ex. Basque (0)	109	0.52
German (137)	486	2.32
Greek (16)	40	0.19
Irish (31)	163	0.78
Italian (16)	187	0.89
Norwegian (0)	34	0.16
Polish (19)	19	0.09
Portuguese (0)	5	0.02
Scotch-Irish (0)	35	0.17
Scottish (0)	14	0.07
Swedish (0)	36	0.17
Welsh (0)	38	0.18

Hispanic Origin	Population	%
Hispanic or Latino (of any race)	19,793	94.99
Central American, ex. Mexican	23	0.11
Guatemalan	2	0.01
Honduran	3	0.01
Nicaraguan	3	0.01
Panamanian	4	0.02
Salvadoran	11	0.05
Cuban	26	0.12
Dominican Republic	3	0.01
Mexican	18,778	90.12
Puerto Rican	28	0.13
South American	21	0.10
Argentinean	1	<0.01
Chilean	8	0.04
Colombian	4	0.02
Ecuadorian	1	<0.01
Peruvian	4	0.02
Venezuelan	2	0.01
Other South American	1	<0.01
Other Hispanic or Latino	914	4.39

Race*	Population	%
African-American/Black (75)	103	0.49
Not Hispanic (28)	36	0.17
Hispanic (47)	67	0.32
American Indian/Alaska Native (140)	188	0.90
Not Hispanic (48)	62	0.30
Hispanic (92)	126	0.60
Apache (2)	9	0.04
Cherokee (1)	4	0.02
Chippewa (1)	2	0.01
Creek (1)	1	<0.01
Menominee (1)	1	<0.01
Mexican American Ind. (24)	28	0.13
Navajo (6)	12	0.06
Pima (1)	6	0.03
Pueblo (5)	5	0.02
Sioux (0)	2	0.01
South American Ind. (0)	1	<0.01
Tohono O'Odham (1)	4	0.02
Yaqui (15)	18	0.09
Yuman (1)	1	<0.01
Asian (126)	167	0.80
Not Hispanic (125)	135	0.65
Hispanic (1)	32	0.15
Chinese, ex. Taiwanese (25)	36	0.17
Filipino (8)	12	0.06
Indian (42)	45	0.22
Indonesian (3)	3	0.01
Japanese (2)	6	0.03
Korean (31)	37	0.18
Pakistani (2)	2	0.01
Taiwanese (1)	1	<0.01
Vietnamese (10)	14	0.07
Hawaii Native/Pacific Islander (4)	19	0.09
Not Hispanic (1)	3	0.01
Hispanic (3)	16	0.08
Marshallese (1)	1	<0.01
Native Hawaiian (3)	7	0.03
White (14,933)	15,388	73.85

*Notes: † The Census 2010 population figure is used to calculate the percentages in the Hispanic Origin and Race categories. Ancestry percentages are based on the 2006-2010 American Community Survey population (not shown); ‡ Numbers in parentheses indicate the number of people reporting a single ancestry; * Numbers in parentheses indicate the number of persons reporting this race alone, not in combination with any other race; Please refer to the Explanation of Data for more information.*

Not Hispanic (803)	831	3.99
Hispanic (14,130)	14,557	69.86

Oro Valley

Place Type: Town
County: Pima
Population: 41,011†

Ancestry‡	Population	%
Afghan (0)	13	0.03
African, Sub-Saharan (30)	82	0.21
African (14)	14	0.04
South African (16)	68	0.17
American (1,961)	1,961	4.93
Arab (65)	162	0.41
Arab (18)	18	0.05
Jordanian (10)	10	0.03
Lebanese (37)	125	0.31
Syrian (0)	9	0.02
Armenian (13)	27	0.07
Assyrian/Chaldean/Syriac (13)	13	0.03
Australian (11)	11	0.03
Austrian (44)	230	0.58
Basque (0)	18	0.05
Belgian (24)	78	0.20
Brazilian (0)	16	0.04
British (185)	273	0.69
Cajun (7)	30	0.08
Canadian (83)	249	0.63
Croatian (31)	87	0.22
Czech (110)	247	0.62
Czechoslovakian (33)	63	0.16
Danish (156)	448	1.13
Dutch (211)	780	1.96
Eastern European (160)	160	0.40
English (1,872)	5,972	15.01
Estonian (0)	17	0.04
European (607)	843	2.12
Finnish (48)	276	0.69
French, ex. Basque (202)	1,848	4.65
French Canadian (101)	241	0.61
German (3,192)	10,168	25.56
Greek (64)	203	0.51
Guyanese (0)	22	0.06
Hungarian (199)	506	1.27
Icelander (13)	13	0.03
Iranian (0)	58	0.15
Irish (1,644)	6,017	15.13
Israeli (10)	10	0.03
Italian (1,290)	2,688	6.76
Latvian (28)	28	0.07
Lithuanian (20)	87	0.22
Luxemburger (10)	19	0.05
Maltese (0)	22	0.06
Northern European (66)	78	0.20
Norwegian (408)	1,180	2.97
Polish (695)	1,727	4.34
Portuguese (85)	142	0.36
Romanian (27)	50	0.13
Russian (251)	515	1.29
Scandinavian (55)	186	0.47
Scotch-Irish (246)	804	2.02
Scottish (575)	1,475	3.71
Serbian (25)	71	0.18
Slavic (12)	41	0.10
Slovak (25)	148	0.37
Slovene (20)	41	0.10
Swedish (346)	1,368	3.44
Swiss (111)	239	0.60
Turkish (14)	14	0.04
Ukrainian (39)	107	0.27
Welsh (66)	560	1.41
West Indian, ex. Hispanic (0)	11	0.03
West Indian (0)	11	0.03
Yugoslavian (47)	88	0.22

Hispanic Origin	Population	%
Hispanic or Latino (of any race)	4,731	11.54
Central American, ex. Mexican	130	0.32
Costa Rican	8	0.02
Guatemalan	42	0.10
Honduran	23	0.06
Nicaraguan	9	0.02
Panamanian	9	0.02
Salvadoran	39	0.10
Cuban	76	0.19
Dominican Republic	11	0.03
Mexican	3,518	8.58
Puerto Rican	271	0.66
South American	251	0.61
Argentinean	27	0.07
Bolivian	8	0.02
Chilean	32	0.08
Colombian	63	0.15
Ecuadorian	16	0.04
Paraguayan	1	<0.01
Peruvian	77	0.19
Uruguayan	12	0.03
Venezuelan	13	0.03
Other South American	2	<0.01
Other Hispanic or Latino	474	1.16

Race*	Population	%
African-American/Black (617)	836	2.04
Not Hispanic (559)	728	1.78
Hispanic (58)	108	0.26
American Indian/Alaska Native (179)	393	0.96
Not Hispanic (125)	273	0.67
Hispanic (54)	120	0.29
Aleut *(Alaska Native)* (0)	1	<0.01
Apache (10)	20	0.05
Arapaho (0)	4	0.01
Blackfeet (1)	7	0.02
Canadian/French Am. Ind. (0)	1	<0.01
Cherokee (12)	63	0.15
Cheyenne (0)	1	<0.01
Chickasaw (3)	6	0.01
Chippewa (5)	8	0.02
Choctaw (6)	16	0.04
Comanche (2)	2	<0.01
Cree (0)	1	<0.01
Creek (1)	4	0.01
Crow (0)	1	<0.01
Delaware (0)	1	<0.01
Hopi (1)	1	<0.01
Inupiat *(Alaska Native)* (1)	1	<0.01
Iroquois (4)	5	0.01
Lumbee (0)	1	<0.01
Menominee (1)	1	<0.01
Mexican American Ind. (5)	9	0.02
Navajo (37)	53	0.13
Osage (0)	1	<0.01
Ottawa (1)	1	<0.01
Pima (0)	1	<0.01
Potawatomi (3)	3	0.01
Pueblo (6)	7	0.02
Shoshone (1)	1	<0.01
Sioux (2)	7	0.02
South American Ind. (0)	1	<0.01
Tlingit-Haida *(Alaska Native)* (0)	1	<0.01
Tohono O'Odham (10)	16	0.04
Tsimshian *(Alaska Native)* (1)	1	<0.01
Ute (1)	4	0.01
Yakama (0)	1	<0.01
Yaqui (15)	26	0.06
Yuman (3)	4	0.01
Asian (1,284)	1,667	4.06
Not Hispanic (1,263)	1,588	3.87
Hispanic (21)	79	0.19
Bangladeshi (1)	1	<0.01
Cambodian (0)	4	0.01
Chinese, ex. Taiwanese (289)	388	0.95
Filipino (168)	266	0.65
Indian (256)	281	0.69
Indonesian (8)	18	0.04
Japanese (112)	216	0.53
Korean (200)	243	0.59
Laotian (8)	9	0.02
Pakistani (36)	37	0.09
Sri Lankan (2)	2	<0.01
Taiwanese (23)	27	0.07
Thai (13)	20	0.05
Vietnamese (111)	132	0.32
Hawaii Native/Pacific Islander (54)	131	0.32
Not Hispanic (53)	114	0.28
Hispanic (1)	17	0.04
Guamanian/Chamorro (9)	17	0.04
Marshallese (2)	2	<0.01
Native Hawaiian (18)	55	0.13
Samoan (7)	23	0.06
Tongan (9)	9	0.02
White (36,825)	37,725	91.99
Not Hispanic (33,605)	34,190	83.37
Hispanic (3,220)	3,535	8.62

Paradise Valley

Place Type: Town
County: Maricopa
Population: 12,820†

Ancestry‡	Population	%
American (444)	444	3.36
Arab (66)	151	1.14
Lebanese (37)	65	0.49
Moroccan (14)	71	0.54
Syrian (15)	15	0.11
Austrian (29)	96	0.73
Basque (0)	29	0.22
Belgian (41)	94	0.71
British (120)	288	2.18
Canadian (71)	288	2.18
Croatian (0)	92	0.70
Czech (36)	99	0.75
Czechoslovakian (16)	53	0.40
Danish (44)	113	0.86
Dutch (109)	328	2.49
Eastern European (96)	96	0.73
English (766)	2,218	16.81
European (257)	257	1.95
French, ex. Basque (80)	627	4.75
French Canadian (0)	12	0.09
German (671)	2,163	16.39
Greek (76)	172	1.30
Hungarian (42)	96	0.73
Iranian (181)	281	2.13
Irish (634)	2,151	16.30
Italian (276)	1,179	8.93
Lithuanian (9)	108	0.82
Maltese (12)	26	0.20
Norwegian (81)	325	2.46
Polish (48)	505	3.83
Portuguese (35)	35	0.27
Romanian (20)	47	0.36
Russian (327)	628	4.76
Scandinavian (25)	25	0.19
Scotch-Irish (62)	93	0.70
Scottish (201)	516	3.91
Slovak (13)	55	0.42
Slovene (41)	57	0.43
Swedish (131)	625	4.74
Swiss (27)	55	0.42
Ukrainian (63)	83	0.63
Welsh (23)	54	0.41
West Indian, ex. Hispanic (13)	49	0.37
Trinidadian/Tobagonian (13)	49	0.37
Yugoslavian (63)	63	0.48

Hispanic Origin	Population	%
Hispanic or Latino (of any race)	479	3.74
Central American, ex. Mexican	16	0.12
Guatemalan	9	0.07
Nicaraguan	3	0.02
Salvadoran	4	0.03
Cuban	24	0.19
Dominican Republic	1	0.01
Mexican	282	2.20
Puerto Rican	22	0.17
South American	66	0.51

*Notes: † The Census 2010 population figure is used to calculate the percentages in the Hispanic Origin and Race categories. Ancestry percentages are based on the 2006-2010 American Community Survey population (not shown); ‡ Numbers in parentheses indicate the number of people reporting a single ancestry; * Numbers in parentheses indicate the number of persons reporting this race alone, not in combination with any other race; Please refer to the Explanation of Data for more information.*

	Population	%
Argentinean	15	0.12
Bolivian	8	0.06
Chilean	2	0.02
Colombian	15	0.12
Ecuadorian	11	0.09
Paraguayan	2	0.02
Peruvian	8	0.06
Uruguayan	4	0.03
Venezuelan	1	0.01
Other Hispanic or Latino	68	0.53

Race*	Population	%
African-American/Black (86)	118	0.92
Not Hispanic (83)	102	0.80
Hispanic (3)	16	0.12
American Indian/Alaska Native (28)	71	0.55
Not Hispanic (23)	56	0.44
Hispanic (5)	15	0.12
Apache (1)	2	0.02
Cherokee (3)	11	0.09
Chickasaw (0)	1	0.01
Chippewa (1)	1	0.01
Choctaw (2)	2	0.02
Comanche (1)	1	0.01
Creek (0)	1	0.01
Iroquois (0)	1	0.01
Mexican American Ind. (5)	9	0.07
Navajo (5)	8	0.06
Osage (1)	1	0.01
Pima (2)	2	0.02
Asian (518)	652	5.09
Not Hispanic (516)	642	5.01
Hispanic (2)	10	0.08
Chinese, ex. Taiwanese (143)	189	1.47
Filipino (28)	45	0.35
Indian (215)	239	1.86
Indonesian (1)	1	0.01
Japanese (16)	36	0.28
Korean (37)	43	0.34
Laotian (0)	1	0.01
Pakistani (27)	27	0.21
Sri Lankan (12)	13	0.10
Taiwanese (5)	5	0.04
Thai (4)	6	0.05
Vietnamese (14)	17	0.13
Hawaii Native/Pacific Islander (6)	15	0.12
Not Hispanic (5)	13	0.10
Hispanic (1)	2	0.02
Guamanian/Chamorro (1)	4	0.03
Native Hawaiian (0)	2	0.02
White (11,865)	12,065	94.11
Not Hispanic (11,520)	11,677	91.08
Hispanic (345)	388	3.03

Payson

Place Type: Town
County: Gila
Population: 15,301†

Ancestry‡	Population	%
African, Sub-Saharan (10)	10	0.07
South African (10)	10	0.07
American (854)	854	5.68
Arab (108)	118	0.79
Arab (51)	59	0.39
Lebanese (10)	10	0.07
Syrian (47)	49	0.33
Australian (0)	11	0.07
Austrian (28)	28	0.19
Belgian (32)	52	0.35
British (18)	34	0.23
Croatian (0)	13	0.09
Czech (26)	105	0.70
Czechoslovakian (0)	63	0.42
Danish (64)	156	1.04
Dutch (52)	276	1.84
Eastern European (14)	14	0.09
English (572)	2,233	14.86
European (102)	102	0.68
Finnish (38)	54	0.36
French, ex. Basque (230)	655	4.36
French Canadian (101)	135	0.90
German (824)	3,143	20.92
Greek (27)	82	0.55
Irish (698)	2,462	16.38
Italian (125)	263	1.75
Lithuanian (17)	66	0.44
Norwegian (25)	306	2.04
Pennsylvania German (0)	15	0.10
Polish (134)	307	2.04
Portuguese (68)	283	1.88
Russian (72)	135	0.90
Scandinavian (31)	86	0.57
Scotch-Irish (72)	292	1.94
Scottish (387)	756	5.03
Slovak (41)	41	0.27
Swedish (81)	524	3.49
Swiss (14)	84	0.56
Ukrainian (27)	44	0.29
Welsh (53)	126	0.84

Hispanic Origin	Population	%
Hispanic or Latino (of any race)	1,481	9.68
Central American, ex. Mexican	12	0.08
Guatemalan	2	0.01
Nicaraguan	1	0.01
Panamanian	3	0.02
Salvadoran	6	0.04
Cuban	6	0.04
Dominican Republic	2	0.01
Mexican	1,276	8.34
Puerto Rican	22	0.14
South American	16	0.10
Argentinean	4	0.03
Chilean	3	0.02
Colombian	7	0.05
Peruvian	1	0.01
Venezuelan	1	0.01
Other Hispanic or Latino	147	0.96

Race*	Population	%
African-American/Black (65)	99	0.65
Not Hispanic (50)	79	0.52
Hispanic (15)	20	0.13
American Indian/Alaska Native (355)	509	3.33
Not Hispanic (332)	467	3.05
Hispanic (23)	42	0.27
Aleut *(Alaska Native)* (0)	3	0.02
Apache (113)	134	0.88
Blackfeet (2)	2	0.01
Canadian/French Am. Ind. (0)	1	0.01
Cherokee (14)	48	0.31
Cheyenne (0)	1	0.01
Chickasaw (0)	3	0.02
Chippewa (1)	6	0.04
Choctaw (8)	18	0.12
Comanche (0)	1	0.01
Cree (0)	1	0.01
Creek (0)	4	0.03
Delaware (1)	1	0.01
Hopi (15)	18	0.12
Iroquois (1)	2	0.01
Mexican American Ind. (5)	5	0.03
Navajo (95)	120	0.78
Paiute (0)	2	0.01
Pima (5)	8	0.05
Potawatomi (0)	2	0.01
Pueblo (3)	4	0.03
Puget Sound Salish (0)	2	0.01
Seminole (0)	4	0.03
Sioux (1)	8	0.05
Tlingit-Haida *(Alaska Native)* (2)	6	0.04
Tohono O'Odham (1)	1	0.01
Tsimshian *(Alaska Native)* (0)	4	0.03
Ute (0)	1	0.01
Yaqui (0)	4	0.03
Yuman (3)	6	0.04
Asian (101)	127	0.83
Not Hispanic (98)	120	0.78
Hispanic (3)	7	0.05
Bangladeshi (2)	2	0.01
Chinese, ex. Taiwanese (20)	27	0.18
Filipino (20)	32	0.21
Hmong (1)	1	0.01
Indian (18)	18	0.12
Japanese (13)	21	0.14
Korean (6)	6	0.04
Thai (3)	3	0.02
Vietnamese (8)	10	0.07
Hawaii Native/Pacific Islander (18)	24	0.16
Not Hispanic (13)	18	0.12
Hispanic (5)	6	0.04
Guamanian/Chamorro (1)	1	0.01
Native Hawaiian (5)	10	0.07
Samoan (6)	7	0.05
White (14,021)	14,277	93.31
Not Hispanic (13,126)	13,310	86.99
Hispanic (895)	967	6.32

Peoria

Place Type: City
County: Yavapai
Population: 154,065†

Ancestry‡	Population	%
African, Sub-Saharan (347)	434	0.29
African (105)	145	0.10
Ghanaian (80)	80	0.05
Nigerian (116)	116	0.08
South African (12)	30	0.02
Sudanese (28)	57	0.04
Other Sub-Saharan African (6)	6	<0.01
Albanian (0)	16	0.01
American (15,709)	15,709	10.56
Arab (697)	1,062	0.71
Arab (64)	166	0.11
Egyptian (9)	9	0.01
Iraqi (281)	339	0.23
Jordanian (27)	27	0.02
Lebanese (215)	342	0.23
Syrian (91)	140	0.09
Other Arab (10)	39	0.03
Assyrian/Chaldean/Syriac (232)	277	0.19
Australian (29)	81	0.05
Austrian (104)	424	0.29
Belgian (31)	196	0.13
Brazilian (10)	10	0.01
British (293)	540	0.36
Bulgarian (42)	93	0.06
Canadian (356)	635	0.43
Celtic (0)	49	0.03
Croatian (79)	221	0.15
Czech (219)	942	0.63
Czechoslovakian (50)	135	0.09
Danish (299)	906	0.61
Dutch (623)	2,869	1.93
Eastern European (67)	67	0.05
English (5,216)	15,893	10.69
European (1,844)	2,001	1.35
Finnish (125)	205	0.14
French, ex. Basque (774)	5,022	3.38
French Canadian (356)	1,203	0.81
German (8,659)	28,619	19.25
German Russian (15)	15	0.01
Greek (252)	673	0.45
Hungarian (244)	860	0.58
Icelander (12)	80	0.05
Iranian (224)	252	0.17
Irish (4,341)	17,928	12.06
Israeli (10)	34	0.02
Italian (3,768)	10,027	6.74
Latvian (0)	5	<0.01
Lithuanian (158)	431	0.29
Luxemburger (17)	30	0.02
Macedonian (39)	39	0.03
Northern European (163)	163	0.11
Norwegian (1,481)	3,872	2.60
Pennsylvania German (39)	160	0.11

*Notes: † The Census 2010 population figure is used to calculate the percentages in the Hispanic Origin and Race categories. Ancestry percentages are based on the 2006-2010 American Community Survey population (not shown); ‡ Numbers in parentheses indicate the number of people reporting a single ancestry; * Numbers in parentheses indicate the number of persons reporting this race alone, not in combination with any other race; Please refer to the Explanation of Data for more information.*

Polish (2,154)	5,719	3.85
Portuguese (224)	417	0.28
Romanian (925)	994	0.67
Russian (541)	1,694	1.14
Scandinavian (214)	554	0.37
Scotch-Irish (1,033)	2,473	1.66
Scottish (1,082)	3,189	2.14
Serbian (59)	142	0.10
Slavic (83)	107	0.07
Slovak (56)	241	0.16
Slovene (27)	80	0.05
Swedish (671)	2,539	1.71
Swiss (59)	428	0.29
Turkish (0)	14	0.01
Ukrainian (180)	419	0.28
Welsh (307)	1,002	0.67
West Indian, ex. Hispanic (162)	315	0.21
Bermudan (10)	42	0.03
Haitian (16)	16	0.01
Jamaican (56)	56	0.04
Trinidadian/Tobagonian (52)	140	0.09
West Indian (28)	61	0.04
Yugoslavian (211)	321	0.22

Hispanic Origin	Population	%
Hispanic or Latino (of any race)	28,629	18.58
Central American, ex. Mexican	638	0.41
Costa Rican	32	0.02
Guatemalan	150	0.10
Honduran	91	0.06
Nicaraguan	55	0.04
Panamanian	54	0.04
Salvadoran	228	0.15
Other Central American	28	0.02
Cuban	172	0.11
Dominican Republic	47	0.03
Mexican	23,791	15.44
Puerto Rican	963	0.63
South American	597	0.39
Argentinean	67	0.04
Bolivian	14	0.01
Chilean	76	0.05
Colombian	205	0.13
Ecuadorian	80	0.05
Peruvian	91	0.06
Uruguayan	11	0.01
Venezuelan	48	0.03
Other South American	5	<0.01
Other Hispanic or Latino	2,421	1.57

Race*	Population	%
African-American/Black (5,182)	6,537	4.24
Not Hispanic (4,904)	5,980	3.88
Hispanic (278)	557	0.36
American Indian/Alaska Native (1,471)	2,458	1.60
Not Hispanic (1,102)	1,811	1.18
Hispanic (369)	647	0.42
Alaska Athabascan *(Ala. Nat.)* (2)	2	<0.01
Aleut *(Alaska Native)* (0)	1	<0.01
Apache (58)	100	0.06
Blackfeet (7)	14	0.01
Canadian/French Am. Ind. (2)	7	<0.01
Cherokee (69)	285	0.18
Cheyenne (4)	5	<0.01
Chickasaw (13)	31	0.02
Chippewa (14)	34	0.02
Choctaw (36)	74	0.05
Colville (1)	1	<0.01
Comanche (4)	6	<0.01
Cree (4)	5	<0.01
Creek (8)	20	0.01
Crow (4)	8	0.01
Delaware (3)	3	<0.01
Hopi (19)	40	0.03
Inupiat *(Alaska Native)* (6)	6	<0.01
Iroquois (2)	13	0.01
Kiowa (3)	3	<0.01
Lumbee (1)	1	<0.01
Mexican American Ind. (45)	64	0.04
Navajo (415)	499	0.32
Osage (6)	7	<0.01
Ottawa (2)	5	<0.01
Paiute (3)	5	<0.01
Pima (31)	41	0.03
Potawatomi (6)	11	0.01
Pueblo (43)	47	0.03
Seminole (2)	10	0.01
Shoshone (5)	6	<0.01
Sioux (20)	54	0.04
South American Ind. (2)	8	0.01
Spanish American Ind. (2)	4	<0.01
Tlingit-Haida *(Alaska Native)* (2)	3	<0.01
Tohono O'Odham (30)	42	0.03
Ute (6)	11	0.01
Yakama (0)	1	<0.01
Yaqui (24)	40	0.03
Yuman (11)	22	0.01
Yup'ik *(Alaska Native)* (1)	1	<0.01
Asian (4,971)	6,527	4.24
Not Hispanic (4,832)	6,066	3.94
Hispanic (139)	461	0.30
Bangladeshi (18)	18	0.01
Burmese (14)	17	0.01
Cambodian (107)	124	0.08
Chinese, ex. Taiwanese (773)	1,070	0.69
Filipino (1,112)	1,618	1.05
Hmong (2)	2	<0.01
Indian (845)	967	0.63
Indonesian (18)	45	0.03
Japanese (208)	550	0.36
Korean (579)	789	0.51
Laotian (43)	53	0.03
Malaysian (1)	2	<0.01
Nepalese (1)	2	<0.01
Pakistani (73)	83	0.05
Sri Lankan (5)	6	<0.01
Taiwanese (20)	24	0.02
Thai (101)	156	0.10
Vietnamese (819)	920	0.60
Hawaii Native/Pacific Islander (221)	561	0.36
Not Hispanic (195)	462	0.30
Hispanic (26)	99	0.06
Fijian (5)	7	<0.01
Guamanian/Chamorro (29)	83	0.05
Marshallese (6)	6	<0.01
Native Hawaiian (78)	247	0.16
Samoan (52)	85	0.06
Tongan (2)	6	<0.01
White (126,584)	130,783	84.89
Not Hispanic (111,242)	113,903	73.93
Hispanic (15,342)	16,880	10.96

Phoenix

Place Type: City
County: Maricopa
Population: 1,445,632†

Ancestry‡	Population	%
Afghan (502)	516	0.04
African, Sub-Saharan (9,637)	11,253	0.78
African (4,201)	5,295	0.37
Cape Verdean (0)	18	<0.01
Ethiopian (955)	975	0.07
Ghanaian (182)	193	0.01
Kenyan (138)	161	0.01
Liberian (486)	585	0.04
Nigerian (240)	422	0.03
Sierra Leonean (11)	24	<0.01
Somalian (1,240)	1,261	0.09
South African (362)	395	0.03
Sudanese (1,144)	1,144	0.08
Ugandan (72)	72	<0.01
Zimbabwean (50)	50	<0.01
Other Sub-Saharan African (556)	658	0.05
Albanian (802)	852	0.06
Alsatian (0)	20	<0.01
American (51,759)	51,759	3.57
Arab (6,436)	8,436	0.58
Arab (1,285)	1,525	0.11
Egyptian (321)	362	0.02
Iraqi (1,684)	2,033	0.14
Jordanian (667)	667	0.05
Lebanese (1,181)	2,021	0.14
Moroccan (105)	123	0.01
Palestinian (114)	174	0.01
Syrian (308)	455	0.03
Other Arab (771)	1,076	0.07
Armenian (1,335)	1,825	0.13
Assyrian/Chaldean/Syriac (1,110)	1,205	0.08
Australian (208)	377	0.03
Austrian (637)	2,553	0.18
Basque (89)	285	0.02
Belgian (431)	1,393	0.10
Brazilian (381)	636	0.04
British (2,632)	4,800	0.33
Bulgarian (646)	716	0.05
Cajun (176)	302	0.02
Canadian (1,780)	3,054	0.21
Celtic (146)	223	0.02
Croatian (866)	1,912	0.13
Cypriot (23)	32	<0.01
Czech (1,450)	6,161	0.42
Czechoslovakian (589)	1,066	0.07
Danish (1,832)	6,271	0.43
Dutch (4,192)	17,964	1.24
Eastern European (972)	1,201	0.08
English (33,375)	104,093	7.18
Estonian (63)	144	0.01
European (10,457)	11,745	0.81
Finnish (1,061)	2,568	0.18
French, ex. Basque (5,904)	34,228	2.36
French Canadian (2,768)	6,161	0.42
German (57,334)	188,756	13.02
German Russian (27)	27	<0.01
Greek (2,216)	5,234	0.36
Guyanese (9)	18	<0.01
Hungarian (2,186)	6,414	0.44
Icelander (14)	217	0.01
Iranian (1,378)	1,585	0.11
Irish (34,800)	130,005	8.96
Israeli (243)	288	0.02
Italian (25,082)	59,753	4.12
Latvian (96)	227	0.02
Lithuanian (959)	2,661	0.18
Luxemburger (105)	338	0.02
Macedonian (77)	127	0.01
Maltese (73)	217	0.01
New Zealander (7)	22	<0.01
Northern European (1,029)	1,234	0.09
Norwegian (7,041)	19,701	1.36
Pennsylvania German (261)	535	0.04
Polish (10,623)	33,636	2.32
Portuguese (1,334)	3,044	0.21
Romanian (2,592)	3,727	0.26
Russian (5,776)	13,664	0.94
Scandinavian (1,673)	3,409	0.24
Scotch-Irish (6,215)	17,582	1.21
Scottish (7,465)	22,689	1.56
Serbian (1,096)	1,547	0.11
Slavic (192)	541	0.04
Slovak (928)	2,214	0.15
Slovene (262)	713	0.05
Swedish (4,986)	17,706	1.22
Swiss (730)	2,842	0.20
Turkish (281)	505	0.03
Ukrainian (1,281)	3,010	0.21
Welsh (1,717)	7,431	0.51
West Indian, ex. Hispanic (1,301)	1,788	0.12
Bahamian (44)	61	<0.01
Barbadian (8)	8	<0.01
Belizean (103)	139	0.01
Bermudan (10)	10	<0.01
Dutch West Indian (31)	122	0.01
Haitian (149)	201	0.01
Jamaican (686)	910	0.06
Trinidadian/Tobagonian (181)	181	0.01
West Indian (89)	156	0.01
Yugoslavian (3,955)	5,305	0.37

*Notes: † The Census 2010 population figure is used to calculate the percentages in the Hispanic Origin and Race categories. Ancestry percentages are based on the 2006-2010 American Community Survey population (not shown); ‡ Numbers in parentheses indicate the number of people reporting a single ancestry; * Numbers in parentheses indicate the number of persons reporting this race alone, not in combination with any other race; Please refer to the Explanation of Data for more information.*

Hispanic Origin	Population	%
Hispanic or Latino (of any race)	589,877	40.80
Central American, ex. Mexican	14,788	1.02
Costa Rican	348	0.02
Guatemalan	6,722	0.46
Honduran	1,535	0.11
Nicaraguan	888	0.06
Panamanian	444	0.03
Salvadoran	4,697	0.32
Other Central American	154	0.01
Cuban	3,975	0.27
Dominican Republic	865	0.06
Mexican	519,635	35.95
Puerto Rican	8,103	0.56
South American	5,116	0.35
Argentinean	608	0.04
Bolivian	180	0.01
Chilean	320	0.02
Colombian	1,687	0.12
Ecuadorian	628	0.04
Paraguayan	45	<0.01
Peruvian	1,048	0.07
Uruguayan	106	0.01
Venezuelan	434	0.03
Other South American	60	<0.01
Other Hispanic or Latino	37,395	2.59

Race*	Population	%
African-American/Black (93,608)	109,544	7.58
Not Hispanic (86,788)	98,091	6.79
Hispanic (6,820)	11,453	0.79
American Indian/Alaska Native (32,366)	43,724	3.02
Not Hispanic (23,327)	30,204	2.09
Hispanic (9,039)	13,520	0.94
Alaska Athabascan *(Ala. Nat.)* (20)	35	<0.01
Aleut *(Alaska Native)* (15)	34	<0.01
Apache (1,357)	1,905	0.13
Arapaho (25)	42	<0.01
Blackfeet (34)	306	0.02
Canadian/French Am. Ind. (12)	38	<0.01
Central American Ind. (48)	63	<0.01
Cherokee (509)	1,881	0.13
Cheyenne (50)	81	0.01
Chickasaw (99)	198	0.01
Chippewa (193)	391	0.03
Choctaw (292)	682	0.05
Colville (26)	29	<0.01
Comanche (59)	107	0.01
Cree (16)	37	<0.01
Creek (70)	216	0.01
Crow (17)	30	<0.01
Delaware (21)	42	<0.01
Hopi (1,224)	1,648	0.11
Inupiat *(Alaska Native)* (33)	51	<0.01
Iroquois (104)	250	0.02
Kiowa (57)	90	0.01
Lumbee (24)	38	<0.01
Menominee (17)	23	<0.01
Mexican American Ind. (1,253)	1,725	0.12
Navajo (10,689)	12,260	0.85
Osage (22)	64	<0.01
Ottawa (11)	24	<0.01
Paiute (67)	91	0.01
Pima (2,042)	2,614	0.18
Potawatomi (80)	137	0.01
Pueblo (338)	501	0.03
Puget Sound Salish (3)	17	<0.01
Seminole (26)	72	<0.01
Shoshone (41)	71	<0.01
Sioux (374)	669	0.05
South American Ind. (25)	67	<0.01
Spanish American Ind. (108)	141	0.01
Tlingit-Haida *(Alaska Native)* (39)	74	0.01
Tohono O'Odham (1,152)	1,448	0.10
Tsimshian *(Alaska Native)* (6)	11	<0.01
Ute (27)	49	<0.01
Yakama (11)	15	<0.01
Yaqui (1,486)	1,945	0.13
Yuman (369)	494	0.03
Yup'ik *(Alaska Native)* (13)	23	<0.01
Asian (45,597)	57,619	3.99
Not Hispanic (43,894)	53,095	3.67
Hispanic (1,703)	4,524	0.31
Bangladeshi (280)	322	0.02
Bhutanese (503)	609	0.04
Burmese (1,965)	2,184	0.15
Cambodian (604)	744	0.05
Chinese, ex. Taiwanese (6,977)	8,958	0.62
Filipino (7,606)	11,428	0.79
Hmong (23)	36	<0.01
Indian (12,101)	13,308	0.92
Indonesian (205)	330	0.02
Japanese (1,712)	3,731	0.26
Korean (2,892)	4,028	0.28
Laotian (613)	777	0.05
Malaysian (54)	100	0.01
Nepalese (208)	310	0.02
Pakistani (527)	608	0.04
Sri Lankan (96)	122	0.01
Taiwanese (286)	339	0.02
Thai (587)	964	0.07
Vietnamese (6,270)	7,091	0.49
Hawaii Native/Pacific Islander (2,555)	5,180	0.36
Not Hispanic (2,055)	3,828	0.26
Hispanic (500)	1,352	0.09
Fijian (31)	45	<0.01
Guamanian/Chamorro (583)	917	0.06
Marshallese (118)	127	0.01
Native Hawaiian (629)	1,675	0.12
Samoan (430)	768	0.05
Tongan (305)	385	0.03
White (951,958)	995,467	68.86
Not Hispanic (672,573)	693,617	47.98
Hispanic (279,385)	301,850	20.88

Picture Rocks

Place Type: CDP
County: Pima
Population: 9,563†

Ancestry‡	Population	%
American (580)	580	6.92
Arab (0)	23	0.27
Lebanese (0)	23	0.27
British (14)	14	0.17
Canadian (50)	65	0.78
Dutch (60)	235	2.80
English (323)	1,128	13.46
European (14)	14	0.17
Finnish (0)	11	0.13
French, ex. Basque (45)	292	3.48
French Canadian (12)	12	0.14
German (869)	2,193	26.17
Hungarian (31)	70	0.84
Irish (442)	1,236	14.75
Italian (110)	224	2.67
Lithuanian (0)	21	0.25
Norwegian (40)	207	2.47
Polish (173)	387	4.62
Portuguese (8)	8	0.10
Russian (52)	90	1.07
Scandinavian (29)	61	0.73
Scotch-Irish (104)	338	4.03
Scottish (60)	189	2.26
Serbian (11)	11	0.13
Swedish (45)	215	2.57
Swiss (0)	34	0.41
Ukrainian (0)	24	0.29
Welsh (57)	113	1.35

Hispanic Origin	Population	%
Hispanic or Latino (of any race)	1,558	16.29
Central American, ex. Mexican	12	0.13
Honduran	5	0.05
Nicaraguan	5	0.05
Panamanian	2	0.02
Cuban	19	0.20
Mexican	1,363	14.25
Puerto Rican	34	0.36
South American	10	0.10
Ecuadorian	4	0.04
Peruvian	5	0.05
Other South American	1	0.01
Other Hispanic or Latino	120	1.25

Race*	Population	%
African-American/Black (72)	139	1.45
Not Hispanic (68)	125	1.31
Hispanic (4)	14	0.15
American Indian/Alaska Native (138)	270	2.82
Not Hispanic (97)	203	2.12
Hispanic (41)	67	0.70
Apache (9)	12	0.13
Blackfeet (0)	1	0.01
Canadian/French Am. Ind. (1)	1	0.01
Cherokee (14)	54	0.56
Chickasaw (5)	5	0.05
Chippewa (2)	10	0.10
Choctaw (1)	15	0.16
Comanche (0)	1	0.01
Cree (0)	1	0.01
Creek (0)	1	0.01
Crow (1)	1	0.01
Delaware (1)	2	0.02
Houma (1)	1	0.01
Iroquois (3)	8	0.08
Lumbee (0)	1	0.01
Menominee (0)	1	0.01
Mexican American Ind. (5)	9	0.09
Navajo (24)	27	0.28
Paiute (1)	1	0.01
Pima (0)	1	0.01
Pueblo (0)	1	0.01
Seminole (0)	1	0.01
Shoshone (2)	2	0.02
Sioux (2)	3	0.03
Tohono O'Odham (14)	19	0.20
Yaqui (23)	32	0.33
Asian (44)	85	0.89
Not Hispanic (44)	71	0.74
Hispanic (0)	14	0.15
Chinese, ex. Taiwanese (5)	11	0.12
Filipino (16)	29	0.30
Indian (4)	8	0.08
Indonesian (1)	1	0.01
Japanese (10)	24	0.25
Korean (3)	8	0.08
Pakistani (0)	1	0.01
Thai (1)	4	0.04
Vietnamese (3)	4	0.04
Hawaii Native/Pacific Islander (8)	16	0.17
Not Hispanic (1)	4	0.04
Hispanic (7)	12	0.13
Guamanian/Chamorro (0)	2	0.02
Native Hawaiian (6)	10	0.10
White (8,541)	8,811	92.14
Not Hispanic (7,580)	7,761	81.16
Hispanic (961)	1,050	10.98

Prescott Valley

Place Type: Town
County: Yavapai
Population: 38,822†

Ancestry‡	Population	%
African, Sub-Saharan (104)	104	0.28
African (47)	47	0.13
Nigerian (32)	32	0.09
South African (25)	25	0.07
American (1,805)	1,805	4.84
Arab (0)	12	0.03
Lebanese (0)	12	0.03
Armenian (56)	56	0.15
Australian (14)	14	0.04
Austrian (53)	140	0.38
Belgian (0)	25	0.07
Brazilian (7)	7	0.02
British (168)	228	0.61

*Notes: † The Census 2010 population figure is used to calculate the percentages in the Hispanic Origin and Race categories. Ancestry percentages are based on the 2006-2010 American Community Survey population (not shown); ‡ Numbers in parentheses indicate the number of people reporting a single ancestry; * Numbers in parentheses indicate the number of persons reporting this race alone, not in combination with any other race; Please refer to the Explanation of Data for more information.*

Ancestry	Population	%
Canadian (149)	171	0.46
Celtic (38)	56	0.15
Croatian (0)	29	0.08
Czech (84)	227	0.61
Czechoslovakian (0)	13	0.03
Danish (73)	246	0.66
Dutch (164)	739	1.98
English (1,474)	5,028	13.49
European (484)	576	1.55
Finnish (65)	146	0.39
French, ex. Basque (234)	1,789	4.80
French Canadian (145)	303	0.81
German (2,668)	7,864	21.09
Greek (57)	88	0.24
Hungarian (133)	262	0.70
Icelander (8)	8	0.02
Iranian (9)	9	0.02
Irish (1,405)	6,112	16.39
Italian (781)	2,336	6.27
Latvian (12)	26	0.07
Lithuanian (31)	91	0.24
Luxemburger (13)	13	0.03
New Zealander (0)	12	0.03
Norwegian (386)	1,021	2.74
Pennsylvania German (0)	14	0.04
Polish (783)	1,440	3.86
Portuguese (100)	195	0.52
Romanian (0)	38	0.10
Russian (202)	326	0.87
Scandinavian (95)	182	0.49
Scotch-Irish (242)	635	1.70
Scottish (298)	755	2.03
Serbian (8)	8	0.02
Slovak (52)	76	0.20
Slovene (9)	23	0.06
Swedish (116)	944	2.53
Swiss (54)	232	0.62
Turkish (0)	27	0.07
Ukrainian (133)	170	0.46
Welsh (38)	285	0.76
Yugoslavian (0)	63	0.17

Hispanic Origin	Population	%
Hispanic or Latino (of any race)	6,484	16.70
Central American, ex. Mexican	96	0.25
Costa Rican	10	0.03
Guatemalan	31	0.08
Honduran	7	0.02
Nicaraguan	4	0.01
Panamanian	7	0.02
Salvadoran	37	0.10
Cuban	34	0.09
Dominican Republic	2	0.01
Mexican	5,416	13.95
Puerto Rican	163	0.42
South American	129	0.33
Argentinean	5	0.01
Bolivian	4	0.01
Chilean	10	0.03
Colombian	21	0.05
Ecuadorian	13	0.03
Peruvian	62	0.16
Uruguayan	7	0.02
Venezuelan	5	0.01
Other South American	2	0.01
Other Hispanic or Latino	644	1.66

Race*	Population	%
African-American/Black (324)	556	1.43
Not Hispanic (278)	458	1.18
Hispanic (46)	98	0.25
American Indian/Alaska Native (453)	808	2.08
Not Hispanic (336)	605	1.56
Hispanic (117)	203	0.52
Alaska Athabascan *(Ala. Nat.)* (4)	5	0.01
Apache (13)	30	0.08
Arapaho (1)	1	<0.01
Blackfeet (2)	7	0.02
Canadian/French Am. Ind. (1)	4	0.01
Central American Ind. (0)	1	<0.01
Cherokee (39)	118	0.30
Cheyenne (0)	1	<0.01
Chickasaw (2)	4	0.01
Chippewa (7)	14	0.04
Choctaw (21)	46	0.12
Comanche (3)	5	0.01
Creek (1)	4	0.01
Crow (1)	4	0.01
Delaware (0)	1	<0.01
Hopi (10)	20	0.05
Inupiat *(Alaska Native)* (1)	1	<0.01
Iroquois (2)	10	0.03
Kiowa (1)	5	0.01
Lumbee (0)	1	<0.01
Menominee (4)	4	0.01
Mexican American Ind. (13)	21	0.05
Navajo (83)	115	0.30
Osage (1)	1	<0.01
Ottawa (1)	1	<0.01
Paiute (3)	3	0.01
Pima (6)	9	0.02
Potawatomi (0)	1	<0.01
Pueblo (3)	8	0.02
Puget Sound Salish (0)	3	0.01
Seminole (1)	2	0.01
Shoshone (4)	6	0.02
Sioux (6)	18	0.05
South American Ind. (0)	2	0.01
Tohono O'Odham (8)	12	0.03
Tsimshian *(Alaska Native)* (0)	1	<0.01
Ute (1)	2	0.01
Yaqui (5)	7	0.02
Yuman (34)	37	0.10
Yup'ik *(Alaska Native)* (1)	1	<0.01
Asian (465)	670	1.73
Not Hispanic (435)	589	1.52
Hispanic (30)	81	0.21
Chinese, ex. Taiwanese (51)	75	0.19
Filipino (136)	212	0.55
Hmong (16)	16	0.04
Indian (64)	85	0.22
Indonesian (13)	20	0.05
Japanese (56)	126	0.32
Korean (35)	49	0.13
Laotian (1)	1	<0.01
Thai (24)	30	0.08
Vietnamese (48)	54	0.14
Hawaii Native/Pacific Islander (61)	158	0.41
Not Hispanic (46)	121	0.31
Hispanic (15)	37	0.10
Fijian (1)	1	<0.01
Guamanian/Chamorro (18)	31	0.08
Native Hawaiian (17)	54	0.14
Samoan (11)	17	0.04
Tongan (2)	2	0.01
White (34,187)	35,167	90.59
Not Hispanic (30,588)	31,171	80.29
Hispanic (3,599)	3,996	10.29

Prescott

Place Type: City
County: Yavapai
Population: 39,843†

Ancestry‡	Population	%
African, Sub-Saharan (15)	43	0.11
African (15)	43	0.11
American (1,852)	1,852	4.64
Arab (95)	95	0.24
Arab (65)	65	0.16
Lebanese (30)	30	0.08
Armenian (25)	37	0.09
Australian (17)	17	0.04
Austrian (53)	168	0.42
Basque (0)	26	0.07
Belgian (51)	89	0.22
Brazilian (0)	29	0.07
British (193)	292	0.73
Cajun (41)	41	0.10
Canadian (52)	93	0.23
Croatian (25)	104	0.26
Czech (83)	172	0.43
Czechoslovakian (39)	113	0.28
Danish (113)	424	1.06
Dutch (247)	1,020	2.55
Eastern European (47)	100	0.25
English (2,323)	7,109	17.80
European (581)	593	1.48
Finnish (41)	67	0.17
French, ex. Basque (350)	2,083	5.22
French Canadian (173)	385	0.96
German (3,086)	9,372	23.47
Greek (49)	115	0.29
Hungarian (132)	212	0.53
Irish (1,880)	6,739	16.87
Israeli (12)	12	0.03
Italian (895)	1,985	4.97
Latvian (0)	8	0.02
Lithuanian (26)	63	0.16
Luxemburger (30)	42	0.11
Northern European (60)	132	0.33
Norwegian (529)	1,275	3.19
Pennsylvania German (51)	51	0.13
Polish (394)	927	2.32
Portuguese (37)	50	0.13
Romanian (14)	31	0.08
Russian (159)	528	1.32
Scandinavian (61)	103	0.26
Scotch-Irish (664)	1,301	3.26
Scottish (731)	1,901	4.76
Serbian (40)	68	0.17
Slavic (0)	10	0.03
Slovak (48)	137	0.34
Slovene (11)	11	0.03
Swedish (328)	1,171	2.93
Swiss (65)	211	0.53
Ukrainian (22)	61	0.15
Welsh (61)	438	1.10
West Indian, ex. Hispanic (0)	78	0.20
Jamaican (0)	78	0.20
Yugoslavian (10)	33	0.08

Hispanic Origin	Population	%
Hispanic or Latino (of any race)	3,442	8.64
Central American, ex. Mexican	85	0.21
Costa Rican	3	0.01
Guatemalan	28	0.07
Honduran	6	0.02
Nicaraguan	11	0.03
Panamanian	13	0.03
Salvadoran	24	0.06
Cuban	49	0.12
Dominican Republic	3	0.01
Mexican	2,696	6.77
Puerto Rican	101	0.25
South American	106	0.27
Argentinean	12	0.03
Bolivian	13	0.03
Chilean	14	0.04
Colombian	21	0.05
Ecuadorian	14	0.04
Paraguayan	3	0.01
Peruvian	17	0.04
Venezuelan	11	0.03
Other South American	1	<0.01
Other Hispanic or Latino	402	1.01

Race*	Population	%
African-American/Black (265)	417	1.05
Not Hispanic (242)	358	0.90
Hispanic (23)	59	0.15
American Indian/Alaska Native (451)	818	2.05
Not Hispanic (358)	615	1.54
Hispanic (93)	203	0.51
Alaska Athabascan *(Ala. Nat.)* (1)	3	0.01
Aleut *(Alaska Native)* (0)	1	<0.01
Apache (21)	27	0.07
Blackfeet (3)	11	0.03
Canadian/French Am. Ind. (4)	7	0.02

*Notes: † The Census 2010 population figure is used to calculate the percentages in the Hispanic Origin and Race categories. Ancestry percentages are based on the 2006-2010 American Community Survey population (not shown); ‡ Numbers in parentheses indicate the number of people reporting a single ancestry; * Numbers in parentheses indicate the number of persons reporting this race alone, not in combination with any other race; Please refer to the Explanation of Data for more information.*

Cherokee (19)	96	0.24
Cheyenne (0)	1	<0.01
Chickasaw (2)	4	0.01
Chippewa (2)	4	0.01
Choctaw (3)	17	0.04
Comanche (3)	8	0.02
Creek (5)	6	0.02
Crow (0)	1	<0.01
Delaware (0)	1	<0.01
Hopi (19)	29	0.07
Inupiat *(Alaska Native)* (0)	2	0.01
Iroquois (3)	10	0.03
Kiowa (2)	5	0.01
Mexican American Ind. (8)	12	0.03
Navajo (117)	144	0.36
Osage (5)	8	0.02
Paiute (5)	13	0.03
Pima (2)	5	0.01
Potawatomi (4)	7	0.02
Pueblo (13)	14	0.04
Puget Sound Salish (1)	1	<0.01
Seminole (0)	1	<0.01
Shoshone (3)	4	0.01
Sioux (8)	18	0.05
South American Ind. (3)	3	0.01
Spanish American Ind. (1)	1	<0.01
Tlingit-Haida *(Alaska Native)* (0)	1	<0.01
Tohono O'Odham (2)	2	0.01
Ute (1)	2	0.01
Yakama (0)	1	<0.01
Yaqui (1)	15	0.04
Yuman (11)	32	0.08
Asian (492)	741	1.86
Not Hispanic (481)	676	1.70
Hispanic (11)	65	0.16
Burmese (1)	1	<0.01
Cambodian (3)	4	0.01
Chinese, ex. Taiwanese (105)	147	0.37
Filipino (111)	194	0.49
Hmong (1)	1	<0.01
Indian (79)	89	0.22
Indonesian (2)	11	0.03
Japanese (76)	134	0.34
Korean (47)	77	0.19
Laotian (1)	1	<0.01
Nepalese (3)	5	0.01
Pakistani (1)	2	0.01
Sri Lankan (0)	1	<0.01
Thai (14)	19	0.05
Vietnamese (30)	40	0.10
Hawaii Native/Pacific Islander (48)	122	0.31
Not Hispanic (45)	95	0.24
Hispanic (3)	27	0.07
Fijian (0)	2	0.01
Guamanian/Chamorro (12)	20	0.05
Native Hawaiian (17)	61	0.15
Samoan (11)	16	0.04
Tongan (1)	1	<0.01
White (36,713)	37,550	94.24
Not Hispanic (34,690)	35,186	88.31
Hispanic (2,023)	2,364	5.93

Queen Creek

Place Type: Town
County: Maricopa
Population: 26,361†

Ancestry‡	Population	%
African, Sub-Saharan (207)	207	0.90
African (176)	176	0.76
Ghanaian (15)	15	0.07
Nigerian (16)	16	0.07
American (766)	766	3.32
Arab (103)	103	0.45
Arab (20)	20	0.09
Egyptian (50)	50	0.22
Jordanian (24)	24	0.10
Lebanese (9)	9	0.04
Austrian (0)	22	0.10
British (72)	143	0.62
Canadian (54)	73	0.32
Celtic (12)	32	0.14
Czech (0)	79	0.34
Czechoslovakian (9)	9	0.04
Danish (43)	409	1.77
Dutch (147)	573	2.49
Eastern European (13)	39	0.17
English (1,422)	3,680	15.96
European (270)	285	1.24
Finnish (29)	110	0.48
French, ex. Basque (207)	1,134	4.92
French Canadian (14)	31	0.13
German (1,451)	4,410	19.13
Greek (200)	387	1.68
Guyanese (11)	11	0.05
Hungarian (16)	112	0.49
Irish (807)	3,590	15.57
Italian (476)	1,187	5.15
Lithuanian (0)	34	0.15
Norwegian (85)	346	1.50
Pennsylvania German (14)	28	0.12
Polish (172)	370	1.60
Portuguese (28)	109	0.47
Romanian (14)	126	0.55
Russian (27)	139	0.60
Scandinavian (39)	39	0.17
Scotch-Irish (205)	384	1.67
Scottish (298)	696	3.02
Serbian (16)	16	0.07
Slovak (0)	39	0.17
Swedish (36)	317	1.37
Swiss (8)	16	0.07
Ukrainian (18)	51	0.22
Welsh (15)	158	0.69
West Indian, ex. Hispanic (16)	16	0.07
Jamaican (16)	16	0.07
Yugoslavian (0)	39	0.17

Hispanic Origin	Population	%
Hispanic or Latino (of any race)	4,566	17.32
Central American, ex. Mexican	122	0.46
Costa Rican	10	0.04
Guatemalan	55	0.21
Honduran	6	0.02
Nicaraguan	10	0.04
Panamanian	7	0.03
Salvadoran	34	0.13
Cuban	41	0.16
Dominican Republic	31	0.12
Mexican	3,685	13.98
Puerto Rican	204	0.77
South American	113	0.43
Argentinean	12	0.05
Bolivian	1	<0.01
Chilean	15	0.06
Colombian	32	0.12
Ecuadorian	9	0.03
Paraguayan	5	0.02
Peruvian	24	0.09
Uruguayan	7	0.03
Venezuelan	8	0.03
Other Hispanic or Latino	370	1.40

Race*	Population	%
African-American/Black (895)	1,183	4.49
Not Hispanic (841)	1,075	4.08
Hispanic (54)	108	0.41
American Indian/Alaska Native (189)	343	1.30
Not Hispanic (123)	225	0.85
Hispanic (66)	118	0.45
Aleut *(Alaska Native)* (0)	4	0.02
Apache (6)	7	0.03
Blackfeet (2)	4	0.02
Canadian/French Am. Ind. (2)	2	0.01
Cherokee (12)	24	0.09
Cheyenne (1)	1	<0.01
Chickasaw (1)	5	0.02
Chippewa (2)	4	0.02
Choctaw (2)	8	0.03
Creek (5)	5	0.02
Crow (1)	1	<0.01
Delaware (0)	5	0.02
Hopi (1)	2	0.01
Iroquois (1)	4	0.02
Mexican American Ind. (12)	19	0.07
Navajo (30)	45	0.17
Ottawa (0)	3	0.01
Pima (9)	29	0.11
Potawatomi (1)	1	<0.01
Pueblo (6)	6	0.02
Seminole (1)	4	0.02
Sioux (7)	12	0.05
South American Ind. (1)	1	<0.01
Spanish American Ind. (4)	4	0.02
Tohono O'Odham (0)	1	<0.01
Yaqui (2)	9	0.03
Yuman (1)	1	<0.01
Asian (732)	1,022	3.88
Not Hispanic (709)	938	3.56
Hispanic (23)	84	0.32
Bangladeshi (13)	14	0.05
Cambodian (22)	25	0.09
Chinese, ex. Taiwanese (80)	109	0.41
Filipino (218)	316	1.20
Hmong (1)	2	0.01
Indian (63)	74	0.28
Indonesian (1)	4	0.02
Japanese (31)	83	0.31
Korean (80)	135	0.51
Laotian (8)	12	0.05
Pakistani (17)	19	0.07
Sri Lankan (7)	7	0.03
Taiwanese (6)	6	0.02
Thai (11)	35	0.13
Vietnamese (132)	159	0.60
Hawaii Native/Pacific Islander (39)	123	0.47
Not Hispanic (31)	92	0.35
Hispanic (8)	31	0.12
Guamanian/Chamorro (11)	21	0.08
Marshallese (1)	1	<0.01
Native Hawaiian (16)	48	0.18
Samoan (8)	25	0.09
Tongan (0)	5	0.02
White (22,043)	22,890	86.83
Not Hispanic (19,516)	20,021	75.95
Hispanic (2,527)	2,869	10.88

Rio Rico

Place Type: CDP
County: Santa Cruz
Population: 18,962†

Ancestry‡	Population	%
American (535)	535	2.78
Arab (0)	13	0.07
Moroccan (0)	13	0.07
Austrian (12)	34	0.18
British (38)	38	0.20
Canadian (0)	61	0.32
Croatian (0)	31	0.16
Czech (16)	16	0.08
Danish (0)	15	0.08
Dutch (0)	67	0.35
English (50)	477	2.48
European (62)	62	0.32
French, ex. Basque (0)	35	0.18
French Canadian (0)	27	0.14
German (206)	848	4.40
Hungarian (20)	44	0.23
Irish (190)	799	4.15
Italian (389)	480	2.49
Lithuanian (9)	97	0.50
Norwegian (38)	98	0.51
Polish (0)	66	0.34
Portuguese (19)	44	0.23
Russian (64)	95	0.49
Scandinavian (0)	19	0.10
Scotch-Irish (57)	88	0.46

SECTION TWO

*Notes: † The Census 2010 population figure is used to calculate the percentages in the Hispanic Origin and Race categories. Ancestry percentages are based on the 2006-2010 American Community Survey population (not shown); ‡ Numbers in parentheses indicate the number of people reporting a single ancestry; * Numbers in parentheses indicate the number of persons reporting this race alone, not in combination with any other race; Please refer to the Explanation of Data for more information.*

Scottish (64)	154	0.80
Ukrainian (17)	17	0.09
Welsh (21)	21	0.11

Hispanic Origin	Population	%
Hispanic or Latino (of any race)	16,179	85.32
Central American, ex. Mexican	55	0.29
Costa Rican	1	0.01
Guatemalan	7	0.04
Honduran	12	0.06
Nicaraguan	3	0.02
Panamanian	5	0.03
Salvadoran	27	0.14
Cuban	20	0.11
Dominican Republic	7	0.04
Mexican	15,245	80.40
Puerto Rican	104	0.55
South American	54	0.28
Argentinean	13	0.07
Chilean	9	0.05
Colombian	10	0.05
Ecuadorian	14	0.07
Peruvian	5	0.03
Venezuelan	3	0.02
Other Hispanic or Latino	694	3.66

Race*	Population	%
African-American/Black (75)	98	0.52
Not Hispanic (38)	49	0.26
Hispanic (37)	49	0.26
American Indian/Alaska Native (121)	160	0.84
Not Hispanic (33)	54	0.28
Hispanic (88)	106	0.56
Apache (2)	3	0.02
Canadian/French Am. Ind. (0)	3	0.02
Cherokee (2)	4	0.02
Chickasaw (1)	1	0.01
Choctaw (2)	2	0.01
Houma (1)	1	0.01
Iroquois (1)	1	0.01
Kiowa (0)	1	0.01
Mexican American Ind. (22)	24	0.13
Navajo (2)	3	0.02
Pima (1)	3	0.02
Potawatomi (1)	1	0.01
Pueblo (6)	8	0.04
Sioux (0)	1	0.01
Spanish American Ind. (1)	1	0.01
Tlingit-Haida *(Alaska Native)* (1)	1	0.01
Tohono O'Odham (17)	17	0.09
Yaqui (14)	14	0.07
Asian (94)	115	0.61
Not Hispanic (76)	87	0.46
Hispanic (18)	28	0.15
Cambodian (2)	2	0.01
Chinese, ex. Taiwanese (8)	14	0.07
Filipino (9)	15	0.08
Indian (8)	11	0.06
Japanese (6)	13	0.07
Korean (49)	53	0.28
Thai (2)	2	0.01
Vietnamese (2)	2	0.01
Hawaii Native/Pacific Islander (10)	23	0.12
Not Hispanic (5)	11	0.06
Hispanic (5)	12	0.06
Guamanian/Chamorro (0)	1	0.01
Native Hawaiian (8)	10	0.05
Samoan (1)	2	0.01
White (13,472)	13,797	72.76
Not Hispanic (2,578)	2,622	13.83
Hispanic (10,894)	11,175	58.93

Saddlebrooke

Place Type: CDP
County: Pinal
Population: 9,614†

Ancestry‡	Population	%
American (382)	382	4.24
Arab (17)	35	0.39
Lebanese (17)	35	0.39
Armenian (0)	14	0.16
Austrian (0)	69	0.77
Belgian (28)	28	0.31
Brazilian (0)	13	0.14
British (46)	71	0.79
Canadian (0)	13	0.14
Czech (9)	52	0.58
Czechoslovakian (24)	24	0.27
Danish (61)	162	1.80
Dutch (89)	296	3.29
English (600)	1,808	20.08
European (179)	179	1.99
Finnish (0)	27	0.30
French, ex. Basque (48)	361	4.01
French Canadian (16)	16	0.18
German (1,049)	2,520	27.98
Greek (15)	25	0.28
Hungarian (9)	27	0.30
Irish (373)	1,448	16.08
Italian (334)	479	5.32
Lithuanian (30)	59	0.66
Luxemburger (0)	15	0.17
Norwegian (116)	324	3.60
Polish (187)	460	5.11
Portuguese (19)	34	0.38
Romanian (13)	13	0.14
Russian (89)	155	1.72
Scandinavian (0)	25	0.28
Scotch-Irish (53)	132	1.47
Scottish (87)	324	3.60
Serbian (9)	34	0.38
Slovak (27)	50	0.56
Slovene (0)	10	0.11
Swedish (143)	439	4.88
Swiss (23)	135	1.50
Ukrainian (12)	12	0.13
Welsh (74)	156	1.73
Yugoslavian (29)	29	0.32

Hispanic Origin	Population	%
Hispanic or Latino (of any race)	468	4.87
Central American, ex. Mexican	9	0.09
Costa Rican	1	0.01
Guatemalan	3	0.03
Honduran	1	0.01
Panamanian	1	0.01
Salvadoran	3	0.03
Cuban	8	0.08
Dominican Republic	7	0.07
Mexican	322	3.35
Puerto Rican	27	0.28
South American	21	0.22
Argentinean	3	0.03
Bolivian	1	0.01
Chilean	2	0.02
Colombian	5	0.05
Ecuadorian	2	0.02
Peruvian	4	0.04
Uruguayan	2	0.02
Other South American	2	0.02
Other Hispanic or Latino	74	0.77

Race*	Population	%
African-American/Black (76)	96	1.00
Not Hispanic (68)	80	0.83
Hispanic (8)	16	0.17
American Indian/Alaska Native (23)	54	0.56
Not Hispanic (17)	40	0.42
Hispanic (6)	14	0.15
Apache (0)	1	0.01
Blackfeet (0)	1	0.01
Cherokee (2)	11	0.11
Choctaw (4)	5	0.05
Delaware (0)	2	0.02
Iroquois (0)	1	0.01
Mexican American Ind. (1)	1	0.01
Navajo (1)	2	0.02
Pima (0)	1	0.01
Pueblo (1)	1	0.01
Sioux (1)	1	0.01
Tohono O'Odham (0)	1	0.01
Asian (84)	107	1.11
Not Hispanic (81)	96	1.00
Hispanic (3)	11	0.11
Chinese, ex. Taiwanese (12)	16	0.17
Filipino (15)	23	0.24
Indian (9)	9	0.09
Indonesian (0)	3	0.03
Japanese (20)	22	0.23
Korean (21)	28	0.29
Thai (2)	2	0.02
Vietnamese (1)	1	0.01
Hawaii Native/Pacific Islander (1)	9	0.09
Not Hispanic (1)	6	0.06
Hispanic (0)	3	0.03
Native Hawaiian (0)	3	0.03
Samoan (1)	2	0.02
White (9,211)	9,291	96.64
Not Hispanic (8,924)	8,974	93.34
Hispanic (287)	317	3.30

Safford

Place Type: City
County: Graham
Population: 9,566†

Ancestry‡	Population	%
African, Sub-Saharan (0)	45	0.48
African (0)	45	0.48
American (270)	270	2.89
Arab (13)	13	0.14
Jordanian (13)	13	0.14
Austrian (0)	49	0.52
Czech (0)	12	0.13
Danish (0)	159	1.70
Dutch (0)	196	2.09
English (565)	1,279	13.67
European (66)	86	0.92
French, ex. Basque (14)	222	2.37
German (236)	1,061	11.34
Greek (0)	8	0.09
Irish (268)	800	8.55
Italian (151)	359	3.84
Norwegian (81)	105	1.12
Polish (51)	85	0.91
Russian (0)	10	0.11
Scandinavian (23)	57	0.61
Scotch-Irish (9)	45	0.48
Scottish (12)	112	1.20
Swedish (42)	361	3.86
Swiss (16)	67	0.72
Ukrainian (0)	52	0.56
Welsh (0)	28	0.30
Yugoslavian (18)	25	0.27

Hispanic Origin	Population	%
Hispanic or Latino (of any race)	4,166	43.55
Central American, ex. Mexican	4	0.04
Guatemalan	2	0.02
Panamanian	1	0.01
Salvadoran	1	0.01
Cuban	2	0.02
Mexican	3,725	38.94
Puerto Rican	15	0.16
South American	20	0.21
Chilean	9	0.09
Colombian	3	0.03
Ecuadorian	1	0.01
Peruvian	7	0.07
Other Hispanic or Latino	400	4.18

Race*	Population	%
African-American/Black (116)	207	2.16
Not Hispanic (104)	158	1.65
Hispanic (12)	49	0.51
American Indian/Alaska Native (153)	254	2.66
Not Hispanic (92)	159	1.66

*Notes: † The Census 2010 population figure is used to calculate the percentages in the Hispanic Origin and Race categories. Ancestry percentages are based on the 2006-2010 American Community Survey population (not shown); ‡ Numbers in parentheses indicate the number of people reporting a single ancestry; * Numbers in parentheses indicate the number of persons reporting this race alone, not in combination with any other race; Please refer to the Explanation of Data for more information.*

Hispanic (61)	95	0.99
Apache (35)	53	0.55
Blackfeet (1)	2	0.02
Cherokee (3)	11	0.11
Chickasaw (4)	4	0.04
Chippewa (1)	5	0.05
Choctaw (5)	12	0.13
Cree (1)	1	0.01
Creek (0)	3	0.03
Hopi (1)	1	0.01
Mexican American Ind. (7)	12	0.13
Navajo (28)	40	0.42
Potawatomi (1)	1	0.01
Sioux (1)	1	0.01
Tohono O'Odham (6)	6	0.06
Ute (1)	1	0.01
Yaqui (13)	13	0.14
Yuman (1)	1	0.01
Yup'ik *(Alaska Native)* (1)	1	0.01
Asian (85)	125	1.31
Not Hispanic (85)	110	1.15
Hispanic (0)	15	0.16
Chinese, ex. Taiwanese (36)	41	0.43
Filipino (12)	24	0.25
Indian (12)	15	0.16
Indonesian (8)	8	0.08
Japanese (1)	8	0.08
Korean (3)	5	0.05
Thai (0)	1	0.01
Vietnamese (12)	12	0.13
Hawaii Native/Pacific Islander (5)	13	0.14
Not Hispanic (5)	9	0.09
Hispanic (0)	4	0.04
Guamanian/Chamorro (1)	1	0.01
Native Hawaiian (2)	9	0.09
Samoan (2)	2	0.02
White (7,789)	8,107	84.75
Not Hispanic (4,958)	5,088	53.19
Hispanic (2,831)	3,019	31.56

Sahuarita

Place Type: Town
County: Pima
Population: 25,259†

Ancestry‡	Population	%
African, Sub-Saharan (10)	10	0.05
South African (10)	10	0.05
American (550)	550	2.55
Arab (69)	94	0.44
Arab (61)	61	0.28
Lebanese (8)	33	0.15
Austrian (28)	71	0.33
Belgian (6)	63	0.29
British (32)	145	0.67
Cajun (9)	9	0.04
Canadian (8)	161	0.75
Croatian (0)	33	0.15
Czech (37)	164	0.76
Czechoslovakian (0)	12	0.06
Danish (10)	216	1.00
Dutch (226)	512	2.37
English (680)	2,566	11.88
European (412)	472	2.18
Finnish (37)	47	0.22
French, ex. Basque (101)	905	4.19
French Canadian (91)	232	1.07
German (1,591)	3,886	17.98
German Russian (0)	17	0.08
Greek (18)	62	0.29
Hungarian (37)	79	0.37
Iranian (19)	19	0.09
Irish (665)	2,368	10.96
Italian (400)	949	4.39
Latvian (0)	7	0.03
Lithuanian (58)	77	0.36
Maltese (12)	12	0.06
Norwegian (177)	386	1.79
Polish (307)	731	3.38
Portuguese (17)	55	0.25
Romanian (0)	24	0.11
Russian (131)	390	1.80
Scandinavian (37)	72	0.33
Scotch-Irish (128)	321	1.49
Scottish (90)	596	2.76
Slavic (0)	28	0.13
Slovak (0)	9	0.04
Slovene (0)	18	0.08
Swedish (109)	367	1.70
Ukrainian (0)	10	0.05
Welsh (43)	168	0.78
West Indian, ex. Hispanic (33)	72	0.33
Jamaican (33)	72	0.33
Yugoslavian (0)	42	0.19

Hispanic Origin	Population	%
Hispanic or Latino (of any race)	8,077	31.98
Central American, ex. Mexican	141	0.56
Costa Rican	2	0.01
Guatemalan	15	0.06
Honduran	14	0.06
Nicaraguan	17	0.07
Panamanian	14	0.06
Salvadoran	73	0.29
Other Central American	6	0.02
Cuban	49	0.19
Dominican Republic	33	0.13
Mexican	6,979	27.63
Puerto Rican	265	1.05
South American	141	0.56
Argentinean	9	0.04
Bolivian	13	0.05
Chilean	23	0.09
Colombian	34	0.13
Ecuadorian	19	0.08
Peruvian	24	0.10
Venezuelan	11	0.04
Other South American	8	0.03
Other Hispanic or Latino	469	1.86

Race*	Population	%
African-American/Black (742)	1,021	4.04
Not Hispanic (661)	865	3.42
Hispanic (81)	156	0.62
American Indian/Alaska Native (334)	542	2.15
Not Hispanic (188)	291	1.15
Hispanic (146)	251	0.99
Apache (10)	14	0.06
Blackfeet (7)	9	0.04
Cherokee (19)	40	0.16
Chickasaw (7)	7	0.03
Chippewa (8)	11	0.04
Choctaw (4)	15	0.06
Comanche (2)	3	0.01
Cree (0)	3	0.01
Creek (2)	2	0.01
Delaware (3)	7	0.03
Hopi (2)	7	0.03
Inupiat *(Alaska Native)* (1)	2	0.01
Iroquois (1)	2	0.01
Lumbee (0)	1	<0.01
Mexican American Ind. (8)	12	0.05
Navajo (34)	45	0.18
Osage (1)	1	<0.01
Paiute (0)	1	<0.01
Pima (7)	9	0.04
Potawatomi (1)	1	<0.01
Pueblo (9)	16	0.06
Puget Sound Salish (0)	1	<0.01
Sioux (3)	6	0.02
South American Ind. (1)	6	0.02
Tohono O'Odham (60)	68	0.27
Ute (1)	2	0.01
Yaqui (26)	49	0.19
Yuman (3)	4	0.02
Asian (499)	861	3.41
Not Hispanic (463)	718	2.84
Hispanic (36)	143	0.57
Bangladeshi (3)	3	0.01
Burmese (1)	1	<0.01
Cambodian (0)	2	0.01
Chinese, ex. Taiwanese (85)	160	0.63
Filipino (133)	296	1.17
Indian (96)	113	0.45
Indonesian (3)	15	0.06
Japanese (32)	92	0.36
Korean (43)	88	0.35
Laotian (3)	8	0.03
Malaysian (0)	1	<0.01
Pakistani (18)	20	0.08
Taiwanese (2)	2	0.01
Thai (14)	26	0.10
Vietnamese (39)	48	0.19
Hawaii Native/Pacific Islander (31)	109	0.43
Not Hispanic (28)	93	0.37
Hispanic (3)	16	0.06
Guamanian/Chamorro (1)	8	0.03
Marshallese (5)	5	0.02
Native Hawaiian (10)	36	0.14
Samoan (10)	33	0.13
Tongan (1)	3	0.01
White (20,280)	21,241	84.09
Not Hispanic (15,249)	15,753	62.37
Hispanic (5,031)	5,488	21.73

San Luis

Place Type: City
County: Yuma
Population: 25,505†

Ancestry‡	Population	%
American (40)	40	0.17
Danish (0)	9	0.04
Dutch (10)	34	0.14
English (69)	117	0.49
European (0)	16	0.07
French, ex. Basque (0)	54	0.23
German (195)	434	1.82
Greek (6)	6	0.03
Irish (166)	361	1.51
Italian (90)	136	0.57
Norwegian (17)	39	0.16
Polish (9)	17	0.07
Scotch-Irish (0)	19	0.08
Scottish (6)	32	0.13
Swedish (56)	62	0.26
Welsh (0)	6	0.03
West Indian, ex. Hispanic (0)	9	0.04
Jamaican (0)	9	0.04

Hispanic Origin	Population	%
Hispanic or Latino (of any race)	25,171	98.69
Central American, ex. Mexican	48	0.19
Guatemalan	10	0.04
Honduran	3	0.01
Nicaraguan	3	0.01
Salvadoran	31	0.12
Other Central American	1	<0.01
Cuban	8	0.03
Dominican Republic	4	0.02
Mexican	24,543	96.23
Puerto Rican	29	0.11
South American	12	0.05
Bolivian	1	<0.01
Colombian	4	0.02
Ecuadorian	1	<0.01
Peruvian	2	0.01
Uruguayan	1	<0.01
Venezuelan	3	0.01
Other Hispanic or Latino	527	2.07

Race*	Population	%
African-American/Black (86)	111	0.44
Not Hispanic (25)	30	0.12
Hispanic (61)	81	0.32
American Indian/Alaska Native (122)	157	0.62
Not Hispanic (21)	25	0.10
Hispanic (101)	132	0.52

*Notes: † The Census 2010 population figure is used to calculate the percentages in the Hispanic Origin and Race categories. Ancestry percentages are based on the 2006-2010 American Community Survey population (not shown); ‡ Numbers in parentheses indicate the number of people reporting a single ancestry; * Numbers in parentheses indicate the number of persons reporting this race alone, not in combination with any other race; Please refer to the Explanation of Data for more information.*

Cherokee (0)	1	<0.01
Lumbee (1)	3	0.01
Mexican American Ind. (39)	43	0.17
Navajo (7)	7	0.03
Sioux (1)	1	<0.01
Spanish American Ind. (7)	8	0.03
Tohono O'Odham (7)	7	0.03
Yaqui (1)	1	<0.01
Yuman (6)	6	0.02
Asian (47)	83	0.33
Not Hispanic (37)	39	0.15
Hispanic (10)	44	0.17
Cambodian (0)	1	<0.01
Chinese, ex. Taiwanese (14)	18	0.07
Filipino (6)	18	0.07
Indian (19)	35	0.14
Indonesian (1)	1	<0.01
Japanese (2)	2	0.01
Pakistani (4)	4	0.02
Hawaii Native/Pacific Islander (17)	22	0.09
Hispanic (17)	22	0.09
Guamanian/Chamorro (6)	6	0.02
Native Hawaiian (10)	14	0.05
White (16,120)	16,788	65.82
Not Hispanic (242)	247	0.97
Hispanic (15,878)	16,541	64.85

San Tan Valley

Place Type: CDP
County: Pinal
Population: 81,321†

Ancestry‡	Population	%
African, Sub-Saharan (135)	158	0.25
African (34)	57	0.09
Nigerian (63)	63	0.10
South African (38)	38	0.06
Alsatian (7)	7	0.01
American (1,674)	1,674	2.61
Arab (123)	191	0.30
Arab (66)	66	0.10
Egyptian (47)	47	0.07
Lebanese (10)	78	0.12
Armenian (73)	81	0.13
Austrian (70)	100	0.16
Belgian (0)	26	0.04
Brazilian (13)	101	0.16
British (149)	310	0.48
Canadian (12)	91	0.14
Croatian (24)	39	0.06
Czech (89)	179	0.28
Czechoslovakian (12)	21	0.03
Danish (110)	616	0.96
Dutch (223)	1,149	1.79
English (2,349)	7,534	11.76
European (402)	489	0.76
Finnish (82)	138	0.22
French, ex. Basque (631)	2,540	3.96
French Canadian (139)	279	0.44
German (3,241)	11,876	18.53
Greek (114)	1,003	1.57
Hungarian (21)	263	0.41
Icelander (0)	12	0.02
Iranian (19)	44	0.07
Irish (2,196)	8,153	12.72
Italian (1,672)	4,327	6.75
Lithuanian (30)	123	0.19
Northern European (124)	124	0.19
Norwegian (383)	1,277	1.99
Polish (443)	1,980	3.09
Portuguese (114)	391	0.61
Romanian (0)	9	0.01
Russian (211)	598	0.93
Scandinavian (86)	404	0.63
Scotch-Irish (489)	1,099	1.71
Scottish (435)	1,843	2.88
Serbian (0)	48	0.07
Slavic (9)	37	0.06
Slovak (52)	246	0.38
Slovene (11)	11	0.02
Swedish (374)	1,096	1.71
Swiss (36)	260	0.41
Turkish (64)	64	0.10
Ukrainian (101)	195	0.30
Welsh (118)	350	0.55
West Indian, ex. Hispanic (208)	208	0.32
Haitian (74)	74	0.12
Jamaican (65)	65	0.10
Trinidadian/Tobagonian (29)	29	0.05
West Indian (40)	40	0.06
Yugoslavian (9)	44	0.07

Hispanic Origin	Population	%
Hispanic or Latino (of any race)	18,995	23.36
Central American, ex. Mexican	519	0.64
Costa Rican	48	0.06
Guatemalan	118	0.15
Honduran	52	0.06
Nicaraguan	76	0.09
Panamanian	25	0.03
Salvadoran	196	0.24
Other Central American	4	<0.01
Cuban	118	0.15
Dominican Republic	129	0.16
Mexican	15,678	19.28
Puerto Rican	697	0.86
South American	444	0.55
Argentinean	49	0.06
Bolivian	2	<0.01
Chilean	45	0.06
Colombian	114	0.14
Ecuadorian	51	0.06
Paraguayan	9	0.01
Peruvian	131	0.16
Venezuelan	42	0.05
Other South American	1	<0.01
Other Hispanic or Latino	1,410	1.73

Race*	Population	%
African-American/Black (4,102)	5,262	6.47
Not Hispanic (3,824)	4,716	5.80
Hispanic (278)	546	0.67
American Indian/Alaska Native (946)	1,582	1.95
Not Hispanic (698)	1,152	1.42
Hispanic (248)	430	0.53
Alaska Athabascan *(Ala. Nat.)* (2)	2	<0.01
Aleut *(Alaska Native)* (4)	7	0.01
Apache (36)	67	0.08
Blackfeet (17)	43	0.05
Canadian/French Am. Ind. (2)	4	<0.01
Central American Ind. (3)	5	0.01
Cherokee (34)	144	0.18
Cheyenne (0)	1	<0.01
Chickasaw (3)	4	<0.01
Chippewa (13)	23	0.03
Choctaw (14)	34	0.04
Colville (2)	4	<0.01
Comanche (3)	9	0.01
Cree (1)	5	0.01
Creek (6)	6	0.01
Crow (1)	7	0.01
Delaware (3)	4	<0.01
Hopi (7)	19	0.02
Inupiat *(Alaska Native)* (1)	5	0.01
Iroquois (4)	14	0.02
Kiowa (0)	2	<0.01
Lumbee (0)	2	<0.01
Mexican American Ind. (16)	32	0.04
Navajo (245)	314	0.39
Osage (3)	3	<0.01
Ottawa (1)	1	<0.01
Pima (56)	71	0.09
Potawatomi (1)	4	<0.01
Pueblo (12)	14	0.02
Seminole (1)	3	<0.01
Shoshone (0)	3	<0.01
Sioux (31)	64	0.08
South American Ind. (1)	5	0.01
Spanish American Ind. (2)	2	<0.01
Tlingit-Haida *(Alaska Native)* (2)	2	<0.01
Tohono O'Odham (25)	50	0.06
Yakama (0)	2	<0.01
Yaqui (14)	32	0.04
Yuman (10)	11	0.01
Yup'ik *(Alaska Native)* (1)	1	<0.01
Asian (1,734)	2,630	3.23
Not Hispanic (1,666)	2,357	2.90
Hispanic (68)	273	0.34
Bangladeshi (19)	22	0.03
Burmese (1)	2	<0.01
Cambodian (33)	44	0.05
Chinese, ex. Taiwanese (166)	333	0.41
Filipino (741)	1,105	1.36
Hmong (5)	7	0.01
Indian (132)	179	0.22
Indonesian (3)	12	0.01
Japanese (77)	277	0.34
Korean (75)	155	0.19
Laotian (42)	61	0.08
Malaysian (0)	1	<0.01
Pakistani (16)	20	0.02
Sri Lankan (1)	1	<0.01
Taiwanese (3)	6	0.01
Thai (20)	55	0.07
Vietnamese (278)	332	0.41
Hawaii Native/Pacific Islander (240)	546	0.67
Not Hispanic (221)	465	0.57
Hispanic (19)	81	0.10
Fijian (3)	6	0.01
Guamanian/Chamorro (22)	53	0.07
Marshallese (1)	3	<0.01
Native Hawaiian (73)	236	0.29
Samoan (60)	114	0.14
Tongan (41)	90	0.11
White (63,635)	66,629	81.93
Not Hispanic (53,831)	55,548	68.31
Hispanic (9,804)	11,081	13.63

Scottsdale

Place Type: City
County: Maricopa
Population: 217,385†

Ancestry‡	Population	%
Afghan (40)	40	0.02
African, Sub-Saharan (404)	549	0.25
African (126)	233	0.11
Ethiopian (23)	23	0.01
Nigerian (52)	52	0.02
South African (203)	226	0.10
Other Sub-Saharan African (0)	15	0.01
Albanian (309)	345	0.16
Alsatian (18)	32	0.01
American (10,175)	10,175	4.65
Arab (1,240)	2,012	0.92
Arab (37)	175	0.08
Egyptian (67)	179	0.08
Iraqi (59)	66	0.03
Jordanian (17)	55	0.03
Lebanese (600)	879	0.40
Moroccan (101)	144	0.07
Palestinian (111)	175	0.08
Syrian (170)	241	0.11
Other Arab (78)	98	0.04
Armenian (280)	636	0.29
Assyrian/Chaldean/Syriac (312)	312	0.14
Australian (85)	85	0.04
Austrian (340)	1,456	0.67
Basque (19)	68	0.03
Belgian (76)	323	0.15
Brazilian (73)	73	0.03
British (823)	1,682	0.77
Bulgarian (13)	31	0.01
Canadian (1,380)	1,742	0.80
Carpatho Rusyn (14)	43	0.02
Celtic (30)	49	0.02
Croatian (187)	476	0.22
Czech (775)	2,352	1.08

*Notes: † The Census 2010 population figure is used to calculate the percentages in the Hispanic Origin and Race categories. Ancestry percentages are based on the 2006-2010 American Community Survey population (not shown); ‡ Numbers in parentheses indicate the number of people reporting a single ancestry; * Numbers in parentheses indicate the number of persons reporting this race alone, not in combination with any other race; Please refer to the Explanation of Data for more information.*

Czechoslovakian (205)	454	0.21
Danish (628)	1,820	0.83
Dutch (1,326)	4,409	2.02
Eastern European (852)	941	0.43
English (9,576)	28,279	12.93
Estonian (14)	25	0.01
European (2,892)	3,094	1.41
Finnish (207)	622	0.28
French, ex. Basque (1,566)	8,225	3.76
French Canadian (731)	1,489	0.68
German (15,516)	45,292	20.70
Greek (758)	1,675	0.77
Hungarian (727)	2,210	1.01
Icelander (30)	65	0.03
Iranian (1,180)	1,314	0.60
Irish (10,210)	31,781	14.53
Israeli (119)	213	0.10
Italian (9,046)	18,298	8.36
Latvian (156)	181	0.08
Lithuanian (487)	1,161	0.53
Luxemburger (23)	36	0.02
Macedonian (27)	60	0.03
Maltese (151)	165	0.08
New Zealander (13)	58	0.03
Northern European (255)	276	0.13
Norwegian (2,604)	6,064	2.77
Pennsylvania German (13)	46	0.02
Polish (3,947)	10,499	4.80
Portuguese (442)	791	0.36
Romanian (271)	835	0.38
Russian (2,937)	6,802	3.11
Scandinavian (448)	840	0.38
Scotch-Irish (1,980)	4,446	2.03
Scottish (1,958)	6,598	3.02
Serbian (279)	392	0.18
Slavic (118)	140	0.06
Slovak (209)	699	0.32
Slovene (35)	143	0.07
Swedish (1,799)	5,842	2.67
Swiss (430)	1,463	0.67
Turkish (102)	214	0.10
Ukrainian (532)	1,173	0.54
Welsh (310)	1,906	0.87
West Indian, ex. Hispanic (110)	217	0.10
Haitian (17)	32	0.01
Jamaican (51)	90	0.04
Trinidadian/Tobagonian (0)	19	0.01
West Indian (42)	76	0.03
Yugoslavian (259)	384	0.18

Hispanic Origin	Population	%
Hispanic or Latino (of any race)	19,225	8.84
Central American, ex. Mexican	461	0.21
Costa Rican	49	0.02
Guatemalan	138	0.06
Honduran	50	0.02
Nicaraguan	54	0.02
Panamanian	56	0.03
Salvadoran	99	0.05
Other Central American	15	0.01
Cuban	317	0.15
Dominican Republic	85	0.04
Mexican	14,398	6.62
Puerto Rican	827	0.38
South American	1,093	0.50
Argentinean	172	0.08
Bolivian	21	0.01
Chilean	93	0.04
Colombian	392	0.18
Ecuadorian	84	0.04
Paraguayan	14	0.01
Peruvian	191	0.09
Uruguayan	16	0.01
Venezuelan	98	0.05
Other South American	12	0.01
Other Hispanic or Latino	2,044	0.94

Race*	Population	%
African-American/Black (3,652)	4,882	2.25
Not Hispanic (3,484)	4,499	2.07
Hispanic (168)	383	0.18
American Indian/Alaska Native (1,741)	2,793	1.28
Not Hispanic (1,462)	2,236	1.03
Hispanic (279)	557	0.26
Alaska Athabascan *(Ala. Nat.)* (8)	10	<0.01
Aleut *(Alaska Native)* (1)	1	<0.01
Apache (72)	105	0.05
Arapaho (2)	2	<0.01
Blackfeet (3)	28	0.01
Canadian/French Am. Ind. (2)	5	<0.01
Central American Ind. (2)	3	<0.01
Cherokee (49)	228	0.10
Chickasaw (12)	25	0.01
Chippewa (30)	52	0.02
Choctaw (30)	73	0.03
Colville (1)	2	<0.01
Comanche (4)	9	<0.01
Cree (1)	4	<0.01
Creek (19)	32	0.01
Crow (6)	8	<0.01
Delaware (5)	14	0.01
Hopi (58)	80	0.04
Houma (0)	1	<0.01
Inupiat *(Alaska Native)* (2)	3	<0.01
Iroquois (10)	18	0.01
Kiowa (9)	15	0.01
Lumbee (5)	5	<0.01
Menominee (0)	2	<0.01
Mexican American Ind. (23)	52	0.02
Navajo (503)	610	0.28
Osage (6)	17	0.01
Paiute (0)	1	<0.01
Pima (114)	144	0.07
Potawatomi (9)	12	0.01
Pueblo (18)	35	0.02
Puget Sound Salish (0)	2	<0.01
Seminole (1)	10	<0.01
Shoshone (1)	4	<0.01
Sioux (41)	62	0.03
South American Ind. (3)	14	0.01
Spanish American Ind. (7)	10	<0.01
Tlingit-Haida *(Alaska Native)* (5)	8	<0.01
Tohono O'Odham (27)	41	0.02
Tsimshian *(Alaska Native)* (2)	2	<0.01
Ute (0)	2	<0.01
Yakama (2)	2	<0.01
Yaqui (147)	192	0.09
Yuman (8)	13	0.01
Asian (7,239)	9,366	4.31
Not Hispanic (7,128)	9,037	4.16
Hispanic (111)	329	0.15
Bangladeshi (22)	22	0.01
Burmese (45)	50	0.02
Cambodian (29)	35	0.02
Chinese, ex. Taiwanese (1,487)	1,953	0.90
Filipino (862)	1,350	0.62
Indian (2,286)	2,535	1.17
Indonesian (38)	74	0.03
Japanese (510)	889	0.41
Korean (853)	1,088	0.50
Laotian (28)	36	0.02
Malaysian (8)	24	0.01
Nepalese (19)	19	0.01
Pakistani (179)	190	0.09
Sri Lankan (28)	40	0.02
Taiwanese (76)	96	0.04
Thai (112)	166	0.08
Vietnamese (387)	504	0.23
Hawaii Native/Pacific Islander (208)	482	0.22
Not Hispanic (189)	421	0.19
Hispanic (19)	61	0.03
Guamanian/Chamorro (58)	84	0.04
Marshallese (9)	9	<0.01
Native Hawaiian (58)	188	0.09
Samoan (31)	58	0.03
Tongan (14)	20	0.01
White (194,062)	198,503	91.31
Not Hispanic (182,011)	185,299	85.24
Hispanic (12,051)	13,204	6.07

Sedona

Place Type: City
County: Yavapai
Population: 10,031†

Ancestry‡	Population	%
African, Sub-Saharan (12)	25	0.24
South African (12)	25	0.24
American (389)	389	3.77
Arab (57)	111	1.08
Lebanese (57)	111	1.08
Armenian (11)	11	0.11
Australian (0)	7	0.07
Austrian (9)	23	0.22
Belgian (0)	10	0.10
British (45)	74	0.72
Canadian (49)	56	0.54
Celtic (0)	11	0.11
Croatian (11)	44	0.43
Czech (35)	47	0.46
Danish (60)	99	0.96
Dutch (37)	172	1.67
Eastern European (15)	15	0.15
English (569)	1,707	16.56
European (178)	192	1.86
French, ex. Basque (123)	573	5.56
French Canadian (27)	45	0.44
German (673)	2,416	23.44
Greek (46)	82	0.80
Hungarian (129)	254	2.46
Irish (207)	1,214	11.78
Italian (493)	917	8.90
Lithuanian (16)	36	0.35
Luxemburger (10)	10	0.10
Northern European (21)	31	0.30
Norwegian (99)	361	3.50
Polish (132)	393	3.81
Portuguese (0)	73	0.71
Romanian (33)	45	0.44
Russian (76)	347	3.37
Scandinavian (0)	19	0.18
Scotch-Irish (93)	436	4.23
Scottish (119)	349	3.39
Slovak (24)	84	0.81
Swedish (198)	452	4.39
Swiss (18)	93	0.90
Welsh (0)	97	0.94
Yugoslavian (17)	17	0.16

Hispanic Origin	Population	%
Hispanic or Latino (of any race)	1,438	14.34
Central American, ex. Mexican	16	0.16
Costa Rican	1	0.01
Guatemalan	2	0.02
Honduran	2	0.02
Panamanian	1	0.01
Salvadoran	10	0.10
Cuban	9	0.09
Mexican	1,229	12.25
Puerto Rican	26	0.26
South American	51	0.51
Argentinean	15	0.15
Bolivian	8	0.08
Chilean	5	0.05
Colombian	6	0.06
Ecuadorian	4	0.04
Peruvian	12	0.12
Venezuelan	1	0.01
Other Hispanic or Latino	107	1.07

Race*	Population	%
African-American/Black (49)	69	0.69
Not Hispanic (46)	66	0.66
Hispanic (3)	3	0.03
American Indian/Alaska Native (61)	127	1.27
Not Hispanic (49)	101	1.01
Hispanic (12)	26	0.26
Apache (2)	2	0.02
Canadian/French Am. Ind. (0)	1	0.01

*Notes: † The Census 2010 population figure is used to calculate the percentages in the Hispanic Origin and Race categories. Ancestry percentages are based on the 2006-2010 American Community Survey population (not shown); ‡ Numbers in parentheses indicate the number of people reporting a single ancestry; * Numbers in parentheses indicate the number of persons reporting this race alone, not in combination with any other race; Please refer to the Explanation of Data for more information.*

Cherokee (4)	17	0.17
Chickasaw (1)	2	0.02
Chippewa (3)	3	0.03
Choctaw (1)	3	0.03
Creek (0)	2	0.02
Delaware (0)	1	0.01
Hopi (1)	1	0.01
Inupiat *(Alaska Native)* (2)	2	0.02
Iroquois (1)	7	0.07
Menominee (1)	1	0.01
Mexican American Ind. (2)	6	0.06
Navajo (17)	22	0.22
Ottawa (1)	2	0.02
Pueblo (0)	1	0.01
Sioux (2)	5	0.05
Yaqui (1)	1	0.01
Yuman (1)	3	0.03
Asian (186)	235	2.34
Not Hispanic (182)	227	2.26
Hispanic (4)	8	0.08
Cambodian (2)	2	0.02
Chinese, ex. Taiwanese (33)	48	0.48
Filipino (18)	28	0.28
Indian (27)	32	0.32
Indonesian (1)	1	0.01
Japanese (44)	55	0.55
Korean (35)	42	0.42
Nepalese (6)	6	0.06
Pakistani (1)	1	0.01
Taiwanese (3)	3	0.03
Thai (4)	4	0.04
Vietnamese (8)	8	0.08
Hawaii Native/Pacific Islander (14)	25	0.25
Not Hispanic (7)	17	0.17
Hispanic (7)	8	0.08
Guamanian/Chamorro (6)	8	0.08
Native Hawaiian (7)	15	0.15
Samoan (1)	2	0.02
White (9,036)	9,195	91.67
Not Hispanic (8,181)	8,288	82.62
Hispanic (855)	907	9.04

Show Low

Place Type: City
County: Navajo
Population: 10,660†

Ancestry‡	Population	%
Alsatian (11)	11	0.11
American (547)	547	5.30
British (0)	28	0.27
Canadian (26)	41	0.40
Czech (38)	53	0.51
Danish (0)	91	0.88
Dutch (38)	220	2.13
Eastern European (17)	17	0.16
English (552)	1,522	14.75
European (179)	179	1.73
French, ex. Basque (192)	517	5.01
French Canadian (86)	124	1.20
German (909)	2,590	25.10
Greek (0)	35	0.34
Hungarian (15)	26	0.25
Iranian (14)	45	0.44
Irish (514)	1,312	12.71
Italian (130)	385	3.73
Lithuanian (114)	114	1.10
Norwegian (98)	110	1.07
Polish (131)	271	2.63
Portuguese (0)	14	0.14
Russian (15)	15	0.15
Scandinavian (15)	15	0.15
Scotch-Irish (125)	293	2.84
Scottish (67)	445	4.31
Slavic (0)	9	0.09
Slovak (53)	53	0.51
Swedish (44)	88	0.85
Swiss (0)	25	0.24
Welsh (15)	226	2.19
West Indian, ex. Hispanic (0)	20	0.19
Dutch West Indian (0)	20	0.19
Yugoslavian (0)	8	0.08

Hispanic Origin	Population	%
Hispanic or Latino (of any race)	1,360	12.76
Central American, ex. Mexican	18	0.17
Guatemalan	12	0.11
Nicaraguan	3	0.03
Panamanian	1	0.01
Salvadoran	2	0.02
Cuban	3	0.03
Dominican Republic	1	0.01
Mexican	1,117	10.48
Puerto Rican	21	0.20
South American	11	0.10
Chilean	6	0.06
Colombian	3	0.03
Peruvian	1	0.01
Venezuelan	1	0.01
Other Hispanic or Latino	189	1.77

Race*	Population	%
African-American/Black (47)	94	0.88
Not Hispanic (42)	78	0.73
Hispanic (5)	16	0.15
American Indian/Alaska Native (438)	589	5.53
Not Hispanic (406)	517	4.85
Hispanic (32)	72	0.68
Apache (51)	65	0.61
Blackfeet (1)	3	0.03
Cherokee (10)	26	0.24
Chickasaw (0)	3	0.03
Chippewa (2)	3	0.03
Choctaw (10)	19	0.18
Crow (1)	2	0.02
Hopi (13)	17	0.16
Inupiat *(Alaska Native)* (1)	2	0.02
Iroquois (0)	1	0.01
Kiowa (4)	4	0.04
Mexican American Ind. (4)	7	0.07
Navajo (167)	207	1.94
Osage (3)	4	0.04
Pima (2)	2	0.02
Potawatomi (3)	4	0.04
Pueblo (3)	5	0.05
Shoshone (1)	1	0.01
Sioux (8)	17	0.16
Spanish American Ind. (1)	1	0.01
Yaqui (1)	7	0.07
Asian (84)	117	1.10
Not Hispanic (79)	105	0.98
Hispanic (5)	12	0.11
Chinese, ex. Taiwanese (19)	20	0.19
Filipino (24)	33	0.31
Indian (20)	25	0.23
Japanese (5)	14	0.13
Korean (4)	7	0.07
Vietnamese (9)	10	0.09
Hawaii Native/Pacific Islander (16)	31	0.29
Not Hispanic (10)	25	0.23
Hispanic (6)	6	0.06
Fijian (0)	3	0.03
Guamanian/Chamorro (5)	6	0.06
Native Hawaiian (6)	13	0.12
Samoan (1)	4	0.04
Tongan (2)	6	0.06
White (9,341)	9,601	90.07
Not Hispanic (8,586)	8,751	82.09
Hispanic (755)	850	7.97

Sierra Vista Southeast

Place Type: CDP
County: Cochise
Population: 14,797†

Ancestry‡	Population	%
American (1,133)	1,133	7.41
Arab (0)	19	0.12
Lebanese (0)	19	0.12
Australian (0)	10	0.07
Austrian (11)	72	0.47
British (105)	118	0.77
Canadian (22)	22	0.14
Czech (27)	149	0.97
Czechoslovakian (12)	47	0.31
Danish (0)	83	0.54
Dutch (52)	370	2.42
English (709)	1,802	11.78
Estonian (0)	11	0.07
European (233)	233	1.52
Finnish (16)	30	0.20
French, ex. Basque (99)	596	3.90
French Canadian (58)	159	1.04
German (744)	2,917	19.07
Greek (16)	49	0.32
Hungarian (12)	25	0.16
Irish (643)	2,357	15.41
Italian (107)	643	4.20
Lithuanian (0)	11	0.07
Northern European (32)	32	0.21
Norwegian (91)	325	2.12
Pennsylvania German (10)	10	0.07
Polish (151)	453	2.96
Portuguese (18)	57	0.37
Russian (29)	240	1.57
Scandinavian (0)	16	0.10
Scotch-Irish (179)	424	2.77
Scottish (288)	704	4.60
Slovak (0)	13	0.08
Swedish (59)	150	0.98
Swiss (0)	65	0.42
Ukrainian (0)	56	0.37
Welsh (0)	135	0.88

Hispanic Origin	Population	%
Hispanic or Latino (of any race)	2,612	17.65
Central American, ex. Mexican	39	0.26
Costa Rican	2	0.01
Guatemalan	11	0.07
Honduran	5	0.03
Nicaraguan	4	0.03
Panamanian	13	0.09
Salvadoran	4	0.03
Cuban	24	0.16
Dominican Republic	2	0.01
Mexican	2,186	14.77
Puerto Rican	112	0.76
South American	38	0.26
Argentinean	7	0.05
Bolivian	5	0.03
Chilean	2	0.01
Colombian	7	0.05
Ecuadorian	9	0.06
Peruvian	7	0.05
Uruguayan	1	0.01
Other Hispanic or Latino	211	1.43

Race*	Population	%
African-American/Black (259)	399	2.70
Not Hispanic (228)	334	2.26
Hispanic (31)	65	0.44
American Indian/Alaska Native (151)	276	1.87
Not Hispanic (101)	209	1.41
Hispanic (50)	67	0.45
Alaska Athabascan *(Ala. Nat.)* (0)	1	0.01
Apache (11)	16	0.11
Blackfeet (1)	8	0.05
Cherokee (12)	55	0.37
Cheyenne (0)	1	0.01
Chickasaw (1)	2	0.01
Chippewa (0)	5	0.03
Choctaw (2)	9	0.06
Creek (1)	2	0.01
Crow (2)	2	0.01
Hopi (4)	4	0.03
Inupiat *(Alaska Native)* (1)	1	0.01
Iroquois (5)	8	0.05
Lumbee (1)	1	0.01

*Notes: † The Census 2010 population figure is used to calculate the percentages in the Hispanic Origin and Race categories. Ancestry percentages are based on the 2006-2010 American Community Survey population (not shown); ‡ Numbers in parentheses indicate the number of people reporting a single ancestry; * Numbers in parentheses indicate the number of persons reporting this race alone, not in combination with any other race; Please refer to the Explanation of Data for more information.*

Mexican American Ind. (5)	5	0.03
Navajo (9)	11	0.07
Potawatomi (4)	4	0.03
Pueblo (7)	8	0.05
Seminole (1)	1	0.01
Sioux (7)	9	0.06
Spanish American Ind. (2)	2	0.01
Yaqui (3)	5	0.03
Asian (231)	403	2.72
Not Hispanic (222)	358	2.42
Hispanic (9)	45	0.30
Chinese, ex. Taiwanese (16)	37	0.25
Filipino (74)	136	0.92
Indian (3)	5	0.03
Indonesian (1)	3	0.02
Japanese (47)	92	0.62
Korean (57)	88	0.59
Laotian (1)	3	0.02
Taiwanese (1)	2	0.01
Thai (10)	19	0.13
Vietnamese (14)	20	0.14
Hawaii Native/Pacific Islander (33)	69	0.47
Not Hispanic (30)	62	0.42
Hispanic (3)	7	0.05
Guamanian/Chamorro (9)	19	0.13
Native Hawaiian (16)	40	0.27
Samoan (4)	9	0.06
White (12,857)	13,318	90.00
Not Hispanic (11,249)	11,547	78.04
Hispanic (1,608)	1,771	11.97

Sierra Vista

Place Type: City
County: Cochise
Population: 43,888†

Ancestry‡	Population	%
African, Sub-Saharan (68)	92	0.21
African (38)	62	0.14
Nigerian (30)	30	0.07
Alsatian (11)	11	0.03
American (1,855)	1,855	4.32
Arab (33)	94	0.22
Arab (8)	8	0.02
Egyptian (10)	29	0.07
Lebanese (15)	57	0.13
Armenian (28)	113	0.26
Australian (21)	21	0.05
Austrian (54)	109	0.25
Basque (15)	58	0.14
Belgian (11)	11	0.03
Brazilian (21)	21	0.05
British (52)	95	0.22
Bulgarian (0)	3	0.01
Cajun (50)	50	0.12
Canadian (15)	62	0.14
Croatian (0)	11	0.03
Czech (73)	175	0.41
Danish (73)	236	0.55
Dutch (101)	727	1.69
Eastern European (23)	23	0.05
English (1,146)	3,787	8.83
European (690)	766	1.79
Finnish (0)	94	0.22
French, ex. Basque (311)	1,050	2.45
French Canadian (125)	216	0.50
German (2,971)	8,221	19.16
German Russian (0)	57	0.13
Greek (21)	212	0.49
Guyanese (41)	73	0.17
Hungarian (58)	87	0.20
Irish (965)	5,396	12.58
Israeli (10)	10	0.02
Italian (587)	2,007	4.68
Lithuanian (29)	99	0.23
Northern European (54)	54	0.13
Norwegian (420)	718	1.67
Pennsylvania German (2)	2	<0.01
Polish (306)	863	2.01
Portuguese (23)	89	0.21
Romanian (33)	47	0.11
Russian (87)	160	0.37
Scandinavian (140)	226	0.53
Scotch-Irish (321)	748	1.74
Scottish (179)	857	2.00
Serbian (0)	10	0.02
Slovak (67)	192	0.45
Slovene (25)	35	0.08
Swedish (108)	580	1.35
Swiss (0)	91	0.21
Turkish (15)	18	0.04
Ukrainian (46)	106	0.25
Welsh (136)	351	0.82
West Indian, ex. Hispanic (89)	231	0.54
Belizean (10)	10	0.02
Dutch West Indian (0)	21	0.05
Jamaican (29)	94	0.22
Trinidadian/Tobagonian (17)	27	0.06
U.S. Virgin Islander (7)	7	0.02
West Indian (26)	72	0.17

Hispanic Origin	Population	%
Hispanic or Latino (of any race)	8,527	19.43
Central American, ex. Mexican	334	0.76
Costa Rican	27	0.06
Guatemalan	33	0.08
Honduran	36	0.08
Nicaraguan	34	0.08
Panamanian	145	0.33
Salvadoran	56	0.13
Other Central American	3	0.01
Cuban	99	0.23
Dominican Republic	56	0.13
Mexican	6,193	14.11
Puerto Rican	1,004	2.29
South American	162	0.37
Argentinean	19	0.04
Bolivian	6	0.01
Chilean	16	0.04
Colombian	52	0.12
Ecuadorian	22	0.05
Paraguayan	3	0.01
Peruvian	32	0.07
Venezuelan	11	0.03
Other South American	1	<0.01
Other Hispanic or Latino	679	1.55

Race*	Population	%
African-American/Black (3,951)	4,842	11.03
Not Hispanic (3,637)	4,339	9.89
Hispanic (314)	503	1.15
American Indian/Alaska Native (467)	999	2.28
Not Hispanic (307)	693	1.58
Hispanic (160)	306	0.70
Alaska Athabascan *(Ala. Nat.)* (1)	3	0.01
Apache (33)	59	0.13
Blackfeet (8)	23	0.05
Canadian/French Am. Ind. (1)	2	<0.01
Central American Ind. (2)	6	0.01
Cherokee (41)	173	0.39
Cheyenne (3)	3	0.01
Chickasaw (4)	4	0.01
Chippewa (4)	12	0.03
Choctaw (14)	19	0.04
Colville (0)	1	<0.01
Comanche (2)	6	0.01
Cree (0)	5	0.01
Creek (3)	10	0.02
Crow (0)	1	<0.01
Delaware (1)	2	<0.01
Hopi (2)	9	0.02
Inupiat *(Alaska Native)* (2)	3	0.01
Iroquois (15)	25	0.06
Lumbee (0)	5	0.01
Mexican American Ind. (13)	27	0.06
Navajo (69)	98	0.22
Osage (0)	2	<0.01
Ottawa (3)	6	0.01
Paiute (1)	4	0.01
Pima (3)	4	0.01
Potawatomi (1)	1	<0.01
Pueblo (5)	5	0.01
Puget Sound Salish (1)	3	0.01
Seminole (1)	5	0.01
Shoshone (2)	7	0.02
Sioux (4)	11	0.03
South American Ind. (3)	5	0.01
Tlingit-Haida *(Alaska Native)* (3)	3	0.01
Tohono O'Odham (9)	12	0.03
Yaqui (12)	19	0.04
Yuman (1)	1	<0.01
Yup'ik *(Alaska Native)* (0)	1	<0.01
Asian (1,781)	2,771	6.31
Not Hispanic (1,733)	2,578	5.87
Hispanic (48)	193	0.44
Bangladeshi (3)	3	0.01
Burmese (4)	4	0.01
Cambodian (17)	17	0.04
Chinese, ex. Taiwanese (112)	204	0.46
Filipino (456)	750	1.71
Hmong (3)	4	0.01
Indian (72)	107	0.24
Indonesian (6)	8	0.02
Japanese (165)	369	0.84
Korean (573)	876	2.00
Laotian (12)	21	0.05
Malaysian (3)	6	0.01
Nepalese (2)	2	<0.01
Pakistani (24)	34	0.08
Sri Lankan (2)	5	0.01
Taiwanese (9)	19	0.04
Thai (54)	103	0.23
Vietnamese (187)	234	0.53
Hawaii Native/Pacific Islander (269)	497	1.13
Not Hispanic (260)	438	1.00
Hispanic (9)	59	0.13
Fijian (7)	18	0.04
Guamanian/Chamorro (126)	197	0.45
Native Hawaiian (41)	147	0.33
Samoan (42)	73	0.17
Tongan (1)	9	0.02
White (32,695)	34,827	79.35
Not Hispanic (27,550)	29,092	66.29
Hispanic (5,145)	5,735	13.07

Somerton

Place Type: City
County: Yuma
Population: 14,287†

Ancestry‡	Population	%
American (95)	95	0.72
Arab (250)	250	1.89
Arab (250)	250	1.89
English (21)	52	0.39
French, ex. Basque (0)	85	0.64
German (40)	359	2.71
Hungarian (11)	11	0.08
Irish (0)	92	0.70
Italian (0)	13	0.10
Portuguese (0)	28	0.21
Scotch-Irish (0)	18	0.14
Scottish (199)	222	1.68
Swedish (0)	34	0.26

Hispanic Origin	Population	%
Hispanic or Latino (of any race)	13,708	95.95
Central American, ex. Mexican	39	0.27
Costa Rican	7	0.05
Guatemalan	5	0.03
Honduran	8	0.06
Nicaraguan	1	0.01
Panamanian	1	0.01
Salvadoran	17	0.12
Cuban	8	0.06
Dominican Republic	6	0.04
Mexican	13,311	93.17
Puerto Rican	37	0.26

*Notes: † The Census 2010 population figure is used to calculate the percentages in the Hispanic Origin and Race categories. Ancestry percentages are based on the 2006-2010 American Community Survey population (not shown); ‡ Numbers in parentheses indicate the number of people reporting a single ancestry; * Numbers in parentheses indicate the number of persons reporting this race alone, not in combination with any other race; Please refer to the Explanation of Data for more information.*

South American	13	0.09
Chilean	2	0.01
Colombian	3	0.02
Ecuadorian	2	0.01
Peruvian	2	0.01
Venezuelan	4	0.03
Other Hispanic or Latino	294	2.06

Race*	Population	%
African-American/Black (122)	153	1.07
Not Hispanic (43)	47	0.33
Hispanic (79)	106	0.74
American Indian/Alaska Native (112)	163	1.14
Not Hispanic (57)	66	0.46
Hispanic (55)	97	0.68
Apache (1)	4	0.03
Blackfeet (0)	2	0.01
Canadian/French Am. Ind. (1)	1	0.01
Central American Ind. (0)	7	0.05
Cherokee (0)	1	0.01
Cheyenne (1)	1	0.01
Chickasaw (7)	7	0.05
Chippewa (0)	1	0.01
Choctaw (0)	1	0.01
Crow (5)	5	0.03
Mexican American Ind. (19)	36	0.25
Navajo (4)	5	0.03
Pima (4)	5	0.03
Sioux (5)	5	0.03
Spanish American Ind. (0)	1	0.01
Tohono O'Odham (13)	13	0.09
Yaqui (6)	6	0.04
Yuman (23)	23	0.16
Asian (55)	97	0.68
Not Hispanic (30)	39	0.27
Hispanic (25)	58	0.41
Chinese, ex. Taiwanese (5)	9	0.06
Filipino (29)	38	0.27
Indian (2)	4	0.03
Japanese (4)	15	0.10
Korean (0)	1	0.01
Thai (11)	18	0.13
Vietnamese (3)	6	0.04
Hawaii Native/Pacific Islander (8)	25	0.17
Not Hispanic (2)	2	0.01
Hispanic (6)	23	0.16
Guamanian/Chamorro (5)	5	0.03
Native Hawaiian (1)	1	0.01
Samoan (1)	1	0.01
White (9,196)	9,508	66.55
Not Hispanic (411)	431	3.02
Hispanic (8,785)	9,077	63.53

Sun City

Place Type: CDP
County: Maricopa
Population: 37,499†

Ancestry‡	Population	%
African, Sub-Saharan (14)	14	0.04
African (14)	14	0.04
American (2,723)	2,723	7.10
Arab (0)	13	0.03
Lebanese (0)	13	0.03
Armenian (31)	31	0.08
Austrian (29)	96	0.25
Basque (16)	16	0.04
Belgian (40)	69	0.18
British (116)	162	0.42
Bulgarian (12)	12	0.03
Canadian (94)	201	0.52
Celtic (15)	15	0.04
Croatian (76)	139	0.36
Czech (229)	451	1.18
Czechoslovakian (116)	116	0.30
Danish (68)	321	0.84
Dutch (580)	1,509	3.94
English (3,209)	7,962	20.77
European (392)	408	1.06
Finnish (70)	165	0.43
French, ex. Basque (345)	1,726	4.50
French Canadian (176)	327	0.85
German (4,565)	10,618	27.70
Greek (15)	27	0.07
Hungarian (235)	347	0.91
Irish (1,567)	5,436	14.18
Italian (1,291)	1,871	4.88
Lithuanian (99)	147	0.38
Luxemburger (38)	53	0.14
Maltese (0)	13	0.03
Norwegian (772)	1,683	4.39
Pennsylvania German (49)	49	0.13
Polish (1,122)	1,733	4.52
Portuguese (65)	142	0.37
Romanian (0)	45	0.12
Russian (79)	328	0.86
Scandinavian (102)	149	0.39
Scotch-Irish (432)	1,154	3.01
Scottish (366)	1,183	3.09
Serbian (14)	14	0.04
Slavic (0)	15	0.04
Slovak (30)	114	0.30
Slovene (27)	51	0.13
Swedish (532)	1,580	4.12
Swiss (106)	379	0.99
Ukrainian (202)	202	0.53
Welsh (124)	528	1.38
Yugoslavian (15)	51	0.13

Hispanic Origin	Population	%
Hispanic or Latino (of any race)	1,034	2.76
Central American, ex. Mexican	25	0.07
Costa Rican	3	0.01
Guatemalan	4	0.01
Honduran	3	0.01
Nicaraguan	2	0.01
Panamanian	4	0.01
Salvadoran	8	0.02
Other Central American	1	<0.01
Cuban	12	0.03
Dominican Republic	1	<0.01
Mexican	716	1.91
Puerto Rican	82	0.22
South American	43	0.11
Argentinean	9	0.02
Bolivian	1	<0.01
Chilean	1	<0.01
Colombian	20	0.05
Ecuadorian	4	0.01
Peruvian	6	0.02
Venezuelan	1	<0.01
Other South American	1	<0.01
Other Hispanic or Latino	155	0.41

Race*	Population	%
African-American/Black (528)	598	1.59
Not Hispanic (520)	581	1.55
Hispanic (8)	17	0.05
American Indian/Alaska Native (89)	202	0.54
Not Hispanic (74)	181	0.48
Hispanic (15)	21	0.06
Alaska Athabascan *(Ala. Nat.)* (3)	4	0.01
Apache (2)	3	0.01
Blackfeet (0)	1	<0.01
Canadian/French Am. Ind. (0)	1	<0.01
Cherokee (12)	47	0.13
Cheyenne (0)	1	<0.01
Chickasaw (2)	5	0.01
Chippewa (3)	9	0.02
Choctaw (10)	14	0.04
Cree (1)	1	<0.01
Creek (1)	1	<0.01
Inupiat *(Alaska Native)* (1)	1	<0.01
Iroquois (2)	4	0.01
Lumbee (1)	1	<0.01
Mexican American Ind. (5)	5	0.01
Navajo (2)	3	0.01
Osage (0)	1	<0.01
Pima (0)	1	<0.01
Potawatomi (2)	2	0.01
Pueblo (1)	1	<0.01
Puget Sound Salish (2)	2	0.01
Seminole (0)	1	<0.01
Sioux (1)	4	0.01
Tohono O'Odham (1)	1	<0.01
Yakama (0)	1	<0.01
Yaqui (4)	4	0.01
Asian (244)	295	0.79
Not Hispanic (237)	285	0.76
Hispanic (7)	10	0.03
Cambodian (1)	1	<0.01
Chinese, ex. Taiwanese (21)	31	0.08
Filipino (78)	87	0.23
Indian (15)	20	0.05
Indonesian (6)	9	0.02
Japanese (74)	89	0.24
Korean (18)	26	0.07
Laotian (3)	3	0.01
Malaysian (0)	1	<0.01
Pakistani (1)	1	<0.01
Thai (7)	8	0.02
Vietnamese (15)	18	0.05
Hawaii Native/Pacific Islander (10)	22	0.06
Not Hispanic (10)	21	0.06
Hispanic (0)	1	<0.01
Guamanian/Chamorro (4)	5	0.01
Native Hawaiian (3)	10	0.03
Samoan (1)	1	<0.01
Tongan (0)	1	<0.01
White (36,177)	36,385	97.03
Not Hispanic (35,409)	35,592	94.91
Hispanic (768)	793	2.11

Sun City West

Place Type: CDP
County: Maricopa
Population: 24,535†

Ancestry‡	Population	%
American (2,527)	2,527	9.80
Arab (16)	29	0.11
Lebanese (0)	13	0.05
Palestinian (16)	16	0.06
Austrian (74)	183	0.71
Basque (16)	16	0.06
Belgian (14)	41	0.16
Brazilian (14)	14	0.05
British (149)	177	0.69
Canadian (169)	214	0.83
Croatian (47)	77	0.30
Czech (227)	445	1.73
Czechoslovakian (31)	60	0.23
Danish (154)	293	1.14
Dutch (315)	697	2.70
English (1,864)	4,936	19.13
European (134)	134	0.52
Finnish (30)	70	0.27
French, ex. Basque (200)	960	3.72
French Canadian (110)	200	0.78
German (3,543)	7,470	28.96
Greek (94)	137	0.53
Hungarian (139)	273	1.06
Irish (1,223)	3,511	13.61
Italian (908)	1,302	5.05
Latvian (24)	24	0.09
Lithuanian (86)	154	0.60
Luxemburger (35)	35	0.14
Norwegian (827)	1,484	5.75
Pennsylvania German (14)	14	0.05
Polish (875)	1,484	5.75
Portuguese (0)	14	0.05
Romanian (63)	90	0.35
Russian (140)	291	1.13
Scandinavian (73)	86	0.33
Scotch-Irish (310)	701	2.72
Scottish (217)	626	2.43
Serbian (38)	38	0.15
Slovak (129)	185	0.72

*Notes: † The Census 2010 population figure is used to calculate the percentages in the Hispanic Origin and Race categories. Ancestry percentages are based on the 2006-2010 American Community Survey population (not shown); ‡ Numbers in parentheses indicate the number of people reporting a single ancestry; * Numbers in parentheses indicate the number of persons reporting this race alone, not in combination with any other race; Please refer to the Explanation of Data for more information.*

Slovene (27)	42	0.16
Swedish (438)	1,029	3.99
Swiss (69)	323	1.25
Ukrainian (122)	150	0.58
Welsh (53)	253	0.98
Yugoslavian (12)	42	0.16

Hispanic Origin	Population	%
Hispanic or Latino (of any race)	300	1.22
Central American, ex. Mexican	6	0.02
Guatemalan	1	<0.01
Honduran	1	<0.01
Panamanian	2	0.01
Salvadoran	2	0.01
Cuban	15	0.06
Dominican Republic	2	0.01
Mexican	172	0.70
Puerto Rican	26	0.11
South American	26	0.11
Argentinean	9	0.04
Bolivian	2	0.01
Colombian	8	0.03
Ecuadorian	3	0.01
Peruvian	2	0.01
Venezuelan	2	0.01
Other Hispanic or Latino	53	0.22

Race*	Population	%
African-American/Black (198)	226	0.92
Not Hispanic (194)	215	0.88
Hispanic (4)	11	0.04
American Indian/Alaska Native (37)	87	0.35
Not Hispanic (33)	78	0.32
Hispanic (4)	9	0.04
Alaska Athabascan *(Ala. Nat.)* (1)	2	0.01
Aleut *(Alaska Native)* (0)	1	<0.01
Apache (0)	1	<0.01
Blackfeet (1)	3	0.01
Canadian/French Am. Ind. (0)	2	0.01
Cherokee (5)	12	0.05
Chippewa (3)	7	0.03
Choctaw (4)	5	0.02
Cree (0)	1	<0.01
Creek (1)	2	0.01
Iroquois (0)	1	<0.01
Lumbee (1)	1	<0.01
Osage (0)	1	<0.01
Potawatomi (0)	1	<0.01
Shoshone (2)	2	0.01
Sioux (0)	3	0.01
Tlingit-Haida *(Alaska Native)* (2)	3	0.01
Yaqui (1)	1	<0.01
Yuman (1)	1	<0.01
Asian (147)	172	0.70
Not Hispanic (145)	170	0.69
Hispanic (2)	2	0.01
Chinese, ex. Taiwanese (35)	39	0.16
Filipino (23)	32	0.13
Indian (8)	10	0.04
Japanese (59)	61	0.25
Korean (13)	16	0.07
Taiwanese (1)	1	<0.01
Thai (1)	1	<0.01
Vietnamese (3)	4	0.02
Hawaii Native/Pacific Islander (14)	25	0.10
Not Hispanic (14)	23	0.09
Hispanic (0)	2	0.01
Guamanian/Chamorro (3)	3	0.01
Native Hawaiian (7)	13	0.05
Samoan (1)	1	<0.01
White (23,986)	24,093	98.20
Not Hispanic (23,749)	23,840	97.17
Hispanic (237)	253	1.03

Sun Lakes

Place Type: CDP
County: Maricopa
Population: 13,975†

Ancestry‡	Population	%
African, Sub-Saharan (13)	13	0.10
African (13)	13	0.10
American (783)	783	5.80
Arab (20)	20	0.15
Lebanese (20)	20	0.15
Armenian (13)	13	0.10
Austrian (10)	38	0.28
Belgian (0)	13	0.10
British (37)	64	0.47
Canadian (23)	82	0.61
Carpatho Rusyn (0)	14	0.10
Croatian (39)	70	0.52
Czech (140)	217	1.61
Czechoslovakian (26)	26	0.19
Danish (82)	170	1.26
Dutch (141)	472	3.50
Eastern European (14)	14	0.10
English (907)	2,602	19.27
Estonian (0)	12	0.09
European (41)	41	0.30
Finnish (49)	62	0.46
French, ex. Basque (167)	532	3.94
French Canadian (115)	131	0.97
German (1,504)	3,738	27.68
Greek (55)	78	0.58
Hungarian (24)	60	0.44
Irish (589)	2,143	15.87
Italian (464)	675	5.00
Latvian (14)	26	0.19
Lithuanian (59)	121	0.90
Luxemburger (0)	13	0.10
Northern European (13)	13	0.10
Norwegian (192)	456	3.38
Pennsylvania German (0)	14	0.10
Polish (381)	739	5.47
Portuguese (61)	120	0.89
Russian (185)	377	2.79
Scandinavian (11)	11	0.08
Scotch-Irish (284)	690	5.11
Scottish (131)	441	3.27
Serbian (0)	15	0.11
Slavic (13)	26	0.19
Slovak (26)	40	0.30
Swedish (197)	556	4.12
Swiss (26)	116	0.86
Ukrainian (8)	32	0.24
Welsh (26)	167	1.24
West Indian, ex. Hispanic (34)	34	0.25
Trinidadian/Tobagonian (15)	15	0.11
West Indian (19)	19	0.14

Hispanic Origin	Population	%
Hispanic or Latino (of any race)	249	1.78
Central American, ex. Mexican	6	0.04
Guatemalan	3	0.02
Panamanian	1	0.01
Salvadoran	2	0.01
Cuban	4	0.03
Dominican Republic	1	0.01
Mexican	163	1.17
Puerto Rican	10	0.07
South American	19	0.14
Argentinean	8	0.06
Chilean	1	0.01
Colombian	5	0.04
Ecuadorian	1	0.01
Peruvian	3	0.02
Venezuelan	1	0.01
Other Hispanic or Latino	46	0.33

Race*	Population	%
African-American/Black (170)	183	1.31
Not Hispanic (169)	182	1.30
Hispanic (1)	1	0.01
American Indian/Alaska Native (28)	56	0.40
Not Hispanic (26)	50	0.36
Hispanic (2)	6	0.04
Canadian/French Am. Ind. (0)	1	0.01
Cherokee (0)	11	0.08
Cheyenne (1)	1	0.01
Chickasaw (1)	1	0.01
Chippewa (1)	1	0.01
Choctaw (0)	2	0.01
Creek (1)	1	0.01
Crow (0)	1	0.01
Iroquois (1)	2	0.01
Lumbee (1)	1	0.01
Mexican American Ind. (0)	1	0.01
Navajo (4)	4	0.03
Osage (0)	1	0.01
Pima (3)	4	0.03
Puget Sound Salish (1)	1	0.01
Seminole (0)	1	0.01
Sioux (1)	1	0.01
South American Ind. (1)	1	0.01
Ute (1)	1	0.01
Yaqui (1)	1	0.01
Asian (118)	140	1.00
Not Hispanic (118)	138	0.99
Hispanic (0)	2	0.01
Chinese, ex. Taiwanese (30)	36	0.26
Filipino (21)	26	0.19
Indian (15)	18	0.13
Indonesian (0)	1	0.01
Japanese (18)	21	0.15
Korean (19)	21	0.15
Malaysian (1)	1	0.01
Pakistani (1)	1	0.01
Taiwanese (4)	4	0.03
Thai (6)	6	0.04
Hawaii Native/Pacific Islander (3)	9	0.06
Not Hispanic (3)	9	0.06
Native Hawaiian (0)	5	0.04
Tongan (1)	1	0.01
White (13,558)	13,611	97.40
Not Hispanic (13,351)	13,395	95.85
Hispanic (207)	216	1.55

Surprise

Place Type: City
County: Maricopa
Population: 117,517†

Ancestry‡	Population	%
African, Sub-Saharan (182)	298	0.29
African (81)	89	0.09
Nigerian (65)	119	0.11
Sierra Leonean (18)	72	0.07
South African (18)	18	0.02
Albanian (263)	263	0.25
American (21,370)	21,370	20.59
Arab (224)	413	0.40
Arab (27)	48	0.05
Egyptian (0)	41	0.04
Iraqi (130)	150	0.14
Jordanian (10)	10	0.01
Lebanese (27)	86	0.08
Palestinian (0)	23	0.02
Syrian (18)	31	0.03
Other Arab (12)	24	0.02
Armenian (214)	265	0.26
Assyrian/Chaldean/Syriac (93)	113	0.11
Austrian (176)	351	0.34
Basque (11)	11	0.01
Belgian (45)	112	0.11
Brazilian (54)	81	0.08
British (224)	396	0.38
Bulgarian (46)	78	0.08
Canadian (392)	589	0.57
Croatian (81)	221	0.21
Czech (187)	512	0.49
Czechoslovakian (14)	35	0.03
Danish (385)	969	0.93
Dutch (410)	1,576	1.52
Eastern European (81)	81	0.08
English (2,487)	8,488	8.18
Estonian (14)	14	0.01
European (1,204)	1,449	1.40

*Notes: † The Census 2010 population figure is used to calculate the percentages in the Hispanic Origin and Race categories. Ancestry percentages are based on the 2006-2010 American Community Survey population (not shown); ‡ Numbers in parentheses indicate the number of people reporting a single ancestry; * Numbers in parentheses indicate the number of persons reporting this race alone, not in combination with any other race; Please refer to the Explanation of Data for more information.*

SECTION TWO

Finnish (138)	382	0.37
French, ex. Basque (462)	2,409	2.32
French Canadian (346)	701	0.68
German (5,756)	17,128	16.51
Greek (161)	328	0.32
Guyanese (33)	33	0.03
Hungarian (180)	592	0.57
Iranian (36)	110	0.11
Irish (2,876)	10,364	9.99
Israeli (0)	12	0.01
Italian (2,409)	5,337	5.14
Lithuanian (74)	219	0.21
Luxemburger (42)	42	0.04
Macedonian (15)	15	0.01
Northern European (82)	82	0.08
Norwegian (912)	2,258	2.18
Pennsylvania German (10)	22	0.02
Polish (1,527)	3,460	3.33
Portuguese (190)	344	0.33
Romanian (662)	855	0.82
Russian (511)	1,213	1.17
Scandinavian (124)	254	0.24
Scotch-Irish (653)	1,632	1.57
Scottish (624)	2,263	2.18
Serbian (130)	159	0.15
Slavic (46)	72	0.07
Slovak (135)	270	0.26
Slovene (27)	40	0.04
Swedish (519)	2,011	1.94
Swiss (48)	251	0.24
Ukrainian (71)	165	0.16
Welsh (153)	543	0.52
West Indian, ex. Hispanic (95)	134	0.13
Belizean (42)	42	0.04
Haitian (13)	40	0.04
Jamaican (40)	52	0.05
Yugoslavian (222)	294	0.28

Hispanic Origin	Population	%
Hispanic or Latino (of any race)	21,724	18.49
Central American, ex. Mexican	662	0.56
Costa Rican	30	0.03
Guatemalan	183	0.16
Honduran	63	0.05
Nicaraguan	37	0.03
Panamanian	52	0.04
Salvadoran	293	0.25
Other Central American	4	<0.01
Cuban	173	0.15
Dominican Republic	88	0.07
Mexican	17,481	14.88
Puerto Rican	978	0.83
South American	405	0.34
Argentinean	61	0.05
Bolivian	14	0.01
Chilean	28	0.02
Colombian	140	0.12
Ecuadorian	74	0.06
Paraguayan	4	<0.01
Peruvian	58	0.05
Uruguayan	3	<0.01
Venezuelan	16	0.01
Other South American	7	0.01
Other Hispanic or Latino	1,937	1.65

Race*	Population	%
African-American/Black (6,018)	7,498	6.38
Not Hispanic (5,648)	6,794	5.78
Hispanic (370)	704	0.60
American Indian/Alaska Native (801)	1,650	1.40
Not Hispanic (543)	1,142	0.97
Hispanic (258)	508	0.43
Alaska Athabascan *(Ala. Nat.)* (1)	2	<0.01
Aleut *(Alaska Native)* (5)	8	0.01
Apache (30)	63	0.05
Arapaho (1)	2	<0.01
Blackfeet (3)	46	0.04
Canadian/French Am. Ind. (0)	3	<0.01
Central American Ind. (2)	3	<0.01
Cherokee (55)	210	0.18
Cheyenne (1)	2	<0.01
Chickasaw (7)	17	0.01
Chippewa (6)	19	0.02
Choctaw (27)	68	0.06
Comanche (8)	15	0.01
Creek (7)	19	0.02
Crow (1)	2	<0.01
Delaware (0)	1	<0.01
Hopi (18)	34	0.03
Inupiat *(Alaska Native)* (1)	1	<0.01
Iroquois (14)	30	0.03
Kiowa (2)	2	<0.01
Lumbee (1)	5	<0.01
Menominee (3)	3	<0.01
Mexican American Ind. (42)	78	0.07
Navajo (145)	191	0.16
Osage (4)	8	0.01
Pima (26)	45	0.04
Potawatomi (3)	8	0.01
Pueblo (15)	20	0.02
Puget Sound Salish (2)	7	0.01
Seminole (0)	3	<0.01
Shoshone (2)	5	<0.01
Sioux (14)	33	0.03
South American Ind. (1)	2	<0.01
Spanish American Ind. (4)	6	0.01
Tlingit-Haida *(Alaska Native)* (4)	5	<0.01
Tohono O'Odham (25)	42	0.04
Ute (3)	4	<0.01
Yakama (1)	1	<0.01
Yaqui (8)	13	0.01
Yuman (5)	14	0.01
Yup'ik *(Alaska Native)* (4)	5	<0.01
Asian (3,020)	4,356	3.71
Not Hispanic (2,884)	3,956	3.37
Hispanic (136)	400	0.34
Bangladeshi (15)	15	0.01
Burmese (6)	6	0.01
Cambodian (63)	89	0.08
Chinese, ex. Taiwanese (288)	458	0.39
Filipino (1,308)	1,889	1.61
Hmong (26)	30	0.03
Indian (243)	329	0.28
Indonesian (15)	42	0.04
Japanese (150)	360	0.31
Korean (240)	401	0.34
Laotian (30)	42	0.04
Malaysian (1)	3	<0.01
Nepalese (5)	5	<0.01
Pakistani (29)	33	0.03
Sri Lankan (2)	4	<0.01
Taiwanese (15)	18	0.02
Thai (53)	92	0.08
Vietnamese (380)	461	0.39
Hawaii Native/Pacific Islander (233)	523	0.45
Not Hispanic (211)	448	0.38
Hispanic (22)	75	0.06
Fijian (2)	4	<0.01
Guamanian/Chamorro (66)	116	0.10
Native Hawaiian (61)	206	0.18
Samoan (48)	77	0.07
Tongan (9)	15	0.01
White (94,747)	98,643	83.94
Not Hispanic (83,677)	86,055	73.23
Hispanic (11,070)	12,588	10.71

Tanque Verde

Place Type: CDP
County: Pima
Population: 16,901†

Ancestry‡	Population	%
African, Sub-Saharan (0)	11	0.07
Ethiopian (0)	11	0.07
Alsatian (0)	11	0.07
American (747)	747	4.47
Arab (19)	27	0.16
Arab (8)	8	0.05
Lebanese (11)	11	0.07
Other Arab (0)	8	0.05
Armenian (8)	80	0.48
Australian (0)	5	0.03
Austrian (55)	144	0.86
Belgian (0)	10	0.06
Brazilian (0)	5	0.03
British (49)	102	0.61
Bulgarian (0)	12	0.07
Cajun (11)	11	0.07
Canadian (6)	21	0.13
Croatian (0)	26	0.16
Czech (54)	219	1.31
Czechoslovakian (11)	16	0.10
Danish (22)	171	1.02
Dutch (70)	261	1.56
Eastern European (51)	75	0.45
English (737)	3,025	18.10
Estonian (35)	35	0.21
European (290)	321	1.92
Finnish (21)	34	0.20
French, ex. Basque (162)	780	4.67
French Canadian (103)	244	1.46
German (1,253)	4,252	25.44
Greek (78)	95	0.57
Hungarian (28)	129	0.77
Icelander (0)	15	0.09
Irish (420)	2,484	14.86
Israeli (8)	8	0.05
Italian (461)	1,085	6.49
Latvian (12)	12	0.07
Lithuanian (41)	217	1.30
Luxemburger (0)	10	0.06
Northern European (76)	76	0.45
Norwegian (161)	468	2.80
Pennsylvania German (0)	12	0.07
Polish (156)	405	2.42
Portuguese (28)	68	0.41
Romanian (26)	69	0.41
Russian (29)	166	0.99
Scandinavian (10)	29	0.17
Scotch-Irish (127)	577	3.45
Scottish (205)	596	3.57
Slovak (37)	88	0.53
Slovene (35)	35	0.21
Swedish (141)	547	3.27
Swiss (29)	121	0.72
Turkish (22)	22	0.13
Ukrainian (40)	80	0.48
Welsh (49)	137	0.82
Yugoslavian (0)	12	0.07

Hispanic Origin	Population	%
Hispanic or Latino (of any race)	1,619	9.58
Central American, ex. Mexican	26	0.15
Costa Rican	3	0.02
Guatemalan	10	0.06
Honduran	1	0.01
Nicaraguan	6	0.04
Panamanian	4	0.02
Salvadoran	2	0.01
Cuban	23	0.14
Dominican Republic	3	0.02
Mexican	1,283	7.59
Puerto Rican	57	0.34
South American	48	0.28
Argentinean	8	0.05
Bolivian	2	0.01
Chilean	5	0.03
Colombian	18	0.11
Ecuadorian	8	0.05
Peruvian	2	0.01
Uruguayan	4	0.02
Venezuelan	1	0.01
Other Hispanic or Latino	179	1.06

Race*	Population	%
African-American/Black (152)	252	1.49
Not Hispanic (142)	236	1.40
Hispanic (10)	16	0.09
American Indian/Alaska Native (169)	282	1.67

*Notes: † The Census 2010 population figure is used to calculate the percentages in the Hispanic Origin and Race categories. Ancestry percentages are based on the 2006-2010 American Community Survey population (not shown); ‡ Numbers in parentheses indicate the number of people reporting a single ancestry; * Numbers in parentheses indicate the number of persons reporting this race alone, not in combination with any other race; Please refer to the Explanation of Data for more information.*

Not Hispanic (132)	224	1.33
Hispanic (37)	58	0.34
Alaska Athabascan *(Ala. Nat.)* (0)	4	0.02
Aleut *(Alaska Native)* (3)	3	0.02
Apache (11)	15	0.09
Blackfeet (0)	1	0.01
Cherokee (7)	27	0.16
Chickasaw (0)	2	0.01
Chippewa (3)	6	0.04
Choctaw (7)	11	0.07
Colville (1)	1	0.01
Comanche (0)	1	0.01
Cree (1)	1	0.01
Creek (0)	2	0.01
Hopi (5)	5	0.03
Inupiat *(Alaska Native)* (1)	2	0.01
Iroquois (2)	2	0.01
Mexican American Ind. (6)	10	0.06
Navajo (50)	52	0.31
Osage (3)	7	0.04
Ottawa (2)	3	0.02
Pima (9)	9	0.05
Potawatomi (1)	1	0.01
Puget Sound Salish (1)	1	0.01
Sioux (6)	9	0.05
South American Ind. (0)	6	0.04
Tlingit-Haida *(Alaska Native)* (0)	1	0.01
Tohono O'Odham (4)	5	0.03
Yaqui (7)	7	0.04
Yuman (2)	2	0.01
Asian (276)	403	2.38
Not Hispanic (267)	376	2.22
Hispanic (9)	27	0.16
Cambodian (1)	1	0.01
Chinese, ex. Taiwanese (58)	77	0.46
Filipino (53)	83	0.49
Indian (39)	51	0.30
Indonesian (1)	2	0.01
Japanese (60)	108	0.64
Korean (24)	39	0.23
Pakistani (6)	6	0.04
Sri Lankan (3)	4	0.02
Taiwanese (0)	1	0.01
Thai (6)	8	0.05
Vietnamese (12)	15	0.09
Hawaii Native/Pacific Islander (7)	35	0.21
Not Hispanic (6)	32	0.19
Hispanic (1)	3	0.02
Guamanian/Chamorro (3)	4	0.02
Native Hawaiian (3)	26	0.15
White (15,586)	15,928	94.24
Not Hispanic (14,426)	14,675	86.83
Hispanic (1,160)	1,253	7.41

Tempe

Place Type: City
County: Maricopa
Population: 161,719[†]

Ancestry[‡]	Population	%
African, Sub-Saharan (864)	938	0.57
African (123)	158	0.10
Cape Verdean (37)	37	0.02
Ethiopian (11)	36	0.02
Kenyan (147)	147	0.09
Nigerian (22)	22	0.01
Somalian (404)	404	0.25
South African (18)	32	0.02
Sudanese (28)	28	0.02
Other Sub-Saharan African (74)	74	0.05
Albanian (573)	592	0.36
American (3,976)	3,976	2.42
Arab (1,322)	1,962	1.20
Arab (432)	472	0.29
Egyptian (75)	243	0.15
Jordanian (15)	43	0.03
Lebanese (334)	650	0.40
Moroccan (13)	30	0.02
Palestinian (14)	14	0.01
Syrian (84)	141	0.09
Other Arab (355)	369	0.22
Armenian (197)	386	0.24
Assyrian/Chaldean/Syriac (26)	26	0.02
Australian (51)	51	0.03
Austrian (209)	492	0.30
Basque (13)	24	0.01
Belgian (106)	210	0.13
Brazilian (21)	33	0.02
British (423)	873	0.53
Bulgarian (48)	83	0.05
Cajun (0)	22	0.01
Canadian (156)	311	0.19
Celtic (34)	73	0.04
Croatian (77)	322	0.20
Czech (122)	787	0.48
Czechoslovakian (55)	140	0.09
Danish (373)	1,408	0.86
Dutch (587)	2,935	1.79
Eastern European (233)	310	0.19
English (5,082)	17,066	10.40
Estonian (0)	16	0.01
European (1,851)	2,072	1.26
Finnish (86)	277	0.17
French, ex. Basque (1,113)	5,367	3.27
French Canadian (533)	1,195	0.73
German (8,557)	28,371	17.28
Greek (425)	838	0.51
Hungarian (241)	956	0.58
Icelander (0)	52	0.03
Iranian (412)	536	0.33
Irish (4,565)	19,332	11.78
Israeli (80)	128	0.08
Italian (2,708)	8,665	5.28
Latvian (16)	16	0.01
Lithuanian (78)	288	0.18
Luxemburger (0)	25	0.02
Macedonian (30)	30	0.02
Northern European (187)	201	0.12
Norwegian (1,191)	3,175	1.93
Pennsylvania German (45)	45	0.03
Polish (1,635)	5,573	3.40
Portuguese (114)	572	0.35
Romanian (192)	409	0.25
Russian (832)	2,203	1.34
Scandinavian (339)	564	0.34
Scotch-Irish (1,111)	3,553	2.16
Scottish (745)	2,954	1.80
Serbian (102)	190	0.12
Slavic (20)	28	0.02
Slovak (23)	95	0.06
Slovene (20)	70	0.04
Swedish (810)	3,121	1.90
Swiss (80)	670	0.41
Turkish (248)	326	0.20
Ukrainian (178)	559	0.34
Welsh (307)	1,791	1.09
West Indian, ex. Hispanic (112)	262	0.16
Dutch West Indian (0)	7	<0.01
Haitian (0)	67	0.04
Jamaican (102)	161	0.10
U.S. Virgin Islander (10)	10	0.01
West Indian (0)	17	0.01
Yugoslavian (332)	440	0.27

Hispanic Origin	Population	%
Hispanic or Latino (of any race)	34,092	21.08
Central American, ex. Mexican	679	0.42
Costa Rican	66	0.04
Guatemalan	181	0.11
Honduran	69	0.04
Nicaraguan	79	0.05
Panamanian	82	0.05
Salvadoran	193	0.12
Other Central American	9	0.01
Cuban	324	0.20
Dominican Republic	97	0.06
Mexican	28,204	17.44
Puerto Rican	1,040	0.64
South American	914	0.57
Argentinean	134	0.08
Bolivian	43	0.03
Chilean	66	0.04
Colombian	285	0.18
Ecuadorian	95	0.06
Paraguayan	12	0.01
Peruvian	188	0.12
Uruguayan	13	0.01
Venezuelan	71	0.04
Other South American	7	<0.01
Other Hispanic or Latino	2,834	1.75

Race*	Population	%
African-American/Black (9,551)	11,719	7.25
Not Hispanic (9,021)	10,740	6.64
Hispanic (530)	979	0.61
American Indian/Alaska Native (4,671)	6,238	3.86
Not Hispanic (3,870)	4,865	3.01
Hispanic (801)	1,373	0.85
Alaska Athabascan *(Ala. Nat.)* (4)	4	<0.01
Aleut *(Alaska Native)* (2)	2	<0.01
Apache (205)	302	0.19
Arapaho (2)	7	<0.01
Blackfeet (4)	42	0.03
Canadian/French Am. Ind. (2)	8	<0.01
Central American Ind. (3)	10	0.01
Cherokee (65)	288	0.18
Cheyenne (7)	13	0.01
Chickasaw (7)	20	0.01
Chippewa (29)	60	0.04
Choctaw (34)	90	0.06
Colville (2)	2	<0.01
Comanche (4)	8	<0.01
Cree (8)	15	0.01
Creek (7)	19	0.01
Crow (2)	7	<0.01
Delaware (1)	10	0.01
Hopi (120)	161	0.10
Houma (1)	1	<0.01
Inupiat *(Alaska Native)* (7)	9	0.01
Iroquois (12)	28	0.02
Kiowa (14)	15	0.01
Lumbee (4)	4	<0.01
Mexican American Ind. (62)	92	0.06
Navajo (2,018)	2,234	1.38
Osage (3)	8	<0.01
Ottawa (2)	3	<0.01
Paiute (9)	19	0.01
Pima (161)	234	0.14
Potawatomi (21)	28	0.02
Pueblo (57)	66	0.04
Puget Sound Salish (2)	4	<0.01
Seminole (8)	15	0.01
Shoshone (7)	8	<0.01
Sioux (84)	130	0.08
South American Ind. (11)	18	0.01
Spanish American Ind. (2)	7	<0.01
Tlingit-Haida *(Alaska Native)* (0)	2	<0.01
Tohono O'Odham (79)	101	0.06
Ute (10)	11	0.01
Yakama (1)	3	<0.01
Yaqui (534)	670	0.41
Yuman (36)	44	0.03
Yup'ik *(Alaska Native)* (2)	7	<0.01
Asian (9,217)	11,209	6.93
Not Hispanic (9,035)	10,723	6.63
Hispanic (182)	486	0.30
Bangladeshi (81)	87	0.05
Burmese (22)	25	0.02
Cambodian (164)	190	0.12
Chinese, ex. Taiwanese (2,389)	2,834	1.75
Filipino (813)	1,340	0.83
Hmong (1)	1	<0.01
Indian (2,705)	2,883	1.78
Indonesian (105)	127	0.08
Japanese (415)	827	0.51
Korean (822)	1,042	0.64
Laotian (62)	75	0.05
Malaysian (13)	20	0.01
Nepalese (53)	54	0.03

*Notes: † The Census 2010 population figure is used to calculate the percentages in the Hispanic Origin and Race categories. Ancestry percentages are based on the 2006-2010 American Community Survey population (not shown); ‡ Numbers in parentheses indicate the number of people reporting a single ancestry; * Numbers in parentheses indicate the number of persons reporting this race alone, not in combination with any other race; Please refer to the Explanation of Data for more information.*

	Population	%
Pakistani (205)	228	0.14
Sri Lankan (38)	42	0.03
Taiwanese (235)	259	0.16
Thai (88)	144	0.09
Vietnamese (710)	815	0.50
Hawaii Native/Pacific Islander (645)	1,008	0.62
Not Hispanic (618)	907	0.56
Hispanic (27)	101	0.06
Fijian (2)	3	<0.01
Guamanian/Chamorro (94)	161	0.10
Marshallese (129)	131	0.08
Native Hawaiian (137)	328	0.20
Samoan (88)	127	0.08
Tongan (52)	70	0.04
White (117,457)	122,818	75.95
Not Hispanic (100,711)	104,218	64.44
Hispanic (16,746)	18,600	11.50

Tuba City

Place Type: CDP
County: Coconino
Population: 8,611†

Ancestry‡	Population	%
American (133)	133	1.50
Dutch (0)	24	0.27
English (20)	80	0.90
European (17)	17	0.19
French Canadian (0)	35	0.39
German (38)	177	1.99
Hungarian (0)	83	0.93
Irish (12)	92	1.04
Italian (39)	73	0.82
Lithuanian (0)	49	0.55
Norwegian (0)	51	0.57
Polish (17)	32	0.36
Scotch-Irish (20)	55	0.62
Slovak (0)	25	0.28
Swedish (0)	87	0.98

Hispanic Origin	Population	%
Hispanic or Latino (of any race)	287	3.33
Central American, ex. Mexican	1	0.01
Other Central American	1	0.01
Cuban	4	0.05
Mexican	216	2.51
Puerto Rican	26	0.30
South American	3	0.03
Venezuelan	3	0.03
Other Hispanic or Latino	37	0.43

Race*	Population	%
African-American/Black (27)	46	0.53
Not Hispanic (27)	44	0.51
Hispanic (0)	2	0.02
American Indian/Alaska Native (7,955)	8,089	93.94
Not Hispanic (7,777)	7,889	91.62
Hispanic (178)	200	2.32
Apache (18)	43	0.50
Arapaho (4)	5	0.06
Blackfeet (4)	4	0.05
Cherokee (11)	11	0.13
Cheyenne (4)	4	0.05
Chippewa (2)	5	0.06
Choctaw (0)	1	0.01
Comanche (2)	3	0.03
Cree (2)	2	0.02
Creek (0)	4	0.05
Crow (4)	5	0.06
Hopi (293)	403	4.68
Inupiat *(Alaska Native)* (4)	9	0.10
Navajo (6,809)	7,050	81.87
Paiute (20)	34	0.39
Pima (14)	22	0.26
Pueblo (6)	17	0.20
Puget Sound Salish (0)	2	0.02
Seminole (1)	1	0.01
Shoshone (1)	6	0.07
Sioux (7)	15	0.17
Tlingit-Haida *(Alaska Native)* (0)	2	0.02
Tohono O'Odham (0)	2	0.02
Ute (1)	1	0.01
Yaqui (15)	20	0.23
Yuman (4)	6	0.07
Asian (69)	80	0.93
Not Hispanic (69)	79	0.92
Hispanic (0)	1	0.01
Chinese, ex. Taiwanese (8)	11	0.13
Filipino (43)	46	0.53
Indian (9)	13	0.15
Indonesian (1)	3	0.03
Japanese (1)	3	0.03
Korean (2)	4	0.05
Hawaii Native/Pacific Islander (3)	3	0.03
Hispanic (3)	3	0.03
Guamanian/Chamorro (3)	3	0.03
White (375)	507	5.89
Not Hispanic (326)	439	5.10
Hispanic (49)	68	0.79

Tucson Estates

Place Type: CDP
County: Pima
Population: 12,192†

Ancestry‡	Population	%
American (413)	413	3.41
Arab (0)	36	0.30
Lebanese (0)	23	0.19
Syrian (0)	13	0.11
Armenian (0)	10	0.08
Austrian (0)	7	0.06
British (10)	10	0.08
Canadian (11)	75	0.62
Celtic (0)	19	0.16
Czech (0)	42	0.35
Czechoslovakian (0)	15	0.12
Danish (71)	95	0.78
Dutch (98)	254	2.10
Eastern European (18)	18	0.15
English (442)	1,606	13.27
European (45)	45	0.37
Finnish (45)	71	0.59
French, ex. Basque (26)	426	3.52
French Canadian (103)	284	2.35
German (727)	2,158	17.83
Greek (7)	22	0.18
Irish (367)	1,300	10.74
Italian (170)	393	3.25
Lithuanian (7)	37	0.31
Northern European (24)	24	0.20
Norwegian (58)	359	2.97
Polish (63)	206	1.70
Russian (52)	67	0.55
Scandinavian (0)	49	0.40
Scotch-Irish (160)	276	2.28
Scottish (64)	410	3.39
Serbian (13)	13	0.11
Slovak (31)	55	0.45
Swedish (76)	262	2.16
Swiss (27)	92	0.76
Welsh (9)	54	0.45
West Indian, ex. Hispanic (29)	29	0.24
Jamaican (29)	29	0.24

Hispanic Origin	Population	%
Hispanic or Latino (of any race)	3,948	32.38
Central American, ex. Mexican	18	0.15
Guatemalan	3	0.02
Honduran	4	0.03
Panamanian	7	0.06
Salvadoran	4	0.03
Cuban	10	0.08
Dominican Republic	3	0.02
Mexican	3,569	29.27
Puerto Rican	72	0.59
South American	28	0.23
Argentinean	5	0.04
Chilean	1	0.01
Colombian	2	0.02
Ecuadorian	4	0.03
Peruvian	12	0.10
Uruguayan	1	0.01
Venezuelan	3	0.02
Other Hispanic or Latino	248	2.03

Race*	Population	%
African-American/Black (193)	268	2.20
Not Hispanic (157)	206	1.69
Hispanic (36)	62	0.51
American Indian/Alaska Native (250)	354	2.90
Not Hispanic (146)	208	1.71
Hispanic (104)	146	1.20
Apache (6)	9	0.07
Blackfeet (1)	5	0.04
Canadian/French Am. Ind. (1)	1	0.01
Cherokee (12)	27	0.22
Chippewa (4)	7	0.06
Choctaw (4)	6	0.05
Comanche (0)	2	0.02
Creek (2)	2	0.02
Delaware (1)	1	0.01
Iroquois (1)	3	0.02
Kiowa (1)	1	0.01
Mexican American Ind. (7)	9	0.07
Navajo (18)	27	0.22
Osage (1)	2	0.02
Ottawa (1)	3	0.02
Pima (2)	2	0.02
Pueblo (9)	10	0.08
Sioux (7)	11	0.09
Tlingit-Haida *(Alaska Native)* (1)	1	0.01
Tohono O'Odham (38)	47	0.39
Yakama (0)	1	0.01
Yaqui (58)	68	0.56
Yuman (2)	2	0.02
Asian (130)	214	1.76
Not Hispanic (120)	184	1.51
Hispanic (10)	30	0.25
Cambodian (8)	8	0.07
Chinese, ex. Taiwanese (24)	54	0.44
Filipino (36)	60	0.49
Indian (3)	7	0.06
Indonesian (1)	1	0.01
Japanese (13)	31	0.25
Korean (12)	31	0.25
Malaysian (1)	1	0.01
Thai (6)	8	0.07
Vietnamese (16)	23	0.19
Hawaii Native/Pacific Islander (14)	34	0.28
Not Hispanic (10)	21	0.17
Hispanic (4)	13	0.11
Guamanian/Chamorro (3)	9	0.07
Native Hawaiian (3)	9	0.07
Samoan (1)	4	0.03
Tongan (4)	4	0.03
White (9,752)	10,052	82.45
Not Hispanic (7,643)	7,782	63.83
Hispanic (2,109)	2,270	18.62

Tucson

Place Type: City
County: Pima
Population: 520,116†

Ancestry‡	Population	%
Afghan (305)	320	0.06
African, Sub-Saharan (3,475)	4,324	0.83
African (1,449)	1,955	0.38
Cape Verdean (0)	60	0.01
Ethiopian (36)	204	0.04
Ghanaian (74)	74	0.01
Kenyan (91)	138	0.03
Nigerian (271)	283	0.05
Senegalese (15)	15	<0.01
Somalian (607)	607	0.12
South African (124)	139	0.03

*Notes: † The Census 2010 population figure is used to calculate the percentages in the Hispanic Origin and Race categories. Ancestry percentages are based on the 2006-2010 American Community Survey population (not shown); ‡ Numbers in parentheses indicate the number of people reporting a single ancestry; * Numbers in parentheses indicate the number of persons reporting this race alone, not in combination with any other race; Please refer to the Explanation of Data for more information.*

Sudanese (274)	315	0.06
Other Sub-Saharan African (534)	534	0.10
Albanian (49)	61	0.01
Alsatian (0)	10	<0.01
American (11,664)	11,664	2.25
Arab (2,291)	3,263	0.63
Arab (250)	432	0.08
Egyptian (176)	218	0.04
Iraqi (607)	687	0.13
Jordanian (36)	36	0.01
Lebanese (669)	951	0.18
Moroccan (0)	33	0.01
Palestinian (232)	240	0.05
Syrian (224)	557	0.11
Other Arab (97)	109	0.02
Armenian (193)	321	0.06
Assyrian/Chaldean/Syriac (29)	29	0.01
Australian (122)	179	0.03
Austrian (205)	1,160	0.22
Basque (85)	261	0.05
Belgian (109)	442	0.09
Brazilian (126)	275	0.05
British (922)	2,300	0.44
Bulgarian (83)	174	0.03
Cajun (15)	156	0.03
Canadian (443)	1,007	0.19
Celtic (30)	140	0.03
Croatian (321)	785	0.15
Czech (586)	2,371	0.46
Czechoslovakian (321)	545	0.11
Danish (575)	2,604	0.50
Dutch (1,699)	7,333	1.41
Eastern European (639)	714	0.14
English (12,513)	42,792	8.25
European (5,559)	6,941	1.34
Finnish (304)	881	0.17
French, ex. Basque (2,578)	14,770	2.85
French Canadian (837)	2,501	0.48
German (22,490)	73,191	14.12
German Russian (79)	222	0.04
Greek (898)	2,136	0.41
Hungarian (735)	2,169	0.42
Icelander (67)	67	0.01
Iranian (466)	634	0.12
Irish (14,069)	52,307	10.09
Israeli (110)	175	0.03
Italian (8,324)	22,347	4.31
Latvian (89)	157	0.03
Lithuanian (274)	931	0.18
Luxemburger (0)	182	0.04
Macedonian (10)	10	<0.01
Maltese (60)	105	0.02
New Zealander (14)	60	0.01
Northern European (432)	471	0.09
Norwegian (2,398)	7,557	1.46
Pennsylvania German (165)	371	0.07
Polish (3,390)	12,427	2.40
Portuguese (380)	966	0.19
Romanian (154)	471	0.09
Russian (1,847)	5,201	1.00
Scandinavian (734)	1,378	0.27
Scotch-Irish (3,034)	8,731	1.68
Scottish (3,142)	10,796	2.08
Serbian (52)	223	0.04
Slavic (53)	241	0.05
Slovak (275)	803	0.15
Slovene (24)	105	0.02
Swedish (1,693)	6,478	1.25
Swiss (244)	1,426	0.28
Turkish (147)	232	0.04
Ukrainian (469)	1,223	0.24
Welsh (457)	3,631	0.70
West Indian, ex. Hispanic (576)	892	0.17
Barbadian (27)	27	0.01
Belizean (61)	61	0.01
British West Indian (37)	37	0.01
Dutch West Indian (14)	102	0.02
Haitian (36)	86	0.02
Jamaican (315)	475	0.09
U.S. Virgin Islander (20)	20	<0.01
West Indian (66)	84	0.02
Yugoslavian (320)	514	0.10

Hispanic Origin	Population	%
Hispanic or Latino (of any race)	216,308	41.59
Central American, ex. Mexican	2,527	0.49
Costa Rican	125	0.02
Guatemalan	672	0.13
Honduran	336	0.06
Nicaraguan	277	0.05
Panamanian	319	0.06
Salvadoran	778	0.15
Other Central American	20	<0.01
Cuban	992	0.19
Dominican Republic	223	0.04
Mexican	193,994	37.30
Puerto Rican	3,359	0.65
South American	1,973	0.38
Argentinean	265	0.05
Bolivian	103	0.02
Chilean	293	0.06
Colombian	570	0.11
Ecuadorian	147	0.03
Paraguayan	17	<0.01
Peruvian	382	0.07
Uruguayan	28	0.01
Venezuelan	153	0.03
Other South American	15	<0.01
Other Hispanic or Latino	13,240	2.55

Race*	Population	%
African-American/Black (26,000)	32,361	6.22
Not Hispanic (23,362)	27,643	5.31
Hispanic (2,638)	4,718	0.91
American Indian/Alaska Native (14,154)	19,903	3.83
Not Hispanic (8,776)	11,821	2.27
Hispanic (5,378)	8,082	1.55
Alaska Athabascan *(Ala. Nat.)* (10)	14	<0.01
Aleut *(Alaska Native)* (9)	18	<0.01
Apache (440)	744	0.14
Arapaho (9)	13	<0.01
Blackfeet (35)	154	0.03
Canadian/French Am. Ind. (17)	38	0.01
Central American Ind. (22)	39	0.01
Cherokee (279)	1,019	0.20
Cheyenne (5)	20	<0.01
Chickasaw (24)	75	0.01
Chippewa (75)	197	0.04
Choctaw (88)	246	0.05
Colville (4)	7	<0.01
Comanche (14)	32	0.01
Cree (9)	18	<0.01
Creek (15)	58	0.01
Crow (8)	16	<0.01
Delaware (8)	17	<0.01
Hopi (152)	219	0.04
Inupiat *(Alaska Native)* (11)	22	<0.01
Iroquois (42)	117	0.02
Kiowa (4)	7	<0.01
Lumbee (16)	20	<0.01
Menominee (7)	11	<0.01
Mexican American Ind. (519)	831	0.16
Navajo (1,482)	1,840	0.35
Osage (6)	26	<0.01
Ottawa (4)	10	<0.01
Paiute (20)	30	0.01
Pima (202)	266	0.05
Potawatomi (20)	39	0.01
Pueblo (106)	156	0.03
Puget Sound Salish (5)	16	<0.01
Seminole (7)	34	0.01
Shoshone (26)	35	0.01
Sioux (143)	318	0.06
South American Ind. (17)	49	0.01
Spanish American Ind. (28)	41	0.01
Tlingit-Haida *(Alaska Native)* (22)	32	0.01
Tohono O'Odham (3,086)	3,636	0.70
Tsimshian *(Alaska Native)* (0)	1	<0.01
Ute (30)	39	0.01
Yakama (1)	5	<0.01
Yaqui (3,006)	3,852	0.74
Yuman (70)	101	0.02
Yup'ik *(Alaska Native)* (2)	25	<0.01
Asian (14,920)	20,448	3.93
Not Hispanic (14,211)	18,307	3.52
Hispanic (709)	2,141	0.41
Bangladeshi (35)	43	0.01
Bhutanese (477)	571	0.11
Burmese (52)	55	0.01
Cambodian (69)	94	0.02
Chinese, ex. Taiwanese (3,442)	4,413	0.85
Filipino (2,435)	4,024	0.77
Hmong (6)	7	<0.01
Indian (1,808)	2,198	0.42
Indonesian (51)	103	0.02
Japanese (921)	2,085	0.40
Korean (1,264)	1,892	0.36
Laotian (262)	323	0.06
Malaysian (24)	35	0.01
Nepalese (199)	274	0.05
Pakistani (186)	216	0.04
Sri Lankan (103)	114	0.02
Taiwanese (170)	210	0.04
Thai (354)	611	0.12
Vietnamese (2,198)	2,547	0.49
Hawaii Native/Pacific Islander (1,147)	2,080	0.40
Not Hispanic (951)	1,596	0.31
Hispanic (196)	484	0.09
Fijian (24)	35	0.01
Guamanian/Chamorro (318)	457	0.09
Marshallese (158)	177	0.03
Native Hawaiian (325)	704	0.14
Samoan (88)	169	0.03
Tongan (20)	37	0.01
White (362,649)	380,875	73.23
Not Hispanic (245,323)	254,236	48.88
Hispanic (117,326)	126,639	24.35

Vail

Place Type: CDP
County: Pima
Population: 10,208[†]

Ancestry[‡]	Population	%
American (376)	376	4.07
Arab (0)	9	0.10
Lebanese (0)	9	0.10
Austrian (11)	48	0.52
Belgian (0)	15	0.16
British (63)	63	0.68
Cajun (0)	31	0.34
Canadian (20)	73	0.79
Czech (11)	11	0.12
Czechoslovakian (11)	21	0.23
Danish (0)	15	0.16
Dutch (4)	33	0.36
Eastern European (9)	9	0.10
English (101)	650	7.04
European (127)	127	1.37
French, ex. Basque (6)	264	2.86
French Canadian (19)	78	0.84
German (1,134)	2,347	25.41
Greek (32)	92	1.00
Hungarian (43)	43	0.47
Iranian (12)	12	0.13
Irish (236)	992	10.74
Italian (163)	671	7.26
Lithuanian (0)	6	0.06
Norwegian (99)	149	1.61
Polish (54)	265	2.87
Portuguese (7)	59	0.64
Russian (80)	168	1.82
Scandinavian (22)	56	0.61
Scotch-Irish (34)	116	1.26
Scottish (38)	165	1.79
Swedish (0)	74	0.80
Swiss (0)	15	0.16
Turkish (0)	10	0.11
Ukrainian (0)	11	0.12

*Notes: † The Census 2010 population figure is used to calculate the percentages in the Hispanic Origin and Race categories. Ancestry percentages are based on the 2006-2010 American Community Survey population (not shown); ‡ Numbers in parentheses indicate the number of people reporting a single ancestry; * Numbers in parentheses indicate the number of persons reporting this race alone, not in combination with any other race; Please refer to the Explanation of Data for more information.*

Welsh (10)	88	0.95
Yugoslavian (0)	11	0.12

Hispanic Origin	Population	%
Hispanic or Latino (of any race)	1,983	19.43
Central American, ex. Mexican	36	0.35
Costa Rican	4	0.04
Guatemalan	5	0.05
Honduran	2	0.02
Nicaraguan	1	0.01
Panamanian	1	0.01
Salvadoran	23	0.23
Cuban	24	0.24
Dominican Republic	19	0.19
Mexican	1,587	15.55
Puerto Rican	90	0.88
South American	53	0.52
Argentinean	1	0.01
Chilean	10	0.10
Colombian	20	0.20
Ecuadorian	11	0.11
Peruvian	9	0.09
Uruguayan	1	0.01
Venezuelan	1	0.01
Other Hispanic or Latino	174	1.70

Race*	Population	%
African-American/Black (334)	475	4.65
Not Hispanic (317)	431	4.22
Hispanic (17)	44	0.43
American Indian/Alaska Native (87)	186	1.82
Not Hispanic (51)	123	1.20
Hispanic (36)	63	0.62
Apache (5)	7	0.07
Cherokee (3)	17	0.17
Chickasaw (1)	1	0.01
Choctaw (7)	11	0.11
Creek (2)	3	0.03
Crow (0)	1	0.01
Iroquois (1)	7	0.07
Lumbee (0)	4	0.04
Mexican American Ind. (5)	7	0.07
Navajo (4)	4	0.04
Paiute (1)	1	0.01
Potawatomi (5)	6	0.06
Pueblo (3)	5	0.05
Shoshone (0)	2	0.02
Sioux (1)	9	0.09
South American Ind. (1)	3	0.03
Spanish American Ind. (4)	4	0.04
Tohono O'Odham (5)	6	0.06
Yaqui (7)	10	0.10
Yuman (1)	1	0.01
Asian (249)	399	3.91
Not Hispanic (223)	351	3.44
Hispanic (26)	48	0.47
Cambodian (2)	2	0.02
Chinese, ex. Taiwanese (28)	62	0.61
Filipino (59)	130	1.27
Indian (9)	14	0.14
Indonesian (3)	4	0.04
Japanese (25)	65	0.64
Korean (29)	39	0.38
Laotian (1)	1	0.01
Malaysian (1)	1	0.01
Sri Lankan (1)	1	0.01
Taiwanese (3)	3	0.03
Thai (8)	20	0.20
Vietnamese (54)	64	0.63
Hawaii Native/Pacific Islander (15)	51	0.50
Not Hispanic (15)	51	0.50
Guamanian/Chamorro (7)	12	0.12
Native Hawaiian (6)	26	0.25
Samoan (1)	4	0.04
Tongan (1)	4	0.04
White (8,596)	8,963	87.80
Not Hispanic (7,308)	7,559	74.05
Hispanic (1,288)	1,404	13.75

Valencia West

Place Type: CDP
County: Pima
Population: 9,355†

Ancestry‡	Population	%
African, Sub-Saharan (33)	33	0.36
African (23)	23	0.25
Other Sub-Saharan African (10)	10	0.11
American (216)	216	2.36
Arab (0)	44	0.48
Jordanian (0)	22	0.24
Other Arab (0)	22	0.24
British (4)	4	0.04
Croatian (34)	34	0.37
Danish (0)	22	0.24
Dutch (15)	83	0.91
English (59)	256	2.80
European (108)	117	1.28
French, ex. Basque (10)	32	0.35
French Canadian (0)	56	0.61
German (157)	505	5.52
Hungarian (12)	12	0.13
Irish (64)	279	3.05
Italian (67)	180	1.97
Norwegian (13)	38	0.42
Pennsylvania German (10)	10	0.11
Polish (66)	90	0.98
Portuguese (0)	11	0.12
Romanian (0)	7	0.08
Russian (11)	21	0.23
Scotch-Irish (11)	150	1.64
Scottish (0)	93	1.02
Swedish (0)	42	0.46
Swiss (0)	7	0.08

Hispanic Origin	Population	%
Hispanic or Latino (of any race)	6,089	65.09
Central American, ex. Mexican	52	0.56
Costa Rican	2	0.02
Guatemalan	13	0.14
Honduran	3	0.03
Nicaraguan	8	0.09
Panamanian	5	0.05
Salvadoran	21	0.22
Cuban	11	0.12
Mexican	5,784	61.83
Puerto Rican	47	0.50
South American	25	0.27
Argentinean	1	0.01
Bolivian	2	0.02
Chilean	2	0.02
Colombian	5	0.05
Ecuadorian	5	0.05
Peruvian	3	0.03
Venezuelan	3	0.03
Other South American	4	0.04
Other Hispanic or Latino	170	1.82

Race*	Population	%
African-American/Black (305)	375	4.01
Not Hispanic (254)	295	3.15
Hispanic (51)	80	0.86
American Indian/Alaska Native (389)	501	5.36
Not Hispanic (185)	235	2.51
Hispanic (204)	266	2.84
Aleut *(Alaska Native)* (3)	3	0.03
Apache (11)	23	0.25
Arapaho (0)	1	0.01
Blackfeet (2)	3	0.03
Cherokee (4)	17	0.18
Chickasaw (0)	1	0.01
Chippewa (0)	1	0.01
Choctaw (1)	3	0.03
Comanche (0)	4	0.04
Cree (0)	3	0.03
Creek (0)	1	0.01
Iroquois (1)	1	0.01
Mexican American Ind. (9)	29	0.31
Navajo (24)	26	0.28
Pima (0)	3	0.03
Sioux (4)	11	0.12
Tohono O'Odham (84)	91	0.97
Yaqui (136)	155	1.66
Yuman (0)	3	0.03
Asian (146)	224	2.39
Not Hispanic (121)	169	1.81
Hispanic (25)	55	0.59
Cambodian (2)	7	0.07
Chinese, ex. Taiwanese (12)	25	0.27
Filipino (52)	87	0.93
Indian (10)	12	0.13
Japanese (15)	28	0.30
Korean (5)	5	0.05
Laotian (3)	7	0.07
Malaysian (1)	2	0.02
Taiwanese (8)	9	0.10
Thai (2)	6	0.06
Vietnamese (25)	30	0.32
Hawaii Native/Pacific Islander (20)	24	0.26
Not Hispanic (14)	16	0.17
Hispanic (6)	8	0.09
Native Hawaiian (16)	16	0.17
Samoan (3)	3	0.03
White (5,671)	5,987	64.00
Not Hispanic (2,527)	2,646	28.28
Hispanic (3,144)	3,341	35.71

Verde Village

Place Type: CDP
County: Yavapai
Population: 11,605†

Ancestry‡	Population	%
American (768)	768	5.93
Arab (0)	12	0.09
Lebanese (0)	12	0.09
Australian (0)	20	0.15
Austrian (0)	15	0.12
Basque (22)	22	0.17
British (12)	12	0.09
Celtic (0)	13	0.10
Czech (0)	15	0.12
Danish (117)	317	2.45
Dutch (72)	285	2.20
English (290)	1,259	9.72
European (55)	55	0.42
Finnish (0)	16	0.12
French, ex. Basque (0)	377	2.91
French Canadian (99)	140	1.08
German (905)	2,809	21.69
Greek (33)	274	2.12
Irish (415)	1,471	11.36
Israeli (18)	18	0.14
Italian (240)	696	5.37
Lithuanian (34)	34	0.26
Luxemburger (0)	15	0.12
Norwegian (27)	310	2.39
Polish (210)	515	3.98
Portuguese (11)	11	0.08
Romanian (0)	15	0.12
Russian (0)	181	1.40
Scandinavian (38)	38	0.29
Scotch-Irish (111)	454	3.51
Scottish (97)	285	2.20
Serbian (18)	60	0.46
Swedish (51)	183	1.41
Swiss (0)	51	0.39
Welsh (19)	169	1.30

Hispanic Origin	Population	%
Hispanic or Latino (of any race)	2,512	21.65
Central American, ex. Mexican	17	0.15
Costa Rican	4	0.03
Guatemalan	4	0.03
Honduran	1	0.01
Nicaraguan	1	0.01
Panamanian	3	0.03

*Notes: † The Census 2010 population figure is used to calculate the percentages in the Hispanic Origin and Race categories. Ancestry percentages are based on the 2006-2010 American Community Survey population (not shown); ‡ Numbers in parentheses indicate the number of people reporting a single ancestry; * Numbers in parentheses indicate the number of persons reporting this race alone, not in combination with any other race; Please refer to the Explanation of Data for more information.*

Salvadoran	4	0.03
Cuban	11	0.09
Dominican Republic	3	0.03
Mexican	2,223	19.16
Puerto Rican	37	0.32
South American	18	0.16
Argentinean	5	0.04
Bolivian	2	0.02
Colombian	6	0.05
Ecuadorian	1	0.01
Peruvian	2	0.02
Venezuelan	2	0.02
Other Hispanic or Latino	203	1.75

Race*	Population	%
African-American/Black (58)	100	0.86
Not Hispanic (58)	96	0.83
Hispanic (0)	4	0.03
American Indian/Alaska Native (192)	310	2.67
Not Hispanic (141)	228	1.96
Hispanic (51)	82	0.71
Apache (9)	21	0.18
Blackfeet (0)	5	0.04
Central American Ind. (1)	1	0.01
Cherokee (7)	39	0.34
Chickasaw (0)	1	0.01
Choctaw (5)	10	0.09
Creek (0)	9	0.08
Hopi (3)	7	0.06
Iroquois (3)	4	0.03
Kiowa (2)	2	0.02
Menominee (3)	3	0.03
Mexican American Ind. (9)	12	0.10
Navajo (52)	55	0.47
Pima (0)	5	0.04
Potawatomi (4)	5	0.04
Pueblo (6)	7	0.06
Shoshone (1)	1	0.01
Sioux (4)	6	0.05
Spanish American Ind. (1)	1	0.01
Tlingit-Haida *(Alaska Native)* (0)	1	0.01
Tohono O'Odham (3)	5	0.04
Ute (0)	3	0.03
Yaqui (8)	9	0.08
Yuman (9)	12	0.10
Asian (57)	109	0.94
Not Hispanic (52)	98	0.84
Hispanic (5)	11	0.09
Chinese, ex. Taiwanese (12)	17	0.15
Filipino (24)	42	0.36
Indian (2)	10	0.09
Indonesian (0)	1	0.01
Japanese (4)	9	0.08
Korean (9)	17	0.15
Pakistani (0)	1	0.01
Taiwanese (1)	1	0.01
Thai (0)	1	0.01
Vietnamese (2)	7	0.06
Hawaii Native/Pacific Islander (10)	21	0.18
Not Hispanic (10)	21	0.18
Fijian (0)	1	0.01
Guamanian/Chamorro (1)	1	0.01
Native Hawaiian (6)	13	0.11
Samoan (0)	2	0.02
White (9,942)	10,222	88.08
Not Hispanic (8,647)	8,819	75.99
Hispanic (1,295)	1,403	12.09

Winslow

Place Type: City
County: Navajo
Population: 9,655†

Ancestry‡	Population	%
American (287)	287	2.95
Austrian (0)	69	0.71
Belgian (6)	6	0.06
British (8)	13	0.13
Croatian (0)	29	0.30
Danish (35)	102	1.05
Dutch (31)	122	1.25
Eastern European (6)	6	0.06
English (135)	874	8.98
European (60)	60	0.62
French, ex. Basque (29)	293	3.01
French Canadian (8)	8	0.08
German (274)	974	10.00
Irish (155)	1,148	11.79
Israeli (0)	12	0.12
Italian (59)	305	3.13
Lithuanian (19)	19	0.20
Northern European (5)	5	0.05
Norwegian (20)	33	0.34
Polish (104)	155	1.59
Portuguese (41)	159	1.63
Russian (0)	11	0.11
Scandinavian (0)	8	0.08
Scotch-Irish (48)	119	1.22
Scottish (32)	106	1.09
Slovak (10)	10	0.10
Swedish (58)	144	1.48
Swiss (0)	24	0.25
Welsh (0)	22	0.23
West Indian, ex. Hispanic (11)	16	0.16
Barbadian (11)	11	0.11
West Indian (0)	5	0.05

Hispanic Origin	Population	%
Hispanic or Latino (of any race)	3,171	32.84
Central American, ex. Mexican	14	0.15
Guatemalan	11	0.11
Honduran	3	0.03
Cuban	1	0.01
Dominican Republic	2	0.02
Mexican	2,686	27.82
Puerto Rican	9	0.09
South American	6	0.06
Colombian	1	0.01
Ecuadorian	2	0.02
Paraguayan	1	0.01
Peruvian	2	0.02
Other Hispanic or Latino	453	4.69

Race*	Population	%
African-American/Black (547)	653	6.76
Not Hispanic (501)	574	5.95
Hispanic (46)	79	0.82
American Indian/Alaska Native (2,478)	2,788	28.88
Not Hispanic (2,288)	2,499	25.88
Hispanic (190)	289	2.99
Apache (20)	42	0.44
Blackfeet (0)	1	0.01
Cherokee (4)	6	0.06
Cheyenne (2)	2	0.02
Choctaw (6)	20	0.21
Comanche (0)	1	0.01
Cree (4)	4	0.04
Creek (6)	6	0.06
Crow (0)	1	0.01
Delaware (0)	2	0.02
Hopi (191)	244	2.53
Inupiat *(Alaska Native)* (0)	1	0.01
Iroquois (4)	7	0.07
Kiowa (0)	3	0.03
Mexican American Ind. (2)	2	0.02
Navajo (1,611)	1,845	19.11
Paiute (1)	1	0.01
Pima (1)	4	0.04
Pueblo (56)	66	0.68
Puget Sound Salish (1)	3	0.03
Shoshone (1)	1	0.01
Sioux (12)	17	0.18
Spanish American Ind. (0)	1	0.01
Tohono O'Odham (28)	37	0.38
Ute (1)	3	0.03
Yakama (0)	1	0.01
Yaqui (20)	25	0.26
Yuman (3)	7	0.07
Asian (96)	118	1.22
Not Hispanic (94)	113	1.17
Hispanic (2)	5	0.05
Chinese, ex. Taiwanese (24)	27	0.28
Filipino (19)	25	0.26
Indian (32)	38	0.39
Indonesian (1)	1	0.01
Japanese (7)	8	0.08
Korean (3)	3	0.03
Malaysian (1)	1	0.01
Thai (4)	8	0.08
Vietnamese (2)	3	0.03
Hawaii Native/Pacific Islander (11)	21	0.22
Not Hispanic (10)	19	0.20
Hispanic (1)	2	0.02
Guamanian/Chamorro (4)	5	0.05
Native Hawaiian (5)	10	0.10
Samoan (0)	1	0.01
Tongan (2)	3	0.03
White (5,155)	5,528	57.26
Not Hispanic (3,328)	3,523	36.49
Hispanic (1,827)	2,005	20.77

Yuma

Place Type: City
County: Yuma
Population: 93,064†

Ancestry‡	Population	%
African, Sub-Saharan (134)	165	0.18
African (78)	109	0.12
Sudanese (56)	56	0.06
American (3,360)	3,360	3.69
Arab (121)	151	0.17
Arab (20)	28	0.03
Iraqi (23)	23	0.03
Jordanian (50)	50	0.05
Lebanese (0)	13	0.01
Syrian (0)	9	0.01
Other Arab (28)	28	0.03
Assyrian/Chaldean/Syriac (14)	14	0.02
Austrian (8)	61	0.07
Basque (13)	13	0.01
Belgian (0)	54	0.06
Brazilian (14)	33	0.04
British (145)	258	0.28
Cajun (29)	29	0.03
Canadian (405)	500	0.55
Croatian (7)	56	0.06
Czech (94)	258	0.28
Czechoslovakian (36)	78	0.09
Danish (89)	447	0.49
Dutch (188)	1,165	1.28
Eastern European (10)	10	0.01
English (2,236)	6,299	6.91
European (249)	393	0.43
Finnish (9)	35	0.04
French, ex. Basque (256)	1,840	2.02
French Canadian (226)	389	0.43
German (3,523)	10,259	11.25
Greek (31)	75	0.08
Hungarian (55)	180	0.20
Icelander (0)	15	0.02
Irish (2,283)	7,122	7.81
Israeli (8)	24	0.03
Italian (829)	2,017	2.21
Latvian (13)	53	0.06
Lithuanian (29)	71	0.08
Northern European (140)	140	0.15
Norwegian (517)	1,420	1.56
Pennsylvania German (12)	38	0.04
Polish (252)	1,070	1.17
Portuguese (162)	241	0.26
Romanian (49)	218	0.24
Russian (86)	284	0.31
Scandinavian (83)	132	0.14
Scotch-Irish (441)	1,074	1.18
Scottish (305)	1,214	1.33
Slavic (0)	14	0.02
Slovak (12)	27	0.03

*Notes: † The Census 2010 population figure is used to calculate the percentages in the Hispanic Origin and Race categories. Ancestry percentages are based on the 2006-2010 American Community Survey population (not shown); ‡ Numbers in parentheses indicate the number of people reporting a single ancestry; * Numbers in parentheses indicate the number of persons reporting this race alone, not in combination with any other race; Please refer to the Explanation of Data for more information.*

SECTION TWO

Ancestry	Population	%
Swedish (296)	945	1.04
Swiss (32)	275	0.30
Ukrainian (154)	200	0.22
Welsh (55)	293	0.32
West Indian, ex. Hispanic (58)	113	0.12
Barbadian (44)	44	0.05
Dutch West Indian (0)	44	0.05
Haitian (14)	14	0.02
Jamaican (0)	11	0.01
Yugoslavian (0)	18	0.02

Hispanic Origin	Population	%
Hispanic or Latino (of any race)	51,033	54.84
Central American, ex. Mexican	447	0.48
Costa Rican	21	0.02
Guatemalan	61	0.07
Honduran	55	0.06
Nicaraguan	26	0.03
Panamanian	35	0.04
Salvadoran	246	0.26
Other Central American	3	<0.01
Cuban	105	0.11
Dominican Republic	47	0.05
Mexican	47,190	50.71
Puerto Rican	669	0.72
South American	233	0.25
Argentinean	10	0.01
Chilean	27	0.03
Colombian	97	0.10
Ecuadorian	34	0.04
Paraguayan	4	<0.01
Peruvian	38	0.04
Uruguayan	9	0.01
Venezuelan	14	0.02
Other Hispanic or Latino	2,342	2.52

Race*	Population	%
African-American/Black (3,010)	3,854	4.14
Not Hispanic (2,532)	3,004	3.23
Hispanic (478)	850	0.91
American Indian/Alaska Native (1,644)	2,463	2.65
Not Hispanic (992)	1,410	1.52
Hispanic (652)	1,053	1.13
Alaska Athabascan *(Ala. Nat.)* (3)	8	0.01
Aleut *(Alaska Native)* (0)	1	<0.01
Apache (33)	74	0.08
Arapaho (0)	4	<0.01
Blackfeet (11)	26	0.03
Canadian/French Am. Ind. (2)	6	0.01
Central American Ind. (1)	5	0.01
Cherokee (49)	155	0.17
Chickasaw (6)	12	0.01
Chippewa (11)	27	0.03
Choctaw (32)	69	0.07
Comanche (19)	24	0.03
Cree (1)	5	0.01
Creek (3)	6	0.01
Crow (1)	1	<0.01
Delaware (0)	2	<0.01
Hopi (8)	17	0.02
Inupiat *(Alaska Native)* (2)	2	<0.01
Iroquois (5)	14	0.02
Kiowa (7)	7	0.01
Lumbee (6)	8	0.01
Mexican American Ind. (75)	117	0.13
Navajo (125)	170	0.18
Osage (1)	2	<0.01
Ottawa (0)	1	<0.01
Paiute (4)	7	0.01
Pima (61)	81	0.09
Potawatomi (4)	8	0.01
Pueblo (13)	20	0.02
Puget Sound Salish (3)	4	<0.01
Seminole (9)	10	0.01
Shoshone (2)	4	<0.01
Sioux (27)	44	0.05
South American Ind. (7)	12	0.01
Spanish American Ind. (6)	8	0.01
Tlingit-Haida *(Alaska Native)* (1)	3	<0.01
Tohono O'Odham (67)	84	0.09
Ute (1)	3	<0.01
Yakama (6)	6	0.01
Yaqui (98)	183	0.20
Yuman (308)	407	0.44
Yup'ik *(Alaska Native)* (3)	3	<0.01
Asian (1,730)	2,592	2.79
Not Hispanic (1,561)	2,132	2.29
Hispanic (169)	460	0.49
Burmese (8)	10	0.01
Cambodian (24)	30	0.03
Chinese, ex. Taiwanese (184)	327	0.35
Filipino (628)	1,023	1.10
Hmong (11)	11	0.01
Indian (252)	281	0.30
Indonesian (12)	16	0.02
Japanese (145)	322	0.35
Korean (134)	204	0.22
Laotian (11)	11	0.01
Malaysian (1)	12	0.01
Nepalese (2)	2	<0.01
Pakistani (23)	29	0.03
Sri Lankan (1)	1	<0.01
Taiwanese (8)	12	0.01
Thai (24)	51	0.05
Vietnamese (192)	221	0.24
Hawaii Native/Pacific Islander (205)	443	0.48
Not Hispanic (143)	297	0.32
Hispanic (62)	146	0.16
Fijian (0)	1	<0.01
Guamanian/Chamorro (95)	131	0.14
Marshallese (2)	2	<0.01
Native Hawaiian (55)	193	0.21
Samoan (26)	48	0.05
Tongan (4)	4	<0.01
White (64,013)	67,624	72.66
Not Hispanic (35,306)	36,473	39.19
Hispanic (28,707)	31,151	33.47

*Notes: † The Census 2010 population figure is used to calculate the percentages in the Hispanic Origin and Race categories. Ancestry percentages are based on the 2006-2010 American Community Survey population (not shown); ‡ Numbers in parentheses indicate the number of people reporting a single ancestry; * Numbers in parentheses indicate the number of persons reporting this race alone, not in combination with any other race; Please refer to the Explanation of Data for more information.*

ARKANSAS

Place Type: State
Population: 2,915,918[†]

Ancestry[‡]	Population	%
Afghan (10)	10	<0.01
African, Sub-Saharan (9,298)	10,636	0.37
African (8,109)	9,178	0.32
Cape Verdean (0)	8	<0.01
Ethiopian (44)	120	<0.01
Ghanaian (75)	75	<0.01
Kenyan (68)	85	<0.01
Liberian (40)	40	<0.01
Nigerian (475)	534	0.02
Sierra Leonean (0)	11	<0.01
Somalian (79)	114	<0.01
South African (88)	124	<0.01
Sudanese (16)	16	<0.01
Other Sub-Saharan African (304)	331	0.01
Albanian (17)	17	<0.01
Alsatian (13)	27	<0.01
American (309,378)	309,378	10.77
Arab (2,852)	4,529	0.16
Arab (743)	1,044	0.04
Egyptian (191)	248	0.01
Iraqi (186)	205	0.01
Jordanian (366)	434	0.02
Lebanese (456)	1,145	0.04
Moroccan (60)	136	<0.01
Palestinian (76)	212	0.01
Syrian (297)	520	0.02
Other Arab (477)	585	0.02
Armenian (45)	400	0.01
Assyrian/Chaldean/Syriac (84)	110	<0.01
Australian (235)	500	0.02
Austrian (670)	1,972	0.07
Basque (220)	288	0.01
Belgian (601)	1,275	0.04
Brazilian (438)	547	0.02
British (5,842)	10,712	0.37
Bulgarian (199)	284	0.01
Cajun (773)	1,619	0.06
Canadian (1,116)	2,252	0.08
Carpatho Rusyn (0)	15	<0.01
Celtic (219)	391	0.01
Croatian (366)	826	0.03
Cypriot (22)	22	<0.01
Czech (2,061)	6,665	0.23
Czechoslovakian (1,201)	2,087	0.07
Danish (1,870)	5,934	0.21
Dutch (10,485)	54,436	1.89
Eastern European (214)	252	0.01
English (136,972)	294,987	10.27
Estonian (57)	120	<0.01
European (18,326)	21,677	0.75
Finnish (411)	1,435	0.05
French, ex. Basque (15,203)	66,023	2.30
French Canadian (3,439)	6,437	0.22
German (119,781)	350,425	12.20
German Russian (4)	71	<0.01
Greek (1,462)	3,592	0.13
Hungarian (1,352)	3,909	0.14
Icelander (81)	90	<0.01
Iranian (461)	685	0.02
Irish (122,950)	381,337	13.27
Israeli (76)	196	0.01
Italian (19,681)	48,955	1.70
Latvian (92)	187	0.01
Lithuanian (423)	1,202	0.04
Luxemburger (14)	131	<0.01
Macedonian (12)	42	<0.01
Maltese (35)	48	<0.01
New Zealander (0)	20	<0.01
Northern European (861)	955	0.03
Norwegian (5,051)	13,691	0.48
Pennsylvania German (273)	925	0.03
Polish (8,163)	24,848	0.86
Portuguese (1,137)	2,665	0.09
Romanian (711)	1,270	0.04
Russian (1,382)	5,047	0.18
Scandinavian (1,084)	3,145	0.11
Scotch-Irish (28,808)	58,485	2.04
Scottish (20,445)	53,087	1.85
Serbian (247)	406	0.01
Slavic (155)	445	0.02
Slovak (449)	1,056	0.04
Slovene (41)	102	<0.01
Soviet Union (6)	6	<0.01
Swedish (5,716)	18,687	0.65
Swiss (1,295)	5,805	0.20
Turkish (329)	438	0.02
Ukrainian (554)	1,286	0.04
Welsh (3,438)	13,110	0.46
West Indian, ex. Hispanic (1,603)	4,974	0.17
Bahamian (103)	168	0.01
Barbadian (62)	84	<0.01
Belizean (12)	12	<0.01
Bermudan (12)	12	<0.01
British West Indian (40)	40	<0.01
Dutch West Indian (585)	3,076	0.11
Haitian (216)	423	0.01
Jamaican (395)	840	0.03
Trinidadian/Tobagonian (92)	140	<0.01
West Indian (69)	162	0.01
Other West Indian (17)	17	<0.01
Yugoslavian (259)	480	0.02

Hispanic Origin	Population	%
Hispanic or Latino (of any race)	186,050	6.38
Central American, ex. Mexican	23,216	0.80
Costa Rican	333	0.01
Guatemalan	4,533	0.16
Honduran	2,076	0.07
Nicaraguan	704	0.02
Panamanian	485	0.02
Salvadoran	14,980	0.51
Other Central American	105	<0.01
Cuban	1,493	0.05
Dominican Republic	384	0.01
Mexican	138,194	4.74
Puerto Rican	4,789	0.16
South American	3,028	0.10
Argentinean	338	0.01
Bolivian	260	0.01
Chilean	219	0.01
Colombian	888	0.03
Ecuadorian	302	0.01
Paraguayan	24	<0.01
Peruvian	650	0.02
Uruguayan	25	<0.01
Venezuelan	300	0.01
Other South American	22	<0.01
Other Hispanic or Latino	14,946	0.51

Race*	Population	%
African-American/Black (449,895)	468,710	16.07
Not Hispanic (447,102)	464,242	15.92
Hispanic (2,793)	4,468	0.15
American Indian/Alaska Native (22,248)	47,588	1.63
Not Hispanic (20,183)	43,527	1.49
Hispanic (2,065)	4,061	0.14
Alaska Athabascan *(Ala. Nat.)* (42)	67	<0.01
Aleut *(Alaska Native)* (28)	41	<0.01
Apache (224)	627	0.02
Arapaho (7)	27	<0.01
Blackfeet (136)	799	0.03
Canadian/French Am. Ind. (17)	49	<0.01
Central American Ind. (46)	67	<0.01
Cherokee (8,659)	20,330	0.70
Cheyenne (45)	121	<0.01
Chickasaw (318)	613	0.02
Chippewa (190)	374	0.01
Choctaw (2,702)	4,840	0.17
Colville (10)	15	<0.01
Comanche (98)	203	0.01
Cree (13)	44	<0.01
Creek (579)	1,059	0.04
Crow (6)	68	<0.01
Delaware (71)	140	<0.01
Hopi (12)	29	<0.01
Houma (37)	49	<0.01
Inupiat *(Alaska Native)* (33)	64	<0.01
Iroquois (153)	310	0.01
Kiowa (67)	106	<0.01
Lumbee (68)	100	<0.01
Menominee (7)	13	<0.01
Mexican American Ind. (484)	727	0.02
Navajo (171)	331	0.01
Osage (169)	379	0.01
Ottawa (46)	77	<0.01
Paiute (17)	30	<0.01
Pima (9)	18	<0.01
Potawatomi (228)	325	0.01
Pueblo (53)	96	<0.01
Puget Sound Salish (7)	20	<0.01
Seminole (81)	216	0.01
Shoshone (28)	47	<0.01
Sioux (265)	609	0.02
South American Ind. (28)	61	<0.01
Spanish American Ind. (33)	62	<0.01
Tlingit-Haida *(Alaska Native)* (30)	47	<0.01
Tohono O'Odham (18)	25	<0.01
Tsimshian *(Alaska Native)* (2)	2	<0.01
Ute (7)	31	<0.01
Yakama (5)	16	<0.01
Yaqui (36)	73	<0.01
Yuman (5)	8	<0.01
Yup'ik *(Alaska Native)* (30)	69	<0.01
Asian (36,102)	44,943	1.54
Not Hispanic (35,647)	43,589	1.49
Hispanic (455)	1,354	0.05
Bangladeshi (185)	210	0.01
Burmese (48)	53	<0.01
Cambodian (185)	230	0.01
Chinese, ex. Taiwanese (4,849)	5,936	0.20
Filipino (3,937)	6,396	0.22
Hmong (2,063)	2,143	0.07
Indian (7,973)	9,101	0.31
Indonesian (166)	229	0.01
Japanese (1,111)	2,384	0.08
Korean (2,269)	3,247	0.11
Laotian (3,903)	4,614	0.16
Malaysian (76)	111	<0.01
Nepalese (118)	122	<0.01
Pakistani (715)	815	0.03
Sri Lankan (101)	122	<0.01
Taiwanese (295)	380	0.01
Thai (617)	1,018	0.03
Vietnamese (5,515)	6,302	0.22
Hawaii Native/Pacific Islander (5,863)	7,849	0.27
Not Hispanic (5,509)	7,116	0.24
Hispanic (354)	733	0.03
Fijian (21)	27	<0.01
Guamanian/Chamorro (442)	719	0.02
Marshallese (4,121)	4,324	0.15
Native Hawaiian (537)	1,251	0.04
Samoan (178)	371	0.01
Tongan (18)	34	<0.01
White (2,245,229)	2,296,665	78.76
Not Hispanic (2,173,469)	2,215,467	75.98
Hispanic (71,760)	81,198	2.78

*Notes: † The Census 2010 population figure is used to calculate the percentages in the Hispanic Origin and Race categories. Ancestry percentages are based on the 2006-2010 American Community Survey population (not shown); ‡ Numbers in parentheses indicate the number of people reporting a single ancestry; * Numbers in parentheses indicate the number of persons reporting this race alone, not in combination with any other race; Please refer to the Explanation of Data for more information.*

Arkadelphia

Place Type: City
County: Clark
Population: 10,714†

Ancestry‡	Population	%
African, Sub-Saharan (16)	16	0.15
African (16)	16	0.15
American (427)	427	3.99
Australian (27)	27	0.25
Austrian (9)	47	0.44
British (0)	27	0.25
Canadian (0)	33	0.31
Czech (15)	37	0.35
Dutch (57)	190	1.78
English (372)	984	9.20
European (86)	96	0.90
French, ex. Basque (29)	387	3.62
German (332)	1,276	11.93
Greek (0)	37	0.35
Irish (687)	1,284	12.00
Italian (71)	107	1.00
Norwegian (27)	99	0.93
Polish (47)	179	1.67
Romanian (0)	35	0.33
Russian (8)	41	0.38
Scandinavian (6)	6	0.06
Scotch-Irish (115)	254	2.37
Scottish (76)	450	4.21
Slovak (0)	10	0.09
Swedish (124)	343	3.21
Swiss (0)	48	0.45
Ukrainian (0)	13	0.12
Welsh (22)	79	0.74

Hispanic Origin	Population	%
Hispanic or Latino (of any race)	347	3.24
Central American, ex. Mexican	24	0.22
Costa Rican	2	0.02
Guatemalan	4	0.04
Honduran	1	0.01
Panamanian	1	0.01
Salvadoran	16	0.15
Cuban	4	0.04
Mexican	270	2.52
Puerto Rican	10	0.09
South American	13	0.12
Argentinean	2	0.02
Colombian	5	0.05
Ecuadorian	3	0.03
Peruvian	2	0.02
Venezuelan	1	0.01
Other Hispanic or Latino	26	0.24

Race*	Population	%
African-American/Black (3,244)	3,341	31.18
Not Hispanic (3,215)	3,308	30.88
Hispanic (29)	33	0.31
American Indian/Alaska Native (52)	102	0.95
Not Hispanic (38)	86	0.80
Hispanic (14)	16	0.15
Cherokee (2)	20	0.19
Chickasaw (0)	3	0.03
Chippewa (0)	2	0.02
Choctaw (10)	15	0.14
Cree (1)	1	0.01
Iroquois (0)	1	0.01
Potawatomi (0)	1	0.01
Pueblo (2)	3	0.03
Seminole (0)	1	0.01
Asian (85)	115	1.07
Not Hispanic (85)	109	1.02
Hispanic (0)	6	0.06
Cambodian (2)	2	0.02
Chinese, ex. Taiwanese (31)	32	0.30
Filipino (8)	16	0.15
Indian (6)	7	0.07
Indonesian (1)	1	0.01
Japanese (3)	6	0.06
Korean (13)	16	0.15
Taiwanese (4)	4	0.04
Vietnamese (8)	14	0.13
Hawaii Native/Pacific Islander (3)	7	0.07
Not Hispanic (3)	7	0.07
Guamanian/Chamorro (1)	3	0.03
Native Hawaiian (1)	1	0.01
Samoan (1)	3	0.03
White (7,020)	7,177	66.99
Not Hispanic (6,860)	7,002	65.35
Hispanic (160)	175	1.63

Batesville

Place Type: City
County: Independence
Population: 10,248†

Ancestry‡	Population	%
African, Sub-Saharan (14)	14	0.14
Other Sub-Saharan African (14)	14	0.14
American (1,137)	1,137	11.32
British (29)	48	0.48
Croatian (8)	8	0.08
Czech (5)	32	0.32
Czechoslovakian (8)	8	0.08
Dutch (61)	233	2.32
English (588)	1,049	10.44
European (106)	106	1.06
French, ex. Basque (41)	175	1.74
French Canadian (0)	8	0.08
German (510)	1,201	11.96
Greek (0)	12	0.12
Hungarian (48)	48	0.48
Irish (361)	994	9.90
Italian (0)	20	0.20
Northern European (0)	16	0.16
Norwegian (30)	30	0.30
Polish (13)	73	0.73
Portuguese (35)	55	0.55
Russian (0)	14	0.14
Scotch-Irish (124)	191	1.90
Scottish (159)	315	3.14
Swedish (0)	76	0.76
Swiss (0)	16	0.16
Welsh (0)	29	0.29

Hispanic Origin	Population	%
Hispanic or Latino (of any race)	1,379	13.46
Central American, ex. Mexican	306	2.99
Guatemalan	284	2.77
Honduran	12	0.12
Salvadoran	10	0.10
Cuban	3	0.03
Mexican	923	9.01
Puerto Rican	14	0.14
South American	13	0.13
Colombian	5	0.05
Ecuadorian	5	0.05
Peruvian	1	0.01
Other South American	2	0.02
Other Hispanic or Latino	120	1.17

Race*	Population	%
African-American/Black (438)	530	5.17
Not Hispanic (432)	519	5.06
Hispanic (6)	11	0.11
American Indian/Alaska Native (62)	106	1.03
Not Hispanic (47)	88	0.86
Hispanic (15)	18	0.18
Blackfeet (1)	2	0.02
Cherokee (24)	40	0.39
Chickasaw (0)	1	0.01
Chippewa (0)	3	0.03
Choctaw (2)	5	0.05
Creek (2)	2	0.02
Mexican American Ind. (2)	2	0.02
Ottawa (0)	4	0.04
Potawatomi (1)	1	0.01
Sioux (0)	2	0.02
Asian (158)	190	1.85
Not Hispanic (156)	182	1.78
Hispanic (2)	8	0.08
Bangladeshi (2)	2	0.02
Cambodian (1)	3	0.03
Chinese, ex. Taiwanese (15)	17	0.17
Filipino (16)	28	0.27
Hmong (5)	5	0.05
Indian (15)	16	0.16
Japanese (7)	12	0.12
Korean (1)	2	0.02
Pakistani (6)	7	0.07
Taiwanese (4)	4	0.04
Thai (1)	1	0.01
Vietnamese (75)	81	0.79
Hawaii Native/Pacific Islander (34)	49	0.48
Not Hispanic (13)	23	0.22
Hispanic (21)	26	0.25
Guamanian/Chamorro (26)	28	0.27
Native Hawaiian (1)	8	0.08
Samoan (2)	6	0.06
White (8,527)	8,714	85.03
Not Hispanic (8,053)	8,198	80.00
Hispanic (474)	516	5.04

Bella Vista

Place Type: Town
County: Benton
Population: 26,461†

Ancestry‡	Population	%
African, Sub-Saharan (0)	12	0.05
African (0)	12	0.05
American (2,433)	2,433	9.89
Australian (0)	20	0.08
Austrian (19)	48	0.20
Belgian (22)	40	0.16
British (72)	225	0.91
Canadian (45)	66	0.27
Croatian (15)	15	0.06
Czech (77)	236	0.96
Czechoslovakian (24)	24	0.10
Danish (160)	269	1.09
Dutch (101)	569	2.31
English (1,528)	4,229	17.18
European (101)	161	0.65
Finnish (0)	36	0.15
French, ex. Basque (219)	943	3.83
French Canadian (32)	104	0.42
German (2,696)	6,498	26.40
Greek (0)	48	0.20
Hungarian (12)	66	0.27
Irish (886)	3,074	12.49
Italian (257)	746	3.03
Lithuanian (12)	24	0.10
Luxemburger (0)	12	0.05
Northern European (12)	12	0.05
Norwegian (420)	818	3.32
Pennsylvania German (28)	41	0.17
Polish (160)	578	2.35
Portuguese (15)	27	0.11
Romanian (2)	2	0.01
Russian (0)	71	0.29
Scandinavian (12)	44	0.18
Scotch-Irish (439)	968	3.93
Scottish (323)	882	3.58
Serbian (15)	29	0.12
Slavic (0)	9	0.04
Swedish (262)	563	2.29
Swiss (56)	92	0.37
Turkish (0)	9	0.04
Ukrainian (13)	39	0.16
Welsh (113)	217	0.88

Hispanic Origin	Population	%
Hispanic or Latino (of any race)	688	2.60
Central American, ex. Mexican	69	0.26
Costa Rican	1	<0.01
Guatemalan	11	0.04

*Notes: † The Census 2010 population figure is used to calculate the percentages in the Hispanic Origin and Race categories. Ancestry percentages are based on the 2006-2010 American Community Survey population (not shown); ‡ Numbers in parentheses indicate the number of people reporting a single ancestry; * Numbers in parentheses indicate the number of persons reporting this race alone, not in combination with any other race; Please refer to the Explanation of Data for more information.*

Honduran	3	0.01
Nicaraguan	2	0.01
Panamanian	9	0.03
Salvadoran	43	0.16
Cuban	24	0.09
Dominican Republic	1	<0.01
Mexican	427	1.61
Puerto Rican	39	0.15
South American	47	0.18
Argentinean	8	0.03
Bolivian	3	0.01
Chilean	1	<0.01
Colombian	21	0.08
Paraguayan	4	0.02
Peruvian	6	0.02
Venezuelan	4	0.02
Other Hispanic or Latino	81	0.31

Race*	Population	%
African-American/Black (174)	215	0.81
Not Hispanic (169)	208	0.79
Hispanic (5)	7	0.03
American Indian/Alaska Native (272)	485	1.83
Not Hispanic (258)	458	1.73
Hispanic (14)	27	0.10
Aleut *(Alaska Native)* (2)	2	0.01
Apache (0)	3	0.01
Arapaho (0)	1	<0.01
Blackfeet (1)	4	0.02
Cherokee (121)	237	0.90
Chickasaw (10)	13	0.05
Chippewa (5)	5	0.02
Choctaw (19)	39	0.15
Colville (0)	1	<0.01
Comanche (3)	3	0.01
Creek (12)	18	0.07
Delaware (1)	4	0.02
Inupiat *(Alaska Native)* (0)	1	<0.01
Iroquois (2)	3	0.01
Kiowa (5)	5	0.02
Mexican American Ind. (7)	10	0.04
Navajo (1)	1	<0.01
Osage (3)	5	0.02
Ottawa (1)	1	<0.01
Potawatomi (17)	18	0.07
Pueblo (1)	1	<0.01
Seminole (0)	1	<0.01
Sioux (2)	4	0.02
Tlingit-Haida *(Alaska Native)* (1)	1	<0.01
Yaqui (1)	3	0.01
Asian (124)	192	0.73
Not Hispanic (122)	188	0.71
Hispanic (2)	4	0.02
Bangladeshi (1)	1	<0.01
Chinese, ex. Taiwanese (18)	28	0.11
Filipino (32)	52	0.20
Hmong (6)	6	0.02
Indian (19)	21	0.08
Indonesian (2)	2	0.01
Japanese (8)	17	0.06
Korean (23)	31	0.12
Laotian (2)	2	0.01
Sri Lankan (3)	3	0.01
Thai (1)	3	0.01
Vietnamese (6)	18	0.07
Hawaii Native/Pacific Islander (15)	23	0.09
Not Hispanic (11)	18	0.07
Hispanic (4)	5	0.02
Guamanian/Chamorro (1)	2	0.01
Native Hawaiian (6)	7	0.03
Samoan (5)	7	0.03
White (25,363)	25,691	97.09
Not Hispanic (24,881)	25,177	95.15
Hispanic (482)	514	1.94

Benton

Place Type: City
County: Saline
Population: 30,681†

Ancestry‡	Population	%
African, Sub-Saharan (6)	6	0.02
African (6)	6	0.02
American (2,933)	2,933	10.07
Arab (12)	23	0.08
Arab (12)	23	0.08
Assyrian/Chaldean/Syriac (8)	8	0.03
British (155)	226	0.78
Canadian (0)	56	0.19
Celtic (0)	16	0.05
Czech (0)	97	0.33
Danish (22)	34	0.12
Dutch (15)	386	1.33
Eastern European (13)	13	0.04
English (1,471)	3,362	11.55
European (172)	213	0.73
Finnish (8)	16	0.05
French, ex. Basque (186)	893	3.07
French Canadian (79)	135	0.46
German (1,131)	4,046	13.90
Greek (0)	21	0.07
Hungarian (0)	45	0.15
Irish (1,492)	4,125	14.17
Italian (168)	722	2.48
Norwegian (10)	94	0.32
Polish (64)	129	0.44
Portuguese (36)	36	0.12
Russian (8)	24	0.08
Scandinavian (21)	60	0.21
Scotch-Irish (319)	670	2.30
Scottish (328)	812	2.79
Slavic (22)	22	0.08
Slovak (7)	21	0.07
Swedish (173)	248	0.85
Swiss (13)	27	0.09
Ukrainian (9)	9	0.03
Welsh (0)	206	0.71
West Indian, ex. Hispanic (0)	44	0.15
Dutch West Indian (0)	44	0.15

Hispanic Origin	Population	%
Hispanic or Latino (of any race)	1,390	4.53
Central American, ex. Mexican	183	0.60
Guatemalan	29	0.09
Honduran	67	0.22
Nicaraguan	5	0.02
Panamanian	7	0.02
Salvadoran	75	0.24
Cuban	23	0.07
Dominican Republic	2	0.01
Mexican	922	3.01
Puerto Rican	88	0.29
South American	28	0.09
Argentinean	1	<0.01
Bolivian	1	<0.01
Chilean	4	0.01
Colombian	19	0.06
Peruvian	1	<0.01
Venezuelan	2	0.01
Other Hispanic or Latino	144	0.47

Race*	Population	%
African-American/Black (1,848)	2,046	6.67
Not Hispanic (1,821)	2,012	6.56
Hispanic (27)	34	0.11
American Indian/Alaska Native (158)	321	1.05
Not Hispanic (136)	295	0.96
Hispanic (22)	26	0.08
Blackfeet (1)	4	0.01
Cherokee (49)	116	0.38
Chickasaw (2)	7	0.02
Chippewa (1)	2	0.01
Choctaw (31)	39	0.13
Colville (0)	1	<0.01
Comanche (0)	3	0.01
Creek (1)	1	<0.01
Crow (0)	1	<0.01
Hopi (0)	4	0.01
Iroquois (1)	3	0.01
Mexican American Ind. (5)	5	0.02
Navajo (3)	5	0.02
Osage (1)	1	<0.01
Ottawa (1)	1	<0.01
Potawatomi (3)	3	0.01
Sioux (1)	2	0.01
Spanish American Ind. (0)	1	<0.01
Asian (275)	357	1.16
Not Hispanic (274)	350	1.14
Hispanic (1)	7	0.02
Bangladeshi (4)	4	0.01
Cambodian (10)	10	0.03
Chinese, ex. Taiwanese (33)	40	0.13
Filipino (40)	63	0.21
Hmong (1)	1	<0.01
Indian (34)	43	0.14
Indonesian (2)	4	0.01
Japanese (10)	23	0.07
Korean (35)	42	0.14
Laotian (7)	15	0.05
Malaysian (0)	1	<0.01
Pakistani (4)	6	0.02
Taiwanese (7)	7	0.02
Thai (8)	17	0.06
Vietnamese (71)	81	0.26
Hawaii Native/Pacific Islander (6)	28	0.09
Not Hispanic (4)	20	0.07
Hispanic (2)	8	0.03
Guamanian/Chamorro (3)	3	0.01
Native Hawaiian (2)	9	0.03
Samoan (0)	2	0.01
White (27,235)	27,666	90.17
Not Hispanic (26,627)	27,002	88.01
Hispanic (608)	664	2.16

Bentonville

Place Type: City
County: Benton
Population: 35,301†

Ancestry‡	Population	%
African, Sub-Saharan (21)	21	0.06
Other Sub-Saharan African (21)	21	0.06
American (2,586)	2,586	7.91
Arab (0)	59	0.18
Lebanese (0)	38	0.12
Syrian (0)	21	0.06
Austrian (0)	13	0.04
Belgian (0)	15	0.05
British (116)	123	0.38
Canadian (12)	12	0.04
Celtic (12)	12	0.04
Cypriot (15)	15	0.05
Czech (29)	40	0.12
Czechoslovakian (0)	40	0.12
Danish (0)	50	0.15
Dutch (248)	785	2.40
English (1,540)	3,610	11.04
European (316)	435	1.33
Finnish (11)	33	0.10
French, ex. Basque (298)	890	2.72
French Canadian (30)	190	0.58
German (1,613)	5,228	16.00
Greek (0)	21	0.06
Hungarian (34)	69	0.21
Iranian (10)	10	0.03
Irish (1,517)	4,392	13.44
Italian (255)	1,144	3.50
Lithuanian (8)	43	0.13
Luxemburger (0)	41	0.13
Norwegian (116)	411	1.26
Pennsylvania German (0)	14	0.04
Polish (182)	555	1.70
Portuguese (0)	35	0.11
Romanian (0)	46	0.14
Russian (116)	225	0.69
Scandinavian (0)	57	0.17
Scotch-Irish (352)	686	2.10
Scottish (303)	843	2.58
Slavic (0)	27	0.08

*Notes: † The Census 2010 population figure is used to calculate the percentages in the Hispanic Origin and Race categories. Ancestry percentages are based on the 2006-2010 American Community Survey population (not shown); ‡ Numbers in parentheses indicate the number of people reporting a single ancestry; * Numbers in parentheses indicate the number of persons reporting this race alone, not in combination with any other race; Please refer to the Explanation of Data for more information.*

Slovak (10)	10	0.03
Swedish (135)	464	1.42
Swiss (60)	137	0.42
Ukrainian (9)	40	0.12
Welsh (37)	405	1.24
West Indian, ex. Hispanic (0)	55	0.17
Bahamian (0)	15	0.05
Barbadian (0)	15	0.05
Dutch West Indian (0)	25	0.08

Hispanic Origin	Population	%
Hispanic or Latino (of any race)	3,074	8.71
Central American, ex. Mexican	479	1.36
Costa Rican	20	0.06
Guatemalan	53	0.15
Honduran	23	0.07
Nicaraguan	14	0.04
Panamanian	4	0.01
Salvadoran	365	1.03
Cuban	54	0.15
Dominican Republic	20	0.06
Mexican	1,982	5.61
Puerto Rican	144	0.41
South American	142	0.40
Argentinean	17	0.05
Bolivian	13	0.04
Chilean	5	0.01
Colombian	51	0.14
Ecuadorian	18	0.05
Peruvian	29	0.08
Venezuelan	9	0.03
Other Hispanic or Latino	253	0.72

Race*	Population	%
African-American/Black (876)	1,036	2.93
Not Hispanic (850)	1,003	2.84
Hispanic (26)	33	0.09
American Indian/Alaska Native (436)	775	2.20
Not Hispanic (417)	739	2.09
Hispanic (19)	36	0.10
Aleut *(Alaska Native)* (1)	2	0.01
Apache (5)	7	0.02
Blackfeet (0)	5	0.01
Canadian/French Am. Ind. (0)	1	<0.01
Central American Ind. (0)	1	<0.01
Cherokee (178)	322	0.91
Chickasaw (4)	8	0.02
Chippewa (6)	6	0.02
Choctaw (47)	96	0.27
Comanche (4)	8	0.02
Cree (0)	1	<0.01
Creek (17)	30	0.08
Delaware (2)	5	0.01
Hopi (1)	2	0.01
Iroquois (5)	5	0.01
Kiowa (1)	1	<0.01
Menominee (1)	1	<0.01
Mexican American Ind. (2)	3	0.01
Navajo (15)	17	0.05
Osage (3)	11	0.03
Ottawa (6)	6	0.02
Paiute (0)	1	<0.01
Potawatomi (14)	14	0.04
Seminole (4)	9	0.03
Shoshone (2)	4	0.01
Sioux (5)	10	0.03
South American Ind. (0)	4	0.01
Yup'ik *(Alaska Native)* (1)	1	<0.01
Asian (2,936)	3,214	9.10
Not Hispanic (2,919)	3,180	9.01
Hispanic (17)	34	0.10
Bangladeshi (10)	10	0.03
Cambodian (4)	4	0.01
Chinese, ex. Taiwanese (171)	214	0.61
Filipino (100)	178	0.50
Hmong (30)	31	0.09
Indian (2,038)	2,094	5.93
Indonesian (4)	5	0.01
Japanese (18)	66	0.19
Korean (56)	99	0.28
Laotian (100)	119	0.34
Malaysian (0)	2	0.01
Nepalese (3)	3	0.01
Pakistani (21)	23	0.07
Sri Lankan (21)	24	0.07
Taiwanese (15)	15	0.04
Thai (10)	19	0.05
Vietnamese (275)	316	0.90
Hawaii Native/Pacific Islander (78)	134	0.38
Not Hispanic (69)	123	0.35
Hispanic (9)	11	0.03
Guamanian/Chamorro (17)	23	0.07
Marshallese (16)	29	0.08
Native Hawaiian (17)	49	0.14
Samoan (7)	9	0.03
White (28,720)	29,520	83.62
Not Hispanic (27,193)	27,845	78.88
Hispanic (1,527)	1,675	4.74

Blytheville

Place Type: City
County: Mississippi
Population: 15,620†

Ancestry‡	Population	%
African, Sub-Saharan (180)	196	1.23
African (131)	131	0.83
Nigerian (49)	65	0.41
American (814)	814	5.13
British (92)	131	0.83
Canadian (30)	30	0.19
Czech (0)	7	0.04
Czechoslovakian (3)	3	0.02
Danish (0)	23	0.14
Dutch (0)	54	0.34
English (507)	753	4.74
European (119)	131	0.83
French, ex. Basque (34)	166	1.05
German (480)	970	6.11
Irish (396)	1,034	6.51
Italian (120)	175	1.10
Norwegian (0)	27	0.17
Polish (30)	72	0.45
Portuguese (16)	16	0.10
Scotch-Irish (162)	248	1.56
Scottish (69)	204	1.29
Swedish (17)	71	0.45
Welsh (9)	75	0.47
West Indian, ex. Hispanic (48)	48	0.30
Haitian (41)	41	0.26
Jamaican (7)	7	0.04

Hispanic Origin	Population	%
Hispanic or Latino (of any race)	465	2.98
Central American, ex. Mexican	9	0.06
Guatemalan	3	0.02
Honduran	5	0.03
Salvadoran	1	0.01
Cuban	4	0.03
Dominican Republic	9	0.06
Mexican	358	2.29
Puerto Rican	16	0.10
South American	12	0.08
Argentinean	3	0.02
Colombian	3	0.02
Ecuadorian	1	0.01
Peruvian	2	0.01
Venezuelan	3	0.02
Other Hispanic or Latino	57	0.36

Race*	Population	%
African-American/Black (8,771)	8,928	57.16
Not Hispanic (8,736)	8,873	56.81
Hispanic (35)	55	0.35
American Indian/Alaska Native (42)	97	0.62
Not Hispanic (38)	89	0.57
Hispanic (4)	8	0.05
Canadian/French Am. Ind. (1)	1	0.01
Cherokee (3)	13	0.08
Chickasaw (0)	1	0.01
Choctaw (2)	6	0.04
Iroquois (0)	3	0.02
Asian (125)	147	0.94
Not Hispanic (125)	143	0.92
Hispanic (0)	4	0.03
Chinese, ex. Taiwanese (13)	14	0.09
Filipino (13)	20	0.13
Indian (48)	56	0.36
Japanese (16)	20	0.13
Korean (3)	3	0.02
Laotian (2)	2	0.01
Thai (4)	4	0.03
Vietnamese (25)	27	0.17
Hawaii Native/Pacific Islander (0)	4	0.03
Not Hispanic (0)	4	0.03
Guamanian/Chamorro (0)	1	0.01
White (6,216)	6,410	41.04
Not Hispanic (6,053)	6,211	39.76
Hispanic (163)	199	1.27

Bryant

Place Type: City
County: Saline
Population: 16,688†

Ancestry‡	Population	%
American (1,648)	1,648	10.46
Arab (184)	184	1.17
Arab (138)	138	0.88
Jordanian (46)	46	0.29
Austrian (0)	19	0.12
British (36)	93	0.59
Czech (0)	81	0.51
Czechoslovakian (52)	52	0.33
Dutch (101)	375	2.38
English (851)	1,736	11.02
European (437)	492	3.12
French, ex. Basque (259)	594	3.77
French Canadian (12)	12	0.08
German (824)	2,187	13.88
Greek (10)	10	0.06
Hungarian (0)	6	0.04
Irish (575)	1,984	12.59
Italian (155)	295	1.87
Norwegian (15)	26	0.17
Polish (84)	163	1.03
Portuguese (7)	7	0.04
Russian (0)	21	0.13
Scandinavian (36)	45	0.29
Scotch-Irish (200)	394	2.50
Scottish (132)	240	1.52
Serbian (16)	16	0.10
Swedish (13)	39	0.25
Swiss (18)	27	0.17
Turkish (98)	98	0.62
Welsh (25)	87	0.55
West Indian, ex. Hispanic (0)	18	0.11
Dutch West Indian (0)	18	0.11

Hispanic Origin	Population	%
Hispanic or Latino (of any race)	786	4.71
Central American, ex. Mexican	89	0.53
Costa Rican	12	0.07
Guatemalan	35	0.21
Honduran	20	0.12
Nicaraguan	1	0.01
Panamanian	2	0.01
Salvadoran	14	0.08
Other Central American	5	0.03
Cuban	7	0.04
Mexican	543	3.25
Puerto Rican	49	0.29
South American	26	0.16
Argentinean	6	0.04
Bolivian	3	0.02
Chilean	2	0.01
Colombian	7	0.04
Ecuadorian	1	0.01

*Notes: † The Census 2010 population figure is used to calculate the percentages in the Hispanic Origin and Race categories. Ancestry percentages are based on the 2006-2010 American Community Survey population (not shown); ‡ Numbers in parentheses indicate the number of people reporting a single ancestry; * Numbers in parentheses indicate the number of persons reporting this race alone, not in combination with any other race; Please refer to the Explanation of Data for more information.*

Peruvian	7	0.04
Other Hispanic or Latino	72	0.43

Race*	Population	%
African-American/Black (1,125)	1,213	7.27
Not Hispanic (1,120)	1,200	7.19
Hispanic (5)	13	0.08
American Indian/Alaska Native (75)	164	0.98
Not Hispanic (74)	156	0.93
Hispanic (1)	8	0.05
Apache (0)	6	0.04
Blackfeet (0)	3	0.02
Central American Ind. (1)	1	0.01
Cherokee (23)	68	0.41
Chickasaw (0)	1	0.01
Chippewa (0)	1	0.01
Choctaw (18)	24	0.14
Creek (1)	2	0.01
Delaware (1)	4	0.02
Houma (1)	1	0.01
Iroquois (7)	7	0.04
Osage (4)	9	0.05
Potawatomi (3)	3	0.02
Seminole (2)	2	0.01
Sioux (0)	1	0.01
Tlingit-Haida *(Alaska Native)* (1)	1	0.01
Asian (272)	351	2.10
Not Hispanic (267)	332	1.99
Hispanic (5)	19	0.11
Bangladeshi (1)	1	0.01
Burmese (3)	3	0.02
Chinese, ex. Taiwanese (35)	45	0.27
Filipino (26)	48	0.29
Indian (69)	70	0.42
Indonesian (3)	4	0.02
Japanese (9)	25	0.15
Korean (47)	55	0.33
Laotian (9)	9	0.05
Nepalese (2)	2	0.01
Pakistani (5)	8	0.05
Thai (6)	10	0.06
Vietnamese (48)	52	0.31
Hawaii Native/Pacific Islander (0)	3	0.02
Not Hispanic (0)	3	0.02
Native Hawaiian (0)	3	0.02
White (14,517)	14,753	88.40
Not Hispanic (14,199)	14,398	86.28
Hispanic (318)	355	2.13

Cabot

Place Type: City
County: Lonoke
Population: 23,776†

Ancestry‡	Population	%
American (3,483)	3,483	15.60
Arab (0)	7	0.03
Syrian (0)	7	0.03
Belgian (0)	42	0.19
British (62)	112	0.50
Celtic (9)	9	0.04
Croatian (23)	28	0.13
Czech (0)	95	0.43
Danish (7)	71	0.32
Dutch (76)	315	1.41
English (1,179)	2,839	12.71
European (456)	493	2.21
Finnish (12)	55	0.25
French, ex. Basque (124)	802	3.59
French Canadian (0)	35	0.16
German (1,192)	3,903	17.48
Greek (17)	63	0.28
Hungarian (11)	11	0.05
Irish (849)	3,318	14.86
Italian (252)	644	2.88
Lithuanian (9)	9	0.04
Norwegian (37)	125	0.56
Polish (159)	433	1.94
Romanian (11)	11	0.05
Russian (8)	45	0.20
Scandinavian (26)	26	0.12
Scotch-Irish (351)	946	4.24
Scottish (246)	464	2.08
Serbian (0)	35	0.16
Slavic (0)	10	0.04
Slovak (0)	13	0.06
Swedish (38)	207	0.93
Swiss (0)	16	0.07
Turkish (7)	7	0.03
Welsh (8)	106	0.47
West Indian, ex. Hispanic (0)	71	0.32
Dutch West Indian (0)	46	0.21
Jamaican (0)	25	0.11

Hispanic Origin	Population	%
Hispanic or Latino (of any race)	983	4.13
Central American, ex. Mexican	86	0.36
Costa Rican	5	0.02
Guatemalan	23	0.10
Honduran	10	0.04
Nicaraguan	14	0.06
Panamanian	12	0.05
Salvadoran	22	0.09
Cuban	20	0.08
Dominican Republic	2	0.01
Mexican	634	2.67
Puerto Rican	106	0.45
South American	28	0.12
Argentinean	7	0.03
Bolivian	1	<0.01
Chilean	3	0.01
Colombian	6	0.03
Ecuadorian	2	0.01
Peruvian	3	0.01
Venezuelan	4	0.02
Other South American	2	0.01
Other Hispanic or Latino	107	0.45

Race*	Population	%
African-American/Black (374)	498	2.09
Not Hispanic (366)	476	2.00
Hispanic (8)	22	0.09
American Indian/Alaska Native (131)	277	1.17
Not Hispanic (119)	237	1.00
Hispanic (12)	40	0.17
Alaska Athabascan *(Ala. Nat.)* (2)	2	0.01
Aleut *(Alaska Native)* (1)	1	<0.01
Apache (3)	12	0.05
Blackfeet (1)	4	0.02
Cherokee (41)	87	0.37
Cheyenne (0)	1	<0.01
Chickasaw (3)	7	0.03
Chippewa (5)	12	0.05
Choctaw (22)	29	0.12
Comanche (0)	1	<0.01
Creek (4)	6	0.03
Houma (3)	3	0.01
Inupiat *(Alaska Native)* (1)	1	<0.01
Iroquois (1)	1	<0.01
Lumbee (4)	9	0.04
Mexican American Ind. (1)	10	0.04
Navajo (1)	2	0.01
Potawatomi (2)	3	0.01
Puget Sound Salish (0)	1	<0.01
Seminole (0)	2	0.01
Sioux (1)	1	<0.01
Yakama (0)	1	<0.01
Yaqui (0)	1	<0.01
Asian (351)	540	2.27
Not Hispanic (347)	523	2.20
Hispanic (4)	17	0.07
Cambodian (3)	3	0.01
Chinese, ex. Taiwanese (34)	51	0.21
Filipino (110)	205	0.86
Indian (25)	35	0.15
Japanese (35)	68	0.29
Korean (38)	66	0.28
Laotian (4)	4	0.02
Malaysian (1)	1	<0.01
Pakistani (11)	14	0.06
Taiwanese (4)	4	0.02
Thai (17)	37	0.16
Vietnamese (43)	50	0.21
Hawaii Native/Pacific Islander (11)	43	0.18
Not Hispanic (11)	36	0.15
Hispanic (0)	7	0.03
Guamanian/Chamorro (2)	5	0.02
Native Hawaiian (7)	30	0.13
Samoan (0)	1	<0.01
White (22,137)	22,622	95.15
Not Hispanic (21,534)	21,920	92.19
Hispanic (603)	702	2.95

Camden

Place Type: City
County: Ouachita
Population: 12,183†

Ancestry‡	Population	%
African, Sub-Saharan (43)	55	0.45
African (43)	55	0.45
American (755)	755	6.17
Arab (0)	51	0.42
Lebanese (0)	51	0.42
British (14)	14	0.11
Canadian (0)	6	0.05
Czechoslovakian (7)	7	0.06
Danish (0)	15	0.12
Dutch (36)	83	0.68
English (492)	840	6.86
European (51)	51	0.42
French, ex. Basque (38)	211	1.72
German (255)	686	5.60
Irish (368)	929	7.59
Italian (188)	254	2.07
Scotch-Irish (159)	335	2.74
Scottish (84)	207	1.69
Swedish (0)	6	0.05
Swiss (0)	8	0.07
Welsh (0)	14	0.11

Hispanic Origin	Population	%
Hispanic or Latino (of any race)	192	1.58
Central American, ex. Mexican	10	0.08
Guatemalan	4	0.03
Panamanian	1	0.01
Other Central American	5	0.04
Cuban	4	0.03
Dominican Republic	1	0.01
Mexican	136	1.12
Puerto Rican	7	0.06
South American	2	0.02
Ecuadorian	2	0.02
Other Hispanic or Latino	32	0.26

Race*	Population	%
African-American/Black (6,828)	7,005	57.50
Not Hispanic (6,805)	6,965	57.17
Hispanic (23)	40	0.33
American Indian/Alaska Native (38)	104	0.85
Not Hispanic (35)	93	0.76
Hispanic (3)	11	0.09
Apache (3)	3	0.02
Blackfeet (2)	3	0.02
Cherokee (5)	23	0.19
Cheyenne (0)	3	0.02
Choctaw (1)	3	0.02
Creek (1)	2	0.02
Iroquois (0)	3	0.02
Navajo (0)	1	0.01
Potawatomi (3)	3	0.02
Sioux (0)	5	0.04
Asian (62)	76	0.62
Not Hispanic (62)	76	0.62
Cambodian (4)	4	0.03
Chinese, ex. Taiwanese (14)	19	0.16
Filipino (9)	14	0.11
Indian (14)	17	0.14

*Notes: † The Census 2010 population figure is used to calculate the percentages in the Hispanic Origin and Race categories. Ancestry percentages are based on the 2006-2010 American Community Survey population (not shown); ‡ Numbers in parentheses indicate the number of people reporting a single ancestry; * Numbers in parentheses indicate the number of persons reporting this race alone, not in combination with any other race; Please refer to the Explanation of Data for more information.*

Japanese (3)	3	0.02
Korean (5)	6	0.05
Pakistani (1)	2	0.02
Thai (2)	3	0.02
Vietnamese (9)	13	0.11
Hawaii Native/Pacific Islander (4)	9	0.07
Not Hispanic (2)	7	0.06
Hispanic (2)	2	0.02
Samoan (3)	5	0.04
White (4,957)	5,138	42.17
Not Hispanic (4,876)	5,044	41.40
Hispanic (81)	94	0.77

Centerton

Place Type: City
County: Benton
Population: 9,515†

Ancestry‡	Population	%
African, Sub-Saharan (111)	111	1.34
African (87)	87	1.05
Nigerian (24)	24	0.29
American (455)	455	5.47
Austrian (0)	10	0.12
British (72)	100	1.20
Czech (0)	14	0.17
Dutch (48)	163	1.96
English (274)	727	8.74
European (137)	147	1.77
Finnish (0)	46	0.55
French, ex. Basque (108)	241	2.90
German (496)	1,323	15.91
Greek (0)	28	0.34
Irish (168)	532	6.40
Italian (128)	465	5.59
Lithuanian (6)	6	0.07
Norwegian (25)	59	0.71
Polish (10)	110	1.32
Russian (0)	43	0.52
Scandinavian (0)	57	0.69
Scotch-Irish (16)	73	0.88
Scottish (0)	208	2.50
Ukrainian (10)	10	0.12
Welsh (24)	70	0.84

Hispanic Origin	Population	%
Hispanic or Latino (of any race)	1,161	12.20
Central American, ex. Mexican	219	2.30
Costa Rican	1	0.01
Guatemalan	24	0.25
Honduran	4	0.04
Nicaraguan	9	0.09
Panamanian	5	0.05
Salvadoran	176	1.85
Cuban	18	0.19
Dominican Republic	5	0.05
Mexican	749	7.87
Puerto Rican	56	0.59
South American	20	0.21
Argentinean	1	0.01
Chilean	1	0.01
Colombian	11	0.12
Paraguayan	2	0.02
Peruvian	4	0.04
Venezuelan	1	0.01
Other Hispanic or Latino	94	0.99

Race*	Population	%
African-American/Black (339)	396	4.16
Not Hispanic (334)	382	4.01
Hispanic (5)	14	0.15
American Indian/Alaska Native (115)	217	2.28
Not Hispanic (105)	195	2.05
Hispanic (10)	22	0.23
Apache (1)	1	0.01
Canadian/French Am. Ind. (0)	1	0.01
Central American Ind. (0)	1	0.01
Cherokee (40)	77	0.81
Chickasaw (1)	1	0.01
Chippewa (0)	2	0.02
Choctaw (24)	30	0.32
Creek (3)	8	0.08
Iroquois (0)	3	0.03
Menominee (0)	1	0.01
Mexican American Ind. (5)	5	0.05
Osage (5)	5	0.05
Ottawa (3)	3	0.03
Potawatomi (3)	6	0.06
Pueblo (1)	1	0.01
Puget Sound Salish (0)	5	0.05
Seminole (0)	1	0.01
Sioux (1)	5	0.05
Yup'ik *(Alaska Native)* (0)	2	0.02
Asian (218)	283	2.97
Not Hispanic (218)	280	2.94
Hispanic (0)	3	0.03
Cambodian (5)	7	0.07
Chinese, ex. Taiwanese (20)	25	0.26
Filipino (19)	26	0.27
Hmong (40)	41	0.43
Indian (42)	54	0.57
Indonesian (2)	2	0.02
Japanese (5)	15	0.16
Korean (9)	21	0.22
Laotian (14)	18	0.19
Pakistani (1)	1	0.01
Taiwanese (2)	6	0.06
Thai (1)	3	0.03
Vietnamese (45)	52	0.55
Hawaii Native/Pacific Islander (8)	20	0.21
Not Hispanic (8)	20	0.21
Guamanian/Chamorro (8)	9	0.09
Native Hawaiian (0)	5	0.05
White (7,995)	8,224	86.43
Not Hispanic (7,487)	7,673	80.64
Hispanic (508)	551	5.79

Clarksville

Place Type: City
County: Johnson
Population: 9,178†

Ancestry‡	Population	%
African, Sub-Saharan (0)	65	0.72
Ethiopian (0)	65	0.72
American (1,738)	1,738	19.30
British (31)	37	0.41
Canadian (0)	10	0.11
Danish (6)	6	0.07
Dutch (0)	46	0.51
English (323)	684	7.60
European (95)	112	1.24
French, ex. Basque (35)	131	1.45
German (408)	1,107	12.29
Hungarian (46)	52	0.58
Irish (512)	1,019	11.32
Italian (0)	91	1.01
Northern European (18)	18	0.20
Norwegian (6)	23	0.26
Polish (33)	63	0.70
Russian (0)	11	0.12
Scotch-Irish (78)	133	1.48
Scottish (42)	155	1.72
Slovak (0)	5	0.06
Swedish (0)	28	0.31
Welsh (18)	87	0.97
West Indian, ex. Hispanic (0)	10	0.11
Dutch West Indian (0)	10	0.11

Hispanic Origin	Population	%
Hispanic or Latino (of any race)	2,359	25.70
Central American, ex. Mexican	70	0.76
Costa Rican	6	0.07
Guatemalan	12	0.13
Honduran	19	0.21
Nicaraguan	7	0.08
Panamanian	3	0.03
Salvadoran	23	0.25
Cuban	33	0.36
Dominican Republic	1	0.01
Mexican	2,074	22.60
Puerto Rican	15	0.16
South American	9	0.10
Chilean	2	0.02
Colombian	1	0.01
Ecuadorian	1	0.01
Peruvian	4	0.04
Venezuelan	1	0.01
Other Hispanic or Latino	157	1.71

Race*	Population	%
African-American/Black (273)	321	3.50
Not Hispanic (257)	290	3.16
Hispanic (16)	31	0.34
American Indian/Alaska Native (77)	144	1.57
Not Hispanic (62)	123	1.34
Hispanic (15)	21	0.23
Apache (2)	2	0.02
Blackfeet (0)	2	0.02
Cherokee (27)	56	0.61
Choctaw (6)	13	0.14
Creek (7)	7	0.08
Iroquois (1)	2	0.02
Mexican American Ind. (0)	1	0.01
Osage (2)	2	0.02
Potawatomi (0)	3	0.03
Sioux (0)	2	0.02
Asian (87)	124	1.35
Not Hispanic (87)	113	1.23
Hispanic (0)	11	0.12
Cambodian (8)	8	0.09
Chinese, ex. Taiwanese (31)	34	0.37
Filipino (6)	19	0.21
Hmong (10)	11	0.12
Indian (16)	17	0.19
Japanese (3)	9	0.10
Korean (5)	7	0.08
Malaysian (4)	4	0.04
Thai (2)	2	0.02
Hawaii Native/Pacific Islander (13)	21	0.23
Not Hispanic (12)	17	0.19
Hispanic (1)	4	0.04
Guamanian/Chamorro (0)	1	0.01
Marshallese (3)	7	0.08
Native Hawaiian (6)	6	0.07
Samoan (1)	1	0.01
White (6,932)	7,089	77.24
Not Hispanic (6,276)	6,381	69.52
Hispanic (656)	708	7.71

Conway

Place Type: City
County: Faulkner
Population: 58,908†

Ancestry‡	Population	%
African, Sub-Saharan (1,058)	1,058	1.88
African (943)	943	1.68
Other Sub-Saharan African (115)	115	0.20
American (4,916)	4,916	8.74
Arab (0)	16	0.03
Lebanese (0)	16	0.03
Armenian (0)	14	0.02
Assyrian/Chaldean/Syriac (31)	31	0.06
Australian (0)	35	0.06
Austrian (28)	49	0.09
Belgian (27)	27	0.05
British (174)	315	0.56
Canadian (51)	51	0.09
Celtic (14)	14	0.02
Croatian (10)	50	0.09
Czech (21)	184	0.33
Czechoslovakian (19)	19	0.03
Danish (103)	335	0.60
Dutch (156)	680	1.21
Eastern European (14)	14	0.02
English (2,670)	6,588	11.71

*Notes: † The Census 2010 population figure is used to calculate the percentages in the Hispanic Origin and Race categories. Ancestry percentages are based on the 2006-2010 American Community Survey population (not shown); ‡ Numbers in parentheses indicate the number of people reporting a single ancestry; * Numbers in parentheses indicate the number of persons reporting this race alone, not in combination with any other race; Please refer to the Explanation of Data for more information.*

European (1,187)	1,332	2.37
French, ex. Basque (238)	1,825	3.24
French Canadian (62)	91	0.16
German (3,147)	9,183	16.32
Greek (6)	57	0.10
Hungarian (0)	118	0.21
Icelander (39)	39	0.07
Irish (2,947)	8,000	14.22
Italian (630)	1,317	2.34
Lithuanian (0)	11	0.02
Northern European (27)	27	0.05
Norwegian (104)	526	0.94
Polish (251)	957	1.70
Portuguese (33)	33	0.06
Romanian (36)	121	0.22
Russian (92)	249	0.44
Scandinavian (0)	83	0.15
Scotch-Irish (837)	1,346	2.39
Scottish (553)	1,480	2.63
Serbian (30)	30	0.05
Slavic (0)	12	0.02
Slovak (27)	27	0.05
Swedish (160)	622	1.11
Swiss (18)	387	0.69
Turkish (12)	12	0.02
Ukrainian (0)	15	0.03
Welsh (141)	331	0.59
West Indian, ex. Hispanic (35)	63	0.11
Dutch West Indian (0)	14	0.02
Jamaican (35)	35	0.06
Trinidadian/Tobagonian (0)	14	0.02
Yugoslavian (28)	34	0.06

Hispanic Origin	Population	%
Hispanic or Latino (of any race)	2,998	5.09
Central American, ex. Mexican	315	0.53
Costa Rican	4	0.01
Guatemalan	101	0.17
Honduran	91	0.15
Nicaraguan	14	0.02
Panamanian	12	0.02
Salvadoran	88	0.15
Other Central American	5	0.01
Cuban	44	0.07
Dominican Republic	5	0.01
Mexican	2,129	3.61
Puerto Rican	110	0.19
South American	88	0.15
Argentinean	9	0.02
Bolivian	9	0.02
Chilean	2	<0.01
Colombian	22	0.04
Ecuadorian	4	0.01
Peruvian	20	0.03
Venezuelan	22	0.04
Other Hispanic or Latino	307	0.52

Race*	Population	%
African-American/Black (9,177)	9,766	16.58
Not Hispanic (9,112)	9,661	16.40
Hispanic (65)	105	0.18
American Indian/Alaska Native (260)	632	1.07
Not Hispanic (243)	587	1.00
Hispanic (17)	45	0.08
Alaska Athabascan *(Ala. Nat.)* (3)	3	0.01
Apache (1)	10	0.02
Blackfeet (4)	13	0.02
Central American Ind. (1)	1	<0.01
Cherokee (72)	216	0.37
Cheyenne (0)	2	<0.01
Chickasaw (2)	7	0.01
Chippewa (2)	2	<0.01
Choctaw (26)	50	0.08
Comanche (1)	2	<0.01
Cree (1)	2	<0.01
Creek (5)	22	0.04
Crow (0)	1	<0.01
Hopi (0)	1	<0.01
Inupiat *(Alaska Native)* (1)	1	<0.01
Iroquois (1)	6	0.01
Kiowa (2)	4	0.01
Lumbee (0)	1	<0.01
Mexican American Ind. (2)	6	0.01
Navajo (1)	4	0.01
Osage (7)	13	0.02
Ottawa (2)	3	0.01
Potawatomi (9)	9	0.02
Seminole (2)	6	0.01
Shoshone (1)	1	<0.01
Sioux (6)	17	0.03
Tlingit-Haida *(Alaska Native)* (1)	2	<0.01
Ute (1)	3	0.01
Yaqui (0)	1	<0.01
Yuman (1)	1	<0.01
Asian (1,120)	1,428	2.42
Not Hispanic (1,113)	1,409	2.39
Hispanic (7)	19	0.03
Bangladeshi (8)	11	0.02
Burmese (6)	6	0.01
Cambodian (16)	17	0.03
Chinese, ex. Taiwanese (339)	378	0.64
Filipino (76)	145	0.25
Hmong (4)	4	0.01
Indian (228)	253	0.43
Indonesian (2)	2	<0.01
Japanese (86)	124	0.21
Korean (85)	115	0.20
Laotian (8)	12	0.02
Malaysian (8)	11	0.02
Nepalese (4)	4	0.01
Pakistani (41)	49	0.08
Sri Lankan (0)	1	<0.01
Taiwanese (34)	34	0.06
Thai (7)	15	0.03
Vietnamese (113)	124	0.21
Hawaii Native/Pacific Islander (32)	157	0.27
Not Hispanic (28)	148	0.25
Hispanic (4)	9	0.02
Guamanian/Chamorro (3)	6	0.01
Native Hawaiian (9)	29	0.05
Samoan (4)	6	0.01
Tongan (1)	3	0.01
White (45,610)	46,708	79.29
Not Hispanic (44,223)	45,144	76.63
Hispanic (1,387)	1,564	2.65

El Dorado

Place Type: City
County: Union
Population: 18,884†

Ancestry‡	Population	%
African, Sub-Saharan (81)	94	0.49
African (81)	94	0.49
American (1,619)	1,619	8.40
Brazilian (9)	9	0.05
Cajun (5)	5	0.03
Danish (11)	11	0.06
Dutch (27)	108	0.56
English (664)	1,237	6.42
European (118)	129	0.67
French, ex. Basque (82)	248	1.29
French Canadian (24)	60	0.31
German (244)	715	3.71
Irish (626)	1,347	6.99
Italian (49)	175	0.91
Norwegian (0)	25	0.13
Polish (9)	65	0.34
Portuguese (0)	11	0.06
Russian (10)	10	0.05
Scandinavian (0)	36	0.19
Scotch-Irish (305)	508	2.64
Scottish (133)	297	1.54
Swedish (29)	29	0.15
Swiss (6)	37	0.19
Ukrainian (7)	7	0.04
Welsh (14)	103	0.53
West Indian, ex. Hispanic (7)	7	0.04
Trinidadian/Tobagonian (7)	7	0.04

Hispanic Origin	Population	%
Hispanic or Latino (of any race)	809	4.28
Central American, ex. Mexican	72	0.38
Guatemalan	31	0.16
Honduran	14	0.07
Nicaraguan	16	0.08
Panamanian	1	0.01
Salvadoran	9	0.05
Other Central American	1	0.01
Cuban	2	0.01
Dominican Republic	7	0.04
Mexican	656	3.47
Puerto Rican	15	0.08
South American	17	0.09
Argentinean	7	0.04
Colombian	1	0.01
Peruvian	3	0.02
Venezuelan	5	0.03
Other South American	1	0.01
Other Hispanic or Latino	40	0.21

Race*	Population	%
African-American/Black (9,417)	9,554	50.59
Not Hispanic (9,385)	9,509	50.35
Hispanic (32)	45	0.24
American Indian/Alaska Native (56)	156	0.83
Not Hispanic (48)	135	0.71
Hispanic (8)	21	0.11
Alaska Athabascan *(Ala. Nat.)* (1)	1	0.01
Apache (3)	3	0.02
Blackfeet (2)	5	0.03
Central American Ind. (1)	2	0.01
Cherokee (17)	50	0.26
Chickasaw (1)	4	0.02
Choctaw (1)	8	0.04
Mexican American Ind. (0)	8	0.04
Potawatomi (1)	4	0.02
Sioux (1)	2	0.01
South American Ind. (3)	3	0.02
Asian (160)	187	0.99
Not Hispanic (156)	181	0.96
Hispanic (4)	6	0.03
Cambodian (5)	5	0.03
Chinese, ex. Taiwanese (31)	34	0.18
Filipino (34)	38	0.20
Indian (52)	56	0.30
Japanese (3)	7	0.04
Korean (10)	11	0.06
Pakistani (5)	6	0.03
Thai (2)	4	0.02
Vietnamese (11)	15	0.08
Hawaii Native/Pacific Islander (5)	15	0.08
Not Hispanic (5)	13	0.07
Hispanic (0)	2	0.01
Guamanian/Chamorro (2)	4	0.02
Native Hawaiian (3)	3	0.02
Samoan (0)	2	0.01
White (8,522)	8,731	46.23
Not Hispanic (8,260)	8,434	44.66
Hispanic (262)	297	1.57

Fayetteville

Place Type: City
County: Washington
Population: 73,580†

Ancestry‡	Population	%
African, Sub-Saharan (146)	205	0.29
African (49)	58	0.08
Ethiopian (12)	12	0.02
Ghanaian (58)	58	0.08
Kenyan (18)	18	0.03
Nigerian (0)	15	0.02
Somalian (0)	35	0.05
Other Sub-Saharan African (9)	9	0.01
American (4,740)	4,740	6.60
Arab (142)	308	0.43
Arab (30)	30	0.04
Iraqi (48)	67	0.09

*Notes: † The Census 2010 population figure is used to calculate the percentages in the Hispanic Origin and Race categories. Ancestry percentages are based on the 2006-2010 American Community Survey population (not shown); ‡ Numbers in parentheses indicate the number of people reporting a single ancestry; * Numbers in parentheses indicate the number of persons reporting this race alone, not in combination with any other race; Please refer to the Explanation of Data for more information.*

Lebanese (0)	130	0.18
Syrian (26)	43	0.06
Other Arab (38)	38	0.05
Armenian (0)	31	0.04
Austrian (20)	114	0.16
Basque (213)	213	0.30
Belgian (0)	12	0.02
British (198)	524	0.73
Bulgarian (10)	10	0.01
Cajun (64)	64	0.09
Canadian (16)	43	0.06
Croatian (0)	13	0.02
Czech (10)	252	0.35
Czechoslovakian (108)	115	0.16
Danish (112)	382	0.53
Dutch (528)	1,626	2.27
Eastern European (31)	31	0.04
English (3,973)	9,475	13.20
European (921)	1,141	1.59
Finnish (53)	119	0.17
French, ex. Basque (677)	2,589	3.61
French Canadian (58)	100	0.14
German (4,216)	13,081	18.23
Greek (169)	258	0.36
Hungarian (43)	92	0.13
Iranian (45)	90	0.13
Irish (4,248)	11,418	15.91
Italian (917)	2,380	3.32
Latvian (35)	35	0.05
Lithuanian (0)	14	0.02
Luxemburger (0)	9	0.01
Northern European (119)	133	0.19
Norwegian (219)	683	0.95
Pennsylvania German (0)	13	0.02
Polish (337)	1,167	1.63
Portuguese (12)	51	0.07
Romanian (0)	26	0.04
Russian (131)	305	0.42
Scandinavian (66)	292	0.41
Scotch-Irish (886)	2,102	2.93
Scottish (1,180)	2,682	3.74
Serbian (8)	8	0.01
Slavic (12)	12	0.02
Slovak (53)	154	0.21
Slovene (14)	14	0.02
Swedish (450)	919	1.28
Swiss (49)	359	0.50
Ukrainian (6)	6	0.01
Welsh (75)	466	0.65
West Indian, ex. Hispanic (34)	141	0.20
Bermudan (12)	12	0.02
Dutch West Indian (0)	79	0.11
Haitian (0)	9	0.01
Jamaican (22)	41	0.06
Yugoslavian (34)	67	0.09

Hispanic Origin	Population	%
Hispanic or Latino (of any race)	4,725	6.42
Central American, ex. Mexican	366	0.50
Costa Rican	26	0.04
Guatemalan	48	0.07
Honduran	43	0.06
Nicaraguan	30	0.04
Panamanian	31	0.04
Salvadoran	187	0.25
Other Central American	1	<0.01
Cuban	49	0.07
Dominican Republic	16	0.02
Mexican	3,204	4.35
Puerto Rican	199	0.27
South American	365	0.50
Argentinean	33	0.04
Bolivian	107	0.15
Chilean	27	0.04
Colombian	101	0.14
Ecuadorian	22	0.03
Peruvian	46	0.06
Uruguayan	3	<0.01
Venezuelan	26	0.04
Other Hispanic or Latino	526	0.71

Race*	Population	%
African-American/Black (4,379)	5,145	6.99
Not Hispanic (4,301)	5,008	6.81
Hispanic (78)	137	0.19
American Indian/Alaska Native (785)	1,674	2.28
Not Hispanic (734)	1,559	2.12
Hispanic (51)	115	0.16
Alaska Athabascan *(Ala. Nat.)* (3)	3	<0.01
Apache (8)	19	0.03
Blackfeet (2)	16	0.02
Canadian/French Am. Ind. (1)	1	<0.01
Central American Ind. (2)	6	0.01
Cherokee (328)	750	1.02
Cheyenne (2)	2	<0.01
Chickasaw (19)	36	0.05
Chippewa (9)	12	0.02
Choctaw (72)	152	0.21
Colville (0)	1	<0.01
Comanche (0)	8	0.01
Cree (0)	3	<0.01
Creek (25)	46	0.06
Crow (0)	3	<0.01
Delaware (3)	7	0.01
Hopi (1)	1	<0.01
Inupiat *(Alaska Native)* (1)	3	<0.01
Iroquois (7)	12	0.02
Kiowa (2)	3	<0.01
Lumbee (0)	1	<0.01
Menominee (1)	2	<0.01
Mexican American Ind. (11)	14	0.02
Navajo (7)	21	0.03
Osage (17)	40	0.05
Ottawa (3)	3	<0.01
Paiute (2)	2	<0.01
Pima (1)	2	<0.01
Potawatomi (9)	14	0.02
Pueblo (0)	2	<0.01
Seminole (0)	9	0.01
Sioux (7)	19	0.03
South American Ind. (2)	3	<0.01
Tlingit-Haida *(Alaska Native)* (1)	2	<0.01
Ute (2)	2	<0.01
Yakama (0)	1	<0.01
Yaqui (5)	12	0.02
Yuman (1)	1	<0.01
Asian (2,267)	2,787	3.79
Not Hispanic (2,255)	2,732	3.71
Hispanic (12)	55	0.07
Bangladeshi (36)	38	0.05
Burmese (5)	5	0.01
Cambodian (8)	10	0.01
Chinese, ex. Taiwanese (600)	671	0.91
Filipino (161)	290	0.39
Hmong (43)	46	0.06
Indian (445)	498	0.68
Indonesian (35)	44	0.06
Japanese (115)	181	0.25
Korean (226)	278	0.38
Laotian (84)	112	0.15
Malaysian (22)	33	0.04
Nepalese (22)	23	0.03
Pakistani (22)	25	0.03
Sri Lankan (19)	23	0.03
Taiwanese (43)	46	0.06
Thai (25)	44	0.06
Vietnamese (243)	279	0.38
Hawaii Native/Pacific Islander (172)	255	0.35
Not Hispanic (155)	216	0.29
Hispanic (17)	39	0.05
Fijian (1)	7	0.01
Guamanian/Chamorro (9)	29	0.04
Marshallese (98)	103	0.14
Native Hawaiian (15)	40	0.05
Samoan (14)	21	0.03
Tongan (4)	13	0.02
White (61,661)	63,780	86.68
Not Hispanic (59,398)	61,220	83.20
Hispanic (2,263)	2,560	3.48

Forrest City

Place Type: City
County: St. Francis
Population: 15,371†

Ancestry‡	Population	%
African, Sub-Saharan (229)	229	1.51
African (201)	201	1.32
Ethiopian (14)	14	0.09
Nigerian (14)	14	0.09
American (1,049)	1,049	6.91
Austrian (0)	15	0.10
Dutch (12)	96	0.63
English (276)	478	3.15
European (54)	54	0.36
Finnish (29)	29	0.19
French, ex. Basque (28)	150	0.99
German (141)	506	3.33
Irish (100)	408	2.69
Israeli (0)	13	0.09
Italian (22)	82	0.54
Norwegian (0)	13	0.09
Pennsylvania German (14)	14	0.09
Portuguese (14)	14	0.09
Romanian (0)	9	0.06
Scotch-Irish (70)	162	1.07
Scottish (61)	110	0.72
Welsh (13)	13	0.09
West Indian, ex. Hispanic (48)	84	0.55
Barbadian (48)	48	0.32
Jamaican (0)	36	0.24

Hispanic Origin	Population	%
Hispanic or Latino (of any race)	912	5.93
Central American, ex. Mexican	30	0.20
Guatemalan	6	0.04
Honduran	7	0.05
Nicaraguan	4	0.03
Panamanian	6	0.04
Salvadoran	7	0.05
Cuban	38	0.25
Dominican Republic	6	0.04
Mexican	680	4.42
Puerto Rican	66	0.43
South American	28	0.18
Chilean	1	0.01
Colombian	23	0.15
Ecuadorian	1	0.01
Uruguayan	1	0.01
Venezuelan	2	0.01
Other Hispanic or Latino	64	0.42

Race*	Population	%
African-American/Black (10,350)	10,511	68.38
Not Hispanic (10,264)	10,399	67.65
Hispanic (86)	112	0.73
American Indian/Alaska Native (107)	171	1.11
Not Hispanic (88)	137	0.89
Hispanic (19)	34	0.22
Apache (5)	8	0.05
Blackfeet (0)	3	0.02
Cherokee (22)	41	0.27
Chickasaw (3)	3	0.02
Chippewa (2)	2	0.01
Choctaw (9)	17	0.11
Mexican American Ind. (8)	11	0.07
Navajo (3)	3	0.02
Osage (0)	2	0.01
Shoshone (2)	2	0.01
Sioux (12)	13	0.08
South American Ind. (0)	1	0.01
Spanish American Ind. (0)	1	0.01
Yaqui (0)	1	0.01
Asian (101)	138	0.90
Not Hispanic (98)	129	0.84
Hispanic (3)	9	0.06
Cambodian (6)	6	0.04
Chinese, ex. Taiwanese (17)	21	0.14
Filipino (11)	16	0.10

*Notes: † The Census 2010 population figure is used to calculate the percentages in the Hispanic Origin and Race categories. Ancestry percentages are based on the 2006-2010 American Community Survey population (not shown); ‡ Numbers in parentheses indicate the number of people reporting a single ancestry; * Numbers in parentheses indicate the number of persons reporting this race alone, not in combination with any other race; Please refer to the Explanation of Data for more information.*

Indian (20)	24	0.16
Japanese (6)	10	0.07
Korean (8)	12	0.08
Laotian (10)	10	0.07
Pakistani (0)	2	0.01
Taiwanese (1)	1	0.01
Thai (1)	2	0.01
Vietnamese (13)	14	0.09
Hawaii Native/Pacific Islander (7)	28	0.18
Not Hispanic (7)	23	0.15
Hispanic (0)	5	0.03
Guamanian/Chamorro (1)	1	0.01
Native Hawaiian (6)	14	0.09
Samoan (0)	2	0.01
White (4,244)	4,420	28.76
Not Hispanic (3,821)	3,942	25.65
Hispanic (423)	478	3.11

Fort Smith

Place Type: City
County: Sebastian
Population: 86,209†

Ancestry‡	Population	%
African, Sub-Saharan (61)	67	0.08
African (47)	53	0.06
Nigerian (14)	14	0.02
American (6,521)	6,521	7.65
Arab (94)	166	0.19
Arab (64)	64	0.08
Lebanese (30)	30	0.04
Syrian (0)	26	0.03
Other Arab (0)	46	0.05
Australian (6)	13	0.02
Austrian (17)	80	0.09
Belgian (26)	34	0.04
British (94)	159	0.19
Canadian (92)	92	0.11
Celtic (0)	15	0.02
Croatian (0)	12	0.01
Czech (29)	181	0.21
Czechoslovakian (58)	95	0.11
Danish (12)	70	0.08
Dutch (112)	1,577	1.85
English (2,948)	10,035	11.78
European (351)	479	0.56
Finnish (0)	47	0.06
French, ex. Basque (221)	1,828	2.15
French Canadian (123)	186	0.22
German (3,696)	10,096	11.85
Greek (41)	149	0.17
Hungarian (72)	325	0.38
Iranian (17)	67	0.08
Irish (2,443)	10,564	12.40
Italian (400)	1,690	1.98
Lithuanian (0)	41	0.05
Luxemburger (0)	28	0.03
Northern European (101)	101	0.12
Norwegian (109)	275	0.32
Polish (112)	480	0.56
Portuguese (42)	78	0.09
Romanian (46)	46	0.05
Russian (61)	178	0.21
Scandinavian (116)	116	0.14
Scotch-Irish (633)	1,644	1.93
Scottish (331)	1,281	1.50
Slavic (57)	94	0.11
Slovak (0)	18	0.02
Swedish (65)	386	0.45
Swiss (0)	201	0.24
Ukrainian (3)	26	0.03
Welsh (79)	393	0.46
West Indian, ex. Hispanic (78)	233	0.27
British West Indian (26)	26	0.03
Dutch West Indian (25)	156	0.18
Jamaican (27)	51	0.06
Yugoslavian (0)	14	0.02

Hispanic Origin	Population	%
Hispanic or Latino (of any race)	14,190	16.46
Central American, ex. Mexican	2,444	2.83
Costa Rican	11	0.01
Guatemalan	367	0.43
Honduran	174	0.20
Nicaraguan	19	0.02
Panamanian	6	0.01
Salvadoran	1,855	2.15
Other Central American	12	0.01
Cuban	129	0.15
Dominican Republic	23	0.03
Mexican	10,032	11.64
Puerto Rican	246	0.29
South American	152	0.18
Argentinean	1	<0.01
Bolivian	4	<0.01
Chilean	4	<0.01
Colombian	46	0.05
Ecuadorian	6	0.01
Paraguayan	1	<0.01
Peruvian	76	0.09
Uruguayan	6	0.01
Venezuelan	5	0.01
Other South American	3	<0.01
Other Hispanic or Latino	1,164	1.35

Race*	Population	%
African-American/Black (7,789)	9,042	10.49
Not Hispanic (7,621)	8,739	10.14
Hispanic (168)	303	0.35
American Indian/Alaska Native (1,555)	3,037	3.52
Not Hispanic (1,408)	2,727	3.16
Hispanic (147)	310	0.36
Alaska Athabascan *(Ala. Nat.)* (2)	5	0.01
Aleut *(Alaska Native)* (2)	2	<0.01
Apache (15)	29	0.03
Arapaho (2)	7	0.01
Blackfeet (4)	21	0.02
Canadian/French Am. Ind. (0)	2	<0.01
Central American Ind. (7)	10	0.01
Cherokee (645)	1,370	1.59
Cheyenne (7)	14	0.02
Chickasaw (14)	39	0.05
Chippewa (6)	8	0.01
Choctaw (299)	535	0.62
Comanche (2)	3	<0.01
Cree (1)	1	<0.01
Creek (36)	63	0.07
Delaware (2)	5	0.01
Hopi (0)	1	<0.01
Inupiat *(Alaska Native)* (0)	4	<0.01
Iroquois (5)	11	0.01
Kiowa (8)	10	0.01
Mexican American Ind. (49)	66	0.08
Navajo (4)	12	0.01
Osage (5)	9	0.01
Ottawa (2)	4	<0.01
Paiute (1)	3	<0.01
Potawatomi (4)	5	0.01
Pueblo (0)	3	<0.01
Seminole (7)	15	0.02
Sioux (2)	20	0.02
South American Ind. (1)	1	<0.01
Spanish American Ind. (1)	2	<0.01
Tlingit-Haida *(Alaska Native)* (1)	2	<0.01
Asian (4,578)	5,167	5.99
Not Hispanic (4,524)	5,026	5.83
Hispanic (54)	141	0.16
Burmese (3)	4	<0.01
Cambodian (8)	14	0.02
Chinese, ex. Taiwanese (108)	179	0.21
Filipino (180)	292	0.34
Hmong (71)	75	0.09
Indian (254)	361	0.42
Indonesian (16)	18	0.02
Japanese (40)	111	0.13
Korean (53)	98	0.11
Laotian (1,501)	1,726	2.00
Malaysian (0)	3	<0.01
Nepalese (4)	4	<0.01
Pakistani (44)	45	0.05
Taiwanese (5)	9	0.01
Thai (58)	79	0.09
Vietnamese (1,917)	2,124	2.46
Hawaii Native/Pacific Islander (96)	180	0.21
Not Hispanic (59)	107	0.12
Hispanic (37)	73	0.08
Guamanian/Chamorro (37)	47	0.05
Marshallese (9)	9	0.01
Native Hawaiian (28)	58	0.07
Samoan (6)	8	0.01
White (59,724)	62,888	72.95
Not Hispanic (55,654)	58,082	67.37
Hispanic (4,070)	4,806	5.57

Greenwood

Place Type: City
County: Sebastian
Population: 8,952†

Ancestry‡	Population	%
American (980)	980	11.35
Arab (0)	43	0.50
Syrian (0)	43	0.50
British (0)	40	0.46
Czech (0)	16	0.19
Czechoslovakian (22)	22	0.25
Danish (19)	33	0.38
Dutch (38)	237	2.74
English (231)	1,338	15.50
European (84)	84	0.97
French, ex. Basque (45)	177	2.05
French Canadian (0)	11	0.13
German (346)	1,181	13.68
Hungarian (16)	16	0.19
Irish (308)	1,449	16.78
Italian (57)	77	0.89
Norwegian (9)	17	0.20
Polish (0)	48	0.56
Russian (0)	14	0.16
Scandinavian (16)	16	0.19
Scotch-Irish (91)	104	1.20
Scottish (22)	112	1.30
Swedish (23)	38	0.44
Swiss (0)	29	0.34
West Indian, ex. Hispanic (0)	15	0.17
Dutch West Indian (0)	15	0.17

Hispanic Origin	Population	%
Hispanic or Latino (of any race)	315	3.52
Central American, ex. Mexican	20	0.22
Guatemalan	3	0.03
Honduran	5	0.06
Nicaraguan	1	0.01
Panamanian	3	0.03
Salvadoran	8	0.09
Cuban	2	0.02
Mexican	233	2.60
Puerto Rican	19	0.21
South American	8	0.09
Colombian	5	0.06
Peruvian	1	0.01
Venezuelan	2	0.02
Other Hispanic or Latino	33	0.37

Race*	Population	%
African-American/Black (24)	44	0.49
Not Hispanic (23)	40	0.45
Hispanic (1)	4	0.04
American Indian/Alaska Native (231)	346	3.87
Not Hispanic (217)	322	3.60
Hispanic (14)	24	0.27
Apache (1)	3	0.03
Blackfeet (1)	4	0.04
Cherokee (92)	162	1.81
Cheyenne (6)	6	0.07
Chickasaw (8)	8	0.09
Choctaw (46)	71	0.79

*Notes: † The Census 2010 population figure is used to calculate the percentages in the Hispanic Origin and Race categories. Ancestry percentages are based on the 2006-2010 American Community Survey population (not shown); ‡ Numbers in parentheses indicate the number of people reporting a single ancestry; * Numbers in parentheses indicate the number of persons reporting this race alone, not in combination with any other race; Please refer to the Explanation of Data for more information.*

Creek (11)	13	0.15
Crow (0)	2	0.02
Mexican American Ind. (1)	2	0.02
Ottawa (2)	2	0.02
Potawatomi (8)	9	0.10
Seminole (1)	1	0.01
Spanish American Ind. (1)	1	0.01
Tlingit-Haida *(Alaska Native)* (0)	2	0.02
Asian (75)	118	1.32
Not Hispanic (75)	114	1.27
Hispanic (0)	4	0.04
Cambodian (3)	3	0.03
Chinese, ex. Taiwanese (10)	12	0.13
Filipino (14)	24	0.27
Hmong (7)	7	0.08
Indian (2)	6	0.07
Indonesian (0)	3	0.03
Japanese (2)	13	0.15
Korean (4)	13	0.15
Laotian (14)	18	0.20
Pakistani (12)	12	0.13
Thai (1)	1	0.01
Vietnamese (2)	5	0.06
Hawaii Native/Pacific Islander (2)	3	0.03
Not Hispanic (1)	2	0.02
Hispanic (1)	1	0.01
Guamanian/Chamorro (0)	1	0.01
Native Hawaiian (2)	2	0.02
White (8,329)	8,535	95.34
Not Hispanic (8,155)	8,315	92.88
Hispanic (174)	220	2.46

Harrison

Place Type: City
County: Boone
Population: 12,943†

Ancestry‡	Population	%
American (1,513)	1,513	11.70
Arab (0)	49	0.38
Lebanese (0)	49	0.38
British (0)	29	0.22
Czech (17)	85	0.66
Czechoslovakian (0)	12	0.09
Danish (0)	29	0.22
Dutch (19)	185	1.43
English (629)	1,462	11.31
European (16)	46	0.36
Finnish (0)	13	0.10
French, ex. Basque (26)	308	2.38
French Canadian (0)	57	0.44
German (530)	1,969	15.23
Greek (0)	22	0.17
Hungarian (0)	42	0.32
Irish (574)	2,145	16.59
Italian (102)	187	1.45
Luxemburger (14)	14	0.11
Norwegian (15)	46	0.36
Pennsylvania German (15)	15	0.12
Polish (24)	118	0.91
Portuguese (18)	18	0.14
Scotch-Irish (82)	219	1.69
Scottish (126)	484	3.74
Swedish (15)	87	0.67
Swiss (0)	31	0.24
Welsh (23)	50	0.39
West Indian, ex. Hispanic (0)	11	0.09
Dutch West Indian (0)	11	0.09

Hispanic Origin	Population	%
Hispanic or Latino (of any race)	286	2.21
Central American, ex. Mexican	15	0.12
Costa Rican	1	0.01
Guatemalan	4	0.03
Panamanian	8	0.06
Salvadoran	2	0.02
Cuban	6	0.05
Mexican	213	1.65
Puerto Rican	14	0.11
South American	10	0.08
Argentinean	4	0.03
Colombian	2	0.02
Ecuadorian	1	0.01
Paraguayan	2	0.02
Peruvian	1	0.01
Other Hispanic or Latino	28	0.22

Race*	Population	%
African-American/Black (34)	59	0.46
Not Hispanic (32)	56	0.43
Hispanic (2)	3	0.02
American Indian/Alaska Native (84)	226	1.75
Not Hispanic (82)	215	1.66
Hispanic (2)	11	0.08
Aleut *(Alaska Native)* (0)	1	0.01
Apache (1)	2	0.02
Blackfeet (1)	4	0.03
Cherokee (22)	96	0.74
Cheyenne (0)	1	0.01
Chickasaw (2)	5	0.04
Chippewa (0)	2	0.02
Choctaw (9)	10	0.08
Cree (0)	2	0.02
Creek (5)	9	0.07
Delaware (1)	1	0.01
Iroquois (0)	4	0.03
Osage (1)	2	0.02
Potawatomi (1)	1	0.01
Sioux (16)	24	0.19
South American Ind. (0)	1	0.01
Ute (0)	1	0.01
Yup'ik *(Alaska Native)* (0)	1	0.01
Asian (95)	121	0.93
Not Hispanic (94)	117	0.90
Hispanic (1)	4	0.03
Bangladeshi (2)	2	0.02
Chinese, ex. Taiwanese (18)	22	0.17
Filipino (25)	34	0.26
Indian (18)	22	0.17
Indonesian (0)	1	0.01
Japanese (4)	4	0.03
Korean (7)	9	0.07
Taiwanese (0)	2	0.02
Thai (5)	6	0.05
Vietnamese (14)	14	0.11
Hawaii Native/Pacific Islander (5)	20	0.15
Not Hispanic (5)	18	0.14
Hispanic (0)	2	0.02
Guamanian/Chamorro (0)	4	0.03
Native Hawaiian (4)	7	0.05
Samoan (0)	4	0.03
White (12,448)	12,652	97.75
Not Hispanic (12,245)	12,434	96.07
Hispanic (203)	218	1.68

Helena-West Helena

Place Type: City
County: Phillips
Population: 12,282†

Ancestry‡	Population	%
African, Sub-Saharan (175)	212	1.68
African (175)	212	1.68
American (234)	234	1.85
Arab (10)	10	0.08
Lebanese (10)	10	0.08
Belgian (6)	21	0.17
British (7)	7	0.06
Danish (9)	9	0.07
Dutch (70)	116	0.92
English (202)	376	2.97
European (46)	46	0.36
French, ex. Basque (16)	54	0.43
German (195)	440	3.48
Greek (0)	22	0.17
Irish (182)	484	3.83
Italian (103)	125	0.99
Polish (0)	11	0.09
Romanian (33)	33	0.26
Russian (8)	8	0.06
Scotch-Irish (22)	39	0.31
Scottish (80)	100	0.79
Swiss (0)	11	0.09
Welsh (22)	22	0.17

Hispanic Origin	Population	%
Hispanic or Latino (of any race)	145	1.18
Cuban	3	0.02
Dominican Republic	2	0.02
Mexican	94	0.77
Puerto Rican	15	0.12
South American	4	0.03
Colombian	2	0.02
Ecuadorian	2	0.02
Other Hispanic or Latino	27	0.22

Race*	Population	%
African-American/Black (9,152)	9,217	75.04
Not Hispanic (9,105)	9,155	74.54
Hispanic (47)	62	0.50
American Indian/Alaska Native (31)	60	0.49
Not Hispanic (26)	53	0.43
Hispanic (5)	7	0.06
Blackfeet (1)	2	0.02
Cherokee (5)	10	0.08
Crow (0)	1	0.01
Delaware (1)	3	0.02
Mexican American Ind. (5)	5	0.04
Sioux (1)	3	0.02
Tlingit-Haida *(Alaska Native)* (1)	1	0.01
Asian (44)	55	0.45
Not Hispanic (43)	52	0.42
Hispanic (1)	3	0.02
Bangladeshi (3)	3	0.02
Chinese, ex. Taiwanese (27)	29	0.24
Filipino (0)	1	0.01
Indian (6)	11	0.09
Japanese (3)	5	0.04
Korean (3)	3	0.02
Taiwanese (0)	1	0.01
Vietnamese (1)	1	0.01
Hawaii Native/Pacific Islander (1)	3	0.02
Not Hispanic (1)	3	0.02
Samoan (1)	2	0.02
White (2,930)	2,988	24.33
Not Hispanic (2,892)	2,939	23.93
Hispanic (38)	49	0.40

Hope

Place Type: City
County: Hempstead
Population: 10,095†

Ancestry‡	Population	%
African, Sub-Saharan (0)	13	0.13
African (0)	13	0.13
American (384)	384	3.76
Dutch (108)	152	1.49
English (487)	707	6.93
European (5)	11	0.11
French, ex. Basque (38)	140	1.37
French Canadian (56)	56	0.55
German (50)	151	1.48
Hungarian (4)	29	0.28
Irish (412)	682	6.68
Italian (28)	81	0.79
Norwegian (0)	21	0.21
Polish (8)	28	0.27
Scotch-Irish (20)	47	0.46
Scottish (20)	20	0.20
Swiss (0)	17	0.17
Welsh (7)	18	0.18

Hispanic Origin	Population	%
Hispanic or Latino (of any race)	2,096	20.76
Central American, ex. Mexican	19	0.19
Costa Rican	1	0.01

*Notes: † The Census 2010 population figure is used to calculate the percentages in the Hispanic Origin and Race categories. Ancestry percentages are based on the 2006-2010 American Community Survey population (not shown); ‡ Numbers in parentheses indicate the number of people reporting a single ancestry; * Numbers in parentheses indicate the number of persons reporting this race alone, not in combination with any other race; Please refer to the Explanation of Data for more information.*

	Population	%
Guatemalan	1	0.01
Honduran	12	0.12
Panamanian	1	0.01
Salvadoran	4	0.04
Cuban	1	0.01
Dominican Republic	1	0.01
Mexican	1,919	19.01
Puerto Rican	12	0.12
South American	4	0.04
Argentinean	1	0.01
Colombian	1	0.01
Peruvian	1	0.01
Venezuelan	1	0.01
Other Hispanic or Latino	140	1.39

Race*	Population	%
African-American/Black (4,376)	4,493	44.51
Not Hispanic (4,359)	4,461	44.19
Hispanic (17)	32	0.32
American Indian/Alaska Native (26)	85	0.84
Not Hispanic (23)	76	0.75
Hispanic (3)	9	0.09
Blackfeet (2)	7	0.07
Cherokee (4)	16	0.16
Choctaw (0)	4	0.04
Mexican American Ind. (0)	5	0.05
Navajo (3)	5	0.05
Pima (1)	1	0.01
Seminole (0)	3	0.03
Spanish American Ind. (1)	1	0.01
Asian (20)	39	0.39
Not Hispanic (20)	32	0.32
Hispanic (0)	7	0.07
Cambodian (2)	2	0.02
Chinese, ex. Taiwanese (3)	5	0.05
Filipino (1)	11	0.11
Indian (1)	4	0.04
Japanese (2)	3	0.03
Korean (2)	2	0.02
Thai (5)	7	0.07
Vietnamese (2)	2	0.02
Hawaii Native/Pacific Islander (7)	9	0.09
Not Hispanic (6)	7	0.07
Hispanic (1)	2	0.02
Native Hawaiian (0)	1	0.01
Samoan (1)	1	0.01
White (3,942)	4,132	40.93
Not Hispanic (3,437)	3,554	35.21
Hispanic (505)	578	5.73

Hot Springs Village

Place Type: CDP
County: Garland
Population: 12,807†

Ancestry‡	Population	%
African, Sub-Saharan (11)	23	0.18
African (11)	23	0.18
Alsatian (13)	13	0.10
American (1,041)	1,041	8.31
Arab (14)	14	0.11
Lebanese (14)	14	0.11
Austrian (13)	54	0.43
Brazilian (12)	12	0.10
British (44)	58	0.46
Canadian (16)	16	0.13
Czech (0)	62	0.50
Czechoslovakian (30)	90	0.72
Danish (70)	162	1.29
Dutch (127)	252	2.01
English (866)	2,109	16.84
European (122)	133	1.06
Finnish (0)	14	0.11
French, ex. Basque (173)	526	4.20
French Canadian (82)	82	0.65
German (1,655)	3,500	27.95
Greek (18)	18	0.14
Hungarian (40)	184	1.47
Irish (637)	1,830	14.61
Italian (111)	270	2.16
Latvian (15)	15	0.12
Lithuanian (42)	42	0.34
Luxemburger (0)	13	0.10
Northern European (29)	29	0.23
Norwegian (122)	293	2.34
Polish (186)	407	3.25
Romanian (0)	13	0.10
Russian (42)	136	1.09
Scandinavian (15)	15	0.12
Scotch-Irish (325)	625	4.99
Scottish (330)	744	5.94
Slovak (15)	51	0.41
Slovene (0)	30	0.24
Swedish (200)	415	3.31
Swiss (21)	95	0.76
Ukrainian (0)	11	0.09
Welsh (73)	221	1.76
Yugoslavian (0)	15	0.12

Hispanic Origin	Population	%
Hispanic or Latino (of any race)	197	1.54
Central American, ex. Mexican	39	0.30
Guatemalan	2	0.02
Honduran	25	0.20
Nicaraguan	1	0.01
Panamanian	7	0.05
Salvadoran	4	0.03
Cuban	6	0.05
Mexican	107	0.84
Puerto Rican	16	0.12
South American	5	0.04
Argentinean	3	0.02
Colombian	2	0.02
Other Hispanic or Latino	24	0.19

Race*	Population	%
African-American/Black (145)	161	1.26
Not Hispanic (142)	157	1.23
Hispanic (3)	4	0.03
American Indian/Alaska Native (20)	101	0.79
Not Hispanic (17)	94	0.73
Hispanic (3)	7	0.05
Apache (0)	1	0.01
Blackfeet (0)	2	0.02
Cherokee (7)	51	0.40
Chickasaw (1)	1	0.01
Chippewa (1)	1	0.01
Choctaw (4)	7	0.05
Comanche (0)	1	0.01
Creek (0)	2	0.02
Iroquois (1)	1	0.01
Mexican American Ind. (1)	1	0.01
Potawatomi (1)	1	0.01
Seminole (1)	3	0.02
Yaqui (2)	2	0.02
Asian (49)	57	0.45
Not Hispanic (49)	56	0.44
Hispanic (0)	1	0.01
Chinese, ex. Taiwanese (6)	9	0.07
Filipino (20)	23	0.18
Indian (1)	3	0.02
Japanese (8)	9	0.07
Korean (2)	3	0.02
Taiwanese (3)	3	0.02
Thai (2)	2	0.02
Vietnamese (5)	5	0.04
Hawaii Native/Pacific Islander (2)	6	0.05
Not Hispanic (2)	5	0.04
Hispanic (0)	1	0.01
Guamanian/Chamorro (0)	1	0.01
Native Hawaiian (2)	6	0.05
Samoan (0)	1	0.01
White (12,428)	12,535	97.88
Not Hispanic (12,292)	12,393	96.77
Hispanic (136)	142	1.11

Hot Springs

Place Type: City
County: Garland
Population: 35,193†

Ancestry‡	Population	%
African, Sub-Saharan (11)	11	0.03
African (11)	11	0.03
American (2,585)	2,585	7.26
Arab (0)	28	0.08
Arab (0)	28	0.08
Assyrian/Chaldean/Syriac (13)	13	0.04
Australian (9)	17	0.05
Austrian (0)	34	0.10
Basque (0)	30	0.08
Belgian (0)	14	0.04
Brazilian (13)	13	0.04
British (113)	151	0.42
Cajun (10)	29	0.08
Canadian (19)	19	0.05
Croatian (21)	21	0.06
Czech (79)	128	0.36
Czechoslovakian (0)	33	0.09
Danish (60)	164	0.46
Dutch (179)	855	2.40
English (1,664)	4,905	13.78
European (103)	103	0.29
Finnish (0)	9	0.03
French, ex. Basque (204)	962	2.70
French Canadian (70)	106	0.30
German (1,409)	4,712	13.23
Greek (80)	142	0.40
Hungarian (11)	133	0.37
Irish (1,284)	6,305	17.71
Italian (193)	526	1.48
Lithuanian (29)	29	0.08
Northern European (9)	9	0.03
Norwegian (55)	176	0.49
Polish (70)	310	0.87
Portuguese (0)	218	0.61
Romanian (99)	112	0.31
Russian (8)	60	0.17
Scandinavian (24)	70	0.20
Scotch-Irish (382)	912	2.56
Scottish (408)	930	2.61
Serbian (43)	54	0.15
Slavic (0)	13	0.04
Slovak (0)	14	0.04
Swedish (120)	286	0.80
Swiss (26)	105	0.29
Ukrainian (22)	44	0.12
Welsh (51)	126	0.35
West Indian, ex. Hispanic (29)	52	0.15
Dutch West Indian (19)	42	0.12
Jamaican (10)	10	0.03
Yugoslavian (28)	38	0.11

Hispanic Origin	Population	%
Hispanic or Latino (of any race)	2,631	7.48
Central American, ex. Mexican	222	0.63
Costa Rican	5	0.01
Guatemalan	12	0.03
Honduran	30	0.09
Nicaraguan	1	<0.01
Panamanian	5	0.01
Salvadoran	166	0.47
Other Central American	3	0.01
Cuban	29	0.08
Dominican Republic	1	<0.01
Mexican	2,074	5.89
Puerto Rican	76	0.22
South American	33	0.09
Argentinean	10	0.03
Bolivian	2	0.01
Chilean	1	<0.01
Colombian	5	0.01
Ecuadorian	7	0.02
Peruvian	3	0.01
Venezuelan	5	0.01

*Notes: † The Census 2010 population figure is used to calculate the percentages in the Hispanic Origin and Race categories. Ancestry percentages are based on the 2006-2010 American Community Survey population (not shown); ‡ Numbers in parentheses indicate the number of people reporting a single ancestry; * Numbers in parentheses indicate the number of persons reporting this race alone, not in combination with any other race; Please refer to the Explanation of Data for more information.*

Other Hispanic or Latino	196	0.56

Race*	Population	%
African-American/Black (5,926)	6,475	18.40
Not Hispanic (5,880)	6,377	18.12
Hispanic (46)	98	0.28
American Indian/Alaska Native (219)	549	1.56
Not Hispanic (196)	493	1.40
Hispanic (23)	56	0.16
Alaska Athabascan *(Ala. Nat.)* (0)	2	0.01
Aleut *(Alaska Native)* (0)	1	<0.01
Apache (1)	9	0.03
Blackfeet (1)	15	0.04
Canadian/French Am. Ind. (1)	2	0.01
Cherokee (64)	178	0.51
Chickasaw (1)	2	0.01
Chippewa (5)	9	0.03
Choctaw (20)	34	0.10
Colville (0)	1	<0.01
Comanche (3)	7	0.02
Cree (0)	2	0.01
Creek (5)	16	0.05
Crow (0)	2	0.01
Houma (2)	2	0.01
Inupiat *(Alaska Native)* (1)	2	0.01
Iroquois (1)	3	0.01
Lumbee (0)	2	0.01
Mexican American Ind. (5)	7	0.02
Navajo (8)	12	0.03
Osage (2)	8	0.02
Ottawa (1)	1	<0.01
Potawatomi (0)	3	0.01
Pueblo (0)	1	<0.01
Seminole (1)	2	0.01
Sioux (1)	5	0.01
Tlingit-Haida *(Alaska Native)* (1)	1	<0.01
Yaqui (0)	1	<0.01
Asian (301)	440	1.25
Not Hispanic (300)	432	1.23
Hispanic (1)	8	0.02
Burmese (0)	1	<0.01
Cambodian (2)	5	0.01
Chinese, ex. Taiwanese (45)	56	0.16
Filipino (50)	82	0.23
Hmong (0)	1	<0.01
Indian (86)	100	0.28
Indonesian (1)	3	0.01
Japanese (19)	49	0.14
Korean (14)	34	0.10
Laotian (2)	2	0.01
Pakistani (4)	5	0.01
Sri Lankan (2)	2	0.01
Taiwanese (2)	2	0.01
Thai (6)	11	0.03
Vietnamese (59)	69	0.20
Hawaii Native/Pacific Islander (13)	53	0.15
Not Hispanic (8)	40	0.11
Hispanic (5)	13	0.04
Guamanian/Chamorro (6)	9	0.03
Native Hawaiian (2)	24	0.07
Samoan (4)	5	0.01
White (26,537)	27,488	78.11
Not Hispanic (25,269)	26,082	74.11
Hispanic (1,268)	1,406	4.00

Jacksonville

Place Type: City
County: Pulaski
Population: 28,364†

Ancestry‡	Population	%
African, Sub-Saharan (25)	108	0.38
African (25)	108	0.38
American (2,147)	2,147	7.53
Armenian (23)	123	0.43
Australian (29)	29	0.10
Austrian (0)	11	0.04
British (26)	59	0.21
Bulgarian (0)	6	0.02
Canadian (31)	64	0.22
Czech (0)	45	0.16
Danish (15)	86	0.30
Dutch (88)	334	1.17
English (970)	2,370	8.32
European (85)	169	0.59
French, ex. Basque (175)	771	2.71
French Canadian (50)	157	0.55
German (1,261)	3,573	12.54
Greek (45)	122	0.43
Hungarian (16)	42	0.15
Irish (802)	3,464	12.16
Italian (420)	857	3.01
Latvian (0)	36	0.13
Norwegian (50)	128	0.45
Pennsylvania German (0)	3	0.01
Polish (86)	385	1.35
Portuguese (0)	25	0.09
Romanian (0)	26	0.09
Russian (0)	31	0.11
Scandinavian (0)	9	0.03
Scotch-Irish (238)	463	1.62
Scottish (163)	352	1.24
Slavic (0)	11	0.04
Slovak (47)	56	0.20
Swedish (23)	138	0.48
Swiss (0)	5	0.02
Welsh (12)	93	0.33
West Indian, ex. Hispanic (46)	125	0.44
Dutch West Indian (0)	79	0.28
Haitian (46)	46	0.16

Hispanic Origin	Population	%
Hispanic or Latino (of any race)	1,890	6.66
Central American, ex. Mexican	143	0.50
Costa Rican	9	0.03
Guatemalan	23	0.08
Honduran	23	0.08
Nicaraguan	16	0.06
Panamanian	22	0.08
Salvadoran	48	0.17
Other Central American	2	0.01
Cuban	21	0.07
Dominican Republic	14	0.05
Mexican	1,270	4.48
Puerto Rican	234	0.82
South American	27	0.10
Bolivian	2	0.01
Colombian	12	0.04
Ecuadorian	6	0.02
Peruvian	5	0.02
Uruguayan	1	<0.01
Venezuelan	1	<0.01
Other Hispanic or Latino	181	0.64

Race*	Population	%
African-American/Black (9,272)	9,927	35.00
Not Hispanic (9,184)	9,763	34.42
Hispanic (88)	164	0.58
American Indian/Alaska Native (169)	481	1.70
Not Hispanic (133)	397	1.40
Hispanic (36)	84	0.30
Alaska Athabascan *(Ala. Nat.)* (0)	1	<0.01
Aleut *(Alaska Native)* (3)	3	0.01
Apache (3)	9	0.03
Blackfeet (0)	12	0.04
Cherokee (38)	154	0.54
Chickasaw (3)	4	0.01
Chippewa (2)	4	0.01
Choctaw (11)	19	0.07
Comanche (3)	3	0.01
Creek (0)	1	<0.01
Delaware (1)	1	<0.01
Inupiat *(Alaska Native)* (4)	4	0.01
Iroquois (1)	4	0.01
Lumbee (2)	5	0.02
Mexican American Ind. (2)	6	0.02
Navajo (6)	12	0.04
Osage (2)	4	0.01
Paiute (2)	2	0.01
Potawatomi (3)	9	0.03
Pueblo (1)	1	<0.01
Seminole (0)	1	<0.01
Shoshone (0)	1	<0.01
Sioux (3)	6	0.02
South American Ind. (0)	4	0.01
Tlingit-Haida *(Alaska Native)* (1)	5	0.02
Ute (0)	3	0.01
Yakama (0)	1	<0.01
Yaqui (2)	5	0.02
Asian (597)	877	3.09
Not Hispanic (576)	821	2.89
Hispanic (21)	56	0.20
Burmese (0)	1	<0.01
Chinese, ex. Taiwanese (44)	66	0.23
Filipino (222)	362	1.28
Hmong (3)	3	0.01
Indian (17)	32	0.11
Indonesian (1)	1	<0.01
Japanese (57)	101	0.36
Korean (104)	156	0.55
Laotian (16)	20	0.07
Malaysian (2)	2	0.01
Taiwanese (11)	13	0.05
Thai (53)	72	0.25
Vietnamese (32)	43	0.15
Hawaii Native/Pacific Islander (34)	78	0.27
Not Hispanic (24)	57	0.20
Hispanic (10)	21	0.07
Guamanian/Chamorro (18)	31	0.11
Native Hawaiian (4)	22	0.08
Samoan (3)	5	0.02
White (16,364)	17,325	61.08
Not Hispanic (15,594)	16,370	57.71
Hispanic (770)	955	3.37

Jonesboro

Place Type: City
County: Craighead
Population: 67,263†

Ancestry‡	Population	%
African, Sub-Saharan (108)	181	0.28
African (94)	142	0.22
South African (14)	39	0.06
Alsatian (0)	14	0.02
American (6,060)	6,060	9.35
Arab (186)	216	0.33
Jordanian (151)	151	0.23
Lebanese (0)	30	0.05
Other Arab (35)	35	0.05
Australian (11)	11	0.02
Austrian (37)	65	0.10
Basque (0)	17	0.03
Belgian (53)	64	0.10
British (87)	234	0.36
Canadian (59)	67	0.10
Celtic (33)	33	0.05
Croatian (0)	16	0.02
Czech (43)	121	0.19
Czechoslovakian (14)	14	0.02
Danish (0)	68	0.10
Dutch (314)	1,659	2.56
Eastern European (16)	28	0.04
English (2,946)	6,406	9.89
Estonian (14)	14	0.02
European (421)	519	0.80
French, ex. Basque (364)	1,261	1.95
French Canadian (143)	161	0.25
German (2,628)	7,370	11.37
Greek (18)	18	0.03
Hungarian (36)	157	0.24
Iranian (110)	129	0.20
Irish (2,907)	8,271	12.76
Italian (408)	1,086	1.68
Norwegian (145)	244	0.38
Polish (114)	451	0.70
Portuguese (28)	37	0.06
Romanian (0)	80	0.12

*Notes: † The Census 2010 population figure is used to calculate the percentages in the Hispanic Origin and Race categories. Ancestry percentages are based on the 2006-2010 American Community Survey population (not shown); ‡ Numbers in parentheses indicate the number of people reporting a single ancestry; * Numbers in parentheses indicate the number of persons reporting this race alone, not in combination with any other race; Please refer to the Explanation of Data for more information.*

Russian (71)	190	0.29
Scandinavian (0)	47	0.07
Scotch-Irish (811)	1,684	2.60
Scottish (586)	1,116	1.72
Serbian (0)	10	0.02
Slovak (11)	21	0.03
Swedish (80)	247	0.38
Swiss (125)	191	0.29
Turkish (15)	15	0.02
Welsh (129)	471	0.73
West Indian, ex. Hispanic (53)	128	0.20
Haitian (0)	43	0.07
Jamaican (12)	25	0.04
Trinidadian/Tobagonian (41)	60	0.09
Yugoslavian (16)	16	0.02

Hispanic Origin	Population	%
Hispanic or Latino (of any race)	3,503	5.21
Central American, ex. Mexican	179	0.27
Costa Rican	16	0.02
Guatemalan	47	0.07
Honduran	32	0.05
Nicaraguan	7	0.01
Panamanian	9	0.01
Salvadoran	68	0.10
Cuban	14	0.02
Dominican Republic	21	0.03
Mexican	2,879	4.28
Puerto Rican	101	0.15
South American	84	0.12
Argentinean	2	<0.01
Bolivian	3	<0.01
Chilean	11	0.02
Colombian	26	0.04
Ecuadorian	7	0.01
Peruvian	31	0.05
Venezuelan	4	0.01
Other Hispanic or Latino	225	0.33

Race*	Population	%
African-American/Black (12,384)	13,088	19.46
Not Hispanic (12,319)	12,957	19.26
Hispanic (65)	131	0.19
American Indian/Alaska Native (242)	605	0.90
Not Hispanic (190)	520	0.77
Hispanic (52)	85	0.13
Apache (2)	14	0.02
Blackfeet (3)	15	0.02
Central American Ind. (0)	1	<0.01
Cherokee (86)	259	0.39
Chickasaw (0)	3	<0.01
Chippewa (1)	5	0.01
Choctaw (11)	43	0.06
Comanche (3)	5	0.01
Creek (0)	2	<0.01
Houma (1)	1	<0.01
Inupiat *(Alaska Native)* (1)	2	<0.01
Iroquois (2)	2	<0.01
Kiowa (3)	3	<0.01
Lumbee (4)	5	0.01
Mexican American Ind. (7)	9	0.01
Navajo (2)	5	0.01
Osage (2)	3	<0.01
Paiute (1)	2	<0.01
Pima (2)	2	<0.01
Potawatomi (3)	4	0.01
Pueblo (2)	2	<0.01
Seminole (1)	7	0.01
Sioux (4)	9	0.01
South American Ind. (1)	1	<0.01
Spanish American Ind. (0)	8	0.01
Asian (1,017)	1,225	1.82
Not Hispanic (1,011)	1,204	1.79
Hispanic (6)	21	0.03
Bangladeshi (5)	5	0.01
Burmese (1)	2	<0.01
Cambodian (1)	1	<0.01
Chinese, ex. Taiwanese (366)	410	0.61
Filipino (99)	143	0.21
Hmong (12)	12	0.02
Indian (236)	261	0.39
Indonesian (13)	15	0.02
Japanese (31)	58	0.09
Korean (43)	71	0.11
Laotian (7)	9	0.01
Malaysian (4)	6	0.01
Nepalese (10)	10	0.01
Pakistani (33)	37	0.06
Sri Lankan (5)	5	0.01
Taiwanese (12)	17	0.03
Thai (17)	22	0.03
Vietnamese (67)	75	0.11
Hawaii Native/Pacific Islander (29)	74	0.11
Not Hispanic (23)	52	0.08
Hispanic (6)	22	0.03
Fijian (1)	1	<0.01
Guamanian/Chamorro (13)	15	0.02
Native Hawaiian (6)	27	0.04
Samoan (6)	9	0.01
Tongan (1)	1	<0.01
White (50,251)	51,463	76.51
Not Hispanic (49,062)	50,068	74.44
Hispanic (1,189)	1,395	2.07

Little Rock

Place Type: City
County: Pulaski
Population: 193,524†

Ancestry‡	Population	%
African, Sub-Saharan (1,768)	2,040	1.07
African (1,324)	1,557	0.82
Ghanaian (9)	9	<0.01
Kenyan (19)	36	0.02
Liberian (40)	40	0.02
Nigerian (320)	320	0.17
Sierra Leonean (0)	11	0.01
South African (0)	11	0.01
Other Sub-Saharan African (56)	56	0.03
American (9,399)	9,399	4.93
Arab (1,068)	1,092	0.57
Arab (261)	261	0.14
Egyptian (102)	126	0.07
Iraqi (122)	122	0.06
Jordanian (56)	56	0.03
Lebanese (60)	60	0.03
Moroccan (30)	30	0.02
Palestinian (45)	45	0.02
Syrian (13)	13	0.01
Other Arab (379)	379	0.20
Armenian (0)	8	<0.01
Australian (58)	58	0.03
Austrian (56)	164	0.09
Belgian (43)	136	0.07
Brazilian (20)	58	0.03
British (490)	942	0.49
Bulgarian (16)	16	0.01
Cajun (46)	71	0.04
Canadian (80)	127	0.07
Celtic (44)	61	0.03
Croatian (7)	22	0.01
Czech (148)	387	0.20
Czechoslovakian (67)	227	0.12
Danish (70)	207	0.11
Dutch (358)	1,775	0.93
Eastern European (21)	30	0.02
English (8,221)	19,158	10.05
European (1,714)	2,012	1.05
Finnish (33)	50	0.03
French, ex. Basque (1,047)	4,244	2.23
French Canadian (118)	301	0.16
German (5,578)	17,244	9.04
Greek (153)	327	0.17
Hungarian (140)	305	0.16
Iranian (108)	108	0.06
Irish (4,844)	15,596	8.18
Italian (1,322)	2,967	1.56
Lithuanian (55)	96	0.05
New Zealander (0)	16	0.01
Northern European (70)	86	0.05
Norwegian (201)	892	0.47
Pennsylvania German (10)	10	0.01
Polish (520)	1,454	0.76
Portuguese (15)	58	0.03
Romanian (27)	37	0.02
Russian (124)	384	0.20
Scandinavian (68)	230	0.12
Scotch-Irish (2,800)	4,785	2.51
Scottish (1,265)	3,635	1.91
Serbian (0)	26	0.01
Slavic (14)	14	0.01
Slovak (76)	132	0.07
Swedish (284)	1,056	0.55
Swiss (47)	359	0.19
Turkish (47)	80	0.04
Ukrainian (9)	83	0.04
Welsh (229)	834	0.44
West Indian, ex. Hispanic (246)	389	0.20
Bahamian (34)	34	0.02
British West Indian (14)	14	0.01
Dutch West Indian (14)	14	0.01
Haitian (53)	53	0.03
Jamaican (47)	175	0.09
Trinidadian/Tobagonian (26)	41	0.02
West Indian (46)	46	0.02
Other West Indian (12)	12	0.01
Yugoslavian (0)	14	0.01

Hispanic Origin	Population	%
Hispanic or Latino (of any race)	13,076	6.76
Central American, ex. Mexican	1,529	0.79
Costa Rican	21	0.01
Guatemalan	694	0.36
Honduran	257	0.13
Nicaraguan	147	0.08
Panamanian	47	0.02
Salvadoran	357	0.18
Other Central American	6	<0.01
Cuban	151	0.08
Dominican Republic	32	0.02
Mexican	9,714	5.02
Puerto Rican	342	0.18
South American	343	0.18
Argentinean	83	0.04
Bolivian	27	0.01
Chilean	30	0.02
Colombian	90	0.05
Ecuadorian	32	0.02
Paraguayan	2	<0.01
Peruvian	22	0.01
Venezuelan	56	0.03
Other South American	1	<0.01
Other Hispanic or Latino	965	0.50

Race*	Population	%
African-American/Black (81,889)	83,613	43.21
Not Hispanic (81,572)	83,115	42.95
Hispanic (317)	498	0.26
American Indian/Alaska Native (686)	1,621	0.84
Not Hispanic (519)	1,326	0.69
Hispanic (167)	295	0.15
Alaska Athabascan *(Ala. Nat.)* (5)	5	<0.01
Aleut *(Alaska Native)* (2)	2	<0.01
Apache (4)	15	0.01
Arapaho (1)	1	<0.01
Blackfeet (4)	54	0.03
Canadian/French Am. Ind. (0)	1	<0.01
Central American Ind. (2)	2	<0.01
Cherokee (170)	470	0.24
Cheyenne (1)	1	<0.01
Chickasaw (10)	17	0.01
Chippewa (3)	7	<0.01
Choctaw (51)	103	0.05
Colville (0)	1	<0.01
Comanche (4)	8	<0.01
Cree (0)	5	<0.01
Creek (9)	21	0.01
Crow (0)	3	<0.01
Delaware (4)	4	<0.01

SECTION TWO

*Notes: † The Census 2010 population figure is used to calculate the percentages in the Hispanic Origin and Race categories. Ancestry percentages are based on the 2006-2010 American Community Survey population (not shown); ‡ Numbers in parentheses indicate the number of people reporting a single ancestry; * Numbers in parentheses indicate the number of persons reporting this race alone, not in combination with any other race; Please refer to the Explanation of Data for more information.*

Inupiat *(Alaska Native)* (0)	1	<0.01
Iroquois (5)	6	<0.01
Kiowa (2)	2	<0.01
Lumbee (6)	6	<0.01
Mexican American Ind. (49)	66	0.03
Navajo (6)	13	0.01
Osage (4)	6	<0.01
Ottawa (1)	1	<0.01
Pima (0)	3	<0.01
Potawatomi (8)	14	0.01
Pueblo (10)	14	0.01
Seminole (7)	10	0.01
Shoshone (0)	1	<0.01
Sioux (10)	21	0.01
South American Ind. (1)	5	<0.01
Spanish American Ind. (1)	2	<0.01
Yuman (0)	1	<0.01
Asian (5,131)	5,943	3.07
Not Hispanic (5,098)	5,857	3.03
Hispanic (33)	86	0.04
Bangladeshi (54)	55	0.03
Burmese (9)	9	<0.01
Cambodian (21)	24	0.01
Chinese, ex. Taiwanese (944)	1,083	0.56
Filipino (505)	698	0.36
Hmong (11)	12	0.01
Indian (1,878)	2,038	1.05
Indonesian (38)	46	0.02
Japanese (111)	200	0.10
Korean (418)	505	0.26
Laotian (50)	68	0.04
Malaysian (11)	11	0.01
Nepalese (38)	41	0.02
Pakistani (301)	346	0.18
Sri Lankan (36)	43	0.02
Taiwanese (49)	62	0.03
Thai (33)	52	0.03
Vietnamese (394)	444	0.23
Hawaii Native/Pacific Islander (153)	281	0.15
Not Hispanic (54)	152	0.08
Hispanic (99)	129	0.07
Fijian (2)	2	<0.01
Guamanian/Chamorro (94)	108	0.06
Marshallese (1)	1	<0.01
Native Hawaiian (19)	51	0.03
Samoan (14)	44	0.02
Tongan (0)	2	<0.01
White (94,665)	97,278	50.27
Not Hispanic (90,297)	92,351	47.72
Hispanic (4,368)	4,927	2.55

Magnolia

Place Type: City
County: Columbia
Population: 11,577†

Ancestry‡	Population	%
African, Sub-Saharan (74)	74	0.64
African (59)	59	0.51
Kenyan (15)	15	0.13
Albanian (17)	17	0.15
American (705)	705	6.05
Bulgarian (10)	10	0.09
Danish (33)	33	0.28
Dutch (0)	94	0.81
English (318)	750	6.44
European (240)	286	2.46
French, ex. Basque (12)	119	1.02
French Canadian (62)	62	0.53
German (196)	718	6.16
Iranian (9)	38	0.33
Irish (433)	816	7.01
Italian (30)	47	0.40
Polish (0)	98	0.84
Russian (31)	31	0.27
Scotch-Irish (219)	262	2.25
Scottish (40)	319	2.74
Swedish (33)	64	0.55
Swiss (8)	8	0.07
Welsh (0)	38	0.33
West Indian, ex. Hispanic (0)	15	0.13
Dutch West Indian (0)	15	0.13

Hispanic Origin	Population	%
Hispanic or Latino (of any race)	256	2.21
Central American, ex. Mexican	25	0.22
Guatemalan	3	0.03
Nicaraguan	2	0.02
Panamanian	1	0.01
Salvadoran	19	0.16
Mexican	167	1.44
Puerto Rican	11	0.10
South American	4	0.03
Ecuadorian	2	0.02
Peruvian	1	0.01
Venezuelan	1	0.01
Other Hispanic or Latino	49	0.42

Race*	Population	%
African-American/Black (4,852)	4,946	42.72
Not Hispanic (4,822)	4,910	42.41
Hispanic (30)	36	0.31
American Indian/Alaska Native (43)	92	0.79
Not Hispanic (35)	78	0.67
Hispanic (8)	14	0.12
Blackfeet (0)	7	0.06
Cherokee (9)	28	0.24
Choctaw (4)	6	0.05
Comanche (0)	1	0.01
Crow (0)	1	0.01
Mexican American Ind. (0)	6	0.05
Sioux (2)	3	0.03
Yaqui (0)	1	0.01
Asian (144)	160	1.38
Not Hispanic (144)	160	1.38
Bangladeshi (1)	1	0.01
Chinese, ex. Taiwanese (32)	33	0.29
Filipino (2)	3	0.03
Indian (36)	40	0.35
Japanese (5)	8	0.07
Korean (16)	19	0.16
Laotian (3)	3	0.03
Malaysian (1)	1	0.01
Nepalese (9)	9	0.08
Pakistani (4)	4	0.03
Thai (2)	2	0.02
Vietnamese (16)	17	0.15
Hawaii Native/Pacific Islander (4)	13	0.11
Not Hispanic (3)	11	0.10
Hispanic (1)	2	0.02
Guamanian/Chamorro (1)	1	0.01
Native Hawaiian (3)	9	0.08
White (6,245)	6,370	55.02
Not Hispanic (6,174)	6,281	54.25
Hispanic (71)	89	0.77

Malvern

Place Type: City
County: Hot Spring
Population: 10,318†

Ancestry‡	Population	%
African, Sub-Saharan (17)	17	0.17
African (17)	17	0.17
American (922)	922	8.97
Czechoslovakian (44)	44	0.43
Danish (0)	57	0.55
Dutch (67)	263	2.56
English (555)	850	8.27
French, ex. Basque (136)	303	2.95
French Canadian (0)	12	0.12
German (253)	815	7.93
Greek (0)	8	0.08
Irish (281)	891	8.67
Italian (37)	64	0.62
Lithuanian (11)	11	0.11
Norwegian (0)	9	0.09
Polish (12)	46	0.45
Russian (0)	11	0.11
Scandinavian (19)	19	0.18
Scotch-Irish (146)	204	1.99
Scottish (19)	27	0.26
Swedish (12)	35	0.34
Welsh (0)	35	0.34
West Indian, ex. Hispanic (9)	9	0.09
Haitian (9)	9	0.09

Hispanic Origin	Population	%
Hispanic or Latino (of any race)	445	4.31
Central American, ex. Mexican	3	0.03
Honduran	2	0.02
Salvadoran	1	0.01
Cuban	3	0.03
Mexican	357	3.46
Puerto Rican	18	0.17
South American	11	0.11
Argentinean	3	0.03
Ecuadorian	7	0.07
Venezuelan	1	0.01
Other Hispanic or Latino	53	0.51

Race*	Population	%
African-American/Black (3,088)	3,218	31.19
Not Hispanic (3,071)	3,198	30.99
Hispanic (17)	20	0.19
American Indian/Alaska Native (42)	123	1.19
Not Hispanic (40)	118	1.14
Hispanic (2)	5	0.05
Apache (1)	1	0.01
Blackfeet (0)	5	0.05
Cherokee (8)	46	0.45
Cheyenne (5)	6	0.06
Chickasaw (0)	2	0.02
Choctaw (4)	11	0.11
Creek (0)	2	0.02
Crow (0)	1	0.01
Hopi (0)	1	0.01
Iroquois (1)	9	0.09
Lumbee (1)	1	0.01
Asian (37)	73	0.71
Not Hispanic (36)	65	0.63
Hispanic (1)	8	0.08
Cambodian (1)	2	0.02
Chinese, ex. Taiwanese (8)	12	0.12
Filipino (5)	19	0.18
Indian (13)	23	0.22
Japanese (2)	8	0.08
Korean (0)	1	0.01
Hawaii Native/Pacific Islander (5)	11	0.11
Not Hispanic (5)	9	0.09
Hispanic (0)	2	0.02
Native Hawaiian (5)	8	0.08
Samoan (0)	2	0.02
White (6,713)	6,960	67.45
Not Hispanic (6,490)	6,701	64.94
Hispanic (223)	259	2.51

Marion

Place Type: City
County: Crittenden
Population: 12,345†

Ancestry‡	Population	%
African, Sub-Saharan (45)	74	0.63
African (29)	58	0.50
Kenyan (16)	16	0.14
American (1,072)	1,072	9.17
Arab (0)	9	0.08
Syrian (0)	9	0.08
Austrian (78)	78	0.67
British (18)	18	0.15
Czech (25)	42	0.36
Dutch (87)	195	1.67
English (434)	689	5.89
European (95)	95	0.81
Finnish (0)	9	0.08
French, ex. Basque (98)	206	1.76

*Notes: † The Census 2010 population figure is used to calculate the percentages in the Hispanic Origin and Race categories. Ancestry percentages are based on the 2006-2010 American Community Survey population (not shown); ‡ Numbers in parentheses indicate the number of people reporting a single ancestry; * Numbers in parentheses indicate the number of persons reporting this race alone, not in combination with any other race; Please refer to the Explanation of Data for more information.*

French Canadian (52)	52	0.44
German (619)	1,183	10.12
Hungarian (0)	8	0.07
Irish (399)	941	8.05
Italian (196)	278	2.38
Latvian (9)	9	0.08
Lithuanian (0)	7	0.06
Norwegian (8)	28	0.24
Polish (8)	44	0.38
Romanian (0)	22	0.19
Russian (0)	85	0.73
Scandinavian (0)	13	0.11
Scotch-Irish (81)	137	1.17
Scottish (93)	123	1.05
Serbian (0)	8	0.07
Slavic (0)	17	0.15
Swedish (0)	94	0.80
Welsh (0)	33	0.28
West Indian, ex. Hispanic (19)	19	0.16
Jamaican (19)	19	0.16

Hispanic Origin	Population	%
Hispanic or Latino (of any race)	250	2.03
Central American, ex. Mexican	9	0.07
Guatemalan	1	0.01
Honduran	6	0.05
Nicaraguan	2	0.02
Cuban	1	0.01
Mexican	204	1.65
Puerto Rican	7	0.06
South American	8	0.06
Colombian	1	0.01
Ecuadorian	4	0.03
Peruvian	1	0.01
Venezuelan	2	0.02
Other Hispanic or Latino	21	0.17

Race*	Population	%
African-American/Black (3,452)	3,523	28.54
Not Hispanic (3,434)	3,497	28.33
Hispanic (18)	26	0.21
American Indian/Alaska Native (53)	106	0.86
Not Hispanic (51)	100	0.81
Hispanic (2)	6	0.05
Blackfeet (0)	8	0.06
Cherokee (22)	39	0.32
Choctaw (3)	6	0.05
Iroquois (0)	3	0.02
Mexican American Ind. (1)	1	0.01
Osage (0)	1	0.01
Potawatomi (1)	1	0.01
Asian (180)	212	1.72
Not Hispanic (180)	212	1.72
Bangladeshi (1)	5	0.04
Chinese, ex. Taiwanese (28)	34	0.28
Filipino (42)	45	0.36
Indian (54)	63	0.51
Japanese (9)	13	0.11
Korean (11)	14	0.11
Pakistani (15)	15	0.12
Thai (1)	1	0.01
Vietnamese (6)	10	0.08
Hawaii Native/Pacific Islander (1)	13	0.11
Not Hispanic (1)	9	0.07
Hispanic (0)	4	0.03
Guamanian/Chamorro (0)	1	0.01
Native Hawaiian (1)	3	0.02
Samoan (0)	5	0.04
White (8,409)	8,549	69.25
Not Hispanic (8,299)	8,411	68.13
Hispanic (110)	138	1.12

Maumelle

Place Type: City
County: Pulaski
Population: 17,163†

Ancestry‡	Population	%
African, Sub-Saharan (0)	11	0.07
African (0)	11	0.07
American (1,506)	1,506	9.46
Arab (40)	63	0.40
Arab (14)	14	0.09
Iraqi (16)	16	0.10
Lebanese (10)	33	0.21
Austrian (0)	14	0.09
Belgian (21)	21	0.13
British (49)	90	0.57
Cajun (16)	16	0.10
Canadian (24)	24	0.15
Czech (34)	98	0.62
Czechoslovakian (15)	15	0.09
Danish (0)	6	0.04
Dutch (55)	203	1.28
English (1,120)	2,316	14.55
European (140)	140	0.88
French, ex. Basque (83)	376	2.36
French Canadian (27)	65	0.41
German (946)	2,562	16.09
Greek (0)	14	0.09
Hungarian (16)	33	0.21
Irish (1,025)	2,586	16.25
Italian (142)	462	2.90
Latvian (0)	26	0.16
Northern European (27)	27	0.17
Norwegian (32)	87	0.55
Polish (105)	385	2.42
Portuguese (14)	49	0.31
Russian (13)	37	0.23
Scotch-Irish (376)	518	3.25
Scottish (243)	522	3.28
Swedish (22)	235	1.48
Swiss (0)	30	0.19
Turkish (50)	50	0.31
Welsh (55)	121	0.76
Yugoslavian (16)	16	0.10

Hispanic Origin	Population	%
Hispanic or Latino (of any race)	417	2.43
Central American, ex. Mexican	40	0.23
Costa Rican	1	0.01
Guatemalan	2	0.01
Honduran	25	0.15
Nicaraguan	4	0.02
Panamanian	3	0.02
Salvadoran	5	0.03
Cuban	18	0.10
Dominican Republic	6	0.03
Mexican	258	1.50
Puerto Rican	35	0.20
South American	30	0.17
Argentinean	2	0.01
Bolivian	3	0.02
Colombian	14	0.08
Ecuadorian	6	0.03
Paraguayan	1	0.01
Peruvian	3	0.02
Venezuelan	1	0.01
Other Hispanic or Latino	30	0.17

Race*	Population	%
African-American/Black (2,074)	2,203	12.84
Not Hispanic (2,061)	2,170	12.64
Hispanic (13)	33	0.19
American Indian/Alaska Native (61)	124	0.72
Not Hispanic (60)	118	0.69
Hispanic (1)	6	0.03
Apache (2)	2	0.01
Cherokee (16)	44	0.26
Chickasaw (3)	3	0.02
Choctaw (15)	17	0.10
Creek (0)	1	0.01
Iroquois (1)	1	0.01
Kiowa (1)	1	0.01
Mexican American Ind. (0)	2	0.01
Osage (1)	4	0.02
Pueblo (1)	1	0.01
Seminole (1)	1	0.01
Sioux (2)	3	0.02
Tlingit-Haida *(Alaska Native)* (1)	1	0.01
Yaqui (1)	3	0.02
Yup'ik *(Alaska Native)* (1)	3	0.02
Asian (395)	481	2.80
Not Hispanic (390)	469	2.73
Hispanic (5)	12	0.07
Cambodian (1)	1	0.01
Chinese, ex. Taiwanese (82)	103	0.60
Filipino (50)	69	0.40
Indian (91)	103	0.60
Indonesian (0)	1	0.01
Japanese (6)	17	0.10
Korean (59)	73	0.43
Laotian (7)	9	0.05
Nepalese (4)	4	0.02
Pakistani (6)	8	0.05
Thai (1)	2	0.01
Vietnamese (75)	81	0.47
Hawaii Native/Pacific Islander (9)	25	0.15
Not Hispanic (9)	22	0.13
Hispanic (0)	3	0.02
Guamanian/Chamorro (2)	4	0.02
Native Hawaiian (6)	10	0.06
Samoan (1)	8	0.05
White (14,220)	14,487	84.41
Not Hispanic (13,960)	14,185	82.65
Hispanic (260)	302	1.76

Monticello

Place Type: City
County: Drew
Population: 9,467†

Ancestry‡	Population	%
American (633)	633	6.70
Arab (0)	22	0.23
Lebanese (0)	9	0.10
Syrian (0)	13	0.14
British (32)	124	1.31
Czech (49)	49	0.52
Dutch (29)	290	3.07
English (508)	863	9.14
European (44)	55	0.58
French, ex. Basque (245)	362	3.83
German (227)	836	8.85
Iranian (37)	37	0.39
Irish (686)	1,341	14.20
Italian (32)	62	0.66
Lithuanian (0)	20	0.21
Norwegian (0)	38	0.40
Polish (0)	7	0.07
Scotch-Irish (80)	80	0.85
Scottish (16)	110	1.17
Slovak (12)	19	0.20
Swedish (0)	43	0.46

Hispanic Origin	Population	%
Hispanic or Latino (of any race)	217	2.29
Central American, ex. Mexican	2	0.02
Nicaraguan	1	0.01
Other Central American	1	0.01
Mexican	187	1.98
Puerto Rican	10	0.11
South American	6	0.06
Argentinean	1	0.01
Colombian	3	0.03
Peruvian	1	0.01
Venezuelan	1	0.01
Other Hispanic or Latino	12	0.13

Race*	Population	%
African-American/Black (3,443)	3,516	37.14
Not Hispanic (3,438)	3,507	37.04
Hispanic (5)	9	0.10
American Indian/Alaska Native (21)	55	0.58
Not Hispanic (20)	54	0.57
Hispanic (1)	1	0.01
Apache (0)	1	0.01
Cherokee (6)	14	0.15

*Notes: † The Census 2010 population figure is used to calculate the percentages in the Hispanic Origin and Race categories. Ancestry percentages are based on the 2006-2010 American Community Survey population (not shown); ‡ Numbers in parentheses indicate the number of people reporting a single ancestry; * Numbers in parentheses indicate the number of persons reporting this race alone, not in combination with any other race; Please refer to the Explanation of Data for more information.*

Chippewa (1)	1	0.01
Choctaw (8)	11	0.12
Potawatomi (1)	1	0.01
Asian (70)	82	0.87
Not Hispanic (70)	82	0.87
Bangladeshi (1)	1	0.01
Chinese, ex. Taiwanese (22)	22	0.23
Filipino (25)	31	0.33
Indian (3)	3	0.03
Japanese (1)	3	0.03
Korean (5)	8	0.08
Laotian (1)	1	0.01
Malaysian (1)	1	0.01
Nepalese (1)	1	0.01
Sri Lankan (1)	1	0.01
Vietnamese (7)	7	0.07
Hawaii Native/Pacific Islander (4)	4	0.04
Not Hispanic (2)	2	0.02
Hispanic (2)	2	0.02
Guamanian/Chamorro (2)	2	0.02
Native Hawaiian (1)	2	0.02
White (5,691)	5,793	61.19
Not Hispanic (5,612)	5,706	60.27
Hispanic (79)	87	0.92

Mountain Home

Place Type: City
County: Baxter
Population: 12,448†

Ancestry‡	Population	%
American (1,031)	1,031	8.35
Austrian (29)	50	0.41
Belgian (39)	39	0.32
British (40)	63	0.51
Canadian (12)	35	0.28
Czech (32)	157	1.27
Czechoslovakian (67)	67	0.54
Danish (43)	91	0.74
Dutch (32)	298	2.41
English (543)	1,766	14.31
European (46)	46	0.37
Finnish (14)	14	0.11
French, ex. Basque (37)	388	3.14
French Canadian (24)	36	0.29
German (1,073)	2,941	23.82
Hungarian (41)	90	0.73
Irish (765)	2,274	18.42
Italian (121)	327	2.65
Lithuanian (23)	33	0.27
Norwegian (85)	167	1.35
Pennsylvania German (0)	13	0.11
Polish (284)	618	5.01
Romanian (15)	15	0.12
Russian (0)	70	0.57
Scandinavian (17)	34	0.28
Scotch-Irish (147)	374	3.03
Scottish (87)	219	1.77
Slovak (22)	33	0.27
Swedish (84)	169	1.37
Swiss (0)	48	0.39
Welsh (0)	54	0.44
West Indian, ex. Hispanic (0)	18	0.15
Dutch West Indian (0)	18	0.15

Hispanic Origin	Population	%
Hispanic or Latino (of any race)	245	1.97
Central American, ex. Mexican	18	0.14
Costa Rican	1	0.01
Nicaraguan	16	0.13
Salvadoran	1	0.01
Cuban	7	0.06
Mexican	148	1.19
Puerto Rican	25	0.20
South American	8	0.06
Chilean	1	0.01
Colombian	2	0.02
Ecuadorian	2	0.02
Paraguayan	3	0.02
Other Hispanic or Latino	39	0.31

Race*	Population	%
African-American/Black (35)	60	0.48
Not Hispanic (32)	55	0.44
Hispanic (3)	5	0.04
American Indian/Alaska Native (63)	158	1.27
Not Hispanic (57)	141	1.13
Hispanic (6)	17	0.14
Apache (2)	2	0.02
Blackfeet (1)	3	0.02
Cherokee (20)	60	0.48
Choctaw (0)	6	0.05
Comanche (4)	4	0.03
Creek (1)	4	0.03
Delaware (0)	1	0.01
Iroquois (1)	1	0.01
Mexican American Ind. (1)	3	0.02
Osage (0)	2	0.02
Potawatomi (1)	1	0.01
Pueblo (0)	1	0.01
Seminole (0)	1	0.01
Sioux (0)	7	0.06
Asian (72)	118	0.95
Not Hispanic (71)	117	0.94
Hispanic (1)	1	0.01
Chinese, ex. Taiwanese (10)	10	0.08
Filipino (25)	40	0.32
Indian (9)	16	0.13
Japanese (3)	15	0.12
Korean (14)	17	0.14
Pakistani (5)	9	0.07
Thai (1)	2	0.02
Vietnamese (4)	4	0.03
Hawaii Native/Pacific Islander (7)	15	0.12
Not Hispanic (6)	12	0.10
Hispanic (1)	3	0.02
Native Hawaiian (7)	14	0.11
Samoan (0)	1	0.01
White (12,022)	12,199	98.00
Not Hispanic (11,886)	12,031	96.65
Hispanic (136)	168	1.35

Newport

Place Type: City
County: Jackson
Population: 7,879†

Ancestry‡	Population	%
African, Sub-Saharan (17)	17	0.22
African (17)	17	0.22
American (665)	665	8.44
Canadian (0)	9	0.11
Czech (0)	9	0.11
Dutch (22)	237	3.01
English (483)	788	10.00
French, ex. Basque (30)	193	2.45
French Canadian (17)	17	0.22
German (280)	628	7.97
Hungarian (0)	8	0.10
Irish (251)	901	11.43
Italian (51)	78	0.99
Norwegian (0)	24	0.30
Polish (0)	73	0.93
Scotch-Irish (31)	72	0.91
Scottish (9)	52	0.66
Swedish (21)	54	0.69
Ukrainian (11)	11	0.14

Hispanic Origin	Population	%
Hispanic or Latino (of any race)	201	2.55
Central American, ex. Mexican	4	0.05
Salvadoran	4	0.05
Cuban	4	0.05
Dominican Republic	1	0.01
Mexican	170	2.16
Puerto Rican	5	0.06
South American	3	0.04
Colombian	3	0.04
Other Hispanic or Latino	14	0.18

Race*	Population	%
African-American/Black (2,274)	2,344	29.75
Not Hispanic (2,263)	2,326	29.52
Hispanic (11)	18	0.23
American Indian/Alaska Native (42)	85	1.08
Not Hispanic (39)	79	1.00
Hispanic (3)	6	0.08
Apache (0)	1	0.01
Blackfeet (0)	2	0.03
Cherokee (21)	36	0.46
Cheyenne (0)	1	0.01
Chickasaw (2)	2	0.03
Choctaw (2)	9	0.11
Creek (2)	2	0.03
Iroquois (1)	2	0.03
Osage (1)	2	0.03
Asian (38)	58	0.74
Not Hispanic (38)	54	0.69
Hispanic (0)	4	0.05
Chinese, ex. Taiwanese (14)	19	0.24
Filipino (3)	9	0.11
Indian (0)	4	0.05
Japanese (6)	7	0.09
Korean (4)	8	0.10
Laotian (4)	4	0.05
Pakistani (2)	2	0.03
Vietnamese (4)	6	0.08
Hawaii Native/Pacific Islander (16)	22	0.28
Not Hispanic (16)	19	0.24
Hispanic (0)	3	0.04
Guamanian/Chamorro (0)	3	0.04
Marshallese (15)	15	0.19
Native Hawaiian (1)	2	0.03
Samoan (0)	1	0.01
White (5,303)	5,411	68.68
Not Hispanic (5,216)	5,310	67.39
Hispanic (87)	101	1.28

North Little Rock

Place Type: City
County: Pulaski
Population: 62,304†

Ancestry‡	Population	%
Afghan (10)	10	0.02
African, Sub-Saharan (86)	113	0.18
African (86)	104	0.17
Other Sub-Saharan African (0)	9	0.01
American (4,645)	4,645	7.53
Arab (31)	51	0.08
Arab (18)	18	0.03
Egyptian (9)	9	0.01
Lebanese (0)	8	0.01
Moroccan (4)	4	0.01
Other Arab (0)	12	0.02
Armenian (0)	18	0.03
Austrian (0)	13	0.02
Brazilian (42)	42	0.07
British (139)	253	0.41
Bulgarian (35)	35	0.06
Canadian (35)	134	0.22
Celtic (29)	47	0.08
Croatian (0)	15	0.02
Czech (0)	54	0.09
Danish (58)	112	0.18
Dutch (180)	820	1.33
Eastern European (20)	20	0.03
English (2,001)	4,846	7.85
European (838)	913	1.48
Finnish (22)	22	0.04
French, ex. Basque (283)	1,256	2.04
French Canadian (149)	204	0.33
German (1,888)	5,360	8.69
Greek (93)	125	0.20
Hungarian (44)	50	0.08
Iranian (28)	28	0.05
Irish (1,774)	5,716	9.26

*Notes: † The Census 2010 population figure is used to calculate the percentages in the Hispanic Origin and Race categories. Ancestry percentages are based on the 2006-2010 American Community Survey population (not shown); ‡ Numbers in parentheses indicate the number of people reporting a single ancestry; * Numbers in parentheses indicate the number of persons reporting this race alone, not in combination with any other race; Please refer to the Explanation of Data for more information.*

Italian (335)	793	1.29
Lithuanian (10)	10	0.02
Northern European (0)	37	0.06
Norwegian (122)	238	0.39
Polish (186)	527	0.85
Portuguese (0)	9	0.01
Russian (53)	73	0.12
Scandinavian (39)	65	0.11
Scotch-Irish (668)	1,266	2.05
Scottish (368)	979	1.59
Swedish (35)	265	0.43
Swiss (14)	98	0.16
Welsh (55)	228	0.37
West Indian, ex. Hispanic (10)	10	0.02
West Indian (10)	10	0.02

Hispanic Origin	Population	%
Hispanic or Latino (of any race)	3,557	5.71
Central American, ex. Mexican	349	0.56
Costa Rican	6	0.01
Guatemalan	147	0.24
Honduran	116	0.19
Nicaraguan	7	0.01
Panamanian	13	0.02
Salvadoran	60	0.10
Cuban	51	0.08
Dominican Republic	5	0.01
Mexican	2,594	4.16
Puerto Rican	193	0.31
South American	80	0.13
Argentinean	10	0.02
Chilean	31	0.05
Colombian	22	0.04
Ecuadorian	2	<0.01
Peruvian	10	0.02
Venezuelan	5	0.01
Other Hispanic or Latino	285	0.46

Race*	Population	%
African-American/Black (24,754)	25,486	40.91
Not Hispanic (24,648)	25,307	40.62
Hispanic (106)	179	0.29
American Indian/Alaska Native (244)	732	1.17
Not Hispanic (209)	623	1.00
Hispanic (35)	109	0.17
Alaska Athabascan *(Ala. Nat.)* (0)	1	<0.01
Apache (3)	4	0.01
Blackfeet (4)	18	0.03
Canadian/French Am. Ind. (0)	1	<0.01
Cherokee (64)	199	0.32
Cheyenne (0)	2	<0.01
Chickasaw (4)	8	0.01
Chippewa (4)	6	0.01
Choctaw (23)	41	0.07
Comanche (7)	7	0.01
Creek (5)	11	0.02
Crow (0)	2	<0.01
Iroquois (0)	7	0.01
Menominee (1)	1	<0.01
Mexican American Ind. (9)	11	0.02
Navajo (0)	2	<0.01
Osage (3)	9	0.01
Ottawa (0)	1	<0.01
Potawatomi (5)	5	0.01
Pueblo (1)	2	<0.01
Seminole (2)	8	0.01
Sioux (7)	8	0.01
South American Ind. (0)	7	0.01
Spanish American Ind. (2)	8	0.01
Tohono O'Odham (4)	4	0.01
Ute (0)	1	<0.01
Asian (584)	842	1.35
Not Hispanic (571)	803	1.29
Hispanic (13)	39	0.06
Burmese (2)	2	<0.01
Cambodian (6)	6	0.01
Chinese, ex. Taiwanese (82)	119	0.19
Filipino (85)	143	0.23
Hmong (1)	1	<0.01
Indian (129)	150	0.24
Indonesian (2)	2	<0.01
Japanese (26)	65	0.10
Korean (110)	145	0.23
Laotian (8)	11	0.02
Malaysian (1)	2	<0.01
Nepalese (1)	1	<0.01
Pakistani (14)	14	0.02
Taiwanese (5)	25	0.04
Thai (13)	26	0.04
Vietnamese (81)	93	0.15
Hawaii Native/Pacific Islander (42)	75	0.12
Not Hispanic (37)	61	0.10
Hispanic (5)	14	0.02
Fijian (1)	1	<0.01
Guamanian/Chamorro (6)	14	0.02
Native Hawaiian (7)	16	0.03
Samoan (23)	23	0.04
White (33,655)	34,709	55.71
Not Hispanic (32,126)	33,004	52.97
Hispanic (1,529)	1,705	2.74

Osceola

Place Type: City
County: Mississippi
Population: 7,757†

Ancestry‡	Population	%
African, Sub-Saharan (37)	37	0.47
African (22)	22	0.28
Nigerian (15)	15	0.19
American (669)	669	8.51
Arab (21)	21	0.27
Lebanese (21)	21	0.27
British (20)	20	0.25
Canadian (0)	13	0.17
Dutch (0)	10	0.13
English (147)	299	3.81
European (37)	37	0.47
French, ex. Basque (9)	9	0.11
German (349)	592	7.53
Irish (52)	300	3.82
Italian (13)	13	0.17
Polish (0)	5	0.06
Scotch-Irish (20)	39	0.50
Scottish (21)	46	0.59
Swedish (26)	26	0.33
Ukrainian (8)	8	0.10

Hispanic Origin	Population	%
Hispanic or Latino (of any race)	191	2.46
Central American, ex. Mexican	4	0.05
Guatemalan	3	0.04
Salvadoran	1	0.01
Cuban	1	0.01
Mexican	165	2.13
Puerto Rican	10	0.13
South American	2	0.03
Argentinean	1	0.01
Colombian	1	0.01
Other Hispanic or Latino	9	0.12

Race*	Population	%
African-American/Black (4,184)	4,271	55.06
Not Hispanic (4,178)	4,257	54.88
Hispanic (6)	14	0.18
American Indian/Alaska Native (9)	30	0.39
Not Hispanic (8)	26	0.34
Hispanic (1)	4	0.05
Cherokee (3)	9	0.12
Cheyenne (0)	2	0.03
Choctaw (0)	1	0.01
Creek (2)	2	0.03
Delaware (1)	1	0.01
Potawatomi (1)	1	0.01
Asian (18)	35	0.45
Not Hispanic (18)	34	0.44
Hispanic (0)	1	0.01
Chinese, ex. Taiwanese (13)	15	0.19
Filipino (1)	3	0.04
Indian (1)	8	0.10
Japanese (3)	4	0.05
Thai (0)	1	0.01
Hawaii Native/Pacific Islander (1)	10	0.13
Not Hispanic (0)	5	0.06
Hispanic (1)	5	0.06
Native Hawaiian (1)	5	0.06
Samoan (0)	1	0.01
White (3,312)	3,407	43.92
Not Hispanic (3,253)	3,336	43.01
Hispanic (59)	71	0.92

Paragould

Place Type: City
County: Greene
Population: 26,113†

Ancestry‡	Population	%
American (7,771)	7,771	30.57
Australian (0)	12	0.05
British (66)	88	0.35
Cajun (56)	56	0.22
Canadian (9)	9	0.04
Czech (27)	27	0.11
Dutch (64)	560	2.20
English (899)	1,992	7.84
Estonian (0)	63	0.25
European (54)	85	0.33
French, ex. Basque (340)	763	3.00
French Canadian (26)	86	0.34
German (1,011)	2,809	11.05
Greek (17)	17	0.07
Irish (749)	3,627	14.27
Italian (28)	201	0.79
Norwegian (59)	74	0.29
Pennsylvania German (0)	15	0.06
Polish (90)	190	0.75
Portuguese (0)	26	0.10
Scotch-Irish (139)	319	1.25
Scottish (158)	366	1.44
Swedish (43)	94	0.37
Welsh (0)	67	0.26

Hispanic Origin	Population	%
Hispanic or Latino (of any race)	743	2.85
Central American, ex. Mexican	72	0.28
Costa Rican	1	<0.01
Guatemalan	35	0.13
Honduran	3	0.01
Nicaraguan	3	0.01
Salvadoran	30	0.11
Cuban	4	0.02
Mexican	553	2.12
Puerto Rican	13	0.05
South American	6	0.02
Colombian	3	0.01
Peruvian	3	0.01
Other Hispanic or Latino	95	0.36

Race*	Population	%
African-American/Black (199)	321	1.23
Not Hispanic (198)	315	1.21
Hispanic (1)	6	0.02
American Indian/Alaska Native (130)	289	1.11
Not Hispanic (115)	263	1.01
Hispanic (15)	26	0.10
Aleut *(Alaska Native)* (1)	1	<0.01
Apache (3)	3	0.01
Blackfeet (4)	17	0.07
Cherokee (46)	127	0.49
Cheyenne (0)	1	<0.01
Chickasaw (4)	4	0.02
Chippewa (2)	6	0.02
Choctaw (2)	10	0.04
Comanche (0)	1	<0.01
Creek (9)	10	0.04
Kiowa (0)	1	<0.01
Menominee (1)	1	<0.01
Mexican American Ind. (1)	1	<0.01

*Notes: † The Census 2010 population figure is used to calculate the percentages in the Hispanic Origin and Race categories. Ancestry percentages are based on the 2006-2010 American Community Survey population (not shown); ‡ Numbers in parentheses indicate the number of people reporting a single ancestry; * Numbers in parentheses indicate the number of persons reporting this race alone, not in combination with any other race; Please refer to the Explanation of Data for more information.*

Navajo (1)	2	0.01
Osage (6)	7	0.03
Potawatomi (0)	2	0.01
Sioux (3)	5	0.02
Yakama (0)	1	<0.01
Asian (89)	136	0.52
Not Hispanic (89)	136	0.52
Chinese, ex. Taiwanese (21)	25	0.10
Filipino (9)	17	0.07
Indian (15)	19	0.07
Indonesian (3)	7	0.03
Japanese (8)	22	0.08
Korean (7)	15	0.06
Pakistani (4)	4	0.02
Thai (2)	2	0.01
Vietnamese (17)	22	0.08
Hawaii Native/Pacific Islander (6)	20	0.08
Not Hispanic (6)	15	0.06
Hispanic (0)	5	0.02
Guamanian/Chamorro (0)	7	0.03
Native Hawaiian (6)	11	0.04
Samoan (0)	1	<0.01
White (24,972)	25,342	97.05
Not Hispanic (24,643)	24,942	95.52
Hispanic (329)	400	1.53

Pine Bluff

Place Type: City
County: Jefferson
Population: 49,083†

Ancestry‡	Population	%
African, Sub-Saharan (681)	722	1.44
African (615)	635	1.27
Ghanaian (8)	8	0.02
Nigerian (32)	53	0.11
Other Sub-Saharan African (26)	26	0.05
American (1,979)	1,979	3.95
Arab (15)	63	0.13
Arab (15)	63	0.13
Australian (0)	11	0.02
Austrian (0)	33	0.07
Belgian (29)	29	0.06
Brazilian (0)	9	0.02
British (9)	22	0.04
Canadian (23)	34	0.07
Celtic (29)	29	0.06
Dutch (38)	219	0.44
Eastern European (15)	15	0.03
English (1,387)	2,134	4.26
European (62)	64	0.13
Finnish (12)	12	0.02
French, ex. Basque (46)	351	0.70
French Canadian (4)	4	0.01
German (570)	1,828	3.65
Greek (25)	25	0.05
Hungarian (9)	16	0.03
Icelander (16)	16	0.03
Irish (500)	1,792	3.58
Italian (253)	457	0.91
Norwegian (10)	10	0.02
Polish (23)	64	0.13
Portuguese (0)	8	0.02
Russian (29)	36	0.07
Scandinavian (5)	30	0.06
Scotch-Irish (188)	479	0.96
Scottish (147)	363	0.73
Swedish (34)	44	0.09
Swiss (0)	37	0.07
Turkish (7)	7	0.01
Welsh (0)	64	0.13
West Indian, ex. Hispanic (51)	259	0.52
Bahamian (8)	8	0.02
Haitian (24)	59	0.12
Jamaican (19)	162	0.32
West Indian (0)	30	0.06

Hispanic Origin	Population	%
Hispanic or Latino (of any race)	712	1.45
Central American, ex. Mexican	27	0.06
Guatemalan	16	0.03
Honduran	6	0.01
Panamanian	1	<0.01
Salvadoran	4	0.01
Cuban	11	0.02
Dominican Republic	11	0.02
Mexican	499	1.02
Puerto Rican	36	0.07
South American	17	0.03
Chilean	1	<0.01
Colombian	4	0.01
Ecuadorian	4	0.01
Peruvian	3	0.01
Venezuelan	5	0.01
Other Hispanic or Latino	111	0.23

Race*	Population	%
African-American/Black (37,083)	37,497	76.40
Not Hispanic (36,946)	37,337	76.07
Hispanic (137)	160	0.33
American Indian/Alaska Native (90)	285	0.58
Not Hispanic (81)	263	0.54
Hispanic (9)	22	0.04
Apache (0)	3	0.01
Blackfeet (1)	6	0.01
Cherokee (14)	88	0.18
Chickasaw (3)	3	0.01
Choctaw (1)	15	0.03
Houma (1)	1	<0.01
Mexican American Ind. (2)	2	<0.01
Osage (1)	3	0.01
Pueblo (0)	6	0.01
Seminole (2)	5	0.01
Sioux (1)	3	0.01
Spanish American Ind. (2)	2	<0.01
Tohono O'Odham (1)	1	<0.01
Asian (308)	371	0.76
Not Hispanic (306)	360	0.73
Hispanic (2)	11	0.02
Bangladeshi (21)	23	0.05
Cambodian (4)	4	0.01
Chinese, ex. Taiwanese (61)	73	0.15
Filipino (62)	79	0.16
Indian (82)	102	0.21
Indonesian (3)	5	0.01
Japanese (6)	20	0.04
Korean (4)	7	0.01
Laotian (0)	1	<0.01
Nepalese (4)	4	0.01
Pakistani (18)	25	0.05
Taiwanese (3)	3	0.01
Thai (1)	1	<0.01
Vietnamese (20)	23	0.05
Hawaii Native/Pacific Islander (4)	20	0.04
Not Hispanic (4)	18	0.04
Hispanic (0)	2	<0.01
Guamanian/Chamorro (0)	2	<0.01
Native Hawaiian (1)	5	0.01
Samoan (0)	1	<0.01
Tongan (0)	1	<0.01
White (10,699)	11,111	22.64
Not Hispanic (10,489)	10,863	22.13
Hispanic (210)	248	0.51

Rogers

Place Type: City
County: Benton
Population: 55,964†

Ancestry‡	Population	%
African, Sub-Saharan (24)	24	0.05
African (24)	24	0.05
American (3,714)	3,714	6.98
Arab (48)	142	0.27
Arab (12)	93	0.17
Egyptian (36)	36	0.07
Lebanese (0)	13	0.02
Australian (15)	29	0.05
Austrian (12)	12	0.02
Belgian (15)	30	0.06
British (67)	146	0.27
Bulgarian (10)	10	0.02
Cajun (53)	53	0.10
Canadian (135)	237	0.45
Croatian (14)	14	0.03
Czech (85)	470	0.88
Czechoslovakian (10)	50	0.09
Danish (37)	190	0.36
Dutch (155)	741	1.39
Eastern European (31)	31	0.06
English (2,555)	5,303	9.97
Estonian (11)	11	0.02
European (135)	219	0.41
Finnish (6)	47	0.09
French, ex. Basque (143)	773	1.45
French Canadian (77)	81	0.15
German (2,248)	6,821	12.82
Greek (135)	205	0.39
Hungarian (27)	115	0.22
Iranian (10)	10	0.02
Irish (1,625)	4,662	8.76
Italian (416)	1,011	1.90
Lithuanian (0)	14	0.03
Norwegian (299)	672	1.26
Pennsylvania German (0)	11	0.02
Polish (119)	552	1.04
Romanian (0)	22	0.04
Russian (29)	212	0.40
Scandinavian (72)	205	0.39
Scotch-Irish (427)	977	1.84
Scottish (412)	1,177	2.21
Swedish (168)	383	0.72
Swiss (0)	84	0.16
Ukrainian (38)	38	0.07
Welsh (267)	465	0.87
West Indian, ex. Hispanic (0)	45	0.08
Haitian (0)	45	0.08
Yugoslavian (0)	5	0.01

Hispanic Origin	Population	%
Hispanic or Latino (of any race)	17,619	31.48
Central American, ex. Mexican	3,612	6.45
Costa Rican	19	0.03
Guatemalan	373	0.67
Honduran	121	0.22
Nicaraguan	83	0.15
Panamanian	48	0.09
Salvadoran	2,951	5.27
Other Central American	17	0.03
Cuban	60	0.11
Dominican Republic	33	0.06
Mexican	12,414	22.18
Puerto Rican	180	0.32
South American	238	0.43
Argentinean	26	0.05
Bolivian	9	0.02
Chilean	21	0.04
Colombian	53	0.09
Ecuadorian	24	0.04
Peruvian	81	0.14
Venezuelan	24	0.04
Other Hispanic or Latino	1,082	1.93

Race*	Population	%
African-American/Black (801)	1,081	1.93
Not Hispanic (716)	928	1.66
Hispanic (85)	153	0.27
American Indian/Alaska Native (580)	1,050	1.88
Not Hispanic (468)	856	1.53
Hispanic (112)	194	0.35
Alaska Athabascan *(Ala. Nat.)* (1)	1	<0.01
Aleut *(Alaska Native)* (2)	2	<0.01
Apache (12)	26	0.05
Blackfeet (0)	9	0.02
Central American Ind. (3)	6	0.01
Cherokee (206)	392	0.70
Cheyenne (2)	4	0.01
Chickasaw (9)	15	0.03

*Notes: † The Census 2010 population figure is used to calculate the percentages in the Hispanic Origin and Race categories. Ancestry percentages are based on the 2006-2010 American Community Survey population (not shown); ‡ Numbers in parentheses indicate the number of people reporting a single ancestry; * Numbers in parentheses indicate the number of persons reporting this race alone, not in combination with any other race; Please refer to the Explanation of Data for more information.*

Race* (cont.)	Population	%
Chippewa (4)	12	0.02
Choctaw (57)	83	0.15
Cree (0)	1	<0.01
Creek (21)	44	0.08
Crow (4)	4	0.01
Delaware (1)	7	0.01
Iroquois (8)	13	0.02
Kiowa (6)	10	0.02
Mexican American Ind. (57)	74	0.13
Navajo (9)	11	0.02
Osage (3)	7	0.01
Potawatomi (4)	5	0.01
Seminole (1)	5	0.01
Sioux (13)	19	0.03
South American Ind. (1)	6	0.01
Spanish American Ind. (1)	1	<0.01
Yup'ik *(Alaska Native)* (0)	7	0.01
Asian (1,431)	1,724	3.08
Not Hispanic (1,400)	1,625	2.90
Hispanic (31)	99	0.18
Bangladeshi (6)	9	0.02
Burmese (2)	2	<0.01
Cambodian (2)	3	0.01
Chinese, ex. Taiwanese (137)	192	0.34
Filipino (79)	158	0.28
Hmong (49)	49	0.09
Indian (586)	616	1.10
Indonesian (0)	1	<0.01
Japanese (27)	51	0.09
Korean (81)	108	0.19
Laotian (51)	78	0.14
Malaysian (4)	4	0.01
Nepalese (8)	8	0.01
Pakistani (19)	22	0.04
Taiwanese (12)	12	0.02
Thai (12)	24	0.04
Vietnamese (282)	329	0.59
Hawaii Native/Pacific Islander (143)	237	0.42
Not Hispanic (135)	208	0.37
Hispanic (8)	29	0.05
Fijian (3)	3	0.01
Guamanian/Chamorro (14)	28	0.05
Marshallese (89)	98	0.18
Native Hawaiian (5)	37	0.07
Samoan (0)	6	0.01
White (41,223)	42,704	76.31
Not Hispanic (34,718)	35,470	63.38
Hispanic (6,505)	7,234	12.93

Russellville

Place Type: City
County: Pope
Population: 27,920†

Ancestry‡	Population	%
American (2,693)	2,693	9.86
Arab (0)	37	0.14
Arab (0)	22	0.08
Lebanese (0)	15	0.05
Belgian (0)	10	0.04
British (32)	98	0.36
Bulgarian (61)	61	0.22
Czech (71)	123	0.45
Czechoslovakian (108)	223	0.82
Danish (0)	22	0.08
Dutch (130)	645	2.36
English (1,874)	3,575	13.10
European (352)	409	1.50
French, ex. Basque (101)	693	2.54
French Canadian (10)	19	0.07
German (1,343)	3,838	14.06
Greek (44)	64	0.23
Hungarian (9)	88	0.32
Irish (1,958)	4,357	15.96
Italian (325)	661	2.42
Lithuanian (0)	14	0.05
Northern European (26)	26	0.10
Norwegian (131)	264	0.97
Polish (0)	83	0.30
Portuguese (22)	34	0.12
Russian (0)	57	0.21
Scandinavian (17)	17	0.06
Scotch-Irish (346)	581	2.13
Scottish (130)	411	1.51
Slovene (0)	15	0.05
Swedish (31)	69	0.25
Swiss (7)	51	0.19
Welsh (51)	101	0.37
West Indian, ex. Hispanic (0)	83	0.30
Bahamian (0)	13	0.05
Dutch West Indian (0)	70	0.26

Hispanic Origin	Population	%
Hispanic or Latino (of any race)	3,279	11.74
Central American, ex. Mexican	838	3.00
Costa Rican	12	0.04
Guatemalan	69	0.25
Honduran	81	0.29
Nicaraguan	12	0.04
Panamanian	5	0.02
Salvadoran	656	2.35
Other Central American	3	0.01
Cuban	7	0.03
Dominican Republic	3	0.01
Mexican	2,078	7.44
Puerto Rican	48	0.17
South American	36	0.13
Argentinean	2	0.01
Chilean	2	0.01
Colombian	13	0.05
Ecuadorian	2	0.01
Peruvian	7	0.03
Uruguayan	2	0.01
Venezuelan	7	0.03
Other South American	1	<0.01
Other Hispanic or Latino	269	0.96

Race*	Population	%
African-American/Black (1,536)	1,753	6.28
Not Hispanic (1,505)	1,707	6.11
Hispanic (31)	46	0.16
American Indian/Alaska Native (182)	420	1.50
Not Hispanic (133)	340	1.22
Hispanic (49)	80	0.29
Alaska Athabascan *(Ala. Nat.)* (0)	1	<0.01
Apache (3)	12	0.04
Blackfeet (0)	5	0.02
Central American Ind. (1)	1	<0.01
Cherokee (52)	141	0.51
Chickasaw (7)	16	0.06
Chippewa (1)	2	0.01
Choctaw (13)	23	0.08
Creek (1)	6	0.02
Crow (0)	1	<0.01
Delaware (1)	2	0.01
Houma (2)	2	0.01
Inupiat *(Alaska Native)* (0)	2	0.01
Iroquois (0)	2	0.01
Kiowa (0)	2	0.01
Mexican American Ind. (20)	24	0.09
Osage (1)	2	0.01
Potawatomi (4)	5	0.02
Pueblo (1)	1	<0.01
Puget Sound Salish (0)	1	<0.01
Seminole (1)	2	0.01
Shoshone (0)	1	<0.01
Sioux (1)	3	0.01
Asian (433)	552	1.98
Not Hispanic (427)	528	1.89
Hispanic (6)	24	0.09
Bangladeshi (5)	5	0.02
Chinese, ex. Taiwanese (95)	111	0.40
Filipino (46)	80	0.29
Hmong (9)	9	0.03
Indian (92)	100	0.36
Japanese (19)	36	0.13
Korean (14)	25	0.09
Laotian (40)	55	0.20
Malaysian (2)	2	0.01
Nepalese (3)	3	0.01
Pakistani (6)	6	0.02
Taiwanese (20)	25	0.09
Thai (13)	19	0.07
Vietnamese (43)	48	0.17
Hawaii Native/Pacific Islander (11)	23	0.08
Not Hispanic (10)	19	0.07
Hispanic (1)	4	0.01
Guamanian/Chamorro (7)	7	0.03
Native Hawaiian (0)	4	0.01
Samoan (2)	4	0.01
Tongan (0)	1	<0.01
White (23,238)	23,848	85.42
Not Hispanic (22,060)	22,522	80.67
Hispanic (1,178)	1,326	4.75

Searcy

Place Type: City
County: White
Population: 22,858†

Ancestry‡	Population	%
African, Sub-Saharan (68)	81	0.37
African (30)	43	0.19
South African (17)	17	0.08
Sudanese (16)	16	0.07
Other Sub-Saharan African (5)	5	0.02
American (3,596)	3,596	16.25
Arab (31)	142	0.64
Egyptian (19)	19	0.09
Lebanese (12)	123	0.56
Belgian (10)	10	0.05
Brazilian (0)	14	0.06
British (20)	98	0.44
Bulgarian (34)	34	0.15
Canadian (0)	7	0.03
Czech (27)	40	0.18
Danish (0)	68	0.31
Dutch (156)	525	2.37
Eastern European (12)	12	0.05
English (1,365)	2,722	12.30
European (308)	385	1.74
French, ex. Basque (66)	308	1.39
French Canadian (32)	32	0.14
German (1,065)	3,001	13.56
Greek (23)	23	0.10
Irish (1,120)	3,269	14.77
Italian (43)	268	1.21
Lithuanian (0)	8	0.04
Norwegian (24)	34	0.15
Polish (71)	196	0.89
Portuguese (14)	49	0.22
Scandinavian (11)	105	0.47
Scotch-Irish (260)	667	3.01
Scottish (133)	490	2.21
Swedish (54)	125	0.56
Swiss (43)	77	0.35
Ukrainian (0)	37	0.17
Welsh (41)	222	1.00
West Indian, ex. Hispanic (6)	32	0.14
Bahamian (0)	13	0.06
Jamaican (0)	13	0.06
Trinidadian/Tobagonian (6)	6	0.03

Hispanic Origin	Population	%
Hispanic or Latino (of any race)	1,041	4.55
Central American, ex. Mexican	69	0.30
Costa Rican	2	0.01
Guatemalan	19	0.08
Honduran	8	0.03
Nicaraguan	6	0.03
Panamanian	4	0.02
Salvadoran	30	0.13
Cuban	16	0.07
Dominican Republic	3	0.01
Mexican	810	3.54
Puerto Rican	35	0.15
South American	22	0.10
Argentinean	1	<0.01

*Notes: † The Census 2010 population figure is used to calculate the percentages in the Hispanic Origin and Race categories. Ancestry percentages are based on the 2006-2010 American Community Survey population (not shown); ‡ Numbers in parentheses indicate the number of people reporting a single ancestry; * Numbers in parentheses indicate the number of persons reporting this race alone, not in combination with any other race; Please refer to the Explanation of Data for more information.*

Bolivian	1	<0.01
Colombian	6	0.03
Ecuadorian	1	<0.01
Peruvian	4	0.02
Uruguayan	1	<0.01
Venezuelan	8	0.03
Other Hispanic or Latino	86	0.38

Race*	Population	%
African-American/Black (1,711)	1,972	8.63
Not Hispanic (1,697)	1,939	8.48
Hispanic (14)	33	0.14
American Indian/Alaska Native (115)	236	1.03
Not Hispanic (114)	220	0.96
Hispanic (1)	16	0.07
Blackfeet (0)	4	0.02
Canadian/French Am. Ind. (1)	1	<0.01
Cherokee (33)	72	0.31
Cheyenne (0)	2	0.01
Chickasaw (2)	5	0.02
Chippewa (0)	5	0.02
Choctaw (11)	20	0.09
Creek (7)	8	0.03
Delaware (0)	1	<0.01
Iroquois (0)	1	<0.01
Mexican American Ind. (0)	1	<0.01
Navajo (2)	2	0.01
Ottawa (0)	2	0.01
Potawatomi (1)	1	<0.01
Pueblo (1)	1	<0.01
Puget Sound Salish (1)	3	0.01
Seminole (1)	3	0.01
Sioux (0)	1	<0.01
Tohono O'Odham (0)	2	0.01
Yaqui (0)	2	0.01
Asian (287)	343	1.50
Not Hispanic (282)	336	1.47
Hispanic (5)	7	0.03
Chinese, ex. Taiwanese (135)	138	0.60
Filipino (35)	53	0.23
Indian (31)	37	0.16
Indonesian (3)	4	0.02
Japanese (7)	20	0.09
Korean (17)	24	0.10
Pakistani (1)	1	<0.01
Taiwanese (3)	3	0.01
Thai (3)	4	0.02
Vietnamese (41)	43	0.19
Hawaii Native/Pacific Islander (17)	28	0.12
Not Hispanic (15)	26	0.11
Hispanic (2)	2	0.01
Guamanian/Chamorro (6)	7	0.03
Native Hawaiian (0)	6	0.03
Samoan (1)	3	0.01
White (19,839)	20,247	88.58
Not Hispanic (19,307)	19,670	86.05
Hispanic (532)	577	2.52

Sherwood

Place Type: City
County: Pulaski
Population: 29,523†

Ancestry‡	Population	%
African, Sub-Saharan (44)	44	0.15
African (44)	44	0.15
American (3,825)	3,825	13.33
Arab (55)	64	0.22
Arab (25)	25	0.09
Jordanian (12)	12	0.04
Lebanese (18)	27	0.09
Austrian (24)	24	0.08
Brazilian (62)	62	0.22
British (109)	109	0.38
Carpatho Rusyn (0)	15	0.05
Czech (17)	26	0.09
Czechoslovakian (0)	6	0.02
Danish (7)	7	0.02
Dutch (100)	445	1.55
English (1,334)	3,218	11.22
European (427)	582	2.03
Finnish (22)	36	0.13
French, ex. Basque (84)	358	1.25
French Canadian (24)	35	0.12
German (1,372)	3,296	11.49
Greek (16)	88	0.31
Irish (978)	2,973	10.36
Italian (158)	407	1.42
Northern European (31)	31	0.11
Norwegian (52)	237	0.83
Polish (198)	372	1.30
Portuguese (17)	46	0.16
Russian (66)	89	0.31
Scandinavian (4)	56	0.20
Scotch-Irish (384)	669	2.33
Scottish (212)	496	1.73
Slovak (12)	18	0.06
Swedish (63)	162	0.56
Swiss (0)	19	0.07
Turkish (43)	43	0.15
Ukrainian (32)	82	0.29
Welsh (29)	145	0.51
West Indian, ex. Hispanic (22)	51	0.18
Jamaican (22)	22	0.08
West Indian (0)	29	0.10

Hispanic Origin	Population	%
Hispanic or Latino (of any race)	1,181	4.00
Central American, ex. Mexican	94	0.32
Costa Rican	2	0.01
Guatemalan	21	0.07
Honduran	35	0.12
Nicaraguan	1	<0.01
Panamanian	7	0.02
Salvadoran	28	0.09
Cuban	24	0.08
Dominican Republic	5	0.02
Mexican	807	2.73
Puerto Rican	105	0.36
South American	39	0.13
Argentinean	7	0.02
Chilean	2	0.01
Colombian	11	0.04
Ecuadorian	2	0.01
Paraguayan	4	0.01
Peruvian	13	0.04
Other Hispanic or Latino	107	0.36

Race*	Population	%
African-American/Black (5,464)	5,806	19.67
Not Hispanic (5,439)	5,735	19.43
Hispanic (25)	71	0.24
American Indian/Alaska Native (155)	344	1.17
Not Hispanic (137)	300	1.02
Hispanic (18)	44	0.15
Alaska Athabascan *(Ala. Nat.)* (2)	2	0.01
Aleut *(Alaska Native)* (1)	1	<0.01
Apache (3)	9	0.03
Arapaho (0)	2	0.01
Blackfeet (0)	4	0.01
Central American Ind. (0)	1	<0.01
Cherokee (43)	123	0.42
Cheyenne (0)	1	<0.01
Chickasaw (1)	4	0.01
Chippewa (5)	5	0.02
Choctaw (17)	28	0.09
Comanche (0)	2	0.01
Creek (5)	5	0.02
Delaware (5)	5	0.02
Iroquois (2)	3	0.01
Kiowa (0)	2	0.01
Lumbee (4)	4	0.01
Mexican American Ind. (4)	5	0.02
Navajo (1)	1	<0.01
Osage (1)	3	0.01
Pima (1)	1	<0.01
Potawatomi (3)	3	0.01
Pueblo (1)	1	<0.01
Sioux (6)	9	0.03
South American Ind. (1)	1	<0.01
Spanish American Ind. (3)	3	0.01
Yakama (0)	2	0.01
Yup'ik *(Alaska Native)* (1)	1	<0.01
Asian (464)	627	2.12
Not Hispanic (461)	608	2.06
Hispanic (3)	19	0.06
Burmese (4)	4	0.01
Chinese, ex. Taiwanese (36)	54	0.18
Filipino (105)	162	0.55
Hmong (9)	9	0.03
Indian (61)	75	0.25
Indonesian (1)	1	<0.01
Japanese (21)	47	0.16
Korean (89)	126	0.43
Laotian (3)	3	0.01
Pakistani (4)	4	0.01
Taiwanese (11)	16	0.05
Thai (11)	23	0.08
Vietnamese (80)	97	0.33
Hawaii Native/Pacific Islander (20)	33	0.11
Not Hispanic (18)	29	0.10
Hispanic (2)	4	0.01
Fijian (2)	2	0.01
Guamanian/Chamorro (6)	6	0.02
Native Hawaiian (10)	20	0.07
White (22,232)	22,864	77.44
Not Hispanic (21,681)	22,195	75.18
Hispanic (551)	669	2.27

Siloam Springs

Place Type: City
County: Benton
Population: 15,039†

Ancestry‡	Population	%
African, Sub-Saharan (0)	9	0.06
African (0)	9	0.06
American (970)	970	6.75
Arab (32)	108	0.75
Moroccan (21)	97	0.68
Syrian (11)	11	0.08
Austrian (13)	13	0.09
Belgian (49)	64	0.45
British (21)	59	0.41
Canadian (0)	14	0.10
Czech (0)	26	0.18
Danish (0)	28	0.19
Dutch (8)	126	0.88
English (386)	1,056	7.35
European (68)	68	0.47
French, ex. Basque (48)	319	2.22
French Canadian (25)	25	0.17
German (526)	2,028	14.11
Greek (0)	58	0.40
Irish (358)	1,738	12.09
Italian (33)	224	1.56
Norwegian (41)	96	0.67
Pennsylvania German (0)	11	0.08
Polish (109)	226	1.57
Portuguese (14)	14	0.10
Russian (0)	14	0.10
Scotch-Irish (46)	194	1.35
Scottish (136)	471	3.28
Slovak (0)	9	0.06
Slovene (0)	9	0.06
Swedish (28)	176	1.22
Swiss (0)	70	0.49
Welsh (36)	85	0.59
West Indian, ex. Hispanic (26)	26	0.18
Jamaican (14)	14	0.10
Trinidadian/Tobagonian (12)	12	0.08

Hispanic Origin	Population	%
Hispanic or Latino (of any race)	3,128	20.80
Central American, ex. Mexican	1,094	7.27
Costa Rican	8	0.05
Guatemalan	198	1.32
Honduran	49	0.33

*Notes: † The Census 2010 population figure is used to calculate the percentages in the Hispanic Origin and Race categories. Ancestry percentages are based on the 2006-2010 American Community Survey population (not shown); ‡ Numbers in parentheses indicate the number of people reporting a single ancestry; * Numbers in parentheses indicate the number of persons reporting this race alone, not in combination with any other race; Please refer to the Explanation of Data for more information.*

Nicaraguan	29	0.19
Panamanian	13	0.09
Salvadoran	796	5.29
Other Central American	1	0.01
Cuban	4	0.03
Dominican Republic	2	0.01
Mexican	1,686	11.21
Puerto Rican	16	0.11
South American	42	0.28
Argentinean	2	0.01
Bolivian	3	0.02
Colombian	8	0.05
Ecuadorian	21	0.14
Peruvian	5	0.03
Venezuelan	3	0.02
Other Hispanic or Latino	284	1.89

Race*	Population	%
African-American/Black (119)	168	1.12
Not Hispanic (111)	156	1.04
Hispanic (8)	12	0.08
American Indian/Alaska Native (695)	1,200	7.98
Not Hispanic (651)	1,122	7.46
Hispanic (44)	78	0.52
Aleut *(Alaska Native)* (0)	1	0.01
Apache (4)	8	0.05
Blackfeet (1)	2	0.01
Cherokee (489)	873	5.80
Chickasaw (2)	2	0.01
Choctaw (28)	52	0.35
Comanche (3)	5	0.03
Creek (24)	40	0.27
Delaware (7)	7	0.05
Iroquois (1)	4	0.03
Menominee (0)	1	0.01
Mexican American Ind. (6)	11	0.07
Navajo (5)	6	0.04
Osage (5)	11	0.07
Pima (0)	1	0.01
Potawatomi (8)	11	0.07
Pueblo (0)	1	0.01
Seminole (2)	2	0.01
Sioux (5)	18	0.12
Asian (234)	329	2.19
Not Hispanic (227)	298	1.98
Hispanic (7)	31	0.21
Cambodian (4)	4	0.03
Chinese, ex. Taiwanese (14)	25	0.17
Filipino (58)	92	0.61
Hmong (60)	61	0.41
Indian (19)	27	0.18
Japanese (11)	29	0.19
Korean (22)	27	0.18
Laotian (4)	9	0.06
Sri Lankan (4)	4	0.03
Thai (4)	15	0.10
Vietnamese (11)	12	0.08
Hawaii Native/Pacific Islander (7)	16	0.11
Not Hispanic (6)	12	0.08
Hispanic (1)	4	0.03
Guamanian/Chamorro (5)	7	0.05
Native Hawaiian (0)	3	0.02
Samoan (1)	2	0.01
White (11,153)	11,869	78.92
Not Hispanic (10,314)	10,877	72.33
Hispanic (839)	992	6.60

Springdale

Place Type: City
County: Washington
Population: 69,797[†]

Ancestry[‡]	Population	%
African, Sub-Saharan (13)	13	0.02
African (13)	13	0.02
American (5,332)	5,332	8.02
Arab (50)	142	0.21
Arab (0)	40	0.06
Jordanian (19)	19	0.03
Lebanese (15)	27	0.04
Palestinian (0)	40	0.06
Other Arab (16)	16	0.02
Armenian (0)	30	0.05
Australian (0)	10	0.02
Brazilian (37)	37	0.06
British (148)	171	0.26
Cajun (25)	45	0.07
Canadian (0)	22	0.03
Croatian (0)	11	0.02
Czech (72)	142	0.21
Danish (36)	88	0.13
Dutch (90)	684	1.03
English (2,284)	4,812	7.24
European (171)	231	0.35
Finnish (8)	8	0.01
French, ex. Basque (379)	1,176	1.77
French Canadian (36)	73	0.11
German (2,582)	6,927	10.42
Greek (10)	10	0.02
Hungarian (38)	38	0.06
Irish (2,812)	7,119	10.71
Israeli (51)	51	0.08
Italian (454)	1,182	1.78
Lithuanian (0)	15	0.02
Luxemburger (0)	10	0.02
Norwegian (43)	272	0.41
Polish (127)	383	0.58
Portuguese (80)	138	0.21
Russian (12)	49	0.07
Scandinavian (79)	207	0.31
Scotch-Irish (468)	758	1.14
Scottish (591)	1,100	1.66
Slavic (10)	10	0.02
Swedish (67)	403	0.61
Swiss (0)	54	0.08
Turkish (0)	10	0.02
Ukrainian (36)	58	0.09
Welsh (38)	159	0.24
West Indian, ex. Hispanic (12)	12	0.02
Belizean (12)	12	0.02

Hispanic Origin	Population	%
Hispanic or Latino (of any race)	24,692	35.38
Central American, ex. Mexican	4,092	5.86
Costa Rican	37	0.05
Guatemalan	455	0.65
Honduran	188	0.27
Nicaraguan	70	0.10
Panamanian	17	0.02
Salvadoran	3,316	4.75
Other Central American	9	0.01
Cuban	57	0.08
Dominican Republic	20	0.03
Mexican	18,404	26.37
Puerto Rican	305	0.44
South American	182	0.26
Argentinean	3	<0.01
Bolivian	13	0.02
Chilean	7	0.01
Colombian	60	0.09
Ecuadorian	39	0.06
Peruvian	53	0.08
Venezuelan	7	0.01
Other Hispanic or Latino	1,632	2.34

Race*	Population	%
African-American/Black (1,251)	1,634	2.34
Not Hispanic (1,160)	1,482	2.12
Hispanic (91)	152	0.22
American Indian/Alaska Native (679)	1,401	2.01
Not Hispanic (534)	1,144	1.64
Hispanic (145)	257	0.37
Alaska Athabascan *(Ala. Nat.)* (2)	2	<0.01
Aleut *(Alaska Native)* (0)	1	<0.01
Apache (5)	14	0.02
Blackfeet (0)	7	0.01
Canadian/French Am. Ind. (1)	1	<0.01
Central American Ind. (9)	10	0.01
Cherokee (252)	567	0.81
Cheyenne (6)	9	0.01
Chickasaw (13)	19	0.03
Chippewa (4)	12	0.02
Choctaw (34)	81	0.12
Comanche (1)	3	<0.01
Cree (1)	2	<0.01
Creek (28)	43	0.06
Delaware (6)	23	0.03
Hopi (4)	4	0.01
Houma (0)	3	<0.01
Iroquois (4)	8	0.01
Kiowa (6)	8	0.01
Mexican American Ind. (37)	47	0.07
Navajo (10)	21	0.03
Osage (8)	14	0.02
Potawatomi (3)	5	0.01
Pueblo (2)	4	0.01
Puget Sound Salish (1)	1	<0.01
Seminole (3)	6	0.01
Sioux (4)	13	0.02
South American Ind. (3)	3	<0.01
Yaqui (1)	2	<0.01
Yup'ik *(Alaska Native)* (19)	42	0.06
Asian (1,363)	1,655	2.37
Not Hispanic (1,336)	1,575	2.26
Hispanic (27)	80	0.11
Bangladeshi (1)	7	0.01
Cambodian (3)	4	0.01
Chinese, ex. Taiwanese (64)	89	0.13
Filipino (112)	171	0.24
Hmong (42)	47	0.07
Indian (155)	204	0.29
Indonesian (3)	6	0.01
Japanese (26)	67	0.10
Korean (70)	98	0.14
Laotian (622)	696	1.00
Malaysian (5)	5	0.01
Pakistani (9)	9	0.01
Taiwanese (13)	13	0.02
Thai (36)	60	0.09
Vietnamese (114)	129	0.18
Hawaii Native/Pacific Islander (3,976)	4,172	5.98
Not Hispanic (3,967)	4,152	5.95
Hispanic (9)	20	0.03
Fijian (4)	4	0.01
Guamanian/Chamorro (16)	25	0.04
Marshallese (3,603)	3,740	5.36
Native Hawaiian (96)	118	0.17
Samoan (4)	5	0.01
Tongan (8)	8	0.01
White (45,185)	46,889	67.18
Not Hispanic (36,798)	37,805	54.16
Hispanic (8,387)	9,084	13.01

Stuttgart

Place Type: City
County: Arkansas
Population: 9,326[†]

Ancestry[‡]	Population	%
African, Sub-Saharan (69)	69	0.73
African (69)	69	0.73
American (645)	645	6.86
Arab (0)	16	0.17
Syrian (0)	16	0.17
British (12)	12	0.13
Cajun (28)	28	0.30
Czech (21)	21	0.22
Danish (8)	16	0.17
Dutch (30)	144	1.53
English (247)	524	5.57
European (53)	60	0.64
Finnish (8)	8	0.09
French, ex. Basque (66)	191	2.03
German (729)	1,302	13.85
Hungarian (36)	36	0.38
Irish (159)	911	9.69
Italian (24)	68	0.72
Norwegian (12)	30	0.32

*Notes: † The Census 2010 population figure is used to calculate the percentages in the Hispanic Origin and Race categories. Ancestry percentages are based on the 2006-2010 American Community Survey population (not shown); ‡ Numbers in parentheses indicate the number of people reporting a single ancestry; * Numbers in parentheses indicate the number of persons reporting this race alone, not in combination with any other race; Please refer to the Explanation of Data for more information.*

Ancestry	Population	%
Polish (0)	68	0.72
Russian (0)	8	0.09
Scotch-Irish (47)	91	0.97
Scottish (51)	161	1.71
Slovak (28)	67	0.71
Slovene (10)	10	0.11
Swedish (6)	33	0.35
Swiss (8)	8	0.09
Welsh (13)	46	0.49

Hispanic Origin	Population	%
Hispanic or Latino (of any race)	329	3.53
Central American, ex. Mexican	7	0.08
Honduran	2	0.02
Panamanian	5	0.05
Mexican	296	3.17
Puerto Rican	2	0.02
South American	1	0.01
Other South American	1	0.01
Other Hispanic or Latino	23	0.25

Race*	Population	%
African-American/Black (3,408)	3,488	37.40
Not Hispanic (3,396)	3,475	37.26
Hispanic (12)	13	0.14
American Indian/Alaska Native (17)	61	0.65
Not Hispanic (16)	59	0.63
Hispanic (1)	2	0.02
Apache (0)	1	0.01
Blackfeet (0)	1	0.01
Cherokee (3)	16	0.17
Choctaw (1)	2	0.02
Kiowa (1)	1	0.01
Mexican American Ind. (1)	1	0.01
Asian (69)	81	0.87
Not Hispanic (69)	81	0.87
Bangladeshi (1)	1	0.01
Chinese, ex. Taiwanese (15)	17	0.18
Filipino (4)	10	0.11
Indian (3)	4	0.04
Japanese (0)	1	0.01
Korean (4)	5	0.05
Laotian (6)	6	0.06
Thai (11)	11	0.12
Vietnamese (22)	22	0.24
Hawaii Native/Pacific Islander (0)	4	0.04
Not Hispanic (0)	4	0.04
Guamanian/Chamorro (0)	1	0.01
Native Hawaiian (0)	1	0.01
White (5,477)	5,588	59.92
Not Hispanic (5,386)	5,490	58.87
Hispanic (91)	98	1.05

Texarkana

Place Type: City
County: Miller
Population: 29,919†

Ancestry‡	Population	%
African, Sub-Saharan (1,433)	1,488	5.00
African (1,433)	1,488	5.00
American (3,108)	3,108	10.43
Australian (0)	16	0.05
Austrian (20)	20	0.07
Belgian (10)	10	0.03
British (82)	90	0.30
Celtic (5)	5	0.02
Czech (0)	10	0.03
Dutch (64)	461	1.55
Eastern European (0)	17	0.06
English (1,126)	2,524	8.47
European (54)	108	0.36
French, ex. Basque (23)	414	1.39
French Canadian (20)	20	0.07
German (830)	2,136	7.17
Greek (5)	5	0.02
Hungarian (7)	7	0.02
Irish (1,195)	3,139	10.54
Italian (366)	746	2.50
Polish (9)	24	0.08
Russian (8)	8	0.03
Scotch-Irish (251)	494	1.66
Scottish (236)	422	1.42
Slovak (15)	15	0.05
Swedish (22)	153	0.51
Ukrainian (27)	79	0.27
Welsh (57)	149	0.50
West Indian, ex. Hispanic (0)	5	0.02
Dutch West Indian (0)	5	0.02

Hispanic Origin	Population	%
Hispanic or Latino (of any race)	844	2.82
Central American, ex. Mexican	24	0.08
Costa Rican	3	0.01
Guatemalan	2	0.01
Honduran	9	0.03
Nicaraguan	1	<0.01
Panamanian	4	0.01
Salvadoran	3	0.01
Other Central American	2	0.01
Cuban	11	0.04
Dominican Republic	4	0.01
Mexican	627	2.10
Puerto Rican	52	0.17
South American	7	0.02
Colombian	2	0.01
Peruvian	4	0.01
Venezuelan	1	<0.01
Other Hispanic or Latino	119	0.40

Race*	Population	%
African-American/Black (9,928)	10,262	34.30
Not Hispanic (9,853)	10,148	33.92
Hispanic (75)	114	0.38
American Indian/Alaska Native (170)	364	1.22
Not Hispanic (160)	323	1.08
Hispanic (10)	41	0.14
Alaska Athabascan *(Ala. Nat.)* (1)	1	<0.01
Apache (3)	4	0.01
Blackfeet (5)	8	0.03
Canadian/French Am. Ind. (0)	3	0.01
Cherokee (38)	109	0.36
Cheyenne (1)	2	0.01
Chickasaw (1)	2	0.01
Chippewa (3)	6	0.02
Choctaw (40)	62	0.21
Comanche (2)	4	0.01
Creek (6)	7	0.02
Crow (0)	1	<0.01
Lumbee (1)	1	<0.01
Mexican American Ind. (2)	2	0.01
Navajo (6)	6	0.02
Sioux (0)	3	0.01
Spanish American Ind. (1)	2	0.01
Tohono O'Odham (0)	1	<0.01
Ute (0)	1	<0.01
Asian (167)	255	0.85
Not Hispanic (166)	243	0.81
Hispanic (1)	12	0.04
Bangladeshi (3)	3	0.01
Cambodian (1)	3	0.01
Chinese, ex. Taiwanese (16)	27	0.09
Filipino (28)	54	0.18
Indian (27)	32	0.11
Indonesian (0)	1	<0.01
Japanese (6)	18	0.06
Korean (13)	23	0.08
Laotian (0)	2	0.01
Pakistani (9)	9	0.03
Thai (6)	14	0.05
Vietnamese (51)	52	0.17
Hawaii Native/Pacific Islander (15)	40	0.13
Not Hispanic (15)	38	0.13
Hispanic (0)	2	0.01
Guamanian/Chamorro (2)	6	0.02
Native Hawaiian (10)	21	0.07
Samoan (3)	4	0.01
White (18,674)	19,184	64.12
Not Hispanic (18,356)	18,794	62.82
Hispanic (318)	390	1.30

Van Buren

Place Type: City
County: Crawford
Population: 22,791†

Ancestry‡	Population	%
American (1,954)	1,954	8.79
British (41)	41	0.18
Czech (12)	64	0.29
Czechoslovakian (0)	31	0.14
Dutch (43)	745	3.35
English (874)	2,675	12.03
European (119)	119	0.54
Finnish (32)	32	0.14
French, ex. Basque (31)	178	0.80
French Canadian (32)	32	0.14
German (800)	2,616	11.76
Greek (14)	14	0.06
Hungarian (0)	24	0.11
Iranian (12)	70	0.31
Irish (819)	2,944	13.24
Italian (46)	126	0.57
Norwegian (11)	43	0.19
Polish (49)	303	1.36
Portuguese (21)	21	0.09
Russian (0)	23	0.10
Scotch-Irish (17)	76	0.34
Scottish (102)	286	1.29
Slavic (0)	64	0.29
Swedish (13)	34	0.15
Swiss (0)	16	0.07
Welsh (16)	109	0.49
West Indian, ex. Hispanic (39)	64	0.29
Dutch West Indian (28)	46	0.21
Jamaican (11)	18	0.08

Hispanic Origin	Population	%
Hispanic or Latino (of any race)	2,653	11.64
Central American, ex. Mexican	1,040	4.56
Guatemalan	75	0.33
Honduran	50	0.22
Nicaraguan	2	0.01
Panamanian	2	0.01
Salvadoran	903	3.96
Other Central American	8	0.04
Cuban	26	0.11
Dominican Republic	3	0.01
Mexican	1,261	5.53
Puerto Rican	72	0.32
South American	38	0.17
Colombian	8	0.04
Ecuadorian	2	0.01
Peruvian	19	0.08
Uruguayan	1	<0.01
Venezuelan	8	0.04
Other Hispanic or Latino	213	0.93

Race*	Population	%
African-American/Black (490)	656	2.88
Not Hispanic (467)	610	2.68
Hispanic (23)	46	0.20
American Indian/Alaska Native (539)	909	3.99
Not Hispanic (517)	855	3.75
Hispanic (22)	54	0.24
Alaska Athabascan *(Ala. Nat.)* (1)	1	<0.01
Apache (3)	10	0.04
Blackfeet (0)	3	0.01
Central American Ind. (6)	6	0.03
Cherokee (297)	494	2.17
Chickasaw (4)	8	0.04
Chippewa (2)	4	0.02
Choctaw (81)	131	0.57
Comanche (1)	1	<0.01
Creek (10)	28	0.12
Crow (0)	2	0.01
Delaware (1)	1	<0.01
Hopi (0)	2	0.01

*Notes: † The Census 2010 population figure is used to calculate the percentages in the Hispanic Origin and Race categories. Ancestry percentages are based on the 2006-2010 American Community Survey population (not shown); ‡ Numbers in parentheses indicate the number of people reporting a single ancestry; * Numbers in parentheses indicate the number of persons reporting this race alone, not in combination with any other race; Please refer to the Explanation of Data for more information.*

	Population	%
Kiowa (2)	2	0.01
Mexican American Ind. (0)	4	0.02
Navajo (4)	4	0.02
Osage (0)	3	0.01
Ottawa (4)	4	0.02
Potawatomi (2)	2	0.01
Pueblo (1)	1	<0.01
Seminole (4)	6	0.03
Sioux (3)	6	0.03
Asian (712)	849	3.73
Not Hispanic (700)	824	3.62
Hispanic (12)	25	0.11
Cambodian (7)	7	0.03
Chinese, ex. Taiwanese (44)	52	0.23
Filipino (51)	81	0.36
Indian (29)	30	0.13
Indonesian (2)	3	0.01
Japanese (6)	18	0.08
Korean (19)	30	0.13
Laotian (334)	385	1.69
Sri Lankan (0)	4	0.02
Thai (4)	10	0.04
Vietnamese (188)	211	0.93
Hawaii Native/Pacific Islander (12)	30	0.13
Not Hispanic (11)	25	0.11
Hispanic (1)	5	0.02
Guamanian/Chamorro (0)	1	<0.01
Marshallese (1)	1	<0.01
Native Hawaiian (4)	14	0.06
Samoan (4)	7	0.03
White (18,752)	19,506	85.59
Not Hispanic (17,835)	18,394	80.71
Hispanic (917)	1,112	4.88

West Memphis

Place Type: City
County: Crittenden
Population: 26,245†

Ancestry‡	Population	%
African, Sub-Saharan (65)	65	0.25
African (65)	65	0.25
American (1,413)	1,413	5.35
Brazilian (7)	7	0.03
British (12)	63	0.24
Celtic (0)	12	0.05
Czech (12)	12	0.05
Dutch (22)	142	0.54
English (759)	1,163	4.41
European (53)	53	0.20
French, ex. Basque (53)	326	1.24
German (510)	1,463	5.54
Irish (531)	1,572	5.96
Italian (110)	196	0.74
Norwegian (0)	10	0.04
Polish (46)	157	0.59
Portuguese (47)	47	0.18
Romanian (0)	4	0.02
Russian (19)	19	0.07
Scotch-Irish (164)	230	0.87
Scottish (30)	109	0.41
Swedish (12)	28	0.11
Swiss (9)	9	0.03
Welsh (70)	89	0.34
West Indian, ex. Hispanic (48)	48	0.18
Jamaican (38)	38	0.14
West Indian (10)	10	0.04

Hispanic Origin	Population	%
Hispanic or Latino (of any race)	419	1.60
Central American, ex. Mexican	28	0.11
Costa Rican	3	0.01
Guatemalan	2	0.01
Honduran	4	0.02
Nicaraguan	8	0.03
Panamanian	5	0.02
Salvadoran	6	0.02
Cuban	7	0.03
Dominican Republic	2	0.01
Mexican	292	1.11
Puerto Rican	27	0.10
Other Hispanic or Latino	63	0.24

Race*	Population	%
African-American/Black (16,667)	16,850	64.20
Not Hispanic (16,608)	16,775	63.92
Hispanic (59)	75	0.29
American Indian/Alaska Native (52)	110	0.42
Not Hispanic (39)	95	0.36
Hispanic (13)	15	0.06
Blackfeet (2)	2	0.01
Cherokee (15)	37	0.14
Chippewa (1)	1	<0.01
Choctaw (1)	2	0.01
Mexican American Ind. (5)	5	0.02
Navajo (1)	1	<0.01
Potawatomi (0)	1	<0.01
Asian (103)	145	0.55
Not Hispanic (103)	142	0.54
Hispanic (0)	3	0.01
Chinese, ex. Taiwanese (44)	47	0.18
Filipino (12)	22	0.08
Indian (14)	23	0.09
Japanese (4)	10	0.04
Korean (19)	20	0.08
Pakistani (4)	4	0.02
Thai (0)	1	<0.01
Vietnamese (2)	7	0.03
Hawaii Native/Pacific Islander (6)	13	0.05
Not Hispanic (4)	10	0.04
Hispanic (2)	3	0.01
Guamanian/Chamorro (0)	1	<0.01
Native Hawaiian (5)	9	0.03
Samoan (0)	1	<0.01
White (9,020)	9,204	35.07
Not Hispanic (8,843)	9,000	34.29
Hispanic (177)	204	0.78

Wynne

Place Type: City
County: Cross
Population: 8,367†

Ancestry‡	Population	%
African, Sub-Saharan (51)	51	0.61
African (51)	51	0.61
American (981)	981	11.67
British (11)	349	4.15
English (554)	875	10.41
European (72)	72	0.86
Finnish (9)	9	0.11
French, ex. Basque (0)	57	0.68
German (246)	599	7.12
Greek (0)	13	0.15
Irish (311)	758	9.02
Italian (10)	124	1.47
Polish (0)	132	1.57
Scotch-Irish (95)	164	1.95
Scottish (37)	56	0.67
Welsh (0)	23	0.27

Hispanic Origin	Population	%
Hispanic or Latino (of any race)	160	1.91
Cuban	1	0.01
Dominican Republic	1	0.01
Mexican	142	1.70
Puerto Rican	5	0.06
South American	1	0.01
Uruguayan	1	0.01
Other Hispanic or Latino	10	0.12

Race*	Population	%
African-American/Black (2,631)	2,685	32.09
Not Hispanic (2,628)	2,681	32.04
Hispanic (3)	4	0.05
American Indian/Alaska Native (15)	41	0.49
Not Hispanic (15)	39	0.47
Hispanic (0)	2	0.02
Blackfeet (0)	1	0.01
Cherokee (2)	16	0.19
Choctaw (1)	1	0.01
Creek (0)	2	0.02
Iroquois (0)	3	0.04
Asian (73)	87	1.04
Not Hispanic (73)	87	1.04
Cambodian (2)	2	0.02
Chinese, ex. Taiwanese (13)	16	0.19
Filipino (8)	16	0.19
Indian (24)	24	0.29
Japanese (8)	10	0.12
Korean (3)	3	0.04
Taiwanese (1)	1	0.01
Vietnamese (13)	16	0.19
Hawaii Native/Pacific Islander (0)	1	0.01
Not Hispanic (0)	1	0.01
Guamanian/Chamorro (0)	1	0.01
White (5,498)	5,586	66.76
Not Hispanic (5,409)	5,480	65.50
Hispanic (89)	106	1.27

*Notes: † The Census 2010 population figure is used to calculate the percentages in the Hispanic Origin and Race categories. Ancestry percentages are based on the 2006-2010 American Community Survey population (not shown); ‡ Numbers in parentheses indicate the number of people reporting a single ancestry; * Numbers in parentheses indicate the number of persons reporting this race alone, not in combination with any other race; Please refer to the Explanation of Data for more information.*

CALIFORNIA

Place Type: State
Population: 37,253,956†

Ancestry‡	Population	%
Afghan (31,291)	33,216	0.09
African, Sub-Saharan (211,499)	265,745	0.73
African (138,676)	181,250	0.49
Cape Verdean (1,322)	2,514	0.01
Ethiopian (22,305)	24,586	0.07
Ghanaian (2,126)	2,383	0.01
Kenyan (3,027)	3,397	0.01
Liberian (1,031)	1,184	<0.01
Nigerian (19,694)	21,824	0.06
Senegalese (473)	644	<0.01
Sierra Leonean (458)	667	<0.01
Somalian (6,660)	7,150	0.02
South African (5,978)	8,602	0.02
Sudanese (2,776)	3,028	0.01
Ugandan (1,082)	1,202	<0.01
Zimbabwean (525)	726	<0.01
Other Sub-Saharan African (5,366)	6,588	0.02
Albanian (2,159)	3,854	0.01
Alsatian (256)	926	<0.01
American (889,435)	889,435	2.43
Arab (178,290)	247,243	0.67
Arab (31,197)	41,438	0.11
Egyptian (31,633)	37,531	0.10
Iraqi (11,109)	15,029	0.04
Jordanian (10,962)	13,108	0.04
Lebanese (33,893)	58,107	0.16
Moroccan (5,465)	8,147	0.02
Palestinian (14,035)	18,442	0.05
Syrian (11,044)	19,307	0.05
Other Arab (28,952)	36,134	0.10
Armenian (199,725)	241,323	0.66
Assyrian/Chaldean/Syriac (22,514)	27,563	0.08
Australian (9,511)	19,471	0.05
Austrian (21,461)	81,470	0.22
Basque (8,463)	20,606	0.06
Belgian (9,074)	27,884	0.08
Brazilian (19,862)	30,167	0.08
British (80,256)	150,588	0.41
Bulgarian (7,944)	11,242	0.03
Cajun (1,411)	2,987	0.01
Canadian (44,744)	90,905	0.25
Carpatho Rusyn (64)	374	<0.01
Celtic (3,816)	7,889	0.02
Croatian (19,225)	45,537	0.12
Cypriot (474)	604	<0.01
Czech (25,930)	94,047	0.26
Czechoslovakian (11,160)	25,946	0.07
Danish (52,530)	194,960	0.53
Dutch (105,296)	422,077	1.15
Eastern European (48,975)	56,408	0.15
English (696,517)	2,482,263	6.78
Estonian (1,725)	3,744	0.01
European (387,618)	469,275	1.28
Finnish (17,635)	54,331	0.15
French, ex. Basque (126,540)	775,213	2.12
French Canadian (47,219)	117,231	0.32
German (933,090)	3,506,466	9.57
German Russian (612)	1,616	<0.01
Greek (60,205)	138,194	0.38
Guyanese (1,916)	2,932	0.01
Hungarian (45,512)	131,741	0.36
Icelander (3,058)	7,372	0.02
Iranian (175,122)	203,656	0.56
Irish (678,425)	2,748,155	7.50
Israeli (21,339)	28,074	0.08
Italian (570,968)	1,543,300	4.21
Latvian (4,764)	11,443	0.03
Lithuanian (17,224)	51,747	0.14
Luxemburger (782)	2,948	0.01
Macedonian (1,545)	2,776	0.01
Maltese (3,742)	7,582	0.02
New Zealander (2,696)	4,604	0.01
Northern European (41,001)	45,938	0.13
Norwegian (125,259)	401,548	1.10
Pennsylvania German (3,427)	7,691	0.02
Polish (154,032)	515,633	1.41
Portuguese (170,785)	374,875	1.02
Romanian (38,673)	67,491	0.18
Russian (204,639)	446,376	1.22
Scandinavian (31,728)	67,697	0.18
Scotch-Irish (147,602)	435,810	1.19
Scottish (155,163)	565,334	1.54
Serbian (7,715)	15,315	0.04
Slavic (4,984)	13,137	0.04
Slovak (9,123)	24,859	0.07
Slovene (2,813)	8,956	0.02
Soviet Union (293)	334	<0.01
Swedish (113,350)	456,603	1.25
Swiss (27,062)	114,687	0.31
Turkish (13,579)	22,091	0.06
Ukrainian (56,056)	93,449	0.26
Welsh (30,899)	180,792	0.49
West Indian, ex. Hispanic (46,550)	73,694	0.20
Bahamian (424)	775	<0.01
Barbadian (734)	1,235	<0.01
Belizean (14,852)	19,627	0.05
Bermudan (177)	308	<0.01
British West Indian (1,147)	1,757	<0.01
Dutch West Indian (625)	2,806	0.01
Haitian (4,912)	7,538	0.02
Jamaican (16,117)	25,882	0.07
Trinidadian/Tobagonian (2,671)	4,439	0.01
U.S. Virgin Islander (305)	450	<0.01
West Indian (4,457)	8,589	0.02
Other West Indian (129)	288	<0.01
Yugoslavian (18,028)	37,235	0.10

Hispanic Origin	Population	%
Hispanic or Latino (of any race)	14,013,719	37.62
Central American, ex. Mexican	1,132,520	3.04
Costa Rican	22,469	0.06
Guatemalan	332,737	0.89
Honduran	72,795	0.20
Nicaraguan	100,790	0.27
Panamanian	17,768	0.05
Salvadoran	573,956	1.54
Other Central American	12,005	0.03
Cuban	88,607	0.24
Dominican Republic	11,455	0.03
Mexican	11,423,146	30.66
Puerto Rican	189,945	0.51
South American	293,880	0.79
Argentinean	44,410	0.12
Bolivian	13,351	0.04
Chilean	24,006	0.06
Colombian	64,416	0.17
Ecuadorian	35,750	0.10
Paraguayan	1,228	<0.01
Peruvian	91,511	0.25
Uruguayan	4,110	0.01
Venezuelan	11,100	0.03
Other South American	3,998	0.01
Other Hispanic or Latino	874,166	2.35

Race*	Population	%
African-American/Black (2,299,072)	2,683,914	7.20
Not Hispanic (2,163,804)	2,436,082	6.54
Hispanic (135,268)	247,832	0.67
American Indian/Alaska Native (362,801)	723,225	1.94
Not Hispanic (162,250)	383,957	1.03
Hispanic (200,551)	339,268	0.91
Alaska Athabascan *(Ala. Nat.)* (378)	697	<0.01
Aleut *(Alaska Native)* (488)	1,107	<0.01
Apache (10,803)	24,799	0.07
Arapaho (316)	727	<0.01
Blackfeet (2,498)	15,420	0.04
Canadian/French Am. Ind. (597)	1,645	<0.01
Central American Ind. (2,412)	4,329	0.01
Cherokee (20,969)	92,246	0.25
Cheyenne (543)	1,546	<0.01
Chickasaw (1,822)	4,827	0.01
Chippewa (3,095)	7,250	0.02
Choctaw (7,389)	23,403	0.06
Colville (211)	368	<0.01
Comanche (1,150)	2,920	0.01
Cree (221)	1,053	<0.01
Creek (2,213)	6,195	0.02
Crow (283)	866	<0.01
Delaware (487)	1,289	<0.01
Hopi (1,022)	2,238	0.01
Houma (72)	137	<0.01
Inupiat *(Alaska Native)* (469)	1,019	<0.01
Iroquois (1,636)	5,443	0.01
Kiowa (388)	784	<0.01
Lumbee (413)	855	<0.01
Menominee (148)	316	<0.01
Mexican American Ind. (45,933)	66,424	0.18
Navajo (8,796)	17,080	0.05
Osage (657)	2,168	0.01
Ottawa (286)	651	<0.01
Paiute (2,390)	4,153	0.01
Pima (1,192)	2,127	0.01
Potawatomi (1,393)	2,962	0.01
Pueblo (2,973)	5,569	0.01
Puget Sound Salish (401)	749	<0.01
Seminole (640)	2,992	0.01
Shoshone (1,011)	2,217	0.01
Sioux (5,075)	12,439	0.03
South American Ind. (1,592)	4,121	0.01
Spanish American Ind. (2,854)	4,271	0.01
Tlingit-Haida *(Alaska Native)* (739)	1,571	<0.01
Tohono O'Odham (1,408)	2,359	0.01
Tsimshian *(Alaska Native)* (73)	190	<0.01
Ute (440)	1,111	<0.01
Yakama (168)	385	<0.01
Yaqui (5,279)	10,375	0.03
Yuman (2,263)	2,988	0.01
Yup'ik *(Alaska Native)* (157)	323	<0.01
Asian (4,861,007)	5,556,592	14.92
Not Hispanic (4,775,070)	5,324,591	14.29
Hispanic (85,937)	232,001	0.62
Bangladeshi (9,268)	10,494	0.03
Bhutanese (694)	750	<0.01
Burmese (15,035)	17,978	0.05
Cambodian (86,244)	102,317	0.27
Chinese, ex. Taiwanese (1,150,206)	1,349,111	3.62
Filipino (1,195,580)	1,474,707	3.96
Hmong (86,989)	91,224	0.24
Indian (528,176)	590,445	1.58
Indonesian (25,398)	39,506	0.11
Japanese (272,528)	428,014	1.15
Korean (451,892)	505,225	1.36
Laotian (58,424)	69,303	0.19
Malaysian (2,979)	5,595	0.02
Nepalese (5,618)	6,231	0.02
Pakistani (46,780)	53,474	0.14
Sri Lankan (10,240)	11,929	0.03
Taiwanese (96,009)	109,928	0.30
Thai (51,509)	67,707	0.18
Vietnamese (581,946)	647,589	1.74
Hawaii Native/Pacific Islander (144,386)	286,145	0.77
Not Hispanic (128,577)	233,405	0.63
Hispanic (15,809)	52,740	0.14
Fijian (19,355)	24,059	0.06
Guamanian/Chamorro (24,299)	44,425	0.12
Marshallese (1,559)	1,761	<0.01
Native Hawaiian (21,423)	74,932	0.20
Samoan (40,900)	60,876	0.16
Tongan (18,329)	22,893	0.06
White (21,453,934)	22,953,374	61.61
Not Hispanic (14,956,253)	15,763,625	42.31
Hispanic (6,497,681)	7,189,749	19.30

*Notes: † The Census 2010 population figure is used to calculate the percentages in the Hispanic Origin and Race categories. Ancestry percentages are based on the 2006-2010 American Community Survey population (not shown); ‡ Numbers in parentheses indicate the number of people reporting a single ancestry; * Numbers in parentheses indicate the number of persons reporting this race alone, not in combination with any other race; Please refer to the Explanation of Data for more information.*

Acton

Place Type: CDP
County: Los Angeles
Population: 7,596†

Ancestry‡	Population	%
Alsatian (0)	5	0.07
American (227)	227	3.17
Armenian (43)	43	0.60
Austrian (13)	53	0.74
Belgian (0)	20	0.28
British (11)	36	0.50
Bulgarian (0)	15	0.21
Canadian (41)	193	2.70
Croatian (0)	97	1.36
Danish (25)	91	1.27
Dutch (12)	241	3.37
English (168)	988	13.82
European (109)	109	1.52
Finnish (9)	62	0.87
French, ex. Basque (25)	330	4.62
French Canadian (51)	51	0.71
German (467)	1,735	24.27
Greek (23)	38	0.53
Hungarian (25)	32	0.45
Irish (178)	947	13.24
Italian (264)	705	9.86
Lithuanian (9)	9	0.13
Northern European (189)	189	2.64
Norwegian (22)	220	3.08
Pennsylvania German (0)	20	0.28
Polish (101)	287	4.01
Portuguese (11)	32	0.45
Romanian (34)	34	0.48
Russian (40)	93	1.30
Scandinavian (12)	48	0.67
Scotch-Irish (67)	114	1.59
Scottish (128)	422	5.90
Slovak (0)	11	0.15
Slovene (0)	15	0.21
Swedish (87)	155	2.17
Ukrainian (0)	11	0.15
Welsh (0)	91	1.27

Hispanic Origin	Population	%
Hispanic or Latino (of any race)	1,373	18.08
Central American, ex. Mexican	100	1.32
Costa Rican	11	0.14
Guatemalan	15	0.20
Honduran	1	0.01
Nicaraguan	10	0.13
Salvadoran	63	0.83
Cuban	40	0.53
Dominican Republic	1	0.01
Mexican	1,013	13.34
Puerto Rican	23	0.30
South American	48	0.63
Argentinean	12	0.16
Bolivian	1	0.01
Chilean	3	0.04
Colombian	11	0.14
Ecuadorian	8	0.11
Peruvian	11	0.14
Other South American	2	0.03
Other Hispanic or Latino	148	1.95

Race*	Population	%
African-American/Black (57)	104	1.37
Not Hispanic (54)	88	1.16
Hispanic (3)	16	0.21
American Indian/Alaska Native (70)	185	2.44
Not Hispanic (38)	119	1.57
Hispanic (32)	66	0.87
Apache (3)	9	0.12
Blackfeet (4)	12	0.16
Cherokee (6)	46	0.61
Choctaw (3)	5	0.07
Comanche (0)	1	0.01
Creek (4)	6	0.08
Iroquois (1)	1	0.01
Mexican American Ind. (2)	13	0.17
Navajo (0)	1	0.01
Osage (0)	4	0.05
Paiute (1)	1	0.01
Shoshone (1)	1	0.01
Spanish American Ind. (6)	6	0.08
Ute (1)	3	0.04
Yakama (0)	1	0.01
Yaqui (4)	4	0.05
Asian (155)	242	3.19
Not Hispanic (151)	218	2.87
Hispanic (4)	24	0.32
Cambodian (6)	8	0.11
Chinese, ex. Taiwanese (7)	35	0.46
Filipino (71)	101	1.33
Indian (16)	16	0.21
Indonesian (0)	4	0.05
Japanese (13)	34	0.45
Korean (29)	34	0.45
Taiwanese (3)	3	0.04
Thai (3)	6	0.08
Hawaii Native/Pacific Islander (5)	29	0.38
Not Hispanic (2)	21	0.28
Hispanic (3)	8	0.11
Guamanian/Chamorro (3)	3	0.04
Native Hawaiian (1)	17	0.22
Samoan (1)	4	0.05
White (6,564)	6,833	89.96
Not Hispanic (5,782)	5,950	78.33
Hispanic (782)	883	11.62

Adelanto

Place Type: City
County: San Bernardino
Population: 31,765†

Ancestry‡	Population	%
African, Sub-Saharan (107)	146	0.49
African (107)	118	0.40
Nigerian (0)	28	0.09
American (950)	950	3.19
Arab (23)	49	0.16
Lebanese (12)	38	0.13
Other Arab (11)	11	0.04
Armenian (161)	161	0.54
British (12)	12	0.04
Canadian (13)	26	0.09
Czech (0)	10	0.03
Dutch (0)	36	0.12
English (127)	407	1.37
European (102)	120	0.40
French, ex. Basque (37)	457	1.54
French Canadian (13)	72	0.24
German (235)	1,142	3.84
Hungarian (12)	24	0.08
Irish (121)	1,232	4.14
Italian (162)	594	2.00
Northern European (0)	105	0.35
Norwegian (0)	188	0.63
Pennsylvania German (0)	28	0.09
Polish (644)	695	2.34
Russian (0)	16	0.05
Scandinavian (64)	126	0.42
Scotch-Irish (84)	151	0.51
Scottish (40)	186	0.62
Slovak (16)	16	0.05
Swedish (30)	70	0.24
Swiss (0)	38	0.13
Ukrainian (39)	67	0.23
Welsh (0)	95	0.32
West Indian, ex. Hispanic (100)	112	0.38
Belizean (100)	100	0.34
Jamaican (0)	12	0.04

Hispanic Origin	Population	%
Hispanic or Latino (of any race)	18,513	58.28
Central American, ex. Mexican	1,244	3.92
Costa Rican	18	0.06
Guatemalan	298	0.94
Honduran	104	0.33
Nicaraguan	80	0.25
Panamanian	24	0.08
Salvadoran	707	2.23
Other Central American	13	0.04
Cuban	93	0.29
Dominican Republic	6	0.02
Mexican	15,471	48.70
Puerto Rican	240	0.76
South American	120	0.38
Argentinean	22	0.07
Bolivian	10	0.03
Chilean	10	0.03
Colombian	19	0.06
Ecuadorian	16	0.05
Peruvian	26	0.08
Uruguayan	1	<0.01
Venezuelan	8	0.03
Other South American	8	0.03
Other Hispanic or Latino	1,339	4.22

Race*	Population	%
African-American/Black (6,511)	7,259	22.85
Not Hispanic (6,196)	6,697	21.08
Hispanic (315)	562	1.77
American Indian/Alaska Native (411)	771	2.43
Not Hispanic (101)	303	0.95
Hispanic (310)	468	1.47
Aleut *(Alaska Native)* (1)	1	<0.01
Apache (27)	53	0.17
Blackfeet (1)	24	0.08
Cherokee (24)	103	0.32
Cheyenne (0)	1	<0.01
Chickasaw (0)	1	<0.01
Chippewa (4)	7	0.02
Choctaw (4)	12	0.04
Colville (2)	3	0.01
Comanche (4)	5	0.02
Creek (1)	2	0.01
Hopi (4)	4	0.01
Iroquois (1)	3	0.01
Mexican American Ind. (54)	74	0.23
Navajo (2)	7	0.02
Osage (0)	3	0.01
Ottawa (0)	1	<0.01
Paiute (1)	2	0.01
Pima (0)	6	0.02
Potawatomi (0)	1	<0.01
Pueblo (8)	10	0.03
Sioux (7)	15	0.05
South American Ind. (0)	1	<0.01
Spanish American Ind. (7)	7	0.02
Tohono O'Odham (4)	4	0.01
Yaqui (2)	3	0.01
Yuman (6)	11	0.03
Asian (617)	911	2.87
Not Hispanic (522)	700	2.20
Hispanic (95)	211	0.66
Bangladeshi (7)	11	0.03
Cambodian (39)	56	0.18
Chinese, ex. Taiwanese (33)	68	0.21
Filipino (288)	419	1.32
Indian (39)	55	0.17
Indonesian (13)	19	0.06
Japanese (25)	83	0.26
Korean (46)	71	0.22
Laotian (8)	22	0.07
Pakistani (13)	18	0.06
Sri Lankan (0)	2	0.01
Taiwanese (0)	1	<0.01
Thai (13)	34	0.11
Vietnamese (56)	85	0.27
Hawaii Native/Pacific Islander (194)	302	0.95
Not Hispanic (177)	259	0.82
Hispanic (17)	43	0.14
Guamanian/Chamorro (24)	42	0.13
Native Hawaiian (35)	64	0.20
Samoan (72)	101	0.32
Tongan (57)	83	0.26

*Notes: † The Census 2010 population figure is used to calculate the percentages in the Hispanic Origin and Race categories. Ancestry percentages are based on the 2006-2010 American Community Survey population (not shown); ‡ Numbers in parentheses indicate the number of people reporting a single ancestry; * Numbers in parentheses indicate the number of persons reporting this race alone, not in combination with any other race; Please refer to the Explanation of Data for more information.*

White (13,909)	15,289	48.13
Not Hispanic (5,395)	5,981	18.83
Hispanic (8,514)	9,308	29.30

Agoura Hills

Place Type: City
County: Los Angeles
Population: 20,330†

Ancestry‡	Population	%
Afghan (33)	33	0.16
African, Sub-Saharan (23)	23	0.11
Sudanese (23)	23	0.11
American (1,043)	1,043	5.13
Arab (124)	236	1.16
Arab (0)	12	0.06
Iraqi (42)	42	0.21
Lebanese (46)	91	0.45
Syrian (19)	19	0.09
Other Arab (17)	72	0.35
Armenian (89)	234	1.15
Austrian (51)	235	1.16
Basque (0)	8	0.04
Belgian (16)	16	0.08
Brazilian (13)	25	0.12
British (30)	128	0.63
Bulgarian (19)	41	0.20
Canadian (57)	173	0.85
Croatian (59)	59	0.29
Czech (16)	139	0.68
Czechoslovakian (27)	44	0.22
Danish (48)	230	1.13
Dutch (36)	210	1.03
Eastern European (645)	663	3.26
English (408)	1,385	6.81
European (522)	620	3.05
Finnish (14)	26	0.13
French, ex. Basque (18)	261	1.28
French Canadian (13)	59	0.29
German (972)	3,334	16.40
Greek (150)	251	1.23
Hungarian (186)	420	2.07
Iranian (203)	203	1.00
Irish (842)	2,366	11.64
Israeli (165)	215	1.06
Italian (553)	1,572	7.73
Latvian (0)	131	0.64
Lithuanian (34)	138	0.68
New Zealander (0)	13	0.06
Northern European (180)	180	0.89
Norwegian (106)	349	1.72
Polish (409)	1,380	6.79
Portuguese (14)	92	0.45
Romanian (30)	113	0.56
Russian (825)	1,725	8.49
Scotch-Irish (153)	473	2.33
Scottish (64)	383	1.88
Swedish (228)	491	2.42
Swiss (0)	244	1.20
Turkish (0)	22	0.11
Ukrainian (47)	130	0.64
Welsh (0)	84	0.41

Hispanic Origin	Population	%
Hispanic or Latino (of any race)	1,936	9.52
Central American, ex. Mexican	185	0.91
Costa Rican	8	0.04
Guatemalan	58	0.29
Honduran	11	0.05
Nicaraguan	16	0.08
Panamanian	13	0.06
Salvadoran	76	0.37
Other Central American	3	0.01
Cuban	59	0.29
Dominican Republic	5	0.02
Mexican	1,080	5.31
Puerto Rican	93	0.46
South American	295	1.45
Argentinean	99	0.49
Bolivian	5	0.02
Chilean	26	0.13
Colombian	50	0.25
Ecuadorian	35	0.17
Paraguayan	4	0.02
Peruvian	62	0.30
Uruguayan	5	0.02
Venezuelan	9	0.04
Other Hispanic or Latino	219	1.08

Race*	Population	%
African-American/Black (267)	414	2.04
Not Hispanic (256)	372	1.83
Hispanic (11)	42	0.21
American Indian/Alaska Native (51)	182	0.90
Not Hispanic (26)	132	0.65
Hispanic (25)	50	0.25
Apache (1)	2	0.01
Blackfeet (0)	5	0.02
Cherokee (8)	47	0.23
Chickasaw (0)	4	0.02
Chippewa (1)	6	0.03
Choctaw (3)	7	0.03
Comanche (0)	2	0.01
Cree (1)	1	<0.01
Delaware (0)	1	<0.01
Hopi (1)	1	<0.01
Iroquois (0)	3	0.01
Kiowa (1)	1	<0.01
Mexican American Ind. (8)	9	0.04
Navajo (3)	3	0.01
Seminole (0)	2	0.01
Shoshone (3)	3	0.01
Sioux (3)	8	0.04
Spanish American Ind. (1)	3	0.01
Yaqui (1)	4	0.02
Asian (1,521)	1,918	9.43
Not Hispanic (1,503)	1,867	9.18
Hispanic (18)	51	0.25
Bangladeshi (5)	6	0.03
Burmese (6)	8	0.04
Cambodian (3)	5	0.02
Chinese, ex. Taiwanese (390)	495	2.43
Filipino (228)	314	1.54
Indian (264)	288	1.42
Indonesian (6)	9	0.04
Japanese (169)	274	1.35
Korean (251)	298	1.47
Laotian (1)	2	0.01
Malaysian (2)	4	0.02
Pakistani (25)	30	0.15
Sri Lankan (3)	3	0.01
Taiwanese (40)	48	0.24
Thai (8)	10	0.05
Vietnamese (74)	77	0.38
Hawaii Native/Pacific Islander (24)	62	0.30
Not Hispanic (22)	51	0.25
Hispanic (2)	11	0.05
Fijian (1)	3	0.01
Guamanian/Chamorro (1)	2	0.01
Native Hawaiian (10)	33	0.16
Samoan (1)	2	0.01
Tongan (3)	4	0.02
White (17,147)	17,814	87.62
Not Hispanic (15,971)	16,500	81.16
Hispanic (1,176)	1,314	6.46

Alameda

Place Type: City
County: Alameda
Population: 73,812†

Ancestry‡	Population	%
Afghan (290)	337	0.46
African, Sub-Saharan (573)	586	0.81
African (69)	82	0.11
Ethiopian (326)	326	0.45
Liberian (8)	8	0.01
Nigerian (71)	71	0.10
Other Sub-Saharan African (99)	99	0.14
Albanian (0)	25	0.03
Alsatian (0)	12	0.02
American (837)	837	1.15
Arab (268)	478	0.66
Lebanese (0)	100	0.14
Moroccan (69)	119	0.16
Palestinian (136)	136	0.19
Syrian (0)	32	0.04
Other Arab (63)	91	0.13
Armenian (93)	127	0.18
Assyrian/Chaldean/Syriac (0)	9	0.01
Australian (0)	45	0.06
Austrian (44)	221	0.30
Basque (89)	119	0.16
Belgian (8)	27	0.04
Brazilian (33)	52	0.07
British (371)	578	0.80
Bulgarian (25)	43	0.06
Canadian (39)	126	0.17
Celtic (11)	50	0.07
Croatian (62)	104	0.14
Cypriot (51)	51	0.07
Czech (20)	139	0.19
Czechoslovakian (0)	7	0.01
Danish (117)	599	0.83
Dutch (306)	1,050	1.45
Eastern European (240)	341	0.47
English (1,325)	6,400	8.83
Estonian (27)	27	0.04
European (1,216)	1,553	2.14
Finnish (9)	222	0.31
French, ex. Basque (220)	1,806	2.49
French Canadian (83)	347	0.48
German (1,719)	7,596	10.48
Greek (40)	262	0.36
Hungarian (105)	298	0.41
Iranian (0)	13	0.02
Irish (1,927)	7,529	10.38
Italian (1,237)	3,647	5.03
Lithuanian (14)	128	0.18
New Zealander (25)	62	0.09
Northern European (249)	269	0.37
Norwegian (378)	1,270	1.75
Pennsylvania German (0)	17	0.02
Polish (348)	1,627	2.24
Portuguese (396)	1,093	1.51
Romanian (54)	93	0.13
Russian (444)	1,295	1.79
Scandinavian (45)	210	0.29
Scotch-Irish (442)	1,426	1.97
Scottish (296)	1,309	1.81
Serbian (6)	35	0.05
Slavic (11)	25	0.03
Slovak (0)	23	0.03
Slovene (47)	47	0.06
Swedish (214)	1,104	1.52
Swiss (38)	317	0.44
Turkish (15)	57	0.08
Ukrainian (106)	215	0.30
Welsh (146)	596	0.82
West Indian, ex. Hispanic (160)	190	0.26
Haitian (65)	65	0.09
Jamaican (48)	78	0.11
West Indian (47)	47	0.06
Yugoslavian (144)	226	0.31

Hispanic Origin	Population	%
Hispanic or Latino (of any race)	8,092	10.96
Central American, ex. Mexican	841	1.14
Costa Rican	18	0.02
Guatemalan	178	0.24
Honduran	41	0.06
Nicaraguan	213	0.29
Panamanian	33	0.04
Salvadoran	352	0.48
Other Central American	6	0.01
Cuban	158	0.21
Dominican Republic	36	0.05
Mexican	4,765	6.46

*Notes: † The Census 2010 population figure is used to calculate the percentages in the Hispanic Origin and Race categories. Ancestry percentages are based on the 2006-2010 American Community Survey population (not shown); ‡ Numbers in parentheses indicate the number of people reporting a single ancestry; * Numbers in parentheses indicate the number of persons reporting this race alone, not in combination with any other race; Please refer to the Explanation of Data for more information.*

Puerto Rican	487	0.66
South American	701	0.95
Argentinean	50	0.07
Bolivian	16	0.02
Chilean	74	0.10
Colombian	172	0.23
Ecuadorian	41	0.06
Paraguayan	2	<0.01
Peruvian	285	0.39
Uruguayan	8	0.01
Venezuelan	40	0.05
Other South American	13	0.02
Other Hispanic or Latino	1,104	1.50

Race*	Population	%
African-American/Black (4,759)	6,149	8.33
Not Hispanic (4,516)	5,645	7.65
Hispanic (243)	504	0.68
American Indian/Alaska Native (426)	1,397	1.89
Not Hispanic (247)	916	1.24
Hispanic (179)	481	0.65
Alaska Athabascan *(Ala. Nat.)* (1)	1	<0.01
Aleut *(Alaska Native)* (4)	4	0.01
Apache (15)	56	0.08
Arapaho (1)	1	<0.01
Blackfeet (5)	61	0.08
Canadian/French Am. Ind. (3)	5	0.01
Central American Ind. (4)	9	0.01
Cherokee (15)	206	0.28
Cheyenne (1)	8	0.01
Chickasaw (3)	9	0.01
Chippewa (7)	20	0.03
Choctaw (8)	60	0.08
Colville (0)	1	<0.01
Comanche (4)	8	0.01
Cree (0)	2	<0.01
Creek (4)	20	0.03
Crow (0)	1	<0.01
Delaware (2)	10	0.01
Hopi (1)	6	0.01
Inupiat *(Alaska Native)* (1)	2	<0.01
Iroquois (3)	22	0.03
Kiowa (1)	1	<0.01
Mexican American Ind. (29)	65	0.09
Navajo (27)	60	0.08
Osage (0)	5	0.01
Paiute (7)	10	0.01
Pima (2)	4	0.01
Pueblo (4)	9	0.01
Seminole (1)	10	0.01
Shoshone (0)	1	<0.01
Sioux (27)	53	0.07
South American Ind. (3)	12	0.02
Spanish American Ind. (3)	8	0.01
Tlingit-Haida *(Alaska Native)* (3)	11	0.01
Tohono O'Odham (1)	1	<0.01
Ute (0)	2	<0.01
Yaqui (4)	10	0.01
Yuman (1)	2	<0.01
Yup'ik *(Alaska Native)* (1)	2	<0.01
Asian (23,058)	26,240	35.55
Not Hispanic (22,822)	25,552	34.62
Hispanic (236)	688	0.93
Bangladeshi (9)	9	0.01
Bhutanese (59)	71	0.10
Burmese (21)	28	0.04
Cambodian (127)	175	0.24
Chinese, ex. Taiwanese (10,485)	11,760	15.93
Filipino (5,419)	6,809	9.22
Hmong (7)	7	0.01
Indian (793)	954	1.29
Indonesian (40)	84	0.11
Japanese (836)	1,496	2.03
Korean (1,496)	1,751	2.37
Laotian (71)	96	0.13
Malaysian (11)	28	0.04
Nepalese (79)	99	0.13
Pakistani (59)	73	0.10
Sri Lankan (16)	24	0.03
Taiwanese (136)	179	0.24
Thai (92)	141	0.19
Vietnamese (2,041)	2,379	3.22
Hawaii Native/Pacific Islander (381)	834	1.13
Not Hispanic (342)	708	0.96
Hispanic (39)	126	0.17
Fijian (20)	27	0.04
Guamanian/Chamorro (129)	223	0.30
Native Hawaiian (77)	307	0.42
Samoan (86)	150	0.20
Tongan (24)	36	0.05
White (37,460)	41,810	56.64
Not Hispanic (33,468)	36,910	50.01
Hispanic (3,992)	4,900	6.64

Alamo

Place Type: CDP
County: Contra Costa
Population: 14,570†

Ancestry‡	Population	%
African, Sub-Saharan (24)	24	0.16
South African (24)	24	0.16
Albanian (0)	12	0.08
American (811)	811	5.34
Arab (35)	103	0.68
Lebanese (35)	103	0.68
Armenian (136)	174	1.15
Australian (22)	39	0.26
Austrian (38)	126	0.83
Basque (24)	94	0.62
Belgian (0)	22	0.14
Brazilian (18)	18	0.12
British (119)	160	1.05
Canadian (45)	62	0.41
Croatian (24)	67	0.44
Czech (7)	65	0.43
Czechoslovakian (11)	22	0.14
Danish (59)	188	1.24
Dutch (162)	368	2.42
English (942)	3,093	20.38
European (336)	373	2.46
Finnish (16)	73	0.48
French, ex. Basque (53)	495	3.26
French Canadian (16)	48	0.32
German (536)	2,566	16.91
Greek (24)	195	1.28
Hungarian (23)	171	1.13
Icelander (0)	10	0.07
Iranian (291)	320	2.11
Irish (462)	2,506	16.51
Italian (673)	1,715	11.30
Latvian (0)	23	0.15
Lithuanian (8)	34	0.22
Maltese (0)	15	0.10
Northern European (222)	222	1.46
Norwegian (104)	476	3.14
Polish (52)	314	2.07
Portuguese (114)	356	2.35
Russian (115)	205	1.35
Scandinavian (25)	71	0.47
Scotch-Irish (88)	408	2.69
Scottish (95)	417	2.75
Slavic (8)	17	0.11
Slovak (11)	11	0.07
Swedish (149)	557	3.67
Swiss (56)	93	0.61
Welsh (11)	31	0.20
Yugoslavian (32)	56	0.37

Hispanic Origin	Population	%
Hispanic or Latino (of any race)	839	5.76
Central American, ex. Mexican	86	0.59
Costa Rican	3	0.02
Guatemalan	10	0.07
Honduran	8	0.05
Nicaraguan	29	0.20
Panamanian	6	0.04
Salvadoran	30	0.21
Cuban	22	0.15
Dominican Republic	3	0.02
Mexican	446	3.06
Puerto Rican	40	0.27
South American	80	0.55
Argentinean	7	0.05
Bolivian	7	0.05
Chilean	11	0.08
Colombian	22	0.15
Ecuadorian	5	0.03
Paraguayan	3	0.02
Peruvian	23	0.16
Venezuelan	2	0.01
Other Hispanic or Latino	162	1.11

Race*	Population	%
African-American/Black (73)	127	0.87
Not Hispanic (71)	117	0.80
Hispanic (2)	10	0.07
American Indian/Alaska Native (18)	112	0.77
Not Hispanic (7)	69	0.47
Hispanic (11)	43	0.30
Apache (1)	2	0.01
Blackfeet (0)	2	0.01
Cherokee (1)	20	0.14
Chickasaw (1)	1	0.01
Chippewa (1)	1	0.01
Choctaw (0)	2	0.01
Creek (0)	1	0.01
Delaware (0)	1	0.01
Iroquois (1)	2	0.01
Lumbee (0)	1	0.01
Mexican American Ind. (1)	5	0.03
Navajo (0)	3	0.02
Osage (1)	6	0.04
Potawatomi (0)	1	0.01
Shoshone (0)	3	0.02
Sioux (0)	4	0.03
South American Ind. (1)	4	0.03
Spanish American Ind. (1)	1	0.01
Asian (1,190)	1,471	10.10
Not Hispanic (1,177)	1,429	9.81
Hispanic (13)	42	0.29
Cambodian (1)	3	0.02
Chinese, ex. Taiwanese (478)	616	4.23
Filipino (172)	248	1.70
Indian (159)	179	1.23
Indonesian (6)	10	0.07
Japanese (111)	197	1.35
Korean (102)	145	1.00
Laotian (3)	3	0.02
Malaysian (0)	1	0.01
Pakistani (9)	11	0.08
Sri Lankan (2)	3	0.02
Taiwanese (47)	47	0.32
Thai (5)	7	0.05
Vietnamese (24)	32	0.22
Hawaii Native/Pacific Islander (22)	67	0.46
Not Hispanic (13)	51	0.35
Hispanic (9)	16	0.11
Guamanian/Chamorro (7)	10	0.07
Native Hawaiian (5)	34	0.23
Samoan (1)	6	0.04
Tongan (2)	2	0.01
White (12,662)	13,115	90.01
Not Hispanic (12,067)	12,412	85.19
Hispanic (595)	703	4.82

Albany

Place Type: City
County: Alameda
Population: 18,539†

Ancestry‡	Population	%
African, Sub-Saharan (113)	142	0.79
African (0)	29	0.16
Kenyan (113)	113	0.63
American (385)	385	2.15
Arab (16)	117	0.65
Arab (0)	10	0.06

*Notes: † The Census 2010 population figure is used to calculate the percentages in the Hispanic Origin and Race categories. Ancestry percentages are based on the 2006-2010 American Community Survey population (not shown); ‡ Numbers in parentheses indicate the number of people reporting a single ancestry; * Numbers in parentheses indicate the number of persons reporting this race alone, not in combination with any other race; Please refer to the Explanation of Data for more information.*

Egyptian (10)	10	0.06
Lebanese (6)	64	0.36
Syrian (0)	33	0.18
Armenian (7)	37	0.21
Australian (0)	34	0.19
Austrian (13)	80	0.45
Basque (0)	21	0.12
Belgian (0)	23	0.13
Brazilian (88)	135	0.75
British (92)	181	1.01
Canadian (20)	56	0.31
Croatian (12)	41	0.23
Czech (14)	64	0.36
Czechoslovakian (12)	12	0.07
Danish (48)	192	1.07
Dutch (37)	215	1.20
Eastern European (142)	142	0.79
English (205)	1,132	6.32
European (706)	807	4.50
Finnish (17)	17	0.09
French, ex. Basque (73)	422	2.35
French Canadian (24)	111	0.62
German (515)	1,733	9.67
Greek (38)	71	0.40
Hungarian (35)	106	0.59
Icelander (0)	37	0.21
Iranian (266)	318	1.77
Irish (358)	1,362	7.60
Israeli (97)	97	0.54
Italian (331)	960	5.36
Latvian (0)	6	0.03
Lithuanian (76)	110	0.61
Northern European (92)	92	0.51
Norwegian (76)	204	1.14
Polish (213)	493	2.75
Portuguese (50)	148	0.83
Romanian (0)	28	0.16
Russian (118)	306	1.71
Scandinavian (24)	45	0.25
Scotch-Irish (31)	261	1.46
Scottish (78)	425	2.37
Slavic (8)	8	0.04
Slovene (0)	19	0.11
Swedish (87)	358	2.00
Swiss (31)	96	0.54
Turkish (17)	38	0.21
Ukrainian (51)	124	0.69
Welsh (7)	122	0.68
West Indian, ex. Hispanic (0)	36	0.20
West Indian (0)	36	0.20
Yugoslavian (17)	44	0.25

Hispanic Origin	Population	%
Hispanic or Latino (of any race)	1,891	10.20
Central American, ex. Mexican	195	1.05
Costa Rican	6	0.03
Guatemalan	33	0.18
Honduran	13	0.07
Nicaraguan	36	0.19
Panamanian	15	0.08
Salvadoran	91	0.49
Other Central American	1	0.01
Cuban	32	0.17
Dominican Republic	1	0.01
Mexican	1,017	5.49
Puerto Rican	59	0.32
South American	376	2.03
Argentinean	24	0.13
Bolivian	16	0.09
Chilean	112	0.60
Colombian	39	0.21
Ecuadorian	32	0.17
Peruvian	113	0.61
Uruguayan	9	0.05
Venezuelan	23	0.12
Other South American	8	0.04
Other Hispanic or Latino	211	1.14

Race*	Population	%
African-American/Black (645)	938	5.06
Not Hispanic (621)	861	4.64
Hispanic (24)	77	0.42
American Indian/Alaska Native (88)	292	1.58
Not Hispanic (44)	170	0.92
Hispanic (44)	122	0.66
Apache (8)	13	0.07
Blackfeet (1)	10	0.05
Central American Ind. (2)	4	0.02
Cherokee (1)	31	0.17
Chippewa (1)	1	0.01
Choctaw (0)	11	0.06
Comanche (0)	2	0.01
Cree (0)	2	0.01
Creek (1)	2	0.01
Delaware (0)	3	0.02
Hopi (0)	1	0.01
Iroquois (0)	7	0.04
Lumbee (2)	2	0.01
Mexican American Ind. (16)	23	0.12
Navajo (0)	1	0.01
Paiute (0)	1	0.01
Pima (2)	3	0.02
Potawatomi (1)	1	0.01
Seminole (0)	1	0.01
Sioux (3)	4	0.02
South American Ind. (4)	14	0.08
Tohono O'Odham (0)	1	0.01
Yaqui (1)	3	0.02
Yuman (0)	1	0.01
Yup'ik *(Alaska Native)* (0)	3	0.02
Asian (5,790)	6,568	35.43
Not Hispanic (5,754)	6,431	34.69
Hispanic (36)	137	0.74
Bangladeshi (13)	13	0.07
Burmese (12)	12	0.06
Cambodian (17)	21	0.11
Chinese, ex. Taiwanese (2,732)	3,066	16.54
Filipino (219)	379	2.04
Hmong (10)	10	0.05
Indian (340)	405	2.18
Indonesian (27)	39	0.21
Japanese (557)	853	4.60
Korean (1,042)	1,105	5.96
Laotian (11)	19	0.10
Malaysian (6)	14	0.08
Nepalese (67)	77	0.42
Pakistani (42)	53	0.29
Sri Lankan (23)	27	0.15
Taiwanese (182)	215	1.16
Thai (62)	79	0.43
Vietnamese (87)	123	0.66
Hawaii Native/Pacific Islander (37)	81	0.44
Not Hispanic (32)	73	0.39
Hispanic (5)	8	0.04
Fijian (3)	3	0.02
Guamanian/Chamorro (4)	17	0.09
Native Hawaiian (13)	29	0.16
Samoan (4)	9	0.05
Tongan (4)	5	0.03
White (10,128)	11,246	60.66
Not Hispanic (9,136)	10,011	54.00
Hispanic (992)	1,235	6.66

Alhambra

Place Type: City
County: Los Angeles
Population: 83,089†

Ancestry‡	Population	%
Afghan (8)	8	0.01
African, Sub-Saharan (62)	72	0.09
African (24)	34	0.04
South African (15)	15	0.02
Other Sub-Saharan African (23)	23	0.03
Albanian (73)	73	0.09
American (366)	366	0.44
Arab (111)	158	0.19
Egyptian (46)	93	0.11
Lebanese (65)	65	0.08
Armenian (23)	142	0.17
Assyrian/Chaldean/Syriac (12)	12	0.01
Australian (0)	8	0.01
Austrian (20)	46	0.06
Basque (14)	35	0.04
Belgian (21)	59	0.07
Brazilian (53)	53	0.06
British (34)	62	0.07
Canadian (64)	102	0.12
Celtic (9)	9	0.01
Croatian (42)	64	0.08
Czech (0)	7	0.01
Danish (59)	112	0.13
Dutch (22)	178	0.21
Eastern European (8)	8	0.01
English (315)	1,360	1.63
Estonian (10)	10	0.01
European (244)	308	0.37
Finnish (0)	7	0.01
French, ex. Basque (37)	534	0.64
French Canadian (0)	71	0.09
German (384)	1,376	1.65
Greek (63)	203	0.24
Hungarian (50)	134	0.16
Icelander (6)	6	0.01
Iranian (213)	384	0.46
Irish (293)	1,140	1.37
Italian (936)	1,521	1.82
Latvian (18)	72	0.09
Lithuanian (50)	57	0.07
Norwegian (108)	200	0.24
Polish (148)	364	0.44
Portuguese (61)	212	0.25
Romanian (81)	108	0.13
Russian (93)	206	0.25
Scandinavian (16)	16	0.02
Scotch-Irish (77)	329	0.39
Scottish (94)	233	0.28
Slavic (36)	36	0.04
Slovak (26)	26	0.03
Swedish (17)	218	0.26
Swiss (0)	47	0.06
Ukrainian (59)	142	0.17
Welsh (14)	14	0.02
West Indian, ex. Hispanic (16)	16	0.02
Belizean (16)	16	0.02
Yugoslavian (46)	63	0.08

Hispanic Origin	Population	%
Hispanic or Latino (of any race)	28,582	34.40
Central American, ex. Mexican	2,842	3.42
Costa Rican	110	0.13
Guatemalan	713	0.86
Honduran	128	0.15
Nicaraguan	509	0.61
Panamanian	45	0.05
Salvadoran	1,286	1.55
Other Central American	51	0.06
Cuban	417	0.50
Dominican Republic	21	0.03
Mexican	22,159	26.67
Puerto Rican	346	0.42
South American	961	1.16
Argentinean	112	0.13
Bolivian	19	0.02
Chilean	47	0.06
Colombian	225	0.27
Ecuadorian	249	0.30
Paraguayan	7	0.01
Peruvian	248	0.30
Uruguayan	2	<0.01
Venezuelan	40	0.05
Other South American	12	0.01
Other Hispanic or Latino	1,836	2.21

Race*	Population	%
African-American/Black (1,281)	1,703	2.05
Not Hispanic (1,078)	1,308	1.57
Hispanic (203)	395	0.48
American Indian/Alaska Native (538)	1,037	1.25

*Notes: † The Census 2010 population figure is used to calculate the percentages in the Hispanic Origin and Race categories. Ancestry percentages are based on the 2006-2010 American Community Survey population (not shown); ‡ Numbers in parentheses indicate the number of people reporting a single ancestry; * Numbers in parentheses indicate the number of persons reporting this race alone, not in combination with any other race; Please refer to the Explanation of Data for more information.*

Not Hispanic (116)	301	0.36
Hispanic (422)	736	0.89
Alaska Athabascan *(Ala. Nat.)* (2)	2	<0.01
Aleut *(Alaska Native)* (0)	1	<0.01
Apache (34)	66	0.08
Arapaho (1)	1	<0.01
Blackfeet (2)	22	0.03
Central American Ind. (5)	11	0.01
Cherokee (12)	55	0.07
Cheyenne (1)	2	<0.01
Chickasaw (0)	3	<0.01
Chippewa (1)	1	<0.01
Choctaw (9)	20	0.02
Colville (0)	1	<0.01
Comanche (3)	5	0.01
Creek (1)	2	<0.01
Crow (0)	3	<0.01
Delaware (2)	2	<0.01
Hopi (4)	17	0.02
Inupiat *(Alaska Native)* (0)	1	<0.01
Iroquois (0)	4	<0.01
Lumbee (9)	9	0.01
Menominee (0)	1	<0.01
Mexican American Ind. (82)	133	0.16
Navajo (9)	26	0.03
Pima (1)	1	<0.01
Potawatomi (2)	2	<0.01
Pueblo (7)	24	0.03
Seminole (2)	12	0.01
Shoshone (1)	1	<0.01
Sioux (8)	13	0.02
South American Ind. (4)	7	0.01
Spanish American Ind. (22)	28	0.03
Tohono O'Odham (4)	4	<0.01
Tsimshian *(Alaska Native)* (0)	1	<0.01
Yaqui (19)	36	0.04
Yuman (0)	1	<0.01
Asian (43,957)	45,395	54.63
Not Hispanic (43,614)	44,579	53.65
Hispanic (343)	816	0.98
Bangladeshi (13)	17	0.02
Burmese (433)	528	0.64
Cambodian (342)	497	0.60
Chinese, ex. Taiwanese (29,201)	31,493	37.90
Filipino (2,109)	2,592	3.12
Hmong (9)	9	0.01
Indian (451)	557	0.67
Indonesian (508)	647	0.78
Japanese (1,224)	1,642	1.98
Korean (844)	969	1.17
Laotian (51)	85	0.10
Malaysian (35)	57	0.07
Nepalese (49)	51	0.06
Pakistani (50)	56	0.07
Sri Lankan (35)	43	0.05
Taiwanese (1,659)	1,866	2.25
Thai (494)	561	0.68
Vietnamese (4,212)	5,348	6.44
Hawaii Native/Pacific Islander (81)	308	0.37
Not Hispanic (54)	213	0.26
Hispanic (27)	95	0.11
Guamanian/Chamorro (17)	40	0.05
Marshallese (1)	2	<0.01
Native Hawaiian (31)	94	0.11
Samoan (23)	39	0.05
Tongan (1)	2	<0.01
White (23,521)	25,700	30.93
Not Hispanic (8,346)	9,217	11.09
Hispanic (15,175)	16,483	19.84

Aliso Viejo

Place Type: City
County: Orange
Population: 47,823†

Ancestry‡	Population	%
Afghan (262)	262	0.57
African, Sub-Saharan (98)	252	0.54
African (71)	184	0.40
Kenyan (12)	12	0.03
South African (15)	56	0.12
Albanian (8)	8	0.02
American (1,229)	1,229	2.65
Arab (361)	545	1.18
Arab (49)	49	0.11
Egyptian (215)	279	0.60
Lebanese (26)	83	0.18
Palestinian (17)	17	0.04
Syrian (0)	51	0.11
Other Arab (54)	66	0.14
Armenian (56)	185	0.40
Australian (17)	17	0.04
Austrian (104)	184	0.40
Belgian (7)	77	0.17
Brazilian (116)	116	0.25
British (315)	647	1.40
Canadian (131)	184	0.40
Croatian (35)	77	0.17
Czech (74)	262	0.57
Czechoslovakian (32)	104	0.22
Danish (62)	332	0.72
Dutch (59)	547	1.18
Eastern European (72)	72	0.16
English (1,506)	4,866	10.50
European (347)	535	1.15
Finnish (15)	47	0.10
French, ex. Basque (221)	1,462	3.16
French Canadian (25)	89	0.19
German (1,879)	7,280	15.71
Greek (111)	319	0.69
Hungarian (160)	350	0.76
Iranian (1,886)	1,977	4.27
Irish (1,206)	5,068	10.94
Israeli (26)	46	0.10
Italian (862)	2,879	6.21
Latvian (0)	15	0.03
Lithuanian (0)	101	0.22
Macedonian (14)	30	0.06
Maltese (16)	16	0.03
New Zealander (10)	10	0.02
Northern European (146)	146	0.32
Norwegian (295)	923	1.99
Polish (503)	1,699	3.67
Portuguese (74)	344	0.74
Romanian (108)	168	0.36
Russian (301)	831	1.79
Scandinavian (43)	153	0.33
Scotch-Irish (138)	494	1.07
Scottish (423)	1,337	2.89
Serbian (82)	110	0.24
Slavic (0)	9	0.02
Slovak (19)	37	0.08
Slovene (12)	37	0.08
Swedish (111)	733	1.58
Swiss (12)	233	0.50
Turkish (64)	72	0.16
Ukrainian (44)	90	0.19
Welsh (107)	238	0.51
West Indian, ex. Hispanic (17)	64	0.14
Belizean (8)	55	0.12
Jamaican (9)	9	0.02
Yugoslavian (90)	139	0.30

Hispanic Origin	Population	%
Hispanic or Latino (of any race)	8,164	17.07
Central American, ex. Mexican	437	0.91
Costa Rican	44	0.09
Guatemalan	108	0.23
Honduran	35	0.07
Nicaraguan	48	0.10
Panamanian	29	0.06
Salvadoran	171	0.36
Other Central American	2	<0.01
Cuban	192	0.40
Dominican Republic	32	0.07
Mexican	5,712	11.94
Puerto Rican	269	0.56
South American	859	1.80
Argentinean	148	0.31
Bolivian	27	0.06
Chilean	57	0.12
Colombian	268	0.56
Ecuadorian	86	0.18
Paraguayan	2	<0.01
Peruvian	208	0.43
Uruguayan	7	0.01
Venezuelan	45	0.09
Other South American	11	0.02
Other Hispanic or Latino	663	1.39

Race*	Population	%
African-American/Black (967)	1,368	2.86
Not Hispanic (892)	1,197	2.50
Hispanic (75)	171	0.36
American Indian/Alaska Native (151)	446	0.93
Not Hispanic (82)	270	0.56
Hispanic (69)	176	0.37
Apache (7)	31	0.06
Blackfeet (6)	13	0.03
Canadian/French Am. Ind. (0)	1	<0.01
Central American Ind. (0)	2	<0.01
Cherokee (14)	74	0.15
Cheyenne (0)	1	<0.01
Chickasaw (3)	3	0.01
Chippewa (5)	9	0.02
Choctaw (6)	16	0.03
Comanche (2)	2	<0.01
Cree (1)	3	0.01
Creek (3)	4	0.01
Hopi (0)	2	<0.01
Inupiat *(Alaska Native)* (1)	3	0.01
Iroquois (1)	1	<0.01
Mexican American Ind. (5)	9	0.02
Navajo (11)	19	0.04
Osage (0)	1	<0.01
Ottawa (0)	1	<0.01
Potawatomi (1)	3	0.01
Seminole (1)	8	0.02
Shoshone (1)	1	<0.01
Sioux (3)	8	0.02
South American Ind. (3)	5	0.01
Tlingit-Haida *(Alaska Native)* (0)	1	<0.01
Yaqui (1)	7	0.01
Yuman (1)	1	<0.01
Asian (6,996)	8,761	18.32
Not Hispanic (6,902)	8,455	17.68
Hispanic (94)	306	0.64
Bangladeshi (25)	28	0.06
Burmese (5)	6	0.01
Cambodian (25)	38	0.08
Chinese, ex. Taiwanese (1,023)	1,441	3.01
Filipino (1,548)	2,046	4.28
Hmong (8)	9	0.02
Indian (1,043)	1,163	2.43
Indonesian (76)	106	0.22
Japanese (874)	1,357	2.84
Korean (956)	1,137	2.38
Laotian (12)	17	0.04
Malaysian (7)	9	0.02
Nepalese (9)	9	0.02
Pakistani (62)	76	0.16
Sri Lankan (29)	38	0.08
Taiwanese (107)	124	0.26
Thai (68)	103	0.22
Vietnamese (791)	947	1.98
Hawaii Native/Pacific Islander (89)	323	0.68
Not Hispanic (75)	272	0.57
Hispanic (14)	51	0.11
Fijian (0)	5	0.01
Guamanian/Chamorro (17)	30	0.06
Native Hawaiian (35)	164	0.34
Samoan (14)	37	0.08
Tongan (0)	1	<0.01
White (34,437)	36,869	77.09
Not Hispanic (29,538)	31,393	65.64
Hispanic (4,899)	5,476	11.45

*Notes: † The Census 2010 population figure is used to calculate the percentages in the Hispanic Origin and Race categories. Ancestry percentages are based on the 2006-2010 American Community Survey population (not shown); ‡ Numbers in parentheses indicate the number of people reporting a single ancestry; * Numbers in parentheses indicate the number of persons reporting this race alone, not in combination with any other race; Please refer to the Explanation of Data for more information.*

Alondra Park

Place Type: CDP
County: Los Angeles
Population: 8,592†

Ancestry‡	Population	%
African, Sub-Saharan (61)	61	0.69
African (61)	61	0.69
American (696)	696	7.89
Arab (77)	77	0.87
Arab (31)	31	0.35
Jordanian (46)	46	0.52
Austrian (27)	27	0.31
British (11)	20	0.23
Celtic (0)	9	0.10
Czech (0)	64	0.73
Dutch (6)	31	0.35
English (37)	247	2.80
European (89)	89	1.01
French, ex. Basque (0)	62	0.70
French Canadian (0)	12	0.14
German (170)	352	3.99
Guyanese (25)	25	0.28
Iranian (0)	13	0.15
Irish (54)	190	2.15
Italian (43)	222	2.52
Norwegian (25)	35	0.40
Polish (27)	141	1.60
Portuguese (21)	21	0.24
Russian (32)	32	0.36
Scotch-Irish (35)	66	0.75
Scottish (14)	22	0.25
Slovak (9)	9	0.10
Slovene (0)	12	0.14
Swedish (7)	32	0.36
Turkish (0)	14	0.16
Ukrainian (69)	69	0.78
West Indian, ex. Hispanic (31)	31	0.35
Belizean (17)	17	0.19
Trinidadian/Tobagonian (14)	14	0.16
Yugoslavian (12)	12	0.14

Hispanic Origin	Population	%
Hispanic or Latino (of any race)	4,304	50.09
Central American, ex. Mexican	633	7.37
Costa Rican	24	0.28
Guatemalan	315	3.67
Honduran	31	0.36
Nicaraguan	36	0.42
Panamanian	4	0.05
Salvadoran	219	2.55
Other Central American	4	0.05
Cuban	43	0.50
Dominican Republic	2	0.02
Mexican	3,160	36.78
Puerto Rican	52	0.61
South American	188	2.19
Argentinean	20	0.23
Bolivian	3	0.03
Chilean	4	0.05
Colombian	31	0.36
Ecuadorian	40	0.47
Peruvian	86	1.00
Venezuelan	3	0.03
Other South American	1	0.01
Other Hispanic or Latino	226	2.63

Race*	Population	%
African-American/Black (806)	896	10.43
Not Hispanic (787)	853	9.93
Hispanic (19)	43	0.50
American Indian/Alaska Native (32)	97	1.13
Not Hispanic (14)	52	0.61
Hispanic (18)	45	0.52
Apache (1)	4	0.05
Central American Ind. (2)	3	0.03
Cherokee (3)	14	0.16
Chickasaw (0)	3	0.03
Chippewa (1)	1	0.01
Choctaw (4)	4	0.05
Delaware (0)	1	0.01
Mexican American Ind. (2)	9	0.10
Pima (0)	1	0.01
Pueblo (0)	6	0.07
Sioux (0)	1	0.01
South American Ind. (5)	8	0.09
Tohono O'Odham (0)	2	0.02
Yakama (1)	1	0.01
Asian (1,396)	1,554	18.09
Not Hispanic (1,348)	1,469	17.10
Hispanic (48)	85	0.99
Cambodian (6)	7	0.08
Chinese, ex. Taiwanese (135)	175	2.04
Filipino (360)	422	4.91
Indian (56)	63	0.73
Indonesian (12)	18	0.21
Japanese (117)	170	1.98
Korean (85)	96	1.12
Laotian (2)	4	0.05
Nepalese (4)	4	0.05
Pakistani (7)	8	0.09
Sri Lankan (9)	9	0.10
Taiwanese (6)	10	0.12
Thai (18)	20	0.23
Vietnamese (526)	561	6.53
Hawaii Native/Pacific Islander (48)	95	1.11
Not Hispanic (46)	76	0.88
Hispanic (2)	19	0.22
Guamanian/Chamorro (6)	12	0.14
Native Hawaiian (9)	21	0.24
Samoan (17)	26	0.30
Tongan (10)	23	0.27
White (3,716)	4,045	47.08
Not Hispanic (1,869)	2,015	23.45
Hispanic (1,847)	2,030	23.63

Alpine

Place Type: CDP
County: San Diego
Population: 14,236†

Ancestry‡	Population	%
American (711)	711	5.34
Arab (0)	81	0.61
Arab (0)	81	0.61
Assyrian/Chaldean/Syriac (28)	28	0.21
Austrian (23)	33	0.25
Belgian (10)	42	0.32
British (46)	96	0.72
Canadian (0)	55	0.41
Celtic (4)	4	0.03
Croatian (10)	28	0.21
Czech (97)	136	1.02
Czechoslovakian (11)	21	0.16
Danish (0)	144	1.08
Dutch (35)	166	1.25
Eastern European (23)	39	0.29
English (571)	2,033	15.26
European (278)	278	2.09
Finnish (0)	9	0.07
French, ex. Basque (79)	521	3.91
French Canadian (22)	32	0.24
German (729)	3,375	25.33
Greek (26)	70	0.53
Hungarian (19)	51	0.38
Icelander (35)	35	0.26
Iranian (19)	36	0.27
Irish (342)	2,004	15.04
Italian (331)	980	7.35
Lithuanian (13)	80	0.60
Northern European (41)	41	0.31
Norwegian (93)	255	1.91
Polish (164)	566	4.25
Portuguese (72)	166	1.25
Russian (38)	97	0.73
Scandinavian (54)	83	0.62
Scotch-Irish (124)	334	2.51
Scottish (201)	398	2.99
Serbian (72)	72	0.54
Slavic (21)	21	0.16
Slovene (0)	58	0.44
Swedish (76)	340	2.55
Swiss (0)	33	0.25
Welsh (64)	264	1.98

Hispanic Origin	Population	%
Hispanic or Latino (of any race)	2,081	14.62
Central American, ex. Mexican	56	0.39
Costa Rican	7	0.05
Guatemalan	9	0.06
Honduran	9	0.06
Nicaraguan	3	0.02
Panamanian	4	0.03
Salvadoran	24	0.17
Cuban	24	0.17
Dominican Republic	1	0.01
Mexican	1,689	11.86
Puerto Rican	57	0.40
South American	40	0.28
Argentinean	10	0.07
Chilean	2	0.01
Colombian	14	0.10
Ecuadorian	1	0.01
Paraguayan	2	0.01
Peruvian	9	0.06
Venezuelan	2	0.01
Other Hispanic or Latino	214	1.50

Race*	Population	%
African-American/Black (167)	244	1.71
Not Hispanic (154)	213	1.50
Hispanic (13)	31	0.22
American Indian/Alaska Native (222)	364	2.56
Not Hispanic (176)	275	1.93
Hispanic (46)	89	0.63
Aleut *(Alaska Native)* (1)	1	0.01
Apache (5)	11	0.08
Blackfeet (3)	4	0.03
Cherokee (19)	43	0.30
Cheyenne (1)	1	0.01
Chickasaw (9)	13	0.09
Chippewa (0)	4	0.03
Choctaw (6)	13	0.09
Comanche (0)	1	0.01
Creek (1)	4	0.03
Hopi (0)	5	0.04
Iroquois (0)	4	0.03
Mexican American Ind. (3)	10	0.07
Navajo (4)	6	0.04
Osage (0)	2	0.01
Ottawa (0)	1	0.01
Paiute (0)	2	0.01
Potawatomi (2)	3	0.02
Pueblo (2)	3	0.02
Seminole (2)	4	0.03
Shoshone (3)	3	0.02
Sioux (2)	4	0.03
South American Ind. (0)	1	0.01
Yaqui (3)	3	0.02
Yup'ik *(Alaska Native)* (0)	1	0.01
Asian (319)	500	3.51
Not Hispanic (298)	439	3.08
Hispanic (21)	61	0.43
Cambodian (8)	9	0.06
Chinese, ex. Taiwanese (23)	56	0.39
Filipino (161)	256	1.80
Hmong (0)	1	0.01
Indian (35)	42	0.30
Indonesian (0)	10	0.07
Japanese (35)	83	0.58
Korean (11)	18	0.13
Pakistani (2)	2	0.01
Taiwanese (1)	1	0.01
Thai (10)	16	0.11
Vietnamese (19)	21	0.15
Hawaii Native/Pacific Islander (39)	83	0.58
Not Hispanic (33)	68	0.48
Hispanic (6)	15	0.11

*Notes: † The Census 2010 population figure is used to calculate the percentages in the Hispanic Origin and Race categories. Ancestry percentages are based on the 2006-2010 American Community Survey population (not shown); ‡ Numbers in parentheses indicate the number of people reporting a single ancestry; * Numbers in parentheses indicate the number of persons reporting this race alone, not in combination with any other race; Please refer to the Explanation of Data for more information.*

Guamanian/Chamorro (10)	24	0.17
Marshallese (1)	1	0.01
Native Hawaiian (6)	21	0.15
Samoan (11)	16	0.11
Tongan (0)	1	0.01
White (12,424)	12,879	90.47
Not Hispanic (11,183)	11,463	80.52
Hispanic (1,241)	1,416	9.95

Altadena

Place Type: CDP
County: Los Angeles
Population: 42,777†

Ancestry‡	Population	%
African, Sub-Saharan (693)	749	1.65
African (639)	695	1.53
Kenyan (16)	16	0.04
Liberian (12)	12	0.03
Nigerian (10)	10	0.02
Other Sub-Saharan African (16)	16	0.04
American (1,336)	1,336	2.94
Arab (102)	219	0.48
Arab (14)	14	0.03
Egyptian (14)	44	0.10
Lebanese (50)	124	0.27
Moroccan (10)	10	0.02
Syrian (14)	27	0.06
Armenian (2,077)	2,354	5.18
Assyrian/Chaldean/Syriac (0)	33	0.07
Austrian (2)	36	0.08
Basque (14)	55	0.12
Belgian (0)	19	0.04
Brazilian (148)	155	0.34
British (225)	364	0.80
Bulgarian (35)	35	0.08
Canadian (87)	150	0.33
Celtic (16)	16	0.04
Croatian (21)	76	0.17
Czech (92)	172	0.38
Czechoslovakian (0)	8	0.02
Danish (29)	146	0.32
Dutch (190)	522	1.15
Eastern European (74)	74	0.16
English (564)	2,651	5.83
Estonian (0)	9	0.02
European (695)	813	1.79
Finnish (13)	66	0.15
French, ex. Basque (112)	665	1.46
French Canadian (57)	106	0.23
German (798)	3,359	7.39
Greek (140)	202	0.44
Hungarian (73)	128	0.28
Iranian (102)	184	0.40
Irish (796)	3,160	6.95
Israeli (13)	13	0.03
Italian (492)	1,600	3.52
Latvian (0)	15	0.03
Lithuanian (23)	62	0.14
New Zealander (18)	33	0.07
Northern European (105)	177	0.39
Norwegian (170)	442	0.97
Pennsylvania German (0)	10	0.02
Polish (100)	575	1.27
Portuguese (79)	249	0.55
Romanian (0)	32	0.07
Russian (302)	591	1.30
Scandinavian (19)	95	0.21
Scotch-Irish (130)	553	1.22
Scottish (187)	802	1.76
Serbian (0)	40	0.09
Slovak (0)	9	0.02
Slovene (0)	18	0.04
Swedish (176)	443	0.97
Swiss (9)	309	0.68
Ukrainian (0)	64	0.14
Welsh (12)	334	0.73
West Indian, ex. Hispanic (315)	417	0.92
Belizean (126)	126	0.28
Jamaican (189)	291	0.64
Yugoslavian (21)	21	0.05

Hispanic Origin	Population	%
Hispanic or Latino (of any race)	11,502	26.89
Central American, ex. Mexican	1,496	3.50
Costa Rican	82	0.19
Guatemalan	275	0.64
Honduran	185	0.43
Nicaraguan	102	0.24
Panamanian	53	0.12
Salvadoran	783	1.83
Other Central American	16	0.04
Cuban	170	0.40
Dominican Republic	10	0.02
Mexican	8,477	19.82
Puerto Rican	196	0.46
South American	459	1.07
Argentinean	114	0.27
Bolivian	13	0.03
Chilean	33	0.08
Colombian	139	0.32
Ecuadorian	52	0.12
Paraguayan	1	<0.01
Peruvian	75	0.18
Venezuelan	17	0.04
Other South American	15	0.04
Other Hispanic or Latino	694	1.62

Race*	Population	%
African-American/Black (10,136)	11,328	26.48
Not Hispanic (9,816)	10,717	25.05
Hispanic (320)	611	1.43
American Indian/Alaska Native (300)	986	2.30
Not Hispanic (85)	573	1.34
Hispanic (215)	413	0.97
Alaska Athabascan *(Ala. Nat.)* (0)	1	<0.01
Apache (10)	26	0.06
Blackfeet (6)	44	0.10
Central American Ind. (4)	4	0.01
Cherokee (9)	143	0.33
Cheyenne (0)	1	<0.01
Chickasaw (0)	9	0.02
Chippewa (4)	16	0.04
Choctaw (4)	43	0.10
Comanche (0)	1	<0.01
Cree (0)	10	0.02
Creek (2)	16	0.04
Crow (0)	1	<0.01
Iroquois (0)	15	0.04
Mexican American Ind. (59)	89	0.21
Navajo (2)	18	0.04
Osage (0)	3	0.01
Ottawa (0)	4	0.01
Paiute (0)	4	0.01
Potawatomi (1)	2	<0.01
Pueblo (2)	3	0.01
Seminole (0)	7	0.02
Shoshone (1)	5	0.01
Sioux (4)	16	0.04
South American Ind. (1)	15	0.04
Tohono O'Odham (4)	4	0.01
Yaqui (2)	6	0.01
Yuman (2)	2	<0.01
Asian (2,307)	3,154	7.37
Not Hispanic (2,231)	2,942	6.88
Hispanic (76)	212	0.50
Burmese (2)	2	<0.01
Cambodian (14)	24	0.06
Chinese, ex. Taiwanese (448)	728	1.70
Filipino (606)	852	1.99
Hmong (5)	5	0.01
Indian (163)	244	0.57
Indonesian (18)	55	0.13
Japanese (478)	741	1.73
Korean (213)	272	0.64
Laotian (5)	5	0.01
Malaysian (3)	6	0.01
Nepalese (5)	6	0.01
Pakistani (9)	14	0.03
Sri Lankan (24)	31	0.07
Taiwanese (27)	40	0.09
Thai (32)	50	0.12
Vietnamese (105)	138	0.32
Hawaii Native/Pacific Islander (71)	214	0.50
Not Hispanic (65)	186	0.43
Hispanic (6)	28	0.07
Fijian (0)	1	<0.01
Guamanian/Chamorro (8)	20	0.05
Native Hawaiian (11)	64	0.15
Samoan (7)	17	0.04
Tongan (1)	3	0.01
White (22,569)	24,517	57.31
Not Hispanic (17,231)	18,515	43.28
Hispanic (5,338)	6,002	14.03

Alum Rock

Place Type: CDP
County: Santa Clara
Population: 15,536†

Ancestry‡	Population	%
American (91)	91	0.57
Arab (15)	24	0.15
Egyptian (15)	15	0.09
Other Arab (0)	9	0.06
British (27)	27	0.17
Croatian (87)	87	0.54
Dutch (6)	20	0.12
English (30)	298	1.86
European (0)	14	0.09
Finnish (0)	22	0.14
French, ex. Basque (14)	44	0.27
French Canadian (17)	17	0.11
German (112)	284	1.77
Hungarian (14)	14	0.09
Irish (7)	334	2.08
Italian (219)	305	1.90
Latvian (26)	26	0.16
Norwegian (0)	12	0.07
Polish (0)	29	0.18
Portuguese (384)	507	3.16
Scotch-Irish (0)	47	0.29
Scottish (0)	48	0.30
Swedish (11)	76	0.47
Swiss (66)	66	0.41

Hispanic Origin	Population	%
Hispanic or Latino (of any race)	10,977	70.66
Central American, ex. Mexican	384	2.47
Costa Rican	1	0.01
Guatemalan	61	0.39
Honduran	26	0.17
Nicaraguan	63	0.41
Panamanian	3	0.02
Salvadoran	228	1.47
Other Central American	2	0.01
Cuban	16	0.10
Mexican	10,024	64.52
Puerto Rican	127	0.82
South American	68	0.44
Argentinean	6	0.04
Bolivian	4	0.03
Chilean	12	0.08
Colombian	18	0.12
Ecuadorian	4	0.03
Peruvian	22	0.14
Venezuelan	2	0.01
Other Hispanic or Latino	358	2.30

Race*	Population	%
African-American/Black (207)	314	2.02
Not Hispanic (166)	206	1.33
Hispanic (41)	108	0.70
American Indian/Alaska Native (298)	492	3.17
Not Hispanic (80)	146	0.94
Hispanic (218)	346	2.23
Apache (18)	44	0.28
Blackfeet (1)	2	0.01

*Notes: † The Census 2010 population figure is used to calculate the percentages in the Hispanic Origin and Race categories. Ancestry percentages are based on the 2006-2010 American Community Survey population (not shown); ‡ Numbers in parentheses indicate the number of people reporting a single ancestry; * Numbers in parentheses indicate the number of persons reporting this race alone, not in combination with any other race; Please refer to the Explanation of Data for more information.*

Canadian/French Am. Ind. (4)	4	0.03
Cherokee (7)	31	0.20
Cheyenne (1)	1	0.01
Chippewa (5)	7	0.05
Choctaw (2)	6	0.04
Comanche (1)	8	0.05
Cree (0)	1	0.01
Creek (0)	2	0.01
Delaware (0)	1	0.01
Hopi (0)	3	0.02
Mexican American Ind. (52)	79	0.51
Navajo (15)	20	0.13
Osage (0)	1	0.01
Pima (1)	1	0.01
Potawatomi (2)	5	0.03
Pueblo (3)	4	0.03
Puget Sound Salish (3)	3	0.02
Seminole (0)	1	0.01
Shoshone (0)	2	0.01
Sioux (17)	18	0.12
South American Ind. (4)	6	0.04
Ute (1)	1	0.01
Yaqui (13)	25	0.16
Asian (2,039)	2,287	14.72
Not Hispanic (1,988)	2,118	13.63
Hispanic (51)	169	1.09
Bangladeshi (2)	2	0.01
Burmese (1)	1	0.01
Cambodian (60)	71	0.46
Chinese, ex. Taiwanese (138)	202	1.30
Filipino (637)	769	4.95
Indian (66)	93	0.60
Indonesian (2)	2	0.01
Japanese (80)	97	0.62
Korean (17)	28	0.18
Laotian (14)	15	0.10
Malaysian (1)	1	0.01
Pakistani (14)	17	0.11
Sri Lankan (2)	3	0.02
Taiwanese (1)	1	0.01
Thai (3)	4	0.03
Vietnamese (957)	998	6.42
Hawaii Native/Pacific Islander (70)	126	0.81
Not Hispanic (61)	86	0.55
Hispanic (9)	40	0.26
Fijian (8)	11	0.07
Guamanian/Chamorro (1)	8	0.05
Native Hawaiian (2)	27	0.17
Samoan (52)	59	0.38
Tongan (1)	2	0.01
White (6,581)	7,282	46.87
Not Hispanic (2,028)	2,204	14.19
Hispanic (4,553)	5,078	32.69

American Canyon

Place Type: City
County: Napa
Population: 19,454†

Ancestry‡	Population	%
African, Sub-Saharan (14)	14	0.08
Nigerian (14)	14	0.08
American (369)	369	2.09
Arab (0)	11	0.06
Lebanese (0)	11	0.06
Australian (52)	52	0.29
Austrian (0)	21	0.12
British (58)	88	0.50
Canadian (12)	48	0.27
Croatian (0)	18	0.10
Czech (7)	20	0.11
Czechoslovakian (56)	56	0.32
Danish (9)	55	0.31
Dutch (19)	203	1.15
English (196)	693	3.92
European (127)	227	1.28
French, ex. Basque (35)	230	1.30
French Canadian (31)	31	0.18
German (214)	943	5.33
Greek (0)	12	0.07
Hungarian (9)	29	0.16
Iranian (11)	70	0.40
Irish (656)	1,296	7.33
Italian (165)	664	3.75
New Zealander (87)	129	0.73
Norwegian (30)	76	0.43
Pennsylvania German (0)	18	0.10
Polish (20)	143	0.81
Portuguese (160)	230	1.30
Russian (30)	68	0.38
Scandinavian (8)	17	0.10
Scotch-Irish (147)	307	1.74
Scottish (87)	197	1.11
Slovene (0)	11	0.06
Swedish (0)	37	0.21
Swiss (0)	13	0.07
Welsh (13)	38	0.21

Hispanic Origin	Population	%
Hispanic or Latino (of any race)	5,009	25.75
Central American, ex. Mexican	483	2.48
Costa Rican	2	0.01
Guatemalan	120	0.62
Honduran	6	0.03
Nicaraguan	86	0.44
Panamanian	6	0.03
Salvadoran	262	1.35
Other Central American	1	0.01
Cuban	37	0.19
Dominican Republic	2	0.01
Mexican	3,843	19.75
Puerto Rican	149	0.77
South American	92	0.47
Argentinean	8	0.04
Bolivian	2	0.01
Chilean	13	0.07
Colombian	7	0.04
Ecuadorian	4	0.02
Paraguayan	1	0.01
Peruvian	44	0.23
Uruguayan	4	0.02
Venezuelan	8	0.04
Other South American	1	0.01
Other Hispanic or Latino	403	2.07

Race*	Population	%
African-American/Black (1,535)	1,851	9.51
Not Hispanic (1,477)	1,731	8.90
Hispanic (58)	120	0.62
American Indian/Alaska Native (142)	356	1.83
Not Hispanic (74)	229	1.18
Hispanic (68)	127	0.65
Alaska Athabascan *(Ala. Nat.)* (1)	1	0.01
Apache (7)	9	0.05
Blackfeet (0)	19	0.10
Central American Ind. (0)	1	0.01
Cherokee (10)	64	0.33
Chickasaw (0)	3	0.02
Chippewa (1)	5	0.03
Choctaw (4)	8	0.04
Colville (1)	1	0.01
Creek (1)	3	0.02
Crow (2)	5	0.03
Delaware (4)	4	0.02
Mexican American Ind. (5)	20	0.10
Navajo (0)	5	0.03
Osage (4)	4	0.02
Ottawa (0)	1	0.01
Potawatomi (1)	1	0.01
Pueblo (0)	1	0.01
Sioux (5)	15	0.08
Tlingit-Haida *(Alaska Native)* (3)	3	0.02
Tohono O'Odham (0)	1	0.01
Asian (6,396)	7,145	36.73
Not Hispanic (6,261)	6,849	35.21
Hispanic (135)	296	1.52
Bangladeshi (6)	6	0.03
Burmese (15)	17	0.09
Cambodian (20)	34	0.17
Chinese, ex. Taiwanese (378)	530	2.72
Filipino (4,938)	5,572	28.64
Hmong (5)	7	0.04
Indian (415)	453	2.33
Indonesian (6)	9	0.05
Japanese (38)	123	0.63
Korean (71)	98	0.50
Laotian (52)	58	0.30
Malaysian (1)	8	0.04
Nepalese (2)	2	0.01
Pakistani (48)	52	0.27
Taiwanese (4)	5	0.03
Thai (26)	36	0.19
Vietnamese (190)	238	1.22
Hawaii Native/Pacific Islander (176)	331	1.70
Not Hispanic (156)	289	1.49
Hispanic (20)	42	0.22
Fijian (4)	10	0.05
Guamanian/Chamorro (104)	150	0.77
Native Hawaiian (15)	58	0.30
Samoan (30)	50	0.26
Tongan (2)	2	0.01
White (7,564)	8,557	43.99
Not Hispanic (5,543)	6,228	32.01
Hispanic (2,021)	2,329	11.97

Anaheim

Place Type: City
County: Orange
Population: 336,265†

Ancestry‡	Population	%
Afghan (200)	308	0.09
African, Sub-Saharan (1,449)	1,577	0.47
African (387)	474	0.14
Ethiopian (642)	642	0.19
Kenyan (60)	60	0.02
Nigerian (104)	104	0.03
Somalian (72)	72	0.02
South African (0)	27	0.01
Zimbabwean (9)	9	<0.01
Other Sub-Saharan African (175)	189	0.06
Albanian (182)	207	0.06
American (5,167)	5,167	1.55
Arab (3,389)	4,077	1.22
Arab (404)	607	0.18
Egyptian (1,042)	1,072	0.32
Iraqi (89)	89	0.03
Jordanian (548)	575	0.17
Lebanese (590)	816	0.25
Moroccan (31)	31	0.01
Palestinian (199)	226	0.07
Syrian (344)	399	0.12
Other Arab (142)	262	0.08
Armenian (568)	802	0.24
Assyrian/Chaldean/Syriac (34)	85	0.03
Australian (9)	49	0.01
Austrian (133)	609	0.18
Basque (34)	71	0.02
Belgian (139)	254	0.08
Brazilian (271)	387	0.12
British (398)	629	0.19
Bulgarian (111)	147	0.04
Canadian (412)	756	0.23
Celtic (18)	81	0.02
Croatian (134)	232	0.07
Czech (215)	680	0.20
Czechoslovakian (112)	234	0.07
Danish (188)	945	0.28
Dutch (858)	2,724	0.82
Eastern European (106)	146	0.04
English (4,688)	15,386	4.62
Estonian (0)	9	<0.01
European (1,666)	2,073	0.62
Finnish (88)	256	0.08
French, ex. Basque (1,036)	5,575	1.67
French Canadian (331)	662	0.20
German (7,063)	23,531	7.07
Greek (607)	908	0.27

Notes: † The Census 2010 population figure is used to calculate the percentages in the Hispanic Origin and Race categories. Ancestry percentages are based on the 2006-2010 American Community Survey population (not shown); ‡ Numbers in parentheses indicate the number of people reporting a single ancestry; * Numbers in parentheses indicate the number of persons reporting this race alone, not in combination with any other race; Please refer to the Explanation of Data for more information.

Guyanese (44)	44	0.01
Hungarian (348)	834	0.25
Icelander (0)	9	<0.01
Iranian (1,814)	2,070	0.62
Irish (4,205)	17,503	5.26
Israeli (43)	104	0.03
Italian (4,368)	9,767	2.93
Latvian (35)	68	0.02
Lithuanian (108)	278	0.08
Luxemburger (44)	44	0.01
Macedonian (67)	87	0.03
New Zealander (0)	13	<0.01
Northern European (75)	126	0.04
Norwegian (1,047)	2,965	0.89
Pennsylvania German (36)	64	0.02
Polish (941)	3,304	0.99
Portuguese (516)	1,035	0.31
Romanian (1,567)	1,744	0.52
Russian (642)	1,973	0.59
Scandinavian (124)	281	0.08
Scotch-Irish (844)	2,321	0.70
Scottish (744)	2,711	0.81
Serbian (42)	158	0.05
Slavic (36)	68	0.02
Slovak (87)	176	0.05
Slovene (25)	43	0.01
Swedish (711)	2,803	0.84
Swiss (71)	491	0.15
Turkish (31)	59	0.02
Ukrainian (88)	218	0.07
Welsh (223)	930	0.28
West Indian, ex. Hispanic (284)	345	0.10
Belizean (24)	24	0.01
British West Indian (6)	6	<0.01
Haitian (15)	15	<0.01
Jamaican (215)	225	0.07
Trinidadian/Tobagonian (13)	13	<0.01
West Indian (11)	62	0.02
Yugoslavian (216)	258	0.08

Hispanic Origin	Population	%
Hispanic or Latino (of any race)	177,467	52.78
Central American, ex. Mexican	9,074	2.70
Costa Rican	296	0.09
Guatemalan	3,474	1.03
Honduran	636	0.19
Nicaraguan	543	0.16
Panamanian	100	0.03
Salvadoran	3,957	1.18
Other Central American	68	0.02
Cuban	945	0.28
Dominican Republic	114	0.03
Mexican	154,554	45.96
Puerto Rican	1,439	0.43
South American	3,763	1.12
Argentinean	519	0.15
Bolivian	211	0.06
Chilean	181	0.05
Colombian	884	0.26
Ecuadorian	417	0.12
Paraguayan	9	<0.01
Peruvian	1,365	0.41
Uruguayan	66	0.02
Venezuelan	80	0.02
Other South American	31	0.01
Other Hispanic or Latino	7,578	2.25

Race*	Population	%
African-American/Black (9,347)	11,478	3.41
Not Hispanic (8,209)	9,560	2.84
Hispanic (1,138)	1,918	0.57
American Indian/Alaska Native (2,648)	4,684	1.39
Not Hispanic (743)	1,773	0.53
Hispanic (1,905)	2,911	0.87
Alaska Athabascan *(Ala. Nat.)* (0)	3	<0.01
Aleut *(Alaska Native)* (6)	9	<0.01
Apache (113)	228	0.07
Arapaho (0)	3	<0.01
Blackfeet (9)	68	0.02
Canadian/French Am. Ind. (7)	14	<0.01
Central American Ind. (7)	14	<0.01
Cherokee (92)	408	0.12
Cheyenne (5)	9	<0.01
Chickasaw (8)	25	0.01
Chippewa (16)	25	0.01
Choctaw (24)	72	0.02
Colville (4)	5	<0.01
Comanche (4)	16	<0.01
Cree (0)	5	<0.01
Creek (12)	37	0.01
Crow (2)	6	<0.01
Delaware (2)	6	<0.01
Hopi (13)	25	0.01
Inupiat *(Alaska Native)* (0)	1	<0.01
Iroquois (4)	32	0.01
Kiowa (5)	8	<0.01
Lumbee (4)	7	<0.01
Menominee (10)	10	<0.01
Mexican American Ind. (450)	592	0.18
Navajo (71)	149	0.04
Osage (3)	10	<0.01
Ottawa (2)	8	<0.01
Paiute (5)	17	0.01
Pima (12)	18	0.01
Potawatomi (6)	23	0.01
Pueblo (21)	34	0.01
Puget Sound Salish (3)	3	<0.01
Seminole (3)	21	0.01
Shoshone (20)	30	0.01
Sioux (17)	51	0.02
South American Ind. (11)	27	0.01
Spanish American Ind. (34)	46	0.01
Tlingit-Haida *(Alaska Native)* (6)	9	<0.01
Tohono O'Odham (10)	23	0.01
Tsimshian *(Alaska Native)* (2)	3	<0.01
Ute (1)	2	<0.01
Yakama (3)	6	<0.01
Yaqui (50)	84	0.02
Yuman (22)	26	0.01
Asian (49,857)	55,024	16.36
Not Hispanic (49,210)	53,269	15.84
Hispanic (647)	1,755	0.52
Bangladeshi (227)	240	0.07
Burmese (85)	97	0.03
Cambodian (680)	831	0.25
Chinese, ex. Taiwanese (4,042)	5,374	1.60
Filipino (11,956)	13,813	4.11
Hmong (118)	132	0.04
Indian (4,456)	4,915	1.46
Indonesian (306)	462	0.14
Japanese (2,082)	3,145	0.94
Korean (6,575)	6,999	2.08
Laotian (648)	749	0.22
Malaysian (22)	53	0.02
Nepalese (79)	80	0.02
Pakistani (705)	782	0.23
Sri Lankan (214)	237	0.07
Taiwanese (657)	740	0.22
Thai (480)	632	0.19
Vietnamese (14,706)	15,674	4.66
Hawaii Native/Pacific Islander (1,607)	2,778	0.83
Not Hispanic (1,437)	2,238	0.67
Hispanic (170)	540	0.16
Fijian (35)	65	0.02
Guamanian/Chamorro (184)	328	0.10
Native Hawaiian (227)	653	0.19
Samoan (766)	1,023	0.30
Tongan (209)	259	0.08
White (177,237)	189,689	56.41
Not Hispanic (92,362)	97,490	28.99
Hispanic (84,875)	92,199	27.42

Anderson

Place Type: City
County: Shasta
Population: 9,932†

Ancestry‡	Population	%
African, Sub-Saharan (21)	38	0.38
Nigerian (21)	38	0.38
American (924)	924	9.32
Arab (42)	93	0.94
Arab (12)	12	0.12
Iraqi (0)	19	0.19
Lebanese (30)	62	0.63
Austrian (0)	10	0.10
Belgian (0)	13	0.13
British (0)	30	0.30
Canadian (25)	46	0.46
Czech (15)	38	0.38
Danish (0)	21	0.21
Dutch (47)	224	2.26
English (228)	770	7.77
European (73)	73	0.74
Finnish (13)	28	0.28
French, ex. Basque (73)	482	4.86
French Canadian (27)	38	0.38
German (848)	2,399	24.21
Hungarian (0)	13	0.13
Irish (417)	1,681	16.96
Italian (220)	489	4.93
Norwegian (53)	315	3.18
Pennsylvania German (41)	54	0.54
Polish (20)	43	0.43
Portuguese (43)	86	0.87
Russian (0)	87	0.88
Scotch-Irish (21)	247	2.49
Scottish (53)	237	2.39
Slovak (11)	11	0.11
Swedish (39)	247	2.49
Swiss (20)	172	1.74
Welsh (8)	89	0.90

Hispanic Origin	Population	%
Hispanic or Latino (of any race)	1,070	10.77
Central American, ex. Mexican	33	0.33
Costa Rican	6	0.06
Guatemalan	9	0.09
Honduran	1	0.01
Nicaraguan	1	0.01
Panamanian	6	0.06
Salvadoran	10	0.10
Cuban	10	0.10
Dominican Republic	2	0.02
Mexican	887	8.93
Puerto Rican	19	0.19
South American	9	0.09
Argentinean	1	0.01
Colombian	2	0.02
Ecuadorian	4	0.04
Peruvian	1	0.01
Uruguayan	1	0.01
Other Hispanic or Latino	110	1.11

Race*	Population	%
African-American/Black (70)	145	1.46
Not Hispanic (64)	120	1.21
Hispanic (6)	25	0.25
American Indian/Alaska Native (426)	775	7.80
Not Hispanic (369)	641	6.45
Hispanic (57)	134	1.35
Aleut *(Alaska Native)* (3)	6	0.06
Apache (4)	13	0.13
Blackfeet (0)	10	0.10
Canadian/French Am. Ind. (3)	3	0.03
Cherokee (23)	95	0.96
Cheyenne (0)	1	0.01
Chickasaw (0)	6	0.06
Chippewa (2)	8	0.08
Choctaw (15)	37	0.37
Cree (0)	2	0.02
Creek (0)	2	0.02
Inupiat *(Alaska Native)* (1)	1	0.01
Iroquois (2)	6	0.06
Lumbee (0)	1	0.01
Mexican American Ind. (2)	2	0.02
Navajo (6)	16	0.16
Osage (0)	4	0.04
Ottawa (0)	1	0.01

*Notes: † The Census 2010 population figure is used to calculate the percentages in the Hispanic Origin and Race categories. Ancestry percentages are based on the 2006-2010 American Community Survey population (not shown); ‡ Numbers in parentheses indicate the number of people reporting a single ancestry; * Numbers in parentheses indicate the number of persons reporting this race alone, not in combination with any other race; Please refer to the Explanation of Data for more information.*

Paiute (6)	7	0.07
Potawatomi (1)	6	0.06
Pueblo (3)	3	0.03
Puget Sound Salish (1)	1	0.01
Shoshone (2)	3	0.03
Sioux (5)	9	0.09
Tlingit-Haida *(Alaska Native)* (3)	3	0.03
Ute (1)	2	0.02
Yaqui (0)	3	0.03
Asian (256)	338	3.40
Not Hispanic (243)	309	3.11
Hispanic (13)	29	0.29
Cambodian (6)	7	0.07
Chinese, ex. Taiwanese (13)	34	0.34
Filipino (54)	93	0.94
Hmong (10)	10	0.10
Indian (30)	33	0.33
Indonesian (0)	1	0.01
Japanese (3)	14	0.14
Korean (3)	6	0.06
Laotian (112)	119	1.20
Thai (4)	9	0.09
Vietnamese (7)	11	0.11
Hawaii Native/Pacific Islander (17)	36	0.36
Not Hispanic (17)	32	0.32
Hispanic (0)	4	0.04
Guamanian/Chamorro (9)	12	0.12
Native Hawaiian (7)	16	0.16
Samoan (1)	1	0.01
White (8,273)	8,784	88.44
Not Hispanic (7,775)	8,153	82.09
Hispanic (498)	631	6.35

Antelope

Place Type: CDP
County: Sacramento
Population: 45,770†

Ancestry‡	Population	%
African, Sub-Saharan (222)	593	1.30
African (114)	470	1.03
Ethiopian (0)	15	0.03
Nigerian (84)	84	0.18
Sudanese (24)	24	0.05
American (1,331)	1,331	2.91
Arab (38)	62	0.14
Egyptian (15)	27	0.06
Lebanese (12)	12	0.03
Moroccan (11)	23	0.05
Armenian (0)	13	0.03
Assyrian/Chaldean/Syriac (0)	16	0.04
Australian (0)	16	0.04
Austrian (0)	9	0.02
Basque (14)	14	0.03
Belgian (14)	51	0.11
British (120)	201	0.44
Bulgarian (4)	4	0.01
Canadian (13)	62	0.14
Celtic (0)	13	0.03
Croatian (42)	42	0.09
Czech (35)	114	0.25
Czechoslovakian (25)	54	0.12
Danish (20)	216	0.47
Dutch (23)	246	0.54
English (861)	3,291	7.20
European (287)	554	1.21
Finnish (34)	48	0.11
French, ex. Basque (278)	1,422	3.11
French Canadian (41)	137	0.30
German (1,887)	5,420	11.86
Greek (98)	285	0.62
Hungarian (0)	67	0.15
Iranian (62)	77	0.17
Irish (936)	4,375	9.58
Italian (753)	2,012	4.40
Latvian (14)	14	0.03
Lithuanian (21)	49	0.11
Northern European (45)	55	0.12
Norwegian (142)	686	1.50
Polish (117)	300	0.66
Portuguese (233)	462	1.01
Romanian (672)	714	1.56
Russian (1,420)	1,628	3.56
Scandinavian (21)	42	0.09
Scotch-Irish (216)	651	1.42
Scottish (150)	742	1.62
Serbian (26)	26	0.06
Slavic (21)	21	0.05
Slovak (13)	22	0.05
Swedish (118)	956	2.09
Swiss (8)	41	0.09
Turkish (114)	114	0.25
Ukrainian (3,086)	3,301	7.22
Welsh (12)	111	0.24
West Indian, ex. Hispanic (16)	25	0.05
Barbadian (8)	8	0.02
Jamaican (8)	8	0.02
U.S. Virgin Islander (0)	9	0.02
Yugoslavian (55)	95	0.21

Hispanic Origin	Population	%
Hispanic or Latino (of any race)	6,635	14.50
Central American, ex. Mexican	421	0.92
Costa Rican	8	0.02
Guatemalan	66	0.14
Honduran	20	0.04
Nicaraguan	91	0.20
Panamanian	37	0.08
Salvadoran	195	0.43
Other Central American	4	0.01
Cuban	54	0.12
Dominican Republic	13	0.03
Mexican	4,907	10.72
Puerto Rican	334	0.73
South American	188	0.41
Argentinean	25	0.05
Chilean	20	0.04
Colombian	46	0.10
Ecuadorian	13	0.03
Peruvian	63	0.14
Venezuelan	19	0.04
Other South American	2	<0.01
Other Hispanic or Latino	718	1.57

Race*	Population	%
African-American/Black (4,039)	5,198	11.36
Not Hispanic (3,853)	4,754	10.39
Hispanic (186)	444	0.97
American Indian/Alaska Native (402)	1,072	2.34
Not Hispanic (261)	736	1.61
Hispanic (141)	336	0.73
Aleut *(Alaska Native)* (0)	2	<0.01
Apache (11)	50	0.11
Blackfeet (5)	35	0.08
Canadian/French Am. Ind. (2)	5	0.01
Central American Ind. (5)	7	0.02
Cherokee (42)	167	0.36
Cheyenne (5)	6	0.01
Chickasaw (7)	20	0.04
Chippewa (1)	9	0.02
Choctaw (17)	55	0.12
Comanche (1)	2	<0.01
Cree (2)	3	0.01
Creek (9)	18	0.04
Delaware (0)	2	<0.01
Hopi (0)	1	<0.01
Iroquois (4)	9	0.02
Kiowa (0)	4	0.01
Mexican American Ind. (16)	25	0.05
Navajo (17)	46	0.10
Osage (0)	6	0.01
Ottawa (6)	9	0.02
Paiute (4)	11	0.02
Potawatomi (6)	7	0.02
Pueblo (11)	19	0.04
Puget Sound Salish (1)	1	<0.01
Seminole (2)	12	0.03
Shoshone (3)	6	0.01
Sioux (12)	18	0.04
Spanish American Ind. (0)	1	<0.01
Tlingit-Haida *(Alaska Native)* (1)	1	<0.01
Tsimshian *(Alaska Native)* (0)	5	0.01
Ute (0)	1	<0.01
Yakama (0)	1	<0.01
Yaqui (0)	6	0.01
Asian (6,090)	7,548	16.49
Not Hispanic (5,949)	7,169	15.66
Hispanic (141)	379	0.83
Bangladeshi (5)	6	0.01
Burmese (4)	4	0.01
Cambodian (34)	43	0.09
Chinese, ex. Taiwanese (320)	543	1.19
Filipino (1,805)	2,430	5.31
Hmong (88)	102	0.22
Indian (1,929)	2,173	4.75
Indonesian (9)	20	0.04
Japanese (130)	355	0.78
Korean (193)	331	0.72
Laotian (342)	372	0.81
Malaysian (0)	1	<0.01
Nepalese (7)	8	0.02
Pakistani (79)	80	0.17
Sri Lankan (9)	11	0.02
Taiwanese (8)	24	0.05
Thai (74)	146	0.32
Vietnamese (820)	892	1.95
Hawaii Native/Pacific Islander (407)	798	1.74
Not Hispanic (370)	688	1.50
Hispanic (37)	110	0.24
Fijian (121)	164	0.36
Guamanian/Chamorro (102)	168	0.37
Marshallese (2)	3	0.01
Native Hawaiian (40)	169	0.37
Samoan (53)	72	0.16
Tongan (47)	63	0.14
White (29,200)	31,903	69.70
Not Hispanic (26,268)	28,162	61.53
Hispanic (2,932)	3,741	8.17

Antioch

Place Type: City
County: Contra Costa
Population: 102,372†

Ancestry‡	Population	%
Afghan (706)	725	0.73
African, Sub-Saharan (1,577)	2,459	2.47
African (836)	1,700	1.70
Ethiopian (217)	217	0.22
Ghanaian (20)	20	0.02
Nigerian (504)	522	0.52
American (1,716)	1,716	1.72
Arab (514)	695	0.70
Arab (61)	87	0.09
Egyptian (206)	206	0.21
Lebanese (18)	143	0.14
Palestinian (212)	229	0.23
Syrian (17)	30	0.03
Armenian (110)	110	0.11
Australian (14)	14	0.01
Austrian (0)	70	0.07
Basque (0)	122	0.12
Belgian (23)	52	0.05
Brazilian (196)	239	0.24
British (95)	446	0.45
Cajun (40)	40	0.04
Canadian (39)	79	0.08
Croatian (12)	90	0.09
Czech (44)	199	0.20
Czechoslovakian (0)	110	0.11
Danish (143)	664	0.67
Dutch (246)	2,152	2.16
Eastern European (10)	18	0.02
English (1,520)	5,508	5.52
European (706)	938	0.94
Finnish (19)	236	0.24
French, ex. Basque (335)	1,789	1.79
French Canadian (30)	318	0.32

*Notes: † The Census 2010 population figure is used to calculate the percentages in the Hispanic Origin and Race categories. Ancestry percentages are based on the 2006-2010 American Community Survey population (not shown); ‡ Numbers in parentheses indicate the number of people reporting a single ancestry; * Numbers in parentheses indicate the number of persons reporting this race alone, not in combination with any other race; Please refer to the Explanation of Data for more information.*

German (2,025)	10,160	10.19
Greek (76)	282	0.28
Guyanese (40)	40	0.04
Hungarian (49)	145	0.15
Icelander (14)	14	0.01
Iranian (90)	90	0.09
Irish (1,479)	8,778	8.80
Israeli (13)	13	0.01
Italian (1,870)	4,791	4.80
Lithuanian (4)	43	0.04
Maltese (30)	40	0.04
New Zealander (38)	38	0.04
Northern European (17)	36	0.04
Norwegian (216)	730	0.73
Pennsylvania German (9)	9	0.01
Polish (212)	954	0.96
Portuguese (709)	1,994	2.00
Romanian (23)	64	0.06
Russian (137)	426	0.43
Scandinavian (31)	174	0.17
Scotch-Irish (363)	1,142	1.15
Scottish (301)	1,711	1.72
Serbian (0)	23	0.02
Slavic (0)	13	0.01
Slovak (0)	21	0.02
Slovene (0)	8	0.01
Swedish (103)	1,179	1.18
Swiss (21)	102	0.10
Ukrainian (52)	78	0.08
Welsh (20)	587	0.59
West Indian, ex. Hispanic (97)	358	0.36
Bahamian (0)	33	0.03
Barbadian (10)	93	0.09
Belizean (9)	9	0.01
Dutch West Indian (0)	10	0.01
Jamaican (20)	79	0.08
Trinidadian/Tobagonian (37)	37	0.04
West Indian (21)	97	0.10
Yugoslavian (0)	96	0.10

Hispanic Origin	Population	%
Hispanic or Latino (of any race)	32,436	31.68
Central American, ex. Mexican	4,289	4.19
Costa Rican	94	0.09
Guatemalan	452	0.44
Honduran	150	0.15
Nicaraguan	1,269	1.24
Panamanian	85	0.08
Salvadoran	2,212	2.16
Other Central American	27	0.03
Cuban	185	0.18
Dominican Republic	61	0.06
Mexican	23,110	22.57
Puerto Rican	1,204	1.18
South American	1,083	1.06
Argentinean	47	0.05
Bolivian	54	0.05
Chilean	46	0.04
Colombian	86	0.08
Ecuadorian	46	0.04
Paraguayan	3	<0.01
Peruvian	748	0.73
Uruguayan	11	0.01
Venezuelan	32	0.03
Other South American	10	0.01
Other Hispanic or Latino	2,504	2.45

Race*	Population	%
African-American/Black (17,667)	20,329	19.86
Not Hispanic (17,045)	19,064	18.62
Hispanic (622)	1,265	1.24
American Indian/Alaska Native (887)	2,514	2.46
Not Hispanic (455)	1,532	1.50
Hispanic (432)	982	0.96
Aleut *(Alaska Native)* (1)	2	<0.01
Apache (23)	64	0.06
Arapaho (5)	5	<0.01
Blackfeet (13)	89	0.09
Canadian/French Am. Ind. (0)	6	0.01
Central American Ind. (5)	9	0.01
Cherokee (65)	489	0.48
Cheyenne (4)	9	0.01
Chickasaw (3)	8	0.01
Chippewa (11)	26	0.03
Choctaw (24)	136	0.13
Comanche (2)	3	<0.01
Creek (8)	31	0.03
Delaware (5)	10	0.01
Hopi (11)	19	0.02
Inupiat *(Alaska Native)* (0)	8	0.01
Iroquois (6)	11	0.01
Kiowa (0)	3	<0.01
Lumbee (1)	7	0.01
Mexican American Ind. (130)	224	0.22
Navajo (13)	49	0.05
Osage (2)	3	<0.01
Ottawa (0)	7	0.01
Paiute (16)	27	0.03
Pima (5)	7	0.01
Potawatomi (2)	14	0.01
Pueblo (10)	12	0.01
Puget Sound Salish (0)	1	<0.01
Seminole (6)	13	0.01
Shoshone (0)	1	<0.01
Sioux (15)	46	0.04
South American Ind. (8)	12	0.01
Spanish American Ind. (9)	13	0.01
Tlingit-Haida *(Alaska Native)* (1)	5	<0.01
Tohono O'Odham (2)	10	0.01
Ute (4)	9	0.01
Yakama (0)	3	<0.01
Yaqui (20)	37	0.04
Yuman (2)	2	<0.01
Asian (10,709)	13,704	13.39
Not Hispanic (10,322)	12,608	12.32
Hispanic (387)	1,096	1.07
Bangladeshi (43)	43	0.04
Burmese (48)	53	0.05
Cambodian (148)	198	0.19
Chinese, ex. Taiwanese (1,356)	1,953	1.91
Filipino (5,850)	7,541	7.37
Hmong (16)	16	0.02
Indian (964)	1,197	1.17
Indonesian (76)	116	0.11
Japanese (212)	604	0.59
Korean (214)	306	0.30
Laotian (153)	204	0.20
Malaysian (9)	13	0.01
Nepalese (10)	10	0.01
Pakistani (223)	272	0.27
Sri Lankan (30)	32	0.03
Taiwanese (35)	42	0.04
Thai (95)	147	0.14
Vietnamese (733)	886	0.87
Hawaii Native/Pacific Islander (817)	1,529	1.49
Not Hispanic (743)	1,271	1.24
Hispanic (74)	258	0.25
Fijian (109)	139	0.14
Guamanian/Chamorro (137)	272	0.27
Native Hawaiian (81)	352	0.34
Samoan (210)	325	0.32
Tongan (178)	226	0.22
White (50,083)	56,308	55.00
Not Hispanic (36,490)	40,125	39.20
Hispanic (13,593)	16,183	15.81

Apple Valley

Place Type: Town
County: San Bernardino
Population: 69,135†

Ancestry‡	Population	%
African, Sub-Saharan (627)	656	0.97
African (570)	588	0.87
Ethiopian (33)	33	0.05
Nigerian (24)	24	0.04
South African (0)	11	0.02
Albanian (10)	10	0.01
American (2,597)	2,597	3.85
Arab (305)	332	0.49
Arab (7)	7	0.01
Egyptian (178)	178	0.26
Jordanian (11)	22	0.03
Lebanese (0)	16	0.02
Other Arab (109)	109	0.16
Armenian (72)	148	0.22
Australian (26)	26	0.04
Austrian (57)	88	0.13
Basque (0)	70	0.10
Belgian (0)	70	0.10
Brazilian (14)	24	0.04
British (68)	149	0.22
Canadian (62)	212	0.31
Celtic (0)	20	0.03
Croatian (0)	51	0.08
Czech (24)	156	0.23
Czechoslovakian (18)	25	0.04
Danish (111)	418	0.62
Dutch (286)	1,143	1.70
Eastern European (18)	18	0.03
English (3,110)	8,389	12.45
European (524)	706	1.05
Finnish (82)	116	0.17
French, ex. Basque (387)	2,805	4.16
French Canadian (167)	497	0.74
German (2,383)	9,749	14.47
Greek (0)	64	0.09
Guyanese (16)	16	0.02
Hungarian (17)	168	0.25
Icelander (0)	27	0.04
Iranian (65)	65	0.10
Irish (2,094)	7,835	11.63
Italian (1,470)	4,017	5.96
Lithuanian (8)	38	0.06
Luxemburger (0)	9	0.01
New Zealander (0)	6	0.01
Northern European (13)	38	0.06
Norwegian (390)	1,319	1.96
Pennsylvania German (54)	68	0.10
Polish (251)	1,530	2.27
Portuguese (63)	239	0.35
Romanian (81)	91	0.14
Russian (161)	399	0.59
Scandinavian (64)	143	0.21
Scotch-Irish (339)	912	1.35
Scottish (178)	1,144	1.70
Slavic (0)	45	0.07
Slovak (8)	29	0.04
Swedish (232)	1,023	1.52
Swiss (28)	239	0.35
Ukrainian (0)	58	0.09
Welsh (85)	459	0.68
West Indian, ex. Hispanic (39)	39	0.06
Belizean (10)	10	0.01
British West Indian (12)	12	0.02
Trinidadian/Tobagonian (17)	17	0.03
Yugoslavian (74)	74	0.11

Hispanic Origin	Population	%
Hispanic or Latino (of any race)	20,156	29.15
Central American, ex. Mexican	986	1.43
Costa Rican	47	0.07
Guatemalan	329	0.48
Honduran	58	0.08
Nicaraguan	76	0.11
Panamanian	37	0.05
Salvadoran	421	0.61
Other Central American	18	0.03
Cuban	214	0.31
Dominican Republic	19	0.03
Mexican	16,217	23.46
Puerto Rican	518	0.75
South American	288	0.42
Argentinean	54	0.08
Bolivian	3	<0.01
Chilean	16	0.02
Colombian	89	0.13
Ecuadorian	61	0.09
Paraguayan	2	<0.01

*Notes: † The Census 2010 population figure is used to calculate the percentages in the Hispanic Origin and Race categories. Ancestry percentages are based on the 2006-2010 American Community Survey population (not shown); ‡ Numbers in parentheses indicate the number of people reporting a single ancestry; * Numbers in parentheses indicate the number of persons reporting this race alone, not in combination with any other race; Please refer to the Explanation of Data for more information.*

Peruvian	52	0.08
Venezuelan	7	0.01
Other South American	4	0.01
Other Hispanic or Latino	1,914	2.77

Race*	Population	%
African-American/Black (6,321)	7,434	10.75
Not Hispanic (5,967)	6,802	9.84
Hispanic (354)	632	0.91
American Indian/Alaska Native (779)	1,871	2.71
Not Hispanic (363)	1,060	1.53
Hispanic (416)	811	1.17
Aleut *(Alaska Native)* (1)	1	<0.01
Apache (37)	84	0.12
Arapaho (1)	9	0.01
Blackfeet (5)	54	0.08
Canadian/French Am. Ind. (2)	7	0.01
Central American Ind. (1)	3	<0.01
Cherokee (52)	287	0.42
Cheyenne (5)	15	0.02
Chickasaw (1)	19	0.03
Chippewa (10)	23	0.03
Choctaw (32)	67	0.10
Colville (0)	1	<0.01
Comanche (3)	7	0.01
Cree (0)	2	<0.01
Creek (2)	7	0.01
Crow (1)	2	<0.01
Delaware (1)	2	<0.01
Hopi (2)	14	0.02
Inupiat *(Alaska Native)* (1)	1	<0.01
Iroquois (10)	22	0.03
Lumbee (0)	1	<0.01
Menominee (0)	1	<0.01
Mexican American Ind. (59)	119	0.17
Navajo (36)	60	0.09
Osage (3)	8	0.01
Paiute (5)	16	0.02
Pima (5)	7	0.01
Potawatomi (12)	15	0.02
Pueblo (30)	58	0.08
Puget Sound Salish (0)	2	<0.01
Seminole (5)	10	0.01
Shoshone (5)	15	0.02
Sioux (11)	40	0.06
South American Ind. (1)	2	<0.01
Spanish American Ind. (2)	10	0.01
Tlingit-Haida *(Alaska Native)* (1)	1	<0.01
Tohono O'Odham (5)	8	0.01
Ute (1)	1	<0.01
Yaqui (11)	30	0.04
Yuman (6)	11	0.02
Asian (2,020)	2,782	4.02
Not Hispanic (1,934)	2,497	3.61
Hispanic (86)	285	0.41
Bangladeshi (6)	8	0.01
Cambodian (50)	57	0.08
Chinese, ex. Taiwanese (179)	290	0.42
Filipino (741)	1,088	1.57
Indian (272)	323	0.47
Indonesian (11)	32	0.05
Japanese (154)	324	0.47
Korean (327)	385	0.56
Laotian (3)	7	0.01
Malaysian (1)	6	0.01
Pakistani (25)	29	0.04
Sri Lankan (12)	13	0.02
Taiwanese (16)	21	0.03
Thai (37)	47	0.07
Vietnamese (122)	147	0.21
Hawaii Native/Pacific Islander (294)	508	0.73
Not Hispanic (265)	431	0.62
Hispanic (29)	77	0.11
Guamanian/Chamorro (45)	79	0.11
Native Hawaiian (78)	157	0.23
Samoan (141)	188	0.27
Tongan (17)	20	0.03
White (47,762)	50,821	73.51
Not Hispanic (38,374)	40,088	57.99
Hispanic (9,388)	10,733	15.52

Arcadia

Place Type: City
County: Los Angeles
Population: 56,364†

Ancestry‡	Population	%
African, Sub-Saharan (35)	45	0.08
African (13)	23	0.04
Ethiopian (11)	11	0.02
Nigerian (11)	11	0.02
American (874)	874	1.57
Arab (347)	506	0.91
Arab (7)	24	0.04
Egyptian (196)	275	0.49
Jordanian (13)	66	0.12
Lebanese (45)	55	0.10
Syrian (30)	30	0.05
Other Arab (56)	56	0.10
Armenian (260)	287	0.52
Australian (3)	34	0.06
Austrian (26)	52	0.09
Basque (11)	11	0.02
Belgian (0)	12	0.02
Brazilian (0)	31	0.06
British (91)	136	0.24
Bulgarian (11)	11	0.02
Canadian (109)	210	0.38
Croatian (44)	44	0.08
Czech (16)	27	0.05
Czechoslovakian (0)	9	0.02
Danish (33)	139	0.25
Dutch (127)	470	0.84
Eastern European (62)	62	0.11
English (862)	2,810	5.04
European (256)	316	0.57
Finnish (10)	10	0.02
French, ex. Basque (42)	792	1.42
French Canadian (53)	63	0.11
German (974)	3,062	5.50
Greek (190)	275	0.49
Hungarian (62)	81	0.15
Iranian (202)	211	0.38
Irish (488)	2,040	3.66
Israeli (36)	36	0.06
Italian (785)	1,823	3.27
Latvian (10)	24	0.04
Lithuanian (30)	93	0.17
Northern European (38)	38	0.07
Norwegian (132)	536	0.96
Pennsylvania German (0)	5	0.01
Polish (161)	421	0.76
Portuguese (27)	35	0.06
Romanian (61)	71	0.13
Russian (101)	232	0.42
Scandinavian (0)	31	0.06
Scotch-Irish (110)	413	0.74
Scottish (168)	599	1.08
Slovak (0)	32	0.06
Swedish (78)	249	0.45
Swiss (11)	75	0.13
Ukrainian (23)	36	0.06
Welsh (31)	86	0.15
West Indian, ex. Hispanic (21)	21	0.04
Trinidadian/Tobagonian (21)	21	0.04
Yugoslavian (0)	65	0.12

Hispanic Origin	Population	%
Hispanic or Latino (of any race)	6,799	12.06
Central American, ex. Mexican	490	0.87
Costa Rican	16	0.03
Guatemalan	140	0.25
Honduran	26	0.05
Nicaraguan	71	0.13
Panamanian	20	0.04
Salvadoran	211	0.37
Other Central American	6	0.01
Cuban	131	0.23
Dominican Republic	3	0.01
Mexican	4,438	7.87
Puerto Rican	141	0.25
South American	516	0.92
Argentinean	124	0.22
Bolivian	28	0.05
Chilean	31	0.05
Colombian	126	0.22
Ecuadorian	48	0.09
Paraguayan	6	0.01
Peruvian	134	0.24
Uruguayan	2	<0.01
Venezuelan	11	0.02
Other South American	6	0.01
Other Hispanic or Latino	1,080	1.92

Race*	Population	%
African-American/Black (681)	896	1.59
Not Hispanic (628)	778	1.38
Hispanic (53)	118	0.21
American Indian/Alaska Native (186)	426	0.76
Not Hispanic (73)	200	0.35
Hispanic (113)	226	0.40
Aleut *(Alaska Native)* (0)	1	<0.01
Apache (5)	9	0.02
Arapaho (0)	1	<0.01
Blackfeet (0)	5	0.01
Canadian/French Am. Ind. (1)	4	0.01
Cherokee (9)	31	0.05
Cheyenne (0)	2	<0.01
Chickasaw (0)	1	<0.01
Chippewa (1)	8	0.01
Choctaw (0)	3	0.01
Creek (0)	2	<0.01
Hopi (1)	1	<0.01
Iroquois (0)	1	<0.01
Lumbee (0)	1	<0.01
Mexican American Ind. (47)	49	0.09
Navajo (3)	11	0.02
Osage (0)	2	<0.01
Ottawa (0)	1	<0.01
Paiute (0)	2	<0.01
Potawatomi (1)	1	<0.01
Pueblo (1)	5	0.01
Seminole (0)	1	<0.01
Sioux (5)	10	0.02
South American Ind. (3)	11	0.02
Tlingit-Haida *(Alaska Native)* (1)	1	<0.01
Ute (1)	6	0.01
Yaqui (1)	4	0.01
Asian (33,353)	34,416	61.06
Not Hispanic (33,224)	34,096	60.49
Hispanic (129)	320	0.57
Bangladeshi (41)	41	0.07
Burmese (325)	376	0.67
Cambodian (64)	98	0.17
Chinese, ex. Taiwanese (20,345)	21,744	38.58
Filipino (1,087)	1,342	2.38
Hmong (1)	1	<0.01
Indian (1,377)	1,473	2.61
Indonesian (328)	422	0.75
Japanese (883)	1,235	2.19
Korean (1,937)	2,094	3.72
Laotian (17)	25	0.04
Malaysian (59)	80	0.14
Nepalese (2)	3	0.01
Pakistani (97)	111	0.20
Sri Lankan (59)	67	0.12
Taiwanese (4,400)	4,846	8.60
Thai (248)	301	0.53
Vietnamese (776)	1,042	1.85
Hawaii Native/Pacific Islander (16)	191	0.34
Not Hispanic (15)	168	0.30
Hispanic (1)	23	0.04
Fijian (3)	8	0.01
Guamanian/Chamorro (2)	11	0.02
Native Hawaiian (4)	28	0.05
Samoan (3)	5	0.01
White (18,191)	19,390	34.40
Not Hispanic (14,467)	15,275	27.10
Hispanic (3,724)	4,115	7.30

*Notes: † The Census 2010 population figure is used to calculate the percentages in the Hispanic Origin and Race categories. Ancestry percentages are based on the 2006-2010 American Community Survey population (not shown); ‡ Numbers in parentheses indicate the number of people reporting a single ancestry; * Numbers in parentheses indicate the number of persons reporting this race alone, not in combination with any other race; Please refer to the Explanation of Data for more information.*

Arcata

Place Type: City
County: Humboldt
Population: 17,231†

Ancestry‡	Population	%
African, Sub-Saharan (45)	90	0.53
African (40)	85	0.50
Ghanaian (5)	5	0.03
American (485)	485	2.84
Arab (0)	58	0.34
Lebanese (0)	58	0.34
Armenian (0)	30	0.18
Austrian (6)	57	0.33
Belgian (0)	11	0.06
British (38)	141	0.82
Canadian (37)	88	0.51
Celtic (16)	16	0.09
Croatian (112)	112	0.65
Czech (0)	47	0.27
Czechoslovakian (13)	13	0.08
Danish (126)	233	1.36
Dutch (39)	272	1.59
Eastern European (35)	47	0.27
English (440)	2,106	12.32
European (1,351)	1,637	9.57
Finnish (27)	72	0.42
French, ex. Basque (102)	695	4.06
French Canadian (124)	169	0.99
German (404)	2,782	16.27
Greek (24)	24	0.14
Hungarian (32)	61	0.36
Icelander (17)	17	0.10
Iranian (52)	60	0.35
Irish (475)	2,235	13.07
Italian (429)	964	5.64
Lithuanian (28)	35	0.20
New Zealander (0)	6	0.04
Northern European (70)	70	0.41
Norwegian (114)	311	1.82
Polish (68)	254	1.49
Portuguese (209)	495	2.89
Russian (311)	543	3.18
Scandinavian (16)	32	0.19
Scotch-Irish (107)	407	2.38
Scottish (33)	536	3.13
Slovak (11)	26	0.15
Swedish (131)	558	3.26
Swiss (33)	290	1.70
Ukrainian (64)	73	0.43
Welsh (25)	102	0.60
West Indian, ex. Hispanic (0)	72	0.42
Trinidadian/Tobagonian (0)	29	0.17
West Indian (0)	43	0.25
Yugoslavian (17)	30	0.18

Hispanic Origin	Population	%
Hispanic or Latino (of any race)	2,000	11.61
Central American, ex. Mexican	147	0.85
Costa Rican	4	0.02
Guatemalan	29	0.17
Honduran	19	0.11
Nicaraguan	24	0.14
Panamanian	7	0.04
Salvadoran	62	0.36
Other Central American	2	0.01
Cuban	37	0.21
Dominican Republic	8	0.05
Mexican	1,419	8.24
Puerto Rican	75	0.44
South American	88	0.51
Argentinean	12	0.07
Bolivian	5	0.03
Chilean	9	0.05
Colombian	17	0.10
Ecuadorian	10	0.06
Peruvian	19	0.11
Uruguayan	4	0.02
Venezuelan	8	0.05
Other South American	4	0.02
Other Hispanic or Latino	226	1.31

Race*	Population	%
African-American/Black (351)	624	3.62
Not Hispanic (323)	541	3.14
Hispanic (28)	83	0.48
American Indian/Alaska Native (393)	889	5.16
Not Hispanic (323)	727	4.22
Hispanic (70)	162	0.94
Aleut *(Alaska Native)* (1)	4	0.02
Apache (14)	22	0.13
Blackfeet (2)	22	0.13
Canadian/French Am. Ind. (2)	2	0.01
Central American Ind. (0)	2	0.01
Cherokee (18)	129	0.75
Cheyenne (1)	5	0.03
Chickasaw (3)	11	0.06
Chippewa (3)	9	0.05
Choctaw (3)	28	0.16
Comanche (0)	2	0.01
Cree (0)	2	0.01
Creek (1)	3	0.02
Crow (0)	2	0.01
Inupiat *(Alaska Native)* (5)	5	0.03
Iroquois (5)	14	0.08
Kiowa (1)	2	0.01
Menominee (0)	1	0.01
Mexican American Ind. (11)	16	0.09
Navajo (7)	15	0.09
Osage (0)	4	0.02
Paiute (2)	4	0.02
Potawatomi (2)	2	0.01
Pueblo (3)	4	0.02
Sioux (9)	13	0.08
South American Ind. (0)	4	0.02
Tlingit-Haida *(Alaska Native)* (4)	4	0.02
Tohono O'Odham (2)	5	0.03
Yaqui (7)	10	0.06
Yuman (3)	6	0.03
Asian (454)	807	4.68
Not Hispanic (434)	742	4.31
Hispanic (20)	65	0.38
Bhutanese (1)	1	0.01
Burmese (1)	1	0.01
Cambodian (7)	8	0.05
Chinese, ex. Taiwanese (143)	243	1.41
Filipino (62)	161	0.93
Hmong (15)	16	0.09
Indian (22)	43	0.25
Indonesian (4)	10	0.06
Japanese (71)	186	1.08
Korean (31)	57	0.33
Laotian (14)	21	0.12
Malaysian (0)	1	0.01
Pakistani (1)	4	0.02
Taiwanese (4)	4	0.02
Thai (17)	23	0.13
Vietnamese (28)	47	0.27
Hawaii Native/Pacific Islander (35)	108	0.63
Not Hispanic (31)	94	0.55
Hispanic (4)	14	0.08
Fijian (1)	2	0.01
Guamanian/Chamorro (6)	12	0.07
Native Hawaiian (16)	51	0.30
Samoan (8)	20	0.12
Tongan (0)	2	0.01
White (14,094)	15,149	87.92
Not Hispanic (13,153)	13,966	81.05
Hispanic (941)	1,183	6.87

Arden-Arcade

Place Type: CDP
County: Sacramento
Population: 92,186†

Ancestry‡	Population	%
Afghan (26)	26	0.03
African, Sub-Saharan (446)	575	0.63
African (316)	350	0.38
Cape Verdean (15)	31	0.03
Ethiopian (55)	71	0.08
Kenyan (19)	19	0.02
Nigerian (24)	39	0.04
Ugandan (8)	40	0.04
Other Sub-Saharan African (9)	25	0.03
Alsatian (15)	23	0.03
American (3,234)	3,234	3.56
Arab (185)	335	0.37
Arab (111)	111	0.12
Egyptian (31)	31	0.03
Lebanese (27)	106	0.12
Palestinian (16)	29	0.03
Syrian (0)	13	0.01
Other Arab (0)	45	0.05
Armenian (303)	337	0.37
Assyrian/Chaldean/Syriac (19)	30	0.03
Australian (53)	53	0.06
Austrian (105)	230	0.25
Basque (50)	159	0.17
Belgian (34)	67	0.07
Brazilian (31)	31	0.03
British (157)	327	0.36
Bulgarian (17)	17	0.02
Canadian (196)	265	0.29
Celtic (17)	205	0.23
Croatian (191)	471	0.52
Czech (93)	450	0.49
Czechoslovakian (46)	180	0.20
Danish (245)	826	0.91
Dutch (279)	1,654	1.82
Eastern European (243)	273	0.30
English (2,973)	10,809	11.89
Estonian (0)	7	0.01
European (1,031)	1,324	1.46
Finnish (51)	208	0.23
French, ex. Basque (266)	3,429	3.77
French Canadian (190)	454	0.50
German (3,662)	13,842	15.22
Greek (176)	390	0.43
Hungarian (114)	373	0.41
Icelander (0)	30	0.03
Iranian (368)	461	0.51
Irish (2,278)	10,656	11.72
Israeli (94)	94	0.10
Italian (1,992)	5,574	6.13
Lithuanian (19)	121	0.13
Luxemburger (0)	9	0.01
Maltese (10)	22	0.02
Northern European (268)	285	0.31
Norwegian (586)	1,936	2.13
Polish (657)	1,804	1.98
Portuguese (328)	1,403	1.54
Romanian (239)	297	0.33
Russian (974)	1,489	1.64
Scandinavian (229)	481	0.53
Scotch-Irish (1,032)	2,677	2.94
Scottish (709)	2,817	3.10
Serbian (15)	60	0.07
Slavic (9)	60	0.07
Slovak (19)	70	0.08
Swedish (525)	1,652	1.82
Swiss (167)	523	0.58
Turkish (29)	45	0.05
Ukrainian (597)	761	0.84
Welsh (86)	693	0.76
West Indian, ex. Hispanic (39)	62	0.07
Bermudan (0)	10	0.01
Dutch West Indian (16)	23	0.03
Haitian (14)	20	0.02
Jamaican (9)	9	0.01
Yugoslavian (92)	201	0.22

Hispanic Origin	Population	%
Hispanic or Latino (of any race)	17,147	18.60
Central American, ex. Mexican	952	1.03
Costa Rican	35	0.04
Guatemalan	178	0.19
Honduran	171	0.19

*Notes: † The Census 2010 population figure is used to calculate the percentages in the Hispanic Origin and Race categories. Ancestry percentages are based on the 2006-2010 American Community Survey population (not shown); ‡ Numbers in parentheses indicate the number of people reporting a single ancestry; * Numbers in parentheses indicate the number of persons reporting this race alone, not in combination with any other race; Please refer to the Explanation of Data for more information.*

Nicaraguan	118	0.13
Panamanian	53	0.06
Salvadoran	382	0.41
Other Central American	15	0.02
Cuban	135	0.15
Dominican Republic	20	0.02
Mexican	13,469	14.61
Puerto Rican	548	0.59
South American	455	0.49
Argentinean	36	0.04
Bolivian	14	0.02
Chilean	58	0.06
Colombian	90	0.10
Ecuadorian	24	0.03
Paraguayan	3	<0.01
Peruvian	178	0.19
Uruguayan	9	0.01
Venezuelan	32	0.03
Other South American	11	0.01
Other Hispanic or Latino	1,568	1.70

Race*	Population	%
African-American/Black (7,977)	9,974	10.82
Not Hispanic (7,527)	9,091	9.86
Hispanic (450)	883	0.96
American Indian/Alaska Native (948)	2,418	2.62
Not Hispanic (584)	1,628	1.77
Hispanic (364)	790	0.86
Alaska Athabascan *(Ala. Nat.)* (1)	2	<0.01
Aleut *(Alaska Native)* (5)	6	0.01
Apache (27)	52	0.06
Arapaho (0)	2	<0.01
Blackfeet (4)	77	0.08
Canadian/French Am. Ind. (2)	5	0.01
Central American Ind. (0)	1	<0.01
Cherokee (91)	441	0.48
Cheyenne (1)	13	0.01
Chickasaw (4)	16	0.02
Chippewa (22)	34	0.04
Choctaw (16)	90	0.10
Colville (0)	1	<0.01
Comanche (5)	5	0.01
Cree (0)	4	<0.01
Creek (4)	20	0.02
Crow (1)	9	0.01
Delaware (4)	5	0.01
Hopi (0)	6	0.01
Houma (0)	3	<0.01
Inupiat *(Alaska Native)* (2)	4	<0.01
Iroquois (12)	36	0.04
Kiowa (1)	2	<0.01
Lumbee (2)	2	<0.01
Menominee (2)	3	<0.01
Mexican American Ind. (64)	108	0.12
Navajo (15)	39	0.04
Osage (1)	11	0.01
Ottawa (1)	1	<0.01
Paiute (8)	11	0.01
Pima (9)	11	0.01
Potawatomi (6)	9	0.01
Pueblo (11)	20	0.02
Puget Sound Salish (2)	3	<0.01
Seminole (3)	11	0.01
Shoshone (4)	14	0.02
Sioux (34)	76	0.08
South American Ind. (1)	10	0.01
Spanish American Ind. (1)	5	0.01
Tlingit-Haida *(Alaska Native)* (4)	8	0.01
Tohono O'Odham (3)	6	0.01
Tsimshian *(Alaska Native)* (0)	4	<0.01
Yakama (0)	1	<0.01
Yaqui (8)	28	0.03
Yup'ik *(Alaska Native)* (0)	3	<0.01
Asian (5,152)	6,976	7.57
Not Hispanic (4,990)	6,493	7.04
Hispanic (162)	483	0.52
Bangladeshi (5)	5	0.01
Bhutanese (135)	142	0.15
Burmese (9)	12	0.01
Cambodian (57)	75	0.08
Chinese, ex. Taiwanese (893)	1,213	1.32
Filipino (1,233)	1,926	2.09
Hmong (261)	292	0.32
Indian (569)	713	0.77
Indonesian (35)	62	0.07
Japanese (468)	868	0.94
Korean (351)	488	0.53
Laotian (183)	209	0.23
Malaysian (5)	7	0.01
Nepalese (20)	41	0.04
Pakistani (63)	76	0.08
Sri Lankan (10)	11	0.01
Taiwanese (65)	81	0.09
Thai (90)	129	0.14
Vietnamese (366)	434	0.47
Hawaii Native/Pacific Islander (531)	988	1.07
Not Hispanic (491)	857	0.93
Hispanic (40)	131	0.14
Fijian (224)	262	0.28
Guamanian/Chamorro (60)	103	0.11
Marshallese (0)	1	<0.01
Native Hawaiian (62)	253	0.27
Samoan (76)	146	0.16
Tongan (54)	74	0.08
White (64,688)	69,251	75.12
Not Hispanic (57,529)	60,628	65.77
Hispanic (7,159)	8,623	9.35

Arroyo Grande

Place Type: City
County: San Luis Obispo
Population: 17,252†

Ancestry‡	Population	%
African, Sub-Saharan (18)	18	0.11
African (18)	18	0.11
American (687)	687	4.04
Arab (16)	26	0.15
Egyptian (16)	16	0.09
Lebanese (0)	10	0.06
Armenian (0)	53	0.31
Australian (30)	30	0.18
Austrian (0)	75	0.44
Basque (0)	23	0.14
Belgian (0)	32	0.19
Brazilian (0)	42	0.25
British (114)	128	0.75
Bulgarian (0)	9	0.05
Cajun (28)	28	0.16
Canadian (46)	98	0.58
Celtic (0)	15	0.09
Croatian (25)	149	0.88
Czech (21)	83	0.49
Czechoslovakian (34)	34	0.20
Danish (137)	289	1.70
Dutch (31)	410	2.41
Eastern European (30)	30	0.18
English (780)	2,658	15.64
European (242)	242	1.42
Finnish (31)	31	0.18
French, ex. Basque (147)	612	3.60
French Canadian (32)	76	0.45
German (843)	3,017	17.76
Greek (33)	51	0.30
Hungarian (33)	51	0.30
Iranian (108)	108	0.64
Irish (654)	2,246	13.22
Italian (423)	1,226	7.22
Lithuanian (20)	40	0.24
Norwegian (181)	548	3.23
Pennsylvania German (0)	14	0.08
Polish (171)	570	3.35
Portuguese (201)	390	2.30
Russian (84)	276	1.62
Scandinavian (15)	67	0.39
Scotch-Irish (121)	498	2.93
Scottish (133)	522	3.07
Swedish (136)	361	2.12
Swiss (17)	133	0.78
Ukrainian (0)	14	0.08
Welsh (13)	115	0.68

Hispanic Origin	Population	%
Hispanic or Latino (of any race)	2,707	15.69
Central American, ex. Mexican	68	0.39
Costa Rican	3	0.02
Guatemalan	18	0.10
Honduran	2	0.01
Nicaraguan	8	0.05
Panamanian	2	0.01
Salvadoran	33	0.19
Other Central American	2	0.01
Cuban	16	0.09
Dominican Republic	2	0.01
Mexican	2,229	12.92
Puerto Rican	71	0.41
South American	43	0.25
Argentinean	11	0.06
Bolivian	1	0.01
Chilean	8	0.05
Colombian	7	0.04
Ecuadorian	1	0.01
Peruvian	14	0.08
Other South American	1	0.01
Other Hispanic or Latino	278	1.61

Race*	Population	%
African-American/Black (156)	265	1.54
Not Hispanic (124)	202	1.17
Hispanic (32)	63	0.37
American Indian/Alaska Native (125)	371	2.15
Not Hispanic (63)	221	1.28
Hispanic (62)	150	0.87
Aleut *(Alaska Native)* (0)	2	0.01
Apache (3)	8	0.05
Blackfeet (1)	6	0.03
Central American Ind. (0)	4	0.02
Cherokee (11)	87	0.50
Chickasaw (1)	1	0.01
Choctaw (1)	15	0.09
Cree (0)	1	0.01
Creek (1)	5	0.03
Iroquois (2)	2	0.01
Mexican American Ind. (12)	27	0.16
Navajo (0)	11	0.06
Osage (0)	4	0.02
Paiute (0)	1	0.01
Potawatomi (3)	6	0.03
Pueblo (2)	7	0.04
Seminole (2)	3	0.02
Shoshone (0)	2	0.01
Sioux (1)	4	0.02
South American Ind. (3)	5	0.03
Spanish American Ind. (1)	1	0.01
Tlingit-Haida *(Alaska Native)* (2)	2	0.01
Ute (1)	1	0.01
Yaqui (6)	11	0.06
Asian (595)	916	5.31
Not Hispanic (557)	819	4.75
Hispanic (38)	97	0.56
Bangladeshi (3)	3	0.02
Cambodian (4)	8	0.05
Chinese, ex. Taiwanese (74)	131	0.76
Filipino (187)	358	2.08
Indian (55)	64	0.37
Indonesian (5)	10	0.06
Japanese (141)	241	1.40
Korean (54)	73	0.42
Laotian (4)	4	0.02
Pakistani (1)	5	0.03
Sri Lankan (3)	3	0.02
Taiwanese (1)	3	0.02
Thai (11)	24	0.14
Vietnamese (18)	28	0.16
Hawaii Native/Pacific Islander (14)	65	0.38
Not Hispanic (14)	56	0.32
Hispanic (0)	9	0.05
Guamanian/Chamorro (2)	7	0.04
Native Hawaiian (4)	31	0.18

*Notes: † The Census 2010 population figure is used to calculate the percentages in the Hispanic Origin and Race categories. Ancestry percentages are based on the 2006-2010 American Community Survey population (not shown); ‡ Numbers in parentheses indicate the number of people reporting a single ancestry; * Numbers in parentheses indicate the number of persons reporting this race alone, not in combination with any other race; Please refer to the Explanation of Data for more information.*

SECTION TWO

Samoan (2)	8	0.05
White (14,710)	15,429	89.43
Not Hispanic (13,266)	13,730	79.58
Hispanic (1,444)	1,699	9.85

Artesia

Place Type: City
County: Los Angeles
Population: 16,522†

Ancestry‡	Population	%
American (346)	346	2.10
Arab (0)	17	0.10
Lebanese (0)	17	0.10
Brazilian (12)	24	0.15
Danish (0)	18	0.11
Dutch (564)	737	4.47
English (58)	202	1.23
European (61)	79	0.48
French, ex. Basque (19)	350	2.12
French Canadian (25)	143	0.87
German (143)	465	2.82
Iranian (29)	29	0.18
Irish (164)	444	2.69
Italian (68)	102	0.62
Norwegian (43)	55	0.33
Pennsylvania German (11)	11	0.07
Polish (35)	78	0.47
Portuguese (1,278)	1,378	8.36
Russian (42)	59	0.36
Scandinavian (13)	13	0.08
Scotch-Irish (21)	157	0.95
Scottish (30)	119	0.72
Swedish (10)	16	0.10
Swiss (0)	10	0.06
Turkish (14)	14	0.08
Welsh (0)	36	0.22

Hispanic Origin	Population	%
Hispanic or Latino (of any race)	5,910	35.77
Central American, ex. Mexican	286	1.73
Costa Rican	12	0.07
Guatemalan	61	0.37
Honduran	18	0.11
Nicaraguan	26	0.16
Panamanian	11	0.07
Salvadoran	152	0.92
Other Central American	6	0.04
Cuban	37	0.22
Dominican Republic	1	0.01
Mexican	5,144	31.13
Puerto Rican	44	0.27
South American	139	0.84
Argentinean	16	0.10
Bolivian	16	0.10
Chilean	6	0.04
Colombian	13	0.08
Ecuadorian	36	0.22
Peruvian	46	0.28
Uruguayan	1	0.01
Venezuelan	5	0.03
Other Hispanic or Latino	259	1.57

Race*	Population	%
African-American/Black (589)	691	4.18
Not Hispanic (543)	627	3.79
Hispanic (46)	64	0.39
American Indian/Alaska Native (94)	174	1.05
Not Hispanic (36)	91	0.55
Hispanic (58)	83	0.50
Apache (2)	9	0.05
Blackfeet (0)	9	0.05
Canadian/French Am. Ind. (1)	1	0.01
Cherokee (5)	23	0.14
Chickasaw (1)	1	0.01
Choctaw (1)	2	0.01
Creek (0)	5	0.03
Hopi (0)	3	0.02
Iroquois (2)	2	0.01
Mexican American Ind. (8)	12	0.07
Sioux (2)	5	0.03
South American Ind. (1)	1	0.01
Spanish American Ind. (4)	4	0.02
Tlingit-Haida *(Alaska Native)* (1)	1	0.01
Yaqui (1)	4	0.02
Asian (6,131)	6,408	38.78
Not Hispanic (6,092)	6,322	38.26
Hispanic (39)	86	0.52
Bangladeshi (32)	36	0.22
Cambodian (154)	202	1.22
Chinese, ex. Taiwanese (794)	938	5.68
Filipino (2,014)	2,158	13.06
Hmong (2)	2	0.01
Indian (1,299)	1,407	8.52
Indonesian (50)	58	0.35
Japanese (57)	87	0.53
Korean (816)	830	5.02
Laotian (7)	7	0.04
Malaysian (6)	6	0.04
Nepalese (215)	226	1.37
Pakistani (68)	75	0.45
Sri Lankan (12)	12	0.07
Taiwanese (217)	233	1.41
Thai (68)	76	0.46
Vietnamese (119)	165	1.00
Hawaii Native/Pacific Islander (40)	73	0.44
Not Hispanic (37)	66	0.40
Hispanic (3)	7	0.04
Fijian (14)	14	0.08
Guamanian/Chamorro (7)	9	0.05
Native Hawaiian (5)	14	0.08
Samoan (7)	13	0.08
Tongan (1)	2	0.01
White (6,446)	6,843	41.42
Not Hispanic (3,518)	3,678	22.26
Hispanic (2,928)	3,165	19.16

Arvin

Place Type: City
County: Kern
Population: 19,304†

Ancestry‡	Population	%
American (111)	111	0.61
Arab (1,089)	1,089	5.94
Arab (782)	782	4.27
Other Arab (307)	307	1.67
Czech (0)	10	0.05
English (116)	230	1.25
European (10)	19	0.10
French, ex. Basque (0)	11	0.06
German (0)	69	0.38
Irish (33)	95	0.52
Italian (0)	14	0.08
Norwegian (9)	9	0.05
Portuguese (0)	9	0.05
Scotch-Irish (14)	14	0.08
Scottish (15)	29	0.16
Swiss (10)	10	0.05

Hispanic Origin	Population	%
Hispanic or Latino (of any race)	17,892	92.69
Central American, ex. Mexican	148	0.77
Costa Rican	8	0.04
Guatemalan	37	0.19
Honduran	21	0.11
Nicaraguan	4	0.02
Salvadoran	78	0.40
Cuban	1	0.01
Mexican	17,133	88.75
Puerto Rican	70	0.36
South American	8	0.04
Chilean	1	0.01
Colombian	1	0.01
Ecuadorian	1	0.01
Peruvian	5	0.03
Other Hispanic or Latino	532	2.76

Race*	Population	%
African-American/Black (192)	268	1.39
Not Hispanic (102)	139	0.72
Hispanic (90)	129	0.67
American Indian/Alaska Native (240)	372	1.93
Not Hispanic (41)	75	0.39
Hispanic (199)	297	1.54
Apache (0)	2	0.01
Blackfeet (0)	2	0.01
Cherokee (5)	31	0.16
Comanche (2)	2	0.01
Delaware (1)	1	0.01
Hopi (1)	1	0.01
Iroquois (4)	4	0.02
Mexican American Ind. (123)	156	0.81
Navajo (1)	1	0.01
Paiute (4)	10	0.05
Pima (3)	3	0.02
Shoshone (1)	1	0.01
Sioux (2)	4	0.02
Spanish American Ind. (0)	1	0.01
Yuman (2)	3	0.02
Asian (155)	275	1.42
Not Hispanic (135)	196	1.02
Hispanic (20)	79	0.41
Chinese, ex. Taiwanese (6)	11	0.06
Filipino (72)	107	0.55
Indian (48)	56	0.29
Japanese (0)	6	0.03
Korean (2)	2	0.01
Laotian (8)	15	0.08
Thai (10)	10	0.05
Vietnamese (1)	1	0.01
Hawaii Native/Pacific Islander (6)	31	0.16
Not Hispanic (2)	8	0.04
Hispanic (4)	23	0.12
Native Hawaiian (4)	8	0.04
Samoan (2)	11	0.06
White (10,247)	10,918	56.56
Not Hispanic (985)	1,092	5.66
Hispanic (9,262)	9,826	50.90

Ashland

Place Type: CDP
County: Alameda
Population: 21,925†

Ancestry‡	Population	%
African, Sub-Saharan (394)	394	1.78
African (284)	284	1.29
Kenyan (42)	42	0.19
Nigerian (26)	26	0.12
Sierra Leonean (38)	38	0.17
South African (4)	4	0.02
American (166)	166	0.75
Arab (24)	37	0.17
Arab (24)	37	0.17
Australian (18)	30	0.14
Basque (11)	11	0.05
Belgian (0)	18	0.08
Brazilian (0)	28	0.13
British (16)	16	0.07
Canadian (39)	39	0.18
Czech (27)	35	0.16
Czechoslovakian (28)	36	0.16
Danish (9)	33	0.15
Dutch (28)	67	0.30
English (266)	522	2.36
European (37)	94	0.43
Finnish (0)	12	0.05
French, ex. Basque (270)	495	2.24
French Canadian (20)	34	0.15
German (133)	519	2.35
Greek (0)	64	0.29
Hungarian (0)	15	0.07
Iranian (32)	32	0.14
Irish (239)	610	2.76
Italian (186)	497	2.25

*Notes: † The Census 2010 population figure is used to calculate the percentages in the Hispanic Origin and Race categories. Ancestry percentages are based on the 2006-2010 American Community Survey population (not shown); ‡ Numbers in parentheses indicate the number of people reporting a single ancestry; * Numbers in parentheses indicate the number of persons reporting this race alone, not in combination with any other race; Please refer to the Explanation of Data for more information.*

Northern European (9)	9	0.04
Norwegian (7)	86	0.39
Polish (11)	60	0.27
Portuguese (255)	691	3.13
Romanian (102)	138	0.62
Russian (48)	80	0.36
Scandinavian (39)	47	0.21
Scotch-Irish (31)	152	0.69
Scottish (21)	69	0.31
Swedish (55)	168	0.76
Swiss (0)	14	0.06
Welsh (4)	23	0.10
Yugoslavian (57)	57	0.26

Hispanic Origin	Population	%
Hispanic or Latino (of any race)	9,394	42.85
Central American, ex. Mexican	984	4.49
Costa Rican	15	0.07
Guatemalan	176	0.80
Honduran	112	0.51
Nicaraguan	218	0.99
Panamanian	3	0.01
Salvadoran	453	2.07
Other Central American	7	0.03
Cuban	24	0.11
Dominican Republic	4	0.02
Mexican	7,081	32.30
Puerto Rican	304	1.39
South American	185	0.84
Argentinean	27	0.12
Bolivian	9	0.04
Chilean	6	0.03
Colombian	33	0.15
Ecuadorian	14	0.06
Peruvian	82	0.37
Uruguayan	1	<0.01
Venezuelan	11	0.05
Other South American	2	0.01
Other Hispanic or Latino	812	3.70

Race*	Population	%
African-American/Black (4,269)	4,737	21.61
Not Hispanic (4,085)	4,428	20.20
Hispanic (184)	309	1.41
American Indian/Alaska Native (232)	494	2.25
Not Hispanic (95)	262	1.19
Hispanic (137)	232	1.06
Apache (13)	22	0.10
Blackfeet (5)	18	0.08
Central American Ind. (2)	3	0.01
Cherokee (15)	67	0.31
Cheyenne (0)	3	0.01
Chickasaw (3)	3	0.01
Chippewa (7)	9	0.04
Choctaw (4)	11	0.05
Comanche (6)	6	0.03
Cree (0)	2	0.01
Creek (6)	7	0.03
Hopi (2)	6	0.03
Inupiat *(Alaska Native)* (2)	4	0.02
Iroquois (3)	5	0.02
Mexican American Ind. (36)	44	0.20
Navajo (8)	13	0.06
Osage (0)	1	<0.01
Paiute (1)	9	0.04
Pima (2)	2	0.01
Potawatomi (0)	4	0.02
Pueblo (3)	5	0.02
Seminole (0)	3	0.01
Sioux (0)	10	0.05
South American Ind. (2)	5	0.02
Spanish American Ind. (1)	2	0.01
Ute (0)	1	<0.01
Yakama (0)	2	0.01
Yaqui (3)	11	0.05
Asian (4,031)	4,446	20.28
Not Hispanic (3,967)	4,272	19.48
Hispanic (64)	174	0.79
Burmese (1)	6	0.03
Cambodian (73)	87	0.40
Chinese, ex. Taiwanese (1,587)	1,720	7.84
Filipino (1,508)	1,734	7.91
Hmong (6)	11	0.05
Indian (137)	190	0.87
Indonesian (13)	21	0.10
Japanese (71)	108	0.49
Korean (93)	107	0.49
Laotian (26)	40	0.18
Malaysian (3)	8	0.04
Nepalese (5)	5	0.02
Pakistani (11)	13	0.06
Sri Lankan (6)	7	0.03
Taiwanese (10)	14	0.06
Thai (6)	8	0.04
Vietnamese (357)	409	1.87
Hawaii Native/Pacific Islander (260)	425	1.94
Not Hispanic (239)	367	1.67
Hispanic (21)	58	0.26
Fijian (53)	79	0.36
Guamanian/Chamorro (38)	70	0.32
Native Hawaiian (10)	61	0.28
Samoan (86)	126	0.57
Tongan (39)	48	0.22
White (6,705)	7,642	34.86
Not Hispanic (3,413)	3,867	17.64
Hispanic (3,292)	3,775	17.22

Atascadero

Place Type: City
County: San Luis Obispo
Population: 28,310†

Ancestry‡	Population	%
African, Sub-Saharan (7)	7	0.03
African (7)	7	0.03
Alsatian (0)	11	0.04
American (1,194)	1,194	4.27
Arab (163)	242	0.86
Arab (0)	11	0.04
Jordanian (116)	116	0.41
Palestinian (29)	58	0.21
Syrian (18)	57	0.20
Armenian (5)	21	0.08
Assyrian/Chaldean/Syriac (14)	26	0.09
Austrian (0)	150	0.54
Basque (0)	16	0.06
Belgian (3)	16	0.06
Brazilian (44)	44	0.16
British (61)	152	0.54
Cajun (14)	14	0.05
Canadian (109)	122	0.44
Celtic (7)	7	0.03
Croatian (34)	56	0.20
Czech (10)	218	0.78
Czechoslovakian (0)	11	0.04
Danish (151)	428	1.53
Dutch (388)	1,023	3.66
Eastern European (15)	15	0.05
English (1,265)	4,083	14.59
Estonian (0)	13	0.05
European (580)	654	2.34
Finnish (12)	43	0.15
French, ex. Basque (242)	1,088	3.89
French Canadian (49)	178	0.64
German (1,562)	5,253	18.77
Greek (48)	200	0.71
Hungarian (0)	99	0.35
Iranian (13)	52	0.19
Irish (1,010)	3,516	12.57
Italian (642)	1,684	6.02
Lithuanian (42)	84	0.30
Northern European (28)	28	0.10
Norwegian (170)	439	1.57
Pennsylvania German (18)	49	0.18
Polish (246)	565	2.02
Portuguese (192)	515	1.84
Romanian (0)	5	0.02
Russian (65)	183	0.65
Scandinavian (172)	264	0.94
Scotch-Irish (170)	595	2.13
Scottish (120)	798	2.85
Slavic (0)	8	0.03
Slovene (10)	96	0.34
Swedish (160)	351	1.25
Swiss (17)	283	1.01
Ukrainian (8)	26	0.09
Welsh (55)	257	0.92
Yugoslavian (10)	32	0.11

Hispanic Origin	Population	%
Hispanic or Latino (of any race)	4,429	15.64
Central American, ex. Mexican	114	0.40
Costa Rican	13	0.05
Guatemalan	35	0.12
Honduran	4	0.01
Nicaraguan	10	0.04
Panamanian	5	0.02
Salvadoran	47	0.17
Cuban	24	0.08
Dominican Republic	6	0.02
Mexican	3,678	12.99
Puerto Rican	99	0.35
South American	108	0.38
Argentinean	22	0.08
Bolivian	4	0.01
Chilean	12	0.04
Colombian	12	0.04
Ecuadorian	10	0.04
Peruvian	40	0.14
Venezuelan	6	0.02
Other South American	2	0.01
Other Hispanic or Latino	400	1.41

Race*	Population	%
African-American/Black (585)	774	2.73
Not Hispanic (551)	695	2.45
Hispanic (34)	79	0.28
American Indian/Alaska Native (295)	704	2.49
Not Hispanic (179)	468	1.65
Hispanic (116)	236	0.83
Aleut *(Alaska Native)* (0)	3	0.01
Apache (6)	13	0.05
Blackfeet (3)	32	0.11
Canadian/French Am. Ind. (1)	2	0.01
Cherokee (29)	130	0.46
Cheyenne (0)	1	<0.01
Chickasaw (2)	6	0.02
Chippewa (1)	9	0.03
Choctaw (13)	34	0.12
Comanche (1)	2	0.01
Creek (1)	7	0.02
Crow (0)	1	<0.01
Delaware (0)	2	0.01
Hopi (1)	3	0.01
Iroquois (0)	1	<0.01
Menominee (0)	1	<0.01
Mexican American Ind. (22)	33	0.12
Navajo (6)	19	0.07
Osage (0)	3	0.01
Ottawa (1)	2	0.01
Paiute (0)	1	<0.01
Potawatomi (2)	5	0.02
Pueblo (1)	4	0.01
Seminole (0)	2	0.01
Shoshone (0)	1	<0.01
Sioux (13)	21	0.07
South American Ind. (2)	3	0.01
Spanish American Ind. (0)	2	0.01
Tohono O'Odham (5)	5	0.02
Ute (0)	2	0.01
Yaqui (6)	19	0.07
Yuman (1)	1	<0.01
Asian (685)	997	3.52
Not Hispanic (642)	908	3.21
Hispanic (43)	89	0.31
Burmese (1)	1	<0.01
Cambodian (14)	16	0.06
Chinese, ex. Taiwanese (86)	126	0.45
Filipino (264)	408	1.44

*Notes: † The Census 2010 population figure is used to calculate the percentages in the Hispanic Origin and Race categories. Ancestry percentages are based on the 2006-2010 American Community Survey population (not shown); ‡ Numbers in parentheses indicate the number of people reporting a single ancestry; * Numbers in parentheses indicate the number of persons reporting this race alone, not in combination with any other race; Please refer to the Explanation of Data for more information.*

Indian (58)	77	0.27
Indonesian (11)	29	0.10
Japanese (76)	145	0.51
Korean (61)	95	0.34
Laotian (3)	5	0.02
Pakistani (2)	7	0.02
Sri Lankan (6)	8	0.03
Taiwanese (6)	9	0.03
Thai (14)	24	0.08
Vietnamese (31)	41	0.14
Hawaii Native/Pacific Islander (57)	118	0.42
Not Hispanic (51)	97	0.34
Hispanic (6)	21	0.07
Guamanian/Chamorro (5)	10	0.04
Marshallese (1)	1	<0.01
Native Hawaiian (17)	40	0.14
Samoan (20)	24	0.08
White (24,457)	25,403	89.73
Not Hispanic (21,742)	22,385	79.07
Hispanic (2,715)	3,018	10.66

Atwater

Place Type: City
County: Merced
Population: 28,168†

Ancestry‡	Population	%
African, Sub-Saharan (89)	115	0.42
African (75)	101	0.37
Nigerian (14)	14	0.05
American (979)	979	3.55
Arab (27)	42	0.15
Arab (27)	27	0.10
Other Arab (0)	15	0.05
Armenian (0)	17	0.06
British (60)	102	0.37
Cajun (0)	29	0.11
Canadian (14)	38	0.14
Czech (25)	48	0.17
Czechoslovakian (0)	6	0.02
Danish (29)	127	0.46
Dutch (55)	209	0.76
English (225)	1,253	4.54
European (205)	240	0.87
Finnish (6)	63	0.23
French, ex. Basque (50)	339	1.23
French Canadian (60)	140	0.51
German (334)	1,567	5.68
Greek (12)	19	0.07
Hungarian (29)	61	0.22
Irish (568)	1,787	6.48
Italian (369)	758	2.75
Lithuanian (28)	38	0.14
Norwegian (118)	208	0.75
Polish (23)	157	0.57
Portuguese (432)	686	2.49
Romanian (0)	22	0.08
Russian (33)	135	0.49
Scandinavian (0)	15	0.05
Scotch-Irish (179)	366	1.33
Scottish (120)	462	1.67
Swedish (14)	209	0.76
Swiss (14)	28	0.10
Turkish (12)	12	0.04
Ukrainian (0)	15	0.05
Welsh (14)	40	0.14
West Indian, ex. Hispanic (34)	34	0.12
Jamaican (34)	34	0.12
Yugoslavian (9)	9	0.03

Hispanic Origin	Population	%
Hispanic or Latino (of any race)	14,808	52.57
Central American, ex. Mexican	159	0.56
Costa Rican	9	0.03
Guatemalan	25	0.09
Honduran	15	0.05
Nicaraguan	39	0.14
Panamanian	14	0.05
Salvadoran	57	0.20
Cuban	12	0.04
Dominican Republic	1	<0.01
Mexican	13,829	49.09
Puerto Rican	132	0.47
South American	28	0.10
Argentinean	6	0.02
Bolivian	1	<0.01
Colombian	8	0.03
Peruvian	11	0.04
Venezuelan	2	0.01
Other Hispanic or Latino	647	2.30

Race*	Population	%
African-American/Black (1,225)	1,514	5.37
Not Hispanic (1,087)	1,284	4.56
Hispanic (138)	230	0.82
American Indian/Alaska Native (364)	613	2.18
Not Hispanic (132)	302	1.07
Hispanic (232)	311	1.10
Aleut *(Alaska Native)* (3)	3	0.01
Apache (8)	18	0.06
Blackfeet (5)	16	0.06
Cherokee (34)	96	0.34
Cheyenne (0)	1	<0.01
Chickasaw (1)	5	0.02
Chippewa (4)	5	0.02
Choctaw (5)	11	0.04
Creek (3)	4	0.01
Crow (2)	2	0.01
Delaware (1)	1	<0.01
Hopi (0)	1	<0.01
Iroquois (1)	1	<0.01
Mexican American Ind. (47)	62	0.22
Navajo (4)	7	0.02
Osage (2)	2	0.01
Paiute (1)	1	<0.01
Potawatomi (3)	7	0.02
Seminole (0)	4	0.01
Sioux (0)	6	0.02
Spanish American Ind. (8)	8	0.03
Tlingit-Haida *(Alaska Native)* (0)	4	0.01
Tohono O'Odham (6)	6	0.02
Ute (1)	2	0.01
Yaqui (7)	11	0.04
Asian (1,416)	1,809	6.42
Not Hispanic (1,347)	1,608	5.71
Hispanic (69)	201	0.71
Cambodian (7)	11	0.04
Chinese, ex. Taiwanese (85)	123	0.44
Filipino (242)	400	1.42
Hmong (472)	489	1.74
Indian (313)	350	1.24
Indonesian (1)	2	0.01
Japanese (62)	138	0.49
Korean (60)	94	0.33
Laotian (51)	64	0.23
Pakistani (4)	4	0.01
Taiwanese (1)	2	0.01
Thai (47)	78	0.28
Vietnamese (39)	57	0.20
Hawaii Native/Pacific Islander (76)	185	0.66
Not Hispanic (66)	135	0.48
Hispanic (10)	50	0.18
Guamanian/Chamorro (34)	41	0.15
Native Hawaiian (23)	80	0.28
Samoan (4)	11	0.04
Tongan (0)	1	<0.01
White (18,410)	19,603	69.59
Not Hispanic (10,085)	10,586	37.58
Hispanic (8,325)	9,017	32.01

Auburn

Place Type: City
County: Placer
Population: 13,330†

Ancestry‡	Population	%
African, Sub-Saharan (0)	40	0.30
African (0)	40	0.30
Alsatian (15)	15	0.11
American (413)	413	3.07
Arab (45)	131	0.97
Arab (45)	89	0.66
Lebanese (0)	33	0.25
Syrian (0)	9	0.07
Armenian (13)	48	0.36
Assyrian/Chaldean/Syriac (12)	12	0.09
Austrian (8)	22	0.16
British (82)	131	0.97
Canadian (0)	83	0.62
Czech (21)	21	0.16
Czechoslovakian (22)	22	0.16
Danish (91)	243	1.81
Dutch (34)	333	2.48
English (1,001)	3,120	23.20
European (428)	466	3.46
Finnish (35)	50	0.37
French, ex. Basque (96)	856	6.36
French Canadian (24)	57	0.42
German (677)	3,029	22.52
Greek (0)	69	0.51
Hungarian (14)	14	0.10
Iranian (38)	38	0.28
Irish (339)	2,321	17.26
Italian (175)	789	5.87
Lithuanian (12)	22	0.16
Northern European (27)	27	0.20
Norwegian (60)	302	2.25
Polish (131)	506	3.76
Portuguese (84)	322	2.39
Romanian (36)	36	0.27
Russian (57)	184	1.37
Scandinavian (45)	75	0.56
Scotch-Irish (190)	460	3.42
Scottish (248)	543	4.04
Swedish (71)	548	4.07
Swiss (95)	145	1.08
Turkish (0)	11	0.08
Ukrainian (29)	149	1.11
Welsh (34)	169	1.26
Yugoslavian (12)	12	0.09

Hispanic Origin	Population	%
Hispanic or Latino (of any race)	1,331	9.98
Central American, ex. Mexican	91	0.68
Costa Rican	5	0.04
Guatemalan	21	0.16
Honduran	6	0.05
Nicaraguan	14	0.11
Panamanian	6	0.05
Salvadoran	39	0.29
Cuban	4	0.03
Dominican Republic	4	0.03
Mexican	924	6.93
Puerto Rican	56	0.42
South American	32	0.24
Argentinean	4	0.03
Chilean	7	0.05
Colombian	8	0.06
Ecuadorian	4	0.03
Paraguayan	1	0.01
Peruvian	6	0.05
Venezuelan	2	0.02
Other Hispanic or Latino	220	1.65

Race*	Population	%
African-American/Black (100)	200	1.50
Not Hispanic (99)	180	1.35
Hispanic (1)	20	0.15
American Indian/Alaska Native (129)	400	3.00
Not Hispanic (95)	312	2.34
Hispanic (34)	88	0.66
Apache (0)	2	0.02
Blackfeet (0)	10	0.08
Canadian/French Am. Ind. (1)	4	0.03
Cherokee (23)	100	0.75
Chickasaw (0)	4	0.03
Chippewa (6)	13	0.10
Choctaw (10)	17	0.13

*Notes: † The Census 2010 population figure is used to calculate the percentages in the Hispanic Origin and Race categories. Ancestry percentages are based on the 2006-2010 American Community Survey population (not shown); ‡ Numbers in parentheses indicate the number of people reporting a single ancestry; * Numbers in parentheses indicate the number of persons reporting this race alone, not in combination with any other race; Please refer to the Explanation of Data for more information.*

Creek (1)	4	0.03
Crow (0)	3	0.02
Delaware (0)	5	0.04
Iroquois (2)	12	0.09
Menominee (0)	1	0.01
Mexican American Ind. (0)	2	0.02
Navajo (0)	4	0.03
Osage (1)	6	0.05
Ottawa (0)	2	0.02
Paiute (3)	3	0.02
Pima (2)	3	0.02
Potawatomi (0)	2	0.02
Pueblo (2)	5	0.04
Puget Sound Salish (0)	3	0.02
Seminole (0)	2	0.02
Sioux (0)	6	0.05
South American Ind. (1)	1	0.01
Tlingit-Haida *(Alaska Native)* (0)	1	0.01
Yakama (0)	1	0.01
Asian (240)	391	2.93
Not Hispanic (231)	374	2.81
Hispanic (9)	17	0.13
Burmese (2)	3	0.02
Cambodian (2)	3	0.02
Chinese, ex. Taiwanese (68)	106	0.80
Filipino (52)	89	0.67
Indian (28)	36	0.27
Indonesian (4)	10	0.08
Japanese (48)	89	0.67
Korean (16)	16	0.12
Nepalese (1)	1	0.01
Sri Lankan (0)	2	0.02
Taiwanese (0)	1	0.01
Thai (7)	10	0.08
Vietnamese (3)	6	0.05
Hawaii Native/Pacific Islander (9)	50	0.38
Not Hispanic (9)	42	0.32
Hispanic (0)	8	0.06
Guamanian/Chamorro (1)	5	0.04
Native Hawaiian (5)	31	0.23
Samoan (0)	6	0.05
Tongan (1)	1	0.01
White (11,863)	12,405	93.06
Not Hispanic (11,113)	11,517	86.40
Hispanic (750)	888	6.66

August

Place Type: CDP
County: San Joaquin
Population: 8,390†

Ancestry‡	Population	%
American (90)	90	1.08
Arab (11)	11	0.13
Arab (11)	11	0.13
Dutch (0)	35	0.42
English (80)	200	2.40
French, ex. Basque (28)	151	1.81
French Canadian (10)	10	0.12
German (119)	722	8.67
Hungarian (0)	13	0.16
Irish (0)	472	5.66
Italian (55)	150	1.80
Norwegian (39)	70	0.84
Polish (97)	156	1.87
Portuguese (0)	24	0.29
Russian (17)	30	0.36
Scotch-Irish (0)	33	0.40
Scottish (14)	14	0.17
Swedish (21)	33	0.40
Welsh (0)	12	0.14

Hispanic Origin	Population	%
Hispanic or Latino (of any race)	5,897	70.29
Central American, ex. Mexican	76	0.91
Guatemalan	29	0.35
Honduran	6	0.07
Nicaraguan	7	0.08
Panamanian	1	0.01
Salvadoran	33	0.39
Cuban	2	0.02
Mexican	5,531	65.92
Puerto Rican	36	0.43
South American	6	0.07
Argentinean	4	0.05
Chilean	2	0.02
Other Hispanic or Latino	246	2.93

Race*	Population	%
African-American/Black (224)	308	3.67
Not Hispanic (190)	244	2.91
Hispanic (34)	64	0.76
American Indian/Alaska Native (183)	326	3.89
Not Hispanic (81)	180	2.15
Hispanic (102)	146	1.74
Apache (11)	18	0.21
Blackfeet (0)	1	0.01
Central American Ind. (3)	3	0.04
Cherokee (20)	51	0.61
Choctaw (5)	15	0.18
Comanche (0)	2	0.02
Delaware (2)	5	0.06
Hopi (0)	2	0.02
Iroquois (1)	4	0.05
Mexican American Ind. (18)	34	0.41
Navajo (1)	2	0.02
Osage (0)	1	0.01
Ottawa (1)	2	0.02
Paiute (2)	2	0.02
Potawatomi (1)	1	0.01
Sioux (6)	8	0.10
Spanish American Ind. (4)	4	0.05
Tlingit-Haida *(Alaska Native)* (0)	4	0.05
Ute (1)	1	0.01
Yaqui (7)	7	0.08
Yuman (0)	2	0.02
Asian (358)	512	6.10
Not Hispanic (325)	398	4.74
Hispanic (33)	114	1.36
Cambodian (52)	63	0.75
Chinese, ex. Taiwanese (9)	14	0.17
Filipino (82)	199	2.37
Hmong (42)	50	0.60
Indian (4)	23	0.27
Japanese (12)	16	0.19
Korean (0)	4	0.05
Laotian (21)	25	0.30
Pakistani (77)	78	0.93
Thai (1)	1	0.01
Vietnamese (13)	20	0.24
Hawaii Native/Pacific Islander (20)	56	0.67
Not Hispanic (17)	27	0.32
Hispanic (3)	29	0.35
Fijian (1)	4	0.05
Guamanian/Chamorro (6)	7	0.08
Native Hawaiian (2)	19	0.23
Samoan (7)	8	0.10
Tongan (1)	2	0.02
White (3,914)	4,399	52.43
Not Hispanic (1,679)	1,851	22.06
Hispanic (2,235)	2,548	30.37

Avenal

Place Type: City
County: Kings
Population: 15,505†

Ancestry‡	Population	%
American (585)	585	3.71
Armenian (8)	8	0.05
Basque (0)	9	0.06
British (51)	114	0.72
Dutch (0)	9	0.06
English (61)	184	1.17
European (6)	32	0.20
French, ex. Basque (0)	17	0.11
German (78)	162	1.03
Irish (428)	516	3.28
Italian (7)	48	0.30
Norwegian (0)	20	0.13
Polish (29)	59	0.37
Portuguese (0)	13	0.08
Russian (0)	30	0.19
Scandinavian (0)	2	0.01
Scotch-Irish (0)	45	0.29
Scottish (34)	58	0.37
Serbian (37)	37	0.23
Swedish (53)	53	0.34
Welsh (0)	24	0.15
West Indian, ex. Hispanic (0)	5	0.03
Jamaican (0)	5	0.03

Hispanic Origin	Population	%
Hispanic or Latino (of any race)	11,130	71.78
Central American, ex. Mexican	117	0.75
Guatemalan	23	0.15
Honduran	30	0.19
Nicaraguan	2	0.01
Salvadoran	55	0.35
Other Central American	7	0.05
Cuban	14	0.09
Dominican Republic	1	0.01
Mexican	9,481	61.15
Puerto Rican	24	0.15
South American	7	0.05
Bolivian	1	0.01
Colombian	1	0.01
Ecuadorian	3	0.02
Peruvian	2	0.01
Other Hispanic or Latino	1,486	9.58

Race*	Population	%
African-American/Black (1,625)	1,670	10.77
Not Hispanic (1,540)	1,556	10.04
Hispanic (85)	114	0.74
American Indian/Alaska Native (186)	224	1.44
Not Hispanic (82)	90	0.58
Hispanic (104)	134	0.86
Apache (8)	9	0.06
Canadian/French Am. Ind. (1)	1	0.01
Cherokee (2)	5	0.03
Cheyenne (1)	1	0.01
Chippewa (4)	4	0.03
Choctaw (3)	4	0.03
Mexican American Ind. (19)	24	0.15
Navajo (1)	1	0.01
Paiute (1)	1	0.01
Spanish American Ind. (2)	2	0.01
Tlingit-Haida *(Alaska Native)* (0)	1	0.01
Yaqui (1)	1	0.01
Asian (108)	173	1.12
Not Hispanic (102)	141	0.91
Hispanic (6)	32	0.21
Cambodian (2)	2	0.01
Chinese, ex. Taiwanese (11)	16	0.10
Filipino (31)	36	0.23
Hmong (9)	9	0.06
Indian (24)	44	0.28
Japanese (6)	10	0.06
Korean (4)	9	0.06
Laotian (5)	6	0.04
Vietnamese (5)	6	0.04
Hawaii Native/Pacific Islander (6)	35	0.23
Not Hispanic (4)	12	0.08
Hispanic (2)	23	0.15
Fijian (1)	1	0.01
Guamanian/Chamorro (0)	1	0.01
Native Hawaiian (0)	8	0.05
Samoan (1)	1	0.01
White (6,044)	6,332	40.84
Not Hispanic (2,387)	2,442	15.75
Hispanic (3,657)	3,890	25.09

Avocado Heights

Place Type: CDP
County: Los Angeles
Population: 15,411†

*Notes: † The Census 2010 population figure is used to calculate the percentages in the Hispanic Origin and Race categories. Ancestry percentages are based on the 2006-2010 American Community Survey population (not shown); ‡ Numbers in parentheses indicate the number of people reporting a single ancestry; * Numbers in parentheses indicate the number of persons reporting this race alone, not in combination with any other race; Please refer to the Explanation of Data for more information.*

Ancestry‡	Population	%
African, Sub-Saharan (107)	118	0.76
African (107)	118	0.76
American (97)	97	0.63
Arab (37)	37	0.24
Arab (8)	8	0.05
Egyptian (29)	29	0.19
Belgian (8)	19	0.12
Canadian (8)	18	0.12
Danish (12)	39	0.25
Dutch (13)	36	0.23
English (31)	173	1.12
European (23)	23	0.15
French, ex. Basque (0)	128	0.83
French Canadian (22)	22	0.14
German (148)	396	2.56
Greek (0)	8	0.05
Hungarian (23)	48	0.31
Irish (47)	179	1.16
Italian (26)	64	0.41
Norwegian (0)	13	0.08
Polish (92)	119	0.77
Portuguese (33)	110	0.71
Russian (7)	56	0.36
Scotch-Irish (0)	23	0.15
Scottish (0)	19	0.12
Slovak (0)	43	0.28
Swedish (0)	35	0.23
Swiss (12)	12	0.08
Ukrainian (0)	31	0.20
West Indian, ex. Hispanic (0)	21	0.14
Belizean (0)	21	0.14
Yugoslavian (0)	11	0.07

Hispanic Origin	Population	%
Hispanic or Latino (of any race)	12,648	82.07
Central American, ex. Mexican	575	3.73
Costa Rican	19	0.12
Guatemalan	186	1.21
Honduran	24	0.16
Nicaraguan	78	0.51
Panamanian	4	0.03
Salvadoran	254	1.65
Other Central American	10	0.06
Cuban	56	0.36
Dominican Republic	6	0.04
Mexican	11,245	72.97
Puerto Rican	70	0.45
South American	127	0.82
Argentinean	26	0.17
Bolivian	1	0.01
Chilean	6	0.04
Colombian	37	0.24
Ecuadorian	34	0.22
Paraguayan	1	0.01
Peruvian	15	0.10
Uruguayan	3	0.02
Venezuelan	4	0.03
Other Hispanic or Latino	569	3.69

Race*	Population	%
African-American/Black (136)	181	1.17
Not Hispanic (100)	111	0.72
Hispanic (36)	70	0.45
American Indian/Alaska Native (107)	191	1.24
Not Hispanic (19)	38	0.25
Hispanic (88)	153	0.99
Apache (7)	7	0.05
Blackfeet (0)	3	0.02
Canadian/French Am. Ind. (0)	1	0.01
Cherokee (1)	11	0.07
Choctaw (1)	3	0.02
Colville (1)	1	0.01
Creek (1)	1	0.01
Delaware (0)	1	0.01
Hopi (2)	2	0.01
Iroquois (3)	3	0.02
Mexican American Ind. (19)	23	0.15
Navajo (1)	3	0.02
Paiute (0)	1	0.01
Pueblo (1)	1	0.01
Sioux (3)	5	0.03
Tohono O'Odham (0)	3	0.02
Yaqui (2)	4	0.03
Asian (1,359)	1,495	9.70
Not Hispanic (1,324)	1,380	8.95
Hispanic (35)	115	0.75
Bangladeshi (1)	1	0.01
Cambodian (31)	36	0.23
Chinese, ex. Taiwanese (376)	433	2.81
Filipino (345)	393	2.55
Indian (23)	32	0.21
Indonesian (1)	6	0.04
Japanese (186)	227	1.47
Korean (87)	93	0.60
Malaysian (16)	16	0.10
Sri Lankan (3)	3	0.02
Taiwanese (20)	22	0.14
Thai (89)	102	0.66
Vietnamese (131)	163	1.06
Hawaii Native/Pacific Islander (13)	33	0.21
Not Hispanic (8)	18	0.12
Hispanic (5)	15	0.10
Fijian (2)	2	0.01
Guamanian/Chamorro (4)	6	0.04
Native Hawaiian (0)	2	0.01
Samoan (7)	10	0.06
White (8,564)	8,993	58.35
Not Hispanic (1,199)	1,264	8.20
Hispanic (7,365)	7,729	50.15

Azusa

Place Type: City
County: Los Angeles
Population: 46,361†

Ancestry‡	Population	%
African, Sub-Saharan (90)	170	0.37
African (58)	138	0.30
Ethiopian (11)	11	0.02
Other Sub-Saharan African (21)	21	0.05
American (435)	435	0.95
Arab (158)	233	0.51
Arab (9)	9	0.02
Egyptian (92)	92	0.20
Lebanese (0)	46	0.10
Palestinian (48)	48	0.10
Syrian (9)	38	0.08
Armenian (41)	72	0.16
Austrian (0)	35	0.08
Belgian (0)	34	0.07
Brazilian (18)	39	0.08
British (0)	94	0.20
Canadian (12)	45	0.10
Celtic (0)	9	0.02
Czech (0)	14	0.03
Czechoslovakian (14)	42	0.09
Danish (28)	130	0.28
Dutch (158)	665	1.45
Eastern European (14)	14	0.03
English (223)	1,484	3.23
European (40)	40	0.09
Finnish (6)	64	0.14
French, ex. Basque (24)	390	0.85
French Canadian (9)	59	0.13
German (611)	2,765	6.01
Greek (38)	86	0.19
Hungarian (25)	214	0.47
Iranian (22)	34	0.07
Irish (230)	1,512	3.29
Italian (329)	1,111	2.41
Lithuanian (11)	43	0.09
Northern European (10)	10	0.02
Norwegian (122)	250	0.54
Pennsylvania German (11)	11	0.02
Polish (165)	343	0.75
Portuguese (0)	12	0.03
Romanian (0)	10	0.02
Russian (28)	74	0.16
Scandinavian (0)	83	0.18
Scotch-Irish (79)	312	0.68
Scottish (23)	332	0.72
Slovak (24)	33	0.07
Swedish (27)	341	0.74
Swiss (9)	17	0.04
Turkish (23)	23	0.05
Ukrainian (38)	47	0.10
Welsh (0)	80	0.17
West Indian, ex. Hispanic (40)	46	0.10
Belizean (40)	40	0.09
West Indian (0)	6	0.01
Yugoslavian (15)	71	0.15

Hispanic Origin	Population	%
Hispanic or Latino (of any race)	31,328	67.57
Central American, ex. Mexican	1,630	3.52
Costa Rican	51	0.11
Guatemalan	513	1.11
Honduran	112	0.24
Nicaraguan	207	0.45
Panamanian	22	0.05
Salvadoran	707	1.52
Other Central American	18	0.04
Cuban	157	0.34
Dominican Republic	10	0.02
Mexican	27,377	59.05
Puerto Rican	230	0.50
South American	581	1.25
Argentinean	131	0.28
Bolivian	11	0.02
Chilean	63	0.14
Colombian	91	0.20
Ecuadorian	86	0.19
Paraguayan	5	0.01
Peruvian	179	0.39
Uruguayan	5	0.01
Venezuelan	9	0.02
Other South American	1	<0.01
Other Hispanic or Latino	1,343	2.90

Race*	Population	%
African-American/Black (1,499)	1,836	3.96
Not Hispanic (1,293)	1,491	3.22
Hispanic (206)	345	0.74
American Indian/Alaska Native (562)	910	1.96
Not Hispanic (114)	221	0.48
Hispanic (448)	689	1.49
Apache (23)	59	0.13
Blackfeet (2)	6	0.01
Canadian/French Am. Ind. (2)	5	0.01
Central American Ind. (1)	4	0.01
Cherokee (21)	66	0.14
Cheyenne (2)	2	<0.01
Chickasaw (0)	3	0.01
Chippewa (7)	9	0.02
Choctaw (3)	8	0.02
Comanche (7)	7	0.02
Creek (0)	1	<0.01
Hopi (0)	1	<0.01
Iroquois (0)	5	0.01
Lumbee (1)	1	<0.01
Mexican American Ind. (85)	114	0.25
Navajo (15)	26	0.06
Osage (0)	2	<0.01
Ottawa (1)	1	<0.01
Paiute (1)	1	<0.01
Pima (1)	5	0.01
Pueblo (4)	4	0.01
Shoshone (2)	2	<0.01
South American Ind. (3)	4	0.01
Spanish American Ind. (19)	27	0.06
Tlingit-Haida *(Alaska Native)* (1)	4	0.01
Tohono O'Odham (7)	7	0.02
Yaqui (9)	22	0.05
Yuman (1)	2	<0.01
Asian (4,054)	4,739	10.22
Not Hispanic (3,896)	4,314	9.31
Hispanic (158)	425	0.92
Bangladeshi (10)	10	0.02

*Notes: † The Census 2010 population figure is used to calculate the percentages in the Hispanic Origin and Race categories. Ancestry percentages are based on the 2006-2010 American Community Survey population (not shown); ‡ Numbers in parentheses indicate the number of people reporting a single ancestry; * Numbers in parentheses indicate the number of persons reporting this race alone, not in combination with any other race; Please refer to the Explanation of Data for more information.*

	Population	%
Burmese (11)	12	0.03
Cambodian (35)	40	0.09
Chinese, ex. Taiwanese (635)	801	1.73
Filipino (1,887)	2,186	4.72
Hmong (3)	3	0.01
Indian (325)	378	0.82
Indonesian (83)	116	0.25
Japanese (225)	414	0.89
Korean (286)	330	0.71
Laotian (2)	3	0.01
Malaysian (4)	5	0.01
Nepalese (2)	5	0.01
Pakistani (23)	24	0.05
Sri Lankan (19)	19	0.04
Taiwanese (106)	115	0.25
Thai (84)	108	0.23
Vietnamese (177)	218	0.47
Hawaii Native/Pacific Islander (87)	202	0.44
Not Hispanic (67)	128	0.28
Hispanic (20)	74	0.16
Fijian (5)	11	0.02
Guamanian/Chamorro (15)	18	0.04
Native Hawaiian (23)	79	0.17
Samoan (23)	39	0.08
Tongan (7)	17	0.04
White (26,715)	28,522	61.52
Not Hispanic (8,955)	9,483	20.45
Hispanic (17,760)	19,039	41.07

Bakersfield

Place Type: City
County: Kern
Population: 347,483†

Ancestry‡	Population	%
Afghan (41)	41	0.01
African, Sub-Saharan (1,554)	1,907	0.57
African (834)	1,163	0.35
Ethiopian (162)	162	0.05
Nigerian (416)	440	0.13
Somalian (58)	58	0.02
South African (66)	66	0.02
Other Sub-Saharan African (18)	18	0.01
Albanian (0)	9	<0.01
American (8,205)	8,205	2.47
Arab (1,749)	2,702	0.81
Arab (788)	1,040	0.31
Egyptian (291)	364	0.11
Iraqi (0)	8	<0.01
Jordanian (105)	352	0.11
Lebanese (199)	359	0.11
Moroccan (17)	40	0.01
Palestinian (56)	165	0.05
Syrian (38)	103	0.03
Other Arab (255)	271	0.08
Armenian (310)	557	0.17
Assyrian/Chaldean/Syriac (63)	63	0.02
Australian (9)	58	0.02
Austrian (40)	218	0.07
Basque (602)	1,084	0.33
Belgian (29)	110	0.03
Brazilian (96)	166	0.05
British (401)	632	0.19
Bulgarian (29)	42	0.01
Cajun (40)	139	0.04
Canadian (388)	598	0.18
Celtic (55)	86	0.03
Croatian (95)	284	0.09
Czech (124)	578	0.17
Czechoslovakian (47)	177	0.05
Danish (416)	1,382	0.42
Dutch (599)	4,032	1.21
Eastern European (33)	71	0.02
English (6,915)	21,066	6.35
Estonian (19)	38	0.01
European (3,013)	3,718	1.12
Finnish (59)	298	0.09
French, ex. Basque (902)	5,286	1.59
French Canadian (321)	934	0.28
German (9,945)	31,918	9.62
German Russian (8)	8	<0.01
Greek (272)	1,029	0.31
Guyanese (38)	121	0.04
Hungarian (152)	408	0.12
Iranian (562)	641	0.19
Irish (6,524)	25,483	7.68
Israeli (0)	36	0.01
Italian (3,512)	9,902	2.98
Latvian (9)	35	0.01
Lithuanian (100)	286	0.09
Luxemburger (9)	9	<0.01
Maltese (9)	9	<0.01
New Zealander (8)	8	<0.01
Northern European (125)	152	0.05
Norwegian (744)	2,750	0.83
Pennsylvania German (9)	72	0.02
Polish (569)	2,502	0.75
Portuguese (545)	1,586	0.48
Romanian (66)	184	0.06
Russian (336)	948	0.29
Scandinavian (171)	543	0.16
Scotch-Irish (1,166)	3,607	1.09
Scottish (1,140)	4,779	1.44
Serbian (0)	9	<0.01
Slavic (43)	65	0.02
Slovak (14)	37	0.01
Swedish (904)	4,065	1.22
Swiss (154)	750	0.23
Turkish (25)	73	0.02
Ukrainian (142)	285	0.09
Welsh (259)	1,244	0.37
West Indian, ex. Hispanic (160)	425	0.13
Dutch West Indian (18)	201	0.06
Haitian (71)	71	0.02
Jamaican (43)	80	0.02
Trinidadian/Tobagonian (0)	45	0.01
West Indian (19)	19	0.01
Other West Indian (9)	9	<0.01
Yugoslavian (260)	365	0.11

Hispanic Origin	Population	%
Hispanic or Latino (of any race)	158,205	45.53
Central American, ex. Mexican	7,497	2.16
Costa Rican	139	0.04
Guatemalan	1,804	0.52
Honduran	545	0.16
Nicaraguan	239	0.07
Panamanian	66	0.02
Salvadoran	4,654	1.34
Other Central American	50	0.01
Cuban	405	0.12
Dominican Republic	77	0.02
Mexican	137,102	39.46
Puerto Rican	1,860	0.54
South American	1,747	0.50
Argentinean	212	0.06
Bolivian	50	0.01
Chilean	89	0.03
Colombian	425	0.12
Ecuadorian	136	0.04
Peruvian	534	0.15
Uruguayan	21	0.01
Venezuelan	259	0.07
Other South American	21	0.01
Other Hispanic or Latino	9,517	2.74

Race*	Population	%
African-American/Black (28,368)	32,437	9.33
Not Hispanic (26,677)	29,390	8.46
Hispanic (1,691)	3,047	0.88
American Indian/Alaska Native (5,102)	9,097	2.62
Not Hispanic (2,265)	4,742	1.36
Hispanic (2,837)	4,355	1.25
Alaska Athabascan *(Ala. Nat.)* (3)	11	<0.01
Aleut *(Alaska Native)* (1)	1	<0.01
Apache (173)	336	0.10
Arapaho (6)	13	<0.01
Blackfeet (54)	186	0.05
Canadian/French Am. Ind. (2)	6	<0.01
Central American Ind. (12)	29	0.01
Cherokee (497)	1,444	0.42
Cheyenne (12)	15	<0.01
Chickasaw (53)	112	0.03
Chippewa (13)	47	0.01
Choctaw (202)	467	0.13
Colville (4)	6	<0.01
Comanche (36)	57	0.02
Cree (1)	6	<0.01
Creek (53)	143	0.04
Crow (3)	7	<0.01
Delaware (2)	4	<0.01
Hopi (18)	27	0.01
Houma (0)	1	<0.01
Inupiat *(Alaska Native)* (9)	11	<0.01
Iroquois (4)	20	0.01
Kiowa (6)	19	0.01
Lumbee (3)	6	<0.01
Mexican American Ind. (338)	474	0.14
Navajo (104)	176	0.05
Osage (5)	19	0.01
Ottawa (3)	5	<0.01
Paiute (125)	214	0.06
Pima (23)	41	0.01
Potawatomi (35)	52	0.01
Pueblo (35)	58	0.02
Puget Sound Salish (11)	14	<0.01
Seminole (11)	42	0.01
Shoshone (22)	45	0.01
Sioux (42)	99	0.03
South American Ind. (15)	24	0.01
Spanish American Ind. (19)	24	0.01
Tlingit-Haida *(Alaska Native)* (3)	4	<0.01
Tohono O'Odham (26)	32	0.01
Ute (3)	5	<0.01
Yakama (0)	4	<0.01
Yaqui (88)	154	0.04
Yuman (1)	3	<0.01
Yup'ik *(Alaska Native)* (0)	2	<0.01
Asian (21,432)	25,815	7.43
Not Hispanic (20,496)	23,435	6.74
Hispanic (936)	2,380	0.68
Bangladeshi (44)	44	0.01
Bhutanese (2)	2	<0.01
Burmese (255)	294	0.08
Cambodian (396)	520	0.15
Chinese, ex. Taiwanese (1,721)	2,341	0.67
Filipino (7,046)	9,074	2.61
Hmong (15)	21	0.01
Indian (7,328)	7,896	2.27
Indonesian (123)	167	0.05
Japanese (551)	1,128	0.32
Korean (1,352)	1,619	0.47
Laotian (204)	297	0.09
Malaysian (14)	24	0.01
Nepalese (7)	8	<0.01
Pakistani (245)	289	0.08
Sri Lankan (31)	45	0.01
Taiwanese (92)	110	0.03
Thai (188)	264	0.08
Vietnamese (1,140)	1,368	0.39
Hawaii Native/Pacific Islander (478)	1,202	0.35
Not Hispanic (357)	792	0.23
Hispanic (121)	410	0.12
Fijian (12)	21	0.01
Guamanian/Chamorro (111)	221	0.06
Marshallese (15)	16	<0.01
Native Hawaiian (132)	408	0.12
Samoan (104)	224	0.06
Tongan (21)	29	0.01
White (197,349)	211,351	60.82
Not Hispanic (131,311)	137,595	39.60
Hispanic (66,038)	73,756	21.23

Baldwin Park

Place Type: City
County: Los Angeles
Population: 75,390†

*Notes: † The Census 2010 population figure is used to calculate the percentages in the Hispanic Origin and Race categories. Ancestry percentages are based on the 2006-2010 American Community Survey population (not shown); ‡ Numbers in parentheses indicate the number of people reporting a single ancestry; * Numbers in parentheses indicate the number of persons reporting this race alone, not in combination with any other race; Please refer to the Explanation of Data for more information.*

Ancestry‡	Population	%
African, Sub-Saharan (106)	116	0.15
African (14)	24	0.03
Nigerian (92)	92	0.12
American (501)	501	0.66
Arab (37)	37	0.05
Syrian (37)	37	0.05
Armenian (50)	50	0.07
Austrian (0)	27	0.04
Belgian (0)	9	0.01
British (32)	53	0.07
Bulgarian (60)	93	0.12
Danish (0)	73	0.10
Dutch (17)	278	0.37
Eastern European (12)	12	0.02
English (89)	366	0.49
European (9)	30	0.04
French, ex. Basque (41)	250	0.33
French Canadian (4)	18	0.02
German (147)	722	0.96
Greek (11)	47	0.06
Hungarian (0)	36	0.05
Iranian (17)	60	0.08
Irish (237)	731	0.97
Italian (108)	407	0.54
Norwegian (39)	81	0.11
Polish (60)	159	0.21
Portuguese (5)	39	0.05
Russian (41)	96	0.13
Scotch-Irish (25)	242	0.32
Scottish (44)	161	0.21
Swedish (16)	44	0.06
Swiss (0)	63	0.08
Turkish (7)	7	0.01
Ukrainian (18)	18	0.02
Welsh (33)	160	0.21
Yugoslavian (0)	14	0.02

Hispanic Origin	Population	%
Hispanic or Latino (of any race)	60,403	80.12
Central American, ex. Mexican	4,065	5.39
Costa Rican	70	0.09
Guatemalan	924	1.23
Honduran	262	0.35
Nicaraguan	440	0.58
Panamanian	30	0.04
Salvadoran	2,272	3.01
Other Central American	67	0.09
Cuban	173	0.23
Dominican Republic	21	0.03
Mexican	52,803	70.04
Puerto Rican	267	0.35
South American	526	0.70
Argentinean	42	0.06
Bolivian	44	0.06
Chilean	20	0.03
Colombian	147	0.19
Ecuadorian	113	0.15
Paraguayan	4	0.01
Peruvian	144	0.19
Uruguayan	8	0.01
Venezuelan	4	0.01
Other Hispanic or Latino	2,548	3.38

Race*	Population	%
African-American/Black (913)	1,142	1.51
Not Hispanic (662)	737	0.98
Hispanic (251)	405	0.54
American Indian/Alaska Native (674)	1,134	1.50
Not Hispanic (91)	169	0.22
Hispanic (583)	965	1.28
Apache (28)	66	0.09
Blackfeet (2)	14	0.02
Central American Ind. (4)	14	0.02
Cherokee (11)	36	0.05
Chickasaw (3)	5	0.01
Chippewa (3)	3	<0.01
Choctaw (6)	10	0.01
Comanche (7)	8	0.01
Creek (0)	3	<0.01
Crow (0)	1	<0.01
Lumbee (1)	1	<0.01
Mexican American Ind. (106)	175	0.23
Navajo (8)	23	0.03
Osage (0)	1	<0.01
Paiute (4)	4	0.01
Pima (2)	2	<0.01
Potawatomi (0)	5	0.01
Pueblo (13)	21	0.03
Shoshone (7)	7	0.01
Sioux (7)	10	0.01
South American Ind. (1)	5	0.01
Spanish American Ind. (12)	16	0.02
Tohono O'Odham (1)	3	<0.01
Yaqui (8)	21	0.03
Yuman (10)	10	0.01
Asian (10,696)	11,190	14.84
Not Hispanic (10,495)	10,715	14.21
Hispanic (201)	475	0.63
Burmese (90)	97	0.13
Cambodian (312)	350	0.46
Chinese, ex. Taiwanese (3,654)	4,086	5.42
Filipino (3,439)	3,733	4.95
Hmong (3)	3	<0.01
Indian (62)	109	0.14
Indonesian (47)	79	0.10
Japanese (122)	188	0.25
Korean (119)	132	0.18
Laotian (104)	114	0.15
Malaysian (0)	10	0.01
Pakistani (6)	6	0.01
Sri Lankan (6)	6	0.01
Taiwanese (217)	259	0.34
Thai (155)	169	0.22
Vietnamese (1,895)	2,178	2.89
Hawaii Native/Pacific Islander (85)	178	0.24
Not Hispanic (66)	125	0.17
Hispanic (19)	53	0.07
Guamanian/Chamorro (15)	20	0.03
Native Hawaiian (12)	30	0.04
Samoan (24)	35	0.05
Tongan (6)	7	0.01
White (33,119)	35,388	46.94
Not Hispanic (3,232)	3,464	4.59
Hispanic (29,887)	31,924	42.35

Banning

Place Type: City
County: Riverside
Population: 29,603†

Ancestry‡	Population	%
African, Sub-Saharan (77)	77	0.27
African (77)	77	0.27
American (921)	921	3.17
Arab (42)	42	0.14
Egyptian (7)	7	0.02
Lebanese (35)	35	0.12
Armenian (16)	41	0.14
Austrian (0)	74	0.25
Brazilian (0)	10	0.03
British (92)	101	0.35
Canadian (50)	73	0.25
Croatian (14)	64	0.22
Czech (49)	88	0.30
Czechoslovakian (0)	14	0.05
Danish (37)	162	0.56
Dutch (98)	360	1.24
Eastern European (10)	10	0.03
English (1,181)	2,949	10.16
Estonian (0)	16	0.06
European (75)	75	0.26
Finnish (40)	86	0.30
French, ex. Basque (134)	640	2.20
French Canadian (65)	90	0.31
German (916)	3,121	10.75
Greek (99)	112	0.39
Hungarian (69)	142	0.49
Irish (726)	2,712	9.34
Italian (540)	914	3.15
Lithuanian (0)	30	0.10
Northern European (14)	14	0.05
Norwegian (131)	296	1.02
Polish (174)	353	1.22
Portuguese (31)	59	0.20
Romanian (57)	109	0.38
Russian (77)	152	0.52
Scandinavian (21)	21	0.07
Scotch-Irish (181)	395	1.36
Scottish (157)	692	2.38
Serbian (32)	32	0.11
Slovak (31)	31	0.11
Slovene (14)	14	0.05
Swedish (191)	440	1.52
Swiss (44)	115	0.40
Ukrainian (62)	72	0.25
Welsh (19)	127	0.44
Yugoslavian (13)	13	0.04

Hispanic Origin	Population	%
Hispanic or Latino (of any race)	12,181	41.15
Central American, ex. Mexican	310	1.05
Costa Rican	11	0.04
Guatemalan	71	0.24
Honduran	45	0.15
Nicaraguan	38	0.13
Panamanian	7	0.02
Salvadoran	137	0.46
Other Central American	1	<0.01
Cuban	27	0.09
Dominican Republic	4	0.01
Mexican	10,855	36.67
Puerto Rican	110	0.37
South American	81	0.27
Argentinean	18	0.06
Bolivian	5	0.02
Colombian	37	0.12
Ecuadorian	3	0.01
Peruvian	15	0.05
Uruguayan	2	0.01
Venezuelan	1	<0.01
Other Hispanic or Latino	794	2.68

Race*	Population	%
African-American/Black (2,165)	2,570	8.68
Not Hispanic (2,023)	2,290	7.74
Hispanic (142)	280	0.95
American Indian/Alaska Native (641)	1,050	3.55
Not Hispanic (365)	600	2.03
Hispanic (276)	450	1.52
Alaska Athabascan *(Ala. Nat.)* (1)	1	<0.01
Aleut *(Alaska Native)* (1)	1	<0.01
Apache (14)	31	0.10
Arapaho (0)	1	<0.01
Blackfeet (0)	15	0.05
Cherokee (11)	70	0.24
Cheyenne (0)	2	0.01
Chickasaw (10)	11	0.04
Chippewa (4)	6	0.02
Choctaw (24)	50	0.17
Comanche (1)	1	<0.01
Cree (1)	1	<0.01
Creek (3)	9	0.03
Hopi (1)	1	<0.01
Iroquois (0)	1	<0.01
Mexican American Ind. (35)	57	0.19
Navajo (7)	16	0.05
Osage (0)	4	0.01
Paiute (1)	1	<0.01
Pima (1)	3	0.01
Potawatomi (0)	2	0.01
Pueblo (4)	4	0.01
Seminole (0)	5	0.02
Sioux (12)	25	0.08
Spanish American Ind. (2)	8	0.03
Tlingit-Haida *(Alaska Native)* (1)	1	<0.01
Tohono O'Odham (24)	27	0.09
Yaqui (4)	26	0.09
Yuman (13)	13	0.04

*Notes: † The Census 2010 population figure is used to calculate the percentages in the Hispanic Origin and Race categories. Ancestry percentages are based on the 2006-2010 American Community Survey population (not shown); ‡ Numbers in parentheses indicate the number of people reporting a single ancestry; * Numbers in parentheses indicate the number of persons reporting this race alone, not in combination with any other race; Please refer to the Explanation of Data for more information.*

Asian (1,549)	1,787	6.04
Not Hispanic (1,510)	1,677	5.66
Hispanic (39)	110	0.37
Burmese (3)	3	0.01
Cambodian (26)	31	0.10
Chinese, ex. Taiwanese (59)	79	0.27
Filipino (312)	389	1.31
Hmong (537)	591	2.00
Indian (26)	63	0.21
Indonesian (21)	32	0.11
Japanese (61)	103	0.35
Korean (82)	92	0.31
Laotian (252)	276	0.93
Pakistani (21)	21	0.07
Sri Lankan (5)	5	0.02
Taiwanese (5)	6	0.02
Thai (37)	51	0.17
Vietnamese (16)	21	0.07
Hawaii Native/Pacific Islander (39)	98	0.33
Not Hispanic (34)	74	0.25
Hispanic (5)	24	0.08
Guamanian/Chamorro (4)	11	0.04
Native Hawaiian (11)	38	0.13
Samoan (16)	30	0.10
Tongan (0)	2	0.01
White (19,164)	20,370	68.81
Not Hispanic (12,858)	13,363	45.14
Hispanic (6,306)	7,007	23.67

Barstow

Place Type: City
County: San Bernardino
Population: 22,639†

Ancestry‡	Population	%
African, Sub-Saharan (158)	215	0.94
African (142)	199	0.87
Nigerian (16)	16	0.07
American (994)	994	4.32
Arab (0)	56	0.24
Arab (0)	56	0.24
Armenian (30)	30	0.13
Assyrian/Chaldean/Syriac (15)	15	0.07
British (57)	99	0.43
Croatian (0)	12	0.05
Czech (68)	68	0.30
Czechoslovakian (21)	21	0.09
Danish (14)	55	0.24
Dutch (32)	149	0.65
English (234)	1,058	4.60
European (68)	75	0.33
Finnish (0)	13	0.06
French, ex. Basque (149)	405	1.76
French Canadian (19)	46	0.20
German (793)	2,079	9.05
Greek (28)	55	0.24
Hungarian (0)	62	0.27
Irish (361)	1,296	5.64
Italian (177)	548	2.38
Latvian (14)	14	0.06
Norwegian (28)	166	0.72
Polish (101)	243	1.06
Portuguese (0)	13	0.06
Romanian (7)	14	0.06
Russian (43)	143	0.62
Scandinavian (16)	16	0.07
Scotch-Irish (136)	388	1.69
Scottish (77)	232	1.01
Serbian (0)	10	0.04
Swedish (58)	421	1.83
Swiss (14)	52	0.23
Ukrainian (15)	55	0.24
Welsh (69)	199	0.87
West Indian, ex. Hispanic (69)	190	0.83
Haitian (14)	14	0.06
Jamaican (55)	176	0.77
Yugoslavian (0)	12	0.05

Hispanic Origin	Population	%
Hispanic or Latino (of any race)	9,700	42.85
Central American, ex. Mexican	200	0.88
Costa Rican	1	<0.01
Guatemalan	50	0.22
Honduran	19	0.08
Nicaraguan	16	0.07
Panamanian	32	0.14
Salvadoran	77	0.34
Other Central American	5	0.02
Cuban	63	0.28
Dominican Republic	9	0.04
Mexican	7,802	34.46
Puerto Rican	285	1.26
South American	69	0.30
Argentinean	5	0.02
Bolivian	3	0.01
Chilean	11	0.05
Colombian	14	0.06
Ecuadorian	4	0.02
Peruvian	17	0.08
Uruguayan	4	0.02
Venezuelan	9	0.04
Other South American	2	0.01
Other Hispanic or Latino	1,272	5.62

Race*	Population	%
African-American/Black (3,313)	4,018	17.75
Not Hispanic (3,132)	3,596	15.88
Hispanic (181)	422	1.86
American Indian/Alaska Native (477)	969	4.28
Not Hispanic (260)	563	2.49
Hispanic (217)	406	1.79
Alaska Athabascan *(Ala. Nat.)* (0)	1	<0.01
Aleut *(Alaska Native)* (0)	1	<0.01
Apache (16)	44	0.19
Arapaho (3)	4	0.02
Blackfeet (3)	21	0.09
Canadian/French Am. Ind. (0)	4	0.02
Cherokee (20)	107	0.47
Chickasaw (9)	13	0.06
Chippewa (3)	3	0.01
Choctaw (12)	23	0.10
Comanche (1)	3	0.01
Creek (0)	1	<0.01
Crow (1)	1	<0.01
Hopi (1)	4	0.02
Inupiat *(Alaska Native)* (0)	3	0.01
Iroquois (0)	1	<0.01
Mexican American Ind. (23)	37	0.16
Navajo (76)	127	0.56
Osage (0)	1	<0.01
Paiute (1)	1	<0.01
Pima (3)	8	0.04
Potawatomi (1)	1	<0.01
Pueblo (82)	131	0.58
Puget Sound Salish (1)	1	<0.01
Seminole (0)	6	0.03
Sioux (8)	13	0.06
South American Ind. (1)	4	0.02
Spanish American Ind. (5)	5	0.02
Tohono O'Odham (1)	2	0.01
Ute (0)	5	0.02
Yaqui (3)	15	0.07
Yuman (2)	7	0.03
Asian (723)	1,107	4.89
Not Hispanic (659)	928	4.10
Hispanic (64)	179	0.79
Bangladeshi (3)	3	0.01
Cambodian (12)	17	0.08
Chinese, ex. Taiwanese (69)	116	0.51
Filipino (375)	527	2.33
Indian (28)	49	0.22
Japanese (60)	130	0.57
Korean (99)	155	0.68
Laotian (10)	10	0.04
Pakistani (8)	8	0.04
Taiwanese (11)	11	0.05
Thai (12)	22	0.10
Vietnamese (19)	27	0.12
Hawaii Native/Pacific Islander (278)	421	1.86
Not Hispanic (249)	344	1.52
Hispanic (29)	77	0.34
Fijian (0)	2	0.01
Guamanian/Chamorro (121)	195	0.86
Native Hawaiian (15)	56	0.25
Samoan (124)	155	0.68
Tongan (1)	1	<0.01
White (11,840)	13,199	58.30
Not Hispanic (7,746)	8,427	37.22
Hispanic (4,094)	4,772	21.08

Bay Point

Place Type: CDP
County: Contra Costa
Population: 21,349†

Ancestry‡	Population	%
African, Sub-Saharan (188)	339	1.60
African (93)	222	1.05
Ghanaian (13)	35	0.17
Nigerian (82)	82	0.39
American (306)	306	1.44
Arab (57)	57	0.27
Egyptian (57)	57	0.27
Austrian (0)	9	0.04
British (0)	28	0.13
Croatian (20)	20	0.09
Czech (0)	17	0.08
Danish (0)	73	0.34
Dutch (44)	205	0.97
English (145)	717	3.38
European (76)	116	0.55
Finnish (0)	32	0.15
French, ex. Basque (97)	453	2.14
French Canadian (16)	16	0.08
German (364)	1,201	5.67
Greek (22)	22	0.10
Hungarian (10)	10	0.05
Iranian (28)	28	0.13
Irish (79)	1,152	5.43
Italian (188)	619	2.92
Lithuanian (0)	10	0.05
Northern European (16)	52	0.25
Norwegian (13)	120	0.57
Polish (21)	88	0.42
Portuguese (110)	180	0.85
Russian (40)	81	0.38
Scandinavian (16)	44	0.21
Scotch-Irish (52)	151	0.71
Scottish (29)	126	0.59
Swedish (48)	486	2.29
Welsh (7)	25	0.12
West Indian, ex. Hispanic (0)	18	0.08
Haitian (0)	9	0.04
Jamaican (0)	9	0.04
Yugoslavian (0)	112	0.53

Hispanic Origin	Population	%
Hispanic or Latino (of any race)	11,730	54.94
Central American, ex. Mexican	1,335	6.25
Costa Rican	11	0.05
Guatemalan	103	0.48
Honduran	24	0.11
Nicaraguan	186	0.87
Panamanian	19	0.09
Salvadoran	984	4.61
Other Central American	8	0.04
Cuban	34	0.16
Dominican Republic	3	0.01
Mexican	9,242	43.29
Puerto Rican	170	0.80
South American	197	0.92
Argentinean	11	0.05
Bolivian	4	0.02
Chilean	18	0.08
Colombian	48	0.22
Ecuadorian	9	0.04
Peruvian	98	0.46

*Notes: † The Census 2010 population figure is used to calculate the percentages in the Hispanic Origin and Race categories. Ancestry percentages are based on the 2006-2010 American Community Survey population (not shown); ‡ Numbers in parentheses indicate the number of people reporting a single ancestry; * Numbers in parentheses indicate the number of persons reporting this race alone, not in combination with any other race; Please refer to the Explanation of Data for more information.*

Uruguayan	2	0.01
Venezuelan	6	0.03
Other South American	1	<0.01
Other Hispanic or Latino	749	3.51

Race*	Population	%
African-American/Black (2,469)	2,847	13.34
Not Hispanic (2,330)	2,585	12.11
Hispanic (139)	262	1.23
American Indian/Alaska Native (225)	487	2.28
Not Hispanic (77)	227	1.06
Hispanic (148)	260	1.22
Alaska Athabascan *(Ala. Nat.)* (0)	4	0.02
Aleut *(Alaska Native)* (0)	1	<0.01
Apache (3)	10	0.05
Blackfeet (3)	16	0.07
Central American Ind. (5)	5	0.02
Cherokee (13)	67	0.31
Chickasaw (0)	1	<0.01
Chippewa (4)	15	0.07
Choctaw (15)	34	0.16
Comanche (0)	1	<0.01
Creek (1)	1	<0.01
Delaware (1)	1	<0.01
Houma (0)	2	0.01
Inupiat *(Alaska Native)* (2)	2	0.01
Iroquois (0)	3	0.01
Lumbee (2)	2	0.01
Mexican American Ind. (46)	62	0.29
Navajo (4)	13	0.06
Osage (1)	3	0.01
Pueblo (1)	3	0.01
Seminole (0)	3	0.01
Sioux (3)	16	0.07
South American Ind. (2)	4	0.02
Spanish American Ind. (2)	7	0.03
Tohono O'Odham (5)	5	0.02
Yaqui (1)	6	0.03
Yuman (0)	1	<0.01
Asian (2,121)	2,482	11.63
Not Hispanic (2,071)	2,336	10.94
Hispanic (50)	146	0.68
Bangladeshi (1)	1	<0.01
Burmese (21)	23	0.11
Cambodian (11)	11	0.05
Chinese, ex. Taiwanese (204)	279	1.31
Filipino (1,156)	1,329	6.23
Indian (191)	223	1.04
Indonesian (10)	12	0.06
Japanese (41)	96	0.45
Korean (26)	36	0.17
Laotian (24)	24	0.11
Malaysian (3)	9	0.04
Nepalese (6)	9	0.04
Pakistani (50)	55	0.26
Sri Lankan (2)	2	0.01
Taiwanese (4)	4	0.02
Thai (6)	16	0.07
Vietnamese (318)	337	1.58
Hawaii Native/Pacific Islander (147)	248	1.16
Not Hispanic (127)	191	0.89
Hispanic (20)	57	0.27
Fijian (12)	13	0.06
Guamanian/Chamorro (24)	36	0.17
Native Hawaiian (7)	46	0.22
Samoan (21)	41	0.19
Tongan (52)	65	0.30
White (8,848)	9,997	46.83
Not Hispanic (4,374)	4,866	22.79
Hispanic (4,474)	5,131	24.03

Beaumont

Place Type: City
County: Riverside
Population: 36,877†

Ancestry‡	Population	%
African, Sub-Saharan (95)	95	0.29
African (54)	54	0.16
Kenyan (41)	41	0.12
American (998)	998	3.04
Armenian (17)	17	0.05
Australian (10)	10	0.03
Austrian (47)	120	0.37
Basque (0)	37	0.11
Brazilian (9)	9	0.03
British (12)	12	0.04
Bulgarian (0)	26	0.08
Canadian (94)	133	0.40
Celtic (24)	24	0.07
Croatian (14)	14	0.04
Czech (0)	18	0.05
Czechoslovakian (26)	44	0.13
Danish (48)	213	0.65
Dutch (139)	515	1.57
Eastern European (21)	21	0.06
English (817)	2,277	6.93
Estonian (10)	10	0.03
European (191)	254	0.77
Finnish (0)	22	0.07
French, ex. Basque (88)	522	1.59
French Canadian (112)	338	1.03
German (1,415)	3,635	11.07
German Russian (11)	11	0.03
Greek (93)	135	0.41
Hungarian (0)	32	0.10
Icelander (8)	8	0.02
Irish (1,030)	3,135	9.54
Italian (599)	1,287	3.92
Macedonian (11)	11	0.03
New Zealander (17)	17	0.05
Northern European (10)	10	0.03
Norwegian (196)	290	0.88
Pennsylvania German (0)	8	0.02
Polish (134)	423	1.29
Portuguese (0)	8	0.02
Russian (20)	146	0.44
Scandinavian (51)	51	0.16
Scotch-Irish (116)	315	0.96
Scottish (222)	666	2.03
Serbian (0)	10	0.03
Slovak (9)	9	0.03
Slovene (0)	15	0.05
Swedish (135)	356	1.08
Swiss (16)	46	0.14
Ukrainian (0)	61	0.19
Welsh (11)	118	0.36
West Indian, ex. Hispanic (39)	47	0.14
Dutch West Indian (0)	8	0.02
Jamaican (39)	39	0.12

Hispanic Origin	Population	%
Hispanic or Latino (of any race)	14,864	40.31
Central American, ex. Mexican	622	1.69
Costa Rican	20	0.05
Guatemalan	176	0.48
Honduran	25	0.07
Nicaraguan	73	0.20
Panamanian	4	0.01
Salvadoran	317	0.86
Other Central American	7	0.02
Cuban	124	0.34
Dominican Republic	17	0.05
Mexican	12,727	34.51
Puerto Rican	189	0.51
South American	225	0.61
Argentinean	29	0.08
Bolivian	9	0.02
Chilean	7	0.02
Colombian	75	0.20
Ecuadorian	28	0.08
Peruvian	68	0.18
Venezuelan	4	0.01
Other South American	5	0.01
Other Hispanic or Latino	960	2.60

Race*	Population	%
African-American/Black (2,276)	2,704	7.33
Not Hispanic (2,155)	2,437	6.61
Hispanic (121)	267	0.72
American Indian/Alaska Native (544)	960	2.60
Not Hispanic (282)	518	1.40
Hispanic (262)	442	1.20
Alaska Athabascan *(Ala. Nat.)* (5)	5	0.01
Aleut *(Alaska Native)* (1)	1	<0.01
Apache (14)	26	0.07
Blackfeet (5)	19	0.05
Canadian/French Am. Ind. (1)	5	0.01
Central American Ind. (0)	1	<0.01
Cherokee (24)	107	0.29
Cheyenne (0)	2	0.01
Chickasaw (3)	4	0.01
Chippewa (2)	6	0.02
Choctaw (7)	18	0.05
Colville (1)	1	<0.01
Comanche (0)	2	0.01
Creek (2)	11	0.03
Delaware (3)	4	0.01
Hopi (0)	3	0.01
Iroquois (3)	16	0.04
Kiowa (1)	1	<0.01
Lumbee (1)	1	<0.01
Mexican American Ind. (40)	54	0.15
Navajo (18)	30	0.08
Osage (2)	17	0.05
Paiute (2)	5	0.01
Pima (3)	5	0.01
Potawatomi (0)	4	0.01
Pueblo (6)	8	0.02
Seminole (1)	4	0.01
Shoshone (3)	3	0.01
Sioux (4)	9	0.02
Spanish American Ind. (7)	7	0.02
Ute (0)	1	<0.01
Yaqui (9)	10	0.03
Yuman (1)	4	0.01
Asian (2,845)	3,420	9.27
Not Hispanic (2,745)	3,163	8.58
Hispanic (100)	257	0.70
Bangladeshi (8)	8	0.02
Cambodian (65)	86	0.23
Chinese, ex. Taiwanese (321)	410	1.11
Filipino (1,206)	1,481	4.02
Hmong (85)	107	0.29
Indian (186)	240	0.65
Indonesian (69)	88	0.24
Japanese (92)	178	0.48
Korean (261)	318	0.86
Laotian (35)	51	0.14
Malaysian (3)	3	0.01
Nepalese (3)	7	0.02
Pakistani (70)	73	0.20
Sri Lankan (1)	1	<0.01
Taiwanese (38)	45	0.12
Thai (92)	123	0.33
Vietnamese (170)	204	0.55
Hawaii Native/Pacific Islander (83)	212	0.57
Not Hispanic (65)	154	0.42
Hispanic (18)	58	0.16
Fijian (1)	1	<0.01
Guamanian/Chamorro (37)	53	0.14
Native Hawaiian (19)	94	0.25
Samoan (8)	19	0.05
Tongan (4)	4	0.01
White (23,163)	24,770	67.17
Not Hispanic (15,831)	16,556	44.90
Hispanic (7,332)	8,214	22.27

Bell Gardens

Place Type: City
County: Los Angeles
Population: 42,072†

Ancestry‡	Population	%
American (499)	499	1.18
Arab (180)	180	0.42
Arab (50)	50	0.12
Other Arab (130)	130	0.31

*Notes: † The Census 2010 population figure is used to calculate the percentages in the Hispanic Origin and Race categories. Ancestry percentages are based on the 2006-2010 American Community Survey population (not shown); ‡ Numbers in parentheses indicate the number of people reporting a single ancestry; * Numbers in parentheses indicate the number of persons reporting this race alone, not in combination with any other race; Please refer to the Explanation of Data for more information.*

British (14)	14	0.03
Czech (0)	12	0.03
Danish (0)	13	0.03
English (16)	55	0.13
European (7)	7	0.02
French, ex. Basque (11)	20	0.05
German (53)	113	0.27
Greek (8)	8	0.02
Iranian (9)	9	0.02
Irish (69)	151	0.36
Israeli (13)	13	0.03
Italian (20)	118	0.28
Norwegian (0)	24	0.06
Polish (0)	12	0.03
Welsh (0)	9	0.02
West Indian, ex. Hispanic (12)	12	0.03
Jamaican (12)	12	0.03

Hispanic Origin	Population	%
Hispanic or Latino (of any race)	40,271	95.72
Central American, ex. Mexican	3,670	8.72
Costa Rican	34	0.08
Guatemalan	934	2.22
Honduran	257	0.61
Nicaraguan	414	0.98
Panamanian	6	0.01
Salvadoran	1,967	4.68
Other Central American	58	0.14
Cuban	149	0.35
Dominican Republic	9	0.02
Mexican	34,509	82.02
Puerto Rican	131	0.31
South American	258	0.61
Argentinean	10	0.02
Bolivian	5	0.01
Chilean	6	0.01
Colombian	55	0.13
Ecuadorian	64	0.15
Paraguayan	1	<0.01
Peruvian	107	0.25
Uruguayan	5	0.01
Venezuelan	4	0.01
Other South American	1	<0.01
Other Hispanic or Latino	1,545	3.67

Race*	Population	%
African-American/Black (377)	475	1.13
Not Hispanic (201)	215	0.51
Hispanic (176)	260	0.62
American Indian/Alaska Native (476)	597	1.42
Not Hispanic (97)	121	0.29
Hispanic (379)	476	1.13
Apache (21)	21	0.05
Blackfeet (0)	2	<0.01
Central American Ind. (1)	7	0.02
Cherokee (11)	19	0.05
Cheyenne (1)	1	<0.01
Chickasaw (2)	2	<0.01
Chippewa (1)	5	0.01
Choctaw (12)	12	0.03
Comanche (0)	1	<0.01
Creek (1)	4	0.01
Hopi (1)	2	<0.01
Kiowa (1)	3	0.01
Mexican American Ind. (91)	96	0.23
Navajo (36)	38	0.09
Ottawa (0)	1	<0.01
Paiute (1)	1	<0.01
Pima (1)	1	<0.01
Shoshone (1)	1	<0.01
Sioux (8)	9	0.02
Spanish American Ind. (16)	17	0.04
Tohono O'Odham (1)	1	<0.01
Yaqui (4)	6	0.01
Yuman (1)	1	<0.01
Asian (261)	348	0.83
Not Hispanic (226)	247	0.59
Hispanic (35)	101	0.24
Bangladeshi (3)	3	0.01
Cambodian (24)	38	0.09
Chinese, ex. Taiwanese (29)	45	0.11
Filipino (72)	96	0.23
Indian (13)	18	0.04
Japanese (12)	27	0.06
Korean (37)	42	0.10
Taiwanese (0)	1	<0.01
Thai (4)	5	0.01
Vietnamese (40)	43	0.10
Hawaii Native/Pacific Islander (37)	72	0.17
Not Hispanic (28)	34	0.08
Hispanic (9)	38	0.09
Guamanian/Chamorro (7)	7	0.02
Native Hawaiian (5)	7	0.02
Samoan (25)	34	0.08
White (20,824)	21,979	52.24
Not Hispanic (1,133)	1,185	2.82
Hispanic (19,691)	20,794	49.42

Bell

Place Type: City
County: Los Angeles
Population: 35,477†

Ancestry‡	Population	%
African, Sub-Saharan (0)	22	0.06
African (0)	22	0.06
American (845)	845	2.37
Arab (849)	857	2.40
Arab (7)	7	0.02
Jordanian (85)	85	0.24
Lebanese (440)	444	1.25
Palestinian (144)	144	0.40
Other Arab (173)	177	0.50
British (0)	23	0.06
Danish (10)	52	0.15
Dutch (0)	11	0.03
English (65)	181	0.51
French, ex. Basque (33)	69	0.19
French Canadian (14)	14	0.04
German (72)	317	0.89
Hungarian (0)	9	0.03
Irish (116)	324	0.91
Italian (81)	148	0.42
Norwegian (14)	26	0.07
Polish (11)	23	0.06
Portuguese (0)	27	0.08
Romanian (63)	63	0.18
Russian (27)	44	0.12
Scotch-Irish (0)	45	0.13
Scottish (0)	39	0.11
Swedish (0)	12	0.03
Welsh (12)	66	0.19
West Indian, ex. Hispanic (0)	58	0.16
Haitian (0)	58	0.16

Hispanic Origin	Population	%
Hispanic or Latino (of any race)	33,028	93.10
Central American, ex. Mexican	3,894	10.98
Costa Rican	45	0.13
Guatemalan	1,041	2.93
Honduran	268	0.76
Nicaraguan	381	1.07
Panamanian	4	0.01
Salvadoran	2,082	5.87
Other Central American	73	0.21
Cuban	774	2.18
Dominican Republic	8	0.02
Mexican	26,606	75.00
Puerto Rican	139	0.39
South American	293	0.83
Argentinean	28	0.08
Bolivian	2	0.01
Chilean	8	0.02
Colombian	53	0.15
Ecuadorian	73	0.21
Paraguayan	1	<0.01
Peruvian	118	0.33
Uruguayan	2	0.01
Venezuelan	7	0.02
Other South American	1	<0.01
Other Hispanic or Latino	1,314	3.70

Race*	Population	%
African-American/Black (337)	413	1.16
Not Hispanic (214)	233	0.66
Hispanic (123)	180	0.51
American Indian/Alaska Native (315)	516	1.45
Not Hispanic (64)	98	0.28
Hispanic (251)	418	1.18
Apache (9)	19	0.05
Blackfeet (0)	3	0.01
Central American Ind. (2)	7	0.02
Cherokee (5)	11	0.03
Chippewa (1)	1	<0.01
Choctaw (12)	14	0.04
Creek (1)	2	0.01
Hopi (1)	1	<0.01
Iroquois (0)	1	<0.01
Kiowa (6)	6	0.02
Mexican American Ind. (62)	95	0.27
Navajo (28)	47	0.13
Ottawa (0)	1	<0.01
Pima (3)	3	0.01
Pueblo (5)	5	0.01
Sioux (2)	7	0.02
South American Ind. (0)	5	0.01
Spanish American Ind. (0)	2	0.01
Tohono O'Odham (10)	10	0.03
Yaqui (2)	6	0.02
Yuman (1)	8	0.02
Asian (259)	436	1.23
Not Hispanic (229)	318	0.90
Hispanic (30)	118	0.33
Bangladeshi (4)	4	0.01
Cambodian (3)	3	0.01
Chinese, ex. Taiwanese (18)	34	0.10
Filipino (116)	141	0.40
Indian (20)	36	0.10
Indonesian (0)	1	<0.01
Japanese (12)	24	0.07
Korean (54)	59	0.17
Taiwanese (2)	2	0.01
Thai (3)	3	0.01
Vietnamese (11)	17	0.05
Hawaii Native/Pacific Islander (8)	29	0.08
Not Hispanic (2)	11	0.03
Hispanic (6)	18	0.05
Guamanian/Chamorro (1)	1	<0.01
Native Hawaiian (5)	11	0.03
Samoan (2)	4	0.01
Tongan (0)	1	<0.01
White (19,098)	20,468	57.69
Not Hispanic (1,728)	1,854	5.23
Hispanic (17,370)	18,614	52.47

Bellflower

Place Type: City
County: Los Angeles
Population: 76,616†

Ancestry‡	Population	%
African, Sub-Saharan (640)	704	0.93
African (215)	270	0.36
Ghanaian (0)	9	0.01
Nigerian (402)	402	0.53
South African (12)	12	0.02
Other Sub-Saharan African (11)	11	0.01
American (1,467)	1,467	1.93
Arab (476)	594	0.78
Arab (17)	17	0.02
Egyptian (415)	494	0.65
Lebanese (27)	51	0.07
Syrian (0)	5	0.01
Other Arab (17)	27	0.04
Armenian (13)	24	0.03
Assyrian/Chaldean/Syriac (0)	69	0.09
Austrian (10)	48	0.06
Belgian (21)	21	0.03

*Notes: † The Census 2010 population figure is used to calculate the percentages in the Hispanic Origin and Race categories. Ancestry percentages are based on the 2006-2010 American Community Survey population (not shown); ‡ Numbers in parentheses indicate the number of people reporting a single ancestry; * Numbers in parentheses indicate the number of persons reporting this race alone, not in combination with any other race; Please refer to the Explanation of Data for more information.*

British (64)	91	0.12
Cajun (11)	11	0.01
Canadian (28)	57	0.08
Czech (52)	128	0.17
Czechoslovakian (0)	5	0.01
Danish (21)	120	0.16
Dutch (1,081)	1,961	2.58
Eastern European (21)	21	0.03
English (766)	2,373	3.12
European (168)	214	0.28
Finnish (5)	30	0.04
French, ex. Basque (116)	753	0.99
French Canadian (180)	340	0.45
German (828)	3,485	4.59
German Russian (13)	13	0.02
Greek (0)	28	0.04
Hungarian (0)	129	0.17
Irish (732)	2,761	3.64
Italian (498)	1,449	1.91
Latvian (0)	25	0.03
Lithuanian (114)	114	0.15
Norwegian (48)	189	0.25
Pennsylvania German (0)	9	0.01
Polish (107)	338	0.45
Portuguese (45)	143	0.19
Romanian (71)	145	0.19
Russian (17)	68	0.09
Scandinavian (59)	127	0.17
Scotch-Irish (94)	267	0.35
Scottish (21)	270	0.36
Slovak (0)	4	0.01
Swedish (121)	368	0.48
Swiss (0)	45	0.06
Turkish (18)	28	0.04
Ukrainian (4)	4	0.01
Welsh (49)	135	0.18
West Indian, ex. Hispanic (108)	108	0.14
British West Indian (56)	56	0.07
Jamaican (26)	26	0.03
Trinidadian/Tobagonian (12)	12	0.02
U.S. Virgin Islander (14)	14	0.02
Yugoslavian (28)	49	0.06

Hispanic Origin	Population	%
Hispanic or Latino (of any race)	40,085	52.32
Central American, ex. Mexican	3,104	4.05
Costa Rican	74	0.10
Guatemalan	898	1.17
Honduran	184	0.24
Nicaraguan	297	0.39
Panamanian	62	0.08
Salvadoran	1,563	2.04
Other Central American	26	0.03
Cuban	295	0.39
Dominican Republic	44	0.06
Mexican	32,587	42.53
Puerto Rican	445	0.58
South American	867	1.13
Argentinean	116	0.15
Bolivian	22	0.03
Chilean	58	0.08
Colombian	203	0.26
Ecuadorian	174	0.23
Paraguayan	3	<0.01
Peruvian	250	0.33
Uruguayan	6	0.01
Venezuelan	23	0.03
Other South American	12	0.02
Other Hispanic or Latino	2,743	3.58

Race*	Population	%
African-American/Black (10,760)	11,788	15.39
Not Hispanic (10,374)	11,032	14.40
Hispanic (386)	756	0.99
American Indian/Alaska Native (731)	1,286	1.68
Not Hispanic (229)	543	0.71
Hispanic (502)	743	0.97
Alaska Athabascan *(Ala. Nat.)* (2)	2	<0.01
Apache (21)	34	0.04
Arapaho (1)	1	<0.01
Blackfeet (9)	21	0.03
Canadian/French Am. Ind. (4)	8	0.01
Central American Ind. (5)	7	0.01
Cherokee (51)	137	0.18
Cheyenne (5)	8	0.01
Chickasaw (1)	3	<0.01
Chippewa (3)	13	0.02
Choctaw (27)	50	0.07
Comanche (7)	9	0.01
Cree (0)	1	<0.01
Creek (4)	11	0.01
Crow (0)	7	0.01
Delaware (1)	6	0.01
Hopi (4)	4	0.01
Iroquois (2)	11	0.01
Kiowa (0)	3	<0.01
Lumbee (0)	1	<0.01
Mexican American Ind. (113)	152	0.20
Navajo (28)	50	0.07
Osage (0)	5	0.01
Ottawa (0)	1	<0.01
Paiute (2)	3	<0.01
Pima (3)	4	0.01
Potawatomi (1)	1	<0.01
Pueblo (12)	16	0.02
Seminole (0)	9	0.01
Shoshone (0)	2	<0.01
Sioux (4)	13	0.02
South American Ind. (1)	2	<0.01
Spanish American Ind. (11)	14	0.02
Ute (1)	1	<0.01
Yakama (2)	2	<0.01
Yaqui (3)	10	0.01
Asian (8,865)	9,846	12.85
Not Hispanic (8,720)	9,404	12.27
Hispanic (145)	442	0.58
Bangladeshi (51)	55	0.07
Burmese (4)	4	0.01
Cambodian (810)	978	1.28
Chinese, ex. Taiwanese (453)	710	0.93
Filipino (4,563)	5,088	6.64
Hmong (3)	4	0.01
Indian (416)	515	0.67
Indonesian (75)	109	0.14
Japanese (195)	337	0.44
Korean (826)	866	1.13
Laotian (13)	25	0.03
Malaysian (4)	4	0.01
Nepalese (6)	7	0.01
Pakistani (52)	57	0.07
Sri Lankan (36)	37	0.05
Taiwanese (30)	33	0.04
Thai (485)	552	0.72
Vietnamese (453)	538	0.70
Hawaii Native/Pacific Islander (615)	954	1.25
Not Hispanic (567)	805	1.05
Hispanic (48)	149	0.19
Fijian (34)	52	0.07
Guamanian/Chamorro (45)	90	0.12
Marshallese (0)	1	<0.01
Native Hawaiian (38)	135	0.18
Samoan (400)	507	0.66
Tongan (57)	81	0.11
White (32,337)	35,015	45.70
Not Hispanic (14,971)	16,072	20.98
Hispanic (17,366)	18,943	24.72

Belmont

Place Type: City
County: San Mateo
Population: 25,835†

Ancestry‡	Population	%
African, Sub-Saharan (14)	14	0.06
African (14)	14	0.06
Albanian (13)	13	0.05
American (346)	346	1.37
Arab (174)	234	0.93
Arab (46)	46	0.18
Lebanese (62)	81	0.32
Syrian (66)	107	0.42
Armenian (45)	61	0.24
Assyrian/Chaldean/Syriac (20)	38	0.15
Australian (49)	49	0.19
Austrian (36)	89	0.35
Basque (0)	13	0.05
Belgian (12)	34	0.13
British (187)	316	1.25
Canadian (78)	132	0.52
Croatian (11)	11	0.04
Czech (43)	135	0.53
Danish (73)	341	1.35
Dutch (53)	319	1.26
Eastern European (14)	29	0.11
English (577)	2,475	9.79
European (417)	482	1.91
Finnish (0)	65	0.26
French, ex. Basque (102)	492	1.95
French Canadian (66)	179	0.71
German (781)	3,766	14.90
Greek (340)	453	1.79
Hungarian (28)	74	0.29
Icelander (0)	13	0.05
Iranian (418)	424	1.68
Irish (636)	2,848	11.27
Israeli (0)	26	0.10
Italian (761)	2,270	8.98
Lithuanian (14)	44	0.17
Maltese (30)	30	0.12
Northern European (68)	68	0.27
Norwegian (106)	308	1.22
Polish (249)	715	2.83
Portuguese (28)	157	0.62
Romanian (91)	113	0.45
Russian (422)	833	3.29
Scandinavian (12)	12	0.05
Scotch-Irish (64)	367	1.45
Scottish (112)	521	2.06
Serbian (0)	19	0.08
Slavic (11)	11	0.04
Slovak (11)	11	0.04
Swedish (103)	499	1.97
Swiss (23)	147	0.58
Turkish (20)	20	0.08
Ukrainian (316)	379	1.50
Welsh (0)	114	0.45
West Indian, ex. Hispanic (96)	96	0.38
Haitian (27)	27	0.11
Jamaican (54)	54	0.21
Trinidadian/Tobagonian (9)	9	0.04
Other West Indian (6)	6	0.02
Yugoslavian (0)	13	0.05

Hispanic Origin	Population	%
Hispanic or Latino (of any race)	2,977	11.52
Central American, ex. Mexican	541	2.09
Costa Rican	19	0.07
Guatemalan	117	0.45
Honduran	9	0.03
Nicaraguan	121	0.47
Panamanian	9	0.03
Salvadoran	258	1.00
Other Central American	8	0.03
Cuban	52	0.20
Dominican Republic	4	0.02
Mexican	1,452	5.62
Puerto Rican	106	0.41
South American	389	1.51
Argentinean	48	0.19
Bolivian	15	0.06
Chilean	32	0.12
Colombian	43	0.17
Ecuadorian	9	0.03
Peruvian	208	0.81
Uruguayan	3	0.01
Venezuelan	21	0.08
Other South American	10	0.04
Other Hispanic or Latino	433	1.68

*Notes: † The Census 2010 population figure is used to calculate the percentages in the Hispanic Origin and Race categories. Ancestry percentages are based on the 2006-2010 American Community Survey population (not shown); ‡ Numbers in parentheses indicate the number of people reporting a single ancestry; * Numbers in parentheses indicate the number of persons reporting this race alone, not in combination with any other race; Please refer to the Explanation of Data for more information.*

Race*	Population	%
African-American/Black (423)	630	2.44
Not Hispanic (402)	572	2.21
Hispanic (21)	58	0.22
American Indian/Alaska Native (72)	271	1.05
Not Hispanic (44)	169	0.65
Hispanic (28)	102	0.39
Aleut *(Alaska Native)* (0)	1	<0.01
Apache (4)	9	0.03
Blackfeet (0)	3	0.01
Canadian/French Am. Ind. (1)	2	0.01
Cherokee (1)	40	0.15
Chickasaw (4)	5	0.02
Chippewa (1)	5	0.02
Choctaw (1)	4	0.02
Creek (0)	4	0.02
Delaware (1)	3	0.01
Hopi (1)	1	<0.01
Houma (0)	1	<0.01
Iroquois (4)	5	0.02
Mexican American Ind. (9)	23	0.09
Navajo (6)	10	0.04
Pima (0)	1	<0.01
Potawatomi (1)	1	<0.01
Pueblo (1)	1	<0.01
Puget Sound Salish (0)	1	<0.01
Seminole (1)	1	<0.01
Shoshone (0)	3	0.01
Sioux (0)	4	0.02
South American Ind. (0)	4	0.02
Spanish American Ind. (0)	2	0.01
Tlingit-Haida *(Alaska Native)* (3)	4	0.02
Yuman (0)	4	0.02
Asian (5,151)	6,140	23.77
Not Hispanic (5,100)	5,963	23.08
Hispanic (51)	177	0.69
Bangladeshi (5)	5	0.02
Burmese (14)	17	0.07
Cambodian (8)	17	0.07
Chinese, ex. Taiwanese (2,123)	2,614	10.12
Filipino (782)	1,054	4.08
Hmong (9)	9	0.03
Indian (979)	1,097	4.25
Indonesian (17)	29	0.11
Japanese (461)	722	2.79
Korean (204)	286	1.11
Laotian (2)	3	0.01
Malaysian (10)	13	0.05
Nepalese (12)	13	0.05
Pakistani (45)	53	0.21
Sri Lankan (7)	11	0.04
Taiwanese (106)	125	0.48
Thai (26)	48	0.19
Vietnamese (107)	155	0.60
Hawaii Native/Pacific Islander (198)	387	1.50
Not Hispanic (180)	349	1.35
Hispanic (18)	38	0.15
Fijian (12)	25	0.10
Guamanian/Chamorro (19)	38	0.15
Marshallese (2)	2	0.01
Native Hawaiian (30)	116	0.45
Samoan (13)	45	0.17
Tongan (101)	128	0.50
White (17,455)	18,864	73.02
Not Hispanic (15,831)	16,924	65.51
Hispanic (1,624)	1,940	7.51

Benicia

Place Type: City
County: Solano
Population: 26,997†

Ancestry‡	Population	%
African, Sub-Saharan (35)	41	0.15
African (35)	41	0.15
American (854)	854	3.17
Arab (72)	228	0.85
Arab (45)	59	0.22
Egyptian (19)	93	0.34
Lebanese (8)	76	0.28
Armenian (0)	8	0.03
Assyrian/Chaldean/Syriac (0)	10	0.04
Austrian (17)	51	0.19
Basque (24)	38	0.14
Belgian (15)	61	0.23
British (72)	164	0.61
Bulgarian (0)	13	0.05
Canadian (23)	114	0.42
Celtic (25)	36	0.13
Croatian (43)	67	0.25
Czech (11)	75	0.28
Czechoslovakian (21)	21	0.08
Danish (224)	447	1.66
Dutch (35)	329	1.22
Eastern European (26)	26	0.10
English (1,471)	4,228	15.68
European (851)	949	3.52
Finnish (88)	313	1.16
French, ex. Basque (44)	886	3.29
French Canadian (73)	160	0.59
German (1,024)	4,552	16.88
Greek (97)	149	0.55
Hungarian (76)	336	1.25
Iranian (38)	46	0.17
Irish (937)	4,067	15.09
Italian (502)	1,786	6.62
Latvian (37)	65	0.24
Lithuanian (23)	62	0.23
Luxemburger (0)	11	0.04
Northern European (49)	61	0.23
Norwegian (182)	694	2.57
Polish (237)	694	2.57
Portuguese (256)	706	2.62
Romanian (43)	56	0.21
Russian (133)	445	1.65
Scandinavian (13)	98	0.36
Scotch-Irish (201)	525	1.95
Scottish (355)	863	3.20
Slovak (11)	211	0.78
Slovene (0)	43	0.16
Swedish (180)	635	2.36
Swiss (12)	73	0.27
Turkish (7)	15	0.06
Ukrainian (46)	73	0.27
Welsh (52)	448	1.66
West Indian, ex. Hispanic (67)	116	0.43
Jamaican (38)	38	0.14
Trinidadian/Tobagonian (29)	29	0.11
West Indian (0)	49	0.18
Yugoslavian (0)	42	0.16

Hispanic Origin	Population	%
Hispanic or Latino (of any race)	3,248	12.03
Central American, ex. Mexican	279	1.03
Costa Rican	9	0.03
Guatemalan	32	0.12
Honduran	4	0.01
Nicaraguan	93	0.34
Panamanian	14	0.05
Salvadoran	122	0.45
Other Central American	5	0.02
Cuban	60	0.22
Dominican Republic	7	0.03
Mexican	2,078	7.70
Puerto Rican	190	0.70
South American	177	0.66
Argentinean	44	0.16
Bolivian	4	0.01
Chilean	20	0.07
Colombian	27	0.10
Ecuadorian	5	0.02
Paraguayan	1	<0.01
Peruvian	50	0.19
Uruguayan	1	<0.01
Venezuelan	24	0.09
Other South American	1	<0.01
Other Hispanic or Latino	457	1.69

Race*	Population	%
African-American/Black (1,510)	1,970	7.30
Not Hispanic (1,427)	1,796	6.65
Hispanic (83)	174	0.64
American Indian/Alaska Native (135)	553	2.05
Not Hispanic (93)	411	1.52
Hispanic (42)	142	0.53
Alaska Athabascan *(Ala. Nat.)* (0)	1	<0.01
Aleut *(Alaska Native)* (0)	5	0.02
Apache (4)	6	0.02
Arapaho (0)	2	0.01
Blackfeet (1)	10	0.04
Canadian/French Am. Ind. (0)	1	<0.01
Cherokee (8)	103	0.38
Chippewa (8)	12	0.04
Choctaw (3)	27	0.10
Comanche (0)	1	<0.01
Cree (1)	2	0.01
Creek (2)	4	0.01
Crow (0)	1	<0.01
Delaware (0)	3	0.01
Hopi (1)	6	0.02
Inupiat *(Alaska Native)* (0)	1	<0.01
Iroquois (2)	9	0.03
Menominee (0)	1	<0.01
Mexican American Ind. (5)	16	0.06
Navajo (2)	9	0.03
Osage (3)	7	0.03
Paiute (1)	5	0.02
Potawatomi (1)	4	0.01
Pueblo (2)	5	0.02
Seminole (3)	4	0.01
Sioux (3)	15	0.06
South American Ind. (1)	1	<0.01
Tlingit-Haida *(Alaska Native)* (1)	2	0.01
Yaqui (0)	2	0.01
Yuman (0)	4	0.01
Yup'ik *(Alaska Native)* (1)	1	<0.01
Asian (2,989)	3,915	14.50
Not Hispanic (2,901)	3,675	13.61
Hispanic (88)	240	0.89
Bangladeshi (5)	5	0.02
Burmese (4)	4	0.01
Cambodian (6)	6	0.02
Chinese, ex. Taiwanese (486)	717	2.66
Filipino (1,666)	2,255	8.35
Indian (242)	282	1.04
Indonesian (5)	34	0.13
Japanese (152)	375	1.39
Korean (142)	188	0.70
Laotian (13)	26	0.10
Malaysian (3)	4	0.01
Nepalese (8)	9	0.03
Pakistani (13)	13	0.05
Taiwanese (12)	14	0.05
Thai (12)	24	0.09
Vietnamese (82)	114	0.42
Hawaii Native/Pacific Islander (102)	304	1.13
Not Hispanic (96)	274	1.01
Hispanic (6)	30	0.11
Fijian (2)	3	0.01
Guamanian/Chamorro (41)	104	0.39
Native Hawaiian (19)	118	0.44
Samoan (13)	39	0.14
Tongan (6)	12	0.04
White (19,568)	21,104	78.17
Not Hispanic (17,835)	19,000	70.38
Hispanic (1,733)	2,104	7.79

Berkeley

Place Type: City
County: Alameda
Population: 112,580†

Ancestry‡	Population	%
Afghan (8)	29	0.03
African, Sub-Saharan (1,047)	1,312	1.20
African (437)	668	0.61

SECTION TWO

*Notes: † The Census 2010 population figure is used to calculate the percentages in the Hispanic Origin and Race categories. Ancestry percentages are based on the 2006-2010 American Community Survey population (not shown); ‡ Numbers in parentheses indicate the number of people reporting a single ancestry; * Numbers in parentheses indicate the number of persons reporting this race alone, not in combination with any other race; Please refer to the Explanation of Data for more information.*

Ethiopian (217)	222	0.20
Kenyan (70)	70	0.06
Nigerian (36)	65	0.06
Sierra Leonean (23)	23	0.02
South African (92)	92	0.08
Other Sub-Saharan African (172)	172	0.16
Alsatian (0)	19	0.02
American (1,220)	1,220	1.12
Arab (672)	882	0.81
Arab (153)	157	0.14
Egyptian (41)	41	0.04
Iraqi (17)	26	0.02
Jordanian (50)	50	0.05
Lebanese (49)	93	0.09
Moroccan (101)	136	0.12
Palestinian (34)	47	0.04
Syrian (10)	29	0.03
Other Arab (217)	303	0.28
Armenian (256)	381	0.35
Assyrian/Chaldean/Syriac (51)	51	0.05
Australian (47)	58	0.05
Austrian (108)	539	0.49
Basque (0)	22	0.02
Belgian (86)	209	0.19
Brazilian (118)	229	0.21
British (349)	975	0.89
Bulgarian (40)	72	0.07
Cajun (6)	6	0.01
Canadian (171)	307	0.28
Carpatho Rusyn (0)	11	0.01
Celtic (38)	86	0.08
Croatian (28)	158	0.14
Czech (53)	502	0.46
Czechoslovakian (10)	36	0.03
Danish (153)	851	0.78
Dutch (193)	1,041	0.95
Eastern European (869)	1,046	0.96
English (1,717)	8,474	7.75
Estonian (9)	57	0.05
European (2,467)	2,914	2.66
Finnish (63)	327	0.30
French, ex. Basque (707)	3,051	2.79
French Canadian (66)	282	0.26
German (1,772)	9,475	8.66
Greek (294)	648	0.59
Guyanese (8)	8	0.01
Hungarian (187)	640	0.58
Icelander (0)	68	0.06
Iranian (741)	925	0.85
Irish (1,927)	7,959	7.27
Israeli (153)	214	0.20
Italian (999)	4,172	3.81
Latvian (78)	100	0.09
Lithuanian (105)	302	0.28
Macedonian (0)	41	0.04
Maltese (10)	30	0.03
New Zealander (10)	36	0.03
Northern European (263)	305	0.28
Norwegian (286)	1,315	1.20
Pennsylvania German (8)	8	0.01
Polish (759)	3,058	2.80
Portuguese (258)	793	0.72
Romanian (195)	449	0.41
Russian (1,605)	4,125	3.77
Scandinavian (225)	399	0.36
Scotch-Irish (356)	1,478	1.35
Scottish (435)	2,473	2.26
Serbian (19)	25	0.02
Slavic (23)	128	0.12
Slovak (39)	220	0.20
Slovene (23)	57	0.05
Swedish (321)	1,340	1.22
Swiss (132)	784	0.72
Turkish (64)	86	0.08
Ukrainian (139)	561	0.51
Welsh (63)	795	0.73
West Indian, ex. Hispanic (142)	248	0.23
Haitian (54)	64	0.06
Jamaican (19)	32	0.03
Trinidadian/Tobagonian (10)	23	0.02
West Indian (59)	129	0.12
Yugoslavian (9)	68	0.06

Hispanic Origin	Population	%
Hispanic or Latino (of any race)	12,209	10.84
Central American, ex. Mexican	1,220	1.08
Costa Rican	76	0.07
Guatemalan	346	0.31
Honduran	81	0.07
Nicaraguan	186	0.17
Panamanian	63	0.06
Salvadoran	451	0.40
Other Central American	17	0.02
Cuban	248	0.22
Dominican Republic	59	0.05
Mexican	7,680	6.82
Puerto Rican	521	0.46
South American	1,319	1.17
Argentinean	232	0.21
Bolivian	41	0.04
Chilean	201	0.18
Colombian	236	0.21
Ecuadorian	84	0.07
Paraguayan	7	0.01
Peruvian	382	0.34
Uruguayan	21	0.02
Venezuelan	91	0.08
Other South American	24	0.02
Other Hispanic or Latino	1,162	1.03

Race*	Population	%
African-American/Black (11,241)	13,317	11.83
Not Hispanic (10,896)	12,524	11.12
Hispanic (345)	793	0.70
American Indian/Alaska Native (479)	1,836	1.63
Not Hispanic (228)	1,119	0.99
Hispanic (251)	717	0.64
Alaska Athabascan *(Ala. Nat.)* (0)	1	<0.01
Aleut *(Alaska Native)* (2)	4	<0.01
Apache (20)	57	0.05
Arapaho (0)	1	<0.01
Blackfeet (10)	45	0.04
Canadian/French Am. Ind. (2)	6	0.01
Central American Ind. (11)	22	0.02
Cherokee (21)	257	0.23
Cheyenne (0)	5	<0.01
Chickasaw (1)	6	0.01
Chippewa (4)	19	0.02
Choctaw (8)	107	0.10
Colville (0)	1	<0.01
Comanche (2)	3	<0.01
Cree (1)	8	0.01
Creek (3)	23	0.02
Crow (0)	1	<0.01
Delaware (1)	1	<0.01
Hopi (4)	4	<0.01
Inupiat *(Alaska Native)* (1)	7	0.01
Iroquois (8)	43	0.04
Kiowa (4)	6	0.01
Lumbee (0)	7	0.01
Menominee (0)	1	<0.01
Mexican American Ind. (81)	164	0.15
Navajo (19)	44	0.04
Osage (0)	7	0.01
Pima (1)	6	0.01
Potawatomi (5)	13	0.01
Pueblo (2)	14	0.01
Puget Sound Salish (0)	1	<0.01
Seminole (0)	15	0.01
Shoshone (1)	3	<0.01
Sioux (19)	44	0.04
South American Ind. (6)	47	0.04
Spanish American Ind. (5)	9	0.01
Tlingit-Haida *(Alaska Native)* (1)	2	<0.01
Tohono O'Odham (4)	5	<0.01
Tsimshian *(Alaska Native)* (0)	1	<0.01
Ute (1)	2	<0.01
Yaqui (14)	29	0.03
Yuman (2)	5	<0.01
Yup'ik *(Alaska Native)* (0)	1	<0.01
Asian (21,690)	25,707	22.83
Not Hispanic (21,499)	25,158	22.35
Hispanic (191)	549	0.49
Bangladeshi (64)	72	0.06
Bhutanese (2)	2	<0.01
Burmese (43)	66	0.06
Cambodian (100)	132	0.12
Chinese, ex. Taiwanese (8,655)	10,374	9.21
Filipino (1,640)	2,446	2.17
Hmong (56)	59	0.05
Indian (2,712)	3,197	2.84
Indonesian (94)	179	0.16
Japanese (1,752)	2,948	2.62
Korean (2,392)	2,754	2.45
Laotian (84)	101	0.09
Malaysian (20)	47	0.04
Nepalese (190)	211	0.19
Pakistani (349)	428	0.38
Sri Lankan (57)	71	0.06
Taiwanese (918)	1,066	0.95
Thai (323)	410	0.36
Vietnamese (1,110)	1,394	1.24
Hawaii Native/Pacific Islander (186)	577	0.51
Not Hispanic (170)	496	0.44
Hispanic (16)	81	0.07
Fijian (21)	36	0.03
Guamanian/Chamorro (30)	53	0.05
Native Hawaiian (30)	195	0.17
Samoan (43)	77	0.07
Tongan (31)	48	0.04
White (66,996)	72,950	64.80
Not Hispanic (61,539)	66,337	58.92
Hispanic (5,457)	6,613	5.87

Beverly Hills

Place Type: City
County: Los Angeles
Population: 34,109†

Ancestry‡	Population	%
African, Sub-Saharan (65)	104	0.31
African (56)	85	0.25
Ethiopian (9)	19	0.06
Alsatian (0)	19	0.06
American (1,560)	1,560	4.59
Arab (664)	1,295	3.81
Egyptian (23)	23	0.07
Iraqi (126)	146	0.43
Lebanese (235)	284	0.84
Moroccan (118)	451	1.33
Syrian (56)	69	0.20
Other Arab (106)	322	0.95
Armenian (43)	219	0.64
Australian (15)	15	0.04
Austrian (133)	554	1.63
Belgian (0)	39	0.11
Brazilian (61)	75	0.22
British (158)	238	0.70
Canadian (26)	84	0.25
Czech (51)	111	0.33
Czechoslovakian (12)	12	0.04
Danish (58)	348	1.02
Dutch (40)	223	0.66
Eastern European (522)	535	1.57
English (565)	1,984	5.84
European (499)	535	1.57
Finnish (0)	76	0.22
French, ex. Basque (398)	1,224	3.60
French Canadian (7)	31	0.09
German (488)	2,056	6.05
Greek (35)	154	0.45
Hungarian (280)	592	1.74
Iranian (8,690)	9,158	26.95
Irish (268)	1,629	4.79
Israeli (651)	920	2.71
Italian (656)	1,396	4.11
Latvian (0)	124	0.36
Lithuanian (47)	186	0.55
Northern European (13)	13	0.04

*Notes: † The Census 2010 population figure is used to calculate the percentages in the Hispanic Origin and Race categories. Ancestry percentages are based on the 2006-2010 American Community Survey population (not shown); ‡ Numbers in parentheses indicate the number of people reporting a single ancestry; * Numbers in parentheses indicate the number of persons reporting this race alone, not in combination with any other race; Please refer to the Explanation of Data for more information.*

Norwegian (40)	235	0.69
Polish (713)	2,004	5.90
Portuguese (53)	141	0.41
Romanian (162)	316	0.93
Russian (1,400)	3,343	9.84
Scandinavian (0)	48	0.14
Scotch-Irish (64)	333	0.98
Scottish (219)	447	1.32
Serbian (86)	141	0.41
Slavic (34)	34	0.10
Slovak (0)	9	0.03
Slovene (0)	14	0.04
Swedish (73)	302	0.89
Swiss (45)	91	0.27
Turkish (35)	56	0.16
Ukrainian (81)	210	0.62
Welsh (0)	35	0.10
West Indian, ex. Hispanic (40)	74	0.22
Haitian (0)	34	0.10
Jamaican (40)	40	0.12
Yugoslavian (13)	13	0.04

Hispanic Origin	Population	%
Hispanic or Latino (of any race)	1,941	5.69
Central American, ex. Mexican	313	0.92
Costa Rican	18	0.05
Guatemalan	98	0.29
Honduran	16	0.05
Nicaraguan	28	0.08
Panamanian	8	0.02
Salvadoran	143	0.42
Other Central American	2	0.01
Cuban	81	0.24
Dominican Republic	12	0.04
Mexican	834	2.45
Puerto Rican	70	0.21
South American	369	1.08
Argentinean	120	0.35
Bolivian	14	0.04
Chilean	26	0.08
Colombian	76	0.22
Ecuadorian	38	0.11
Paraguayan	2	0.01
Peruvian	48	0.14
Uruguayan	12	0.04
Venezuelan	22	0.06
Other South American	11	0.03
Other Hispanic or Latino	262	0.77

Race*	Population	%
African-American/Black (746)	918	2.69
Not Hispanic (725)	876	2.57
Hispanic (21)	42	0.12
American Indian/Alaska Native (48)	164	0.48
Not Hispanic (29)	128	0.38
Hispanic (19)	36	0.11
Apache (1)	7	0.02
Blackfeet (1)	3	0.01
Cherokee (2)	34	0.10
Chickasaw (0)	2	0.01
Choctaw (7)	12	0.04
Creek (0)	5	0.01
Iroquois (1)	4	0.01
Lumbee (0)	1	<0.01
Mexican American Ind. (3)	3	0.01
Navajo (1)	2	0.01
Osage (0)	1	<0.01
Paiute (1)	1	<0.01
Potawatomi (0)	3	0.01
Pueblo (0)	1	<0.01
Sioux (1)	4	0.01
Spanish American Ind. (3)	3	0.01
Tlingit-Haida *(Alaska Native)* (1)	2	0.01
Yaqui (0)	2	0.01
Yuman (2)	2	0.01
Asian (3,032)	4,257	12.48
Not Hispanic (3,009)	4,208	12.34
Hispanic (23)	49	0.14
Bangladeshi (5)	5	0.01
Burmese (2)	3	0.01
Cambodian (6)	11	0.03
Chinese, ex. Taiwanese (545)	649	1.90
Filipino (340)	421	1.23
Indian (235)	267	0.78
Indonesian (39)	46	0.13
Japanese (267)	341	1.00
Korean (1,350)	1,399	4.10
Laotian (3)	4	0.01
Malaysian (1)	2	0.01
Nepalese (2)	2	0.01
Pakistani (15)	17	0.05
Sri Lankan (7)	7	0.02
Taiwanese (63)	66	0.19
Thai (30)	39	0.11
Vietnamese (51)	68	0.20
Hawaii Native/Pacific Islander (12)	118	0.35
Not Hispanic (10)	106	0.31
Hispanic (2)	12	0.04
Fijian (1)	2	0.01
Guamanian/Chamorro (4)	13	0.04
Native Hawaiian (3)	20	0.06
Samoan (1)	4	0.01
White (28,112)	29,705	87.09
Not Hispanic (26,794)	28,244	82.81
Hispanic (1,318)	1,461	4.28

Big Bear City

Place Type: CDP
County: San Bernardino
Population: 12,304†

Ancestry‡	Population	%
American (239)	239	2.00
Armenian (14)	40	0.34
Assyrian/Chaldean/Syriac (30)	30	0.25
Austrian (0)	11	0.09
Belgian (0)	15	0.13
British (43)	43	0.36
Canadian (14)	16	0.13
Croatian (14)	20	0.17
Danish (49)	117	0.98
Dutch (131)	273	2.29
English (1,244)	1,939	16.24
European (175)	180	1.51
Finnish (0)	14	0.12
French, ex. Basque (136)	404	3.38
French Canadian (15)	15	0.13
German (804)	1,779	14.90
Guyanese (31)	31	0.26
Hungarian (39)	39	0.33
Irish (833)	1,844	15.45
Italian (241)	319	2.67
Lithuanian (0)	11	0.09
New Zealander (0)	30	0.25
Northern European (90)	90	0.75
Norwegian (61)	130	1.09
Polish (75)	258	2.16
Portuguese (0)	13	0.11
Romanian (0)	29	0.24
Russian (32)	46	0.39
Scandinavian (44)	92	0.77
Scotch-Irish (229)	301	2.52
Scottish (258)	417	3.49
Slovak (103)	103	0.86
Swedish (217)	246	2.06
Swiss (48)	75	0.63
Ukrainian (57)	57	0.48
Welsh (11)	46	0.39

Hispanic Origin	Population	%
Hispanic or Latino (of any race)	2,323	18.88
Central American, ex. Mexican	50	0.41
Costa Rican	1	0.01
Guatemalan	24	0.20
Honduran	1	0.01
Nicaraguan	1	0.01
Salvadoran	19	0.15
Other Central American	4	0.03
Cuban	5	0.04
Mexican	1,923	15.63
Puerto Rican	53	0.43
South American	25	0.20
Argentinean	3	0.02
Chilean	2	0.02
Colombian	3	0.02
Ecuadorian	1	0.01
Peruvian	8	0.07
Uruguayan	1	0.01
Other South American	7	0.06
Other Hispanic or Latino	267	2.17

Race*	Population	%
African-American/Black (83)	153	1.24
Not Hispanic (72)	128	1.04
Hispanic (11)	25	0.20
American Indian/Alaska Native (202)	455	3.70
Not Hispanic (125)	318	2.58
Hispanic (77)	137	1.11
Aleut *(Alaska Native)* (1)	1	0.01
Apache (13)	23	0.19
Blackfeet (2)	18	0.15
Cherokee (34)	102	0.83
Cheyenne (1)	2	0.02
Chickasaw (7)	10	0.08
Chippewa (3)	10	0.08
Choctaw (4)	9	0.07
Colville (1)	1	0.01
Comanche (1)	1	0.01
Creek (1)	2	0.02
Hopi (0)	1	0.01
Inupiat *(Alaska Native)* (2)	2	0.02
Iroquois (5)	14	0.11
Menominee (0)	2	0.02
Mexican American Ind. (15)	17	0.14
Navajo (3)	18	0.15
Osage (0)	2	0.02
Pima (1)	4	0.03
Potawatomi (3)	3	0.02
Pueblo (2)	3	0.02
Seminole (2)	2	0.02
Shoshone (0)	4	0.03
Sioux (5)	12	0.10
Spanish American Ind. (1)	1	0.01
Tlingit-Haida *(Alaska Native)* (0)	1	0.01
Tohono O'Odham (0)	1	0.01
Yaqui (1)	4	0.03
Yuman (2)	3	0.02
Asian (103)	198	1.61
Not Hispanic (98)	173	1.41
Hispanic (5)	25	0.20
Cambodian (2)	2	0.02
Chinese, ex. Taiwanese (27)	38	0.31
Filipino (30)	46	0.37
Indian (5)	15	0.12
Indonesian (5)	18	0.15
Japanese (16)	52	0.42
Korean (5)	8	0.07
Thai (1)	6	0.05
Vietnamese (4)	6	0.05
Hawaii Native/Pacific Islander (31)	57	0.46
Not Hispanic (17)	40	0.33
Hispanic (14)	17	0.14
Guamanian/Chamorro (2)	6	0.05
Native Hawaiian (21)	36	0.29
Samoan (4)	5	0.04
White (10,252)	10,765	87.49
Not Hispanic (9,322)	9,643	78.37
Hispanic (930)	1,122	9.12

Blackhawk

Place Type: CDP
County: Contra Costa
Population: 9,354†

Ancestry‡	Population	%
Afghan (83)	83	0.86
African, Sub-Saharan (70)	70	0.73
African (70)	70	0.73

*Notes: † The Census 2010 population figure is used to calculate the percentages in the Hispanic Origin and Race categories. Ancestry percentages are based on the 2006-2010 American Community Survey population (not shown); ‡ Numbers in parentheses indicate the number of people reporting a single ancestry; * Numbers in parentheses indicate the number of persons reporting this race alone, not in combination with any other race; Please refer to the Explanation of Data for more information.*

American (161)	161	1.68
Arab (18)	18	0.19
Other Arab (18)	18	0.19
Armenian (29)	29	0.30
Assyrian/Chaldean/Syriac (53)	53	0.55
Austrian (0)	14	0.15
Basque (7)	14	0.15
Belgian (16)	48	0.50
Brazilian (69)	69	0.72
British (85)	139	1.45
Canadian (13)	55	0.57
Croatian (16)	32	0.33
Czech (25)	39	0.41
Danish (88)	292	3.04
Dutch (0)	96	1.00
English (375)	1,578	16.43
European (196)	223	2.32
Finnish (0)	18	0.19
French, ex. Basque (112)	337	3.51
French Canadian (22)	75	0.78
German (368)	1,478	15.38
Greek (0)	50	0.52
Hungarian (43)	63	0.66
Iranian (193)	193	2.01
Irish (434)	1,409	14.67
Italian (333)	804	8.37
Lithuanian (0)	54	0.56
Luxemburger (16)	16	0.17
Norwegian (114)	354	3.68
Polish (129)	310	3.23
Portuguese (47)	149	1.55
Romanian (0)	33	0.34
Russian (89)	115	1.20
Scandinavian (14)	42	0.44
Scotch-Irish (31)	86	0.90
Scottish (37)	305	3.17
Slavic (0)	40	0.42
Swedish (56)	131	1.36
Swiss (12)	69	0.72
Ukrainian (0)	41	0.43
Welsh (0)	55	0.57
West Indian, ex. Hispanic (0)	12	0.12
West Indian (0)	12	0.12

Hispanic Origin	Population	%
Hispanic or Latino (of any race)	464	4.96
Central American, ex. Mexican	27	0.29
Costa Rican	1	0.01
Guatemalan	4	0.04
Honduran	1	0.01
Nicaraguan	3	0.03
Panamanian	4	0.04
Salvadoran	13	0.14
Other Central American	1	0.01
Cuban	20	0.21
Dominican Republic	2	0.02
Mexican	234	2.50
Puerto Rican	20	0.21
South American	48	0.51
Argentinean	7	0.07
Bolivian	2	0.02
Chilean	2	0.02
Colombian	20	0.21
Ecuadorian	4	0.04
Peruvian	8	0.09
Venezuelan	5	0.05
Other Hispanic or Latino	113	1.21

Race*	Population	%
African-American/Black (172)	225	2.41
Not Hispanic (167)	216	2.31
Hispanic (5)	9	0.10
American Indian/Alaska Native (15)	43	0.46
Not Hispanic (10)	32	0.34
Hispanic (5)	11	0.12
Blackfeet (0)	2	0.02
Canadian/French Am. Ind. (0)	1	0.01
Cherokee (1)	8	0.09
Chippewa (0)	1	0.01
Creek (2)	2	0.02
Iroquois (0)	1	0.01
Mexican American Ind. (4)	4	0.04
Potawatomi (0)	1	0.01
Yaqui (1)	1	0.01
Asian (1,801)	2,104	22.49
Not Hispanic (1,786)	2,063	22.05
Hispanic (15)	41	0.44
Burmese (9)	9	0.10
Chinese, ex. Taiwanese (648)	750	8.02
Filipino (202)	262	2.80
Indian (437)	476	5.09
Indonesian (12)	18	0.19
Japanese (83)	147	1.57
Korean (175)	216	2.31
Malaysian (1)	1	0.01
Pakistani (54)	54	0.58
Taiwanese (50)	60	0.64
Thai (6)	6	0.06
Vietnamese (59)	70	0.75
Hawaii Native/Pacific Islander (8)	33	0.35
Not Hispanic (8)	28	0.30
Hispanic (0)	5	0.05
Native Hawaiian (1)	15	0.16
Tongan (5)	5	0.05
White (6,882)	7,227	77.26
Not Hispanic (6,562)	6,853	73.26
Hispanic (320)	374	4.00

Bloomington

Place Type: CDP
County: San Bernardino
Population: 23,851†

Ancestry‡	Population	%
African, Sub-Saharan (29)	29	0.12
African (29)	29	0.12
American (485)	485	1.94
Arab (188)	188	0.75
Lebanese (51)	51	0.20
Other Arab (137)	137	0.55
Armenian (0)	30	0.12
Australian (24)	24	0.10
Belgian (0)	30	0.12
Canadian (0)	29	0.12
Celtic (0)	16	0.06
Czech (0)	56	0.22
Dutch (0)	114	0.46
English (250)	466	1.87
Estonian (17)	17	0.07
European (11)	11	0.04
French, ex. Basque (47)	357	1.43
French Canadian (25)	52	0.21
German (275)	1,202	4.81
German Russian (0)	11	0.04
Greek (0)	70	0.28
Hungarian (0)	83	0.33
Irish (18)	354	1.42
Italian (180)	372	1.49
Norwegian (6)	101	0.40
Polish (77)	114	0.46
Portuguese (0)	13	0.05
Romanian (18)	59	0.24
Scandinavian (19)	59	0.24
Scotch-Irish (22)	62	0.25
Scottish (17)	58	0.23
Swedish (0)	113	0.45
Swiss (0)	20	0.08
Ukrainian (15)	15	0.06
Welsh (0)	6	0.02
Yugoslavian (0)	30	0.12

Hispanic Origin	Population	%
Hispanic or Latino (of any race)	19,326	81.03
Central American, ex. Mexican	803	3.37
Costa Rican	16	0.07
Guatemalan	212	0.89
Honduran	54	0.23
Nicaraguan	86	0.36
Panamanian	7	0.03
Salvadoran	423	1.77
Other Central American	5	0.02
Cuban	37	0.16
Dominican Republic	1	<0.01
Mexican	17,441	73.12
Puerto Rican	123	0.52
South American	130	0.55
Argentinean	9	0.04
Bolivian	1	<0.01
Chilean	6	0.03
Colombian	33	0.14
Ecuadorian	28	0.12
Peruvian	53	0.22
Other Hispanic or Latino	791	3.32

Race*	Population	%
African-American/Black (649)	830	3.48
Not Hispanic (555)	636	2.67
Hispanic (94)	194	0.81
American Indian/Alaska Native (309)	498	2.09
Not Hispanic (70)	157	0.66
Hispanic (239)	341	1.43
Apache (16)	27	0.11
Blackfeet (0)	9	0.04
Canadian/French Am. Ind. (5)	5	0.02
Central American Ind. (4)	5	0.02
Cherokee (15)	48	0.20
Chickasaw (0)	1	<0.01
Chippewa (1)	1	<0.01
Choctaw (2)	9	0.04
Comanche (0)	5	0.02
Creek (1)	1	<0.01
Delaware (0)	5	0.02
Hopi (0)	3	0.01
Iroquois (2)	2	0.01
Mexican American Ind. (47)	70	0.29
Navajo (13)	21	0.09
Osage (0)	1	<0.01
Sioux (4)	4	0.02
South American Ind. (0)	3	0.01
Spanish American Ind. (2)	4	0.02
Tohono O'Odham (2)	2	0.01
Yaqui (6)	10	0.04
Yuman (2)	5	0.02
Asian (330)	430	1.80
Not Hispanic (283)	329	1.38
Hispanic (47)	101	0.42
Cambodian (10)	11	0.05
Chinese, ex. Taiwanese (37)	44	0.18
Filipino (113)	156	0.65
Hmong (11)	11	0.05
Indian (39)	48	0.20
Indonesian (17)	20	0.08
Japanese (9)	29	0.12
Korean (7)	15	0.06
Pakistani (4)	4	0.02
Taiwanese (13)	13	0.05
Thai (11)	19	0.08
Vietnamese (40)	44	0.18
Hawaii Native/Pacific Islander (47)	61	0.26
Not Hispanic (39)	46	0.19
Hispanic (8)	15	0.06
Guamanian/Chamorro (8)	8	0.03
Native Hawaiian (3)	8	0.03
Samoan (5)	10	0.04
Tongan (14)	19	0.08
White (12,988)	13,761	57.70
Not Hispanic (3,369)	3,521	14.76
Hispanic (9,619)	10,240	42.93

Blythe

Place Type: City
County: Riverside
Population: 20,817†

Ancestry‡	Population	%
African, Sub-Saharan (200)	224	1.06
African (200)	224	1.06
Albanian (16)	16	0.08

*Notes: † The Census 2010 population figure is used to calculate the percentages in the Hispanic Origin and Race categories. Ancestry percentages are based on the 2006-2010 American Community Survey population (not shown); ‡ Numbers in parentheses indicate the number of people reporting a single ancestry; * Numbers in parentheses indicate the number of persons reporting this race alone, not in combination with any other race; Please refer to the Explanation of Data for more information.*

American (348)	348	1.64
Arab (7)	26	0.12
Iraqi (7)	7	0.03
Moroccan (0)	9	0.04
Palestinian (0)	10	0.05
Armenian (16)	16	0.08
Brazilian (0)	8	0.04
British (0)	8	0.04
Canadian (29)	29	0.14
Celtic (10)	10	0.05
Czech (0)	8	0.04
Danish (0)	36	0.17
Dutch (19)	103	0.49
English (437)	806	3.81
European (68)	80	0.38
French, ex. Basque (38)	163	0.77
French Canadian (17)	38	0.18
German (460)	1,432	6.77
Greek (125)	125	0.59
Guyanese (7)	7	0.03
Icelander (9)	9	0.04
Irish (247)	1,016	4.80
Israeli (0)	9	0.04
Italian (166)	414	1.96
Lithuanian (0)	12	0.06
New Zealander (8)	8	0.04
Norwegian (19)	102	0.48
Polish (18)	105	0.50
Portuguese (52)	114	0.54
Russian (0)	31	0.15
Scandinavian (16)	16	0.08
Scotch-Irish (30)	114	0.54
Scottish (59)	193	0.91
Swedish (13)	167	0.79
Swiss (17)	17	0.08
Ukrainian (0)	11	0.05
Welsh (0)	23	0.11
West Indian, ex. Hispanic (17)	42	0.20
Belizean (0)	7	0.03
Haitian (8)	8	0.04
Jamaican (9)	27	0.13
Yugoslavian (0)	13	0.06

Hispanic Origin	Population	%
Hispanic or Latino (of any race)	11,068	53.17
Central American, ex. Mexican	67	0.32
Costa Rican	1	<0.01
Guatemalan	13	0.06
Honduran	13	0.06
Nicaraguan	1	<0.01
Panamanian	6	0.03
Salvadoran	32	0.15
Other Central American	1	<0.01
Cuban	11	0.05
Dominican Republic	3	0.01
Mexican	9,530	45.78
Puerto Rican	70	0.34
South American	15	0.07
Argentinean	1	<0.01
Chilean	2	0.01
Colombian	5	0.02
Ecuadorian	2	0.01
Peruvian	1	<0.01
Uruguayan	4	0.02
Other Hispanic or Latino	1,372	6.59

Race*	Population	%
African-American/Black (3,126)	3,331	16.00
Not Hispanic (3,020)	3,134	15.06
Hispanic (106)	197	0.95
American Indian/Alaska Native (243)	385	1.85
Not Hispanic (147)	223	1.07
Hispanic (96)	162	0.78
Apache (2)	3	0.01
Blackfeet (0)	3	0.01
Cherokee (10)	39	0.19
Chickasaw (5)	15	0.07
Chippewa (4)	4	0.02
Choctaw (6)	10	0.05
Comanche (0)	1	<0.01
Cree (0)	4	0.02
Creek (0)	18	0.09
Hopi (0)	2	0.01
Mexican American Ind. (9)	17	0.08
Navajo (10)	23	0.11
Paiute (3)	3	0.01
Pima (1)	4	0.02
Pueblo (1)	1	<0.01
Seminole (1)	13	0.06
Sioux (2)	2	0.01
Spanish American Ind. (1)	3	0.01
Tohono O'Odham (6)	8	0.04
Yaqui (3)	17	0.08
Yuman (0)	3	0.01
Asian (319)	384	1.84
Not Hispanic (291)	329	1.58
Hispanic (28)	55	0.26
Cambodian (8)	8	0.04
Chinese, ex. Taiwanese (21)	26	0.12
Filipino (150)	179	0.86
Hmong (3)	3	0.01
Indian (41)	49	0.24
Indonesian (2)	4	0.02
Japanese (13)	23	0.11
Korean (16)	23	0.11
Laotian (4)	4	0.02
Pakistani (2)	3	0.01
Thai (7)	9	0.04
Vietnamese (28)	31	0.15
Hawaii Native/Pacific Islander (32)	62	0.30
Not Hispanic (25)	38	0.18
Hispanic (7)	24	0.12
Guamanian/Chamorro (3)	3	0.01
Native Hawaiian (16)	19	0.09
Samoan (9)	11	0.05
White (12,396)	12,936	62.14
Not Hispanic (5,894)	6,065	29.13
Hispanic (6,502)	6,871	33.01

Bonadelle Ranchos-Madera Ranchos

Place Type: CDP
County: Madera
Population: 8,569†

Ancestry‡	Population	%
American (291)	291	3.26
Arab (40)	100	1.12
Lebanese (40)	40	0.45
Syrian (0)	60	0.67
Armenian (24)	89	1.00
Assyrian/Chaldean/Syriac (28)	79	0.88
Basque (14)	14	0.16
British (7)	43	0.48
Czech (0)	64	0.72
Czechoslovakian (31)	31	0.35
Danish (0)	7	0.08
Dutch (38)	192	2.15
English (131)	639	7.15
European (62)	102	1.14
French, ex. Basque (22)	228	2.55
French Canadian (18)	48	0.54
German (438)	1,372	15.35
German Russian (0)	11	0.12
Greek (9)	25	0.28
Hungarian (6)	28	0.31
Iranian (15)	46	0.51
Irish (140)	596	6.67
Italian (122)	325	3.64
Lithuanian (0)	81	0.91
Norwegian (33)	108	1.21
Polish (33)	44	0.49
Portuguese (170)	234	2.62
Romanian (0)	31	0.35
Russian (24)	116	1.30
Scotch-Irish (43)	155	1.73
Scottish (83)	300	3.36
Swedish (63)	107	1.20
Swiss (7)	43	0.48
Ukrainian (9)	9	0.10
Welsh (46)	129	1.44
West Indian, ex. Hispanic (0)	12	0.13
Dutch West Indian (0)	12	0.13

Hispanic Origin	Population	%
Hispanic or Latino (of any race)	2,305	26.90
Central American, ex. Mexican	52	0.61
Guatemalan	7	0.08
Honduran	7	0.08
Nicaraguan	16	0.19
Panamanian	2	0.02
Salvadoran	20	0.23
Cuban	4	0.05
Dominican Republic	1	0.01
Mexican	2,051	23.94
Puerto Rican	36	0.42
South American	41	0.48
Argentinean	7	0.08
Chilean	8	0.09
Colombian	13	0.15
Ecuadorian	5	0.06
Peruvian	8	0.09
Other Hispanic or Latino	120	1.40

Race*	Population	%
African-American/Black (114)	150	1.75
Not Hispanic (95)	115	1.34
Hispanic (19)	35	0.41
American Indian/Alaska Native (120)	212	2.47
Not Hispanic (72)	127	1.48
Hispanic (48)	85	0.99
Blackfeet (1)	1	0.01
Canadian/French Am. Ind. (0)	1	0.01
Central American Ind. (2)	2	0.02
Cherokee (13)	33	0.39
Choctaw (5)	9	0.11
Comanche (0)	1	0.01
Creek (2)	2	0.02
Mexican American Ind. (12)	21	0.25
Navajo (0)	1	0.01
Osage (3)	3	0.04
Potawatomi (2)	3	0.04
Seminole (1)	2	0.02
Shoshone (1)	2	0.02
South American Ind. (2)	2	0.02
Yaqui (1)	3	0.04
Yuman (1)	1	0.01
Asian (207)	285	3.33
Not Hispanic (189)	246	2.87
Hispanic (18)	39	0.46
Burmese (2)	2	0.02
Cambodian (2)	2	0.02
Chinese, ex. Taiwanese (22)	29	0.34
Filipino (56)	87	1.02
Hmong (44)	44	0.51
Indian (23)	41	0.48
Indonesian (1)	1	0.01
Japanese (21)	39	0.46
Korean (10)	11	0.13
Laotian (4)	4	0.05
Pakistani (7)	7	0.08
Thai (1)	1	0.01
Vietnamese (5)	9	0.11
Hawaii Native/Pacific Islander (4)	27	0.32
Not Hispanic (4)	16	0.19
Hispanic (0)	11	0.13
Guamanian/Chamorro (1)	4	0.05
Marshallese (1)	1	0.01
Native Hawaiian (0)	13	0.15
Samoan (0)	4	0.05
Tongan (1)	2	0.02
White (7,034)	7,276	84.91
Not Hispanic (5,752)	5,877	68.58
Hispanic (1,282)	1,399	16.33

*Notes: † The Census 2010 population figure is used to calculate the percentages in the Hispanic Origin and Race categories. Ancestry percentages are based on the 2006-2010 American Community Survey population (not shown); ‡ Numbers in parentheses indicate the number of people reporting a single ancestry; * Numbers in parentheses indicate the number of persons reporting this race alone, not in combination with any other race; Please refer to the Explanation of Data for more information.*

Bonita

Place Type: CDP
County: San Diego
Population: 12,538†

Ancestry‡	Population	%
African, Sub-Saharan (27)	27	0.19
African (27)	27	0.19
American (444)	444	3.16
Arab (154)	154	1.09
Arab (105)	105	0.75
Iraqi (40)	40	0.28
Lebanese (9)	9	0.06
Armenian (36)	50	0.36
Assyrian/Chaldean/Syriac (242)	242	1.72
Austrian (11)	36	0.26
Belgian (0)	51	0.36
Brazilian (20)	20	0.14
British (19)	29	0.21
Czech (22)	49	0.35
Danish (38)	47	0.33
Dutch (0)	11	0.08
Eastern European (56)	56	0.40
English (321)	822	5.84
European (99)	99	0.70
French, ex. Basque (38)	406	2.89
French Canadian (9)	31	0.22
German (308)	1,136	8.08
Greek (0)	8	0.06
Hungarian (0)	17	0.12
Iranian (43)	56	0.40
Irish (130)	637	4.53
Italian (250)	555	3.95
Lithuanian (9)	25	0.18
Northern European (23)	23	0.16
Norwegian (42)	138	0.98
Polish (20)	270	1.92
Portuguese (49)	49	0.35
Russian (92)	136	0.97
Scandinavian (0)	34	0.24
Scotch-Irish (67)	144	1.02
Scottish (88)	269	1.91
Swedish (20)	147	1.05
Swiss (24)	58	0.41
Turkish (0)	16	0.11
Welsh (0)	36	0.26
West Indian, ex. Hispanic (23)	23	0.16
Jamaican (23)	23	0.16

Hispanic Origin	Population	%
Hispanic or Latino (of any race)	5,106	40.72
Central American, ex. Mexican	56	0.45
Costa Rican	12	0.10
Guatemalan	3	0.02
Honduran	1	0.01
Nicaraguan	8	0.06
Panamanian	15	0.12
Salvadoran	17	0.14
Cuban	40	0.32
Dominican Republic	9	0.07
Mexican	4,591	36.62
Puerto Rican	81	0.65
South American	88	0.70
Argentinean	18	0.14
Bolivian	1	0.01
Chilean	2	0.02
Colombian	22	0.18
Ecuadorian	9	0.07
Peruvian	34	0.27
Uruguayan	1	0.01
Venezuelan	1	0.01
Other Hispanic or Latino	241	1.92

Race*	Population	%
African-American/Black (466)	583	4.65
Not Hispanic (438)	509	4.06
Hispanic (28)	74	0.59
American Indian/Alaska Native (109)	195	1.56
Not Hispanic (54)	105	0.84
Hispanic (55)	90	0.72
Aleut *(Alaska Native)* (1)	1	0.01
Apache (6)	7	0.06
Blackfeet (0)	2	0.02
Canadian/French Am. Ind. (2)	2	0.02
Central American Ind. (1)	1	0.01
Cherokee (3)	9	0.07
Chickasaw (0)	2	0.02
Chippewa (0)	2	0.02
Choctaw (3)	7	0.06
Inupiat *(Alaska Native)* (1)	1	0.01
Iroquois (2)	8	0.06
Mexican American Ind. (11)	14	0.11
Navajo (1)	3	0.02
Osage (2)	2	0.02
Seminole (0)	1	0.01
Sioux (0)	1	0.01
Spanish American Ind. (0)	3	0.02
Tohono O'Odham (0)	1	0.01
Ute (0)	1	0.01
Asian (1,200)	1,510	12.04
Not Hispanic (1,143)	1,357	10.82
Hispanic (57)	153	1.22
Cambodian (4)	4	0.03
Chinese, ex. Taiwanese (71)	117	0.93
Filipino (826)	1,030	8.22
Indian (27)	33	0.26
Indonesian (1)	8	0.06
Japanese (122)	185	1.48
Korean (49)	57	0.45
Laotian (6)	7	0.06
Malaysian (0)	2	0.02
Pakistani (0)	5	0.04
Taiwanese (6)	8	0.06
Thai (7)	9	0.07
Vietnamese (47)	54	0.43
Hawaii Native/Pacific Islander (80)	140	1.12
Not Hispanic (70)	108	0.86
Hispanic (10)	32	0.26
Fijian (1)	3	0.02
Guamanian/Chamorro (58)	79	0.63
Native Hawaiian (12)	29	0.23
Samoan (7)	11	0.09
White (8,382)	8,887	70.88
Not Hispanic (5,387)	5,662	45.16
Hispanic (2,995)	3,225	25.72

Bostonia

Place Type: CDP
County: San Diego
Population: 15,379†

Ancestry‡	Population	%
African, Sub-Saharan (0)	19	0.13
African (0)	19	0.13
American (400)	400	2.76
Arab (346)	357	2.46
Arab (24)	35	0.24
Iraqi (322)	322	2.22
Armenian (30)	30	0.21
Assyrian/Chaldean/Syriac (106)	106	0.73
Austrian (0)	21	0.14
British (15)	15	0.10
Bulgarian (13)	13	0.09
Canadian (28)	28	0.19
Croatian (0)	17	0.12
Czech (42)	157	1.08
Czechoslovakian (58)	58	0.40
Danish (117)	172	1.18
Dutch (26)	176	1.21
English (410)	1,698	11.70
European (112)	135	0.93
Finnish (0)	8	0.06
French, ex. Basque (38)	419	2.89
French Canadian (26)	26	0.18
German (732)	2,693	18.55
Greek (0)	19	0.13
Hungarian (0)	27	0.19
Icelander (16)	16	0.11
Iranian (12)	12	0.08
Irish (362)	2,239	15.43
Israeli (0)	9	0.06
Italian (189)	561	3.86
Northern European (0)	8	0.06
Norwegian (31)	116	0.80
Pennsylvania German (30)	30	0.21
Polish (219)	469	3.23
Portuguese (51)	132	0.91
Russian (24)	68	0.47
Scandinavian (41)	62	0.43
Scotch-Irish (135)	228	1.57
Scottish (28)	213	1.47
Slovak (7)	17	0.12
Swedish (58)	265	1.83
Swiss (82)	133	0.92
Turkish (20)	20	0.14
Welsh (29)	217	1.50
West Indian, ex. Hispanic (0)	26	0.18
Belizean (0)	26	0.18
Yugoslavian (31)	31	0.21

Hispanic Origin	Population	%
Hispanic or Latino (of any race)	3,941	25.63
Central American, ex. Mexican	98	0.64
Costa Rican	3	0.02
Guatemalan	23	0.15
Honduran	10	0.07
Nicaraguan	22	0.14
Panamanian	11	0.07
Salvadoran	26	0.17
Other Central American	3	0.02
Cuban	21	0.14
Dominican Republic	11	0.07
Mexican	3,416	22.21
Puerto Rican	131	0.85
South American	42	0.27
Argentinean	3	0.02
Bolivian	1	0.01
Chilean	6	0.04
Colombian	20	0.13
Ecuadorian	2	0.01
Peruvian	9	0.06
Venezuelan	1	0.01
Other Hispanic or Latino	222	1.44

Race*	Population	%
African-American/Black (1,011)	1,334	8.67
Not Hispanic (954)	1,193	7.76
Hispanic (57)	141	0.92
American Indian/Alaska Native (102)	319	2.07
Not Hispanic (67)	233	1.52
Hispanic (35)	86	0.56
Alaska Athabascan *(Ala. Nat.)* (1)	3	0.02
Aleut *(Alaska Native)* (1)	1	0.01
Apache (5)	8	0.05
Blackfeet (0)	5	0.03
Canadian/French Am. Ind. (0)	3	0.02
Central American Ind. (6)	6	0.04
Cherokee (4)	60	0.39
Chickasaw (0)	4	0.03
Chippewa (2)	5	0.03
Choctaw (1)	17	0.11
Comanche (0)	1	0.01
Creek (4)	4	0.03
Delaware (1)	1	0.01
Iroquois (0)	1	0.01
Mexican American Ind. (0)	8	0.05
Navajo (8)	12	0.08
Osage (0)	4	0.03
Ottawa (0)	3	0.02
Pima (1)	1	0.01
Potawatomi (0)	1	0.01
Pueblo (0)	2	0.01
Puget Sound Salish (0)	1	0.01
Shoshone (0)	1	0.01
Sioux (1)	7	0.05
Tlingit-Haida *(Alaska Native)* (1)	1	0.01
Yaqui (1)	3	0.02
Yuman (2)	2	0.01

*Notes: † The Census 2010 population figure is used to calculate the percentages in the Hispanic Origin and Race categories. Ancestry percentages are based on the 2006-2010 American Community Survey population (not shown); ‡ Numbers in parentheses indicate the number of people reporting a single ancestry; * Numbers in parentheses indicate the number of persons reporting this race alone, not in combination with any other race; Please refer to the Explanation of Data for more information.*

Yup'ik *(Alaska Native)* (0)	2	0.01
Asian (375)	770	5.01
Not Hispanic (358)	688	4.47
Hispanic (17)	82	0.53
Burmese (0)	1	0.01
Cambodian (13)	26	0.17
Chinese, ex. Taiwanese (57)	94	0.61
Filipino (159)	321	2.09
Hmong (1)	1	0.01
Indian (23)	32	0.21
Indonesian (1)	4	0.03
Japanese (39)	109	0.71
Korean (8)	35	0.23
Laotian (5)	5	0.03
Pakistani (3)	10	0.07
Taiwanese (1)	3	0.02
Thai (7)	10	0.07
Vietnamese (36)	49	0.32
Hawaii Native/Pacific Islander (89)	200	1.30
Not Hispanic (79)	153	0.99
Hispanic (10)	47	0.31
Guamanian/Chamorro (36)	55	0.36
Native Hawaiian (16)	48	0.31
Samoan (26)	33	0.21
Tongan (1)	5	0.03
White (10,891)	11,891	77.32
Not Hispanic (9,252)	9,889	64.30
Hispanic (1,639)	2,002	13.02

Brawley

Place Type: City
County: Imperial
Population: 24,953†

Ancestry‡	Population	%
African, Sub-Saharan (26)	26	0.11
African (26)	26	0.11
American (277)	277	1.14
Arab (11)	11	0.05
Other Arab (11)	11	0.05
Austrian (0)	34	0.14
British (11)	11	0.05
Czech (12)	12	0.05
Czechoslovakian (9)	9	0.04
Danish (0)	4	0.02
Dutch (6)	119	0.49
English (95)	506	2.08
European (29)	42	0.17
French, ex. Basque (50)	356	1.47
French Canadian (13)	13	0.05
German (209)	916	3.77
Irish (229)	754	3.10
Italian (72)	159	0.65
Luxemburger (0)	10	0.04
Norwegian (0)	18	0.07
Polish (29)	40	0.16
Portuguese (0)	29	0.12
Russian (0)	36	0.15
Scotch-Irish (49)	159	0.65
Scottish (84)	205	0.84
Swedish (4)	55	0.23
Swiss (40)	49	0.20
Ukrainian (14)	28	0.12
Welsh (0)	29	0.12
West Indian, ex. Hispanic (0)	17	0.07
Belizean (0)	17	0.07

Hispanic Origin	Population	%
Hispanic or Latino (of any race)	20,344	81.53
Central American, ex. Mexican	160	0.64
Guatemalan	19	0.08
Honduran	2	0.01
Nicaraguan	16	0.06
Panamanian	2	0.01
Salvadoran	121	0.48
Cuban	9	0.04
Dominican Republic	1	<0.01
Mexican	19,317	77.41
Puerto Rican	85	0.34
South American	24	0.10
Chilean	5	0.02
Colombian	1	<0.01
Ecuadorian	2	0.01
Peruvian	13	0.05
Venezuelan	3	0.01
Other Hispanic or Latino	748	3.00

Race*	Population	%
African-American/Black (510)	658	2.64
Not Hispanic (369)	424	1.70
Hispanic (141)	234	0.94
American Indian/Alaska Native (241)	412	1.65
Not Hispanic (86)	144	0.58
Hispanic (155)	268	1.07
Apache (3)	6	0.02
Blackfeet (4)	4	0.02
Canadian/French Am. Ind. (0)	2	0.01
Cherokee (6)	20	0.08
Chickasaw (1)	1	<0.01
Chippewa (3)	6	0.02
Choctaw (5)	10	0.04
Comanche (1)	1	<0.01
Creek (2)	2	0.01
Inupiat *(Alaska Native)* (1)	1	<0.01
Mexican American Ind. (36)	44	0.18
Navajo (11)	11	0.04
Osage (0)	1	<0.01
Shoshone (0)	3	0.01
Sioux (4)	8	0.03
Spanish American Ind. (0)	2	0.01
Tlingit-Haida *(Alaska Native)* (0)	1	<0.01
Yaqui (18)	25	0.10
Yuman (4)	4	0.02
Asian (349)	595	2.38
Not Hispanic (235)	306	1.23
Hispanic (114)	289	1.16
Cambodian (4)	6	0.02
Chinese, ex. Taiwanese (53)	81	0.32
Filipino (208)	352	1.41
Indian (37)	50	0.20
Japanese (8)	22	0.09
Korean (12)	26	0.10
Laotian (1)	4	0.02
Pakistani (8)	9	0.04
Taiwanese (1)	3	0.01
Thai (2)	6	0.02
Vietnamese (8)	22	0.09
Hawaii Native/Pacific Islander (32)	64	0.26
Not Hispanic (7)	19	0.08
Hispanic (25)	45	0.18
Guamanian/Chamorro (13)	13	0.05
Native Hawaiian (4)	16	0.06
Samoan (9)	11	0.04
White (13,570)	14,340	57.47
Not Hispanic (3,724)	3,866	15.49
Hispanic (9,846)	10,474	41.97

Brea

Place Type: City
County: Orange
Population: 39,282†

Ancestry‡	Population	%
American (1,297)	1,297	3.38
Arab (175)	183	0.48
Arab (20)	20	0.05
Egyptian (73)	73	0.19
Lebanese (9)	17	0.04
Syrian (40)	40	0.10
Other Arab (33)	33	0.09
Armenian (82)	102	0.27
Assyrian/Chaldean/Syriac (13)	13	0.03
Austrian (35)	72	0.19
Basque (7)	21	0.05
Belgian (30)	30	0.08
Brazilian (0)	11	0.03
British (207)	262	0.68
Canadian (74)	225	0.59
Celtic (35)	78	0.20
Croatian (9)	59	0.15
Czech (0)	74	0.19
Czechoslovakian (13)	21	0.05
Danish (98)	189	0.49
Dutch (151)	537	1.40
Eastern European (26)	26	0.07
English (1,638)	4,442	11.56
Estonian (12)	12	0.03
European (418)	459	1.19
Finnish (0)	13	0.03
French, ex. Basque (120)	1,009	2.63
French Canadian (53)	133	0.35
German (1,646)	6,117	15.92
Greek (118)	208	0.54
Hungarian (20)	89	0.23
Icelander (0)	13	0.03
Iranian (128)	128	0.33
Irish (672)	4,102	10.67
Israeli (54)	54	0.14
Italian (1,114)	2,479	6.45
Lithuanian (11)	68	0.18
New Zealander (9)	9	0.02
Northern European (242)	267	0.69
Norwegian (241)	738	1.92
Pennsylvania German (0)	44	0.11
Polish (238)	843	2.19
Portuguese (19)	66	0.17
Romanian (61)	100	0.26
Russian (161)	413	1.07
Scandinavian (0)	46	0.12
Scotch-Irish (273)	852	2.22
Scottish (144)	828	2.15
Serbian (0)	10	0.03
Slavic (15)	49	0.13
Slovak (7)	16	0.04
Swedish (273)	665	1.73
Swiss (22)	73	0.19
Turkish (44)	64	0.17
Ukrainian (35)	121	0.31
Welsh (23)	251	0.65
West Indian, ex. Hispanic (48)	121	0.31
Haitian (17)	60	0.16
Jamaican (17)	32	0.08
Trinidadian/Tobagonian (14)	29	0.08
Yugoslavian (4)	23	0.06

Hispanic Origin	Population	%
Hispanic or Latino (of any race)	9,817	24.99
Central American, ex. Mexican	370	0.94
Costa Rican	27	0.07
Guatemalan	105	0.27
Honduran	32	0.08
Nicaraguan	49	0.12
Panamanian	9	0.02
Salvadoran	146	0.37
Other Central American	2	0.01
Cuban	139	0.35
Dominican Republic	8	0.02
Mexican	8,000	20.37
Puerto Rican	190	0.48
South American	444	1.13
Argentinean	88	0.22
Bolivian	14	0.04
Chilean	20	0.05
Colombian	95	0.24
Ecuadorian	46	0.12
Peruvian	150	0.38
Uruguayan	8	0.02
Venezuelan	14	0.04
Other South American	9	0.02
Other Hispanic or Latino	666	1.70

Race*	Population	%
African-American/Black (549)	784	2.00
Not Hispanic (499)	671	1.71
Hispanic (50)	113	0.29
American Indian/Alaska Native (190)	467	1.19
Not Hispanic (90)	259	0.66
Hispanic (100)	208	0.53

*Notes: † The Census 2010 population figure is used to calculate the percentages in the Hispanic Origin and Race categories. Ancestry percentages are based on the 2006-2010 American Community Survey population (not shown); ‡ Numbers in parentheses indicate the number of people reporting a single ancestry; * Numbers in parentheses indicate the number of persons reporting this race alone, not in combination with any other race; Please refer to the Explanation of Data for more information.*

SECTION TWO

Apache (5)	15	0.04
Blackfeet (2)	9	0.02
Canadian/French Am. Ind. (0)	2	0.01
Cherokee (16)	81	0.21
Chickasaw (9)	16	0.04
Chippewa (1)	3	0.01
Choctaw (8)	33	0.08
Colville (4)	4	0.01
Cree (0)	1	<0.01
Creek (2)	12	0.03
Delaware (2)	5	0.01
Hopi (2)	3	0.01
Iroquois (2)	5	0.01
Lumbee (0)	2	0.01
Mexican American Ind. (18)	24	0.06
Navajo (6)	20	0.05
Osage (1)	5	0.01
Potawatomi (6)	6	0.02
Pueblo (1)	3	0.01
Seminole (0)	1	<0.01
Shoshone (0)	1	<0.01
Sioux (1)	11	0.03
South American Ind. (6)	7	0.02
Ute (0)	1	<0.01
Yaqui (4)	8	0.02
Asian (7,144)	7,966	20.28
Not Hispanic (7,068)	7,719	19.65
Hispanic (76)	247	0.63
Bangladeshi (4)	4	0.01
Burmese (3)	8	0.02
Cambodian (50)	57	0.15
Chinese, ex. Taiwanese (1,104)	1,372	3.49
Filipino (1,031)	1,310	3.33
Hmong (1)	1	<0.01
Indian (801)	861	2.19
Indonesian (40)	65	0.17
Japanese (423)	708	1.80
Korean (2,592)	2,676	6.81
Laotian (25)	31	0.08
Malaysian (6)	11	0.03
Pakistani (125)	146	0.37
Sri Lankan (28)	30	0.08
Taiwanese (248)	281	0.72
Thai (33)	60	0.15
Vietnamese (373)	445	1.13
Hawaii Native/Pacific Islander (69)	213	0.54
Not Hispanic (62)	178	0.45
Hispanic (7)	35	0.09
Guamanian/Chamorro (10)	23	0.06
Native Hawaiian (22)	84	0.21
Samoan (11)	34	0.09
Tongan (5)	7	0.02
White (26,363)	27,858	70.92
Not Hispanic (20,690)	21,538	54.83
Hispanic (5,673)	6,320	16.09

Brentwood

Place Type: City
County: Contra Costa
Population: 51,481†

Ancestry‡	Population	%
Afghan (200)	200	0.43
African, Sub-Saharan (137)	174	0.38
African (28)	35	0.08
Nigerian (109)	109	0.24
Somalian (0)	30	0.06
American (984)	984	2.13
Arab (223)	336	0.73
Arab (53)	164	0.35
Egyptian (76)	78	0.17
Lebanese (14)	14	0.03
Palestinian (80)	80	0.17
Armenian (11)	93	0.20
Australian (13)	13	0.03
Austrian (15)	175	0.38
Brazilian (17)	17	0.04
British (68)	213	0.46
Canadian (29)	87	0.19
Celtic (0)	12	0.03
Croatian (24)	133	0.29
Czech (0)	76	0.16
Czechoslovakian (2)	19	0.04
Danish (62)	365	0.79
Dutch (204)	747	1.61
Eastern European (11)	11	0.02
English (975)	4,704	10.16
European (719)	913	1.97
Finnish (22)	87	0.19
French, ex. Basque (54)	1,423	3.07
French Canadian (181)	283	0.61
German (1,388)	6,490	14.02
Greek (15)	133	0.29
Hungarian (53)	89	0.19
Iranian (116)	116	0.25
Irish (1,189)	5,755	12.43
Italian (1,248)	3,962	8.56
Latvian (0)	25	0.05
Lithuanian (0)	39	0.08
Luxemburger (0)	11	0.02
Northern European (38)	38	0.08
Norwegian (184)	863	1.86
Polish (145)	965	2.08
Portuguese (897)	2,149	4.64
Romanian (0)	61	0.13
Russian (72)	427	0.92
Scandinavian (124)	287	0.62
Scotch-Irish (170)	439	0.95
Scottish (223)	803	1.73
Serbian (22)	66	0.14
Slavic (14)	41	0.09
Slovak (13)	22	0.05
Slovene (0)	30	0.06
Swedish (271)	1,111	2.40
Swiss (37)	240	0.52
Ukrainian (72)	85	0.18
Welsh (38)	268	0.58
West Indian, ex. Hispanic (141)	193	0.42
Belizean (0)	34	0.07
Jamaican (141)	159	0.34
Yugoslavian (14)	14	0.03

Hispanic Origin	Population	%
Hispanic or Latino (of any race)	13,779	26.77
Central American, ex. Mexican	934	1.81
Costa Rican	17	0.03
Guatemalan	183	0.36
Honduran	34	0.07
Nicaraguan	233	0.45
Panamanian	29	0.06
Salvadoran	438	0.85
Cuban	82	0.16
Dominican Republic	10	0.02
Mexican	10,521	20.44
Puerto Rican	618	1.20
South American	348	0.68
Argentinean	50	0.10
Bolivian	32	0.06
Chilean	48	0.09
Colombian	46	0.09
Ecuadorian	30	0.06
Peruvian	112	0.22
Uruguayan	6	0.01
Venezuelan	15	0.03
Other South American	9	0.02
Other Hispanic or Latino	1,266	2.46

Race*	Population	%
African-American/Black (3,389)	4,184	8.13
Not Hispanic (3,197)	3,825	7.43
Hispanic (192)	359	0.70
American Indian/Alaska Native (333)	992	1.93
Not Hispanic (178)	633	1.23
Hispanic (155)	359	0.70
Apache (5)	28	0.05
Blackfeet (2)	34	0.07
Canadian/French Am. Ind. (0)	1	<0.01
Central American Ind. (3)	5	0.01
Cherokee (35)	192	0.37
Chickasaw (1)	13	0.03
Chippewa (13)	22	0.04
Choctaw (16)	67	0.13
Colville (0)	2	<0.01
Comanche (3)	9	0.02
Cree (0)	1	<0.01
Creek (1)	18	0.03
Crow (0)	7	0.01
Delaware (0)	2	<0.01
Hopi (0)	5	0.01
Iroquois (0)	10	0.02
Kiowa (0)	8	0.02
Lumbee (1)	1	<0.01
Mexican American Ind. (14)	37	0.07
Navajo (12)	34	0.07
Osage (0)	2	<0.01
Paiute (1)	2	<0.01
Pima (1)	1	<0.01
Potawatomi (2)	2	<0.01
Pueblo (2)	11	0.02
Puget Sound Salish (5)	8	0.02
Seminole (1)	7	0.01
Shoshone (2)	6	0.01
Sioux (6)	19	0.04
South American Ind. (1)	1	<0.01
Spanish American Ind. (4)	6	0.01
Tohono O'Odham (1)	1	<0.01
Ute (1)	4	0.01
Yaqui (5)	9	0.02
Asian (4,051)	5,630	10.94
Not Hispanic (3,903)	5,151	10.01
Hispanic (148)	479	0.93
Bangladeshi (12)	15	0.03
Burmese (13)	15	0.03
Cambodian (29)	38	0.07
Chinese, ex. Taiwanese (459)	740	1.44
Filipino (2,159)	2,958	5.75
Hmong (11)	11	0.02
Indian (441)	530	1.03
Indonesian (24)	46	0.09
Japanese (141)	434	0.84
Korean (166)	231	0.45
Laotian (18)	38	0.07
Malaysian (2)	2	<0.01
Nepalese (2)	2	<0.01
Pakistani (82)	87	0.17
Sri Lankan (3)	3	0.01
Taiwanese (33)	36	0.07
Thai (17)	45	0.09
Vietnamese (224)	303	0.59
Hawaii Native/Pacific Islander (202)	560	1.09
Not Hispanic (170)	461	0.90
Hispanic (32)	99	0.19
Fijian (20)	40	0.08
Guamanian/Chamorro (54)	119	0.23
Native Hawaiian (45)	238	0.46
Samoan (28)	70	0.14
Tongan (16)	26	0.05
White (34,969)	38,011	73.84
Not Hispanic (27,944)	29,819	57.92
Hispanic (7,025)	8,192	15.91

Buena Park

Place Type: City
County: Orange
Population: 80,530†

Ancestry‡	Population	%
Afghan (89)	89	0.11
African, Sub-Saharan (39)	39	0.05
African (39)	39	0.05
American (1,428)	1,428	1.79
Arab (344)	464	0.58
Arab (113)	113	0.14
Egyptian (40)	40	0.05
Jordanian (121)	142	0.18
Lebanese (17)	52	0.07
Moroccan (27)	27	0.03
Syrian (0)	43	0.05

*Notes: † The Census 2010 population figure is used to calculate the percentages in the Hispanic Origin and Race categories. Ancestry percentages are based on the 2006-2010 American Community Survey population (not shown); ‡ Numbers in parentheses indicate the number of people reporting a single ancestry; * Numbers in parentheses indicate the number of persons reporting this race alone, not in combination with any other race; Please refer to the Explanation of Data for more information.*

Other Arab (26)	47	0.06
Armenian (0)	27	0.03
Austrian (45)	78	0.10
Belgian (7)	44	0.06
Brazilian (70)	70	0.09
British (116)	176	0.22
Canadian (82)	102	0.13
Celtic (0)	26	0.03
Czech (10)	32	0.04
Czechoslovakian (36)	45	0.06
Danish (59)	186	0.23
Dutch (259)	900	1.13
Eastern European (17)	17	0.02
English (960)	3,677	4.61
European (318)	318	0.40
Finnish (17)	71	0.09
French, ex. Basque (177)	1,236	1.55
French Canadian (78)	225	0.28
German (1,743)	6,207	7.78
Greek (152)	270	0.34
Hungarian (111)	336	0.42
Icelander (9)	19	0.02
Iranian (160)	178	0.22
Irish (1,232)	5,376	6.74
Italian (973)	2,728	3.42
Lithuanian (0)	9	0.01
Norwegian (223)	642	0.81
Polish (317)	1,005	1.26
Portuguese (154)	439	0.55
Romanian (274)	274	0.34
Russian (121)	260	0.33
Scandinavian (125)	219	0.27
Scotch-Irish (182)	702	0.88
Scottish (198)	737	0.92
Serbian (33)	146	0.18
Slovak (0)	120	0.15
Swedish (167)	715	0.90
Swiss (16)	25	0.03
Ukrainian (56)	91	0.11
Welsh (0)	312	0.39
West Indian, ex. Hispanic (38)	46	0.06
British West Indian (4)	4	0.01
Jamaican (34)	42	0.05
Yugoslavian (0)	108	0.14

Hispanic Origin	Population	%
Hispanic or Latino (of any race)	31,638	39.29
Central American, ex. Mexican	1,700	2.11
Costa Rican	47	0.06
Guatemalan	592	0.74
Honduran	119	0.15
Nicaraguan	206	0.26
Panamanian	22	0.03
Salvadoran	679	0.84
Other Central American	35	0.04
Cuban	261	0.32
Dominican Republic	20	0.02
Mexican	26,549	32.97
Puerto Rican	422	0.52
South American	930	1.15
Argentinean	112	0.14
Bolivian	22	0.03
Chilean	40	0.05
Colombian	209	0.26
Ecuadorian	146	0.18
Paraguayan	6	0.01
Peruvian	374	0.46
Uruguayan	1	<0.01
Venezuelan	15	0.02
Other South American	5	0.01
Other Hispanic or Latino	1,756	2.18

Race*	Population	%
African-American/Black (3,073)	3,761	4.67
Not Hispanic (2,809)	3,239	4.02
Hispanic (264)	522	0.65
American Indian/Alaska Native (862)	1,602	1.99
Not Hispanic (188)	473	0.59
Hispanic (674)	1,129	1.40
Aleut *(Alaska Native)* (0)	1	<0.01
Apache (28)	67	0.08
Blackfeet (5)	29	0.04
Canadian/French Am. Ind. (1)	2	<0.01
Central American Ind. (2)	3	<0.01
Cherokee (33)	143	0.18
Chickasaw (0)	8	0.01
Chippewa (4)	10	0.01
Choctaw (11)	25	0.03
Comanche (1)	6	0.01
Creek (6)	8	0.01
Hopi (5)	12	0.01
Iroquois (4)	6	0.01
Menominee (1)	1	<0.01
Mexican American Ind. (93)	142	0.18
Navajo (15)	44	0.05
Osage (0)	1	<0.01
Pima (2)	2	<0.01
Potawatomi (4)	6	0.01
Pueblo (3)	11	0.01
Shoshone (7)	10	0.01
Sioux (8)	20	0.02
South American Ind. (0)	2	<0.01
Spanish American Ind. (2)	2	<0.01
Tlingit-Haida *(Alaska Native)* (7)	7	0.01
Tohono O'Odham (3)	6	0.01
Ute (1)	8	0.01
Yaqui (10)	28	0.03
Yuman (4)	6	0.01
Asian (21,488)	23,063	28.64
Not Hispanic (21,232)	22,417	27.84
Hispanic (256)	646	0.80
Bangladeshi (32)	32	0.04
Burmese (47)	52	0.06
Cambodian (227)	282	0.35
Chinese, ex. Taiwanese (1,179)	1,538	1.91
Filipino (6,767)	7,506	9.32
Hmong (26)	27	0.03
Indian (2,054)	2,247	2.79
Indonesian (60)	123	0.15
Japanese (636)	996	1.24
Korean (7,806)	8,001	9.94
Laotian (92)	97	0.12
Malaysian (3)	3	<0.01
Nepalese (16)	16	0.02
Pakistani (169)	197	0.24
Sri Lankan (43)	45	0.06
Taiwanese (296)	332	0.41
Thai (255)	288	0.36
Vietnamese (1,317)	1,479	1.84
Hawaii Native/Pacific Islander (455)	814	1.01
Not Hispanic (389)	653	0.81
Hispanic (66)	161	0.20
Fijian (44)	50	0.06
Guamanian/Chamorro (80)	118	0.15
Native Hawaiian (62)	182	0.23
Samoan (173)	241	0.30
Tongan (43)	59	0.07
White (36,454)	39,761	49.37
Not Hispanic (22,302)	23,728	29.46
Hispanic (14,152)	16,033	19.91

Burbank

Place Type: City
County: Los Angeles
Population: 103,340†

Ancestry‡	Population	%
African, Sub-Saharan (60)	102	0.10
African (60)	82	0.08
South African (0)	20	0.02
Albanian (12)	30	0.03
American (2,962)	2,962	2.88
Arab (1,402)	1,768	1.72
Arab (334)	383	0.37
Egyptian (157)	244	0.24
Jordanian (47)	47	0.05
Lebanese (333)	470	0.46
Palestinian (28)	70	0.07
Syrian (373)	409	0.40
Other Arab (130)	145	0.14
Armenian (11,652)	12,490	12.16
Assyrian/Chaldean/Syriac (49)	74	0.07
Australian (9)	20	0.02
Austrian (115)	450	0.44
Basque (0)	12	0.01
Belgian (93)	176	0.17
Brazilian (34)	49	0.05
British (199)	465	0.45
Bulgarian (84)	84	0.08
Canadian (173)	292	0.28
Croatian (49)	110	0.11
Czech (95)	271	0.26
Czechoslovakian (93)	156	0.15
Danish (162)	591	0.58
Dutch (72)	1,006	0.98
Eastern European (58)	80	0.08
English (1,652)	6,949	6.76
European (1,096)	1,652	1.61
Finnish (61)	223	0.22
French, ex. Basque (331)	2,066	2.01
French Canadian (116)	424	0.41
German (2,257)	9,613	9.36
Greek (412)	766	0.75
Guyanese (8)	8	0.01
Hungarian (225)	523	0.51
Icelander (0)	12	0.01
Iranian (915)	1,583	1.54
Irish (1,958)	8,539	8.31
Israeli (18)	39	0.04
Italian (3,124)	6,982	6.80
Latvian (15)	15	0.01
Lithuanian (89)	231	0.22
Luxemburger (0)	30	0.03
Macedonian (34)	47	0.05
New Zealander (24)	24	0.02
Northern European (220)	220	0.21
Norwegian (332)	891	0.87
Pennsylvania German (7)	25	0.02
Polish (401)	1,721	1.68
Portuguese (133)	376	0.37
Romanian (83)	222	0.22
Russian (461)	1,617	1.57
Scandinavian (70)	148	0.14
Scotch-Irish (607)	1,680	1.64
Scottish (710)	2,020	1.97
Serbian (198)	198	0.19
Slovak (82)	136	0.13
Slovene (13)	55	0.05
Swedish (356)	1,536	1.50
Swiss (69)	339	0.33
Turkish (114)	161	0.16
Ukrainian (151)	288	0.28
Welsh (147)	631	0.61
West Indian, ex. Hispanic (145)	280	0.27
Barbadian (13)	13	0.01
Haitian (10)	80	0.08
Jamaican (122)	179	0.17
West Indian (0)	8	0.01
Yugoslavian (15)	73	0.07

Hispanic Origin	Population	%
Hispanic or Latino (of any race)	25,310	24.49
Central American, ex. Mexican	4,331	4.19
Costa Rican	199	0.19
Guatemalan	1,238	1.20
Honduran	165	0.16
Nicaraguan	406	0.39
Panamanian	66	0.06
Salvadoran	2,231	2.16
Other Central American	26	0.03
Cuban	1,087	1.05
Dominican Republic	62	0.06
Mexican	14,706	14.23
Puerto Rican	601	0.58
South American	2,548	2.47
Argentinean	406	0.39
Bolivian	208	0.20
Chilean	165	0.16
Colombian	677	0.66

*Notes: † The Census 2010 population figure is used to calculate the percentages in the Hispanic Origin and Race categories. Ancestry percentages are based on the 2006-2010 American Community Survey population (not shown); ‡ Numbers in parentheses indicate the number of people reporting a single ancestry; * Numbers in parentheses indicate the number of persons reporting this race alone, not in combination with any other race; Please refer to the Explanation of Data for more information.*

Ecuadorian	376	0.36
Paraguayan	7	0.01
Peruvian	589	0.57
Uruguayan	24	0.02
Venezuelan	65	0.06
Other South American	31	0.03
Other Hispanic or Latino	1,975	1.91

Race*	Population	%
African-American/Black (2,600)	3,478	3.37
Not Hispanic (2,443)	3,098	3.00
Hispanic (157)	380	0.37
American Indian/Alaska Native (486)	1,210	1.17
Not Hispanic (196)	609	0.59
Hispanic (290)	601	0.58
Aleut *(Alaska Native)* (1)	1	<0.01
Apache (25)	47	0.05
Arapaho (2)	2	<0.01
Blackfeet (1)	13	0.01
Canadian/French Am. Ind. (0)	1	<0.01
Central American Ind. (1)	5	<0.01
Cherokee (21)	171	0.17
Chickasaw (1)	11	0.01
Chippewa (9)	15	0.01
Choctaw (11)	46	0.04
Comanche (1)	5	<0.01
Cree (0)	3	<0.01
Creek (7)	19	0.02
Crow (6)	11	0.01
Delaware (2)	2	<0.01
Hopi (4)	6	0.01
Inupiat *(Alaska Native)* (1)	1	<0.01
Iroquois (7)	20	0.02
Kiowa (0)	1	<0.01
Lumbee (1)	1	<0.01
Mexican American Ind. (81)	130	0.13
Navajo (25)	35	0.03
Osage (3)	7	0.01
Paiute (2)	8	0.01
Pima (1)	1	<0.01
Potawatomi (2)	15	0.01
Pueblo (9)	15	0.01
Puget Sound Salish (2)	3	<0.01
Seminole (1)	9	0.01
Shoshone (1)	1	<0.01
Sioux (6)	40	0.04
South American Ind. (12)	23	0.02
Spanish American Ind. (2)	3	<0.01
Tlingit-Haida *(Alaska Native)* (0)	1	<0.01
Tohono O'Odham (5)	7	0.01
Ute (2)	4	<0.01
Yaqui (5)	13	0.01
Yuman (0)	2	<0.01
Yup'ik *(Alaska Native)* (0)	1	<0.01
Asian (12,007)	14,398	13.93
Not Hispanic (11,753)	13,797	13.35
Hispanic (254)	601	0.58
Bangladeshi (15)	17	0.02
Burmese (0)	4	<0.01
Cambodian (30)	55	0.05
Chinese, ex. Taiwanese (1,029)	1,520	1.47
Filipino (4,835)	5,612	5.43
Hmong (0)	1	<0.01
Indian (1,502)	1,643	1.59
Indonesian (37)	72	0.07
Japanese (716)	1,102	1.07
Korean (2,140)	2,324	2.25
Laotian (5)	11	0.01
Malaysian (5)	14	0.01
Nepalese (10)	10	0.01
Pakistani (35)	41	0.04
Sri Lankan (62)	82	0.08
Taiwanese (55)	74	0.07
Thai (470)	538	0.52
Vietnamese (673)	763	0.74
Hawaii Native/Pacific Islander (89)	405	0.39
Not Hispanic (76)	332	0.32
Hispanic (13)	73	0.07
Fijian (4)	6	0.01
Guamanian/Chamorro (13)	46	0.04
Native Hawaiian (28)	150	0.15
Samoan (14)	29	0.03
Tongan (0)	1	<0.01
White (75,167)	79,609	77.04
Not Hispanic (60,265)	63,038	61.00
Hispanic (14,902)	16,571	16.04

Burlingame

Place Type: City
County: San Mateo
Population: 28,806†

Ancestry‡	Population	%
African, Sub-Saharan (80)	102	0.36
African (9)	9	0.03
Kenyan (0)	22	0.08
Liberian (62)	62	0.22
South African (9)	9	0.03
American (600)	600	2.13
Arab (251)	418	1.48
Arab (32)	32	0.11
Egyptian (8)	8	0.03
Iraqi (24)	24	0.09
Lebanese (53)	80	0.28
Moroccan (0)	11	0.04
Syrian (10)	10	0.04
Other Arab (124)	253	0.90
Armenian (217)	286	1.01
Assyrian/Chaldean/Syriac (11)	44	0.16
Australian (25)	38	0.13
Austrian (0)	125	0.44
Basque (44)	73	0.26
Belgian (0)	17	0.06
Brazilian (323)	381	1.35
British (133)	143	0.51
Bulgarian (0)	12	0.04
Canadian (48)	85	0.30
Celtic (11)	11	0.04
Croatian (76)	193	0.68
Cypriot (0)	9	0.03
Czech (38)	134	0.48
Czechoslovakian (48)	83	0.29
Danish (20)	127	0.45
Dutch (36)	396	1.40
Eastern European (157)	204	0.72
English (534)	2,380	8.44
Estonian (10)	30	0.11
European (663)	768	2.72
Finnish (22)	73	0.26
French, ex. Basque (229)	918	3.25
French Canadian (0)	75	0.27
German (949)	3,724	13.20
Greek (37)	229	0.81
Hungarian (52)	136	0.48
Icelander (0)	54	0.19
Iranian (266)	313	1.11
Irish (1,128)	4,041	14.33
Italian (1,097)	3,245	11.51
Latvian (0)	33	0.12
Lithuanian (10)	116	0.41
Maltese (35)	35	0.12
Northern European (134)	134	0.48
Norwegian (96)	455	1.61
Polish (131)	597	2.12
Portuguese (105)	208	0.74
Romanian (0)	56	0.20
Russian (272)	563	2.00
Scandinavian (40)	68	0.24
Scotch-Irish (156)	416	1.47
Scottish (200)	585	2.07
Serbian (33)	51	0.18
Slovak (0)	23	0.08
Swedish (62)	445	1.58
Swiss (48)	209	0.74
Turkish (41)	181	0.64
Ukrainian (116)	176	0.62
Welsh (13)	59	0.21
Yugoslavian (51)	108	0.38

Hispanic Origin	Population	%
Hispanic or Latino (of any race)	3,966	13.77
Central American, ex. Mexican	885	3.07
Costa Rican	18	0.06
Guatemalan	142	0.49
Honduran	53	0.18
Nicaraguan	184	0.64
Panamanian	22	0.08
Salvadoran	459	1.59
Other Central American	7	0.02
Cuban	44	0.15
Dominican Republic	2	0.01
Mexican	1,721	5.97
Puerto Rican	134	0.47
South American	630	2.19
Argentinean	100	0.35
Bolivian	19	0.07
Chilean	58	0.20
Colombian	96	0.33
Ecuadorian	37	0.13
Paraguayan	5	0.02
Peruvian	274	0.95
Uruguayan	5	0.02
Venezuelan	20	0.07
Other South American	16	0.06
Other Hispanic or Latino	550	1.91

Race*	Population	%
African-American/Black (360)	543	1.89
Not Hispanic (327)	472	1.64
Hispanic (33)	71	0.25
American Indian/Alaska Native (74)	219	0.76
Not Hispanic (34)	106	0.37
Hispanic (40)	113	0.39
Apache (2)	7	0.02
Blackfeet (0)	8	0.03
Cherokee (6)	28	0.10
Chickasaw (0)	1	<0.01
Chippewa (1)	5	0.02
Choctaw (3)	10	0.03
Delaware (0)	1	<0.01
Iroquois (1)	2	0.01
Mexican American Ind. (9)	10	0.03
Navajo (0)	2	0.01
Paiute (1)	2	0.01
Pueblo (2)	5	0.02
Seminole (0)	1	<0.01
Shoshone (1)	1	<0.01
Sioux (0)	1	<0.01
South American Ind. (0)	4	0.01
Tlingit-Haida *(Alaska Native)* (1)	1	<0.01
Yaqui (5)	8	0.03
Asian (5,841)	6,759	23.46
Not Hispanic (5,773)	6,556	22.76
Hispanic (68)	203	0.70
Bangladeshi (4)	4	0.01
Burmese (9)	13	0.05
Cambodian (13)	21	0.07
Chinese, ex. Taiwanese (2,692)	3,126	10.85
Filipino (1,167)	1,515	5.26
Hmong (3)	6	0.02
Indian (486)	580	2.01
Indonesian (24)	34	0.12
Japanese (471)	675	2.34
Korean (375)	474	1.65
Laotian (10)	12	0.04
Malaysian (4)	5	0.02
Nepalese (9)	9	0.03
Pakistani (17)	29	0.10
Sri Lankan (1)	1	<0.01
Taiwanese (171)	198	0.69
Thai (30)	50	0.17
Vietnamese (91)	155	0.54
Hawaii Native/Pacific Islander (139)	242	0.84
Not Hispanic (129)	210	0.73
Hispanic (10)	32	0.11
Fijian (25)	27	0.09
Guamanian/Chamorro (7)	10	0.03
Native Hawaiian (29)	82	0.28
Samoan (17)	36	0.12

*Notes: † The Census 2010 population figure is used to calculate the percentages in the Hispanic Origin and Race categories. Ancestry percentages are based on the 2006-2010 American Community Survey population (not shown); ‡ Numbers in parentheses indicate the number of people reporting a single ancestry; * Numbers in parentheses indicate the number of persons reporting this race alone, not in combination with any other race; Please refer to the Explanation of Data for more information.*

	Population	%
Tongan (42)	50	0.17
White (19,510)	20,778	72.13
Not Hispanic (17,434)	18,321	63.60
Hispanic (2,076)	2,457	8.53

Calabasas

Place Type: City
County: Los Angeles
Population: 23,058†

Ancestry‡	Population	%
African, Sub-Saharan (16)	16	0.07
South African (16)	16	0.07
American (1,355)	1,355	5.97
Arab (436)	581	2.56
Arab (9)	9	0.04
Egyptian (71)	81	0.36
Iraqi (179)	179	0.79
Lebanese (16)	74	0.33
Moroccan (38)	38	0.17
Syrian (9)	48	0.21
Other Arab (114)	152	0.67
Armenian (13)	115	0.51
Australian (0)	16	0.07
Austrian (56)	304	1.34
Basque (13)	13	0.06
Belgian (36)	44	0.19
Brazilian (25)	54	0.24
British (93)	198	0.87
Bulgarian (12)	12	0.05
Canadian (96)	151	0.67
Celtic (12)	12	0.05
Croatian (45)	55	0.24
Czech (22)	70	0.31
Czechoslovakian (21)	43	0.19
Danish (67)	124	0.55
Dutch (85)	244	1.08
Eastern European (408)	416	1.83
English (745)	1,800	7.93
Estonian (0)	9	0.04
European (599)	643	2.83
Finnish (0)	10	0.04
French, ex. Basque (46)	404	1.78
German (575)	1,978	8.72
Greek (103)	141	0.62
Hungarian (139)	349	1.54
Iranian (1,690)	1,747	7.70
Irish (622)	1,709	7.53
Israeli (280)	443	1.95
Italian (450)	1,363	6.01
Latvian (0)	14	0.06
Lithuanian (14)	47	0.21
Norwegian (35)	175	0.77
Pennsylvania German (9)	9	0.04
Polish (366)	1,389	6.12
Portuguese (0)	11	0.05
Romanian (26)	197	0.87
Russian (1,357)	2,509	11.06
Scotch-Irish (251)	434	1.91
Scottish (110)	330	1.45
Serbian (67)	67	0.30
Slovak (0)	13	0.06
Swedish (63)	227	1.00
Swiss (0)	64	0.28
Turkish (19)	119	0.52
Ukrainian (136)	188	0.83
Welsh (33)	169	0.74
Yugoslavian (33)	79	0.35

Hispanic Origin	Population	%
Hispanic or Latino (of any race)	1,481	6.42
Central American, ex. Mexican	162	0.70
Costa Rican	15	0.07
Guatemalan	36	0.16
Honduran	6	0.03
Nicaraguan	23	0.10
Panamanian	16	0.07
Salvadoran	65	0.28
Other Central American	1	<0.01
Cuban	59	0.26
Dominican Republic	9	0.04
Mexican	764	3.31
Puerto Rican	94	0.41
South American	225	0.98
Argentinean	64	0.28
Bolivian	5	0.02
Chilean	11	0.05
Colombian	59	0.26
Ecuadorian	9	0.04
Paraguayan	2	0.01
Peruvian	50	0.22
Uruguayan	10	0.04
Venezuelan	13	0.06
Other South American	2	0.01
Other Hispanic or Latino	168	0.73

Race*	Population	%
African-American/Black (375)	507	2.20
Not Hispanic (356)	470	2.04
Hispanic (19)	37	0.16
American Indian/Alaska Native (48)	129	0.56
Not Hispanic (30)	98	0.43
Hispanic (18)	31	0.13
Apache (2)	7	0.03
Blackfeet (2)	2	0.01
Canadian/French Am. Ind. (3)	3	0.01
Cherokee (7)	19	0.08
Chickasaw (0)	1	<0.01
Choctaw (3)	5	0.02
Creek (5)	5	0.02
Hopi (1)	4	0.02
Mexican American Ind. (6)	10	0.04
Navajo (2)	6	0.03
Osage (0)	3	0.01
Seminole (1)	1	<0.01
Sioux (0)	1	<0.01
South American Ind. (1)	2	0.01
Ute (2)	2	0.01
Yakama (1)	1	<0.01
Asian (1,993)	2,654	11.51
Not Hispanic (1,977)	2,611	11.32
Hispanic (16)	43	0.19
Bangladeshi (12)	13	0.06
Burmese (2)	5	0.02
Cambodian (2)	3	0.01
Chinese, ex. Taiwanese (490)	646	2.80
Filipino (203)	315	1.37
Indian (457)	514	2.23
Indonesian (22)	37	0.16
Japanese (160)	257	1.11
Korean (411)	476	2.06
Malaysian (1)	2	0.01
Pakistani (19)	20	0.09
Sri Lankan (13)	16	0.07
Taiwanese (34)	36	0.16
Thai (16)	20	0.09
Vietnamese (74)	92	0.40
Hawaii Native/Pacific Islander (8)	36	0.16
Not Hispanic (6)	29	0.13
Hispanic (2)	7	0.03
Guamanian/Chamorro (1)	7	0.03
Native Hawaiian (5)	23	0.10
Samoan (1)	1	<0.01
White (19,341)	20,207	87.64
Not Hispanic (18,332)	19,102	82.84
Hispanic (1,009)	1,105	4.79

Calexico

Place Type: City
County: Imperial
Population: 38,572†

Ancestry‡	Population	%
American (69)	69	0.19
Arab (382)	394	1.09
Arab (17)	17	0.05
Egyptian (0)	12	0.03
Other Arab (365)	365	1.01
British (11)	11	0.03
Dutch (13)	35	0.10
Eastern European (9)	18	0.05
English (0)	8	0.02
European (0)	9	0.02
French, ex. Basque (0)	10	0.03
German (16)	109	0.30
Greek (0)	10	0.03
Hungarian (0)	26	0.07
Irish (20)	100	0.28
Italian (23)	174	0.48
Northern European (78)	78	0.21
Scotch-Irish (0)	10	0.03
Swedish (0)	9	0.02

Hispanic Origin	Population	%
Hispanic or Latino (of any race)	37,354	96.84
Central American, ex. Mexican	68	0.18
Costa Rican	3	0.01
Guatemalan	11	0.03
Honduran	3	0.01
Nicaraguan	15	0.04
Panamanian	2	0.01
Salvadoran	32	0.08
Other Central American	2	0.01
Cuban	22	0.06
Mexican	36,443	94.48
Puerto Rican	39	0.10
South American	41	0.11
Argentinean	2	0.01
Bolivian	1	<0.01
Chilean	20	0.05
Colombian	9	0.02
Ecuadorian	2	0.01
Peruvian	4	0.01
Venezuelan	3	0.01
Other Hispanic or Latino	741	1.92

Race*	Population	%
African-American/Black (134)	215	0.56
Not Hispanic (50)	54	0.14
Hispanic (84)	161	0.42
American Indian/Alaska Native (204)	303	0.79
Not Hispanic (26)	30	0.08
Hispanic (178)	273	0.71
Apache (1)	1	<0.01
Arapaho (5)	6	0.02
Cherokee (1)	2	0.01
Cheyenne (3)	3	0.01
Chickasaw (2)	2	0.01
Iroquois (1)	1	<0.01
Mexican American Ind. (38)	61	0.16
Navajo (2)	5	0.01
Pima (2)	2	0.01
Spanish American Ind. (2)	13	0.03
Tohono O'Odham (4)	4	0.01
Yaqui (36)	39	0.10
Yuman (7)	10	0.03
Asian (504)	710	1.84
Not Hispanic (416)	442	1.15
Hispanic (88)	268	0.69
Cambodian (1)	3	0.01
Chinese, ex. Taiwanese (311)	422	1.09
Filipino (43)	71	0.18
Indian (14)	27	0.07
Japanese (10)	33	0.09
Korean (81)	83	0.22
Taiwanese (22)	22	0.06
Vietnamese (14)	18	0.05
Hawaii Native/Pacific Islander (21)	53	0.14
Not Hispanic (1)	5	0.01
Hispanic (20)	48	0.12
Guamanian/Chamorro (4)	7	0.02
Native Hawaiian (6)	10	0.03
Samoan (3)	5	0.01
White (23,150)	24,605	63.79
Not Hispanic (649)	674	1.75
Hispanic (22,501)	23,931	62.04

*Notes: † The Census 2010 population figure is used to calculate the percentages in the Hispanic Origin and Race categories. Ancestry percentages are based on the 2006-2010 American Community Survey population (not shown); ‡ Numbers in parentheses indicate the number of people reporting a single ancestry; * Numbers in parentheses indicate the number of persons reporting this race alone, not in combination with any other race; Please refer to the Explanation of Data for more information.*

California City

Place Type: City
County: Kern
Population: 14,120†

Ancestry‡	Population	%
African, Sub-Saharan (0)	14	0.11
African (0)	14	0.11
American (251)	251	1.89
Armenian (42)	42	0.32
Austrian (0)	15	0.11
Belgian (53)	68	0.51
British (16)	16	0.12
Croatian (0)	33	0.25
Czech (0)	27	0.20
Danish (51)	160	1.21
Dutch (44)	327	2.47
English (276)	1,032	7.78
European (43)	70	0.53
French, ex. Basque (17)	255	1.92
French Canadian (23)	75	0.57
German (674)	1,656	12.48
Hungarian (0)	10	0.08
Irish (483)	1,384	10.43
Italian (89)	425	3.20
Lithuanian (0)	16	0.12
Norwegian (70)	120	0.90
Pennsylvania German (13)	37	0.28
Polish (75)	200	1.51
Portuguese (0)	129	0.97
Romanian (26)	41	0.31
Scandinavian (0)	63	0.47
Scotch-Irish (26)	185	1.39
Scottish (15)	161	1.21
Slovak (0)	29	0.22
Swedish (0)	137	1.03
Swiss (0)	14	0.11
Ukrainian (70)	70	0.53
Welsh (53)	108	0.81

Hispanic Origin	Population	%
Hispanic or Latino (of any race)	5,385	38.14
Central American, ex. Mexican	269	1.91
Costa Rican	9	0.06
Guatemalan	80	0.57
Honduran	13	0.09
Nicaraguan	11	0.08
Panamanian	14	0.10
Salvadoran	138	0.98
Other Central American	4	0.03
Cuban	14	0.10
Dominican Republic	8	0.06
Mexican	2,134	15.11
Puerto Rican	147	1.04
South American	23	0.16
Argentinean	1	0.01
Colombian	5	0.04
Ecuadorian	2	0.01
Paraguayan	1	0.01
Peruvian	12	0.08
Uruguayan	2	0.01
Other Hispanic or Latino	2,790	19.76

Race*	Population	%
African-American/Black (2,150)	2,494	17.66
Not Hispanic (2,028)	2,327	16.48
Hispanic (122)	167	1.18
American Indian/Alaska Native (132)	373	2.64
Not Hispanic (73)	266	1.88
Hispanic (59)	107	0.76
Aleut *(Alaska Native)* (1)	1	0.01
Apache (12)	23	0.16
Blackfeet (0)	11	0.08
Cherokee (7)	90	0.64
Chickasaw (2)	3	0.02
Chippewa (1)	3	0.02
Choctaw (1)	9	0.06
Comanche (2)	2	0.01
Creek (1)	2	0.01
Crow (0)	2	0.01
Delaware (1)	1	0.01
Hopi (1)	1	0.01
Iroquois (0)	1	0.01
Lumbee (2)	2	0.01
Mexican American Ind. (6)	8	0.06
Navajo (1)	1	0.01
Paiute (4)	6	0.04
Potawatomi (0)	4	0.03
Pueblo (0)	4	0.03
Seminole (0)	3	0.02
Sioux (0)	7	0.05
Spanish American Ind. (2)	2	0.01
Yaqui (4)	5	0.04
Asian (367)	581	4.11
Not Hispanic (341)	508	3.60
Hispanic (26)	73	0.52
Cambodian (1)	1	0.01
Chinese, ex. Taiwanese (29)	58	0.41
Filipino (183)	305	2.16
Indian (3)	9	0.06
Indonesian (0)	1	0.01
Japanese (15)	63	0.45
Korean (39)	59	0.42
Laotian (3)	3	0.02
Malaysian (1)	3	0.02
Pakistani (0)	1	0.01
Thai (21)	31	0.22
Vietnamese (13)	16	0.11
Hawaii Native/Pacific Islander (59)	112	0.79
Not Hispanic (53)	93	0.66
Hispanic (6)	19	0.13
Guamanian/Chamorro (17)	25	0.18
Native Hawaiian (21)	45	0.32
Samoan (4)	9	0.06
Tongan (9)	15	0.11
White (9,188)	9,851	69.77
Not Hispanic (5,640)	6,111	43.28
Hispanic (3,548)	3,740	26.49

Calimesa

Place Type: City
County: Riverside
Population: 7,879†

Ancestry‡	Population	%
American (381)	381	4.84
Arab (148)	148	1.88
Lebanese (122)	122	1.55
Syrian (26)	26	0.33
Austrian (0)	204	2.59
British (52)	106	1.35
Canadian (0)	65	0.83
Czech (0)	195	2.48
Danish (34)	54	0.69
Dutch (105)	217	2.76
English (258)	1,136	14.44
European (17)	180	2.29
French, ex. Basque (93)	493	6.27
French Canadian (14)	26	0.33
German (426)	2,069	26.29
Greek (7)	29	0.37
Hungarian (27)	32	0.41
Irish (113)	696	8.84
Italian (203)	311	3.95
Norwegian (77)	143	1.82
Polish (40)	177	2.25
Portuguese (15)	96	1.22
Romanian (0)	18	0.23
Russian (0)	108	1.37
Scotch-Irish (65)	135	1.72
Scottish (44)	218	2.77
Swedish (95)	149	1.89
Swiss (0)	10	0.13
Welsh (0)	42	0.53
West Indian, ex. Hispanic (29)	41	0.52
Bermudan (13)	13	0.17
Jamaican (16)	28	0.36

Hispanic Origin	Population	%
Hispanic or Latino (of any race)	1,762	22.36
Central American, ex. Mexican	39	0.49
Costa Rican	3	0.04
Guatemalan	11	0.14
Honduran	9	0.11
Nicaraguan	1	0.01
Panamanian	1	0.01
Salvadoran	14	0.18
Cuban	7	0.09
Mexican	1,542	19.57
Puerto Rican	25	0.32
South American	13	0.16
Colombian	1	0.01
Ecuadorian	3	0.04
Paraguayan	1	0.01
Peruvian	7	0.09
Other South American	1	0.01
Other Hispanic or Latino	136	1.73

Race*	Population	%
African-American/Black (88)	139	1.76
Not Hispanic (75)	113	1.43
Hispanic (13)	26	0.33
American Indian/Alaska Native (99)	189	2.40
Not Hispanic (67)	134	1.70
Hispanic (32)	55	0.70
Apache (2)	2	0.03
Blackfeet (0)	3	0.04
Central American Ind. (1)	1	0.01
Cherokee (10)	34	0.43
Chickasaw (4)	6	0.08
Chippewa (3)	6	0.08
Choctaw (7)	13	0.16
Comanche (1)	1	0.01
Creek (1)	2	0.03
Iroquois (2)	2	0.03
Kiowa (1)	1	0.01
Mexican American Ind. (9)	10	0.13
Navajo (3)	3	0.04
Pima (1)	2	0.03
Potawatomi (1)	1	0.01
Pueblo (2)	3	0.04
Seminole (0)	1	0.01
Sioux (2)	5	0.06
South American Ind. (1)	4	0.05
Tohono O'Odham (0)	3	0.04
Yaqui (2)	2	0.03
Yuman (1)	1	0.01
Asian (100)	150	1.90
Not Hispanic (93)	132	1.68
Hispanic (7)	18	0.23
Burmese (1)	1	0.01
Cambodian (0)	1	0.01
Chinese, ex. Taiwanese (10)	23	0.29
Filipino (18)	37	0.47
Hmong (6)	7	0.09
Indian (11)	16	0.20
Indonesian (5)	12	0.15
Japanese (14)	22	0.28
Korean (22)	25	0.32
Laotian (3)	3	0.04
Thai (3)	4	0.05
Vietnamese (4)	4	0.05
Hawaii Native/Pacific Islander (10)	31	0.39
Not Hispanic (10)	28	0.36
Hispanic (0)	3	0.04
Guamanian/Chamorro (1)	5	0.06
Native Hawaiian (1)	13	0.16
Samoan (6)	6	0.08
White (6,777)	6,998	88.82
Not Hispanic (5,730)	5,856	74.32
Hispanic (1,047)	1,142	14.49

Calipatria

Place Type: City
County: Imperial
Population: 7,705†

*Notes: † The Census 2010 population figure is used to calculate the percentages in the Hispanic Origin and Race categories. Ancestry percentages are based on the 2006-2010 American Community Survey population (not shown); ‡ Numbers in parentheses indicate the number of people reporting a single ancestry; * Numbers in parentheses indicate the number of persons reporting this race alone, not in combination with any other race; Please refer to the Explanation of Data for more information.*

Ancestry‡	Population	%
Dutch (0)	29	0.42
English (12)	12	0.17
Finnish (0)	31	0.45
French, ex. Basque (0)	215	3.09
German (103)	549	7.90
Irish (0)	221	3.18
Italian (0)	19	0.27
Polish (0)	201	2.89
Russian (0)	36	0.52
Scottish (75)	151	2.17
Swedish (0)	31	0.45
Welsh (0)	14	0.20
West Indian, ex. Hispanic (19)	19	0.27
British West Indian (19)	19	0.27

Hispanic Origin	Population	%
Hispanic or Latino (of any race)	4,940	64.11
Central American, ex. Mexican	23	0.30
Costa Rican	1	0.01
Guatemalan	4	0.05
Honduran	1	0.01
Nicaraguan	1	0.01
Panamanian	1	0.01
Salvadoran	15	0.19
Cuban	2	0.03
Dominican Republic	1	0.01
Mexican	4,828	62.66
Puerto Rican	8	0.10
South American	2	0.03
Ecuadorian	1	0.01
Peruvian	1	0.01
Other Hispanic or Latino	76	0.99

Race*	Population	%
African-American/Black (1,612)	1,656	21.49
Not Hispanic (1,588)	1,602	20.79
Hispanic (24)	54	0.70
American Indian/Alaska Native (79)	156	2.02
Not Hispanic (49)	70	0.91
Hispanic (30)	86	1.12
Apache (0)	7	0.09
Blackfeet (1)	2	0.03
Cherokee (4)	27	0.35
Chickasaw (1)	2	0.03
Choctaw (1)	5	0.06
Comanche (2)	2	0.03
Lumbee (0)	3	0.04
Mexican American Ind. (2)	7	0.09
Navajo (3)	12	0.16
Paiute (6)	7	0.09
Pueblo (0)	1	0.01
Sioux (0)	4	0.05
Yaqui (3)	15	0.19
Yuman (1)	1	0.01
Asian (95)	177	2.30
Not Hispanic (72)	98	1.27
Hispanic (23)	79	1.03
Cambodian (10)	10	0.13
Chinese, ex. Taiwanese (6)	15	0.19
Filipino (36)	99	1.28
Hmong (2)	2	0.03
Indian (4)	8	0.10
Japanese (8)	9	0.12
Korean (3)	7	0.09
Laotian (4)	4	0.05
Thai (0)	1	0.01
Vietnamese (20)	22	0.29
Hawaii Native/Pacific Islander (25)	42	0.55
Not Hispanic (21)	26	0.34
Hispanic (4)	16	0.21
Fijian (1)	3	0.04
Guamanian/Chamorro (2)	3	0.04
Native Hawaiian (6)	16	0.21
Samoan (8)	10	0.13
Tongan (5)	6	0.08
White (3,212)	3,381	43.88
Not Hispanic (964)	1,001	12.99
Hispanic (2,248)	2,380	30.89

Camarillo

Place Type: City
County: Ventura
Population: 65,201†

Ancestry‡	Population	%
African, Sub-Saharan (89)	147	0.23
African (37)	80	0.13
Somalian (24)	24	0.04
South African (28)	43	0.07
American (2,022)	2,022	3.18
Arab (415)	568	0.89
Arab (196)	233	0.37
Egyptian (61)	61	0.10
Iraqi (0)	15	0.02
Lebanese (80)	147	0.23
Palestinian (10)	10	0.02
Syrian (25)	46	0.07
Other Arab (43)	56	0.09
Armenian (269)	390	0.61
Austrian (139)	271	0.43
Basque (7)	34	0.05
Belgian (0)	16	0.03
British (296)	386	0.61
Canadian (103)	418	0.66
Croatian (21)	78	0.12
Czech (83)	214	0.34
Czechoslovakian (6)	42	0.07
Danish (80)	375	0.59
Dutch (345)	1,169	1.84
Eastern European (164)	190	0.30
English (1,755)	7,679	12.07
European (921)	1,152	1.81
Finnish (53)	243	0.38
French, ex. Basque (225)	2,257	3.55
French Canadian (120)	467	0.73
German (2,680)	11,389	17.91
Greek (47)	235	0.37
Hungarian (85)	338	0.53
Icelander (10)	28	0.04
Iranian (241)	267	0.42
Irish (1,729)	7,412	11.65
Israeli (7)	17	0.03
Italian (1,324)	3,773	5.93
Lithuanian (44)	151	0.24
Luxemburger (0)	7	0.01
Macedonian (0)	49	0.08
New Zealander (11)	11	0.02
Northern European (101)	101	0.16
Norwegian (354)	1,167	1.83
Pennsylvania German (0)	24	0.04
Polish (597)	2,076	3.26
Portuguese (164)	382	0.60
Romanian (146)	185	0.29
Russian (557)	1,682	2.64
Scandinavian (90)	124	0.19
Scotch-Irish (380)	1,198	1.88
Scottish (367)	1,525	2.40
Slavic (28)	42	0.07
Slovak (8)	27	0.04
Slovene (22)	57	0.09
Swedish (249)	1,247	1.96
Swiss (63)	219	0.34
Turkish (23)	23	0.04
Ukrainian (55)	186	0.29
Welsh (153)	510	0.80
West Indian, ex. Hispanic (0)	12	0.02
Belizean (0)	12	0.02
Yugoslavian (226)	301	0.47

Hispanic Origin	Population	%
Hispanic or Latino (of any race)	14,958	22.94
Central American, ex. Mexican	502	0.77
Costa Rican	20	0.03
Guatemalan	156	0.24
Honduran	30	0.05
Nicaraguan	84	0.13
Panamanian	27	0.04
Salvadoran	183	0.28
Other Central American	2	<0.01
Cuban	100	0.15
Dominican Republic	12	0.02
Mexican	12,613	19.34
Puerto Rican	271	0.42
South American	487	0.75
Argentinean	88	0.13
Bolivian	24	0.04
Chilean	57	0.09
Colombian	91	0.14
Ecuadorian	52	0.08
Paraguayan	1	<0.01
Peruvian	116	0.18
Uruguayan	9	0.01
Venezuelan	36	0.06
Other South American	13	0.02
Other Hispanic or Latino	973	1.49

Race*	Population	%
African-American/Black (1,216)	1,760	2.70
Not Hispanic (1,106)	1,519	2.33
Hispanic (110)	241	0.37
American Indian/Alaska Native (397)	1,018	1.56
Not Hispanic (139)	521	0.80
Hispanic (258)	497	0.76
Alaska Athabascan *(Ala. Nat.)* (0)	1	<0.01
Apache (26)	52	0.08
Arapaho (1)	3	<0.01
Blackfeet (4)	19	0.03
Canadian/French Am. Ind. (1)	1	<0.01
Central American Ind. (0)	1	<0.01
Cherokee (26)	162	0.25
Cheyenne (1)	4	0.01
Chickasaw (2)	6	0.01
Chippewa (8)	17	0.03
Choctaw (16)	45	0.07
Colville (2)	6	0.01
Comanche (1)	2	<0.01
Creek (2)	7	0.01
Crow (0)	1	<0.01
Delaware (1)	2	<0.01
Hopi (1)	6	0.01
Inupiat *(Alaska Native)* (0)	3	<0.01
Iroquois (7)	13	0.02
Lumbee (0)	1	<0.01
Mexican American Ind. (37)	79	0.12
Navajo (4)	12	0.02
Osage (3)	9	0.01
Ottawa (1)	1	<0.01
Paiute (1)	2	<0.01
Potawatomi (10)	13	0.02
Pueblo (4)	12	0.02
Puget Sound Salish (1)	1	<0.01
Seminole (1)	3	<0.01
Sioux (6)	24	0.04
South American Ind. (0)	1	<0.01
Spanish American Ind. (3)	7	0.01
Tlingit-Haida *(Alaska Native)* (0)	5	0.01
Ute (0)	1	<0.01
Yaqui (2)	8	0.01
Asian (6,633)	8,150	12.50
Not Hispanic (6,491)	7,751	11.89
Hispanic (142)	399	0.61
Bangladeshi (17)	20	0.03
Bhutanese (1)	3	<0.01
Burmese (10)	13	0.02
Cambodian (32)	54	0.08
Chinese, ex. Taiwanese (945)	1,306	2.00
Filipino (2,437)	3,087	4.73
Hmong (14)	14	0.02
Indian (795)	876	1.34
Indonesian (22)	61	0.09
Japanese (777)	1,266	1.94
Korean (614)	768	1.18
Laotian (27)	39	0.06
Malaysian (3)	12	0.02
Nepalese (5)	5	0.01
Pakistani (37)	48	0.07
Sri Lankan (9)	12	0.02
Taiwanese (113)	133	0.20

SECTION TWO

*Notes: † The Census 2010 population figure is used to calculate the percentages in the Hispanic Origin and Race categories. Ancestry percentages are based on the 2006-2010 American Community Survey population (not shown); ‡ Numbers in parentheses indicate the number of people reporting a single ancestry; * Numbers in parentheses indicate the number of persons reporting this race alone, not in combination with any other race; Please refer to the Explanation of Data for more information.*

Thai (72)	110	0.17
Vietnamese (451)	516	0.79
Hawaii Native/Pacific Islander (116)	365	0.56
Not Hispanic (107)	307	0.47
Hispanic (9)	58	0.09
Fijian (3)	3	<0.01
Guamanian/Chamorro (48)	91	0.14
Native Hawaiian (23)	127	0.19
Samoan (24)	55	0.08
Tongan (6)	9	0.01
White (48,947)	51,689	79.28
Not Hispanic (40,324)	42,083	64.54
Hispanic (8,623)	9,606	14.73

Cameron Park

Place Type: CDP
County: El Dorado
Population: 18,228†

Ancestry‡	Population	%
African, Sub-Saharan (24)	24	0.14
African (24)	24	0.14
Albanian (0)	9	0.05
American (643)	643	3.74
Armenian (9)	9	0.05
Austrian (0)	30	0.17
Belgian (0)	11	0.06
British (65)	192	1.12
Canadian (33)	58	0.34
Croatian (88)	88	0.51
Czech (25)	92	0.53
Czechoslovakian (34)	34	0.20
Danish (51)	325	1.89
Dutch (61)	464	2.70
English (531)	2,291	13.31
European (250)	286	1.66
Finnish (17)	17	0.10
French, ex. Basque (110)	912	5.30
French Canadian (48)	67	0.39
German (971)	3,718	21.60
Greek (60)	103	0.60
Hungarian (48)	64	0.37
Icelander (12)	12	0.07
Irish (467)	2,098	12.19
Israeli (36)	36	0.21
Italian (371)	1,365	7.93
Latvian (0)	16	0.09
Lithuanian (0)	19	0.11
Northern European (33)	33	0.19
Norwegian (313)	609	3.54
Polish (108)	325	1.89
Portuguese (132)	387	2.25
Romanian (18)	18	0.10
Russian (50)	167	0.97
Scandinavian (40)	40	0.23
Scotch-Irish (175)	526	3.06
Scottish (193)	643	3.74
Serbian (0)	26	0.15
Slavic (15)	37	0.21
Slovak (13)	27	0.16
Slovene (0)	14	0.08
Swedish (179)	659	3.83
Swiss (9)	59	0.34
Ukrainian (11)	62	0.36
Welsh (23)	226	1.31
Yugoslavian (26)	42	0.24

Hispanic Origin	Population	%
Hispanic or Latino (of any race)	2,056	11.28
Central American, ex. Mexican	98	0.54
Costa Rican	5	0.03
Guatemalan	31	0.17
Honduran	13	0.07
Nicaraguan	9	0.05
Panamanian	6	0.03
Salvadoran	31	0.17
Other Central American	3	0.02
Cuban	10	0.05
Dominican Republic	1	0.01
Mexican	1,479	8.11
Puerto Rican	81	0.44
South American	67	0.37
Argentinean	25	0.14
Bolivian	1	0.01
Chilean	11	0.06
Colombian	9	0.05
Ecuadorian	7	0.04
Peruvian	10	0.05
Venezuelan	3	0.02
Other South American	1	0.01
Other Hispanic or Latino	320	1.76

Race*	Population	%
African-American/Black (143)	269	1.48
Not Hispanic (132)	235	1.29
Hispanic (11)	34	0.19
American Indian/Alaska Native (194)	458	2.51
Not Hispanic (149)	360	1.97
Hispanic (45)	98	0.54
Alaska Athabascan *(Ala. Nat.)* (1)	1	0.01
Aleut *(Alaska Native)* (2)	2	0.01
Apache (5)	11	0.06
Blackfeet (3)	14	0.08
Canadian/French Am. Ind. (6)	6	0.03
Cherokee (29)	94	0.52
Cheyenne (0)	1	0.01
Chickasaw (4)	8	0.04
Chippewa (4)	10	0.05
Choctaw (2)	8	0.04
Comanche (0)	3	0.02
Creek (0)	2	0.01
Crow (0)	5	0.03
Delaware (2)	2	0.01
Hopi (0)	3	0.02
Iroquois (7)	14	0.08
Kiowa (0)	1	0.01
Mexican American Ind. (8)	13	0.07
Navajo (2)	3	0.02
Osage (1)	1	0.01
Paiute (1)	1	0.01
Pima (3)	3	0.02
Potawatomi (0)	4	0.02
Pueblo (2)	2	0.01
Seminole (0)	1	0.01
Shoshone (2)	6	0.03
Sioux (9)	23	0.13
Spanish American Ind. (1)	1	0.01
Tlingit-Haida *(Alaska Native)* (0)	3	0.02
Tohono O'Odham (0)	4	0.02
Yaqui (1)	2	0.01
Yup'ik *(Alaska Native)* (0)	1	0.01
Asian (425)	696	3.82
Not Hispanic (415)	636	3.49
Hispanic (10)	60	0.33
Cambodian (15)	17	0.09
Chinese, ex. Taiwanese (93)	139	0.76
Filipino (98)	201	1.10
Hmong (5)	7	0.04
Indian (58)	64	0.35
Indonesian (1)	13	0.07
Japanese (49)	124	0.68
Korean (54)	85	0.47
Laotian (6)	6	0.03
Taiwanese (1)	6	0.03
Thai (3)	6	0.03
Vietnamese (22)	48	0.26
Hawaii Native/Pacific Islander (36)	109	0.60
Not Hispanic (33)	91	0.50
Hispanic (3)	18	0.10
Fijian (2)	2	0.01
Guamanian/Chamorro (8)	19	0.10
Native Hawaiian (12)	49	0.27
Samoan (2)	4	0.02
White (16,242)	16,899	92.71
Not Hispanic (14,912)	15,370	84.32
Hispanic (1,330)	1,529	8.39

Camp Pendleton South

Place Type: CDP
County: San Diego
Population: 10,616†

Ancestry‡	Population	%
African, Sub-Saharan (616)	684	5.10
African (584)	652	4.86
Zimbabwean (32)	32	0.24
American (124)	124	0.93
Arab (12)	23	0.17
Lebanese (12)	23	0.17
Australian (0)	14	0.10
Austrian (0)	14	0.10
Belgian (13)	13	0.10
British (0)	19	0.14
Cajun (25)	74	0.55
Canadian (21)	21	0.16
Czech (25)	55	0.41
Danish (12)	189	1.41
Dutch (13)	47	0.35
English (161)	893	6.66
Estonian (14)	14	0.10
European (296)	437	3.26
Finnish (0)	36	0.27
French, ex. Basque (68)	301	2.25
French Canadian (0)	12	0.09
German (732)	3,321	24.78
Greek (0)	13	0.10
Hungarian (12)	47	0.35
Irish (277)	1,903	14.20
Italian (101)	948	7.07
Norwegian (32)	202	1.51
Polish (57)	196	1.46
Portuguese (83)	169	1.26
Russian (0)	15	0.11
Scandinavian (6)	20	0.15
Scotch-Irish (60)	185	1.38
Scottish (65)	248	1.85
Serbian (0)	8	0.06
Slavic (13)	13	0.10
Slovak (0)	60	0.45
Swedish (10)	372	2.78
Swiss (0)	8	0.06
Turkish (10)	36	0.27
Welsh (0)	13	0.10

Hispanic Origin	Population	%
Hispanic or Latino (of any race)	2,586	24.36
Central American, ex. Mexican	137	1.29
Costa Rican	5	0.05
Guatemalan	36	0.34
Honduran	18	0.17
Nicaraguan	15	0.14
Panamanian	6	0.06
Salvadoran	57	0.54
Cuban	63	0.59
Dominican Republic	24	0.23
Mexican	1,798	16.94
Puerto Rican	261	2.46
South American	65	0.61
Bolivian	4	0.04
Chilean	4	0.04
Colombian	31	0.29
Ecuadorian	7	0.07
Peruvian	9	0.08
Uruguayan	1	0.01
Venezuelan	8	0.08
Other South American	1	0.01
Other Hispanic or Latino	238	2.24

Race*	Population	%
African-American/Black (992)	1,327	12.50
Not Hispanic (934)	1,172	11.04
Hispanic (58)	155	1.46
American Indian/Alaska Native (146)	324	3.05
Not Hispanic (109)	242	2.28
Hispanic (37)	82	0.77
Apache (4)	12	0.11

*Notes: † The Census 2010 population figure is used to calculate the percentages in the Hispanic Origin and Race categories. Ancestry percentages are based on the 2006-2010 American Community Survey population (not shown); ‡ Numbers in parentheses indicate the number of people reporting a single ancestry; * Numbers in parentheses indicate the number of persons reporting this race alone, not in combination with any other race; Please refer to the Explanation of Data for more information.*

Blackfeet (2)	9	0.08
Canadian/French Am. Ind. (3)	5	0.05
Cherokee (3)	36	0.34
Cheyenne (4)	5	0.05
Chippewa (0)	6	0.06
Choctaw (4)	8	0.08
Comanche (3)	3	0.03
Creek (0)	1	0.01
Crow (1)	1	0.01
Iroquois (2)	6	0.06
Lumbee (0)	1	0.01
Menominee (4)	9	0.08
Mexican American Ind. (2)	6	0.06
Navajo (24)	39	0.37
Osage (0)	3	0.03
Potawatomi (5)	5	0.05
Pueblo (3)	3	0.03
Shoshone (1)	3	0.03
Sioux (0)	3	0.03
Tlingit-Haida *(Alaska Native)* (1)	1	0.01
Asian (299)	619	5.83
Not Hispanic (270)	530	4.99
Hispanic (29)	89	0.84
Cambodian (6)	8	0.08
Chinese, ex. Taiwanese (12)	42	0.40
Filipino (132)	282	2.66
Hmong (2)	3	0.03
Indian (7)	16	0.15
Indonesian (4)	4	0.04
Japanese (31)	122	1.15
Korean (13)	43	0.41
Laotian (3)	17	0.16
Taiwanese (1)	2	0.02
Thai (5)	27	0.25
Vietnamese (36)	49	0.46
Hawaii Native/Pacific Islander (41)	116	1.09
Not Hispanic (35)	91	0.86
Hispanic (6)	25	0.24
Fijian (0)	3	0.03
Guamanian/Chamorro (6)	18	0.17
Marshallese (0)	2	0.02
Native Hawaiian (18)	66	0.62
Samoan (7)	16	0.15
White (7,530)	8,243	77.65
Not Hispanic (6,144)	6,571	61.90
Hispanic (1,386)	1,672	15.75

Campbell

Place Type: City
County: Santa Clara
Population: 39,349†

Ancestry‡	Population	%
Afghan (16)	16	0.04
African, Sub-Saharan (157)	187	0.48
African (74)	104	0.27
Ethiopian (42)	42	0.11
Nigerian (41)	41	0.11
Albanian (29)	29	0.07
American (908)	908	2.35
Arab (73)	230	0.59
Arab (0)	20	0.05
Lebanese (73)	210	0.54
Armenian (125)	125	0.32
Assyrian/Chaldean/Syriac (14)	21	0.05
Austrian (0)	160	0.41
Basque (16)	50	0.13
Belgian (7)	14	0.04
Brazilian (0)	15	0.04
British (227)	282	0.73
Canadian (78)	96	0.25
Celtic (0)	27	0.07
Croatian (63)	146	0.38
Czech (62)	354	0.91
Czechoslovakian (111)	132	0.34
Danish (99)	439	1.13
Dutch (220)	693	1.79
Eastern European (20)	54	0.14
English (799)	3,386	8.75
Estonian (0)	14	0.04
European (787)	939	2.43
Finnish (76)	219	0.57
French, ex. Basque (210)	1,186	3.07
French Canadian (46)	139	0.36
German (1,489)	5,579	14.42
Greek (228)	409	1.06
Hungarian (24)	71	0.18
Iranian (514)	532	1.37
Irish (970)	4,108	10.62
Israeli (12)	12	0.03
Italian (1,063)	3,525	9.11
Latvian (12)	12	0.03
Lithuanian (37)	59	0.15
Luxemburger (0)	16	0.04
Maltese (40)	40	0.10
Northern European (33)	39	0.10
Norwegian (203)	835	2.16
Pennsylvania German (0)	12	0.03
Polish (315)	854	2.21
Portuguese (326)	930	2.40
Romanian (50)	50	0.13
Russian (597)	1,272	3.29
Scandinavian (27)	36	0.09
Scotch-Irish (233)	561	1.45
Scottish (303)	1,063	2.75
Serbian (10)	10	0.03
Slovak (19)	34	0.09
Slovene (13)	13	0.03
Swedish (80)	514	1.33
Swiss (47)	242	0.63
Turkish (22)	60	0.16
Ukrainian (118)	290	0.75
Welsh (108)	311	0.80
West Indian, ex. Hispanic (47)	76	0.20
Haitian (47)	76	0.20
Yugoslavian (17)	27	0.07

Hispanic Origin	Population	%
Hispanic or Latino (of any race)	7,247	18.42
Central American, ex. Mexican	458	1.16
Costa Rican	21	0.05
Guatemalan	73	0.19
Honduran	73	0.19
Nicaraguan	98	0.25
Panamanian	15	0.04
Salvadoran	176	0.45
Other Central American	2	0.01
Cuban	80	0.20
Dominican Republic	13	0.03
Mexican	5,489	13.95
Puerto Rican	186	0.47
South American	399	1.01
Argentinean	51	0.13
Bolivian	17	0.04
Chilean	59	0.15
Colombian	81	0.21
Ecuadorian	22	0.06
Paraguayan	1	<0.01
Peruvian	131	0.33
Uruguayan	1	<0.01
Venezuelan	26	0.07
Other South American	10	0.03
Other Hispanic or Latino	622	1.58

Race*	Population	%
African-American/Black (1,158)	1,573	4.00
Not Hispanic (1,109)	1,409	3.58
Hispanic (49)	164	0.42
American Indian/Alaska Native (275)	706	1.79
Not Hispanic (101)	354	0.90
Hispanic (174)	352	0.89
Alaska Athabascan *(Ala. Nat.)* (0)	3	0.01
Apache (15)	42	0.11
Blackfeet (3)	17	0.04
Canadian/French Am. Ind. (0)	3	0.01
Central American Ind. (3)	3	0.01
Cherokee (9)	113	0.29
Cheyenne (1)	5	0.01
Chickasaw (1)	3	0.01
Chippewa (3)	13	0.03
Choctaw (4)	18	0.05
Comanche (1)	1	<0.01
Creek (1)	13	0.03
Crow (0)	4	0.01
Delaware (0)	1	<0.01
Hopi (2)	2	0.01
Iroquois (0)	6	0.02
Mexican American Ind. (45)	66	0.17
Navajo (7)	20	0.05
Osage (2)	7	0.02
Paiute (5)	7	0.02
Pima (1)	1	<0.01
Potawatomi (3)	11	0.03
Pueblo (2)	4	0.01
Puget Sound Salish (0)	1	<0.01
Seminole (0)	4	0.01
Shoshone (2)	4	0.01
Sioux (4)	10	0.03
South American Ind. (1)	8	0.02
Spanish American Ind. (0)	1	<0.01
Tlingit-Haida *(Alaska Native)* (0)	4	0.01
Tohono O'Odham (2)	4	0.01
Tsimshian *(Alaska Native)* (1)	1	<0.01
Yaqui (2)	11	0.03
Asian (6,320)	7,635	19.40
Not Hispanic (6,222)	7,308	18.57
Hispanic (98)	327	0.83
Bangladeshi (13)	13	0.03
Burmese (6)	7	0.02
Cambodian (20)	33	0.08
Chinese, ex. Taiwanese (1,647)	2,091	5.31
Filipino (735)	1,149	2.92
Indian (957)	1,051	2.67
Indonesian (12)	31	0.08
Japanese (698)	1,058	2.69
Korean (734)	855	2.17
Laotian (26)	29	0.07
Malaysian (5)	16	0.04
Nepalese (3)	3	0.01
Pakistani (38)	53	0.13
Sri Lankan (29)	31	0.08
Taiwanese (156)	180	0.46
Thai (37)	49	0.12
Vietnamese (913)	1,074	2.73
Hawaii Native/Pacific Islander (161)	345	0.88
Not Hispanic (140)	277	0.70
Hispanic (21)	68	0.17
Fijian (33)	43	0.11
Guamanian/Chamorro (27)	57	0.14
Native Hawaiian (33)	120	0.30
Samoan (30)	38	0.10
Tongan (11)	14	0.04
White (26,315)	28,429	72.25
Not Hispanic (22,866)	24,306	61.77
Hispanic (3,449)	4,123	10.48

Canyon Lake

Place Type: City
County: Riverside
Population: 10,561†

Ancestry‡	Population	%
American (804)	804	7.57
Arab (50)	137	1.29
Egyptian (50)	95	0.89
Jordanian (0)	31	0.29
Lebanese (0)	11	0.10
Armenian (0)	26	0.24
Austrian (0)	43	0.40
Belgian (0)	39	0.37
Brazilian (65)	79	0.74
British (62)	76	0.72
Canadian (7)	28	0.26
Czech (0)	3	0.03
Czechoslovakian (31)	31	0.29
Danish (91)	163	1.54
Dutch (107)	442	4.16
English (541)	1,786	16.82

*Notes: † The Census 2010 population figure is used to calculate the percentages in the Hispanic Origin and Race categories. Ancestry percentages are based on the 2006-2010 American Community Survey population (not shown); ‡ Numbers in parentheses indicate the number of people reporting a single ancestry; * Numbers in parentheses indicate the number of persons reporting this race alone, not in combination with any other race; Please refer to the Explanation of Data for more information.*

SECTION TWO

Estonian (13)	13	0.12
European (250)	314	2.96
Finnish (23)	61	0.57
French, ex. Basque (73)	621	5.85
French Canadian (0)	68	0.64
German (676)	2,132	20.08
Greek (46)	46	0.43
Hungarian (0)	24	0.23
Iranian (9)	9	0.08
Irish (576)	1,891	17.81
Italian (344)	787	7.41
Lithuanian (0)	19	0.18
Northern European (14)	14	0.13
Norwegian (83)	201	1.89
Pennsylvania German (7)	28	0.26
Polish (84)	362	3.41
Portuguese (12)	80	0.75
Romanian (0)	37	0.35
Russian (58)	214	2.02
Scotch-Irish (101)	353	3.32
Scottish (59)	349	3.29
Slavic (7)	7	0.07
Slovene (12)	12	0.11
Swedish (93)	355	3.34
Swiss (9)	49	0.46
Welsh (55)	167	1.57

Hispanic Origin	Population	%
Hispanic or Latino (of any race)	1,303	12.34
Central American, ex. Mexican	56	0.53
Costa Rican	9	0.09
Guatemalan	15	0.14
Nicaraguan	9	0.09
Panamanian	3	0.03
Salvadoran	20	0.19
Cuban	27	0.26
Dominican Republic	5	0.05
Mexican	971	9.19
Puerto Rican	38	0.36
South American	58	0.55
Argentinean	12	0.11
Chilean	4	0.04
Colombian	26	0.25
Ecuadorian	4	0.04
Paraguayan	1	0.01
Peruvian	7	0.07
Uruguayan	2	0.02
Venezuelan	2	0.02
Other Hispanic or Latino	148	1.40

Race*	Population	%
African-American/Black (128)	184	1.74
Not Hispanic (122)	175	1.66
Hispanic (6)	9	0.09
American Indian/Alaska Native (61)	156	1.48
Not Hispanic (40)	113	1.07
Hispanic (21)	43	0.41
Apache (1)	10	0.09
Blackfeet (2)	3	0.03
Cherokee (7)	33	0.31
Chippewa (8)	12	0.11
Choctaw (0)	5	0.05
Comanche (0)	1	0.01
Creek (1)	4	0.04
Delaware (1)	1	0.01
Iroquois (2)	4	0.04
Lumbee (0)	1	0.01
Mexican American Ind. (1)	4	0.04
Navajo (0)	1	0.01
Osage (1)	4	0.04
Pima (2)	4	0.04
Potawatomi (1)	1	0.01
Pueblo (6)	7	0.07
Seminole (0)	6	0.06
Sioux (1)	2	0.02
Yakama (0)	1	0.01
Yaqui (0)	4	0.04
Asian (190)	308	2.92
Not Hispanic (184)	281	2.66
Hispanic (6)	27	0.26
Burmese (1)	1	0.01
Cambodian (1)	7	0.07
Chinese, ex. Taiwanese (37)	63	0.60
Filipino (54)	88	0.83
Indian (12)	14	0.13
Indonesian (5)	13	0.12
Japanese (25)	60	0.57
Korean (15)	22	0.21
Laotian (2)	2	0.02
Sri Lankan (1)	1	0.01
Taiwanese (9)	9	0.09
Thai (2)	4	0.04
Vietnamese (14)	28	0.27
Hawaii Native/Pacific Islander (36)	88	0.83
Not Hispanic (33)	76	0.72
Hispanic (3)	12	0.11
Fijian (0)	1	0.01
Guamanian/Chamorro (4)	8	0.08
Native Hawaiian (10)	43	0.41
Samoan (6)	12	0.11
White (9,495)	9,780	92.60
Not Hispanic (8,630)	8,828	83.59
Hispanic (865)	952	9.01

Capitola

Place Type: City
County: Santa Cruz
Population: 9,918†

Ancestry‡	Population	%
American (194)	194	1.98
Arab (13)	27	0.28
Arab (0)	14	0.14
Palestinian (13)	13	0.13
Armenian (0)	44	0.45
Austrian (0)	22	0.22
Belgian (15)	15	0.15
Brazilian (0)	104	1.06
British (28)	73	0.74
Bulgarian (28)	28	0.29
Canadian (38)	51	0.52
Czech (0)	49	0.50
Czechoslovakian (11)	11	0.11
Danish (30)	183	1.87
Dutch (57)	209	2.13
English (201)	1,361	13.89
European (410)	453	4.62
Finnish (16)	54	0.55
French, ex. Basque (46)	626	6.39
French Canadian (29)	46	0.47
German (635)	1,969	20.09
Greek (0)	58	0.59
Irish (284)	1,346	13.73
Italian (143)	804	8.20
Northern European (162)	162	1.65
Norwegian (108)	259	2.64
Pennsylvania German (0)	5	0.05
Polish (25)	167	1.70
Portuguese (50)	192	1.96
Russian (16)	115	1.17
Scandinavian (0)	13	0.13
Scotch-Irish (38)	245	2.50
Scottish (203)	390	3.98
Slavic (0)	44	0.45
Slovak (16)	16	0.16
Swedish (62)	329	3.36
Swiss (19)	120	1.22
Turkish (91)	91	0.93
Ukrainian (63)	83	0.85
Welsh (61)	146	1.49

Hispanic Origin	Population	%
Hispanic or Latino (of any race)	1,957	19.73
Central American, ex. Mexican	127	1.28
Costa Rican	7	0.07
Guatemalan	5	0.05
Honduran	6	0.06
Nicaraguan	15	0.15
Panamanian	7	0.07
Salvadoran	85	0.86
Other Central American	2	0.02
Cuban	17	0.17
Dominican Republic	4	0.04
Mexican	1,559	15.72
Puerto Rican	26	0.26
South American	66	0.67
Argentinean	13	0.13
Bolivian	1	0.01
Chilean	11	0.11
Colombian	16	0.16
Ecuadorian	3	0.03
Paraguayan	2	0.02
Peruvian	17	0.17
Venezuelan	3	0.03
Other Hispanic or Latino	158	1.59

Race*	Population	%
African-American/Black (123)	213	2.15
Not Hispanic (109)	176	1.77
Hispanic (14)	37	0.37
American Indian/Alaska Native (59)	185	1.87
Not Hispanic (30)	116	1.17
Hispanic (29)	69	0.70
Apache (2)	14	0.14
Blackfeet (0)	6	0.06
Canadian/French Am. Ind. (0)	3	0.03
Cherokee (1)	39	0.39
Chippewa (2)	3	0.03
Choctaw (2)	13	0.13
Cree (0)	1	0.01
Creek (0)	5	0.05
Iroquois (0)	3	0.03
Mexican American Ind. (7)	8	0.08
Navajo (0)	7	0.07
Paiute (3)	3	0.03
Seminole (0)	1	0.01
Sioux (1)	4	0.04
Spanish American Ind. (1)	1	0.01
Asian (424)	603	6.08
Not Hispanic (407)	564	5.69
Hispanic (17)	39	0.39
Cambodian (12)	16	0.16
Chinese, ex. Taiwanese (63)	109	1.10
Filipino (141)	214	2.16
Indian (52)	63	0.64
Indonesian (10)	18	0.18
Japanese (44)	98	0.99
Korean (33)	45	0.45
Nepalese (2)	2	0.02
Pakistani (0)	2	0.02
Sri Lankan (3)	3	0.03
Taiwanese (1)	1	0.01
Thai (16)	19	0.19
Vietnamese (29)	33	0.33
Hawaii Native/Pacific Islander (10)	64	0.65
Not Hispanic (8)	57	0.57
Hispanic (2)	7	0.07
Guamanian/Chamorro (3)	6	0.06
Native Hawaiian (4)	31	0.31
Samoan (1)	9	0.09
White (7,963)	8,388	84.57
Not Hispanic (7,075)	7,360	74.21
Hispanic (888)	1,028	10.36

Carlsbad

Place Type: City
County: San Diego
Population: 105,328†

Ancestry‡	Population	%
Afghan (278)	302	0.30
African, Sub-Saharan (21)	90	0.09
African (13)	22	0.02
South African (8)	68	0.07
Albanian (28)	40	0.04
American (2,866)	2,866	2.87
Arab (429)	811	0.81
Arab (35)	61	0.06

*Notes: † The Census 2010 population figure is used to calculate the percentages in the Hispanic Origin and Race categories. Ancestry percentages are based on the 2006-2010 American Community Survey population (not shown); ‡ Numbers in parentheses indicate the number of people reporting a single ancestry; * Numbers in parentheses indicate the number of persons reporting this race alone, not in combination with any other race; Please refer to the Explanation of Data for more information.*

Egyptian (85)	96	0.10
Lebanese (124)	443	0.44
Moroccan (0)	9	0.01
Palestinian (23)	23	0.02
Syrian (65)	82	0.08
Other Arab (97)	97	0.10
Armenian (129)	265	0.27
Australian (92)	101	0.10
Austrian (179)	596	0.60
Basque (0)	152	0.15
Belgian (17)	82	0.08
Brazilian (76)	166	0.17
British (286)	710	0.71
Bulgarian (30)	30	0.03
Canadian (216)	525	0.53
Celtic (20)	44	0.04
Croatian (68)	257	0.26
Cypriot (18)	18	0.02
Czech (114)	593	0.59
Czechoslovakian (56)	189	0.19
Danish (429)	1,413	1.42
Dutch (569)	1,883	1.89
Eastern European (216)	267	0.27
English (6,452)	16,407	16.45
Estonian (9)	22	0.02
European (2,439)	2,706	2.71
Finnish (109)	298	0.30
French, ex. Basque (401)	3,531	3.54
French Canadian (202)	850	0.85
German (4,403)	17,307	17.35
Greek (160)	619	0.62
Guyanese (0)	10	0.01
Hungarian (289)	885	0.89
Icelander (8)	83	0.08
Iranian (469)	598	0.60
Irish (3,209)	13,677	13.71
Israeli (15)	54	0.05
Italian (2,890)	7,825	7.84
Latvian (38)	70	0.07
Lithuanian (74)	212	0.21
Luxemburger (0)	24	0.02
Macedonian (116)	127	0.13
Maltese (0)	45	0.05
New Zealander (0)	8	0.01
Northern European (91)	91	0.09
Norwegian (804)	2,375	2.38
Pennsylvania German (19)	19	0.02
Polish (1,202)	3,666	3.68
Portuguese (181)	696	0.70
Romanian (56)	146	0.15
Russian (879)	2,346	2.35
Scandinavian (242)	325	0.33
Scotch-Irish (511)	1,837	1.84
Scottish (643)	2,720	2.73
Serbian (235)	288	0.29
Slavic (29)	93	0.09
Slovak (63)	151	0.15
Slovene (9)	18	0.02
Swedish (701)	2,833	2.84
Swiss (135)	577	0.58
Turkish (58)	94	0.09
Ukrainian (554)	832	0.83
Welsh (184)	963	0.97
West Indian, ex. Hispanic (0)	9	0.01
Belizean (0)	9	0.01
Yugoslavian (28)	191	0.19

Hispanic Origin	**Population**	**%**
Hispanic or Latino (of any race)	13,988	13.28
Central American, ex. Mexican	471	0.45
Costa Rican	41	0.04
Guatemalan	129	0.12
Honduran	56	0.05
Nicaraguan	69	0.07
Panamanian	52	0.05
Salvadoran	117	0.11
Other Central American	7	0.01
Cuban	213	0.20
Dominican Republic	34	0.03
Mexican	10,695	10.15
Puerto Rican	449	0.43
South American	898	0.85
Argentinean	124	0.12
Bolivian	35	0.03
Chilean	113	0.11
Colombian	208	0.20
Ecuadorian	90	0.09
Paraguayan	14	0.01
Peruvian	221	0.21
Uruguayan	4	<0.01
Venezuelan	67	0.06
Other South American	22	0.02
Other Hispanic or Latino	1,228	1.17

Race*	**Population**	**%**
African-American/Black (1,379)	2,048	1.94
Not Hispanic (1,232)	1,796	1.71
Hispanic (147)	252	0.24
American Indian/Alaska Native (514)	1,111	1.05
Not Hispanic (271)	665	0.63
Hispanic (243)	446	0.42
Aleut *(Alaska Native)* (1)	2	<0.01
Apache (8)	30	0.03
Blackfeet (1)	16	0.02
Canadian/French Am. Ind. (2)	3	<0.01
Cherokee (40)	163	0.15
Chickasaw (5)	7	0.01
Chippewa (9)	17	0.02
Choctaw (17)	41	0.04
Comanche (1)	3	<0.01
Cree (0)	1	<0.01
Creek (3)	5	<0.01
Crow (1)	2	<0.01
Delaware (2)	2	<0.01
Hopi (0)	1	<0.01
Inupiat *(Alaska Native)* (0)	1	<0.01
Iroquois (7)	17	0.02
Kiowa (1)	1	<0.01
Lumbee (0)	3	<0.01
Mexican American Ind. (64)	81	0.08
Navajo (8)	20	0.02
Osage (2)	6	0.01
Ottawa (3)	3	<0.01
Paiute (1)	7	0.01
Pima (0)	2	<0.01
Potawatomi (5)	13	0.01
Pueblo (5)	8	0.01
Seminole (0)	6	0.01
Shoshone (2)	3	<0.01
Sioux (7)	20	0.02
South American Ind. (7)	17	0.02
Spanish American Ind. (1)	8	0.01
Tohono O'Odham (1)	2	<0.01
Ute (1)	3	<0.01
Yakama (0)	1	<0.01
Yaqui (5)	7	0.01
Yuman (1)	1	<0.01
Asian (7,460)	10,058	9.55
Not Hispanic (7,336)	9,624	9.14
Hispanic (124)	434	0.41
Bangladeshi (27)	27	0.03
Burmese (6)	6	0.01
Cambodian (33)	41	0.04
Chinese, ex. Taiwanese (1,815)	2,420	2.30
Filipino (1,225)	2,049	1.95
Hmong (2)	3	<0.01
Indian (1,195)	1,401	1.33
Indonesian (27)	84	0.08
Japanese (852)	1,528	1.45
Korean (926)	1,173	1.11
Laotian (16)	27	0.03
Malaysian (5)	11	0.01
Nepalese (2)	3	<0.01
Pakistani (49)	63	0.06
Sri Lankan (8)	12	0.01
Taiwanese (182)	215	0.20
Thai (89)	132	0.13
Vietnamese (675)	817	0.78
Hawaii Native/Pacific Islander (198)	607	0.58
Not Hispanic (182)	500	0.47
Hispanic (16)	107	0.10
Fijian (5)	11	0.01
Guamanian/Chamorro (45)	103	0.10
Native Hawaiian (56)	271	0.26
Samoan (51)	122	0.12
Tongan (1)	16	0.02
White (87,205)	91,202	86.59
Not Hispanic (78,879)	81,860	77.72
Hispanic (8,326)	9,342	8.87

Carmichael

Place Type: CDP
County: Sacramento
Population: 61,762[†]

Ancestry[‡]	**Population**	**%**
African, Sub-Saharan (467)	794	1.28
African (276)	500	0.81
Cape Verdean (0)	22	0.04
South African (128)	152	0.25
Other Sub-Saharan African (63)	120	0.19
Albanian (102)	102	0.17
American (1,894)	1,894	3.06
Arab (293)	407	0.66
Arab (45)	73	0.12
Iraqi (12)	12	0.02
Jordanian (24)	24	0.04
Lebanese (42)	73	0.12
Moroccan (59)	87	0.14
Syrian (8)	35	0.06
Other Arab (103)	103	0.17
Armenian (240)	266	0.43
Australian (0)	12	0.02
Austrian (33)	94	0.15
Basque (24)	123	0.20
Belgian (36)	145	0.23
British (73)	280	0.45
Bulgarian (30)	30	0.05
Canadian (22)	68	0.11
Celtic (8)	20	0.03
Croatian (46)	150	0.24
Czech (63)	271	0.44
Czechoslovakian (50)	133	0.22
Danish (154)	503	0.81
Dutch (151)	1,299	2.10
Eastern European (56)	56	0.09
English (2,303)	9,670	15.65
European (941)	1,322	2.14
Finnish (62)	134	0.22
French, ex. Basque (234)	2,078	3.36
French Canadian (97)	207	0.33
German (2,567)	11,501	18.61
German Russian (11)	11	0.02
Greek (158)	337	0.55
Hungarian (87)	302	0.49
Icelander (38)	88	0.14
Iranian (256)	420	0.68
Irish (2,308)	9,857	15.95
Israeli (0)	24	0.04
Italian (1,860)	4,932	7.98
Latvian (0)	11	0.02
Lithuanian (13)	64	0.10
Maltese (7)	7	0.01
Northern European (94)	105	0.17
Norwegian (278)	1,301	2.10
Pennsylvania German (0)	43	0.07
Polish (310)	1,041	1.68
Portuguese (483)	1,497	2.42
Romanian (455)	629	1.02
Russian (515)	1,052	1.70
Scandinavian (53)	149	0.24
Scotch-Irish (413)	1,728	2.80
Scottish (448)	1,827	2.96
Serbian (47)	47	0.08
Slavic (29)	55	0.09
Slovak (20)	43	0.07
Slovene (16)	50	0.08
Swedish (366)	1,233	1.99
Swiss (103)	509	0.82

*Notes: † The Census 2010 population figure is used to calculate the percentages in the Hispanic Origin and Race categories. Ancestry percentages are based on the 2006-2010 American Community Survey population (not shown); ‡ Numbers in parentheses indicate the number of people reporting a single ancestry; * Numbers in parentheses indicate the number of persons reporting this race alone, not in combination with any other race; Please refer to the Explanation of Data for more information.*

Turkish (58)	80	0.13
Ukrainian (581)	819	1.33
Welsh (204)	664	1.07
West Indian, ex. Hispanic (14)	110	0.18
Belizean (0)	33	0.05
British West Indian (2)	12	0.02
Haitian (0)	17	0.03
Jamaican (0)	36	0.06
West Indian (12)	12	0.02
Yugoslavian (250)	272	0.44

Hispanic Origin	Population	%
Hispanic or Latino (of any race)	7,218	11.69
Central American, ex. Mexican	372	0.60
Costa Rican	26	0.04
Guatemalan	87	0.14
Honduran	18	0.03
Nicaraguan	60	0.10
Panamanian	28	0.05
Salvadoran	138	0.22
Other Central American	15	0.02
Cuban	90	0.15
Dominican Republic	19	0.03
Mexican	5,130	8.31
Puerto Rican	335	0.54
South American	257	0.42
Argentinean	49	0.08
Bolivian	11	0.02
Chilean	28	0.05
Colombian	73	0.12
Ecuadorian	19	0.03
Paraguayan	2	<0.01
Peruvian	54	0.09
Uruguayan	8	0.01
Venezuelan	9	0.01
Other South American	4	0.01
Other Hispanic or Latino	1,015	1.64

Race*	Population	%
African-American/Black (2,972)	4,101	6.64
Not Hispanic (2,795)	3,694	5.98
Hispanic (177)	407	0.66
American Indian/Alaska Native (546)	1,530	2.48
Not Hispanic (382)	1,114	1.80
Hispanic (164)	416	0.67
Alaska Athabascan *(Ala. Nat.)* (2)	2	<0.01
Aleut *(Alaska Native)* (0)	2	<0.01
Apache (23)	51	0.08
Arapaho (0)	1	<0.01
Blackfeet (11)	65	0.11
Canadian/French Am. Ind. (0)	7	0.01
Central American Ind. (0)	2	<0.01
Cherokee (61)	303	0.49
Cheyenne (2)	9	0.01
Chickasaw (9)	22	0.04
Chippewa (16)	38	0.06
Choctaw (19)	54	0.09
Colville (3)	4	0.01
Comanche (1)	5	0.01
Cree (0)	4	0.01
Creek (5)	26	0.04
Crow (1)	3	<0.01
Delaware (0)	5	0.01
Hopi (1)	1	<0.01
Inupiat *(Alaska Native)* (2)	8	0.01
Iroquois (10)	24	0.04
Kiowa (3)	3	<0.01
Lumbee (3)	3	<0.01
Menominee (0)	1	<0.01
Mexican American Ind. (21)	45	0.07
Navajo (18)	38	0.06
Osage (0)	2	<0.01
Ottawa (4)	5	0.01
Paiute (3)	6	0.01
Potawatomi (9)	17	0.03
Pueblo (8)	14	0.02
Puget Sound Salish (5)	5	0.01
Seminole (5)	10	0.02
Shoshone (7)	14	0.02
Sioux (13)	42	0.07
South American Ind. (0)	2	<0.01
Spanish American Ind. (1)	2	<0.01
Tlingit-Haida *(Alaska Native)* (2)	7	0.01
Tohono O'Odham (2)	4	0.01
Tsimshian *(Alaska Native)* (1)	1	<0.01
Ute (2)	2	<0.01
Yakama (2)	4	0.01
Yaqui (8)	11	0.02
Yuman (4)	4	0.01
Asian (2,653)	3,865	6.26
Not Hispanic (2,546)	3,563	5.77
Hispanic (107)	302	0.49
Bangladeshi (2)	2	<0.01
Bhutanese (20)	24	0.04
Burmese (5)	6	0.01
Cambodian (16)	31	0.05
Chinese, ex. Taiwanese (505)	725	1.17
Filipino (566)	1,055	1.71
Hmong (43)	49	0.08
Indian (330)	408	0.66
Indonesian (31)	45	0.07
Japanese (319)	643	1.04
Korean (363)	430	0.70
Laotian (15)	26	0.04
Malaysian (2)	8	0.01
Nepalese (7)	12	0.02
Pakistani (22)	31	0.05
Sri Lankan (9)	9	0.01
Taiwanese (29)	29	0.05
Thai (26)	49	0.08
Vietnamese (198)	240	0.39
Hawaii Native/Pacific Islander (287)	532	0.86
Not Hispanic (250)	429	0.69
Hispanic (37)	103	0.17
Fijian (50)	61	0.10
Guamanian/Chamorro (67)	115	0.19
Marshallese (2)	2	<0.01
Native Hawaiian (62)	168	0.27
Samoan (60)	103	0.17
Tongan (16)	28	0.05
White (49,776)	52,877	85.61
Not Hispanic (45,979)	48,212	78.06
Hispanic (3,797)	4,665	7.55

Carpinteria

Place Type: City
County: Santa Barbara
Population: 13,040†

Ancestry‡	Population	%
American (234)	234	1.78
Arab (39)	83	0.63
Arab (25)	69	0.53
Other Arab (14)	14	0.11
Austrian (8)	52	0.40
Basque (14)	14	0.11
Brazilian (12)	12	0.09
British (73)	170	1.30
Canadian (24)	62	0.47
Croatian (18)	18	0.14
Czech (0)	23	0.18
Czechoslovakian (7)	7	0.05
Danish (163)	250	1.91
Dutch (25)	160	1.22
Eastern European (12)	12	0.09
English (217)	1,133	8.63
European (185)	219	1.67
Finnish (0)	40	0.30
French, ex. Basque (194)	861	6.56
French Canadian (13)	37	0.28
German (277)	1,413	10.77
Greek (0)	8	0.06
Irish (212)	1,160	8.84
Italian (228)	671	5.11
Northern European (12)	12	0.09
Norwegian (107)	338	2.58
Pennsylvania German (11)	31	0.24
Polish (50)	196	1.49
Portuguese (13)	53	0.40
Russian (66)	258	1.97
Scotch-Irish (127)	425	3.24
Scottish (54)	253	1.93
Slovak (0)	8	0.06
Swedish (83)	230	1.75
Swiss (36)	53	0.40
Ukrainian (10)	24	0.18
Welsh (0)	115	0.88
West Indian, ex. Hispanic (14)	38	0.29
Jamaican (14)	38	0.29

Hispanic Origin	Population	%
Hispanic or Latino (of any race)	6,351	48.70
Central American, ex. Mexican	86	0.66
Costa Rican	7	0.05
Guatemalan	28	0.21
Honduran	13	0.10
Nicaraguan	19	0.15
Panamanian	1	0.01
Salvadoran	17	0.13
Other Central American	1	0.01
Cuban	17	0.13
Dominican Republic	2	0.02
Mexican	5,925	45.44
Puerto Rican	24	0.18
South American	69	0.53
Argentinean	19	0.15
Bolivian	7	0.05
Chilean	11	0.08
Colombian	9	0.07
Ecuadorian	8	0.06
Peruvian	13	0.10
Venezuelan	2	0.02
Other Hispanic or Latino	228	1.75

Race*	Population	%
African-American/Black (109)	186	1.43
Not Hispanic (76)	118	0.90
Hispanic (33)	68	0.52
American Indian/Alaska Native (144)	273	2.09
Not Hispanic (40)	74	0.57
Hispanic (104)	199	1.53
Apache (9)	14	0.11
Cherokee (4)	26	0.20
Chickasaw (0)	5	0.04
Choctaw (1)	2	0.02
Comanche (2)	5	0.04
Crow (0)	1	0.01
Inupiat *(Alaska Native)* (1)	1	0.01
Iroquois (0)	6	0.05
Mexican American Ind. (25)	33	0.25
Navajo (6)	11	0.08
Osage (1)	1	0.01
Paiute (4)	4	0.03
Pueblo (0)	4	0.03
Sioux (2)	5	0.04
Spanish American Ind. (1)	1	0.01
Tohono O'Odham (0)	2	0.02
Yaqui (0)	3	0.02
Asian (296)	436	3.34
Not Hispanic (287)	381	2.92
Hispanic (9)	55	0.42
Chinese, ex. Taiwanese (32)	70	0.54
Filipino (47)	124	0.95
Indian (37)	50	0.38
Indonesian (6)	9	0.07
Japanese (82)	125	0.96
Korean (30)	42	0.32
Nepalese (8)	8	0.06
Pakistani (2)	3	0.02
Taiwanese (3)	3	0.02
Thai (8)	8	0.06
Vietnamese (25)	26	0.20
Hawaii Native/Pacific Islander (15)	53	0.41
Not Hispanic (11)	42	0.32
Hispanic (4)	11	0.08
Fijian (0)	1	0.01
Guamanian/Chamorro (1)	2	0.02
Native Hawaiian (9)	32	0.25
Samoan (1)	2	0.02

*Notes: † The Census 2010 population figure is used to calculate the percentages in the Hispanic Origin and Race categories. Ancestry percentages are based on the 2006-2010 American Community Survey population (not shown); ‡ Numbers in parentheses indicate the number of people reporting a single ancestry; * Numbers in parentheses indicate the number of persons reporting this race alone, not in combination with any other race; Please refer to the Explanation of Data for more information.*

White (9,348)	9,818	75.29
Not Hispanic (6,081)	6,239	47.85
Hispanic (3,267)	3,579	27.45

Carson

Place Type: City
County: Los Angeles
Population: 91,714†

Ancestry‡	Population	%
Afghan (61)	61	0.07
African, Sub-Saharan (3,966)	4,806	5.26
African (3,517)	4,332	4.74
Ethiopian (64)	79	0.09
Nigerian (359)	369	0.40
Somalian (26)	26	0.03
American (4,135)	4,135	4.53
Arab (133)	210	0.23
Arab (18)	50	0.05
Egyptian (10)	10	0.01
Jordanian (44)	69	0.08
Lebanese (0)	12	0.01
Palestinian (38)	46	0.05
Syrian (23)	23	0.03
Armenian (0)	16	0.02
Australian (10)	10	0.01
Austrian (15)	15	0.02
Belgian (0)	31	0.03
Brazilian (13)	13	0.01
British (54)	90	0.10
Canadian (31)	70	0.08
Croatian (0)	27	0.03
Czech (20)	65	0.07
Danish (6)	32	0.04
Dutch (40)	147	0.16
English (261)	1,196	1.31
European (77)	176	0.19
Finnish (11)	59	0.06
French, ex. Basque (272)	805	0.88
French Canadian (39)	78	0.09
German (401)	2,300	2.52
German Russian (31)	88	0.10
Greek (20)	29	0.03
Hungarian (12)	32	0.04
Iranian (19)	19	0.02
Irish (179)	1,115	1.22
Italian (235)	1,033	1.13
Norwegian (61)	227	0.25
Polish (139)	248	0.27
Portuguese (42)	117	0.13
Romanian (0)	14	0.02
Russian (40)	52	0.06
Scotch-Irish (94)	313	0.34
Scottish (35)	246	0.27
Slavic (4)	4	<0.01
Slovak (23)	31	0.03
Swedish (40)	222	0.24
Swiss (0)	10	0.01
Turkish (19)	19	0.02
Ukrainian (16)	74	0.08
Welsh (13)	23	0.03
West Indian, ex. Hispanic (203)	316	0.35
Barbadian (0)	25	0.03
Belizean (44)	47	0.05
Jamaican (159)	198	0.22
West Indian (0)	46	0.05

Hispanic Origin	Population	%
Hispanic or Latino (of any race)	35,417	38.62
Central American, ex. Mexican	2,402	2.62
Costa Rican	88	0.10
Guatemalan	896	0.98
Honduran	170	0.19
Nicaraguan	113	0.12
Panamanian	81	0.09
Salvadoran	1,033	1.13
Other Central American	21	0.02
Cuban	274	0.30
Dominican Republic	24	0.03
Mexican	29,896	32.60
Puerto Rican	576	0.63
South American	627	0.68
Argentinean	69	0.08
Bolivian	14	0.02
Chilean	48	0.05
Colombian	110	0.12
Ecuadorian	139	0.15
Paraguayan	8	0.01
Peruvian	204	0.22
Uruguayan	2	<0.01
Venezuelan	18	0.02
Other South American	15	0.02
Other Hispanic or Latino	1,618	1.76

Race*	Population	%
African-American/Black (21,856)	23,090	25.18
Not Hispanic (21,385)	22,263	24.27
Hispanic (471)	827	0.90
American Indian/Alaska Native (518)	1,207	1.32
Not Hispanic (152)	581	0.63
Hispanic (366)	626	0.68
Aleut *(Alaska Native)* (0)	1	<0.01
Apache (15)	36	0.04
Arapaho (8)	8	0.01
Blackfeet (1)	43	0.05
Canadian/French Am. Ind. (1)	1	<0.01
Central American Ind. (14)	16	0.02
Cherokee (21)	134	0.15
Chickasaw (0)	2	<0.01
Chippewa (6)	7	0.01
Choctaw (6)	50	0.05
Cree (0)	1	<0.01
Creek (2)	20	0.02
Delaware (2)	2	<0.01
Houma (0)	2	<0.01
Inupiat *(Alaska Native)* (0)	1	<0.01
Iroquois (0)	1	<0.01
Lumbee (0)	1	<0.01
Mexican American Ind. (66)	105	0.11
Navajo (30)	49	0.05
Osage (1)	3	<0.01
Ottawa (1)	7	0.01
Paiute (1)	4	<0.01
Pima (0)	2	<0.01
Potawatomi (1)	6	0.01
Pueblo (3)	9	0.01
Seminole (0)	4	<0.01
Shoshone (3)	3	<0.01
Sioux (16)	30	0.03
South American Ind. (1)	8	0.01
Spanish American Ind. (13)	17	0.02
Tlingit-Haida *(Alaska Native)* (0)	2	<0.01
Tohono O'Odham (0)	2	<0.01
Ute (4)	6	0.01
Yaqui (11)	27	0.03
Yuman (0)	1	<0.01
Asian (23,522)	25,296	27.58
Not Hispanic (23,105)	24,363	26.56
Hispanic (417)	933	1.02
Bangladeshi (9)	10	0.01
Burmese (4)	7	0.01
Cambodian (209)	236	0.26
Chinese, ex. Taiwanese (397)	719	0.78
Filipino (20,092)	21,539	23.48
Hmong (1)	2	<0.01
Indian (275)	381	0.42
Indonesian (34)	69	0.08
Japanese (730)	1,079	1.18
Korean (754)	822	0.90
Laotian (15)	37	0.04
Malaysian (2)	8	0.01
Nepalese (19)	23	0.03
Pakistani (86)	92	0.10
Sri Lankan (47)	47	0.05
Taiwanese (28)	41	0.04
Thai (61)	94	0.10
Vietnamese (325)	417	0.45
Hawaii Native/Pacific Islander (2,386)	3,088	3.37
Not Hispanic (2,291)	2,773	3.02
Hispanic (95)	315	0.34
Fijian (33)	43	0.05
Guamanian/Chamorro (148)	261	0.28
Native Hawaiian (109)	355	0.39
Samoan (1,982)	2,352	2.56
Tongan (24)	40	0.04
White (21,864)	24,707	26.94
Not Hispanic (7,022)	8,238	8.98
Hispanic (14,842)	16,469	17.96

Casa de Oro-Mount Helix

Place Type: CDP
County: San Diego
Population: 18,762†

Ancestry‡	Population	%
African, Sub-Saharan (217)	269	1.41
African (217)	256	1.34
Cape Verdean (0)	13	0.07
Alsatian (9)	9	0.05
American (696)	696	3.64
Arab (166)	197	1.03
Arab (14)	39	0.20
Iraqi (86)	86	0.45
Syrian (0)	6	0.03
Other Arab (66)	66	0.35
Armenian (0)	19	0.10
Assyrian/Chaldean/Syriac (95)	228	1.19
Australian (0)	8	0.04
Austrian (0)	7	0.04
Belgian (0)	60	0.31
British (36)	36	0.19
Canadian (160)	202	1.06
Croatian (0)	54	0.28
Czech (42)	97	0.51
Czechoslovakian (0)	15	0.08
Danish (35)	315	1.65
Dutch (89)	208	1.09
Eastern European (27)	71	0.37
English (746)	2,624	13.73
European (157)	157	0.82
Finnish (18)	46	0.24
French, ex. Basque (92)	1,032	5.40
French Canadian (24)	147	0.77
German (1,028)	3,810	19.93
Greek (101)	183	0.96
Hungarian (0)	46	0.24
Icelander (59)	59	0.31
Iranian (33)	33	0.17
Irish (556)	2,966	15.51
Israeli (11)	11	0.06
Italian (503)	1,263	6.61
Latvian (23)	23	0.12
Lithuanian (0)	74	0.39
New Zealander (7)	27	0.14
Northern European (185)	185	0.97
Norwegian (110)	451	2.36
Polish (168)	683	3.57
Portuguese (32)	90	0.47
Russian (72)	296	1.55
Scandinavian (35)	130	0.68
Scotch-Irish (153)	441	2.31
Scottish (192)	598	3.13
Serbian (0)	10	0.05
Slovak (8)	25	0.13
Swedish (99)	381	1.99
Swiss (86)	194	1.01
Ukrainian (0)	21	0.11
Welsh (33)	125	0.65
West Indian, ex. Hispanic (84)	94	0.49
Belizean (0)	10	0.05
Haitian (31)	31	0.16
West Indian (53)	53	0.28
Yugoslavian (0)	11	0.06

Hispanic Origin	Population	%
Hispanic or Latino (of any race)	3,235	17.24
Central American, ex. Mexican	76	0.41
Costa Rican	18	0.10

*Notes: † The Census 2010 population figure is used to calculate the percentages in the Hispanic Origin and Race categories. Ancestry percentages are based on the 2006-2010 American Community Survey population (not shown); ‡ Numbers in parentheses indicate the number of people reporting a single ancestry; * Numbers in parentheses indicate the number of persons reporting this race alone, not in combination with any other race; Please refer to the Explanation of Data for more information.*

Guatemalan	18	0.10
Honduran	5	0.03
Nicaraguan	3	0.02
Panamanian	9	0.05
Salvadoran	22	0.12
Other Central American	1	0.01
Cuban	35	0.19
Dominican Republic	9	0.05
Mexican	2,715	14.47
Puerto Rican	102	0.54
South American	76	0.41
Argentinean	8	0.04
Bolivian	6	0.03
Chilean	19	0.10
Colombian	23	0.12
Ecuadorian	5	0.03
Peruvian	8	0.04
Uruguayan	2	0.01
Venezuelan	5	0.03
Other Hispanic or Latino	222	1.18

Race*	Population	%
African-American/Black (1,108)	1,396	7.44
Not Hispanic (1,064)	1,282	6.83
Hispanic (44)	114	0.61
American Indian/Alaska Native (89)	299	1.59
Not Hispanic (69)	230	1.23
Hispanic (20)	69	0.37
Aleut *(Alaska Native)* (4)	4	0.02
Apache (2)	9	0.05
Blackfeet (0)	1	0.01
Cherokee (7)	62	0.33
Chickasaw (4)	5	0.03
Chippewa (0)	3	0.02
Choctaw (6)	15	0.08
Creek (2)	3	0.02
Delaware (0)	3	0.02
Hopi (1)	1	0.01
Inupiat *(Alaska Native)* (0)	2	0.01
Iroquois (0)	1	0.01
Kiowa (0)	1	0.01
Mexican American Ind. (3)	8	0.04
Navajo (9)	11	0.06
Osage (0)	1	0.01
Pima (1)	4	0.02
Potawatomi (0)	1	0.01
Seminole (2)	4	0.02
Shoshone (0)	1	0.01
Sioux (2)	8	0.04
Yaqui (3)	3	0.02
Yuman (5)	5	0.03
Yup'ik *(Alaska Native)* (0)	1	0.01
Asian (593)	991	5.28
Not Hispanic (566)	882	4.70
Hispanic (27)	109	0.58
Burmese (3)	3	0.02
Cambodian (20)	21	0.11
Chinese, ex. Taiwanese (60)	105	0.56
Filipino (241)	409	2.18
Hmong (6)	7	0.04
Indian (40)	60	0.32
Indonesian (5)	8	0.04
Japanese (70)	137	0.73
Korean (19)	30	0.16
Laotian (4)	5	0.03
Nepalese (7)	7	0.04
Pakistani (5)	5	0.03
Sri Lankan (1)	1	0.01
Taiwanese (10)	14	0.07
Thai (9)	10	0.05
Vietnamese (65)	87	0.46
Hawaii Native/Pacific Islander (96)	202	1.08
Not Hispanic (86)	159	0.85
Hispanic (10)	43	0.23
Fijian (2)	2	0.01
Guamanian/Chamorro (43)	88	0.47
Native Hawaiian (11)	40	0.21
Samoan (29)	45	0.24
Tongan (0)	2	0.01
White (14,881)	15,722	83.80
Not Hispanic (13,061)	13,643	72.72
Hispanic (1,820)	2,079	11.08

Castaic

Place Type: CDP
County: Los Angeles
Population: 19,015†

Ancestry‡	Population	%
African, Sub-Saharan (85)	85	0.47
African (33)	33	0.18
Sierra Leonean (52)	52	0.29
American (569)	569	3.14
Arab (124)	257	1.42
Egyptian (85)	102	0.56
Lebanese (20)	61	0.34
Syrian (19)	19	0.10
Other Arab (0)	75	0.41
Armenian (107)	135	0.74
Australian (41)	41	0.23
Austrian (15)	40	0.22
British (188)	211	1.16
Canadian (10)	56	0.31
Croatian (9)	46	0.25
Czech (0)	63	0.35
Czechoslovakian (0)	28	0.15
Danish (89)	255	1.41
Dutch (40)	557	3.07
English (539)	1,774	9.78
European (417)	417	2.30
Finnish (10)	21	0.12
French, ex. Basque (16)	363	2.00
French Canadian (55)	211	1.16
German (608)	2,852	15.73
Hungarian (95)	301	1.66
Iranian (21)	21	0.12
Irish (360)	2,163	11.93
Italian (439)	1,508	8.32
Lithuanian (0)	42	0.23
Norwegian (176)	505	2.78
Polish (129)	392	2.16
Portuguese (26)	26	0.14
Romanian (29)	113	0.62
Russian (101)	453	2.50
Scotch-Irish (63)	201	1.11
Scottish (59)	204	1.12
Serbian (0)	37	0.20
Swedish (99)	465	2.56
Welsh (0)	98	0.54
West Indian, ex. Hispanic (31)	45	0.25
Belizean (13)	13	0.07
Jamaican (18)	32	0.18
Yugoslavian (21)	84	0.46

Hispanic Origin	Population	%
Hispanic or Latino (of any race)	4,716	24.80
Central American, ex. Mexican	441	2.32
Costa Rican	27	0.14
Guatemalan	123	0.65
Honduran	16	0.08
Nicaraguan	32	0.17
Panamanian	5	0.03
Salvadoran	235	1.24
Other Central American	3	0.02
Cuban	110	0.58
Dominican Republic	17	0.09
Mexican	3,247	17.08
Puerto Rican	172	0.90
South American	353	1.86
Argentinean	53	0.28
Bolivian	9	0.05
Chilean	28	0.15
Colombian	87	0.46
Ecuadorian	45	0.24
Peruvian	121	0.64
Uruguayan	2	0.01
Venezuelan	4	0.02
Other South American	4	0.02
Other Hispanic or Latino	376	1.98

Race*	Population	%
African-American/Black (630)	819	4.31
Not Hispanic (589)	745	3.92
Hispanic (41)	74	0.39
American Indian/Alaska Native (119)	291	1.53
Not Hispanic (45)	155	0.82
Hispanic (74)	136	0.72
Apache (4)	6	0.03
Arapaho (0)	1	0.01
Blackfeet (0)	4	0.02
Canadian/French Am. Ind. (0)	1	0.01
Cherokee (5)	46	0.24
Chickasaw (1)	1	0.01
Chippewa (0)	1	0.01
Choctaw (1)	6	0.03
Comanche (6)	9	0.05
Creek (2)	2	0.01
Delaware (0)	1	0.01
Hopi (2)	2	0.01
Inupiat *(Alaska Native)* (1)	1	0.01
Iroquois (1)	5	0.03
Kiowa (1)	1	0.01
Lumbee (1)	2	0.01
Mexican American Ind. (15)	21	0.11
Paiute (2)	2	0.01
Potawatomi (4)	4	0.02
Pueblo (2)	11	0.06
Shoshone (0)	2	0.01
Sioux (1)	1	0.01
South American Ind. (4)	7	0.04
Spanish American Ind. (0)	2	0.01
Tlingit-Haida *(Alaska Native)* (0)	6	0.03
Yaqui (0)	12	0.06
Yuman (1)	1	0.01
Asian (2,162)	2,631	13.84
Not Hispanic (2,123)	2,515	13.23
Hispanic (39)	116	0.61
Bangladeshi (4)	4	0.02
Burmese (2)	2	0.01
Cambodian (19)	25	0.13
Chinese, ex. Taiwanese (176)	267	1.40
Filipino (1,081)	1,322	6.95
Indian (187)	219	1.15
Indonesian (5)	20	0.11
Japanese (94)	221	1.16
Korean (284)	332	1.75
Laotian (4)	5	0.03
Malaysian (3)	3	0.02
Nepalese (5)	5	0.03
Pakistani (23)	29	0.15
Sri Lankan (26)	28	0.15
Taiwanese (5)	14	0.07
Thai (52)	61	0.32
Vietnamese (109)	128	0.67
Hawaii Native/Pacific Islander (26)	88	0.46
Not Hispanic (23)	72	0.38
Hispanic (3)	16	0.08
Fijian (3)	4	0.02
Guamanian/Chamorro (6)	16	0.08
Native Hawaiian (7)	36	0.19
Samoan (3)	5	0.03
Tongan (2)	2	0.01
White (13,607)	14,520	76.36
Not Hispanic (10,864)	11,440	60.16
Hispanic (2,743)	3,080	16.20

Castro Valley

Place Type: CDP
County: Alameda
Population: 61,388†

Ancestry‡	Population	%
Afghan (316)	316	0.52
African, Sub-Saharan (586)	638	1.05
African (422)	461	0.76
Ethiopian (13)	13	0.02
Kenyan (29)	42	0.07
Nigerian (122)	122	0.20

*Notes: † The Census 2010 population figure is used to calculate the percentages in the Hispanic Origin and Race categories. Ancestry percentages are based on the 2006-2010 American Community Survey population (not shown); ‡ Numbers in parentheses indicate the number of people reporting a single ancestry; * Numbers in parentheses indicate the number of persons reporting this race alone, not in combination with any other race; Please refer to the Explanation of Data for more information.*

American (1,191)	1,191	1.96
Arab (364)	530	0.87
Arab (35)	76	0.13
Egyptian (134)	151	0.25
Jordanian (66)	66	0.11
Lebanese (24)	35	0.06
Palestinian (11)	55	0.09
Syrian (9)	51	0.08
Other Arab (85)	96	0.16
Armenian (79)	142	0.23
Assyrian/Chaldean/Syriac (21)	21	0.03
Austrian (105)	230	0.38
Belgian (41)	216	0.36
Brazilian (0)	20	0.03
British (226)	363	0.60
Canadian (24)	60	0.10
Celtic (0)	21	0.03
Croatian (29)	101	0.17
Czech (92)	276	0.46
Czechoslovakian (12)	28	0.05
Danish (141)	720	1.19
Dutch (162)	946	1.56
Eastern European (24)	24	0.04
English (1,294)	5,839	9.63
Estonian (21)	21	0.03
European (1,135)	1,372	2.26
Finnish (26)	56	0.09
French, ex. Basque (238)	1,685	2.78
French Canadian (67)	288	0.48
German (1,613)	7,285	12.02
Greek (233)	409	0.67
Hungarian (199)	334	0.55
Icelander (0)	21	0.03
Iranian (330)	410	0.68
Irish (1,306)	6,837	11.28
Israeli (0)	40	0.07
Italian (1,484)	4,134	6.82
Latvian (0)	30	0.05
Lithuanian (101)	180	0.30
Maltese (13)	41	0.07
Northern European (19)	46	0.08
Norwegian (200)	1,178	1.94
Pennsylvania German (0)	3	<0.01
Polish (227)	719	1.19
Portuguese (1,246)	2,665	4.40
Romanian (61)	112	0.18
Russian (429)	777	1.28
Scandinavian (32)	77	0.13
Scotch-Irish (195)	1,119	1.85
Scottish (413)	1,147	1.89
Serbian (12)	23	0.04
Slovak (0)	54	0.09
Swedish (151)	738	1.22
Swiss (46)	280	0.46
Turkish (0)	21	0.03
Ukrainian (135)	177	0.29
Welsh (37)	351	0.58
West Indian, ex. Hispanic (111)	158	0.26
Belizean (51)	51	0.08
Jamaican (60)	60	0.10
West Indian (0)	47	0.08
Yugoslavian (132)	161	0.27

Hispanic Origin	Population	%
Hispanic or Latino (of any race)	10,689	17.41
Central American, ex. Mexican	984	1.60
Costa Rican	27	0.04
Guatemalan	137	0.22
Honduran	36	0.06
Nicaraguan	335	0.55
Panamanian	23	0.04
Salvadoran	403	0.66
Other Central American	23	0.04
Cuban	90	0.15
Dominican Republic	12	0.02
Mexican	6,929	11.29
Puerto Rican	665	1.08
South American	522	0.85
Argentinean	53	0.09
Bolivian	22	0.04
Chilean	39	0.06
Colombian	81	0.13
Ecuadorian	26	0.04
Peruvian	284	0.46
Uruguayan	2	<0.01
Venezuelan	12	0.02
Other South American	3	<0.01
Other Hispanic or Latino	1,487	2.42

Race*	Population	%
African-American/Black (4,260)	5,171	8.42
Not Hispanic (4,064)	4,740	7.72
Hispanic (196)	431	0.70
American Indian/Alaska Native (329)	1,106	1.80
Not Hispanic (160)	659	1.07
Hispanic (169)	447	0.73
Aleut *(Alaska Native)* (3)	6	0.01
Apache (24)	70	0.11
Blackfeet (13)	46	0.07
Canadian/French Am. Ind. (0)	7	0.01
Central American Ind. (1)	1	<0.01
Cherokee (30)	190	0.31
Cheyenne (2)	8	0.01
Chickasaw (1)	14	0.02
Chippewa (8)	21	0.03
Choctaw (27)	68	0.11
Comanche (3)	3	<0.01
Cree (0)	3	<0.01
Creek (1)	3	<0.01
Hopi (1)	2	<0.01
Inupiat *(Alaska Native)* (1)	3	<0.01
Iroquois (1)	9	0.01
Kiowa (3)	6	0.01
Mexican American Ind. (35)	63	0.10
Navajo (8)	21	0.03
Osage (0)	2	<0.01
Paiute (3)	7	0.01
Pima (3)	4	0.01
Potawatomi (1)	2	<0.01
Pueblo (1)	7	0.01
Puget Sound Salish (0)	2	<0.01
Seminole (0)	4	0.01
Shoshone (1)	2	<0.01
Sioux (9)	38	0.06
South American Ind. (6)	13	0.02
Spanish American Ind. (1)	3	<0.01
Tlingit-Haida *(Alaska Native)* (0)	4	0.01
Tohono O'Odham (0)	4	0.01
Ute (0)	1	<0.01
Yaqui (0)	8	0.01
Asian (13,140)	15,080	24.57
Not Hispanic (12,975)	14,567	23.73
Hispanic (165)	513	0.84
Bangladeshi (13)	13	0.02
Burmese (12)	13	0.02
Cambodian (103)	126	0.21
Chinese, ex. Taiwanese (6,919)	7,718	12.57
Filipino (1,938)	2,794	4.55
Hmong (6)	6	0.01
Indian (1,008)	1,177	1.92
Indonesian (57)	90	0.15
Japanese (536)	1,009	1.64
Korean (969)	1,088	1.77
Laotian (61)	86	0.14
Malaysian (8)	29	0.05
Nepalese (52)	53	0.09
Pakistani (42)	55	0.09
Sri Lankan (12)	13	0.02
Taiwanese (139)	161	0.26
Thai (57)	77	0.13
Vietnamese (673)	826	1.35
Hawaii Native/Pacific Islander (417)	818	1.33
Not Hispanic (374)	688	1.12
Hispanic (43)	130	0.21
Fijian (85)	110	0.18
Guamanian/Chamorro (57)	112	0.18
Native Hawaiian (57)	258	0.42
Samoan (48)	81	0.13
Tongan (99)	129	0.21
White (35,602)	38,920	63.40
Not Hispanic (30,398)	32,622	53.14
Hispanic (5,204)	6,298	10.26

Cathedral City

Place Type: City
County: Riverside
Population: 51,200†

Ancestry‡	Population	%
African, Sub-Saharan (69)	103	0.20
African (24)	24	0.05
Cape Verdean (2)	16	0.03
Nigerian (17)	19	0.04
South African (26)	26	0.05
Other Sub-Saharan African (0)	18	0.04
American (1,580)	1,580	3.12
Arab (54)	74	0.15
Arab (0)	11	0.02
Lebanese (39)	46	0.09
Syrian (12)	14	0.03
Other Arab (3)	3	0.01
Armenian (46)	84	0.17
Assyrian/Chaldean/Syriac (21)	24	0.05
Australian (10)	10	0.02
Austrian (120)	174	0.34
Basque (9)	9	0.02
Belgian (5)	5	0.01
Brazilian (38)	60	0.12
British (70)	235	0.46
Bulgarian (0)	11	0.02
Cajun (4)	17	0.03
Canadian (300)	404	0.80
Croatian (13)	79	0.16
Czech (53)	122	0.24
Czechoslovakian (21)	21	0.04
Danish (31)	202	0.40
Dutch (93)	481	0.95
Eastern European (30)	30	0.06
English (931)	3,120	6.17
European (311)	395	0.78
Finnish (6)	21	0.04
French, ex. Basque (202)	840	1.66
French Canadian (185)	299	0.59
German (1,303)	4,032	7.97
Greek (46)	152	0.30
Hungarian (88)	255	0.50
Icelander (11)	11	0.02
Iranian (20)	23	0.05
Irish (1,210)	3,584	7.08
Italian (963)	1,724	3.41
Latvian (2)	4	0.01
Lithuanian (57)	98	0.19
Maltese (0)	70	0.14
Northern European (28)	28	0.06
Norwegian (241)	494	0.98
Pennsylvania German (0)	19	0.04
Polish (217)	540	1.07
Portuguese (65)	127	0.25
Romanian (125)	156	0.31
Russian (236)	536	1.06
Scandinavian (99)	99	0.20
Scotch-Irish (110)	421	0.83
Scottish (189)	528	1.04
Serbian (0)	61	0.12
Slavic (5)	5	0.01
Slovak (2)	34	0.07
Slovene (20)	24	0.05
Swedish (107)	484	0.96
Swiss (10)	103	0.20
Turkish (0)	11	0.02
Ukrainian (21)	80	0.16
Welsh (20)	230	0.45
West Indian, ex. Hispanic (75)	83	0.16
Belizean (37)	45	0.09
West Indian (38)	38	0.08
Yugoslavian (2)	21	0.04

Hispanic Origin	Population	%
Hispanic or Latino (of any race)	30,085	58.76

*Notes: † The Census 2010 population figure is used to calculate the percentages in the Hispanic Origin and Race categories. Ancestry percentages are based on the 2006-2010 American Community Survey population (not shown); ‡ Numbers in parentheses indicate the number of people reporting a single ancestry; * Numbers in parentheses indicate the number of persons reporting this race alone, not in combination with any other race; Please refer to the Explanation of Data for more information.*

	Population	%
Central American, ex. Mexican	1,927	3.76
Costa Rican	6	0.01
Guatemalan	994	1.94
Honduran	70	0.14
Nicaraguan	122	0.24
Panamanian	22	0.04
Salvadoran	704	1.38
Other Central American	9	0.02
Cuban	91	0.18
Dominican Republic	5	0.01
Mexican	26,165	51.10
Puerto Rican	222	0.43
South American	390	0.76
Argentinean	51	0.10
Bolivian	2	<0.01
Chilean	54	0.11
Colombian	62	0.12
Ecuadorian	17	0.03
Paraguayan	7	0.01
Peruvian	159	0.31
Uruguayan	22	0.04
Venezuelan	15	0.03
Other South American	1	<0.01
Other Hispanic or Latino	1,285	2.51

Race*	Population	%
African-American/Black (1,344)	1,737	3.39
Not Hispanic (1,108)	1,329	2.60
Hispanic (236)	408	0.80
American Indian/Alaska Native (540)	902	1.76
Not Hispanic (228)	406	0.79
Hispanic (312)	496	0.97
Alaska Athabascan *(Ala. Nat.)* (1)	1	<0.01
Apache (9)	18	0.04
Blackfeet (1)	14	0.03
Canadian/French Am. Ind. (1)	2	<0.01
Central American Ind. (2)	2	<0.01
Cherokee (32)	95	0.19
Chickasaw (6)	7	0.01
Chippewa (1)	8	0.02
Choctaw (7)	21	0.04
Comanche (4)	5	0.01
Creek (6)	11	0.02
Hopi (0)	1	<0.01
Houma (0)	1	<0.01
Inupiat *(Alaska Native)* (2)	2	<0.01
Iroquois (3)	4	0.01
Kiowa (7)	7	0.01
Mexican American Ind. (73)	104	0.20
Navajo (11)	18	0.04
Osage (5)	5	0.01
Paiute (1)	5	0.01
Pima (0)	2	<0.01
Potawatomi (1)	9	0.02
Pueblo (3)	7	0.01
Puget Sound Salish (2)	2	<0.01
Seminole (0)	2	<0.01
Shoshone (0)	1	<0.01
Sioux (1)	7	0.01
South American Ind. (9)	16	0.03
Spanish American Ind. (8)	16	0.03
Yaqui (15)	17	0.03
Yuman (1)	1	<0.01
Yup'ik *(Alaska Native)* (0)	1	<0.01
Asian (2,562)	3,035	5.93
Not Hispanic (2,449)	2,734	5.34
Hispanic (113)	301	0.59
Bangladeshi (1)	1	<0.01
Burmese (1)	1	<0.01
Cambodian (17)	25	0.05
Chinese, ex. Taiwanese (168)	233	0.46
Filipino (1,771)	2,083	4.07
Indian (131)	174	0.34
Indonesian (11)	15	0.03
Japanese (70)	147	0.29
Korean (61)	71	0.14
Laotian (12)	16	0.03
Malaysian (0)	3	0.01
Nepalese (1)	2	<0.01
Pakistani (11)	17	0.03
Sri Lankan (26)	38	0.07
Taiwanese (1)	4	0.01
Thai (16)	21	0.04
Vietnamese (189)	197	0.38
Hawaii Native/Pacific Islander (55)	154	0.30
Not Hispanic (47)	116	0.23
Hispanic (8)	38	0.07
Guamanian/Chamorro (16)	31	0.06
Native Hawaiian (12)	51	0.10
Samoan (12)	17	0.03
Tongan (0)	1	<0.01
White (32,537)	34,379	67.15
Not Hispanic (16,531)	17,129	33.46
Hispanic (16,006)	17,250	33.69

Ceres

Place Type: City
County: Stanislaus
Population: 45,417†

Ancestry‡	Population	%
African, Sub-Saharan (114)	170	0.39
African (72)	72	0.16
Cape Verdean (0)	33	0.07
Nigerian (42)	42	0.10
Other Sub-Saharan African (0)	23	0.05
American (1,488)	1,488	3.37
Arab (141)	219	0.50
Arab (60)	71	0.16
Iraqi (23)	33	0.07
Other Arab (58)	115	0.26
Armenian (8)	17	0.04
Assyrian/Chaldean/Syriac (172)	262	0.59
Australian (8)	8	0.02
Austrian (0)	21	0.05
Belgian (13)	21	0.05
British (12)	33	0.07
Cajun (0)	11	0.02
Canadian (0)	36	0.08
Czech (9)	51	0.12
Czechoslovakian (10)	10	0.02
Danish (57)	226	0.51
Dutch (103)	391	0.89
Eastern European (15)	15	0.03
English (646)	1,977	4.48
European (59)	88	0.20
French, ex. Basque (76)	833	1.89
French Canadian (17)	59	0.13
German (647)	3,498	7.92
Greek (123)	154	0.35
Hungarian (13)	20	0.05
Irish (634)	3,010	6.82
Italian (200)	980	2.22
Lithuanian (0)	45	0.10
Northern European (31)	31	0.07
Norwegian (85)	303	0.69
Polish (13)	254	0.58
Portuguese (877)	1,490	3.37
Russian (77)	164	0.37
Scandinavian (9)	17	0.04
Scotch-Irish (189)	366	0.83
Scottish (216)	541	1.23
Serbian (0)	8	0.02
Slavic (0)	10	0.02
Slovak (0)	21	0.05
Slovene (0)	10	0.02
Swedish (63)	320	0.72
Swiss (21)	146	0.33
Turkish (0)	6	0.01
Welsh (32)	108	0.24
West Indian, ex. Hispanic (53)	53	0.12
Dutch West Indian (33)	33	0.07
Jamaican (20)	20	0.05

Hispanic Origin	Population	%
Hispanic or Latino (of any race)	25,436	56.01
Central American, ex. Mexican	572	1.26
Costa Rican	6	0.01
Guatemalan	105	0.23
Honduran	31	0.07
Nicaraguan	137	0.30
Panamanian	21	0.05
Salvadoran	256	0.56
Other Central American	16	0.04
Cuban	39	0.09
Dominican Republic	9	0.02
Mexican	23,232	51.15
Puerto Rican	278	0.61
South American	115	0.25
Argentinean	7	0.02
Bolivian	1	<0.01
Chilean	7	0.02
Colombian	48	0.11
Ecuadorian	4	0.01
Paraguayan	3	0.01
Peruvian	36	0.08
Venezuelan	8	0.02
Other South American	1	<0.01
Other Hispanic or Latino	1,191	2.62

Race*	Population	%
African-American/Black (1,185)	1,536	3.38
Not Hispanic (995)	1,225	2.70
Hispanic (190)	311	0.68
American Indian/Alaska Native (609)	1,178	2.59
Not Hispanic (289)	684	1.51
Hispanic (320)	494	1.09
Apache (14)	27	0.06
Arapaho (4)	4	0.01
Blackfeet (4)	26	0.06
Cherokee (90)	254	0.56
Cheyenne (0)	1	<0.01
Chickasaw (7)	12	0.03
Chippewa (2)	11	0.02
Choctaw (24)	84	0.18
Colville (1)	1	<0.01
Comanche (1)	2	<0.01
Cree (0)	2	<0.01
Creek (17)	43	0.09
Crow (5)	5	0.01
Delaware (0)	2	<0.01
Hopi (3)	3	0.01
Inupiat *(Alaska Native)* (4)	6	0.01
Iroquois (0)	1	<0.01
Kiowa (0)	1	<0.01
Mexican American Ind. (51)	69	0.15
Navajo (7)	22	0.05
Osage (1)	1	<0.01
Ottawa (0)	2	<0.01
Paiute (5)	6	0.01
Pima (4)	4	0.01
Potawatomi (2)	3	0.01
Pueblo (3)	6	0.01
Seminole (0)	6	0.01
Shoshone (1)	1	<0.01
Sioux (22)	42	0.09
South American Ind. (0)	4	0.01
Spanish American Ind. (1)	2	<0.01
Tlingit-Haida *(Alaska Native)* (0)	1	<0.01
Tohono O'Odham (5)	5	0.01
Yaqui (14)	21	0.05
Yuman (7)	7	0.02
Asian (3,093)	3,840	8.45
Not Hispanic (2,967)	3,465	7.63
Hispanic (126)	375	0.83
Cambodian (346)	383	0.84
Chinese, ex. Taiwanese (130)	175	0.39
Filipino (393)	651	1.43
Hmong (111)	115	0.25
Indian (1,544)	1,741	3.83
Indonesian (1)	8	0.02
Japanese (33)	115	0.25
Korean (22)	54	0.12
Laotian (308)	348	0.77
Pakistani (52)	58	0.13
Thai (11)	23	0.05
Vietnamese (57)	66	0.15
Hawaii Native/Pacific Islander (346)	614	1.35
Not Hispanic (300)	466	1.03

*Notes: † The Census 2010 population figure is used to calculate the percentages in the Hispanic Origin and Race categories. Ancestry percentages are based on the 2006-2010 American Community Survey population (not shown); ‡ Numbers in parentheses indicate the number of people reporting a single ancestry; * Numbers in parentheses indicate the number of persons reporting this race alone, not in combination with any other race; Please refer to the Explanation of Data for more information.*

Hispanic (46)	148	0.33
Fijian (109)	133	0.29
Guamanian/Chamorro (26)	46	0.10
Native Hawaiian (35)	123	0.27
Samoan (128)	150	0.33
Tongan (3)	4	0.01
White (26,217)	28,210	62.11
Not Hispanic (14,277)	15,106	33.26
Hispanic (11,940)	13,104	28.85

Cerritos

Place Type: City
County: Los Angeles
Population: 49,041†

Ancestry‡	Population	%
African, Sub-Saharan (444)	581	1.18
African (197)	279	0.56
Ethiopian (111)	111	0.22
Nigerian (121)	176	0.36
Sudanese (15)	15	0.03
Albanian (9)	9	0.02
American (1,013)	1,013	2.05
Arab (351)	501	1.01
Arab (116)	235	0.48
Egyptian (86)	94	0.19
Iraqi (9)	9	0.02
Jordanian (65)	65	0.13
Lebanese (0)	11	0.02
Palestinian (48)	48	0.10
Other Arab (27)	39	0.08
Armenian (9)	9	0.02
Assyrian/Chaldean/Syriac (27)	27	0.05
Austrian (10)	55	0.11
Basque (6)	6	0.01
Belgian (15)	15	0.03
Brazilian (14)	14	0.03
British (34)	108	0.22
Canadian (18)	32	0.06
Croatian (42)	42	0.08
Czech (69)	108	0.22
Czechoslovakian (12)	12	0.02
Danish (11)	102	0.21
Dutch (102)	170	0.34
Eastern European (13)	13	0.03
English (440)	1,143	2.31
European (135)	176	0.36
French, ex. Basque (53)	352	0.71
French Canadian (0)	12	0.02
German (474)	1,287	2.60
Greek (114)	149	0.30
Hungarian (59)	138	0.28
Iranian (117)	197	0.40
Irish (239)	972	1.97
Israeli (18)	18	0.04
Italian (304)	509	1.03
Lithuanian (12)	44	0.09
Northern European (19)	19	0.04
Norwegian (86)	242	0.49
Pennsylvania German (0)	10	0.02
Polish (39)	130	0.26
Portuguese (277)	294	0.59
Russian (30)	50	0.10
Scandinavian (0)	7	0.01
Scotch-Irish (125)	200	0.40
Scottish (147)	242	0.49
Swedish (65)	341	0.69
Swiss (0)	11	0.02
Ukrainian (100)	100	0.20
Welsh (9)	57	0.12
West Indian, ex. Hispanic (37)	148	0.30
Haitian (13)	98	0.20
Jamaican (11)	24	0.05
Trinidadian/Tobagonian (13)	26	0.05

Hispanic Origin	Population	%
Hispanic or Latino (of any race)	5,883	12.00
Central American, ex. Mexican	409	0.83
Costa Rican	60	0.12
Guatemalan	83	0.17
Honduran	21	0.04
Nicaraguan	51	0.10
Panamanian	17	0.03
Salvadoran	172	0.35
Other Central American	5	0.01
Cuban	157	0.32
Dominican Republic	11	0.02
Mexican	4,201	8.57
Puerto Rican	157	0.32
South American	523	1.07
Argentinean	73	0.15
Bolivian	13	0.03
Chilean	39	0.08
Colombian	141	0.29
Ecuadorian	106	0.22
Peruvian	126	0.26
Uruguayan	12	0.02
Venezuelan	7	0.01
Other South American	6	0.01
Other Hispanic or Latino	425	0.87

Race*	Population	%
African-American/Black (3,388)	3,733	7.61
Not Hispanic (3,283)	3,540	7.22
Hispanic (105)	193	0.39
American Indian/Alaska Native (131)	331	0.67
Not Hispanic (51)	183	0.37
Hispanic (80)	148	0.30
Aleut *(Alaska Native)* (0)	1	<0.01
Apache (5)	6	0.01
Arapaho (1)	2	<0.01
Blackfeet (3)	5	0.01
Canadian/French Am. Ind. (0)	1	<0.01
Central American Ind. (1)	2	<0.01
Cherokee (7)	29	0.06
Chickasaw (0)	9	0.02
Chippewa (0)	11	0.02
Choctaw (4)	12	0.02
Colville (1)	1	<0.01
Creek (2)	8	0.02
Hopi (0)	1	<0.01
Kiowa (0)	1	<0.01
Lumbee (0)	1	<0.01
Mexican American Ind. (18)	34	0.07
Navajo (8)	12	0.02
Paiute (1)	2	<0.01
Pima (1)	1	<0.01
Potawatomi (0)	2	<0.01
Pueblo (2)	3	0.01
Seminole (3)	5	0.01
Sioux (0)	5	0.01
South American Ind. (5)	7	0.01
Yuman (0)	2	<0.01
Asian (30,363)	31,691	64.62
Not Hispanic (30,163)	31,229	63.68
Hispanic (200)	462	0.94
Bangladeshi (61)	67	0.14
Burmese (36)	40	0.08
Cambodian (291)	349	0.71
Chinese, ex. Taiwanese (5,515)	6,267	12.78
Filipino (7,155)	7,917	16.14
Hmong (1)	3	0.01
Indian (3,771)	3,983	8.12
Indonesian (128)	177	0.36
Japanese (1,533)	1,951	3.98
Korean (7,240)	7,451	15.19
Laotian (32)	39	0.08
Malaysian (22)	24	0.05
Nepalese (11)	11	0.02
Pakistani (225)	253	0.52
Sri Lankan (79)	95	0.19
Taiwanese (1,750)	1,945	3.97
Thai (574)	651	1.33
Vietnamese (1,021)	1,185	2.42
Hawaii Native/Pacific Islander (138)	366	0.75
Not Hispanic (119)	322	0.66
Hispanic (19)	44	0.09
Fijian (6)	10	0.02
Guamanian/Chamorro (49)	108	0.22
Native Hawaiian (35)	83	0.17
Samoan (33)	52	0.11
Tongan (5)	5	0.01
White (11,341)	12,570	25.63
Not Hispanic (8,141)	9,032	18.42
Hispanic (3,200)	3,538	7.21

Charter Oak

Place Type: CDP
County: Los Angeles
Population: 9,310†

Ancestry‡	Population	%
African, Sub-Saharan (36)	36	0.39
African (36)	36	0.39
American (249)	249	2.68
Arab (191)	196	2.11
Arab (49)	49	0.53
Jordanian (142)	142	1.53
Lebanese (0)	5	0.05
Armenian (0)	154	1.66
Basque (15)	15	0.16
Belgian (0)	11	0.12
Canadian (15)	15	0.16
Czech (15)	15	0.16
Czechoslovakian (13)	31	0.33
Danish (12)	36	0.39
Dutch (0)	76	0.82
English (98)	438	4.71
European (68)	81	0.87
French, ex. Basque (61)	303	3.26
French Canadian (21)	115	1.24
German (292)	1,201	12.92
Greek (0)	14	0.15
Hungarian (0)	20	0.22
Irish (166)	485	5.22
Italian (205)	614	6.60
Lithuanian (0)	93	1.00
Norwegian (120)	208	2.24
Polish (44)	122	1.31
Portuguese (33)	75	0.81
Romanian (15)	39	0.42
Russian (0)	88	0.95
Scotch-Irish (9)	102	1.10
Scottish (10)	49	0.53
Swedish (66)	160	1.72
Turkish (0)	14	0.15
Ukrainian (0)	12	0.13
Welsh (0)	24	0.26
West Indian, ex. Hispanic (12)	12	0.13
Jamaican (12)	12	0.13

Hispanic Origin	Population	%
Hispanic or Latino (of any race)	4,546	48.83
Central American, ex. Mexican	369	3.96
Costa Rican	17	0.18
Guatemalan	110	1.18
Honduran	21	0.23
Nicaraguan	76	0.82
Panamanian	2	0.02
Salvadoran	137	1.47
Other Central American	6	0.06
Cuban	72	0.77
Mexican	3,587	38.53
Puerto Rican	81	0.87
South American	145	1.56
Argentinean	17	0.18
Bolivian	14	0.15
Chilean	11	0.12
Colombian	40	0.43
Ecuadorian	30	0.32
Peruvian	25	0.27
Uruguayan	2	0.02
Venezuelan	6	0.06
Other Hispanic or Latino	292	3.14

Race*	Population	%
African-American/Black (405)	484	5.20
Not Hispanic (369)	410	4.40

*Notes: † The Census 2010 population figure is used to calculate the percentages in the Hispanic Origin and Race categories. Ancestry percentages are based on the 2006-2010 American Community Survey population (not shown); ‡ Numbers in parentheses indicate the number of people reporting a single ancestry; * Numbers in parentheses indicate the number of persons reporting this race alone, not in combination with any other race; Please refer to the Explanation of Data for more information.*

Hispanic (36)	74	0.79
American Indian/Alaska Native (85)	180	1.93
Not Hispanic (32)	81	0.87
Hispanic (53)	99	1.06
Apache (3)	6	0.06
Cherokee (1)	12	0.13
Chippewa (1)	1	0.01
Choctaw (1)	2	0.02
Creek (7)	7	0.08
Iroquois (1)	1	0.01
Mexican American Ind. (13)	21	0.23
Navajo (1)	6	0.06
Paiute (0)	2	0.02
Potawatomi (2)	4	0.04
Seminole (0)	1	0.01
Sioux (0)	6	0.06
South American Ind. (1)	1	0.01
Spanish American Ind. (0)	1	0.01
Tlingit-Haida *(Alaska Native)* (1)	1	0.01
Tohono O'Odham (3)	6	0.06
Yaqui (4)	4	0.04
Asian (1,035)	1,201	12.90
Not Hispanic (975)	1,078	11.58
Hispanic (60)	123	1.32
Burmese (17)	18	0.19
Cambodian (20)	23	0.25
Chinese, ex. Taiwanese (179)	224	2.41
Filipino (429)	503	5.40
Indian (134)	151	1.62
Indonesian (2)	17	0.18
Japanese (72)	123	1.32
Korean (33)	41	0.44
Laotian (1)	2	0.02
Malaysian (2)	2	0.02
Pakistani (7)	7	0.08
Sri Lankan (20)	27	0.29
Taiwanese (11)	11	0.12
Thai (6)	6	0.06
Vietnamese (48)	62	0.67
Hawaii Native/Pacific Islander (18)	49	0.53
Not Hispanic (14)	30	0.32
Hispanic (4)	19	0.20
Guamanian/Chamorro (2)	4	0.04
Native Hawaiian (9)	23	0.25
Samoan (0)	1	0.01
Tongan (1)	4	0.04
White (5,602)	5,985	64.29
Not Hispanic (3,169)	3,314	35.60
Hispanic (2,433)	2,671	28.69

Cherryland

Place Type: CDP
County: Alameda
Population: 14,728†

Ancestry‡	Population	%
African, Sub-Saharan (59)	59	0.44
Ethiopian (45)	45	0.34
Nigerian (14)	14	0.11
American (159)	159	1.19
Brazilian (65)	65	0.49
British (58)	109	0.82
Czech (0)	26	0.20
Danish (0)	27	0.20
Dutch (27)	122	0.92
Eastern European (0)	21	0.16
English (237)	649	4.87
European (195)	195	1.46
Finnish (0)	16	0.12
French, ex. Basque (57)	198	1.49
French Canadian (0)	11	0.08
German (170)	593	4.45
Hungarian (0)	19	0.14
Irish (116)	448	3.36
Italian (111)	283	2.12
Norwegian (35)	159	1.19
Polish (23)	58	0.44
Portuguese (461)	717	5.38
Romanian (0)	22	0.17
Russian (0)	21	0.16
Scotch-Irish (0)	6	0.05
Scottish (22)	80	0.60
Slavic (15)	15	0.11
Swedish (35)	95	0.71
Welsh (0)	31	0.23
Yugoslavian (9)	9	0.07

Hispanic Origin	Population	%
Hispanic or Latino (of any race)	7,955	54.01
Central American, ex. Mexican	612	4.16
Costa Rican	10	0.07
Guatemalan	126	0.86
Honduran	17	0.12
Nicaraguan	126	0.86
Panamanian	14	0.10
Salvadoran	318	2.16
Other Central American	1	0.01
Cuban	33	0.22
Mexican	6,433	43.68
Puerto Rican	268	1.82
South American	174	1.18
Argentinean	8	0.05
Bolivian	5	0.03
Chilean	22	0.15
Colombian	20	0.14
Ecuadorian	4	0.03
Peruvian	111	0.75
Venezuelan	4	0.03
Other Hispanic or Latino	435	2.95

Race*	Population	%
African-American/Black (1,698)	1,954	13.27
Not Hispanic (1,585)	1,740	11.81
Hispanic (113)	214	1.45
American Indian/Alaska Native (200)	366	2.49
Not Hispanic (62)	158	1.07
Hispanic (138)	208	1.41
Aleut *(Alaska Native)* (0)	1	0.01
Apache (7)	17	0.12
Blackfeet (1)	17	0.12
Central American Ind. (0)	1	0.01
Cherokee (14)	51	0.35
Chickasaw (1)	1	0.01
Chippewa (2)	2	0.01
Choctaw (6)	17	0.12
Comanche (1)	1	0.01
Delaware (1)	1	0.01
Hopi (4)	5	0.03
Iroquois (1)	2	0.01
Mexican American Ind. (29)	37	0.25
Navajo (3)	8	0.05
Pueblo (1)	1	0.01
Seminole (0)	1	0.01
Sioux (0)	2	0.01
South American Ind. (0)	3	0.02
Spanish American Ind. (3)	4	0.03
Tohono O'Odham (1)	1	0.01
Yaqui (1)	8	0.05
Asian (1,404)	1,687	11.45
Not Hispanic (1,354)	1,550	10.52
Hispanic (50)	137	0.93
Burmese (3)	4	0.03
Cambodian (17)	23	0.16
Chinese, ex. Taiwanese (264)	312	2.12
Filipino (649)	771	5.23
Indian (115)	134	0.91
Indonesian (6)	15	0.10
Japanese (52)	99	0.67
Korean (33)	45	0.31
Laotian (12)	15	0.10
Pakistani (8)	15	0.10
Taiwanese (7)	9	0.06
Thai (16)	17	0.12
Vietnamese (183)	203	1.38
Hawaii Native/Pacific Islander (310)	440	2.99
Not Hispanic (277)	363	2.46
Hispanic (33)	77	0.52
Fijian (82)	93	0.63
Guamanian/Chamorro (23)	45	0.31
Native Hawaiian (35)	94	0.64
Samoan (52)	83	0.56
Tongan (77)	95	0.65
White (6,035)	6,838	46.43
Not Hispanic (3,071)	3,355	22.78
Hispanic (2,964)	3,483	23.65

Chico

Place Type: City
County: Butte
Population: 86,187†

Ancestry‡	Population	%
African, Sub-Saharan (201)	280	0.33
African (163)	226	0.27
Ethiopian (9)	22	0.03
Kenyan (29)	29	0.03
Other Sub-Saharan African (0)	3	<0.01
American (5,798)	5,798	6.81
Arab (236)	356	0.42
Arab (13)	13	0.02
Egyptian (11)	11	0.01
Iraqi (0)	22	0.03
Jordanian (4)	4	<0.01
Lebanese (0)	83	0.10
Moroccan (31)	31	0.04
Palestinian (22)	22	0.03
Syrian (30)	45	0.05
Other Arab (125)	125	0.15
Armenian (150)	266	0.31
Assyrian/Chaldean/Syriac (15)	28	0.03
Australian (65)	83	0.10
Austrian (106)	305	0.36
Basque (46)	55	0.06
Belgian (0)	44	0.05
Brazilian (0)	51	0.06
British (172)	449	0.53
Bulgarian (187)	187	0.22
Canadian (137)	455	0.53
Croatian (96)	201	0.24
Czech (135)	442	0.52
Czechoslovakian (43)	106	0.12
Danish (248)	1,185	1.39
Dutch (282)	1,808	2.12
Eastern European (61)	61	0.07
English (2,206)	10,783	12.67
European (1,466)	1,705	2.00
Finnish (46)	168	0.20
French, ex. Basque (322)	3,374	3.96
French Canadian (204)	488	0.57
German (4,083)	16,596	19.49
Greek (250)	808	0.95
Guyanese (0)	50	0.06
Hungarian (116)	308	0.36
Icelander (38)	64	0.08
Iranian (15)	66	0.08
Irish (2,818)	12,531	14.72
Italian (2,050)	6,333	7.44
Latvian (6)	6	0.01
Lithuanian (33)	233	0.27
Maltese (17)	73	0.09
Northern European (135)	136	0.16
Norwegian (525)	2,139	2.51
Polish (385)	1,428	1.68
Portuguese (800)	2,352	2.76
Romanian (52)	116	0.14
Russian (110)	812	0.95
Scandinavian (128)	336	0.39
Scotch-Irish (641)	2,302	2.70
Scottish (478)	2,710	3.18
Serbian (0)	4	<0.01
Slavic (44)	44	0.05
Slovak (0)	65	0.08
Slovene (9)	59	0.07
Swedish (458)	1,980	2.33
Swiss (82)	467	0.55
Turkish (20)	53	0.06
Ukrainian (44)	171	0.20
Welsh (109)	736	0.86

*Notes: † The Census 2010 population figure is used to calculate the percentages in the Hispanic Origin and Race categories. Ancestry percentages are based on the 2006-2010 American Community Survey population (not shown); ‡ Numbers in parentheses indicate the number of people reporting a single ancestry; * Numbers in parentheses indicate the number of persons reporting this race alone, not in combination with any other race; Please refer to the Explanation of Data for more information.*

West Indian, ex. Hispanic (65)	79	0.09
Haitian (5)	19	0.02
Trinidadian/Tobagonian (27)	27	0.03
West Indian (33)	33	0.04
Yugoslavian (25)	148	0.17

Hispanic Origin	Population	%
Hispanic or Latino (of any race)	13,315	15.45
Central American, ex. Mexican	391	0.45
Costa Rican	37	0.04
Guatemalan	89	0.10
Honduran	29	0.03
Nicaraguan	80	0.09
Panamanian	20	0.02
Salvadoran	127	0.15
Other Central American	9	0.01
Cuban	91	0.11
Dominican Republic	11	0.01
Mexican	11,051	12.82
Puerto Rican	322	0.37
South American	286	0.33
Argentinean	28	0.03
Bolivian	18	0.02
Chilean	49	0.06
Colombian	60	0.07
Ecuadorian	16	0.02
Paraguayan	3	<0.01
Peruvian	77	0.09
Uruguayan	4	<0.01
Venezuelan	24	0.03
Other South American	7	0.01
Other Hispanic or Latino	1,163	1.35

Race*	Population	%
African-American/Black (1,771)	2,798	3.25
Not Hispanic (1,636)	2,468	2.86
Hispanic (135)	330	0.38
American Indian/Alaska Native (1,167)	2,666	3.09
Not Hispanic (791)	1,922	2.23
Hispanic (376)	744	0.86
Alaska Athabascan *(Ala. Nat.)* (6)	6	0.01
Aleut *(Alaska Native)* (3)	4	<0.01
Apache (21)	56	0.06
Arapaho (4)	7	0.01
Blackfeet (6)	81	0.09
Canadian/French Am. Ind. (0)	4	<0.01
Central American Ind. (1)	5	0.01
Cherokee (107)	431	0.50
Cheyenne (3)	7	0.01
Chickasaw (7)	26	0.03
Chippewa (19)	46	0.05
Choctaw (22)	96	0.11
Colville (2)	2	<0.01
Comanche (1)	3	<0.01
Cree (3)	6	0.01
Creek (5)	24	0.03
Crow (0)	2	<0.01
Delaware (2)	7	0.01
Inupiat *(Alaska Native)* (1)	3	<0.01
Iroquois (4)	15	0.02
Kiowa (0)	2	<0.01
Lumbee (0)	1	<0.01
Menominee (0)	1	<0.01
Mexican American Ind. (54)	84	0.10
Navajo (20)	41	0.05
Osage (5)	18	0.02
Ottawa (1)	1	<0.01
Paiute (5)	17	0.02
Pima (1)	1	<0.01
Potawatomi (9)	22	0.03
Pueblo (8)	16	0.02
Puget Sound Salish (2)	3	<0.01
Seminole (3)	10	0.01
Shoshone (9)	23	0.03
Sioux (38)	89	0.10
South American Ind. (1)	4	<0.01
Spanish American Ind. (1)	3	<0.01
Tlingit-Haida *(Alaska Native)* (6)	11	0.01
Tohono O'Odham (1)	2	<0.01
Tsimshian *(Alaska Native)* (7)	7	0.01
Ute (1)	2	<0.01
Yakama (0)	5	0.01
Yaqui (7)	31	0.04
Yuman (2)	2	<0.01
Yup'ik *(Alaska Native)* (2)	3	<0.01
Asian (3,656)	4,948	5.74
Not Hispanic (3,589)	4,700	5.45
Hispanic (67)	248	0.29
Bangladeshi (4)	4	<0.01
Burmese (4)	6	0.01
Cambodian (27)	42	0.05
Chinese, ex. Taiwanese (584)	806	0.94
Filipino (419)	800	0.93
Hmong (1,157)	1,225	1.42
Indian (325)	413	0.48
Indonesian (10)	21	0.02
Japanese (293)	642	0.74
Korean (174)	264	0.31
Laotian (141)	177	0.21
Malaysian (5)	7	0.01
Nepalese (6)	7	0.01
Pakistani (89)	97	0.11
Sri Lankan (25)	25	0.03
Taiwanese (28)	41	0.05
Thai (30)	57	0.07
Vietnamese (164)	195	0.23
Hawaii Native/Pacific Islander (210)	516	0.60
Not Hispanic (189)	434	0.50
Hispanic (21)	82	0.10
Fijian (6)	16	0.02
Guamanian/Chamorro (48)	78	0.09
Marshallese (0)	5	0.01
Native Hawaiian (44)	192	0.22
Samoan (40)	58	0.07
Tongan (5)	5	0.01
White (69,606)	73,535	85.32
Not Hispanic (63,561)	66,261	76.88
Hispanic (6,045)	7,274	8.44

Chino Hills

Place Type: City
County: San Bernardino
Population: 74,799†

Ancestry‡	Population	%
Afghan (41)	41	0.06
African, Sub-Saharan (323)	534	0.72
African (125)	271	0.36
Ethiopian (0)	65	0.09
Ghanaian (35)	35	0.05
Nigerian (148)	148	0.20
Other Sub-Saharan African (15)	15	0.02
American (2,017)	2,017	2.71
Arab (1,231)	1,497	2.01
Arab (184)	405	0.54
Egyptian (340)	371	0.50
Jordanian (15)	15	0.02
Lebanese (369)	383	0.51
Palestinian (175)	175	0.24
Syrian (11)	11	0.01
Other Arab (137)	137	0.18
Armenian (154)	248	0.33
Assyrian/Chaldean/Syriac (8)	26	0.03
Austrian (0)	55	0.07
Basque (18)	65	0.09
Belgian (0)	26	0.03
Brazilian (21)	32	0.04
British (80)	142	0.19
Bulgarian (30)	30	0.04
Canadian (160)	385	0.52
Croatian (11)	70	0.09
Czech (34)	117	0.16
Czechoslovakian (12)	21	0.03
Danish (80)	422	0.57
Dutch (244)	1,384	1.86
Eastern European (39)	39	0.05
English (1,282)	4,488	6.03
European (832)	1,235	1.66
Finnish (13)	57	0.08
French, ex. Basque (170)	1,267	1.70
French Canadian (42)	364	0.49
German (1,361)	6,506	8.74
Greek (127)	277	0.37
Hungarian (152)	239	0.32
Icelander (0)	9	0.01
Iranian (131)	187	0.25
Irish (879)	4,584	6.16
Israeli (91)	91	0.12
Italian (1,322)	3,811	5.12
Lithuanian (22)	35	0.05
New Zealander (8)	8	0.01
Northern European (51)	51	0.07
Norwegian (249)	740	0.99
Pennsylvania German (15)	47	0.06
Polish (186)	881	1.18
Portuguese (49)	181	0.24
Romanian (39)	60	0.08
Russian (121)	560	0.75
Scandinavian (159)	270	0.36
Scotch-Irish (430)	1,089	1.46
Scottish (341)	1,236	1.66
Serbian (14)	53	0.07
Slavic (0)	13	0.02
Slovak (27)	52	0.07
Swedish (141)	674	0.91
Swiss (65)	214	0.29
Ukrainian (68)	226	0.30
Welsh (65)	347	0.47
West Indian, ex. Hispanic (170)	193	0.26
Belizean (116)	116	0.16
Haitian (27)	41	0.06
Jamaican (27)	36	0.05
Yugoslavian (10)	10	0.01

Hispanic Origin	Population	%
Hispanic or Latino (of any race)	21,802	29.15
Central American, ex. Mexican	1,180	1.58
Costa Rican	92	0.12
Guatemalan	278	0.37
Honduran	51	0.07
Nicaraguan	169	0.23
Panamanian	20	0.03
Salvadoran	547	0.73
Other Central American	23	0.03
Cuban	383	0.51
Dominican Republic	23	0.03
Mexican	17,678	23.63
Puerto Rican	389	0.52
South American	965	1.29
Argentinean	167	0.22
Bolivian	23	0.03
Chilean	73	0.10
Colombian	273	0.36
Ecuadorian	191	0.26
Paraguayan	7	0.01
Peruvian	171	0.23
Uruguayan	8	0.01
Venezuelan	33	0.04
Other South American	19	0.03
Other Hispanic or Latino	1,184	1.58

Race*	Population	%
African-American/Black (3,415)	3,986	5.33
Not Hispanic (3,225)	3,644	4.87
Hispanic (190)	342	0.46
American Indian/Alaska Native (379)	816	1.09
Not Hispanic (143)	350	0.47
Hispanic (236)	466	0.62
Apache (13)	42	0.06
Blackfeet (7)	18	0.02
Canadian/French Am. Ind. (1)	2	<0.01
Cherokee (25)	105	0.14
Cheyenne (0)	1	<0.01
Chickasaw (4)	17	0.02
Chippewa (1)	6	0.01
Choctaw (11)	28	0.04
Comanche (3)	8	0.01
Creek (0)	4	0.01
Crow (5)	5	0.01

*Notes: † The Census 2010 population figure is used to calculate the percentages in the Hispanic Origin and Race categories. Ancestry percentages are based on the 2006-2010 American Community Survey population (not shown); ‡ Numbers in parentheses indicate the number of people reporting a single ancestry; * Numbers in parentheses indicate the number of persons reporting this race alone, not in combination with any other race; Please refer to the Explanation of Data for more information.*

Delaware (1)	4	0.01
Hopi (3)	5	0.01
Iroquois (0)	3	<0.01
Mexican American Ind. (30)	50	0.07
Navajo (15)	40	0.05
Paiute (1)	1	<0.01
Pima (4)	10	0.01
Potawatomi (3)	4	0.01
Pueblo (7)	21	0.03
Seminole (0)	1	<0.01
Sioux (7)	15	0.02
South American Ind. (0)	3	<0.01
Spanish American Ind. (6)	9	0.01
Yaqui (6)	12	0.02
Asian (22,676)	24,637	32.94
Not Hispanic (22,351)	23,813	31.84
Hispanic (325)	824	1.10
Bangladeshi (26)	32	0.04
Burmese (41)	51	0.07
Cambodian (106)	145	0.19
Chinese, ex. Taiwanese (6,012)	6,895	9.22
Filipino (6,277)	7,257	9.70
Hmong (8)	9	0.01
Indian (2,003)	2,139	2.86
Indonesian (288)	389	0.52
Japanese (660)	1,162	1.55
Korean (3,401)	3,662	4.90
Laotian (70)	79	0.11
Malaysian (27)	34	0.05
Nepalese (5)	5	0.01
Pakistani (334)	375	0.50
Sri Lankan (42)	47	0.06
Taiwanese (1,242)	1,422	1.90
Thai (244)	323	0.43
Vietnamese (996)	1,168	1.56
Hawaii Native/Pacific Islander (115)	360	0.48
Not Hispanic (99)	291	0.39
Hispanic (16)	69	0.09
Fijian (5)	8	0.01
Guamanian/Chamorro (25)	43	0.06
Native Hawaiian (36)	118	0.16
Samoan (28)	44	0.06
White (38,035)	41,076	54.92
Not Hispanic (25,017)	26,656	35.64
Hispanic (13,018)	14,420	19.28

Chino

Place Type: City
County: San Bernardino
Population: 77,983†

Ancestry‡	Population	%
African, Sub-Saharan (296)	433	0.56
African (165)	242	0.31
Ethiopian (81)	133	0.17
Nigerian (50)	50	0.06
South African (0)	8	0.01
American (2,824)	2,824	3.63
Arab (187)	313	0.40
Arab (7)	16	0.02
Egyptian (7)	7	0.01
Lebanese (42)	99	0.13
Moroccan (0)	8	0.01
Palestinian (0)	9	0.01
Syrian (131)	174	0.22
Armenian (117)	143	0.18
Assyrian/Chaldean/Syriac (13)	22	0.03
Australian (33)	59	0.08
Austrian (21)	95	0.12
Basque (66)	103	0.13
Belgian (0)	20	0.03
Brazilian (4)	4	0.01
Canadian (68)	210	0.27
Croatian (0)	13	0.02
Czech (0)	49	0.06
Czechoslovakian (8)	8	0.01
Danish (76)	200	0.26
Dutch (631)	1,087	1.40
Eastern European (15)	15	0.02
English (1,260)	3,717	4.78
European (469)	730	0.94
Finnish (0)	135	0.17
French, ex. Basque (169)	1,185	1.52
French Canadian (237)	282	0.36
German (1,466)	5,550	7.14
Greek (29)	98	0.13
Guyanese (19)	19	0.02
Hungarian (58)	115	0.15
Icelander (5)	5	0.01
Iranian (44)	53	0.07
Irish (980)	4,246	5.46
Italian (758)	2,698	3.47
Lithuanian (18)	49	0.06
Northern European (26)	26	0.03
Norwegian (173)	461	0.59
Polish (193)	721	0.93
Portuguese (729)	1,174	1.51
Romanian (153)	153	0.20
Russian (97)	254	0.33
Scandinavian (17)	26	0.03
Scotch-Irish (255)	678	0.87
Scottish (375)	827	1.06
Serbian (0)	7	0.01
Slavic (16)	69	0.09
Swedish (60)	414	0.53
Swiss (8)	66	0.08
Ukrainian (0)	26	0.03
Welsh (20)	235	0.30
West Indian, ex. Hispanic (77)	167	0.21
Belizean (24)	93	0.12
Jamaican (13)	21	0.03
Trinidadian/Tobagonian (0)	8	0.01
West Indian (40)	45	0.06
Yugoslavian (0)	34	0.04

Hispanic Origin	Population	%
Hispanic or Latino (of any race)	41,993	53.85
Central American, ex. Mexican	1,792	2.30
Costa Rican	106	0.14
Guatemalan	432	0.55
Honduran	145	0.19
Nicaraguan	221	0.28
Panamanian	28	0.04
Salvadoran	849	1.09
Other Central American	11	0.01
Cuban	355	0.46
Dominican Republic	17	0.02
Mexican	36,069	46.25
Puerto Rican	490	0.63
South American	874	1.12
Argentinean	229	0.29
Bolivian	20	0.03
Chilean	41	0.05
Colombian	182	0.23
Ecuadorian	151	0.19
Paraguayan	2	<0.01
Peruvian	213	0.27
Uruguayan	6	0.01
Venezuelan	17	0.02
Other South American	13	0.02
Other Hispanic or Latino	2,396	3.07

Race*	Population	%
African-American/Black (4,829)	5,459	7.00
Not Hispanic (4,529)	4,913	6.30
Hispanic (300)	546	0.70
American Indian/Alaska Native (786)	1,381	1.77
Not Hispanic (256)	536	0.69
Hispanic (530)	845	1.08
Alaska Athabascan *(Ala. Nat.)* (1)	1	<0.01
Apache (25)	68	0.09
Arapaho (1)	1	<0.01
Blackfeet (6)	27	0.03
Canadian/French Am. Ind. (0)	2	<0.01
Central American Ind. (4)	4	0.01
Cherokee (38)	144	0.18
Cheyenne (4)	6	0.01
Chickasaw (1)	3	<0.01
Chippewa (2)	4	0.01
Choctaw (13)	40	0.05
Comanche (3)	3	<0.01
Cree (0)	1	<0.01
Creek (18)	20	0.03
Crow (2)	4	0.01
Delaware (1)	1	<0.01
Hopi (0)	2	<0.01
Inupiat *(Alaska Native)* (3)	5	0.01
Iroquois (0)	4	0.01
Kiowa (2)	2	<0.01
Lumbee (1)	2	<0.01
Mexican American Ind. (76)	108	0.14
Navajo (22)	44	0.06
Osage (3)	3	<0.01
Paiute (2)	3	<0.01
Pima (5)	9	0.01
Potawatomi (4)	4	0.01
Pueblo (6)	16	0.02
Seminole (1)	4	0.01
Shoshone (3)	9	0.01
Sioux (15)	34	0.04
South American Ind. (11)	11	0.01
Spanish American Ind. (1)	5	0.01
Tlingit-Haida *(Alaska Native)* (6)	10	0.01
Tohono O'Odham (3)	8	0.01
Ute (0)	6	0.01
Yaqui (20)	37	0.05
Yuman (8)	11	0.01
Asian (8,159)	9,279	11.90
Not Hispanic (7,932)	8,632	11.07
Hispanic (227)	647	0.83
Bangladeshi (39)	45	0.06
Bhutanese (5)	5	0.01
Burmese (25)	28	0.04
Cambodian (102)	116	0.15
Chinese, ex. Taiwanese (1,909)	2,258	2.90
Filipino (2,821)	3,361	4.31
Hmong (4)	4	0.01
Indian (626)	710	0.91
Indonesian (99)	177	0.23
Japanese (244)	516	0.66
Korean (606)	683	0.88
Laotian (46)	58	0.07
Malaysian (21)	30	0.04
Nepalese (0)	1	<0.01
Pakistani (96)	118	0.15
Sri Lankan (13)	18	0.02
Taiwanese (448)	503	0.65
Thai (99)	136	0.17
Vietnamese (537)	652	0.84
Hawaii Native/Pacific Islander (168)	419	0.54
Not Hispanic (112)	261	0.33
Hispanic (56)	158	0.20
Fijian (4)	6	0.01
Guamanian/Chamorro (33)	56	0.07
Native Hawaiian (35)	138	0.18
Samoan (62)	104	0.13
Tongan (20)	21	0.03
White (43,981)	46,869	60.10
Not Hispanic (21,659)	22,700	29.11
Hispanic (22,322)	24,169	30.99

Chowchilla

Place Type: City
County: Madera
Population: 18,720†

Ancestry‡	Population	%
African, Sub-Saharan (5)	13	0.07
African (5)	13	0.07
Albanian (0)	9	0.05
American (244)	244	1.35
Arab (208)	233	1.29
Arab (10)	10	0.06
Jordanian (87)	87	0.48
Lebanese (0)	10	0.06
Palestinian (111)	126	0.70
Armenian (0)	22	0.12
Austrian (0)	33	0.18

*Notes: † The Census 2010 population figure is used to calculate the percentages in the Hispanic Origin and Race categories. Ancestry percentages are based on the 2006-2010 American Community Survey population (not shown); ‡ Numbers in parentheses indicate the number of people reporting a single ancestry; * Numbers in parentheses indicate the number of persons reporting this race alone, not in combination with any other race; Please refer to the Explanation of Data for more information.*

Basque (51)	51	0.28
British (1)	2	0.01
Canadian (35)	35	0.19
Czech (0)	42	0.23
Danish (2)	56	0.31
Dutch (33)	108	0.60
English (283)	721	3.99
European (40)	67	0.37
French, ex. Basque (45)	262	1.45
French Canadian (0)	44	0.24
German (297)	1,377	7.61
Greek (5)	47	0.26
Hungarian (0)	23	0.13
Irish (224)	1,192	6.59
Italian (220)	749	4.14
Norwegian (49)	107	0.59
Polish (0)	64	0.35
Portuguese (283)	455	2.52
Russian (3)	28	0.15
Scandinavian (0)	8	0.04
Scotch-Irish (31)	116	0.64
Scottish (38)	104	0.57
Swedish (6)	43	0.24
Swiss (0)	33	0.18
Ukrainian (14)	27	0.15
Welsh (34)	128	0.71
West Indian, ex. Hispanic (9)	47	0.26
Belizean (0)	9	0.05
Dutch West Indian (0)	29	0.16
Jamaican (9)	9	0.05
Yugoslavian (0)	6	0.03

Hispanic Origin	Population	%
Hispanic or Latino (of any race)	7,073	37.78
Central American, ex. Mexican	64	0.34
Costa Rican	2	0.01
Guatemalan	10	0.05
Honduran	4	0.02
Nicaraguan	6	0.03
Panamanian	3	0.02
Salvadoran	37	0.20
Other Central American	2	0.01
Cuban	14	0.07
Dominican Republic	1	0.01
Mexican	5,828	31.13
Puerto Rican	62	0.33
South American	18	0.10
Chilean	2	0.01
Colombian	4	0.02
Peruvian	8	0.04
Uruguayan	1	0.01
Venezuelan	3	0.02
Other Hispanic or Latino	1,086	5.80

Race*	Population	%
African-American/Black (2,358)	2,456	13.12
Not Hispanic (2,309)	2,373	12.68
Hispanic (49)	83	0.44
American Indian/Alaska Native (376)	610	3.26
Not Hispanic (251)	404	2.16
Hispanic (125)	206	1.10
Apache (3)	14	0.07
Blackfeet (3)	7	0.04
Cherokee (44)	131	0.70
Chickasaw (1)	1	0.01
Chippewa (0)	7	0.04
Choctaw (14)	27	0.14
Creek (1)	5	0.03
Delaware (5)	12	0.06
Hopi (0)	1	0.01
Iroquois (1)	1	0.01
Kiowa (0)	1	0.01
Mexican American Ind. (11)	31	0.17
Navajo (3)	6	0.03
Paiute (1)	1	0.01
Pima (0)	1	0.01
Sioux (12)	13	0.07
South American Ind. (0)	2	0.01
Tohono O'Odham (0)	1	0.01
Tsimshian *(Alaska Native)* (1)	1	0.01
Yaqui (2)	11	0.06
Asian (395)	512	2.74
Not Hispanic (373)	446	2.38
Hispanic (22)	66	0.35
Cambodian (11)	13	0.07
Chinese, ex. Taiwanese (32)	54	0.29
Filipino (104)	146	0.78
Hmong (6)	7	0.04
Indian (161)	179	0.96
Japanese (12)	29	0.15
Korean (21)	22	0.12
Laotian (7)	9	0.05
Pakistani (1)	2	0.01
Taiwanese (1)	1	0.01
Thai (0)	2	0.01
Vietnamese (16)	21	0.11
Hawaii Native/Pacific Islander (37)	71	0.38
Not Hispanic (30)	41	0.22
Hispanic (7)	30	0.16
Guamanian/Chamorro (3)	6	0.03
Native Hawaiian (5)	17	0.09
Samoan (18)	25	0.13
White (11,533)	12,142	64.86
Not Hispanic (7,887)	8,165	43.62
Hispanic (3,646)	3,977	21.24

Chula Vista

Place Type: City
County: San Diego
Population: 243,916†

Ancestry‡	Population	%
Afghan (39)	39	0.02
African, Sub-Saharan (633)	806	0.35
African (344)	517	0.23
Cape Verdean (8)	8	<0.01
Ethiopian (209)	209	0.09
Nigerian (25)	25	0.01
South African (27)	27	0.01
Ugandan (20)	20	0.01
American (3,413)	3,413	1.49
Arab (479)	892	0.39
Arab (23)	134	0.06
Egyptian (0)	34	0.01
Iraqi (56)	77	0.03
Jordanian (22)	22	0.01
Lebanese (86)	219	0.10
Moroccan (95)	113	0.05
Palestinian (34)	52	0.02
Syrian (0)	10	<0.01
Other Arab (163)	231	0.10
Armenian (113)	218	0.09
Assyrian/Chaldean/Syriac (15)	37	0.02
Australian (26)	78	0.03
Austrian (51)	287	0.12
Basque (42)	80	0.03
Belgian (0)	40	0.02
Brazilian (35)	35	0.02
British (682)	895	0.39
Bulgarian (49)	61	0.03
Canadian (232)	288	0.13
Celtic (28)	34	0.01
Croatian (10)	36	0.02
Czech (89)	422	0.18
Czechoslovakian (21)	101	0.04
Danish (170)	625	0.27
Dutch (168)	996	0.43
Eastern European (39)	39	0.02
English (2,584)	8,433	3.67
European (1,437)	1,658	0.72
Finnish (38)	166	0.07
French, ex. Basque (483)	3,717	1.62
French Canadian (206)	463	0.20
German (4,095)	14,147	6.16
Greek (152)	657	0.29
Guyanese (16)	46	0.02
Hungarian (29)	385	0.17
Icelander (16)	16	0.01
Iranian (153)	350	0.15
Irish (3,144)	11,613	5.06
Israeli (44)	44	0.02
Italian (2,180)	5,093	2.22
Latvian (24)	32	0.01
Lithuanian (0)	106	0.05
Luxemburger (0)	8	<0.01
Macedonian (0)	28	0.01
Northern European (45)	55	0.02
Norwegian (557)	1,588	0.69
Pennsylvania German (35)	35	0.02
Polish (517)	1,875	0.82
Portuguese (533)	1,363	0.59
Romanian (39)	101	0.04
Russian (125)	580	0.25
Scandinavian (58)	198	0.09
Scotch-Irish (630)	1,819	0.79
Scottish (603)	1,755	0.76
Serbian (11)	32	0.01
Slavic (35)	35	0.02
Slovak (32)	128	0.06
Slovene (8)	25	0.01
Swedish (392)	1,254	0.55
Swiss (129)	277	0.12
Turkish (58)	169	0.07
Ukrainian (90)	192	0.08
Welsh (255)	703	0.31
West Indian, ex. Hispanic (341)	600	0.26
Barbadian (12)	12	0.01
Belizean (0)	15	0.01
British West Indian (13)	34	0.01
Dutch West Indian (0)	13	0.01
Haitian (18)	104	0.05
Jamaican (298)	345	0.15
Trinidadian/Tobagonian (0)	14	0.01
U.S. Virgin Islander (0)	16	0.01
West Indian (0)	47	0.02
Yugoslavian (16)	46	0.02

Hispanic Origin	Population	%
Hispanic or Latino (of any race)	142,066	58.24
Central American, ex. Mexican	1,619	0.66
Costa Rican	181	0.07
Guatemalan	320	0.13
Honduran	176	0.07
Nicaraguan	236	0.10
Panamanian	203	0.08
Salvadoran	489	0.20
Other Central American	14	0.01
Cuban	532	0.22
Dominican Republic	193	0.08
Mexican	130,413	53.47
Puerto Rican	2,282	0.94
South American	1,763	0.72
Argentinean	202	0.08
Bolivian	113	0.05
Chilean	168	0.07
Colombian	572	0.23
Ecuadorian	176	0.07
Paraguayan	4	<0.01
Peruvian	408	0.17
Uruguayan	25	0.01
Venezuelan	81	0.03
Other South American	14	0.01
Other Hispanic or Latino	5,264	2.16

Race*	Population	%
African-American/Black (11,219)	14,196	5.82
Not Hispanic (9,972)	11,893	4.88
Hispanic (1,247)	2,303	0.94
American Indian/Alaska Native (1,880)	3,421	1.40
Not Hispanic (600)	1,420	0.58
Hispanic (1,280)	2,001	0.82
Alaska Athabascan *(Ala. Nat.)* (5)	5	<0.01
Aleut *(Alaska Native)* (3)	5	<0.01
Apache (45)	128	0.05
Blackfeet (12)	63	0.03
Canadian/French Am. Ind. (2)	6	<0.01
Central American Ind. (8)	13	0.01
Cherokee (68)	296	0.12
Cheyenne (2)	9	<0.01

*Notes: † The Census 2010 population figure is used to calculate the percentages in the Hispanic Origin and Race categories. Ancestry percentages are based on the 2006-2010 American Community Survey population (not shown); ‡ Numbers in parentheses indicate the number of people reporting a single ancestry; * Numbers in parentheses indicate the number of persons reporting this race alone, not in combination with any other race; Please refer to the Explanation of Data for more information.*

Chickasaw (19)	25	0.01
Chippewa (10)	24	0.01
Choctaw (39)	89	0.04
Comanche (12)	25	0.01
Cree (2)	3	<0.01
Creek (9)	26	0.01
Crow (4)	13	0.01
Delaware (0)	2	<0.01
Hopi (3)	3	<0.01
Houma (1)	2	<0.01
Inupiat *(Alaska Native)* (3)	8	<0.01
Iroquois (16)	36	0.01
Kiowa (2)	6	<0.01
Lumbee (3)	7	<0.01
Mexican American Ind. (296)	451	0.18
Navajo (100)	158	0.06
Osage (5)	8	<0.01
Ottawa (1)	2	<0.01
Paiute (0)	2	<0.01
Pima (9)	14	0.01
Potawatomi (4)	6	<0.01
Pueblo (23)	35	0.01
Puget Sound Salish (2)	5	<0.01
Seminole (1)	5	<0.01
Shoshone (0)	4	<0.01
Sioux (15)	34	0.01
South American Ind. (3)	11	<0.01
Spanish American Ind. (8)	10	<0.01
Tlingit-Haida *(Alaska Native)* (1)	2	<0.01
Tohono O'Odham (20)	28	0.01
Tsimshian *(Alaska Native)* (2)	3	<0.01
Ute (1)	1	<0.01
Yakama (0)	3	<0.01
Yaqui (34)	77	0.03
Yuman (6)	10	<0.01
Yup'ik *(Alaska Native)* (1)	3	<0.01
Asian (35,042)	41,840	17.15
Not Hispanic (33,581)	38,101	15.62
Hispanic (1,461)	3,739	1.53
Bangladeshi (19)	20	0.01
Burmese (13)	15	0.01
Cambodian (95)	135	0.06
Chinese, ex. Taiwanese (1,558)	2,441	1.00
Filipino (26,597)	31,344	12.85
Hmong (3)	6	<0.01
Indian (582)	784	0.32
Indonesian (33)	74	0.03
Japanese (1,951)	3,369	1.38
Korean (2,028)	2,397	0.98
Laotian (113)	162	0.07
Malaysian (8)	32	0.01
Nepalese (11)	13	0.01
Pakistani (105)	145	0.06
Sri Lankan (41)	46	0.02
Taiwanese (116)	164	0.07
Thai (102)	191	0.08
Vietnamese (888)	1,108	0.45
Hawaii Native/Pacific Islander (1,351)	2,746	1.13
Not Hispanic (1,105)	1,993	0.82
Hispanic (246)	753	0.31
Fijian (10)	11	<0.01
Guamanian/Chamorro (780)	1,389	0.57
Marshallese (1)	6	<0.01
Native Hawaiian (155)	577	0.24
Samoan (237)	396	0.16
Tongan (61)	72	0.03
White (130,991)	142,343	58.36
Not Hispanic (49,641)	54,966	22.53
Hispanic (81,350)	87,377	35.82

Citrus

Place Type: CDP
County: Los Angeles
Population: 10,866†

Ancestry‡	Population	%
African, Sub-Saharan (0)	12	0.12
African (0)	12	0.12
American (125)	125	1.24
Arab (196)	207	2.05
Egyptian (189)	189	1.87
Jordanian (7)	7	0.07
Syrian (0)	11	0.11
Armenian (0)	33	0.33
British (0)	16	0.16
Canadian (0)	58	0.57
Czech (6)	6	0.06
Danish (0)	9	0.09
Dutch (0)	115	1.14
English (85)	315	3.12
European (43)	43	0.43
French, ex. Basque (30)	84	0.83
French Canadian (0)	30	0.30
German (129)	450	4.45
Greek (0)	10	0.10
Hungarian (6)	21	0.21
Iranian (24)	24	0.24
Irish (80)	507	5.02
Italian (142)	241	2.38
Lithuanian (6)	15	0.15
Norwegian (15)	66	0.65
Polish (10)	30	0.30
Russian (0)	14	0.14
Scotch-Irish (15)	58	0.57
Scottish (55)	132	1.31
Swedish (65)	157	1.55
Welsh (0)	10	0.10
West Indian, ex. Hispanic (35)	35	0.35
West Indian (35)	35	0.35
Yugoslavian (15)	34	0.34

Hispanic Origin	Population	%
Hispanic or Latino (of any race)	7,911	72.81
Central American, ex. Mexican	424	3.90
Costa Rican	11	0.10
Guatemalan	85	0.78
Honduran	18	0.17
Nicaraguan	50	0.46
Panamanian	12	0.11
Salvadoran	246	2.26
Other Central American	2	0.02
Cuban	32	0.29
Mexican	7,030	64.70
Puerto Rican	73	0.67
South American	127	1.17
Argentinean	25	0.23
Bolivian	15	0.14
Chilean	4	0.04
Colombian	7	0.06
Ecuadorian	28	0.26
Peruvian	40	0.37
Venezuelan	1	0.01
Other South American	7	0.06
Other Hispanic or Latino	225	2.07

Race*	Population	%
African-American/Black (240)	296	2.72
Not Hispanic (198)	231	2.13
Hispanic (42)	65	0.60
American Indian/Alaska Native (120)	202	1.86
Not Hispanic (22)	55	0.51
Hispanic (98)	147	1.35
Alaska Athabascan *(Ala. Nat.)* (0)	2	0.02
Apache (5)	11	0.10
Blackfeet (4)	5	0.05
Central American Ind. (1)	2	0.02
Cherokee (0)	2	0.02
Choctaw (0)	3	0.03
Creek (0)	4	0.04
Delaware (0)	1	0.01
Hopi (0)	1	0.01
Iroquois (0)	1	0.01
Mexican American Ind. (27)	37	0.34
Navajo (11)	18	0.17
Ottawa (0)	1	0.01
Pima (3)	3	0.03
Potawatomi (0)	8	0.07
Shoshone (0)	2	0.02
Sioux (0)	1	0.01
Tohono O'Odham (2)	2	0.02
Yaqui (2)	6	0.06
Asian (860)	973	8.95
Not Hispanic (837)	899	8.27
Hispanic (23)	74	0.68
Burmese (4)	4	0.04
Cambodian (2)	2	0.02
Chinese, ex. Taiwanese (92)	111	1.02
Filipino (333)	369	3.40
Indian (244)	252	2.32
Indonesian (28)	52	0.48
Japanese (38)	65	0.60
Korean (14)	16	0.15
Laotian (0)	5	0.05
Pakistani (1)	1	0.01
Taiwanese (23)	23	0.21
Thai (29)	38	0.35
Vietnamese (39)	46	0.42
Hawaii Native/Pacific Islander (4)	37	0.34
Not Hispanic (4)	20	0.18
Hispanic (0)	17	0.16
Fijian (1)	1	0.01
Native Hawaiian (1)	10	0.09
White (5,898)	6,267	57.68
Not Hispanic (1,748)	1,859	17.11
Hispanic (4,150)	4,408	40.57

Citrus Heights

Place Type: City
County: Sacramento
Population: 83,301†

Ancestry‡	Population	%
African, Sub-Saharan (131)	197	0.23
African (90)	148	0.18
Cape Verdean (7)	7	0.01
Ethiopian (21)	29	0.03
Liberian (13)	13	0.02
Alsatian (0)	14	0.02
American (2,380)	2,380	2.82
Arab (208)	280	0.33
Arab (6)	40	0.05
Egyptian (11)	11	0.01
Iraqi (39)	39	0.05
Lebanese (9)	9	0.01
Moroccan (29)	29	0.03
Other Arab (114)	152	0.18
Armenian (123)	234	0.28
Assyrian/Chaldean/Syriac (0)	37	0.04
Australian (0)	80	0.09
Austrian (88)	122	0.14
Basque (35)	44	0.05
Belgian (0)	49	0.06
Brazilian (68)	105	0.12
British (226)	349	0.41
Bulgarian (0)	14	0.02
Canadian (124)	294	0.35
Carpatho Rusyn (0)	19	0.02
Celtic (8)	8	0.01
Croatian (55)	211	0.25
Czech (78)	290	0.34
Czechoslovakian (52)	75	0.09
Danish (209)	1,123	1.33
Dutch (451)	2,006	2.38
English (3,422)	11,463	13.59
European (940)	1,044	1.24
Finnish (116)	226	0.27
French, ex. Basque (252)	2,853	3.38
French Canadian (130)	286	0.34
German (4,168)	15,987	18.95
Greek (191)	547	0.65
Hungarian (152)	522	0.62
Icelander (12)	63	0.07
Iranian (240)	339	0.40
Irish (2,736)	12,491	14.81
Italian (1,647)	5,358	6.35
Lithuanian (21)	75	0.09
Maltese (0)	27	0.03
Northern European (139)	139	0.16

*Notes: † The Census 2010 population figure is used to calculate the percentages in the Hispanic Origin and Race categories. Ancestry percentages are based on the 2006-2010 American Community Survey population (not shown); ‡ Numbers in parentheses indicate the number of people reporting a single ancestry; * Numbers in parentheses indicate the number of persons reporting this race alone, not in combination with any other race; Please refer to the Explanation of Data for more information.*

Norwegian (561)	2,043	2.42
Pennsylvania German (34)	75	0.09
Polish (310)	1,260	1.49
Portuguese (427)	1,645	1.95
Romanian (462)	533	0.63
Russian (1,283)	1,916	2.27
Scandinavian (125)	318	0.38
Scotch-Irish (778)	1,532	1.82
Scottish (692)	1,893	2.24
Serbian (45)	54	0.06
Slavic (19)	82	0.10
Slovak (29)	87	0.10
Swedish (350)	1,968	2.33
Swiss (18)	289	0.34
Turkish (38)	72	0.09
Ukrainian (1,796)	1,833	2.17
Welsh (114)	766	0.91
Yugoslavian (321)	447	0.53

Hispanic Origin	**Population**	**%**
Hispanic or Latino (of any race)	13,734	16.49
Central American, ex. Mexican	775	0.93
Costa Rican	18	0.02
Guatemalan	290	0.35
Honduran	25	0.03
Nicaraguan	102	0.12
Panamanian	45	0.05
Salvadoran	290	0.35
Other Central American	5	0.01
Cuban	102	0.12
Dominican Republic	18	0.02
Mexican	10,321	12.39
Puerto Rican	458	0.55
South American	332	0.40
Argentinean	51	0.06
Bolivian	4	<0.01
Chilean	66	0.08
Colombian	54	0.06
Ecuadorian	32	0.04
Paraguayan	3	<0.01
Peruvian	92	0.11
Uruguayan	8	0.01
Venezuelan	17	0.02
Other South American	5	0.01
Other Hispanic or Latino	1,728	2.07

Race*	**Population**	**%**
African-American/Black (2,751)	3,849	4.62
Not Hispanic (2,542)	3,416	4.10
Hispanic (209)	433	0.52
American Indian/Alaska Native (753)	2,187	2.63
Not Hispanic (507)	1,579	1.90
Hispanic (246)	608	0.73
Alaska Athabascan *(Ala. Nat.)* (1)	3	<0.01
Aleut *(Alaska Native)* (1)	5	0.01
Apache (18)	69	0.08
Blackfeet (11)	62	0.07
Canadian/French Am. Ind. (2)	4	<0.01
Central American Ind. (6)	6	0.01
Cherokee (83)	439	0.53
Cheyenne (1)	6	0.01
Chickasaw (6)	27	0.03
Chippewa (10)	32	0.04
Choctaw (16)	102	0.12
Colville (3)	3	<0.01
Comanche (1)	25	0.03
Cree (2)	3	<0.01
Creek (8)	28	0.03
Crow (0)	1	<0.01
Delaware (1)	2	<0.01
Hopi (2)	4	<0.01
Houma (2)	2	<0.01
Inupiat *(Alaska Native)* (2)	4	<0.01
Iroquois (7)	18	0.02
Lumbee (0)	1	<0.01
Menominee (1)	2	<0.01
Mexican American Ind. (35)	60	0.07
Navajo (15)	36	0.04
Osage (1)	8	0.01
Ottawa (2)	2	<0.01
Paiute (11)	18	0.02
Pima (1)	1	<0.01
Potawatomi (13)	25	0.03
Pueblo (7)	14	0.02
Puget Sound Salish (2)	2	<0.01
Seminole (3)	14	0.02
Shoshone (5)	15	0.02
Sioux (28)	62	0.07
South American Ind. (3)	8	0.01
Spanish American Ind. (5)	11	0.01
Tlingit-Haida *(Alaska Native)* (4)	7	0.01
Tohono O'Odham (9)	15	0.02
Tsimshian *(Alaska Native)* (0)	1	<0.01
Yakama (1)	1	<0.01
Yaqui (8)	15	0.02
Yuman (1)	2	<0.01
Yup'ik *(Alaska Native)* (1)	1	<0.01
Asian (2,714)	4,218	5.06
Not Hispanic (2,577)	3,805	4.57
Hispanic (137)	413	0.50
Bangladeshi (4)	4	<0.01
Burmese (1)	1	<0.01
Cambodian (34)	48	0.06
Chinese, ex. Taiwanese (309)	532	0.64
Filipino (1,027)	1,627	1.95
Hmong (51)	57	0.07
Indian (338)	431	0.52
Indonesian (10)	27	0.03
Japanese (280)	664	0.80
Korean (180)	286	0.34
Laotian (37)	60	0.07
Malaysian (4)	4	<0.01
Nepalese (5)	7	0.01
Pakistani (40)	54	0.06
Sri Lankan (9)	9	0.01
Taiwanese (9)	19	0.02
Thai (44)	83	0.10
Vietnamese (200)	261	0.31
Hawaii Native/Pacific Islander (363)	766	0.92
Not Hispanic (325)	623	0.75
Hispanic (38)	143	0.17
Fijian (50)	58	0.07
Guamanian/Chamorro (103)	164	0.20
Marshallese (7)	7	0.01
Native Hawaiian (58)	273	0.33
Samoan (52)	86	0.10
Tongan (52)	62	0.07
White (66,856)	70,911	85.13
Not Hispanic (60,438)	63,235	75.91
Hispanic (6,418)	7,676	9.21

Claremont

Place Type: City
County: Los Angeles
Population: 34,926†

Ancestry‡	**Population**	**%**
Afghan (0)	45	0.13
African, Sub-Saharan (278)	335	0.97
African (141)	141	0.41
Ethiopian (0)	14	0.04
Ghanaian (13)	13	0.04
Kenyan (13)	13	0.04
Nigerian (0)	18	0.05
Senegalese (83)	83	0.24
South African (15)	28	0.08
Other Sub-Saharan African (13)	25	0.07
Albanian (27)	77	0.22
American (982)	982	2.83
Arab (379)	510	1.47
Arab (0)	24	0.07
Egyptian (125)	163	0.47
Lebanese (23)	78	0.22
Syrian (109)	123	0.35
Other Arab (122)	122	0.35
Armenian (71)	163	0.47
Australian (62)	62	0.18
Austrian (8)	111	0.32
Basque (0)	7	0.02
Belgian (7)	17	0.05
Brazilian (53)	107	0.31
British (174)	438	1.26
Bulgarian (19)	29	0.08
Cajun (0)	14	0.04
Canadian (64)	302	0.87
Croatian (26)	109	0.31
Czech (52)	157	0.45
Czechoslovakian (0)	22	0.06
Danish (43)	191	0.55
Dutch (196)	798	2.30
Eastern European (117)	117	0.34
English (987)	4,198	12.09
European (548)	641	1.85
Finnish (0)	55	0.16
French, ex. Basque (57)	1,194	3.44
French Canadian (82)	185	0.53
German (1,270)	5,149	14.83
Greek (102)	230	0.66
Hungarian (141)	297	0.86
Iranian (171)	196	0.56
Irish (756)	3,210	9.25
Israeli (0)	14	0.04
Italian (647)	2,025	5.83
Latvian (9)	20	0.06
Lithuanian (0)	64	0.18
Maltese (9)	15	0.04
Northern European (62)	71	0.20
Norwegian (183)	507	1.46
Polish (246)	689	1.98
Portuguese (0)	12	0.03
Romanian (0)	50	0.14
Russian (223)	691	1.99
Scandinavian (72)	142	0.41
Scotch-Irish (144)	503	1.45
Scottish (257)	986	2.84
Serbian (0)	41	0.12
Slovak (12)	24	0.07
Slovene (0)	8	0.02
Swedish (233)	738	2.13
Swiss (94)	184	0.53
Turkish (36)	45	0.13
Ukrainian (41)	174	0.50
Welsh (46)	310	0.89
West Indian, ex. Hispanic (13)	51	0.15
Belizean (0)	18	0.05
Haitian (13)	19	0.05
Jamaican (0)	14	0.04
Yugoslavian (9)	9	0.03

Hispanic Origin	**Population**	**%**
Hispanic or Latino (of any race)	6,919	19.81
Central American, ex. Mexican	458	1.31
Costa Rican	32	0.09
Guatemalan	129	0.37
Honduran	19	0.05
Nicaraguan	64	0.18
Panamanian	16	0.05
Salvadoran	192	0.55
Other Central American	6	0.02
Cuban	200	0.57
Dominican Republic	20	0.06
Mexican	5,091	14.58
Puerto Rican	173	0.50
South American	431	1.23
Argentinean	118	0.34
Bolivian	21	0.06
Chilean	25	0.07
Colombian	112	0.32
Ecuadorian	47	0.13
Paraguayan	5	0.01
Peruvian	56	0.16
Uruguayan	10	0.03
Venezuelan	28	0.08
Other South American	9	0.03
Other Hispanic or Latino	546	1.56

Race*	**Population**	**%**
African-American/Black (1,651)	2,030	5.81
Not Hispanic (1,560)	1,849	5.29

*Notes: † The Census 2010 population figure is used to calculate the percentages in the Hispanic Origin and Race categories. Ancestry percentages are based on the 2006-2010 American Community Survey population (not shown); ‡ Numbers in parentheses indicate the number of people reporting a single ancestry; * Numbers in parentheses indicate the number of persons reporting this race alone, not in combination with any other race; Please refer to the Explanation of Data for more information.*

Hispanic (91)	181	0.52
American Indian/Alaska Native (172)	496	1.42
Not Hispanic (80)	283	0.81
Hispanic (92)	213	0.61
Apache (8)	19	0.05
Blackfeet (1)	3	0.01
Central American Ind. (0)	4	0.01
Cherokee (15)	92	0.26
Chickasaw (1)	2	0.01
Chippewa (2)	3	0.01
Choctaw (11)	19	0.05
Comanche (2)	6	0.02
Cree (1)	7	0.02
Creek (1)	10	0.03
Delaware (0)	2	0.01
Iroquois (1)	6	0.02
Mexican American Ind. (13)	28	0.08
Navajo (3)	12	0.03
Osage (0)	3	0.01
Paiute (1)	2	0.01
Pima (2)	3	0.01
Potawatomi (0)	1	<0.01
Pueblo (2)	2	0.01
Puget Sound Salish (0)	1	<0.01
Seminole (0)	1	<0.01
Shoshone (0)	1	<0.01
Sioux (1)	7	0.02
South American Ind. (3)	8	0.02
Spanish American Ind. (0)	2	0.01
Ute (0)	3	0.01
Yakama (1)	1	<0.01
Yaqui (1)	10	0.03
Yuman (6)	6	0.02
Asian (4,564)	5,480	15.69
Not Hispanic (4,500)	5,263	15.07
Hispanic (64)	217	0.62
Bangladeshi (8)	8	0.02
Burmese (13)	18	0.05
Cambodian (5)	14	0.04
Chinese, ex. Taiwanese (1,308)	1,732	4.96
Filipino (428)	628	1.80
Indian (571)	652	1.87
Indonesian (68)	103	0.29
Japanese (289)	580	1.66
Korean (767)	853	2.44
Laotian (2)	12	0.03
Malaysian (3)	8	0.02
Nepalese (3)	4	0.01
Pakistani (50)	55	0.16
Sri Lankan (38)	46	0.13
Taiwanese (272)	317	0.91
Thai (100)	131	0.38
Vietnamese (390)	457	1.31
Hawaii Native/Pacific Islander (38)	161	0.46
Not Hispanic (35)	129	0.37
Hispanic (3)	32	0.09
Fijian (6)	6	0.02
Guamanian/Chamorro (5)	12	0.03
Native Hawaiian (6)	61	0.17
Samoan (7)	20	0.06
Tongan (2)	2	0.01
White (24,666)	26,262	75.19
Not Hispanic (20,568)	21,651	61.99
Hispanic (4,098)	4,611	13.20

Clayton

Place Type: City
County: Contra Costa
Population: 10,897†

Ancestry‡	Population	%
African, Sub-Saharan (35)	44	0.41
African (0)	9	0.08
Zimbabwean (35)	35	0.32
American (255)	255	2.36
Armenian (5)	5	0.05
Brazilian (30)	30	0.28
British (201)	256	2.37
Bulgarian (30)	30	0.28
Canadian (55)	147	1.36
Croatian (26)	26	0.24
Czech (10)	56	0.52
Czechoslovakian (6)	6	0.06
Danish (31)	252	2.33
Dutch (9)	271	2.50
Eastern European (41)	41	0.38
English (645)	1,870	17.28
European (472)	480	4.44
Finnish (41)	81	0.75
French, ex. Basque (0)	357	3.30
French Canadian (11)	20	0.18
German (444)	2,067	19.11
Greek (39)	49	0.45
Hungarian (0)	41	0.38
Iranian (147)	152	1.40
Irish (341)	1,666	15.40
Italian (547)	1,268	11.72
Lithuanian (0)	9	0.08
Maltese (52)	62	0.57
Northern European (104)	104	0.96
Norwegian (31)	173	1.60
Polish (61)	166	1.53
Portuguese (165)	284	2.63
Romanian (0)	21	0.19
Russian (10)	38	0.35
Scandinavian (16)	33	0.31
Scotch-Irish (48)	366	3.38
Scottish (185)	496	4.58
Slovak (0)	14	0.13
Swedish (64)	406	3.75
Swiss (82)	153	1.41
Welsh (16)	207	1.91
West Indian, ex. Hispanic (22)	22	0.20
Haitian (22)	22	0.20
Yugoslavian (0)	9	0.08

Hispanic Origin	Population	%
Hispanic or Latino (of any race)	982	9.01
Central American, ex. Mexican	130	1.19
Costa Rican	8	0.07
Guatemalan	28	0.26
Honduran	5	0.05
Nicaraguan	38	0.35
Panamanian	4	0.04
Salvadoran	47	0.43
Cuban	14	0.13
Dominican Republic	1	0.01
Mexican	518	4.75
Puerto Rican	35	0.32
South American	124	1.14
Argentinean	7	0.06
Bolivian	8	0.07
Chilean	9	0.08
Colombian	9	0.08
Ecuadorian	18	0.17
Peruvian	66	0.61
Venezuelan	7	0.06
Other Hispanic or Latino	160	1.47

Race*	Population	%
African-American/Black (146)	203	1.86
Not Hispanic (144)	191	1.75
Hispanic (2)	12	0.11
American Indian/Alaska Native (34)	114	1.05
Not Hispanic (30)	85	0.78
Hispanic (4)	29	0.27
Apache (0)	1	0.01
Blackfeet (1)	8	0.07
Cherokee (7)	23	0.21
Cheyenne (0)	3	0.03
Chippewa (2)	2	0.02
Choctaw (7)	9	0.08
Colville (0)	2	0.02
Iroquois (0)	1	0.01
Mexican American Ind. (0)	5	0.05
Navajo (0)	1	0.01
Potawatomi (0)	1	0.01
South American Ind. (0)	1	0.01
Yaqui (0)	1	0.01
Asian (717)	999	9.17
Not Hispanic (707)	947	8.69
Hispanic (10)	52	0.48
Chinese, ex. Taiwanese (159)	241	2.21
Filipino (217)	316	2.90
Indian (96)	113	1.04
Indonesian (4)	13	0.12
Japanese (95)	158	1.45
Korean (58)	72	0.66
Malaysian (2)	2	0.02
Pakistani (9)	12	0.11
Sri Lankan (2)	2	0.02
Taiwanese (0)	3	0.03
Thai (15)	16	0.15
Vietnamese (22)	24	0.22
Hawaii Native/Pacific Islander (16)	56	0.51
Not Hispanic (14)	48	0.44
Hispanic (2)	8	0.07
Fijian (2)	2	0.02
Guamanian/Chamorro (7)	15	0.14
Marshallese (0)	1	0.01
Native Hawaiian (4)	26	0.24
Samoan (0)	2	0.02
White (9,273)	9,707	89.08
Not Hispanic (8,640)	8,970	82.32
Hispanic (633)	737	6.76

Clearlake

Place Type: City
County: Lake
Population: 15,250†

Ancestry‡	Population	%
African, Sub-Saharan (72)	127	0.84
African (72)	127	0.84
American (522)	522	3.46
Arab (14)	57	0.38
Egyptian (14)	14	0.09
Iraqi (0)	12	0.08
Syrian (0)	31	0.21
Belgian (72)	72	0.48
British (47)	47	0.31
Czech (0)	22	0.15
Danish (43)	75	0.50
Dutch (53)	204	1.35
English (324)	1,804	11.97
European (123)	153	1.01
Finnish (0)	13	0.09
French, ex. Basque (118)	687	4.56
French Canadian (0)	106	0.70
German (555)	2,491	16.53
Greek (134)	206	1.37
Hungarian (0)	47	0.31
Iranian (14)	53	0.35
Irish (369)	2,411	15.99
Italian (414)	1,225	8.13
Maltese (54)	54	0.36
Norwegian (166)	389	2.58
Pennsylvania German (0)	20	0.13
Polish (0)	64	0.42
Portuguese (67)	327	2.17
Russian (0)	22	0.15
Scandinavian (0)	33	0.22
Scotch-Irish (203)	519	3.44
Scottish (75)	191	1.27
Swedish (12)	351	2.33
Swiss (40)	78	0.52
Ukrainian (0)	11	0.07
Welsh (0)	85	0.56
West Indian, ex. Hispanic (24)	24	0.16
Belizean (24)	24	0.16

Hispanic Origin	Population	%
Hispanic or Latino (of any race)	3,248	21.30
Central American, ex. Mexican	61	0.40
Costa Rican	1	0.01
Guatemalan	20	0.13
Honduran	5	0.03
Nicaraguan	8	0.05

*Notes: † The Census 2010 population figure is used to calculate the percentages in the Hispanic Origin and Race categories. Ancestry percentages are based on the 2006-2010 American Community Survey population (not shown); ‡ Numbers in parentheses indicate the number of people reporting a single ancestry; * Numbers in parentheses indicate the number of persons reporting this race alone, not in combination with any other race; Please refer to the Explanation of Data for more information.*

Salvadoran	27	0.18
Cuban	10	0.07
Dominican Republic	2	0.01
Mexican	2,794	18.32
Puerto Rican	65	0.43
South American	25	0.16
Argentinean	2	0.01
Chilean	4	0.03
Colombian	5	0.03
Peruvian	10	0.07
Uruguayan	2	0.01
Venezuelan	1	0.01
Other South American	1	0.01
Other Hispanic or Latino	291	1.91

Race*	Population	%
African-American/Black (614)	841	5.51
Not Hispanic (592)	785	5.15
Hispanic (22)	56	0.37
American Indian/Alaska Native (400)	923	6.05
Not Hispanic (292)	691	4.53
Hispanic (108)	232	1.52
Alaska Athabascan *(Ala. Nat.)* (4)	4	0.03
Aleut *(Alaska Native)* (9)	9	0.06
Apache (8)	26	0.17
Blackfeet (6)	27	0.18
Canadian/French Am. Ind. (0)	3	0.02
Central American Ind. (5)	5	0.03
Cherokee (38)	195	1.28
Cheyenne (0)	3	0.02
Chickasaw (1)	3	0.02
Chippewa (0)	4	0.03
Choctaw (16)	47	0.31
Comanche (0)	5	0.03
Cree (0)	7	0.05
Creek (5)	6	0.04
Crow (1)	1	0.01
Delaware (0)	1	0.01
Hopi (1)	2	0.01
Inupiat *(Alaska Native)* (8)	13	0.09
Iroquois (3)	6	0.04
Mexican American Ind. (7)	20	0.13
Navajo (12)	25	0.16
Osage (0)	7	0.05
Ottawa (1)	3	0.02
Paiute (7)	11	0.07
Pima (5)	7	0.05
Potawatomi (1)	5	0.03
Pueblo (1)	1	0.01
Seminole (0)	7	0.05
Shoshone (1)	8	0.05
Sioux (5)	14	0.09
Tlingit-Haida *(Alaska Native)* (2)	3	0.02
Yakama (0)	1	0.01
Yaqui (0)	3	0.02
Asian (161)	273	1.79
Not Hispanic (154)	239	1.57
Hispanic (7)	34	0.22
Cambodian (9)	9	0.06
Chinese, ex. Taiwanese (30)	38	0.25
Filipino (52)	111	0.73
Indian (19)	26	0.17
Japanese (17)	51	0.33
Korean (5)	14	0.09
Laotian (9)	11	0.07
Thai (8)	10	0.07
Vietnamese (6)	6	0.04
Hawaii Native/Pacific Islander (27)	132	0.87
Not Hispanic (26)	107	0.70
Hispanic (1)	25	0.16
Guamanian/Chamorro (1)	6	0.04
Native Hawaiian (18)	94	0.62
Samoan (5)	14	0.09
White (11,262)	12,131	79.55
Not Hispanic (10,254)	10,856	71.19
Hispanic (1,008)	1,275	8.36

Cloverdale

Place Type: City
County: Sonoma
Population: 8,618†

Ancestry‡	Population	%
American (255)	255	3.11
Arab (237)	268	3.26
Arab (0)	31	0.38
Egyptian (221)	221	2.69
Moroccan (16)	16	0.19
Armenian (0)	46	0.56
Australian (24)	24	0.29
Austrian (0)	14	0.17
Belgian (7)	7	0.09
British (53)	64	0.78
Croatian (0)	16	0.19
Czech (3)	100	1.22
Danish (28)	196	2.39
Dutch (15)	150	1.83
English (222)	928	11.30
European (81)	126	1.53
Finnish (38)	53	0.65
French, ex. Basque (34)	349	4.25
French Canadian (16)	16	0.19
German (170)	1,472	17.92
Greek (16)	16	0.19
Hungarian (4)	4	0.05
Irish (281)	941	11.46
Italian (512)	949	11.56
Maltese (15)	15	0.18
Norwegian (43)	141	1.72
Polish (14)	226	2.75
Portuguese (102)	229	2.79
Russian (0)	48	0.58
Scandinavian (0)	24	0.29
Scotch-Irish (36)	192	2.34
Scottish (44)	343	4.18
Swedish (107)	345	4.20
Swiss (11)	51	0.62
Welsh (0)	39	0.47
Yugoslavian (16)	16	0.19

Hispanic Origin	Population	%
Hispanic or Latino (of any race)	2,824	32.77
Central American, ex. Mexican	49	0.57
Costa Rican	1	0.01
Guatemalan	5	0.06
Honduran	3	0.03
Nicaraguan	14	0.16
Panamanian	2	0.02
Salvadoran	24	0.28
Cuban	6	0.07
Dominican Republic	3	0.03
Mexican	2,546	29.54
Puerto Rican	29	0.34
South American	17	0.20
Chilean	1	0.01
Colombian	9	0.10
Ecuadorian	2	0.02
Peruvian	5	0.06
Other Hispanic or Latino	174	2.02

Race*	Population	%
African-American/Black (48)	84	0.97
Not Hispanic (33)	65	0.75
Hispanic (15)	19	0.22
American Indian/Alaska Native (156)	286	3.32
Not Hispanic (109)	191	2.22
Hispanic (47)	95	1.10
Blackfeet (2)	3	0.03
Canadian/French Am. Ind. (1)	1	0.01
Cherokee (7)	27	0.31
Chippewa (4)	4	0.05
Choctaw (9)	21	0.24
Creek (0)	1	0.01
Delaware (0)	2	0.02
Kiowa (0)	2	0.02
Mexican American Ind. (4)	5	0.06
Navajo (2)	6	0.07
Osage (0)	2	0.02
Ottawa (1)	1	0.01
Paiute (2)	3	0.03
Pima (1)	2	0.02
Potawatomi (0)	1	0.01
Pueblo (1)	1	0.01
Puget Sound Salish (0)	1	0.01
Shoshone (4)	5	0.06
Sioux (1)	3	0.03
Yaqui (1)	1	0.01
Asian (98)	171	1.98
Not Hispanic (95)	144	1.67
Hispanic (3)	27	0.31
Cambodian (0)	2	0.02
Chinese, ex. Taiwanese (25)	39	0.45
Filipino (23)	55	0.64
Indian (14)	16	0.19
Japanese (12)	35	0.41
Korean (5)	6	0.07
Taiwanese (2)	2	0.02
Thai (7)	12	0.14
Vietnamese (8)	15	0.17
Hawaii Native/Pacific Islander (7)	20	0.23
Not Hispanic (6)	13	0.15
Hispanic (1)	7	0.08
Fijian (2)	2	0.02
Guamanian/Chamorro (1)	2	0.02
Native Hawaiian (2)	10	0.12
Samoan (1)	4	0.05
Tongan (1)	1	0.01
White (6,458)	6,754	78.37
Not Hispanic (5,386)	5,529	64.16
Hispanic (1,072)	1,225	14.21

Clovis

Place Type: City
County: Fresno
Population: 95,631†

Ancestry‡	Population	%
African, Sub-Saharan (438)	482	0.53
African (140)	164	0.18
Ethiopian (66)	66	0.07
Ghanaian (0)	20	0.02
Nigerian (232)	232	0.25
American (2,525)	2,525	2.77
Arab (559)	676	0.74
Arab (235)	253	0.28
Egyptian (78)	78	0.09
Jordanian (75)	75	0.08
Lebanese (37)	95	0.10
Moroccan (11)	23	0.03
Syrian (13)	42	0.05
Other Arab (110)	110	0.12
Armenian (602)	984	1.08
Assyrian/Chaldean/Syriac (43)	108	0.12
Austrian (36)	141	0.15
Basque (86)	100	0.11
Belgian (24)	82	0.09
Brazilian (55)	350	0.38
British (186)	351	0.39
Canadian (73)	155	0.17
Croatian (21)	51	0.06
Czech (181)	329	0.36
Czechoslovakian (87)	275	0.30
Danish (355)	812	0.89
Dutch (142)	1,248	1.37
English (2,126)	8,109	8.89
European (1,368)	1,560	1.71
Finnish (84)	148	0.16
French, ex. Basque (302)	2,289	2.51
French Canadian (188)	388	0.43
German (3,493)	13,881	15.23
German Russian (12)	12	0.01
Greek (65)	235	0.26
Hungarian (95)	142	0.16
Icelander (9)	53	0.06
Iranian (132)	234	0.26

*Notes: † The Census 2010 population figure is used to calculate the percentages in the Hispanic Origin and Race categories. Ancestry percentages are based on the 2006-2010 American Community Survey population (not shown); ‡ Numbers in parentheses indicate the number of people reporting a single ancestry; * Numbers in parentheses indicate the number of persons reporting this race alone, not in combination with any other race; Please refer to the Explanation of Data for more information.*

Ancestry	Population	%
Irish (2,460)	9,216	10.11
Israeli (0)	17	0.02
Italian (2,246)	6,461	7.09
Latvian (0)	41	0.04
Lithuanian (7)	26	0.03
Macedonian (0)	9	0.01
New Zealander (23)	23	0.03
Northern European (128)	185	0.20
Norwegian (304)	1,114	1.22
Pennsylvania German (122)	122	0.13
Polish (110)	907	0.99
Portuguese (540)	1,490	1.63
Romanian (85)	162	0.18
Russian (196)	759	0.83
Scandinavian (35)	48	0.05
Scotch-Irish (555)	1,955	2.14
Scottish (442)	1,829	2.01
Serbian (0)	26	0.03
Slavic (89)	96	0.11
Slovak (9)	57	0.06
Slovene (0)	14	0.02
Swedish (343)	1,423	1.56
Swiss (76)	596	0.65
Turkish (11)	11	0.01
Ukrainian (291)	369	0.40
Welsh (80)	788	0.86
West Indian, ex. Hispanic (66)	117	0.13
Bahamian (66)	66	0.07
Belizean (0)	27	0.03
Dutch West Indian (0)	10	0.01
West Indian (0)	14	0.02
Yugoslavian (20)	76	0.08

Hispanic Origin	Population	%
Hispanic or Latino (of any race)	24,514	25.63
Central American, ex. Mexican	556	0.58
Costa Rican	59	0.06
Guatemalan	96	0.10
Honduran	38	0.04
Nicaraguan	85	0.09
Panamanian	34	0.04
Salvadoran	230	0.24
Other Central American	14	0.01
Cuban	66	0.07
Dominican Republic	8	0.01
Mexican	21,360	22.34
Puerto Rican	307	0.32
South American	275	0.29
Argentinean	41	0.04
Bolivian	11	0.01
Chilean	38	0.04
Colombian	86	0.09
Ecuadorian	21	0.02
Paraguayan	1	<0.01
Peruvian	50	0.05
Uruguayan	11	0.01
Venezuelan	16	0.02
Other Hispanic or Latino	1,942	2.03

Race*	Population	%
African-American/Black (2,618)	3,481	3.64
Not Hispanic (2,360)	3,002	3.14
Hispanic (258)	479	0.50
American Indian/Alaska Native (1,320)	2,580	2.70
Not Hispanic (754)	1,616	1.69
Hispanic (566)	964	1.01
Alaska Athabascan *(Ala. Nat.)* (0)	1	<0.01
Aleut *(Alaska Native)* (4)	4	<0.01
Apache (61)	95	0.10
Blackfeet (10)	53	0.06
Canadian/French Am. Ind. (2)	6	0.01
Central American Ind. (1)	4	<0.01
Cherokee (129)	405	0.42
Cheyenne (1)	12	0.01
Chickasaw (9)	28	0.03
Chippewa (5)	16	0.02
Choctaw (75)	150	0.16
Colville (4)	5	0.01
Comanche (5)	18	0.02
Cree (2)	2	<0.01
Creek (10)	31	0.03
Crow (3)	7	0.01
Delaware (4)	4	<0.01
Hopi (6)	8	0.01
Inupiat *(Alaska Native)* (0)	3	<0.01
Iroquois (10)	29	0.03
Kiowa (2)	3	<0.01
Lumbee (0)	7	0.01
Mexican American Ind. (67)	110	0.12
Navajo (10)	26	0.03
Osage (1)	7	0.01
Paiute (9)	18	0.02
Pima (8)	8	0.01
Potawatomi (7)	14	0.01
Pueblo (16)	20	0.02
Puget Sound Salish (2)	2	<0.01
Seminole (2)	7	0.01
Shoshone (2)	6	0.01
Sioux (15)	42	0.04
South American Ind. (0)	2	<0.01
Spanish American Ind. (3)	4	<0.01
Tlingit-Haida *(Alaska Native)* (0)	1	<0.01
Tohono O'Odham (2)	4	<0.01
Ute (1)	1	<0.01
Yaqui (15)	31	0.03
Yup'ik *(Alaska Native)* (2)	2	<0.01
Asian (10,233)	11,971	12.52
Not Hispanic (9,965)	11,264	11.78
Hispanic (268)	707	0.74
Bangladeshi (2)	2	<0.01
Burmese (9)	12	0.01
Cambodian (208)	254	0.27
Chinese, ex. Taiwanese (920)	1,216	1.27
Filipino (1,826)	2,407	2.52
Hmong (2,887)	3,001	3.14
Indian (1,553)	1,750	1.83
Indonesian (42)	69	0.07
Japanese (660)	1,111	1.16
Korean (318)	428	0.45
Laotian (359)	417	0.44
Malaysian (1)	3	<0.01
Pakistani (87)	106	0.11
Sri Lankan (27)	33	0.03
Taiwanese (17)	18	0.02
Thai (103)	148	0.15
Vietnamese (721)	836	0.87
Hawaii Native/Pacific Islander (218)	493	0.52
Not Hispanic (187)	390	0.41
Hispanic (31)	103	0.11
Fijian (31)	36	0.04
Guamanian/Chamorro (57)	87	0.09
Native Hawaiian (49)	184	0.19
Samoan (55)	93	0.10
White (67,758)	71,689	74.96
Not Hispanic (55,021)	57,330	59.95
Hispanic (12,737)	14,359	15.02

Coachella

Place Type: City
County: Riverside
Population: 40,704†

Ancestry‡	Population	%
American (225)	225	0.59
Arab (61)	77	0.20
Arab (0)	10	0.03
Lebanese (19)	19	0.05
Syrian (42)	42	0.11
Other Arab (0)	6	0.02
Dutch (0)	11	0.03
English (68)	150	0.39
Finnish (10)	35	0.09
French, ex. Basque (16)	71	0.19
German (120)	279	0.73
Irish (33)	96	0.25
Norwegian (0)	15	0.04
Polish (55)	75	0.20
Scottish (0)	29	0.08
West Indian, ex. Hispanic (14)	14	0.04
Jamaican (14)	14	0.04

Hispanic Origin	Population	%
Hispanic or Latino (of any race)	39,254	96.44
Central American, ex. Mexican	522	1.28
Guatemalan	84	0.21
Honduran	48	0.12
Nicaraguan	37	0.09
Salvadoran	351	0.86
Other Central American	2	<0.01
Cuban	17	0.04
Dominican Republic	1	<0.01
Mexican	37,265	91.55
Puerto Rican	71	0.17
South American	42	0.10
Argentinean	5	0.01
Chilean	7	0.02
Colombian	14	0.03
Ecuadorian	3	0.01
Paraguayan	1	<0.01
Peruvian	11	0.03
Venezuelan	1	<0.01
Other Hispanic or Latino	1,336	3.28

Race*	Population	%
African-American/Black (320)	406	1.00
Not Hispanic (140)	164	0.40
Hispanic (180)	242	0.59
American Indian/Alaska Native (290)	390	0.96
Not Hispanic (54)	92	0.23
Hispanic (236)	298	0.73
Apache (2)	5	0.01
Blackfeet (1)	3	0.01
Central American Ind. (1)	1	<0.01
Cherokee (3)	3	0.01
Choctaw (0)	1	<0.01
Comanche (0)	1	<0.01
Mexican American Ind. (56)	67	0.16
Navajo (2)	6	0.01
Paiute (0)	1	<0.01
Pima (7)	10	0.02
Potawatomi (3)	3	0.01
Sioux (2)	2	<0.01
Yaqui (6)	6	0.01
Asian (266)	416	1.02
Not Hispanic (168)	213	0.52
Hispanic (98)	203	0.50
Chinese, ex. Taiwanese (18)	24	0.06
Filipino (188)	266	0.65
Indian (17)	28	0.07
Indonesian (0)	2	<0.01
Japanese (8)	11	0.03
Korean (3)	3	0.01
Laotian (1)	1	<0.01
Sri Lankan (2)	2	<0.01
Thai (1)	3	0.01
Vietnamese (24)	24	0.06
Hawaii Native/Pacific Islander (34)	83	0.20
Not Hispanic (13)	17	0.04
Hispanic (21)	66	0.16
Guamanian/Chamorro (10)	18	0.04
Native Hawaiian (3)	6	0.01
Samoan (13)	19	0.05
White (19,576)	20,468	50.28
Not Hispanic (933)	1,034	2.54
Hispanic (18,643)	19,434	47.74

Coalinga

Place Type: City
County: Fresno
Population: 13,380†

Ancestry‡	Population	%
African, Sub-Saharan (7)	25	0.19
African (7)	25	0.19
American (423)	423	3.23
Arab (36)	44	0.34
Egyptian (0)	8	0.06
Iraqi (8)	8	0.06

*Notes: † The Census 2010 population figure is used to calculate the percentages in the Hispanic Origin and Race categories. Ancestry percentages are based on the 2006-2010 American Community Survey population (not shown); ‡ Numbers in parentheses indicate the number of people reporting a single ancestry; * Numbers in parentheses indicate the number of persons reporting this race alone, not in combination with any other race; Please refer to the Explanation of Data for more information.*

Ancestry (cont.)	Population	%
Syrian (28)	28	0.21
Armenian (38)	46	0.35
Austrian (0)	7	0.05
Basque (0)	6	0.05
Belgian (7)	26	0.20
British (8)	14	0.11
Canadian (14)	24	0.18
Celtic (0)	10	0.08
Croatian (0)	10	0.08
Czech (8)	17	0.13
Danish (0)	9	0.07
Dutch (5)	117	0.89
Eastern European (6)	6	0.05
English (114)	488	3.73
European (8)	15	0.11
French, ex. Basque (13)	187	1.43
French Canadian (7)	30	0.23
German (352)	1,103	8.43
Greek (7)	7	0.05
Iranian (0)	9	0.07
Irish (313)	1,027	7.85
Italian (96)	216	1.65
Northern European (46)	46	0.35
Norwegian (48)	146	1.12
Polish (27)	54	0.41
Portuguese (41)	77	0.59
Russian (21)	51	0.39
Scandinavian (8)	15	0.11
Scotch-Irish (53)	134	1.02
Scottish (94)	223	1.70
Slavic (7)	7	0.05
Swedish (32)	100	0.76
Swiss (0)	14	0.11
Ukrainian (0)	8	0.06
Welsh (16)	52	0.40
West Indian, ex. Hispanic (0)	8	0.06
Barbadian (0)	8	0.06

Hispanic Origin	Population	%
Hispanic or Latino (of any race)	7,161	53.52
Central American, ex. Mexican	161	1.20
Costa Rican	3	0.02
Guatemalan	12	0.09
Honduran	22	0.16
Nicaraguan	5	0.04
Panamanian	2	0.01
Salvadoran	117	0.87
Cuban	11	0.08
Mexican	6,643	49.65
Puerto Rican	35	0.26
South American	23	0.17
Argentinean	3	0.02
Bolivian	1	0.01
Chilean	2	0.01
Colombian	7	0.05
Ecuadorian	3	0.02
Peruvian	7	0.05
Other Hispanic or Latino	288	2.15

Race*	Population	%
African-American/Black (549)	626	4.68
Not Hispanic (513)	555	4.15
Hispanic (36)	71	0.53
American Indian/Alaska Native (171)	275	2.06
Not Hispanic (85)	147	1.10
Hispanic (86)	128	0.96
Apache (5)	17	0.13
Arapaho (1)	1	0.01
Central American Ind. (0)	1	0.01
Cherokee (12)	35	0.26
Chickasaw (1)	4	0.03
Chippewa (2)	2	0.01
Choctaw (10)	17	0.13
Comanche (2)	4	0.03
Cree (1)	1	0.01
Creek (1)	1	0.01
Iroquois (1)	3	0.02
Mexican American Ind. (10)	12	0.09
Navajo (0)	2	0.01
Osage (0)	3	0.02
Sioux (2)	2	0.01
Ute (1)	1	0.01
Yaqui (18)	20	0.15
Yuman (1)	1	0.01
Asian (407)	507	3.79
Not Hispanic (385)	437	3.27
Hispanic (22)	70	0.52
Bangladeshi (2)	2	0.01
Cambodian (17)	23	0.17
Chinese, ex. Taiwanese (88)	105	0.78
Filipino (137)	173	1.29
Hmong (9)	9	0.07
Indian (52)	64	0.48
Indonesian (1)	2	0.01
Japanese (40)	64	0.48
Korean (13)	15	0.11
Laotian (7)	7	0.05
Malaysian (0)	1	0.01
Pakistani (10)	10	0.07
Thai (6)	8	0.06
Vietnamese (12)	16	0.12
Hawaii Native/Pacific Islander (36)	62	0.46
Not Hispanic (23)	36	0.27
Hispanic (13)	26	0.19
Guamanian/Chamorro (0)	5	0.04
Native Hawaiian (15)	32	0.24
Samoan (13)	14	0.10
White (7,734)	8,207	61.34
Not Hispanic (5,044)	5,182	38.73
Hispanic (2,690)	3,025	22.61

Colton

Place Type: City
County: San Bernardino
Population: 52,154†

Ancestry‡	Population	%
African, Sub-Saharan (530)	585	1.12
African (195)	226	0.43
Nigerian (335)	335	0.64
South African (0)	24	0.05
American (610)	610	1.17
Arab (301)	331	0.63
Arab (34)	34	0.07
Egyptian (177)	189	0.36
Jordanian (44)	44	0.08
Lebanese (13)	31	0.06
Syrian (33)	33	0.06
Armenian (122)	122	0.23
Basque (0)	53	0.10
Brazilian (22)	34	0.07
British (70)	111	0.21
Cajun (0)	22	0.04
Czech (13)	46	0.09
Danish (13)	79	0.15
Dutch (53)	178	0.34
English (143)	684	1.31
European (110)	110	0.21
Finnish (0)	50	0.10
French, ex. Basque (156)	384	0.74
German (477)	1,525	2.92
Hungarian (35)	54	0.10
Iranian (54)	54	0.10
Irish (352)	1,431	2.74
Italian (458)	998	1.91
Norwegian (14)	175	0.34
Polish (50)	172	0.33
Portuguese (64)	224	0.43
Romanian (184)	184	0.35
Russian (0)	20	0.04
Scandinavian (7)	27	0.05
Scotch-Irish (55)	259	0.50
Scottish (196)	347	0.66
Slavic (11)	11	0.02
Slovak (0)	9	0.02
Swedish (82)	182	0.35
Ukrainian (11)	20	0.04
Welsh (0)	42	0.08
West Indian, ex. Hispanic (178)	218	0.42
Belizean (56)	96	0.18
Dutch West Indian (13)	13	0.02
Haitian (46)	46	0.09
Jamaican (63)	63	0.12
Yugoslavian (9)	37	0.07

Hispanic Origin	Population	%
Hispanic or Latino (of any race)	37,039	71.02
Central American, ex. Mexican	1,397	2.68
Costa Rican	21	0.04
Guatemalan	406	0.78
Honduran	93	0.18
Nicaraguan	157	0.30
Panamanian	40	0.08
Salvadoran	656	1.26
Other Central American	24	0.05
Cuban	119	0.23
Dominican Republic	26	0.05
Mexican	32,985	63.25
Puerto Rican	397	0.76
South American	289	0.55
Argentinean	32	0.06
Bolivian	13	0.02
Chilean	13	0.02
Colombian	83	0.16
Ecuadorian	44	0.08
Peruvian	80	0.15
Uruguayan	7	0.01
Venezuelan	16	0.03
Other South American	1	<0.01
Other Hispanic or Latino	1,826	3.50

Race*	Population	%
African-American/Black (5,055)	5,750	11.03
Not Hispanic (4,648)	5,060	9.70
Hispanic (407)	690	1.32
American Indian/Alaska Native (661)	1,122	2.15
Not Hispanic (126)	334	0.64
Hispanic (535)	788	1.51
Alaska Athabascan *(Ala. Nat.)* (3)	3	0.01
Aleut *(Alaska Native)* (0)	3	0.01
Apache (29)	53	0.10
Blackfeet (4)	18	0.03
Canadian/French Am. Ind. (2)	2	<0.01
Central American Ind. (5)	14	0.03
Cherokee (20)	108	0.21
Cheyenne (2)	3	0.01
Chickasaw (1)	6	0.01
Chippewa (2)	11	0.02
Choctaw (10)	28	0.05
Comanche (3)	5	0.01
Creek (8)	16	0.03
Hopi (0)	1	<0.01
Iroquois (2)	6	0.01
Mexican American Ind. (88)	134	0.26
Navajo (12)	29	0.06
Osage (0)	1	<0.01
Ottawa (1)	1	<0.01
Paiute (0)	2	<0.01
Pima (4)	4	0.01
Potawatomi (2)	7	0.01
Pueblo (5)	6	0.01
Shoshone (0)	1	<0.01
Sioux (10)	13	0.02
South American Ind. (0)	1	<0.01
Spanish American Ind. (7)	7	0.01
Tohono O'Odham (0)	1	<0.01
Yaqui (20)	29	0.06
Yuman (6)	14	0.03
Asian (2,590)	3,151	6.04
Not Hispanic (2,430)	2,780	5.33
Hispanic (160)	371	0.71
Bangladeshi (10)	14	0.03
Burmese (6)	6	0.01
Cambodian (57)	76	0.15
Chinese, ex. Taiwanese (191)	283	0.54
Filipino (943)	1,160	2.22
Hmong (16)	16	0.03
Indian (257)	338	0.65
Indonesian (319)	429	0.82

*Notes: † The Census 2010 population figure is used to calculate the percentages in the Hispanic Origin and Race categories. Ancestry percentages are based on the 2006-2010 American Community Survey population (not shown); ‡ Numbers in parentheses indicate the number of people reporting a single ancestry; * Numbers in parentheses indicate the number of persons reporting this race alone, not in combination with any other race; Please refer to the Explanation of Data for more information.*

Japanese (73)	140	0.27
Korean (149)	186	0.36
Laotian (15)	21	0.04
Malaysian (0)	2	<0.01
Nepalese (6)	6	0.01
Pakistani (30)	40	0.08
Sri Lankan (3)	6	0.01
Taiwanese (6)	6	0.01
Thai (38)	54	0.10
Vietnamese (308)	343	0.66
Hawaii Native/Pacific Islander (176)	337	0.65
Not Hispanic (136)	232	0.44
Hispanic (40)	105	0.20
Fijian (1)	1	<0.01
Guamanian/Chamorro (24)	39	0.07
Native Hawaiian (29)	73	0.14
Samoan (67)	101	0.19
Tongan (41)	49	0.09
White (22,613)	24,634	47.23
Not Hispanic (6,803)	7,413	14.21
Hispanic (15,810)	17,221	33.02

Commerce

Place Type: City
County: Los Angeles
Population: 12,823†

Ancestry‡	Population	%
African, Sub-Saharan (0)	10	0.08
African (0)	10	0.08
American (105)	105	0.82
Canadian (13)	13	0.10
English (9)	9	0.07
French, ex. Basque (3)	18	0.14
German (9)	58	0.45
Hungarian (7)	7	0.05
Iranian (0)	6	0.05
Irish (49)	79	0.62
Italian (64)	114	0.89
Scottish (21)	21	0.16

Hispanic Origin	Population	%
Hispanic or Latino (of any race)	12,114	94.47
Central American, ex. Mexican	688	5.37
Costa Rican	13	0.10
Guatemalan	190	1.48
Honduran	41	0.32
Nicaraguan	60	0.47
Panamanian	1	0.01
Salvadoran	370	2.89
Other Central American	13	0.10
Cuban	57	0.44
Dominican Republic	2	0.02
Mexican	10,758	83.90
Puerto Rican	26	0.20
South American	87	0.68
Argentinean	10	0.08
Chilean	2	0.02
Colombian	9	0.07
Ecuadorian	22	0.17
Peruvian	37	0.29
Uruguayan	1	0.01
Venezuelan	4	0.03
Other South American	2	0.02
Other Hispanic or Latino	496	3.87

Race*	Population	%
African-American/Black (96)	153	1.19
Not Hispanic (66)	72	0.56
Hispanic (30)	81	0.63
American Indian/Alaska Native (161)	248	1.93
Not Hispanic (48)	59	0.46
Hispanic (113)	189	1.47
Apache (6)	7	0.05
Blackfeet (0)	2	0.02
Cherokee (5)	8	0.06
Chippewa (0)	1	0.01
Colville (3)	3	0.02
Creek (0)	2	0.02
Inupiat *(Alaska Native)* (1)	1	0.01
Mexican American Ind. (17)	46	0.36
Navajo (19)	24	0.19
Pima (1)	1	0.01
Seminole (0)	2	0.02
South American Ind. (1)	2	0.02
Tohono O'Odham (0)	1	0.01
Yuman (3)	3	0.02
Asian (140)	202	1.58
Not Hispanic (134)	145	1.13
Hispanic (6)	57	0.44
Cambodian (1)	1	0.01
Chinese, ex. Taiwanese (22)	29	0.23
Filipino (58)	81	0.63
Indian (17)	32	0.25
Indonesian (1)	1	0.01
Japanese (19)	31	0.24
Korean (8)	11	0.09
Pakistani (3)	6	0.05
Taiwanese (0)	1	0.01
Thai (3)	3	0.02
Vietnamese (1)	2	0.02
Hawaii Native/Pacific Islander (9)	42	0.33
Not Hispanic (7)	13	0.10
Hispanic (2)	29	0.23
Fijian (1)	4	0.03
Guamanian/Chamorro (0)	1	0.01
Native Hawaiian (2)	3	0.02
Samoan (3)	14	0.11
White (6,930)	7,438	58.01
Not Hispanic (402)	423	3.30
Hispanic (6,528)	7,015	54.71

Compton

Place Type: City
County: Los Angeles
Population: 96,455†

Ancestry‡	Population	%
African, Sub-Saharan (3,208)	4,191	4.38
African (3,199)	4,112	4.29
Ethiopian (9)	9	0.01
Nigerian (0)	70	0.07
American (1,113)	1,113	1.16
British (48)	58	0.06
Czech (0)	14	0.01
Danish (0)	20	0.02
Dutch (0)	31	0.03
English (51)	127	0.13
European (23)	149	0.16
Finnish (0)	11	0.01
French, ex. Basque (5)	80	0.08
German (8)	71	0.07
Greek (7)	7	0.01
Guyanese (64)	64	0.07
Hungarian (9)	9	0.01
Irish (28)	162	0.17
Italian (48)	182	0.19
Northern European (12)	51	0.05
Norwegian (35)	35	0.04
Portuguese (24)	110	0.11
Scottish (0)	8	0.01
West Indian, ex. Hispanic (192)	458	0.48
Bahamian (11)	11	0.01
Belizean (158)	308	0.32
Jamaican (23)	122	0.13
West Indian (0)	17	0.02

Hispanic Origin	Population	%
Hispanic or Latino (of any race)	62,669	64.97
Central American, ex. Mexican	4,910	5.09
Costa Rican	39	0.04
Guatemalan	1,471	1.53
Honduran	571	0.59
Nicaraguan	215	0.22
Panamanian	30	0.03
Salvadoran	2,470	2.56
Other Central American	114	0.12
Cuban	77	0.08
Dominican Republic	27	0.03
Mexican	54,084	56.07
Puerto Rican	218	0.23
South American	209	0.22
Argentinean	12	0.01
Bolivian	7	0.01
Chilean	15	0.02
Colombian	46	0.05
Ecuadorian	54	0.06
Paraguayan	1	<0.01
Peruvian	66	0.07
Venezuelan	3	<0.01
Other South American	5	0.01
Other Hispanic or Latino	3,144	3.26

Race*	Population	%
African-American/Black (31,688)	32,800	34.01
Not Hispanic (30,992)	31,687	32.85
Hispanic (696)	1,113	1.15
American Indian/Alaska Native (655)	1,182	1.23
Not Hispanic (175)	468	0.49
Hispanic (480)	714	0.74
Apache (7)	14	0.01
Blackfeet (3)	42	0.04
Canadian/French Am. Ind. (13)	13	0.01
Central American Ind. (4)	8	0.01
Cherokee (23)	88	0.09
Cheyenne (0)	4	<0.01
Chippewa (1)	4	<0.01
Choctaw (19)	47	0.05
Cree (0)	1	<0.01
Creek (1)	8	0.01
Iroquois (0)	1	<0.01
Mexican American Ind. (127)	185	0.19
Navajo (29)	31	0.03
Paiute (3)	3	<0.01
Pima (2)	4	<0.01
Pueblo (3)	4	<0.01
Seminole (0)	2	<0.01
Sioux (7)	11	0.01
South American Ind. (4)	4	<0.01
Spanish American Ind. (28)	31	0.03
Yaqui (3)	8	0.01
Yuman (3)	3	<0.01
Asian (292)	617	0.64
Not Hispanic (222)	391	0.41
Hispanic (70)	226	0.23
Burmese (0)	1	<0.01
Cambodian (11)	25	0.03
Chinese, ex. Taiwanese (18)	59	0.06
Filipino (137)	257	0.27
Hmong (1)	1	<0.01
Indian (31)	67	0.07
Indonesian (3)	9	0.01
Japanese (23)	46	0.05
Korean (13)	26	0.03
Laotian (1)	3	<0.01
Pakistani (11)	11	0.01
Sri Lankan (2)	2	<0.01
Taiwanese (0)	1	<0.01
Thai (8)	9	0.01
Vietnamese (23)	30	0.03
Hawaii Native/Pacific Islander (718)	899	0.93
Not Hispanic (684)	805	0.83
Hispanic (34)	94	0.10
Fijian (1)	1	<0.01
Guamanian/Chamorro (6)	18	0.02
Native Hawaiian (9)	52	0.05
Samoan (624)	735	0.76
Tongan (33)	42	0.04
White (24,942)	27,200	28.20
Not Hispanic (782)	1,117	1.16
Hispanic (24,160)	26,083	27.04

Concord

Place Type: City
County: Contra Costa
Population: 122,067†

*Notes: † The Census 2010 population figure is used to calculate the percentages in the Hispanic Origin and Race categories. Ancestry percentages are based on the 2006-2010 American Community Survey population (not shown); ‡ Numbers in parentheses indicate the number of people reporting a single ancestry; * Numbers in parentheses indicate the number of persons reporting this race alone, not in combination with any other race; Please refer to the Explanation of Data for more information.*

Ancestry‡	Population	%
Afghan (1,608)	1,655	1.36
African, Sub-Saharan (736)	931	0.77
African (229)	347	0.29
Cape Verdean (89)	114	0.09
Ethiopian (55)	55	0.05
Kenyan (17)	38	0.03
Liberian (64)	64	0.05
Nigerian (104)	135	0.11
South African (100)	100	0.08
Ugandan (66)	66	0.05
Other Sub-Saharan African (12)	12	0.01
Alsatian (29)	29	0.02
American (4,147)	4,147	3.42
Arab (145)	182	0.15
Egyptian (10)	10	0.01
Lebanese (28)	56	0.05
Palestinian (60)	60	0.05
Syrian (0)	9	0.01
Other Arab (47)	47	0.04
Armenian (66)	205	0.17
Australian (62)	95	0.08
Austrian (92)	211	0.17
Basque (0)	30	0.02
Belgian (30)	154	0.13
Brazilian (271)	327	0.27
British (217)	585	0.48
Bulgarian (149)	294	0.24
Cajun (16)	16	0.01
Canadian (121)	216	0.18
Celtic (7)	21	0.02
Croatian (87)	175	0.14
Czech (106)	379	0.31
Czechoslovakian (0)	10	0.01
Danish (215)	892	0.74
Dutch (273)	1,529	1.26
Eastern European (108)	119	0.10
English (2,562)	10,528	8.68
European (1,816)	2,204	1.82
Finnish (13)	80	0.07
French, ex. Basque (403)	3,477	2.87
French Canadian (189)	517	0.43
German (3,705)	14,696	12.11
Greek (180)	813	0.67
Guyanese (71)	71	0.06
Hungarian (134)	633	0.52
Icelander (16)	16	0.01
Iranian (589)	714	0.59
Irish (2,774)	12,170	10.03
Israeli (109)	109	0.09
Italian (2,759)	7,426	6.12
Latvian (0)	28	0.02
Lithuanian (98)	231	0.19
Luxemburger (0)	16	0.01
Macedonian (0)	37	0.03
Maltese (24)	166	0.14
New Zealander (0)	13	0.01
Northern European (164)	180	0.15
Norwegian (860)	2,059	1.70
Pennsylvania German (0)	13	0.01
Polish (577)	1,834	1.51
Portuguese (832)	2,291	1.89
Romanian (124)	164	0.14
Russian (1,443)	2,149	1.77
Scandinavian (323)	517	0.43
Scotch-Irish (753)	2,110	1.74
Scottish (639)	2,161	1.78
Serbian (15)	29	0.02
Slavic (22)	51	0.04
Slovak (122)	194	0.16
Slovene (0)	17	0.01
Swedish (562)	1,845	1.52
Swiss (46)	288	0.24
Turkish (41)	49	0.04
Ukrainian (287)	529	0.44
Welsh (131)	975	0.80
West Indian, ex. Hispanic (51)	131	0.11
British West Indian (10)	10	0.01
Jamaican (11)	74	0.06
Trinidadian/Tobagonian (12)	12	0.01
West Indian (18)	35	0.03
Yugoslavian (16)	48	0.04

Hispanic Origin	Population	%
Hispanic or Latino (of any race)	37,311	30.57
Central American, ex. Mexican	4,761	3.90
Costa Rican	118	0.10
Guatemalan	592	0.48
Honduran	116	0.10
Nicaraguan	886	0.73
Panamanian	119	0.10
Salvadoran	2,904	2.38
Other Central American	26	0.02
Cuban	214	0.18
Dominican Republic	30	0.02
Mexican	26,779	21.94
Puerto Rican	892	0.73
South American	1,845	1.51
Argentinean	146	0.12
Bolivian	53	0.04
Chilean	101	0.08
Colombian	279	0.23
Ecuadorian	111	0.09
Paraguayan	9	0.01
Peruvian	1,056	0.87
Uruguayan	15	0.01
Venezuelan	55	0.05
Other South American	20	0.02
Other Hispanic or Latino	2,790	2.29

Race*	Population	%
African-American/Black (4,371)	5,791	4.74
Not Hispanic (3,991)	5,064	4.15
Hispanic (380)	727	0.60
American Indian/Alaska Native (852)	2,298	1.88
Not Hispanic (366)	1,287	1.05
Hispanic (486)	1,011	0.83
Alaska Athabascan *(Ala. Nat.)* (1)	2	<0.01
Aleut *(Alaska Native)* (2)	4	<0.01
Apache (38)	95	0.08
Arapaho (1)	8	0.01
Blackfeet (8)	79	0.06
Canadian/French Am. Ind. (2)	6	<0.01
Central American Ind. (3)	21	0.02
Cherokee (64)	438	0.36
Cheyenne (1)	5	<0.01
Chickasaw (9)	25	0.02
Chippewa (8)	35	0.03
Choctaw (28)	111	0.09
Colville (0)	2	<0.01
Comanche (6)	14	0.01
Cree (0)	3	<0.01
Creek (3)	12	0.01
Crow (0)	1	<0.01
Delaware (6)	7	0.01
Hopi (2)	4	<0.01
Iroquois (17)	27	0.02
Kiowa (2)	4	<0.01
Menominee (0)	1	<0.01
Mexican American Ind. (105)	160	0.13
Navajo (35)	77	0.06
Osage (2)	6	<0.01
Paiute (8)	15	0.01
Potawatomi (12)	15	0.01
Pueblo (15)	27	0.02
Puget Sound Salish (1)	4	<0.01
Seminole (2)	9	0.01
Shoshone (0)	4	<0.01
Sioux (20)	70	0.06
South American Ind. (9)	24	0.02
Spanish American Ind. (2)	5	<0.01
Tlingit-Haida *(Alaska Native)* (3)	8	0.01
Tohono O'Odham (4)	5	<0.01
Tsimshian *(Alaska Native)* (0)	2	<0.01
Ute (7)	16	0.01
Yakama (2)	3	<0.01
Yaqui (5)	18	0.01
Yuman (0)	2	<0.01
Asian (13,538)	17,105	14.01
Not Hispanic (13,219)	16,144	13.23
Hispanic (319)	961	0.79
Bangladeshi (8)	9	0.01
Burmese (75)	96	0.08
Cambodian (48)	68	0.06
Chinese, ex. Taiwanese (2,795)	3,601	2.95
Filipino (5,333)	6,837	5.60
Hmong (8)	9	0.01
Indian (1,628)	1,872	1.53
Indonesian (132)	201	0.16
Japanese (749)	1,382	1.13
Korean (686)	873	0.72
Laotian (101)	121	0.10
Malaysian (4)	17	0.01
Nepalese (16)	17	0.01
Pakistani (188)	218	0.18
Sri Lankan (34)	39	0.03
Taiwanese (99)	126	0.10
Thai (112)	162	0.13
Vietnamese (799)	944	0.77
Hawaii Native/Pacific Islander (816)	1,445	1.18
Not Hispanic (744)	1,172	0.96
Hispanic (72)	273	0.22
Fijian (28)	36	0.03
Guamanian/Chamorro (90)	161	0.13
Native Hawaiian (88)	369	0.30
Samoan (121)	232	0.19
Tongan (341)	380	0.31
White (78,767)	85,528	70.07
Not Hispanic (61,416)	65,567	53.71
Hispanic (17,351)	19,961	16.35

Corcoran

Place Type: City
County: Kings
Population: 24,813†

Ancestry‡	Population	%
Afghan (7)	7	0.03
African, Sub-Saharan (159)	222	0.88
African (141)	204	0.81
Ethiopian (18)	18	0.07
American (333)	333	1.32
Armenian (36)	42	0.17
Austrian (0)	16	0.06
Basque (0)	35	0.14
Belgian (7)	7	0.03
Brazilian (0)	11	0.04
British (0)	27	0.11
Canadian (0)	9	0.04
Czech (7)	7	0.03
Czechoslovakian (10)	10	0.04
Danish (0)	24	0.10
Dutch (24)	79	0.31
English (282)	581	2.31
European (61)	72	0.29
French, ex. Basque (14)	167	0.66
French Canadian (0)	22	0.09
German (345)	964	3.84
German Russian (0)	8	0.03
Greek (0)	28	0.11
Iranian (11)	11	0.04
Irish (290)	1,139	4.53
Italian (90)	389	1.55
Lithuanian (0)	8	0.03
Norwegian (34)	115	0.46
Polish (8)	52	0.21
Portuguese (39)	132	0.53
Romanian (8)	8	0.03
Russian (0)	6	0.02
Scandinavian (9)	18	0.07
Scotch-Irish (33)	57	0.23
Scottish (8)	55	0.22
Slovak (0)	10	0.04
Slovene (0)	9	0.04
Swedish (21)	111	0.44
Ukrainian (0)	8	0.03
Welsh (7)	36	0.14
West Indian, ex. Hispanic (21)	28	0.11

SECTION TWO

*Notes: † The Census 2010 population figure is used to calculate the percentages in the Hispanic Origin and Race categories. Ancestry percentages are based on the 2006-2010 American Community Survey population (not shown); ‡ Numbers in parentheses indicate the number of people reporting a single ancestry; * Numbers in parentheses indicate the number of persons reporting this race alone, not in combination with any other race; Please refer to the Explanation of Data for more information.*

Belizean (14)	14	0.06
Haitian (7)	7	0.03
Jamaican (0)	7	0.03
Yugoslavian (9)	17	0.07

Hispanic Origin	Population	%
Hispanic or Latino (of any race)	15,545	62.65
Central American, ex. Mexican	63	0.25
Costa Rican	1	<0.01
Guatemalan	18	0.07
Honduran	6	0.02
Nicaraguan	7	0.03
Salvadoran	31	0.12
Cuban	14	0.06
Dominican Republic	1	<0.01
Mexican	13,686	55.16
Puerto Rican	29	0.12
South American	29	0.12
Colombian	4	0.02
Ecuadorian	7	0.03
Peruvian	18	0.07
Other Hispanic or Latino	1,723	6.94

Race*	Population	%
African-American/Black (3,725)	3,846	15.50
Not Hispanic (3,617)	3,676	14.81
Hispanic (108)	170	0.69
American Indian/Alaska Native (349)	469	1.89
Not Hispanic (133)	196	0.79
Hispanic (216)	273	1.10
Apache (10)	18	0.07
Central American Ind. (0)	1	<0.01
Cherokee (11)	24	0.10
Chickasaw (0)	4	0.02
Choctaw (3)	9	0.04
Comanche (0)	3	0.01
Creek (9)	10	0.04
Hopi (1)	1	<0.01
Mexican American Ind. (31)	42	0.17
Navajo (1)	1	<0.01
Pima (4)	4	0.02
Potawatomi (3)	6	0.02
Puget Sound Salish (1)	1	<0.01
Seminole (1)	1	<0.01
South American Ind. (3)	3	0.01
Spanish American Ind. (1)	2	0.01
Tohono O'Odham (1)	1	<0.01
Ute (0)	2	0.01
Yakama (1)	1	<0.01
Yaqui (16)	16	0.06
Asian (193)	263	1.06
Not Hispanic (179)	218	0.88
Hispanic (14)	45	0.18
Cambodian (12)	14	0.06
Chinese, ex. Taiwanese (36)	49	0.20
Filipino (74)	93	0.37
Hmong (8)	8	0.03
Indian (30)	45	0.18
Indonesian (1)	1	<0.01
Japanese (5)	7	0.03
Korean (5)	7	0.03
Laotian (3)	3	0.01
Thai (4)	7	0.03
Vietnamese (5)	6	0.02
Hawaii Native/Pacific Islander (17)	32	0.13
Not Hispanic (11)	22	0.09
Hispanic (6)	10	0.04
Guamanian/Chamorro (5)	5	0.02
Native Hawaiian (4)	13	0.05
Samoan (3)	7	0.03
Tongan (0)	1	<0.01
White (8,940)	9,457	38.11
Not Hispanic (4,818)	4,943	19.92
Hispanic (4,122)	4,514	18.19

Corning

Place Type: City
County: Tehama
Population: 7,663†

Ancestry‡	Population	%
American (449)	449	5.95
British (0)	11	0.15
Czech (14)	14	0.19
Czechoslovakian (0)	26	0.34
Dutch (16)	64	0.85
English (425)	920	12.19
European (62)	79	1.05
French, ex. Basque (17)	77	1.02
German (227)	949	12.58
Irish (258)	811	10.75
Italian (51)	165	2.19
Norwegian (43)	159	2.11
Polish (0)	65	0.86
Portuguese (58)	138	1.83
Russian (0)	28	0.37
Scandinavian (0)	17	0.23
Scotch-Irish (10)	94	1.25
Scottish (0)	140	1.86
Swedish (30)	80	1.06
Welsh (0)	22	0.29
Yugoslavian (0)	11	0.15

Hispanic Origin	Population	%
Hispanic or Latino (of any race)	3,271	42.69
Central American, ex. Mexican	55	0.72
Costa Rican	10	0.13
Guatemalan	3	0.04
Nicaraguan	4	0.05
Panamanian	1	0.01
Salvadoran	37	0.48
Cuban	2	0.03
Mexican	3,045	39.74
Puerto Rican	21	0.27
South American	21	0.27
Bolivian	1	0.01
Chilean	6	0.08
Colombian	2	0.03
Peruvian	6	0.08
Venezuelan	6	0.08
Other Hispanic or Latino	127	1.66

Race*	Population	%
African-American/Black (44)	80	1.04
Not Hispanic (27)	50	0.65
Hispanic (17)	30	0.39
American Indian/Alaska Native (201)	346	4.52
Not Hispanic (118)	242	3.16
Hispanic (83)	104	1.36
Apache (0)	1	0.01
Blackfeet (1)	2	0.03
Cherokee (9)	29	0.38
Chickasaw (1)	3	0.04
Chippewa (3)	13	0.17
Choctaw (8)	15	0.20
Cree (1)	3	0.04
Creek (0)	1	0.01
Delaware (3)	3	0.04
Hopi (0)	1	0.01
Inupiat *(Alaska Native)* (1)	1	0.01
Kiowa (0)	1	0.01
Lumbee (0)	4	0.05
Mexican American Ind. (26)	28	0.37
Navajo (3)	3	0.04
Seminole (5)	8	0.10
Sioux (2)	5	0.07
Spanish American Ind. (5)	5	0.07
Tlingit Haida *(Alaska Native)* (0)	1	0.01
Ute (2)	2	0.03
Yakama (0)	1	0.01
Yaqui (1)	4	0.05
Asian (82)	116	1.51
Not Hispanic (76)	98	1.28
Hispanic (6)	18	0.23
Chinese, ex. Taiwanese (8)	9	0.12
Filipino (18)	32	0.42
Hmong (12)	14	0.18
Indian (17)	21	0.27
Indonesian (4)	4	0.05
Japanese (1)	6	0.08
Korean (3)	5	0.07
Laotian (7)	10	0.13
Pakistani (0)	1	0.01
Taiwanese (1)	1	0.01
Vietnamese (6)	6	0.08
Hawaii Native/Pacific Islander (11)	26	0.34
Not Hispanic (11)	24	0.31
Hispanic (0)	2	0.03
Native Hawaiian (3)	11	0.14
Samoan (6)	7	0.09
White (5,510)	5,809	75.81
Not Hispanic (3,976)	4,137	53.99
Hispanic (1,534)	1,672	21.82

Corona

Place Type: City
County: Riverside
Population: 152,374†

Ancestry‡	Population	%
Afghan (22)	94	0.06
African, Sub-Saharan (398)	600	0.40
African (237)	407	0.27
Ethiopian (26)	26	0.02
Nigerian (65)	82	0.05
Sudanese (40)	40	0.03
Zimbabwean (30)	30	0.02
Other Sub-Saharan African (0)	15	0.01
American (3,027)	3,027	2.01
Arab (2,818)	3,365	2.24
Arab (379)	463	0.31
Egyptian (1,053)	1,103	0.73
Iraqi (151)	239	0.16
Jordanian (58)	88	0.06
Lebanese (715)	845	0.56
Moroccan (148)	148	0.10
Palestinian (149)	195	0.13
Syrian (0)	46	0.03
Other Arab (165)	238	0.16
Armenian (187)	313	0.21
Assyrian/Chaldean/Syriac (34)	34	0.02
Australian (0)	47	0.03
Austrian (46)	137	0.09
Basque (37)	57	0.04
Belgian (28)	71	0.05
Brazilian (83)	183	0.12
British (182)	309	0.21
Bulgarian (6)	20	0.01
Cajun (0)	27	0.02
Canadian (103)	296	0.20
Celtic (0)	6	<0.01
Croatian (12)	80	0.05
Czech (178)	286	0.19
Czechoslovakian (27)	49	0.03
Danish (256)	758	0.50
Dutch (365)	1,911	1.27
Eastern European (0)	10	0.01
English (2,697)	8,970	5.96
European (1,754)	2,049	1.36
Finnish (43)	153	0.10
French, ex. Basque (649)	3,872	2.57
French Canadian (456)	892	0.59
German (4,083)	16,019	10.64
Greek (140)	725	0.48
Guyanese (0)	11	0.01
Hungarian (220)	458	0.30
Icelander (9)	23	0.02
Iranian (961)	1,065	0.71
Irish (2,074)	11,652	7.74
Israeli (32)	62	0.04
Italian (1,921)	6,284	4.18
Latvian (69)	78	0.05
Lithuanian (100)	223	0.15
Luxemburger (11)	11	0.01
Macedonian (34)	49	0.03
New Zealander (8)	24	0.02
Northern European (30)	43	0.03
Norwegian (429)	1,808	1.20
Polish (912)	2,224	1.48

*Notes: † The Census 2010 population figure is used to calculate the percentages in the Hispanic Origin and Race categories. Ancestry percentages are based on the 2006-2010 American Community Survey population (not shown); ‡ Numbers in parentheses indicate the number of people reporting a single ancestry; * Numbers in parentheses indicate the number of persons reporting this race alone, not in combination with any other race; Please refer to the Explanation of Data for more information.*

Portuguese (209)	639	0.42
Romanian (145)	221	0.15
Russian (269)	776	0.52
Scandinavian (257)	681	0.45
Scotch-Irish (486)	1,758	1.17
Scottish (518)	1,904	1.27
Serbian (0)	95	0.06
Slavic (0)	36	0.02
Slovak (24)	107	0.07
Slovene (12)	29	0.02
Swedish (380)	1,857	1.23
Swiss (59)	168	0.11
Turkish (0)	19	0.01
Ukrainian (78)	136	0.09
Welsh (49)	466	0.31
West Indian, ex. Hispanic (67)	101	0.07
Barbadian (8)	8	0.01
Belizean (20)	20	0.01
Jamaican (13)	47	0.03
West Indian (26)	26	0.02
Yugoslavian (20)	115	0.08

Hispanic Origin	Population	%
Hispanic or Latino (of any race)	66,447	43.61
Central American, ex. Mexican	3,118	2.05
Costa Rican	173	0.11
Guatemalan	934	0.61
Honduran	215	0.14
Nicaraguan	296	0.19
Panamanian	111	0.07
Salvadoran	1,350	0.89
Other Central American	39	0.03
Cuban	651	0.43
Dominican Republic	54	0.04
Mexican	56,979	37.39
Puerto Rican	899	0.59
South American	1,740	1.14
Argentinean	244	0.16
Bolivian	82	0.05
Chilean	140	0.09
Colombian	396	0.26
Ecuadorian	239	0.16
Peruvian	513	0.34
Uruguayan	27	0.02
Venezuelan	70	0.05
Other South American	29	0.02
Other Hispanic or Latino	3,006	1.97

Race*	Population	%
African-American/Black (8,934)	10,450	6.86
Not Hispanic (8,333)	9,399	6.17
Hispanic (601)	1,051	0.69
American Indian/Alaska Native (1,153)	2,256	1.48
Not Hispanic (422)	992	0.65
Hispanic (731)	1,264	0.83
Aleut *(Alaska Native)* (0)	2	<0.01
Apache (46)	86	0.06
Blackfeet (13)	41	0.03
Canadian/French Am. Ind. (0)	1	<0.01
Central American Ind. (3)	3	<0.01
Cherokee (75)	265	0.17
Cheyenne (1)	1	<0.01
Chickasaw (24)	32	0.02
Chippewa (15)	23	0.02
Choctaw (29)	81	0.05
Colville (1)	1	<0.01
Comanche (3)	17	0.01
Cree (1)	1	<0.01
Creek (9)	16	0.01
Crow (5)	9	0.01
Hopi (8)	14	0.01
Iroquois (6)	23	0.02
Kiowa (6)	7	<0.01
Lumbee (1)	2	<0.01
Menominee (1)	1	<0.01
Mexican American Ind. (117)	171	0.11
Navajo (33)	66	0.04
Osage (4)	9	0.01
Paiute (2)	9	0.01
Pima (6)	7	<0.01
Potawatomi (3)	4	<0.01
Pueblo (6)	13	0.01
Seminole (1)	19	0.01
Shoshone (1)	3	<0.01
Sioux (16)	40	0.03
South American Ind. (6)	15	0.01
Spanish American Ind. (5)	35	0.02
Tlingit-Haida *(Alaska Native)* (0)	1	<0.01
Tohono O'Odham (5)	8	0.01
Ute (4)	12	0.01
Yakama (0)	1	<0.01
Yaqui (27)	56	0.04
Yuman (6)	11	0.01
Asian (15,048)	17,899	11.75
Not Hispanic (14,650)	16,857	11.06
Hispanic (398)	1,042	0.68
Bangladeshi (55)	77	0.05
Burmese (11)	17	0.01
Cambodian (284)	332	0.22
Chinese, ex. Taiwanese (1,287)	1,843	1.21
Filipino (4,570)	5,660	3.71
Hmong (21)	34	0.02
Indian (2,436)	2,693	1.77
Indonesian (153)	227	0.15
Japanese (465)	1,012	0.66
Korean (1,756)	1,993	1.31
Laotian (139)	182	0.12
Malaysian (2)	8	0.01
Nepalese (2)	2	<0.01
Pakistani (666)	731	0.48
Sri Lankan (86)	88	0.06
Taiwanese (156)	172	0.11
Thai (130)	198	0.13
Vietnamese (2,215)	2,520	1.65
Hawaii Native/Pacific Islander (552)	1,098	0.72
Not Hispanic (496)	887	0.58
Hispanic (56)	211	0.14
Fijian (38)	47	0.03
Guamanian/Chamorro (127)	222	0.15
Marshallese (5)	5	<0.01
Native Hawaiian (101)	301	0.20
Samoan (161)	260	0.17
Tongan (50)	58	0.04
White (90,925)	97,516	64.00
Not Hispanic (58,087)	61,175	40.15
Hispanic (32,838)	36,341	23.85

Coronado

Place Type: City
County: San Diego
Population: 18,912†

Ancestry‡	Population	%
African, Sub-Saharan (11)	71	0.36
African (0)	52	0.26
Cape Verdean (8)	8	0.04
Ethiopian (3)	3	0.02
South African (0)	8	0.04
American (495)	495	2.51
Arab (113)	133	0.67
Arab (76)	76	0.39
Lebanese (37)	57	0.29
Armenian (0)	11	0.06
Australian (164)	175	0.89
Austrian (68)	101	0.51
Basque (0)	8	0.04
Belgian (0)	8	0.04
British (63)	128	0.65
Canadian (5)	34	0.17
Celtic (6)	25	0.13
Croatian (0)	15	0.08
Czech (73)	261	1.32
Czechoslovakian (12)	16	0.08
Danish (58)	252	1.28
Dutch (73)	295	1.50
Eastern European (26)	35	0.18
English (842)	3,225	16.35
European (435)	493	2.50
Finnish (12)	12	0.06
French, ex. Basque (139)	861	4.37
French Canadian (58)	113	0.57
German (807)	3,593	18.22
Greek (84)	128	0.65
Hungarian (38)	157	0.80
Icelander (0)	17	0.09
Iranian (14)	16	0.08
Irish (1,078)	3,079	15.61
Italian (431)	971	4.92
Latvian (0)	85	0.43
Lithuanian (0)	53	0.27
New Zealander (6)	6	0.03
Northern European (17)	17	0.09
Norwegian (107)	423	2.14
Polish (228)	645	3.27
Portuguese (21)	110	0.56
Romanian (0)	25	0.13
Russian (113)	323	1.64
Scandinavian (30)	114	0.58
Scotch-Irish (160)	508	2.58
Scottish (197)	732	3.71
Slavic (0)	9	0.05
Slovak (39)	39	0.20
Slovene (6)	64	0.32
Swedish (38)	205	1.04
Swiss (10)	43	0.22
Ukrainian (11)	56	0.28
Welsh (13)	204	1.03
West Indian, ex. Hispanic (8)	8	0.04
Jamaican (8)	8	0.04

Hispanic Origin	Population	%
Hispanic or Latino (of any race)	2,302	12.17
Central American, ex. Mexican	85	0.45
Costa Rican	11	0.06
Guatemalan	20	0.11
Honduran	12	0.06
Nicaraguan	13	0.07
Panamanian	15	0.08
Salvadoran	11	0.06
Other Central American	3	0.02
Cuban	28	0.15
Dominican Republic	11	0.06
Mexican	1,688	8.93
Puerto Rican	133	0.70
South American	99	0.52
Argentinean	14	0.07
Bolivian	1	0.01
Chilean	11	0.06
Colombian	34	0.18
Ecuadorian	8	0.04
Paraguayan	1	0.01
Peruvian	16	0.08
Uruguayan	3	0.02
Venezuelan	11	0.06
Other Hispanic or Latino	258	1.36

Race*	Population	%
African-American/Black (399)	554	2.93
Not Hispanic (370)	505	2.67
Hispanic (29)	49	0.26
American Indian/Alaska Native (103)	255	1.35
Not Hispanic (75)	194	1.03
Hispanic (28)	61	0.32
Apache (6)	13	0.07
Blackfeet (1)	8	0.04
Canadian/French Am. Ind. (1)	1	0.01
Central American Ind. (1)	1	0.01
Cherokee (10)	49	0.26
Cheyenne (0)	1	0.01
Chickasaw (5)	9	0.05
Chippewa (3)	4	0.02
Choctaw (7)	8	0.04
Colville (0)	1	0.01
Delaware (0)	1	0.01
Hopi (1)	1	0.01
Inupiat *(Alaska Native)* (0)	1	0.01
Iroquois (2)	5	0.03
Mexican American Ind. (6)	16	0.08
Navajo (7)	10	0.05

*Notes: † The Census 2010 population figure is used to calculate the percentages in the Hispanic Origin and Race categories. Ancestry percentages are based on the 2006-2010 American Community Survey population (not shown); ‡ Numbers in parentheses indicate the number of people reporting a single ancestry; * Numbers in parentheses indicate the number of persons reporting this race alone, not in combination with any other race; Please refer to the Explanation of Data for more information.*

Osage (1)	1	0.01
Potawatomi (5)	5	0.03
Pueblo (2)	6	0.03
Seminole (1)	3	0.02
Sioux (3)	4	0.02
South American Ind. (0)	2	0.01
Tlingit-Haida *(Alaska Native)* (0)	1	0.01
Tohono O'Odham (1)	1	0.01
Yaqui (1)	1	0.01
Asian (572)	897	4.74
Not Hispanic (547)	844	4.46
Hispanic (25)	53	0.28
Burmese (5)	5	0.03
Cambodian (4)	5	0.03
Chinese, ex. Taiwanese (100)	177	0.94
Filipino (245)	360	1.90
Hmong (2)	2	0.01
Indian (26)	42	0.22
Indonesian (3)	9	0.05
Japanese (74)	149	0.79
Korean (40)	86	0.45
Laotian (1)	1	0.01
Malaysian (0)	1	0.01
Taiwanese (4)	7	0.04
Thai (6)	7	0.04
Vietnamese (30)	38	0.20
Hawaii Native/Pacific Islander (55)	127	0.67
Not Hispanic (51)	115	0.61
Hispanic (4)	12	0.06
Fijian (1)	1	0.01
Guamanian/Chamorro (13)	34	0.18
Native Hawaiian (15)	48	0.25
Samoan (2)	5	0.03
Tongan (5)	5	0.03
White (16,668)	17,260	91.26
Not Hispanic (15,016)	15,490	81.91
Hispanic (1,652)	1,770	9.36

Corte Madera

Place Type: Town
County: Marin
Population: 9,253†

Ancestry‡	Population	%
American (357)	357	3.92
Arab (14)	14	0.15
Other Arab (14)	14	0.15
Armenian (50)	69	0.76
Australian (13)	13	0.14
Austrian (14)	120	1.32
Basque (20)	20	0.22
Brazilian (21)	21	0.23
British (77)	105	1.15
Bulgarian (0)	50	0.55
Canadian (68)	136	1.49
Croatian (67)	105	1.15
Czech (0)	143	1.57
Danish (61)	156	1.71
Dutch (16)	72	0.79
Eastern European (130)	145	1.59
English (373)	1,342	14.73
European (195)	212	2.33
Finnish (53)	53	0.58
French, ex. Basque (15)	447	4.91
French Canadian (13)	58	0.64
German (332)	1,452	15.94
Greek (82)	82	0.90
Hungarian (20)	39	0.43
Icelander (33)	47	0.52
Iranian (211)	211	2.32
Irish (248)	1,033	11.34
Italian (465)	975	10.70
Lithuanian (0)	16	0.18
Northern European (39)	53	0.58
Norwegian (53)	261	2.86
Polish (100)	188	2.06
Portuguese (56)	76	0.83
Romanian (13)	47	0.52
Russian (83)	233	2.56
Scandinavian (0)	29	0.32
Scotch-Irish (10)	136	1.49
Scottish (96)	431	4.73
Slovene (15)	15	0.16
Swedish (78)	331	3.63
Swiss (90)	147	1.61
Ukrainian (16)	16	0.18
Welsh (17)	87	0.95
Yugoslavian (18)	33	0.36

Hispanic Origin	Population	%
Hispanic or Latino (of any race)	772	8.34
Central American, ex. Mexican	157	1.70
Costa Rican	3	0.03
Guatemalan	68	0.73
Nicaraguan	9	0.10
Panamanian	4	0.04
Salvadoran	71	0.77
Other Central American	2	0.02
Cuban	19	0.21
Dominican Republic	14	0.15
Mexican	330	3.57
Puerto Rican	43	0.46
South American	92	0.99
Argentinean	14	0.15
Chilean	7	0.08
Colombian	18	0.19
Ecuadorian	13	0.14
Peruvian	32	0.35
Uruguayan	3	0.03
Venezuelan	3	0.03
Other South American	2	0.02
Other Hispanic or Latino	117	1.26

Race*	Population	%
African-American/Black (87)	155	1.68
Not Hispanic (79)	131	1.42
Hispanic (8)	24	0.26
American Indian/Alaska Native (15)	87	0.94
Not Hispanic (4)	56	0.61
Hispanic (11)	31	0.34
Apache (1)	1	0.01
Blackfeet (1)	4	0.04
Central American Ind. (0)	2	0.02
Cherokee (0)	9	0.10
Chickasaw (0)	4	0.04
Chippewa (0)	1	0.01
Choctaw (1)	4	0.04
Crow (0)	1	0.01
Mexican American Ind. (6)	9	0.10
Navajo (0)	1	0.01
Osage (0)	1	0.01
Pima (0)	2	0.02
Pueblo (0)	3	0.03
Sioux (0)	3	0.03
South American Ind. (1)	2	0.02
Asian (625)	882	9.53
Not Hispanic (616)	855	9.24
Hispanic (9)	27	0.29
Chinese, ex. Taiwanese (216)	311	3.36
Filipino (58)	103	1.11
Indian (91)	108	1.17
Indonesian (5)	7	0.08
Japanese (97)	172	1.86
Korean (75)	116	1.25
Laotian (1)	3	0.03
Malaysian (1)	1	0.01
Pakistani (3)	3	0.03
Taiwanese (11)	13	0.14
Thai (11)	15	0.16
Vietnamese (14)	25	0.27
Hawaii Native/Pacific Islander (29)	53	0.57
Not Hispanic (26)	45	0.49
Hispanic (3)	8	0.09
Fijian (16)	18	0.19
Guamanian/Chamorro (5)	7	0.08
Native Hawaiian (3)	17	0.18
Samoan (0)	2	0.02
White (7,808)	8,210	88.73
Not Hispanic (7,364)	7,692	83.13
Hispanic (444)	518	5.60

Costa Mesa

Place Type: City
County: Orange
Population: 109,960†

Ancestry‡	Population	%
Afghan (9)	9	0.01
African, Sub-Saharan (119)	155	0.14
African (77)	95	0.09
South African (8)	26	0.02
Other Sub-Saharan African (34)	34	0.03
Alsatian (0)	33	0.03
American (2,803)	2,803	2.56
Arab (615)	746	0.68
Arab (138)	181	0.17
Egyptian (206)	206	0.19
Jordanian (53)	53	0.05
Lebanese (96)	136	0.12
Moroccan (7)	7	0.01
Palestinian (53)	53	0.05
Syrian (9)	25	0.02
Other Arab (53)	85	0.08
Armenian (221)	674	0.62
Australian (13)	95	0.09
Austrian (43)	256	0.23
Basque (9)	23	0.02
Belgian (17)	44	0.04
Brazilian (134)	193	0.18
British (394)	826	0.76
Bulgarian (25)	38	0.03
Canadian (147)	482	0.44
Celtic (19)	19	0.02
Croatian (124)	201	0.18
Czech (92)	533	0.49
Czechoslovakian (9)	42	0.04
Danish (86)	513	0.47
Dutch (395)	1,668	1.53
Eastern European (205)	237	0.22
English (2,957)	9,779	8.95
Estonian (12)	12	0.01
European (1,178)	1,511	1.38
Finnish (59)	170	0.16
French, ex. Basque (284)	3,000	2.74
French Canadian (232)	661	0.60
German (3,505)	14,780	13.52
Greek (247)	727	0.67
Hungarian (131)	640	0.59
Icelander (27)	35	0.03
Iranian (244)	361	0.33
Irish (2,670)	10,915	9.98
Israeli (54)	84	0.08
Italian (2,113)	5,902	5.40
Latvian (25)	60	0.05
Lithuanian (98)	245	0.22
Macedonian (8)	8	0.01
Maltese (11)	11	0.01
New Zealander (55)	55	0.05
Northern European (158)	171	0.16
Norwegian (500)	1,924	1.76
Pennsylvania German (0)	15	0.01
Polish (912)	2,415	2.21
Portuguese (183)	704	0.64
Romanian (39)	93	0.09
Russian (437)	1,496	1.37
Scandinavian (161)	473	0.43
Scotch-Irish (567)	1,748	1.60
Scottish (568)	2,293	2.10
Serbian (32)	32	0.03
Slavic (10)	21	0.02
Slovak (128)	207	0.19
Slovene (7)	48	0.04
Swedish (615)	2,201	2.01
Swiss (141)	467	0.43
Turkish (54)	78	0.07
Ukrainian (100)	211	0.19
Welsh (138)	710	0.65
West Indian, ex. Hispanic (151)	218	0.20

*Notes: † The Census 2010 population figure is used to calculate the percentages in the Hispanic Origin and Race categories. Ancestry percentages are based on the 2006-2010 American Community Survey population (not shown); ‡ Numbers in parentheses indicate the number of people reporting a single ancestry; * Numbers in parentheses indicate the number of persons reporting this race alone, not in combination with any other race; Please refer to the Explanation of Data for more information.*

Barbadian (8)	8	0.01
British West Indian (61)	61	0.06
Jamaican (48)	115	0.11
Trinidadian/Tobagonian (34)	34	0.03
Yugoslavian (50)	112	0.10

Hispanic Origin	Population	%
Hispanic or Latino (of any race)	39,403	35.83
Central American, ex. Mexican	3,497	3.18
Costa Rican	47	0.04
Guatemalan	1,134	1.03
Honduran	174	0.16
Nicaraguan	108	0.10
Panamanian	22	0.02
Salvadoran	1,983	1.80
Other Central American	29	0.03
Cuban	233	0.21
Dominican Republic	23	0.02
Mexican	31,646	28.78
Puerto Rican	433	0.39
South American	1,146	1.04
Argentinean	239	0.22
Bolivian	70	0.06
Chilean	54	0.05
Colombian	299	0.27
Ecuadorian	153	0.14
Paraguayan	8	0.01
Peruvian	251	0.23
Uruguayan	35	0.03
Venezuelan	22	0.02
Other South American	15	0.01
Other Hispanic or Latino	2,425	2.21

Race*	Population	%
African-American/Black (1,640)	2,337	2.13
Not Hispanic (1,352)	1,895	1.72
Hispanic (288)	442	0.40
American Indian/Alaska Native (686)	1,651	1.50
Not Hispanic (266)	772	0.70
Hispanic (420)	879	0.80
Aleut *(Alaska Native)* (5)	6	0.01
Apache (21)	49	0.04
Arapaho (2)	2	<0.01
Blackfeet (4)	35	0.03
Canadian/French Am. Ind. (1)	1	<0.01
Central American Ind. (1)	1	<0.01
Cherokee (63)	252	0.23
Chickasaw (4)	16	0.01
Chippewa (2)	15	0.01
Choctaw (16)	52	0.05
Colville (2)	2	<0.01
Comanche (1)	5	<0.01
Cree (1)	4	<0.01
Creek (0)	6	0.01
Crow (0)	1	<0.01
Delaware (2)	3	<0.01
Hopi (3)	5	<0.01
Inupiat *(Alaska Native)* (0)	1	<0.01
Iroquois (1)	6	0.01
Lumbee (2)	3	<0.01
Mexican American Ind. (100)	197	0.18
Navajo (20)	41	0.04
Osage (3)	7	0.01
Paiute (5)	7	0.01
Pima (3)	6	0.01
Potawatomi (5)	8	0.01
Pueblo (6)	9	0.01
Puget Sound Salish (5)	6	0.01
Seminole (4)	8	0.01
Shoshone (1)	6	0.01
Sioux (4)	10	0.01
South American Ind. (11)	18	0.02
Spanish American Ind. (7)	10	0.01
Tlingit-Haida *(Alaska Native)* (1)	2	<0.01
Tohono O'Odham (0)	2	<0.01
Ute (2)	2	<0.01
Yakama (0)	4	<0.01
Yaqui (12)	21	0.02
Yuman (4)	5	<0.01
Yup'ik *(Alaska Native)* (1)	1	<0.01
Asian (8,654)	10,662	9.70
Not Hispanic (8,483)	10,160	9.24
Hispanic (171)	502	0.46
Bangladeshi (10)	10	0.01
Burmese (8)	9	0.01
Cambodian (93)	137	0.12
Chinese, ex. Taiwanese (981)	1,427	1.30
Filipino (1,814)	2,500	2.27
Hmong (14)	18	0.02
Indian (617)	740	0.67
Indonesian (57)	131	0.12
Japanese (1,312)	1,905	1.73
Korean (730)	907	0.82
Laotian (24)	25	0.02
Malaysian (9)	9	0.01
Nepalese (7)	8	0.01
Pakistani (61)	84	0.08
Sri Lankan (48)	51	0.05
Taiwanese (112)	137	0.12
Thai (121)	167	0.15
Vietnamese (2,255)	2,475	2.25
Hawaii Native/Pacific Islander (527)	995	0.90
Not Hispanic (486)	879	0.80
Hispanic (41)	116	0.11
Fijian (9)	15	0.01
Guamanian/Chamorro (42)	87	0.08
Marshallese (164)	177	0.16
Native Hawaiian (140)	380	0.35
Samoan (86)	155	0.14
Tongan (4)	6	0.01
White (75,335)	79,899	72.66
Not Hispanic (56,993)	59,439	54.06
Hispanic (18,342)	20,460	18.61

Coto de Caza

Place Type: CDP
County: Orange
Population: 14,866†

Ancestry‡	Population	%
Afghan (39)	39	0.25
African, Sub-Saharan (0)	24	0.16
African (0)	24	0.16
Albanian (0)	18	0.12
American (961)	961	6.22
Arab (189)	239	1.55
Arab (54)	54	0.35
Egyptian (20)	20	0.13
Lebanese (0)	50	0.32
Palestinian (97)	97	0.63
Syrian (18)	18	0.12
Armenian (16)	59	0.38
Assyrian/Chaldean/Syriac (12)	12	0.08
Austrian (7)	140	0.91
Belgian (7)	27	0.17
Brazilian (15)	40	0.26
British (269)	614	3.97
Canadian (32)	91	0.59
Celtic (8)	24	0.16
Croatian (0)	20	0.13
Czech (0)	83	0.54
Czechoslovakian (0)	6	0.04
Danish (39)	81	0.52
Dutch (27)	285	1.84
Eastern European (10)	73	0.47
English (691)	2,231	14.44
European (418)	442	2.86
Finnish (11)	59	0.38
French, ex. Basque (29)	439	2.84
French Canadian (20)	111	0.72
German (833)	3,249	21.03
Greek (87)	161	1.04
Hungarian (43)	260	1.68
Iranian (258)	258	1.67
Irish (708)	2,784	18.02
Italian (344)	1,245	8.06
Lithuanian (17)	43	0.28
Northern European (80)	92	0.60
Norwegian (121)	427	2.76
Polish (106)	581	3.76
Portuguese (16)	60	0.39
Romanian (16)	21	0.14
Russian (84)	275	1.78
Scandinavian (0)	96	0.62
Scotch-Irish (53)	263	1.70
Scottish (118)	321	2.08
Serbian (19)	50	0.32
Slovak (0)	13	0.08
Slovene (0)	7	0.05
Swedish (117)	504	3.26
Swiss (11)	11	0.07
Ukrainian (18)	51	0.33
Welsh (42)	232	1.50
Yugoslavian (0)	49	0.32

Hispanic Origin	Population	%
Hispanic or Latino (of any race)	1,170	7.87
Central American, ex. Mexican	64	0.43
Costa Rican	8	0.05
Guatemalan	7	0.05
Honduran	3	0.02
Nicaraguan	17	0.11
Panamanian	6	0.04
Salvadoran	21	0.14
Other Central American	2	0.01
Cuban	57	0.38
Dominican Republic	1	0.01
Mexican	730	4.91
Puerto Rican	39	0.26
South American	136	0.91
Argentinean	33	0.22
Bolivian	14	0.09
Chilean	6	0.04
Colombian	31	0.21
Ecuadorian	6	0.04
Peruvian	36	0.24
Uruguayan	1	0.01
Venezuelan	7	0.05
Other South American	2	0.01
Other Hispanic or Latino	143	0.96

Race*	Population	%
African-American/Black (132)	213	1.43
Not Hispanic (129)	200	1.35
Hispanic (3)	13	0.09
American Indian/Alaska Native (26)	83	0.56
Not Hispanic (23)	64	0.43
Hispanic (3)	19	0.13
Apache (0)	4	0.03
Blackfeet (0)	1	0.01
Cherokee (10)	23	0.15
Chickasaw (1)	1	0.01
Chippewa (0)	1	0.01
Choctaw (2)	5	0.03
Hopi (1)	1	0.01
Iroquois (0)	1	0.01
Lumbee (3)	6	0.04
Mexican American Ind. (1)	3	0.02
Navajo (0)	4	0.03
Ottawa (1)	3	0.02
Pueblo (0)	1	0.01
Sioux (0)	1	0.01
Yaqui (0)	2	0.01
Asian (878)	1,222	8.22
Not Hispanic (860)	1,171	7.88
Hispanic (18)	51	0.34
Burmese (1)	1	0.01
Cambodian (12)	12	0.08
Chinese, ex. Taiwanese (158)	259	1.74
Filipino (218)	325	2.19
Indian (107)	151	1.02
Indonesian (3)	4	0.03
Japanese (94)	214	1.44
Korean (147)	187	1.26
Malaysian (0)	1	0.01
Pakistani (6)	10	0.07
Sri Lankan (3)	3	0.02
Taiwanese (11)	13	0.09
Thai (5)	10	0.07

*Notes: † The Census 2010 population figure is used to calculate the percentages in the Hispanic Origin and Race categories. Ancestry percentages are based on the 2006-2010 American Community Survey population (not shown); ‡ Numbers in parentheses indicate the number of people reporting a single ancestry; * Numbers in parentheses indicate the number of persons reporting this race alone, not in combination with any other race; Please refer to the Explanation of Data for more information.*

Vietnamese (54)	72	0.48
Hawaii Native/Pacific Islander (20)	82	0.55
Not Hispanic (20)	64	0.43
Hispanic (0)	18	0.12
Fijian (1)	1	0.01
Guamanian/Chamorro (2)	12	0.08
Native Hawaiian (9)	45	0.30
White (13,094)	13,570	91.28
Not Hispanic (12,219)	12,598	84.74
Hispanic (875)	972	6.54

Country Club

Place Type: CDP
County: San Joaquin
Population: 9,379†

Ancestry‡	Population	%
American (499)	499	5.66
Basque (6)	6	0.07
Belgian (0)	6	0.07
British (23)	29	0.33
Canadian (0)	7	0.08
Czech (36)	36	0.41
Danish (22)	39	0.44
Dutch (22)	344	3.90
English (112)	489	5.54
European (59)	91	1.03
French, ex. Basque (56)	207	2.35
French Canadian (42)	42	0.48
German (544)	1,221	13.85
Greek (12)	18	0.20
Irish (124)	824	9.34
Italian (84)	325	3.69
Norwegian (27)	93	1.05
Polish (8)	18	0.20
Portuguese (131)	173	1.96
Romanian (19)	29	0.33
Russian (0)	7	0.08
Scandinavian (0)	16	0.18
Scotch-Irish (6)	187	2.12
Scottish (14)	74	0.84
Slovak (0)	23	0.26
Swedish (10)	98	1.11
Swiss (0)	7	0.08
Ukrainian (0)	10	0.11
Welsh (0)	14	0.16
West Indian, ex. Hispanic (0)	39	0.44
Dutch West Indian (0)	39	0.44

Hispanic Origin	Population	%
Hispanic or Latino (of any race)	3,790	40.41
Central American, ex. Mexican	62	0.66
Costa Rican	1	0.01
Guatemalan	10	0.11
Nicaraguan	17	0.18
Panamanian	2	0.02
Salvadoran	32	0.34
Cuban	9	0.10
Mexican	3,378	36.02
Puerto Rican	74	0.79
South American	36	0.38
Argentinean	3	0.03
Chilean	10	0.11
Colombian	8	0.09
Ecuadorian	2	0.02
Paraguayan	4	0.04
Peruvian	8	0.09
Venezuelan	1	0.01
Other Hispanic or Latino	231	2.46

Race*	Population	%
African-American/Black (472)	655	6.98
Not Hispanic (422)	544	5.80
Hispanic (50)	111	1.18
American Indian/Alaska Native (159)	348	3.71
Not Hispanic (41)	152	1.62
Hispanic (118)	196	2.09
Aleut *(Alaska Native)* (0)	1	0.01
Apache (11)	23	0.25
Blackfeet (0)	3	0.03
Cherokee (6)	56	0.60
Chickasaw (0)	4	0.04
Choctaw (2)	15	0.16
Comanche (1)	2	0.02
Creek (2)	7	0.07
Hopi (0)	4	0.04
Iroquois (0)	3	0.03
Mexican American Ind. (29)	36	0.38
Navajo (5)	7	0.07
Osage (0)	1	0.01
Puget Sound Salish (0)	1	0.01
Seminole (0)	2	0.02
Sioux (1)	5	0.05
Spanish American Ind. (0)	1	0.01
Tlingit-Haida *(Alaska Native)* (3)	8	0.09
Tohono O'Odham (0)	3	0.03
Ute (2)	2	0.02
Yaqui (6)	8	0.09
Asian (628)	959	10.22
Not Hispanic (502)	696	7.42
Hispanic (126)	263	2.80
Cambodian (51)	60	0.64
Chinese, ex. Taiwanese (53)	91	0.97
Filipino (329)	574	6.12
Hmong (46)	46	0.49
Indian (10)	23	0.25
Indonesian (4)	5	0.05
Japanese (80)	129	1.38
Korean (7)	13	0.14
Laotian (11)	16	0.17
Pakistani (3)	6	0.06
Taiwanese (1)	1	0.01
Thai (1)	9	0.10
Vietnamese (11)	13	0.14
Hawaii Native/Pacific Islander (42)	114	1.22
Not Hispanic (30)	71	0.76
Hispanic (12)	43	0.46
Fijian (1)	2	0.02
Guamanian/Chamorro (13)	31	0.33
Marshallese (1)	4	0.04
Native Hawaiian (12)	42	0.45
Samoan (11)	16	0.17
Tongan (0)	3	0.03
White (5,744)	6,369	67.91
Not Hispanic (4,193)	4,515	48.14
Hispanic (1,551)	1,854	19.77

Covina

Place Type: City
County: Los Angeles
Population: 47,796†

Ancestry‡	Population	%
African, Sub-Saharan (100)	127	0.27
African (71)	98	0.21
Nigerian (22)	22	0.05
Other Sub-Saharan African (7)	7	0.01
American (1,216)	1,216	2.56
Arab (208)	308	0.65
Egyptian (27)	27	0.06
Jordanian (8)	8	0.02
Lebanese (43)	143	0.30
Syrian (108)	108	0.23
Other Arab (22)	22	0.05
Armenian (325)	379	0.80
Austrian (15)	44	0.09
Basque (151)	159	0.33
Belgian (9)	9	0.02
British (39)	49	0.10
Canadian (44)	208	0.44
Croatian (24)	33	0.07
Czech (0)	82	0.17
Danish (56)	188	0.40
Dutch (33)	200	0.42
Eastern European (0)	16	0.03
English (960)	3,260	6.86
European (197)	265	0.56
French, ex. Basque (234)	724	1.52
French Canadian (55)	187	0.39
German (905)	4,271	8.99
Greek (44)	83	0.17
Hungarian (85)	216	0.45
Irish (922)	4,064	8.55
Italian (553)	1,915	4.03
Lithuanian (0)	24	0.05
Luxemburger (0)	21	0.04
Macedonian (15)	15	0.03
Northern European (2)	2	<0.01
Norwegian (93)	215	0.45
Polish (167)	529	1.11
Portuguese (29)	50	0.11
Russian (126)	270	0.57
Scotch-Irish (111)	453	0.95
Scottish (126)	550	1.16
Serbian (41)	132	0.28
Slavic (0)	41	0.09
Slovak (0)	14	0.03
Swedish (89)	377	0.79
Swiss (0)	66	0.14
Ukrainian (0)	7	0.01
Welsh (36)	178	0.37
West Indian, ex. Hispanic (123)	237	0.50
Belizean (9)	123	0.26
Haitian (41)	41	0.09
Jamaican (14)	14	0.03
Trinidadian/Tobagonian (11)	11	0.02
West Indian (48)	48	0.10
Yugoslavian (33)	42	0.09

Hispanic Origin	Population	%
Hispanic or Latino (of any race)	25,030	52.37
Central American, ex. Mexican	1,680	3.51
Costa Rican	69	0.14
Guatemalan	424	0.89
Honduran	87	0.18
Nicaraguan	256	0.54
Panamanian	39	0.08
Salvadoran	779	1.63
Other Central American	26	0.05
Cuban	281	0.59
Dominican Republic	15	0.03
Mexican	20,430	42.74
Puerto Rican	431	0.90
South American	880	1.84
Argentinean	145	0.30
Bolivian	17	0.04
Chilean	44	0.09
Colombian	184	0.38
Ecuadorian	186	0.39
Paraguayan	4	0.01
Peruvian	279	0.58
Uruguayan	11	0.02
Venezuelan	5	0.01
Other South American	5	0.01
Other Hispanic or Latino	1,313	2.75

Race*	Population	%
African-American/Black (2,013)	2,452	5.13
Not Hispanic (1,806)	2,075	4.34
Hispanic (207)	377	0.79
American Indian/Alaska Native (532)	973	2.04
Not Hispanic (128)	328	0.69
Hispanic (404)	645	1.35
Aleut *(Alaska Native)* (1)	1	<0.01
Apache (21)	61	0.13
Arapaho (7)	8	0.02
Blackfeet (3)	21	0.04
Canadian/French Am. Ind. (0)	2	<0.01
Central American Ind. (1)	7	0.01
Cherokee (11)	81	0.17
Cheyenne (0)	1	<0.01
Chickasaw (2)	5	0.01
Chippewa (0)	1	<0.01
Choctaw (0)	14	0.03
Comanche (4)	5	0.01
Creek (1)	1	<0.01
Crow (0)	1	<0.01
Delaware (0)	3	0.01

*Notes: † The Census 2010 population figure is used to calculate the percentages in the Hispanic Origin and Race categories. Ancestry percentages are based on the 2006-2010 American Community Survey population (not shown); ‡ Numbers in parentheses indicate the number of people reporting a single ancestry; * Numbers in parentheses indicate the number of persons reporting this race alone, not in combination with any other race; Please refer to the Explanation of Data for more information.*

Hopi (2)	3	0.01
Iroquois (1)	10	0.02
Mexican American Ind. (51)	78	0.16
Navajo (10)	28	0.06
Osage (1)	1	<0.01
Pima (1)	4	0.01
Potawatomi (0)	1	<0.01
Pueblo (3)	13	0.03
Puget Sound Salish (2)	2	<0.01
Seminole (0)	1	<0.01
Shoshone (0)	2	<0.01
Sioux (4)	14	0.03
South American Ind. (1)	1	<0.01
Spanish American Ind. (3)	6	0.01
Tohono O'Odham (4)	7	0.01
Ute (2)	2	<0.01
Yaqui (21)	34	0.07
Asian (5,684)	6,488	13.57
Not Hispanic (5,492)	6,000	12.55
Hispanic (192)	488	1.02
Bangladeshi (4)	4	0.01
Burmese (64)	77	0.16
Cambodian (41)	47	0.10
Chinese, ex. Taiwanese (1,220)	1,453	3.04
Filipino (2,213)	2,594	5.43
Hmong (6)	6	0.01
Indian (433)	459	0.96
Indonesian (128)	178	0.37
Japanese (375)	544	1.14
Korean (177)	231	0.48
Laotian (9)	17	0.04
Malaysian (1)	1	<0.01
Nepalese (3)	6	0.01
Pakistani (38)	46	0.10
Sri Lankan (42)	46	0.10
Taiwanese (242)	273	0.57
Thai (100)	128	0.27
Vietnamese (387)	456	0.95
Hawaii Native/Pacific Islander (104)	255	0.53
Not Hispanic (85)	179	0.37
Hispanic (19)	76	0.16
Fijian (1)	1	<0.01
Guamanian/Chamorro (19)	31	0.06
Marshallese (1)	1	<0.01
Native Hawaiian (39)	103	0.22
Samoan (25)	38	0.08
Tongan (0)	2	<0.01
White (27,937)	29,818	62.39
Not Hispanic (14,288)	15,035	31.46
Hispanic (13,649)	14,783	30.93

Crescent City

Place Type: City
County: Del Norte
Population: 7,643†

Ancestry‡	Population	%
African, Sub-Saharan (81)	101	1.32
African (81)	101	1.32
American (389)	389	5.07
British (0)	21	0.27
Canadian (18)	18	0.23
Czech (0)	5	0.07
Danish (0)	11	0.14
Dutch (21)	47	0.61
English (155)	595	7.75
European (15)	15	0.20
French, ex. Basque (0)	74	0.96
French Canadian (18)	18	0.23
German (225)	954	12.43
Greek (25)	82	1.07
Hungarian (11)	11	0.14
Irish (209)	752	9.80
Italian (82)	262	3.41
Polish (0)	10	0.13
Portuguese (0)	47	0.61
Scandinavian (10)	10	0.13
Scotch-Irish (108)	222	2.89
Scottish (63)	201	2.62
Swedish (31)	269	3.50
Welsh (14)	14	0.18
West Indian, ex. Hispanic (7)	7	0.09
Belizean (7)	7	0.09

Hispanic Origin	Population	%
Hispanic or Latino (of any race)	2,342	30.64
Central American, ex. Mexican	12	0.16
Guatemalan	1	0.01
Honduran	1	0.01
Nicaraguan	1	0.01
Salvadoran	9	0.12
Cuban	1	0.01
Mexican	1,907	24.95
Puerto Rican	19	0.25
South American	15	0.20
Argentinean	5	0.07
Bolivian	3	0.04
Colombian	6	0.08
Peruvian	1	0.01
Other Hispanic or Latino	388	5.08

Race*	Population	%
African-American/Black (910)	948	12.40
Not Hispanic (891)	927	12.13
Hispanic (19)	21	0.27
American Indian/Alaska Native (370)	509	6.66
Not Hispanic (304)	412	5.39
Hispanic (66)	97	1.27
Aleut *(Alaska Native)* (1)	2	0.03
Apache (1)	5	0.07
Blackfeet (0)	2	0.03
Central American Ind. (2)	2	0.03
Cherokee (19)	40	0.52
Chippewa (3)	3	0.04
Choctaw (3)	8	0.10
Comanche (2)	2	0.03
Hopi (2)	2	0.03
Iroquois (2)	2	0.03
Mexican American Ind. (6)	10	0.13
Paiute (5)	5	0.07
Pueblo (4)	5	0.07
Shoshone (1)	1	0.01
Sioux (2)	2	0.03
Tlingit-Haida *(Alaska Native)* (0)	2	0.03
Ute (1)	1	0.01
Asian (333)	399	5.22
Not Hispanic (325)	375	4.91
Hispanic (8)	24	0.31
Chinese, ex. Taiwanese (20)	27	0.35
Filipino (25)	49	0.64
Hmong (220)	228	2.98
Indian (8)	10	0.13
Japanese (2)	13	0.17
Korean (3)	10	0.13
Laotian (18)	22	0.29
Thai (2)	2	0.03
Vietnamese (12)	16	0.21
Hawaii Native/Pacific Islander (7)	20	0.26
Not Hispanic (5)	13	0.17
Hispanic (2)	7	0.09
Native Hawaiian (3)	8	0.10
Samoan (4)	6	0.08
White (5,052)	5,298	69.32
Not Hispanic (3,455)	3,625	47.43
Hispanic (1,597)	1,673	21.89

Crestline

Place Type: CDP
County: San Bernardino
Population: 10,770†

Ancestry‡	Population	%
African, Sub-Saharan (112)	112	1.25
South African (112)	112	1.25
American (190)	190	2.13
Armenian (32)	42	0.47
Belgian (21)	21	0.24
Brazilian (28)	28	0.31
British (28)	132	1.48
Canadian (0)	29	0.32
Czech (14)	14	0.16
Danish (57)	87	0.97
Dutch (27)	228	2.55
English (653)	1,232	13.79
European (134)	165	1.85
French, ex. Basque (168)	409	4.58
French Canadian (22)	22	0.25
German (902)	2,086	23.34
Greek (0)	20	0.22
Hungarian (0)	13	0.15
Irish (810)	1,725	19.30
Italian (164)	462	5.17
Norwegian (36)	119	1.33
Polish (82)	261	2.92
Portuguese (0)	9	0.10
Russian (80)	190	2.13
Scandinavian (0)	27	0.30
Scotch-Irish (139)	223	2.50
Scottish (120)	270	3.02
Swedish (177)	191	2.14
Swiss (54)	88	0.98
Welsh (26)	44	0.49

Hispanic Origin	Population	%
Hispanic or Latino (of any race)	1,775	16.48
Central American, ex. Mexican	88	0.82
Costa Rican	5	0.05
Guatemalan	42	0.39
Nicaraguan	12	0.11
Panamanian	2	0.02
Salvadoran	16	0.15
Other Central American	11	0.10
Cuban	27	0.25
Dominican Republic	3	0.03
Mexican	1,288	11.96
Puerto Rican	50	0.46
South American	42	0.39
Argentinean	13	0.12
Chilean	10	0.09
Colombian	11	0.10
Ecuadorian	2	0.02
Peruvian	1	0.01
Uruguayan	1	0.01
Venezuelan	4	0.04
Other Hispanic or Latino	277	2.57

Race*	Population	%
African-American/Black (107)	213	1.98
Not Hispanic (91)	164	1.52
Hispanic (16)	49	0.45
American Indian/Alaska Native (135)	413	3.83
Not Hispanic (102)	322	2.99
Hispanic (33)	91	0.84
Apache (2)	10	0.09
Blackfeet (6)	23	0.21
Canadian/French Am. Ind. (2)	2	0.02
Central American Ind. (2)	2	0.02
Cherokee (23)	95	0.88
Chickasaw (0)	3	0.03
Chippewa (2)	7	0.06
Choctaw (8)	22	0.20
Comanche (4)	4	0.04
Creek (0)	2	0.02
Crow (0)	1	0.01
Hopi (1)	2	0.02
Inupiat *(Alaska Native)* (1)	3	0.03
Iroquois (2)	10	0.09
Kiowa (1)	1	0.01
Mexican American Ind. (5)	16	0.15
Navajo (6)	11	0.10
Osage (1)	2	0.02
Paiute (0)	3	0.03
Pima (4)	7	0.06
Potawatomi (2)	4	0.04
Pueblo (0)	2	0.02
Seminole (2)	4	0.04
Shoshone (1)	1	0.01
Sioux (1)	12	0.11

*Notes: † The Census 2010 population figure is used to calculate the percentages in the Hispanic Origin and Race categories. Ancestry percentages are based on the 2006-2010 American Community Survey population (not shown); ‡ Numbers in parentheses indicate the number of people reporting a single ancestry; * Numbers in parentheses indicate the number of persons reporting this race alone, not in combination with any other race; Please refer to the Explanation of Data for more information.*

Yaqui (2)	3	0.03
Yuman (0)	1	0.01
Asian (96)	207	1.92
Not Hispanic (91)	184	1.71
Hispanic (5)	23	0.21
Cambodian (1)	1	0.01
Chinese, ex. Taiwanese (8)	30	0.28
Filipino (39)	83	0.77
Indian (7)	10	0.09
Japanese (18)	59	0.55
Korean (12)	15	0.14
Pakistani (0)	1	0.01
Thai (2)	5	0.05
Vietnamese (6)	9	0.08
Hawaii Native/Pacific Islander (20)	41	0.38
Not Hispanic (13)	33	0.31
Hispanic (7)	8	0.07
Guamanian/Chamorro (6)	8	0.07
Native Hawaiian (7)	16	0.15
Samoan (5)	13	0.12
Tongan (0)	1	0.01
White (9,289)	9,848	91.44
Not Hispanic (8,297)	8,664	80.45
Hispanic (992)	1,184	10.99

Cudahy

Place Type: City
County: Los Angeles
Population: 23,805†

Ancestry‡	Population	%
African, Sub-Saharan (0)	28	0.12
African (0)	28	0.12
American (806)	806	3.38
Australian (0)	10	0.04
Danish (0)	10	0.04
Dutch (0)	19	0.08
English (26)	99	0.42
French, ex. Basque (8)	25	0.10
French Canadian (0)	10	0.04
German (8)	51	0.21
Irish (0)	153	0.64
Italian (93)	147	0.62
Portuguese (0)	11	0.05
Russian (40)	50	0.21
Swedish (0)	23	0.10

Hispanic Origin	Population	%
Hispanic or Latino (of any race)	22,850	95.99
Central American, ex. Mexican	3,198	13.43
Costa Rican	25	0.11
Guatemalan	902	3.79
Honduran	249	1.05
Nicaraguan	349	1.47
Panamanian	1	<0.01
Salvadoran	1,634	6.86
Other Central American	38	0.16
Cuban	197	0.83
Dominican Republic	12	0.05
Mexican	18,073	75.92
Puerto Rican	83	0.35
South American	244	1.02
Argentinean	9	0.04
Chilean	6	0.03
Colombian	81	0.34
Ecuadorian	74	0.31
Peruvian	69	0.29
Uruguayan	2	0.01
Venezuelan	2	0.01
Other South American	1	<0.01
Other Hispanic or Latino	1,043	4.38

Race*	Population	%
African-American/Black (333)	393	1.65
Not Hispanic (193)	207	0.87
Hispanic (140)	186	0.78
American Indian/Alaska Native (246)	343	1.44
Not Hispanic (46)	58	0.24
Hispanic (200)	285	1.20
Apache (10)	12	0.05
Blackfeet (0)	5	0.02
Central American Ind. (5)	5	0.02
Cherokee (3)	7	0.03
Chickasaw (2)	2	0.01
Choctaw (0)	2	0.01
Creek (3)	3	0.01
Crow (4)	4	0.02
Mexican American Ind. (72)	94	0.39
Navajo (6)	7	0.03
Pima (0)	2	0.01
Pueblo (0)	4	0.02
Sioux (3)	3	0.01
South American Ind. (1)	3	0.01
Spanish American Ind. (1)	4	0.02
Tsimshian *(Alaska Native)* (1)	1	<0.01
Yaqui (0)	2	0.01
Yuman (5)	5	0.02
Asian (137)	199	0.84
Not Hispanic (110)	125	0.53
Hispanic (27)	74	0.31
Cambodian (16)	16	0.07
Chinese, ex. Taiwanese (10)	12	0.05
Filipino (45)	59	0.25
Indian (13)	20	0.08
Japanese (6)	16	0.07
Korean (11)	11	0.05
Laotian (0)	6	0.03
Pakistani (1)	1	<0.01
Taiwanese (6)	7	0.03
Thai (4)	4	0.02
Vietnamese (6)	8	0.03
Hawaii Native/Pacific Islander (24)	63	0.26
Not Hispanic (8)	17	0.07
Hispanic (16)	46	0.19
Guamanian/Chamorro (11)	18	0.08
Native Hawaiian (1)	10	0.04
Samoan (12)	18	0.08
White (11,708)	12,598	52.92
Not Hispanic (505)	541	2.27
Hispanic (11,203)	12,057	50.65

Culver City

Place Type: City
County: Los Angeles
Population: 38,883†

Ancestry‡	Population	%
African, Sub-Saharan (681)	746	1.92
African (200)	255	0.66
Ethiopian (456)	456	1.17
Nigerian (16)	16	0.04
South African (9)	19	0.05
American (1,165)	1,165	3.00
Arab (268)	406	1.05
Arab (7)	7	0.02
Egyptian (22)	37	0.10
Iraqi (24)	24	0.06
Lebanese (146)	157	0.40
Palestinian (29)	40	0.10
Syrian (26)	101	0.26
Other Arab (14)	40	0.10
Armenian (46)	46	0.12
Australian (7)	7	0.02
Austrian (53)	205	0.53
Basque (36)	53	0.14
Belgian (37)	66	0.17
Brazilian (54)	165	0.42
British (171)	288	0.74
Bulgarian (83)	83	0.21
Canadian (102)	225	0.58
Celtic (9)	9	0.02
Croatian (42)	100	0.26
Czech (49)	125	0.32
Czechoslovakian (25)	54	0.14
Danish (26)	153	0.39
Dutch (108)	407	1.05
Eastern European (146)	146	0.38
English (1,179)	3,888	10.01
Estonian (20)	20	0.05
European (639)	918	2.36
Finnish (21)	58	0.15
French, ex. Basque (158)	774	1.99
French Canadian (41)	181	0.47
German (892)	3,660	9.43
Greek (50)	169	0.44
Hungarian (211)	366	0.94
Icelander (0)	12	0.03
Iranian (153)	153	0.39
Irish (780)	2,735	7.04
Israeli (31)	43	0.11
Italian (589)	1,654	4.26
Latvian (0)	10	0.03
Lithuanian (104)	138	0.36
New Zealander (15)	15	0.04
Northern European (32)	32	0.08
Norwegian (172)	484	1.25
Pennsylvania German (0)	11	0.03
Polish (301)	1,006	2.59
Portuguese (29)	292	0.75
Romanian (111)	111	0.29
Russian (825)	1,856	4.78
Scandinavian (24)	101	0.26
Scotch-Irish (108)	351	0.90
Scottish (183)	764	1.97
Serbian (0)	8	0.02
Slavic (11)	46	0.12
Slovak (0)	84	0.22
Slovene (0)	37	0.10
Swedish (218)	632	1.63
Swiss (91)	212	0.55
Turkish (12)	26	0.07
Ukrainian (12)	85	0.22
Welsh (39)	258	0.66
West Indian, ex. Hispanic (276)	355	0.91
Belizean (155)	155	0.40
British West Indian (24)	28	0.07
Jamaican (97)	148	0.38
West Indian (0)	7	0.02
Other West Indian (0)	17	0.04
Yugoslavian (45)	59	0.15

Hispanic Origin	Population	%
Hispanic or Latino (of any race)	9,025	23.21
Central American, ex. Mexican	1,047	2.69
Costa Rican	61	0.16
Guatemalan	276	0.71
Honduran	100	0.26
Nicaraguan	72	0.19
Panamanian	37	0.10
Salvadoran	479	1.23
Other Central American	22	0.06
Cuban	414	1.06
Dominican Republic	11	0.03
Mexican	6,004	15.44
Puerto Rican	159	0.41
South American	699	1.80
Argentinean	190	0.49
Bolivian	21	0.05
Chilean	71	0.18
Colombian	150	0.39
Ecuadorian	86	0.22
Paraguayan	3	0.01
Peruvian	112	0.29
Uruguayan	28	0.07
Venezuelan	29	0.07
Other South American	9	0.02
Other Hispanic or Latino	691	1.78

Race*	Population	%
African-American/Black (3,694)	4,431	11.40
Not Hispanic (3,587)	4,157	10.69
Hispanic (107)	274	0.70
American Indian/Alaska Native (191)	570	1.47
Not Hispanic (65)	313	0.80
Hispanic (126)	257	0.66
Alaska Athabascan *(Ala. Nat.)* (1)	2	0.01
Aleut *(Alaska Native)* (1)	1	<0.01
Apache (3)	12	0.03

*Notes: † The Census 2010 population figure is used to calculate the percentages in the Hispanic Origin and Race categories. Ancestry percentages are based on the 2006-2010 American Community Survey population (not shown); ‡ Numbers in parentheses indicate the number of people reporting a single ancestry; * Numbers in parentheses indicate the number of persons reporting this race alone, not in combination with any other race; Please refer to the Explanation of Data for more information.*

Blackfeet (2)	22	0.06
Central American Ind. (7)	11	0.03
Cherokee (6)	87	0.22
Cheyenne (0)	5	0.01
Chickasaw (0)	3	0.01
Chippewa (0)	3	0.01
Choctaw (0)	25	0.06
Colville (1)	3	0.01
Cree (0)	2	0.01
Creek (6)	9	0.02
Hopi (1)	1	<0.01
Iroquois (1)	7	0.02
Lumbee (2)	3	0.01
Mexican American Ind. (34)	48	0.12
Navajo (13)	25	0.06
Ottawa (0)	1	<0.01
Pima (2)	5	0.01
Potawatomi (0)	1	<0.01
Pueblo (4)	5	0.01
Puget Sound Salish (0)	2	0.01
Seminole (1)	7	0.02
Shoshone (1)	1	<0.01
Sioux (3)	13	0.03
South American Ind. (3)	4	0.01
Spanish American Ind. (1)	4	0.01
Ute (0)	1	<0.01
Yaqui (1)	4	0.01
Asian (5,742)	6,906	17.76
Not Hispanic (5,656)	6,628	17.05
Hispanic (86)	278	0.71
Bangladeshi (7)	7	0.02
Burmese (111)	114	0.29
Cambodian (11)	13	0.03
Chinese, ex. Taiwanese (968)	1,310	3.37
Filipino (829)	1,135	2.92
Hmong (5)	5	0.01
Indian (915)	1,037	2.67
Indonesian (17)	29	0.07
Japanese (1,406)	1,898	4.88
Korean (629)	745	1.92
Laotian (4)	8	0.02
Malaysian (1)	3	0.01
Nepalese (8)	11	0.03
Pakistani (205)	216	0.56
Sri Lankan (18)	25	0.06
Taiwanese (88)	109	0.28
Thai (74)	88	0.23
Vietnamese (155)	216	0.56
Hawaii Native/Pacific Islander (81)	255	0.66
Not Hispanic (70)	197	0.51
Hispanic (11)	58	0.15
Fijian (22)	34	0.09
Guamanian/Chamorro (7)	14	0.04
Native Hawaiian (25)	107	0.28
Samoan (5)	14	0.04
Tongan (6)	8	0.02
White (23,450)	25,408	65.34
Not Hispanic (18,649)	19,988	51.41
Hispanic (4,801)	5,420	13.94

Cupertino

Place Type: City
County: Santa Clara
Population: 58,302†

Ancestry‡	Population	%
Afghan (60)	60	0.11
African, Sub-Saharan (17)	95	0.17
African (0)	34	0.06
Ethiopian (17)	61	0.11
Albanian (13)	25	0.04
American (594)	594	1.05
Arab (307)	399	0.71
Arab (0)	13	0.02
Egyptian (205)	227	0.40
Jordanian (25)	25	0.04
Lebanese (14)	40	0.07
Syrian (63)	94	0.17
Armenian (162)	201	0.36
Assyrian/Chaldean/Syriac (168)	168	0.30
Austrian (59)	102	0.18
Belgian (21)	51	0.09
Brazilian (14)	14	0.02
British (145)	272	0.48
Bulgarian (55)	55	0.10
Canadian (75)	133	0.24
Celtic (11)	11	0.02
Croatian (102)	228	0.40
Czech (128)	319	0.56
Czechoslovakian (8)	31	0.05
Danish (29)	226	0.40
Dutch (37)	463	0.82
Eastern European (79)	79	0.14
English (716)	2,908	5.15
European (619)	678	1.20
Finnish (0)	124	0.22
French, ex. Basque (151)	1,037	1.84
French Canadian (73)	162	0.29
German (1,074)	3,754	6.64
Greek (109)	303	0.54
Hungarian (63)	122	0.22
Iranian (1,005)	1,005	1.78
Irish (595)	2,479	4.39
Israeli (354)	363	0.64
Italian (802)	1,477	2.61
Latvian (29)	60	0.11
Lithuanian (16)	63	0.11
Macedonian (44)	44	0.08
Northern European (111)	124	0.22
Norwegian (207)	492	0.87
Polish (146)	595	1.05
Portuguese (105)	320	0.57
Romanian (22)	76	0.13
Russian (792)	1,192	2.11
Scandinavian (34)	58	0.10
Scotch-Irish (162)	553	0.98
Scottish (216)	629	1.11
Serbian (15)	30	0.05
Slavic (0)	45	0.08
Slovak (39)	39	0.07
Slovene (14)	14	0.02
Swedish (90)	373	0.66
Swiss (119)	274	0.48
Turkish (11)	11	0.02
Ukrainian (190)	240	0.42
Welsh (51)	96	0.17
West Indian, ex. Hispanic (54)	77	0.14
Haitian (54)	54	0.10
Jamaican (0)	23	0.04
Yugoslavian (149)	194	0.34

Hispanic Origin	Population	%
Hispanic or Latino (of any race)	2,113	3.62
Central American, ex. Mexican	111	0.19
Costa Rican	7	0.01
Guatemalan	28	0.05
Honduran	4	0.01
Nicaraguan	24	0.04
Panamanian	4	0.01
Salvadoran	41	0.07
Other Central American	3	0.01
Cuban	26	0.04
Dominican Republic	3	0.01
Mexican	1,373	2.35
Puerto Rican	70	0.12
South American	241	0.41
Argentinean	28	0.05
Bolivian	23	0.04
Chilean	23	0.04
Colombian	56	0.10
Ecuadorian	12	0.02
Peruvian	62	0.11
Uruguayan	7	0.01
Venezuelan	27	0.05
Other South American	3	0.01
Other Hispanic or Latino	289	0.50

Race*	Population	%
African-American/Black (344)	515	0.88
Not Hispanic (322)	473	0.81
Hispanic (22)	42	0.07
American Indian/Alaska Native (117)	310	0.53
Not Hispanic (80)	228	0.39
Hispanic (37)	82	0.14
Alaska Athabascan *(Ala. Nat.)* (1)	1	<0.01
Apache (1)	2	<0.01
Blackfeet (1)	11	0.02
Canadian/French Am. Ind. (0)	1	<0.01
Central American Ind. (2)	2	<0.01
Cherokee (7)	41	0.07
Chippewa (1)	7	0.01
Choctaw (7)	15	0.03
Colville (1)	1	<0.01
Comanche (1)	2	<0.01
Creek (2)	2	<0.01
Delaware (0)	3	0.01
Inupiat *(Alaska Native)* (0)	1	<0.01
Iroquois (2)	5	0.01
Mexican American Ind. (3)	8	0.01
Navajo (2)	7	0.01
Osage (0)	1	<0.01
Pueblo (2)	2	<0.01
Puget Sound Salish (0)	2	<0.01
Sioux (1)	4	0.01
South American Ind. (1)	5	0.01
Ute (0)	1	<0.01
Yakama (0)	1	<0.01
Yaqui (2)	10	0.02
Asian (36,895)	38,503	66.04
Not Hispanic (36,815)	38,342	65.76
Hispanic (80)	161	0.28
Bangladeshi (66)	67	0.11
Burmese (52)	59	0.10
Cambodian (18)	27	0.05
Chinese, ex. Taiwanese (13,953)	14,930	25.61
Filipino (535)	777	1.33
Hmong (3)	4	0.01
Indian (13,179)	13,415	23.01
Indonesian (74)	110	0.19
Japanese (1,951)	2,489	4.27
Korean (2,709)	2,876	4.93
Laotian (2)	2	<0.01
Malaysian (27)	38	0.07
Nepalese (25)	25	0.04
Pakistani (233)	248	0.43
Sri Lankan (32)	37	0.06
Taiwanese (2,467)	2,753	4.72
Thai (70)	102	0.17
Vietnamese (745)	850	1.46
Hawaii Native/Pacific Islander (54)	191	0.33
Not Hispanic (39)	162	0.28
Hispanic (15)	29	0.05
Fijian (2)	2	<0.01
Guamanian/Chamorro (21)	39	0.07
Native Hawaiian (13)	43	0.07
Samoan (8)	10	0.02
Tongan (2)	3	0.01
White (18,270)	19,846	34.04
Not Hispanic (17,085)	18,483	31.70
Hispanic (1,185)	1,363	2.34

Cypress

Place Type: City
County: Orange
Population: 47,802†

Ancestry‡	Population	%
Afghan (71)	71	0.15
African, Sub-Saharan (17)	17	0.04
Sudanese (17)	17	0.04
Albanian (13)	13	0.03
American (1,218)	1,218	2.57
Arab (540)	590	1.25
Arab (179)	179	0.38
Egyptian (94)	94	0.20
Iraqi (99)	99	0.21
Lebanese (78)	128	0.27
Syrian (46)	46	0.10

*Notes: † The Census 2010 population figure is used to calculate the percentages in the Hispanic Origin and Race categories. Ancestry percentages are based on the 2006-2010 American Community Survey population (not shown); ‡ Numbers in parentheses indicate the number of people reporting a single ancestry; * Numbers in parentheses indicate the number of persons reporting this race alone, not in combination with any other race; Please refer to the Explanation of Data for more information.*

Other Arab (44)	44	0.09
Armenian (153)	182	0.38
Australian (79)	79	0.17
Austrian (22)	166	0.35
Basque (0)	16	0.03
Belgian (13)	57	0.12
British (123)	174	0.37
Canadian (47)	77	0.16
Celtic (10)	32	0.07
Croatian (0)	65	0.14
Czech (6)	96	0.20
Czechoslovakian (9)	25	0.05
Danish (106)	278	0.59
Dutch (329)	862	1.82
Eastern European (53)	53	0.11
English (1,161)	4,157	8.79
European (488)	584	1.23
Finnish (30)	53	0.11
French, ex. Basque (253)	1,283	2.71
French Canadian (69)	153	0.32
German (1,567)	5,166	10.92
Greek (142)	268	0.57
Hungarian (36)	163	0.34
Icelander (18)	28	0.06
Iranian (107)	119	0.25
Irish (1,053)	4,208	8.89
Israeli (0)	4	0.01
Italian (612)	1,749	3.70
Lithuanian (71)	144	0.30
Maltese (69)	69	0.15
Northern European (97)	97	0.21
Norwegian (307)	722	1.53
Pennsylvania German (7)	7	0.01
Polish (277)	626	1.32
Portuguese (147)	306	0.65
Romanian (17)	26	0.05
Russian (151)	536	1.13
Scandinavian (37)	138	0.29
Scotch-Irish (196)	482	1.02
Scottish (185)	623	1.32
Serbian (55)	95	0.20
Slavic (34)	76	0.16
Slovak (0)	8	0.02
Swedish (209)	966	2.04
Swiss (6)	70	0.15
Turkish (0)	19	0.04
Ukrainian (21)	61	0.13
Welsh (36)	177	0.37
West Indian, ex. Hispanic (35)	65	0.14
Trinidadian/Tobagonian (35)	65	0.14
Yugoslavian (13)	21	0.04

Hispanic Origin	Population	%
Hispanic or Latino (of any race)	8,779	18.37
Central American, ex. Mexican	472	0.99
Costa Rican	41	0.09
Guatemalan	161	0.34
Honduran	19	0.04
Nicaraguan	70	0.15
Panamanian	17	0.04
Salvadoran	162	0.34
Other Central American	2	<0.01
Cuban	161	0.34
Dominican Republic	5	0.01
Mexican	6,745	14.11
Puerto Rican	259	0.54
South American	451	0.94
Argentinean	71	0.15
Bolivian	6	0.01
Chilean	27	0.06
Colombian	97	0.20
Ecuadorian	70	0.15
Peruvian	151	0.32
Uruguayan	3	0.01
Venezuelan	25	0.05
Other South American	1	<0.01
Other Hispanic or Latino	686	1.44

Race*	Population	%
African-American/Black (1,444)	1,893	3.96
Not Hispanic (1,376)	1,718	3.59
Hispanic (68)	175	0.37
American Indian/Alaska Native (289)	676	1.41
Not Hispanic (142)	387	0.81
Hispanic (147)	289	0.60
Apache (9)	25	0.05
Arapaho (2)	2	<0.01
Blackfeet (1)	21	0.04
Cherokee (17)	98	0.21
Chickasaw (0)	1	<0.01
Chippewa (4)	8	0.02
Choctaw (6)	17	0.04
Comanche (0)	3	0.01
Creek (1)	5	0.01
Delaware (0)	3	0.01
Hopi (7)	7	0.01
Houma (0)	1	<0.01
Inupiat *(Alaska Native)* (1)	1	<0.01
Iroquois (1)	6	0.01
Mexican American Ind. (22)	38	0.08
Navajo (3)	8	0.02
Ottawa (1)	1	<0.01
Potawatomi (3)	5	0.01
Pueblo (3)	5	0.01
Seminole (1)	5	0.01
Shoshone (1)	4	0.01
Sioux (1)	17	0.04
South American Ind. (1)	8	0.02
Spanish American Ind. (2)	2	<0.01
Tlingit-Haida *(Alaska Native)* (0)	1	<0.01
Tohono O'Odham (2)	3	0.01
Yakama (1)	2	<0.01
Yaqui (13)	16	0.03
Asian (14,978)	16,239	33.97
Not Hispanic (14,850)	15,864	33.19
Hispanic (128)	375	0.78
Bangladeshi (19)	21	0.04
Burmese (12)	25	0.05
Cambodian (144)	198	0.41
Chinese, ex. Taiwanese (1,723)	2,214	4.63
Filipino (2,783)	3,363	7.04
Hmong (8)	8	0.02
Indian (1,117)	1,214	2.54
Indonesian (63)	104	0.22
Japanese (1,179)	1,588	3.32
Korean (5,698)	5,878	12.30
Laotian (1)	9	0.02
Malaysian (11)	14	0.03
Nepalese (22)	23	0.05
Pakistani (168)	188	0.39
Sri Lankan (43)	48	0.10
Taiwanese (417)	453	0.95
Thai (152)	197	0.41
Vietnamese (939)	1,049	2.19
Hawaii Native/Pacific Islander (234)	483	1.01
Not Hispanic (204)	403	0.84
Hispanic (30)	80	0.17
Fijian (8)	8	0.02
Guamanian/Chamorro (94)	137	0.29
Native Hawaiian (33)	139	0.29
Samoan (80)	113	0.24
Tongan (2)	4	0.01
White (26,000)	27,964	58.50
Not Hispanic (20,865)	22,127	46.29
Hispanic (5,135)	5,837	12.21

Daly City

Place Type: City
County: San Mateo
Population: 101,123†

Ancestry‡	Population	%
African, Sub-Saharan (215)	358	0.36
African (179)	322	0.32
Nigerian (16)	16	0.02
Other Sub-Saharan African (20)	20	0.02
American (434)	434	0.43
Arab (2,071)	2,327	2.33
Arab (929)	991	0.99
Egyptian (70)	70	0.07
Iraqi (230)	230	0.23
Jordanian (62)	97	0.10
Lebanese (102)	191	0.19
Palestinian (511)	555	0.56
Syrian (0)	26	0.03
Other Arab (167)	167	0.17
Armenian (183)	183	0.18
Australian (0)	16	0.02
Austrian (12)	55	0.06
Basque (25)	99	0.10
Brazilian (274)	311	0.31
British (150)	164	0.16
Bulgarian (40)	40	0.04
Canadian (56)	141	0.14
Celtic (15)	15	0.02
Croatian (32)	102	0.10
Czech (43)	105	0.11
Czechoslovakian (16)	47	0.05
Danish (59)	136	0.14
Dutch (103)	289	0.29
English (159)	1,064	1.07
Estonian (20)	20	0.02
European (699)	962	0.96
Finnish (0)	47	0.05
French, ex. Basque (171)	654	0.66
French Canadian (13)	44	0.04
German (604)	2,613	2.62
Greek (104)	197	0.20
Hungarian (41)	172	0.17
Icelander (11)	19	0.02
Iranian (150)	179	0.18
Irish (683)	2,435	2.44
Italian (1,150)	2,546	2.55
Latvian (0)	5	0.01
Lithuanian (0)	12	0.01
New Zealander (14)	14	0.01
Norwegian (101)	216	0.22
Polish (129)	516	0.52
Portuguese (184)	404	0.40
Romanian (0)	25	0.03
Russian (429)	527	0.53
Scandinavian (0)	27	0.03
Scotch-Irish (69)	396	0.40
Scottish (134)	280	0.28
Serbian (0)	14	0.01
Slavic (0)	7	0.01
Slovak (0)	22	0.02
Slovene (0)	27	0.03
Swedish (103)	425	0.43
Swiss (34)	97	0.10
Turkish (0)	14	0.01
Ukrainian (85)	100	0.10
Welsh (0)	96	0.10
West Indian, ex. Hispanic (11)	23	0.02
Belizean (0)	12	0.01
Jamaican (11)	11	0.01
Yugoslavian (83)	142	0.14

Hispanic Origin	Population	%
Hispanic or Latino (of any race)	23,929	23.66
Central American, ex. Mexican	9,813	9.70
Costa Rican	79	0.08
Guatemalan	1,363	1.35
Honduran	479	0.47
Nicaraguan	2,764	2.73
Panamanian	48	0.05
Salvadoran	5,000	4.94
Other Central American	80	0.08
Cuban	131	0.13
Dominican Republic	20	0.02
Mexican	9,535	9.43
Puerto Rican	684	0.68
South American	1,233	1.22
Argentinean	61	0.06
Bolivian	87	0.09
Chilean	64	0.06
Colombian	143	0.14
Ecuadorian	67	0.07
Paraguayan	2	<0.01

*Notes: † The Census 2010 population figure is used to calculate the percentages in the Hispanic Origin and Race categories. Ancestry percentages are based on the 2006-2010 American Community Survey population (not shown); ‡ Numbers in parentheses indicate the number of people reporting a single ancestry; * Numbers in parentheses indicate the number of persons reporting this race alone, not in combination with any other race; Please refer to the Explanation of Data for more information.*

Peruvian	738	0.73
Uruguayan	6	0.01
Venezuelan	32	0.03
Other South American	33	0.03
Other Hispanic or Latino	2,513	2.49

Race*	Population	%
African-American/Black (3,600)	4,612	4.56
Not Hispanic (3,284)	4,005	3.96
Hispanic (316)	607	0.60
American Indian/Alaska Native (404)	992	0.98
Not Hispanic (115)	453	0.45
Hispanic (289)	539	0.53
Alaska Athabascan *(Ala. Nat.)* (0)	4	<0.01
Aleut *(Alaska Native)* (2)	3	<0.01
Apache (12)	35	0.03
Arapaho (3)	5	<0.01
Blackfeet (1)	34	0.03
Canadian/French Am. Ind. (1)	1	<0.01
Central American Ind. (4)	11	0.01
Cherokee (6)	113	0.11
Cheyenne (0)	2	<0.01
Chickasaw (0)	1	<0.01
Chippewa (4)	11	0.01
Choctaw (4)	17	0.02
Comanche (0)	2	<0.01
Creek (0)	5	<0.01
Delaware (0)	1	<0.01
Inupiat *(Alaska Native)* (1)	1	<0.01
Iroquois (0)	12	0.01
Lumbee (0)	1	<0.01
Mexican American Ind. (71)	108	0.11
Navajo (16)	33	0.03
Osage (0)	8	0.01
Paiute (2)	7	0.01
Potawatomi (1)	1	<0.01
Pueblo (6)	9	0.01
Seminole (2)	8	0.01
Shoshone (1)	1	<0.01
Sioux (15)	23	0.02
South American Ind. (9)	16	0.02
Spanish American Ind. (14)	23	0.02
Tlingit-Haida *(Alaska Native)* (0)	4	<0.01
Tohono O'Odham (6)	6	0.01
Ute (0)	3	<0.01
Yaqui (4)	6	0.01
Yuman (1)	1	<0.01
Asian (56,267)	59,093	58.44
Not Hispanic (55,711)	57,841	57.20
Hispanic (556)	1,252	1.24
Bangladeshi (11)	12	0.01
Bhutanese (2)	2	<0.01
Burmese (1,829)	2,023	2.00
Cambodian (98)	135	0.13
Chinese, ex. Taiwanese (15,438)	16,992	16.80
Filipino (33,649)	36,028	35.63
Hmong (23)	30	0.03
Indian (637)	851	0.84
Indonesian (217)	281	0.28
Japanese (611)	1,022	1.01
Korean (629)	764	0.76
Laotian (44)	62	0.06
Malaysian (22)	47	0.05
Nepalese (29)	30	0.03
Pakistani (169)	189	0.19
Sri Lankan (17)	20	0.02
Taiwanese (167)	185	0.18
Thai (200)	257	0.25
Vietnamese (1,037)	1,331	1.32
Hawaii Native/Pacific Islander (805)	1,396	1.38
Not Hispanic (752)	1,203	1.19
Hispanic (53)	193	0.19
Fijian (126)	178	0.18
Guamanian/Chamorro (43)	123	0.12
Marshallese (2)	6	0.01
Native Hawaiian (58)	230	0.23
Samoan (467)	603	0.60
Tongan (16)	37	0.04
White (23,842)	27,266	26.96
Not Hispanic (14,031)	15,942	15.76
Hispanic (9,811)	11,324	11.20

Dana Point

Place Type: City
County: Orange
Population: 33,351†

Ancestry‡	Population	%
African, Sub-Saharan (47)	72	0.22
African (31)	56	0.17
Kenyan (5)	5	0.01
Nigerian (11)	11	0.03
Albanian (102)	102	0.30
American (1,055)	1,055	3.15
Arab (219)	316	0.94
Egyptian (149)	160	0.48
Lebanese (52)	138	0.41
Palestinian (18)	18	0.05
Armenian (188)	304	0.91
Australian (17)	34	0.10
Austrian (144)	211	0.63
Basque (0)	29	0.09
Belgian (0)	37	0.11
Brazilian (38)	38	0.11
British (167)	225	0.67
Bulgarian (59)	59	0.18
Canadian (14)	101	0.30
Croatian (38)	47	0.14
Czech (93)	265	0.79
Czechoslovakian (0)	19	0.06
Danish (245)	404	1.21
Dutch (224)	683	2.04
Eastern European (57)	57	0.17
English (1,876)	4,928	14.72
European (326)	431	1.29
Finnish (68)	104	0.31
French, ex. Basque (422)	1,442	4.31
French Canadian (134)	197	0.59
German (2,191)	7,264	21.69
Greek (57)	192	0.57
Guyanese (0)	13	0.04
Hungarian (64)	253	0.76
Icelander (0)	13	0.04
Iranian (68)	68	0.20
Irish (1,695)	5,750	17.17
Israeli (0)	24	0.07
Italian (1,031)	2,637	7.88
Lithuanian (15)	45	0.13
Macedonian (18)	24	0.07
Northern European (70)	81	0.24
Norwegian (156)	681	2.03
Pennsylvania German (13)	13	0.04
Polish (167)	703	2.10
Portuguese (86)	221	0.66
Romanian (37)	73	0.22
Russian (222)	579	1.73
Scandinavian (96)	163	0.49
Scotch-Irish (290)	566	1.69
Scottish (381)	1,023	3.06
Slovak (32)	32	0.10
Swedish (399)	884	2.64
Swiss (26)	201	0.60
Turkish (17)	27	0.08
Ukrainian (85)	138	0.41
Welsh (103)	342	1.02
West Indian, ex. Hispanic (13)	13	0.04
Jamaican (13)	13	0.04
Yugoslavian (0)	34	0.10

Hispanic Origin	Population	%
Hispanic or Latino (of any race)	5,662	16.98
Central American, ex. Mexican	191	0.57
Costa Rican	13	0.04
Guatemalan	68	0.20
Honduran	14	0.04
Nicaraguan	18	0.05
Panamanian	12	0.04
Salvadoran	62	0.19
Other Central American	4	0.01
Cuban	100	0.30
Dominican Republic	8	0.02
Mexican	4,405	13.21
Puerto Rican	93	0.28
South American	325	0.97
Argentinean	88	0.26
Bolivian	9	0.03
Chilean	15	0.04
Colombian	67	0.20
Ecuadorian	46	0.14
Paraguayan	1	<0.01
Peruvian	76	0.23
Uruguayan	3	0.01
Venezuelan	14	0.04
Other South American	6	0.02
Other Hispanic or Latino	540	1.62

Race*	Population	%
African-American/Black (294)	441	1.32
Not Hispanic (255)	367	1.10
Hispanic (39)	74	0.22
American Indian/Alaska Native (229)	518	1.55
Not Hispanic (110)	327	0.98
Hispanic (119)	191	0.57
Apache (5)	9	0.03
Blackfeet (1)	12	0.04
Canadian/French Am. Ind. (0)	1	<0.01
Cherokee (20)	83	0.25
Chickasaw (3)	4	0.01
Chippewa (3)	5	0.01
Choctaw (7)	17	0.05
Comanche (5)	9	0.03
Creek (3)	13	0.04
Delaware (0)	2	0.01
Hopi (1)	2	0.01
Iroquois (8)	11	0.03
Lumbee (2)	2	0.01
Mexican American Ind. (22)	34	0.10
Navajo (5)	7	0.02
Osage (6)	7	0.02
Potawatomi (1)	1	<0.01
Pueblo (1)	1	<0.01
Seminole (0)	1	<0.01
Shoshone (1)	3	0.01
Sioux (4)	11	0.03
South American Ind. (0)	3	0.01
Tohono O'Odham (1)	1	<0.01
Yaqui (1)	9	0.03
Yuman (0)	2	0.01
Asian (1,064)	1,507	4.52
Not Hispanic (1,037)	1,410	4.23
Hispanic (27)	97	0.29
Burmese (2)	2	0.01
Cambodian (15)	16	0.05
Chinese, ex. Taiwanese (211)	326	0.98
Filipino (228)	356	1.07
Indian (106)	134	0.40
Indonesian (17)	22	0.07
Japanese (187)	323	0.97
Korean (79)	123	0.37
Laotian (1)	4	0.01
Nepalese (1)	3	0.01
Pakistani (8)	12	0.04
Sri Lankan (1)	1	<0.01
Taiwanese (29)	33	0.10
Thai (20)	23	0.07
Vietnamese (97)	122	0.37
Hawaii Native/Pacific Islander (37)	126	0.38
Not Hispanic (37)	112	0.34
Hispanic (0)	14	0.04
Fijian (2)	2	0.01
Guamanian/Chamorro (7)	10	0.03
Marshallese (0)	2	0.01
Native Hawaiian (19)	72	0.22
Samoan (4)	11	0.03
Tongan (1)	1	<0.01
White (28,701)	29,682	89.00
Not Hispanic (25,468)	26,135	78.36
Hispanic (3,233)	3,547	10.64

*Notes: † The Census 2010 population figure is used to calculate the percentages in the Hispanic Origin and Race categories. Ancestry percentages are based on the 2006-2010 American Community Survey population (not shown); ‡ Numbers in parentheses indicate the number of people reporting a single ancestry; * Numbers in parentheses indicate the number of persons reporting this race alone, not in combination with any other race; Please refer to the Explanation of Data for more information.*

Danville

Place Type: Town
County: Contra Costa
Population: 42,039†

Ancestry‡	Population	%
African, Sub-Saharan (81)	95	0.23
African (31)	45	0.11
Ethiopian (20)	20	0.05
Nigerian (14)	14	0.03
South African (16)	16	0.04
Alsatian (13)	13	0.03
American (1,480)	1,480	3.55
Arab (340)	410	0.98
Arab (0)	5	0.01
Egyptian (218)	218	0.52
Jordanian (16)	16	0.04
Lebanese (52)	101	0.24
Other Arab (54)	70	0.17
Armenian (39)	39	0.09
Assyrian/Chaldean/Syriac (13)	13	0.03
Australian (39)	143	0.34
Austrian (55)	184	0.44
Basque (0)	24	0.06
Belgian (39)	66	0.16
Brazilian (26)	26	0.06
British (167)	644	1.54
Bulgarian (16)	16	0.04
Canadian (111)	197	0.47
Croatian (21)	173	0.41
Czech (42)	189	0.45
Czechoslovakian (29)	29	0.07
Danish (106)	523	1.25
Dutch (175)	664	1.59
Eastern European (116)	184	0.44
English (1,729)	6,111	14.64
Estonian (0)	12	0.03
European (720)	769	1.84
Finnish (13)	221	0.53
French, ex. Basque (339)	1,565	3.75
French Canadian (87)	199	0.48
German (1,914)	7,198	17.25
Greek (158)	340	0.81
Hungarian (105)	298	0.71
Iranian (456)	607	1.45
Irish (1,247)	6,359	15.24
Italian (1,538)	4,523	10.84
Latvian (15)	42	0.10
Lithuanian (65)	145	0.35
Maltese (80)	217	0.52
Northern European (177)	209	0.50
Norwegian (520)	1,290	3.09
Polish (264)	1,160	2.78
Portuguese (583)	1,538	3.68
Romanian (10)	60	0.14
Russian (524)	942	2.26
Scandinavian (168)	283	0.68
Scotch-Irish (228)	975	2.34
Scottish (384)	1,437	3.44
Serbian (7)	24	0.06
Slavic (0)	55	0.13
Slovak (16)	73	0.17
Swedish (362)	1,286	3.08
Swiss (13)	268	0.64
Ukrainian (122)	158	0.38
Welsh (76)	485	1.16
Yugoslavian (63)	146	0.35

Hispanic Origin	Population	%
Hispanic or Latino (of any race)	2,879	6.85
Central American, ex. Mexican	211	0.50
Costa Rican	25	0.06
Guatemalan	29	0.07
Honduran	10	0.02
Nicaraguan	45	0.11
Panamanian	8	0.02
Salvadoran	93	0.22
Other Central American	1	<0.01
Cuban	76	0.18
Dominican Republic	4	0.01
Mexican	1,518	3.61
Puerto Rican	156	0.37
South American	351	0.83
Argentinean	34	0.08
Bolivian	8	0.02
Chilean	54	0.13
Colombian	74	0.18
Ecuadorian	10	0.02
Peruvian	136	0.32
Uruguayan	7	0.02
Venezuelan	26	0.06
Other South American	2	<0.01
Other Hispanic or Latino	563	1.34

Race*	Population	%
African-American/Black (372)	545	1.30
Not Hispanic (355)	496	1.18
Hispanic (17)	49	0.12
American Indian/Alaska Native (67)	296	0.70
Not Hispanic (47)	223	0.53
Hispanic (20)	73	0.17
Alaska Athabascan *(Ala. Nat.)* (0)	1	<0.01
Apache (2)	15	0.04
Arapaho (0)	4	0.01
Blackfeet (0)	5	0.01
Cherokee (11)	66	0.16
Cheyenne (0)	1	<0.01
Chickasaw (0)	2	<0.01
Chippewa (3)	9	0.02
Choctaw (0)	13	0.03
Comanche (3)	5	0.01
Creek (3)	7	0.02
Hopi (1)	1	<0.01
Inupiat *(Alaska Native)* (0)	1	<0.01
Iroquois (0)	4	0.01
Lumbee (0)	4	0.01
Mexican American Ind. (1)	12	0.03
Navajo (1)	2	<0.01
Osage (2)	4	0.01
Paiute (1)	1	<0.01
Potawatomi (1)	1	<0.01
Pueblo (0)	4	0.01
Seminole (0)	3	0.01
South American Ind. (0)	1	<0.01
Ute (0)	3	0.01
Asian (4,417)	5,604	13.33
Not Hispanic (4,360)	5,438	12.94
Hispanic (57)	166	0.39
Bangladeshi (0)	5	0.01
Burmese (0)	9	0.02
Cambodian (13)	21	0.05
Chinese, ex. Taiwanese (1,726)	2,183	5.19
Filipino (611)	1,032	2.45
Hmong (2)	3	0.01
Indian (745)	824	1.96
Indonesian (27)	51	0.12
Japanese (315)	654	1.56
Korean (289)	414	0.98
Laotian (10)	16	0.04
Malaysian (3)	7	0.02
Nepalese (3)	5	0.01
Pakistani (116)	134	0.32
Sri Lankan (22)	29	0.07
Taiwanese (140)	169	0.40
Thai (16)	34	0.08
Vietnamese (126)	173	0.41
Hawaii Native/Pacific Islander (68)	215	0.51
Not Hispanic (61)	184	0.44
Hispanic (7)	31	0.07
Fijian (8)	8	0.02
Guamanian/Chamorro (10)	36	0.09
Native Hawaiian (19)	85	0.20
Samoan (11)	23	0.05
Tongan (8)	11	0.03
White (34,942)	36,481	86.78
Not Hispanic (32,834)	34,138	81.21
Hispanic (2,108)	2,343	5.57

Davis

Place Type: City
County: Yolo
Population: 65,622†

Ancestry‡	Population	%
Afghan (154)	154	0.24
African, Sub-Saharan (434)	531	0.82
African (285)	340	0.52
Ethiopian (49)	74	0.11
Ghanaian (0)	17	0.03
Nigerian (9)	9	0.01
Somalian (91)	91	0.14
Albanian (0)	40	0.06
Alsatian (12)	12	0.02
American (992)	992	1.53
Arab (272)	370	0.57
Arab (45)	50	0.08
Egyptian (0)	14	0.02
Jordanian (23)	23	0.04
Lebanese (57)	111	0.17
Palestinian (32)	32	0.05
Syrian (0)	13	0.02
Other Arab (115)	127	0.20
Armenian (122)	192	0.30
Australian (50)	269	0.41
Austrian (50)	273	0.42
Basque (65)	77	0.12
Belgian (60)	136	0.21
Brazilian (67)	86	0.13
British (227)	551	0.85
Bulgarian (0)	9	0.01
Cajun (0)	9	0.01
Canadian (49)	190	0.29
Celtic (0)	21	0.03
Croatian (27)	104	0.16
Cypriot (11)	11	0.02
Czech (113)	307	0.47
Czechoslovakian (0)	27	0.04
Danish (87)	410	0.63
Dutch (276)	988	1.52
Eastern European (199)	235	0.36
English (2,047)	8,175	12.61
Estonian (12)	12	0.02
European (2,445)	3,038	4.69
Finnish (34)	121	0.19
French, ex. Basque (381)	1,809	2.79
French Canadian (101)	249	0.38
German (1,961)	9,304	14.35
Greek (105)	363	0.56
Hungarian (26)	275	0.42
Icelander (12)	12	0.02
Iranian (447)	530	0.82
Irish (1,860)	7,023	10.83
Israeli (104)	104	0.16
Italian (869)	3,874	5.97
Latvian (41)	60	0.09
Lithuanian (60)	202	0.31
Macedonian (0)	11	0.02
New Zealander (27)	27	0.04
Northern European (295)	337	0.52
Norwegian (234)	959	1.48
Pennsylvania German (13)	13	0.02
Polish (342)	1,591	2.45
Portuguese (302)	659	1.02
Romanian (54)	247	0.38
Russian (533)	1,289	1.99
Scandinavian (85)	209	0.32
Scotch-Irish (387)	1,809	2.79
Scottish (268)	1,993	3.07
Serbian (13)	21	0.03
Slavic (33)	67	0.10
Slovak (25)	61	0.09
Slovene (0)	32	0.05
Swedish (284)	1,200	1.85
Swiss (128)	722	1.11
Turkish (126)	163	0.25
Ukrainian (155)	259	0.40

*Notes: † The Census 2010 population figure is used to calculate the percentages in the Hispanic Origin and Race categories. Ancestry percentages are based on the 2006-2010 American Community Survey population (not shown); ‡ Numbers in parentheses indicate the number of people reporting a single ancestry; * Numbers in parentheses indicate the number of persons reporting this race alone, not in combination with any other race; Please refer to the Explanation of Data for more information.*

Welsh (140)	742	1.14
West Indian, ex. Hispanic (41)	45	0.07
Jamaican (41)	41	0.06
Trinidadian/Tobagonian (0)	4	0.01
Yugoslavian (31)	61	0.09

Hispanic Origin	Population	%
Hispanic or Latino (of any race)	8,172	12.45
Central American, ex. Mexican	708	1.08
Costa Rican	40	0.06
Guatemalan	182	0.28
Honduran	24	0.04
Nicaraguan	97	0.15
Panamanian	24	0.04
Salvadoran	336	0.51
Other Central American	5	0.01
Cuban	80	0.12
Dominican Republic	14	0.02
Mexican	5,618	8.56
Puerto Rican	221	0.34
South American	711	1.08
Argentinean	128	0.20
Bolivian	19	0.03
Chilean	123	0.19
Colombian	141	0.21
Ecuadorian	57	0.09
Paraguayan	4	0.01
Peruvian	159	0.24
Uruguayan	17	0.03
Venezuelan	58	0.09
Other South American	5	0.01
Other Hispanic or Latino	820	1.25

Race*	Population	%
African-American/Black (1,528)	2,086	3.18
Not Hispanic (1,415)	1,859	2.83
Hispanic (113)	227	0.35
American Indian/Alaska Native (339)	983	1.50
Not Hispanic (166)	602	0.92
Hispanic (173)	381	0.58
Alaska Athabascan *(Ala. Nat.)* (1)	1	<0.01
Apache (24)	44	0.07
Blackfeet (2)	22	0.03
Canadian/French Am. Ind. (3)	4	0.01
Central American Ind. (4)	8	0.01
Cherokee (24)	163	0.25
Cheyenne (0)	4	0.01
Chickasaw (6)	10	0.02
Chippewa (2)	7	0.01
Choctaw (11)	52	0.08
Colville (0)	1	<0.01
Comanche (0)	4	0.01
Cree (0)	6	0.01
Creek (4)	10	0.02
Delaware (1)	1	<0.01
Houma (0)	1	<0.01
Iroquois (4)	14	0.02
Mexican American Ind. (40)	65	0.10
Navajo (15)	27	0.04
Osage (1)	7	0.01
Ottawa (0)	5	0.01
Paiute (0)	4	0.01
Pima (0)	1	<0.01
Potawatomi (2)	3	<0.01
Pueblo (0)	5	0.01
Puget Sound Salish (0)	1	<0.01
Seminole (1)	2	<0.01
Shoshone (1)	3	<0.01
Sioux (11)	26	0.04
South American Ind. (2)	14	0.02
Spanish American Ind. (6)	7	0.01
Tlingit-Haida *(Alaska Native)* (2)	3	<0.01
Yakama (1)	1	<0.01
Yaqui (4)	9	0.01
Yup'ik *(Alaska Native)* (1)	3	<0.01
Asian (14,355)	16,574	25.26
Not Hispanic (14,213)	16,170	24.64
Hispanic (142)	404	0.62
Bangladeshi (41)	41	0.06
Bhutanese (1)	1	<0.01
Burmese (30)	50	0.08
Cambodian (63)	87	0.13
Chinese, ex. Taiwanese (5,969)	7,009	10.68
Filipino (1,033)	1,615	2.46
Hmong (201)	204	0.31
Indian (1,631)	1,793	2.73
Indonesian (55)	76	0.12
Japanese (953)	1,674	2.55
Korean (1,560)	1,766	2.69
Laotian (90)	97	0.15
Malaysian (14)	19	0.03
Nepalese (134)	150	0.23
Pakistani (172)	194	0.30
Sri Lankan (59)	64	0.10
Taiwanese (394)	446	0.68
Thai (104)	148	0.23
Vietnamese (1,185)	1,403	2.14
Hawaii Native/Pacific Islander (136)	344	0.52
Not Hispanic (120)	279	0.43
Hispanic (16)	65	0.10
Fijian (35)	42	0.06
Guamanian/Chamorro (23)	60	0.09
Marshallese (6)	6	0.01
Native Hawaiian (22)	113	0.17
Samoan (19)	41	0.06
Tongan (2)	5	0.01
White (42,571)	45,794	69.78
Not Hispanic (38,641)	41,141	62.69
Hispanic (3,930)	4,653	7.09

Del Aire

Place Type: CDP
County: Los Angeles
Population: 10,001†

Ancestry‡	Population	%
African, Sub-Saharan (12)	12	0.13
African (12)	12	0.13
American (1,815)	1,815	18.94
Arab (153)	194	2.02
Arab (0)	14	0.15
Egyptian (145)	145	1.51
Syrian (8)	26	0.27
Other Arab (0)	9	0.09
Armenian (46)	46	0.48
Austrian (0)	26	0.27
British (8)	8	0.08
Czech (0)	27	0.28
Danish (0)	24	0.25
Dutch (51)	144	1.50
Eastern European (0)	14	0.15
English (164)	733	7.65
European (0)	33	0.34
Finnish (0)	9	0.09
French, ex. Basque (23)	177	1.85
French Canadian (12)	29	0.30
German (160)	737	7.69
Greek (0)	13	0.14
Hungarian (71)	129	1.35
Irish (55)	458	4.78
Italian (112)	251	2.62
Norwegian (0)	22	0.23
Polish (27)	94	0.98
Portuguese (9)	68	0.71
Romanian (21)	146	1.52
Russian (13)	13	0.14
Scotch-Irish (70)	121	1.26
Scottish (29)	180	1.88
Serbian (12)	12	0.13
Slavic (10)	10	0.10
Swedish (20)	107	1.12
Welsh (12)	74	0.77
West Indian, ex. Hispanic (29)	29	0.30
Belizean (9)	9	0.09
Haitian (20)	20	0.21
Yugoslavian (0)	41	0.43

Hispanic Origin	Population	%
Hispanic or Latino (of any race)	4,724	47.24
Central American, ex. Mexican	578	5.78
Costa Rican	47	0.47
Guatemalan	222	2.22
Honduran	20	0.20
Nicaraguan	39	0.39
Panamanian	4	0.04
Salvadoran	238	2.38
Other Central American	8	0.08
Cuban	219	2.19
Dominican Republic	6	0.06
Mexican	3,188	31.88
Puerto Rican	110	1.10
South American	330	3.30
Argentinean	41	0.41
Bolivian	5	0.05
Chilean	18	0.18
Colombian	87	0.87
Ecuadorian	61	0.61
Peruvian	102	1.02
Uruguayan	5	0.05
Venezuelan	5	0.05
Other South American	6	0.06
Other Hispanic or Latino	293	2.93

Race*	Population	%
African-American/Black (458)	598	5.98
Not Hispanic (431)	532	5.32
Hispanic (27)	66	0.66
American Indian/Alaska Native (60)	142	1.42
Not Hispanic (24)	78	0.78
Hispanic (36)	64	0.64
Alaska Athabascan *(Ala. Nat.)* (0)	1	0.01
Apache (1)	4	0.04
Blackfeet (1)	11	0.11
Cherokee (1)	13	0.13
Chippewa (0)	1	0.01
Choctaw (4)	8	0.08
Creek (2)	2	0.02
Iroquois (0)	2	0.02
Mexican American Ind. (10)	11	0.11
Navajo (1)	2	0.02
Osage (2)	2	0.02
Potawatomi (2)	2	0.02
Pueblo (1)	1	0.01
Puget Sound Salish (1)	1	0.01
Sioux (2)	2	0.02
Asian (922)	1,132	11.32
Not Hispanic (901)	1,056	10.56
Hispanic (21)	76	0.76
Bangladeshi (7)	8	0.08
Burmese (1)	4	0.04
Cambodian (10)	12	0.12
Chinese, ex. Taiwanese (125)	162	1.62
Filipino (288)	378	3.78
Indian (82)	100	1.00
Indonesian (15)	27	0.27
Japanese (87)	134	1.34
Korean (64)	82	0.82
Laotian (1)	1	0.01
Malaysian (2)	5	0.05
Nepalese (1)	1	0.01
Pakistani (21)	24	0.24
Sri Lankan (5)	5	0.05
Taiwanese (13)	13	0.13
Thai (30)	34	0.34
Vietnamese (140)	149	1.49
Hawaii Native/Pacific Islander (131)	179	1.79
Not Hispanic (128)	169	1.69
Hispanic (3)	10	0.10
Fijian (30)	33	0.33
Guamanian/Chamorro (1)	2	0.02
Native Hawaiian (10)	24	0.24
Samoan (35)	51	0.51
Tongan (44)	52	0.52
White (6,052)	6,503	65.02
Not Hispanic (3,458)	3,690	36.90
Hispanic (2,594)	2,813	28.13

*Notes: † The Census 2010 population figure is used to calculate the percentages in the Hispanic Origin and Race categories. Ancestry percentages are based on the 2006-2010 American Community Survey population (not shown); ‡ Numbers in parentheses indicate the number of people reporting a single ancestry; * Numbers in parentheses indicate the number of persons reporting this race alone, not in combination with any other race; Please refer to the Explanation of Data for more information.*

Delano

Place Type: City
County: Kern
Population: 53,041†

Ancestry‡	Population	%
African, Sub-Saharan (51)	58	0.11
African (40)	47	0.09
Other Sub-Saharan African (11)	11	0.02
American (355)	355	0.69
Arab (84)	110	0.21
Arab (7)	24	0.05
Jordanian (32)	32	0.06
Palestinian (8)	8	0.02
Other Arab (37)	46	0.09
Armenian (41)	57	0.11
Austrian (0)	16	0.03
Brazilian (9)	9	0.02
British (0)	18	0.04
Canadian (14)	22	0.04
Croatian (23)	23	0.04
Czech (0)	8	0.02
Danish (10)	47	0.09
Dutch (47)	121	0.24
English (176)	502	0.98
European (129)	137	0.27
Finnish (10)	20	0.04
French, ex. Basque (26)	185	0.36
French Canadian (11)	27	0.05
German (151)	916	1.79
Greek (0)	37	0.07
Hungarian (0)	5	0.01
Iranian (15)	15	0.03
Irish (174)	936	1.82
Italian (182)	538	1.05
Maltese (8)	8	0.02
Northern European (9)	9	0.02
Norwegian (9)	68	0.13
Polish (17)	83	0.16
Portuguese (63)	104	0.20
Romanian (23)	38	0.07
Russian (23)	70	0.14
Scandinavian (0)	15	0.03
Scotch-Irish (52)	128	0.25
Scottish (16)	135	0.26
Swedish (0)	23	0.04
Welsh (0)	59	0.11
West Indian, ex. Hispanic (20)	71	0.14
Belizean (8)	33	0.06
Haitian (12)	12	0.02
Jamaican (0)	26	0.05

Hispanic Origin	Population	%
Hispanic or Latino (of any race)	37,913	71.48
Central American, ex. Mexican	427	0.81
Costa Rican	13	0.02
Guatemalan	121	0.23
Honduran	37	0.07
Nicaraguan	12	0.02
Panamanian	5	0.01
Salvadoran	238	0.45
Other Central American	1	<0.01
Cuban	14	0.03
Mexican	34,658	65.34
Puerto Rican	197	0.37
South American	34	0.06
Argentinean	1	<0.01
Bolivian	1	<0.01
Chilean	10	0.02
Ecuadorian	10	0.02
Peruvian	7	0.01
Venezuelan	5	0.01
Other Hispanic or Latino	2,583	4.87

Race*	Population	%
African-American/Black (4,191)	4,360	8.22
Not Hispanic (4,007)	4,088	7.71
Hispanic (184)	272	0.51
American Indian/Alaska Native (501)	666	1.26
Not Hispanic (154)	220	0.41
Hispanic (347)	446	0.84
Aleut *(Alaska Native)* (1)	2	<0.01
Apache (14)	19	0.04
Blackfeet (0)	1	<0.01
Cherokee (7)	21	0.04
Cheyenne (0)	1	<0.01
Chickasaw (3)	3	0.01
Choctaw (8)	13	0.02
Creek (4)	5	0.01
Mexican American Ind. (95)	111	0.21
Navajo (6)	18	0.03
Paiute (3)	10	0.02
Potawatomi (1)	1	<0.01
Pueblo (7)	8	0.02
Seminole (4)	4	0.01
Sioux (1)	1	<0.01
Tlingit-Haida *(Alaska Native)* (1)	1	<0.01
Tohono O'Odham (2)	4	0.01
Yaqui (28)	33	0.06
Yuman (4)	8	0.02
Yup'ik *(Alaska Native)* (1)	2	<0.01
Asian (6,757)	7,493	14.13
Not Hispanic (6,436)	6,795	12.81
Hispanic (321)	698	1.32
Bangladeshi (3)	3	0.01
Cambodian (19)	25	0.05
Chinese, ex. Taiwanese (34)	62	0.12
Filipino (6,280)	6,927	13.06
Hmong (1)	3	0.01
Indian (324)	375	0.71
Japanese (21)	36	0.07
Korean (28)	28	0.05
Laotian (5)	6	0.01
Vietnamese (7)	9	0.02
Hawaii Native/Pacific Islander (30)	156	0.29
Not Hispanic (22)	89	0.17
Hispanic (8)	67	0.13
Guamanian/Chamorro (9)	25	0.05
Native Hawaiian (8)	45	0.08
Samoan (1)	9	0.02
Tongan (0)	1	<0.01
White (19,304)	20,721	39.07
Not Hispanic (3,980)	4,243	8.00
Hispanic (15,324)	16,478	31.07

Delhi

Place Type: CDP
County: Merced
Population: 10,755†

Ancestry‡	Population	%
Afghan (19)	79	0.75
American (52)	52	0.50
Basque (16)	16	0.15
Dutch (100)	169	1.61
English (249)	356	3.40
European (99)	99	0.94
French, ex. Basque (0)	101	0.96
German (70)	517	4.93
Greek (20)	20	0.19
Irish (130)	528	5.04
Italian (48)	142	1.35
Portuguese (249)	301	2.87
Scotch-Irish (0)	11	0.10
Scottish (23)	34	0.32
Swedish (39)	99	0.94
Swiss (0)	37	0.35
Welsh (0)	14	0.13
Yugoslavian (0)	15	0.14

Hispanic Origin	Population	%
Hispanic or Latino (of any race)	7,706	71.65
Central American, ex. Mexican	83	0.77
Guatemalan	29	0.27
Honduran	4	0.04
Nicaraguan	9	0.08
Panamanian	5	0.05
Salvadoran	36	0.33
Cuban	2	0.02
Mexican	7,369	68.52
Puerto Rican	40	0.37
South American	6	0.06
Colombian	1	0.01
Peruvian	4	0.04
Venezuelan	1	0.01
Other Hispanic or Latino	206	1.92

Race*	Population	%
African-American/Black (118)	169	1.57
Not Hispanic (87)	117	1.09
Hispanic (31)	52	0.48
American Indian/Alaska Native (157)	233	2.17
Not Hispanic (37)	98	0.91
Hispanic (120)	135	1.26
Alaska Athabascan *(Ala. Nat.)* (0)	1	0.01
Aleut *(Alaska Native)* (1)	1	0.01
Apache (2)	5	0.05
Cherokee (3)	28	0.26
Choctaw (0)	4	0.04
Cree (0)	1	0.01
Creek (2)	2	0.02
Delaware (1)	3	0.03
Mexican American Ind. (19)	25	0.23
Navajo (0)	5	0.05
Ottawa (1)	1	0.01
Paiute (3)	3	0.03
Pima (1)	1	0.01
Potawatomi (3)	5	0.05
Seminole (0)	2	0.02
Sioux (1)	1	0.01
Spanish American Ind. (46)	46	0.43
Yaqui (6)	7	0.07
Asian (405)	501	4.66
Not Hispanic (386)	460	4.28
Hispanic (19)	41	0.38
Chinese, ex. Taiwanese (11)	16	0.15
Filipino (45)	80	0.74
Hmong (57)	63	0.59
Indian (256)	295	2.74
Japanese (1)	16	0.15
Korean (2)	3	0.03
Laotian (13)	13	0.12
Malaysian (1)	1	0.01
Pakistani (1)	1	0.01
Vietnamese (9)	16	0.15
Hawaii Native/Pacific Islander (30)	51	0.47
Not Hispanic (28)	38	0.35
Hispanic (2)	13	0.12
Fijian (8)	10	0.09
Guamanian/Chamorro (1)	2	0.02
Native Hawaiian (8)	14	0.13
Samoan (9)	9	0.08
White (5,655)	6,051	56.26
Not Hispanic (2,338)	2,466	22.93
Hispanic (3,317)	3,585	33.33

Desert Hot Springs

Place Type: City
County: Riverside
Population: 25,938†

Ancestry‡	Population	%
African, Sub-Saharan (146)	210	0.85
African (146)	210	0.85
American (437)	437	1.77
Arab (32)	42	0.17
Lebanese (11)	11	0.04
Other Arab (21)	31	0.13
Assyrian/Chaldean/Syriac (17)	72	0.29
Austrian (45)	61	0.25
Basque (13)	13	0.05
Belgian (0)	18	0.07
British (43)	58	0.24
Canadian (71)	71	0.29
Croatian (14)	24	0.10
Czech (59)	59	0.24
Czechoslovakian (0)	21	0.09

*Notes: † The Census 2010 population figure is used to calculate the percentages in the Hispanic Origin and Race categories. Ancestry percentages are based on the 2006-2010 American Community Survey population (not shown); ‡ Numbers in parentheses indicate the number of people reporting a single ancestry; * Numbers in parentheses indicate the number of persons reporting this race alone, not in combination with any other race; Please refer to the Explanation of Data for more information.*

Danish (30)	77	0.31
Dutch (12)	203	0.82
English (613)	1,440	5.84
European (347)	530	2.15
Finnish (30)	30	0.12
French, ex. Basque (184)	531	2.15
French Canadian (10)	57	0.23
German (499)	1,497	6.07
Greek (22)	22	0.09
Hungarian (129)	478	1.94
Irish (636)	1,713	6.94
Italian (293)	960	3.89
Lithuanian (69)	87	0.35
Norwegian (38)	206	0.83
Pennsylvania German (14)	14	0.06
Polish (146)	292	1.18
Portuguese (66)	81	0.33
Romanian (110)	152	0.62
Russian (67)	155	0.63
Scandinavian (0)	22	0.09
Scotch-Irish (0)	49	0.20
Scottish (23)	158	0.64
Slavic (0)	19	0.08
Swedish (81)	288	1.17
Swiss (9)	41	0.17
Turkish (12)	12	0.05
Ukrainian (32)	66	0.27
Welsh (34)	127	0.51

Hispanic Origin	Population	%
Hispanic or Latino (of any race)	13,646	52.61
Central American, ex. Mexican	789	3.04
Costa Rican	5	0.02
Guatemalan	303	1.17
Honduran	28	0.11
Nicaraguan	62	0.24
Panamanian	13	0.05
Salvadoran	373	1.44
Other Central American	5	0.02
Cuban	50	0.19
Dominican Republic	12	0.05
Mexican	11,775	45.40
Puerto Rican	161	0.62
South American	88	0.34
Argentinean	33	0.13
Chilean	7	0.03
Colombian	17	0.07
Ecuadorian	9	0.03
Peruvian	13	0.05
Uruguayan	2	0.01
Venezuelan	4	0.02
Other South American	3	0.01
Other Hispanic or Latino	771	2.97

Race*	Population	%
African-American/Black (2,133)	2,524	9.73
Not Hispanic (1,948)	2,231	8.60
Hispanic (185)	293	1.13
American Indian/Alaska Native (357)	640	2.47
Not Hispanic (161)	319	1.23
Hispanic (196)	321	1.24
Alaska Athabascan *(Ala. Nat.)* (1)	1	<0.01
Aleut *(Alaska Native)* (0)	5	0.02
Apache (18)	29	0.11
Blackfeet (2)	5	0.02
Canadian/French Am. Ind. (0)	1	<0.01
Central American Ind. (1)	2	0.01
Cherokee (20)	71	0.27
Cheyenne (0)	1	<0.01
Chickasaw (1)	3	0.01
Chippewa (0)	3	0.01
Choctaw (3)	12	0.05
Comanche (6)	6	0.02
Cree (1)	1	<0.01
Creek (1)	1	<0.01
Inupiat *(Alaska Native)* (0)	4	0.02
Iroquois (5)	12	0.05
Mexican American Ind. (26)	52	0.20
Navajo (10)	20	0.08
Osage (0)	6	0.02
Ottawa (10)	10	0.04
Paiute (0)	2	0.01
Potawatomi (2)	3	0.01
Pueblo (1)	2	0.01
Puget Sound Salish (0)	3	0.01
Seminole (0)	2	0.01
Shoshone (0)	1	<0.01
Sioux (6)	13	0.05
Spanish American Ind. (0)	2	0.01
Tlingit-Haida *(Alaska Native)* (5)	7	0.03
Tohono O'Odham (12)	15	0.06
Yaqui (14)	24	0.09
Yup'ik *(Alaska Native)* (0)	3	0.01
Asian (675)	938	3.62
Not Hispanic (604)	770	2.97
Hispanic (71)	168	0.65
Burmese (1)	1	<0.01
Cambodian (21)	24	0.09
Chinese, ex. Taiwanese (61)	95	0.37
Filipino (333)	482	1.86
Hmong (10)	11	0.04
Indian (38)	62	0.24
Indonesian (7)	12	0.05
Japanese (36)	66	0.25
Korean (47)	62	0.24
Laotian (8)	9	0.03
Nepalese (0)	1	<0.01
Pakistani (14)	17	0.07
Sri Lankan (1)	1	<0.01
Thai (24)	29	0.11
Vietnamese (42)	52	0.20
Hawaii Native/Pacific Islander (84)	200	0.77
Not Hispanic (71)	136	0.52
Hispanic (13)	64	0.25
Guamanian/Chamorro (15)	30	0.12
Native Hawaiian (21)	79	0.30
Samoan (32)	56	0.22
White (15,053)	16,079	61.99
Not Hispanic (8,930)	9,381	36.17
Hispanic (6,123)	6,698	25.82

Diamond Bar

Place Type: City
County: Los Angeles
Population: 55,544†

Ancestry‡	Population	%
African, Sub-Saharan (286)	355	0.64
African (268)	326	0.59
Nigerian (18)	18	0.03
Other Sub-Saharan African (0)	11	0.02
American (1,298)	1,298	2.33
Arab (357)	461	0.83
Arab (150)	156	0.28
Egyptian (100)	100	0.18
Lebanese (54)	110	0.20
Other Arab (53)	95	0.17
Armenian (312)	447	0.80
Austrian (31)	63	0.11
Basque (0)	72	0.13
Belgian (0)	31	0.06
British (73)	83	0.15
Bulgarian (23)	23	0.04
Canadian (8)	58	0.10
Celtic (10)	22	0.04
Croatian (14)	42	0.08
Czech (0)	102	0.18
Czechoslovakian (0)	55	0.10
Danish (24)	145	0.26
Dutch (100)	521	0.94
Eastern European (120)	120	0.22
English (632)	2,450	4.40
European (224)	420	0.75
Finnish (8)	25	0.04
French, ex. Basque (79)	537	0.96
French Canadian (110)	129	0.23
German (724)	3,311	5.94
Greek (143)	325	0.58
Guyanese (13)	13	0.02
Hungarian (27)	104	0.19
Iranian (128)	128	0.23
Irish (660)	2,305	4.14
Italian (649)	1,832	3.29
Lithuanian (0)	24	0.04
Macedonian (0)	19	0.03
Northern European (11)	17	0.03
Norwegian (64)	194	0.35
Pennsylvania German (8)	16	0.03
Polish (152)	499	0.90
Portuguese (60)	123	0.22
Romanian (9)	21	0.04
Russian (94)	241	0.43
Scandinavian (8)	71	0.13
Scotch-Irish (70)	396	0.71
Scottish (253)	641	1.15
Serbian (10)	10	0.02
Slovene (13)	13	0.02
Swedish (63)	197	0.35
Swiss (30)	76	0.14
Turkish (0)	26	0.05
Ukrainian (11)	48	0.09
Welsh (15)	85	0.15
West Indian, ex. Hispanic (36)	36	0.06
Belizean (9)	9	0.02
Haitian (12)	12	0.02
Trinidadian/Tobagonian (15)	15	0.03
Yugoslavian (0)	9	0.02

Hispanic Origin	Population	%
Hispanic or Latino (of any race)	11,138	20.05
Central American, ex. Mexican	675	1.22
Costa Rican	54	0.10
Guatemalan	174	0.31
Honduran	41	0.07
Nicaraguan	118	0.21
Panamanian	20	0.04
Salvadoran	255	0.46
Other Central American	13	0.02
Cuban	193	0.35
Dominican Republic	6	0.01
Mexican	8,766	15.78
Puerto Rican	185	0.33
South American	640	1.15
Argentinean	86	0.15
Bolivian	16	0.03
Chilean	50	0.09
Colombian	163	0.29
Ecuadorian	120	0.22
Paraguayan	1	<0.01
Peruvian	174	0.31
Uruguayan	7	0.01
Venezuelan	21	0.04
Other South American	2	<0.01
Other Hispanic or Latino	673	1.21

Race*	Population	%
African-American/Black (2,288)	2,620	4.72
Not Hispanic (2,194)	2,437	4.39
Hispanic (94)	183	0.33
American Indian/Alaska Native (178)	455	0.82
Not Hispanic (67)	203	0.37
Hispanic (111)	252	0.45
Alaska Athabascan *(Ala. Nat.)* (0)	1	<0.01
Aleut *(Alaska Native)* (0)	1	<0.01
Apache (10)	22	0.04
Blackfeet (1)	4	0.01
Central American Ind. (0)	1	<0.01
Cherokee (8)	34	0.06
Chickasaw (2)	3	0.01
Chippewa (1)	1	<0.01
Choctaw (5)	17	0.03
Cree (0)	1	<0.01
Creek (0)	5	0.01
Crow (0)	1	<0.01
Hopi (0)	2	<0.01
Mexican American Ind. (5)	13	0.02
Navajo (8)	32	0.06
Osage (1)	2	<0.01
Pima (5)	5	0.01

*Notes: † The Census 2010 population figure is used to calculate the percentages in the Hispanic Origin and Race categories. Ancestry percentages are based on the 2006-2010 American Community Survey population (not shown); ‡ Numbers in parentheses indicate the number of people reporting a single ancestry; * Numbers in parentheses indicate the number of persons reporting this race alone, not in combination with any other race; Please refer to the Explanation of Data for more information.*

Potawatomi (2)	2	<0.01
Pueblo (0)	2	<0.01
Seminole (1)	6	0.01
Shoshone (1)	3	0.01
Sioux (1)	6	0.01
South American Ind. (1)	7	0.01
Spanish American Ind. (8)	8	0.01
Tohono O'Odham (1)	2	<0.01
Yaqui (1)	4	0.01
Yuman (2)	2	<0.01
Asian (29,144)	30,478	54.87
Not Hispanic (28,883)	29,892	53.82
Hispanic (261)	586	1.06
Bangladeshi (27)	27	0.05
Burmese (131)	166	0.30
Cambodian (63)	100	0.18
Chinese, ex. Taiwanese (11,587)	12,547	22.59
Filipino (3,277)	3,767	6.78
Hmong (3)	3	0.01
Indian (2,086)	2,205	3.97
Indonesian (277)	350	0.63
Japanese (870)	1,194	2.15
Korean (5,782)	5,961	10.73
Laotian (19)	31	0.06
Malaysian (17)	31	0.06
Nepalese (4)	4	0.01
Pakistani (301)	337	0.61
Sri Lankan (42)	43	0.08
Taiwanese (2,808)	3,162	5.69
Thai (170)	203	0.37
Vietnamese (717)	906	1.63
Hawaii Native/Pacific Islander (106)	335	0.60
Not Hispanic (92)	287	0.52
Hispanic (14)	48	0.09
Fijian (2)	9	0.02
Guamanian/Chamorro (18)	20	0.04
Native Hawaiian (28)	84	0.15
Samoan (44)	52	0.09
Tongan (3)	8	0.01
White (18,434)	20,044	36.09
Not Hispanic (11,812)	12,743	22.94
Hispanic (6,622)	7,301	13.14

Diamond Springs

Place Type: CDP
County: El Dorado
Population: 11,037†

Ancestry‡	Population	%
American (637)	637	5.62
Austrian (17)	31	0.27
Belgian (22)	55	0.49
British (22)	35	0.31
Canadian (10)	17	0.15
Croatian (12)	12	0.11
Czech (0)	24	0.21
Danish (95)	370	3.27
Dutch (35)	270	2.38
English (637)	1,807	15.95
European (183)	191	1.69
Finnish (9)	83	0.73
French, ex. Basque (54)	477	4.21
French Canadian (49)	56	0.49
German (634)	2,220	19.60
Greek (0)	63	0.56
Hungarian (0)	122	1.08
Irish (299)	1,463	12.92
Italian (156)	730	6.44
Norwegian (211)	371	3.28
Polish (44)	252	2.22
Portuguese (107)	318	2.81
Russian (5)	39	0.34
Scandinavian (12)	12	0.11
Scotch-Irish (110)	329	2.90
Scottish (98)	516	4.56
Slovak (10)	10	0.09
Swedish (113)	513	4.53
Swiss (12)	93	0.82
Welsh (81)	89	0.79
Yugoslavian (0)	24	0.21

Hispanic Origin	Population	%
Hispanic or Latino (of any race)	1,377	12.48
Central American, ex. Mexican	39	0.35
Costa Rican	2	0.02
Guatemalan	6	0.05
Honduran	2	0.02
Nicaraguan	7	0.06
Salvadoran	22	0.20
Cuban	3	0.03
Mexican	1,111	10.07
Puerto Rican	22	0.20
South American	31	0.28
Argentinean	11	0.10
Bolivian	1	0.01
Chilean	5	0.05
Colombian	8	0.07
Ecuadorian	1	0.01
Paraguayan	1	0.01
Peruvian	4	0.04
Other Hispanic or Latino	171	1.55

Race*	Population	%
African-American/Black (39)	92	0.83
Not Hispanic (37)	82	0.74
Hispanic (2)	10	0.09
American Indian/Alaska Native (176)	443	4.01
Not Hispanic (129)	346	3.13
Hispanic (47)	97	0.88
Alaska Athabascan *(Ala. Nat.)* (1)	2	0.02
Aleut *(Alaska Native)* (0)	3	0.03
Apache (4)	10	0.09
Blackfeet (2)	11	0.10
Central American Ind. (1)	1	0.01
Cherokee (23)	97	0.88
Chickasaw (2)	2	0.02
Chippewa (1)	5	0.05
Choctaw (9)	24	0.22
Cree (1)	4	0.04
Creek (1)	6	0.05
Crow (1)	2	0.02
Delaware (0)	5	0.05
Inupiat *(Alaska Native)* (1)	3	0.03
Iroquois (0)	3	0.03
Kiowa (3)	3	0.03
Mexican American Ind. (7)	10	0.09
Navajo (3)	6	0.05
Osage (0)	4	0.04
Pima (0)	3	0.03
Potawatomi (0)	1	0.01
Pueblo (0)	4	0.04
Puget Sound Salish (0)	2	0.02
Seminole (0)	1	0.01
Sioux (0)	9	0.08
Tlingit-Haida *(Alaska Native)* (2)	2	0.02
Yaqui (1)	1	0.01
Asian (110)	174	1.58
Not Hispanic (108)	163	1.48
Hispanic (2)	11	0.10
Chinese, ex. Taiwanese (21)	31	0.28
Filipino (31)	67	0.61
Indian (18)	22	0.20
Indonesian (1)	1	0.01
Japanese (12)	32	0.29
Korean (12)	13	0.12
Sri Lankan (1)	4	0.04
Taiwanese (6)	6	0.05
Vietnamese (2)	2	0.02
Hawaii Native/Pacific Islander (6)	37	0.34
Not Hispanic (6)	28	0.25
Hispanic (0)	9	0.08
Guamanian/Chamorro (2)	5	0.05
Native Hawaiian (3)	15	0.14
Samoan (0)	3	0.03
Tongan (1)	8	0.07
White (9,743)	10,170	92.14
Not Hispanic (9,025)	9,352	84.73
Hispanic (718)	818	7.41

Dinuba

Place Type: City
County: Tulare
Population: 21,453†

Ancestry‡	Population	%
American (44)	44	0.21
Arab (262)	276	1.33
Arab (142)	142	0.68
Lebanese (10)	10	0.05
Palestinian (110)	110	0.53
Syrian (0)	14	0.07
Armenian (25)	25	0.12
Basque (21)	57	0.27
British (8)	8	0.04
Canadian (8)	8	0.04
Celtic (10)	10	0.05
Dutch (9)	48	0.23
English (147)	272	1.31
European (32)	61	0.29
French, ex. Basque (9)	118	0.57
French Canadian (11)	11	0.05
German (158)	336	1.61
Irish (130)	372	1.79
Italian (7)	7	0.03
Northern European (15)	15	0.07
Norwegian (0)	7	0.03
Portuguese (9)	94	0.45
Russian (24)	33	0.16
Scotch-Irish (22)	36	0.17
Scottish (25)	46	0.22
Swedish (21)	30	0.14
Swiss (0)	18	0.09
Ukrainian (0)	9	0.04

Hispanic Origin	Population	%
Hispanic or Latino (of any race)	18,114	84.44
Central American, ex. Mexican	117	0.55
Costa Rican	1	<0.01
Guatemalan	33	0.15
Honduran	9	0.04
Nicaraguan	23	0.11
Panamanian	9	0.04
Salvadoran	40	0.19
Other Central American	2	0.01
Cuban	13	0.06
Dominican Republic	1	<0.01
Mexican	17,316	80.72
Puerto Rican	30	0.14
South American	10	0.05
Argentinean	3	0.01
Chilean	2	0.01
Colombian	5	0.02
Other Hispanic or Latino	627	2.92

Race*	Population	%
African-American/Black (141)	203	0.95
Not Hispanic (29)	44	0.21
Hispanic (112)	159	0.74
American Indian/Alaska Native (193)	320	1.49
Not Hispanic (52)	97	0.45
Hispanic (141)	223	1.04
Apache (7)	14	0.07
Blackfeet (0)	1	<0.01
Canadian/French Am. Ind. (3)	3	0.01
Cherokee (15)	26	0.12
Choctaw (10)	12	0.06
Colville (0)	2	0.01
Creek (2)	4	0.02
Iroquois (1)	1	<0.01
Mexican American Ind. (30)	43	0.20
Navajo (1)	6	0.03
Osage (0)	1	<0.01
Seminole (1)	1	<0.01
Spanish American Ind. (3)	6	0.03
Tohono O'Odham (1)	1	<0.01
Yaqui (3)	8	0.04
Asian (454)	618	2.88
Not Hispanic (411)	484	2.26

*Notes: † The Census 2010 population figure is used to calculate the percentages in the Hispanic Origin and Race categories. Ancestry percentages are based on the 2006-2010 American Community Survey population (not shown); ‡ Numbers in parentheses indicate the number of people reporting a single ancestry; * Numbers in parentheses indicate the number of persons reporting this race alone, not in combination with any other race; Please refer to the Explanation of Data for more information.*

Hispanic (43)	134	0.62
Cambodian (13)	14	0.07
Chinese, ex. Taiwanese (67)	82	0.38
Filipino (198)	265	1.24
Hmong (9)	9	0.04
Indian (71)	85	0.40
Japanese (52)	72	0.34
Korean (7)	19	0.09
Laotian (4)	6	0.03
Pakistani (0)	2	0.01
Thai (1)	2	0.01
Vietnamese (24)	24	0.11
Hawaii Native/Pacific Islander (17)	52	0.24
Not Hispanic (9)	22	0.10
Hispanic (8)	30	0.14
Guamanian/Chamorro (1)	1	<0.01
Native Hawaiian (4)	14	0.07
Samoan (6)	8	0.04
White (11,166)	11,864	55.30
Not Hispanic (2,682)	2,795	13.03
Hispanic (8,484)	9,069	42.27

Discovery Bay

Place Type: CDP
County: Contra Costa
Population: 13,352†

Ancestry‡	Population	%
African, Sub-Saharan (36)	48	0.42
African (21)	21	0.18
Nigerian (15)	15	0.13
South African (0)	12	0.10
American (498)	498	4.35
Arab (28)	107	0.94
Egyptian (28)	28	0.24
Lebanese (0)	79	0.69
Austrian (12)	22	0.19
Belgian (0)	18	0.16
British (24)	120	1.05
Canadian (0)	19	0.17
Czech (19)	118	1.03
Danish (15)	36	0.31
Dutch (42)	317	2.77
English (258)	796	6.96
European (193)	193	1.69
Finnish (12)	24	0.21
French, ex. Basque (21)	677	5.92
German (716)	2,402	21.00
Greek (30)	216	1.89
Hungarian (0)	15	0.13
Iranian (12)	12	0.10
Irish (444)	1,497	13.09
Italian (682)	1,404	12.27
Maltese (0)	16	0.14
Northern European (15)	15	0.13
Norwegian (69)	360	3.15
Polish (0)	36	0.31
Portuguese (377)	632	5.53
Russian (67)	78	0.68
Scandinavian (85)	85	0.74
Scotch-Irish (178)	303	2.65
Scottish (402)	632	5.53
Swedish (112)	250	2.19
Swiss (58)	73	0.64
Welsh (39)	189	1.65

Hispanic Origin	Population	%
Hispanic or Latino (of any race)	2,074	15.53
Central American, ex. Mexican	148	1.11
Costa Rican	5	0.04
Guatemalan	17	0.13
Honduran	4	0.03
Nicaraguan	51	0.38
Panamanian	9	0.07
Salvadoran	62	0.46
Cuban	39	0.29
Dominican Republic	6	0.04
Mexican	1,353	10.13
Puerto Rican	138	1.03
South American	67	0.50
Argentinean	9	0.07
Bolivian	4	0.03
Chilean	4	0.03
Colombian	18	0.13
Ecuadorian	4	0.03
Peruvian	23	0.17
Uruguayan	2	0.01
Other South American	3	0.02
Other Hispanic or Latino	323	2.42

Race*	Population	%
African-American/Black (550)	673	5.04
Not Hispanic (530)	615	4.61
Hispanic (20)	58	0.43
American Indian/Alaska Native (86)	228	1.71
Not Hispanic (67)	187	1.40
Hispanic (19)	41	0.31
Apache (2)	2	0.01
Blackfeet (6)	12	0.09
Cherokee (22)	53	0.40
Cheyenne (2)	2	0.01
Chippewa (7)	10	0.07
Choctaw (8)	18	0.13
Comanche (5)	5	0.04
Creek (1)	1	0.01
Delaware (1)	2	0.01
Iroquois (1)	8	0.06
Mexican American Ind. (1)	5	0.04
Navajo (0)	1	0.01
Osage (1)	4	0.03
Paiute (0)	1	0.01
Pueblo (3)	3	0.02
Seminole (0)	3	0.02
Sioux (0)	4	0.03
Yaqui (0)	1	0.01
Asian (522)	868	6.50
Not Hispanic (509)	766	5.74
Hispanic (13)	102	0.76
Cambodian (7)	14	0.10
Chinese, ex. Taiwanese (86)	151	1.13
Filipino (250)	443	3.32
Indian (40)	46	0.34
Indonesian (3)	7	0.05
Japanese (43)	128	0.96
Korean (13)	21	0.16
Laotian (3)	6	0.04
Pakistani (2)	2	0.01
Sri Lankan (1)	1	0.01
Taiwanese (1)	1	0.01
Thai (2)	10	0.07
Vietnamese (44)	59	0.44
Hawaii Native/Pacific Islander (51)	150	1.12
Not Hispanic (41)	113	0.85
Hispanic (10)	37	0.28
Fijian (14)	17	0.13
Guamanian/Chamorro (3)	13	0.10
Native Hawaiian (26)	87	0.65
Samoan (1)	9	0.07
White (10,909)	11,589	86.80
Not Hispanic (9,659)	10,064	75.37
Hispanic (1,250)	1,525	11.42

Dixon

Place Type: City
County: Solano
Population: 18,351†

Ancestry‡	Population	%
Afghan (41)	41	0.23
American (364)	364	2.03
Arab (24)	24	0.13
Egyptian (12)	12	0.07
Lebanese (12)	12	0.07
Austrian (8)	8	0.04
Basque (9)	40	0.22
Brazilian (0)	18	0.10
British (79)	134	0.75
Canadian (18)	26	0.15
Croatian (0)	25	0.14
Czech (15)	28	0.16
Czechoslovakian (0)	13	0.07
Danish (79)	174	0.97
Dutch (16)	116	0.65
English (296)	1,608	8.97
European (560)	964	5.38
Finnish (0)	12	0.07
French, ex. Basque (22)	505	2.82
French Canadian (23)	59	0.33
German (547)	2,129	11.88
Greek (126)	338	1.89
Irish (473)	2,372	13.23
Italian (202)	780	4.35
Lithuanian (0)	30	0.17
Norwegian (17)	201	1.12
Polish (76)	183	1.02
Portuguese (202)	456	2.54
Russian (14)	64	0.36
Scandinavian (12)	58	0.32
Scotch-Irish (68)	169	0.94
Scottish (148)	369	2.06
Swedish (29)	113	0.63
Swiss (48)	83	0.46
Welsh (0)	154	0.86
Yugoslavian (13)	31	0.17

Hispanic Origin	Population	%
Hispanic or Latino (of any race)	7,426	40.47
Central American, ex. Mexican	183	1.00
Costa Rican	1	0.01
Guatemalan	50	0.27
Honduran	5	0.03
Nicaraguan	44	0.24
Panamanian	16	0.09
Salvadoran	65	0.35
Other Central American	2	0.01
Cuban	30	0.16
Dominican Republic	4	0.02
Mexican	6,667	36.33
Puerto Rican	105	0.57
South American	74	0.40
Argentinean	4	0.02
Bolivian	12	0.07
Chilean	6	0.03
Colombian	10	0.05
Ecuadorian	3	0.02
Peruvian	31	0.17
Venezuelan	4	0.02
Other South American	4	0.02
Other Hispanic or Latino	363	1.98

Race*	Population	%
African-American/Black (562)	765	4.17
Not Hispanic (498)	658	3.59
Hispanic (64)	107	0.58
American Indian/Alaska Native (184)	344	1.87
Not Hispanic (102)	217	1.18
Hispanic (82)	127	0.69
Alaska Athabascan *(Ala. Nat.)* (4)	5	0.03
Aleut *(Alaska Native)* (2)	3	0.02
Apache (4)	15	0.08
Arapaho (0)	1	0.01
Blackfeet (1)	4	0.02
Cherokee (9)	67	0.37
Chickasaw (3)	5	0.03
Chippewa (1)	1	0.01
Choctaw (6)	21	0.11
Cree (0)	2	0.01
Creek (2)	5	0.03
Crow (4)	4	0.02
Delaware (1)	2	0.01
Hopi (0)	2	0.01
Inupiat *(Alaska Native)* (0)	3	0.02
Iroquois (2)	5	0.03
Lumbee (1)	2	0.01
Mexican American Ind. (32)	37	0.20
Navajo (10)	13	0.07
Potawatomi (2)	4	0.02
Puget Sound Salish (2)	2	0.01

*Notes: † The Census 2010 population figure is used to calculate the percentages in the Hispanic Origin and Race categories. Ancestry percentages are based on the 2006-2010 American Community Survey population (not shown); ‡ Numbers in parentheses indicate the number of people reporting a single ancestry; * Numbers in parentheses indicate the number of persons reporting this race alone, not in combination with any other race; Please refer to the Explanation of Data for more information.*

Sioux (0)	8	0.04
South American Ind. (0)	3	0.02
Yakama (0)	1	0.01
Yuman (0)	1	0.01
Asian (671)	1,087	5.92
Not Hispanic (635)	966	5.26
Hispanic (36)	121	0.66
Bangladeshi (0)	3	0.02
Burmese (3)	3	0.02
Cambodian (0)	1	0.01
Chinese, ex. Taiwanese (105)	160	0.87
Filipino (295)	480	2.62
Hmong (4)	4	0.02
Indian (82)	103	0.56
Indonesian (2)	13	0.07
Japanese (57)	143	0.78
Korean (28)	55	0.30
Laotian (5)	12	0.07
Pakistani (2)	6	0.03
Sri Lankan (2)	2	0.01
Taiwanese (4)	5	0.03
Thai (12)	29	0.16
Vietnamese (34)	42	0.23
Hawaii Native/Pacific Islander (58)	155	0.84
Not Hispanic (50)	119	0.65
Hispanic (8)	36	0.20
Fijian (3)	3	0.02
Guamanian/Chamorro (16)	36	0.20
Native Hawaiian (11)	51	0.28
Samoan (16)	29	0.16
Tongan (2)	3	0.02
White (13,023)	13,925	75.88
Not Hispanic (9,038)	9,564	52.12
Hispanic (3,985)	4,361	23.76

Downey

Place Type: City
County: Los Angeles
Population: 111,772†

Ancestry‡	Population	%
African, Sub-Saharan (343)	402	0.36
African (197)	226	0.20
Ethiopian (7)	7	0.01
Ghanaian (93)	93	0.08
Kenyan (0)	23	0.02
Nigerian (46)	46	0.04
Other Sub-Saharan African (0)	7	0.01
Albanian (43)	52	0.05
American (1,718)	1,718	1.55
Arab (792)	1,007	0.91
Arab (40)	92	0.08
Egyptian (549)	603	0.54
Lebanese (62)	137	0.12
Moroccan (23)	48	0.04
Syrian (55)	64	0.06
Other Arab (63)	63	0.06
Armenian (133)	178	0.16
Austrian (37)	37	0.03
Basque (15)	15	0.01
Belgian (9)	39	0.04
Brazilian (11)	45	0.04
British (59)	118	0.11
Cajun (7)	7	0.01
Canadian (66)	111	0.10
Croatian (0)	41	0.04
Czech (72)	157	0.14
Czechoslovakian (55)	84	0.08
Danish (53)	151	0.14
Dutch (167)	477	0.43
English (1,021)	3,050	2.75
European (340)	409	0.37
French, ex. Basque (171)	1,126	1.02
French Canadian (190)	273	0.25
German (1,220)	4,386	3.95
Greek (461)	579	0.52
Guyanese (22)	22	0.02
Hungarian (78)	111	0.10
Iranian (365)	379	0.34
Irish (585)	2,704	2.44
Italian (1,234)	2,250	2.03
Latvian (17)	17	0.02
Lithuanian (28)	28	0.03
Luxemburger (0)	15	0.01
Northern European (33)	33	0.03
Norwegian (87)	523	0.47
Pennsylvania German (14)	43	0.04
Polish (328)	620	0.56
Portuguese (32)	253	0.23
Romanian (62)	75	0.07
Russian (393)	600	0.54
Scandinavian (36)	54	0.05
Scotch-Irish (165)	631	0.57
Scottish (211)	637	0.57
Slavic (0)	78	0.07
Slovak (0)	21	0.02
Slovene (0)	6	0.01
Swedish (120)	473	0.43
Swiss (43)	104	0.09
Welsh (58)	154	0.14
West Indian, ex. Hispanic (72)	109	0.10
Belizean (0)	4	<0.01
Jamaican (61)	71	0.06
Trinidadian/Tobagonian (11)	11	0.01
West Indian (0)	23	0.02
Yugoslavian (184)	201	0.18

Hispanic Origin	Population	%
Hispanic or Latino (of any race)	78,996	70.68
Central American, ex. Mexican	8,546	7.65
Costa Rican	263	0.24
Guatemalan	2,180	1.95
Honduran	505	0.45
Nicaraguan	1,092	0.98
Panamanian	71	0.06
Salvadoran	4,356	3.90
Other Central American	79	0.07
Cuban	2,283	2.04
Dominican Republic	70	0.06
Mexican	60,331	53.98
Puerto Rican	745	0.67
South American	3,506	3.14
Argentinean	429	0.38
Bolivian	134	0.12
Chilean	120	0.11
Colombian	733	0.66
Ecuadorian	678	0.61
Paraguayan	4	<0.01
Peruvian	1,277	1.14
Uruguayan	29	0.03
Venezuelan	67	0.06
Other South American	35	0.03
Other Hispanic or Latino	3,515	3.14

Race*	Population	%
African-American/Black (4,329)	4,933	4.41
Not Hispanic (3,834)	4,105	3.67
Hispanic (495)	828	0.74
American Indian/Alaska Native (820)	1,439	1.29
Not Hispanic (212)	408	0.37
Hispanic (608)	1,031	0.92
Aleut *(Alaska Native)* (1)	2	<0.01
Apache (30)	52	0.05
Blackfeet (10)	21	0.02
Canadian/French Am. Ind. (2)	5	<0.01
Central American Ind. (5)	15	0.01
Cherokee (26)	93	0.08
Cheyenne (2)	3	<0.01
Chickasaw (2)	7	0.01
Chippewa (7)	10	0.01
Choctaw (29)	51	0.05
Comanche (10)	11	0.01
Creek (7)	16	0.01
Crow (0)	1	<0.01
Delaware (4)	4	<0.01
Hopi (12)	17	0.02
Inupiat *(Alaska Native)* (0)	1	<0.01
Iroquois (2)	4	<0.01
Kiowa (3)	3	<0.01
Lumbee (1)	1	<0.01
Menominee (1)	1	<0.01
Mexican American Ind. (119)	158	0.14
Navajo (51)	80	0.07
Osage (0)	3	<0.01
Paiute (1)	1	<0.01
Pima (7)	11	0.01
Potawatomi (0)	2	<0.01
Pueblo (9)	15	0.01
Seminole (0)	3	<0.01
Shoshone (1)	14	0.01
Sioux (8)	16	0.01
South American Ind. (13)	19	0.02
Spanish American Ind. (11)	18	0.02
Tlingit-Haida *(Alaska Native)* (0)	1	<0.01
Tohono O'Odham (6)	9	0.01
Yakama (1)	3	<0.01
Yaqui (11)	28	0.03
Yuman (5)	6	0.01
Asian (7,804)	8,898	7.96
Not Hispanic (7,484)	8,088	7.24
Hispanic (320)	810	0.72
Bangladeshi (37)	52	0.05
Burmese (13)	25	0.02
Cambodian (145)	217	0.19
Chinese, ex. Taiwanese (477)	671	0.60
Filipino (2,470)	2,869	2.57
Hmong (5)	9	0.01
Indian (657)	771	0.69
Indonesian (30)	51	0.05
Japanese (322)	557	0.50
Korean (2,508)	2,619	2.34
Laotian (10)	11	0.01
Malaysian (1)	3	<0.01
Nepalese (5)	5	<0.01
Pakistani (129)	155	0.14
Sri Lankan (23)	24	0.02
Taiwanese (106)	115	0.10
Thai (254)	289	0.26
Vietnamese (367)	423	0.38
Hawaii Native/Pacific Islander (221)	494	0.44
Not Hispanic (170)	327	0.29
Hispanic (51)	167	0.15
Fijian (20)	28	0.03
Guamanian/Chamorro (33)	61	0.05
Native Hawaiian (46)	149	0.13
Samoan (83)	133	0.12
Tongan (10)	14	0.01
White (63,255)	66,983	59.93
Not Hispanic (19,786)	20,652	18.48
Hispanic (43,469)	46,331	41.45

Duarte

Place Type: City
County: Los Angeles
Population: 21,321†

Ancestry‡	Population	%
African, Sub-Saharan (12)	22	0.10
African (12)	22	0.10
American (201)	201	0.94
Arab (360)	423	1.98
Arab (25)	34	0.16
Egyptian (105)	105	0.49
Lebanese (221)	239	1.12
Syrian (0)	26	0.12
Other Arab (9)	19	0.09
Armenian (350)	473	2.21
British (34)	44	0.21
Canadian (32)	58	0.27
Celtic (22)	22	0.10
Czech (10)	25	0.12
Czechoslovakian (13)	13	0.06
Danish (0)	38	0.18
Dutch (14)	54	0.25
English (145)	897	4.20
European (79)	79	0.37
Finnish (0)	9	0.04
French, ex. Basque (72)	251	1.17

*Notes: † The Census 2010 population figure is used to calculate the percentages in the Hispanic Origin and Race categories. Ancestry percentages are based on the 2006-2010 American Community Survey population (not shown); ‡ Numbers in parentheses indicate the number of people reporting a single ancestry; * Numbers in parentheses indicate the number of persons reporting this race alone, not in combination with any other race; Please refer to the Explanation of Data for more information.*

French Canadian (29)	41	0.19
German (198)	1,021	4.78
Hungarian (44)	90	0.42
Iranian (25)	43	0.20
Irish (209)	852	3.99
Italian (339)	586	2.74
Latvian (9)	9	0.04
Lithuanian (0)	19	0.09
Norwegian (8)	122	0.57
Polish (120)	221	1.03
Portuguese (12)	32	0.15
Russian (34)	67	0.31
Scotch-Irish (147)	307	1.44
Scottish (42)	269	1.26
Soviet Union (14)	14	0.07
Swedish (9)	144	0.67
Swiss (0)	67	0.31
Turkish (88)	98	0.46
Ukrainian (0)	10	0.05
Welsh (11)	39	0.18
West Indian, ex. Hispanic (18)	26	0.12
Belizean (0)	8	0.04
Trinidadian/Tobagonian (18)	18	0.08
Yugoslavian (46)	54	0.25

Hispanic Origin	Population	%
Hispanic or Latino (of any race)	10,190	47.79
Central American, ex. Mexican	723	3.39
Costa Rican	28	0.13
Guatemalan	162	0.76
Honduran	65	0.30
Nicaraguan	70	0.33
Panamanian	14	0.07
Salvadoran	383	1.80
Other Central American	1	<0.01
Cuban	100	0.47
Dominican Republic	10	0.05
Mexican	8,328	39.06
Puerto Rican	95	0.45
South American	392	1.84
Argentinean	81	0.38
Bolivian	7	0.03
Chilean	23	0.11
Colombian	99	0.46
Ecuadorian	49	0.23
Peruvian	105	0.49
Uruguayan	7	0.03
Venezuelan	20	0.09
Other South American	1	<0.01
Other Hispanic or Latino	542	2.54

Race*	Population	%
African-American/Black (1,587)	1,794	8.41
Not Hispanic (1,486)	1,621	7.60
Hispanic (101)	173	0.81
American Indian/Alaska Native (179)	322	1.51
Not Hispanic (63)	144	0.68
Hispanic (116)	178	0.83
Apache (2)	10	0.05
Blackfeet (4)	9	0.04
Canadian/French Am. Ind. (0)	2	0.01
Central American Ind. (1)	1	<0.01
Cherokee (10)	40	0.19
Chickasaw (0)	3	0.01
Chippewa (0)	2	0.01
Choctaw (1)	10	0.05
Crow (1)	4	0.02
Hopi (1)	4	0.02
Iroquois (6)	8	0.04
Mexican American Ind. (15)	32	0.15
Navajo (11)	18	0.08
Paiute (1)	1	<0.01
Pima (1)	1	<0.01
Pueblo (0)	2	0.01
Puget Sound Salish (2)	3	0.01
Sioux (0)	5	0.02
South American Ind. (1)	2	0.01
Tlingit-Haida *(Alaska Native)* (0)	1	<0.01
Ute (1)	1	<0.01
Yaqui (3)	3	0.01
Asian (3,361)	3,784	17.75
Not Hispanic (3,287)	3,602	16.89
Hispanic (74)	182	0.85
Bangladeshi (13)	13	0.06
Burmese (17)	17	0.08
Cambodian (7)	11	0.05
Chinese, ex. Taiwanese (761)	889	4.17
Filipino (1,583)	1,765	8.28
Indian (253)	288	1.35
Indonesian (29)	53	0.25
Japanese (112)	191	0.90
Korean (109)	134	0.63
Laotian (2)	2	0.01
Malaysian (9)	16	0.08
Pakistani (68)	71	0.33
Sri Lankan (37)	42	0.20
Taiwanese (75)	82	0.38
Thai (63)	82	0.38
Vietnamese (119)	135	0.63
Hawaii Native/Pacific Islander (26)	93	0.44
Not Hispanic (24)	72	0.34
Hispanic (2)	21	0.10
Guamanian/Chamorro (2)	6	0.03
Native Hawaiian (5)	33	0.15
Samoan (10)	14	0.07
White (11,076)	11,836	55.51
Not Hispanic (5,729)	6,098	28.60
Hispanic (5,347)	5,738	26.91

Dublin

Place Type: City
County: Alameda
Population: 46,036†

Ancestry‡	Population	%
Afghan (411)	428	1.00
African, Sub-Saharan (227)	368	0.86
African (179)	304	0.71
Ethiopian (29)	37	0.09
Ghanaian (11)	11	0.03
Sudanese (8)	16	0.04
American (910)	910	2.13
Arab (160)	167	0.39
Arab (35)	35	0.08
Lebanese (36)	43	0.10
Palestinian (69)	69	0.16
Other Arab (20)	20	0.05
Armenian (79)	133	0.31
Assyrian/Chaldean/Syriac (28)	28	0.07
Australian (12)	31	0.07
Austrian (6)	155	0.36
Belgian (0)	9	0.02
Brazilian (0)	9	0.02
British (93)	231	0.54
Bulgarian (11)	11	0.03
Canadian (20)	111	0.26
Celtic (0)	15	0.04
Croatian (80)	114	0.27
Czech (54)	86	0.20
Czechoslovakian (0)	22	0.05
Danish (63)	276	0.65
Dutch (92)	447	1.05
Eastern European (19)	34	0.08
English (550)	3,547	8.32
European (626)	656	1.54
Finnish (24)	62	0.15
French, ex. Basque (204)	1,039	2.44
French Canadian (50)	155	0.36
German (997)	4,824	11.31
Greek (127)	362	0.85
Hungarian (39)	130	0.30
Icelander (68)	68	0.16
Iranian (601)	614	1.44
Irish (1,121)	3,960	9.28
Israeli (12)	12	0.03
Italian (739)	2,590	6.07
Lithuanian (11)	40	0.09
Maltese (20)	20	0.05
Norwegian (38)	367	0.86
Polish (195)	940	2.20
Portuguese (763)	1,945	4.56
Romanian (111)	127	0.30
Russian (334)	728	1.71
Scandinavian (52)	130	0.30
Scotch-Irish (128)	407	0.95
Scottish (91)	636	1.49
Serbian (34)	41	0.10
Slavic (0)	15	0.04
Slovak (0)	20	0.05
Swedish (104)	446	1.05
Swiss (167)	289	0.68
Turkish (147)	147	0.34
Ukrainian (0)	46	0.11
Welsh (31)	296	0.69
West Indian, ex. Hispanic (9)	9	0.02
West Indian (9)	9	0.02
Yugoslavian (23)	23	0.05

Hispanic Origin	Population	%
Hispanic or Latino (of any race)	6,663	14.47
Central American, ex. Mexican	402	0.87
Costa Rican	19	0.04
Guatemalan	55	0.12
Honduran	18	0.04
Nicaraguan	131	0.28
Panamanian	21	0.05
Salvadoran	157	0.34
Other Central American	1	<0.01
Cuban	96	0.21
Dominican Republic	36	0.08
Mexican	4,745	10.31
Puerto Rican	379	0.82
South American	356	0.77
Argentinean	33	0.07
Bolivian	14	0.03
Chilean	17	0.04
Colombian	95	0.21
Ecuadorian	41	0.09
Peruvian	130	0.28
Uruguayan	3	0.01
Venezuelan	18	0.04
Other South American	5	0.01
Other Hispanic or Latino	649	1.41

Race*	Population	%
African-American/Black (4,347)	4,835	10.50
Not Hispanic (4,214)	4,606	10.01
Hispanic (133)	229	0.50
American Indian/Alaska Native (246)	612	1.33
Not Hispanic (164)	431	0.94
Hispanic (82)	181	0.39
Apache (8)	28	0.06
Arapaho (4)	4	0.01
Blackfeet (6)	21	0.05
Canadian/French Am. Ind. (1)	6	0.01
Central American Ind. (1)	2	<0.01
Cherokee (13)	74	0.16
Cheyenne (1)	1	<0.01
Chickasaw (3)	8	0.02
Chippewa (4)	15	0.03
Choctaw (3)	15	0.03
Colville (1)	1	<0.01
Comanche (2)	9	0.02
Cree (0)	2	<0.01
Creek (0)	5	0.01
Crow (3)	6	0.01
Delaware (0)	1	<0.01
Inupiat *(Alaska Native)* (0)	1	<0.01
Iroquois (0)	3	0.01
Kiowa (1)	2	<0.01
Mexican American Ind. (15)	39	0.08
Navajo (11)	20	0.04
Osage (0)	3	0.01
Pima (2)	3	0.01
Potawatomi (0)	1	<0.01
Pueblo (4)	8	0.02
Puget Sound Salish (0)	1	<0.01
Seminole (0)	6	0.01
Shoshone (3)	3	0.01

*Notes: † The Census 2010 population figure is used to calculate the percentages in the Hispanic Origin and Race categories. Ancestry percentages are based on the 2006-2010 American Community Survey population (not shown); ‡ Numbers in parentheses indicate the number of people reporting a single ancestry; * Numbers in parentheses indicate the number of persons reporting this race alone, not in combination with any other race; Please refer to the Explanation of Data for more information.*

Sioux (6)	12	0.03
South American Ind. (2)	8	0.02
Tlingit-Haida *(Alaska Native)* (0)	5	0.01
Tohono O'Odham (17)	18	0.04
Ute (3)	7	0.02
Yakama (1)	1	<0.01
Yaqui (1)	6	0.01
Yuman (0)	1	<0.01
Asian (12,321)	14,050	30.52
Not Hispanic (12,170)	13,683	29.72
Hispanic (151)	367	0.80
Bangladeshi (23)	24	0.05
Burmese (18)	31	0.07
Cambodian (42)	76	0.17
Chinese, ex. Taiwanese (3,431)	4,016	8.72
Filipino (2,562)	3,251	7.06
Hmong (2)	2	<0.01
Indian (3,116)	3,323	7.22
Indonesian (56)	80	0.17
Japanese (376)	724	1.57
Korean (940)	1,082	2.35
Laotian (31)	40	0.09
Malaysian (7)	8	0.02
Nepalese (7)	11	0.02
Pakistani (191)	209	0.45
Sri Lankan (4)	4	0.01
Taiwanese (180)	215	0.47
Thai (58)	84	0.18
Vietnamese (720)	859	1.87
Hawaii Native/Pacific Islander (287)	546	1.19
Not Hispanic (277)	488	1.06
Hispanic (10)	58	0.13
Fijian (39)	50	0.11
Guamanian/Chamorro (66)	107	0.23
Native Hawaiian (84)	208	0.45
Samoan (53)	63	0.14
Tongan (32)	35	0.08
White (23,634)	25,947	56.36
Not Hispanic (20,380)	22,100	48.01
Hispanic (3,254)	3,847	8.36

Earlimart

Place Type: CDP
County: Tulare
Population: 8,537†

Ancestry‡	Population	%
American (29)	29	0.44
Dutch (0)	8	0.12
English (39)	56	0.85
French, ex. Basque (0)	18	0.27
German (14)	23	0.35
Irish (9)	28	0.42
Northern European (0)	14	0.21
Polish (0)	10	0.15
Scottish (0)	18	0.27
Welsh (0)	14	0.21

Hispanic Origin	Population	%
Hispanic or Latino (of any race)	7,805	91.43
Central American, ex. Mexican	32	0.37
Guatemalan	10	0.12
Honduran	8	0.09
Nicaraguan	1	0.01
Salvadoran	13	0.15
Cuban	1	0.01
Mexican	7,427	87.00
Puerto Rican	40	0.47
Other Hispanic or Latino	305	3.57

Race*	Population	%
African-American/Black (67)	99	1.16
Not Hispanic (39)	43	0.50
Hispanic (28)	56	0.66
American Indian/Alaska Native (45)	84	0.98
Not Hispanic (10)	21	0.25
Hispanic (35)	63	0.74
Apache (0)	1	0.01
Cherokee (4)	4	0.05
Choctaw (0)	1	0.01
Mexican American Ind. (10)	14	0.16
Navajo (4)	4	0.05
Pueblo (0)	2	0.02
Tohono O'Odham (4)	9	0.11
Yaqui (3)	4	0.05
Asian (536)	616	7.22
Not Hispanic (502)	522	6.11
Hispanic (34)	94	1.10
Cambodian (1)	1	0.01
Chinese, ex. Taiwanese (4)	5	0.06
Filipino (522)	583	6.83
Indian (8)	10	0.12
Japanese (1)	6	0.07
Hawaii Native/Pacific Islander (0)	14	0.16
Not Hispanic (0)	5	0.06
Hispanic (0)	9	0.11
Native Hawaiian (0)	6	0.07
Samoan (0)	1	0.01
White (3,193)	3,501	41.01
Not Hispanic (143)	165	1.93
Hispanic (3,050)	3,336	39.08

East Foothills

Place Type: CDP
County: Santa Clara
Population: 8,269†

Ancestry‡	Population	%
African, Sub-Saharan (19)	26	0.34
African (19)	26	0.34
American (156)	156	2.03
Australian (11)	11	0.14
Austrian (9)	18	0.23
Basque (15)	15	0.20
British (14)	14	0.18
Croatian (0)	46	0.60
Czech (0)	62	0.81
Danish (0)	120	1.56
Dutch (22)	24	0.31
English (130)	363	4.73
European (100)	110	1.43
Finnish (9)	27	0.35
French, ex. Basque (12)	151	1.97
French Canadian (39)	52	0.68
German (323)	728	9.49
Hungarian (32)	65	0.85
Irish (182)	553	7.21
Italian (359)	670	8.73
Northern European (57)	57	0.74
Norwegian (27)	111	1.45
Polish (8)	102	1.33
Portuguese (259)	331	4.31
Russian (12)	62	0.81
Scotch-Irish (0)	66	0.86
Scottish (9)	48	0.63
Slavic (28)	28	0.36
Swedish (51)	102	1.33
Swiss (0)	18	0.23
Welsh (12)	22	0.29
Yugoslavian (0)	18	0.23

Hispanic Origin	Population	%
Hispanic or Latino (of any race)	3,118	37.71
Central American, ex. Mexican	93	1.12
Costa Rican	2	0.02
Guatemalan	3	0.04
Honduran	2	0.02
Nicaraguan	19	0.23
Panamanian	1	0.01
Salvadoran	54	0.65
Other Central American	12	0.15
Cuban	12	0.15
Mexican	2,690	32.53
Puerto Rican	51	0.62
South American	74	0.89
Argentinean	15	0.18
Bolivian	1	0.01
Chilean	6	0.07
Colombian	16	0.19
Ecuadorian	4	0.05
Peruvian	30	0.36
Venezuelan	1	0.01
Other South American	1	0.01
Other Hispanic or Latino	198	2.39

Race*	Population	%
African-American/Black (205)	276	3.34
Not Hispanic (192)	243	2.94
Hispanic (13)	33	0.40
American Indian/Alaska Native (78)	151	1.83
Not Hispanic (16)	51	0.62
Hispanic (62)	100	1.21
Apache (7)	10	0.12
Blackfeet (0)	4	0.05
Cherokee (6)	24	0.29
Chippewa (3)	3	0.04
Choctaw (2)	3	0.04
Creek (1)	1	0.01
Hopi (2)	3	0.04
Mexican American Ind. (9)	21	0.25
Navajo (0)	1	0.01
Pueblo (1)	2	0.02
Seminole (0)	1	0.01
South American Ind. (1)	1	0.01
Yaqui (6)	8	0.10
Asian (1,445)	1,655	20.01
Not Hispanic (1,393)	1,548	18.72
Hispanic (52)	107	1.29
Bangladeshi (1)	1	0.01
Burmese (4)	4	0.05
Cambodian (11)	15	0.18
Chinese, ex. Taiwanese (189)	265	3.20
Filipino (350)	465	5.62
Indian (115)	126	1.52
Indonesian (1)	4	0.05
Japanese (107)	136	1.64
Korean (36)	45	0.54
Laotian (3)	8	0.10
Malaysian (3)	3	0.04
Pakistani (18)	18	0.22
Sri Lankan (2)	7	0.08
Taiwanese (32)	38	0.46
Thai (3)	5	0.06
Vietnamese (500)	574	6.94
Hawaii Native/Pacific Islander (41)	68	0.82
Not Hispanic (32)	49	0.59
Hispanic (9)	19	0.23
Fijian (6)	7	0.08
Guamanian/Chamorro (0)	5	0.06
Native Hawaiian (9)	29	0.35
Samoan (25)	28	0.34
White (4,853)	5,212	63.03
Not Hispanic (3,282)	3,466	41.92
Hispanic (1,571)	1,746	21.12

East Hemet

Place Type: CDP
County: Riverside
Population: 17,418†

Ancestry‡	Population	%
African, Sub-Saharan (0)	17	0.09
South African (0)	17	0.09
American (755)	755	3.78
Arab (33)	41	0.21
Arab (33)	41	0.21
Belgian (3)	3	0.02
British (12)	23	0.12
Canadian (12)	48	0.24
Czech (0)	17	0.09
Danish (21)	134	0.67
Dutch (45)	416	2.08
English (659)	2,357	11.81
European (89)	147	0.74
Finnish (0)	28	0.14
French, ex. Basque (160)	754	3.78
French Canadian (42)	117	0.59

*Notes: † The Census 2010 population figure is used to calculate the percentages in the Hispanic Origin and Race categories. Ancestry percentages are based on the 2006-2010 American Community Survey population (not shown); ‡ Numbers in parentheses indicate the number of people reporting a single ancestry; * Numbers in parentheses indicate the number of persons reporting this race alone, not in combination with any other race; Please refer to the Explanation of Data for more information.*

German (989)	3,333	16.70
Greek (38)	94	0.47
Hungarian (0)	47	0.24
Iranian (10)	18	0.09
Irish (264)	1,926	9.65
Italian (232)	764	3.83
Luxemburger (24)	48	0.24
Norwegian (98)	315	1.58
Polish (22)	35	0.18
Portuguese (10)	49	0.25
Romanian (121)	136	0.68
Russian (239)	320	1.60
Scandinavian (16)	85	0.43
Scotch-Irish (203)	383	1.92
Scottish (95)	498	2.49
Slovak (10)	10	0.05
Swedish (222)	659	3.30
Swiss (11)	11	0.06
Ukrainian (29)	29	0.15
Welsh (0)	29	0.15

Hispanic Origin	Population	%
Hispanic or Latino (of any race)	6,778	38.91
Central American, ex. Mexican	290	1.66
Costa Rican	10	0.06
Guatemalan	116	0.67
Honduran	18	0.10
Nicaraguan	28	0.16
Panamanian	11	0.06
Salvadoran	101	0.58
Other Central American	6	0.03
Cuban	31	0.18
Dominican Republic	2	0.01
Mexican	5,837	33.51
Puerto Rican	92	0.53
South American	68	0.39
Argentinean	11	0.06
Bolivian	5	0.03
Chilean	11	0.06
Colombian	14	0.08
Ecuadorian	1	0.01
Peruvian	20	0.11
Venezuelan	6	0.03
Other Hispanic or Latino	458	2.63

Race*	Population	%
African-American/Black (679)	836	4.80
Not Hispanic (609)	705	4.05
Hispanic (70)	131	0.75
American Indian/Alaska Native (323)	570	3.27
Not Hispanic (177)	307	1.76
Hispanic (146)	263	1.51
Apache (17)	42	0.24
Arapaho (0)	1	0.01
Blackfeet (0)	8	0.05
Central American Ind. (5)	6	0.03
Cherokee (8)	42	0.24
Cheyenne (1)	2	0.01
Chickasaw (8)	9	0.05
Chippewa (2)	5	0.03
Choctaw (10)	18	0.10
Creek (2)	2	0.01
Crow (0)	2	0.01
Inupiat *(Alaska Native)* (0)	1	0.01
Iroquois (0)	1	0.01
Lumbee (4)	4	0.02
Mexican American Ind. (9)	15	0.09
Navajo (5)	16	0.09
Osage (1)	3	0.02
Paiute (8)	8	0.05
Pima (0)	1	0.01
Potawatomi (0)	1	0.01
Pueblo (3)	4	0.02
Sioux (3)	11	0.06
Tohono O'Odham (0)	2	0.01
Yaqui (9)	17	0.10
Yuman (3)	3	0.02
Asian (275)	445	2.55
Not Hispanic (262)	364	2.09
Hispanic (13)	81	0.47
Cambodian (14)	16	0.09
Chinese, ex. Taiwanese (24)	50	0.29
Filipino (94)	161	0.92
Hmong (16)	16	0.09
Indian (45)	53	0.30
Indonesian (7)	9	0.05
Japanese (13)	58	0.33
Korean (14)	26	0.15
Laotian (13)	15	0.09
Pakistani (5)	5	0.03
Sri Lankan (0)	1	0.01
Taiwanese (9)	9	0.05
Thai (9)	12	0.07
Vietnamese (2)	10	0.06
Hawaii Native/Pacific Islander (29)	87	0.50
Not Hispanic (26)	63	0.36
Hispanic (3)	24	0.14
Guamanian/Chamorro (4)	10	0.06
Native Hawaiian (12)	49	0.28
Samoan (6)	21	0.12
White (12,257)	12,994	74.60
Not Hispanic (9,232)	9,530	54.71
Hispanic (3,025)	3,464	19.89

East La Mirada

Place Type: CDP
County: Los Angeles
Population: 9,757†

Ancestry‡	Population	%
American (343)	343	3.37
Arab (173)	229	2.25
Arab (56)	112	1.10
Egyptian (50)	50	0.49
Jordanian (67)	67	0.66
Australian (14)	14	0.14
Austrian (0)	238	2.34
British (60)	81	0.80
Croatian (8)	8	0.08
Danish (23)	76	0.75
Dutch (0)	58	0.57
English (146)	797	7.83
European (68)	103	1.01
French, ex. Basque (0)	136	1.34
French Canadian (12)	76	0.75
German (372)	1,160	11.40
Greek (0)	43	0.42
Hungarian (41)	55	0.54
Iranian (20)	20	0.20
Irish (252)	623	6.12
Italian (300)	648	6.37
Norwegian (41)	83	0.82
Pennsylvania German (0)	17	0.17
Polish (71)	119	1.17
Romanian (18)	18	0.18
Russian (7)	47	0.46
Scandinavian (23)	23	0.23
Scotch-Irish (22)	186	1.83
Scottish (64)	165	1.62
Swedish (37)	99	0.97
Ukrainian (0)	6	0.06
Welsh (81)	106	1.04
West Indian, ex. Hispanic (0)	9	0.09
Jamaican (0)	9	0.09

Hispanic Origin	Population	%
Hispanic or Latino (of any race)	4,907	50.29
Central American, ex. Mexican	216	2.21
Costa Rican	22	0.23
Guatemalan	56	0.57
Honduran	14	0.14
Nicaraguan	28	0.29
Salvadoran	90	0.92
Other Central American	6	0.06
Cuban	87	0.89
Dominican Republic	3	0.03
Mexican	4,160	42.64
Puerto Rican	82	0.84
South American	122	1.25
Argentinean	19	0.19
Bolivian	4	0.04
Chilean	5	0.05
Colombian	14	0.14
Ecuadorian	36	0.37
Paraguayan	2	0.02
Peruvian	42	0.43
Other Hispanic or Latino	237	2.43

Race*	Population	%
African-American/Black (178)	249	2.55
Not Hispanic (160)	206	2.11
Hispanic (18)	43	0.44
American Indian/Alaska Native (78)	146	1.50
Not Hispanic (21)	55	0.56
Hispanic (57)	91	0.93
Alaska Athabascan *(Ala. Nat.)* (0)	1	0.01
Apache (0)	5	0.05
Arapaho (0)	1	0.01
Blackfeet (0)	1	0.01
Cherokee (4)	28	0.29
Choctaw (1)	1	0.01
Hopi (0)	1	0.01
Lumbee (2)	2	0.02
Mexican American Ind. (3)	3	0.03
Navajo (1)	3	0.03
Pueblo (4)	8	0.08
Seminole (10)	10	0.10
Sioux (0)	1	0.01
South American Ind. (1)	1	0.01
Spanish American Ind. (0)	2	0.02
Tohono O'Odham (2)	2	0.02
Yaqui (2)	10	0.10
Asian (462)	600	6.15
Not Hispanic (444)	529	5.42
Hispanic (18)	71	0.73
Cambodian (4)	6	0.06
Chinese, ex. Taiwanese (49)	85	0.87
Filipino (154)	213	2.18
Indian (3)	11	0.11
Indonesian (12)	16	0.16
Japanese (71)	119	1.22
Korean (106)	121	1.24
Laotian (12)	12	0.12
Taiwanese (0)	1	0.01
Thai (4)	7	0.07
Vietnamese (21)	34	0.35
Hawaii Native/Pacific Islander (20)	58	0.59
Not Hispanic (11)	31	0.32
Hispanic (9)	27	0.28
Guamanian/Chamorro (0)	7	0.07
Native Hawaiian (9)	38	0.39
Samoan (8)	14	0.14
White (7,022)	7,410	75.95
Not Hispanic (4,046)	4,186	42.90
Hispanic (2,976)	3,224	33.04

East Los Angeles

Place Type: CDP
County: Los Angeles
Population: 126,496†

Ancestry‡	Population	%
African, Sub-Saharan (0)	13	0.01
African (0)	13	0.01
American (2,082)	2,082	1.69
Arab (13)	60	0.05
Arab (13)	60	0.05
Armenian (59)	70	0.06
Basque (22)	22	0.02
Czech (0)	3	<0.01
Danish (6)	6	<0.01
English (71)	191	0.16
European (0)	89	0.07
French, ex. Basque (8)	134	0.11
French Canadian (0)	23	0.02
German (117)	335	0.27
Greek (8)	8	0.01
Hungarian (7)	27	0.02

*Notes: † The Census 2010 population figure is used to calculate the percentages in the Hispanic Origin and Race categories. Ancestry percentages are based on the 2006-2010 American Community Survey population (not shown); ‡ Numbers in parentheses indicate the number of people reporting a single ancestry; * Numbers in parentheses indicate the number of persons reporting this race alone, not in combination with any other race; Please refer to the Explanation of Data for more information.*

Irish (23)	117	0.10
Italian (33)	190	0.15
New Zealander (23)	23	0.02
Norwegian (0)	17	0.01
Polish (141)	176	0.14
Portuguese (0)	12	0.01
Russian (89)	97	0.08
Scandinavian (13)	13	0.01
Scottish (36)	121	0.10
Serbian (15)	15	0.01
Swedish (0)	10	0.01
Ukrainian (32)	32	0.03
Welsh (0)	37	0.03
West Indian, ex. Hispanic (56)	111	0.09
Haitian (49)	104	0.08
West Indian (7)	7	0.01
Yugoslavian (0)	26	0.02

Hispanic Origin	Population	%
Hispanic or Latino (of any race)	122,784	97.07
Central American, ex. Mexican	5,994	4.74
Costa Rican	29	0.02
Guatemalan	1,825	1.44
Honduran	494	0.39
Nicaraguan	283	0.22
Panamanian	21	0.02
Salvadoran	3,274	2.59
Other Central American	68	0.05
Cuban	132	0.10
Dominican Republic	9	0.01
Mexican	111,441	88.10
Puerto Rican	264	0.21
South American	458	0.36
Argentinean	43	0.03
Bolivian	11	0.01
Chilean	29	0.02
Colombian	90	0.07
Ecuadorian	163	0.13
Peruvian	100	0.08
Uruguayan	11	0.01
Venezuelan	3	<0.01
Other South American	8	0.01
Other Hispanic or Latino	4,486	3.55

Race*	Population	%
African-American/Black (817)	1,073	0.85
Not Hispanic (322)	354	0.28
Hispanic (495)	719	0.57
American Indian/Alaska Native (1,549)	2,088	1.65
Not Hispanic (167)	219	0.17
Hispanic (1,382)	1,869	1.48
Apache (58)	74	0.06
Blackfeet (1)	5	<0.01
Central American Ind. (10)	21	0.02
Cherokee (27)	71	0.06
Cheyenne (0)	1	<0.01
Chippewa (8)	9	0.01
Choctaw (4)	7	0.01
Comanche (3)	3	<0.01
Creek (3)	4	<0.01
Crow (1)	1	<0.01
Hopi (4)	8	0.01
Inupiat *(Alaska Native)* (1)	2	<0.01
Iroquois (1)	1	<0.01
Mexican American Ind. (384)	487	0.38
Navajo (40)	69	0.05
Paiute (6)	6	<0.01
Pima (11)	12	0.01
Pueblo (22)	26	0.02
Shoshone (1)	1	<0.01
Sioux (9)	10	0.01
South American Ind. (1)	3	<0.01
Spanish American Ind. (26)	33	0.03
Tohono O'Odham (7)	16	0.01
Ute (4)	4	<0.01
Yaqui (45)	66	0.05
Yuman (4)	4	<0.01
Asian (1,144)	1,531	1.21
Not Hispanic (962)	1,045	0.83
Hispanic (182)	486	0.38
Burmese (2)	2	<0.01
Cambodian (14)	16	0.01
Chinese, ex. Taiwanese (377)	453	0.36
Filipino (209)	311	0.25
Indian (38)	66	0.05
Indonesian (4)	7	0.01
Japanese (258)	335	0.26
Korean (60)	75	0.06
Laotian (14)	21	0.02
Malaysian (2)	2	<0.01
Pakistani (4)	5	<0.01
Sri Lankan (0)	1	<0.01
Taiwanese (7)	10	0.01
Thai (20)	29	0.02
Vietnamese (73)	90	0.07
Hawaii Native/Pacific Islander (63)	149	0.12
Not Hispanic (13)	21	0.02
Hispanic (50)	128	0.10
Guamanian/Chamorro (25)	31	0.02
Native Hawaiian (21)	49	0.04
Samoan (8)	20	0.02
White (63,934)	67,508	53.37
Not Hispanic (1,917)	2,062	1.63
Hispanic (62,017)	65,446	51.74

East Palo Alto

Place Type: City
County: San Mateo
Population: 28,155†

Ancestry‡	Population	%
African, Sub-Saharan (190)	208	0.75
African (64)	82	0.29
Ethiopian (100)	100	0.36
Ghanaian (10)	10	0.04
Kenyan (8)	8	0.03
Other Sub-Saharan African (8)	8	0.03
American (276)	276	0.99
Arab (66)	74	0.27
Arab (7)	7	0.03
Jordanian (29)	29	0.10
Syrian (16)	24	0.09
Other Arab (14)	14	0.05
Brazilian (26)	26	0.09
British (0)	12	0.04
Bulgarian (0)	8	0.03
Croatian (0)	9	0.03
Danish (21)	33	0.12
Dutch (18)	25	0.09
English (135)	438	1.57
European (113)	221	0.79
French, ex. Basque (109)	355	1.27
German (98)	206	0.74
Greek (0)	29	0.10
Hungarian (16)	16	0.06
Irish (140)	246	0.88
Italian (55)	239	0.86
Macedonian (0)	16	0.06
Maltese (62)	93	0.33
New Zealander (31)	31	0.11
Northern European (28)	72	0.26
Norwegian (43)	91	0.33
Polish (10)	34	0.12
Portuguese (0)	14	0.05
Russian (99)	99	0.35
Scandinavian (12)	12	0.04
Scotch-Irish (0)	42	0.15
Scottish (0)	12	0.04
Swedish (28)	87	0.31
Ukrainian (38)	38	0.14
Welsh (12)	36	0.13
West Indian, ex. Hispanic (136)	175	0.63
Belizean (18)	18	0.06
Haitian (61)	61	0.22
Jamaican (13)	35	0.13
Trinidadian/Tobagonian (26)	43	0.15
West Indian (18)	18	0.06
Yugoslavian (22)	22	0.08

Hispanic Origin	Population	%
Hispanic or Latino (of any race)	18,147	64.45
Central American, ex. Mexican	1,877	6.67
Costa Rican	13	0.05
Guatemalan	431	1.53
Honduran	43	0.15
Nicaraguan	151	0.54
Panamanian	27	0.10
Salvadoran	1,202	4.27
Other Central American	10	0.04
Cuban	23	0.08
Dominican Republic	6	0.02
Mexican	15,319	54.41
Puerto Rican	69	0.25
South American	127	0.45
Argentinean	6	0.02
Bolivian	12	0.04
Chilean	12	0.04
Colombian	16	0.06
Ecuadorian	6	0.02
Peruvian	66	0.23
Uruguayan	1	<0.01
Venezuelan	3	0.01
Other South American	5	0.02
Other Hispanic or Latino	726	2.58

Race*	Population	%
African-American/Black (4,704)	5,114	18.16
Not Hispanic (4,458)	4,738	16.83
Hispanic (246)	376	1.34
American Indian/Alaska Native (120)	366	1.30
Not Hispanic (30)	184	0.65
Hispanic (90)	182	0.65
Apache (2)	6	0.02
Blackfeet (0)	13	0.05
Canadian/French Am. Ind. (1)	1	<0.01
Central American Ind. (1)	12	0.04
Cherokee (5)	47	0.17
Cheyenne (0)	3	0.01
Chickasaw (0)	1	<0.01
Chippewa (0)	8	0.03
Choctaw (1)	15	0.05
Comanche (0)	1	<0.01
Creek (2)	3	0.01
Delaware (0)	1	<0.01
Hopi (1)	1	<0.01
Iroquois (0)	3	0.01
Lumbee (0)	1	<0.01
Mexican American Ind. (34)	41	0.15
Navajo (8)	15	0.05
Pima (0)	4	0.01
Seminole (0)	7	0.02
Sioux (0)	3	0.01
South American Ind. (2)	6	0.02
Spanish American Ind. (1)	1	<0.01
Yaqui (1)	7	0.02
Yuman (1)	4	0.01
Asian (1,057)	1,392	4.94
Not Hispanic (1,025)	1,292	4.59
Hispanic (32)	100	0.36
Burmese (5)	8	0.03
Cambodian (1)	2	0.01
Chinese, ex. Taiwanese (310)	369	1.31
Filipino (247)	313	1.11
Indian (240)	382	1.36
Indonesian (0)	2	0.01
Japanese (66)	98	0.35
Korean (62)	75	0.27
Laotian (5)	7	0.02
Malaysian (0)	1	<0.01
Nepalese (3)	3	0.01
Pakistani (4)	7	0.02
Taiwanese (11)	13	0.05
Thai (2)	2	0.01
Vietnamese (78)	83	0.29
Hawaii Native/Pacific Islander (2,118)	2,386	8.47
Not Hispanic (2,083)	2,310	8.20
Hispanic (35)	76	0.27
Fijian (164)	208	0.74
Guamanian/Chamorro (1)	6	0.02

*Notes: † The Census 2010 population figure is used to calculate the percentages in the Hispanic Origin and Race categories. Ancestry percentages are based on the 2006-2010 American Community Survey population (not shown); ‡ Numbers in parentheses indicate the number of people reporting a single ancestry; * Numbers in parentheses indicate the number of persons reporting this race alone, not in combination with any other race; Please refer to the Explanation of Data for more information.*

Native Hawaiian (18)	37	0.13
Samoan (344)	430	1.53
Tongan (1,406)	1,526	5.42
White (8,104)	8,995	31.95
Not Hispanic (1,754)	2,071	7.36
Hispanic (6,350)	6,924	24.59

East Rancho Dominguez

Place Type: CDP
County: Los Angeles
Population: 15,135†

Ancestry‡	Population	%
African, Sub-Saharan (137)	207	1.52
African (137)	207	1.52
American (138)	138	1.01
English (53)	151	1.11
European (0)	23	0.17
French, ex. Basque (0)	12	0.09
Irish (0)	9	0.07
Italian (22)	217	1.60
Portuguese (26)	26	0.19
Scotch-Irish (0)	80	0.59
Scottish (0)	26	0.19
West Indian, ex. Hispanic (11)	11	0.08
Belizean (11)	11	0.08

Hispanic Origin	Population	%
Hispanic or Latino (of any race)	12,407	81.98
Central American, ex. Mexican	850	5.62
Costa Rican	7	0.05
Guatemalan	234	1.55
Honduran	105	0.69
Nicaraguan	12	0.08
Panamanian	9	0.06
Salvadoran	472	3.12
Other Central American	11	0.07
Cuban	8	0.05
Mexican	10,864	71.78
Puerto Rican	40	0.26
South American	33	0.22
Chilean	3	0.02
Colombian	15	0.10
Ecuadorian	11	0.07
Peruvian	3	0.02
Venezuelan	1	0.01
Other Hispanic or Latino	612	4.04

Race*	Population	%
African-American/Black (2,404)	2,528	16.70
Not Hispanic (2,320)	2,380	15.73
Hispanic (84)	148	0.98
American Indian/Alaska Native (133)	174	1.15
Not Hispanic (11)	35	0.23
Hispanic (122)	139	0.92
Apache (4)	6	0.04
Blackfeet (0)	1	0.01
Cherokee (3)	4	0.03
Choctaw (0)	1	0.01
Comanche (0)	1	0.01
Mexican American Ind. (28)	35	0.23
Navajo (2)	4	0.03
Asian (33)	77	0.51
Not Hispanic (19)	37	0.24
Hispanic (14)	40	0.26
Cambodian (2)	2	0.01
Chinese, ex. Taiwanese (11)	12	0.08
Filipino (6)	13	0.09
Indian (10)	14	0.09
Japanese (0)	6	0.04
Korean (0)	5	0.03
Thai (1)	2	0.01
Vietnamese (0)	2	0.01
Hawaii Native/Pacific Islander (109)	133	0.88
Not Hispanic (105)	122	0.81
Hispanic (4)	11	0.07
Guamanian/Chamorro (4)	8	0.05
Native Hawaiian (2)	7	0.05
Samoan (85)	106	0.70
Tongan (8)	13	0.09
White (4,774)	5,196	34.33
Not Hispanic (174)	218	1.44
Hispanic (4,600)	4,978	32.89

East San Gabriel

Place Type: CDP
County: Los Angeles
Population: 14,874†

Ancestry‡	Population	%
African, Sub-Saharan (15)	15	0.10
Sudanese (15)	15	0.10
American (149)	149	0.98
Arab (119)	131	0.87
Egyptian (8)	14	0.09
Jordanian (22)	22	0.15
Lebanese (60)	60	0.40
Syrian (15)	15	0.10
Other Arab (14)	20	0.13
Armenian (89)	104	0.69
Austrian (9)	38	0.25
Basque (12)	12	0.08
Belgian (16)	16	0.11
Brazilian (0)	22	0.15
British (34)	49	0.32
Canadian (15)	44	0.29
Czech (0)	27	0.18
Czechoslovakian (12)	12	0.08
Danish (0)	11	0.07
Dutch (9)	48	0.32
Eastern European (19)	19	0.13
English (353)	808	5.34
European (57)	68	0.45
French, ex. Basque (19)	128	0.85
French Canadian (20)	20	0.13
German (161)	818	5.41
Greek (27)	42	0.28
Hungarian (9)	33	0.22
Icelander (0)	32	0.21
Iranian (19)	65	0.43
Irish (100)	692	4.57
Italian (257)	521	3.44
Northern European (11)	11	0.07
Norwegian (11)	115	0.76
Polish (39)	179	1.18
Portuguese (69)	83	0.55
Russian (44)	134	0.89
Scotch-Irish (34)	119	0.79
Scottish (34)	89	0.59
Slovak (0)	9	0.06
Swedish (26)	56	0.37
Swiss (10)	64	0.42
Turkish (11)	11	0.07
Ukrainian (36)	48	0.32
Welsh (15)	36	0.24

Hispanic Origin	Population	%
Hispanic or Latino (of any race)	3,700	24.88
Central American, ex. Mexican	314	2.11
Costa Rican	13	0.09
Guatemalan	88	0.59
Honduran	22	0.15
Nicaraguan	53	0.36
Panamanian	17	0.11
Salvadoran	121	0.81
Cuban	61	0.41
Dominican Republic	1	0.01
Mexican	2,930	19.70
Puerto Rican	45	0.30
South American	160	1.08
Argentinean	39	0.26
Chilean	10	0.07
Colombian	40	0.27
Ecuadorian	25	0.17
Paraguayan	2	0.01
Peruvian	38	0.26
Venezuelan	3	0.02
Other South American	3	0.02
Other Hispanic or Latino	189	1.27

Race*	Population	%
African-American/Black (243)	284	1.91
Not Hispanic (216)	246	1.65
Hispanic (27)	38	0.26
American Indian/Alaska Native (58)	137	0.92
Not Hispanic (16)	52	0.35
Hispanic (42)	85	0.57
Alaska Athabascan *(Ala. Nat.)* (1)	1	0.01
Apache (1)	3	0.02
Arapaho (0)	1	0.01
Blackfeet (0)	1	0.01
Cherokee (0)	23	0.15
Choctaw (0)	1	0.01
Mexican American Ind. (6)	12	0.08
Navajo (3)	6	0.04
Pima (0)	1	0.01
Pueblo (1)	4	0.03
South American Ind. (1)	2	0.01
Asian (7,421)	7,739	52.03
Not Hispanic (7,372)	7,610	51.16
Hispanic (49)	129	0.87
Bangladeshi (14)	14	0.09
Burmese (33)	40	0.27
Cambodian (22)	37	0.25
Chinese, ex. Taiwanese (4,593)	4,965	33.38
Filipino (288)	369	2.48
Indian (152)	177	1.19
Indonesian (98)	118	0.79
Japanese (366)	448	3.01
Korean (273)	319	2.14
Laotian (5)	10	0.07
Malaysian (7)	10	0.07
Pakistani (19)	24	0.16
Sri Lankan (18)	25	0.17
Taiwanese (733)	809	5.44
Thai (65)	75	0.50
Vietnamese (419)	536	3.60
Hawaii Native/Pacific Islander (3)	44	0.30
Not Hispanic (3)	42	0.28
Hispanic (0)	2	0.01
Guamanian/Chamorro (0)	1	0.01
Native Hawaiian (3)	11	0.07
White (5,037)	5,434	36.53
Not Hispanic (3,251)	3,488	23.45
Hispanic (1,786)	1,946	13.08

Eastvale

Place Type: CDP
County: Riverside
Population: 53,668†

Ancestry‡	Population	%
African, Sub-Saharan (791)	811	1.65
African (197)	217	0.44
Ethiopian (29)	29	0.06
Nigerian (565)	565	1.15
American (1,166)	1,166	2.37
Arab (327)	403	0.82
Egyptian (261)	308	0.63
Lebanese (18)	47	0.10
Other Arab (48)	48	0.10
Armenian (48)	85	0.17
Austrian (0)	97	0.20
Belgian (0)	12	0.02
Brazilian (0)	27	0.05
British (38)	68	0.14
Canadian (90)	162	0.33
Croatian (0)	10	0.02
Czech (0)	17	0.03
Czechoslovakian (10)	33	0.07
Danish (11)	148	0.30
Dutch (156)	460	0.94
Eastern European (21)	21	0.04
English (250)	1,608	3.27
European (367)	560	1.14
Finnish (0)	9	0.02
French, ex. Basque (73)	837	1.70

*Notes: † The Census 2010 population figure is used to calculate the percentages in the Hispanic Origin and Race categories. Ancestry percentages are based on the 2006-2010 American Community Survey population (not shown); ‡ Numbers in parentheses indicate the number of people reporting a single ancestry; * Numbers in parentheses indicate the number of persons reporting this race alone, not in combination with any other race; Please refer to the Explanation of Data for more information.*

French Canadian (28)	173	0.35
German (841)	3,555	7.24
Greek (20)	30	0.06
Hungarian (69)	152	0.31
Iranian (105)	116	0.24
Irish (564)	2,485	5.06
Italian (383)	1,433	2.92
Latvian (0)	6	0.01
Northern European (63)	63	0.13
Norwegian (113)	292	0.59
Polish (53)	280	0.57
Portuguese (182)	344	0.70
Romanian (88)	88	0.18
Russian (62)	161	0.33
Scandinavian (45)	87	0.18
Scotch-Irish (51)	212	0.43
Scottish (8)	359	0.73
Swedish (52)	154	0.31
Swiss (12)	56	0.11
Ukrainian (36)	57	0.12
Welsh (0)	115	0.23
West Indian, ex. Hispanic (62)	62	0.13
British West Indian (24)	24	0.05
Jamaican (19)	19	0.04
West Indian (19)	19	0.04
Yugoslavian (13)	163	0.33

Hispanic Origin	Population	%
Hispanic or Latino (of any race)	21,445	39.96
Central American, ex. Mexican	1,198	2.23
Costa Rican	53	0.10
Guatemalan	311	0.58
Honduran	69	0.13
Nicaraguan	149	0.28
Panamanian	43	0.08
Salvadoran	561	1.05
Other Central American	12	0.02
Cuban	277	0.52
Dominican Republic	10	0.02
Mexican	17,575	32.75
Puerto Rican	356	0.66
South American	739	1.38
Argentinean	76	0.14
Bolivian	44	0.08
Chilean	43	0.08
Colombian	200	0.37
Ecuadorian	145	0.27
Peruvian	199	0.37
Uruguayan	12	0.02
Venezuelan	16	0.03
Other South American	4	0.01
Other Hispanic or Latino	1,290	2.40

Race*	Population	%
African-American/Black (5,190)	5,892	10.98
Not Hispanic (4,914)	5,411	10.08
Hispanic (276)	481	0.90
American Indian/Alaska Native (290)	650	1.21
Not Hispanic (102)	321	0.60
Hispanic (188)	329	0.61
Aleut *(Alaska Native)* (3)	3	0.01
Apache (10)	32	0.06
Arapaho (2)	2	<0.01
Blackfeet (1)	16	0.03
Canadian/French Am. Ind. (0)	2	<0.01
Central American Ind. (0)	1	<0.01
Cherokee (15)	85	0.16
Chickasaw (7)	21	0.04
Chippewa (5)	9	0.02
Choctaw (7)	19	0.04
Comanche (1)	1	<0.01
Delaware (0)	4	0.01
Hopi (0)	2	<0.01
Iroquois (2)	7	0.01
Mexican American Ind. (25)	37	0.07
Navajo (6)	16	0.03
Pima (0)	1	<0.01
Potawatomi (4)	4	0.01
Pueblo (5)	17	0.03
Seminole (1)	2	<0.01
Sioux (0)	3	0.01
South American Ind. (1)	1	<0.01
Spanish American Ind. (6)	6	0.01
Tlingit-Haida *(Alaska Native)* (0)	1	<0.01
Tohono O'Odham (3)	3	0.01
Asian (13,003)	14,244	26.54
Not Hispanic (12,770)	13,719	25.56
Hispanic (233)	525	0.98
Bangladeshi (19)	23	0.04
Burmese (9)	10	0.02
Cambodian (291)	367	0.68
Chinese, ex. Taiwanese (3,158)	3,625	6.75
Filipino (3,417)	3,973	7.40
Hmong (71)	75	0.14
Indian (1,456)	1,593	2.97
Indonesian (109)	172	0.32
Japanese (128)	334	0.62
Korean (1,108)	1,194	2.22
Laotian (148)	167	0.31
Malaysian (11)	15	0.03
Nepalese (22)	22	0.04
Pakistani (319)	342	0.64
Sri Lankan (39)	42	0.08
Taiwanese (518)	622	1.16
Thai (112)	153	0.29
Vietnamese (1,517)	1,756	3.27
Hawaii Native/Pacific Islander (198)	443	0.83
Not Hispanic (156)	322	0.60
Hispanic (42)	121	0.23
Fijian (4)	5	0.01
Guamanian/Chamorro (31)	52	0.10
Native Hawaiian (13)	75	0.14
Samoan (62)	99	0.18
Tongan (62)	69	0.13
White (22,998)	25,136	46.84
Not Hispanic (12,712)	13,792	25.70
Hispanic (10,286)	11,344	21.14

El Cajon

Place Type: City
County: San Diego
Population: 99,478†

Ancestry‡	Population	%
Afghan (403)	484	0.49
African, Sub-Saharan (330)	459	0.47
African (306)	377	0.38
Cape Verdean (14)	14	0.01
Nigerian (10)	10	0.01
Somalian (0)	48	0.05
Other Sub-Saharan African (0)	10	0.01
American (2,287)	2,287	2.34
Arab (3,598)	4,795	4.90
Arab (386)	560	0.57
Egyptian (37)	37	0.04
Iraqi (2,221)	3,081	3.15
Jordanian (49)	49	0.05
Lebanese (49)	62	0.06
Palestinian (38)	38	0.04
Syrian (10)	10	0.01
Other Arab (808)	958	0.98
Armenian (161)	169	0.17
Assyrian/Chaldean/Syriac (3,849)	4,776	4.88
Australian (13)	24	0.02
Austrian (21)	167	0.17
Basque (21)	21	0.02
Belgian (0)	45	0.05
Brazilian (0)	9	0.01
British (93)	287	0.29
Bulgarian (0)	31	0.03
Canadian (26)	330	0.34
Croatian (20)	57	0.06
Czech (118)	368	0.38
Czechoslovakian (35)	46	0.05
Danish (110)	373	0.38
Dutch (237)	1,371	1.40
Eastern European (22)	22	0.02
English (1,724)	7,754	7.92
European (724)	791	0.81
Finnish (14)	134	0.14
French, ex. Basque (381)	2,749	2.81
French Canadian (284)	433	0.44
German (3,319)	13,339	13.62
Greek (208)	376	0.38
Hungarian (64)	302	0.31
Icelander (0)	56	0.06
Iranian (138)	158	0.16
Irish (2,105)	10,107	10.32
Israeli (9)	22	0.02
Italian (2,033)	5,053	5.16
Latvian (0)	41	0.04
Lithuanian (74)	222	0.23
Luxemburger (12)	12	0.01
Maltese (0)	39	0.04
New Zealander (0)	17	0.02
Northern European (27)	27	0.03
Norwegian (285)	1,066	1.09
Pennsylvania German (15)	47	0.05
Polish (426)	1,672	1.71
Portuguese (151)	427	0.44
Romanian (9)	22	0.02
Russian (297)	812	0.83
Scandinavian (93)	310	0.32
Scotch-Irish (377)	1,493	1.52
Scottish (452)	1,771	1.81
Serbian (13)	13	0.01
Slavic (18)	86	0.09
Slovak (8)	52	0.05
Slovene (26)	26	0.03
Swedish (368)	1,478	1.51
Swiss (7)	150	0.15
Ukrainian (107)	257	0.26
Welsh (150)	634	0.65
West Indian, ex. Hispanic (127)	224	0.23
Belizean (21)	36	0.04
Haitian (17)	94	0.10
Jamaican (7)	7	0.01
West Indian (82)	87	0.09
Yugoslavian (105)	116	0.12

Hispanic Origin	Population	%
Hispanic or Latino (of any race)	28,036	28.18
Central American, ex. Mexican	694	0.70
Costa Rican	54	0.05
Guatemalan	225	0.23
Honduran	51	0.05
Nicaraguan	62	0.06
Panamanian	67	0.07
Salvadoran	219	0.22
Other Central American	16	0.02
Cuban	99	0.10
Dominican Republic	37	0.04
Mexican	24,534	24.66
Puerto Rican	646	0.65
South American	339	0.34
Argentinean	30	0.03
Bolivian	15	0.02
Chilean	44	0.04
Colombian	99	0.10
Ecuadorian	34	0.03
Peruvian	97	0.10
Uruguayan	2	<0.01
Venezuelan	18	0.02
Other Hispanic or Latino	1,687	1.70

Race*	Population	%
African-American/Black (6,306)	8,058	8.10
Not Hispanic (5,939)	7,213	7.25
Hispanic (367)	845	0.85
American Indian/Alaska Native (835)	2,017	2.03
Not Hispanic (455)	1,236	1.24
Hispanic (380)	781	0.79
Alaska Athabascan *(Ala. Nat.)* (1)	2	<0.01
Aleut *(Alaska Native)* (0)	3	<0.01
Apache (27)	61	0.06
Arapaho (2)	8	0.01
Blackfeet (10)	66	0.07
Canadian/French Am. Ind. (2)	13	0.01
Central American Ind. (5)	7	0.01

*Notes: † The Census 2010 population figure is used to calculate the percentages in the Hispanic Origin and Race categories. Ancestry percentages are based on the 2006-2010 American Community Survey population (not shown); ‡ Numbers in parentheses indicate the number of people reporting a single ancestry; * Numbers in parentheses indicate the number of persons reporting this race alone, not in combination with any other race; Please refer to the Explanation of Data for more information.*

Cherokee (61)	306	0.31
Cheyenne (7)	12	0.01
Chickasaw (3)	10	0.01
Chippewa (21)	30	0.03
Choctaw (20)	63	0.06
Comanche (3)	7	0.01
Cree (1)	8	0.01
Creek (1)	24	0.02
Crow (1)	3	<0.01
Delaware (0)	1	<0.01
Hopi (1)	3	<0.01
Inupiat *(Alaska Native)* (0)	1	<0.01
Iroquois (5)	17	0.02
Kiowa (2)	2	<0.01
Lumbee (1)	3	<0.01
Menominee (2)	2	<0.01
Mexican American Ind. (55)	105	0.11
Navajo (14)	34	0.03
Osage (1)	8	0.01
Ottawa (6)	6	0.01
Paiute (2)	2	<0.01
Pima (2)	5	0.01
Potawatomi (0)	2	<0.01
Pueblo (17)	37	0.04
Puget Sound Salish (0)	3	<0.01
Seminole (1)	6	0.01
Shoshone (2)	7	0.01
Sioux (18)	47	0.05
South American Ind. (3)	6	0.01
Spanish American Ind. (4)	5	0.01
Tohono O'Odham (3)	8	0.01
Yakama (1)	3	<0.01
Yaqui (23)	45	0.05
Yuman (7)	8	0.01
Asian (3,561)	6,496	6.53
Not Hispanic (3,375)	5,904	5.93
Hispanic (186)	592	0.60
Bhutanese (2)	2	<0.01
Burmese (122)	124	0.12
Cambodian (102)	132	0.13
Chinese, ex. Taiwanese (443)	638	0.64
Filipino (1,740)	2,678	2.69
Hmong (7)	10	0.01
Indian (119)	229	0.23
Indonesian (27)	39	0.04
Japanese (193)	536	0.54
Korean (88)	180	0.18
Laotian (28)	41	0.04
Malaysian (2)	2	<0.01
Pakistani (32)	36	0.04
Sri Lankan (6)	15	0.02
Taiwanese (10)	12	0.01
Thai (43)	73	0.07
Vietnamese (412)	520	0.52
Hawaii Native/Pacific Islander (495)	1,210	1.22
Not Hispanic (440)	978	0.98
Hispanic (55)	232	0.23
Fijian (1)	3	<0.01
Guamanian/Chamorro (230)	404	0.41
Native Hawaiian (72)	258	0.26
Samoan (120)	227	0.23
Tongan (4)	13	0.01
White (68,897)	74,773	75.17
Not Hispanic (56,462)	60,466	60.78
Hispanic (12,435)	14,307	14.38

El Centro

Place Type: City
County: Imperial
Population: 42,598†

Ancestry‡	Population	%
African, Sub-Saharan (21)	44	0.11
African (21)	44	0.11
American (563)	563	1.35
Arab (104)	109	0.26
Lebanese (19)	24	0.06
Syrian (85)	85	0.20
Basque (0)	75	0.18
British (44)	93	0.22
Canadian (4)	38	0.09
Croatian (11)	11	0.03
Czech (0)	23	0.06
Danish (10)	28	0.07
Dutch (29)	167	0.40
Eastern European (9)	9	0.02
English (580)	1,286	3.09
European (63)	116	0.28
Finnish (0)	9	0.02
French, ex. Basque (8)	308	0.74
French Canadian (6)	6	0.01
German (559)	1,671	4.02
Greek (9)	16	0.04
Hungarian (0)	96	0.23
Irish (375)	1,221	2.94
Italian (277)	1,000	2.40
Latvian (0)	40	0.10
Northern European (18)	18	0.04
Norwegian (65)	166	0.40
Polish (161)	328	0.79
Portuguese (4)	9	0.02
Russian (20)	67	0.16
Scandinavian (49)	49	0.12
Scotch-Irish (34)	146	0.35
Scottish (63)	208	0.50
Slavic (8)	8	0.02
Slovak (0)	11	0.03
Swedish (52)	98	0.24
Swiss (16)	111	0.27
Ukrainian (0)	51	0.12
Welsh (0)	193	0.46
West Indian, ex. Hispanic (0)	6	0.01
Dutch West Indian (0)	6	0.01
Yugoslavian (8)	8	0.02

Hispanic Origin	Population	%
Hispanic or Latino (of any race)	34,751	81.58
Central American, ex. Mexican	143	0.34
Costa Rican	5	0.01
Guatemalan	14	0.03
Honduran	7	0.02
Nicaraguan	30	0.07
Panamanian	6	0.01
Salvadoran	76	0.18
Other Central American	5	0.01
Cuban	32	0.08
Dominican Republic	12	0.03
Mexican	33,206	77.95
Puerto Rican	138	0.32
South American	73	0.17
Argentinean	11	0.03
Bolivian	2	<0.01
Chilean	5	0.01
Colombian	21	0.05
Ecuadorian	10	0.02
Paraguayan	1	<0.01
Peruvian	22	0.05
Other South American	1	<0.01
Other Hispanic or Latino	1,147	2.69

Race*	Population	%
African-American/Black (1,081)	1,324	3.11
Not Hispanic (864)	966	2.27
Hispanic (217)	358	0.84
American Indian/Alaska Native (554)	783	1.84
Not Hispanic (95)	165	0.39
Hispanic (459)	618	1.45
Apache (8)	15	0.04
Blackfeet (7)	12	0.03
Central American Ind. (4)	5	0.01
Cherokee (12)	33	0.08
Chickasaw (3)	3	0.01
Choctaw (8)	17	0.04
Creek (1)	1	<0.01
Hopi (0)	1	<0.01
Mexican American Ind. (71)	104	0.24
Navajo (6)	18	0.04
Osage (0)	1	<0.01
Pima (5)	5	0.01
Pueblo (2)	2	<0.01
Sioux (1)	6	0.01
South American Ind. (0)	3	0.01
Spanish American Ind. (1)	4	0.01
Tohono O'Odham (4)	4	0.01
Yaqui (18)	41	0.10
Yuman (8)	12	0.03
Asian (965)	1,290	3.03
Not Hispanic (785)	911	2.14
Hispanic (180)	379	0.89
Cambodian (22)	23	0.05
Chinese, ex. Taiwanese (169)	222	0.52
Filipino (295)	458	1.08
Hmong (1)	1	<0.01
Indian (156)	215	0.50
Japanese (39)	64	0.15
Korean (180)	200	0.47
Laotian (3)	4	0.01
Pakistani (4)	4	0.01
Sri Lankan (2)	2	<0.01
Taiwanese (3)	7	0.02
Thai (1)	3	0.01
Vietnamese (68)	78	0.18
Hawaii Native/Pacific Islander (34)	89	0.21
Not Hispanic (19)	38	0.09
Hispanic (15)	51	0.12
Fijian (1)	1	<0.01
Guamanian/Chamorro (8)	11	0.03
Native Hawaiian (5)	20	0.05
Samoan (11)	24	0.06
Tongan (1)	1	<0.01
White (25,376)	27,311	64.11
Not Hispanic (5,758)	5,977	14.03
Hispanic (19,618)	21,334	50.08

El Cerrito

Place Type: City
County: Contra Costa
Population: 23,549†

Ancestry‡	Population	%
Afghan (9)	9	0.04
African, Sub-Saharan (165)	187	0.80
African (37)	50	0.21
Ethiopian (21)	21	0.09
Nigerian (85)	94	0.40
Other Sub-Saharan African (22)	22	0.09
American (390)	390	1.67
Arab (118)	151	0.65
Arab (27)	27	0.12
Egyptian (10)	10	0.04
Lebanese (0)	33	0.14
Other Arab (81)	81	0.35
Armenian (67)	83	0.36
Assyrian/Chaldean/Syriac (0)	6	0.03
Australian (8)	8	0.03
Austrian (9)	65	0.28
Belgian (11)	11	0.05
Brazilian (69)	108	0.46
British (148)	230	0.99
Bulgarian (21)	21	0.09
Canadian (6)	61	0.26
Croatian (12)	19	0.08
Czech (0)	39	0.17
Czechoslovakian (16)	22	0.09
Danish (70)	183	0.78
Dutch (53)	284	1.22
Eastern European (149)	149	0.64
English (356)	2,069	8.87
Estonian (7)	20	0.09
European (689)	823	3.53
Finnish (4)	40	0.17
French, ex. Basque (56)	673	2.89
French Canadian (18)	72	0.31
German (495)	2,510	10.76
Greek (18)	48	0.21
Hungarian (56)	143	0.61
Icelander (0)	9	0.04
Iranian (409)	409	1.75

*Notes: † The Census 2010 population figure is used to calculate the percentages in the Hispanic Origin and Race categories. Ancestry percentages are based on the 2006-2010 American Community Survey population (not shown); ‡ Numbers in parentheses indicate the number of people reporting a single ancestry; * Numbers in parentheses indicate the number of persons reporting this race alone, not in combination with any other race; Please refer to the Explanation of Data for more information.*

Ancestry	Population	%
Irish (418)	1,661	7.12
Israeli (12)	34	0.15
Italian (645)	1,323	5.67
Latvian (25)	56	0.24
Lithuanian (24)	98	0.42
Northern European (40)	40	0.17
Norwegian (38)	168	0.72
Polish (149)	476	2.04
Portuguese (111)	325	1.39
Romanian (21)	41	0.18
Russian (96)	386	1.66
Scandinavian (10)	35	0.15
Scotch-Irish (93)	420	1.80
Scottish (64)	571	2.45
Serbian (11)	11	0.05
Slavic (9)	9	0.04
Slovak (0)	7	0.03
Slovene (0)	10	0.04
Swedish (42)	385	1.65
Swiss (30)	149	0.64
Turkish (77)	77	0.33
Ukrainian (97)	192	0.82
Welsh (5)	142	0.61
West Indian, ex. Hispanic (49)	113	0.48
Jamaican (36)	57	0.24
Trinidadian/Tobagonian (13)	13	0.06
West Indian (0)	22	0.09
Other West Indian (0)	21	0.09
Yugoslavian (19)	25	0.11

Hispanic Origin	Population	%
Hispanic or Latino (of any race)	2,621	11.13
Central American, ex. Mexican	313	1.33
Costa Rican	10	0.04
Guatemalan	63	0.27
Honduran	21	0.09
Nicaraguan	68	0.29
Panamanian	11	0.05
Salvadoran	139	0.59
Other Central American	1	<0.01
Cuban	50	0.21
Dominican Republic	6	0.03
Mexican	1,482	6.29
Puerto Rican	89	0.38
South American	445	1.89
Argentinean	72	0.31
Bolivian	11	0.05
Chilean	62	0.26
Colombian	36	0.15
Ecuadorian	29	0.12
Paraguayan	5	0.02
Peruvian	204	0.87
Uruguayan	7	0.03
Venezuelan	18	0.08
Other South American	1	<0.01
Other Hispanic or Latino	236	1.00

Race*	Population	%
African-American/Black (1,819)	2,246	9.54
Not Hispanic (1,773)	2,133	9.06
Hispanic (46)	113	0.48
American Indian/Alaska Native (107)	359	1.52
Not Hispanic (66)	243	1.03
Hispanic (41)	116	0.49
Apache (3)	8	0.03
Blackfeet (0)	7	0.03
Canadian/French Am. Ind. (0)	1	<0.01
Cherokee (8)	54	0.23
Chickasaw (2)	2	0.01
Chippewa (2)	4	0.02
Choctaw (1)	15	0.06
Creek (0)	1	<0.01
Crow (0)	1	<0.01
Delaware (0)	2	0.01
Iroquois (1)	6	0.03
Menominee (1)	1	<0.01
Mexican American Ind. (15)	27	0.11
Navajo (1)	1	<0.01
Osage (0)	3	0.01
Paiute (1)	1	<0.01
Pueblo (3)	5	0.02
Seminole (2)	11	0.05
Shoshone (3)	4	0.02
Sioux (2)	7	0.03
South American Ind. (8)	17	0.07
Spanish American Ind. (3)	4	0.02
Tlingit-Haida *(Alaska Native)* (1)	1	<0.01
Tsimshian *(Alaska Native)* (1)	1	<0.01
Ute (1)	3	0.01
Asian (6,439)	7,357	31.24
Not Hispanic (6,389)	7,198	30.57
Hispanic (50)	159	0.68
Bangladeshi (15)	16	0.07
Bhutanese (1)	3	0.01
Burmese (12)	14	0.06
Cambodian (28)	38	0.16
Chinese, ex. Taiwanese (2,886)	3,309	14.05
Filipino (501)	747	3.17
Hmong (15)	15	0.06
Indian (430)	522	2.22
Indonesian (26)	39	0.17
Japanese (923)	1,247	5.30
Korean (310)	387	1.64
Laotian (52)	72	0.31
Malaysian (7)	14	0.06
Nepalese (209)	222	0.94
Pakistani (155)	161	0.68
Sri Lankan (20)	22	0.09
Taiwanese (232)	287	1.22
Thai (102)	131	0.56
Vietnamese (140)	195	0.83
Hawaii Native/Pacific Islander (37)	129	0.55
Not Hispanic (36)	119	0.51
Hispanic (1)	10	0.04
Fijian (16)	26	0.11
Guamanian/Chamorro (6)	19	0.08
Native Hawaiian (12)	44	0.19
Samoan (2)	11	0.05
Tongan (0)	3	0.01
White (12,543)	13,814	58.66
Not Hispanic (11,364)	12,363	52.50
Hispanic (1,179)	1,451	6.16

El Dorado Hills

Place Type: CDP
County: El Dorado
Population: 42,108†

Ancestry‡	Population	%
African, Sub-Saharan (78)	190	0.44
African (64)	159	0.37
Nigerian (0)	17	0.04
South African (14)	14	0.03
American (1,438)	1,438	3.33
Arab (117)	336	0.78
Arab (0)	21	0.05
Egyptian (0)	9	0.02
Lebanese (87)	162	0.38
Syrian (0)	27	0.06
Other Arab (30)	117	0.27
Armenian (95)	155	0.36
Assyrian/Chaldean/Syriac (25)	25	0.06
Australian (14)	14	0.03
Austrian (35)	110	0.25
Basque (0)	159	0.37
Belgian (16)	47	0.11
Brazilian (26)	26	0.06
British (177)	455	1.05
Bulgarian (127)	148	0.34
Canadian (103)	177	0.41
Celtic (13)	13	0.03
Croatian (81)	173	0.40
Czech (20)	120	0.28
Czechoslovakian (0)	39	0.09
Danish (82)	589	1.36
Dutch (134)	651	1.51
Eastern European (47)	47	0.11
English (1,836)	6,438	14.91
European (655)	809	1.87
Finnish (9)	172	0.40
French, ex. Basque (170)	1,331	3.08
French Canadian (114)	316	0.73
German (2,087)	8,547	19.79
Greek (162)	420	0.97
Hungarian (154)	343	0.79
Icelander (0)	30	0.07
Iranian (609)	609	1.41
Irish (1,299)	5,783	13.39
Israeli (0)	15	0.03
Italian (1,254)	3,998	9.26
Latvian (0)	21	0.05
Macedonian (0)	4	0.01
New Zealander (0)	51	0.12
Northern European (78)	104	0.24
Norwegian (303)	1,174	2.72
Polish (257)	1,054	2.44
Portuguese (228)	745	1.73
Romanian (70)	122	0.28
Russian (179)	727	1.68
Scandinavian (77)	212	0.49
Scotch-Irish (294)	812	1.88
Scottish (364)	1,709	3.96
Slavic (0)	9	0.02
Slovak (0)	18	0.04
Slovene (20)	20	0.05
Swedish (335)	1,423	3.30
Swiss (141)	466	1.08
Turkish (78)	82	0.19
Ukrainian (80)	243	0.56
Welsh (124)	631	1.46
Yugoslavian (21)	48	0.11

Hispanic Origin	Population	%
Hispanic or Latino (of any race)	3,802	9.03
Central American, ex. Mexican	240	0.57
Costa Rican	15	0.04
Guatemalan	21	0.05
Honduran	11	0.03
Nicaraguan	51	0.12
Panamanian	29	0.07
Salvadoran	113	0.27
Cuban	64	0.15
Dominican Republic	10	0.02
Mexican	2,507	5.95
Puerto Rican	177	0.42
South American	193	0.46
Argentinean	33	0.08
Bolivian	12	0.03
Chilean	13	0.03
Colombian	69	0.16
Ecuadorian	13	0.03
Paraguayan	2	<0.01
Peruvian	29	0.07
Uruguayan	1	<0.01
Venezuelan	8	0.02
Other South American	13	0.03
Other Hispanic or Latino	611	1.45

Race*	Population	%
African-American/Black (615)	827	1.96
Not Hispanic (593)	772	1.83
Hispanic (22)	55	0.13
American Indian/Alaska Native (196)	557	1.32
Not Hispanic (145)	407	0.97
Hispanic (51)	150	0.36
Apache (3)	6	0.01
Blackfeet (4)	10	0.02
Cherokee (32)	118	0.28
Cheyenne (0)	1	<0.01
Chickasaw (0)	4	0.01
Chippewa (1)	9	0.02
Choctaw (12)	33	0.08
Creek (0)	5	0.01
Crow (1)	2	<0.01
Delaware (0)	2	<0.01
Inupiat *(Alaska Native)* (2)	4	0.01
Iroquois (2)	13	0.03
Mexican American Ind. (13)	23	0.05
Navajo (2)	11	0.03

*Notes: † The Census 2010 population figure is used to calculate the percentages in the Hispanic Origin and Race categories. Ancestry percentages are based on the 2006-2010 American Community Survey population (not shown); ‡ Numbers in parentheses indicate the number of people reporting a single ancestry; * Numbers in parentheses indicate the number of persons reporting this race alone, not in combination with any other race; Please refer to the Explanation of Data for more information.*

Osage (0)	3	0.01
Ottawa (1)	1	<0.01
Paiute (0)	3	0.01
Potawatomi (4)	6	0.01
Pueblo (9)	11	0.03
Shoshone (2)	5	0.01
Sioux (1)	13	0.03
South American Ind. (2)	2	<0.01
Spanish American Ind. (2)	4	0.01
Ute (0)	3	0.01
Yaqui (1)	4	0.01
Asian (3,563)	4,676	11.10
Not Hispanic (3,492)	4,460	10.59
Hispanic (71)	216	0.51
Bangladeshi (15)	15	0.04
Burmese (11)	12	0.03
Cambodian (24)	32	0.08
Chinese, ex. Taiwanese (704)	951	2.26
Filipino (838)	1,240	2.94
Hmong (40)	44	0.10
Indian (787)	856	2.03
Indonesian (14)	34	0.08
Japanese (207)	491	1.17
Korean (387)	521	1.24
Laotian (2)	8	0.02
Malaysian (1)	2	<0.01
Nepalese (1)	2	<0.01
Pakistani (53)	56	0.13
Sri Lankan (6)	6	0.01
Taiwanese (37)	37	0.09
Thai (15)	29	0.07
Vietnamese (291)	358	0.85
Hawaii Native/Pacific Islander (71)	230	0.55
Not Hispanic (67)	196	0.47
Hispanic (4)	34	0.08
Fijian (7)	8	0.02
Guamanian/Chamorro (20)	46	0.11
Native Hawaiian (23)	101	0.24
Samoan (4)	13	0.03
Tongan (6)	8	0.02
White (35,089)	36,859	87.53
Not Hispanic (32,481)	33,843	80.37
Hispanic (2,608)	3,016	7.16

El Monte

Place Type: City
County: Los Angeles
Population: 113,475†

Ancestry‡	Population	%
African, Sub-Saharan (120)	132	0.12
African (29)	41	0.04
Ethiopian (36)	36	0.03
Nigerian (55)	55	0.05
American (547)	547	0.48
Arab (22)	22	0.02
Egyptian (10)	10	0.01
Lebanese (12)	12	0.01
Armenian (8)	34	0.03
Austrian (0)	5	<0.01
Basque (0)	19	0.02
Brazilian (21)	21	0.02
British (0)	6	0.01
Bulgarian (11)	26	0.02
Canadian (5)	5	<0.01
Czech (7)	27	0.02
Czechoslovakian (13)	13	0.01
Danish (0)	39	0.03
Dutch (20)	251	0.22
English (240)	708	0.62
European (110)	115	0.10
Finnish (0)	51	0.04
French, ex. Basque (94)	336	0.30
French Canadian (18)	18	0.02
German (297)	1,228	1.08
Greek (0)	23	0.02
Hungarian (13)	22	0.02
Iranian (11)	11	0.01
Irish (236)	826	0.73
Italian (160)	539	0.47
Lithuanian (17)	60	0.05
Norwegian (45)	92	0.08
Polish (13)	43	0.04
Portuguese (34)	34	0.03
Russian (48)	76	0.07
Scandinavian (7)	17	0.01
Scotch-Irish (51)	137	0.12
Scottish (0)	37	0.03
Swedish (24)	194	0.17
Swiss (0)	23	0.02
West Indian, ex. Hispanic (37)	59	0.05
Belizean (25)	25	0.02
Jamaican (12)	34	0.03

Hispanic Origin	Population	%
Hispanic or Latino (of any race)	78,317	69.02
Central American, ex. Mexican	4,961	4.37
Costa Rican	67	0.06
Guatemalan	1,393	1.23
Honduran	388	0.34
Nicaraguan	450	0.40
Panamanian	31	0.03
Salvadoran	2,570	2.26
Other Central American	62	0.05
Cuban	350	0.31
Dominican Republic	8	0.01
Mexican	69,053	60.85
Puerto Rican	232	0.20
South American	565	0.50
Argentinean	103	0.09
Bolivian	9	0.01
Chilean	17	0.01
Colombian	93	0.08
Ecuadorian	102	0.09
Paraguayan	1	<0.01
Peruvian	209	0.18
Uruguayan	12	0.01
Venezuelan	7	0.01
Other South American	12	0.01
Other Hispanic or Latino	3,148	2.77

Race*	Population	%
African-American/Black (870)	1,178	1.04
Not Hispanic (502)	582	0.51
Hispanic (368)	596	0.53
American Indian/Alaska Native (1,083)	1,569	1.38
Not Hispanic (133)	272	0.24
Hispanic (950)	1,297	1.14
Aleut *(Alaska Native)* (1)	1	<0.01
Apache (29)	61	0.05
Arapaho (1)	1	<0.01
Blackfeet (2)	2	<0.01
Central American Ind. (16)	29	0.03
Cherokee (10)	52	0.05
Cheyenne (10)	10	0.01
Chickasaw (0)	4	<0.01
Chippewa (4)	7	0.01
Choctaw (2)	6	0.01
Creek (3)	6	0.01
Hopi (4)	6	0.01
Iroquois (1)	5	<0.01
Mexican American Ind. (200)	277	0.24
Navajo (9)	19	0.02
Osage (1)	1	<0.01
Paiute (2)	3	<0.01
Pima (7)	7	0.01
Potawatomi (1)	1	<0.01
Pueblo (2)	11	0.01
Seminole (0)	3	<0.01
Sioux (5)	10	0.01
South American Ind. (3)	5	<0.01
Spanish American Ind. (19)	27	0.02
Tohono O'Odham (5)	7	0.01
Yaqui (31)	55	0.05
Yuman (5)	10	0.01
Asian (28,503)	29,188	25.72
Not Hispanic (28,264)	28,605	25.21
Hispanic (239)	583	0.51
Bangladeshi (1)	11	0.01
Burmese (225)	241	0.21
Cambodian (481)	632	0.56
Chinese, ex. Taiwanese (14,665)	16,151	14.23
Filipino (1,384)	1,565	1.38
Hmong (0)	1	<0.01
Indian (184)	282	0.25
Indonesian (113)	135	0.12
Japanese (210)	320	0.28
Korean (199)	236	0.21
Laotian (40)	65	0.06
Malaysian (24)	42	0.04
Nepalese (24)	24	0.02
Pakistani (14)	18	0.02
Sri Lankan (12)	16	0.01
Taiwanese (730)	816	0.72
Thai (201)	230	0.20
Vietnamese (8,433)	9,667	8.52
Hawaii Native/Pacific Islander (131)	282	0.25
Not Hispanic (84)	153	0.13
Hispanic (47)	129	0.11
Fijian (0)	1	<0.01
Guamanian/Chamorro (21)	30	0.03
Native Hawaiian (39)	78	0.07
Samoan (37)	59	0.05
Tongan (5)	7	0.01
White (44,058)	47,011	41.43
Not Hispanic (5,556)	5,890	5.19
Hispanic (38,502)	41,121	36.24

El Paso de Robles (Paso Robles)

Place Type: City
County: San Luis Obispo
Population: 29,793†

Ancestry‡	Population	%
African, Sub-Saharan (22)	22	0.08
African (22)	22	0.08
American (650)	650	2.26
Arab (0)	9	0.03
Egyptian (0)	9	0.03
Armenian (12)	39	0.14
Assyrian/Chaldean/Syriac (0)	12	0.04
Australian (47)	47	0.16
Austrian (27)	48	0.17
Basque (10)	33	0.11
Belgian (0)	11	0.04
British (83)	198	0.69
Cajun (0)	13	0.05
Canadian (71)	148	0.51
Croatian (0)	12	0.04
Czech (53)	129	0.45
Czechoslovakian (11)	11	0.04
Danish (67)	410	1.42
Dutch (298)	665	2.31
English (858)	3,307	11.49
European (547)	731	2.54
Finnish (0)	25	0.09
French, ex. Basque (139)	1,100	3.82
French Canadian (31)	106	0.37
German (1,106)	4,309	14.96
German Russian (0)	4	0.01
Greek (33)	140	0.49
Hungarian (25)	174	0.60
Icelander (8)	8	0.03
Irish (539)	3,184	11.06
Italian (573)	1,333	4.63
Lithuanian (8)	87	0.30
Maltese (0)	7	0.02
Northern European (13)	13	0.05
Norwegian (92)	377	1.31
Pennsylvania German (29)	29	0.10
Polish (80)	228	0.79
Portuguese (138)	382	1.33
Russian (120)	319	1.11
Scandinavian (24)	32	0.11
Scotch-Irish (335)	710	2.47
Scottish (256)	790	2.74

*Notes: † The Census 2010 population figure is used to calculate the percentages in the Hispanic Origin and Race categories. Ancestry percentages are based on the 2006-2010 American Community Survey population (not shown); ‡ Numbers in parentheses indicate the number of people reporting a single ancestry; * Numbers in parentheses indicate the number of persons reporting this race alone, not in combination with any other race; Please refer to the Explanation of Data for more information.*

Slavic (41)	56	0.19
Slovak (38)	38	0.13
Swedish (104)	476	1.65
Swiss (29)	177	0.61
Ukrainian (37)	37	0.13
Welsh (25)	143	0.50
West Indian, ex. Hispanic (9)	99	0.34
Dutch West Indian (0)	16	0.06
Haitian (0)	20	0.07
Jamaican (9)	63	0.22
Yugoslavian (0)	8	0.03

Hispanic Origin	Population	%
Hispanic or Latino (of any race)	10,275	34.49
Central American, ex. Mexican	217	0.73
Costa Rican	13	0.04
Guatemalan	37	0.12
Honduran	21	0.07
Nicaraguan	32	0.11
Panamanian	9	0.03
Salvadoran	99	0.33
Other Central American	6	0.02
Cuban	20	0.07
Dominican Republic	3	0.01
Mexican	9,131	30.65
Puerto Rican	109	0.37
South American	90	0.30
Argentinean	14	0.05
Bolivian	3	0.01
Chilean	11	0.04
Colombian	29	0.10
Ecuadorian	6	0.02
Peruvian	25	0.08
Other South American	2	0.01
Other Hispanic or Latino	705	2.37

Race*	Population	%
African-American/Black (622)	896	3.01
Not Hispanic (529)	715	2.40
Hispanic (93)	181	0.61
American Indian/Alaska Native (297)	653	2.19
Not Hispanic (150)	367	1.23
Hispanic (147)	286	0.96
Alaska Athabascan *(Ala. Nat.)* (0)	1	<0.01
Apache (7)	20	0.07
Blackfeet (4)	18	0.06
Cherokee (25)	106	0.36
Cheyenne (0)	1	<0.01
Chickasaw (1)	3	0.01
Chippewa (5)	8	0.03
Choctaw (10)	30	0.10
Comanche (2)	3	0.01
Cree (0)	3	0.01
Creek (3)	8	0.03
Delaware (0)	1	<0.01
Hopi (0)	2	0.01
Iroquois (0)	11	0.04
Menominee (1)	1	<0.01
Mexican American Ind. (26)	32	0.11
Navajo (8)	14	0.05
Osage (2)	2	0.01
Ottawa (0)	1	<0.01
Paiute (6)	6	0.02
Potawatomi (4)	4	0.01
Pueblo (3)	9	0.03
Seminole (2)	4	0.01
Shoshone (1)	1	<0.01
Sioux (7)	15	0.05
South American Ind. (1)	6	0.02
Spanish American Ind. (0)	2	0.01
Tlingit-Haida *(Alaska Native)* (0)	3	0.01
Tohono O'Odham (1)	1	<0.01
Yakama (3)	7	0.02
Yaqui (5)	12	0.04
Yuman (1)	1	<0.01
Asian (593)	878	2.95
Not Hispanic (552)	756	2.54
Hispanic (41)	122	0.41
Cambodian (15)	15	0.05
Chinese, ex. Taiwanese (49)	87	0.29
Filipino (195)	325	1.09
Hmong (1)	1	<0.01
Indian (40)	62	0.21
Indonesian (8)	11	0.04
Japanese (56)	113	0.38
Korean (93)	122	0.41
Laotian (3)	4	0.01
Malaysian (2)	2	0.01
Nepalese (1)	4	0.01
Pakistani (12)	15	0.05
Sri Lankan (6)	6	0.02
Taiwanese (2)	2	0.01
Thai (8)	16	0.05
Vietnamese (61)	70	0.23
Hawaii Native/Pacific Islander (56)	126	0.42
Not Hispanic (49)	101	0.34
Hispanic (7)	25	0.08
Fijian (8)	8	0.03
Guamanian/Chamorro (6)	11	0.04
Native Hawaiian (9)	44	0.15
Samoan (9)	21	0.07
Tongan (9)	11	0.04
White (23,158)	24,183	81.17
Not Hispanic (17,605)	18,145	60.90
Hispanic (5,553)	6,038	20.27

El Segundo

Place Type: City
County: Los Angeles
Population: 16,654[†]

Ancestry[‡]	Population	%
African, Sub-Saharan (110)	178	1.08
African (0)	58	0.35
Nigerian (96)	106	0.64
South African (14)	14	0.08
American (1,110)	1,110	6.71
Arab (16)	51	0.31
Arab (0)	8	0.05
Lebanese (16)	16	0.10
Other Arab (0)	27	0.16
Armenian (17)	86	0.52
Assyrian/Chaldean/Syriac (11)	11	0.07
Australian (22)	22	0.13
Austrian (11)	22	0.13
Basque (0)	13	0.08
Belgian (0)	65	0.39
British (96)	261	1.58
Bulgarian (9)	9	0.05
Canadian (49)	153	0.93
Croatian (0)	45	0.27
Czech (33)	53	0.32
Czechoslovakian (25)	40	0.24
Danish (14)	133	0.80
Dutch (53)	212	1.28
Eastern European (59)	59	0.36
English (659)	2,337	14.13
European (412)	564	3.41
Finnish (34)	34	0.21
French, ex. Basque (115)	780	4.72
French Canadian (44)	100	0.60
German (690)	3,067	18.55
Greek (14)	128	0.77
Hungarian (82)	311	1.88
Iranian (10)	10	0.06
Irish (727)	2,391	14.46
Israeli (22)	36	0.22
Italian (447)	1,446	8.75
Lithuanian (0)	61	0.37
Macedonian (22)	22	0.13
Northern European (73)	73	0.44
Norwegian (91)	247	1.49
Polish (140)	404	2.44
Portuguese (40)	102	0.62
Romanian (0)	10	0.06
Russian (109)	222	1.34
Scandinavian (10)	37	0.22
Scotch-Irish (161)	332	2.01
Scottish (91)	406	2.46
Serbian (23)	23	0.14
Slovak (9)	29	0.18
Slovene (13)	13	0.08
Swedish (32)	272	1.65
Swiss (0)	122	0.74
Ukrainian (38)	49	0.30
Welsh (0)	125	0.76
West Indian, ex. Hispanic (13)	86	0.52
Barbadian (13)	28	0.17
West Indian (0)	58	0.35
Yugoslavian (0)	10	0.06

Hispanic Origin	Population	%
Hispanic or Latino (of any race)	2,609	15.67
Central American, ex. Mexican	236	1.42
Costa Rican	30	0.18
Guatemalan	67	0.40
Honduran	8	0.05
Nicaraguan	34	0.20
Panamanian	13	0.08
Salvadoran	82	0.49
Other Central American	2	0.01
Cuban	100	0.60
Dominican Republic	5	0.03
Mexican	1,613	9.69
Puerto Rican	110	0.66
South American	255	1.53
Argentinean	61	0.37
Bolivian	4	0.02
Chilean	30	0.18
Colombian	49	0.29
Ecuadorian	33	0.20
Peruvian	65	0.39
Uruguayan	1	0.01
Venezuelan	8	0.05
Other South American	4	0.02
Other Hispanic or Latino	290	1.74

Race*	Population	%
African-American/Black (337)	491	2.95
Not Hispanic (321)	443	2.66
Hispanic (16)	48	0.29
American Indian/Alaska Native (68)	226	1.36
Not Hispanic (40)	149	0.89
Hispanic (28)	77	0.46
Apache (7)	15	0.09
Arapaho (1)	1	0.01
Blackfeet (1)	9	0.05
Canadian/French Am. Ind. (0)	2	0.01
Cherokee (4)	26	0.16
Chickasaw (3)	4	0.02
Chippewa (1)	2	0.01
Choctaw (3)	13	0.08
Comanche (0)	1	0.01
Iroquois (0)	6	0.04
Mexican American Ind. (1)	11	0.07
Navajo (9)	10	0.06
Osage (0)	4	0.02
Paiute (3)	3	0.02
Pueblo (1)	2	0.01
Shoshone (1)	1	0.01
Sioux (1)	1	0.01
Ute (0)	2	0.01
Yakama (1)	3	0.02
Yaqui (3)	4	0.02
Asian (1,458)	1,986	11.93
Not Hispanic (1,427)	1,885	11.32
Hispanic (31)	101	0.61
Bangladeshi (4)	6	0.04
Burmese (0)	5	0.03
Cambodian (4)	4	0.02
Chinese, ex. Taiwanese (274)	429	2.58
Filipino (255)	395	2.37
Indian (275)	316	1.90
Indonesian (27)	48	0.29
Japanese (229)	416	2.50
Korean (96)	157	0.94
Laotian (1)	1	0.01
Malaysian (5)	8	0.05
Pakistani (60)	63	0.38

*Notes: † The Census 2010 population figure is used to calculate the percentages in the Hispanic Origin and Race categories. Ancestry percentages are based on the 2006-2010 American Community Survey population (not shown); ‡ Numbers in parentheses indicate the number of people reporting a single ancestry; * Numbers in parentheses indicate the number of persons reporting this race alone, not in combination with any other race; Please refer to the Explanation of Data for more information.*

Sri Lankan (17)	20	0.12
Taiwanese (30)	37	0.22
Thai (43)	53	0.32
Vietnamese (53)	89	0.53
Hawaii Native/Pacific Islander (38)	115	0.69
Not Hispanic (30)	95	0.57
Hispanic (8)	20	0.12
Fijian (4)	5	0.03
Guamanian/Chamorro (5)	6	0.04
Native Hawaiian (21)	61	0.37
Samoan (4)	12	0.07
Tongan (2)	6	0.04
White (12,997)	13,858	83.21
Not Hispanic (11,515)	12,105	72.69
Hispanic (1,482)	1,753	10.53

El Sobrante

Place Type: CDP
County: Contra Costa
Population: 12,669†

Ancestry‡	Population	%
African, Sub-Saharan (217)	226	1.68
African (42)	42	0.31
Ghanaian (11)	11	0.08
Nigerian (152)	152	1.13
Other Sub-Saharan African (12)	21	0.16
American (115)	115	0.85
Arab (92)	92	0.68
Arab (14)	14	0.10
Moroccan (25)	25	0.19
Palestinian (17)	17	0.13
Syrian (36)	36	0.27
Armenian (0)	29	0.21
Australian (16)	38	0.28
Austrian (0)	27	0.20
Basque (50)	50	0.37
Belgian (0)	26	0.19
Brazilian (0)	15	0.11
Croatian (0)	24	0.18
Czech (0)	12	0.09
Danish (28)	64	0.47
Dutch (65)	156	1.16
Eastern European (0)	9	0.07
English (182)	782	5.80
European (737)	792	5.87
Finnish (0)	34	0.25
French, ex. Basque (146)	456	3.38
French Canadian (23)	46	0.34
German (566)	1,951	14.46
Greek (0)	11	0.08
Hungarian (9)	88	0.65
Iranian (98)	104	0.77
Irish (238)	1,267	9.39
Italian (332)	734	5.44
Latvian (0)	10	0.07
Lithuanian (20)	30	0.22
Norwegian (111)	207	1.53
Pennsylvania German (0)	7	0.05
Polish (27)	207	1.53
Portuguese (106)	263	1.95
Russian (131)	157	1.16
Scandinavian (12)	26	0.19
Scotch-Irish (67)	164	1.22
Scottish (20)	185	1.37
Slovene (9)	9	0.07
Swedish (40)	127	0.94
Swiss (19)	54	0.40
Ukrainian (13)	13	0.10
Welsh (0)	63	0.47
West Indian, ex. Hispanic (0)	13	0.10
Trinidadian/Tobagonian (0)	13	0.10
Yugoslavian (16)	38	0.28

Hispanic Origin	Population	%
Hispanic or Latino (of any race)	3,036	23.96
Central American, ex. Mexican	566	4.47
Costa Rican	3	0.02
Guatemalan	98	0.77
Honduran	27	0.21
Nicaraguan	144	1.14
Panamanian	5	0.04
Salvadoran	285	2.25
Other Central American	4	0.03
Cuban	27	0.21
Dominican Republic	5	0.04
Mexican	1,890	14.92
Puerto Rican	85	0.67
South American	151	1.19
Argentinean	21	0.17
Bolivian	3	0.02
Chilean	3	0.02
Colombian	30	0.24
Ecuadorian	8	0.06
Peruvian	82	0.65
Venezuelan	3	0.02
Other South American	1	0.01
Other Hispanic or Latino	312	2.46

Race*	Population	%
African-American/Black (1,673)	1,977	15.61
Not Hispanic (1,614)	1,849	14.59
Hispanic (59)	128	1.01
American Indian/Alaska Native (127)	326	2.57
Not Hispanic (56)	195	1.54
Hispanic (71)	131	1.03
Apache (1)	2	0.02
Blackfeet (1)	4	0.03
Central American Ind. (1)	2	0.02
Cherokee (5)	35	0.28
Chickasaw (2)	9	0.07
Choctaw (0)	5	0.04
Creek (1)	5	0.04
Hopi (1)	1	0.01
Iroquois (0)	2	0.02
Lumbee (0)	2	0.02
Mexican American Ind. (18)	31	0.24
Navajo (2)	5	0.04
Osage (0)	1	0.01
Potawatomi (1)	2	0.02
Pueblo (10)	10	0.08
Sioux (2)	3	0.02
South American Ind. (4)	10	0.08
Spanish American Ind. (0)	5	0.04
Asian (1,986)	2,368	18.69
Not Hispanic (1,948)	2,260	17.84
Hispanic (38)	108	0.85
Burmese (9)	12	0.09
Cambodian (21)	27	0.21
Chinese, ex. Taiwanese (396)	483	3.81
Filipino (551)	703	5.55
Indian (476)	553	4.36
Indonesian (5)	12	0.09
Japanese (68)	132	1.04
Korean (69)	82	0.65
Laotian (96)	117	0.92
Malaysian (0)	1	0.01
Nepalese (14)	14	0.11
Pakistani (64)	69	0.54
Sri Lankan (3)	3	0.02
Taiwanese (13)	19	0.15
Thai (16)	17	0.13
Vietnamese (99)	115	0.91
Hawaii Native/Pacific Islander (113)	218	1.72
Not Hispanic (110)	186	1.47
Hispanic (3)	32	0.25
Fijian (35)	46	0.36
Guamanian/Chamorro (19)	29	0.23
Native Hawaiian (12)	45	0.36
Samoan (11)	20	0.16
Tongan (22)	29	0.23
White (6,405)	7,165	56.56
Not Hispanic (5,214)	5,686	44.88
Hispanic (1,191)	1,479	11.67

El Sobrante

Place Type: CDP
County: Riverside
Population: 12,723†

Ancestry‡	Population	%
African, Sub-Saharan (9)	13	0.12
African (0)	4	0.04
South African (9)	9	0.08
American (351)	351	3.16
Arab (268)	304	2.73
Arab (95)	95	0.85
Egyptian (78)	114	1.02
Lebanese (77)	77	0.69
Palestinian (18)	18	0.16
Armenian (0)	13	0.12
Austrian (0)	26	0.23
Czech (0)	48	0.43
Danish (12)	33	0.30
Dutch (90)	233	2.09
English (296)	1,199	10.78
European (40)	61	0.55
French, ex. Basque (10)	181	1.63
French Canadian (8)	43	0.39
German (591)	1,580	14.21
Greek (0)	21	0.19
Hungarian (44)	44	0.40
Iranian (15)	15	0.13
Irish (112)	586	5.27
Italian (109)	423	3.80
Lithuanian (0)	29	0.26
Norwegian (12)	209	1.88
Polish (44)	169	1.52
Portuguese (18)	35	0.31
Romanian (110)	165	1.48
Russian (17)	49	0.44
Scandinavian (19)	57	0.51
Scotch-Irish (34)	146	1.31
Scottish (35)	282	2.54
Slavic (18)	18	0.16
Swedish (10)	82	0.74
Ukrainian (0)	15	0.13
Welsh (0)	21	0.19
West Indian, ex. Hispanic (14)	14	0.13
Haitian (14)	14	0.13
Yugoslavian (11)	11	0.10

Hispanic Origin	Population	%
Hispanic or Latino (of any race)	3,626	28.50
Central American, ex. Mexican	185	1.45
Costa Rican	13	0.10
Guatemalan	36	0.28
Honduran	36	0.28
Nicaraguan	24	0.19
Panamanian	8	0.06
Salvadoran	68	0.53
Cuban	71	0.56
Dominican Republic	16	0.13
Mexican	2,845	22.36
Puerto Rican	111	0.87
South American	167	1.31
Argentinean	22	0.17
Bolivian	11	0.09
Chilean	9	0.07
Colombian	54	0.42
Ecuadorian	10	0.08
Peruvian	55	0.43
Uruguayan	1	0.01
Venezuelan	3	0.02
Other South American	2	0.02
Other Hispanic or Latino	231	1.82

Race*	Population	%
African-American/Black (1,010)	1,138	8.94
Not Hispanic (957)	1,041	8.18
Hispanic (53)	97	0.76
American Indian/Alaska Native (73)	170	1.34
Not Hispanic (24)	72	0.57
Hispanic (49)	98	0.77

*Notes: † The Census 2010 population figure is used to calculate the percentages in the Hispanic Origin and Race categories. Ancestry percentages are based on the 2006-2010 American Community Survey population (not shown); ‡ Numbers in parentheses indicate the number of people reporting a single ancestry; * Numbers in parentheses indicate the number of persons reporting this race alone, not in combination with any other race; Please refer to the Explanation of Data for more information.*

Aleut *(Alaska Native)* (0)	3	0.02
Apache (1)	1	0.01
Blackfeet (0)	1	0.01
Cherokee (3)	9	0.07
Chippewa (0)	4	0.03
Choctaw (0)	1	0.01
Cree (2)	3	0.02
Creek (1)	5	0.04
Delaware (3)	3	0.02
Mexican American Ind. (5)	7	0.06
Pima (0)	4	0.03
Potawatomi (2)	5	0.04
Pueblo (3)	3	0.02
Puget Sound Salish (3)	3	0.02
Seminole (5)	5	0.04
Sioux (0)	4	0.03
Spanish American Ind. (1)	2	0.02
Tlingit-Haida *(Alaska Native)* (2)	2	0.02
Ute (0)	3	0.02
Yaqui (5)	9	0.07
Asian (2,240)	2,524	19.84
Not Hispanic (2,170)	2,402	18.88
Hispanic (70)	122	0.96
Bangladeshi (10)	10	0.08
Burmese (5)	6	0.05
Cambodian (36)	63	0.50
Chinese, ex. Taiwanese (232)	307	2.41
Filipino (794)	926	7.28
Hmong (9)	9	0.07
Indian (228)	246	1.93
Indonesian (31)	40	0.31
Japanese (68)	116	0.91
Korean (316)	339	2.66
Laotian (24)	31	0.24
Malaysian (6)	6	0.05
Pakistani (29)	33	0.26
Sri Lankan (2)	2	0.02
Taiwanese (36)	36	0.28
Thai (6)	8	0.06
Vietnamese (325)	364	2.86
Hawaii Native/Pacific Islander (36)	105	0.83
Not Hispanic (31)	83	0.65
Hispanic (5)	22	0.17
Fijian (4)	4	0.03
Guamanian/Chamorro (5)	13	0.10
Native Hawaiian (3)	17	0.13
Samoan (18)	40	0.31
Tongan (1)	1	0.01
White (7,435)	7,939	62.40
Not Hispanic (5,521)	5,808	45.65
Hispanic (1,914)	2,131	16.75

Elk Grove

Place Type: City
County: Sacramento
Population: 153,015†

Ancestry‡	Population	%
Afghan (1,204)	1,211	0.86
African, Sub-Saharan (1,669)	2,477	1.75
African (619)	1,331	0.94
Cape Verdean (38)	106	0.08
Ethiopian (486)	492	0.35
Ghanaian (10)	10	0.01
Nigerian (354)	363	0.26
Somalian (148)	148	0.10
South African (14)	14	0.01
Other Sub-Saharan African (0)	13	0.01
Albanian (0)	8	0.01
American (2,130)	2,130	1.51
Arab (1,044)	1,444	1.02
Arab (132)	206	0.15
Egyptian (101)	110	0.08
Iraqi (46)	46	0.03
Jordanian (115)	115	0.08
Lebanese (233)	397	0.28
Palestinian (267)	396	0.28
Syrian (80)	80	0.06
Other Arab (70)	94	0.07
Armenian (53)	202	0.14
Assyrian/Chaldean/Syriac (13)	13	0.01
Australian (26)	48	0.03
Austrian (109)	317	0.22
Basque (52)	52	0.04
Belgian (13)	45	0.03
Brazilian (34)	73	0.05
British (70)	463	0.33
Canadian (127)	446	0.32
Celtic (0)	15	0.01
Croatian (64)	231	0.16
Czech (76)	261	0.18
Czechoslovakian (22)	62	0.04
Danish (127)	739	0.52
Dutch (349)	1,801	1.28
Eastern European (22)	48	0.03
English (2,030)	9,477	6.71
European (1,024)	1,413	1.00
Finnish (25)	120	0.08
French, ex. Basque (309)	3,063	2.17
French Canadian (209)	740	0.52
German (3,692)	15,493	10.97
Greek (247)	837	0.59
Guyanese (23)	23	0.02
Hungarian (81)	286	0.20
Icelander (8)	8	0.01
Iranian (221)	271	0.19
Irish (1,957)	11,046	7.82
Italian (2,182)	6,741	4.77
Latvian (0)	15	0.01
Lithuanian (25)	75	0.05
Maltese (10)	47	0.03
New Zealander (8)	8	0.01
Northern European (177)	200	0.14
Norwegian (477)	1,360	0.96
Polish (249)	1,258	0.89
Portuguese (865)	2,750	1.95
Romanian (132)	400	0.28
Russian (344)	945	0.67
Scandinavian (142)	321	0.23
Scotch-Irish (536)	1,675	1.19
Scottish (412)	2,583	1.83
Serbian (8)	17	0.01
Slavic (0)	40	0.03
Slovak (0)	63	0.04
Slovene (0)	39	0.03
Swedish (386)	2,091	1.48
Swiss (38)	322	0.23
Turkish (0)	8	0.01
Ukrainian (271)	385	0.27
Welsh (222)	1,020	0.72
West Indian, ex. Hispanic (154)	387	0.27
Bahamian (44)	44	0.03
Bermudan (0)	15	0.01
Dutch West Indian (0)	42	0.03
Haitian (0)	53	0.04
Jamaican (37)	51	0.04
Trinidadian/Tobagonian (23)	79	0.06
West Indian (50)	103	0.07
Yugoslavian (119)	358	0.25

Hispanic Origin	Population	%
Hispanic or Latino (of any race)	27,581	18.03
Central American, ex. Mexican	1,882	1.23
Costa Rican	73	0.05
Guatemalan	255	0.17
Honduran	73	0.05
Nicaraguan	453	0.30
Panamanian	175	0.11
Salvadoran	831	0.54
Other Central American	22	0.01
Cuban	222	0.15
Dominican Republic	56	0.04
Mexican	21,186	13.85
Puerto Rican	1,064	0.70
South American	699	0.46
Argentinean	63	0.04
Bolivian	39	0.03
Chilean	63	0.04
Colombian	140	0.09
Ecuadorian	55	0.04
Paraguayan	2	<0.01
Peruvian	275	0.18
Uruguayan	8	0.01
Venezuelan	50	0.03
Other South American	4	<0.01
Other Hispanic or Latino	2,472	1.62

Race*	Population	%
African-American/Black (17,172)	20,952	13.69
Not Hispanic (16,462)	19,426	12.70
Hispanic (710)	1,526	1.00
American Indian/Alaska Native (965)	2,996	1.96
Not Hispanic (507)	1,962	1.28
Hispanic (458)	1,034	0.68
Alaska Athabascan *(Ala. Nat.)* (1)	2	<0.01
Aleut *(Alaska Native)* (0)	8	0.01
Apache (36)	96	0.06
Blackfeet (10)	95	0.06
Canadian/French Am. Ind. (1)	2	<0.01
Central American Ind. (3)	5	<0.01
Cherokee (93)	555	0.36
Cheyenne (0)	6	<0.01
Chickasaw (7)	18	0.01
Chippewa (14)	36	0.02
Choctaw (18)	137	0.09
Colville (1)	1	<0.01
Comanche (1)	12	0.01
Cree (1)	8	0.01
Creek (10)	44	0.03
Delaware (5)	8	0.01
Hopi (0)	8	0.01
Inupiat *(Alaska Native)* (1)	2	<0.01
Iroquois (7)	21	0.01
Kiowa (2)	5	<0.01
Lumbee (2)	3	<0.01
Mexican American Ind. (65)	108	0.07
Navajo (18)	63	0.04
Osage (1)	4	<0.01
Ottawa (3)	3	<0.01
Paiute (6)	17	0.01
Pima (0)	1	<0.01
Potawatomi (8)	19	0.01
Pueblo (3)	13	0.01
Puget Sound Salish (0)	1	<0.01
Seminole (5)	20	0.01
Shoshone (3)	7	<0.01
Sioux (22)	58	0.04
South American Ind. (4)	16	0.01
Spanish American Ind. (3)	8	0.01
Tlingit-Haida *(Alaska Native)* (5)	17	0.01
Tohono O'Odham (2)	2	<0.01
Tsimshian *(Alaska Native)* (1)	4	<0.01
Yakama (1)	1	<0.01
Yaqui (18)	32	0.02
Yuman (5)	7	<0.01
Yup'ik *(Alaska Native)* (0)	6	<0.01
Asian (40,261)	46,861	30.63
Not Hispanic (39,479)	44,901	29.34
Hispanic (782)	1,960	1.28
Bangladeshi (13)	20	0.01
Burmese (24)	30	0.02
Cambodian (311)	384	0.25
Chinese, ex. Taiwanese (8,806)	10,629	6.95
Filipino (11,769)	14,891	9.73
Hmong (1,696)	1,789	1.17
Indian (4,968)	5,856	3.83
Indonesian (65)	125	0.08
Japanese (1,346)	2,725	1.78
Korean (658)	1,028	0.67
Laotian (777)	937	0.61
Malaysian (16)	26	0.02
Nepalese (28)	31	0.02
Pakistani (581)	645	0.42
Sri Lankan (35)	41	0.03
Taiwanese (150)	198	0.13
Thai (118)	257	0.17
Vietnamese (7,024)	7,796	5.09
Hawaii Native/Pacific Islander (1,807)	3,319	2.17
Not Hispanic (1,731)	3,048	1.99

*Notes: † The Census 2010 population figure is used to calculate the percentages in the Hispanic Origin and Race categories. Ancestry percentages are based on the 2006-2010 American Community Survey population (not shown); ‡ Numbers in parentheses indicate the number of people reporting a single ancestry; * Numbers in parentheses indicate the number of persons reporting this race alone, not in combination with any other race; Please refer to the Explanation of Data for more information.*

Hispanic (76)	271	0.18
Fijian (1,103)	1,279	0.84
Guamanian/Chamorro (171)	350	0.23
Marshallese (18)	26	0.02
Native Hawaiian (77)	402	0.26
Samoan (99)	191	0.12
Tongan (101)	133	0.09
White (70,478)	79,401	51.89
Not Hispanic (58,305)	64,620	42.23
Hispanic (12,173)	14,781	9.66

Emeryville

Place Type: City
County: Alameda
Population: 10,080†

Ancestry‡	Population	%
Afghan (0)	24	0.26
African, Sub-Saharan (13)	13	0.14
African (13)	13	0.14
American (65)	65	0.69
Arab (56)	90	0.96
Lebanese (16)	50	0.53
Palestinian (40)	40	0.43
Armenian (0)	17	0.18
Assyrian/Chaldean/Syriac (16)	16	0.17
Austrian (0)	12	0.13
Basque (0)	18	0.19
British (18)	53	0.56
Canadian (30)	58	0.62
Czech (0)	49	0.52
Danish (14)	14	0.15
Dutch (0)	56	0.60
Eastern European (24)	24	0.26
English (101)	511	5.44
European (264)	300	3.19
French, ex. Basque (92)	278	2.96
French Canadian (0)	15	0.16
German (133)	617	6.57
Greek (57)	57	0.61
Guyanese (13)	13	0.14
Iranian (31)	41	0.44
Irish (213)	728	7.75
Italian (130)	325	3.46
Northern European (35)	48	0.51
Norwegian (18)	135	1.44
Pennsylvania German (0)	19	0.20
Polish (54)	113	1.20
Portuguese (32)	70	0.75
Romanian (0)	23	0.24
Russian (90)	216	2.30
Scandinavian (18)	29	0.31
Scotch-Irish (26)	157	1.67
Scottish (13)	66	0.70
Slavic (12)	12	0.13
Slovak (0)	13	0.14
Swedish (0)	43	0.46
Swiss (0)	33	0.35
Turkish (15)	15	0.16
Ukrainian (39)	39	0.42
Welsh (10)	91	0.97
West Indian, ex. Hispanic (0)	10	0.11
Jamaican (0)	10	0.11
Yugoslavian (19)	53	0.56

Hispanic Origin	Population	%
Hispanic or Latino (of any race)	927	9.20
Central American, ex. Mexican	98	0.97
Costa Rican	2	0.02
Guatemalan	10	0.10
Honduran	2	0.02
Nicaraguan	29	0.29
Panamanian	6	0.06
Salvadoran	44	0.44
Other Central American	5	0.05
Cuban	23	0.23
Dominican Republic	5	0.05
Mexican	554	5.50
Puerto Rican	66	0.65
South American	102	1.01
Argentinean	19	0.19
Bolivian	9	0.09
Chilean	8	0.08
Colombian	21	0.21
Ecuadorian	7	0.07
Peruvian	25	0.25
Uruguayan	2	0.02
Venezuelan	11	0.11
Other Hispanic or Latino	79	0.78

Race*	Population	%
African-American/Black (1,764)	2,011	19.95
Not Hispanic (1,733)	1,929	19.14
Hispanic (31)	82	0.81
American Indian/Alaska Native (44)	174	1.73
Not Hispanic (19)	117	1.16
Hispanic (25)	57	0.57
Aleut *(Alaska Native)* (0)	1	0.01
Apache (0)	1	0.01
Blackfeet (0)	15	0.15
Central American Ind. (0)	1	0.01
Cherokee (2)	43	0.43
Chickasaw (0)	4	0.04
Chippewa (0)	1	0.01
Choctaw (2)	2	0.02
Creek (0)	1	0.01
Iroquois (0)	1	0.01
Mexican American Ind. (5)	6	0.06
Paiute (1)	1	0.01
Pueblo (2)	2	0.02
Seminole (1)	2	0.02
Shoshone (2)	2	0.02
Sioux (0)	4	0.04
South American Ind. (3)	4	0.04
Tlingit-Haida *(Alaska Native)* (1)	1	0.01
Tsimshian *(Alaska Native)* (0)	1	0.01
Asian (2,775)	3,144	31.19
Not Hispanic (2,756)	3,090	30.65
Hispanic (19)	54	0.54
Bangladeshi (2)	2	0.02
Burmese (9)	17	0.17
Cambodian (7)	13	0.13
Chinese, ex. Taiwanese (851)	1,006	9.98
Filipino (399)	520	5.16
Hmong (5)	5	0.05
Indian (424)	477	4.73
Indonesian (17)	28	0.28
Japanese (159)	243	2.41
Korean (415)	455	4.51
Laotian (8)	10	0.10
Malaysian (2)	3	0.03
Nepalese (2)	2	0.02
Pakistani (40)	53	0.53
Sri Lankan (9)	13	0.13
Taiwanese (110)	121	1.20
Thai (38)	53	0.53
Vietnamese (120)	150	1.49
Hawaii Native/Pacific Islander (16)	58	0.58
Not Hispanic (16)	51	0.51
Hispanic (0)	7	0.07
Fijian (1)	1	0.01
Guamanian/Chamorro (4)	9	0.09
Native Hawaiian (6)	23	0.23
Samoan (1)	5	0.05
Tongan (1)	1	0.01
White (4,490)	4,960	49.21
Not Hispanic (4,057)	4,445	44.10
Hispanic (433)	515	5.11

Encinitas

Place Type: City
County: San Diego
Population: 59,518†

Ancestry‡	Population	%
Albanian (0)	28	0.05
American (1,648)	1,648	2.80
Arab (100)	249	0.42
Arab (17)	17	0.03
Iraqi (0)	27	0.05
Lebanese (53)	146	0.25
Moroccan (7)	30	0.05
Syrian (23)	29	0.05
Armenian (24)	59	0.10
Australian (118)	133	0.23
Austrian (66)	184	0.31
Basque (8)	31	0.05
Belgian (0)	24	0.04
Brazilian (74)	111	0.19
British (283)	666	1.13
Canadian (123)	214	0.36
Celtic (30)	30	0.05
Croatian (28)	85	0.14
Czech (95)	252	0.43
Czechoslovakian (74)	114	0.19
Danish (94)	407	0.69
Dutch (209)	665	1.13
Eastern European (181)	220	0.37
English (3,152)	9,494	16.16
European (1,158)	1,308	2.23
Finnish (12)	21	0.04
French, ex. Basque (434)	2,779	4.73
French Canadian (218)	482	0.82
German (2,452)	10,401	17.70
Greek (193)	395	0.67
Hungarian (152)	478	0.81
Icelander (10)	22	0.04
Iranian (306)	393	0.67
Irish (2,059)	7,825	13.32
Israeli (25)	25	0.04
Italian (1,591)	4,259	7.25
Latvian (21)	66	0.11
Lithuanian (58)	190	0.32
New Zealander (8)	8	0.01
Northern European (183)	183	0.31
Norwegian (706)	1,880	3.20
Pennsylvania German (69)	69	0.12
Polish (461)	1,809	3.08
Portuguese (268)	450	0.77
Romanian (14)	106	0.18
Russian (935)	1,863	3.17
Scandinavian (144)	377	0.64
Scotch-Irish (490)	1,740	2.96
Scottish (734)	2,179	3.71
Serbian (21)	81	0.14
Slavic (0)	64	0.11
Slovak (51)	160	0.27
Slovene (0)	14	0.02
Swedish (336)	1,466	2.49
Swiss (54)	251	0.43
Turkish (52)	52	0.09
Ukrainian (47)	205	0.35
Welsh (45)	575	0.98
West Indian, ex. Hispanic (15)	30	0.05
Barbadian (0)	15	0.03
Jamaican (15)	15	0.03
Yugoslavian (34)	87	0.15

Hispanic Origin	Population	%
Hispanic or Latino (of any race)	8,138	13.67
Central American, ex. Mexican	403	0.68
Costa Rican	24	0.04
Guatemalan	205	0.34
Honduran	34	0.06
Nicaraguan	22	0.04
Panamanian	27	0.05
Salvadoran	85	0.14
Other Central American	6	0.01
Cuban	91	0.15
Dominican Republic	12	0.02
Mexican	6,412	10.77
Puerto Rican	186	0.31
South American	366	0.61
Argentinean	64	0.11
Bolivian	13	0.02
Chilean	50	0.08
Colombian	105	0.18
Ecuadorian	20	0.03

*Notes: † The Census 2010 population figure is used to calculate the percentages in the Hispanic Origin and Race categories. Ancestry percentages are based on the 2006-2010 American Community Survey population (not shown); ‡ Numbers in parentheses indicate the number of people reporting a single ancestry; * Numbers in parentheses indicate the number of persons reporting this race alone, not in combination with any other race; Please refer to the Explanation of Data for more information.*

Peruvian	69	0.12
Venezuelan	39	0.07
Other South American	6	0.01
Other Hispanic or Latino	668	1.12

Race*	Population	%
African-American/Black (361)	618	1.04
Not Hispanic (316)	515	0.87
Hispanic (45)	103	0.17
American Indian/Alaska Native (301)	729	1.22
Not Hispanic (159)	437	0.73
Hispanic (142)	292	0.49
Alaska Athabascan *(Ala. Nat.)* (1)	4	0.01
Apache (7)	22	0.04
Blackfeet (2)	14	0.02
Canadian/French Am. Ind. (0)	2	<0.01
Central American Ind. (0)	1	<0.01
Cherokee (19)	96	0.16
Chickasaw (2)	6	0.01
Chippewa (4)	16	0.03
Choctaw (6)	23	0.04
Comanche (1)	1	<0.01
Creek (2)	3	0.01
Crow (2)	2	<0.01
Hopi (1)	3	0.01
Iroquois (6)	14	0.02
Lumbee (3)	3	0.01
Mexican American Ind. (60)	85	0.14
Navajo (3)	14	0.02
Osage (0)	4	0.01
Paiute (2)	2	<0.01
Potawatomi (0)	1	<0.01
Pueblo (3)	8	0.01
Puget Sound Salish (6)	7	0.01
Seminole (1)	6	0.01
Sioux (10)	19	0.03
South American Ind. (1)	8	0.01
Spanish American Ind. (0)	1	<0.01
Tlingit-Haida *(Alaska Native)* (3)	4	0.01
Tohono O'Odham (0)	2	<0.01
Tsimshian *(Alaska Native)* (1)	1	<0.01
Yaqui (3)	6	0.01
Yup'ik *(Alaska Native)* (1)	1	<0.01
Asian (2,323)	3,390	5.70
Not Hispanic (2,291)	3,258	5.47
Hispanic (32)	132	0.22
Bangladeshi (4)	6	0.01
Burmese (4)	4	0.01
Cambodian (8)	10	0.02
Chinese, ex. Taiwanese (546)	804	1.35
Filipino (353)	634	1.07
Indian (351)	422	0.71
Indonesian (9)	39	0.07
Japanese (447)	816	1.37
Korean (218)	326	0.55
Laotian (13)	17	0.03
Malaysian (2)	3	0.01
Nepalese (1)	1	<0.01
Pakistani (10)	23	0.04
Sri Lankan (8)	9	0.02
Taiwanese (52)	62	0.10
Thai (44)	58	0.10
Vietnamese (136)	191	0.32
Hawaii Native/Pacific Islander (91)	253	0.43
Not Hispanic (81)	225	0.38
Hispanic (10)	28	0.05
Fijian (1)	3	0.01
Guamanian/Chamorro (21)	48	0.08
Native Hawaiian (39)	120	0.20
Samoan (2)	6	0.01
Tongan (1)	4	0.01
White (51,067)	52,974	89.01
Not Hispanic (46,881)	48,279	81.12
Hispanic (4,186)	4,695	7.89

Escondido

Place Type: City
County: San Diego
Population: 143,911†

Ancestry‡	Population	%
Afghan (47)	63	0.04
African, Sub-Saharan (365)	511	0.36
African (47)	193	0.14
Ethiopian (16)	16	0.01
Ghanaian (8)	8	0.01
Nigerian (90)	90	0.06
South African (60)	60	0.04
Ugandan (11)	11	0.01
Other Sub-Saharan African (133)	133	0.09
Albanian (11)	11	0.01
American (2,997)	2,997	2.13
Arab (432)	612	0.43
Arab (68)	128	0.09
Egyptian (125)	125	0.09
Iraqi (49)	71	0.05
Lebanese (33)	46	0.03
Palestinian (26)	51	0.04
Syrian (75)	127	0.09
Other Arab (56)	64	0.05
Armenian (44)	78	0.06
Assyrian/Chaldean/Syriac (0)	7	<0.01
Australian (0)	10	0.01
Austrian (71)	254	0.18
Basque (0)	60	0.04
Belgian (21)	114	0.08
Brazilian (60)	118	0.08
British (322)	564	0.40
Bulgarian (54)	54	0.04
Canadian (145)	270	0.19
Carpatho Rusyn (0)	49	0.03
Celtic (8)	8	0.01
Croatian (4)	60	0.04
Czech (91)	357	0.25
Czechoslovakian (21)	57	0.04
Danish (185)	785	0.56
Dutch (553)	1,634	1.16
Eastern European (41)	53	0.04
English (4,576)	12,343	8.75
Estonian (0)	10	0.01
European (1,014)	1,168	0.83
Finnish (59)	232	0.16
French, ex. Basque (632)	3,026	2.15
French Canadian (240)	465	0.33
German (4,627)	14,458	10.25
German Russian (0)	12	0.01
Greek (203)	513	0.36
Hungarian (248)	456	0.32
Iranian (408)	500	0.35
Irish (2,276)	9,651	6.84
Israeli (18)	46	0.03
Italian (1,959)	5,156	3.66
Latvian (10)	10	0.01
Lithuanian (29)	215	0.15
Luxemburger (0)	26	0.02
Maltese (10)	10	0.01
Northern European (176)	176	0.12
Norwegian (634)	1,880	1.33
Pennsylvania German (18)	37	0.03
Polish (877)	2,368	1.68
Portuguese (253)	889	0.63
Romanian (252)	303	0.21
Russian (316)	858	0.61
Scandinavian (72)	132	0.09
Scotch-Irish (783)	1,965	1.39
Scottish (618)	2,609	1.85
Serbian (83)	105	0.07
Slavic (10)	36	0.03
Slovak (93)	117	0.08
Slovene (17)	98	0.07
Swedish (494)	1,894	1.34
Swiss (123)	442	0.31
Turkish (0)	28	0.02
Ukrainian (11)	130	0.09
Welsh (168)	918	0.65
West Indian, ex. Hispanic (30)	55	0.04
Belizean (9)	9	0.01
Haitian (0)	8	0.01
Jamaican (7)	24	0.02
Trinidadian/Tobagonian (14)	14	0.01
Yugoslavian (137)	210	0.15

Hispanic Origin	Population	%
Hispanic or Latino (of any race)	70,326	48.87
Central American, ex. Mexican	1,816	1.26
Costa Rican	66	0.05
Guatemalan	872	0.61
Honduran	101	0.07
Nicaraguan	79	0.05
Panamanian	46	0.03
Salvadoran	616	0.43
Other Central American	36	0.03
Cuban	173	0.12
Dominican Republic	57	0.04
Mexican	63,552	44.16
Puerto Rican	863	0.60
South American	535	0.37
Argentinean	68	0.05
Bolivian	21	0.01
Chilean	33	0.02
Colombian	155	0.11
Ecuadorian	67	0.05
Paraguayan	4	<0.01
Peruvian	126	0.09
Uruguayan	15	0.01
Venezuelan	43	0.03
Other South American	3	<0.01
Other Hispanic or Latino	3,330	2.31

Race*	Population	%
African-American/Black (3,585)	4,844	3.37
Not Hispanic (3,046)	3,894	2.71
Hispanic (539)	950	0.66
American Indian/Alaska Native (1,472)	2,829	1.97
Not Hispanic (577)	1,242	0.86
Hispanic (895)	1,587	1.10
Aleut *(Alaska Native)* (2)	3	<0.01
Apache (28)	69	0.05
Arapaho (1)	1	<0.01
Blackfeet (7)	28	0.02
Canadian/French Am. Ind. (1)	3	<0.01
Central American Ind. (12)	26	0.02
Cherokee (67)	237	0.16
Cheyenne (0)	2	<0.01
Chickasaw (2)	11	0.01
Chippewa (14)	29	0.02
Choctaw (10)	49	0.03
Colville (3)	6	<0.01
Comanche (4)	6	<0.01
Creek (7)	16	0.01
Crow (5)	6	<0.01
Delaware (4)	5	<0.01
Hopi (5)	6	<0.01
Inupiat *(Alaska Native)* (5)	7	<0.01
Iroquois (16)	41	0.03
Kiowa (0)	1	<0.01
Lumbee (3)	3	<0.01
Menominee (0)	1	<0.01
Mexican American Ind. (278)	374	0.26
Navajo (47)	66	0.05
Osage (0)	8	0.01
Ottawa (1)	1	<0.01
Pima (2)	3	<0.01
Potawatomi (4)	4	<0.01
Pueblo (9)	14	0.01
Puget Sound Salish (1)	1	<0.01
Seminole (1)	6	<0.01
Shoshone (4)	14	0.01
Sioux (12)	34	0.02
South American Ind. (6)	11	0.01
Spanish American Ind. (13)	16	0.01
Tlingit-Haida *(Alaska Native)* (2)	2	<0.01
Tohono O'Odham (8)	13	0.01
Ute (1)	6	<0.01
Yaqui (21)	44	0.03
Yuman (5)	5	<0.01
Asian (8,740)	10,679	7.42
Not Hispanic (8,491)	9,970	6.93
Hispanic (249)	709	0.49

*Notes: † The Census 2010 population figure is used to calculate the percentages in the Hispanic Origin and Race categories. Ancestry percentages are based on the 2006-2010 American Community Survey population (not shown); ‡ Numbers in parentheses indicate the number of people reporting a single ancestry; * Numbers in parentheses indicate the number of persons reporting this race alone, not in combination with any other race; Please refer to the Explanation of Data for more information.*

Bangladeshi (2)	12	0.01
Burmese (12)	13	0.01
Cambodian (72)	98	0.07
Chinese, ex. Taiwanese (691)	993	0.69
Filipino (3,807)	4,768	3.31
Hmong (25)	25	0.02
Indian (479)	626	0.43
Indonesian (17)	42	0.03
Japanese (381)	739	0.51
Korean (382)	527	0.37
Laotian (489)	557	0.39
Malaysian (4)	6	<0.01
Pakistani (71)	79	0.05
Sri Lankan (7)	9	0.01
Taiwanese (51)	72	0.05
Thai (128)	158	0.11
Vietnamese (1,755)	1,947	1.35
Hawaii Native/Pacific Islander (350)	761	0.53
Not Hispanic (306)	576	0.40
Hispanic (44)	185	0.13
Fijian (1)	1	<0.01
Guamanian/Chamorro (112)	209	0.15
Marshallese (2)	2	<0.01
Native Hawaiian (91)	246	0.17
Samoan (95)	157	0.11
Tongan (7)	11	0.01
White (86,876)	92,390	64.20
Not Hispanic (58,142)	60,637	42.14
Hispanic (28,734)	31,753	22.06

Eureka

Place Type: City
County: Humboldt
Population: 27,191†

Ancestry‡	Population	%
Afghan (141)	141	0.52
African, Sub-Saharan (135)	194	0.72
African (65)	124	0.46
Nigerian (70)	70	0.26
Alsatian (0)	35	0.13
American (898)	898	3.33
Arab (30)	59	0.22
Egyptian (14)	14	0.05
Lebanese (16)	45	0.17
Armenian (10)	10	0.04
Australian (15)	33	0.12
Austrian (33)	209	0.78
Belgian (0)	61	0.23
Brazilian (49)	49	0.18
British (85)	158	0.59
Canadian (46)	149	0.55
Celtic (0)	8	0.03
Croatian (0)	35	0.13
Czech (13)	139	0.52
Czechoslovakian (22)	85	0.32
Danish (43)	336	1.25
Dutch (64)	468	1.74
Eastern European (0)	8	0.03
English (547)	2,873	10.66
European (1,067)	1,496	5.55
Finnish (51)	67	0.25
French, ex. Basque (130)	1,146	4.25
French Canadian (80)	152	0.56
German (1,119)	3,926	14.57
Greek (0)	99	0.37
Hungarian (28)	94	0.35
Irish (1,346)	4,294	15.93
Italian (971)	2,226	8.26
Lithuanian (0)	18	0.07
Northern European (32)	32	0.12
Norwegian (236)	815	3.02
Pennsylvania German (0)	4	0.01
Polish (104)	405	1.50
Portuguese (231)	604	2.24
Romanian (0)	18	0.07
Russian (82)	204	0.76
Scandinavian (190)	261	0.97
Scotch-Irish (412)	928	3.44
Scottish (292)	893	3.31
Slavic (12)	37	0.14
Slovak (0)	33	0.12
Swedish (161)	785	2.91
Swiss (66)	156	0.58
Ukrainian (13)	24	0.09
Welsh (56)	260	0.96
West Indian, ex. Hispanic (8)	45	0.17
Dutch West Indian (0)	37	0.14
Jamaican (8)	8	0.03
Yugoslavian (38)	38	0.14

Hispanic Origin	Population	%
Hispanic or Latino (of any race)	3,143	11.56
Central American, ex. Mexican	105	0.39
Costa Rican	14	0.05
Guatemalan	38	0.14
Honduran	2	0.01
Nicaraguan	15	0.06
Panamanian	2	0.01
Salvadoran	32	0.12
Other Central American	2	0.01
Cuban	35	0.13
Dominican Republic	1	<0.01
Mexican	2,548	9.37
Puerto Rican	90	0.33
South American	48	0.18
Argentinean	4	0.01
Bolivian	5	0.02
Chilean	6	0.02
Colombian	16	0.06
Ecuadorian	5	0.02
Peruvian	9	0.03
Venezuelan	3	0.01
Other Hispanic or Latino	316	1.16

Race*	Population	%
African-American/Black (514)	799	2.94
Not Hispanic (497)	727	2.67
Hispanic (17)	72	0.26
American Indian/Alaska Native (1,011)	1,904	7.00
Not Hispanic (903)	1,679	6.17
Hispanic (108)	225	0.83
Alaska Athabascan *(Ala. Nat.)* (5)	5	0.02
Aleut *(Alaska Native)* (4)	7	0.03
Apache (14)	30	0.11
Blackfeet (5)	52	0.19
Canadian/French Am. Ind. (2)	4	0.01
Central American Ind. (1)	1	<0.01
Cherokee (34)	216	0.79
Cheyenne (1)	4	0.01
Chickasaw (1)	7	0.03
Chippewa (5)	15	0.06
Choctaw (14)	51	0.19
Comanche (2)	12	0.04
Cree (0)	4	0.01
Creek (1)	10	0.04
Crow (3)	4	0.01
Delaware (1)	1	<0.01
Hopi (3)	4	0.01
Inupiat *(Alaska Native)* (0)	1	<0.01
Iroquois (2)	16	0.06
Lumbee (1)	1	<0.01
Mexican American Ind. (20)	27	0.10
Navajo (16)	25	0.09
Osage (3)	6	0.02
Ottawa (2)	2	0.01
Paiute (4)	7	0.03
Pima (2)	2	0.01
Potawatomi (3)	6	0.02
Pueblo (0)	1	<0.01
Seminole (0)	4	0.01
Shoshone (2)	2	0.01
Sioux (18)	41	0.15
South American Ind. (1)	4	0.01
Spanish American Ind. (1)	2	0.01
Tlingit-Haida *(Alaska Native)* (2)	3	0.01
Tohono O'Odham (0)	2	0.01
Tsimshian *(Alaska Native)* (1)	1	<0.01
Ute (2)	2	0.01
Yakama (1)	1	<0.01
Yaqui (4)	10	0.04
Yuman (1)	1	<0.01
Yup'ik *(Alaska Native)* (0)	1	<0.01
Asian (1,153)	1,478	5.44
Not Hispanic (1,124)	1,394	5.13
Hispanic (29)	84	0.31
Burmese (1)	1	<0.01
Cambodian (5)	6	0.02
Chinese, ex. Taiwanese (112)	154	0.57
Filipino (84)	204	0.75
Hmong (502)	515	1.89
Indian (68)	93	0.34
Indonesian (2)	6	0.02
Japanese (68)	132	0.49
Korean (47)	81	0.30
Laotian (143)	174	0.64
Malaysian (1)	1	<0.01
Nepalese (1)	2	0.01
Pakistani (5)	10	0.04
Sri Lankan (2)	3	0.01
Taiwanese (1)	4	0.01
Thai (15)	26	0.10
Vietnamese (51)	64	0.24
Hawaii Native/Pacific Islander (176)	298	1.10
Not Hispanic (169)	263	0.97
Hispanic (7)	35	0.13
Fijian (0)	2	0.01
Guamanian/Chamorro (4)	15	0.06
Native Hawaiian (34)	95	0.35
Samoan (27)	56	0.21
Tongan (3)	7	0.03
White (21,565)	23,018	84.65
Not Hispanic (20,081)	21,218	78.03
Hispanic (1,484)	1,800	6.62

Exeter

Place Type: City
County: Tulare
Population: 10,334†

Ancestry‡	Population	%
American (263)	263	2.59
Armenian (42)	42	0.41
Australian (0)	10	0.10
Belgian (0)	10	0.10
British (9)	9	0.09
Canadian (11)	31	0.31
Croatian (11)	11	0.11
Danish (0)	16	0.16
Dutch (57)	196	1.93
English (320)	919	9.06
European (88)	130	1.28
French, ex. Basque (18)	108	1.07
French Canadian (8)	8	0.08
German (311)	729	7.19
Greek (13)	13	0.13
Hungarian (13)	13	0.13
Irish (311)	877	8.65
Italian (30)	101	1.00
Norwegian (60)	129	1.27
Polish (19)	56	0.55
Portuguese (40)	83	0.82
Russian (0)	9	0.09
Scandinavian (10)	10	0.10
Scotch-Irish (67)	121	1.19
Scottish (81)	129	1.27
Swiss (0)	10	0.10
Welsh (10)	18	0.18

Hispanic Origin	Population	%
Hispanic or Latino (of any race)	4,703	45.51
Central American, ex. Mexican	8	0.08
Guatemalan	1	0.01
Honduran	2	0.02
Nicaraguan	1	0.01
Salvadoran	4	0.04
Cuban	6	0.06
Mexican	4,358	42.17

*Notes: † The Census 2010 population figure is used to calculate the percentages in the Hispanic Origin and Race categories. Ancestry percentages are based on the 2006-2010 American Community Survey population (not shown); ‡ Numbers in parentheses indicate the number of people reporting a single ancestry; * Numbers in parentheses indicate the number of persons reporting this race alone, not in combination with any other race; Please refer to the Explanation of Data for more information.*

Puerto Rican	20	0.19
South American	13	0.13
Argentinean	4	0.04
Colombian	2	0.02
Peruvian	2	0.02
Uruguayan	5	0.05
Other Hispanic or Latino	298	2.88

Race*	Population	%
African-American/Black (67)	109	1.05
Not Hispanic (53)	85	0.82
Hispanic (14)	24	0.23
American Indian/Alaska Native (171)	291	2.82
Not Hispanic (80)	164	1.59
Hispanic (91)	127	1.23
Apache (7)	13	0.13
Blackfeet (1)	2	0.02
Cherokee (18)	46	0.45
Chickasaw (4)	4	0.04
Choctaw (8)	13	0.13
Creek (1)	3	0.03
Iroquois (0)	1	0.01
Lumbee (0)	1	0.01
Mexican American Ind. (19)	20	0.19
Navajo (0)	5	0.05
Paiute (6)	6	0.06
Potawatomi (0)	3	0.03
Seminole (0)	1	0.01
Sioux (2)	8	0.08
Spanish American Ind. (0)	1	0.01
Tohono O'Odham (0)	1	0.01
Asian (138)	201	1.95
Not Hispanic (126)	175	1.69
Hispanic (12)	26	0.25
Cambodian (4)	4	0.04
Chinese, ex. Taiwanese (31)	51	0.49
Filipino (50)	82	0.79
Hmong (3)	7	0.07
Indian (23)	24	0.23
Indonesian (2)	4	0.04
Japanese (11)	19	0.18
Korean (5)	9	0.09
Laotian (0)	2	0.02
Pakistani (1)	1	0.01
Vietnamese (1)	1	0.01
Hawaii Native/Pacific Islander (8)	30	0.29
Not Hispanic (7)	16	0.15
Hispanic (1)	14	0.14
Guamanian/Chamorro (0)	6	0.06
Native Hawaiian (1)	5	0.05
Samoan (0)	5	0.05
Tongan (1)	1	0.01
White (7,150)	7,517	72.74
Not Hispanic (5,171)	5,343	51.70
Hispanic (1,979)	2,174	21.04

Fair Oaks

Place Type: CDP
County: Sacramento
Population: 30,912†

Ancestry‡	Population	%
African, Sub-Saharan (11)	11	0.04
African (11)	11	0.04
American (947)	947	3.08
Arab (108)	300	0.98
Arab (31)	31	0.10
Egyptian (51)	51	0.17
Lebanese (26)	104	0.34
Syrian (0)	114	0.37
Armenian (15)	40	0.13
Austrian (0)	33	0.11
Belgian (0)	25	0.08
Brazilian (0)	24	0.08
British (171)	282	0.92
Canadian (19)	141	0.46
Croatian (16)	79	0.26
Czech (70)	130	0.42
Czechoslovakian (11)	43	0.14
Danish (103)	349	1.14
Dutch (110)	429	1.40
Eastern European (42)	42	0.14
English (1,255)	4,296	13.99
European (477)	536	1.75
Finnish (35)	70	0.23
French, ex. Basque (226)	1,220	3.97
French Canadian (90)	167	0.54
German (1,808)	6,552	21.33
Greek (83)	166	0.54
Hungarian (88)	181	0.59
Iranian (255)	277	0.90
Irish (976)	4,367	14.22
Italian (643)	2,150	7.00
Lithuanian (10)	147	0.48
Maltese (0)	13	0.04
Northern European (124)	181	0.59
Norwegian (265)	709	2.31
Pennsylvania German (0)	39	0.13
Polish (264)	1,005	3.27
Portuguese (329)	728	2.37
Romanian (380)	430	1.40
Russian (446)	829	2.70
Scandinavian (42)	110	0.36
Scotch-Irish (289)	612	1.99
Scottish (279)	1,316	4.28
Serbian (40)	82	0.27
Slavic (0)	15	0.05
Slovene (0)	33	0.11
Swedish (216)	713	2.32
Swiss (18)	292	0.95
Turkish (0)	9	0.03
Ukrainian (671)	869	2.83
Welsh (95)	326	1.06
Yugoslavian (23)	59	0.19

Hispanic Origin	Population	%
Hispanic or Latino (of any race)	2,954	9.56
Central American, ex. Mexican	150	0.49
Costa Rican	8	0.03
Guatemalan	44	0.14
Honduran	9	0.03
Nicaraguan	25	0.08
Panamanian	10	0.03
Salvadoran	54	0.17
Cuban	36	0.12
Dominican Republic	3	0.01
Mexican	2,062	6.67
Puerto Rican	144	0.47
South American	118	0.38
Argentinean	31	0.10
Bolivian	4	0.01
Chilean	16	0.05
Colombian	15	0.05
Ecuadorian	19	0.06
Paraguayan	2	0.01
Peruvian	27	0.09
Venezuelan	4	0.01
Other Hispanic or Latino	441	1.43

Race*	Population	%
African-American/Black (729)	1,064	3.44
Not Hispanic (678)	943	3.05
Hispanic (51)	121	0.39
American Indian/Alaska Native (255)	609	1.97
Not Hispanic (186)	474	1.53
Hispanic (69)	135	0.44
Aleut *(Alaska Native)* (0)	1	<0.01
Apache (10)	16	0.05
Arapaho (0)	3	0.01
Blackfeet (2)	23	0.07
Canadian/French Am. Ind. (2)	5	0.02
Cherokee (34)	122	0.39
Chickasaw (4)	8	0.03
Chippewa (11)	13	0.04
Choctaw (13)	44	0.14
Cree (1)	1	<0.01
Creek (1)	1	<0.01
Crow (2)	2	0.01
Delaware (0)	2	0.01
Hopi (0)	1	<0.01
Inupiat *(Alaska Native)* (3)	3	0.01
Iroquois (7)	19	0.06
Kiowa (1)	1	<0.01
Mexican American Ind. (3)	8	0.03
Navajo (10)	15	0.05
Osage (0)	2	0.01
Ottawa (5)	7	0.02
Paiute (3)	5	0.02
Pima (1)	1	<0.01
Potawatomi (1)	3	0.01
Pueblo (4)	4	0.01
Puget Sound Salish (2)	2	0.01
Seminole (0)	5	0.02
Shoshone (2)	6	0.02
Sioux (10)	25	0.08
South American Ind. (0)	7	0.02
Spanish American Ind. (3)	7	0.02
Tlingit-Haida *(Alaska Native)* (2)	2	0.01
Yakama (1)	1	<0.01
Yaqui (2)	3	0.01
Yup'ik *(Alaska Native)* (0)	1	<0.01
Asian (1,289)	1,928	6.24
Not Hispanic (1,252)	1,809	5.85
Hispanic (37)	119	0.38
Burmese (1)	1	<0.01
Cambodian (14)	14	0.05
Chinese, ex. Taiwanese (260)	410	1.33
Filipino (250)	458	1.48
Hmong (23)	23	0.07
Indian (163)	194	0.63
Indonesian (6)	11	0.04
Japanese (214)	381	1.23
Korean (164)	208	0.67
Laotian (7)	12	0.04
Malaysian (2)	2	0.01
Pakistani (6)	16	0.05
Sri Lankan (1)	3	0.01
Taiwanese (11)	16	0.05
Thai (28)	33	0.11
Vietnamese (95)	133	0.43
Hawaii Native/Pacific Islander (57)	158	0.51
Not Hispanic (48)	128	0.41
Hispanic (9)	30	0.10
Fijian (5)	7	0.02
Guamanian/Chamorro (8)	49	0.16
Native Hawaiian (17)	54	0.17
Samoan (6)	16	0.05
Tongan (11)	12	0.04
White (26,479)	27,722	89.68
Not Hispanic (24,694)	25,663	83.02
Hispanic (1,785)	2,059	6.66

Fairfield

Place Type: City
County: Solano
Population: 105,321†

Ancestry‡	Population	%
Afghan (213)	271	0.26
African, Sub-Saharan (1,989)	2,343	2.26
African (1,706)	2,042	1.97
Cape Verdean (57)	57	0.05
Ethiopian (32)	41	0.04
Kenyan (135)	135	0.13
Nigerian (31)	40	0.04
Sudanese (28)	28	0.03
American (1,938)	1,938	1.87
Arab (489)	898	0.87
Egyptian (37)	135	0.13
Iraqi (12)	12	0.01
Jordanian (107)	113	0.11
Lebanese (69)	163	0.16
Moroccan (0)	9	0.01
Palestinian (191)	226	0.22
Syrian (19)	88	0.08
Other Arab (54)	152	0.15
Armenian (28)	83	0.08
Austrian (48)	122	0.12

*Notes: † The Census 2010 population figure is used to calculate the percentages in the Hispanic Origin and Race categories. Ancestry percentages are based on the 2006-2010 American Community Survey population (not shown); ‡ Numbers in parentheses indicate the number of people reporting a single ancestry; * Numbers in parentheses indicate the number of persons reporting this race alone, not in combination with any other race; Please refer to the Explanation of Data for more information.*

Basque (28)	62	0.06
Belgian (12)	42	0.04
Brazilian (127)	127	0.12
British (141)	248	0.24
Canadian (116)	200	0.19
Croatian (32)	43	0.04
Czech (22)	152	0.15
Czechoslovakian (0)	36	0.03
Danish (83)	435	0.42
Dutch (176)	915	0.88
Eastern European (51)	68	0.07
English (1,747)	5,395	5.20
European (1,472)	1,595	1.54
Finnish (0)	58	0.06
French, ex. Basque (223)	1,914	1.85
French Canadian (109)	396	0.38
German (2,662)	8,597	8.29
German Russian (19)	19	0.02
Greek (237)	516	0.50
Guyanese (0)	16	0.02
Hungarian (82)	236	0.23
Icelander (15)	49	0.05
Iranian (62)	120	0.12
Irish (1,847)	7,191	6.93
Italian (1,375)	3,714	3.58
Latvian (29)	29	0.03
Lithuanian (17)	49	0.05
Luxemburger (14)	14	0.01
Maltese (25)	32	0.03
Northern European (53)	53	0.05
Norwegian (405)	1,515	1.46
Pennsylvania German (25)	43	0.04
Polish (255)	1,196	1.15
Portuguese (470)	1,208	1.16
Russian (49)	233	0.22
Scandinavian (66)	206	0.20
Scotch-Irish (273)	1,080	1.04
Scottish (513)	1,715	1.65
Serbian (0)	11	0.01
Slavic (65)	128	0.12
Slovak (0)	160	0.15
Soviet Union (7)	7	0.01
Swedish (250)	1,213	1.17
Swiss (31)	173	0.17
Turkish (80)	103	0.10
Ukrainian (50)	89	0.09
Welsh (17)	321	0.31
West Indian, ex. Hispanic (88)	245	0.24
Jamaican (88)	229	0.22
Trinidadian/Tobagonian (0)	16	0.02
Yugoslavian (0)	94	0.09

Hispanic Origin	Population	%
Hispanic or Latino (of any race)	28,789	27.33
Central American, ex. Mexican	2,099	1.99
Costa Rican	63	0.06
Guatemalan	275	0.26
Honduran	106	0.10
Nicaraguan	478	0.45
Panamanian	89	0.08
Salvadoran	1,068	1.01
Other Central American	20	0.02
Cuban	179	0.17
Dominican Republic	60	0.06
Mexican	22,360	21.23
Puerto Rican	1,184	1.12
South American	566	0.54
Argentinean	31	0.03
Bolivian	12	0.01
Chilean	45	0.04
Colombian	136	0.13
Ecuadorian	38	0.04
Paraguayan	4	<0.01
Peruvian	254	0.24
Uruguayan	4	<0.01
Venezuelan	30	0.03
Other South American	12	0.01
Other Hispanic or Latino	2,341	2.22

Race*	Population	%
African-American/Black (16,586)	20,028	19.02
Not Hispanic (15,979)	18,660	17.72
Hispanic (607)	1,368	1.30
American Indian/Alaska Native (869)	2,529	2.40
Not Hispanic (462)	1,683	1.60
Hispanic (407)	846	0.80
Alaska Athabascan *(Ala. Nat.)* (1)	3	<0.01
Aleut *(Alaska Native)* (2)	3	<0.01
Apache (40)	84	0.08
Blackfeet (2)	70	0.07
Canadian/French Am. Ind. (0)	3	<0.01
Central American Ind. (0)	6	0.01
Cherokee (76)	414	0.39
Cheyenne (0)	2	<0.01
Chickasaw (7)	16	0.02
Chippewa (16)	34	0.03
Choctaw (21)	111	0.11
Colville (1)	1	<0.01
Comanche (0)	9	0.01
Cree (0)	6	0.01
Creek (7)	35	0.03
Crow (1)	4	<0.01
Delaware (0)	1	<0.01
Hopi (1)	3	<0.01
Inupiat *(Alaska Native)* (2)	7	0.01
Iroquois (8)	23	0.02
Kiowa (2)	2	<0.01
Menominee (1)	1	<0.01
Mexican American Ind. (58)	109	0.10
Navajo (37)	54	0.05
Osage (0)	7	0.01
Paiute (6)	18	0.02
Potawatomi (12)	13	0.01
Pueblo (9)	10	0.01
Puget Sound Salish (1)	2	<0.01
Seminole (3)	16	0.02
Shoshone (2)	5	<0.01
Sioux (17)	55	0.05
South American Ind. (3)	10	0.01
Spanish American Ind. (6)	7	0.01
Tlingit-Haida *(Alaska Native)* (2)	9	0.01
Tohono O'Odham (5)	9	0.01
Tsimshian *(Alaska Native)* (0)	1	<0.01
Ute (1)	2	<0.01
Yaqui (4)	18	0.02
Yuman (4)	4	<0.01
Yup'ik *(Alaska Native)* (0)	1	<0.01
Asian (15,700)	20,062	19.05
Not Hispanic (15,265)	18,804	17.85
Hispanic (435)	1,258	1.19
Bangladeshi (2)	5	<0.01
Burmese (9)	16	0.02
Cambodian (37)	63	0.06
Chinese, ex. Taiwanese (1,049)	1,783	1.69
Filipino (9,590)	12,265	11.65
Hmong (141)	170	0.16
Indian (1,846)	2,051	1.95
Indonesian (24)	47	0.04
Japanese (616)	1,452	1.38
Korean (446)	775	0.74
Laotian (357)	437	0.41
Malaysian (5)	8	0.01
Nepalese (22)	23	0.02
Pakistani (121)	137	0.13
Sri Lankan (8)	10	0.01
Taiwanese (63)	92	0.09
Thai (161)	323	0.31
Vietnamese (632)	808	0.77
Hawaii Native/Pacific Islander (1,149)	2,503	2.38
Not Hispanic (1,049)	2,140	2.03
Hispanic (100)	363	0.34
Fijian (143)	183	0.17
Guamanian/Chamorro (539)	1,013	0.96
Marshallese (4)	5	<0.01
Native Hawaiian (119)	668	0.63
Samoan (194)	348	0.33
Tongan (44)	57	0.05
White (48,407)	55,602	52.79
Not Hispanic (37,091)	42,174	40.04
Hispanic (11,316)	13,428	12.75

Fairview

Place Type: CDP
County: Alameda
Population: 10,003†

Ancestry‡	Population	%
Afghan (78)	78	0.79
African, Sub-Saharan (85)	103	1.05
African (12)	30	0.31
Nigerian (73)	73	0.74
American (15)	15	0.15
Austrian (0)	39	0.40
Belgian (0)	23	0.23
British (58)	68	0.69
Bulgarian (23)	44	0.45
Canadian (15)	15	0.15
Celtic (0)	49	0.50
Croatian (12)	12	0.12
Danish (18)	42	0.43
Dutch (28)	202	2.06
Eastern European (11)	11	0.11
English (188)	650	6.62
European (185)	216	2.20
Finnish (0)	17	0.17
French, ex. Basque (26)	276	2.81
French Canadian (0)	18	0.18
German (196)	1,036	10.56
Greek (0)	9	0.09
Hungarian (15)	44	0.45
Iranian (27)	47	0.48
Irish (137)	832	8.48
Italian (144)	349	3.56
Lithuanian (7)	15	0.15
Northern European (59)	68	0.69
Norwegian (40)	183	1.87
Pennsylvania German (0)	9	0.09
Polish (21)	67	0.68
Portuguese (140)	611	6.23
Russian (23)	23	0.23
Scandinavian (0)	18	0.18
Scotch-Irish (48)	150	1.53
Scottish (8)	133	1.36
Slavic (37)	49	0.50
Swedish (32)	137	1.40
Swiss (0)	73	0.74
Welsh (11)	46	0.47

Hispanic Origin	Population	%
Hispanic or Latino (of any race)	2,171	21.70
Central American, ex. Mexican	215	2.15
Costa Rican	4	0.04
Guatemalan	29	0.29
Honduran	8	0.08
Nicaraguan	70	0.70
Panamanian	11	0.11
Salvadoran	93	0.93
Cuban	14	0.14
Dominican Republic	7	0.07
Mexican	1,549	15.49
Puerto Rican	106	1.06
South American	94	0.94
Argentinean	4	0.04
Bolivian	1	0.01
Chilean	11	0.11
Colombian	7	0.07
Ecuadorian	3	0.03
Paraguayan	1	0.01
Peruvian	57	0.57
Venezuelan	10	0.10
Other Hispanic or Latino	186	1.86

Race*	Population	%
African-American/Black (2,105)	2,366	23.65
Not Hispanic (2,047)	2,246	22.45
Hispanic (58)	120	1.20
American Indian/Alaska Native (76)	217	2.17

*Notes: † The Census 2010 population figure is used to calculate the percentages in the Hispanic Origin and Race categories. Ancestry percentages are based on the 2006-2010 American Community Survey population (not shown); ‡ Numbers in parentheses indicate the number of people reporting a single ancestry; * Numbers in parentheses indicate the number of persons reporting this race alone, not in combination with any other race; Please refer to the Explanation of Data for more information.*

Not Hispanic (45)	131	1.31
Hispanic (31)	86	0.86
Apache (0)	4	0.04
Blackfeet (2)	5	0.05
Canadian/French Am. Ind. (1)	4	0.04
Cherokee (1)	32	0.32
Chickasaw (3)	3	0.03
Chippewa (2)	3	0.03
Choctaw (2)	6	0.06
Colville (3)	3	0.03
Comanche (1)	1	0.01
Cree (0)	1	0.01
Creek (1)	2	0.02
Inupiat *(Alaska Native)* (1)	1	0.01
Lumbee (1)	1	0.01
Mexican American Ind. (7)	13	0.13
Navajo (3)	3	0.03
Osage (2)	2	0.02
Potawatomi (0)	4	0.04
Sioux (2)	3	0.03
South American Ind. (0)	1	0.01
Tlingit-Haida *(Alaska Native)* (0)	3	0.03
Tsimshian *(Alaska Native)* (0)	3	0.03
Asian (1,525)	1,885	18.84
Not Hispanic (1,484)	1,778	17.77
Hispanic (41)	107	1.07
Bangladeshi (4)	4	0.04
Burmese (2)	2	0.02
Cambodian (21)	24	0.24
Chinese, ex. Taiwanese (370)	460	4.60
Filipino (573)	747	7.47
Indian (184)	229	2.29
Indonesian (4)	7	0.07
Japanese (92)	151	1.51
Korean (51)	64	0.64
Laotian (10)	14	0.14
Malaysian (1)	2	0.02
Pakistani (24)	27	0.27
Taiwanese (16)	17	0.17
Thai (15)	21	0.21
Vietnamese (91)	111	1.11
Hawaii Native/Pacific Islander (129)	233	2.33
Not Hispanic (114)	202	2.02
Hispanic (15)	31	0.31
Fijian (50)	52	0.52
Guamanian/Chamorro (2)	11	0.11
Native Hawaiian (9)	44	0.44
Samoan (27)	39	0.39
Tongan (27)	32	0.32
White (4,499)	5,058	50.56
Not Hispanic (3,618)	3,992	39.91
Hispanic (881)	1,066	10.66

Fallbrook

Place Type: CDP
County: San Diego
Population: 30,534†

Ancestry‡	Population	%
African, Sub-Saharan (232)	307	1.03
African (232)	307	1.03
American (880)	880	2.94
Arab (17)	123	0.41
Arab (0)	32	0.11
Lebanese (0)	9	0.03
Moroccan (0)	9	0.03
Syrian (17)	73	0.24
Austrian (22)	140	0.47
Basque (28)	28	0.09
Belgian (7)	28	0.09
British (119)	170	0.57
Bulgarian (18)	32	0.11
Canadian (58)	129	0.43
Czech (54)	164	0.55
Czechoslovakian (9)	9	0.03
Danish (48)	123	0.41
Dutch (125)	362	1.21
English (1,048)	3,203	10.72
European (594)	902	3.02
Finnish (23)	47	0.16
French, ex. Basque (119)	680	2.27
French Canadian (103)	151	0.51
German (1,206)	4,310	14.42
Greek (66)	114	0.38
Guyanese (35)	35	0.12
Hungarian (71)	138	0.46
Iranian (52)	63	0.21
Irish (1,104)	3,534	11.82
Italian (531)	982	3.29
Latvian (8)	8	0.03
Lithuanian (37)	67	0.22
Macedonian (12)	19	0.06
Norwegian (221)	489	1.64
Pennsylvania German (0)	11	0.04
Polish (92)	530	1.77
Portuguese (22)	107	0.36
Romanian (0)	13	0.04
Russian (21)	108	0.36
Scandinavian (0)	45	0.15
Scotch-Irish (77)	457	1.53
Scottish (103)	908	3.04
Slavic (0)	21	0.07
Slovene (26)	26	0.09
Swedish (121)	415	1.39
Swiss (62)	181	0.61
Ukrainian (22)	53	0.18
Welsh (32)	169	0.57
West Indian, ex. Hispanic (36)	36	0.12
Haitian (36)	36	0.12

Hispanic Origin	Population	%
Hispanic or Latino (of any race)	13,800	45.20
Central American, ex. Mexican	911	2.98
Costa Rican	17	0.06
Guatemalan	815	2.67
Honduran	26	0.09
Nicaraguan	9	0.03
Panamanian	4	0.01
Salvadoran	33	0.11
Other Central American	7	0.02
Cuban	36	0.12
Dominican Republic	14	0.05
Mexican	12,033	39.41
Puerto Rican	148	0.48
South American	104	0.34
Argentinean	12	0.04
Chilean	10	0.03
Colombian	27	0.09
Ecuadorian	16	0.05
Peruvian	22	0.07
Uruguayan	5	0.02
Venezuelan	6	0.02
Other South American	6	0.02
Other Hispanic or Latino	554	1.81

Race*	Population	%
African-American/Black (489)	675	2.21
Not Hispanic (411)	518	1.70
Hispanic (78)	157	0.51
American Indian/Alaska Native (233)	510	1.67
Not Hispanic (107)	274	0.90
Hispanic (126)	236	0.77
Alaska Athabascan *(Ala. Nat.)* (0)	1	<0.01
Apache (5)	9	0.03
Arapaho (1)	1	<0.01
Blackfeet (0)	9	0.03
Canadian/French Am. Ind. (2)	2	0.01
Central American Ind. (15)	24	0.08
Cherokee (11)	56	0.18
Chickasaw (0)	3	0.01
Chippewa (4)	8	0.03
Choctaw (1)	20	0.07
Comanche (3)	5	0.02
Creek (0)	2	0.01
Hopi (0)	11	0.04
Inupiat *(Alaska Native)* (1)	1	<0.01
Iroquois (4)	11	0.04
Mexican American Ind. (60)	93	0.30
Navajo (6)	16	0.05
Osage (3)	5	0.02
Ottawa (1)	1	<0.01
Pima (0)	2	0.01
Pueblo (1)	4	0.01
Sioux (2)	11	0.04
Spanish American Ind. (1)	2	0.01
Tlingit-Haida *(Alaska Native)* (3)	3	0.01
Yaqui (1)	14	0.05
Asian (592)	925	3.03
Not Hispanic (550)	815	2.67
Hispanic (42)	110	0.36
Burmese (2)	2	0.01
Cambodian (15)	18	0.06
Chinese, ex. Taiwanese (54)	108	0.35
Filipino (256)	377	1.23
Hmong (16)	16	0.05
Indian (31)	43	0.14
Indonesian (1)	5	0.02
Japanese (94)	196	0.64
Korean (40)	57	0.19
Laotian (5)	11	0.04
Malaysian (0)	1	<0.01
Sri Lankan (4)	4	0.01
Taiwanese (1)	2	0.01
Thai (14)	28	0.09
Vietnamese (34)	62	0.20
Hawaii Native/Pacific Islander (71)	197	0.65
Not Hispanic (57)	148	0.48
Hispanic (14)	49	0.16
Guamanian/Chamorro (20)	60	0.20
Marshallese (0)	1	<0.01
Native Hawaiian (18)	73	0.24
Samoan (25)	36	0.12
Tongan (1)	6	0.02
White (20,454)	21,629	70.84
Not Hispanic (15,006)	15,513	50.81
Hispanic (5,448)	6,116	20.03

Farmersville

Place Type: City
County: Tulare
Population: 10,588†

Ancestry‡	Population	%
American (27)	27	0.26
Austrian (14)	14	0.14
Czech (0)	5	0.05
Dutch (0)	9	0.09
English (48)	102	0.99
French, ex. Basque (30)	64	0.62
German (35)	247	2.40
Greek (0)	10	0.10
Irish (66)	184	1.79
Italian (81)	216	2.10
Polish (14)	14	0.14
Portuguese (53)	118	1.15
Scotch-Irish (10)	18	0.18
Scottish (0)	28	0.27
Swedish (10)	28	0.27

Hispanic Origin	Population	%
Hispanic or Latino (of any race)	8,876	83.83
Central American, ex. Mexican	109	1.03
Guatemalan	7	0.07
Honduran	5	0.05
Nicaraguan	3	0.03
Panamanian	3	0.03
Salvadoran	91	0.86
Cuban	2	0.02
Dominican Republic	1	0.01
Mexican	8,339	78.76
Puerto Rican	36	0.34
South American	13	0.12
Argentinean	6	0.06
Chilean	4	0.04
Peruvian	3	0.03
Other Hispanic or Latino	376	3.55

*Notes: † The Census 2010 population figure is used to calculate the percentages in the Hispanic Origin and Race categories. Ancestry percentages are based on the 2006-2010 American Community Survey population (not shown); ‡ Numbers in parentheses indicate the number of people reporting a single ancestry; * Numbers in parentheses indicate the number of persons reporting this race alone, not in combination with any other race; Please refer to the Explanation of Data for more information.*

Race*	Population	%
African-American/Black (60)	98	0.93
Not Hispanic (15)	32	0.30
Hispanic (45)	66	0.62
American Indian/Alaska Native (213)	324	3.06
Not Hispanic (51)	115	1.09
Hispanic (162)	209	1.97
Apache (5)	11	0.10
Blackfeet (0)	6	0.06
Canadian/French Am. Ind. (0)	1	0.01
Cherokee (7)	32	0.30
Chickasaw (0)	6	0.06
Choctaw (7)	21	0.20
Comanche (1)	1	0.01
Creek (4)	5	0.05
Mexican American Ind. (95)	106	1.00
Navajo (0)	3	0.03
Paiute (0)	2	0.02
Potawatomi (1)	2	0.02
Sioux (1)	2	0.02
Ute (1)	1	0.01
Yaqui (4)	5	0.05
Asian (72)	111	1.05
Not Hispanic (69)	87	0.82
Hispanic (3)	24	0.23
Chinese, ex. Taiwanese (5)	12	0.11
Filipino (23)	38	0.36
Indian (2)	4	0.04
Japanese (1)	8	0.08
Korean (1)	3	0.03
Laotian (12)	12	0.11
Thai (18)	18	0.17
Vietnamese (1)	5	0.05
Hawaii Native/Pacific Islander (5)	20	0.19
Not Hispanic (4)	13	0.12
Hispanic (1)	7	0.07
Guamanian/Chamorro (3)	3	0.03
Native Hawaiian (2)	6	0.06
White (5,295)	5,696	53.80
Not Hispanic (1,455)	1,556	14.70
Hispanic (3,840)	4,140	39.10

Fillmore

Place Type: City
County: Ventura
Population: 15,002†

Ancestry‡	Population	%
American (426)	426	2.89
Arab (25)	25	0.17
Syrian (25)	25	0.17
Assyrian/Chaldean/Syriac (0)	15	0.10
Austrian (0)	17	0.12
Canadian (0)	29	0.20
Danish (15)	112	0.76
Dutch (12)	112	0.76
English (215)	693	4.71
European (58)	111	0.75
Finnish (0)	9	0.06
French, ex. Basque (15)	219	1.49
French Canadian (15)	15	0.10
German (158)	670	4.55
Greek (0)	12	0.08
Hungarian (9)	9	0.06
Iranian (0)	15	0.10
Irish (80)	648	4.40
Italian (44)	157	1.07
Lithuanian (13)	13	0.09
Northern European (10)	10	0.07
Norwegian (0)	42	0.29
Polish (32)	221	1.50
Portuguese (0)	66	0.45
Romanian (13)	13	0.09
Russian (42)	42	0.29
Scandinavian (0)	74	0.50
Scotch-Irish (63)	164	1.11
Scottish (235)	406	2.76
Swedish (55)	169	1.15
Swiss (0)	29	0.20
Welsh (7)	15	0.10

Hispanic Origin	Population	%
Hispanic or Latino (of any race)	11,212	74.74
Central American, ex. Mexican	139	0.93
Costa Rican	11	0.07
Guatemalan	53	0.35
Honduran	13	0.09
Nicaraguan	2	0.01
Panamanian	2	0.01
Salvadoran	58	0.39
Cuban	24	0.16
Dominican Republic	2	0.01
Mexican	10,565	70.42
Puerto Rican	42	0.28
South American	28	0.19
Argentinean	2	0.01
Bolivian	1	0.01
Chilean	10	0.07
Colombian	2	0.01
Ecuadorian	10	0.07
Peruvian	3	0.02
Other Hispanic or Latino	412	2.75

Race*	Population	%
African-American/Black (75)	118	0.79
Not Hispanic (44)	59	0.39
Hispanic (31)	59	0.39
American Indian/Alaska Native (180)	306	2.04
Not Hispanic (42)	94	0.63
Hispanic (138)	212	1.41
Apache (2)	9	0.06
Central American Ind. (0)	1	0.01
Cherokee (13)	44	0.29
Chickasaw (0)	2	0.01
Choctaw (4)	14	0.09
Creek (0)	1	0.01
Crow (0)	1	0.01
Mexican American Ind. (34)	38	0.25
Navajo (9)	9	0.06
Paiute (0)	3	0.02
Potawatomi (0)	1	0.01
Pueblo (3)	3	0.02
Shoshone (1)	1	0.01
Sioux (2)	9	0.06
Tohono O'Odham (0)	2	0.01
Yaqui (0)	6	0.04
Asian (155)	282	1.88
Not Hispanic (125)	187	1.25
Hispanic (30)	95	0.63
Cambodian (8)	9	0.06
Chinese, ex. Taiwanese (19)	34	0.23
Filipino (49)	96	0.64
Indian (22)	33	0.22
Indonesian (1)	1	0.01
Japanese (20)	41	0.27
Korean (14)	19	0.13
Laotian (8)	9	0.06
Taiwanese (0)	2	0.01
Thai (0)	4	0.03
Vietnamese (6)	7	0.05
Hawaii Native/Pacific Islander (12)	32	0.21
Not Hispanic (8)	18	0.12
Hispanic (4)	14	0.09
Fijian (0)	4	0.03
Guamanian/Chamorro (0)	1	0.01
Native Hawaiian (5)	19	0.13
Samoan (0)	10	0.07
White (8,581)	9,289	61.92
Not Hispanic (3,400)	3,532	23.54
Hispanic (5,181)	5,757	38.37

Firebaugh

Place Type: City
County: Fresno
Population: 7,549†

Ancestry‡	Population	%
American (16)	16	0.22
Arab (206)	206	2.79
Arab (93)	93	1.26
Other Arab (113)	113	1.53
Austrian (0)	11	0.15
Basque (0)	10	0.14
Danish (12)	12	0.16
English (94)	128	1.74
French, ex. Basque (25)	39	0.53
German (46)	63	0.85
Irish (0)	34	0.46
Italian (53)	70	0.95
Polish (0)	14	0.19
Portuguese (26)	26	0.35
Russian (0)	11	0.15
Scotch-Irish (12)	22	0.30

Hispanic Origin	Population	%
Hispanic or Latino (of any race)	6,887	91.23
Central American, ex. Mexican	232	3.07
Guatemalan	8	0.11
Honduran	9	0.12
Nicaraguan	16	0.21
Salvadoran	198	2.62
Other Central American	1	0.01
Mexican	6,434	85.23
Puerto Rican	1	0.01
South American	2	0.03
Ecuadorian	1	0.01
Peruvian	1	0.01
Other Hispanic or Latino	218	2.89

Race*	Population	%
African-American/Black (70)	87	1.15
Not Hispanic (25)	26	0.34
Hispanic (45)	61	0.81
American Indian/Alaska Native (116)	139	1.84
Not Hispanic (18)	21	0.28
Hispanic (98)	118	1.56
Apache (3)	3	0.04
Cherokee (2)	5	0.07
Choctaw (4)	6	0.08
Iroquois (0)	2	0.03
Mexican American Ind. (23)	23	0.30
Navajo (2)	2	0.03
South American Ind. (0)	1	0.01
Spanish American Ind. (3)	3	0.04
Asian (40)	61	0.81
Not Hispanic (35)	40	0.53
Hispanic (5)	21	0.28
Chinese, ex. Taiwanese (9)	11	0.15
Filipino (2)	8	0.11
Indian (22)	23	0.30
Japanese (1)	2	0.03
Korean (2)	2	0.03
Hawaii Native/Pacific Islander (0)	15	0.20
Not Hispanic (0)	4	0.05
Hispanic (0)	11	0.15
Guamanian/Chamorro (0)	4	0.05
White (4,715)	4,919	65.16
Not Hispanic (564)	579	7.67
Hispanic (4,151)	4,340	57.49

Florence-Graham

Place Type: CDP
County: Los Angeles
Population: 63,387†

Ancestry‡	Population	%
African, Sub-Saharan (167)	167	0.27
African (161)	161	0.26
Nigerian (6)	6	0.01
American (497)	497	0.82
Arab (7)	22	0.04
Moroccan (0)	6	0.01
Other Arab (7)	16	0.03
British (20)	20	0.03
Dutch (0)	57	0.09

*Notes: † The Census 2010 population figure is used to calculate the percentages in the Hispanic Origin and Race categories. Ancestry percentages are based on the 2006-2010 American Community Survey population (not shown); ‡ Numbers in parentheses indicate the number of people reporting a single ancestry; * Numbers in parentheses indicate the number of persons reporting this race alone, not in combination with any other race; Please refer to the Explanation of Data for more information.*

Eastern European (27)	27	0.04
French, ex. Basque (10)	136	0.22
German (0)	99	0.16
Irish (11)	94	0.15
Italian (8)	16	0.03
Lithuanian (8)	18	0.03
Scottish (18)	18	0.03
West Indian, ex. Hispanic (33)	72	0.12
Belizean (11)	50	0.08
Haitian (22)	22	0.04

Hispanic Origin	Population	%
Hispanic or Latino (of any race)	57,066	90.03
Central American, ex. Mexican	5,736	9.05
Costa Rican	11	0.02
Guatemalan	1,685	2.66
Honduran	505	0.80
Nicaraguan	196	0.31
Panamanian	4	0.01
Salvadoran	3,239	5.11
Other Central American	96	0.15
Cuban	47	0.07
Dominican Republic	4	0.01
Mexican	47,862	75.51
Puerto Rican	143	0.23
South American	120	0.19
Argentinean	10	0.02
Bolivian	1	<0.01
Chilean	12	0.02
Colombian	9	0.01
Ecuadorian	43	0.07
Peruvian	41	0.06
Other South American	4	0.01
Other Hispanic or Latino	3,154	4.98

Race*	Population	%
African-American/Black (5,861)	6,163	9.72
Not Hispanic (5,517)	5,620	8.87
Hispanic (344)	543	0.86
American Indian/Alaska Native (498)	788	1.24
Not Hispanic (50)	100	0.16
Hispanic (448)	688	1.09
Apache (2)	4	0.01
Arapaho (0)	2	<0.01
Blackfeet (1)	5	0.01
Canadian/French Am. Ind. (0)	1	<0.01
Central American Ind. (9)	26	0.04
Cherokee (9)	26	0.04
Choctaw (4)	11	0.02
Cree (1)	1	<0.01
Creek (1)	3	<0.01
Kiowa (6)	6	0.01
Lumbee (5)	5	0.01
Mexican American Ind. (154)	213	0.34
Navajo (8)	11	0.02
Osage (0)	1	<0.01
Pima (3)	3	<0.01
Seminole (0)	1	<0.01
South American Ind. (4)	5	0.01
Spanish American Ind. (13)	34	0.05
Tlingit-Haida *(Alaska Native)* (0)	3	<0.01
Tohono O'Odham (2)	2	<0.01
Yaqui (2)	3	<0.01
Yuman (1)	1	<0.01
Asian (150)	290	0.46
Not Hispanic (91)	110	0.17
Hispanic (59)	180	0.28
Bangladeshi (0)	12	0.02
Cambodian (5)	9	0.01
Chinese, ex. Taiwanese (15)	22	0.03
Filipino (40)	67	0.11
Indian (23)	41	0.06
Japanese (22)	43	0.07
Korean (11)	19	0.03
Laotian (4)	4	0.01
Thai (2)	2	<0.01
Vietnamese (1)	1	<0.01
Hawaii Native/Pacific Islander (25)	89	0.14
Not Hispanic (9)	22	0.03
Hispanic (16)	67	0.11
Guamanian/Chamorro (6)	10	0.02
Native Hawaiian (10)	16	0.03
Samoan (7)	17	0.03
White (23,895)	25,713	40.57
Not Hispanic (422)	496	0.78
Hispanic (23,473)	25,217	39.78

Florin

Place Type: CDP
County: Sacramento
Population: 47,513†

Ancestry‡	Population	%
Afghan (42)	42	0.09
African, Sub-Saharan (278)	454	0.95
African (168)	304	0.64
Cape Verdean (77)	77	0.16
Ethiopian (33)	64	0.13
Nigerian (0)	9	0.02
American (738)	738	1.54
Arab (265)	297	0.62
Arab (227)	227	0.47
Egyptian (17)	17	0.04
Iraqi (0)	32	0.07
Jordanian (21)	21	0.04
Australian (0)	10	0.02
Austrian (0)	17	0.04
Basque (10)	17	0.04
British (42)	106	0.22
Bulgarian (0)	20	0.04
Canadian (28)	79	0.17
Czech (0)	17	0.04
Czechoslovakian (18)	28	0.06
Danish (17)	75	0.16
Dutch (8)	426	0.89
English (432)	1,909	3.99
European (160)	174	0.36
Finnish (0)	30	0.06
French, ex. Basque (92)	901	1.88
French Canadian (75)	134	0.28
German (691)	2,802	5.85
Greek (51)	141	0.29
Hungarian (0)	39	0.08
Iranian (39)	39	0.08
Irish (510)	2,477	5.17
Israeli (0)	34	0.07
Italian (222)	1,368	2.86
Lithuanian (0)	8	0.02
Norwegian (116)	266	0.56
Polish (112)	293	0.61
Portuguese (246)	1,204	2.52
Romanian (13)	56	0.12
Russian (135)	296	0.62
Scandinavian (42)	91	0.19
Scotch-Irish (210)	483	1.01
Scottish (152)	445	0.93
Serbian (10)	37	0.08
Slavic (83)	83	0.17
Swedish (63)	316	0.66
Swiss (24)	39	0.08
Turkish (0)	38	0.08
Ukrainian (88)	88	0.18
Welsh (31)	129	0.27
West Indian, ex. Hispanic (64)	80	0.17
Jamaican (64)	80	0.17
Yugoslavian (22)	22	0.05

Hispanic Origin	Population	%
Hispanic or Latino (of any race)	13,048	27.46
Central American, ex. Mexican	616	1.30
Costa Rican	9	0.02
Guatemalan	134	0.28
Honduran	50	0.11
Nicaraguan	140	0.29
Panamanian	33	0.07
Salvadoran	246	0.52
Other Central American	4	0.01
Cuban	69	0.15
Dominican Republic	11	0.02
Mexican	11,196	23.56
Puerto Rican	337	0.71
South American	72	0.15
Argentinean	3	0.01
Chilean	9	0.02
Colombian	9	0.02
Ecuadorian	5	0.01
Peruvian	38	0.08
Venezuelan	8	0.02
Other Hispanic or Latino	747	1.57

Race*	Population	%
African-American/Black (7,521)	8,788	18.50
Not Hispanic (7,188)	8,111	17.07
Hispanic (333)	677	1.42
American Indian/Alaska Native (543)	1,232	2.59
Not Hispanic (246)	721	1.52
Hispanic (297)	511	1.08
Alaska Athabascan *(Ala. Nat.)* (3)	3	0.01
Aleut *(Alaska Native)* (0)	1	<0.01
Apache (24)	51	0.11
Arapaho (0)	1	<0.01
Blackfeet (7)	42	0.09
Canadian/French Am. Ind. (2)	4	0.01
Central American Ind. (2)	2	<0.01
Cherokee (48)	179	0.38
Chickasaw (4)	9	0.02
Chippewa (6)	14	0.03
Choctaw (16)	63	0.13
Comanche (1)	1	<0.01
Creek (2)	3	0.01
Crow (1)	3	0.01
Delaware (1)	1	<0.01
Houma (0)	2	<0.01
Iroquois (0)	6	0.01
Lumbee (4)	4	0.01
Menominee (0)	1	<0.01
Mexican American Ind. (53)	72	0.15
Navajo (24)	33	0.07
Osage (1)	2	<0.01
Paiute (3)	9	0.02
Pima (0)	1	<0.01
Potawatomi (3)	4	0.01
Pueblo (2)	4	0.01
Seminole (3)	6	0.01
Shoshone (1)	5	0.01
Sioux (10)	23	0.05
South American Ind. (0)	1	<0.01
Spanish American Ind. (8)	9	0.02
Tlingit-Haida *(Alaska Native)* (0)	3	0.01
Tsimshian *(Alaska Native)* (0)	1	<0.01
Yaqui (0)	1	<0.01
Yuman (0)	1	<0.01
Asian (13,605)	14,937	31.44
Not Hispanic (13,415)	14,420	30.35
Hispanic (190)	517	1.09
Bangladeshi (0)	1	<0.01
Burmese (3)	15	0.03
Cambodian (285)	357	0.75
Chinese, ex. Taiwanese (2,073)	2,400	5.05
Filipino (2,026)	2,586	5.44
Hmong (2,829)	2,933	6.17
Indian (980)	1,350	2.84
Indonesian (25)	32	0.07
Japanese (173)	375	0.79
Korean (79)	117	0.25
Laotian (991)	1,128	2.37
Malaysian (3)	6	0.01
Pakistani (280)	304	0.64
Taiwanese (10)	20	0.04
Thai (45)	90	0.19
Vietnamese (3,126)	3,461	7.28
Hawaii Native/Pacific Islander (815)	1,388	2.92
Not Hispanic (783)	1,271	2.68
Hispanic (32)	117	0.25
Fijian (420)	500	1.05
Guamanian/Chamorro (79)	114	0.24
Marshallese (37)	37	0.08
Native Hawaiian (27)	152	0.32
Samoan (72)	107	0.23

*Notes: † The Census 2010 population figure is used to calculate the percentages in the Hispanic Origin and Race categories. Ancestry percentages are based on the 2006-2010 American Community Survey population (not shown); ‡ Numbers in parentheses indicate the number of people reporting a single ancestry; * Numbers in parentheses indicate the number of persons reporting this race alone, not in combination with any other race; Please refer to the Explanation of Data for more information.*

Tongan (104)	119	0.25
White (15,034)	17,075	35.94
Not Hispanic (10,650)	11,906	25.06
Hispanic (4,384)	5,169	10.88

Folsom

Place Type: City
County: Sacramento
Population: 72,203†

Ancestry‡	Population	%
Afghan (17)	17	0.02
African, Sub-Saharan (222)	266	0.39
African (189)	233	0.34
Ethiopian (10)	10	0.01
Nigerian (13)	13	0.02
South African (10)	10	0.01
Albanian (11)	33	0.05
American (1,838)	1,838	2.66
Arab (166)	359	0.52
Arab (29)	29	0.04
Egyptian (44)	93	0.13
Lebanese (24)	168	0.24
Moroccan (11)	11	0.02
Palestinian (29)	29	0.04
Other Arab (29)	29	0.04
Armenian (70)	179	0.26
Australian (13)	27	0.04
Austrian (11)	114	0.17
Basque (12)	12	0.02
Belgian (16)	79	0.11
British (179)	353	0.51
Bulgarian (0)	58	0.08
Canadian (131)	239	0.35
Celtic (28)	28	0.04
Croatian (43)	134	0.19
Czech (48)	329	0.48
Czechoslovakian (0)	45	0.07
Danish (219)	823	1.19
Dutch (358)	1,411	2.04
Eastern European (24)	40	0.06
English (1,923)	7,950	11.51
European (998)	1,269	1.84
Finnish (0)	148	0.21
French, ex. Basque (207)	1,979	2.87
French Canadian (150)	391	0.57
German (3,744)	12,307	17.82
Greek (132)	308	0.45
Hungarian (52)	258	0.37
Icelander (0)	33	0.05
Iranian (444)	531	0.77
Irish (1,793)	9,088	13.16
Italian (1,857)	6,013	8.71
Latvian (21)	65	0.09
Lithuanian (24)	89	0.13
Northern European (158)	168	0.24
Norwegian (540)	1,785	2.58
Pennsylvania German (0)	39	0.06
Polish (399)	1,910	2.77
Portuguese (411)	1,023	1.48
Romanian (41)	77	0.11
Russian (226)	740	1.07
Scandinavian (76)	190	0.28
Scotch-Irish (448)	984	1.42
Scottish (549)	1,948	2.82
Slavic (8)	54	0.08
Slovak (33)	42	0.06
Slovene (27)	44	0.06
Swedish (328)	1,282	1.86
Swiss (32)	355	0.51
Turkish (18)	29	0.04
Ukrainian (284)	343	0.50
Welsh (128)	634	0.92
West Indian, ex. Hispanic (37)	151	0.22
Belizean (14)	23	0.03
Jamaican (23)	38	0.06
West Indian (0)	90	0.13
Yugoslavian (88)	144	0.21

Hispanic Origin	Population	%
Hispanic or Latino (of any race)	8,064	11.17
Central American, ex. Mexican	392	0.54
Costa Rican	57	0.08
Guatemalan	43	0.06
Honduran	27	0.04
Nicaraguan	78	0.11
Panamanian	25	0.03
Salvadoran	158	0.22
Other Central American	4	0.01
Cuban	63	0.09
Dominican Republic	16	0.02
Mexican	5,422	7.51
Puerto Rican	283	0.39
South American	381	0.53
Argentinean	58	0.08
Bolivian	20	0.03
Chilean	30	0.04
Colombian	117	0.16
Ecuadorian	23	0.03
Paraguayan	3	<0.01
Peruvian	90	0.12
Uruguayan	7	0.01
Venezuelan	26	0.04
Other South American	7	0.01
Other Hispanic or Latino	1,507	2.09

Race*	Population	%
African-American/Black (4,140)	4,587	6.35
Not Hispanic (4,080)	4,436	6.14
Hispanic (60)	151	0.21
American Indian/Alaska Native (427)	1,011	1.40
Not Hispanic (289)	728	1.01
Hispanic (138)	283	0.39
Aleut *(Alaska Native)* (0)	1	<0.01
Apache (15)	39	0.05
Arapaho (1)	3	<0.01
Blackfeet (4)	16	0.02
Cherokee (46)	168	0.23
Cheyenne (0)	1	<0.01
Chickasaw (2)	7	0.01
Chippewa (11)	18	0.02
Choctaw (19)	38	0.05
Comanche (0)	1	<0.01
Creek (2)	12	0.02
Delaware (1)	5	0.01
Hopi (0)	4	0.01
Inupiat *(Alaska Native)* (2)	3	<0.01
Iroquois (2)	12	0.02
Kiowa (1)	1	<0.01
Menominee (2)	2	<0.01
Mexican American Ind. (26)	40	0.06
Navajo (4)	12	0.02
Osage (0)	5	0.01
Paiute (6)	6	0.01
Pima (1)	1	<0.01
Potawatomi (2)	4	0.01
Pueblo (4)	5	0.01
Seminole (0)	3	<0.01
Shoshone (0)	1	<0.01
Sioux (7)	26	0.04
South American Ind. (2)	7	0.01
Spanish American Ind. (3)	5	0.01
Tlingit-Haida *(Alaska Native)* (4)	12	0.02
Yakama (3)	4	0.01
Yaqui (3)	8	0.01
Yuman (1)	1	<0.01
Yup'ik *(Alaska Native)* (1)	1	<0.01
Asian (9,000)	10,710	14.83
Not Hispanic (8,917)	10,393	14.39
Hispanic (83)	317	0.44
Bangladeshi (95)	99	0.14
Bhutanese (4)	4	0.01
Burmese (8)	11	0.02
Cambodian (29)	43	0.06
Chinese, ex. Taiwanese (1,530)	1,974	2.73
Filipino (1,128)	1,738	2.41
Hmong (19)	24	0.03
Indian (3,801)	3,981	5.51
Indonesian (26)	43	0.06
Japanese (347)	762	1.06
Korean (734)	868	1.20
Laotian (22)	32	0.04
Malaysian (30)	38	0.05
Nepalese (38)	38	0.05
Pakistani (146)	168	0.23
Sri Lankan (62)	66	0.09
Taiwanese (86)	108	0.15
Thai (50)	72	0.10
Vietnamese (463)	587	0.81
Hawaii Native/Pacific Islander (173)	447	0.62
Not Hispanic (156)	382	0.53
Hispanic (17)	65	0.09
Fijian (71)	79	0.11
Guamanian/Chamorro (32)	70	0.10
Native Hawaiian (37)	160	0.22
Samoan (3)	9	0.01
Tongan (9)	13	0.02
White (53,627)	56,318	78.00
Not Hispanic (48,009)	50,013	69.27
Hispanic (5,618)	6,305	8.73

Fontana

Place Type: City
County: San Bernardino
Population: 196,069†

Ancestry‡	Population	%
Afghan (238)	238	0.13
African, Sub-Saharan (1,756)	2,139	1.13
African (1,360)	1,703	0.90
Cape Verdean (68)	96	0.05
Ethiopian (48)	48	0.03
Ghanaian (35)	47	0.02
Nigerian (180)	180	0.10
Other Sub-Saharan African (65)	65	0.03
American (3,822)	3,822	2.02
Arab (676)	1,107	0.58
Arab (110)	368	0.19
Egyptian (95)	164	0.09
Iraqi (17)	49	0.03
Jordanian (5)	5	<0.01
Lebanese (34)	59	0.03
Moroccan (132)	132	0.07
Palestinian (131)	131	0.07
Syrian (0)	13	0.01
Other Arab (152)	186	0.10
Armenian (49)	49	0.03
Assyrian/Chaldean/Syriac (60)	60	0.03
Austrian (31)	130	0.07
Basque (12)	12	0.01
Belgian (57)	112	0.06
Brazilian (0)	31	0.02
British (77)	208	0.11
Bulgarian (0)	54	0.03
Canadian (29)	233	0.12
Croatian (14)	14	0.01
Czech (46)	144	0.08
Czechoslovakian (0)	22	0.01
Danish (33)	228	0.12
Dutch (144)	846	0.45
Eastern European (56)	56	0.03
English (1,144)	4,852	2.56
European (697)	1,048	0.55
Finnish (16)	34	0.02
French, ex. Basque (491)	1,887	1.00
French Canadian (103)	292	0.15
German (1,723)	8,399	4.43
Greek (47)	198	0.10
Hungarian (167)	381	0.20
Icelander (47)	47	0.02
Iranian (127)	171	0.09
Irish (997)	6,960	3.67
Israeli (0)	10	0.01
Italian (1,451)	4,478	2.36
Lithuanian (0)	75	0.04
Luxemburger (0)	13	0.01
Northern European (16)	16	0.01
Norwegian (222)	618	0.33

*Notes: † The Census 2010 population figure is used to calculate the percentages in the Hispanic Origin and Race categories. Ancestry percentages are based on the 2006-2010 American Community Survey population (not shown); ‡ Numbers in parentheses indicate the number of people reporting a single ancestry; * Numbers in parentheses indicate the number of persons reporting this race alone, not in combination with any other race; Please refer to the Explanation of Data for more information.*

Polish (193)	1,072	0.57
Portuguese (199)	620	0.33
Romanian (87)	118	0.06
Russian (132)	351	0.19
Scandinavian (17)	198	0.10
Scotch-Irish (153)	564	0.30
Scottish (283)	1,204	0.64
Serbian (50)	82	0.04
Slavic (0)	8	<0.01
Slovak (0)	55	0.03
Slovene (36)	76	0.04
Swedish (83)	401	0.21
Swiss (0)	247	0.13
Ukrainian (14)	24	0.01
Welsh (46)	371	0.20
West Indian, ex. Hispanic (531)	618	0.33
Barbadian (56)	72	0.04
Belizean (198)	198	0.10
British West Indian (8)	27	0.01
Haitian (13)	13	0.01
Jamaican (199)	251	0.13
U.S. Virgin Islander (24)	24	0.01
West Indian (33)	33	0.02
Yugoslavian (51)	151	0.08

Hispanic Origin	Population	%
Hispanic or Latino (of any race)	130,957	66.79
Central American, ex. Mexican	8,860	4.52
Costa Rican	187	0.10
Guatemalan	2,230	1.14
Honduran	636	0.32
Nicaraguan	1,152	0.59
Panamanian	179	0.09
Salvadoran	4,382	2.23
Other Central American	94	0.05
Cuban	617	0.31
Dominican Republic	42	0.02
Mexican	111,818	57.03
Puerto Rican	1,344	0.69
South American	2,245	1.15
Argentinean	323	0.16
Bolivian	58	0.03
Chilean	134	0.07
Colombian	545	0.28
Ecuadorian	415	0.21
Paraguayan	10	0.01
Peruvian	646	0.33
Uruguayan	54	0.03
Venezuelan	34	0.02
Other South American	26	0.01
Other Hispanic or Latino	6,031	3.08

Race*	Population	%
African-American/Black (19,574)	21,881	11.16
Not Hispanic (18,157)	19,507	9.95
Hispanic (1,417)	2,374	1.21
American Indian/Alaska Native (1,957)	3,482	1.78
Not Hispanic (454)	1,084	0.55
Hispanic (1,503)	2,398	1.22
Alaska Athabascan *(Ala. Nat.)* (0)	1	<0.01
Aleut *(Alaska Native)* (0)	1	<0.01
Apache (67)	162	0.08
Blackfeet (19)	84	0.04
Canadian/French Am. Ind. (2)	2	<0.01
Central American Ind. (12)	23	0.01
Cherokee (60)	309	0.16
Cheyenne (2)	9	<0.01
Chickasaw (4)	9	<0.01
Chippewa (15)	22	0.01
Choctaw (25)	78	0.04
Comanche (5)	10	0.01
Creek (3)	19	0.01
Crow (0)	2	<0.01
Delaware (1)	3	<0.01
Hopi (1)	8	<0.01
Houma (0)	4	<0.01
Iroquois (3)	21	0.01
Kiowa (4)	6	<0.01
Lumbee (0)	3	<0.01
Mexican American Ind. (254)	374	0.19
Navajo (57)	100	0.05
Osage (8)	13	0.01
Ottawa (2)	2	<0.01
Pima (4)	8	<0.01
Potawatomi (4)	9	<0.01
Pueblo (45)	56	0.03
Seminole (8)	18	0.01
Shoshone (11)	13	0.01
Sioux (30)	46	0.02
South American Ind. (6)	15	0.01
Spanish American Ind. (23)	37	0.02
Tlingit-Haida *(Alaska Native)* (0)	1	<0.01
Tohono O'Odham (15)	21	0.01
Ute (5)	5	<0.01
Yaqui (50)	86	0.04
Yuman (10)	17	0.01
Asian (12,948)	15,084	7.69
Not Hispanic (12,456)	13,826	7.05
Hispanic (492)	1,258	0.64
Bangladeshi (64)	73	0.04
Burmese (43)	48	0.02
Cambodian (290)	358	0.18
Chinese, ex. Taiwanese (1,347)	1,783	0.91
Filipino (6,047)	7,014	3.58
Hmong (3)	5	<0.01
Indian (1,294)	1,455	0.74
Indonesian (398)	503	0.26
Japanese (270)	659	0.34
Korean (1,022)	1,174	0.60
Laotian (89)	122	0.06
Malaysian (3)	6	<0.01
Nepalese (3)	3	<0.01
Pakistani (195)	221	0.11
Sri Lankan (40)	48	0.02
Taiwanese (123)	152	0.08
Thai (133)	200	0.10
Vietnamese (1,095)	1,252	0.64
Hawaii Native/Pacific Islander (547)	1,032	0.53
Not Hispanic (474)	764	0.39
Hispanic (73)	268	0.14
Fijian (16)	22	0.01
Guamanian/Chamorro (50)	95	0.05
Native Hawaiian (77)	241	0.12
Samoan (195)	290	0.15
Tongan (157)	176	0.09
White (92,978)	100,668	51.34
Not Hispanic (30,279)	32,526	16.59
Hispanic (62,699)	68,142	34.75

Foothill Farms

Place Type: CDP
County: Sacramento
Population: 33,121†

Ancestry‡	Population	%
African, Sub-Saharan (427)	445	1.36
African (217)	235	0.72
Kenyan (106)	106	0.32
Nigerian (73)	73	0.22
Other Sub-Saharan African (31)	31	0.09
American (1,094)	1,094	3.34
Arab (193)	193	0.59
Arab (8)	8	0.02
Egyptian (10)	10	0.03
Lebanese (9)	9	0.03
Other Arab (166)	166	0.51
Armenian (26)	60	0.18
Australian (0)	18	0.05
Austrian (41)	51	0.16
Belgian (0)	11	0.03
British (95)	140	0.43
Bulgarian (29)	29	0.09
Canadian (27)	27	0.08
Croatian (9)	94	0.29
Czech (17)	43	0.13
Czechoslovakian (0)	31	0.09
Danish (10)	39	0.12
Dutch (99)	841	2.56
English (666)	2,579	7.86
European (277)	277	0.84
Finnish (14)	26	0.08
French, ex. Basque (65)	800	2.44
French Canadian (84)	133	0.41
German (1,044)	4,782	14.58
German Russian (0)	50	0.15
Greek (184)	377	1.15
Hungarian (162)	199	0.61
Iranian (41)	41	0.13
Irish (547)	3,352	10.22
Italian (922)	1,942	5.92
Latvian (0)	15	0.05
Lithuanian (0)	25	0.08
Northern European (7)	7	0.02
Norwegian (126)	277	0.84
Polish (87)	425	1.30
Portuguese (105)	540	1.65
Romanian (378)	420	1.28
Russian (795)	936	2.85
Scandinavian (46)	46	0.14
Scotch-Irish (264)	523	1.59
Scottish (333)	633	1.93
Slovak (0)	12	0.04
Slovene (32)	32	0.10
Swedish (22)	263	0.80
Swiss (0)	66	0.20
Ukrainian (987)	1,082	3.30
Welsh (45)	212	0.65
West Indian, ex. Hispanic (101)	101	0.31
Belizean (69)	69	0.21
Jamaican (32)	32	0.10
Yugoslavian (17)	28	0.09

Hispanic Origin	Population	%
Hispanic or Latino (of any race)	7,579	22.88
Central American, ex. Mexican	513	1.55
Costa Rican	8	0.02
Guatemalan	93	0.28
Honduran	32	0.10
Nicaraguan	50	0.15
Panamanian	14	0.04
Salvadoran	315	0.95
Other Central American	1	<0.01
Cuban	23	0.07
Dominican Republic	19	0.06
Mexican	6,006	18.13
Puerto Rican	314	0.95
South American	122	0.37
Argentinean	14	0.04
Bolivian	3	0.01
Chilean	9	0.03
Colombian	26	0.08
Ecuadorian	9	0.03
Paraguayan	1	<0.01
Peruvian	54	0.16
Venezuelan	5	0.02
Other South American	1	<0.01
Other Hispanic or Latino	582	1.76

Race*	Population	%
African-American/Black (3,628)	4,739	14.31
Not Hispanic (3,459)	4,322	13.05
Hispanic (169)	417	1.26
American Indian/Alaska Native (357)	995	3.00
Not Hispanic (211)	677	2.04
Hispanic (146)	318	0.96
Aleut *(Alaska Native)* (3)	5	0.02
Apache (16)	48	0.14
Arapaho (0)	7	0.02
Blackfeet (9)	58	0.18
Canadian/French Am. Ind. (2)	5	0.02
Cherokee (38)	164	0.50
Cheyenne (1)	1	<0.01
Chickasaw (0)	7	0.02
Chippewa (11)	21	0.06
Choctaw (4)	27	0.08
Comanche (0)	1	<0.01
Cree (0)	3	0.01
Creek (2)	11	0.03
Crow (2)	6	0.02

*Notes: † The Census 2010 population figure is used to calculate the percentages in the Hispanic Origin and Race categories. Ancestry percentages are based on the 2006-2010 American Community Survey population (not shown); ‡ Numbers in parentheses indicate the number of people reporting a single ancestry; * Numbers in parentheses indicate the number of persons reporting this race alone, not in combination with any other race; Please refer to the Explanation of Data for more information.*

Hopi (0)	2	0.01
Inupiat *(Alaska Native)* (0)	1	<0.01
Iroquois (4)	7	0.02
Menominee (0)	1	<0.01
Mexican American Ind. (5)	24	0.07
Navajo (25)	30	0.09
Osage (1)	4	0.01
Paiute (6)	9	0.03
Potawatomi (1)	4	0.01
Pueblo (0)	2	0.01
Seminole (1)	3	0.01
Shoshone (6)	13	0.04
Sioux (11)	28	0.08
South American Ind. (0)	1	<0.01
Spanish American Ind. (1)	3	0.01
Tlingit-Haida *(Alaska Native)* (1)	2	0.01
Tohono O'Odham (3)	3	0.01
Yakama (0)	1	<0.01
Yaqui (0)	8	0.02
Asian (1,731)	2,526	7.63
Not Hispanic (1,642)	2,271	6.86
Hispanic (89)	255	0.77
Bangladeshi (5)	5	0.02
Burmese (1)	1	<0.01
Cambodian (16)	24	0.07
Chinese, ex. Taiwanese (103)	203	0.61
Filipino (534)	867	2.62
Hmong (95)	104	0.31
Indian (276)	340	1.03
Indonesian (8)	18	0.05
Japanese (104)	275	0.83
Korean (74)	161	0.49
Laotian (126)	155	0.47
Malaysian (0)	2	0.01
Nepalese (3)	4	0.01
Pakistani (3)	12	0.04
Sri Lankan (6)	7	0.02
Taiwanese (5)	7	0.02
Thai (37)	66	0.20
Vietnamese (256)	288	0.87
Hawaii Native/Pacific Islander (208)	432	1.30
Not Hispanic (189)	353	1.07
Hispanic (19)	79	0.24
Fijian (48)	58	0.18
Guamanian/Chamorro (30)	62	0.19
Native Hawaiian (37)	146	0.44
Samoan (53)	90	0.27
Tongan (17)	25	0.08
White (21,249)	23,387	70.61
Not Hispanic (18,283)	19,715	59.52
Hispanic (2,966)	3,672	11.09

Fort Irwin

Place Type: CDP
County: San Bernardino
Population: 8,845†

Ancestry‡	Population	%
African, Sub-Saharan (14)	14	0.15
African (14)	14	0.15
American (236)	236	2.59
Arab (41)	41	0.45
Iraqi (27)	27	0.30
Other Arab (14)	14	0.15
Austrian (41)	50	0.55
British (48)	55	0.60
Canadian (6)	6	0.07
Croatian (0)	38	0.42
Czech (13)	39	0.43
Dutch (60)	79	0.87
English (144)	420	4.61
European (55)	87	0.96
Finnish (0)	19	0.21
French, ex. Basque (103)	353	3.88
French Canadian (7)	31	0.34
German (412)	1,491	16.37
Greek (0)	23	0.25
Guyanese (10)	10	0.11
Hungarian (0)	16	0.18
Irish (533)	1,080	11.86
Italian (268)	520	5.71
Norwegian (0)	11	0.12
Polish (37)	93	1.02
Portuguese (0)	19	0.21
Russian (0)	19	0.21
Scandinavian (0)	20	0.22
Scotch-Irish (123)	303	3.33
Scottish (31)	65	0.71
Swedish (106)	115	1.26
Ukrainian (26)	26	0.29

Hispanic Origin	Population	%
Hispanic or Latino (of any race)	2,261	25.56
Central American, ex. Mexican	152	1.72
Costa Rican	8	0.09
Guatemalan	47	0.53
Honduran	2	0.02
Nicaraguan	18	0.20
Panamanian	28	0.32
Salvadoran	49	0.55
Cuban	37	0.42
Dominican Republic	39	0.44
Mexican	1,500	16.96
Puerto Rican	291	3.29
South American	69	0.78
Argentinean	2	0.02
Bolivian	1	0.01
Chilean	5	0.06
Colombian	18	0.20
Ecuadorian	8	0.09
Paraguayan	1	0.01
Peruvian	18	0.20
Uruguayan	7	0.08
Venezuelan	9	0.10
Other Hispanic or Latino	173	1.96

Race*	Population	%
African-American/Black (1,086)	1,384	15.65
Not Hispanic (1,008)	1,203	13.60
Hispanic (78)	181	2.05
American Indian/Alaska Native (103)	229	2.59
Not Hispanic (67)	160	1.81
Hispanic (36)	69	0.78
Alaska Athabascan *(Ala. Nat.)* (1)	1	0.01
Apache (0)	11	0.12
Blackfeet (2)	8	0.09
Canadian/French Am. Ind. (3)	3	0.03
Central American Ind. (6)	6	0.07
Cherokee (4)	29	0.33
Chippewa (3)	6	0.07
Choctaw (2)	11	0.12
Comanche (0)	1	0.01
Creek (3)	5	0.06
Kiowa (1)	1	0.01
Lumbee (0)	3	0.03
Menominee (0)	3	0.03
Mexican American Ind. (8)	10	0.11
Navajo (7)	11	0.12
Osage (1)	1	0.01
Ottawa (1)	2	0.02
Paiute (0)	1	0.01
Pima (2)	2	0.02
Pueblo (4)	4	0.05
Sioux (4)	13	0.15
Tlingit-Haida *(Alaska Native)* (1)	2	0.02
Ute (0)	1	0.01
Yup'ik *(Alaska Native)* (9)	9	0.10
Asian (402)	612	6.92
Not Hispanic (379)	537	6.07
Hispanic (23)	75	0.85
Cambodian (19)	24	0.27
Chinese, ex. Taiwanese (23)	45	0.51
Filipino (214)	328	3.71
Hmong (1)	1	0.01
Indian (4)	11	0.12
Indonesian (1)	1	0.01
Japanese (9)	30	0.34
Korean (45)	92	1.04
Laotian (6)	6	0.07
Malaysian (0)	2	0.02
Pakistani (2)	3	0.03
Taiwanese (4)	6	0.07
Thai (10)	13	0.15
Vietnamese (28)	29	0.33
Hawaii Native/Pacific Islander (120)	191	2.16
Not Hispanic (110)	160	1.81
Hispanic (10)	31	0.35
Guamanian/Chamorro (45)	56	0.63
Native Hawaiian (16)	27	0.31
Samoan (37)	55	0.62
Tongan (2)	2	0.02
White (5,481)	6,069	68.62
Not Hispanic (4,567)	4,928	55.72
Hispanic (914)	1,141	12.90

Fortuna

Place Type: City
County: Humboldt
Population: 11,926†

Ancestry‡	Population	%
African, Sub-Saharan (0)	12	0.10
African (0)	12	0.10
American (320)	320	2.75
Australian (0)	20	0.17
Austrian (0)	23	0.20
Belgian (19)	19	0.16
British (14)	110	0.94
Canadian (0)	15	0.13
Celtic (0)	11	0.09
Danish (78)	265	2.28
Dutch (30)	195	1.67
English (480)	1,308	11.23
European (1,393)	1,684	14.46
Finnish (13)	44	0.38
French, ex. Basque (105)	657	5.64
French Canadian (0)	6	0.05
German (561)	1,650	14.17
Greek (10)	28	0.24
Hungarian (0)	21	0.18
Irish (230)	1,009	8.66
Italian (79)	277	2.38
Lithuanian (0)	15	0.13
Norwegian (17)	261	2.24
Pennsylvania German (0)	14	0.12
Polish (64)	139	1.19
Portuguese (150)	312	2.68
Russian (55)	151	1.30
Scandinavian (0)	9	0.08
Scotch-Irish (105)	273	2.34
Scottish (121)	342	2.94
Slovak (49)	85	0.73
Swedish (99)	331	2.84
Swiss (48)	127	1.09
Welsh (11)	22	0.19

Hispanic Origin	Population	%
Hispanic or Latino (of any race)	2,032	17.04
Central American, ex. Mexican	41	0.34
Costa Rican	4	0.03
Guatemalan	16	0.13
Honduran	11	0.09
Nicaraguan	4	0.03
Salvadoran	5	0.04
Other Central American	1	0.01
Cuban	16	0.13
Mexican	1,770	14.84
Puerto Rican	23	0.19
South American	11	0.09
Argentinean	1	0.01
Chilean	8	0.07
Colombian	1	0.01
Peruvian	1	0.01
Other Hispanic or Latino	171	1.43

Race*	Population	%
African-American/Black (73)	166	1.39
Not Hispanic (65)	133	1.12

*Notes: † The Census 2010 population figure is used to calculate the percentages in the Hispanic Origin and Race categories. Ancestry percentages are based on the 2006-2010 American Community Survey population (not shown); ‡ Numbers in parentheses indicate the number of people reporting a single ancestry; * Numbers in parentheses indicate the number of persons reporting this race alone, not in combination with any other race; Please refer to the Explanation of Data for more information.*

Hispanic (8)	33	0.28
American Indian/Alaska Native (444)	770	6.46
Not Hispanic (381)	655	5.49
Hispanic (63)	115	0.96
Alaska Athabascan *(Ala. Nat.)* (2)	4	0.03
Aleut *(Alaska Native)* (2)	3	0.03
Apache (4)	9	0.08
Blackfeet (5)	9	0.08
Canadian/French Am. Ind. (1)	2	0.02
Cherokee (23)	103	0.86
Cheyenne (0)	2	0.02
Chickasaw (6)	10	0.08
Chippewa (4)	5	0.04
Choctaw (17)	32	0.27
Creek (1)	5	0.04
Hopi (2)	2	0.02
Inupiat *(Alaska Native)* (2)	4	0.03
Iroquois (0)	7	0.06
Mexican American Ind. (8)	16	0.13
Navajo (6)	7	0.06
Ottawa (1)	1	0.01
Paiute (4)	6	0.05
Potawatomi (3)	3	0.03
Puget Sound Salish (1)	1	0.01
Shoshone (0)	6	0.05
Sioux (0)	5	0.04
Spanish American Ind. (0)	1	0.01
Tlingit-Haida *(Alaska Native)* (1)	2	0.02
Ute (2)	2	0.02
Yakama (0)	1	0.01
Yaqui (2)	3	0.03
Yup'ik *(Alaska Native)* (1)	1	0.01
Asian (106)	176	1.48
Not Hispanic (102)	158	1.32
Hispanic (4)	18	0.15
Bangladeshi (5)	5	0.04
Burmese (1)	1	0.01
Cambodian (1)	1	0.01
Chinese, ex. Taiwanese (28)	42	0.35
Filipino (29)	48	0.40
Indian (4)	7	0.06
Indonesian (0)	1	0.01
Japanese (13)	35	0.29
Korean (8)	10	0.08
Laotian (5)	8	0.07
Pakistani (6)	6	0.05
Vietnamese (4)	8	0.07
Hawaii Native/Pacific Islander (9)	32	0.27
Not Hispanic (8)	27	0.23
Hispanic (1)	5	0.04
Guamanian/Chamorro (0)	4	0.03
Native Hawaiian (5)	21	0.18
Samoan (4)	5	0.04
White (9,686)	10,186	85.41
Not Hispanic (8,926)	9,301	77.99
Hispanic (760)	885	7.42

Foster City

Place Type: City
County: San Mateo
Population: 30,567†

Ancestry‡	Population	%
Afghan (24)	24	0.08
African, Sub-Saharan (64)	110	0.37
African (32)	32	0.11
Liberian (0)	46	0.15
South African (32)	32	0.11
American (286)	286	0.96
Arab (703)	750	2.52
Arab (34)	47	0.16
Egyptian (245)	245	0.82
Jordanian (14)	14	0.05
Lebanese (326)	360	1.21
Moroccan (35)	35	0.12
Palestinian (12)	12	0.04
Syrian (3)	3	0.01
Other Arab (34)	34	0.11
Armenian (70)	139	0.47
Assyrian/Chaldean/Syriac (10)	10	0.03
Austrian (0)	79	0.27
Basque (0)	18	0.06
Belgian (0)	12	0.04
Brazilian (20)	20	0.07
British (154)	193	0.65
Canadian (77)	86	0.29
Celtic (0)	9	0.03
Croatian (32)	44	0.15
Czech (8)	123	0.41
Czechoslovakian (31)	55	0.18
Danish (58)	125	0.42
Dutch (42)	237	0.80
Eastern European (94)	94	0.32
English (479)	1,677	5.64
European (436)	516	1.73
Finnish (14)	22	0.07
French, ex. Basque (26)	817	2.75
French Canadian (12)	57	0.19
German (892)	2,923	9.83
Greek (98)	175	0.59
Guyanese (0)	10	0.03
Hungarian (18)	28	0.09
Iranian (572)	572	1.92
Irish (503)	1,818	6.11
Israeli (11)	25	0.08
Italian (677)	1,693	5.69
Lithuanian (0)	27	0.09
Maltese (21)	21	0.07
Northern European (7)	7	0.02
Norwegian (117)	324	1.09
Polish (259)	649	2.18
Portuguese (51)	243	0.82
Romanian (0)	16	0.05
Russian (822)	1,168	3.93
Scandinavian (11)	11	0.04
Scotch-Irish (100)	211	0.71
Scottish (72)	414	1.39
Serbian (12)	12	0.04
Slovak (49)	64	0.22
Slovene (13)	13	0.04
Swedish (80)	352	1.18
Swiss (26)	142	0.48
Turkish (83)	127	0.43
Ukrainian (102)	173	0.58
Welsh (46)	164	0.55
West Indian, ex. Hispanic (23)	53	0.18
Jamaican (23)	34	0.11
Trinidadian/Tobagonian (0)	10	0.03
West Indian (0)	9	0.03

Hispanic Origin	Population	%
Hispanic or Latino (of any race)	1,995	6.53
Central American, ex. Mexican	389	1.27
Costa Rican	18	0.06
Guatemalan	52	0.17
Honduran	7	0.02
Nicaraguan	125	0.41
Panamanian	4	0.01
Salvadoran	177	0.58
Other Central American	6	0.02
Cuban	48	0.16
Dominican Republic	12	0.04
Mexican	755	2.47
Puerto Rican	98	0.32
South American	400	1.31
Argentinean	32	0.10
Bolivian	12	0.04
Chilean	53	0.17
Colombian	64	0.21
Ecuadorian	32	0.10
Paraguayan	3	0.01
Peruvian	170	0.56
Uruguayan	10	0.03
Venezuelan	16	0.05
Other South American	8	0.03
Other Hispanic or Latino	293	0.96

Race*	Population	%
African-American/Black (576)	762	2.49
Not Hispanic (545)	684	2.24
Hispanic (31)	78	0.26
American Indian/Alaska Native (29)	180	0.59
Not Hispanic (17)	121	0.40
Hispanic (12)	59	0.19
Aleut *(Alaska Native)* (0)	1	<0.01
Blackfeet (0)	4	0.01
Central American Ind. (1)	1	<0.01
Cherokee (0)	28	0.09
Chippewa (1)	2	0.01
Choctaw (1)	3	0.01
Comanche (0)	2	0.01
Creek (0)	1	<0.01
Delaware (0)	3	0.01
Hopi (0)	4	0.01
Iroquois (1)	6	0.02
Kiowa (0)	4	0.01
Mexican American Ind. (3)	7	0.02
Navajo (2)	7	0.02
Paiute (0)	2	0.01
Potawatomi (0)	1	<0.01
Pueblo (0)	2	0.01
Shoshone (1)	1	<0.01
Sioux (1)	8	0.03
South American Ind. (0)	1	<0.01
Spanish American Ind. (2)	5	0.02
Tlingit-Haida *(Alaska Native)* (0)	1	<0.01
Asian (13,746)	14,910	48.78
Not Hispanic (13,691)	14,701	48.09
Hispanic (55)	209	0.68
Bangladeshi (10)	11	0.04
Burmese (10)	16	0.05
Cambodian (11)	17	0.06
Chinese, ex. Taiwanese (6,112)	6,701	21.92
Filipino (1,322)	1,784	5.84
Hmong (9)	9	0.03
Indian (3,461)	3,593	11.75
Indonesian (38)	62	0.20
Japanese (1,222)	1,588	5.20
Korean (481)	587	1.92
Laotian (7)	16	0.05
Malaysian (5)	8	0.03
Nepalese (4)	8	0.03
Pakistani (68)	76	0.25
Sri Lankan (11)	11	0.04
Taiwanese (335)	378	1.24
Thai (43)	68	0.22
Vietnamese (164)	210	0.69
Hawaii Native/Pacific Islander (189)	338	1.11
Not Hispanic (182)	301	0.98
Hispanic (7)	37	0.12
Fijian (69)	77	0.25
Guamanian/Chamorro (21)	38	0.12
Native Hawaiian (21)	93	0.30
Samoan (13)	21	0.07
Tongan (43)	48	0.16
White (13,912)	15,210	49.76
Not Hispanic (12,829)	13,861	45.35
Hispanic (1,083)	1,349	4.41

Fountain Valley

Place Type: City
County: Orange
Population: 55,313†

Ancestry‡	Population	%
Afghan (54)	54	0.10
African, Sub-Saharan (103)	214	0.39
African (103)	214	0.39
American (1,134)	1,134	2.06
Arab (564)	636	1.16
Arab (252)	252	0.46
Egyptian (72)	80	0.15
Jordanian (92)	92	0.17
Lebanese (36)	85	0.15
Palestinian (13)	28	0.05
Other Arab (99)	99	0.18
Armenian (335)	378	0.69
Australian (32)	70	0.13

*Notes: † The Census 2010 population figure is used to calculate the percentages in the Hispanic Origin and Race categories. Ancestry percentages are based on the 2006-2010 American Community Survey population (not shown); ‡ Numbers in parentheses indicate the number of people reporting a single ancestry; * Numbers in parentheses indicate the number of persons reporting this race alone, not in combination with any other race; Please refer to the Explanation of Data for more information.*

Austrian (66)	203	0.37
Belgian (82)	82	0.15
Brazilian (34)	34	0.06
British (120)	274	0.50
Cajun (14)	29	0.05
Canadian (39)	146	0.27
Croatian (118)	198	0.36
Czech (71)	235	0.43
Czechoslovakian (24)	50	0.09
Danish (63)	440	0.80
Dutch (290)	923	1.68
Eastern European (66)	66	0.12
English (1,440)	5,281	9.61
European (785)	880	1.60
Finnish (14)	129	0.23
French, ex. Basque (258)	1,420	2.58
French Canadian (123)	264	0.48
German (1,742)	6,635	12.07
Greek (89)	272	0.49
Guyanese (19)	59	0.11
Hungarian (50)	195	0.35
Icelander (0)	21	0.04
Iranian (63)	63	0.11
Irish (1,253)	5,738	10.44
Israeli (9)	9	0.02
Italian (1,099)	2,448	4.45
Latvian (0)	10	0.02
Lithuanian (11)	82	0.15
New Zealander (10)	24	0.04
Northern European (73)	73	0.13
Norwegian (235)	989	1.80
Polish (360)	1,160	2.11
Portuguese (83)	199	0.36
Romanian (147)	196	0.36
Russian (232)	804	1.46
Scandinavian (9)	33	0.06
Scotch-Irish (161)	864	1.57
Scottish (381)	1,341	2.44
Serbian (0)	14	0.03
Slavic (0)	12	0.02
Slovene (6)	21	0.04
Swedish (306)	1,089	1.98
Swiss (82)	157	0.29
Turkish (136)	136	0.25
Ukrainian (28)	82	0.15
Welsh (89)	440	0.80
West Indian, ex. Hispanic (49)	49	0.09
Belizean (8)	8	0.01
Jamaican (41)	41	0.07
Yugoslavian (51)	51	0.09

Hispanic Origin	Population	%
Hispanic or Latino (of any race)	7,250	13.11
Central American, ex. Mexican	337	0.61
Costa Rican	25	0.05
Guatemalan	73	0.13
Honduran	30	0.05
Nicaraguan	42	0.08
Panamanian	23	0.04
Salvadoran	135	0.24
Other Central American	9	0.02
Cuban	154	0.28
Dominican Republic	6	0.01
Mexican	5,463	9.88
Puerto Rican	175	0.32
South American	503	0.91
Argentinean	97	0.18
Bolivian	40	0.07
Chilean	41	0.07
Colombian	107	0.19
Ecuadorian	64	0.12
Peruvian	137	0.25
Uruguayan	5	0.01
Venezuelan	4	0.01
Other South American	8	0.01
Other Hispanic or Latino	612	1.11

Race*	Population	%
African-American/Black (510)	767	1.39
Not Hispanic (473)	681	1.23
Hispanic (37)	86	0.16
American Indian/Alaska Native (229)	635	1.15
Not Hispanic (127)	403	0.73
Hispanic (102)	232	0.42
Aleut *(Alaska Native)* (0)	1	<0.01
Apache (11)	26	0.05
Blackfeet (5)	16	0.03
Canadian/French Am. Ind. (5)	6	0.01
Cherokee (30)	152	0.27
Cheyenne (4)	4	0.01
Chickasaw (3)	11	0.02
Chippewa (1)	2	<0.01
Choctaw (8)	29	0.05
Comanche (0)	4	0.01
Cree (0)	1	<0.01
Creek (0)	11	0.02
Delaware (0)	2	<0.01
Iroquois (0)	7	0.01
Lumbee (3)	3	0.01
Mexican American Ind. (32)	39	0.07
Navajo (3)	10	0.02
Ottawa (1)	1	<0.01
Paiute (0)	1	<0.01
Pima (0)	1	<0.01
Potawatomi (2)	3	0.01
Pueblo (5)	13	0.02
Seminole (0)	1	<0.01
Sioux (7)	18	0.03
South American Ind. (0)	3	0.01
Spanish American Ind. (2)	2	<0.01
Yaqui (6)	16	0.03
Yup'ik *(Alaska Native)* (0)	5	0.01
Asian (18,418)	19,755	35.71
Not Hispanic (18,324)	19,481	35.22
Hispanic (94)	274	0.50
Bangladeshi (10)	10	0.02
Burmese (23)	32	0.06
Cambodian (120)	170	0.31
Chinese, ex. Taiwanese (1,851)	2,421	4.38
Filipino (838)	1,190	2.15
Hmong (56)	59	0.11
Indian (544)	608	1.10
Indonesian (45)	86	0.16
Japanese (1,312)	1,817	3.28
Korean (894)	1,019	1.84
Laotian (62)	79	0.14
Malaysian (2)	6	0.01
Pakistani (111)	134	0.24
Sri Lankan (4)	4	0.01
Taiwanese (483)	529	0.96
Thai (63)	92	0.17
Vietnamese (11,431)	11,861	21.44
Hawaii Native/Pacific Islander (171)	435	0.79
Not Hispanic (159)	384	0.69
Hispanic (12)	51	0.09
Fijian (2)	2	<0.01
Guamanian/Chamorro (27)	56	0.10
Marshallese (2)	2	<0.01
Native Hawaiian (38)	169	0.31
Samoan (73)	108	0.20
Tongan (13)	26	0.05
White (31,225)	33,287	60.18
Not Hispanic (27,234)	28,713	51.91
Hispanic (3,991)	4,574	8.27

Fremont

Place Type: City
County: Alameda
Population: 214,089†

Ancestry‡	Population	%
Afghan (2,638)	2,760	1.32
African, Sub-Saharan (890)	1,187	0.57
African (629)	795	0.38
Cape Verdean (0)	13	0.01
Ethiopian (97)	125	0.06
Ghanaian (20)	20	0.01
Kenyan (0)	42	0.02
Somalian (0)	20	0.01
South African (4)	32	0.02
Sudanese (27)	27	0.01
Other Sub-Saharan African (113)	113	0.05
American (2,512)	2,512	1.20
Arab (1,877)	2,346	1.12
Arab (322)	396	0.19
Egyptian (268)	391	0.19
Iraqi (71)	110	0.05
Jordanian (14)	14	0.01
Lebanese (348)	454	0.22
Palestinian (300)	391	0.19
Other Arab (554)	590	0.28
Armenian (161)	247	0.12
Assyrian/Chaldean/Syriac (81)	81	0.04
Australian (5)	5	<0.01
Austrian (109)	281	0.13
Basque (27)	38	0.02
Belgian (31)	133	0.06
Brazilian (82)	105	0.05
British (771)	1,345	0.64
Bulgarian (49)	56	0.03
Cajun (0)	11	0.01
Canadian (163)	493	0.24
Celtic (80)	80	0.04
Croatian (81)	187	0.09
Czech (56)	233	0.11
Czechoslovakian (26)	84	0.04
Danish (118)	1,000	0.48
Dutch (517)	1,554	0.74
Eastern European (32)	61	0.03
English (2,243)	9,623	4.60
Estonian (12)	36	0.02
European (1,577)	1,837	0.88
Finnish (68)	289	0.14
French, ex. Basque (483)	2,524	1.21
French Canadian (206)	449	0.21
German (3,496)	14,843	7.09
Greek (211)	590	0.28
Hungarian (117)	419	0.20
Iranian (652)	800	0.38
Irish (2,636)	9,938	4.75
Israeli (0)	34	0.02
Italian (2,010)	5,357	2.56
Latvian (0)	44	0.02
Lithuanian (79)	306	0.15
Luxemburger (0)	30	0.01
Northern European (254)	297	0.14
Norwegian (251)	1,499	0.72
Pennsylvania German (0)	10	<0.01
Polish (618)	2,165	1.03
Portuguese (2,427)	4,754	2.27
Romanian (134)	164	0.08
Russian (828)	1,958	0.94
Scandinavian (125)	238	0.11
Scotch-Irish (634)	2,074	0.99
Scottish (686)	2,689	1.29
Serbian (0)	29	0.01
Slavic (45)	45	0.02
Slovak (40)	98	0.05
Slovene (21)	21	0.01
Swedish (743)	2,362	1.13
Swiss (24)	307	0.15
Turkish (56)	74	0.04
Ukrainian (184)	465	0.22
Welsh (81)	537	0.26
West Indian, ex. Hispanic (87)	126	0.06
Jamaican (41)	46	0.02
Trinidadian/Tobagonian (34)	68	0.03
West Indian (12)	12	0.01
Yugoslavian (70)	140	0.07

Hispanic Origin	Population	%
Hispanic or Latino (of any race)	31,698	14.81
Central American, ex. Mexican	2,429	1.13
Costa Rican	63	0.03
Guatemalan	430	0.20
Honduran	73	0.03
Nicaraguan	645	0.30
Panamanian	94	0.04
Salvadoran	1,102	0.51

SECTION TWO

*Notes: † The Census 2010 population figure is used to calculate the percentages in the Hispanic Origin and Race categories. Ancestry percentages are based on the 2006-2010 American Community Survey population (not shown); ‡ Numbers in parentheses indicate the number of people reporting a single ancestry; * Numbers in parentheses indicate the number of persons reporting this race alone, not in combination with any other race; Please refer to the Explanation of Data for more information.*

Other Central American	22	0.01
Cuban	165	0.08
Dominican Republic	26	0.01
Mexican	23,600	11.02
Puerto Rican	1,241	0.58
South American	1,344	0.63
Argentinean	103	0.05
Bolivian	80	0.04
Chilean	124	0.06
Colombian	228	0.11
Ecuadorian	80	0.04
Paraguayan	2	<0.01
Peruvian	616	0.29
Uruguayan	22	0.01
Venezuelan	78	0.04
Other South American	11	0.01
Other Hispanic or Latino	2,893	1.35

Race*	Population	%
African-American/Black (7,103)	8,842	4.13
Not Hispanic (6,743)	8,086	3.78
Hispanic (360)	756	0.35
American Indian/Alaska Native (976)	2,463	1.15
Not Hispanic (458)	1,436	0.67
Hispanic (518)	1,027	0.48
Alaska Athabascan *(Ala. Nat.)* (2)	3	<0.01
Aleut *(Alaska Native)* (3)	9	<0.01
Apache (29)	98	0.05
Arapaho (0)	2	<0.01
Blackfeet (10)	70	0.03
Canadian/French Am. Ind. (1)	6	<0.01
Central American Ind. (0)	3	<0.01
Cherokee (56)	374	0.17
Cheyenne (0)	6	<0.01
Chickasaw (11)	22	0.01
Chippewa (10)	34	0.02
Choctaw (20)	77	0.04
Comanche (6)	16	0.01
Cree (0)	6	<0.01
Creek (8)	24	0.01
Delaware (3)	5	<0.01
Hopi (2)	7	<0.01
Inupiat *(Alaska Native)* (2)	5	<0.01
Iroquois (4)	15	0.01
Kiowa (8)	9	<0.01
Mexican American Ind. (113)	179	0.08
Navajo (30)	63	0.03
Osage (4)	7	<0.01
Paiute (3)	8	<0.01
Pima (0)	2	<0.01
Potawatomi (5)	13	0.01
Pueblo (11)	25	0.01
Seminole (2)	12	0.01
Shoshone (2)	2	<0.01
Sioux (17)	53	0.02
South American Ind. (4)	12	0.01
Spanish American Ind. (15)	20	0.01
Tlingit-Haida *(Alaska Native)* (9)	20	0.01
Tohono O'Odham (7)	10	<0.01
Tsimshian *(Alaska Native)* (0)	1	<0.01
Ute (0)	4	<0.01
Yaqui (9)	37	0.02
Yuman (1)	1	<0.01
Yup'ik *(Alaska Native)* (0)	1	<0.01
Asian (108,332)	116,755	54.54
Not Hispanic (107,679)	115,097	53.76
Hispanic (653)	1,658	0.77
Bangladeshi (216)	231	0.11
Burmese (1,314)	1,450	0.68
Cambodian (153)	215	0.10
Chinese, ex. Taiwanese (33,706)	36,484	17.04
Filipino (14,285)	17,070	7.97
Hmong (112)	117	0.05
Indian (38,711)	40,010	18.69
Indonesian (237)	360	0.17
Japanese (1,716)	2,852	1.33
Korean (3,059)	3,459	1.62
Laotian (152)	208	0.10
Malaysian (96)	158	0.07
Nepalese (142)	152	0.07
Pakistani (2,081)	2,242	1.05
Sri Lankan (151)	172	0.08
Taiwanese (4,131)	4,572	2.14
Thai (264)	400	0.19
Vietnamese (5,249)	5,952	2.78
Hawaii Native/Pacific Islander (1,169)	2,514	1.17
Not Hispanic (1,064)	2,174	1.02
Hispanic (105)	340	0.16
Fijian (291)	348	0.16
Guamanian/Chamorro (238)	458	0.21
Marshallese (11)	17	0.01
Native Hawaiian (195)	735	0.34
Samoan (166)	255	0.12
Tongan (149)	192	0.09
White (70,320)	80,195	37.46
Not Hispanic (56,766)	64,017	29.90
Hispanic (13,554)	16,178	7.56

French Valley

Place Type: CDP
County: Riverside
Population: 23,067†

Ancestry‡	Population	%
African, Sub-Saharan (36)	113	0.54
African (36)	113	0.54
American (656)	656	3.12
Arab (12)	33	0.16
Arab (12)	12	0.06
Egyptian (0)	21	0.10
Armenian (11)	35	0.17
Assyrian/Chaldean/Syriac (12)	12	0.06
Australian (0)	25	0.12
Austrian (0)	79	0.38
Brazilian (62)	62	0.30
British (65)	75	0.36
Canadian (25)	25	0.12
Croatian (0)	14	0.07
Czech (0)	31	0.15
Danish (0)	11	0.05
Dutch (110)	345	1.64
English (392)	1,972	9.39
European (476)	636	3.03
Finnish (15)	23	0.11
French, ex. Basque (12)	515	2.45
French Canadian (97)	106	0.50
German (632)	2,886	13.74
Greek (0)	9	0.04
Guyanese (9)	9	0.04
Hungarian (69)	149	0.71
Irish (505)	2,466	11.74
Italian (515)	1,298	6.18
Lithuanian (0)	21	0.10
Norwegian (21)	240	1.14
Polish (51)	186	0.89
Portuguese (40)	140	0.67
Romanian (10)	54	0.26
Russian (16)	51	0.24
Scotch-Irish (93)	487	2.32
Scottish (60)	352	1.68
Serbian (0)	14	0.07
Slavic (49)	49	0.23
Slovak (7)	7	0.03
Swedish (51)	401	1.91
Turkish (11)	11	0.05
Welsh (12)	71	0.34
West Indian, ex. Hispanic (11)	42	0.20
Belizean (0)	31	0.15
Trinidadian/Tobagonian (11)	11	0.05

Hispanic Origin	Population	%
Hispanic or Latino (of any race)	6,318	27.39
Central American, ex. Mexican	225	0.98
Costa Rican	15	0.07
Guatemalan	42	0.18
Honduran	11	0.05
Nicaraguan	21	0.09
Panamanian	22	0.10
Salvadoran	108	0.47
Other Central American	6	0.03
Cuban	123	0.53
Dominican Republic	29	0.13
Mexican	5,114	22.17
Puerto Rican	261	1.13
South American	190	0.82
Argentinean	18	0.08
Bolivian	21	0.09
Chilean	16	0.07
Colombian	36	0.16
Ecuadorian	23	0.10
Peruvian	58	0.25
Uruguayan	1	<0.01
Venezuelan	13	0.06
Other South American	4	0.02
Other Hispanic or Latino	376	1.63

Race*	Population	%
African-American/Black (1,828)	2,245	9.73
Not Hispanic (1,700)	2,019	8.75
Hispanic (128)	226	0.98
American Indian/Alaska Native (229)	470	2.04
Not Hispanic (114)	264	1.14
Hispanic (115)	206	0.89
Alaska Athabascan *(Ala. Nat.)* (4)	4	0.02
Apache (12)	15	0.07
Blackfeet (0)	8	0.03
Cherokee (9)	44	0.19
Chippewa (1)	4	0.02
Choctaw (2)	9	0.04
Comanche (1)	1	<0.01
Creek (10)	10	0.04
Crow (0)	1	<0.01
Delaware (1)	1	<0.01
Hopi (3)	3	0.01
Iroquois (2)	4	0.02
Mexican American Ind. (14)	21	0.09
Navajo (1)	4	0.02
Osage (0)	1	<0.01
Paiute (3)	6	0.03
Pueblo (2)	3	0.01
Puget Sound Salish (1)	1	<0.01
Seminole (0)	1	<0.01
Sioux (8)	16	0.07
South American Ind. (3)	6	0.03
Spanish American Ind. (0)	1	<0.01
Yaqui (5)	6	0.03
Yuman (2)	2	0.01
Asian (2,672)	3,378	14.64
Not Hispanic (2,592)	3,178	13.78
Hispanic (80)	200	0.87
Burmese (4)	6	0.03
Cambodian (52)	71	0.31
Chinese, ex. Taiwanese (111)	234	1.01
Filipino (1,722)	2,159	9.36
Hmong (3)	5	0.02
Indian (129)	154	0.67
Indonesian (7)	28	0.12
Japanese (83)	207	0.90
Korean (70)	127	0.55
Laotian (107)	127	0.55
Pakistani (3)	5	0.02
Sri Lankan (2)	7	0.03
Taiwanese (4)	10	0.04
Thai (22)	40	0.17
Vietnamese (227)	280	1.21
Hawaii Native/Pacific Islander (134)	328	1.42
Not Hispanic (118)	261	1.13
Hispanic (16)	67	0.29
Guamanian/Chamorro (45)	89	0.39
Native Hawaiian (30)	117	0.51
Samoan (39)	69	0.30
Tongan (4)	4	0.02
White (14,827)	16,087	69.74
Not Hispanic (11,235)	12,057	52.27
Hispanic (3,592)	4,030	17.47

*Notes: † The Census 2010 population figure is used to calculate the percentages in the Hispanic Origin and Race categories. Ancestry percentages are based on the 2006-2010 American Community Survey population (not shown); ‡ Numbers in parentheses indicate the number of people reporting a single ancestry; * Numbers in parentheses indicate the number of persons reporting this race alone, not in combination with any other race; Please refer to the Explanation of Data for more information.*

Fresno

Place Type: City
County: Fresno
Population: 494,665†

Ancestry‡	Population	%
Afghan (46)	58	0.01
African, Sub-Saharan (1,907)	2,412	0.50
African (1,344)	1,818	0.38
Ethiopian (221)	240	0.05
Ghanaian (5)	5	<0.01
Nigerian (157)	157	0.03
South African (7)	19	<0.01
Sudanese (109)	109	0.02
Other Sub-Saharan African (64)	64	0.01
Albanian (0)	23	<0.01
American (6,280)	6,280	1.30
Arab (3,658)	4,301	0.89
Arab (1,557)	1,720	0.36
Egyptian (305)	313	0.06
Iraqi (91)	91	0.02
Jordanian (708)	708	0.15
Lebanese (153)	372	0.08
Palestinian (123)	170	0.04
Syrian (203)	363	0.07
Other Arab (518)	564	0.12
Armenian (5,389)	7,000	1.45
Assyrian/Chaldean/Syriac (52)	79	0.02
Australian (23)	39	0.01
Austrian (129)	451	0.09
Basque (203)	359	0.07
Belgian (42)	195	0.04
Brazilian (71)	142	0.03
British (211)	841	0.17
Cajun (4)	36	0.01
Canadian (535)	874	0.18
Celtic (55)	183	0.04
Croatian (76)	154	0.03
Czech (207)	825	0.17
Czechoslovakian (104)	213	0.04
Danish (678)	2,292	0.47
Dutch (878)	4,720	0.98
Eastern European (119)	165	0.03
English (6,805)	24,262	5.01
Estonian (20)	28	0.01
European (2,498)	3,030	0.63
Finnish (81)	640	0.13
French, ex. Basque (1,231)	7,784	1.61
French Canadian (441)	914	0.19
German (11,561)	39,420	8.14
German Russian (9)	23	<0.01
Greek (505)	1,082	0.22
Hungarian (58)	465	0.10
Iranian (695)	995	0.21
Irish (6,748)	26,731	5.52
Israeli (193)	231	0.05
Italian (5,935)	16,181	3.34
Latvian (10)	21	<0.01
Lithuanian (29)	168	0.03
Luxemburger (0)	25	0.01
Macedonian (0)	13	<0.01
New Zealander (0)	42	0.01
Northern European (362)	387	0.08
Norwegian (991)	2,869	0.59
Pennsylvania German (55)	82	0.02
Polish (924)	2,612	0.54
Portuguese (2,751)	5,315	1.10
Romanian (98)	235	0.05
Russian (1,323)	3,100	0.64
Scandinavian (177)	487	0.10
Scotch-Irish (1,672)	4,450	0.92
Scottish (1,729)	4,988	1.03
Serbian (31)	91	0.02
Slavic (39)	144	0.03
Slovak (33)	80	0.02
Slovene (12)	42	0.01
Swedish (1,055)	4,491	0.93
Swiss (186)	1,010	0.21
Turkish (87)	87	0.02
Ukrainian (891)	1,067	0.22
Welsh (437)	1,973	0.41
West Indian, ex. Hispanic (122)	510	0.11
Barbadian (0)	6	<0.01
Belizean (0)	12	<0.01
Dutch West Indian (16)	133	0.03
Jamaican (95)	231	0.05
West Indian (11)	115	0.02
Other West Indian (0)	13	<0.01
Yugoslavian (57)	119	0.02

Hispanic Origin	Population	%
Hispanic or Latino (of any race)	232,055	46.91
Central American, ex. Mexican	3,381	0.68
Costa Rican	98	0.02
Guatemalan	678	0.14
Honduran	318	0.06
Nicaraguan	320	0.06
Panamanian	107	0.02
Salvadoran	1,833	0.37
Other Central American	27	0.01
Cuban	406	0.08
Dominican Republic	79	0.02
Mexican	211,431	42.74
Puerto Rican	1,825	0.37
South American	1,084	0.22
Argentinean	148	0.03
Bolivian	47	0.01
Chilean	113	0.02
Colombian	318	0.06
Ecuadorian	88	0.02
Paraguayan	7	<0.01
Peruvian	283	0.06
Uruguayan	15	<0.01
Venezuelan	49	0.01
Other South American	16	<0.01
Other Hispanic or Latino	13,849	2.80

Race*	Population	%
African-American/Black (40,960)	46,895	9.48
Not Hispanic (37,885)	41,526	8.39
Hispanic (3,075)	5,369	1.09
American Indian/Alaska Native (8,525)	14,161	2.86
Not Hispanic (3,127)	6,241	1.26
Hispanic (5,398)	7,920	1.60
Alaska Athabascan *(Ala. Nat.)* (7)	7	<0.01
Aleut *(Alaska Native)* (7)	8	<0.01
Apache (355)	648	0.13
Arapaho (0)	4	<0.01
Blackfeet (44)	216	0.04
Canadian/French Am. Ind. (14)	21	<0.01
Central American Ind. (19)	34	0.01
Cherokee (422)	1,408	0.28
Cheyenne (9)	22	<0.01
Chickasaw (13)	71	0.01
Chippewa (33)	68	0.01
Choctaw (136)	411	0.08
Colville (5)	6	<0.01
Comanche (41)	77	0.02
Cree (5)	15	<0.01
Creek (52)	162	0.03
Crow (11)	18	<0.01
Delaware (10)	16	<0.01
Hopi (12)	45	0.01
Houma (1)	3	<0.01
Inupiat *(Alaska Native)* (3)	5	<0.01
Iroquois (23)	44	0.01
Kiowa (13)	21	<0.01
Lumbee (4)	7	<0.01
Menominee (6)	6	<0.01
Mexican American Ind. (1,282)	1,666	0.34
Navajo (165)	294	0.06
Osage (6)	24	<0.01
Ottawa (4)	7	<0.01
Paiute (19)	67	0.01
Pima (24)	41	0.01
Potawatomi (29)	47	0.01
Pueblo (37)	68	0.01
Puget Sound Salish (3)	7	<0.01
Seminole (19)	49	0.01
Shoshone (25)	36	0.01
Sioux (68)	149	0.03
South American Ind. (9)	22	<0.01
Spanish American Ind. (46)	58	0.01
Tlingit-Haida *(Alaska Native)* (1)	5	<0.01
Tohono O'Odham (43)	62	0.01
Tsimshian *(Alaska Native)* (1)	1	<0.01
Ute (9)	20	<0.01
Yakama (1)	3	<0.01
Yaqui (353)	522	0.11
Yuman (15)	26	0.01
Yup'ik *(Alaska Native)* (1)	4	<0.01
Asian (62,528)	69,765	14.10
Not Hispanic (60,939)	65,854	13.31
Hispanic (1,589)	3,911	0.79
Bangladeshi (28)	30	0.01
Bhutanese (1)	1	<0.01
Burmese (50)	66	0.01
Cambodian (4,310)	4,798	0.97
Chinese, ex. Taiwanese (3,605)	4,726	0.96
Filipino (6,359)	8,726	1.76
Hmong (23,449)	24,328	4.92
Indian (8,814)	9,825	1.99
Indonesian (158)	253	0.05
Japanese (2,401)	3,787	0.77
Korean (1,106)	1,434	0.29
Laotian (6,007)	6,733	1.36
Malaysian (30)	43	0.01
Nepalese (29)	34	0.01
Pakistani (326)	378	0.08
Sri Lankan (35)	45	0.01
Taiwanese (140)	154	0.03
Thai (337)	515	0.10
Vietnamese (2,093)	2,412	0.49
Hawaii Native/Pacific Islander (849)	2,133	0.43
Not Hispanic (663)	1,431	0.29
Hispanic (186)	702	0.14
Fijian (93)	114	0.02
Guamanian/Chamorro (152)	264	0.05
Marshallese (5)	6	<0.01
Native Hawaiian (164)	608	0.12
Samoan (234)	388	0.08
Tongan (23)	48	0.01
White (245,306)	263,929	53.36
Not Hispanic (148,598)	156,548	31.65
Hispanic (96,708)	107,381	21.71

Fullerton

Place Type: City
County: Orange
Population: 135,161†

Ancestry‡	Population	%
Afghan (176)	188	0.14
African, Sub-Saharan (304)	607	0.46
African (77)	126	0.09
Ethiopian (94)	139	0.10
Nigerian (119)	119	0.09
South African (14)	198	0.15
Other Sub-Saharan African (0)	25	0.02
Alsatian (0)	9	0.01
American (2,569)	2,569	1.93
Arab (447)	770	0.58
Arab (0)	238	0.18
Egyptian (60)	74	0.06
Iraqi (27)	33	0.02
Jordanian (15)	20	0.02
Lebanese (232)	280	0.21
Palestinian (41)	41	0.03
Syrian (0)	12	0.01
Other Arab (72)	72	0.05
Armenian (215)	338	0.25
Assyrian/Chaldean/Syriac (0)	8	0.01
Australian (24)	46	0.03
Austrian (31)	370	0.28
Basque (50)	50	0.04
Belgian (50)	161	0.12
Brazilian (16)	37	0.03

*Notes: † The Census 2010 population figure is used to calculate the percentages in the Hispanic Origin and Race categories. Ancestry percentages are based on the 2006-2010 American Community Survey population (not shown); ‡ Numbers in parentheses indicate the number of people reporting a single ancestry; * Numbers in parentheses indicate the number of persons reporting this race alone, not in combination with any other race; Please refer to the Explanation of Data for more information.*

Ancestry	Population	%
British (200)	634	0.48
Canadian (270)	474	0.36
Celtic (37)	111	0.08
Croatian (85)	190	0.14
Czech (34)	193	0.15
Czechoslovakian (0)	107	0.08
Danish (125)	638	0.48
Dutch (724)	1,891	1.42
Eastern European (29)	67	0.05
English (2,822)	9,591	7.22
European (758)	950	0.71
Finnish (82)	211	0.16
French, ex. Basque (310)	2,297	1.73
French Canadian (254)	442	0.33
German (3,722)	13,529	10.18
German Russian (7)	7	0.01
Greek (496)	828	0.62
Hungarian (208)	770	0.58
Icelander (0)	53	0.04
Iranian (528)	537	0.40
Irish (2,271)	9,523	7.17
Israeli (53)	53	0.04
Italian (1,793)	4,838	3.64
Latvian (0)	15	0.01
Lithuanian (27)	83	0.06
Luxemburger (0)	12	0.01
New Zealander (16)	51	0.04
Northern European (127)	127	0.10
Norwegian (410)	1,353	1.02
Pennsylvania German (0)	10	0.01
Polish (496)	1,688	1.27
Portuguese (252)	539	0.41
Romanian (574)	663	0.50
Russian (508)	989	0.74
Scandinavian (98)	257	0.19
Scotch-Irish (725)	2,049	1.54
Scottish (402)	1,926	1.45
Serbian (62)	80	0.06
Slavic (47)	75	0.06
Slovak (70)	86	0.06
Slovene (24)	49	0.04
Swedish (481)	1,929	1.45
Swiss (43)	302	0.23
Turkish (60)	74	0.06
Ukrainian (105)	314	0.24
Welsh (171)	986	0.74
West Indian, ex. Hispanic (16)	80	0.06
Belizean (0)	31	0.02
Haitian (0)	21	0.02
Trinidadian/Tobagonian (0)	2	<0.01
West Indian (0)	10	0.01
Other West Indian (16)	16	0.01
Yugoslavian (30)	59	0.04

Hispanic Origin	Population	%
Hispanic or Latino (of any race)	46,501	34.40
Central American, ex. Mexican	2,039	1.51
Costa Rican	117	0.09
Guatemalan	594	0.44
Honduran	163	0.12
Nicaraguan	274	0.20
Panamanian	31	0.02
Salvadoran	800	0.59
Other Central American	60	0.04
Cuban	413	0.31
Dominican Republic	24	0.02
Mexican	39,718	29.39
Puerto Rican	594	0.44
South American	1,291	0.96
Argentinean	244	0.18
Bolivian	49	0.04
Chilean	70	0.05
Colombian	269	0.20
Ecuadorian	161	0.12
Paraguayan	7	0.01
Peruvian	423	0.31
Uruguayan	10	0.01
Venezuelan	15	0.01
Other South American	43	0.03
Other Hispanic or Latino	2,422	1.79

Race*	Population	%
African-American/Black (3,138)	3,968	2.94
Not Hispanic (2,791)	3,321	2.46
Hispanic (347)	647	0.48
American Indian/Alaska Native (842)	1,859	1.38
Not Hispanic (251)	796	0.59
Hispanic (591)	1,063	0.79
Alaska Athabascan *(Ala. Nat.)* (0)	1	<0.01
Aleut *(Alaska Native)* (0)	1	<0.01
Apache (34)	77	0.06
Arapaho (0)	3	<0.01
Blackfeet (7)	43	0.03
Canadian/French Am. Ind. (0)	2	<0.01
Central American Ind. (2)	4	<0.01
Cherokee (50)	238	0.18
Cheyenne (2)	4	<0.01
Chickasaw (1)	5	<0.01
Chippewa (4)	9	0.01
Choctaw (10)	48	0.04
Colville (0)	2	<0.01
Comanche (6)	13	0.01
Cree (0)	1	<0.01
Creek (3)	27	0.02
Delaware (1)	5	<0.01
Hopi (1)	2	<0.01
Inupiat *(Alaska Native)* (1)	2	<0.01
Iroquois (3)	15	0.01
Kiowa (4)	5	<0.01
Lumbee (1)	1	<0.01
Menominee (0)	1	<0.01
Mexican American Ind. (114)	172	0.13
Navajo (25)	52	0.04
Osage (2)	4	<0.01
Paiute (3)	5	<0.01
Pima (5)	8	0.01
Potawatomi (3)	17	0.01
Pueblo (11)	19	0.01
Puget Sound Salish (1)	1	<0.01
Seminole (0)	8	0.01
Shoshone (1)	6	<0.01
Sioux (12)	46	0.03
South American Ind. (3)	7	0.01
Spanish American Ind. (9)	15	0.01
Tohono O'Odham (4)	6	<0.01
Ute (0)	2	<0.01
Yaqui (21)	53	0.04
Yuman (1)	1	<0.01
Asian (30,788)	33,256	24.60
Not Hispanic (30,486)	32,479	24.03
Hispanic (302)	777	0.57
Bangladeshi (49)	54	0.04
Burmese (51)	67	0.05
Cambodian (153)	215	0.16
Chinese, ex. Taiwanese (3,339)	4,235	3.13
Filipino (3,380)	4,263	3.15
Hmong (20)	25	0.02
Indian (2,494)	2,714	2.01
Indonesian (194)	278	0.21
Japanese (1,260)	1,966	1.45
Korean (15,544)	16,004	11.84
Laotian (157)	196	0.15
Malaysian (24)	37	0.03
Nepalese (20)	20	0.01
Pakistani (254)	306	0.23
Sri Lankan (51)	55	0.04
Taiwanese (697)	782	0.58
Thai (218)	284	0.21
Vietnamese (1,945)	2,277	1.68
Hawaii Native/Pacific Islander (321)	790	0.58
Not Hispanic (270)	653	0.48
Hispanic (51)	137	0.10
Fijian (3)	7	0.01
Guamanian/Chamorro (40)	112	0.08
Native Hawaiian (77)	271	0.20
Samoan (132)	196	0.15
Tongan (15)	24	0.02
White (72,845)	77,699	57.49
Not Hispanic (51,656)	54,164	40.07
Hispanic (21,189)	23,535	17.41

Galt

Place Type: City
County: Sacramento
Population: 23,647†

Ancestry‡	Population	%
African, Sub-Saharan (14)	14	0.06
Nigerian (14)	14	0.06
American (695)	695	3.01
Arab (259)	259	1.12
Lebanese (27)	27	0.12
Palestinian (200)	200	0.87
Other Arab (32)	32	0.14
Armenian (179)	179	0.78
Australian (7)	21	0.09
Austrian (12)	25	0.11
British (28)	152	0.66
Canadian (14)	25	0.11
Czech (25)	36	0.16
Danish (67)	173	0.75
Dutch (147)	293	1.27
English (724)	1,879	8.14
European (60)	100	0.43
Finnish (17)	34	0.15
French, ex. Basque (98)	757	3.28
French Canadian (16)	73	0.32
German (1,194)	3,343	14.49
Greek (21)	46	0.20
Hungarian (0)	16	0.07
Iranian (39)	39	0.17
Irish (198)	1,867	8.09
Italian (316)	1,321	5.73
New Zealander (12)	12	0.05
Norwegian (34)	276	1.20
Polish (23)	202	0.88
Portuguese (365)	715	3.10
Russian (60)	291	1.26
Scandinavian (90)	124	0.54
Scotch-Irish (144)	317	1.37
Scottish (110)	368	1.59
Slavic (0)	8	0.03
Slovak (32)	32	0.14
Swedish (82)	220	0.95
Swiss (0)	29	0.13
Welsh (0)	201	0.87
West Indian, ex. Hispanic (0)	18	0.08
British West Indian (0)	18	0.08

Hispanic Origin	Population	%
Hispanic or Latino (of any race)	10,113	42.77
Central American, ex. Mexican	128	0.54
Costa Rican	2	0.01
Guatemalan	23	0.10
Honduran	10	0.04
Nicaraguan	22	0.09
Panamanian	3	0.01
Salvadoran	67	0.28
Other Central American	1	<0.01
Cuban	15	0.06
Dominican Republic	2	0.01
Mexican	9,212	38.96
Puerto Rican	91	0.38
South American	49	0.21
Argentinean	3	0.01
Chilean	10	0.04
Colombian	12	0.05
Ecuadorian	13	0.05
Peruvian	9	0.04
Venezuelan	2	0.01
Other Hispanic or Latino	616	2.60

Race*	Population	%
African-American/Black (430)	668	2.82
Not Hispanic (367)	528	2.23
Hispanic (63)	140	0.59
American Indian/Alaska Native (361)	774	3.27
Not Hispanic (142)	390	1.65
Hispanic (219)	384	1.62
Apache (8)	21	0.09

*Notes: † The Census 2010 population figure is used to calculate the percentages in the Hispanic Origin and Race categories. Ancestry percentages are based on the 2006-2010 American Community Survey population (not shown); ‡ Numbers in parentheses indicate the number of people reporting a single ancestry; * Numbers in parentheses indicate the number of persons reporting this race alone, not in combination with any other race; Please refer to the Explanation of Data for more information.*

Arapaho (2)	2	0.01
Blackfeet (1)	19	0.08
Cherokee (22)	118	0.50
Cheyenne (0)	2	0.01
Chickasaw (2)	5	0.02
Choctaw (16)	47	0.20
Comanche (0)	6	0.03
Cree (0)	1	<0.01
Creek (7)	8	0.03
Delaware (1)	2	0.01
Hopi (0)	4	0.02
Inupiat *(Alaska Native)* (0)	1	<0.01
Iroquois (1)	2	0.01
Lumbee (4)	4	0.02
Mexican American Ind. (5)	20	0.08
Navajo (1)	12	0.05
Paiute (0)	7	0.03
Potawatomi (0)	8	0.03
Pueblo (2)	4	0.02
Seminole (0)	3	0.01
Sioux (7)	14	0.06
Spanish American Ind. (1)	1	<0.01
Ute (0)	1	<0.01
Yakama (1)	2	0.01
Yup'ik *(Alaska Native)* (2)	2	0.01
Asian (815)	1,256	5.31
Not Hispanic (745)	1,041	4.40
Hispanic (70)	215	0.91
Cambodian (16)	22	0.09
Chinese, ex. Taiwanese (78)	142	0.60
Filipino (324)	621	2.63
Hmong (34)	36	0.15
Indian (134)	149	0.63
Indonesian (1)	6	0.03
Japanese (65)	126	0.53
Korean (31)	54	0.23
Laotian (23)	24	0.10
Pakistani (37)	39	0.16
Taiwanese (2)	2	0.01
Thai (8)	13	0.05
Vietnamese (31)	40	0.17
Hawaii Native/Pacific Islander (108)	210	0.89
Not Hispanic (82)	143	0.60
Hispanic (26)	67	0.28
Fijian (24)	32	0.14
Guamanian/Chamorro (15)	31	0.13
Native Hawaiian (19)	64	0.27
Samoan (25)	38	0.16
Tongan (16)	22	0.09
White (15,639)	16,889	71.42
Not Hispanic (11,513)	12,099	51.17
Hispanic (4,126)	4,790	20.26

Garden Acres

Place Type: CDP
County: San Joaquin
Population: 10,648†

Ancestry‡	Population	%
American (122)	122	1.17
Arab (0)	18	0.17
Moroccan (0)	18	0.17
Austrian (8)	8	0.08
Brazilian (0)	55	0.53
Czech (0)	9	0.09
Danish (0)	10	0.10
Dutch (0)	5	0.05
English (44)	172	1.64
European (55)	66	0.63
Finnish (0)	17	0.16
French, ex. Basque (12)	301	2.87
French Canadian (11)	11	0.11
German (428)	905	8.64
Hungarian (0)	20	0.19
Irish (60)	784	7.49
Italian (137)	268	2.56
Northern European (15)	15	0.14
Norwegian (11)	36	0.34
Pennsylvania German (16)	16	0.15
Polish (7)	22	0.21
Portuguese (31)	31	0.30
Scotch-Irish (0)	137	1.31
Scottish (0)	85	0.81
Swedish (13)	63	0.60
Swiss (0)	36	0.34

Hispanic Origin	Population	%
Hispanic or Latino (of any race)	7,338	68.91
Central American, ex. Mexican	71	0.67
Costa Rican	3	0.03
Guatemalan	37	0.35
Honduran	2	0.02
Nicaraguan	6	0.06
Panamanian	2	0.02
Salvadoran	21	0.20
Cuban	8	0.08
Mexican	6,916	64.95
Puerto Rican	48	0.45
South American	10	0.09
Chilean	1	0.01
Colombian	3	0.03
Peruvian	5	0.05
Uruguayan	1	0.01
Other Hispanic or Latino	285	2.68

Race*	Population	%
African-American/Black (233)	325	3.05
Not Hispanic (155)	198	1.86
Hispanic (78)	127	1.19
American Indian/Alaska Native (172)	348	3.27
Not Hispanic (65)	179	1.68
Hispanic (107)	169	1.59
Apache (23)	27	0.25
Blackfeet (2)	10	0.09
Cherokee (20)	95	0.89
Chickasaw (2)	5	0.05
Choctaw (5)	15	0.14
Comanche (1)	1	0.01
Creek (0)	4	0.04
Hopi (2)	5	0.05
Kiowa (1)	2	0.02
Mexican American Ind. (14)	35	0.33
Navajo (1)	11	0.10
Osage (0)	1	0.01
Ottawa (1)	1	0.01
Paiute (3)	3	0.03
Potawatomi (2)	3	0.03
Pueblo (5)	5	0.05
Puget Sound Salish (8)	10	0.09
Sioux (1)	4	0.04
South American Ind. (0)	1	0.01
Tlingit-Haida *(Alaska Native)* (1)	1	0.01
Asian (358)	524	4.92
Not Hispanic (318)	402	3.78
Hispanic (40)	122	1.15
Cambodian (17)	22	0.21
Chinese, ex. Taiwanese (7)	19	0.18
Filipino (83)	187	1.76
Hmong (151)	158	1.48
Indian (4)	17	0.16
Japanese (8)	34	0.32
Korean (1)	4	0.04
Laotian (49)	54	0.51
Pakistani (16)	17	0.16
Vietnamese (4)	6	0.06
Hawaii Native/Pacific Islander (40)	76	0.71
Not Hispanic (28)	52	0.49
Hispanic (12)	24	0.23
Fijian (9)	9	0.08
Guamanian/Chamorro (8)	14	0.13
Native Hawaiian (9)	26	0.24
Samoan (0)	1	0.01
Tongan (8)	8	0.08
White (5,244)	5,833	54.78
Not Hispanic (2,496)	2,687	25.23
Hispanic (2,748)	3,146	29.55

Garden Grove

Place Type: City
County: Orange
Population: 170,883†

Ancestry‡	Population	%
Afghan (434)	434	0.26
African, Sub-Saharan (87)	131	0.08
African (68)	86	0.05
South African (0)	26	0.02
Sudanese (8)	8	<0.01
Other Sub-Saharan African (11)	11	0.01
Albanian (0)	8	<0.01
American (3,323)	3,323	1.97
Arab (509)	585	0.35
Arab (20)	20	0.01
Egyptian (118)	118	0.07
Iraqi (9)	9	0.01
Jordanian (69)	69	0.04
Lebanese (3)	40	0.02
Moroccan (108)	108	0.06
Palestinian (60)	60	0.04
Syrian (113)	113	0.07
Other Arab (9)	48	0.03
Armenian (88)	165	0.10
Assyrian/Chaldean/Syriac (29)	29	0.02
Australian (42)	62	0.04
Austrian (11)	79	0.05
Basque (12)	31	0.02
Belgian (9)	56	0.03
Brazilian (47)	47	0.03
British (225)	369	0.22
Bulgarian (0)	22	0.01
Canadian (119)	217	0.13
Celtic (7)	19	0.01
Croatian (40)	81	0.05
Czech (23)	195	0.12
Czechoslovakian (8)	82	0.05
Danish (78)	434	0.26
Dutch (295)	1,260	0.75
Eastern European (27)	27	0.02
English (2,038)	7,102	4.20
European (592)	786	0.47
Finnish (26)	103	0.06
French, ex. Basque (480)	2,112	1.25
French Canadian (176)	394	0.23
German (2,843)	10,090	5.97
German Russian (10)	10	0.01
Greek (228)	376	0.22
Hungarian (80)	342	0.20
Iranian (81)	86	0.05
Irish (1,980)	7,908	4.68
Israeli (10)	10	0.01
Italian (1,194)	2,886	1.71
Latvian (0)	34	0.02
Lithuanian (87)	174	0.10
Maltese (0)	21	0.01
Northern European (17)	17	0.01
Norwegian (321)	848	0.50
Pennsylvania German (15)	26	0.02
Polish (658)	1,608	0.95
Portuguese (146)	461	0.27
Romanian (325)	355	0.21
Russian (254)	679	0.40
Scandinavian (103)	141	0.08
Scotch-Irish (375)	1,179	0.70
Scottish (359)	1,354	0.80
Serbian (29)	29	0.02
Slavic (14)	27	0.02
Slovak (40)	53	0.03
Swedish (359)	1,052	0.62
Swiss (60)	225	0.13
Turkish (121)	165	0.10
Ukrainian (97)	138	0.08
Welsh (174)	486	0.29
West Indian, ex. Hispanic (67)	96	0.06
Belizean (0)	6	<0.01
Jamaican (67)	90	0.05

*Notes: † The Census 2010 population figure is used to calculate the percentages in the Hispanic Origin and Race categories. Ancestry percentages are based on the 2006-2010 American Community Survey population (not shown); ‡ Numbers in parentheses indicate the number of people reporting a single ancestry; * Numbers in parentheses indicate the number of persons reporting this race alone, not in combination with any other race; Please refer to the Explanation of Data for more information.*

Yugoslavian (13)	65	0.04

Hispanic Origin	Population	%
Hispanic or Latino (of any race)	63,079	36.91
Central American, ex. Mexican	2,968	1.74
Costa Rican	89	0.05
Guatemalan	841	0.49
Honduran	210	0.12
Nicaraguan	156	0.09
Panamanian	55	0.03
Salvadoran	1,609	0.94
Other Central American	8	<0.01
Cuban	341	0.20
Dominican Republic	44	0.03
Mexican	54,565	31.93
Puerto Rican	524	0.31
South American	1,465	0.86
Argentinean	169	0.10
Bolivian	110	0.06
Chilean	88	0.05
Colombian	327	0.19
Ecuadorian	149	0.09
Paraguayan	2	<0.01
Peruvian	569	0.33
Uruguayan	19	0.01
Venezuelan	23	0.01
Other South American	9	0.01
Other Hispanic or Latino	3,172	1.86

Race*	Population	%
African-American/Black (2,155)	2,919	1.71
Not Hispanic (1,752)	2,267	1.33
Hispanic (403)	652	0.38
American Indian/Alaska Native (983)	1,826	1.07
Not Hispanic (286)	724	0.42
Hispanic (697)	1,102	0.64
Apache (33)	88	0.05
Arapaho (0)	2	<0.01
Blackfeet (3)	15	0.01
Canadian/French Am. Ind. (0)	3	<0.01
Central American Ind. (3)	3	<0.01
Cherokee (54)	153	0.09
Cheyenne (3)	10	0.01
Chickasaw (9)	10	0.01
Chippewa (8)	16	0.01
Choctaw (9)	29	0.02
Comanche (2)	4	<0.01
Cree (0)	2	<0.01
Creek (1)	3	<0.01
Crow (0)	3	<0.01
Delaware (4)	7	<0.01
Hopi (4)	10	0.01
Iroquois (7)	23	0.01
Kiowa (1)	1	<0.01
Lumbee (0)	4	<0.01
Menominee (0)	1	<0.01
Mexican American Ind. (126)	175	0.10
Navajo (22)	51	0.03
Osage (0)	5	<0.01
Ottawa (0)	1	<0.01
Paiute (1)	2	<0.01
Pima (7)	10	0.01
Pueblo (5)	14	0.01
Puget Sound Salish (4)	4	<0.01
Seminole (7)	10	0.01
Shoshone (2)	4	<0.01
Sioux (12)	24	0.01
South American Ind. (2)	5	<0.01
Spanish American Ind. (20)	23	0.01
Tlingit-Haida *(Alaska Native)* (0)	2	<0.01
Tohono O'Odham (5)	6	<0.01
Yaqui (3)	20	0.01
Yuman (2)	2	<0.01
Yup'ik *(Alaska Native)* (0)	2	<0.01
Asian (63,451)	65,923	38.58
Not Hispanic (63,118)	65,071	38.08
Hispanic (333)	852	0.50
Bangladeshi (42)	47	0.03
Burmese (99)	104	0.06
Cambodian (627)	753	0.44
Chinese, ex. Taiwanese (2,084)	3,035	1.78
Filipino (3,177)	3,944	2.31
Hmong (200)	212	0.12
Indian (676)	895	0.52
Indonesian (152)	223	0.13
Japanese (895)	1,297	0.76
Korean (5,717)	5,951	3.48
Laotian (355)	412	0.24
Malaysian (8)	20	0.01
Nepalese (3)	3	<0.01
Pakistani (384)	416	0.24
Sri Lankan (50)	60	0.04
Taiwanese (106)	134	0.08
Thai (202)	256	0.15
Vietnamese (47,331)	48,774	28.54
Hawaii Native/Pacific Islander (1,110)	1,673	0.98
Not Hispanic (1,030)	1,460	0.85
Hispanic (80)	213	0.12
Fijian (8)	10	0.01
Guamanian/Chamorro (140)	218	0.13
Marshallese (103)	109	0.06
Native Hawaiian (134)	366	0.21
Samoan (617)	760	0.44
Tongan (48)	56	0.03
White (68,149)	73,273	42.88
Not Hispanic (38,558)	40,865	23.91
Hispanic (29,591)	32,408	18.97

Gardena

Place Type: City
County: Los Angeles
Population: 58,829†

Ancestry‡	Population	%
African, Sub-Saharan (531)	580	0.99
African (428)	477	0.81
Ethiopian (23)	23	0.04
Nigerian (80)	80	0.14
American (1,792)	1,792	3.05
Arab (37)	37	0.06
Egyptian (18)	18	0.03
Lebanese (11)	11	0.02
Other Arab (8)	8	0.01
Armenian (10)	10	0.02
Austrian (6)	28	0.05
Brazilian (9)	9	0.02
British (66)	129	0.22
Cajun (8)	8	0.01
Canadian (26)	42	0.07
Croatian (22)	33	0.06
Czechoslovakian (10)	10	0.02
Danish (17)	25	0.04
Dutch (18)	192	0.33
English (217)	1,001	1.71
European (99)	119	0.20
French, ex. Basque (25)	257	0.44
French Canadian (36)	36	0.06
German (526)	1,768	3.01
Hungarian (19)	47	0.08
Iranian (42)	53	0.09
Irish (235)	1,390	2.37
Italian (371)	608	1.04
Norwegian (49)	209	0.36
Polish (69)	92	0.16
Portuguese (34)	131	0.22
Russian (59)	93	0.16
Scandinavian (0)	7	0.01
Scotch-Irish (10)	111	0.19
Scottish (26)	151	0.26
Serbian (0)	24	0.04
Slovak (10)	21	0.04
Swedish (23)	170	0.29
Swiss (5)	65	0.11
Ukrainian (11)	18	0.03
Welsh (7)	83	0.14
West Indian, ex. Hispanic (226)	332	0.57
Belizean (203)	203	0.35
British West Indian (0)	16	0.03
Jamaican (9)	9	0.02
Trinidadian/Tobagonian (14)	75	0.13
West Indian (0)	29	0.05

Hispanic Origin	Population	%
Hispanic or Latino (of any race)	22,151	37.65
Central American, ex. Mexican	2,934	4.99
Costa Rican	69	0.12
Guatemalan	1,080	1.84
Honduran	170	0.29
Nicaraguan	190	0.32
Panamanian	48	0.08
Salvadoran	1,341	2.28
Other Central American	36	0.06
Cuban	225	0.38
Dominican Republic	36	0.06
Mexican	16,462	27.98
Puerto Rican	356	0.61
South American	867	1.47
Argentinean	51	0.09
Bolivian	13	0.02
Chilean	36	0.06
Colombian	122	0.21
Ecuadorian	176	0.30
Paraguayan	2	<0.01
Peruvian	439	0.75
Uruguayan	3	0.01
Venezuelan	16	0.03
Other South American	9	0.02
Other Hispanic or Latino	1,271	2.16

Race*	Population	%
African-American/Black (14,352)	15,136	25.73
Not Hispanic (14,034)	14,571	24.77
Hispanic (318)	565	0.96
American Indian/Alaska Native (348)	735	1.25
Not Hispanic (100)	333	0.57
Hispanic (248)	402	0.68
Apache (11)	16	0.03
Blackfeet (1)	18	0.03
Canadian/French Am. Ind. (0)	1	<0.01
Central American Ind. (5)	11	0.02
Cherokee (12)	56	0.10
Cheyenne (1)	1	<0.01
Chickasaw (1)	3	0.01
Chippewa (9)	10	0.02
Choctaw (7)	28	0.05
Comanche (3)	4	0.01
Creek (0)	4	0.01
Houma (0)	3	0.01
Inupiat *(Alaska Native)* (0)	1	<0.01
Mexican American Ind. (45)	78	0.13
Navajo (11)	27	0.05
Osage (1)	4	0.01
Ottawa (0)	1	<0.01
Paiute (1)	1	<0.01
Pima (1)	1	<0.01
Potawatomi (0)	1	<0.01
Pueblo (7)	16	0.03
Seminole (0)	2	<0.01
Shoshone (0)	1	<0.01
Sioux (8)	9	0.02
South American Ind. (5)	12	0.02
Spanish American Ind. (5)	7	0.01
Tohono O'Odham (6)	10	0.02
Yakama (0)	1	<0.01
Yaqui (1)	2	<0.01
Yup'ik *(Alaska Native)* (0)	4	0.01
Asian (15,400)	16,602	28.22
Not Hispanic (15,149)	16,023	27.24
Hispanic (251)	579	0.98
Burmese (18)	23	0.04
Cambodian (86)	96	0.16
Chinese, ex. Taiwanese (957)	1,316	2.24
Filipino (2,346)	2,853	4.85
Hmong (1)	1	<0.01
Indian (193)	277	0.47
Indonesian (50)	74	0.13
Japanese (5,726)	6,584	11.19
Korean (3,457)	3,636	6.18
Laotian (8)	14	0.02

*Notes: † The Census 2010 population figure is used to calculate the percentages in the Hispanic Origin and Race categories. Ancestry percentages are based on the 2006-2010 American Community Survey population (not shown); ‡ Numbers in parentheses indicate the number of people reporting a single ancestry; * Numbers in parentheses indicate the number of persons reporting this race alone, not in combination with any other race; Please refer to the Explanation of Data for more information.*

Malaysian (2)	6	0.01
Nepalese (20)	23	0.04
Pakistani (30)	32	0.05
Sri Lankan (61)	66	0.11
Taiwanese (95)	113	0.19
Thai (175)	210	0.36
Vietnamese (1,624)	1,737	2.95
Hawaii Native/Pacific Islander (426)	767	1.30
Not Hispanic (382)	643	1.09
Hispanic (44)	124	0.21
Fijian (14)	19	0.03
Guamanian/Chamorro (28)	46	0.08
Marshallese (1)	1	<0.01
Native Hawaiian (122)	324	0.55
Samoan (191)	269	0.46
Tongan (40)	51	0.09
White (14,498)	16,293	27.70
Not Hispanic (5,484)	6,344	10.78
Hispanic (9,014)	9,949	16.91

Garnet

Place Type: CDP
County: Riverside
Population: 7,543†

Ancestry‡	Population	%
American (203)	203	3.08
Arab (14)	14	0.21
Syrian (14)	14	0.21
Belgian (0)	27	0.41
British (0)	9	0.14
Cajun (13)	13	0.20
Canadian (0)	8	0.12
Dutch (0)	86	1.30
English (64)	314	4.76
French, ex. Basque (93)	366	5.55
French Canadian (15)	15	0.23
German (127)	312	4.73
Hungarian (13)	29	0.44
Iranian (0)	14	0.21
Irish (136)	542	8.22
Italian (74)	90	1.36
Lithuanian (56)	56	0.85
Norwegian (52)	101	1.53
Polish (0)	43	0.65
Romanian (0)	25	0.38
Russian (43)	59	0.89
Scotch-Irish (0)	38	0.58
Scottish (35)	35	0.53
Swedish (20)	110	1.67
Welsh (0)	9	0.14

Hispanic Origin	Population	%
Hispanic or Latino (of any race)	5,580	73.98
Central American, ex. Mexican	408	5.41
Costa Rican	12	0.16
Guatemalan	217	2.88
Honduran	14	0.19
Nicaraguan	18	0.24
Panamanian	1	0.01
Salvadoran	145	1.92
Other Central American	1	0.01
Cuban	10	0.13
Dominican Republic	4	0.05
Mexican	4,891	64.84
Puerto Rican	24	0.32
South American	27	0.36
Argentinean	2	0.03
Bolivian	4	0.05
Colombian	2	0.03
Ecuadorian	9	0.12
Peruvian	8	0.11
Venezuelan	2	0.03
Other Hispanic or Latino	216	2.86

Race*	Population	%
African-American/Black (203)	252	3.34
Not Hispanic (167)	178	2.36
Hispanic (36)	74	0.98
American Indian/Alaska Native (96)	132	1.75
Not Hispanic (30)	49	0.65
Hispanic (66)	83	1.10
Apache (0)	2	0.03
Blackfeet (0)	5	0.07
Cherokee (0)	5	0.07
Chippewa (1)	1	0.01
Choctaw (1)	4	0.05
Comanche (0)	1	0.01
Hopi (1)	1	0.01
Mexican American Ind. (9)	12	0.16
Navajo (0)	2	0.03
Paiute (0)	1	0.01
Pima (1)	1	0.01
Pueblo (5)	7	0.09
Shoshone (2)	2	0.03
Sioux (2)	3	0.04
South American Ind. (0)	1	0.01
Yaqui (8)	9	0.12
Asian (62)	99	1.31
Not Hispanic (53)	75	0.99
Hispanic (9)	24	0.32
Cambodian (10)	10	0.13
Chinese, ex. Taiwanese (4)	11	0.15
Filipino (28)	44	0.58
Indian (5)	5	0.07
Indonesian (1)	1	0.01
Japanese (2)	8	0.11
Korean (6)	6	0.08
Nepalese (1)	1	0.01
Thai (3)	4	0.05
Vietnamese (2)	2	0.03
Hawaii Native/Pacific Islander (10)	24	0.32
Not Hispanic (4)	7	0.09
Hispanic (6)	17	0.23
Native Hawaiian (2)	8	0.11
Samoan (8)	9	0.12
White (4,247)	4,489	59.51
Not Hispanic (1,654)	1,696	22.48
Hispanic (2,593)	2,793	37.03

Gilroy

Place Type: City
County: Santa Clara
Population: 48,821†

Ancestry‡	Population	%
Afghan (26)	26	0.06
African, Sub-Saharan (131)	176	0.38
African (120)	165	0.35
Somalian (11)	11	0.02
American (711)	711	1.52
Arab (52)	60	0.13
Arab (20)	20	0.04
Jordanian (21)	21	0.04
Lebanese (11)	11	0.02
Other Arab (0)	8	0.02
Armenian (11)	92	0.20
Australian (51)	51	0.11
Austrian (0)	40	0.09
Basque (0)	12	0.03
Brazilian (45)	62	0.13
British (26)	64	0.14
Canadian (113)	173	0.37
Celtic (11)	11	0.02
Croatian (20)	79	0.17
Czech (42)	69	0.15
Czechoslovakian (11)	26	0.06
Danish (100)	331	0.71
Dutch (58)	314	0.67
Eastern European (0)	16	0.03
English (745)	2,536	5.42
European (367)	443	0.95
Finnish (0)	13	0.03
French, ex. Basque (188)	893	1.91
French Canadian (10)	171	0.37
German (906)	3,764	8.04
Greek (71)	158	0.34
Hungarian (46)	94	0.20
Iranian (104)	194	0.41
Irish (780)	3,355	7.17
Italian (1,116)	2,576	5.50
Lithuanian (0)	14	0.03
Maltese (0)	24	0.05
Northern European (58)	78	0.17
Norwegian (88)	345	0.74
Polish (166)	429	0.92
Portuguese (452)	861	1.84
Romanian (0)	29	0.06
Russian (44)	193	0.41
Scandinavian (0)	103	0.22
Scotch-Irish (83)	238	0.51
Scottish (326)	943	2.01
Serbian (58)	58	0.12
Slavic (0)	15	0.03
Slovak (29)	58	0.12
Swedish (56)	442	0.94
Swiss (30)	156	0.33
Ukrainian (31)	87	0.19
Welsh (51)	162	0.35
West Indian, ex. Hispanic (11)	25	0.05
Haitian (11)	25	0.05
Yugoslavian (96)	156	0.33

Hispanic Origin	Population	%
Hispanic or Latino (of any race)	28,214	57.79
Central American, ex. Mexican	577	1.18
Costa Rican	28	0.06
Guatemalan	120	0.25
Honduran	63	0.13
Nicaraguan	87	0.18
Panamanian	9	0.02
Salvadoran	265	0.54
Other Central American	5	0.01
Cuban	76	0.16
Dominican Republic	21	0.04
Mexican	25,617	52.47
Puerto Rican	258	0.53
South American	213	0.44
Argentinean	13	0.03
Bolivian	5	0.01
Chilean	21	0.04
Colombian	70	0.14
Ecuadorian	21	0.04
Paraguayan	3	0.01
Peruvian	57	0.12
Uruguayan	1	<0.01
Venezuelan	18	0.04
Other South American	4	0.01
Other Hispanic or Latino	1,452	2.97

Race*	Population	%
African-American/Black (942)	1,285	2.63
Not Hispanic (709)	925	1.89
Hispanic (233)	360	0.74
American Indian/Alaska Native (831)	1,387	2.84
Not Hispanic (180)	373	0.76
Hispanic (651)	1,014	2.08
Alaska Athabascan *(Ala. Nat.)* (2)	2	<0.01
Apache (41)	98	0.20
Arapaho (1)	4	0.01
Blackfeet (0)	14	0.03
Canadian/French Am. Ind. (1)	2	<0.01
Central American Ind. (6)	7	0.01
Cherokee (37)	118	0.24
Cheyenne (3)	4	0.01
Chickasaw (2)	2	<0.01
Chippewa (17)	29	0.06
Choctaw (1)	12	0.02
Colville (0)	1	<0.01
Comanche (2)	2	<0.01
Cree (2)	3	0.01
Creek (6)	8	0.02
Crow (3)	8	0.02
Hopi (4)	4	0.01
Inupiat *(Alaska Native)* (1)	3	0.01
Iroquois (0)	2	<0.01
Mexican American Ind. (127)	174	0.36
Navajo (8)	36	0.07

*Notes: † The Census 2010 population figure is used to calculate the percentages in the Hispanic Origin and Race categories. Ancestry percentages are based on the 2006-2010 American Community Survey population (not shown); ‡ Numbers in parentheses indicate the number of people reporting a single ancestry; * Numbers in parentheses indicate the number of persons reporting this race alone, not in combination with any other race; Please refer to the Explanation of Data for more information.*

Paiute (1)	6	0.01
Pima (4)	4	0.01
Potawatomi (3)	7	0.01
Pueblo (18)	31	0.06
Seminole (0)	2	<0.01
Shoshone (0)	8	0.02
Sioux (5)	13	0.03
South American Ind. (1)	3	0.01
Spanish American Ind. (6)	8	0.02
Tlingit-Haida *(Alaska Native)* (3)	3	0.01
Tohono O'Odham (3)	3	0.01
Ute (2)	6	0.01
Yakama (0)	2	<0.01
Yaqui (21)	36	0.07
Asian (3,448)	4,367	8.94
Not Hispanic (3,265)	3,866	7.92
Hispanic (183)	501	1.03
Bangladeshi (5)	6	0.01
Burmese (11)	11	0.02
Cambodian (76)	89	0.18
Chinese, ex. Taiwanese (499)	656	1.34
Filipino (1,216)	1,665	3.41
Hmong (1)	2	<0.01
Indian (418)	484	0.99
Indonesian (3)	14	0.03
Japanese (316)	546	1.12
Korean (190)	256	0.52
Laotian (7)	10	0.02
Malaysian (5)	16	0.03
Nepalese (22)	23	0.05
Pakistani (24)	28	0.06
Sri Lankan (6)	6	0.01
Taiwanese (23)	38	0.08
Thai (8)	17	0.03
Vietnamese (464)	531	1.09
Hawaii Native/Pacific Islander (111)	282	0.58
Not Hispanic (86)	201	0.41
Hispanic (25)	81	0.17
Fijian (8)	9	0.02
Guamanian/Chamorro (18)	59	0.12
Marshallese (9)	9	0.02
Native Hawaiian (24)	89	0.18
Samoan (20)	30	0.06
Tongan (11)	21	0.04
White (28,674)	30,768	63.02
Not Hispanic (15,335)	16,187	33.16
Hispanic (13,339)	14,581	29.87

Glen Avon

Place Type: CDP
County: Riverside
Population: 20,199†

Ancestry‡	Population	%
American (451)	451	2.30
Austrian (0)	13	0.07
Basque (0)	12	0.06
Canadian (13)	21	0.11
Czech (0)	13	0.07
Danish (4)	30	0.15
Dutch (42)	157	0.80
English (228)	948	4.84
European (56)	56	0.29
Finnish (0)	9	0.05
French, ex. Basque (7)	230	1.17
French Canadian (107)	132	0.67
German (551)	1,756	8.97
Hungarian (15)	15	0.08
Iranian (0)	17	0.09
Irish (304)	1,176	6.00
Italian (145)	306	1.56
Lithuanian (0)	23	0.12
Norwegian (30)	103	0.53
Pennsylvania German (12)	12	0.06
Polish (24)	45	0.23
Portuguese (0)	52	0.27
Russian (11)	56	0.29
Scandinavian (28)	41	0.21
Scotch-Irish (13)	85	0.43
Scottish (85)	153	0.78
Swedish (0)	48	0.25
Swiss (10)	10	0.05
Welsh (9)	18	0.09
West Indian, ex. Hispanic (32)	48	0.25
Jamaican (12)	28	0.14
West Indian (20)	20	0.10

Hispanic Origin	Population	%
Hispanic or Latino (of any race)	13,766	68.15
Central American, ex. Mexican	384	1.90
Costa Rican	9	0.04
Guatemalan	94	0.47
Honduran	33	0.16
Nicaraguan	39	0.19
Panamanian	3	0.01
Salvadoran	205	1.01
Other Central American	1	<0.01
Cuban	48	0.24
Dominican Republic	8	0.04
Mexican	12,282	60.80
Puerto Rican	119	0.59
South American	133	0.66
Argentinean	24	0.12
Bolivian	4	0.02
Chilean	8	0.04
Colombian	38	0.19
Ecuadorian	20	0.10
Peruvian	31	0.15
Uruguayan	3	0.01
Venezuelan	3	0.01
Other South American	2	0.01
Other Hispanic or Latino	792	3.92

Race*	Population	%
African-American/Black (805)	944	4.67
Not Hispanic (734)	814	4.03
Hispanic (71)	130	0.64
American Indian/Alaska Native (216)	369	1.83
Not Hispanic (58)	156	0.77
Hispanic (158)	213	1.05
Apache (9)	23	0.11
Arapaho (1)	1	<0.01
Blackfeet (2)	8	0.04
Canadian/French Am. Ind. (0)	2	0.01
Cherokee (12)	37	0.18
Chickasaw (0)	1	<0.01
Choctaw (8)	13	0.06
Creek (0)	1	<0.01
Delaware (2)	4	0.02
Hopi (1)	1	<0.01
Inupiat *(Alaska Native)* (1)	2	0.01
Iroquois (5)	5	0.02
Lumbee (5)	5	0.02
Mexican American Ind. (19)	35	0.17
Navajo (5)	16	0.08
Potawatomi (1)	3	0.01
Pueblo (1)	1	<0.01
Sioux (4)	6	0.03
Spanish American Ind. (6)	6	0.03
Yuman (0)	1	<0.01
Asian (462)	586	2.90
Not Hispanic (439)	514	2.54
Hispanic (23)	72	0.36
Cambodian (13)	13	0.06
Chinese, ex. Taiwanese (40)	64	0.32
Filipino (146)	170	0.84
Indian (102)	122	0.60
Indonesian (13)	17	0.08
Japanese (28)	61	0.30
Korean (53)	58	0.29
Laotian (10)	11	0.05
Taiwanese (5)	5	0.02
Thai (10)	16	0.08
Vietnamese (25)	37	0.18
Hawaii Native/Pacific Islander (34)	85	0.42
Not Hispanic (23)	45	0.22
Hispanic (11)	40	0.20
Fijian (0)	4	0.02
Guamanian/Chamorro (0)	2	0.01
Native Hawaiian (11)	23	0.11
Samoan (12)	23	0.11
Tongan (6)	9	0.04
White (10,272)	10,969	54.30
Not Hispanic (4,917)	5,109	25.29
Hispanic (5,355)	5,860	29.01

Glendale

Place Type: City
County: Los Angeles
Population: 191,719†

Ancestry‡	Population	%
Afghan (92)	92	0.05
African, Sub-Saharan (273)	342	0.18
African (67)	109	0.06
Nigerian (109)	109	0.06
Sierra Leonean (34)	34	0.02
South African (0)	27	0.01
Sudanese (10)	10	0.01
Other Sub-Saharan African (53)	53	0.03
Albanian (0)	95	0.05
American (3,450)	3,450	1.80
Arab (2,910)	4,218	2.19
Arab (291)	420	0.22
Egyptian (282)	329	0.17
Iraqi (429)	715	0.37
Lebanese (1,470)	2,062	1.07
Moroccan (32)	32	0.02
Palestinian (27)	96	0.05
Syrian (238)	340	0.18
Other Arab (141)	224	0.12
Armenian (58,115)	65,434	34.05
Assyrian/Chaldean/Syriac (121)	235	0.12
Australian (74)	89	0.05
Austrian (125)	402	0.21
Basque (39)	39	0.02
Belgian (21)	69	0.04
Brazilian (109)	120	0.06
British (541)	895	0.47
Bulgarian (35)	115	0.06
Canadian (164)	383	0.20
Celtic (0)	14	0.01
Croatian (95)	190	0.10
Czech (55)	298	0.16
Czechoslovakian (0)	67	0.03
Danish (171)	767	0.40
Dutch (277)	958	0.50
Eastern European (89)	103	0.05
English (1,981)	7,611	3.96
Estonian (18)	18	0.01
European (802)	933	0.49
Finnish (113)	236	0.12
French, ex. Basque (324)	2,100	1.09
French Canadian (66)	362	0.19
German (2,361)	9,882	5.14
Greek (467)	1,214	0.63
Hungarian (257)	512	0.27
Icelander (0)	15	0.01
Iranian (5,079)	10,199	5.31
Irish (2,203)	7,669	3.99
Israeli (20)	92	0.05
Italian (2,119)	5,077	2.64
Latvian (0)	10	0.01
Lithuanian (163)	265	0.14
Luxemburger (0)	86	0.04
Macedonian (11)	22	0.01
New Zealander (11)	11	0.01
Northern European (47)	60	0.03
Norwegian (202)	942	0.49
Pennsylvania German (0)	27	0.01
Polish (561)	1,916	1.00
Portuguese (28)	155	0.08
Romanian (471)	576	0.30
Russian (826)	1,837	0.96
Scandinavian (153)	286	0.15
Scotch-Irish (426)	1,306	0.68
Scottish (674)	1,836	0.96
Serbian (55)	67	0.03

*Notes: † The Census 2010 population figure is used to calculate the percentages in the Hispanic Origin and Race categories. Ancestry percentages are based on the 2006-2010 American Community Survey population (not shown); ‡ Numbers in parentheses indicate the number of people reporting a single ancestry; * Numbers in parentheses indicate the number of persons reporting this race alone, not in combination with any other race; Please refer to the Explanation of Data for more information.*

Ancestry (continued)	Population	%
Slavic (15)	96	0.05
Slovak (55)	124	0.06
Swedish (323)	1,349	0.70
Swiss (34)	231	0.12
Turkish (40)	72	0.04
Ukrainian (319)	541	0.28
Welsh (109)	737	0.38
West Indian, ex. Hispanic (194)	236	0.12
Belizean (38)	38	0.02
British West Indian (15)	31	0.02
Haitian (61)	70	0.04
Jamaican (80)	97	0.05
Yugoslavian (54)	78	0.04

Hispanic Origin	Population	%
Hispanic or Latino (of any race)	33,414	17.43
Central American, ex. Mexican	6,392	3.33
Costa Rican	145	0.08
Guatemalan	1,723	0.90
Honduran	367	0.19
Nicaraguan	526	0.27
Panamanian	72	0.04
Salvadoran	3,481	1.82
Other Central American	78	0.04
Cuban	1,513	0.79
Dominican Republic	69	0.04
Mexican	19,126	9.98
Puerto Rican	575	0.30
South American	3,287	1.71
Argentinean	539	0.28
Bolivian	150	0.08
Chilean	230	0.12
Colombian	841	0.44
Ecuadorian	542	0.28
Paraguayan	20	0.01
Peruvian	803	0.42
Uruguayan	53	0.03
Venezuelan	82	0.04
Other South American	27	0.01
Other Hispanic or Latino	2,452	1.28

Race*	Population	%
African-American/Black (2,573)	3,445	1.80
Not Hispanic (2,325)	2,932	1.53
Hispanic (248)	513	0.27
American Indian/Alaska Native (531)	1,185	0.62
Not Hispanic (192)	567	0.30
Hispanic (339)	618	0.32
Aleut *(Alaska Native)* (0)	4	<0.01
Apache (18)	43	0.02
Arapaho (1)	1	<0.01
Blackfeet (3)	21	0.01
Canadian/French Am. Ind. (1)	1	<0.01
Central American Ind. (14)	16	0.01
Cherokee (21)	122	0.06
Cheyenne (0)	2	<0.01
Chickasaw (0)	7	<0.01
Chippewa (0)	1	<0.01
Choctaw (7)	23	0.01
Colville (1)	1	<0.01
Comanche (5)	8	<0.01
Cree (2)	3	<0.01
Creek (3)	5	<0.01
Delaware (1)	1	<0.01
Hopi (7)	20	0.01
Iroquois (1)	15	0.01
Lumbee (1)	1	<0.01
Mexican American Ind. (75)	131	0.07
Navajo (31)	46	0.02
Osage (4)	11	0.01
Ottawa (1)	1	<0.01
Pima (1)	3	<0.01
Potawatomi (0)	3	<0.01
Pueblo (5)	14	0.01
Puget Sound Salish (0)	3	<0.01
Seminole (0)	4	<0.01
Shoshone (1)	5	<0.01
Sioux (11)	19	0.01
South American Ind. (9)	27	0.01
Spanish American Ind. (5)	18	0.01
Tlingit-Haida *(Alaska Native)* (2)	4	<0.01
Tohono O'Odham (3)	11	0.01
Ute (0)	1	<0.01
Yakama (0)	3	<0.01
Yaqui (7)	19	0.01
Yuman (1)	1	<0.01
Asian (31,434)	36,832	19.21
Not Hispanic (31,073)	35,949	18.75
Hispanic (361)	883	0.46
Bangladeshi (154)	182	0.09
Burmese (34)	41	0.02
Cambodian (32)	51	0.03
Chinese, ex. Taiwanese (2,313)	3,008	1.57
Filipino (13,238)	14,442	7.53
Hmong (0)	1	<0.01
Indian (1,747)	1,996	1.04
Indonesian (77)	137	0.07
Japanese (1,222)	1,785	0.93
Korean (10,315)	10,650	5.56
Laotian (23)	33	0.02
Malaysian (8)	10	0.01
Nepalese (6)	6	<0.01
Pakistani (111)	141	0.07
Sri Lankan (44)	49	0.03
Taiwanese (122)	136	0.07
Thai (525)	592	0.31
Vietnamese (686)	807	0.42
Hawaii Native/Pacific Islander (122)	915	0.48
Not Hispanic (105)	835	0.44
Hispanic (17)	80	0.04
Fijian (5)	9	<0.01
Guamanian/Chamorro (31)	64	0.03
Marshallese (1)	2	<0.01
Native Hawaiian (52)	170	0.09
Samoan (4)	17	0.01
Tongan (2)	5	<0.01
White (136,226)	144,049	75.14
Not Hispanic (117,929)	123,773	64.56
Hispanic (18,297)	20,276	10.58

Glendora

Place Type: City
County: Los Angeles
Population: 50,073†

Ancestry‡	Population	%
African, Sub-Saharan (39)	39	0.08
African (14)	14	0.03
Ethiopian (12)	12	0.02
Nigerian (13)	13	0.03
American (1,867)	1,867	3.74
Arab (1,048)	1,087	2.18
Arab (112)	112	0.22
Egyptian (136)	161	0.32
Lebanese (455)	455	0.91
Palestinian (4)	4	0.01
Syrian (269)	283	0.57
Other Arab (72)	72	0.14
Armenian (192)	315	0.63
Assyrian/Chaldean/Syriac (33)	33	0.07
Australian (13)	13	0.03
Austrian (38)	79	0.16
Basque (52)	106	0.21
Belgian (0)	15	0.03
British (59)	160	0.32
Cajun (0)	18	0.04
Canadian (139)	245	0.49
Celtic (15)	66	0.13
Croatian (31)	40	0.08
Czech (132)	325	0.65
Czechoslovakian (15)	26	0.05
Danish (115)	481	0.96
Dutch (216)	1,481	2.97
Eastern European (16)	16	0.03
English (1,362)	4,870	9.76
European (495)	736	1.48
Finnish (0)	39	0.08
French, ex. Basque (144)	1,500	3.01
French Canadian (87)	159	0.32
German (2,077)	7,755	15.55
Greek (107)	325	0.65
Hungarian (120)	247	0.50
Icelander (0)	10	0.02
Iranian (130)	135	0.27
Irish (1,113)	4,549	9.12
Italian (1,476)	4,208	8.44
Lithuanian (0)	49	0.10
Maltese (10)	10	0.02
Northern European (28)	65	0.13
Norwegian (175)	735	1.47
Pennsylvania German (6)	54	0.11
Polish (371)	1,096	2.20
Portuguese (56)	170	0.34
Romanian (55)	75	0.15
Russian (231)	475	0.95
Scandinavian (38)	223	0.45
Scotch-Irish (340)	927	1.86
Scottish (328)	1,354	2.71
Serbian (23)	23	0.05
Slavic (10)	62	0.12
Slovak (22)	80	0.16
Slovene (9)	9	0.02
Swedish (236)	758	1.52
Swiss (46)	74	0.15
Turkish (75)	75	0.15
Ukrainian (41)	137	0.27
Welsh (105)	297	0.60
West Indian, ex. Hispanic (77)	90	0.18
Jamaican (65)	65	0.13
West Indian (12)	25	0.05
Yugoslavian (23)	128	0.26

Hispanic Origin	Population	%
Hispanic or Latino (of any race)	15,348	30.65
Central American, ex. Mexican	898	1.79
Costa Rican	49	0.10
Guatemalan	205	0.41
Honduran	39	0.08
Nicaraguan	175	0.35
Panamanian	18	0.04
Salvadoran	401	0.80
Other Central American	11	0.02
Cuban	259	0.52
Dominican Republic	16	0.03
Mexican	12,151	24.27
Puerto Rican	274	0.55
South American	622	1.24
Argentinean	142	0.28
Bolivian	25	0.05
Chilean	50	0.10
Colombian	148	0.30
Ecuadorian	83	0.17
Paraguayan	2	<0.01
Peruvian	148	0.30
Uruguayan	3	0.01
Venezuelan	11	0.02
Other South American	10	0.02
Other Hispanic or Latino	1,128	2.25

Race*	Population	%
African-American/Black (930)	1,278	2.55
Not Hispanic (834)	1,068	2.13
Hispanic (96)	210	0.42
American Indian/Alaska Native (345)	759	1.52
Not Hispanic (102)	315	0.63
Hispanic (243)	444	0.89
Aleut *(Alaska Native)* (1)	2	<0.01
Apache (23)	49	0.10
Arapaho (0)	2	<0.01
Blackfeet (0)	10	0.02
Canadian/French Am. Ind. (0)	1	<0.01
Central American Ind. (3)	4	0.01
Cherokee (15)	95	0.19
Cheyenne (0)	5	0.01
Chickasaw (0)	2	<0.01
Chippewa (3)	6	0.01
Choctaw (1)	15	0.03
Comanche (2)	9	0.02
Cree (0)	2	<0.01

*Notes: † The Census 2010 population figure is used to calculate the percentages in the Hispanic Origin and Race categories. Ancestry percentages are based on the 2006-2010 American Community Survey population (not shown); ‡ Numbers in parentheses indicate the number of people reporting a single ancestry; * Numbers in parentheses indicate the number of persons reporting this race alone, not in combination with any other race; Please refer to the Explanation of Data for more information.*

Creek (2)	4	0.01
Delaware (0)	1	<0.01
Hopi (1)	3	0.01
Iroquois (4)	13	0.03
Mexican American Ind. (35)	48	0.10
Navajo (11)	28	0.06
Osage (0)	1	<0.01
Ottawa (1)	2	<0.01
Paiute (3)	5	0.01
Pima (1)	4	0.01
Potawatomi (0)	2	<0.01
Pueblo (2)	3	0.01
Seminole (0)	1	<0.01
Shoshone (1)	1	<0.01
Sioux (10)	14	0.03
South American Ind. (0)	3	0.01
Spanish American Ind. (6)	6	0.01
Tohono O'Odham (7)	12	0.02
Ute (0)	3	0.01
Yaqui (12)	21	0.04
Yuman (2)	5	0.01
Asian (3,999)	4,980	9.95
Not Hispanic (3,898)	4,634	9.25
Hispanic (101)	346	0.69
Bangladeshi (10)	12	0.02
Burmese (3)	6	0.01
Cambodian (18)	26	0.05
Chinese, ex. Taiwanese (944)	1,207	2.41
Filipino (1,352)	1,694	3.38
Hmong (15)	15	0.03
Indian (499)	548	1.09
Indonesian (76)	149	0.30
Japanese (303)	564	1.13
Korean (185)	237	0.47
Laotian (3)	8	0.02
Malaysian (1)	2	<0.01
Nepalese (0)	4	0.01
Pakistani (29)	36	0.07
Sri Lankan (21)	28	0.06
Taiwanese (116)	137	0.27
Thai (80)	95	0.19
Vietnamese (159)	221	0.44
Hawaii Native/Pacific Islander (52)	222	0.44
Not Hispanic (42)	183	0.37
Hispanic (10)	39	0.08
Fijian (1)	1	<0.01
Guamanian/Chamorro (6)	11	0.02
Native Hawaiian (22)	102	0.20
Samoan (7)	35	0.07
Tongan (1)	5	0.01
White (37,582)	39,711	79.31
Not Hispanic (28,565)	29,628	59.17
Hispanic (9,017)	10,083	20.14

Gold River

Place Type: CDP
County: Sacramento
Population: 7,912†

Ancestry‡	Population	%
American (395)	395	4.74
Arab (80)	80	0.96
Arab (80)	80	0.96
Austrian (0)	40	0.48
British (61)	61	0.73
Canadian (24)	33	0.40
Celtic (0)	74	0.89
Czech (14)	36	0.43
Danish (12)	102	1.22
Dutch (23)	115	1.38
Eastern European (17)	17	0.20
English (388)	1,400	16.79
European (135)	155	1.86
French, ex. Basque (51)	260	3.12
French Canadian (8)	8	0.10
German (350)	1,154	13.84
Greek (0)	52	0.62
Hungarian (8)	17	0.20
Icelander (0)	17	0.20
Iranian (136)	156	1.87
Irish (220)	710	8.51
Israeli (30)	30	0.36
Italian (132)	444	5.32
Latvian (0)	17	0.20
Lithuanian (0)	8	0.10
Norwegian (25)	117	1.40
Polish (27)	179	2.15
Portuguese (98)	137	1.64
Russian (99)	201	2.41
Scandinavian (7)	46	0.55
Scotch-Irish (94)	227	2.72
Scottish (65)	378	4.53
Slovak (7)	33	0.40
Swedish (25)	228	2.73
Swiss (22)	22	0.26
Welsh (0)	95	1.14
Yugoslavian (17)	34	0.41

Hispanic Origin	Population	%
Hispanic or Latino (of any race)	515	6.51
Central American, ex. Mexican	46	0.58
Guatemalan	2	0.03
Honduran	4	0.05
Nicaraguan	25	0.32
Panamanian	8	0.10
Salvadoran	7	0.09
Cuban	18	0.23
Mexican	314	3.97
Puerto Rican	35	0.44
South American	19	0.24
Argentinean	1	0.01
Chilean	1	0.01
Colombian	5	0.06
Ecuadorian	2	0.03
Peruvian	9	0.11
Venezuelan	1	0.01
Other Hispanic or Latino	83	1.05

Race*	Population	%
African-American/Black (195)	251	3.17
Not Hispanic (182)	231	2.92
Hispanic (13)	20	0.25
American Indian/Alaska Native (20)	73	0.92
Not Hispanic (15)	66	0.83
Hispanic (5)	7	0.09
Cherokee (0)	15	0.19
Chickasaw (0)	5	0.06
Choctaw (3)	5	0.06
Delaware (0)	4	0.05
Navajo (3)	3	0.04
Ottawa (0)	1	0.01
Pueblo (3)	3	0.04
Seminole (0)	4	0.05
Sioux (0)	1	0.01
Ute (0)	1	0.01
Asian (1,426)	1,626	20.55
Not Hispanic (1,409)	1,585	20.03
Hispanic (17)	41	0.52
Cambodian (17)	17	0.21
Chinese, ex. Taiwanese (276)	324	4.10
Filipino (147)	223	2.82
Indian (338)	353	4.46
Indonesian (6)	12	0.15
Japanese (105)	144	1.82
Korean (317)	345	4.36
Laotian (5)	5	0.06
Nepalese (7)	10	0.13
Pakistani (25)	25	0.32
Sri Lankan (14)	16	0.20
Taiwanese (35)	39	0.49
Thai (6)	10	0.13
Vietnamese (81)	91	1.15
Hawaii Native/Pacific Islander (28)	51	0.64
Not Hispanic (26)	47	0.59
Hispanic (2)	4	0.05
Fijian (4)	5	0.06
Guamanian/Chamorro (2)	3	0.04
Native Hawaiian (4)	11	0.14
Samoan (4)	4	0.05
Tongan (8)	8	0.10
White (5,837)	6,118	77.33
Not Hispanic (5,504)	5,731	72.43
Hispanic (333)	387	4.89

Golden Hills

Place Type: CDP
County: Kern
Population: 8,656†

Ancestry‡	Population	%
American (559)	559	6.52
Arab (84)	183	2.13
Arab (84)	183	2.13
Austrian (44)	115	1.34
British (28)	56	0.65
Cajun (18)	18	0.21
Canadian (13)	49	0.57
Czech (26)	88	1.03
Czechoslovakian (16)	16	0.19
Danish (64)	139	1.62
Dutch (0)	134	1.56
English (306)	1,130	13.18
European (13)	13	0.15
Finnish (18)	18	0.21
French, ex. Basque (58)	163	1.90
French Canadian (0)	128	1.49
German (543)	1,973	23.01
Hungarian (0)	12	0.14
Iranian (31)	31	0.36
Irish (273)	1,201	14.01
Italian (33)	202	2.36
Northern European (42)	42	0.49
Norwegian (33)	99	1.15
Polish (94)	312	3.64
Portuguese (30)	89	1.04
Romanian (0)	17	0.20
Russian (17)	17	0.20
Scandinavian (0)	8	0.09
Scotch-Irish (41)	124	1.45
Scottish (63)	379	4.42
Serbian (0)	13	0.15
Swedish (43)	224	2.61
Swiss (0)	11	0.13
Welsh (0)	32	0.37

Hispanic Origin	Population	%
Hispanic or Latino (of any race)	1,674	19.34
Central American, ex. Mexican	63	0.73
Costa Rican	2	0.02
Guatemalan	21	0.24
Nicaraguan	7	0.08
Salvadoran	33	0.38
Cuban	7	0.08
Dominican Republic	4	0.05
Mexican	1,395	16.12
Puerto Rican	32	0.37
South American	23	0.27
Chilean	1	0.01
Colombian	2	0.02
Ecuadorian	13	0.15
Peruvian	7	0.08
Other Hispanic or Latino	150	1.73

Race*	Population	%
African-American/Black (129)	192	2.22
Not Hispanic (118)	169	1.95
Hispanic (11)	23	0.27
American Indian/Alaska Native (124)	284	3.28
Not Hispanic (78)	217	2.51
Hispanic (46)	67	0.77
Aleut *(Alaska Native)* (1)	3	0.03
Apache (12)	15	0.17
Blackfeet (7)	16	0.18
Cherokee (14)	58	0.67
Chickasaw (6)	6	0.07
Chippewa (2)	5	0.06
Choctaw (8)	18	0.21
Comanche (2)	4	0.05

*Notes: † The Census 2010 population figure is used to calculate the percentages in the Hispanic Origin and Race categories. Ancestry percentages are based on the 2006-2010 American Community Survey population (not shown); ‡ Numbers in parentheses indicate the number of people reporting a single ancestry; * Numbers in parentheses indicate the number of persons reporting this race alone, not in combination with any other race; Please refer to the Explanation of Data for more information.*

Creek (0)	1	0.01
Houma (0)	2	0.02
Iroquois (4)	10	0.12
Mexican American Ind. (4)	5	0.06
Navajo (1)	6	0.07
Osage (0)	1	0.01
Paiute (0)	5	0.06
Pima (1)	1	0.01
Pueblo (3)	3	0.03
Shoshone (0)	2	0.02
Sioux (4)	5	0.06
Tlingit-Haida *(Alaska Native)* (1)	1	0.01
Yaqui (2)	4	0.05
Asian (120)	206	2.38
Not Hispanic (114)	185	2.14
Hispanic (6)	21	0.24
Chinese, ex. Taiwanese (22)	33	0.38
Filipino (39)	87	1.01
Indian (11)	15	0.17
Indonesian (10)	10	0.12
Japanese (9)	24	0.28
Korean (7)	10	0.12
Laotian (1)	3	0.03
Pakistani (1)	1	0.01
Thai (10)	10	0.12
Vietnamese (6)	9	0.10
Hawaii Native/Pacific Islander (15)	26	0.30
Not Hispanic (11)	20	0.23
Hispanic (4)	6	0.07
Guamanian/Chamorro (2)	2	0.02
Native Hawaiian (10)	19	0.22
Samoan (2)	2	0.02
White (7,235)	7,573	87.49
Not Hispanic (6,387)	6,622	76.50
Hispanic (848)	951	10.99

Goleta

Place Type: City
County: Santa Barbara
Population: 29,888†

Ancestry‡	Population	%
Afghan (52)	52	0.18
African, Sub-Saharan (38)	42	0.14
African (38)	42	0.14
American (381)	381	1.30
Arab (304)	354	1.20
Arab (6)	6	0.02
Lebanese (213)	240	0.82
Moroccan (0)	23	0.08
Palestinian (22)	22	0.07
Other Arab (63)	63	0.21
Armenian (35)	35	0.12
Assyrian/Chaldean/Syriac (17)	17	0.06
Australian (44)	104	0.35
Austrian (17)	86	0.29
Basque (0)	27	0.09
Belgian (0)	26	0.09
British (100)	168	0.57
Bulgarian (16)	16	0.05
Canadian (37)	107	0.36
Celtic (17)	17	0.06
Croatian (0)	21	0.07
Czech (27)	148	0.50
Czechoslovakian (47)	123	0.42
Danish (63)	316	1.07
Dutch (120)	404	1.37
Eastern European (39)	76	0.26
English (872)	3,198	10.88
European (477)	557	1.89
Finnish (9)	45	0.15
French, ex. Basque (100)	946	3.22
French Canadian (38)	75	0.26
German (932)	3,452	11.74
Greek (21)	70	0.24
Hungarian (36)	176	0.60
Icelander (0)	31	0.11
Iranian (149)	160	0.54
Irish (749)	3,309	11.26
Israeli (38)	38	0.13
Italian (438)	1,735	5.90
Latvian (0)	13	0.04
Lithuanian (0)	41	0.14
Macedonian (0)	10	0.03
Northern European (29)	38	0.13
Norwegian (208)	487	1.66
Pennsylvania German (7)	7	0.02
Polish (148)	578	1.97
Portuguese (106)	237	0.81
Romanian (0)	55	0.19
Russian (111)	500	1.70
Scandinavian (10)	50	0.17
Scotch-Irish (122)	489	1.66
Scottish (61)	586	1.99
Serbian (77)	77	0.26
Slavic (47)	63	0.21
Slovak (98)	140	0.48
Slovene (7)	7	0.02
Swedish (201)	571	1.94
Swiss (123)	393	1.34
Turkish (10)	20	0.07
Ukrainian (28)	103	0.35
Welsh (0)	338	1.15
Yugoslavian (0)	10	0.03

Hispanic Origin	Population	%
Hispanic or Latino (of any race)	9,824	32.87
Central American, ex. Mexican	292	0.98
Costa Rican	14	0.05
Guatemalan	152	0.51
Honduran	10	0.03
Nicaraguan	15	0.05
Panamanian	7	0.02
Salvadoran	86	0.29
Other Central American	8	0.03
Cuban	26	0.09
Dominican Republic	7	0.02
Mexican	8,690	29.08
Puerto Rican	88	0.29
South American	200	0.67
Argentinean	48	0.16
Bolivian	5	0.02
Chilean	29	0.10
Colombian	41	0.14
Ecuadorian	17	0.06
Peruvian	51	0.17
Uruguayan	4	0.01
Venezuelan	5	0.02
Other Hispanic or Latino	521	1.74

Race*	Population	%
African-American/Black (469)	710	2.38
Not Hispanic (399)	574	1.92
Hispanic (70)	136	0.46
American Indian/Alaska Native (283)	612	2.05
Not Hispanic (104)	273	0.91
Hispanic (179)	339	1.13
Aleut *(Alaska Native)* (0)	2	0.01
Apache (12)	25	0.08
Blackfeet (0)	7	0.02
Canadian/French Am. Ind. (0)	3	0.01
Central American Ind. (1)	1	<0.01
Cherokee (13)	55	0.18
Cheyenne (0)	2	0.01
Chickasaw (0)	4	0.01
Chippewa (0)	14	0.05
Choctaw (5)	14	0.05
Comanche (0)	2	0.01
Cree (0)	1	<0.01
Creek (0)	3	0.01
Crow (0)	2	0.01
Hopi (1)	4	0.01
Inupiat *(Alaska Native)* (1)	1	<0.01
Iroquois (3)	4	0.01
Kiowa (1)	1	<0.01
Mexican American Ind. (26)	59	0.20
Navajo (3)	5	0.02
Osage (0)	4	0.01
Potawatomi (0)	4	0.01
Pueblo (1)	2	0.01
Shoshone (0)	3	0.01
Sioux (1)	9	0.03
South American Ind. (1)	6	0.02
Spanish American Ind. (0)	1	<0.01
Tlingit-Haida *(Alaska Native)* (0)	1	<0.01
Tohono O'Odham (1)	2	0.01
Yakama (3)	3	0.01
Yaqui (3)	9	0.03
Asian (2,728)	3,265	10.92
Not Hispanic (2,681)	3,125	10.46
Hispanic (47)	140	0.47
Bangladeshi (9)	9	0.03
Burmese (2)	6	0.02
Cambodian (20)	22	0.07
Chinese, ex. Taiwanese (724)	879	2.94
Filipino (363)	475	1.59
Hmong (98)	101	0.34
Indian (345)	406	1.36
Indonesian (26)	36	0.12
Japanese (284)	444	1.49
Korean (264)	307	1.03
Laotian (26)	29	0.10
Malaysian (1)	2	0.01
Nepalese (4)	4	0.01
Pakistani (36)	44	0.15
Sri Lankan (16)	16	0.05
Taiwanese (53)	71	0.24
Thai (24)	34	0.11
Vietnamese (339)	382	1.28
Hawaii Native/Pacific Islander (26)	75	0.25
Not Hispanic (25)	69	0.23
Hispanic (1)	6	0.02
Fijian (1)	1	<0.01
Guamanian/Chamorro (4)	7	0.02
Native Hawaiian (10)	38	0.13
Samoan (6)	8	0.03
White (20,833)	22,049	73.77
Not Hispanic (16,020)	16,719	55.94
Hispanic (4,813)	5,330	17.83

Gonzales

Place Type: City
County: Monterey
Population: 8,187†

Ancestry‡	Population	%
American (12)	12	0.15
Armenian (0)	10	0.13
Czech (0)	20	0.25
Dutch (0)	7	0.09
English (0)	14	0.18
French Canadian (24)	24	0.30
German (70)	179	2.25
Greek (0)	10	0.13
Irish (109)	138	1.73
Italian (0)	22	0.28
Polish (0)	8	0.10
Portuguese (38)	155	1.95
Scotch-Irish (20)	96	1.21
Slovak (0)	19	0.24
Swedish (0)	10	0.13
Swiss (25)	67	0.84

Hispanic Origin	Population	%
Hispanic or Latino (of any race)	7,276	88.87
Central American, ex. Mexican	47	0.57
Guatemalan	7	0.09
Nicaraguan	3	0.04
Panamanian	6	0.07
Salvadoran	31	0.38
Cuban	3	0.04
Mexican	6,899	84.27
Puerto Rican	23	0.28
Other Hispanic or Latino	304	3.71

Race*	Population	%
African-American/Black (81)	106	1.29
Not Hispanic (27)	40	0.49

*Notes: † The Census 2010 population figure is used to calculate the percentages in the Hispanic Origin and Race categories. Ancestry percentages are based on the 2006-2010 American Community Survey population (not shown); ‡ Numbers in parentheses indicate the number of people reporting a single ancestry; * Numbers in parentheses indicate the number of persons reporting this race alone, not in combination with any other race; Please refer to the Explanation of Data for more information.*

Hispanic (54)	66	0.81
American Indian/Alaska Native (124)	202	2.47
Not Hispanic (12)	30	0.37
Hispanic (112)	172	2.10
Alaska Athabascan *(Ala. Nat.)* (1)	1	0.01
Apache (3)	8	0.10
Canadian/French Am. Ind. (1)	1	0.01
Central American Ind. (3)	5	0.06
Cherokee (1)	1	0.01
Chickasaw (0)	1	0.01
Hopi (4)	5	0.06
Mexican American Ind. (20)	39	0.48
Navajo (1)	1	0.01
Sioux (1)	4	0.05
Asian (190)	299	3.65
Not Hispanic (133)	179	2.19
Hispanic (57)	120	1.47
Cambodian (2)	3	0.04
Chinese, ex. Taiwanese (9)	19	0.23
Filipino (142)	217	2.65
Indian (9)	12	0.15
Japanese (12)	29	0.35
Korean (5)	10	0.12
Laotian (0)	1	0.01
Taiwanese (0)	2	0.02
Vietnamese (2)	3	0.04
Hawaii Native/Pacific Islander (14)	34	0.42
Not Hispanic (9)	13	0.16
Hispanic (5)	21	0.26
Guamanian/Chamorro (1)	2	0.02
Native Hawaiian (5)	21	0.26
Samoan (5)	11	0.13
White (3,464)	3,757	45.89
Not Hispanic (650)	716	8.75
Hispanic (2,814)	3,041	37.14

Good Hope

Place Type: CDP
County: Riverside
Population: 9,192†

Ancestry‡	Population	%
African, Sub-Saharan (0)	11	0.14
African (0)	11	0.14
American (85)	85	1.05
Czech (7)	7	0.09
English (0)	20	0.25
French, ex. Basque (0)	17	0.21
French Canadian (7)	7	0.09
German (118)	262	3.23
Irish (146)	250	3.08
Italian (93)	144	1.78
Polish (0)	53	0.65
Russian (0)	11	0.14
Scotch-Irish (0)	18	0.22
Slovak (6)	6	0.07
Swedish (0)	10	0.12
Swiss (9)	9	0.11
Welsh (0)	17	0.21

Hispanic Origin	Population	%
Hispanic or Latino (of any race)	7,319	79.62
Central American, ex. Mexican	136	1.48
Guatemalan	65	0.71
Honduran	7	0.08
Nicaraguan	5	0.05
Salvadoran	59	0.64
Cuban	8	0.09
Dominican Republic	3	0.03
Mexican	6,615	71.96
Puerto Rican	51	0.55
South American	22	0.24
Argentinean	7	0.08
Bolivian	3	0.03
Colombian	3	0.03
Ecuadorian	5	0.05
Peruvian	3	0.03
Other South American	1	0.01
Other Hispanic or Latino	484	5.27

Race*	Population	%
African-American/Black (669)	761	8.28
Not Hispanic (608)	663	7.21
Hispanic (61)	98	1.07
American Indian/Alaska Native (98)	141	1.53
Not Hispanic (25)	49	0.53
Hispanic (73)	92	1.00
Apache (5)	5	0.05
Blackfeet (0)	1	0.01
Cherokee (2)	11	0.12
Chippewa (4)	4	0.04
Choctaw (1)	3	0.03
Mexican American Ind. (20)	20	0.22
Navajo (1)	4	0.04
Pueblo (1)	1	0.01
Seminole (2)	4	0.04
Yaqui (1)	4	0.04
Asian (64)	96	1.04
Not Hispanic (59)	73	0.79
Hispanic (5)	23	0.25
Chinese, ex. Taiwanese (3)	5	0.05
Filipino (18)	30	0.33
Indian (2)	2	0.02
Japanese (4)	9	0.10
Korean (4)	5	0.05
Taiwanese (4)	4	0.04
Vietnamese (29)	31	0.34
Hawaii Native/Pacific Islander (4)	13	0.14
Not Hispanic (3)	4	0.04
Hispanic (1)	9	0.10
Guamanian/Chamorro (3)	3	0.03
Samoan (1)	10	0.11
White (4,156)	4,426	48.15
Not Hispanic (1,095)	1,165	12.67
Hispanic (3,061)	3,261	35.48

Grand Terrace

Place Type: City
County: San Bernardino
Population: 12,040†

Ancestry‡	Population	%
African, Sub-Saharan (31)	31	0.26
African (31)	31	0.26
American (406)	406	3.35
Arab (208)	226	1.87
Arab (0)	9	0.07
Egyptian (29)	29	0.24
Lebanese (74)	74	0.61
Palestinian (67)	76	0.63
Other Arab (38)	38	0.31
Armenian (39)	39	0.32
Australian (0)	8	0.07
Austrian (0)	20	0.17
Basque (0)	11	0.09
British (15)	15	0.12
Canadian (8)	17	0.14
Czech (10)	31	0.26
Czechoslovakian (0)	22	0.18
Danish (40)	168	1.39
Dutch (39)	86	0.71
English (394)	978	8.07
European (188)	196	1.62
French, ex. Basque (106)	250	2.06
French Canadian (12)	19	0.16
German (535)	1,115	9.20
Greek (57)	138	1.14
Hungarian (28)	68	0.56
Irish (491)	1,244	10.27
Italian (203)	374	3.09
Northern European (55)	55	0.45
Norwegian (9)	62	0.51
Pennsylvania German (0)	36	0.30
Polish (68)	89	0.73
Portuguese (0)	21	0.17
Russian (18)	49	0.40
Scandinavian (40)	40	0.33
Scotch-Irish (82)	174	1.44
Scottish (89)	172	1.42
Swedish (28)	76	0.63
Welsh (0)	10	0.08
West Indian, ex. Hispanic (42)	42	0.35
Dutch West Indian (9)	9	0.07
Jamaican (33)	33	0.27
Yugoslavian (11)	26	0.21

Hispanic Origin	Population	%
Hispanic or Latino (of any race)	4,708	39.10
Central American, ex. Mexican	111	0.92
Costa Rican	1	0.01
Guatemalan	22	0.18
Honduran	7	0.06
Nicaraguan	18	0.15
Panamanian	3	0.02
Salvadoran	60	0.50
Cuban	18	0.15
Dominican Republic	6	0.05
Mexican	4,167	34.61
Puerto Rican	77	0.64
South American	70	0.58
Argentinean	20	0.17
Bolivian	3	0.02
Chilean	4	0.03
Colombian	10	0.08
Ecuadorian	6	0.05
Peruvian	21	0.17
Uruguayan	5	0.04
Venezuelan	1	0.01
Other Hispanic or Latino	259	2.15

Race*	Population	%
African-American/Black (673)	816	6.78
Not Hispanic (641)	734	6.10
Hispanic (32)	82	0.68
American Indian/Alaska Native (120)	240	1.99
Not Hispanic (42)	103	0.86
Hispanic (78)	137	1.14
Apache (6)	22	0.18
Blackfeet (5)	13	0.11
Cherokee (5)	40	0.33
Cheyenne (1)	2	0.02
Chickasaw (0)	1	0.01
Chippewa (0)	3	0.02
Choctaw (2)	6	0.05
Creek (1)	1	0.01
Delaware (0)	1	0.01
Iroquois (1)	1	0.01
Mexican American Ind. (13)	22	0.18
Navajo (6)	7	0.06
Osage (0)	3	0.02
Pima (0)	1	0.01
Pueblo (3)	4	0.03
Sioux (3)	6	0.05
Yaqui (3)	12	0.10
Asian (778)	979	8.13
Not Hispanic (739)	882	7.33
Hispanic (39)	97	0.81
Bangladeshi (1)	1	0.01
Burmese (1)	5	0.04
Cambodian (9)	9	0.07
Chinese, ex. Taiwanese (83)	107	0.89
Filipino (252)	320	2.66
Indian (99)	121	1.00
Indonesian (78)	85	0.71
Japanese (48)	72	0.60
Korean (65)	90	0.75
Laotian (1)	2	0.02
Malaysian (2)	4	0.03
Pakistani (22)	26	0.22
Sri Lankan (8)	12	0.10
Taiwanese (0)	1	0.01
Thai (34)	46	0.38
Vietnamese (38)	47	0.39
Hawaii Native/Pacific Islander (32)	83	0.69
Not Hispanic (21)	51	0.42
Hispanic (11)	32	0.27
Fijian (0)	3	0.02
Guamanian/Chamorro (2)	15	0.12

*Notes: † The Census 2010 population figure is used to calculate the percentages in the Hispanic Origin and Race categories. Ancestry percentages are based on the 2006-2010 American Community Survey population (not shown); ‡ Numbers in parentheses indicate the number of people reporting a single ancestry; * Numbers in parentheses indicate the number of persons reporting this race alone, not in combination with any other race; Please refer to the Explanation of Data for more information.*

Native Hawaiian (14)	31	0.26
Samoan (11)	19	0.16
Tongan (2)	4	0.03
White (7,912)	8,437	70.07
Not Hispanic (5,582)	5,807	48.23
Hispanic (2,330)	2,630	21.84

Granite Bay

Place Type: CDP
County: Placer
Population: 20,402†

Ancestry‡	Population	%
African, Sub-Saharan (0)	41	0.18
African (0)	41	0.18
American (780)	780	3.44
Arab (75)	292	1.29
Egyptian (26)	26	0.11
Lebanese (49)	266	1.17
Armenian (12)	12	0.05
Assyrian/Chaldean/Syriac (13)	13	0.06
Austrian (31)	131	0.58
Basque (0)	24	0.11
Belgian (0)	10	0.04
British (74)	163	0.72
Canadian (40)	172	0.76
Croatian (0)	16	0.07
Czech (11)	52	0.23
Czechoslovakian (0)	15	0.07
Danish (66)	281	1.24
Dutch (132)	455	2.01
Eastern European (50)	50	0.22
English (1,124)	4,781	21.08
European (499)	574	2.53
Finnish (22)	32	0.14
French, ex. Basque (191)	1,304	5.75
French Canadian (24)	24	0.11
German (695)	4,055	17.88
Greek (66)	127	0.56
Hungarian (56)	110	0.48
Iranian (379)	379	1.67
Irish (831)	3,955	17.44
Italian (805)	2,532	11.16
Lithuanian (16)	78	0.34
New Zealander (23)	23	0.10
Northern European (30)	30	0.13
Norwegian (269)	661	2.91
Pennsylvania German (21)	43	0.19
Polish (109)	537	2.37
Portuguese (137)	442	1.95
Russian (71)	250	1.10
Scandinavian (45)	85	0.37
Scotch-Irish (253)	415	1.83
Scottish (204)	729	3.21
Slavic (8)	36	0.16
Slovak (15)	27	0.12
Slovene (23)	45	0.20
Swedish (165)	801	3.53
Swiss (31)	129	0.57
Turkish (51)	75	0.33
Ukrainian (33)	82	0.36
Welsh (34)	164	0.72
West Indian, ex. Hispanic (13)	13	0.06
West Indian (8)	8	0.04
Other West Indian (5)	5	0.02
Yugoslavian (14)	59	0.26

Hispanic Origin	Population	%
Hispanic or Latino (of any race)	1,260	6.18
Central American, ex. Mexican	73	0.36
Costa Rican	10	0.05
Guatemalan	9	0.04
Honduran	1	<0.01
Nicaraguan	22	0.11
Panamanian	11	0.05
Salvadoran	20	0.10
Cuban	21	0.10
Mexican	823	4.03
Puerto Rican	66	0.32
South American	68	0.33
Argentinean	18	0.09
Bolivian	4	0.02
Chilean	11	0.05
Colombian	14	0.07
Paraguayan	1	<0.01
Peruvian	18	0.09
Venezuelan	2	0.01
Other Hispanic or Latino	209	1.02

Race*	Population	%
African-American/Black (148)	228	1.12
Not Hispanic (140)	215	1.05
Hispanic (8)	13	0.06
American Indian/Alaska Native (138)	361	1.77
Not Hispanic (96)	271	1.33
Hispanic (42)	90	0.44
Aleut *(Alaska Native)* (3)	7	0.03
Apache (8)	17	0.08
Blackfeet (0)	11	0.05
Cherokee (15)	69	0.34
Chickasaw (2)	10	0.05
Chippewa (1)	2	0.01
Choctaw (16)	33	0.16
Creek (0)	2	0.01
Iroquois (0)	2	0.01
Menominee (0)	3	0.01
Mexican American Ind. (1)	5	0.02
Navajo (1)	3	0.01
Osage (0)	1	<0.01
Seminole (0)	4	0.02
Sioux (4)	17	0.08
South American Ind. (1)	1	<0.01
Spanish American Ind. (2)	2	0.01
Tlingit-Haida *(Alaska Native)* (2)	5	0.02
Ute (3)	3	0.01
Yaqui (0)	2	0.01
Asian (1,152)	1,564	7.67
Not Hispanic (1,143)	1,515	7.43
Hispanic (9)	49	0.24
Bangladeshi (2)	5	0.02
Burmese (1)	2	0.01
Cambodian (2)	11	0.05
Chinese, ex. Taiwanese (304)	419	2.05
Filipino (110)	216	1.06
Hmong (3)	3	0.01
Indian (306)	335	1.64
Indonesian (9)	11	0.05
Japanese (144)	264	1.29
Korean (69)	84	0.41
Laotian (0)	1	<0.01
Malaysian (0)	1	<0.01
Nepalese (0)	1	<0.01
Pakistani (26)	28	0.14
Taiwanese (15)	15	0.07
Thai (6)	18	0.09
Vietnamese (89)	103	0.50
Hawaii Native/Pacific Islander (28)	75	0.37
Not Hispanic (27)	69	0.34
Hispanic (1)	6	0.03
Fijian (0)	2	0.01
Guamanian/Chamorro (8)	18	0.09
Native Hawaiian (9)	31	0.15
White (17,960)	18,668	91.50
Not Hispanic (17,075)	17,649	86.51
Hispanic (885)	1,019	4.99

Grass Valley

Place Type: City
County: Nevada
Population: 12,860†

Ancestry‡	Population	%
American (465)	465	3.64
Armenian (8)	31	0.24
Australian (0)	33	0.26
Austrian (0)	35	0.27
Belgian (0)	7	0.05
British (57)	80	0.63
Canadian (10)	162	1.27
Czechoslovakian (0)	40	0.31
Danish (0)	41	0.32
Dutch (22)	236	1.85
Eastern European (11)	11	0.09
English (821)	2,180	17.08
European (237)	271	2.12
Finnish (39)	155	1.21
French, ex. Basque (42)	556	4.36
French Canadian (29)	61	0.48
German (498)	2,182	17.09
Greek (39)	137	1.07
Hungarian (0)	33	0.26
Irish (457)	1,839	14.41
Italian (494)	1,020	7.99
Luxemburger (13)	13	0.10
Norwegian (137)	282	2.21
Polish (26)	90	0.71
Portuguese (199)	301	2.36
Romanian (0)	10	0.08
Russian (0)	43	0.34
Scandinavian (0)	23	0.18
Scotch-Irish (86)	451	3.53
Scottish (206)	595	4.66
Slavic (0)	10	0.08
Slovak (0)	10	0.08
Swedish (63)	292	2.29
Swiss (0)	72	0.56
Turkish (0)	7	0.05
Ukrainian (0)	141	1.10
Welsh (56)	150	1.18

Hispanic Origin	Population	%
Hispanic or Latino (of any race)	1,341	10.43
Central American, ex. Mexican	50	0.39
Guatemalan	6	0.05
Honduran	10	0.08
Nicaraguan	12	0.09
Panamanian	2	0.02
Salvadoran	19	0.15
Other Central American	1	0.01
Cuban	4	0.03
Dominican Republic	6	0.05
Mexican	1,082	8.41
Puerto Rican	59	0.46
South American	17	0.13
Argentinean	3	0.02
Bolivian	2	0.02
Chilean	6	0.05
Colombian	4	0.03
Peruvian	2	0.02
Other Hispanic or Latino	123	0.96

Race*	Population	%
African-American/Black (46)	121	0.94
Not Hispanic (36)	103	0.80
Hispanic (10)	18	0.14
American Indian/Alaska Native (208)	509	3.96
Not Hispanic (148)	393	3.06
Hispanic (60)	116	0.90
Aleut *(Alaska Native)* (1)	1	0.01
Apache (6)	13	0.10
Blackfeet (4)	24	0.19
Canadian/French Am. Ind. (0)	1	0.01
Cherokee (23)	105	0.82
Chickasaw (0)	4	0.03
Chippewa (5)	10	0.08
Choctaw (3)	21	0.16
Comanche (0)	4	0.03
Creek (2)	4	0.03
Crow (1)	1	0.01
Iroquois (2)	3	0.02
Kiowa (0)	2	0.02
Mexican American Ind. (11)	13	0.10
Navajo (2)	6	0.05
Osage (2)	2	0.02
Paiute (7)	12	0.09
Pima (1)	1	0.01
Potawatomi (1)	6	0.05
Pueblo (2)	6	0.05

*Notes: † The Census 2010 population figure is used to calculate the percentages in the Hispanic Origin and Race categories. Ancestry percentages are based on the 2006-2010 American Community Survey population (not shown); ‡ Numbers in parentheses indicate the number of people reporting a single ancestry; * Numbers in parentheses indicate the number of persons reporting this race alone, not in combination with any other race; Please refer to the Explanation of Data for more information.*

Puget Sound Salish (8)	9	0.07
Shoshone (4)	6	0.05
Sioux (7)	10	0.08
Spanish American Ind. (1)	1	0.01
Tsimshian *(Alaska Native)* (0)	2	0.02
Yaqui (6)	6	0.05
Asian (188)	264	2.05
Not Hispanic (185)	252	1.96
Hispanic (3)	12	0.09
Burmese (3)	3	0.02
Cambodian (1)	2	0.02
Chinese, ex. Taiwanese (51)	65	0.51
Filipino (21)	45	0.35
Indian (49)	64	0.50
Indonesian (6)	7	0.05
Japanese (17)	33	0.26
Korean (5)	8	0.06
Nepalese (7)	7	0.05
Pakistani (3)	8	0.06
Taiwanese (1)	1	0.01
Thai (9)	9	0.07
Vietnamese (7)	7	0.05
Hawaii Native/Pacific Islander (9)	41	0.32
Not Hispanic (9)	30	0.23
Hispanic (0)	11	0.09
Fijian (0)	1	0.01
Guamanian/Chamorro (0)	1	0.01
Native Hawaiian (3)	24	0.19
Tongan (4)	4	0.03
White (11,493)	11,946	92.89
Not Hispanic (10,764)	11,106	86.36
Hispanic (729)	840	6.53

Greenfield

Place Type: City
County: Monterey
Population: 16,330†

Ancestry‡	Population	%
American (23)	23	0.15
British (31)	31	0.20
Dutch (0)	31	0.20
English (29)	180	1.16
European (31)	41	0.26
Finnish (0)	13	0.08
French, ex. Basque (39)	83	0.54
German (17)	95	0.61
Irish (21)	94	0.61
Italian (51)	103	0.67
Portuguese (79)	130	0.84
Scotch-Irish (41)	105	0.68
Scottish (0)	22	0.14
Swedish (0)	11	0.07
Swiss (0)	57	0.37
Welsh (0)	20	0.13

Hispanic Origin	Population	%
Hispanic or Latino (of any race)	14,917	91.35
Central American, ex. Mexican	101	0.62
Costa Rican	1	0.01
Guatemalan	18	0.11
Honduran	6	0.04
Nicaraguan	3	0.02
Panamanian	3	0.02
Salvadoran	69	0.42
Other Central American	1	0.01
Cuban	9	0.06
Mexican	14,164	86.74
Puerto Rican	26	0.16
South American	14	0.09
Argentinean	1	0.01
Colombian	4	0.02
Ecuadorian	4	0.02
Peruvian	1	0.01
Uruguayan	3	0.02
Venezuelan	1	0.01
Other Hispanic or Latino	603	3.69

Race*	Population	%
African-American/Black (183)	268	1.64
Not Hispanic (134)	168	1.03
Hispanic (49)	100	0.61
American Indian/Alaska Native (878)	989	6.06
Not Hispanic (52)	82	0.50
Hispanic (826)	907	5.55
Apache (3)	5	0.03
Blackfeet (1)	10	0.06
Cherokee (8)	16	0.10
Chickasaw (5)	5	0.03
Chippewa (1)	2	0.01
Choctaw (0)	2	0.01
Comanche (1)	1	0.01
Hopi (1)	1	0.01
Iroquois (6)	6	0.04
Mexican American Ind. (730)	765	4.68
Navajo (4)	4	0.02
Potawatomi (1)	1	0.01
Pueblo (3)	3	0.02
Shoshone (1)	2	0.01
Sioux (1)	3	0.02
South American Ind. (0)	1	0.01
Spanish American Ind. (6)	6	0.04
Yaqui (1)	3	0.02
Asian (179)	306	1.87
Not Hispanic (150)	209	1.28
Hispanic (29)	97	0.59
Cambodian (3)	3	0.02
Chinese, ex. Taiwanese (10)	16	0.10
Filipino (122)	190	1.16
Indian (21)	32	0.20
Japanese (2)	16	0.10
Korean (11)	22	0.13
Nepalese (1)	1	0.01
Pakistani (1)	1	0.01
Thai (4)	5	0.03
Vietnamese (2)	8	0.05
Hawaii Native/Pacific Islander (13)	21	0.13
Not Hispanic (12)	16	0.10
Hispanic (1)	5	0.03
Fijian (9)	9	0.06
Guamanian/Chamorro (1)	2	0.01
Native Hawaiian (2)	3	0.02
Samoan (0)	1	0.01
White (5,976)	6,493	39.76
Not Hispanic (935)	1,019	6.24
Hispanic (5,041)	5,474	33.52

Grover Beach

Place Type: City
County: San Luis Obispo
Population: 13,156†

Ancestry‡	Population	%
American (713)	713	5.43
Arab (44)	60	0.46
Arab (32)	32	0.24
Lebanese (12)	28	0.21
Basque (30)	59	0.45
British (12)	39	0.30
Canadian (10)	10	0.08
Celtic (9)	9	0.07
Croatian (0)	40	0.30
Czech (31)	105	0.80
Czechoslovakian (14)	28	0.21
Danish (54)	130	0.99
Dutch (22)	492	3.75
English (473)	1,428	10.87
European (313)	331	2.52
Finnish (6)	33	0.25
French, ex. Basque (55)	539	4.10
French Canadian (16)	101	0.77
German (510)	1,689	12.86
German Russian (0)	13	0.10
Greek (28)	40	0.30
Hungarian (47)	47	0.36
Icelander (10)	10	0.08
Irish (386)	1,845	14.04
Italian (207)	661	5.03
Latvian (15)	15	0.11
Lithuanian (10)	23	0.18
Northern European (49)	54	0.41
Norwegian (103)	406	3.09
Pennsylvania German (0)	25	0.19
Polish (46)	209	1.59
Portuguese (561)	727	5.53
Romanian (27)	27	0.21
Russian (0)	55	0.42
Scandinavian (21)	21	0.16
Scotch-Irish (198)	376	2.86
Scottish (89)	195	1.48
Serbian (0)	9	0.07
Slovak (0)	18	0.14
Swedish (27)	130	0.99
Swiss (10)	50	0.38
Welsh (0)	57	0.43
Yugoslavian (0)	19	0.14

Hispanic Origin	Population	%
Hispanic or Latino (of any race)	3,840	29.19
Central American, ex. Mexican	77	0.59
Costa Rican	2	0.02
Guatemalan	13	0.10
Honduran	10	0.08
Nicaraguan	6	0.05
Panamanian	13	0.10
Salvadoran	33	0.25
Cuban	12	0.09
Dominican Republic	1	0.01
Mexican	3,412	25.93
Puerto Rican	58	0.44
South American	37	0.28
Argentinean	4	0.03
Chilean	3	0.02
Colombian	8	0.06
Ecuadorian	5	0.04
Peruvian	16	0.12
Other South American	1	0.01
Other Hispanic or Latino	243	1.85

Race*	Population	%
African-American/Black (146)	249	1.89
Not Hispanic (113)	190	1.44
Hispanic (33)	59	0.45
American Indian/Alaska Native (186)	413	3.14
Not Hispanic (74)	202	1.54
Hispanic (112)	211	1.60
Apache (6)	17	0.13
Blackfeet (2)	7	0.05
Canadian/French Am. Ind. (0)	1	0.01
Cherokee (19)	67	0.51
Cheyenne (2)	2	0.02
Chickasaw (5)	10	0.08
Chippewa (1)	2	0.02
Choctaw (6)	13	0.10
Comanche (1)	2	0.02
Delaware (1)	1	0.01
Iroquois (3)	3	0.02
Kiowa (0)	1	0.01
Mexican American Ind. (18)	51	0.39
Navajo (10)	14	0.11
Osage (0)	3	0.02
Paiute (0)	1	0.01
Potawatomi (0)	2	0.02
Pueblo (0)	2	0.02
Puget Sound Salish (2)	2	0.02
Seminole (2)	3	0.02
Sioux (0)	7	0.05
Spanish American Ind. (1)	1	0.01
Tohono O'Odham (0)	1	0.01
Yaqui (4)	11	0.08
Asian (542)	748	5.69
Not Hispanic (525)	681	5.18
Hispanic (17)	67	0.51
Cambodian (8)	8	0.06
Chinese, ex. Taiwanese (64)	86	0.65
Filipino (315)	434	3.30

*Notes: † The Census 2010 population figure is used to calculate the percentages in the Hispanic Origin and Race categories. Ancestry percentages are based on the 2006-2010 American Community Survey population (not shown); ‡ Numbers in parentheses indicate the number of people reporting a single ancestry; * Numbers in parentheses indicate the number of persons reporting this race alone, not in combination with any other race; Please refer to the Explanation of Data for more information.*

Indian (18)	22	0.17
Indonesian (2)	4	0.03
Japanese (54)	104	0.79
Korean (32)	37	0.28
Laotian (2)	3	0.02
Malaysian (0)	1	0.01
Pakistani (0)	2	0.02
Taiwanese (1)	3	0.02
Thai (13)	17	0.13
Vietnamese (16)	27	0.21
Hawaii Native/Pacific Islander (35)	98	0.74
Not Hispanic (22)	70	0.53
Hispanic (13)	28	0.21
Guamanian/Chamorro (7)	13	0.10
Native Hawaiian (5)	51	0.39
Samoan (14)	35	0.27
White (9,964)	10,593	80.52
Not Hispanic (8,190)	8,520	64.76
Hispanic (1,774)	2,073	15.76

Hacienda Heights

Place Type: CDP
County: Los Angeles
Population: 54,038†

Ancestry‡	Population	%
African, Sub-Saharan (30)	30	0.06
African (30)	30	0.06
American (1,338)	1,338	2.49
Arab (235)	260	0.48
Arab (82)	82	0.15
Egyptian (143)	143	0.27
Lebanese (0)	25	0.05
Other Arab (10)	10	0.02
Armenian (146)	173	0.32
Australian (0)	7	0.01
Austrian (18)	74	0.14
Belgian (0)	6	0.01
Brazilian (11)	11	0.02
British (10)	10	0.02
Cajun (47)	47	0.09
Canadian (83)	147	0.27
Celtic (0)	11	0.02
Croatian (10)	50	0.09
Czech (0)	50	0.09
Czechoslovakian (15)	26	0.05
Danish (17)	75	0.14
Dutch (37)	429	0.80
Eastern European (7)	7	0.01
English (316)	1,152	2.15
Estonian (21)	21	0.04
European (150)	196	0.37
Finnish (19)	113	0.21
French, ex. Basque (33)	367	0.68
French Canadian (17)	54	0.10
German (638)	2,335	4.35
Greek (188)	229	0.43
Hungarian (25)	51	0.10
Iranian (113)	126	0.23
Irish (258)	1,584	2.95
Italian (406)	1,068	1.99
Latvian (11)	11	0.02
Northern European (7)	7	0.01
Norwegian (53)	134	0.25
Polish (151)	373	0.70
Portuguese (59)	114	0.21
Romanian (28)	38	0.07
Russian (194)	250	0.47
Scandinavian (27)	39	0.07
Scotch-Irish (57)	275	0.51
Scottish (156)	418	0.78
Slavic (0)	15	0.03
Slovak (8)	19	0.04
Slovene (0)	8	0.01
Swedish (70)	401	0.75
Swiss (0)	31	0.06
Ukrainian (35)	63	0.12
Welsh (13)	62	0.12
West Indian, ex. Hispanic (90)	113	0.21
Belizean (15)	38	0.07
Haitian (46)	46	0.09
West Indian (29)	29	0.05
Yugoslavian (12)	12	0.02

Hispanic Origin	Population	%
Hispanic or Latino (of any race)	24,608	45.54
Central American, ex. Mexican	1,511	2.80
Costa Rican	64	0.12
Guatemalan	378	0.70
Honduran	69	0.13
Nicaraguan	157	0.29
Panamanian	12	0.02
Salvadoran	807	1.49
Other Central American	24	0.04
Cuban	157	0.29
Dominican Republic	6	0.01
Mexican	20,994	38.85
Puerto Rican	215	0.40
South American	660	1.22
Argentinean	117	0.22
Bolivian	30	0.06
Chilean	31	0.06
Colombian	142	0.26
Ecuadorian	135	0.25
Paraguayan	1	<0.01
Peruvian	182	0.34
Uruguayan	7	0.01
Venezuelan	11	0.02
Other South American	4	0.01
Other Hispanic or Latino	1,065	1.97

Race*	Population	%
African-American/Black (743)	916	1.70
Not Hispanic (644)	726	1.34
Hispanic (99)	190	0.35
American Indian/Alaska Native (315)	567	1.05
Not Hispanic (69)	175	0.32
Hispanic (246)	392	0.73
Apache (13)	37	0.07
Blackfeet (4)	10	0.02
Canadian/French Am. Ind. (0)	2	<0.01
Cherokee (4)	33	0.06
Cheyenne (1)	1	<0.01
Chickasaw (0)	4	0.01
Chippewa (9)	9	0.02
Choctaw (2)	7	0.01
Colville (0)	1	<0.01
Cree (0)	1	<0.01
Creek (0)	4	0.01
Delaware (1)	1	<0.01
Hopi (5)	5	0.01
Inupiat *(Alaska Native)* (1)	1	<0.01
Iroquois (2)	4	0.01
Kiowa (1)	1	<0.01
Mexican American Ind. (52)	67	0.12
Navajo (11)	17	0.03
Osage (1)	1	<0.01
Paiute (2)	3	0.01
Pima (1)	4	0.01
Pueblo (6)	12	0.02
Puget Sound Salish (1)	1	<0.01
Seminole (0)	2	<0.01
Shoshone (3)	3	0.01
South American Ind. (2)	5	0.01
Spanish American Ind. (8)	15	0.03
Tlingit-Haida *(Alaska Native)* (1)	1	<0.01
Tohono O'Odham (5)	10	0.02
Ute (5)	5	0.01
Yaqui (3)	7	0.01
Yup'ik *(Alaska Native)* (5)	5	0.01
Asian (20,065)	20,891	38.66
Not Hispanic (19,878)	20,414	37.78
Hispanic (187)	477	0.88
Bangladeshi (7)	9	0.02
Burmese (49)	57	0.11
Cambodian (96)	115	0.21
Chinese, ex. Taiwanese (10,497)	11,348	21.00
Filipino (1,212)	1,504	2.78
Hmong (8)	8	0.01
Indian (265)	319	0.59
Indonesian (147)	205	0.38
Japanese (1,158)	1,449	2.68
Korean (2,483)	2,609	4.83
Laotian (43)	47	0.09
Malaysian (19)	39	0.07
Pakistani (41)	42	0.08
Sri Lankan (5)	9	0.02
Taiwanese (2,547)	2,944	5.45
Thai (231)	287	0.53
Vietnamese (417)	563	1.04
Hawaii Native/Pacific Islander (99)	290	0.54
Not Hispanic (63)	212	0.39
Hispanic (36)	78	0.14
Fijian (4)	7	0.01
Guamanian/Chamorro (7)	11	0.02
Native Hawaiian (30)	69	0.13
Samoan (29)	47	0.09
Tongan (19)	20	0.04
White (21,873)	23,196	42.93
Not Hispanic (8,035)	8,495	15.72
Hispanic (13,838)	14,701	27.20

Half Moon Bay

Place Type: City
County: San Mateo
Population: 11,324†

Ancestry‡	Population	%
American (259)	259	2.33
Arab (0)	33	0.30
Arab (0)	12	0.11
Lebanese (0)	21	0.19
Australian (0)	7	0.06
Austrian (14)	58	0.52
Belgian (7)	38	0.34
British (49)	64	0.58
Bulgarian (12)	25	0.22
Canadian (12)	12	0.11
Croatian (13)	52	0.47
Czech (0)	77	0.69
Danish (94)	131	1.18
Dutch (34)	166	1.49
Eastern European (14)	14	0.13
English (350)	1,190	10.70
Estonian (0)	11	0.10
European (214)	214	1.92
Finnish (24)	38	0.34
French, ex. Basque (18)	232	2.09
French Canadian (51)	71	0.64
German (509)	1,363	12.25
Greek (49)	179	1.61
Hungarian (42)	92	0.83
Irish (336)	1,305	11.73
Italian (360)	1,154	10.37
Latvian (0)	13	0.12
Maltese (30)	126	1.13
Northern European (106)	106	0.95
Norwegian (38)	139	1.25
Polish (129)	270	2.43
Portuguese (155)	297	2.67
Romanian (0)	15	0.13
Russian (36)	94	0.84
Scandinavian (66)	66	0.59
Scotch-Irish (113)	241	2.17
Scottish (37)	335	3.01
Swedish (60)	157	1.41
Swiss (0)	60	0.54
Ukrainian (15)	111	1.00
Welsh (27)	72	0.65
Yugoslavian (0)	16	0.14

Hispanic Origin	Population	%
Hispanic or Latino (of any race)	3,563	31.46
Central American, ex. Mexican	107	0.94
Costa Rican	4	0.04
Guatemalan	22	0.19
Honduran	3	0.03
Nicaraguan	17	0.15

SECTION TWO

*Notes: † The Census 2010 population figure is used to calculate the percentages in the Hispanic Origin and Race categories. Ancestry percentages are based on the 2006-2010 American Community Survey population (not shown); ‡ Numbers in parentheses indicate the number of people reporting a single ancestry; * Numbers in parentheses indicate the number of persons reporting this race alone, not in combination with any other race; Please refer to the Explanation of Data for more information.*

Panamanian	6	0.05
Salvadoran	53	0.47
Other Central American	2	0.02
Cuban	7	0.06
Dominican Republic	1	0.01
Mexican	3,153	27.84
Puerto Rican	39	0.34
South American	58	0.51
Argentinean	16	0.14
Bolivian	11	0.10
Chilean	9	0.08
Colombian	5	0.04
Ecuadorian	2	0.02
Paraguayan	1	0.01
Peruvian	14	0.12
Other Hispanic or Latino	198	1.75

Race*	Population	%
African-American/Black (82)	121	1.07
Not Hispanic (65)	97	0.86
Hispanic (17)	24	0.21
American Indian/Alaska Native (71)	145	1.28
Not Hispanic (20)	62	0.55
Hispanic (51)	83	0.73
Aleut *(Alaska Native)* (1)	1	0.01
Apache (1)	1	0.01
Blackfeet (0)	3	0.03
Cherokee (5)	20	0.18
Chippewa (0)	7	0.06
Choctaw (4)	9	0.08
Comanche (0)	4	0.04
Creek (1)	1	0.01
Iroquois (1)	2	0.02
Mexican American Ind. (16)	22	0.19
Osage (0)	1	0.01
Sioux (0)	3	0.03
South American Ind. (1)	1	0.01
Yaqui (0)	2	0.02
Asian (490)	631	5.57
Not Hispanic (472)	596	5.26
Hispanic (18)	35	0.31
Burmese (1)	4	0.04
Cambodian (3)	3	0.03
Chinese, ex. Taiwanese (117)	176	1.55
Filipino (179)	225	1.99
Indian (33)	39	0.34
Indonesian (4)	8	0.07
Japanese (76)	112	0.99
Korean (17)	29	0.26
Nepalese (1)	1	0.01
Pakistani (5)	8	0.07
Taiwanese (1)	2	0.02
Thai (12)	12	0.11
Vietnamese (19)	19	0.17
Hawaii Native/Pacific Islander (9)	43	0.38
Not Hispanic (8)	36	0.32
Hispanic (1)	7	0.06
Fijian (2)	2	0.02
Guamanian/Chamorro (2)	4	0.04
Native Hawaiian (0)	19	0.17
Samoan (1)	4	0.04
White (8,580)	8,927	78.83
Not Hispanic (6,977)	7,170	63.32
Hispanic (1,603)	1,757	15.52

Hanford

Place Type: City
County: Kings
Population: 53,967†

Ancestry‡	Population	%
African, Sub-Saharan (252)	287	0.55
African (130)	165	0.32
Ethiopian (28)	28	0.05
Other Sub-Saharan African (94)	94	0.18
American (1,723)	1,723	3.29
Arab (160)	177	0.34
Arab (41)	41	0.08
Egyptian (7)	7	0.01
Lebanese (4)	21	0.04
Other Arab (108)	108	0.21
Armenian (10)	19	0.04
Australian (19)	29	0.06
Austrian (14)	27	0.05
Basque (27)	65	0.12
Belgian (0)	33	0.06
British (38)	98	0.19
Cajun (8)	13	0.02
Canadian (54)	54	0.10
Celtic (45)	45	0.09
Croatian (26)	32	0.06
Czech (0)	123	0.24
Czechoslovakian (14)	53	0.10
Danish (68)	245	0.47
Dutch (415)	1,162	2.22
English (1,228)	3,523	6.73
European (487)	551	1.05
Finnish (17)	176	0.34
French, ex. Basque (187)	944	1.80
French Canadian (10)	39	0.07
German (1,412)	4,900	9.37
Greek (39)	150	0.29
Guyanese (0)	20	0.04
Hungarian (18)	74	0.14
Irish (1,196)	3,870	7.40
Italian (618)	1,825	3.49
New Zealander (0)	57	0.11
Northern European (48)	48	0.09
Norwegian (36)	244	0.47
Polish (91)	299	0.57
Portuguese (2,268)	3,147	6.02
Romanian (8)	8	0.02
Russian (21)	80	0.15
Scotch-Irish (225)	852	1.63
Scottish (186)	550	1.05
Slovak (18)	18	0.03
Swedish (68)	402	0.77
Swiss (31)	102	0.19
Turkish (16)	16	0.03
Ukrainian (12)	12	0.02
Welsh (10)	270	0.52
West Indian, ex. Hispanic (35)	63	0.12
Barbadian (19)	19	0.04
Dutch West Indian (0)	28	0.05
Trinidadian/Tobagonian (16)	16	0.03
Yugoslavian (0)	14	0.03

Hispanic Origin	Population	%
Hispanic or Latino (of any race)	25,419	47.10
Central American, ex. Mexican	282	0.52
Costa Rican	7	0.01
Guatemalan	60	0.11
Honduran	47	0.09
Nicaraguan	36	0.07
Panamanian	15	0.03
Salvadoran	117	0.22
Cuban	40	0.07
Dominican Republic	16	0.03
Mexican	23,269	43.12
Puerto Rican	180	0.33
South American	93	0.17
Argentinean	8	0.01
Bolivian	11	0.02
Chilean	7	0.01
Colombian	18	0.03
Ecuadorian	10	0.02
Paraguayan	1	<0.01
Peruvian	36	0.07
Venezuelan	2	<0.01
Other Hispanic or Latino	1,539	2.85

Race*	Population	%
African-American/Black (2,632)	3,320	6.15
Not Hispanic (2,367)	2,837	5.26
Hispanic (265)	483	0.89
American Indian/Alaska Native (712)	1,247	2.31
Not Hispanic (331)	612	1.13
Hispanic (381)	635	1.18
Apache (24)	58	0.11
Arapaho (2)	4	0.01
Blackfeet (4)	15	0.03
Canadian/French Am. Ind. (0)	6	0.01
Cherokee (57)	185	0.34
Chickasaw (3)	6	0.01
Chippewa (6)	6	0.01
Choctaw (33)	45	0.08
Comanche (2)	2	<0.01
Cree (2)	5	0.01
Creek (8)	13	0.02
Crow (1)	1	<0.01
Delaware (0)	1	<0.01
Hopi (1)	3	0.01
Iroquois (4)	5	0.01
Lumbee (0)	1	<0.01
Mexican American Ind. (63)	75	0.14
Navajo (14)	26	0.05
Osage (0)	3	0.01
Ottawa (0)	1	<0.01
Paiute (3)	5	0.01
Pima (23)	25	0.05
Pueblo (0)	2	<0.01
Puget Sound Salish (2)	2	<0.01
Shoshone (5)	7	0.01
Sioux (4)	12	0.02
South American Ind. (1)	1	<0.01
Spanish American Ind. (1)	1	<0.01
Tlingit-Haida *(Alaska Native)* (1)	2	<0.01
Tohono O'Odham (2)	3	0.01
Ute (1)	2	<0.01
Yaqui (12)	22	0.04
Asian (2,322)	3,071	5.69
Not Hispanic (2,205)	2,738	5.07
Hispanic (117)	333	0.62
Bangladeshi (2)	4	0.01
Cambodian (33)	40	0.07
Chinese, ex. Taiwanese (214)	317	0.59
Filipino (1,354)	1,751	3.24
Hmong (104)	126	0.23
Indian (217)	274	0.51
Indonesian (7)	8	0.01
Japanese (117)	238	0.44
Korean (41)	72	0.13
Laotian (26)	38	0.07
Malaysian (0)	1	<0.01
Pakistani (18)	23	0.04
Sri Lankan (4)	5	0.01
Taiwanese (3)	4	0.01
Thai (15)	27	0.05
Vietnamese (66)	104	0.19
Hawaii Native/Pacific Islander (53)	205	0.38
Not Hispanic (43)	150	0.28
Hispanic (10)	55	0.10
Guamanian/Chamorro (8)	18	0.03
Marshallese (3)	3	0.01
Native Hawaiian (19)	79	0.15
Samoan (8)	17	0.03
White (33,713)	36,283	67.23
Not Hispanic (22,205)	23,331	43.23
Hispanic (11,508)	12,952	24.00

Hawaiian Gardens

Place Type: City
County: Los Angeles
Population: 14,254†

Ancestry‡	Population	%
African, Sub-Saharan (53)	66	0.46
African (53)	66	0.46
American (204)	204	1.42
Arab (94)	94	0.66
Lebanese (45)	45	0.31
Moroccan (49)	49	0.34
Austrian (0)	11	0.08
Canadian (9)	19	0.13
Danish (0)	49	0.34
Dutch (0)	23	0.16
English (124)	220	1.54
French, ex. Basque (0)	80	0.56

*Notes: † The Census 2010 population figure is used to calculate the percentages in the Hispanic Origin and Race categories. Ancestry percentages are based on the 2006-2010 American Community Survey population (not shown); ‡ Numbers in parentheses indicate the number of people reporting a single ancestry; * Numbers in parentheses indicate the number of persons reporting this race alone, not in combination with any other race; Please refer to the Explanation of Data for more information.*

German (64)	273	1.91
Iranian (18)	62	0.43
Irish (8)	318	2.22
Italian (92)	228	1.59
Norwegian (10)	59	0.41
Portuguese (0)	49	0.34
Romanian (0)	9	0.06
Russian (0)	9	0.06
Scottish (10)	29	0.20
Swedish (140)	152	1.06
Turkish (13)	13	0.09
Ukrainian (10)	10	0.07

Hispanic Origin	Population	%
Hispanic or Latino (of any race)	11,010	77.24
Central American, ex. Mexican	522	3.66
Costa Rican	9	0.06
Guatemalan	201	1.41
Honduran	51	0.36
Nicaraguan	27	0.19
Panamanian	2	0.01
Salvadoran	226	1.59
Other Central American	6	0.04
Cuban	16	0.11
Dominican Republic	3	0.02
Mexican	9,955	69.84
Puerto Rican	32	0.22
South American	39	0.27
Chilean	4	0.03
Colombian	11	0.08
Ecuadorian	6	0.04
Peruvian	12	0.08
Venezuelan	5	0.04
Other South American	1	0.01
Other Hispanic or Latino	443	3.11

Race*	Population	%
African-American/Black (546)	643	4.51
Not Hispanic (482)	537	3.77
Hispanic (64)	106	0.74
American Indian/Alaska Native (178)	260	1.82
Not Hispanic (46)	76	0.53
Hispanic (132)	184	1.29
Apache (10)	12	0.08
Blackfeet (1)	4	0.03
Cherokee (4)	22	0.15
Chippewa (1)	1	0.01
Choctaw (3)	7	0.05
Comanche (0)	1	0.01
Cree (0)	1	0.01
Hopi (0)	2	0.01
Mexican American Ind. (23)	27	0.19
Navajo (1)	1	0.01
Potawatomi (1)	1	0.01
Pueblo (1)	1	0.01
Seminole (1)	1	0.01
Sioux (3)	3	0.02
Spanish American Ind. (0)	1	0.01
Tlingit-Haida *(Alaska Native)* (1)	1	0.01
Yaqui (1)	1	0.01
Asian (1,513)	1,616	11.34
Not Hispanic (1,491)	1,552	10.89
Hispanic (22)	64	0.45
Bangladeshi (30)	30	0.21
Cambodian (106)	125	0.88
Chinese, ex. Taiwanese (121)	150	1.05
Filipino (297)	350	2.46
Indian (49)	57	0.40
Indonesian (6)	10	0.07
Japanese (28)	38	0.27
Korean (743)	754	5.29
Pakistani (0)	1	0.01
Taiwanese (14)	14	0.10
Thai (26)	27	0.19
Vietnamese (51)	59	0.41
Hawaii Native/Pacific Islander (57)	98	0.69
Not Hispanic (49)	65	0.46
Hispanic (8)	33	0.23
Fijian (3)	3	0.02
Guamanian/Chamorro (8)	9	0.06
Native Hawaiian (15)	22	0.15
Samoan (28)	40	0.28
Tongan (2)	2	0.01
White (6,477)	6,931	48.62
Not Hispanic (1,044)	1,124	7.89
Hispanic (5,433)	5,807	40.74

Hawthorne

Place Type: City
County: Los Angeles
Population: 84,293†

Ancestry‡	Population	%
Afghan (113)	113	0.13
African, Sub-Saharan (2,260)	2,790	3.31
African (1,323)	1,719	2.04
Ethiopian (409)	409	0.49
Ghanaian (69)	69	0.08
Kenyan (5)	5	0.01
Nigerian (325)	447	0.53
Sierra Leonean (27)	27	0.03
South African (0)	12	0.01
Sudanese (102)	102	0.12
Albanian (0)	9	0.01
American (12,456)	12,456	14.79
Arab (595)	717	0.85
Arab (54)	78	0.09
Egyptian (305)	329	0.39
Jordanian (7)	7	0.01
Lebanese (0)	49	0.06
Moroccan (33)	33	0.04
Palestinian (89)	89	0.11
Syrian (0)	25	0.03
Other Arab (107)	107	0.13
Armenian (78)	87	0.10
Assyrian/Chaldean/Syriac (22)	22	0.03
Austrian (0)	21	0.02
Brazilian (97)	108	0.13
British (72)	78	0.09
Canadian (12)	32	0.04
Croatian (0)	12	0.01
Czech (22)	99	0.12
Czechoslovakian (0)	6	0.01
Danish (0)	80	0.10
Dutch (41)	230	0.27
English (212)	984	1.17
European (145)	238	0.28
French, ex. Basque (66)	301	0.36
French Canadian (44)	101	0.12
German (532)	1,993	2.37
Greek (32)	58	0.07
Hungarian (44)	126	0.15
Icelander (0)	26	0.03
Iranian (64)	64	0.08
Irish (136)	1,248	1.48
Italian (386)	878	1.04
Lithuanian (0)	9	0.01
Luxemburger (9)	17	0.02
New Zealander (17)	17	0.02
Northern European (22)	22	0.03
Norwegian (0)	28	0.03
Polish (52)	298	0.35
Portuguese (18)	129	0.15
Romanian (21)	21	0.02
Russian (21)	132	0.16
Scandinavian (11)	53	0.06
Scotch-Irish (53)	152	0.18
Scottish (17)	117	0.14
Serbian (29)	29	0.03
Slovak (0)	11	0.01
Swedish (33)	270	0.32
Swiss (0)	43	0.05
Turkish (10)	10	0.01
Ukrainian (34)	48	0.06
Welsh (0)	24	0.03
West Indian, ex. Hispanic (556)	645	0.77
Belizean (292)	341	0.41
Haitian (42)	42	0.05
Jamaican (183)	201	0.24
Trinidadian/Tobagonian (0)	22	0.03
West Indian (39)	39	0.05

Hispanic Origin	Population	%
Hispanic or Latino (of any race)	44,572	52.88
Central American, ex. Mexican	8,547	10.14
Costa Rican	169	0.20
Guatemalan	3,669	4.35
Honduran	584	0.69
Nicaraguan	556	0.66
Panamanian	130	0.15
Salvadoran	3,335	3.96
Other Central American	104	0.12
Cuban	752	0.89
Dominican Republic	55	0.07
Mexican	29,371	34.84
Puerto Rican	689	0.82
South American	1,826	2.17
Argentinean	123	0.15
Bolivian	31	0.04
Chilean	61	0.07
Colombian	487	0.58
Ecuadorian	280	0.33
Paraguayan	3	<0.01
Peruvian	768	0.91
Uruguayan	29	0.03
Venezuelan	29	0.03
Other South American	15	0.02
Other Hispanic or Latino	3,332	3.95

Race*	Population	%
African-American/Black (23,385)	24,674	29.27
Not Hispanic (22,579)	23,386	27.74
Hispanic (806)	1,288	1.53
American Indian/Alaska Native (565)	1,214	1.44
Not Hispanic (172)	449	0.53
Hispanic (393)	765	0.91
Apache (15)	34	0.04
Arapaho (0)	1	<0.01
Blackfeet (4)	36	0.04
Canadian/French Am. Ind. (1)	2	<0.01
Central American Ind. (6)	20	0.02
Cherokee (26)	95	0.11
Chickasaw (0)	5	0.01
Chippewa (2)	8	0.01
Choctaw (1)	28	0.03
Colville (1)	3	<0.01
Comanche (5)	8	0.01
Creek (0)	5	0.01
Delaware (0)	1	<0.01
Hopi (2)	2	<0.01
Inupiat *(Alaska Native)* (0)	4	<0.01
Iroquois (1)	9	0.01
Mexican American Ind. (130)	203	0.24
Navajo (13)	23	0.03
Osage (0)	3	<0.01
Pima (1)	7	0.01
Pueblo (7)	15	0.02
Seminole (0)	18	0.02
Shoshone (0)	1	<0.01
Sioux (11)	17	0.02
South American Ind. (6)	22	0.03
Spanish American Ind. (7)	13	0.02
Tohono O'Odham (3)	4	<0.01
Ute (2)	2	<0.01
Yaqui (9)	16	0.02
Yuman (0)	4	<0.01
Asian (5,642)	6,624	7.86
Not Hispanic (5,492)	6,203	7.36
Hispanic (150)	421	0.50
Bangladeshi (31)	31	0.04
Burmese (31)	34	0.04
Cambodian (21)	28	0.03
Chinese, ex. Taiwanese (392)	583	0.69
Filipino (2,317)	2,697	3.20
Hmong (1)	1	<0.01
Indian (519)	663	0.79
Indonesian (36)	67	0.08
Japanese (339)	533	0.63
Korean (308)	363	0.43

*Notes: † The Census 2010 population figure is used to calculate the percentages in the Hispanic Origin and Race categories. Ancestry percentages are based on the 2006-2010 American Community Survey population (not shown); ‡ Numbers in parentheses indicate the number of people reporting a single ancestry; * Numbers in parentheses indicate the number of persons reporting this race alone, not in combination with any other race; Please refer to the Explanation of Data for more information.*

	Population	%
Laotian (2)	2	<0.01
Malaysian (2)	5	0.01
Nepalese (13)	13	0.02
Pakistani (246)	288	0.34
Sri Lankan (29)	36	0.04
Taiwanese (18)	26	0.03
Thai (63)	77	0.09
Vietnamese (1,058)	1,136	1.35
Hawaii Native/Pacific Islander (974)	1,337	1.59
Not Hispanic (919)	1,176	1.40
Hispanic (55)	161	0.19
Fijian (108)	126	0.15
Guamanian/Chamorro (33)	42	0.05
Native Hawaiian (51)	164	0.19
Samoan (123)	214	0.25
Tongan (575)	656	0.78
White (27,678)	30,467	36.14
Not Hispanic (8,642)	9,609	11.40
Hispanic (19,036)	20,858	24.74

Hayward

Place Type: City
County: Alameda
Population: 144,186†

Ancestry‡	Population	%
Afghan (798)	826	0.58
African, Sub-Saharan (1,732)	1,985	1.40
African (682)	840	0.59
Ethiopian (260)	331	0.23
Ghanaian (43)	43	0.03
Kenyan (54)	66	0.05
Liberian (129)	129	0.09
Nigerian (543)	543	0.38
Ugandan (21)	21	0.01
Other Sub-Saharan African (0)	12	0.01
American (1,373)	1,373	0.97
Arab (500)	580	0.41
Arab (157)	157	0.11
Egyptian (140)	140	0.10
Iraqi (15)	15	0.01
Lebanese (0)	9	0.01
Palestinian (150)	165	0.12
Syrian (21)	77	0.05
Other Arab (17)	17	0.01
Armenian (63)	119	0.08
Australian (9)	31	0.02
Austrian (13)	79	0.06
Basque (10)	17	0.01
Belgian (17)	61	0.04
Brazilian (28)	75	0.05
British (159)	357	0.25
Bulgarian (0)	12	0.01
Canadian (41)	135	0.10
Celtic (28)	28	0.02
Croatian (103)	119	0.08
Czech (34)	113	0.08
Czechoslovakian (22)	44	0.03
Danish (78)	580	0.41
Dutch (363)	1,029	0.73
Eastern European (49)	49	0.03
English (940)	4,609	3.26
Estonian (8)	8	0.01
European (743)	916	0.65
Finnish (43)	133	0.09
French, ex. Basque (319)	1,623	1.15
French Canadian (75)	118	0.08
German (1,716)	6,298	4.45
Greek (134)	420	0.30
Hungarian (42)	223	0.16
Iranian (300)	353	0.25
Irish (1,107)	5,694	4.02
Israeli (0)	22	0.02
Italian (993)	2,611	1.85
Lithuanian (0)	19	0.01
Maltese (11)	11	0.01
Northern European (8)	8	0.01
Norwegian (125)	500	0.35
Pennsylvania German (0)	9	0.01
Polish (279)	736	0.52
Portuguese (2,043)	4,390	3.10
Romanian (113)	244	0.17
Russian (242)	601	0.42
Scandinavian (44)	54	0.04
Scotch-Irish (249)	880	0.62
Scottish (193)	805	0.57
Serbian (0)	8	0.01
Slavic (18)	18	0.01
Slovak (10)	54	0.04
Slovene (0)	13	0.01
Swedish (209)	904	0.64
Swiss (11)	108	0.08
Turkish (100)	108	0.08
Ukrainian (49)	114	0.08
Welsh (47)	202	0.14
West Indian, ex. Hispanic (47)	154	0.11
Bahamian (0)	16	0.01
Haitian (15)	64	0.05
Jamaican (32)	58	0.04
West Indian (0)	16	0.01
Yugoslavian (72)	83	0.06

Hispanic Origin	Population	%
Hispanic or Latino (of any race)	58,730	40.73
Central American, ex. Mexican	7,505	5.21
Costa Rican	96	0.07
Guatemalan	1,504	1.04
Honduran	329	0.23
Nicaraguan	1,745	1.21
Panamanian	100	0.07
Salvadoran	3,676	2.55
Other Central American	55	0.04
Cuban	217	0.15
Dominican Republic	40	0.03
Mexican	43,597	30.24
Puerto Rican	2,232	1.55
South American	1,300	0.90
Argentinean	65	0.05
Bolivian	86	0.06
Chilean	82	0.06
Colombian	196	0.14
Ecuadorian	61	0.04
Paraguayan	3	<0.01
Peruvian	761	0.53
Uruguayan	4	<0.01
Venezuelan	28	0.02
Other South American	14	0.01
Other Hispanic or Latino	3,839	2.66

Race*	Population	%
African-American/Black (17,099)	19,451	13.49
Not Hispanic (16,297)	17,898	12.41
Hispanic (802)	1,553	1.08
American Indian/Alaska Native (1,396)	2,973	2.06
Not Hispanic (492)	1,414	0.98
Hispanic (904)	1,559	1.08
Aleut *(Alaska Native)* (1)	3	<0.01
Apache (45)	118	0.08
Arapaho (6)	10	0.01
Blackfeet (9)	79	0.05
Canadian/French Am. Ind. (1)	3	<0.01
Central American Ind. (8)	16	0.01
Cherokee (39)	303	0.21
Cheyenne (6)	9	0.01
Chickasaw (1)	9	0.01
Chippewa (15)	22	0.02
Choctaw (10)	68	0.05
Colville (3)	3	<0.01
Comanche (9)	14	0.01
Creek (3)	13	0.01
Crow (1)	6	<0.01
Delaware (0)	1	<0.01
Hopi (7)	20	0.01
Inupiat *(Alaska Native)* (1)	4	<0.01
Iroquois (2)	20	0.01
Kiowa (1)	4	<0.01
Lumbee (0)	2	<0.01
Mexican American Ind. (202)	309	0.21
Navajo (50)	104	0.07
Osage (0)	3	<0.01
Paiute (14)	21	0.01
Pima (5)	6	<0.01
Potawatomi (1)	6	<0.01
Pueblo (22)	34	0.02
Seminole (3)	17	0.01
Shoshone (2)	4	<0.01
Sioux (43)	84	0.06
South American Ind. (6)	14	0.01
Spanish American Ind. (8)	15	0.01
Tlingit-Haida *(Alaska Native)* (3)	10	0.01
Tohono O'Odham (3)	9	0.01
Tsimshian *(Alaska Native)* (3)	4	<0.01
Ute (3)	5	<0.01
Yakama (1)	5	<0.01
Yaqui (7)	26	0.02
Yuman (1)	2	<0.01
Yup'ik *(Alaska Native)* (1)	1	<0.01
Asian (31,666)	36,334	25.20
Not Hispanic (31,090)	34,827	24.15
Hispanic (576)	1,507	1.05
Bangladeshi (19)	20	0.01
Burmese (105)	120	0.08
Cambodian (229)	312	0.22
Chinese, ex. Taiwanese (5,421)	6,398	4.44
Filipino (15,058)	17,134	11.88
Hmong (37)	38	0.03
Indian (4,260)	5,409	3.75
Indonesian (121)	195	0.14
Japanese (715)	1,276	0.88
Korean (662)	846	0.59
Laotian (73)	106	0.07
Malaysian (23)	43	0.03
Nepalese (59)	63	0.04
Pakistani (183)	224	0.16
Sri Lankan (18)	19	0.01
Taiwanese (169)	206	0.14
Thai (120)	170	0.12
Vietnamese (3,416)	3,712	2.57
Hawaii Native/Pacific Islander (4,535)	6,708	4.65
Not Hispanic (4,290)	6,093	4.23
Hispanic (245)	615	0.43
Fijian (2,188)	2,535	1.76
Guamanian/Chamorro (271)	470	0.33
Marshallese (0)	2	<0.01
Native Hawaiian (261)	784	0.54
Samoan (673)	859	0.60
Tongan (627)	719	0.50
White (49,309)	56,207	38.98
Not Hispanic (27,178)	30,682	21.28
Hispanic (22,131)	25,525	17.70

Healdsburg

Place Type: City
County: Sonoma
Population: 11,254†

Ancestry‡	Population	%
African, Sub-Saharan (9)	9	0.08
African (9)	9	0.08
American (248)	248	2.24
Arab (0)	43	0.39
Arab (0)	25	0.23
Lebanese (0)	18	0.16
Austrian (21)	35	0.32
Basque (8)	8	0.07
British (13)	66	0.60
Canadian (0)	26	0.23
Croatian (11)	23	0.21
Czech (11)	86	0.78
Czechoslovakian (12)	32	0.29
Danish (25)	72	0.65
Dutch (11)	127	1.15
Eastern European (12)	12	0.11
English (529)	1,391	12.55
European (237)	282	2.54
Finnish (7)	53	0.48
French, ex. Basque (38)	246	2.22
French Canadian (50)	50	0.45

*Notes: † The Census 2010 population figure is used to calculate the percentages in the Hispanic Origin and Race categories. Ancestry percentages are based on the 2006-2010 American Community Survey population (not shown); ‡ Numbers in parentheses indicate the number of people reporting a single ancestry; * Numbers in parentheses indicate the number of persons reporting this race alone, not in combination with any other race; Please refer to the Explanation of Data for more information.*

Ancestry	Population	%
German (469)	1,737	15.67
Greek (0)	40	0.36
Hungarian (14)	34	0.31
Icelander (0)	10	0.09
Irish (341)	1,228	11.08
Italian (610)	1,668	15.05
Lithuanian (16)	85	0.77
Northern European (23)	33	0.30
Norwegian (47)	202	1.82
Polish (29)	131	1.18
Portuguese (41)	186	1.68
Russian (21)	77	0.69
Scandinavian (12)	62	0.56
Scotch-Irish (83)	189	1.71
Scottish (54)	311	2.81
Slovak (8)	8	0.07
Swedish (68)	190	1.71
Swiss (30)	146	1.32
Ukrainian (0)	9	0.08
Welsh (19)	151	1.36

Hispanic Origin	Population	%
Hispanic or Latino (of any race)	3,820	33.94
Central American, ex. Mexican	46	0.41
Costa Rican	4	0.04
Guatemalan	14	0.12
Honduran	6	0.05
Nicaraguan	14	0.12
Panamanian	1	0.01
Salvadoran	7	0.06
Cuban	19	0.17
Dominican Republic	1	0.01
Mexican	3,506	31.15
Puerto Rican	25	0.22
South American	28	0.25
Argentinean	4	0.04
Bolivian	6	0.05
Chilean	2	0.02
Colombian	5	0.04
Ecuadorian	6	0.05
Peruvian	5	0.04
Other Hispanic or Latino	195	1.73

Race*	Population	%
African-American/Black (56)	90	0.80
Not Hispanic (43)	74	0.66
Hispanic (13)	16	0.14
American Indian/Alaska Native (205)	316	2.81
Not Hispanic (66)	109	0.97
Hispanic (139)	207	1.84
Aleut *(Alaska Native)* (0)	2	0.02
Apache (4)	6	0.05
Blackfeet (1)	3	0.03
Cherokee (10)	24	0.21
Chippewa (0)	5	0.04
Choctaw (1)	8	0.07
Comanche (0)	1	0.01
Creek (0)	1	0.01
Hopi (1)	2	0.02
Houma (0)	1	0.01
Iroquois (0)	1	0.01
Mexican American Ind. (71)	81	0.72
Navajo (0)	2	0.02
Osage (0)	1	0.01
Spanish American Ind. (3)	7	0.06
Yaqui (1)	1	0.01
Asian (125)	212	1.88
Not Hispanic (112)	174	1.55
Hispanic (13)	38	0.34
Burmese (2)	2	0.02
Chinese, ex. Taiwanese (24)	50	0.44
Filipino (19)	44	0.39
Indian (15)	21	0.19
Indonesian (0)	2	0.02
Japanese (24)	50	0.44
Korean (4)	8	0.07
Nepalese (4)	4	0.04
Pakistani (7)	13	0.12
Taiwanese (2)	2	0.02
Thai (3)	8	0.07
Vietnamese (9)	14	0.12
Hawaii Native/Pacific Islander (18)	52	0.46
Not Hispanic (10)	22	0.20
Hispanic (8)	30	0.27
Fijian (8)	8	0.07
Guamanian/Chamorro (2)	4	0.04
Native Hawaiian (1)	13	0.12
Samoan (1)	1	0.01
White (8,334)	8,666	77.00
Not Hispanic (7,038)	7,179	63.79
Hispanic (1,296)	1,487	13.21

Hemet

Place Type: City
County: Riverside
Population: 78,657†

Ancestry‡	Population	%
African, Sub-Saharan (73)	212	0.28
African (36)	130	0.17
Ugandan (37)	37	0.05
Other Sub-Saharan African (0)	45	0.06
Albanian (12)	32	0.04
American (2,937)	2,937	3.84
Arab (131)	155	0.20
Arab (9)	33	0.04
Egyptian (9)	9	0.01
Jordanian (100)	100	0.13
Lebanese (13)	13	0.02
Armenian (11)	61	0.08
Assyrian/Chaldean/Syriac (0)	13	0.02
Australian (49)	57	0.07
Austrian (94)	231	0.30
Basque (0)	146	0.19
Belgian (25)	99	0.13
Brazilian (26)	26	0.03
British (224)	255	0.33
Canadian (235)	358	0.47
Celtic (0)	12	0.02
Croatian (19)	28	0.04
Czech (92)	237	0.31
Czechoslovakian (64)	112	0.15
Danish (178)	479	0.63
Dutch (345)	1,094	1.43
English (2,926)	8,359	10.94
European (345)	572	0.75
Finnish (18)	113	0.15
French, ex. Basque (394)	2,368	3.10
French Canadian (312)	470	0.62
German (2,855)	9,886	12.94
Greek (91)	201	0.26
Hungarian (126)	395	0.52
Icelander (15)	15	0.02
Irish (2,050)	7,059	9.24
Italian (1,430)	2,635	3.45
Latvian (44)	78	0.10
Lithuanian (84)	231	0.30
Luxemburger (7)	7	0.01
Northern European (22)	30	0.04
Norwegian (531)	1,283	1.68
Pennsylvania German (32)	71	0.09
Polish (377)	1,184	1.55
Portuguese (122)	326	0.43
Romanian (171)	229	0.30
Russian (166)	358	0.47
Scandinavian (195)	265	0.35
Scotch-Irish (348)	1,333	1.74
Scottish (296)	1,238	1.62
Serbian (15)	25	0.03
Slovak (77)	113	0.15
Soviet Union (34)	34	0.04
Swedish (351)	1,443	1.89
Swiss (9)	117	0.15
Turkish (12)	34	0.04
Ukrainian (137)	153	0.20
Welsh (160)	548	0.72
West Indian, ex. Hispanic (66)	119	0.16
Belizean (0)	12	0.02
Haitian (0)	27	0.04
Jamaican (66)	66	0.09
Trinidadian/Tobagonian (0)	14	0.02
Yugoslavian (6)	71	0.09

Hispanic Origin	Population	%
Hispanic or Latino (of any race)	28,150	35.79
Central American, ex. Mexican	788	1.00
Costa Rican	34	0.04
Guatemalan	235	0.30
Honduran	42	0.05
Nicaraguan	102	0.13
Panamanian	38	0.05
Salvadoran	330	0.42
Other Central American	7	0.01
Cuban	203	0.26
Dominican Republic	22	0.03
Mexican	24,271	30.86
Puerto Rican	627	0.80
South American	357	0.45
Argentinean	53	0.07
Bolivian	17	0.02
Chilean	11	0.01
Colombian	101	0.13
Ecuadorian	48	0.06
Paraguayan	3	<0.01
Peruvian	98	0.12
Uruguayan	8	0.01
Venezuelan	9	0.01
Other South American	9	0.01
Other Hispanic or Latino	1,882	2.39

Race*	Population	%
African-American/Black (5,049)	6,236	7.93
Not Hispanic (4,711)	5,503	7.00
Hispanic (338)	733	0.93
American Indian/Alaska Native (1,223)	2,237	2.84
Not Hispanic (549)	1,176	1.50
Hispanic (674)	1,061	1.35
Alaska Athabascan *(Ala. Nat.)* (6)	6	0.01
Aleut *(Alaska Native)* (1)	2	<0.01
Apache (58)	109	0.14
Arapaho (0)	8	0.01
Blackfeet (8)	54	0.07
Canadian/French Am. Ind. (5)	6	0.01
Central American Ind. (1)	3	<0.01
Cherokee (54)	267	0.34
Cheyenne (1)	10	0.01
Chickasaw (7)	15	0.02
Chippewa (9)	17	0.02
Choctaw (21)	81	0.10
Colville (1)	1	<0.01
Comanche (5)	7	0.01
Creek (15)	22	0.03
Crow (0)	2	<0.01
Delaware (0)	1	<0.01
Hopi (0)	7	0.01
Iroquois (3)	14	0.02
Lumbee (4)	11	0.01
Menominee (6)	6	0.01
Mexican American Ind. (81)	115	0.15
Navajo (39)	64	0.08
Osage (4)	9	0.01
Ottawa (8)	15	0.02
Paiute (10)	14	0.02
Pima (3)	5	0.01
Potawatomi (4)	5	0.01
Pueblo (1)	9	0.01
Seminole (2)	7	0.01
Shoshone (2)	5	0.01
Sioux (12)	25	0.03
South American Ind. (1)	1	<0.01
Spanish American Ind. (11)	13	0.02
Tlingit-Haida *(Alaska Native)* (1)	1	<0.01
Tohono O'Odham (4)	4	0.01
Ute (1)	7	0.01
Yaqui (7)	37	0.05
Yuman (14)	14	0.02
Asian (2,352)	3,324	4.23
Not Hispanic (2,197)	2,876	3.66
Hispanic (155)	448	0.57

SECTION TWO

*Notes: † The Census 2010 population figure is used to calculate the percentages in the Hispanic Origin and Race categories. Ancestry percentages are based on the 2006-2010 American Community Survey population (not shown); ‡ Numbers in parentheses indicate the number of people reporting a single ancestry; * Numbers in parentheses indicate the number of persons reporting this race alone, not in combination with any other race; Please refer to the Explanation of Data for more information.*

Bangladeshi (1)	1	<0.01
Burmese (5)	9	0.01
Cambodian (82)	108	0.14
Chinese, ex. Taiwanese (202)	284	0.36
Filipino (1,233)	1,733	2.20
Hmong (14)	15	0.02
Indian (176)	218	0.28
Indonesian (21)	57	0.07
Japanese (137)	313	0.40
Korean (78)	130	0.17
Laotian (41)	50	0.06
Malaysian (3)	6	0.01
Nepalese (3)	3	<0.01
Pakistani (29)	32	0.04
Sri Lankan (3)	5	0.01
Taiwanese (25)	25	0.03
Thai (44)	82	0.10
Vietnamese (166)	207	0.26
Hawaii Native/Pacific Islander (284)	606	0.77
Not Hispanic (239)	474	0.60
Hispanic (45)	132	0.17
Fijian (0)	1	<0.01
Guamanian/Chamorro (61)	129	0.16
Native Hawaiian (72)	187	0.24
Samoan (82)	133	0.17
Tongan (28)	50	0.06
White (53,259)	56,784	72.19
Not Hispanic (40,723)	42,479	54.01
Hispanic (12,536)	14,305	18.19

Hercules

Place Type: City
County: Contra Costa
Population: 24,060†

Ancestry‡	Population	%
African, Sub-Saharan (660)	660	2.86
African (257)	257	1.11
Ethiopian (182)	182	0.79
Liberian (30)	30	0.13
Nigerian (184)	184	0.80
Somalian (7)	7	0.03
American (105)	105	0.46
Arab (255)	293	1.27
Arab (13)	51	0.22
Egyptian (15)	15	0.07
Iraqi (100)	100	0.43
Palestinian (127)	127	0.55
Armenian (11)	28	0.12
Austrian (17)	30	0.13
Belgian (27)	27	0.12
Brazilian (139)	139	0.60
British (0)	66	0.29
Canadian (12)	12	0.05
Czech (0)	38	0.16
Czechoslovakian (10)	32	0.14
Danish (13)	39	0.17
Dutch (0)	94	0.41
English (163)	738	3.20
European (332)	450	1.95
Finnish (14)	60	0.26
French, ex. Basque (0)	244	1.06
French Canadian (0)	33	0.14
German (355)	1,136	4.93
Hungarian (0)	10	0.04
Iranian (11)	11	0.05
Irish (279)	878	3.81
Italian (132)	782	3.39
Latvian (13)	13	0.06
Lithuanian (0)	46	0.20
Northern European (20)	65	0.28
Norwegian (22)	108	0.47
Polish (11)	23	0.10
Portuguese (101)	334	1.45
Russian (88)	139	0.60
Scotch-Irish (14)	138	0.60
Scottish (86)	308	1.34
Slovak (0)	10	0.04
Slovene (10)	10	0.04
Swedish (45)	199	0.86
Swiss (0)	28	0.12
Turkish (8)	16	0.07
Ukrainian (0)	13	0.06
Welsh (0)	90	0.39
West Indian, ex. Hispanic (120)	133	0.58
Jamaican (0)	13	0.06
West Indian (120)	120	0.52
Yugoslavian (9)	9	0.04

Hispanic Origin	Population	%
Hispanic or Latino (of any race)	3,508	14.58
Central American, ex. Mexican	641	2.66
Costa Rican	7	0.03
Guatemalan	48	0.20
Honduran	22	0.09
Nicaraguan	182	0.76
Panamanian	15	0.06
Salvadoran	360	1.50
Other Central American	7	0.03
Cuban	31	0.13
Dominican Republic	9	0.04
Mexican	2,164	8.99
Puerto Rican	138	0.57
South American	231	0.96
Argentinean	16	0.07
Bolivian	7	0.03
Chilean	37	0.15
Colombian	26	0.11
Ecuadorian	4	0.02
Peruvian	118	0.49
Uruguayan	1	<0.01
Venezuelan	15	0.06
Other South American	7	0.03
Other Hispanic or Latino	294	1.22

Race*	Population	%
African-American/Black (4,547)	5,028	20.90
Not Hispanic (4,434)	4,826	20.06
Hispanic (113)	202	0.84
American Indian/Alaska Native (102)	296	1.23
Not Hispanic (65)	200	0.83
Hispanic (37)	96	0.40
Apache (2)	3	0.01
Blackfeet (2)	9	0.04
Canadian/French Am. Ind. (0)	2	0.01
Central American Ind. (0)	1	<0.01
Cherokee (3)	37	0.15
Chippewa (2)	7	0.03
Choctaw (1)	6	0.02
Comanche (0)	1	<0.01
Creek (2)	10	0.04
Iroquois (0)	3	0.01
Mexican American Ind. (11)	19	0.08
Navajo (1)	4	0.02
Paiute (0)	2	0.01
Potawatomi (0)	2	0.01
Pueblo (1)	3	0.01
Sioux (1)	2	0.01
South American Ind. (0)	1	<0.01
Spanish American Ind. (0)	1	<0.01
Tohono O'Odham (1)	4	0.02
Yaqui (3)	3	0.01
Asian (10,956)	11,815	49.11
Not Hispanic (10,801)	11,490	47.76
Hispanic (155)	325	1.35
Bangladeshi (14)	15	0.06
Burmese (30)	38	0.16
Cambodian (81)	110	0.46
Chinese, ex. Taiwanese (1,986)	2,363	9.82
Filipino (6,034)	6,670	27.72
Indian (1,083)	1,182	4.91
Indonesian (25)	37	0.15
Japanese (226)	347	1.44
Korean (259)	308	1.28
Laotian (228)	255	1.06
Malaysian (2)	19	0.08
Nepalese (6)	6	0.02
Pakistani (101)	117	0.49
Sri Lankan (9)	9	0.04
Taiwanese (47)	53	0.22
Thai (35)	57	0.24
Vietnamese (401)	471	1.96
Hawaii Native/Pacific Islander (101)	245	1.02
Not Hispanic (92)	227	0.94
Hispanic (9)	18	0.07
Fijian (31)	39	0.16
Guamanian/Chamorro (9)	32	0.13
Native Hawaiian (18)	56	0.23
Samoan (24)	42	0.17
Tongan (5)	11	0.05
White (5,302)	6,345	26.37
Not Hispanic (4,026)	4,737	19.69
Hispanic (1,276)	1,608	6.68

Hermosa Beach

Place Type: City
County: Los Angeles
Population: 19,506†

Ancestry‡	Population	%
Afghan (98)	98	0.51
African, Sub-Saharan (51)	51	0.26
African (51)	51	0.26
American (746)	746	3.85
Arab (46)	157	0.81
Egyptian (21)	21	0.11
Lebanese (0)	35	0.18
Syrian (25)	101	0.52
Armenian (184)	230	1.19
Australian (28)	48	0.25
Austrian (0)	197	1.02
Basque (0)	14	0.07
Brazilian (102)	102	0.53
British (96)	190	0.98
Canadian (36)	82	0.42
Celtic (10)	10	0.05
Croatian (16)	27	0.14
Czech (15)	130	0.67
Danish (55)	168	0.87
Dutch (68)	440	2.27
Eastern European (67)	99	0.51
English (653)	2,663	13.76
European (428)	552	2.85
Finnish (70)	124	0.64
French, ex. Basque (270)	1,000	5.17
French Canadian (0)	85	0.44
German (1,067)	4,061	20.98
Greek (12)	174	0.90
Hungarian (28)	157	0.81
Icelander (22)	55	0.28
Irish (1,188)	3,317	17.14
Italian (723)	1,608	8.31
Lithuanian (39)	142	0.73
Northern European (127)	127	0.66
Norwegian (51)	265	1.37
Polish (78)	511	2.64
Portuguese (0)	27	0.14
Romanian (0)	12	0.06
Russian (100)	289	1.49
Scandinavian (10)	10	0.05
Scotch-Irish (192)	340	1.76
Scottish (120)	585	3.02
Serbian (8)	16	0.08
Slovak (15)	29	0.15
Slovene (14)	25	0.13
Swedish (134)	573	2.96
Swiss (57)	138	0.71
Turkish (11)	11	0.06
Ukrainian (31)	108	0.56
Welsh (67)	152	0.79
West Indian, ex. Hispanic (24)	24	0.12
Haitian (12)	12	0.06
Jamaican (12)	12	0.06
Yugoslavian (44)	44	0.23

Hispanic Origin	Population	%
Hispanic or Latino (of any race)	1,632	8.37
Central American, ex. Mexican	120	0.62

*Notes: † The Census 2010 population figure is used to calculate the percentages in the Hispanic Origin and Race categories. Ancestry percentages are based on the 2006-2010 American Community Survey population (not shown); ‡ Numbers in parentheses indicate the number of people reporting a single ancestry; * Numbers in parentheses indicate the number of persons reporting this race alone, not in combination with any other race; Please refer to the Explanation of Data for more information.*

Costa Rican	30	0.15
Guatemalan	30	0.15
Honduran	5	0.03
Nicaraguan	10	0.05
Panamanian	6	0.03
Salvadoran	35	0.18
Other Central American	4	0.02
Cuban	64	0.33
Dominican Republic	8	0.04
Mexican	933	4.78
Puerto Rican	77	0.39
South American	200	1.03
Argentinean	32	0.16
Bolivian	9	0.05
Chilean	16	0.08
Colombian	57	0.29
Ecuadorian	30	0.15
Peruvian	47	0.24
Uruguayan	1	0.01
Venezuelan	4	0.02
Other South American	4	0.02
Other Hispanic or Latino	230	1.18

Race*	Population	%
African-American/Black (229)	336	1.72
Not Hispanic (216)	290	1.49
Hispanic (13)	46	0.24
American Indian/Alaska Native (49)	170	0.87
Not Hispanic (28)	116	0.59
Hispanic (21)	54	0.28
Aleut *(Alaska Native)* (1)	1	0.01
Apache (1)	8	0.04
Blackfeet (0)	7	0.04
Central American Ind. (1)	2	0.01
Cherokee (0)	34	0.17
Chickasaw (1)	1	0.01
Chippewa (1)	3	0.02
Choctaw (1)	5	0.03
Comanche (0)	2	0.01
Hopi (2)	2	0.01
Inupiat *(Alaska Native)* (1)	1	0.01
Iroquois (0)	2	0.01
Mexican American Ind. (4)	5	0.03
Navajo (2)	6	0.03
Paiute (0)	2	0.01
Pima (2)	2	0.01
Potawatomi (3)	3	0.02
Pueblo (1)	1	0.01
Seminole (0)	1	0.01
Sioux (1)	1	0.01
South American Ind. (1)	1	0.01
Ute (0)	1	0.01
Yakama (0)	1	0.01
Yaqui (0)	2	0.01
Asian (1,111)	1,623	8.32
Not Hispanic (1,097)	1,576	8.08
Hispanic (14)	47	0.24
Burmese (1)	1	0.01
Cambodian (1)	7	0.04
Chinese, ex. Taiwanese (282)	440	2.26
Filipino (173)	294	1.51
Hmong (1)	1	0.01
Indian (102)	136	0.70
Indonesian (6)	21	0.11
Japanese (229)	362	1.86
Korean (122)	175	0.90
Laotian (3)	4	0.02
Malaysian (2)	3	0.02
Pakistani (5)	5	0.03
Sri Lankan (0)	1	0.01
Taiwanese (30)	40	0.21
Thai (20)	31	0.16
Vietnamese (77)	110	0.56
Hawaii Native/Pacific Islander (46)	96	0.49
Not Hispanic (43)	84	0.43
Hispanic (3)	12	0.06
Fijian (2)	2	0.01
Guamanian/Chamorro (5)	13	0.07
Native Hawaiian (27)	40	0.21
Samoan (4)	12	0.06
White (16,928)	17,704	90.76
Not Hispanic (15,780)	16,408	84.12
Hispanic (1,148)	1,296	6.64

Hesperia

Place Type: City
County: San Bernardino
Population: 90,173†

Ancestry‡	Population	%
Afghan (40)	40	0.05
African, Sub-Saharan (129)	176	0.20
African (97)	144	0.17
Ethiopian (32)	32	0.04
American (2,195)	2,195	2.54
Arab (150)	150	0.17
Arab (43)	43	0.05
Egyptian (39)	39	0.05
Jordanian (46)	46	0.05
Lebanese (22)	22	0.03
Armenian (11)	36	0.04
Australian (0)	38	0.04
Austrian (64)	110	0.13
Basque (26)	44	0.05
Belgian (17)	17	0.02
Brazilian (22)	31	0.04
British (115)	213	0.25
Canadian (54)	131	0.15
Celtic (31)	31	0.04
Croatian (43)	78	0.09
Czech (26)	170	0.20
Czechoslovakian (0)	12	0.01
Danish (81)	265	0.31
Dutch (218)	1,308	1.51
English (2,453)	6,901	7.99
European (858)	910	1.05
Finnish (0)	31	0.04
French, ex. Basque (380)	2,174	2.52
French Canadian (88)	289	0.33
German (2,408)	9,140	10.58
Greek (44)	393	0.45
Hungarian (78)	132	0.15
Irish (1,701)	7,883	9.12
Italian (1,108)	3,697	4.28
Lithuanian (10)	77	0.09
Maltese (0)	21	0.02
Northern European (13)	13	0.02
Norwegian (218)	930	1.08
Pennsylvania German (31)	63	0.07
Polish (235)	1,045	1.21
Portuguese (302)	504	0.58
Romanian (0)	37	0.04
Russian (255)	547	0.63
Scandinavian (7)	76	0.09
Scotch-Irish (233)	743	0.86
Scottish (359)	998	1.16
Slavic (0)	27	0.03
Slovak (24)	56	0.06
Swedish (179)	882	1.02
Swiss (28)	127	0.15
Ukrainian (0)	19	0.02
Welsh (0)	287	0.33
West Indian, ex. Hispanic (93)	162	0.19
Belizean (0)	17	0.02
Jamaican (93)	145	0.17

Hispanic Origin	Population	%
Hispanic or Latino (of any race)	44,091	48.90
Central American, ex. Mexican	2,847	3.16
Costa Rican	55	0.06
Guatemalan	863	0.96
Honduran	183	0.20
Nicaraguan	202	0.22
Panamanian	39	0.04
Salvadoran	1,450	1.61
Other Central American	55	0.06
Cuban	237	0.26
Dominican Republic	18	0.02
Mexican	36,486	40.46
Puerto Rican	626	0.69
South American	454	0.50
Argentinean	86	0.10
Bolivian	13	0.01
Chilean	37	0.04
Colombian	107	0.12
Ecuadorian	65	0.07
Peruvian	128	0.14
Uruguayan	3	<0.01
Venezuelan	8	0.01
Other South American	7	0.01
Other Hispanic or Latino	3,423	3.80

Race*	Population	%
African-American/Black (5,226)	6,214	6.89
Not Hispanic (4,853)	5,484	6.08
Hispanic (373)	730	0.81
American Indian/Alaska Native (1,118)	2,050	2.27
Not Hispanic (412)	923	1.02
Hispanic (706)	1,127	1.25
Aleut *(Alaska Native)* (1)	1	<0.01
Apache (66)	126	0.14
Arapaho (0)	1	<0.01
Blackfeet (2)	30	0.03
Canadian/French Am. Ind. (0)	1	<0.01
Central American Ind. (2)	6	0.01
Cherokee (75)	281	0.31
Cheyenne (3)	8	0.01
Chickasaw (2)	18	0.02
Chippewa (12)	20	0.02
Choctaw (22)	50	0.06
Comanche (2)	6	0.01
Cree (0)	1	<0.01
Creek (6)	16	0.02
Delaware (3)	4	<0.01
Hopi (15)	17	0.02
Inupiat *(Alaska Native)* (0)	3	<0.01
Iroquois (1)	12	0.01
Kiowa (0)	4	<0.01
Lumbee (2)	2	<0.01
Mexican American Ind. (118)	164	0.18
Navajo (25)	49	0.05
Osage (2)	2	<0.01
Ottawa (0)	1	<0.01
Paiute (3)	9	0.01
Pima (14)	20	0.02
Potawatomi (8)	14	0.02
Pueblo (10)	21	0.02
Seminole (2)	5	0.01
Shoshone (3)	8	0.01
Sioux (19)	40	0.04
South American Ind. (3)	5	0.01
Spanish American Ind. (11)	15	0.02
Tlingit-Haida *(Alaska Native)* (9)	9	0.01
Tohono O'Odham (9)	19	0.02
Ute (5)	6	0.01
Yaqui (32)	59	0.07
Yuman (2)	3	<0.01
Yup'ik *(Alaska Native)* (0)	1	<0.01
Asian (1,884)	2,851	3.16
Not Hispanic (1,704)	2,337	2.59
Hispanic (180)	514	0.57
Bangladeshi (7)	7	0.01
Burmese (0)	2	<0.01
Cambodian (89)	105	0.12
Chinese, ex. Taiwanese (129)	244	0.27
Filipino (604)	954	1.06
Indian (194)	268	0.30
Indonesian (41)	71	0.08
Japanese (143)	371	0.41
Korean (249)	348	0.39
Laotian (6)	9	0.01
Malaysian (6)	14	0.02
Pakistani (8)	11	0.01
Sri Lankan (6)	6	0.01
Taiwanese (0)	5	0.01
Thai (20)	57	0.06
Vietnamese (309)	349	0.39
Hawaii Native/Pacific Islander (270)	563	0.62
Not Hispanic (205)	395	0.44

*Notes: † The Census 2010 population figure is used to calculate the percentages in the Hispanic Origin and Race categories. Ancestry percentages are based on the 2006-2010 American Community Survey population (not shown); ‡ Numbers in parentheses indicate the number of people reporting a single ancestry; * Numbers in parentheses indicate the number of persons reporting this race alone, not in combination with any other race; Please refer to the Explanation of Data for more information.*

Hispanic (65)	168	0.19
Fijian (1)	3	<0.01
Guamanian/Chamorro (35)	71	0.08
Native Hawaiian (78)	175	0.19
Samoan (95)	163	0.18
Tongan (24)	32	0.04
White (55,129)	58,853	65.27
Not Hispanic (37,027)	38,508	42.70
Hispanic (18,102)	20,345	22.56

Highland

Place Type: City
County: San Bernardino
Population: 53,104†

Ancestry‡	Population	%
African, Sub-Saharan (291)	385	0.74
African (25)	75	0.14
Ghanaian (41)	41	0.08
Nigerian (180)	180	0.34
Somalian (0)	44	0.08
Other Sub-Saharan African (45)	45	0.09
American (1,040)	1,040	1.99
Arab (410)	466	0.89
Arab (184)	184	0.35
Jordanian (33)	33	0.06
Lebanese (66)	109	0.21
Palestinian (16)	16	0.03
Syrian (106)	117	0.22
Other Arab (5)	7	0.01
Armenian (10)	68	0.13
Australian (11)	11	0.02
Austrian (0)	27	0.05
Basque (46)	79	0.15
Belgian (0)	9	0.02
British (4)	91	0.17
Canadian (32)	39	0.07
Croatian (0)	15	0.03
Czech (32)	69	0.13
Czechoslovakian (0)	48	0.09
Danish (0)	85	0.16
Dutch (56)	495	0.95
English (735)	2,809	5.37
European (136)	163	0.31
Finnish (0)	5	0.01
French, ex. Basque (122)	1,103	2.11
French Canadian (132)	188	0.36
German (1,212)	4,860	9.29
Greek (0)	21	0.04
Hungarian (29)	241	0.46
Icelander (28)	28	0.05
Iranian (0)	23	0.04
Irish (1,025)	3,993	7.63
Italian (611)	1,689	3.23
Latvian (0)	13	0.02
Lithuanian (96)	96	0.18
Northern European (36)	36	0.07
Norwegian (172)	681	1.30
Polish (166)	663	1.27
Portuguese (16)	197	0.38
Romanian (49)	49	0.09
Russian (276)	455	0.87
Scandinavian (0)	48	0.09
Scotch-Irish (73)	375	0.72
Scottish (145)	555	1.06
Slavic (3)	14	0.03
Slovak (22)	22	0.04
Slovene (0)	15	0.03
Swedish (86)	302	0.58
Swiss (11)	22	0.04
Ukrainian (10)	34	0.06
Welsh (0)	193	0.37
West Indian, ex. Hispanic (41)	55	0.11
British West Indian (12)	12	0.02
Haitian (21)	21	0.04
West Indian (8)	22	0.04
Yugoslavian (74)	74	0.14

Hispanic Origin	Population	%
Hispanic or Latino (of any race)	25,556	48.12
Central American, ex. Mexican	911	1.72
Costa Rican	35	0.07
Guatemalan	278	0.52
Honduran	94	0.18
Nicaraguan	113	0.21
Panamanian	25	0.05
Salvadoran	352	0.66
Other Central American	14	0.03
Cuban	156	0.29
Dominican Republic	15	0.03
Mexican	22,430	42.24
Puerto Rican	294	0.55
South American	252	0.47
Argentinean	45	0.08
Bolivian	5	0.01
Chilean	23	0.04
Colombian	45	0.08
Ecuadorian	39	0.07
Peruvian	72	0.14
Uruguayan	10	0.02
Venezuelan	11	0.02
Other South American	2	<0.01
Other Hispanic or Latino	1,498	2.82

Race*	Population	%
African-American/Black (5,887)	6,795	12.80
Not Hispanic (5,584)	6,220	11.71
Hispanic (303)	575	1.08
American Indian/Alaska Native (542)	1,092	2.06
Not Hispanic (233)	543	1.02
Hispanic (309)	549	1.03
Alaska Athabascan *(Ala. Nat.)* (1)	3	0.01
Aleut *(Alaska Native)* (0)	2	<0.01
Apache (26)	38	0.07
Arapaho (1)	2	<0.01
Blackfeet (10)	62	0.12
Canadian/French Am. Ind. (0)	2	<0.01
Central American Ind. (1)	1	<0.01
Cherokee (33)	116	0.22
Cheyenne (2)	2	<0.01
Chickasaw (0)	7	0.01
Chippewa (6)	16	0.03
Choctaw (6)	39	0.07
Colville (1)	1	<0.01
Comanche (0)	1	<0.01
Creek (7)	14	0.03
Hopi (2)	7	0.01
Iroquois (5)	7	0.01
Mexican American Ind. (55)	77	0.14
Navajo (18)	24	0.05
Osage (1)	3	0.01
Ottawa (0)	1	<0.01
Paiute (3)	3	0.01
Pima (1)	1	<0.01
Potawatomi (2)	5	0.01
Pueblo (11)	16	0.03
Seminole (2)	7	0.01
Shoshone (0)	2	<0.01
Sioux (10)	22	0.04
South American Ind. (1)	3	0.01
Spanish American Ind. (0)	1	<0.01
Tlingit-Haida *(Alaska Native)* (1)	1	<0.01
Tohono O'Odham (4)	8	0.02
Yaqui (21)	30	0.06
Asian (3,954)	4,775	8.99
Not Hispanic (3,812)	4,431	8.34
Hispanic (142)	344	0.65
Bangladeshi (35)	35	0.07
Burmese (1)	1	<0.01
Cambodian (186)	230	0.43
Chinese, ex. Taiwanese (278)	425	0.80
Filipino (1,044)	1,405	2.65
Indian (328)	379	0.71
Indonesian (163)	206	0.39
Japanese (120)	264	0.50
Korean (198)	250	0.47
Laotian (21)	33	0.06
Malaysian (3)	7	0.01
Pakistani (70)	92	0.17
Taiwanese (18)	24	0.05
Thai (126)	158	0.30
Vietnamese (1,222)	1,312	2.47
Hawaii Native/Pacific Islander (168)	370	0.70
Not Hispanic (159)	287	0.54
Hispanic (9)	83	0.16
Fijian (14)	14	0.03
Guamanian/Chamorro (20)	51	0.10
Native Hawaiian (28)	108	0.20
Samoan (80)	121	0.23
Tongan (11)	14	0.03
White (27,836)	30,159	56.79
Not Hispanic (16,347)	17,384	32.74
Hispanic (11,489)	12,775	24.06

Hillsborough

Place Type: Town
County: San Mateo
Population: 10,825†

Ancestry‡	Population	%
African, Sub-Saharan (0)	11	0.10
African (0)	11	0.10
American (241)	241	2.26
Arab (246)	422	3.96
Arab (11)	11	0.10
Lebanese (102)	278	2.61
Palestinian (84)	84	0.79
Syrian (8)	8	0.08
Other Arab (41)	41	0.38
Armenian (94)	130	1.22
Austrian (37)	177	1.66
Belgian (17)	70	0.66
British (75)	113	1.06
Canadian (32)	41	0.38
Croatian (0)	26	0.24
Czech (34)	34	0.32
Czechoslovakian (9)	9	0.08
Danish (26)	141	1.32
Dutch (13)	79	0.74
Eastern European (46)	46	0.43
English (409)	1,397	13.12
European (305)	324	3.04
French, ex. Basque (42)	424	3.98
French Canadian (0)	30	0.28
German (389)	1,416	13.30
Greek (127)	201	1.89
Hungarian (48)	140	1.31
Iranian (235)	235	2.21
Irish (225)	1,235	11.60
Israeli (12)	12	0.11
Italian (375)	853	8.01
Latvian (0)	16	0.15
Lithuanian (0)	30	0.28
Macedonian (8)	8	0.08
Maltese (38)	116	1.09
Northern European (34)	34	0.32
Norwegian (23)	123	1.15
Polish (126)	234	2.20
Portuguese (8)	70	0.66
Russian (98)	244	2.29
Scandinavian (7)	25	0.23
Scotch-Irish (58)	98	0.92
Scottish (23)	156	1.46
Slovak (29)	38	0.36
Swedish (53)	174	1.63
Swiss (0)	47	0.44
Ukrainian (11)	40	0.38
Welsh (0)	23	0.22

Hispanic Origin	Population	%
Hispanic or Latino (of any race)	373	3.45
Central American, ex. Mexican	53	0.49
Guatemalan	8	0.07
Nicaraguan	11	0.10
Panamanian	4	0.04
Salvadoran	30	0.28
Cuban	20	0.18

*Notes: † The Census 2010 population figure is used to calculate the percentages in the Hispanic Origin and Race categories. Ancestry percentages are based on the 2006-2010 American Community Survey population (not shown); ‡ Numbers in parentheses indicate the number of people reporting a single ancestry; * Numbers in parentheses indicate the number of persons reporting this race alone, not in combination with any other race; Please refer to the Explanation of Data for more information.*

Dominican Republic	3	0.03
Mexican	145	1.34
Puerto Rican	12	0.11
South American	61	0.56
Argentinean	16	0.15
Bolivian	1	0.01
Chilean	7	0.06
Colombian	10	0.09
Ecuadorian	1	0.01
Peruvian	18	0.17
Venezuelan	5	0.05
Other South American	3	0.03
Other Hispanic or Latino	79	0.73

Race*	Population	%
African-American/Black (42)	71	0.66
Not Hispanic (40)	64	0.59
Hispanic (2)	7	0.06
American Indian/Alaska Native (7)	42	0.39
Not Hispanic (3)	25	0.23
Hispanic (4)	17	0.16
Cherokee (1)	9	0.08
Choctaw (0)	3	0.03
Lumbee (0)	4	0.04
Navajo (0)	1	0.01
Paiute (0)	5	0.05
Seminole (0)	1	0.01
Tlingit-Haida *(Alaska Native)* (1)	4	0.04
Asian (3,044)	3,382	31.24
Not Hispanic (3,030)	3,339	30.85
Hispanic (14)	43	0.40
Bangladeshi (2)	2	0.02
Burmese (12)	12	0.11
Cambodian (0)	1	0.01
Chinese, ex. Taiwanese (1,859)	2,100	19.40
Filipino (241)	341	3.15
Indian (272)	291	2.69
Indonesian (4)	9	0.08
Japanese (157)	250	2.31
Korean (138)	180	1.66
Laotian (2)	4	0.04
Pakistani (21)	22	0.20
Sri Lankan (2)	3	0.03
Taiwanese (147)	170	1.57
Thai (10)	13	0.12
Vietnamese (34)	46	0.42
Hawaii Native/Pacific Islander (23)	48	0.44
Not Hispanic (23)	45	0.42
Hispanic (0)	3	0.03
Fijian (4)	7	0.06
Guamanian/Chamorro (1)	1	0.01
Native Hawaiian (0)	7	0.06
Samoan (1)	1	0.01
Tongan (16)	18	0.17
White (7,178)	7,565	69.88
Not Hispanic (6,955)	7,294	67.38
Hispanic (223)	271	2.50

Hollister

Place Type: City
County: San Benito
Population: 34,928†

Ancestry‡	Population	%
African, Sub-Saharan (0)	45	0.13
African (0)	45	0.13
American (875)	875	2.53
Arab (161)	187	0.54
Arab (48)	74	0.21
Lebanese (113)	113	0.33
Australian (84)	84	0.24
Basque (28)	111	0.32
British (93)	169	0.49
Cajun (0)	31	0.09
Canadian (15)	57	0.17
Celtic (16)	16	0.05
Croatian (0)	18	0.05
Czech (75)	256	0.74
Danish (40)	176	0.51
Dutch (39)	165	0.48
Eastern European (0)	17	0.05
English (296)	2,041	5.91
European (247)	568	1.64
Finnish (0)	15	0.04
French, ex. Basque (9)	721	2.09
French Canadian (0)	67	0.19
German (419)	2,436	7.05
Greek (11)	11	0.03
Hungarian (0)	28	0.08
Irish (667)	2,404	6.96
Italian (699)	2,089	6.05
Lithuanian (0)	87	0.25
Maltese (8)	8	0.02
Northern European (14)	14	0.04
Norwegian (19)	174	0.50
Pennsylvania German (18)	18	0.05
Polish (20)	217	0.63
Portuguese (156)	949	2.75
Russian (7)	61	0.18
Scandinavian (25)	25	0.07
Scotch-Irish (170)	350	1.01
Scottish (122)	593	1.72
Swedish (48)	251	0.73
Swiss (33)	86	0.25
Ukrainian (12)	12	0.03
Welsh (0)	60	0.17
Yugoslavian (0)	6	0.02

Hispanic Origin	Population	%
Hispanic or Latino (of any race)	22,965	65.75
Central American, ex. Mexican	310	0.89
Costa Rican	13	0.04
Guatemalan	63	0.18
Honduran	46	0.13
Nicaraguan	43	0.12
Panamanian	7	0.02
Salvadoran	137	0.39
Other Central American	1	<0.01
Cuban	10	0.03
Dominican Republic	4	0.01
Mexican	21,304	60.99
Puerto Rican	171	0.49
South American	80	0.23
Argentinean	7	0.02
Bolivian	1	<0.01
Chilean	15	0.04
Colombian	20	0.06
Ecuadorian	5	0.01
Paraguayan	1	<0.01
Peruvian	24	0.07
Uruguayan	1	<0.01
Venezuelan	6	0.02
Other Hispanic or Latino	1,086	3.11

Race*	Population	%
African-American/Black (341)	571	1.63
Not Hispanic (247)	347	0.99
Hispanic (94)	224	0.64
American Indian/Alaska Native (617)	1,080	3.09
Not Hispanic (118)	298	0.85
Hispanic (499)	782	2.24
Apache (14)	40	0.11
Arapaho (1)	1	<0.01
Blackfeet (3)	25	0.07
Canadian/French Am. Ind. (1)	6	0.02
Cherokee (24)	103	0.29
Chickasaw (1)	2	0.01
Chippewa (5)	19	0.05
Choctaw (2)	10	0.03
Comanche (2)	3	0.01
Cree (0)	1	<0.01
Creek (1)	2	0.01
Hopi (6)	10	0.03
Inupiat *(Alaska Native)* (1)	3	0.01
Iroquois (1)	1	<0.01
Mexican American Ind. (206)	268	0.77
Navajo (5)	14	0.04
Osage (0)	4	0.01
Paiute (2)	3	0.01
Pima (2)	10	0.03
Potawatomi (3)	11	0.03
Pueblo (1)	11	0.03
Puget Sound Salish (1)	7	0.02
Seminole (1)	1	<0.01
Shoshone (1)	1	<0.01
Sioux (7)	11	0.03
South American Ind. (1)	1	<0.01
Spanish American Ind. (7)	21	0.06
Yaqui (5)	18	0.05
Asian (929)	1,444	4.13
Not Hispanic (824)	1,112	3.18
Hispanic (105)	332	0.95
Bangladeshi (1)	1	<0.01
Burmese (0)	3	0.01
Cambodian (12)	16	0.05
Chinese, ex. Taiwanese (84)	148	0.42
Filipino (519)	818	2.34
Indian (90)	107	0.31
Indonesian (0)	19	0.05
Japanese (92)	198	0.57
Korean (30)	46	0.13
Laotian (1)	1	<0.01
Pakistani (5)	7	0.02
Taiwanese (2)	7	0.02
Thai (5)	6	0.02
Vietnamese (47)	68	0.19
Hawaii Native/Pacific Islander (63)	166	0.48
Not Hispanic (38)	85	0.24
Hispanic (25)	81	0.23
Guamanian/Chamorro (17)	27	0.08
Native Hawaiian (18)	71	0.20
Samoan (4)	6	0.02
Tongan (1)	2	0.01
White (20,761)	22,239	63.67
Not Hispanic (10,163)	10,625	30.42
Hispanic (10,598)	11,614	33.25

Home Gardens

Place Type: CDP
County: Riverside
Population: 11,570†

Ancestry‡	Population	%
African, Sub-Saharan (71)	92	0.84
African (11)	11	0.10
Ethiopian (38)	59	0.54
Nigerian (14)	14	0.13
Other Sub-Saharan African (8)	8	0.07
American (123)	123	1.12
Arab (42)	63	0.58
Egyptian (22)	43	0.39
Lebanese (20)	20	0.18
British (0)	11	0.10
Canadian (0)	7	0.06
Czech (18)	51	0.47
Danish (15)	22	0.20
Dutch (24)	89	0.81
English (104)	335	3.06
European (69)	69	0.63
French, ex. Basque (13)	173	1.58
German (198)	626	5.72
Greek (0)	14	0.13
Hungarian (10)	10	0.09
Iranian (19)	19	0.17
Irish (22)	347	3.17
Italian (15)	94	0.86
Norwegian (63)	63	0.58
Polish (11)	17	0.16
Portuguese (29)	29	0.26
Romanian (16)	16	0.15
Russian (0)	12	0.11
Scandinavian (15)	60	0.55
Scotch-Irish (69)	117	1.07
Scottish (24)	53	0.48
Swedish (0)	73	0.67
Welsh (9)	36	0.33

SECTION TWO

*Notes: † The Census 2010 population figure is used to calculate the percentages in the Hispanic Origin and Race categories. Ancestry percentages are based on the 2006-2010 American Community Survey population (not shown); ‡ Numbers in parentheses indicate the number of people reporting a single ancestry; * Numbers in parentheses indicate the number of persons reporting this race alone, not in combination with any other race; Please refer to the Explanation of Data for more information.*

Hispanic Origin	Population	%
Hispanic or Latino (of any race)	8,524	73.67
Central American, ex. Mexican	451	3.90
Costa Rican	1	0.01
Guatemalan	281	2.43
Honduran	23	0.20
Nicaraguan	17	0.15
Panamanian	7	0.06
Salvadoran	108	0.93
Other Central American	14	0.12
Cuban	17	0.15
Dominican Republic	3	0.03
Mexican	7,647	66.09
Puerto Rican	35	0.30
South American	72	0.62
Argentinean	5	0.04
Colombian	21	0.18
Ecuadorian	9	0.08
Peruvian	33	0.29
Venezuelan	1	0.01
Other South American	3	0.03
Other Hispanic or Latino	299	2.58

Race*	Population	%
African-American/Black (364)	452	3.91
Not Hispanic (299)	359	3.10
Hispanic (65)	93	0.80
American Indian/Alaska Native (126)	212	1.83
Not Hispanic (35)	69	0.60
Hispanic (91)	143	1.24
Alaska Athabascan *(Ala. Nat.)* (1)	1	0.01
Apache (2)	5	0.04
Central American Ind. (8)	11	0.10
Cherokee (7)	11	0.10
Chickasaw (0)	1	0.01
Choctaw (0)	3	0.03
Crow (0)	1	0.01
Iroquois (3)	3	0.03
Kiowa (0)	2	0.02
Mexican American Ind. (25)	37	0.32
Navajo (3)	6	0.05
Pueblo (2)	2	0.02
Yaqui (0)	5	0.04
Asian (667)	780	6.74
Not Hispanic (648)	716	6.19
Hispanic (19)	64	0.55
Bangladeshi (4)	5	0.04
Cambodian (10)	13	0.11
Chinese, ex. Taiwanese (24)	42	0.36
Filipino (292)	332	2.87
Hmong (2)	2	0.02
Indian (73)	88	0.76
Indonesian (28)	34	0.29
Japanese (17)	39	0.34
Korean (26)	27	0.23
Laotian (13)	16	0.14
Pakistani (19)	25	0.22
Sri Lankan (11)	11	0.10
Taiwanese (3)	4	0.03
Thai (8)	18	0.16
Vietnamese (119)	128	1.11
Hawaii Native/Pacific Islander (51)	85	0.73
Not Hispanic (42)	65	0.56
Hispanic (9)	20	0.17
Fijian (3)	3	0.03
Guamanian/Chamorro (15)	25	0.22
Native Hawaiian (8)	20	0.17
Samoan (17)	19	0.16
Tongan (7)	9	0.08
White (5,275)	5,774	49.90
Not Hispanic (1,866)	1,967	17.00
Hispanic (3,409)	3,807	32.90

Huntington Beach

Place Type: City
County: Orange
Population: 189,992†

Ancestry‡	Population	%
Afghan (24)	24	0.01
African, Sub-Saharan (156)	268	0.14
African (82)	183	0.10
Ethiopian (10)	10	0.01
Nigerian (0)	11	0.01
South African (48)	48	0.03
Other Sub-Saharan African (16)	16	0.01
Albanian (0)	15	0.01
Alsatian (0)	10	0.01
American (6,150)	6,150	3.26
Arab (1,895)	2,455	1.30
Arab (197)	255	0.13
Egyptian (1,048)	1,048	0.55
Iraqi (9)	46	0.02
Jordanian (171)	171	0.09
Lebanese (158)	453	0.24
Moroccan (0)	80	0.04
Palestinian (53)	98	0.05
Syrian (88)	114	0.06
Other Arab (171)	190	0.10
Armenian (472)	695	0.37
Assyrian/Chaldean/Syriac (16)	16	0.01
Australian (110)	391	0.21
Austrian (198)	728	0.39
Basque (11)	23	0.01
Belgian (29)	168	0.09
Brazilian (307)	450	0.24
British (597)	1,185	0.63
Bulgarian (9)	60	0.03
Cajun (17)	28	0.01
Canadian (256)	799	0.42
Celtic (14)	21	0.01
Croatian (169)	618	0.33
Czech (333)	1,079	0.57
Czechoslovakian (46)	214	0.11
Danish (483)	1,987	1.05
Dutch (1,103)	4,608	2.44
Eastern European (251)	274	0.15
English (6,172)	21,837	11.56
Estonian (0)	11	0.01
European (2,703)	3,207	1.70
Finnish (41)	445	0.24
French, ex. Basque (950)	6,793	3.60
French Canadian (401)	1,008	0.53
German (9,715)	32,622	17.27
Greek (561)	1,199	0.63
Hungarian (605)	1,920	1.02
Icelander (54)	61	0.03
Iranian (435)	478	0.25
Irish (6,383)	24,675	13.06
Israeli (48)	197	0.10
Italian (6,522)	15,311	8.10
Latvian (0)	77	0.04
Lithuanian (154)	629	0.33
Luxemburger (15)	73	0.04
Macedonian (0)	48	0.03
Maltese (9)	49	0.03
New Zealander (7)	80	0.04
Northern European (199)	273	0.14
Norwegian (1,463)	3,981	2.11
Pennsylvania German (35)	94	0.05
Polish (1,553)	4,968	2.63
Portuguese (473)	1,256	0.66
Romanian (408)	1,012	0.54
Russian (1,461)	3,421	1.81
Scandinavian (230)	539	0.29
Scotch-Irish (1,179)	3,816	2.02
Scottish (1,735)	5,014	2.65
Serbian (46)	75	0.04
Slavic (35)	95	0.05
Slovak (188)	427	0.23
Slovene (23)	159	0.08
Swedish (882)	4,208	2.23
Swiss (177)	688	0.36
Turkish (161)	185	0.10
Ukrainian (296)	732	0.39
Welsh (258)	1,786	0.95
West Indian, ex. Hispanic (32)	71	0.04
Haitian (0)	23	0.01
Jamaican (15)	15	0.01
West Indian (17)	33	0.02
Yugoslavian (208)	514	0.27

Hispanic Origin	Population	%
Hispanic or Latino (of any race)	32,411	17.06
Central American, ex. Mexican	1,216	0.64
Costa Rican	118	0.06
Guatemalan	373	0.20
Honduran	107	0.06
Nicaraguan	137	0.07
Panamanian	62	0.03
Salvadoran	397	0.21
Other Central American	22	0.01
Cuban	633	0.33
Dominican Republic	38	0.02
Mexican	25,139	13.23
Puerto Rican	844	0.44
South American	1,805	0.95
Argentinean	394	0.21
Bolivian	75	0.04
Chilean	159	0.08
Colombian	418	0.22
Ecuadorian	216	0.11
Paraguayan	4	<0.01
Peruvian	411	0.22
Uruguayan	34	0.02
Venezuelan	67	0.04
Other South American	27	0.01
Other Hispanic or Latino	2,736	1.44

Race*	Population	%
African-American/Black (1,813)	2,774	1.46
Not Hispanic (1,635)	2,400	1.26
Hispanic (178)	374	0.20
American Indian/Alaska Native (992)	2,759	1.45
Not Hispanic (532)	1,778	0.94
Hispanic (460)	981	0.52
Alaska Athabascan *(Ala. Nat.)* (0)	2	<0.01
Aleut *(Alaska Native)* (2)	6	<0.01
Apache (50)	138	0.07
Blackfeet (8)	79	0.04
Canadian/French Am. Ind. (6)	13	0.01
Central American Ind. (0)	2	<0.01
Cherokee (93)	470	0.25
Cheyenne (4)	7	<0.01
Chickasaw (8)	20	0.01
Chippewa (29)	68	0.04
Choctaw (30)	139	0.07
Colville (0)	1	<0.01
Comanche (4)	21	0.01
Cree (2)	6	<0.01
Creek (19)	40	0.02
Crow (0)	8	<0.01
Delaware (4)	12	0.01
Hopi (7)	14	0.01
Inupiat *(Alaska Native)* (7)	12	0.01
Iroquois (5)	37	0.02
Kiowa (1)	3	<0.01
Lumbee (8)	10	0.01
Menominee (0)	3	<0.01
Mexican American Ind. (104)	147	0.08
Navajo (26)	64	0.03
Osage (4)	21	0.01
Ottawa (2)	3	<0.01
Paiute (2)	8	<0.01
Pima (5)	7	<0.01
Potawatomi (12)	19	0.01
Pueblo (12)	26	0.01
Puget Sound Salish (2)	3	<0.01
Seminole (6)	19	0.01
Shoshone (8)	25	0.01
Sioux (25)	61	0.03
South American Ind. (3)	14	0.01
Spanish American Ind. (2)	8	<0.01
Tlingit-Haida *(Alaska Native)* (2)	5	<0.01
Tohono O'Odham (2)	7	<0.01
Ute (2)	2	<0.01
Yakama (1)	1	<0.01

*Notes: † The Census 2010 population figure is used to calculate the percentages in the Hispanic Origin and Race categories. Ancestry percentages are based on the 2006-2010 American Community Survey population (not shown); ‡ Numbers in parentheses indicate the number of people reporting a single ancestry; * Numbers in parentheses indicate the number of persons reporting this race alone, not in combination with any other race; Please refer to the Explanation of Data for more information.*

Yaqui (16)	46	0.02
Yuman (7)	11	0.01
Yup'ik *(Alaska Native)* (2)	5	<0.01
Asian (21,070)	25,619	13.48
Not Hispanic (20,792)	24,694	13.00
Hispanic (278)	925	0.49
Bangladeshi (17)	18	0.01
Burmese (29)	32	0.02
Cambodian (171)	227	0.12
Chinese, ex. Taiwanese (3,203)	4,507	2.37
Filipino (2,474)	3,863	2.03
Hmong (25)	32	0.02
Indian (967)	1,173	0.62
Indonesian (98)	263	0.14
Japanese (2,953)	4,451	2.34
Korean (1,610)	1,990	1.05
Laotian (45)	64	0.03
Malaysian (22)	33	0.02
Nepalese (2)	2	<0.01
Pakistani (145)	161	0.08
Sri Lankan (55)	66	0.03
Taiwanese (503)	548	0.29
Thai (293)	403	0.21
Vietnamese (7,585)	8,215	4.32
Hawaii Native/Pacific Islander (635)	1,578	0.83
Not Hispanic (595)	1,374	0.72
Hispanic (40)	204	0.11
Fijian (2)	7	<0.01
Guamanian/Chamorro (105)	209	0.11
Marshallese (19)	24	0.01
Native Hawaiian (183)	668	0.35
Samoan (195)	327	0.17
Tongan (46)	61	0.03
White (145,661)	153,515	80.80
Not Hispanic (127,640)	133,155	70.08
Hispanic (18,021)	20,360	10.72

Huntington Park

Place Type: City
County: Los Angeles
Population: 58,114†

Ancestry‡	Population	%
African, Sub-Saharan (23)	23	0.04
African (23)	23	0.04
American (707)	707	1.21
Armenian (0)	36	0.06
British (11)	11	0.02
Bulgarian (11)	11	0.02
Canadian (8)	8	0.01
Dutch (0)	72	0.12
English (0)	39	0.07
Estonian (14)	14	0.02
French, ex. Basque (0)	42	0.07
German (28)	170	0.29
Iranian (0)	23	0.04
Irish (61)	75	0.13
Italian (34)	148	0.25
Polish (22)	22	0.04
Portuguese (34)	34	0.06
Scotch-Irish (0)	7	0.01
Scottish (0)	16	0.03
Swedish (4)	4	0.01
Turkish (19)	40	0.07
Welsh (0)	9	0.02

Hispanic Origin	Population	%
Hispanic or Latino (of any race)	56,445	97.13
Central American, ex. Mexican	6,404	11.02
Costa Rican	79	0.14
Guatemalan	1,822	3.14
Honduran	487	0.84
Nicaraguan	546	0.94
Panamanian	18	0.03
Salvadoran	3,381	5.82
Other Central American	71	0.12
Cuban	442	0.76
Dominican Republic	13	0.02
Mexican	46,467	79.96
Puerto Rican	188	0.32
South American	447	0.77
Argentinean	39	0.07
Bolivian	17	0.03
Chilean	16	0.03
Colombian	115	0.20
Ecuadorian	142	0.24
Paraguayan	2	<0.01
Peruvian	112	0.19
Uruguayan	1	<0.01
Venezuelan	3	0.01
Other Hispanic or Latino	2,484	4.27

Race*	Population	%
African-American/Black (440)	572	0.98
Not Hispanic (211)	228	0.39
Hispanic (229)	344	0.59
American Indian/Alaska Native (752)	1,000	1.72
Not Hispanic (29)	46	0.08
Hispanic (723)	954	1.64
Apache (8)	16	0.03
Blackfeet (3)	11	0.02
Central American Ind. (11)	21	0.04
Cherokee (5)	18	0.03
Chippewa (1)	1	<0.01
Choctaw (1)	2	<0.01
Comanche (4)	4	0.01
Mexican American Ind. (243)	286	0.49
Navajo (6)	11	0.02
Pima (4)	7	0.01
Pueblo (5)	12	0.02
Shoshone (3)	3	0.01
Sioux (7)	8	0.01
South American Ind. (1)	4	0.01
Spanish American Ind. (5)	12	0.02
Tohono O'Odham (6)	12	0.02
Yaqui (3)	5	0.01
Yuman (0)	3	0.01
Asian (393)	529	0.91
Not Hispanic (320)	343	0.59
Hispanic (73)	186	0.32
Bangladeshi (4)	4	0.01
Cambodian (3)	5	0.01
Chinese, ex. Taiwanese (34)	51	0.09
Filipino (187)	222	0.38
Hmong (1)	1	<0.01
Indian (45)	72	0.12
Japanese (13)	17	0.03
Korean (19)	23	0.04
Laotian (7)	7	0.01
Taiwanese (4)	4	0.01
Thai (12)	16	0.03
Vietnamese (48)	54	0.09
Hawaii Native/Pacific Islander (28)	78	0.13
Not Hispanic (15)	29	0.05
Hispanic (13)	49	0.08
Fijian (2)	3	0.01
Guamanian/Chamorro (5)	15	0.03
Native Hawaiian (11)	21	0.04
Samoan (7)	12	0.02
Tongan (0)	1	<0.01
White (29,776)	31,657	54.47
Not Hispanic (935)	979	1.68
Hispanic (28,841)	30,678	52.79

Imperial Beach

Place Type: City
County: San Diego
Population: 26,324†

Ancestry‡	Population	%
African, Sub-Saharan (195)	195	0.74
African (36)	36	0.14
Ethiopian (29)	29	0.11
South African (14)	14	0.05
Other Sub-Saharan African (116)	116	0.44
Albanian (14)	14	0.05
American (767)	767	2.92
Arab (0)	20	0.08
Arab (0)	20	0.08
Armenian (8)	8	0.03
Australian (15)	15	0.06
British (81)	81	0.31
Cajun (0)	7	0.03
Canadian (29)	29	0.11
Celtic (14)	36	0.14
Czech (21)	69	0.26
Czechoslovakian (16)	53	0.20
Danish (17)	207	0.79
Dutch (57)	210	0.80
English (644)	1,453	5.53
European (199)	221	0.84
French, ex. Basque (131)	584	2.22
French Canadian (29)	94	0.36
German (856)	3,104	11.82
Greek (0)	52	0.20
Hungarian (13)	22	0.08
Iranian (17)	17	0.06
Irish (796)	2,523	9.61
Italian (212)	692	2.64
Maltese (25)	25	0.10
New Zealander (12)	12	0.05
Northern European (9)	9	0.03
Norwegian (69)	236	0.90
Pennsylvania German (9)	9	0.03
Polish (74)	286	1.09
Portuguese (37)	125	0.48
Romanian (0)	10	0.04
Russian (30)	75	0.29
Scandinavian (0)	16	0.06
Scotch-Irish (128)	243	0.93
Scottish (106)	365	1.39
Serbian (0)	11	0.04
Slovene (0)	9	0.03
Swedish (28)	177	0.67
Swiss (12)	97	0.37
Ukrainian (18)	26	0.10
Welsh (30)	210	0.80
West Indian, ex. Hispanic (8)	80	0.30
British West Indian (0)	15	0.06
Haitian (0)	57	0.22
Jamaican (8)	8	0.03
Yugoslavian (37)	37	0.14

Hispanic Origin	Population	%
Hispanic or Latino (of any race)	12,893	48.98
Central American, ex. Mexican	131	0.50
Costa Rican	9	0.03
Guatemalan	25	0.09
Honduran	14	0.05
Nicaraguan	21	0.08
Panamanian	13	0.05
Salvadoran	49	0.19
Cuban	54	0.21
Dominican Republic	22	0.08
Mexican	11,732	44.57
Puerto Rican	314	1.19
South American	89	0.34
Argentinean	8	0.03
Bolivian	5	0.02
Chilean	12	0.05
Colombian	24	0.09
Ecuadorian	17	0.06
Peruvian	15	0.06
Venezuelan	5	0.02
Other South American	3	0.01
Other Hispanic or Latino	551	2.09

Race*	Population	%
African-American/Black (1,170)	1,605	6.10
Not Hispanic (1,063)	1,337	5.08
Hispanic (107)	268	1.02
American Indian/Alaska Native (266)	607	2.31
Not Hispanic (136)	310	1.18
Hispanic (130)	297	1.13
Alaska Athabascan *(Ala. Nat.)* (0)	3	0.01
Apache (9)	23	0.09
Blackfeet (1)	16	0.06
Canadian/French Am. Ind. (1)	1	<0.01

*Notes: † The Census 2010 population figure is used to calculate the percentages in the Hispanic Origin and Race categories. Ancestry percentages are based on the 2006-2010 American Community Survey population (not shown); ‡ Numbers in parentheses indicate the number of people reporting a single ancestry; * Numbers in parentheses indicate the number of persons reporting this race alone, not in combination with any other race; Please refer to the Explanation of Data for more information.*

Cherokee (11)	71	0.27
Cheyenne (1)	7	0.03
Chickasaw (1)	6	0.02
Chippewa (4)	5	0.02
Choctaw (5)	23	0.09
Comanche (1)	1	<0.01
Creek (6)	21	0.08
Crow (0)	2	0.01
Delaware (2)	3	0.01
Hopi (0)	1	<0.01
Inupiat *(Alaska Native)* (1)	1	<0.01
Iroquois (6)	9	0.03
Kiowa (0)	1	<0.01
Lumbee (3)	3	0.01
Mexican American Ind. (45)	62	0.24
Navajo (19)	35	0.13
Osage (0)	1	<0.01
Potawatomi (2)	2	0.01
Pueblo (10)	10	0.04
Puget Sound Salish (1)	7	0.03
Seminole (0)	3	0.01
Shoshone (2)	7	0.03
Sioux (3)	10	0.04
South American Ind. (0)	4	0.02
Spanish American Ind. (1)	1	<0.01
Tlingit-Haida *(Alaska Native)* (1)	3	0.01
Yakama (0)	1	<0.01
Yaqui (8)	27	0.10
Asian (1,731)	2,538	9.64
Not Hispanic (1,624)	2,192	8.33
Hispanic (107)	346	1.31
Cambodian (9)	14	0.05
Chinese, ex. Taiwanese (45)	100	0.38
Filipino (1,387)	1,930	7.33
Hmong (1)	1	<0.01
Indian (40)	51	0.19
Indonesian (0)	4	0.02
Japanese (122)	284	1.08
Korean (14)	36	0.14
Laotian (4)	5	0.02
Malaysian (0)	3	0.01
Pakistani (2)	2	0.01
Sri Lankan (4)	4	0.02
Taiwanese (1)	1	<0.01
Thai (15)	37	0.14
Vietnamese (24)	52	0.20
Hawaii Native/Pacific Islander (188)	388	1.47
Not Hispanic (156)	284	1.08
Hispanic (32)	104	0.40
Fijian (1)	2	0.01
Guamanian/Chamorro (70)	128	0.49
Native Hawaiian (54)	126	0.48
Samoan (27)	64	0.24
Tongan (8)	16	0.06
White (16,467)	17,859	67.84
Not Hispanic (9,487)	10,241	38.90
Hispanic (6,980)	7,618	28.94

Imperial

Place Type: City
County: Imperial
Population: 14,758†

Ancestry‡	Population	%
American (347)	347	2.59
Arab (0)	18	0.13
Lebanese (0)	9	0.07
Palestinian (0)	9	0.07
Danish (11)	24	0.18
Dutch (0)	45	0.34
English (84)	333	2.48
European (80)	96	0.72
French, ex. Basque (33)	182	1.36
French Canadian (11)	21	0.16
German (163)	519	3.87
Greek (20)	49	0.37
Hungarian (0)	22	0.16
Irish (75)	321	2.39
Italian (56)	234	1.75
Norwegian (26)	26	0.19
Portuguese (0)	10	0.07
Scotch-Irish (58)	110	0.82
Scottish (13)	13	0.10
Swedish (38)	105	0.78
Welsh (0)	11	0.08

Hispanic Origin	Population	%
Hispanic or Latino (of any race)	11,046	74.85
Central American, ex. Mexican	81	0.55
Costa Rican	2	0.01
Guatemalan	11	0.07
Honduran	1	0.01
Nicaraguan	15	0.10
Panamanian	6	0.04
Salvadoran	46	0.31
Cuban	10	0.07
Dominican Republic	4	0.03
Mexican	10,525	71.32
Puerto Rican	92	0.62
South American	45	0.30
Argentinean	4	0.03
Chilean	1	0.01
Colombian	26	0.18
Ecuadorian	5	0.03
Peruvian	6	0.04
Venezuelan	3	0.02
Other Hispanic or Latino	289	1.96

Race*	Population	%
African-American/Black (331)	440	2.98
Not Hispanic (258)	292	1.98
Hispanic (73)	148	1.00
American Indian/Alaska Native (154)	256	1.73
Not Hispanic (31)	75	0.51
Hispanic (123)	181	1.23
Apache (3)	8	0.05
Blackfeet (0)	2	0.01
Cherokee (11)	25	0.17
Choctaw (7)	14	0.09
Hopi (1)	1	0.01
Iroquois (1)	1	0.01
Mexican American Ind. (26)	37	0.25
Navajo (1)	1	0.01
Paiute (1)	1	0.01
Pima (1)	1	0.01
Pueblo (1)	1	0.01
Sioux (1)	1	0.01
Spanish American Ind. (1)	1	0.01
Yaqui (11)	22	0.15
Yuman (5)	5	0.03
Asian (370)	542	3.67
Not Hispanic (294)	354	2.40
Hispanic (76)	188	1.27
Bangladeshi (5)	5	0.03
Burmese (2)	2	0.01
Cambodian (1)	1	0.01
Chinese, ex. Taiwanese (30)	50	0.34
Filipino (166)	265	1.80
Indian (32)	45	0.30
Indonesian (3)	3	0.02
Japanese (33)	54	0.37
Korean (42)	53	0.36
Laotian (1)	2	0.01
Malaysian (1)	1	0.01
Pakistani (9)	18	0.12
Vietnamese (31)	33	0.22
Hawaii Native/Pacific Islander (13)	41	0.28
Not Hispanic (8)	20	0.14
Hispanic (5)	21	0.14
Guamanian/Chamorro (5)	11	0.07
Native Hawaiian (0)	17	0.12
Samoan (5)	5	0.03
White (9,298)	9,981	67.63
Not Hispanic (2,982)	3,078	20.86
Hispanic (6,316)	6,903	46.77

Indio

Place Type: City
County: Riverside
Population: 76,036†

Ancestry‡	Population	%
African, Sub-Saharan (430)	508	0.70
African (367)	445	0.61
Liberian (26)	26	0.04
South African (37)	37	0.05
American (1,476)	1,476	2.04
Arab (9)	18	0.02
Lebanese (0)	9	0.01
Palestinian (9)	9	0.01
Armenian (21)	31	0.04
Australian (0)	10	0.01
Austrian (6)	60	0.08
Basque (5)	5	0.01
Belgian (23)	23	0.03
British (80)	229	0.32
Canadian (99)	153	0.21
Croatian (21)	29	0.04
Czech (36)	49	0.07
Czechoslovakian (0)	11	0.02
Danish (117)	375	0.52
Dutch (192)	724	1.00
Eastern European (46)	46	0.06
English (1,272)	3,682	5.08
Estonian (10)	10	0.01
European (211)	225	0.31
Finnish (55)	66	0.09
French, ex. Basque (206)	1,054	1.45
French Canadian (39)	94	0.13
German (1,498)	4,555	6.28
Greek (30)	137	0.19
Hungarian (69)	186	0.26
Irish (1,312)	3,517	4.85
Italian (962)	1,829	2.52
Latvian (0)	14	0.02
Lithuanian (52)	114	0.16
Northern European (20)	20	0.03
Norwegian (139)	563	0.78
Polish (263)	706	0.97
Portuguese (127)	253	0.35
Romanian (0)	61	0.08
Russian (236)	508	0.70
Scandinavian (48)	66	0.09
Scotch-Irish (279)	646	0.89
Scottish (228)	555	0.77
Slavic (0)	42	0.06
Slovak (26)	71	0.10
Slovene (0)	9	0.01
Swedish (236)	504	0.70
Swiss (65)	119	0.16
Turkish (0)	26	0.04
Ukrainian (55)	74	0.10
Welsh (35)	169	0.23
West Indian, ex. Hispanic (0)	11	0.02
West Indian (0)	11	0.02
Yugoslavian (0)	11	0.02

Hispanic Origin	Population	%
Hispanic or Latino (of any race)	51,540	67.78
Central American, ex. Mexican	876	1.15
Costa Rican	20	0.03
Guatemalan	180	0.24
Honduran	43	0.06
Nicaraguan	88	0.12
Panamanian	39	0.05
Salvadoran	492	0.65
Other Central American	14	0.02
Cuban	91	0.12
Dominican Republic	12	0.02
Mexican	48,095	63.25
Puerto Rican	232	0.31
South American	289	0.38
Argentinean	74	0.10
Bolivian	8	0.01
Chilean	35	0.05

*Notes: † The Census 2010 population figure is used to calculate the percentages in the Hispanic Origin and Race categories. Ancestry percentages are based on the 2006-2010 American Community Survey population (not shown); ‡ Numbers in parentheses indicate the number of people reporting a single ancestry; * Numbers in parentheses indicate the number of persons reporting this race alone, not in combination with any other race; Please refer to the Explanation of Data for more information.*

Colombian	80	0.11
Ecuadorian	27	0.04
Paraguayan	2	<0.01
Peruvian	46	0.06
Uruguayan	7	0.01
Venezuelan	8	0.01
Other South American	2	<0.01
Other Hispanic or Latino	1,945	2.56

Race*	Population	%
African-American/Black (1,805)	2,264	2.98
Not Hispanic (1,521)	1,752	2.30
Hispanic (284)	512	0.67
American Indian/Alaska Native (741)	1,121	1.47
Not Hispanic (209)	349	0.46
Hispanic (532)	772	1.02
Aleut *(Alaska Native)* (2)	2	<0.01
Apache (20)	44	0.06
Blackfeet (3)	20	0.03
Canadian/French Am. Ind. (0)	1	<0.01
Central American Ind. (9)	17	0.02
Cherokee (26)	82	0.11
Chickasaw (3)	10	0.01
Chippewa (2)	5	0.01
Choctaw (12)	27	0.04
Comanche (0)	2	<0.01
Creek (5)	11	0.01
Delaware (0)	1	<0.01
Inupiat *(Alaska Native)* (1)	1	<0.01
Iroquois (2)	2	<0.01
Mexican American Ind. (124)	179	0.24
Navajo (26)	40	0.05
Ottawa (1)	6	0.01
Paiute (0)	3	<0.01
Pima (14)	15	0.02
Potawatomi (1)	2	<0.01
Puget Sound Salish (3)	3	<0.01
Seminole (2)	3	<0.01
Shoshone (0)	2	<0.01
Sioux (4)	10	0.01
South American Ind. (1)	2	<0.01
Spanish American Ind. (9)	12	0.02
Tohono O'Odham (5)	7	0.01
Ute (0)	1	<0.01
Yaqui (14)	25	0.03
Yuman (4)	5	0.01
Yup'ik *(Alaska Native)* (0)	1	<0.01
Asian (1,693)	2,314	3.04
Not Hispanic (1,467)	1,784	2.35
Hispanic (226)	530	0.70
Burmese (1)	1	<0.01
Cambodian (28)	36	0.05
Chinese, ex. Taiwanese (212)	291	0.38
Filipino (765)	1,093	1.44
Indian (166)	198	0.26
Indonesian (20)	31	0.04
Japanese (112)	200	0.26
Korean (101)	130	0.17
Laotian (1)	5	0.01
Malaysian (1)	1	<0.01
Pakistani (13)	22	0.03
Sri Lankan (9)	10	0.01
Taiwanese (10)	17	0.02
Thai (20)	38	0.05
Vietnamese (151)	179	0.24
Hawaii Native/Pacific Islander (55)	174	0.23
Not Hispanic (40)	93	0.12
Hispanic (15)	81	0.11
Fijian (2)	2	<0.01
Guamanian/Chamorro (12)	36	0.05
Native Hawaiian (21)	72	0.09
Samoan (3)	10	0.01
White (46,735)	48,900	64.31
Not Hispanic (20,512)	21,090	27.74
Hispanic (26,223)	27,810	36.57

Inglewood

Place Type: City
County: Los Angeles
Population: 109,673†

Ancestry‡	Population	%
African, Sub-Saharan (2,554)	3,108	2.82
African (1,767)	2,163	1.97
Cape Verdean (0)	16	0.01
Ethiopian (316)	399	0.36
Ghanaian (15)	15	0.01
Liberian (9)	9	0.01
Nigerian (356)	415	0.38
Other Sub-Saharan African (91)	91	0.08
American (2,663)	2,663	2.42
Arab (235)	328	0.30
Arab (115)	148	0.13
Egyptian (97)	129	0.12
Lebanese (23)	51	0.05
Armenian (41)	130	0.12
Austrian (0)	33	0.03
Basque (0)	15	0.01
Belgian (0)	8	0.01
Brazilian (84)	264	0.24
British (0)	82	0.07
Canadian (0)	27	0.02
Celtic (15)	15	0.01
Croatian (0)	57	0.05
Czech (0)	8	0.01
Czechoslovakian (0)	14	0.01
Danish (18)	18	0.02
Dutch (37)	100	0.09
Eastern European (13)	13	0.01
English (190)	663	0.60
Estonian (55)	55	0.05
European (106)	208	0.19
French, ex. Basque (14)	644	0.59
French Canadian (0)	35	0.03
German (229)	1,216	1.10
Greek (8)	17	0.02
Guyanese (40)	53	0.05
Hungarian (14)	119	0.11
Iranian (8)	8	0.01
Irish (253)	958	0.87
Italian (168)	543	0.49
Northern European (7)	7	0.01
Norwegian (25)	55	0.05
Polish (34)	129	0.12
Portuguese (0)	26	0.02
Romanian (11)	11	0.01
Russian (7)	7	0.01
Scandinavian (30)	30	0.03
Scotch-Irish (105)	277	0.25
Scottish (38)	126	0.11
Swedish (18)	71	0.06
Swiss (7)	7	0.01
Turkish (0)	39	0.04
Ukrainian (17)	17	0.02
Welsh (0)	91	0.08
West Indian, ex. Hispanic (1,362)	1,770	1.61
Bahamian (88)	88	0.08
Barbadian (16)	16	0.01
Belizean (505)	711	0.65
Haitian (48)	48	0.04
Jamaican (612)	766	0.70
Trinidadian/Tobagonian (14)	14	0.01
U.S. Virgin Islander (22)	46	0.04
West Indian (57)	81	0.07
Yugoslavian (90)	102	0.09

Hispanic Origin	Population	%
Hispanic or Latino (of any race)	55,449	50.56
Central American, ex. Mexican	8,697	7.93
Costa Rican	70	0.06
Guatemalan	3,593	3.28
Honduran	649	0.59
Nicaraguan	337	0.31
Panamanian	119	0.11
Salvadoran	3,869	3.53
Other Central American	60	0.05
Cuban	362	0.33
Dominican Republic	74	0.07
Mexican	41,983	38.28
Puerto Rican	578	0.53
South American	505	0.46
Argentinean	45	0.04
Bolivian	18	0.02
Chilean	14	0.01
Colombian	140	0.13
Ecuadorian	105	0.10
Paraguayan	3	<0.01
Peruvian	161	0.15
Uruguayan	3	<0.01
Venezuelan	13	0.01
Other South American	3	<0.01
Other Hispanic or Latino	3,250	2.96

Race*	Population	%
African-American/Black (48,164)	50,219	45.79
Not Hispanic (47,029)	48,512	44.23
Hispanic (1,135)	1,707	1.56
American Indian/Alaska Native (751)	1,699	1.55
Not Hispanic (220)	846	0.77
Hispanic (531)	853	0.78
Apache (3)	17	0.02
Blackfeet (7)	70	0.06
Canadian/French Am. Ind. (0)	4	<0.01
Central American Ind. (4)	33	0.03
Cherokee (23)	208	0.19
Chickasaw (0)	9	0.01
Chippewa (1)	2	<0.01
Choctaw (11)	57	0.05
Comanche (1)	3	<0.01
Cree (2)	2	<0.01
Creek (2)	18	0.02
Delaware (1)	1	<0.01
Hopi (0)	5	<0.01
Iroquois (0)	4	<0.01
Mexican American Ind. (178)	268	0.24
Navajo (19)	30	0.03
Paiute (1)	1	<0.01
Pima (1)	1	<0.01
Potawatomi (0)	1	<0.01
Pueblo (8)	10	0.01
Seminole (4)	12	0.01
Shoshone (0)	1	<0.01
Sioux (2)	13	0.01
South American Ind. (2)	11	0.01
Spanish American Ind. (6)	9	0.01
Tlingit-Haida *(Alaska Native)* (4)	6	0.01
Tohono O'Odham (11)	14	0.01
Yakama (1)	1	<0.01
Yaqui (12)	23	0.02
Yuman (0)	3	<0.01
Asian (1,484)	2,104	1.92
Not Hispanic (1,374)	1,815	1.65
Hispanic (110)	289	0.26
Bangladeshi (14)	15	0.01
Burmese (14)	15	0.01
Cambodian (15)	21	0.02
Chinese, ex. Taiwanese (92)	168	0.15
Filipino (593)	771	0.70
Hmong (2)	4	<0.01
Indian (257)	364	0.33
Indonesian (19)	35	0.03
Japanese (150)	271	0.25
Korean (51)	84	0.08
Laotian (3)	21	0.02
Nepalese (0)	2	<0.01
Pakistani (106)	135	0.12
Sri Lankan (42)	44	0.04
Taiwanese (10)	10	0.01
Thai (23)	37	0.03
Vietnamese (28)	47	0.04
Hawaii Native/Pacific Islander (350)	597	0.54
Not Hispanic (323)	497	0.45
Hispanic (27)	100	0.09
Fijian (62)	75	0.07
Guamanian/Chamorro (14)	16	0.01

SECTION TWO

*Notes: † The Census 2010 population figure is used to calculate the percentages in the Hispanic Origin and Race categories. Ancestry percentages are based on the 2006-2010 American Community Survey population (not shown); ‡ Numbers in parentheses indicate the number of people reporting a single ancestry; * Numbers in parentheses indicate the number of persons reporting this race alone, not in combination with any other race; Please refer to the Explanation of Data for more information.*

Native Hawaiian (11)	54	0.05
Samoan (33)	67	0.06
Tongan (196)	221	0.20
White (25,562)	28,634	26.11
Not Hispanic (3,165)	4,080	3.72
Hispanic (22,397)	24,554	22.39

Ione

Place Type: City
County: Amador
Population: 7,918†

Ancestry‡	Population	%
African, Sub-Saharan (17)	49	0.62
African (17)	49	0.62
American (235)	235	3.00
Arab (16)	22	0.28
Arab (8)	8	0.10
Egyptian (8)	8	0.10
Palestinian (0)	6	0.08
Basque (9)	9	0.11
Belgian (22)	22	0.28
British (0)	29	0.37
Canadian (8)	8	0.10
Croatian (8)	8	0.10
Czech (17)	25	0.32
Czechoslovakian (0)	15	0.19
Danish (0)	15	0.19
Dutch (23)	150	1.91
English (133)	665	8.48
European (72)	103	1.31
French, ex. Basque (72)	492	6.27
French Canadian (4)	20	0.25
German (241)	1,209	15.41
Greek (16)	29	0.37
Hungarian (0)	8	0.10
Irish (245)	1,172	14.94
Italian (131)	902	11.50
Lithuanian (0)	3	0.04
Norwegian (29)	130	1.66
Polish (27)	66	0.84
Portuguese (29)	74	0.94
Russian (16)	24	0.31
Scandinavian (36)	36	0.46
Scotch-Irish (52)	163	2.08
Scottish (33)	248	3.16
Swedish (16)	124	1.58
Swiss (0)	46	0.59
Ukrainian (0)	16	0.20
Welsh (20)	64	0.82
West Indian, ex. Hispanic (0)	8	0.10
Dutch West Indian (0)	8	0.10
Yugoslavian (11)	11	0.14

Hispanic Origin	Population	%
Hispanic or Latino (of any race)	1,991	25.15
Central American, ex. Mexican	15	0.19
Costa Rican	1	0.01
Guatemalan	1	0.01
Honduran	4	0.05
Nicaraguan	1	0.01
Salvadoran	8	0.10
Cuban	11	0.14
Mexican	1,699	21.46
Puerto Rican	17	0.21
South American	6	0.08
Chilean	4	0.05
Ecuadorian	1	0.01
Peruvian	1	0.01
Other Hispanic or Latino	243	3.07

Race*	Population	%
African-American/Black (824)	864	10.91
Not Hispanic (809)	840	10.61
Hispanic (15)	24	0.30
American Indian/Alaska Native (173)	309	3.90
Not Hispanic (139)	229	2.89
Hispanic (34)	80	1.01
Apache (9)	12	0.15
Blackfeet (0)	3	0.04
Cherokee (20)	53	0.67
Cheyenne (0)	1	0.01
Chickasaw (0)	2	0.03
Choctaw (0)	11	0.14
Comanche (1)	5	0.06
Hopi (1)	1	0.01
Mexican American Ind. (3)	5	0.06
Navajo (1)	2	0.03
Paiute (0)	1	0.01
Potawatomi (4)	4	0.05
Pueblo (1)	1	0.01
Sioux (1)	4	0.05
Tlingit-Haida *(Alaska Native)* (4)	4	0.05
Yaqui (1)	2	0.03
Yuman (1)	1	0.01
Asian (110)	171	2.16
Not Hispanic (103)	146	1.84
Hispanic (7)	25	0.32
Burmese (0)	3	0.04
Cambodian (1)	1	0.01
Chinese, ex. Taiwanese (17)	19	0.24
Filipino (27)	54	0.68
Indian (13)	15	0.19
Japanese (11)	19	0.24
Korean (4)	9	0.11
Pakistani (1)	1	0.01
Taiwanese (0)	1	0.01
Thai (1)	12	0.15
Vietnamese (7)	8	0.10
Hawaii Native/Pacific Islander (21)	33	0.42
Not Hispanic (18)	23	0.29
Hispanic (3)	10	0.13
Guamanian/Chamorro (2)	2	0.03
Native Hawaiian (9)	17	0.21
Samoan (2)	4	0.05
Tongan (1)	1	0.01
White (5,826)	6,078	76.76
Not Hispanic (4,608)	4,755	60.05
Hispanic (1,218)	1,323	16.71

Irvine

Place Type: City
County: Orange
Population: 212,375†

Ancestry‡	Population	%
Afghan (1,177)	1,177	0.59
African, Sub-Saharan (763)	879	0.44
African (284)	350	0.18
Cape Verdean (15)	15	0.01
Ethiopian (33)	33	0.02
Nigerian (54)	54	0.03
Somalian (75)	75	0.04
South African (302)	339	0.17
Zimbabwean (0)	13	0.01
Albanian (12)	27	0.01
American (7,327)	7,327	3.68
Arab (2,568)	3,229	1.62
Arab (557)	667	0.33
Egyptian (448)	463	0.23
Iraqi (41)	59	0.03
Jordanian (154)	239	0.12
Lebanese (558)	661	0.33
Moroccan (98)	133	0.07
Palestinian (35)	61	0.03
Syrian (161)	346	0.17
Other Arab (516)	600	0.30
Armenian (556)	838	0.42
Assyrian/Chaldean/Syriac (69)	87	0.04
Australian (164)	256	0.13
Austrian (160)	463	0.23
Basque (37)	111	0.06
Belgian (150)	271	0.14
Brazilian (58)	73	0.04
British (435)	1,176	0.59
Bulgarian (141)	141	0.07
Cajun (4)	4	<0.01
Canadian (460)	1,087	0.55
Celtic (36)	48	0.02
Croatian (90)	243	0.12
Czech (322)	775	0.39
Czechoslovakian (116)	169	0.08
Danish (197)	858	0.43
Dutch (511)	1,650	0.83
Eastern European (724)	851	0.43
English (3,487)	12,960	6.51
European (2,728)	3,236	1.63
Finnish (124)	303	0.15
French, ex. Basque (946)	4,184	2.10
French Canadian (307)	655	0.33
German (4,413)	17,426	8.75
Greek (320)	835	0.42
Guyanese (24)	24	0.01
Hungarian (391)	1,365	0.69
Icelander (16)	57	0.03
Iranian (7,475)	7,908	3.97
Irish (3,783)	12,827	6.44
Israeli (442)	525	0.26
Italian (2,730)	7,135	3.58
Latvian (51)	131	0.07
Lithuanian (124)	335	0.17
Luxemburger (0)	7	<0.01
Macedonian (17)	31	0.02
Maltese (10)	10	0.01
New Zealander (7)	7	<0.01
Northern European (134)	164	0.08
Norwegian (546)	1,936	0.97
Pennsylvania German (8)	8	<0.01
Polish (1,202)	3,697	1.86
Portuguese (273)	743	0.37
Romanian (340)	617	0.31
Russian (2,106)	4,120	2.07
Scandinavian (168)	294	0.15
Scotch-Irish (735)	1,932	0.97
Scottish (614)	2,827	1.42
Serbian (96)	223	0.11
Slavic (10)	37	0.02
Slovak (26)	128	0.06
Slovene (32)	66	0.03
Swedish (916)	2,808	1.41
Swiss (241)	835	0.42
Turkish (496)	612	0.31
Ukrainian (272)	465	0.23
Welsh (165)	736	0.37
West Indian, ex. Hispanic (46)	104	0.05
Haitian (0)	9	<0.01
Jamaican (46)	58	0.03
Trinidadian/Tobagonian (0)	28	0.01
West Indian (0)	9	<0.01
Yugoslavian (121)	176	0.09

Hispanic Origin	Population	%
Hispanic or Latino (of any race)	19,621	9.24
Central American, ex. Mexican	1,461	0.69
Costa Rican	172	0.08
Guatemalan	334	0.16
Honduran	84	0.04
Nicaraguan	176	0.08
Panamanian	99	0.05
Salvadoran	585	0.28
Other Central American	11	0.01
Cuban	467	0.22
Dominican Republic	69	0.03
Mexican	12,807	6.03
Puerto Rican	641	0.30
South American	2,418	1.14
Argentinean	440	0.21
Bolivian	123	0.06
Chilean	198	0.09
Colombian	662	0.31
Ecuadorian	249	0.12
Paraguayan	8	<0.01
Peruvian	557	0.26
Uruguayan	26	0.01
Venezuelan	115	0.05
Other South American	40	0.02
Other Hispanic or Latino	1,758	0.83

*Notes: † The Census 2010 population figure is used to calculate the percentages in the Hispanic Origin and Race categories. Ancestry percentages are based on the 2006-2010 American Community Survey population (not shown); ‡ Numbers in parentheses indicate the number of people reporting a single ancestry; * Numbers in parentheses indicate the number of persons reporting this race alone, not in combination with any other race; Please refer to the Explanation of Data for more information.*

Race*	Population	%
African-American/Black (3,718)	5,104	2.40
Not Hispanic (3,494)	4,618	2.17
Hispanic (224)	486	0.23
American Indian/Alaska Native (355)	1,362	0.64
Not Hispanic (199)	889	0.42
Hispanic (156)	473	0.22
Aleut *(Alaska Native)* (3)	8	<0.01
Apache (16)	57	0.03
Arapaho (0)	1	<0.01
Blackfeet (1)	29	0.01
Canadian/French Am. Ind. (0)	3	<0.01
Central American Ind. (0)	1	<0.01
Cherokee (38)	260	0.12
Cheyenne (2)	5	<0.01
Chickasaw (6)	14	0.01
Chippewa (4)	20	0.01
Choctaw (10)	41	0.02
Comanche (3)	10	<0.01
Cree (0)	3	<0.01
Creek (4)	20	0.01
Crow (0)	6	<0.01
Delaware (1)	1	<0.01
Hopi (3)	6	<0.01
Houma (1)	1	<0.01
Iroquois (1)	16	0.01
Kiowa (1)	6	<0.01
Lumbee (2)	3	<0.01
Menominee (0)	2	<0.01
Mexican American Ind. (43)	75	0.04
Navajo (13)	40	0.02
Osage (5)	17	0.01
Ottawa (2)	2	<0.01
Paiute (2)	2	<0.01
Pima (0)	3	<0.01
Potawatomi (0)	3	<0.01
Pueblo (4)	9	<0.01
Seminole (2)	5	<0.01
Shoshone (3)	6	<0.01
Sioux (10)	30	0.01
South American Ind. (5)	31	0.01
Spanish American Ind. (2)	2	<0.01
Tlingit-Haida *(Alaska Native)* (1)	1	<0.01
Tsimshian *(Alaska Native)* (0)	1	<0.01
Yaqui (8)	16	0.01
Asian (83,176)	91,896	43.27
Not Hispanic (82,722)	90,762	42.74
Hispanic (454)	1,134	0.53
Bangladeshi (122)	136	0.06
Burmese (93)	127	0.06
Cambodian (234)	336	0.16
Chinese, ex. Taiwanese (21,783)	25,177	11.85
Filipino (6,192)	8,085	3.81
Hmong (50)	56	0.03
Indian (10,687)	11,325	5.33
Indonesian (320)	498	0.23
Japanese (6,474)	8,797	4.14
Korean (18,445)	19,473	9.17
Laotian (74)	117	0.06
Malaysian (52)	84	0.04
Nepalese (50)	62	0.03
Pakistani (1,490)	1,631	0.77
Sri Lankan (195)	217	0.10
Taiwanese (5,284)	5,790	2.73
Thai (464)	598	0.28
Vietnamese (7,882)	9,000	4.24
Hawaii Native/Pacific Islander (334)	1,067	0.50
Not Hispanic (295)	953	0.45
Hispanic (39)	114	0.05
Fijian (18)	23	0.01
Guamanian/Chamorro (94)	163	0.08
Marshallese (8)	9	<0.01
Native Hawaiian (75)	347	0.16
Samoan (85)	146	0.07
Tongan (11)	18	0.01
White (107,215)	117,576	55.36
Not Hispanic (95,822)	104,511	49.21
Hispanic (11,393)	13,065	6.15

Isla Vista

Place Type: CDP
County: Santa Barbara
Population: 23,096†

Ancestry‡	Population	%
Afghan (19)	19	0.08
African, Sub-Saharan (70)	156	0.66
African (30)	52	0.22
Ethiopian (0)	13	0.05
Nigerian (13)	30	0.13
South African (15)	49	0.21
Other Sub-Saharan African (12)	12	0.05
American (221)	221	0.93
Arab (97)	261	1.10
Arab (26)	40	0.17
Egyptian (0)	40	0.17
Lebanese (24)	93	0.39
Moroccan (18)	19	0.08
Palestinian (0)	5	0.02
Syrian (18)	45	0.19
Other Arab (11)	19	0.08
Armenian (43)	51	0.21
Australian (0)	54	0.23
Austrian (14)	71	0.30
Belgian (13)	38	0.16
Brazilian (20)	90	0.38
British (86)	133	0.56
Bulgarian (14)	14	0.06
Cajun (27)	27	0.11
Canadian (8)	144	0.61
Croatian (51)	133	0.56
Czech (0)	102	0.43
Czechoslovakian (0)	22	0.09
Danish (47)	204	0.86
Dutch (43)	332	1.40
English (389)	1,981	8.33
Estonian (0)	11	0.05
European (378)	460	1.93
Finnish (26)	95	0.40
French, ex. Basque (131)	624	2.62
French Canadian (0)	32	0.13
German (684)	2,752	11.57
Greek (40)	179	0.75
Hungarian (80)	188	0.79
Iranian (128)	206	0.87
Irish (676)	2,975	12.51
Israeli (101)	140	0.59
Italian (604)	1,692	7.12
Lithuanian (15)	68	0.29
Macedonian (0)	13	0.05
New Zealander (0)	25	0.11
Norwegian (128)	390	1.64
Pennsylvania German (0)	23	0.10
Polish (145)	950	4.00
Portuguese (83)	333	1.40
Romanian (0)	50	0.21
Russian (195)	710	2.99
Scandinavian (10)	24	0.10
Scotch-Irish (139)	303	1.27
Scottish (155)	505	2.12
Serbian (14)	14	0.06
Slovak (15)	29	0.12
Swedish (161)	429	1.80
Swiss (21)	148	0.62
Turkish (67)	111	0.47
Ukrainian (0)	80	0.34
Welsh (0)	156	0.66
West Indian, ex. Hispanic (15)	16	0.07
British West Indian (0)	1	<0.01
Jamaican (1)	1	<0.01
West Indian (14)	14	0.06
Yugoslavian (0)	13	0.05

Hispanic Origin	Population	%
Hispanic or Latino (of any race)	5,265	22.80
Central American, ex. Mexican	528	2.29
Costa Rican	21	0.09
Guatemalan	159	0.69
Honduran	21	0.09
Nicaraguan	44	0.19
Panamanian	16	0.07
Salvadoran	264	1.14
Other Central American	3	0.01
Cuban	73	0.32
Dominican Republic	9	0.04
Mexican	3,947	17.09
Puerto Rican	68	0.29
South American	278	1.20
Argentinean	50	0.22
Bolivian	5	0.02
Chilean	52	0.23
Colombian	57	0.25
Ecuadorian	19	0.08
Paraguayan	8	0.03
Peruvian	62	0.27
Uruguayan	4	0.02
Venezuelan	15	0.06
Other South American	6	0.03
Other Hispanic or Latino	362	1.57

Race*	Population	%
African-American/Black (594)	822	3.56
Not Hispanic (521)	692	3.00
Hispanic (73)	130	0.56
American Indian/Alaska Native (104)	330	1.43
Not Hispanic (42)	161	0.70
Hispanic (62)	169	0.73
Alaska Athabascan *(Ala. Nat.)* (1)	1	<0.01
Aleut *(Alaska Native)* (0)	2	0.01
Apache (1)	10	0.04
Blackfeet (1)	1	<0.01
Canadian/French Am. Ind. (0)	2	0.01
Cherokee (6)	41	0.18
Chickasaw (1)	4	0.02
Chippewa (0)	2	0.01
Choctaw (1)	9	0.04
Cree (0)	1	<0.01
Creek (0)	2	0.01
Crow (0)	1	<0.01
Hopi (0)	1	<0.01
Inupiat *(Alaska Native)* (0)	1	<0.01
Iroquois (0)	3	0.01
Mexican American Ind. (14)	23	0.10
Navajo (1)	7	0.03
Osage (1)	2	0.01
Pima (0)	1	<0.01
Potawatomi (1)	2	0.01
Pueblo (2)	3	0.01
Seminole (0)	1	<0.01
Sioux (2)	8	0.03
South American Ind. (0)	3	0.01
Spanish American Ind. (1)	1	<0.01
Tohono O'Odham (0)	1	<0.01
Yakama (1)	2	0.01
Yaqui (0)	5	0.02
Asian (3,387)	4,212	18.24
Not Hispanic (3,316)	4,054	17.55
Hispanic (71)	158	0.68
Bangladeshi (2)	3	0.01
Bhutanese (1)	1	<0.01
Cambodian (28)	46	0.20
Chinese, ex. Taiwanese (1,156)	1,512	6.55
Filipino (347)	589	2.55
Hmong (35)	37	0.16
Indian (327)	387	1.68
Indonesian (12)	24	0.10
Japanese (199)	458	1.98
Korean (423)	491	2.13
Laotian (20)	24	0.10
Malaysian (3)	9	0.04
Nepalese (3)	3	0.01
Pakistani (20)	28	0.12
Sri Lankan (6)	8	0.03
Taiwanese (149)	169	0.73
Thai (44)	58	0.25
Vietnamese (362)	455	1.97
Hawaii Native/Pacific Islander (45)	123	0.53
Not Hispanic (38)	103	0.45

*Notes: † The Census 2010 population figure is used to calculate the percentages in the Hispanic Origin and Race categories. Ancestry percentages are based on the 2006-2010 American Community Survey population (not shown); ‡ Numbers in parentheses indicate the number of people reporting a single ancestry; * Numbers in parentheses indicate the number of persons reporting this race alone, not in combination with any other race; Please refer to the Explanation of Data for more information.*

Hispanic (7)	20	0.09
Fijian (3)	7	0.03
Guamanian/Chamorro (9)	22	0.10
Native Hawaiian (15)	41	0.18
Samoan (8)	15	0.06
Tongan (4)	6	0.03
White (14,875)	16,119	69.79
Not Hispanic (12,854)	13,765	59.60
Hispanic (2,021)	2,354	10.19

Kerman

Place Type: City
County: Fresno
Population: 13,544†

Ancestry‡	Population	%
American (382)	382	3.01
Armenian (0)	28	0.22
Basque (0)	15	0.12
Belgian (0)	20	0.16
Danish (63)	148	1.16
Dutch (25)	56	0.44
English (42)	238	1.87
European (127)	138	1.09
French, ex. Basque (0)	126	0.99
French Canadian (47)	47	0.37
German (70)	561	4.41
Greek (9)	26	0.20
Irish (125)	472	3.71
Italian (22)	191	1.50
Norwegian (0)	23	0.18
Polish (58)	58	0.46
Portuguese (246)	304	2.39
Russian (11)	11	0.09
Scotch-Irish (41)	65	0.51
Scottish (0)	53	0.42
Swedish (0)	16	0.13
Welsh (0)	31	0.24
West Indian, ex. Hispanic (0)	13	0.10
Dutch West Indian (0)	13	0.10

Hispanic Origin	Population	%
Hispanic or Latino (of any race)	9,711	71.70
Central American, ex. Mexican	139	1.03
Costa Rican	2	0.01
Guatemalan	19	0.14
Honduran	3	0.02
Nicaraguan	4	0.03
Salvadoran	111	0.82
Cuban	6	0.04
Mexican	9,043	66.77
Puerto Rican	34	0.25
South American	16	0.12
Argentinean	2	0.01
Chilean	5	0.04
Colombian	9	0.07
Other Hispanic or Latino	473	3.49

Race*	Population	%
African-American/Black (68)	112	0.83
Not Hispanic (41)	61	0.45
Hispanic (27)	51	0.38
American Indian/Alaska Native (173)	277	2.05
Not Hispanic (56)	95	0.70
Hispanic (117)	182	1.34
Alaska Athabascan *(Ala. Nat.)* (0)	4	0.03
Apache (4)	7	0.05
Blackfeet (1)	1	0.01
Cherokee (9)	17	0.13
Chippewa (2)	5	0.04
Choctaw (3)	11	0.08
Crow (0)	1	0.01
Mexican American Ind. (32)	42	0.31
Navajo (0)	3	0.02
Paiute (0)	5	0.04
Pima (1)	1	0.01
Shoshone (6)	6	0.04
Sioux (4)	4	0.03
South American Ind. (0)	1	0.01
Yaqui (10)	12	0.09
Asian (1,091)	1,241	9.16
Not Hispanic (1,075)	1,177	8.69
Hispanic (16)	64	0.47
Chinese, ex. Taiwanese (35)	45	0.33
Filipino (21)	46	0.34
Hmong (35)	35	0.26
Indian (971)	1,037	7.66
Indonesian (2)	3	0.02
Japanese (8)	11	0.08
Korean (4)	14	0.10
Laotian (1)	2	0.01
Pakistani (6)	12	0.09
Vietnamese (4)	4	0.03
Hawaii Native/Pacific Islander (14)	48	0.35
Not Hispanic (5)	18	0.13
Hispanic (9)	30	0.22
Guamanian/Chamorro (0)	3	0.02
Native Hawaiian (7)	13	0.10
Samoan (0)	3	0.02
White (6,860)	7,373	54.44
Not Hispanic (2,465)	2,553	18.85
Hispanic (4,395)	4,820	35.59

King City

Place Type: City
County: Monterey
Population: 12,874†

Ancestry‡	Population	%
American (26)	26	0.21
Dutch (0)	31	0.25
English (12)	315	2.54
European (0)	16	0.13
French, ex. Basque (12)	46	0.37
French Canadian (12)	12	0.10
German (118)	347	2.80
Greek (11)	23	0.19
Irish (67)	208	1.68
Italian (40)	83	0.67
Norwegian (12)	44	0.35
Polish (0)	18	0.15
Portuguese (11)	72	0.58
Scotch-Irish (12)	35	0.28
Scottish (10)	29	0.23
Swedish (0)	60	0.48
Swiss (58)	145	1.17
Welsh (12)	12	0.10

Hispanic Origin	Population	%
Hispanic or Latino (of any race)	11,266	87.51
Central American, ex. Mexican	151	1.17
Costa Rican	1	0.01
Guatemalan	18	0.14
Honduran	34	0.26
Nicaraguan	4	0.03
Panamanian	1	0.01
Salvadoran	90	0.70
Other Central American	3	0.02
Mexican	10,573	82.13
Puerto Rican	30	0.23
South American	5	0.04
Bolivian	1	0.01
Colombian	1	0.01
Ecuadorian	1	0.01
Peruvian	1	0.01
Venezuelan	1	0.01
Other Hispanic or Latino	507	3.94

Race*	Population	%
African-American/Black (150)	186	1.44
Not Hispanic (49)	55	0.43
Hispanic (101)	131	1.02
American Indian/Alaska Native (347)	483	3.75
Not Hispanic (46)	82	0.64
Hispanic (301)	401	3.11
Apache (5)	9	0.07
Blackfeet (0)	2	0.02
Central American Ind. (0)	1	0.01
Cherokee (5)	21	0.16
Chickasaw (0)	1	0.01
Choctaw (3)	5	0.04
Cree (1)	1	0.01
Creek (5)	5	0.04
Iroquois (0)	1	0.01
Mexican American Ind. (81)	112	0.87
Navajo (3)	5	0.04
Potawatomi (3)	3	0.02
Pueblo (0)	1	0.01
Spanish American Ind. (4)	6	0.05
Yaqui (0)	1	0.01
Yuman (6)	9	0.07
Asian (172)	240	1.86
Not Hispanic (166)	192	1.49
Hispanic (6)	48	0.37
Chinese, ex. Taiwanese (10)	13	0.10
Filipino (96)	128	0.99
Indian (39)	49	0.38
Indonesian (1)	2	0.02
Japanese (4)	9	0.07
Korean (20)	30	0.23
Vietnamese (1)	1	0.01
Hawaii Native/Pacific Islander (8)	23	0.18
Not Hispanic (7)	10	0.08
Hispanic (1)	13	0.10
Guamanian/Chamorro (0)	3	0.02
Native Hawaiian (1)	8	0.06
Samoan (1)	4	0.03
Tongan (1)	2	0.02
White (6,173)	6,669	51.80
Not Hispanic (1,251)	1,310	10.18
Hispanic (4,922)	5,359	41.63

Kingsburg

Place Type: City
County: Fresno
Population: 11,382†

Ancestry‡	Population	%
Albanian (4)	4	0.04
American (270)	270	2.45
Arab (0)	8	0.07
Lebanese (0)	8	0.07
Armenian (66)	129	1.17
British (39)	39	0.35
Canadian (9)	19	0.17
Czech (9)	21	0.19
Danish (88)	168	1.52
Dutch (35)	207	1.87
English (383)	960	8.69
European (20)	26	0.24
Finnish (0)	17	0.15
French, ex. Basque (0)	91	0.82
French Canadian (12)	60	0.54
German (419)	1,343	12.16
Hungarian (5)	43	0.39
Irish (120)	1,134	10.27
Italian (141)	379	3.43
Norwegian (0)	142	1.29
Polish (0)	22	0.20
Portuguese (102)	174	1.58
Russian (12)	12	0.11
Scandinavian (10)	10	0.09
Scotch-Irish (62)	120	1.09
Scottish (36)	119	1.08
Swedish (227)	620	5.62
Swiss (16)	80	0.72
Welsh (0)	32	0.29
West Indian, ex. Hispanic (0)	12	0.11
Dutch West Indian (0)	12	0.11
Yugoslavian (12)	12	0.11

Hispanic Origin	Population	%
Hispanic or Latino (of any race)	4,883	42.90
Central American, ex. Mexican	23	0.20
Guatemalan	7	0.06
Honduran	4	0.04
Nicaraguan	1	0.01

*Notes: † The Census 2010 population figure is used to calculate the percentages in the Hispanic Origin and Race categories. Ancestry percentages are based on the 2006-2010 American Community Survey population (not shown); ‡ Numbers in parentheses indicate the number of people reporting a single ancestry; * Numbers in parentheses indicate the number of persons reporting this race alone, not in combination with any other race; Please refer to the Explanation of Data for more information.*

Panamanian	2	0.02
Salvadoran	9	0.08
Cuban	9	0.08
Dominican Republic	1	0.01
Mexican	4,569	40.14
Puerto Rican	32	0.28
South American	15	0.13
Argentinean	2	0.02
Colombian	2	0.02
Ecuadorian	6	0.05
Peruvian	5	0.04
Other Hispanic or Latino	234	2.06

Race*	Population	%
African-American/Black (62)	140	1.23
Not Hispanic (38)	91	0.80
Hispanic (24)	49	0.43
American Indian/Alaska Native (146)	282	2.48
Not Hispanic (58)	140	1.23
Hispanic (88)	142	1.25
Apache (0)	3	0.03
Blackfeet (1)	2	0.02
Cherokee (19)	48	0.42
Chickasaw (1)	4	0.04
Choctaw (5)	11	0.10
Comanche (0)	3	0.03
Creek (7)	15	0.13
Iroquois (1)	1	0.01
Kiowa (1)	1	0.01
Mexican American Ind. (19)	28	0.25
Navajo (8)	10	0.09
Paiute (3)	3	0.03
Potawatomi (1)	8	0.07
Pueblo (2)	2	0.02
Seminole (5)	5	0.04
South American Ind. (1)	1	0.01
Asian (383)	527	4.63
Not Hispanic (374)	460	4.04
Hispanic (9)	67	0.59
Cambodian (6)	8	0.07
Chinese, ex. Taiwanese (81)	93	0.82
Filipino (17)	52	0.46
Hmong (1)	1	0.01
Indian (180)	201	1.77
Indonesian (2)	4	0.04
Japanese (81)	134	1.18
Korean (2)	10	0.09
Laotian (5)	9	0.08
Pakistani (2)	2	0.02
Vietnamese (1)	2	0.02
Hawaii Native/Pacific Islander (21)	37	0.33
Not Hispanic (6)	20	0.18
Hispanic (15)	17	0.15
Fijian (0)	1	0.01
Guamanian/Chamorro (12)	14	0.12
Native Hawaiian (2)	6	0.05
Samoan (1)	1	0.01
White (8,576)	8,993	79.01
Not Hispanic (5,776)	5,971	52.46
Hispanic (2,800)	3,022	26.55

La Cañada Flintridge

Place Type: City
County: Los Angeles
Population: 20,246†

Ancestry‡	Population	%
Alsatian (0)	11	0.05
American (777)	777	3.84
Arab (87)	304	1.50
Arab (14)	44	0.22
Egyptian (23)	82	0.40
Iraqi (10)	67	0.33
Lebanese (13)	84	0.41
Syrian (14)	14	0.07
Other Arab (13)	13	0.06
Armenian (836)	925	4.57
Assyrian/Chaldean/Syriac (11)	11	0.05
Australian (12)	12	0.06
Austrian (20)	157	0.78
Brazilian (0)	30	0.15
British (55)	188	0.93
Bulgarian (46)	46	0.23
Canadian (65)	181	0.89
Croatian (24)	66	0.33
Czech (54)	116	0.57
Czechoslovakian (16)	16	0.08
Danish (24)	159	0.79
Dutch (9)	246	1.21
Eastern European (52)	52	0.26
English (838)	2,962	14.62
European (631)	668	3.30
Finnish (9)	20	0.10
French, ex. Basque (37)	487	2.40
French Canadian (13)	63	0.31
German (475)	2,431	12.00
Greek (42)	127	0.63
Guyanese (9)	9	0.04
Hungarian (65)	115	0.57
Iranian (254)	307	1.52
Irish (439)	1,862	9.19
Italian (567)	1,011	4.99
Lithuanian (49)	111	0.55
New Zealander (67)	67	0.33
Northern European (91)	101	0.50
Norwegian (83)	364	1.80
Polish (159)	471	2.33
Portuguese (28)	99	0.49
Romanian (41)	41	0.20
Russian (309)	586	2.89
Scandinavian (34)	124	0.61
Scotch-Irish (127)	283	1.40
Scottish (175)	769	3.80
Slovak (32)	32	0.16
Swedish (243)	479	2.36
Swiss (12)	57	0.28
Turkish (27)	58	0.29
Welsh (0)	70	0.35
Yugoslavian (0)	29	0.14

Hispanic Origin	Population	%
Hispanic or Latino (of any race)	1,267	6.26
Central American, ex. Mexican	112	0.55
Costa Rican	6	0.03
Guatemalan	40	0.20
Honduran	10	0.05
Nicaraguan	11	0.05
Panamanian	5	0.02
Salvadoran	40	0.20
Cuban	122	0.60
Dominican Republic	10	0.05
Mexican	695	3.43
Puerto Rican	44	0.22
South American	144	0.71
Argentinean	35	0.17
Bolivian	12	0.06
Chilean	9	0.04
Colombian	24	0.12
Ecuadorian	11	0.05
Peruvian	28	0.14
Uruguayan	4	0.02
Venezuelan	21	0.10
Other Hispanic or Latino	140	0.69

Race*	Population	%
African-American/Black (109)	173	0.85
Not Hispanic (101)	149	0.74
Hispanic (8)	24	0.12
American Indian/Alaska Native (24)	106	0.52
Not Hispanic (4)	72	0.36
Hispanic (20)	34	0.17
Apache (0)	5	0.02
Canadian/French Am. Ind. (1)	1	<0.01
Cherokee (0)	31	0.15
Chickasaw (0)	5	0.02
Chippewa (1)	1	<0.01
Choctaw (0)	3	0.01
Iroquois (1)	1	<0.01
Mexican American Ind. (4)	7	0.03
Navajo (1)	3	0.01
Potawatomi (0)	2	0.01
Pueblo (0)	3	0.01
Seminole (0)	1	<0.01
South American Ind. (0)	3	0.01
Yakama (0)	4	0.02
Yaqui (3)	8	0.04
Asian (5,214)	5,711	28.21
Not Hispanic (5,181)	5,623	27.77
Hispanic (33)	88	0.43
Bangladeshi (8)	8	0.04
Burmese (4)	10	0.05
Cambodian (1)	3	0.01
Chinese, ex. Taiwanese (1,037)	1,260	6.22
Filipino (221)	314	1.55
Indian (286)	334	1.65
Indonesian (1)	7	0.03
Japanese (348)	508	2.51
Korean (2,941)	3,030	14.97
Nepalese (3)	3	0.01
Pakistani (33)	35	0.17
Sri Lankan (23)	30	0.15
Taiwanese (71)	78	0.39
Thai (31)	38	0.19
Vietnamese (51)	72	0.36
Hawaii Native/Pacific Islander (5)	31	0.15
Not Hispanic (4)	22	0.11
Hispanic (1)	9	0.04
Guamanian/Chamorro (2)	4	0.02
Native Hawaiian (1)	12	0.06
Samoan (0)	1	<0.01
White (13,959)	14,603	72.13
Not Hispanic (13,094)	13,608	67.21
Hispanic (865)	995	4.91

La Crescenta-Montrose

Place Type: CDP
County: Los Angeles
Population: 19,653†

Ancestry‡	Population	%
African, Sub-Saharan (17)	26	0.13
African (0)	9	0.05
South African (17)	17	0.09
American (459)	459	2.30
Arab (133)	231	1.16
Egyptian (0)	33	0.17
Lebanese (118)	151	0.76
Palestinian (0)	20	0.10
Syrian (15)	27	0.14
Armenian (1,859)	2,171	10.89
Australian (0)	12	0.06
Austrian (0)	25	0.13
Belgian (14)	100	0.50
British (6)	103	0.52
Bulgarian (63)	63	0.32
Canadian (61)	111	0.56
Croatian (16)	29	0.15
Czechoslovakian (14)	14	0.07
Danish (40)	294	1.48
Dutch (74)	226	1.13
Eastern European (17)	62	0.31
English (356)	1,579	7.92
European (105)	122	0.61
Finnish (0)	8	0.04
French, ex. Basque (91)	520	2.61
French Canadian (31)	182	0.91
German (480)	2,362	11.85
Greek (10)	125	0.63
Hungarian (18)	34	0.17
Iranian (161)	478	2.40
Irish (439)	1,756	8.81
Italian (224)	804	4.03
Latvian (0)	13	0.07
Lithuanian (22)	46	0.23
Luxemburger (0)	9	0.05
Maltese (0)	18	0.09
Northern European (9)	9	0.05
Norwegian (132)	313	1.57

*Notes: † The Census 2010 population figure is used to calculate the percentages in the Hispanic Origin and Race categories. Ancestry percentages are based on the 2006-2010 American Community Survey population (not shown); ‡ Numbers in parentheses indicate the number of people reporting a single ancestry; * Numbers in parentheses indicate the number of persons reporting this race alone, not in combination with any other race; Please refer to the Explanation of Data for more information.*

Pennsylvania German (15)	24	0.12
Polish (104)	253	1.27
Portuguese (14)	56	0.28
Romanian (13)	27	0.14
Russian (34)	254	1.27
Scandinavian (35)	41	0.21
Scotch-Irish (60)	289	1.45
Scottish (90)	338	1.70
Serbian (29)	59	0.30
Slovak (36)	36	0.18
Swedish (106)	254	1.27
Swiss (9)	28	0.14
Ukrainian (0)	85	0.43
Welsh (11)	86	0.43

Hispanic Origin	Population	%
Hispanic or Latino (of any race)	2,232	11.36
Central American, ex. Mexican	330	1.68
Costa Rican	26	0.13
Guatemalan	122	0.62
Honduran	5	0.03
Nicaraguan	23	0.12
Panamanian	7	0.04
Salvadoran	143	0.73
Other Central American	4	0.02
Cuban	132	0.67
Dominican Republic	1	0.01
Mexican	1,265	6.44
Puerto Rican	53	0.27
South American	242	1.23
Argentinean	71	0.36
Bolivian	12	0.06
Chilean	19	0.10
Colombian	62	0.32
Ecuadorian	19	0.10
Peruvian	50	0.25
Uruguayan	4	0.02
Venezuelan	4	0.02
Other South American	1	0.01
Other Hispanic or Latino	209	1.06

Race*	Population	%
African-American/Black (142)	207	1.05
Not Hispanic (130)	184	0.94
Hispanic (12)	23	0.12
American Indian/Alaska Native (70)	167	0.85
Not Hispanic (35)	96	0.49
Hispanic (35)	71	0.36
Apache (3)	4	0.02
Blackfeet (2)	7	0.04
Canadian/French Am. Ind. (1)	2	0.01
Central American Ind. (0)	2	0.01
Cherokee (9)	29	0.15
Chickasaw (0)	1	0.01
Chippewa (1)	5	0.03
Choctaw (3)	6	0.03
Colville (2)	2	0.01
Cree (0)	1	0.01
Creek (1)	2	0.01
Mexican American Ind. (6)	8	0.04
Navajo (3)	3	0.02
Osage (1)	1	0.01
Potawatomi (1)	3	0.02
Pueblo (0)	1	0.01
Spanish American Ind. (0)	1	0.01
Tlingit-Haida *(Alaska Native)* (1)	1	0.01
Yaqui (3)	3	0.02
Asian (5,375)	5,830	29.66
Not Hispanic (5,339)	5,726	29.14
Hispanic (36)	104	0.53
Bangladeshi (14)	18	0.09
Burmese (2)	2	0.01
Cambodian (2)	2	0.01
Chinese, ex. Taiwanese (250)	361	1.84
Filipino (510)	617	3.14
Indian (166)	209	1.06
Indonesian (18)	31	0.16
Japanese (189)	303	1.54
Korean (3,977)	4,058	20.65
Laotian (1)	1	0.01
Pakistani (17)	20	0.10
Sri Lankan (14)	16	0.08
Taiwanese (18)	22	0.11
Thai (56)	66	0.34
Vietnamese (44)	59	0.30
Hawaii Native/Pacific Islander (12)	57	0.29
Not Hispanic (9)	44	0.22
Hispanic (3)	13	0.07
Guamanian/Chamorro (4)	10	0.05
Native Hawaiian (7)	21	0.11
Samoan (1)	1	0.01
Tongan (0)	1	0.01
White (12,807)	13,440	68.39
Not Hispanic (11,376)	11,837	60.23
Hispanic (1,431)	1,603	8.16

La Habra

Place Type: City
County: Orange
Population: 60,239†

Ancestry‡	Population	%
Afghan (77)	77	0.13
African, Sub-Saharan (12)	12	0.02
African (12)	12	0.02
Albanian (0)	12	0.02
American (1,343)	1,343	2.25
Arab (84)	179	0.30
Arab (10)	46	0.08
Egyptian (10)	18	0.03
Lebanese (30)	51	0.09
Palestinian (0)	20	0.03
Syrian (34)	44	0.07
Armenian (194)	244	0.41
Assyrian/Chaldean/Syriac (33)	85	0.14
Austrian (26)	144	0.24
Basque (35)	67	0.11
Brazilian (17)	28	0.05
British (90)	185	0.31
Canadian (75)	104	0.17
Celtic (21)	21	0.04
Croatian (0)	12	0.02
Czech (58)	206	0.34
Czechoslovakian (9)	17	0.03
Danish (47)	444	0.74
Dutch (301)	764	1.28
English (857)	3,431	5.74
Estonian (0)	16	0.03
European (582)	604	1.01
Finnish (31)	69	0.12
French, ex. Basque (143)	854	1.43
French Canadian (157)	203	0.34
German (1,324)	5,078	8.50
Greek (46)	64	0.11
Hungarian (95)	177	0.30
Iranian (202)	202	0.34
Irish (966)	4,339	7.26
Israeli (0)	25	0.04
Italian (634)	1,696	2.84
Lithuanian (0)	13	0.02
Maltese (13)	13	0.02
Northern European (28)	45	0.08
Norwegian (118)	545	0.91
Pennsylvania German (35)	35	0.06
Polish (124)	577	0.97
Portuguese (63)	136	0.23
Romanian (48)	98	0.16
Russian (274)	426	0.71
Scandinavian (24)	34	0.06
Scotch-Irish (222)	553	0.93
Scottish (105)	598	1.00
Serbian (43)	43	0.07
Slavic (41)	41	0.07
Slovak (14)	62	0.10
Swedish (115)	644	1.08
Swiss (0)	43	0.07
Turkish (0)	26	0.04
Ukrainian (5)	35	0.06
Welsh (43)	170	0.28
West Indian, ex. Hispanic (64)	64	0.11
Belizean (49)	49	0.08
Dutch West Indian (10)	10	0.02
Jamaican (5)	5	0.01
Yugoslavian (41)	74	0.12

Hispanic Origin	Population	%
Hispanic or Latino (of any race)	34,449	57.19
Central American, ex. Mexican	1,283	2.13
Costa Rican	83	0.14
Guatemalan	418	0.69
Honduran	52	0.09
Nicaraguan	119	0.20
Panamanian	15	0.02
Salvadoran	577	0.96
Other Central American	19	0.03
Cuban	279	0.46
Dominican Republic	15	0.02
Mexican	30,316	50.33
Puerto Rican	313	0.52
South American	634	1.05
Argentinean	123	0.20
Bolivian	32	0.05
Chilean	30	0.05
Colombian	162	0.27
Ecuadorian	101	0.17
Paraguayan	7	0.01
Peruvian	151	0.25
Uruguayan	10	0.02
Venezuelan	8	0.01
Other South American	10	0.02
Other Hispanic or Latino	1,609	2.67

Race*	Population	%
African-American/Black (1,025)	1,349	2.24
Not Hispanic (836)	1,018	1.69
Hispanic (189)	331	0.55
American Indian/Alaska Native (531)	960	1.59
Not Hispanic (148)	368	0.61
Hispanic (383)	592	0.98
Alaska Athabascan *(Ala. Nat.)* (1)	1	<0.01
Apache (15)	55	0.09
Arapaho (0)	1	<0.01
Blackfeet (0)	13	0.02
Central American Ind. (7)	8	0.01
Cherokee (28)	129	0.21
Chickasaw (10)	13	0.02
Chippewa (7)	8	0.01
Choctaw (13)	38	0.06
Comanche (1)	3	<0.01
Creek (3)	11	0.02
Crow (1)	1	<0.01
Delaware (0)	7	0.01
Hopi (2)	6	0.01
Inupiat *(Alaska Native)* (0)	1	<0.01
Iroquois (0)	4	0.01
Kiowa (3)	3	<0.01
Lumbee (3)	7	0.01
Mexican American Ind. (56)	79	0.13
Navajo (28)	47	0.08
Osage (5)	7	0.01
Paiute (5)	5	0.01
Pima (7)	10	0.02
Potawatomi (5)	5	0.01
Pueblo (14)	15	0.02
Puget Sound Salish (5)	5	0.01
Seminole (1)	1	<0.01
Sioux (8)	17	0.03
South American Ind. (1)	4	0.01
Spanish American Ind. (4)	4	0.01
Tlingit-Haida *(Alaska Native)* (0)	4	0.01
Tohono O'Odham (2)	6	0.01
Ute (1)	1	<0.01
Yaqui (7)	17	0.03
Yuman (1)	1	<0.01
Asian (5,653)	6,415	10.65
Not Hispanic (5,501)	6,021	10.00
Hispanic (152)	394	0.65
Bangladeshi (15)	21	0.03
Burmese (15)	17	0.03

*Notes: † The Census 2010 population figure is used to calculate the percentages in the Hispanic Origin and Race categories. Ancestry percentages are based on the 2006-2010 American Community Survey population (not shown); ‡ Numbers in parentheses indicate the number of people reporting a single ancestry; * Numbers in parentheses indicate the number of persons reporting this race alone, not in combination with any other race; Please refer to the Explanation of Data for more information.*

Cambodian (43)	64	0.11
Chinese, ex. Taiwanese (695)	856	1.42
Filipino (1,137)	1,421	2.36
Hmong (2)	6	0.01
Indian (384)	430	0.71
Indonesian (61)	86	0.14
Japanese (352)	561	0.93
Korean (2,306)	2,375	3.94
Laotian (17)	18	0.03
Malaysian (5)	6	0.01
Nepalese (5)	5	0.01
Pakistani (37)	52	0.09
Sri Lankan (12)	12	0.02
Taiwanese (119)	148	0.25
Thai (83)	110	0.18
Vietnamese (197)	235	0.39
Hawaii Native/Pacific Islander (103)	288	0.48
Not Hispanic (80)	210	0.35
Hispanic (23)	78	0.13
Fijian (2)	3	<0.01
Guamanian/Chamorro (24)	39	0.06
Native Hawaiian (44)	129	0.21
Samoan (26)	47	0.08
Tongan (3)	6	0.01
White (35,147)	37,363	62.02
Not Hispanic (18,178)	19,022	31.58
Hispanic (16,969)	18,341	30.45

La Mesa

Place Type: City
County: San Diego
Population: 57,065†

Ancestry‡	Population	%
Afghan (73)	73	0.13
African, Sub-Saharan (608)	729	1.30
African (178)	281	0.50
Ethiopian (133)	133	0.24
Nigerian (64)	64	0.11
Somalian (233)	233	0.41
South African (0)	18	0.03
American (1,485)	1,485	2.64
Arab (233)	307	0.55
Arab (25)	25	0.04
Egyptian (49)	62	0.11
Iraqi (12)	12	0.02
Jordanian (79)	79	0.14
Lebanese (30)	56	0.10
Syrian (0)	11	0.02
Other Arab (38)	62	0.11
Armenian (74)	144	0.26
Assyrian/Chaldean/Syriac (94)	94	0.17
Australian (19)	62	0.11
Austrian (43)	103	0.18
Belgian (40)	141	0.25
Brazilian (0)	28	0.05
British (129)	318	0.57
Bulgarian (10)	10	0.02
Canadian (55)	261	0.46
Celtic (39)	39	0.07
Croatian (27)	27	0.05
Czech (34)	291	0.52
Czechoslovakian (88)	104	0.18
Danish (60)	404	0.72
Dutch (175)	854	1.52
Eastern European (12)	12	0.02
English (1,480)	6,214	11.05
European (491)	617	1.10
Finnish (0)	168	0.30
French, ex. Basque (246)	1,923	3.42
French Canadian (116)	283	0.50
German (2,222)	10,278	18.27
German Russian (0)	43	0.08
Greek (73)	271	0.48
Hungarian (109)	421	0.75
Icelander (0)	14	0.02
Iranian (190)	277	0.49
Irish (2,145)	7,663	13.62
Israeli (12)	30	0.05
Italian (1,237)	3,706	6.59
Latvian (17)	17	0.03
Lithuanian (70)	166	0.30
Macedonian (0)	18	0.03
New Zealander (15)	15	0.03
Northern European (16)	16	0.03
Norwegian (441)	1,179	2.10
Pennsylvania German (32)	62	0.11
Polish (526)	1,674	2.98
Portuguese (267)	604	1.07
Romanian (51)	84	0.15
Russian (532)	917	1.63
Scandinavian (0)	320	0.57
Scotch-Irish (299)	1,262	2.24
Scottish (596)	1,903	3.38
Serbian (18)	18	0.03
Slavic (0)	16	0.03
Slovak (59)	116	0.21
Slovene (0)	14	0.02
Swedish (407)	1,513	2.69
Swiss (29)	221	0.39
Turkish (19)	28	0.05
Ukrainian (146)	194	0.34
Welsh (103)	470	0.84
West Indian, ex. Hispanic (239)	419	0.74
Barbadian (12)	23	0.04
Belizean (65)	65	0.12
Haitian (89)	89	0.16
Jamaican (73)	147	0.26
West Indian (0)	95	0.17
Yugoslavian (45)	83	0.15

Hispanic Origin	Population	%
Hispanic or Latino (of any race)	11,696	20.50
Central American, ex. Mexican	339	0.59
Costa Rican	48	0.08
Guatemalan	66	0.12
Honduran	40	0.07
Nicaraguan	38	0.07
Panamanian	75	0.13
Salvadoran	69	0.12
Other Central American	3	0.01
Cuban	124	0.22
Dominican Republic	59	0.10
Mexican	9,496	16.64
Puerto Rican	402	0.70
South American	349	0.61
Argentinean	39	0.07
Bolivian	9	0.02
Chilean	28	0.05
Colombian	114	0.20
Ecuadorian	38	0.07
Paraguayan	1	<0.01
Peruvian	108	0.19
Venezuelan	10	0.02
Other South American	2	<0.01
Other Hispanic or Latino	927	1.62

Race*	Population	%
African-American/Black (4,399)	5,458	9.56
Not Hispanic (4,102)	4,914	8.61
Hispanic (297)	544	0.95
American Indian/Alaska Native (431)	1,104	1.93
Not Hispanic (249)	676	1.18
Hispanic (182)	428	0.75
Alaska Athabascan *(Ala. Nat.)* (1)	1	<0.01
Aleut *(Alaska Native)* (4)	4	0.01
Apache (18)	33	0.06
Blackfeet (7)	34	0.06
Canadian/French Am. Ind. (1)	2	<0.01
Central American Ind. (1)	3	0.01
Cherokee (22)	158	0.28
Cheyenne (0)	6	0.01
Chickasaw (4)	9	0.02
Chippewa (9)	19	0.03
Choctaw (11)	36	0.06
Comanche (4)	6	0.01
Cree (0)	1	<0.01
Creek (5)	17	0.03
Crow (1)	1	<0.01
Delaware (3)	5	0.01
Hopi (0)	4	0.01
Inupiat *(Alaska Native)* (1)	1	<0.01
Iroquois (9)	23	0.04
Kiowa (1)	3	0.01
Lumbee (2)	2	<0.01
Mexican American Ind. (26)	46	0.08
Navajo (9)	30	0.05
Osage (6)	6	0.01
Paiute (2)	2	<0.01
Pima (4)	5	0.01
Potawatomi (3)	3	0.01
Pueblo (6)	12	0.02
Puget Sound Salish (1)	1	<0.01
Seminole (1)	7	0.01
Sioux (21)	33	0.06
South American Ind. (0)	4	0.01
Spanish American Ind. (5)	11	0.02
Tlingit-Haida *(Alaska Native)* (4)	5	0.01
Tohono O'Odham (1)	2	<0.01
Ute (0)	7	0.01
Yaqui (9)	29	0.05
Yuman (3)	4	0.01
Asian (3,289)	4,584	8.03
Not Hispanic (3,152)	4,192	7.35
Hispanic (137)	392	0.69
Burmese (1)	7	0.01
Cambodian (71)	97	0.17
Chinese, ex. Taiwanese (560)	756	1.32
Filipino (994)	1,591	2.79
Hmong (4)	4	0.01
Indian (206)	283	0.50
Indonesian (28)	46	0.08
Japanese (328)	641	1.12
Korean (186)	256	0.45
Laotian (58)	68	0.12
Malaysian (0)	1	<0.01
Nepalese (11)	11	0.02
Pakistani (16)	25	0.04
Sri Lankan (2)	3	0.01
Taiwanese (28)	33	0.06
Thai (61)	106	0.19
Vietnamese (567)	660	1.16
Hawaii Native/Pacific Islander (318)	622	1.09
Not Hispanic (272)	519	0.91
Hispanic (46)	103	0.18
Fijian (4)	4	0.01
Guamanian/Chamorro (149)	241	0.42
Native Hawaiian (36)	121	0.21
Samoan (92)	162	0.28
Tongan (2)	8	0.01
White (40,964)	43,761	76.69
Not Hispanic (35,295)	37,130	65.07
Hispanic (5,669)	6,631	11.62

La Mirada

Place Type: City
County: Los Angeles
Population: 48,527†

Ancestry‡	Population	%
African, Sub-Saharan (84)	84	0.17
African (50)	50	0.10
Ethiopian (20)	20	0.04
South African (14)	14	0.03
American (816)	816	1.69
Arab (130)	182	0.38
Arab (0)	21	0.04
Egyptian (94)	106	0.22
Jordanian (8)	18	0.04
Lebanese (28)	28	0.06
Syrian (0)	9	0.02
Armenian (86)	97	0.20
Austrian (14)	27	0.06
Basque (0)	12	0.02
Belgian (0)	3	0.01
Brazilian (25)	25	0.05
British (21)	54	0.11
Canadian (66)	171	0.35

*Notes: † The Census 2010 population figure is used to calculate the percentages in the Hispanic Origin and Race categories. Ancestry percentages are based on the 2006-2010 American Community Survey population (not shown); ‡ Numbers in parentheses indicate the number of people reporting a single ancestry; * Numbers in parentheses indicate the number of persons reporting this race alone, not in combination with any other race; Please refer to the Explanation of Data for more information.*

Croatian (70)	140	0.29
Czech (53)	219	0.45
Czechoslovakian (13)	22	0.05
Danish (14)	140	0.29
Dutch (259)	788	1.64
English (1,056)	3,053	6.34
European (242)	288	0.60
Finnish (10)	22	0.05
French, ex. Basque (97)	965	2.00
French Canadian (32)	111	0.23
German (1,285)	4,401	9.14
Greek (83)	211	0.44
Hungarian (61)	86	0.18
Iranian (78)	87	0.18
Irish (615)	2,815	5.84
Italian (865)	1,814	3.77
Latvian (19)	19	0.04
Lithuanian (57)	144	0.30
New Zealander (0)	14	0.03
Northern European (49)	63	0.13
Norwegian (204)	594	1.23
Polish (180)	521	1.08
Portuguese (49)	108	0.22
Romanian (123)	156	0.32
Russian (230)	469	0.97
Scandinavian (15)	28	0.06
Scotch-Irish (148)	476	0.99
Scottish (277)	659	1.37
Slovak (11)	23	0.05
Swedish (183)	783	1.63
Swiss (83)	201	0.42
Turkish (0)	11	0.02
Ukrainian (0)	11	0.02
Welsh (40)	231	0.48
West Indian, ex. Hispanic (28)	45	0.09
Jamaican (0)	17	0.04
Trinidadian/Tobagonian (28)	28	0.06
Yugoslavian (84)	114	0.24

Hispanic Origin	Population	%
Hispanic or Latino (of any race)	19,272	39.71
Central American, ex. Mexican	1,067	2.20
Costa Rican	68	0.14
Guatemalan	258	0.53
Honduran	55	0.11
Nicaraguan	153	0.32
Panamanian	26	0.05
Salvadoran	498	1.03
Other Central American	9	0.02
Cuban	352	0.73
Dominican Republic	20	0.04
Mexican	15,796	32.55
Puerto Rican	321	0.66
South American	635	1.31
Argentinean	98	0.20
Bolivian	11	0.02
Chilean	33	0.07
Colombian	133	0.27
Ecuadorian	119	0.25
Paraguayan	1	<0.01
Peruvian	204	0.42
Uruguayan	15	0.03
Venezuelan	15	0.03
Other South American	6	0.01
Other Hispanic or Latino	1,081	2.23

Race*	Population	%
African-American/Black (1,099)	1,377	2.84
Not Hispanic (1,010)	1,183	2.44
Hispanic (89)	194	0.40
American Indian/Alaska Native (394)	831	1.71
Not Hispanic (138)	313	0.65
Hispanic (256)	518	1.07
Aleut *(Alaska Native)* (3)	3	0.01
Apache (12)	20	0.04
Blackfeet (4)	9	0.02
Canadian/French Am. Ind. (0)	3	0.01
Central American Ind. (3)	6	0.01
Cherokee (22)	72	0.15
Cheyenne (0)	1	<0.01
Chickasaw (0)	4	0.01
Chippewa (1)	8	0.02
Choctaw (9)	24	0.05
Creek (1)	2	<0.01
Hopi (1)	1	<0.01
Iroquois (0)	13	0.03
Kiowa (2)	2	<0.01
Mexican American Ind. (40)	73	0.15
Navajo (13)	28	0.06
Osage (0)	8	0.02
Ottawa (0)	1	<0.01
Pima (2)	3	0.01
Potawatomi (7)	14	0.03
Pueblo (9)	23	0.05
Puget Sound Salish (1)	2	<0.01
Seminole (2)	5	0.01
Sioux (3)	10	0.02
South American Ind. (1)	2	<0.01
Spanish American Ind. (1)	4	0.01
Tlingit-Haida *(Alaska Native)* (2)	2	<0.01
Tohono O'Odham (3)	9	0.02
Yaqui (15)	35	0.07
Yuman (7)	7	0.01
Asian (8,650)	9,481	19.54
Not Hispanic (8,530)	9,129	18.81
Hispanic (120)	352	0.73
Bangladeshi (13)	13	0.03
Burmese (0)	3	0.01
Cambodian (63)	71	0.15
Chinese, ex. Taiwanese (717)	946	1.95
Filipino (2,410)	2,797	5.76
Hmong (1)	4	0.01
Indian (532)	596	1.23
Indonesian (36)	78	0.16
Japanese (362)	582	1.20
Korean (3,671)	3,791	7.81
Laotian (17)	28	0.06
Nepalese (5)	5	0.01
Pakistani (36)	37	0.08
Sri Lankan (18)	23	0.05
Taiwanese (109)	118	0.24
Thai (89)	110	0.23
Vietnamese (319)	365	0.75
Hawaii Native/Pacific Islander (142)	353	0.73
Not Hispanic (114)	270	0.56
Hispanic (28)	83	0.17
Fijian (9)	12	0.02
Guamanian/Chamorro (30)	56	0.12
Marshallese (2)	2	<0.01
Native Hawaiian (28)	104	0.21
Samoan (45)	76	0.16
Tongan (11)	13	0.03
White (29,462)	31,237	64.37
Not Hispanic (18,418)	19,198	39.56
Hispanic (11,044)	12,039	24.81

La Palma

Place Type: City
County: Orange
Population: 15,568†

Ancestry‡	Population	%
African, Sub-Saharan (166)	166	1.07
African (31)	31	0.20
Ethiopian (110)	110	0.71
Nigerian (25)	25	0.16
American (241)	241	1.56
Arab (151)	240	1.55
Arab (65)	111	0.72
Egyptian (64)	64	0.41
Jordanian (22)	22	0.14
Palestinian (0)	30	0.19
Syrian (0)	13	0.08
Armenian (24)	24	0.16
Australian (0)	11	0.07
Austrian (23)	23	0.15
Canadian (12)	26	0.17
Croatian (0)	27	0.17
Czech (10)	10	0.06
Czechoslovakian (11)	21	0.14
Danish (0)	85	0.55
Dutch (59)	256	1.65
Eastern European (15)	15	0.10
English (228)	983	6.35
European (116)	129	0.83
French, ex. Basque (123)	483	3.12
French Canadian (12)	23	0.15
German (395)	1,508	9.74
Greek (0)	10	0.06
Hungarian (43)	70	0.45
Iranian (30)	76	0.49
Irish (198)	1,180	7.62
Israeli (45)	45	0.29
Italian (208)	403	2.60
Lithuanian (0)	11	0.07
Macedonian (10)	22	0.14
Norwegian (0)	43	0.28
Polish (67)	163	1.05
Portuguese (111)	177	1.14
Russian (12)	12	0.08
Scotch-Irish (44)	122	0.79
Scottish (43)	156	1.01
Slavic (0)	25	0.16
Slovak (18)	29	0.19
Swedish (51)	160	1.03
Swiss (0)	7	0.05
Turkish (25)	47	0.30
Welsh (0)	49	0.32

Hispanic Origin	Population	%
Hispanic or Latino (of any race)	2,487	15.98
Central American, ex. Mexican	128	0.82
Costa Rican	16	0.10
Guatemalan	30	0.19
Honduran	8	0.05
Nicaraguan	12	0.08
Panamanian	8	0.05
Salvadoran	52	0.33
Other Central American	2	0.01
Cuban	52	0.33
Dominican Republic	5	0.03
Mexican	1,866	11.99
Puerto Rican	63	0.40
South American	189	1.21
Argentinean	24	0.15
Bolivian	12	0.08
Chilean	7	0.04
Colombian	58	0.37
Ecuadorian	25	0.16
Peruvian	52	0.33
Uruguayan	1	0.01
Venezuelan	4	0.03
Other South American	6	0.04
Other Hispanic or Latino	184	1.18

Race*	Population	%
African-American/Black (802)	933	5.99
Not Hispanic (773)	872	5.60
Hispanic (29)	61	0.39
American Indian/Alaska Native (56)	131	0.84
Not Hispanic (26)	71	0.46
Hispanic (30)	60	0.39
Aleut *(Alaska Native)* (1)	1	0.01
Apache (4)	6	0.04
Blackfeet (3)	4	0.03
Canadian/French Am. Ind. (1)	2	0.01
Central American Ind. (1)	1	0.01
Cherokee (4)	11	0.07
Chickasaw (0)	1	0.01
Chippewa (0)	4	0.03
Choctaw (0)	1	0.01
Iroquois (0)	2	0.01
Mexican American Ind. (6)	12	0.08
Navajo (0)	2	0.01
Pima (0)	1	0.01
Potawatomi (4)	7	0.04
Pueblo (1)	3	0.02
Shoshone (1)	2	0.01
Sioux (0)	1	0.01

*Notes: † The Census 2010 population figure is used to calculate the percentages in the Hispanic Origin and Race categories. Ancestry percentages are based on the 2006-2010 American Community Survey population (not shown); ‡ Numbers in parentheses indicate the number of people reporting a single ancestry; * Numbers in parentheses indicate the number of persons reporting this race alone, not in combination with any other race; Please refer to the Explanation of Data for more information.*

South American Ind. (0)	1	0.01
Yaqui (2)	2	0.01
Asian (7,483)	7,896	50.72
Not Hispanic (7,432)	7,771	49.92
Hispanic (51)	125	0.80
Bangladeshi (8)	8	0.05
Cambodian (70)	76	0.49
Chinese, ex. Taiwanese (966)	1,146	7.36
Filipino (1,447)	1,684	10.82
Hmong (1)	1	0.01
Indian (842)	868	5.58
Indonesian (14)	21	0.13
Japanese (695)	886	5.69
Korean (2,587)	2,656	17.06
Laotian (1)	2	0.01
Malaysian (1)	2	0.01
Pakistani (61)	68	0.44
Sri Lankan (11)	15	0.10
Taiwanese (220)	259	1.66
Thai (63)	70	0.45
Vietnamese (295)	325	2.09
Hawaii Native/Pacific Islander (41)	132	0.85
Not Hispanic (36)	113	0.73
Hispanic (5)	19	0.12
Fijian (6)	7	0.04
Guamanian/Chamorro (8)	24	0.15
Native Hawaiian (11)	41	0.26
Samoan (12)	25	0.16
Tongan (2)	6	0.04
White (5,762)	6,259	40.20
Not Hispanic (4,329)	4,668	29.98
Hispanic (1,433)	1,591	10.22

La Presa

Place Type: CDP
County: San Diego
Population: 34,169†

Ancestry‡	Population	%
Afghan (37)	58	0.17
African, Sub-Saharan (1,399)	1,504	4.31
African (960)	1,065	3.05
Nigerian (27)	27	0.08
Somalian (388)	388	1.11
Other Sub-Saharan African (24)	24	0.07
Albanian (8)	8	0.02
American (435)	435	1.25
Arab (250)	259	0.74
Arab (10)	10	0.03
Iraqi (138)	138	0.40
Lebanese (9)	18	0.05
Syrian (40)	40	0.11
Other Arab (53)	53	0.15
Armenian (0)	9	0.03
Assyrian/Chaldean/Syriac (77)	77	0.22
Austrian (8)	8	0.02
Belgian (0)	11	0.03
Brazilian (0)	10	0.03
British (49)	93	0.27
Czech (53)	68	0.19
Czechoslovakian (0)	8	0.02
Danish (35)	126	0.36
Dutch (94)	366	1.05
English (521)	1,867	5.35
European (82)	110	0.32
Finnish (15)	40	0.11
French, ex. Basque (68)	715	2.05
French Canadian (43)	104	0.30
German (525)	2,647	7.59
Greek (0)	57	0.16
Hungarian (0)	16	0.05
Iranian (44)	44	0.13
Irish (396)	2,042	5.85
Italian (241)	1,196	3.43
Lithuanian (0)	12	0.03
Maltese (0)	13	0.04
Norwegian (45)	298	0.85
Polish (49)	255	0.73
Portuguese (43)	109	0.31
Romanian (0)	27	0.08
Russian (37)	153	0.44
Scandinavian (56)	56	0.16
Scotch-Irish (136)	343	0.98
Scottish (176)	489	1.40
Slavic (14)	14	0.04
Swedish (92)	345	0.99
Swiss (17)	51	0.15
Ukrainian (12)	25	0.07
Welsh (10)	92	0.26
West Indian, ex. Hispanic (119)	157	0.45
Belizean (39)	39	0.11
Jamaican (36)	74	0.21
Trinidadian/Tobagonian (33)	33	0.09
West Indian (11)	11	0.03

Hispanic Origin	Population	%
Hispanic or Latino (of any race)	16,150	47.27
Central American, ex. Mexican	253	0.74
Costa Rican	18	0.05
Guatemalan	45	0.13
Honduran	44	0.13
Nicaraguan	47	0.14
Panamanian	39	0.11
Salvadoran	55	0.16
Other Central American	5	0.01
Cuban	78	0.23
Dominican Republic	22	0.06
Mexican	14,443	42.27
Puerto Rican	314	0.92
South American	151	0.44
Argentinean	3	0.01
Bolivian	4	0.01
Chilean	9	0.03
Colombian	54	0.16
Ecuadorian	9	0.03
Peruvian	60	0.18
Uruguayan	2	0.01
Venezuelan	6	0.02
Other South American	4	0.01
Other Hispanic or Latino	889	2.60

Race*	Population	%
African-American/Black (4,428)	5,313	15.55
Not Hispanic (4,146)	4,745	13.89
Hispanic (282)	568	1.66
American Indian/Alaska Native (282)	630	1.84
Not Hispanic (94)	308	0.90
Hispanic (188)	322	0.94
Apache (3)	19	0.06
Arapaho (1)	1	<0.01
Blackfeet (1)	5	0.01
Canadian/French Am. Ind. (1)	1	<0.01
Central American Ind. (0)	2	0.01
Cherokee (10)	61	0.18
Chickasaw (1)	2	0.01
Chippewa (2)	3	0.01
Choctaw (0)	11	0.03
Comanche (1)	4	0.01
Cree (1)	2	0.01
Creek (1)	3	0.01
Delaware (2)	2	0.01
Houma (1)	1	<0.01
Iroquois (4)	12	0.04
Kiowa (1)	1	<0.01
Lumbee (1)	1	<0.01
Menominee (0)	3	0.01
Mexican American Ind. (51)	64	0.19
Navajo (6)	20	0.06
Osage (1)	4	0.01
Paiute (0)	1	<0.01
Pima (0)	3	0.01
Pueblo (1)	2	0.01
Seminole (0)	4	0.01
Shoshone (1)	1	<0.01
Sioux (4)	13	0.04
South American Ind. (5)	5	0.01
Spanish American Ind. (0)	1	<0.01
Tohono O'Odham (5)	8	0.02
Yaqui (2)	11	0.03
Yuman (1)	4	0.01
Asian (3,212)	4,221	12.35
Not Hispanic (3,064)	3,800	11.12
Hispanic (148)	421	1.23
Cambodian (62)	79	0.23
Chinese, ex. Taiwanese (95)	187	0.55
Filipino (2,533)	3,280	9.60
Hmong (8)	8	0.02
Indian (44)	70	0.20
Indonesian (0)	8	0.02
Japanese (138)	313	0.92
Korean (57)	90	0.26
Laotian (19)	25	0.07
Malaysian (2)	11	0.03
Nepalese (2)	2	0.01
Pakistani (1)	1	<0.01
Taiwanese (12)	13	0.04
Thai (15)	30	0.09
Vietnamese (126)	167	0.49
Hawaii Native/Pacific Islander (410)	668	1.95
Not Hispanic (362)	543	1.59
Hispanic (48)	125	0.37
Guamanian/Chamorro (198)	312	0.91
Marshallese (1)	1	<0.01
Native Hawaiian (40)	90	0.26
Samoan (151)	205	0.60
Tongan (1)	5	0.01
White (15,064)	16,984	49.71
Not Hispanic (8,950)	10,002	29.27
Hispanic (6,114)	6,982	20.43

La Puente

Place Type: City
County: Los Angeles
Population: 39,816†

Ancestry‡	Population	%
American (305)	305	0.76
Arab (15)	37	0.09
Lebanese (15)	26	0.06
Syrian (0)	11	0.03
Austrian (23)	23	0.06
Basque (11)	11	0.03
British (27)	27	0.07
Dutch (18)	74	0.18
English (38)	356	0.89
French, ex. Basque (5)	90	0.22
French Canadian (0)	67	0.17
German (60)	523	1.31
Greek (0)	33	0.08
Hungarian (0)	4	0.01
Irish (52)	435	1.09
Italian (82)	370	0.92
Maltese (12)	12	0.03
Norwegian (0)	17	0.04
Polish (16)	28	0.07
Portuguese (10)	21	0.05
Russian (29)	43	0.11
Scottish (37)	171	0.43
Slovene (0)	33	0.08
Swedish (0)	142	0.35
Welsh (0)	9	0.02
West Indian, ex. Hispanic (0)	8	0.02
Barbadian (0)	8	0.02
Yugoslavian (0)	11	0.03

Hispanic Origin	Population	%
Hispanic or Latino (of any race)	33,896	85.13
Central American, ex. Mexican	2,362	5.93
Costa Rican	24	0.06
Guatemalan	683	1.72
Honduran	90	0.23
Nicaraguan	250	0.63
Panamanian	7	0.02
Salvadoran	1,292	3.24
Other Central American	16	0.04
Cuban	65	0.16
Dominican Republic	3	0.01
Mexican	29,607	74.36

*Notes: † The Census 2010 population figure is used to calculate the percentages in the Hispanic Origin and Race categories. Ancestry percentages are based on the 2006-2010 American Community Survey population (not shown); ‡ Numbers in parentheses indicate the number of people reporting a single ancestry; * Numbers in parentheses indicate the number of persons reporting this race alone, not in combination with any other race; Please refer to the Explanation of Data for more information.*

Puerto Rican	167	0.42
South American	358	0.90
Argentinean	40	0.10
Bolivian	11	0.03
Chilean	12	0.03
Colombian	77	0.19
Ecuadorian	107	0.27
Paraguayan	4	0.01
Peruvian	85	0.21
Uruguayan	5	0.01
Venezuelan	5	0.01
Other South American	12	0.03
Other Hispanic or Latino	1,334	3.35

Race*	Population	%
African-American/Black (558)	738	1.85
Not Hispanic (451)	522	1.31
Hispanic (107)	216	0.54
American Indian/Alaska Native (430)	614	1.54
Not Hispanic (75)	110	0.28
Hispanic (355)	504	1.27
Apache (9)	14	0.04
Blackfeet (0)	2	0.01
Central American Ind. (4)	4	0.01
Cherokee (6)	24	0.06
Cheyenne (1)	1	<0.01
Choctaw (6)	9	0.02
Comanche (2)	4	0.01
Creek (0)	2	0.01
Inupiat *(Alaska Native)* (0)	3	0.01
Kiowa (2)	2	0.01
Mexican American Ind. (83)	109	0.27
Navajo (21)	30	0.08
Ottawa (1)	1	<0.01
Pima (6)	6	0.02
Pueblo (6)	11	0.03
Shoshone (5)	6	0.02
Sioux (10)	12	0.03
South American Ind. (0)	2	0.01
Spanish American Ind. (19)	23	0.06
Tohono O'Odham (1)	7	0.02
Ute (1)	1	<0.01
Yaqui (6)	10	0.03
Asian (3,356)	3,657	9.18
Not Hispanic (3,270)	3,397	8.53
Hispanic (86)	260	0.65
Bangladeshi (11)	12	0.03
Burmese (10)	10	0.03
Cambodian (44)	48	0.12
Chinese, ex. Taiwanese (910)	1,010	2.54
Filipino (1,244)	1,366	3.43
Indian (84)	109	0.27
Indonesian (22)	50	0.13
Japanese (71)	95	0.24
Korean (201)	218	0.55
Laotian (41)	46	0.12
Malaysian (5)	7	0.02
Pakistani (2)	2	0.01
Sri Lankan (7)	9	0.02
Taiwanese (74)	86	0.22
Thai (59)	80	0.20
Vietnamese (468)	527	1.32
Hawaii Native/Pacific Islander (42)	145	0.36
Not Hispanic (31)	93	0.23
Hispanic (11)	52	0.13
Fijian (4)	7	0.02
Guamanian/Chamorro (5)	6	0.02
Native Hawaiian (12)	52	0.13
Samoan (18)	29	0.07
Tongan (0)	2	0.01
White (19,658)	20,815	52.28
Not Hispanic (1,835)	1,968	4.94
Hispanic (17,823)	18,847	47.34

La Quinta

Place Type: City
County: Riverside
Population: 37,467†

Ancestry‡	Population	%
African, Sub-Saharan (240)	248	0.70
African (225)	225	0.63
Ethiopian (15)	15	0.04
South African (0)	8	0.02
American (1,130)	1,130	3.17
Arab (67)	67	0.19
Egyptian (30)	30	0.08
Lebanese (24)	24	0.07
Other Arab (13)	13	0.04
Armenian (148)	281	0.79
Assyrian/Chaldean/Syriac (0)	13	0.04
Austrian (23)	55	0.15
Basque (12)	12	0.03
Belgian (18)	28	0.08
Brazilian (55)	55	0.15
British (130)	187	0.52
Bulgarian (0)	14	0.04
Canadian (65)	79	0.22
Celtic (13)	13	0.04
Croatian (107)	131	0.37
Czech (90)	169	0.47
Czechoslovakian (32)	59	0.17
Danish (128)	180	0.50
Dutch (88)	333	0.93
Eastern European (13)	13	0.04
English (1,526)	4,106	11.51
Estonian (31)	31	0.09
European (241)	257	0.72
Finnish (66)	66	0.19
French, ex. Basque (122)	714	2.00
French Canadian (114)	195	0.55
German (1,979)	6,173	17.31
Greek (90)	198	0.56
Hungarian (112)	242	0.68
Icelander (11)	11	0.03
Iranian (45)	58	0.16
Irish (1,302)	4,212	11.81
Italian (843)	1,938	5.43
Lithuanian (27)	95	0.27
Norwegian (189)	626	1.76
Polish (277)	953	2.67
Portuguese (12)	96	0.27
Romanian (35)	68	0.19
Russian (253)	789	2.21
Scandinavian (66)	83	0.23
Scotch-Irish (187)	513	1.44
Scottish (305)	833	2.34
Serbian (0)	21	0.06
Slavic (13)	30	0.08
Slovak (13)	35	0.10
Swedish (314)	1,114	3.12
Swiss (38)	77	0.22
Turkish (13)	28	0.08
Ukrainian (84)	120	0.34
Welsh (67)	196	0.55
Yugoslavian (24)	77	0.22

Hispanic Origin	Population	%
Hispanic or Latino (of any race)	11,339	30.26
Central American, ex. Mexican	244	0.65
Costa Rican	6	0.02
Guatemalan	43	0.11
Honduran	20	0.05
Nicaraguan	25	0.07
Panamanian	14	0.04
Salvadoran	134	0.36
Other Central American	2	0.01
Cuban	42	0.11
Dominican Republic	8	0.02
Mexican	10,122	27.02
Puerto Rican	134	0.36
South American	195	0.52
Argentinean	29	0.08
Bolivian	1	<0.01
Chilean	21	0.06
Colombian	69	0.18
Ecuadorian	30	0.08
Peruvian	32	0.09
Uruguayan	1	<0.01
Venezuelan	9	0.02
Other South American	3	0.01
Other Hispanic or Latino	594	1.59

Race*	Population	%
African-American/Black (713)	959	2.56
Not Hispanic (607)	755	2.02
Hispanic (106)	204	0.54
American Indian/Alaska Native (230)	484	1.29
Not Hispanic (98)	231	0.62
Hispanic (132)	253	0.68
Apache (15)	29	0.08
Arapaho (1)	1	<0.01
Blackfeet (0)	2	0.01
Canadian/French Am. Ind. (0)	5	0.01
Cherokee (9)	54	0.14
Chickasaw (1)	5	0.01
Chippewa (2)	9	0.02
Choctaw (9)	18	0.05
Cree (0)	2	0.01
Creek (0)	1	<0.01
Delaware (1)	1	<0.01
Hopi (0)	3	0.01
Iroquois (1)	2	0.01
Mexican American Ind. (18)	34	0.09
Navajo (9)	15	0.04
Osage (1)	2	0.01
Paiute (0)	2	0.01
Pima (1)	1	<0.01
Potawatomi (0)	1	<0.01
Pueblo (1)	1	<0.01
Sioux (1)	5	0.01
South American Ind. (1)	1	<0.01
Tlingit-Haida *(Alaska Native)* (2)	2	0.01
Tohono O'Odham (2)	2	0.01
Yakama (0)	2	0.01
Yaqui (7)	17	0.05
Yuman (1)	5	0.01
Asian (1,176)	1,581	4.22
Not Hispanic (1,093)	1,387	3.70
Hispanic (83)	194	0.52
Burmese (3)	5	0.01
Cambodian (2)	2	0.01
Chinese, ex. Taiwanese (152)	210	0.56
Filipino (362)	569	1.52
Hmong (1)	1	<0.01
Indian (105)	118	0.31
Indonesian (13)	16	0.04
Japanese (131)	231	0.62
Korean (176)	189	0.50
Laotian (7)	9	0.02
Nepalese (3)	3	0.01
Pakistani (4)	6	0.02
Taiwanese (10)	15	0.04
Thai (28)	39	0.10
Vietnamese (123)	136	0.36
Hawaii Native/Pacific Islander (41)	112	0.30
Not Hispanic (25)	70	0.19
Hispanic (16)	42	0.11
Guamanian/Chamorro (7)	18	0.05
Native Hawaiian (22)	67	0.18
Samoan (6)	14	0.04
White (29,489)	30,571	81.59
Not Hispanic (23,648)	24,214	64.63
Hispanic (5,841)	6,357	16.97

La Riviera

Place Type: CDP
County: Sacramento
Population: 10,802†

Ancestry‡	Population	%
African, Sub-Saharan (86)	121	1.09
African (86)	86	0.77
Cape Verdean (0)	35	0.31
Albanian (0)	35	0.31
American (227)	227	2.04
Arab (11)	11	0.10
Lebanese (11)	11	0.10

*Notes: † The Census 2010 population figure is used to calculate the percentages in the Hispanic Origin and Race categories. Ancestry percentages are based on the 2006-2010 American Community Survey population (not shown); ‡ Numbers in parentheses indicate the number of people reporting a single ancestry; * Numbers in parentheses indicate the number of persons reporting this race alone, not in combination with any other race; Please refer to the Explanation of Data for more information.*

Ancestry (cont.)	Population	%
Armenian (10)	10	0.09
Assyrian/Chaldean/Syriac (26)	26	0.23
Australian (0)	26	0.23
Austrian (0)	34	0.30
Basque (28)	28	0.25
British (25)	51	0.46
Danish (9)	67	0.60
Dutch (60)	178	1.60
English (258)	1,386	12.43
Estonian (0)	24	0.22
European (203)	223	2.00
Finnish (0)	37	0.33
French, ex. Basque (8)	260	2.33
French Canadian (11)	54	0.48
German (352)	1,970	17.67
Greek (62)	93	0.83
Hungarian (46)	115	1.03
Iranian (114)	114	1.02
Irish (174)	1,021	9.16
Italian (313)	781	7.01
Lithuanian (0)	30	0.27
Northern European (19)	46	0.41
Norwegian (74)	193	1.73
Pennsylvania German (0)	16	0.14
Polish (28)	129	1.16
Portuguese (73)	186	1.67
Russian (146)	178	1.60
Scandinavian (22)	36	0.32
Scotch-Irish (51)	175	1.57
Scottish (109)	531	4.76
Slavic (22)	22	0.20
Slovak (14)	14	0.13
Swedish (35)	300	2.69
Swiss (19)	45	0.40
Ukrainian (7)	21	0.19
Welsh (41)	156	1.40
Yugoslavian (13)	29	0.26

Hispanic Origin	Population	%
Hispanic or Latino (of any race)	1,756	16.26
Central American, ex. Mexican	119	1.10
Costa Rican	5	0.05
Guatemalan	20	0.19
Honduran	14	0.13
Nicaraguan	11	0.10
Panamanian	8	0.07
Salvadoran	57	0.53
Other Central American	4	0.04
Cuban	14	0.13
Dominican Republic	4	0.04
Mexican	1,315	12.17
Puerto Rican	75	0.69
South American	49	0.45
Argentinean	6	0.06
Bolivian	7	0.06
Chilean	4	0.04
Colombian	9	0.08
Peruvian	18	0.17
Uruguayan	4	0.04
Venezuelan	1	0.01
Other Hispanic or Latino	180	1.67

Race*	Population	%
African-American/Black (1,084)	1,342	12.42
Not Hispanic (1,030)	1,240	11.48
Hispanic (54)	102	0.94
American Indian/Alaska Native (76)	275	2.55
Not Hispanic (39)	171	1.58
Hispanic (37)	104	0.96
Apache (2)	10	0.09
Arapaho (0)	3	0.03
Blackfeet (2)	7	0.06
Cherokee (5)	52	0.48
Cheyenne (0)	1	0.01
Chippewa (0)	1	0.01
Choctaw (0)	8	0.07
Colville (0)	1	0.01
Comanche (1)	1	0.01
Crow (0)	1	0.01
Iroquois (0)	4	0.04
Menominee (1)	1	0.01
Mexican American Ind. (3)	11	0.10
Navajo (1)	19	0.18
Pueblo (1)	2	0.02
Puget Sound Salish (0)	1	0.01
Seminole (1)	1	0.01
Sioux (2)	6	0.06
South American Ind. (1)	2	0.02
Tlingit-Haida *(Alaska Native)* (0)	1	0.01
Yaqui (0)	1	0.01
Asian (766)	1,104	10.22
Not Hispanic (755)	1,036	9.59
Hispanic (11)	68	0.63
Cambodian (6)	11	0.10
Chinese, ex. Taiwanese (138)	202	1.87
Filipino (220)	355	3.29
Hmong (29)	32	0.30
Indian (34)	53	0.49
Indonesian (0)	11	0.10
Japanese (96)	190	1.76
Korean (81)	104	0.96
Laotian (17)	18	0.17
Malaysian (0)	1	0.01
Nepalese (1)	1	0.01
Pakistani (5)	7	0.06
Sri Lankan (6)	6	0.06
Taiwanese (19)	21	0.19
Thai (8)	21	0.19
Vietnamese (70)	81	0.75
Hawaii Native/Pacific Islander (87)	147	1.36
Not Hispanic (85)	130	1.20
Hispanic (2)	17	0.16
Fijian (22)	23	0.21
Guamanian/Chamorro (10)	19	0.18
Marshallese (10)	10	0.09
Native Hawaiian (9)	38	0.35
Samoan (22)	31	0.29
Tongan (2)	4	0.04
White (7,315)	7,995	74.01
Not Hispanic (6,569)	7,055	65.31
Hispanic (746)	940	8.70

La Verne

Place Type: City
County: Los Angeles
Population: 31,063†

Ancestry‡	Population	%
African, Sub-Saharan (163)	163	0.52
African (163)	163	0.52
American (718)	718	2.30
Arab (670)	793	2.54
Arab (140)	164	0.53
Egyptian (99)	109	0.35
Jordanian (230)	243	0.78
Lebanese (77)	109	0.35
Moroccan (31)	31	0.10
Palestinian (15)	15	0.05
Syrian (56)	100	0.32
Other Arab (22)	22	0.07
Armenian (292)	334	1.07
Australian (9)	9	0.03
Austrian (0)	30	0.10
Basque (12)	49	0.16
Brazilian (172)	172	0.55
British (48)	198	0.64
Canadian (126)	228	0.73
Croatian (14)	24	0.08
Czech (33)	83	0.27
Czechoslovakian (35)	35	0.11
Danish (47)	215	0.69
Dutch (187)	742	2.38
Eastern European (10)	10	0.03
English (1,073)	3,506	11.25
European (574)	739	2.37
Finnish (13)	63	0.20
French, ex. Basque (76)	768	2.46
French Canadian (140)	241	0.77
German (1,522)	4,958	15.90
Greek (144)	144	0.46
Hungarian (11)	35	0.11
Iranian (396)	396	1.27
Irish (733)	3,366	10.80
Italian (985)	2,260	7.25
Lithuanian (18)	41	0.13
Northern European (31)	31	0.10
Norwegian (210)	740	2.37
Polish (155)	749	2.40
Portuguese (17)	35	0.11
Romanian (0)	12	0.04
Russian (42)	280	0.90
Scandinavian (65)	74	0.24
Scotch-Irish (157)	472	1.51
Scottish (153)	877	2.81
Serbian (0)	10	0.03
Slavic (0)	73	0.23
Slovak (8)	46	0.15
Swedish (139)	621	1.99
Swiss (7)	70	0.22
Turkish (0)	14	0.04
Ukrainian (61)	107	0.34
Welsh (61)	177	0.57
West Indian, ex. Hispanic (23)	54	0.17
Belizean (23)	54	0.17
Yugoslavian (12)	12	0.04

Hispanic Origin	Population	%
Hispanic or Latino (of any race)	9,635	31.02
Central American, ex. Mexican	519	1.67
Costa Rican	36	0.12
Guatemalan	145	0.47
Honduran	32	0.10
Nicaraguan	113	0.36
Panamanian	11	0.04
Salvadoran	178	0.57
Other Central American	4	0.01
Cuban	182	0.59
Dominican Republic	14	0.05
Mexican	7,627	24.55
Puerto Rican	180	0.58
South American	425	1.37
Argentinean	121	0.39
Bolivian	29	0.09
Chilean	25	0.08
Colombian	86	0.28
Ecuadorian	70	0.23
Paraguayan	4	0.01
Peruvian	75	0.24
Uruguayan	4	0.01
Venezuelan	5	0.02
Other South American	6	0.02
Other Hispanic or Latino	688	2.21

Race*	Population	%
African-American/Black (1,065)	1,297	4.18
Not Hispanic (992)	1,153	3.71
Hispanic (73)	144	0.46
American Indian/Alaska Native (265)	554	1.78
Not Hispanic (98)	278	0.89
Hispanic (167)	276	0.89
Apache (14)	18	0.06
Arapaho (0)	2	0.01
Blackfeet (0)	4	0.01
Canadian/French Am. Ind. (1)	4	0.01
Central American Ind. (0)	2	0.01
Cherokee (13)	72	0.23
Chickasaw (0)	1	<0.01
Chippewa (2)	16	0.05
Choctaw (9)	20	0.06
Cree (0)	1	<0.01
Creek (2)	4	0.01
Crow (0)	1	<0.01
Delaware (1)	2	0.01
Hopi (6)	9	0.03
Iroquois (1)	9	0.03
Kiowa (0)	1	<0.01
Mexican American Ind. (13)	23	0.07
Navajo (7)	19	0.06
Osage (1)	1	<0.01

*Notes: † The Census 2010 population figure is used to calculate the percentages in the Hispanic Origin and Race categories. Ancestry percentages are based on the 2006-2010 American Community Survey population (not shown); ‡ Numbers in parentheses indicate the number of people reporting a single ancestry; * Numbers in parentheses indicate the number of persons reporting this race alone, not in combination with any other race; Please refer to the Explanation of Data for more information.*

Ottawa (1)	4	0.01
Paiute (0)	2	0.01
Pima (0)	4	0.01
Potawatomi (0)	1	<0.01
Pueblo (1)	1	<0.01
Seminole (0)	2	0.01
Sioux (3)	7	0.02
South American Ind. (2)	2	0.01
Spanish American Ind. (11)	19	0.06
Tlingit-Haida *(Alaska Native)* (0)	2	0.01
Yaqui (0)	5	0.02
Yuman (1)	1	<0.01
Asian (2,381)	2,921	9.40
Not Hispanic (2,310)	2,717	8.75
Hispanic (71)	204	0.66
Bangladeshi (9)	12	0.04
Burmese (2)	2	0.01
Cambodian (32)	43	0.14
Chinese, ex. Taiwanese (564)	707	2.28
Filipino (701)	868	2.79
Indian (289)	322	1.04
Indonesian (40)	92	0.30
Japanese (215)	361	1.16
Korean (156)	184	0.59
Malaysian (0)	1	<0.01
Pakistani (30)	34	0.11
Sri Lankan (15)	19	0.06
Taiwanese (67)	72	0.23
Thai (40)	48	0.15
Vietnamese (134)	172	0.55
Hawaii Native/Pacific Islander (61)	173	0.56
Not Hispanic (54)	130	0.42
Hispanic (7)	43	0.14
Guamanian/Chamorro (14)	25	0.08
Native Hawaiian (27)	67	0.22
Samoan (6)	22	0.07
Tongan (1)	3	0.01
White (23,057)	24,289	78.19
Not Hispanic (17,197)	17,833	57.41
Hispanic (5,860)	6,456	20.78

Ladera Ranch

Place Type: CDP
County: Orange
Population: 22,980†

Ancestry‡	Population	%
Afghan (73)	97	0.53
African, Sub-Saharan (17)	17	0.09
South African (17)	17	0.09
American (570)	570	3.14
Arab (161)	223	1.23
Egyptian (139)	139	0.76
Lebanese (0)	19	0.10
Moroccan (22)	22	0.12
Syrian (0)	43	0.24
Armenian (12)	12	0.07
Australian (14)	14	0.08
Austrian (0)	96	0.53
Basque (0)	11	0.06
Belgian (25)	81	0.45
Brazilian (62)	76	0.42
British (95)	221	1.22
Bulgarian (8)	17	0.09
Canadian (0)	27	0.15
Croatian (11)	18	0.10
Czech (26)	104	0.57
Czechoslovakian (146)	154	0.85
Danish (166)	224	1.23
Dutch (101)	487	2.68
Eastern European (121)	121	0.67
English (602)	1,957	10.77
European (196)	292	1.61
French, ex. Basque (75)	396	2.18
French Canadian (29)	59	0.32
German (948)	3,213	17.68
Greek (94)	120	0.66
Hungarian (38)	234	1.29
Iranian (324)	468	2.58
Irish (727)	3,036	16.71
Israeli (18)	18	0.10
Italian (514)	1,891	10.41
Latvian (8)	8	0.04
Lithuanian (12)	33	0.18
Maltese (0)	5	0.03
New Zealander (12)	36	0.20
Norwegian (80)	242	1.33
Polish (172)	650	3.58
Portuguese (0)	52	0.29
Romanian (115)	115	0.63
Russian (138)	404	2.22
Scandinavian (0)	51	0.28
Scotch-Irish (159)	269	1.48
Scottish (175)	439	2.42
Slovene (0)	26	0.14
Swedish (147)	315	1.73
Swiss (37)	160	0.88
Turkish (0)	11	0.06
Ukrainian (0)	11	0.06
Welsh (77)	234	1.29
West Indian, ex. Hispanic (7)	7	0.04
West Indian (7)	7	0.04
Yugoslavian (0)	22	0.12

Hispanic Origin	Population	%
Hispanic or Latino (of any race)	2,952	12.85
Central American, ex. Mexican	125	0.54
Costa Rican	13	0.06
Guatemalan	21	0.09
Honduran	10	0.04
Nicaraguan	7	0.03
Panamanian	7	0.03
Salvadoran	65	0.28
Other Central American	2	0.01
Cuban	74	0.32
Dominican Republic	6	0.03
Mexican	1,950	8.49
Puerto Rican	140	0.61
South American	332	1.44
Argentinean	74	0.32
Bolivian	10	0.04
Chilean	12	0.05
Colombian	121	0.53
Ecuadorian	5	0.02
Peruvian	70	0.30
Uruguayan	5	0.02
Venezuelan	33	0.14
Other South American	2	0.01
Other Hispanic or Latino	325	1.41

Race*	Population	%
African-American/Black (335)	547	2.38
Not Hispanic (312)	473	2.06
Hispanic (23)	74	0.32
American Indian/Alaska Native (54)	176	0.77
Not Hispanic (33)	128	0.56
Hispanic (21)	48	0.21
Apache (0)	2	0.01
Blackfeet (2)	7	0.03
Cherokee (5)	36	0.16
Chickasaw (2)	3	0.01
Choctaw (2)	7	0.03
Colville (0)	1	<0.01
Hopi (0)	4	0.02
Iroquois (1)	3	0.01
Lumbee (0)	4	0.02
Mexican American Ind. (4)	5	0.02
Navajo (1)	1	<0.01
Osage (2)	2	0.01
Potawatomi (2)	2	0.01
Pueblo (0)	2	0.01
Puget Sound Salish (0)	3	0.01
Sioux (1)	4	0.02
South American Ind. (1)	5	0.02
Tlingit-Haida *(Alaska Native)* (1)	2	0.01
Yaqui (0)	1	<0.01
Asian (2,774)	3,565	15.51
Not Hispanic (2,734)	3,419	14.88
Hispanic (40)	146	0.64
Bangladeshi (4)	4	0.02
Burmese (0)	3	0.01
Cambodian (11)	21	0.09
Chinese, ex. Taiwanese (477)	644	2.80
Filipino (632)	909	3.96
Hmong (1)	3	0.01
Indian (407)	458	1.99
Indonesian (26)	41	0.18
Japanese (174)	376	1.64
Korean (431)	528	2.30
Laotian (4)	4	0.02
Malaysian (2)	3	0.01
Nepalese (1)	1	<0.01
Pakistani (31)	40	0.17
Sri Lankan (7)	7	0.03
Taiwanese (46)	53	0.23
Thai (22)	44	0.19
Vietnamese (349)	470	2.05
Hawaii Native/Pacific Islander (27)	113	0.49
Not Hispanic (27)	97	0.42
Hispanic (0)	16	0.07
Guamanian/Chamorro (1)	5	0.02
Native Hawaiian (11)	60	0.26
Samoan (2)	18	0.08
White (17,899)	19,084	83.05
Not Hispanic (15,939)	16,852	73.33
Hispanic (1,960)	2,232	9.71

Lafayette

Place Type: City
County: Contra Costa
Population: 23,893†

Ancestry‡	Population	%
African, Sub-Saharan (42)	76	0.32
African (0)	20	0.08
South African (25)	25	0.11
Other Sub-Saharan African (17)	31	0.13
Alsatian (0)	10	0.04
American (1,511)	1,511	6.36
Arab (60)	124	0.52
Iraqi (32)	32	0.13
Lebanese (28)	92	0.39
Armenian (54)	95	0.40
Austrian (12)	174	0.73
Basque (23)	72	0.30
Belgian (0)	36	0.15
British (123)	173	0.73
Bulgarian (14)	14	0.06
Canadian (6)	32	0.13
Celtic (12)	34	0.14
Croatian (77)	98	0.41
Czech (28)	175	0.74
Danish (157)	447	1.88
Dutch (187)	348	1.46
Eastern European (157)	172	0.72
English (1,365)	4,353	18.31
European (508)	595	2.50
Finnish (91)	210	0.88
French, ex. Basque (63)	740	3.11
French Canadian (59)	136	0.57
German (1,094)	4,388	18.46
Greek (230)	324	1.36
Hungarian (47)	122	0.51
Icelander (0)	17	0.07
Iranian (151)	176	0.74
Irish (869)	3,581	15.07
Italian (407)	1,432	6.02
Latvian (0)	55	0.23
Lithuanian (71)	136	0.57
Luxemburger (0)	8	0.03
Maltese (22)	47	0.20
New Zealander (0)	27	0.11
Northern European (511)	511	2.15
Norwegian (144)	598	2.52
Pennsylvania German (12)	12	0.05
Polish (141)	544	2.29
Portuguese (89)	238	1.00
Romanian (13)	22	0.09

*Notes: † The Census 2010 population figure is used to calculate the percentages in the Hispanic Origin and Race categories. Ancestry percentages are based on the 2006-2010 American Community Survey population (not shown); ‡ Numbers in parentheses indicate the number of people reporting a single ancestry; * Numbers in parentheses indicate the number of persons reporting this race alone, not in combination with any other race; Please refer to the Explanation of Data for more information.*

Russian (227)	585	2.46
Scandinavian (30)	130	0.55
Scotch-Irish (182)	789	3.32
Scottish (147)	757	3.18
Slavic (14)	32	0.13
Slovak (0)	27	0.11
Swedish (186)	621	2.61
Swiss (86)	272	1.14
Ukrainian (53)	106	0.45
Welsh (67)	259	1.09
Yugoslavian (13)	31	0.13

Hispanic Origin	Population	%
Hispanic or Latino (of any race)	1,388	5.81
Central American, ex. Mexican	166	0.69
Costa Rican	11	0.05
Guatemalan	33	0.14
Honduran	12	0.05
Nicaraguan	31	0.13
Panamanian	5	0.02
Salvadoran	65	0.27
Other Central American	9	0.04
Cuban	26	0.11
Dominican Republic	1	<0.01
Mexican	735	3.08
Puerto Rican	74	0.31
South American	172	0.72
Argentinean	27	0.11
Bolivian	5	0.02
Chilean	28	0.12
Colombian	39	0.16
Ecuadorian	7	0.03
Paraguayan	2	0.01
Peruvian	46	0.19
Uruguayan	1	<0.01
Venezuelan	16	0.07
Other South American	1	<0.01
Other Hispanic or Latino	214	0.90

Race*	Population	%
African-American/Black (166)	291	1.22
Not Hispanic (154)	262	1.10
Hispanic (12)	29	0.12
American Indian/Alaska Native (66)	205	0.86
Not Hispanic (41)	139	0.58
Hispanic (25)	66	0.28
Apache (1)	11	0.05
Blackfeet (2)	10	0.04
Cherokee (11)	54	0.23
Chippewa (4)	5	0.02
Choctaw (2)	7	0.03
Comanche (0)	2	0.01
Cree (0)	1	<0.01
Crow (1)	1	<0.01
Iroquois (0)	2	0.01
Mexican American Ind. (7)	11	0.05
Navajo (0)	1	<0.01
Osage (0)	1	<0.01
Pima (0)	3	0.01
Potawatomi (0)	2	0.01
Pueblo (3)	3	0.01
Puget Sound Salish (2)	2	0.01
Seminole (1)	2	0.01
Sioux (2)	4	0.02
South American Ind. (2)	4	0.02
Spanish American Ind. (0)	2	0.01
Yaqui (0)	1	<0.01
Asian (2,162)	2,884	12.07
Not Hispanic (2,133)	2,801	11.72
Hispanic (29)	83	0.35
Bangladeshi (1)	1	<0.01
Burmese (1)	4	0.02
Cambodian (5)	5	0.02
Chinese, ex. Taiwanese (950)	1,228	5.14
Filipino (224)	402	1.68
Hmong (4)	4	0.02
Indian (226)	300	1.26
Indonesian (3)	13	0.05
Japanese (248)	434	1.82
Korean (256)	324	1.36
Laotian (1)	1	<0.01
Malaysian (6)	6	0.03
Nepalese (1)	2	0.01
Pakistani (22)	31	0.13
Sri Lankan (3)	4	0.02
Taiwanese (37)	41	0.17
Thai (12)	24	0.10
Vietnamese (49)	75	0.31
Hawaii Native/Pacific Islander (27)	92	0.39
Not Hispanic (26)	83	0.35
Hispanic (1)	9	0.04
Fijian (2)	2	0.01
Guamanian/Chamorro (6)	9	0.04
Native Hawaiian (6)	48	0.20
Samoan (1)	6	0.03
Tongan (2)	2	0.01
White (20,232)	21,166	88.59
Not Hispanic (19,246)	20,045	83.89
Hispanic (986)	1,121	4.69

Laguna Beach

Place Type: City
County: Orange
Population: 22,723†

Ancestry‡	Population	%
African, Sub-Saharan (69)	69	0.30
South African (69)	69	0.30
American (885)	885	3.88
Arab (12)	49	0.22
Egyptian (12)	12	0.05
Lebanese (0)	21	0.09
Moroccan (0)	16	0.07
Armenian (52)	92	0.40
Assyrian/Chaldean/Syriac (26)	26	0.11
Australian (10)	18	0.08
Austrian (76)	179	0.79
Belgian (58)	75	0.33
Brazilian (0)	2	0.01
British (143)	210	0.92
Bulgarian (0)	10	0.04
Canadian (42)	142	0.62
Croatian (8)	26	0.11
Czech (12)	75	0.33
Czechoslovakian (31)	70	0.31
Danish (159)	354	1.55
Dutch (355)	699	3.07
Eastern European (76)	110	0.48
English (1,138)	3,522	15.46
Estonian (12)	12	0.05
European (479)	505	2.22
Finnish (0)	61	0.27
French, ex. Basque (274)	1,145	5.02
French Canadian (92)	187	0.82
German (1,207)	4,544	19.94
Greek (22)	160	0.70
Hungarian (50)	197	0.86
Iranian (266)	266	1.17
Irish (898)	3,148	13.81
Israeli (31)	31	0.14
Italian (855)	2,126	9.33
Latvian (11)	11	0.05
Lithuanian (9)	94	0.41
Northern European (149)	190	0.83
Norwegian (264)	458	2.01
Pennsylvania German (0)	8	0.04
Polish (407)	949	4.16
Portuguese (29)	113	0.50
Romanian (42)	89	0.39
Russian (309)	567	2.49
Scandinavian (19)	63	0.28
Scotch-Irish (208)	564	2.47
Scottish (315)	997	4.38
Serbian (28)	28	0.12
Slavic (13)	13	0.06
Slovak (26)	35	0.15
Slovene (23)	23	0.10
Swedish (195)	634	2.78
Swiss (28)	127	0.56
Turkish (0)	16	0.07
Ukrainian (49)	134	0.59
Welsh (108)	251	1.10
West Indian, ex. Hispanic (32)	68	0.30
Jamaican (32)	32	0.14
West Indian (0)	36	0.16

Hispanic Origin	Population	%
Hispanic or Latino (of any race)	1,650	7.26
Central American, ex. Mexican	57	0.25
Costa Rican	9	0.04
Guatemalan	13	0.06
Honduran	9	0.04
Nicaraguan	9	0.04
Panamanian	5	0.02
Salvadoran	12	0.05
Cuban	52	0.23
Dominican Republic	8	0.04
Mexican	1,121	4.93
Puerto Rican	63	0.28
South American	164	0.72
Argentinean	47	0.21
Bolivian	3	0.01
Chilean	16	0.07
Colombian	56	0.25
Ecuadorian	9	0.04
Paraguayan	1	<0.01
Peruvian	16	0.07
Uruguayan	5	0.02
Venezuelan	10	0.04
Other South American	1	<0.01
Other Hispanic or Latino	185	0.81

Race*	Population	%
African-American/Black (178)	280	1.23
Not Hispanic (158)	251	1.10
Hispanic (20)	29	0.13
American Indian/Alaska Native (61)	202	0.89
Not Hispanic (34)	142	0.62
Hispanic (27)	60	0.26
Apache (3)	9	0.04
Blackfeet (1)	4	0.02
Canadian/French Am. Ind. (1)	1	<0.01
Cherokee (6)	57	0.25
Chickasaw (1)	1	<0.01
Chippewa (1)	7	0.03
Choctaw (1)	6	0.03
Cree (0)	2	0.01
Creek (3)	5	0.02
Iroquois (0)	2	0.01
Mexican American Ind. (3)	4	0.02
Navajo (3)	5	0.02
Osage (2)	6	0.03
Potawatomi (0)	1	<0.01
Pueblo (0)	1	<0.01
Sioux (1)	2	0.01
South American Ind. (1)	1	<0.01
Spanish American Ind. (1)	1	<0.01
Tlingit-Haida *(Alaska Native)* (1)	2	0.01
Ute (0)	1	<0.01
Yaqui (0)	2	0.01
Asian (811)	1,196	5.26
Not Hispanic (797)	1,154	5.08
Hispanic (14)	42	0.18
Burmese (0)	1	<0.01
Cambodian (3)	5	0.02
Chinese, ex. Taiwanese (215)	303	1.33
Filipino (127)	207	0.91
Hmong (1)	3	0.01
Indian (99)	132	0.58
Indonesian (9)	16	0.07
Japanese (129)	235	1.03
Korean (73)	110	0.48
Laotian (2)	4	0.02
Malaysian (1)	1	<0.01
Pakistani (8)	10	0.04
Sri Lankan (1)	1	<0.01
Taiwanese (18)	26	0.11
Thai (14)	17	0.07
Vietnamese (73)	94	0.41

SECTION TWO

*Notes: † The Census 2010 population figure is used to calculate the percentages in the Hispanic Origin and Race categories. Ancestry percentages are based on the 2006-2010 American Community Survey population (not shown); ‡ Numbers in parentheses indicate the number of people reporting a single ancestry; * Numbers in parentheses indicate the number of persons reporting this race alone, not in combination with any other race; Please refer to the Explanation of Data for more information.*

Hawaii Native/Pacific Islander (15)	63	0.28
Not Hispanic (13)	56	0.25
Hispanic (2)	7	0.03
Guamanian/Chamorro (2)	5	0.02
Native Hawaiian (7)	28	0.12
Samoan (1)	6	0.03
Tongan (2)	2	0.01
White (20,645)	21,264	93.58
Not Hispanic (19,472)	19,993	87.99
Hispanic (1,173)	1,271	5.59

Laguna Hills

Place Type: City
County: Orange
Population: 30,344†

Ancestry‡	Population	%
African, Sub-Saharan (9)	17	0.06
African (9)	17	0.06
Albanian (0)	9	0.03
American (600)	600	1.97
Arab (116)	228	0.75
Arab (10)	44	0.14
Egyptian (45)	79	0.26
Lebanese (38)	38	0.12
Palestinian (3)	3	0.01
Syrian (0)	34	0.11
Other Arab (20)	30	0.10
Armenian (30)	62	0.20
Assyrian/Chaldean/Syriac (26)	26	0.09
Australian (43)	51	0.17
Austrian (9)	54	0.18
Basque (0)	10	0.03
Belgian (40)	40	0.13
British (100)	303	1.00
Canadian (56)	102	0.34
Celtic (0)	14	0.05
Croatian (0)	50	0.16
Czech (59)	144	0.47
Czechoslovakian (18)	26	0.09
Danish (82)	299	0.98
Dutch (159)	628	2.06
English (746)	3,077	10.12
European (469)	513	1.69
Finnish (17)	89	0.29
French, ex. Basque (129)	1,046	3.44
French Canadian (101)	193	0.63
German (1,596)	5,844	19.21
Greek (44)	122	0.40
Hungarian (28)	129	0.42
Iranian (939)	1,043	3.43
Irish (1,119)	3,879	12.75
Italian (928)	2,322	7.63
Latvian (0)	9	0.03
Lithuanian (0)	23	0.08
Luxemburger (8)	8	0.03
Northern European (10)	10	0.03
Norwegian (211)	529	1.74
Pennsylvania German (8)	8	0.03
Polish (299)	748	2.46
Portuguese (136)	201	0.66
Romanian (31)	57	0.19
Russian (211)	585	1.92
Scandinavian (12)	61	0.20
Scotch-Irish (173)	335	1.10
Scottish (207)	798	2.62
Serbian (31)	31	0.10
Slovak (0)	116	0.38
Swedish (133)	426	1.40
Swiss (22)	50	0.16
Ukrainian (48)	70	0.23
Welsh (34)	269	0.88
West Indian, ex. Hispanic (9)	47	0.15
Jamaican (0)	38	0.12
West Indian (9)	9	0.03
Yugoslavian (33)	95	0.31

Hispanic Origin	Population	%
Hispanic or Latino (of any race)	6,242	20.57
Central American, ex. Mexican	292	0.96
Costa Rican	28	0.09
Guatemalan	106	0.35
Honduran	6	0.02
Nicaraguan	31	0.10
Panamanian	7	0.02
Salvadoran	114	0.38
Cuban	95	0.31
Dominican Republic	4	0.01
Mexican	4,822	15.89
Puerto Rican	119	0.39
South American	487	1.60
Argentinean	71	0.23
Bolivian	32	0.11
Chilean	21	0.07
Colombian	160	0.53
Ecuadorian	34	0.11
Paraguayan	1	<0.01
Peruvian	139	0.46
Uruguayan	1	<0.01
Venezuelan	16	0.05
Other South American	12	0.04
Other Hispanic or Latino	423	1.39

Race*	Population	%
African-American/Black (420)	588	1.94
Not Hispanic (373)	507	1.67
Hispanic (47)	81	0.27
American Indian/Alaska Native (101)	270	0.89
Not Hispanic (53)	170	0.56
Hispanic (48)	100	0.33
Apache (2)	5	0.02
Arapaho (1)	1	<0.01
Blackfeet (0)	8	0.03
Cherokee (18)	42	0.14
Cheyenne (0)	5	0.02
Chippewa (1)	5	0.02
Choctaw (6)	6	0.02
Comanche (1)	1	<0.01
Creek (0)	1	<0.01
Delaware (0)	2	0.01
Inupiat *(Alaska Native)* (1)	2	0.01
Iroquois (1)	11	0.04
Mexican American Ind. (7)	12	0.04
Navajo (5)	12	0.04
Osage (0)	3	0.01
Potawatomi (0)	1	<0.01
Pueblo (0)	5	0.02
Puget Sound Salish (1)	1	<0.01
Sioux (2)	2	0.01
Spanish American Ind. (0)	2	0.01
Tohono O'Odham (0)	1	<0.01
Yaqui (2)	2	0.01
Asian (3,829)	4,714	15.54
Not Hispanic (3,790)	4,588	15.12
Hispanic (39)	126	0.42
Bangladeshi (5)	5	0.02
Burmese (3)	7	0.02
Cambodian (17)	18	0.06
Chinese, ex. Taiwanese (567)	733	2.42
Filipino (1,106)	1,303	4.29
Hmong (8)	8	0.03
Indian (385)	440	1.45
Indonesian (75)	107	0.35
Japanese (331)	528	1.74
Korean (397)	466	1.54
Laotian (11)	13	0.04
Malaysian (7)	10	0.03
Nepalese (2)	2	0.01
Pakistani (62)	72	0.24
Sri Lankan (7)	8	0.03
Taiwanese (123)	144	0.47
Thai (45)	56	0.18
Vietnamese (534)	606	2.00
Hawaii Native/Pacific Islander (58)	149	0.49
Not Hispanic (45)	114	0.38
Hispanic (13)	35	0.12
Fijian (2)	4	0.01
Guamanian/Chamorro (18)	23	0.08
Native Hawaiian (12)	51	0.17
Samoan (5)	13	0.04
Tongan (11)	11	0.04
White (22,045)	23,328	76.88
Not Hispanic (18,725)	19,704	64.94
Hispanic (3,320)	3,624	11.94

Laguna Niguel

Place Type: City
County: Orange
Population: 62,979†

Ancestry‡	Population	%
Afghan (178)	178	0.28
African, Sub-Saharan (110)	116	0.19
African (23)	29	0.05
South African (78)	78	0.12
Sudanese (9)	9	0.01
Albanian (0)	16	0.03
American (1,805)	1,805	2.88
Arab (527)	730	1.17
Arab (53)	53	0.08
Egyptian (156)	211	0.34
Iraqi (36)	51	0.08
Jordanian (14)	14	0.02
Lebanese (157)	258	0.41
Palestinian (9)	9	0.01
Syrian (65)	97	0.15
Other Arab (37)	37	0.06
Armenian (233)	387	0.62
Assyrian/Chaldean/Syriac (10)	10	0.02
Australian (0)	20	0.03
Austrian (119)	298	0.48
Basque (51)	67	0.11
Belgian (63)	91	0.15
Brazilian (50)	90	0.14
British (273)	778	1.24
Bulgarian (72)	72	0.11
Canadian (98)	206	0.33
Croatian (60)	123	0.20
Czech (173)	337	0.54
Czechoslovakian (26)	60	0.10
Danish (175)	342	0.55
Dutch (258)	1,061	1.69
Eastern European (188)	188	0.30
English (2,540)	7,457	11.91
Estonian (11)	19	0.03
European (1,145)	1,430	2.28
Finnish (82)	228	0.36
French, ex. Basque (452)	2,235	3.57
French Canadian (93)	255	0.41
German (3,686)	10,822	17.28
Greek (326)	557	0.89
Hungarian (224)	419	0.67
Iranian (3,045)	3,258	5.20
Irish (2,506)	8,818	14.08
Israeli (0)	20	0.03
Italian (1,851)	4,797	7.66
Latvian (11)	11	0.02
Lithuanian (86)	227	0.36
Luxemburger (6)	6	0.01
Maltese (14)	41	0.07
New Zealander (50)	60	0.10
Northern European (59)	59	0.09
Norwegian (248)	845	1.35
Pennsylvania German (0)	18	0.03
Polish (751)	2,004	3.20
Portuguese (358)	526	0.84
Romanian (170)	421	0.67
Russian (809)	1,915	3.06
Scandinavian (43)	64	0.10
Scotch-Irish (428)	1,122	1.79
Scottish (378)	1,251	2.00
Serbian (0)	9	0.01
Slavic (58)	117	0.19
Slovak (33)	140	0.22
Slovene (0)	37	0.06
Swedish (286)	1,257	2.01
Swiss (41)	289	0.46
Turkish (10)	48	0.08

*Notes: † The Census 2010 population figure is used to calculate the percentages in the Hispanic Origin and Race categories. Ancestry percentages are based on the 2006-2010 American Community Survey population (not shown); ‡ Numbers in parentheses indicate the number of people reporting a single ancestry; * Numbers in parentheses indicate the number of persons reporting this race alone, not in combination with any other race; Please refer to the Explanation of Data for more information.*

Ukrainian (102)	272	0.43
Welsh (57)	423	0.68
West Indian, ex. Hispanic (42)	61	0.10
Barbadian (17)	17	0.03
Dutch West Indian (25)	44	0.07
Yugoslavian (48)	64	0.10

Hispanic Origin	Population	%
Hispanic or Latino (of any race)	8,761	13.91
Central American, ex. Mexican	479	0.76
Costa Rican	34	0.05
Guatemalan	191	0.30
Honduran	18	0.03
Nicaraguan	62	0.10
Panamanian	39	0.06
Salvadoran	115	0.18
Other Central American	20	0.03
Cuban	212	0.34
Dominican Republic	18	0.03
Mexican	6,264	9.95
Puerto Rican	214	0.34
South American	813	1.29
Argentinean	159	0.25
Bolivian	39	0.06
Chilean	42	0.07
Colombian	196	0.31
Ecuadorian	78	0.12
Paraguayan	1	<0.01
Peruvian	240	0.38
Uruguayan	3	<0.01
Venezuelan	38	0.06
Other South American	17	0.03
Other Hispanic or Latino	761	1.21

Race*	Population	%
African-American/Black (777)	1,113	1.77
Not Hispanic (693)	952	1.51
Hispanic (84)	161	0.26
American Indian/Alaska Native (219)	571	0.91
Not Hispanic (115)	355	0.56
Hispanic (104)	216	0.34
Alaska Athabascan *(Ala. Nat.)* (1)	1	<0.01
Apache (7)	33	0.05
Blackfeet (0)	12	0.02
Canadian/French Am. Ind. (1)	1	<0.01
Cherokee (13)	96	0.15
Cheyenne (1)	2	<0.01
Chickasaw (2)	7	0.01
Chippewa (3)	14	0.02
Choctaw (7)	23	0.04
Colville (0)	3	<0.01
Comanche (4)	12	0.02
Cree (1)	1	<0.01
Creek (1)	1	<0.01
Delaware (0)	7	0.01
Hopi (2)	5	0.01
Inupiat *(Alaska Native)* (1)	1	<0.01
Iroquois (0)	1	<0.01
Mexican American Ind. (18)	41	0.07
Navajo (10)	13	0.02
Osage (2)	2	<0.01
Ottawa (2)	2	<0.01
Paiute (0)	1	<0.01
Pima (1)	1	<0.01
Potawatomi (0)	3	<0.01
Pueblo (5)	6	0.01
Puget Sound Salish (0)	1	<0.01
Seminole (0)	1	<0.01
Shoshone (1)	3	<0.01
Sioux (0)	6	0.01
South American Ind. (1)	5	0.01
Tlingit-Haida *(Alaska Native)* (0)	2	<0.01
Ute (1)	4	0.01
Yaqui (2)	4	0.01
Asian (5,459)	7,236	11.49
Not Hispanic (5,390)	7,000	11.11
Hispanic (69)	236	0.37
Bangladeshi (6)	11	0.02
Burmese (2)	3	<0.01
Cambodian (32)	56	0.09
Chinese, ex. Taiwanese (1,225)	1,558	2.47
Filipino (1,125)	1,529	2.43
Hmong (2)	2	<0.01
Indian (488)	547	0.87
Indonesian (83)	116	0.18
Japanese (779)	1,151	1.83
Korean (573)	699	1.11
Laotian (13)	16	0.03
Malaysian (6)	13	0.02
Nepalese (6)	9	0.01
Pakistani (60)	74	0.12
Sri Lankan (16)	16	0.03
Taiwanese (201)	235	0.37
Thai (78)	106	0.17
Vietnamese (520)	642	1.02
Hawaii Native/Pacific Islander (87)	290	0.46
Not Hispanic (79)	262	0.42
Hispanic (8)	28	0.04
Fijian (3)	9	0.01
Guamanian/Chamorro (9)	24	0.04
Native Hawaiian (31)	102	0.16
Samoan (17)	49	0.08
Tongan (6)	10	0.02
White (50,625)	53,168	84.42
Not Hispanic (45,682)	47,688	75.72
Hispanic (4,943)	5,480	8.70

Laguna Woods

Place Type: City
County: Orange
Population: 16,192†

Ancestry‡	Population	%
African, Sub-Saharan (46)	58	0.36
African (46)	46	0.28
South African (0)	12	0.07
American (981)	981	6.02
Arab (88)	88	0.54
Lebanese (40)	40	0.25
Other Arab (48)	48	0.29
Armenian (9)	9	0.06
Austrian (116)	292	1.79
Belgian (0)	13	0.08
British (119)	131	0.80
Bulgarian (12)	12	0.07
Canadian (68)	140	0.86
Croatian (12)	30	0.18
Czech (36)	171	1.05
Czechoslovakian (22)	35	0.21
Danish (15)	81	0.50
Dutch (99)	410	2.52
Eastern European (76)	76	0.47
English (933)	2,413	14.81
European (265)	287	1.76
Finnish (0)	36	0.22
French, ex. Basque (119)	732	4.49
French Canadian (65)	77	0.47
German (884)	2,597	15.94
Greek (66)	128	0.79
Hungarian (151)	284	1.74
Iranian (306)	306	1.88
Irish (720)	1,753	10.76
Italian (445)	726	4.46
Latvian (15)	23	0.14
Lithuanian (15)	57	0.35
Maltese (13)	13	0.08
Norwegian (132)	322	1.98
Polish (447)	831	5.10
Portuguese (62)	106	0.65
Romanian (101)	149	0.91
Russian (643)	918	5.63
Scandinavian (0)	15	0.09
Scotch-Irish (121)	376	2.31
Scottish (131)	628	3.85
Serbian (12)	12	0.07
Slavic (11)	11	0.07
Slovak (0)	12	0.07
Slovene (0)	18	0.11
Soviet Union (14)	14	0.09
Swedish (147)	342	2.10
Swiss (38)	88	0.54
Turkish (14)	44	0.27
Ukrainian (94)	112	0.69
Welsh (15)	93	0.57
Yugoslavian (38)	38	0.23

Hispanic Origin	Population	%
Hispanic or Latino (of any race)	650	4.01
Central American, ex. Mexican	34	0.21
Costa Rican	2	0.01
Guatemalan	5	0.03
Honduran	1	0.01
Nicaraguan	10	0.06
Panamanian	7	0.04
Salvadoran	9	0.06
Cuban	42	0.26
Dominican Republic	4	0.02
Mexican	318	1.96
Puerto Rican	30	0.19
South American	112	0.69
Argentinean	31	0.19
Bolivian	11	0.07
Chilean	17	0.10
Colombian	25	0.15
Ecuadorian	11	0.07
Peruvian	14	0.09
Uruguayan	1	0.01
Venezuelan	2	0.01
Other Hispanic or Latino	110	0.68

Race*	Population	%
African-American/Black (110)	140	0.86
Not Hispanic (105)	132	0.82
Hispanic (5)	8	0.05
American Indian/Alaska Native (24)	75	0.46
Not Hispanic (17)	64	0.40
Hispanic (7)	11	0.07
Blackfeet (0)	2	0.01
Canadian/French Am. Ind. (1)	2	0.01
Cherokee (5)	19	0.12
Chippewa (0)	4	0.02
Choctaw (0)	1	0.01
Comanche (0)	1	0.01
Creek (1)	1	0.01
Crow (1)	1	0.01
Mexican American Ind. (1)	1	0.01
Navajo (2)	3	0.02
Osage (1)	1	0.01
Potawatomi (0)	1	0.01
Sioux (1)	4	0.02
South American Ind. (0)	1	0.01
Asian (1,624)	1,739	10.74
Not Hispanic (1,613)	1,722	10.63
Hispanic (11)	17	0.10
Chinese, ex. Taiwanese (393)	420	2.59
Filipino (273)	299	1.85
Indian (68)	74	0.46
Indonesian (18)	34	0.21
Japanese (185)	205	1.27
Korean (503)	517	3.19
Malaysian (1)	1	0.01
Pakistani (4)	4	0.02
Sri Lankan (1)	1	0.01
Taiwanese (111)	119	0.73
Thai (11)	13	0.08
Vietnamese (31)	31	0.19
Hawaii Native/Pacific Islander (10)	28	0.17
Not Hispanic (10)	28	0.17
Fijian (1)	1	0.01
Guamanian/Chamorro (4)	4	0.02
Native Hawaiian (5)	9	0.06
White (14,133)	14,300	88.32
Not Hispanic (13,600)	13,749	84.91
Hispanic (533)	551	3.40

*Notes: † The Census 2010 population figure is used to calculate the percentages in the Hispanic Origin and Race categories. Ancestry percentages are based on the 2006-2010 American Community Survey population (not shown); ‡ Numbers in parentheses indicate the number of people reporting a single ancestry; * Numbers in parentheses indicate the number of persons reporting this race alone, not in combination with any other race; Please refer to the Explanation of Data for more information.*

Lake Arrowhead

Place Type: CDP
County: San Bernardino
Population: 12,424†

Ancestry‡	Population	%
American (99)	99	1.03
Arab (0)	69	0.72
Lebanese (0)	15	0.16
Palestinian (0)	39	0.41
Other Arab (0)	15	0.16
Armenian (34)	75	0.78
Australian (0)	19	0.20
Belgian (0)	16	0.17
British (9)	9	0.09
Croatian (0)	15	0.16
Czech (17)	17	0.18
Dutch (45)	118	1.23
Eastern European (0)	39	0.41
English (427)	1,335	13.94
European (78)	199	2.08
Finnish (0)	15	0.16
French, ex. Basque (98)	408	4.26
French Canadian (0)	15	0.16
German (539)	1,768	18.46
Hungarian (167)	182	1.90
Irish (1,193)	2,312	24.14
Italian (121)	289	3.02
Northern European (217)	217	2.27
Norwegian (71)	149	1.56
Polish (42)	72	0.75
Russian (118)	201	2.10
Scandinavian (110)	110	1.15
Scotch-Irish (108)	229	2.39
Scottish (88)	297	3.10
Slovene (12)	12	0.13
Swedish (212)	363	3.79
Welsh (0)	50	0.52

Hispanic Origin	Population	%
Hispanic or Latino (of any race)	2,709	21.80
Central American, ex. Mexican	114	0.92
Costa Rican	2	0.02
Guatemalan	61	0.49
Honduran	4	0.03
Nicaraguan	13	0.10
Salvadoran	26	0.21
Other Central American	8	0.06
Cuban	19	0.15
Mexican	2,201	17.72
Puerto Rican	35	0.28
South American	31	0.25
Argentinean	7	0.06
Chilean	5	0.04
Colombian	3	0.02
Ecuadorian	10	0.08
Peruvian	4	0.03
Uruguayan	2	0.02
Other Hispanic or Latino	309	2.49

Race*	Population	%
African-American/Black (95)	161	1.30
Not Hispanic (90)	148	1.19
Hispanic (5)	13	0.10
American Indian/Alaska Native (93)	299	2.41
Not Hispanic (58)	218	1.75
Hispanic (35)	81	0.65
Aleut *(Alaska Native)* (0)	3	0.02
Apache (2)	15	0.12
Arapaho (0)	2	0.02
Blackfeet (0)	16	0.13
Canadian/French Am. Ind. (1)	1	0.01
Cherokee (11)	71	0.57
Chippewa (1)	4	0.03
Choctaw (9)	14	0.11
Comanche (1)	3	0.02
Creek (0)	2	0.02
Crow (1)	7	0.06
Delaware (0)	3	0.02
Iroquois (3)	7	0.06
Mexican American Ind. (9)	14	0.11
Navajo (3)	6	0.05
Osage (0)	4	0.03
Paiute (1)	1	0.01
Pima (2)	2	0.02
Potawatomi (5)	12	0.10
Seminole (0)	3	0.02
Shoshone (0)	1	0.01
Sioux (0)	9	0.07
South American Ind. (1)	1	0.01
Tlingit-Haida *(Alaska Native)* (0)	1	0.01
Tohono O'Odham (0)	1	0.01
Yaqui (0)	1	0.01
Yuman (5)	5	0.04
Asian (152)	270	2.17
Not Hispanic (137)	238	1.92
Hispanic (15)	32	0.26
Burmese (0)	5	0.04
Cambodian (0)	1	0.01
Chinese, ex. Taiwanese (38)	60	0.48
Filipino (27)	65	0.52
Indian (15)	27	0.22
Japanese (24)	45	0.36
Korean (12)	31	0.25
Malaysian (3)	5	0.04
Nepalese (2)	2	0.02
Pakistani (1)	1	0.01
Sri Lankan (0)	2	0.02
Taiwanese (0)	1	0.01
Thai (4)	6	0.05
Vietnamese (11)	21	0.17
Hawaii Native/Pacific Islander (33)	57	0.46
Not Hispanic (28)	49	0.39
Hispanic (5)	8	0.06
Guamanian/Chamorro (11)	18	0.14
Native Hawaiian (11)	23	0.19
Samoan (10)	12	0.10
White (10,729)	11,173	89.93
Not Hispanic (9,069)	9,368	75.40
Hispanic (1,660)	1,805	14.53

Lake Elsinore

Place Type: City
County: Riverside
Population: 51,821†

Ancestry‡	Population	%
Afghan (0)	12	0.02
African, Sub-Saharan (129)	366	0.75
African (53)	244	0.50
Nigerian (76)	76	0.16
Somalian (0)	46	0.09
American (1,132)	1,132	2.33
Arab (121)	281	0.58
Arab (11)	11	0.02
Egyptian (0)	27	0.06
Jordanian (29)	29	0.06
Lebanese (15)	130	0.27
Palestinian (25)	25	0.05
Syrian (41)	59	0.12
Armenian (12)	120	0.25
Austrian (22)	46	0.09
Brazilian (0)	26	0.05
British (33)	51	0.10
Bulgarian (0)	9	0.02
Canadian (147)	176	0.36
Croatian (34)	45	0.09
Czech (60)	205	0.42
Czechoslovakian (0)	6	0.01
Danish (14)	365	0.75
Dutch (411)	1,108	2.28
Eastern European (22)	22	0.05
English (911)	2,988	6.14
European (317)	456	0.94
Finnish (51)	111	0.23
French, ex. Basque (394)	1,370	2.82
French Canadian (62)	202	0.42
German (1,297)	4,777	9.82
Greek (18)	132	0.27
Hungarian (70)	175	0.36
Icelander (0)	7	0.01
Iranian (12)	53	0.11
Irish (623)	3,621	7.44
Italian (909)	2,321	4.77
Lithuanian (0)	14	0.03
New Zealander (0)	40	0.08
Norwegian (198)	552	1.13
Polish (251)	668	1.37
Portuguese (41)	134	0.28
Romanian (26)	45	0.09
Russian (42)	197	0.40
Scandinavian (60)	126	0.26
Scotch-Irish (154)	490	1.01
Scottish (152)	510	1.05
Slovak (0)	21	0.04
Slovene (0)	6	0.01
Swedish (36)	496	1.02
Swiss (9)	105	0.22
Ukrainian (26)	54	0.11
Welsh (28)	189	0.39
West Indian, ex. Hispanic (166)	297	0.61
Belizean (17)	111	0.23
Jamaican (149)	186	0.38
Yugoslavian (25)	40	0.08

Hispanic Origin	Population	%
Hispanic or Latino (of any race)	25,073	48.38
Central American, ex. Mexican	1,935	3.73
Costa Rican	46	0.09
Guatemalan	1,268	2.45
Honduran	49	0.09
Nicaraguan	73	0.14
Panamanian	51	0.10
Salvadoran	433	0.84
Other Central American	15	0.03
Cuban	150	0.29
Dominican Republic	23	0.04
Mexican	20,497	39.55
Puerto Rican	319	0.62
South American	558	1.08
Argentinean	142	0.27
Bolivian	16	0.03
Chilean	29	0.06
Colombian	136	0.26
Ecuadorian	71	0.14
Paraguayan	9	0.02
Peruvian	130	0.25
Uruguayan	6	0.01
Venezuelan	18	0.03
Other South American	1	<0.01
Other Hispanic or Latino	1,591	3.07

Race*	Population	%
African-American/Black (2,738)	3,544	6.84
Not Hispanic (2,488)	3,011	5.81
Hispanic (250)	533	1.03
American Indian/Alaska Native (483)	1,054	2.03
Not Hispanic (190)	515	0.99
Hispanic (293)	539	1.04
Aleut *(Alaska Native)* (6)	6	0.01
Apache (20)	48	0.09
Blackfeet (5)	33	0.06
Canadian/French Am. Ind. (3)	3	0.01
Central American Ind. (5)	5	0.01
Cherokee (17)	130	0.25
Cheyenne (3)	7	0.01
Chickasaw (1)	4	0.01
Chippewa (4)	11	0.02
Choctaw (4)	27	0.05
Comanche (3)	11	0.02
Creek (5)	14	0.03
Crow (0)	2	<0.01
Delaware (5)	8	0.02
Hopi (1)	5	0.01
Inupiat *(Alaska Native)* (0)	1	<0.01
Iroquois (2)	10	0.02
Lumbee (0)	1	<0.01
Mexican American Ind. (71)	103	0.20

*Notes: † The Census 2010 population figure is used to calculate the percentages in the Hispanic Origin and Race categories. Ancestry percentages are based on the 2006-2010 American Community Survey population (not shown); ‡ Numbers in parentheses indicate the number of people reporting a single ancestry; * Numbers in parentheses indicate the number of persons reporting this race alone, not in combination with any other race; Please refer to the Explanation of Data for more information.*

Navajo (11)	14	0.03
Osage (1)	4	0.01
Ottawa (0)	2	<0.01
Paiute (0)	1	<0.01
Pima (0)	1	<0.01
Pueblo (4)	6	0.01
Puget Sound Salish (5)	5	0.01
Seminole (3)	4	0.01
Shoshone (3)	9	0.02
Sioux (9)	29	0.06
South American Ind. (0)	2	<0.01
Spanish American Ind. (1)	1	<0.01
Tlingit-Haida *(Alaska Native)* (0)	1	<0.01
Tohono O'Odham (1)	4	0.01
Tsimshian *(Alaska Native)* (0)	1	<0.01
Yaqui (12)	20	0.04
Yuman (3)	3	0.01
Asian (2,996)	3,768	7.27
Not Hispanic (2,895)	3,431	6.62
Hispanic (101)	337	0.65
Burmese (6)	7	0.01
Cambodian (213)	230	0.44
Chinese, ex. Taiwanese (258)	383	0.74
Filipino (1,272)	1,681	3.24
Hmong (8)	9	0.02
Indian (153)	173	0.33
Indonesian (8)	24	0.05
Japanese (118)	271	0.52
Korean (270)	333	0.64
Laotian (51)	62	0.12
Malaysian (2)	7	0.01
Nepalese (1)	1	<0.01
Pakistani (47)	54	0.10
Sri Lankan (2)	4	0.01
Taiwanese (9)	12	0.02
Thai (38)	60	0.12
Vietnamese (427)	504	0.97
Hawaii Native/Pacific Islander (174)	409	0.79
Not Hispanic (144)	309	0.60
Hispanic (30)	100	0.19
Fijian (4)	8	0.02
Guamanian/Chamorro (22)	50	0.10
Native Hawaiian (47)	155	0.30
Samoan (71)	141	0.27
Tongan (4)	4	0.01
White (31,067)	33,819	65.26
Not Hispanic (19,604)	20,757	40.06
Hispanic (11,463)	13,062	25.21

Lake Forest

Place Type: City
County: Orange
Population: 77,264†

Ancestry‡	Population	%
Afghan (106)	150	0.20
African, Sub-Saharan (250)	250	0.33
African (148)	148	0.19
Somalian (46)	46	0.06
South African (56)	56	0.07
Albanian (11)	11	0.01
Alsatian (0)	16	0.02
American (2,803)	2,803	3.65
Arab (365)	481	0.63
Arab (46)	46	0.06
Egyptian (132)	186	0.24
Lebanese (151)	213	0.28
Syrian (17)	17	0.02
Other Arab (19)	19	0.02
Armenian (164)	269	0.35
Australian (42)	112	0.15
Austrian (26)	209	0.27
Basque (0)	19	0.02
Belgian (37)	109	0.14
Brazilian (66)	92	0.12
British (381)	891	1.16
Canadian (138)	263	0.34
Croatian (61)	153	0.20
Czech (96)	255	0.33
Czechoslovakian (21)	47	0.06
Danish (88)	400	0.52
Dutch (468)	1,646	2.15
Eastern European (128)	141	0.18
English (2,574)	7,581	9.88
European (989)	1,247	1.63
Finnish (49)	243	0.32
French, ex. Basque (524)	2,611	3.40
French Canadian (214)	423	0.55
German (3,106)	11,350	14.79
Greek (131)	366	0.48
Hungarian (126)	325	0.42
Icelander (16)	16	0.02
Iranian (984)	1,167	1.52
Irish (2,297)	8,071	10.52
Israeli (57)	57	0.07
Italian (1,754)	4,292	5.59
Latvian (0)	13	0.02
Lithuanian (0)	79	0.10
Maltese (0)	31	0.04
Northern European (57)	92	0.12
Norwegian (493)	1,272	1.66
Polish (444)	1,967	2.56
Portuguese (80)	255	0.33
Romanian (199)	250	0.33
Russian (570)	1,310	1.71
Scandinavian (150)	230	0.30
Scotch-Irish (454)	1,120	1.46
Scottish (369)	1,503	1.96
Serbian (7)	33	0.04
Slavic (8)	18	0.02
Slovak (0)	44	0.06
Slovene (0)	7	0.01
Swedish (386)	1,761	2.30
Swiss (4)	340	0.44
Turkish (52)	100	0.13
Ukrainian (48)	148	0.19
Welsh (67)	508	0.66
West Indian, ex. Hispanic (14)	14	0.02
Jamaican (14)	14	0.02
Yugoslavian (0)	82	0.11

Hispanic Origin	Population	%
Hispanic or Latino (of any race)	19,024	24.62
Central American, ex. Mexican	1,595	2.06
Costa Rican	70	0.09
Guatemalan	855	1.11
Honduran	60	0.08
Nicaraguan	83	0.11
Panamanian	38	0.05
Salvadoran	474	0.61
Other Central American	15	0.02
Cuban	200	0.26
Dominican Republic	13	0.02
Mexican	14,299	18.51
Puerto Rican	354	0.46
South American	1,430	1.85
Argentinean	261	0.34
Bolivian	85	0.11
Chilean	60	0.08
Colombian	454	0.59
Ecuadorian	120	0.16
Paraguayan	2	<0.01
Peruvian	371	0.48
Uruguayan	19	0.02
Venezuelan	39	0.05
Other South American	19	0.02
Other Hispanic or Latino	1,133	1.47

Race*	Population	%
African-American/Black (1,295)	1,794	2.32
Not Hispanic (1,158)	1,544	2.00
Hispanic (137)	250	0.32
American Indian/Alaska Native (384)	951	1.23
Not Hispanic (195)	548	0.71
Hispanic (189)	403	0.52
Alaska Athabascan *(Ala. Nat.)* (1)	1	<0.01
Aleut *(Alaska Native)* (0)	2	<0.01
Apache (7)	29	0.04
Arapaho (1)	1	<0.01
Blackfeet (6)	26	0.03
Canadian/French Am. Ind. (5)	8	0.01
Central American Ind. (0)	4	0.01
Cherokee (23)	164	0.21
Cheyenne (0)	2	<0.01
Chickasaw (0)	7	0.01
Chippewa (7)	11	0.01
Choctaw (10)	36	0.05
Comanche (0)	3	<0.01
Creek (6)	11	0.01
Delaware (1)	6	0.01
Hopi (0)	2	<0.01
Iroquois (9)	12	0.02
Kiowa (0)	6	0.01
Lumbee (1)	1	<0.01
Menominee (1)	1	<0.01
Mexican American Ind. (44)	70	0.09
Navajo (9)	18	0.02
Osage (9)	20	0.03
Paiute (1)	2	<0.01
Pima (0)	1	<0.01
Potawatomi (3)	8	0.01
Pueblo (10)	20	0.03
Seminole (0)	5	0.01
Shoshone (0)	2	<0.01
Sioux (4)	15	0.02
South American Ind. (4)	13	0.02
Spanish American Ind. (3)	9	0.01
Tohono O'Odham (1)	1	<0.01
Ute (1)	1	<0.01
Yaqui (5)	11	0.01
Asian (10,115)	12,091	15.65
Not Hispanic (9,985)	11,699	15.14
Hispanic (130)	392	0.51
Bangladeshi (8)	13	0.02
Burmese (5)	13	0.02
Cambodian (35)	51	0.07
Chinese, ex. Taiwanese (1,432)	1,946	2.52
Filipino (2,625)	3,232	4.18
Hmong (15)	17	0.02
Indian (1,610)	1,739	2.25
Indonesian (189)	266	0.34
Japanese (764)	1,267	1.64
Korean (827)	983	1.27
Laotian (61)	72	0.09
Malaysian (16)	24	0.03
Pakistani (116)	127	0.16
Sri Lankan (93)	100	0.13
Taiwanese (228)	293	0.38
Thai (108)	145	0.19
Vietnamese (1,617)	1,819	2.35
Hawaii Native/Pacific Islander (191)	509	0.66
Not Hispanic (172)	425	0.55
Hispanic (19)	84	0.11
Fijian (2)	2	<0.01
Guamanian/Chamorro (43)	92	0.12
Native Hawaiian (59)	182	0.24
Samoan (46)	73	0.09
Tongan (2)	4	0.01
White (54,341)	57,595	74.54
Not Hispanic (44,177)	46,333	59.97
Hispanic (10,164)	11,262	14.58

Lake Los Angeles

Place Type: CDP
County: Los Angeles
Population: 12,328†

Ancestry‡	Population	%
African, Sub-Saharan (483)	495	3.96
African (483)	495	3.96
American (293)	293	2.34
Austrian (30)	45	0.36
British (18)	18	0.14
Canadian (31)	57	0.46
Czech (0)	14	0.11
Danish (0)	7	0.06
Dutch (0)	70	0.56
English (419)	640	5.12

*Notes: † The Census 2010 population figure is used to calculate the percentages in the Hispanic Origin and Race categories. Ancestry percentages are based on the 2006-2010 American Community Survey population (not shown); ‡ Numbers in parentheses indicate the number of people reporting a single ancestry; * Numbers in parentheses indicate the number of persons reporting this race alone, not in combination with any other race; Please refer to the Explanation of Data for more information.*

SECTION TWO

European (36)	76	0.61
French, ex. Basque (20)	136	1.09
French Canadian (14)	38	0.30
German (158)	774	6.19
Hungarian (0)	18	0.14
Irish (531)	946	7.56
Italian (313)	603	4.82
Lithuanian (0)	30	0.24
Northern European (188)	188	1.50
Norwegian (41)	71	0.57
Polish (67)	125	1.00
Portuguese (81)	173	1.38
Scotch-Irish (0)	63	0.50
Swedish (0)	67	0.54
Swiss (0)	48	0.38

Hispanic Origin	Population	%
Hispanic or Latino (of any race)	6,604	53.57
Central American, ex. Mexican	658	5.34
Costa Rican	10	0.08
Guatemalan	203	1.65
Honduran	31	0.25
Nicaraguan	26	0.21
Panamanian	6	0.05
Salvadoran	376	3.05
Other Central American	6	0.05
Cuban	36	0.29
Dominican Republic	4	0.03
Mexican	5,174	41.97
Puerto Rican	108	0.88
South American	56	0.45
Argentinean	7	0.06
Chilean	5	0.04
Colombian	18	0.15
Ecuadorian	17	0.14
Paraguayan	1	0.01
Peruvian	8	0.06
Other Hispanic or Latino	568	4.61

Race*	Population	%
African-American/Black (1,388)	1,564	12.69
Not Hispanic (1,310)	1,425	11.56
Hispanic (78)	139	1.13
American Indian/Alaska Native (178)	379	3.07
Not Hispanic (75)	204	1.65
Hispanic (103)	175	1.42
Apache (5)	18	0.15
Blackfeet (3)	15	0.12
Canadian/French Am. Ind. (6)	10	0.08
Central American Ind. (1)	1	0.01
Cherokee (23)	61	0.49
Cheyenne (1)	3	0.02
Chippewa (2)	3	0.02
Choctaw (3)	5	0.04
Comanche (0)	1	0.01
Creek (3)	3	0.02
Hopi (2)	2	0.02
Iroquois (1)	1	0.01
Mexican American Ind. (30)	49	0.40
Navajo (0)	1	0.01
Osage (1)	6	0.05
Paiute (0)	1	0.01
Pima (2)	2	0.02
Potawatomi (2)	3	0.02
Pueblo (0)	4	0.03
Seminole (0)	5	0.04
Sioux (1)	11	0.09
Spanish American Ind. (0)	2	0.02
Tohono O'Odham (1)	5	0.04
Ute (2)	2	0.02
Yaqui (0)	2	0.02
Asian (116)	210	1.70
Not Hispanic (99)	152	1.23
Hispanic (17)	58	0.47
Cambodian (6)	8	0.06
Chinese, ex. Taiwanese (5)	19	0.15
Filipino (55)	84	0.68
Indian (7)	11	0.09
Indonesian (5)	11	0.09
Japanese (6)	22	0.18
Korean (6)	13	0.11
Laotian (4)	9	0.07
Thai (15)	20	0.16
Vietnamese (3)	3	0.02
Hawaii Native/Pacific Islander (27)	55	0.45
Not Hispanic (25)	46	0.37
Hispanic (2)	9	0.07
Fijian (0)	2	0.02
Guamanian/Chamorro (3)	6	0.05
Native Hawaiian (11)	22	0.18
Samoan (12)	19	0.15
Tongan (0)	2	0.02
White (6,862)	7,448	60.42
Not Hispanic (3,937)	4,146	33.63
Hispanic (2,925)	3,302	26.78

Lakeland Village

Place Type: CDP
County: Riverside
Population: 11,541†

Ancestry‡	Population	%
American (680)	680	5.61
Arab (0)	7	0.06
Lebanese (0)	7	0.06
Austrian (0)	14	0.12
British (0)	44	0.36
Canadian (16)	31	0.26
Czech (0)	17	0.14
Danish (23)	23	0.19
Dutch (56)	139	1.15
Eastern European (19)	19	0.16
English (446)	1,148	9.47
European (235)	235	1.94
Finnish (0)	107	0.88
French, ex. Basque (44)	337	2.78
French Canadian (32)	71	0.59
German (325)	1,517	12.51
Greek (33)	77	0.64
Hungarian (0)	99	0.82
Irish (199)	1,338	11.04
Italian (231)	551	4.54
Lithuanian (16)	31	0.26
Norwegian (32)	165	1.36
Polish (25)	105	0.87
Portuguese (10)	18	0.15
Russian (55)	124	1.02
Scotch-Irish (21)	96	0.79
Scottish (0)	90	0.74
Slovak (32)	32	0.26
Swedish (11)	190	1.57
Swiss (9)	21	0.17
Welsh (0)	19	0.16

Hispanic Origin	Population	%
Hispanic or Latino (of any race)	5,114	44.31
Central American, ex. Mexican	161	1.40
Costa Rican	8	0.07
Guatemalan	76	0.66
Honduran	5	0.04
Nicaraguan	6	0.05
Panamanian	7	0.06
Salvadoran	59	0.51
Cuban	17	0.15
Dominican Republic	6	0.05
Mexican	4,447	38.53
Puerto Rican	69	0.60
South American	67	0.58
Argentinean	7	0.06
Chilean	5	0.04
Colombian	10	0.09
Ecuadorian	16	0.14
Paraguayan	3	0.03
Peruvian	16	0.14
Uruguayan	2	0.02
Venezuelan	2	0.02
Other South American	6	0.05
Other Hispanic or Latino	347	3.01

Race*	Population	%
African-American/Black (285)	421	3.65
Not Hispanic (257)	347	3.01
Hispanic (28)	74	0.64
American Indian/Alaska Native (131)	297	2.57
Not Hispanic (50)	167	1.45
Hispanic (81)	130	1.13
Apache (0)	11	0.10
Blackfeet (1)	4	0.03
Canadian/French Am. Ind. (0)	1	0.01
Central American Ind. (0)	4	0.03
Cherokee (6)	55	0.48
Chippewa (1)	2	0.02
Choctaw (4)	7	0.06
Comanche (1)	3	0.03
Cree (1)	1	0.01
Creek (0)	1	0.01
Crow (0)	1	0.01
Delaware (1)	1	0.01
Hopi (0)	2	0.02
Iroquois (0)	1	0.01
Kiowa (0)	4	0.03
Mexican American Ind. (11)	17	0.15
Navajo (2)	9	0.08
Pima (1)	1	0.01
Pueblo (0)	1	0.01
Seminole (6)	6	0.05
Shoshone (0)	1	0.01
Sioux (1)	3	0.03
Spanish American Ind. (0)	1	0.01
Tohono O'Odham (0)	2	0.02
Ute (0)	6	0.05
Yaqui (0)	3	0.03
Asian (168)	275	2.38
Not Hispanic (142)	216	1.87
Hispanic (26)	59	0.51
Burmese (2)	2	0.02
Cambodian (3)	3	0.03
Chinese, ex. Taiwanese (13)	22	0.19
Filipino (59)	95	0.82
Indian (7)	16	0.14
Indonesian (4)	5	0.04
Japanese (14)	44	0.38
Korean (8)	16	0.14
Laotian (1)	1	0.01
Pakistani (3)	9	0.08
Thai (8)	17	0.15
Vietnamese (33)	34	0.29
Hawaii Native/Pacific Islander (21)	59	0.51
Not Hispanic (17)	45	0.39
Hispanic (4)	14	0.12
Guamanian/Chamorro (6)	13	0.11
Native Hawaiian (6)	23	0.20
Samoan (8)	15	0.13
White (7,764)	8,305	71.96
Not Hispanic (5,662)	5,913	51.23
Hispanic (2,102)	2,392	20.73

Lakeside

Place Type: CDP
County: San Diego
Population: 20,648†

Ancestry‡	Population	%
African, Sub-Saharan (124)	124	0.60
African (124)	124	0.60
American (847)	847	4.13
Arab (125)	172	0.84
Arab (15)	15	0.07
Iraqi (100)	100	0.49
Lebanese (0)	20	0.10
Palestinian (0)	27	0.13
Other Arab (10)	10	0.05
Armenian (9)	9	0.04
Australian (0)	27	0.13
Austrian (0)	71	0.35
Belgian (13)	83	0.40
British (0)	10	0.05

*Notes: † The Census 2010 population figure is used to calculate the percentages in the Hispanic Origin and Race categories. Ancestry percentages are based on the 2006-2010 American Community Survey population (not shown); ‡ Numbers in parentheses indicate the number of people reporting a single ancestry; * Numbers in parentheses indicate the number of persons reporting this race alone, not in combination with any other race; Please refer to the Explanation of Data for more information.*

Ancestry	Population	%
Bulgarian (38)	205	1.00
Canadian (21)	49	0.24
Croatian (16)	70	0.34
Czech (35)	220	1.07
Czechoslovakian (59)	90	0.44
Danish (0)	91	0.44
Dutch (46)	510	2.49
English (772)	2,386	11.64
European (417)	507	2.47
French, ex. Basque (66)	818	3.99
French Canadian (93)	209	1.02
German (1,057)	4,579	22.33
Greek (53)	121	0.59
Hungarian (0)	64	0.31
Irish (648)	3,311	16.15
Italian (527)	1,438	7.01
Lithuanian (8)	39	0.19
Maltese (9)	9	0.04
Northern European (9)	9	0.04
Norwegian (169)	442	2.16
Pennsylvania German (9)	9	0.04
Polish (238)	681	3.32
Portuguese (39)	150	0.73
Russian (79)	288	1.40
Scandinavian (29)	131	0.64
Scotch-Irish (184)	548	2.67
Scottish (83)	406	1.98
Swedish (75)	313	1.53
Swiss (11)	22	0.11
Ukrainian (9)	25	0.12
Welsh (87)	305	1.49

Hispanic Origin	Population	%
Hispanic or Latino (of any race)	3,627	17.57
Central American, ex. Mexican	62	0.30
Costa Rican	17	0.08
Guatemalan	17	0.08
Honduran	4	0.02
Nicaraguan	5	0.02
Panamanian	2	0.01
Salvadoran	17	0.08
Cuban	23	0.11
Dominican Republic	2	0.01
Mexican	3,084	14.94
Puerto Rican	109	0.53
South American	28	0.14
Argentinean	2	0.01
Chilean	1	<0.01
Colombian	8	0.04
Ecuadorian	11	0.05
Peruvian	2	0.01
Venezuelan	1	<0.01
Other South American	3	0.01
Other Hispanic or Latino	319	1.54

Race*	Population	%
African-American/Black (235)	359	1.74
Not Hispanic (220)	311	1.51
Hispanic (15)	48	0.23
American Indian/Alaska Native (181)	462	2.24
Not Hispanic (135)	340	1.65
Hispanic (46)	122	0.59
Aleut *(Alaska Native)* (1)	5	0.02
Apache (10)	16	0.08
Blackfeet (0)	19	0.09
Canadian/French Am. Ind. (2)	3	0.01
Cherokee (17)	81	0.39
Chickasaw (3)	5	0.02
Chippewa (2)	15	0.07
Choctaw (5)	25	0.12
Comanche (1)	1	<0.01
Creek (5)	5	0.02
Iroquois (3)	9	0.04
Kiowa (0)	1	<0.01
Mexican American Ind. (0)	6	0.03
Navajo (10)	13	0.06
Osage (1)	4	0.02
Ottawa (1)	1	<0.01
Paiute (0)	1	<0.01
Pima (2)	2	0.01
Potawatomi (0)	1	<0.01
Pueblo (1)	1	<0.01
Shoshone (1)	2	0.01
Sioux (2)	9	0.04
Tlingit-Haida *(Alaska Native)* (1)	1	<0.01
Tohono O'Odham (2)	4	0.02
Ute (1)	1	<0.01
Yaqui (4)	14	0.07
Yuman (4)	6	0.03
Yup'ik *(Alaska Native)* (0)	1	<0.01
Asian (351)	631	3.06
Not Hispanic (333)	553	2.68
Hispanic (18)	78	0.38
Cambodian (25)	25	0.12
Chinese, ex. Taiwanese (35)	74	0.36
Filipino (175)	320	1.55
Hmong (5)	5	0.02
Indian (15)	20	0.10
Indonesian (2)	3	0.01
Japanese (28)	103	0.50
Korean (20)	37	0.18
Laotian (6)	11	0.05
Pakistani (4)	4	0.02
Thai (1)	6	0.03
Vietnamese (24)	32	0.15
Hawaii Native/Pacific Islander (53)	172	0.83
Not Hispanic (44)	125	0.61
Hispanic (9)	47	0.23
Guamanian/Chamorro (26)	69	0.33
Native Hawaiian (14)	70	0.34
Samoan (7)	19	0.09
Tongan (1)	1	<0.01
White (17,545)	18,430	89.26
Not Hispanic (15,726)	16,251	78.70
Hispanic (1,819)	2,179	10.55

Lakewood

Place Type: City
County: Los Angeles
Population: 80,048†

Ancestry‡	Population	%
African, Sub-Saharan (457)	542	0.68
African (242)	302	0.38
Cape Verdean (25)	50	0.06
Nigerian (45)	45	0.06
South African (12)	12	0.02
Other Sub-Saharan African (133)	133	0.17
American (1,588)	1,588	1.99
Arab (461)	668	0.84
Arab (110)	147	0.18
Egyptian (93)	129	0.16
Jordanian (52)	68	0.09
Lebanese (34)	45	0.06
Moroccan (121)	149	0.19
Palestinian (0)	16	0.02
Syrian (38)	63	0.08
Other Arab (13)	51	0.06
Armenian (80)	216	0.27
Australian (45)	45	0.06
Austrian (12)	171	0.21
Belgian (0)	23	0.03
Brazilian (41)	41	0.05
British (77)	158	0.20
Canadian (135)	253	0.32
Celtic (11)	23	0.03
Croatian (0)	39	0.05
Cypriot (11)	11	0.01
Czech (11)	124	0.16
Czechoslovakian (24)	42	0.05
Danish (136)	436	0.55
Dutch (557)	1,430	1.79
Eastern European (84)	84	0.11
English (1,789)	5,414	6.78
European (900)	1,113	1.39
Finnish (77)	160	0.20
French, ex. Basque (190)	1,245	1.56
French Canadian (101)	241	0.30
German (2,537)	8,127	10.18
Greek (11)	115	0.14
Guyanese (23)	45	0.06
Hungarian (56)	392	0.49
Icelander (64)	64	0.08
Iranian (17)	39	0.05
Irish (1,401)	6,044	7.57
Israeli (29)	29	0.04
Italian (851)	2,493	3.12
Latvian (11)	11	0.01
Lithuanian (0)	39	0.05
Northern European (33)	43	0.05
Norwegian (270)	992	1.24
Pennsylvania German (36)	48	0.06
Polish (342)	922	1.15
Portuguese (161)	443	0.55
Romanian (123)	185	0.23
Russian (308)	624	0.78
Scandinavian (85)	130	0.16
Scotch-Irish (115)	823	1.03
Scottish (385)	1,067	1.34
Serbian (0)	12	0.02
Slovene (0)	35	0.04
Swedish (273)	821	1.03
Swiss (54)	170	0.21
Turkish (13)	26	0.03
Ukrainian (10)	38	0.05
Welsh (56)	249	0.31
West Indian, ex. Hispanic (257)	321	0.40
Belizean (153)	153	0.19
Jamaican (75)	75	0.09
Trinidadian/Tobagonian (9)	9	0.01
West Indian (20)	84	0.11
Yugoslavian (19)	54	0.07

Hispanic Origin	Population	%
Hispanic or Latino (of any race)	24,101	30.11
Central American, ex. Mexican	1,566	1.96
Costa Rican	106	0.13
Guatemalan	394	0.49
Honduran	153	0.19
Nicaraguan	170	0.21
Panamanian	65	0.08
Salvadoran	662	0.83
Other Central American	16	0.02
Cuban	315	0.39
Dominican Republic	63	0.08
Mexican	19,252	24.05
Puerto Rican	537	0.67
South American	824	1.03
Argentinean	151	0.19
Bolivian	18	0.02
Chilean	57	0.07
Colombian	193	0.24
Ecuadorian	136	0.17
Peruvian	227	0.28
Uruguayan	24	0.03
Venezuelan	9	0.01
Other South American	9	0.01
Other Hispanic or Latino	1,544	1.93

Race*	Population	%
African-American/Black (6,973)	8,044	10.05
Not Hispanic (6,663)	7,424	9.27
Hispanic (310)	620	0.77
American Indian/Alaska Native (564)	1,320	1.65
Not Hispanic (234)	704	0.88
Hispanic (330)	616	0.77
Apache (20)	62	0.08
Arapaho (1)	3	<0.01
Blackfeet (5)	31	0.04
Canadian/French Am. Ind. (1)	2	<0.01
Central American Ind. (0)	3	<0.01
Cherokee (46)	209	0.26
Cheyenne (2)	7	0.01
Chickasaw (7)	25	0.03
Chippewa (15)	33	0.04
Choctaw (11)	53	0.07
Comanche (1)	6	0.01
Cree (4)	7	0.01
Creek (11)	20	0.02

SECTION TWO

*Notes: † The Census 2010 population figure is used to calculate the percentages in the Hispanic Origin and Race categories. Ancestry percentages are based on the 2006-2010 American Community Survey population (not shown); ‡ Numbers in parentheses indicate the number of people reporting a single ancestry; * Numbers in parentheses indicate the number of persons reporting this race alone, not in combination with any other race; Please refer to the Explanation of Data for more information.*

Crow (0)	4	<0.01
Delaware (4)	4	<0.01
Hopi (0)	7	0.01
Inupiat *(Alaska Native)* (0)	10	0.01
Iroquois (4)	16	0.02
Kiowa (3)	5	0.01
Lumbee (5)	8	0.01
Menominee (0)	1	<0.01
Mexican American Ind. (63)	81	0.10
Navajo (32)	57	0.07
Osage (2)	3	<0.01
Ottawa (0)	1	<0.01
Paiute (0)	1	<0.01
Pima (0)	1	<0.01
Potawatomi (1)	8	0.01
Pueblo (5)	10	0.01
Puget Sound Salish (0)	2	<0.01
Seminole (0)	5	0.01
Shoshone (2)	3	<0.01
Sioux (17)	30	0.04
South American Ind. (8)	13	0.02
Spanish American Ind. (6)	10	0.01
Tlingit-Haida *(Alaska Native)* (2)	7	0.01
Tohono O'Odham (0)	4	<0.01
Tsimshian *(Alaska Native)* (2)	2	<0.01
Ute (1)	1	<0.01
Yaqui (3)	12	0.01
Yuman (6)	6	0.01
Yup'ik *(Alaska Native)* (3)	3	<0.01
Asian (13,115)	15,136	18.91
Not Hispanic (12,811)	14,352	17.93
Hispanic (304)	784	0.98
Bangladeshi (17)	19	0.02
Burmese (5)	14	0.02
Cambodian (1,144)	1,317	1.65
Chinese, ex. Taiwanese (1,042)	1,561	1.95
Filipino (6,504)	7,715	9.64
Hmong (9)	9	0.01
Indian (509)	590	0.74
Indonesian (69)	130	0.16
Japanese (571)	1,039	1.30
Korean (1,177)	1,327	1.66
Laotian (41)	67	0.08
Malaysian (8)	10	0.01
Nepalese (4)	6	0.01
Pakistani (59)	65	0.08
Sri Lankan (42)	53	0.07
Taiwanese (116)	131	0.16
Thai (299)	386	0.48
Vietnamese (947)	1,101	1.38
Hawaii Native/Pacific Islander (744)	1,265	1.58
Not Hispanic (686)	1,100	1.37
Hispanic (58)	165	0.21
Fijian (7)	7	0.01
Guamanian/Chamorro (148)	275	0.34
Marshallese (1)	1	<0.01
Native Hawaiian (93)	288	0.36
Samoan (403)	534	0.67
Tongan (48)	57	0.07
White (44,820)	48,522	60.62
Not Hispanic (32,774)	34,872	43.56
Hispanic (12,046)	13,650	17.05

Lamont

Place Type: CDP
County: Kern
Population: 15,120†

Ancestry‡	Population	%
American (21)	21	0.14
Arab (93)	93	0.61
Other Arab (93)	93	0.61
Armenian (16)	16	0.10
Dutch (0)	6	0.04
German (14)	94	0.61
Irish (0)	157	1.02
Italian (0)	13	0.08
Portuguese (5)	5	0.03
Scottish (0)	13	0.08
Swedish (19)	19	0.12

Hispanic Origin	Population	%
Hispanic or Latino (of any race)	14,293	94.53
Central American, ex. Mexican	354	2.34
Guatemalan	148	0.98
Honduran	39	0.26
Nicaraguan	14	0.09
Salvadoran	147	0.97
Other Central American	6	0.04
Cuban	6	0.04
Mexican	13,154	87.00
Puerto Rican	233	1.54
South American	14	0.09
Argentinean	7	0.05
Colombian	4	0.03
Ecuadorian	1	0.01
Peruvian	2	0.01
Other Hispanic or Latino	532	3.52

Race*	Population	%
African-American/Black (130)	151	1.00
Not Hispanic (20)	22	0.15
Hispanic (110)	129	0.85
American Indian/Alaska Native (230)	285	1.88
Not Hispanic (30)	44	0.29
Hispanic (200)	241	1.59
Aleut *(Alaska Native)* (1)	1	0.01
Apache (5)	8	0.05
Cherokee (13)	21	0.14
Chickasaw (0)	1	0.01
Chippewa (1)	1	0.01
Choctaw (2)	5	0.03
Comanche (0)	1	0.01
Mexican American Ind. (80)	90	0.60
Navajo (3)	7	0.05
Pueblo (0)	4	0.03
Shoshone (1)	1	0.01
South American Ind. (0)	1	0.01
Yaqui (6)	9	0.06
Asian (72)	142	0.94
Not Hispanic (51)	57	0.38
Hispanic (21)	85	0.56
Chinese, ex. Taiwanese (5)	8	0.05
Filipino (48)	88	0.58
Indian (12)	21	0.14
Japanese (0)	2	0.01
Korean (2)	2	0.01
Hawaii Native/Pacific Islander (9)	49	0.32
Not Hispanic (2)	3	0.02
Hispanic (7)	46	0.30
Guamanian/Chamorro (1)	4	0.03
Native Hawaiian (1)	4	0.03
Samoan (0)	4	0.03
White (6,677)	7,228	47.80
Not Hispanic (694)	715	4.73
Hispanic (5,983)	6,513	43.08

Lancaster

Place Type: City
County: Los Angeles
Population: 156,633†

Ancestry‡	Population	%
African, Sub-Saharan (1,621)	2,125	1.42
African (1,357)	1,803	1.20
Cape Verdean (17)	17	0.01
Ethiopian (26)	36	0.02
Kenyan (17)	34	0.02
Nigerian (138)	151	0.10
Somalian (22)	32	0.02
South African (44)	44	0.03
Other Sub-Saharan African (0)	8	0.01
American (2,966)	2,966	1.98
Arab (1,011)	1,111	0.74
Arab (133)	153	0.10
Egyptian (152)	152	0.10
Jordanian (7)	7	<0.01
Lebanese (154)	213	0.14
Syrian (515)	536	0.36
Other Arab (50)	50	0.03
Armenian (315)	576	0.38
Austrian (154)	318	0.21
Basque (29)	29	0.02
Belgian (20)	50	0.03
British (275)	455	0.30
Bulgarian (20)	26	0.02
Cajun (20)	20	0.01
Canadian (292)	631	0.42
Croatian (23)	110	0.07
Czech (143)	288	0.19
Czechoslovakian (0)	46	0.03
Danish (99)	694	0.46
Dutch (346)	1,398	0.93
Eastern European (134)	160	0.11
English (2,398)	8,112	5.42
Estonian (27)	110	0.07
European (1,118)	1,245	0.83
Finnish (33)	155	0.10
French, ex. Basque (711)	3,197	2.14
French Canadian (152)	361	0.24
German (3,738)	12,246	8.18
German Russian (0)	27	0.02
Greek (169)	357	0.24
Guyanese (17)	52	0.03
Hungarian (177)	377	0.25
Icelander (0)	10	0.01
Iranian (65)	268	0.18
Irish (2,004)	8,889	5.94
Italian (2,827)	5,661	3.78
Lithuanian (0)	58	0.04
Northern European (42)	42	0.03
Norwegian (529)	1,007	0.67
Pennsylvania German (6)	31	0.02
Polish (379)	1,418	0.95
Portuguese (222)	512	0.34
Romanian (106)	179	0.12
Russian (152)	718	0.48
Scandinavian (70)	194	0.13
Scotch-Irish (619)	1,311	0.88
Scottish (527)	2,064	1.38
Serbian (0)	87	0.06
Slavic (24)	67	0.04
Slovak (0)	23	0.02
Slovene (9)	9	0.01
Swedish (268)	1,047	0.70
Swiss (83)	351	0.23
Ukrainian (89)	211	0.14
Welsh (125)	426	0.28
West Indian, ex. Hispanic (618)	1,053	0.70
Barbadian (0)	10	0.01
Belizean (567)	876	0.59
British West Indian (22)	22	0.01
Dutch West Indian (0)	7	<0.01
Haitian (18)	18	0.01
Jamaican (0)	46	0.03
Trinidadian/Tobagonian (0)	34	0.02
West Indian (11)	40	0.03
Yugoslavian (70)	104	0.07

Hispanic Origin	Population	%
Hispanic or Latino (of any race)	59,596	38.05
Central American, ex. Mexican	8,114	5.18
Costa Rican	156	0.10
Guatemalan	2,075	1.32
Honduran	474	0.30
Nicaraguan	442	0.28
Panamanian	170	0.11
Salvadoran	4,713	3.01
Other Central American	84	0.05
Cuban	514	0.33
Dominican Republic	63	0.04
Mexican	42,115	26.89
Puerto Rican	1,105	0.71
South American	1,345	0.86
Argentinean	204	0.13
Bolivian	25	0.02
Chilean	162	0.10
Colombian	227	0.14

*Notes: † The Census 2010 population figure is used to calculate the percentages in the Hispanic Origin and Race categories. Ancestry percentages are based on the 2006-2010 American Community Survey population (not shown); ‡ Numbers in parentheses indicate the number of people reporting a single ancestry; * Numbers in parentheses indicate the number of persons reporting this race alone, not in combination with any other race; Please refer to the Explanation of Data for more information.*

Ecuadorian	181	0.12
Paraguayan	3	<0.01
Peruvian	457	0.29
Uruguayan	29	0.02
Venezuelan	29	0.02
Other South American	28	0.02
Other Hispanic or Latino	6,340	4.05

Race*	Population	%
African-American/Black (32,083)	35,558	22.70
Not Hispanic (30,859)	33,469	21.37
Hispanic (1,224)	2,089	1.33
American Indian/Alaska Native (1,519)	3,310	2.11
Not Hispanic (663)	1,843	1.18
Hispanic (856)	1,467	0.94
Alaska Athabascan *(Ala. Nat.)* (1)	1	<0.01
Aleut *(Alaska Native)* (1)	4	<0.01
Apache (46)	151	0.10
Arapaho (7)	12	0.01
Blackfeet (20)	168	0.11
Canadian/French Am. Ind. (8)	12	0.01
Central American Ind. (13)	22	0.01
Cherokee (105)	487	0.31
Cheyenne (2)	12	0.01
Chickasaw (11)	28	0.02
Chippewa (9)	16	0.01
Choctaw (28)	99	0.06
Comanche (2)	9	0.01
Cree (1)	2	<0.01
Creek (8)	41	0.03
Crow (0)	3	<0.01
Delaware (0)	3	<0.01
Hopi (8)	13	0.01
Inupiat *(Alaska Native)* (8)	12	0.01
Iroquois (4)	36	0.02
Kiowa (0)	1	<0.01
Menominee (0)	2	<0.01
Mexican American Ind. (159)	245	0.16
Navajo (58)	85	0.05
Osage (6)	13	0.01
Ottawa (8)	11	0.01
Paiute (7)	18	0.01
Pima (4)	5	<0.01
Potawatomi (5)	9	0.01
Pueblo (7)	16	0.01
Seminole (9)	25	0.02
Shoshone (2)	25	0.02
Sioux (21)	56	0.04
South American Ind. (3)	9	0.01
Spanish American Ind. (12)	14	0.01
Tlingit-Haida *(Alaska Native)* (0)	4	<0.01
Tohono O'Odham (5)	7	<0.01
Ute (1)	6	<0.01
Yaqui (34)	62	0.04
Yuman (1)	4	<0.01
Asian (6,810)	8,839	5.64
Not Hispanic (6,474)	7,925	5.06
Hispanic (336)	914	0.58
Bangladeshi (26)	26	0.02
Burmese (6)	10	0.01
Cambodian (147)	165	0.11
Chinese, ex. Taiwanese (581)	874	0.56
Filipino (3,444)	4,399	2.81
Hmong (21)	21	0.01
Indian (593)	716	0.46
Indonesian (47)	89	0.06
Japanese (297)	718	0.46
Korean (503)	691	0.44
Laotian (22)	33	0.02
Malaysian (1)	1	<0.01
Nepalese (5)	5	<0.01
Pakistani (59)	65	0.04
Sri Lankan (96)	107	0.07
Taiwanese (25)	28	0.02
Thai (106)	160	0.10
Vietnamese (529)	616	0.39
Hawaii Native/Pacific Islander (362)	877	0.56
Not Hispanic (295)	632	0.40
Hispanic (67)	245	0.16
Fijian (7)	18	0.01
Guamanian/Chamorro (112)	160	0.10
Native Hawaiian (93)	290	0.19
Samoan (81)	176	0.11
Tongan (34)	48	0.03
White (77,734)	84,210	53.76
Not Hispanic (53,576)	57,150	36.49
Hispanic (24,158)	27,060	17.28

Larkfield-Wikiup

Place Type: CDP
County: Sonoma
Population: 8,884†

Ancestry‡	Population	%
African, Sub-Saharan (12)	28	0.32
Sierra Leonean (0)	16	0.19
South African (12)	12	0.14
American (349)	349	4.04
Arab (16)	25	0.29
Lebanese (16)	16	0.19
Syrian (0)	9	0.10
Austrian (0)	51	0.59
Basque (44)	44	0.51
Belgian (0)	23	0.27
British (86)	119	1.38
Bulgarian (15)	15	0.17
Canadian (37)	68	0.79
Croatian (27)	27	0.31
Czech (18)	37	0.43
Czechoslovakian (34)	69	0.80
Danish (42)	79	0.91
Dutch (0)	146	1.69
English (220)	1,101	12.74
Estonian (31)	31	0.36
European (312)	312	3.61
Finnish (24)	40	0.46
French, ex. Basque (23)	221	2.56
German (408)	1,565	18.11
Greek (14)	57	0.66
Hungarian (16)	16	0.19
Irish (285)	1,106	12.80
Italian (396)	980	11.34
Lithuanian (6)	6	0.07
Maltese (0)	23	0.27
Northern European (23)	23	0.27
Norwegian (86)	179	2.07
Polish (45)	227	2.63
Portuguese (162)	206	2.38
Romanian (0)	11	0.13
Russian (17)	152	1.76
Scandinavian (39)	39	0.45
Scotch-Irish (35)	79	0.91
Scottish (49)	164	1.90
Swedish (46)	112	1.30
Swiss (0)	72	0.83
Ukrainian (30)	30	0.35
Welsh (14)	71	0.82
Yugoslavian (25)	25	0.29

Hispanic Origin	Population	%
Hispanic or Latino (of any race)	1,979	22.28
Central American, ex. Mexican	92	1.04
Costa Rican	8	0.09
Guatemalan	14	0.16
Honduran	1	0.01
Nicaraguan	14	0.16
Panamanian	4	0.05
Salvadoran	51	0.57
Cuban	8	0.09
Dominican Republic	3	0.03
Mexican	1,679	18.90
Puerto Rican	39	0.44
South American	42	0.47
Argentinean	6	0.07
Chilean	4	0.05
Colombian	19	0.21
Ecuadorian	4	0.05
Peruvian	8	0.09
Venezuelan	1	0.01
Other Hispanic or Latino	116	1.31

Race*	Population	%
African-American/Black (81)	152	1.71
Not Hispanic (76)	123	1.38
Hispanic (5)	29	0.33
American Indian/Alaska Native (168)	308	3.47
Not Hispanic (107)	190	2.14
Hispanic (61)	118	1.33
Aleut *(Alaska Native)* (0)	4	0.05
Apache (4)	4	0.05
Blackfeet (1)	4	0.05
Canadian/French Am. Ind. (1)	1	0.01
Cherokee (4)	47	0.53
Chippewa (5)	6	0.07
Choctaw (3)	11	0.12
Comanche (1)	1	0.01
Mexican American Ind. (13)	25	0.28
Navajo (3)	9	0.10
Osage (4)	7	0.08
Paiute (2)	2	0.02
Pima (1)	1	0.01
Potawatomi (1)	1	0.01
Pueblo (5)	8	0.09
Shoshone (0)	3	0.03
Sioux (1)	2	0.02
South American Ind. (1)	1	0.01
Spanish American Ind. (5)	5	0.06
Tsimshian *(Alaska Native)* (0)	4	0.05
Yaqui (1)	6	0.07
Asian (292)	427	4.81
Not Hispanic (274)	385	4.33
Hispanic (18)	42	0.47
Cambodian (8)	14	0.16
Chinese, ex. Taiwanese (60)	91	1.02
Filipino (91)	138	1.55
Hmong (1)	1	0.01
Indian (28)	33	0.37
Indonesian (8)	11	0.12
Japanese (30)	53	0.60
Korean (9)	13	0.15
Laotian (15)	17	0.19
Pakistani (2)	2	0.02
Sri Lankan (4)	4	0.05
Thai (3)	8	0.09
Vietnamese (21)	21	0.24
Hawaii Native/Pacific Islander (19)	49	0.55
Not Hispanic (18)	45	0.51
Hispanic (1)	4	0.05
Fijian (7)	8	0.09
Guamanian/Chamorro (1)	6	0.07
Native Hawaiian (8)	21	0.24
Samoan (1)	6	0.07
White (7,042)	7,408	83.39
Not Hispanic (6,171)	6,392	71.95
Hispanic (871)	1,016	11.44

Larkspur

Place Type: City
County: Marin
Population: 11,926†

Ancestry‡	Population	%
African, Sub-Saharan (17)	34	0.29
Ethiopian (17)	17	0.14
Other Sub-Saharan African (0)	17	0.14
Albanian (11)	11	0.09
American (283)	283	2.40
Arab (12)	23	0.19
Syrian (0)	11	0.09
Other Arab (12)	12	0.10
Austrian (0)	47	0.40
Belgian (19)	33	0.28
British (89)	142	1.20
Bulgarian (38)	38	0.32
Canadian (28)	71	0.60
Celtic (17)	32	0.27
Croatian (128)	180	1.52
Czech (50)	50	0.42

*Notes: † The Census 2010 population figure is used to calculate the percentages in the Hispanic Origin and Race categories. Ancestry percentages are based on the 2006-2010 American Community Survey population (not shown); ‡ Numbers in parentheses indicate the number of people reporting a single ancestry; * Numbers in parentheses indicate the number of persons reporting this race alone, not in combination with any other race; Please refer to the Explanation of Data for more information.*

Czechoslovakian (0)	15	0.13
Danish (24)	140	1.19
Dutch (68)	228	1.93
Eastern European (41)	56	0.47
English (483)	1,695	14.36
Estonian (37)	37	0.31
European (189)	189	1.60
Finnish (0)	15	0.13
French, ex. Basque (157)	390	3.30
French Canadian (13)	73	0.62
German (732)	1,618	13.71
Greek (28)	79	0.67
Hungarian (64)	130	1.10
Iranian (38)	131	1.11
Irish (741)	1,999	16.93
Israeli (22)	22	0.19
Italian (373)	1,123	9.51
Lithuanian (17)	52	0.44
Luxemburger (13)	13	0.11
Macedonian (42)	85	0.72
Northern European (14)	14	0.12
Norwegian (129)	362	3.07
Pennsylvania German (32)	32	0.27
Polish (70)	225	1.91
Portuguese (57)	165	1.40
Romanian (92)	92	0.78
Russian (304)	453	3.84
Scandinavian (68)	132	1.12
Scotch-Irish (100)	266	2.25
Scottish (157)	439	3.72
Serbian (60)	72	0.61
Slavic (0)	11	0.09
Swedish (102)	340	2.88
Swiss (19)	59	0.50
Ukrainian (29)	29	0.25
Welsh (6)	107	0.91
Yugoslavian (29)	57	0.48

Hispanic Origin	Population	%
Hispanic or Latino (of any race)	918	7.70
Central American, ex. Mexican	148	1.24
Costa Rican	7	0.06
Guatemalan	55	0.46
Honduran	6	0.05
Nicaraguan	17	0.14
Panamanian	2	0.02
Salvadoran	61	0.51
Cuban	31	0.26
Dominican Republic	7	0.06
Mexican	398	3.34
Puerto Rican	51	0.43
South American	159	1.33
Argentinean	26	0.22
Bolivian	6	0.05
Chilean	10	0.08
Colombian	49	0.41
Ecuadorian	11	0.09
Peruvian	47	0.39
Uruguayan	3	0.03
Venezuelan	3	0.03
Other South American	4	0.03
Other Hispanic or Latino	124	1.04

Race*	Population	%
African-American/Black (186)	281	2.36
Not Hispanic (174)	259	2.17
Hispanic (12)	22	0.18
American Indian/Alaska Native (26)	111	0.93
Not Hispanic (16)	78	0.65
Hispanic (10)	33	0.28
Alaska Athabascan *(Ala. Nat.)* (1)	1	0.01
Blackfeet (0)	3	0.03
Central American Ind. (0)	1	0.01
Cherokee (3)	17	0.14
Chippewa (0)	3	0.03
Choctaw (0)	9	0.08
Creek (1)	1	0.01
Iroquois (0)	1	0.01
Mexican American Ind. (9)	10	0.08
Navajo (1)	1	0.01
Potawatomi (0)	1	0.01
Puget Sound Salish (0)	1	0.01
South American Ind. (0)	1	0.01
Tlingit-Haida *(Alaska Native)* (0)	2	0.02
Yakama (0)	2	0.02
Asian (563)	808	6.78
Not Hispanic (562)	791	6.63
Hispanic (1)	17	0.14
Burmese (0)	1	0.01
Cambodian (0)	1	0.01
Chinese, ex. Taiwanese (180)	272	2.28
Filipino (68)	120	1.01
Indian (101)	112	0.94
Indonesian (1)	1	0.01
Japanese (93)	153	1.28
Korean (38)	60	0.50
Laotian (2)	2	0.02
Nepalese (1)	1	0.01
Pakistani (2)	3	0.03
Taiwanese (9)	9	0.08
Thai (8)	14	0.12
Vietnamese (24)	31	0.26
Hawaii Native/Pacific Islander (13)	49	0.41
Not Hispanic (13)	45	0.38
Hispanic (0)	4	0.03
Fijian (3)	3	0.03
Guamanian/Chamorro (1)	5	0.04
Native Hawaiian (5)	26	0.22
Samoan (0)	2	0.02
Tongan (1)	3	0.03
White (10,311)	10,760	90.22
Not Hispanic (9,791)	10,147	85.08
Hispanic (520)	613	5.14

Lathrop

Place Type: City
County: San Joaquin
Population: 18,023†

Ancestry‡	Population	%
Afghan (140)	140	0.82
African, Sub-Saharan (135)	135	0.79
African (54)	54	0.32
Cape Verdean (28)	28	0.16
Nigerian (53)	53	0.31
American (446)	446	2.62
Arab (7)	7	0.04
Palestinian (7)	7	0.04
Armenian (0)	11	0.06
Assyrian/Chaldean/Syriac (6)	6	0.04
Belgian (0)	8	0.05
British (0)	72	0.42
Canadian (29)	29	0.17
Czech (0)	28	0.16
Danish (0)	73	0.43
Dutch (9)	146	0.86
Eastern European (0)	9	0.05
English (75)	431	2.53
European (33)	33	0.19
French, ex. Basque (21)	224	1.31
French Canadian (27)	123	0.72
German (157)	1,126	6.61
Greek (0)	38	0.22
Iranian (114)	165	0.97
Irish (189)	795	4.67
Israeli (0)	9	0.05
Italian (183)	486	2.85
Latvian (14)	14	0.08
Lithuanian (6)	6	0.04
Norwegian (0)	83	0.49
Polish (14)	43	0.25
Portuguese (204)	432	2.54
Russian (9)	37	0.22
Scandinavian (0)	14	0.08
Scotch-Irish (13)	110	0.65
Scottish (0)	138	0.81
Swedish (0)	53	0.31
Swiss (39)	68	0.40
Welsh (0)	40	0.23
West Indian, ex. Hispanic (0)	26	0.15
Jamaican (0)	26	0.15

Hispanic Origin	Population	%
Hispanic or Latino (of any race)	7,674	42.58
Central American, ex. Mexican	291	1.61
Costa Rican	5	0.03
Guatemalan	35	0.19
Honduran	21	0.12
Nicaraguan	80	0.44
Panamanian	8	0.04
Salvadoran	139	0.77
Other Central American	3	0.02
Cuban	24	0.13
Dominican Republic	2	0.01
Mexican	6,623	36.75
Puerto Rican	203	1.13
South American	155	0.86
Argentinean	39	0.22
Bolivian	2	0.01
Chilean	18	0.10
Colombian	9	0.05
Ecuadorian	5	0.03
Peruvian	70	0.39
Venezuelan	4	0.02
Other South American	8	0.04
Other Hispanic or Latino	376	2.09

Race*	Population	%
African-American/Black (1,300)	1,545	8.57
Not Hispanic (1,214)	1,380	7.66
Hispanic (86)	165	0.92
American Indian/Alaska Native (231)	414	2.30
Not Hispanic (102)	192	1.07
Hispanic (129)	222	1.23
Alaska Athabascan *(Ala. Nat.)* (1)	3	0.02
Apache (0)	6	0.03
Blackfeet (7)	10	0.06
Canadian/French Am. Ind. (2)	2	0.01
Cherokee (18)	54	0.30
Cheyenne (1)	1	0.01
Chickasaw (7)	8	0.04
Chippewa (1)	1	0.01
Choctaw (13)	17	0.09
Colville (1)	1	0.01
Cree (1)	1	0.01
Creek (4)	4	0.02
Hopi (0)	2	0.01
Mexican American Ind. (34)	36	0.20
Navajo (6)	9	0.05
Paiute (3)	6	0.03
Pima (2)	2	0.01
Potawatomi (0)	1	0.01
Shoshone (0)	3	0.02
Sioux (3)	7	0.04
South American Ind. (6)	7	0.04
Spanish American Ind. (1)	1	0.01
Tohono O'Odham (2)	5	0.03
Yaqui (1)	1	0.01
Asian (3,968)	4,498	24.96
Not Hispanic (3,863)	4,235	23.50
Hispanic (105)	263	1.46
Burmese (10)	15	0.08
Cambodian (110)	118	0.65
Chinese, ex. Taiwanese (126)	169	0.94
Filipino (2,393)	2,736	15.18
Hmong (41)	41	0.23
Indian (868)	926	5.14
Indonesian (10)	18	0.10
Japanese (40)	79	0.44
Korean (23)	38	0.21
Laotian (75)	96	0.53
Pakistani (29)	36	0.20
Taiwanese (0)	4	0.02
Thai (13)	24	0.13
Vietnamese (119)	143	0.79
Hawaii Native/Pacific Islander (144)	254	1.41
Not Hispanic (128)	203	1.13
Hispanic (16)	51	0.28
Fijian (60)	69	0.38

*Notes: † The Census 2010 population figure is used to calculate the percentages in the Hispanic Origin and Race categories. Ancestry percentages are based on the 2006-2010 American Community Survey population (not shown); ‡ Numbers in parentheses indicate the number of people reporting a single ancestry; * Numbers in parentheses indicate the number of persons reporting this race alone, not in combination with any other race; Please refer to the Explanation of Data for more information.*

Guamanian/Chamorro (37)	49	0.27
Native Hawaiian (17)	58	0.32
Samoan (20)	31	0.17
Tongan (1)	1	0.01
White (7,410)	8,370	46.44
Not Hispanic (4,430)	4,871	27.03
Hispanic (2,980)	3,499	19.41

Lawndale

Place Type: City
County: Los Angeles
Population: 32,769†

Ancestry‡	Population	%
Afghan (73)	73	0.22
African, Sub-Saharan (340)	380	1.17
African (225)	253	0.78
Ethiopian (11)	11	0.03
Nigerian (99)	99	0.30
Other Sub-Saharan African (5)	17	0.05
American (2,403)	2,403	7.38
Arab (175)	261	0.80
Arab (27)	41	0.13
Egyptian (55)	55	0.17
Jordanian (34)	56	0.17
Lebanese (11)	61	0.19
Palestinian (5)	5	0.02
Other Arab (43)	43	0.13
Armenian (125)	125	0.38
Australian (11)	11	0.03
Austrian (0)	27	0.08
Brazilian (0)	105	0.32
British (31)	49	0.15
Canadian (8)	37	0.11
Croatian (0)	105	0.32
Czech (9)	30	0.09
Danish (6)	38	0.12
Dutch (5)	113	0.35
English (151)	764	2.35
European (64)	128	0.39
Finnish (0)	17	0.05
French, ex. Basque (0)	116	0.36
French Canadian (14)	47	0.14
German (455)	1,351	4.15
Hungarian (51)	93	0.29
Iranian (120)	208	0.64
Irish (270)	943	2.90
Italian (231)	568	1.74
Lithuanian (0)	20	0.06
Norwegian (60)	75	0.23
Pennsylvania German (17)	17	0.05
Polish (55)	167	0.51
Portuguese (30)	61	0.19
Russian (40)	166	0.51
Scandinavian (15)	15	0.05
Scotch-Irish (51)	147	0.45
Scottish (58)	168	0.52
Swedish (13)	23	0.07
Turkish (11)	11	0.03
Ukrainian (30)	71	0.22
Welsh (0)	21	0.06
West Indian, ex. Hispanic (254)	320	0.98
Belizean (73)	73	0.22
British West Indian (31)	31	0.10
Jamaican (150)	189	0.58
West Indian (0)	27	0.08
Yugoslavian (0)	13	0.04

Hispanic Origin	Population	%
Hispanic or Latino (of any race)	20,002	61.04
Central American, ex. Mexican	3,568	10.89
Costa Rican	87	0.27
Guatemalan	1,953	5.96
Honduran	200	0.61
Nicaraguan	264	0.81
Panamanian	36	0.11
Salvadoran	1,005	3.07
Other Central American	23	0.07
Cuban	276	0.84
Dominican Republic	37	0.11
Mexican	13,300	40.59
Puerto Rican	302	0.92
South American	1,092	3.33
Argentinean	69	0.21
Bolivian	15	0.05
Chilean	55	0.17
Colombian	191	0.58
Ecuadorian	191	0.58
Paraguayan	1	<0.01
Peruvian	525	1.60
Uruguayan	15	0.05
Venezuelan	26	0.08
Other South American	4	0.01
Other Hispanic or Latino	1,427	4.35

Race*	Population	%
African-American/Black (3,320)	3,674	11.21
Not Hispanic (3,054)	3,297	10.06
Hispanic (266)	377	1.15
American Indian/Alaska Native (301)	544	1.66
Not Hispanic (95)	188	0.57
Hispanic (206)	356	1.09
Aleut *(Alaska Native)* (0)	1	<0.01
Apache (7)	14	0.04
Blackfeet (2)	9	0.03
Central American Ind. (9)	14	0.04
Cherokee (4)	28	0.09
Cheyenne (1)	1	<0.01
Chippewa (1)	6	0.02
Choctaw (4)	12	0.04
Comanche (2)	3	0.01
Cree (1)	2	0.01
Delaware (5)	5	0.02
Hopi (1)	3	0.01
Houma (1)	1	<0.01
Iroquois (3)	4	0.01
Kiowa (1)	1	<0.01
Lumbee (1)	1	<0.01
Menominee (0)	1	<0.01
Mexican American Ind. (52)	86	0.26
Navajo (17)	22	0.07
Osage (3)	3	0.01
Paiute (1)	1	<0.01
Pima (1)	1	<0.01
Potawatomi (3)	7	0.02
Pueblo (2)	5	0.02
Seminole (0)	1	<0.01
Shoshone (0)	5	0.02
Sioux (7)	18	0.05
South American Ind. (2)	7	0.02
Spanish American Ind. (8)	8	0.02
Yaqui (2)	14	0.04
Asian (3,269)	3,804	11.61
Not Hispanic (3,142)	3,521	10.74
Hispanic (127)	283	0.86
Bangladeshi (15)	15	0.05
Burmese (17)	17	0.05
Cambodian (17)	26	0.08
Chinese, ex. Taiwanese (207)	310	0.95
Filipino (728)	939	2.87
Hmong (1)	1	<0.01
Indian (184)	259	0.79
Indonesian (35)	41	0.13
Japanese (153)	261	0.80
Korean (137)	179	0.55
Laotian (2)	3	0.01
Malaysian (1)	6	0.02
Nepalese (5)	5	0.02
Pakistani (161)	184	0.56
Sri Lankan (12)	16	0.05
Taiwanese (9)	13	0.04
Thai (66)	73	0.22
Vietnamese (1,391)	1,453	4.43
Hawaii Native/Pacific Islander (367)	510	1.56
Not Hispanic (343)	440	1.34
Hispanic (24)	70	0.21
Fijian (12)	13	0.04
Guamanian/Chamorro (19)	31	0.09
Marshallese (0)	1	<0.01
Native Hawaiian (25)	78	0.24
Samoan (137)	187	0.57
Tongan (133)	170	0.52
White (14,274)	15,785	48.17
Not Hispanic (5,311)	5,837	17.81
Hispanic (8,963)	9,948	30.36

Lemon Grove

Place Type: City
County: San Diego
Population: 25,320†

Ancestry‡	Population	%
African, Sub-Saharan (599)	637	2.54
African (199)	207	0.83
Ethiopian (198)	213	0.85
Somalian (202)	202	0.81
Other Sub-Saharan African (0)	15	0.06
American (1,883)	1,883	7.51
Arab (8)	19	0.08
Palestinian (8)	19	0.08
Australian (0)	35	0.14
Austrian (0)	9	0.04
Basque (12)	12	0.05
British (39)	71	0.28
Bulgarian (0)	19	0.08
Canadian (10)	10	0.04
Celtic (0)	15	0.06
Czech (0)	28	0.11
Czechoslovakian (0)	8	0.03
Danish (27)	69	0.28
Dutch (26)	275	1.10
Eastern European (0)	13	0.05
English (359)	1,450	5.78
European (210)	290	1.16
Finnish (15)	15	0.06
French, ex. Basque (113)	608	2.42
French Canadian (36)	77	0.31
German (657)	1,989	7.93
Greek (17)	17	0.07
Hungarian (0)	32	0.13
Icelander (8)	21	0.08
Irish (502)	1,775	7.08
Italian (283)	611	2.44
Lithuanian (6)	24	0.10
Northern European (6)	27	0.11
Norwegian (94)	301	1.20
Pennsylvania German (0)	10	0.04
Polish (99)	271	1.08
Portuguese (18)	167	0.67
Romanian (58)	68	0.27
Russian (65)	87	0.35
Scandinavian (0)	51	0.20
Scotch-Irish (196)	458	1.83
Scottish (133)	420	1.68
Slavic (0)	18	0.07
Slovene (0)	11	0.04
Swedish (81)	278	1.11
Swiss (0)	44	0.18
Ukrainian (25)	77	0.31
Welsh (7)	66	0.26
West Indian, ex. Hispanic (101)	110	0.44
Belizean (40)	40	0.16
Haitian (61)	61	0.24
Trinidadian/Tobagonian (0)	9	0.04
Yugoslavian (15)	33	0.13

Hispanic Origin	Population	%
Hispanic or Latino (of any race)	10,435	41.21
Central American, ex. Mexican	194	0.77
Costa Rican	22	0.09
Guatemalan	63	0.25
Honduran	25	0.10
Nicaraguan	19	0.08
Panamanian	33	0.13
Salvadoran	32	0.13
Cuban	50	0.20
Dominican Republic	19	0.08
Mexican	9,395	37.11

*Notes: † The Census 2010 population figure is used to calculate the percentages in the Hispanic Origin and Race categories. Ancestry percentages are based on the 2006-2010 American Community Survey population (not shown); ‡ Numbers in parentheses indicate the number of people reporting a single ancestry; * Numbers in parentheses indicate the number of persons reporting this race alone, not in combination with any other race; Please refer to the Explanation of Data for more information.*

Puerto Rican	240	0.95
South American	123	0.49
Argentinean	11	0.04
Bolivian	17	0.07
Chilean	8	0.03
Colombian	33	0.13
Ecuadorian	18	0.07
Paraguayan	1	<0.01
Peruvian	30	0.12
Venezuelan	5	0.02
Other Hispanic or Latino	414	1.64

Race*	Population	%
African-American/Black (3,495)	4,079	16.11
Not Hispanic (3,277)	3,695	14.59
Hispanic (218)	384	1.52
American Indian/Alaska Native (225)	520	2.05
Not Hispanic (109)	285	1.13
Hispanic (116)	235	0.93
Aleut *(Alaska Native)* (3)	3	0.01
Apache (4)	12	0.05
Blackfeet (5)	14	0.06
Central American Ind. (1)	2	0.01
Cherokee (12)	72	0.28
Chippewa (2)	5	0.02
Choctaw (5)	15	0.06
Colville (0)	1	<0.01
Crow (0)	1	<0.01
Iroquois (2)	5	0.02
Mexican American Ind. (20)	35	0.14
Navajo (4)	12	0.05
Osage (4)	4	0.02
Paiute (1)	1	<0.01
Pima (1)	2	0.01
Potawatomi (3)	3	0.01
Pueblo (3)	3	0.01
Shoshone (0)	4	0.02
Sioux (10)	21	0.08
South American Ind. (7)	14	0.06
Spanish American Ind. (5)	5	0.02
Tlingit-Haida *(Alaska Native)* (0)	1	<0.01
Ute (2)	2	0.01
Yaqui (10)	14	0.06
Asian (1,624)	2,246	8.87
Not Hispanic (1,545)	1,946	7.69
Hispanic (79)	300	1.18
Burmese (0)	1	<0.01
Cambodian (57)	71	0.28
Chinese, ex. Taiwanese (69)	155	0.61
Filipino (721)	1,112	4.39
Hmong (2)	2	0.01
Indian (18)	27	0.11
Indonesian (0)	2	0.01
Japanese (127)	248	0.98
Korean (20)	43	0.17
Laotian (71)	88	0.35
Malaysian (1)	1	<0.01
Pakistani (5)	5	0.02
Taiwanese (11)	13	0.05
Thai (12)	26	0.10
Vietnamese (432)	465	1.84
Hawaii Native/Pacific Islander (275)	481	1.90
Not Hispanic (244)	387	1.53
Hispanic (31)	94	0.37
Guamanian/Chamorro (135)	229	0.90
Marshallese (0)	4	0.02
Native Hawaiian (29)	86	0.34
Samoan (95)	132	0.52
Tongan (1)	2	0.01
White (13,072)	14,437	57.02
Not Hispanic (8,787)	9,469	37.40
Hispanic (4,285)	4,968	19.62

Lemon Hill

Place Type: CDP
County: Sacramento
Population: 13,729†

Ancestry‡	Population	%
African, Sub-Saharan (62)	62	0.46
African (62)	62	0.46
American (79)	79	0.59
Armenian (6)	6	0.04
Dutch (15)	116	0.86
Eastern European (40)	40	0.30
English (148)	334	2.49
Estonian (20)	20	0.15
European (39)	52	0.39
French, ex. Basque (45)	129	0.96
German (281)	902	6.72
Irish (93)	801	5.97
Italian (31)	162	1.21
Northern European (14)	14	0.10
Norwegian (0)	9	0.07
Pennsylvania German (16)	16	0.12
Polish (0)	28	0.21
Portuguese (64)	148	1.10
Romanian (33)	33	0.25
Russian (140)	140	1.04
Scotch-Irish (31)	104	0.77
Scottish (87)	109	0.81
Slovene (0)	7	0.05
Swedish (0)	59	0.44
Ukrainian (61)	61	0.45
West Indian, ex. Hispanic (73)	73	0.54
Jamaican (73)	73	0.54
Yugoslavian (0)	9	0.07

Hispanic Origin	Population	%
Hispanic or Latino (of any race)	6,790	49.46
Central American, ex. Mexican	215	1.57
Guatemalan	83	0.60
Honduran	16	0.12
Nicaraguan	23	0.17
Panamanian	2	0.01
Salvadoran	90	0.66
Other Central American	1	0.01
Cuban	15	0.11
Mexican	6,191	45.09
Puerto Rican	84	0.61
South American	16	0.12
Argentinean	2	0.01
Chilean	3	0.02
Colombian	2	0.01
Peruvian	6	0.04
Venezuelan	3	0.02
Other Hispanic or Latino	269	1.96

Race*	Population	%
African-American/Black (1,493)	1,806	13.15
Not Hispanic (1,390)	1,595	11.62
Hispanic (103)	211	1.54
American Indian/Alaska Native (246)	482	3.51
Not Hispanic (89)	226	1.65
Hispanic (157)	256	1.86
Apache (14)	20	0.15
Blackfeet (1)	10	0.07
Cherokee (12)	79	0.58
Cheyenne (0)	1	0.01
Chickasaw (0)	1	0.01
Chippewa (8)	15	0.11
Choctaw (1)	8	0.06
Comanche (4)	6	0.04
Creek (1)	1	0.01
Crow (0)	1	0.01
Delaware (1)	3	0.02
Hopi (3)	3	0.02
Inupiat *(Alaska Native)* (0)	3	0.02
Iroquois (0)	4	0.03
Kiowa (1)	3	0.02
Mexican American Ind. (56)	69	0.50
Navajo (3)	9	0.07
Paiute (4)	4	0.03
Seminole (0)	3	0.02
Shoshone (5)	5	0.04
Sioux (4)	18	0.13
South American Ind. (1)	5	0.04
Ute (1)	1	0.01
Yaqui (2)	6	0.04
Yuman (1)	1	0.01
Yup'ik *(Alaska Native)* (1)	2	0.01
Asian (2,394)	2,617	19.06
Not Hispanic (2,369)	2,523	18.38
Hispanic (25)	94	0.68
Burmese (17)	17	0.12
Cambodian (57)	68	0.50
Chinese, ex. Taiwanese (287)	369	2.69
Filipino (96)	165	1.20
Hmong (978)	1,009	7.35
Indian (44)	79	0.58
Indonesian (1)	1	0.01
Japanese (29)	59	0.43
Korean (9)	19	0.14
Laotian (444)	497	3.62
Pakistani (32)	32	0.23
Thai (6)	14	0.10
Vietnamese (235)	303	2.21
Hawaii Native/Pacific Islander (196)	260	1.89
Not Hispanic (183)	225	1.64
Hispanic (13)	35	0.25
Fijian (27)	35	0.25
Guamanian/Chamorro (6)	12	0.09
Marshallese (82)	84	0.61
Native Hawaiian (13)	34	0.25
Samoan (21)	21	0.15
Tongan (34)	36	0.26
White (5,091)	5,684	41.40
Not Hispanic (2,484)	2,775	20.21
Hispanic (2,607)	2,909	21.19

Lemoore

Place Type: City
County: Kings
Population: 24,531†

Ancestry‡	Population	%
African, Sub-Saharan (75)	113	0.47
African (75)	113	0.47
American (546)	546	2.28
Australian (12)	21	0.09
Basque (29)	70	0.29
Belgian (0)	5	0.02
Brazilian (23)	23	0.10
British (54)	54	0.23
Canadian (7)	7	0.03
Czech (22)	22	0.09
Czechoslovakian (36)	49	0.21
Danish (29)	68	0.28
Dutch (59)	245	1.03
Eastern European (12)	12	0.05
English (738)	1,569	6.56
European (282)	296	1.24
Finnish (9)	9	0.04
French, ex. Basque (70)	457	1.91
French Canadian (19)	30	0.13
German (723)	1,828	7.65
Greek (15)	15	0.06
Hungarian (0)	26	0.11
Iranian (33)	33	0.14
Irish (463)	2,051	8.58
Italian (158)	611	2.56
Norwegian (48)	222	0.93
Pennsylvania German (0)	21	0.09
Polish (171)	328	1.37
Portuguese (549)	797	3.33
Russian (0)	47	0.20
Scotch-Irish (53)	208	0.87
Scottish (118)	218	0.91
Slovak (11)	11	0.05
Swedish (24)	223	0.93
Swiss (29)	92	0.38
Welsh (0)	25	0.10
West Indian, ex. Hispanic (46)	81	0.34
West Indian (46)	81	0.34

Hispanic Origin	Population	%
Hispanic or Latino (of any race)	9,820	40.03

*Notes: † The Census 2010 population figure is used to calculate the percentages in the Hispanic Origin and Race categories. Ancestry percentages are based on the 2006-2010 American Community Survey population (not shown); ‡ Numbers in parentheses indicate the number of people reporting a single ancestry; * Numbers in parentheses indicate the number of persons reporting this race alone, not in combination with any other race; Please refer to the Explanation of Data for more information.*

Central American, ex. Mexican	189	0.77
Costa Rican	2	0.01
Guatemalan	42	0.17
Honduran	42	0.17
Nicaraguan	25	0.10
Panamanian	21	0.09
Salvadoran	41	0.17
Other Central American	16	0.07
Cuban	19	0.08
Dominican Republic	10	0.04
Mexican	8,878	36.19
Puerto Rican	150	0.61
South American	75	0.31
Argentinean	5	0.02
Bolivian	5	0.02
Chilean	8	0.03
Colombian	12	0.05
Ecuadorian	8	0.03
Peruvian	22	0.09
Venezuelan	10	0.04
Other South American	5	0.02
Other Hispanic or Latino	499	2.03

Race*	Population	%
African-American/Black (1,566)	1,972	8.04
Not Hispanic (1,450)	1,744	7.11
Hispanic (116)	228	0.93
American Indian/Alaska Native (333)	594	2.42
Not Hispanic (200)	367	1.50
Hispanic (133)	227	0.93
Apache (8)	14	0.06
Blackfeet (0)	14	0.06
Central American Ind. (3)	6	0.02
Cherokee (29)	95	0.39
Chickasaw (1)	3	0.01
Chippewa (2)	3	0.01
Choctaw (21)	48	0.20
Comanche (3)	8	0.03
Crow (0)	1	<0.01
Delaware (0)	1	<0.01
Hopi (0)	1	<0.01
Iroquois (0)	4	0.02
Lumbee (1)	2	0.01
Mexican American Ind. (12)	28	0.11
Navajo (9)	18	0.07
Osage (1)	1	<0.01
Paiute (5)	6	0.02
Pima (6)	6	0.02
Potawatomi (2)	2	0.01
Pueblo (2)	3	0.01
Seminole (0)	1	<0.01
Shoshone (2)	2	0.01
Sioux (4)	8	0.03
South American Ind. (0)	1	<0.01
Spanish American Ind. (2)	2	0.01
Tlingit-Haida *(Alaska Native)* (1)	1	<0.01
Ute (1)	1	<0.01
Yaqui (2)	3	0.01
Asian (2,010)	2,709	11.04
Not Hispanic (1,924)	2,482	10.12
Hispanic (86)	227	0.93
Burmese (1)	1	<0.01
Cambodian (25)	30	0.12
Chinese, ex. Taiwanese (63)	129	0.53
Filipino (1,644)	2,161	8.81
Hmong (8)	10	0.04
Indian (72)	85	0.35
Indonesian (0)	3	0.01
Japanese (66)	183	0.75
Korean (33)	75	0.31
Laotian (12)	14	0.06
Pakistani (4)	4	0.02
Sri Lankan (3)	3	0.01
Taiwanese (2)	5	0.02
Thai (9)	16	0.07
Vietnamese (21)	31	0.13
Hawaii Native/Pacific Islander (102)	214	0.87
Not Hispanic (89)	169	0.69
Hispanic (13)	45	0.18
Fijian (1)	1	<0.01
Guamanian/Chamorro (35)	61	0.25
Native Hawaiian (25)	66	0.27
Samoan (23)	39	0.16
Tongan (1)	1	<0.01
White (13,925)	15,323	62.46
Not Hispanic (10,068)	10,893	44.41
Hispanic (3,857)	4,430	18.06

Lennox

Place Type: CDP
County: Los Angeles
Population: 22,753†

Ancestry‡	Population	%
African, Sub-Saharan (78)	78	0.36
African (49)	49	0.23
Ethiopian (29)	29	0.13
American (526)	526	2.44
Armenian (10)	10	0.05
Czechoslovakian (0)	12	0.06
English (0)	25	0.12
European (0)	30	0.14
French, ex. Basque (0)	32	0.15
German (0)	56	0.26
Irish (9)	52	0.24
Israeli (7)	23	0.11
Italian (0)	30	0.14
Polish (7)	7	0.03
Scotch-Irish (26)	72	0.33
Ukrainian (0)	10	0.05
West Indian, ex. Hispanic (98)	193	0.89
Belizean (0)	31	0.14
Jamaican (98)	162	0.75

Hispanic Origin	Population	%
Hispanic or Latino (of any race)	21,162	93.01
Central American, ex. Mexican	3,045	13.38
Costa Rican	23	0.10
Guatemalan	1,474	6.48
Honduran	206	0.91
Nicaraguan	145	0.64
Panamanian	3	0.01
Salvadoran	1,151	5.06
Other Central American	43	0.19
Cuban	156	0.69
Dominican Republic	2	0.01
Mexican	16,817	73.91
Puerto Rican	53	0.23
South American	164	0.72
Argentinean	9	0.04
Bolivian	6	0.03
Chilean	1	<0.01
Colombian	22	0.10
Ecuadorian	27	0.12
Peruvian	86	0.38
Uruguayan	9	0.04
Venezuelan	4	0.02
Other Hispanic or Latino	925	4.07

Race*	Population	%
African-American/Black (765)	849	3.73
Not Hispanic (682)	715	3.14
Hispanic (83)	134	0.59
American Indian/Alaska Native (199)	299	1.31
Not Hispanic (24)	41	0.18
Hispanic (175)	258	1.13
Apache (7)	7	0.03
Blackfeet (0)	1	<0.01
Central American Ind. (3)	4	0.02
Cherokee (2)	3	0.01
Chippewa (0)	2	0.01
Choctaw (3)	4	0.02
Hopi (1)	1	<0.01
Mexican American Ind. (61)	74	0.33
Navajo (3)	3	0.01
Pueblo (2)	6	0.03
Sioux (0)	1	<0.01
South American Ind. (1)	4	0.02
Spanish American Ind. (17)	19	0.08
Yaqui (0)	1	<0.01
Asian (177)	253	1.11
Not Hispanic (159)	186	0.82
Hispanic (18)	67	0.29
Bangladeshi (3)	3	0.01
Cambodian (1)	1	<0.01
Chinese, ex. Taiwanese (9)	10	0.04
Filipino (105)	121	0.53
Indian (20)	44	0.19
Indonesian (2)	6	0.03
Japanese (3)	13	0.06
Korean (2)	2	0.01
Laotian (6)	6	0.03
Pakistani (4)	4	0.02
Thai (1)	1	<0.01
Vietnamese (12)	12	0.05
Hawaii Native/Pacific Islander (188)	218	0.96
Not Hispanic (184)	193	0.85
Hispanic (4)	25	0.11
Native Hawaiian (5)	9	0.04
Samoan (14)	16	0.07
Tongan (131)	154	0.68
White (8,623)	9,437	41.48
Not Hispanic (435)	469	2.06
Hispanic (8,188)	8,968	39.41

Lincoln

Place Type: City
County: Placer
Population: 42,819†

Ancestry‡	Population	%
Albanian (26)	26	0.07
American (1,474)	1,474	3.90
Arab (22)	56	0.15
Arab (8)	8	0.02
Iraqi (14)	14	0.04
Lebanese (0)	34	0.09
Armenian (29)	117	0.31
Assyrian/Chaldean/Syriac (44)	44	0.12
Australian (9)	9	0.02
Austrian (22)	77	0.20
Belgian (38)	38	0.10
Brazilian (46)	46	0.12
British (141)	246	0.65
Bulgarian (29)	29	0.08
Canadian (35)	125	0.33
Croatian (17)	30	0.08
Czech (25)	73	0.19
Czechoslovakian (18)	33	0.09
Danish (125)	616	1.63
Dutch (194)	858	2.27
Eastern European (34)	34	0.09
English (1,374)	4,906	12.99
European (703)	799	2.12
Finnish (83)	176	0.47
French, ex. Basque (197)	1,210	3.20
French Canadian (111)	162	0.43
German (1,914)	6,946	18.39
Greek (220)	286	0.76
Hungarian (63)	138	0.37
Iranian (118)	118	0.31
Irish (1,353)	5,528	14.64
Israeli (11)	11	0.03
Italian (1,175)	3,133	8.29
Lithuanian (24)	24	0.06
Luxemburger (0)	9	0.02
Maltese (7)	7	0.02
Norwegian (288)	909	2.41
Pennsylvania German (0)	8	0.02
Polish (130)	679	1.80
Portuguese (250)	623	1.65
Romanian (7)	42	0.11
Russian (115)	395	1.05
Scandinavian (22)	91	0.24
Scotch-Irish (229)	713	1.89
Scottish (274)	1,074	2.84
Serbian (0)	19	0.05
Slavic (9)	21	0.06

*Notes: † The Census 2010 population figure is used to calculate the percentages in the Hispanic Origin and Race categories. Ancestry percentages are based on the 2006-2010 American Community Survey population (not shown); ‡ Numbers in parentheses indicate the number of people reporting a single ancestry; * Numbers in parentheses indicate the number of persons reporting this race alone, not in combination with any other race; Please refer to the Explanation of Data for more information.*

Slovak (8)	26	0.07
Slovene (9)	9	0.02
Swedish (430)	1,054	2.79
Swiss (50)	196	0.52
Turkish (8)	8	0.02
Ukrainian (42)	153	0.41
Welsh (108)	365	0.97
West Indian, ex. Hispanic (15)	29	0.08
Haitian (0)	14	0.04
Trinidadian/Tobagonian (15)	15	0.04
Yugoslavian (15)	107	0.28

Hispanic Origin	Population	%
Hispanic or Latino (of any race)	7,597	17.74
Central American, ex. Mexican	316	0.74
Costa Rican	10	0.02
Guatemalan	55	0.13
Honduran	11	0.03
Nicaraguan	60	0.14
Panamanian	25	0.06
Salvadoran	146	0.34
Other Central American	9	0.02
Cuban	50	0.12
Dominican Republic	10	0.02
Mexican	6,159	14.38
Puerto Rican	206	0.48
South American	184	0.43
Argentinean	23	0.05
Bolivian	7	0.02
Chilean	17	0.04
Colombian	44	0.10
Ecuadorian	5	0.01
Peruvian	68	0.16
Venezuelan	17	0.04
Other South American	3	0.01
Other Hispanic or Latino	672	1.57

Race*	Population	%
African-American/Black (629)	914	2.13
Not Hispanic (576)	815	1.90
Hispanic (53)	99	0.23
American Indian/Alaska Native (399)	842	1.97
Not Hispanic (247)	557	1.30
Hispanic (152)	285	0.67
Alaska Athabascan *(Ala. Nat.)* (2)	5	0.01
Aleut *(Alaska Native)* (2)	2	<0.01
Apache (6)	22	0.05
Blackfeet (3)	23	0.05
Central American Ind. (2)	2	<0.01
Cherokee (66)	201	0.47
Chickasaw (7)	11	0.03
Chippewa (2)	15	0.04
Choctaw (25)	48	0.11
Comanche (1)	1	<0.01
Creek (3)	8	0.02
Delaware (0)	4	0.01
Hopi (1)	5	0.01
Houma (0)	1	<0.01
Iroquois (4)	4	0.01
Lumbee (5)	6	0.01
Mexican American Ind. (26)	33	0.08
Navajo (5)	8	0.02
Osage (0)	1	<0.01
Ottawa (0)	1	<0.01
Paiute (5)	8	0.02
Pima (1)	2	<0.01
Potawatomi (10)	13	0.03
Pueblo (7)	7	0.02
Shoshone (1)	1	<0.01
Sioux (7)	9	0.02
South American Ind. (2)	3	0.01
Spanish American Ind. (12)	12	0.03
Tlingit-Haida *(Alaska Native)* (1)	5	0.01
Ute (1)	1	<0.01
Yaqui (2)	9	0.02
Yuman (0)	1	<0.01
Asian (2,663)	3,430	8.01
Not Hispanic (2,597)	3,246	7.58
Hispanic (66)	184	0.43
Burmese (4)	4	0.01
Cambodian (5)	10	0.02
Chinese, ex. Taiwanese (269)	401	0.94
Filipino (1,094)	1,433	3.35
Hmong (24)	27	0.06
Indian (489)	561	1.31
Indonesian (9)	14	0.03
Japanese (205)	381	0.89
Korean (170)	219	0.51
Laotian (18)	29	0.07
Malaysian (0)	1	<0.01
Pakistani (25)	28	0.07
Sri Lankan (11)	12	0.03
Taiwanese (18)	21	0.05
Thai (22)	54	0.13
Vietnamese (190)	221	0.52
Hawaii Native/Pacific Islander (115)	276	0.64
Not Hispanic (111)	240	0.56
Hispanic (4)	36	0.08
Fijian (6)	7	0.02
Guamanian/Chamorro (21)	55	0.13
Native Hawaiian (34)	117	0.27
Samoan (14)	27	0.06
Tongan (12)	14	0.03
White (34,087)	35,715	83.41
Not Hispanic (30,434)	31,514	73.60
Hispanic (3,653)	4,201	9.81

Linda

Place Type: CDP
County: Yuba
Population: 17,773†

Ancestry‡	Population	%
Afghan (60)	60	0.34
African, Sub-Saharan (0)	24	0.14
African (0)	24	0.14
American (1,529)	1,529	8.78
Brazilian (18)	27	0.16
British (9)	9	0.05
Canadian (0)	13	0.07
Croatian (26)	37	0.21
Czech (0)	9	0.05
Czechoslovakian (10)	10	0.06
Danish (0)	21	0.12
Dutch (13)	272	1.56
Eastern European (8)	8	0.05
English (284)	1,165	6.69
European (71)	71	0.41
French, ex. Basque (30)	469	2.69
French Canadian (33)	79	0.45
German (294)	1,947	11.19
Greek (0)	79	0.45
Hungarian (51)	51	0.29
Irish (336)	1,651	9.49
Italian (362)	591	3.40
Latvian (10)	10	0.06
Lithuanian (0)	42	0.24
Luxemburger (9)	18	0.10
New Zealander (0)	13	0.07
Northern European (0)	19	0.11
Norwegian (64)	243	1.40
Polish (58)	186	1.07
Portuguese (253)	474	2.72
Romanian (21)	28	0.16
Russian (21)	33	0.19
Scandinavian (0)	9	0.05
Scotch-Irish (95)	514	2.95
Scottish (65)	174	1.00
Swedish (0)	114	0.65
Swiss (0)	17	0.10
Welsh (12)	97	0.56
West Indian, ex. Hispanic (0)	9	0.05
Dutch West Indian (0)	9	0.05
Yugoslavian (26)	52	0.30

Hispanic Origin	Population	%
Hispanic or Latino (of any race)	5,779	32.52
Central American, ex. Mexican	123	0.69
Guatemalan	10	0.06
Honduran	19	0.11
Nicaraguan	17	0.10
Panamanian	15	0.08
Salvadoran	62	0.35
Cuban	9	0.05
Dominican Republic	3	0.02
Mexican	5,124	28.83
Puerto Rican	84	0.47
South American	19	0.11
Argentinean	1	0.01
Chilean	2	0.01
Colombian	5	0.03
Ecuadorian	1	0.01
Peruvian	10	0.06
Other Hispanic or Latino	417	2.35

Race*	Population	%
African-American/Black (722)	1,084	6.10
Not Hispanic (625)	877	4.93
Hispanic (97)	207	1.16
American Indian/Alaska Native (361)	903	5.08
Not Hispanic (266)	662	3.72
Hispanic (95)	241	1.36
Aleut *(Alaska Native)* (0)	4	0.02
Apache (6)	18	0.10
Arapaho (0)	1	0.01
Blackfeet (4)	27	0.15
Canadian/French Am. Ind. (0)	4	0.02
Cherokee (77)	234	1.32
Cheyenne (0)	1	0.01
Chickasaw (2)	7	0.04
Chippewa (3)	24	0.14
Choctaw (14)	30	0.17
Colville (1)	1	0.01
Comanche (1)	4	0.02
Creek (19)	28	0.16
Iroquois (1)	4	0.02
Menominee (2)	2	0.01
Mexican American Ind. (21)	24	0.14
Navajo (5)	18	0.10
Paiute (4)	5	0.03
Potawatomi (8)	9	0.05
Pueblo (0)	6	0.03
Shoshone (2)	4	0.02
Sioux (8)	22	0.12
South American Ind. (1)	6	0.03
Spanish American Ind. (1)	1	0.01
Yakama (0)	2	0.01
Yaqui (1)	5	0.03
Asian (2,304)	2,644	14.88
Not Hispanic (2,271)	2,538	14.28
Hispanic (33)	106	0.60
Cambodian (19)	25	0.14
Chinese, ex. Taiwanese (40)	76	0.43
Filipino (207)	360	2.03
Hmong (1,690)	1,742	9.80
Indian (54)	94	0.53
Indonesian (0)	1	0.01
Japanese (46)	109	0.61
Korean (22)	60	0.34
Laotian (74)	96	0.54
Pakistani (18)	22	0.12
Sri Lankan (2)	2	0.01
Taiwanese (0)	3	0.02
Thai (25)	48	0.27
Vietnamese (35)	41	0.23
Hawaii Native/Pacific Islander (80)	152	0.86
Not Hispanic (75)	130	0.73
Hispanic (5)	22	0.12
Fijian (7)	8	0.05
Guamanian/Chamorro (34)	56	0.32
Native Hawaiian (12)	42	0.24
Samoan (11)	22	0.12
Tongan (6)	10	0.06
White (9,973)	11,083	62.36
Not Hispanic (7,944)	8,647	48.65
Hispanic (2,029)	2,436	13.71

*Notes: † The Census 2010 population figure is used to calculate the percentages in the Hispanic Origin and Race categories. Ancestry percentages are based on the 2006-2010 American Community Survey population (not shown); ‡ Numbers in parentheses indicate the number of people reporting a single ancestry; * Numbers in parentheses indicate the number of persons reporting this race alone, not in combination with any other race; Please refer to the Explanation of Data for more information.*

Lindsay

Place Type: City
County: Tulare
Population: 11,768†

Ancestry‡	Population	%
American (231)	231	2.00
Arab (0)	10	0.09
Arab (0)	10	0.09
Dutch (65)	84	0.73
English (66)	206	1.79
European (8)	8	0.07
Finnish (0)	18	0.16
French, ex. Basque (0)	18	0.16
German (49)	116	1.01
Irish (31)	134	1.16
Italian (0)	9	0.08
Norwegian (32)	76	0.66
Russian (7)	7	0.06
Scotch-Irish (0)	25	0.22
Scottish (10)	10	0.09
Swiss (49)	85	0.74
Welsh (15)	15	0.13
West Indian, ex. Hispanic (0)	21	0.18
Dutch West Indian (0)	21	0.18

Hispanic Origin	Population	%
Hispanic or Latino (of any race)	10,056	85.45
Central American, ex. Mexican	56	0.48
Guatemalan	1	0.01
Honduran	19	0.16
Nicaraguan	9	0.08
Salvadoran	27	0.23
Cuban	9	0.08
Dominican Republic	4	0.03
Mexican	9,533	81.01
Puerto Rican	57	0.48
South American	1	0.01
Argentinean	1	0.01
Other Hispanic or Latino	396	3.37

Race*	Population	%
African-American/Black (85)	121	1.03
Not Hispanic (24)	33	0.28
Hispanic (61)	88	0.75
American Indian/Alaska Native (128)	169	1.44
Not Hispanic (34)	48	0.41
Hispanic (94)	121	1.03
Alaska Athabascan *(Ala. Nat.)* (1)	2	0.02
Apache (1)	1	0.01
Canadian/French Am. Ind. (2)	2	0.02
Cherokee (4)	15	0.13
Chickasaw (1)	3	0.03
Choctaw (1)	5	0.04
Colville (2)	2	0.02
Mexican American Ind. (17)	21	0.18
Navajo (1)	2	0.02
Potawatomi (0)	6	0.05
Sioux (5)	5	0.04
Spanish American Ind. (1)	1	0.01
Yaqui (2)	2	0.02
Asian (267)	314	2.67
Not Hispanic (253)	267	2.27
Hispanic (14)	47	0.40
Bangladeshi (1)	1	0.01
Burmese (0)	3	0.03
Cambodian (2)	2	0.02
Chinese, ex. Taiwanese (19)	26	0.22
Filipino (10)	21	0.18
Hmong (36)	37	0.31
Indian (27)	32	0.27
Japanese (11)	12	0.10
Korean (1)	3	0.03
Laotian (4)	13	0.11
Nepalese (0)	3	0.03
Pakistani (4)	4	0.03
Thai (130)	134	1.14
Vietnamese (2)	6	0.05
Hawaii Native/Pacific Islander (4)	14	0.12
Not Hispanic (4)	5	0.04
Hispanic (0)	9	0.08
Native Hawaiian (0)	2	0.02
Samoan (4)	4	0.03
White (6,480)	6,882	58.48
Not Hispanic (1,349)	1,384	11.76
Hispanic (5,131)	5,498	46.72

Live Oak

Place Type: CDP
County: Santa Cruz
Population: 17,158†

Ancestry‡	Population	%
African, Sub-Saharan (12)	30	0.18
African (12)	30	0.18
American (264)	264	1.61
Arab (13)	26	0.16
Lebanese (13)	26	0.16
Armenian (12)	12	0.07
Austrian (71)	109	0.66
Basque (12)	12	0.07
Belgian (11)	58	0.35
Brazilian (0)	11	0.07
British (46)	56	0.34
Bulgarian (0)	42	0.26
Canadian (5)	18	0.11
Croatian (0)	65	0.40
Czech (12)	51	0.31
Czechoslovakian (0)	35	0.21
Danish (59)	168	1.02
Dutch (27)	226	1.37
Eastern European (50)	103	0.63
English (504)	1,989	12.10
European (295)	339	2.06
Finnish (7)	45	0.27
French, ex. Basque (66)	452	2.75
French Canadian (36)	125	0.76
German (441)	2,355	14.33
Greek (52)	123	0.75
Hungarian (0)	186	1.13
Icelander (19)	19	0.12
Iranian (7)	7	0.04
Irish (433)	1,648	10.02
Italian (599)	1,235	7.51
Macedonian (0)	28	0.17
Northern European (80)	112	0.68
Norwegian (71)	197	1.20
Polish (89)	303	1.84
Portuguese (83)	235	1.43
Romanian (36)	79	0.48
Russian (86)	382	2.32
Scandinavian (10)	25	0.15
Scotch-Irish (86)	363	2.21
Scottish (79)	520	3.16
Slavic (7)	7	0.04
Slovak (12)	12	0.07
Slovene (0)	11	0.07
Swedish (34)	319	1.94
Swiss (25)	133	0.81
Turkish (0)	53	0.32
Ukrainian (12)	21	0.13
Welsh (0)	151	0.92
West Indian, ex. Hispanic (0)	18	0.11
Trinidadian/Tobagonian (0)	18	0.11
Yugoslavian (0)	25	0.15

Hispanic Origin	Population	%
Hispanic or Latino (of any race)	4,796	27.95
Central American, ex. Mexican	317	1.85
Costa Rican	7	0.04
Guatemalan	19	0.11
Honduran	4	0.02
Nicaraguan	5	0.03
Panamanian	6	0.03
Salvadoran	276	1.61
Cuban	13	0.08
Dominican Republic	3	0.02
Mexican	4,105	23.92
Puerto Rican	49	0.29
South American	63	0.37
Argentinean	12	0.07
Bolivian	1	0.01
Chilean	7	0.04
Colombian	12	0.07
Ecuadorian	1	0.01
Peruvian	25	0.15
Uruguayan	1	0.01
Venezuelan	2	0.01
Other South American	2	0.01
Other Hispanic or Latino	246	1.43

Race*	Population	%
African-American/Black (240)	407	2.37
Not Hispanic (208)	342	1.99
Hispanic (32)	65	0.38
American Indian/Alaska Native (171)	401	2.34
Not Hispanic (75)	220	1.28
Hispanic (96)	181	1.05
Aleut *(Alaska Native)* (0)	2	0.01
Apache (5)	13	0.08
Blackfeet (1)	4	0.02
Canadian/French Am. Ind. (1)	2	0.01
Central American Ind. (1)	1	0.01
Cherokee (9)	54	0.31
Chippewa (6)	8	0.05
Choctaw (2)	19	0.11
Comanche (5)	5	0.03
Cree (0)	1	0.01
Creek (0)	3	0.02
Iroquois (3)	5	0.03
Lumbee (1)	1	0.01
Mexican American Ind. (26)	37	0.22
Navajo (2)	6	0.03
Ottawa (1)	2	0.01
Pima (1)	1	0.01
Potawatomi (5)	5	0.03
Pueblo (0)	6	0.03
Seminole (0)	1	0.01
Sioux (2)	8	0.05
South American Ind. (1)	6	0.03
Ute (0)	1	0.01
Yaqui (7)	12	0.07
Yup'ik *(Alaska Native)* (0)	1	0.01
Asian (773)	1,032	6.01
Not Hispanic (752)	957	5.58
Hispanic (21)	75	0.44
Cambodian (61)	62	0.36
Chinese, ex. Taiwanese (169)	251	1.46
Filipino (203)	288	1.68
Hmong (2)	2	0.01
Indian (52)	68	0.40
Indonesian (8)	8	0.05
Japanese (95)	171	1.00
Korean (47)	61	0.36
Malaysian (2)	4	0.02
Nepalese (0)	1	0.01
Pakistani (3)	8	0.05
Sri Lankan (1)	2	0.01
Taiwanese (2)	7	0.04
Thai (11)	13	0.08
Vietnamese (79)	100	0.58
Hawaii Native/Pacific Islander (41)	87	0.51
Not Hispanic (38)	74	0.43
Hispanic (3)	13	0.08
Fijian (3)	3	0.02
Guamanian/Chamorro (2)	15	0.09
Native Hawaiian (15)	33	0.19
Samoan (2)	14	0.08
Tongan (2)	2	0.01
White (12,636)	13,414	78.18
Not Hispanic (10,782)	11,225	65.42
Hispanic (1,854)	2,189	12.76

Live Oak

Place Type: City
County: Sutter
Population: 8,392†

*Notes: † The Census 2010 population figure is used to calculate the percentages in the Hispanic Origin and Race categories. Ancestry percentages are based on the 2006-2010 American Community Survey population (not shown); ‡ Numbers in parentheses indicate the number of people reporting a single ancestry; * Numbers in parentheses indicate the number of persons reporting this race alone, not in combination with any other race; Please refer to the Explanation of Data for more information.*

SECTION TWO

Ancestry‡	Population	%
African, Sub-Saharan (0)	7	0.09
African (0)	7	0.09
American (691)	691	8.50
Canadian (0)	21	0.26
Czech (11)	11	0.14
Czechoslovakian (0)	12	0.15
Danish (115)	241	2.96
Dutch (12)	12	0.15
English (96)	319	3.92
European (8)	8	0.10
French, ex. Basque (60)	164	2.02
French Canadian (10)	51	0.63
German (28)	649	7.98
Irish (62)	363	4.47
Italian (34)	184	2.26
Norwegian (0)	222	2.73
Polish (20)	20	0.25
Portuguese (42)	128	1.57
Romanian (0)	11	0.14
Russian (0)	83	1.02
Scandinavian (20)	20	0.25
Scotch-Irish (9)	20	0.25
Scottish (0)	145	1.78
Swedish (0)	23	0.28
Swiss (0)	11	0.14
Welsh (0)	8	0.10

Hispanic Origin	Population	%
Hispanic or Latino (of any race)	4,093	48.77
Central American, ex. Mexican	56	0.67
Guatemalan	1	0.01
Honduran	14	0.17
Nicaraguan	11	0.13
Salvadoran	30	0.36
Cuban	8	0.10
Mexican	3,702	44.11
Puerto Rican	37	0.44
South American	8	0.10
Argentinean	1	0.01
Colombian	6	0.07
Ecuadorian	1	0.01
Other Hispanic or Latino	282	3.36

Race*	Population	%
African-American/Black (138)	190	2.26
Not Hispanic (120)	156	1.86
Hispanic (18)	34	0.41
American Indian/Alaska Native (130)	226	2.69
Not Hispanic (74)	141	1.68
Hispanic (56)	85	1.01
Apache (6)	7	0.08
Blackfeet (1)	4	0.05
Central American Ind. (1)	1	0.01
Cherokee (27)	37	0.44
Choctaw (0)	3	0.04
Creek (1)	5	0.06
Crow (0)	1	0.01
Delaware (0)	3	0.04
Hopi (0)	1	0.01
Mexican American Ind. (4)	6	0.07
Navajo (3)	7	0.08
Osage (0)	1	0.01
Pueblo (1)	7	0.08
Shoshone (2)	3	0.04
Tlingit-Haida *(Alaska Native)* (0)	1	0.01
Asian (978)	1,092	13.01
Not Hispanic (953)	1,034	12.32
Hispanic (25)	58	0.69
Cambodian (9)	11	0.13
Chinese, ex. Taiwanese (9)	22	0.26
Filipino (46)	83	0.99
Hmong (50)	50	0.60
Indian (647)	696	8.29
Indonesian (2)	2	0.02
Japanese (16)	34	0.41
Korean (4)	8	0.10
Laotian (9)	15	0.18
Pakistani (128)	158	1.88
Vietnamese (11)	14	0.17
Hawaii Native/Pacific Islander (17)	51	0.61
Not Hispanic (14)	36	0.43
Hispanic (3)	15	0.18
Fijian (4)	4	0.05
Guamanian/Chamorro (6)	10	0.12
Native Hawaiian (4)	17	0.20
White (4,491)	4,879	58.14
Not Hispanic (2,940)	3,083	36.74
Hispanic (1,551)	1,796	21.40

Livermore

Place Type: City
County: Alameda
Population: 80,968†

Ancestry‡	Population	%
Afghan (179)	179	0.23
African, Sub-Saharan (291)	419	0.53
African (197)	231	0.29
Nigerian (79)	136	0.17
Sierra Leonean (15)	52	0.07
American (2,742)	2,742	3.49
Arab (273)	682	0.87
Arab (33)	33	0.04
Jordanian (73)	250	0.32
Lebanese (115)	169	0.22
Palestinian (32)	100	0.13
Syrian (20)	24	0.03
Other Arab (0)	106	0.13
Armenian (152)	304	0.39
Assyrian/Chaldean/Syriac (62)	62	0.08
Australian (8)	8	0.01
Austrian (32)	171	0.22
Basque (139)	156	0.20
Belgian (0)	58	0.07
Brazilian (122)	122	0.16
British (168)	322	0.41
Cajun (17)	17	0.02
Canadian (154)	361	0.46
Celtic (9)	9	0.01
Croatian (69)	261	0.33
Czech (10)	227	0.29
Czechoslovakian (13)	83	0.11
Danish (154)	1,107	1.41
Dutch (338)	1,350	1.72
Eastern European (8)	16	0.02
English (2,607)	9,374	11.94
European (1,365)	1,485	1.89
Finnish (46)	167	0.21
French, ex. Basque (633)	2,682	3.42
French Canadian (355)	541	0.69
German (2,823)	12,945	16.49
Greek (110)	471	0.60
Hungarian (171)	492	0.63
Icelander (23)	35	0.04
Iranian (288)	288	0.37
Irish (2,140)	9,994	12.73
Italian (1,865)	6,299	8.02
Lithuanian (80)	255	0.32
Maltese (18)	18	0.02
Northern European (156)	156	0.20
Norwegian (433)	1,586	2.02
Pennsylvania German (12)	12	0.02
Polish (404)	1,492	1.90
Portuguese (1,100)	2,934	3.74
Romanian (35)	189	0.24
Russian (319)	637	0.81
Scandinavian (169)	322	0.41
Scotch-Irish (569)	2,051	2.61
Scottish (526)	2,365	3.01
Serbian (0)	36	0.05
Slavic (9)	18	0.02
Slovak (21)	107	0.14
Slovene (14)	79	0.10
Swedish (365)	2,279	2.90
Swiss (60)	247	0.31
Turkish (8)	15	0.02
Ukrainian (10)	100	0.13
Welsh (117)	796	1.01
West Indian, ex. Hispanic (11)	11	0.01
Barbadian (11)	11	0.01
Yugoslavian (13)	103	0.13

Hispanic Origin	Population	%
Hispanic or Latino (of any race)	16,920	20.90
Central American, ex. Mexican	730	0.90
Costa Rican	18	0.02
Guatemalan	73	0.09
Honduran	27	0.03
Nicaraguan	174	0.21
Panamanian	42	0.05
Salvadoran	385	0.48
Other Central American	11	0.01
Cuban	105	0.13
Dominican Republic	12	0.01
Mexican	13,296	16.42
Puerto Rican	586	0.72
South American	499	0.62
Argentinean	57	0.07
Bolivian	38	0.05
Chilean	40	0.05
Colombian	109	0.13
Ecuadorian	26	0.03
Paraguayan	1	<0.01
Peruvian	195	0.24
Uruguayan	5	0.01
Venezuelan	14	0.02
Other South American	14	0.02
Other Hispanic or Latino	1,692	2.09

Race*	Population	%
African-American/Black (1,702)	2,365	2.92
Not Hispanic (1,562)	2,058	2.54
Hispanic (140)	307	0.38
American Indian/Alaska Native (476)	1,312	1.62
Not Hispanic (251)	789	0.97
Hispanic (225)	523	0.65
Alaska Athabascan *(Ala. Nat.)* (0)	1	<0.01
Aleut *(Alaska Native)* (2)	7	0.01
Apache (21)	74	0.09
Arapaho (0)	3	<0.01
Blackfeet (4)	37	0.05
Canadian/French Am. Ind. (0)	5	0.01
Central American Ind. (4)	4	<0.01
Cherokee (45)	250	0.31
Chickasaw (2)	6	0.01
Chippewa (13)	24	0.03
Choctaw (12)	62	0.08
Comanche (6)	10	0.01
Cree (1)	1	<0.01
Creek (2)	6	0.01
Crow (0)	2	<0.01
Hopi (0)	2	<0.01
Iroquois (3)	14	0.02
Kiowa (0)	7	0.01
Menominee (0)	1	<0.01
Mexican American Ind. (30)	53	0.07
Navajo (9)	24	0.03
Osage (2)	6	0.01
Paiute (6)	9	0.01
Pima (2)	2	<0.01
Potawatomi (4)	5	0.01
Pueblo (5)	15	0.02
Puget Sound Salish (2)	2	<0.01
Seminole (1)	9	0.01
Shoshone (3)	9	0.01
Sioux (11)	28	0.03
South American Ind. (4)	7	0.01
Spanish American Ind. (3)	4	<0.01
Tlingit-Haida *(Alaska Native)* (8)	14	0.02
Ute (1)	11	0.01
Yaqui (4)	14	0.02
Yup'ik *(Alaska Native)* (1)	1	<0.01
Asian (6,802)	8,916	11.01
Not Hispanic (6,643)	8,390	10.36
Hispanic (159)	526	0.65
Bangladeshi (8)	8	0.01
Burmese (4)	6	0.01
Cambodian (37)	60	0.07

*Notes: † The Census 2010 population figure is used to calculate the percentages in the Hispanic Origin and Race categories. Ancestry percentages are based on the 2006-2010 American Community Survey population (not shown); ‡ Numbers in parentheses indicate the number of people reporting a single ancestry; * Numbers in parentheses indicate the number of persons reporting this race alone, not in combination with any other race; Please refer to the Explanation of Data for more information.*

Chinese, ex. Taiwanese (1,223)	1,712	2.11
Filipino (2,245)	3,153	3.89
Hmong (4)	4	<0.01
Indian (1,578)	1,729	2.14
Indonesian (20)	36	0.04
Japanese (379)	825	1.02
Korean (346)	519	0.64
Laotian (6)	8	0.01
Malaysian (12)	20	0.02
Nepalese (6)	6	0.01
Pakistani (103)	115	0.14
Sri Lankan (25)	25	0.03
Taiwanese (73)	91	0.11
Thai (60)	81	0.10
Vietnamese (393)	504	0.62
Hawaii Native/Pacific Islander (277)	684	0.84
Not Hispanic (231)	524	0.65
Hispanic (46)	160	0.20
Fijian (32)	56	0.07
Guamanian/Chamorro (66)	106	0.13
Native Hawaiian (90)	326	0.40
Samoan (50)	87	0.11
Tongan (14)	20	0.02
White (60,418)	64,320	79.44
Not Hispanic (52,397)	54,902	67.81
Hispanic (8,021)	9,418	11.63

Livingston

Place Type: City
County: Merced
Population: 13,058†

Ancestry‡	Population	%
African, Sub-Saharan (0)	22	0.17
African (0)	22	0.17
American (88)	88	0.69
Assyrian/Chaldean/Syriac (0)	28	0.22
Croatian (0)	9	0.07
Dutch (8)	8	0.06
English (14)	53	0.42
European (40)	40	0.31
French, ex. Basque (0)	25	0.20
French Canadian (7)	7	0.05
German (80)	181	1.42
Hungarian (0)	32	0.25
Irish (67)	206	1.62
Italian (0)	24	0.19
Norwegian (0)	7	0.05
Polish (0)	33	0.26
Portuguese (300)	310	2.43
Russian (0)	15	0.12
Scottish (9)	9	0.07
Slovak (0)	9	0.07

Hispanic Origin	Population	%
Hispanic or Latino (of any race)	9,547	73.11
Central American, ex. Mexican	60	0.46
Costa Rican	3	0.02
Guatemalan	17	0.13
Honduran	7	0.05
Nicaraguan	3	0.02
Panamanian	3	0.02
Salvadoran	27	0.21
Cuban	1	0.01
Dominican Republic	1	0.01
Mexican	9,244	70.79
Puerto Rican	15	0.11
South American	4	0.03
Colombian	1	0.01
Peruvian	3	0.02
Other Hispanic or Latino	222	1.70

Race*	Population	%
African-American/Black (106)	145	1.11
Not Hispanic (60)	76	0.58
Hispanic (46)	69	0.53
American Indian/Alaska Native (348)	446	3.42
Not Hispanic (37)	61	0.47
Hispanic (311)	385	2.95
Apache (14)	22	0.17
Blackfeet (0)	3	0.02
Central American Ind. (0)	1	0.01
Cherokee (1)	15	0.11
Chippewa (0)	1	0.01
Choctaw (3)	18	0.14
Hopi (4)	4	0.03
Mexican American Ind. (51)	70	0.54
Navajo (1)	1	0.01
Potawatomi (1)	1	0.01
Pueblo (2)	2	0.02
Spanish American Ind. (86)	87	0.67
Yaqui (1)	1	0.01
Asian (2,223)	2,380	18.23
Not Hispanic (2,193)	2,293	17.56
Hispanic (30)	87	0.67
Cambodian (6)	6	0.05
Chinese, ex. Taiwanese (10)	26	0.20
Filipino (131)	180	1.38
Hmong (29)	29	0.22
Indian (1,962)	2,039	15.61
Indonesian (2)	2	0.02
Japanese (6)	20	0.15
Laotian (4)	4	0.03
Pakistani (31)	38	0.29
Sri Lankan (5)	5	0.04
Thai (2)	5	0.04
Vietnamese (4)	6	0.05
Hawaii Native/Pacific Islander (18)	47	0.36
Not Hispanic (16)	32	0.25
Hispanic (2)	15	0.11
Fijian (5)	8	0.06
Guamanian/Chamorro (8)	12	0.09
Native Hawaiian (4)	12	0.09
Samoan (1)	1	0.01
White (5,263)	5,679	43.49
Not Hispanic (1,039)	1,102	8.44
Hispanic (4,224)	4,577	35.05

Lodi

Place Type: City
County: San Joaquin
Population: 62,134†

Ancestry‡	Population	%
African, Sub-Saharan (131)	227	0.36
African (131)	227	0.36
American (1,479)	1,479	2.38
Arab (502)	640	1.03
Jordanian (21)	21	0.03
Lebanese (12)	52	0.08
Palestinian (464)	464	0.75
Syrian (5)	103	0.17
Armenian (16)	93	0.15
Australian (0)	29	0.05
Austrian (14)	96	0.15
Basque (0)	56	0.09
Belgian (31)	89	0.14
British (51)	153	0.25
Canadian (72)	214	0.34
Croatian (9)	52	0.08
Czech (35)	225	0.36
Czechoslovakian (37)	37	0.06
Danish (69)	489	0.79
Dutch (171)	1,050	1.69
Eastern European (24)	29	0.05
English (1,257)	4,928	7.92
European (418)	532	0.85
Finnish (55)	72	0.12
French, ex. Basque (266)	1,373	2.21
French Canadian (178)	228	0.37
German (5,630)	12,805	20.58
Greek (105)	327	0.53
Hungarian (21)	45	0.07
Iranian (167)	205	0.33
Irish (1,434)	6,226	10.01
Italian (1,589)	4,435	7.13
Maltese (17)	17	0.03
Northern European (86)	86	0.14
Norwegian (253)	1,021	1.64
Polish (139)	584	0.94
Portuguese (552)	1,106	1.78
Romanian (7)	20	0.03
Russian (65)	500	0.80
Scandinavian (21)	85	0.14
Scotch-Irish (321)	1,106	1.78
Scottish (325)	978	1.57
Slavic (63)	90	0.14
Slovak (11)	11	0.02
Slovene (0)	11	0.02
Swedish (231)	1,055	1.70
Swiss (27)	294	0.47
Ukrainian (6)	49	0.08
Welsh (30)	351	0.56
Yugoslavian (43)	72	0.12

Hispanic Origin	Population	%
Hispanic or Latino (of any race)	22,613	36.39
Central American, ex. Mexican	285	0.46
Costa Rican	15	0.02
Guatemalan	77	0.12
Honduran	24	0.04
Nicaraguan	48	0.08
Panamanian	5	0.01
Salvadoran	115	0.19
Other Central American	1	<0.01
Cuban	39	0.06
Dominican Republic	3	<0.01
Mexican	20,579	33.12
Puerto Rican	246	0.40
South American	91	0.15
Argentinean	14	0.02
Bolivian	3	<0.01
Chilean	8	0.01
Colombian	26	0.04
Ecuadorian	6	0.01
Peruvian	26	0.04
Uruguayan	4	0.01
Venezuelan	3	<0.01
Other South American	1	<0.01
Other Hispanic or Latino	1,370	2.20

Race*	Population	%
African-American/Black (517)	834	1.34
Not Hispanic (388)	587	0.94
Hispanic (129)	247	0.40
American Indian/Alaska Native (560)	1,255	2.02
Not Hispanic (248)	724	1.17
Hispanic (312)	531	0.85
Aleut *(Alaska Native)* (3)	4	0.01
Apache (13)	36	0.06
Blackfeet (4)	17	0.03
Cherokee (40)	201	0.32
Cheyenne (0)	2	<0.01
Chickasaw (4)	16	0.03
Chippewa (7)	9	0.01
Choctaw (13)	52	0.08
Colville (0)	1	<0.01
Comanche (3)	5	0.01
Cree (2)	7	0.01
Creek (3)	7	0.01
Crow (0)	1	<0.01
Delaware (0)	3	<0.01
Inupiat *(Alaska Native)* (1)	1	<0.01
Iroquois (0)	2	<0.01
Kiowa (2)	3	<0.01
Lumbee (0)	4	0.01
Mexican American Ind. (109)	142	0.23
Navajo (4)	12	0.02
Osage (5)	6	0.01
Paiute (1)	4	0.01
Pima (0)	1	<0.01
Potawatomi (1)	3	<0.01
Pueblo (2)	4	0.01
Puget Sound Salish (3)	4	0.01
Seminole (1)	1	<0.01
Shoshone (1)	5	0.01
Sioux (10)	26	0.04
South American Ind. (0)	1	<0.01

*Notes: † The Census 2010 population figure is used to calculate the percentages in the Hispanic Origin and Race categories. Ancestry percentages are based on the 2006-2010 American Community Survey population (not shown); ‡ Numbers in parentheses indicate the number of people reporting a single ancestry; * Numbers in parentheses indicate the number of persons reporting this race alone, not in combination with any other race; Please refer to the Explanation of Data for more information.*

Spanish American Ind. (1)	2	<0.01
Tlingit-Haida *(Alaska Native)* (3)	8	0.01
Tohono O'Odham (2)	2	<0.01
Ute (1)	5	0.01
Yakama (7)	11	0.02
Yaqui (8)	16	0.03
Yuman (0)	6	0.01
Asian (4,293)	5,250	8.45
Not Hispanic (4,167)	4,834	7.78
Hispanic (126)	416	0.67
Burmese (12)	16	0.03
Cambodian (34)	39	0.06
Chinese, ex. Taiwanese (206)	299	0.48
Filipino (706)	1,162	1.87
Hmong (27)	28	0.05
Indian (812)	914	1.47
Indonesian (4)	16	0.03
Japanese (482)	663	1.07
Korean (67)	106	0.17
Laotian (39)	43	0.07
Malaysian (2)	2	<0.01
Nepalese (9)	9	0.01
Pakistani (1,603)	1,709	2.75
Sri Lankan (4)	9	0.01
Taiwanese (5)	5	0.01
Thai (9)	14	0.02
Vietnamese (72)	96	0.15
Hawaii Native/Pacific Islander (105)	302	0.49
Not Hispanic (88)	233	0.37
Hispanic (17)	69	0.11
Fijian (29)	37	0.06
Guamanian/Chamorro (17)	39	0.06
Native Hawaiian (45)	122	0.20
Samoan (1)	21	0.03
Tongan (0)	6	0.01
White (42,662)	45,122	72.62
Not Hispanic (33,194)	34,352	55.29
Hispanic (9,468)	10,770	17.33

Loma Linda

Place Type: City
County: San Bernardino
Population: 23,261†

Ancestry‡	Population	%
African, Sub-Saharan (492)	580	2.54
African (230)	318	1.39
Ethiopian (16)	16	0.07
Nigerian (205)	205	0.90
Zimbabwean (22)	22	0.10
Other Sub-Saharan African (19)	19	0.08
American (339)	339	1.48
Arab (319)	330	1.45
Arab (83)	83	0.36
Iraqi (10)	10	0.04
Jordanian (78)	78	0.34
Lebanese (0)	11	0.05
Syrian (15)	15	0.07
Other Arab (133)	133	0.58
Armenian (53)	70	0.31
Australian (44)	44	0.19
Belgian (0)	96	0.42
British (30)	46	0.20
Canadian (39)	39	0.17
Czech (51)	82	0.36
Danish (55)	147	0.64
Dutch (126)	458	2.01
English (327)	1,172	5.13
European (312)	355	1.55
Finnish (18)	18	0.08
French, ex. Basque (16)	254	1.11
French Canadian (48)	71	0.31
German (618)	1,938	8.49
Greek (47)	47	0.21
Hungarian (70)	112	0.49
Iranian (219)	219	0.96
Irish (366)	1,160	5.08
Italian (155)	635	2.78
Lithuanian (0)	9	0.04
Norwegian (135)	212	0.93
Polish (147)	179	0.78
Portuguese (141)	239	1.05
Romanian (449)	512	2.24
Russian (53)	135	0.59
Scandinavian (23)	38	0.17
Scotch-Irish (113)	292	1.28
Scottish (140)	269	1.18
Slovak (0)	16	0.07
Swedish (112)	374	1.64
Swiss (0)	33	0.14
Turkish (0)	42	0.18
Ukrainian (0)	12	0.05
Welsh (0)	21	0.09
West Indian, ex. Hispanic (139)	227	0.99
Haitian (47)	47	0.21
Jamaican (43)	131	0.57
Trinidadian/Tobagonian (49)	49	0.21
Yugoslavian (9)	9	0.04

Hispanic Origin	Population	%
Hispanic or Latino (of any race)	5,171	22.23
Central American, ex. Mexican	331	1.42
Costa Rican	21	0.09
Guatemalan	75	0.32
Honduran	34	0.15
Nicaraguan	65	0.28
Panamanian	40	0.17
Salvadoran	90	0.39
Other Central American	6	0.03
Cuban	61	0.26
Dominican Republic	25	0.11
Mexican	3,666	15.76
Puerto Rican	209	0.90
South American	443	1.90
Argentinean	78	0.34
Bolivian	20	0.09
Chilean	24	0.10
Colombian	73	0.31
Ecuadorian	65	0.28
Paraguayan	1	<0.01
Peruvian	148	0.64
Uruguayan	13	0.06
Venezuelan	19	0.08
Other South American	2	0.01
Other Hispanic or Latino	436	1.87

Race*	Population	%
African-American/Black (2,032)	2,363	10.16
Not Hispanic (1,932)	2,169	9.32
Hispanic (100)	194	0.83
American Indian/Alaska Native (97)	254	1.09
Not Hispanic (52)	155	0.67
Hispanic (45)	99	0.43
Aleut *(Alaska Native)* (2)	3	0.01
Apache (6)	9	0.04
Blackfeet (1)	6	0.03
Central American Ind. (0)	1	<0.01
Cherokee (3)	30	0.13
Cheyenne (1)	1	<0.01
Chickasaw (0)	1	<0.01
Chippewa (1)	3	0.01
Choctaw (3)	8	0.03
Comanche (0)	2	0.01
Creek (0)	2	0.01
Hopi (1)	1	<0.01
Kiowa (0)	2	0.01
Menominee (0)	1	<0.01
Mexican American Ind. (5)	12	0.05
Navajo (4)	4	0.02
Osage (1)	1	<0.01
Potawatomi (3)	3	0.01
Seminole (0)	1	<0.01
Sioux (3)	4	0.02
South American Ind. (2)	5	0.02
Spanish American Ind. (0)	1	<0.01
Yaqui (3)	3	0.01
Asian (6,589)	7,231	31.09
Not Hispanic (6,509)	7,040	30.27
Hispanic (80)	191	0.82
Bangladeshi (75)	93	0.40
Burmese (22)	26	0.11
Cambodian (68)	89	0.38
Chinese, ex. Taiwanese (676)	880	3.78
Filipino (2,207)	2,505	10.77
Hmong (2)	2	0.01
Indian (809)	929	3.99
Indonesian (814)	929	3.99
Japanese (166)	248	1.07
Korean (844)	931	4.00
Laotian (5)	5	0.02
Malaysian (11)	20	0.09
Nepalese (3)	3	0.01
Pakistani (135)	155	0.67
Sri Lankan (12)	17	0.07
Taiwanese (51)	56	0.24
Thai (144)	178	0.77
Vietnamese (246)	275	1.18
Hawaii Native/Pacific Islander (154)	284	1.22
Not Hispanic (139)	238	1.02
Hispanic (15)	46	0.20
Fijian (1)	5	0.02
Guamanian/Chamorro (19)	33	0.14
Marshallese (8)	8	0.03
Native Hawaiian (20)	47	0.20
Samoan (92)	107	0.46
Tongan (3)	12	0.05
White (11,122)	12,048	51.79
Not Hispanic (8,600)	9,184	39.48
Hispanic (2,522)	2,864	12.31

Lomita

Place Type: City
County: Los Angeles
Population: 20,256†

Ancestry‡	Population	%
African, Sub-Saharan (0)	160	0.79
African (0)	135	0.67
Cape Verdean (0)	25	0.12
American (981)	981	4.86
Arab (56)	71	0.35
Arab (11)	11	0.05
Lebanese (31)	31	0.15
Syrian (14)	29	0.14
Armenian (14)	14	0.07
Brazilian (41)	41	0.20
British (114)	178	0.88
Bulgarian (11)	11	0.05
Canadian (18)	18	0.09
Croatian (75)	352	1.74
Czech (9)	17	0.08
Czechoslovakian (9)	9	0.04
Danish (22)	114	0.56
Dutch (34)	97	0.48
English (280)	1,276	6.32
European (228)	369	1.83
Finnish (9)	9	0.04
French, ex. Basque (107)	658	3.26
French Canadian (42)	185	0.92
German (749)	2,572	12.74
Greek (24)	26	0.13
Hungarian (28)	122	0.60
Iranian (29)	29	0.14
Irish (416)	1,830	9.07
Italian (460)	1,176	5.83
Lithuanian (11)	11	0.05
Northern European (20)	20	0.10
Norwegian (72)	352	1.74
Polish (17)	305	1.51
Portuguese (174)	174	0.86
Russian (72)	177	0.88
Scandinavian (0)	17	0.08
Scotch-Irish (36)	215	1.07
Scottish (36)	225	1.11
Serbian (13)	42	0.21
Slavic (21)	21	0.10
Slovak (13)	13	0.06
Swedish (34)	327	1.62

*Notes: † The Census 2010 population figure is used to calculate the percentages in the Hispanic Origin and Race categories. Ancestry percentages are based on the 2006-2010 American Community Survey population (not shown); ‡ Numbers in parentheses indicate the number of people reporting a single ancestry; * Numbers in parentheses indicate the number of persons reporting this race alone, not in combination with any other race; Please refer to the Explanation of Data for more information.*

Swiss (8)	102	0.51
Ukrainian (8)	51	0.25
Welsh (23)	94	0.47
West Indian, ex. Hispanic (12)	28	0.14
Jamaican (12)	28	0.14
Yugoslavian (20)	20	0.10

Hispanic Origin	Population	%
Hispanic or Latino (of any race)	6,652	32.84
Central American, ex. Mexican	574	2.83
Costa Rican	33	0.16
Guatemalan	201	0.99
Honduran	23	0.11
Nicaraguan	57	0.28
Panamanian	15	0.07
Salvadoran	236	1.17
Other Central American	9	0.04
Cuban	122	0.60
Dominican Republic	9	0.04
Mexican	4,925	24.31
Puerto Rican	152	0.75
South American	388	1.92
Argentinean	59	0.29
Bolivian	1	<0.01
Chilean	31	0.15
Colombian	101	0.50
Ecuadorian	44	0.22
Peruvian	137	0.68
Uruguayan	6	0.03
Venezuelan	8	0.04
Other South American	1	<0.01
Other Hispanic or Latino	482	2.38

Race*	Population	%
African-American/Black (1,075)	1,319	6.51
Not Hispanic (964)	1,140	5.63
Hispanic (111)	179	0.88
American Indian/Alaska Native (174)	425	2.10
Not Hispanic (76)	221	1.09
Hispanic (98)	204	1.01
Alaska Athabascan *(Ala. Nat.)* (3)	4	0.02
Aleut *(Alaska Native)* (1)	1	<0.01
Apache (7)	29	0.14
Arapaho (1)	3	0.01
Blackfeet (2)	8	0.04
Central American Ind. (0)	2	0.01
Cherokee (10)	52	0.26
Cheyenne (0)	1	<0.01
Chickasaw (0)	2	0.01
Chippewa (6)	6	0.03
Choctaw (2)	11	0.05
Creek (6)	12	0.06
Delaware (0)	2	0.01
Hopi (2)	5	0.02
Iroquois (0)	2	0.01
Menominee (0)	3	0.01
Mexican American Ind. (15)	25	0.12
Navajo (3)	9	0.04
Osage (0)	1	<0.01
Paiute (0)	3	0.01
Pima (2)	10	0.05
Potawatomi (0)	3	0.01
Pueblo (4)	11	0.05
Seminole (0)	2	0.01
Shoshone (0)	3	0.01
Sioux (9)	17	0.08
South American Ind. (2)	2	0.01
Spanish American Ind. (1)	1	<0.01
Tohono O'Odham (0)	2	0.01
Yaqui (0)	4	0.02
Asian (2,923)	3,507	17.31
Not Hispanic (2,850)	3,298	16.28
Hispanic (73)	209	1.03
Bangladeshi (11)	11	0.05
Burmese (2)	5	0.02
Cambodian (18)	24	0.12
Chinese, ex. Taiwanese (393)	523	2.58
Filipino (644)	905	4.47
Indian (264)	295	1.46
Indonesian (16)	25	0.12
Japanese (722)	937	4.63
Korean (435)	497	2.45
Laotian (2)	4	0.02
Malaysian (1)	4	0.02
Nepalese (5)	5	0.02
Pakistani (82)	83	0.41
Sri Lankan (34)	38	0.19
Taiwanese (82)	100	0.49
Thai (24)	30	0.15
Vietnamese (74)	99	0.49
Hawaii Native/Pacific Islander (140)	256	1.26
Not Hispanic (112)	200	0.99
Hispanic (28)	56	0.28
Fijian (4)	4	0.02
Guamanian/Chamorro (19)	27	0.13
Native Hawaiian (26)	79	0.39
Samoan (74)	100	0.49
Tongan (6)	6	0.03
White (11,987)	13,073	64.54
Not Hispanic (8,797)	9,432	46.56
Hispanic (3,190)	3,641	17.97

Lompoc

Place Type: City
County: Santa Barbara
Population: 42,434†

Ancestry‡	Population	%
African, Sub-Saharan (212)	227	0.54
African (161)	176	0.42
Ethiopian (36)	36	0.09
Kenyan (8)	8	0.02
Nigerian (7)	7	0.02
American (1,184)	1,184	2.83
Arab (20)	90	0.21
Arab (11)	73	0.17
Palestinian (9)	17	0.04
Armenian (19)	19	0.05
Assyrian/Chaldean/Syriac (8)	8	0.02
Austrian (0)	47	0.11
Basque (0)	55	0.13
Belgian (0)	92	0.22
British (102)	117	0.28
Cajun (4)	38	0.09
Canadian (32)	188	0.45
Celtic (0)	7	0.02
Croatian (34)	34	0.08
Czech (23)	111	0.27
Czechoslovakian (53)	96	0.23
Danish (111)	246	0.59
Dutch (27)	385	0.92
Eastern European (16)	26	0.06
English (528)	2,158	5.15
European (207)	325	0.78
Finnish (0)	21	0.05
French, ex. Basque (170)	934	2.23
French Canadian (53)	133	0.32
German (1,450)	4,439	10.60
German Russian (0)	12	0.03
Greek (131)	182	0.43
Guyanese (80)	80	0.19
Hungarian (20)	74	0.18
Icelander (0)	36	0.09
Iranian (28)	28	0.07
Irish (700)	3,407	8.14
Italian (360)	998	2.38
Lithuanian (18)	36	0.09
Maltese (7)	28	0.07
Northern European (64)	182	0.43
Norwegian (288)	561	1.34
Pennsylvania German (8)	8	0.02
Polish (128)	226	0.54
Portuguese (195)	555	1.33
Romanian (0)	9	0.02
Russian (18)	126	0.30
Scandinavian (11)	53	0.13
Scotch-Irish (236)	482	1.15
Scottish (150)	459	1.10
Slovak (0)	22	0.05
Slovene (8)	8	0.02
Swedish (112)	423	1.01
Swiss (0)	68	0.16
Turkish (40)	40	0.10
Ukrainian (25)	32	0.08
Welsh (30)	266	0.64
West Indian, ex. Hispanic (105)	286	0.68
British West Indian (42)	103	0.25
Haitian (9)	20	0.05
Jamaican (45)	154	0.37
West Indian (9)	9	0.02
Yugoslavian (69)	69	0.16

Hispanic Origin	Population	%
Hispanic or Latino (of any race)	21,557	50.80
Central American, ex. Mexican	531	1.25
Costa Rican	12	0.03
Guatemalan	214	0.50
Honduran	75	0.18
Nicaraguan	39	0.09
Panamanian	5	0.01
Salvadoran	183	0.43
Other Central American	3	0.01
Cuban	52	0.12
Dominican Republic	3	0.01
Mexican	19,252	45.37
Puerto Rican	262	0.62
South American	127	0.30
Argentinean	24	0.06
Bolivian	5	0.01
Chilean	21	0.05
Colombian	40	0.09
Ecuadorian	4	0.01
Paraguayan	1	<0.01
Peruvian	25	0.06
Venezuelan	7	0.02
Other Hispanic or Latino	1,330	3.13

Race*	Population	%
African-American/Black (2,432)	3,144	7.41
Not Hispanic (2,204)	2,725	6.42
Hispanic (228)	419	0.99
American Indian/Alaska Native (750)	1,416	3.34
Not Hispanic (325)	671	1.58
Hispanic (425)	745	1.76
Alaska Athabascan *(Ala. Nat.)* (3)	3	0.01
Aleut *(Alaska Native)* (0)	2	<0.01
Apache (15)	40	0.09
Arapaho (1)	2	<0.01
Blackfeet (2)	22	0.05
Canadian/French Am. Ind. (0)	4	0.01
Central American Ind. (2)	2	<0.01
Cherokee (32)	138	0.33
Cheyenne (2)	6	0.01
Chickasaw (11)	16	0.04
Chippewa (3)	9	0.02
Choctaw (9)	40	0.09
Colville (0)	1	<0.01
Comanche (2)	7	0.02
Creek (11)	20	0.05
Crow (1)	2	<0.01
Delaware (2)	2	<0.01
Hopi (0)	2	<0.01
Iroquois (2)	11	0.03
Lumbee (1)	1	<0.01
Mexican American Ind. (89)	130	0.31
Navajo (18)	26	0.06
Osage (3)	8	0.02
Paiute (2)	3	0.01
Pima (9)	14	0.03
Pueblo (12)	14	0.03
Puget Sound Salish (3)	3	0.01
Seminole (1)	2	<0.01
Shoshone (1)	2	<0.01
Sioux (8)	35	0.08
South American Ind. (4)	5	0.01
Tlingit-Haida *(Alaska Native)* (6)	8	0.02
Tohono O'Odham (3)	11	0.03
Tsimshian *(Alaska Native)* (1)	1	<0.01
Yakama (1)	1	<0.01

*Notes: † The Census 2010 population figure is used to calculate the percentages in the Hispanic Origin and Race categories. Ancestry percentages are based on the 2006-2010 American Community Survey population (not shown); ‡ Numbers in parentheses indicate the number of people reporting a single ancestry; * Numbers in parentheses indicate the number of persons reporting this race alone, not in combination with any other race; Please refer to the Explanation of Data for more information.*

Yaqui (18)	25	0.06
Yuman (3)	7	0.02
Yup'ik *(Alaska Native)* (5)	6	0.01
Asian (1,615)	2,354	5.55
Not Hispanic (1,505)	1,995	4.70
Hispanic (110)	359	0.85
Bangladeshi (4)	4	0.01
Burmese (1)	1	<0.01
Cambodian (16)	18	0.04
Chinese, ex. Taiwanese (90)	198	0.47
Filipino (576)	942	2.22
Hmong (296)	309	0.73
Indian (81)	102	0.24
Indonesian (20)	34	0.08
Japanese (115)	284	0.67
Korean (77)	135	0.32
Laotian (76)	82	0.19
Malaysian (2)	10	0.02
Pakistani (7)	8	0.02
Sri Lankan (9)	11	0.03
Taiwanese (0)	5	0.01
Thai (44)	68	0.16
Vietnamese (122)	161	0.38
Hawaii Native/Pacific Islander (186)	369	0.87
Not Hispanic (156)	257	0.61
Hispanic (30)	112	0.26
Fijian (1)	1	<0.01
Guamanian/Chamorro (100)	131	0.31
Marshallese (2)	2	<0.01
Native Hawaiian (47)	141	0.33
Samoan (27)	38	0.09
Tongan (4)	8	0.02
White (25,950)	28,002	65.99
Not Hispanic (15,424)	16,412	38.68
Hispanic (10,526)	11,590	27.31

Long Beach

Place Type: City
County: Los Angeles
Population: 462,257†

Ancestry‡	Population	%
Afghan (18)	18	<0.01
African, Sub-Saharan (7,542)	10,870	2.35
African (6,339)	9,464	2.05
Cape Verdean (6)	47	0.01
Ethiopian (142)	229	0.05
Ghanaian (9)	9	<0.01
Kenyan (100)	117	0.03
Nigerian (485)	528	0.11
Sierra Leonean (12)	27	0.01
South African (59)	59	0.01
Sudanese (126)	126	0.03
Ugandan (29)	29	0.01
Other Sub-Saharan African (235)	235	0.05
Albanian (16)	63	0.01
American (7,230)	7,230	1.57
Arab (1,478)	2,244	0.49
Arab (321)	537	0.12
Egyptian (250)	263	0.06
Iraqi (0)	18	<0.01
Jordanian (10)	22	<0.01
Lebanese (340)	588	0.13
Moroccan (37)	51	0.01
Palestinian (42)	111	0.02
Syrian (50)	68	0.01
Other Arab (428)	586	0.13
Armenian (467)	889	0.19
Assyrian/Chaldean/Syriac (43)	65	0.01
Australian (32)	165	0.04
Austrian (222)	617	0.13
Basque (39)	153	0.03
Belgian (53)	267	0.06
Brazilian (232)	281	0.06
British (800)	1,611	0.35
Bulgarian (60)	95	0.02
Cajun (31)	157	0.03
Canadian (435)	887	0.19
Carpatho Rusyn (0)	34	0.01
Celtic (117)	170	0.04
Croatian (220)	485	0.11
Cypriot (70)	94	0.02
Czech (243)	854	0.18
Czechoslovakian (127)	369	0.08
Danish (340)	1,179	0.26
Dutch (1,498)	4,630	1.00
Eastern European (262)	285	0.06
English (7,163)	23,359	5.06
European (4,306)	5,522	1.20
Finnish (158)	479	0.10
French, ex. Basque (1,221)	8,425	1.82
French Canadian (470)	1,161	0.25
German (8,982)	33,099	7.17
German Russian (11)	50	0.01
Greek (832)	1,580	0.34
Guyanese (15)	15	<0.01
Hungarian (830)	1,825	0.40
Icelander (58)	76	0.02
Iranian (507)	613	0.13
Irish (8,000)	27,445	5.94
Israeli (98)	208	0.05
Italian (5,745)	14,721	3.19
Latvian (50)	99	0.02
Lithuanian (113)	463	0.10
Luxemburger (15)	15	<0.01
New Zealander (11)	11	<0.01
Northern European (460)	485	0.11
Norwegian (1,542)	4,263	0.92
Pennsylvania German (23)	65	0.01
Polish (1,909)	6,373	1.38
Portuguese (441)	1,460	0.32
Romanian (302)	621	0.13
Russian (1,491)	4,610	1.00
Scandinavian (304)	561	0.12
Scotch-Irish (1,750)	4,933	1.07
Scottish (1,699)	6,072	1.31
Serbian (110)	263	0.06
Slavic (11)	157	0.03
Slovak (23)	183	0.04
Slovene (37)	105	0.02
Swedish (864)	4,170	0.90
Swiss (142)	763	0.17
Turkish (254)	288	0.06
Ukrainian (193)	552	0.12
Welsh (520)	1,823	0.39
West Indian, ex. Hispanic (1,055)	1,815	0.39
Bahamian (17)	92	0.02
Belizean (240)	336	0.07
British West Indian (43)	69	0.01
Dutch West Indian (0)	47	0.01
Haitian (49)	102	0.02
Jamaican (320)	557	0.12
Trinidadian/Tobagonian (163)	168	0.04
U.S. Virgin Islander (37)	37	0.01
West Indian (186)	407	0.09
Yugoslavian (73)	238	0.05

Hispanic Origin	Population	%
Hispanic or Latino (of any race)	188,412	40.76
Central American, ex. Mexican	16,486	3.57
Costa Rican	467	0.10
Guatemalan	5,134	1.11
Honduran	2,696	0.58
Nicaraguan	1,007	0.22
Panamanian	313	0.07
Salvadoran	6,657	1.44
Other Central American	212	0.05
Cuban	1,264	0.27
Dominican Republic	194	0.04
Mexican	151,983	32.88
Puerto Rican	3,025	0.65
South American	4,123	0.89
Argentinean	650	0.14
Bolivian	125	0.03
Chilean	288	0.06
Colombian	1,037	0.22
Ecuadorian	679	0.15
Paraguayan	12	<0.01
Peruvian	1,109	0.24
Uruguayan	51	0.01
Venezuelan	123	0.03
Other South American	49	0.01
Other Hispanic or Latino	11,337	2.45

Race*	Population	%
African-American/Black (62,603)	69,744	15.09
Not Hispanic (59,925)	65,067	14.08
Hispanic (2,678)	4,677	1.01
American Indian/Alaska Native (3,458)	7,958	1.72
Not Hispanic (1,349)	4,002	0.87
Hispanic (2,109)	3,956	0.86
Alaska Athabascan *(Ala. Nat.)* (9)	11	<0.01
Aleut *(Alaska Native)* (2)	13	<0.01
Apache (89)	244	0.05
Arapaho (5)	6	<0.01
Blackfeet (27)	214	0.05
Canadian/French Am. Ind. (4)	30	0.01
Central American Ind. (46)	78	0.02
Cherokee (185)	947	0.20
Cheyenne (13)	22	<0.01
Chickasaw (14)	43	0.01
Chippewa (40)	108	0.02
Choctaw (59)	240	0.05
Comanche (8)	15	<0.01
Cree (2)	13	<0.01
Creek (32)	98	0.02
Crow (4)	6	<0.01
Delaware (5)	13	<0.01
Hopi (7)	22	<0.01
Inupiat *(Alaska Native)* (2)	8	<0.01
Iroquois (23)	79	0.02
Kiowa (3)	5	<0.01
Lumbee (7)	10	<0.01
Menominee (1)	1	<0.01
Mexican American Ind. (578)	840	0.18
Navajo (175)	320	0.07
Osage (13)	29	0.01
Ottawa (4)	7	<0.01
Paiute (7)	7	<0.01
Pima (17)	25	0.01
Potawatomi (11)	27	0.01
Pueblo (34)	83	0.02
Puget Sound Salish (1)	1	<0.01
Seminole (6)	48	0.01
Shoshone (5)	29	0.01
Sioux (56)	166	0.04
South American Ind. (18)	77	0.02
Spanish American Ind. (32)	62	0.01
Tlingit-Haida *(Alaska Native)* (9)	13	<0.01
Tohono O'Odham (5)	18	<0.01
Ute (15)	19	<0.01
Yakama (1)	7	<0.01
Yaqui (61)	130	0.03
Yuman (19)	37	0.01
Yup'ik *(Alaska Native)* (1)	2	<0.01
Asian (59,496)	67,961	14.70
Not Hispanic (58,268)	64,834	14.03
Hispanic (1,228)	3,127	0.68
Bangladeshi (153)	180	0.04
Burmese (69)	89	0.02
Cambodian (18,051)	19,998	4.33
Chinese, ex. Taiwanese (3,478)	5,734	1.24
Filipino (20,964)	24,963	5.40
Hmong (299)	327	0.07
Indian (1,916)	2,591	0.56
Indonesian (143)	304	0.07
Japanese (2,883)	4,683	1.01
Korean (1,888)	2,385	0.52
Laotian (536)	893	0.19
Malaysian (39)	60	0.01
Nepalese (26)	31	0.01
Pakistani (131)	181	0.04
Sri Lankan (176)	212	0.05
Taiwanese (289)	356	0.08
Thai (780)	1,266	0.27
Vietnamese (4,204)	4,952	1.07
Hawaii Native/Pacific Islander (5,253)	7,498	1.62
Not Hispanic (4,915)	6,549	1.42
Hispanic (338)	949	0.21

*Notes: † The Census 2010 population figure is used to calculate the percentages in the Hispanic Origin and Race categories. Ancestry percentages are based on the 2006-2010 American Community Survey population (not shown); ‡ Numbers in parentheses indicate the number of people reporting a single ancestry; * Numbers in parentheses indicate the number of persons reporting this race alone, not in combination with any other race; Please refer to the Explanation of Data for more information.*

Fijian (32)	50	0.01
Guamanian/Chamorro (534)	937	0.20
Native Hawaiian (336)	1,018	0.22
Samoan (3,736)	4,513	0.98
Tongan (295)	371	0.08
White (213,066)	231,897	50.17
Not Hispanic (135,698)	145,170	31.40
Hispanic (77,368)	86,727	18.76

Los Alamitos

Place Type: City
County: Orange
Population: 11,449†

Ancestry‡	Population	%
African, Sub-Saharan (0)	36	0.32
African (0)	36	0.32
American (223)	223	1.95
Arab (76)	98	0.86
Arab (42)	58	0.51
Lebanese (15)	21	0.18
Syrian (19)	19	0.17
Armenian (23)	23	0.20
Austrian (0)	17	0.15
British (92)	101	0.88
Canadian (19)	44	0.39
Czech (19)	59	0.52
Czechoslovakian (0)	9	0.08
Danish (33)	87	0.76
Dutch (60)	199	1.74
English (342)	1,198	10.50
Estonian (0)	9	0.08
European (84)	127	1.11
French, ex. Basque (51)	522	4.57
French Canadian (32)	142	1.24
German (355)	1,844	16.16
Greek (70)	70	0.61
Hungarian (27)	76	0.67
Iranian (29)	39	0.34
Irish (401)	1,500	13.14
Italian (221)	616	5.40
Lithuanian (102)	118	1.03
Northern European (27)	27	0.24
Norwegian (46)	263	2.30
Polish (91)	304	2.66
Portuguese (10)	48	0.42
Romanian (24)	24	0.21
Russian (51)	85	0.74
Scandinavian (0)	30	0.26
Scotch-Irish (40)	200	1.75
Scottish (90)	252	2.21
Serbian (0)	11	0.10
Slovak (21)	29	0.25
Swedish (65)	152	1.33
Swiss (10)	59	0.52
Turkish (0)	47	0.41
Ukrainian (17)	17	0.15
Welsh (17)	70	0.61
Yugoslavian (30)	30	0.26

Hispanic Origin	Population	%
Hispanic or Latino (of any race)	2,418	21.12
Central American, ex. Mexican	110	0.96
Costa Rican	14	0.12
Guatemalan	28	0.24
Honduran	10	0.09
Nicaraguan	8	0.07
Panamanian	5	0.04
Salvadoran	44	0.38
Other Central American	1	0.01
Cuban	33	0.29
Dominican Republic	6	0.05
Mexican	1,793	15.66
Puerto Rican	64	0.56
South American	187	1.63
Argentinean	17	0.15
Bolivian	4	0.03
Chilean	6	0.05
Colombian	46	0.40
Ecuadorian	12	0.10
Paraguayan	2	0.02
Peruvian	94	0.82
Venezuelan	6	0.05
Other Hispanic or Latino	225	1.97

Race*	Population	%
African-American/Black (324)	489	4.27
Not Hispanic (300)	415	3.62
Hispanic (24)	74	0.65
American Indian/Alaska Native (51)	207	1.81
Not Hispanic (22)	118	1.03
Hispanic (29)	89	0.78
Aleut *(Alaska Native)* (0)	1	0.01
Apache (1)	16	0.14
Blackfeet (1)	3	0.03
Cherokee (5)	36	0.31
Cheyenne (1)	4	0.03
Chippewa (1)	1	0.01
Choctaw (1)	4	0.03
Colville (2)	2	0.02
Creek (3)	3	0.03
Iroquois (0)	10	0.09
Lumbee (0)	2	0.02
Mexican American Ind. (4)	8	0.07
Navajo (3)	4	0.03
Potawatomi (4)	4	0.03
Pueblo (0)	7	0.06
Sioux (0)	2	0.02
Spanish American Ind. (1)	1	0.01
Yaqui (2)	2	0.02
Asian (1,471)	1,797	15.70
Not Hispanic (1,447)	1,713	14.96
Hispanic (24)	84	0.73
Bangladeshi (4)	4	0.03
Burmese (8)	10	0.09
Cambodian (19)	28	0.24
Chinese, ex. Taiwanese (219)	279	2.44
Filipino (304)	463	4.04
Indian (81)	87	0.76
Indonesian (1)	5	0.04
Japanese (149)	251	2.19
Korean (495)	518	4.52
Malaysian (1)	1	0.01
Nepalese (4)	4	0.03
Pakistani (8)	8	0.07
Sri Lankan (2)	5	0.04
Taiwanese (40)	42	0.37
Thai (23)	33	0.29
Vietnamese (59)	79	0.69
Hawaii Native/Pacific Islander (50)	103	0.90
Not Hispanic (47)	90	0.79
Hispanic (3)	13	0.11
Fijian (0)	4	0.03
Guamanian/Chamorro (13)	16	0.14
Native Hawaiian (10)	37	0.32
Samoan (24)	34	0.30
Tongan (0)	2	0.02
White (8,131)	8,752	76.44
Not Hispanic (6,721)	7,122	62.21
Hispanic (1,410)	1,630	14.24

Los Altos Hills

Place Type: Town
County: Santa Clara
Population: 7,922†

Ancestry‡	Population	%
African, Sub-Saharan (14)	14	0.18
Senegalese (14)	14	0.18
American (131)	131	1.67
Arab (0)	12	0.15
Arab (0)	12	0.15
Armenian (43)	43	0.55
Austrian (22)	29	0.37
Belgian (19)	19	0.24
British (32)	43	0.55
Canadian (45)	45	0.57
Croatian (0)	13	0.17
Czech (12)	12	0.15
Czechoslovakian (0)	42	0.53
Danish (36)	50	0.64
Dutch (45)	88	1.12
Eastern European (15)	15	0.19
English (358)	849	10.80
European (141)	141	1.79
Finnish (58)	113	1.44
French, ex. Basque (13)	292	3.72
French Canadian (11)	11	0.14
German (275)	1,163	14.80
Greek (16)	45	0.57
Hungarian (13)	13	0.17
Iranian (215)	228	2.90
Irish (119)	555	7.06
Israeli (26)	68	0.87
Italian (183)	378	4.81
Lithuanian (22)	60	0.76
Northern European (70)	70	0.89
Norwegian (47)	90	1.15
Polish (116)	287	3.65
Portuguese (15)	85	1.08
Romanian (0)	52	0.66
Russian (88)	171	2.18
Scandinavian (5)	5	0.06
Scotch-Irish (80)	129	1.64
Scottish (34)	217	2.76
Swedish (72)	225	2.86
Swiss (9)	56	0.71
Ukrainian (42)	65	0.83
Welsh (0)	128	1.63
Yugoslavian (15)	70	0.89

Hispanic Origin	Population	%
Hispanic or Latino (of any race)	213	2.69
Central American, ex. Mexican	25	0.32
Costa Rican	5	0.06
Guatemalan	2	0.03
Honduran	5	0.06
Nicaraguan	1	0.01
Panamanian	1	0.01
Salvadoran	10	0.13
Other Central American	1	0.01
Cuban	21	0.27
Dominican Republic	2	0.03
Mexican	90	1.14
Puerto Rican	3	0.04
South American	24	0.30
Argentinean	9	0.11
Chilean	6	0.08
Colombian	2	0.03
Peruvian	7	0.09
Other Hispanic or Latino	48	0.61

Race*	Population	%
African-American/Black (37)	55	0.69
Not Hispanic (37)	53	0.67
Hispanic (0)	2	0.03
American Indian/Alaska Native (4)	32	0.40
Not Hispanic (2)	29	0.37
Hispanic (2)	3	0.04
Apache (0)	3	0.04
Blackfeet (0)	1	0.01
Cherokee (0)	5	0.06
Chickasaw (1)	1	0.01
Choctaw (1)	1	0.01
Mexican American Ind. (1)	1	0.01
Osage (0)	1	0.01
Potawatomi (0)	2	0.03
South American Ind. (0)	1	0.01
Asian (2,109)	2,360	29.79
Not Hispanic (2,108)	2,356	29.74
Hispanic (1)	4	0.05
Burmese (4)	6	0.08
Chinese, ex. Taiwanese (1,028)	1,158	14.62
Filipino (48)	84	1.06
Indian (532)	571	7.21
Indonesian (0)	1	0.01
Japanese (119)	164	2.07
Korean (125)	152	1.92

SECTION TWO

*Notes: † The Census 2010 population figure is used to calculate the percentages in the Hispanic Origin and Race categories. Ancestry percentages are based on the 2006-2010 American Community Survey population (not shown); ‡ Numbers in parentheses indicate the number of people reporting a single ancestry; * Numbers in parentheses indicate the number of persons reporting this race alone, not in combination with any other race; Please refer to the Explanation of Data for more information.*

Nepalese (1)	1	0.01
Pakistani (15)	17	0.21
Sri Lankan (2)	5	0.06
Taiwanese (114)	122	1.54
Thai (5)	5	0.06
Vietnamese (62)	82	1.04
Hawaii Native/Pacific Islander (8)	17	0.21
Not Hispanic (8)	17	0.21
Fijian (1)	1	0.01
Guamanian/Chamorro (3)	6	0.08
Native Hawaiian (0)	3	0.04
Tongan (4)	4	0.05
White (5,417)	5,691	71.84
Not Hispanic (5,239)	5,503	69.46
Hispanic (178)	188	2.37

Los Altos

Place Type: City
County: Santa Clara
Population: 28,976†

Ancestry‡	Population	%
African, Sub-Saharan (0)	23	0.08
African (0)	23	0.08
American (620)	620	2.18
Arab (232)	299	1.05
Arab (7)	7	0.02
Egyptian (173)	186	0.65
Lebanese (0)	23	0.08
Moroccan (4)	19	0.07
Palestinian (13)	13	0.05
Other Arab (35)	51	0.18
Armenian (58)	87	0.31
Australian (10)	22	0.08
Austrian (24)	140	0.49
Belgian (51)	198	0.70
Brazilian (22)	22	0.08
British (91)	268	0.94
Bulgarian (0)	9	0.03
Canadian (203)	237	0.83
Carpatho Rusyn (57)	57	0.20
Celtic (0)	7	0.02
Croatian (52)	83	0.29
Czech (77)	207	0.73
Czechoslovakian (57)	66	0.23
Danish (148)	347	1.22
Dutch (166)	464	1.63
Eastern European (141)	153	0.54
English (932)	3,509	12.35
European (948)	1,037	3.65
Finnish (44)	108	0.38
French, ex. Basque (286)	1,172	4.13
French Canadian (39)	91	0.32
German (1,055)	4,535	15.96
Greek (47)	282	0.99
Hungarian (35)	167	0.59
Iranian (336)	379	1.33
Irish (796)	3,052	10.74
Israeli (158)	158	0.56
Italian (799)	1,996	7.03
Latvian (47)	59	0.21
Lithuanian (21)	246	0.87
Maltese (14)	14	0.05
New Zealander (9)	9	0.03
Northern European (287)	294	1.03
Norwegian (175)	631	2.22
Polish (170)	773	2.72
Portuguese (116)	273	0.96
Romanian (91)	146	0.51
Russian (468)	872	3.07
Scandinavian (10)	36	0.13
Scotch-Irish (118)	476	1.68
Scottish (133)	877	3.09
Serbian (0)	17	0.06
Slovak (12)	76	0.27
Slovene (10)	10	0.04
Swedish (148)	516	1.82
Swiss (107)	310	1.09
Turkish (0)	7	0.02
Ukrainian (90)	193	0.68
Welsh (22)	274	0.96
West Indian, ex. Hispanic (10)	33	0.12
Jamaican (0)	23	0.08
West Indian (10)	10	0.04
Yugoslavian (51)	101	0.36

Hispanic Origin	Population	%
Hispanic or Latino (of any race)	1,132	3.91
Central American, ex. Mexican	106	0.37
Costa Rican	11	0.04
Guatemalan	29	0.10
Honduran	2	0.01
Nicaraguan	23	0.08
Salvadoran	39	0.13
Other Central American	2	0.01
Cuban	32	0.11
Dominican Republic	4	0.01
Mexican	541	1.87
Puerto Rican	58	0.20
South American	194	0.67
Argentinean	44	0.15
Bolivian	12	0.04
Chilean	22	0.08
Colombian	39	0.13
Ecuadorian	11	0.04
Peruvian	50	0.17
Uruguayan	3	0.01
Venezuelan	10	0.03
Other South American	3	0.01
Other Hispanic or Latino	197	0.68

Race*	Population	%
African-American/Black (148)	238	0.82
Not Hispanic (137)	210	0.72
Hispanic (11)	28	0.10
American Indian/Alaska Native (48)	159	0.55
Not Hispanic (21)	99	0.34
Hispanic (27)	60	0.21
Alaska Athabascan *(Ala. Nat.)* (0)	1	<0.01
Apache (0)	10	0.03
Blackfeet (0)	1	<0.01
Cherokee (2)	17	0.06
Chickasaw (1)	1	<0.01
Chippewa (1)	7	0.02
Choctaw (2)	5	0.02
Colville (0)	3	0.01
Cree (0)	1	<0.01
Creek (0)	6	0.02
Delaware (1)	1	<0.01
Iroquois (1)	2	0.01
Mexican American Ind. (10)	11	0.04
Navajo (1)	1	<0.01
Pima (1)	1	<0.01
Potawatomi (1)	1	<0.01
Pueblo (4)	7	0.02
Shoshone (0)	1	<0.01
Sioux (2)	3	0.01
South American Ind. (0)	1	<0.01
Tsimshian *(Alaska Native)* (1)	1	<0.01
Ute (3)	3	0.01
Yuman (0)	1	<0.01
Asian (6,815)	7,854	27.11
Not Hispanic (6,795)	7,789	26.88
Hispanic (20)	65	0.22
Bangladeshi (3)	3	0.01
Burmese (5)	9	0.03
Cambodian (16)	20	0.07
Chinese, ex. Taiwanese (3,011)	3,576	12.34
Filipino (178)	298	1.03
Hmong (1)	3	0.01
Indian (1,552)	1,686	5.82
Indonesian (4)	15	0.05
Japanese (620)	938	3.24
Korean (493)	636	2.19
Laotian (1)	7	0.02
Malaysian (8)	16	0.06
Pakistani (54)	62	0.21
Sri Lankan (28)	32	0.11
Taiwanese (345)	398	1.37
Thai (15)	21	0.07
Vietnamese (190)	266	0.92
Hawaii Native/Pacific Islander (59)	107	0.37
Not Hispanic (56)	101	0.35
Hispanic (3)	6	0.02
Fijian (3)	4	0.01
Guamanian/Chamorro (10)	15	0.05
Native Hawaiian (3)	20	0.07
Samoan (7)	10	0.03
Tongan (27)	29	0.10
White (20,459)	21,647	74.71
Not Hispanic (19,642)	20,716	71.49
Hispanic (817)	931	3.21

Los Angeles

Place Type: City
County: Los Angeles
Population: 3,792,621†

Ancestry‡	Population	%
Afghan (2,245)	2,434	0.06
African, Sub-Saharan (44,842)	51,431	1.36
African (34,439)	39,515	1.05
Cape Verdean (118)	198	0.01
Ethiopian (3,611)	3,896	0.10
Ghanaian (548)	587	0.02
Kenyan (327)	336	0.01
Liberian (76)	76	<0.01
Nigerian (2,870)	3,268	0.09
Senegalese (164)	164	<0.01
Sierra Leonean (82)	121	<0.01
South African (1,120)	1,463	0.04
Sudanese (109)	184	<0.01
Ugandan (455)	491	0.01
Zimbabwean (74)	101	<0.01
Other Sub-Saharan African (849)	1,031	0.03
Albanian (164)	335	0.01
Alsatian (20)	78	<0.01
American (68,094)	68,094	1.81
Arab (20,422)	30,066	0.80
Arab (2,382)	3,096	0.08
Egyptian (4,964)	6,033	0.16
Iraqi (659)	1,444	0.04
Jordanian (1,094)	1,238	0.03
Lebanese (4,390)	8,079	0.21
Moroccan (1,441)	2,098	0.06
Palestinian (625)	947	0.03
Syrian (1,761)	2,954	0.08
Other Arab (3,106)	4,177	0.11
Armenian (67,869)	73,256	1.94
Assyrian/Chaldean/Syriac (1,238)	1,479	0.04
Australian (1,627)	2,486	0.07
Austrian (3,249)	11,090	0.29
Basque (195)	741	0.02
Belgian (819)	2,001	0.05
Brazilian (2,864)	3,962	0.11
British (6,774)	12,180	0.32
Bulgarian (1,850)	2,293	0.06
Cajun (50)	153	<0.01
Canadian (4,548)	7,817	0.21
Carpatho Rusyn (7)	80	<0.01
Celtic (192)	654	0.02
Croatian (3,875)	6,277	0.17
Cypriot (52)	69	<0.01
Czech (1,893)	6,899	0.18
Czechoslovakian (816)	1,806	0.05
Danish (2,465)	9,510	0.25
Dutch (4,418)	17,897	0.47
Eastern European (12,383)	14,001	0.37
English (32,884)	129,873	3.44
Estonian (186)	347	0.01
European (27,406)	33,149	0.88
Finnish (1,054)	2,919	0.08
French, ex. Basque (9,775)	46,698	1.24
French Canadian (3,034)	6,978	0.18
German (45,269)	177,061	4.69
German Russian (111)	145	<0.01
Greek (6,423)	12,497	0.33
Guyanese (250)	437	0.01

*Notes: † The Census 2010 population figure is used to calculate the percentages in the Hispanic Origin and Race categories. Ancestry percentages are based on the 2006-2010 American Community Survey population (not shown); ‡ Numbers in parentheses indicate the number of people reporting a single ancestry; * Numbers in parentheses indicate the number of persons reporting this race alone, not in combination with any other race; Please refer to the Explanation of Data for more information.*

Hungarian (6,434)	16,285	0.43
Icelander (269)	380	0.01
Iranian (47,100)	51,547	1.37
Irish (36,683)	147,342	3.91
Israeli (9,984)	12,294	0.33
Italian (39,779)	101,064	2.68
Latvian (1,116)	2,043	0.05
Lithuanian (2,509)	6,875	0.18
Luxemburger (73)	253	0.01
Macedonian (352)	473	0.01
Maltese (164)	279	0.01
New Zealander (351)	502	0.01
Northern European (1,712)	1,975	0.05
Norwegian (6,731)	20,565	0.55
Pennsylvania German (196)	440	0.01
Polish (17,994)	60,010	1.59
Portuguese (2,915)	7,722	0.20
Romanian (5,610)	10,676	0.28
Russian (49,568)	96,251	2.55
Scandinavian (2,082)	4,130	0.11
Scotch-Irish (7,498)	21,996	0.58
Scottish (7,629)	29,120	0.77
Serbian (774)	1,315	0.03
Slavic (271)	742	0.02
Slovak (654)	1,904	0.05
Slovene (175)	730	0.02
Soviet Union (82)	105	<0.01
Swedish (6,007)	23,723	0.63
Swiss (1,678)	5,328	0.14
Turkish (1,961)	3,354	0.09
Ukrainian (7,070)	11,493	0.30
Welsh (1,655)	10,583	0.28
West Indian, ex. Hispanic (13,757)	17,886	0.47
Bahamian (88)	166	<0.01
Barbadian (128)	202	0.01
Belizean (7,369)	8,719	0.23
Bermudan (80)	118	<0.01
British West Indian (235)	308	0.01
Dutch West Indian (0)	71	<0.01
Haitian (1,109)	1,526	0.04
Jamaican (3,172)	4,559	0.12
Trinidadian/Tobagonian (469)	631	0.02
U.S. Virgin Islander (33)	77	<0.01
West Indian (1,056)	1,476	0.04
Other West Indian (18)	33	<0.01
Yugoslavian (1,137)	2,313	0.06

Hispanic Origin	Population	%
Hispanic or Latino (of any race)	1,838,822	48.48
Central American, ex. Mexican	415,913	10.97
Costa Rican	3,182	0.08
Guatemalan	138,139	3.64
Honduran	23,919	0.63
Nicaraguan	15,572	0.41
Panamanian	2,131	0.06
Salvadoran	228,990	6.04
Other Central American	3,980	0.10
Cuban	13,494	0.36
Dominican Republic	1,602	0.04
Mexican	1,209,573	31.89
Puerto Rican	15,565	0.41
South American	49,352	1.30
Argentinean	8,570	0.23
Bolivian	2,561	0.07
Chilean	4,112	0.11
Colombian	9,766	0.26
Ecuadorian	7,314	0.19
Paraguayan	180	<0.01
Peruvian	14,033	0.37
Uruguayan	697	0.02
Venezuelan	1,490	0.04
Other South American	629	0.02
Other Hispanic or Latino	133,323	3.52

Race*	Population	%
African-American/Black (365,118)	402,448	10.61
Not Hispanic (347,380)	372,821	9.83
Hispanic (17,738)	29,627	0.78
American Indian/Alaska Native (28,215)	54,236	1.43
Not Hispanic (6,589)	19,510	0.51
Hispanic (21,626)	34,726	0.92
Alaska Athabascan *(Ala. Nat.)* (23)	49	<0.01
Aleut *(Alaska Native)* (14)	35	<0.01
Apache (691)	1,531	0.04
Arapaho (10)	24	<0.01
Blackfeet (108)	966	0.03
Canadian/French Am. Ind. (57)	119	<0.01
Central American Ind. (959)	1,602	0.04
Cherokee (881)	4,661	0.12
Cheyenne (22)	77	<0.01
Chickasaw (65)	207	0.01
Chippewa (134)	331	0.01
Choctaw (243)	1,133	0.03
Colville (12)	27	<0.01
Comanche (58)	145	<0.01
Cree (15)	66	<0.01
Creek (108)	334	0.01
Crow (11)	44	<0.01
Delaware (28)	80	<0.01
Hopi (85)	163	<0.01
Houma (0)	10	<0.01
Inupiat *(Alaska Native)* (23)	56	<0.01
Iroquois (112)	321	0.01
Kiowa (35)	49	<0.01
Lumbee (20)	59	<0.01
Menominee (11)	18	<0.01
Mexican American Ind. (6,740)	9,589	0.25
Navajo (740)	1,260	0.03
Osage (27)	107	<0.01
Ottawa (9)	24	<0.01
Paiute (45)	86	<0.01
Pima (69)	152	<0.01
Potawatomi (40)	115	<0.01
Pueblo (261)	493	0.01
Puget Sound Salish (7)	22	<0.01
Seminole (41)	234	0.01
Shoshone (74)	116	<0.01
Sioux (267)	661	0.02
South American Ind. (243)	595	0.02
Spanish American Ind. (351)	564	0.01
Tlingit-Haida *(Alaska Native)* (30)	69	<0.01
Tohono O'Odham (150)	220	0.01
Tsimshian *(Alaska Native)* (6)	14	<0.01
Ute (27)	48	<0.01
Yakama (7)	15	<0.01
Yaqui (314)	647	0.02
Yuman (75)	105	<0.01
Yup'ik *(Alaska Native)* (5)	17	<0.01
Asian (426,959)	483,585	12.75
Not Hispanic (420,212)	465,942	12.29
Hispanic (6,747)	17,643	0.47
Bangladeshi (3,098)	3,483	0.09
Bhutanese (35)	36	<0.01
Burmese (673)	842	0.02
Cambodian (3,446)	4,280	0.11
Chinese, ex. Taiwanese (61,950)	75,827	2.00
Filipino (122,787)	139,859	3.69
Hmong (131)	149	<0.01
Indian (32,996)	38,574	1.02
Indonesian (2,544)	3,670	0.10
Japanese (32,619)	43,978	1.16
Korean (108,282)	114,140	3.01
Laotian (635)	871	0.02
Malaysian (190)	342	0.01
Nepalese (347)	387	0.01
Pakistani (3,411)	3,973	0.10
Sri Lankan (2,058)	2,358	0.06
Taiwanese (4,559)	5,282	0.14
Thai (12,349)	14,122	0.37
Vietnamese (19,969)	23,325	0.62
Hawaii Native/Pacific Islander (5,577)	15,031	0.40
Not Hispanic (4,300)	10,779	0.28
Hispanic (1,277)	4,252	0.11
Fijian (329)	420	0.01
Guamanian/Chamorro (1,103)	1,840	0.05
Marshallese (2)	3	<0.01
Native Hawaiian (1,209)	4,062	0.11
Samoan (1,504)	2,480	0.07
Tongan (502)	649	0.02
White (1,888,158)	2,031,586	53.57
Not Hispanic (1,086,908)	1,148,305	30.28
Hispanic (801,250)	883,281	23.29

Los Banos

Place Type: City
County: Merced
Population: 35,972†

Ancestry‡	Population	%
Afghan (18)	18	0.05
American (391)	391	1.13
Arab (8)	8	0.02
Lebanese (8)	8	0.02
Basque (11)	24	0.07
Brazilian (15)	15	0.04
British (29)	50	0.14
Canadian (16)	16	0.05
Czech (16)	16	0.05
Czechoslovakian (0)	35	0.10
Danish (12)	31	0.09
Dutch (12)	81	0.23
English (450)	1,210	3.50
European (60)	111	0.32
French, ex. Basque (82)	359	1.04
French Canadian (0)	13	0.04
German (488)	1,812	5.24
Greek (0)	34	0.10
Hungarian (32)	32	0.09
Iranian (46)	46	0.13
Irish (308)	1,479	4.28
Italian (367)	1,086	3.14
Norwegian (48)	333	0.96
Polish (131)	183	0.53
Portuguese (1,309)	1,870	5.41
Russian (0)	7	0.02
Scandinavian (13)	13	0.04
Scotch-Irish (23)	87	0.25
Scottish (10)	106	0.31
Swedish (45)	235	0.68
Swiss (0)	79	0.23
Welsh (0)	29	0.08

Hispanic Origin	Population	%
Hispanic or Latino (of any race)	23,346	64.90
Central American, ex. Mexican	531	1.48
Costa Rican	11	0.03
Guatemalan	77	0.21
Honduran	47	0.13
Nicaraguan	65	0.18
Panamanian	11	0.03
Salvadoran	312	0.87
Other Central American	8	0.02
Cuban	47	0.13
Dominican Republic	1	<0.01
Mexican	21,344	59.34
Puerto Rican	226	0.63
South American	160	0.44
Argentinean	16	0.04
Bolivian	9	0.03
Chilean	15	0.04
Colombian	28	0.08
Ecuadorian	10	0.03
Peruvian	70	0.19
Uruguayan	4	0.01
Other South American	8	0.02
Other Hispanic or Latino	1,037	2.88

Race*	Population	%
African-American/Black (1,354)	1,669	4.64
Not Hispanic (1,154)	1,328	3.69
Hispanic (200)	341	0.95
American Indian/Alaska Native (512)	878	2.44
Not Hispanic (142)	314	0.87
Hispanic (370)	564	1.57
Apache (35)	69	0.19
Blackfeet (1)	14	0.04
Canadian/French Am. Ind. (0)	3	0.01
Central American Ind. (1)	1	<0.01
Cherokee (30)	99	0.28

*Notes: † The Census 2010 population figure is used to calculate the percentages in the Hispanic Origin and Race categories. Ancestry percentages are based on the 2006-2010 American Community Survey population (not shown); ‡ Numbers in parentheses indicate the number of people reporting a single ancestry; * Numbers in parentheses indicate the number of persons reporting this race alone, not in combination with any other race; Please refer to the Explanation of Data for more information.*

Chickasaw (1)	3	0.01
Chippewa (3)	3	0.01
Choctaw (14)	22	0.06
Comanche (6)	7	0.02
Creek (0)	3	0.01
Delaware (1)	1	<0.01
Hopi (0)	2	0.01
Mexican American Ind. (77)	116	0.32
Navajo (2)	12	0.03
Osage (1)	3	0.01
Paiute (3)	3	0.01
Pima (0)	6	0.02
Potawatomi (2)	12	0.03
Pueblo (1)	1	<0.01
Seminole (1)	4	0.01
Sioux (8)	9	0.03
South American Ind. (0)	2	0.01
Spanish American Ind. (9)	9	0.03
Tlingit-Haida *(Alaska Native)* (1)	1	<0.01
Yaqui (9)	16	0.04
Asian (1,162)	1,611	4.48
Not Hispanic (1,004)	1,249	3.47
Hispanic (158)	362	1.01
Cambodian (40)	49	0.14
Chinese, ex. Taiwanese (129)	191	0.53
Filipino (507)	751	2.09
Hmong (1)	1	<0.01
Indian (257)	307	0.85
Indonesian (8)	19	0.05
Japanese (60)	116	0.32
Korean (39)	62	0.17
Laotian (12)	14	0.04
Pakistani (4)	4	0.01
Taiwanese (4)	5	0.01
Thai (3)	10	0.03
Vietnamese (63)	73	0.20
Hawaii Native/Pacific Islander (134)	305	0.85
Not Hispanic (116)	222	0.62
Hispanic (18)	83	0.23
Fijian (2)	2	0.01
Guamanian/Chamorro (24)	40	0.11
Native Hawaiian (19)	76	0.21
Samoan (69)	113	0.31
Tongan (10)	15	0.04
White (20,846)	22,362	62.17
Not Hispanic (9,521)	10,029	27.88
Hispanic (11,325)	12,333	34.28

Los Gatos

Place Type: Town
County: Santa Clara
Population: 29,413†

Ancestry‡	Population	%
African, Sub-Saharan (27)	27	0.09
Ethiopian (27)	27	0.09
Albanian (10)	10	0.03
Alsatian (7)	7	0.02
American (838)	838	2.90
Arab (128)	176	0.61
Arab (16)	16	0.06
Egyptian (20)	20	0.07
Lebanese (72)	110	0.38
Syrian (6)	6	0.02
Other Arab (14)	24	0.08
Armenian (9)	9	0.03
Assyrian/Chaldean/Syriac (67)	67	0.23
Australian (13)	13	0.05
Austrian (69)	118	0.41
Basque (0)	18	0.06
Belgian (14)	44	0.15
Brazilian (68)	68	0.24
British (224)	334	1.16
Bulgarian (25)	25	0.09
Canadian (101)	119	0.41
Celtic (10)	10	0.03
Croatian (77)	205	0.71
Czech (17)	131	0.45
Czechoslovakian (16)	32	0.11
Danish (160)	399	1.38
Dutch (213)	390	1.35
Eastern European (146)	146	0.51
English (1,012)	3,983	13.79
Estonian (12)	61	0.21
European (630)	732	2.53
Finnish (0)	82	0.28
French, ex. Basque (442)	1,251	4.33
French Canadian (58)	149	0.52
German (1,258)	5,618	19.45
Greek (158)	337	1.17
Hungarian (60)	126	0.44
Icelander (0)	20	0.07
Iranian (434)	446	1.54
Irish (1,306)	3,979	13.78
Israeli (10)	17	0.06
Italian (926)	2,569	8.90
Latvian (0)	8	0.03
Lithuanian (12)	73	0.25
Luxemburger (0)	9	0.03
Northern European (266)	273	0.95
Norwegian (160)	654	2.26
Pennsylvania German (0)	24	0.08
Polish (194)	612	2.12
Portuguese (262)	605	2.10
Romanian (0)	14	0.05
Russian (711)	951	3.29
Scandinavian (58)	181	0.63
Scotch-Irish (176)	581	2.01
Scottish (362)	890	3.08
Serbian (19)	120	0.42
Slavic (43)	43	0.15
Slovak (27)	52	0.18
Slovene (11)	35	0.12
Swedish (175)	794	2.75
Swiss (117)	353	1.22
Turkish (84)	84	0.29
Ukrainian (46)	119	0.41
Welsh (120)	473	1.64
Yugoslavian (44)	114	0.39

Hispanic Origin	Population	%
Hispanic or Latino (of any race)	2,120	7.21
Central American, ex. Mexican	129	0.44
Costa Rican	7	0.02
Guatemalan	26	0.09
Honduran	18	0.06
Nicaraguan	26	0.09
Panamanian	8	0.03
Salvadoran	43	0.15
Other Central American	1	<0.01
Cuban	40	0.14
Dominican Republic	4	0.01
Mexican	1,295	4.40
Puerto Rican	79	0.27
South American	227	0.77
Argentinean	36	0.12
Bolivian	15	0.05
Chilean	16	0.05
Colombian	41	0.14
Ecuadorian	16	0.05
Peruvian	81	0.28
Uruguayan	4	0.01
Venezuelan	13	0.04
Other South American	5	0.02
Other Hispanic or Latino	346	1.18

Race*	Population	%
African-American/Black (269)	385	1.31
Not Hispanic (254)	349	1.19
Hispanic (15)	36	0.12
American Indian/Alaska Native (86)	314	1.07
Not Hispanic (51)	206	0.70
Hispanic (35)	108	0.37
Apache (3)	10	0.03
Blackfeet (0)	1	<0.01
Canadian/French Am. Ind. (0)	1	<0.01
Cherokee (6)	53	0.18
Chickasaw (3)	3	0.01
Chippewa (1)	5	0.02
Choctaw (3)	17	0.06
Creek (1)	6	0.02
Hopi (1)	1	<0.01
Iroquois (1)	13	0.04
Mexican American Ind. (8)	16	0.05
Navajo (2)	3	0.01
Paiute (3)	3	0.01
Potawatomi (1)	1	<0.01
Pueblo (1)	2	0.01
Seminole (0)	1	<0.01
Shoshone (1)	1	<0.01
Sioux (1)	8	0.03
South American Ind. (1)	4	0.01
Tlingit-Haida *(Alaska Native)* (2)	2	0.01
Tohono O'Odham (0)	1	<0.01
Yaqui (2)	6	0.02
Asian (3,203)	4,052	13.78
Not Hispanic (3,177)	3,965	13.48
Hispanic (26)	87	0.30
Bangladeshi (10)	12	0.04
Cambodian (11)	13	0.04
Chinese, ex. Taiwanese (932)	1,201	4.08
Filipino (267)	435	1.48
Indian (600)	679	2.31
Indonesian (8)	21	0.07
Japanese (437)	648	2.20
Korean (321)	383	1.30
Laotian (12)	16	0.05
Malaysian (2)	5	0.02
Nepalese (3)	4	0.01
Pakistani (34)	43	0.15
Sri Lankan (18)	19	0.06
Taiwanese (100)	132	0.45
Thai (9)	14	0.05
Vietnamese (312)	373	1.27
Hawaii Native/Pacific Islander (52)	140	0.48
Not Hispanic (43)	117	0.40
Hispanic (9)	23	0.08
Fijian (2)	3	0.01
Guamanian/Chamorro (9)	19	0.06
Native Hawaiian (15)	56	0.19
Samoan (4)	4	0.01
Tongan (10)	10	0.03
White (24,060)	25,259	85.88
Not Hispanic (22,657)	23,644	80.39
Hispanic (1,403)	1,615	5.49

Los Osos

Place Type: CDP
County: San Luis Obispo
Population: 14,276†

Ancestry‡	Population	%
American (507)	507	3.40
Arab (31)	91	0.61
Lebanese (0)	60	0.40
Other Arab (31)	31	0.21
Armenian (24)	24	0.16
Austrian (22)	110	0.74
Belgian (0)	14	0.09
British (45)	130	0.87
Canadian (48)	48	0.32
Croatian (17)	17	0.11
Czech (11)	41	0.27
Czechoslovakian (0)	9	0.06
Danish (24)	239	1.60
Dutch (107)	329	2.20
Eastern European (48)	48	0.32
English (793)	2,311	15.49
European (320)	388	2.60
Finnish (39)	77	0.52
French, ex. Basque (155)	675	4.52
French Canadian (13)	87	0.58
German (909)	3,180	21.31
Greek (23)	23	0.15
Hungarian (19)	63	0.42
Irish (386)	2,035	13.64
Italian (400)	911	6.10
Latvian (13)	13	0.09

*Notes: † The Census 2010 population figure is used to calculate the percentages in the Hispanic Origin and Race categories. Ancestry percentages are based on the 2006-2010 American Community Survey population (not shown); ‡ Numbers in parentheses indicate the number of people reporting a single ancestry; * Numbers in parentheses indicate the number of persons reporting this race alone, not in combination with any other race; Please refer to the Explanation of Data for more information.*

Northern European (80)	80	0.54
Norwegian (90)	228	1.53
Pennsylvania German (0)	9	0.06
Polish (24)	130	0.87
Portuguese (31)	108	0.72
Romanian (0)	26	0.17
Russian (102)	185	1.24
Scandinavian (106)	201	1.35
Scotch-Irish (121)	527	3.53
Scottish (230)	660	4.42
Serbian (0)	15	0.10
Slavic (0)	12	0.08
Slovak (9)	9	0.06
Swedish (184)	445	2.98
Swiss (10)	97	0.65
Ukrainian (10)	19	0.13
Welsh (0)	90	0.60

Hispanic Origin	Population	%
Hispanic or Latino (of any race)	1,977	13.85
Central American, ex. Mexican	54	0.38
Costa Rican	2	0.01
Guatemalan	24	0.17
Honduran	3	0.02
Nicaraguan	4	0.03
Panamanian	1	0.01
Salvadoran	20	0.14
Cuban	17	0.12
Mexican	1,647	11.54
Puerto Rican	36	0.25
South American	58	0.41
Argentinean	11	0.08
Chilean	8	0.06
Colombian	11	0.08
Ecuadorian	13	0.09
Peruvian	10	0.07
Uruguayan	1	0.01
Venezuelan	2	0.01
Other South American	2	0.01
Other Hispanic or Latino	165	1.16

Race*	Population	%
African-American/Black (79)	141	0.99
Not Hispanic (65)	109	0.76
Hispanic (14)	32	0.22
American Indian/Alaska Native (97)	279	1.95
Not Hispanic (50)	183	1.28
Hispanic (47)	96	0.67
Apache (2)	9	0.06
Blackfeet (8)	16	0.11
Central American Ind. (2)	2	0.01
Cherokee (6)	36	0.25
Cheyenne (5)	5	0.04
Chickasaw (0)	6	0.04
Chippewa (5)	6	0.04
Choctaw (5)	22	0.15
Comanche (0)	1	0.01
Cree (1)	2	0.01
Creek (0)	1	0.01
Crow (0)	1	0.01
Hopi (0)	1	0.01
Iroquois (1)	3	0.02
Mexican American Ind. (4)	8	0.06
Navajo (4)	7	0.05
Paiute (2)	7	0.05
Potawatomi (2)	4	0.03
Pueblo (1)	3	0.02
Seminole (0)	1	0.01
Sioux (0)	1	0.01
Tlingit-Haida *(Alaska Native)* (1)	1	0.01
Yaqui (1)	2	0.01
Asian (748)	921	6.45
Not Hispanic (728)	868	6.08
Hispanic (20)	53	0.37
Bhutanese (3)	3	0.02
Burmese (1)	4	0.03
Chinese, ex. Taiwanese (48)	87	0.61
Filipino (536)	602	4.22
Indian (24)	35	0.25
Indonesian (4)	12	0.08
Japanese (79)	138	0.97
Korean (17)	20	0.14
Laotian (1)	2	0.01
Malaysian (0)	1	0.01
Taiwanese (2)	10	0.07
Thai (6)	6	0.04
Vietnamese (8)	11	0.08
Hawaii Native/Pacific Islander (18)	62	0.43
Not Hispanic (16)	49	0.34
Hispanic (2)	13	0.09
Fijian (2)	4	0.03
Guamanian/Chamorro (0)	4	0.03
Native Hawaiian (11)	34	0.24
Samoan (2)	4	0.03
White (12,304)	12,763	89.40
Not Hispanic (11,092)	11,409	79.92
Hispanic (1,212)	1,354	9.48

Lynwood

Place Type: City
County: Los Angeles
Population: 69,772†

Ancestry‡	Population	%
African, Sub-Saharan (525)	662	0.95
African (525)	662	0.95
American (1,380)	1,380	1.98
Arab (34)	62	0.09
Iraqi (28)	28	0.04
Lebanese (6)	6	0.01
Other Arab (0)	28	0.04
Armenian (6)	6	0.01
Czech (10)	10	0.01
Danish (0)	9	0.01
Dutch (0)	9	0.01
English (113)	263	0.38
European (0)	9	0.01
French, ex. Basque (8)	75	0.11
French Canadian (8)	14	0.02
German (189)	390	0.56
Greek (22)	30	0.04
Hungarian (0)	16	0.02
Iranian (6)	6	0.01
Irish (29)	307	0.44
Israeli (0)	8	0.01
Italian (36)	186	0.27
Norwegian (0)	42	0.06
Pennsylvania German (0)	11	0.02
Polish (55)	84	0.12
Portuguese (0)	28	0.04
Russian (93)	101	0.14
Scotch-Irish (28)	28	0.04
Scottish (0)	75	0.11
Swedish (0)	14	0.02
Ukrainian (0)	8	0.01
Welsh (0)	7	0.01
West Indian, ex. Hispanic (68)	120	0.17
Belizean (40)	48	0.07
Jamaican (16)	16	0.02
Trinidadian/Tobagonian (0)	44	0.06
West Indian (12)	12	0.02

Hispanic Origin	Population	%
Hispanic or Latino (of any race)	60,452	86.64
Central American, ex. Mexican	5,761	8.26
Costa Rican	15	0.02
Guatemalan	1,754	2.51
Honduran	420	0.60
Nicaraguan	315	0.45
Panamanian	25	0.04
Salvadoran	3,154	4.52
Other Central American	78	0.11
Cuban	110	0.16
Dominican Republic	13	0.02
Mexican	51,021	73.13
Puerto Rican	192	0.28
South American	349	0.50
Argentinean	26	0.04
Bolivian	13	0.02
Chilean	9	0.01
Colombian	29	0.04
Ecuadorian	128	0.18
Peruvian	137	0.20
Uruguayan	3	<0.01
Venezuelan	3	<0.01
Other South American	1	<0.01
Other Hispanic or Latino	3,006	4.31

Race*	Population	%
African-American/Black (7,168)	7,602	10.90
Not Hispanic (6,752)	6,922	9.92
Hispanic (416)	680	0.97
American Indian/Alaska Native (464)	753	1.08
Not Hispanic (76)	152	0.22
Hispanic (388)	601	0.86
Apache (3)	7	0.01
Blackfeet (0)	3	<0.01
Canadian/French Am. Ind. (0)	1	<0.01
Central American Ind. (6)	10	0.01
Cherokee (9)	37	0.05
Chippewa (0)	4	0.01
Choctaw (8)	15	0.02
Cree (0)	3	<0.01
Creek (0)	1	<0.01
Delaware (1)	2	<0.01
Mexican American Ind. (128)	190	0.27
Navajo (9)	18	0.03
Pima (1)	3	<0.01
Pueblo (3)	7	0.01
Sioux (3)	3	<0.01
South American Ind. (1)	1	<0.01
Spanish American Ind. (4)	13	0.02
Tohono O'Odham (6)	6	0.01
Yuman (0)	3	<0.01
Asian (457)	603	0.86
Not Hispanic (390)	442	0.63
Hispanic (67)	161	0.23
Cambodian (6)	8	0.01
Chinese, ex. Taiwanese (31)	50	0.07
Filipino (120)	174	0.25
Indian (91)	106	0.15
Indonesian (5)	6	0.01
Japanese (12)	18	0.03
Korean (44)	51	0.07
Laotian (67)	73	0.10
Pakistani (1)	1	<0.01
Taiwanese (0)	1	<0.01
Thai (40)	57	0.08
Vietnamese (18)	19	0.03
Hawaii Native/Pacific Islander (206)	294	0.42
Not Hispanic (170)	204	0.29
Hispanic (36)	90	0.13
Fijian (0)	1	<0.01
Guamanian/Chamorro (10)	21	0.03
Native Hawaiian (6)	23	0.03
Samoan (171)	198	0.28
Tongan (12)	14	0.02
White (27,444)	29,384	42.11
Not Hispanic (1,539)	1,673	2.40
Hispanic (25,905)	27,711	39.72

Madera Acres

Place Type: CDP
County: Madera
Population: 9,163†

Ancestry‡	Population	%
American (111)	111	1.22
Arab (109)	109	1.20
Other Arab (109)	109	1.20
Danish (26)	68	0.75
Dutch (17)	112	1.24
English (103)	380	4.19
European (31)	48	0.53
French, ex. Basque (0)	160	1.77
French Canadian (9)	9	0.10
German (183)	723	7.98
Greek (12)	12	0.13

*Notes: † The Census 2010 population figure is used to calculate the percentages in the Hispanic Origin and Race categories. Ancestry percentages are based on the 2006-2010 American Community Survey population (not shown); ‡ Numbers in parentheses indicate the number of people reporting a single ancestry; * Numbers in parentheses indicate the number of persons reporting this race alone, not in combination with any other race; Please refer to the Explanation of Data for more information.*

Ancestry	Population	%
Irish (127)	525	5.79
Italian (164)	231	2.55
Latvian (0)	44	0.49
Norwegian (31)	31	0.34
Polish (0)	11	0.12
Portuguese (6)	6	0.07
Russian (42)	53	0.58
Scotch-Irish (37)	105	1.16
Scottish (23)	53	0.58
Swedish (9)	18	0.20
Welsh (0)	14	0.15

Hispanic Origin	Population	%
Hispanic or Latino (of any race)	5,985	65.32
Central American, ex. Mexican	124	1.35
Costa Rican	3	0.03
Guatemalan	29	0.32
Honduran	13	0.14
Nicaraguan	2	0.02
Panamanian	1	0.01
Salvadoran	74	0.81
Other Central American	2	0.02
Cuban	2	0.02
Mexican	5,469	59.69
Puerto Rican	66	0.72
South American	17	0.19
Argentinean	6	0.07
Chilean	1	0.01
Colombian	6	0.07
Ecuadorian	1	0.01
Peruvian	3	0.03
Other Hispanic or Latino	307	3.35

Race*	Population	%
African-American/Black (241)	303	3.31
Not Hispanic (204)	234	2.55
Hispanic (37)	69	0.75
American Indian/Alaska Native (161)	229	2.50
Not Hispanic (55)	96	1.05
Hispanic (106)	133	1.45
Apache (3)	10	0.11
Arapaho (0)	1	0.01
Blackfeet (1)	2	0.02
Cherokee (10)	30	0.33
Chickasaw (1)	2	0.02
Chippewa (1)	1	0.01
Choctaw (6)	10	0.11
Creek (2)	2	0.02
Mexican American Ind. (33)	33	0.36
Osage (1)	1	0.01
Puget Sound Salish (1)	1	0.01
Seminole (1)	1	0.01
Sioux (1)	1	0.01
South American Ind. (6)	6	0.07
Ute (0)	1	0.01
Yaqui (1)	4	0.04
Yup'ik *(Alaska Native)* (0)	1	0.01
Asian (114)	175	1.91
Not Hispanic (100)	146	1.59
Hispanic (14)	29	0.32
Chinese, ex. Taiwanese (10)	24	0.26
Filipino (24)	47	0.51
Hmong (33)	34	0.37
Indian (19)	26	0.28
Japanese (9)	19	0.21
Korean (7)	11	0.12
Laotian (4)	4	0.04
Malaysian (0)	1	0.01
Taiwanese (2)	3	0.03
Vietnamese (5)	5	0.05
Hawaii Native/Pacific Islander (5)	24	0.26
Not Hispanic (1)	9	0.10
Hispanic (4)	15	0.16
Fijian (1)	1	0.01
Guamanian/Chamorro (1)	1	0.01
Native Hawaiian (3)	11	0.12
Tongan (0)	2	0.02
White (5,838)	6,147	67.09
Not Hispanic (2,696)	2,793	30.48
Hispanic (3,142)	3,354	36.60

Madera

Place Type: City
County: Madera
Population: 61,416†

Ancestry‡	Population	%
African, Sub-Saharan (15)	111	0.19
African (15)	111	0.19
American (565)	565	0.96
Arab (103)	148	0.25
Arab (91)	111	0.19
Lebanese (12)	37	0.06
Armenian (0)	40	0.07
Basque (28)	28	0.05
British (10)	121	0.21
Canadian (0)	11	0.02
Czech (0)	19	0.03
Danish (36)	140	0.24
Dutch (152)	447	0.76
English (402)	1,229	2.08
European (177)	240	0.41
French, ex. Basque (107)	350	0.59
French Canadian (97)	141	0.24
German (517)	1,921	3.26
Greek (0)	25	0.04
Irish (960)	2,219	3.76
Italian (515)	881	1.49
Maltese (16)	16	0.03
Northern European (0)	9	0.02
Norwegian (83)	225	0.38
Polish (88)	117	0.20
Portuguese (573)	827	1.40
Russian (44)	135	0.23
Scandinavian (26)	39	0.07
Scotch-Irish (62)	256	0.43
Scottish (11)	262	0.44
Slovak (0)	11	0.02
Swedish (53)	211	0.36
Swiss (39)	98	0.17
Ukrainian (18)	40	0.07
Welsh (9)	141	0.24

Hispanic Origin	Population	%
Hispanic or Latino (of any race)	47,103	76.69
Central American, ex. Mexican	491	0.80
Costa Rican	4	0.01
Guatemalan	104	0.17
Honduran	53	0.09
Nicaraguan	33	0.05
Panamanian	6	0.01
Salvadoran	287	0.47
Other Central American	4	0.01
Cuban	48	0.08
Dominican Republic	4	0.01
Mexican	44,444	72.37
Puerto Rican	227	0.37
South American	96	0.16
Argentinean	25	0.04
Bolivian	6	0.01
Chilean	5	0.01
Colombian	13	0.02
Ecuadorian	7	0.01
Peruvian	31	0.05
Uruguayan	2	<0.01
Venezuelan	7	0.01
Other Hispanic or Latino	1,793	2.92

Race*	Population	%
African-American/Black (2,069)	2,477	4.03
Not Hispanic (1,661)	1,861	3.03
Hispanic (408)	616	1.00
American Indian/Alaska Native (1,933)	2,471	4.02
Not Hispanic (335)	567	0.92
Hispanic (1,598)	1,904	3.10
Apache (32)	59	0.10
Blackfeet (3)	9	0.01
Canadian/French Am. Ind. (2)	2	<0.01
Central American Ind. (8)	10	0.02
Cherokee (28)	110	0.18
Cheyenne (0)	3	<0.01
Chickasaw (1)	1	<0.01
Chippewa (9)	13	0.02
Choctaw (23)	43	0.07
Comanche (5)	11	0.02
Cree (1)	1	<0.01
Creek (4)	5	0.01
Delaware (0)	1	<0.01
Hopi (1)	1	<0.01
Iroquois (2)	3	<0.01
Kiowa (2)	2	<0.01
Mexican American Ind. (780)	891	1.45
Navajo (18)	28	0.05
Paiute (11)	13	0.02
Pima (0)	4	0.01
Potawatomi (1)	2	<0.01
Pueblo (4)	9	0.01
Seminole (0)	1	<0.01
Shoshone (1)	1	<0.01
Sioux (6)	14	0.02
South American Ind. (9)	9	0.01
Spanish American Ind. (7)	7	0.01
Tohono O'Odham (1)	1	<0.01
Yakama (6)	6	0.01
Yaqui (14)	27	0.04
Yuman (4)	7	0.01
Yup'ik *(Alaska Native)* (0)	3	<0.01
Asian (1,369)	1,825	2.97
Not Hispanic (1,199)	1,452	2.36
Hispanic (170)	373	0.61
Cambodian (32)	40	0.07
Chinese, ex. Taiwanese (109)	147	0.24
Filipino (328)	510	0.83
Hmong (48)	51	0.08
Indian (563)	638	1.04
Indonesian (8)	17	0.03
Japanese (46)	105	0.17
Korean (39)	62	0.10
Laotian (16)	16	0.03
Pakistani (80)	86	0.14
Thai (11)	20	0.03
Vietnamese (30)	37	0.06
Hawaii Native/Pacific Islander (72)	207	0.34
Not Hispanic (35)	75	0.12
Hispanic (37)	132	0.21
Fijian (3)	6	0.01
Guamanian/Chamorro (4)	11	0.02
Native Hawaiian (33)	69	0.11
Samoan (16)	25	0.04
Tongan (0)	1	<0.01
White (30,640)	32,872	53.52
Not Hispanic (10,402)	10,927	17.79
Hispanic (20,238)	21,945	35.73

Magalia

Place Type: CDP
County: Butte
Population: 11,310†

Ancestry‡	Population	%
African, Sub-Saharan (34)	34	0.29
African (34)	34	0.29
American (560)	560	4.81
Armenian (22)	22	0.19
Austrian (83)	83	0.71
Canadian (10)	29	0.25
Czech (0)	14	0.12
Danish (28)	220	1.89
Dutch (86)	378	3.25
English (480)	2,232	19.18
European (652)	694	5.96
Finnish (17)	91	0.78
French, ex. Basque (50)	681	5.85
French Canadian (12)	62	0.53
German (1,166)	3,290	28.26
Greek (12)	12	0.10
Hungarian (0)	34	0.29
Irish (355)	1,802	15.48
Italian (286)	582	5.00

*Notes: † The Census 2010 population figure is used to calculate the percentages in the Hispanic Origin and Race categories. Ancestry percentages are based on the 2006-2010 American Community Survey population (not shown); ‡ Numbers in parentheses indicate the number of people reporting a single ancestry; * Numbers in parentheses indicate the number of persons reporting this race alone, not in combination with any other race; Please refer to the Explanation of Data for more information.*

Lithuanian (0)	21	0.18
Northern European (47)	47	0.40
Norwegian (198)	334	2.87
Polish (115)	217	1.86
Portuguese (27)	107	0.92
Russian (0)	46	0.40
Scandinavian (14)	42	0.36
Scotch-Irish (99)	229	1.97
Scottish (107)	404	3.47
Slovak (0)	17	0.15
Swedish (121)	311	2.67
Swiss (20)	59	0.51
Welsh (0)	242	2.08
Yugoslavian (14)	14	0.12

Hispanic Origin	Population	%
Hispanic or Latino (of any race)	765	6.76
Central American, ex. Mexican	35	0.31
Costa Rican	6	0.05
Guatemalan	11	0.10
Honduran	1	0.01
Nicaraguan	3	0.03
Salvadoran	14	0.12
Cuban	1	0.01
Mexican	564	4.99
Puerto Rican	41	0.36
South American	15	0.13
Argentinean	1	0.01
Bolivian	3	0.03
Chilean	4	0.04
Colombian	1	0.01
Ecuadorian	3	0.03
Peruvian	2	0.02
Uruguayan	1	0.01
Other Hispanic or Latino	109	0.96

Race*	Population	%
African-American/Black (40)	77	0.68
Not Hispanic (39)	71	0.63
Hispanic (1)	6	0.05
American Indian/Alaska Native (141)	408	3.61
Not Hispanic (118)	358	3.17
Hispanic (23)	50	0.44
Alaska Athabascan *(Ala. Nat.)* (0)	1	0.01
Apache (2)	8	0.07
Blackfeet (4)	23	0.20
Cherokee (28)	104	0.92
Chickasaw (1)	3	0.03
Chippewa (1)	11	0.10
Choctaw (4)	18	0.16
Cree (5)	8	0.07
Creek (2)	6	0.05
Crow (1)	2	0.02
Delaware (4)	5	0.04
Hopi (0)	1	0.01
Iroquois (2)	5	0.04
Mexican American Ind. (2)	10	0.09
Navajo (0)	3	0.03
Paiute (4)	5	0.04
Potawatomi (0)	1	0.01
Seminole (1)	1	0.01
Sioux (3)	17	0.15
Spanish American Ind. (0)	1	0.01
Tlingit-Haida *(Alaska Native)* (1)	4	0.04
Yaqui (3)	4	0.04
Asian (90)	201	1.78
Not Hispanic (87)	183	1.62
Hispanic (3)	18	0.16
Chinese, ex. Taiwanese (12)	25	0.22
Filipino (23)	64	0.57
Hmong (3)	5	0.04
Indian (9)	18	0.16
Indonesian (3)	3	0.03
Japanese (15)	39	0.34
Korean (13)	26	0.23
Malaysian (1)	2	0.02
Thai (5)	6	0.05
Vietnamese (2)	10	0.09
Hawaii Native/Pacific Islander (17)	38	0.34
Not Hispanic (17)	35	0.31
Hispanic (0)	3	0.03
Fijian (3)	3	0.03
Guamanian/Chamorro (1)	1	0.01
Native Hawaiian (8)	21	0.19
Samoan (2)	2	0.02
White (10,398)	10,872	96.13
Not Hispanic (9,893)	10,260	90.72
Hispanic (505)	612	5.41

Malibu

Place Type: City
County: Los Angeles
Population: 12,645†

Ancestry‡	Population	%
African, Sub-Saharan (0)	38	0.30
African (0)	22	0.17
South African (0)	16	0.13
Albanian (10)	10	0.08
American (831)	831	6.50
Arab (33)	59	0.46
Arab (20)	20	0.16
Iraqi (13)	13	0.10
Lebanese (0)	18	0.14
Other Arab (0)	8	0.06
Australian (38)	38	0.30
Austrian (71)	163	1.27
Belgian (0)	53	0.41
Brazilian (14)	14	0.11
British (109)	208	1.63
Bulgarian (0)	17	0.13
Canadian (60)	68	0.53
Croatian (0)	11	0.09
Czech (57)	93	0.73
Danish (14)	120	0.94
Dutch (10)	147	1.15
Eastern European (72)	94	0.73
English (377)	2,156	16.85
Estonian (0)	25	0.20
European (511)	519	4.06
Finnish (0)	13	0.10
French, ex. Basque (79)	415	3.24
French Canadian (19)	27	0.21
German (444)	2,036	15.91
Greek (176)	228	1.78
Guyanese (0)	38	0.30
Hungarian (40)	146	1.14
Icelander (0)	36	0.28
Iranian (175)	175	1.37
Irish (424)	1,894	14.80
Italian (380)	948	7.41
Latvian (0)	25	0.20
Lithuanian (9)	24	0.19
Northern European (16)	16	0.13
Norwegian (60)	236	1.84
Polish (145)	408	3.19
Portuguese (14)	75	0.59
Romanian (24)	37	0.29
Russian (324)	699	5.46
Scotch-Irish (66)	264	2.06
Scottish (78)	552	4.31
Serbian (11)	18	0.14
Slovak (10)	20	0.16
Swedish (75)	324	2.53
Swiss (70)	143	1.12
Turkish (29)	55	0.43
Ukrainian (0)	41	0.32
Welsh (13)	186	1.45
Yugoslavian (17)	36	0.28

Hispanic Origin	Population	%
Hispanic or Latino (of any race)	769	6.08
Central American, ex. Mexican	88	0.70
Costa Rican	4	0.03
Guatemalan	24	0.19
Honduran	1	0.01
Nicaraguan	6	0.05
Panamanian	2	0.02
Salvadoran	51	0.40
Cuban	29	0.23
Mexican	450	3.56
Puerto Rican	26	0.21
South American	81	0.64
Argentinean	28	0.22
Bolivian	3	0.02
Chilean	14	0.11
Colombian	18	0.14
Ecuadorian	1	0.01
Peruvian	12	0.09
Uruguayan	1	0.01
Venezuelan	4	0.03
Other Hispanic or Latino	95	0.75

Race*	Population	%
African-American/Black (148)	210	1.66
Not Hispanic (137)	191	1.51
Hispanic (11)	19	0.15
American Indian/Alaska Native (20)	115	0.91
Not Hispanic (17)	95	0.75
Hispanic (3)	20	0.16
Apache (0)	3	0.02
Cherokee (4)	25	0.20
Chickasaw (0)	1	0.01
Chippewa (2)	2	0.02
Choctaw (0)	1	0.01
Comanche (0)	2	0.02
Iroquois (0)	1	0.01
Menominee (2)	2	0.02
Mexican American Ind. (0)	2	0.02
Osage (0)	1	0.01
Ottawa (1)	1	0.01
Pima (0)	3	0.02
Pueblo (0)	1	0.01
Sioux (1)	3	0.02
South American Ind. (0)	1	0.01
Yaqui (3)	4	0.03
Asian (328)	537	4.25
Not Hispanic (323)	514	4.06
Hispanic (5)	23	0.18
Bangladeshi (1)	1	0.01
Cambodian (1)	1	0.01
Chinese, ex. Taiwanese (88)	137	1.08
Filipino (63)	111	0.88
Indian (34)	49	0.39
Indonesian (2)	5	0.04
Japanese (54)	88	0.70
Korean (38)	64	0.51
Malaysian (0)	8	0.06
Pakistani (1)	3	0.02
Sri Lankan (1)	2	0.02
Taiwanese (11)	12	0.09
Thai (6)	6	0.05
Vietnamese (18)	21	0.17
Hawaii Native/Pacific Islander (15)	47	0.37
Not Hispanic (15)	44	0.35
Hispanic (0)	3	0.02
Native Hawaiian (13)	23	0.18
Samoan (1)	5	0.04
White (11,565)	11,910	94.19
Not Hispanic (11,046)	11,331	89.61
Hispanic (519)	579	4.58

Mammoth Lakes

Place Type: Town
County: Mono
Population: 8,234†

Ancestry‡	Population	%
American (42)	42	0.52
Arab (42)	42	0.52
Lebanese (42)	42	0.52
Armenian (122)	122	1.52
Austrian (0)	17	0.21
Basque (0)	206	2.57
British (27)	27	0.34
Canadian (0)	55	0.69
Croatian (16)	63	0.79
Danish (0)	28	0.35

*Notes: † The Census 2010 population figure is used to calculate the percentages in the Hispanic Origin and Race categories. Ancestry percentages are based on the 2006-2010 American Community Survey population (not shown); ‡ Numbers in parentheses indicate the number of people reporting a single ancestry; * Numbers in parentheses indicate the number of persons reporting this race alone, not in combination with any other race; Please refer to the Explanation of Data for more information.*

SECTION TWO

Dutch (145)	163	2.04
English (238)	849	10.61
European (37)	98	1.22
French, ex. Basque (100)	120	1.50
French Canadian (0)	13	0.16
German (314)	1,077	13.45
Greek (36)	36	0.45
Icelander (35)	35	0.44
Irish (431)	1,234	15.42
Italian (61)	429	5.36
Lithuanian (55)	55	0.69
Norwegian (0)	83	1.04
Pennsylvania German (53)	118	1.47
Polish (12)	67	0.84
Russian (219)	244	3.05
Scotch-Irish (62)	276	3.45
Scottish (139)	252	3.15
Slovene (0)	21	0.26
Swedish (81)	242	3.02
Swiss (0)	69	0.86

Hispanic Origin	Population	%
Hispanic or Latino (of any race)	2,772	33.67
Central American, ex. Mexican	45	0.55
Costa Rican	2	0.02
Guatemalan	6	0.07
Honduran	12	0.15
Nicaraguan	1	0.01
Salvadoran	24	0.29
Cuban	13	0.16
Dominican Republic	2	0.02
Mexican	2,413	29.31
Puerto Rican	13	0.16
South American	60	0.73
Argentinean	9	0.11
Chilean	31	0.38
Colombian	9	0.11
Ecuadorian	1	0.01
Peruvian	6	0.07
Uruguayan	3	0.04
Venezuelan	1	0.01
Other Hispanic or Latino	226	2.74

Race*	Population	%
African-American/Black (29)	60	0.73
Not Hispanic (29)	57	0.69
Hispanic (0)	3	0.04
American Indian/Alaska Native (49)	93	1.13
Not Hispanic (32)	58	0.70
Hispanic (17)	35	0.43
Blackfeet (1)	1	0.01
Cherokee (3)	7	0.09
Choctaw (0)	1	0.01
Comanche (0)	1	0.01
Hopi (0)	4	0.05
Inupiat *(Alaska Native)* (1)	1	0.01
Iroquois (1)	1	0.01
Mexican American Ind. (7)	11	0.13
Navajo (0)	1	0.01
Paiute (13)	19	0.23
Pueblo (0)	1	0.01
Sioux (1)	3	0.04
Yaqui (1)	1	0.01
Asian (128)	189	2.30
Not Hispanic (128)	181	2.20
Hispanic (0)	8	0.10
Cambodian (1)	1	0.01
Chinese, ex. Taiwanese (17)	42	0.51
Filipino (13)	32	0.39
Hmong (8)	8	0.10
Indian (11)	12	0.15
Indonesian (1)	3	0.04
Japanese (36)	60	0.73
Korean (18)	19	0.23
Laotian (0)	1	0.01
Sri Lankan (1)	1	0.01
Thai (4)	10	0.12
Vietnamese (1)	6	0.07
Hawaii Native/Pacific Islander (5)	19	0.23
Not Hispanic (5)	16	0.19
Hispanic (0)	3	0.04
Native Hawaiian (3)	13	0.16
White (6,643)	6,858	83.29
Not Hispanic (5,143)	5,253	63.80
Hispanic (1,500)	1,605	19.49

Manhattan Beach

Place Type: City
County: Los Angeles
Population: 35,135†

Ancestry‡	Population	%
Afghan (38)	38	0.11
African, Sub-Saharan (17)	168	0.48
African (17)	30	0.09
South African (0)	138	0.40
American (1,871)	1,871	5.37
Arab (100)	246	0.71
Arab (21)	21	0.06
Egyptian (12)	12	0.03
Iraqi (5)	5	0.01
Jordanian (7)	21	0.06
Lebanese (52)	86	0.25
Moroccan (3)	3	0.01
Palestinian (0)	12	0.03
Syrian (0)	79	0.23
Other Arab (0)	7	0.02
Armenian (83)	91	0.26
Australian (16)	34	0.10
Austrian (73)	249	0.71
Basque (0)	32	0.09
Belgian (12)	36	0.10
British (168)	284	0.81
Canadian (83)	183	0.52
Celtic (0)	44	0.13
Croatian (36)	174	0.50
Czech (33)	254	0.73
Czechoslovakian (13)	33	0.09
Danish (57)	485	1.39
Dutch (105)	517	1.48
Eastern European (194)	194	0.56
English (1,199)	5,271	15.12
European (1,184)	1,314	3.77
Finnish (0)	126	0.36
French, ex. Basque (222)	1,155	3.31
French Canadian (72)	159	0.46
German (1,392)	6,574	18.85
Greek (160)	532	1.53
Hungarian (123)	350	1.00
Iranian (295)	295	0.85
Irish (1,509)	5,994	17.19
Israeli (42)	86	0.25
Italian (816)	3,032	8.70
Lithuanian (39)	86	0.25
Luxemburger (0)	8	0.02
New Zealander (31)	31	0.09
Northern European (79)	79	0.23
Norwegian (156)	852	2.44
Pennsylvania German (12)	12	0.03
Polish (408)	1,459	4.18
Portuguese (157)	198	0.57
Romanian (60)	259	0.74
Russian (546)	1,620	4.65
Scandinavian (24)	60	0.17
Scotch-Irish (293)	538	1.54
Scottish (248)	1,625	4.66
Slavic (8)	8	0.02
Slovak (0)	149	0.43
Slovene (79)	123	0.35
Soviet Union (13)	13	0.04
Swedish (195)	897	2.57
Swiss (26)	333	0.96
Turkish (35)	35	0.10
Ukrainian (95)	227	0.65
Welsh (53)	235	0.67
Yugoslavian (0)	9	0.03

Hispanic Origin	Population	%
Hispanic or Latino (of any race)	2,440	6.94
Central American, ex. Mexican	160	0.46
Costa Rican	32	0.09
Guatemalan	37	0.11
Honduran	9	0.03
Nicaraguan	26	0.07
Panamanian	10	0.03
Salvadoran	46	0.13
Cuban	118	0.34
Dominican Republic	6	0.02
Mexican	1,363	3.88
Puerto Rican	126	0.36
South American	343	0.98
Argentinean	100	0.28
Bolivian	9	0.03
Chilean	29	0.08
Colombian	82	0.23
Ecuadorian	46	0.13
Peruvian	68	0.19
Uruguayan	1	<0.01
Venezuelan	6	0.02
Other South American	2	0.01
Other Hispanic or Latino	324	0.92

Race*	Population	%
African-American/Black (290)	498	1.42
Not Hispanic (282)	471	1.34
Hispanic (8)	27	0.08
American Indian/Alaska Native (59)	234	0.67
Not Hispanic (44)	175	0.50
Hispanic (15)	59	0.17
Alaska Athabascan *(Ala. Nat.)* (3)	3	0.01
Apache (5)	12	0.03
Blackfeet (2)	12	0.03
Canadian/French Am. Ind. (0)	3	0.01
Cherokee (4)	39	0.11
Chickasaw (0)	2	0.01
Chippewa (5)	8	0.02
Choctaw (2)	13	0.04
Comanche (1)	1	<0.01
Cree (0)	5	0.01
Creek (1)	5	0.01
Delaware (0)	2	0.01
Hopi (0)	4	0.01
Inupiat *(Alaska Native)* (1)	1	<0.01
Iroquois (0)	6	0.02
Lumbee (1)	1	<0.01
Mexican American Ind. (3)	11	0.03
Navajo (3)	5	0.01
Paiute (2)	2	0.01
Pima (1)	1	<0.01
Potawatomi (0)	1	<0.01
Pueblo (1)	1	<0.01
Sioux (3)	3	0.01
South American Ind. (1)	2	0.01
Tlingit-Haida *(Alaska Native)* (2)	4	0.01
Tsimshian *(Alaska Native)* (0)	3	0.01
Yuman (0)	1	<0.01
Asian (3,023)	4,192	11.93
Not Hispanic (2,992)	4,061	11.56
Hispanic (31)	131	0.37
Bangladeshi (1)	1	<0.01
Burmese (4)	8	0.02
Cambodian (3)	4	0.01
Chinese, ex. Taiwanese (784)	1,223	3.48
Filipino (244)	545	1.55
Indian (307)	376	1.07
Indonesian (6)	18	0.05
Japanese (665)	1,111	3.16
Korean (450)	644	1.83
Laotian (2)	5	0.01
Nepalese (4)	4	0.01
Pakistani (35)	40	0.11
Sri Lankan (9)	19	0.05
Taiwanese (98)	116	0.33
Thai (44)	72	0.20
Vietnamese (168)	219	0.62
Hawaii Native/Pacific Islander (49)	169	0.48
Not Hispanic (44)	150	0.43
Hispanic (5)	19	0.05
Fijian (2)	2	0.01

*Notes: † The Census 2010 population figure is used to calculate the percentages in the Hispanic Origin and Race categories. Ancestry percentages are based on the 2006-2010 American Community Survey population (not shown); ‡ Numbers in parentheses indicate the number of people reporting a single ancestry; * Numbers in parentheses indicate the number of persons reporting this race alone, not in combination with any other race; Please refer to the Explanation of Data for more information.*

Guamanian/Chamorro (3)	15	0.04
Marshallese (0)	1	<0.01
Native Hawaiian (24)	106	0.30
Samoan (7)	8	0.02
Tongan (8)	10	0.03
White (29,686)	31,204	88.81
Not Hispanic (27,873)	29,180	83.05
Hispanic (1,813)	2,024	5.76

Manteca

Place Type: City
County: San Joaquin
Population: 67,096†

Ancestry‡	Population	%
Afghan (313)	416	0.64
African, Sub-Saharan (45)	70	0.11
African (17)	42	0.06
Sierra Leonean (28)	28	0.04
American (1,786)	1,786	2.75
Arab (122)	140	0.22
Egyptian (30)	30	0.05
Moroccan (9)	18	0.03
Other Arab (83)	92	0.14
Armenian (44)	90	0.14
Assyrian/Chaldean/Syriac (0)	31	0.05
Australian (0)	30	0.05
Austrian (8)	61	0.09
Basque (0)	11	0.02
Belgian (27)	83	0.13
Brazilian (0)	47	0.07
British (95)	213	0.33
Canadian (59)	167	0.26
Celtic (0)	7	0.01
Croatian (27)	197	0.30
Czech (0)	126	0.19
Czechoslovakian (18)	24	0.04
Danish (37)	245	0.38
Dutch (361)	1,269	1.95
English (1,343)	4,615	7.10
European (595)	671	1.03
Finnish (0)	14	0.02
French, ex. Basque (196)	1,558	2.40
French Canadian (42)	185	0.28
German (2,084)	9,462	14.57
Greek (92)	250	0.38
Hungarian (41)	183	0.28
Icelander (10)	34	0.05
Irish (1,540)	6,490	9.99
Italian (1,313)	4,017	6.18
Lithuanian (0)	38	0.06
Maltese (0)	14	0.02
Northern European (27)	27	0.04
Norwegian (262)	924	1.42
Pennsylvania German (0)	11	0.02
Polish (109)	546	0.84
Portuguese (1,563)	3,310	5.10
Romanian (36)	36	0.06
Russian (37)	265	0.41
Scandinavian (0)	23	0.04
Scotch-Irish (185)	671	1.03
Scottish (204)	818	1.26
Slavic (0)	117	0.18
Slovak (51)	151	0.23
Slovene (0)	17	0.03
Swedish (204)	844	1.30
Swiss (91)	323	0.50
Turkish (20)	75	0.12
Ukrainian (0)	44	0.07
Welsh (47)	141	0.22
West Indian, ex. Hispanic (83)	122	0.19
Belizean (0)	16	0.02
Jamaican (0)	23	0.04
Trinidadian/Tobagonian (83)	83	0.13
Yugoslavian (8)	25	0.04

Hispanic Origin	Population	%
Hispanic or Latino (of any race)	25,317	37.73
Central American, ex. Mexican	882	1.31
Costa Rican	18	0.03
Guatemalan	175	0.26
Honduran	52	0.08
Nicaraguan	210	0.31
Panamanian	22	0.03
Salvadoran	396	0.59
Other Central American	9	0.01
Cuban	88	0.13
Dominican Republic	24	0.04
Mexican	20,962	31.24
Puerto Rican	844	1.26
South American	315	0.47
Argentinean	19	0.03
Bolivian	7	0.01
Chilean	27	0.04
Colombian	42	0.06
Ecuadorian	35	0.05
Paraguayan	1	<0.01
Peruvian	173	0.26
Uruguayan	3	<0.01
Venezuelan	7	0.01
Other South American	1	<0.01
Other Hispanic or Latino	2,202	3.28

Race*	Population	%
African-American/Black (2,869)	3,724	5.55
Not Hispanic (2,669)	3,204	4.78
Hispanic (200)	520	0.78
American Indian/Alaska Native (735)	1,801	2.68
Not Hispanic (359)	941	1.40
Hispanic (376)	860	1.28
Alaska Athabascan *(Ala. Nat.)* (1)	1	<0.01
Aleut *(Alaska Native)* (1)	4	0.01
Apache (27)	87	0.13
Blackfeet (4)	39	0.06
Canadian/French Am. Ind. (0)	9	0.01
Central American Ind. (1)	2	<0.01
Cherokee (68)	343	0.51
Cheyenne (0)	1	<0.01
Chickasaw (6)	8	0.01
Chippewa (9)	29	0.04
Choctaw (34)	102	0.15
Colville (2)	2	<0.01
Comanche (1)	2	<0.01
Creek (3)	8	0.01
Delaware (0)	2	<0.01
Hopi (0)	5	0.01
Houma (1)	5	0.01
Inupiat *(Alaska Native)* (0)	3	<0.01
Iroquois (1)	19	0.03
Kiowa (3)	5	0.01
Mexican American Ind. (47)	95	0.14
Navajo (14)	40	0.06
Osage (6)	12	0.02
Paiute (19)	33	0.05
Potawatomi (3)	12	0.02
Pueblo (6)	13	0.02
Puget Sound Salish (5)	7	0.01
Seminole (6)	17	0.03
Shoshone (1)	7	0.01
Sioux (29)	52	0.08
South American Ind. (5)	13	0.02
Spanish American Ind. (7)	8	0.01
Tlingit-Haida *(Alaska Native)* (1)	1	<0.01
Ute (3)	18	0.03
Yakama (1)	4	0.01
Yaqui (20)	37	0.06
Yuman (2)	2	<0.01
Asian (4,780)	6,532	9.74
Not Hispanic (4,549)	5,757	8.58
Hispanic (231)	775	1.16
Burmese (17)	19	0.03
Cambodian (134)	164	0.24
Chinese, ex. Taiwanese (349)	571	0.85
Filipino (1,899)	2,953	4.40
Hmong (49)	52	0.08
Indian (1,622)	1,746	2.60
Indonesian (15)	36	0.05
Japanese (133)	351	0.52
Korean (86)	146	0.22
Laotian (72)	95	0.14
Malaysian (1)	3	<0.01
Pakistani (40)	54	0.08
Sri Lankan (0)	1	<0.01
Taiwanese (4)	6	0.01
Thai (18)	42	0.06
Vietnamese (167)	226	0.34
Hawaii Native/Pacific Islander (384)	890	1.33
Not Hispanic (302)	624	0.93
Hispanic (82)	266	0.40
Fijian (99)	106	0.16
Guamanian/Chamorro (81)	182	0.27
Native Hawaiian (93)	340	0.51
Samoan (51)	106	0.16
Tongan (9)	16	0.02
White (41,840)	45,863	68.35
Not Hispanic (31,476)	33,402	49.78
Hispanic (10,364)	12,461	18.57

Marina

Place Type: City
County: Monterey
Population: 19,718†

Ancestry‡	Population	%
African, Sub-Saharan (0)	121	0.62
African (0)	85	0.44
Ethiopian (0)	36	0.18
American (237)	237	1.21
Arab (110)	160	0.82
Egyptian (8)	8	0.04
Iraqi (48)	65	0.33
Palestinian (11)	11	0.06
Syrian (43)	60	0.31
Other Arab (0)	16	0.08
Armenian (35)	48	0.25
Assyrian/Chaldean/Syriac (67)	67	0.34
Austrian (28)	39	0.20
British (34)	80	0.41
Canadian (15)	46	0.24
Croatian (0)	26	0.13
Danish (21)	69	0.35
Dutch (21)	204	1.04
Eastern European (11)	11	0.06
English (317)	1,209	6.19
Estonian (15)	15	0.08
European (168)	183	0.94
Finnish (28)	41	0.21
French, ex. Basque (56)	573	2.93
French Canadian (31)	42	0.22
German (478)	2,009	10.29
German Russian (15)	15	0.08
Guyanese (23)	23	0.12
Hungarian (47)	73	0.37
Icelander (0)	16	0.08
Irish (260)	1,496	7.66
Italian (186)	818	4.19
Latvian (0)	17	0.09
Lithuanian (0)	53	0.27
Northern European (39)	45	0.23
Norwegian (70)	129	0.66
Polish (265)	517	2.65
Portuguese (72)	252	1.29
Russian (31)	160	0.82
Scotch-Irish (74)	441	2.26
Scottish (95)	279	1.43
Swedish (25)	80	0.41
Swiss (23)	107	0.55
Turkish (34)	50	0.26
Ukrainian (8)	30	0.15
Welsh (17)	53	0.27
West Indian, ex. Hispanic (12)	64	0.33
Barbadian (0)	26	0.13
Jamaican (0)	26	0.13
Trinidadian/Tobagonian (12)	12	0.06
Yugoslavian (8)	28	0.14

Hispanic Origin	Population	%
Hispanic or Latino (of any race)	5,372	27.24

*Notes: † The Census 2010 population figure is used to calculate the percentages in the Hispanic Origin and Race categories. Ancestry percentages are based on the 2006-2010 American Community Survey population (not shown); ‡ Numbers in parentheses indicate the number of people reporting a single ancestry; * Numbers in parentheses indicate the number of persons reporting this race alone, not in combination with any other race; Please refer to the Explanation of Data for more information.*

Central American, ex. Mexican	561	2.85
Costa Rican	7	0.04
Guatemalan	27	0.14
Honduran	50	0.25
Nicaraguan	27	0.14
Panamanian	28	0.14
Salvadoran	417	2.11
Other Central American	5	0.03
Cuban	21	0.11
Dominican Republic	6	0.03
Mexican	3,940	19.98
Puerto Rican	272	1.38
South American	91	0.46
Argentinean	10	0.05
Bolivian	3	0.02
Chilean	5	0.03
Colombian	13	0.07
Ecuadorian	6	0.03
Paraguayan	1	0.01
Peruvian	38	0.19
Venezuelan	11	0.06
Other South American	4	0.02
Other Hispanic or Latino	481	2.44

Race*	Population	%
African-American/Black (1,487)	2,066	10.48
Not Hispanic (1,413)	1,846	9.36
Hispanic (74)	220	1.12
American Indian/Alaska Native (140)	472	2.39
Not Hispanic (60)	279	1.41
Hispanic (80)	193	0.98
Apache (5)	20	0.10
Blackfeet (1)	13	0.07
Canadian/French Am. Ind. (0)	1	0.01
Central American Ind. (1)	2	0.01
Cherokee (11)	69	0.35
Cheyenne (0)	2	0.01
Chippewa (1)	8	0.04
Choctaw (5)	17	0.09
Comanche (0)	3	0.02
Cree (1)	2	0.01
Creek (0)	4	0.02
Crow (0)	1	0.01
Inupiat *(Alaska Native)* (4)	6	0.03
Iroquois (1)	3	0.02
Kiowa (0)	1	0.01
Mexican American Ind. (11)	19	0.10
Navajo (0)	12	0.06
Osage (0)	1	0.01
Paiute (0)	1	0.01
Pueblo (3)	13	0.07
Puget Sound Salish (0)	2	0.01
Seminole (0)	3	0.02
Sioux (3)	6	0.03
Spanish American Ind. (1)	6	0.03
Tlingit-Haida *(Alaska Native)* (0)	1	0.01
Ute (1)	1	0.01
Yaqui (0)	1	0.01
Yup'ik *(Alaska Native)* (0)	1	0.01
Asian (3,931)	5,071	25.72
Not Hispanic (3,826)	4,762	24.15
Hispanic (105)	309	1.57
Burmese (4)	4	0.02
Cambodian (9)	9	0.05
Chinese, ex. Taiwanese (218)	362	1.84
Filipino (1,371)	1,849	9.38
Hmong (1)	1	0.01
Indian (106)	189	0.96
Indonesian (22)	46	0.23
Japanese (271)	600	3.04
Korean (793)	1,058	5.37
Nepalese (12)	15	0.08
Pakistani (4)	4	0.02
Taiwanese (17)	27	0.14
Thai (53)	69	0.35
Vietnamese (707)	799	4.05
Hawaii Native/Pacific Islander (544)	903	4.58
Not Hispanic (507)	805	4.08
Hispanic (37)	98	0.50
Fijian (81)	102	0.52
Guamanian/Chamorro (136)	231	1.17
Native Hawaiian (51)	183	0.93
Samoan (164)	256	1.30
Tongan (47)	58	0.29
White (8,904)	10,371	52.60
Not Hispanic (7,112)	8,136	41.26
Hispanic (1,792)	2,235	11.33

Marina del Rey

Place Type: CDP
County: Los Angeles
Population: 8,866†

Ancestry‡	Population	%
African, Sub-Saharan (256)	267	2.90
African (35)	35	0.38
Ethiopian (65)	65	0.71
Nigerian (7)	7	0.08
South African (0)	11	0.12
Other Sub-Saharan African (149)	149	1.62
American (241)	241	2.62
Arab (0)	14	0.15
Lebanese (0)	14	0.15
Armenian (13)	13	0.14
Australian (110)	110	1.20
Austrian (36)	118	1.28
Belgian (32)	32	0.35
Brazilian (60)	73	0.79
British (41)	93	1.01
Canadian (56)	56	0.61
Czech (0)	31	0.34
Czechoslovakian (20)	51	0.55
Danish (0)	58	0.63
Dutch (67)	113	1.23
Eastern European (116)	116	1.26
English (284)	784	8.53
European (117)	117	1.27
French, ex. Basque (93)	319	3.47
French Canadian (55)	92	1.00
German (413)	1,505	16.37
Greek (51)	74	0.80
Hungarian (24)	83	0.90
Iranian (287)	287	3.12
Irish (333)	1,135	12.34
Israeli (59)	59	0.64
Italian (291)	833	9.06
Latvian (34)	34	0.37
Lithuanian (42)	98	1.07
Norwegian (43)	155	1.69
Polish (169)	407	4.43
Portuguese (14)	67	0.73
Romanian (0)	25	0.27
Russian (485)	789	8.58
Scandinavian (13)	13	0.14
Scotch-Irish (29)	74	0.80
Scottish (61)	263	2.86
Slavic (0)	46	0.50
Swedish (97)	305	3.32
Swiss (0)	10	0.11
Turkish (21)	21	0.23
Ukrainian (63)	76	0.83
Welsh (31)	82	0.89
Yugoslavian (28)	28	0.30

Hispanic Origin	Population	%
Hispanic or Latino (of any race)	686	7.74
Central American, ex. Mexican	69	0.78
Costa Rican	7	0.08
Guatemalan	9	0.10
Honduran	3	0.03
Nicaraguan	6	0.07
Panamanian	5	0.06
Salvadoran	38	0.43
Other Central American	1	0.01
Cuban	32	0.36
Dominican Republic	9	0.10
Mexican	311	3.51
Puerto Rican	34	0.38
South American	155	1.75
Argentinean	44	0.50
Bolivian	4	0.05
Chilean	8	0.09
Colombian	41	0.46
Ecuadorian	8	0.09
Peruvian	31	0.35
Uruguayan	4	0.05
Venezuelan	15	0.17
Other Hispanic or Latino	76	0.86

Race*	Population	%
African-American/Black (465)	592	6.68
Not Hispanic (453)	558	6.29
Hispanic (12)	34	0.38
American Indian/Alaska Native (31)	117	1.32
Not Hispanic (16)	84	0.95
Hispanic (15)	33	0.37
Apache (2)	3	0.03
Blackfeet (0)	5	0.06
Canadian/French Am. Ind. (0)	1	0.01
Cherokee (3)	26	0.29
Cheyenne (0)	1	0.01
Chickasaw (0)	1	0.01
Chippewa (1)	1	0.01
Choctaw (0)	3	0.03
Creek (1)	1	0.01
Iroquois (0)	1	0.01
Mexican American Ind. (2)	2	0.02
Navajo (2)	3	0.03
Osage (0)	6	0.07
Potawatomi (0)	1	0.01
Seminole (0)	2	0.02
Sioux (3)	13	0.15
South American Ind. (0)	3	0.03
Tlingit-Haida *(Alaska Native)* (1)	1	0.01
Yaqui (0)	1	0.01
Asian (749)	935	10.55
Not Hispanic (736)	907	10.23
Hispanic (13)	28	0.32
Bangladeshi (2)	2	0.02
Burmese (1)	1	0.01
Cambodian (3)	3	0.03
Chinese, ex. Taiwanese (148)	186	2.10
Filipino (92)	137	1.55
Hmong (1)	1	0.01
Indian (136)	146	1.65
Indonesian (3)	6	0.07
Japanese (170)	224	2.53
Korean (116)	135	1.52
Malaysian (0)	2	0.02
Nepalese (1)	1	0.01
Pakistani (8)	10	0.11
Taiwanese (5)	7	0.08
Thai (17)	21	0.24
Vietnamese (16)	29	0.33
Hawaii Native/Pacific Islander (10)	25	0.28
Not Hispanic (10)	23	0.26
Hispanic (0)	2	0.02
Guamanian/Chamorro (2)	3	0.03
Native Hawaiian (4)	11	0.12
Samoan (2)	2	0.02
White (7,071)	7,408	83.56
Not Hispanic (6,624)	6,910	77.94
Hispanic (447)	498	5.62

Martinez

Place Type: City
County: Contra Costa
Population: 35,824†

Ancestry‡	Population	%
Afghan (163)	163	0.46
African, Sub-Saharan (28)	79	0.22
African (13)	64	0.18
South African (15)	15	0.04
Albanian (0)	13	0.04
American (1,833)	1,833	5.15
Arab (78)	161	0.45
Arab (37)	37	0.10

*Notes: † The Census 2010 population figure is used to calculate the percentages in the Hispanic Origin and Race categories. Ancestry percentages are based on the 2006-2010 American Community Survey population (not shown); ‡ Numbers in parentheses indicate the number of people reporting a single ancestry; * Numbers in parentheses indicate the number of persons reporting this race alone, not in combination with any other race; Please refer to the Explanation of Data for more information.*

Egyptian (0)	64	0.18
Iraqi (0)	19	0.05
Lebanese (33)	33	0.09
Other Arab (8)	8	0.02
Armenian (36)	74	0.21
Australian (0)	6	0.02
Austrian (60)	103	0.29
Basque (62)	144	0.40
Belgian (18)	43	0.12
Brazilian (31)	31	0.09
British (119)	217	0.61
Croatian (42)	172	0.48
Czech (126)	399	1.12
Czechoslovakian (0)	21	0.06
Danish (77)	214	0.60
Dutch (114)	449	1.26
Eastern European (48)	48	0.13
English (1,091)	4,245	11.92
European (873)	981	2.75
Finnish (76)	130	0.36
French, ex. Basque (123)	1,532	4.30
French Canadian (44)	126	0.35
German (1,352)	5,276	14.81
Greek (132)	241	0.68
Hungarian (16)	83	0.23
Icelander (15)	15	0.04
Iranian (127)	127	0.36
Irish (1,165)	4,435	12.45
Italian (1,284)	3,183	8.94
Latvian (0)	17	0.05
Lithuanian (21)	34	0.10
Luxemburger (12)	28	0.08
Maltese (61)	61	0.17
Northern European (359)	359	1.01
Norwegian (207)	682	1.91
Polish (246)	643	1.81
Portuguese (405)	1,123	3.15
Romanian (13)	57	0.16
Russian (190)	384	1.08
Scandinavian (44)	76	0.21
Scotch-Irish (139)	678	1.90
Scottish (152)	921	2.59
Serbian (17)	33	0.09
Slavic (7)	7	0.02
Slovene (29)	37	0.10
Swedish (194)	786	2.21
Swiss (25)	168	0.47
Ukrainian (69)	124	0.35
Welsh (66)	533	1.50
West Indian, ex. Hispanic (96)	216	0.61
Belizean (0)	10	0.03
Dutch West Indian (0)	19	0.05
Jamaican (96)	187	0.52
Yugoslavian (20)	52	0.15

Hispanic Origin	**Population**	**%**
Hispanic or Latino (of any race)	5,258	14.68
Central American, ex. Mexican	499	1.39
Costa Rican	27	0.08
Guatemalan	35	0.10
Honduran	13	0.04
Nicaraguan	174	0.49
Panamanian	9	0.03
Salvadoran	229	0.64
Other Central American	12	0.03
Cuban	61	0.17
Dominican Republic	15	0.04
Mexican	3,509	9.80
Puerto Rican	215	0.60
South American	300	0.84
Argentinean	28	0.08
Bolivian	13	0.04
Chilean	34	0.09
Colombian	57	0.16
Ecuadorian	16	0.04
Paraguayan	1	<0.01
Peruvian	136	0.38
Venezuelan	9	0.03
Other South American	6	0.02
Other Hispanic or Latino	659	1.84

Race*	**Population**	**%**
African-American/Black (1,303)	1,713	4.78
Not Hispanic (1,263)	1,596	4.46
Hispanic (40)	117	0.33
American Indian/Alaska Native (255)	840	2.34
Not Hispanic (163)	596	1.66
Hispanic (92)	244	0.68
Alaska Athabascan *(Ala. Nat.)* (1)	1	<0.01
Apache (12)	38	0.11
Arapaho (0)	1	<0.01
Blackfeet (2)	26	0.07
Canadian/French Am. Ind. (0)	2	0.01
Cherokee (26)	181	0.51
Cheyenne (0)	3	0.01
Chickasaw (4)	10	0.03
Chippewa (7)	13	0.04
Choctaw (18)	46	0.13
Comanche (0)	1	<0.01
Cree (0)	1	<0.01
Creek (4)	18	0.05
Delaware (1)	4	0.01
Hopi (1)	3	0.01
Iroquois (0)	4	0.01
Kiowa (0)	1	<0.01
Lumbee (0)	1	<0.01
Menominee (1)	1	<0.01
Mexican American Ind. (18)	33	0.09
Navajo (6)	23	0.06
Osage (3)	4	0.01
Ottawa (2)	2	0.01
Paiute (2)	5	0.01
Potawatomi (2)	5	0.01
Pueblo (1)	4	0.01
Puget Sound Salish (4)	5	0.01
Seminole (0)	2	0.01
Shoshone (0)	3	0.01
Sioux (10)	29	0.08
South American Ind. (3)	6	0.02
Spanish American Ind. (1)	4	0.01
Tlingit-Haida *(Alaska Native)* (1)	7	0.02
Tsimshian *(Alaska Native)* (1)	1	<0.01
Ute (3)	3	0.01
Yaqui (5)	9	0.03
Asian (2,876)	3,906	10.90
Not Hispanic (2,810)	3,681	10.28
Hispanic (66)	225	0.63
Bangladeshi (0)	1	<0.01
Burmese (12)	12	0.03
Cambodian (4)	10	0.03
Chinese, ex. Taiwanese (574)	836	2.33
Filipino (1,118)	1,629	4.55
Indian (329)	400	1.12
Indonesian (16)	42	0.12
Japanese (239)	432	1.21
Korean (213)	259	0.72
Laotian (30)	41	0.11
Malaysian (2)	5	0.01
Nepalese (11)	12	0.03
Pakistani (9)	13	0.04
Sri Lankan (12)	12	0.03
Taiwanese (23)	27	0.08
Thai (32)	44	0.12
Vietnamese (80)	117	0.33
Hawaii Native/Pacific Islander (121)	360	1.00
Not Hispanic (99)	291	0.81
Hispanic (22)	69	0.19
Fijian (4)	11	0.03
Guamanian/Chamorro (32)	70	0.20
Native Hawaiian (33)	142	0.40
Samoan (16)	32	0.09
Tongan (11)	20	0.06
White (27,603)	29,576	82.56
Not Hispanic (24,604)	26,016	72.62
Hispanic (2,999)	3,560	9.94

Marysville

Place Type: City
County: Yuba
Population: 12,072†

Ancestry‡	**Population**	**%**
African, Sub-Saharan (54)	75	0.61
African (54)	75	0.61
American (1,038)	1,038	8.44
Armenian (11)	11	0.09
Austrian (0)	9	0.07
Basque (6)	85	0.69
Brazilian (0)	7	0.06
British (45)	55	0.45
Cajun (13)	23	0.19
Canadian (0)	17	0.14
Czech (11)	39	0.32
Czechoslovakian (12)	22	0.18
Danish (89)	189	1.54
Dutch (11)	200	1.63
English (298)	991	8.06
European (25)	25	0.20
Finnish (12)	12	0.10
French, ex. Basque (61)	408	3.32
French Canadian (14)	27	0.22
German (336)	1,604	13.05
Greek (8)	88	0.72
Hungarian (12)	12	0.10
Irish (168)	1,274	10.36
Italian (116)	419	3.41
Lithuanian (0)	10	0.08
Norwegian (30)	123	1.00
Polish (33)	142	1.15
Portuguese (114)	128	1.04
Romanian (17)	17	0.14
Russian (22)	66	0.54
Scotch-Irish (148)	309	2.51
Scottish (29)	130	1.06
Swedish (0)	38	0.31
Swiss (0)	36	0.29
Ukrainian (0)	42	0.34
Welsh (36)	36	0.29

Hispanic Origin	**Population**	**%**
Hispanic or Latino (of any race)	2,920	24.19
Central American, ex. Mexican	23	0.19
Honduran	6	0.05
Nicaraguan	4	0.03
Panamanian	5	0.04
Salvadoran	7	0.06
Other Central American	1	0.01
Cuban	7	0.06
Mexican	2,579	21.36
Puerto Rican	60	0.50
South American	21	0.17
Argentinean	2	0.02
Chilean	1	0.01
Colombian	1	0.01
Ecuadorian	1	0.01
Peruvian	13	0.11
Venezuelan	3	0.02
Other Hispanic or Latino	230	1.91

Race*	**Population**	**%**
African-American/Black (522)	768	6.36
Not Hispanic (493)	689	5.71
Hispanic (29)	79	0.65
American Indian/Alaska Native (298)	643	5.33
Not Hispanic (207)	474	3.93
Hispanic (91)	169	1.40
Alaska Athabascan *(Ala. Nat.)* (1)	1	0.01
Apache (5)	18	0.15
Blackfeet (3)	17	0.14
Canadian/French Am. Ind. (0)	1	0.01
Cherokee (55)	158	1.31
Chickasaw (1)	4	0.03
Chippewa (10)	20	0.17
Choctaw (12)	44	0.36
Comanche (1)	3	0.02

SECTION TWO

*Notes: † The Census 2010 population figure is used to calculate the percentages in the Hispanic Origin and Race categories. Ancestry percentages are based on the 2006-2010 American Community Survey population (not shown); ‡ Numbers in parentheses indicate the number of people reporting a single ancestry; * Numbers in parentheses indicate the number of persons reporting this race alone, not in combination with any other race; Please refer to the Explanation of Data for more information.*

Creek (0)	2	0.02
Delaware (1)	1	0.01
Hopi (1)	1	0.01
Inupiat *(Alaska Native)* (1)	3	0.02
Iroquois (2)	6	0.05
Mexican American Ind. (7)	23	0.19
Navajo (1)	3	0.02
Osage (0)	1	0.01
Paiute (0)	4	0.03
Potawatomi (2)	4	0.03
Pueblo (2)	3	0.02
Seminole (1)	1	0.01
Shoshone (0)	1	0.01
Sioux (5)	9	0.07
Tlingit-Haida *(Alaska Native)* (0)	1	0.01
Yaqui (4)	7	0.06
Asian (498)	682	5.65
Not Hispanic (464)	603	5.00
Hispanic (34)	79	0.65
Cambodian (6)	6	0.05
Chinese, ex. Taiwanese (106)	135	1.12
Filipino (100)	165	1.37
Hmong (104)	109	0.90
Indian (59)	82	0.68
Japanese (57)	91	0.75
Korean (11)	35	0.29
Laotian (13)	17	0.14
Pakistani (3)	16	0.13
Taiwanese (0)	2	0.02
Thai (2)	7	0.06
Vietnamese (6)	17	0.14
Hawaii Native/Pacific Islander (38)	86	0.71
Not Hispanic (30)	69	0.57
Hispanic (8)	17	0.14
Fijian (1)	1	0.01
Guamanian/Chamorro (16)	25	0.21
Native Hawaiian (13)	31	0.26
Samoan (0)	3	0.02
Tongan (0)	5	0.04
White (8,576)	9,361	77.54
Not Hispanic (7,399)	7,874	65.23
Hispanic (1,177)	1,487	12.32

Maywood

Place Type: City
County: Los Angeles
Population: 27,395†

Ancestry‡	Population	%
American (375)	375	1.36
Czech (0)	79	0.29
Dutch (0)	24	0.09
European (18)	18	0.07
German (48)	88	0.32
Irish (16)	143	0.52
Italian (0)	33	0.12
Lithuanian (15)	15	0.05
Norwegian (0)	19	0.07
Polish (10)	10	0.04

Hispanic Origin	Population	%
Hispanic or Latino (of any race)	26,696	97.45
Central American, ex. Mexican	2,460	8.98
Costa Rican	7	0.03
Guatemalan	609	2.22
Honduran	178	0.65
Nicaraguan	263	0.96
Panamanian	10	0.04
Salvadoran	1,354	4.94
Other Central American	39	0.14
Cuban	193	0.70
Dominican Republic	2	0.01
Mexican	22,719	82.93
Puerto Rican	65	0.24
South American	162	0.59
Argentinean	7	0.03
Bolivian	4	0.01
Chilean	9	0.03
Colombian	25	0.09
Ecuadorian	46	0.17
Peruvian	68	0.25
Uruguayan	1	<0.01
Other South American	2	0.01
Other Hispanic or Latino	1,095	4.00

Race*	Population	%
African-American/Black (166)	229	0.84
Not Hispanic (49)	55	0.20
Hispanic (117)	174	0.64
American Indian/Alaska Native (208)	299	1.09
Not Hispanic (24)	31	0.11
Hispanic (184)	268	0.98
Apache (1)	10	0.04
Central American Ind. (0)	3	0.01
Cherokee (1)	5	0.02
Cheyenne (3)	3	0.01
Chippewa (3)	3	0.01
Choctaw (2)	3	0.01
Comanche (1)	1	<0.01
Crow (1)	1	<0.01
Hopi (3)	8	0.03
Mexican American Ind. (53)	75	0.27
Navajo (3)	3	0.01
Pueblo (5)	5	0.02
Sioux (1)	1	<0.01
South American Ind. (1)	1	<0.01
Spanish American Ind. (2)	6	0.02
Tohono O'Odham (7)	7	0.03
Yaqui (1)	1	<0.01
Asian (87)	146	0.53
Not Hispanic (61)	73	0.27
Hispanic (26)	73	0.27
Bangladeshi (2)	5	0.02
Cambodian (2)	2	0.01
Chinese, ex. Taiwanese (4)	5	0.02
Filipino (41)	59	0.22
Indian (2)	10	0.04
Indonesian (4)	4	0.01
Japanese (2)	11	0.04
Korean (9)	11	0.04
Malaysian (1)	1	<0.01
Thai (5)	6	0.02
Vietnamese (1)	4	0.01
Hawaii Native/Pacific Islander (20)	84	0.31
Not Hispanic (14)	15	0.05
Hispanic (6)	69	0.25
Guamanian/Chamorro (1)	2	0.01
Native Hawaiian (5)	6	0.02
Samoan (11)	12	0.04
White (14,244)	15,285	55.79
Not Hispanic (498)	518	1.89
Hispanic (13,746)	14,767	53.90

McFarland

Place Type: City
County: Kern
Population: 12,707†

Ancestry‡	Population	%
African, Sub-Saharan (17)	17	0.14
African (9)	9	0.07
South African (8)	8	0.07
American (23)	23	0.19
Arab (87)	87	0.71
Other Arab (87)	87	0.71
Dutch (0)	11	0.09
English (54)	71	0.58
French, ex. Basque (8)	42	0.34
French Canadian (0)	12	0.10
German (30)	129	1.05
Hungarian (8)	8	0.07
Irish (98)	210	1.71
Italian (27)	70	0.57
Norwegian (9)	15	0.12
Portuguese (6)	21	0.17
Scotch-Irish (25)	47	0.38
Scottish (27)	44	0.36
Swedish (0)	6	0.05

Hispanic Origin	Population	%
Hispanic or Latino (of any race)	11,625	91.49
Central American, ex. Mexican	80	0.63
Costa Rican	1	0.01
Guatemalan	18	0.14
Honduran	5	0.04
Nicaraguan	26	0.20
Salvadoran	30	0.24
Cuban	5	0.04
Mexican	10,839	85.30
Puerto Rican	24	0.19
South American	11	0.09
Argentinean	6	0.05
Colombian	4	0.03
Ecuadorian	1	0.01
Other Hispanic or Latino	666	5.24

Race*	Population	%
African-American/Black (236)	262	2.06
Not Hispanic (171)	175	1.38
Hispanic (65)	87	0.68
American Indian/Alaska Native (171)	260	2.05
Not Hispanic (13)	26	0.20
Hispanic (158)	234	1.84
Apache (3)	3	0.02
Canadian/French Am. Ind. (0)	1	0.01
Cherokee (4)	6	0.05
Choctaw (6)	6	0.05
Creek (0)	1	0.01
Mexican American Ind. (69)	106	0.83
Navajo (2)	3	0.02
Puget Sound Salish (1)	1	0.01
Sioux (1)	1	0.01
Spanish American Ind. (1)	2	0.02
Yaqui (5)	5	0.04
Asian (84)	118	0.93
Not Hispanic (68)	73	0.57
Hispanic (16)	45	0.35
Cambodian (3)	4	0.03
Chinese, ex. Taiwanese (24)	25	0.20
Filipino (34)	48	0.38
Indian (9)	15	0.12
Japanese (7)	9	0.07
Laotian (3)	3	0.02
Pakistani (0)	7	0.06
Vietnamese (1)	1	0.01
Hawaii Native/Pacific Islander (6)	38	0.30
Not Hispanic (5)	8	0.06
Hispanic (1)	30	0.24
Guamanian/Chamorro (0)	1	0.01
Native Hawaiian (1)	3	0.02
Samoan (4)	7	0.06
Tongan (0)	6	0.05
White (5,433)	5,788	45.55
Not Hispanic (743)	759	5.97
Hispanic (4,690)	5,029	39.58

McKinleyville

Place Type: CDP
County: Humboldt
Population: 15,177†

Ancestry‡	Population	%
American (1,169)	1,169	6.92
Arab (85)	85	0.50
Arab (85)	85	0.50
Assyrian/Chaldean/Syriac (12)	12	0.07
Austrian (11)	45	0.27
Basque (0)	13	0.08
Belgian (25)	95	0.56
British (95)	95	0.56
Canadian (8)	69	0.41
Croatian (0)	19	0.11
Czech (10)	62	0.37
Czechoslovakian (0)	66	0.39
Danish (43)	109	0.65
Dutch (63)	385	2.28
Eastern European (0)	11	0.07
English (461)	1,818	10.76

*Notes: † The Census 2010 population figure is used to calculate the percentages in the Hispanic Origin and Race categories. Ancestry percentages are based on the 2006-2010 American Community Survey population (not shown); ‡ Numbers in parentheses indicate the number of people reporting a single ancestry; * Numbers in parentheses indicate the number of persons reporting this race alone, not in combination with any other race; Please refer to the Explanation of Data for more information.*

Ancestry (continued)	Population	%
European (1,127)	1,276	7.55
Finnish (0)	27	0.16
French, ex. Basque (34)	792	4.69
French Canadian (26)	195	1.15
German (611)	2,958	17.51
Greek (46)	46	0.27
Hungarian (24)	89	0.53
Irish (521)	2,876	17.02
Italian (522)	1,306	7.73
Lithuanian (38)	38	0.22
Northern European (32)	32	0.19
Norwegian (118)	613	3.63
Pennsylvania German (0)	13	0.08
Polish (80)	286	1.69
Portuguese (270)	420	2.49
Romanian (18)	18	0.11
Russian (62)	207	1.23
Scandinavian (48)	56	0.33
Scotch-Irish (251)	538	3.18
Scottish (114)	691	4.09
Slavic (0)	21	0.12
Slovak (26)	26	0.15
Slovene (0)	9	0.05
Swedish (97)	444	2.63
Swiss (0)	41	0.24
Turkish (4)	8	0.05
Ukrainian (38)	38	0.22
Welsh (43)	149	0.88
West Indian, ex. Hispanic (48)	71	0.42
Dutch West Indian (48)	48	0.28
Trinidadian/Tobagonian (0)	23	0.14
Yugoslavian (14)	14	0.08

Hispanic Origin	Population	%
Hispanic or Latino (of any race)	1,081	7.12
Central American, ex. Mexican	32	0.21
Costa Rican	1	0.01
Guatemalan	9	0.06
Honduran	5	0.03
Nicaraguan	5	0.03
Panamanian	3	0.02
Salvadoran	9	0.06
Cuban	9	0.06
Dominican Republic	2	0.01
Mexican	780	5.14
Puerto Rican	53	0.35
South American	60	0.40
Argentinean	6	0.04
Bolivian	3	0.02
Chilean	21	0.14
Colombian	4	0.03
Ecuadorian	14	0.09
Paraguayan	2	0.01
Peruvian	8	0.05
Venezuelan	2	0.01
Other Hispanic or Latino	145	0.96

Race*	Population	%
African-American/Black (103)	207	1.36
Not Hispanic (95)	185	1.22
Hispanic (8)	22	0.14
American Indian/Alaska Native (700)	1,162	7.66
Not Hispanic (623)	992	6.54
Hispanic (77)	170	1.12
Aleut *(Alaska Native)* (2)	2	0.01
Apache (4)	19	0.13
Arapaho (0)	3	0.02
Blackfeet (6)	15	0.10
Canadian/French Am. Ind. (6)	7	0.05
Central American Ind. (3)	6	0.04
Cherokee (36)	100	0.66
Cheyenne (0)	3	0.02
Chickasaw (3)	9	0.06
Chippewa (1)	2	0.01
Choctaw (6)	21	0.14
Comanche (1)	5	0.03
Creek (0)	2	0.01
Crow (0)	4	0.03
Hopi (3)	3	0.02
Inupiat *(Alaska Native)* (1)	1	0.01
Iroquois (6)	11	0.07
Lumbee (1)	1	0.01
Mexican American Ind. (9)	16	0.11
Navajo (2)	2	0.01
Osage (4)	5	0.03
Ottawa (1)	2	0.01
Paiute (2)	2	0.01
Pima (2)	2	0.01
Potawatomi (5)	5	0.03
Pueblo (1)	3	0.02
Puget Sound Salish (3)	3	0.02
Seminole (0)	3	0.02
Shoshone (0)	1	0.01
Sioux (4)	11	0.07
South American Ind. (1)	10	0.07
Tlingit-Haida *(Alaska Native)* (3)	6	0.04
Ute (1)	2	0.01
Yaqui (2)	4	0.03
Asian (211)	416	2.74
Not Hispanic (205)	375	2.47
Hispanic (6)	41	0.27
Bangladeshi (1)	1	0.01
Burmese (3)	3	0.02
Chinese, ex. Taiwanese (59)	98	0.65
Filipino (40)	106	0.70
Hmong (1)	1	0.01
Indian (11)	19	0.13
Indonesian (3)	3	0.02
Japanese (40)	111	0.73
Korean (21)	42	0.28
Laotian (2)	3	0.02
Nepalese (1)	1	0.01
Pakistani (6)	9	0.06
Thai (3)	6	0.04
Vietnamese (6)	12	0.08
Hawaii Native/Pacific Islander (17)	53	0.35
Not Hispanic (15)	49	0.32
Hispanic (2)	4	0.03
Fijian (2)	2	0.01
Guamanian/Chamorro (3)	3	0.02
Native Hawaiian (6)	17	0.11
Samoan (3)	14	0.09
Tongan (1)	1	0.01
White (13,010)	13,765	90.70
Not Hispanic (12,499)	13,099	86.31
Hispanic (511)	666	4.39

Mead Valley

Place Type: CDP
County: Riverside
Population: 18,510†

Ancestry‡	Population	%
African, Sub-Saharan (48)	121	0.69
African (30)	103	0.58
Sudanese (18)	18	0.10
American (183)	183	1.04
Arab (0)	33	0.19
Arab (0)	33	0.19
Austrian (0)	15	0.09
Belgian (0)	8	0.05
Czech (24)	47	0.27
Dutch (27)	59	0.33
English (163)	333	1.89
European (8)	8	0.05
Finnish (0)	21	0.12
French, ex. Basque (17)	44	0.25
French Canadian (53)	82	0.47
German (150)	477	2.71
Greek (71)	82	0.47
Hungarian (0)	5	0.03
Icelander (0)	13	0.07
Irish (206)	403	2.29
Italian (55)	170	0.97
Norwegian (42)	136	0.77
Polish (13)	28	0.16
Portuguese (3)	3	0.02
Romanian (196)	231	1.31
Scotch-Irish (9)	9	0.05
Scottish (34)	179	1.02
Slavic (0)	10	0.06
Swedish (11)	39	0.22
Welsh (0)	106	0.60
Yugoslavian (0)	29	0.16

Hispanic Origin	Population	%
Hispanic or Latino (of any race)	13,395	72.37
Central American, ex. Mexican	446	2.41
Costa Rican	7	0.04
Guatemalan	261	1.41
Honduran	17	0.09
Nicaraguan	18	0.10
Panamanian	7	0.04
Salvadoran	131	0.71
Other Central American	5	0.03
Cuban	29	0.16
Dominican Republic	11	0.06
Mexican	11,958	64.60
Puerto Rican	75	0.41
South American	71	0.38
Argentinean	7	0.04
Bolivian	18	0.10
Chilean	1	0.01
Colombian	11	0.06
Ecuadorian	13	0.07
Peruvian	12	0.06
Uruguayan	8	0.04
Venezuelan	1	0.01
Other Hispanic or Latino	805	4.35

Race*	Population	%
African-American/Black (1,515)	1,672	9.03
Not Hispanic (1,422)	1,541	8.33
Hispanic (93)	131	0.71
American Indian/Alaska Native (179)	289	1.56
Not Hispanic (45)	99	0.53
Hispanic (134)	190	1.03
Aleut *(Alaska Native)* (0)	1	0.01
Apache (5)	16	0.09
Blackfeet (0)	5	0.03
Central American Ind. (5)	8	0.04
Cherokee (6)	18	0.10
Chippewa (1)	1	0.01
Choctaw (3)	8	0.04
Comanche (0)	1	0.01
Creek (1)	1	0.01
Crow (0)	2	0.01
Hopi (3)	3	0.02
Iroquois (2)	2	0.01
Mexican American Ind. (23)	30	0.16
Navajo (2)	2	0.01
Paiute (1)	2	0.01
Pueblo (1)	1	0.01
Sioux (2)	7	0.04
South American Ind. (5)	8	0.04
Spanish American Ind. (2)	2	0.01
Yaqui (1)	1	0.01
Asian (259)	339	1.83
Not Hispanic (249)	301	1.63
Hispanic (10)	38	0.21
Bangladeshi (1)	3	0.02
Chinese, ex. Taiwanese (10)	18	0.10
Filipino (103)	143	0.77
Hmong (1)	1	0.01
Indian (14)	22	0.12
Indonesian (2)	4	0.02
Japanese (11)	27	0.15
Korean (42)	43	0.23
Laotian (1)	1	0.01
Malaysian (0)	2	0.01
Pakistani (0)	1	0.01
Taiwanese (2)	2	0.01
Thai (9)	9	0.05
Vietnamese (56)	57	0.31
Hawaii Native/Pacific Islander (17)	55	0.30
Not Hispanic (11)	42	0.23
Hispanic (6)	13	0.07
Guamanian/Chamorro (10)	15	0.08
Native Hawaiian (3)	17	0.09

*Notes: † The Census 2010 population figure is used to calculate the percentages in the Hispanic Origin and Race categories. Ancestry percentages are based on the 2006-2010 American Community Survey population (not shown); ‡ Numbers in parentheses indicate the number of people reporting a single ancestry; * Numbers in parentheses indicate the number of persons reporting this race alone, not in combination with any other race; Please refer to the Explanation of Data for more information.*

Samoan (2)	10	0.05
White (8,383)	8,944	48.32
Not Hispanic (3,142)	3,287	17.76
Hispanic (5,241)	5,657	30.56

Mecca

Place Type: CDP
County: Riverside
Population: 8,577†

Ancestry‡	Population	%
American (16)	16	0.20
English (0)	22	0.28
Irish (0)	11	0.14
Russian (0)	13	0.17

Hispanic Origin	Population	%
Hispanic or Latino (of any race)	8,462	98.66
Central American, ex. Mexican	420	4.90
Costa Rican	1	0.01
Guatemalan	11	0.13
Honduran	9	0.10
Nicaraguan	3	0.03
Salvadoran	396	4.62
Cuban	1	0.01
Mexican	7,815	91.12
Puerto Rican	6	0.07
South American	4	0.05
Argentinean	1	0.01
Peruvian	3	0.03
Other Hispanic or Latino	216	2.52

Race*	Population	%
African-American/Black (40)	51	0.59
Not Hispanic (9)	11	0.13
Hispanic (31)	40	0.47
American Indian/Alaska Native (47)	63	0.73
Not Hispanic (11)	16	0.19
Hispanic (36)	47	0.55
Canadian/French Am. Ind. (0)	1	0.01
Mexican American Ind. (9)	18	0.21
Spanish American Ind. (7)	7	0.08
Yaqui (3)	3	0.03
Asian (17)	35	0.41
Not Hispanic (14)	15	0.17
Hispanic (3)	20	0.23
Filipino (16)	24	0.28
Laotian (1)	1	0.01
Hawaii Native/Pacific Islander (7)	13	0.15
Not Hispanic (6)	6	0.07
Hispanic (1)	7	0.08
Fijian (6)	6	0.07
Native Hawaiian (0)	2	0.02
White (2,686)	2,899	33.80
Not Hispanic (57)	63	0.73
Hispanic (2,629)	2,836	33.07

Mendota

Place Type: City
County: Fresno
Population: 11,014†

Ancestry‡	Population	%

Hispanic Origin	Population	%
Hispanic or Latino (of any race)	10,643	96.63
Central American, ex. Mexican	2,885	26.19
Guatemalan	43	0.39
Honduran	416	3.78
Nicaraguan	6	0.05
Salvadoran	2,411	21.89
Other Central American	9	0.08
Mexican	7,183	65.22
Puerto Rican	9	0.08
South American	3	0.03
Chilean	2	0.02
Colombian	1	0.01
Other Hispanic or Latino	563	5.11

Race*	Population	%
African-American/Black (107)	155	1.41
Not Hispanic (28)	30	0.27
Hispanic (79)	125	1.13
American Indian/Alaska Native (153)	202	1.83
Not Hispanic (26)	33	0.30
Hispanic (127)	169	1.53
Apache (1)	4	0.04
Blackfeet (1)	1	0.01
Central American Ind. (7)	7	0.06
Cherokee (3)	6	0.05
Chickasaw (1)	1	0.01
Choctaw (3)	3	0.03
Iroquois (0)	1	0.01
Mexican American Ind. (14)	28	0.25
Navajo (0)	1	0.01
Paiute (1)	1	0.01
Spanish American Ind. (2)	2	0.02
Asian (82)	100	0.91
Not Hispanic (43)	44	0.40
Hispanic (39)	56	0.51
Cambodian (7)	7	0.06
Chinese, ex. Taiwanese (17)	17	0.15
Filipino (2)	3	0.03
Hmong (1)	1	0.01
Indian (31)	31	0.28
Japanese (2)	2	0.02
Korean (1)	1	0.01
Laotian (12)	13	0.12
Vietnamese (3)	3	0.03
Hawaii Native/Pacific Islander (5)	11	0.10
Not Hispanic (1)	1	0.01
Hispanic (4)	10	0.09
Fijian (1)	1	0.01
Guamanian/Chamorro (0)	1	0.01
Native Hawaiian (4)	4	0.04
White (5,823)	6,126	55.62
Not Hispanic (243)	250	2.27
Hispanic (5,580)	5,876	53.35

Menifee

Place Type: City
County: Riverside
Population: 77,519†

Ancestry‡	Population	%
Afghan (11)	11	0.02
African, Sub-Saharan (266)	289	0.40
African (266)	289	0.40
American (2,194)	2,194	3.03
Arab (233)	266	0.37
Arab (10)	10	0.01
Iraqi (8)	8	0.01
Jordanian (163)	163	0.22
Lebanese (0)	19	0.03
Syrian (0)	14	0.02
Other Arab (52)	52	0.07
Armenian (57)	76	0.10
Australian (13)	75	0.10
Austrian (49)	144	0.20
Basque (85)	85	0.12
Belgian (13)	45	0.06
Brazilian (8)	37	0.05
British (157)	226	0.31
Bulgarian (26)	26	0.04
Canadian (113)	325	0.45
Celtic (0)	32	0.04
Croatian (68)	100	0.14
Czech (70)	256	0.35
Czechoslovakian (23)	33	0.05
Danish (121)	433	0.60
Dutch (381)	2,084	2.87
Eastern European (21)	21	0.03
English (2,163)	7,360	10.15
European (762)	997	1.38
Finnish (82)	251	0.35
French, ex. Basque (351)	2,493	3.44
French Canadian (190)	556	0.77
German (3,084)	10,602	14.62
Greek (121)	241	0.33
Guyanese (41)	53	0.07
Hungarian (117)	278	0.38
Icelander (0)	9	0.01
Iranian (0)	20	0.03
Irish (1,896)	6,860	9.46
Italian (1,717)	3,985	5.50
Lithuanian (13)	62	0.09
Luxemburger (13)	26	0.04
Macedonian (23)	23	0.03
Maltese (34)	34	0.05
Northern European (11)	24	0.03
Norwegian (652)	1,218	1.68
Pennsylvania German (13)	28	0.04
Polish (649)	1,414	1.95
Portuguese (77)	232	0.32
Romanian (235)	386	0.53
Russian (268)	550	0.76
Scandinavian (62)	106	0.15
Scotch-Irish (402)	1,449	2.00
Scottish (351)	1,348	1.86
Serbian (15)	27	0.04
Slavic (39)	39	0.05
Slovak (25)	78	0.11
Slovene (0)	10	0.01
Swedish (398)	1,169	1.61
Swiss (34)	149	0.21
Ukrainian (64)	176	0.24
Welsh (77)	412	0.57
West Indian, ex. Hispanic (133)	218	0.30
Belizean (121)	121	0.17
Haitian (0)	14	0.02
Jamaican (12)	83	0.11
Yugoslavian (51)	69	0.10

Hispanic Origin	Population	%
Hispanic or Latino (of any race)	25,551	32.96
Central American, ex. Mexican	730	0.94
Costa Rican	33	0.04
Guatemalan	194	0.25
Honduran	51	0.07
Nicaraguan	117	0.15
Panamanian	46	0.06
Salvadoran	284	0.37
Other Central American	5	0.01
Cuban	212	0.27
Dominican Republic	15	0.02
Mexican	21,690	27.98
Puerto Rican	591	0.76
South American	488	0.63
Argentinean	75	0.10
Bolivian	21	0.03
Chilean	27	0.03
Colombian	163	0.21
Ecuadorian	73	0.09
Peruvian	92	0.12
Uruguayan	13	0.02
Venezuelan	13	0.02
Other South American	11	0.01
Other Hispanic or Latino	1,825	2.35

Race*	Population	%
African-American/Black (3,858)	4,717	6.08
Not Hispanic (3,630)	4,288	5.53
Hispanic (228)	429	0.55
American Indian/Alaska Native (655)	1,483	1.91
Not Hispanic (314)	852	1.10
Hispanic (341)	631	0.81
Alaska Athabascan *(Ala. Nat.)* (1)	2	<0.01
Aleut *(Alaska Native)* (2)	2	<0.01
Apache (21)	48	0.06
Blackfeet (5)	30	0.04
Canadian/French Am. Ind. (1)	7	0.01
Central American Ind. (4)	4	0.01
Cherokee (46)	169	0.22
Cheyenne (0)	2	<0.01
Chickasaw (4)	13	0.02
Chippewa (15)	27	0.03
Choctaw (17)	43	0.06

*Notes: † The Census 2010 population figure is used to calculate the percentages in the Hispanic Origin and Race categories. Ancestry percentages are based on the 2006-2010 American Community Survey population (not shown); ‡ Numbers in parentheses indicate the number of people reporting a single ancestry; * Numbers in parentheses indicate the number of persons reporting this race alone, not in combination with any other race; Please refer to the Explanation of Data for more information.*

Colville (0)	1	<0.01
Comanche (2)	6	0.01
Creek (6)	15	0.02
Crow (0)	2	<0.01
Delaware (4)	12	0.02
Hopi (7)	8	0.01
Inupiat *(Alaska Native)* (0)	1	<0.01
Iroquois (2)	12	0.02
Lumbee (2)	5	0.01
Mexican American Ind. (42)	77	0.10
Navajo (14)	44	0.06
Osage (0)	2	<0.01
Paiute (5)	5	0.01
Pima (3)	5	0.01
Potawatomi (3)	9	0.01
Pueblo (3)	5	0.01
Sioux (15)	30	0.04
South American Ind. (2)	6	0.01
Tlingit-Haida *(Alaska Native)* (1)	1	<0.01
Tohono O'Odham (5)	5	0.01
Ute (1)	2	<0.01
Yakama (1)	1	<0.01
Yaqui (6)	21	0.03
Yuman (1)	1	<0.01
Asian (3,788)	5,094	6.57
Not Hispanic (3,597)	4,559	5.88
Hispanic (191)	535	0.69
Bangladeshi (3)	11	0.01
Burmese (1)	2	<0.01
Cambodian (137)	157	0.20
Chinese, ex. Taiwanese (232)	394	0.51
Filipino (2,042)	2,690	3.47
Hmong (3)	3	<0.01
Indian (162)	243	0.31
Indonesian (33)	85	0.11
Japanese (231)	498	0.64
Korean (138)	214	0.28
Laotian (150)	181	0.23
Malaysian (0)	7	0.01
Nepalese (0)	1	<0.01
Pakistani (23)	35	0.05
Sri Lankan (9)	10	0.01
Taiwanese (8)	11	0.01
Thai (58)	101	0.13
Vietnamese (424)	484	0.62
Hawaii Native/Pacific Islander (295)	609	0.79
Not Hispanic (262)	513	0.66
Hispanic (33)	96	0.12
Fijian (6)	7	0.01
Guamanian/Chamorro (93)	142	0.18
Native Hawaiian (42)	188	0.24
Samoan (72)	130	0.17
Tongan (43)	52	0.07
White (55,444)	58,760	75.80
Not Hispanic (41,988)	43,744	56.43
Hispanic (13,456)	15,016	19.37

Menlo Park

Place Type: City
County: San Mateo
Population: 32,026†

Ancestry‡	Population	%
African, Sub-Saharan (85)	119	0.38
African (48)	59	0.19
Ethiopian (10)	10	0.03
Kenyan (0)	10	0.03
South African (6)	19	0.06
Other Sub-Saharan African (21)	21	0.07
American (774)	774	2.47
Arab (15)	127	0.41
Arab (0)	17	0.05
Lebanese (15)	67	0.21
Moroccan (0)	11	0.04
Syrian (0)	13	0.04
Other Arab (0)	19	0.06
Armenian (50)	64	0.20
Assyrian/Chaldean/Syriac (13)	13	0.04
Austrian (127)	258	0.82
Basque (0)	24	0.08
Belgian (21)	30	0.10
Brazilian (28)	45	0.14
British (313)	540	1.72
Bulgarian (12)	12	0.04
Canadian (133)	169	0.54
Celtic (9)	9	0.03
Czech (30)	96	0.31
Czechoslovakian (12)	29	0.09
Danish (41)	216	0.69
Dutch (152)	510	1.63
Eastern European (157)	157	0.50
English (986)	4,089	13.06
Estonian (11)	11	0.04
European (1,305)	1,356	4.33
Finnish (0)	14	0.04
French, ex. Basque (276)	1,259	4.02
French Canadian (22)	22	0.07
German (1,102)	4,393	14.03
Greek (138)	339	1.08
Hungarian (122)	252	0.80
Iranian (276)	336	1.07
Irish (817)	3,653	11.66
Israeli (67)	67	0.21
Italian (447)	1,961	6.26
Lithuanian (13)	79	0.25
Luxemburger (0)	7	0.02
Macedonian (0)	9	0.03
Maltese (14)	14	0.04
New Zealander (40)	40	0.13
Northern European (81)	97	0.31
Norwegian (204)	736	2.35
Polish (276)	801	2.56
Portuguese (36)	126	0.40
Romanian (16)	105	0.34
Russian (260)	789	2.52
Scandinavian (123)	171	0.55
Scotch-Irish (211)	589	1.88
Scottish (303)	1,040	3.32
Serbian (0)	11	0.04
Slovak (14)	28	0.09
Swedish (236)	780	2.49
Swiss (56)	298	0.95
Turkish (78)	78	0.25
Ukrainian (39)	89	0.28
Welsh (33)	251	0.80
West Indian, ex. Hispanic (23)	23	0.07
Jamaican (23)	23	0.07
Yugoslavian (0)	25	0.08

Hispanic Origin	Population	%
Hispanic or Latino (of any race)	5,902	18.43
Central American, ex. Mexican	763	2.38
Costa Rican	8	0.02
Guatemalan	154	0.48
Honduran	8	0.02
Nicaraguan	75	0.23
Panamanian	19	0.06
Salvadoran	486	1.52
Other Central American	13	0.04
Cuban	35	0.11
Dominican Republic	2	0.01
Mexican	4,303	13.44
Puerto Rican	78	0.24
South American	289	0.90
Argentinean	61	0.19
Bolivian	7	0.02
Chilean	35	0.11
Colombian	57	0.18
Ecuadorian	10	0.03
Peruvian	85	0.27
Uruguayan	16	0.05
Venezuelan	14	0.04
Other South American	4	0.01
Other Hispanic or Latino	432	1.35

Race*	Population	%
African-American/Black (1,551)	1,815	5.67
Not Hispanic (1,482)	1,692	5.28
Hispanic (69)	123	0.38
American Indian/Alaska Native (156)	365	1.14
Not Hispanic (43)	177	0.55
Hispanic (113)	188	0.59
Aleut *(Alaska Native)* (0)	4	0.01
Apache (12)	21	0.07
Blackfeet (1)	4	0.01
Cherokee (11)	34	0.11
Cheyenne (0)	1	<0.01
Chickasaw (0)	1	<0.01
Chippewa (0)	4	0.01
Choctaw (5)	19	0.06
Comanche (0)	3	0.01
Creek (0)	3	0.01
Hopi (3)	4	0.01
Iroquois (0)	1	<0.01
Lumbee (0)	4	0.01
Mexican American Ind. (25)	34	0.11
Navajo (2)	6	0.02
Osage (0)	6	0.02
Ottawa (1)	1	<0.01
Paiute (1)	1	<0.01
Seminole (0)	2	0.01
Sioux (3)	13	0.04
South American Ind. (0)	8	0.02
Spanish American Ind. (2)	3	0.01
Tlingit-Haida *(Alaska Native)* (1)	1	<0.01
Yaqui (1)	1	<0.01
Asian (3,157)	4,052	12.65
Not Hispanic (3,132)	3,966	12.38
Hispanic (25)	86	0.27
Bangladeshi (4)	4	0.01
Burmese (2)	3	0.01
Cambodian (0)	4	0.01
Chinese, ex. Taiwanese (1,208)	1,565	4.89
Filipino (300)	460	1.44
Hmong (0)	1	<0.01
Indian (612)	738	2.30
Indonesian (9)	21	0.07
Japanese (381)	576	1.80
Korean (273)	363	1.13
Laotian (3)	6	0.02
Malaysian (4)	5	0.02
Nepalese (0)	2	0.01
Pakistani (28)	42	0.13
Sri Lankan (11)	18	0.06
Taiwanese (67)	86	0.27
Thai (25)	46	0.14
Vietnamese (81)	111	0.35
Hawaii Native/Pacific Islander (454)	566	1.77
Not Hispanic (446)	551	1.72
Hispanic (8)	15	0.05
Fijian (39)	52	0.16
Guamanian/Chamorro (7)	10	0.03
Native Hawaiian (8)	44	0.14
Samoan (61)	73	0.23
Tongan (300)	326	1.02
White (22,494)	23,764	74.20
Not Hispanic (19,841)	20,832	65.05
Hispanic (2,653)	2,932	9.16

Mentone

Place Type: CDP
County: San Bernardino
Population: 8,720†

Ancestry‡	Population	%
African, Sub-Saharan (193)	193	2.18
African (151)	151	1.71
Other Sub-Saharan African (42)	42	0.47
American (156)	156	1.76
Czechoslovakian (20)	20	0.23
Danish (0)	61	0.69
Dutch (16)	110	1.24
English (146)	811	9.16
European (102)	109	1.23
Finnish (41)	95	1.07
French, ex. Basque (26)	244	2.76
French Canadian (73)	154	1.74
German (230)	1,718	19.40

*Notes: † The Census 2010 population figure is used to calculate the percentages in the Hispanic Origin and Race categories. Ancestry percentages are based on the 2006-2010 American Community Survey population (not shown); ‡ Numbers in parentheses indicate the number of people reporting a single ancestry; * Numbers in parentheses indicate the number of persons reporting this race alone, not in combination with any other race; Please refer to the Explanation of Data for more information.*

Icelander (12)	12	0.14
Irish (471)	1,298	14.66
Italian (234)	485	5.48
Lithuanian (0)	14	0.16
Norwegian (56)	154	1.74
Polish (32)	90	1.02
Portuguese (17)	17	0.19
Russian (7)	37	0.42
Scotch-Irish (47)	178	2.01
Scottish (28)	227	2.56
Swedish (13)	65	0.73
Welsh (0)	23	0.26
West Indian, ex. Hispanic (0)	64	0.72
Dutch West Indian (0)	11	0.12
Jamaican (0)	53	0.60
Yugoslavian (0)	50	0.56

Hispanic Origin	Population	%
Hispanic or Latino (of any race)	3,085	35.38
Central American, ex. Mexican	91	1.04
Costa Rican	4	0.05
Guatemalan	21	0.24
Honduran	4	0.05
Nicaraguan	23	0.26
Panamanian	5	0.06
Salvadoran	34	0.39
Cuban	19	0.22
Dominican Republic	7	0.08
Mexican	2,658	30.48
Puerto Rican	61	0.70
South American	72	0.83
Argentinean	15	0.17
Bolivian	1	0.01
Chilean	4	0.05
Colombian	12	0.14
Ecuadorian	11	0.13
Peruvian	18	0.21
Uruguayan	5	0.06
Venezuelan	6	0.07
Other Hispanic or Latino	177	2.03

Race*	Population	%
African-American/Black (438)	521	5.97
Not Hispanic (405)	456	5.23
Hispanic (33)	65	0.75
American Indian/Alaska Native (122)	214	2.45
Not Hispanic (52)	115	1.32
Hispanic (70)	99	1.14
Alaska Athabascan *(Ala. Nat.)* (0)	1	0.01
Aleut *(Alaska Native)* (0)	1	0.01
Apache (8)	10	0.11
Blackfeet (1)	6	0.07
Canadian/French Am. Ind. (1)	2	0.02
Cherokee (15)	34	0.39
Chippewa (2)	4	0.05
Choctaw (3)	12	0.14
Comanche (2)	2	0.02
Crow (1)	1	0.01
Delaware (1)	1	0.01
Hopi (3)	3	0.03
Iroquois (3)	4	0.05
Kiowa (1)	1	0.01
Lumbee (1)	2	0.02
Menominee (1)	1	0.01
Mexican American Ind. (10)	17	0.19
Navajo (5)	9	0.10
Pueblo (1)	1	0.01
Puget Sound Salish (1)	1	0.01
Seminole (0)	1	0.01
Sioux (1)	2	0.02
Spanish American Ind. (0)	2	0.02
Ute (1)	1	0.01
Yaqui (8)	8	0.09
Asian (352)	513	5.88
Not Hispanic (337)	450	5.16
Hispanic (15)	63	0.72
Bangladeshi (5)	10	0.11
Cambodian (6)	8	0.09
Chinese, ex. Taiwanese (40)	71	0.81
Filipino (96)	165	1.89
Indian (32)	46	0.53
Indonesian (40)	51	0.58
Japanese (20)	41	0.47
Korean (29)	38	0.44
Malaysian (0)	5	0.06
Pakistani (21)	27	0.31
Taiwanese (4)	4	0.05
Thai (12)	25	0.29
Vietnamese (17)	25	0.29
Hawaii Native/Pacific Islander (32)	63	0.72
Not Hispanic (26)	47	0.54
Hispanic (6)	16	0.18
Guamanian/Chamorro (3)	5	0.06
Native Hawaiian (14)	22	0.25
Samoan (8)	9	0.10
Tongan (4)	6	0.07
White (6,114)	6,479	74.30
Not Hispanic (4,568)	4,764	54.63
Hispanic (1,546)	1,715	19.67

Merced

Place Type: City
County: Merced
Population: 78,958†

Ancestry‡	Population	%
African, Sub-Saharan (108)	119	0.15
African (76)	87	0.11
Nigerian (12)	12	0.02
South African (20)	20	0.03
Albanian (0)	6	0.01
Alsatian (0)	12	0.02
American (1,590)	1,590	2.06
Arab (103)	164	0.21
Iraqi (0)	8	0.01
Lebanese (0)	10	0.01
Moroccan (0)	10	0.01
Palestinian (38)	38	0.05
Syrian (7)	40	0.05
Other Arab (58)	58	0.08
Armenian (10)	35	0.05
Australian (33)	33	0.04
Austrian (8)	40	0.05
Basque (46)	53	0.07
Belgian (0)	41	0.05
Brazilian (0)	57	0.07
British (107)	128	0.17
Canadian (19)	36	0.05
Celtic (26)	26	0.03
Croatian (0)	8	0.01
Czech (19)	38	0.05
Czechoslovakian (0)	8	0.01
Danish (54)	259	0.34
Dutch (61)	455	0.59
Eastern European (47)	57	0.07
English (810)	3,102	4.02
European (263)	321	0.42
Finnish (60)	94	0.12
French, ex. Basque (266)	1,482	1.92
French Canadian (38)	174	0.23
German (1,214)	4,733	6.14
Greek (0)	102	0.13
Hungarian (32)	150	0.19
Icelander (0)	13	0.02
Iranian (75)	75	0.10
Irish (926)	4,161	5.40
Italian (439)	1,718	2.23
Lithuanian (12)	56	0.07
Norwegian (322)	658	0.85
Polish (52)	272	0.35
Portuguese (733)	1,645	2.13
Russian (156)	251	0.33
Scandinavian (41)	50	0.06
Scotch-Irish (126)	492	0.64
Scottish (257)	674	0.87
Swedish (108)	378	0.49
Swiss (68)	224	0.29
Welsh (16)	224	0.29
West Indian, ex. Hispanic (11)	11	0.01
West Indian (11)	11	0.01

Hispanic Origin	Population	%
Hispanic or Latino (of any race)	39,140	49.57
Central American, ex. Mexican	502	0.64
Costa Rican	18	0.02
Guatemalan	57	0.07
Honduran	37	0.05
Nicaraguan	120	0.15
Panamanian	17	0.02
Salvadoran	248	0.31
Other Central American	5	0.01
Cuban	75	0.09
Dominican Republic	7	0.01
Mexican	35,593	45.08
Puerto Rican	384	0.49
South American	152	0.19
Argentinean	31	0.04
Bolivian	4	0.01
Chilean	19	0.02
Colombian	32	0.04
Ecuadorian	3	<0.01
Paraguayan	1	<0.01
Peruvian	41	0.05
Uruguayan	5	0.01
Venezuelan	15	0.02
Other South American	1	<0.01
Other Hispanic or Latino	2,427	3.07

Race*	Population	%
African-American/Black (4,958)	6,059	7.67
Not Hispanic (4,483)	5,200	6.59
Hispanic (475)	859	1.09
American Indian/Alaska Native (1,153)	2,091	2.65
Not Hispanic (399)	966	1.22
Hispanic (754)	1,125	1.42
Apache (42)	75	0.09
Blackfeet (11)	36	0.05
Central American Ind. (5)	5	0.01
Cherokee (91)	332	0.42
Cheyenne (1)	6	0.01
Chickasaw (2)	12	0.02
Chippewa (11)	17	0.02
Choctaw (28)	77	0.10
Comanche (0)	1	<0.01
Cree (1)	4	0.01
Creek (5)	12	0.02
Crow (3)	6	0.01
Delaware (0)	3	<0.01
Hopi (1)	3	<0.01
Iroquois (2)	5	0.01
Mexican American Ind. (121)	176	0.22
Navajo (24)	32	0.04
Osage (3)	6	0.01
Paiute (17)	32	0.04
Pima (3)	5	0.01
Potawatomi (2)	4	0.01
Pueblo (2)	4	0.01
Puget Sound Salish (1)	1	<0.01
Seminole (1)	9	0.01
Shoshone (4)	10	0.01
Sioux (17)	40	0.05
South American Ind. (1)	1	<0.01
Spanish American Ind. (18)	26	0.03
Tlingit-Haida *(Alaska Native)* (5)	9	0.01
Tohono O'Odham (3)	4	0.01
Ute (2)	3	<0.01
Yaqui (23)	35	0.04
Yuman (1)	1	<0.01
Asian (9,342)	10,509	13.31
Not Hispanic (9,116)	9,934	12.58
Hispanic (226)	575	0.73
Burmese (9)	10	0.01
Cambodian (31)	43	0.05
Chinese, ex. Taiwanese (535)	684	0.87
Filipino (1,046)	1,451	1.84
Hmong (4,552)	4,741	6.00
Indian (597)	725	0.92
Indonesian (6)	16	0.02
Japanese (223)	391	0.50

*Notes: † The Census 2010 population figure is used to calculate the percentages in the Hispanic Origin and Race categories. Ancestry percentages are based on the 2006-2010 American Community Survey population (not shown); ‡ Numbers in parentheses indicate the number of people reporting a single ancestry; * Numbers in parentheses indicate the number of persons reporting this race alone, not in combination with any other race; Please refer to the Explanation of Data for more information.*

	Population	%
Korean (137)	201	0.25
Laotian (1,323)	1,482	1.88
Nepalese (8)	8	0.01
Pakistani (54)	69	0.09
Sri Lankan (5)	6	0.01
Taiwanese (41)	50	0.06
Thai (63)	137	0.17
Vietnamese (188)	225	0.28
Hawaii Native/Pacific Islander (174)	392	0.50
Not Hispanic (131)	259	0.33
Hispanic (43)	133	0.17
Fijian (18)	27	0.03
Guamanian/Chamorro (38)	66	0.08
Marshallese (3)	3	<0.01
Native Hawaiian (43)	132	0.17
Samoan (33)	55	0.07
White (41,177)	44,776	56.71
Not Hispanic (23,702)	25,220	31.94
Hispanic (17,475)	19,556	24.77

Midway City

Place Type: CDP
County: Orange
Population: 8,485†

Ancestry‡	Population	%
American (106)	106	1.36
Arab (116)	116	1.49
Egyptian (116)	116	1.49
Austrian (0)	7	0.09
Belgian (11)	11	0.14
British (17)	17	0.22
Czechoslovakian (19)	19	0.24
Danish (0)	13	0.17
Dutch (0)	51	0.65
English (76)	288	3.69
European (40)	40	0.51
French, ex. Basque (115)	145	1.86
German (82)	349	4.47
Greek (13)	70	0.90
Iranian (34)	34	0.44
Irish (91)	186	2.38
Italian (77)	93	1.19
Northern European (0)	30	0.38
Norwegian (13)	13	0.17
Polish (72)	72	0.92
Romanian (15)	32	0.41
Russian (56)	56	0.72
Scandinavian (0)	27	0.35
Scotch-Irish (67)	111	1.42
Scottish (0)	36	0.46
Swedish (0)	51	0.65

Hispanic Origin	Population	%
Hispanic or Latino (of any race)	2,467	29.07
Central American, ex. Mexican	82	0.97
Costa Rican	1	0.01
Guatemalan	29	0.34
Honduran	3	0.04
Nicaraguan	3	0.04
Panamanian	3	0.04
Salvadoran	43	0.51
Cuban	15	0.18
Dominican Republic	1	0.01
Mexican	2,182	25.72
Puerto Rican	14	0.16
South American	49	0.58
Argentinean	6	0.07
Chilean	7	0.08
Colombian	15	0.18
Ecuadorian	5	0.06
Peruvian	14	0.16
Uruguayan	2	0.02
Other Hispanic or Latino	124	1.46

Race*	Population	%
African-American/Black (71)	113	1.33
Not Hispanic (62)	96	1.13
Hispanic (9)	17	0.20
American Indian/Alaska Native (65)	126	1.48
Not Hispanic (24)	51	0.60
Hispanic (41)	75	0.88
Apache (4)	7	0.08
Blackfeet (0)	1	0.01
Cherokee (4)	22	0.26
Choctaw (1)	3	0.04
Mexican American Ind. (13)	18	0.21
Navajo (1)	2	0.02
Paiute (2)	2	0.02
Potawatomi (0)	1	0.01
Sioux (3)	6	0.07
Yaqui (0)	3	0.04
Asian (3,994)	4,110	48.44
Not Hispanic (3,960)	4,068	47.94
Hispanic (34)	42	0.49
Bangladeshi (1)	1	0.01
Bhutanese (1)	1	0.01
Cambodian (14)	22	0.26
Chinese, ex. Taiwanese (84)	158	1.86
Filipino (94)	131	1.54
Indian (15)	37	0.44
Indonesian (0)	6	0.07
Japanese (43)	52	0.61
Korean (90)	93	1.10
Laotian (19)	19	0.22
Malaysian (0)	1	0.01
Pakistani (4)	11	0.13
Taiwanese (1)	6	0.07
Thai (16)	20	0.24
Vietnamese (3,511)	3,651	43.03
Hawaii Native/Pacific Islander (40)	62	0.73
Not Hispanic (38)	58	0.68
Hispanic (2)	4	0.05
Guamanian/Chamorro (10)	15	0.18
Native Hawaiian (8)	20	0.24
Samoan (21)	23	0.27
White (2,884)	3,113	36.69
Not Hispanic (1,776)	1,899	22.38
Hispanic (1,108)	1,214	14.31

Mill Valley

Place Type: City
County: Marin
Population: 13,903†

Ancestry‡	Population	%
African, Sub-Saharan (47)	47	0.34
African (47)	47	0.34
Alsatian (0)	13	0.09
American (301)	301	2.20
Arab (49)	60	0.44
Jordanian (14)	14	0.10
Moroccan (6)	6	0.04
Palestinian (10)	21	0.15
Other Arab (19)	19	0.14
Armenian (16)	52	0.38
Australian (49)	49	0.36
Austrian (25)	98	0.72
Basque (18)	35	0.26
Belgian (24)	68	0.50
British (164)	288	2.10
Canadian (19)	91	0.66
Celtic (46)	78	0.57
Czech (68)	158	1.15
Czechoslovakian (0)	46	0.34
Danish (153)	224	1.63
Dutch (0)	146	1.07
Eastern European (197)	197	1.44
English (554)	2,287	16.69
Estonian (11)	21	0.15
European (361)	372	2.71
Finnish (15)	28	0.20
French, ex. Basque (199)	697	5.09
French Canadian (30)	103	0.75
German (653)	2,437	17.79
Greek (12)	50	0.36
Hungarian (19)	77	0.56
Iranian (12)	12	0.09
Irish (325)	1,878	13.71
Italian (511)	1,289	9.41
Latvian (0)	12	0.09
Lithuanian (17)	98	0.72
Luxemburger (0)	12	0.09
New Zealander (83)	83	0.61
Northern European (326)	326	2.38
Norwegian (13)	222	1.62
Pennsylvania German (0)	36	0.26
Polish (131)	334	2.44
Portuguese (12)	79	0.58
Romanian (15)	135	0.99
Russian (398)	802	5.85
Scandinavian (21)	21	0.15
Scotch-Irish (123)	315	2.30
Scottish (160)	824	6.01
Slovak (37)	53	0.39
Swedish (61)	436	3.18
Swiss (41)	146	1.07
Ukrainian (27)	38	0.28
Welsh (0)	49	0.36

Hispanic Origin	Population	%
Hispanic or Latino (of any race)	622	4.47
Central American, ex. Mexican	103	0.74
Costa Rican	1	0.01
Guatemalan	29	0.21
Honduran	5	0.04
Nicaraguan	16	0.12
Panamanian	7	0.05
Salvadoran	45	0.32
Cuban	24	0.17
Dominican Republic	2	0.01
Mexican	255	1.83
Puerto Rican	28	0.20
South American	111	0.80
Argentinean	24	0.17
Bolivian	2	0.01
Chilean	13	0.09
Colombian	35	0.25
Ecuadorian	8	0.06
Peruvian	16	0.12
Uruguayan	1	0.01
Venezuelan	9	0.06
Other South American	3	0.02
Other Hispanic or Latino	99	0.71

Race*	Population	%
African-American/Black (118)	179	1.29
Not Hispanic (109)	164	1.18
Hispanic (9)	15	0.11
American Indian/Alaska Native (23)	116	0.83
Not Hispanic (15)	80	0.58
Hispanic (8)	36	0.26
Apache (1)	2	0.01
Canadian/French Am. Ind. (1)	2	0.01
Central American Ind. (1)	2	0.01
Cherokee (4)	21	0.15
Cheyenne (0)	1	0.01
Chickasaw (1)	1	0.01
Chippewa (0)	1	0.01
Choctaw (1)	2	0.01
Comanche (0)	1	0.01
Delaware (0)	3	0.02
Iroquois (0)	1	0.01
Lumbee (1)	1	0.01
Mexican American Ind. (3)	4	0.03
Navajo (0)	1	0.01
Osage (1)	1	0.01
Seminole (0)	1	0.01
Shoshone (0)	2	0.01
Sioux (0)	1	0.01
South American Ind. (0)	2	0.01
Spanish American Ind. (1)	1	0.01
Yuman (0)	1	0.01
Asian (755)	1,077	7.75
Not Hispanic (740)	1,047	7.53
Hispanic (15)	30	0.22
Bangladeshi (1)	1	0.01
Burmese (0)	1	0.01

*Notes: † The Census 2010 population figure is used to calculate the percentages in the Hispanic Origin and Race categories. Ancestry percentages are based on the 2006-2010 American Community Survey population (not shown); ‡ Numbers in parentheses indicate the number of people reporting a single ancestry; * Numbers in parentheses indicate the number of persons reporting this race alone, not in combination with any other race; Please refer to the Explanation of Data for more information.*

Cambodian (3)	3	0.02
Chinese, ex. Taiwanese (222)	347	2.50
Filipino (54)	93	0.67
Indian (195)	227	1.63
Indonesian (1)	3	0.02
Japanese (130)	218	1.57
Korean (74)	113	0.81
Nepalese (6)	6	0.04
Pakistani (6)	9	0.06
Sri Lankan (4)	6	0.04
Taiwanese (3)	4	0.03
Thai (16)	20	0.14
Vietnamese (19)	26	0.19
Hawaii Native/Pacific Islander (14)	28	0.20
Not Hispanic (14)	25	0.18
Hispanic (0)	3	0.02
Fijian (12)	12	0.09
Native Hawaiian (0)	8	0.06
Samoan (0)	1	0.01
White (12,341)	12,808	92.12
Not Hispanic (11,934)	12,341	88.77
Hispanic (407)	467	3.36

Millbrae

Place Type: City
County: San Mateo
Population: 21,532†

Ancestry‡	Population	%
Afghan (7)	21	0.10
African, Sub-Saharan (9)	25	0.12
Ethiopian (9)	9	0.04
Nigerian (0)	16	0.08
Albanian (3)	3	0.01
American (330)	330	1.57
Arab (512)	600	2.86
Arab (88)	88	0.42
Iraqi (6)	6	0.03
Jordanian (243)	243	1.16
Lebanese (20)	108	0.51
Palestinian (112)	112	0.53
Other Arab (43)	43	0.20
Armenian (296)	316	1.50
Assyrian/Chaldean/Syriac (12)	12	0.06
Australian (15)	26	0.12
Austrian (0)	81	0.39
Belgian (11)	11	0.05
British (7)	38	0.18
Canadian (16)	73	0.35
Celtic (14)	14	0.07
Croatian (37)	66	0.31
Czech (0)	26	0.12
Danish (5)	70	0.33
Dutch (42)	99	0.47
English (238)	1,174	5.59
Estonian (11)	11	0.05
European (138)	154	0.73
Finnish (0)	8	0.04
French, ex. Basque (56)	408	1.94
French Canadian (11)	11	0.05
German (395)	1,768	8.42
Greek (192)	270	1.29
Hungarian (6)	80	0.38
Iranian (52)	58	0.28
Irish (567)	2,510	11.95
Israeli (6)	6	0.03
Italian (877)	2,345	11.16
Latvian (0)	22	0.10
Lithuanian (22)	22	0.10
Maltese (142)	191	0.91
Norwegian (50)	293	1.39
Polish (60)	182	0.87
Portuguese (12)	108	0.51
Russian (106)	233	1.11
Scotch-Irish (41)	153	0.73
Scottish (64)	261	1.24
Slovak (13)	13	0.06
Slovene (0)	12	0.06
Swedish (36)	324	1.54
Swiss (22)	39	0.19
Ukrainian (8)	25	0.12
Welsh (14)	189	0.90
West Indian, ex. Hispanic (28)	66	0.31
Barbadian (10)	10	0.05
Jamaican (18)	56	0.27
Yugoslavian (0)	33	0.16

Hispanic Origin	Population	%
Hispanic or Latino (of any race)	2,555	11.87
Central American, ex. Mexican	586	2.72
Costa Rican	15	0.07
Guatemalan	62	0.29
Honduran	13	0.06
Nicaraguan	211	0.98
Panamanian	17	0.08
Salvadoran	262	1.22
Other Central American	6	0.03
Cuban	18	0.08
Dominican Republic	3	0.01
Mexican	1,245	5.78
Puerto Rican	125	0.58
South American	241	1.12
Argentinean	17	0.08
Bolivian	16	0.07
Chilean	14	0.07
Colombian	45	0.21
Ecuadorian	14	0.07
Peruvian	121	0.56
Venezuelan	10	0.05
Other South American	4	0.02
Other Hispanic or Latino	337	1.57

Race*	Population	%
African-American/Black (179)	284	1.32
Not Hispanic (158)	244	1.13
Hispanic (21)	40	0.19
American Indian/Alaska Native (33)	125	0.58
Not Hispanic (11)	61	0.28
Hispanic (22)	64	0.30
Alaska Athabascan *(Ala. Nat.)* (0)	1	<0.01
Apache (1)	4	0.02
Blackfeet (0)	10	0.05
Cherokee (4)	23	0.11
Chippewa (1)	2	0.01
Choctaw (2)	2	0.01
Cree (0)	1	<0.01
Hopi (0)	3	0.01
Mexican American Ind. (0)	3	0.01
Navajo (1)	5	0.02
Pueblo (0)	1	<0.01
Sioux (1)	1	<0.01
South American Ind. (0)	4	0.02
Yaqui (0)	1	<0.01
Asian (9,205)	9,866	45.82
Not Hispanic (9,155)	9,708	45.09
Hispanic (50)	158	0.73
Bangladeshi (3)	5	0.02
Bhutanese (1)	1	<0.01
Burmese (40)	42	0.20
Cambodian (10)	13	0.06
Chinese, ex. Taiwanese (5,930)	6,268	29.11
Filipino (1,225)	1,499	6.96
Hmong (7)	11	0.05
Indian (303)	348	1.62
Indonesian (37)	50	0.23
Japanese (317)	463	2.15
Korean (602)	660	3.07
Laotian (7)	7	0.03
Malaysian (1)	3	0.01
Nepalese (4)	4	0.02
Pakistani (22)	25	0.12
Sri Lankan (10)	14	0.07
Taiwanese (277)	300	1.39
Thai (65)	79	0.37
Vietnamese (91)	130	0.60
Hawaii Native/Pacific Islander (214)	317	1.47
Not Hispanic (197)	277	1.29
Hispanic (17)	40	0.19
Fijian (45)	51	0.24
Guamanian/Chamorro (11)	22	0.10
Native Hawaiian (24)	65	0.30
Samoan (16)	28	0.13
Tongan (105)	107	0.50
White (10,177)	10,996	51.07
Not Hispanic (8,736)	9,327	43.32
Hispanic (1,441)	1,669	7.75

Milpitas

Place Type: City
County: Santa Clara
Population: 66,790†

Ancestry‡	Population	%
Afghan (444)	454	0.70
African, Sub-Saharan (325)	336	0.52
African (94)	103	0.16
Ethiopian (91)	91	0.14
Liberian (104)	104	0.16
Nigerian (0)	2	<0.01
Somalian (36)	36	0.06
American (413)	413	0.63
Arab (180)	256	0.39
Arab (73)	83	0.13
Iraqi (11)	11	0.02
Lebanese (39)	52	0.08
Moroccan (0)	10	0.02
Palestinian (9)	52	0.08
Syrian (43)	43	0.07
Other Arab (5)	5	0.01
Armenian (23)	36	0.06
Assyrian/Chaldean/Syriac (31)	62	0.10
Australian (11)	11	0.02
Austrian (12)	40	0.06
Belgian (0)	23	0.04
British (113)	302	0.46
Bulgarian (30)	38	0.06
Croatian (7)	7	0.01
Czech (10)	45	0.07
Czechoslovakian (12)	12	0.02
Danish (5)	86	0.13
Dutch (59)	456	0.70
English (361)	1,722	2.64
Estonian (3)	3	<0.01
European (224)	321	0.49
Finnish (0)	22	0.03
French, ex. Basque (97)	1,203	1.85
French Canadian (11)	33	0.05
German (715)	3,221	4.94
Greek (37)	54	0.08
Hungarian (56)	103	0.16
Iranian (217)	217	0.33
Irish (536)	2,065	3.17
Israeli (15)	60	0.09
Italian (437)	1,411	2.17
Lithuanian (13)	13	0.02
Northern European (10)	10	0.02
Norwegian (99)	447	0.69
Polish (144)	360	0.55
Portuguese (236)	530	0.81
Romanian (84)	106	0.16
Russian (50)	96	0.15
Scandinavian (19)	68	0.10
Scotch-Irish (60)	382	0.59
Scottish (97)	284	0.44
Slavic (15)	15	0.02
Slovak (21)	105	0.16
Slovene (15)	15	0.02
Swedish (39)	325	0.50
Swiss (17)	48	0.07
Turkish (63)	63	0.10
Ukrainian (9)	45	0.07
Welsh (5)	127	0.19
West Indian, ex. Hispanic (54)	75	0.12
Jamaican (54)	60	0.09
West Indian (0)	15	0.02
Yugoslavian (15)	15	0.02

*Notes: † The Census 2010 population figure is used to calculate the percentages in the Hispanic Origin and Race categories. Ancestry percentages are based on the 2006-2010 American Community Survey population (not shown); ‡ Numbers in parentheses indicate the number of people reporting a single ancestry; * Numbers in parentheses indicate the number of persons reporting this race alone, not in combination with any other race; Please refer to the Explanation of Data for more information.*

Hispanic Origin	Population	%
Hispanic or Latino (of any race)	11,240	16.83
Central American, ex. Mexican	608	0.91
Costa Rican	20	0.03
Guatemalan	70	0.10
Honduran	23	0.03
Nicaraguan	237	0.35
Panamanian	31	0.05
Salvadoran	217	0.32
Other Central American	10	0.01
Cuban	44	0.07
Dominican Republic	21	0.03
Mexican	9,257	13.86
Puerto Rican	209	0.31
South American	315	0.47
Argentinean	66	0.10
Bolivian	5	0.01
Chilean	25	0.04
Colombian	26	0.04
Ecuadorian	16	0.02
Peruvian	139	0.21
Uruguayan	3	<0.01
Venezuelan	28	0.04
Other South American	7	0.01
Other Hispanic or Latino	786	1.18

Race*	Population	%
African-American/Black (1,969)	2,588	3.87
Not Hispanic (1,836)	2,290	3.43
Hispanic (133)	298	0.45
American Indian/Alaska Native (309)	792	1.19
Not Hispanic (137)	434	0.65
Hispanic (172)	358	0.54
Aleut *(Alaska Native)* (2)	6	0.01
Apache (19)	36	0.05
Blackfeet (4)	30	0.04
Canadian/French Am. Ind. (1)	3	<0.01
Central American Ind. (1)	1	<0.01
Cherokee (14)	82	0.12
Cheyenne (1)	1	<0.01
Chickasaw (1)	3	<0.01
Chippewa (5)	29	0.04
Choctaw (1)	25	0.04
Creek (0)	7	0.01
Crow (0)	1	<0.01
Delaware (1)	6	0.01
Hopi (1)	1	<0.01
Inupiat *(Alaska Native)* (1)	1	<0.01
Iroquois (7)	12	0.02
Kiowa (3)	3	<0.01
Menominee (5)	5	0.01
Mexican American Ind. (13)	36	0.05
Navajo (13)	23	0.03
Osage (2)	2	<0.01
Paiute (1)	3	<0.01
Potawatomi (3)	3	<0.01
Pueblo (0)	1	<0.01
Puget Sound Salish (1)	1	<0.01
Seminole (1)	3	<0.01
Shoshone (0)	2	<0.01
Sioux (2)	17	0.03
South American Ind. (1)	4	0.01
Spanish American Ind. (1)	3	<0.01
Tlingit-Haida *(Alaska Native)* (1)	6	0.01
Tohono O'Odham (2)	2	<0.01
Ute (1)	4	0.01
Yakama (1)	2	<0.01
Yaqui (8)	19	0.03
Yup'ik *(Alaska Native)* (3)	3	<0.01
Asian (41,536)	43,466	65.08
Not Hispanic (41,308)	42,929	64.27
Hispanic (228)	537	0.80
Bangladeshi (56)	58	0.09
Burmese (123)	135	0.20
Cambodian (177)	220	0.33
Chinese, ex. Taiwanese (9,182)	10,156	15.21
Filipino (11,546)	12,649	18.94
Hmong (31)	35	0.05
Indian (6,351)	6,602	9.88
Indonesian (52)	79	0.12
Japanese (404)	681	1.02
Korean (711)	816	1.22
Laotian (101)	146	0.22
Malaysian (43)	81	0.12
Nepalese (21)	23	0.03
Pakistani (380)	408	0.61
Sri Lankan (13)	16	0.02
Taiwanese (758)	860	1.29
Thai (92)	124	0.19
Vietnamese (10,356)	11,042	16.53
Hawaii Native/Pacific Islander (346)	739	1.11
Not Hispanic (316)	619	0.93
Hispanic (30)	120	0.18
Fijian (42)	57	0.09
Guamanian/Chamorro (107)	177	0.27
Native Hawaiian (30)	145	0.22
Samoan (78)	126	0.19
Tongan (39)	50	0.07
White (13,725)	15,892	23.79
Not Hispanic (9,751)	11,226	16.81
Hispanic (3,974)	4,666	6.99

Mira Loma

Place Type: CDP
County: Riverside
Population: 21,930†

Ancestry‡	Population	%
American (386)	386	1.92
Australian (38)	38	0.19
Austrian (0)	74	0.37
British (26)	71	0.35
Canadian (0)	12	0.06
Czech (8)	32	0.16
Danish (62)	195	0.97
Dutch (89)	333	1.65
English (286)	919	4.56
Estonian (0)	37	0.18
European (35)	35	0.17
French, ex. Basque (21)	352	1.75
French Canadian (0)	48	0.24
German (402)	1,518	7.54
Greek (12)	12	0.06
Guyanese (20)	68	0.34
Hungarian (0)	65	0.32
Iranian (28)	28	0.14
Irish (198)	1,003	4.98
Italian (127)	580	2.88
Lithuanian (8)	20	0.10
Norwegian (64)	122	0.61
Polish (104)	535	2.66
Portuguese (88)	232	1.15
Russian (41)	121	0.60
Scotch-Irish (0)	50	0.25
Scottish (18)	122	0.61
Swedish (52)	64	0.32
Swiss (35)	81	0.40
Ukrainian (0)	35	0.17
Welsh (0)	32	0.16

Hispanic Origin	Population	%
Hispanic or Latino (of any race)	14,846	67.70
Central American, ex. Mexican	388	1.77
Costa Rican	10	0.05
Guatemalan	73	0.33
Honduran	57	0.26
Nicaraguan	45	0.21
Panamanian	2	0.01
Salvadoran	198	0.90
Other Central American	3	0.01
Cuban	56	0.26
Dominican Republic	2	0.01
Mexican	13,503	61.57
Puerto Rican	86	0.39
South American	99	0.45
Argentinean	17	0.08
Colombian	30	0.14
Ecuadorian	28	0.13
Paraguayan	5	0.02
Peruvian	16	0.07
Uruguayan	1	<0.01
Other South American	2	0.01
Other Hispanic or Latino	712	3.25

Race*	Population	%
African-American/Black (383)	506	2.31
Not Hispanic (339)	414	1.89
Hispanic (44)	92	0.42
American Indian/Alaska Native (240)	453	2.07
Not Hispanic (76)	180	0.82
Hispanic (164)	273	1.24
Apache (19)	22	0.10
Blackfeet (1)	14	0.06
Central American Ind. (1)	3	0.01
Cherokee (12)	38	0.17
Choctaw (3)	8	0.04
Colville (1)	1	<0.01
Comanche (3)	5	0.02
Cree (0)	1	<0.01
Creek (5)	5	0.02
Crow (1)	1	<0.01
Inupiat *(Alaska Native)* (11)	11	0.05
Iroquois (5)	13	0.06
Mexican American Ind. (13)	36	0.16
Navajo (9)	11	0.05
Osage (0)	3	0.01
Paiute (1)	1	<0.01
Potawatomi (0)	3	0.01
Pueblo (1)	1	<0.01
Seminole (0)	2	0.01
Sioux (1)	16	0.07
South American Ind. (0)	1	<0.01
Spanish American Ind. (3)	4	0.02
Tlingit-Haida *(Alaska Native)* (1)	1	<0.01
Tohono O'Odham (2)	2	0.01
Yaqui (1)	1	<0.01
Asian (465)	629	2.87
Not Hispanic (439)	550	2.51
Hispanic (26)	79	0.36
Cambodian (11)	19	0.09
Chinese, ex. Taiwanese (87)	117	0.53
Filipino (125)	199	0.91
Hmong (10)	12	0.05
Indian (41)	49	0.22
Indonesian (5)	12	0.05
Japanese (16)	47	0.21
Korean (47)	55	0.25
Laotian (2)	9	0.04
Pakistani (21)	22	0.10
Taiwanese (6)	7	0.03
Thai (4)	8	0.04
Vietnamese (60)	64	0.29
Hawaii Native/Pacific Islander (43)	113	0.52
Not Hispanic (29)	85	0.39
Hispanic (14)	28	0.13
Fijian (1)	2	0.01
Guamanian/Chamorro (9)	13	0.06
Native Hawaiian (5)	33	0.15
Samoan (14)	40	0.18
Tongan (8)	10	0.05
White (12,577)	13,418	61.19
Not Hispanic (5,882)	6,112	27.87
Hispanic (6,695)	7,306	33.32

Mission Viejo

Place Type: City
County: Orange
Population: 93,305†

Ancestry‡	Population	%
Afghan (55)	55	0.06
African, Sub-Saharan (292)	325	0.35
African (189)	193	0.21
Nigerian (17)	17	0.02
Senegalese (0)	17	0.02
South African (65)	77	0.08
Other Sub-Saharan African (21)	21	0.02
American (4,003)	4,003	4.32

*Notes: † The Census 2010 population figure is used to calculate the percentages in the Hispanic Origin and Race categories. Ancestry percentages are based on the 2006-2010 American Community Survey population (not shown); ‡ Numbers in parentheses indicate the number of people reporting a single ancestry; * Numbers in parentheses indicate the number of persons reporting this race alone, not in combination with any other race; Please refer to the Explanation of Data for more information.*

Arab (962)	1,264	1.36
Arab (314)	324	0.35
Egyptian (161)	177	0.19
Jordanian (37)	57	0.06
Lebanese (360)	507	0.55
Palestinian (30)	66	0.07
Syrian (0)	35	0.04
Other Arab (60)	98	0.11
Armenian (386)	462	0.50
Australian (0)	17	0.02
Austrian (90)	401	0.43
Basque (31)	122	0.13
Belgian (16)	92	0.10
Brazilian (11)	17	0.02
British (543)	1,204	1.30
Bulgarian (17)	17	0.02
Cajun (33)	33	0.04
Canadian (351)	559	0.60
Celtic (16)	16	0.02
Croatian (47)	214	0.23
Czech (115)	480	0.52
Czechoslovakian (0)	69	0.07
Danish (228)	942	1.02
Dutch (563)	1,707	1.84
Eastern European (161)	173	0.19
English (3,141)	11,373	12.28
Estonian (11)	25	0.03
European (1,439)	1,673	1.81
Finnish (45)	211	0.23
French, ex. Basque (629)	3,375	3.64
French Canadian (254)	553	0.60
German (4,059)	15,874	17.14
Greek (185)	547	0.59
Guyanese (0)	28	0.03
Hungarian (128)	754	0.81
Icelander (0)	32	0.03
Iranian (2,404)	2,460	2.66
Irish (3,696)	13,315	14.38
Israeli (9)	9	0.01
Italian (2,530)	6,660	7.19
Latvian (27)	60	0.06
Lithuanian (99)	388	0.42
Luxemburger (8)	20	0.02
Macedonian (0)	14	0.02
Maltese (11)	20	0.02
New Zealander (22)	22	0.02
Northern European (74)	74	0.08
Norwegian (526)	1,730	1.87
Polish (781)	3,283	3.54
Portuguese (102)	243	0.26
Romanian (247)	592	0.64
Russian (834)	2,070	2.24
Scandinavian (100)	315	0.34
Scotch-Irish (736)	1,675	1.81
Scottish (1,029)	2,724	2.94
Serbian (64)	88	0.10
Slavic (20)	20	0.02
Slovak (13)	181	0.20
Slovene (27)	65	0.07
Swedish (280)	2,055	2.22
Swiss (110)	346	0.37
Turkish (98)	122	0.13
Ukrainian (71)	201	0.22
Welsh (251)	763	0.82
West Indian, ex. Hispanic (23)	78	0.08
Barbadian (6)	22	0.02
Belizean (7)	7	0.01
British West Indian (0)	12	0.01
Jamaican (10)	10	0.01
West Indian (0)	27	0.03
Yugoslavian (50)	172	0.19

Hispanic Origin	Population	%
Hispanic or Latino (of any race)	15,877	17.02
Central American, ex. Mexican	823	0.88
Costa Rican	71	0.08
Guatemalan	300	0.32
Honduran	50	0.05
Nicaraguan	78	0.08
Panamanian	40	0.04
Salvadoran	276	0.30
Other Central American	8	0.01
Cuban	325	0.35
Dominican Republic	32	0.03
Mexican	11,559	12.39
Puerto Rican	396	0.42
South American	1,569	1.68
Argentinean	313	0.34
Bolivian	72	0.08
Chilean	92	0.10
Colombian	446	0.48
Ecuadorian	173	0.19
Paraguayan	3	<0.01
Peruvian	379	0.41
Uruguayan	18	0.02
Venezuelan	50	0.05
Other South American	23	0.02
Other Hispanic or Latino	1,173	1.26

Race*	Population	%
African-American/Black (1,210)	1,847	1.98
Not Hispanic (1,129)	1,654	1.77
Hispanic (81)	193	0.21
American Indian/Alaska Native (379)	925	0.99
Not Hispanic (176)	568	0.61
Hispanic (203)	357	0.38
Aleut *(Alaska Native)* (0)	3	<0.01
Apache (8)	19	0.02
Arapaho (1)	1	<0.01
Blackfeet (4)	29	0.03
Central American Ind. (1)	2	<0.01
Cherokee (35)	171	0.18
Cheyenne (1)	2	<0.01
Chickasaw (4)	9	0.01
Chippewa (3)	4	<0.01
Choctaw (7)	26	0.03
Colville (1)	1	<0.01
Comanche (1)	2	<0.01
Cree (1)	1	<0.01
Creek (6)	8	0.01
Hopi (0)	1	<0.01
Houma (2)	2	<0.01
Inupiat *(Alaska Native)* (1)	1	<0.01
Iroquois (7)	13	0.01
Kiowa (2)	2	<0.01
Lumbee (2)	2	<0.01
Menominee (1)	1	<0.01
Mexican American Ind. (35)	58	0.06
Navajo (19)	34	0.04
Osage (4)	8	0.01
Ottawa (1)	6	0.01
Paiute (1)	5	0.01
Pima (1)	2	<0.01
Potawatomi (1)	8	0.01
Pueblo (7)	9	0.01
Puget Sound Salish (3)	3	<0.01
Seminole (0)	4	<0.01
Shoshone (0)	1	<0.01
Sioux (5)	13	0.01
South American Ind. (1)	8	0.01
Spanish American Ind. (2)	3	<0.01
Tohono O'Odham (2)	4	<0.01
Ute (0)	5	0.01
Yaqui (3)	7	0.01
Yup'ik *(Alaska Native)* (1)	1	<0.01
Asian (8,462)	11,030	11.82
Not Hispanic (8,312)	10,616	11.38
Hispanic (150)	414	0.44
Bangladeshi (24)	24	0.03
Burmese (24)	33	0.04
Cambodian (71)	91	0.10
Chinese, ex. Taiwanese (1,403)	1,889	2.02
Filipino (2,240)	2,946	3.16
Hmong (5)	5	0.01
Indian (852)	990	1.06
Indonesian (97)	172	0.18
Japanese (959)	1,639	1.76
Korean (743)	931	1.00
Laotian (12)	13	0.01
Malaysian (1)	2	<0.01
Nepalese (13)	13	0.01
Pakistani (143)	175	0.19
Sri Lankan (40)	45	0.05
Taiwanese (171)	201	0.22
Thai (120)	159	0.17
Vietnamese (1,146)	1,315	1.41
Hawaii Native/Pacific Islander (153)	437	0.47
Not Hispanic (146)	403	0.43
Hispanic (7)	34	0.04
Fijian (7)	9	0.01
Guamanian/Chamorro (38)	73	0.08
Native Hawaiian (47)	191	0.20
Samoan (26)	55	0.06
Tongan (7)	9	0.01
White (74,493)	78,381	84.01
Not Hispanic (64,276)	67,222	72.05
Hispanic (10,217)	11,159	11.96

Modesto

Place Type: City
County: Stanislaus
Population: 201,165†

Ancestry‡	Population	%
Afghan (256)	256	0.13
African, Sub-Saharan (211)	387	0.19
African (98)	274	0.14
Ethiopian (76)	76	0.04
Nigerian (37)	37	0.02
American (6,546)	6,546	3.24
Arab (1,267)	1,485	0.74
Arab (108)	223	0.11
Egyptian (25)	41	0.02
Iraqi (491)	547	0.27
Lebanese (49)	59	0.03
Moroccan (0)	12	0.01
Palestinian (270)	270	0.13
Syrian (75)	75	0.04
Other Arab (249)	258	0.13
Armenian (341)	565	0.28
Assyrian/Chaldean/Syriac (2,367)	2,553	1.26
Australian (40)	94	0.05
Austrian (10)	243	0.12
Basque (63)	116	0.06
Belgian (13)	66	0.03
Brazilian (50)	98	0.05
British (205)	393	0.19
Bulgarian (0)	13	0.01
Cajun (0)	16	0.01
Canadian (184)	271	0.13
Celtic (15)	50	0.02
Croatian (26)	81	0.04
Czech (72)	254	0.13
Czechoslovakian (28)	113	0.06
Danish (270)	1,066	0.53
Dutch (1,198)	4,037	2.00
Eastern European (107)	116	0.06
English (4,395)	14,727	7.29
Estonian (23)	54	0.03
European (1,640)	2,029	1.00
Finnish (62)	368	0.18
French, ex. Basque (604)	5,489	2.72
French Canadian (155)	501	0.25
German (6,429)	22,747	11.27
German Russian (0)	21	0.01
Greek (330)	820	0.41
Hungarian (154)	380	0.19
Icelander (47)	96	0.05
Iranian (393)	554	0.27
Irish (4,509)	19,237	9.53
Israeli (0)	17	0.01
Italian (3,470)	8,823	4.37
Lithuanian (35)	147	0.07
Luxemburger (0)	21	0.01
Maltese (0)	28	0.01
New Zealander (9)	9	<0.01
Northern European (93)	93	0.05
Norwegian (812)	2,570	1.27
Pennsylvania German (15)	42	0.02

*Notes: † The Census 2010 population figure is used to calculate the percentages in the Hispanic Origin and Race categories. Ancestry percentages are based on the 2006-2010 American Community Survey population (not shown); ‡ Numbers in parentheses indicate the number of people reporting a single ancestry; * Numbers in parentheses indicate the number of persons reporting this race alone, not in combination with any other race; Please refer to the Explanation of Data for more information.*

Polish (633)	1,744	0.86
Portuguese (3,878)	7,250	3.59
Romanian (747)	791	0.39
Russian (259)	756	0.37
Scandinavian (213)	375	0.19
Scotch-Irish (1,083)	3,409	1.69
Scottish (890)	2,625	1.30
Serbian (0)	53	0.03
Slavic (24)	37	0.02
Slovak (0)	17	0.01
Slovene (0)	32	0.02
Swedish (888)	3,260	1.61
Swiss (371)	1,072	0.53
Turkish (0)	5	<0.01
Ukrainian (160)	320	0.16
Welsh (175)	1,523	0.75
West Indian, ex. Hispanic (67)	179	0.09
Belizean (0)	58	0.03
Dutch West Indian (0)	24	0.01
Haitian (0)	20	0.01
Jamaican (54)	64	0.03
West Indian (13)	13	0.01
Yugoslavian (43)	78	0.04

Hispanic Origin	Population	%
Hispanic or Latino (of any race)	71,381	35.48
Central American, ex. Mexican	2,341	1.16
Costa Rican	55	0.03
Guatemalan	421	0.21
Honduran	126	0.06
Nicaraguan	510	0.25
Panamanian	82	0.04
Salvadoran	1,134	0.56
Other Central American	13	0.01
Cuban	196	0.10
Dominican Republic	18	0.01
Mexican	62,010	30.83
Puerto Rican	1,447	0.72
South American	749	0.37
Argentinean	73	0.04
Bolivian	29	0.01
Chilean	97	0.05
Colombian	239	0.12
Ecuadorian	38	0.02
Peruvian	230	0.11
Uruguayan	15	0.01
Venezuelan	24	0.01
Other South American	4	<0.01
Other Hispanic or Latino	4,620	2.30

Race*	Population	%
African-American/Black (8,396)	11,151	5.54
Not Hispanic (7,539)	9,455	4.70
Hispanic (857)	1,696	0.84
American Indian/Alaska Native (2,494)	5,569	2.77
Not Hispanic (1,141)	3,080	1.53
Hispanic (1,353)	2,489	1.24
Alaska Athabascan *(Ala. Nat.)* (0)	16	0.01
Aleut *(Alaska Native)* (11)	16	0.01
Apache (97)	266	0.13
Arapaho (0)	1	<0.01
Blackfeet (10)	129	0.06
Canadian/French Am. Ind. (2)	4	<0.01
Central American Ind. (0)	4	<0.01
Cherokee (277)	1,004	0.50
Cheyenne (3)	12	0.01
Chickasaw (31)	76	0.04
Chippewa (9)	50	0.02
Choctaw (130)	385	0.19
Colville (3)	5	<0.01
Comanche (4)	24	0.01
Cree (4)	8	<0.01
Creek (28)	85	0.04
Crow (0)	1	<0.01
Delaware (5)	7	<0.01
Hopi (7)	11	0.01
Houma (0)	1	<0.01
Inupiat *(Alaska Native)* (3)	5	<0.01
Iroquois (14)	41	0.02
Kiowa (1)	5	<0.01
Lumbee (0)	1	<0.01
Mexican American Ind. (212)	323	0.16
Navajo (70)	158	0.08
Osage (2)	15	0.01
Ottawa (0)	2	<0.01
Paiute (39)	70	0.03
Pima (7)	20	0.01
Potawatomi (12)	22	0.01
Pueblo (12)	37	0.02
Puget Sound Salish (2)	6	<0.01
Seminole (7)	27	0.01
Shoshone (3)	13	0.01
Sioux (39)	105	0.05
South American Ind. (9)	21	0.01
Spanish American Ind. (19)	27	0.01
Tlingit-Haida *(Alaska Native)* (3)	4	<0.01
Tohono O'Odham (10)	21	0.01
Ute (1)	6	<0.01
Yaqui (51)	100	0.05
Yuman (1)	4	<0.01
Yup'ik *(Alaska Native)* (0)	1	<0.01
Asian (13,557)	17,695	8.80
Not Hispanic (12,899)	15,978	7.94
Hispanic (658)	1,717	0.85
Bangladeshi (1)	7	<0.01
Burmese (29)	30	0.01
Cambodian (2,402)	2,752	1.37
Chinese, ex. Taiwanese (1,358)	1,901	0.94
Filipino (3,021)	4,614	2.29
Hmong (261)	287	0.14
Indian (2,599)	3,403	1.69
Indonesian (12)	37	0.02
Japanese (356)	924	0.46
Korean (314)	450	0.22
Laotian (1,035)	1,257	0.62
Malaysian (2)	7	<0.01
Nepalese (4)	4	<0.01
Pakistani (132)	157	0.08
Sri Lankan (3)	5	<0.01
Taiwanese (48)	63	0.03
Thai (88)	162	0.08
Vietnamese (1,183)	1,394	0.69
Hawaii Native/Pacific Islander (1,924)	3,467	1.72
Not Hispanic (1,747)	2,976	1.48
Hispanic (177)	491	0.24
Fijian (1,109)	1,355	0.67
Guamanian/Chamorro (144)	324	0.16
Marshallese (0)	1	<0.01
Native Hawaiian (173)	567	0.28
Samoan (202)	334	0.17
Tongan (22)	34	0.02
White (130,833)	140,979	70.08
Not Hispanic (99,347)	104,608	52.00
Hispanic (31,486)	36,371	18.08

Monrovia

Place Type: City
County: Los Angeles
Population: 36,590†

Ancestry‡	Population	%
African, Sub-Saharan (196)	323	0.88
African (196)	282	0.77
Cape Verdean (0)	41	0.11
American (884)	884	2.41
Arab (97)	163	0.45
Arab (21)	21	0.06
Egyptian (27)	52	0.14
Jordanian (15)	15	0.04
Lebanese (18)	18	0.05
Syrian (0)	41	0.11
Other Arab (16)	16	0.04
Armenian (96)	109	0.30
Austrian (10)	130	0.36
Basque (0)	10	0.03
Belgian (9)	9	0.02
British (146)	255	0.70
Canadian (23)	83	0.23
Croatian (65)	65	0.18
Czech (0)	67	0.18
Czechoslovakian (43)	53	0.14
Danish (130)	298	0.81
Dutch (81)	559	1.53
Eastern European (37)	37	0.10
English (443)	2,438	6.66
European (360)	412	1.13
Finnish (46)	86	0.23
French, ex. Basque (64)	499	1.36
French Canadian (84)	159	0.43
German (1,164)	3,875	10.58
Greek (70)	145	0.40
Hungarian (28)	59	0.16
Iranian (63)	63	0.17
Irish (457)	2,685	7.33
Israeli (1)	1	<0.01
Italian (505)	1,396	3.81
Latvian (0)	9	0.02
Lithuanian (0)	63	0.17
Maltese (0)	7	0.02
Northern European (65)	65	0.18
Norwegian (89)	414	1.13
Pennsylvania German (0)	13	0.04
Polish (69)	391	1.07
Portuguese (24)	171	0.47
Romanian (9)	62	0.17
Russian (210)	336	0.92
Scandinavian (42)	53	0.14
Scotch-Irish (168)	466	1.27
Scottish (125)	608	1.66
Slavic (0)	14	0.04
Slovene (0)	21	0.06
Swedish (151)	414	1.13
Swiss (34)	44	0.12
Ukrainian (57)	88	0.24
Welsh (13)	194	0.53
West Indian, ex. Hispanic (0)	15	0.04
Belizean (0)	15	0.04
Yugoslavian (24)	73	0.20

Hispanic Origin	Population	%
Hispanic or Latino (of any race)	14,043	38.38
Central American, ex. Mexican	986	2.69
Costa Rican	45	0.12
Guatemalan	245	0.67
Honduran	109	0.30
Nicaraguan	113	0.31
Panamanian	26	0.07
Salvadoran	446	1.22
Other Central American	2	0.01
Cuban	287	0.78
Dominican Republic	15	0.04
Mexican	11,123	30.40
Puerto Rican	196	0.54
South American	561	1.53
Argentinean	139	0.38
Bolivian	14	0.04
Chilean	30	0.08
Colombian	126	0.34
Ecuadorian	61	0.17
Peruvian	141	0.39
Uruguayan	5	0.01
Venezuelan	23	0.06
Other South American	22	0.06
Other Hispanic or Latino	875	2.39

Race*	Population	%
African-American/Black (2,500)	2,942	8.04
Not Hispanic (2,346)	2,644	7.23
Hispanic (154)	298	0.81
American Indian/Alaska Native (279)	703	1.92
Not Hispanic (89)	323	0.88
Hispanic (190)	380	1.04
Alaska Athabascan *(Ala. Nat.)* (1)	1	<0.01
Apache (31)	39	0.11
Arapaho (0)	1	<0.01
Blackfeet (4)	21	0.06
Canadian/French Am. Ind. (0)	2	0.01
Central American Ind. (2)	4	0.01
Cherokee (15)	84	0.23

SECTION TWO

*Notes: † The Census 2010 population figure is used to calculate the percentages in the Hispanic Origin and Race categories. Ancestry percentages are based on the 2006-2010 American Community Survey population (not shown); ‡ Numbers in parentheses indicate the number of people reporting a single ancestry; * Numbers in parentheses indicate the number of persons reporting this race alone, not in combination with any other race; Please refer to the Explanation of Data for more information.*

Cheyenne (0)	3	0.01
Chickasaw (0)	8	0.02
Chippewa (2)	3	0.01
Choctaw (12)	26	0.07
Creek (1)	7	0.02
Crow (0)	1	<0.01
Delaware (0)	2	0.01
Hopi (1)	4	0.01
Inupiat *(Alaska Native)* (0)	1	<0.01
Iroquois (4)	6	0.02
Mexican American Ind. (15)	38	0.10
Navajo (9)	28	0.08
Osage (0)	5	0.01
Ottawa (0)	3	0.01
Paiute (1)	1	<0.01
Pima (3)	7	0.02
Potawatomi (4)	6	0.02
Pueblo (2)	4	0.01
Shoshone (0)	1	<0.01
Sioux (14)	32	0.09
South American Ind. (2)	2	0.01
Tohono O'Odham (1)	4	0.01
Ute (0)	3	0.01
Yakama (1)	1	<0.01
Yaqui (6)	9	0.02
Asian (4,107)	4,752	12.99
Not Hispanic (3,997)	4,480	12.24
Hispanic (110)	272	0.74
Bangladeshi (2)	2	0.01
Burmese (6)	12	0.03
Cambodian (20)	25	0.07
Chinese, ex. Taiwanese (1,365)	1,605	4.39
Filipino (1,189)	1,463	4.00
Hmong (1)	1	<0.01
Indian (245)	285	0.78
Indonesian (93)	130	0.36
Japanese (314)	495	1.35
Korean (158)	202	0.55
Laotian (3)	7	0.02
Malaysian (5)	10	0.03
Nepalese (0)	1	<0.01
Pakistani (19)	24	0.07
Sri Lankan (20)	24	0.07
Taiwanese (181)	199	0.54
Thai (126)	155	0.42
Vietnamese (181)	220	0.60
Hawaii Native/Pacific Islander (76)	174	0.48
Not Hispanic (69)	135	0.37
Hispanic (7)	39	0.11
Fijian (1)	1	<0.01
Guamanian/Chamorro (2)	7	0.02
Native Hawaiian (20)	55	0.15
Samoan (38)	53	0.14
Tongan (0)	1	<0.01
White (21,932)	23,505	64.24
Not Hispanic (15,023)	15,821	43.24
Hispanic (6,909)	7,684	21.00

Montclair

Place Type: City
County: San Bernardino
Population: 36,664†

Ancestry‡	Population	%
Afghan (40)	40	0.11
African, Sub-Saharan (51)	125	0.34
African (43)	109	0.30
Kenyan (8)	16	0.04
American (885)	885	2.41
Arab (103)	139	0.38
Lebanese (33)	33	0.09
Moroccan (16)	25	0.07
Syrian (22)	22	0.06
Other Arab (32)	59	0.16
Armenian (0)	11	0.03
Australian (15)	15	0.04
Belgian (34)	34	0.09
British (23)	23	0.06
Bulgarian (0)	10	0.03
Croatian (0)	15	0.04
Czech (0)	82	0.22
Danish (0)	79	0.22
Dutch (15)	92	0.25
Eastern European (8)	8	0.02
English (348)	850	2.32
European (43)	55	0.15
French, ex. Basque (77)	660	1.80
French Canadian (19)	19	0.05
German (379)	1,627	4.43
Greek (8)	18	0.05
Hungarian (7)	35	0.10
Iranian (192)	192	0.52
Irish (204)	1,064	2.90
Italian (252)	741	2.02
Lithuanian (15)	36	0.10
Norwegian (32)	58	0.16
Polish (19)	108	0.29
Portuguese (0)	102	0.28
Romanian (7)	7	0.02
Russian (30)	57	0.16
Scotch-Irish (27)	141	0.38
Scottish (29)	75	0.20
Slovak (0)	9	0.02
Swedish (16)	282	0.77
Swiss (11)	11	0.03
Ukrainian (4)	4	0.01
Welsh (0)	27	0.07
West Indian, ex. Hispanic (153)	153	0.42
Belizean (131)	131	0.36
Haitian (10)	10	0.03
Jamaican (12)	12	0.03
Yugoslavian (0)	15	0.04

Hispanic Origin	Population	%
Hispanic or Latino (of any race)	25,744	70.22
Central American, ex. Mexican	1,764	4.81
Costa Rican	33	0.09
Guatemalan	513	1.40
Honduran	159	0.43
Nicaraguan	182	0.50
Panamanian	32	0.09
Salvadoran	834	2.27
Other Central American	11	0.03
Cuban	147	0.40
Dominican Republic	6	0.02
Mexican	21,893	59.71
Puerto Rican	176	0.48
South American	382	1.04
Argentinean	78	0.21
Bolivian	11	0.03
Chilean	17	0.05
Colombian	100	0.27
Ecuadorian	55	0.15
Peruvian	110	0.30
Uruguayan	3	0.01
Venezuelan	8	0.02
Other Hispanic or Latino	1,376	3.75

Race*	Population	%
African-American/Black (1,908)	2,206	6.02
Not Hispanic (1,702)	1,867	5.09
Hispanic (206)	339	0.92
American Indian/Alaska Native (434)	677	1.85
Not Hispanic (93)	180	0.49
Hispanic (341)	497	1.36
Apache (14)	28	0.08
Arapaho (1)	1	<0.01
Blackfeet (6)	10	0.03
Cherokee (14)	50	0.14
Cheyenne (0)	3	0.01
Chickasaw (0)	2	0.01
Chippewa (3)	4	0.01
Choctaw (1)	5	0.01
Comanche (0)	3	0.01
Creek (4)	4	0.01
Hopi (1)	1	<0.01
Inupiat *(Alaska Native)* (0)	2	0.01
Lumbee (2)	5	0.01
Mexican American Ind. (99)	117	0.32
Navajo (14)	24	0.07
Pima (1)	1	<0.01
Pueblo (3)	8	0.02
Seminole (0)	5	0.01
Sioux (1)	6	0.02
South American Ind. (1)	2	0.01
Spanish American Ind. (7)	9	0.02
Tlingit-Haida *(Alaska Native)* (1)	2	0.01
Tohono O'Odham (0)	2	0.01
Ute (2)	2	0.01
Yaqui (10)	17	0.05
Yuman (2)	2	0.01
Asian (3,425)	3,790	10.34
Not Hispanic (3,275)	3,490	9.52
Hispanic (150)	300	0.82
Burmese (5)	5	0.01
Cambodian (69)	84	0.23
Chinese, ex. Taiwanese (483)	605	1.65
Filipino (865)	978	2.67
Hmong (1)	1	<0.01
Indian (92)	130	0.35
Indonesian (172)	224	0.61
Japanese (58)	126	0.34
Korean (79)	94	0.26
Laotian (74)	91	0.25
Malaysian (1)	8	0.02
Pakistani (44)	46	0.13
Sri Lankan (3)	3	0.01
Taiwanese (63)	65	0.18
Thai (96)	111	0.30
Vietnamese (1,149)	1,241	3.38
Hawaii Native/Pacific Islander (74)	165	0.45
Not Hispanic (60)	120	0.33
Hispanic (14)	45	0.12
Fijian (2)	5	0.01
Guamanian/Chamorro (15)	25	0.07
Native Hawaiian (5)	25	0.07
Samoan (17)	31	0.08
Tongan (23)	24	0.07
White (19,337)	20,614	56.22
Not Hispanic (5,293)	5,605	15.29
Hispanic (14,044)	15,009	40.94

Montebello

Place Type: City
County: Los Angeles
Population: 62,500†

Ancestry‡	Population	%
African, Sub-Saharan (13)	39	0.06
African (13)	39	0.06
American (922)	922	1.48
Arab (77)	151	0.24
Egyptian (18)	18	0.03
Lebanese (6)	46	0.07
Palestinian (45)	45	0.07
Syrian (8)	28	0.04
Other Arab (0)	14	0.02
Armenian (1,686)	1,885	3.02
Austrian (9)	9	0.01
Basque (0)	17	0.03
Belgian (22)	22	0.04
British (0)	27	0.04
Bulgarian (16)	16	0.03
Dutch (36)	122	0.20
Eastern European (2)	2	<0.01
English (117)	411	0.66
European (78)	201	0.32
Finnish (0)	5	0.01
French, ex. Basque (12)	117	0.19
French Canadian (22)	30	0.05
German (133)	559	0.90
Greek (75)	96	0.15
Hungarian (13)	19	0.03
Iranian (98)	172	0.28
Irish (123)	495	0.79
Italian (400)	935	1.50
Northern European (2)	2	<0.01
Norwegian (7)	24	0.04

*Notes: † The Census 2010 population figure is used to calculate the percentages in the Hispanic Origin and Race categories. Ancestry percentages are based on the 2006-2010 American Community Survey population (not shown); ‡ Numbers in parentheses indicate the number of people reporting a single ancestry; * Numbers in parentheses indicate the number of persons reporting this race alone, not in combination with any other race; Please refer to the Explanation of Data for more information.*

Pennsylvania German (0)	9	0.01
Polish (46)	80	0.13
Portuguese (0)	36	0.06
Romanian (14)	42	0.07
Russian (206)	316	0.51
Scotch-Irish (40)	86	0.14
Scottish (15)	60	0.10
Serbian (7)	7	0.01
Slovene (16)	16	0.03
Swedish (0)	8	0.01
Swiss (10)	17	0.03
Turkish (18)	30	0.05
Ukrainian (38)	38	0.06
Welsh (0)	9	0.01
West Indian, ex. Hispanic (31)	40	0.06
British West Indian (31)	31	0.05
Haitian (0)	9	0.01
Yugoslavian (0)	11	0.02

Hispanic Origin	Population	%
Hispanic or Latino (of any race)	49,578	79.32
Central American, ex. Mexican	3,219	5.15
Costa Rican	53	0.08
Guatemalan	789	1.26
Honduran	210	0.34
Nicaraguan	341	0.55
Panamanian	3	<0.01
Salvadoran	1,780	2.85
Other Central American	43	0.07
Cuban	127	0.20
Dominican Republic	14	0.02
Mexican	43,662	69.86
Puerto Rican	212	0.34
South American	654	1.05
Argentinean	106	0.17
Bolivian	28	0.04
Chilean	39	0.06
Colombian	128	0.20
Ecuadorian	124	0.20
Paraguayan	10	0.02
Peruvian	194	0.31
Uruguayan	7	0.01
Venezuelan	13	0.02
Other South American	5	0.01
Other Hispanic or Latino	1,690	2.70

Race*	Population	%
African-American/Black (567)	781	1.25
Not Hispanic (380)	431	0.69
Hispanic (187)	350	0.56
American Indian/Alaska Native (634)	948	1.52
Not Hispanic (99)	167	0.27
Hispanic (535)	781	1.25
Apache (40)	61	0.10
Blackfeet (11)	12	0.02
Canadian/French Am. Ind. (0)	1	<0.01
Cherokee (26)	57	0.09
Cheyenne (2)	2	<0.01
Chippewa (0)	4	0.01
Choctaw (2)	6	0.01
Comanche (1)	1	<0.01
Cree (1)	1	<0.01
Creek (0)	1	<0.01
Crow (0)	1	<0.01
Delaware (1)	2	<0.01
Hopi (6)	10	0.02
Iroquois (0)	1	<0.01
Mexican American Ind. (109)	162	0.26
Navajo (37)	51	0.08
Paiute (4)	4	0.01
Pima (5)	7	0.01
Potawatomi (0)	1	<0.01
Pueblo (2)	4	0.01
Sioux (7)	10	0.02
South American Ind. (0)	1	<0.01
Spanish American Ind. (9)	10	0.02
Tohono O'Odham (16)	16	0.03
Tsimshian *(Alaska Native)* (3)	4	0.01
Yaqui (18)	34	0.05
Asian (6,850)	7,359	11.77
Not Hispanic (6,646)	6,886	11.02
Hispanic (204)	473	0.76
Bangladeshi (50)	54	0.09
Burmese (16)	21	0.03
Cambodian (54)	98	0.16
Chinese, ex. Taiwanese (2,469)	2,749	4.40
Filipino (932)	1,132	1.81
Indian (481)	517	0.83
Indonesian (24)	25	0.04
Japanese (1,462)	1,669	2.67
Korean (586)	624	1.00
Laotian (5)	6	0.01
Malaysian (9)	11	0.02
Nepalese (2)	2	<0.01
Pakistani (5)	7	0.01
Sri Lankan (3)	3	<0.01
Taiwanese (74)	82	0.13
Thai (143)	175	0.28
Vietnamese (231)	287	0.46
Hawaii Native/Pacific Islander (58)	190	0.30
Not Hispanic (37)	101	0.16
Hispanic (21)	89	0.14
Fijian (0)	1	<0.01
Guamanian/Chamorro (17)	26	0.04
Native Hawaiian (12)	39	0.06
Samoan (22)	36	0.06
White (33,633)	35,555	56.89
Not Hispanic (5,325)	5,613	8.98
Hispanic (28,308)	29,942	47.91

Montecito

Place Type: CDP
County: Santa Barbara
Population: 8,965[†]

Ancestry[‡]	Population	%
African, Sub-Saharan (28)	28	0.30
South African (28)	28	0.30
Albanian (8)	8	0.09
American (283)	283	3.06
Arab (0)	41	0.44
Lebanese (0)	41	0.44
Armenian (50)	120	1.30
Australian (8)	8	0.09
Austrian (13)	94	1.02
Basque (0)	10	0.11
Belgian (5)	5	0.05
Brazilian (8)	8	0.09
British (156)	288	3.12
Canadian (56)	71	0.77
Croatian (0)	35	0.38
Czech (0)	53	0.57
Czechoslovakian (0)	23	0.25
Danish (39)	184	1.99
Dutch (103)	318	3.44
Eastern European (127)	127	1.37
English (371)	1,743	18.86
European (332)	369	3.99
Finnish (27)	53	0.57
French, ex. Basque (90)	530	5.74
French Canadian (0)	50	0.54
German (563)	1,601	17.32
Greek (40)	76	0.82
Hungarian (14)	187	2.02
Icelander (0)	18	0.19
Iranian (26)	26	0.28
Irish (428)	1,251	13.54
Italian (230)	684	7.40
Lithuanian (8)	61	0.66
New Zealander (9)	23	0.25
Northern European (14)	42	0.45
Norwegian (94)	259	2.80
Polish (110)	276	2.99
Portuguese (0)	27	0.29
Romanian (35)	59	0.64
Russian (204)	501	5.42
Scandinavian (33)	71	0.77
Scotch-Irish (105)	254	2.75
Scottish (81)	328	3.55
Serbian (0)	14	0.15
Slovak (0)	8	0.09
Swedish (130)	451	4.88
Swiss (26)	97	1.05
Ukrainian (21)	84	0.91
Welsh (35)	209	2.26
West Indian, ex. Hispanic (0)	1	0.01
Haitian (0)	1	0.01
Yugoslavian (14)	14	0.15

Hispanic Origin	Population	%
Hispanic or Latino (of any race)	605	6.75
Central American, ex. Mexican	42	0.47
Costa Rican	4	0.04
Guatemalan	9	0.10
Honduran	1	0.01
Nicaraguan	7	0.08
Panamanian	5	0.06
Salvadoran	16	0.18
Cuban	20	0.22
Dominican Republic	2	0.02
Mexican	403	4.50
Puerto Rican	6	0.07
South American	59	0.66
Argentinean	12	0.13
Bolivian	1	0.01
Chilean	13	0.15
Colombian	21	0.23
Ecuadorian	1	0.01
Paraguayan	2	0.02
Peruvian	8	0.09
Venezuelan	1	0.01
Other Hispanic or Latino	73	0.81

Race*	Population	%
African-American/Black (55)	89	0.99
Not Hispanic (46)	71	0.79
Hispanic (9)	18	0.20
American Indian/Alaska Native (38)	95	1.06
Not Hispanic (32)	59	0.66
Hispanic (6)	36	0.40
Aleut *(Alaska Native)* (1)	1	0.01
Apache (1)	1	0.01
Blackfeet (0)	2	0.02
Cherokee (2)	9	0.10
Chickasaw (0)	1	0.01
Chippewa (0)	1	0.01
Choctaw (1)	2	0.02
Comanche (0)	1	0.01
Hopi (0)	1	0.01
Houma (0)	1	0.01
Inupiat *(Alaska Native)* (0)	2	0.02
Mexican American Ind. (1)	4	0.04
Navajo (0)	1	0.01
Osage (0)	3	0.03
Sioux (0)	1	0.01
South American Ind. (0)	2	0.02
Yaqui (0)	2	0.02
Asian (218)	329	3.67
Not Hispanic (215)	313	3.49
Hispanic (3)	16	0.18
Cambodian (1)	1	0.01
Chinese, ex. Taiwanese (50)	92	1.03
Filipino (33)	56	0.62
Indian (15)	24	0.27
Indonesian (1)	3	0.03
Japanese (41)	69	0.77
Korean (33)	42	0.47
Laotian (1)	1	0.01
Malaysian (0)	2	0.02
Nepalese (1)	1	0.01
Pakistani (2)	2	0.02
Sri Lankan (1)	1	0.01
Taiwanese (1)	1	0.01
Thai (3)	11	0.12
Vietnamese (8)	14	0.16
Hawaii Native/Pacific Islander (6)	25	0.28
Not Hispanic (6)	25	0.28
Fijian (0)	1	0.01
Guamanian/Chamorro (1)	1	0.01

*Notes: † The Census 2010 population figure is used to calculate the percentages in the Hispanic Origin and Race categories. Ancestry percentages are based on the 2006-2010 American Community Survey population (not shown); ‡ Numbers in parentheses indicate the number of people reporting a single ancestry; * Numbers in parentheses indicate the number of persons reporting this race alone, not in combination with any other race. Please refer to the Explanation of Data for more information.*

	Population	%
Native Hawaiian (1)	18	0.20
White (8,267)	8,481	94.60
Not Hispanic (7,891)	8,041	89.69
Hispanic (376)	440	4.91

Monterey Park

Place Type: City
County: Los Angeles
Population: 60,269†

Ancestry‡	Population	%
American (225)	225	0.37
Arab (171)	268	0.45
Iraqi (20)	40	0.07
Lebanese (151)	212	0.35
Other Arab (0)	16	0.03
Armenian (273)	273	0.45
Brazilian (18)	18	0.03
British (12)	12	0.02
Canadian (0)	37	0.06
Croatian (7)	7	0.01
Czech (9)	9	0.01
Danish (47)	74	0.12
Dutch (6)	35	0.06
Eastern European (18)	37	0.06
English (76)	263	0.44
European (72)	154	0.26
French, ex. Basque (0)	270	0.45
German (150)	887	1.47
Greek (15)	18	0.03
Guyanese (22)	22	0.04
Hungarian (6)	18	0.03
Iranian (11)	11	0.02
Irish (185)	508	0.84
Israeli (0)	8	0.01
Italian (165)	479	0.80
Lithuanian (0)	23	0.04
Norwegian (11)	11	0.02
Polish (26)	54	0.09
Portuguese (28)	41	0.07
Romanian (31)	54	0.09
Russian (64)	72	0.12
Scotch-Irish (96)	150	0.25
Scottish (31)	65	0.11
Serbian (0)	51	0.08
Swedish (31)	47	0.08
Swiss (11)	11	0.02
Ukrainian (0)	14	0.02
Welsh (11)	72	0.12
West Indian, ex. Hispanic (15)	15	0.02
Belizean (15)	15	0.02
Yugoslavian (12)	12	0.02

Hispanic Origin	Population	%
Hispanic or Latino (of any race)	16,218	26.91
Central American, ex. Mexican	1,183	1.96
Costa Rican	19	0.03
Guatemalan	275	0.46
Honduran	52	0.09
Nicaraguan	164	0.27
Panamanian	16	0.03
Salvadoran	641	1.06
Other Central American	16	0.03
Cuban	108	0.18
Dominican Republic	2	<0.01
Mexican	13,659	22.66
Puerto Rican	124	0.21
South American	326	0.54
Argentinean	33	0.05
Bolivian	10	0.02
Chilean	10	0.02
Colombian	60	0.10
Ecuadorian	103	0.17
Peruvian	96	0.16
Venezuelan	9	0.01
Other South American	5	0.01
Other Hispanic or Latino	816	1.35

Race*	Population	%
African-American/Black (252)	458	0.76
Not Hispanic (194)	301	0.50
Hispanic (58)	157	0.26
American Indian/Alaska Native (242)	516	0.86
Not Hispanic (51)	181	0.30
Hispanic (191)	335	0.56
Apache (16)	22	0.04
Blackfeet (4)	14	0.02
Canadian/French Am. Ind. (0)	2	<0.01
Central American Ind. (0)	1	<0.01
Cherokee (2)	33	0.05
Cheyenne (0)	4	0.01
Choctaw (0)	2	<0.01
Colville (0)	3	<0.01
Comanche (0)	1	<0.01
Hopi (1)	5	0.01
Iroquois (3)	6	0.01
Mexican American Ind. (29)	80	0.13
Navajo (34)	43	0.07
Paiute (0)	1	<0.01
Pima (1)	3	<0.01
Pueblo (2)	4	0.01
Seminole (0)	1	<0.01
Sioux (7)	10	0.02
South American Ind. (0)	3	<0.01
Spanish American Ind. (1)	5	0.01
Tlingit-Haida *(Alaska Native)* (0)	1	<0.01
Tohono O'Odham (3)	6	0.01
Tsimshian *(Alaska Native)* (0)	2	<0.01
Yakama (1)	1	<0.01
Yaqui (4)	10	0.02
Yuman (3)	7	0.01
Asian (40,301)	41,284	68.50
Not Hispanic (39,974)	40,660	67.46
Hispanic (327)	624	1.04
Bangladeshi (8)	8	0.01
Burmese (236)	279	0.46
Cambodian (495)	676	1.12
Chinese, ex. Taiwanese (27,734)	29,537	49.01
Filipino (1,165)	1,437	2.38
Indian (152)	217	0.36
Indonesian (223)	284	0.47
Japanese (3,515)	4,034	6.69
Korean (768)	890	1.48
Laotian (51)	68	0.11
Malaysian (29)	49	0.08
Nepalese (1)	2	<0.01
Pakistani (6)	8	0.01
Sri Lankan (9)	10	0.02
Taiwanese (1,025)	1,233	2.05
Thai (529)	569	0.94
Vietnamese (2,629)	3,323	5.51
Hawaii Native/Pacific Islander (28)	176	0.29
Not Hispanic (19)	149	0.25
Hispanic (9)	27	0.04
Fijian (4)	4	0.01
Guamanian/Chamorro (7)	12	0.02
Marshallese (0)	2	<0.01
Native Hawaiian (8)	58	0.10
Samoan (2)	5	0.01
White (11,680)	12,942	21.47
Not Hispanic (2,998)	3,504	5.81
Hispanic (8,682)	9,438	15.66

Monterey

Place Type: City
County: Monterey
Population: 27,810†

Ancestry‡	Population	%
Afghan (16)	16	0.06
African, Sub-Saharan (203)	236	0.85
African (43)	63	0.23
Cape Verdean (6)	6	0.02
Kenyan (0)	3	0.01
Nigerian (23)	23	0.08
Senegalese (131)	131	0.47
Zimbabwean (0)	10	0.04
American (680)	680	2.44
Arab (230)	283	1.02
Arab (45)	45	0.16
Egyptian (26)	26	0.09
Iraqi (0)	28	0.10
Lebanese (47)	47	0.17
Moroccan (43)	43	0.15
Palestinian (10)	35	0.13
Other Arab (59)	59	0.21
Armenian (29)	103	0.37
Assyrian/Chaldean/Syriac (8)	8	0.03
Austrian (70)	153	0.55
Basque (0)	21	0.08
Belgian (0)	25	0.09
Brazilian (22)	43	0.15
British (111)	249	0.89
Canadian (41)	102	0.37
Croatian (0)	11	0.04
Czech (75)	329	1.18
Danish (66)	394	1.42
Dutch (86)	346	1.24
Eastern European (103)	190	0.68
English (910)	3,406	12.24
Estonian (40)	40	0.14
European (582)	772	2.77
Finnish (0)	50	0.18
French, ex. Basque (174)	868	3.12
French Canadian (102)	214	0.77
German (1,253)	4,655	16.73
Greek (101)	267	0.96
Guyanese (0)	4	0.01
Hungarian (79)	156	0.56
Icelander (0)	8	0.03
Iranian (63)	63	0.23
Irish (977)	3,772	13.56
Italian (1,690)	3,041	10.93
Latvian (0)	30	0.11
Lithuanian (28)	95	0.34
Northern European (161)	161	0.58
Norwegian (157)	514	1.85
Pennsylvania German (0)	38	0.14
Polish (253)	838	3.01
Portuguese (156)	335	1.20
Romanian (39)	39	0.14
Russian (314)	554	1.99
Scandinavian (0)	133	0.48
Scotch-Irish (166)	790	2.84
Scottish (178)	884	3.18
Serbian (0)	11	0.04
Slavic (5)	5	0.02
Slovak (35)	183	0.66
Slovene (0)	9	0.03
Swedish (42)	626	2.25
Swiss (29)	446	1.60
Turkish (77)	77	0.28
Ukrainian (57)	104	0.37
Welsh (63)	284	1.02
West Indian, ex. Hispanic (10)	53	0.19
Jamaican (10)	49	0.18
West Indian (0)	4	0.01
Yugoslavian (78)	78	0.28

Hispanic Origin	Population	%
Hispanic or Latino (of any race)	3,817	13.73
Central American, ex. Mexican	315	1.13
Costa Rican	7	0.03
Guatemalan	25	0.09
Honduran	16	0.06
Nicaraguan	17	0.06
Panamanian	45	0.16
Salvadoran	202	0.73
Other Central American	3	0.01
Cuban	50	0.18
Dominican Republic	8	0.03
Mexican	2,591	9.32
Puerto Rican	172	0.62
South American	207	0.74
Argentinean	31	0.11
Bolivian	8	0.03

*Notes: † The Census 2010 population figure is used to calculate the percentages in the Hispanic Origin and Race categories. Ancestry percentages are based on the 2006-2010 American Community Survey population (not shown); ‡ Numbers in parentheses indicate the number of people reporting a single ancestry; * Numbers in parentheses indicate the number of persons reporting this race alone, not in combination with any other race; Please refer to the Explanation of Data for more information.*

Chilean	25	0.09
Colombian	61	0.22
Ecuadorian	14	0.05
Paraguayan	8	0.03
Peruvian	46	0.17
Venezuelan	10	0.04
Other South American	4	0.01
Other Hispanic or Latino	474	1.70

Race*	Population	%
African-American/Black (777)	1,063	3.82
Not Hispanic (734)	980	3.52
Hispanic (43)	83	0.30
American Indian/Alaska Native (149)	476	1.71
Not Hispanic (99)	326	1.17
Hispanic (50)	150	0.54
Aleut *(Alaska Native)* (0)	1	<0.01
Apache (4)	10	0.04
Blackfeet (0)	15	0.05
Central American Ind. (0)	5	0.02
Cherokee (7)	80	0.29
Chickasaw (2)	4	0.01
Chippewa (3)	9	0.03
Choctaw (5)	11	0.04
Creek (3)	5	0.02
Crow (1)	3	0.01
Delaware (3)	4	0.01
Hopi (1)	1	<0.01
Inupiat *(Alaska Native)* (1)	1	<0.01
Iroquois (1)	2	0.01
Menominee (1)	1	<0.01
Mexican American Ind. (9)	30	0.11
Navajo (4)	9	0.03
Osage (1)	1	<0.01
Paiute (1)	2	0.01
Pima (1)	1	<0.01
Potawatomi (0)	7	0.03
Pueblo (3)	7	0.03
Puget Sound Salish (0)	2	0.01
Seminole (0)	1	<0.01
Shoshone (1)	1	<0.01
Sioux (3)	15	0.05
South American Ind. (0)	1	<0.01
Spanish American Ind. (1)	1	<0.01
Tlingit-Haida *(Alaska Native)* (1)	1	<0.01
Yakama (0)	3	0.01
Yaqui (3)	6	0.02
Yup'ik *(Alaska Native)* (1)	1	<0.01
Asian (2,204)	2,958	10.64
Not Hispanic (2,157)	2,832	10.18
Hispanic (47)	126	0.45
Bangladeshi (3)	3	0.01
Burmese (3)	5	0.02
Cambodian (11)	11	0.04
Chinese, ex. Taiwanese (413)	522	1.88
Filipino (407)	660	2.37
Hmong (2)	2	0.01
Indian (294)	352	1.27
Indonesian (32)	37	0.13
Japanese (314)	533	1.92
Korean (394)	491	1.77
Laotian (3)	3	0.01
Malaysian (1)	3	0.01
Nepalese (22)	23	0.08
Pakistani (35)	48	0.17
Sri Lankan (6)	6	0.02
Taiwanese (47)	58	0.21
Thai (44)	60	0.22
Vietnamese (62)	80	0.29
Hawaii Native/Pacific Islander (91)	231	0.83
Not Hispanic (89)	212	0.76
Hispanic (2)	19	0.07
Fijian (6)	7	0.03
Guamanian/Chamorro (15)	44	0.16
Marshallese (1)	1	<0.01
Native Hawaiian (18)	88	0.32
Samoan (11)	34	0.12
Tongan (11)	14	0.05
White (21,788)	23,058	82.91
Not Hispanic (19,786)	20,744	74.59
Hispanic (2,002)	2,314	8.32

Moorpark

Place Type: City
County: Ventura
Population: 34,421†

Ancestry‡	Population	%
Afghan (106)	106	0.31
African, Sub-Saharan (0)	7	0.02
African (0)	7	0.02
Albanian (11)	35	0.10
American (2,217)	2,217	6.56
Arab (354)	426	1.26
Arab (38)	55	0.16
Egyptian (32)	32	0.09
Jordanian (122)	122	0.36
Lebanese (40)	57	0.17
Palestinian (26)	26	0.08
Syrian (40)	78	0.23
Other Arab (56)	56	0.17
Armenian (214)	305	0.90
Australian (19)	35	0.10
Austrian (31)	203	0.60
Basque (14)	70	0.21
Belgian (0)	37	0.11
British (122)	277	0.82
Canadian (42)	173	0.51
Croatian (0)	24	0.07
Czech (23)	258	0.76
Czechoslovakian (17)	17	0.05
Danish (102)	213	0.63
Dutch (68)	415	1.23
Eastern European (83)	103	0.30
English (1,236)	3,390	10.03
European (520)	569	1.68
Finnish (0)	25	0.07
French, ex. Basque (78)	682	2.02
French Canadian (45)	95	0.28
German (1,017)	4,660	13.78
Greek (62)	135	0.40
Hungarian (78)	229	0.68
Iranian (91)	91	0.27
Irish (1,093)	3,642	10.77
Israeli (9)	26	0.08
Italian (701)	2,431	7.19
Latvian (0)	9	0.03
Lithuanian (38)	76	0.22
New Zealander (3)	3	0.01
Northern European (13)	13	0.04
Norwegian (149)	594	1.76
Polish (189)	975	2.88
Portuguese (64)	70	0.21
Romanian (0)	94	0.28
Russian (103)	395	1.17
Scandinavian (146)	196	0.58
Scotch-Irish (72)	460	1.36
Scottish (395)	1,060	3.14
Slovak (0)	34	0.10
Swedish (143)	774	2.29
Swiss (0)	135	0.40
Turkish (36)	107	0.32
Ukrainian (35)	61	0.18
Welsh (59)	227	0.67
West Indian, ex. Hispanic (86)	114	0.34
Jamaican (73)	101	0.30
West Indian (13)	13	0.04
Yugoslavian (14)	14	0.04

Hispanic Origin	Population	%
Hispanic or Latino (of any race)	10,813	31.41
Central American, ex. Mexican	424	1.23
Costa Rican	41	0.12
Guatemalan	148	0.43
Honduran	44	0.13
Nicaraguan	16	0.05
Panamanian	9	0.03
Salvadoran	160	0.46
Other Central American	6	0.02
Cuban	108	0.31
Dominican Republic	10	0.03
Mexican	9,244	26.86
Puerto Rican	126	0.37
South American	327	0.95
Argentinean	40	0.12
Bolivian	8	0.02
Chilean	36	0.10
Colombian	102	0.30
Ecuadorian	46	0.13
Paraguayan	1	<0.01
Peruvian	76	0.22
Uruguayan	3	0.01
Venezuelan	10	0.03
Other South American	5	0.01
Other Hispanic or Latino	574	1.67

Race*	Population	%
African-American/Black (533)	772	2.24
Not Hispanic (486)	658	1.91
Hispanic (47)	114	0.33
American Indian/Alaska Native (248)	544	1.58
Not Hispanic (76)	245	0.71
Hispanic (172)	299	0.87
Apache (8)	18	0.05
Blackfeet (4)	20	0.06
Canadian/French Am. Ind. (1)	2	0.01
Cherokee (19)	99	0.29
Cheyenne (0)	1	<0.01
Chippewa (0)	1	<0.01
Choctaw (5)	25	0.07
Creek (7)	7	0.02
Delaware (2)	2	0.01
Hopi (2)	3	0.01
Inupiat *(Alaska Native)* (0)	2	0.01
Iroquois (1)	5	0.01
Menominee (2)	4	0.01
Mexican American Ind. (60)	90	0.26
Navajo (6)	11	0.03
Osage (2)	2	0.01
Potawatomi (3)	4	0.01
Pueblo (7)	9	0.03
Shoshone (0)	12	0.03
Sioux (5)	16	0.05
Tlingit-Haida *(Alaska Native)* (0)	2	0.01
Tohono O'Odham (3)	7	0.02
Yaqui (5)	11	0.03
Asian (2,352)	3,117	9.06
Not Hispanic (2,309)	2,960	8.60
Hispanic (43)	157	0.46
Bangladeshi (6)	6	0.02
Burmese (3)	3	0.01
Cambodian (34)	45	0.13
Chinese, ex. Taiwanese (408)	564	1.64
Filipino (470)	685	1.99
Hmong (6)	6	0.02
Indian (523)	608	1.77
Indonesian (26)	47	0.14
Japanese (208)	426	1.24
Korean (193)	255	0.74
Malaysian (4)	9	0.03
Pakistani (48)	59	0.17
Sri Lankan (13)	22	0.06
Taiwanese (23)	28	0.08
Thai (23)	29	0.08
Vietnamese (261)	311	0.90
Hawaii Native/Pacific Islander (50)	151	0.44
Not Hispanic (38)	115	0.33
Hispanic (12)	36	0.10
Fijian (1)	2	0.01
Guamanian/Chamorro (6)	11	0.03
Native Hawaiian (25)	65	0.19
Samoan (6)	23	0.07
Tongan (2)	5	0.01
White (25,860)	27,331	79.40
Not Hispanic (19,654)	20,534	59.66
Hispanic (6,206)	6,797	19.75

*Notes: † The Census 2010 population figure is used to calculate the percentages in the Hispanic Origin and Race categories. Ancestry percentages are based on the 2006-2010 American Community Survey population (not shown); ‡ Numbers in parentheses indicate the number of people reporting a single ancestry; * Numbers in parentheses indicate the number of persons reporting this race alone, not in combination with any other race; Please refer to the Explanation of Data for more information.*

Moraga

Place Type: Town
County: Contra Costa
Population: 16,016†

Ancestry‡	Population	%
African, Sub-Saharan (73)	73	0.46
Nigerian (41)	41	0.26
South African (32)	32	0.20
American (522)	522	3.27
Arab (0)	164	1.03
Arab (0)	85	0.53
Egyptian (0)	18	0.11
Lebanese (0)	20	0.13
Moroccan (0)	25	0.16
Other Arab (0)	16	0.10
Armenian (68)	78	0.49
Assyrian/Chaldean/Syriac (12)	12	0.08
Austrian (43)	93	0.58
Basque (10)	10	0.06
Belgian (0)	25	0.16
Brazilian (0)	59	0.37
British (130)	183	1.15
Bulgarian (0)	51	0.32
Canadian (11)	11	0.07
Celtic (16)	16	0.10
Croatian (44)	44	0.28
Czech (7)	50	0.31
Czechoslovakian (61)	61	0.38
Danish (66)	207	1.30
Dutch (52)	239	1.50
Eastern European (91)	91	0.57
English (561)	2,314	14.49
European (380)	400	2.50
Finnish (0)	37	0.23
French, ex. Basque (30)	551	3.45
French Canadian (7)	59	0.37
German (544)	2,190	13.71
Greek (70)	215	1.35
Guyanese (13)	13	0.08
Hungarian (0)	58	0.36
Icelander (13)	13	0.08
Iranian (203)	244	1.53
Irish (554)	2,687	16.82
Israeli (0)	69	0.43
Italian (417)	1,258	7.87
Lithuanian (0)	38	0.24
Maltese (0)	35	0.22
Northern European (32)	32	0.20
Norwegian (125)	351	2.20
Polish (118)	407	2.55
Portuguese (41)	63	0.39
Romanian (0)	29	0.18
Russian (251)	498	3.12
Scandinavian (56)	166	1.04
Scotch-Irish (106)	426	2.67
Scottish (133)	584	3.66
Serbian (0)	15	0.09
Slavic (0)	36	0.23
Slovak (0)	17	0.11
Slovene (9)	9	0.06
Swedish (55)	290	1.82
Swiss (32)	106	0.66
Turkish (13)	13	0.08
Ukrainian (7)	27	0.17
Welsh (46)	177	1.11
West Indian, ex. Hispanic (0)	13	0.08
Haitian (0)	13	0.08
Yugoslavian (20)	20	0.13

Hispanic Origin	Population	%
Hispanic or Latino (of any race)	1,123	7.01
Central American, ex. Mexican	100	0.62
Costa Rican	2	0.01
Guatemalan	8	0.05
Honduran	3	0.02
Nicaraguan	19	0.12
Panamanian	1	0.01
Salvadoran	64	0.40
Other Central American	3	0.02
Cuban	32	0.20
Dominican Republic	5	0.03
Mexican	631	3.94
Puerto Rican	27	0.17
South American	129	0.81
Argentinean	11	0.07
Bolivian	3	0.02
Chilean	18	0.11
Colombian	30	0.19
Ecuadorian	16	0.10
Paraguayan	1	0.01
Peruvian	44	0.27
Uruguayan	1	0.01
Venezuelan	4	0.02
Other South American	1	0.01
Other Hispanic or Latino	199	1.24

Race*	Population	%
African-American/Black (277)	365	2.28
Not Hispanic (258)	335	2.09
Hispanic (19)	30	0.19
American Indian/Alaska Native (31)	119	0.74
Not Hispanic (16)	79	0.49
Hispanic (15)	40	0.25
Apache (0)	3	0.02
Blackfeet (0)	3	0.02
Cherokee (2)	13	0.08
Chippewa (0)	1	0.01
Choctaw (4)	5	0.03
Creek (0)	1	0.01
Mexican American Ind. (5)	10	0.06
Navajo (3)	5	0.03
Pueblo (1)	1	0.01
Puget Sound Salish (0)	1	0.01
Seminole (0)	3	0.02
South American Ind. (0)	1	0.01
Tlingit-Haida *(Alaska Native)* (1)	1	0.01
Tsimshian *(Alaska Native)* (0)	1	0.01
Yaqui (1)	1	0.01
Asian (2,393)	3,007	18.77
Not Hispanic (2,371)	2,923	18.25
Hispanic (22)	84	0.52
Bhutanese (1)	1	0.01
Burmese (1)	2	0.01
Cambodian (5)	5	0.03
Chinese, ex. Taiwanese (1,174)	1,470	9.18
Filipino (212)	370	2.31
Indian (205)	243	1.52
Indonesian (3)	11	0.07
Japanese (222)	396	2.47
Korean (226)	278	1.74
Laotian (3)	8	0.05
Malaysian (1)	1	0.01
Pakistani (16)	20	0.12
Sri Lankan (11)	14	0.09
Taiwanese (102)	120	0.75
Thai (19)	32	0.20
Vietnamese (52)	83	0.52
Hawaii Native/Pacific Islander (25)	72	0.45
Not Hispanic (24)	61	0.38
Hispanic (1)	11	0.07
Guamanian/Chamorro (2)	5	0.03
Marshallese (0)	2	0.01
Native Hawaiian (7)	31	0.19
Samoan (7)	8	0.05
Tongan (2)	2	0.01
White (12,201)	12,952	80.87
Not Hispanic (11,509)	12,150	75.86
Hispanic (692)	802	5.01

Moreno Valley

Place Type: City
County: Riverside
Population: 193,365†

Ancestry‡	Population	%
Afghan (245)	337	0.18
African, Sub-Saharan (1,207)	1,405	0.75
African (941)	1,113	0.59
Ethiopian (106)	106	0.06
Kenyan (25)	51	0.03
Nigerian (135)	135	0.07
American (2,619)	2,619	1.40
Arab (957)	1,107	0.59
Arab (241)	241	0.13
Egyptian (189)	271	0.14
Iraqi (12)	12	0.01
Jordanian (35)	35	0.02
Lebanese (195)	195	0.10
Palestinian (230)	259	0.14
Syrian (12)	19	0.01
Other Arab (43)	75	0.04
Armenian (28)	64	0.03
Austrian (0)	57	0.03
Belgian (3)	63	0.03
Brazilian (6)	6	<0.01
British (113)	320	0.17
Bulgarian (8)	8	<0.01
Canadian (100)	336	0.18
Celtic (0)	24	0.01
Croatian (20)	97	0.05
Czech (25)	93	0.05
Czechoslovakian (17)	47	0.03
Danish (159)	437	0.23
Dutch (341)	1,238	0.66
Eastern European (9)	9	<0.01
English (1,547)	5,560	2.97
European (687)	935	0.50
Finnish (13)	82	0.04
French, ex. Basque (514)	2,513	1.34
French Canadian (300)	863	0.46
German (2,632)	9,981	5.33
Greek (42)	133	0.07
Guyanese (10)	10	0.01
Hungarian (36)	247	0.13
Icelander (50)	50	0.03
Iranian (263)	263	0.14
Irish (1,546)	6,755	3.60
Italian (1,157)	3,337	1.78
Lithuanian (10)	92	0.05
Macedonian (10)	10	0.01
Northern European (62)	62	0.03
Norwegian (235)	943	0.50
Pennsylvania German (13)	62	0.03
Polish (441)	1,186	0.63
Portuguese (214)	570	0.30
Romanian (50)	50	0.03
Russian (221)	531	0.28
Scandinavian (49)	155	0.08
Scotch-Irish (147)	688	0.37
Scottish (372)	1,029	0.55
Serbian (0)	53	0.03
Slavic (0)	102	0.05
Slovak (13)	16	0.01
Swedish (205)	1,010	0.54
Swiss (32)	141	0.08
Ukrainian (63)	168	0.09
Welsh (26)	367	0.20
West Indian, ex. Hispanic (439)	717	0.38
Bahamian (0)	8	<0.01
Belizean (144)	236	0.13
British West Indian (10)	10	0.01
Dutch West Indian (8)	23	0.01
Jamaican (226)	353	0.19
Trinidadian/Tobagonian (0)	11	0.01
West Indian (51)	76	0.04
Yugoslavian (16)	55	0.03

Hispanic Origin	Population	%
Hispanic or Latino (of any race)	105,169	54.39
Central American, ex. Mexican	5,710	2.95
Costa Rican	185	0.10
Guatemalan	1,562	0.81
Honduran	386	0.20
Nicaraguan	528	0.27
Panamanian	186	0.10
Salvadoran	2,794	1.44
Other Central American	69	0.04

*Notes: † The Census 2010 population figure is used to calculate the percentages in the Hispanic Origin and Race categories. Ancestry percentages are based on the 2006-2010 American Community Survey population (not shown); ‡ Numbers in parentheses indicate the number of people reporting a single ancestry; * Numbers in parentheses indicate the number of persons reporting this race alone, not in combination with any other race; Please refer to the Explanation of Data for more information.*

Cuban	606	0.31
Dominican Republic	65	0.03
Mexican	90,054	46.57
Puerto Rican	1,636	0.85
South American	1,587	0.82
Argentinean	233	0.12
Bolivian	85	0.04
Chilean	59	0.03
Colombian	355	0.18
Ecuadorian	296	0.15
Paraguayan	4	<0.01
Peruvian	463	0.24
Uruguayan	39	0.02
Venezuelan	39	0.02
Other South American	14	0.01
Other Hispanic or Latino	5,511	2.85

Race*	Population	%
African-American/Black (34,889)	39,019	20.18
Not Hispanic (33,195)	36,134	18.69
Hispanic (1,694)	2,885	1.49
American Indian/Alaska Native (1,721)	3,611	1.87
Not Hispanic (573)	1,681	0.87
Hispanic (1,148)	1,930	1.00
Alaska Athabascan *(Ala. Nat.)* (2)	2	<0.01
Aleut *(Alaska Native)* (2)	8	<0.01
Apache (55)	125	0.06
Arapaho (1)	2	<0.01
Blackfeet (16)	77	0.04
Canadian/French Am. Ind. (6)	12	0.01
Central American Ind. (10)	11	0.01
Cherokee (96)	367	0.19
Cheyenne (3)	6	<0.01
Chickasaw (2)	8	<0.01
Chippewa (14)	38	0.02
Choctaw (36)	136	0.07
Comanche (2)	2	<0.01
Cree (0)	7	<0.01
Creek (9)	38	0.02
Crow (2)	5	<0.01
Delaware (1)	5	<0.01
Hopi (4)	7	<0.01
Iroquois (2)	14	0.01
Kiowa (1)	1	<0.01
Lumbee (5)	7	<0.01
Menominee (1)	4	<0.01
Mexican American Ind. (237)	338	0.17
Navajo (84)	146	0.08
Osage (5)	9	<0.01
Ottawa (2)	4	<0.01
Paiute (6)	20	0.01
Pima (0)	6	<0.01
Potawatomi (5)	10	0.01
Pueblo (7)	12	0.01
Puget Sound Salish (1)	1	<0.01
Seminole (3)	36	0.02
Shoshone (4)	7	<0.01
Sioux (17)	53	0.03
South American Ind. (9)	21	0.01
Spanish American Ind. (27)	30	0.02
Tlingit-Haida *(Alaska Native)* (2)	4	<0.01
Tohono O'Odham (12)	27	0.01
Tsimshian *(Alaska Native)* (1)	3	<0.01
Ute (0)	4	<0.01
Yaqui (27)	59	0.03
Yuman (3)	11	0.01
Yup'ik *(Alaska Native)* (0)	3	<0.01
Asian (11,867)	14,814	7.66
Not Hispanic (11,423)	13,509	6.99
Hispanic (444)	1,305	0.67
Bangladeshi (105)	115	0.06
Burmese (14)	15	0.01
Cambodian (398)	496	0.26
Chinese, ex. Taiwanese (831)	1,301	0.67
Filipino (5,437)	6,788	3.51
Hmong (138)	143	0.07
Indian (794)	999	0.52
Indonesian (98)	149	0.08
Japanese (362)	874	0.45
Korean (678)	920	0.48
Laotian (396)	454	0.23
Malaysian (8)	18	0.01
Nepalese (3)	3	<0.01
Pakistani (264)	298	0.15
Sri Lankan (26)	28	0.01
Taiwanese (88)	102	0.05
Thai (277)	427	0.22
Vietnamese (1,394)	1,604	0.83
Hawaii Native/Pacific Islander (1,117)	1,760	0.91
Not Hispanic (990)	1,409	0.73
Hispanic (127)	351	0.18
Fijian (20)	30	0.02
Guamanian/Chamorro (220)	344	0.18
Marshallese (0)	1	<0.01
Native Hawaiian (138)	372	0.19
Samoan (455)	628	0.32
Tongan (158)	187	0.10
White (80,969)	89,407	46.24
Not Hispanic (36,573)	40,399	20.89
Hispanic (44,396)	49,008	25.34

Morgan Hill

Place Type: City
County: Santa Clara
Population: 37,882†

Ancestry‡	Population	%
Afghan (27)	27	0.07
African, Sub-Saharan (46)	108	0.29
African (40)	57	0.16
Ethiopian (6)	14	0.04
Somalian (0)	37	0.10
American (764)	764	2.09
Arab (117)	130	0.35
Lebanese (16)	19	0.05
Palestinian (42)	42	0.11
Syrian (0)	10	0.03
Other Arab (59)	59	0.16
Armenian (61)	97	0.26
Australian (0)	10	0.03
Austrian (0)	59	0.16
Basque (10)	10	0.03
Belgian (10)	31	0.08
British (212)	252	0.69
Canadian (70)	133	0.36
Croatian (51)	207	0.57
Czech (35)	107	0.29
Czechoslovakian (25)	25	0.07
Danish (24)	319	0.87
Dutch (56)	417	1.14
Eastern European (15)	30	0.08
English (884)	3,253	8.88
Estonian (12)	12	0.03
European (333)	514	1.40
Finnish (27)	145	0.40
French, ex. Basque (179)	973	2.66
French Canadian (130)	273	0.75
German (1,196)	4,842	13.22
Greek (14)	56	0.15
Hungarian (12)	65	0.18
Iranian (299)	357	0.97
Irish (906)	3,420	9.34
Italian (1,056)	2,872	7.84
Lithuanian (0)	86	0.23
Northern European (49)	57	0.16
Norwegian (287)	738	2.01
Polish (93)	490	1.34
Portuguese (307)	892	2.44
Romanian (37)	55	0.15
Russian (78)	154	0.42
Scandinavian (31)	50	0.14
Scotch-Irish (53)	385	1.05
Scottish (165)	833	2.27
Serbian (0)	53	0.14
Slovak (0)	23	0.06
Swedish (74)	583	1.59
Swiss (39)	153	0.42
Turkish (14)	14	0.04
Ukrainian (25)	100	0.27
Welsh (20)	363	0.99
West Indian, ex. Hispanic (34)	34	0.09
Jamaican (34)	34	0.09
Yugoslavian (0)	34	0.09

Hispanic Origin	Population	%
Hispanic or Latino (of any race)	12,863	33.96
Central American, ex. Mexican	411	1.08
Costa Rican	15	0.04
Guatemalan	84	0.22
Honduran	38	0.10
Nicaraguan	63	0.17
Panamanian	11	0.03
Salvadoran	199	0.53
Other Central American	1	<0.01
Cuban	57	0.15
Dominican Republic	16	0.04
Mexican	10,821	28.57
Puerto Rican	206	0.54
South American	311	0.82
Argentinean	35	0.09
Bolivian	36	0.10
Chilean	35	0.09
Colombian	72	0.19
Ecuadorian	21	0.06
Peruvian	80	0.21
Uruguayan	5	0.01
Venezuelan	24	0.06
Other South American	3	0.01
Other Hispanic or Latino	1,041	2.75

Race*	Population	%
African-American/Black (746)	1,082	2.86
Not Hispanic (667)	901	2.38
Hispanic (79)	181	0.48
American Indian/Alaska Native (335)	773	2.04
Not Hispanic (125)	348	0.92
Hispanic (210)	425	1.12
Alaska Athabascan *(Ala. Nat.)* (0)	1	<0.01
Apache (16)	48	0.13
Blackfeet (1)	13	0.03
Canadian/French Am. Ind. (0)	6	0.02
Central American Ind. (3)	4	0.01
Cherokee (10)	83	0.22
Cheyenne (1)	1	<0.01
Chickasaw (3)	4	0.01
Chippewa (3)	9	0.02
Choctaw (11)	30	0.08
Colville (0)	2	0.01
Comanche (0)	1	<0.01
Cree (0)	1	<0.01
Creek (1)	9	0.02
Hopi (0)	2	0.01
Inupiat *(Alaska Native)* (1)	1	<0.01
Iroquois (1)	4	0.01
Kiowa (1)	5	0.01
Lumbee (1)	1	<0.01
Mexican American Ind. (39)	58	0.15
Navajo (13)	24	0.06
Osage (1)	3	0.01
Ottawa (0)	2	0.01
Paiute (4)	4	0.01
Pima (2)	2	0.01
Potawatomi (1)	7	0.02
Pueblo (10)	17	0.04
Shoshone (3)	12	0.03
Sioux (14)	20	0.05
South American Ind. (2)	2	0.01
Spanish American Ind. (1)	1	<0.01
Tohono O'Odham (0)	3	0.01
Tsimshian *(Alaska Native)* (0)	1	<0.01
Ute (0)	1	<0.01
Yaqui (8)	15	0.04
Asian (3,852)	4,945	13.05
Not Hispanic (3,712)	4,523	11.94
Hispanic (140)	422	1.11
Burmese (4)	4	0.01
Cambodian (51)	65	0.17
Chinese, ex. Taiwanese (718)	961	2.54
Filipino (886)	1,279	3.38

SECTION TWO

*Notes: † The Census 2010 population figure is used to calculate the percentages in the Hispanic Origin and Race categories. Ancestry percentages are based on the 2006-2010 American Community Survey population (not shown); ‡ Numbers in parentheses indicate the number of people reporting a single ancestry; * Numbers in parentheses indicate the number of persons reporting this race alone, not in combination with any other race; Please refer to the Explanation of Data for more information.*

Hmong (1)	1	<0.01
Indian (650)	726	1.92
Indonesian (6)	21	0.06
Japanese (364)	648	1.71
Korean (191)	282	0.74
Laotian (13)	16	0.04
Malaysian (2)	9	0.02
Nepalese (1)	1	<0.01
Pakistani (35)	44	0.12
Sri Lankan (9)	15	0.04
Taiwanese (33)	45	0.12
Thai (19)	31	0.08
Vietnamese (708)	837	2.21
Hawaii Native/Pacific Islander (125)	348	0.92
Not Hispanic (107)	265	0.70
Hispanic (18)	83	0.22
Fijian (5)	11	0.03
Guamanian/Chamorro (39)	89	0.23
Native Hawaiian (27)	117	0.31
Samoan (19)	31	0.08
Tongan (31)	37	0.10
White (24,713)	26,680	70.43
Not Hispanic (19,073)	20,175	53.26
Hispanic (5,640)	6,505	17.17

Morro Bay

Place Type: City
County: San Luis Obispo
Population: 10,234†

Ancestry‡	Population	%
American (466)	466	4.54
Arab (34)	34	0.33
Arab (9)	9	0.09
Syrian (25)	25	0.24
Armenian (19)	54	0.53
Belgian (0)	14	0.14
British (25)	77	0.75
Canadian (26)	64	0.62
Celtic (0)	14	0.14
Croatian (14)	36	0.35
Czech (13)	37	0.36
Czechoslovakian (23)	23	0.22
Danish (20)	132	1.29
Dutch (70)	301	2.94
Eastern European (14)	14	0.14
English (520)	1,908	18.61
European (113)	113	1.10
French, ex. Basque (78)	515	5.02
French Canadian (0)	16	0.16
German (646)	2,138	20.85
Greek (13)	13	0.13
Irish (318)	1,284	12.52
Italian (83)	523	5.10
Lithuanian (0)	25	0.24
Northern European (65)	65	0.63
Norwegian (53)	395	3.85
Polish (129)	283	2.76
Portuguese (46)	57	0.56
Romanian (28)	42	0.41
Russian (13)	112	1.09
Scandinavian (20)	34	0.33
Scotch-Irish (165)	465	4.53
Scottish (58)	324	3.16
Serbian (16)	16	0.16
Slavic (0)	12	0.12
Slovak (0)	34	0.33
Swedish (71)	379	3.70
Swiss (12)	50	0.49
Welsh (28)	163	1.59
West Indian, ex. Hispanic (0)	4	0.04
Dutch West Indian (0)	4	0.04

Hispanic Origin	Population	%
Hispanic or Latino (of any race)	1,526	14.91
Central American, ex. Mexican	26	0.25
Costa Rican	2	0.02
Guatemalan	8	0.08
Panamanian	2	0.02
Salvadoran	14	0.14
Cuban	6	0.06
Dominican Republic	2	0.02
Mexican	1,292	12.62
Puerto Rican	25	0.24
South American	32	0.31
Argentinean	6	0.06
Chilean	8	0.08
Colombian	4	0.04
Ecuadorian	5	0.05
Paraguayan	1	0.01
Peruvian	4	0.04
Venezuelan	3	0.03
Other South American	1	0.01
Other Hispanic or Latino	143	1.40

Race*	Population	%
African-American/Black (44)	86	0.84
Not Hispanic (39)	74	0.72
Hispanic (5)	12	0.12
American Indian/Alaska Native (92)	216	2.11
Not Hispanic (63)	162	1.58
Hispanic (29)	54	0.53
Apache (4)	10	0.10
Arapaho (1)	1	0.01
Blackfeet (0)	10	0.10
Cherokee (7)	39	0.38
Chickasaw (1)	1	0.01
Chippewa (1)	1	0.01
Choctaw (8)	15	0.15
Comanche (0)	1	0.01
Creek (0)	1	0.01
Inupiat *(Alaska Native)* (0)	1	0.01
Iroquois (0)	3	0.03
Lumbee (0)	1	0.01
Mexican American Ind. (8)	9	0.09
Navajo (1)	5	0.05
Osage (1)	5	0.05
Paiute (1)	1	0.01
Pueblo (0)	1	0.01
Seminole (0)	1	0.01
Sioux (4)	4	0.04
Tlingit-Haida *(Alaska Native)* (2)	2	0.02
Yaqui (5)	7	0.07
Asian (258)	347	3.39
Not Hispanic (251)	327	3.20
Hispanic (7)	20	0.20
Burmese (1)	1	0.01
Cambodian (6)	6	0.06
Chinese, ex. Taiwanese (40)	50	0.49
Filipino (89)	139	1.36
Indian (31)	36	0.35
Indonesian (1)	1	0.01
Japanese (35)	56	0.55
Korean (23)	30	0.29
Laotian (1)	4	0.04
Pakistani (0)	2	0.02
Thai (10)	12	0.12
Vietnamese (14)	17	0.17
Hawaii Native/Pacific Islander (9)	21	0.21
Not Hispanic (9)	19	0.19
Hispanic (0)	2	0.02
Native Hawaiian (5)	9	0.09
Samoan (2)	6	0.06
White (8,909)	9,196	89.86
Not Hispanic (8,123)	8,329	81.39
Hispanic (786)	867	8.47

Mountain House

Place Type: CDP
County: San Joaquin
Population: 9,675†

Ancestry‡	Population	%
Afghan (253)	284	3.79
African, Sub-Saharan (193)	240	3.20
African (32)	47	0.63
Ethiopian (2)	2	0.03
Nigerian (91)	123	1.64
Somalian (6)	6	0.08
Sudanese (62)	62	0.83
Austrian (0)	21	0.28
British (9)	9	0.12
Canadian (3)	6	0.08
Celtic (2)	2	0.03
Danish (0)	39	0.52
Dutch (14)	23	0.31
English (159)	647	8.63
European (46)	46	0.61
French, ex. Basque (9)	174	2.32
German (13)	458	6.11
Greek (0)	10	0.13
Iranian (14)	41	0.55
Irish (68)	457	6.10
Italian (58)	229	3.05
Lithuanian (12)	26	0.35
Northern European (35)	35	0.47
Norwegian (0)	58	0.77
Polish (41)	50	0.67
Portuguese (46)	129	1.72
Romanian (124)	124	1.65
Scotch-Irish (13)	56	0.75
Scottish (23)	50	0.67
Swedish (20)	33	0.44
Welsh (0)	65	0.87

Hispanic Origin	Population	%
Hispanic or Latino (of any race)	1,637	16.92
Central American, ex. Mexican	132	1.36
Costa Rican	5	0.05
Guatemalan	4	0.04
Honduran	4	0.04
Nicaraguan	37	0.38
Panamanian	14	0.14
Salvadoran	65	0.67
Other Central American	3	0.03
Cuban	1	0.01
Dominican Republic	13	0.13
Mexican	1,203	12.43
Puerto Rican	73	0.75
South American	87	0.90
Argentinean	16	0.17
Bolivian	4	0.04
Chilean	1	0.01
Colombian	23	0.24
Ecuadorian	4	0.04
Peruvian	23	0.24
Uruguayan	2	0.02
Venezuelan	14	0.14
Other Hispanic or Latino	128	1.32

Race*	Population	%
African-American/Black (903)	1,074	11.10
Not Hispanic (873)	1,012	10.46
Hispanic (30)	62	0.64
American Indian/Alaska Native (45)	114	1.18
Not Hispanic (33)	82	0.85
Hispanic (12)	32	0.33
Apache (2)	2	0.02
Blackfeet (0)	3	0.03
Cherokee (2)	10	0.10
Choctaw (4)	6	0.06
Cree (0)	1	0.01
Creek (2)	2	0.02
Inupiat *(Alaska Native)* (1)	1	0.01
Iroquois (1)	1	0.01
Navajo (0)	4	0.04
Paiute (2)	2	0.02
Pima (0)	2	0.02
Seminole (0)	3	0.03
Sioux (0)	1	0.01
Spanish American Ind. (0)	2	0.02
Yuman (4)	4	0.04
Asian (3,830)	4,289	44.33
Not Hispanic (3,765)	4,178	43.18
Hispanic (65)	111	1.15
Bangladeshi (4)	7	0.07
Cambodian (54)	58	0.60
Chinese, ex. Taiwanese (397)	518	5.35

*Notes: † The Census 2010 population figure is used to calculate the percentages in the Hispanic Origin and Race categories. Ancestry percentages are based on the 2006-2010 American Community Survey population (not shown); ‡ Numbers in parentheses indicate the number of people reporting a single ancestry; * Numbers in parentheses indicate the number of persons reporting this race alone, not in combination with any other race; Please refer to the Explanation of Data for more information.*

Filipino (1,793)	2,037	21.05
Hmong (5)	6	0.06
Indian (959)	1,015	10.49
Indonesian (5)	5	0.05
Japanese (28)	79	0.82
Korean (99)	122	1.26
Laotian (13)	17	0.18
Malaysian (0)	3	0.03
Nepalese (22)	22	0.23
Pakistani (91)	96	0.99
Sri Lankan (4)	5	0.05
Taiwanese (10)	13	0.13
Thai (10)	13	0.13
Vietnamese (199)	234	2.42
Hawaii Native/Pacific Islander (71)	134	1.39
Not Hispanic (67)	115	1.19
Hispanic (4)	19	0.20
Fijian (16)	20	0.21
Guamanian/Chamorro (10)	27	0.28
Native Hawaiian (25)	49	0.51
Samoan (13)	15	0.16
Tongan (6)	6	0.06
White (3,467)	3,995	41.29
Not Hispanic (2,731)	3,147	32.53
Hispanic (736)	848	8.76

Mountain View

Place Type: City
County: Santa Clara
Population: 74,066†

Ancestry‡	Population	%
African, Sub-Saharan (268)	479	0.66
African (90)	231	0.32
Ethiopian (7)	7	0.01
Ghanaian (0)	16	0.02
Kenyan (55)	74	0.10
Nigerian (9)	9	0.01
South African (48)	83	0.11
Sudanese (40)	40	0.06
Other Sub-Saharan African (19)	19	0.03
American (924)	924	1.27
Arab (530)	756	1.04
Arab (96)	129	0.18
Egyptian (51)	79	0.11
Lebanese (46)	83	0.11
Moroccan (15)	101	0.14
Palestinian (186)	193	0.27
Other Arab (136)	171	0.24
Armenian (90)	99	0.14
Australian (39)	78	0.11
Austrian (34)	114	0.16
Basque (5)	14	0.02
Belgian (10)	49	0.07
Brazilian (97)	139	0.19
British (508)	927	1.28
Bulgarian (108)	108	0.15
Canadian (71)	186	0.26
Celtic (50)	50	0.07
Croatian (75)	194	0.27
Czech (50)	125	0.17
Czechoslovakian (19)	43	0.06
Danish (98)	783	1.08
Dutch (301)	1,158	1.60
Eastern European (165)	189	0.26
English (1,373)	5,882	8.11
Estonian (11)	26	0.04
European (1,527)	1,647	2.27
Finnish (47)	139	0.19
French, ex. Basque (601)	2,008	2.77
French Canadian (140)	320	0.44
German (1,944)	7,661	10.57
German Russian (0)	8	0.01
Greek (108)	249	0.34
Guyanese (0)	24	0.03
Hungarian (341)	690	0.95
Iranian (506)	606	0.84
Irish (1,217)	5,012	6.91
Israeli (96)	134	0.18
Italian (1,046)	3,361	4.64
Latvian (23)	31	0.04
Lithuanian (55)	113	0.16
Maltese (6)	6	0.01
New Zealander (8)	8	0.01
Northern European (86)	86	0.12
Norwegian (264)	1,278	1.76
Pennsylvania German (0)	13	0.02
Polish (402)	1,195	1.65
Portuguese (314)	765	1.06
Romanian (100)	231	0.32
Russian (1,191)	1,976	2.73
Scandinavian (119)	343	0.47
Scotch-Irish (248)	970	1.34
Scottish (415)	1,478	2.04
Serbian (91)	135	0.19
Slavic (0)	49	0.07
Slovak (67)	109	0.15
Slovene (22)	53	0.07
Swedish (221)	971	1.34
Swiss (107)	591	0.82
Turkish (131)	163	0.22
Ukrainian (610)	680	0.94
Welsh (108)	498	0.69
West Indian, ex. Hispanic (45)	69	0.10
Jamaican (29)	53	0.07
Trinidadian/Tobagonian (8)	8	0.01
West Indian (8)	8	0.01
Yugoslavian (180)	180	0.25

Hispanic Origin	Population	%
Hispanic or Latino (of any race)	16,071	21.70
Central American, ex. Mexican	1,910	2.58
Costa Rican	28	0.04
Guatemalan	474	0.64
Honduran	81	0.11
Nicaraguan	109	0.15
Panamanian	46	0.06
Salvadoran	1,155	1.56
Other Central American	17	0.02
Cuban	90	0.12
Dominican Republic	24	0.03
Mexican	11,523	15.56
Puerto Rican	338	0.46
South American	874	1.18
Argentinean	96	0.13
Bolivian	53	0.07
Chilean	91	0.12
Colombian	137	0.18
Ecuadorian	41	0.06
Paraguayan	3	<0.01
Peruvian	395	0.53
Uruguayan	11	0.01
Venezuelan	32	0.04
Other South American	15	0.02
Other Hispanic or Latino	1,312	1.77

Race*	Population	%
African-American/Black (1,629)	2,201	2.97
Not Hispanic (1,468)	1,906	2.57
Hispanic (161)	295	0.40
American Indian/Alaska Native (344)	823	1.11
Not Hispanic (116)	396	0.53
Hispanic (228)	427	0.58
Aleut *(Alaska Native)* (0)	2	<0.01
Apache (8)	20	0.03
Blackfeet (1)	17	0.02
Canadian/French Am. Ind. (2)	2	<0.01
Central American Ind. (1)	1	<0.01
Cherokee (22)	105	0.14
Cheyenne (0)	2	<0.01
Chickasaw (2)	5	0.01
Chippewa (4)	11	0.01
Choctaw (4)	19	0.03
Colville (1)	1	<0.01
Cree (1)	2	<0.01
Creek (1)	7	0.01
Delaware (1)	2	<0.01
Inupiat *(Alaska Native)* (1)	3	<0.01
Iroquois (5)	16	0.02
Kiowa (2)	4	0.01
Menominee (0)	1	<0.01
Mexican American Ind. (60)	92	0.12
Navajo (7)	29	0.04
Osage (0)	2	<0.01
Ottawa (0)	1	<0.01
Paiute (0)	2	<0.01
Potawatomi (2)	3	<0.01
Pueblo (8)	10	0.01
Seminole (1)	8	0.01
Shoshone (0)	6	0.01
Sioux (6)	11	0.01
South American Ind. (5)	12	0.02
Spanish American Ind. (1)	1	<0.01
Tlingit-Haida *(Alaska Native)* (1)	2	<0.01
Tohono O'Odham (0)	1	<0.01
Tsimshian *(Alaska Native)* (1)	1	<0.01
Ute (0)	1	<0.01
Yaqui (5)	16	0.02
Yup'ik *(Alaska Native)* (0)	1	<0.01
Asian (19,232)	21,527	29.06
Not Hispanic (19,064)	21,116	28.51
Hispanic (168)	411	0.55
Bangladeshi (11)	11	0.01
Bhutanese (1)	1	<0.01
Burmese (47)	73	0.10
Cambodian (23)	27	0.04
Chinese, ex. Taiwanese (7,303)	8,277	11.18
Filipino (2,499)	3,086	4.17
Hmong (7)	7	0.01
Indian (4,344)	4,612	6.23
Indonesian (89)	136	0.18
Japanese (1,548)	2,091	2.82
Korean (1,031)	1,236	1.67
Laotian (12)	15	0.02
Malaysian (17)	23	0.03
Nepalese (101)	108	0.15
Pakistani (136)	163	0.22
Sri Lankan (53)	65	0.09
Taiwanese (648)	757	1.02
Thai (126)	162	0.22
Vietnamese (694)	798	1.08
Hawaii Native/Pacific Islander (391)	694	0.94
Not Hispanic (372)	612	0.83
Hispanic (19)	82	0.11
Fijian (56)	64	0.09
Guamanian/Chamorro (44)	77	0.10
Native Hawaiian (29)	161	0.22
Samoan (43)	69	0.09
Tongan (171)	202	0.27
White (41,468)	44,694	60.34
Not Hispanic (34,052)	36,381	49.12
Hispanic (7,416)	8,313	11.22

Murrieta

Place Type: City
County: Riverside
Population: 103,466†

Ancestry‡	Population	%
Afghan (165)	165	0.17
African, Sub-Saharan (1,218)	1,396	1.46
African (995)	1,154	1.21
Kenyan (48)	48	0.05
South African (99)	118	0.12
Other Sub-Saharan African (76)	76	0.08
Alsatian (0)	12	0.01
American (2,317)	2,317	2.42
Arab (176)	424	0.44
Arab (0)	10	0.01
Iraqi (15)	42	0.04
Lebanese (65)	215	0.22
Moroccan (0)	37	0.04
Palestinian (35)	47	0.05
Syrian (42)	42	0.04
Other Arab (19)	31	0.03
Armenian (37)	137	0.14
Assyrian/Chaldean/Syriac (20)	76	0.08
Australian (28)	295	0.31

*Notes: † The Census 2010 population figure is used to calculate the percentages in the Hispanic Origin and Race categories. Ancestry percentages are based on the 2006-2010 American Community Survey population (not shown); ‡ Numbers in parentheses indicate the number of people reporting a single ancestry; * Numbers in parentheses indicate the number of persons reporting this race alone, not in combination with any other race; Please refer to the Explanation of Data for more information.*

Austrian (0)	189	0.20
Belgian (0)	91	0.10
Brazilian (9)	55	0.06
British (323)	528	0.55
Bulgarian (48)	69	0.07
Canadian (251)	324	0.34
Croatian (25)	57	0.06
Czech (25)	174	0.18
Czechoslovakian (16)	86	0.09
Danish (149)	777	0.81
Dutch (274)	1,801	1.88
Eastern European (83)	167	0.17
English (2,434)	9,682	10.12
European (2,043)	2,477	2.59
Finnish (39)	171	0.18
French, ex. Basque (457)	3,255	3.40
French Canadian (331)	745	0.78
German (3,542)	15,477	16.18
Greek (64)	293	0.31
Guyanese (23)	23	0.02
Hungarian (152)	521	0.54
Icelander (0)	21	0.02
Iranian (228)	361	0.38
Irish (2,002)	10,350	10.82
Israeli (19)	60	0.06
Italian (2,076)	6,261	6.54
Latvian (31)	51	0.05
Lithuanian (55)	196	0.20
Maltese (17)	37	0.04
Northern European (27)	27	0.03
Norwegian (639)	2,314	2.42
Pennsylvania German (12)	38	0.04
Polish (340)	1,615	1.69
Portuguese (137)	324	0.34
Romanian (73)	179	0.19
Russian (206)	791	0.83
Scandinavian (92)	173	0.18
Scotch-Irish (558)	1,431	1.50
Scottish (516)	2,207	2.31
Serbian (13)	16	0.02
Slavic (0)	49	0.05
Slovak (38)	70	0.07
Slovene (0)	32	0.03
Swedish (472)	1,401	1.46
Swiss (118)	325	0.34
Ukrainian (75)	216	0.23
Welsh (24)	563	0.59
West Indian, ex. Hispanic (81)	183	0.19
Barbadian (0)	16	0.02
Dutch West Indian (17)	17	0.02
Haitian (10)	60	0.06
Jamaican (28)	56	0.06
Trinidadian/Tobagonian (26)	26	0.03
West Indian (0)	8	0.01
Yugoslavian (11)	91	0.10

Hispanic Origin	**Population**	**%**
Hispanic or Latino (of any race)	26,792	25.89
Central American, ex. Mexican	1,151	1.11
Costa Rican	96	0.09
Guatemalan	273	0.26
Honduran	82	0.08
Nicaraguan	123	0.12
Panamanian	121	0.12
Salvadoran	445	0.43
Other Central American	11	0.01
Cuban	375	0.36
Dominican Republic	61	0.06
Mexican	21,400	20.68
Puerto Rican	1,025	0.99
South American	905	0.87
Argentinean	144	0.14
Bolivian	28	0.03
Chilean	63	0.06
Colombian	228	0.22
Ecuadorian	137	0.13
Paraguayan	3	<0.01
Peruvian	240	0.23
Uruguayan	18	0.02
Venezuelan	35	0.03
Other South American	9	0.01
Other Hispanic or Latino	1,875	1.81

Race*	**Population**	**%**
African-American/Black (5,601)	7,178	6.94
Not Hispanic (5,162)	6,335	6.12
Hispanic (439)	843	0.81
American Indian/Alaska Native (741)	1,753	1.69
Not Hispanic (389)	1,001	0.97
Hispanic (352)	752	0.73
Alaska Athabascan *(Ala. Nat.)* (4)	5	<0.01
Aleut *(Alaska Native)* (1)	2	<0.01
Apache (13)	62	0.06
Arapaho (0)	3	<0.01
Blackfeet (10)	42	0.04
Canadian/French Am. Ind. (0)	7	0.01
Central American Ind. (10)	17	0.02
Cherokee (52)	248	0.24
Cheyenne (2)	5	<0.01
Chickasaw (2)	7	0.01
Chippewa (5)	27	0.03
Choctaw (10)	40	0.04
Colville (3)	3	<0.01
Comanche (2)	2	<0.01
Cree (1)	2	<0.01
Creek (11)	20	0.02
Hopi (6)	8	0.01
Houma (1)	1	<0.01
Iroquois (7)	32	0.03
Kiowa (0)	1	<0.01
Lumbee (2)	2	<0.01
Menominee (2)	2	<0.01
Mexican American Ind. (58)	102	0.10
Navajo (32)	67	0.06
Osage (1)	2	<0.01
Ottawa (0)	1	<0.01
Paiute (0)	1	<0.01
Pima (3)	12	0.01
Potawatomi (1)	6	0.01
Pueblo (23)	36	0.03
Puget Sound Salish (5)	7	0.01
Seminole (0)	3	<0.01
Shoshone (2)	5	<0.01
Sioux (14)	35	0.03
South American Ind. (6)	11	0.01
Spanish American Ind. (3)	5	<0.01
Tlingit-Haida *(Alaska Native)* (6)	7	0.01
Tohono O'Odham (0)	2	<0.01
Ute (0)	5	<0.01
Yakama (0)	3	<0.01
Yaqui (17)	22	0.02
Yup'ik *(Alaska Native)* (1)	1	<0.01
Asian (9,556)	12,457	12.04
Not Hispanic (9,304)	11,498	11.11
Hispanic (252)	959	0.93
Bangladeshi (15)	15	0.01
Burmese (14)	26	0.03
Cambodian (234)	268	0.26
Chinese, ex. Taiwanese (639)	1,092	1.06
Filipino (4,966)	6,449	6.23
Hmong (35)	43	0.04
Indian (464)	577	0.56
Indonesian (45)	112	0.11
Japanese (390)	1,048	1.01
Korean (748)	931	0.90
Laotian (323)	402	0.39
Malaysian (4)	11	0.01
Nepalese (2)	2	<0.01
Pakistani (63)	84	0.08
Sri Lankan (15)	20	0.02
Taiwanese (50)	71	0.07
Thai (119)	185	0.18
Vietnamese (1,045)	1,248	1.21
Hawaii Native/Pacific Islander (391)	923	0.89
Not Hispanic (332)	750	0.72
Hispanic (59)	173	0.17
Fijian (5)	5	<0.01
Guamanian/Chamorro (176)	296	0.29
Native Hawaiian (73)	298	0.29
Samoan (80)	161	0.16
Tongan (16)	28	0.03
White (72,137)	77,562	74.96
Not Hispanic (57,590)	60,850	58.81
Hispanic (14,547)	16,712	16.15

Muscoy

Place Type: CDP
County: San Bernardino
Population: 10,644†

Ancestry‡	**Population**	**%**
African, Sub-Saharan (25)	39	0.35
African (25)	39	0.35
American (24)	24	0.21
Dutch (0)	91	0.81
English (32)	161	1.43
French, ex. Basque (0)	26	0.23
German (59)	381	3.37
Irish (37)	178	1.58
Italian (0)	28	0.25
Norwegian (0)	18	0.16
Russian (0)	40	0.35
Scotch-Irish (0)	45	0.40
Swedish (13)	75	0.66
Swiss (0)	21	0.19

Hispanic Origin	**Population**	**%**
Hispanic or Latino (of any race)	8,824	82.90
Central American, ex. Mexican	255	2.40
Costa Rican	1	0.01
Guatemalan	91	0.85
Honduran	18	0.17
Nicaraguan	40	0.38
Salvadoran	103	0.97
Other Central American	2	0.02
Cuban	9	0.08
Dominican Republic	3	0.03
Mexican	8,076	75.87
Puerto Rican	51	0.48
South American	11	0.10
Argentinean	1	0.01
Peruvian	6	0.06
Venezuelan	3	0.03
Other South American	1	0.01
Other Hispanic or Latino	419	3.94

Race*	**Population**	**%**
African-American/Black (454)	548	5.15
Not Hispanic (397)	457	4.29
Hispanic (57)	91	0.85
American Indian/Alaska Native (125)	223	2.10
Not Hispanic (27)	65	0.61
Hispanic (98)	158	1.48
Apache (5)	17	0.16
Blackfeet (0)	3	0.03
Canadian/French Am. Ind. (0)	1	0.01
Central American Ind. (0)	4	0.04
Cherokee (3)	19	0.18
Choctaw (0)	12	0.11
Comanche (0)	1	0.01
Hopi (1)	4	0.04
Mexican American Ind. (25)	47	0.44
Navajo (0)	2	0.02
Ottawa (0)	1	0.01
Pima (0)	1	0.01
Seminole (4)	4	0.04
Sioux (0)	1	0.01
Tohono O'Odham (7)	7	0.07
Yaqui (1)	1	0.01
Asian (101)	145	1.36
Not Hispanic (80)	102	0.96
Hispanic (21)	43	0.40
Cambodian (21)	21	0.20
Chinese, ex. Taiwanese (6)	12	0.11
Filipino (25)	36	0.34
Indian (6)	7	0.07
Indonesian (0)	1	0.01
Japanese (10)	19	0.18
Korean (3)	5	0.05

*Notes: † The Census 2010 population figure is used to calculate the percentages in the Hispanic Origin and Race categories. Ancestry percentages are based on the 2006-2010 American Community Survey population (not shown); ‡ Numbers in parentheses indicate the number of people reporting a single ancestry; * Numbers in parentheses indicate the number of persons reporting this race alone, not in combination with any other race; Please refer to the Explanation of Data for more information.*

Laotian (5)	6	0.06
Malaysian (1)	1	0.01
Thai (7)	7	0.07
Vietnamese (12)	15	0.14
Hawaii Native/Pacific Islander (16)	47	0.44
Not Hispanic (14)	23	0.22
Hispanic (2)	24	0.23
Guamanian/Chamorro (0)	4	0.04
Marshallese (1)	1	0.01
Native Hawaiian (2)	4	0.04
Samoan (2)	2	0.02
Tongan (4)	8	0.08
White (4,459)	4,872	45.77
Not Hispanic (1,174)	1,258	11.82
Hispanic (3,285)	3,614	33.95

Napa

Place Type: City
County: Napa
Population: 76,915†

Ancestry‡	Population	%
African, Sub-Saharan (139)	147	0.19
African (7)	7	0.01
Cape Verdean (36)	36	0.05
Ghanaian (15)	15	0.02
Nigerian (52)	52	0.07
South African (8)	16	0.02
Other Sub-Saharan African (21)	21	0.03
American (2,121)	2,121	2.79
Arab (91)	238	0.31
Arab (18)	64	0.08
Egyptian (13)	13	0.02
Lebanese (14)	65	0.09
Palestinian (0)	6	0.01
Syrian (17)	61	0.08
Other Arab (29)	29	0.04
Armenian (35)	97	0.13
Australian (12)	28	0.04
Austrian (56)	292	0.38
Basque (32)	130	0.17
Belgian (32)	69	0.09
Brazilian (9)	24	0.03
British (220)	341	0.45
Bulgarian (0)	10	0.01
Canadian (48)	194	0.26
Celtic (0)	10	0.01
Croatian (33)	121	0.16
Czech (83)	153	0.20
Czechoslovakian (28)	94	0.12
Danish (225)	821	1.08
Dutch (302)	1,285	1.69
Eastern European (104)	104	0.14
English (1,491)	6,981	9.18
Estonian (0)	20	0.03
European (1,169)	1,297	1.71
Finnish (54)	110	0.14
French, ex. Basque (474)	2,562	3.37
French Canadian (79)	237	0.31
German (2,248)	10,127	13.32
Greek (125)	340	0.45
Hungarian (6)	236	0.31
Icelander (0)	12	0.02
Iranian (26)	26	0.03
Irish (1,819)	7,872	10.36
Italian (1,721)	4,849	6.38
Latvian (0)	26	0.03
Lithuanian (0)	68	0.09
Luxemburger (14)	26	0.03
Maltese (11)	11	0.01
Northern European (135)	135	0.18
Norwegian (649)	1,587	2.09
Polish (198)	835	1.10
Portuguese (330)	1,298	1.71
Romanian (0)	60	0.08
Russian (336)	659	0.87
Scandinavian (229)	303	0.40
Scotch-Irish (442)	1,489	1.96
Scottish (355)	1,823	2.40
Serbian (12)	38	0.05
Slavic (0)	8	0.01
Slovene (58)	73	0.10
Swedish (326)	1,424	1.87
Swiss (106)	425	0.56
Turkish (48)	91	0.12
Ukrainian (30)	178	0.23
Welsh (132)	853	1.12
West Indian, ex. Hispanic (0)	10	0.01
Trinidadian/Tobagonian (0)	10	0.01
Yugoslavian (143)	257	0.34

Hispanic Origin	Population	%
Hispanic or Latino (of any race)	28,923	37.60
Central American, ex. Mexican	693	0.90
Costa Rican	51	0.07
Guatemalan	258	0.34
Honduran	47	0.06
Nicaraguan	75	0.10
Panamanian	10	0.01
Salvadoran	248	0.32
Other Central American	4	0.01
Cuban	70	0.09
Dominican Republic	12	0.02
Mexican	26,246	34.12
Puerto Rican	220	0.29
South American	268	0.35
Argentinean	23	0.03
Bolivian	5	0.01
Chilean	48	0.06
Colombian	69	0.09
Ecuadorian	19	0.02
Peruvian	81	0.11
Uruguayan	5	0.01
Venezuelan	15	0.02
Other South American	3	<0.01
Other Hispanic or Latino	1,414	1.84

Race*	Population	%
African-American/Black (486)	808	1.05
Not Hispanic (370)	617	0.80
Hispanic (116)	191	0.25
American Indian/Alaska Native (637)	1,419	1.84
Not Hispanic (312)	856	1.11
Hispanic (325)	563	0.73
Alaska Athabascan *(Ala. Nat.)* (0)	1	<0.01
Aleut *(Alaska Native)* (0)	1	<0.01
Apache (6)	32	0.04
Blackfeet (2)	30	0.04
Canadian/French Am. Ind. (0)	3	<0.01
Central American Ind. (1)	1	<0.01
Cherokee (58)	244	0.32
Cheyenne (1)	1	<0.01
Chickasaw (4)	10	0.01
Chippewa (9)	13	0.02
Choctaw (30)	70	0.09
Colville (0)	1	<0.01
Comanche (0)	5	0.01
Cree (3)	5	0.01
Creek (5)	7	0.01
Crow (0)	9	0.01
Delaware (2)	5	0.01
Houma (3)	3	<0.01
Iroquois (5)	15	0.02
Kiowa (1)	3	<0.01
Lumbee (0)	3	<0.01
Menominee (3)	3	<0.01
Mexican American Ind. (97)	124	0.16
Navajo (5)	16	0.02
Osage (4)	4	0.01
Ottawa (4)	9	0.01
Paiute (2)	4	0.01
Pima (1)	2	<0.01
Potawatomi (11)	11	0.01
Pueblo (4)	5	0.01
Seminole (1)	6	0.01
Shoshone (0)	1	<0.01
Sioux (9)	24	0.03
South American Ind. (3)	6	0.01
Spanish American Ind. (6)	12	0.02
Tlingit-Haida *(Alaska Native)* (1)	1	<0.01
Tohono O'Odham (0)	3	<0.01
Yaqui (2)	2	<0.01
Yup'ik *(Alaska Native)* (2)	3	<0.01
Asian (1,755)	2,535	3.30
Not Hispanic (1,685)	2,302	2.99
Hispanic (70)	233	0.30
Bangladeshi (5)	5	0.01
Burmese (7)	12	0.02
Cambodian (6)	6	0.01
Chinese, ex. Taiwanese (282)	455	0.59
Filipino (551)	866	1.13
Hmong (1)	2	<0.01
Indian (186)	253	0.33
Indonesian (16)	30	0.04
Japanese (302)	486	0.63
Korean (153)	217	0.28
Laotian (4)	7	0.01
Malaysian (0)	7	0.01
Pakistani (44)	46	0.06
Sri Lankan (5)	7	0.01
Taiwanese (17)	18	0.02
Thai (19)	27	0.04
Vietnamese (75)	96	0.12
Hawaii Native/Pacific Islander (144)	345	0.45
Not Hispanic (116)	261	0.34
Hispanic (28)	84	0.11
Fijian (6)	6	0.01
Guamanian/Chamorro (51)	94	0.12
Native Hawaiian (46)	147	0.19
Samoan (3)	24	0.03
Tongan (12)	21	0.03
White (57,754)	60,375	78.50
Not Hispanic (43,963)	45,310	58.91
Hispanic (13,791)	15,065	19.59

National City

Place Type: City
County: San Diego
Population: 58,582†

Ancestry‡	Population	%
African, Sub-Saharan (106)	130	0.23
African (96)	109	0.19
Nigerian (10)	21	0.04
American (456)	456	0.80
Arab (143)	203	0.35
Arab (143)	143	0.25
Lebanese (0)	48	0.08
Syrian (0)	12	0.02
Armenian (0)	12	0.02
Austrian (25)	50	0.09
Belgian (21)	21	0.04
British (0)	55	0.10
Canadian (0)	19	0.03
Czech (0)	1	<0.01
Danish (0)	66	0.12
Dutch (28)	148	0.26
English (371)	1,349	2.35
European (12)	34	0.06
French, ex. Basque (57)	349	0.61
French Canadian (0)	10	0.02
German (370)	1,402	2.44
Greek (0)	37	0.06
Hungarian (10)	67	0.12
Iranian (0)	9	0.02
Irish (169)	1,270	2.21
Israeli (15)	15	0.03
Italian (169)	639	1.11
Lithuanian (10)	10	0.02
Norwegian (59)	256	0.45
Polish (48)	162	0.28
Portuguese (32)	239	0.42
Romanian (0)	10	0.02
Russian (34)	44	0.08
Scandinavian (0)	9	0.02
Scotch-Irish (148)	273	0.48
Scottish (54)	272	0.47
Slovene (0)	30	0.05

SECTION TWO

*Notes: † The Census 2010 population figure is used to calculate the percentages in the Hispanic Origin and Race categories. Ancestry percentages are based on the 2006-2010 American Community Survey population (not shown); ‡ Numbers in parentheses indicate the number of people reporting a single ancestry; * Numbers in parentheses indicate the number of persons reporting this race alone, not in combination with any other race; Please refer to the Explanation of Data for more information.*

Swedish (115)	220	0.38
Ukrainian (25)	25	0.04
Welsh (0)	24	0.04
West Indian, ex. Hispanic (15)	71	0.12
Jamaican (0)	39	0.07
Trinidadian/Tobagonian (0)	17	0.03
West Indian (15)	15	0.03
Yugoslavian (41)	41	0.07

Hispanic Origin	Population	%
Hispanic or Latino (of any race)	36,911	63.01
Central American, ex. Mexican	504	0.86
Costa Rican	47	0.08
Guatemalan	101	0.17
Honduran	97	0.17
Nicaraguan	55	0.09
Panamanian	60	0.10
Salvadoran	141	0.24
Other Central American	3	0.01
Cuban	109	0.19
Dominican Republic	54	0.09
Mexican	34,473	58.85
Puerto Rican	489	0.83
South American	206	0.35
Argentinean	25	0.04
Bolivian	33	0.06
Chilean	12	0.02
Colombian	54	0.09
Ecuadorian	26	0.04
Peruvian	37	0.06
Uruguayan	4	0.01
Venezuelan	14	0.02
Other South American	1	<0.01
Other Hispanic or Latino	1,076	1.84

Race*	Population	%
African-American/Black (3,054)	3,638	6.21
Not Hispanic (2,660)	3,023	5.16
Hispanic (394)	615	1.05
American Indian/Alaska Native (618)	1,006	1.72
Not Hispanic (168)	367	0.63
Hispanic (450)	639	1.09
Alaska Athabascan *(Ala. Nat.)* (0)	1	<0.01
Apache (32)	52	0.09
Arapaho (1)	4	0.01
Blackfeet (2)	15	0.03
Canadian/French Am. Ind. (0)	1	<0.01
Central American Ind. (0)	1	<0.01
Cherokee (19)	67	0.11
Chickasaw (1)	7	0.01
Chippewa (8)	14	0.02
Choctaw (9)	12	0.02
Comanche (0)	2	<0.01
Cree (1)	1	<0.01
Creek (3)	4	0.01
Crow (1)	3	0.01
Delaware (0)	1	<0.01
Hopi (1)	1	<0.01
Inupiat *(Alaska Native)* (2)	3	0.01
Iroquois (1)	4	0.01
Lumbee (1)	1	<0.01
Mexican American Ind. (71)	106	0.18
Navajo (29)	38	0.06
Ottawa (1)	2	<0.01
Pima (0)	1	<0.01
Potawatomi (0)	1	<0.01
Pueblo (5)	6	0.01
Seminole (0)	4	0.01
Shoshone (1)	4	0.01
Sioux (2)	10	0.02
South American Ind. (6)	7	0.01
Spanish American Ind. (3)	4	0.01
Tlingit-Haida *(Alaska Native)* (2)	2	<0.01
Tohono O'Odham (2)	3	0.01
Yaqui (6)	8	0.01
Yuman (2)	2	<0.01
Yup'ik *(Alaska Native)* (0)	1	<0.01
Asian (10,699)	11,771	20.09
Not Hispanic (10,401)	11,148	19.03
Hispanic (298)	623	1.06
Bangladeshi (1)	1	<0.01
Burmese (1)	1	<0.01
Cambodian (33)	46	0.08
Chinese, ex. Taiwanese (165)	255	0.44
Filipino (9,772)	10,695	18.26
Hmong (19)	20	0.03
Indian (68)	123	0.21
Indonesian (6)	11	0.02
Japanese (120)	286	0.49
Korean (72)	100	0.17
Laotian (111)	139	0.24
Malaysian (1)	21	0.04
Nepalese (1)	1	<0.01
Pakistani (5)	8	0.01
Sri Lankan (0)	4	0.01
Taiwanese (2)	4	0.01
Thai (11)	20	0.03
Vietnamese (127)	145	0.25
Hawaii Native/Pacific Islander (482)	777	1.33
Not Hispanic (413)	604	1.03
Hispanic (69)	173	0.30
Fijian (1)	2	<0.01
Guamanian/Chamorro (212)	303	0.52
Marshallese (12)	12	0.02
Native Hawaiian (27)	90	0.15
Samoan (176)	238	0.41
Tongan (14)	24	0.04
White (24,725)	26,830	45.80
Not Hispanic (6,872)	7,597	12.97
Hispanic (17,853)	19,233	32.83

Newark

Place Type: City
County: Alameda
Population: 42,573[†]

Ancestry[‡]	Population	%
Afghan (474)	474	1.13
African, Sub-Saharan (186)	247	0.59
African (111)	159	0.38
Ethiopian (23)	23	0.05
Senegalese (0)	13	0.03
Other Sub-Saharan African (52)	52	0.12
Albanian (21)	21	0.05
American (630)	630	1.50
Arab (233)	311	0.74
Arab (30)	68	0.16
Egyptian (152)	181	0.43
Lebanese (8)	8	0.02
Other Arab (43)	54	0.13
Armenian (16)	24	0.06
Austrian (63)	146	0.35
Belgian (17)	33	0.08
British (114)	339	0.81
Cajun (0)	14	0.03
Canadian (0)	31	0.07
Croatian (0)	15	0.04
Czech (0)	41	0.10
Czechoslovakian (23)	41	0.10
Danish (17)	187	0.45
Dutch (48)	218	0.52
Eastern European (60)	60	0.14
English (259)	1,705	4.06
European (407)	539	1.28
Finnish (0)	19	0.05
French, ex. Basque (32)	883	2.10
French Canadian (16)	53	0.13
German (610)	3,238	7.71
Greek (249)	264	0.63
Hungarian (0)	47	0.11
Iranian (150)	150	0.36
Irish (679)	3,167	7.54
Italian (373)	1,190	2.83
Latvian (17)	17	0.04
Lithuanian (16)	16	0.04
Luxemburger (22)	44	0.10
Maltese (9)	27	0.06
Northern European (47)	47	0.11
Norwegian (185)	546	1.30
Polish (83)	477	1.14
Portuguese (1,083)	1,640	3.91
Russian (114)	161	0.38
Scandinavian (23)	61	0.15
Scotch-Irish (32)	208	0.50
Scottish (154)	455	1.08
Slovak (0)	202	0.48
Slovene (0)	31	0.07
Swedish (124)	519	1.24
Swiss (11)	66	0.16
Ukrainian (9)	9	0.02
Welsh (0)	60	0.14
West Indian, ex. Hispanic (5)	17	0.04
Barbadian (5)	5	0.01
Jamaican (0)	12	0.03

Hispanic Origin	Population	%
Hispanic or Latino (of any race)	14,994	35.22
Central American, ex. Mexican	992	2.33
Costa Rican	16	0.04
Guatemalan	186	0.44
Honduran	27	0.06
Nicaraguan	221	0.52
Panamanian	17	0.04
Salvadoran	504	1.18
Other Central American	21	0.05
Cuban	56	0.13
Dominican Republic	7	0.02
Mexican	12,221	28.71
Puerto Rican	352	0.83
South American	363	0.85
Argentinean	37	0.09
Bolivian	57	0.13
Chilean	15	0.04
Colombian	58	0.14
Ecuadorian	19	0.04
Paraguayan	4	0.01
Peruvian	147	0.35
Uruguayan	7	0.02
Venezuelan	10	0.02
Other South American	9	0.02
Other Hispanic or Latino	1,003	2.36

Race*	Population	%
African-American/Black (2,002)	2,426	5.70
Not Hispanic (1,908)	2,191	5.15
Hispanic (94)	235	0.55
American Indian/Alaska Native (279)	647	1.52
Not Hispanic (95)	315	0.74
Hispanic (184)	332	0.78
Aleut *(Alaska Native)* (0)	1	<0.01
Apache (7)	19	0.04
Arapaho (4)	4	0.01
Blackfeet (6)	14	0.03
Central American Ind. (0)	6	0.01
Cherokee (21)	98	0.23
Cheyenne (1)	5	0.01
Chickasaw (4)	4	0.01
Chippewa (3)	10	0.02
Choctaw (2)	18	0.04
Comanche (2)	3	0.01
Creek (1)	3	0.01
Inupiat *(Alaska Native)* (0)	1	<0.01
Iroquois (0)	6	0.01
Mexican American Ind. (41)	59	0.14
Navajo (6)	14	0.03
Paiute (2)	4	0.01
Potawatomi (1)	3	0.01
Pueblo (5)	7	0.02
Puget Sound Salish (0)	1	<0.01
Seminole (1)	2	<0.01
Shoshone (8)	10	0.02
Sioux (4)	11	0.03
South American Ind. (1)	1	<0.01
Spanish American Ind. (0)	1	<0.01
Tlingit-Haida *(Alaska Native)* (2)	2	<0.01
Ute (1)	4	0.01
Yaqui (2)	2	<0.01
Asian (11,571)	13,163	30.92
Not Hispanic (11,404)	12,711	29.86

*Notes: † The Census 2010 population figure is used to calculate the percentages in the Hispanic Origin and Race categories. Ancestry percentages are based on the 2006-2010 American Community Survey population (not shown); ‡ Numbers in parentheses indicate the number of people reporting a single ancestry; * Numbers in parentheses indicate the number of persons reporting this race alone, not in combination with any other race; Please refer to the Explanation of Data for more information.*

Hispanic (167)	452	1.06
Bangladeshi (14)	16	0.04
Burmese (126)	145	0.34
Cambodian (40)	48	0.11
Chinese, ex. Taiwanese (2,458)	2,852	6.70
Filipino (4,054)	4,775	11.22
Hmong (13)	13	0.03
Indian (2,500)	2,716	6.38
Indonesian (20)	33	0.08
Japanese (252)	475	1.12
Korean (261)	311	0.73
Laotian (92)	96	0.23
Malaysian (5)	5	0.01
Nepalese (30)	32	0.08
Pakistani (199)	215	0.51
Sri Lankan (25)	27	0.06
Taiwanese (134)	167	0.39
Thai (53)	63	0.15
Vietnamese (980)	1,068	2.51
Hawaii Native/Pacific Islander (621)	1,141	2.68
Not Hispanic (601)	1,030	2.42
Hispanic (20)	111	0.26
Fijian (206)	247	0.58
Guamanian/Chamorro (56)	119	0.28
Native Hawaiian (31)	192	0.45
Samoan (119)	198	0.47
Tongan (130)	172	0.40
White (17,566)	19,685	46.24
Not Hispanic (11,726)	13,018	30.58
Hispanic (5,840)	6,667	15.66

Newman

Place Type: City
County: Stanislaus
Population: 10,224†

Ancestry‡	Population	%
American (256)	256	2.61
Armenian (53)	53	0.54
Belgian (0)	12	0.12
British (28)	28	0.29
Danish (40)	135	1.38
Dutch (17)	83	0.85
English (118)	331	3.38
European (24)	24	0.24
French, ex. Basque (24)	44	0.45
German (150)	868	8.85
Hungarian (0)	44	0.45
Irish (66)	604	6.16
Italian (35)	290	2.96
Norwegian (0)	99	1.01
Polish (0)	66	0.67
Portuguese (565)	978	9.97
Scotch-Irish (24)	38	0.39
Scottish (0)	91	0.93
Swedish (0)	150	1.53
Swiss (0)	50	0.51
Welsh (15)	29	0.30
Yugoslavian (0)	35	0.36

Hispanic Origin	Population	%
Hispanic or Latino (of any race)	6,299	61.61
Central American, ex. Mexican	115	1.12
Costa Rican	1	0.01
Guatemalan	5	0.05
Honduran	18	0.18
Nicaraguan	13	0.13
Salvadoran	78	0.76
Cuban	4	0.04
Mexican	5,907	57.78
Puerto Rican	60	0.59
South American	20	0.20
Argentinean	1	0.01
Bolivian	1	0.01
Chilean	1	0.01
Colombian	5	0.05
Ecuadorian	1	0.01
Peruvian	11	0.11
Other Hispanic or Latino	193	1.89

Race*	Population	%
African-American/Black (234)	300	2.93
Not Hispanic (215)	243	2.38
Hispanic (19)	57	0.56
American Indian/Alaska Native (106)	222	2.17
Not Hispanic (42)	94	0.92
Hispanic (64)	128	1.25
Aleut *(Alaska Native)* (2)	6	0.06
Apache (4)	11	0.11
Canadian/French Am. Ind. (1)	1	0.01
Central American Ind. (0)	1	0.01
Cherokee (10)	47	0.46
Chickasaw (1)	1	0.01
Chippewa (2)	7	0.07
Choctaw (3)	13	0.13
Comanche (0)	3	0.03
Creek (0)	1	0.01
Mexican American Ind. (16)	22	0.22
Navajo (1)	1	0.01
Paiute (0)	1	0.01
Seminole (0)	1	0.01
Sioux (1)	3	0.03
South American Ind. (0)	1	0.01
Spanish American Ind. (5)	5	0.05
Tlingit-Haida *(Alaska Native)* (2)	2	0.02
Yaqui (1)	4	0.04
Asian (191)	299	2.92
Not Hispanic (154)	221	2.16
Hispanic (37)	78	0.76
Cambodian (1)	2	0.02
Chinese, ex. Taiwanese (24)	39	0.38
Filipino (86)	143	1.40
Indian (40)	51	0.50
Indonesian (1)	3	0.03
Japanese (4)	14	0.14
Korean (7)	9	0.09
Laotian (6)	6	0.06
Malaysian (3)	5	0.05
Pakistani (1)	1	0.01
Thai (1)	7	0.07
Vietnamese (12)	16	0.16
Hawaii Native/Pacific Islander (40)	93	0.91
Not Hispanic (29)	62	0.61
Hispanic (11)	31	0.30
Guamanian/Chamorro (5)	12	0.12
Native Hawaiian (24)	54	0.53
Samoan (3)	5	0.05
Tongan (7)	9	0.09
White (6,812)	7,265	71.06
Not Hispanic (3,319)	3,446	33.71
Hispanic (3,493)	3,819	37.35

Newport Beach

Place Type: City
County: Orange
Population: 85,186†

Ancestry‡	Population	%
African, Sub-Saharan (160)	314	0.38
African (50)	151	0.18
South African (83)	125	0.15
Other Sub-Saharan African (27)	38	0.05
Albanian (0)	7	0.01
American (3,741)	3,741	4.48
Arab (603)	997	1.19
Arab (12)	12	0.01
Egyptian (77)	160	0.19
Iraqi (35)	83	0.10
Jordanian (17)	49	0.06
Lebanese (175)	301	0.36
Palestinian (36)	36	0.04
Syrian (28)	59	0.07
Other Arab (223)	297	0.36
Armenian (332)	581	0.70
Australian (17)	17	0.02
Austrian (293)	601	0.72
Basque (0)	20	0.02
Belgian (54)	192	0.23
Brazilian (20)	20	0.02
British (333)	734	0.88
Bulgarian (28)	54	0.06
Cajun (0)	5	0.01
Canadian (258)	516	0.62
Carpatho Rusyn (0)	13	0.02
Croatian (58)	197	0.24
Czech (122)	356	0.43
Czechoslovakian (30)	167	0.20
Danish (205)	702	0.84
Dutch (359)	1,588	1.90
Eastern European (148)	148	0.18
English (4,258)	14,515	17.37
Estonian (11)	11	0.01
European (2,170)	2,427	2.90
Finnish (26)	96	0.11
French, ex. Basque (490)	3,333	3.99
French Canadian (175)	459	0.55
German (3,890)	15,533	18.59
Greek (272)	560	0.67
Hungarian (434)	870	1.04
Iranian (2,099)	2,378	2.85
Irish (2,968)	12,812	15.33
Israeli (96)	123	0.15
Italian (2,721)	7,119	8.52
Latvian (11)	24	0.03
Lithuanian (24)	304	0.36
Luxemburger (0)	11	0.01
New Zealander (21)	33	0.04
Northern European (107)	132	0.16
Norwegian (595)	1,963	2.35
Polish (666)	2,431	2.91
Portuguese (144)	484	0.58
Romanian (126)	312	0.37
Russian (964)	1,996	2.39
Scandinavian (80)	205	0.25
Scotch-Irish (1,112)	2,750	3.29
Scottish (877)	2,846	3.41
Serbian (9)	20	0.02
Slavic (0)	63	0.08
Slovak (28)	91	0.11
Slovene (13)	38	0.05
Swedish (543)	2,439	2.92
Swiss (184)	730	0.87
Turkish (142)	204	0.24
Ukrainian (238)	362	0.43
Welsh (162)	1,134	1.36
West Indian, ex. Hispanic (24)	24	0.03
Barbadian (24)	24	0.03
Yugoslavian (100)	143	0.17

Hispanic Origin	Population	%
Hispanic or Latino (of any race)	6,174	7.25
Central American, ex. Mexican	350	0.41
Costa Rican	36	0.04
Guatemalan	108	0.13
Honduran	14	0.02
Nicaraguan	58	0.07
Panamanian	21	0.02
Salvadoran	98	0.12
Other Central American	15	0.02
Cuban	216	0.25
Dominican Republic	19	0.02
Mexican	3,861	4.53
Puerto Rican	220	0.26
South American	628	0.74
Argentinean	141	0.17
Bolivian	30	0.04
Chilean	66	0.08
Colombian	155	0.18
Ecuadorian	80	0.09
Paraguayan	3	<0.01
Peruvian	87	0.10
Uruguayan	18	0.02
Venezuelan	33	0.04
Other South American	15	0.02
Other Hispanic or Latino	880	1.03

Race*	Population	%
African-American/Black (616)	880	1.03

*Notes: † The Census 2010 population figure is used to calculate the percentages in the Hispanic Origin and Race categories. Ancestry percentages are based on the 2006-2010 American Community Survey population (not shown); ‡ Numbers in parentheses indicate the number of people reporting a single ancestry; * Numbers in parentheses indicate the number of persons reporting this race alone, not in combination with any other race; Please refer to the Explanation of Data for more information.*

SECTION TWO

	Population	%
Not Hispanic (571)	795	0.93
Hispanic (45)	85	0.10
American Indian/Alaska Native (223)	603	0.71
Not Hispanic (152)	414	0.49
Hispanic (71)	189	0.22
Alaska Athabascan *(Ala. Nat.)* (0)	1	<0.01
Apache (11)	24	0.03
Arapaho (1)	1	<0.01
Blackfeet (2)	16	0.02
Canadian/French Am. Ind. (4)	5	0.01
Cherokee (29)	110	0.13
Cheyenne (0)	1	<0.01
Chickasaw (4)	6	0.01
Chippewa (6)	11	0.01
Choctaw (9)	19	0.02
Colville (0)	1	<0.01
Creek (3)	6	0.01
Crow (2)	2	<0.01
Delaware (1)	2	<0.01
Iroquois (3)	15	0.02
Lumbee (1)	2	<0.01
Mexican American Ind. (4)	22	0.03
Navajo (13)	21	0.02
Osage (0)	4	<0.01
Ottawa (2)	3	<0.01
Paiute (3)	4	<0.01
Potawatomi (2)	3	<0.01
Pueblo (2)	9	0.01
Puget Sound Salish (1)	4	<0.01
Shoshone (1)	1	<0.01
Sioux (1)	13	0.02
South American Ind. (0)	1	<0.01
Tohono O'Odham (1)	1	<0.01
Tsimshian *(Alaska Native)* (0)	1	<0.01
Yaqui (2)	7	0.01
Asian (5,982)	7,587	8.91
Not Hispanic (5,925)	7,382	8.67
Hispanic (57)	205	0.24
Bangladeshi (11)	11	0.01
Burmese (13)	20	0.02
Cambodian (15)	29	0.03
Chinese, ex. Taiwanese (1,480)	1,945	2.28
Filipino (619)	918	1.08
Hmong (3)	3	<0.01
Indian (691)	826	0.97
Indonesian (17)	48	0.06
Japanese (821)	1,230	1.44
Korean (843)	1,030	1.21
Laotian (7)	13	0.02
Malaysian (4)	13	0.02
Pakistani (54)	66	0.08
Sri Lankan (11)	13	0.02
Taiwanese (320)	369	0.43
Thai (69)	89	0.10
Vietnamese (668)	815	0.96
Hawaii Native/Pacific Islander (114)	327	0.38
Not Hispanic (95)	274	0.32
Hispanic (19)	53	0.06
Fijian (1)	3	<0.01
Guamanian/Chamorro (20)	42	0.05
Native Hawaiian (49)	150	0.18
Samoan (22)	40	0.05
Tongan (2)	2	<0.01
White (74,357)	76,656	89.99
Not Hispanic (70,142)	71,976	84.49
Hispanic (4,215)	4,680	5.49

Nipomo

Place Type: CDP
County: San Luis Obispo
Population: 16,714†

Ancestry‡	Population	%
American (789)	789	4.88
Arab (18)	48	0.30
Lebanese (0)	15	0.09
Syrian (0)	15	0.09
Other Arab (18)	18	0.11
Armenian (24)	49	0.30
Austrian (13)	23	0.14
Belgian (9)	9	0.06
British (44)	44	0.27
Canadian (34)	50	0.31
Croatian (0)	20	0.12
Czech (10)	28	0.17
Czechoslovakian (0)	119	0.74
Danish (47)	240	1.48
Dutch (103)	316	1.95
English (368)	1,334	8.25
European (320)	320	1.98
Finnish (11)	24	0.15
French, ex. Basque (35)	535	3.31
French Canadian (45)	122	0.75
German (600)	2,567	15.87
Greek (50)	153	0.95
Hungarian (32)	45	0.28
Icelander (0)	8	0.05
Irish (461)	1,808	11.17
Italian (349)	768	4.75
Norwegian (84)	304	1.88
Polish (32)	221	1.37
Portuguese (131)	204	1.26
Romanian (0)	17	0.11
Russian (31)	79	0.49
Scotch-Irish (132)	365	2.26
Scottish (97)	415	2.57
Serbian (0)	14	0.09
Slavic (9)	24	0.15
Swedish (119)	271	1.68
Swiss (0)	90	0.56
Welsh (65)	93	0.57

Hispanic Origin	Population	%
Hispanic or Latino (of any race)	6,645	39.76
Central American, ex. Mexican	67	0.40
Costa Rican	5	0.03
Guatemalan	18	0.11
Honduran	9	0.05
Nicaraguan	9	0.05
Panamanian	4	0.02
Salvadoran	21	0.13
Other Central American	1	0.01
Cuban	22	0.13
Dominican Republic	1	0.01
Mexican	6,126	36.65
Puerto Rican	56	0.34
South American	46	0.28
Argentinean	7	0.04
Bolivian	2	0.01
Chilean	2	0.01
Colombian	7	0.04
Ecuadorian	4	0.02
Peruvian	16	0.10
Uruguayan	2	0.01
Venezuelan	6	0.04
Other Hispanic or Latino	327	1.96

Race*	Population	%
African-American/Black (177)	286	1.71
Not Hispanic (141)	212	1.27
Hispanic (36)	74	0.44
American Indian/Alaska Native (200)	489	2.93
Not Hispanic (87)	240	1.44
Hispanic (113)	249	1.49
Aleut *(Alaska Native)* (0)	1	0.01
Apache (7)	15	0.09
Blackfeet (2)	8	0.05
Central American Ind. (1)	2	0.01
Cherokee (14)	71	0.42
Cheyenne (0)	1	0.01
Chickasaw (1)	5	0.03
Chippewa (6)	8	0.05
Choctaw (6)	27	0.16
Cree (0)	1	0.01
Creek (0)	7	0.04
Iroquois (5)	12	0.07
Mexican American Ind. (49)	72	0.43
Navajo (4)	18	0.11
Osage (2)	2	0.01
Ottawa (2)	2	0.01
Paiute (1)	1	0.01
Potawatomi (2)	6	0.04
Pueblo (1)	4	0.02
Sioux (3)	12	0.07
South American Ind. (1)	1	0.01
Tlingit-Haida *(Alaska Native)* (3)	3	0.02
Ute (0)	1	0.01
Yaqui (4)	10	0.06
Asian (421)	674	4.03
Not Hispanic (366)	485	2.90
Hispanic (55)	189	1.13
Cambodian (12)	13	0.08
Chinese, ex. Taiwanese (29)	57	0.34
Filipino (212)	359	2.15
Hmong (1)	3	0.02
Indian (26)	34	0.20
Indonesian (2)	2	0.01
Japanese (40)	89	0.53
Korean (39)	59	0.35
Laotian (20)	23	0.14
Taiwanese (1)	1	0.01
Thai (7)	8	0.05
Vietnamese (13)	18	0.11
Hawaii Native/Pacific Islander (33)	84	0.50
Not Hispanic (33)	65	0.39
Hispanic (0)	19	0.11
Fijian (4)	4	0.02
Guamanian/Chamorro (0)	2	0.01
Native Hawaiian (8)	42	0.25
Samoan (12)	21	0.13
White (12,281)	12,942	77.43
Not Hispanic (9,075)	9,396	56.22
Hispanic (3,206)	3,546	21.22

Norco

Place Type: City
County: Riverside
Population: 27,063†

Ancestry‡	Population	%
African, Sub-Saharan (87)	126	0.47
African (71)	102	0.38
Ethiopian (8)	8	0.03
Nigerian (8)	16	0.06
American (971)	971	3.60
Arab (101)	131	0.49
Jordanian (0)	8	0.03
Lebanese (101)	101	0.37
Palestinian (0)	8	0.03
Syrian (0)	8	0.03
Other Arab (0)	6	0.02
Armenian (21)	49	0.18
Austrian (24)	24	0.09
Belgian (9)	148	0.55
Brazilian (0)	62	0.23
British (71)	109	0.40
Canadian (59)	68	0.25
Czech (0)	80	0.30
Czechoslovakian (57)	57	0.21
Danish (174)	396	1.47
Dutch (250)	1,001	3.71
English (707)	2,723	10.09
European (353)	494	1.83
Finnish (0)	18	0.07
French, ex. Basque (155)	867	3.21
French Canadian (97)	229	0.85
German (1,407)	4,217	15.63
Greek (19)	114	0.42
Hungarian (123)	254	0.94
Icelander (0)	22	0.08
Iranian (8)	8	0.03
Irish (677)	2,348	8.70
Italian (494)	1,572	5.83
Lithuanian (29)	120	0.44
Maltese (12)	12	0.04
Northern European (18)	18	0.07
Norwegian (155)	256	0.95
Pennsylvania German (7)	7	0.03

*Notes: † The Census 2010 population figure is used to calculate the percentages in the Hispanic Origin and Race categories. Ancestry percentages are based on the 2006-2010 American Community Survey population (not shown); ‡ Numbers in parentheses indicate the number of people reporting a single ancestry; * Numbers in parentheses indicate the number of persons reporting this race alone, not in combination with any other race; Please refer to the Explanation of Data for more information.*

Polish (103)	272	1.01
Portuguese (152)	335	1.24
Romanian (16)	157	0.58
Russian (21)	170	0.63
Scandinavian (8)	25	0.09
Scotch-Irish (222)	403	1.49
Scottish (87)	587	2.18
Swedish (77)	476	1.76
Swiss (16)	85	0.32
Turkish (0)	15	0.06
Ukrainian (0)	8	0.03
Welsh (49)	146	0.54
West Indian, ex. Hispanic (47)	55	0.20
Belizean (7)	15	0.06
Jamaican (8)	8	0.03
Trinidadian/Tobagonian (32)	32	0.12

Hispanic Origin	Population	%
Hispanic or Latino (of any race)	8,405	31.06
Central American, ex. Mexican	195	0.72
Costa Rican	10	0.04
Guatemalan	37	0.14
Honduran	16	0.06
Nicaraguan	29	0.11
Panamanian	3	0.01
Salvadoran	98	0.36
Other Central American	2	0.01
Cuban	86	0.32
Dominican Republic	3	0.01
Mexican	7,354	27.17
Puerto Rican	103	0.38
South American	135	0.50
Argentinean	29	0.11
Bolivian	1	<0.01
Chilean	9	0.03
Colombian	38	0.14
Ecuadorian	5	0.02
Paraguayan	1	<0.01
Peruvian	38	0.14
Venezuelan	11	0.04
Other South American	3	0.01
Other Hispanic or Latino	529	1.95

Race*	Population	%
African-American/Black (1,893)	2,017	7.45
Not Hispanic (1,858)	1,950	7.21
Hispanic (35)	67	0.25
American Indian/Alaska Native (248)	502	1.85
Not Hispanic (150)	312	1.15
Hispanic (98)	190	0.70
Aleut *(Alaska Native)* (1)	2	0.01
Apache (21)	31	0.11
Blackfeet (1)	14	0.05
Canadian/French Am. Ind. (1)	1	<0.01
Cherokee (25)	62	0.23
Chippewa (0)	3	0.01
Choctaw (6)	18	0.07
Comanche (3)	8	0.03
Cree (0)	2	0.01
Creek (1)	5	0.02
Delaware (0)	5	0.02
Hopi (4)	6	0.02
Iroquois (2)	3	0.01
Kiowa (0)	4	0.01
Mexican American Ind. (21)	28	0.10
Navajo (6)	21	0.08
Ottawa (0)	4	0.01
Puget Sound Salish (1)	1	<0.01
Seminole (0)	1	<0.01
Sioux (4)	12	0.04
South American Ind. (2)	2	0.01
Spanish American Ind. (1)	1	<0.01
Tohono O'Odham (0)	1	<0.01
Ute (0)	1	<0.01
Yaqui (1)	1	<0.01
Yuman (1)	1	<0.01
Asian (844)	1,109	4.10
Not Hispanic (828)	1,037	3.83
Hispanic (16)	72	0.27
Burmese (2)	2	0.01
Cambodian (20)	20	0.07
Chinese, ex. Taiwanese (95)	133	0.49
Filipino (250)	362	1.34
Indian (78)	93	0.34
Indonesian (6)	13	0.05
Japanese (63)	132	0.49
Korean (96)	129	0.48
Laotian (13)	13	0.05
Malaysian (0)	1	<0.01
Pakistani (18)	22	0.08
Sri Lankan (4)	4	0.01
Taiwanese (18)	19	0.07
Thai (12)	15	0.06
Vietnamese (125)	153	0.57
Hawaii Native/Pacific Islander (59)	110	0.41
Not Hispanic (52)	91	0.34
Hispanic (7)	19	0.07
Guamanian/Chamorro (12)	20	0.07
Native Hawaiian (28)	43	0.16
Samoan (14)	19	0.07
Tongan (0)	2	0.01
White (20,641)	21,409	79.11
Not Hispanic (15,275)	15,696	58.00
Hispanic (5,366)	5,713	21.11

North Auburn

Place Type: CDP
County: Placer
Population: 13,022†

Ancestry‡	Population	%
African, Sub-Saharan (50)	50	0.40
African (50)	50	0.40
American (624)	624	4.97
Arab (17)	31	0.25
Arab (9)	9	0.07
Jordanian (8)	8	0.06
Lebanese (0)	14	0.11
Austrian (8)	62	0.49
Belgian (9)	9	0.07
British (44)	63	0.50
Canadian (15)	25	0.20
Croatian (0)	15	0.12
Czech (12)	39	0.31
Danish (14)	34	0.27
Dutch (73)	297	2.36
Eastern European (5)	5	0.04
English (535)	1,732	13.79
Estonian (0)	9	0.07
European (193)	226	1.80
Finnish (0)	9	0.07
French, ex. Basque (82)	406	3.23
French Canadian (0)	20	0.16
German (986)	2,782	22.15
Greek (54)	132	1.05
Hungarian (28)	45	0.36
Iranian (73)	73	0.58
Irish (554)	2,049	16.31
Italian (205)	665	5.29
Lithuanian (9)	9	0.07
Norwegian (56)	251	2.00
Pennsylvania German (12)	12	0.10
Polish (44)	96	0.76
Portuguese (121)	293	2.33
Russian (23)	77	0.61
Scandinavian (51)	67	0.53
Scotch-Irish (89)	334	2.66
Scottish (49)	289	2.30
Slavic (0)	25	0.20
Slovak (0)	19	0.15
Slovene (46)	46	0.37
Swedish (147)	367	2.92
Swiss (0)	24	0.19
Ukrainian (35)	35	0.28
Welsh (22)	142	1.13
West Indian, ex. Hispanic (0)	18	0.14
Dutch West Indian (0)	18	0.14
Yugoslavian (11)	22	0.18

Hispanic Origin	Population	%
Hispanic or Latino (of any race)	2,108	16.19
Central American, ex. Mexican	237	1.82
Costa Rican	4	0.03
Guatemalan	42	0.32
Honduran	8	0.06
Nicaraguan	8	0.06
Panamanian	1	0.01
Salvadoran	174	1.34
Cuban	5	0.04
Mexican	1,510	11.60
Puerto Rican	60	0.46
South American	26	0.20
Argentinean	2	0.02
Chilean	11	0.08
Colombian	6	0.05
Ecuadorian	2	0.02
Peruvian	4	0.03
Other South American	1	0.01
Other Hispanic or Latino	270	2.07

Race*	Population	%
African-American/Black (115)	192	1.47
Not Hispanic (111)	182	1.40
Hispanic (4)	10	0.08
American Indian/Alaska Native (172)	360	2.76
Not Hispanic (125)	269	2.07
Hispanic (47)	91	0.70
Aleut *(Alaska Native)* (2)	4	0.03
Apache (2)	4	0.03
Blackfeet (2)	8	0.06
Canadian/French Am. Ind. (0)	1	0.01
Central American Ind. (2)	2	0.02
Cherokee (18)	80	0.61
Chickasaw (0)	2	0.02
Chippewa (4)	5	0.04
Choctaw (6)	22	0.17
Comanche (0)	1	0.01
Cree (0)	1	0.01
Creek (1)	3	0.02
Hopi (0)	1	0.01
Iroquois (1)	3	0.02
Menominee (0)	1	0.01
Mexican American Ind. (1)	1	0.01
Navajo (2)	7	0.05
Osage (1)	3	0.02
Paiute (3)	5	0.04
Pima (1)	1	0.01
Potawatomi (1)	2	0.02
Pueblo (1)	2	0.02
Shoshone (3)	3	0.02
Sioux (7)	8	0.06
Spanish American Ind. (2)	6	0.05
Tohono O'Odham (0)	2	0.02
Ute (0)	2	0.02
Yaqui (1)	1	0.01
Asian (298)	412	3.16
Not Hispanic (285)	375	2.88
Hispanic (13)	37	0.28
Cambodian (0)	1	0.01
Chinese, ex. Taiwanese (41)	55	0.42
Filipino (125)	184	1.41
Hmong (1)	2	0.02
Indian (26)	31	0.24
Indonesian (3)	8	0.06
Japanese (39)	73	0.56
Korean (16)	20	0.15
Laotian (2)	2	0.02
Malaysian (0)	3	0.02
Nepalese (4)	4	0.03
Pakistani (8)	8	0.06
Taiwanese (1)	2	0.02
Thai (3)	9	0.07
Vietnamese (2)	2	0.02
Hawaii Native/Pacific Islander (13)	35	0.27
Not Hispanic (12)	31	0.24
Hispanic (1)	4	0.03
Guamanian/Chamorro (4)	6	0.05
Native Hawaiian (4)	15	0.12
Samoan (3)	4	0.03

*Notes: † The Census 2010 population figure is used to calculate the percentages in the Hispanic Origin and Race categories. Ancestry percentages are based on the 2006-2010 American Community Survey population (not shown); ‡ Numbers in parentheses indicate the number of people reporting a single ancestry; * Numbers in parentheses indicate the number of persons reporting this race alone, not in combination with any other race; Please refer to the Explanation of Data for more information.*

White (11,081)	11,506	88.36
Not Hispanic (10,066)	10,353	79.50
Hispanic (1,015)	1,153	8.85

North Fair Oaks

Place Type: CDP
County: San Mateo
Population: 14,687[†]

Ancestry[‡]	Population	%
African, Sub-Saharan (17)	17	0.12
Kenyan (17)	17	0.12
American (178)	178	1.25
Arab (125)	125	0.88
Egyptian (29)	29	0.20
Lebanese (19)	19	0.13
Other Arab (77)	77	0.54
Austrian (8)	8	0.06
British (56)	120	0.84
Canadian (9)	42	0.29
Croatian (29)	29	0.20
Czechoslovakian (0)	13	0.09
Danish (0)	38	0.27
Dutch (0)	45	0.32
English (194)	508	3.56
European (206)	240	1.68
Finnish (19)	66	0.46
French, ex. Basque (48)	104	0.73
French Canadian (10)	37	0.26
German (211)	627	4.39
Greek (8)	31	0.22
Hungarian (63)	79	0.55
Icelander (11)	11	0.08
Irish (135)	470	3.29
Italian (106)	260	1.82
Maltese (6)	6	0.04
Northern European (32)	32	0.22
Norwegian (0)	118	0.83
Polish (27)	78	0.55
Portuguese (0)	16	0.11
Russian (16)	72	0.50
Scandinavian (0)	12	0.08
Scotch-Irish (0)	42	0.29
Scottish (0)	109	0.76
Slovene (0)	7	0.05
Swedish (48)	125	0.88
Swiss (16)	47	0.33
Turkish (6)	6	0.04
Ukrainian (0)	10	0.07
Welsh (0)	17	0.12

Hispanic Origin	Population	%
Hispanic or Latino (of any race)	10,731	73.06
Central American, ex. Mexican	1,296	8.82
Costa Rican	1	0.01
Guatemalan	552	3.76
Honduran	21	0.14
Nicaraguan	41	0.28
Panamanian	2	0.01
Salvadoran	673	4.58
Other Central American	6	0.04
Cuban	21	0.14
Mexican	8,691	59.17
Puerto Rican	57	0.39
South American	140	0.95
Argentinean	18	0.12
Bolivian	11	0.07
Chilean	10	0.07
Colombian	17	0.12
Ecuadorian	4	0.03
Paraguayan	1	0.01
Peruvian	72	0.49
Uruguayan	2	0.01
Venezuelan	5	0.03
Other Hispanic or Latino	526	3.58

Race*	Population	%
African-American/Black (235)	341	2.32
Not Hispanic (163)	213	1.45
Hispanic (72)	128	0.87
American Indian/Alaska Native (143)	241	1.64
Not Hispanic (33)	74	0.50
Hispanic (110)	167	1.14
Apache (1)	4	0.03
Cherokee (3)	13	0.09
Chippewa (1)	1	0.01
Iroquois (1)	4	0.03
Kiowa (0)	1	0.01
Mexican American Ind. (25)	38	0.26
Navajo (7)	13	0.09
South American Ind. (1)	1	0.01
Tlingit-Haida *(Alaska Native)* (0)	3	0.02
Yaqui (0)	1	0.01
Asian (548)	713	4.85
Not Hispanic (526)	650	4.43
Hispanic (22)	63	0.43
Burmese (2)	2	0.01
Cambodian (0)	2	0.01
Chinese, ex. Taiwanese (139)	180	1.23
Filipino (130)	164	1.12
Indian (84)	130	0.89
Indonesian (4)	8	0.05
Japanese (35)	63	0.43
Korean (17)	36	0.25
Laotian (31)	32	0.22
Malaysian (0)	3	0.02
Nepalese (1)	1	0.01
Pakistani (7)	9	0.06
Taiwanese (15)	19	0.13
Thai (5)	5	0.03
Vietnamese (51)	59	0.40
Hawaii Native/Pacific Islander (219)	286	1.95
Not Hispanic (193)	240	1.63
Hispanic (26)	46	0.31
Fijian (20)	21	0.14
Guamanian/Chamorro (8)	10	0.07
Native Hawaiian (3)	22	0.15
Samoan (8)	11	0.07
Tongan (139)	157	1.07
White (7,060)	7,681	52.30
Not Hispanic (2,793)	2,975	20.26
Hispanic (4,267)	4,706	32.04

North Highlands

Place Type: CDP
County: Sacramento
Population: 42,694[†]

Ancestry[‡]	Population	%
African, Sub-Saharan (113)	471	1.10
African (106)	464	1.09
Ethiopian (7)	7	0.02
American (1,497)	1,497	3.51
Arab (13)	63	0.15
Arab (13)	13	0.03
Lebanese (0)	25	0.06
Syrian (0)	25	0.06
Armenian (54)	64	0.15
Australian (0)	80	0.19
Austrian (13)	63	0.15
Belgian (114)	114	0.27
British (75)	130	0.30
Bulgarian (12)	17	0.04
Canadian (32)	54	0.13
Celtic (0)	10	0.02
Croatian (19)	58	0.14
Czech (14)	27	0.06
Czechoslovakian (12)	12	0.03
Danish (77)	142	0.33
Dutch (12)	383	0.90
English (871)	2,447	5.73
European (157)	287	0.67
Finnish (22)	80	0.19
French, ex. Basque (192)	770	1.80
French Canadian (15)	27	0.06
German (955)	4,319	10.12
Greek (27)	65	0.15
Hungarian (15)	69	0.16
Icelander (20)	20	0.05
Irish (1,077)	3,101	7.27
Italian (663)	1,356	3.18
Latvian (21)	21	0.05
Lithuanian (22)	52	0.12
Luxemburger (0)	7	0.02
Macedonian (0)	14	0.03
Northern European (10)	20	0.05
Norwegian (138)	414	0.97
Polish (181)	483	1.13
Portuguese (335)	801	1.88
Romanian (190)	356	0.83
Russian (1,097)	1,491	3.49
Scandinavian (27)	48	0.11
Scotch-Irish (388)	757	1.77
Scottish (281)	799	1.87
Slavic (32)	32	0.07
Slovak (0)	14	0.03
Swedish (116)	422	0.99
Swiss (15)	140	0.33
Ukrainian (1,954)	2,401	5.63
Welsh (64)	226	0.53
Yugoslavian (64)	86	0.20

Hispanic Origin	Population	%
Hispanic or Latino (of any race)	10,077	23.60
Central American, ex. Mexican	516	1.21
Costa Rican	16	0.04
Guatemalan	106	0.25
Honduran	48	0.11
Nicaraguan	44	0.10
Panamanian	48	0.11
Salvadoran	252	0.59
Other Central American	2	<0.01
Cuban	116	0.27
Dominican Republic	13	0.03
Mexican	8,147	19.08
Puerto Rican	377	0.88
South American	93	0.22
Argentinean	17	0.04
Bolivian	3	0.01
Chilean	3	0.01
Colombian	10	0.02
Ecuadorian	8	0.02
Peruvian	43	0.10
Venezuelan	9	0.02
Other Hispanic or Latino	815	1.91

Race*	Population	%
African-American/Black (4,883)	6,239	14.61
Not Hispanic (4,609)	5,651	13.24
Hispanic (274)	588	1.38
American Indian/Alaska Native (603)	1,523	3.57
Not Hispanic (381)	1,039	2.43
Hispanic (222)	484	1.13
Alaska Athabascan *(Ala. Nat.)* (4)	4	0.01
Apache (10)	49	0.11
Arapaho (1)	3	0.01
Blackfeet (9)	64	0.15
Cherokee (69)	294	0.69
Cheyenne (2)	6	0.01
Chickasaw (4)	9	0.02
Chippewa (4)	20	0.05
Choctaw (15)	59	0.14
Comanche (1)	5	0.01
Cree (0)	7	0.02
Creek (1)	7	0.02
Crow (1)	4	0.01
Delaware (0)	7	0.02
Hopi (2)	9	0.02
Inupiat *(Alaska Native)* (4)	6	0.01
Iroquois (3)	12	0.03
Lumbee (2)	2	<0.01
Menominee (1)	1	<0.01
Mexican American Ind. (52)	79	0.19
Navajo (14)	24	0.06
Osage (3)	4	0.01
Ottawa (0)	2	<0.01
Paiute (15)	15	0.04
Pima (4)	7	0.02

*Notes: † The Census 2010 population figure is used to calculate the percentages in the Hispanic Origin and Race categories. Ancestry percentages are based on the 2006-2010 American Community Survey population (not shown); ‡ Numbers in parentheses indicate the number of people reporting a single ancestry; * Numbers in parentheses indicate the number of persons reporting this race alone, not in combination with any other race; Please refer to the Explanation of Data for more information.*

Potawatomi (2)	4	0.01
Pueblo (6)	11	0.03
Seminole (3)	8	0.02
Shoshone (1)	15	0.04
Sioux (17)	38	0.09
South American Ind. (1)	2	<0.01
Spanish American Ind. (5)	7	0.02
Tlingit-Haida *(Alaska Native)* (3)	6	0.01
Tohono O'Odham (2)	5	0.01
Tsimshian *(Alaska Native)* (0)	1	<0.01
Yakama (0)	1	<0.01
Yaqui (0)	7	0.02
Yuman (3)	6	0.01
Asian (2,067)	2,924	6.85
Not Hispanic (1,997)	2,635	6.17
Hispanic (70)	289	0.68
Bangladeshi (0)	2	<0.01
Burmese (1)	1	<0.01
Cambodian (16)	26	0.06
Chinese, ex. Taiwanese (106)	193	0.45
Filipino (605)	936	2.19
Hmong (154)	166	0.39
Indian (121)	200	0.47
Indonesian (13)	28	0.07
Japanese (151)	312	0.73
Korean (81)	125	0.29
Laotian (353)	382	0.89
Malaysian (0)	1	<0.01
Nepalese (5)	6	0.01
Pakistani (16)	23	0.05
Taiwanese (5)	6	0.01
Thai (65)	96	0.22
Vietnamese (280)	322	0.75
Hawaii Native/Pacific Islander (300)	598	1.40
Not Hispanic (289)	495	1.16
Hispanic (11)	103	0.24
Fijian (80)	90	0.21
Guamanian/Chamorro (45)	78	0.18
Native Hawaiian (40)	155	0.36
Samoan (68)	99	0.23
Tongan (29)	34	0.08
White (27,000)	29,552	69.22
Not Hispanic (23,211)	24,929	58.39
Hispanic (3,789)	4,623	10.83

North Tustin

Place Type: CDP
County: Orange
Population: 24,917†

Ancestry‡	Population	%
Afghan (12)	12	0.05
American (1,129)	1,129	4.60
Arab (197)	287	1.17
Egyptian (0)	17	0.07
Lebanese (183)	245	1.00
Moroccan (0)	8	0.03
Syrian (14)	17	0.07
Armenian (157)	333	1.36
Austrian (14)	93	0.38
Basque (0)	15	0.06
Belgian (14)	40	0.16
British (174)	216	0.88
Cajun (15)	29	0.12
Canadian (25)	99	0.40
Celtic (0)	17	0.07
Croatian (9)	9	0.04
Czech (66)	180	0.73
Czechoslovakian (13)	32	0.13
Danish (19)	104	0.42
Dutch (197)	463	1.89
Eastern European (75)	122	0.50
English (1,059)	3,977	16.22
European (556)	687	2.80
Finnish (15)	68	0.28
French, ex. Basque (171)	703	2.87
French Canadian (45)	139	0.57
German (1,406)	4,351	17.74
Greek (82)	130	0.53
Hungarian (221)	414	1.69
Irish (718)	3,027	12.35
Israeli (15)	121	0.49
Italian (711)	1,961	8.00
Lithuanian (33)	106	0.43
Luxemburger (0)	16	0.07
Northern European (88)	142	0.58
Norwegian (148)	577	2.35
Polish (183)	636	2.59
Portuguese (14)	78	0.32
Romanian (16)	72	0.29
Russian (125)	538	2.19
Scandinavian (111)	173	0.71
Scotch-Irish (239)	560	2.28
Scottish (206)	609	2.48
Serbian (8)	8	0.03
Slavic (10)	31	0.13
Slovak (0)	14	0.06
Swedish (138)	589	2.40
Swiss (20)	154	0.63
Turkish (74)	149	0.61
Ukrainian (41)	118	0.48
Welsh (11)	297	1.21
West Indian, ex. Hispanic (0)	15	0.06
Haitian (0)	15	0.06
Yugoslavian (13)	13	0.05

Hispanic Origin	Population	%
Hispanic or Latino (of any race)	3,260	13.08
Central American, ex. Mexican	111	0.45
Costa Rican	20	0.08
Guatemalan	20	0.08
Honduran	15	0.06
Nicaraguan	19	0.08
Panamanian	2	0.01
Salvadoran	35	0.14
Cuban	78	0.31
Dominican Republic	3	0.01
Mexican	2,396	9.62
Puerto Rican	74	0.30
South American	267	1.07
Argentinean	52	0.21
Bolivian	42	0.17
Chilean	16	0.06
Colombian	40	0.16
Ecuadorian	26	0.10
Paraguayan	2	0.01
Peruvian	75	0.30
Uruguayan	5	0.02
Venezuelan	5	0.02
Other South American	4	0.02
Other Hispanic or Latino	331	1.33

Race*	Population	%
African-American/Black (148)	207	0.83
Not Hispanic (138)	183	0.73
Hispanic (10)	24	0.10
American Indian/Alaska Native (104)	215	0.86
Not Hispanic (58)	127	0.51
Hispanic (46)	88	0.35
Apache (0)	5	0.02
Central American Ind. (0)	4	0.02
Cherokee (20)	45	0.18
Chickasaw (1)	2	0.01
Chippewa (1)	3	0.01
Choctaw (3)	4	0.02
Comanche (0)	2	0.01
Creek (4)	10	0.04
Crow (0)	1	<0.01
Hopi (0)	5	0.02
Iroquois (3)	6	0.02
Menominee (0)	1	<0.01
Mexican American Ind. (10)	15	0.06
Navajo (4)	7	0.03
Osage (0)	2	0.01
Potawatomi (0)	1	<0.01
Pueblo (1)	1	<0.01
Shoshone (1)	1	<0.01
South American Ind. (0)	4	0.02
Spanish American Ind. (1)	1	<0.01
Asian (1,994)	2,513	10.09
Not Hispanic (1,975)	2,433	9.76
Hispanic (19)	80	0.32
Bangladeshi (12)	14	0.06
Burmese (1)	2	0.01
Cambodian (29)	34	0.14
Chinese, ex. Taiwanese (438)	600	2.41
Filipino (244)	395	1.59
Indian (203)	225	0.90
Indonesian (10)	30	0.12
Japanese (272)	448	1.80
Korean (233)	285	1.14
Laotian (4)	4	0.02
Malaysian (2)	2	0.01
Pakistani (20)	24	0.10
Sri Lankan (13)	15	0.06
Taiwanese (106)	113	0.45
Thai (25)	28	0.11
Vietnamese (285)	343	1.38
Hawaii Native/Pacific Islander (52)	138	0.55
Not Hispanic (47)	116	0.47
Hispanic (5)	22	0.09
Guamanian/Chamorro (2)	7	0.03
Native Hawaiian (8)	46	0.18
Samoan (19)	30	0.12
Tongan (6)	11	0.04
White (20,836)	21,634	86.82
Not Hispanic (18,784)	19,336	77.60
Hispanic (2,052)	2,298	9.22

Norwalk

Place Type: City
County: Los Angeles
Population: 105,549†

Ancestry‡	Population	%
African, Sub-Saharan (244)	319	0.30
African (244)	319	0.30
American (1,903)	1,903	1.81
Arab (184)	209	0.20
Egyptian (114)	114	0.11
Lebanese (46)	60	0.06
Syrian (0)	11	0.01
Other Arab (24)	24	0.02
Armenian (44)	65	0.06
Belgian (17)	42	0.04
Brazilian (0)	15	0.01
British (0)	43	0.04
Bulgarian (8)	8	0.01
Cajun (15)	15	0.01
Canadian (25)	71	0.07
Croatian (7)	14	0.01
Czech (5)	38	0.04
Danish (57)	118	0.11
Dutch (180)	675	0.64
English (851)	2,538	2.41
Estonian (22)	22	0.02
European (152)	152	0.14
Finnish (11)	35	0.03
French, ex. Basque (254)	938	0.89
French Canadian (31)	42	0.04
German (644)	2,455	2.34
Greek (0)	49	0.05
Hungarian (94)	143	0.14
Iranian (152)	198	0.19
Irish (474)	2,447	2.33
Italian (519)	1,477	1.41
Latvian (104)	104	0.10
Lithuanian (0)	21	0.02
New Zealander (9)	9	0.01
Norwegian (200)	462	0.44
Polish (198)	539	0.51
Portuguese (169)	366	0.35
Romanian (66)	66	0.06
Russian (87)	187	0.18
Scandinavian (14)	14	0.01
Scotch-Irish (76)	322	0.31
Scottish (122)	420	0.40
Slovak (17)	17	0.02

*Notes: † The Census 2010 population figure is used to calculate the percentages in the Hispanic Origin and Race categories. Ancestry percentages are based on the 2006-2010 American Community Survey population (not shown); ‡ Numbers in parentheses indicate the number of people reporting a single ancestry; * Numbers in parentheses indicate the number of persons reporting this race alone, not in combination with any other race; Please refer to the Explanation of Data for more information.*

Swedish (62)	235	0.22
Swiss (0)	7	0.01
Ukrainian (17)	17	0.02
Welsh (12)	111	0.11
West Indian, ex. Hispanic (58)	90	0.09
Belizean (16)	16	0.02
British West Indian (0)	21	0.02
West Indian (42)	53	0.05

Hispanic Origin	Population	%
Hispanic or Latino (of any race)	74,041	70.15
Central American, ex. Mexican	5,460	5.17
Costa Rican	158	0.15
Guatemalan	1,411	1.34
Honduran	330	0.31
Nicaraguan	603	0.57
Panamanian	52	0.05
Salvadoran	2,871	2.72
Other Central American	35	0.03
Cuban	386	0.37
Dominican Republic	49	0.05
Mexican	63,299	59.97
Puerto Rican	488	0.46
South American	1,333	1.26
Argentinean	120	0.11
Bolivian	26	0.02
Chilean	42	0.04
Colombian	303	0.29
Ecuadorian	325	0.31
Peruvian	453	0.43
Uruguayan	22	0.02
Venezuelan	24	0.02
Other South American	18	0.02
Other Hispanic or Latino	3,026	2.87

Race*	Population	%
African-American/Black (4,593)	5,240	4.96
Not Hispanic (4,135)	4,451	4.22
Hispanic (458)	789	0.75
American Indian/Alaska Native (1,213)	1,916	1.82
Not Hispanic (281)	570	0.54
Hispanic (932)	1,346	1.28
Alaska Athabascan *(Ala. Nat.)* (1)	3	<0.01
Aleut *(Alaska Native)* (2)	2	<0.01
Apache (46)	100	0.09
Arapaho (1)	4	<0.01
Blackfeet (3)	31	0.03
Central American Ind. (10)	17	0.02
Cherokee (27)	110	0.10
Cheyenne (0)	1	<0.01
Chickasaw (3)	6	0.01
Chippewa (10)	15	0.01
Choctaw (19)	40	0.04
Colville (9)	9	0.01
Comanche (9)	12	0.01
Cree (0)	1	<0.01
Creek (20)	23	0.02
Crow (0)	1	<0.01
Delaware (0)	2	<0.01
Hopi (16)	18	0.02
Inupiat *(Alaska Native)* (0)	2	<0.01
Iroquois (1)	1	<0.01
Kiowa (1)	1	<0.01
Lumbee (1)	1	<0.01
Menominee (0)	4	<0.01
Mexican American Ind. (155)	232	0.22
Navajo (40)	96	0.09
Ottawa (1)	1	<0.01
Paiute (10)	10	0.01
Pima (14)	18	0.02
Potawatomi (0)	1	<0.01
Pueblo (11)	19	0.02
Seminole (5)	10	0.01
Shoshone (0)	4	<0.01
Sioux (16)	37	0.04
South American Ind. (4)	8	0.01
Spanish American Ind. (13)	18	0.02
Tohono O'Odham (8)	12	0.01
Ute (1)	4	<0.01
Yaqui (7)	25	0.02
Yup'ik *(Alaska Native)* (0)	1	<0.01
Asian (12,700)	13,787	13.06
Not Hispanic (12,387)	13,032	12.35
Hispanic (313)	755	0.72
Bangladeshi (31)	41	0.04
Bhutanese (2)	2	<0.01
Burmese (19)	22	0.02
Cambodian (677)	743	0.70
Chinese, ex. Taiwanese (813)	1,047	0.99
Filipino (5,581)	6,135	5.81
Hmong (6)	17	0.02
Indian (870)	997	0.94
Indonesian (67)	105	0.10
Japanese (260)	427	0.40
Korean (2,610)	2,678	2.54
Laotian (31)	42	0.04
Malaysian (2)	8	0.01
Nepalese (49)	49	0.05
Pakistani (78)	89	0.08
Sri Lankan (34)	45	0.04
Taiwanese (88)	112	0.11
Thai (282)	344	0.33
Vietnamese (822)	900	0.85
Hawaii Native/Pacific Islander (431)	752	0.71
Not Hispanic (366)	559	0.53
Hispanic (65)	193	0.18
Fijian (22)	30	0.03
Guamanian/Chamorro (55)	98	0.09
Native Hawaiian (62)	148	0.14
Samoan (173)	252	0.24
Tongan (65)	74	0.07
White (52,089)	55,720	52.79
Not Hispanic (13,007)	13,808	13.08
Hispanic (39,082)	41,912	39.71

Novato

Place Type: City
County: Marin
Population: 51,904†

Ancestry‡	Population	%
African, Sub-Saharan (271)	320	0.63
African (108)	145	0.29
Kenyan (101)	101	0.20
South African (21)	33	0.07
Other Sub-Saharan African (41)	41	0.08
American (918)	918	1.82
Arab (103)	337	0.67
Egyptian (0)	29	0.06
Lebanese (0)	115	0.23
Moroccan (50)	108	0.21
Palestinian (0)	19	0.04
Syrian (33)	33	0.07
Other Arab (20)	33	0.07
Armenian (97)	97	0.19
Australian (16)	28	0.06
Austrian (78)	272	0.54
Basque (11)	78	0.15
Belgian (123)	164	0.32
Brazilian (316)	316	0.63
British (389)	521	1.03
Bulgarian (84)	84	0.17
Canadian (208)	539	1.07
Celtic (14)	27	0.05
Croatian (116)	269	0.53
Czech (42)	245	0.49
Czechoslovakian (50)	91	0.18
Danish (160)	675	1.34
Dutch (139)	576	1.14
Eastern European (116)	155	0.31
English (1,224)	5,507	10.91
Estonian (0)	37	0.07
European (1,274)	1,496	2.96
Finnish (60)	84	0.17
French, ex. Basque (365)	1,751	3.47
French Canadian (113)	261	0.52
German (1,873)	7,318	14.49
Greek (166)	396	0.78
Hungarian (49)	262	0.52
Iranian (476)	500	0.99
Irish (2,372)	7,264	14.39
Israeli (19)	19	0.04
Italian (1,977)	5,410	10.72
Latvian (57)	89	0.18
Lithuanian (38)	98	0.19
Maltese (18)	18	0.04
New Zealander (0)	16	0.03
Northern European (47)	68	0.13
Norwegian (197)	1,014	2.01
Polish (244)	1,011	2.00
Portuguese (469)	1,163	2.30
Romanian (56)	180	0.36
Russian (413)	1,297	2.57
Scandinavian (46)	122	0.24
Scotch-Irish (336)	1,315	2.60
Scottish (231)	1,496	2.96
Serbian (0)	11	0.02
Slavic (0)	22	0.04
Slovak (42)	66	0.13
Slovene (0)	58	0.11
Swedish (332)	1,525	3.02
Swiss (90)	319	0.63
Turkish (0)	12	0.02
Ukrainian (161)	263	0.52
Welsh (59)	396	0.78
West Indian, ex. Hispanic (138)	145	0.29
Haitian (50)	50	0.10
Jamaican (88)	88	0.17
Trinidadian/Tobagonian (0)	7	0.01
Yugoslavian (23)	37	0.07

Hispanic Origin	Population	%
Hispanic or Latino (of any race)	11,046	21.28
Central American, ex. Mexican	2,892	5.57
Costa Rican	30	0.06
Guatemalan	1,412	2.72
Honduran	36	0.07
Nicaraguan	206	0.40
Panamanian	9	0.02
Salvadoran	1,156	2.23
Other Central American	43	0.08
Cuban	70	0.13
Dominican Republic	13	0.03
Mexican	5,941	11.45
Puerto Rican	239	0.46
South American	829	1.60
Argentinean	64	0.12
Bolivian	28	0.05
Chilean	38	0.07
Colombian	103	0.20
Ecuadorian	31	0.06
Paraguayan	4	0.01
Peruvian	496	0.96
Uruguayan	32	0.06
Venezuelan	20	0.04
Other South American	13	0.03
Other Hispanic or Latino	1,062	2.05

Race*	Population	%
African-American/Black (1,419)	1,971	3.80
Not Hispanic (1,321)	1,785	3.44
Hispanic (98)	186	0.36
American Indian/Alaska Native (286)	759	1.46
Not Hispanic (108)	425	0.82
Hispanic (178)	334	0.64
Alaska Athabascan *(Ala. Nat.)* (1)	1	<0.01
Aleut *(Alaska Native)* (0)	4	0.01
Apache (2)	7	0.01
Blackfeet (3)	19	0.04
Canadian/French Am. Ind. (0)	1	<0.01
Cherokee (28)	103	0.20
Cheyenne (1)	3	0.01
Chickasaw (1)	2	<0.01
Chippewa (6)	11	0.02
Choctaw (7)	19	0.04
Comanche (0)	3	0.01
Cree (0)	3	0.01
Creek (2)	5	0.01
Crow (0)	1	<0.01

*Notes: † The Census 2010 population figure is used to calculate the percentages in the Hispanic Origin and Race categories. Ancestry percentages are based on the 2006-2010 American Community Survey population (not shown); ‡ Numbers in parentheses indicate the number of people reporting a single ancestry; * Numbers in parentheses indicate the number of persons reporting this race alone, not in combination with any other race; Please refer to the Explanation of Data for more information.*

Delaware (1)	2	<0.01
Hopi (0)	1	<0.01
Inupiat *(Alaska Native)* (1)	1	<0.01
Iroquois (0)	9	0.02
Mexican American Ind. (59)	89	0.17
Navajo (5)	17	0.03
Osage (0)	2	<0.01
Paiute (0)	1	<0.01
Pima (2)	2	<0.01
Potawatomi (1)	4	0.01
Pueblo (2)	2	<0.01
Puget Sound Salish (1)	1	<0.01
Seminole (1)	9	0.02
Shoshone (0)	2	<0.01
Sioux (0)	6	0.01
South American Ind. (1)	5	0.01
Spanish American Ind. (14)	15	0.03
Tlingit-Haida *(Alaska Native)* (1)	1	<0.01
Tohono O'Odham (1)	8	0.02
Ute (0)	1	<0.01
Yaqui (0)	8	0.02
Asian (3,428)	4,541	8.75
Not Hispanic (3,367)	4,310	8.30
Hispanic (61)	231	0.45
Bangladeshi (3)	3	0.01
Burmese (6)	13	0.03
Cambodian (66)	75	0.14
Chinese, ex. Taiwanese (1,009)	1,390	2.68
Filipino (608)	956	1.84
Indian (578)	644	1.24
Indonesian (11)	26	0.05
Japanese (301)	595	1.15
Korean (237)	319	0.61
Laotian (20)	24	0.05
Malaysian (0)	2	<0.01
Nepalese (3)	3	0.01
Pakistani (37)	41	0.08
Sri Lankan (3)	4	0.01
Taiwanese (30)	61	0.12
Thai (69)	106	0.20
Vietnamese (283)	354	0.68
Hawaii Native/Pacific Islander (117)	286	0.55
Not Hispanic (103)	230	0.44
Hispanic (14)	56	0.11
Fijian (33)	38	0.07
Guamanian/Chamorro (14)	28	0.05
Native Hawaiian (35)	123	0.24
Samoan (15)	38	0.07
Tongan (5)	8	0.02
White (39,443)	41,688	80.32
Not Hispanic (34,141)	35,651	68.69
Hispanic (5,302)	6,037	11.63

Oak Hills

Place Type: CDP
County: San Bernardino
Population: 8,879†

Ancestry‡	Population	%
African, Sub-Saharan (25)	25	0.31
African (14)	14	0.17
Nigerian (11)	11	0.14
American (225)	225	2.79
Arab (14)	14	0.17
Arab (14)	14	0.17
Armenian (10)	10	0.12
Austrian (0)	29	0.36
Belgian (0)	43	0.53
British (36)	49	0.61
Bulgarian (0)	11	0.14
Danish (24)	48	0.60
Dutch (0)	33	0.41
English (404)	1,209	15.01
European (382)	392	4.87
Finnish (12)	12	0.15
French, ex. Basque (21)	334	4.15
French Canadian (25)	56	0.70
German (327)	1,320	16.39
Irish (143)	767	9.52
Israeli (9)	37	0.46
Italian (113)	269	3.34
Latvian (20)	20	0.25
Luxemburger (9)	9	0.11
Norwegian (12)	130	1.61
Polish (44)	94	1.17
Portuguese (0)	100	1.24
Romanian (0)	9	0.11
Russian (0)	12	0.15
Scandinavian (16)	102	1.27
Scotch-Irish (73)	175	2.17
Scottish (25)	142	1.76
Slavic (0)	15	0.19
Swedish (9)	145	1.80
Swiss (11)	11	0.14
Welsh (15)	29	0.36

Hispanic Origin	Population	%
Hispanic or Latino (of any race)	2,719	30.62
Central American, ex. Mexican	108	1.22
Costa Rican	3	0.03
Guatemalan	18	0.20
Honduran	11	0.12
Nicaraguan	9	0.10
Panamanian	1	0.01
Salvadoran	64	0.72
Other Central American	2	0.02
Cuban	11	0.12
Dominican Republic	4	0.05
Mexican	2,233	25.15
Puerto Rican	57	0.64
South American	52	0.59
Argentinean	24	0.27
Bolivian	6	0.07
Chilean	1	0.01
Colombian	7	0.08
Ecuadorian	5	0.06
Peruvian	5	0.06
Venezuelan	4	0.05
Other Hispanic or Latino	254	2.86

Race*	Population	%
African-American/Black (266)	316	3.56
Not Hispanic (243)	265	2.98
Hispanic (23)	51	0.57
American Indian/Alaska Native (100)	188	2.12
Not Hispanic (62)	119	1.34
Hispanic (38)	69	0.78
Aleut *(Alaska Native)* (0)	2	0.02
Apache (2)	8	0.09
Blackfeet (1)	6	0.07
Cherokee (6)	37	0.42
Cheyenne (0)	1	0.01
Chickasaw (0)	1	0.01
Chippewa (1)	2	0.02
Choctaw (0)	5	0.06
Comanche (1)	1	0.01
Crow (0)	2	0.02
Delaware (1)	1	0.01
Iroquois (0)	1	0.01
Mexican American Ind. (18)	20	0.23
Navajo (1)	3	0.03
Osage (0)	1	0.01
Pueblo (2)	2	0.02
Puget Sound Salish (1)	1	0.01
Tohono O'Odham (4)	4	0.05
Asian (226)	298	3.36
Not Hispanic (217)	256	2.88
Hispanic (9)	42	0.47
Cambodian (1)	1	0.01
Chinese, ex. Taiwanese (26)	45	0.51
Filipino (59)	90	1.01
Indian (40)	47	0.53
Indonesian (4)	7	0.08
Japanese (8)	31	0.35
Korean (53)	53	0.60
Taiwanese (5)	5	0.06
Thai (4)	4	0.05
Vietnamese (22)	24	0.27
Hawaii Native/Pacific Islander (28)	42	0.47
Not Hispanic (24)	36	0.41
Hispanic (4)	6	0.07
Fijian (5)	7	0.08
Guamanian/Chamorro (6)	10	0.11
Native Hawaiian (3)	8	0.09
Samoan (1)	1	0.01
Tongan (12)	14	0.16
White (6,796)	7,066	79.58
Not Hispanic (5,475)	5,591	62.97
Hispanic (1,321)	1,475	16.61

Oak Park

Place Type: CDP
County: Ventura
Population: 13,811†

Ancestry‡	Population	%
African, Sub-Saharan (18)	18	0.13
South African (18)	18	0.13
American (1,264)	1,264	9.00
Arab (102)	102	0.73
Lebanese (46)	46	0.33
Other Arab (56)	56	0.40
Armenian (74)	134	0.95
Assyrian/Chaldean/Syriac (42)	42	0.30
Austrian (70)	177	1.26
Basque (10)	10	0.07
Belgian (0)	14	0.10
Brazilian (17)	103	0.73
British (61)	82	0.58
Canadian (40)	82	0.58
Czech (60)	174	1.24
Czechoslovakian (0)	21	0.15
Danish (0)	54	0.38
Dutch (31)	195	1.39
Eastern European (62)	62	0.44
English (393)	1,850	13.17
Estonian (0)	28	0.20
European (529)	541	3.85
Finnish (29)	43	0.31
French, ex. Basque (105)	669	4.76
French Canadian (48)	65	0.46
German (514)	2,715	19.33
Greek (0)	25	0.18
Hungarian (66)	151	1.08
Iranian (363)	388	2.76
Irish (278)	1,856	13.22
Israeli (77)	77	0.55
Italian (328)	1,276	9.09
Latvian (0)	14	0.10
Lithuanian (31)	152	1.08
Macedonian (0)	13	0.09
Northern European (41)	41	0.29
Norwegian (79)	301	2.14
Polish (180)	720	5.13
Portuguese (0)	41	0.29
Romanian (40)	73	0.52
Russian (591)	1,297	9.24
Scandinavian (0)	19	0.14
Scotch-Irish (0)	163	1.16
Scottish (23)	157	1.12
Slovak (0)	10	0.07
Swedish (130)	308	2.19
Swiss (15)	65	0.46
Ukrainian (28)	90	0.64
Welsh (10)	89	0.63
Yugoslavian (0)	39	0.28

Hispanic Origin	Population	%
Hispanic or Latino (of any race)	826	5.98
Central American, ex. Mexican	85	0.62
Costa Rican	9	0.07
Guatemalan	26	0.19
Honduran	7	0.05
Nicaraguan	13	0.09
Panamanian	1	0.01
Salvadoran	29	0.21
Cuban	43	0.31
Mexican	472	3.42

*Notes: † The Census 2010 population figure is used to calculate the percentages in the Hispanic Origin and Race categories. Ancestry percentages are based on the 2006-2010 American Community Survey population (not shown); ‡ Numbers in parentheses indicate the number of people reporting a single ancestry; * Numbers in parentheses indicate the number of persons reporting this race alone, not in combination with any other race; Please refer to the Explanation of Data for more information.*

Puerto Rican	24	0.17
South American	107	0.77
Argentinean	34	0.25
Bolivian	2	0.01
Chilean	22	0.16
Colombian	20	0.14
Ecuadorian	12	0.09
Peruvian	14	0.10
Uruguayan	2	0.01
Venezuelan	1	0.01
Other Hispanic or Latino	95	0.69

Race*	Population	%
African-American/Black (141)	199	1.44
Not Hispanic (138)	192	1.39
Hispanic (3)	7	0.05
American Indian/Alaska Native (32)	83	0.60
Not Hispanic (15)	44	0.32
Hispanic (17)	39	0.28
Apache (0)	7	0.05
Blackfeet (0)	3	0.02
Canadian/French Am. Ind. (0)	2	0.01
Cherokee (0)	20	0.14
Chickasaw (3)	3	0.02
Choctaw (1)	2	0.01
Comanche (0)	4	0.03
Mexican American Ind. (3)	4	0.03
Navajo (3)	6	0.04
Pima (0)	1	0.01
Potawatomi (1)	1	0.01
Sioux (0)	2	0.01
Yaqui (2)	2	0.01
Asian (1,556)	1,864	13.50
Not Hispanic (1,553)	1,832	13.26
Hispanic (3)	32	0.23
Bangladeshi (3)	3	0.02
Burmese (3)	3	0.02
Cambodian (0)	3	0.02
Chinese, ex. Taiwanese (463)	571	4.13
Filipino (94)	140	1.01
Indian (460)	481	3.48
Indonesian (9)	9	0.07
Japanese (112)	205	1.48
Korean (192)	216	1.56
Laotian (5)	5	0.04
Malaysian (0)	4	0.03
Pakistani (15)	16	0.12
Taiwanese (75)	84	0.61
Thai (6)	11	0.08
Vietnamese (64)	73	0.53
Hawaii Native/Pacific Islander (9)	33	0.24
Not Hispanic (8)	27	0.20
Hispanic (1)	6	0.04
Guamanian/Chamorro (1)	3	0.02
Native Hawaiian (7)	18	0.13
Samoan (1)	3	0.02
White (11,473)	11,880	86.02
Not Hispanic (10,903)	11,235	81.35
Hispanic (570)	645	4.67

Oakdale

Place Type: City
County: Stanislaus
Population: 20,675†

Ancestry‡	Population	%
American (1,567)	1,567	7.81
Armenian (23)	23	0.11
Austrian (0)	103	0.51
Belgian (21)	43	0.21
British (52)	52	0.26
Canadian (29)	29	0.14
Croatian (27)	27	0.13
Czech (0)	11	0.05
Danish (25)	194	0.97
Dutch (248)	671	3.34
English (690)	1,849	9.21
European (531)	546	2.72
French, ex. Basque (79)	241	1.20
French Canadian (53)	67	0.33
German (816)	2,528	12.59
Greek (40)	40	0.20
Hungarian (15)	26	0.13
Irish (671)	2,584	12.87
Italian (364)	1,023	5.10
Luxemburger (22)	22	0.11
Maltese (0)	12	0.06
Norwegian (162)	364	1.81
Polish (72)	235	1.17
Portuguese (646)	1,461	7.28
Scandinavian (0)	7	0.03
Scotch-Irish (275)	445	2.22
Scottish (168)	455	2.27
Swedish (152)	439	2.19
Swiss (0)	39	0.19
Turkish (0)	30	0.15
Ukrainian (0)	86	0.43
Welsh (73)	161	0.80
West Indian, ex. Hispanic (0)	10	0.05
Dutch West Indian (0)	10	0.05
Yugoslavian (77)	77	0.38

Hispanic Origin	Population	%
Hispanic or Latino (of any race)	5,398	26.11
Central American, ex. Mexican	118	0.57
Costa Rican	28	0.14
Guatemalan	18	0.09
Honduran	5	0.02
Nicaraguan	20	0.10
Panamanian	1	<0.01
Salvadoran	46	0.22
Cuban	20	0.10
Dominican Republic	1	<0.01
Mexican	4,691	22.69
Puerto Rican	103	0.50
South American	45	0.22
Argentinean	2	0.01
Bolivian	4	0.02
Chilean	8	0.04
Colombian	11	0.05
Ecuadorian	15	0.07
Peruvian	3	0.01
Uruguayan	1	<0.01
Venezuelan	1	<0.01
Other Hispanic or Latino	420	2.03

Race*	Population	%
African-American/Black (163)	256	1.24
Not Hispanic (150)	215	1.04
Hispanic (13)	41	0.20
American Indian/Alaska Native (210)	524	2.53
Not Hispanic (133)	375	1.81
Hispanic (77)	149	0.72
Aleut *(Alaska Native)* (1)	1	<0.01
Apache (6)	22	0.11
Blackfeet (2)	15	0.07
Cherokee (35)	146	0.71
Cheyenne (0)	2	0.01
Chickasaw (2)	7	0.03
Chippewa (1)	2	0.01
Choctaw (10)	26	0.13
Comanche (2)	2	0.01
Creek (4)	11	0.05
Hopi (1)	1	<0.01
Inupiat *(Alaska Native)* (1)	2	0.01
Iroquois (0)	9	0.04
Kiowa (1)	1	<0.01
Mexican American Ind. (9)	10	0.05
Navajo (3)	11	0.05
Osage (2)	4	0.02
Paiute (2)	3	0.01
Potawatomi (5)	5	0.02
Pueblo (2)	2	0.01
Shoshone (0)	3	0.01
Sioux (1)	8	0.04
South American Ind. (0)	1	<0.01
Tohono O'Odham (2)	4	0.02
Yaqui (1)	5	0.02
Yup'ik *(Alaska Native)* (0)	1	<0.01
Asian (463)	677	3.27
Not Hispanic (419)	562	2.72
Hispanic (44)	115	0.56
Cambodian (21)	22	0.11
Chinese, ex. Taiwanese (79)	113	0.55
Filipino (212)	327	1.58
Indian (77)	81	0.39
Indonesian (2)	5	0.02
Japanese (23)	72	0.35
Korean (8)	22	0.11
Laotian (0)	4	0.02
Malaysian (0)	2	0.01
Pakistani (5)	5	0.02
Thai (2)	2	0.01
Vietnamese (23)	30	0.15
Hawaii Native/Pacific Islander (37)	92	0.44
Not Hispanic (31)	65	0.31
Hispanic (6)	27	0.13
Fijian (9)	12	0.06
Guamanian/Chamorro (5)	12	0.06
Native Hawaiian (16)	44	0.21
Samoan (4)	15	0.07
Tongan (0)	1	<0.01
White (16,558)	17,364	83.99
Not Hispanic (14,074)	14,514	70.20
Hispanic (2,484)	2,850	13.78

Oakland

Place Type: City
County: Alameda
Population: 390,724†

Ancestry‡	Population	%
Afghan (536)	551	0.14
African, Sub-Saharan (7,268)	8,436	2.18
African (4,055)	4,978	1.29
Cape Verdean (99)	115	0.03
Ethiopian (1,867)	1,983	0.51
Ghanaian (69)	79	0.02
Kenyan (115)	115	0.03
Liberian (89)	89	0.02
Nigerian (509)	542	0.14
Senegalese (10)	10	<0.01
Somalian (54)	105	0.03
South African (32)	32	0.01
Sudanese (78)	78	0.02
Other Sub-Saharan African (291)	310	0.08
Albanian (8)	22	0.01
Alsatian (10)	10	<0.01
American (3,822)	3,822	0.99
Arab (2,249)	2,646	0.68
Arab (446)	515	0.13
Egyptian (20)	65	0.02
Iraqi (42)	42	0.01
Jordanian (21)	21	0.01
Lebanese (118)	237	0.06
Moroccan (27)	78	0.02
Palestinian (125)	137	0.04
Syrian (0)	31	0.01
Other Arab (1,450)	1,520	0.39
Armenian (186)	359	0.09
Assyrian/Chaldean/Syriac (0)	11	<0.01
Australian (105)	216	0.06
Austrian (132)	843	0.22
Basque (14)	24	0.01
Belgian (259)	370	0.10
Brazilian (149)	347	0.09
British (780)	1,790	0.46
Bulgarian (61)	61	0.02
Cajun (10)	47	0.01
Canadian (287)	558	0.14
Carpatho Rusyn (0)	37	0.01
Celtic (43)	235	0.06
Croatian (106)	455	0.12
Czech (61)	719	0.19
Czechoslovakian (60)	123	0.03
Danish (260)	1,221	0.32
Dutch (417)	2,131	0.55
Eastern European (1,444)	1,717	0.44

*Notes: † The Census 2010 population figure is used to calculate the percentages in the Hispanic Origin and Race categories. Ancestry percentages are based on the 2006-2010 American Community Survey population (not shown); ‡ Numbers in parentheses indicate the number of people reporting a single ancestry; * Numbers in parentheses indicate the number of persons reporting this race alone, not in combination with any other race; Please refer to the Explanation of Data for more information.*

English (3,496)	15,955	4.12
Estonian (14)	65	0.02
European (5,453)	6,403	1.65
Finnish (190)	514	0.13
French, ex. Basque (1,070)	5,368	1.39
French Canadian (173)	1,004	0.26
German (4,317)	21,071	5.45
German Russian (0)	23	0.01
Greek (710)	1,246	0.32
Guyanese (78)	106	0.03
Hungarian (206)	939	0.24
Icelander (12)	57	0.01
Iranian (798)	1,056	0.27
Irish (4,548)	18,855	4.87
Israeli (183)	235	0.06
Italian (3,259)	10,620	2.74
Latvian (67)	201	0.05
Lithuanian (179)	701	0.18
Luxemburger (0)	46	0.01
Macedonian (21)	21	0.01
Maltese (8)	44	0.01
New Zealander (34)	63	0.02
Northern European (699)	853	0.22
Norwegian (466)	2,538	0.66
Pennsylvania German (11)	26	0.01
Polish (929)	4,296	1.11
Portuguese (1,028)	2,276	0.59
Romanian (117)	466	0.12
Russian (1,984)	5,358	1.38
Scandinavian (192)	419	0.11
Scotch-Irish (977)	3,269	0.84
Scottish (950)	4,325	1.12
Serbian (11)	99	0.03
Slavic (16)	54	0.01
Slovak (175)	359	0.09
Slovene (23)	66	0.02
Swedish (1,029)	3,653	0.94
Swiss (149)	856	0.22
Turkish (299)	575	0.15
Ukrainian (204)	579	0.15
Welsh (65)	1,353	0.35
West Indian, ex. Hispanic (1,073)	1,774	0.46
Barbadian (9)	9	<0.01
Belizean (12)	61	0.02
Bermudan (11)	39	0.01
British West Indian (0)	29	0.01
Haitian (45)	102	0.03
Jamaican (393)	705	0.18
Trinidadian/Tobagonian (229)	387	0.10
U.S. Virgin Islander (16)	16	<0.01
West Indian (358)	426	0.11
Yugoslavian (125)	277	0.07

Hispanic Origin	Population	%
Hispanic or Latino (of any race)	99,068	25.35
Central American, ex. Mexican	15,387	3.94
Costa Rican	145	0.04
Guatemalan	5,223	1.34
Honduran	1,160	0.30
Nicaraguan	1,156	0.30
Panamanian	301	0.08
Salvadoran	7,246	1.85
Other Central American	156	0.04
Cuban	862	0.22
Dominican Republic	183	0.05
Mexican	70,799	18.12
Puerto Rican	2,737	0.70
South American	2,371	0.61
Argentinean	334	0.09
Bolivian	93	0.02
Chilean	297	0.08
Colombian	493	0.13
Ecuadorian	193	0.05
Paraguayan	9	<0.01
Peruvian	690	0.18
Uruguayan	42	0.01
Venezuelan	176	0.05
Other South American	44	0.01
Other Hispanic or Latino	6,729	1.72

Race*	Population	%
African-American/Black (109,471)	119,122	30.49
Not Hispanic (106,637)	114,212	29.23
Hispanic (2,834)	4,910	1.26
American Indian/Alaska Native (3,040)	8,322	2.13
Not Hispanic (1,214)	4,795	1.23
Hispanic (1,826)	3,527	0.90
Alaska Athabascan *(Ala. Nat.)* (6)	11	<0.01
Aleut *(Alaska Native)* (2)	9	<0.01
Apache (69)	174	0.04
Arapaho (6)	16	<0.01
Blackfeet (30)	328	0.08
Canadian/French Am. Ind. (4)	27	0.01
Central American Ind. (111)	199	0.05
Cherokee (94)	971	0.25
Cheyenne (11)	28	0.01
Chickasaw (5)	45	0.01
Chippewa (33)	80	0.02
Choctaw (36)	282	0.07
Colville (0)	1	<0.01
Comanche (4)	24	0.01
Cree (3)	14	<0.01
Creek (13)	97	0.02
Crow (13)	22	0.01
Delaware (5)	18	<0.01
Hopi (10)	26	0.01
Houma (1)	2	<0.01
Inupiat *(Alaska Native)* (10)	26	0.01
Iroquois (21)	95	0.02
Kiowa (9)	11	<0.01
Lumbee (3)	7	<0.01
Menominee (1)	2	<0.01
Mexican American Ind. (621)	945	0.24
Navajo (111)	184	0.05
Osage (6)	13	<0.01
Ottawa (4)	6	<0.01
Paiute (14)	31	0.01
Pima (14)	25	0.01
Potawatomi (5)	21	0.01
Pueblo (45)	83	0.02
Puget Sound Salish (3)	9	<0.01
Seminole (7)	86	0.02
Shoshone (13)	29	0.01
Sioux (94)	213	0.05
South American Ind. (49)	134	0.03
Spanish American Ind. (21)	32	0.01
Tlingit-Haida *(Alaska Native)* (5)	16	<0.01
Tohono O'Odham (13)	29	0.01
Tsimshian *(Alaska Native)* (0)	2	<0.01
Ute (5)	8	<0.01
Yakama (6)	7	<0.01
Yaqui (33)	67	0.02
Yuman (4)	15	<0.01
Yup'ik *(Alaska Native)* (0)	1	<0.01
Asian (65,811)	73,775	18.88
Not Hispanic (65,127)	71,892	18.40
Hispanic (684)	1,883	0.48
Bangladeshi (23)	33	0.01
Bhutanese (255)	272	0.07
Burmese (335)	377	0.10
Cambodian (2,746)	3,175	0.81
Chinese, ex. Taiwanese (33,734)	37,235	9.53
Filipino (6,070)	8,661	2.22
Hmong (40)	49	0.01
Indian (2,114)	2,879	0.74
Indonesian (102)	196	0.05
Japanese (2,031)	3,667	0.94
Korean (2,446)	3,096	0.79
Laotian (2,815)	3,071	0.79
Malaysian (19)	55	0.01
Nepalese (171)	204	0.05
Pakistani (187)	243	0.06
Sri Lankan (71)	97	0.02
Taiwanese (308)	401	0.10
Thai (308)	472	0.12
Vietnamese (8,766)	10,038	2.57
Hawaii Native/Pacific Islander (2,222)	3,574	0.91
Not Hispanic (2,081)	3,073	0.79
Hispanic (141)	501	0.13
Fijian (107)	174	0.04
Guamanian/Chamorro (142)	305	0.08
Marshallese (2)	4	<0.01
Native Hawaiian (168)	664	0.17
Samoan (238)	460	0.12
Tongan (1,299)	1,463	0.37
White (134,925)	151,162	38.69
Not Hispanic (101,308)	111,751	28.60
Hispanic (33,617)	39,411	10.09

Oakley

Place Type: City
County: Contra Costa
Population: 35,432†

Ancestry‡	Population	%
Afghan (133)	133	0.40
African, Sub-Saharan (52)	88	0.26
African (46)	82	0.24
Nigerian (6)	6	0.02
American (634)	634	1.89
Arab (155)	235	0.70
Palestinian (0)	63	0.19
Other Arab (155)	172	0.51
Australian (0)	27	0.08
Austrian (0)	15	0.04
Brazilian (22)	22	0.07
British (77)	148	0.44
Bulgarian (12)	12	0.04
Canadian (38)	145	0.43
Celtic (0)	12	0.04
Czech (41)	114	0.34
Czechoslovakian (20)	62	0.19
Danish (38)	162	0.48
Dutch (41)	316	0.94
English (301)	1,649	4.92
European (431)	492	1.47
French, ex. Basque (82)	1,024	3.06
French Canadian (17)	31	0.09
German (726)	4,677	13.96
Greek (283)	500	1.49
Hungarian (14)	154	0.46
Iranian (0)	6	0.02
Irish (532)	3,880	11.58
Italian (580)	2,160	6.45
Latvian (0)	54	0.16
Lithuanian (0)	5	0.01
Norwegian (135)	551	1.64
Polish (175)	498	1.49
Portuguese (362)	1,582	4.72
Russian (58)	174	0.52
Scandinavian (31)	86	0.26
Scotch-Irish (142)	706	2.11
Scottish (44)	369	1.10
Swedish (71)	380	1.13
Swiss (20)	214	0.64
Turkish (0)	11	0.03
Ukrainian (14)	14	0.04
Welsh (16)	195	0.58
Yugoslavian (34)	64	0.19

Hispanic Origin	Population	%
Hispanic or Latino (of any race)	12,364	34.90
Central American, ex. Mexican	835	2.36
Costa Rican	42	0.12
Guatemalan	110	0.31
Honduran	17	0.05
Nicaraguan	194	0.55
Panamanian	18	0.05
Salvadoran	449	1.27
Other Central American	5	0.01
Cuban	45	0.13
Dominican Republic	5	0.01
Mexican	9,960	28.11
Puerto Rican	469	1.32
South American	157	0.44
Argentinean	8	0.02
Bolivian	9	0.03
Chilean	12	0.03

*Notes: † The Census 2010 population figure is used to calculate the percentages in the Hispanic Origin and Race categories. Ancestry percentages are based on the 2006-2010 American Community Survey population (not shown); ‡ Numbers in parentheses indicate the number of people reporting a single ancestry; * Numbers in parentheses indicate the number of persons reporting this race alone, not in combination with any other race; Please refer to the Explanation of Data for more information.*

Colombian	27	0.08
Ecuadorian	7	0.02
Peruvian	78	0.22
Uruguayan	2	0.01
Venezuelan	12	0.03
Other South American	2	0.01
Other Hispanic or Latino	893	2.52

Race*	Population	%
African-American/Black (2,582)	3,128	8.83
Not Hispanic (2,460)	2,837	8.01
Hispanic (122)	291	0.82
American Indian/Alaska Native (314)	776	2.19
Not Hispanic (177)	493	1.39
Hispanic (137)	283	0.80
Alaska Athabascan *(Ala. Nat.)* (0)	1	<0.01
Apache (9)	26	0.07
Arapaho (1)	1	<0.01
Blackfeet (5)	29	0.08
Canadian/French Am. Ind. (1)	1	<0.01
Central American Ind. (3)	3	0.01
Cherokee (23)	134	0.38
Chickasaw (0)	1	<0.01
Chippewa (3)	12	0.03
Choctaw (19)	44	0.12
Comanche (0)	3	0.01
Cree (0)	2	0.01
Creek (1)	4	0.01
Delaware (3)	5	0.01
Houma (9)	9	0.03
Inupiat *(Alaska Native)* (1)	1	<0.01
Iroquois (0)	3	0.01
Lumbee (2)	2	0.01
Mexican American Ind. (27)	44	0.12
Navajo (8)	29	0.08
Osage (0)	6	0.02
Paiute (5)	11	0.03
Pima (0)	9	0.03
Potawatomi (8)	9	0.03
Pueblo (1)	13	0.04
Puget Sound Salish (3)	3	0.01
Shoshone (1)	2	0.01
Sioux (2)	10	0.03
South American Ind. (2)	3	0.01
Spanish American Ind. (0)	3	0.01
Tohono O'Odham (5)	5	0.01
Ute (1)	6	0.02
Yaqui (5)	12	0.03
Yuman (5)	5	0.01
Asian (2,236)	3,223	9.10
Not Hispanic (2,098)	2,807	7.92
Hispanic (138)	416	1.17
Bangladeshi (2)	2	0.01
Burmese (3)	3	0.01
Cambodian (52)	58	0.16
Chinese, ex. Taiwanese (206)	386	1.09
Filipino (1,306)	1,909	5.39
Hmong (7)	7	0.02
Indian (217)	253	0.71
Indonesian (6)	25	0.07
Japanese (61)	222	0.63
Korean (36)	66	0.19
Laotian (54)	61	0.17
Nepalese (1)	1	<0.01
Pakistani (40)	42	0.12
Taiwanese (11)	11	0.03
Thai (12)	28	0.08
Vietnamese (110)	146	0.41
Hawaii Native/Pacific Islander (142)	362	1.02
Not Hispanic (119)	255	0.72
Hispanic (23)	107	0.30
Fijian (13)	21	0.06
Guamanian/Chamorro (34)	65	0.18
Native Hawaiian (30)	123	0.35
Samoan (34)	70	0.20
Tongan (18)	28	0.08
White (22,641)	24,809	70.02
Not Hispanic (16,815)	17,976	50.73
Hispanic (5,826)	6,833	19.28

Oceanside

Place Type: City
County: San Diego
Population: 167,086†

Ancestry‡	Population	%
Afghan (12)	12	0.01
African, Sub-Saharan (1,447)	2,090	1.27
African (1,070)	1,713	1.04
Ethiopian (208)	208	0.13
Nigerian (13)	13	0.01
Somalian (139)	139	0.08
Other Sub-Saharan African (17)	17	0.01
Albanian (11)	11	0.01
American (3,408)	3,408	2.07
Arab (266)	543	0.33
Arab (67)	112	0.07
Egyptian (11)	11	0.01
Iraqi (94)	141	0.09
Lebanese (52)	172	0.10
Moroccan (0)	18	0.01
Palestinian (29)	58	0.04
Syrian (0)	18	0.01
Other Arab (13)	13	0.01
Armenian (93)	275	0.17
Australian (21)	21	0.01
Austrian (110)	373	0.23
Basque (30)	54	0.03
Belgian (36)	420	0.25
Brazilian (86)	133	0.08
British (408)	781	0.47
Bulgarian (0)	12	0.01
Cajun (0)	74	0.04
Canadian (291)	517	0.31
Celtic (13)	103	0.06
Croatian (54)	146	0.09
Czech (159)	679	0.41
Czechoslovakian (35)	35	0.02
Danish (358)	1,549	0.94
Dutch (538)	2,641	1.60
Eastern European (37)	37	0.02
English (4,137)	14,231	8.64
European (2,290)	2,689	1.63
Finnish (47)	295	0.18
French, ex. Basque (870)	4,599	2.79
French Canadian (300)	656	0.40
German (6,091)	21,019	12.76
Greek (227)	693	0.42
Hungarian (162)	939	0.57
Icelander (0)	24	0.01
Iranian (263)	326	0.20
Irish (3,927)	16,680	10.13
Italian (2,681)	7,600	4.61
Latvian (8)	105	0.06
Lithuanian (127)	277	0.17
Luxemburger (19)	31	0.02
Macedonian (34)	34	0.02
Northern European (213)	213	0.13
Norwegian (646)	2,418	1.47
Pennsylvania German (7)	20	0.01
Polish (1,195)	3,389	2.06
Portuguese (345)	923	0.56
Romanian (87)	199	0.12
Russian (701)	1,689	1.03
Scandinavian (192)	376	0.23
Scotch-Irish (1,099)	2,838	1.72
Scottish (851)	3,104	1.88
Serbian (31)	91	0.06
Slavic (26)	71	0.04
Slovak (33)	78	0.05
Slovene (0)	11	0.01
Swedish (655)	2,512	1.53
Swiss (60)	354	0.21
Turkish (99)	139	0.08
Ukrainian (262)	406	0.25
Welsh (130)	1,055	0.64
West Indian, ex. Hispanic (122)	219	0.13
Barbadian (0)	9	0.01
Belizean (0)	40	0.02
Haitian (40)	40	0.02
Jamaican (82)	106	0.06
Trinidadian/Tobagonian (0)	12	0.01
West Indian (0)	12	0.01
Yugoslavian (69)	95	0.06

Hispanic Origin	Population	%
Hispanic or Latino (of any race)	59,947	35.88
Central American, ex. Mexican	1,547	0.93
Costa Rican	131	0.08
Guatemalan	371	0.22
Honduran	138	0.08
Nicaraguan	127	0.08
Panamanian	175	0.10
Salvadoran	589	0.35
Other Central American	16	0.01
Cuban	288	0.17
Dominican Republic	154	0.09
Mexican	52,217	31.25
Puerto Rican	1,602	0.96
South American	1,084	0.65
Argentinean	116	0.07
Bolivian	46	0.03
Chilean	64	0.04
Colombian	316	0.19
Ecuadorian	130	0.08
Paraguayan	3	<0.01
Peruvian	301	0.18
Uruguayan	12	0.01
Venezuelan	77	0.05
Other South American	19	0.01
Other Hispanic or Latino	3,055	1.83

Race*	Population	%
African-American/Black (7,873)	10,278	6.15
Not Hispanic (7,101)	8,838	5.29
Hispanic (772)	1,440	0.86
American Indian/Alaska Native (1,385)	2,998	1.79
Not Hispanic (613)	1,563	0.94
Hispanic (772)	1,435	0.86
Aleut *(Alaska Native)* (2)	4	<0.01
Apache (56)	124	0.07
Arapaho (1)	1	<0.01
Blackfeet (8)	45	0.03
Canadian/French Am. Ind. (7)	11	0.01
Central American Ind. (11)	19	0.01
Cherokee (62)	335	0.20
Cheyenne (0)	3	<0.01
Chickasaw (12)	32	0.02
Chippewa (16)	30	0.02
Choctaw (30)	84	0.05
Colville (2)	3	<0.01
Comanche (4)	14	0.01
Cree (0)	7	<0.01
Creek (8)	23	0.01
Crow (1)	2	<0.01
Delaware (1)	4	<0.01
Hopi (8)	14	0.01
Inupiat *(Alaska Native)* (5)	6	<0.01
Iroquois (5)	24	0.01
Lumbee (3)	8	<0.01
Menominee (0)	1	<0.01
Mexican American Ind. (229)	338	0.20
Navajo (64)	101	0.06
Osage (2)	6	<0.01
Ottawa (2)	5	<0.01
Paiute (8)	10	0.01
Pima (1)	4	<0.01
Potawatomi (2)	3	<0.01
Pueblo (19)	33	0.02
Puget Sound Salish (4)	5	<0.01
Seminole (6)	21	0.01
Shoshone (4)	14	0.01
Sioux (20)	59	0.04
South American Ind. (7)	19	0.01
Spanish American Ind. (18)	23	0.01
Tlingit-Haida *(Alaska Native)* (4)	7	<0.01
Tohono O'Odham (1)	1	<0.01
Ute (1)	7	<0.01

*Notes: † The Census 2010 population figure is used to calculate the percentages in the Hispanic Origin and Race categories. Ancestry percentages are based on the 2006-2010 American Community Survey population (not shown); ‡ Numbers in parentheses indicate the number of people reporting a single ancestry; * Numbers in parentheses indicate the number of persons reporting this race alone, not in combination with any other race; Please refer to the Explanation of Data for more information.*

Yakama (1)	1	<0.01
Yaqui (9)	29	0.02
Yuman (5)	9	0.01
Yup'ik *(Alaska Native)* (1)	1	<0.01
Asian (11,081)	15,112	9.04
Not Hispanic (10,638)	13,827	8.28
Hispanic (443)	1,285	0.77
Bangladeshi (8)	8	<0.01
Burmese (33)	42	0.03
Cambodian (98)	126	0.08
Chinese, ex. Taiwanese (929)	1,548	0.93
Filipino (5,705)	7,853	4.70
Hmong (28)	30	0.02
Indian (407)	531	0.32
Indonesian (52)	104	0.06
Japanese (1,243)	2,376	1.42
Korean (609)	874	0.52
Laotian (61)	87	0.05
Malaysian (13)	17	0.01
Nepalese (16)	21	0.01
Pakistani (24)	27	0.02
Sri Lankan (15)	15	0.01
Taiwanese (79)	106	0.06
Thai (132)	198	0.12
Vietnamese (1,178)	1,388	0.83
Hawaii Native/Pacific Islander (2,144)	3,428	2.05
Not Hispanic (1,999)	2,962	1.77
Hispanic (145)	466	0.28
Fijian (3)	11	0.01
Guamanian/Chamorro (325)	525	0.31
Marshallese (3)	3	<0.01
Native Hawaiian (261)	877	0.52
Samoan (1,330)	1,781	1.07
Tongan (33)	60	0.04
White (109,020)	117,020	70.04
Not Hispanic (80,849)	85,536	51.19
Hispanic (28,171)	31,484	18.84

Oildale

Place Type: CDP
County: Kern
Population: 32,684†

Ancestry‡	Population	%
African, Sub-Saharan (0)	15	0.05
African (0)	15	0.05
American (1,641)	1,641	5.01
Arab (88)	88	0.27
Arab (40)	40	0.12
Jordanian (48)	48	0.15
Armenian (13)	13	0.04
Australian (11)	11	0.03
Austrian (0)	46	0.14
Basque (32)	32	0.10
British (64)	102	0.31
Canadian (26)	135	0.41
Czech (14)	106	0.32
Czechoslovakian (20)	124	0.38
Danish (103)	197	0.60
Dutch (104)	891	2.72
Eastern European (23)	23	0.07
English (1,360)	3,314	10.12
European (87)	307	0.94
Finnish (29)	83	0.25
French, ex. Basque (345)	1,030	3.14
French Canadian (150)	203	0.62
German (1,848)	5,056	15.44
Greek (12)	70	0.21
Hungarian (13)	77	0.24
Irish (1,229)	4,910	14.99
Italian (505)	1,186	3.62
Maltese (29)	29	0.09
Northern European (14)	14	0.04
Norwegian (127)	445	1.36
Pennsylvania German (35)	47	0.14
Polish (15)	195	0.60
Portuguese (49)	196	0.60
Romanian (0)	10	0.03
Russian (90)	164	0.50
Scandinavian (27)	142	0.43
Scotch-Irish (287)	631	1.93
Scottish (349)	1,016	3.10
Slavic (0)	39	0.12
Swedish (107)	262	0.80
Swiss (21)	50	0.15
Turkish (5)	46	0.14
Ukrainian (10)	10	0.03
Welsh (0)	296	0.90
West Indian, ex. Hispanic (0)	206	0.63
Dutch West Indian (0)	206	0.63

Hispanic Origin	Population	%
Hispanic or Latino (of any race)	6,301	19.28
Central American, ex. Mexican	206	0.63
Costa Rican	6	0.02
Guatemalan	32	0.10
Honduran	12	0.04
Nicaraguan	4	0.01
Panamanian	5	0.02
Salvadoran	144	0.44
Other Central American	3	0.01
Cuban	25	0.08
Dominican Republic	4	0.01
Mexican	5,419	16.58
Puerto Rican	88	0.27
South American	69	0.21
Argentinean	6	0.02
Chilean	1	<0.01
Colombian	8	0.02
Ecuadorian	4	0.01
Peruvian	48	0.15
Venezuelan	2	0.01
Other Hispanic or Latino	490	1.50

Race*	Population	%
African-American/Black (255)	426	1.30
Not Hispanic (217)	343	1.05
Hispanic (38)	83	0.25
American Indian/Alaska Native (590)	1,319	4.04
Not Hispanic (433)	1,000	3.06
Hispanic (157)	319	0.98
Aleut *(Alaska Native)* (1)	1	<0.01
Apache (15)	47	0.14
Arapaho (1)	3	0.01
Blackfeet (14)	48	0.15
Canadian/French Am. Ind. (1)	1	<0.01
Cherokee (133)	381	1.17
Cheyenne (0)	3	0.01
Chickasaw (12)	39	0.12
Chippewa (2)	7	0.02
Choctaw (66)	145	0.44
Colville (0)	1	<0.01
Comanche (4)	8	0.02
Cree (0)	1	<0.01
Creek (14)	42	0.13
Crow (0)	1	<0.01
Delaware (0)	6	0.02
Hopi (1)	1	<0.01
Inupiat *(Alaska Native)* (0)	2	0.01
Iroquois (0)	1	<0.01
Kiowa (2)	4	0.01
Lumbee (10)	11	0.03
Mexican American Ind. (12)	25	0.08
Navajo (25)	31	0.09
Paiute (14)	43	0.13
Pima (2)	3	0.01
Potawatomi (6)	14	0.04
Pueblo (2)	2	0.01
Seminole (0)	6	0.02
Shoshone (2)	4	0.01
Sioux (4)	7	0.02
South American Ind. (1)	3	0.01
Spanish American Ind. (0)	2	0.01
Tlingit-Haida *(Alaska Native)* (0)	3	0.01
Tohono O'Odham (1)	3	0.01
Ute (4)	6	0.02
Yaqui (10)	14	0.04
Yuman (1)	1	<0.01
Yup'ik *(Alaska Native)* (1)	2	0.01
Asian (316)	523	1.60
Not Hispanic (292)	435	1.33
Hispanic (24)	88	0.27
Bangladeshi (1)	4	0.01
Burmese (2)	2	0.01
Cambodian (4)	5	0.02
Chinese, ex. Taiwanese (20)	44	0.13
Filipino (146)	259	0.79
Hmong (8)	8	0.02
Indian (44)	60	0.18
Indonesian (4)	6	0.02
Japanese (18)	41	0.13
Korean (12)	27	0.08
Laotian (3)	8	0.02
Pakistani (7)	7	0.02
Taiwanese (1)	1	<0.01
Thai (1)	3	0.01
Vietnamese (30)	45	0.14
Hawaii Native/Pacific Islander (30)	74	0.23
Not Hispanic (20)	41	0.13
Hispanic (10)	33	0.10
Fijian (0)	2	0.01
Guamanian/Chamorro (9)	12	0.04
Native Hawaiian (12)	29	0.09
Samoan (6)	11	0.03
White (27,463)	28,766	88.01
Not Hispanic (24,548)	25,357	77.58
Hispanic (2,915)	3,409	10.43

Olivehurst

Place Type: CDP
County: Yuba
Population: 13,656†

Ancestry‡	Population	%
American (851)	851	6.40
British (0)	42	0.32
Canadian (0)	34	0.26
Celtic (38)	38	0.29
Danish (0)	188	1.41
Dutch (50)	153	1.15
Eastern European (0)	15	0.11
English (324)	844	6.35
European (32)	44	0.33
Finnish (0)	13	0.10
French, ex. Basque (101)	160	1.20
French Canadian (6)	16	0.12
German (379)	1,089	8.19
Greek (31)	87	0.65
Irish (175)	1,162	8.74
Italian (146)	233	1.75
Norwegian (14)	104	0.78
Polish (31)	117	0.88
Portuguese (100)	165	1.24
Romanian (587)	587	4.41
Scandinavian (0)	289	2.17
Scotch-Irish (43)	134	1.01
Scottish (0)	42	0.32
Serbian (0)	18	0.14
Slovak (9)	17	0.13
Swedish (0)	8	0.06
Swiss (20)	20	0.15
Welsh (0)	14	0.11

Hispanic Origin	Population	%
Hispanic or Latino (of any race)	4,994	36.57
Central American, ex. Mexican	68	0.50
Guatemalan	9	0.07
Honduran	6	0.04
Nicaraguan	8	0.06
Panamanian	10	0.07
Salvadoran	35	0.26
Cuban	2	0.01
Mexican	4,558	33.38
Puerto Rican	41	0.30
South American	19	0.14
Bolivian	1	0.01
Chilean	2	0.01
Colombian	6	0.04

*Notes: † The Census 2010 population figure is used to calculate the percentages in the Hispanic Origin and Race categories. Ancestry percentages are based on the 2006-2010 American Community Survey population (not shown); ‡ Numbers in parentheses indicate the number of people reporting a single ancestry; * Numbers in parentheses indicate the number of persons reporting this race alone, not in combination with any other race; Please refer to the Explanation of Data for more information.*

Ecuadorian	2	0.01
Peruvian	8	0.06
Other Hispanic or Latino	306	2.24

Race*	Population	%
African-American/Black (322)	506	3.71
Not Hispanic (286)	434	3.18
Hispanic (36)	72	0.53
American Indian/Alaska Native (399)	824	6.03
Not Hispanic (297)	628	4.60
Hispanic (102)	196	1.44
Apache (8)	27	0.20
Blackfeet (2)	26	0.19
Canadian/French Am. Ind. (0)	2	0.01
Cherokee (89)	253	1.85
Cheyenne (0)	1	0.01
Chickasaw (3)	3	0.02
Chippewa (7)	11	0.08
Choctaw (31)	60	0.44
Cree (3)	5	0.04
Creek (2)	5	0.04
Delaware (2)	2	0.01
Iroquois (0)	1	0.01
Menominee (1)	1	0.01
Mexican American Ind. (27)	29	0.21
Navajo (3)	6	0.04
Osage (0)	1	0.01
Paiute (1)	4	0.03
Potawatomi (0)	2	0.01
Pueblo (2)	3	0.02
Shoshone (1)	2	0.01
Sioux (6)	15	0.11
Spanish American Ind. (5)	5	0.04
Ute (0)	2	0.01
Yaqui (6)	13	0.10
Asian (772)	943	6.91
Not Hispanic (736)	858	6.28
Hispanic (36)	85	0.62
Cambodian (30)	33	0.24
Chinese, ex. Taiwanese (26)	54	0.40
Filipino (77)	134	0.98
Hmong (441)	466	3.41
Indian (74)	97	0.71
Indonesian (1)	1	0.01
Japanese (16)	61	0.45
Korean (16)	27	0.20
Laotian (16)	16	0.12
Pakistani (17)	19	0.14
Thai (7)	19	0.14
Vietnamese (3)	12	0.09
Hawaii Native/Pacific Islander (61)	96	0.70
Not Hispanic (60)	88	0.64
Hispanic (1)	8	0.06
Fijian (3)	3	0.02
Guamanian/Chamorro (27)	35	0.26
Native Hawaiian (3)	28	0.21
Samoan (18)	26	0.19
Tongan (1)	5	0.04
White (8,534)	9,380	68.69
Not Hispanic (6,704)	7,221	52.88
Hispanic (1,830)	2,159	15.81

Ontario

Place Type: City
County: San Bernardino
Population: 163,924†

Ancestry‡	Population	%
Afghan (63)	63	0.04
African, Sub-Saharan (777)	916	0.55
African (480)	609	0.37
Nigerian (297)	307	0.19
Alsatian (0)	25	0.02
American (4,023)	4,023	2.44
Arab (376)	451	0.27
Arab (57)	57	0.03
Egyptian (79)	79	0.05
Lebanese (81)	100	0.06
Palestinian (78)	90	0.05
Syrian (81)	125	0.08
Armenian (102)	134	0.08
Assyrian/Chaldean/Syriac (77)	77	0.05
Austrian (0)	130	0.08
Basque (33)	116	0.07
Brazilian (98)	107	0.06
British (83)	237	0.14
Cajun (0)	48	0.03
Canadian (57)	267	0.16
Croatian (71)	82	0.05
Czech (29)	135	0.08
Czechoslovakian (0)	21	0.01
Danish (34)	472	0.29
Dutch (1,120)	1,980	1.20
Eastern European (27)	27	0.02
English (1,471)	5,887	3.56
European (784)	1,108	0.67
Finnish (38)	120	0.07
French, ex. Basque (243)	2,359	1.43
French Canadian (188)	270	0.16
German (2,077)	8,373	5.07
Greek (19)	137	0.08
Hungarian (101)	554	0.34
Icelander (75)	75	0.05
Iranian (138)	157	0.10
Irish (1,320)	6,161	3.73
Italian (1,213)	4,032	2.44
Lithuanian (11)	106	0.06
Northern European (26)	37	0.02
Norwegian (434)	1,328	0.80
Pennsylvania German (41)	80	0.05
Polish (344)	1,301	0.79
Portuguese (459)	597	0.36
Romanian (0)	13	0.01
Russian (49)	328	0.20
Scandinavian (0)	37	0.02
Scotch-Irish (377)	851	0.52
Scottish (261)	1,583	0.96
Serbian (0)	15	0.01
Slavic (24)	24	0.01
Slovak (0)	41	0.02
Slovene (0)	17	0.01
Swedish (240)	1,152	0.70
Swiss (22)	170	0.10
Turkish (15)	86	0.05
Ukrainian (28)	141	0.09
Welsh (106)	349	0.21
West Indian, ex. Hispanic (249)	591	0.36
Belizean (52)	155	0.09
British West Indian (107)	107	0.06
Jamaican (69)	162	0.10
U.S. Virgin Islander (12)	12	0.01
West Indian (9)	155	0.09
Yugoslavian (39)	127	0.08

Hispanic Origin	Population	%
Hispanic or Latino (of any race)	113,085	68.99
Central American, ex. Mexican	6,264	3.82
Costa Rican	175	0.11
Guatemalan	1,676	1.02
Honduran	793	0.48
Nicaraguan	658	0.40
Panamanian	102	0.06
Salvadoran	2,791	1.70
Other Central American	69	0.04
Cuban	592	0.36
Dominican Republic	56	0.03
Mexican	98,596	60.15
Puerto Rican	1,001	0.61
South American	1,519	0.93
Argentinean	243	0.15
Bolivian	62	0.04
Chilean	65	0.04
Colombian	376	0.23
Ecuadorian	270	0.16
Paraguayan	6	<0.01
Peruvian	404	0.25
Uruguayan	30	0.02
Venezuelan	36	0.02
Other South American	27	0.02
Other Hispanic or Latino	5,057	3.08

Race*	Population	%
African-American/Black (10,561)	12,096	7.38
Not Hispanic (9,598)	10,529	6.42
Hispanic (963)	1,567	0.96
American Indian/Alaska Native (1,686)	2,949	1.80
Not Hispanic (361)	848	0.52
Hispanic (1,325)	2,101	1.28
Alaska Athabascan *(Ala. Nat.)* (1)	1	<0.01
Apache (59)	98	0.06
Arapaho (7)	7	<0.01
Blackfeet (12)	60	0.04
Canadian/French Am. Ind. (1)	7	<0.01
Central American Ind. (14)	20	0.01
Cherokee (82)	264	0.16
Cheyenne (1)	3	<0.01
Chickasaw (9)	16	0.01
Chippewa (6)	20	0.01
Choctaw (15)	57	0.03
Comanche (10)	15	0.01
Creek (2)	3	<0.01
Delaware (4)	7	<0.01
Hopi (6)	12	0.01
Iroquois (2)	5	<0.01
Kiowa (3)	4	<0.01
Lumbee (3)	3	<0.01
Mexican American Ind. (211)	417	0.25
Navajo (61)	98	0.06
Osage (0)	8	<0.01
Ottawa (3)	4	<0.01
Paiute (6)	6	<0.01
Pima (9)	12	0.01
Potawatomi (5)	7	<0.01
Pueblo (15)	25	0.02
Seminole (2)	10	0.01
Shoshone (6)	8	<0.01
Sioux (18)	37	0.02
South American Ind. (7)	7	<0.01
Spanish American Ind. (21)	29	0.02
Tlingit-Haida *(Alaska Native)* (1)	2	<0.01
Tohono O'Odham (10)	10	0.01
Ute (0)	2	<0.01
Yaqui (53)	84	0.05
Yuman (3)	16	0.01
Asian (8,453)	10,009	6.11
Not Hispanic (8,078)	8,965	5.47
Hispanic (375)	1,044	0.64
Bangladeshi (59)	64	0.04
Burmese (20)	27	0.02
Cambodian (276)	309	0.19
Chinese, ex. Taiwanese (1,074)	1,422	0.87
Filipino (2,909)	3,566	2.18
Hmong (37)	38	0.02
Indian (640)	757	0.46
Indonesian (267)	344	0.21
Japanese (263)	543	0.33
Korean (488)	610	0.37
Laotian (33)	48	0.03
Malaysian (3)	9	0.01
Pakistani (129)	163	0.10
Sri Lankan (15)	16	0.01
Taiwanese (174)	197	0.12
Thai (107)	157	0.10
Vietnamese (1,612)	1,752	1.07
Hawaii Native/Pacific Islander (514)	962	0.59
Not Hispanic (448)	686	0.42
Hispanic (66)	276	0.17
Fijian (10)	13	0.01
Guamanian/Chamorro (45)	79	0.05
Marshallese (1)	2	<0.01
Native Hawaiian (69)	228	0.14
Samoan (128)	206	0.13
Tongan (200)	237	0.14
White (83,683)	89,915	54.85
Not Hispanic (29,898)	31,518	19.23
Hispanic (53,785)	58,397	35.62

*Notes: † The Census 2010 population figure is used to calculate the percentages in the Hispanic Origin and Race categories. Ancestry percentages are based on the 2006-2010 American Community Survey population (not shown); ‡ Numbers in parentheses indicate the number of people reporting a single ancestry; * Numbers in parentheses indicate the number of persons reporting this race alone, not in combination with any other race; Please refer to the Explanation of Data for more information.*

Orange Cove

Place Type: City
County: Fresno
Population: 9,078†

Ancestry‡	Population	%
Dutch (0)	13	0.15
English (26)	26	0.30
Finnish (0)	14	0.16
German (10)	44	0.50
Irish (20)	78	0.89
Italian (4)	4	0.05
Scotch-Irish (0)	16	0.18
Swedish (16)	16	0.18

Hispanic Origin	Population	%
Hispanic or Latino (of any race)	8,413	92.67
Central American, ex. Mexican	293	3.23
Costa Rican	1	0.01
Guatemalan	8	0.09
Honduran	3	0.03
Salvadoran	280	3.08
Other Central American	1	0.01
Cuban	7	0.08
Mexican	7,669	84.48
Puerto Rican	12	0.13
South American	5	0.06
Chilean	3	0.03
Peruvian	2	0.02
Other Hispanic or Latino	427	4.70

Race*	Population	%
African-American/Black (72)	93	1.02
Not Hispanic (21)	32	0.35
Hispanic (51)	61	0.67
American Indian/Alaska Native (131)	182	2.00
Not Hispanic (28)	40	0.44
Hispanic (103)	142	1.56
Apache (5)	16	0.18
Canadian/French Am. Ind. (0)	6	0.07
Cherokee (1)	2	0.02
Creek (3)	3	0.03
Mexican American Ind. (33)	37	0.41
Navajo (4)	4	0.04
Potawatomi (2)	2	0.02
Sioux (11)	11	0.12
South American Ind. (0)	1	0.01
Tohono O'Odham (1)	1	0.01
Yaqui (1)	3	0.03
Asian (101)	181	1.99
Not Hispanic (86)	117	1.29
Hispanic (15)	64	0.71
Cambodian (0)	1	0.01
Chinese, ex. Taiwanese (23)	24	0.26
Filipino (49)	73	0.80
Hmong (20)	20	0.22
Indian (0)	8	0.09
Japanese (3)	5	0.06
Laotian (4)	5	0.06
Vietnamese (0)	1	0.01
Hawaii Native/Pacific Islander (3)	21	0.23
Not Hispanic (2)	3	0.03
Hispanic (1)	18	0.20
Native Hawaiian (2)	10	0.11
White (3,940)	4,216	46.44
Not Hispanic (457)	507	5.58
Hispanic (3,483)	3,709	40.86

Orange

Place Type: City
County: Orange
Population: 136,416†

Ancestry‡	Population	%
Afghan (42)	42	0.03
African, Sub-Saharan (156)	194	0.14
African (97)	128	0.10
Ethiopian (2)	2	<0.01
Nigerian (12)	19	0.01
Sudanese (21)	21	0.02
Other Sub-Saharan African (24)	24	0.02
Albanian (20)	41	0.03
American (10,395)	10,395	7.72
Arab (870)	1,076	0.80
Arab (37)	37	0.03
Egyptian (76)	89	0.07
Iraqi (39)	39	0.03
Jordanian (187)	219	0.16
Lebanese (196)	309	0.23
Syrian (244)	268	0.20
Other Arab (91)	115	0.09
Armenian (650)	781	0.58
Assyrian/Chaldean/Syriac (0)	38	0.03
Australian (3)	20	0.01
Austrian (34)	271	0.20
Basque (8)	22	0.02
Belgian (19)	124	0.09
Brazilian (14)	14	0.01
British (359)	640	0.48
Bulgarian (18)	27	0.02
Canadian (127)	254	0.19
Celtic (10)	49	0.04
Croatian (38)	132	0.10
Czech (48)	407	0.30
Czechoslovakian (64)	106	0.08
Danish (189)	572	0.43
Dutch (488)	1,907	1.42
Eastern European (146)	146	0.11
English (2,686)	9,623	7.15
Estonian (17)	17	0.01
European (1,034)	1,228	0.91
Finnish (122)	239	0.18
French, ex. Basque (371)	2,532	1.88
French Canadian (209)	409	0.30
German (4,069)	14,807	11.00
Greek (366)	670	0.50
Guyanese (0)	13	0.01
Hungarian (108)	400	0.30
Icelander (0)	22	0.02
Iranian (503)	626	0.47
Irish (2,322)	10,224	7.60
Israeli (10)	10	0.01
Italian (2,072)	5,575	4.14
Latvian (64)	113	0.08
Lithuanian (22)	125	0.09
Maltese (10)	35	0.03
New Zealander (0)	7	0.01
Northern European (105)	135	0.10
Norwegian (488)	1,652	1.23
Polish (525)	1,808	1.34
Portuguese (81)	437	0.32
Romanian (377)	549	0.41
Russian (379)	978	0.73
Scandinavian (107)	289	0.21
Scotch-Irish (569)	1,558	1.16
Scottish (530)	2,126	1.58
Serbian (24)	83	0.06
Slavic (17)	61	0.05
Slovak (54)	95	0.07
Slovene (12)	51	0.04
Swedish (390)	1,764	1.31
Swiss (46)	289	0.21
Turkish (102)	123	0.09
Ukrainian (67)	150	0.11
Welsh (184)	589	0.44
West Indian, ex. Hispanic (102)	187	0.14
Belizean (14)	14	0.01
Haitian (2)	2	<0.01
Jamaican (66)	127	0.09
West Indian (20)	44	0.03
Yugoslavian (64)	116	0.09

Hispanic Origin	Population	%
Hispanic or Latino (of any race)	52,014	38.13
Central American, ex. Mexican	2,152	1.58
Costa Rican	94	0.07
Guatemalan	790	0.58
Honduran	163	0.12
Nicaraguan	163	0.12
Panamanian	55	0.04
Salvadoran	851	0.62
Other Central American	36	0.03
Cuban	414	0.30
Dominican Republic	49	0.04
Mexican	45,074	33.04
Puerto Rican	488	0.36
South American	1,349	0.99
Argentinean	257	0.19
Bolivian	157	0.12
Chilean	72	0.05
Colombian	257	0.19
Ecuadorian	158	0.12
Paraguayan	3	<0.01
Peruvian	371	0.27
Uruguayan	25	0.02
Venezuelan	32	0.02
Other South American	17	0.01
Other Hispanic or Latino	2,488	1.82

Race*	Population	%
African-American/Black (2,227)	3,007	2.20
Not Hispanic (1,895)	2,425	1.78
Hispanic (332)	582	0.43
American Indian/Alaska Native (993)	1,939	1.42
Not Hispanic (357)	869	0.64
Hispanic (636)	1,070	0.78
Alaska Athabascan *(Ala. Nat.)* (0)	1	<0.01
Aleut *(Alaska Native)* (3)	8	0.01
Apache (60)	106	0.08
Arapaho (2)	5	<0.01
Blackfeet (10)	42	0.03
Canadian/French Am. Ind. (0)	6	<0.01
Central American Ind. (3)	13	0.01
Cherokee (51)	249	0.18
Cheyenne (4)	5	<0.01
Chickasaw (9)	17	0.01
Chippewa (6)	29	0.02
Choctaw (20)	63	0.05
Comanche (5)	10	0.01
Cree (0)	1	<0.01
Creek (4)	16	0.01
Crow (2)	4	<0.01
Hopi (0)	2	<0.01
Inupiat *(Alaska Native)* (2)	4	<0.01
Iroquois (13)	20	0.01
Lumbee (3)	3	<0.01
Mexican American Ind. (129)	179	0.13
Navajo (31)	47	0.03
Osage (3)	7	0.01
Paiute (0)	5	<0.01
Pima (4)	11	0.01
Potawatomi (10)	12	0.01
Pueblo (4)	8	0.01
Puget Sound Salish (2)	3	<0.01
Seminole (2)	6	<0.01
Shoshone (8)	13	0.01
Sioux (10)	32	0.02
South American Ind. (1)	14	0.01
Spanish American Ind. (10)	19	0.01
Tlingit-Haida *(Alaska Native)* (1)	3	<0.01
Tohono O'Odham (5)	11	0.01
Ute (0)	2	<0.01
Yaqui (15)	30	0.02
Asian (15,350)	17,473	12.81
Not Hispanic (15,116)	16,795	12.31
Hispanic (234)	678	0.50
Bangladeshi (22)	22	0.02
Burmese (9)	21	0.02
Cambodian (313)	351	0.26
Chinese, ex. Taiwanese (1,791)	2,444	1.79
Filipino (2,892)	3,607	2.64
Hmong (12)	18	0.01
Indian (1,460)	1,597	1.17
Indonesian (114)	162	0.12
Japanese (1,106)	1,772	1.30
Korean (1,830)	2,039	1.49
Laotian (41)	51	0.04
Malaysian (4)	15	0.01

SECTION TWO

*Notes: † The Census 2010 population figure is used to calculate the percentages in the Hispanic Origin and Race categories. Ancestry percentages are based on the 2006-2010 American Community Survey population (not shown); ‡ Numbers in parentheses indicate the number of people reporting a single ancestry; * Numbers in parentheses indicate the number of persons reporting this race alone, not in combination with any other race; Please refer to the Explanation of Data for more information.*

Nepalese (1)	2	<0.01
Pakistani (170)	194	0.14
Sri Lankan (67)	70	0.05
Taiwanese (420)	477	0.35
Thai (144)	185	0.14
Vietnamese (4,310)	4,664	3.42
Hawaii Native/Pacific Islander (352)	720	0.53
Not Hispanic (321)	604	0.44
Hispanic (31)	116	0.09
Fijian (4)	7	0.01
Guamanian/Chamorro (59)	99	0.07
Marshallese (5)	8	0.01
Native Hawaiian (98)	270	0.20
Samoan (99)	155	0.11
Tongan (41)	58	0.04
White (91,522)	96,270	70.57
Not Hispanic (63,805)	66,180	48.51
Hispanic (27,717)	30,090	22.06

Orangevale

Place Type: CDP
County: Sacramento
Population: 33,960†

Ancestry‡	Population	%
African, Sub-Saharan (0)	8	0.02
African (0)	8	0.02
American (1,264)	1,264	3.70
Arab (38)	58	0.17
Arab (30)	30	0.09
Lebanese (8)	28	0.08
Armenian (0)	9	0.03
Austrian (8)	83	0.24
Basque (0)	15	0.04
Belgian (0)	47	0.14
Brazilian (7)	7	0.02
British (142)	187	0.55
Canadian (62)	265	0.77
Croatian (9)	40	0.12
Czech (10)	156	0.46
Czechoslovakian (55)	55	0.16
Danish (45)	214	0.63
Dutch (100)	733	2.14
English (1,389)	5,027	14.70
European (539)	571	1.67
Finnish (104)	148	0.43
French, ex. Basque (255)	1,310	3.83
French Canadian (33)	233	0.68
German (1,958)	7,175	20.98
Greek (9)	90	0.26
Hungarian (38)	238	0.70
Iranian (128)	128	0.37
Irish (1,267)	4,988	14.58
Italian (1,274)	3,154	9.22
Lithuanian (13)	50	0.15
Luxemburger (0)	56	0.16
Macedonian (0)	9	0.03
Northern European (55)	55	0.16
Norwegian (227)	846	2.47
Pennsylvania German (0)	8	0.02
Polish (218)	797	2.33
Portuguese (145)	854	2.50
Romanian (236)	257	0.75
Russian (378)	546	1.60
Scandinavian (175)	226	0.66
Scotch-Irish (304)	908	2.65
Scottish (190)	808	2.36
Slovak (34)	34	0.10
Swedish (311)	984	2.88
Swiss (37)	143	0.42
Ukrainian (405)	447	1.31
Welsh (98)	545	1.59
Yugoslavian (36)	61	0.18

Hispanic Origin	Population	%
Hispanic or Latino (of any race)	3,448	10.15
Central American, ex. Mexican	144	0.42
Costa Rican	10	0.03
Guatemalan	27	0.08
Honduran	14	0.04
Nicaraguan	43	0.13
Panamanian	8	0.02
Salvadoran	42	0.12
Cuban	37	0.11
Dominican Republic	4	0.01
Mexican	2,536	7.47
Puerto Rican	147	0.43
South American	134	0.39
Argentinean	23	0.07
Bolivian	13	0.04
Chilean	24	0.07
Colombian	19	0.06
Ecuadorian	12	0.04
Peruvian	29	0.09
Uruguayan	1	<0.01
Venezuelan	10	0.03
Other South American	3	0.01
Other Hispanic or Latino	446	1.31

Race*	Population	%
African-American/Black (463)	742	2.18
Not Hispanic (440)	662	1.95
Hispanic (23)	80	0.24
American Indian/Alaska Native (316)	845	2.49
Not Hispanic (214)	639	1.88
Hispanic (102)	206	0.61
Alaska Athabascan *(Ala. Nat.)* (1)	2	0.01
Apache (9)	31	0.09
Arapaho (0)	1	<0.01
Blackfeet (1)	24	0.07
Central American Ind. (2)	2	0.01
Cherokee (36)	175	0.52
Chickasaw (0)	3	0.01
Chippewa (6)	12	0.04
Choctaw (19)	44	0.13
Comanche (3)	3	0.01
Cree (1)	5	0.01
Creek (2)	6	0.02
Crow (2)	5	0.01
Delaware (1)	2	0.01
Hopi (1)	1	<0.01
Iroquois (1)	8	0.02
Menominee (0)	2	0.01
Mexican American Ind. (9)	9	0.03
Navajo (10)	29	0.09
Paiute (2)	6	0.02
Potawatomi (2)	10	0.03
Pueblo (2)	4	0.01
Puget Sound Salish (1)	1	<0.01
Shoshone (1)	4	0.01
Sioux (9)	17	0.05
South American Ind. (3)	4	0.01
Tlingit-Haida *(Alaska Native)* (0)	1	<0.01
Tohono O'Odham (0)	2	0.01
Ute (0)	1	<0.01
Yaqui (6)	7	0.02
Asian (1,040)	1,587	4.67
Not Hispanic (999)	1,450	4.27
Hispanic (41)	137	0.40
Burmese (13)	14	0.04
Cambodian (5)	5	0.01
Chinese, ex. Taiwanese (203)	309	0.91
Filipino (284)	466	1.37
Hmong (6)	8	0.02
Indian (165)	211	0.62
Indonesian (3)	8	0.02
Japanese (124)	282	0.83
Korean (79)	113	0.33
Laotian (7)	7	0.02
Malaysian (4)	5	0.01
Nepalese (1)	2	0.01
Pakistani (11)	11	0.03
Sri Lankan (3)	5	0.01
Taiwanese (7)	10	0.03
Thai (11)	33	0.10
Vietnamese (83)	100	0.29
Hawaii Native/Pacific Islander (75)	237	0.70
Not Hispanic (64)	181	0.53
Hispanic (11)	56	0.16
Fijian (14)	27	0.08
Guamanian/Chamorro (26)	65	0.19
Marshallese (1)	1	<0.01
Native Hawaiian (20)	84	0.25
Samoan (3)	14	0.04
Tongan (2)	7	0.02
White (29,679)	31,072	91.50
Not Hispanic (27,665)	28,664	84.41
Hispanic (2,014)	2,408	7.09

Orcutt

Place Type: CDP
County: Santa Barbara
Population: 28,905†

Ancestry‡	Population	%
African, Sub-Saharan (12)	12	0.04
Cape Verdean (12)	12	0.04
American (1,326)	1,326	4.62
Arab (182)	182	0.63
Arab (134)	134	0.47
Egyptian (8)	8	0.03
Lebanese (40)	40	0.14
Armenian (0)	13	0.05
Austrian (15)	93	0.32
Basque (51)	95	0.33
Belgian (12)	49	0.17
Brazilian (9)	18	0.06
British (123)	158	0.55
Canadian (51)	147	0.51
Croatian (0)	143	0.50
Czech (30)	230	0.80
Czechoslovakian (10)	50	0.17
Danish (132)	373	1.30
Dutch (209)	590	2.06
Eastern European (18)	18	0.06
English (1,242)	4,093	14.26
European (627)	650	2.27
Finnish (15)	29	0.10
French, ex. Basque (146)	1,103	3.84
French Canadian (107)	227	0.79
German (1,519)	5,946	20.72
Greek (177)	242	0.84
Hungarian (27)	71	0.25
Iranian (91)	91	0.32
Irish (1,169)	4,256	14.83
Italian (510)	1,960	6.83
Latvian (0)	12	0.04
Lithuanian (24)	24	0.08
Northern European (9)	9	0.03
Norwegian (206)	527	1.84
Polish (189)	566	1.97
Portuguese (343)	577	2.01
Russian (57)	178	0.62
Scandinavian (17)	34	0.12
Scotch-Irish (210)	573	2.00
Scottish (224)	548	1.91
Slavic (10)	20	0.07
Slovak (0)	17	0.06
Swedish (207)	531	1.85
Swiss (9)	194	0.68
Welsh (24)	248	0.86
West Indian, ex. Hispanic (20)	57	0.20
Dutch West Indian (0)	14	0.05
Haitian (0)	14	0.05
Jamaican (9)	18	0.06
Trinidadian/Tobagonian (11)	11	0.04

Hispanic Origin	Population	%
Hispanic or Latino (of any race)	6,870	23.77
Central American, ex. Mexican	141	0.49
Costa Rican	26	0.09
Guatemalan	20	0.07
Honduran	24	0.08
Nicaraguan	16	0.06
Panamanian	13	0.04
Salvadoran	39	0.13
Other Central American	3	0.01
Cuban	4	0.01

*Notes: † The Census 2010 population figure is used to calculate the percentages in the Hispanic Origin and Race categories. Ancestry percentages are based on the 2006-2010 American Community Survey population (not shown); ‡ Numbers in parentheses indicate the number of people reporting a single ancestry; * Numbers in parentheses indicate the number of persons reporting this race alone, not in combination with any other race; Please refer to the Explanation of Data for more information.*

Dominican Republic	5	0.02
Mexican	6,023	20.84
Puerto Rican	130	0.45
South American	107	0.37
Argentinean	33	0.11
Bolivian	1	<0.01
Chilean	23	0.08
Colombian	19	0.07
Ecuadorian	5	0.02
Paraguayan	1	<0.01
Peruvian	16	0.06
Uruguayan	1	<0.01
Venezuelan	8	0.03
Other Hispanic or Latino	460	1.59

Race*	Population	%
African-American/Black (394)	602	2.08
Not Hispanic (375)	529	1.83
Hispanic (19)	73	0.25
American Indian/Alaska Native (347)	670	2.32
Not Hispanic (162)	338	1.17
Hispanic (185)	332	1.15
Alaska Athabascan *(Ala. Nat.)* (1)	1	<0.01
Aleut *(Alaska Native)* (2)	5	0.02
Apache (7)	18	0.06
Blackfeet (2)	5	0.02
Canadian/French Am. Ind. (0)	1	<0.01
Cherokee (23)	90	0.31
Cheyenne (1)	1	<0.01
Chickasaw (2)	4	0.01
Chippewa (3)	10	0.03
Choctaw (34)	57	0.20
Comanche (1)	3	0.01
Creek (1)	9	0.03
Hopi (0)	1	<0.01
Inupiat *(Alaska Native)* (4)	4	0.01
Iroquois (6)	10	0.03
Lumbee (1)	1	<0.01
Menominee (1)	1	<0.01
Mexican American Ind. (30)	39	0.13
Navajo (2)	6	0.02
Osage (1)	3	0.01
Paiute (2)	2	0.01
Potawatomi (0)	3	0.01
Pueblo (1)	2	0.01
Puget Sound Salish (0)	1	<0.01
Shoshone (1)	5	0.02
Sioux (3)	11	0.04
South American Ind. (1)	1	<0.01
Spanish American Ind. (2)	2	0.01
Tlingit-Haida *(Alaska Native)* (1)	3	0.01
Ute (2)	2	0.01
Yaqui (8)	19	0.07
Yuman (0)	1	<0.01
Asian (1,129)	1,681	5.82
Not Hispanic (1,012)	1,394	4.82
Hispanic (117)	287	0.99
Bangladeshi (4)	4	0.01
Burmese (1)	1	<0.01
Cambodian (0)	1	<0.01
Chinese, ex. Taiwanese (114)	190	0.66
Filipino (416)	709	2.45
Hmong (8)	8	0.03
Indian (80)	93	0.32
Indonesian (3)	14	0.05
Japanese (185)	325	1.12
Korean (202)	227	0.79
Laotian (5)	6	0.02
Malaysian (0)	2	0.01
Pakistani (14)	17	0.06
Sri Lankan (7)	15	0.05
Taiwanese (3)	3	0.01
Thai (27)	39	0.13
Vietnamese (36)	53	0.18
Hawaii Native/Pacific Islander (59)	172	0.60
Not Hispanic (54)	137	0.47
Hispanic (5)	35	0.12
Guamanian/Chamorro (12)	18	0.06
Marshallese (2)	2	0.01
Native Hawaiian (28)	87	0.30
Samoan (6)	13	0.04
Tongan (0)	3	0.01
White (23,677)	24,831	85.91
Not Hispanic (19,667)	20,340	70.37
Hispanic (4,010)	4,491	15.54

Orinda

Place Type: City
County: Contra Costa
Population: 17,643†

Ancestry‡	Population	%
Afghan (57)	57	0.33
African, Sub-Saharan (13)	23	0.13
African (0)	10	0.06
Ethiopian (13)	13	0.07
American (488)	488	2.79
Arab (32)	104	0.59
Egyptian (0)	8	0.05
Iraqi (22)	66	0.38
Other Arab (10)	30	0.17
Armenian (121)	163	0.93
Australian (16)	67	0.38
Austrian (31)	55	0.31
Belgian (0)	17	0.10
Brazilian (104)	104	0.59
British (61)	143	0.82
Bulgarian (9)	9	0.05
Canadian (16)	80	0.46
Croatian (16)	65	0.37
Czech (16)	102	0.58
Czechoslovakian (11)	24	0.14
Danish (74)	185	1.06
Dutch (107)	468	2.68
Eastern European (158)	167	0.96
English (995)	4,072	23.29
European (763)	866	4.95
Finnish (110)	155	0.89
French, ex. Basque (40)	613	3.51
French Canadian (14)	35	0.20
German (669)	3,162	18.08
Greek (54)	96	0.55
Hungarian (0)	54	0.31
Iranian (139)	166	0.95
Irish (545)	3,020	17.27
Italian (319)	1,322	7.56
Latvian (0)	22	0.13
Lithuanian (18)	27	0.15
Northern European (35)	43	0.25
Norwegian (79)	444	2.54
Polish (185)	575	3.29
Portuguese (117)	259	1.48
Romanian (12)	23	0.13
Russian (188)	487	2.79
Scandinavian (12)	36	0.21
Scotch-Irish (103)	440	2.52
Scottish (89)	690	3.95
Serbian (0)	43	0.25
Slovak (0)	35	0.20
Swedish (183)	660	3.77
Swiss (0)	234	1.34
Turkish (10)	10	0.06
Ukrainian (27)	144	0.82
Welsh (12)	178	1.02
West Indian, ex. Hispanic (8)	8	0.05
Jamaican (8)	8	0.05

Hispanic Origin	Population	%
Hispanic or Latino (of any race)	807	4.57
Central American, ex. Mexican	74	0.42
Costa Rican	5	0.03
Guatemalan	5	0.03
Honduran	1	0.01
Nicaraguan	27	0.15
Panamanian	6	0.03
Salvadoran	28	0.16
Other Central American	2	0.01
Cuban	10	0.06
Dominican Republic	1	0.01
Mexican	413	2.34
Puerto Rican	44	0.25
South American	142	0.80
Argentinean	27	0.15
Bolivian	10	0.06
Chilean	13	0.07
Colombian	26	0.15
Ecuadorian	15	0.09
Paraguayan	4	0.02
Peruvian	36	0.20
Uruguayan	4	0.02
Venezuelan	7	0.04
Other Hispanic or Latino	123	0.70

Race*	Population	%
African-American/Black (149)	216	1.22
Not Hispanic (143)	201	1.14
Hispanic (6)	15	0.09
American Indian/Alaska Native (22)	139	0.79
Not Hispanic (16)	111	0.63
Hispanic (6)	28	0.16
Aleut *(Alaska Native)* (1)	3	0.02
Apache (1)	3	0.02
Blackfeet (0)	2	0.01
Cherokee (1)	36	0.20
Chickasaw (0)	1	0.01
Chippewa (2)	8	0.05
Choctaw (0)	5	0.03
Comanche (0)	4	0.02
Cree (0)	1	0.01
Creek (0)	5	0.03
Inupiat *(Alaska Native)* (1)	1	0.01
Iroquois (0)	2	0.01
Lumbee (1)	1	0.01
Mexican American Ind. (3)	4	0.02
Sioux (0)	2	0.01
South American Ind. (0)	3	0.02
Spanish American Ind. (0)	1	0.01
Yaqui (0)	2	0.01
Asian (2,016)	2,596	14.71
Not Hispanic (2,009)	2,556	14.49
Hispanic (7)	40	0.23
Burmese (0)	3	0.02
Cambodian (1)	1	0.01
Chinese, ex. Taiwanese (1,067)	1,406	7.97
Filipino (120)	230	1.30
Indian (184)	229	1.30
Indonesian (6)	14	0.08
Japanese (170)	315	1.79
Korean (159)	223	1.26
Laotian (0)	1	0.01
Malaysian (0)	2	0.01
Nepalese (1)	1	0.01
Pakistani (32)	39	0.22
Sri Lankan (3)	8	0.05
Taiwanese (53)	60	0.34
Thai (11)	23	0.13
Vietnamese (58)	85	0.48
Hawaii Native/Pacific Islander (24)	71	0.40
Not Hispanic (24)	65	0.37
Hispanic (0)	6	0.03
Fijian (5)	6	0.03
Guamanian/Chamorro (2)	8	0.05
Native Hawaiian (1)	30	0.17
Samoan (1)	7	0.04
Tongan (14)	14	0.08
White (14,533)	15,276	86.58
Not Hispanic (13,910)	14,563	82.54
Hispanic (623)	713	4.04

Orosi

Place Type: CDP
County: Tulare
Population: 8,770†

Ancestry‡	Population	%
American (17)	17	0.19
English (6)	55	0.63
French, ex. Basque (0)	13	0.15

*Notes: † The Census 2010 population figure is used to calculate the percentages in the Hispanic Origin and Race categories. Ancestry percentages are based on the 2006-2010 American Community Survey population (not shown); ‡ Numbers in parentheses indicate the number of people reporting a single ancestry; * Numbers in parentheses indicate the number of persons reporting this race alone, not in combination with any other race; Please refer to the Explanation of Data for more information.*

French Canadian (11)	11	0.13
German (16)	108	1.23
Irish (5)	12	0.14
Portuguese (13)	13	0.15
Scotch-Irish (0)	31	0.35
Swedish (0)	13	0.15

Hispanic Origin	Population	%
Hispanic or Latino (of any race)	7,606	86.73
Central American, ex. Mexican	30	0.34
Guatemalan	9	0.10
Honduran	1	0.01
Nicaraguan	6	0.07
Salvadoran	14	0.16
Cuban	1	0.01
Mexican	7,209	82.20
Puerto Rican	9	0.10
Other Hispanic or Latino	357	4.07

Race*	Population	%
African-American/Black (65)	75	0.86
Not Hispanic (8)	14	0.16
Hispanic (57)	61	0.70
American Indian/Alaska Native (57)	110	1.25
Not Hispanic (19)	38	0.43
Hispanic (38)	72	0.82
Apache (2)	3	0.03
Cherokee (3)	7	0.08
Iroquois (4)	4	0.05
Mexican American Ind. (11)	27	0.31
Navajo (1)	1	0.01
Seminole (2)	2	0.02
Yaqui (0)	1	0.01
Yuman (1)	1	0.01
Asian (803)	868	9.90
Not Hispanic (768)	798	9.10
Hispanic (35)	70	0.80
Cambodian (4)	4	0.05
Chinese, ex. Taiwanese (4)	6	0.07
Filipino (663)	717	8.18
Hmong (2)	6	0.07
Indian (15)	18	0.21
Indonesian (0)	2	0.02
Japanese (12)	15	0.17
Korean (0)	4	0.05
Laotian (2)	4	0.05
Thai (83)	87	0.99
Hawaii Native/Pacific Islander (1)	11	0.13
Not Hispanic (1)	10	0.11
Hispanic (0)	1	0.01
Guamanian/Chamorro (0)	1	0.01
Native Hawaiian (1)	1	0.01
White (3,861)	4,136	47.16
Not Hispanic (301)	332	3.79
Hispanic (3,560)	3,804	43.38

Oroville East

Place Type: CDP
County: Butte
Population: 8,280†

Ancestry‡	Population	%
American (792)	792	9.21
Arab (14)	14	0.16
Lebanese (14)	14	0.16
Belgian (17)	17	0.20
British (42)	61	0.71
Canadian (13)	44	0.51
Czechoslovakian (13)	13	0.15
Danish (19)	154	1.79
Dutch (126)	258	3.00
English (398)	1,258	14.63
European (61)	70	0.81
Finnish (16)	16	0.19
French, ex. Basque (101)	356	4.14
French Canadian (24)	34	0.40
German (462)	1,462	17.00
Irish (180)	1,037	12.06
Italian (162)	416	4.84
Lithuanian (0)	18	0.21
Northern European (14)	14	0.16
Norwegian (102)	212	2.47
Polish (10)	74	0.86
Portuguese (22)	71	0.83
Russian (64)	98	1.14
Scandinavian (0)	23	0.27
Scotch-Irish (59)	129	1.50
Scottish (45)	162	1.88
Swedish (91)	181	2.10
Swiss (126)	214	2.49
Ukrainian (0)	10	0.12
Welsh (11)	61	0.71

Hispanic Origin	Population	%
Hispanic or Latino (of any race)	702	8.48
Central American, ex. Mexican	19	0.23
Guatemalan	2	0.02
Honduran	1	0.01
Nicaraguan	3	0.04
Panamanian	1	0.01
Salvadoran	9	0.11
Other Central American	3	0.04
Cuban	10	0.12
Mexican	532	6.43
Puerto Rican	34	0.41
South American	7	0.08
Argentinean	2	0.02
Colombian	4	0.05
Peruvian	1	0.01
Other Hispanic or Latino	100	1.21

Race*	Population	%
African-American/Black (126)	212	2.56
Not Hispanic (119)	188	2.27
Hispanic (7)	24	0.29
American Indian/Alaska Native (477)	689	8.32
Not Hispanic (428)	601	7.26
Hispanic (49)	88	1.06
Apache (2)	3	0.04
Blackfeet (1)	5	0.06
Cherokee (25)	71	0.86
Cheyenne (0)	1	0.01
Chickasaw (3)	5	0.06
Chippewa (1)	2	0.02
Choctaw (9)	18	0.22
Cree (0)	1	0.01
Crow (1)	1	0.01
Hopi (1)	1	0.01
Inupiat *(Alaska Native)* (1)	1	0.01
Iroquois (0)	1	0.01
Mexican American Ind. (2)	5	0.06
Navajo (2)	5	0.06
Osage (1)	1	0.01
Paiute (3)	8	0.10
Potawatomi (3)	5	0.06
Seminole (1)	2	0.02
Shoshone (1)	2	0.02
Sioux (3)	7	0.08
Tlingit-Haida *(Alaska Native)* (1)	1	0.01
Asian (294)	379	4.58
Not Hispanic (292)	371	4.48
Hispanic (2)	8	0.10
Cambodian (1)	1	0.01
Chinese, ex. Taiwanese (25)	32	0.39
Filipino (28)	39	0.47
Hmong (121)	140	1.69
Indian (8)	15	0.18
Indonesian (0)	2	0.02
Japanese (12)	26	0.31
Korean (7)	14	0.17
Laotian (57)	64	0.77
Pakistani (0)	2	0.02
Thai (1)	1	0.01
Vietnamese (5)	7	0.08
Hawaii Native/Pacific Islander (8)	31	0.37
Not Hispanic (7)	25	0.30
Hispanic (1)	6	0.07
Native Hawaiian (4)	12	0.14
Samoan (3)	11	0.13
White (6,830)	7,188	86.81
Not Hispanic (6,417)	6,699	80.91
Hispanic (413)	489	5.91

Oroville

Place Type: City
County: Butte
Population: 15,546†

Ancestry‡	Population	%
African, Sub-Saharan (0)	12	0.08
African (0)	12	0.08
American (1,658)	1,658	10.79
Arab (0)	31	0.20
Lebanese (0)	31	0.20
Armenian (10)	46	0.30
Assyrian/Chaldean/Syriac (20)	20	0.13
Austrian (0)	50	0.33
British (10)	10	0.07
Canadian (9)	9	0.06
Czech (0)	90	0.59
Czechoslovakian (8)	8	0.05
Danish (121)	236	1.54
Dutch (144)	873	5.68
English (524)	1,868	12.15
European (227)	245	1.59
Finnish (8)	8	0.05
French, ex. Basque (92)	813	5.29
French Canadian (68)	79	0.51
German (931)	2,833	18.43
Greek (15)	62	0.40
Hungarian (10)	54	0.35
Irish (399)	1,932	12.57
Israeli (0)	7	0.05
Italian (290)	1,327	8.63
Norwegian (55)	311	2.02
Pennsylvania German (8)	8	0.05
Polish (0)	91	0.59
Portuguese (241)	370	2.41
Romanian (9)	44	0.29
Russian (52)	134	0.87
Scandinavian (32)	160	1.04
Scotch-Irish (68)	508	3.31
Scottish (52)	162	1.05
Swedish (31)	139	0.90
Swiss (0)	42	0.27
Welsh (49)	71	0.46
West Indian, ex. Hispanic (16)	23	0.15
Dutch West Indian (16)	16	0.10
Haitian (0)	7	0.05
Yugoslavian (0)	19	0.12

Hispanic Origin	Population	%
Hispanic or Latino (of any race)	1,945	12.51
Central American, ex. Mexican	48	0.31
Guatemalan	10	0.06
Honduran	9	0.06
Nicaraguan	11	0.07
Panamanian	3	0.02
Salvadoran	15	0.10
Cuban	18	0.12
Dominican Republic	1	0.01
Mexican	1,537	9.89
Puerto Rican	71	0.46
South American	14	0.09
Argentinean	2	0.01
Colombian	4	0.03
Peruvian	6	0.04
Other South American	2	0.01
Other Hispanic or Latino	256	1.65

Race*	Population	%
African-American/Black (453)	715	4.60
Not Hispanic (426)	647	4.16
Hispanic (27)	68	0.44
American Indian/Alaska Native (573)	1,041	6.70
Not Hispanic (453)	850	5.47
Hispanic (120)	191	1.23
Aleut *(Alaska Native)* (3)	3	0.02

*Notes: † The Census 2010 population figure is used to calculate the percentages in the Hispanic Origin and Race categories. Ancestry percentages are based on the 2006-2010 American Community Survey population (not shown); ‡ Numbers in parentheses indicate the number of people reporting a single ancestry; * Numbers in parentheses indicate the number of persons reporting this race alone, not in combination with any other race; Please refer to the Explanation of Data for more information.*

Apache (12)	21	0.14
Blackfeet (5)	25	0.16
Cherokee (62)	179	1.15
Cheyenne (2)	3	0.02
Chickasaw (1)	5	0.03
Chippewa (1)	4	0.03
Choctaw (9)	20	0.13
Comanche (1)	4	0.03
Cree (1)	2	0.01
Creek (0)	6	0.04
Crow (1)	1	0.01
Hopi (0)	1	0.01
Iroquois (0)	3	0.02
Lumbee (0)	1	0.01
Mexican American Ind. (5)	7	0.05
Navajo (5)	7	0.05
Osage (0)	1	0.01
Ottawa (1)	3	0.02
Paiute (2)	7	0.05
Potawatomi (3)	10	0.06
Puget Sound Salish (0)	1	0.01
Seminole (0)	1	0.01
Shoshone (1)	1	0.01
Sioux (9)	17	0.11
Tlingit-Haida *(Alaska Native)* (1)	2	0.01
Tohono O'Odham (2)	2	0.01
Tsimshian *(Alaska Native)* (1)	2	0.01
Yaqui (0)	4	0.03
Yuman (1)	2	0.01
Yup'ik *(Alaska Native)* (6)	6	0.04
Asian (1,238)	1,409	9.06
Not Hispanic (1,224)	1,363	8.77
Hispanic (14)	46	0.30
Burmese (4)	4	0.03
Cambodian (3)	7	0.05
Chinese, ex. Taiwanese (28)	54	0.35
Filipino (90)	170	1.09
Hmong (740)	773	4.97
Indian (84)	98	0.63
Indonesian (0)	4	0.03
Japanese (9)	37	0.24
Korean (5)	9	0.06
Laotian (132)	145	0.93
Malaysian (1)	1	0.01
Pakistani (7)	10	0.06
Taiwanese (2)	2	0.01
Thai (4)	6	0.04
Vietnamese (22)	47	0.30
Hawaii Native/Pacific Islander (56)	144	0.93
Not Hispanic (55)	117	0.75
Hispanic (1)	27	0.17
Fijian (5)	5	0.03
Guamanian/Chamorro (5)	11	0.07
Native Hawaiian (23)	67	0.43
Samoan (6)	22	0.14
Tongan (16)	16	0.10
White (11,686)	12,555	80.76
Not Hispanic (10,727)	11,354	73.03
Hispanic (959)	1,201	7.73

Oxnard

Place Type: City
County: Ventura
Population: 197,899†

Ancestry‡	Population	%
Afghan (32)	32	0.02
African, Sub-Saharan (434)	496	0.26
African (385)	439	0.23
Nigerian (15)	23	0.01
South African (34)	34	0.02
Albanian (31)	31	0.02
American (1,962)	1,962	1.02
Arab (137)	170	0.09
Arab (45)	45	0.02
Egyptian (13)	35	0.02
Lebanese (0)	11	0.01
Syrian (16)	16	0.01
Other Arab (63)	63	0.03
Armenian (34)	67	0.03
Australian (7)	24	0.01
Austrian (64)	226	0.12
Basque (8)	48	0.02
Belgian (8)	87	0.05
Brazilian (0)	27	0.01
British (196)	353	0.18
Bulgarian (83)	106	0.06
Canadian (69)	245	0.13
Croatian (93)	110	0.06
Czech (37)	127	0.07
Czechoslovakian (0)	19	0.01
Danish (68)	405	0.21
Dutch (108)	753	0.39
Eastern European (88)	107	0.06
English (1,691)	5,380	2.79
European (573)	807	0.42
Finnish (56)	56	0.03
French, ex. Basque (172)	1,779	0.92
French Canadian (77)	251	0.13
German (2,491)	8,448	4.39
German Russian (0)	6	<0.01
Greek (85)	138	0.07
Guyanese (12)	29	0.02
Hungarian (115)	336	0.17
Icelander (12)	12	0.01
Iranian (150)	181	0.09
Irish (1,706)	7,202	3.74
Italian (905)	2,897	1.50
Lithuanian (84)	119	0.06
Macedonian (0)	19	0.01
Maltese (0)	21	0.01
New Zealander (11)	28	0.01
Northern European (80)	113	0.06
Norwegian (306)	774	0.40
Pennsylvania German (13)	13	0.01
Polish (318)	1,543	0.80
Portuguese (117)	550	0.29
Romanian (0)	41	0.02
Russian (396)	1,056	0.55
Scandinavian (33)	111	0.06
Scotch-Irish (392)	1,253	0.65
Scottish (374)	1,368	0.71
Serbian (7)	85	0.04
Slavic (9)	51	0.03
Slovak (26)	62	0.03
Swedish (391)	1,002	0.52
Swiss (35)	171	0.09
Turkish (9)	9	<0.01
Ukrainian (54)	117	0.06
Welsh (38)	345	0.18
West Indian, ex. Hispanic (177)	232	0.12
Dutch West Indian (6)	6	<0.01
Haitian (0)	6	<0.01
Jamaican (89)	116	0.06
Trinidadian/Tobagonian (82)	104	0.05
Yugoslavian (0)	82	0.04

Hispanic Origin	Population	%
Hispanic or Latino (of any race)	145,551	73.55
Central American, ex. Mexican	2,288	1.16
Costa Rican	52	0.03
Guatemalan	630	0.32
Honduran	204	0.10
Nicaraguan	138	0.07
Panamanian	72	0.04
Salvadoran	1,172	0.59
Other Central American	20	0.01
Cuban	166	0.08
Dominican Republic	39	0.02
Mexican	136,991	69.22
Puerto Rican	678	0.34
South American	686	0.35
Argentinean	105	0.05
Bolivian	36	0.02
Chilean	80	0.04
Colombian	183	0.09
Ecuadorian	55	0.03
Peruvian	185	0.09
Uruguayan	25	0.01
Venezuelan	13	0.01
Other South American	4	<0.01
Other Hispanic or Latino	4,703	2.38

Race*	Population	%
African-American/Black (5,771)	7,324	3.70
Not Hispanic (4,754)	5,591	2.83
Hispanic (1,017)	1,733	0.88
American Indian/Alaska Native (2,953)	4,494	2.27
Not Hispanic (424)	1,023	0.52
Hispanic (2,529)	3,471	1.75
Alaska Athabascan *(Ala. Nat.)* (0)	2	<0.01
Aleut *(Alaska Native)* (4)	5	<0.01
Apache (55)	146	0.07
Blackfeet (9)	52	0.03
Canadian/French Am. Ind. (1)	3	<0.01
Central American Ind. (8)	11	0.01
Cherokee (80)	295	0.15
Cheyenne (4)	4	<0.01
Chickasaw (7)	9	<0.01
Chippewa (11)	18	0.01
Choctaw (22)	48	0.02
Comanche (17)	20	0.01
Cree (1)	1	<0.01
Creek (2)	11	0.01
Crow (0)	2	<0.01
Delaware (3)	8	<0.01
Hopi (5)	15	0.01
Iroquois (4)	12	0.01
Kiowa (3)	10	0.01
Lumbee (0)	1	<0.01
Mexican American Ind. (1,129)	1,377	0.70
Navajo (35)	59	0.03
Osage (2)	15	0.01
Ottawa (1)	2	<0.01
Paiute (7)	14	0.01
Pima (0)	4	<0.01
Potawatomi (0)	1	<0.01
Pueblo (21)	36	0.02
Seminole (3)	17	0.01
Shoshone (0)	1	<0.01
Sioux (23)	54	0.03
South American Ind. (8)	24	0.01
Spanish American Ind. (16)	32	0.02
Tlingit-Haida *(Alaska Native)* (0)	4	<0.01
Tohono O'Odham (9)	20	0.01
Ute (2)	5	<0.01
Yakama (1)	1	<0.01
Yaqui (49)	91	0.05
Yuman (4)	4	<0.01
Yup'ik *(Alaska Native)* (2)	2	<0.01
Asian (14,550)	17,273	8.73
Not Hispanic (14,084)	15,805	7.99
Hispanic (466)	1,468	0.74
Bangladeshi (31)	33	0.02
Burmese (6)	6	<0.01
Cambodian (81)	107	0.05
Chinese, ex. Taiwanese (605)	948	0.48
Filipino (10,166)	11,788	5.96
Hmong (8)	9	<0.01
Indian (586)	741	0.37
Indonesian (25)	47	0.02
Japanese (801)	1,411	0.71
Korean (465)	570	0.29
Laotian (92)	113	0.06
Malaysian (1)	21	0.01
Nepalese (13)	19	0.01
Pakistani (9)	12	0.01
Sri Lankan (20)	26	0.01
Taiwanese (47)	65	0.03
Thai (78)	129	0.07
Vietnamese (1,203)	1,343	0.68
Hawaii Native/Pacific Islander (658)	1,241	0.63
Not Hispanic (537)	867	0.44
Hispanic (121)	374	0.19
Fijian (4)	8	<0.01
Guamanian/Chamorro (172)	275	0.14
Native Hawaiian (87)	262	0.13
Samoan (327)	474	0.24
Tongan (7)	11	0.01

*Notes: † The Census 2010 population figure is used to calculate the percentages in the Hispanic Origin and Race categories. Ancestry percentages are based on the 2006-2010 American Community Survey population (not shown); ‡ Numbers in parentheses indicate the number of people reporting a single ancestry; * Numbers in parentheses indicate the number of persons reporting this race alone, not in combination with any other race; Please refer to the Explanation of Data for more information.*

White (95,346)	102,814	51.95
Not Hispanic (29,410)	31,821	16.08
Hispanic (65,936)	70,993	35.87

Pacific Grove

Place Type: City
County: Monterey
Population: 15,041†

Ancestry‡	Population	%
African, Sub-Saharan (14)	14	0.09
African (8)	8	0.05
Ethiopian (6)	6	0.04
American (520)	520	3.49
Arab (225)	226	1.52
Egyptian (138)	138	0.93
Lebanese (30)	31	0.21
Moroccan (39)	39	0.26
Syrian (18)	18	0.12
Armenian (14)	14	0.09
Australian (0)	8	0.05
Austrian (8)	79	0.53
Basque (9)	56	0.38
Belgian (9)	31	0.21
British (58)	108	0.72
Canadian (22)	43	0.29
Croatian (19)	50	0.34
Czech (61)	130	0.87
Czechoslovakian (0)	12	0.08
Danish (44)	199	1.34
Dutch (43)	294	1.97
Eastern European (40)	40	0.27
English (447)	2,312	15.51
European (272)	315	2.11
Finnish (0)	11	0.07
French, ex. Basque (87)	574	3.85
French Canadian (78)	185	1.24
German (528)	2,417	16.22
German Russian (14)	14	0.09
Greek (55)	113	0.76
Hungarian (7)	138	0.93
Iranian (73)	73	0.49
Irish (677)	2,772	18.60
Italian (788)	1,539	10.33
Latvian (11)	24	0.16
Lithuanian (7)	54	0.36
Maltese (9)	9	0.06
Northern European (110)	110	0.74
Norwegian (124)	324	2.17
Pennsylvania German (0)	11	0.07
Polish (98)	393	2.64
Portuguese (240)	447	3.00
Romanian (9)	9	0.06
Russian (81)	265	1.78
Scandinavian (51)	59	0.40
Scotch-Irish (267)	606	4.07
Scottish (112)	666	4.47
Slavic (0)	4	0.03
Slovak (0)	20	0.13
Slovene (25)	71	0.48
Swedish (32)	267	1.79
Swiss (42)	94	0.63
Turkish (9)	46	0.31
Ukrainian (48)	75	0.50
Welsh (128)	315	2.11
West Indian, ex. Hispanic (7)	7	0.05
Jamaican (7)	7	0.05
Yugoslavian (8)	8	0.05

Hispanic Origin	Population	%
Hispanic or Latino (of any race)	1,615	10.74
Central American, ex. Mexican	98	0.65
Costa Rican	6	0.04
Guatemalan	13	0.09
Honduran	8	0.05
Nicaraguan	5	0.03
Panamanian	11	0.07
Salvadoran	55	0.37
Cuban	12	0.08
Dominican Republic	2	0.01
Mexican	1,100	7.31
Puerto Rican	49	0.33
South American	117	0.78
Argentinean	11	0.07
Bolivian	7	0.05
Chilean	18	0.12
Colombian	22	0.15
Ecuadorian	8	0.05
Paraguayan	15	0.10
Peruvian	24	0.16
Venezuelan	8	0.05
Other South American	4	0.03
Other Hispanic or Latino	237	1.58

Race*	Population	%
African-American/Black (199)	318	2.11
Not Hispanic (191)	296	1.97
Hispanic (8)	22	0.15
American Indian/Alaska Native (78)	245	1.63
Not Hispanic (53)	163	1.08
Hispanic (25)	82	0.55
Apache (2)	8	0.05
Blackfeet (0)	5	0.03
Cherokee (9)	48	0.32
Cheyenne (0)	1	0.01
Chickasaw (2)	2	0.01
Choctaw (0)	10	0.07
Colville (3)	3	0.02
Comanche (1)	2	0.01
Creek (0)	2	0.01
Crow (1)	1	0.01
Hopi (1)	2	0.01
Iroquois (1)	3	0.02
Menominee (0)	1	0.01
Mexican American Ind. (3)	6	0.04
Navajo (3)	7	0.05
Paiute (1)	2	0.01
Potawatomi (1)	1	0.01
Puget Sound Salish (0)	1	0.01
Shoshone (1)	1	0.01
Sioux (2)	4	0.03
South American Ind. (1)	2	0.01
Spanish American Ind. (1)	1	0.01
Tlingit-Haida *(Alaska Native)* (1)	1	0.01
Tohono O'Odham (0)	1	0.01
Yaqui (0)	1	0.01
Asian (872)	1,208	8.03
Not Hispanic (859)	1,151	7.65
Hispanic (13)	57	0.38
Bangladeshi (1)	1	0.01
Burmese (3)	4	0.03
Chinese, ex. Taiwanese (127)	178	1.18
Filipino (141)	264	1.76
Indian (43)	58	0.39
Indonesian (13)	22	0.15
Japanese (160)	265	1.76
Korean (258)	298	1.98
Laotian (1)	1	0.01
Malaysian (1)	1	0.01
Nepalese (20)	20	0.13
Pakistani (5)	8	0.05
Sri Lankan (11)	11	0.07
Taiwanese (20)	24	0.16
Thai (19)	30	0.20
Vietnamese (18)	24	0.16
Hawaii Native/Pacific Islander (49)	98	0.65
Not Hispanic (41)	81	0.54
Hispanic (8)	17	0.11
Fijian (7)	13	0.09
Guamanian/Chamorro (10)	29	0.19
Native Hawaiian (3)	16	0.11
Samoan (4)	4	0.03
Tongan (12)	13	0.09
White (12,710)	13,321	88.56
Not Hispanic (11,767)	12,224	81.27
Hispanic (943)	1,097	7.29

Pacifica

Place Type: City
County: San Mateo
Population: 37,234†

Ancestry‡	Population	%
African, Sub-Saharan (111)	170	0.46
African (12)	30	0.08
Ethiopian (10)	20	0.05
Liberian (12)	12	0.03
Nigerian (26)	26	0.07
South African (44)	75	0.20
Other Sub-Saharan African (7)	7	0.02
Alsatian (0)	15	0.04
American (990)	990	2.69
Arab (335)	472	1.28
Arab (50)	147	0.40
Iraqi (134)	134	0.36
Jordanian (30)	30	0.08
Lebanese (12)	36	0.10
Palestinian (109)	125	0.34
Armenian (50)	73	0.20
Australian (0)	25	0.07
Austrian (68)	191	0.52
Basque (80)	213	0.58
Belgian (14)	27	0.07
Brazilian (150)	209	0.57
British (109)	251	0.68
Canadian (39)	93	0.25
Croatian (0)	33	0.09
Czech (18)	92	0.25
Czechoslovakian (25)	41	0.11
Danish (43)	360	0.98
Dutch (147)	587	1.59
Eastern European (37)	37	0.10
English (824)	3,524	9.57
Estonian (10)	22	0.06
European (663)	763	2.07
Finnish (41)	180	0.49
French, ex. Basque (219)	1,261	3.43
French Canadian (13)	50	0.14
German (914)	4,609	12.52
Greek (81)	154	0.42
Hungarian (70)	135	0.37
Icelander (0)	11	0.03
Iranian (153)	211	0.57
Irish (1,356)	5,512	14.98
Italian (1,283)	3,437	9.34
Latvian (9)	9	0.02
Lithuanian (39)	70	0.19
Maltese (33)	84	0.23
New Zealander (32)	32	0.09
Northern European (63)	109	0.30
Norwegian (52)	324	0.88
Polish (146)	658	1.79
Portuguese (115)	607	1.65
Romanian (26)	36	0.10
Russian (430)	862	2.34
Scandinavian (32)	70	0.19
Scotch-Irish (242)	532	1.45
Scottish (190)	813	2.21
Serbian (5)	57	0.15
Slavic (0)	10	0.03
Slovak (0)	24	0.07
Slovene (0)	18	0.05
Swedish (151)	900	2.45
Swiss (10)	138	0.37
Turkish (11)	24	0.07
Ukrainian (83)	115	0.31
Welsh (46)	189	0.51
West Indian, ex. Hispanic (32)	49	0.13
Haitian (32)	32	0.09
Jamaican (0)	17	0.05
Yugoslavian (22)	56	0.15

Hispanic Origin	Population	%
Hispanic or Latino (of any race)	6,243	16.77
Central American, ex. Mexican	1,507	4.05
Costa Rican	54	0.15

*Notes: † The Census 2010 population figure is used to calculate the percentages in the Hispanic Origin and Race categories. Ancestry percentages are based on the 2006-2010 American Community Survey population (not shown); ‡ Numbers in parentheses indicate the number of people reporting a single ancestry; * Numbers in parentheses indicate the number of persons reporting this race alone, not in combination with any other race; Please refer to the Explanation of Data for more information.*

Guatemalan	135	0.36
Honduran	25	0.07
Nicaraguan	519	1.39
Panamanian	10	0.03
Salvadoran	747	2.01
Other Central American	17	0.05
Cuban	93	0.25
Dominican Republic	8	0.02
Mexican	2,854	7.67
Puerto Rican	362	0.97
South American	432	1.16
Argentinean	56	0.15
Bolivian	25	0.07
Chilean	43	0.12
Colombian	62	0.17
Ecuadorian	41	0.11
Paraguayan	3	0.01
Peruvian	158	0.42
Uruguayan	1	<0.01
Venezuelan	26	0.07
Other South American	17	0.05
Other Hispanic or Latino	987	2.65

Race*	Population	%
African-American/Black (976)	1,397	3.75
Not Hispanic (902)	1,225	3.29
Hispanic (74)	172	0.46
American Indian/Alaska Native (206)	606	1.63
Not Hispanic (123)	358	0.96
Hispanic (83)	248	0.67
Alaska Athabascan *(Ala. Nat.)* (1)	1	<0.01
Apache (6)	30	0.08
Arapaho (17)	25	0.07
Blackfeet (2)	20	0.05
Canadian/French Am. Ind. (2)	4	0.01
Central American Ind. (2)	5	0.01
Cherokee (17)	78	0.21
Cheyenne (1)	1	<0.01
Chickasaw (0)	2	0.01
Chippewa (4)	9	0.02
Choctaw (3)	21	0.06
Comanche (1)	2	0.01
Creek (0)	7	0.02
Hopi (1)	2	0.01
Iroquois (0)	14	0.04
Kiowa (0)	2	0.01
Mexican American Ind. (19)	38	0.10
Navajo (10)	24	0.06
Ottawa (0)	1	<0.01
Paiute (1)	2	0.01
Pima (1)	1	<0.01
Potawatomi (0)	1	<0.01
Pueblo (3)	6	0.02
Puget Sound Salish (1)	1	<0.01
Seminole (0)	4	0.01
Sioux (2)	15	0.04
South American Ind. (1)	9	0.02
Tlingit-Haida *(Alaska Native)* (0)	1	<0.01
Ute (0)	2	0.01
Yaqui (5)	13	0.03
Yuman (1)	1	<0.01
Asian (7,230)	8,793	23.62
Not Hispanic (7,045)	8,316	22.33
Hispanic (185)	477	1.28
Burmese (35)	46	0.12
Cambodian (17)	29	0.08
Chinese, ex. Taiwanese (1,830)	2,496	6.70
Filipino (3,931)	4,881	13.11
Hmong (1)	4	0.01
Indian (212)	319	0.86
Indonesian (46)	67	0.18
Japanese (317)	646	1.73
Korean (191)	271	0.73
Laotian (14)	25	0.07
Malaysian (8)	13	0.03
Nepalese (6)	6	0.02
Pakistani (32)	33	0.09
Sri Lankan (4)	11	0.03
Taiwanese (22)	25	0.07
Thai (48)	71	0.19
Vietnamese (169)	257	0.69
Hawaii Native/Pacific Islander (315)	631	1.69
Not Hispanic (285)	521	1.40
Hispanic (30)	110	0.30
Fijian (44)	64	0.17
Guamanian/Chamorro (26)	62	0.17
Marshallese (6)	6	0.02
Native Hawaiian (36)	203	0.55
Samoan (116)	156	0.42
Tongan (53)	68	0.18
White (24,166)	26,423	70.96
Not Hispanic (20,703)	22,257	59.78
Hispanic (3,463)	4,166	11.19

Palm Desert

Place Type: City
County: Riverside
Population: 48,445†

Ancestry‡	Population	%
African, Sub-Saharan (15)	38	0.08
African (0)	23	0.05
Cape Verdean (15)	15	0.03
American (2,226)	2,226	4.59
Arab (330)	455	0.94
Egyptian (112)	112	0.23
Lebanese (190)	259	0.53
Moroccan (28)	28	0.06
Syrian (0)	12	0.02
Other Arab (0)	44	0.09
Armenian (137)	154	0.32
Austrian (87)	235	0.48
Belgian (21)	21	0.04
Brazilian (63)	94	0.19
British (399)	526	1.08
Canadian (397)	641	1.32
Celtic (0)	14	0.03
Croatian (79)	149	0.31
Czech (56)	298	0.61
Czechoslovakian (17)	27	0.06
Danish (209)	511	1.05
Dutch (360)	930	1.92
Eastern European (143)	143	0.29
English (2,304)	7,343	15.13
European (427)	549	1.13
Finnish (17)	32	0.07
French, ex. Basque (347)	1,607	3.31
French Canadian (227)	369	0.76
German (2,217)	7,617	15.69
Greek (157)	290	0.60
Hungarian (379)	662	1.36
Icelander (18)	18	0.04
Iranian (120)	120	0.25
Irish (2,510)	6,379	13.14
Israeli (39)	39	0.08
Italian (1,323)	2,455	5.06
Lithuanian (25)	39	0.08
Luxemburger (0)	13	0.03
Northern European (38)	38	0.08
Norwegian (403)	1,151	2.37
Pennsylvania German (10)	57	0.12
Polish (390)	889	1.83
Portuguese (111)	287	0.59
Romanian (24)	157	0.32
Russian (714)	1,218	2.51
Scandinavian (73)	104	0.21
Scotch-Irish (627)	1,433	2.95
Scottish (483)	1,542	3.18
Slavic (35)	35	0.07
Slovak (75)	75	0.15
Slovene (10)	24	0.05
Swedish (340)	1,174	2.42
Swiss (49)	198	0.41
Turkish (33)	46	0.09
Ukrainian (77)	145	0.30
Welsh (277)	843	1.74
Yugoslavian (45)	83	0.17

Hispanic Origin	Population	%
Hispanic or Latino (of any race)	11,038	22.78
Central American, ex. Mexican	542	1.12
Costa Rican	6	0.01
Guatemalan	108	0.22
Honduran	46	0.09
Nicaraguan	99	0.20
Panamanian	10	0.02
Salvadoran	267	0.55
Other Central American	6	0.01
Cuban	111	0.23
Dominican Republic	20	0.04
Mexican	9,147	18.88
Puerto Rican	152	0.31
South American	330	0.68
Argentinean	35	0.07
Bolivian	4	0.01
Chilean	28	0.06
Colombian	106	0.22
Ecuadorian	27	0.06
Peruvian	110	0.23
Venezuelan	15	0.03
Other South American	5	0.01
Other Hispanic or Latino	736	1.52

Race*	Population	%
African-American/Black (875)	1,124	2.32
Not Hispanic (782)	962	1.99
Hispanic (93)	162	0.33
American Indian/Alaska Native (249)	492	1.02
Not Hispanic (143)	313	0.65
Hispanic (106)	179	0.37
Aleut *(Alaska Native)* (0)	1	<0.01
Apache (10)	24	0.05
Blackfeet (1)	10	0.02
Canadian/French Am. Ind. (1)	1	<0.01
Cherokee (10)	74	0.15
Cheyenne (2)	2	<0.01
Chickasaw (1)	3	0.01
Chippewa (3)	10	0.02
Choctaw (2)	13	0.03
Comanche (0)	6	0.01
Creek (7)	10	0.02
Delaware (1)	2	<0.01
Iroquois (1)	3	0.01
Kiowa (0)	1	<0.01
Lumbee (1)	3	0.01
Mexican American Ind. (21)	34	0.07
Navajo (5)	11	0.02
Paiute (2)	2	<0.01
Pima (1)	1	<0.01
Potawatomi (1)	4	0.01
Pueblo (6)	9	0.02
Puget Sound Salish (3)	4	0.01
Seminole (1)	2	<0.01
Shoshone (2)	2	<0.01
Sioux (4)	11	0.02
South American Ind. (1)	2	<0.01
Tlingit-Haida *(Alaska Native)* (1)	1	<0.01
Yaqui (8)	9	0.02
Yuman (1)	1	<0.01
Asian (1,647)	2,050	4.23
Not Hispanic (1,587)	1,919	3.96
Hispanic (60)	131	0.27
Bangladeshi (3)	3	0.01
Bhutanese (1)	1	<0.01
Burmese (8)	11	0.02
Cambodian (14)	14	0.03
Chinese, ex. Taiwanese (272)	337	0.70
Filipino (459)	617	1.27
Hmong (2)	2	<0.01
Indian (139)	168	0.35
Indonesian (12)	39	0.08
Japanese (177)	261	0.54
Korean (211)	237	0.49
Laotian (2)	3	0.01
Malaysian (0)	4	0.01
Nepalese (2)	2	<0.01
Pakistani (16)	25	0.05
Sri Lankan (14)	14	0.03

*Notes: † The Census 2010 population figure is used to calculate the percentages in the Hispanic Origin and Race categories. Ancestry percentages are based on the 2006-2010 American Community Survey population (not shown); ‡ Numbers in parentheses indicate the number of people reporting a single ancestry; * Numbers in parentheses indicate the number of persons reporting this race alone, not in combination with any other race; Please refer to the Explanation of Data for more information.*

Taiwanese (23)	25	0.05
Thai (30)	35	0.07
Vietnamese (206)	221	0.46
Hawaii Native/Pacific Islander (55)	148	0.31
Not Hispanic (49)	121	0.25
Hispanic (6)	27	0.06
Fijian (1)	1	<0.01
Guamanian/Chamorro (4)	12	0.02
Native Hawaiian (21)	57	0.12
Samoan (8)	16	0.03
Tongan (4)	4	0.01
White (39,957)	41,038	84.71
Not Hispanic (34,115)	34,700	71.63
Hispanic (5,842)	6,338	13.08

Palm Springs

Place Type: City
County: Riverside
Population: 44,552†

Ancestry‡	Population	%
Afghan (8)	8	0.02
African, Sub-Saharan (97)	108	0.24
African (67)	78	0.17
Liberian (3)	3	0.01
Senegalese (7)	7	0.02
South African (20)	20	0.04
American (1,057)	1,057	2.35
Arab (82)	127	0.28
Arab (30)	30	0.07
Egyptian (10)	10	0.02
Jordanian (10)	10	0.02
Lebanese (14)	38	0.08
Moroccan (6)	6	0.01
Palestinian (0)	10	0.02
Syrian (4)	9	0.02
Other Arab (8)	14	0.03
Armenian (132)	153	0.34
Australian (4)	16	0.04
Austrian (107)	349	0.78
Basque (17)	46	0.10
Belgian (43)	96	0.21
Brazilian (3)	10	0.02
British (158)	215	0.48
Bulgarian (6)	28	0.06
Cajun (4)	4	0.01
Canadian (218)	290	0.64
Celtic (2)	2	<0.01
Croatian (40)	65	0.14
Czech (54)	198	0.44
Czechoslovakian (33)	48	0.11
Danish (131)	265	0.59
Dutch (271)	711	1.58
Eastern European (45)	47	0.10
English (1,864)	5,821	12.93
Estonian (5)	7	0.02
European (400)	418	0.93
Finnish (66)	123	0.27
French, ex. Basque (308)	1,633	3.63
French Canadian (187)	354	0.79
German (2,018)	6,138	13.64
Greek (202)	271	0.60
Guyanese (13)	13	0.03
Hungarian (190)	399	0.89
Icelander (5)	9	0.02
Iranian (139)	149	0.33
Irish (1,540)	5,051	11.22
Israeli (37)	37	0.08
Italian (1,361)	2,601	5.78
Latvian (0)	2	<0.01
Lithuanian (111)	212	0.47
Luxemburger (15)	15	0.03
Macedonian (13)	13	0.03
New Zealander (0)	2	<0.01
Northern European (30)	30	0.07
Norwegian (482)	1,086	2.41
Pennsylvania German (20)	37	0.08
Polish (518)	1,084	2.41
Portuguese (129)	290	0.64
Romanian (55)	157	0.35
Russian (373)	813	1.81
Scandinavian (83)	121	0.27
Scotch-Irish (579)	972	2.16
Scottish (500)	1,193	2.65
Serbian (11)	14	0.03
Slavic (43)	45	0.10
Slovak (27)	86	0.19
Slovene (10)	12	0.03
Swedish (395)	1,174	2.61
Swiss (78)	189	0.42
Turkish (3)	29	0.06
Ukrainian (64)	118	0.26
Welsh (223)	458	1.02
West Indian, ex. Hispanic (2)	6	0.01
Jamaican (2)	2	<0.01
West Indian (0)	4	0.01
Yugoslavian (31)	76	0.17

Hispanic Origin	Population	%
Hispanic or Latino (of any race)	11,286	25.33
Central American, ex. Mexican	634	1.42
Costa Rican	23	0.05
Guatemalan	299	0.67
Honduran	30	0.07
Nicaraguan	46	0.10
Panamanian	6	0.01
Salvadoran	220	0.49
Other Central American	10	0.02
Cuban	127	0.29
Dominican Republic	19	0.04
Mexican	9,144	20.52
Puerto Rican	214	0.48
South American	347	0.78
Argentinean	45	0.10
Bolivian	1	<0.01
Chilean	26	0.06
Colombian	50	0.11
Ecuadorian	26	0.06
Paraguayan	1	<0.01
Peruvian	168	0.38
Uruguayan	6	0.01
Venezuelan	22	0.05
Other South American	2	<0.01
Other Hispanic or Latino	801	1.80

Race*	Population	%
African-American/Black (1,982)	2,329	5.23
Not Hispanic (1,850)	2,101	4.72
Hispanic (132)	228	0.51
American Indian/Alaska Native (467)	858	1.93
Not Hispanic (273)	548	1.23
Hispanic (194)	310	0.70
Apache (9)	18	0.04
Arapaho (1)	1	<0.01
Blackfeet (0)	11	0.02
Canadian/French Am. Ind. (2)	6	0.01
Central American Ind. (2)	3	0.01
Cherokee (33)	125	0.28
Chickasaw (3)	5	0.01
Chippewa (5)	9	0.02
Choctaw (12)	25	0.06
Comanche (2)	6	0.01
Creek (3)	7	0.02
Crow (0)	1	<0.01
Hopi (3)	4	0.01
Iroquois (2)	7	0.02
Lumbee (2)	8	0.02
Mexican American Ind. (49)	66	0.15
Navajo (5)	14	0.03
Pima (0)	4	0.01
Potawatomi (0)	5	0.01
Pueblo (1)	2	<0.01
Puget Sound Salish (1)	2	<0.01
Seminole (2)	3	0.01
Shoshone (1)	1	<0.01
Sioux (8)	13	0.03
South American Ind. (0)	3	0.01
Spanish American Ind. (5)	5	0.01
Tlingit-Haida *(Alaska Native)* (3)	3	0.01
Tohono O'Odham (1)	1	<0.01
Yaqui (10)	16	0.04
Yuman (1)	1	<0.01
Asian (1,971)	2,358	5.29
Not Hispanic (1,917)	2,223	4.99
Hispanic (54)	135	0.30
Burmese (2)	2	<0.01
Cambodian (19)	20	0.04
Chinese, ex. Taiwanese (146)	202	0.45
Filipino (1,258)	1,438	3.23
Hmong (1)	2	<0.01
Indian (126)	167	0.37
Indonesian (12)	14	0.03
Japanese (113)	168	0.38
Korean (64)	85	0.19
Laotian (4)	12	0.03
Malaysian (0)	3	0.01
Nepalese (2)	2	<0.01
Pakistani (9)	10	0.02
Sri Lankan (67)	78	0.18
Taiwanese (7)	10	0.02
Thai (44)	51	0.11
Vietnamese (55)	62	0.14
Hawaii Native/Pacific Islander (71)	158	0.35
Not Hispanic (60)	125	0.28
Hispanic (11)	33	0.07
Fijian (2)	3	0.01
Guamanian/Chamorro (13)	31	0.07
Native Hawaiian (24)	70	0.16
Samoan (10)	13	0.03
Tongan (1)	1	<0.01
White (33,720)	34,867	78.26
Not Hispanic (28,313)	28,979	65.05
Hispanic (5,407)	5,888	13.22

Palmdale

Place Type: City
County: Los Angeles
Population: 152,750†

Ancestry‡	Population	%
African, Sub-Saharan (2,709)	3,168	2.17
African (2,530)	2,924	2.00
Ethiopian (99)	99	0.07
Nigerian (50)	50	0.03
South African (30)	83	0.06
Other Sub-Saharan African (0)	12	0.01
American (2,904)	2,904	1.99
Arab (615)	840	0.57
Arab (80)	137	0.09
Egyptian (277)	277	0.19
Jordanian (66)	66	0.05
Lebanese (64)	204	0.14
Moroccan (10)	28	0.02
Syrian (59)	69	0.05
Other Arab (59)	59	0.04
Armenian (456)	776	0.53
Assyrian/Chaldean/Syriac (26)	26	0.02
Australian (10)	57	0.04
Austrian (0)	29	0.02
Belgian (23)	129	0.09
British (289)	366	0.25
Bulgarian (0)	9	0.01
Canadian (265)	441	0.30
Croatian (16)	90	0.06
Czech (55)	228	0.16
Czechoslovakian (26)	96	0.07
Danish (122)	436	0.30
Dutch (260)	1,408	0.96
Eastern European (61)	101	0.07
English (1,994)	6,570	4.49
European (896)	1,113	0.76
Finnish (47)	140	0.10
French, ex. Basque (295)	1,925	1.32
French Canadian (278)	585	0.40
German (1,873)	8,673	5.93
German Russian (0)	21	0.01
Greek (119)	303	0.21
Hungarian (258)	526	0.36

*Notes: † The Census 2010 population figure is used to calculate the percentages in the Hispanic Origin and Race categories. Ancestry percentages are based on the 2006-2010 American Community Survey population (not shown); ‡ Numbers in parentheses indicate the number of people reporting a single ancestry; * Numbers in parentheses indicate the number of persons reporting this race alone, not in combination with any other race; Please refer to the Explanation of Data for more information.*

Ancestry	Population	%
Icelander (204)	204	0.14
Iranian (294)	321	0.22
Irish (1,648)	7,527	5.15
Israeli (12)	12	0.01
Italian (1,232)	4,553	3.11
Latvian (15)	15	0.01
Macedonian (63)	63	0.04
Maltese (0)	14	0.01
Norwegian (433)	1,327	0.91
Pennsylvania German (12)	12	0.01
Polish (407)	1,434	0.98
Portuguese (83)	188	0.13
Romanian (11)	34	0.02
Russian (355)	882	0.60
Scandinavian (22)	22	0.02
Scotch-Irish (240)	1,169	0.80
Scottish (321)	1,567	1.07
Serbian (0)	9	0.01
Slovak (0)	11	0.01
Slovene (0)	13	0.01
Swedish (297)	1,308	0.89
Swiss (42)	107	0.07
Turkish (35)	35	0.02
Ukrainian (67)	141	0.10
Welsh (30)	558	0.38
West Indian, ex. Hispanic (176)	535	0.37
Belizean (89)	128	0.09
Dutch West Indian (0)	27	0.02
Jamaican (67)	344	0.24
Trinidadian/Tobagonian (20)	20	0.01
West Indian (0)	16	0.01
Yugoslavian (72)	224	0.15

Hispanic Origin	Population	%
Hispanic or Latino (of any race)	83,097	54.40
Central American, ex. Mexican	14,815	9.70
Costa Rican	176	0.12
Guatemalan	3,618	2.37
Honduran	656	0.43
Nicaraguan	650	0.43
Panamanian	124	0.08
Salvadoran	9,488	6.21
Other Central American	103	0.07
Cuban	705	0.46
Dominican Republic	48	0.03
Mexican	58,207	38.11
Puerto Rican	1,138	0.75
South American	1,951	1.28
Argentinean	307	0.20
Bolivian	58	0.04
Chilean	172	0.11
Colombian	385	0.25
Ecuadorian	385	0.25
Peruvian	573	0.38
Uruguayan	22	0.01
Venezuelan	31	0.02
Other South American	18	0.01
Other Hispanic or Latino	6,233	4.08

Race*	Population	%
African-American/Black (22,677)	25,272	16.54
Not Hispanic (21,595)	23,302	15.25
Hispanic (1,082)	1,970	1.29
American Indian/Alaska Native (1,316)	2,842	1.86
Not Hispanic (477)	1,403	0.92
Hispanic (839)	1,439	0.94
Alaska Athabascan *(Ala. Nat.)* (3)	5	<0.01
Apache (52)	121	0.08
Arapaho (0)	1	<0.01
Blackfeet (13)	107	0.07
Canadian/French Am. Ind. (4)	7	<0.01
Central American Ind. (9)	18	0.01
Cherokee (90)	406	0.27
Cheyenne (10)	16	0.01
Chickasaw (13)	21	0.01
Chippewa (8)	23	0.02
Choctaw (26)	97	0.06
Comanche (2)	4	<0.01
Cree (1)	2	<0.01
Creek (9)	34	0.02
Crow (0)	4	<0.01
Delaware (4)	8	0.01
Hopi (11)	23	0.02
Inupiat *(Alaska Native)* (2)	5	<0.01
Iroquois (0)	17	0.01
Kiowa (0)	2	<0.01
Lumbee (2)	7	<0.01
Mexican American Ind. (150)	212	0.14
Navajo (41)	78	0.05
Osage (2)	10	0.01
Ottawa (3)	5	<0.01
Paiute (10)	14	0.01
Pima (2)	4	<0.01
Potawatomi (0)	10	0.01
Pueblo (23)	33	0.02
Puget Sound Salish (0)	2	<0.01
Seminole (1)	11	0.01
Shoshone (1)	6	<0.01
Sioux (22)	49	0.03
South American Ind. (4)	11	0.01
Spanish American Ind. (10)	20	0.01
Tlingit-Haida *(Alaska Native)* (1)	1	<0.01
Tohono O'Odham (15)	19	0.01
Yaqui (38)	51	0.03
Yuman (2)	8	0.01
Asian (6,548)	8,430	5.52
Not Hispanic (6,223)	7,479	4.90
Hispanic (325)	951	0.62
Bangladeshi (32)	38	0.02
Burmese (22)	27	0.02
Cambodian (63)	72	0.05
Chinese, ex. Taiwanese (422)	689	0.45
Filipino (3,394)	4,273	2.80
Hmong (4)	6	<0.01
Indian (621)	779	0.51
Indonesian (48)	106	0.07
Japanese (265)	620	0.41
Korean (609)	776	0.51
Laotian (20)	31	0.02
Malaysian (7)	8	0.01
Nepalese (14)	14	0.01
Pakistani (126)	145	0.09
Sri Lankan (87)	88	0.06
Taiwanese (27)	31	0.02
Thai (130)	172	0.11
Vietnamese (414)	495	0.32
Hawaii Native/Pacific Islander (335)	763	0.50
Not Hispanic (211)	472	0.31
Hispanic (124)	291	0.19
Fijian (13)	14	0.01
Guamanian/Chamorro (97)	155	0.10
Native Hawaiian (85)	240	0.16
Samoan (38)	112	0.07
Tongan (29)	36	0.02
White (74,901)	81,397	53.29
Not Hispanic (37,390)	40,028	26.20
Hispanic (37,511)	41,369	27.08

Palo Alto

Place Type: City
County: Santa Clara
Population: 64,403†

Ancestry‡	Population	%
Afghan (65)	65	0.10
African, Sub-Saharan (408)	642	1.03
African (175)	175	0.28
Cape Verdean (0)	10	0.02
Ethiopian (220)	360	0.58
South African (13)	97	0.16
American (1,058)	1,058	1.69
Arab (265)	680	1.09
Arab (9)	9	0.01
Egyptian (17)	108	0.17
Iraqi (15)	58	0.09
Jordanian (21)	21	0.03
Lebanese (5)	42	0.07
Moroccan (88)	181	0.29
Palestinian (10)	28	0.04
Syrian (22)	50	0.08
Other Arab (78)	183	0.29
Armenian (131)	200	0.32
Assyrian/Chaldean/Syriac (87)	126	0.20
Australian (21)	71	0.11
Austrian (153)	343	0.55
Belgian (97)	141	0.23
Brazilian (63)	73	0.12
British (538)	1,004	1.61
Bulgarian (24)	76	0.12
Cajun (0)	11	0.02
Canadian (262)	324	0.52
Celtic (6)	13	0.02
Croatian (41)	144	0.23
Czech (359)	554	0.89
Czechoslovakian (20)	46	0.07
Danish (187)	546	0.87
Dutch (402)	934	1.49
Eastern European (431)	452	0.72
English (2,149)	7,653	12.25
European (2,509)	2,712	4.34
Finnish (78)	130	0.21
French, ex. Basque (811)	2,308	3.69
French Canadian (95)	239	0.38
German (1,994)	7,260	11.62
Greek (125)	375	0.60
Guyanese (16)	68	0.11
Hungarian (106)	452	0.72
Icelander (0)	11	0.02
Iranian (599)	720	1.15
Irish (988)	4,757	7.61
Israeli (356)	421	0.67
Italian (845)	2,273	3.64
Latvian (36)	49	0.08
Lithuanian (62)	185	0.30
Luxemburger (0)	30	0.05
Macedonian (27)	39	0.06
New Zealander (78)	103	0.16
Northern European (369)	369	0.59
Norwegian (327)	1,072	1.72
Pennsylvania German (0)	19	0.03
Polish (492)	1,629	2.61
Portuguese (126)	364	0.58
Romanian (48)	159	0.25
Russian (1,390)	2,425	3.88
Scandinavian (88)	206	0.33
Scotch-Irish (256)	953	1.53
Scottish (391)	1,822	2.92
Serbian (29)	51	0.08
Slavic (0)	13	0.02
Slovak (16)	38	0.06
Slovene (0)	42	0.07
Soviet Union (0)	9	0.01
Swedish (411)	1,522	2.44
Swiss (187)	490	0.78
Turkish (92)	144	0.23
Ukrainian (341)	563	0.90
Welsh (47)	510	0.82
West Indian, ex. Hispanic (94)	146	0.23
Jamaican (74)	126	0.20
West Indian (20)	20	0.03
Yugoslavian (23)	54	0.09

Hispanic Origin	Population	%
Hispanic or Latino (of any race)	3,974	6.17
Central American, ex. Mexican	414	0.64
Costa Rican	25	0.04
Guatemalan	87	0.14
Honduran	30	0.05
Nicaraguan	51	0.08
Panamanian	17	0.03
Salvadoran	194	0.30
Other Central American	10	0.02
Cuban	82	0.13
Dominican Republic	18	0.03
Mexican	2,265	3.52
Puerto Rican	113	0.18
South American	588	0.91
Argentinean	111	0.17
Bolivian	37	0.06

*Notes: † The Census 2010 population figure is used to calculate the percentages in the Hispanic Origin and Race categories. Ancestry percentages are based on the 2006-2010 American Community Survey population (not shown); ‡ Numbers in parentheses indicate the number of people reporting a single ancestry; * Numbers in parentheses indicate the number of persons reporting this race alone, not in combination with any other race; Please refer to the Explanation of Data for more information.*

Chilean	82	0.13
Colombian	94	0.15
Ecuadorian	37	0.06
Paraguayan	4	0.01
Peruvian	157	0.24
Uruguayan	19	0.03
Venezuelan	44	0.07
Other South American	3	<0.01
Other Hispanic or Latino	494	0.77

Race*	Population	%
African-American/Black (1,197)	1,559	2.42
Not Hispanic (1,131)	1,441	2.24
Hispanic (66)	118	0.18
American Indian/Alaska Native (121)	371	0.58
Not Hispanic (65)	269	0.42
Hispanic (56)	102	0.16
Alaska Athabascan *(Ala. Nat.)* (0)	5	0.01
Aleut *(Alaska Native)* (0)	6	0.01
Apache (5)	6	0.01
Blackfeet (2)	11	0.02
Canadian/French Am. Ind. (0)	1	<0.01
Central American Ind. (2)	7	0.01
Cherokee (7)	68	0.11
Chickasaw (0)	5	0.01
Chippewa (0)	2	<0.01
Choctaw (4)	14	0.02
Comanche (1)	1	<0.01
Cree (1)	2	<0.01
Creek (4)	4	0.01
Delaware (0)	2	<0.01
Inupiat *(Alaska Native)* (1)	2	<0.01
Iroquois (1)	4	0.01
Mexican American Ind. (15)	26	0.04
Navajo (4)	11	0.02
Osage (0)	1	<0.01
Ottawa (0)	1	<0.01
Paiute (0)	4	0.01
Potawatomi (0)	6	0.01
Seminole (1)	1	<0.01
Sioux (2)	7	0.01
South American Ind. (2)	3	<0.01
Spanish American Ind. (1)	1	<0.01
Tlingit-Haida *(Alaska Native)* (5)	6	0.01
Tohono O'Odham (0)	1	<0.01
Ute (1)	1	<0.01
Yaqui (1)	2	<0.01
Yuman (1)	1	<0.01
Yup'ik *(Alaska Native)* (0)	1	<0.01
Asian (17,461)	19,492	30.27
Not Hispanic (17,404)	19,336	30.02
Hispanic (57)	156	0.24
Bangladeshi (10)	17	0.03
Burmese (20)	26	0.04
Cambodian (18)	26	0.04
Chinese, ex. Taiwanese (8,695)	9,739	15.12
Filipino (581)	852	1.32
Indian (2,776)	3,099	4.81
Indonesian (44)	58	0.09
Japanese (1,319)	1,831	2.84
Korean (1,791)	1,978	3.07
Laotian (8)	14	0.02
Malaysian (5)	29	0.05
Nepalese (18)	21	0.03
Pakistani (159)	200	0.31
Sri Lankan (32)	43	0.07
Taiwanese (946)	1,061	1.65
Thai (109)	135	0.21
Vietnamese (401)	514	0.80
Hawaii Native/Pacific Islander (142)	295	0.46
Not Hispanic (135)	272	0.42
Hispanic (7)	23	0.04
Fijian (13)	16	0.02
Guamanian/Chamorro (12)	25	0.04
Native Hawaiian (16)	80	0.12
Samoan (20)	27	0.04
Tongan (68)	85	0.13
White (41,359)	43,815	68.03
Not Hispanic (39,052)	41,247	64.05
Hispanic (2,307)	2,568	3.99

Palos Verdes Estates

Place Type: City
County: Los Angeles
Population: 13,438†

Ancestry‡	Population	%
African, Sub-Saharan (21)	21	0.16
Nigerian (21)	21	0.16
Albanian (0)	13	0.10
American (668)	668	4.98
Arab (0)	43	0.32
Egyptian (0)	30	0.22
Lebanese (0)	13	0.10
Armenian (171)	247	1.84
Austrian (11)	34	0.25
Basque (13)	13	0.10
Belgian (0)	50	0.37
Brazilian (0)	9	0.07
British (71)	184	1.37
Bulgarian (42)	42	0.31
Canadian (0)	8	0.06
Celtic (15)	15	0.11
Croatian (21)	33	0.25
Czech (0)	41	0.31
Danish (21)	220	1.64
Dutch (66)	174	1.30
Eastern European (50)	50	0.37
English (699)	2,029	15.14
European (295)	295	2.20
Finnish (0)	43	0.32
French, ex. Basque (48)	395	2.95
French Canadian (0)	123	0.92
German (386)	1,868	13.93
Greek (82)	172	1.28
Hungarian (64)	140	1.04
Iranian (82)	82	0.61
Irish (385)	1,433	10.69
Italian (356)	1,029	7.68
Lithuanian (0)	58	0.43
Northern European (127)	139	1.04
Norwegian (61)	202	1.51
Polish (81)	308	2.30
Portuguese (0)	22	0.16
Romanian (15)	15	0.11
Russian (124)	300	2.24
Scandinavian (46)	46	0.34
Scotch-Irish (74)	274	2.04
Scottish (124)	495	3.69
Slavic (0)	13	0.10
Slovak (41)	207	1.54
Swedish (164)	498	3.71
Swiss (16)	108	0.81
Ukrainian (10)	36	0.27
Welsh (62)	311	2.32
West Indian, ex. Hispanic (0)	12	0.09
Barbadian (0)	12	0.09
Yugoslavian (39)	64	0.48

Hispanic Origin	Population	%
Hispanic or Latino (of any race)	631	4.70
Central American, ex. Mexican	43	0.32
Costa Rican	7	0.05
Guatemalan	10	0.07
Honduran	1	0.01
Nicaraguan	7	0.05
Panamanian	1	0.01
Salvadoran	17	0.13
Cuban	30	0.22
Dominican Republic	2	0.01
Mexican	351	2.61
Puerto Rican	20	0.15
South American	107	0.80
Argentinean	30	0.22
Chilean	7	0.05
Colombian	7	0.05
Ecuadorian	24	0.18
Peruvian	36	0.27
Uruguayan	1	0.01
Venezuelan	2	0.01
Other Hispanic or Latino	78	0.58

Race*	Population	%
African-American/Black (161)	193	1.44
Not Hispanic (156)	182	1.35
Hispanic (5)	11	0.08
American Indian/Alaska Native (21)	61	0.45
Not Hispanic (14)	51	0.38
Hispanic (7)	10	0.07
Alaska Athabascan *(Ala. Nat.)* (2)	2	0.01
Apache (1)	2	0.01
Canadian/French Am. Ind. (0)	1	0.01
Cherokee (5)	14	0.10
Chickasaw (0)	1	0.01
Chippewa (1)	2	0.01
Choctaw (1)	3	0.02
Mexican American Ind. (0)	1	0.01
Paiute (0)	1	0.01
Sioux (0)	1	0.01
Yaqui (1)	3	0.02
Yuman (1)	1	0.01
Asian (2,322)	2,705	20.13
Not Hispanic (2,306)	2,669	19.86
Hispanic (16)	36	0.27
Burmese (1)	1	0.01
Cambodian (2)	3	0.02
Chinese, ex. Taiwanese (632)	768	5.72
Filipino (139)	201	1.50
Indian (241)	270	2.01
Indonesian (3)	5	0.04
Japanese (484)	634	4.72
Korean (428)	471	3.50
Nepalese (1)	2	0.01
Pakistani (14)	14	0.10
Sri Lankan (4)	7	0.05
Taiwanese (219)	246	1.83
Thai (11)	13	0.10
Vietnamese (53)	73	0.54
Hawaii Native/Pacific Islander (8)	52	0.39
Not Hispanic (8)	50	0.37
Hispanic (0)	2	0.01
Fijian (1)	1	0.01
Guamanian/Chamorro (4)	8	0.06
Native Hawaiian (0)	13	0.10
Samoan (1)	5	0.04
White (10,346)	10,789	80.29
Not Hispanic (9,868)	10,265	76.39
Hispanic (478)	524	3.90

Paradise

Place Type: Town
County: Butte
Population: 26,218†

Ancestry‡	Population	%
American (1,772)	1,772	6.71
Arab (21)	21	0.08
Arab (21)	21	0.08
Armenian (0)	15	0.06
Austrian (55)	145	0.55
Belgian (0)	79	0.30
Brazilian (0)	24	0.09
British (187)	220	0.83
Canadian (35)	265	1.00
Croatian (17)	17	0.06
Czech (44)	254	0.96
Czechoslovakian (18)	18	0.07
Danish (122)	731	2.77
Dutch (100)	753	2.85
English (1,036)	4,780	18.09
European (374)	389	1.47
Finnish (19)	63	0.24
French, ex. Basque (155)	1,246	4.72
French Canadian (79)	156	0.59
German (1,721)	6,197	23.45
Greek (31)	68	0.26
Hungarian (17)	119	0.45
Iranian (60)	60	0.23
Irish (1,094)	4,022	15.22

*Notes: † The Census 2010 population figure is used to calculate the percentages in the Hispanic Origin and Race categories. Ancestry percentages are based on the 2006-2010 American Community Survey population (not shown); ‡ Numbers in parentheses indicate the number of people reporting a single ancestry; * Numbers in parentheses indicate the number of persons reporting this race alone, not in combination with any other race; Please refer to the Explanation of Data for more information.*

Italian (450)	1,416	5.36
Latvian (14)	26	0.10
Lithuanian (0)	11	0.04
Luxemburger (12)	12	0.05
Northern European (178)	178	0.67
Norwegian (207)	716	2.71
Pennsylvania German (11)	11	0.04
Polish (10)	280	1.06
Portuguese (245)	687	2.60
Romanian (29)	29	0.11
Russian (119)	251	0.95
Scandinavian (95)	281	1.06
Scotch-Irish (387)	1,238	4.68
Scottish (168)	730	2.76
Slovak (0)	53	0.20
Slovene (0)	15	0.06
Swedish (138)	720	2.72
Swiss (40)	149	0.56
Ukrainian (25)	78	0.30
Welsh (22)	300	1.14
Yugoslavian (28)	54	0.20

Hispanic Origin	Population	%
Hispanic or Latino (of any race)	1,836	7.00
Central American, ex. Mexican	73	0.28
Costa Rican	5	0.02
Guatemalan	2	0.01
Honduran	3	0.01
Nicaraguan	16	0.06
Panamanian	3	0.01
Salvadoran	44	0.17
Cuban	17	0.06
Mexican	1,357	5.18
Puerto Rican	60	0.23
South American	54	0.21
Argentinean	9	0.03
Bolivian	10	0.04
Chilean	5	0.02
Colombian	7	0.03
Ecuadorian	7	0.03
Peruvian	13	0.05
Uruguayan	1	<0.01
Venezuelan	1	<0.01
Other South American	1	<0.01
Other Hispanic or Latino	275	1.05

Race*	Population	%
African-American/Black (112)	211	0.80
Not Hispanic (98)	182	0.69
Hispanic (14)	29	0.11
American Indian/Alaska Native (301)	822	3.14
Not Hispanic (239)	655	2.50
Hispanic (62)	167	0.64
Alaska Athabascan *(Ala. Nat.)* (2)	2	0.01
Apache (14)	33	0.13
Arapaho (1)	3	0.01
Blackfeet (5)	31	0.12
Canadian/French Am. Ind. (1)	3	0.01
Cherokee (57)	202	0.77
Cheyenne (0)	3	0.01
Chippewa (11)	14	0.05
Choctaw (12)	55	0.21
Comanche (0)	1	<0.01
Cree (1)	1	<0.01
Creek (3)	3	0.01
Crow (1)	5	0.02
Delaware (0)	1	<0.01
Hopi (0)	1	<0.01
Houma (6)	6	0.02
Inupiat *(Alaska Native)* (3)	6	0.02
Iroquois (0)	6	0.02
Lumbee (1)	2	0.01
Mexican American Ind. (4)	27	0.10
Navajo (1)	7	0.03
Osage (1)	3	0.01
Ottawa (1)	2	0.01
Paiute (0)	2	0.01
Pima (0)	5	0.02
Potawatomi (2)	4	0.02
Pueblo (2)	3	0.01
Puget Sound Salish (0)	1	<0.01
Seminole (1)	3	0.01
Shoshone (8)	8	0.03
Sioux (6)	25	0.10
Spanish American Ind. (1)	2	0.01
Tlingit-Haida *(Alaska Native)* (0)	2	0.01
Tohono O'Odham (1)	1	<0.01
Yaqui (5)	8	0.03
Asian (330)	520	1.98
Not Hispanic (317)	476	1.82
Hispanic (13)	44	0.17
Burmese (3)	3	0.01
Cambodian (5)	6	0.02
Chinese, ex. Taiwanese (70)	90	0.34
Filipino (80)	172	0.66
Hmong (1)	1	<0.01
Indian (23)	34	0.13
Indonesian (2)	5	0.02
Japanese (47)	105	0.40
Korean (56)	65	0.25
Laotian (7)	8	0.03
Malaysian (0)	3	0.01
Sri Lankan (0)	1	<0.01
Thai (6)	8	0.03
Vietnamese (18)	31	0.12
Hawaii Native/Pacific Islander (24)	90	0.34
Not Hispanic (22)	79	0.30
Hispanic (2)	11	0.04
Fijian (0)	1	<0.01
Guamanian/Chamorro (4)	14	0.05
Native Hawaiian (16)	48	0.18
Samoan (0)	2	0.01
White (24,129)	24,997	95.34
Not Hispanic (23,004)	23,666	90.27
Hispanic (1,125)	1,331	5.08

Paramount

Place Type: City
County: Los Angeles
Population: 54,098†

Ancestry‡	Population	%
African, Sub-Saharan (363)	407	0.75
African (222)	266	0.49
Ethiopian (141)	141	0.26
American (672)	672	1.24
Arab (397)	431	0.80
Egyptian (364)	364	0.67
Lebanese (33)	46	0.08
Palestinian (0)	21	0.04
Armenian (30)	30	0.06
Australian (0)	26	0.05
British (10)	21	0.04
Czech (0)	47	0.09
Danish (45)	84	0.16
Dutch (21)	129	0.24
English (87)	337	0.62
European (29)	174	0.32
French, ex. Basque (26)	281	0.52
French Canadian (10)	30	0.06
German (337)	1,101	2.03
German Russian (0)	13	0.02
Hungarian (44)	66	0.12
Iranian (8)	8	0.01
Irish (208)	643	1.19
Israeli (53)	53	0.10
Italian (202)	596	1.10
Norwegian (30)	67	0.12
Polish (80)	190	0.35
Portuguese (20)	20	0.04
Scotch-Irish (10)	69	0.13
Scottish (11)	128	0.24
Serbian (0)	14	0.03
Swedish (10)	32	0.06
Welsh (0)	86	0.16
West Indian, ex. Hispanic (167)	197	0.36
Belizean (58)	77	0.14
Jamaican (109)	109	0.20
Trinidadian/Tobagonian (0)	11	0.02
Yugoslavian (0)	9	0.02

Hispanic Origin	Population	%
Hispanic or Latino (of any race)	42,547	78.65
Central American, ex. Mexican	2,962	5.48
Costa Rican	32	0.06
Guatemalan	943	1.74
Honduran	206	0.38
Nicaraguan	249	0.46
Panamanian	38	0.07
Salvadoran	1,463	2.70
Other Central American	31	0.06
Cuban	133	0.25
Dominican Republic	29	0.05
Mexican	37,077	68.54
Puerto Rican	234	0.43
South American	426	0.79
Argentinean	24	0.04
Bolivian	10	0.02
Chilean	22	0.04
Colombian	90	0.17
Ecuadorian	95	0.18
Paraguayan	3	0.01
Peruvian	169	0.31
Uruguayan	6	0.01
Venezuelan	7	0.01
Other Hispanic or Latino	1,686	3.12

Race*	Population	%
African-American/Black (6,334)	6,748	12.47
Not Hispanic (5,980)	6,230	11.52
Hispanic (354)	518	0.96
American Indian/Alaska Native (440)	716	1.32
Not Hispanic (86)	211	0.39
Hispanic (354)	505	0.93
Apache (10)	19	0.04
Blackfeet (0)	10	0.02
Central American Ind. (5)	13	0.02
Cherokee (7)	25	0.05
Cheyenne (0)	2	<0.01
Chickasaw (0)	2	<0.01
Chippewa (1)	8	0.01
Choctaw (0)	8	0.01
Comanche (3)	3	0.01
Creek (2)	3	0.01
Crow (0)	1	<0.01
Iroquois (2)	4	0.01
Lumbee (1)	1	<0.01
Mexican American Ind. (90)	159	0.29
Navajo (13)	16	0.03
Paiute (2)	2	<0.01
Pueblo (4)	6	0.01
Seminole (0)	3	0.01
Sioux (4)	7	0.01
South American Ind. (1)	7	0.01
Spanish American Ind. (5)	6	0.01
Tohono O'Odham (0)	1	<0.01
Yaqui (1)	7	0.01
Yuman (0)	3	0.01
Asian (1,629)	1,999	3.70
Not Hispanic (1,531)	1,727	3.19
Hispanic (98)	272	0.50
Bangladeshi (9)	15	0.03
Cambodian (249)	275	0.51
Chinese, ex. Taiwanese (69)	123	0.23
Filipino (731)	859	1.59
Hmong (8)	8	0.01
Indian (113)	146	0.27
Indonesian (5)	10	0.02
Japanese (63)	114	0.21
Korean (100)	114	0.21
Laotian (20)	26	0.05
Nepalese (2)	3	0.01
Pakistani (28)	33	0.06
Sri Lankan (4)	4	0.01
Taiwanese (0)	3	0.01
Thai (88)	115	0.21
Vietnamese (54)	63	0.12
Hawaii Native/Pacific Islander (419)	574	1.06
Not Hispanic (396)	508	0.94

*Notes: † The Census 2010 population figure is used to calculate the percentages in the Hispanic Origin and Race categories. Ancestry percentages are based on the 2006-2010 American Community Survey population (not shown); ‡ Numbers in parentheses indicate the number of people reporting a single ancestry; * Numbers in parentheses indicate the number of persons reporting this race alone, not in combination with any other race; Please refer to the Explanation of Data for more information.*

Hispanic (23)	66	0.12
Fijian (6)	7	0.01
Guamanian/Chamorro (38)	53	0.10
Native Hawaiian (14)	47	0.09
Samoan (318)	360	0.67
Tongan (15)	23	0.04
White (22,988)	24,788	45.82
Not Hispanic (3,015)	3,295	6.09
Hispanic (19,973)	21,493	39.73

Parkway

Place Type: CDP
County: Sacramento
Population: 14,670†

Ancestry‡	Population	%
Afghan (19)	19	0.13
African, Sub-Saharan (14)	72	0.51
African (14)	40	0.28
Ethiopian (0)	17	0.12
Sierra Leonean (0)	15	0.11
American (167)	167	1.18
Arab (13)	96	0.68
Arab (13)	39	0.28
Lebanese (0)	57	0.40
Armenian (14)	14	0.10
Assyrian/Chaldean/Syriac (0)	8	0.06
Austrian (8)	15	0.11
British (0)	8	0.06
Canadian (37)	52	0.37
Czech (0)	19	0.13
Czechoslovakian (15)	15	0.11
Danish (18)	42	0.30
Dutch (32)	108	0.76
English (238)	560	3.96
European (68)	82	0.58
Finnish (8)	18	0.13
French, ex. Basque (9)	193	1.36
French Canadian (0)	67	0.47
German (205)	770	5.44
Hungarian (66)	82	0.58
Irish (50)	514	3.63
Italian (207)	416	2.94
Lithuanian (12)	38	0.27
Norwegian (22)	39	0.28
Polish (9)	37	0.26
Portuguese (59)	189	1.34
Russian (15)	36	0.25
Scandinavian (7)	28	0.20
Scotch-Irish (38)	82	0.58
Scottish (31)	129	0.91
Swedish (47)	115	0.81
Swiss (9)	18	0.13
Ukrainian (14)	40	0.28
Welsh (9)	54	0.38

Hispanic Origin	Population	%
Hispanic or Latino (of any race)	6,185	42.16
Central American, ex. Mexican	236	1.61
Costa Rican	6	0.04
Guatemalan	81	0.55
Honduran	15	0.10
Nicaraguan	27	0.18
Panamanian	9	0.06
Salvadoran	95	0.65
Other Central American	3	0.02
Cuban	9	0.06
Dominican Republic	1	0.01
Mexican	5,534	37.72
Puerto Rican	129	0.88
South American	18	0.12
Argentinean	3	0.02
Chilean	4	0.03
Colombian	4	0.03
Peruvian	5	0.03
Venezuelan	2	0.01
Other Hispanic or Latino	258	1.76

Race*	Population	%
African-American/Black (2,696)	3,157	21.52
Not Hispanic (2,546)	2,889	19.69
Hispanic (150)	268	1.83
American Indian/Alaska Native (182)	522	3.56
Not Hispanic (69)	288	1.96
Hispanic (113)	234	1.60
Apache (4)	21	0.14
Blackfeet (3)	32	0.22
Central American Ind. (4)	6	0.04
Cherokee (7)	100	0.68
Chickasaw (0)	2	0.01
Chippewa (4)	4	0.03
Choctaw (3)	29	0.20
Cree (1)	1	0.01
Creek (0)	1	0.01
Iroquois (0)	5	0.03
Mexican American Ind. (6)	12	0.08
Navajo (8)	12	0.08
Osage (0)	2	0.01
Paiute (4)	4	0.03
Pueblo (0)	2	0.01
Seminole (0)	8	0.05
Shoshone (0)	3	0.02
Sioux (5)	9	0.06
South American Ind. (1)	2	0.01
Tlingit-Haida *(Alaska Native)* (0)	4	0.03
Tohono O'Odham (1)	1	0.01
Tsimshian *(Alaska Native)* (1)	1	0.01
Yakama (3)	4	0.03
Yaqui (1)	2	0.01
Asian (1,997)	2,322	15.83
Not Hispanic (1,915)	2,153	14.68
Hispanic (82)	169	1.15
Burmese (2)	2	0.01
Cambodian (72)	91	0.62
Chinese, ex. Taiwanese (225)	273	1.86
Filipino (287)	420	2.86
Hmong (733)	779	5.31
Indian (75)	135	0.92
Indonesian (5)	6	0.04
Japanese (71)	109	0.74
Korean (8)	18	0.12
Laotian (155)	190	1.30
Pakistani (13)	19	0.13
Taiwanese (4)	4	0.03
Thai (2)	7	0.05
Vietnamese (266)	302	2.06
Hawaii Native/Pacific Islander (300)	400	2.73
Not Hispanic (289)	371	2.53
Hispanic (11)	29	0.20
Fijian (80)	94	0.64
Guamanian/Chamorro (8)	20	0.14
Marshallese (160)	161	1.10
Native Hawaiian (12)	29	0.20
Samoan (11)	18	0.12
Tongan (18)	23	0.16
White (5,225)	5,987	40.81
Not Hispanic (3,033)	3,413	23.27
Hispanic (2,192)	2,574	17.55

Parlier

Place Type: City
County: Fresno
Population: 14,494†

Ancestry‡	Population	%
American (112)	112	0.80
English (17)	25	0.18
European (0)	10	0.07
French, ex. Basque (0)	51	0.37
German (42)	117	0.84
Irish (0)	116	0.83
Italian (0)	25	0.18
Polish (0)	9	0.06

Hispanic Origin	Population	%
Hispanic or Latino (of any race)	14,137	97.54
Central American, ex. Mexican	86	0.59
Costa Rican	1	0.01
Guatemalan	26	0.18
Honduran	4	0.03
Salvadoran	55	0.38
Cuban	2	0.01
Mexican	13,445	92.76
Puerto Rican	18	0.12
South American	1	0.01
Paraguayan	1	0.01
Other Hispanic or Latino	585	4.04

Race*	Population	%
African-American/Black (85)	122	0.84
Not Hispanic (14)	23	0.16
Hispanic (71)	99	0.68
American Indian/Alaska Native (180)	224	1.55
Not Hispanic (15)	15	0.10
Hispanic (165)	209	1.44
Apache (0)	2	0.01
Central American Ind. (2)	2	0.01
Cherokee (0)	10	0.07
Choctaw (2)	7	0.05
Creek (1)	1	0.01
Iroquois (1)	1	0.01
Mexican American Ind. (50)	55	0.38
Navajo (3)	3	0.02
Yaqui (2)	5	0.03
Asian (77)	127	0.88
Not Hispanic (46)	51	0.35
Hispanic (31)	76	0.52
Chinese, ex. Taiwanese (1)	5	0.03
Filipino (32)	47	0.32
Hmong (1)	1	0.01
Indian (10)	13	0.09
Japanese (28)	31	0.21
Laotian (0)	1	0.01
Vietnamese (0)	4	0.03
Hawaii Native/Pacific Islander (9)	33	0.23
Not Hispanic (4)	7	0.05
Hispanic (5)	26	0.18
Guamanian/Chamorro (1)	2	0.01
Native Hawaiian (0)	1	0.01
Samoan (0)	1	0.01
White (7,251)	7,679	52.98
Not Hispanic (242)	260	1.79
Hispanic (7,009)	7,419	51.19

Pasadena

Place Type: City
County: Los Angeles
Population: 137,122†

Ancestry‡	Population	%
African, Sub-Saharan (757)	900	0.66
African (506)	616	0.45
Ethiopian (116)	116	0.09
Kenyan (11)	11	0.01
Nigerian (19)	37	0.03
South African (0)	15	0.01
Zimbabwean (105)	105	0.08
American (1,965)	1,965	1.44
Arab (1,410)	2,003	1.47
Arab (170)	383	0.28
Egyptian (98)	98	0.07
Jordanian (325)	356	0.26
Lebanese (254)	467	0.34
Palestinian (73)	79	0.06
Syrian (333)	428	0.31
Other Arab (157)	192	0.14
Armenian (4,606)	5,017	3.68
Australian (0)	43	0.03
Austrian (104)	383	0.28
Basque (0)	72	0.05
Belgian (36)	134	0.10
Brazilian (108)	176	0.13
British (365)	812	0.60
Bulgarian (116)	116	0.09
Cajun (6)	6	<0.01
Canadian (15)	134	0.10

*Notes: † The Census 2010 population figure is used to calculate the percentages in the Hispanic Origin and Race categories. Ancestry percentages are based on the 2006-2010 American Community Survey population (not shown); ‡ Numbers in parentheses indicate the number of people reporting a single ancestry; * Numbers in parentheses indicate the number of persons reporting this race alone, not in combination with any other race; Please refer to the Explanation of Data for more information.*

Celtic (21)	37	0.03
Croatian (40)	77	0.06
Czech (30)	217	0.16
Czechoslovakian (11)	45	0.03
Danish (187)	569	0.42
Dutch (454)	1,370	1.00
Eastern European (144)	168	0.12
English (2,727)	9,624	7.05
Estonian (0)	27	0.02
European (1,322)	1,616	1.18
Finnish (87)	280	0.21
French, ex. Basque (508)	3,027	2.22
French Canadian (84)	389	0.29
German (2,679)	9,864	7.23
Greek (279)	709	0.52
Guyanese (36)	36	0.03
Hungarian (179)	558	0.41
Icelander (23)	31	0.02
Iranian (519)	573	0.42
Irish (2,776)	8,963	6.57
Israeli (25)	31	0.02
Italian (1,654)	5,139	3.77
Latvian (24)	24	0.02
Lithuanian (58)	192	0.14
Luxemburger (37)	37	0.03
Maltese (9)	29	0.02
New Zealander (15)	15	0.01
Northern European (229)	242	0.18
Norwegian (310)	1,113	0.82
Polish (761)	2,127	1.56
Portuguese (13)	129	0.09
Romanian (434)	517	0.38
Russian (597)	1,461	1.07
Scandinavian (149)	307	0.22
Scotch-Irish (600)	1,644	1.20
Scottish (640)	2,177	1.60
Serbian (29)	62	0.05
Slavic (26)	49	0.04
Slovak (45)	90	0.07
Slovene (20)	101	0.07
Swedish (339)	1,383	1.01
Swiss (70)	494	0.36
Turkish (10)	21	0.02
Ukrainian (103)	298	0.22
Welsh (104)	726	0.53
West Indian, ex. Hispanic (136)	159	0.12
Barbadian (14)	14	0.01
Belizean (23)	23	0.02
Bermudan (8)	8	0.01
Dutch West Indian (0)	6	<0.01
Haitian (16)	16	0.01
Jamaican (73)	90	0.07
West Indian (2)	2	<0.01
Yugoslavian (85)	108	0.08

Hispanic Origin	Population	%
Hispanic or Latino (of any race)	46,174	33.67
Central American, ex. Mexican	5,724	4.17
Costa Rican	178	0.13
Guatemalan	1,367	1.00
Honduran	897	0.65
Nicaraguan	357	0.26
Panamanian	170	0.12
Salvadoran	2,689	1.96
Other Central American	66	0.05
Cuban	627	0.46
Dominican Republic	48	0.04
Mexican	34,168	24.92
Puerto Rican	624	0.46
South American	2,283	1.66
Argentinean	404	0.29
Bolivian	101	0.07
Chilean	171	0.12
Colombian	540	0.39
Ecuadorian	334	0.24
Paraguayan	4	<0.01
Peruvian	584	0.43
Uruguayan	15	0.01
Venezuelan	100	0.07
Other South American	30	0.02
Other Hispanic or Latino	2,700	1.97

Race*	Population	%
African-American/Black (14,650)	16,498	12.03
Not Hispanic (13,912)	15,192	11.08
Hispanic (738)	1,306	0.95
American Indian/Alaska Native (827)	2,033	1.48
Not Hispanic (211)	874	0.64
Hispanic (616)	1,159	0.85
Aleut *(Alaska Native)* (2)	2	<0.01
Apache (24)	62	0.05
Arapaho (4)	9	0.01
Blackfeet (6)	45	0.03
Canadian/French Am. Ind. (4)	6	<0.01
Central American Ind. (8)	20	0.01
Cherokee (18)	219	0.16
Cheyenne (1)	1	<0.01
Chickasaw (1)	15	0.01
Chippewa (3)	16	0.01
Choctaw (5)	32	0.02
Colville (2)	2	<0.01
Comanche (2)	8	0.01
Cree (1)	8	0.01
Creek (2)	13	0.01
Crow (0)	1	<0.01
Delaware (0)	1	<0.01
Hopi (5)	11	0.01
Houma (0)	1	<0.01
Inupiat *(Alaska Native)* (0)	1	<0.01
Iroquois (3)	13	0.01
Lumbee (0)	1	<0.01
Menominee (0)	3	<0.01
Mexican American Ind. (135)	249	0.18
Navajo (18)	36	0.03
Osage (0)	7	0.01
Ottawa (4)	4	<0.01
Paiute (3)	8	0.01
Pima (8)	17	0.01
Potawatomi (2)	5	<0.01
Pueblo (3)	11	0.01
Puget Sound Salish (0)	3	<0.01
Seminole (0)	12	0.01
Shoshone (3)	5	<0.01
Sioux (15)	30	0.02
South American Ind. (6)	23	0.02
Spanish American Ind. (11)	26	0.02
Tlingit-Haida *(Alaska Native)* (0)	4	<0.01
Tohono O'Odham (2)	2	<0.01
Ute (1)	3	<0.01
Yaqui (9)	26	0.02
Yuman (5)	8	0.01
Asian (19,595)	22,513	16.42
Not Hispanic (19,293)	21,709	15.83
Hispanic (302)	804	0.59
Bangladeshi (28)	30	0.02
Burmese (42)	58	0.04
Cambodian (36)	63	0.05
Chinese, ex. Taiwanese (6,168)	7,316	5.34
Filipino (3,692)	4,632	3.38
Hmong (1)	2	<0.01
Indian (1,742)	2,008	1.46
Indonesian (230)	325	0.24
Japanese (2,013)	2,808	2.05
Korean (2,709)	3,017	2.20
Laotian (10)	18	0.01
Malaysian (15)	34	0.02
Nepalese (17)	20	0.01
Pakistani (143)	165	0.12
Sri Lankan (169)	182	0.13
Taiwanese (777)	887	0.65
Thai (261)	347	0.25
Vietnamese (632)	812	0.59
Hawaii Native/Pacific Islander (134)	476	0.35
Not Hispanic (106)	387	0.28
Hispanic (28)	89	0.06
Fijian (2)	4	<0.01
Guamanian/Chamorro (21)	47	0.03
Native Hawaiian (50)	180	0.13
Samoan (13)	21	0.02
Tongan (1)	3	<0.01
White (76,550)	81,968	59.78
Not Hispanic (53,135)	56,332	41.08
Hispanic (23,415)	25,636	18.70

Patterson

Place Type: City
County: Stanislaus
Population: 20,413†

Ancestry‡	Population	%
African, Sub-Saharan (92)	92	0.48
African (70)	70	0.37
Somalian (22)	22	0.12
American (115)	115	0.60
Arab (8)	51	0.27
Lebanese (8)	51	0.27
Australian (0)	30	0.16
Basque (8)	19	0.10
Canadian (0)	80	0.42
Danish (0)	65	0.34
Dutch (48)	231	1.21
English (176)	925	4.84
European (93)	129	0.68
Finnish (0)	9	0.05
French, ex. Basque (40)	408	2.14
French Canadian (0)	30	0.16
German (122)	892	4.67
German Russian (0)	33	0.17
Greek (9)	18	0.09
Hungarian (91)	91	0.48
Irish (216)	1,130	5.91
Italian (161)	632	3.31
Luxemburger (0)	13	0.07
Norwegian (20)	133	0.70
Polish (14)	318	1.66
Portuguese (381)	932	4.88
Russian (11)	237	1.24
Scandinavian (9)	21	0.11
Scotch-Irish (38)	147	0.77
Scottish (0)	100	0.52
Swedish (47)	177	0.93
Swiss (15)	41	0.21
Welsh (0)	43	0.23
Yugoslavian (41)	66	0.35

Hispanic Origin	Population	%
Hispanic or Latino (of any race)	11,971	58.64
Central American, ex. Mexican	527	2.58
Costa Rican	10	0.05
Guatemalan	130	0.64
Honduran	25	0.12
Nicaraguan	54	0.26
Panamanian	4	0.02
Salvadoran	304	1.49
Cuban	10	0.05
Dominican Republic	1	<0.01
Mexican	10,510	51.49
Puerto Rican	195	0.96
South American	89	0.44
Argentinean	1	<0.01
Bolivian	1	<0.01
Chilean	7	0.03
Colombian	27	0.13
Ecuadorian	10	0.05
Peruvian	40	0.20
Venezuelan	2	0.01
Other South American	1	<0.01
Other Hispanic or Latino	639	3.13

Race*	Population	%
African-American/Black (1,291)	1,563	7.66
Not Hispanic (1,176)	1,338	6.55
Hispanic (115)	225	1.10
American Indian/Alaska Native (221)	414	2.03
Not Hispanic (91)	190	0.93
Hispanic (130)	224	1.10
Apache (11)	22	0.11
Blackfeet (9)	13	0.06
Canadian/French Am. Ind. (1)	1	<0.01

*Notes: † The Census 2010 population figure is used to calculate the percentages in the Hispanic Origin and Race categories. Ancestry percentages are based on the 2006-2010 American Community Survey population (not shown); ‡ Numbers in parentheses indicate the number of people reporting a single ancestry; * Numbers in parentheses indicate the number of persons reporting this race alone, not in combination with any other race; Please refer to the Explanation of Data for more information.*

Cherokee (21)	65	0.32
Chickasaw (12)	15	0.07
Chippewa (1)	1	<0.01
Choctaw (6)	11	0.05
Creek (2)	2	0.01
Inupiat *(Alaska Native)* (1)	2	0.01
Iroquois (1)	2	0.01
Lumbee (1)	1	<0.01
Mexican American Ind. (12)	20	0.10
Navajo (2)	5	0.02
Osage (0)	1	<0.01
Ottawa (1)	2	0.01
Paiute (5)	10	0.05
Pueblo (0)	2	0.01
Shoshone (4)	4	0.02
Sioux (2)	11	0.05
South American Ind. (6)	8	0.04
Spanish American Ind. (0)	1	<0.01
Tohono O'Odham (2)	2	0.01
Ute (4)	7	0.03
Yaqui (3)	4	0.02
Yuman (0)	3	0.01
Asian (1,069)	1,459	7.15
Not Hispanic (1,000)	1,292	6.33
Hispanic (69)	167	0.82
Bangladeshi (5)	5	0.02
Burmese (2)	5	0.02
Cambodian (50)	64	0.31
Chinese, ex. Taiwanese (104)	150	0.73
Filipino (521)	747	3.66
Indian (171)	199	0.97
Indonesian (5)	6	0.03
Japanese (21)	63	0.31
Korean (31)	56	0.27
Laotian (20)	23	0.11
Pakistani (8)	8	0.04
Taiwanese (2)	2	0.01
Thai (16)	20	0.10
Vietnamese (76)	85	0.42
Hawaii Native/Pacific Islander (280)	419	2.05
Not Hispanic (247)	323	1.58
Hispanic (33)	96	0.47
Fijian (42)	45	0.22
Guamanian/Chamorro (17)	32	0.16
Native Hawaiian (32)	93	0.46
Samoan (111)	139	0.68
Tongan (58)	71	0.35
White (10,117)	11,087	54.31
Not Hispanic (5,346)	5,797	28.40
Hispanic (4,771)	5,290	25.91

Pedley

Place Type: CDP
County: Riverside
Population: 12,672†

Ancestry‡	Population	%
African, Sub-Saharan (16)	16	0.13
African (16)	16	0.13
American (323)	323	2.72
Arab (33)	113	0.95
Lebanese (33)	66	0.55
Syrian (0)	47	0.40
Armenian (0)	24	0.20
Austrian (0)	51	0.43
Basque (42)	59	0.50
Belgian (0)	25	0.21
British (27)	27	0.23
Canadian (37)	37	0.31
Czech (0)	88	0.74
Czechoslovakian (0)	12	0.10
Danish (9)	27	0.23
Dutch (551)	652	5.48
English (112)	667	5.61
European (112)	234	1.97
French, ex. Basque (0)	168	1.41
French Canadian (33)	77	0.65
German (213)	1,082	9.10
Greek (36)	36	0.30
Irish (393)	1,262	10.61
Italian (111)	408	3.43
Northern European (17)	17	0.14
Norwegian (52)	199	1.67
Polish (127)	304	2.56
Portuguese (13)	34	0.29
Scandinavian (25)	40	0.34
Scotch-Irish (53)	91	0.77
Scottish (0)	45	0.38
Slovak (0)	13	0.11
Swedish (0)	124	1.04
Welsh (36)	58	0.49
West Indian, ex. Hispanic (42)	42	0.35
Jamaican (42)	42	0.35

Hispanic Origin	Population	%
Hispanic or Latino (of any race)	6,773	53.45
Central American, ex. Mexican	250	1.97
Costa Rican	6	0.05
Guatemalan	69	0.54
Honduran	26	0.21
Nicaraguan	33	0.26
Salvadoran	112	0.88
Other Central American	4	0.03
Cuban	28	0.22
Dominican Republic	3	0.02
Mexican	6,034	47.62
Puerto Rican	50	0.39
South American	95	0.75
Argentinean	23	0.18
Bolivian	5	0.04
Chilean	4	0.03
Colombian	24	0.19
Ecuadorian	12	0.09
Peruvian	21	0.17
Uruguayan	4	0.03
Venezuelan	2	0.02
Other Hispanic or Latino	313	2.47

Race*	Population	%
African-American/Black (381)	481	3.80
Not Hispanic (342)	401	3.16
Hispanic (39)	80	0.63
American Indian/Alaska Native (119)	233	1.84
Not Hispanic (37)	92	0.73
Hispanic (82)	141	1.11
Apache (9)	18	0.14
Arapaho (0)	1	0.01
Blackfeet (0)	2	0.02
Canadian/French Am. Ind. (1)	3	0.02
Cherokee (3)	26	0.21
Chickasaw (0)	1	0.01
Chippewa (1)	1	0.01
Choctaw (6)	14	0.11
Comanche (0)	1	0.01
Cree (0)	1	0.01
Crow (0)	2	0.02
Inupiat *(Alaska Native)* (0)	1	0.01
Iroquois (1)	2	0.02
Lumbee (0)	2	0.02
Mexican American Ind. (11)	17	0.13
Osage (0)	2	0.02
Potawatomi (2)	2	0.02
Pueblo (3)	8	0.06
Sioux (3)	6	0.05
Tlingit-Haida *(Alaska Native)* (0)	1	0.01
Tohono O'Odham (3)	3	0.02
Yakama (0)	1	0.01
Yaqui (3)	3	0.02
Asian (554)	674	5.32
Not Hispanic (542)	613	4.84
Hispanic (12)	61	0.48
Bangladeshi (0)	2	0.02
Cambodian (19)	25	0.20
Chinese, ex. Taiwanese (52)	80	0.63
Filipino (184)	225	1.78
Indian (72)	90	0.71
Indonesian (5)	5	0.04
Japanese (23)	50	0.39
Korean (67)	83	0.65
Laotian (10)	10	0.08
Malaysian (1)	2	0.02
Pakistani (15)	20	0.16
Sri Lankan (2)	3	0.02
Taiwanese (2)	2	0.02
Thai (10)	11	0.09
Vietnamese (69)	78	0.62
Hawaii Native/Pacific Islander (48)	71	0.56
Not Hispanic (38)	49	0.39
Hispanic (10)	22	0.17
Fijian (4)	6	0.05
Guamanian/Chamorro (5)	11	0.09
Native Hawaiian (16)	31	0.24
Samoan (14)	16	0.13
Tongan (5)	5	0.04
White (7,509)	7,976	62.94
Not Hispanic (4,727)	4,885	38.55
Hispanic (2,782)	3,091	24.39

Perris

Place Type: City
County: Riverside
Population: 68,386†

Ancestry‡	Population	%
African, Sub-Saharan (386)	386	0.61
African (343)	343	0.54
Nigerian (43)	43	0.07
American (653)	653	1.03
Arab (209)	284	0.45
Arab (12)	12	0.02
Egyptian (115)	115	0.18
Iraqi (41)	41	0.06
Syrian (18)	93	0.15
Other Arab (23)	23	0.04
Austrian (0)	12	0.02
Basque (0)	29	0.05
Belgian (0)	63	0.10
Brazilian (59)	59	0.09
British (18)	42	0.07
Canadian (28)	132	0.21
Croatian (13)	33	0.05
Czech (11)	45	0.07
Danish (16)	36	0.06
Dutch (32)	210	0.33
Eastern European (47)	47	0.07
English (329)	1,015	1.59
European (302)	445	0.70
Finnish (0)	16	0.03
French, ex. Basque (12)	311	0.49
French Canadian (21)	134	0.21
German (786)	2,855	4.49
Greek (0)	13	0.02
Hungarian (28)	44	0.07
Iranian (21)	101	0.16
Irish (393)	1,637	2.57
Italian (161)	711	1.12
Lithuanian (11)	22	0.03
Norwegian (64)	377	0.59
Pennsylvania German (0)	16	0.03
Polish (187)	394	0.62
Portuguese (14)	103	0.16
Romanian (13)	27	0.04
Russian (80)	215	0.34
Scandinavian (0)	14	0.02
Scotch-Irish (38)	433	0.68
Scottish (19)	241	0.38
Serbian (0)	10	0.02
Slavic (0)	8	0.01
Swedish (7)	28	0.04
Turkish (0)	36	0.06
Ukrainian (0)	14	0.02
Welsh (11)	64	0.10
West Indian, ex. Hispanic (241)	255	0.40
Belizean (80)	80	0.13
Dutch West Indian (0)	14	0.02
Jamaican (67)	67	0.11
Trinidadian/Tobagonian (74)	74	0.12
West Indian (20)	20	0.03

*Notes: † The Census 2010 population figure is used to calculate the percentages in the Hispanic Origin and Race categories. Ancestry percentages are based on the 2006-2010 American Community Survey population (not shown); ‡ Numbers in parentheses indicate the number of people reporting a single ancestry; * Numbers in parentheses indicate the number of persons reporting this race alone, not in combination with any other race; Please refer to the Explanation of Data for more information.*

Yugoslavian (0)	9	0.01

Hispanic Origin	Population	%
Hispanic or Latino (of any race)	49,079	71.77
Central American, ex. Mexican	2,089	3.05
Costa Rican	36	0.05
Guatemalan	704	1.03
Honduran	102	0.15
Nicaraguan	195	0.29
Panamanian	40	0.06
Salvadoran	997	1.46
Other Central American	15	0.02
Cuban	211	0.31
Dominican Republic	18	0.03
Mexican	43,641	63.82
Puerto Rican	410	0.60
South American	403	0.59
Argentinean	43	0.06
Bolivian	28	0.04
Chilean	13	0.02
Colombian	98	0.14
Ecuadorian	76	0.11
Peruvian	119	0.17
Venezuelan	21	0.03
Other South American	5	0.01
Other Hispanic or Latino	2,307	3.37

Race*	Population	%
African-American/Black (8,307)	9,393	13.74
Not Hispanic (7,763)	8,471	12.39
Hispanic (544)	922	1.35
American Indian/Alaska Native (589)	1,070	1.56
Not Hispanic (154)	387	0.57
Hispanic (435)	683	1.00
Apache (9)	36	0.05
Blackfeet (0)	26	0.04
Canadian/French Am. Ind. (0)	9	0.01
Central American Ind. (6)	6	0.01
Cherokee (19)	103	0.15
Chickasaw (1)	5	0.01
Chippewa (2)	3	<0.01
Choctaw (9)	28	0.04
Creek (0)	2	<0.01
Crow (0)	1	<0.01
Delaware (0)	1	<0.01
Hopi (3)	3	<0.01
Inupiat *(Alaska Native)* (1)	1	<0.01
Iroquois (0)	6	0.01
Mexican American Ind. (102)	141	0.21
Navajo (21)	35	0.05
Osage (0)	1	<0.01
Ottawa (0)	4	0.01
Paiute (4)	8	0.01
Pima (1)	4	0.01
Potawatomi (0)	1	<0.01
Pueblo (11)	11	0.02
Puget Sound Salish (2)	2	<0.01
Shoshone (6)	6	0.01
Sioux (8)	10	0.01
South American Ind. (1)	3	<0.01
Spanish American Ind. (3)	14	0.02
Tlingit-Haida *(Alaska Native)* (0)	1	<0.01
Tohono O'Odham (0)	1	<0.01
Ute (0)	4	0.01
Yaqui (6)	6	0.01
Yuman (0)	3	<0.01
Asian (2,461)	3,166	4.63
Not Hispanic (2,285)	2,747	4.02
Hispanic (176)	419	0.61
Bangladeshi (27)	38	0.06
Cambodian (80)	100	0.15
Chinese, ex. Taiwanese (159)	280	0.41
Filipino (1,172)	1,512	2.21
Hmong (7)	8	0.01
Indian (193)	272	0.40
Indonesian (13)	28	0.04
Japanese (54)	145	0.21
Korean (49)	99	0.14
Laotian (60)	98	0.14
Nepalese (3)	3	<0.01
Pakistani (64)	77	0.11
Sri Lankan (5)	5	0.01
Taiwanese (19)	20	0.03
Thai (46)	73	0.11
Vietnamese (354)	397	0.58
Hawaii Native/Pacific Islander (286)	504	0.74
Not Hispanic (259)	409	0.60
Hispanic (27)	95	0.14
Fijian (32)	33	0.05
Guamanian/Chamorro (28)	61	0.09
Native Hawaiian (23)	77	0.11
Samoan (140)	192	0.28
Tongan (33)	40	0.06
White (28,937)	31,662	46.30
Not Hispanic (7,499)	8,387	12.26
Hispanic (21,438)	23,275	34.03

Petaluma

Place Type: City
County: Sonoma
Population: 57,941†

Ancestry‡	Population	%
Afghan (16)	16	0.03
African, Sub-Saharan (27)	27	0.05
African (27)	27	0.05
Albanian (0)	10	0.02
Alsatian (11)	11	0.02
American (1,354)	1,354	2.39
Arab (162)	245	0.43
Arab (17)	17	0.03
Jordanian (0)	11	0.02
Lebanese (9)	58	0.10
Palestinian (98)	109	0.19
Other Arab (38)	50	0.09
Armenian (58)	113	0.20
Assyrian/Chaldean/Syriac (31)	31	0.05
Australian (0)	54	0.10
Austrian (20)	137	0.24
Basque (0)	6	0.01
Belgian (23)	99	0.17
British (358)	492	0.87
Canadian (95)	165	0.29
Celtic (16)	25	0.04
Croatian (46)	112	0.20
Czech (34)	195	0.34
Czechoslovakian (10)	79	0.14
Danish (199)	845	1.49
Dutch (115)	913	1.61
Eastern European (188)	198	0.35
English (1,377)	6,894	12.16
Estonian (8)	20	0.04
European (1,247)	1,396	2.46
Finnish (0)	107	0.19
French, ex. Basque (271)	2,369	4.18
French Canadian (69)	283	0.50
German (2,634)	9,221	16.27
Greek (138)	383	0.68
Hungarian (93)	375	0.66
Iranian (174)	213	0.38
Irish (1,995)	9,046	15.96
Israeli (84)	93	0.16
Italian (1,718)	5,480	9.67
Latvian (14)	28	0.05
Lithuanian (45)	131	0.23
Maltese (65)	99	0.17
Northern European (102)	155	0.27
Norwegian (234)	1,109	1.96
Pennsylvania German (0)	13	0.02
Polish (278)	872	1.54
Portuguese (538)	1,755	3.10
Romanian (18)	138	0.24
Russian (540)	1,179	2.08
Scandinavian (82)	190	0.34
Scotch-Irish (715)	1,773	3.13
Scottish (363)	1,355	2.39
Serbian (0)	41	0.07
Slovak (0)	17	0.03
Slovene (15)	22	0.04
Swedish (265)	1,230	2.17
Swiss (103)	697	1.23
Turkish (79)	114	0.20
Ukrainian (0)	9	0.02
Welsh (105)	636	1.12
West Indian, ex. Hispanic (229)	229	0.40
Haitian (229)	229	0.40
Yugoslavian (21)	81	0.14

Hispanic Origin	Population	%
Hispanic or Latino (of any race)	12,453	21.49
Central American, ex. Mexican	1,342	2.32
Costa Rican	25	0.04
Guatemalan	375	0.65
Honduran	46	0.08
Nicaraguan	178	0.31
Panamanian	16	0.03
Salvadoran	688	1.19
Other Central American	14	0.02
Cuban	40	0.07
Dominican Republic	8	0.01
Mexican	9,378	16.19
Puerto Rican	164	0.28
South American	472	0.81
Argentinean	31	0.05
Bolivian	4	0.01
Chilean	43	0.07
Colombian	135	0.23
Ecuadorian	30	0.05
Paraguayan	4	0.01
Peruvian	200	0.35
Uruguayan	6	0.01
Venezuelan	11	0.02
Other South American	8	0.01
Other Hispanic or Latino	1,049	1.81

Race*	Population	%
African-American/Black (801)	1,167	2.01
Not Hispanic (719)	1,028	1.77
Hispanic (82)	139	0.24
American Indian/Alaska Native (353)	924	1.59
Not Hispanic (198)	602	1.04
Hispanic (155)	322	0.56
Alaska Athabascan *(Ala. Nat.)* (1)	2	<0.01
Aleut *(Alaska Native)* (0)	4	0.01
Apache (10)	40	0.07
Blackfeet (3)	21	0.04
Central American Ind. (5)	6	0.01
Cherokee (34)	144	0.25
Cheyenne (2)	3	0.01
Chickasaw (1)	8	0.01
Chippewa (7)	23	0.04
Choctaw (17)	55	0.09
Comanche (2)	2	<0.01
Cree (0)	1	<0.01
Creek (2)	4	0.01
Crow (0)	1	<0.01
Delaware (0)	4	0.01
Hopi (0)	1	<0.01
Houma (0)	2	<0.01
Inupiat *(Alaska Native)* (0)	2	<0.01
Iroquois (1)	8	0.01
Lumbee (6)	6	0.01
Mexican American Ind. (49)	64	0.11
Navajo (4)	17	0.03
Osage (2)	7	0.01
Paiute (1)	6	0.01
Pima (1)	1	<0.01
Potawatomi (3)	6	0.01
Pueblo (2)	2	<0.01
Puget Sound Salish (0)	5	0.01
Seminole (1)	3	0.01
Shoshone (0)	2	<0.01
Sioux (3)	18	0.03
South American Ind. (3)	4	0.01
Spanish American Ind. (2)	3	0.01
Tlingit-Haida *(Alaska Native)* (1)	1	<0.01
Ute (0)	2	<0.01
Yakama (0)	1	<0.01
Yaqui (4)	9	0.02

*Notes: † The Census 2010 population figure is used to calculate the percentages in the Hispanic Origin and Race categories. Ancestry percentages are based on the 2006-2010 American Community Survey population (not shown); ‡ Numbers in parentheses indicate the number of people reporting a single ancestry; * Numbers in parentheses indicate the number of persons reporting this race alone, not in combination with any other race; Please refer to the Explanation of Data for more information.*

Asian (2,607)	3,571	6.16
Not Hispanic (2,550)	3,382	5.84
Hispanic (57)	189	0.33
Bangladeshi (7)	7	0.01
Burmese (9)	13	0.02
Cambodian (23)	27	0.05
Chinese, ex. Taiwanese (727)	979	1.69
Filipino (546)	881	1.52
Hmong (18)	21	0.04
Indian (444)	492	0.85
Indonesian (22)	32	0.06
Japanese (211)	473	0.82
Korean (127)	193	0.33
Laotian (62)	68	0.12
Malaysian (0)	3	0.01
Nepalese (6)	6	0.01
Pakistani (66)	73	0.13
Sri Lankan (7)	13	0.02
Taiwanese (35)	42	0.07
Thai (42)	67	0.12
Vietnamese (152)	188	0.32
Hawaii Native/Pacific Islander (129)	362	0.62
Not Hispanic (119)	299	0.52
Hispanic (10)	63	0.11
Fijian (34)	46	0.08
Guamanian/Chamorro (21)	49	0.08
Marshallese (1)	1	<0.01
Native Hawaiian (29)	181	0.31
Samoan (15)	31	0.05
Tongan (3)	17	0.03
White (46,566)	48,767	84.17
Not Hispanic (40,226)	41,698	71.97
Hispanic (6,340)	7,069	12.20

Phelan

Place Type: CDP
County: San Bernardino
Population: 14,304†

Ancestry‡	Population	%
American (472)	472	3.37
Austrian (0)	15	0.11
British (54)	54	0.39
Canadian (92)	103	0.73
Celtic (33)	33	0.24
Croatian (0)	10	0.07
Czech (37)	62	0.44
Danish (0)	49	0.35
Dutch (82)	440	3.14
English (253)	1,837	13.11
European (13)	13	0.09
Finnish (12)	39	0.28
French, ex. Basque (90)	382	2.73
French Canadian (48)	79	0.56
German (500)	2,638	18.82
Hungarian (0)	201	1.43
Irish (181)	1,857	13.25
Italian (87)	243	1.73
Northern European (4)	4	0.03
Norwegian (36)	167	1.19
Polish (59)	266	1.90
Portuguese (12)	12	0.09
Romanian (16)	31	0.22
Russian (14)	215	1.53
Scotch-Irish (161)	491	3.50
Scottish (232)	310	2.21
Slovak (0)	27	0.19
Swedish (92)	148	1.06
Swiss (0)	15	0.11
Ukrainian (10)	29	0.21
Welsh (44)	192	1.37

Hispanic Origin	Population	%
Hispanic or Latino (of any race)	4,128	28.86
Central American, ex. Mexican	155	1.08
Costa Rican	4	0.03
Guatemalan	29	0.20
Honduran	4	0.03
Nicaraguan	43	0.30
Panamanian	6	0.04
Salvadoran	67	0.47
Other Central American	2	0.01
Cuban	31	0.22
Mexican	3,428	23.97
Puerto Rican	59	0.41
South American	27	0.19
Argentinean	9	0.06
Colombian	13	0.09
Ecuadorian	2	0.01
Uruguayan	2	0.01
Venezuelan	1	0.01
Other Hispanic or Latino	428	2.99

Race*	Population	%
African-American/Black (276)	362	2.53
Not Hispanic (250)	317	2.22
Hispanic (26)	45	0.31
American Indian/Alaska Native (139)	365	2.55
Not Hispanic (70)	231	1.61
Hispanic (69)	134	0.94
Alaska Athabascan *(Ala. Nat.)* (0)	1	0.01
Aleut *(Alaska Native)* (1)	1	0.01
Apache (9)	19	0.13
Blackfeet (3)	9	0.06
Central American Ind. (0)	2	0.01
Cherokee (17)	61	0.43
Chickasaw (0)	3	0.02
Chippewa (0)	1	0.01
Choctaw (2)	14	0.10
Colville (0)	1	0.01
Comanche (2)	5	0.03
Creek (1)	1	0.01
Inupiat *(Alaska Native)* (3)	3	0.02
Iroquois (2)	4	0.03
Kiowa (2)	4	0.03
Menominee (0)	3	0.02
Mexican American Ind. (13)	19	0.13
Navajo (8)	14	0.10
Osage (0)	3	0.02
Ottawa (0)	7	0.05
Paiute (0)	1	0.01
Pima (1)	1	0.01
Pueblo (2)	5	0.03
Shoshone (3)	3	0.02
Sioux (4)	6	0.04
Tlingit-Haida *(Alaska Native)* (0)	3	0.02
Yaqui (0)	1	0.01
Yuman (3)	3	0.02
Asian (446)	571	3.99
Not Hispanic (425)	525	3.67
Hispanic (21)	46	0.32
Cambodian (2)	3	0.02
Chinese, ex. Taiwanese (20)	44	0.31
Filipino (29)	67	0.47
Indian (22)	27	0.19
Indonesian (4)	17	0.12
Japanese (22)	60	0.42
Korean (322)	341	2.38
Taiwanese (1)	1	0.01
Thai (4)	4	0.03
Vietnamese (3)	9	0.06
Hawaii Native/Pacific Islander (20)	55	0.38
Not Hispanic (13)	39	0.27
Hispanic (7)	16	0.11
Fijian (1)	2	0.01
Guamanian/Chamorro (4)	9	0.06
Native Hawaiian (6)	24	0.17
Samoan (4)	5	0.03
Tongan (2)	3	0.02
White (10,807)	11,379	79.55
Not Hispanic (9,060)	9,371	65.51
Hispanic (1,747)	2,008	14.04

Pico Rivera

Place Type: City
County: Los Angeles
Population: 62,942†

Ancestry‡	Population	%
African, Sub-Saharan (79)	122	0.19
African (79)	122	0.19
American (459)	459	0.73
Arab (82)	82	0.13
Egyptian (82)	82	0.13
Armenian (227)	272	0.43
Austrian (9)	60	0.10
Basque (0)	25	0.04
British (36)	58	0.09
Canadian (40)	45	0.07
Celtic (9)	9	0.01
Croatian (11)	11	0.02
Czechoslovakian (0)	12	0.02
Danish (0)	12	0.02
Dutch (40)	87	0.14
English (222)	638	1.01
French, ex. Basque (64)	270	0.43
French Canadian (11)	24	0.04
German (124)	698	1.11
Greek (14)	22	0.03
Hungarian (12)	25	0.04
Iranian (9)	9	0.01
Irish (140)	579	0.92
Italian (156)	521	0.83
Norwegian (0)	64	0.10
Pennsylvania German (0)	9	0.01
Polish (0)	24	0.04
Portuguese (26)	152	0.24
Russian (40)	50	0.08
Scandinavian (0)	21	0.03
Scotch-Irish (0)	102	0.16
Scottish (29)	100	0.16
Serbian (0)	19	0.03
Slovak (0)	27	0.04
Swedish (26)	136	0.22
Swiss (0)	12	0.02
Ukrainian (28)	47	0.07
Welsh (14)	33	0.05
West Indian, ex. Hispanic (0)	11	0.02
Belizean (0)	11	0.02

Hispanic Origin	Population	%
Hispanic or Latino (of any race)	57,400	91.20
Central American, ex. Mexican	3,059	4.86
Costa Rican	66	0.10
Guatemalan	761	1.21
Honduran	154	0.24
Nicaraguan	281	0.45
Panamanian	14	0.02
Salvadoran	1,733	2.75
Other Central American	50	0.08
Cuban	166	0.26
Dominican Republic	13	0.02
Mexican	51,337	81.56
Puerto Rican	268	0.43
South American	530	0.84
Argentinean	65	0.10
Bolivian	12	0.02
Chilean	12	0.02
Colombian	154	0.24
Ecuadorian	114	0.18
Peruvian	155	0.25
Uruguayan	7	0.01
Venezuelan	7	0.01
Other South American	4	0.01
Other Hispanic or Latino	2,027	3.22

Race*	Population	%
African-American/Black (602)	834	1.33
Not Hispanic (366)	424	0.67
Hispanic (236)	410	0.65
American Indian/Alaska Native (871)	1,207	1.92
Not Hispanic (114)	170	0.27
Hispanic (757)	1,037	1.65
Alaska Athabascan *(Ala. Nat.)* (2)	2	<0.01
Apache (55)	90	0.14
Arapaho (2)	2	<0.01
Blackfeet (0)	1	<0.01
Canadian/French Am. Ind. (2)	2	<0.01

*Notes: † The Census 2010 population figure is used to calculate the percentages in the Hispanic Origin and Race categories. Ancestry percentages are based on the 2006-2010 American Community Survey population (not shown); ‡ Numbers in parentheses indicate the number of people reporting a single ancestry; * Numbers in parentheses indicate the number of persons reporting this race alone, not in combination with any other race; Please refer to the Explanation of Data for more information.*

Cherokee (13)	43	0.07
Cheyenne (1)	2	<0.01
Chickasaw (0)	7	0.01
Chippewa (2)	6	0.01
Choctaw (7)	12	0.02
Comanche (7)	7	0.01
Creek (0)	1	<0.01
Crow (1)	5	0.01
Hopi (1)	3	<0.01
Kiowa (4)	9	0.01
Mexican American Ind. (152)	189	0.30
Navajo (20)	35	0.06
Paiute (2)	9	0.01
Pima (7)	9	0.01
Pueblo (1)	1	<0.01
Seminole (0)	5	0.01
Shoshone (2)	2	<0.01
Sioux (13)	16	0.03
South American Ind. (0)	4	0.01
Spanish American Ind. (5)	15	0.02
Tlingit-Haida *(Alaska Native)* (0)	3	<0.01
Tohono O'Odham (2)	3	<0.01
Ute (1)	4	0.01
Yaqui (33)	56	0.09
Yuman (1)	2	<0.01
Asian (1,614)	1,921	3.05
Not Hispanic (1,463)	1,579	2.51
Hispanic (151)	342	0.54
Bangladeshi (3)	3	<0.01
Burmese (11)	11	0.02
Cambodian (67)	80	0.13
Chinese, ex. Taiwanese (218)	255	0.41
Filipino (772)	900	1.43
Hmong (0)	1	<0.01
Indian (69)	99	0.16
Indonesian (1)	6	0.01
Japanese (134)	223	0.35
Korean (64)	84	0.13
Laotian (0)	3	<0.01
Malaysian (2)	2	<0.01
Nepalese (3)	3	<0.01
Pakistani (3)	6	0.01
Sri Lankan (1)	2	<0.01
Taiwanese (25)	27	0.04
Thai (48)	50	0.08
Vietnamese (144)	166	0.26
Hawaii Native/Pacific Islander (42)	160	0.25
Not Hispanic (15)	65	0.10
Hispanic (27)	95	0.15
Fijian (1)	1	<0.01
Guamanian/Chamorro (13)	18	0.03
Native Hawaiian (15)	61	0.10
Samoan (5)	21	0.03
Tongan (1)	4	0.01
White (37,411)	39,388	62.58
Not Hispanic (3,281)	3,467	5.51
Hispanic (34,130)	35,921	57.07

Piedmont

Place Type: City
County: Alameda
Population: 10,667†

Ancestry‡	Population	%
Albanian (0)	82	0.78
American (135)	135	1.28
Arab (0)	27	0.26
Moroccan (0)	27	0.26
Armenian (0)	10	0.09
Australian (14)	26	0.25
Austrian (8)	61	0.58
Basque (0)	23	0.22
Belgian (65)	119	1.13
British (9)	61	0.58
Canadian (64)	78	0.74
Croatian (0)	27	0.26
Czech (0)	27	0.26
Danish (36)	178	1.68
Dutch (17)	230	2.18
Eastern European (167)	167	1.58
English (316)	1,798	17.01
European (449)	468	4.43
Finnish (18)	58	0.55
French, ex. Basque (41)	289	2.73
French Canadian (0)	37	0.35
German (280)	1,591	15.05
Greek (22)	34	0.32
Hungarian (33)	64	0.61
Icelander (9)	9	0.09
Irish (293)	1,261	11.93
Italian (207)	610	5.77
Lithuanian (12)	35	0.33
Luxemburger (0)	8	0.08
Northern European (113)	125	1.18
Norwegian (20)	147	1.39
Polish (65)	392	3.71
Portuguese (38)	128	1.21
Romanian (0)	13	0.12
Russian (251)	605	5.72
Scandinavian (32)	44	0.42
Scotch-Irish (101)	251	2.37
Scottish (74)	382	3.61
Slovak (0)	19	0.18
Slovene (0)	43	0.41
Swedish (12)	282	2.67
Swiss (36)	125	1.18
Turkish (9)	9	0.09
Ukrainian (0)	11	0.10
Welsh (22)	83	0.79
Yugoslavian (0)	24	0.23

Hispanic Origin	Population	%
Hispanic or Latino (of any race)	421	3.95
Central American, ex. Mexican	30	0.28
Guatemalan	3	0.03
Honduran	1	0.01
Nicaraguan	10	0.09
Salvadoran	16	0.15
Cuban	11	0.10
Dominican Republic	7	0.07
Mexican	210	1.97
Puerto Rican	9	0.08
South American	73	0.68
Argentinean	22	0.21
Bolivian	2	0.02
Chilean	16	0.15
Colombian	6	0.06
Ecuadorian	1	0.01
Peruvian	18	0.17
Uruguayan	2	0.02
Venezuelan	6	0.06
Other Hispanic or Latino	81	0.76

Race*	Population	%
African-American/Black (144)	252	2.36
Not Hispanic (136)	234	2.19
Hispanic (8)	18	0.17
American Indian/Alaska Native (6)	54	0.51
Not Hispanic (4)	41	0.38
Hispanic (2)	13	0.12
Cherokee (0)	15	0.14
Choctaw (0)	8	0.07
Hopi (1)	3	0.03
Mexican American Ind. (1)	4	0.04
Asian (1,939)	2,374	22.26
Not Hispanic (1,924)	2,318	21.73
Hispanic (15)	56	0.52
Cambodian (1)	1	0.01
Chinese, ex. Taiwanese (1,230)	1,475	13.83
Filipino (85)	153	1.43
Indian (107)	150	1.41
Indonesian (0)	8	0.07
Japanese (150)	290	2.72
Korean (142)	197	1.85
Laotian (1)	4	0.04
Malaysian (0)	1	0.01
Pakistani (16)	21	0.20
Sri Lankan (1)	6	0.06
Taiwanese (49)	65	0.61
Thai (5)	11	0.10
Vietnamese (52)	73	0.68
Hawaii Native/Pacific Islander (13)	27	0.25
Not Hispanic (11)	24	0.22
Hispanic (2)	3	0.03
Guamanian/Chamorro (4)	6	0.06
Native Hawaiian (3)	11	0.10
Samoan (3)	3	0.03
Tongan (3)	3	0.03
White (7,917)	8,435	79.08
Not Hispanic (7,632)	8,094	75.88
Hispanic (285)	341	3.20

Pinole

Place Type: City
County: Contra Costa
Population: 18,390†

Ancestry‡	Population	%
African, Sub-Saharan (198)	211	1.14
African (11)	11	0.06
Ethiopian (187)	187	1.01
Nigerian (0)	13	0.07
American (303)	303	1.64
Arab (48)	77	0.42
Arab (13)	13	0.07
Lebanese (0)	29	0.16
Other Arab (35)	35	0.19
Armenian (0)	12	0.07
Austrian (11)	54	0.29
British (10)	38	0.21
Canadian (19)	33	0.18
Czech (11)	20	0.11
Danish (48)	129	0.70
Dutch (35)	149	0.81
Eastern European (14)	14	0.08
English (342)	920	4.98
Estonian (15)	15	0.08
European (667)	731	3.96
Finnish (50)	155	0.84
French, ex. Basque (73)	384	2.08
French Canadian (28)	67	0.36
German (224)	1,550	8.40
Greek (0)	63	0.34
Hungarian (15)	15	0.08
Iranian (36)	36	0.20
Irish (230)	1,244	6.74
Italian (417)	778	4.21
Lithuanian (11)	11	0.06
Luxemburger (0)	64	0.35
Northern European (73)	73	0.40
Norwegian (18)	335	1.81
Polish (126)	325	1.76
Portuguese (374)	759	4.11
Romanian (0)	47	0.25
Russian (117)	194	1.05
Scandinavian (0)	103	0.56
Scotch-Irish (79)	183	0.99
Scottish (60)	340	1.84
Slavic (9)	31	0.17
Slovak (27)	46	0.25
Swedish (69)	267	1.45
Swiss (0)	93	0.50
Ukrainian (26)	26	0.14
Welsh (0)	58	0.31

Hispanic Origin	Population	%
Hispanic or Latino (of any race)	4,005	21.78
Central American, ex. Mexican	775	4.21
Costa Rican	4	0.02
Guatemalan	101	0.55
Honduran	24	0.13
Nicaraguan	189	1.03
Panamanian	9	0.05
Salvadoran	448	2.44
Cuban	26	0.14
Dominican Republic	3	0.02
Mexican	2,533	13.77
Puerto Rican	108	0.59

SECTION TWO

*Notes: † The Census 2010 population figure is used to calculate the percentages in the Hispanic Origin and Race categories. Ancestry percentages are based on the 2006-2010 American Community Survey population (not shown); ‡ Numbers in parentheses indicate the number of people reporting a single ancestry; * Numbers in parentheses indicate the number of persons reporting this race alone, not in combination with any other race; Please refer to the Explanation of Data for more information.*

South American	223	1.21
Argentinean	11	0.06
Bolivian	4	0.02
Chilean	9	0.05
Colombian	27	0.15
Ecuadorian	10	0.05
Peruvian	156	0.85
Venezuelan	1	0.01
Other South American	5	0.03
Other Hispanic or Latino	337	1.83

Race*	Population	%
African-American/Black (2,458)	2,820	15.33
Not Hispanic (2,397)	2,680	14.57
Hispanic (61)	140	0.76
American Indian/Alaska Native (147)	390	2.12
Not Hispanic (60)	233	1.27
Hispanic (87)	157	0.85
Aleut *(Alaska Native)* (2)	4	0.02
Apache (6)	11	0.06
Blackfeet (1)	24	0.13
Central American Ind. (1)	1	0.01
Cherokee (19)	77	0.42
Chickasaw (0)	9	0.05
Chippewa (2)	14	0.08
Choctaw (3)	21	0.11
Comanche (1)	1	0.01
Creek (0)	2	0.01
Delaware (0)	2	0.01
Iroquois (0)	5	0.03
Mexican American Ind. (18)	28	0.15
Navajo (3)	10	0.05
Ottawa (0)	7	0.04
Paiute (1)	5	0.03
Pueblo (3)	10	0.05
Seminole (0)	5	0.03
Sioux (3)	12	0.07
South American Ind. (0)	3	0.02
Spanish American Ind. (11)	11	0.06
Tlingit-Haida *(Alaska Native)* (0)	2	0.01
Ute (1)	1	0.01
Yaqui (1)	2	0.01
Asian (4,220)	4,800	26.10
Not Hispanic (4,156)	4,618	25.11
Hispanic (64)	182	0.99
Burmese (8)	11	0.06
Cambodian (60)	76	0.41
Chinese, ex. Taiwanese (906)	1,105	6.01
Filipino (1,805)	2,101	11.42
Hmong (2)	2	0.01
Indian (322)	374	2.03
Indonesian (28)	38	0.21
Japanese (189)	314	1.71
Korean (141)	165	0.90
Laotian (158)	166	0.90
Malaysian (1)	4	0.02
Nepalese (11)	11	0.06
Pakistani (64)	75	0.41
Sri Lankan (7)	9	0.05
Taiwanese (20)	25	0.14
Thai (39)	50	0.27
Vietnamese (285)	320	1.74
Hawaii Native/Pacific Islander (64)	187	1.02
Not Hispanic (62)	158	0.86
Hispanic (2)	29	0.16
Fijian (9)	17	0.09
Guamanian/Chamorro (6)	20	0.11
Native Hawaiian (14)	70	0.38
Samoan (12)	22	0.12
Tongan (15)	25	0.14
White (8,488)	9,508	51.70
Not Hispanic (6,814)	7,469	40.61
Hispanic (1,674)	2,039	11.09

Pismo Beach

Place Type: City
County: San Luis Obispo
Population: 7,655†

Ancestry‡	Population	%
African, Sub-Saharan (26)	26	0.33
South African (26)	26	0.33
American (281)	281	3.60
Arab (14)	28	0.36
Lebanese (14)	28	0.36
Armenian (16)	16	0.21
Assyrian/Chaldean/Syriac (10)	10	0.13
Belgian (0)	16	0.21
British (18)	40	0.51
Canadian (13)	13	0.17
Czech (11)	11	0.14
Czechoslovakian (21)	33	0.42
Danish (88)	205	2.63
Dutch (21)	190	2.44
Eastern European (28)	28	0.36
English (354)	1,266	16.23
European (239)	250	3.20
Finnish (0)	13	0.17
French, ex. Basque (27)	366	4.69
French Canadian (56)	92	1.18
German (613)	1,757	22.52
Greek (47)	92	1.18
Hungarian (0)	62	0.79
Irish (296)	1,059	13.57
Italian (241)	614	7.87
Lithuanian (13)	25	0.32
Northern European (36)	36	0.46
Norwegian (110)	291	3.73
Pennsylvania German (0)	12	0.15
Polish (12)	143	1.83
Portuguese (134)	208	2.67
Romanian (13)	29	0.37
Russian (20)	240	3.08
Scotch-Irish (12)	64	0.82
Scottish (100)	351	4.50
Slovak (14)	14	0.18
Swedish (66)	228	2.92
Swiss (0)	24	0.31
Ukrainian (0)	14	0.18
Welsh (17)	120	1.54

Hispanic Origin	Population	%
Hispanic or Latino (of any race)	715	9.34
Central American, ex. Mexican	14	0.18
Guatemalan	8	0.10
Panamanian	1	0.01
Salvadoran	4	0.05
Other Central American	1	0.01
Cuban	4	0.05
Dominican Republic	1	0.01
Mexican	554	7.24
Puerto Rican	29	0.38
South American	36	0.47
Argentinean	4	0.05
Bolivian	1	0.01
Chilean	4	0.05
Colombian	11	0.14
Ecuadorian	3	0.04
Peruvian	11	0.14
Venezuelan	2	0.03
Other Hispanic or Latino	77	1.01

Race*	Population	%
African-American/Black (50)	64	0.84
Not Hispanic (47)	61	0.80
Hispanic (3)	3	0.04
American Indian/Alaska Native (41)	110	1.44
Not Hispanic (30)	79	1.03
Hispanic (11)	31	0.40
Apache (0)	1	0.01
Blackfeet (0)	3	0.04
Cherokee (7)	35	0.46
Chickasaw (0)	1	0.01
Choctaw (2)	5	0.07
Comanche (1)	2	0.03
Creek (0)	1	0.01
Delaware (1)	1	0.01
Mexican American Ind. (0)	1	0.01
Navajo (1)	3	0.04
Osage (0)	1	0.01
Potawatomi (3)	3	0.04
Pueblo (1)	1	0.01
Seminole (0)	1	0.01
Sioux (0)	2	0.03
South American Ind. (0)	2	0.03
Ute (1)	1	0.01
Yaqui (2)	2	0.03
Asian (203)	280	3.66
Not Hispanic (192)	252	3.29
Hispanic (11)	28	0.37
Cambodian (9)	10	0.13
Chinese, ex. Taiwanese (40)	57	0.74
Filipino (47)	82	1.07
Indian (27)	31	0.40
Indonesian (3)	3	0.04
Japanese (38)	50	0.65
Korean (17)	28	0.37
Laotian (1)	1	0.01
Taiwanese (0)	3	0.04
Thai (1)	2	0.03
Vietnamese (7)	8	0.10
Hawaii Native/Pacific Islander (11)	29	0.38
Not Hispanic (11)	26	0.34
Hispanic (0)	3	0.04
Guamanian/Chamorro (6)	6	0.08
Native Hawaiian (3)	12	0.16
Samoan (2)	2	0.03
White (6,976)	7,158	93.51
Not Hispanic (6,510)	6,628	86.58
Hispanic (466)	530	6.92

Pittsburg

Place Type: City
County: Contra Costa
Population: 63,264†

Ancestry‡	Population	%
Afghan (147)	147	0.24
African, Sub-Saharan (864)	1,533	2.48
African (478)	1,147	1.86
Nigerian (84)	84	0.14
South African (41)	41	0.07
Ugandan (55)	55	0.09
Other Sub-Saharan African (206)	206	0.33
American (582)	582	0.94
Arab (218)	218	0.35
Arab (123)	123	0.20
Egyptian (47)	47	0.08
Lebanese (15)	15	0.02
Moroccan (12)	12	0.02
Other Arab (21)	21	0.03
Armenian (11)	11	0.02
Austrian (15)	65	0.11
Basque (53)	87	0.14
British (42)	161	0.26
Croatian (0)	11	0.02
Czech (23)	94	0.15
Danish (22)	265	0.43
Dutch (202)	460	0.75
Eastern European (10)	10	0.02
English (288)	1,695	2.75
European (126)	200	0.32
Finnish (0)	15	0.02
French, ex. Basque (69)	683	1.11
French Canadian (30)	49	0.08
German (555)	2,679	4.34
German Russian (23)	23	0.04
Greek (10)	64	0.10
Guyanese (18)	18	0.03
Hungarian (63)	135	0.22
Iranian (31)	31	0.05
Irish (503)	2,638	4.27
Italian (1,209)	2,501	4.05
Lithuanian (0)	44	0.07
Norwegian (99)	293	0.47
Pennsylvania German (0)	9	0.01
Polish (168)	385	0.62
Portuguese (223)	1,176	1.91

*Notes: † The Census 2010 population figure is used to calculate the percentages in the Hispanic Origin and Race categories. Ancestry percentages are based on the 2006-2010 American Community Survey population (not shown); ‡ Numbers in parentheses indicate the number of people reporting a single ancestry; * Numbers in parentheses indicate the number of persons reporting this race alone, not in combination with any other race; Please refer to the Explanation of Data for more information.*

Romanian (0)	14	0.02
Russian (38)	158	0.26
Scandinavian (73)	126	0.20
Scotch-Irish (278)	576	0.93
Scottish (141)	425	0.69
Slovak (27)	27	0.04
Swedish (26)	376	0.61
Swiss (0)	34	0.06
Ukrainian (26)	40	0.06
Welsh (16)	105	0.17
West Indian, ex. Hispanic (66)	66	0.11
Jamaican (57)	57	0.09
West Indian (9)	9	0.01
Yugoslavian (117)	174	0.28

Hispanic Origin	Population	%
Hispanic or Latino (of any race)	26,841	42.43
Central American, ex. Mexican	3,513	5.55
Costa Rican	37	0.06
Guatemalan	354	0.56
Honduran	91	0.14
Nicaraguan	879	1.39
Panamanian	54	0.09
Salvadoran	2,076	3.28
Other Central American	22	0.03
Cuban	98	0.15
Dominican Republic	30	0.05
Mexican	20,109	31.79
Puerto Rican	890	1.41
South American	610	0.96
Argentinean	21	0.03
Bolivian	28	0.04
Chilean	33	0.05
Colombian	112	0.18
Ecuadorian	24	0.04
Paraguayan	4	0.01
Peruvian	348	0.55
Uruguayan	5	0.01
Venezuelan	31	0.05
Other South American	4	0.01
Other Hispanic or Latino	1,591	2.51

Race*	Population	%
African-American/Black (11,187)	12,770	20.19
Not Hispanic (10,756)	11,831	18.70
Hispanic (431)	939	1.48
American Indian/Alaska Native (517)	1,263	2.00
Not Hispanic (202)	638	1.01
Hispanic (315)	625	0.99
Aleut *(Alaska Native)* (1)	1	<0.01
Apache (19)	62	0.10
Blackfeet (2)	43	0.07
Canadian/French Am. Ind. (0)	1	<0.01
Central American Ind. (1)	2	<0.01
Cherokee (26)	148	0.23
Cheyenne (0)	8	0.01
Chickasaw (0)	3	<0.01
Chippewa (1)	3	<0.01
Choctaw (8)	33	0.05
Comanche (0)	5	0.01
Cree (0)	4	0.01
Creek (8)	12	0.02
Crow (0)	2	<0.01
Hopi (2)	6	0.01
Houma (1)	1	<0.01
Inupiat *(Alaska Native)* (3)	4	0.01
Iroquois (0)	5	0.01
Kiowa (0)	4	0.01
Mexican American Ind. (99)	146	0.23
Navajo (8)	23	0.04
Osage (3)	7	0.01
Ottawa (2)	5	0.01
Paiute (0)	9	0.01
Pima (1)	1	<0.01
Potawatomi (1)	1	<0.01
Pueblo (0)	3	<0.01
Seminole (1)	4	0.01
Shoshone (1)	3	<0.01
Sioux (13)	35	0.06
South American Ind. (4)	9	0.01
Spanish American Ind. (1)	2	<0.01
Tohono O'Odham (0)	5	0.01
Ute (2)	6	0.01
Yaqui (2)	13	0.02
Yuman (3)	4	0.01
Asian (9,891)	11,659	18.43
Not Hispanic (9,654)	10,933	17.28
Hispanic (237)	726	1.15
Bangladeshi (17)	18	0.03
Burmese (9)	11	0.02
Cambodian (128)	146	0.23
Chinese, ex. Taiwanese (721)	995	1.57
Filipino (6,253)	7,301	11.54
Hmong (1)	3	<0.01
Indian (1,251)	1,465	2.32
Indonesian (33)	66	0.10
Japanese (114)	310	0.49
Korean (120)	198	0.31
Laotian (92)	117	0.18
Malaysian (1)	7	0.01
Nepalese (8)	8	0.01
Pakistani (99)	116	0.18
Sri Lankan (7)	7	0.01
Taiwanese (12)	16	0.03
Thai (54)	87	0.14
Vietnamese (717)	787	1.24
Hawaii Native/Pacific Islander (645)	1,126	1.78
Not Hispanic (614)	976	1.54
Hispanic (31)	150	0.24
Fijian (175)	234	0.37
Guamanian/Chamorro (42)	116	0.18
Native Hawaiian (42)	184	0.29
Samoan (108)	164	0.26
Tongan (202)	235	0.37
White (23,106)	26,446	41.80
Not Hispanic (12,684)	14,289	22.59
Hispanic (10,422)	12,157	19.22

Placentia

Place Type: City
County: Orange
Population: 50,533†

Ancestry‡	Population	%
Afghan (8)	8	0.02
African, Sub-Saharan (233)	260	0.52
African (30)	42	0.08
Ethiopian (15)	15	0.03
Nigerian (175)	175	0.35
South African (13)	28	0.06
American (1,409)	1,409	2.84
Arab (274)	407	0.82
Arab (40)	40	0.08
Egyptian (0)	33	0.07
Iraqi (0)	23	0.05
Jordanian (110)	118	0.24
Lebanese (80)	149	0.30
Syrian (31)	31	0.06
Other Arab (13)	13	0.03
Armenian (101)	196	0.40
Austrian (26)	90	0.18
Belgian (0)	14	0.03
Brazilian (16)	16	0.03
British (88)	218	0.44
Bulgarian (0)	9	0.02
Canadian (160)	213	0.43
Croatian (33)	117	0.24
Czech (30)	167	0.34
Czechoslovakian (32)	80	0.16
Danish (115)	435	0.88
Dutch (161)	533	1.08
Eastern European (38)	84	0.17
English (1,022)	3,982	8.03
European (517)	613	1.24
Finnish (23)	33	0.07
French, ex. Basque (113)	983	1.98
French Canadian (54)	148	0.30
German (1,664)	6,630	13.38
Greek (49)	196	0.40
Hungarian (145)	429	0.87
Icelander (0)	17	0.03
Iranian (280)	287	0.58
Irish (1,085)	4,986	10.06
Italian (937)	2,352	4.75
Lithuanian (56)	77	0.16
Northern European (64)	64	0.13
Norwegian (276)	533	1.08
Pennsylvania German (9)	31	0.06
Polish (329)	1,097	2.21
Portuguese (35)	49	0.10
Romanian (94)	148	0.30
Russian (206)	388	0.78
Scandinavian (43)	55	0.11
Scotch-Irish (189)	611	1.23
Scottish (216)	909	1.83
Serbian (9)	9	0.02
Slavic (10)	70	0.14
Slovak (28)	93	0.19
Slovene (0)	21	0.04
Swedish (78)	814	1.64
Swiss (0)	55	0.11
Ukrainian (52)	136	0.27
Welsh (0)	152	0.31
West Indian, ex. Hispanic (32)	32	0.06
Belizean (22)	22	0.04
Haitian (10)	10	0.02
Yugoslavian (0)	16	0.03

Hispanic Origin	Population	%
Hispanic or Latino (of any race)	18,416	36.44
Central American, ex. Mexican	934	1.85
Costa Rican	32	0.06
Guatemalan	492	0.97
Honduran	34	0.07
Nicaraguan	73	0.14
Panamanian	21	0.04
Salvadoran	272	0.54
Other Central American	10	0.02
Cuban	172	0.34
Dominican Republic	13	0.03
Mexican	15,464	30.60
Puerto Rican	163	0.32
South American	554	1.10
Argentinean	93	0.18
Bolivian	30	0.06
Chilean	37	0.07
Colombian	129	0.26
Ecuadorian	63	0.12
Paraguayan	4	0.01
Peruvian	179	0.35
Uruguayan	5	0.01
Venezuelan	7	0.01
Other South American	7	0.01
Other Hispanic or Latino	1,116	2.21

Race*	Population	%
African-American/Black (914)	1,185	2.35
Not Hispanic (818)	997	1.97
Hispanic (96)	188	0.37
American Indian/Alaska Native (386)	722	1.43
Not Hispanic (123)	289	0.57
Hispanic (263)	433	0.86
Aleut *(Alaska Native)* (1)	4	0.01
Apache (6)	25	0.05
Blackfeet (1)	6	0.01
Canadian/French Am. Ind. (2)	3	0.01
Cherokee (24)	80	0.16
Cheyenne (1)	4	0.01
Chickasaw (1)	4	0.01
Chippewa (3)	9	0.02
Choctaw (4)	30	0.06
Comanche (2)	2	<0.01
Creek (1)	6	0.01
Hopi (2)	3	0.01
Iroquois (1)	3	0.01
Kiowa (4)	4	0.01
Lumbee (0)	3	0.01
Mexican American Ind. (39)	63	0.12
Navajo (13)	19	0.04

*Notes: † The Census 2010 population figure is used to calculate the percentages in the Hispanic Origin and Race categories. Ancestry percentages are based on the 2006-2010 American Community Survey population (not shown); ‡ Numbers in parentheses indicate the number of people reporting a single ancestry; * Numbers in parentheses indicate the number of persons reporting this race alone, not in combination with any other race; Please refer to the Explanation of Data for more information.*

Osage (1)	1	<0.01
Ottawa (1)	1	<0.01
Paiute (0)	1	<0.01
Potawatomi (3)	5	0.01
Pueblo (2)	7	0.01
Shoshone (2)	3	0.01
Sioux (1)	1	<0.01
South American Ind. (0)	1	<0.01
Spanish American Ind. (5)	9	0.02
Tlingit-Haida *(Alaska Native)* (0)	2	<0.01
Tohono O'Odham (4)	5	0.01
Tsimshian *(Alaska Native)* (0)	1	<0.01
Ute (1)	3	0.01
Yakama (1)	1	<0.01
Yaqui (6)	13	0.03
Asian (7,531)	8,389	16.60
Not Hispanic (7,457)	8,122	16.07
Hispanic (74)	267	0.53
Bangladeshi (14)	17	0.03
Burmese (10)	13	0.03
Cambodian (76)	95	0.19
Chinese, ex. Taiwanese (1,135)	1,438	2.85
Filipino (1,569)	1,894	3.75
Hmong (9)	11	0.02
Indian (922)	1,007	1.99
Indonesian (90)	146	0.29
Japanese (506)	762	1.51
Korean (978)	1,055	2.09
Laotian (32)	47	0.09
Malaysian (16)	18	0.04
Nepalese (3)	3	0.01
Pakistani (60)	75	0.15
Sri Lankan (29)	29	0.06
Taiwanese (331)	358	0.71
Thai (73)	93	0.18
Vietnamese (1,349)	1,467	2.90
Hawaii Native/Pacific Islander (74)	179	0.35
Not Hispanic (58)	135	0.27
Hispanic (16)	44	0.09
Fijian (7)	7	0.01
Guamanian/Chamorro (12)	21	0.04
Native Hawaiian (23)	68	0.13
Samoan (17)	25	0.05
Tongan (5)	5	0.01
White (31,373)	33,091	65.48
Not Hispanic (22,590)	23,449	46.40
Hispanic (8,783)	9,642	19.08

Placerville

Place Type: City
County: El Dorado
Population: 10,389†

Ancestry‡	Population	%
American (365)	365	3.52
Australian (0)	30	0.29
Austrian (0)	8	0.08
Belgian (0)	13	0.13
British (24)	38	0.37
Canadian (0)	16	0.15
Croatian (14)	14	0.13
Czech (8)	8	0.08
Czechoslovakian (25)	25	0.24
Danish (86)	197	1.90
Dutch (12)	203	1.95
English (257)	1,218	11.73
European (143)	190	1.83
Finnish (13)	13	0.13
French, ex. Basque (141)	526	5.07
French Canadian (63)	225	2.17
German (438)	2,210	21.28
Greek (29)	60	0.58
Hungarian (12)	62	0.60
Irish (227)	1,385	13.34
Italian (233)	757	7.29
Latvian (0)	11	0.11
Lithuanian (11)	11	0.11
Maltese (0)	13	0.13
Northern European (11)	11	0.11
Norwegian (82)	165	1.59
Pennsylvania German (9)	9	0.09
Polish (0)	157	1.51
Portuguese (61)	111	1.07
Russian (0)	10	0.10
Scandinavian (57)	119	1.15
Scotch-Irish (96)	373	3.59
Scottish (91)	319	3.07
Serbian (0)	7	0.07
Swedish (9)	126	1.21
Swiss (0)	161	1.55
Welsh (0)	39	0.38

Hispanic Origin	Population	%
Hispanic or Latino (of any race)	1,863	17.93
Central American, ex. Mexican	56	0.54
Costa Rican	3	0.03
Guatemalan	19	0.18
Nicaraguan	7	0.07
Panamanian	1	0.01
Salvadoran	26	0.25
Dominican Republic	1	0.01
Mexican	1,573	15.14
Puerto Rican	23	0.22
South American	20	0.19
Argentinean	3	0.03
Bolivian	2	0.02
Chilean	4	0.04
Colombian	5	0.05
Peruvian	5	0.05
Venezuelan	1	0.01
Other Hispanic or Latino	190	1.83

Race*	Population	%
African-American/Black (80)	145	1.40
Not Hispanic (78)	115	1.11
Hispanic (2)	30	0.29
American Indian/Alaska Native (162)	397	3.82
Not Hispanic (122)	309	2.97
Hispanic (40)	88	0.85
Apache (3)	13	0.13
Arapaho (0)	1	0.01
Blackfeet (1)	12	0.12
Canadian/French Am. Ind. (1)	2	0.02
Cherokee (18)	94	0.90
Chickasaw (3)	3	0.03
Chippewa (15)	16	0.15
Choctaw (7)	24	0.23
Cree (1)	1	0.01
Creek (3)	5	0.05
Crow (0)	1	0.01
Iroquois (1)	8	0.08
Mexican American Ind. (6)	11	0.11
Navajo (2)	10	0.10
Paiute (0)	1	0.01
Pueblo (1)	1	0.01
Seminole (0)	3	0.03
Sioux (4)	12	0.12
South American Ind. (1)	1	0.01
Spanish American Ind. (4)	4	0.04
Yaqui (1)	2	0.02
Asian (98)	187	1.80
Not Hispanic (88)	143	1.38
Hispanic (10)	44	0.42
Cambodian (2)	2	0.02
Chinese, ex. Taiwanese (17)	28	0.27
Filipino (25)	55	0.53
Indian (24)	46	0.44
Indonesian (2)	2	0.02
Japanese (15)	46	0.44
Korean (3)	5	0.05
Thai (4)	4	0.04
Hawaii Native/Pacific Islander (13)	38	0.37
Not Hispanic (13)	32	0.31
Hispanic (0)	6	0.06
Guamanian/Chamorro (2)	8	0.08
Native Hawaiian (7)	20	0.19
Samoan (2)	9	0.09
White (8,716)	9,132	87.90
Not Hispanic (7,938)	8,194	78.87
Hispanic (778)	938	9.03

Pleasant Hill

Place Type: City
County: Contra Costa
Population: 33,152†

Ancestry‡	Population	%
Afghan (81)	113	0.34
African, Sub-Saharan (57)	57	0.17
African (37)	37	0.11
South African (20)	20	0.06
Albanian (29)	29	0.09
American (1,409)	1,409	4.29
Arab (262)	358	1.09
Arab (0)	6	0.02
Egyptian (7)	21	0.06
Iraqi (38)	38	0.12
Lebanese (9)	36	0.11
Moroccan (71)	104	0.32
Palestinian (86)	86	0.26
Syrian (0)	16	0.05
Other Arab (51)	51	0.16
Armenian (11)	72	0.22
Australian (0)	11	0.03
Austrian (0)	45	0.14
Basque (0)	13	0.04
Belgian (13)	40	0.12
Brazilian (14)	29	0.09
British (81)	233	0.71
Bulgarian (51)	51	0.16
Cajun (36)	36	0.11
Celtic (44)	52	0.16
Croatian (18)	70	0.21
Czech (66)	171	0.52
Czechoslovakian (11)	33	0.10
Danish (64)	410	1.25
Dutch (103)	652	1.99
Eastern European (35)	35	0.11
English (858)	3,883	11.83
Estonian (13)	13	0.04
European (601)	747	2.28
Finnish (46)	102	0.31
French, ex. Basque (124)	1,039	3.17
French Canadian (67)	225	0.69
German (1,197)	5,822	17.74
German Russian (9)	9	0.03
Greek (107)	166	0.51
Hungarian (55)	279	0.85
Iranian (303)	340	1.04
Irish (1,108)	4,712	14.35
Israeli (200)	200	0.61
Italian (913)	2,433	7.41
Latvian (0)	8	0.02
Lithuanian (61)	115	0.35
Northern European (119)	119	0.36
Norwegian (214)	712	2.17
Polish (153)	522	1.59
Portuguese (210)	625	1.90
Romanian (0)	34	0.10
Russian (380)	702	2.14
Scandinavian (157)	206	0.63
Scotch-Irish (211)	582	1.77
Scottish (262)	833	2.54
Serbian (25)	37	0.11
Slavic (32)	43	0.13
Slovene (0)	26	0.08
Swedish (177)	779	2.37
Swiss (43)	136	0.41
Ukrainian (41)	90	0.27
Welsh (85)	325	0.99
West Indian, ex. Hispanic (0)	40	0.12
Haitian (0)	20	0.06
Jamaican (0)	20	0.06

Hispanic Origin	Population	%
Hispanic or Latino (of any race)	4,009	12.09
Central American, ex. Mexican	557	1.68
Costa Rican	31	0.09

*Notes: † The Census 2010 population figure is used to calculate the percentages in the Hispanic Origin and Race categories. Ancestry percentages are based on the 2006-2010 American Community Survey population (not shown); ‡ Numbers in parentheses indicate the number of people reporting a single ancestry; * Numbers in parentheses indicate the number of persons reporting this race alone, not in combination with any other race; Please refer to the Explanation of Data for more information.*

Guatemalan	61	0.18
Honduran	10	0.03
Nicaraguan	148	0.45
Panamanian	20	0.06
Salvadoran	287	0.87
Cuban	41	0.12
Dominican Republic	12	0.04
Mexican	2,266	6.84
Puerto Rican	205	0.62
South American	455	1.37
Argentinean	36	0.11
Bolivian	14	0.04
Chilean	23	0.07
Colombian	78	0.24
Ecuadorian	23	0.07
Paraguayan	6	0.02
Peruvian	260	0.78
Uruguayan	1	<0.01
Venezuelan	12	0.04
Other South American	2	0.01
Other Hispanic or Latino	473	1.43

Race*	Population	%
African-American/Black (686)	996	3.00
Not Hispanic (656)	905	2.73
Hispanic (30)	91	0.27
American Indian/Alaska Native (127)	472	1.42
Not Hispanic (68)	306	0.92
Hispanic (59)	166	0.50
Alaska Athabascan *(Ala. Nat.)* (1)	1	<0.01
Aleut *(Alaska Native)* (0)	3	0.01
Apache (7)	14	0.04
Blackfeet (0)	9	0.03
Canadian/French Am. Ind. (0)	3	0.01
Cherokee (15)	101	0.30
Chickasaw (0)	2	0.01
Chippewa (2)	7	0.02
Choctaw (6)	30	0.09
Creek (2)	12	0.04
Crow (1)	2	0.01
Inupiat *(Alaska Native)* (0)	1	<0.01
Iroquois (3)	11	0.03
Kiowa (0)	1	<0.01
Mexican American Ind. (5)	13	0.04
Navajo (3)	13	0.04
Osage (0)	3	0.01
Ottawa (0)	1	<0.01
Paiute (1)	5	0.02
Pima (1)	1	<0.01
Potawatomi (1)	1	<0.01
Pueblo (1)	3	0.01
Seminole (0)	9	0.03
Shoshone (2)	3	0.01
Sioux (3)	15	0.05
South American Ind. (0)	11	0.03
Spanish American Ind. (1)	1	<0.01
Tlingit-Haida *(Alaska Native)* (1)	2	0.01
Tohono O'Odham (0)	4	0.01
Tsimshian *(Alaska Native)* (0)	3	0.01
Ute (1)	1	<0.01
Yaqui (1)	1	<0.01
Asian (4,516)	5,588	16.86
Not Hispanic (4,447)	5,378	16.22
Hispanic (69)	210	0.63
Bangladeshi (1)	1	<0.01
Burmese (13)	22	0.07
Cambodian (18)	18	0.05
Chinese, ex. Taiwanese (1,365)	1,740	5.25
Filipino (1,017)	1,407	4.24
Indian (367)	426	1.28
Indonesian (147)	177	0.53
Japanese (423)	637	1.92
Korean (571)	658	1.98
Laotian (13)	22	0.07
Malaysian (2)	6	0.02
Nepalese (5)	5	0.02
Pakistani (44)	51	0.15
Sri Lankan (4)	5	0.02
Taiwanese (71)	88	0.27
Thai (37)	53	0.16
Vietnamese (200)	255	0.77
Hawaii Native/Pacific Islander (66)	178	0.54
Not Hispanic (62)	153	0.46
Hispanic (4)	25	0.08
Fijian (3)	8	0.02
Guamanian/Chamorro (16)	29	0.09
Native Hawaiian (15)	72	0.22
Samoan (1)	7	0.02
Tongan (12)	14	0.04
White (24,846)	26,518	79.99
Not Hispanic (22,498)	23,775	71.72
Hispanic (2,348)	2,743	8.27

Pleasanton

Place Type: City
County: Alameda
Population: 70,285†

Ancestry‡	Population	%
Afghan (121)	153	0.22
African, Sub-Saharan (59)	167	0.24
African (59)	167	0.24
American (1,331)	1,331	1.95
Arab (225)	345	0.51
Egyptian (86)	86	0.13
Lebanese (33)	86	0.13
Palestinian (78)	117	0.17
Syrian (9)	21	0.03
Other Arab (19)	35	0.05
Armenian (88)	177	0.26
Assyrian/Chaldean/Syriac (10)	40	0.06
Australian (0)	67	0.10
Austrian (19)	155	0.23
Basque (20)	28	0.04
Belgian (46)	148	0.22
Brazilian (65)	87	0.13
British (393)	655	0.96
Canadian (135)	227	0.33
Croatian (70)	224	0.33
Cypriot (10)	10	0.01
Czech (26)	273	0.40
Czechoslovakian (31)	80	0.12
Danish (98)	768	1.13
Dutch (82)	746	1.09
Eastern European (104)	104	0.15
English (1,740)	8,006	11.74
European (1,011)	1,320	1.94
Finnish (47)	107	0.16
French, ex. Basque (230)	2,067	3.03
French Canadian (108)	263	0.39
German (2,021)	9,821	14.40
Greek (172)	489	0.72
Hungarian (76)	258	0.38
Icelander (0)	8	0.01
Iranian (862)	870	1.28
Irish (1,774)	8,737	12.81
Israeli (62)	62	0.09
Italian (1,866)	5,716	8.38
Lithuanian (109)	135	0.20
Luxemburger (0)	10	0.01
New Zealander (34)	34	0.05
Northern European (234)	234	0.34
Norwegian (331)	1,137	1.67
Pennsylvania German (9)	23	0.03
Polish (206)	1,037	1.52
Portuguese (396)	1,733	2.54
Romanian (141)	184	0.27
Russian (313)	713	1.05
Scandinavian (84)	151	0.22
Scotch-Irish (332)	1,218	1.79
Scottish (376)	1,738	2.55
Serbian (0)	22	0.03
Slavic (0)	6	0.01
Slovak (33)	106	0.16
Slovene (16)	16	0.02
Swedish (207)	1,893	2.78
Swiss (123)	308	0.45
Turkish (32)	32	0.05
Ukrainian (74)	224	0.33
Welsh (58)	543	0.80
West Indian, ex. Hispanic (39)	96	0.14
West Indian (39)	96	0.14
Yugoslavian (111)	252	0.37

Hispanic Origin	Population	%
Hispanic or Latino (of any race)	7,264	10.34
Central American, ex. Mexican	418	0.59
Costa Rican	24	0.03
Guatemalan	60	0.09
Honduran	24	0.03
Nicaraguan	101	0.14
Panamanian	39	0.06
Salvadoran	166	0.24
Other Central American	4	0.01
Cuban	98	0.14
Dominican Republic	17	0.02
Mexican	4,903	6.98
Puerto Rican	331	0.47
South American	470	0.67
Argentinean	68	0.10
Bolivian	22	0.03
Chilean	55	0.08
Colombian	128	0.18
Ecuadorian	22	0.03
Paraguayan	3	<0.01
Peruvian	148	0.21
Venezuelan	20	0.03
Other South American	4	0.01
Other Hispanic or Latino	1,027	1.46

Race*	Population	%
African-American/Black (1,190)	1,616	2.30
Not Hispanic (1,116)	1,456	2.07
Hispanic (74)	160	0.23
American Indian/Alaska Native (226)	713	1.01
Not Hispanic (143)	488	0.69
Hispanic (83)	225	0.32
Alaska Athabascan *(Ala. Nat.)* (0)	1	<0.01
Apache (2)	14	0.02
Arapaho (2)	2	<0.01
Blackfeet (4)	10	0.01
Canadian/French Am. Ind. (1)	3	<0.01
Central American Ind. (0)	2	<0.01
Cherokee (22)	134	0.19
Cheyenne (0)	2	<0.01
Chickasaw (1)	3	<0.01
Chippewa (4)	12	0.02
Choctaw (7)	41	0.06
Colville (1)	1	<0.01
Comanche (1)	5	0.01
Cree (0)	1	<0.01
Creek (5)	8	0.01
Crow (0)	5	0.01
Delaware (3)	5	0.01
Hopi (0)	3	<0.01
Iroquois (1)	6	0.01
Kiowa (0)	2	<0.01
Mexican American Ind. (17)	29	0.04
Navajo (8)	14	0.02
Osage (0)	2	<0.01
Paiute (2)	3	<0.01
Pima (1)	3	<0.01
Potawatomi (3)	10	0.01
Pueblo (0)	1	<0.01
Puget Sound Salish (1)	1	<0.01
Seminole (1)	4	0.01
Shoshone (0)	1	<0.01
Sioux (3)	10	0.01
South American Ind. (3)	7	0.01
Tohono O'Odham (1)	1	<0.01
Ute (0)	3	<0.01
Yakama (0)	2	<0.01
Yaqui (1)	5	0.01
Yup'ik *(Alaska Native)* (0)	3	<0.01
Asian (16,322)	18,484	26.30
Not Hispanic (16,209)	18,108	25.76
Hispanic (113)	376	0.53
Bangladeshi (34)	36	0.05
Burmese (35)	42	0.06

*Notes: † The Census 2010 population figure is used to calculate the percentages in the Hispanic Origin and Race categories. Ancestry percentages are based on the 2006-2010 American Community Survey population (not shown); ‡ Numbers in parentheses indicate the number of people reporting a single ancestry; * Numbers in parentheses indicate the number of persons reporting this race alone, not in combination with any other race; Please refer to the Explanation of Data for more information.*

Cambodian (27)	37	0.05
Chinese, ex. Taiwanese (5,198)	5,928	8.43
Filipino (1,521)	2,234	3.18
Hmong (6)	6	0.01
Indian (5,214)	5,476	7.79
Indonesian (62)	107	0.15
Japanese (624)	1,155	1.64
Korean (1,882)	2,046	2.91
Laotian (19)	27	0.04
Malaysian (7)	21	0.03
Nepalese (10)	14	0.02
Pakistani (262)	299	0.43
Sri Lankan (33)	34	0.05
Taiwanese (438)	478	0.68
Thai (56)	80	0.11
Vietnamese (429)	528	0.75
Hawaii Native/Pacific Islander (134)	393	0.56
Not Hispanic (125)	345	0.49
Hispanic (9)	48	0.07
Fijian (21)	25	0.04
Guamanian/Chamorro (29)	70	0.10
Native Hawaiian (32)	191	0.27
Samoan (11)	23	0.03
Tongan (20)	25	0.04
White (47,058)	50,027	71.18
Not Hispanic (42,738)	44,995	64.02
Hispanic (4,320)	5,032	7.16

Pomona

Place Type: City
County: Los Angeles
Population: 149,058†

Ancestry‡	Population	%
Afghan (72)	72	0.05
African, Sub-Saharan (516)	574	0.39
African (233)	272	0.18
Cape Verdean (0)	12	0.01
Ethiopian (61)	61	0.04
Ghanaian (10)	10	0.01
Kenyan (36)	36	0.02
Nigerian (28)	28	0.02
Somalian (99)	99	0.07
Other Sub-Saharan African (49)	56	0.04
American (2,429)	2,429	1.63
Arab (962)	1,005	0.68
Arab (14)	14	0.01
Egyptian (18)	18	0.01
Jordanian (15)	28	0.02
Lebanese (905)	935	0.63
Other Arab (10)	10	0.01
Armenian (78)	78	0.05
Austrian (13)	113	0.08
Basque (16)	28	0.02
Belgian (0)	111	0.07
Brazilian (9)	21	0.01
British (71)	129	0.09
Bulgarian (0)	18	0.01
Canadian (73)	120	0.08
Croatian (0)	17	0.01
Czech (0)	35	0.02
Danish (74)	173	0.12
Dutch (165)	672	0.45
Eastern European (8)	16	0.01
English (883)	3,009	2.02
European (250)	297	0.20
Finnish (62)	132	0.09
French, ex. Basque (194)	1,165	0.78
French Canadian (80)	146	0.10
German (1,009)	4,622	3.11
Greek (75)	119	0.08
Hungarian (77)	180	0.12
Iranian (485)	508	0.34
Irish (629)	3,841	2.58
Italian (687)	2,572	1.73
Maltese (10)	10	0.01
Norwegian (146)	450	0.30
Polish (247)	492	0.33
Portuguese (90)	204	0.14
Romanian (0)	30	0.02
Russian (229)	472	0.32
Scandinavian (42)	42	0.03
Scotch-Irish (112)	343	0.23
Scottish (110)	597	0.40
Slavic (0)	9	0.01
Slovak (0)	31	0.02
Swedish (132)	337	0.23
Swiss (0)	53	0.04
Turkish (26)	64	0.04
Ukrainian (86)	118	0.08
Welsh (44)	152	0.10
West Indian, ex. Hispanic (166)	286	0.19
Belizean (36)	67	0.05
Jamaican (117)	206	0.14
Trinidadian/Tobagonian (13)	13	0.01
Yugoslavian (8)	21	0.01

Hispanic Origin	Population	%
Hispanic or Latino (of any race)	105,135	70.53
Central American, ex. Mexican	6,907	4.63
Costa Rican	85	0.06
Guatemalan	1,885	1.26
Honduran	632	0.42
Nicaraguan	625	0.42
Panamanian	75	0.05
Salvadoran	3,518	2.36
Other Central American	87	0.06
Cuban	404	0.27
Dominican Republic	23	0.02
Mexican	90,988	61.04
Puerto Rican	725	0.49
South American	1,007	0.68
Argentinean	154	0.10
Bolivian	33	0.02
Chilean	47	0.03
Colombian	200	0.13
Ecuadorian	219	0.15
Paraguayan	2	<0.01
Peruvian	288	0.19
Uruguayan	11	0.01
Venezuelan	28	0.02
Other South American	25	0.02
Other Hispanic or Latino	5,081	3.41

Race*	Population	%
African-American/Black (10,924)	12,276	8.24
Not Hispanic (10,107)	10,915	7.32
Hispanic (817)	1,361	0.91
American Indian/Alaska Native (1,763)	2,949	1.98
Not Hispanic (320)	769	0.52
Hispanic (1,443)	2,180	1.46
Aleut *(Alaska Native)* (0)	7	<0.01
Apache (66)	129	0.09
Arapaho (5)	5	<0.01
Blackfeet (8)	46	0.03
Canadian/French Am. Ind. (1)	3	<0.01
Central American Ind. (11)	28	0.02
Cherokee (47)	183	0.12
Cheyenne (1)	3	<0.01
Chickasaw (4)	19	0.01
Chippewa (5)	14	0.01
Choctaw (10)	35	0.02
Comanche (10)	13	0.01
Cree (1)	3	<0.01
Creek (3)	9	0.01
Delaware (1)	4	<0.01
Hopi (5)	15	0.01
Inupiat *(Alaska Native)* (2)	7	<0.01
Iroquois (2)	4	<0.01
Kiowa (0)	1	<0.01
Lumbee (1)	2	<0.01
Menominee (0)	2	<0.01
Mexican American Ind. (265)	355	0.24
Navajo (61)	114	0.08
Osage (2)	3	<0.01
Paiute (1)	4	<0.01
Pima (8)	12	0.01
Potawatomi (3)	3	<0.01
Pueblo (8)	30	0.02
Puget Sound Salish (0)	1	<0.01
Seminole (4)	9	0.01
Shoshone (10)	11	0.01
Sioux (20)	38	0.03
South American Ind. (6)	15	0.01
Spanish American Ind. (27)	33	0.02
Tohono O'Odham (7)	8	0.01
Ute (0)	4	<0.01
Yakama (0)	1	<0.01
Yaqui (13)	21	0.01
Yuman (14)	19	0.01
Asian (12,688)	14,312	9.60
Not Hispanic (12,303)	13,374	8.97
Hispanic (385)	938	0.63
Bangladeshi (35)	39	0.03
Burmese (41)	44	0.03
Cambodian (768)	836	0.56
Chinese, ex. Taiwanese (2,945)	3,460	2.32
Filipino (3,250)	3,879	2.60
Hmong (37)	41	0.03
Indian (684)	807	0.54
Indonesian (150)	219	0.15
Japanese (400)	740	0.50
Korean (1,038)	1,130	0.76
Laotian (217)	244	0.16
Malaysian (30)	41	0.03
Nepalese (3)	3	<0.01
Pakistani (148)	163	0.11
Sri Lankan (16)	22	0.01
Taiwanese (378)	445	0.30
Thai (245)	312	0.21
Vietnamese (1,777)	1,966	1.32
Hawaii Native/Pacific Islander (282)	681	0.46
Not Hispanic (240)	474	0.32
Hispanic (42)	207	0.14
Fijian (13)	15	0.01
Guamanian/Chamorro (30)	59	0.04
Native Hawaiian (58)	147	0.10
Samoan (135)	224	0.15
Tongan (23)	33	0.02
White (71,564)	76,897	51.59
Not Hispanic (18,672)	20,142	13.51
Hispanic (52,892)	56,755	38.08

Port Hueneme

Place Type: City
County: Ventura
Population: 21,723†

Ancestry‡	Population	%
African, Sub-Saharan (47)	52	0.24
African (26)	31	0.14
Kenyan (12)	12	0.06
Nigerian (9)	9	0.04
American (477)	477	2.20
Arab (24)	46	0.21
Egyptian (12)	27	0.12
Lebanese (12)	19	0.09
Armenian (16)	16	0.07
Austrian (0)	28	0.13
Belgian (0)	19	0.09
British (36)	158	0.73
Canadian (33)	93	0.43
Celtic (0)	13	0.06
Czech (0)	44	0.20
Czechoslovakian (11)	11	0.05
Danish (6)	152	0.70
Dutch (77)	252	1.16
English (376)	1,037	4.77
European (152)	182	0.84
Finnish (0)	14	0.06
French, ex. Basque (91)	576	2.65
French Canadian (69)	119	0.55
German (573)	2,066	9.51
Greek (19)	31	0.14
Hungarian (40)	82	0.38
Irish (369)	1,507	6.94
Italian (197)	1,030	4.74
Latvian (0)	10	0.05

*Notes: † The Census 2010 population figure is used to calculate the percentages in the Hispanic Origin and Race categories. Ancestry percentages are based on the 2006-2010 American Community Survey population (not shown); ‡ Numbers in parentheses indicate the number of people reporting a single ancestry; * Numbers in parentheses indicate the number of persons reporting this race alone, not in combination with any other race; Please refer to the Explanation of Data for more information.*

Norwegian (89)	332	1.53
Polish (153)	410	1.89
Portuguese (11)	74	0.34
Russian (25)	189	0.87
Scandinavian (12)	12	0.06
Scotch-Irish (190)	426	1.96
Scottish (104)	372	1.71
Slavic (0)	11	0.05
Swedish (0)	112	0.52
Swiss (36)	122	0.56
Ukrainian (6)	21	0.10
Welsh (13)	134	0.62
West Indian, ex. Hispanic (9)	59	0.27
Jamaican (0)	50	0.23
West Indian (9)	9	0.04

Hispanic Origin	Population	%
Hispanic or Latino (of any race)	11,360	52.29
Central American, ex. Mexican	223	1.03
Costa Rican	12	0.06
Guatemalan	53	0.24
Honduran	18	0.08
Nicaraguan	18	0.08
Panamanian	19	0.09
Salvadoran	101	0.46
Other Central American	2	0.01
Cuban	25	0.12
Dominican Republic	22	0.10
Mexican	10,232	47.10
Puerto Rican	156	0.72
South American	98	0.45
Argentinean	14	0.06
Bolivian	3	0.01
Chilean	13	0.06
Colombian	28	0.13
Ecuadorian	8	0.04
Peruvian	21	0.10
Uruguayan	1	<0.01
Venezuelan	10	0.05
Other Hispanic or Latino	604	2.78

Race*	Population	%
African-American/Black (1,111)	1,405	6.47
Not Hispanic (1,002)	1,189	5.47
Hispanic (109)	216	0.99
American Indian/Alaska Native (295)	556	2.56
Not Hispanic (103)	247	1.14
Hispanic (192)	309	1.42
Alaska Athabascan *(Ala. Nat.)* (1)	1	<0.01
Aleut *(Alaska Native)* (0)	1	<0.01
Apache (17)	40	0.18
Blackfeet (4)	12	0.06
Cherokee (23)	67	0.31
Cheyenne (3)	6	0.03
Chippewa (0)	5	0.02
Choctaw (7)	15	0.07
Comanche (1)	8	0.04
Creek (2)	3	0.01
Crow (4)	5	0.02
Delaware (1)	1	<0.01
Hopi (6)	7	0.03
Iroquois (0)	7	0.03
Lumbee (1)	2	0.01
Mexican American Ind. (35)	48	0.22
Navajo (8)	10	0.05
Pima (0)	2	0.01
Pueblo (2)	5	0.02
Seminole (0)	3	0.01
Shoshone (1)	3	0.01
Sioux (6)	13	0.06
South American Ind. (1)	1	<0.01
Tohono O'Odham (0)	3	0.01
Yaqui (4)	10	0.05
Asian (1,299)	1,756	8.08
Not Hispanic (1,213)	1,539	7.08
Hispanic (86)	217	1.00
Burmese (4)	4	0.02
Cambodian (13)	16	0.07
Chinese, ex. Taiwanese (65)	118	0.54
Filipino (872)	1,147	5.28
Indian (47)	62	0.29
Indonesian (0)	2	0.01
Japanese (131)	266	1.22
Korean (33)	58	0.27
Laotian (1)	4	0.02
Malaysian (1)	1	<0.01
Pakistani (3)	3	0.01
Sri Lankan (1)	1	<0.01
Thai (21)	26	0.12
Vietnamese (63)	73	0.34
Hawaii Native/Pacific Islander (119)	235	1.08
Not Hispanic (95)	171	0.79
Hispanic (24)	64	0.29
Fijian (4)	4	0.02
Guamanian/Chamorro (26)	51	0.23
Native Hawaiian (35)	88	0.41
Samoan (33)	57	0.26
Tongan (0)	4	0.02
White (12,357)	13,450	61.92
Not Hispanic (7,291)	7,808	35.94
Hispanic (5,066)	5,642	25.97

Porterville

Place Type: City
County: Tulare
Population: 54,165†

Ancestry‡	Population	%
African, Sub-Saharan (24)	24	0.05
African (12)	12	0.02
Nigerian (12)	12	0.02
American (1,683)	1,683	3.19
Arab (77)	77	0.15
Arab (44)	44	0.08
Lebanese (33)	33	0.06
Armenian (0)	25	0.05
Australian (12)	12	0.02
Austrian (13)	55	0.10
Belgian (0)	32	0.06
Brazilian (31)	36	0.07
British (0)	28	0.05
Canadian (0)	10	0.02
Croatian (9)	9	0.02
Czech (0)	14	0.03
Czechoslovakian (12)	53	0.10
Danish (18)	112	0.21
Dutch (89)	369	0.70
English (788)	2,382	4.51
European (230)	280	0.53
Finnish (115)	167	0.32
French, ex. Basque (159)	694	1.32
French Canadian (24)	112	0.21
German (1,219)	3,829	7.26
Greek (27)	74	0.14
Hungarian (0)	36	0.07
Icelander (0)	33	0.06
Irish (816)	2,918	5.53
Italian (248)	1,314	2.49
Norwegian (185)	250	0.47
Pennsylvania German (0)	8	0.02
Polish (40)	145	0.27
Portuguese (93)	108	0.20
Russian (52)	130	0.25
Scandinavian (26)	97	0.18
Scotch-Irish (73)	388	0.74
Scottish (10)	393	0.74
Serbian (0)	11	0.02
Slavic (15)	49	0.09
Slovak (10)	10	0.02
Swedish (131)	393	0.74
Swiss (9)	26	0.05
Ukrainian (7)	7	0.01
Welsh (0)	265	0.50
West Indian, ex. Hispanic (60)	109	0.21
Dutch West Indian (60)	109	0.21
Yugoslavian (24)	24	0.05

Hispanic Origin	Population	%
Hispanic or Latino (of any race)	33,549	61.94
Central American, ex. Mexican	236	0.44
Costa Rican	12	0.02
Guatemalan	57	0.11
Honduran	26	0.05
Nicaraguan	20	0.04
Panamanian	15	0.03
Salvadoran	104	0.19
Other Central American	2	<0.01
Cuban	30	0.06
Dominican Republic	5	0.01
Mexican	31,421	58.01
Puerto Rican	173	0.32
South American	40	0.07
Argentinean	2	<0.01
Bolivian	2	<0.01
Chilean	5	0.01
Colombian	10	0.02
Peruvian	21	0.04
Other Hispanic or Latino	1,644	3.04

Race*	Population	%
African-American/Black (673)	960	1.77
Not Hispanic (454)	586	1.08
Hispanic (219)	374	0.69
American Indian/Alaska Native (1,007)	1,675	3.09
Not Hispanic (461)	824	1.52
Hispanic (546)	851	1.57
Aleut *(Alaska Native)* (1)	4	0.01
Apache (11)	20	0.04
Arapaho (3)	4	0.01
Blackfeet (4)	14	0.03
Canadian/French Am. Ind. (1)	3	0.01
Central American Ind. (1)	1	<0.01
Cherokee (57)	190	0.35
Cheyenne (2)	2	<0.01
Chickasaw (2)	5	0.01
Chippewa (5)	5	0.01
Choctaw (17)	42	0.08
Colville (0)	1	<0.01
Comanche (1)	5	0.01
Creek (1)	10	0.02
Delaware (3)	4	0.01
Hopi (6)	9	0.02
Inupiat *(Alaska Native)* (1)	4	0.01
Iroquois (0)	2	<0.01
Kiowa (2)	19	0.04
Mexican American Ind. (66)	105	0.19
Navajo (4)	8	0.01
Ottawa (0)	1	<0.01
Paiute (7)	10	0.02
Pima (15)	23	0.04
Potawatomi (1)	5	0.01
Pueblo (1)	5	0.01
Shoshone (3)	9	0.02
Sioux (10)	21	0.04
Spanish American Ind. (8)	9	0.02
Tlingit-Haida *(Alaska Native)* (2)	6	0.01
Tohono O'Odham (5)	5	0.01
Ute (1)	4	0.01
Yaqui (18)	25	0.05
Yuman (12)	17	0.03
Asian (2,521)	3,153	5.82
Not Hispanic (2,349)	2,707	5.00
Hispanic (172)	446	0.82
Bangladeshi (2)	2	<0.01
Burmese (2)	2	<0.01
Cambodian (23)	34	0.06
Chinese, ex. Taiwanese (124)	170	0.31
Filipino (1,256)	1,643	3.03
Hmong (192)	203	0.37
Indian (218)	266	0.49
Indonesian (1)	5	0.01
Japanese (38)	98	0.18
Korean (35)	57	0.11
Laotian (352)	429	0.79
Malaysian (3)	3	0.01
Pakistani (63)	73	0.13
Sri Lankan (1)	1	<0.01
Taiwanese (1)	7	0.01
Thai (22)	63	0.12

SECTION TWO

*Notes: † The Census 2010 population figure is used to calculate the percentages in the Hispanic Origin and Race categories. Ancestry percentages are based on the 2006-2010 American Community Survey population (not shown); ‡ Numbers in parentheses indicate the number of people reporting a single ancestry; * Numbers in parentheses indicate the number of persons reporting this race alone, not in combination with any other race; Please refer to the Explanation of Data for more information.*

Vietnamese (38)	43	0.08
Hawaii Native/Pacific Islander (64)	157	0.29
Not Hispanic (49)	98	0.18
Hispanic (15)	59	0.11
Fijian (1)	1	<0.01
Guamanian/Chamorro (5)	13	0.02
Marshallese (5)	5	0.01
Native Hawaiian (19)	59	0.11
Samoan (21)	27	0.05
White (31,847)	34,025	62.82
Not Hispanic (16,423)	17,160	31.68
Hispanic (15,424)	16,865	31.14

Poway

Place Type: City
County: San Diego
Population: 47,811†

Ancestry‡	Population	%
African, Sub-Saharan (267)	316	0.67
African (172)	206	0.43
Nigerian (40)	40	0.08
South African (55)	70	0.15
American (1,934)	1,934	4.07
Arab (387)	649	1.37
Arab (20)	34	0.07
Egyptian (37)	77	0.16
Iraqi (9)	33	0.07
Lebanese (132)	214	0.45
Moroccan (9)	9	0.02
Syrian (51)	148	0.31
Other Arab (129)	134	0.28
Armenian (55)	196	0.41
Assyrian/Chaldean/Syriac (107)	121	0.25
Australian (33)	33	0.07
Austrian (28)	228	0.48
Belgian (33)	74	0.16
Brazilian (19)	59	0.12
British (107)	139	0.29
Bulgarian (0)	13	0.03
Canadian (39)	126	0.27
Celtic (204)	204	0.43
Croatian (0)	44	0.09
Czech (58)	330	0.70
Czechoslovakian (41)	99	0.21
Danish (167)	396	0.83
Dutch (119)	695	1.46
Eastern European (139)	139	0.29
English (1,987)	5,636	11.87
European (773)	980	2.06
Finnish (20)	217	0.46
French, ex. Basque (364)	1,910	4.02
French Canadian (143)	314	0.66
German (1,949)	9,544	20.10
Greek (51)	51	0.11
Hungarian (128)	286	0.60
Icelander (30)	41	0.09
Iranian (318)	390	0.82
Irish (1,377)	6,596	13.89
Italian (811)	3,348	7.05
Latvian (37)	59	0.12
Lithuanian (88)	177	0.37
Luxemburger (0)	8	0.02
Macedonian (16)	16	0.03
Maltese (19)	19	0.04
Northern European (136)	136	0.29
Norwegian (247)	859	1.81
Pennsylvania German (0)	21	0.04
Polish (516)	1,790	3.77
Portuguese (127)	351	0.74
Romanian (24)	50	0.11
Russian (200)	554	1.17
Scandinavian (136)	216	0.45
Scotch-Irish (277)	744	1.57
Scottish (209)	1,102	2.32
Serbian (0)	21	0.04
Slavic (30)	89	0.19
Slovak (53)	106	0.22
Slovene (9)	33	0.07
Swedish (265)	1,364	2.87
Swiss (46)	186	0.39
Turkish (28)	28	0.06
Ukrainian (68)	89	0.19
Welsh (80)	346	0.73
West Indian, ex. Hispanic (0)	23	0.05
Jamaican (0)	23	0.05
Yugoslavian (16)	31	0.07

Hispanic Origin	Population	%
Hispanic or Latino (of any race)	7,508	15.70
Central American, ex. Mexican	196	0.41
Costa Rican	17	0.04
Guatemalan	64	0.13
Honduran	22	0.05
Nicaraguan	20	0.04
Panamanian	23	0.05
Salvadoran	49	0.10
Other Central American	1	<0.01
Cuban	46	0.10
Dominican Republic	15	0.03
Mexican	6,056	12.67
Puerto Rican	295	0.62
South American	250	0.52
Argentinean	27	0.06
Bolivian	19	0.04
Chilean	10	0.02
Colombian	98	0.20
Ecuadorian	28	0.06
Paraguayan	1	<0.01
Peruvian	54	0.11
Uruguayan	3	0.01
Venezuelan	10	0.02
Other Hispanic or Latino	650	1.36

Race*	Population	%
African-American/Black (783)	1,092	2.28
Not Hispanic (722)	958	2.00
Hispanic (61)	134	0.28
American Indian/Alaska Native (265)	677	1.42
Not Hispanic (149)	440	0.92
Hispanic (116)	237	0.50
Aleut *(Alaska Native)* (0)	1	<0.01
Apache (2)	4	0.01
Arapaho (0)	2	<0.01
Blackfeet (6)	15	0.03
Canadian/French Am. Ind. (0)	5	0.01
Cherokee (25)	112	0.23
Cheyenne (1)	1	<0.01
Chickasaw (12)	17	0.04
Chippewa (0)	2	<0.01
Choctaw (6)	18	0.04
Cree (0)	5	0.01
Creek (0)	4	0.01
Delaware (0)	6	0.01
Hopi (1)	9	0.02
Iroquois (0)	7	0.01
Lumbee (0)	1	<0.01
Menominee (1)	2	<0.01
Mexican American Ind. (30)	50	0.10
Navajo (4)	18	0.04
Osage (0)	1	<0.01
Paiute (1)	1	<0.01
Pima (1)	1	<0.01
Potawatomi (1)	3	0.01
Pueblo (1)	3	0.01
Puget Sound Salish (6)	6	0.01
Shoshone (1)	8	0.02
Sioux (12)	22	0.05
South American Ind. (4)	10	0.02
Spanish American Ind. (5)	6	0.01
Tohono O'Odham (0)	5	0.01
Ute (1)	2	<0.01
Yaqui (7)	11	0.02
Asian (4,853)	5,983	12.51
Not Hispanic (4,750)	5,718	11.96
Hispanic (103)	265	0.55
Bangladeshi (7)	7	0.01
Burmese (2)	5	0.01
Cambodian (10)	13	0.03
Chinese, ex. Taiwanese (804)	1,058	2.21
Filipino (1,865)	2,404	5.03
Hmong (1)	3	0.01
Indian (563)	629	1.32
Indonesian (27)	34	0.07
Japanese (317)	594	1.24
Korean (259)	346	0.72
Laotian (29)	37	0.08
Malaysian (0)	4	0.01
Pakistani (33)	34	0.07
Sri Lankan (2)	2	<0.01
Taiwanese (93)	121	0.25
Thai (28)	58	0.12
Vietnamese (635)	697	1.46
Hawaii Native/Pacific Islander (106)	303	0.63
Not Hispanic (101)	254	0.53
Hispanic (5)	49	0.10
Fijian (3)	4	0.01
Guamanian/Chamorro (40)	94	0.20
Marshallese (1)	1	<0.01
Native Hawaiian (36)	129	0.27
Samoan (7)	29	0.06
Tongan (1)	2	<0.01
White (36,781)	38,642	80.82
Not Hispanic (33,041)	34,376	71.90
Hispanic (3,740)	4,266	8.92

Prunedale

Place Type: CDP
County: Monterey
Population: 17,560†

Ancestry‡	Population	%
American (668)	668	3.51
Arab (32)	39	0.20
Arab (11)	11	0.06
Egyptian (21)	21	0.11
Lebanese (0)	7	0.04
Armenian (10)	10	0.05
Australian (13)	13	0.07
Austrian (0)	20	0.11
Basque (0)	24	0.13
British (43)	64	0.34
Canadian (35)	35	0.18
Celtic (8)	8	0.04
Czech (30)	62	0.33
Danish (28)	89	0.47
Dutch (25)	192	1.01
Eastern European (17)	17	0.09
English (425)	1,408	7.39
European (275)	295	1.55
Finnish (16)	93	0.49
French, ex. Basque (28)	493	2.59
French Canadian (0)	52	0.27
German (564)	1,855	9.74
Greek (142)	383	2.01
Hungarian (0)	9	0.05
Iranian (26)	26	0.14
Irish (1,221)	2,540	13.34
Israeli (16)	16	0.08
Italian (332)	1,155	6.06
Lithuanian (9)	9	0.05
New Zealander (11)	11	0.06
Northern European (20)	77	0.40
Norwegian (102)	363	1.91
Polish (27)	111	0.58
Portuguese (247)	487	2.56
Russian (68)	74	0.39
Scandinavian (11)	11	0.06
Scotch-Irish (104)	443	2.33
Scottish (11)	243	1.28
Slavic (9)	27	0.14
Slovene (0)	70	0.37
Swedish (135)	361	1.90
Swiss (34)	184	0.97
Welsh (56)	208	1.09
Yugoslavian (19)	63	0.33

*Notes: † The Census 2010 population figure is used to calculate the percentages in the Hispanic Origin and Race categories. Ancestry percentages are based on the 2006-2010 American Community Survey population (not shown); ‡ Numbers in parentheses indicate the number of people reporting a single ancestry; * Numbers in parentheses indicate the number of persons reporting this race alone, not in combination with any other race; Please refer to the Explanation of Data for more information.*

Hispanic Origin	Population	%
Hispanic or Latino (of any race)	7,322	41.70
Central American, ex. Mexican	96	0.55
Costa Rican	4	0.02
Guatemalan	11	0.06
Honduran	1	0.01
Nicaraguan	7	0.04
Panamanian	13	0.07
Salvadoran	60	0.34
Cuban	12	0.07
Dominican Republic	1	0.01
Mexican	6,729	38.32
Puerto Rican	73	0.42
South American	43	0.24
Argentinean	1	0.01
Chilean	8	0.05
Colombian	6	0.03
Ecuadorian	13	0.07
Paraguayan	1	0.01
Peruvian	14	0.08
Other Hispanic or Latino	368	2.10

Race*	Population	%
African-American/Black (177)	287	1.63
Not Hispanic (148)	226	1.29
Hispanic (29)	61	0.35
American Indian/Alaska Native (199)	489	2.78
Not Hispanic (87)	256	1.46
Hispanic (112)	233	1.33
Aleut *(Alaska Native)* (0)	2	0.01
Apache (7)	16	0.09
Blackfeet (3)	13	0.07
Cherokee (12)	56	0.32
Chickasaw (2)	7	0.04
Chippewa (2)	5	0.03
Choctaw (6)	20	0.11
Creek (2)	2	0.01
Hopi (5)	9	0.05
Iroquois (0)	5	0.03
Kiowa (0)	2	0.01
Mexican American Ind. (25)	41	0.23
Navajo (2)	3	0.02
Osage (4)	7	0.04
Potawatomi (3)	5	0.03
Pueblo (0)	4	0.02
Shoshone (0)	3	0.02
Sioux (4)	13	0.07
South American Ind. (1)	1	0.01
Spanish American Ind. (2)	8	0.05
Yaqui (3)	10	0.06
Asian (672)	1,064	6.06
Not Hispanic (602)	871	4.96
Hispanic (70)	193	1.10
Burmese (0)	4	0.02
Cambodian (9)	9	0.05
Chinese, ex. Taiwanese (55)	87	0.50
Filipino (312)	514	2.93
Hmong (1)	1	0.01
Indian (47)	61	0.35
Indonesian (1)	1	0.01
Japanese (126)	273	1.55
Korean (42)	76	0.43
Taiwanese (5)	5	0.03
Vietnamese (41)	50	0.28
Hawaii Native/Pacific Islander (58)	130	0.74
Not Hispanic (53)	111	0.63
Hispanic (5)	19	0.11
Fijian (7)	8	0.05
Guamanian/Chamorro (9)	21	0.12
Native Hawaiian (16)	51	0.29
Samoan (17)	29	0.17
Tongan (1)	2	0.01
White (11,771)	12,696	72.30
Not Hispanic (8,806)	9,270	52.79
Hispanic (2,965)	3,426	19.51

Quartz Hill

Place Type: CDP
County: Los Angeles
Population: 10,912†

Ancestry‡	Population	%
African, Sub-Saharan (0)	64	0.62
African (0)	34	0.33
Nigerian (0)	30	0.29
American (603)	603	5.80
Arab (73)	74	0.71
Arab (24)	25	0.24
Syrian (49)	49	0.47
Armenian (27)	67	0.64
Austrian (0)	70	0.67
Basque (13)	13	0.13
British (9)	9	0.09
Canadian (26)	45	0.43
Czech (0)	62	0.60
Danish (12)	50	0.48
Dutch (45)	145	1.39
Eastern European (14)	14	0.13
English (357)	1,268	12.19
European (83)	114	1.10
French, ex. Basque (34)	335	3.22
German (459)	1,696	16.31
Greek (0)	9	0.09
Hungarian (11)	21	0.20
Irish (208)	1,133	10.90
Italian (268)	549	5.28
Norwegian (20)	244	2.35
Polish (42)	163	1.57
Romanian (16)	16	0.15
Russian (57)	98	0.94
Scotch-Irish (60)	268	2.58
Scottish (24)	329	3.16
Slavic (0)	12	0.12
Swedish (7)	163	1.57
Swiss (9)	18	0.17
Welsh (9)	110	1.06
West Indian, ex. Hispanic (41)	101	0.97
Jamaican (41)	101	0.97

Hispanic Origin	Population	%
Hispanic or Latino (of any race)	2,689	24.64
Central American, ex. Mexican	246	2.25
Costa Rican	3	0.03
Guatemalan	55	0.50
Honduran	14	0.13
Nicaraguan	18	0.16
Panamanian	6	0.05
Salvadoran	143	1.31
Other Central American	7	0.06
Cuban	38	0.35
Dominican Republic	6	0.05
Mexican	1,956	17.93
Puerto Rican	65	0.60
South American	71	0.65
Argentinean	16	0.15
Chilean	9	0.08
Colombian	10	0.09
Ecuadorian	17	0.16
Peruvian	12	0.11
Uruguayan	1	0.01
Other South American	6	0.05
Other Hispanic or Latino	307	2.81

Race*	Population	%
African-American/Black (795)	920	8.43
Not Hispanic (751)	839	7.69
Hispanic (44)	81	0.74
American Indian/Alaska Native (142)	286	2.62
Not Hispanic (73)	166	1.52
Hispanic (69)	120	1.10
Apache (1)	2	0.02
Arapaho (1)	1	0.01
Blackfeet (0)	8	0.07
Cherokee (20)	63	0.58
Cheyenne (0)	1	0.01
Chickasaw (0)	3	0.03
Chippewa (0)	2	0.02
Choctaw (6)	8	0.07
Colville (1)	1	0.01
Cree (0)	3	0.03
Creek (2)	5	0.05
Hopi (0)	1	0.01
Iroquois (4)	7	0.06
Mexican American Ind. (30)	34	0.31
Navajo (6)	8	0.07
Paiute (4)	10	0.09
Potawatomi (0)	1	0.01
Pueblo (3)	4	0.04
Sioux (0)	2	0.02
South American Ind. (0)	3	0.03
Yaqui (0)	3	0.03
Asian (303)	435	3.99
Not Hispanic (288)	398	3.65
Hispanic (15)	37	0.34
Bangladeshi (4)	4	0.04
Cambodian (13)	16	0.15
Chinese, ex. Taiwanese (41)	62	0.57
Filipino (111)	162	1.48
Indian (38)	50	0.46
Japanese (27)	62	0.57
Korean (41)	47	0.43
Sri Lankan (1)	1	0.01
Taiwanese (0)	3	0.03
Thai (9)	12	0.11
Vietnamese (6)	15	0.14
Hawaii Native/Pacific Islander (28)	79	0.72
Not Hispanic (24)	60	0.55
Hispanic (4)	19	0.17
Guamanian/Chamorro (14)	23	0.21
Native Hawaiian (4)	29	0.27
Samoan (7)	13	0.12
Tongan (1)	3	0.03
White (8,218)	8,616	78.96
Not Hispanic (6,798)	7,045	64.56
Hispanic (1,420)	1,571	14.40

Ramona

Place Type: CDP
County: San Diego
Population: 20,292†

Ancestry‡	Population	%
American (359)	359	1.67
Arab (38)	71	0.33
Lebanese (7)	7	0.03
Syrian (31)	64	0.30
Austrian (0)	20	0.09
Basque (0)	50	0.23
British (31)	70	0.33
Canadian (31)	49	0.23
Croatian (17)	17	0.08
Czech (73)	142	0.66
Czechoslovakian (0)	43	0.20
Danish (93)	115	0.54
Dutch (94)	344	1.60
English (544)	2,174	10.12
European (349)	415	1.93
Finnish (0)	41	0.19
French, ex. Basque (172)	690	3.21
French Canadian (0)	33	0.15
German (1,255)	4,966	23.12
Greek (77)	163	0.76
Hungarian (19)	57	0.27
Iranian (10)	10	0.05
Irish (708)	3,315	15.43
Italian (340)	798	3.71
Lithuanian (0)	82	0.38
Northern European (11)	11	0.05
Norwegian (117)	413	1.92
Pennsylvania German (0)	10	0.05
Polish (122)	492	2.29
Portuguese (100)	130	0.61
Romanian (25)	54	0.25
Russian (17)	114	0.53

SECTION TWO

*Notes: † The Census 2010 population figure is used to calculate the percentages in the Hispanic Origin and Race categories. Ancestry percentages are based on the 2006-2010 American Community Survey population (not shown); ‡ Numbers in parentheses indicate the number of people reporting a single ancestry; * Numbers in parentheses indicate the number of persons reporting this race alone, not in combination with any other race; Please refer to the Explanation of Data for more information.*

Scandinavian (0)	10	0.05
Scotch-Irish (107)	455	2.12
Scottish (130)	523	2.43
Slavic (16)	49	0.23
Swedish (159)	475	2.21
Swiss (20)	113	0.53
Ukrainian (46)	46	0.21
Welsh (11)	83	0.39
Yugoslavian (16)	171	0.80

Hispanic Origin	Population	%
Hispanic or Latino (of any race)	6,334	31.21
Central American, ex. Mexican	161	0.79
Costa Rican	1	<0.01
Guatemalan	91	0.45
Honduran	17	0.08
Nicaraguan	2	0.01
Panamanian	1	<0.01
Salvadoran	48	0.24
Other Central American	1	<0.01
Cuban	21	0.10
Dominican Republic	4	0.02
Mexican	5,731	28.24
Puerto Rican	56	0.28
South American	30	0.15
Argentinean	4	0.02
Chilean	3	0.01
Colombian	12	0.06
Ecuadorian	2	0.01
Peruvian	3	0.01
Uruguayan	1	<0.01
Venezuelan	5	0.02
Other Hispanic or Latino	331	1.63

Race*	Population	%
African-American/Black (139)	260	1.28
Not Hispanic (118)	205	1.01
Hispanic (21)	55	0.27
American Indian/Alaska Native (224)	421	2.07
Not Hispanic (139)	272	1.34
Hispanic (85)	149	0.73
Aleut *(Alaska Native)* (2)	3	0.01
Apache (4)	18	0.09
Blackfeet (2)	13	0.06
Central American Ind. (1)	1	<0.01
Cherokee (8)	49	0.24
Cheyenne (1)	2	0.01
Chickasaw (2)	4	0.02
Chippewa (1)	5	0.02
Choctaw (4)	6	0.03
Comanche (3)	6	0.03
Cree (0)	1	<0.01
Creek (8)	8	0.04
Delaware (0)	2	0.01
Hopi (1)	4	0.02
Inupiat *(Alaska Native)* (2)	2	0.01
Iroquois (1)	4	0.02
Menominee (0)	1	<0.01
Mexican American Ind. (22)	27	0.13
Navajo (5)	8	0.04
Paiute (4)	4	0.02
Potawatomi (0)	1	<0.01
Pueblo (0)	1	<0.01
Puget Sound Salish (0)	2	0.01
Seminole (1)	4	0.02
Sioux (6)	10	0.05
Ute (1)	3	0.01
Yaqui (4)	5	0.02
Yuman (1)	1	<0.01
Asian (279)	435	2.14
Not Hispanic (268)	393	1.94
Hispanic (11)	42	0.21
Cambodian (1)	2	0.01
Chinese, ex. Taiwanese (55)	70	0.34
Filipino (109)	203	1.00
Hmong (12)	17	0.08
Indian (20)	28	0.14
Indonesian (0)	2	0.01
Japanese (37)	54	0.27
Korean (5)	13	0.06
Laotian (2)	3	0.01
Thai (8)	9	0.04
Vietnamese (21)	23	0.11
Hawaii Native/Pacific Islander (71)	146	0.72
Not Hispanic (54)	114	0.56
Hispanic (17)	32	0.16
Guamanian/Chamorro (25)	39	0.19
Native Hawaiian (23)	51	0.25
Samoan (19)	45	0.22
Tongan (0)	1	<0.01
White (15,887)	16,565	81.63
Not Hispanic (12,985)	13,335	65.72
Hispanic (2,902)	3,230	15.92

Rancho Cordova

Place Type: City
County: Sacramento
Population: 64,776†

Ancestry‡	Population	%
Afghan (13)	13	0.02
African, Sub-Saharan (505)	562	0.89
African (224)	281	0.44
Ethiopian (22)	22	0.03
Kenyan (129)	129	0.20
Nigerian (22)	22	0.03
Ugandan (108)	108	0.17
American (1,885)	1,885	2.98
Arab (313)	399	0.63
Arab (8)	8	0.01
Egyptian (52)	52	0.08
Jordanian (33)	33	0.05
Lebanese (10)	10	0.02
Moroccan (44)	59	0.09
Syrian (0)	32	0.05
Other Arab (166)	205	0.32
Armenian (768)	900	1.42
Australian (0)	9	0.01
Austrian (36)	82	0.13
Basque (22)	22	0.03
Belgian (15)	38	0.06
Brazilian (9)	9	0.01
British (158)	291	0.46
Bulgarian (30)	30	0.05
Canadian (89)	166	0.26
Croatian (0)	30	0.05
Cypriot (10)	22	0.03
Czech (20)	215	0.34
Czechoslovakian (24)	62	0.10
Danish (46)	343	0.54
Dutch (91)	832	1.31
English (1,022)	4,461	7.05
European (654)	722	1.14
Finnish (39)	73	0.12
French, ex. Basque (330)	1,573	2.49
French Canadian (85)	251	0.40
German (1,818)	7,424	11.73
Greek (152)	294	0.46
Hungarian (29)	108	0.17
Icelander (14)	14	0.02
Iranian (130)	130	0.21
Irish (1,356)	5,396	8.52
Israeli (0)	38	0.06
Italian (988)	3,128	4.94
Latvian (0)	9	0.01
Lithuanian (0)	57	0.09
Maltese (0)	37	0.06
Northern European (89)	133	0.21
Norwegian (213)	819	1.29
Pennsylvania German (46)	46	0.07
Polish (151)	930	1.47
Portuguese (429)	895	1.41
Romanian (640)	682	1.08
Russian (929)	1,137	1.80
Scandinavian (78)	196	0.31
Scotch-Irish (386)	1,003	1.58
Scottish (366)	1,063	1.68
Slavic (0)	7	0.01
Slovak (17)	46	0.07
Slovene (0)	16	0.03
Swedish (107)	618	0.98
Swiss (7)	87	0.14
Turkish (20)	20	0.03
Ukrainian (2,675)	2,814	4.45
Welsh (19)	491	0.78
West Indian, ex. Hispanic (123)	123	0.19
Bermudan (5)	5	0.01
Jamaican (20)	20	0.03
West Indian (98)	98	0.15
Yugoslavian (0)	85	0.13

Hispanic Origin	Population	%
Hispanic or Latino (of any race)	12,740	19.67
Central American, ex. Mexican	970	1.50
Costa Rican	31	0.05
Guatemalan	225	0.35
Honduran	53	0.08
Nicaraguan	166	0.26
Panamanian	26	0.04
Salvadoran	454	0.70
Other Central American	15	0.02
Cuban	66	0.10
Dominican Republic	23	0.04
Mexican	9,862	15.22
Puerto Rican	468	0.72
South American	260	0.40
Argentinean	23	0.04
Bolivian	26	0.04
Chilean	25	0.04
Colombian	55	0.08
Ecuadorian	17	0.03
Paraguayan	2	<0.01
Peruvian	99	0.15
Venezuelan	13	0.02
Other Hispanic or Latino	1,091	1.68

Race*	Population	%
African-American/Black (6,561)	8,361	12.91
Not Hispanic (6,286)	7,710	11.90
Hispanic (275)	651	1.01
American Indian/Alaska Native (668)	1,651	2.55
Not Hispanic (398)	1,126	1.74
Hispanic (270)	525	0.81
Alaska Athabascan *(Ala. Nat.)* (0)	1	<0.01
Aleut *(Alaska Native)* (2)	5	0.01
Apache (31)	75	0.12
Arapaho (6)	7	0.01
Blackfeet (11)	77	0.12
Canadian/French Am. Ind. (0)	3	<0.01
Central American Ind. (1)	7	0.01
Cherokee (67)	341	0.53
Cheyenne (0)	1	<0.01
Chickasaw (8)	21	0.03
Chippewa (14)	22	0.03
Choctaw (23)	70	0.11
Colville (0)	1	<0.01
Comanche (5)	5	0.01
Cree (0)	6	0.01
Creek (10)	35	0.05
Crow (0)	3	<0.01
Delaware (1)	7	0.01
Hopi (3)	3	<0.01
Inupiat *(Alaska Native)* (1)	3	<0.01
Iroquois (5)	10	0.02
Kiowa (6)	8	0.01
Menominee (1)	3	<0.01
Mexican American Ind. (39)	57	0.09
Navajo (22)	48	0.07
Osage (2)	2	<0.01
Paiute (9)	19	0.03
Pima (2)	2	<0.01
Potawatomi (4)	10	0.02
Pueblo (4)	9	0.01
Seminole (0)	5	0.01
Shoshone (2)	8	0.01
Sioux (26)	56	0.09
South American Ind. (4)	6	0.01
Spanish American Ind. (2)	6	0.01
Tlingit-Haida *(Alaska Native)* (5)	5	0.01

*Notes: † The Census 2010 population figure is used to calculate the percentages in the Hispanic Origin and Race categories. Ancestry percentages are based on the 2006-2010 American Community Survey population (not shown); ‡ Numbers in parentheses indicate the number of people reporting a single ancestry; * Numbers in parentheses indicate the number of persons reporting this race alone, not in combination with any other race; Please refer to the Explanation of Data for more information.*

Tohono O'Odham (1)	1	<0.01
Ute (1)	1	<0.01
Yakama (2)	2	<0.01
Yaqui (2)	6	0.01
Yuman (1)	2	<0.01
Asian (7,831)	9,610	14.84
Not Hispanic (7,645)	9,124	14.09
Hispanic (186)	486	0.75
Bangladeshi (49)	50	0.08
Burmese (1)	1	<0.01
Cambodian (78)	103	0.16
Chinese, ex. Taiwanese (852)	1,197	1.85
Filipino (2,330)	3,110	4.80
Hmong (420)	440	0.68
Indian (1,325)	1,530	2.36
Indonesian (67)	102	0.16
Japanese (269)	639	0.99
Korean (678)	810	1.25
Laotian (131)	154	0.24
Malaysian (19)	27	0.04
Nepalese (8)	9	0.01
Pakistani (100)	122	0.19
Sri Lankan (21)	22	0.03
Taiwanese (22)	28	0.04
Thai (77)	118	0.18
Vietnamese (1,031)	1,188	1.83
Hawaii Native/Pacific Islander (556)	1,044	1.61
Not Hispanic (506)	910	1.40
Hispanic (50)	134	0.21
Fijian (172)	233	0.36
Guamanian/Chamorro (66)	138	0.21
Marshallese (1)	4	0.01
Native Hawaiian (40)	211	0.33
Samoan (89)	168	0.26
Tongan (16)	31	0.05
White (39,123)	42,728	65.96
Not Hispanic (33,863)	36,418	56.22
Hispanic (5,260)	6,310	9.74

Rancho Cucamonga

Place Type: City
County: San Bernardino
Population: 165,269†

Ancestry‡	Population	%
Afghan (219)	219	0.14
African, Sub-Saharan (1,505)	2,103	1.31
African (1,220)	1,716	1.07
Ethiopian (0)	13	0.01
Kenyan (59)	59	0.04
Liberian (15)	15	0.01
Nigerian (200)	277	0.17
Other Sub-Saharan African (11)	23	0.01
Albanian (99)	114	0.07
American (5,809)	5,809	3.61
Arab (1,368)	2,065	1.28
Arab (330)	454	0.28
Egyptian (434)	434	0.27
Iraqi (0)	17	0.01
Jordanian (86)	161	0.10
Lebanese (176)	495	0.31
Moroccan (45)	81	0.05
Palestinian (153)	168	0.10
Syrian (114)	225	0.14
Other Arab (30)	30	0.02
Armenian (279)	444	0.28
Assyrian/Chaldean/Syriac (0)	16	0.01
Australian (53)	150	0.09
Austrian (51)	237	0.15
Basque (87)	221	0.14
Belgian (0)	42	0.03
Brazilian (73)	206	0.13
British (324)	595	0.37
Bulgarian (7)	40	0.02
Canadian (270)	526	0.33
Celtic (13)	26	0.02
Croatian (24)	132	0.08
Czech (158)	627	0.39
Czechoslovakian (116)	165	0.10
Danish (246)	647	0.40
Dutch (594)	2,719	1.69
Eastern European (85)	157	0.10
English (3,195)	11,740	7.30
European (1,576)	2,309	1.44
Finnish (142)	330	0.21
French, ex. Basque (397)	4,318	2.69
French Canadian (166)	846	0.53
German (3,885)	18,604	11.57
Greek (215)	666	0.41
Hungarian (183)	864	0.54
Icelander (47)	87	0.05
Iranian (810)	903	0.56
Irish (2,771)	12,938	8.05
Israeli (80)	80	0.05
Italian (3,668)	10,720	6.67
Lithuanian (103)	239	0.15
Macedonian (0)	2	<0.01
Northern European (87)	97	0.06
Norwegian (622)	1,790	1.11
Pennsylvania German (17)	17	0.01
Polish (790)	2,686	1.67
Portuguese (239)	695	0.43
Romanian (101)	284	0.18
Russian (157)	850	0.53
Scandinavian (148)	395	0.25
Scotch-Irish (253)	1,566	0.97
Scottish (565)	2,037	1.27
Serbian (44)	73	0.05
Slavic (0)	71	0.04
Slovak (0)	35	0.02
Slovene (30)	55	0.03
Swedish (387)	2,344	1.46
Swiss (13)	293	0.18
Turkish (61)	160	0.10
Ukrainian (39)	361	0.22
Welsh (173)	1,323	0.82
West Indian, ex. Hispanic (336)	698	0.43
Bahamian (0)	34	0.02
Barbadian (10)	10	0.01
Belizean (71)	179	0.11
Dutch West Indian (24)	24	0.01
Haitian (26)	95	0.06
Jamaican (70)	145	0.09
Trinidadian/Tobagonian (61)	61	0.04
West Indian (51)	127	0.08
Other West Indian (23)	23	0.01
Yugoslavian (44)	222	0.14

Hispanic Origin	Population	%
Hispanic or Latino (of any race)	57,688	34.91
Central American, ex. Mexican	3,487	2.11
Costa Rican	245	0.15
Guatemalan	907	0.55
Honduran	211	0.13
Nicaraguan	598	0.36
Panamanian	100	0.06
Salvadoran	1,396	0.84
Other Central American	30	0.02
Cuban	820	0.50
Dominican Republic	64	0.04
Mexican	45,369	27.45
Puerto Rican	1,214	0.73
South American	2,823	1.71
Argentinean	561	0.34
Bolivian	75	0.05
Chilean	146	0.09
Colombian	694	0.42
Ecuadorian	399	0.24
Paraguayan	9	0.01
Peruvian	800	0.48
Uruguayan	19	0.01
Venezuelan	73	0.04
Other South American	47	0.03
Other Hispanic or Latino	3,911	2.37

Race*	Population	%
African-American/Black (15,246)	17,582	10.64
Not Hispanic (14,486)	16,162	9.78
Hispanic (760)	1,420	0.86
American Indian/Alaska Native (1,134)	2,611	1.58
Not Hispanic (409)	1,235	0.75
Hispanic (725)	1,376	0.83
Alaska Athabascan *(Ala. Nat.)* (0)	5	<0.01
Aleut *(Alaska Native)* (1)	3	<0.01
Apache (49)	113	0.07
Arapaho (0)	1	<0.01
Blackfeet (8)	80	0.05
Canadian/French Am. Ind. (2)	6	<0.01
Central American Ind. (7)	16	0.01
Cherokee (67)	362	0.22
Cheyenne (1)	4	<0.01
Chickasaw (3)	25	0.02
Chippewa (12)	30	0.02
Choctaw (26)	80	0.05
Colville (2)	8	<0.01
Comanche (4)	16	0.01
Cree (0)	1	<0.01
Creek (8)	37	0.02
Crow (0)	2	<0.01
Delaware (0)	5	<0.01
Hopi (5)	11	0.01
Houma (1)	1	<0.01
Inupiat *(Alaska Native)* (1)	2	<0.01
Iroquois (9)	21	0.01
Kiowa (7)	9	0.01
Lumbee (4)	4	<0.01
Mexican American Ind. (100)	176	0.11
Navajo (46)	92	0.06
Osage (4)	11	0.01
Ottawa (0)	5	<0.01
Paiute (11)	14	0.01
Pima (1)	8	<0.01
Potawatomi (3)	24	0.01
Pueblo (9)	24	0.01
Puget Sound Salish (6)	8	<0.01
Seminole (1)	9	0.01
Shoshone (2)	8	<0.01
Sioux (18)	43	0.03
South American Ind. (12)	16	0.01
Spanish American Ind. (7)	14	0.01
Tlingit-Haida *(Alaska Native)* (1)	1	<0.01
Tohono O'Odham (10)	10	0.01
Ute (6)	9	0.01
Yakama (3)	6	<0.01
Yaqui (30)	73	0.04
Yuman (6)	11	0.01
Yup'ik *(Alaska Native)* (5)	9	0.01
Asian (17,208)	20,512	12.41
Not Hispanic (16,741)	19,216	11.63
Hispanic (467)	1,296	0.78
Bangladeshi (131)	144	0.09
Bhutanese (1)	1	<0.01
Burmese (58)	72	0.04
Cambodian (142)	180	0.11
Chinese, ex. Taiwanese (2,916)	3,715	2.25
Filipino (5,513)	6,762	4.09
Hmong (22)	27	0.02
Indian (1,869)	2,133	1.29
Indonesian (494)	723	0.44
Japanese (559)	1,224	0.74
Korean (2,189)	2,443	1.48
Laotian (36)	42	0.03
Malaysian (22)	31	0.02
Nepalese (8)	8	<0.01
Pakistani (466)	521	0.32
Sri Lankan (42)	49	0.03
Taiwanese (533)	609	0.37
Thai (297)	403	0.24
Vietnamese (1,159)	1,350	0.82
Hawaii Native/Pacific Islander (443)	1,132	0.68
Not Hispanic (383)	909	0.55
Hispanic (60)	223	0.13
Fijian (6)	22	0.01
Guamanian/Chamorro (53)	94	0.06
Native Hawaiian (75)	286	0.17
Samoan (109)	207	0.13
Tongan (145)	195	0.12
White (102,401)	109,730	66.39
Not Hispanic (70,572)	74,326	44.97

*Notes: † The Census 2010 population figure is used to calculate the percentages in the Hispanic Origin and Race categories. Ancestry percentages are based on the 2006-2010 American Community Survey population (not shown); ‡ Numbers in parentheses indicate the number of people reporting a single ancestry; * Numbers in parentheses indicate the number of persons reporting this race alone, not in combination with any other race; Please refer to the Explanation of Data for more information.*

Hispanic (31,829)	35,404	21.42

Rancho Mirage

Place Type: City
County: Riverside
Population: 17,218†

Ancestry‡	Population	%
African, Sub-Saharan (0)	9	0.05
African (0)	9	0.05
Albanian (0)	21	0.13
American (812)	812	4.85
Arab (72)	87	0.52
Lebanese (31)	31	0.19
Moroccan (21)	21	0.13
Syrian (0)	15	0.09
Other Arab (20)	20	0.12
Armenian (61)	84	0.50
Assyrian/Chaldean/Syriac (12)	12	0.07
Australian (2)	2	0.01
Austrian (83)	144	0.86
Brazilian (106)	106	0.63
British (145)	165	0.99
Canadian (61)	97	0.58
Croatian (32)	47	0.28
Czech (29)	73	0.44
Danish (152)	167	1.00
Dutch (84)	503	3.01
Eastern European (134)	134	0.80
English (766)	2,169	12.97
Estonian (6)	6	0.04
European (328)	342	2.04
Finnish (29)	114	0.68
French, ex. Basque (150)	643	3.84
French Canadian (31)	103	0.62
German (811)	2,627	15.71
Greek (151)	170	1.02
Hungarian (88)	124	0.74
Icelander (12)	12	0.07
Iranian (35)	35	0.21
Irish (542)	1,755	10.49
Israeli (29)	29	0.17
Italian (484)	950	5.68
Lithuanian (47)	90	0.54
Northern European (25)	25	0.15
Norwegian (232)	378	2.26
Polish (374)	570	3.41
Portuguese (54)	92	0.55
Romanian (50)	78	0.47
Russian (510)	735	4.39
Scandinavian (21)	33	0.20
Scotch-Irish (231)	447	2.67
Scottish (87)	329	1.97
Slavic (27)	27	0.16
Slovak (18)	34	0.20
Slovene (0)	15	0.09
Swedish (315)	521	3.11
Swiss (15)	58	0.35
Turkish (15)	38	0.23
Ukrainian (5)	33	0.20
Welsh (13)	141	0.84
West Indian, ex. Hispanic (10)	58	0.35
West Indian (10)	58	0.35
Yugoslavian (46)	57	0.34

Hispanic Origin	Population	%
Hispanic or Latino (of any race)	1,964	11.41
Central American, ex. Mexican	100	0.58
Costa Rican	7	0.04
Guatemalan	22	0.13
Honduran	4	0.02
Nicaraguan	11	0.06
Panamanian	5	0.03
Salvadoran	50	0.29
Other Central American	1	0.01
Cuban	20	0.12
Mexican	1,582	9.19
Puerto Rican	40	0.23
South American	74	0.43
Argentinean	26	0.15
Bolivian	2	0.01
Chilean	9	0.05
Colombian	11	0.06
Ecuadorian	7	0.04
Paraguayan	2	0.01
Peruvian	15	0.09
Uruguayan	1	0.01
Venezuelan	1	0.01
Other Hispanic or Latino	148	0.86

Race*	Population	%
African-American/Black (256)	323	1.88
Not Hispanic (235)	286	1.66
Hispanic (21)	37	0.21
American Indian/Alaska Native (94)	151	0.88
Not Hispanic (61)	102	0.59
Hispanic (33)	49	0.28
Apache (1)	2	0.01
Blackfeet (0)	2	0.01
Cherokee (5)	15	0.09
Chippewa (1)	3	0.02
Choctaw (1)	4	0.02
Comanche (0)	1	0.01
Creek (2)	3	0.02
Crow (0)	1	0.01
Delaware (0)	1	0.01
Iroquois (0)	1	0.01
Mexican American Ind. (6)	10	0.06
Navajo (0)	1	0.01
Ottawa (1)	1	0.01
Paiute (2)	2	0.01
Potawatomi (0)	4	0.02
Shoshone (1)	1	0.01
Sioux (0)	1	0.01
South American Ind. (1)	1	0.01
Tlingit-Haida *(Alaska Native)* (1)	1	0.01
Yaqui (4)	4	0.02
Asian (651)	777	4.51
Not Hispanic (639)	745	4.33
Hispanic (12)	32	0.19
Burmese (3)	5	0.03
Chinese, ex. Taiwanese (98)	125	0.73
Filipino (200)	260	1.51
Indian (136)	149	0.87
Indonesian (12)	15	0.09
Japanese (43)	57	0.33
Korean (65)	86	0.50
Malaysian (0)	1	0.01
Pakistani (15)	18	0.10
Sri Lankan (0)	1	0.01
Taiwanese (3)	5	0.03
Thai (7)	8	0.05
Vietnamese (37)	41	0.24
Hawaii Native/Pacific Islander (14)	33	0.19
Not Hispanic (13)	32	0.19
Hispanic (1)	1	0.01
Guamanian/Chamorro (7)	7	0.04
Native Hawaiian (5)	16	0.09
Samoan (1)	2	0.01
White (15,267)	15,568	90.42
Not Hispanic (14,065)	14,252	82.77
Hispanic (1,202)	1,316	7.64

Rancho Palos Verdes

Place Type: City
County: Los Angeles
Population: 41,643†

Ancestry‡	Population	%
Afghan (9)	9	0.02
African, Sub-Saharan (249)	338	0.81
African (30)	91	0.22
Liberian (13)	13	0.03
Nigerian (206)	234	0.56
Alsatian (0)	27	0.07
American (1,157)	1,157	2.79
Arab (217)	272	0.65
Egyptian (40)	40	0.10
Lebanese (169)	214	0.52
Moroccan (8)	8	0.02
Syrian (0)	10	0.02
Armenian (230)	581	1.40
Australian (66)	84	0.20
Austrian (142)	303	0.73
Basque (67)	82	0.20
Belgian (10)	10	0.02
Brazilian (11)	11	0.03
British (192)	269	0.65
Bulgarian (0)	34	0.08
Canadian (83)	157	0.38
Croatian (548)	990	2.38
Czech (62)	281	0.68
Czechoslovakian (34)	99	0.24
Danish (128)	214	0.52
Dutch (120)	530	1.28
Eastern European (161)	161	0.39
English (1,089)	3,724	8.97
Estonian (29)	29	0.07
European (569)	667	1.61
Finnish (14)	54	0.13
French, ex. Basque (185)	1,060	2.55
French Canadian (69)	92	0.22
German (1,297)	5,110	12.30
Greek (240)	382	0.92
Hungarian (81)	274	0.66
Icelander (0)	28	0.07
Iranian (1,157)	1,182	2.85
Irish (1,033)	3,255	7.84
Italian (1,286)	2,964	7.14
Latvian (10)	24	0.06
Lithuanian (33)	148	0.36
Maltese (21)	21	0.05
New Zealander (20)	20	0.05
Northern European (44)	44	0.11
Norwegian (170)	483	1.16
Polish (405)	1,064	2.56
Portuguese (15)	137	0.33
Romanian (31)	42	0.10
Russian (574)	1,264	3.04
Scandinavian (50)	126	0.30
Scotch-Irish (295)	564	1.36
Scottish (210)	833	2.01
Serbian (0)	12	0.03
Slavic (5)	203	0.49
Slovene (0)	14	0.03
Swedish (199)	787	1.89
Swiss (50)	311	0.75
Turkish (10)	10	0.02
Ukrainian (38)	133	0.32
Welsh (43)	223	0.54
West Indian, ex. Hispanic (26)	26	0.06
British West Indian (17)	17	0.04
Dutch West Indian (9)	9	0.02
Yugoslavian (37)	60	0.14

Hispanic Origin	Population	%
Hispanic or Latino (of any race)	3,556	8.54
Central American, ex. Mexican	220	0.53
Costa Rican	24	0.06
Guatemalan	52	0.12
Honduran	18	0.04
Nicaraguan	38	0.09
Panamanian	17	0.04
Salvadoran	71	0.17
Cuban	125	0.30
Dominican Republic	11	0.03
Mexican	2,254	5.41
Puerto Rican	117	0.28
South American	466	1.12
Argentinean	121	0.29
Bolivian	16	0.04
Chilean	50	0.12
Colombian	93	0.22
Ecuadorian	54	0.13
Peruvian	110	0.26
Uruguayan	3	0.01
Venezuelan	12	0.03
Other South American	7	0.02

*Notes: † The Census 2010 population figure is used to calculate the percentages in the Hispanic Origin and Race categories. Ancestry percentages are based on the 2006-2010 American Community Survey population (not shown); ‡ Numbers in parentheses indicate the number of people reporting a single ancestry; * Numbers in parentheses indicate the number of persons reporting this race alone, not in combination with any other race; Please refer to the Explanation of Data for more information.*

Other Hispanic or Latino	363	0.87

Race*	Population	%
African-American/Black (1,015)	1,267	3.04
Not Hispanic (988)	1,201	2.88
Hispanic (27)	66	0.16
American Indian/Alaska Native (80)	277	0.67
Not Hispanic (54)	184	0.44
Hispanic (26)	93	0.22
Alaska Athabascan *(Ala. Nat.)* (1)	4	0.01
Apache (5)	7	0.02
Blackfeet (2)	5	0.01
Canadian/French Am. Ind. (0)	1	<0.01
Central American Ind. (2)	2	<0.01
Cherokee (10)	47	0.11
Cheyenne (0)	1	<0.01
Chickasaw (0)	1	<0.01
Choctaw (1)	4	0.01
Comanche (0)	2	<0.01
Cree (2)	4	0.01
Creek (3)	6	0.01
Delaware (0)	3	0.01
Iroquois (0)	8	0.02
Mexican American Ind. (7)	10	0.02
Navajo (1)	1	<0.01
Osage (1)	2	<0.01
Potawatomi (0)	1	<0.01
Seminole (0)	1	<0.01
Shoshone (2)	2	<0.01
South American Ind. (1)	8	0.02
Spanish American Ind. (2)	4	0.01
Yuman (0)	2	<0.01
Asian (12,077)	13,481	32.37
Not Hispanic (11,998)	13,259	31.84
Hispanic (79)	222	0.53
Bangladeshi (7)	8	0.02
Burmese (5)	12	0.03
Cambodian (23)	28	0.07
Chinese, ex. Taiwanese (2,877)	3,424	8.22
Filipino (920)	1,279	3.07
Indian (782)	898	2.16
Indonesian (24)	41	0.10
Japanese (2,917)	3,577	8.59
Korean (2,825)	3,066	7.36
Laotian (1)	2	<0.01
Malaysian (20)	23	0.06
Nepalese (13)	15	0.04
Pakistani (221)	239	0.57
Sri Lankan (48)	54	0.13
Taiwanese (685)	750	1.80
Thai (40)	70	0.17
Vietnamese (183)	226	0.54
Hawaii Native/Pacific Islander (41)	173	0.42
Not Hispanic (39)	160	0.38
Hispanic (2)	13	0.03
Fijian (1)	1	<0.01
Guamanian/Chamorro (3)	10	0.02
Native Hawaiian (11)	70	0.17
Samoan (6)	18	0.04
Tongan (1)	1	<0.01
White (25,698)	27,466	65.96
Not Hispanic (23,323)	24,771	59.48
Hispanic (2,375)	2,695	6.47

Rancho San Diego

Place Type: CDP
County: San Diego
Population: 21,208†

Ancestry‡	Population	%
African, Sub-Saharan (0)	21	0.10
African (0)	21	0.10
Albanian (0)	28	0.14
American (664)	664	3.28
Arab (662)	717	3.54
Arab (192)	192	0.95
Iraqi (432)	459	2.27
Syrian (0)	28	0.14
Other Arab (38)	38	0.19
Armenian (16)	16	0.08
Assyrian/Chaldean/Syriac (749)	776	3.83
Austrian (49)	126	0.62
British (104)	114	0.56
Bulgarian (0)	24	0.12
Canadian (53)	81	0.40
Czech (13)	59	0.29
Czechoslovakian (27)	70	0.35
Danish (94)	173	0.85
Dutch (44)	189	0.93
English (772)	2,935	14.50
European (408)	487	2.41
French, ex. Basque (179)	1,009	4.98
French Canadian (78)	213	1.05
German (1,066)	3,699	18.27
Greek (90)	250	1.23
Hungarian (53)	136	0.67
Iranian (103)	134	0.66
Irish (403)	2,768	13.67
Italian (594)	1,371	6.77
Lithuanian (0)	47	0.23
Northern European (8)	8	0.04
Norwegian (141)	441	2.18
Polish (203)	497	2.45
Portuguese (12)	36	0.18
Romanian (0)	28	0.14
Russian (50)	184	0.91
Scandinavian (0)	89	0.44
Scotch-Irish (89)	557	2.75
Scottish (78)	513	2.53
Serbian (30)	89	0.44
Slovak (12)	51	0.25
Swedish (91)	547	2.70
Swiss (82)	210	1.04
Ukrainian (31)	45	0.22
Welsh (25)	297	1.47
West Indian, ex. Hispanic (0)	33	0.16
Bahamian (0)	12	0.06
Jamaican (0)	21	0.10
Yugoslavian (111)	111	0.55

Hispanic Origin	Population	%
Hispanic or Latino (of any race)	3,117	14.70
Central American, ex. Mexican	75	0.35
Costa Rican	7	0.03
Guatemalan	18	0.08
Honduran	7	0.03
Nicaraguan	12	0.06
Panamanian	13	0.06
Salvadoran	18	0.08
Cuban	19	0.09
Dominican Republic	10	0.05
Mexican	2,556	12.05
Puerto Rican	75	0.35
South American	97	0.46
Argentinean	10	0.05
Bolivian	1	<0.01
Chilean	16	0.08
Colombian	34	0.16
Ecuadorian	13	0.06
Peruvian	19	0.09
Venezuelan	1	<0.01
Other South American	3	0.01
Other Hispanic or Latino	285	1.34

Race*	Population	%
African-American/Black (817)	994	4.69
Not Hispanic (776)	925	4.36
Hispanic (41)	69	0.33
American Indian/Alaska Native (105)	272	1.28
Not Hispanic (63)	192	0.91
Hispanic (42)	80	0.38
Apache (4)	8	0.04
Blackfeet (0)	5	0.02
Cherokee (8)	48	0.23
Chickasaw (0)	1	<0.01
Chippewa (0)	3	0.01
Choctaw (4)	9	0.04
Creek (0)	1	<0.01
Inupiat *(Alaska Native)* (0)	2	0.01
Iroquois (2)	4	0.02
Kiowa (0)	2	0.01
Lumbee (0)	3	0.01
Mexican American Ind. (6)	9	0.04
Navajo (2)	4	0.02
Osage (1)	1	<0.01
Potawatomi (1)	1	<0.01
Puget Sound Salish (1)	1	<0.01
Sioux (2)	4	0.02
South American Ind. (0)	2	0.01
Yaqui (0)	5	0.02
Asian (940)	1,454	6.86
Not Hispanic (894)	1,353	6.38
Hispanic (46)	101	0.48
Bangladeshi (1)	1	<0.01
Cambodian (11)	11	0.05
Chinese, ex. Taiwanese (129)	199	0.94
Filipino (414)	590	2.78
Indian (74)	87	0.41
Indonesian (3)	7	0.03
Japanese (83)	193	0.91
Korean (64)	84	0.40
Laotian (9)	12	0.06
Malaysian (0)	1	<0.01
Pakistani (5)	5	0.02
Sri Lankan (0)	1	<0.01
Taiwanese (7)	12	0.06
Thai (8)	12	0.06
Vietnamese (90)	101	0.48
Hawaii Native/Pacific Islander (56)	160	0.75
Not Hispanic (45)	131	0.62
Hispanic (11)	29	0.14
Guamanian/Chamorro (30)	54	0.25
Native Hawaiian (16)	49	0.23
Samoan (7)	13	0.06
White (17,535)	18,463	87.06
Not Hispanic (15,503)	16,216	76.46
Hispanic (2,032)	2,247	10.60

Rancho Santa Margarita

Place Type: City
County: Orange
Population: 47,853†

Ancestry‡	Population	%
Afghan (75)	75	0.16
African, Sub-Saharan (45)	72	0.15
African (35)	56	0.12
South African (0)	6	0.01
Zimbabwean (10)	10	0.02
Albanian (0)	34	0.07
American (1,469)	1,469	3.09
Arab (297)	376	0.79
Arab (55)	55	0.12
Egyptian (35)	35	0.07
Iraqi (66)	66	0.14
Jordanian (0)	4	0.01
Lebanese (32)	93	0.20
Palestinian (2)	16	0.03
Other Arab (107)	107	0.23
Armenian (60)	127	0.27
Assyrian/Chaldean/Syriac (0)	28	0.06
Australian (16)	68	0.14
Austrian (78)	170	0.36
Basque (38)	74	0.16
Belgian (9)	9	0.02
British (468)	868	1.83
Bulgarian (0)	34	0.07
Canadian (89)	298	0.63
Celtic (23)	23	0.05
Croatian (19)	76	0.16
Czech (93)	338	0.71
Czechoslovakian (7)	30	0.06
Danish (151)	401	0.84
Dutch (360)	961	2.02
Eastern European (109)	119	0.25
English (1,307)	4,607	9.69
European (1,042)	1,109	2.33
Finnish (15)	230	0.48

*Notes: † The Census 2010 population figure is used to calculate the percentages in the Hispanic Origin and Race categories. Ancestry percentages are based on the 2006-2010 American Community Survey population (not shown); ‡ Numbers in parentheses indicate the number of people reporting a single ancestry; * Numbers in parentheses indicate the number of persons reporting this race alone, not in combination with any other race; Please refer to the Explanation of Data for more information.*

French, ex. Basque (215)	1,470	3.09
French Canadian (103)	329	0.69
German (1,822)	9,193	19.34
Greek (56)	191	0.40
Hungarian (21)	231	0.49
Icelander (48)	71	0.15
Iranian (552)	579	1.22
Irish (1,455)	7,393	15.55
Israeli (74)	100	0.21
Italian (1,402)	3,838	8.07
Latvian (27)	27	0.06
Lithuanian (0)	61	0.13
Luxemburger (0)	16	0.03
Maltese (24)	36	0.08
Northern European (36)	36	0.08
Norwegian (212)	797	1.68
Polish (449)	2,047	4.31
Portuguese (52)	348	0.73
Romanian (0)	21	0.04
Russian (144)	503	1.06
Scandinavian (92)	218	0.46
Scotch-Irish (257)	702	1.48
Scottish (564)	2,192	4.61
Slavic (0)	35	0.07
Slovak (45)	76	0.16
Slovene (0)	27	0.06
Swedish (232)	979	2.06
Swiss (71)	251	0.53
Turkish (14)	38	0.08
Ukrainian (22)	61	0.13
Welsh (49)	278	0.58
West Indian, ex. Hispanic (39)	54	0.11
British West Indian (10)	10	0.02
Jamaican (29)	44	0.09
Yugoslavian (36)	66	0.14

Hispanic Origin	Population	%
Hispanic or Latino (of any race)	8,902	18.60
Central American, ex. Mexican	533	1.11
Costa Rican	51	0.11
Guatemalan	186	0.39
Honduran	31	0.06
Nicaraguan	59	0.12
Panamanian	14	0.03
Salvadoran	192	0.40
Cuban	192	0.40
Dominican Republic	10	0.02
Mexican	6,368	13.31
Puerto Rican	304	0.64
South American	920	1.92
Argentinean	193	0.40
Bolivian	45	0.09
Chilean	65	0.14
Colombian	277	0.58
Ecuadorian	71	0.15
Paraguayan	2	<0.01
Peruvian	219	0.46
Uruguayan	11	0.02
Venezuelan	25	0.05
Other South American	12	0.03
Other Hispanic or Latino	575	1.20

Race*	Population	%
African-American/Black (887)	1,280	2.67
Not Hispanic (788)	1,128	2.36
Hispanic (99)	152	0.32
American Indian/Alaska Native (182)	494	1.03
Not Hispanic (82)	303	0.63
Hispanic (100)	191	0.40
Alaska Athabascan *(Ala. Nat.)* (0)	1	<0.01
Aleut *(Alaska Native)* (1)	1	<0.01
Apache (5)	18	0.04
Blackfeet (6)	15	0.03
Cherokee (13)	85	0.18
Chickasaw (4)	6	0.01
Chippewa (6)	8	0.02
Choctaw (8)	23	0.05
Comanche (1)	1	<0.01
Cree (0)	1	<0.01
Creek (2)	5	0.01
Delaware (0)	1	<0.01
Iroquois (3)	4	0.01
Kiowa (1)	4	0.01
Mexican American Ind. (16)	27	0.06
Navajo (4)	13	0.03
Osage (0)	9	0.02
Ottawa (1)	1	<0.01
Potawatomi (3)	6	0.01
Pueblo (0)	1	<0.01
Shoshone (1)	1	<0.01
Sioux (2)	5	0.01
South American Ind. (1)	1	<0.01
Spanish American Ind. (2)	3	0.01
Tlingit-Haida *(Alaska Native)* (0)	1	<0.01
Ute (0)	1	<0.01
Yaqui (6)	9	0.02
Asian (4,350)	5,596	11.69
Not Hispanic (4,268)	5,346	11.17
Hispanic (82)	250	0.52
Bangladeshi (4)	4	0.01
Burmese (1)	2	<0.01
Cambodian (14)	27	0.06
Chinese, ex. Taiwanese (606)	892	1.86
Filipino (1,461)	1,935	4.04
Hmong (4)	6	0.01
Indian (491)	539	1.13
Indonesian (45)	73	0.15
Japanese (442)	798	1.67
Korean (363)	462	0.97
Laotian (12)	27	0.06
Malaysian (4)	8	0.02
Pakistani (65)	67	0.14
Sri Lankan (38)	39	0.08
Taiwanese (60)	73	0.15
Thai (44)	58	0.12
Vietnamese (455)	567	1.18
Hawaii Native/Pacific Islander (102)	264	0.55
Not Hispanic (88)	219	0.46
Hispanic (14)	45	0.09
Guamanian/Chamorro (26)	50	0.10
Native Hawaiian (52)	133	0.28
Samoan (9)	22	0.05
Tongan (6)	6	0.01
White (37,421)	39,431	82.40
Not Hispanic (32,054)	33,506	70.02
Hispanic (5,367)	5,925	12.38

Red Bluff

Place Type: City
County: Tehama
Population: 14,076†

Ancestry‡	Population	%
African, Sub-Saharan (19)	19	0.14
Cape Verdean (19)	19	0.14
American (462)	462	3.31
Arab (12)	12	0.09
Jordanian (12)	12	0.09
Assyrian/Chaldean/Syriac (22)	93	0.67
Australian (12)	62	0.44
Belgian (0)	9	0.06
Bulgarian (20)	20	0.14
Canadian (9)	9	0.06
Czech (0)	40	0.29
Czechoslovakian (0)	12	0.09
Danish (51)	91	0.65
Dutch (57)	546	3.91
Eastern European (0)	10	0.07
English (358)	1,488	10.65
European (45)	63	0.45
Finnish (23)	58	0.41
French, ex. Basque (85)	642	4.59
French Canadian (17)	17	0.12
German (594)	2,369	16.95
Greek (40)	127	0.91
Hungarian (14)	26	0.19
Iranian (18)	34	0.24
Irish (443)	1,728	12.36
Italian (341)	673	4.82
Lithuanian (0)	12	0.09
Norwegian (75)	344	2.46
Pennsylvania German (15)	25	0.18
Polish (47)	246	1.76
Portuguese (239)	412	2.95
Romanian (0)	83	0.59
Russian (33)	222	1.59
Scandinavian (0)	10	0.07
Scotch-Irish (75)	240	1.72
Scottish (59)	459	3.28
Swedish (39)	407	2.91
Swiss (42)	65	0.47
Ukrainian (0)	32	0.23
Welsh (0)	75	0.54
Yugoslavian (0)	13	0.09

Hispanic Origin	Population	%
Hispanic or Latino (of any race)	3,037	21.58
Central American, ex. Mexican	59	0.42
Guatemalan	6	0.04
Honduran	20	0.14
Nicaraguan	3	0.02
Panamanian	7	0.05
Salvadoran	23	0.16
Cuban	2	0.01
Dominican Republic	1	0.01
Mexican	2,631	18.69
Puerto Rican	68	0.48
South American	10	0.07
Argentinean	5	0.04
Colombian	2	0.01
Peruvian	2	0.01
Venezuelan	1	0.01
Other Hispanic or Latino	266	1.89

Race*	Population	%
African-American/Black (128)	235	1.67
Not Hispanic (112)	205	1.46
Hispanic (16)	30	0.21
American Indian/Alaska Native (438)	788	5.60
Not Hispanic (305)	571	4.06
Hispanic (133)	217	1.54
Alaska Athabascan *(Ala. Nat.)* (2)	2	0.01
Apache (4)	11	0.08
Blackfeet (2)	19	0.13
Canadian/French Am. Ind. (1)	1	0.01
Cherokee (29)	125	0.89
Chickasaw (1)	3	0.02
Chippewa (6)	13	0.09
Choctaw (9)	26	0.18
Comanche (0)	3	0.02
Creek (1)	2	0.01
Inupiat *(Alaska Native)* (0)	1	0.01
Iroquois (2)	5	0.04
Lumbee (0)	1	0.01
Mexican American Ind. (22)	30	0.21
Navajo (9)	21	0.15
Osage (1)	1	0.01
Ottawa (0)	1	0.01
Paiute (0)	6	0.04
Potawatomi (6)	6	0.04
Pueblo (3)	3	0.02
Puget Sound Salish (1)	4	0.03
Shoshone (1)	2	0.01
Sioux (7)	17	0.12
Tlingit-Haida *(Alaska Native)* (3)	3	0.02
Yaqui (3)	8	0.06
Asian (187)	322	2.29
Not Hispanic (178)	281	2.00
Hispanic (9)	41	0.29
Burmese (4)	4	0.03
Chinese, ex. Taiwanese (25)	30	0.21
Filipino (47)	106	0.75
Indian (34)	49	0.35
Japanese (15)	43	0.31
Korean (10)	21	0.15
Laotian (24)	38	0.27
Thai (2)	3	0.02
Vietnamese (17)	18	0.13
Hawaii Native/Pacific Islander (16)	44	0.31

*Notes: † The Census 2010 population figure is used to calculate the percentages in the Hispanic Origin and Race categories. Ancestry percentages are based on the 2006-2010 American Community Survey population (not shown); ‡ Numbers in parentheses indicate the number of people reporting a single ancestry; * Numbers in parentheses indicate the number of persons reporting this race alone, not in combination with any other race; Please refer to the Explanation of Data for more information.*

Not Hispanic (10)	30	0.21
Hispanic (6)	14	0.10
Fijian (0)	2	0.01
Guamanian/Chamorro (0)	2	0.01
Native Hawaiian (4)	20	0.14
Samoan (9)	14	0.10
Tongan (1)	1	0.01
White (11,366)	12,071	85.76
Not Hispanic (9,975)	10,391	73.82
Hispanic (1,391)	1,680	11.94

Redding

Place Type: City
County: Shasta
Population: 89,861†

Ancestry‡	Population	%
Afghan (10)	10	0.01
African, Sub-Saharan (51)	166	0.19
African (0)	72	0.08
Ethiopian (0)	43	0.05
Liberian (34)	34	0.04
South African (17)	17	0.02
American (5,979)	5,979	6.69
Arab (96)	150	0.17
Jordanian (3)	3	<0.01
Lebanese (76)	130	0.15
Syrian (17)	17	0.02
Armenian (159)	171	0.19
Australian (34)	87	0.10
Austrian (66)	239	0.27
Basque (90)	106	0.12
Belgian (0)	9	0.01
Brazilian (25)	35	0.04
British (198)	506	0.57
Bulgarian (0)	13	0.01
Cajun (24)	35	0.04
Canadian (77)	184	0.21
Croatian (37)	119	0.13
Czech (80)	417	0.47
Czechoslovakian (35)	235	0.26
Danish (207)	1,008	1.13
Dutch (489)	2,024	2.26
Eastern European (81)	111	0.12
English (3,773)	12,433	13.91
European (958)	1,111	1.24
Finnish (533)	836	0.94
French, ex. Basque (499)	3,512	3.93
French Canadian (164)	635	0.71
German (5,347)	17,567	19.65
German Russian (0)	61	0.07
Greek (127)	321	0.36
Hungarian (60)	381	0.43
Icelander (0)	6	0.01
Iranian (16)	80	0.09
Irish (3,778)	13,432	15.03
Italian (2,032)	5,117	5.72
Latvian (11)	11	0.01
Lithuanian (48)	72	0.08
Luxemburger (0)	31	0.03
Maltese (0)	18	0.02
Northern European (269)	275	0.31
Norwegian (350)	2,132	2.39
Pennsylvania German (38)	53	0.06
Polish (591)	1,610	1.80
Portuguese (393)	1,436	1.61
Romanian (35)	77	0.09
Russian (551)	1,237	1.38
Scandinavian (297)	428	0.48
Scotch-Irish (676)	2,305	2.58
Scottish (516)	2,023	2.26
Serbian (0)	8	0.01
Slavic (0)	33	0.04
Slovak (0)	29	0.03
Swedish (662)	3,053	3.42
Swiss (54)	280	0.31
Ukrainian (0)	201	0.22
Welsh (131)	853	0.95
West Indian, ex. Hispanic (0)	38	0.04
Dutch West Indian (0)	38	0.04
Yugoslavian (54)	131	0.15

Hispanic Origin	Population	%
Hispanic or Latino (of any race)	7,787	8.67
Central American, ex. Mexican	244	0.27
Costa Rican	20	0.02
Guatemalan	43	0.05
Honduran	15	0.02
Nicaraguan	39	0.04
Panamanian	11	0.01
Salvadoran	113	0.13
Other Central American	3	<0.01
Cuban	56	0.06
Dominican Republic	18	0.02
Mexican	5,767	6.42
Puerto Rican	307	0.34
South American	143	0.16
Argentinean	13	0.01
Bolivian	6	0.01
Chilean	12	0.01
Colombian	41	0.05
Ecuadorian	9	0.01
Paraguayan	1	<0.01
Peruvian	44	0.05
Uruguayan	1	<0.01
Venezuelan	13	0.01
Other South American	3	<0.01
Other Hispanic or Latino	1,252	1.39

Race*	Population	%
African-American/Black (1,092)	1,971	2.19
Not Hispanic (1,025)	1,757	1.96
Hispanic (67)	214	0.24
American Indian/Alaska Native (2,034)	4,059	4.52
Not Hispanic (1,665)	3,383	3.76
Hispanic (369)	676	0.75
Alaska Athabascan *(Ala. Nat.)* (10)	15	0.02
Aleut *(Alaska Native)* (2)	7	0.01
Apache (33)	79	0.09
Arapaho (2)	6	0.01
Blackfeet (21)	94	0.10
Canadian/French Am. Ind. (2)	5	0.01
Central American Ind. (1)	2	<0.01
Cherokee (170)	599	0.67
Cheyenne (6)	9	0.01
Chickasaw (8)	25	0.03
Chippewa (24)	63	0.07
Choctaw (61)	175	0.19
Colville (1)	1	<0.01
Comanche (3)	15	0.02
Cree (1)	5	0.01
Creek (12)	38	0.04
Crow (1)	6	0.01
Delaware (1)	5	0.01
Hopi (3)	7	0.01
Inupiat *(Alaska Native)* (6)	20	0.02
Iroquois (9)	17	0.02
Kiowa (1)	5	0.01
Lumbee (3)	7	0.01
Menominee (0)	1	<0.01
Mexican American Ind. (37)	65	0.07
Navajo (22)	48	0.05
Osage (4)	10	0.01
Ottawa (2)	3	<0.01
Paiute (22)	33	0.04
Pima (2)	5	0.01
Potawatomi (14)	29	0.03
Pueblo (6)	9	0.01
Puget Sound Salish (1)	3	<0.01
Seminole (1)	5	0.01
Shoshone (1)	5	0.01
Sioux (34)	71	0.08
South American Ind. (0)	3	<0.01
Spanish American Ind. (0)	2	<0.01
Tlingit-Haida *(Alaska Native)* (6)	19	0.02
Tohono O'Odham (2)	2	<0.01
Tsimshian *(Alaska Native)* (1)	5	0.01
Ute (0)	1	<0.01
Yakama (3)	4	<0.01
Yaqui (7)	12	0.01
Yuman (4)	6	0.01
Yup'ik *(Alaska Native)* (0)	1	<0.01
Asian (3,034)	3,925	4.37
Not Hispanic (2,974)	3,752	4.18
Hispanic (60)	173	0.19
Bangladeshi (8)	9	0.01
Burmese (5)	6	0.01
Cambodian (29)	49	0.05
Chinese, ex. Taiwanese (390)	566	0.63
Filipino (425)	762	0.85
Hmong (52)	68	0.08
Indian (370)	428	0.48
Indonesian (7)	25	0.03
Japanese (158)	405	0.45
Korean (143)	208	0.23
Laotian (1,023)	1,124	1.25
Nepalese (2)	2	<0.01
Pakistani (25)	27	0.03
Sri Lankan (3)	3	<0.01
Taiwanese (9)	13	0.01
Thai (44)	66	0.07
Vietnamese (120)	156	0.17
Hawaii Native/Pacific Islander (156)	413	0.46
Not Hispanic (128)	334	0.37
Hispanic (28)	79	0.09
Fijian (7)	7	0.01
Guamanian/Chamorro (28)	57	0.06
Marshallese (1)	5	0.01
Native Hawaiian (63)	217	0.24
Samoan (25)	49	0.05
Tongan (3)	6	0.01
White (77,117)	80,967	90.10
Not Hispanic (73,038)	75,994	84.57
Hispanic (4,079)	4,973	5.53

Redlands

Place Type: City
County: San Bernardino
Population: 68,747†

Ancestry‡	Population	%
African, Sub-Saharan (807)	844	1.23
African (706)	727	1.06
Ethiopian (20)	20	0.03
Kenyan (21)	21	0.03
South African (53)	53	0.08
Sudanese (7)	23	0.03
Alsatian (16)	16	0.02
American (1,811)	1,811	2.63
Arab (468)	603	0.88
Egyptian (113)	149	0.22
Iraqi (11)	11	0.02
Jordanian (111)	111	0.16
Lebanese (51)	77	0.11
Palestinian (29)	29	0.04
Syrian (135)	208	0.30
Other Arab (18)	18	0.03
Armenian (71)	153	0.22
Australian (42)	100	0.15
Austrian (29)	207	0.30
Basque (12)	18	0.03
Belgian (0)	35	0.05
Brazilian (1)	14	0.02
British (341)	701	1.02
Bulgarian (0)	17	0.02
Cajun (16)	16	0.02
Canadian (88)	220	0.32
Croatian (0)	29	0.04
Czech (29)	139	0.20
Czechoslovakian (14)	68	0.10
Danish (185)	487	0.71
Dutch (631)	1,575	2.29
Eastern European (30)	41	0.06
English (1,727)	6,746	9.80
European (994)	1,249	1.81
Finnish (51)	142	0.21
French, ex. Basque (457)	1,821	2.64
French Canadian (193)	445	0.65

*Notes: † The Census 2010 population figure is used to calculate the percentages in the Hispanic Origin and Race categories. Ancestry percentages are based on the 2006-2010 American Community Survey population (not shown); ‡ Numbers in parentheses indicate the number of people reporting a single ancestry; * Numbers in parentheses indicate the number of persons reporting this race alone, not in combination with any other race; Please refer to the Explanation of Data for more information.*

German (3,381)	10,844	15.75
Greek (173)	326	0.47
Hungarian (139)	467	0.68
Iranian (186)	186	0.27
Irish (1,672)	7,443	10.81
Israeli (27)	27	0.04
Italian (1,262)	3,665	5.32
Latvian (14)	24	0.03
Lithuanian (25)	118	0.17
New Zealander (0)	18	0.03
Northern European (78)	78	0.11
Norwegian (297)	1,224	1.78
Pennsylvania German (0)	12	0.02
Polish (340)	1,394	2.02
Portuguese (179)	460	0.67
Romanian (162)	168	0.24
Russian (208)	725	1.05
Scandinavian (94)	135	0.20
Scotch-Irish (481)	1,059	1.54
Scottish (316)	1,357	1.97
Serbian (24)	53	0.08
Slavic (19)	38	0.06
Slovak (12)	28	0.04
Slovene (0)	14	0.02
Swedish (545)	1,411	2.05
Swiss (81)	292	0.42
Ukrainian (0)	69	0.10
Welsh (102)	566	0.82
West Indian, ex. Hispanic (52)	140	0.20
Bahamian (0)	23	0.03
Jamaican (38)	103	0.15
West Indian (14)	14	0.02
Yugoslavian (38)	63	0.09

Hispanic Origin	Population	%
Hispanic or Latino (of any race)	20,810	30.27
Central American, ex. Mexican	611	0.89
Costa Rican	56	0.08
Guatemalan	127	0.18
Honduran	51	0.07
Nicaraguan	61	0.09
Panamanian	44	0.06
Salvadoran	255	0.37
Other Central American	17	0.02
Cuban	137	0.20
Dominican Republic	35	0.05
Mexican	17,460	25.40
Puerto Rican	477	0.69
South American	462	0.67
Argentinean	97	0.14
Bolivian	18	0.03
Chilean	45	0.07
Colombian	141	0.21
Ecuadorian	36	0.05
Paraguayan	2	<0.01
Peruvian	106	0.15
Uruguayan	4	0.01
Venezuelan	9	0.01
Other South American	4	0.01
Other Hispanic or Latino	1,628	2.37

Race*	Population	%
African-American/Black (3,564)	4,411	6.42
Not Hispanic (3,326)	3,900	5.67
Hispanic (238)	511	0.74
American Indian/Alaska Native (625)	1,313	1.91
Not Hispanic (236)	636	0.93
Hispanic (389)	677	0.98
Alaska Athabascan *(Ala. Nat.)* (0)	2	<0.01
Aleut *(Alaska Native)* (1)	2	<0.01
Apache (12)	39	0.06
Arapaho (0)	2	<0.01
Blackfeet (6)	27	0.04
Canadian/French Am. Ind. (0)	4	0.01
Central American Ind. (1)	7	0.01
Cherokee (28)	174	0.25
Cheyenne (1)	6	0.01
Chickasaw (2)	5	0.01
Chippewa (6)	17	0.02
Choctaw (19)	54	0.08
Creek (4)	9	0.01
Crow (0)	4	0.01
Delaware (1)	1	<0.01
Hopi (9)	9	0.01
Inupiat *(Alaska Native)* (0)	1	<0.01
Iroquois (4)	8	0.01
Lumbee (1)	4	0.01
Mexican American Ind. (59)	87	0.13
Navajo (28)	44	0.06
Osage (6)	8	0.01
Ottawa (1)	5	0.01
Pima (0)	2	<0.01
Potawatomi (1)	5	0.01
Pueblo (13)	18	0.03
Puget Sound Salish (2)	2	<0.01
Seminole (0)	3	<0.01
Shoshone (1)	2	<0.01
Sioux (10)	22	0.03
South American Ind. (1)	8	0.01
Spanish American Ind. (8)	8	0.01
Tlingit-Haida *(Alaska Native)* (1)	1	<0.01
Tohono O'Odham (5)	8	0.01
Yaqui (23)	47	0.07
Yuman (4)	5	0.01
Asian (5,216)	6,487	9.44
Not Hispanic (5,100)	6,075	8.84
Hispanic (116)	412	0.60
Bangladeshi (53)	71	0.10
Burmese (16)	23	0.03
Cambodian (101)	134	0.19
Chinese, ex. Taiwanese (718)	979	1.42
Filipino (1,209)	1,623	2.36
Indian (856)	1,007	1.46
Indonesian (375)	434	0.63
Japanese (233)	528	0.77
Korean (532)	657	0.96
Laotian (12)	17	0.02
Malaysian (5)	12	0.02
Nepalese (13)	13	0.02
Pakistani (127)	161	0.23
Sri Lankan (17)	21	0.03
Taiwanese (96)	113	0.16
Thai (153)	195	0.28
Vietnamese (456)	528	0.77
Hawaii Native/Pacific Islander (235)	504	0.73
Not Hispanic (201)	403	0.59
Hispanic (34)	101	0.15
Fijian (0)	2	<0.01
Guamanian/Chamorro (18)	50	0.07
Marshallese (0)	2	<0.01
Native Hawaiian (60)	181	0.26
Samoan (102)	143	0.21
Tongan (3)	11	0.02
White (47,452)	50,342	73.23
Not Hispanic (37,103)	38,703	56.30
Hispanic (10,349)	11,639	16.93

Redondo Beach

Place Type: City
County: Los Angeles
Population: 66,748†

Ancestry‡	Population	%
Afghan (210)	210	0.32
African, Sub-Saharan (285)	308	0.47
African (171)	172	0.26
Cape Verdean (32)	32	0.05
Ethiopian (48)	48	0.07
Ghanaian (12)	12	0.02
Kenyan (22)	22	0.03
Nigerian (0)	10	0.02
Other Sub-Saharan African (0)	12	0.02
American (2,768)	2,768	4.19
Arab (550)	795	1.20
Arab (12)	12	0.02
Egyptian (61)	61	0.09
Iraqi (13)	13	0.02
Lebanese (339)	545	0.83
Moroccan (15)	15	0.02
Palestinian (14)	14	0.02
Syrian (82)	105	0.16
Other Arab (14)	30	0.05
Armenian (594)	659	1.00
Assyrian/Chaldean/Syriac (17)	17	0.03
Australian (11)	41	0.06
Austrian (95)	291	0.44
Basque (11)	11	0.02
Belgian (22)	58	0.09
Brazilian (302)	302	0.46
British (392)	730	1.11
Bulgarian (15)	40	0.06
Canadian (141)	265	0.40
Carpatho Rusyn (0)	15	0.02
Celtic (0)	42	0.06
Croatian (66)	95	0.14
Czech (140)	391	0.59
Czechoslovakian (0)	22	0.03
Danish (76)	310	0.47
Dutch (187)	1,197	1.81
Eastern European (365)	380	0.58
English (1,906)	6,401	9.69
Estonian (0)	39	0.06
European (1,530)	1,770	2.68
Finnish (90)	289	0.44
French, ex. Basque (292)	1,768	2.68
French Canadian (253)	574	0.87
German (3,122)	10,689	16.18
Greek (193)	440	0.67
Hungarian (186)	576	0.87
Icelander (0)	14	0.02
Iranian (672)	672	1.02
Irish (2,544)	8,764	13.27
Israeli (18)	18	0.03
Italian (1,331)	4,623	7.00
Latvian (39)	95	0.14
Lithuanian (72)	164	0.25
Luxemburger (0)	1	<0.01
Maltese (8)	17	0.03
Northern European (41)	47	0.07
Norwegian (412)	1,399	2.12
Polish (789)	2,078	3.15
Portuguese (266)	430	0.65
Romanian (33)	212	0.32
Russian (568)	1,509	2.28
Scandinavian (130)	250	0.38
Scotch-Irish (192)	662	1.00
Scottish (296)	1,368	2.07
Serbian (69)	106	0.16
Slavic (98)	110	0.17
Slovak (0)	142	0.21
Slovene (0)	52	0.08
Swedish (258)	1,304	1.97
Swiss (22)	523	0.79
Turkish (132)	139	0.21
Ukrainian (83)	190	0.29
Welsh (84)	499	0.76
West Indian, ex. Hispanic (52)	67	0.10
Belizean (17)	17	0.03
Haitian (10)	10	0.02
Jamaican (11)	11	0.02
West Indian (14)	29	0.04
Yugoslavian (30)	88	0.13

Hispanic Origin	Population	%
Hispanic or Latino (of any race)	10,142	15.19
Central American, ex. Mexican	930	1.39
Costa Rican	73	0.11
Guatemalan	302	0.45
Honduran	69	0.10
Nicaraguan	117	0.18
Panamanian	33	0.05
Salvadoran	305	0.46
Other Central American	31	0.05
Cuban	338	0.51
Dominican Republic	28	0.04
Mexican	6,193	9.28
Puerto Rican	399	0.60
South American	1,230	1.84
Argentinean	232	0.35

*Notes: † The Census 2010 population figure is used to calculate the percentages in the Hispanic Origin and Race categories. Ancestry percentages are based on the 2006-2010 American Community Survey population (not shown); ‡ Numbers in parentheses indicate the number of people reporting a single ancestry; * Numbers in parentheses indicate the number of persons reporting this race alone, not in combination with any other race; Please refer to the Explanation of Data for more information.*

Bolivian	41	0.06
Chilean	104	0.16
Colombian	243	0.36
Ecuadorian	124	0.19
Paraguayan	5	0.01
Peruvian	375	0.56
Uruguayan	29	0.04
Venezuelan	61	0.09
Other South American	16	0.02
Other Hispanic or Latino	1,024	1.53

Race*	Population	%
African-American/Black (1,852)	2,558	3.83
Not Hispanic (1,772)	2,323	3.48
Hispanic (80)	235	0.35
American Indian/Alaska Native (291)	767	1.15
Not Hispanic (163)	494	0.74
Hispanic (128)	273	0.41
Alaska Athabascan *(Ala. Nat.)* (0)	1	<0.01
Aleut *(Alaska Native)* (2)	2	<0.01
Apache (8)	19	0.03
Arapaho (0)	3	<0.01
Blackfeet (10)	23	0.03
Canadian/French Am. Ind. (0)	1	<0.01
Central American Ind. (5)	5	0.01
Cherokee (35)	128	0.19
Cheyenne (2)	6	0.01
Chickasaw (2)	6	0.01
Chippewa (5)	18	0.03
Choctaw (14)	39	0.06
Colville (1)	1	<0.01
Comanche (1)	5	0.01
Cree (1)	4	0.01
Creek (3)	12	0.02
Crow (0)	1	<0.01
Delaware (0)	4	0.01
Hopi (0)	2	<0.01
Inupiat *(Alaska Native)* (2)	2	<0.01
Iroquois (1)	9	0.01
Lumbee (0)	1	<0.01
Menominee (0)	1	<0.01
Mexican American Ind. (16)	30	0.04
Navajo (24)	47	0.07
Osage (0)	1	<0.01
Paiute (1)	3	<0.01
Pima (0)	4	0.01
Potawatomi (1)	4	0.01
Pueblo (6)	10	0.01
Puget Sound Salish (0)	2	<0.01
Seminole (1)	5	0.01
Shoshone (0)	1	<0.01
Sioux (8)	23	0.03
South American Ind. (1)	7	0.01
Spanish American Ind. (3)	3	<0.01
Tlingit-Haida *(Alaska Native)* (0)	2	<0.01
Tohono O'Odham (0)	1	<0.01
Ute (0)	1	<0.01
Yakama (0)	6	0.01
Yaqui (4)	10	0.01
Yuman (2)	2	<0.01
Asian (8,004)	10,324	15.47
Not Hispanic (7,858)	9,865	14.78
Hispanic (146)	459	0.69
Bangladeshi (6)	6	0.01
Burmese (8)	14	0.02
Cambodian (23)	28	0.04
Chinese, ex. Taiwanese (1,567)	2,247	3.37
Filipino (1,159)	1,937	2.90
Hmong (3)	3	<0.01
Indian (736)	870	1.30
Indonesian (55)	114	0.17
Japanese (1,836)	2,658	3.98
Korean (1,020)	1,282	1.92
Laotian (7)	10	0.01
Malaysian (7)	13	0.02
Nepalese (4)	4	0.01
Pakistani (165)	185	0.28
Sri Lankan (15)	26	0.04
Taiwanese (187)	219	0.33
Thai (124)	180	0.27
Vietnamese (599)	746	1.12
Hawaii Native/Pacific Islander (199)	580	0.87
Not Hispanic (177)	469	0.70
Hispanic (22)	111	0.17
Fijian (8)	13	0.02
Guamanian/Chamorro (48)	79	0.12
Native Hawaiian (56)	248	0.37
Samoan (52)	100	0.15
Tongan (10)	19	0.03
White (49,805)	53,210	79.72
Not Hispanic (43,531)	46,077	69.03
Hispanic (6,274)	7,133	10.69

Redwood City

Place Type: City
County: San Mateo
Population: 76,815†

Ancestry‡	Population	%
African, Sub-Saharan (29)	120	0.16
African (13)	95	0.13
South African (9)	18	0.02
Other Sub-Saharan African (7)	7	0.01
Albanian (14)	14	0.02
American (1,474)	1,474	1.96
Arab (533)	695	0.92
Arab (141)	155	0.21
Egyptian (35)	55	0.07
Iraqi (100)	100	0.13
Lebanese (119)	218	0.29
Moroccan (23)	23	0.03
Palestinian (47)	66	0.09
Syrian (20)	30	0.04
Other Arab (48)	48	0.06
Armenian (55)	79	0.11
Assyrian/Chaldean/Syriac (16)	38	0.05
Australian (13)	61	0.08
Austrian (26)	216	0.29
Basque (33)	43	0.06
Belgian (0)	58	0.08
Brazilian (46)	87	0.12
British (269)	409	0.54
Bulgarian (42)	42	0.06
Canadian (124)	299	0.40
Celtic (115)	115	0.15
Croatian (112)	342	0.45
Czech (91)	239	0.32
Czechoslovakian (34)	109	0.14
Danish (99)	698	0.93
Dutch (244)	903	1.20
Eastern European (187)	226	0.30
English (1,454)	5,306	7.06
Estonian (44)	76	0.10
European (924)	1,231	1.64
Finnish (63)	134	0.18
French, ex. Basque (285)	1,924	2.56
French Canadian (56)	147	0.20
German (2,419)	7,186	9.56
Greek (456)	799	1.06
Hungarian (56)	278	0.37
Iranian (485)	491	0.65
Irish (1,866)	6,552	8.71
Israeli (90)	102	0.14
Italian (2,202)	5,505	7.32
Latvian (15)	54	0.07
Lithuanian (27)	70	0.09
Maltese (32)	121	0.16
New Zealander (10)	10	0.01
Northern European (53)	62	0.08
Norwegian (289)	752	1.00
Pennsylvania German (0)	12	0.02
Polish (393)	984	1.31
Portuguese (375)	676	0.90
Romanian (91)	135	0.18
Russian (532)	1,013	1.35
Scandinavian (94)	114	0.15
Scotch-Irish (245)	857	1.14
Scottish (591)	1,603	2.13
Slovak (13)	45	0.06
Slovene (14)	14	0.02
Swedish (266)	1,137	1.51
Swiss (250)	556	0.74
Turkish (223)	283	0.38
Ukrainian (44)	181	0.24
Welsh (45)	414	0.55
West Indian, ex. Hispanic (0)	37	0.05
West Indian (0)	37	0.05
Yugoslavian (117)	169	0.22

Hispanic Origin	Population	%
Hispanic or Latino (of any race)	29,810	38.81
Central American, ex. Mexican	5,032	6.55
Costa Rican	62	0.08
Guatemalan	1,756	2.29
Honduran	135	0.18
Nicaraguan	565	0.74
Panamanian	37	0.05
Salvadoran	2,432	3.17
Other Central American	45	0.06
Cuban	167	0.22
Dominican Republic	24	0.03
Mexican	21,132	27.51
Puerto Rican	384	0.50
South American	1,166	1.52
Argentinean	149	0.19
Bolivian	90	0.12
Chilean	89	0.12
Colombian	133	0.17
Ecuadorian	43	0.06
Peruvian	578	0.75
Uruguayan	21	0.03
Venezuelan	41	0.05
Other South American	22	0.03
Other Hispanic or Latino	1,905	2.48

Race*	Population	%
African-American/Black (1,881)	2,531	3.29
Not Hispanic (1,655)	2,131	2.77
Hispanic (226)	400	0.52
American Indian/Alaska Native (511)	1,101	1.43
Not Hispanic (152)	484	0.63
Hispanic (359)	617	0.80
Aleut *(Alaska Native)* (1)	2	<0.01
Apache (13)	42	0.05
Arapaho (1)	2	<0.01
Blackfeet (4)	20	0.03
Canadian/French Am. Ind. (1)	3	<0.01
Central American Ind. (17)	25	0.03
Cherokee (15)	101	0.13
Chickasaw (2)	9	0.01
Chippewa (5)	13	0.02
Choctaw (5)	30	0.04
Colville (3)	3	<0.01
Comanche (0)	3	<0.01
Creek (3)	4	0.01
Delaware (1)	1	<0.01
Hopi (1)	1	<0.01
Inupiat *(Alaska Native)* (1)	3	<0.01
Iroquois (2)	5	0.01
Kiowa (0)	1	<0.01
Mexican American Ind. (123)	169	0.22
Navajo (8)	33	0.04
Osage (0)	2	<0.01
Ottawa (1)	1	<0.01
Paiute (2)	7	0.01
Potawatomi (0)	1	<0.01
Pueblo (2)	6	0.01
Puget Sound Salish (1)	1	<0.01
Seminole (0)	2	<0.01
Shoshone (0)	3	<0.01
Sioux (8)	25	0.03
South American Ind. (6)	12	0.02
Spanish American Ind. (7)	7	0.01
Tlingit-Haida *(Alaska Native)* (8)	12	0.02
Ute (0)	1	<0.01
Yakama (1)	1	<0.01
Yaqui (3)	8	0.01
Yuman (0)	7	0.01
Asian (8,216)	10,083	13.13

SECTION TWO

*Notes: † The Census 2010 population figure is used to calculate the percentages in the Hispanic Origin and Race categories. Ancestry percentages are based on the 2006-2010 American Community Survey population (not shown); ‡ Numbers in parentheses indicate the number of people reporting a single ancestry; * Numbers in parentheses indicate the number of persons reporting this race alone, not in combination with any other race; Please refer to the Explanation of Data for more information.*

Not Hispanic (8,063)	9,620	12.52
Hispanic (153)	463	0.60
Bangladeshi (4)	5	0.01
Burmese (5)	15	0.02
Cambodian (37)	56	0.07
Chinese, ex. Taiwanese (2,870)	3,628	4.72
Filipino (1,665)	2,331	3.03
Hmong (2)	2	<0.01
Indian (1,440)	1,673	2.18
Indonesian (45)	78	0.10
Japanese (647)	1,038	1.35
Korean (405)	541	0.70
Laotian (22)	34	0.04
Malaysian (5)	13	0.02
Nepalese (6)	6	0.01
Pakistani (69)	84	0.11
Sri Lankan (15)	19	0.02
Taiwanese (179)	227	0.30
Thai (53)	82	0.11
Vietnamese (331)	423	0.55
Hawaii Native/Pacific Islander (795)	1,242	1.62
Not Hispanic (732)	1,092	1.42
Hispanic (63)	150	0.20
Fijian (121)	156	0.20
Guamanian/Chamorro (45)	77	0.10
Native Hawaiian (33)	156	0.20
Samoan (69)	107	0.14
Tongan (459)	539	0.70
White (46,255)	49,787	64.81
Not Hispanic (33,801)	35,757	46.55
Hispanic (12,454)	14,030	18.26

Reedley

Place Type: City
County: Fresno
Population: 24,194†

Ancestry‡	Population	%
Afghan (78)	78	0.33
American (332)	332	1.40
Arab (20)	20	0.08
Palestinian (20)	20	0.08
Armenian (10)	90	0.38
Austrian (0)	8	0.03
Brazilian (11)	11	0.05
Croatian (0)	6	0.03
Danish (34)	44	0.19
Dutch (227)	409	1.73
English (189)	769	3.25
European (127)	141	0.60
French, ex. Basque (51)	158	0.67
French Canadian (18)	18	0.08
German (838)	1,795	7.58
Greek (0)	46	0.19
Irish (114)	689	2.91
Italian (27)	98	0.41
Lithuanian (0)	11	0.05
Norwegian (41)	91	0.38
Polish (21)	34	0.14
Portuguese (82)	109	0.46
Russian (10)	41	0.17
Scandinavian (9)	9	0.04
Scotch-Irish (55)	139	0.59
Scottish (45)	110	0.46
Swedish (141)	239	1.01
Turkish (0)	11	0.05
Ukrainian (11)	11	0.05
Welsh (0)	16	0.07
Yugoslavian (0)	8	0.03

Hispanic Origin	Population	%
Hispanic or Latino (of any race)	18,455	76.28
Central American, ex. Mexican	264	1.09
Costa Rican	5	0.02
Guatemalan	16	0.07
Honduran	7	0.03
Nicaraguan	6	0.02
Panamanian	1	<0.01
Salvadoran	228	0.94
Other Central American	1	<0.01
Cuban	4	0.02
Dominican Republic	1	<0.01
Mexican	17,406	71.94
Puerto Rican	57	0.24
South American	17	0.07
Chilean	3	0.01
Colombian	5	0.02
Paraguayan	4	0.02
Peruvian	4	0.02
Venezuelan	1	<0.01
Other Hispanic or Latino	706	2.92

Race*	Population	%
African-American/Black (169)	228	0.94
Not Hispanic (88)	115	0.48
Hispanic (81)	113	0.47
American Indian/Alaska Native (267)	361	1.49
Not Hispanic (58)	96	0.40
Hispanic (209)	265	1.10
Apache (2)	6	0.02
Cherokee (9)	28	0.12
Choctaw (1)	5	0.02
Comanche (1)	1	<0.01
Creek (3)	6	0.02
Hopi (1)	1	<0.01
Inupiat *(Alaska Native)* (1)	1	<0.01
Menominee (1)	1	<0.01
Mexican American Ind. (63)	74	0.31
Navajo (5)	9	0.04
Potawatomi (1)	4	0.02
Seminole (0)	1	<0.01
South American Ind. (3)	4	0.02
Spanish American Ind. (5)	5	0.02
Yaqui (3)	5	0.02
Asian (797)	1,027	4.24
Not Hispanic (739)	876	3.62
Hispanic (58)	151	0.62
Cambodian (15)	20	0.08
Chinese, ex. Taiwanese (74)	101	0.42
Filipino (303)	391	1.62
Indian (42)	49	0.20
Indonesian (0)	1	<0.01
Japanese (294)	406	1.68
Korean (12)	19	0.08
Laotian (6)	8	0.03
Malaysian (0)	2	0.01
Pakistani (4)	4	0.02
Taiwanese (3)	3	0.01
Thai (0)	1	<0.01
Vietnamese (12)	13	0.05
Hawaii Native/Pacific Islander (8)	51	0.21
Not Hispanic (5)	13	0.05
Hispanic (3)	38	0.16
Fijian (0)	12	0.05
Guamanian/Chamorro (1)	5	0.02
Native Hawaiian (0)	5	0.02
Samoan (5)	5	0.02
White (14,105)	15,002	62.01
Not Hispanic (4,604)	4,791	19.80
Hispanic (9,501)	10,211	42.20

Rialto

Place Type: City
County: San Bernardino
Population: 99,171†

Ancestry‡	Population	%
African, Sub-Saharan (641)	868	0.87
African (544)	771	0.78
Ethiopian (22)	22	0.02
Ghanaian (12)	12	0.01
Kenyan (17)	17	0.02
Nigerian (46)	46	0.05
American (2,257)	2,257	2.27
Arab (397)	421	0.42
Arab (0)	24	0.02
Egyptian (208)	208	0.21
Palestinian (153)	153	0.15
Syrian (36)	36	0.04
Brazilian (36)	95	0.10
British (35)	170	0.17
Canadian (25)	25	0.03
Czech (0)	65	0.07
Czechoslovakian (7)	7	0.01
Danish (22)	131	0.13
Dutch (0)	238	0.24
English (578)	2,205	2.22
European (262)	353	0.36
Finnish (0)	22	0.02
French, ex. Basque (109)	975	0.98
French Canadian (16)	47	0.05
German (1,299)	4,375	4.41
Greek (13)	44	0.04
Hungarian (11)	67	0.07
Irish (817)	2,925	2.95
Italian (429)	1,402	1.41
Lithuanian (46)	71	0.07
Norwegian (32)	398	0.40
Pennsylvania German (16)	16	0.02
Polish (71)	187	0.19
Portuguese (42)	42	0.04
Russian (32)	114	0.11
Scandinavian (40)	50	0.05
Scotch-Irish (81)	260	0.26
Scottish (75)	234	0.24
Slovak (24)	69	0.07
Slovene (25)	33	0.03
Swedish (58)	169	0.17
Swiss (35)	136	0.14
Welsh (9)	40	0.04
West Indian, ex. Hispanic (527)	572	0.58
Barbadian (159)	159	0.16
Belizean (223)	231	0.23
Jamaican (145)	182	0.18

Hispanic Origin	Population	%
Hispanic or Latino (of any race)	67,038	67.60
Central American, ex. Mexican	4,402	4.44
Costa Rican	102	0.10
Guatemalan	1,111	1.12
Honduran	324	0.33
Nicaraguan	482	0.49
Panamanian	86	0.09
Salvadoran	2,246	2.26
Other Central American	51	0.05
Cuban	251	0.25
Dominican Republic	39	0.04
Mexican	57,699	58.18
Puerto Rican	687	0.69
South American	747	0.75
Argentinean	97	0.10
Bolivian	35	0.04
Chilean	35	0.04
Colombian	201	0.20
Ecuadorian	127	0.13
Peruvian	207	0.21
Uruguayan	4	<0.01
Venezuelan	30	0.03
Other South American	11	0.01
Other Hispanic or Latino	3,213	3.24

Race*	Population	%
African-American/Black (16,236)	17,754	17.90
Not Hispanic (15,457)	16,367	16.50
Hispanic (779)	1,387	1.40
American Indian/Alaska Native (1,062)	1,855	1.87
Not Hispanic (237)	640	0.65
Hispanic (825)	1,215	1.23
Aleut *(Alaska Native)* (0)	1	<0.01
Apache (36)	79	0.08
Arapaho (0)	1	<0.01
Blackfeet (3)	56	0.06
Central American Ind. (12)	27	0.03
Cherokee (20)	152	0.15
Chickasaw (2)	16	0.02
Chippewa (11)	17	0.02
Choctaw (13)	32	0.03
Comanche (2)	3	<0.01

*Notes: † The Census 2010 population figure is used to calculate the percentages in the Hispanic Origin and Race categories. Ancestry percentages are based on the 2006-2010 American Community Survey population (not shown); ‡ Numbers in parentheses indicate the number of people reporting a single ancestry; * Numbers in parentheses indicate the number of persons reporting this race alone, not in combination with any other race; Please refer to the Explanation of Data for more information.*

Creek (1)	6	0.01
Crow (0)	1	<0.01
Delaware (1)	4	<0.01
Hopi (3)	7	0.01
Houma (3)	3	<0.01
Inupiat *(Alaska Native)* (1)	1	<0.01
Iroquois (2)	8	0.01
Kiowa (1)	1	<0.01
Mexican American Ind. (141)	198	0.20
Navajo (17)	44	0.04
Osage (4)	11	0.01
Ottawa (0)	5	0.01
Paiute (10)	19	0.02
Pima (5)	7	0.01
Potawatomi (4)	4	<0.01
Pueblo (28)	36	0.04
Seminole (2)	19	0.02
Shoshone (4)	9	0.01
Sioux (11)	25	0.03
South American Ind. (0)	3	<0.01
Spanish American Ind. (13)	13	0.01
Tohono O'Odham (1)	3	<0.01
Yakama (0)	4	<0.01
Yaqui (48)	63	0.06
Yuman (1)	2	<0.01
Asian (2,258)	2,950	2.97
Not Hispanic (2,037)	2,435	2.46
Hispanic (221)	515	0.52
Bangladeshi (4)	4	<0.01
Burmese (25)	26	0.03
Cambodian (257)	310	0.31
Chinese, ex. Taiwanese (185)	324	0.33
Filipino (814)	1,102	1.11
Indian (168)	222	0.22
Indonesian (76)	107	0.11
Japanese (94)	199	0.20
Korean (90)	117	0.12
Laotian (45)	57	0.06
Malaysian (2)	3	<0.01
Pakistani (50)	61	0.06
Sri Lankan (1)	2	<0.01
Taiwanese (18)	20	0.02
Thai (60)	79	0.08
Vietnamese (239)	279	0.28
Hawaii Native/Pacific Islander (361)	635	0.64
Not Hispanic (313)	476	0.48
Hispanic (48)	159	0.16
Fijian (20)	22	0.02
Guamanian/Chamorro (28)	39	0.04
Marshallese (8)	8	0.01
Native Hawaiian (66)	168	0.17
Samoan (139)	209	0.21
Tongan (50)	66	0.07
White (43,592)	47,165	47.56
Not Hispanic (12,475)	13,465	13.58
Hispanic (31,117)	33,700	33.98

Richmond

Place Type: City
County: Contra Costa
Population: 103,701†

Ancestry‡	Population	%
Afghan (12)	12	0.01
African, Sub-Saharan (5,295)	5,853	5.72
African (4,590)	4,973	4.86
Cape Verdean (0)	22	0.02
Ethiopian (321)	474	0.46
Nigerian (326)	326	0.32
Senegalese (11)	11	0.01
Other Sub-Saharan African (47)	47	0.05
American (886)	886	0.87
Arab (624)	670	0.66
Arab (43)	43	0.04
Iraqi (8)	8	0.01
Lebanese (18)	24	0.02
Moroccan (26)	37	0.04
Palestinian (529)	539	0.53
Syrian (0)	10	0.01
Other Arab (0)	9	0.01
Armenian (45)	60	0.06
Australian (10)	32	0.03
Austrian (19)	229	0.22
Basque (11)	11	0.01
Belgian (13)	96	0.09
Brazilian (547)	547	0.53
British (126)	181	0.18
Canadian (26)	43	0.04
Celtic (31)	73	0.07
Croatian (8)	42	0.04
Czech (21)	146	0.14
Czechoslovakian (30)	43	0.04
Danish (100)	237	0.23
Dutch (129)	434	0.42
Eastern European (150)	150	0.15
English (642)	2,649	2.59
European (457)	623	0.61
Finnish (0)	38	0.04
French, ex. Basque (114)	1,261	1.23
French Canadian (32)	82	0.08
German (1,031)	4,058	3.97
Greek (66)	180	0.18
Hungarian (146)	273	0.27
Icelander (0)	20	0.02
Iranian (419)	485	0.47
Irish (596)	2,693	2.63
Israeli (44)	44	0.04
Italian (919)	2,181	2.13
Latvian (9)	9	0.01
Lithuanian (35)	78	0.08
Northern European (187)	187	0.18
Norwegian (100)	494	0.48
Polish (108)	548	0.54
Portuguese (475)	817	0.80
Romanian (42)	63	0.06
Russian (253)	609	0.60
Scandinavian (57)	122	0.12
Scotch-Irish (301)	882	0.86
Scottish (235)	789	0.77
Slavic (63)	75	0.07
Slovak (48)	61	0.06
Slovene (13)	13	0.01
Swedish (151)	703	0.69
Swiss (28)	84	0.08
Ukrainian (61)	115	0.11
Welsh (19)	229	0.22
West Indian, ex. Hispanic (190)	334	0.33
Haitian (77)	101	0.10
Jamaican (98)	177	0.17
West Indian (15)	56	0.05
Yugoslavian (24)	190	0.19

Hispanic Origin	Population	%
Hispanic or Latino (of any race)	40,921	39.46
Central American, ex. Mexican	8,329	8.03
Costa Rican	36	0.03
Guatemalan	1,717	1.66
Honduran	319	0.31
Nicaraguan	1,209	1.17
Panamanian	87	0.08
Salvadoran	4,888	4.71
Other Central American	73	0.07
Cuban	141	0.14
Dominican Republic	27	0.03
Mexican	28,275	27.27
Puerto Rican	534	0.51
South American	942	0.91
Argentinean	53	0.05
Bolivian	22	0.02
Chilean	136	0.13
Colombian	107	0.10
Ecuadorian	37	0.04
Peruvian	548	0.53
Uruguayan	6	0.01
Venezuelan	26	0.03
Other South American	7	0.01
Other Hispanic or Latino	2,673	2.58

Race*	Population	%
African-American/Black (27,542)	29,796	28.73
Not Hispanic (26,872)	28,533	27.51
Hispanic (670)	1,263	1.22
American Indian/Alaska Native (662)	1,735	1.67
Not Hispanic (250)	962	0.93
Hispanic (412)	773	0.75
Alaska Athabascan *(Ala. Nat.)* (1)	1	<0.01
Aleut *(Alaska Native)* (0)	1	<0.01
Apache (18)	50	0.05
Blackfeet (0)	51	0.05
Canadian/French Am. Ind. (1)	6	0.01
Central American Ind. (18)	31	0.03
Cherokee (33)	204	0.20
Chickasaw (2)	13	0.01
Chippewa (5)	7	0.01
Choctaw (13)	64	0.06
Colville (1)	1	<0.01
Comanche (2)	10	0.01
Cree (4)	7	0.01
Creek (5)	15	0.01
Crow (0)	3	<0.01
Delaware (1)	2	<0.01
Hopi (0)	1	<0.01
Houma (2)	2	<0.01
Inupiat *(Alaska Native)* (3)	3	<0.01
Iroquois (7)	19	0.02
Kiowa (1)	1	<0.01
Mexican American Ind. (115)	173	0.17
Navajo (16)	24	0.02
Osage (0)	1	<0.01
Paiute (5)	9	0.01
Pueblo (14)	19	0.02
Puget Sound Salish (0)	1	<0.01
Seminole (0)	10	0.01
Shoshone (0)	1	<0.01
Sioux (11)	24	0.02
South American Ind. (9)	20	0.02
Spanish American Ind. (12)	14	0.01
Tlingit-Haida *(Alaska Native)* (1)	5	<0.01
Tohono O'Odham (1)	3	<0.01
Ute (1)	2	<0.01
Yaqui (13)	25	0.02
Yup'ik *(Alaska Native)* (0)	1	<0.01
Asian (13,984)	15,852	15.29
Not Hispanic (13,783)	15,261	14.72
Hispanic (201)	591	0.57
Bangladeshi (2)	2	<0.01
Burmese (46)	54	0.05
Cambodian (107)	150	0.14
Chinese, ex. Taiwanese (4,009)	4,581	4.42
Filipino (3,678)	4,500	4.34
Hmong (16)	18	0.02
Indian (1,295)	1,469	1.42
Indonesian (46)	84	0.08
Japanese (657)	1,073	1.03
Korean (405)	494	0.48
Laotian (1,703)	1,886	1.82
Malaysian (25)	45	0.04
Nepalese (68)	75	0.07
Pakistani (244)	261	0.25
Sri Lankan (39)	48	0.05
Taiwanese (169)	190	0.18
Thai (137)	217	0.21
Vietnamese (689)	816	0.79
Hawaii Native/Pacific Islander (537)	977	0.94
Not Hispanic (462)	768	0.74
Hispanic (75)	209	0.20
Fijian (110)	132	0.13
Guamanian/Chamorro (58)	111	0.11
Native Hawaiian (47)	189	0.18
Samoan (157)	230	0.22
Tongan (102)	130	0.13
White (32,590)	36,803	35.49
Not Hispanic (17,769)	19,814	19.11
Hispanic (14,821)	16,989	16.38

*Notes: † The Census 2010 population figure is used to calculate the percentages in the Hispanic Origin and Race categories. Ancestry percentages are based on the 2006-2010 American Community Survey population (not shown); ‡ Numbers in parentheses indicate the number of people reporting a single ancestry; * Numbers in parentheses indicate the number of persons reporting this race alone, not in combination with any other race; Please refer to the Explanation of Data for more information.*

Ridgecrest

Place Type: City
County: Kern
Population: 27,616†

Ancestry‡	Population	%
African, Sub-Saharan (257)	287	1.05
African (166)	179	0.65
Kenyan (56)	73	0.27
Nigerian (15)	15	0.05
Sudanese (20)	20	0.07
American (1,680)	1,680	6.13
Arab (29)	29	0.11
Lebanese (29)	29	0.11
Armenian (11)	24	0.09
Australian (15)	46	0.17
Austrian (12)	65	0.24
Belgian (21)	114	0.42
British (103)	310	1.13
Cajun (5)	15	0.05
Canadian (35)	35	0.13
Celtic (0)	16	0.06
Czech (0)	119	0.43
Czechoslovakian (38)	56	0.20
Danish (38)	95	0.35
Dutch (62)	433	1.58
English (945)	2,751	10.05
European (599)	634	2.32
Finnish (39)	160	0.58
French, ex. Basque (171)	662	2.42
French Canadian (21)	118	0.43
German (1,325)	4,648	16.97
Greek (0)	37	0.14
Hungarian (14)	109	0.40
Iranian (23)	23	0.08
Irish (615)	3,134	11.44
Italian (336)	1,267	4.63
Lithuanian (0)	68	0.25
Northern European (54)	54	0.20
Norwegian (265)	784	2.86
Pennsylvania German (7)	33	0.12
Polish (137)	421	1.54
Portuguese (50)	182	0.66
Romanian (0)	9	0.03
Russian (25)	60	0.22
Scandinavian (37)	133	0.49
Scotch-Irish (270)	671	2.45
Scottish (217)	790	2.88
Serbian (20)	20	0.07
Slavic (7)	7	0.03
Slovene (9)	9	0.03
Swedish (221)	768	2.80
Swiss (0)	31	0.11
Ukrainian (43)	126	0.46
Welsh (51)	222	0.81
West Indian, ex. Hispanic (222)	244	0.89
Haitian (151)	151	0.55
Jamaican (71)	93	0.34
Yugoslavian (0)	13	0.05

Hispanic Origin	Population	%
Hispanic or Latino (of any race)	4,941	17.89
Central American, ex. Mexican	268	0.97
Costa Rican	8	0.03
Guatemalan	75	0.27
Honduran	23	0.08
Nicaraguan	18	0.07
Panamanian	13	0.05
Salvadoran	131	0.47
Cuban	28	0.10
Dominican Republic	11	0.04
Mexican	4,007	14.51
Puerto Rican	157	0.57
South American	96	0.35
Argentinean	7	0.03
Bolivian	1	<0.01
Chilean	14	0.05
Colombian	17	0.06
Ecuadorian	11	0.04
Peruvian	38	0.14
Uruguayan	2	0.01
Venezuelan	6	0.02
Other Hispanic or Latino	374	1.35

Race*	Population	%
African-American/Black (1,113)	1,537	5.57
Not Hispanic (1,041)	1,361	4.93
Hispanic (72)	176	0.64
American Indian/Alaska Native (341)	773	2.80
Not Hispanic (245)	566	2.05
Hispanic (96)	207	0.75
Aleut *(Alaska Native)* (2)	2	0.01
Apache (12)	31	0.11
Arapaho (0)	1	<0.01
Blackfeet (2)	11	0.04
Canadian/French Am. Ind. (0)	2	0.01
Central American Ind. (1)	1	<0.01
Cherokee (46)	168	0.61
Chickasaw (2)	6	0.02
Chippewa (6)	11	0.04
Choctaw (17)	59	0.21
Comanche (1)	9	0.03
Creek (1)	8	0.03
Crow (0)	1	<0.01
Delaware (1)	1	<0.01
Iroquois (6)	10	0.04
Lumbee (1)	2	0.01
Menominee (1)	3	0.01
Mexican American Ind. (18)	27	0.10
Navajo (18)	21	0.08
Osage (0)	6	0.02
Paiute (15)	25	0.09
Potawatomi (4)	6	0.02
Pueblo (13)	14	0.05
Shoshone (5)	10	0.04
Sioux (14)	29	0.11
South American Ind. (1)	1	<0.01
Spanish American Ind. (5)	5	0.02
Tlingit-Haida *(Alaska Native)* (2)	4	0.01
Tsimshian *(Alaska Native)* (1)	1	<0.01
Yaqui (9)	13	0.05
Asian (1,209)	1,746	6.32
Not Hispanic (1,188)	1,611	5.83
Hispanic (21)	135	0.49
Bangladeshi (1)	1	<0.01
Cambodian (32)	34	0.12
Chinese, ex. Taiwanese (138)	197	0.71
Filipino (475)	758	2.74
Hmong (15)	15	0.05
Indian (120)	132	0.48
Indonesian (15)	20	0.07
Japanese (93)	258	0.93
Korean (62)	110	0.40
Laotian (2)	4	0.01
Pakistani (30)	37	0.13
Sri Lankan (1)	1	<0.01
Taiwanese (3)	6	0.02
Thai (39)	46	0.17
Vietnamese (139)	169	0.61
Hawaii Native/Pacific Islander (143)	289	1.05
Not Hispanic (127)	240	0.87
Hispanic (16)	49	0.18
Fijian (3)	3	0.01
Guamanian/Chamorro (54)	102	0.37
Native Hawaiian (21)	81	0.29
Samoan (54)	89	0.32
Tongan (0)	6	0.02
White (21,387)	22,776	82.47
Not Hispanic (19,019)	19,907	72.09
Hispanic (2,368)	2,869	10.39

Rio Linda

Place Type: CDP
County: Sacramento
Population: 15,106†

Ancestry‡	Population	%
American (872)	872	5.93
Arab (0)	11	0.07
Lebanese (0)	11	0.07
Armenian (12)	12	0.08
British (11)	16	0.11
Canadian (11)	11	0.07
Celtic (0)	8	0.05
Czech (0)	30	0.20
Czechoslovakian (11)	11	0.07
Danish (37)	157	1.07
Dutch (75)	272	1.85
Eastern European (12)	12	0.08
English (248)	980	6.67
European (363)	409	2.78
Finnish (9)	25	0.17
French, ex. Basque (43)	490	3.33
French Canadian (14)	14	0.10
German (874)	2,543	17.31
German Russian (9)	9	0.06
Greek (14)	22	0.15
Hungarian (14)	24	0.16
Irish (448)	1,383	9.41
Italian (111)	743	5.06
Latvian (0)	25	0.17
Norwegian (52)	304	2.07
Polish (92)	189	1.29
Portuguese (70)	259	1.76
Romanian (85)	109	0.74
Russian (417)	505	3.44
Scandinavian (0)	18	0.12
Scotch-Irish (202)	334	2.27
Scottish (49)	331	2.25
Slavic (0)	13	0.09
Swedish (20)	316	2.15
Swiss (23)	122	0.83
Turkish (0)	37	0.25
Ukrainian (193)	217	1.48
Welsh (0)	26	0.18
Yugoslavian (0)	13	0.09

Hispanic Origin	Population	%
Hispanic or Latino (of any race)	3,033	20.08
Central American, ex. Mexican	73	0.48
Costa Rican	2	0.01
Guatemalan	13	0.09
Honduran	6	0.04
Nicaraguan	11	0.07
Panamanian	8	0.05
Salvadoran	33	0.22
Cuban	12	0.08
Dominican Republic	1	0.01
Mexican	2,597	17.19
Puerto Rican	66	0.44
South American	27	0.18
Argentinean	1	0.01
Colombian	4	0.03
Ecuadorian	1	0.01
Paraguayan	4	0.03
Peruvian	16	0.11
Other South American	1	0.01
Other Hispanic or Latino	257	1.70

Race*	Population	%
African-American/Black (365)	498	3.30
Not Hispanic (339)	442	2.93
Hispanic (26)	56	0.37
American Indian/Alaska Native (235)	568	3.76
Not Hispanic (143)	385	2.55
Hispanic (92)	183	1.21
Alaska Athabascan *(Ala. Nat.)* (4)	4	0.03
Aleut *(Alaska Native)* (0)	1	0.01
Apache (6)	11	0.07
Blackfeet (1)	19	0.13
Canadian/French Am. Ind. (0)	1	0.01
Cherokee (22)	102	0.68
Chickasaw (0)	2	0.01
Chippewa (1)	5	0.03
Choctaw (11)	25	0.17
Comanche (1)	2	0.01
Creek (0)	8	0.05
Crow (0)	1	0.01

*Notes: † The Census 2010 population figure is used to calculate the percentages in the Hispanic Origin and Race categories. Ancestry percentages are based on the 2006-2010 American Community Survey population (not shown); ‡ Numbers in parentheses indicate the number of people reporting a single ancestry; * Numbers in parentheses indicate the number of persons reporting this race alone, not in combination with any other race; Please refer to the Explanation of Data for more information.*

Inupiat *(Alaska Native)* (1)	1	0.01
Iroquois (0)	3	0.02
Menominee (0)	2	0.01
Mexican American Ind. (21)	40	0.26
Navajo (5)	9	0.06
Osage (1)	2	0.01
Ottawa (0)	2	0.01
Paiute (1)	4	0.03
Pima (0)	2	0.01
Potawatomi (0)	2	0.01
Seminole (0)	6	0.04
Sioux (1)	5	0.03
South American Ind. (1)	2	0.01
Tlingit-Haida *(Alaska Native)* (5)	6	0.04
Tohono O'Odham (0)	3	0.02
Tsimshian *(Alaska Native)* (0)	1	0.01
Ute (1)	6	0.04
Yaqui (1)	3	0.02
Asian (665)	862	5.71
Not Hispanic (659)	810	5.36
Hispanic (6)	52	0.34
Cambodian (14)	14	0.09
Chinese, ex. Taiwanese (18)	38	0.25
Filipino (90)	173	1.15
Hmong (251)	256	1.69
Indian (64)	86	0.57
Indonesian (1)	4	0.03
Japanese (36)	77	0.51
Korean (5)	15	0.10
Laotian (72)	74	0.49
Nepalese (2)	2	0.01
Pakistani (7)	11	0.07
Thai (10)	24	0.16
Vietnamese (35)	40	0.26
Hawaii Native/Pacific Islander (62)	139	0.92
Not Hispanic (52)	118	0.78
Hispanic (10)	21	0.14
Fijian (32)	46	0.30
Guamanian/Chamorro (13)	17	0.11
Native Hawaiian (6)	31	0.21
Samoan (7)	19	0.13
Tongan (1)	5	0.03
White (11,654)	12,380	81.95
Not Hispanic (10,362)	10,805	71.53
Hispanic (1,292)	1,575	10.43

Rio del Mar

Place Type: CDP
County: Santa Cruz
Population: 9,216†

Ancestry‡	Population	%
American (322)	322	3.42
Arab (0)	21	0.22
Egyptian (0)	21	0.22
Austrian (51)	51	0.54
Brazilian (28)	122	1.29
British (27)	40	0.42
Canadian (15)	66	0.70
Celtic (0)	11	0.12
Croatian (55)	81	0.86
Czech (8)	61	0.65
Danish (13)	147	1.56
Dutch (37)	276	2.93
Eastern European (9)	19	0.20
English (448)	1,691	17.95
European (219)	257	2.73
Finnish (22)	114	1.21
French, ex. Basque (46)	447	4.74
French Canadian (13)	25	0.27
German (415)	1,813	19.24
Hungarian (0)	5	0.05
Iranian (48)	48	0.51
Irish (323)	1,582	16.79
Italian (364)	1,193	12.66
Lithuanian (0)	26	0.28
Northern European (201)	201	2.13
Norwegian (79)	377	4.00
Polish (75)	314	3.33
Portuguese (42)	150	1.59
Romanian (24)	51	0.54
Russian (96)	167	1.77
Scandinavian (30)	30	0.32
Scotch-Irish (40)	139	1.48
Scottish (38)	301	3.19
Serbian (38)	59	0.63
Slavic (9)	24	0.25
Swedish (61)	297	3.15
Swiss (25)	149	1.58
Ukrainian (9)	22	0.23
Welsh (12)	180	1.91
West Indian, ex. Hispanic (9)	9	0.10
West Indian (9)	9	0.10
Yugoslavian (0)	14	0.15

Hispanic Origin	Population	%
Hispanic or Latino (of any race)	899	9.75
Central American, ex. Mexican	33	0.36
Costa Rican	2	0.02
Guatemalan	7	0.08
Honduran	4	0.04
Nicaraguan	3	0.03
Panamanian	2	0.02
Salvadoran	15	0.16
Cuban	9	0.10
Dominican Republic	2	0.02
Mexican	625	6.78
Puerto Rican	30	0.33
South American	61	0.66
Argentinean	15	0.16
Bolivian	6	0.07
Chilean	6	0.07
Colombian	14	0.15
Ecuadorian	9	0.10
Peruvian	7	0.08
Uruguayan	2	0.02
Venezuelan	1	0.01
Other South American	1	0.01
Other Hispanic or Latino	139	1.51

Race*	Population	%
African-American/Black (61)	108	1.17
Not Hispanic (54)	96	1.04
Hispanic (7)	12	0.13
American Indian/Alaska Native (50)	137	1.49
Not Hispanic (28)	82	0.89
Hispanic (22)	55	0.60
Apache (6)	10	0.11
Blackfeet (0)	3	0.03
Cherokee (4)	39	0.42
Chippewa (0)	3	0.03
Choctaw (1)	1	0.01
Creek (0)	1	0.01
Crow (0)	1	0.01
Hopi (0)	1	0.01
Mexican American Ind. (6)	6	0.07
Navajo (0)	2	0.02
Osage (1)	1	0.01
Seminole (0)	1	0.01
Sioux (2)	8	0.09
Tohono O'Odham (0)	2	0.02
Yaqui (1)	2	0.02
Asian (313)	451	4.89
Not Hispanic (307)	422	4.58
Hispanic (6)	29	0.31
Chinese, ex. Taiwanese (80)	108	1.17
Filipino (43)	95	1.03
Indian (58)	66	0.72
Indonesian (1)	4	0.04
Japanese (77)	114	1.24
Korean (19)	27	0.29
Laotian (2)	2	0.02
Malaysian (1)	1	0.01
Pakistani (0)	1	0.01
Sri Lankan (2)	4	0.04
Taiwanese (2)	2	0.02
Thai (4)	4	0.04
Vietnamese (13)	16	0.17
Hawaii Native/Pacific Islander (7)	21	0.23
Not Hispanic (6)	18	0.20
Hispanic (1)	3	0.03
Guamanian/Chamorro (1)	1	0.01
Native Hawaiian (3)	13	0.14
Samoan (0)	1	0.01
Tongan (0)	2	0.02
White (8,310)	8,566	92.95
Not Hispanic (7,704)	7,888	85.59
Hispanic (606)	678	7.36

Ripon

Place Type: City
County: San Joaquin
Population: 14,297†

Ancestry‡	Population	%
Afghan (251)	251	1.82
American (658)	658	4.77
Arab (82)	92	0.67
Lebanese (71)	71	0.51
Other Arab (11)	21	0.15
Austrian (0)	36	0.26
Basque (0)	16	0.12
Belgian (0)	12	0.09
Brazilian (10)	31	0.22
British (56)	64	0.46
Canadian (14)	14	0.10
Croatian (4)	4	0.03
Czech (10)	30	0.22
Danish (28)	142	1.03
Dutch (829)	1,123	8.14
English (223)	1,270	9.21
European (56)	125	0.91
Finnish (4)	13	0.09
French, ex. Basque (33)	142	1.03
French Canadian (68)	140	1.02
German (554)	2,040	14.79
Greek (7)	13	0.09
Hungarian (39)	99	0.72
Icelander (8)	8	0.06
Iranian (14)	40	0.29
Irish (228)	1,148	8.32
Italian (386)	996	7.22
Lithuanian (0)	50	0.36
New Zealander (10)	44	0.32
Northern European (10)	44	0.32
Norwegian (48)	217	1.57
Polish (12)	150	1.09
Portuguese (367)	732	5.31
Russian (97)	123	0.89
Scandinavian (28)	77	0.56
Scotch-Irish (42)	253	1.83
Scottish (55)	293	2.12
Slavic (0)	13	0.09
Swedish (79)	255	1.85
Swiss (120)	340	2.47
Ukrainian (0)	28	0.20
Welsh (0)	88	0.64
Yugoslavian (25)	103	0.75

Hispanic Origin	Population	%
Hispanic or Latino (of any race)	3,177	22.22
Central American, ex. Mexican	70	0.49
Costa Rican	6	0.04
Guatemalan	13	0.09
Honduran	4	0.03
Nicaraguan	6	0.04
Panamanian	3	0.02
Salvadoran	28	0.20
Other Central American	10	0.07
Cuban	15	0.10
Mexican	2,691	18.82
Puerto Rican	76	0.53
South American	39	0.27
Argentinean	2	0.01
Bolivian	1	0.01
Chilean	4	0.03
Colombian	5	0.03
Ecuadorian	10	0.07

*Notes: † The Census 2010 population figure is used to calculate the percentages in the Hispanic Origin and Race categories. Ancestry percentages are based on the 2006-2010 American Community Survey population (not shown); ‡ Numbers in parentheses indicate the number of people reporting a single ancestry; * Numbers in parentheses indicate the number of persons reporting this race alone, not in combination with any other race; Please refer to the Explanation of Data for more information.*

Peruvian	13	0.09
Venezuelan	4	0.03
Other Hispanic or Latino	286	2.00

Race*	Population	%
African-American/Black (221)	310	2.17
Not Hispanic (199)	264	1.85
Hispanic (22)	46	0.32
American Indian/Alaska Native (125)	319	2.23
Not Hispanic (69)	198	1.38
Hispanic (56)	121	0.85
Apache (2)	11	0.08
Blackfeet (6)	13	0.09
Canadian/French Am. Ind. (0)	1	0.01
Cherokee (8)	57	0.40
Chickasaw (8)	11	0.08
Chippewa (1)	1	0.01
Choctaw (8)	12	0.08
Comanche (1)	6	0.04
Creek (4)	7	0.05
Delaware (0)	1	0.01
Inupiat *(Alaska Native)* (2)	4	0.03
Iroquois (0)	2	0.01
Mexican American Ind. (16)	17	0.12
Navajo (1)	3	0.02
Potawatomi (0)	2	0.01
Pueblo (1)	1	0.01
Puget Sound Salish (3)	3	0.02
Sioux (3)	3	0.02
Tohono O'Odham (0)	1	0.01
Yuman (0)	3	0.02
Asian (599)	871	6.09
Not Hispanic (564)	762	5.33
Hispanic (35)	109	0.76
Cambodian (42)	47	0.33
Chinese, ex. Taiwanese (54)	111	0.78
Filipino (183)	341	2.39
Indian (149)	161	1.13
Indonesian (3)	7	0.05
Japanese (24)	71	0.50
Korean (35)	55	0.38
Laotian (12)	13	0.09
Pakistani (6)	6	0.04
Taiwanese (4)	8	0.06
Thai (2)	2	0.01
Vietnamese (64)	67	0.47
Hawaii Native/Pacific Islander (36)	110	0.77
Not Hispanic (23)	73	0.51
Hispanic (13)	37	0.26
Fijian (4)	4	0.03
Guamanian/Chamorro (18)	35	0.24
Native Hawaiian (11)	54	0.38
Samoan (0)	4	0.03
White (11,392)	12,041	84.22
Not Hispanic (9,855)	10,215	71.45
Hispanic (1,537)	1,826	12.77

Riverbank

Place Type: City
County: Stanislaus
Population: 22,678†

Ancestry‡	Population	%
African, Sub-Saharan (0)	32	0.15
African (0)	13	0.06
South African (0)	19	0.09
American (787)	787	3.61
Arab (419)	493	2.26
Arab (223)	231	1.06
Egyptian (21)	21	0.10
Lebanese (9)	19	0.09
Syrian (24)	76	0.35
Other Arab (142)	146	0.67
Armenian (17)	17	0.08
Assyrian/Chaldean/Syriac (350)	350	1.61
Brazilian (22)	22	0.10
British (23)	32	0.15
Canadian (23)	44	0.20
Czech (10)	10	0.05
Danish (9)	39	0.18
Dutch (38)	230	1.06
English (343)	949	4.36
Estonian (0)	135	0.62
European (78)	135	0.62
Finnish (0)	35	0.16
French, ex. Basque (23)	178	0.82
French Canadian (17)	17	0.08
German (356)	1,837	8.44
Greek (9)	18	0.08
Hungarian (0)	68	0.31
Icelander (47)	47	0.22
Iranian (10)	45	0.21
Irish (234)	1,615	7.42
Italian (226)	682	3.13
New Zealander (0)	8	0.04
Northern European (8)	8	0.04
Norwegian (12)	130	0.60
Polish (24)	73	0.34
Portuguese (540)	823	3.78
Russian (49)	49	0.22
Scandinavian (27)	58	0.27
Scotch-Irish (17)	95	0.44
Scottish (56)	337	1.55
Slovak (20)	20	0.09
Swedish (56)	190	0.87
Swiss (0)	42	0.19
Ukrainian (0)	34	0.16
Welsh (19)	88	0.40

Hispanic Origin	Population	%
Hispanic or Latino (of any race)	11,822	52.13
Central American, ex. Mexican	237	1.05
Costa Rican	7	0.03
Guatemalan	59	0.26
Honduran	16	0.07
Nicaraguan	59	0.26
Panamanian	3	0.01
Salvadoran	89	0.39
Other Central American	4	0.02
Cuban	15	0.07
Mexican	10,824	47.73
Puerto Rican	109	0.48
South American	58	0.26
Argentinean	10	0.04
Bolivian	5	0.02
Chilean	9	0.04
Colombian	11	0.05
Ecuadorian	6	0.03
Paraguayan	1	<0.01
Peruvian	13	0.06
Venezuelan	3	0.01
Other Hispanic or Latino	579	2.55

Race*	Population	%
African-American/Black (480)	666	2.94
Not Hispanic (410)	549	2.42
Hispanic (70)	117	0.52
American Indian/Alaska Native (269)	485	2.14
Not Hispanic (129)	275	1.21
Hispanic (140)	210	0.93
Apache (15)	23	0.10
Blackfeet (0)	8	0.04
Cherokee (36)	108	0.48
Chickasaw (7)	8	0.04
Chippewa (0)	2	0.01
Choctaw (14)	24	0.11
Colville (1)	1	<0.01
Comanche (0)	1	<0.01
Cree (1)	1	<0.01
Creek (0)	1	<0.01
Crow (0)	1	<0.01
Hopi (0)	3	0.01
Inupiat *(Alaska Native)* (1)	1	<0.01
Iroquois (0)	5	0.02
Lumbee (1)	1	<0.01
Mexican American Ind. (18)	29	0.13
Navajo (9)	16	0.07
Osage (1)	1	<0.01
Paiute (5)	5	0.02
Pima (1)	2	0.01
Pueblo (7)	9	0.04
Seminole (0)	2	0.01
Sioux (2)	6	0.03
Spanish American Ind. (5)	5	0.02
Tohono O'Odham (1)	1	<0.01
Tsimshian *(Alaska Native)* (1)	1	<0.01
Yakama (0)	1	<0.01
Asian (770)	1,117	4.93
Not Hispanic (733)	969	4.27
Hispanic (37)	148	0.65
Cambodian (40)	49	0.22
Chinese, ex. Taiwanese (66)	111	0.49
Filipino (326)	476	2.10
Hmong (19)	19	0.08
Indian (126)	154	0.68
Indonesian (1)	4	0.02
Japanese (16)	66	0.29
Korean (29)	41	0.18
Laotian (10)	15	0.07
Pakistani (2)	5	0.02
Sri Lankan (2)	2	0.01
Taiwanese (0)	4	0.02
Thai (3)	12	0.05
Vietnamese (102)	124	0.55
Hawaii Native/Pacific Islander (88)	202	0.89
Not Hispanic (81)	152	0.67
Hispanic (7)	50	0.22
Fijian (48)	56	0.25
Guamanian/Chamorro (9)	29	0.13
Native Hawaiian (13)	55	0.24
Samoan (5)	14	0.06
White (14,951)	15,948	70.32
Not Hispanic (8,964)	9,393	41.42
Hispanic (5,987)	6,555	28.90

Riverside

Place Type: City
County: Riverside
Population: 303,871†

Ancestry‡	Population	%
Afghan (69)	69	0.02
African, Sub-Saharan (1,292)	1,585	0.53
African (846)	1,076	0.36
Kenyan (85)	100	0.03
Nigerian (351)	351	0.12
Somalian (10)	10	<0.01
South African (0)	20	0.01
Ugandan (0)	18	0.01
Other Sub-Saharan African (0)	10	<0.01
American (7,297)	7,297	2.43
Arab (1,846)	2,242	0.75
Arab (127)	127	0.04
Egyptian (320)	349	0.12
Iraqi (237)	258	0.09
Jordanian (367)	367	0.12
Lebanese (567)	789	0.26
Moroccan (28)	28	0.01
Palestinian (12)	21	0.01
Syrian (8)	86	0.03
Other Arab (180)	217	0.07
Armenian (188)	357	0.12
Assyrian/Chaldean/Syriac (22)	99	0.03
Australian (31)	56	0.02
Austrian (251)	607	0.20
Basque (55)	120	0.04
Belgian (165)	285	0.09
Brazilian (97)	166	0.06
British (432)	697	0.23
Bulgarian (116)	130	0.04
Cajun (16)	16	0.01
Canadian (325)	620	0.21
Celtic (9)	9	<0.01
Croatian (32)	164	0.05
Czech (58)	676	0.22
Czechoslovakian (76)	204	0.07
Danish (335)	1,079	0.36
Dutch (754)	3,659	1.22

*Notes: † The Census 2010 population figure is used to calculate the percentages in the Hispanic Origin and Race categories. Ancestry percentages are based on the 2006-2010 American Community Survey population (not shown); ‡ Numbers in parentheses indicate the number of people reporting a single ancestry; * Numbers in parentheses indicate the number of persons reporting this race alone, not in combination with any other race; Please refer to the Explanation of Data for more information.*

Ancestry	Population	%
Eastern European (74)	101	0.03
English (6,029)	18,993	6.32
Estonian (0)	10	<0.01
European (1,634)	2,080	0.69
Finnish (179)	494	0.16
French, ex. Basque (1,101)	7,394	2.46
French Canadian (405)	1,155	0.38
German (7,904)	29,153	9.70
Greek (364)	723	0.24
Guyanese (21)	21	0.01
Hungarian (318)	799	0.27
Iranian (372)	456	0.15
Irish (5,516)	20,754	6.91
Israeli (136)	146	0.05
Italian (4,273)	12,257	4.08
Lithuanian (76)	176	0.06
Maltese (0)	94	0.03
New Zealander (24)	73	0.02
Northern European (273)	295	0.10
Norwegian (818)	2,285	0.76
Pennsylvania German (59)	82	0.03
Polish (911)	3,752	1.25
Portuguese (514)	914	0.30
Romanian (909)	1,063	0.35
Russian (398)	1,525	0.51
Scandinavian (175)	548	0.18
Scotch-Irish (1,349)	3,461	1.15
Scottish (959)	3,263	1.09
Serbian (25)	90	0.03
Slavic (0)	112	0.04
Slovak (113)	178	0.06
Slovene (10)	98	0.03
Swedish (1,140)	3,367	1.12
Swiss (135)	643	0.21
Turkish (59)	59	0.02
Ukrainian (105)	218	0.07
Welsh (304)	1,170	0.39
West Indian, ex. Hispanic (311)	670	0.22
Belizean (13)	13	<0.01
Dutch West Indian (0)	9	<0.01
Haitian (72)	89	0.03
Jamaican (218)	502	0.17
West Indian (8)	57	0.02
Yugoslavian (34)	106	0.04

Hispanic Origin	Population	%
Hispanic or Latino (of any race)	148,953	49.02
Central American, ex. Mexican	7,792	2.56
Costa Rican	249	0.08
Guatemalan	3,338	1.10
Honduran	367	0.12
Nicaraguan	600	0.20
Panamanian	144	0.05
Salvadoran	2,995	0.99
Other Central American	99	0.03
Cuban	912	0.30
Dominican Republic	76	0.03
Mexican	127,165	41.85
Puerto Rican	2,115	0.70
South American	2,540	0.84
Argentinean	379	0.12
Bolivian	102	0.03
Chilean	236	0.08
Colombian	660	0.22
Ecuadorian	317	0.10
Paraguayan	2	<0.01
Peruvian	702	0.23
Uruguayan	19	0.01
Venezuelan	98	0.03
Other South American	25	0.01
Other Hispanic or Latino	8,353	2.75

Race*	Population	%
African-American/Black (21,421)	25,409	8.36
Not Hispanic (19,917)	22,636	7.45
Hispanic (1,504)	2,773	0.91
American Indian/Alaska Native (3,467)	6,447	2.12
Not Hispanic (1,297)	2,862	0.94
Hispanic (2,170)	3,585	1.18
Alaska Athabascan *(Ala. Nat.)* (8)	11	<0.01
Aleut *(Alaska Native)* (4)	5	<0.01
Apache (122)	256	0.08
Arapaho (5)	9	<0.01
Blackfeet (33)	139	0.05
Canadian/French Am. Ind. (4)	5	<0.01
Central American Ind. (19)	32	0.01
Cherokee (182)	693	0.23
Cheyenne (3)	13	<0.01
Chickasaw (13)	34	0.01
Chippewa (10)	42	0.01
Choctaw (68)	182	0.06
Colville (3)	5	<0.01
Comanche (10)	26	0.01
Cree (1)	5	<0.01
Creek (28)	48	0.02
Crow (6)	8	<0.01
Delaware (6)	13	<0.01
Hopi (38)	59	0.02
Houma (2)	2	<0.01
Inupiat *(Alaska Native)* (4)	7	<0.01
Iroquois (3)	35	0.01
Kiowa (3)	4	<0.01
Lumbee (9)	12	<0.01
Menominee (4)	4	<0.01
Mexican American Ind. (400)	633	0.21
Navajo (106)	201	0.07
Osage (8)	20	0.01
Ottawa (2)	2	<0.01
Paiute (10)	17	0.01
Pima (23)	51	0.02
Potawatomi (3)	31	0.01
Pueblo (37)	66	0.02
Puget Sound Salish (1)	1	<0.01
Seminole (12)	43	0.01
Shoshone (6)	15	<0.01
Sioux (43)	93	0.03
South American Ind. (29)	45	0.01
Spanish American Ind. (29)	52	0.02
Tlingit-Haida *(Alaska Native)* (2)	14	<0.01
Tohono O'Odham (21)	29	0.01
Tsimshian *(Alaska Native)* (0)	2	<0.01
Ute (7)	16	0.01
Yaqui (60)	103	0.03
Yuman (38)	48	0.02
Yup'ik *(Alaska Native)* (1)	1	<0.01
Asian (22,566)	26,675	8.78
Not Hispanic (21,934)	24,912	8.20
Hispanic (632)	1,763	0.58
Bangladeshi (69)	76	0.03
Burmese (45)	60	0.02
Cambodian (275)	373	0.12
Chinese, ex. Taiwanese (4,422)	5,471	1.80
Filipino (5,124)	6,761	2.22
Hmong (76)	83	0.03
Indian (2,396)	2,712	0.89
Indonesian (213)	370	0.12
Japanese (948)	1,907	0.63
Korean (3,220)	3,557	1.17
Laotian (303)	369	0.12
Malaysian (14)	25	0.01
Nepalese (17)	18	0.01
Pakistani (331)	377	0.12
Sri Lankan (114)	122	0.04
Taiwanese (484)	547	0.18
Thai (307)	427	0.14
Vietnamese (3,135)	3,544	1.17
Hawaii Native/Pacific Islander (1,219)	2,283	0.75
Not Hispanic (1,019)	1,762	0.58
Hispanic (200)	521	0.17
Fijian (34)	54	0.02
Guamanian/Chamorro (218)	384	0.13
Marshallese (4)	4	<0.01
Native Hawaiian (162)	586	0.19
Samoan (434)	618	0.20
Tongan (240)	281	0.09
White (171,669)	184,386	60.68
Not Hispanic (103,398)	109,018	35.88
Hispanic (68,271)	75,368	24.80

Rocklin

Place Type: City
County: Placer
Population: 56,974†

Ancestry‡	Population	%
Afghan (216)	216	0.40
African, Sub-Saharan (232)	260	0.48
African (96)	110	0.20
Nigerian (11)	11	0.02
South African (77)	77	0.14
Sudanese (48)	48	0.09
Ugandan (0)	14	0.03
Alsatian (0)	12	0.02
American (2,289)	2,289	4.22
Arab (177)	245	0.45
Arab (15)	15	0.03
Egyptian (127)	127	0.23
Lebanese (21)	21	0.04
Palestinian (14)	30	0.06
Syrian (0)	52	0.10
Armenian (80)	137	0.25
Australian (7)	14	0.03
Austrian (12)	152	0.28
Basque (12)	115	0.21
Belgian (55)	133	0.25
Brazilian (43)	43	0.08
British (183)	326	0.60
Bulgarian (11)	21	0.04
Cajun (0)	29	0.05
Canadian (85)	244	0.45
Croatian (23)	39	0.07
Czech (88)	286	0.53
Czechoslovakian (38)	48	0.09
Danish (97)	663	1.22
Dutch (196)	1,019	1.88
Eastern European (42)	63	0.12
English (2,099)	8,010	14.76
Estonian (0)	14	0.03
European (1,281)	1,482	2.73
Finnish (89)	257	0.47
French, ex. Basque (385)	2,223	4.10
French Canadian (58)	237	0.44
German (2,380)	10,333	19.04
Greek (28)	364	0.67
Hungarian (0)	90	0.17
Icelander (12)	26	0.05
Iranian (258)	322	0.59
Irish (1,865)	7,830	14.43
Italian (1,855)	4,789	8.82
Lithuanian (48)	85	0.16
Macedonian (48)	48	0.09
New Zealander (11)	33	0.06
Northern European (66)	66	0.12
Norwegian (546)	1,640	3.02
Polish (289)	1,249	2.30
Portuguese (370)	1,045	1.93
Romanian (147)	224	0.41
Russian (153)	325	0.60
Scandinavian (48)	110	0.20
Scotch-Irish (295)	888	1.64
Scottish (439)	1,480	2.73
Serbian (0)	25	0.05
Slavic (9)	19	0.04
Slovak (0)	38	0.07
Slovene (22)	64	0.12
Swedish (459)	1,645	3.03
Swiss (77)	266	0.49
Turkish (16)	16	0.03
Ukrainian (612)	685	1.26
Welsh (84)	424	0.78
West Indian, ex. Hispanic (26)	26	0.05
Jamaican (12)	12	0.02
West Indian (14)	14	0.03
Yugoslavian (164)	299	0.55

Hispanic Origin	Population	%
Hispanic or Latino (of any race)	6,555	11.51
Central American, ex. Mexican	355	0.62

*Notes: † The Census 2010 population figure is used to calculate the percentages in the Hispanic Origin and Race categories. Ancestry percentages are based on the 2006-2010 American Community Survey population (not shown); ‡ Numbers in parentheses indicate the number of people reporting a single ancestry; * Numbers in parentheses indicate the number of persons reporting this race alone, not in combination with any other race; Please refer to the Explanation of Data for more information.*

Costa Rican	28	0.05
Guatemalan	70	0.12
Honduran	21	0.04
Nicaraguan	73	0.13
Panamanian	21	0.04
Salvadoran	134	0.24
Other Central American	8	0.01
Cuban	83	0.15
Dominican Republic	15	0.03
Mexican	4,685	8.22
Puerto Rican	317	0.56
South American	277	0.49
Argentinean	39	0.07
Bolivian	13	0.02
Chilean	35	0.06
Colombian	75	0.13
Ecuadorian	21	0.04
Peruvian	67	0.12
Uruguayan	8	0.01
Venezuelan	16	0.03
Other South American	3	0.01
Other Hispanic or Latino	823	1.44

Race*	Population	%
African-American/Black (858)	1,262	2.22
Not Hispanic (809)	1,133	1.99
Hispanic (49)	129	0.23
American Indian/Alaska Native (410)	1,042	1.83
Not Hispanic (270)	719	1.26
Hispanic (140)	323	0.57
Alaska Athabascan *(Ala. Nat.)* (1)	2	<0.01
Aleut *(Alaska Native)* (2)	3	0.01
Apache (22)	39	0.07
Arapaho (1)	2	<0.01
Blackfeet (2)	16	0.03
Canadian/French Am. Ind. (0)	1	<0.01
Central American Ind. (1)	2	<0.01
Cherokee (40)	192	0.34
Cheyenne (0)	6	0.01
Chickasaw (4)	13	0.02
Chippewa (4)	18	0.03
Choctaw (4)	29	0.05
Colville (2)	5	0.01
Comanche (1)	4	0.01
Cree (0)	4	0.01
Creek (9)	24	0.04
Crow (0)	3	0.01
Delaware (0)	4	0.01
Hopi (0)	4	0.01
Inupiat *(Alaska Native)* (1)	1	<0.01
Iroquois (3)	17	0.03
Kiowa (1)	2	<0.01
Lumbee (1)	9	0.02
Mexican American Ind. (22)	35	0.06
Navajo (4)	14	0.02
Osage (0)	2	<0.01
Ottawa (0)	1	<0.01
Paiute (4)	9	0.02
Potawatomi (8)	10	0.02
Pueblo (10)	14	0.02
Puget Sound Salish (2)	3	0.01
Seminole (1)	1	<0.01
Shoshone (1)	5	0.01
Sioux (14)	29	0.05
South American Ind. (0)	3	0.01
Spanish American Ind. (1)	1	<0.01
Tlingit-Haida *(Alaska Native)* (1)	1	<0.01
Tohono O'Odham (3)	6	0.01
Ute (6)	6	0.01
Yaqui (4)	8	0.01
Yuman (4)	5	0.01
Asian (4,105)	5,644	9.91
Not Hispanic (4,024)	5,336	9.37
Hispanic (81)	308	0.54
Bangladeshi (8)	12	0.02
Burmese (14)	17	0.03
Cambodian (40)	54	0.09
Chinese, ex. Taiwanese (617)	970	1.70
Filipino (1,051)	1,671	2.93
Hmong (5)	7	0.01
Indian (837)	924	1.62
Indonesian (43)	68	0.12
Japanese (415)	827	1.45
Korean (332)	473	0.83
Laotian (33)	45	0.08
Malaysian (6)	16	0.03
Nepalese (8)	8	0.01
Pakistani (41)	49	0.09
Sri Lankan (25)	25	0.04
Taiwanese (44)	50	0.09
Thai (19)	41	0.07
Vietnamese (328)	407	0.71
Hawaii Native/Pacific Islander (150)	404	0.71
Not Hispanic (138)	323	0.57
Hispanic (12)	81	0.14
Fijian (20)	25	0.04
Guamanian/Chamorro (36)	73	0.13
Marshallese (0)	1	<0.01
Native Hawaiian (30)	174	0.31
Samoan (22)	42	0.07
Tongan (7)	7	0.01
White (47,047)	49,657	87.16
Not Hispanic (43,008)	44,930	78.86
Hispanic (4,039)	4,727	8.30

Rodeo

Place Type: CDP
County: Contra Costa
Population: 8,679†

Ancestry‡	Population	%
African, Sub-Saharan (164)	362	3.97
African (164)	362	3.97
American (129)	129	1.41
Arab (163)	163	1.79
Other Arab (163)	163	1.79
Armenian (126)	126	1.38
Brazilian (89)	89	0.98
British (0)	29	0.32
Czech (0)	32	0.35
Danish (0)	21	0.23
Dutch (45)	98	1.07
English (71)	423	4.63
European (105)	115	1.26
Finnish (0)	73	0.80
French, ex. Basque (10)	66	0.72
French Canadian (0)	23	0.25
German (124)	626	6.86
Greek (0)	51	0.56
Iranian (24)	24	0.26
Irish (60)	577	6.32
Italian (125)	486	5.32
Norwegian (15)	44	0.48
Polish (9)	58	0.64
Portuguese (189)	357	3.91
Romanian (56)	56	0.61
Russian (0)	22	0.24
Scandinavian (11)	23	0.25
Scotch-Irish (26)	222	2.43
Scottish (10)	53	0.58
Slavic (0)	23	0.25
Slovak (0)	17	0.19
Swedish (18)	44	0.48
Swiss (0)	17	0.19
Ukrainian (0)	6	0.07
Welsh (0)	51	0.56
West Indian, ex. Hispanic (67)	114	1.25
Bahamian (18)	18	0.20
British West Indian (0)	14	0.15
Jamaican (25)	44	0.48
Trinidadian/Tobagonian (24)	38	0.42

Hispanic Origin	Population	%
Hispanic or Latino (of any race)	2,134	24.59
Central American, ex. Mexican	350	4.03
Costa Rican	1	0.01
Guatemalan	52	0.60
Honduran	8	0.09
Nicaraguan	78	0.90
Panamanian	5	0.06
Salvadoran	206	2.37
Cuban	14	0.16
Mexican	1,498	17.26
Puerto Rican	48	0.55
South American	42	0.48
Argentinean	1	0.01
Bolivian	1	0.01
Chilean	7	0.08
Colombian	4	0.05
Ecuadorian	3	0.03
Peruvian	23	0.27
Venezuelan	3	0.03
Other Hispanic or Latino	182	2.10

Race*	Population	%
African-American/Black (1,410)	1,657	19.09
Not Hispanic (1,370)	1,564	18.02
Hispanic (40)	93	1.07
American Indian/Alaska Native (53)	192	2.21
Not Hispanic (31)	118	1.36
Hispanic (22)	74	0.85
Apache (3)	9	0.10
Blackfeet (1)	6	0.07
Cherokee (4)	24	0.28
Cheyenne (0)	1	0.01
Chippewa (1)	1	0.01
Choctaw (4)	16	0.18
Creek (0)	1	0.01
Iroquois (0)	1	0.01
Kiowa (0)	2	0.02
Lumbee (1)	1	0.01
Mexican American Ind. (4)	8	0.09
Navajo (1)	2	0.02
Ottawa (3)	4	0.05
Pueblo (0)	2	0.02
Shoshone (0)	4	0.05
Sioux (1)	3	0.03
Spanish American Ind. (1)	3	0.03
Ute (0)	1	0.01
Asian (1,762)	2,047	23.59
Not Hispanic (1,727)	1,956	22.54
Hispanic (35)	91	1.05
Burmese (0)	1	0.01
Cambodian (8)	9	0.10
Chinese, ex. Taiwanese (125)	159	1.83
Filipino (929)	1,093	12.59
Hmong (1)	1	0.01
Indian (365)	429	4.94
Indonesian (3)	7	0.08
Japanese (32)	72	0.83
Korean (14)	18	0.21
Laotian (167)	189	2.18
Malaysian (1)	2	0.02
Pakistani (15)	28	0.32
Thai (2)	3	0.03
Vietnamese (34)	52	0.60
Hawaii Native/Pacific Islander (62)	128	1.47
Not Hispanic (62)	113	1.30
Hispanic (0)	15	0.17
Fijian (6)	7	0.08
Guamanian/Chamorro (4)	10	0.12
Native Hawaiian (16)	48	0.55
Samoan (13)	24	0.28
Tongan (12)	12	0.14
White (3,823)	4,321	49.79
Not Hispanic (2,890)	3,188	36.73
Hispanic (933)	1,133	13.05

Rohnert Park

Place Type: City
County: Sonoma
Population: 40,971†

Ancestry‡	Population	%
African, Sub-Saharan (206)	206	0.51
African (180)	180	0.44
Ethiopian (26)	26	0.06
American (965)	965	2.38

*Notes: † The Census 2010 population figure is used to calculate the percentages in the Hispanic Origin and Race categories. Ancestry percentages are based on the 2006-2010 American Community Survey population (not shown); ‡ Numbers in parentheses indicate the number of people reporting a single ancestry; * Numbers in parentheses indicate the number of persons reporting this race alone, not in combination with any other race; Please refer to the Explanation of Data for more information.*

Arab (131)	152	0.38
Arab (63)	65	0.16
Egyptian (14)	14	0.03
Lebanese (0)	10	0.02
Palestinian (42)	42	0.10
Syrian (0)	9	0.02
Other Arab (12)	12	0.03
Armenian (24)	52	0.13
Assyrian/Chaldean/Syriac (36)	36	0.09
Australian (14)	32	0.08
Austrian (11)	146	0.36
Basque (0)	47	0.12
Belgian (16)	56	0.14
Brazilian (44)	44	0.11
British (42)	160	0.39
Bulgarian (83)	83	0.20
Canadian (46)	76	0.19
Croatian (66)	124	0.31
Czech (26)	163	0.40
Czechoslovakian (57)	161	0.40
Danish (118)	296	0.73
Dutch (154)	590	1.46
Eastern European (43)	72	0.18
English (911)	4,301	10.61
European (698)	867	2.14
Finnish (15)	172	0.42
French, ex. Basque (175)	1,520	3.75
French Canadian (30)	200	0.49
German (1,437)	6,361	15.70
Greek (59)	203	0.50
Hungarian (52)	235	0.58
Icelander (0)	13	0.03
Iranian (45)	45	0.11
Irish (1,078)	5,803	14.32
Israeli (0)	47	0.12
Italian (1,709)	3,956	9.76
Latvian (0)	53	0.13
Lithuanian (17)	114	0.28
Luxemburger (9)	9	0.02
Maltese (0)	30	0.07
Northern European (40)	40	0.10
Norwegian (169)	719	1.77
Polish (249)	1,011	2.50
Portuguese (300)	882	2.18
Romanian (0)	41	0.10
Russian (122)	389	0.96
Scandinavian (75)	137	0.34
Scotch-Irish (332)	900	2.22
Scottish (307)	1,337	3.30
Serbian (24)	74	0.18
Slovak (13)	28	0.07
Swedish (140)	715	1.76
Swiss (21)	181	0.45
Ukrainian (68)	184	0.45
Welsh (42)	166	0.41
West Indian, ex. Hispanic (191)	211	0.52
Dutch West Indian (0)	20	0.05
Haitian (191)	191	0.47
Yugoslavian (64)	178	0.44

Hispanic Origin	Population	%
Hispanic or Latino (of any race)	9,068	22.13
Central American, ex. Mexican	721	1.76
Costa Rican	17	0.04
Guatemalan	147	0.36
Honduran	38	0.09
Nicaraguan	107	0.26
Panamanian	9	0.02
Salvadoran	394	0.96
Other Central American	9	0.02
Cuban	68	0.17
Dominican Republic	15	0.04
Mexican	7,093	17.31
Puerto Rican	241	0.59
South American	268	0.65
Argentinean	13	0.03
Bolivian	2	<0.01
Chilean	19	0.05
Colombian	78	0.19
Ecuadorian	16	0.04
Peruvian	115	0.28
Uruguayan	2	<0.01
Venezuelan	13	0.03
Other South American	10	0.02
Other Hispanic or Latino	662	1.62

Race*	Population	%
African-American/Black (759)	1,268	3.09
Not Hispanic (708)	1,115	2.72
Hispanic (51)	153	0.37
American Indian/Alaska Native (407)	1,022	2.49
Not Hispanic (221)	638	1.56
Hispanic (186)	384	0.94
Aleut *(Alaska Native)* (0)	2	<0.01
Apache (10)	30	0.07
Blackfeet (4)	30	0.07
Canadian/French Am. Ind. (0)	4	0.01
Central American Ind. (0)	2	<0.01
Cherokee (30)	158	0.39
Cheyenne (1)	2	<0.01
Chickasaw (1)	3	0.01
Chippewa (7)	18	0.04
Choctaw (12)	42	0.10
Comanche (1)	8	0.02
Creek (0)	1	<0.01
Crow (0)	1	<0.01
Delaware (0)	4	0.01
Hopi (0)	5	0.01
Inupiat *(Alaska Native)* (2)	4	0.01
Iroquois (3)	9	0.02
Kiowa (0)	1	<0.01
Lumbee (0)	1	<0.01
Mexican American Ind. (32)	51	0.12
Navajo (9)	21	0.05
Osage (2)	2	<0.01
Ottawa (1)	1	<0.01
Paiute (1)	1	<0.01
Potawatomi (4)	5	0.01
Pueblo (1)	2	<0.01
Puget Sound Salish (1)	3	0.01
Seminole (0)	1	<0.01
Shoshone (1)	1	<0.01
Sioux (11)	31	0.08
South American Ind. (2)	10	0.02
Spanish American Ind. (1)	2	<0.01
Tlingit-Haida *(Alaska Native)* (1)	6	0.01
Tsimshian *(Alaska Native)* (1)	3	0.01
Ute (0)	3	0.01
Yakama (1)	3	0.01
Yaqui (2)	3	0.01
Yuman (0)	2	<0.01
Yup'ik *(Alaska Native)* (4)	4	0.01
Asian (2,144)	2,996	7.31
Not Hispanic (2,079)	2,790	6.81
Hispanic (65)	206	0.50
Bangladeshi (3)	3	0.01
Burmese (2)	3	0.01
Cambodian (45)	60	0.15
Chinese, ex. Taiwanese (399)	589	1.44
Filipino (544)	882	2.15
Hmong (11)	13	0.03
Indian (329)	379	0.93
Indonesian (20)	38	0.09
Japanese (162)	373	0.91
Korean (160)	207	0.51
Laotian (97)	129	0.31
Malaysian (8)	12	0.03
Nepalese (22)	27	0.07
Pakistani (13)	17	0.04
Taiwanese (18)	19	0.05
Thai (39)	69	0.17
Vietnamese (175)	213	0.52
Hawaii Native/Pacific Islander (179)	415	1.01
Not Hispanic (167)	356	0.87
Hispanic (12)	59	0.14
Fijian (44)	50	0.12
Guamanian/Chamorro (6)	28	0.07
Marshallese (1)	1	<0.01
Native Hawaiian (39)	160	0.39
Samoan (42)	98	0.24
Tongan (22)	39	0.10
White (31,178)	33,302	81.28
Not Hispanic (27,141)	28,541	69.66
Hispanic (4,037)	4,761	11.62

Rolling Hills Estates

Place Type: City
County: Los Angeles
Population: 8,067†

Ancestry‡	Population	%
Albanian (0)	33	0.41
American (360)	360	4.50
Arab (77)	104	1.30
Lebanese (77)	104	1.30
Armenian (46)	46	0.57
Austrian (0)	13	0.16
Belgian (10)	56	0.70
British (0)	8	0.10
Bulgarian (0)	10	0.12
Canadian (0)	9	0.11
Croatian (0)	46	0.57
Czech (12)	95	1.19
Danish (18)	55	0.69
Dutch (0)	143	1.79
Eastern European (26)	26	0.32
English (420)	1,286	16.07
European (250)	275	3.44
Finnish (12)	12	0.15
French, ex. Basque (73)	216	2.70
French Canadian (9)	9	0.11
German (223)	1,479	18.48
Greek (9)	9	0.11
Hungarian (0)	51	0.64
Iranian (114)	122	1.52
Irish (253)	1,125	14.06
Italian (186)	486	6.07
Lithuanian (10)	45	0.56
Maltese (14)	14	0.17
Norwegian (33)	107	1.34
Polish (151)	301	3.76
Portuguese (0)	40	0.50
Romanian (11)	66	0.82
Russian (103)	280	3.50
Scandinavian (0)	11	0.14
Scotch-Irish (61)	125	1.56
Scottish (92)	182	2.27
Serbian (0)	21	0.26
Swedish (19)	160	2.00
Swiss (9)	43	0.54
Turkish (11)	11	0.14
Ukrainian (10)	56	0.70
Welsh (12)	61	0.76
West Indian, ex. Hispanic (15)	15	0.19
Jamaican (15)	15	0.19

Hispanic Origin	Population	%
Hispanic or Latino (of any race)	499	6.19
Central American, ex. Mexican	18	0.22
Costa Rican	3	0.04
Guatemalan	7	0.09
Salvadoran	8	0.10
Cuban	30	0.37
Mexican	321	3.98
Puerto Rican	8	0.10
South American	61	0.76
Argentinean	30	0.37
Bolivian	1	0.01
Chilean	2	0.02
Colombian	5	0.06
Peruvian	19	0.24
Uruguayan	3	0.04
Venezuelan	1	0.01
Other Hispanic or Latino	61	0.76

Race*	Population	%
African-American/Black (109)	153	1.90
Not Hispanic (107)	141	1.75
Hispanic (2)	12	0.15

*Notes: † The Census 2010 population figure is used to calculate the percentages in the Hispanic Origin and Race categories. Ancestry percentages are based on the 2006-2010 American Community Survey population (not shown); ‡ Numbers in parentheses indicate the number of people reporting a single ancestry; * Numbers in parentheses indicate the number of persons reporting this race alone, not in combination with any other race; Please refer to the Explanation of Data for more information.*

American Indian/Alaska Native (19)	47	0.58
Not Hispanic (12)	30	0.37
Hispanic (7)	17	0.21
Cherokee (0)	3	0.04
Chippewa (1)	1	0.01
Choctaw (1)	1	0.01
Creek (0)	5	0.06
Mexican American Ind. (1)	2	0.02
Navajo (0)	2	0.02
Osage (5)	5	0.06
Seminole (1)	1	0.01
Yaqui (0)	2	0.02
Asian (2,007)	2,262	28.04
Not Hispanic (1,995)	2,227	27.61
Hispanic (12)	35	0.43
Burmese (4)	4	0.05
Cambodian (2)	5	0.06
Chinese, ex. Taiwanese (408)	500	6.20
Filipino (136)	201	2.49
Indian (122)	142	1.76
Indonesian (3)	4	0.05
Japanese (490)	645	8.00
Korean (580)	622	7.71
Laotian (1)	1	0.01
Pakistani (31)	32	0.40
Sri Lankan (11)	11	0.14
Taiwanese (103)	111	1.38
Thai (9)	13	0.16
Vietnamese (24)	34	0.42
Hawaii Native/Pacific Islander (8)	29	0.36
Not Hispanic (8)	26	0.32
Hispanic (0)	3	0.04
Guamanian/Chamorro (2)	2	0.02
Native Hawaiian (1)	13	0.16
Samoan (1)	3	0.04
White (5,463)	5,775	71.59
Not Hispanic (5,134)	5,409	67.05
Hispanic (329)	366	4.54

Rosamond

Place Type: CDP
County: Kern
Population: 18,150†

Ancestry‡	Population	%
African, Sub-Saharan (106)	126	0.74
African (106)	126	0.74
American (492)	492	2.89
Arab (46)	46	0.27
Egyptian (46)	46	0.27
Australian (33)	33	0.19
Austrian (18)	63	0.37
British (0)	27	0.16
Cajun (0)	23	0.14
Canadian (10)	30	0.18
Czech (14)	21	0.12
Danish (65)	135	0.79
Dutch (44)	218	1.28
Eastern European (0)	8	0.05
English (489)	1,105	6.49
European (386)	400	2.35
Finnish (0)	6	0.04
French, ex. Basque (103)	433	2.54
French Canadian (55)	142	0.83
German (904)	2,395	14.06
Greek (10)	10	0.06
Hungarian (0)	28	0.16
Irish (365)	1,482	8.70
Italian (271)	660	3.88
Lithuanian (17)	37	0.22
Norwegian (76)	153	0.90
Polish (95)	223	1.31
Portuguese (173)	173	1.02
Russian (0)	129	0.76
Scandinavian (8)	8	0.05
Scotch-Irish (132)	200	1.17
Scottish (35)	205	1.20
Slovak (13)	13	0.08
Swedish (24)	37	0.22
Swiss (33)	95	0.56
Welsh (0)	82	0.48
West Indian, ex. Hispanic (26)	277	1.63
Dutch West Indian (0)	41	0.24
Haitian (0)	123	0.72
West Indian (26)	113	0.66
Yugoslavian (0)	47	0.28

Hispanic Origin	Population	%
Hispanic or Latino (of any race)	6,230	34.33
Central American, ex. Mexican	548	3.02
Costa Rican	8	0.04
Guatemalan	131	0.72
Honduran	44	0.24
Nicaraguan	40	0.22
Panamanian	12	0.07
Salvadoran	307	1.69
Other Central American	6	0.03
Cuban	34	0.19
Dominican Republic	7	0.04
Mexican	4,884	26.91
Puerto Rican	114	0.63
South American	155	0.85
Argentinean	13	0.07
Bolivian	8	0.04
Chilean	6	0.03
Colombian	38	0.21
Ecuadorian	28	0.15
Peruvian	48	0.26
Uruguayan	4	0.02
Venezuelan	7	0.04
Other South American	3	0.02
Other Hispanic or Latino	488	2.69

Race*	Population	%
African-American/Black (1,476)	1,806	9.95
Not Hispanic (1,430)	1,697	9.35
Hispanic (46)	109	0.60
American Indian/Alaska Native (221)	467	2.57
Not Hispanic (140)	320	1.76
Hispanic (81)	147	0.81
Aleut *(Alaska Native)* (5)	11	0.06
Apache (11)	16	0.09
Blackfeet (1)	8	0.04
Cherokee (21)	78	0.43
Cheyenne (0)	1	0.01
Chickasaw (1)	3	0.02
Chippewa (5)	10	0.06
Choctaw (10)	20	0.11
Comanche (0)	2	0.01
Creek (1)	4	0.02
Delaware (1)	1	0.01
Hopi (0)	1	0.01
Inupiat *(Alaska Native)* (0)	1	0.01
Iroquois (2)	7	0.04
Mexican American Ind. (26)	39	0.21
Navajo (3)	15	0.08
Ottawa (1)	1	0.01
Paiute (2)	11	0.06
Potawatomi (0)	4	0.02
Pueblo (4)	4	0.02
Seminole (3)	7	0.04
Shoshone (0)	3	0.02
Sioux (3)	9	0.05
South American Ind. (0)	2	0.01
Spanish American Ind. (0)	3	0.02
Tlingit-Haida *(Alaska Native)* (3)	3	0.02
Tohono O'Odham (3)	4	0.02
Ute (2)	2	0.01
Yaqui (2)	2	0.01
Yuman (1)	3	0.02
Asian (658)	1,004	5.53
Not Hispanic (623)	881	4.85
Hispanic (35)	123	0.68
Burmese (5)	5	0.03
Cambodian (6)	8	0.04
Chinese, ex. Taiwanese (37)	89	0.49
Filipino (372)	560	3.09
Indian (30)	47	0.26
Indonesian (3)	7	0.04
Japanese (55)	136	0.75
Korean (52)	81	0.45
Pakistani (1)	1	0.01
Taiwanese (2)	2	0.01
Thai (51)	73	0.40
Vietnamese (12)	18	0.10
Hawaii Native/Pacific Islander (66)	176	0.97
Not Hispanic (54)	131	0.72
Hispanic (12)	45	0.25
Guamanian/Chamorro (45)	69	0.38
Native Hawaiian (9)	75	0.41
Samoan (7)	15	0.08
Tongan (1)	1	0.01
White (11,294)	12,268	67.59
Not Hispanic (8,993)	9,520	52.45
Hispanic (2,301)	2,748	15.14

Rosedale

Place Type: CDP
County: Kern
Population: 14,058†

Ancestry‡	Population	%
Albanian (9)	9	0.06
American (855)	855	5.76
Arab (208)	244	1.64
Arab (0)	36	0.24
Syrian (159)	159	1.07
Other Arab (49)	49	0.33
Australian (8)	8	0.05
Basque (71)	206	1.39
Brazilian (9)	9	0.06
British (8)	35	0.24
Canadian (42)	73	0.49
Czech (13)	48	0.32
Czechoslovakian (22)	43	0.29
Danish (10)	73	0.49
Dutch (45)	355	2.39
English (605)	1,474	9.93
European (773)	828	5.58
Finnish (4)	4	0.03
French, ex. Basque (35)	132	0.89
German (673)	1,982	13.35
Greek (27)	79	0.53
Iranian (0)	6	0.04
Irish (612)	1,700	11.45
Italian (287)	713	4.80
Lithuanian (8)	20	0.13
New Zealander (19)	19	0.13
Northern European (51)	51	0.34
Norwegian (54)	190	1.28
Polish (29)	102	0.69
Portuguese (26)	53	0.36
Russian (93)	144	0.97
Scandinavian (0)	11	0.07
Scotch-Irish (84)	143	0.96
Scottish (141)	386	2.60
Swedish (16)	92	0.62
Swiss (63)	124	0.84
Turkish (0)	8	0.05
Ukrainian (9)	18	0.12
Welsh (28)	85	0.57
West Indian, ex. Hispanic (0)	42	0.28
Dutch West Indian (0)	26	0.18
West Indian (0)	16	0.11
Yugoslavian (0)	25	0.17

Hispanic Origin	Population	%
Hispanic or Latino (of any race)	2,495	17.75
Central American, ex. Mexican	106	0.75
Costa Rican	1	0.01
Guatemalan	10	0.07
Honduran	11	0.08
Nicaraguan	10	0.07
Panamanian	4	0.03
Salvadoran	65	0.46
Other Central American	5	0.04
Cuban	16	0.11
Dominican Republic	2	0.01

*Notes: † The Census 2010 population figure is used to calculate the percentages in the Hispanic Origin and Race categories. Ancestry percentages are based on the 2006-2010 American Community Survey population (not shown); ‡ Numbers in parentheses indicate the number of people reporting a single ancestry; * Numbers in parentheses indicate the number of persons reporting this race alone, not in combination with any other race; Please refer to the Explanation of Data for more information.*

Mexican	2,128	15.14
Puerto Rican	44	0.31
South American	55	0.39
Argentinean	8	0.06
Bolivian	3	0.02
Colombian	5	0.04
Ecuadorian	4	0.03
Peruvian	27	0.19
Venezuelan	3	0.02
Other South American	5	0.04
Other Hispanic or Latino	144	1.02

Race*	Population	%
African-American/Black (208)	281	2.00
Not Hispanic (186)	247	1.76
Hispanic (22)	34	0.24
American Indian/Alaska Native (159)	417	2.97
Not Hispanic (100)	289	2.06
Hispanic (59)	128	0.91
Apache (1)	17	0.12
Central American Ind. (2)	2	0.01
Cherokee (25)	103	0.73
Chickasaw (10)	12	0.09
Choctaw (14)	42	0.30
Cree (0)	1	0.01
Creek (3)	10	0.07
Inupiat *(Alaska Native)* (1)	2	0.01
Lumbee (1)	1	0.01
Mexican American Ind. (4)	7	0.05
Navajo (3)	5	0.04
Osage (0)	4	0.03
Ottawa (0)	1	0.01
Paiute (1)	1	0.01
Potawatomi (4)	4	0.03
Seminole (0)	6	0.04
Sioux (1)	1	0.01
South American Ind. (0)	1	0.01
Spanish American Ind. (0)	1	0.01
Tlingit-Haida *(Alaska Native)* (1)	1	0.01
Yaqui (1)	2	0.01
Asian (389)	526	3.74
Not Hispanic (373)	489	3.48
Hispanic (16)	37	0.26
Burmese (4)	4	0.03
Cambodian (23)	29	0.21
Chinese, ex. Taiwanese (49)	82	0.58
Filipino (111)	163	1.16
Hmong (2)	3	0.02
Indian (83)	89	0.63
Indonesian (1)	3	0.02
Japanese (16)	48	0.34
Korean (26)	42	0.30
Laotian (0)	2	0.01
Pakistani (18)	18	0.13
Sri Lankan (0)	1	0.01
Taiwanese (2)	2	0.01
Thai (15)	15	0.11
Vietnamese (18)	30	0.21
Hawaii Native/Pacific Islander (24)	55	0.39
Not Hispanic (15)	42	0.30
Hispanic (9)	13	0.09
Guamanian/Chamorro (1)	8	0.06
Native Hawaiian (18)	36	0.26
White (11,695)	12,244	87.10
Not Hispanic (10,491)	10,846	77.15
Hispanic (1,204)	1,398	9.94

Rosemead

Place Type: City
County: Los Angeles
Population: 53,764†

Ancestry‡	Population	%
African, Sub-Saharan (121)	128	0.24
African (42)	49	0.09
Other Sub-Saharan African (79)	79	0.15
American (281)	281	0.52
Arab (49)	49	0.09
Arab (49)	49	0.09
Armenian (37)	37	0.07
Austrian (7)	7	0.01
Basque (0)	8	0.01
Brazilian (17)	51	0.10
British (8)	19	0.04
Canadian (0)	22	0.04
Czech (5)	16	0.03
Danish (0)	14	0.03
Dutch (0)	23	0.04
Eastern European (21)	21	0.04
English (60)	324	0.60
European (49)	78	0.15
Finnish (0)	35	0.07
French, ex. Basque (31)	240	0.45
German (95)	525	0.98
Irish (107)	533	0.99
Italian (284)	521	0.97
Norwegian (18)	63	0.12
Polish (10)	31	0.06
Portuguese (0)	11	0.02
Romanian (19)	19	0.04
Russian (16)	50	0.09
Scotch-Irish (52)	140	0.26
Scottish (32)	86	0.16
Swedish (9)	44	0.08
Swiss (10)	33	0.06
West Indian, ex. Hispanic (10)	44	0.08
Belizean (10)	44	0.08
Yugoslavian (18)	18	0.03

Hispanic Origin	Population	%
Hispanic or Latino (of any race)	18,147	33.75
Central American, ex. Mexican	1,188	2.21
Costa Rican	24	0.04
Guatemalan	306	0.57
Honduran	81	0.15
Nicaraguan	143	0.27
Panamanian	9	0.02
Salvadoran	594	1.10
Other Central American	31	0.06
Cuban	153	0.28
Dominican Republic	3	0.01
Mexican	15,469	28.77
Puerto Rican	113	0.21
South American	251	0.47
Argentinean	51	0.09
Bolivian	8	0.01
Chilean	5	0.01
Colombian	49	0.09
Ecuadorian	42	0.08
Peruvian	74	0.14
Uruguayan	6	0.01
Venezuelan	11	0.02
Other South American	5	0.01
Other Hispanic or Latino	970	1.80

Race*	Population	%
African-American/Black (273)	363	0.68
Not Hispanic (176)	218	0.41
Hispanic (97)	145	0.27
American Indian/Alaska Native (396)	600	1.12
Not Hispanic (56)	122	0.23
Hispanic (340)	478	0.89
Apache (10)	21	0.04
Blackfeet (1)	4	0.01
Cherokee (17)	25	0.05
Chippewa (1)	3	0.01
Choctaw (0)	4	0.01
Creek (1)	1	<0.01
Iroquois (1)	1	<0.01
Mexican American Ind. (73)	119	0.22
Navajo (8)	23	0.04
Paiute (1)	1	<0.01
Pueblo (8)	9	0.02
Seminole (1)	1	<0.01
Sioux (7)	8	0.01
South American Ind. (0)	1	<0.01
Spanish American Ind. (2)	2	<0.01
Tohono O'Odham (8)	8	0.01
Ute (0)	2	<0.01
Yaqui (9)	20	0.04
Asian (32,617)	33,107	61.58
Not Hispanic (32,439)	32,749	60.91
Hispanic (178)	358	0.67
Bangladeshi (5)	7	0.01
Burmese (336)	376	0.70
Cambodian (749)	994	1.85
Chinese, ex. Taiwanese (18,352)	20,548	38.22
Filipino (816)	974	1.81
Hmong (3)	3	0.01
Indian (202)	269	0.50
Indonesian (71)	100	0.19
Japanese (590)	684	1.27
Korean (270)	293	0.54
Laotian (26)	42	0.08
Malaysian (12)	18	0.03
Nepalese (4)	4	0.01
Pakistani (3)	3	0.01
Sri Lankan (8)	11	0.02
Taiwanese (407)	461	0.86
Thai (205)	235	0.44
Vietnamese (8,268)	10,046	18.69
Hawaii Native/Pacific Islander (32)	92	0.17
Not Hispanic (14)	53	0.10
Hispanic (18)	39	0.07
Guamanian/Chamorro (11)	18	0.03
Native Hawaiian (6)	21	0.04
Samoan (9)	13	0.02
Tongan (1)	2	<0.01
White (11,348)	12,192	22.68
Not Hispanic (2,549)	2,788	5.19
Hispanic (8,799)	9,404	17.49

Rosemont

Place Type: CDP
County: Sacramento
Population: 22,681†

Ancestry‡	Population	%
Afghan (50)	50	0.22
African, Sub-Saharan (256)	294	1.29
African (192)	218	0.95
Ethiopian (11)	11	0.05
Kenyan (29)	29	0.13
Sudanese (24)	36	0.16
American (511)	511	2.24
Arab (198)	288	1.26
Lebanese (115)	115	0.50
Moroccan (0)	9	0.04
Palestinian (14)	14	0.06
Syrian (0)	57	0.25
Other Arab (69)	93	0.41
Armenian (25)	34	0.15
Australian (0)	10	0.04
Austrian (20)	43	0.19
Basque (12)	28	0.12
Brazilian (0)	30	0.13
British (37)	85	0.37
Canadian (22)	22	0.10
Croatian (0)	64	0.28
Czech (24)	38	0.17
Czechoslovakian (17)	26	0.11
Danish (35)	149	0.65
Dutch (9)	439	1.92
English (276)	1,458	6.38
European (155)	199	0.87
Finnish (0)	64	0.28
French, ex. Basque (75)	456	2.00
French Canadian (0)	38	0.17
German (838)	3,214	14.07
Greek (10)	30	0.13
Hungarian (16)	35	0.15
Iranian (22)	51	0.22
Irish (433)	2,371	10.38
Italian (164)	914	4.00
Lithuanian (22)	36	0.16
Norwegian (46)	350	1.53
Polish (24)	383	1.68
Portuguese (139)	668	2.92

*Notes: † The Census 2010 population figure is used to calculate the percentages in the Hispanic Origin and Race categories. Ancestry percentages are based on the 2006-2010 American Community Survey population (not shown); ‡ Numbers in parentheses indicate the number of people reporting a single ancestry; * Numbers in parentheses indicate the number of persons reporting this race alone, not in combination with any other race; Please refer to the Explanation of Data for more information.*

Romanian (41)	78	0.34
Russian (216)	335	1.47
Scandinavian (10)	47	0.21
Scotch-Irish (19)	229	1.00
Scottish (197)	596	2.61
Slavic (0)	9	0.04
Slovak (10)	18	0.08
Swedish (16)	347	1.52
Swiss (0)	36	0.16
Turkish (11)	11	0.05
Ukrainian (738)	768	3.36
Welsh (22)	137	0.60
West Indian, ex. Hispanic (135)	140	0.61
Jamaican (135)	135	0.59
West Indian (0)	5	0.02
Yugoslavian (87)	87	0.38

Hispanic Origin	Population	%
Hispanic or Latino (of any race)	4,587	20.22
Central American, ex. Mexican	239	1.05
Costa Rican	5	0.02
Guatemalan	60	0.26
Honduran	9	0.04
Nicaraguan	34	0.15
Panamanian	14	0.06
Salvadoran	99	0.44
Other Central American	18	0.08
Cuban	34	0.15
Dominican Republic	2	0.01
Mexican	3,600	15.87
Puerto Rican	222	0.98
South American	92	0.41
Argentinean	9	0.04
Bolivian	1	<0.01
Chilean	9	0.04
Colombian	21	0.09
Ecuadorian	7	0.03
Peruvian	36	0.16
Venezuelan	8	0.04
Other South American	1	<0.01
Other Hispanic or Latino	398	1.75

Race*	Population	%
African-American/Black (2,720)	3,416	15.06
Not Hispanic (2,567)	3,134	13.82
Hispanic (153)	282	1.24
American Indian/Alaska Native (310)	798	3.52
Not Hispanic (169)	521	2.30
Hispanic (141)	277	1.22
Aleut *(Alaska Native)* (1)	1	<0.01
Apache (10)	22	0.10
Blackfeet (4)	28	0.12
Canadian/French Am. Ind. (1)	2	0.01
Central American Ind. (0)	3	0.01
Cherokee (23)	131	0.58
Cheyenne (0)	1	<0.01
Chickasaw (0)	11	0.05
Chippewa (2)	14	0.06
Choctaw (7)	41	0.18
Colville (0)	1	<0.01
Comanche (7)	9	0.04
Cree (0)	4	0.02
Creek (1)	5	0.02
Hopi (2)	2	0.01
Inupiat *(Alaska Native)* (0)	1	<0.01
Iroquois (1)	6	0.03
Lumbee (0)	2	0.01
Menominee (1)	1	<0.01
Mexican American Ind. (8)	26	0.11
Navajo (12)	24	0.11
Paiute (6)	7	0.03
Potawatomi (0)	2	0.01
Pueblo (1)	3	0.01
Puget Sound Salish (3)	3	0.01
Shoshone (2)	8	0.04
Sioux (14)	28	0.12
Spanish American Ind. (0)	1	<0.01
Tlingit-Haida *(Alaska Native)* (4)	4	0.02
Tohono O'Odham (1)	1	<0.01
Tsimshian *(Alaska Native)* (0)	3	0.01
Ute (1)	1	<0.01
Yaqui (2)	9	0.04
Yup'ik *(Alaska Native)* (0)	1	<0.01
Asian (2,419)	3,086	13.61
Not Hispanic (2,329)	2,878	12.69
Hispanic (90)	208	0.92
Burmese (6)	6	0.03
Cambodian (11)	20	0.09
Chinese, ex. Taiwanese (291)	368	1.62
Filipino (628)	896	3.95
Hmong (101)	107	0.47
Indian (198)	279	1.23
Indonesian (12)	19	0.08
Japanese (223)	378	1.67
Korean (313)	377	1.66
Laotian (64)	88	0.39
Nepalese (14)	21	0.09
Pakistani (14)	28	0.12
Sri Lankan (2)	2	0.01
Taiwanese (2)	4	0.02
Thai (24)	41	0.18
Vietnamese (407)	447	1.97
Hawaii Native/Pacific Islander (134)	278	1.23
Not Hispanic (118)	237	1.04
Hispanic (16)	41	0.18
Fijian (45)	66	0.29
Guamanian/Chamorro (23)	46	0.20
Native Hawaiian (17)	71	0.31
Samoan (18)	33	0.15
Tongan (4)	7	0.03
White (13,496)	14,997	66.12
Not Hispanic (11,608)	12,628	55.68
Hispanic (1,888)	2,369	10.44

Roseville

Place Type: City
County: Placer
Population: 118,788†

Ancestry‡	Population	%
Afghan (28)	28	0.02
African, Sub-Saharan (110)	121	0.11
African (13)	24	0.02
Cape Verdean (9)	9	0.01
Ghanaian (48)	48	0.04
South African (40)	40	0.04
American (3,835)	3,835	3.37
Arab (319)	604	0.53
Arab (117)	153	0.13
Egyptian (87)	115	0.10
Iraqi (0)	141	0.12
Lebanese (88)	145	0.13
Palestinian (10)	10	0.01
Other Arab (17)	40	0.04
Armenian (150)	229	0.20
Assyrian/Chaldean/Syriac (5)	98	0.09
Australian (162)	256	0.22
Austrian (113)	366	0.32
Basque (39)	57	0.05
Belgian (33)	114	0.10
Brazilian (11)	11	0.01
British (254)	577	0.51
Bulgarian (84)	84	0.07
Cajun (9)	9	0.01
Canadian (143)	383	0.34
Croatian (29)	122	0.11
Czech (208)	597	0.52
Czechoslovakian (21)	101	0.09
Danish (337)	1,567	1.38
Dutch (296)	1,546	1.36
Eastern European (101)	101	0.09
English (4,230)	15,474	13.60
Estonian (12)	12	0.01
European (2,354)	2,574	2.26
Finnish (192)	530	0.47
French, ex. Basque (328)	3,671	3.23
French Canadian (110)	371	0.33
German (5,977)	20,919	18.38
Greek (363)	1,029	0.90
Hungarian (43)	317	0.28
Icelander (12)	12	0.01
Iranian (589)	767	0.67
Irish (3,967)	18,023	15.83
Italian (2,933)	8,689	7.63
Latvian (69)	84	0.07
Lithuanian (41)	217	0.19
Macedonian (33)	33	0.03
Maltese (67)	181	0.16
Northern European (229)	229	0.20
Norwegian (1,062)	3,331	2.93
Pennsylvania German (14)	27	0.02
Polish (569)	2,528	2.22
Portuguese (544)	2,134	1.87
Romanian (309)	415	0.36
Russian (762)	1,431	1.26
Scandinavian (257)	423	0.37
Scotch-Irish (766)	2,143	1.88
Scottish (707)	3,159	2.78
Serbian (0)	31	0.03
Slavic (8)	78	0.07
Slovak (108)	196	0.17
Slovene (9)	25	0.02
Swedish (620)	2,780	2.44
Swiss (171)	691	0.61
Turkish (21)	21	0.02
Ukrainian (748)	830	0.73
Welsh (94)	817	0.72
West Indian, ex. Hispanic (51)	107	0.09
Barbadian (0)	28	0.02
Jamaican (44)	72	0.06
West Indian (7)	7	0.01
Yugoslavian (253)	348	0.31

Hispanic Origin	Population	%
Hispanic or Latino (of any race)	17,359	14.61
Central American, ex. Mexican	837	0.70
Costa Rican	46	0.04
Guatemalan	236	0.20
Honduran	49	0.04
Nicaraguan	130	0.11
Panamanian	40	0.03
Salvadoran	331	0.28
Other Central American	5	<0.01
Cuban	137	0.12
Dominican Republic	23	0.02
Mexican	13,096	11.02
Puerto Rican	619	0.52
South American	504	0.42
Argentinean	58	0.05
Bolivian	19	0.02
Chilean	74	0.06
Colombian	115	0.10
Ecuadorian	32	0.03
Paraguayan	2	<0.01
Peruvian	157	0.13
Uruguayan	7	0.01
Venezuelan	31	0.03
Other South American	9	0.01
Other Hispanic or Latino	2,143	1.80

Race*	Population	%
African-American/Black (2,329)	3,470	2.92
Not Hispanic (2,157)	3,058	2.57
Hispanic (172)	412	0.35
American Indian/Alaska Native (885)	2,157	1.82
Not Hispanic (568)	1,509	1.27
Hispanic (317)	648	0.55
Alaska Athabascan *(Ala. Nat.)* (3)	3	<0.01
Apache (38)	82	0.07
Arapaho (3)	9	0.01
Blackfeet (7)	49	0.04
Canadian/French Am. Ind. (1)	1	<0.01
Cherokee (87)	380	0.32
Cheyenne (7)	12	0.01
Chickasaw (13)	27	0.02
Chippewa (19)	28	0.02
Choctaw (36)	107	0.09
Colville (2)	2	<0.01
Comanche (2)	11	0.01

*Notes: † The Census 2010 population figure is used to calculate the percentages in the Hispanic Origin and Race categories. Ancestry percentages are based on the 2006-2010 American Community Survey population (not shown); ‡ Numbers in parentheses indicate the number of people reporting a single ancestry; * Numbers in parentheses indicate the number of persons reporting this race alone, not in combination with any other race; Please refer to the Explanation of Data for more information.*

Cree (1)	2	<0.01
Creek (9)	29	0.02
Crow (1)	2	<0.01
Delaware (2)	6	0.01
Hopi (4)	10	0.01
Houma (1)	1	<0.01
Inupiat *(Alaska Native)* (1)	1	<0.01
Iroquois (8)	18	0.02
Lumbee (2)	7	0.01
Menominee (0)	1	<0.01
Mexican American Ind. (56)	88	0.07
Navajo (17)	30	0.03
Osage (1)	4	<0.01
Ottawa (1)	8	0.01
Paiute (9)	16	0.01
Pima (1)	2	<0.01
Potawatomi (6)	15	0.01
Pueblo (2)	10	0.01
Puget Sound Salish (1)	4	<0.01
Seminole (0)	7	0.01
Shoshone (8)	15	0.01
Sioux (30)	64	0.05
South American Ind. (1)	8	0.01
Spanish American Ind. (0)	2	<0.01
Tlingit-Haida *(Alaska Native)* (1)	4	<0.01
Tohono O'Odham (1)	3	<0.01
Yakama (1)	2	<0.01
Yaqui (10)	15	0.01
Yuman (4)	10	0.01
Yup'ik *(Alaska Native)* (2)	3	<0.01
Asian (10,026)	12,853	10.82
Not Hispanic (9,785)	12,117	10.20
Hispanic (241)	736	0.62
Bangladeshi (8)	9	0.01
Burmese (26)	37	0.03
Cambodian (45)	64	0.05
Chinese, ex. Taiwanese (1,144)	1,766	1.49
Filipino (3,637)	4,791	4.03
Hmong (52)	71	0.06
Indian (2,337)	2,501	2.11
Indonesian (40)	71	0.06
Japanese (674)	1,400	1.18
Korean (583)	842	0.71
Laotian (38)	50	0.04
Malaysian (9)	10	0.01
Nepalese (5)	5	<0.01
Pakistani (151)	176	0.15
Sri Lankan (26)	30	0.03
Taiwanese (80)	110	0.09
Thai (65)	131	0.11
Vietnamese (676)	834	0.70
Hawaii Native/Pacific Islander (346)	829	0.70
Not Hispanic (294)	653	0.55
Hispanic (52)	176	0.15
Fijian (46)	55	0.05
Guamanian/Chamorro (99)	205	0.17
Marshallese (0)	1	<0.01
Native Hawaiian (95)	337	0.28
Samoan (31)	68	0.06
Tongan (17)	32	0.03
White (94,199)	99,504	83.77
Not Hispanic (84,349)	88,043	74.12
Hispanic (9,850)	11,461	9.65

Rossmoor

Place Type: CDP
County: Orange
Population: 10,244†

Ancestry‡	Population	%
African, Sub-Saharan (12)	12	0.11
Ethiopian (12)	12	0.11
American (534)	534	5.09
Arab (20)	31	0.30
Egyptian (10)	10	0.10
Lebanese (10)	21	0.20
Armenian (28)	28	0.27
Australian (11)	11	0.10
Austrian (0)	66	0.63
Basque (17)	17	0.16
British (148)	207	1.97
Bulgarian (11)	11	0.10
Croatian (15)	47	0.45
Czech (0)	24	0.23
Czechoslovakian (0)	8	0.08
Danish (30)	167	1.59
Dutch (56)	260	2.48
Eastern European (143)	161	1.53
English (386)	1,577	15.03
European (478)	478	4.56
Finnish (0)	8	0.08
French, ex. Basque (64)	429	4.09
French Canadian (7)	14	0.13
German (584)	2,057	19.61
Greek (192)	204	1.94
Hungarian (33)	182	1.73
Iranian (166)	166	1.58
Irish (271)	1,423	13.56
Italian (205)	579	5.52
Latvian (10)	10	0.10
Lithuanian (28)	57	0.54
Macedonian (0)	10	0.10
Northern European (6)	19	0.18
Norwegian (32)	274	2.61
Pennsylvania German (11)	19	0.18
Polish (73)	289	2.75
Portuguese (11)	139	1.32
Romanian (0)	10	0.10
Russian (113)	303	2.89
Scandinavian (0)	10	0.10
Scotch-Irish (184)	454	4.33
Scottish (155)	433	4.13
Serbian (0)	10	0.10
Slovak (0)	25	0.24
Swedish (97)	256	2.44
Swiss (0)	28	0.27
Ukrainian (14)	90	0.86
Welsh (94)	153	1.46
West Indian, ex. Hispanic (0)	10	0.10
Bermudan (0)	10	0.10
Yugoslavian (0)	9	0.09

Hispanic Origin	Population	%
Hispanic or Latino (of any race)	1,174	11.46
Central American, ex. Mexican	55	0.54
Costa Rican	4	0.04
Guatemalan	11	0.11
Honduran	6	0.06
Nicaraguan	7	0.07
Panamanian	3	0.03
Salvadoran	21	0.20
Other Central American	3	0.03
Cuban	52	0.51
Dominican Republic	5	0.05
Mexican	768	7.50
Puerto Rican	28	0.27
South American	100	0.98
Argentinean	16	0.16
Chilean	4	0.04
Colombian	32	0.31
Ecuadorian	23	0.22
Peruvian	25	0.24
Other Hispanic or Latino	166	1.62

Race*	Population	%
African-American/Black (84)	123	1.20
Not Hispanic (76)	108	1.05
Hispanic (8)	15	0.15
American Indian/Alaska Native (36)	113	1.10
Not Hispanic (29)	86	0.84
Hispanic (7)	27	0.26
Apache (1)	3	0.03
Blackfeet (0)	3	0.03
Canadian/French Am. Ind. (0)	2	0.02
Cherokee (5)	29	0.28
Chippewa (2)	2	0.02
Choctaw (3)	8	0.08
Hopi (0)	3	0.03
Iroquois (0)	3	0.03
Lumbee (0)	1	0.01
Mexican American Ind. (3)	5	0.05
Navajo (2)	7	0.07
Osage (0)	1	0.01
Ottawa (5)	5	0.05
Shoshone (2)	2	0.02
Sioux (0)	3	0.03
Tlingit-Haida *(Alaska Native)* (0)	1	0.01
Tohono O'Odham (0)	1	0.01
Yaqui (0)	3	0.03
Asian (838)	1,068	10.43
Not Hispanic (812)	1,001	9.77
Hispanic (26)	67	0.65
Burmese (0)	3	0.03
Cambodian (11)	16	0.16
Chinese, ex. Taiwanese (170)	244	2.38
Filipino (164)	241	2.35
Indian (45)	52	0.51
Indonesian (1)	5	0.05
Japanese (197)	296	2.89
Korean (108)	133	1.30
Laotian (1)	2	0.02
Pakistani (1)	3	0.03
Sri Lankan (6)	7	0.07
Taiwanese (52)	57	0.56
Thai (7)	15	0.15
Vietnamese (13)	26	0.25
Hawaii Native/Pacific Islander (29)	50	0.49
Not Hispanic (21)	37	0.36
Hispanic (8)	13	0.13
Guamanian/Chamorro (9)	14	0.14
Native Hawaiian (6)	15	0.15
Samoan (13)	14	0.14
White (8,691)	9,053	88.37
Not Hispanic (7,845)	8,105	79.12
Hispanic (846)	948	9.25

Rowland Heights

Place Type: CDP
County: Los Angeles
Population: 48,993†

Ancestry‡	Population	%
African, Sub-Saharan (110)	119	0.23
African (62)	71	0.14
Nigerian (48)	48	0.09
American (694)	694	1.35
Arab (235)	247	0.48
Egyptian (13)	13	0.03
Jordanian (60)	60	0.12
Lebanese (34)	46	0.09
Palestinian (80)	80	0.16
Other Arab (48)	48	0.09
Armenian (168)	322	0.62
Austrian (0)	27	0.05
Basque (0)	6	0.01
Brazilian (9)	9	0.02
British (12)	21	0.04
Canadian (29)	67	0.13
Croatian (20)	50	0.10
Czech (13)	32	0.06
Czechoslovakian (0)	9	0.02
Danish (7)	26	0.05
Dutch (53)	295	0.57
English (182)	920	1.78
European (81)	81	0.16
French, ex. Basque (55)	210	0.41
French Canadian (14)	14	0.03
German (207)	1,110	2.15
Greek (23)	85	0.16
Hungarian (19)	66	0.13
Iranian (188)	242	0.47
Irish (265)	909	1.76
Italian (190)	489	0.95
Lithuanian (15)	49	0.10
Norwegian (44)	102	0.20
Polish (33)	112	0.22
Portuguese (20)	37	0.07
Romanian (47)	47	0.09

SECTION TWO

*Notes: † The Census 2010 population figure is used to calculate the percentages in the Hispanic Origin and Race categories. Ancestry percentages are based on the 2006-2010 American Community Survey population (not shown); ‡ Numbers in parentheses indicate the number of people reporting a single ancestry; * Numbers in parentheses indicate the number of persons reporting this race alone, not in combination with any other race; Please refer to the Explanation of Data for more information.*

Russian (94)	121	0.23
Scotch-Irish (61)	215	0.42
Scottish (27)	96	0.19
Swedish (59)	202	0.39
Turkish (10)	21	0.04
Welsh (0)	44	0.09
West Indian, ex. Hispanic (26)	26	0.05
Trinidadian/Tobagonian (26)	26	0.05

Hispanic Origin	Population	%
Hispanic or Latino (of any race)	13,229	27.00
Central American, ex. Mexican	926	1.89
Costa Rican	24	0.05
Guatemalan	327	0.67
Honduran	32	0.07
Nicaraguan	112	0.23
Panamanian	10	0.02
Salvadoran	419	0.86
Other Central American	2	<0.01
Cuban	84	0.17
Mexican	10,976	22.40
Puerto Rican	161	0.33
South American	484	0.99
Argentinean	45	0.09
Bolivian	24	0.05
Chilean	23	0.05
Colombian	91	0.19
Ecuadorian	114	0.23
Peruvian	154	0.31
Uruguayan	8	0.02
Venezuelan	21	0.04
Other South American	4	0.01
Other Hispanic or Latino	598	1.22

Race*	Population	%
African-American/Black (772)	988	2.02
Not Hispanic (683)	808	1.65
Hispanic (89)	180	0.37
American Indian/Alaska Native (175)	437	0.89
Not Hispanic (43)	170	0.35
Hispanic (132)	267	0.54
Alaska Athabascan *(Ala. Nat.)* (0)	1	<0.01
Apache (3)	18	0.04
Blackfeet (0)	13	0.03
Canadian/French Am. Ind. (0)	1	<0.01
Cherokee (3)	19	0.04
Cheyenne (1)	3	0.01
Chickasaw (0)	1	<0.01
Chippewa (1)	7	0.01
Choctaw (0)	4	0.01
Creek (0)	7	0.01
Delaware (0)	1	<0.01
Inupiat *(Alaska Native)* (1)	3	0.01
Iroquois (1)	2	<0.01
Mexican American Ind. (39)	74	0.15
Navajo (10)	16	0.03
Pima (1)	9	0.02
Pueblo (4)	4	0.01
Seminole (0)	1	<0.01
Sioux (2)	9	0.02
South American Ind. (1)	5	0.01
Spanish American Ind. (2)	3	0.01
Tohono O'Odham (0)	1	<0.01
Ute (1)	6	0.01
Yaqui (1)	4	0.01
Yuman (0)	2	<0.01
Asian (29,284)	30,088	61.41
Not Hispanic (29,135)	29,752	60.73
Hispanic (149)	336	0.69
Bangladeshi (13)	15	0.03
Burmese (111)	143	0.29
Cambodian (145)	198	0.40
Chinese, ex. Taiwanese (15,518)	16,563	33.81
Filipino (3,151)	3,487	7.12
Hmong (2)	4	0.01
Indian (559)	617	1.26
Indonesian (375)	459	0.94
Japanese (592)	782	1.60
Korean (3,506)	3,636	7.42
Laotian (29)	47	0.10
Malaysian (40)	57	0.12
Nepalese (29)	39	0.08
Pakistani (109)	124	0.25
Sri Lankan (23)	23	0.05
Taiwanese (3,079)	3,476	7.09
Thai (286)	346	0.71
Vietnamese (699)	902	1.84
Hawaii Native/Pacific Islander (61)	271	0.55
Not Hispanic (60)	242	0.49
Hispanic (1)	29	0.06
Guamanian/Chamorro (1)	4	0.01
Native Hawaiian (5)	51	0.10
Samoan (39)	55	0.11
Tongan (15)	16	0.03
White (11,506)	12,520	25.55
Not Hispanic (5,045)	5,493	11.21
Hispanic (6,461)	7,027	14.34

Rubidoux

Place Type: CDP
County: Riverside
Population: 34,280†

Ancestry‡	Population	%
African, Sub-Saharan (12)	12	0.03
African (12)	12	0.03
American (780)	780	2.09
Arab (20)	20	0.05
Jordanian (20)	20	0.05
Australian (0)	27	0.07
Austrian (0)	18	0.05
Basque (10)	19	0.05
British (47)	56	0.15
Canadian (8)	30	0.08
Croatian (0)	6	0.02
Czech (39)	39	0.10
Danish (23)	76	0.20
Dutch (16)	94	0.25
English (461)	1,390	3.73
European (281)	374	1.00
Finnish (24)	24	0.06
French, ex. Basque (27)	461	1.24
French Canadian (47)	57	0.15
German (628)	1,991	5.34
Greek (0)	25	0.07
Hungarian (41)	71	0.19
Icelander (11)	11	0.03
Iranian (26)	26	0.07
Irish (404)	1,414	3.79
Italian (298)	1,198	3.22
Latvian (15)	30	0.08
Luxemburger (0)	13	0.03
Northern European (25)	25	0.07
Norwegian (113)	283	0.76
Polish (48)	265	0.71
Portuguese (50)	156	0.42
Romanian (46)	58	0.16
Russian (23)	136	0.36
Scandinavian (0)	9	0.02
Scotch-Irish (90)	394	1.06
Scottish (129)	341	0.92
Slavic (6)	6	0.02
Swedish (51)	112	0.30
Swiss (0)	23	0.06
Ukrainian (0)	8	0.02
Welsh (83)	127	0.34
West Indian, ex. Hispanic (73)	73	0.20
Belizean (17)	17	0.05
Jamaican (42)	42	0.11
West Indian (14)	14	0.04
Yugoslavian (0)	6	0.02

Hispanic Origin	Population	%
Hispanic or Latino (of any race)	23,322	68.03
Central American, ex. Mexican	835	2.44
Costa Rican	17	0.05
Guatemalan	250	0.73
Honduran	101	0.29
Nicaraguan	67	0.20
Panamanian	21	0.06
Salvadoran	371	1.08
Other Central American	8	0.02
Cuban	52	0.15
Dominican Republic	7	0.02
Mexican	21,173	61.76
Puerto Rican	186	0.54
South American	149	0.43
Argentinean	21	0.06
Bolivian	7	0.02
Chilean	3	0.01
Colombian	46	0.13
Ecuadorian	21	0.06
Peruvian	38	0.11
Uruguayan	3	0.01
Venezuelan	4	0.01
Other South American	6	0.02
Other Hispanic or Latino	920	2.68

Race*	Population	%
African-American/Black (1,850)	2,138	6.24
Not Hispanic (1,710)	1,862	5.43
Hispanic (140)	276	0.81
American Indian/Alaska Native (391)	676	1.97
Not Hispanic (121)	266	0.78
Hispanic (270)	410	1.20
Apache (15)	29	0.08
Blackfeet (2)	6	0.02
Central American Ind. (10)	12	0.04
Cherokee (22)	68	0.20
Chickasaw (4)	6	0.02
Chippewa (2)	4	0.01
Choctaw (9)	22	0.06
Comanche (2)	3	0.01
Creek (3)	8	0.02
Delaware (0)	1	<0.01
Hopi (5)	10	0.03
Inupiat *(Alaska Native)* (0)	3	0.01
Iroquois (0)	3	0.01
Kiowa (1)	1	<0.01
Lumbee (0)	4	0.01
Mexican American Ind. (33)	57	0.17
Navajo (15)	20	0.06
Osage (1)	1	<0.01
Ottawa (0)	2	0.01
Pima (3)	6	0.02
Pueblo (3)	8	0.02
Puget Sound Salish (4)	4	0.01
Seminole (0)	5	0.01
Shoshone (1)	1	<0.01
Sioux (1)	5	0.01
South American Ind. (2)	3	0.01
Spanish American Ind. (7)	7	0.02
Yakama (1)	1	<0.01
Yaqui (9)	16	0.05
Yuman (3)	3	0.01
Asian (855)	1,135	3.31
Not Hispanic (820)	972	2.84
Hispanic (35)	163	0.48
Cambodian (40)	50	0.15
Chinese, ex. Taiwanese (56)	99	0.29
Filipino (336)	450	1.31
Indian (72)	103	0.30
Indonesian (5)	17	0.05
Japanese (57)	123	0.36
Korean (49)	59	0.17
Laotian (15)	22	0.06
Pakistani (31)	32	0.09
Sri Lankan (5)	5	0.01
Taiwanese (7)	9	0.03
Thai (10)	13	0.04
Vietnamese (118)	139	0.41
Hawaii Native/Pacific Islander (136)	219	0.64
Not Hispanic (121)	163	0.48
Hispanic (15)	56	0.16
Fijian (1)	1	<0.01
Guamanian/Chamorro (17)	27	0.08
Native Hawaiian (14)	43	0.13
Samoan (42)	64	0.19
Tongan (50)	57	0.17

*Notes: † The Census 2010 population figure is used to calculate the percentages in the Hispanic Origin and Race categories. Ancestry percentages are based on the 2006-2010 American Community Survey population (not shown); ‡ Numbers in parentheses indicate the number of people reporting a single ancestry; * Numbers in parentheses indicate the number of persons reporting this race alone, not in combination with any other race; Please refer to the Explanation of Data for more information.*

White (16,935)	18,304	53.40
Not Hispanic (7,703)	8,053	23.49
Hispanic (9,232)	10,251	29.90

Sacramento

Place Type: City
County: Sacramento
Population: 466,488†

Ancestry‡	Population	%
Afghan (580)	580	0.13
African, Sub-Saharan (3,143)	4,175	0.91
African (1,896)	2,618	0.57
Cape Verdean (112)	299	0.07
Ethiopian (605)	692	0.15
Ghanaian (41)	41	0.01
Kenyan (9)	9	<0.01
Nigerian (350)	359	0.08
Somalian (0)	8	<0.01
South African (130)	149	0.03
Albanian (8)	27	0.01
American (7,542)	7,542	1.64
Arab (922)	1,877	0.41
Arab (348)	597	0.13
Egyptian (68)	201	0.04
Iraqi (0)	9	<0.01
Jordanian (152)	199	0.04
Lebanese (101)	323	0.07
Moroccan (23)	46	0.01
Palestinian (105)	159	0.03
Syrian (10)	37	0.01
Other Arab (115)	306	0.07
Armenian (317)	711	0.15
Assyrian/Chaldean/Syriac (85)	151	0.03
Australian (93)	357	0.08
Austrian (116)	709	0.15
Basque (32)	101	0.02
Belgian (19)	205	0.04
Brazilian (26)	175	0.04
British (654)	1,493	0.32
Bulgarian (278)	304	0.07
Cajun (0)	17	<0.01
Canadian (262)	634	0.14
Celtic (56)	97	0.02
Croatian (167)	483	0.11
Czech (303)	1,164	0.25
Czechoslovakian (87)	294	0.06
Danish (409)	1,908	0.42
Dutch (950)	4,826	1.05
Eastern European (370)	414	0.09
English (6,966)	28,086	6.11
Estonian (0)	34	0.01
European (3,938)	5,277	1.15
Finnish (145)	567	0.12
French, ex. Basque (1,089)	9,645	2.10
French Canadian (412)	1,254	0.27
German (10,093)	41,408	9.01
German Russian (14)	38	0.01
Greek (1,009)	2,242	0.49
Hungarian (284)	1,189	0.26
Icelander (87)	189	0.04
Iranian (629)	1,001	0.22
Irish (8,354)	35,916	7.82
Israeli (76)	94	0.02
Italian (6,196)	18,754	4.08
Latvian (52)	101	0.02
Lithuanian (165)	593	0.13
Luxemburger (0)	35	0.01
Maltese (16)	44	0.01
Northern European (479)	493	0.11
Norwegian (1,904)	5,382	1.17
Pennsylvania German (21)	73	0.02
Polish (1,235)	4,573	1.00
Portuguese (2,792)	7,182	1.56
Romanian (888)	1,087	0.24
Russian (2,507)	4,916	1.07
Scandinavian (384)	989	0.22
Scotch-Irish (1,629)	5,314	1.16
Scottish (1,719)	7,694	1.67
Serbian (122)	312	0.07
Slavic (45)	161	0.04
Slovak (33)	179	0.04
Slovene (14)	120	0.03
Swedish (1,103)	5,613	1.22
Swiss (437)	1,686	0.37
Turkish (258)	279	0.06
Ukrainian (1,425)	2,189	0.48
Welsh (289)	2,314	0.50
West Indian, ex. Hispanic (412)	812	0.18
Barbadian (10)	10	<0.01
Belizean (92)	104	0.02
British West Indian (0)	21	<0.01
Haitian (0)	20	<0.01
Jamaican (133)	376	0.08
Trinidadian/Tobagonian (73)	90	0.02
West Indian (104)	191	0.04
Yugoslavian (574)	900	0.20

Hispanic Origin	Population	%
Hispanic or Latino (of any race)	125,276	26.86
Central American, ex. Mexican	5,184	1.11
Costa Rican	162	0.03
Guatemalan	977	0.21
Honduran	357	0.08
Nicaraguan	895	0.19
Panamanian	325	0.07
Salvadoran	2,425	0.52
Other Central American	43	0.01
Cuban	640	0.14
Dominican Republic	190	0.04
Mexican	105,467	22.61
Puerto Rican	3,344	0.72
South American	1,777	0.38
Argentinean	179	0.04
Bolivian	66	0.01
Chilean	205	0.04
Colombian	400	0.09
Ecuadorian	116	0.02
Paraguayan	12	<0.01
Peruvian	614	0.13
Uruguayan	27	0.01
Venezuelan	118	0.03
Other South American	40	0.01
Other Hispanic or Latino	8,674	1.86

Race*	Population	%
African-American/Black (68,335)	80,469	17.25
Not Hispanic (64,967)	74,051	15.87
Hispanic (3,368)	6,418	1.38
American Indian/Alaska Native (5,291)	13,242	2.84
Not Hispanic (2,586)	7,885	1.69
Hispanic (2,705)	5,357	1.15
Alaska Athabascan *(Ala. Nat.)* (7)	11	<0.01
Aleut *(Alaska Native)* (2)	20	<0.01
Apache (197)	476	0.10
Arapaho (1)	10	<0.01
Blackfeet (82)	485	0.10
Canadian/French Am. Ind. (12)	21	<0.01
Central American Ind. (6)	23	<0.01
Cherokee (371)	2,019	0.43
Cheyenne (12)	46	0.01
Chickasaw (27)	96	0.02
Chippewa (65)	151	0.03
Choctaw (84)	426	0.09
Colville (3)	12	<0.01
Comanche (11)	44	0.01
Cree (10)	39	0.01
Creek (22)	114	0.02
Crow (12)	37	0.01
Delaware (8)	20	<0.01
Hopi (12)	28	0.01
Houma (3)	3	<0.01
Inupiat *(Alaska Native)* (14)	27	0.01
Iroquois (31)	92	0.02
Kiowa (7)	15	<0.01
Lumbee (10)	19	<0.01
Menominee (1)	7	<0.01
Mexican American Ind. (469)	746	0.16
Navajo (155)	355	0.08
Osage (3)	30	0.01
Ottawa (1)	6	<0.01
Paiute (62)	107	0.02
Pima (20)	33	0.01
Potawatomi (16)	54	0.01
Pueblo (47)	81	0.02
Puget Sound Salish (11)	21	<0.01
Seminole (10)	63	0.01
Shoshone (17)	49	0.01
Sioux (118)	302	0.06
South American Ind. (12)	43	0.01
Spanish American Ind. (45)	65	0.01
Tlingit-Haida *(Alaska Native)* (20)	55	0.01
Tohono O'Odham (12)	26	0.01
Tsimshian *(Alaska Native)* (1)	5	<0.01
Ute (12)	21	<0.01
Yakama (4)	6	<0.01
Yaqui (125)	207	0.04
Yuman (9)	15	<0.01
Yup'ik *(Alaska Native)* (1)	3	<0.01
Asian (85,503)	98,705	21.16
Not Hispanic (83,841)	94,141	20.18
Hispanic (1,662)	4,564	0.98
Bangladeshi (68)	70	0.02
Bhutanese (8)	8	<0.01
Burmese (49)	71	0.02
Cambodian (840)	1,082	0.23
Chinese, ex. Taiwanese (19,989)	23,350	5.01
Filipino (13,468)	18,503	3.97
Hmong (15,984)	16,676	3.57
Indian (8,514)	10,700	2.29
Indonesian (147)	278	0.06
Japanese (5,730)	8,759	1.88
Korean (1,265)	1,994	0.43
Laotian (5,904)	6,675	1.43
Malaysian (26)	45	0.01
Nepalese (84)	90	0.02
Pakistani (1,927)	2,061	0.44
Sri Lankan (76)	94	0.02
Taiwanese (310)	367	0.08
Thai (415)	784	0.17
Vietnamese (6,682)	7,730	1.66
Hawaii Native/Pacific Islander (6,655)	10,699	2.29
Not Hispanic (6,392)	9,762	2.09
Hispanic (263)	937	0.20
Fijian (2,703)	3,244	0.70
Guamanian/Chamorro (366)	707	0.15
Marshallese (387)	400	0.09
Native Hawaiian (346)	1,236	0.26
Samoan (819)	1,233	0.26
Tongan (1,141)	1,382	0.30
White (210,006)	233,865	50.13
Not Hispanic (161,062)	175,948	37.72
Hispanic (48,944)	57,917	12.42

Salida

Place Type: CDP
County: Stanislaus
Population: 13,722†

Ancestry‡	Population	%
African, Sub-Saharan (168)	168	1.15
African (90)	90	0.62
Kenyan (78)	78	0.53
American (578)	578	3.95
Arab (10)	10	0.07
Arab (10)	10	0.07
Armenian (0)	78	0.53
Austrian (0)	66	0.45
British (0)	59	0.40
Canadian (62)	62	0.42
Czech (0)	14	0.10
Dutch (141)	232	1.59
English (180)	621	4.25
European (129)	225	1.54
French, ex. Basque (0)	124	0.85
French Canadian (12)	56	0.38
German (419)	1,398	9.56
Greek (14)	49	0.34

*Notes: † The Census 2010 population figure is used to calculate the percentages in the Hispanic Origin and Race categories. Ancestry percentages are based on the 2006-2010 American Community Survey population (not shown); ‡ Numbers in parentheses indicate the number of people reporting a single ancestry; * Numbers in parentheses indicate the number of persons reporting this race alone, not in combination with any other race; Please refer to the Explanation of Data for more information.*

Hungarian (0)	47	0.32
Irish (380)	1,336	9.14
Italian (280)	859	5.87
Norwegian (14)	114	0.78
Polish (187)	283	1.94
Portuguese (279)	622	4.25
Romanian (0)	14	0.10
Russian (15)	48	0.33
Scandinavian (0)	24	0.16
Scotch-Irish (65)	158	1.08
Scottish (0)	153	1.05
Swedish (35)	103	0.70
Swiss (14)	82	0.56
Welsh (0)	51	0.35
Yugoslavian (41)	41	0.28

Hispanic Origin	Population	%
Hispanic or Latino (of any race)	6,426	46.83
Central American, ex. Mexican	211	1.54
Costa Rican	8	0.06
Guatemalan	79	0.58
Honduran	16	0.12
Nicaraguan	43	0.31
Panamanian	1	0.01
Salvadoran	61	0.44
Other Central American	3	0.02
Cuban	9	0.07
Mexican	5,667	41.30
Puerto Rican	138	1.01
South American	60	0.44
Argentinean	11	0.08
Bolivian	5	0.04
Chilean	9	0.07
Colombian	13	0.09
Ecuadorian	3	0.02
Paraguayan	2	0.01
Peruvian	15	0.11
Venezuelan	2	0.01
Other Hispanic or Latino	341	2.49

Race*	Population	%
African-American/Black (435)	587	4.28
Not Hispanic (406)	512	3.73
Hispanic (29)	75	0.55
American Indian/Alaska Native (111)	264	1.92
Not Hispanic (47)	132	0.96
Hispanic (64)	132	0.96
Alaska Athabascan *(Ala. Nat.)* (3)	3	0.02
Apache (2)	12	0.09
Blackfeet (0)	9	0.07
Cherokee (8)	31	0.23
Chickasaw (5)	5	0.04
Chippewa (1)	2	0.01
Choctaw (5)	20	0.15
Comanche (0)	1	0.01
Creek (1)	1	0.01
Mexican American Ind. (0)	5	0.04
Osage (0)	3	0.02
Pima (0)	1	0.01
Potawatomi (4)	4	0.03
Pueblo (1)	1	0.01
Sioux (4)	14	0.10
South American Ind. (4)	7	0.05
Spanish American Ind. (1)	1	0.01
Tohono O'Odham (4)	6	0.04
Yaqui (5)	12	0.09
Yup'ik *(Alaska Native)* (0)	1	0.01
Asian (669)	1,002	7.30
Not Hispanic (585)	801	5.84
Hispanic (84)	201	1.46
Cambodian (44)	53	0.39
Chinese, ex. Taiwanese (42)	62	0.45
Filipino (269)	420	3.06
Hmong (3)	6	0.04
Indian (152)	197	1.44
Indonesian (2)	2	0.01
Japanese (26)	79	0.58
Korean (14)	21	0.15
Laotian (16)	25	0.18
Pakistani (29)	35	0.26
Taiwanese (2)	5	0.04
Thai (6)	10	0.07
Vietnamese (31)	58	0.42
Hawaii Native/Pacific Islander (83)	158	1.15
Not Hispanic (68)	125	0.91
Hispanic (15)	33	0.24
Fijian (29)	38	0.28
Guamanian/Chamorro (18)	28	0.20
Native Hawaiian (13)	35	0.26
Samoan (11)	16	0.12
Tongan (0)	3	0.02
White (8,479)	9,144	66.64
Not Hispanic (5,768)	6,093	44.40
Hispanic (2,711)	3,051	22.23

Salinas

Place Type: City
County: Monterey
Population: 150,441†

Ancestry‡	Population	%
Afghan (15)	15	0.01
African, Sub-Saharan (315)	345	0.23
African (242)	272	0.18
Senegalese (20)	20	0.01
South African (38)	38	0.03
Other Sub-Saharan African (15)	15	0.01
American (1,553)	1,553	1.06
Arab (151)	190	0.13
Arab (8)	8	0.01
Egyptian (53)	53	0.04
Lebanese (0)	25	0.02
Palestinian (9)	9	0.01
Syrian (11)	25	0.02
Other Arab (70)	70	0.05
Armenian (24)	69	0.05
Australian (10)	77	0.05
Austrian (30)	153	0.10
Basque (25)	55	0.04
Belgian (0)	27	0.02
Brazilian (0)	86	0.06
British (127)	217	0.15
Bulgarian (0)	15	0.01
Cajun (14)	30	0.02
Canadian (100)	146	0.10
Celtic (0)	28	0.02
Croatian (20)	20	0.01
Czech (39)	133	0.09
Czechoslovakian (9)	81	0.06
Danish (174)	511	0.35
Dutch (117)	760	0.52
Eastern European (12)	12	0.01
English (1,181)	3,789	2.58
European (660)	753	0.51
Finnish (32)	77	0.05
French, ex. Basque (50)	1,160	0.79
French Canadian (61)	166	0.11
German (1,452)	6,020	4.09
German Russian (0)	11	0.01
Greek (20)	119	0.08
Hungarian (57)	169	0.11
Iranian (17)	17	0.01
Irish (1,271)	5,253	3.57
Israeli (0)	39	0.03
Italian (1,257)	3,230	2.20
Lithuanian (7)	7	<0.01
Northern European (58)	69	0.05
Norwegian (173)	491	0.33
Pennsylvania German (12)	12	0.01
Polish (104)	393	0.27
Portuguese (281)	746	0.51
Romanian (88)	111	0.08
Russian (86)	224	0.15
Scandinavian (138)	151	0.10
Scotch-Irish (501)	1,035	0.70
Scottish (236)	895	0.61
Slavic (14)	14	0.01
Slovak (0)	41	0.03
Slovene (0)	10	0.01
Swedish (235)	762	0.52
Swiss (155)	567	0.39
Turkish (85)	85	0.06
Ukrainian (28)	38	0.03
Welsh (19)	290	0.20
West Indian, ex. Hispanic (132)	132	0.09
Jamaican (132)	132	0.09
Yugoslavian (0)	12	0.01

Hispanic Origin	Population	%
Hispanic or Latino (of any race)	112,799	74.98
Central American, ex. Mexican	1,800	1.20
Costa Rican	24	0.02
Guatemalan	177	0.12
Honduran	136	0.09
Nicaraguan	58	0.04
Panamanian	93	0.06
Salvadoran	1,302	0.87
Other Central American	10	0.01
Cuban	94	0.06
Dominican Republic	21	0.01
Mexican	104,237	69.29
Puerto Rican	715	0.48
South American	420	0.28
Argentinean	53	0.04
Bolivian	5	<0.01
Chilean	61	0.04
Colombian	74	0.05
Ecuadorian	36	0.02
Peruvian	179	0.12
Venezuelan	12	0.01
Other Hispanic or Latino	5,512	3.66

Race*	Population	%
African-American/Black (2,993)	4,054	2.69
Not Hispanic (2,343)	2,934	1.95
Hispanic (650)	1,120	0.74
American Indian/Alaska Native (1,888)	3,125	2.08
Not Hispanic (418)	892	0.59
Hispanic (1,470)	2,233	1.48
Alaska Athabascan *(Ala. Nat.)* (0)	2	<0.01
Aleut *(Alaska Native)* (2)	5	<0.01
Apache (50)	93	0.06
Arapaho (0)	4	<0.01
Blackfeet (3)	22	0.01
Canadian/French Am. Ind. (0)	2	<0.01
Central American Ind. (1)	4	<0.01
Cherokee (76)	230	0.15
Cheyenne (1)	1	<0.01
Chickasaw (10)	21	0.01
Chippewa (5)	21	0.01
Choctaw (35)	55	0.04
Comanche (9)	16	0.01
Cree (0)	4	<0.01
Creek (13)	24	0.02
Crow (1)	2	<0.01
Hopi (6)	12	0.01
Inupiat *(Alaska Native)* (1)	2	<0.01
Iroquois (1)	18	0.01
Kiowa (1)	1	<0.01
Lumbee (0)	2	<0.01
Mexican American Ind. (320)	508	0.34
Navajo (23)	32	0.02
Osage (1)	6	<0.01
Paiute (17)	25	0.02
Pima (0)	2	<0.01
Potawatomi (1)	5	<0.01
Pueblo (7)	15	0.01
Puget Sound Salish (2)	3	<0.01
Seminole (1)	5	<0.01
Shoshone (12)	16	0.01
Sioux (12)	18	0.01
South American Ind. (2)	6	<0.01
Spanish American Ind. (8)	12	0.01
Tlingit-Haida *(Alaska Native)* (2)	8	0.01
Tohono O'Odham (5)	8	0.01
Ute (4)	4	<0.01
Yaqui (19)	41	0.03
Yuman (1)	1	<0.01
Yup'ik *(Alaska Native)* (0)	4	<0.01

*Notes: † The Census 2010 population figure is used to calculate the percentages in the Hispanic Origin and Race categories. Ancestry percentages are based on the 2006-2010 American Community Survey population (not shown); ‡ Numbers in parentheses indicate the number of people reporting a single ancestry; * Numbers in parentheses indicate the number of persons reporting this race alone, not in combination with any other race; Please refer to the Explanation of Data for more information.*

Asian (9,438)	12,058	8.02
Not Hispanic (8,677)	10,123	6.73
Hispanic (761)	1,935	1.29
Bangladeshi (4)	4	<0.01
Burmese (30)	35	0.02
Cambodian (18)	26	0.02
Chinese, ex. Taiwanese (815)	1,147	0.76
Filipino (6,041)	7,740	5.14
Hmong (11)	11	0.01
Indian (582)	722	0.48
Indonesian (12)	21	0.01
Japanese (659)	1,193	0.79
Korean (500)	699	0.46
Laotian (5)	11	0.01
Malaysian (0)	6	<0.01
Nepalese (3)	3	<0.01
Pakistani (5)	23	0.02
Sri Lankan (3)	3	<0.01
Taiwanese (15)	22	0.01
Thai (29)	61	0.04
Vietnamese (383)	463	0.31
Hawaii Native/Pacific Islander (478)	1,047	0.70
Not Hispanic (383)	748	0.50
Hispanic (95)	299	0.20
Fijian (17)	17	0.01
Guamanian/Chamorro (158)	281	0.19
Native Hawaiian (92)	349	0.23
Samoan (72)	125	0.08
Tongan (50)	65	0.04
White (68,973)	75,011	49.86
Not Hispanic (23,333)	25,121	16.70
Hispanic (45,640)	49,890	33.16

San Anselmo

Place Type: Town
County: Marin
Population: 12,336†

Ancestry‡	Population	%
African, Sub-Saharan (12)	12	0.10
African (12)	12	0.10
American (310)	310	2.54
Arab (11)	50	0.41
Egyptian (0)	28	0.23
Lebanese (11)	22	0.18
Assyrian/Chaldean/Syriac (13)	13	0.11
Australian (0)	121	0.99
Austrian (30)	42	0.34
Basque (9)	9	0.07
British (156)	221	1.81
Canadian (61)	111	0.91
Croatian (14)	74	0.61
Czech (0)	62	0.51
Czechoslovakian (19)	19	0.16
Danish (15)	109	0.89
Dutch (90)	278	2.28
Eastern European (81)	81	0.66
English (631)	1,953	16.00
European (214)	307	2.52
Finnish (18)	102	0.84
French, ex. Basque (187)	580	4.75
French Canadian (25)	86	0.70
German (296)	2,350	19.26
Greek (88)	133	1.09
Hungarian (17)	48	0.39
Iranian (47)	184	1.51
Irish (623)	2,305	18.89
Italian (589)	1,426	11.69
Lithuanian (8)	8	0.07
New Zealander (15)	15	0.12
Northern European (38)	38	0.31
Norwegian (73)	306	2.51
Polish (94)	512	4.20
Portuguese (15)	43	0.35
Romanian (10)	45	0.37
Russian (284)	590	4.83
Scandinavian (51)	64	0.52
Scotch-Irish (65)	364	2.98
Scottish (114)	398	3.26
Slavic (0)	13	0.11
Slovak (17)	17	0.14
Swedish (29)	404	3.31
Swiss (16)	94	0.77
Welsh (0)	81	0.66
Yugoslavian (0)	30	0.25

Hispanic Origin	Population	%
Hispanic or Latino (of any race)	717	5.81
Central American, ex. Mexican	127	1.03
Costa Rican	2	0.02
Guatemalan	40	0.32
Honduran	3	0.02
Nicaraguan	27	0.22
Panamanian	1	0.01
Salvadoran	54	0.44
Cuban	26	0.21
Dominican Republic	4	0.03
Mexican	324	2.63
Puerto Rican	23	0.19
South American	89	0.72
Argentinean	15	0.12
Bolivian	5	0.04
Chilean	12	0.10
Colombian	19	0.15
Ecuadorian	3	0.02
Peruvian	31	0.25
Uruguayan	1	0.01
Venezuelan	3	0.02
Other Hispanic or Latino	124	1.01

Race*	Population	%
African-American/Black (106)	181	1.47
Not Hispanic (98)	169	1.37
Hispanic (8)	12	0.10
American Indian/Alaska Native (40)	132	1.07
Not Hispanic (24)	95	0.77
Hispanic (16)	37	0.30
Alaska Athabascan *(Ala. Nat.)* (0)	1	0.01
Aleut *(Alaska Native)* (1)	1	0.01
Apache (1)	2	0.02
Arapaho (0)	1	0.01
Blackfeet (1)	2	0.02
Cherokee (8)	29	0.24
Cheyenne (0)	2	0.02
Choctaw (0)	4	0.03
Comanche (2)	6	0.05
Creek (1)	2	0.02
Inupiat *(Alaska Native)* (0)	1	0.01
Iroquois (2)	6	0.05
Mexican American Ind. (7)	9	0.07
Navajo (0)	5	0.04
Osage (0)	2	0.02
Pueblo (1)	2	0.02
Puget Sound Salish (0)	2	0.02
Seminole (0)	1	0.01
Sioux (1)	2	0.02
Asian (437)	662	5.37
Not Hispanic (429)	631	5.12
Hispanic (8)	31	0.25
Bhutanese (4)	4	0.03
Cambodian (1)	2	0.02
Chinese, ex. Taiwanese (90)	168	1.36
Filipino (41)	97	0.79
Indian (38)	60	0.49
Indonesian (1)	2	0.02
Japanese (68)	121	0.98
Korean (136)	153	1.24
Malaysian (1)	3	0.02
Pakistani (0)	1	0.01
Taiwanese (5)	5	0.04
Thai (5)	14	0.11
Vietnamese (21)	34	0.28
Hawaii Native/Pacific Islander (26)	56	0.45
Not Hispanic (26)	51	0.41
Hispanic (0)	5	0.04
Fijian (17)	18	0.15
Guamanian/Chamorro (0)	4	0.03
Native Hawaiian (6)	22	0.18
Samoan (1)	3	0.02
White (11,134)	11,530	93.47
Not Hispanic (10,663)	10,978	88.99
Hispanic (471)	552	4.47

San Bernardino

Place Type: City
County: San Bernardino
Population: 209,924†

Ancestry‡	Population	%
African, Sub-Saharan (815)	955	0.46
African (517)	625	0.30
Cape Verdean (30)	30	0.01
Ethiopian (22)	22	0.01
Ghanaian (56)	56	0.03
Nigerian (148)	148	0.07
South African (5)	5	<0.01
Ugandan (24)	24	0.01
Other Sub-Saharan African (13)	45	0.02
American (2,621)	2,621	1.25
Arab (1,577)	3,403	1.63
Arab (472)	574	0.27
Egyptian (46)	46	0.02
Iraqi (45)	114	0.05
Jordanian (111)	250	0.12
Lebanese (389)	1,107	0.53
Palestinian (70)	670	0.32
Syrian (0)	71	0.03
Other Arab (444)	571	0.27
Armenian (22)	22	0.01
Assyrian/Chaldean/Syriac (38)	51	0.02
Australian (5)	5	<0.01
Austrian (59)	144	0.07
Basque (0)	48	0.02
Belgian (8)	113	0.05
Brazilian (38)	68	0.03
British (93)	237	0.11
Bulgarian (0)	13	0.01
Canadian (109)	199	0.10
Croatian (20)	48	0.02
Czech (55)	166	0.08
Czechoslovakian (13)	47	0.02
Danish (34)	297	0.14
Dutch (305)	984	0.47
Eastern European (35)	35	0.02
English (1,914)	6,889	3.29
Estonian (17)	17	0.01
European (813)	1,029	0.49
Finnish (23)	54	0.03
French, ex. Basque (463)	2,526	1.21
French Canadian (197)	436	0.21
German (3,435)	10,589	5.06
Greek (48)	376	0.18
Guyanese (15)	29	0.01
Hungarian (58)	189	0.09
Icelander (0)	9	<0.01
Iranian (49)	135	0.06
Irish (2,295)	8,158	3.90
Italian (893)	3,379	1.62
Latvian (39)	39	0.02
Lithuanian (0)	49	0.02
Luxemburger (0)	10	<0.01
Northern European (128)	128	0.06
Norwegian (286)	861	0.41
Pennsylvania German (11)	11	0.01
Polish (339)	1,174	0.56
Portuguese (137)	423	0.20
Romanian (63)	63	0.03
Russian (376)	834	0.40
Scandinavian (29)	82	0.04
Scotch-Irish (399)	1,361	0.65
Scottish (386)	1,478	0.71
Slavic (0)	6	<0.01
Slovak (0)	32	0.02
Slovene (44)	94	0.04
Swedish (299)	850	0.41
Swiss (8)	137	0.07
Turkish (37)	80	0.04
Ukrainian (34)	143	0.07

*Notes: † The Census 2010 population figure is used to calculate the percentages in the Hispanic Origin and Race categories. Ancestry percentages are based on the 2006-2010 American Community Survey population (not shown); ‡ Numbers in parentheses indicate the number of people reporting a single ancestry; * Numbers in parentheses indicate the number of persons reporting this race alone, not in combination with any other race; Please refer to the Explanation of Data for more information.*

Welsh (126)	284	0.14
West Indian, ex. Hispanic (150)	213	0.10
Belizean (72)	72	0.03
Jamaican (78)	126	0.06
U.S. Virgin Islander (0)	15	0.01
Yugoslavian (19)	19	0.01

Hispanic Origin	Population	%
Hispanic or Latino (of any race)	125,994	60.02
Central American, ex. Mexican	5,616	2.68
Costa Rican	159	0.08
Guatemalan	1,509	0.72
Honduran	528	0.25
Nicaraguan	559	0.27
Panamanian	152	0.07
Salvadoran	2,641	1.26
Other Central American	68	0.03
Cuban	412	0.20
Dominican Republic	60	0.03
Mexican	109,448	52.14
Puerto Rican	1,495	0.71
South American	764	0.36
Argentinean	132	0.06
Bolivian	20	0.01
Chilean	41	0.02
Colombian	203	0.10
Ecuadorian	106	0.05
Peruvian	205	0.10
Uruguayan	8	<0.01
Venezuelan	36	0.02
Other South American	13	0.01
Other Hispanic or Latino	8,199	3.91

Race*	Population	%
African-American/Black (31,582)	35,348	16.84
Not Hispanic (29,897)	32,292	15.38
Hispanic (1,685)	3,056	1.46
American Indian/Alaska Native (2,822)	4,997	2.38
Not Hispanic (867)	1,993	0.95
Hispanic (1,955)	3,004	1.43
Alaska Athabascan *(Ala. Nat.)* (5)	7	<0.01
Aleut *(Alaska Native)* (5)	11	0.01
Apache (107)	254	0.12
Arapaho (0)	5	<0.01
Blackfeet (26)	112	0.05
Canadian/French Am. Ind. (3)	12	0.01
Central American Ind. (10)	14	0.01
Cherokee (151)	512	0.24
Cheyenne (12)	14	0.01
Chickasaw (0)	13	0.01
Chippewa (25)	34	0.02
Choctaw (28)	146	0.07
Colville (1)	2	<0.01
Comanche (18)	27	0.01
Cree (0)	7	<0.01
Creek (26)	76	0.04
Crow (0)	7	<0.01
Delaware (2)	3	<0.01
Hopi (19)	27	0.01
Inupiat *(Alaska Native)* (3)	7	<0.01
Iroquois (12)	28	0.01
Lumbee (1)	2	<0.01
Menominee (1)	1	<0.01
Mexican American Ind. (372)	540	0.26
Navajo (93)	165	0.08
Osage (4)	14	0.01
Ottawa (2)	3	<0.01
Paiute (8)	20	0.01
Pima (18)	27	0.01
Potawatomi (18)	22	0.01
Pueblo (46)	61	0.03
Puget Sound Salish (1)	1	<0.01
Seminole (2)	10	<0.01
Shoshone (9)	10	<0.01
Sioux (58)	92	0.04
South American Ind. (7)	23	0.01
Spanish American Ind. (19)	25	0.01
Tlingit-Haida *(Alaska Native)* (4)	5	<0.01
Tohono O'Odham (3)	14	0.01
Ute (0)	10	<0.01
Yaqui (63)	108	0.05
Yuman (15)	27	0.01
Asian (8,454)	10,503	5.00
Not Hispanic (8,027)	9,389	4.47
Hispanic (427)	1,114	0.53
Bangladeshi (90)	114	0.05
Burmese (10)	15	0.01
Cambodian (852)	1,014	0.48
Chinese, ex. Taiwanese (642)	968	0.46
Filipino (2,495)	3,260	1.55
Hmong (41)	41	0.02
Indian (584)	786	0.37
Indonesian (650)	769	0.37
Japanese (271)	667	0.32
Korean (429)	578	0.28
Laotian (208)	260	0.12
Nepalese (10)	10	<0.01
Pakistani (103)	134	0.06
Sri Lankan (26)	26	0.01
Taiwanese (47)	57	0.03
Thai (231)	286	0.14
Vietnamese (1,221)	1,397	0.67
Hawaii Native/Pacific Islander (839)	1,497	0.71
Not Hispanic (704)	1,120	0.53
Hispanic (135)	377	0.18
Fijian (35)	51	0.02
Guamanian/Chamorro (130)	186	0.09
Marshallese (15)	16	0.01
Native Hawaiian (107)	303	0.14
Samoan (388)	594	0.28
Tongan (82)	151	0.07
White (95,734)	103,895	49.49
Not Hispanic (39,977)	43,018	20.49
Hispanic (55,757)	60,877	29.00

San Bruno

Place Type: City
County: San Mateo
Population: 41,114†

Ancestry‡	Population	%
African, Sub-Saharan (5)	54	0.13
African (0)	49	0.12
Nigerian (5)	5	0.01
Albanian (0)	10	0.02
American (752)	752	1.87
Arab (953)	1,085	2.70
Arab (255)	286	0.71
Egyptian (30)	30	0.07
Jordanian (48)	48	0.12
Lebanese (21)	41	0.10
Palestinian (417)	471	1.17
Syrian (11)	28	0.07
Other Arab (171)	181	0.45
Armenian (68)	135	0.34
Assyrian/Chaldean/Syriac (22)	22	0.05
Australian (15)	15	0.04
Austrian (0)	44	0.11
Basque (0)	94	0.23
Belgian (12)	26	0.06
Brazilian (359)	438	1.09
British (22)	75	0.19
Canadian (19)	46	0.11
Carpatho Rusyn (0)	18	0.04
Croatian (90)	168	0.42
Cypriot (0)	10	0.02
Czech (0)	65	0.16
Czechoslovakian (0)	33	0.08
Danish (0)	107	0.27
Dutch (7)	336	0.84
English (344)	1,774	4.41
European (321)	430	1.07
Finnish (35)	53	0.13
French, ex. Basque (156)	949	2.36
French Canadian (43)	93	0.23
German (540)	2,475	6.15
Greek (157)	250	0.62
Hungarian (60)	206	0.51
Iranian (55)	55	0.14
Irish (757)	3,082	7.66
Israeli (0)	54	0.13
Italian (1,191)	3,329	8.27
Latvian (8)	8	0.02
Lithuanian (0)	37	0.09
Maltese (227)	275	0.68
New Zealander (0)	36	0.09
Northern European (59)	59	0.15
Norwegian (106)	236	0.59
Polish (137)	381	0.95
Portuguese (100)	314	0.78
Romanian (0)	12	0.03
Russian (605)	891	2.21
Scandinavian (11)	63	0.16
Scotch-Irish (54)	401	1.00
Scottish (109)	323	0.80
Slovak (0)	23	0.06
Swedish (106)	397	0.99
Swiss (80)	193	0.48
Ukrainian (89)	107	0.27
Welsh (22)	210	0.52
West Indian, ex. Hispanic (22)	45	0.11
British West Indian (0)	23	0.06
Jamaican (22)	22	0.05
Yugoslavian (0)	34	0.08

Hispanic Origin	Population	%
Hispanic or Latino (of any race)	12,016	29.23
Central American, ex. Mexican	2,800	6.81
Costa Rican	21	0.05
Guatemalan	341	0.83
Honduran	114	0.28
Nicaraguan	824	2.00
Panamanian	31	0.08
Salvadoran	1,418	3.45
Other Central American	51	0.12
Cuban	74	0.18
Dominican Republic	10	0.02
Mexican	6,990	17.00
Puerto Rican	369	0.90
South American	564	1.37
Argentinean	39	0.09
Bolivian	30	0.07
Chilean	45	0.11
Colombian	67	0.16
Ecuadorian	37	0.09
Paraguayan	3	0.01
Peruvian	308	0.75
Uruguayan	4	0.01
Venezuelan	12	0.03
Other South American	19	0.05
Other Hispanic or Latino	1,209	2.94

Race*	Population	%
African-American/Black (942)	1,315	3.20
Not Hispanic (841)	1,085	2.64
Hispanic (101)	230	0.56
American Indian/Alaska Native (246)	601	1.46
Not Hispanic (89)	280	0.68
Hispanic (157)	321	0.78
Alaska Athabascan *(Ala. Nat.)* (3)	5	0.01
Aleut *(Alaska Native)* (0)	7	0.02
Apache (6)	22	0.05
Blackfeet (0)	24	0.06
Central American Ind. (2)	4	0.01
Cherokee (8)	53	0.13
Cheyenne (0)	1	<0.01
Chickasaw (1)	4	0.01
Chippewa (2)	5	0.01
Choctaw (10)	19	0.05
Comanche (3)	3	0.01
Creek (0)	1	<0.01
Iroquois (1)	4	0.01
Kiowa (0)	1	<0.01
Lumbee (2)	2	<0.01
Mexican American Ind. (28)	67	0.16
Navajo (2)	10	0.02
Ottawa (0)	2	<0.01
Paiute (2)	2	<0.01
Pueblo (0)	4	0.01

*Notes: † The Census 2010 population figure is used to calculate the percentages in the Hispanic Origin and Race categories. Ancestry percentages are based on the 2006-2010 American Community Survey population (not shown); ‡ Numbers in parentheses indicate the number of people reporting a single ancestry; * Numbers in parentheses indicate the number of persons reporting this race alone, not in combination with any other race; Please refer to the Explanation of Data for more information.*

Seminole (0)	4	0.01
Shoshone (1)	1	<0.01
Sioux (5)	12	0.03
South American Ind. (2)	7	0.02
Spanish American Ind. (11)	17	0.04
Tohono O'Odham (1)	9	0.02
Ute (0)	3	0.01
Yaqui (1)	8	0.02
Asian (10,423)	11,867	28.86
Not Hispanic (10,228)	11,349	27.60
Hispanic (195)	518	1.26
Burmese (35)	51	0.12
Cambodian (20)	24	0.06
Chinese, ex. Taiwanese (3,190)	3,688	8.97
Filipino (4,740)	5,548	13.49
Hmong (2)	2	<0.01
Indian (787)	1,037	2.52
Indonesian (34)	66	0.16
Japanese (409)	672	1.63
Korean (435)	517	1.26
Laotian (9)	11	0.03
Malaysian (3)	3	0.01
Nepalese (19)	23	0.06
Pakistani (36)	38	0.09
Sri Lankan (3)	4	0.01
Taiwanese (49)	59	0.14
Thai (64)	83	0.20
Vietnamese (185)	256	0.62
Hawaii Native/Pacific Islander (1,377)	1,934	4.70
Not Hispanic (1,342)	1,792	4.36
Hispanic (35)	142	0.35
Fijian (364)	441	1.07
Guamanian/Chamorro (19)	38	0.09
Native Hawaiian (42)	184	0.45
Samoan (247)	403	0.98
Tongan (529)	612	1.49
White (20,350)	22,329	54.31
Not Hispanic (14,781)	15,865	38.59
Hispanic (5,569)	6,464	15.72

San Buenaventura (Ventura)

Place Type: City
County: Ventura
Population: 106,433†

Ancestry‡	Population	%
African, Sub-Saharan (66)	98	0.09
African (37)	56	0.05
Kenyan (13)	13	0.01
South African (0)	13	0.01
Other Sub-Saharan African (16)	16	0.02
Albanian (10)	10	0.01
American (2,859)	2,859	2.72
Arab (428)	697	0.66
Arab (241)	271	0.26
Egyptian (104)	115	0.11
Lebanese (43)	227	0.22
Syrian (0)	28	0.03
Other Arab (40)	56	0.05
Armenian (122)	152	0.14
Australian (11)	68	0.06
Austrian (65)	458	0.44
Basque (24)	67	0.06
Belgian (65)	100	0.10
Brazilian (27)	39	0.04
British (208)	369	0.35
Canadian (152)	410	0.39
Celtic (0)	12	0.01
Croatian (0)	43	0.04
Czech (61)	389	0.37
Czechoslovakian (36)	36	0.03
Danish (379)	1,189	1.13
Dutch (314)	1,869	1.78
Eastern European (159)	159	0.15
English (3,493)	13,161	12.51
Estonian (0)	10	0.01
European (1,511)	1,777	1.69
Finnish (112)	187	0.18
French, ex. Basque (511)	3,912	3.72
French Canadian (283)	734	0.70
German (3,897)	17,580	16.71
Greek (194)	609	0.58
Hungarian (227)	786	0.75
Icelander (9)	24	0.02
Iranian (157)	317	0.30
Irish (2,917)	12,972	12.33
Israeli (39)	49	0.05
Italian (1,633)	5,364	5.10
Latvian (0)	34	0.03
Lithuanian (41)	197	0.19
Northern European (91)	91	0.09
Norwegian (593)	1,826	1.74
Pennsylvania German (41)	60	0.06
Polish (694)	2,459	2.34
Portuguese (274)	728	0.69
Romanian (41)	278	0.26
Russian (539)	1,625	1.54
Scandinavian (38)	261	0.25
Scotch-Irish (827)	2,369	2.25
Scottish (773)	2,873	2.73
Slavic (27)	153	0.15
Slovak (78)	98	0.09
Swedish (372)	2,104	2.00
Swiss (80)	637	0.61
Turkish (84)	150	0.14
Ukrainian (161)	303	0.29
Welsh (265)	968	0.92
West Indian, ex. Hispanic (47)	130	0.12
Dutch West Indian (0)	75	0.07
Haitian (30)	30	0.03
Jamaican (17)	17	0.02
West Indian (0)	8	0.01
Yugoslavian (120)	247	0.23

Hispanic Origin	Population	%
Hispanic or Latino (of any race)	33,874	31.83
Central American, ex. Mexican	758	0.71
Costa Rican	44	0.04
Guatemalan	277	0.26
Honduran	36	0.03
Nicaraguan	86	0.08
Panamanian	44	0.04
Salvadoran	262	0.25
Other Central American	9	0.01
Cuban	144	0.14
Dominican Republic	24	0.02
Mexican	29,837	28.03
Puerto Rican	396	0.37
South American	674	0.63
Argentinean	111	0.10
Bolivian	28	0.03
Chilean	94	0.09
Colombian	149	0.14
Ecuadorian	40	0.04
Paraguayan	1	<0.01
Peruvian	183	0.17
Uruguayan	19	0.02
Venezuelan	37	0.03
Other South American	12	0.01
Other Hispanic or Latino	2,041	1.92

Race*	Population	%
African-American/Black (1,724)	2,660	2.50
Not Hispanic (1,466)	2,132	2.00
Hispanic (258)	528	0.50
American Indian/Alaska Native (1,287)	2,858	2.69
Not Hispanic (545)	1,512	1.42
Hispanic (742)	1,346	1.26
Alaska Athabascan *(Ala. Nat.)* (1)	1	<0.01
Aleut *(Alaska Native)* (3)	3	<0.01
Apache (52)	131	0.12
Arapaho (0)	1	<0.01
Blackfeet (4)	61	0.06
Canadian/French Am. Ind. (1)	8	0.01
Central American Ind. (2)	6	0.01
Cherokee (128)	536	0.50
Cheyenne (1)	3	<0.01
Chickasaw (9)	27	0.03
Chippewa (13)	33	0.03
Choctaw (38)	155	0.15
Comanche (12)	21	0.02
Cree (0)	2	<0.01
Creek (8)	21	0.02
Crow (0)	7	0.01
Delaware (1)	5	<0.01
Hopi (2)	17	0.02
Inupiat *(Alaska Native)* (1)	1	<0.01
Iroquois (9)	32	0.03
Kiowa (1)	3	<0.01
Lumbee (0)	2	<0.01
Menominee (1)	5	<0.01
Mexican American Ind. (123)	178	0.17
Navajo (16)	53	0.05
Osage (5)	14	0.01
Ottawa (0)	1	<0.01
Paiute (6)	11	0.01
Pima (6)	10	0.01
Potawatomi (7)	19	0.02
Pueblo (17)	27	0.03
Seminole (1)	4	<0.01
Shoshone (4)	5	<0.01
Sioux (25)	51	0.05
South American Ind. (7)	14	0.01
Spanish American Ind. (2)	7	0.01
Tlingit-Haida *(Alaska Native)* (4)	7	0.01
Tohono O'Odham (10)	17	0.02
Ute (1)	4	<0.01
Yakama (2)	2	<0.01
Yaqui (19)	52	0.05
Yuman (2)	2	<0.01
Yup'ik *(Alaska Native)* (0)	1	<0.01
Asian (3,663)	5,321	5.00
Not Hispanic (3,523)	4,769	4.48
Hispanic (140)	552	0.52
Bangladeshi (19)	25	0.02
Burmese (0)	7	0.01
Cambodian (86)	99	0.09
Chinese, ex. Taiwanese (560)	908	0.85
Filipino (930)	1,551	1.46
Hmong (2)	3	<0.01
Indian (467)	576	0.54
Indonesian (21)	57	0.05
Japanese (395)	873	0.82
Korean (450)	550	0.52
Laotian (52)	58	0.05
Malaysian (9)	11	0.01
Nepalese (23)	27	0.03
Pakistani (45)	48	0.05
Sri Lankan (50)	55	0.05
Taiwanese (35)	41	0.04
Thai (70)	97	0.09
Vietnamese (281)	339	0.32
Hawaii Native/Pacific Islander (206)	548	0.51
Not Hispanic (167)	389	0.37
Hispanic (39)	159	0.15
Fijian (4)	4	<0.01
Guamanian/Chamorro (35)	80	0.08
Native Hawaiian (80)	254	0.24
Samoan (36)	96	0.09
Tongan (3)	11	0.01
White (81,553)	86,489	81.26
Not Hispanic (63,879)	66,463	62.45
Hispanic (17,674)	20,026	18.82

San Carlos

Place Type: City
County: San Mateo
Population: 28,406†

Ancestry‡	Population	%
Afghan (92)	92	0.33
African, Sub-Saharan (23)	59	0.21
African (0)	26	0.09
Ghanaian (12)	12	0.04
South African (11)	21	0.08
Albanian (0)	23	0.08

*Notes: † The Census 2010 population figure is used to calculate the percentages in the Hispanic Origin and Race categories. Ancestry percentages are based on the 2006-2010 American Community Survey population (not shown); ‡ Numbers in parentheses indicate the number of people reporting a single ancestry; * Numbers in parentheses indicate the number of persons reporting this race alone, not in combination with any other race; Please refer to the Explanation of Data for more information.*

SECTION TWO

Alsatian (0)	23	0.08
American (580)	580	2.08
Arab (288)	382	1.37
Arab (14)	22	0.08
Egyptian (22)	46	0.17
Jordanian (8)	8	0.03
Lebanese (25)	35	0.13
Palestinian (26)	53	0.19
Syrian (38)	63	0.23
Other Arab (155)	155	0.56
Armenian (109)	139	0.50
Assyrian/Chaldean/Syriac (18)	18	0.06
Australian (37)	54	0.19
Austrian (66)	141	0.51
Basque (19)	51	0.18
Belgian (23)	34	0.12
Brazilian (93)	112	0.40
British (107)	239	0.86
Bulgarian (0)	12	0.04
Canadian (76)	167	0.60
Croatian (24)	24	0.09
Czech (56)	151	0.54
Czechoslovakian (0)	23	0.08
Danish (149)	511	1.84
Dutch (146)	498	1.79
Eastern European (205)	217	0.78
English (755)	3,648	13.11
European (891)	1,204	4.33
Finnish (33)	81	0.29
French, ex. Basque (199)	918	3.30
French Canadian (55)	130	0.47
German (1,246)	5,263	18.91
Greek (342)	671	2.41
Hungarian (81)	191	0.69
Iranian (283)	377	1.35
Irish (823)	4,284	15.39
Israeli (0)	14	0.05
Italian (1,031)	2,895	10.40
Latvian (26)	26	0.09
Lithuanian (16)	107	0.38
Maltese (0)	73	0.26
Northern European (20)	20	0.07
Norwegian (141)	415	1.49
Pennsylvania German (8)	8	0.03
Polish (209)	750	2.69
Portuguese (87)	429	1.54
Romanian (110)	149	0.54
Russian (523)	854	3.07
Scandinavian (47)	120	0.43
Scotch-Irish (96)	350	1.26
Scottish (137)	1,011	3.63
Serbian (21)	55	0.20
Slovak (9)	20	0.07
Swedish (181)	934	3.36
Swiss (122)	228	0.82
Turkish (80)	80	0.29
Ukrainian (7)	49	0.18
Welsh (0)	256	0.92
West Indian, ex. Hispanic (11)	33	0.12
Jamaican (11)	33	0.12
Yugoslavian (37)	77	0.28

Hispanic Origin	Population	%
Hispanic or Latino (of any race)	2,855	10.05
Central American, ex. Mexican	532	1.87
Costa Rican	25	0.09
Guatemalan	108	0.38
Honduran	11	0.04
Nicaraguan	130	0.46
Panamanian	17	0.06
Salvadoran	233	0.82
Other Central American	8	0.03
Cuban	56	0.20
Dominican Republic	4	0.01
Mexican	1,320	4.65
Puerto Rican	111	0.39
South American	403	1.42
Argentinean	45	0.16
Bolivian	31	0.11
Chilean	34	0.12
Colombian	72	0.25
Ecuadorian	16	0.06
Paraguayan	1	<0.01
Peruvian	180	0.63
Uruguayan	5	0.02
Venezuelan	13	0.05
Other South American	6	0.02
Other Hispanic or Latino	429	1.51

Race*	Population	%
African-American/Black (233)	394	1.39
Not Hispanic (214)	346	1.22
Hispanic (19)	48	0.17
American Indian/Alaska Native (65)	243	0.86
Not Hispanic (32)	161	0.57
Hispanic (33)	82	0.29
Apache (4)	8	0.03
Blackfeet (0)	8	0.03
Central American Ind. (1)	4	0.01
Cherokee (5)	47	0.17
Chippewa (1)	4	0.01
Choctaw (0)	11	0.04
Comanche (0)	4	0.01
Creek (1)	3	0.01
Hopi (0)	1	<0.01
Inupiat *(Alaska Native)* (1)	4	0.01
Iroquois (0)	7	0.02
Kiowa (1)	1	<0.01
Mexican American Ind. (5)	7	0.02
Navajo (0)	2	0.01
Osage (1)	4	0.01
Pima (1)	2	0.01
Sioux (3)	11	0.04
South American Ind. (7)	10	0.04
Spanish American Ind. (2)	3	0.01
Tlingit-Haida *(Alaska Native)* (1)	2	0.01
Tsimshian *(Alaska Native)* (1)	1	<0.01
Ute (0)	3	0.01
Asian (3,267)	4,221	14.86
Not Hispanic (3,234)	4,086	14.38
Hispanic (33)	135	0.48
Bangladeshi (8)	13	0.05
Burmese (14)	17	0.06
Cambodian (10)	12	0.04
Chinese, ex. Taiwanese (1,297)	1,768	6.22
Filipino (482)	747	2.63
Hmong (5)	5	0.02
Indian (504)	581	2.05
Indonesian (7)	24	0.08
Japanese (320)	552	1.94
Korean (172)	260	0.92
Laotian (4)	7	0.02
Malaysian (3)	5	0.02
Nepalese (14)	14	0.05
Pakistani (24)	31	0.11
Sri Lankan (6)	7	0.02
Taiwanese (84)	118	0.42
Thai (41)	58	0.20
Vietnamese (89)	130	0.46
Hawaii Native/Pacific Islander (70)	157	0.55
Not Hispanic (67)	131	0.46
Hispanic (3)	26	0.09
Fijian (5)	6	0.02
Guamanian/Chamorro (4)	18	0.06
Native Hawaiian (11)	49	0.17
Samoan (8)	11	0.04
Tongan (32)	42	0.15
White (22,497)	23,829	83.89
Not Hispanic (20,786)	21,830	76.85
Hispanic (1,711)	1,999	7.04

San Clemente

Place Type: City
County: Orange
Population: 63,522†

Ancestry‡	Population	%
Afghan (44)	44	0.07
African, Sub-Saharan (36)	96	0.16
African (36)	57	0.09
Other Sub-Saharan African (0)	39	0.06
American (1,902)	1,902	3.13
Arab (250)	308	0.51
Arab (25)	25	0.04
Egyptian (92)	101	0.17
Iraqi (0)	9	0.01
Jordanian (27)	36	0.06
Lebanese (73)	97	0.16
Syrian (15)	15	0.02
Other Arab (18)	25	0.04
Armenian (161)	267	0.44
Assyrian/Chaldean/Syriac (13)	26	0.04
Australian (42)	147	0.24
Austrian (48)	177	0.29
Basque (0)	18	0.03
Belgian (118)	278	0.46
Brazilian (169)	182	0.30
British (313)	433	0.71
Bulgarian (0)	8	0.01
Canadian (143)	267	0.44
Celtic (22)	22	0.04
Croatian (59)	172	0.28
Czech (21)	140	0.23
Czechoslovakian (47)	61	0.10
Danish (106)	633	1.04
Dutch (492)	1,526	2.51
Eastern European (46)	46	0.08
English (3,284)	8,898	14.64
European (948)	1,142	1.88
Finnish (40)	107	0.18
French, ex. Basque (413)	2,064	3.40
French Canadian (184)	343	0.56
German (3,203)	11,693	19.24
German Russian (0)	8	0.01
Greek (91)	275	0.45
Hungarian (185)	408	0.67
Icelander (0)	14	0.02
Iranian (367)	465	0.77
Irish (2,611)	9,417	15.50
Israeli (19)	19	0.03
Italian (1,774)	5,107	8.40
Latvian (0)	11	0.02
Lithuanian (15)	120	0.20
Luxemburger (0)	12	0.02
Macedonian (14)	50	0.08
Maltese (0)	6	0.01
New Zealander (0)	8	0.01
Northern European (73)	86	0.14
Norwegian (413)	1,175	1.93
Polish (654)	1,824	3.00
Portuguese (118)	225	0.37
Romanian (134)	206	0.34
Russian (524)	1,447	2.38
Scandinavian (126)	256	0.42
Scotch-Irish (671)	1,276	2.10
Scottish (889)	2,113	3.48
Serbian (20)	80	0.13
Slavic (129)	160	0.26
Slovak (39)	85	0.14
Swedish (581)	1,632	2.69
Swiss (48)	156	0.26
Turkish (28)	114	0.19
Ukrainian (13)	79	0.13
Welsh (94)	562	0.92
Yugoslavian (33)	75	0.12

Hispanic Origin	Population	%
Hispanic or Latino (of any race)	10,702	16.85
Central American, ex. Mexican	298	0.47
Costa Rican	34	0.05
Guatemalan	82	0.13
Honduran	16	0.03
Nicaraguan	31	0.05
Panamanian	23	0.04
Salvadoran	110	0.17
Other Central American	2	<0.01
Cuban	148	0.23
Dominican Republic	17	0.03
Mexican	8,471	13.34

*Notes: † The Census 2010 population figure is used to calculate the percentages in the Hispanic Origin and Race categories. Ancestry percentages are based on the 2006-2010 American Community Survey population (not shown); ‡ Numbers in parentheses indicate the number of people reporting a single ancestry; * Numbers in parentheses indicate the number of persons reporting this race alone, not in combination with any other race; Please refer to the Explanation of Data for more information.*

Puerto Rican	260	0.41
South American	606	0.95
Argentinean	162	0.26
Bolivian	24	0.04
Chilean	53	0.08
Colombian	108	0.17
Ecuadorian	62	0.10
Paraguayan	4	0.01
Peruvian	140	0.22
Uruguayan	7	0.01
Venezuelan	40	0.06
Other South American	6	0.01
Other Hispanic or Latino	902	1.42

Race*	Population	%
African-American/Black (411)	689	1.08
Not Hispanic (349)	586	0.92
Hispanic (62)	103	0.16
American Indian/Alaska Native (363)	829	1.31
Not Hispanic (193)	545	0.86
Hispanic (170)	284	0.45
Alaska Athabascan *(Ala. Nat.)* (2)	2	<0.01
Apache (9)	23	0.04
Blackfeet (3)	20	0.03
Canadian/French Am. Ind. (1)	2	<0.01
Central American Ind. (0)	1	<0.01
Cherokee (34)	135	0.21
Chickasaw (2)	7	0.01
Chippewa (4)	13	0.02
Choctaw (13)	35	0.06
Colville (1)	1	<0.01
Comanche (0)	5	0.01
Creek (1)	7	0.01
Delaware (1)	5	0.01
Inupiat *(Alaska Native)* (1)	1	<0.01
Iroquois (3)	18	0.03
Kiowa (3)	3	<0.01
Lumbee (0)	8	0.01
Mexican American Ind. (18)	28	0.04
Navajo (9)	18	0.03
Osage (1)	7	0.01
Ottawa (1)	1	<0.01
Potawatomi (0)	2	<0.01
Pueblo (1)	9	0.01
Puget Sound Salish (1)	1	<0.01
Seminole (0)	10	0.02
Shoshone (3)	3	<0.01
Sioux (12)	18	0.03
South American Ind. (2)	5	0.01
Spanish American Ind. (2)	7	0.01
Tlingit-Haida *(Alaska Native)* (0)	1	<0.01
Tohono O'Odham (1)	3	<0.01
Ute (0)	2	<0.01
Yaqui (3)	8	0.01
Yuman (2)	3	<0.01
Asian (2,333)	3,461	5.45
Not Hispanic (2,269)	3,265	5.14
Hispanic (64)	196	0.31
Bangladeshi (14)	15	0.02
Burmese (1)	2	<0.01
Cambodian (16)	22	0.03
Chinese, ex. Taiwanese (391)	644	1.01
Filipino (550)	887	1.40
Indian (278)	338	0.53
Indonesian (10)	51	0.08
Japanese (318)	618	0.97
Korean (267)	383	0.60
Laotian (4)	7	0.01
Malaysian (3)	3	<0.01
Nepalese (4)	4	0.01
Pakistani (17)	23	0.04
Sri Lankan (3)	3	<0.01
Taiwanese (31)	41	0.06
Thai (62)	92	0.14
Vietnamese (212)	285	0.45
Hawaii Native/Pacific Islander (90)	263	0.41
Not Hispanic (78)	222	0.35
Hispanic (12)	41	0.06
Fijian (6)	8	0.01
Guamanian/Chamorro (9)	24	0.04
Marshallese (1)	2	<0.01
Native Hawaiian (45)	134	0.21
Samoan (12)	30	0.05
Tongan (0)	8	0.01
White (54,605)	56,749	89.34
Not Hispanic (48,254)	49,759	78.33
Hispanic (6,351)	6,990	11.00

San Diego Country Estates

Place Type: CDP
County: San Diego
Population: 10,109†

Ancestry‡	Population	%
American (491)	491	4.61
Austrian (0)	30	0.28
British (67)	89	0.84
Cajun (12)	12	0.11
Czech (0)	37	0.35
Dutch (71)	213	2.00
English (816)	2,279	21.39
European (253)	253	2.37
French, ex. Basque (31)	430	4.03
French Canadian (44)	203	1.90
German (720)	1,811	16.99
Greek (0)	13	0.12
Hungarian (27)	90	0.84
Iranian (0)	60	0.56
Irish (408)	1,618	15.18
Italian (104)	620	5.82
Lithuanian (13)	30	0.28
Northern European (56)	56	0.53
Norwegian (180)	391	3.67
Polish (53)	251	2.36
Portuguese (114)	191	1.79
Romanian (7)	20	0.19
Russian (23)	124	1.16
Scotch-Irish (7)	107	1.00
Scottish (50)	297	2.79
Swedish (169)	495	4.64
Swiss (0)	89	0.84
Ukrainian (0)	35	0.33
Welsh (88)	563	5.28

Hispanic Origin	Population	%
Hispanic or Latino (of any race)	1,126	11.14
Central American, ex. Mexican	22	0.22
Costa Rican	3	0.03
Honduran	1	0.01
Nicaraguan	5	0.05
Panamanian	3	0.03
Salvadoran	10	0.10
Cuban	11	0.11
Dominican Republic	8	0.08
Mexican	890	8.80
Puerto Rican	47	0.46
South American	39	0.39
Argentinean	9	0.09
Chilean	2	0.02
Colombian	7	0.07
Ecuadorian	3	0.03
Peruvian	9	0.09
Uruguayan	8	0.08
Venezuelan	1	0.01
Other Hispanic or Latino	109	1.08

Race*	Population	%
African-American/Black (91)	147	1.45
Not Hispanic (83)	129	1.28
Hispanic (8)	18	0.18
American Indian/Alaska Native (90)	160	1.58
Not Hispanic (66)	122	1.21
Hispanic (24)	38	0.38
Apache (1)	4	0.04
Cherokee (8)	35	0.35
Chickasaw (1)	1	0.01
Chippewa (1)	2	0.02
Choctaw (8)	10	0.10
Comanche (2)	5	0.05
Iroquois (1)	4	0.04
Mexican American Ind. (1)	4	0.04
Navajo (2)	2	0.02
Osage (2)	2	0.02
Ottawa (1)	1	0.01
Pima (2)	2	0.02
Potawatomi (1)	1	0.01
Seminole (0)	1	0.01
Sioux (3)	3	0.03
South American Ind. (0)	1	0.01
Yaqui (0)	2	0.02
Asian (147)	307	3.04
Not Hispanic (133)	258	2.55
Hispanic (14)	49	0.48
Bangladeshi (1)	1	0.01
Cambodian (2)	4	0.04
Chinese, ex. Taiwanese (21)	51	0.50
Filipino (66)	132	1.31
Hmong (1)	1	0.01
Indian (6)	10	0.10
Indonesian (0)	5	0.05
Japanese (21)	74	0.73
Korean (5)	15	0.15
Laotian (2)	2	0.02
Pakistani (2)	8	0.08
Thai (8)	12	0.12
Vietnamese (2)	8	0.08
Hawaii Native/Pacific Islander (34)	73	0.72
Not Hispanic (27)	62	0.61
Hispanic (7)	11	0.11
Guamanian/Chamorro (14)	30	0.30
Native Hawaiian (9)	28	0.28
Samoan (2)	6	0.06
White (9,107)	9,444	93.42
Not Hispanic (8,415)	8,644	85.51
Hispanic (692)	800	7.91

San Diego

Place Type: City
County: San Diego
Population: 1,307,402†

Ancestry‡	Population	%
Afghan (1,808)	1,850	0.14
African, Sub-Saharan (12,871)	15,315	1.19
African (3,942)	5,572	0.43
Cape Verdean (217)	270	0.02
Ethiopian (1,688)	1,985	0.15
Ghanaian (79)	79	0.01
Kenyan (144)	160	0.01
Liberian (40)	40	<0.01
Nigerian (624)	658	0.05
Senegalese (0)	141	0.01
Somalian (4,076)	4,090	0.32
South African (671)	869	0.07
Sudanese (1,036)	1,036	0.08
Zimbabwean (39)	39	<0.01
Other Sub-Saharan African (315)	376	0.03
Albanian (98)	193	0.02
American (32,627)	32,627	2.54
Arab (6,874)	10,030	0.78
Arab (678)	944	0.07
Egyptian (342)	430	0.03
Iraqi (1,155)	1,390	0.11
Jordanian (152)	185	0.01
Lebanese (2,299)	3,545	0.28
Moroccan (540)	611	0.05
Palestinian (448)	828	0.06
Syrian (254)	762	0.06
Other Arab (1,006)	1,335	0.10
Armenian (2,071)	3,045	0.24
Assyrian/Chaldean/Syriac (234)	463	0.04
Australian (713)	1,114	0.09
Austrian (851)	3,861	0.30
Basque (178)	498	0.04
Belgian (536)	1,571	0.12
Brazilian (1,760)	2,350	0.18
British (3,433)	6,683	0.52
Bulgarian (359)	474	0.04

*Notes: † The Census 2010 population figure is used to calculate the percentages in the Hispanic Origin and Race categories. Ancestry percentages are based on the 2006-2010 American Community Survey population (not shown); ‡ Numbers in parentheses indicate the number of people reporting a single ancestry; * Numbers in parentheses indicate the number of persons reporting this race alone, not in combination with any other race; Please refer to the Explanation of Data for more information.*

Cajun (131)	217	0.02
Canadian (1,944)	3,425	0.27
Carpatho Rusyn (0)	12	<0.01
Celtic (109)	224	0.02
Croatian (424)	1,378	0.11
Cypriot (51)	51	<0.01
Czech (1,630)	5,144	0.40
Czechoslovakian (358)	1,044	0.08
Danish (1,455)	5,944	0.46
Dutch (3,510)	14,365	1.12
Eastern European (2,350)	2,599	0.20
English (24,452)	92,418	7.20
Estonian (60)	164	0.01
European (16,404)	19,955	1.56
Finnish (701)	2,374	0.19
French, ex. Basque (6,144)	32,028	2.50
French Canadian (2,164)	5,134	0.40
German (39,229)	140,941	10.99
German Russian (39)	53	<0.01
Greek (2,169)	5,154	0.40
Guyanese (173)	260	0.02
Hungarian (2,197)	6,397	0.50
Icelander (224)	408	0.03
Iranian (6,731)	7,595	0.59
Irish (28,310)	108,215	8.44
Israeli (782)	990	0.08
Italian (22,861)	61,669	4.81
Latvian (250)	596	0.05
Lithuanian (876)	2,852	0.22
Luxemburger (25)	130	0.01
Macedonian (25)	47	<0.01
Maltese (77)	146	0.01
New Zealander (142)	193	0.02
Northern European (1,318)	1,520	0.12
Norwegian (5,525)	16,955	1.32
Pennsylvania German (164)	308	0.02
Polish (8,465)	26,533	2.07
Portuguese (4,518)	9,505	0.74
Romanian (788)	2,000	0.16
Russian (8,529)	18,222	1.42
Scandinavian (1,432)	2,796	0.22
Scotch-Irish (6,291)	17,899	1.40
Scottish (6,292)	24,212	1.89
Serbian (564)	935	0.07
Slavic (248)	468	0.04
Slovak (466)	1,472	0.11
Slovene (203)	455	0.04
Soviet Union (25)	25	<0.01
Swedish (4,230)	17,467	1.36
Swiss (931)	4,165	0.32
Turkish (825)	1,280	0.10
Ukrainian (1,576)	3,425	0.27
Welsh (1,673)	8,167	0.64
West Indian, ex. Hispanic (1,820)	2,607	0.20
Bahamian (60)	74	0.01
Barbadian (31)	39	<0.01
Belizean (83)	122	0.01
Bermudan (46)	46	<0.01
British West Indian (101)	112	0.01
Dutch West Indian (51)	74	0.01
Haitian (355)	413	0.03
Jamaican (703)	1,036	0.08
Trinidadian/Tobagonian (144)	156	0.01
U.S. Virgin Islander (0)	27	<0.01
West Indian (212)	474	0.04
Other West Indian (34)	34	<0.01
Yugoslavian (585)	1,142	0.09

Hispanic Origin	Population	%
Hispanic or Latino (of any race)	376,020	28.76
Central American, ex. Mexican	9,188	0.70
Costa Rican	723	0.06
Guatemalan	2,696	0.21
Honduran	1,293	0.10
Nicaraguan	895	0.07
Panamanian	1,018	0.08
Salvadoran	2,415	0.18
Other Central American	148	0.01
Cuban	2,694	0.21
Dominican Republic	903	0.07
Mexican	325,812	24.92
Puerto Rican	8,220	0.63
South American	8,220	0.63
Argentinean	1,322	0.10
Bolivian	345	0.03
Chilean	876	0.07
Colombian	2,214	0.17
Ecuadorian	737	0.06
Paraguayan	52	<0.01
Peruvian	1,901	0.15
Uruguayan	141	0.01
Venezuelan	525	0.04
Other South American	107	0.01
Other Hispanic or Latino	20,983	1.60

Race*	Population	%
African-American/Black (87,949)	104,374	7.98
Not Hispanic (82,497)	94,818	7.25
Hispanic (5,452)	9,556	0.73
American Indian/Alaska Native (7,696)	17,865	1.37
Not Hispanic (3,545)	10,117	0.77
Hispanic (4,151)	7,748	0.59
Alaska Athabascan *(Ala. Nat.)* (19)	39	<0.01
Aleut *(Alaska Native)* (23)	51	<0.01
Apache (239)	616	0.05
Arapaho (5)	16	<0.01
Blackfeet (64)	426	0.03
Canadian/French Am. Ind. (22)	53	<0.01
Central American Ind. (27)	59	<0.01
Cherokee (456)	2,342	0.18
Cheyenne (13)	31	<0.01
Chickasaw (47)	141	0.01
Chippewa (124)	238	0.02
Choctaw (153)	487	0.04
Colville (1)	3	<0.01
Comanche (27)	79	0.01
Cree (11)	40	<0.01
Creek (49)	163	0.01
Crow (8)	20	<0.01
Delaware (10)	26	<0.01
Hopi (30)	57	<0.01
Houma (3)	12	<0.01
Inupiat *(Alaska Native)* (19)	41	<0.01
Iroquois (61)	183	0.01
Kiowa (7)	16	<0.01
Lumbee (20)	45	<0.01
Menominee (7)	19	<0.01
Mexican American Ind. (1,020)	1,561	0.12
Navajo (314)	532	0.04
Osage (21)	70	0.01
Ottawa (12)	22	<0.01
Paiute (29)	62	<0.01
Pima (24)	44	<0.01
Potawatomi (44)	80	0.01
Pueblo (93)	150	0.01
Puget Sound Salish (16)	32	<0.01
Seminole (28)	114	0.01
Shoshone (18)	51	<0.01
Sioux (138)	335	0.03
South American Ind. (31)	106	0.01
Spanish American Ind. (20)	51	<0.01
Tlingit-Haida *(Alaska Native)* (35)	70	0.01
Tohono O'Odham (27)	69	0.01
Tsimshian *(Alaska Native)* (3)	7	<0.01
Ute (13)	22	<0.01
Yakama (5)	12	<0.01
Yaqui (157)	310	0.02
Yuman (27)	48	<0.01
Yup'ik *(Alaska Native)* (15)	20	<0.01
Asian (207,944)	241,293	18.46
Not Hispanic (204,347)	232,029	17.75
Hispanic (3,597)	9,264	0.71
Bangladeshi (223)	254	0.02
Bhutanese (80)	81	0.01
Burmese (766)	824	0.06
Cambodian (3,922)	4,650	0.36
Chinese, ex. Taiwanese (32,525)	40,557	3.10
Filipino (76,738)	92,828	7.10
Hmong (1,081)	1,166	0.09
Indian (17,255)	19,096	1.46
Indonesian (470)	879	0.07
Japanese (9,625)	16,815	1.29
Korean (13,559)	15,883	1.21
Laotian (5,260)	6,058	0.46
Malaysian (103)	315	0.02
Nepalese (131)	146	0.01
Pakistani (919)	1,132	0.09
Sri Lankan (194)	248	0.02
Taiwanese (2,953)	3,400	0.26
Thai (1,367)	2,061	0.16
Vietnamese (33,149)	36,713	2.81
Hawaii Native/Pacific Islander (5,908)	11,945	0.91
Not Hispanic (5,178)	9,844	0.75
Hispanic (730)	2,101	0.16
Fijian (43)	79	0.01
Guamanian/Chamorro (2,301)	3,999	0.31
Marshallese (145)	164	0.01
Native Hawaiian (1,005)	3,194	0.24
Samoan (1,567)	2,490	0.19
Tongan (115)	180	0.01
White (769,971)	824,542	63.07
Not Hispanic (589,702)	625,399	47.84
Hispanic (180,269)	199,143	15.23

San Dimas

Place Type: City
County: Los Angeles
Population: 33,371†

Ancestry‡	Population	%
African, Sub-Saharan (51)	51	0.15
African (13)	13	0.04
Somalian (38)	38	0.11
American (1,806)	1,806	5.37
Arab (1,073)	1,194	3.55
Arab (488)	488	1.45
Egyptian (206)	206	0.61
Lebanese (292)	337	1.00
Syrian (47)	123	0.37
Other Arab (40)	40	0.12
Armenian (0)	29	0.09
Australian (11)	11	0.03
Austrian (10)	62	0.18
Belgian (0)	27	0.08
Brazilian (15)	45	0.13
British (52)	99	0.29
Canadian (95)	150	0.45
Croatian (9)	9	0.03
Czech (53)	224	0.67
Czechoslovakian (32)	46	0.14
Danish (37)	215	0.64
Dutch (61)	443	1.32
English (832)	2,950	8.77
European (435)	510	1.52
Finnish (38)	38	0.11
French, ex. Basque (100)	1,047	3.11
French Canadian (31)	62	0.18
German (1,255)	3,936	11.70
Greek (22)	173	0.51
Hungarian (0)	26	0.08
Iranian (446)	522	1.55
Irish (579)	2,925	8.70
Italian (662)	2,015	5.99
Latvian (0)	29	0.09
Lithuanian (0)	5	0.01
New Zealander (0)	45	0.13
Norwegian (226)	693	2.06
Polish (242)	703	2.09
Portuguese (56)	112	0.33
Romanian (0)	49	0.15
Russian (24)	208	0.62
Scandinavian (16)	16	0.05
Scotch-Irish (84)	338	1.00
Scottish (122)	606	1.80
Slavic (0)	17	0.05
Slovak (17)	31	0.09
Swedish (195)	689	2.05
Swiss (12)	114	0.34
Turkish (54)	54	0.16

*Notes: † The Census 2010 population figure is used to calculate the percentages in the Hispanic Origin and Race categories. Ancestry percentages are based on the 2006-2010 American Community Survey population (not shown); ‡ Numbers in parentheses indicate the number of people reporting a single ancestry; * Numbers in parentheses indicate the number of persons reporting this race alone, not in combination with any other race; Please refer to the Explanation of Data for more information.*

Ukrainian (16)	16	0.05
Welsh (17)	160	0.48
West Indian, ex. Hispanic (27)	68	0.20
Haitian (0)	12	0.04
Jamaican (9)	23	0.07
West Indian (0)	15	0.04
Other West Indian (18)	18	0.05
Yugoslavian (15)	15	0.04

Hispanic Origin	Population	%
Hispanic or Latino (of any race)	10,491	31.44
Central American, ex. Mexican	587	1.76
Costa Rican	36	0.11
Guatemalan	161	0.48
Honduran	30	0.09
Nicaraguan	93	0.28
Panamanian	15	0.04
Salvadoran	245	0.73
Other Central American	7	0.02
Cuban	267	0.80
Dominican Republic	8	0.02
Mexican	8,085	24.23
Puerto Rican	223	0.67
South American	543	1.63
Argentinean	117	0.35
Bolivian	16	0.05
Chilean	40	0.12
Colombian	151	0.45
Ecuadorian	93	0.28
Paraguayan	1	<0.01
Peruvian	112	0.34
Uruguayan	2	0.01
Venezuelan	5	0.01
Other South American	6	0.02
Other Hispanic or Latino	778	2.33

Race*	Population	%
African-American/Black (1,084)	1,354	4.06
Not Hispanic (1,015)	1,210	3.63
Hispanic (69)	144	0.43
American Indian/Alaska Native (233)	539	1.62
Not Hispanic (77)	279	0.84
Hispanic (156)	260	0.78
Apache (6)	20	0.06
Blackfeet (1)	13	0.04
Canadian/French Am. Ind. (5)	5	0.01
Central American Ind. (1)	3	0.01
Cherokee (6)	68	0.20
Chickasaw (0)	9	0.03
Chippewa (0)	4	0.01
Choctaw (6)	18	0.05
Comanche (3)	5	0.01
Creek (2)	6	0.02
Crow (0)	1	<0.01
Delaware (1)	2	0.01
Hopi (2)	2	0.01
Iroquois (2)	4	0.01
Mexican American Ind. (26)	35	0.10
Navajo (12)	16	0.05
Osage (0)	3	0.01
Ottawa (2)	6	0.02
Pima (2)	4	0.01
Potawatomi (0)	2	0.01
Pueblo (2)	14	0.04
Seminole (0)	3	0.01
Shoshone (7)	9	0.03
Sioux (5)	15	0.04
Spanish American Ind. (5)	7	0.02
Tohono O'Odham (1)	3	0.01
Ute (1)	4	0.01
Yaqui (1)	4	0.01
Yuman (1)	1	<0.01
Asian (3,496)	4,196	12.57
Not Hispanic (3,381)	3,886	11.64
Hispanic (115)	310	0.93
Bangladeshi (5)	7	0.02
Burmese (12)	14	0.04
Cambodian (16)	17	0.05
Chinese, ex. Taiwanese (784)	1,000	3.00
Filipino (1,067)	1,345	4.03
Indian (386)	454	1.36
Indonesian (41)	72	0.22
Japanese (331)	497	1.49
Korean (211)	258	0.77
Laotian (0)	1	<0.01
Malaysian (3)	4	0.01
Pakistani (88)	93	0.28
Sri Lankan (14)	21	0.06
Taiwanese (148)	169	0.51
Thai (85)	112	0.34
Vietnamese (145)	177	0.53
Hawaii Native/Pacific Islander (48)	144	0.43
Not Hispanic (36)	113	0.34
Hispanic (12)	31	0.09
Guamanian/Chamorro (10)	15	0.04
Native Hawaiian (19)	73	0.22
Samoan (13)	24	0.07
White (24,038)	25,482	76.36
Not Hispanic (17,448)	18,208	54.56
Hispanic (6,590)	7,274	21.80

San Fernando

Place Type: City
County: Los Angeles
Population: 23,645†

Ancestry‡	Population	%
American (96)	96	0.41
Armenian (15)	45	0.19
Austrian (19)	19	0.08
Brazilian (0)	16	0.07
Canadian (0)	12	0.05
Czech (18)	36	0.15
Dutch (0)	54	0.23
English (46)	145	0.61
European (22)	22	0.09
Finnish (10)	14	0.06
French, ex. Basque (0)	29	0.12
French Canadian (0)	32	0.14
German (165)	363	1.54
Greek (0)	20	0.08
Hungarian (0)	12	0.05
Irish (88)	273	1.16
Italian (103)	325	1.38
Northern European (8)	8	0.03
Norwegian (12)	56	0.24
Polish (29)	154	0.65
Romanian (0)	5	0.02
Russian (18)	18	0.08
Scotch-Irish (9)	76	0.32
Scottish (14)	118	0.50
Slavic (0)	17	0.07
Swedish (0)	11	0.05
Swiss (0)	19	0.08
Yugoslavian (0)	13	0.06

Hispanic Origin	Population	%
Hispanic or Latino (of any race)	21,867	92.48
Central American, ex. Mexican	1,461	6.18
Costa Rican	27	0.11
Guatemalan	421	1.78
Honduran	85	0.36
Nicaraguan	54	0.23
Panamanian	12	0.05
Salvadoran	855	3.62
Other Central American	7	0.03
Cuban	33	0.14
Dominican Republic	2	0.01
Mexican	19,373	81.93
Puerto Rican	63	0.27
South American	140	0.59
Argentinean	11	0.05
Chilean	16	0.07
Colombian	44	0.19
Ecuadorian	20	0.08
Paraguayan	6	0.03
Peruvian	39	0.16
Uruguayan	1	<0.01
Venezuelan	3	0.01
Other Hispanic or Latino	795	3.36

Race*	Population	%
African-American/Black (222)	313	1.32
Not Hispanic (146)	172	0.73
Hispanic (76)	141	0.60
American Indian/Alaska Native (314)	449	1.90
Not Hispanic (66)	86	0.36
Hispanic (248)	363	1.54
Apache (8)	13	0.05
Blackfeet (1)	2	0.01
Canadian/French Am. Ind. (1)	1	<0.01
Cherokee (3)	5	0.02
Choctaw (4)	4	0.02
Comanche (1)	1	<0.01
Delaware (0)	1	<0.01
Hopi (0)	3	0.01
Kiowa (4)	4	0.02
Mexican American Ind. (55)	75	0.32
Navajo (12)	20	0.08
Paiute (2)	7	0.03
Pima (1)	1	<0.01
Pueblo (7)	7	0.03
Shoshone (0)	5	0.02
Sioux (13)	15	0.06
Spanish American Ind. (7)	7	0.03
Tlingit-Haida *(Alaska Native)* (0)	2	0.01
Tohono O'Odham (2)	5	0.02
Yaqui (13)	16	0.07
Yup'ik *(Alaska Native)* (1)	3	0.01
Asian (248)	367	1.55
Not Hispanic (192)	229	0.97
Hispanic (56)	138	0.58
Cambodian (11)	19	0.08
Chinese, ex. Taiwanese (21)	40	0.17
Filipino (114)	158	0.67
Indian (6)	19	0.08
Indonesian (3)	3	0.01
Japanese (27)	46	0.19
Korean (19)	26	0.11
Laotian (2)	3	0.01
Taiwanese (1)	1	<0.01
Thai (13)	27	0.11
Vietnamese (9)	14	0.06
Hawaii Native/Pacific Islander (33)	68	0.29
Not Hispanic (19)	28	0.12
Hispanic (14)	40	0.17
Fijian (3)	4	0.02
Guamanian/Chamorro (9)	9	0.04
Native Hawaiian (6)	22	0.09
Samoan (8)	14	0.06
White (12,068)	12,818	54.21
Not Hispanic (1,259)	1,330	5.62
Hispanic (10,809)	11,488	48.59

San Francisco

Place Type: City
County: San Francisco
Population: 805,235†

Ancestry‡	Population	%
Afghan (118)	158	0.02
African, Sub-Saharan (3,082)	4,541	0.58
African (1,941)	3,031	0.38
Ethiopian (561)	585	0.07
Ghanaian (91)	123	0.02
Liberian (7)	18	<0.01
Nigerian (170)	211	0.03
Somalian (47)	72	0.01
South African (78)	247	0.03
Sudanese (0)	30	<0.01
Ugandan (6)	6	<0.01
Other Sub-Saharan African (181)	218	0.03
Albanian (53)	143	0.02
Alsatian (24)	49	0.01
American (8,041)	8,041	1.02
Arab (3,899)	5,672	0.72
Arab (727)	1,106	0.14
Egyptian (360)	483	0.06

SECTION TWO

*Notes: † The Census 2010 population figure is used to calculate the percentages in the Hispanic Origin and Race categories. Ancestry percentages are based on the 2006-2010 American Community Survey population (not shown); ‡ Numbers in parentheses indicate the number of people reporting a single ancestry; * Numbers in parentheses indicate the number of persons reporting this race alone, not in combination with any other race; Please refer to the Explanation of Data for more information.*

Iraqi (32)	60	0.01
Jordanian (296)	353	0.04
Lebanese (541)	1,112	0.14
Moroccan (65)	135	0.02
Palestinian (520)	705	0.09
Syrian (77)	159	0.02
Other Arab (1,281)	1,559	0.20
Armenian (1,496)	2,149	0.27
Assyrian/Chaldean/Syriac (154)	196	0.02
Australian (626)	954	0.12
Austrian (916)	3,588	0.45
Basque (206)	508	0.06
Belgian (294)	783	0.10
Brazilian (1,266)	1,569	0.20
British (3,363)	6,050	0.77
Bulgarian (402)	468	0.06
Cajun (155)	219	0.03
Canadian (801)	1,697	0.22
Carpatho Rusyn (0)	16	<0.01
Celtic (91)	194	0.02
Croatian (578)	1,466	0.19
Cypriot (6)	50	0.01
Czech (960)	2,987	0.38
Czechoslovakian (268)	422	0.05
Danish (973)	3,739	0.47
Dutch (1,691)	7,416	0.94
Eastern European (3,092)	3,844	0.49
English (10,682)	45,268	5.74
Estonian (98)	227	0.03
European (13,269)	15,818	2.00
Finnish (390)	1,264	0.16
French, ex. Basque (4,299)	17,757	2.25
French Canadian (1,190)	2,726	0.35
German (16,144)	65,133	8.25
German Russian (0)	16	<0.01
Greek (2,266)	4,216	0.53
Hungarian (1,208)	3,416	0.43
Icelander (67)	223	0.03
Iranian (1,848)	2,263	0.29
Irish (20,894)	64,487	8.17
Israeli (279)	437	0.06
Italian (15,657)	38,913	4.93
Latvian (243)	632	0.08
Lithuanian (500)	1,821	0.23
Luxemburger (0)	126	0.02
Macedonian (68)	156	0.02
Maltese (385)	608	0.08
New Zealander (74)	123	0.02
Northern European (1,907)	2,060	0.26
Norwegian (1,935)	7,582	0.96
Pennsylvania German (19)	111	0.01
Polish (4,793)	16,127	2.04
Portuguese (1,615)	4,497	0.57
Romanian (810)	1,943	0.25
Russian (11,670)	21,435	2.72
Scandinavian (523)	1,088	0.14
Scotch-Irish (2,897)	8,480	1.07
Scottish (3,767)	13,167	1.67
Serbian (204)	435	0.06
Slavic (197)	627	0.08
Slovak (268)	861	0.11
Slovene (187)	400	0.05
Soviet Union (75)	75	0.01
Swedish (2,218)	8,924	1.13
Swiss (906)	3,264	0.41
Turkish (525)	721	0.09
Ukrainian (3,286)	4,917	0.62
Welsh (850)	3,806	0.48
West Indian, ex. Hispanic (689)	1,316	0.17
Bahamian (9)	9	<0.01
Barbadian (0)	20	<0.01
Belizean (90)	140	0.02
British West Indian (27)	36	<0.01
Haitian (49)	49	0.01
Jamaican (399)	714	0.09
Trinidadian/Tobagonian (25)	140	0.02
West Indian (90)	208	0.03
Yugoslavian (279)	538	0.07

Hispanic Origin	Population	%
Hispanic or Latino (of any race)	121,774	15.12
Central American, ex. Mexican	33,834	4.20
Costa Rican	487	0.06
Guatemalan	6,154	0.76
Honduran	2,611	0.32
Nicaraguan	7,604	0.94
Panamanian	399	0.05
Salvadoran	16,165	2.01
Other Central American	414	0.05
Cuban	1,992	0.25
Dominican Republic	289	0.04
Mexican	59,675	7.41
Puerto Rican	4,204	0.52
South American	8,618	1.07
Argentinean	1,100	0.14
Bolivian	416	0.05
Chilean	754	0.09
Colombian	1,717	0.21
Ecuadorian	577	0.07
Paraguayan	43	0.01
Peruvian	3,260	0.40
Uruguayan	118	0.01
Venezuelan	496	0.06
Other South American	137	0.02
Other Hispanic or Latino	13,162	1.63

Race*	Population	%
African-American/Black (48,870)	57,810	7.18
Not Hispanic (46,781)	53,760	6.68
Hispanic (2,089)	4,050	0.50
American Indian/Alaska Native (4,024)	10,873	1.35
Not Hispanic (1,828)	6,241	0.78
Hispanic (2,196)	4,632	0.58
Alaska Athabascan *(Ala. Nat.)* (5)	9	<0.01
Aleut *(Alaska Native)* (10)	30	<0.01
Apache (105)	271	0.03
Arapaho (8)	17	<0.01
Blackfeet (27)	284	0.04
Canadian/French Am. Ind. (9)	42	0.01
Central American Ind. (83)	144	0.02
Cherokee (223)	1,441	0.18
Cheyenne (5)	14	<0.01
Chickasaw (17)	80	0.01
Chippewa (72)	167	0.02
Choctaw (64)	318	0.04
Colville (5)	8	<0.01
Comanche (6)	47	0.01
Cree (5)	35	<0.01
Creek (27)	108	0.01
Crow (9)	23	<0.01
Delaware (5)	38	<0.01
Hopi (8)	23	<0.01
Houma (4)	5	<0.01
Inupiat *(Alaska Native)* (12)	22	<0.01
Iroquois (43)	133	0.02
Kiowa (1)	10	<0.01
Lumbee (5)	11	<0.01
Menominee (1)	3	<0.01
Mexican American Ind. (752)	1,209	0.15
Navajo (151)	242	0.03
Osage (5)	26	<0.01
Ottawa (1)	7	<0.01
Paiute (28)	44	0.01
Pima (19)	36	<0.01
Potawatomi (11)	34	<0.01
Pueblo (19)	83	0.01
Puget Sound Salish (6)	11	<0.01
Seminole (10)	68	0.01
Shoshone (5)	25	<0.01
Sioux (94)	251	0.03
South American Ind. (73)	198	0.02
Spanish American Ind. (27)	41	0.01
Tlingit-Haida *(Alaska Native)* (19)	29	<0.01
Tohono O'Odham (19)	27	<0.01
Tsimshian *(Alaska Native)* (3)	8	<0.01
Ute (5)	18	<0.01
Yakama (2)	7	<0.01
Yaqui (45)	90	0.01
Yuman (6)	10	<0.01
Yup'ik *(Alaska Native)* (3)	5	<0.01
Asian (267,915)	288,529	35.83
Not Hispanic (265,700)	283,435	35.20
Hispanic (2,215)	5,094	0.63
Bangladeshi (98)	113	0.01
Bhutanese (7)	8	<0.01
Burmese (1,296)	1,579	0.20
Cambodian (1,213)	1,518	0.19
Chinese, ex. Taiwanese (169,642)	181,707	22.57
Filipino (36,347)	43,646	5.42
Hmong (95)	109	0.01
Indian (9,747)	11,583	1.44
Indonesian (946)	1,349	0.17
Japanese (10,121)	15,278	1.90
Korean (9,670)	11,558	1.44
Laotian (529)	651	0.08
Malaysian (202)	358	0.04
Nepalese (352)	388	0.05
Pakistani (831)	1,012	0.13
Sri Lankan (141)	191	0.02
Taiwanese (2,332)	2,806	0.35
Thai (2,336)	2,879	0.36
Vietnamese (12,871)	16,075	2.00
Hawaii Native/Pacific Islander (3,359)	6,173	0.77
Not Hispanic (3,128)	5,432	0.67
Hispanic (231)	741	0.09
Fijian (176)	250	0.03
Guamanian/Chamorro (313)	566	0.07
Marshallese (3)	5	<0.01
Native Hawaiian (410)	1,489	0.18
Samoan (1,988)	2,542	0.32
Tongan (163)	220	0.03
White (390,387)	420,823	52.26
Not Hispanic (337,451)	358,844	44.56
Hispanic (52,936)	61,979	7.70

San Gabriel

Place Type: City
County: Los Angeles
Population: 39,718†

Ancestry‡	Population	%
African, Sub-Saharan (18)	36	0.09
Nigerian (18)	36	0.09
American (269)	269	0.68
Arab (0)	36	0.09
Arab (0)	14	0.04
Other Arab (0)	22	0.06
Armenian (127)	137	0.35
Assyrian/Chaldean/Syriac (29)	29	0.07
Austrian (0)	17	0.04
Brazilian (9)	9	0.02
British (19)	29	0.07
Canadian (10)	10	0.03
Celtic (0)	9	0.02
Croatian (27)	114	0.29
Czech (0)	45	0.11
Czechoslovakian (11)	11	0.03
Danish (19)	19	0.05
Dutch (8)	111	0.28
Eastern European (21)	21	0.05
English (196)	689	1.74
European (61)	101	0.25
Finnish (11)	11	0.03
French, ex. Basque (22)	264	0.67
French Canadian (10)	90	0.23
German (268)	1,226	3.09
Greek (27)	27	0.07
Hungarian (8)	28	0.07
Irish (268)	876	2.21
Italian (462)	951	2.40
Lithuanian (21)	30	0.08
Northern European (20)	20	0.05
Norwegian (15)	138	0.35
Polish (53)	189	0.48
Portuguese (0)	113	0.28
Russian (0)	135	0.34
Scandinavian (11)	11	0.03
Scotch-Irish (61)	174	0.44

*Notes: † The Census 2010 population figure is used to calculate the percentages in the Hispanic Origin and Race categories. Ancestry percentages are based on the 2006-2010 American Community Survey population (not shown); ‡ Numbers in parentheses indicate the number of people reporting a single ancestry; * Numbers in parentheses indicate the number of persons reporting this race alone, not in combination with any other race; Please refer to the Explanation of Data for more information.*

	Population	%
Scottish (86)	174	0.44
Slovak (0)	15	0.04
Swedish (32)	138	0.35
Swiss (19)	67	0.17
Ukrainian (7)	22	0.06
Welsh (16)	59	0.15
West Indian, ex. Hispanic (0)	30	0.08
Belizean (0)	30	0.08
Yugoslavian (0)	22	0.06

Hispanic Origin	Population	%
Hispanic or Latino (of any race)	10,189	25.65
Central American, ex. Mexican	739	1.86
Costa Rican	21	0.05
Guatemalan	142	0.36
Honduran	59	0.15
Nicaraguan	124	0.31
Panamanian	9	0.02
Salvadoran	374	0.94
Other Central American	10	0.03
Cuban	119	0.30
Dominican Republic	8	0.02
Mexican	8,433	21.23
Puerto Rican	121	0.30
South American	231	0.58
Argentinean	49	0.12
Bolivian	1	<0.01
Chilean	9	0.02
Colombian	44	0.11
Ecuadorian	47	0.12
Peruvian	61	0.15
Uruguayan	4	0.01
Venezuelan	8	0.02
Other South American	8	0.02
Other Hispanic or Latino	538	1.35

Race*	Population	%
African-American/Black (388)	527	1.33
Not Hispanic (337)	409	1.03
Hispanic (51)	118	0.30
American Indian/Alaska Native (220)	388	0.98
Not Hispanic (55)	130	0.33
Hispanic (165)	258	0.65
Apache (14)	24	0.06
Blackfeet (0)	5	0.01
Canadian/French Am. Ind. (1)	3	0.01
Central American Ind. (5)	6	0.02
Cherokee (3)	27	0.07
Choctaw (3)	8	0.02
Comanche (3)	3	0.01
Delaware (0)	2	0.01
Inupiat *(Alaska Native)* (2)	4	0.01
Iroquois (0)	2	0.01
Lumbee (0)	1	<0.01
Mexican American Ind. (34)	47	0.12
Navajo (6)	9	0.02
Paiute (0)	1	<0.01
Pima (8)	10	0.03
Pueblo (5)	5	0.01
Shoshone (0)	1	<0.01
Sioux (3)	5	0.01
South American Ind. (2)	9	0.02
Spanish American Ind. (2)	5	0.01
Yaqui (2)	9	0.02
Asian (24,091)	24,672	62.12
Not Hispanic (23,994)	24,430	61.51
Hispanic (97)	242	0.61
Bangladeshi (13)	13	0.03
Burmese (237)	261	0.66
Cambodian (281)	382	0.96
Chinese, ex. Taiwanese (15,797)	17,137	43.15
Filipino (962)	1,135	2.86
Hmong (17)	17	0.04
Indian (152)	205	0.52
Indonesian (231)	280	0.70
Japanese (597)	765	1.93
Korean (235)	297	0.75
Laotian (36)	49	0.12
Malaysian (19)	44	0.11
Nepalese (5)	5	0.01
Pakistani (18)	24	0.06
Sri Lankan (7)	7	0.02
Taiwanese (905)	1,009	2.54
Thai (184)	212	0.53
Vietnamese (3,070)	3,834	9.65
Hawaii Native/Pacific Islander (43)	151	0.38
Not Hispanic (26)	99	0.25
Hispanic (17)	52	0.13
Guamanian/Chamorro (6)	13	0.03
Native Hawaiian (20)	41	0.10
Samoan (9)	15	0.04
Tongan (0)	2	0.01
White (10,076)	10,945	27.56
Not Hispanic (4,539)	4,929	12.41
Hispanic (5,537)	6,016	15.15

San Jacinto

Place Type: City
County: Riverside
Population: 44,199†

Ancestry‡	Population	%
African, Sub-Saharan (285)	344	0.83
African (247)	306	0.74
Nigerian (38)	38	0.09
American (1,027)	1,027	2.49
Arab (0)	13	0.03
Arab (0)	6	0.01
Syrian (0)	7	0.02
Armenian (0)	18	0.04
Australian (23)	23	0.06
Austrian (0)	71	0.17
Basque (56)	56	0.14
Belgian (0)	36	0.09
British (0)	15	0.04
Bulgarian (0)	3	0.01
Canadian (22)	97	0.24
Celtic (19)	19	0.05
Croatian (0)	31	0.08
Czech (6)	6	0.01
Czechoslovakian (2)	2	<0.01
Danish (75)	210	0.51
Dutch (398)	684	1.66
English (689)	2,449	5.94
European (143)	212	0.51
Finnish (47)	56	0.14
French, ex. Basque (97)	871	2.11
French Canadian (106)	201	0.49
German (1,064)	3,926	9.53
Greek (73)	186	0.45
Hungarian (28)	180	0.44
Irish (1,075)	3,572	8.67
Italian (452)	1,458	3.54
Latvian (12)	12	0.03
Lithuanian (0)	17	0.04
Northern European (19)	19	0.05
Norwegian (103)	627	1.52
Pennsylvania German (10)	10	0.02
Polish (138)	391	0.95
Portuguese (0)	31	0.08
Romanian (31)	96	0.23
Russian (38)	151	0.37
Scandinavian (16)	73	0.18
Scotch-Irish (350)	632	1.53
Scottish (178)	590	1.43
Slovak (11)	28	0.07
Swedish (80)	344	0.83
Swiss (0)	23	0.06
Ukrainian (52)	88	0.21
Welsh (80)	305	0.74
West Indian, ex. Hispanic (10)	10	0.02
Jamaican (10)	10	0.02
Yugoslavian (8)	8	0.02

Hispanic Origin	Population	%
Hispanic or Latino (of any race)	23,109	52.28
Central American, ex. Mexican	936	2.12
Costa Rican	31	0.07
Guatemalan	319	0.72
Honduran	86	0.19
Nicaraguan	128	0.29
Panamanian	28	0.06
Salvadoran	340	0.77
Other Central American	4	0.01
Cuban	95	0.21
Dominican Republic	11	0.02
Mexican	20,322	45.98
Puerto Rican	386	0.87
South American	226	0.51
Argentinean	41	0.09
Bolivian	17	0.04
Chilean	17	0.04
Colombian	47	0.11
Ecuadorian	40	0.09
Peruvian	53	0.12
Venezuelan	10	0.02
Other South American	1	<0.01
Other Hispanic or Latino	1,133	2.56

Race*	Population	%
African-American/Black (2,928)	3,649	8.26
Not Hispanic (2,702)	3,192	7.22
Hispanic (226)	457	1.03
American Indian/Alaska Native (812)	1,404	3.18
Not Hispanic (405)	760	1.72
Hispanic (407)	644	1.46
Alaska Athabascan *(Ala. Nat.)* (0)	6	0.01
Apache (20)	50	0.11
Blackfeet (1)	12	0.03
Canadian/French Am. Ind. (1)	7	0.02
Central American Ind. (0)	6	0.01
Cherokee (32)	117	0.26
Cheyenne (1)	3	0.01
Chickasaw (2)	4	0.01
Chippewa (29)	38	0.09
Choctaw (25)	46	0.10
Comanche (1)	4	0.01
Cree (0)	5	0.01
Hopi (1)	4	0.01
Iroquois (1)	3	0.01
Lumbee (0)	1	<0.01
Mexican American Ind. (57)	79	0.18
Navajo (18)	37	0.08
Osage (2)	3	0.01
Paiute (0)	6	0.01
Pima (0)	1	<0.01
Potawatomi (2)	7	0.02
Pueblo (2)	10	0.02
Puget Sound Salish (4)	4	0.01
Seminole (1)	4	0.01
Shoshone (3)	3	0.01
Sioux (4)	11	0.02
South American Ind. (3)	5	0.01
Spanish American Ind. (3)	6	0.01
Tohono O'Odham (3)	3	0.01
Ute (2)	2	<0.01
Yaqui (9)	14	0.03
Yuman (2)	2	<0.01
Yup'ik *(Alaska Native)* (0)	1	<0.01
Asian (1,341)	1,892	4.28
Not Hispanic (1,254)	1,614	3.65
Hispanic (87)	278	0.63
Cambodian (46)	67	0.15
Chinese, ex. Taiwanese (73)	155	0.35
Filipino (713)	989	2.24
Hmong (67)	73	0.17
Indian (93)	118	0.27
Indonesian (21)	39	0.09
Japanese (40)	146	0.33
Korean (36)	55	0.12
Laotian (39)	41	0.09
Malaysian (5)	5	0.01
Pakistani (22)	25	0.06
Sri Lankan (1)	2	<0.01
Taiwanese (15)	16	0.04
Thai (17)	26	0.06
Vietnamese (87)	115	0.26
Hawaii Native/Pacific Islander (124)	275	0.62
Not Hispanic (102)	194	0.44

SECTION TWO

*Notes: † The Census 2010 population figure is used to calculate the percentages in the Hispanic Origin and Race categories. Ancestry percentages are based on the 2006-2010 American Community Survey population (not shown); ‡ Numbers in parentheses indicate the number of people reporting a single ancestry; * Numbers in parentheses indicate the number of persons reporting this race alone, not in combination with any other race; Please refer to the Explanation of Data for more information.*

Hispanic (22)	81	0.18
Fijian (3)	3	0.01
Guamanian/Chamorro (37)	48	0.11
Native Hawaiian (19)	89	0.20
Samoan (22)	64	0.14
Tongan (16)	19	0.04
White (25,272)	27,356	61.89
Not Hispanic (15,508)	16,395	37.09
Hispanic (9,764)	10,961	24.80

San Jose

Place Type: City
County: Santa Clara
Population: 945,942†

Ancestry‡	Population	%
Afghan (808)	925	0.10
African, Sub-Saharan (4,478)	5,552	0.60
African (1,313)	1,999	0.22
Cape Verdean (21)	105	0.01
Ethiopian (1,993)	2,008	0.22
Kenyan (69)	69	0.01
Liberian (41)	94	0.01
Nigerian (221)	229	0.02
Sierra Leonean (44)	117	0.01
Somalian (324)	324	0.04
South African (184)	211	0.02
Sudanese (39)	81	0.01
Ugandan (18)	18	<0.01
Other Sub-Saharan African (211)	297	0.03
Albanian (56)	64	0.01
Alsatian (38)	61	0.01
American (11,998)	11,998	1.30
Arab (3,514)	4,802	0.52
Arab (441)	698	0.08
Egyptian (733)	847	0.09
Iraqi (140)	177	0.02
Jordanian (204)	219	0.02
Lebanese (1,025)	1,317	0.14
Moroccan (38)	91	0.01
Palestinian (361)	587	0.06
Syrian (111)	171	0.02
Other Arab (461)	695	0.08
Armenian (1,238)	1,585	0.17
Assyrian/Chaldean/Syriac (1,732)	2,016	0.22
Australian (17)	80	0.01
Austrian (197)	1,045	0.11
Basque (73)	259	0.03
Belgian (274)	693	0.07
Brazilian (470)	683	0.07
British (1,711)	3,157	0.34
Bulgarian (202)	264	0.03
Cajun (13)	68	0.01
Canadian (875)	1,796	0.19
Celtic (60)	243	0.03
Croatian (742)	1,692	0.18
Czech (449)	1,653	0.18
Czechoslovakian (217)	484	0.05
Danish (858)	3,362	0.36
Dutch (2,072)	7,446	0.80
Eastern European (900)	1,162	0.13
English (11,113)	42,150	4.56
Estonian (37)	54	0.01
European (8,084)	9,840	1.06
Finnish (309)	892	0.10
French, ex. Basque (2,199)	14,068	1.52
French Canadian (614)	1,741	0.19
German (15,618)	61,487	6.65
German Russian (7)	7	<0.01
Greek (1,635)	3,018	0.33
Guyanese (59)	59	0.01
Hungarian (651)	1,873	0.20
Icelander (47)	121	0.01
Iranian (6,703)	7,389	0.80
Irish (11,484)	46,086	4.98
Israeli (529)	641	0.07
Italian (16,922)	40,876	4.42
Latvian (29)	155	0.02
Lithuanian (223)	644	0.07
Luxemburger (74)	168	0.02
Macedonian (43)	65	0.01
Maltese (106)	179	0.02
New Zealander (59)	59	0.01
Northern European (958)	1,065	0.12
Norwegian (2,111)	8,087	0.87
Pennsylvania German (49)	60	0.01
Polish (2,946)	8,895	0.96
Portuguese (8,414)	15,480	1.67
Romanian (836)	1,307	0.14
Russian (3,533)	6,163	0.67
Scandinavian (435)	980	0.11
Scotch-Irish (2,309)	7,094	0.77
Scottish (2,187)	9,176	0.99
Serbian (201)	398	0.04
Slavic (57)	235	0.03
Slovak (227)	702	0.08
Slovene (39)	107	0.01
Swedish (1,742)	8,620	0.93
Swiss (541)	2,530	0.27
Turkish (361)	539	0.06
Ukrainian (1,060)	1,748	0.19
Welsh (725)	3,304	0.36
West Indian, ex. Hispanic (356)	684	0.07
Belizean (0)	41	<0.01
Dutch West Indian (0)	14	<0.01
Haitian (87)	87	0.01
Jamaican (123)	252	0.03
Trinidadian/Tobagonian (97)	140	0.02
West Indian (49)	112	0.01
Other West Indian (0)	38	<0.01
Yugoslavian (1,112)	1,585	0.17

Hispanic Origin	Population	%
Hispanic or Latino (of any race)	313,636	33.16
Central American, ex. Mexican	14,697	1.55
Costa Rican	258	0.03
Guatemalan	2,294	0.24
Honduran	1,890	0.20
Nicaraguan	2,917	0.31
Panamanian	371	0.04
Salvadoran	6,829	0.72
Other Central American	138	0.01
Cuban	1,194	0.13
Dominican Republic	235	0.02
Mexican	268,538	28.39
Puerto Rican	4,763	0.50
South American	6,035	0.64
Argentinean	666	0.07
Bolivian	459	0.05
Chilean	632	0.07
Colombian	1,266	0.13
Ecuadorian	368	0.04
Paraguayan	31	<0.01
Peruvian	2,128	0.22
Uruguayan	45	<0.01
Venezuelan	350	0.04
Other South American	90	0.01
Other Hispanic or Latino	18,174	1.92

Race*	Population	%
African-American/Black (30,242)	37,836	4.00
Not Hispanic (27,508)	32,533	3.44
Hispanic (2,734)	5,303	0.56
American Indian/Alaska Native (8,297)	16,064	1.70
Not Hispanic (2,255)	6,164	0.65
Hispanic (6,042)	9,900	1.05
Alaska Athabascan *(Ala. Nat.)* (3)	11	<0.01
Aleut *(Alaska Native)* (21)	33	<0.01
Apache (445)	959	0.10
Arapaho (4)	9	<0.01
Blackfeet (44)	267	0.03
Canadian/French Am. Ind. (16)	45	<0.01
Central American Ind. (32)	51	0.01
Cherokee (331)	1,622	0.17
Cheyenne (4)	16	<0.01
Chickasaw (26)	53	0.01
Chippewa (85)	181	0.02
Choctaw (100)	371	0.04
Colville (7)	7	<0.01
Comanche (52)	91	0.01
Cree (1)	18	<0.01
Creek (36)	115	0.01
Crow (1)	6	<0.01
Delaware (8)	25	<0.01
Hopi (19)	58	0.01
Houma (2)	4	<0.01
Inupiat *(Alaska Native)* (8)	26	<0.01
Iroquois (27)	117	0.01
Kiowa (17)	25	<0.01
Lumbee (4)	11	<0.01
Menominee (4)	9	<0.01
Mexican American Ind. (1,208)	1,697	0.18
Navajo (233)	476	0.05
Osage (8)	35	<0.01
Ottawa (5)	8	<0.01
Paiute (30)	58	0.01
Pima (24)	38	<0.01
Potawatomi (23)	52	0.01
Pueblo (54)	114	0.01
Puget Sound Salish (1)	11	<0.01
Seminole (12)	54	0.01
Shoshone (25)	46	<0.01
Sioux (168)	313	0.03
South American Ind. (50)	133	0.01
Spanish American Ind. (55)	82	0.01
Tlingit-Haida *(Alaska Native)* (18)	40	<0.01
Tohono O'Odham (41)	68	0.01
Tsimshian *(Alaska Native)* (0)	3	<0.01
Ute (6)	17	<0.01
Yakama (5)	7	<0.01
Yaqui (183)	354	0.04
Yuman (28)	41	<0.01
Yup'ik *(Alaska Native)* (2)	3	<0.01
Asian (303,138)	326,627	34.53
Not Hispanic (300,022)	318,607	33.68
Hispanic (3,116)	8,020	0.85
Bangladeshi (519)	576	0.06
Burmese (510)	602	0.06
Cambodian (4,106)	4,934	0.52
Chinese, ex. Taiwanese (57,189)	67,093	7.09
Filipino (53,008)	62,549	6.61
Hmong (199)	219	0.02
Indian (43,827)	46,410	4.91
Indonesian (580)	948	0.10
Japanese (10,998)	16,322	1.73
Korean (11,342)	12,929	1.37
Laotian (1,275)	1,590	0.17
Malaysian (194)	304	0.03
Nepalese (134)	139	0.01
Pakistani (1,890)	2,131	0.23
Sri Lankan (316)	358	0.04
Taiwanese (5,834)	6,579	0.70
Thai (848)	1,178	0.12
Vietnamese (100,486)	106,647	11.27
Hawaii Native/Pacific Islander (4,017)	8,116	0.86
Not Hispanic (3,492)	6,460	0.68
Hispanic (525)	1,656	0.18
Fijian (396)	490	0.05
Guamanian/Chamorro (689)	1,396	0.15
Marshallese (13)	20	<0.01
Native Hawaiian (547)	2,161	0.23
Samoan (1,389)	1,954	0.21
Tongan (381)	526	0.06
White (404,437)	442,231	46.75
Not Hispanic (271,382)	292,431	30.91
Hispanic (133,055)	149,800	15.84

San Juan Capistrano

Place Type: City
County: Orange
Population: 34,593†

Ancestry‡	Population	%
African, Sub-Saharan (0)	16	0.05
African (0)	16	0.05
American (873)	873	2.55
Arab (249)	259	0.76
Lebanese (26)	36	0.11

*Notes: † The Census 2010 population figure is used to calculate the percentages in the Hispanic Origin and Race categories. Ancestry percentages are based on the 2006-2010 American Community Survey population (not shown); ‡ Numbers in parentheses indicate the number of people reporting a single ancestry; * Numbers in parentheses indicate the number of persons reporting this race alone, not in combination with any other race; Please refer to the Explanation of Data for more information.*

Other Arab (223)	223	0.65
Armenian (30)	30	0.09
Australian (10)	10	0.03
Austrian (57)	148	0.43
Basque (13)	13	0.04
Belgian (28)	54	0.16
Brazilian (11)	34	0.10
British (108)	210	0.61
Canadian (84)	314	0.92
Croatian (0)	24	0.07
Czech (53)	136	0.40
Danish (64)	251	0.73
Dutch (70)	484	1.41
Eastern European (49)	49	0.14
English (986)	3,671	10.71
Estonian (0)	34	0.10
European (407)	552	1.61
Finnish (19)	45	0.13
French, ex. Basque (164)	836	2.44
French Canadian (61)	121	0.35
German (1,230)	4,884	14.25
Greek (204)	479	1.40
Hungarian (79)	181	0.53
Icelander (13)	55	0.16
Iranian (126)	136	0.40
Irish (1,100)	3,875	11.31
Israeli (56)	56	0.16
Italian (663)	2,009	5.86
Lithuanian (51)	87	0.25
Luxemburger (0)	16	0.05
Northern European (36)	56	0.16
Norwegian (213)	607	1.77
Pennsylvania German (0)	14	0.04
Polish (135)	555	1.62
Portuguese (116)	138	0.40
Romanian (16)	39	0.11
Russian (183)	441	1.29
Scandinavian (111)	214	0.62
Scotch-Irish (186)	566	1.65
Scottish (387)	954	2.78
Serbian (31)	31	0.09
Slavic (0)	11	0.03
Slovak (44)	181	0.53
Slovene (0)	48	0.14
Swedish (259)	757	2.21
Swiss (0)	73	0.21
Ukrainian (15)	61	0.18
Welsh (61)	278	0.81
West Indian, ex. Hispanic (43)	43	0.13
Belizean (43)	43	0.13
Yugoslavian (0)	48	0.14

Hispanic Origin	Population	%
Hispanic or Latino (of any race)	13,388	38.70
Central American, ex. Mexican	273	0.79
Costa Rican	19	0.05
Guatemalan	111	0.32
Honduran	13	0.04
Nicaraguan	6	0.02
Panamanian	5	0.01
Salvadoran	113	0.33
Other Central American	6	0.02
Cuban	71	0.21
Dominican Republic	7	0.02
Mexican	12,122	35.04
Puerto Rican	91	0.26
South American	314	0.91
Argentinean	81	0.23
Bolivian	5	0.01
Chilean	28	0.08
Colombian	61	0.18
Ecuadorian	53	0.15
Peruvian	65	0.19
Uruguayan	9	0.03
Venezuelan	8	0.02
Other South American	4	0.01
Other Hispanic or Latino	510	1.47

Race*	Population	%
African-American/Black (193)	301	0.87
Not Hispanic (146)	223	0.64
Hispanic (47)	78	0.23
American Indian/Alaska Native (286)	505	1.46
Not Hispanic (156)	280	0.81
Hispanic (130)	225	0.65
Alaska Athabascan *(Ala. Nat.)* (3)	3	0.01
Apache (10)	15	0.04
Blackfeet (1)	3	0.01
Cherokee (15)	56	0.16
Cheyenne (2)	2	0.01
Chickasaw (0)	3	0.01
Chippewa (0)	4	0.01
Choctaw (7)	16	0.05
Comanche (0)	4	0.01
Creek (1)	5	0.01
Crow (0)	1	<0.01
Hopi (0)	1	<0.01
Iroquois (1)	4	0.01
Mexican American Ind. (13)	22	0.06
Navajo (2)	6	0.02
Osage (0)	1	<0.01
Paiute (2)	2	0.01
Pueblo (0)	1	<0.01
Seminole (1)	6	0.02
Shoshone (2)	2	0.01
Sioux (2)	9	0.03
South American Ind. (0)	2	0.01
Ute (1)	1	<0.01
Yaqui (3)	7	0.02
Asian (975)	1,370	3.96
Not Hispanic (952)	1,296	3.75
Hispanic (23)	74	0.21
Burmese (2)	2	0.01
Cambodian (7)	15	0.04
Chinese, ex. Taiwanese (170)	272	0.79
Filipino (235)	351	1.01
Hmong (1)	1	<0.01
Indian (99)	111	0.32
Indonesian (6)	15	0.04
Japanese (161)	262	0.76
Korean (108)	137	0.40
Laotian (1)	1	<0.01
Malaysian (1)	6	0.02
Nepalese (0)	1	<0.01
Pakistani (9)	10	0.03
Sri Lankan (4)	5	0.01
Taiwanese (18)	24	0.07
Thai (6)	8	0.02
Vietnamese (100)	120	0.35
Hawaii Native/Pacific Islander (33)	114	0.33
Not Hispanic (30)	95	0.27
Hispanic (3)	19	0.05
Fijian (1)	1	<0.01
Guamanian/Chamorro (4)	14	0.04
Native Hawaiian (16)	55	0.16
Samoan (6)	12	0.03
Tongan (2)	5	0.01
White (26,664)	27,779	80.30
Not Hispanic (19,312)	19,839	57.35
Hispanic (7,352)	7,940	22.95

San Leandro

Place Type: City
County: Alameda
Population: 84,950†

Ancestry‡	Population	%
Afghan (35)	35	0.04
African, Sub-Saharan (1,952)	2,077	2.51
African (893)	951	1.15
Ethiopian (350)	350	0.42
Nigerian (676)	729	0.88
Senegalese (33)	33	0.04
Sierra Leonean (0)	14	0.02
Albanian (10)	10	0.01
American (1,334)	1,334	1.61
Arab (391)	479	0.58
Arab (67)	99	0.12
Egyptian (66)	66	0.08
Jordanian (26)	26	0.03
Lebanese (6)	40	0.05
Moroccan (19)	19	0.02
Palestinian (55)	55	0.07
Syrian (0)	22	0.03
Other Arab (152)	152	0.18
Armenian (48)	118	0.14
Australian (15)	15	0.02
Austrian (24)	143	0.17
Basque (0)	23	0.03
Belgian (0)	15	0.02
British (30)	67	0.08
Canadian (13)	84	0.10
Croatian (106)	163	0.20
Czech (27)	129	0.16
Czechoslovakian (15)	56	0.07
Danish (62)	298	0.36
Dutch (79)	511	0.62
Eastern European (96)	96	0.12
English (920)	3,223	3.89
Estonian (11)	11	0.01
European (1,214)	1,367	1.65
Finnish (18)	102	0.12
French, ex. Basque (323)	1,355	1.64
French Canadian (53)	72	0.09
German (1,470)	4,418	5.33
Greek (219)	292	0.35
Hungarian (5)	31	0.04
Iranian (23)	47	0.06
Irish (1,451)	4,357	5.26
Italian (1,019)	2,702	3.26
Latvian (61)	61	0.07
Lithuanian (0)	17	0.02
Maltese (37)	37	0.04
Northern European (68)	76	0.09
Norwegian (186)	710	0.86
Polish (514)	1,134	1.37
Portuguese (1,880)	3,314	4.00
Romanian (24)	33	0.04
Russian (208)	459	0.55
Scandinavian (14)	93	0.11
Scotch-Irish (240)	766	0.92
Scottish (91)	690	0.83
Slavic (39)	68	0.08
Slovak (5)	14	0.02
Slovene (0)	16	0.02
Swedish (226)	580	0.70
Swiss (135)	249	0.30
Ukrainian (72)	122	0.15
Welsh (12)	164	0.20
West Indian, ex. Hispanic (14)	37	0.04
Jamaican (14)	28	0.03
West Indian (0)	9	0.01
Yugoslavian (135)	157	0.19

Hispanic Origin	Population	%
Hispanic or Latino (of any race)	23,237	27.35
Central American, ex. Mexican	2,371	2.79
Costa Rican	62	0.07
Guatemalan	455	0.54
Honduran	118	0.14
Nicaraguan	444	0.52
Panamanian	41	0.05
Salvadoran	1,229	1.45
Other Central American	22	0.03
Cuban	121	0.14
Dominican Republic	22	0.03
Mexican	17,102	20.13
Puerto Rican	831	0.98
South American	668	0.79
Argentinean	80	0.09
Bolivian	30	0.04
Chilean	50	0.06
Colombian	135	0.16
Ecuadorian	16	0.02
Paraguayan	1	<0.01
Peruvian	298	0.35
Uruguayan	6	0.01
Venezuelan	39	0.05
Other South American	13	0.02

*Notes: † The Census 2010 population figure is used to calculate the percentages in the Hispanic Origin and Race categories. Ancestry percentages are based on the 2006-2010 American Community Survey population (not shown); ‡ Numbers in parentheses indicate the number of people reporting a single ancestry; * Numbers in parentheses indicate the number of persons reporting this race alone, not in combination with any other race; Please refer to the Explanation of Data for more information.*

Other Hispanic or Latino	2,122	2.50

Race*	Population	%
African-American/Black (10,437)	11,838	13.94
Not Hispanic (10,052)	11,051	13.01
Hispanic (385)	787	0.93
American Indian/Alaska Native (669)	1,578	1.86
Not Hispanic (246)	791	0.93
Hispanic (423)	787	0.93
Alaska Athabascan *(Ala. Nat.)* (0)	1	<0.01
Aleut *(Alaska Native)* (1)	4	<0.01
Apache (28)	60	0.07
Arapaho (1)	1	<0.01
Blackfeet (6)	45	0.05
Canadian/French Am. Ind. (0)	1	<0.01
Central American Ind. (5)	10	0.01
Cherokee (27)	203	0.24
Cheyenne (1)	2	<0.01
Chickasaw (0)	3	<0.01
Chippewa (5)	26	0.03
Choctaw (13)	42	0.05
Colville (0)	2	<0.01
Comanche (5)	10	0.01
Cree (0)	5	0.01
Creek (2)	8	0.01
Delaware (0)	1	<0.01
Hopi (2)	9	0.01
Houma (0)	4	<0.01
Iroquois (6)	17	0.02
Kiowa (2)	4	<0.01
Mexican American Ind. (94)	170	0.20
Navajo (31)	55	0.06
Osage (0)	3	<0.01
Ottawa (1)	1	<0.01
Paiute (3)	14	0.02
Pima (4)	4	<0.01
Potawatomi (1)	1	<0.01
Pueblo (16)	29	0.03
Puget Sound Salish (1)	1	<0.01
Seminole (2)	4	<0.01
Shoshone (1)	3	<0.01
Sioux (15)	33	0.04
South American Ind. (8)	23	0.03
Spanish American Ind. (3)	4	<0.01
Tlingit-Haida *(Alaska Native)* (3)	8	0.01
Tohono O'Odham (4)	6	0.01
Tsimshian *(Alaska Native)* (0)	1	<0.01
Ute (0)	4	<0.01
Yaqui (6)	13	0.02
Yuman (1)	2	<0.01
Yup'ik *(Alaska Native)* (1)	1	<0.01
Asian (25,206)	27,280	32.11
Not Hispanic (24,924)	26,490	31.18
Hispanic (282)	790	0.93
Bangladeshi (2)	2	<0.01
Burmese (37)	57	0.07
Cambodian (277)	335	0.39
Chinese, ex. Taiwanese (11,551)	12,337	14.52
Filipino (7,935)	9,060	10.67
Hmong (2)	2	<0.01
Indian (638)	767	0.90
Indonesian (47)	81	0.10
Japanese (462)	817	0.96
Korean (491)	635	0.75
Laotian (95)	112	0.13
Malaysian (9)	16	0.02
Nepalese (32)	32	0.04
Pakistani (43)	49	0.06
Sri Lankan (11)	11	0.01
Taiwanese (97)	116	0.14
Thai (47)	75	0.09
Vietnamese (2,715)	3,000	3.53
Hawaii Native/Pacific Islander (642)	1,182	1.39
Not Hispanic (596)	996	1.17
Hispanic (46)	186	0.22
Fijian (72)	104	0.12
Guamanian/Chamorro (159)	252	0.30
Native Hawaiian (81)	314	0.37
Samoan (162)	222	0.26
Tongan (88)	109	0.13
White (31,946)	35,526	41.82
Not Hispanic (23,006)	25,040	29.48
Hispanic (8,940)	10,486	12.34

San Lorenzo

Place Type: CDP
County: Alameda
Population: 23,452†

Ancestry‡	Population	%
Afghan (67)	67	0.28
African, Sub-Saharan (240)	257	1.09
African (88)	88	0.37
Ethiopian (11)	11	0.05
Nigerian (97)	97	0.41
Somalian (0)	17	0.07
Zimbabwean (44)	44	0.19
American (539)	539	2.29
Arab (125)	125	0.53
Palestinian (125)	125	0.53
Armenian (33)	33	0.14
Brazilian (24)	47	0.20
British (24)	39	0.17
Canadian (43)	66	0.28
Croatian (0)	12	0.05
Czech (0)	5	0.02
Czechoslovakian (10)	10	0.04
Danish (24)	82	0.35
Dutch (35)	160	0.68
English (291)	1,235	5.24
European (115)	184	0.78
Finnish (0)	10	0.04
French, ex. Basque (0)	492	2.09
French Canadian (23)	39	0.17
German (616)	1,925	8.17
Greek (27)	73	0.31
Hungarian (8)	17	0.07
Iranian (0)	20	0.08
Irish (561)	1,598	6.78
Italian (390)	1,021	4.33
Lithuanian (0)	9	0.04
Northern European (52)	52	0.22
Norwegian (55)	198	0.84
Polish (80)	219	0.93
Portuguese (857)	1,383	5.87
Russian (30)	82	0.35
Scotch-Irish (68)	299	1.27
Scottish (26)	187	0.79
Serbian (0)	5	0.02
Slavic (0)	25	0.11
Swedish (48)	297	1.26
Swiss (0)	17	0.07
Ukrainian (0)	21	0.09
Welsh (0)	20	0.08
West Indian, ex. Hispanic (25)	43	0.18
Jamaican (25)	25	0.11
Trinidadian/Tobagonian (0)	18	0.08
Yugoslavian (10)	21	0.09

Hispanic Origin	Population	%
Hispanic or Latino (of any race)	8,843	37.71
Central American, ex. Mexican	838	3.57
Costa Rican	24	0.10
Guatemalan	103	0.44
Honduran	30	0.13
Nicaraguan	219	0.93
Panamanian	3	0.01
Salvadoran	451	1.92
Other Central American	8	0.03
Cuban	31	0.13
Dominican Republic	14	0.06
Mexican	6,758	28.82
Puerto Rican	336	1.43
South American	247	1.05
Argentinean	30	0.13
Bolivian	12	0.05
Chilean	11	0.05
Colombian	42	0.18
Ecuadorian	12	0.05
Peruvian	131	0.56
Uruguayan	2	0.01
Venezuelan	3	0.01
Other South American	4	0.02
Other Hispanic or Latino	619	2.64

Race*	Population	%
African-American/Black (1,136)	1,468	6.26
Not Hispanic (1,062)	1,273	5.43
Hispanic (74)	195	0.83
American Indian/Alaska Native (228)	528	2.25
Not Hispanic (73)	212	0.90
Hispanic (155)	316	1.35
Aleut *(Alaska Native)* (1)	1	<0.01
Apache (11)	24	0.10
Blackfeet (7)	16	0.07
Central American Ind. (0)	1	<0.01
Cherokee (8)	44	0.19
Cheyenne (0)	1	<0.01
Chickasaw (1)	4	0.02
Chippewa (0)	1	<0.01
Choctaw (1)	10	0.04
Comanche (0)	2	0.01
Creek (0)	3	0.01
Delaware (0)	1	<0.01
Iroquois (2)	6	0.03
Kiowa (3)	4	0.02
Mexican American Ind. (19)	40	0.17
Navajo (10)	19	0.08
Paiute (4)	5	0.02
Potawatomi (0)	2	0.01
Pueblo (2)	4	0.02
Puget Sound Salish (0)	1	<0.01
Shoshone (2)	2	0.01
Sioux (1)	3	0.01
South American Ind. (4)	15	0.06
Spanish American Ind. (2)	7	0.03
Tlingit-Haida *(Alaska Native)* (1)	2	0.01
Tohono O'Odham (0)	1	<0.01
Yakama (1)	1	<0.01
Yaqui (0)	7	0.03
Yup'ik *(Alaska Native)* (1)	1	<0.01
Asian (5,054)	5,623	23.98
Not Hispanic (4,957)	5,359	22.85
Hispanic (97)	264	1.13
Bangladeshi (4)	4	0.02
Burmese (15)	20	0.09
Cambodian (113)	124	0.53
Chinese, ex. Taiwanese (1,690)	1,865	7.95
Filipino (2,059)	2,375	10.13
Indian (174)	214	0.91
Indonesian (13)	23	0.10
Japanese (151)	257	1.10
Korean (62)	92	0.39
Laotian (23)	30	0.13
Malaysian (2)	2	0.01
Nepalese (2)	2	0.01
Pakistani (23)	24	0.10
Sri Lankan (1)	4	0.02
Taiwanese (29)	32	0.14
Thai (17)	24	0.10
Vietnamese (537)	575	2.45
Hawaii Native/Pacific Islander (182)	368	1.57
Not Hispanic (167)	294	1.25
Hispanic (15)	74	0.32
Fijian (24)	30	0.13
Guamanian/Chamorro (17)	49	0.21
Native Hawaiian (27)	112	0.48
Samoan (42)	59	0.25
Tongan (49)	66	0.28
White (11,115)	12,331	52.58
Not Hispanic (7,592)	8,148	34.74
Hispanic (3,523)	4,183	17.84

San Luis Obispo

Place Type: City
County: San Luis Obispo
Population: 45,119†

*Notes: † The Census 2010 population figure is used to calculate the percentages in the Hispanic Origin and Race categories. Ancestry percentages are based on the 2006-2010 American Community Survey population (not shown); ‡ Numbers in parentheses indicate the number of people reporting a single ancestry; * Numbers in parentheses indicate the number of persons reporting this race alone, not in combination with any other race; Please refer to the Explanation of Data for more information.*

Ancestry[‡]	Population	%
African, Sub-Saharan (120)	120	0.27
African (40)	40	0.09
Ethiopian (48)	48	0.11
Ghanaian (16)	16	0.04
South African (16)	16	0.04
Albanian (0)	13	0.03
American (1,263)	1,263	2.81
Arab (165)	315	0.70
Arab (89)	89	0.20
Egyptian (0)	33	0.07
Lebanese (9)	61	0.14
Palestinian (7)	7	0.02
Syrian (0)	26	0.06
Other Arab (60)	99	0.22
Armenian (35)	75	0.17
Austrian (17)	199	0.44
Basque (99)	115	0.26
Belgian (13)	94	0.21
British (173)	429	0.95
Bulgarian (0)	5	0.01
Cajun (19)	19	0.04
Canadian (52)	133	0.30
Celtic (9)	9	0.02
Croatian (60)	70	0.16
Czech (184)	281	0.63
Czechoslovakian (0)	48	0.11
Danish (189)	589	1.31
Dutch (134)	645	1.43
Eastern European (56)	74	0.16
English (1,723)	5,474	12.18
Estonian (14)	14	0.03
European (1,840)	2,135	4.75
Finnish (16)	80	0.18
French, ex. Basque (229)	1,366	3.04
French Canadian (87)	264	0.59
German (2,028)	7,498	16.68
Greek (147)	282	0.63
Hungarian (162)	421	0.94
Icelander (0)	19	0.04
Iranian (11)	72	0.16
Irish (1,439)	5,543	12.33
Israeli (77)	77	0.17
Italian (1,138)	3,316	7.38
Lithuanian (36)	62	0.14
Luxemburger (10)	36	0.08
Northern European (99)	112	0.25
Norwegian (474)	1,110	2.47
Polish (320)	1,036	2.30
Portuguese (446)	1,092	2.43
Romanian (14)	100	0.22
Russian (162)	635	1.41
Scandinavian (103)	231	0.51
Scotch-Irish (194)	930	2.07
Scottish (451)	1,447	3.22
Serbian (0)	22	0.05
Slavic (13)	26	0.06
Slovak (0)	32	0.07
Slovene (0)	17	0.04
Swedish (503)	1,392	3.10
Swiss (172)	703	1.56
Turkish (23)	64	0.14
Ukrainian (11)	216	0.48
Welsh (118)	591	1.31
West Indian, ex. Hispanic (41)	169	0.38
Belizean (0)	26	0.06
Haitian (28)	28	0.06
Jamaican (0)	68	0.15
Trinidadian/Tobagonian (13)	13	0.03
West Indian (0)	34	0.08
Yugoslavian (20)	69	0.15

Hispanic Origin	Population	%
Hispanic or Latino (of any race)	6,626	14.69
Central American, ex. Mexican	276	0.61
Costa Rican	17	0.04
Guatemalan	112	0.25
Honduran	10	0.02
Nicaraguan	42	0.09
Panamanian	12	0.03
Salvadoran	83	0.18
Cuban	81	0.18
Dominican Republic	11	0.02
Mexican	5,194	11.51
Puerto Rican	159	0.35
South American	274	0.61
Argentinean	47	0.10
Bolivian	12	0.03
Chilean	28	0.06
Colombian	47	0.10
Ecuadorian	21	0.05
Peruvian	99	0.22
Venezuelan	15	0.03
Other South American	5	0.01
Other Hispanic or Latino	631	1.40

Race*	Population	%
African-American/Black (523)	803	1.78
Not Hispanic (449)	662	1.47
Hispanic (74)	141	0.31
American Indian/Alaska Native (275)	749	1.66
Not Hispanic (145)	442	0.98
Hispanic (130)	307	0.68
Aleut *(Alaska Native)* (0)	1	<0.01
Apache (11)	23	0.05
Blackfeet (5)	31	0.07
Canadian/French Am. Ind. (0)	1	<0.01
Central American Ind. (0)	1	<0.01
Cherokee (30)	140	0.31
Cheyenne (0)	5	0.01
Chickasaw (1)	3	0.01
Chippewa (6)	11	0.02
Choctaw (7)	22	0.05
Comanche (1)	2	<0.01
Cree (0)	4	0.01
Creek (3)	7	0.02
Crow (0)	1	<0.01
Delaware (0)	1	<0.01
Hopi (0)	2	<0.01
Inupiat *(Alaska Native)* (0)	4	0.01
Iroquois (1)	7	0.02
Mexican American Ind. (20)	35	0.08
Navajo (3)	14	0.03
Osage (4)	7	0.02
Ottawa (0)	2	<0.01
Paiute (6)	8	0.02
Pima (0)	3	0.01
Potawatomi (2)	9	0.02
Pueblo (2)	5	0.01
Puget Sound Salish (0)	1	<0.01
Seminole (4)	7	0.02
Shoshone (0)	2	<0.01
Sioux (5)	7	0.02
South American Ind. (6)	10	0.02
Spanish American Ind. (3)	3	0.01
Tlingit-Haida *(Alaska Native)* (0)	3	0.01
Tsimshian *(Alaska Native)* (0)	2	<0.01
Ute (1)	1	<0.01
Yaqui (9)	11	0.02
Asian (2,350)	3,248	7.20
Not Hispanic (2,284)	3,063	6.79
Hispanic (66)	185	0.41
Bangladeshi (3)	4	0.01
Burmese (8)	12	0.03
Cambodian (16)	31	0.07
Chinese, ex. Taiwanese (673)	989	2.19
Filipino (466)	730	1.62
Hmong (8)	9	0.02
Indian (293)	340	0.75
Indonesian (13)	29	0.06
Japanese (264)	543	1.20
Korean (195)	269	0.60
Laotian (9)	11	0.02
Malaysian (2)	5	0.01
Nepalese (1)	1	<0.01
Pakistani (24)	28	0.06
Sri Lankan (1)	1	<0.01
Taiwanese (40)	47	0.10
Thai (54)	70	0.16
Vietnamese (143)	172	0.38
Hawaii Native/Pacific Islander (65)	199	0.44
Not Hispanic (59)	166	0.37
Hispanic (6)	33	0.07
Fijian (5)	9	0.02
Guamanian/Chamorro (13)	32	0.07
Native Hawaiian (26)	110	0.24
Samoan (11)	20	0.04
Tongan (4)	6	0.01
White (38,117)	39,767	88.14
Not Hispanic (34,193)	35,381	78.42
Hispanic (3,924)	4,386	9.72

San Marcos

Place Type: City
County: San Diego
Population: 83,781[†]

Ancestry[‡]	Population	%
Afghan (47)	47	0.06
African, Sub-Saharan (341)	480	0.61
African (163)	211	0.27
Ethiopian (66)	66	0.08
Ghanaian (11)	11	0.01
Somalian (38)	129	0.17
South African (25)	25	0.03
Other Sub-Saharan African (38)	38	0.05
American (1,241)	1,241	1.59
Arab (525)	535	0.68
Arab (156)	156	0.20
Iraqi (59)	59	0.08
Lebanese (10)	10	0.01
Moroccan (0)	10	0.01
Palestinian (89)	89	0.11
Syrian (98)	98	0.13
Other Arab (113)	113	0.14
Armenian (103)	188	0.24
Assyrian/Chaldean/Syriac (0)	25	0.03
Australian (0)	13	0.02
Austrian (33)	235	0.30
Basque (0)	11	0.01
Belgian (0)	22	0.03
Brazilian (22)	33	0.04
British (181)	277	0.35
Bulgarian (35)	35	0.04
Canadian (71)	224	0.29
Croatian (4)	72	0.09
Czech (72)	259	0.33
Czechoslovakian (16)	57	0.07
Danish (62)	346	0.44
Dutch (545)	1,532	1.96
Eastern European (43)	50	0.06
English (4,414)	10,282	13.16
Estonian (15)	44	0.06
European (1,207)	1,412	1.81
Finnish (16)	127	0.16
French, ex. Basque (346)	1,858	2.38
French Canadian (147)	352	0.45
German (2,706)	9,355	11.97
Greek (149)	360	0.46
Guyanese (0)	8	0.01
Hungarian (70)	467	0.60
Icelander (0)	11	0.01
Iranian (293)	444	0.57
Irish (1,697)	6,333	8.11
Israeli (25)	25	0.03
Italian (1,703)	4,747	6.08
Latvian (19)	34	0.04
Lithuanian (20)	129	0.17
Maltese (10)	19	0.02
New Zealander (11)	11	0.01
Northern European (46)	63	0.08
Norwegian (320)	956	1.22
Polish (648)	1,633	2.09
Portuguese (184)	428	0.55
Romanian (79)	116	0.15
Russian (329)	783	1.00
Scandinavian (127)	234	0.30
Scotch-Irish (300)	881	1.13
Scottish (263)	1,086	1.39

*Notes: † The Census 2010 population figure is used to calculate the percentages in the Hispanic Origin and Race categories. Ancestry percentages are based on the 2006-2010 American Community Survey population (not shown); ‡ Numbers in parentheses indicate the number of people reporting a single ancestry; * Numbers in parentheses indicate the number of persons reporting this race alone, not in combination with any other race; Please refer to the Explanation of Data for more information.*

Serbian (42)	81	0.10
Slavic (12)	51	0.07
Slovak (33)	78	0.10
Swedish (370)	1,059	1.36
Swiss (20)	167	0.21
Turkish (26)	111	0.14
Ukrainian (30)	53	0.07
Welsh (55)	438	0.56
West Indian, ex. Hispanic (124)	222	0.28
Belizean (11)	11	0.01
British West Indian (7)	7	0.01
Haitian (67)	83	0.11
Jamaican (0)	52	0.07
Trinidadian/Tobagonian (9)	17	0.02
West Indian (30)	30	0.04
Other West Indian (0)	22	0.03
Yugoslavian (0)	19	0.02

Hispanic Origin	Population	%
Hispanic or Latino (of any race)	30,697	36.64
Central American, ex. Mexican	634	0.76
Costa Rican	35	0.04
Guatemalan	203	0.24
Honduran	62	0.07
Nicaraguan	53	0.06
Panamanian	35	0.04
Salvadoran	231	0.28
Other Central American	15	0.02
Cuban	170	0.20
Dominican Republic	27	0.03
Mexican	27,350	32.64
Puerto Rican	455	0.54
South American	544	0.65
Argentinean	84	0.10
Bolivian	30	0.04
Chilean	37	0.04
Colombian	156	0.19
Ecuadorian	42	0.05
Paraguayan	2	<0.01
Peruvian	155	0.19
Uruguayan	2	<0.01
Venezuelan	36	0.04
Other Hispanic or Latino	1,517	1.81

Race*	Population	%
African-American/Black (1,967)	2,775	3.31
Not Hispanic (1,756)	2,305	2.75
Hispanic (211)	470	0.56
American Indian/Alaska Native (591)	1,176	1.40
Not Hispanic (255)	596	0.71
Hispanic (336)	580	0.69
Alaska Athabascan *(Ala. Nat.)* (2)	2	<0.01
Aleut *(Alaska Native)* (2)	2	<0.01
Apache (16)	30	0.04
Arapaho (1)	7	0.01
Blackfeet (2)	20	0.02
Canadian/French Am. Ind. (1)	3	<0.01
Cherokee (30)	129	0.15
Chickasaw (1)	11	0.01
Chippewa (13)	17	0.02
Choctaw (12)	31	0.04
Colville (0)	2	<0.01
Comanche (2)	5	0.01
Creek (5)	6	0.01
Crow (1)	2	<0.01
Hopi (1)	5	0.01
Iroquois (4)	9	0.01
Lumbee (2)	6	0.01
Mexican American Ind. (100)	143	0.17
Navajo (6)	16	0.02
Osage (0)	1	<0.01
Paiute (1)	3	<0.01
Pima (1)	6	0.01
Potawatomi (1)	6	0.01
Pueblo (3)	4	<0.01
Puget Sound Salish (0)	1	<0.01
Seminole (1)	4	<0.01
Shoshone (0)	3	<0.01
Sioux (7)	15	0.02
South American Ind. (1)	5	0.01
Tlingit-Haida *(Alaska Native)* (1)	2	<0.01
Tohono O'Odham (0)	4	<0.01
Ute (1)	2	<0.01
Yaqui (6)	19	0.02
Yuman (1)	1	<0.01
Asian (7,518)	9,503	11.34
Not Hispanic (7,363)	9,047	10.80
Hispanic (155)	456	0.54
Bangladeshi (2)	5	0.01
Burmese (5)	8	0.01
Cambodian (40)	64	0.08
Chinese, ex. Taiwanese (1,093)	1,482	1.77
Filipino (2,817)	3,575	4.27
Hmong (10)	12	0.01
Indian (700)	834	1.00
Indonesian (18)	47	0.06
Japanese (451)	897	1.07
Korean (410)	555	0.66
Laotian (200)	248	0.30
Malaysian (5)	13	0.02
Nepalese (0)	1	<0.01
Pakistani (38)	49	0.06
Sri Lankan (11)	19	0.02
Taiwanese (69)	89	0.11
Thai (69)	124	0.15
Vietnamese (1,175)	1,372	1.64
Hawaii Native/Pacific Islander (322)	708	0.85
Not Hispanic (289)	574	0.69
Hispanic (33)	134	0.16
Fijian (11)	15	0.02
Guamanian/Chamorro (80)	142	0.17
Native Hawaiian (57)	225	0.27
Samoan (126)	181	0.22
Tongan (18)	33	0.04
White (53,235)	56,959	67.99
Not Hispanic (40,736)	42,954	51.27
Hispanic (12,499)	14,005	16.72

San Marino

Place Type: City
County: Los Angeles
Population: 13,147†

Ancestry‡	Population	%
American (201)	201	1.53
Arab (72)	72	0.55
Arab (72)	72	0.55
Armenian (15)	15	0.11
Australian (19)	59	0.45
Austrian (0)	25	0.19
Basque (0)	16	0.12
Belgian (47)	47	0.36
British (11)	11	0.08
Bulgarian (10)	20	0.15
Canadian (33)	98	0.75
Croatian (0)	10	0.08
Czech (0)	21	0.16
Czechoslovakian (12)	12	0.09
Danish (17)	55	0.42
Dutch (17)	104	0.79
Eastern European (67)	67	0.51
English (484)	1,235	9.42
European (144)	162	1.24
French, ex. Basque (25)	211	1.61
French Canadian (17)	17	0.13
German (499)	1,279	9.75
Greek (73)	150	1.14
Hungarian (55)	55	0.42
Iranian (14)	28	0.21
Irish (138)	964	7.35
Italian (145)	309	2.36
Lithuanian (17)	38	0.29
Macedonian (0)	12	0.09
Northern European (122)	122	0.93
Norwegian (12)	34	0.26
Polish (24)	190	1.45
Russian (47)	151	1.15
Scandinavian (12)	29	0.22
Scotch-Irish (44)	76	0.58
Scottish (32)	219	1.67
Slavic (0)	12	0.09
Slovak (0)	12	0.09
Swedish (51)	234	1.78
Swiss (12)	39	0.30
Ukrainian (13)	13	0.10
Welsh (16)	85	0.65

Hispanic Origin	Population	%
Hispanic or Latino (of any race)	855	6.50
Central American, ex. Mexican	60	0.46
Costa Rican	2	0.02
Guatemalan	16	0.12
Honduran	1	0.01
Nicaraguan	6	0.05
Panamanian	4	0.03
Salvadoran	31	0.24
Cuban	38	0.29
Mexican	558	4.24
Puerto Rican	26	0.20
South American	87	0.66
Argentinean	18	0.14
Bolivian	5	0.04
Chilean	6	0.05
Colombian	24	0.18
Ecuadorian	10	0.08
Peruvian	23	0.17
Other South American	1	0.01
Other Hispanic or Latino	86	0.65

Race*	Population	%
African-American/Black (55)	103	0.78
Not Hispanic (53)	96	0.73
Hispanic (2)	7	0.05
American Indian/Alaska Native (5)	40	0.30
Not Hispanic (1)	28	0.21
Hispanic (4)	12	0.09
Aleut *(Alaska Native)* (0)	1	0.01
Apache (1)	2	0.02
Central American Ind. (2)	2	0.02
Cherokee (0)	2	0.02
Chippewa (0)	1	0.01
South American Ind. (1)	1	0.01
Asian (7,039)	7,349	55.90
Not Hispanic (7,010)	7,293	55.47
Hispanic (29)	56	0.43
Burmese (23)	35	0.27
Cambodian (14)	18	0.14
Chinese, ex. Taiwanese (4,335)	4,707	35.80
Filipino (87)	138	1.05
Indian (157)	186	1.41
Indonesian (59)	73	0.56
Japanese (229)	371	2.82
Korean (269)	362	2.75
Laotian (3)	3	0.02
Malaysian (17)	24	0.18
Pakistani (6)	6	0.05
Sri Lankan (13)	13	0.10
Taiwanese (1,370)	1,498	11.39
Thai (40)	46	0.35
Vietnamese (109)	142	1.08
Hawaii Native/Pacific Islander (2)	55	0.42
Not Hispanic (2)	53	0.40
Hispanic (0)	2	0.02
Guamanian/Chamorro (0)	2	0.02
Native Hawaiian (1)	3	0.02
Tongan (1)	1	0.01
White (5,434)	5,764	43.84
Not Hispanic (4,872)	5,132	39.04
Hispanic (562)	632	4.81

San Mateo

Place Type: City
County: San Mateo
Population: 97,207†

Ancestry‡	Population	%
Afghan (10)	32	0.03
African, Sub-Saharan (212)	316	0.33

*Notes: † The Census 2010 population figure is used to calculate the percentages in the Hispanic Origin and Race categories. Ancestry percentages are based on the 2006-2010 American Community Survey population (not shown); ‡ Numbers in parentheses indicate the number of people reporting a single ancestry; * Numbers in parentheses indicate the number of persons reporting this race alone, not in combination with any other race; Please refer to the Explanation of Data for more information.*

African (135)	196	0.21
Ethiopian (0)	10	0.01
Liberian (16)	16	0.02
Nigerian (0)	33	0.03
South African (48)	48	0.05
Other Sub-Saharan African (13)	13	0.01
Albanian (0)	28	0.03
Alsatian (7)	7	0.01
American (1,430)	1,430	1.51
Arab (1,101)	1,409	1.49
Arab (127)	162	0.17
Egyptian (90)	121	0.13
Iraqi (61)	61	0.06
Jordanian (134)	134	0.14
Lebanese (150)	273	0.29
Moroccan (78)	78	0.08
Palestinian (219)	265	0.28
Syrian (42)	58	0.06
Other Arab (200)	257	0.27
Armenian (585)	755	0.80
Assyrian/Chaldean/Syriac (37)	37	0.04
Australian (58)	87	0.09
Austrian (84)	281	0.30
Basque (57)	125	0.13
Belgian (56)	124	0.13
Brazilian (83)	164	0.17
British (366)	618	0.65
Bulgarian (29)	29	0.03
Canadian (145)	265	0.28
Celtic (38)	51	0.05
Croatian (133)	302	0.32
Czech (156)	497	0.52
Czechoslovakian (49)	68	0.07
Danish (136)	565	0.60
Dutch (249)	995	1.05
Eastern European (155)	183	0.19
English (1,618)	6,445	6.80
Estonian (19)	36	0.04
European (1,172)	1,261	1.33
Finnish (61)	202	0.21
French, ex. Basque (271)	2,461	2.60
French Canadian (168)	321	0.34
German (2,428)	9,474	10.00
Greek (398)	776	0.82
Guyanese (38)	38	0.04
Hungarian (170)	428	0.45
Icelander (14)	43	0.05
Iranian (884)	1,015	1.07
Irish (2,306)	9,085	9.59
Israeli (0)	49	0.05
Italian (3,176)	7,619	8.04
Latvian (20)	59	0.06
Lithuanian (18)	107	0.11
Maltese (101)	203	0.21
New Zealander (23)	23	0.02
Northern European (111)	111	0.12
Norwegian (202)	864	0.91
Pennsylvania German (8)	8	0.01
Polish (624)	1,746	1.84
Portuguese (486)	947	1.00
Romanian (123)	207	0.22
Russian (1,448)	2,375	2.51
Scandinavian (69)	87	0.09
Scotch-Irish (388)	1,420	1.50
Scottish (527)	1,966	2.07
Serbian (0)	18	0.02
Slavic (21)	37	0.04
Slovak (10)	73	0.08
Slovene (11)	21	0.02
Swedish (331)	1,100	1.16
Swiss (57)	334	0.35
Turkish (401)	501	0.53
Ukrainian (159)	327	0.35
Welsh (64)	410	0.43
West Indian, ex. Hispanic (9)	47	0.05
British West Indian (0)	14	0.01
Jamaican (0)	24	0.03
Trinidadian/Tobagonian (9)	9	0.01
Yugoslavian (10)	42	0.04

Hispanic Origin	Population	%
Hispanic or Latino (of any race)	25,815	26.56
Central American, ex. Mexican	6,575	6.76
Costa Rican	42	0.04
Guatemalan	2,755	2.83
Honduran	189	0.19
Nicaraguan	910	0.94
Panamanian	43	0.04
Salvadoran	2,571	2.64
Other Central American	65	0.07
Cuban	189	0.19
Dominican Republic	34	0.03
Mexican	13,959	14.36
Puerto Rican	519	0.53
South American	2,228	2.29
Argentinean	225	0.23
Bolivian	131	0.13
Chilean	258	0.27
Colombian	244	0.25
Ecuadorian	92	0.09
Paraguayan	10	0.01
Peruvian	1,163	1.20
Uruguayan	22	0.02
Venezuelan	44	0.05
Other South American	39	0.04
Other Hispanic or Latino	2,311	2.38

Race*	Population	%
African-American/Black (2,296)	3,102	3.19
Not Hispanic (2,099)	2,672	2.75
Hispanic (197)	430	0.44
American Indian/Alaska Native (505)	1,173	1.21
Not Hispanic (140)	502	0.52
Hispanic (365)	671	0.69
Alaska Athabascan *(Ala. Nat.)* (0)	1	<0.01
Aleut *(Alaska Native)* (2)	2	<0.01
Apache (9)	29	0.03
Blackfeet (1)	12	0.01
Canadian/French Am. Ind. (1)	5	0.01
Central American Ind. (13)	22	0.02
Cherokee (23)	146	0.15
Cheyenne (1)	2	<0.01
Chickasaw (0)	5	0.01
Chippewa (3)	11	0.01
Choctaw (8)	31	0.03
Colville (0)	2	<0.01
Comanche (0)	2	<0.01
Cree (0)	3	<0.01
Creek (2)	6	0.01
Delaware (0)	4	<0.01
Hopi (1)	1	<0.01
Inupiat *(Alaska Native)* (0)	1	<0.01
Iroquois (0)	10	0.01
Kiowa (2)	5	0.01
Mexican American Ind. (103)	141	0.15
Navajo (18)	36	0.04
Osage (0)	1	<0.01
Potawatomi (2)	4	<0.01
Pueblo (5)	13	0.01
Seminole (1)	4	<0.01
Shoshone (2)	2	<0.01
Sioux (6)	25	0.03
South American Ind. (4)	27	0.03
Spanish American Ind. (1)	2	<0.01
Tlingit-Haida *(Alaska Native)* (4)	8	0.01
Ute (0)	5	0.01
Yakama (1)	1	<0.01
Yaqui (3)	3	<0.01
Yuman (1)	1	<0.01
Asian (18,384)	21,349	21.96
Not Hispanic (18,153)	20,645	21.24
Hispanic (231)	704	0.72
Bangladeshi (3)	3	<0.01
Burmese (38)	52	0.05
Cambodian (47)	63	0.06
Chinese, ex. Taiwanese (7,377)	8,674	8.92
Filipino (4,478)	5,611	5.77
Hmong (7)	7	0.01
Indian (1,713)	2,076	2.14
Indonesian (86)	129	0.13
Japanese (2,093)	2,835	2.92
Korean (776)	1,002	1.03
Laotian (15)	26	0.03
Malaysian (6)	17	0.02
Nepalese (70)	72	0.07
Pakistani (60)	73	0.08
Sri Lankan (20)	25	0.03
Taiwanese (350)	433	0.45
Thai (146)	186	0.19
Vietnamese (336)	475	0.49
Hawaii Native/Pacific Islander (1,998)	2,803	2.88
Not Hispanic (1,937)	2,588	2.66
Hispanic (61)	215	0.22
Fijian (322)	390	0.40
Guamanian/Chamorro (73)	119	0.12
Native Hawaiian (100)	345	0.35
Samoan (161)	261	0.27
Tongan (1,111)	1,324	1.36
White (56,214)	60,800	62.55
Not Hispanic (45,240)	48,139	49.52
Hispanic (10,974)	12,661	13.02

San Pablo

Place Type: City
County: Contra Costa
Population: 29,139†

Ancestry‡	Population	%
African, Sub-Saharan (499)	511	1.75
African (432)	444	1.52
Ghanaian (67)	67	0.23
American (216)	216	0.74
Arab (108)	108	0.37
Arab (92)	92	0.32
Other Arab (16)	16	0.05
Armenian (32)	32	0.11
Australian (15)	15	0.05
Austrian (16)	16	0.05
Brazilian (171)	171	0.59
British (0)	22	0.08
Canadian (8)	8	0.03
Czech (0)	14	0.05
Czechoslovakian (0)	18	0.06
Danish (0)	50	0.17
Dutch (0)	17	0.06
English (122)	295	1.01
European (109)	123	0.42
Finnish (0)	15	0.05
French, ex. Basque (65)	227	0.78
German (157)	604	2.07
Hungarian (21)	66	0.23
Icelander (19)	19	0.07
Iranian (137)	137	0.47
Irish (207)	595	2.04
Italian (96)	393	1.35
Norwegian (16)	107	0.37
Polish (0)	40	0.14
Portuguese (40)	55	0.19
Romanian (18)	18	0.06
Russian (27)	40	0.14
Scandinavian (35)	35	0.12
Scotch-Irish (8)	36	0.12
Scottish (15)	144	0.49
Slovak (9)	22	0.08
Swedish (0)	30	0.10
Welsh (0)	34	0.12
West Indian, ex. Hispanic (298)	338	1.16
Belizean (290)	330	1.13
Jamaican (8)	8	0.03
Yugoslavian (0)	4	0.01

Hispanic Origin	Population	%
Hispanic or Latino (of any race)	16,462	56.49
Central American, ex. Mexican	3,235	11.10
Costa Rican	15	0.05
Guatemalan	667	2.29
Honduran	102	0.35
Nicaraguan	517	1.77
Panamanian	24	0.08

SECTION TWO

*Notes: † The Census 2010 population figure is used to calculate the percentages in the Hispanic Origin and Race categories. Ancestry percentages are based on the 2006-2010 American Community Survey population (not shown); ‡ Numbers in parentheses indicate the number of people reporting a single ancestry; * Numbers in parentheses indicate the number of persons reporting this race alone, not in combination with any other race; Please refer to the Explanation of Data for more information.*

Salvadoran	1,908	6.55
Other Central American	2	0.01
Cuban	39	0.13
Dominican Republic	5	0.02
Mexican	11,960	41.04
Puerto Rican	120	0.41
South American	278	0.95
Argentinean	21	0.07
Bolivian	10	0.03
Chilean	19	0.07
Colombian	20	0.07
Ecuadorian	8	0.03
Peruvian	198	0.68
Venezuelan	2	0.01
Other Hispanic or Latino	825	2.83

Race*	Population	%
African-American/Black (4,600)	5,053	17.34
Not Hispanic (4,446)	4,773	16.38
Hispanic (154)	280	0.96
American Indian/Alaska Native (244)	523	1.79
Not Hispanic (73)	227	0.78
Hispanic (171)	296	1.02
Aleut *(Alaska Native)* (1)	1	<0.01
Apache (1)	8	0.03
Arapaho (1)	2	0.01
Blackfeet (1)	15	0.05
Canadian/French Am. Ind. (1)	6	0.02
Central American Ind. (11)	16	0.05
Cherokee (13)	52	0.18
Chickasaw (0)	2	0.01
Chippewa (0)	2	0.01
Choctaw (7)	17	0.06
Comanche (2)	7	0.02
Creek (0)	4	0.01
Iroquois (2)	7	0.02
Mexican American Ind. (42)	54	0.19
Navajo (6)	12	0.04
Pueblo (4)	6	0.02
Seminole (0)	1	<0.01
Sioux (2)	10	0.03
South American Ind. (1)	4	0.01
Spanish American Ind. (5)	8	0.03
Tlingit-Haida *(Alaska Native)* (0)	1	<0.01
Yaqui (2)	3	0.01
Asian (4,353)	4,800	16.47
Not Hispanic (4,281)	4,626	15.88
Hispanic (72)	174	0.60
Bangladeshi (1)	1	<0.01
Bhutanese (7)	7	0.02
Cambodian (31)	37	0.13
Chinese, ex. Taiwanese (740)	854	2.93
Filipino (1,638)	1,864	6.40
Indian (298)	376	1.29
Indonesian (5)	15	0.05
Japanese (60)	107	0.37
Korean (58)	71	0.24
Laotian (744)	798	2.74
Malaysian (1)	1	<0.01
Nepalese (56)	58	0.20
Pakistani (28)	30	0.10
Taiwanese (9)	19	0.07
Thai (34)	39	0.13
Vietnamese (469)	518	1.78
Hawaii Native/Pacific Islander (172)	308	1.06
Not Hispanic (156)	250	0.86
Hispanic (16)	58	0.20
Fijian (55)	64	0.22
Guamanian/Chamorro (24)	52	0.18
Native Hawaiian (13)	39	0.13
Samoan (38)	46	0.16
Tongan (1)	6	0.02
White (9,391)	10,481	35.97
Not Hispanic (2,944)	3,331	11.43
Hispanic (6,447)	7,150	24.54

San Rafael

Place Type: City
County: Marin
Population: 57,713†

Ancestry‡	Population	%
African, Sub-Saharan (97)	149	0.26
African (34)	55	0.10
Liberian (63)	63	0.11
Nigerian (0)	14	0.02
South African (0)	17	0.03
Albanian (0)	14	0.02
American (1,101)	1,101	1.93
Arab (249)	329	0.58
Egyptian (85)	85	0.15
Jordanian (41)	41	0.07
Lebanese (33)	78	0.14
Palestinian (81)	116	0.20
Other Arab (9)	9	0.02
Armenian (43)	65	0.11
Australian (15)	26	0.05
Austrian (188)	601	1.06
Basque (0)	35	0.06
Belgian (0)	44	0.08
Brazilian (62)	180	0.32
British (436)	672	1.18
Canadian (174)	233	0.41
Celtic (10)	10	0.02
Croatian (27)	112	0.20
Czech (49)	118	0.21
Czechoslovakian (0)	95	0.17
Danish (226)	775	1.36
Dutch (106)	767	1.35
Eastern European (346)	360	0.63
English (1,335)	5,692	10.00
European (958)	1,146	2.01
Finnish (67)	185	0.32
French, ex. Basque (455)	2,043	3.59
French Canadian (40)	115	0.20
German (2,120)	7,191	12.63
Greek (138)	363	0.64
Hungarian (70)	281	0.49
Icelander (15)	29	0.05
Iranian (341)	384	0.67
Irish (2,295)	7,471	13.12
Israeli (35)	52	0.09
Italian (1,545)	4,405	7.74
Lithuanian (184)	450	0.79
Luxemburger (0)	7	0.01
Northern European (149)	175	0.31
Norwegian (215)	865	1.52
Pennsylvania German (0)	13	0.02
Polish (339)	1,346	2.36
Portuguese (166)	471	0.83
Romanian (166)	425	0.75
Russian (777)	2,027	3.56
Scandinavian (193)	293	0.51
Scotch-Irish (487)	1,330	2.34
Scottish (399)	1,490	2.62
Serbian (7)	22	0.04
Slavic (21)	47	0.08
Slovak (15)	15	0.03
Slovene (16)	37	0.06
Swedish (268)	1,493	2.62
Swiss (198)	561	0.99
Turkish (13)	141	0.25
Ukrainian (48)	225	0.40
Welsh (102)	560	0.98
West Indian, ex. Hispanic (171)	240	0.42
Haitian (35)	35	0.06
Jamaican (128)	197	0.35
U.S. Virgin Islander (8)	8	0.01
Yugoslavian (44)	169	0.30

Hispanic Origin	Population	%
Hispanic or Latino (of any race)	17,302	29.98
Central American, ex. Mexican	7,740	13.41
Costa Rican	36	0.06
Guatemalan	5,895	10.21
Honduran	93	0.16
Nicaraguan	175	0.30
Panamanian	19	0.03
Salvadoran	1,478	2.56
Other Central American	44	0.08
Cuban	96	0.17
Dominican Republic	31	0.05
Mexican	7,011	12.15
Puerto Rican	173	0.30
South American	586	1.02
Argentinean	60	0.10
Bolivian	24	0.04
Chilean	55	0.10
Colombian	112	0.19
Ecuadorian	37	0.06
Paraguayan	4	0.01
Peruvian	251	0.43
Uruguayan	17	0.03
Venezuelan	19	0.03
Other South American	7	0.01
Other Hispanic or Latino	1,665	2.88

Race*	Population	%
African-American/Black (1,154)	1,614	2.80
Not Hispanic (1,024)	1,371	2.38
Hispanic (130)	243	0.42
American Indian/Alaska Native (709)	1,417	2.46
Not Hispanic (107)	421	0.73
Hispanic (602)	996	1.73
Aleut *(Alaska Native)* (0)	3	0.01
Apache (6)	17	0.03
Blackfeet (1)	19	0.03
Canadian/French Am. Ind. (0)	3	0.01
Central American Ind. (32)	56	0.10
Cherokee (11)	121	0.21
Cheyenne (0)	3	0.01
Chickasaw (1)	4	0.01
Chippewa (1)	3	0.01
Choctaw (1)	9	0.02
Comanche (1)	6	0.01
Cree (0)	1	<0.01
Creek (2)	4	0.01
Delaware (1)	12	0.02
Hopi (0)	1	<0.01
Inupiat *(Alaska Native)* (2)	2	<0.01
Iroquois (3)	13	0.02
Kiowa (0)	2	<0.01
Menominee (0)	1	<0.01
Mexican American Ind. (182)	248	0.43
Navajo (4)	13	0.02
Osage (0)	4	0.01
Ottawa (1)	1	<0.01
Paiute (1)	2	<0.01
Pima (1)	3	0.01
Pueblo (5)	9	0.02
Puget Sound Salish (0)	2	<0.01
Seminole (0)	2	<0.01
Shoshone (0)	1	<0.01
Sioux (4)	8	0.01
South American Ind. (7)	12	0.02
Spanish American Ind. (1)	3	0.01
Tlingit-Haida *(Alaska Native)* (0)	1	<0.01
Ute (3)	3	0.01
Yakama (1)	1	<0.01
Yaqui (4)	6	0.01
Yuman (4)	4	0.01
Asian (3,513)	4,503	7.80
Not Hispanic (3,463)	4,331	7.50
Hispanic (50)	172	0.30
Bangladeshi (3)	3	0.01
Cambodian (32)	44	0.08
Chinese, ex. Taiwanese (858)	1,242	2.15
Filipino (533)	780	1.35
Hmong (6)	8	0.01
Indian (494)	567	0.98
Indonesian (27)	35	0.06
Japanese (323)	550	0.95
Korean (244)	335	0.58
Laotian (16)	23	0.04
Malaysian (2)	2	<0.01

*Notes: † The Census 2010 population figure is used to calculate the percentages in the Hispanic Origin and Race categories. Ancestry percentages are based on the 2006-2010 American Community Survey population (not shown); ‡ Numbers in parentheses indicate the number of people reporting a single ancestry; * Numbers in parentheses indicate the number of persons reporting this race alone, not in combination with any other race; Please refer to the Explanation of Data for more information.*

Nepalese (15)	15	0.03
Pakistani (25)	28	0.05
Sri Lankan (10)	10	0.02
Taiwanese (35)	37	0.06
Thai (50)	74	0.13
Vietnamese (652)	734	1.27
Hawaii Native/Pacific Islander (126)	290	0.50
Not Hispanic (93)	213	0.37
Hispanic (33)	77	0.13
Fijian (45)	48	0.08
Guamanian/Chamorro (30)	49	0.08
Native Hawaiian (16)	90	0.16
Samoan (15)	30	0.05
Tongan (13)	16	0.03
White (40,734)	43,379	75.16
Not Hispanic (34,031)	35,399	61.34
Hispanic (6,703)	7,980	13.83

San Ramon

Place Type: City
County: Contra Costa
Population: 72,148†

Ancestry‡	Population	%
Afghan (118)	118	0.18
African, Sub-Saharan (417)	457	0.68
African (0)	7	0.01
Ethiopian (13)	13	0.02
Ghanaian (17)	17	0.03
Kenyan (336)	336	0.50
Nigerian (44)	44	0.07
Sudanese (7)	7	0.01
Zimbabwean (0)	33	0.05
American (1,383)	1,383	2.07
Arab (690)	830	1.24
Egyptian (103)	232	0.35
Jordanian (141)	141	0.21
Lebanese (251)	262	0.39
Palestinian (58)	58	0.09
Other Arab (137)	137	0.21
Armenian (219)	256	0.38
Assyrian/Chaldean/Syriac (21)	27	0.04
Australian (59)	59	0.09
Austrian (22)	311	0.47
Basque (9)	176	0.26
Belgian (0)	128	0.19
Brazilian (35)	35	0.05
British (267)	421	0.63
Canadian (204)	307	0.46
Croatian (40)	72	0.11
Czech (44)	245	0.37
Czechoslovakian (0)	9	0.01
Danish (179)	533	0.80
Dutch (189)	687	1.03
Eastern European (81)	97	0.15
English (1,043)	5,990	8.96
Estonian (0)	6	0.01
European (875)	1,042	1.56
Finnish (28)	111	0.17
French, ex. Basque (249)	1,706	2.55
French Canadian (86)	246	0.37
German (1,764)	8,449	12.64
Greek (158)	522	0.78
Hungarian (149)	410	0.61
Icelander (46)	116	0.17
Iranian (934)	973	1.46
Irish (1,482)	6,828	10.22
Israeli (0)	16	0.02
Italian (1,665)	4,640	6.94
Latvian (0)	17	0.03
Lithuanian (41)	171	0.26
Macedonian (25)	25	0.04
Maltese (0)	15	0.02
New Zealander (12)	12	0.02
Northern European (237)	237	0.35
Norwegian (202)	1,035	1.55
Polish (322)	1,360	2.04
Portuguese (493)	1,836	2.75
Romanian (179)	279	0.42
Russian (668)	1,246	1.86
Scandinavian (66)	131	0.20
Scotch-Irish (225)	736	1.10
Scottish (395)	1,297	1.94
Serbian (0)	12	0.02
Slavic (0)	38	0.06
Slovak (0)	55	0.08
Slovene (15)	15	0.02
Swedish (202)	768	1.15
Swiss (85)	289	0.43
Turkish (13)	57	0.09
Ukrainian (143)	379	0.57
Welsh (58)	451	0.67
West Indian, ex. Hispanic (56)	122	0.18
Jamaican (36)	69	0.10
Trinidadian/Tobagonian (20)	53	0.08
Yugoslavian (83)	160	0.24

Hispanic Origin	Population	%
Hispanic or Latino (of any race)	6,250	8.66
Central American, ex. Mexican	586	0.81
Costa Rican	31	0.04
Guatemalan	71	0.10
Honduran	7	0.01
Nicaraguan	176	0.24
Panamanian	45	0.06
Salvadoran	250	0.35
Other Central American	6	0.01
Cuban	111	0.15
Dominican Republic	15	0.02
Mexican	3,729	5.17
Puerto Rican	309	0.43
South American	628	0.87
Argentinean	76	0.11
Bolivian	40	0.06
Chilean	65	0.09
Colombian	140	0.19
Ecuadorian	30	0.04
Peruvian	222	0.31
Uruguayan	6	0.01
Venezuelan	38	0.05
Other South American	11	0.02
Other Hispanic or Latino	872	1.21

Race*	Population	%
African-American/Black (2,043)	2,657	3.68
Not Hispanic (1,946)	2,419	3.35
Hispanic (97)	238	0.33
American Indian/Alaska Native (205)	645	0.89
Not Hispanic (128)	415	0.58
Hispanic (77)	230	0.32
Alaska Athabascan *(Ala. Nat.)* (2)	2	<0.01
Aleut *(Alaska Native)* (1)	4	0.01
Apache (1)	16	0.02
Blackfeet (4)	17	0.02
Canadian/French Am. Ind. (2)	3	<0.01
Cherokee (17)	121	0.17
Chickasaw (2)	5	0.01
Chippewa (1)	7	0.01
Choctaw (10)	38	0.05
Comanche (0)	1	<0.01
Cree (0)	1	<0.01
Creek (1)	5	0.01
Crow (1)	3	<0.01
Delaware (1)	3	<0.01
Hopi (0)	6	0.01
Iroquois (4)	11	0.02
Kiowa (0)	2	<0.01
Lumbee (0)	1	<0.01
Mexican American Ind. (10)	28	0.04
Navajo (1)	7	0.01
Osage (0)	3	<0.01
Pima (3)	3	<0.01
Potawatomi (1)	5	0.01
Pueblo (4)	4	0.01
Puget Sound Salish (1)	1	<0.01
Shoshone (0)	4	0.01
Sioux (7)	25	0.03
South American Ind. (3)	8	0.01
Spanish American Ind. (1)	3	<0.01
Tlingit-Haida *(Alaska Native)* (0)	2	<0.01
Tohono O'Odham (3)	3	<0.01
Ute (1)	5	0.01
Yaqui (2)	7	0.01
Yuman (3)	3	<0.01
Asian (25,713)	28,406	39.37
Not Hispanic (25,531)	27,937	38.72
Hispanic (182)	469	0.65
Bangladeshi (40)	47	0.07
Burmese (27)	35	0.05
Cambodian (44)	57	0.08
Chinese, ex. Taiwanese (8,040)	9,284	12.87
Filipino (3,412)	4,416	6.12
Hmong (6)	9	0.01
Indian (8,179)	8,468	11.74
Indonesian (146)	199	0.28
Japanese (648)	1,266	1.75
Korean (2,285)	2,548	3.53
Laotian (23)	30	0.04
Malaysian (12)	29	0.04
Nepalese (18)	19	0.03
Pakistani (469)	525	0.73
Sri Lankan (49)	58	0.08
Taiwanese (420)	480	0.67
Thai (71)	102	0.14
Vietnamese (827)	1,083	1.50
Hawaii Native/Pacific Islander (156)	502	0.70
Not Hispanic (141)	423	0.59
Hispanic (15)	79	0.11
Fijian (31)	41	0.06
Guamanian/Chamorro (54)	104	0.14
Native Hawaiian (30)	222	0.31
Samoan (8)	28	0.04
Tongan (16)	19	0.03
White (38,639)	41,924	58.11
Not Hispanic (34,956)	37,605	52.12
Hispanic (3,683)	4,319	5.99

Sanger

Place Type: City
County: Fresno
Population: 24,270†

Ancestry‡	Population	%
American (301)	301	1.29
Armenian (39)	102	0.44
Austrian (11)	20	0.09
Basque (0)	10	0.04
British (27)	58	0.25
Czech (0)	20	0.09
Czechoslovakian (0)	22	0.09
Danish (11)	31	0.13
Dutch (0)	74	0.32
English (111)	322	1.38
European (73)	81	0.35
Finnish (13)	13	0.06
French, ex. Basque (10)	276	1.18
French Canadian (0)	9	0.04
German (183)	968	4.14
Greek (24)	24	0.10
Hungarian (0)	7	0.03
Irish (132)	691	2.96
Italian (128)	516	2.21
Norwegian (19)	135	0.58
Polish (10)	101	0.43
Portuguese (24)	102	0.44
Russian (0)	37	0.16
Scandinavian (6)	6	0.03
Scotch-Irish (67)	79	0.34
Scottish (10)	79	0.34
Swedish (43)	206	0.88
Welsh (0)	22	0.09

Hispanic Origin	Population	%
Hispanic or Latino (of any race)	19,537	80.50
Central American, ex. Mexican	161	0.66
Costa Rican	1	<0.01
Guatemalan	33	0.14
Honduran	25	0.10

*Notes: † The Census 2010 population figure is used to calculate the percentages in the Hispanic Origin and Race categories. Ancestry percentages are based on the 2006-2010 American Community Survey population (not shown); ‡ Numbers in parentheses indicate the number of people reporting a single ancestry; * Numbers in parentheses indicate the number of persons reporting this race alone, not in combination with any other race; Please refer to the Explanation of Data for more information.*

Nicaraguan	9	0.04
Panamanian	3	0.01
Salvadoran	90	0.37
Cuban	6	0.02
Mexican	18,469	76.10
Puerto Rican	48	0.20
South American	26	0.11
Argentinean	1	<0.01
Bolivian	2	0.01
Chilean	4	0.02
Colombian	2	0.01
Ecuadorian	9	0.04
Paraguayan	2	0.01
Peruvian	4	0.02
Uruguayan	1	<0.01
Other South American	1	<0.01
Other Hispanic or Latino	827	3.41

Race*	Population	%
African-American/Black (219)	333	1.37
Not Hispanic (118)	159	0.66
Hispanic (101)	174	0.72
American Indian/Alaska Native (311)	483	1.99
Not Hispanic (102)	190	0.78
Hispanic (209)	293	1.21
Apache (17)	21	0.09
Blackfeet (0)	1	<0.01
Cherokee (19)	48	0.20
Cheyenne (3)	3	0.01
Chickasaw (1)	7	0.03
Chippewa (0)	3	0.01
Choctaw (6)	9	0.04
Comanche (1)	2	0.01
Creek (0)	1	<0.01
Iroquois (5)	6	0.02
Lumbee (1)	1	<0.01
Mexican American Ind. (71)	87	0.36
Navajo (10)	13	0.05
Paiute (5)	5	0.02
Potawatomi (1)	1	<0.01
Pueblo (2)	2	0.01
Sioux (4)	6	0.02
Yaqui (10)	12	0.05
Asian (758)	933	3.84
Not Hispanic (705)	805	3.32
Hispanic (53)	128	0.53
Cambodian (30)	37	0.15
Chinese, ex. Taiwanese (53)	86	0.35
Filipino (95)	142	0.59
Hmong (205)	213	0.88
Indian (197)	231	0.95
Indonesian (0)	3	0.01
Japanese (87)	126	0.52
Korean (6)	12	0.05
Laotian (31)	33	0.14
Pakistani (13)	15	0.06
Taiwanese (4)	4	0.02
Thai (1)	4	0.02
Vietnamese (10)	12	0.05
Hawaii Native/Pacific Islander (39)	67	0.28
Not Hispanic (26)	41	0.17
Hispanic (13)	26	0.11
Guamanian/Chamorro (1)	2	0.01
Marshallese (1)	2	0.01
Native Hawaiian (0)	14	0.06
Samoan (22)	22	0.09
Tongan (8)	11	0.05
White (14,454)	15,147	62.41
Not Hispanic (3,546)	3,716	15.31
Hispanic (10,908)	11,431	47.10

Santa Ana

Place Type: City
County: Orange
Population: 324,528†

Ancestry‡	Population	%
Afghan (93)	93	0.03
African, Sub-Saharan (591)	696	0.21
African (259)	339	0.10
Ethiopian (79)	79	0.02
Ghanaian (72)	72	0.02
Kenyan (88)	88	0.03
South African (93)	118	0.04
American (4,922)	4,922	1.51
Arab (759)	951	0.29
Arab (84)	166	0.05
Egyptian (211)	222	0.07
Jordanian (8)	8	<0.01
Lebanese (106)	188	0.06
Moroccan (47)	47	0.01
Palestinian (205)	216	0.07
Syrian (50)	50	0.02
Other Arab (48)	54	0.02
Armenian (100)	186	0.06
Assyrian/Chaldean/Syriac (19)	19	0.01
Australian (7)	7	<0.01
Austrian (16)	95	0.03
Basque (52)	68	0.02
Belgian (15)	37	0.01
Brazilian (17)	41	0.01
British (98)	287	0.09
Bulgarian (18)	18	0.01
Canadian (44)	166	0.05
Celtic (0)	10	<0.01
Croatian (13)	67	0.02
Czech (59)	221	0.07
Czechoslovakian (12)	49	0.02
Danish (47)	372	0.11
Dutch (248)	882	0.27
Eastern European (19)	19	0.01
English (1,483)	4,960	1.53
European (1,024)	1,123	0.35
Finnish (31)	40	0.01
French, ex. Basque (307)	1,971	0.61
French Canadian (102)	251	0.08
German (1,785)	6,659	2.05
Greek (166)	287	0.09
Hungarian (131)	242	0.07
Iranian (245)	251	0.08
Irish (1,396)	4,904	1.51
Israeli (14)	14	<0.01
Italian (1,323)	2,776	0.85
Latvian (2)	5	<0.01
Lithuanian (117)	174	0.05
Northern European (54)	96	0.03
Norwegian (133)	717	0.22
Pennsylvania German (25)	25	0.01
Polish (341)	1,105	0.34
Portuguese (87)	248	0.08
Romanian (93)	115	0.04
Russian (193)	486	0.15
Scandinavian (13)	64	0.02
Scotch-Irish (201)	809	0.25
Scottish (508)	1,520	0.47
Serbian (49)	57	0.02
Slavic (13)	33	0.01
Slovak (23)	67	0.02
Swedish (229)	796	0.24
Swiss (16)	113	0.03
Turkish (72)	131	0.04
Ukrainian (36)	121	0.04
Welsh (105)	470	0.14
West Indian, ex. Hispanic (44)	86	0.03
Haitian (8)	8	<0.01
Jamaican (9)	21	0.01
Trinidadian/Tobagonian (10)	21	0.01
U.S. Virgin Islander (10)	10	<0.01
West Indian (7)	26	0.01
Yugoslavian (38)	61	0.02

Hispanic Origin	Population	%
Hispanic or Latino (of any race)	253,928	78.25
Central American, ex. Mexican	11,011	3.39
Costa Rican	117	0.04
Guatemalan	3,300	1.02
Honduran	663	0.20
Nicaraguan	375	0.12
Panamanian	54	0.02
Salvadoran	6,389	1.97
Other Central American	113	0.03
Cuban	506	0.16
Dominican Republic	36	0.01
Mexican	230,381	70.99
Puerto Rican	667	0.21
South American	2,303	0.71
Argentinean	276	0.09
Bolivian	398	0.12
Chilean	99	0.03
Colombian	532	0.16
Ecuadorian	224	0.07
Paraguayan	3	<0.01
Peruvian	651	0.20
Uruguayan	47	0.01
Venezuelan	38	0.01
Other South American	35	0.01
Other Hispanic or Latino	9,024	2.78

Race*	Population	%
African-American/Black (4,856)	6,162	1.90
Not Hispanic (3,177)	3,659	1.13
Hispanic (1,679)	2,503	0.77
American Indian/Alaska Native (3,260)	4,916	1.51
Not Hispanic (507)	960	0.30
Hispanic (2,753)	3,956	1.22
Alaska Athabascan *(Ala. Nat.)* (0)	3	<0.01
Aleut *(Alaska Native)* (1)	1	<0.01
Apache (62)	143	0.04
Arapaho (1)	1	<0.01
Blackfeet (17)	35	0.01
Canadian/French Am. Ind. (1)	5	<0.01
Central American Ind. (9)	17	0.01
Cherokee (65)	216	0.07
Cheyenne (1)	1	<0.01
Chickasaw (13)	13	<0.01
Chippewa (9)	18	0.01
Choctaw (17)	36	0.01
Comanche (5)	11	<0.01
Creek (4)	10	<0.01
Crow (0)	2	<0.01
Delaware (1)	1	<0.01
Hopi (7)	14	<0.01
Houma (1)	1	<0.01
Inupiat *(Alaska Native)* (0)	2	<0.01
Iroquois (6)	14	<0.01
Kiowa (3)	4	<0.01
Lumbee (2)	3	<0.01
Mexican American Ind. (721)	974	0.30
Navajo (65)	105	0.03
Osage (4)	10	<0.01
Paiute (0)	2	<0.01
Pima (4)	14	<0.01
Potawatomi (0)	1	<0.01
Pueblo (15)	27	0.01
Seminole (2)	13	<0.01
Shoshone (11)	14	<0.01
Sioux (17)	34	0.01
South American Ind. (11)	22	0.01
Spanish American Ind. (107)	170	0.05
Tlingit-Haida *(Alaska Native)* (2)	2	<0.01
Tohono O'Odham (10)	16	<0.01
Tsimshian *(Alaska Native)* (0)	1	<0.01
Ute (1)	3	<0.01
Yaqui (22)	38	0.01
Yuman (2)	7	<0.01
Asian (34,138)	36,324	11.19
Not Hispanic (33,618)	34,961	10.77
Hispanic (520)	1,363	0.42
Bangladeshi (18)	21	0.01
Burmese (27)	47	0.01
Cambodian (1,583)	1,818	0.56
Chinese, ex. Taiwanese (1,874)	2,634	0.81
Filipino (2,512)	3,101	0.96
Hmong (344)	361	0.11
Indian (1,016)	1,241	0.38
Indonesian (59)	116	0.04
Japanese (741)	1,151	0.35
Korean (690)	836	0.26
Laotian (478)	527	0.16

*Notes: † The Census 2010 population figure is used to calculate the percentages in the Hispanic Origin and Race categories. Ancestry percentages are based on the 2006-2010 American Community Survey population (not shown); ‡ Numbers in parentheses indicate the number of people reporting a single ancestry; * Numbers in parentheses indicate the number of persons reporting this race alone, not in combination with any other race; Please refer to the Explanation of Data for more information.*

	Population	%
Malaysian (14)	16	<0.01
Nepalese (11)	12	<0.01
Pakistani (98)	106	0.03
Sri Lankan (34)	35	0.01
Taiwanese (105)	119	0.04
Thai (160)	232	0.07
Vietnamese (23,167)	24,260	7.48
Hawaii Native/Pacific Islander (976)	1,576	0.49
Not Hispanic (826)	1,109	0.34
Hispanic (150)	467	0.14
Fijian (10)	16	<0.01
Guamanian/Chamorro (52)	98	0.03
Marshallese (70)	82	0.03
Native Hawaiian (113)	307	0.09
Samoan (545)	695	0.21
Tongan (92)	104	0.03
White (148,838)	158,778	48.93
Not Hispanic (29,950)	31,646	9.75
Hispanic (118,888)	127,132	39.17

Santa Barbara

Place Type: City
County: Santa Barbara
Population: 88,410†

Ancestry‡	Population	%
Afghan (73)	73	0.08
African, Sub-Saharan (142)	307	0.35
African (68)	209	0.24
Ethiopian (44)	44	0.05
Nigerian (0)	16	0.02
South African (30)	38	0.04
Alsatian (0)	13	0.01
American (2,069)	2,069	2.35
Arab (169)	329	0.37
Arab (10)	21	0.02
Egyptian (49)	68	0.08
Lebanese (48)	112	0.13
Syrian (0)	66	0.08
Other Arab (62)	62	0.07
Armenian (112)	188	0.21
Australian (23)	212	0.24
Austrian (195)	443	0.50
Basque (101)	276	0.31
Belgian (81)	197	0.22
Brazilian (24)	51	0.06
British (371)	773	0.88
Bulgarian (27)	27	0.03
Cajun (0)	9	0.01
Canadian (87)	327	0.37
Croatian (23)	107	0.12
Cypriot (12)	12	0.01
Czech (71)	278	0.32
Czechoslovakian (106)	206	0.23
Danish (382)	743	0.85
Dutch (334)	1,097	1.25
Eastern European (239)	302	0.34
English (2,262)	8,688	9.89
Estonian (0)	38	0.04
European (1,266)	1,428	1.63
Finnish (6)	183	0.21
French, ex. Basque (532)	2,968	3.38
French Canadian (131)	313	0.36
German (2,496)	11,279	12.84
Greek (152)	458	0.52
Hungarian (192)	451	0.51
Iranian (295)	340	0.39
Irish (2,086)	9,140	10.40
Israeli (13)	40	0.05
Italian (1,881)	5,514	6.28
Latvian (40)	70	0.08
Lithuanian (85)	153	0.17
Macedonian (0)	28	0.03
Maltese (0)	15	0.02
Northern European (138)	138	0.16
Norwegian (495)	1,855	2.11
Pennsylvania German (0)	9	0.01
Polish (490)	2,208	2.51
Portuguese (97)	430	0.49
Romanian (34)	214	0.24
Russian (902)	2,018	2.30
Scandinavian (240)	350	0.40
Scotch-Irish (860)	2,241	2.55
Scottish (796)	2,272	2.59
Serbian (22)	76	0.09
Slavic (13)	34	0.04
Slovak (46)	115	0.13
Swedish (690)	2,060	2.34
Swiss (137)	644	0.73
Turkish (183)	226	0.26
Ukrainian (119)	284	0.32
Welsh (127)	1,017	1.16
West Indian, ex. Hispanic (0)	20	0.02
Haitian (0)	20	0.02

Hispanic Origin	Population	%
Hispanic or Latino (of any race)	33,591	37.99
Central American, ex. Mexican	1,013	1.15
Costa Rican	40	0.05
Guatemalan	546	0.62
Honduran	85	0.10
Nicaraguan	54	0.06
Panamanian	27	0.03
Salvadoran	244	0.28
Other Central American	17	0.02
Cuban	106	0.12
Dominican Republic	28	0.03
Mexican	29,502	33.37
Puerto Rican	197	0.22
South American	651	0.74
Argentinean	121	0.14
Bolivian	19	0.02
Chilean	79	0.09
Colombian	151	0.17
Ecuadorian	44	0.05
Paraguayan	4	<0.01
Peruvian	176	0.20
Uruguayan	10	0.01
Venezuelan	36	0.04
Other South American	11	0.01
Other Hispanic or Latino	2,094	2.37

Race*	Population	%
African-American/Black (1,420)	1,977	2.24
Not Hispanic (1,177)	1,530	1.73
Hispanic (243)	447	0.51
American Indian/Alaska Native (892)	1,771	2.00
Not Hispanic (313)	752	0.85
Hispanic (579)	1,019	1.15
Alaska Athabascan *(Ala. Nat.)* (1)	2	<0.01
Aleut *(Alaska Native)* (1)	3	<0.01
Apache (27)	53	0.06
Arapaho (0)	1	<0.01
Blackfeet (4)	24	0.03
Canadian/French Am. Ind. (0)	3	<0.01
Central American Ind. (7)	9	0.01
Cherokee (27)	171	0.19
Cheyenne (1)	8	0.01
Chickasaw (6)	16	0.02
Chippewa (10)	18	0.02
Choctaw (13)	47	0.05
Comanche (7)	18	0.02
Cree (0)	3	<0.01
Creek (4)	9	0.01
Crow (1)	2	<0.01
Delaware (3)	4	<0.01
Hopi (0)	8	0.01
Inupiat *(Alaska Native)* (1)	3	<0.01
Iroquois (0)	13	0.01
Kiowa (1)	2	<0.01
Lumbee (0)	1	<0.01
Mexican American Ind. (98)	155	0.18
Navajo (9)	18	0.02
Osage (1)	3	<0.01
Paiute (2)	5	0.01
Pima (1)	5	0.01
Potawatomi (0)	3	<0.01
Pueblo (4)	11	0.01
Seminole (0)	4	<0.01
Shoshone (1)	5	0.01
Sioux (16)	35	0.04
South American Ind. (6)	9	0.01
Spanish American Ind. (3)	3	<0.01
Tlingit-Haida *(Alaska Native)* (4)	4	<0.01
Tohono O'Odham (0)	4	<0.01
Ute (1)	1	<0.01
Yaqui (19)	33	0.04
Asian (3,062)	4,281	4.84
Not Hispanic (2,927)	3,907	4.42
Hispanic (135)	374	0.42
Bangladeshi (5)	7	0.01
Bhutanese (9)	10	0.01
Burmese (1)	4	<0.01
Cambodian (35)	44	0.05
Chinese, ex. Taiwanese (848)	1,129	1.28
Filipino (554)	894	1.01
Hmong (7)	9	0.01
Indian (326)	434	0.49
Indonesian (30)	46	0.05
Japanese (474)	780	0.88
Korean (335)	431	0.49
Laotian (14)	17	0.02
Malaysian (4)	7	0.01
Nepalese (4)	12	0.01
Pakistani (13)	16	0.02
Sri Lankan (21)	25	0.03
Taiwanese (48)	62	0.07
Thai (66)	87	0.10
Vietnamese (158)	215	0.24
Hawaii Native/Pacific Islander (116)	285	0.32
Not Hispanic (94)	219	0.25
Hispanic (22)	66	0.07
Fijian (3)	7	0.01
Guamanian/Chamorro (18)	33	0.04
Marshallese (0)	1	<0.01
Native Hawaiian (53)	145	0.16
Samoan (18)	36	0.04
Tongan (0)	6	0.01
White (66,411)	69,489	78.60
Not Hispanic (48,417)	49,972	56.52
Hispanic (17,994)	19,517	22.08

Santa Clara

Place Type: City
County: Santa Clara
Population: 116,468†

Ancestry‡	Population	%
Afghan (160)	160	0.14
African, Sub-Saharan (1,007)	1,089	0.97
African (170)	252	0.22
Ethiopian (692)	692	0.62
Kenyan (38)	38	0.03
Nigerian (47)	47	0.04
Sudanese (60)	60	0.05
Albanian (41)	41	0.04
American (1,390)	1,390	1.24
Arab (973)	1,195	1.06
Arab (101)	101	0.09
Egyptian (64)	98	0.09
Iraqi (174)	174	0.15
Jordanian (86)	86	0.08
Lebanese (135)	261	0.23
Moroccan (55)	91	0.08
Palestinian (10)	21	0.02
Syrian (109)	109	0.10
Other Arab (239)	254	0.23
Armenian (174)	253	0.22
Assyrian/Chaldean/Syriac (219)	219	0.19
Australian (22)	22	0.02
Austrian (58)	260	0.23
Basque (17)	116	0.10
Belgian (52)	70	0.06
Brazilian (16)	132	0.12
British (365)	624	0.55
Bulgarian (45)	45	0.04
Canadian (135)	351	0.31
Croatian (52)	142	0.13

*Notes: † The Census 2010 population figure is used to calculate the percentages in the Hispanic Origin and Race categories. Ancestry percentages are based on the 2006-2010 American Community Survey population (not shown); ‡ Numbers in parentheses indicate the number of people reporting a single ancestry; * Numbers in parentheses indicate the number of persons reporting this race alone, not in combination with any other race; Please refer to the Explanation of Data for more information.*

Ancestry	Population	%
Cypriot (115)	115	0.10
Czech (160)	336	0.30
Czechoslovakian (24)	81	0.07
Danish (46)	300	0.27
Dutch (252)	1,268	1.13
Eastern European (111)	111	0.10
English (1,864)	7,015	6.24
Estonian (32)	53	0.05
European (892)	1,074	0.95
Finnish (36)	120	0.11
French, ex. Basque (619)	2,503	2.23
French Canadian (142)	343	0.30
German (2,097)	9,325	8.29
German Russian (15)	15	0.01
Greek (163)	422	0.38
Hungarian (96)	325	0.29
Icelander (0)	10	0.01
Iranian (684)	713	0.63
Irish (2,225)	7,836	6.97
Israeli (27)	76	0.07
Italian (1,708)	4,479	3.98
Latvian (11)	11	0.01
Lithuanian (23)	134	0.12
Luxemburger (0)	14	0.01
New Zealander (0)	32	0.03
Northern European (85)	98	0.09
Norwegian (203)	878	0.78
Pennsylvania German (79)	93	0.08
Polish (572)	1,615	1.44
Portuguese (2,266)	3,654	3.25
Romanian (285)	345	0.31
Russian (588)	1,028	0.91
Scandinavian (65)	122	0.11
Scotch-Irish (266)	1,090	0.97
Scottish (354)	1,603	1.43
Serbian (187)	187	0.17
Slovak (11)	62	0.06
Slovene (8)	35	0.03
Swedish (236)	1,390	1.24
Swiss (60)	301	0.27
Turkish (85)	85	0.08
Ukrainian (195)	289	0.26
Welsh (38)	490	0.44
West Indian, ex. Hispanic (13)	45	0.04
Barbadian (13)	13	0.01
Jamaican (0)	32	0.03
Yugoslavian (161)	264	0.23

Hispanic Origin	Population	%
Hispanic or Latino (of any race)	22,589	19.40
Central American, ex. Mexican	1,668	1.43
Costa Rican	37	0.03
Guatemalan	341	0.29
Honduran	104	0.09
Nicaraguan	368	0.32
Panamanian	48	0.04
Salvadoran	760	0.65
Other Central American	10	0.01
Cuban	216	0.19
Dominican Republic	23	0.02
Mexican	17,037	14.63
Puerto Rican	421	0.36
South American	1,142	0.98
Argentinean	101	0.09
Bolivian	105	0.09
Chilean	112	0.10
Colombian	172	0.15
Ecuadorian	47	0.04
Paraguayan	2	<0.01
Peruvian	503	0.43
Uruguayan	10	0.01
Venezuelan	79	0.07
Other South American	11	0.01
Other Hispanic or Latino	2,082	1.79

Race*	Population	%
African-American/Black (3,154)	4,150	3.56
Not Hispanic (2,929)	3,690	3.17
Hispanic (225)	460	0.39
American Indian/Alaska Native (579)	1,397	1.20
Not Hispanic (240)	706	0.61
Hispanic (339)	691	0.59
Apache (24)	60	0.05
Arapaho (1)	2	<0.01
Blackfeet (3)	29	0.02
Canadian/French Am. Ind. (1)	3	<0.01
Central American Ind. (2)	3	<0.01
Cherokee (29)	185	0.16
Cheyenne (0)	6	0.01
Chickasaw (2)	6	0.01
Chippewa (7)	14	0.01
Choctaw (5)	29	0.02
Comanche (2)	9	0.01
Cree (0)	6	0.01
Creek (2)	8	0.01
Crow (1)	5	<0.01
Delaware (0)	1	<0.01
Inupiat *(Alaska Native)* (0)	1	<0.01
Iroquois (4)	16	0.01
Kiowa (1)	1	<0.01
Lumbee (2)	4	<0.01
Menominee (1)	1	<0.01
Mexican American Ind. (57)	124	0.11
Navajo (18)	30	0.03
Osage (5)	9	0.01
Ottawa (0)	1	<0.01
Paiute (0)	2	<0.01
Pima (1)	1	<0.01
Potawatomi (1)	8	0.01
Pueblo (4)	8	0.01
Puget Sound Salish (0)	5	<0.01
Seminole (2)	12	0.01
Shoshone (2)	2	<0.01
Sioux (8)	46	0.04
South American Ind. (7)	20	0.02
Spanish American Ind. (4)	4	<0.01
Tlingit-Haida *(Alaska Native)* (3)	9	0.01
Tohono O'Odham (10)	17	0.01
Ute (0)	1	<0.01
Yakama (1)	1	<0.01
Yaqui (18)	32	0.03
Yup'ik *(Alaska Native)* (1)	1	<0.01
Asian (43,889)	47,564	40.84
Not Hispanic (43,531)	46,702	40.10
Hispanic (358)	862	0.74
Bangladeshi (159)	177	0.15
Bhutanese (19)	22	0.02
Burmese (96)	115	0.10
Cambodian (92)	119	0.10
Chinese, ex. Taiwanese (7,396)	8,652	7.43
Filipino (7,222)	8,558	7.35
Hmong (31)	38	0.03
Indian (15,890)	16,412	14.09
Indonesian (114)	209	0.18
Japanese (1,731)	2,617	2.25
Korean (3,506)	3,789	3.25
Laotian (44)	73	0.06
Malaysian (47)	71	0.06
Nepalese (69)	80	0.07
Pakistani (904)	974	0.84
Sri Lankan (68)	81	0.07
Taiwanese (718)	862	0.74
Thai (154)	206	0.18
Vietnamese (4,498)	4,924	4.23
Hawaii Native/Pacific Islander (651)	1,248	1.07
Not Hispanic (604)	1,094	0.94
Hispanic (47)	154	0.13
Fijian (97)	123	0.11
Guamanian/Chamorro (116)	164	0.14
Native Hawaiian (88)	359	0.31
Samoan (148)	240	0.21
Tongan (128)	140	0.12
White (52,359)	57,309	49.21
Not Hispanic (42,026)	45,351	38.94
Hispanic (10,333)	11,958	10.27

Santa Clarita

Place Type: City
County: Los Angeles
Population: 176,320†

Ancestry‡	Population	%
Afghan (154)	180	0.10
African, Sub-Saharan (844)	1,039	0.60
African (347)	385	0.22
Liberian (0)	14	0.01
Nigerian (451)	517	0.30
South African (46)	123	0.07
Albanian (7)	7	<0.01
Alsatian (0)	17	0.01
American (5,155)	5,155	2.99
Arab (1,230)	1,891	1.10
Arab (6)	62	0.04
Egyptian (605)	636	0.37
Jordanian (167)	167	0.10
Lebanese (96)	503	0.29
Palestinian (91)	125	0.07
Syrian (130)	252	0.15
Other Arab (135)	146	0.08
Armenian (1,026)	1,403	0.81
Assyrian/Chaldean/Syriac (113)	162	0.09
Australian (38)	166	0.10
Austrian (44)	468	0.27
Basque (15)	50	0.03
Belgian (67)	231	0.13
Brazilian (83)	168	0.10
British (415)	831	0.48
Bulgarian (42)	56	0.03
Cajun (17)	56	0.03
Canadian (223)	540	0.31
Celtic (0)	157	0.09
Croatian (103)	241	0.14
Czech (138)	603	0.35
Czechoslovakian (8)	106	0.06
Danish (245)	1,078	0.63
Dutch (419)	2,024	1.18
Eastern European (268)	365	0.21
English (4,835)	17,821	10.35
Estonian (0)	10	0.01
European (2,306)	2,946	1.71
Finnish (21)	381	0.22
French, ex. Basque (686)	5,259	3.05
French Canadian (448)	860	0.50
German (5,990)	26,730	15.52
Greek (305)	1,243	0.72
Guyanese (12)	21	0.01
Hungarian (501)	1,257	0.73
Icelander (0)	27	0.02
Iranian (647)	799	0.46
Irish (3,607)	19,220	11.16
Israeli (126)	157	0.09
Italian (4,328)	13,153	7.64
Latvian (9)	24	0.01
Lithuanian (241)	411	0.24
Macedonian (0)	13	0.01
Northern European (204)	226	0.13
Norwegian (775)	3,508	2.04
Polish (1,433)	5,110	2.97
Portuguese (262)	912	0.53
Romanian (133)	319	0.19
Russian (1,729)	4,252	2.47
Scandinavian (214)	459	0.27
Scotch-Irish (1,167)	3,817	2.22
Scottish (1,090)	4,327	2.51
Serbian (0)	10	0.01
Slavic (0)	21	0.01
Slovak (80)	192	0.11
Slovene (25)	137	0.08
Swedish (745)	4,096	2.38
Swiss (133)	896	0.52
Turkish (42)	157	0.09
Ukrainian (125)	388	0.23
Welsh (109)	1,502	0.87
West Indian, ex. Hispanic (78)	483	0.28

*Notes: † The Census 2010 population figure is used to calculate the percentages in the Hispanic Origin and Race categories. Ancestry percentages are based on the 2006-2010 American Community Survey population (not shown); ‡ Numbers in parentheses indicate the number of people reporting a single ancestry; * Numbers in parentheses indicate the number of persons reporting this race alone, not in combination with any other race; Please refer to the Explanation of Data for more information.*

Ancestry	Population	%
Bahamian (0)	14	0.01
Belizean (0)	145	0.08
Bermudan (0)	1	<0.01
Dutch West Indian (20)	75	0.04
Haitian (0)	14	0.01
Jamaican (58)	111	0.06
West Indian (0)	123	0.07
Yugoslavian (165)	311	0.18

Hispanic Origin	Population	%
Hispanic or Latino (of any race)	51,941	29.46
Central American, ex. Mexican	5,657	3.21
Costa Rican	185	0.10
Guatemalan	2,410	1.37
Honduran	276	0.16
Nicaraguan	324	0.18
Panamanian	82	0.05
Salvadoran	2,272	1.29
Other Central American	108	0.06
Cuban	1,053	0.60
Dominican Republic	60	0.03
Mexican	36,666	20.80
Puerto Rican	1,004	0.57
South American	3,311	1.88
Argentinean	621	0.35
Bolivian	124	0.07
Chilean	284	0.16
Colombian	773	0.44
Ecuadorian	509	0.29
Paraguayan	6	<0.01
Peruvian	831	0.47
Uruguayan	47	0.03
Venezuelan	57	0.03
Other South American	59	0.03
Other Hispanic or Latino	4,190	2.38

Race*	Population	%
African-American/Black (5,623)	7,209	4.09
Not Hispanic (5,157)	6,337	3.59
Hispanic (466)	872	0.49
American Indian/Alaska Native (1,013)	2,380	1.35
Not Hispanic (435)	1,313	0.74
Hispanic (578)	1,067	0.61
Alaska Athabascan *(Ala. Nat.)* (1)	6	<0.01
Apache (42)	105	0.06
Arapaho (1)	1	<0.01
Blackfeet (10)	59	0.03
Canadian/French Am. Ind. (2)	6	<0.01
Central American Ind. (4)	9	0.01
Cherokee (64)	359	0.20
Cheyenne (0)	2	<0.01
Chickasaw (11)	37	0.02
Chippewa (13)	28	0.02
Choctaw (21)	102	0.06
Comanche (7)	15	0.01
Creek (16)	33	0.02
Crow (0)	2	<0.01
Delaware (2)	2	<0.01
Hopi (2)	8	<0.01
Inupiat *(Alaska Native)* (3)	3	<0.01
Iroquois (17)	37	0.02
Lumbee (1)	3	<0.01
Menominee (1)	1	<0.01
Mexican American Ind. (111)	179	0.10
Navajo (28)	65	0.04
Osage (0)	1	<0.01
Paiute (6)	11	0.01
Pima (4)	6	<0.01
Potawatomi (12)	17	0.01
Pueblo (16)	31	0.02
Puget Sound Salish (1)	3	<0.01
Seminole (1)	15	0.01
Shoshone (2)	4	<0.01
Sioux (24)	54	0.03
South American Ind. (4)	20	0.01
Spanish American Ind. (9)	19	0.01
Tlingit-Haida *(Alaska Native)* (1)	4	<0.01
Tohono O'Odham (5)	10	0.01
Ute (2)	11	0.01
Yakama (2)	2	<0.01
Yaqui (20)	43	0.02
Yup'ik *(Alaska Native)* (3)	3	<0.01
Asian (15,025)	18,381	10.42
Not Hispanic (14,689)	17,448	9.90
Hispanic (336)	933	0.53
Bangladeshi (61)	79	0.04
Bhutanese (2)	3	<0.01
Burmese (41)	47	0.03
Cambodian (39)	58	0.03
Chinese, ex. Taiwanese (1,328)	2,131	1.21
Filipino (6,063)	7,378	4.18
Hmong (4)	7	<0.01
Indian (1,401)	1,601	0.91
Indonesian (133)	236	0.13
Japanese (1,053)	1,892	1.07
Korean (2,937)	3,238	1.84
Laotian (14)	23	0.01
Malaysian (12)	27	0.02
Nepalese (12)	12	0.01
Pakistani (187)	223	0.13
Sri Lankan (129)	147	0.08
Taiwanese (83)	119	0.07
Thai (337)	456	0.26
Vietnamese (484)	643	0.36
Hawaii Native/Pacific Islander (272)	795	0.45
Not Hispanic (235)	642	0.36
Hispanic (37)	153	0.09
Fijian (12)	12	0.01
Guamanian/Chamorro (59)	125	0.07
Marshallese (2)	2	<0.01
Native Hawaiian (85)	308	0.17
Samoan (22)	88	0.05
Tongan (13)	15	0.01
White (125,005)	132,184	74.97
Not Hispanic (98,838)	102,899	58.36
Hispanic (26,167)	29,285	16.61

Santa Cruz

Place Type: City
County: Santa Cruz
Population: 59,946†

Ancestry‡	Population	%
Afghan (91)	91	0.16
African, Sub-Saharan (90)	194	0.33
African (30)	114	0.20
Ethiopian (26)	26	0.04
Nigerian (17)	17	0.03
South African (17)	37	0.06
American (1,492)	1,492	2.56
Arab (146)	364	0.62
Arab (0)	57	0.10
Iraqi (16)	16	0.03
Lebanese (59)	156	0.27
Moroccan (37)	37	0.06
Syrian (0)	50	0.09
Other Arab (34)	48	0.08
Armenian (153)	279	0.48
Australian (14)	60	0.10
Austrian (9)	226	0.39
Basque (36)	73	0.13
Belgian (12)	66	0.11
Brazilian (0)	32	0.05
British (285)	597	1.02
Bulgarian (14)	28	0.05
Canadian (113)	289	0.50
Celtic (35)	89	0.15
Croatian (28)	141	0.24
Czech (24)	337	0.58
Czechoslovakian (46)	60	0.10
Danish (189)	597	1.02
Dutch (357)	1,210	2.08
Eastern European (213)	297	0.51
English (1,509)	7,257	12.45
Estonian (16)	16	0.03
European (1,670)	2,354	4.04
Finnish (71)	148	0.25
French, ex. Basque (291)	2,565	4.40
French Canadian (117)	383	0.66
German (2,172)	9,157	15.72
Greek (137)	389	0.67
Hungarian (117)	414	0.71
Icelander (0)	38	0.07
Iranian (124)	150	0.26
Irish (1,655)	8,382	14.39
Israeli (73)	135	0.23
Italian (1,485)	4,528	7.77
Latvian (0)	14	0.02
Lithuanian (39)	153	0.26
Luxemburger (8)	16	0.03
Maltese (20)	20	0.03
Northern European (970)	1,071	1.84
Norwegian (628)	1,311	2.25
Polish (186)	1,760	3.02
Portuguese (429)	1,273	2.18
Romanian (70)	187	0.32
Russian (514)	1,732	2.97
Scandinavian (212)	451	0.77
Scotch-Irish (704)	1,514	2.60
Scottish (436)	2,581	4.43
Serbian (19)	19	0.03
Slavic (0)	14	0.02
Slovak (0)	41	0.07
Slovene (0)	158	0.27
Swedish (399)	2,135	3.66
Swiss (33)	371	0.64
Turkish (10)	61	0.10
Ukrainian (85)	193	0.33
Welsh (147)	617	1.06
West Indian, ex. Hispanic (1)	28	0.05
Barbadian (1)	2	<0.01
West Indian (0)	26	0.04
Yugoslavian (33)	138	0.24

Hispanic Origin	Population	%
Hispanic or Latino (of any race)	11,624	19.39
Central American, ex. Mexican	943	1.57
Costa Rican	26	0.04
Guatemalan	127	0.21
Honduran	22	0.04
Nicaraguan	73	0.12
Panamanian	18	0.03
Salvadoran	669	1.12
Other Central American	8	0.01
Cuban	117	0.20
Dominican Republic	16	0.03
Mexican	8,953	14.94
Puerto Rican	242	0.40
South American	455	0.76
Argentinean	83	0.14
Bolivian	16	0.03
Chilean	66	0.11
Colombian	96	0.16
Ecuadorian	31	0.05
Peruvian	115	0.19
Uruguayan	10	0.02
Venezuelan	28	0.05
Other South American	10	0.02
Other Hispanic or Latino	898	1.50

Race*	Population	%
African-American/Black (1,071)	1,709	2.85
Not Hispanic (979)	1,501	2.50
Hispanic (92)	208	0.35
American Indian/Alaska Native (440)	1,292	2.16
Not Hispanic (238)	825	1.38
Hispanic (202)	467	0.78
Alaska Athabascan *(Ala. Nat.)* (1)	1	<0.01
Aleut *(Alaska Native)* (1)	4	0.01
Apache (17)	43	0.07
Arapaho (1)	1	<0.01
Blackfeet (3)	31	0.05
Canadian/French Am. Ind. (1)	3	0.01
Central American Ind. (3)	4	0.01
Cherokee (23)	205	0.34
Cheyenne (2)	6	0.01
Chickasaw (2)	7	0.01
Chippewa (3)	10	0.02
Choctaw (13)	44	0.07

*Notes: † The Census 2010 population figure is used to calculate the percentages in the Hispanic Origin and Race categories. Ancestry percentages are based on the 2006-2010 American Community Survey population (not shown); ‡ Numbers in parentheses indicate the number of people reporting a single ancestry; * Numbers in parentheses indicate the number of persons reporting this race alone, not in combination with any other race; Please refer to the Explanation of Data for more information.*

Comanche (4)	13	0.02
Cree (0)	8	0.01
Creek (0)	17	0.03
Crow (0)	1	<0.01
Delaware (0)	2	<0.01
Hopi (2)	3	0.01
Inupiat *(Alaska Native)* (5)	6	0.01
Iroquois (1)	17	0.03
Kiowa (0)	4	0.01
Lumbee (0)	1	<0.01
Menominee (0)	1	<0.01
Mexican American Ind. (47)	78	0.13
Navajo (7)	19	0.03
Osage (1)	3	0.01
Paiute (0)	3	0.01
Potawatomi (3)	12	0.02
Pueblo (2)	4	0.01
Puget Sound Salish (0)	1	<0.01
Seminole (1)	8	0.01
Shoshone (1)	5	0.01
Sioux (7)	31	0.05
South American Ind. (3)	20	0.03
Spanish American Ind. (7)	9	0.02
Tlingit-Haida *(Alaska Native)* (4)	8	0.01
Tohono O'Odham (4)	10	0.02
Tsimshian *(Alaska Native)* (0)	1	<0.01
Ute (0)	3	0.01
Yaqui (11)	23	0.04
Yup'ik *(Alaska Native)* (0)	1	<0.01
Asian (4,591)	6,182	10.31
Not Hispanic (4,476)	5,825	9.72
Hispanic (115)	357	0.60
Bangladeshi (4)	4	0.01
Burmese (5)	8	0.01
Cambodian (18)	27	0.05
Chinese, ex. Taiwanese (1,798)	2,345	3.91
Filipino (666)	1,108	1.85
Hmong (18)	18	0.03
Indian (453)	584	0.97
Indonesian (11)	42	0.07
Japanese (401)	932	1.55
Korean (352)	478	0.80
Laotian (17)	25	0.04
Malaysian (2)	13	0.02
Nepalese (9)	11	0.02
Pakistani (25)	39	0.07
Sri Lankan (13)	15	0.03
Taiwanese (98)	117	0.20
Thai (75)	110	0.18
Vietnamese (315)	431	0.72
Hawaii Native/Pacific Islander (108)	328	0.55
Not Hispanic (97)	282	0.47
Hispanic (11)	46	0.08
Fijian (5)	14	0.02
Guamanian/Chamorro (10)	41	0.07
Native Hawaiian (44)	146	0.24
Samoan (20)	46	0.08
Tongan (5)	8	0.01
White (44,661)	47,737	79.63
Not Hispanic (39,985)	42,171	70.35
Hispanic (4,676)	5,566	9.29

Santa Fe Springs

Place Type: City
County: Los Angeles
Population: 16,223†

Ancestry‡	Population	%
African, Sub-Saharan (81)	81	0.49
African (81)	81	0.49
American (197)	197	1.20
Arab (32)	49	0.30
Egyptian (32)	32	0.20
Other Arab (0)	17	0.10
Austrian (0)	6	0.04
Basque (25)	25	0.15
Belgian (0)	9	0.05
Danish (13)	36	0.22
Dutch (0)	34	0.21
English (113)	219	1.34
Finnish (0)	25	0.15
French, ex. Basque (24)	105	0.64
German (73)	403	2.46
Greek (0)	11	0.07
Hungarian (0)	13	0.08
Iranian (14)	14	0.09
Irish (106)	574	3.51
Italian (159)	350	2.14
Lithuanian (0)	13	0.08
Norwegian (0)	20	0.12
Polish (10)	50	0.31
Portuguese (0)	38	0.23
Russian (11)	105	0.64
Scotch-Irish (9)	52	0.32
Scottish (26)	89	0.54
Slovak (0)	16	0.10
Swedish (21)	76	0.46
Swiss (19)	19	0.12
Welsh (0)	91	0.56

Hispanic Origin	Population	%
Hispanic or Latino (of any race)	13,137	80.98
Central American, ex. Mexican	784	4.83
Costa Rican	32	0.20
Guatemalan	216	1.33
Honduran	30	0.18
Nicaraguan	109	0.67
Panamanian	8	0.05
Salvadoran	372	2.29
Other Central American	17	0.10
Cuban	146	0.90
Dominican Republic	4	0.02
Mexican	11,217	69.14
Puerto Rican	113	0.70
South American	334	2.06
Argentinean	39	0.24
Bolivian	18	0.11
Chilean	9	0.06
Colombian	78	0.48
Ecuadorian	71	0.44
Paraguayan	1	0.01
Peruvian	108	0.67
Uruguayan	1	0.01
Venezuelan	1	0.01
Other South American	8	0.05
Other Hispanic or Latino	539	3.32

Race*	Population	%
African-American/Black (371)	429	2.64
Not Hispanic (305)	326	2.01
Hispanic (66)	103	0.63
American Indian/Alaska Native (233)	357	2.20
Not Hispanic (65)	95	0.59
Hispanic (168)	262	1.61
Apache (9)	28	0.17
Blackfeet (3)	3	0.02
Cherokee (15)	33	0.20
Cheyenne (1)	1	0.01
Chickasaw (3)	3	0.02
Chippewa (1)	3	0.02
Choctaw (2)	5	0.03
Comanche (0)	1	0.01
Creek (5)	5	0.03
Crow (0)	1	0.01
Hopi (4)	4	0.02
Iroquois (1)	5	0.03
Mexican American Ind. (37)	56	0.35
Navajo (13)	24	0.15
Pima (1)	1	0.01
Pueblo (1)	5	0.03
Sioux (1)	3	0.02
South American Ind. (7)	7	0.04
Spanish American Ind. (10)	10	0.06
Tohono O'Odham (4)	6	0.04
Ute (1)	2	0.01
Yaqui (4)	11	0.07
Asian (677)	820	5.05
Not Hispanic (624)	682	4.20
Hispanic (53)	138	0.85
Burmese (1)	1	0.01
Cambodian (10)	12	0.07
Chinese, ex. Taiwanese (63)	97	0.60
Filipino (259)	319	1.97
Hmong (0)	1	0.01
Indian (45)	51	0.31
Indonesian (14)	19	0.12
Japanese (37)	62	0.38
Korean (124)	126	0.78
Laotian (3)	6	0.04
Pakistani (1)	2	0.01
Sri Lankan (6)	6	0.04
Taiwanese (5)	5	0.03
Thai (14)	24	0.15
Vietnamese (72)	79	0.49
Hawaii Native/Pacific Islander (31)	87	0.54
Not Hispanic (20)	39	0.24
Hispanic (11)	48	0.30
Guamanian/Chamorro (3)	10	0.06
Native Hawaiian (4)	13	0.08
Samoan (14)	27	0.17
Tongan (7)	7	0.04
White (9,514)	10,076	62.11
Not Hispanic (1,927)	2,031	12.52
Hispanic (7,587)	8,045	49.59

Santa Maria

Place Type: City
County: Santa Barbara
Population: 99,553†

Ancestry‡	Population	%
Afghan (8)	8	0.01
African, Sub-Saharan (86)	105	0.11
African (86)	105	0.11
American (1,686)	1,686	1.78
Arab (248)	278	0.29
Arab (217)	217	0.23
Egyptian (0)	30	0.03
Moroccan (19)	19	0.02
Palestinian (12)	12	0.01
Armenian (20)	20	0.02
Australian (9)	9	0.01
Austrian (15)	154	0.16
Basque (30)	30	0.03
Belgian (47)	61	0.06
Brazilian (0)	21	0.02
British (56)	89	0.09
Bulgarian (0)	7	0.01
Canadian (68)	88	0.09
Croatian (0)	29	0.03
Czech (33)	86	0.09
Czechoslovakian (42)	42	0.04
Danish (207)	452	0.48
Dutch (231)	508	0.54
Eastern European (0)	9	0.01
English (1,229)	3,622	3.83
European (472)	538	0.57
Finnish (0)	20	0.02
French, ex. Basque (215)	1,041	1.10
French Canadian (105)	317	0.33
German (1,352)	5,411	5.72
Greek (16)	161	0.17
Hungarian (129)	195	0.21
Icelander (0)	10	0.01
Iranian (9)	55	0.06
Irish (1,002)	4,211	4.45
Italian (654)	1,639	1.73
Latvian (25)	54	0.06
Lithuanian (9)	28	0.03
Luxemburger (0)	13	0.01
Northern European (77)	77	0.08
Norwegian (344)	692	0.73
Polish (76)	393	0.42
Portuguese (660)	1,229	1.30
Romanian (0)	21	0.02
Russian (66)	295	0.31
Scandinavian (24)	93	0.10
Scotch-Irish (149)	569	0.60

*Notes: † The Census 2010 population figure is used to calculate the percentages in the Hispanic Origin and Race categories. Ancestry percentages are based on the 2006-2010 American Community Survey population (not shown); ‡ Numbers in parentheses indicate the number of people reporting a single ancestry; * Numbers in parentheses indicate the number of persons reporting this race alone, not in combination with any other race; Please refer to the Explanation of Data for more information.*

Scottish (190)	657	0.69
Slavic (0)	7	0.01
Slovak (9)	9	0.01
Slovene (0)	10	0.01
Swedish (322)	707	0.75
Swiss (22)	332	0.35
Turkish (8)	8	0.01
Ukrainian (97)	144	0.15
Welsh (70)	280	0.30
West Indian, ex. Hispanic (92)	108	0.11
Belizean (0)	16	0.02
Jamaican (92)	92	0.10
Yugoslavian (23)	23	0.02

Hispanic Origin	Population	%
Hispanic or Latino (of any race)	70,114	70.43
Central American, ex. Mexican	962	0.97
Costa Rican	32	0.03
Guatemalan	225	0.23
Honduran	115	0.12
Nicaraguan	26	0.03
Panamanian	16	0.02
Salvadoran	536	0.54
Other Central American	12	0.01
Cuban	63	0.06
Dominican Republic	10	0.01
Mexican	65,188	65.48
Puerto Rican	362	0.36
South American	178	0.18
Argentinean	31	0.03
Bolivian	13	0.01
Chilean	26	0.03
Colombian	57	0.06
Ecuadorian	7	0.01
Peruvian	29	0.03
Uruguayan	1	<0.01
Venezuelan	14	0.01
Other Hispanic or Latino	3,351	3.37

Race*	Population	%
African-American/Black (1,656)	2,260	2.27
Not Hispanic (1,193)	1,516	1.52
Hispanic (463)	744	0.75
American Indian/Alaska Native (1,818)	2,866	2.88
Not Hispanic (345)	727	0.73
Hispanic (1,473)	2,139	2.15
Aleut *(Alaska Native)* (2)	2	<0.01
Apache (46)	69	0.07
Blackfeet (4)	28	0.03
Canadian/French Am. Ind. (5)	7	0.01
Central American Ind. (1)	8	0.01
Cherokee (38)	153	0.15
Cheyenne (3)	5	0.01
Chickasaw (2)	6	0.01
Chippewa (4)	10	0.01
Choctaw (27)	71	0.07
Comanche (2)	3	<0.01
Cree (0)	1	<0.01
Creek (7)	18	0.02
Crow (0)	1	<0.01
Delaware (1)	1	<0.01
Hopi (2)	5	0.01
Inupiat *(Alaska Native)* (2)	2	<0.01
Iroquois (1)	3	<0.01
Kiowa (2)	7	0.01
Lumbee (2)	3	<0.01
Mexican American Ind. (626)	868	0.87
Navajo (13)	38	0.04
Osage (0)	1	<0.01
Paiute (2)	4	<0.01
Pima (2)	4	<0.01
Potawatomi (2)	8	0.01
Pueblo (6)	6	0.01
Puget Sound Salish (1)	2	<0.01
Seminole (1)	3	<0.01
Shoshone (1)	1	<0.01
Sioux (15)	32	0.03
South American Ind. (2)	4	<0.01
Spanish American Ind. (34)	40	0.04
Tlingit-Haida *(Alaska Native)* (5)	12	0.01
Tohono O'Odham (2)	2	<0.01
Ute (1)	2	<0.01
Yaqui (24)	40	0.04
Yuman (5)	5	0.01
Asian (5,054)	6,418	6.45
Not Hispanic (4,652)	5,354	5.38
Hispanic (402)	1,064	1.07
Burmese (1)	3	<0.01
Cambodian (30)	42	0.04
Chinese, ex. Taiwanese (215)	352	0.35
Filipino (3,595)	4,514	4.53
Hmong (4)	5	0.01
Indian (277)	361	0.36
Indonesian (26)	32	0.03
Japanese (289)	521	0.52
Korean (250)	316	0.32
Laotian (29)	34	0.03
Malaysian (1)	2	<0.01
Nepalese (1)	1	<0.01
Pakistani (12)	14	0.01
Sri Lankan (16)	19	0.02
Taiwanese (6)	7	0.01
Thai (28)	46	0.05
Vietnamese (141)	177	0.18
Hawaii Native/Pacific Islander (161)	402	0.40
Not Hispanic (132)	286	0.29
Hispanic (29)	116	0.12
Guamanian/Chamorro (38)	71	0.07
Native Hawaiian (38)	182	0.18
Samoan (35)	71	0.07
Tongan (12)	19	0.02
White (55,983)	60,167	60.44
Not Hispanic (21,626)	22,747	22.85
Hispanic (34,357)	37,420	37.59

Santa Monica

Place Type: City
County: Los Angeles
Population: 89,736†

Ancestry‡	Population	%
African, Sub-Saharan (518)	884	1.00
African (273)	447	0.50
Cape Verdean (0)	67	0.08
Ethiopian (134)	225	0.25
South African (65)	77	0.09
Zimbabwean (46)	46	0.05
Other Sub-Saharan African (0)	22	0.02
Albanian (17)	17	0.02
Alsatian (0)	14	0.02
American (3,633)	3,633	4.10
Arab (716)	1,138	1.28
Arab (24)	24	0.03
Egyptian (263)	278	0.31
Iraqi (36)	71	0.08
Lebanese (122)	323	0.36
Moroccan (54)	82	0.09
Palestinian (0)	19	0.02
Syrian (61)	123	0.14
Other Arab (156)	218	0.25
Armenian (102)	220	0.25
Australian (51)	188	0.21
Austrian (198)	793	0.89
Basque (49)	49	0.06
Belgian (130)	300	0.34
Brazilian (43)	75	0.08
British (533)	914	1.03
Bulgarian (38)	38	0.04
Cajun (0)	14	0.02
Canadian (342)	592	0.67
Celtic (31)	31	0.03
Croatian (149)	427	0.48
Czech (307)	602	0.68
Czechoslovakian (22)	54	0.06
Danish (142)	564	0.64
Dutch (343)	1,320	1.49
Eastern European (875)	988	1.11
English (2,882)	9,074	10.23
Estonian (13)	24	0.03
European (1,280)	1,445	1.63
Finnish (80)	167	0.19
French, ex. Basque (647)	2,837	3.20
French Canadian (245)	379	0.43
German (3,193)	10,958	12.36
Greek (281)	488	0.55
Guyanese (18)	58	0.07
Hungarian (400)	1,147	1.29
Iranian (2,544)	2,587	2.92
Irish (2,989)	10,235	11.54
Israeli (251)	277	0.31
Italian (2,293)	6,432	7.25
Latvian (24)	136	0.15
Lithuanian (494)	1,080	1.22
Luxemburger (0)	19	0.02
Maltese (0)	12	0.01
New Zealander (35)	76	0.09
Northern European (193)	193	0.22
Norwegian (206)	1,013	1.14
Pennsylvania German (0)	22	0.02
Polish (1,642)	4,188	4.72
Portuguese (32)	87	0.10
Romanian (229)	500	0.56
Russian (2,029)	5,142	5.80
Scandinavian (139)	266	0.30
Scotch-Irish (480)	1,249	1.41
Scottish (645)	2,269	2.56
Serbian (31)	163	0.18
Slavic (9)	167	0.19
Slovak (87)	177	0.20
Slovene (26)	51	0.06
Soviet Union (20)	20	0.02
Swedish (579)	1,921	2.17
Swiss (158)	400	0.45
Turkish (131)	165	0.19
Ukrainian (539)	957	1.08
Welsh (203)	1,075	1.21
West Indian, ex. Hispanic (117)	178	0.20
British West Indian (18)	18	0.02
Jamaican (47)	68	0.08
West Indian (52)	92	0.10
Yugoslavian (53)	207	0.23

Hispanic Origin	Population	%
Hispanic or Latino (of any race)	11,716	13.06
Central American, ex. Mexican	1,120	1.25
Costa Rican	49	0.05
Guatemalan	318	0.35
Honduran	75	0.08
Nicaraguan	80	0.09
Panamanian	40	0.04
Salvadoran	543	0.61
Other Central American	15	0.02
Cuban	267	0.30
Dominican Republic	32	0.04
Mexican	7,686	8.57
Puerto Rican	366	0.41
South American	1,152	1.28
Argentinean	271	0.30
Bolivian	28	0.03
Chilean	131	0.15
Colombian	263	0.29
Ecuadorian	105	0.12
Paraguayan	4	<0.01
Peruvian	184	0.21
Uruguayan	36	0.04
Venezuelan	107	0.12
Other South American	23	0.03
Other Hispanic or Latino	1,093	1.22

Race*	Population	%
African-American/Black (3,526)	4,475	4.99
Not Hispanic (3,364)	4,157	4.63
Hispanic (162)	318	0.35
American Indian/Alaska Native (338)	974	1.09
Not Hispanic (173)	646	0.72
Hispanic (165)	328	0.37
Alaska Athabascan *(Ala. Nat.)* (1)	3	<0.01
Aleut *(Alaska Native)* (1)	2	<0.01
Apache (9)	23	0.03

SECTION TWO

*Notes: † The Census 2010 population figure is used to calculate the percentages in the Hispanic Origin and Race categories. Ancestry percentages are based on the 2006-2010 American Community Survey population (not shown); ‡ Numbers in parentheses indicate the number of people reporting a single ancestry; * Numbers in parentheses indicate the number of persons reporting this race alone, not in combination with any other race; Please refer to the Explanation of Data for more information.*

Blackfeet (2)	17	0.02
Canadian/French Am. Ind. (1)	2	<0.01
Central American Ind. (3)	4	<0.01
Cherokee (30)	164	0.18
Cheyenne (2)	2	<0.01
Chickasaw (0)	6	0.01
Chippewa (5)	15	0.02
Choctaw (6)	31	0.03
Colville (1)	1	<0.01
Comanche (1)	6	0.01
Cree (1)	2	<0.01
Creek (4)	12	0.01
Delaware (0)	2	<0.01
Hopi (1)	2	<0.01
Inupiat *(Alaska Native)* (1)	3	<0.01
Iroquois (1)	17	0.02
Kiowa (1)	4	<0.01
Lumbee (1)	2	<0.01
Mexican American Ind. (42)	55	0.06
Navajo (19)	31	0.03
Osage (1)	5	0.01
Pima (3)	4	<0.01
Potawatomi (4)	5	0.01
Pueblo (8)	12	0.01
Puget Sound Salish (0)	2	<0.01
Seminole (1)	9	0.01
Shoshone (0)	2	<0.01
Sioux (6)	22	0.02
South American Ind. (7)	24	0.03
Spanish American Ind. (2)	4	<0.01
Tlingit-Haida *(Alaska Native)* (1)	4	<0.01
Tohono O'Odham (1)	1	<0.01
Tsimshian *(Alaska Native)* (1)	1	<0.01
Ute (0)	3	<0.01
Yaqui (1)	11	0.01
Yuman (3)	3	<0.01
Yup'ik *(Alaska Native)* (1)	1	<0.01
Asian (8,053)	10,262	11.44
Not Hispanic (7,960)	10,015	11.16
Hispanic (93)	247	0.28
Bangladeshi (19)	24	0.03
Bhutanese (1)	1	<0.01
Burmese (9)	13	0.01
Cambodian (27)	40	0.04
Chinese, ex. Taiwanese (2,159)	2,740	3.05
Filipino (829)	1,212	1.35
Hmong (2)	2	<0.01
Indian (1,034)	1,264	1.41
Indonesian (47)	84	0.09
Japanese (1,343)	1,924	2.14
Korean (1,296)	1,541	1.72
Laotian (7)	17	0.02
Malaysian (6)	11	0.01
Nepalese (16)	19	0.02
Pakistani (101)	137	0.15
Sri Lankan (25)	28	0.03
Taiwanese (303)	370	0.41
Thai (120)	148	0.16
Vietnamese (281)	381	0.42
Hawaii Native/Pacific Islander (124)	361	0.40
Not Hispanic (116)	313	0.35
Hispanic (8)	48	0.05
Fijian (34)	38	0.04
Guamanian/Chamorro (9)	24	0.03
Native Hawaiian (31)	115	0.13
Samoan (16)	23	0.03
Tongan (5)	10	0.01
White (69,663)	73,215	81.59
Not Hispanic (62,917)	65,793	73.32
Hispanic (6,746)	7,422	8.27

Santa Paula

Place Type: City
County: Ventura
Population: 29,321†

Ancestry‡	Population	%
Albanian (0)	13	0.04
American (387)	387	1.33
Arab (0)	45	0.15
Lebanese (0)	45	0.15
Armenian (13)	25	0.09
Australian (11)	11	0.04
British (20)	36	0.12
Bulgarian (0)	33	0.11
Canadian (39)	42	0.14
Croatian (0)	20	0.07
Czech (4)	29	0.10
Czechoslovakian (2)	59	0.20
Danish (13)	58	0.20
Dutch (12)	124	0.43
English (324)	1,066	3.66
European (100)	135	0.46
French, ex. Basque (98)	505	1.73
French Canadian (7)	22	0.08
German (266)	1,009	3.46
Greek (10)	16	0.05
Hungarian (23)	77	0.26
Iranian (81)	81	0.28
Irish (381)	1,227	4.21
Italian (67)	226	0.78
Northern European (23)	23	0.08
Norwegian (52)	136	0.47
Polish (33)	158	0.54
Portuguese (12)	24	0.08
Russian (144)	176	0.60
Scandinavian (12)	12	0.04
Scotch-Irish (133)	301	1.03
Scottish (135)	264	0.91
Swedish (18)	99	0.34
Swiss (24)	63	0.22
Welsh (2)	60	0.21
West Indian, ex. Hispanic (0)	57	0.20
Dutch West Indian (0)	57	0.20
Yugoslavian (0)	4	0.01

Hispanic Origin	Population	%
Hispanic or Latino (of any race)	23,299	79.46
Central American, ex. Mexican	271	0.92
Costa Rican	2	0.01
Guatemalan	87	0.30
Honduran	44	0.15
Nicaraguan	12	0.04
Panamanian	5	0.02
Salvadoran	120	0.41
Other Central American	1	<0.01
Cuban	22	0.08
Dominican Republic	2	0.01
Mexican	22,077	75.29
Puerto Rican	55	0.19
South American	50	0.17
Argentinean	20	0.07
Chilean	9	0.03
Colombian	10	0.03
Ecuadorian	3	0.01
Paraguayan	1	<0.01
Peruvian	5	0.02
Venezuelan	2	0.01
Other Hispanic or Latino	822	2.80

Race*	Population	%
African-American/Black (152)	226	0.77
Not Hispanic (92)	119	0.41
Hispanic (60)	107	0.36
American Indian/Alaska Native (460)	653	2.23
Not Hispanic (107)	191	0.65
Hispanic (353)	462	1.58
Apache (21)	33	0.11
Blackfeet (2)	6	0.02
Cherokee (20)	78	0.27
Chickasaw (3)	9	0.03
Chippewa (2)	3	0.01
Choctaw (12)	15	0.05
Comanche (0)	1	<0.01
Creek (1)	2	0.01
Hopi (2)	2	0.01
Houma (2)	2	0.01
Iroquois (0)	1	<0.01
Mexican American Ind. (53)	77	0.26
Navajo (3)	6	0.02
Osage (0)	1	<0.01
Ottawa (2)	2	0.01
Pima (6)	6	0.02
Pueblo (1)	3	0.01
Shoshone (2)	10	0.03
Sioux (0)	2	0.01
Spanish American Ind. (1)	2	0.01
Tohono O'Odham (0)	2	0.01
Yaqui (15)	17	0.06
Asian (216)	329	1.12
Not Hispanic (189)	234	0.80
Hispanic (27)	95	0.32
Bangladeshi (1)	1	<0.01
Cambodian (3)	3	0.01
Chinese, ex. Taiwanese (37)	53	0.18
Filipino (61)	98	0.33
Indian (33)	40	0.14
Indonesian (4)	12	0.04
Japanese (27)	49	0.17
Korean (20)	33	0.11
Laotian (2)	2	0.01
Sri Lankan (8)	8	0.03
Taiwanese (2)	2	0.01
Thai (1)	1	<0.01
Vietnamese (12)	12	0.04
Hawaii Native/Pacific Islander (24)	84	0.29
Not Hispanic (14)	24	0.08
Hispanic (10)	60	0.20
Guamanian/Chamorro (0)	1	<0.01
Native Hawaiian (9)	22	0.08
Samoan (0)	9	0.03
Tongan (2)	15	0.05
White (18,458)	19,431	66.27
Not Hispanic (5,434)	5,590	19.06
Hispanic (13,024)	13,841	47.21

Santa Rosa

Place Type: City
County: Sonoma
Population: 167,815†

Ancestry‡	Population	%
African, Sub-Saharan (844)	1,077	0.66
African (197)	395	0.24
Ethiopian (466)	491	0.30
Kenyan (0)	10	0.01
South African (35)	35	0.02
Ugandan (146)	146	0.09
American (4,123)	4,123	2.53
Arab (156)	335	0.21
Arab (22)	36	0.02
Egyptian (7)	60	0.04
Jordanian (51)	51	0.03
Lebanese (10)	62	0.04
Palestinian (66)	66	0.04
Syrian (0)	46	0.03
Other Arab (0)	14	0.01
Armenian (16)	165	0.10
Assyrian/Chaldean/Syriac (24)	24	0.01
Australian (28)	54	0.03
Austrian (46)	458	0.28
Basque (0)	10	0.01
Belgian (87)	174	0.11
Brazilian (53)	103	0.06
British (542)	857	0.53
Bulgarian (27)	27	0.02
Cajun (38)	56	0.03
Canadian (213)	428	0.26
Celtic (27)	37	0.02
Croatian (64)	194	0.12
Czech (70)	519	0.32
Czechoslovakian (117)	142	0.09
Danish (772)	2,234	1.37
Dutch (514)	2,452	1.51
Eastern European (376)	419	0.26
English (4,071)	15,897	9.77
European (5,651)	6,559	4.03
Finnish (116)	527	0.32

*Notes: † The Census 2010 population figure is used to calculate the percentages in the Hispanic Origin and Race categories. Ancestry percentages are based on the 2006-2010 American Community Survey population (not shown); ‡ Numbers in parentheses indicate the number of people reporting a single ancestry; * Numbers in parentheses indicate the number of persons reporting this race alone, not in combination with any other race; Please refer to the Explanation of Data for more information.*

French, ex. Basque (649)	5,081	3.12
French Canadian (430)	862	0.53
German (5,853)	21,836	13.43
Greek (213)	939	0.58
Hungarian (279)	820	0.50
Icelander (0)	25	0.02
Iranian (487)	586	0.36
Irish (4,991)	18,711	11.50
Israeli (22)	22	0.01
Italian (4,798)	12,226	7.52
Latvian (16)	42	0.03
Lithuanian (143)	411	0.25
Luxemburger (19)	19	0.01
Macedonian (38)	47	0.03
Maltese (0)	56	0.03
New Zealander (96)	96	0.06
Northern European (303)	330	0.20
Norwegian (610)	2,551	1.57
Pennsylvania German (0)	13	0.01
Polish (537)	2,273	1.40
Portuguese (722)	2,415	1.48
Romanian (86)	201	0.12
Russian (484)	1,888	1.16
Scandinavian (315)	542	0.33
Scotch-Irish (1,249)	3,352	2.06
Scottish (1,098)	4,346	2.67
Serbian (0)	72	0.04
Slavic (47)	59	0.04
Slovak (46)	86	0.05
Slovene (25)	70	0.04
Swedish (669)	3,092	1.90
Swiss (151)	924	0.57
Turkish (18)	38	0.02
Ukrainian (179)	318	0.20
Welsh (181)	1,242	0.76
West Indian, ex. Hispanic (34)	131	0.08
Bahamian (9)	9	0.01
Belizean (15)	15	0.01
Dutch West Indian (0)	5	<0.01
Jamaican (10)	85	0.05
West Indian (0)	17	0.01
Yugoslavian (60)	161	0.10

Hispanic Origin	Population	%
Hispanic or Latino (of any race)	47,970	28.59
Central American, ex. Mexican	2,239	1.33
Costa Rican	54	0.03
Guatemalan	348	0.21
Honduran	132	0.08
Nicaraguan	325	0.19
Panamanian	51	0.03
Salvadoran	1,311	0.78
Other Central American	18	0.01
Cuban	178	0.11
Dominican Republic	22	0.01
Mexican	40,889	24.37
Puerto Rican	661	0.39
South American	845	0.50
Argentinean	91	0.05
Bolivian	41	0.02
Chilean	81	0.05
Colombian	207	0.12
Ecuadorian	66	0.04
Paraguayan	11	0.01
Peruvian	290	0.17
Uruguayan	9	0.01
Venezuelan	32	0.02
Other South American	17	0.01
Other Hispanic or Latino	3,136	1.87

Race*	Population	%
African-American/Black (4,079)	5,938	3.54
Not Hispanic (3,660)	5,142	3.06
Hispanic (419)	796	0.47
American Indian/Alaska Native (2,808)	5,575	3.32
Not Hispanic (1,511)	3,221	1.92
Hispanic (1,297)	2,354	1.40
Alaska Athabascan *(Ala. Nat.)* (5)	8	<0.01
Aleut *(Alaska Native)* (6)	21	0.01
Apache (40)	184	0.11
Arapaho (0)	2	<0.01
Blackfeet (9)	97	0.06
Canadian/French Am. Ind. (5)	12	0.01
Central American Ind. (6)	10	0.01
Cherokee (95)	511	0.30
Cheyenne (3)	14	0.01
Chickasaw (12)	35	0.02
Chippewa (20)	62	0.04
Choctaw (50)	143	0.09
Colville (1)	1	<0.01
Comanche (16)	39	0.02
Cree (1)	13	0.01
Creek (10)	26	0.02
Crow (2)	10	0.01
Delaware (0)	11	0.01
Hopi (5)	6	<0.01
Houma (1)	1	<0.01
Inupiat *(Alaska Native)* (6)	20	0.01
Iroquois (9)	32	0.02
Kiowa (1)	1	<0.01
Lumbee (1)	1	<0.01
Menominee (2)	5	<0.01
Mexican American Ind. (267)	410	0.24
Navajo (40)	92	0.05
Osage (1)	14	0.01
Ottawa (0)	4	<0.01
Paiute (5)	12	0.01
Pima (3)	7	<0.01
Potawatomi (4)	13	0.01
Pueblo (11)	26	0.02
Puget Sound Salish (0)	6	<0.01
Seminole (4)	24	0.01
Shoshone (4)	9	0.01
Sioux (36)	97	0.06
South American Ind. (4)	13	0.01
Spanish American Ind. (14)	26	0.02
Tlingit-Haida *(Alaska Native)* (4)	16	0.01
Tohono O'Odham (0)	7	<0.01
Tsimshian *(Alaska Native)* (0)	2	<0.01
Ute (1)	10	0.01
Yakama (0)	2	<0.01
Yaqui (16)	55	0.03
Yuman (4)	7	<0.01
Yup'ik *(Alaska Native)* (4)	5	<0.01
Asian (8,746)	11,319	6.74
Not Hispanic (8,521)	10,606	6.32
Hispanic (225)	713	0.42
Bangladeshi (5)	5	<0.01
Burmese (22)	32	0.02
Cambodian (808)	931	0.55
Chinese, ex. Taiwanese (1,542)	2,144	1.28
Filipino (1,549)	2,451	1.46
Hmong (63)	76	0.05
Indian (941)	1,154	0.69
Indonesian (32)	64	0.04
Japanese (471)	1,016	0.61
Korean (467)	653	0.39
Laotian (698)	849	0.51
Malaysian (9)	12	0.01
Nepalese (137)	153	0.09
Pakistani (82)	94	0.06
Sri Lankan (14)	16	0.01
Taiwanese (68)	96	0.06
Thai (141)	187	0.11
Vietnamese (1,239)	1,431	0.85
Hawaii Native/Pacific Islander (810)	1,420	0.85
Not Hispanic (750)	1,221	0.73
Hispanic (60)	199	0.12
Fijian (375)	419	0.25
Guamanian/Chamorro (47)	78	0.05
Marshallese (1)	2	<0.01
Native Hawaiian (130)	428	0.26
Samoan (157)	264	0.16
Tongan (15)	27	0.02
White (119,158)	126,600	75.44
Not Hispanic (100,126)	104,546	62.30
Hispanic (19,032)	22,054	13.14

Santee

Place Type: City
County: San Diego
Population: 53,413†

Ancestry‡	Population	%
African, Sub-Saharan (109)	141	0.27
African (96)	118	0.22
South African (9)	19	0.04
Other Sub-Saharan African (4)	4	0.01
Albanian (118)	118	0.22
American (1,791)	1,791	3.38
Arab (887)	1,287	2.43
Arab (148)	219	0.41
Egyptian (12)	39	0.07
Iraqi (117)	148	0.28
Jordanian (6)	160	0.30
Lebanese (118)	137	0.26
Moroccan (0)	19	0.04
Syrian (0)	67	0.13
Other Arab (486)	498	0.94
Armenian (103)	135	0.25
Assyrian/Chaldean/Syriac (110)	110	0.21
Australian (0)	15	0.03
Austrian (47)	197	0.37
Basque (0)	13	0.02
Belgian (0)	101	0.19
Brazilian (0)	100	0.19
British (145)	424	0.80
Bulgarian (20)	20	0.04
Canadian (107)	191	0.36
Celtic (15)	23	0.04
Croatian (26)	26	0.05
Czech (72)	392	0.74
Czechoslovakian (22)	22	0.04
Danish (143)	285	0.54
Dutch (121)	926	1.75
Eastern European (11)	22	0.04
English (1,867)	6,595	12.45
European (532)	708	1.34
Finnish (46)	65	0.12
French, ex. Basque (509)	2,200	4.15
French Canadian (159)	452	0.85
German (3,367)	11,882	22.43
Greek (132)	291	0.55
Hungarian (43)	352	0.66
Icelander (14)	14	0.03
Iranian (142)	154	0.29
Irish (1,543)	8,278	15.63
Israeli (0)	33	0.06
Italian (1,077)	3,637	6.87
Lithuanian (17)	52	0.10
Northern European (27)	27	0.05
Norwegian (425)	1,295	2.44
Pennsylvania German (0)	12	0.02
Polish (357)	1,454	2.75
Portuguese (276)	713	1.35
Romanian (61)	73	0.14
Russian (52)	481	0.91
Scandinavian (34)	82	0.15
Scotch-Irish (475)	1,204	2.27
Scottish (378)	1,277	2.41
Serbian (0)	11	0.02
Slovak (37)	114	0.22
Swedish (264)	1,090	2.06
Swiss (0)	88	0.17
Turkish (0)	31	0.06
Ukrainian (49)	100	0.19
Welsh (56)	411	0.78
West Indian, ex. Hispanic (8)	25	0.05
Bermudan (0)	17	0.03
Jamaican (8)	8	0.02
Yugoslavian (16)	43	0.08

Hispanic Origin	Population	%
Hispanic or Latino (of any race)	8,699	16.29
Central American, ex. Mexican	210	0.39
Costa Rican	54	0.10
Guatemalan	43	0.08

*Notes: † The Census 2010 population figure is used to calculate the percentages in the Hispanic Origin and Race categories. Ancestry percentages are based on the 2006-2010 American Community Survey population (not shown); ‡ Numbers in parentheses indicate the number of people reporting a single ancestry; * Numbers in parentheses indicate the number of persons reporting this race alone, not in combination with any other race; Please refer to the Explanation of Data for more information.*

Honduran	12	0.02
Nicaraguan	29	0.05
Panamanian	23	0.04
Salvadoran	45	0.08
Other Central American	4	0.01
Cuban	49	0.09
Dominican Republic	7	0.01
Mexican	7,086	13.27
Puerto Rican	318	0.60
South American	209	0.39
Argentinean	16	0.03
Bolivian	23	0.04
Chilean	33	0.06
Colombian	45	0.08
Ecuadorian	11	0.02
Paraguayan	5	0.01
Peruvian	58	0.11
Uruguayan	5	0.01
Venezuelan	12	0.02
Other South American	1	<0.01
Other Hispanic or Latino	820	1.54

Race*	Population	%
African-American/Black (1,057)	1,620	3.03
Not Hispanic (971)	1,426	2.67
Hispanic (86)	194	0.36
American Indian/Alaska Native (409)	999	1.87
Not Hispanic (290)	676	1.27
Hispanic (119)	323	0.60
Alaska Athabascan *(Ala. Nat.)* (2)	3	0.01
Aleut *(Alaska Native)* (1)	1	<0.01
Apache (17)	48	0.09
Arapaho (0)	1	<0.01
Blackfeet (14)	47	0.09
Canadian/French Am. Ind. (1)	3	0.01
Cherokee (37)	146	0.27
Cheyenne (1)	2	<0.01
Chickasaw (7)	11	0.02
Chippewa (13)	30	0.06
Choctaw (10)	36	0.07
Comanche (0)	9	0.02
Cree (1)	4	0.01
Creek (3)	8	0.01
Delaware (1)	2	<0.01
Inupiat *(Alaska Native)* (2)	2	<0.01
Iroquois (1)	11	0.02
Lumbee (2)	4	0.01
Menominee (1)	1	<0.01
Mexican American Ind. (15)	30	0.06
Navajo (18)	44	0.08
Osage (0)	12	0.02
Ottawa (1)	3	0.01
Paiute (0)	1	<0.01
Potawatomi (2)	12	0.02
Pueblo (6)	10	0.02
Puget Sound Salish (0)	1	<0.01
Seminole (1)	4	0.01
Shoshone (1)	1	<0.01
Sioux (7)	21	0.04
Spanish American Ind. (1)	1	<0.01
Tohono O'Odham (1)	5	0.01
Yaqui (12)	25	0.05
Yuman (3)	6	0.01
Yup'ik *(Alaska Native)* (1)	1	<0.01
Asian (2,044)	3,247	6.08
Not Hispanic (1,974)	2,949	5.52
Hispanic (70)	298	0.56
Bangladeshi (2)	2	<0.01
Cambodian (25)	31	0.06
Chinese, ex. Taiwanese (194)	355	0.66
Filipino (971)	1,605	3.00
Indian (92)	130	0.24
Indonesian (22)	43	0.08
Japanese (168)	475	0.89
Korean (101)	160	0.30
Laotian (32)	46	0.09
Malaysian (3)	4	0.01
Nepalese (2)	3	0.01
Pakistani (4)	8	0.01
Sri Lankan (3)	4	0.01
Taiwanese (16)	22	0.04
Thai (47)	70	0.13
Vietnamese (255)	307	0.57
Hawaii Native/Pacific Islander (253)	632	1.18
Not Hispanic (232)	526	0.98
Hispanic (21)	106	0.20
Fijian (2)	12	0.02
Guamanian/Chamorro (132)	276	0.52
Native Hawaiian (52)	194	0.36
Samoan (34)	88	0.16
Tongan (2)	3	0.01
White (44,083)	46,684	87.40
Not Hispanic (39,312)	41,021	76.80
Hispanic (4,771)	5,663	10.60

Saratoga

Place Type: City
County: Santa Clara
Population: 29,926†

Ancestry‡	Population	%
Afghan (40)	40	0.14
American (958)	958	3.24
Arab (63)	106	0.36
Arab (0)	32	0.11
Egyptian (23)	23	0.08
Lebanese (26)	26	0.09
Other Arab (14)	25	0.08
Armenian (30)	72	0.24
Austrian (0)	46	0.16
Belgian (6)	6	0.02
Brazilian (6)	6	0.02
British (158)	204	0.69
Canadian (171)	192	0.65
Croatian (200)	262	0.89
Czech (46)	74	0.25
Czechoslovakian (32)	52	0.18
Danish (64)	140	0.47
Dutch (116)	301	1.02
English (1,250)	3,513	11.90
European (431)	578	1.96
Finnish (0)	12	0.04
French, ex. Basque (128)	570	1.93
French Canadian (0)	24	0.08
German (1,113)	3,241	10.98
Greek (95)	200	0.68
Hungarian (44)	68	0.23
Iranian (1,038)	1,119	3.79
Irish (539)	2,118	7.17
Israeli (68)	68	0.23
Italian (603)	1,576	5.34
Lithuanian (29)	76	0.26
Maltese (11)	11	0.04
Northern European (115)	115	0.39
Norwegian (118)	410	1.39
Polish (158)	544	1.84
Portuguese (71)	179	0.61
Romanian (21)	31	0.11
Russian (457)	765	2.59
Scotch-Irish (288)	568	1.92
Scottish (177)	651	2.21
Serbian (20)	35	0.12
Slavic (19)	30	0.10
Swedish (200)	621	2.10
Swiss (87)	177	0.60
Ukrainian (30)	130	0.44
Welsh (0)	185	0.63

Hispanic Origin	Population	%
Hispanic or Latino (of any race)	1,034	3.46
Central American, ex. Mexican	62	0.21
Costa Rican	11	0.04
Guatemalan	9	0.03
Honduran	1	<0.01
Nicaraguan	19	0.06
Panamanian	4	0.01
Salvadoran	18	0.06
Cuban	27	0.09
Dominican Republic	1	<0.01
Mexican	627	2.10
Puerto Rican	26	0.09
South American	105	0.35
Argentinean	14	0.05
Bolivian	8	0.03
Chilean	20	0.07
Colombian	16	0.05
Ecuadorian	7	0.02
Paraguayan	3	0.01
Peruvian	26	0.09
Venezuelan	10	0.03
Other South American	1	<0.01
Other Hispanic or Latino	186	0.62

Race*	Population	%
African-American/Black (94)	179	0.60
Not Hispanic (91)	171	0.57
Hispanic (3)	8	0.03
American Indian/Alaska Native (41)	129	0.43
Not Hispanic (24)	96	0.32
Hispanic (17)	33	0.11
Apache (1)	1	<0.01
Blackfeet (0)	4	0.01
Cherokee (4)	29	0.10
Chickasaw (0)	3	0.01
Chippewa (3)	5	0.02
Choctaw (0)	5	0.02
Delaware (0)	4	0.01
Inupiat *(Alaska Native)* (1)	1	<0.01
Iroquois (1)	2	0.01
Mexican American Ind. (0)	1	<0.01
Navajo (0)	2	0.01
Osage (0)	1	<0.01
Puget Sound Salish (1)	1	<0.01
Seminole (0)	1	<0.01
South American Ind. (1)	1	<0.01
Asian (12,376)	13,230	44.21
Not Hispanic (12,331)	13,135	43.89
Hispanic (45)	95	0.32
Bangladeshi (15)	16	0.05
Burmese (4)	10	0.03
Chinese, ex. Taiwanese (5,610)	6,049	20.21
Filipino (221)	337	1.13
Indian (2,935)	3,057	10.22
Indonesian (10)	15	0.05
Japanese (666)	944	3.15
Korean (869)	962	3.21
Laotian (1)	1	<0.01
Malaysian (3)	8	0.03
Nepalese (2)	2	0.01
Pakistani (126)	139	0.46
Sri Lankan (8)	12	0.04
Taiwanese (1,100)	1,233	4.12
Thai (30)	38	0.13
Vietnamese (455)	517	1.73
Hawaii Native/Pacific Islander (23)	94	0.31
Not Hispanic (23)	91	0.30
Hispanic (0)	3	0.01
Fijian (3)	3	0.01
Guamanian/Chamorro (3)	11	0.04
Native Hawaiian (9)	25	0.08
Samoan (0)	2	0.01
Tongan (5)	9	0.03
White (16,125)	17,061	57.01
Not Hispanic (15,431)	16,260	54.33
Hispanic (694)	801	2.68

Scotts Valley

Place Type: City
County: Santa Cruz
Population: 11,580†

Ancestry‡	Population	%
African, Sub-Saharan (0)	14	0.12
African (0)	14	0.12
American (290)	290	2.55
Arab (19)	108	0.95
Egyptian (0)	53	0.47
Other Arab (19)	55	0.48

*Notes: † The Census 2010 population figure is used to calculate the percentages in the Hispanic Origin and Race categories. Ancestry percentages are based on the 2006-2010 American Community Survey population (not shown); ‡ Numbers in parentheses indicate the number of people reporting a single ancestry; * Numbers in parentheses indicate the number of persons reporting this race alone, not in combination with any other race; Please refer to the Explanation of Data for more information.*

Austrian (26)	50	0.44
British (119)	226	1.99
Canadian (30)	46	0.41
Croatian (0)	13	0.11
Czechoslovakian (0)	73	0.64
Danish (16)	153	1.35
Dutch (97)	359	3.16
Eastern European (11)	11	0.10
English (569)	1,816	16.00
Estonian (11)	23	0.20
European (269)	283	2.49
Finnish (18)	18	0.16
French, ex. Basque (53)	574	5.06
French Canadian (0)	72	0.63
German (520)	2,199	19.37
Hungarian (38)	60	0.53
Iranian (28)	120	1.06
Irish (138)	1,299	11.44
Italian (596)	1,540	13.57
Lithuanian (0)	18	0.16
Norwegian (84)	287	2.53
Polish (18)	263	2.32
Portuguese (73)	399	3.52
Romanian (14)	39	0.34
Russian (41)	41	0.36
Scandinavian (16)	41	0.36
Scotch-Irish (114)	343	3.02
Scottish (166)	536	4.72
Swedish (44)	372	3.28
Swiss (0)	46	0.41
Turkish (13)	13	0.11
Ukrainian (12)	12	0.11
Welsh (0)	149	1.31
Yugoslavian (71)	88	0.78

Hispanic Origin	Population	%
Hispanic or Latino (of any race)	1,158	10.00
Central American, ex. Mexican	67	0.58
Costa Rican	8	0.07
Guatemalan	7	0.06
Honduran	4	0.03
Nicaraguan	9	0.08
Panamanian	1	0.01
Salvadoran	37	0.32
Other Central American	1	0.01
Cuban	6	0.05
Dominican Republic	1	0.01
Mexican	772	6.67
Puerto Rican	38	0.33
South American	63	0.54
Argentinean	8	0.07
Bolivian	2	0.02
Chilean	5	0.04
Colombian	8	0.07
Ecuadorian	8	0.07
Peruvian	27	0.23
Venezuelan	5	0.04
Other Hispanic or Latino	211	1.82

Race*	Population	%
African-American/Black (101)	182	1.57
Not Hispanic (90)	159	1.37
Hispanic (11)	23	0.20
American Indian/Alaska Native (57)	202	1.74
Not Hispanic (29)	129	1.11
Hispanic (28)	73	0.63
Apache (4)	16	0.14
Arapaho (0)	2	0.02
Blackfeet (0)	6	0.05
Cherokee (4)	44	0.38
Chickasaw (2)	5	0.04
Chippewa (2)	4	0.03
Choctaw (2)	5	0.04
Comanche (1)	1	0.01
Creek (0)	4	0.03
Delaware (0)	1	0.01
Iroquois (1)	6	0.05
Mexican American Ind. (0)	2	0.02
Navajo (3)	5	0.04
Ottawa (1)	3	0.03
Potawatomi (0)	1	0.01
Seminole (0)	1	0.01
Sioux (0)	3	0.03
South American Ind. (0)	1	0.01
Yakama (0)	3	0.03
Asian (590)	868	7.50
Not Hispanic (580)	834	7.20
Hispanic (10)	34	0.29
Bangladeshi (1)	1	0.01
Cambodian (3)	10	0.09
Chinese, ex. Taiwanese (158)	224	1.93
Filipino (71)	150	1.30
Hmong (1)	2	0.02
Indian (137)	162	1.40
Indonesian (1)	7	0.06
Japanese (70)	155	1.34
Korean (67)	95	0.82
Laotian (1)	1	0.01
Nepalese (3)	4	0.03
Pakistani (12)	15	0.13
Taiwanese (8)	8	0.07
Thai (9)	11	0.09
Vietnamese (21)	30	0.26
Hawaii Native/Pacific Islander (18)	64	0.55
Not Hispanic (15)	56	0.48
Hispanic (3)	8	0.07
Guamanian/Chamorro (8)	20	0.17
Native Hawaiian (5)	27	0.23
Samoan (2)	3	0.03
Tongan (0)	1	0.01
White (9,958)	10,480	90.50
Not Hispanic (9,265)	9,674	83.54
Hispanic (693)	806	6.96

Seal Beach

Place Type: City
County: Orange
Population: 24,168†

Ancestry‡	Population	%
American (614)	614	2.55
Arab (54)	103	0.43
Egyptian (16)	16	0.07
Lebanese (38)	78	0.32
Syrian (0)	9	0.04
Armenian (81)	170	0.71
Austrian (27)	167	0.69
Basque (7)	53	0.22
Belgian (35)	64	0.27
Brazilian (10)	10	0.04
British (221)	419	1.74
Canadian (188)	225	0.93
Celtic (9)	9	0.04
Croatian (47)	131	0.54
Czech (29)	98	0.41
Czechoslovakian (11)	49	0.20
Danish (125)	296	1.23
Dutch (334)	639	2.65
Eastern European (71)	71	0.29
English (1,195)	3,523	14.63
European (543)	566	2.35
Finnish (0)	12	0.05
French, ex. Basque (166)	1,053	4.37
French Canadian (71)	167	0.69
German (1,188)	4,497	18.67
Greek (157)	204	0.85
Hungarian (74)	266	1.10
Iranian (129)	155	0.64
Irish (1,176)	3,586	14.89
Italian (714)	1,567	6.51
Latvian (13)	13	0.05
Lithuanian (26)	93	0.39
Luxemburger (0)	10	0.04
Northern European (7)	7	0.03
Norwegian (283)	604	2.51
Pennsylvania German (12)	12	0.05
Polish (278)	737	3.06
Portuguese (84)	246	1.02
Romanian (35)	67	0.28
Russian (217)	429	1.78
Scandinavian (11)	46	0.19
Scotch-Irish (304)	659	2.74
Scottish (290)	912	3.79
Serbian (11)	32	0.13
Slavic (32)	32	0.13
Slovak (45)	92	0.38
Swedish (238)	786	3.26
Swiss (27)	104	0.43
Turkish (7)	36	0.15
Ukrainian (31)	46	0.19
Welsh (73)	297	1.23
West Indian, ex. Hispanic (0)	43	0.18
Belizean (0)	36	0.15
Jamaican (0)	7	0.03
Yugoslavian (0)	33	0.14

Hispanic Origin	Population	%
Hispanic or Latino (of any race)	2,331	9.64
Central American, ex. Mexican	132	0.55
Costa Rican	20	0.08
Guatemalan	22	0.09
Honduran	12	0.05
Nicaraguan	15	0.06
Panamanian	12	0.05
Salvadoran	50	0.21
Other Central American	1	<0.01
Cuban	139	0.58
Dominican Republic	2	0.01
Mexican	1,452	6.01
Puerto Rican	86	0.36
South American	210	0.87
Argentinean	29	0.12
Bolivian	3	0.01
Chilean	16	0.07
Colombian	49	0.20
Ecuadorian	24	0.10
Paraguayan	1	<0.01
Peruvian	73	0.30
Uruguayan	6	0.02
Venezuelan	9	0.04
Other Hispanic or Latino	310	1.28

Race*	Population	%
African-American/Black (279)	383	1.58
Not Hispanic (255)	337	1.39
Hispanic (24)	46	0.19
American Indian/Alaska Native (65)	210	0.87
Not Hispanic (38)	142	0.59
Hispanic (27)	68	0.28
Alaska Athabascan *(Ala. Nat.)* (0)	1	<0.01
Apache (4)	11	0.05
Blackfeet (1)	4	0.02
Central American Ind. (0)	1	<0.01
Cherokee (5)	41	0.17
Chickasaw (0)	5	0.02
Chippewa (1)	5	0.02
Choctaw (5)	6	0.02
Creek (1)	1	<0.01
Crow (0)	1	<0.01
Delaware (3)	3	0.01
Iroquois (1)	2	0.01
Kiowa (0)	1	<0.01
Mexican American Ind. (4)	7	0.03
Navajo (1)	1	<0.01
Osage (2)	3	0.01
Ottawa (2)	2	0.01
Potawatomi (0)	1	<0.01
Pueblo (1)	1	<0.01
Seminole (0)	2	0.01
Shoshone (2)	5	0.02
Sioux (0)	4	0.02
South American Ind. (1)	5	0.02
Yaqui (2)	7	0.03
Asian (2,309)	2,781	11.51
Not Hispanic (2,273)	2,653	10.98
Hispanic (36)	128	0.53
Bangladeshi (1)	4	0.02
Burmese (1)	1	<0.01
Cambodian (17)	34	0.14

*Notes: † The Census 2010 population figure is used to calculate the percentages in the Hispanic Origin and Race categories. Ancestry percentages are based on the 2006-2010 American Community Survey population (not shown); ‡ Numbers in parentheses indicate the number of people reporting a single ancestry; * Numbers in parentheses indicate the number of persons reporting this race alone, not in combination with any other race; Please refer to the Explanation of Data for more information.*

Chinese, ex. Taiwanese (380)	505	2.09
Filipino (364)	522	2.16
Hmong (6)	6	0.02
Indian (101)	118	0.49
Indonesian (21)	35	0.14
Japanese (442)	597	2.47
Korean (522)	585	2.42
Laotian (4)	4	0.02
Malaysian (2)	5	0.02
Pakistani (8)	11	0.05
Sri Lankan (2)	4	0.02
Taiwanese (63)	65	0.27
Thai (24)	41	0.17
Vietnamese (259)	300	1.24
Hawaii Native/Pacific Islander (58)	161	0.67
Not Hispanic (52)	136	0.56
Hispanic (6)	25	0.10
Guamanian/Chamorro (13)	25	0.10
Native Hawaiian (12)	72	0.30
Samoan (24)	41	0.17
Tongan (0)	6	0.02
White (20,154)	20,898	86.47
Not Hispanic (18,580)	19,098	79.02
Hispanic (1,574)	1,800	7.45

Seaside

Place Type: City
County: Monterey
Population: 33,025†

Ancestry‡	Population	%
Afghan (25)	25	0.08
African, Sub-Saharan (88)	212	0.65
African (88)	212	0.65
American (422)	422	1.30
Arab (128)	221	0.68
Lebanese (0)	46	0.14
Moroccan (14)	61	0.19
Syrian (12)	12	0.04
Other Arab (102)	102	0.31
Austrian (0)	48	0.15
Basque (8)	44	0.14
Belgian (33)	80	0.25
Brazilian (16)	16	0.05
British (57)	92	0.28
Bulgarian (9)	9	0.03
Canadian (35)	107	0.33
Croatian (0)	25	0.08
Czech (23)	157	0.48
Danish (45)	167	0.51
Dutch (22)	142	0.44
Eastern European (0)	22	0.07
English (453)	2,123	6.55
European (375)	486	1.50
French, ex. Basque (99)	578	1.78
French Canadian (77)	150	0.46
German (617)	2,588	7.98
Greek (0)	115	0.35
Hungarian (35)	144	0.44
Iranian (12)	12	0.04
Irish (551)	2,274	7.01
Italian (588)	1,516	4.67
Lithuanian (40)	57	0.18
Northern European (188)	188	0.58
Norwegian (33)	190	0.59
Polish (105)	267	0.82
Portuguese (120)	284	0.88
Romanian (0)	7	0.02
Russian (18)	218	0.67
Scandinavian (36)	36	0.11
Scotch-Irish (112)	371	1.14
Scottish (156)	501	1.54
Serbian (44)	44	0.14
Slovak (31)	105	0.32
Swedish (87)	307	0.95
Swiss (11)	74	0.23
Ukrainian (45)	45	0.14
Welsh (22)	95	0.29
West Indian, ex. Hispanic (97)	97	0.30
Belizean (97)	97	0.30

Hispanic Origin	Population	%
Hispanic or Latino (of any race)	14,347	43.44
Central American, ex. Mexican	1,193	3.61
Costa Rican	17	0.05
Guatemalan	53	0.16
Honduran	35	0.11
Nicaraguan	17	0.05
Panamanian	93	0.28
Salvadoran	971	2.94
Other Central American	7	0.02
Cuban	54	0.16
Dominican Republic	17	0.05
Mexican	11,629	35.21
Puerto Rican	312	0.94
South American	202	0.61
Argentinean	23	0.07
Bolivian	11	0.03
Chilean	26	0.08
Colombian	50	0.15
Ecuadorian	5	0.02
Paraguayan	11	0.03
Peruvian	59	0.18
Uruguayan	4	0.01
Venezuelan	10	0.03
Other South American	3	0.01
Other Hispanic or Latino	940	2.85

Race*	Population	%
African-American/Black (2,783)	3,633	11.00
Not Hispanic (2,603)	3,246	9.83
Hispanic (180)	387	1.17
American Indian/Alaska Native (347)	782	2.37
Not Hispanic (104)	391	1.18
Hispanic (243)	391	1.18
Alaska Athabascan *(Ala. Nat.)* (0)	3	0.01
Apache (5)	20	0.06
Arapaho (1)	4	0.01
Blackfeet (3)	23	0.07
Canadian/French Am. Ind. (0)	5	0.02
Central American Ind. (3)	8	0.02
Cherokee (12)	136	0.41
Cheyenne (1)	1	<0.01
Chickasaw (2)	3	0.01
Chippewa (2)	7	0.02
Choctaw (2)	8	0.02
Comanche (0)	3	0.01
Cree (0)	2	0.01
Creek (8)	9	0.03
Delaware (0)	7	0.02
Hopi (0)	1	<0.01
Iroquois (0)	4	0.01
Mexican American Ind. (65)	84	0.25
Navajo (4)	12	0.04
Pima (1)	4	0.01
Potawatomi (1)	7	0.02
Pueblo (1)	1	<0.01
Puget Sound Salish (1)	1	<0.01
Seminole (0)	10	0.03
Shoshone (0)	6	0.02
Sioux (0)	6	0.02
South American Ind. (0)	3	0.01
Tlingit-Haida *(Alaska Native)* (0)	1	<0.01
Tohono O'Odham (1)	3	0.01
Tsimshian *(Alaska Native)* (0)	1	<0.01
Ute (0)	1	<0.01
Yaqui (0)	6	0.02
Asian (3,206)	4,320	13.08
Not Hispanic (3,100)	4,021	12.18
Hispanic (106)	299	0.91
Burmese (1)	5	0.02
Cambodian (2)	4	0.01
Chinese, ex. Taiwanese (185)	326	0.99
Filipino (1,559)	2,039	6.17
Hmong (8)	10	0.03
Indian (160)	265	0.80
Indonesian (7)	11	0.03
Japanese (311)	610	1.85
Korean (341)	485	1.47
Laotian (2)	3	0.01
Malaysian (0)	2	0.01
Nepalese (5)	6	0.02
Pakistani (21)	29	0.09
Sri Lankan (1)	1	<0.01
Taiwanese (13)	17	0.05
Thai (41)	74	0.22
Vietnamese (315)	371	1.12
Hawaii Native/Pacific Islander (529)	829	2.51
Not Hispanic (511)	770	2.33
Hispanic (18)	59	0.18
Fijian (138)	183	0.55
Guamanian/Chamorro (68)	118	0.36
Marshallese (2)	2	0.01
Native Hawaiian (34)	124	0.38
Samoan (88)	138	0.42
Tongan (120)	130	0.39
White (15,978)	17,986	54.46
Not Hispanic (10,725)	11,905	36.05
Hispanic (5,253)	6,081	18.41

Selma

Place Type: City
County: Fresno
Population: 23,219†

Ancestry‡	Population	%
American (264)	264	1.17
Arab (58)	80	0.35
Arab (48)	70	0.31
Egyptian (10)	10	0.04
Armenian (52)	73	0.32
Austrian (11)	11	0.05
Canadian (0)	19	0.08
Danish (39)	55	0.24
Dutch (28)	67	0.30
English (172)	561	2.48
European (22)	33	0.15
Finnish (7)	16	0.07
French, ex. Basque (34)	78	0.34
French Canadian (0)	7	0.03
German (343)	1,118	4.94
German Russian (8)	8	0.04
Greek (46)	46	0.20
Irish (126)	511	2.26
Italian (46)	155	0.69
Norwegian (33)	52	0.23
Pennsylvania German (0)	10	0.04
Polish (24)	24	0.11
Portuguese (77)	129	0.57
Scotch-Irish (60)	125	0.55
Scottish (71)	95	0.42
Swedish (88)	216	0.96
Welsh (0)	7	0.03

Hispanic Origin	Population	%
Hispanic or Latino (of any race)	18,014	77.58
Central American, ex. Mexican	71	0.31
Costa Rican	1	<0.01
Guatemalan	31	0.13
Honduran	5	0.02
Nicaraguan	10	0.04
Panamanian	1	<0.01
Salvadoran	22	0.09
Other Central American	1	<0.01
Cuban	2	0.01
Mexican	17,061	73.48
Puerto Rican	37	0.16
South American	20	0.09
Argentinean	5	0.02
Colombian	5	0.02
Ecuadorian	7	0.03
Peruvian	1	<0.01
Venezuelan	2	0.01
Other Hispanic or Latino	823	3.54

Race*	Population	%
African-American/Black (284)	383	1.65
Not Hispanic (160)	201	0.87

*Notes: † The Census 2010 population figure is used to calculate the percentages in the Hispanic Origin and Race categories. Ancestry percentages are based on the 2006-2010 American Community Survey population (not shown); ‡ Numbers in parentheses indicate the number of people reporting a single ancestry; * Numbers in parentheses indicate the number of persons reporting this race alone, not in combination with any other race; Please refer to the Explanation of Data for more information.*

Hispanic (124)	182	0.78
American Indian/Alaska Native (479)	688	2.96
Not Hispanic (116)	196	0.84
Hispanic (363)	492	2.12
Apache (13)	22	0.09
Blackfeet (0)	2	0.01
Cherokee (16)	61	0.26
Cheyenne (3)	3	0.01
Chickasaw (2)	8	0.03
Chippewa (4)	4	0.02
Choctaw (22)	29	0.12
Comanche (1)	1	<0.01
Creek (12)	16	0.07
Iroquois (0)	6	0.03
Mexican American Ind. (74)	107	0.46
Navajo (6)	8	0.03
Pima (2)	3	0.01
Potawatomi (0)	7	0.03
Pueblo (2)	2	0.01
Puget Sound Salish (1)	1	<0.01
Seminole (2)	8	0.03
South American Ind. (0)	1	<0.01
Tlingit-Haida *(Alaska Native)* (1)	1	<0.01
Tohono O'Odham (2)	2	0.01
Yaqui (19)	20	0.09
Asian (1,057)	1,247	5.37
Not Hispanic (993)	1,090	4.69
Hispanic (64)	157	0.68
Cambodian (3)	4	0.02
Chinese, ex. Taiwanese (46)	61	0.26
Filipino (74)	119	0.51
Hmong (7)	7	0.03
Indian (755)	817	3.52
Japanese (109)	139	0.60
Korean (5)	15	0.06
Laotian (2)	3	0.01
Pakistani (13)	13	0.06
Taiwanese (2)	5	0.02
Thai (1)	2	0.01
Vietnamese (6)	11	0.05
Hawaii Native/Pacific Islander (9)	49	0.21
Not Hispanic (2)	14	0.06
Hispanic (7)	35	0.15
Guamanian/Chamorro (1)	6	0.03
Native Hawaiian (0)	10	0.04
Samoan (1)	4	0.02
Tongan (1)	5	0.02
White (12,869)	13,586	58.51
Not Hispanic (3,660)	3,823	16.46
Hispanic (9,209)	9,763	42.05

Shafter

Place Type: City
County: Kern
Population: 16,988†

Ancestry‡	Population	%
African, Sub-Saharan (7)	7	0.04
African (7)	7	0.04
American (235)	235	1.43
Arab (77)	141	0.86
Palestinian (0)	64	0.39
Other Arab (77)	77	0.47
Basque (10)	10	0.06
Brazilian (21)	21	0.13
British (0)	4	0.02
Canadian (24)	24	0.15
Croatian (11)	11	0.07
Czech (0)	13	0.08
Danish (0)	13	0.08
Dutch (13)	113	0.69
English (323)	637	3.89
European (7)	47	0.29
Finnish (0)	13	0.08
French, ex. Basque (0)	137	0.84
French Canadian (30)	43	0.26
German (299)	801	4.89
Hungarian (8)	8	0.05
Irish (37)	470	2.87
Italian (71)	153	0.93
Norwegian (33)	205	1.25
Polish (7)	7	0.04
Portuguese (13)	84	0.51
Russian (21)	33	0.20
Scotch-Irish (10)	54	0.33
Scottish (8)	76	0.46
Serbian (0)	8	0.05
Slovene (11)	11	0.07
Swedish (14)	22	0.13
Swiss (0)	17	0.10

Hispanic Origin	Population	%
Hispanic or Latino (of any race)	13,634	80.26
Central American, ex. Mexican	228	1.34
Costa Rican	2	0.01
Guatemalan	44	0.26
Honduran	11	0.06
Nicaraguan	11	0.06
Panamanian	2	0.01
Salvadoran	157	0.92
Other Central American	1	0.01
Cuban	14	0.08
Dominican Republic	3	0.02
Mexican	12,553	73.89
Puerto Rican	64	0.38
South American	17	0.10
Colombian	5	0.03
Ecuadorian	3	0.02
Peruvian	9	0.05
Other Hispanic or Latino	755	4.44

Race*	Population	%
African-American/Black (219)	277	1.63
Not Hispanic (148)	170	1.00
Hispanic (71)	107	0.63
American Indian/Alaska Native (198)	322	1.90
Not Hispanic (73)	117	0.69
Hispanic (125)	205	1.21
Apache (5)	6	0.04
Cherokee (15)	34	0.20
Chickasaw (2)	2	0.01
Choctaw (5)	6	0.04
Comanche (0)	1	0.01
Cree (0)	1	0.01
Creek (0)	1	0.01
Hopi (0)	2	0.01
Mexican American Ind. (18)	29	0.17
Navajo (2)	3	0.02
Pima (7)	11	0.06
Potawatomi (0)	1	0.01
Pueblo (2)	5	0.03
Puget Sound Salish (0)	1	0.01
Spanish American Ind. (1)	1	0.01
Yaqui (1)	7	0.04
Asian (111)	199	1.17
Not Hispanic (107)	152	0.89
Hispanic (4)	47	0.28
Cambodian (8)	8	0.05
Chinese, ex. Taiwanese (7)	11	0.06
Filipino (24)	53	0.31
Hmong (3)	3	0.02
Indian (39)	47	0.28
Japanese (2)	10	0.06
Korean (4)	14	0.08
Laotian (7)	8	0.05
Thai (1)	1	0.01
Vietnamese (8)	9	0.05
Hawaii Native/Pacific Islander (19)	55	0.32
Not Hispanic (17)	26	0.15
Hispanic (2)	29	0.17
Guamanian/Chamorro (9)	12	0.07
Native Hawaiian (3)	11	0.06
Samoan (4)	6	0.04
White (8,150)	8,716	51.31
Not Hispanic (2,884)	2,986	17.58
Hispanic (5,266)	5,730	33.73

Shasta Lake

Place Type: City
County: Shasta
Population: 10,164†

Ancestry‡	Population	%
American (1,059)	1,059	10.50
Austrian (0)	139	1.38
Canadian (27)	27	0.27
Croatian (13)	29	0.29
Czech (18)	57	0.57
Danish (22)	45	0.45
Dutch (33)	120	1.19
English (309)	981	9.73
European (111)	132	1.31
French, ex. Basque (15)	288	2.86
French Canadian (2)	94	0.93
German (363)	1,774	17.60
Greek (12)	12	0.12
Hungarian (11)	11	0.11
Irish (439)	1,607	15.94
Italian (277)	640	6.35
Lithuanian (0)	41	0.41
Norwegian (157)	313	3.10
Polish (31)	176	1.75
Portuguese (31)	39	0.39
Russian (0)	17	0.17
Scotch-Irish (166)	412	4.09
Scottish (107)	270	2.68
Slovene (0)	16	0.16
Swedish (97)	367	3.64
Swiss (0)	64	0.63
Turkish (56)	56	0.56
Welsh (21)	48	0.48
West Indian, ex. Hispanic (0)	32	0.32
Dutch West Indian (0)	15	0.15
Jamaican (0)	8	0.08
West Indian (0)	9	0.09
Yugoslavian (92)	92	0.91

Hispanic Origin	Population	%
Hispanic or Latino (of any race)	865	8.51
Central American, ex. Mexican	33	0.32
Costa Rican	5	0.05
Guatemalan	12	0.12
Nicaraguan	5	0.05
Panamanian	2	0.02
Salvadoran	9	0.09
Cuban	5	0.05
Mexican	662	6.51
Puerto Rican	28	0.28
South American	21	0.21
Bolivian	4	0.04
Chilean	1	0.01
Colombian	1	0.01
Ecuadorian	6	0.06
Peruvian	6	0.06
Venezuelan	3	0.03
Other Hispanic or Latino	116	1.14

Race*	Population	%
African-American/Black (67)	125	1.23
Not Hispanic (60)	111	1.09
Hispanic (7)	14	0.14
American Indian/Alaska Native (389)	728	7.16
Not Hispanic (324)	605	5.95
Hispanic (65)	123	1.21
Alaska Athabascan *(Ala. Nat.)* (1)	6	0.06
Apache (2)	8	0.08
Blackfeet (3)	17	0.17
Cherokee (38)	123	1.21
Cheyenne (1)	3	0.03
Chickasaw (1)	5	0.05
Chippewa (8)	10	0.10
Choctaw (7)	24	0.24
Creek (3)	9	0.09
Crow (1)	7	0.07
Inupiat *(Alaska Native)* (1)	4	0.04
Iroquois (3)	9	0.09

*Notes: † The Census 2010 population figure is used to calculate the percentages in the Hispanic Origin and Race categories. Ancestry percentages are based on the 2006-2010 American Community Survey population (not shown); ‡ Numbers in parentheses indicate the number of people reporting a single ancestry; * Numbers in parentheses indicate the number of persons reporting this race alone, not in combination with any other race; Please refer to the Explanation of Data for more information.*

Mexican American Ind. (9)	15	0.15
Navajo (1)	2	0.02
Osage (0)	2	0.02
Paiute (2)	5	0.05
Pima (0)	4	0.04
Potawatomi (7)	10	0.10
Puget Sound Salish (1)	1	0.01
Seminole (2)	5	0.05
Shoshone (1)	3	0.03
Sioux (12)	21	0.21
Spanish American Ind. (1)	1	0.01
Tlingit-Haida *(Alaska Native)* (6)	9	0.09
Tohono O'Odham (0)	1	0.01
Ute (0)	1	0.01
Yaqui (0)	1	0.01
Yuman (1)	4	0.04
Asian (233)	324	3.19
Not Hispanic (230)	301	2.96
Hispanic (3)	23	0.23
Chinese, ex. Taiwanese (15)	23	0.23
Filipino (17)	57	0.56
Hmong (0)	1	0.01
Indian (11)	24	0.24
Indonesian (0)	1	0.01
Japanese (7)	33	0.32
Korean (4)	11	0.11
Laotian (143)	157	1.54
Thai (10)	15	0.15
Vietnamese (1)	3	0.03
Hawaii Native/Pacific Islander (13)	36	0.35
Not Hispanic (11)	27	0.27
Hispanic (2)	9	0.09
Fijian (1)	1	0.01
Guamanian/Chamorro (3)	3	0.03
Native Hawaiian (7)	27	0.27
White (8,749)	9,231	90.82
Not Hispanic (8,286)	8,658	85.18
Hispanic (463)	573	5.64

Sierra Madre

Place Type: City
County: Los Angeles
Population: 10,917†

Ancestry‡	Population	%
African, Sub-Saharan (0)	13	0.12
African (0)	13	0.12
Alsatian (0)	13	0.12
American (168)	168	1.55
Arab (39)	47	0.43
Egyptian (21)	21	0.19
Lebanese (13)	13	0.12
Palestinian (5)	5	0.05
Other Arab (0)	8	0.07
Armenian (83)	83	0.76
Austrian (0)	81	0.75
Basque (9)	23	0.21
British (29)	157	1.45
Canadian (27)	39	0.36
Croatian (11)	74	0.68
Czech (0)	43	0.40
Czechoslovakian (10)	10	0.09
Danish (10)	111	1.02
Dutch (10)	353	3.25
English (432)	1,481	13.64
European (181)	213	1.96
Finnish (10)	35	0.32
French, ex. Basque (44)	349	3.22
French Canadian (39)	106	0.98
German (268)	1,363	12.56
Greek (188)	227	2.09
Hungarian (47)	60	0.55
Iranian (127)	154	1.42
Irish (310)	1,176	10.83
Italian (109)	499	4.60
Lithuanian (0)	7	0.06
Macedonian (0)	42	0.39
Northern European (22)	22	0.20
Norwegian (36)	169	1.56
Polish (23)	321	2.96
Portuguese (9)	37	0.34
Romanian (34)	34	0.31
Russian (15)	72	0.66
Scandinavian (16)	16	0.15
Scotch-Irish (118)	299	2.75
Scottish (105)	281	2.59
Slovak (0)	13	0.12
Slovene (0)	14	0.13
Swedish (31)	227	2.09
Swiss (15)	106	0.98
Ukrainian (12)	12	0.11
Welsh (0)	53	0.49
West Indian, ex. Hispanic (13)	13	0.12
Barbadian (13)	13	0.12

Hispanic Origin	Population	%
Hispanic or Latino (of any race)	1,628	14.91
Central American, ex. Mexican	86	0.79
Costa Rican	19	0.17
Guatemalan	13	0.12
Honduran	2	0.02
Nicaraguan	13	0.12
Panamanian	8	0.07
Salvadoran	29	0.27
Other Central American	2	0.02
Cuban	56	0.51
Dominican Republic	6	0.05
Mexican	1,156	10.59
Puerto Rican	49	0.45
South American	151	1.38
Argentinean	41	0.38
Bolivian	3	0.03
Chilean	11	0.10
Colombian	43	0.39
Ecuadorian	28	0.26
Peruvian	14	0.13
Uruguayan	3	0.03
Venezuelan	6	0.05
Other South American	2	0.02
Other Hispanic or Latino	124	1.14

Race*	Population	%
African-American/Black (201)	269	2.46
Not Hispanic (191)	250	2.29
Hispanic (10)	19	0.17
American Indian/Alaska Native (44)	134	1.23
Not Hispanic (30)	99	0.91
Hispanic (14)	35	0.32
Aleut *(Alaska Native)* (2)	2	0.02
Apache (3)	5	0.05
Blackfeet (0)	5	0.05
Cherokee (9)	27	0.25
Chippewa (1)	2	0.02
Choctaw (0)	5	0.05
Comanche (1)	3	0.03
Hopi (1)	3	0.03
Iroquois (0)	7	0.06
Mexican American Ind. (2)	4	0.04
Navajo (5)	13	0.12
Pima (1)	1	0.01
Pueblo (0)	1	0.01
Shoshone (0)	1	0.01
Sioux (0)	2	0.02
Tlingit-Haida *(Alaska Native)* (1)	1	0.01
Yaqui (0)	1	0.01
Yuman (0)	1	0.01
Asian (835)	1,079	9.88
Not Hispanic (815)	1,024	9.38
Hispanic (20)	55	0.50
Burmese (3)	3	0.03
Cambodian (4)	6	0.05
Chinese, ex. Taiwanese (349)	427	3.91
Filipino (111)	172	1.58
Indian (45)	69	0.63
Indonesian (15)	23	0.21
Japanese (132)	209	1.91
Korean (57)	86	0.79
Laotian (1)	1	0.01
Malaysian (1)	1	0.01
Nepalese (0)	1	0.01
Pakistani (2)	4	0.04
Sri Lankan (7)	8	0.07
Taiwanese (18)	27	0.25
Thai (10)	10	0.09
Vietnamese (27)	44	0.40
Hawaii Native/Pacific Islander (9)	28	0.26
Not Hispanic (8)	26	0.24
Hispanic (1)	2	0.02
Guamanian/Chamorro (1)	1	0.01
Native Hawaiian (5)	18	0.16
White (8,967)	9,393	86.04
Not Hispanic (7,891)	8,171	74.85
Hispanic (1,076)	1,222	11.19

Signal Hill

Place Type: City
County: Los Angeles
Population: 11,016†

Ancestry‡	Population	%
African, Sub-Saharan (238)	298	2.79
African (221)	264	2.47
Ghanaian (17)	34	0.32
American (76)	76	0.71
Austrian (0)	19	0.18
Brazilian (28)	28	0.26
British (0)	23	0.21
Canadian (0)	26	0.24
Croatian (7)	37	0.35
Danish (0)	23	0.21
Dutch (58)	74	0.69
Eastern European (10)	10	0.09
English (228)	606	5.66
European (78)	250	2.34
Finnish (0)	10	0.09
French, ex. Basque (111)	229	2.14
French Canadian (38)	55	0.51
German (399)	890	8.32
Greek (14)	23	0.21
Hungarian (0)	9	0.08
Iranian (17)	17	0.16
Irish (149)	488	4.56
Italian (109)	263	2.46
Latvian (5)	5	0.05
Lithuanian (19)	46	0.43
Northern European (0)	10	0.09
Norwegian (17)	110	1.03
Polish (72)	150	1.40
Portuguese (24)	81	0.76
Romanian (12)	12	0.11
Russian (40)	88	0.82
Scandinavian (19)	44	0.41
Scotch-Irish (30)	57	0.53
Scottish (0)	78	0.73
Swedish (0)	12	0.11
Swiss (0)	32	0.30
Ukrainian (12)	23	0.21
Welsh (0)	20	0.19
Yugoslavian (0)	17	0.16

Hispanic Origin	Population	%
Hispanic or Latino (of any race)	3,472	31.52
Central American, ex. Mexican	307	2.79
Costa Rican	20	0.18
Guatemalan	112	1.02
Honduran	27	0.25
Nicaraguan	21	0.19
Panamanian	14	0.13
Salvadoran	108	0.98
Other Central American	5	0.05
Cuban	20	0.18
Dominican Republic	11	0.10
Mexican	2,708	24.58
Puerto Rican	63	0.57
South American	99	0.90
Argentinean	10	0.09
Chilean	16	0.15
Colombian	31	0.28

*Notes: † The Census 2010 population figure is used to calculate the percentages in the Hispanic Origin and Race categories. Ancestry percentages are based on the 2006-2010 American Community Survey population (not shown); ‡ Numbers in parentheses indicate the number of people reporting a single ancestry; * Numbers in parentheses indicate the number of persons reporting this race alone, not in combination with any other race; Please refer to the Explanation of Data for more information.*

Ecuadorian	12	0.11
Paraguayan	2	0.02
Peruvian	20	0.18
Venezuelan	8	0.07
Other Hispanic or Latino	264	2.40

Race*	Population	%
African-American/Black (1,502)	1,694	15.38
Not Hispanic (1,427)	1,575	14.30
Hispanic (75)	119	1.08
American Indian/Alaska Native (83)	189	1.72
Not Hispanic (27)	94	0.85
Hispanic (56)	95	0.86
Apache (1)	5	0.05
Blackfeet (0)	5	0.05
Canadian/French Am. Ind. (0)	1	0.01
Cherokee (5)	24	0.22
Chickasaw (0)	1	0.01
Chippewa (0)	1	0.01
Choctaw (0)	9	0.08
Creek (0)	1	0.01
Iroquois (1)	1	0.01
Lumbee (3)	3	0.03
Mexican American Ind. (11)	16	0.15
Navajo (5)	6	0.05
Osage (2)	2	0.02
Potawatomi (0)	4	0.04
Sioux (3)	5	0.05
Yaqui (3)	3	0.03
Yuman (2)	2	0.02
Asian (2,245)	2,503	22.72
Not Hispanic (2,211)	2,420	21.97
Hispanic (34)	83	0.75
Bangladeshi (4)	4	0.04
Cambodian (822)	927	8.42
Chinese, ex. Taiwanese (158)	241	2.19
Filipino (532)	669	6.07
Hmong (2)	3	0.03
Indian (97)	125	1.13
Indonesian (2)	3	0.03
Japanese (86)	124	1.13
Korean (78)	90	0.82
Laotian (17)	37	0.34
Malaysian (0)	2	0.02
Pakistani (4)	4	0.04
Sri Lankan (3)	3	0.03
Taiwanese (11)	14	0.13
Thai (52)	60	0.54
Vietnamese (188)	225	2.04
Hawaii Native/Pacific Islander (135)	226	2.05
Not Hispanic (112)	180	1.63
Hispanic (23)	46	0.42
Fijian (0)	5	0.05
Guamanian/Chamorro (21)	46	0.42
Native Hawaiian (10)	35	0.32
Samoan (84)	125	1.13
Tongan (8)	12	0.11
White (4,650)	5,100	46.30
Not Hispanic (3,340)	3,632	32.97
Hispanic (1,310)	1,468	13.33

Simi Valley

Place Type: City
County: Ventura
Population: 124,237†

Ancestry‡	Population	%
Afghan (625)	638	0.52
African, Sub-Saharan (153)	360	0.30
African (27)	212	0.17
Cape Verdean (24)	46	0.04
Ethiopian (5)	5	<0.01
Nigerian (97)	97	0.08
Albanian (91)	102	0.08
American (11,845)	11,845	9.74
Arab (952)	1,258	1.03
Arab (66)	70	0.06
Egyptian (84)	107	0.09
Iraqi (96)	107	0.09
Jordanian (120)	120	0.10
Lebanese (238)	341	0.28
Moroccan (75)	75	0.06
Palestinian (61)	73	0.06
Syrian (97)	236	0.19
Other Arab (115)	129	0.11
Armenian (459)	599	0.49
Assyrian/Chaldean/Syriac (38)	53	0.04
Australian (39)	66	0.05
Austrian (199)	452	0.37
Basque (8)	19	0.02
Belgian (14)	72	0.06
Brazilian (51)	197	0.16
British (577)	962	0.79
Bulgarian (0)	8	0.01
Canadian (271)	571	0.47
Croatian (55)	188	0.15
Czech (107)	512	0.42
Czechoslovakian (106)	196	0.16
Danish (268)	922	0.76
Dutch (549)	2,067	1.70
Eastern European (187)	246	0.20
English (3,293)	12,807	10.53
Estonian (13)	19	0.02
European (1,642)	1,895	1.56
Finnish (244)	325	0.27
French, ex. Basque (359)	3,650	3.00
French Canadian (271)	768	0.63
German (4,527)	17,975	14.77
Greek (276)	720	0.59
Hungarian (240)	785	0.65
Icelander (0)	40	0.03
Iranian (658)	767	0.63
Irish (2,690)	13,019	10.70
Israeli (22)	123	0.10
Italian (3,376)	8,720	7.17
Latvian (12)	12	0.01
Lithuanian (124)	422	0.35
Macedonian (0)	11	0.01
Northern European (99)	99	0.08
Norwegian (460)	2,034	1.67
Polish (922)	3,350	2.75
Portuguese (169)	483	0.40
Romanian (212)	375	0.31
Russian (1,105)	2,408	1.98
Scandinavian (157)	397	0.33
Scotch-Irish (522)	2,020	1.66
Scottish (536)	2,221	1.83
Serbian (55)	71	0.06
Slavic (30)	51	0.04
Slovak (17)	57	0.05
Slovene (20)	39	0.03
Swedish (559)	2,433	2.00
Swiss (24)	287	0.24
Turkish (36)	57	0.05
Ukrainian (106)	264	0.22
Welsh (152)	899	0.74
West Indian, ex. Hispanic (161)	279	0.23
Barbadian (16)	16	0.01
Belizean (37)	37	0.03
Jamaican (90)	143	0.12
Trinidadian/Tobagonian (8)	50	0.04
West Indian (10)	33	0.03
Yugoslavian (108)	208	0.17

Hispanic Origin	Population	%
Hispanic or Latino (of any race)	28,938	23.29
Central American, ex. Mexican	3,370	2.71
Costa Rican	164	0.13
Guatemalan	1,082	0.87
Honduran	265	0.21
Nicaraguan	234	0.19
Panamanian	55	0.04
Salvadoran	1,520	1.22
Other Central American	50	0.04
Cuban	431	0.35
Dominican Republic	30	0.02
Mexican	20,165	16.23
Puerto Rican	698	0.56
South American	2,077	1.67
Argentinean	351	0.28
Bolivian	52	0.04
Chilean	132	0.11
Colombian	502	0.40
Ecuadorian	226	0.18
Paraguayan	11	0.01
Peruvian	716	0.58
Uruguayan	31	0.02
Venezuelan	28	0.02
Other South American	28	0.02
Other Hispanic or Latino	2,167	1.74

Race*	Population	%
African-American/Black (1,739)	2,588	2.08
Not Hispanic (1,602)	2,224	1.79
Hispanic (137)	364	0.29
American Indian/Alaska Native (761)	2,042	1.64
Not Hispanic (356)	1,228	0.99
Hispanic (405)	814	0.66
Apache (22)	66	0.05
Arapaho (0)	1	<0.01
Blackfeet (8)	50	0.04
Canadian/French Am. Ind. (0)	1	<0.01
Central American Ind. (1)	6	<0.01
Cherokee (80)	439	0.35
Cheyenne (0)	4	<0.01
Chickasaw (3)	12	0.01
Chippewa (16)	31	0.02
Choctaw (18)	99	0.08
Colville (3)	4	<0.01
Comanche (3)	9	0.01
Cree (1)	5	<0.01
Creek (2)	19	0.02
Delaware (0)	1	<0.01
Hopi (1)	2	<0.01
Inupiat *(Alaska Native)* (0)	4	<0.01
Iroquois (12)	40	0.03
Kiowa (1)	2	<0.01
Lumbee (1)	2	<0.01
Mexican American Ind. (95)	150	0.12
Navajo (15)	42	0.03
Osage (9)	15	0.01
Paiute (0)	3	<0.01
Potawatomi (5)	9	0.01
Pueblo (10)	14	0.01
Puget Sound Salish (2)	2	<0.01
Seminole (3)	16	0.01
Shoshone (1)	4	<0.01
Sioux (13)	48	0.04
South American Ind. (7)	15	0.01
Spanish American Ind. (12)	16	0.01
Tohono O'Odham (7)	15	0.01
Ute (2)	8	0.01
Yaqui (7)	17	0.01
Yuman (2)	9	0.01
Asian (11,555)	14,147	11.39
Not Hispanic (11,328)	13,519	10.88
Hispanic (227)	628	0.51
Bangladeshi (30)	30	0.02
Burmese (35)	44	0.04
Cambodian (68)	85	0.07
Chinese, ex. Taiwanese (1,417)	1,957	1.58
Filipino (2,710)	3,612	2.91
Hmong (3)	5	<0.01
Indian (3,381)	3,617	2.91
Indonesian (123)	220	0.18
Japanese (662)	1,220	0.98
Korean (876)	1,101	0.89
Laotian (11)	20	0.02
Malaysian (10)	18	0.01
Nepalese (14)	17	0.01
Pakistani (165)	189	0.15
Sri Lankan (78)	82	0.07
Taiwanese (91)	128	0.10
Thai (243)	308	0.25
Vietnamese (1,240)	1,403	1.13
Hawaii Native/Pacific Islander (178)	546	0.44
Not Hispanic (148)	446	0.36
Hispanic (30)	100	0.08
Fijian (11)	13	0.01

*Notes: † The Census 2010 population figure is used to calculate the percentages in the Hispanic Origin and Race categories. Ancestry percentages are based on the 2006-2010 American Community Survey population (not shown); ‡ Numbers in parentheses indicate the number of people reporting a single ancestry; * Numbers in parentheses indicate the number of persons reporting this race alone, not in combination with any other race; Please refer to the Explanation of Data for more information.*

Guamanian/Chamorro (43)	71	0.06
Marshallese (1)	4	<0.01
Native Hawaiian (67)	210	0.17
Samoan (15)	48	0.04
Tongan (20)	29	0.02
White (93,597)	98,635	79.39
Not Hispanic (78,009)	81,189	65.35
Hispanic (15,588)	17,446	14.04

Solana Beach

Place Type: City
County: San Diego
Population: 12,867†

Ancestry‡	Population	%
African, Sub-Saharan (51)	206	1.61
African (17)	172	1.34
South African (34)	34	0.27
Albanian (0)	11	0.09
American (392)	392	3.06
Arab (50)	133	1.04
Arab (14)	24	0.19
Lebanese (6)	17	0.13
Syrian (13)	23	0.18
Other Arab (17)	69	0.54
Armenian (27)	27	0.21
Australian (7)	7	0.05
Austrian (26)	136	1.06
Belgian (27)	53	0.41
British (68)	125	0.98
Canadian (9)	15	0.12
Croatian (0)	4	0.03
Czech (29)	81	0.63
Danish (40)	190	1.49
Dutch (27)	170	1.33
Eastern European (52)	52	0.41
English (383)	1,538	12.03
European (254)	254	1.99
French, ex. Basque (80)	510	3.99
French Canadian (26)	56	0.44
German (562)	2,324	18.17
Greek (21)	45	0.35
Hungarian (78)	110	0.86
Iranian (90)	116	0.91
Irish (539)	1,898	14.84
Italian (334)	1,172	9.16
Latvian (0)	24	0.19
Lithuanian (13)	80	0.63
New Zealander (12)	12	0.09
Northern European (179)	179	1.40
Norwegian (53)	183	1.43
Pennsylvania German (0)	9	0.07
Polish (71)	277	2.17
Portuguese (0)	24	0.19
Romanian (0)	23	0.18
Russian (203)	412	3.22
Scandinavian (35)	47	0.37
Scotch-Irish (109)	344	2.69
Scottish (197)	493	3.85
Slavic (10)	10	0.08
Slovak (13)	22	0.17
Swedish (135)	463	3.62
Swiss (63)	203	1.59
Ukrainian (24)	39	0.30
Welsh (10)	78	0.61
Yugoslavian (10)	26	0.20

Hispanic Origin	Population	%
Hispanic or Latino (of any race)	2,048	15.92
Central American, ex. Mexican	53	0.41
Costa Rican	3	0.02
Guatemalan	17	0.13
Honduran	7	0.05
Nicaraguan	6	0.05
Panamanian	2	0.02
Salvadoran	18	0.14
Cuban	21	0.16
Dominican Republic	3	0.02
Mexican	1,723	13.39
Puerto Rican	28	0.22
South American	93	0.72
Argentinean	16	0.12
Bolivian	1	0.01
Chilean	3	0.02
Colombian	27	0.21
Ecuadorian	12	0.09
Peruvian	21	0.16
Uruguayan	1	0.01
Venezuelan	12	0.09
Other Hispanic or Latino	127	0.99

Race*	Population	%
African-American/Black (60)	112	0.87
Not Hispanic (56)	96	0.75
Hispanic (4)	16	0.12
American Indian/Alaska Native (62)	136	1.06
Not Hispanic (26)	81	0.63
Hispanic (36)	55	0.43
Apache (3)	5	0.04
Blackfeet (1)	5	0.04
Central American Ind. (0)	1	0.01
Cherokee (7)	21	0.16
Chickasaw (2)	2	0.02
Chippewa (1)	5	0.04
Choctaw (0)	3	0.02
Comanche (1)	2	0.02
Hopi (3)	3	0.02
Iroquois (0)	1	0.01
Menominee (0)	1	0.01
Mexican American Ind. (2)	4	0.03
Navajo (1)	6	0.05
Potawatomi (0)	1	0.01
Pueblo (1)	2	0.02
Sioux (0)	7	0.05
South American Ind. (2)	2	0.02
Tohono O'Odham (1)	1	0.01
Yaqui (3)	3	0.02
Yuman (2)	2	0.02
Asian (513)	682	5.30
Not Hispanic (506)	656	5.10
Hispanic (7)	26	0.20
Cambodian (1)	3	0.02
Chinese, ex. Taiwanese (135)	168	1.31
Filipino (58)	103	0.80
Indian (67)	80	0.62
Indonesian (3)	7	0.05
Japanese (106)	156	1.21
Korean (45)	67	0.52
Laotian (3)	7	0.05
Pakistani (5)	5	0.04
Sri Lankan (0)	2	0.02
Taiwanese (16)	16	0.12
Thai (14)	23	0.18
Vietnamese (39)	49	0.38
Hawaii Native/Pacific Islander (19)	42	0.33
Not Hispanic (19)	41	0.32
Hispanic (0)	1	0.01
Fijian (0)	9	0.07
Guamanian/Chamorro (2)	9	0.07
Native Hawaiian (7)	12	0.09
Tongan (0)	9	0.07
White (11,039)	11,448	88.97
Not Hispanic (9,944)	10,175	79.08
Hispanic (1,095)	1,273	9.89

Soledad

Place Type: City
County: Monterey
Population: 25,738†

Ancestry‡	Population	%
African, Sub-Saharan (263)	286	1.13
African (246)	269	1.06
Cape Verdean (8)	8	0.03
Ethiopian (9)	9	0.04
American (206)	206	0.81
Arab (22)	22	0.09
Egyptian (7)	7	0.03
Jordanian (7)	7	0.03
Other Arab (8)	8	0.03
Armenian (0)	8	0.03
Assyrian/Chaldean/Syriac (7)	7	0.03
Austrian (16)	16	0.06
Belgian (27)	27	0.11
Brazilian (15)	15	0.06
British (0)	20	0.08
Danish (0)	46	0.18
Dutch (50)	197	0.78
Eastern European (8)	8	0.03
English (145)	479	1.89
Estonian (8)	8	0.03
European (32)	32	0.13
Finnish (0)	25	0.10
French, ex. Basque (23)	419	1.65
French Canadian (44)	44	0.17
German (84)	700	2.76
Greek (6)	6	0.02
Hungarian (0)	5	0.02
Icelander (9)	17	0.07
Iranian (8)	8	0.03
Irish (146)	604	2.38
Israeli (8)	8	0.03
Italian (155)	380	1.50
Macedonian (50)	50	0.20
Northern European (31)	31	0.12
Norwegian (31)	106	0.42
Polish (22)	61	0.24
Portuguese (84)	149	0.59
Romanian (0)	9	0.04
Russian (17)	71	0.28
Scandinavian (0)	8	0.03
Scotch-Irish (13)	89	0.35
Scottish (37)	113	0.45
Slovak (8)	8	0.03
Swedish (43)	56	0.22
Swiss (12)	91	0.36
Welsh (7)	30	0.12
West Indian, ex. Hispanic (48)	54	0.21
Belizean (24)	30	0.12
Jamaican (16)	16	0.06
West Indian (8)	8	0.03
Yugoslavian (0)	9	0.04

Hispanic Origin	Population	%
Hispanic or Latino (of any race)	18,308	71.13
Central American, ex. Mexican	125	0.49
Costa Rican	1	<0.01
Guatemalan	18	0.07
Honduran	17	0.07
Nicaraguan	6	0.02
Panamanian	3	0.01
Salvadoran	74	0.29
Other Central American	6	0.02
Cuban	23	0.09
Mexican	16,261	63.18
Puerto Rican	56	0.22
South American	12	0.05
Bolivian	1	<0.01
Chilean	1	<0.01
Colombian	5	0.02
Peruvian	2	0.01
Venezuelan	3	0.01
Other Hispanic or Latino	1,831	7.11

Race*	Population	%
African-American/Black (2,945)	3,019	11.73
Not Hispanic (2,865)	2,889	11.22
Hispanic (80)	130	0.51
American Indian/Alaska Native (367)	484	1.88
Not Hispanic (132)	170	0.66
Hispanic (235)	314	1.22
Apache (4)	8	0.03
Blackfeet (0)	3	0.01
Central American Ind. (1)	1	<0.01
Cherokee (8)	12	0.05
Chickasaw (2)	2	0.01
Choctaw (1)	3	0.01
Comanche (0)	1	<0.01

*Notes: † The Census 2010 population figure is used to calculate the percentages in the Hispanic Origin and Race categories. Ancestry percentages are based on the 2006-2010 American Community Survey population (not shown); ‡ Numbers in parentheses indicate the number of people reporting a single ancestry; * Numbers in parentheses indicate the number of persons reporting this race alone, not in combination with any other race; Please refer to the Explanation of Data for more information.*

Inupiat *(Alaska Native)* (0)	1	<0.01
Iroquois (1)	1	<0.01
Menominee (1)	1	<0.01
Mexican American Ind. (54)	69	0.27
Navajo (7)	17	0.07
Paiute (1)	1	<0.01
Pueblo (4)	5	0.02
Sioux (2)	7	0.03
South American Ind. (0)	1	<0.01
Spanish American Ind. (4)	7	0.03
Yaqui (7)	7	0.03
Asian (757)	973	3.78
Not Hispanic (675)	776	3.01
Hispanic (82)	197	0.77
Cambodian (9)	15	0.06
Chinese, ex. Taiwanese (33)	58	0.23
Filipino (331)	462	1.80
Hmong (3)	3	0.01
Indian (14)	31	0.12
Japanese (10)	32	0.12
Korean (10)	12	0.05
Laotian (1)	1	<0.01
Sri Lankan (0)	4	0.02
Thai (12)	12	0.05
Vietnamese (17)	22	0.09
Hawaii Native/Pacific Islander (103)	135	0.52
Not Hispanic (98)	112	0.44
Hispanic (5)	23	0.09
Fijian (2)	2	0.01
Guamanian/Chamorro (16)	24	0.09
Native Hawaiian (5)	19	0.07
Samoan (6)	10	0.04
Tongan (12)	12	0.05
White (12,625)	13,228	51.39
Not Hispanic (3,418)	3,556	13.82
Hispanic (9,207)	9,672	37.58

Sonoma

Place Type: City
County: Sonoma
Population: 10,648†

Ancestry‡	Population	%
African, Sub-Saharan (20)	20	0.19
African (20)	20	0.19
American (141)	141	1.37
Arab (15)	29	0.28
Lebanese (15)	29	0.28
Australian (14)	14	0.14
Austrian (28)	80	0.78
Basque (17)	42	0.41
British (103)	129	1.25
Canadian (19)	118	1.15
Celtic (0)	18	0.17
Czech (17)	66	0.64
Danish (64)	193	1.88
Dutch (26)	103	1.00
English (542)	1,621	15.75
European (313)	350	3.40
French, ex. Basque (60)	708	6.88
German (420)	1,950	18.95
Greek (19)	68	0.66
Hungarian (13)	77	0.75
Irish (564)	1,622	15.76
Israeli (48)	48	0.47
Italian (441)	1,143	11.11
Latvian (14)	71	0.69
Lithuanian (0)	17	0.17
Northern European (105)	105	1.02
Norwegian (74)	189	1.84
Polish (45)	134	1.30
Portuguese (30)	86	0.84
Romanian (0)	22	0.21
Russian (57)	270	2.62
Scandinavian (25)	25	0.24
Scotch-Irish (134)	274	2.66
Scottish (44)	400	3.89
Serbian (0)	13	0.13
Slavic (0)	24	0.23
Swedish (71)	271	2.63
Swiss (54)	94	0.91
Ukrainian (0)	34	0.33
Welsh (14)	128	1.24
Yugoslavian (77)	77	0.75

Hispanic Origin	Population	%
Hispanic or Latino (of any race)	1,634	15.35
Central American, ex. Mexican	62	0.58
Costa Rican	6	0.06
Guatemalan	14	0.13
Honduran	5	0.05
Nicaraguan	5	0.05
Panamanian	3	0.03
Salvadoran	28	0.26
Other Central American	1	0.01
Cuban	10	0.09
Dominican Republic	1	0.01
Mexican	1,319	12.39
Puerto Rican	49	0.46
South American	67	0.63
Argentinean	18	0.17
Bolivian	8	0.08
Chilean	4	0.04
Colombian	25	0.23
Ecuadorian	1	0.01
Peruvian	6	0.06
Uruguayan	1	0.01
Venezuelan	4	0.04
Other Hispanic or Latino	126	1.18

Race*	Population	%
African-American/Black (52)	104	0.98
Not Hispanic (48)	90	0.85
Hispanic (4)	14	0.13
American Indian/Alaska Native (56)	142	1.33
Not Hispanic (35)	94	0.88
Hispanic (21)	48	0.45
Apache (1)	7	0.07
Blackfeet (5)	6	0.06
Cherokee (8)	31	0.29
Chickasaw (0)	1	0.01
Chippewa (0)	2	0.02
Choctaw (0)	4	0.04
Comanche (0)	1	0.01
Crow (0)	1	0.01
Mexican American Ind. (5)	8	0.08
Osage (0)	1	0.01
Potawatomi (1)	3	0.03
Sioux (0)	1	0.01
South American Ind. (1)	1	0.01
Spanish American Ind. (1)	1	0.01
Ute (4)	4	0.04
Yaqui (1)	1	0.01
Yup'ik *(Alaska Native)* (3)	3	0.03
Asian (300)	377	3.54
Not Hispanic (297)	366	3.44
Hispanic (3)	11	0.10
Burmese (1)	1	0.01
Cambodian (22)	27	0.25
Chinese, ex. Taiwanese (69)	86	0.81
Filipino (50)	78	0.73
Indian (26)	37	0.35
Indonesian (1)	2	0.02
Japanese (27)	45	0.42
Korean (15)	20	0.19
Nepalese (52)	55	0.52
Thai (8)	9	0.08
Vietnamese (9)	9	0.08
Hawaii Native/Pacific Islander (23)	39	0.37
Not Hispanic (21)	35	0.33
Hispanic (2)	4	0.04
Fijian (14)	14	0.13
Guamanian/Chamorro (2)	4	0.04
Native Hawaiian (5)	14	0.13
Tongan (1)	1	0.01
White (9,242)	9,494	89.16
Not Hispanic (8,430)	8,591	80.68
Hispanic (812)	903	8.48

Soquel

Place Type: CDP
County: Santa Cruz
Population: 9,644†

Ancestry‡	Population	%
American (201)	201	2.14
Arab (28)	37	0.39
Palestinian (10)	19	0.20
Other Arab (18)	18	0.19
Armenian (9)	9	0.10
Austrian (21)	103	1.10
Basque (0)	28	0.30
Belgian (0)	27	0.29
British (104)	218	2.32
Bulgarian (0)	6	0.06
Canadian (11)	31	0.33
Croatian (12)	20	0.21
Czech (0)	37	0.39
Czechoslovakian (40)	69	0.73
Danish (32)	58	0.62
Dutch (46)	213	2.27
Eastern European (55)	55	0.59
English (292)	1,287	13.70
European (166)	361	3.84
Finnish (0)	40	0.43
French, ex. Basque (12)	335	3.57
French Canadian (39)	63	0.67
German (309)	1,327	14.13
Greek (85)	218	2.32
Hungarian (0)	73	0.78
Icelander (0)	26	0.28
Irish (161)	1,118	11.90
Italian (366)	1,056	11.24
Lithuanian (0)	11	0.12
Northern European (114)	216	2.30
Norwegian (50)	138	1.47
Polish (30)	295	3.14
Portuguese (79)	325	3.46
Russian (52)	243	2.59
Scandinavian (21)	45	0.48
Scotch-Irish (33)	109	1.16
Scottish (215)	394	4.20
Slovak (0)	7	0.07
Swedish (21)	276	2.94
Swiss (9)	67	0.71
Ukrainian (6)	33	0.35
Welsh (0)	93	0.99

Hispanic Origin	Population	%
Hispanic or Latino (of any race)	1,606	16.65
Central American, ex. Mexican	98	1.02
Costa Rican	5	0.05
Guatemalan	23	0.24
Honduran	1	0.01
Nicaraguan	8	0.08
Panamanian	4	0.04
Salvadoran	56	0.58
Other Central American	1	0.01
Cuban	10	0.10
Dominican Republic	5	0.05
Mexican	1,234	12.80
Puerto Rican	33	0.34
South American	52	0.54
Argentinean	9	0.09
Bolivian	1	0.01
Chilean	7	0.07
Colombian	14	0.15
Ecuadorian	3	0.03
Peruvian	17	0.18
Venezuelan	1	0.01
Other Hispanic or Latino	174	1.80

Race*	Population	%
African-American/Black (85)	202	2.09
Not Hispanic (80)	162	1.68
Hispanic (5)	40	0.41
American Indian/Alaska Native (71)	223	2.31
Not Hispanic (23)	125	1.30

*Notes: † The Census 2010 population figure is used to calculate the percentages in the Hispanic Origin and Race categories. Ancestry percentages are based on the 2006-2010 American Community Survey population (not shown); ‡ Numbers in parentheses indicate the number of people reporting a single ancestry; * Numbers in parentheses indicate the number of persons reporting this race alone, not in combination with any other race; Please refer to the Explanation of Data for more information.*

Hispanic (48)	98	1.02
Apache (4)	6	0.06
Arapaho (0)	1	0.01
Blackfeet (0)	1	0.01
Central American Ind. (0)	1	0.01
Cherokee (5)	32	0.33
Chickasaw (0)	1	0.01
Chippewa (3)	4	0.04
Comanche (0)	1	0.01
Creek (0)	2	0.02
Iroquois (0)	5	0.05
Mexican American Ind. (8)	16	0.17
Navajo (3)	8	0.08
Ottawa (1)	1	0.01
Paiute (1)	3	0.03
Pima (0)	4	0.04
Pueblo (0)	6	0.06
Sioux (2)	7	0.07
South American Ind. (1)	2	0.02
Yaqui (3)	8	0.08
Asian (356)	538	5.58
Not Hispanic (341)	499	5.17
Hispanic (15)	39	0.40
Cambodian (2)	5	0.05
Chinese, ex. Taiwanese (73)	107	1.11
Filipino (98)	167	1.73
Indian (10)	26	0.27
Indonesian (1)	3	0.03
Japanese (59)	114	1.18
Korean (52)	64	0.66
Malaysian (0)	1	0.01
Nepalese (1)	1	0.01
Pakistani (1)	1	0.01
Sri Lankan (1)	1	0.01
Taiwanese (2)	2	0.02
Thai (18)	25	0.26
Vietnamese (26)	28	0.29
Hawaii Native/Pacific Islander (21)	78	0.81
Not Hispanic (16)	59	0.61
Hispanic (5)	19	0.20
Fijian (0)	1	0.01
Guamanian/Chamorro (4)	9	0.09
Native Hawaiian (11)	48	0.50
Samoan (0)	5	0.05
White (7,898)	8,362	86.71
Not Hispanic (7,205)	7,515	77.92
Hispanic (693)	847	8.78

South El Monte

Place Type: City
County: Los Angeles
Population: 20,116†

Ancestry‡	Population	%
American (69)	69	0.34
Belgian (0)	10	0.05
Dutch (0)	13	0.06
English (20)	120	0.59
French, ex. Basque (0)	53	0.26
German (35)	150	0.74
Irish (9)	89	0.44
Italian (69)	132	0.65
Polish (0)	7	0.03
Portuguese (0)	10	0.05
Romanian (11)	25	0.12
Russian (0)	8	0.04
Scandinavian (30)	30	0.15
Scottish (0)	14	0.07

Hispanic Origin	Population	%
Hispanic or Latino (of any race)	17,079	84.90
Central American, ex. Mexican	755	3.75
Costa Rican	11	0.05
Guatemalan	225	1.12
Honduran	94	0.47
Nicaraguan	38	0.19
Panamanian	3	0.01
Salvadoran	370	1.84
Other Central American	14	0.07
Cuban	23	0.11
Mexican	15,606	77.58
Puerto Rican	49	0.24
South American	92	0.46
Argentinean	14	0.07
Bolivian	2	0.01
Colombian	23	0.11
Ecuadorian	21	0.10
Peruvian	32	0.16
Other Hispanic or Latino	554	2.75

Race*	Population	%
African-American/Black (107)	147	0.73
Not Hispanic (33)	39	0.19
Hispanic (74)	108	0.54
American Indian/Alaska Native (250)	334	1.66
Not Hispanic (24)	47	0.23
Hispanic (226)	287	1.43
Apache (15)	20	0.10
Blackfeet (3)	3	0.01
Central American Ind. (8)	12	0.06
Cherokee (2)	12	0.06
Choctaw (2)	3	0.01
Mexican American Ind. (70)	81	0.40
Navajo (14)	19	0.09
Pueblo (1)	2	0.01
Shoshone (1)	1	<0.01
Yaqui (6)	6	0.03
Asian (2,211)	2,326	11.56
Not Hispanic (2,179)	2,228	11.08
Hispanic (32)	98	0.49
Bangladeshi (3)	3	0.01
Cambodian (51)	56	0.28
Chinese, ex. Taiwanese (1,080)	1,222	6.07
Filipino (89)	112	0.56
Indian (18)	22	0.11
Indonesian (0)	3	0.01
Japanese (30)	54	0.27
Korean (12)	16	0.08
Malaysian (3)	8	0.04
Sri Lankan (6)	6	0.03
Taiwanese (24)	33	0.16
Thai (13)	17	0.08
Vietnamese (767)	875	4.35
Hawaii Native/Pacific Islander (12)	46	0.23
Not Hispanic (10)	26	0.13
Hispanic (2)	20	0.10
Guamanian/Chamorro (1)	2	0.01
Native Hawaiian (2)	22	0.11
Samoan (2)	7	0.03
Tongan (1)	1	<0.01
White (10,136)	10,704	53.21
Not Hispanic (683)	737	3.66
Hispanic (9,453)	9,967	49.55

South Gate

Place Type: City
County: Los Angeles
Population: 94,396†

Ancestry‡	Population	%
African, Sub-Saharan (22)	39	0.04
African (22)	39	0.04
American (1,715)	1,715	1.81
Arab (36)	90	0.10
Arab (27)	73	0.08
Egyptian (9)	9	0.01
Lebanese (0)	8	0.01
Austrian (23)	23	0.02
Basque (0)	16	0.02
Brazilian (29)	50	0.05
British (0)	9	0.01
Canadian (0)	13	0.01
Croatian (9)	22	0.02
Czech (6)	6	0.01
Czechoslovakian (15)	15	0.02
Danish (6)	13	0.01
Dutch (0)	64	0.07
English (206)	513	0.54
European (0)	11	0.01
Finnish (0)	12	0.01
French, ex. Basque (134)	235	0.25
French Canadian (46)	77	0.08
German (187)	710	0.75
Greek (119)	131	0.14
Iranian (0)	19	0.02
Irish (138)	732	0.77
Italian (114)	323	0.34
Lithuanian (0)	8	0.01
Norwegian (43)	66	0.07
Polish (14)	86	0.09
Portuguese (34)	63	0.07
Russian (82)	121	0.13
Scandinavian (13)	13	0.01
Scotch-Irish (12)	41	0.04
Scottish (19)	69	0.07
Swedish (26)	33	0.03
Ukrainian (19)	19	0.02
Welsh (0)	26	0.03
West Indian, ex. Hispanic (0)	14	0.01
Trinidadian/Tobagonian (0)	14	0.01
Yugoslavian (0)	31	0.03

Hispanic Origin	Population	%
Hispanic or Latino (of any race)	89,442	94.75
Central American, ex. Mexican	9,777	10.36
Costa Rican	97	0.10
Guatemalan	2,629	2.79
Honduran	507	0.54
Nicaraguan	983	1.04
Panamanian	18	0.02
Salvadoran	5,407	5.73
Other Central American	136	0.14
Cuban	754	0.80
Dominican Republic	25	0.03
Mexican	73,677	78.05
Puerto Rican	464	0.49
South American	1,216	1.29
Argentinean	112	0.12
Bolivian	13	0.01
Chilean	46	0.05
Colombian	237	0.25
Ecuadorian	348	0.37
Paraguayan	1	<0.01
Peruvian	431	0.46
Uruguayan	7	0.01
Venezuelan	12	0.01
Other South American	9	0.01
Other Hispanic or Latino	3,529	3.74

Race*	Population	%
African-American/Black (890)	1,201	1.27
Not Hispanic (585)	630	0.67
Hispanic (305)	571	0.60
American Indian/Alaska Native (878)	1,269	1.34
Not Hispanic (110)	161	0.17
Hispanic (768)	1,108	1.17
Alaska Athabascan *(Ala. Nat.)* (2)	2	<0.01
Apache (16)	24	0.03
Blackfeet (8)	15	0.02
Canadian/French Am. Ind. (2)	2	<0.01
Central American Ind. (12)	20	0.02
Cherokee (9)	47	0.05
Chickasaw (0)	1	<0.01
Chippewa (0)	1	<0.01
Choctaw (4)	15	0.02
Cree (0)	5	0.01
Creek (7)	9	0.01
Crow (3)	3	<0.01
Delaware (0)	1	<0.01
Hopi (2)	5	0.01
Iroquois (0)	2	<0.01
Lumbee (1)	1	<0.01
Menominee (0)	1	<0.01
Mexican American Ind. (215)	290	0.31
Navajo (9)	28	0.03
Paiute (1)	3	<0.01
Pima (15)	15	0.02
Potawatomi (0)	1	<0.01

*Notes: † The Census 2010 population figure is used to calculate the percentages in the Hispanic Origin and Race categories. Ancestry percentages are based on the 2006-2010 American Community Survey population (not shown); ‡ Numbers in parentheses indicate the number of people reporting a single ancestry; * Numbers in parentheses indicate the number of persons reporting this race alone, not in combination with any other race; Please refer to the Explanation of Data for more information.*

Pueblo (16)	21	0.02
Puget Sound Salish (6)	6	0.01
Seminole (1)	1	<0.01
Shoshone (1)	1	<0.01
Sioux (6)	16	0.02
South American Ind. (2)	6	0.01
Spanish American Ind. (14)	17	0.02
Tlingit-Haida *(Alaska Native)* (3)	3	<0.01
Tohono O'Odham (5)	6	0.01
Yaqui (12)	19	0.02
Asian (732)	991	1.05
Not Hispanic (647)	707	0.75
Hispanic (85)	284	0.30
Bangladeshi (2)	2	<0.01
Burmese (5)	5	0.01
Cambodian (29)	31	0.03
Chinese, ex. Taiwanese (40)	70	0.07
Filipino (223)	299	0.32
Hmong (2)	4	<0.01
Indian (95)	118	0.13
Indonesian (2)	3	<0.01
Japanese (39)	74	0.08
Korean (176)	205	0.22
Laotian (16)	18	0.02
Pakistani (2)	2	<0.01
Sri Lankan (1)	1	<0.01
Taiwanese (10)	10	0.01
Thai (50)	58	0.06
Vietnamese (11)	33	0.03
Hawaii Native/Pacific Islander (99)	185	0.20
Not Hispanic (69)	87	0.09
Hispanic (30)	98	0.10
Guamanian/Chamorro (15)	22	0.02
Native Hawaiian (21)	34	0.04
Samoan (44)	66	0.07
Tongan (7)	7	0.01
White (47,645)	50,671	53.68
Not Hispanic (3,233)	3,363	3.56
Hispanic (44,412)	47,308	50.12

South Lake Tahoe

Place Type: City
County: El Dorado
Population: 21,403†

Ancestry‡	Population	%
African, Sub-Saharan (0)	7	0.03
African (0)	7	0.03
Albanian (0)	24	0.11
American (806)	806	3.64
Arab (46)	46	0.21
Other Arab (46)	46	0.21
Armenian (78)	78	0.35
Austrian (30)	114	0.52
Belgian (19)	50	0.23
Brazilian (17)	28	0.13
British (27)	70	0.32
Bulgarian (0)	53	0.24
Canadian (38)	89	0.40
Croatian (23)	72	0.33
Czech (4)	95	0.43
Czechoslovakian (0)	9	0.04
Danish (65)	110	0.50
Dutch (99)	330	1.49
Eastern European (48)	48	0.22
English (672)	2,257	10.21
European (359)	409	1.85
Finnish (0)	10	0.05
French, ex. Basque (185)	893	4.04
French Canadian (141)	212	0.96
German (1,101)	3,168	14.33
Greek (0)	26	0.12
Hungarian (156)	178	0.80
Irish (643)	3,494	15.80
Italian (612)	1,954	8.84
Latvian (0)	11	0.05
Lithuanian (32)	42	0.19
Norwegian (281)	617	2.79
Pennsylvania German (29)	29	0.13
Polish (156)	288	1.30
Portuguese (124)	309	1.40
Romanian (13)	128	0.58
Russian (59)	147	0.66
Scandinavian (17)	17	0.08
Scotch-Irish (156)	513	2.32
Scottish (97)	491	2.22
Serbian (0)	47	0.21
Slovak (44)	44	0.20
Swedish (130)	510	2.31
Swiss (28)	79	0.36
Ukrainian (54)	54	0.24
Welsh (0)	80	0.36
Yugoslavian (14)	33	0.15

Hispanic Origin	Population	%
Hispanic or Latino (of any race)	6,665	31.14
Central American, ex. Mexican	358	1.67
Costa Rican	7	0.03
Guatemalan	33	0.15
Honduran	7	0.03
Nicaraguan	28	0.13
Panamanian	1	<0.01
Salvadoran	279	1.30
Other Central American	3	0.01
Cuban	28	0.13
Dominican Republic	2	0.01
Mexican	5,483	25.62
Puerto Rican	70	0.33
South American	85	0.40
Argentinean	22	0.10
Bolivian	9	0.04
Chilean	23	0.11
Colombian	14	0.07
Ecuadorian	3	0.01
Peruvian	11	0.05
Uruguayan	1	<0.01
Venezuelan	1	<0.01
Other South American	1	<0.01
Other Hispanic or Latino	639	2.99

Race*	Population	%
African-American/Black (182)	261	1.22
Not Hispanic (138)	204	0.95
Hispanic (44)	57	0.27
American Indian/Alaska Native (232)	456	2.13
Not Hispanic (122)	285	1.33
Hispanic (110)	171	0.80
Apache (5)	12	0.06
Arapaho (0)	2	0.01
Blackfeet (1)	10	0.05
Cherokee (18)	70	0.33
Cheyenne (1)	1	<0.01
Chickasaw (0)	6	0.03
Chippewa (2)	4	0.02
Choctaw (7)	26	0.12
Colville (1)	1	<0.01
Creek (1)	2	0.01
Crow (0)	2	0.01
Delaware (1)	1	<0.01
Hopi (0)	1	<0.01
Inupiat *(Alaska Native)* (0)	6	0.03
Mexican American Ind. (45)	53	0.25
Navajo (5)	12	0.06
Osage (0)	3	0.01
Ottawa (0)	1	<0.01
Paiute (3)	11	0.05
Pima (1)	3	0.01
Potawatomi (1)	1	<0.01
Pueblo (2)	3	0.01
Shoshone (3)	10	0.05
Sioux (7)	18	0.08
Spanish American Ind. (1)	1	<0.01
Tlingit-Haida *(Alaska Native)* (1)	7	0.03
Ute (1)	3	0.01
Yaqui (1)	2	0.01
Asian (1,186)	1,430	6.68
Not Hispanic (1,155)	1,362	6.36
Hispanic (31)	68	0.32
Cambodian (4)	4	0.02
Chinese, ex. Taiwanese (112)	163	0.76
Filipino (828)	955	4.46
Indian (96)	114	0.53
Indonesian (1)	3	0.01
Japanese (63)	120	0.56
Korean (35)	51	0.24
Laotian (1)	1	<0.01
Sri Lankan (1)	1	<0.01
Taiwanese (2)	2	0.01
Thai (1)	8	0.04
Vietnamese (18)	35	0.16
Hawaii Native/Pacific Islander (39)	93	0.43
Not Hispanic (32)	69	0.32
Hispanic (7)	24	0.11
Fijian (1)	1	<0.01
Guamanian/Chamorro (9)	23	0.11
Native Hawaiian (25)	49	0.23
Samoan (2)	2	0.01
White (15,733)	16,457	76.89
Not Hispanic (12,818)	13,221	61.77
Hispanic (2,915)	3,236	15.12

South Pasadena

Place Type: City
County: Los Angeles
Population: 25,619†

Ancestry‡	Population	%
African, Sub-Saharan (61)	80	0.32
African (61)	80	0.32
American (334)	334	1.32
Arab (199)	240	0.95
Arab (161)	161	0.63
Egyptian (16)	22	0.09
Lebanese (10)	20	0.08
Other Arab (12)	37	0.15
Armenian (73)	81	0.32
Australian (0)	22	0.09
Austrian (32)	168	0.66
Basque (11)	11	0.04
Belgian (0)	17	0.07
British (111)	280	1.10
Bulgarian (0)	14	0.06
Croatian (25)	50	0.20
Cypriot (13)	27	0.11
Czech (44)	64	0.25
Czechoslovakian (10)	39	0.15
Danish (20)	138	0.54
Dutch (125)	423	1.67
Eastern European (32)	58	0.23
English (586)	1,877	7.40
Estonian (0)	12	0.05
European (623)	644	2.54
Finnish (24)	24	0.09
French, ex. Basque (76)	440	1.73
French Canadian (31)	133	0.52
German (494)	2,371	9.34
Greek (20)	101	0.40
Hungarian (61)	145	0.57
Iranian (57)	57	0.22
Irish (549)	2,035	8.02
Israeli (9)	9	0.04
Italian (533)	1,441	5.68
Latvian (13)	13	0.05
Lithuanian (28)	69	0.27
Macedonian (0)	14	0.06
Northern European (116)	116	0.46
Norwegian (36)	352	1.39
Polish (156)	581	2.29
Portuguese (29)	121	0.48
Romanian (11)	95	0.37
Russian (147)	339	1.34
Scandinavian (10)	46	0.18
Scotch-Irish (64)	174	0.69
Scottish (88)	648	2.55
Serbian (0)	14	0.06
Slovak (71)	71	0.28
Swedish (132)	465	1.83
Swiss (24)	55	0.22

*Notes: † The Census 2010 population figure is used to calculate the percentages in the Hispanic Origin and Race categories. Ancestry percentages are based on the 2006-2010 American Community Survey population (not shown); ‡ Numbers in parentheses indicate the number of people reporting a single ancestry; * Numbers in parentheses indicate the number of persons reporting this race alone, not in combination with any other race; Please refer to the Explanation of Data for more information.*

Turkish (78)	78	0.31
Ukrainian (36)	103	0.41
Welsh (49)	138	0.54
West Indian, ex. Hispanic (0)	69	0.27
Jamaican (0)	69	0.27

Hispanic Origin	Population	%
Hispanic or Latino (of any race)	4,767	18.61
Central American, ex. Mexican	448	1.75
Costa Rican	45	0.18
Guatemalan	107	0.42
Honduran	37	0.14
Nicaraguan	48	0.19
Panamanian	12	0.05
Salvadoran	179	0.70
Other Central American	20	0.08
Cuban	112	0.44
Dominican Republic	8	0.03
Mexican	3,338	13.03
Puerto Rican	112	0.44
South American	355	1.39
Argentinean	63	0.25
Bolivian	18	0.07
Chilean	34	0.13
Colombian	81	0.32
Ecuadorian	36	0.14
Paraguayan	5	0.02
Peruvian	100	0.39
Uruguayan	9	0.04
Venezuelan	7	0.03
Other South American	2	0.01
Other Hispanic or Latino	394	1.54

Race*	Population	%
African-American/Black (771)	1,041	4.06
Not Hispanic (736)	929	3.63
Hispanic (35)	112	0.44
American Indian/Alaska Native (107)	286	1.12
Not Hispanic (26)	114	0.44
Hispanic (81)	172	0.67
Apache (2)	13	0.05
Blackfeet (1)	7	0.03
Canadian/French Am. Ind. (0)	1	<0.01
Central American Ind. (0)	1	<0.01
Cherokee (2)	30	0.12
Chickasaw (1)	1	<0.01
Choctaw (0)	5	0.02
Cree (0)	3	0.01
Creek (0)	1	<0.01
Hopi (1)	7	0.03
Houma (2)	2	0.01
Inupiat *(Alaska Native)* (0)	3	0.01
Iroquois (0)	1	<0.01
Mexican American Ind. (30)	39	0.15
Navajo (3)	12	0.05
Pima (3)	4	0.02
Potawatomi (0)	1	<0.01
Pueblo (1)	2	0.01
Seminole (0)	1	<0.01
Sioux (1)	4	0.02
South American Ind. (1)	5	0.02
Spanish American Ind. (0)	1	<0.01
Tohono O'Odham (0)	2	0.01
Yaqui (1)	2	0.01
Asian (7,973)	8,844	34.52
Not Hispanic (7,904)	8,605	33.59
Hispanic (69)	239	0.93
Bangladeshi (4)	7	0.03
Burmese (10)	16	0.06
Cambodian (8)	11	0.04
Chinese, ex. Taiwanese (3,630)	4,132	16.13
Filipino (491)	695	2.71
Hmong (6)	7	0.03
Indian (329)	384	1.50
Indonesian (23)	47	0.18
Japanese (793)	1,164	4.54
Korean (1,641)	1,774	6.92
Laotian (1)	2	0.01
Malaysian (7)	8	0.03
Nepalese (9)	9	0.04
Pakistani (30)	32	0.12
Sri Lankan (25)	29	0.11
Taiwanese (382)	428	1.67
Thai (101)	111	0.43
Vietnamese (171)	228	0.89
Hawaii Native/Pacific Islander (9)	77	0.30
Not Hispanic (6)	58	0.23
Hispanic (3)	19	0.07
Guamanian/Chamorro (2)	6	0.02
Native Hawaiian (4)	41	0.16
Samoan (0)	3	0.01
White (13,922)	15,159	59.17
Not Hispanic (11,179)	12,014	46.89
Hispanic (2,743)	3,145	12.28

South San Francisco

Place Type: City
County: San Mateo
Population: 63,632†

Ancestry‡	Population	%
African, Sub-Saharan (211)	282	0.45
African (76)	76	0.12
Nigerian (135)	206	0.33
American (491)	491	0.79
Arab (1,028)	1,248	2.01
Arab (353)	363	0.59
Jordanian (107)	278	0.45
Lebanese (132)	132	0.21
Moroccan (16)	33	0.05
Palestinian (298)	320	0.52
Other Arab (122)	122	0.20
Armenian (84)	95	0.15
Assyrian/Chaldean/Syriac (0)	12	0.02
Australian (0)	11	0.02
Austrian (10)	40	0.06
Basque (0)	11	0.02
Brazilian (27)	62	0.10
British (0)	62	0.10
Canadian (23)	23	0.04
Croatian (72)	90	0.15
Cypriot (34)	34	0.05
Czech (30)	45	0.07
Czechoslovakian (29)	76	0.12
Danish (78)	171	0.28
Dutch (35)	188	0.30
Eastern European (0)	22	0.04
English (452)	1,790	2.89
European (280)	301	0.49
Finnish (38)	103	0.17
French, ex. Basque (233)	976	1.57
French Canadian (28)	86	0.14
German (475)	2,398	3.87
German Russian (18)	18	0.03
Greek (342)	486	0.78
Hungarian (45)	85	0.14
Iranian (0)	9	0.01
Irish (671)	2,998	4.83
Italian (1,991)	3,794	6.12
Latvian (22)	37	0.06
Lithuanian (22)	165	0.27
Maltese (69)	100	0.16
Northern European (68)	68	0.11
Norwegian (107)	314	0.51
Pennsylvania German (12)	34	0.05
Polish (172)	453	0.73
Portuguese (154)	400	0.64
Romanian (34)	52	0.08
Russian (115)	316	0.51
Scandinavian (10)	10	0.02
Scotch-Irish (123)	234	0.38
Scottish (102)	312	0.50
Slavic (10)	10	0.02
Swedish (44)	263	0.42
Swiss (33)	42	0.07
Ukrainian (137)	165	0.27
Welsh (13)	144	0.23
West Indian, ex. Hispanic (10)	10	0.02
Jamaican (10)	10	0.02
Yugoslavian (28)	43	0.07

Hispanic Origin	Population	%
Hispanic or Latino (of any race)	21,645	34.02
Central American, ex. Mexican	5,381	8.46
Costa Rican	43	0.07
Guatemalan	576	0.91
Honduran	140	0.22
Nicaraguan	1,639	2.58
Panamanian	36	0.06
Salvadoran	2,897	4.55
Other Central American	50	0.08
Cuban	92	0.14
Dominican Republic	12	0.02
Mexican	13,194	20.73
Puerto Rican	571	0.90
South American	815	1.28
Argentinean	51	0.08
Bolivian	37	0.06
Chilean	34	0.05
Colombian	152	0.24
Ecuadorian	64	0.10
Paraguayan	3	<0.01
Peruvian	424	0.67
Uruguayan	4	0.01
Venezuelan	26	0.04
Other South American	20	0.03
Other Hispanic or Latino	1,580	2.48

Race*	Population	%
African-American/Black (1,625)	2,190	3.44
Not Hispanic (1,480)	1,851	2.91
Hispanic (145)	339	0.53
American Indian/Alaska Native (395)	927	1.46
Not Hispanic (138)	412	0.65
Hispanic (257)	515	0.81
Alaska Athabascan *(Ala. Nat.)* (1)	2	<0.01
Aleut *(Alaska Native)* (0)	1	<0.01
Apache (9)	29	0.05
Arapaho (0)	5	0.01
Blackfeet (3)	28	0.04
Canadian/French Am. Ind. (0)	4	0.01
Central American Ind. (10)	16	0.03
Cherokee (11)	68	0.11
Cheyenne (0)	8	0.01
Chickasaw (1)	6	0.01
Chippewa (13)	19	0.03
Choctaw (21)	41	0.06
Colville (1)	1	<0.01
Comanche (0)	1	<0.01
Creek (6)	11	0.02
Delaware (0)	2	<0.01
Inupiat *(Alaska Native)* (1)	1	<0.01
Iroquois (0)	8	0.01
Menominee (0)	1	<0.01
Mexican American Ind. (38)	72	0.11
Navajo (21)	44	0.07
Osage (1)	1	<0.01
Paiute (2)	3	<0.01
Pima (1)	4	0.01
Potawatomi (0)	1	<0.01
Pueblo (2)	9	0.01
Seminole (1)	11	0.02
Shoshone (0)	2	<0.01
Sioux (9)	16	0.03
South American Ind. (1)	8	0.01
Spanish American Ind. (9)	11	0.02
Tlingit-Haida *(Alaska Native)* (1)	3	<0.01
Tohono O'Odham (0)	2	<0.01
Tsimshian *(Alaska Native)* (1)	2	<0.01
Ute (1)	2	<0.01
Yakama (2)	2	<0.01
Yaqui (5)	5	0.01
Asian (23,293)	25,409	39.93
Not Hispanic (22,923)	24,507	38.51
Hispanic (370)	902	1.42
Burmese (139)	168	0.26
Cambodian (50)	65	0.10
Chinese, ex. Taiwanese (6,843)	7,687	12.08
Filipino (12,829)	14,358	22.56

*Notes: † The Census 2010 population figure is used to calculate the percentages in the Hispanic Origin and Race categories. Ancestry percentages are based on the 2006-2010 American Community Survey population (not shown); ‡ Numbers in parentheses indicate the number of people reporting a single ancestry; * Numbers in parentheses indicate the number of persons reporting this race alone, not in combination with any other race; Please refer to the Explanation of Data for more information.*

Hmong (4)	4	0.01
Indian (989)	1,311	2.06
Indonesian (111)	160	0.25
Japanese (429)	743	1.17
Korean (374)	498	0.78
Laotian (24)	32	0.05
Malaysian (13)	17	0.03
Nepalese (60)	61	0.10
Pakistani (117)	138	0.22
Sri Lankan (7)	7	0.01
Taiwanese (106)	126	0.20
Thai (104)	129	0.20
Vietnamese (395)	515	0.81
Hawaii Native/Pacific Islander (1,111)	1,797	2.82
Not Hispanic (1,054)	1,595	2.51
Hispanic (57)	202	0.32
Fijian (332)	414	0.65
Guamanian/Chamorro (32)	75	0.12
Native Hawaiian (69)	237	0.37
Samoan (340)	473	0.74
Tongan (171)	250	0.39
White (23,760)	26,496	41.64
Not Hispanic (14,016)	15,403	24.21
Hispanic (9,744)	11,093	17.43

South San Gabriel

Place Type: CDP
County: Los Angeles
Population: 8,070†

Ancestry‡	Population	%
American (63)	63	0.77
Armenian (8)	8	0.10
Czech (0)	19	0.23
Dutch (6)	31	0.38
English (11)	28	0.34
French, ex. Basque (0)	3	0.04
German (9)	45	0.55
Greek (7)	7	0.09
Irish (9)	79	0.97
Italian (24)	61	0.75
Polish (7)	13	0.16
Welsh (0)	3	0.04

Hispanic Origin	Population	%
Hispanic or Latino (of any race)	3,444	42.68
Central American, ex. Mexican	271	3.36
Costa Rican	9	0.11
Guatemalan	72	0.89
Honduran	14	0.17
Nicaraguan	21	0.26
Salvadoran	147	1.82
Other Central American	8	0.10
Cuban	19	0.24
Dominican Republic	1	0.01
Mexican	2,954	36.60
Puerto Rican	12	0.15
South American	27	0.33
Argentinean	2	0.02
Chilean	3	0.04
Colombian	5	0.06
Ecuadorian	10	0.12
Peruvian	7	0.09
Other Hispanic or Latino	160	1.98

Race*	Population	%
African-American/Black (83)	128	1.59
Not Hispanic (74)	109	1.35
Hispanic (9)	19	0.24
American Indian/Alaska Native (56)	88	1.09
Not Hispanic (17)	30	0.37
Hispanic (39)	58	0.72
Apache (7)	8	0.10
Cherokee (3)	3	0.04
Comanche (1)	1	0.01
Creek (1)	5	0.06
Hopi (0)	1	0.01
Mexican American Ind. (4)	10	0.12
Navajo (4)	4	0.05
Pima (3)	3	0.04
Pueblo (1)	1	0.01
Seminole (0)	4	0.05
Sioux (1)	1	0.01
Asian (3,990)	4,159	51.54
Not Hispanic (3,974)	4,069	50.42
Hispanic (16)	90	1.12
Burmese (62)	65	0.81
Cambodian (60)	84	1.04
Chinese, ex. Taiwanese (2,147)	2,385	29.55
Filipino (197)	249	3.09
Indian (30)	50	0.62
Indonesian (25)	27	0.33
Japanese (525)	607	7.52
Korean (54)	70	0.87
Laotian (4)	5	0.06
Malaysian (0)	1	0.01
Nepalese (2)	2	0.02
Taiwanese (29)	38	0.47
Thai (55)	58	0.72
Vietnamese (570)	711	8.81
Hawaii Native/Pacific Islander (4)	24	0.30
Not Hispanic (1)	14	0.17
Hispanic (3)	10	0.12
Guamanian/Chamorro (1)	1	0.01
Marshallese (0)	3	0.04
Native Hawaiian (3)	10	0.12
Tongan (0)	1	0.01
White (2,198)	2,415	29.93
Not Hispanic (451)	515	6.38
Hispanic (1,747)	1,900	23.54

South San Jose Hills

Place Type: CDP
County: Los Angeles
Population: 20,551†

Ancestry‡	Population	%
American (153)	153	0.72
Arab (0)	23	0.11
Arab (0)	23	0.11
Canadian (0)	22	0.10
Dutch (0)	23	0.11
English (45)	136	0.64
European (55)	55	0.26
French, ex. Basque (0)	48	0.22
German (104)	205	0.96
Irish (97)	127	0.59
Italian (23)	69	0.32
Norwegian (23)	23	0.11
Polish (0)	34	0.16
Russian (0)	21	0.10
Scotch-Irish (0)	8	0.04
Scottish (0)	34	0.16
Swedish (0)	16	0.07

Hispanic Origin	Population	%
Hispanic or Latino (of any race)	17,713	86.19
Central American, ex. Mexican	1,254	6.10
Costa Rican	24	0.12
Guatemalan	288	1.40
Honduran	69	0.34
Nicaraguan	81	0.39
Panamanian	5	0.02
Salvadoran	770	3.75
Other Central American	17	0.08
Cuban	35	0.17
Dominican Republic	3	0.01
Mexican	15,436	75.11
Puerto Rican	55	0.27
South American	179	0.87
Argentinean	12	0.06
Bolivian	9	0.04
Chilean	4	0.02
Colombian	46	0.22
Ecuadorian	48	0.23
Peruvian	41	0.20
Uruguayan	4	0.02
Venezuelan	7	0.03
Other South American	8	0.04
Other Hispanic or Latino	751	3.65

Race*	Population	%
African-American/Black (304)	385	1.87
Not Hispanic (231)	250	1.22
Hispanic (73)	135	0.66
American Indian/Alaska Native (195)	269	1.31
Not Hispanic (20)	40	0.19
Hispanic (175)	229	1.11
Apache (6)	10	0.05
Arapaho (0)	4	0.02
Central American Ind. (6)	6	0.03
Cherokee (2)	11	0.05
Chippewa (2)	2	0.01
Creek (3)	3	0.01
Iroquois (0)	2	0.01
Kiowa (0)	3	0.01
Mexican American Ind. (26)	37	0.18
Navajo (5)	11	0.05
Paiute (1)	1	<0.01
Pima (0)	1	<0.01
Pueblo (3)	4	0.02
Shoshone (1)	1	<0.01
South American Ind. (1)	2	0.01
Spanish American Ind. (2)	2	0.01
Tlingit-Haida *(Alaska Native)* (1)	1	<0.01
Tohono O'Odham (0)	3	0.01
Yaqui (2)	2	0.01
Asian (1,649)	1,752	8.53
Not Hispanic (1,602)	1,648	8.02
Hispanic (47)	104	0.51
Burmese (9)	9	0.04
Cambodian (5)	9	0.04
Chinese, ex. Taiwanese (533)	566	2.75
Filipino (729)	793	3.86
Indian (53)	57	0.28
Indonesian (19)	29	0.14
Japanese (28)	36	0.18
Korean (19)	22	0.11
Laotian (13)	28	0.14
Pakistani (12)	14	0.07
Sri Lankan (12)	12	0.06
Taiwanese (57)	64	0.31
Thai (17)	25	0.12
Vietnamese (95)	108	0.53
Hawaii Native/Pacific Islander (30)	51	0.25
Not Hispanic (22)	36	0.18
Hispanic (8)	15	0.07
Guamanian/Chamorro (5)	5	0.02
Native Hawaiian (1)	9	0.04
Samoan (23)	25	0.12
White (9,302)	9,815	47.76
Not Hispanic (853)	907	4.41
Hispanic (8,449)	8,908	43.35

South Whittier

Place Type: CDP
County: Los Angeles
Population: 57,156†

Ancestry‡	Population	%
African, Sub-Saharan (56)	151	0.27
African (56)	151	0.27
American (986)	986	1.73
Arab (112)	177	0.31
Arab (0)	15	0.03
Egyptian (47)	54	0.09
Lebanese (37)	80	0.14
Syrian (15)	15	0.03
Other Arab (13)	13	0.02
Armenian (99)	158	0.28
Austrian (6)	18	0.03
Brazilian (137)	137	0.24
British (63)	177	0.31
Canadian (31)	63	0.11
Croatian (10)	36	0.06
Czech (32)	45	0.08
Czechoslovakian (9)	9	0.02

SECTION TWO

*Notes: † The Census 2010 population figure is used to calculate the percentages in the Hispanic Origin and Race categories. Ancestry percentages are based on the 2006-2010 American Community Survey population (not shown); ‡ Numbers in parentheses indicate the number of people reporting a single ancestry; * Numbers in parentheses indicate the number of persons reporting this race alone, not in combination with any other race; Please refer to the Explanation of Data for more information.*

Danish (51)	166	0.29
Dutch (54)	300	0.53
Eastern European (97)	97	0.17
English (421)	1,591	2.80
European (344)	445	0.78
Finnish (11)	19	0.03
French, ex. Basque (31)	450	0.79
French Canadian (33)	176	0.31
German (590)	2,377	4.18
Greek (64)	187	0.33
Hungarian (49)	62	0.11
Irish (376)	1,867	3.28
Italian (254)	872	1.53
Lithuanian (0)	9	0.02
Norwegian (23)	292	0.51
Pennsylvania German (9)	20	0.04
Polish (70)	414	0.73
Portuguese (52)	135	0.24
Russian (170)	300	0.53
Scandinavian (21)	21	0.04
Scotch-Irish (97)	454	0.80
Scottish (156)	373	0.66
Slovak (0)	15	0.03
Swedish (62)	287	0.50
Swiss (44)	153	0.27
Ukrainian (25)	54	0.09
Welsh (34)	133	0.23
West Indian, ex. Hispanic (43)	71	0.12
Belizean (0)	28	0.05
Jamaican (11)	11	0.02
Trinidadian/Tobagonian (8)	8	0.01
West Indian (24)	24	0.04

Hispanic Origin	Population	%
Hispanic or Latino (of any race)	44,094	77.15
Central American, ex. Mexican	2,217	3.88
Costa Rican	59	0.10
Guatemalan	612	1.07
Honduran	103	0.18
Nicaraguan	299	0.52
Panamanian	24	0.04
Salvadoran	1,110	1.94
Other Central American	10	0.02
Cuban	206	0.36
Dominican Republic	10	0.02
Mexican	38,766	67.82
Puerto Rican	354	0.62
South American	548	0.96
Argentinean	70	0.12
Bolivian	11	0.02
Chilean	34	0.06
Colombian	136	0.24
Ecuadorian	108	0.19
Peruvian	170	0.30
Uruguayan	9	0.02
Venezuelan	5	0.01
Other South American	5	0.01
Other Hispanic or Latino	1,993	3.49

Race*	Population	%
African-American/Black (859)	1,176	2.06
Not Hispanic (601)	711	1.24
Hispanic (258)	465	0.81
American Indian/Alaska Native (743)	1,209	2.12
Not Hispanic (139)	276	0.48
Hispanic (604)	933	1.63
Aleut *(Alaska Native)* (2)	2	<0.01
Apache (54)	91	0.16
Arapaho (2)	5	0.01
Blackfeet (13)	26	0.05
Canadian/French Am. Ind. (1)	1	<0.01
Central American Ind. (12)	12	0.02
Cherokee (18)	72	0.13
Cheyenne (2)	2	<0.01
Chickasaw (0)	4	0.01
Chippewa (5)	17	0.03
Choctaw (3)	15	0.03
Colville (1)	1	<0.01
Comanche (3)	10	0.02
Creek (3)	6	0.01
Hopi (5)	10	0.02
Iroquois (2)	3	0.01
Lumbee (0)	5	0.01
Mexican American Ind. (71)	111	0.19
Navajo (27)	46	0.08
Paiute (1)	4	0.01
Pima (5)	7	0.01
Potawatomi (3)	5	0.01
Pueblo (9)	13	0.02
Seminole (1)	7	0.01
Shoshone (1)	1	<0.01
Sioux (7)	14	0.02
South American Ind. (8)	11	0.02
Spanish American Ind. (0)	1	<0.01
Tlingit-Haida *(Alaska Native)* (0)	5	0.01
Tohono O'Odham (15)	22	0.04
Ute (0)	1	<0.01
Yaqui (13)	42	0.07
Yuman (1)	1	<0.01
Asian (2,305)	2,791	4.88
Not Hispanic (2,151)	2,418	4.23
Hispanic (154)	373	0.65
Bangladeshi (4)	4	0.01
Burmese (7)	11	0.02
Cambodian (54)	58	0.10
Chinese, ex. Taiwanese (222)	321	0.56
Filipino (1,164)	1,406	2.46
Indian (103)	135	0.24
Indonesian (13)	21	0.04
Japanese (159)	273	0.48
Korean (165)	185	0.32
Laotian (67)	83	0.15
Nepalese (16)	16	0.03
Pakistani (2)	5	0.01
Sri Lankan (12)	12	0.02
Taiwanese (21)	26	0.05
Thai (78)	113	0.20
Vietnamese (129)	155	0.27
Hawaii Native/Pacific Islander (147)	282	0.49
Not Hispanic (76)	145	0.25
Hispanic (71)	137	0.24
Guamanian/Chamorro (26)	41	0.07
Native Hawaiian (21)	86	0.15
Samoan (43)	74	0.13
Tongan (32)	34	0.06
White (33,663)	35,650	62.37
Not Hispanic (9,526)	9,959	17.42
Hispanic (24,137)	25,691	44.95

Spring Valley

Place Type: CDP
County: San Diego
Population: 28,205†

Ancestry‡	Population	%
African, Sub-Saharan (354)	354	1.30
African (354)	354	1.30
American (509)	509	1.86
Arab (557)	653	2.39
Arab (22)	22	0.08
Iraqi (390)	475	1.74
Moroccan (0)	11	0.04
Other Arab (145)	145	0.53
Armenian (13)	29	0.11
Assyrian/Chaldean/Syriac (369)	448	1.64
Austrian (7)	51	0.19
Belgian (0)	7	0.03
Brazilian (78)	102	0.37
British (96)	105	0.38
Canadian (104)	138	0.51
Czech (24)	78	0.29
Czechoslovakian (7)	16	0.06
Danish (17)	201	0.74
Dutch (50)	345	1.26
English (660)	2,842	10.41
European (105)	134	0.49
Finnish (31)	47	0.17
French, ex. Basque (81)	612	2.24
French Canadian (89)	193	0.71
German (1,322)	4,732	17.33
Greek (36)	153	0.56
Hungarian (16)	76	0.28
Icelander (7)	7	0.03
Iranian (93)	136	0.50
Irish (530)	2,818	10.32
Italian (435)	1,254	4.59
New Zealander (27)	27	0.10
Northern European (47)	47	0.17
Norwegian (133)	372	1.36
Polish (66)	316	1.16
Portuguese (125)	394	1.44
Romanian (0)	29	0.11
Russian (34)	186	0.68
Scandinavian (0)	76	0.28
Scotch-Irish (144)	548	2.01
Scottish (320)	978	3.58
Slovak (0)	44	0.16
Swedish (24)	539	1.97
Swiss (0)	38	0.14
Ukrainian (22)	51	0.19
Welsh (27)	188	0.69
West Indian, ex. Hispanic (30)	30	0.11
Jamaican (30)	30	0.11
Yugoslavian (12)	24	0.09

Hispanic Origin	Population	%
Hispanic or Latino (of any race)	9,196	32.60
Central American, ex. Mexican	163	0.58
Costa Rican	12	0.04
Guatemalan	53	0.19
Honduran	24	0.09
Nicaraguan	14	0.05
Panamanian	21	0.07
Salvadoran	39	0.14
Cuban	34	0.12
Dominican Republic	11	0.04
Mexican	8,231	29.18
Puerto Rican	236	0.84
South American	126	0.45
Argentinean	8	0.03
Bolivian	9	0.03
Chilean	12	0.04
Colombian	54	0.19
Ecuadorian	7	0.02
Peruvian	22	0.08
Venezuelan	8	0.03
Other South American	6	0.02
Other Hispanic or Latino	395	1.40

Race*	Population	%
African-American/Black (3,131)	3,765	13.35
Not Hispanic (2,984)	3,449	12.23
Hispanic (147)	316	1.12
American Indian/Alaska Native (237)	535	1.90
Not Hispanic (105)	295	1.05
Hispanic (132)	240	0.85
Apache (7)	10	0.04
Arapaho (0)	1	<0.01
Blackfeet (1)	15	0.05
Canadian/French Am. Ind. (0)	4	0.01
Cherokee (18)	66	0.23
Cheyenne (1)	2	0.01
Chickasaw (3)	6	0.02
Chippewa (2)	10	0.04
Choctaw (3)	15	0.05
Cree (1)	1	<0.01
Creek (0)	7	0.02
Crow (1)	1	<0.01
Iroquois (0)	3	0.01
Menominee (1)	1	<0.01
Mexican American Ind. (12)	16	0.06
Navajo (10)	10	0.04
Osage (1)	1	<0.01
Ottawa (1)	1	<0.01
Pima (3)	3	0.01
Potawatomi (0)	1	<0.01
Pueblo (2)	5	0.02
Seminole (1)	17	0.06
Sioux (4)	11	0.04

*Notes: † The Census 2010 population figure is used to calculate the percentages in the Hispanic Origin and Race categories. Ancestry percentages are based on the 2006-2010 American Community Survey population (not shown); ‡ Numbers in parentheses indicate the number of people reporting a single ancestry; * Numbers in parentheses indicate the number of persons reporting this race alone, not in combination with any other race; Please refer to the Explanation of Data for more information.*

South American Ind. (1)	1	<0.01
Tlingit-Haida *(Alaska Native)* (1)	1	<0.01
Tsimshian *(Alaska Native)* (1)	1	<0.01
Yaqui (5)	13	0.05
Yuman (1)	1	<0.01
Asian (1,660)	2,405	8.53
Not Hispanic (1,586)	2,187	7.75
Hispanic (74)	218	0.77
Cambodian (40)	53	0.19
Chinese, ex. Taiwanese (85)	191	0.68
Filipino (1,018)	1,469	5.21
Hmong (1)	1	<0.01
Indian (35)	57	0.20
Indonesian (10)	13	0.05
Japanese (104)	224	0.79
Korean (33)	69	0.24
Laotian (36)	43	0.15
Malaysian (1)	2	0.01
Pakistani (5)	8	0.03
Sri Lankan (1)	1	<0.01
Taiwanese (10)	10	0.04
Thai (14)	18	0.06
Vietnamese (198)	227	0.80
Hawaii Native/Pacific Islander (236)	450	1.60
Not Hispanic (206)	369	1.31
Hispanic (30)	81	0.29
Guamanian/Chamorro (110)	204	0.72
Native Hawaiian (37)	104	0.37
Samoan (61)	96	0.34
Tongan (6)	7	0.02
White (16,781)	18,242	64.68
Not Hispanic (12,924)	13,846	49.09
Hispanic (3,857)	4,396	15.59

Spring Valley Lake

Place Type: CDP
County: San Bernardino
Population: 8,220†

Ancestry‡	Population	%
African, Sub-Saharan (29)	29	0.38
Nigerian (29)	29	0.38
American (210)	210	2.75
Arab (436)	436	5.71
Egyptian (55)	55	0.72
Iraqi (154)	154	2.02
Palestinian (227)	227	2.97
Belgian (15)	15	0.20
Canadian (29)	114	1.49
Czech (0)	29	0.38
Czechoslovakian (14)	14	0.18
Danish (25)	50	0.65
Dutch (0)	173	2.26
English (476)	1,306	17.09
European (235)	235	3.08
French, ex. Basque (0)	428	5.60
German (521)	1,404	18.38
Greek (99)	99	1.30
Irish (228)	1,228	16.07
Italian (298)	875	11.45
Maltese (18)	33	0.43
Norwegian (0)	229	3.00
Polish (15)	217	2.84
Portuguese (0)	33	0.43
Russian (0)	58	0.76
Scandinavian (43)	71	0.93
Scotch-Irish (10)	93	1.22
Scottish (0)	61	0.80
Swedish (58)	88	1.15
Swiss (14)	14	0.18
Ukrainian (26)	139	1.82
Welsh (0)	67	0.88

Hispanic Origin	Population	%
Hispanic or Latino (of any race)	1,528	18.59
Central American, ex. Mexican	53	0.64
Costa Rican	6	0.07
Guatemalan	5	0.06
Honduran	2	0.02
Nicaraguan	22	0.27
Panamanian	4	0.05
Salvadoran	14	0.17
Cuban	36	0.44
Dominican Republic	1	0.01
Mexican	1,156	14.06
Puerto Rican	37	0.45
South American	58	0.71
Argentinean	19	0.23
Bolivian	2	0.02
Colombian	6	0.07
Ecuadorian	12	0.15
Peruvian	10	0.12
Venezuelan	9	0.11
Other Hispanic or Latino	187	2.27

Race*	Population	%
African-American/Black (403)	487	5.92
Not Hispanic (390)	453	5.51
Hispanic (13)	34	0.41
American Indian/Alaska Native (55)	141	1.72
Not Hispanic (34)	97	1.18
Hispanic (21)	44	0.54
Alaska Athabascan *(Ala. Nat.)* (0)	1	0.01
Apache (1)	3	0.04
Arapaho (0)	1	0.01
Blackfeet (0)	4	0.05
Cherokee (8)	30	0.36
Chickasaw (0)	1	0.01
Chippewa (0)	2	0.02
Choctaw (0)	4	0.05
Delaware (1)	1	0.01
Iroquois (0)	1	0.01
Mexican American Ind. (1)	6	0.07
Navajo (2)	2	0.02
Osage (1)	2	0.02
Pueblo (2)	4	0.05
Shoshone (0)	1	0.01
Asian (381)	562	6.84
Not Hispanic (363)	501	6.09
Hispanic (18)	61	0.74
Bangladeshi (4)	4	0.05
Cambodian (7)	11	0.13
Chinese, ex. Taiwanese (43)	73	0.89
Filipino (82)	147	1.79
Indian (119)	134	1.63
Indonesian (0)	8	0.10
Japanese (31)	62	0.75
Korean (51)	69	0.84
Pakistani (5)	5	0.06
Taiwanese (5)	6	0.07
Thai (13)	20	0.24
Vietnamese (12)	16	0.19
Hawaii Native/Pacific Islander (23)	63	0.77
Not Hispanic (23)	53	0.64
Hispanic (0)	10	0.12
Guamanian/Chamorro (18)	24	0.29
Native Hawaiian (3)	21	0.26
Samoan (0)	5	0.06
White (6,450)	6,804	82.77
Not Hispanic (5,600)	5,831	70.94
Hispanic (850)	973	11.84

Stanford

Place Type: CDP
County: Santa Clara
Population: 13,809†

Ancestry‡	Population	%
African, Sub-Saharan (87)	184	1.29
African (13)	36	0.25
Ethiopian (16)	16	0.11
Ghanaian (0)	15	0.11
Kenyan (0)	12	0.08
Nigerian (41)	72	0.51
South African (0)	16	0.11
Other Sub-Saharan African (17)	17	0.12
American (104)	104	0.73
Arab (43)	118	0.83
Egyptian (12)	12	0.08
Lebanese (15)	75	0.53
Moroccan (0)	15	0.11
Other Arab (16)	16	0.11
Australian (0)	16	0.11
Austrian (30)	145	1.02
British (116)	235	1.65
Bulgarian (41)	69	0.48
Canadian (51)	85	0.60
Croatian (34)	49	0.34
Cypriot (10)	10	0.07
Czech (31)	47	0.33
Danish (9)	25	0.18
Dutch (108)	256	1.80
Eastern European (256)	327	2.29
English (161)	1,058	7.42
Estonian (11)	11	0.08
European (538)	655	4.59
Finnish (0)	23	0.16
French, ex. Basque (34)	299	2.10
French Canadian (14)	38	0.27
German (155)	1,764	12.37
Greek (10)	38	0.27
Guyanese (0)	16	0.11
Hungarian (29)	145	1.02
Icelander (0)	13	0.09
Iranian (105)	121	0.85
Irish (84)	1,173	8.23
Israeli (56)	67	0.47
Italian (181)	950	6.66
Latvian (0)	105	0.74
Lithuanian (28)	57	0.40
New Zealander (19)	19	0.13
Northern European (42)	42	0.29
Norwegian (85)	368	2.58
Polish (98)	346	2.43
Portuguese (54)	203	1.42
Romanian (19)	64	0.45
Russian (119)	390	2.74
Scandinavian (0)	30	0.21
Scotch-Irish (23)	236	1.66
Scottish (41)	348	2.44
Serbian (15)	31	0.22
Slovak (0)	23	0.16
Slovene (0)	16	0.11
Swedish (75)	235	1.65
Swiss (65)	148	1.04
Turkish (13)	26	0.18
Ukrainian (43)	100	0.70
Welsh (14)	143	1.00
West Indian, ex. Hispanic (118)	168	1.18
Haitian (0)	16	0.11
Jamaican (87)	100	0.70
Trinidadian/Tobagonian (15)	26	0.18
U.S. Virgin Islander (0)	10	0.07
West Indian (16)	16	0.11
Yugoslavian (0)	15	0.11

Hispanic Origin	Population	%
Hispanic or Latino (of any race)	1,439	10.42
Central American, ex. Mexican	85	0.62
Costa Rican	13	0.09
Guatemalan	14	0.10
Honduran	13	0.09
Nicaraguan	11	0.08
Panamanian	8	0.06
Salvadoran	26	0.19
Cuban	84	0.61
Dominican Republic	29	0.21
Mexican	720	5.21
Puerto Rican	89	0.64
South American	320	2.32
Argentinean	68	0.49
Bolivian	22	0.16
Chilean	81	0.59
Colombian	60	0.43
Ecuadorian	19	0.14
Paraguayan	3	0.02
Peruvian	41	0.30
Uruguayan	5	0.04

*Notes: † The Census 2010 population figure is used to calculate the percentages in the Hispanic Origin and Race categories. Ancestry percentages are based on the 2006-2010 American Community Survey population (not shown); ‡ Numbers in parentheses indicate the number of people reporting a single ancestry; * Numbers in parentheses indicate the number of persons reporting this race alone, not in combination with any other race; Please refer to the Explanation of Data for more information.*

Venezuelan	20	0.14
Other South American	1	0.01
Other Hispanic or Latino	112	0.81

Race*	Population	%
African-American/Black (651)	916	6.63
Not Hispanic (621)	852	6.17
Hispanic (30)	64	0.46
American Indian/Alaska Native (86)	263	1.90
Not Hispanic (76)	217	1.57
Hispanic (10)	46	0.33
Alaska Athabascan *(Ala. Nat.)* (0)	1	0.01
Aleut *(Alaska Native)* (0)	1	0.01
Apache (2)	3	0.02
Blackfeet (2)	6	0.04
Canadian/French Am. Ind. (0)	1	0.01
Central American Ind. (0)	2	0.01
Cherokee (3)	27	0.20
Cheyenne (0)	1	0.01
Chickasaw (1)	4	0.03
Chippewa (3)	7	0.05
Choctaw (3)	12	0.09
Comanche (0)	2	0.01
Creek (1)	2	0.01
Delaware (0)	1	0.01
Hopi (1)	3	0.02
Inupiat *(Alaska Native)* (0)	1	0.01
Iroquois (1)	3	0.02
Mexican American Ind. (4)	10	0.07
Navajo (16)	24	0.17
Ottawa (0)	1	0.01
Paiute (0)	1	0.01
Pima (0)	1	0.01
Potawatomi (1)	6	0.04
Pueblo (3)	6	0.04
Puget Sound Salish (0)	1	0.01
Sioux (6)	9	0.07
South American Ind. (0)	2	0.01
Tlingit-Haida *(Alaska Native)* (2)	5	0.04
Tsimshian *(Alaska Native)* (0)	1	0.01
Yup'ik *(Alaska Native)* (1)	2	0.01
Asian (3,777)	4,446	32.20
Not Hispanic (3,746)	4,377	31.70
Hispanic (31)	69	0.50
Bangladeshi (5)	5	0.04
Bhutanese (10)	10	0.07
Burmese (6)	7	0.05
Cambodian (20)	30	0.22
Chinese, ex. Taiwanese (1,539)	1,879	13.61
Filipino (170)	282	2.04
Hmong (15)	15	0.11
Indian (667)	759	5.50
Indonesian (5)	10	0.07
Japanese (128)	305	2.21
Korean (561)	637	4.61
Laotian (4)	8	0.06
Malaysian (9)	14	0.10
Nepalese (9)	12	0.09
Pakistani (39)	49	0.35
Sri Lankan (14)	21	0.15
Taiwanese (146)	178	1.29
Thai (66)	72	0.52
Vietnamese (199)	237	1.72
Hawaii Native/Pacific Islander (28)	125	0.91
Not Hispanic (26)	115	0.83
Hispanic (2)	10	0.07
Fijian (1)	2	0.01
Guamanian/Chamorro (6)	14	0.10
Native Hawaiian (11)	67	0.49
Samoan (5)	16	0.12
Tongan (4)	7	0.05
White (7,932)	8,900	64.45
Not Hispanic (6,937)	7,787	56.39
Hispanic (995)	1,113	8.06

Stanton

Place Type: City
County: Orange
Population: 38,186†

Ancestry‡	Population	%
Afghan (17)	17	0.04
African, Sub-Saharan (100)	135	0.36
African (68)	103	0.27
Nigerian (22)	22	0.06
Sudanese (10)	10	0.03
American (775)	775	2.04
Arab (491)	545	1.43
Arab (159)	183	0.48
Egyptian (64)	64	0.17
Iraqi (9)	9	0.02
Jordanian (9)	9	0.02
Lebanese (135)	135	0.36
Moroccan (18)	18	0.05
Syrian (27)	27	0.07
Other Arab (70)	100	0.26
Armenian (31)	31	0.08
Assyrian/Chaldean/Syriac (64)	64	0.17
Austrian (32)	54	0.14
Brazilian (9)	9	0.02
British (12)	36	0.09
Canadian (35)	35	0.09
Czech (0)	43	0.11
Czechoslovakian (17)	17	0.04
Danish (24)	71	0.19
Dutch (74)	222	0.58
English (473)	1,195	3.15
European (106)	139	0.37
Finnish (0)	12	0.03
French, ex. Basque (53)	506	1.33
French Canadian (19)	49	0.13
German (914)	2,535	6.67
Greek (0)	9	0.02
Hungarian (77)	85	0.22
Iranian (29)	29	0.08
Irish (578)	1,974	5.20
Italian (505)	881	2.32
Lithuanian (28)	37	0.10
Norwegian (64)	231	0.61
Pennsylvania German (28)	28	0.07
Polish (149)	237	0.62
Portuguese (0)	28	0.07
Romanian (96)	96	0.25
Russian (39)	51	0.13
Scandinavian (22)	22	0.06
Scotch-Irish (139)	259	0.68
Scottish (131)	341	0.90
Slavic (0)	25	0.07
Swedish (79)	210	0.55
Swiss (0)	54	0.14
Welsh (0)	40	0.11
West Indian, ex. Hispanic (21)	31	0.08
Jamaican (21)	21	0.06
Trinidadian/Tobagonian (0)	10	0.03
Yugoslavian (0)	21	0.06

Hispanic Origin	Population	%
Hispanic or Latino (of any race)	19,417	50.85
Central American, ex. Mexican	871	2.28
Costa Rican	25	0.07
Guatemalan	302	0.79
Honduran	70	0.18
Nicaraguan	64	0.17
Panamanian	1	<0.01
Salvadoran	396	1.04
Other Central American	13	0.03
Cuban	100	0.26
Dominican Republic	4	0.01
Mexican	16,878	44.20
Puerto Rican	139	0.36
South American	327	0.86
Argentinean	33	0.09
Bolivian	22	0.06
Chilean	8	0.02
Colombian	66	0.17
Ecuadorian	38	0.10
Paraguayan	2	0.01
Peruvian	143	0.37
Uruguayan	8	0.02
Venezuelan	2	0.01
Other South American	5	0.01
Other Hispanic or Latino	1,098	2.88

Race*	Population	%
African-American/Black (858)	1,098	2.88
Not Hispanic (703)	857	2.24
Hispanic (155)	241	0.63
American Indian/Alaska Native (405)	677	1.77
Not Hispanic (107)	235	0.62
Hispanic (298)	442	1.16
Aleut *(Alaska Native)* (1)	1	<0.01
Apache (12)	29	0.08
Blackfeet (1)	2	0.01
Canadian/French Am. Ind. (1)	1	<0.01
Central American Ind. (3)	3	0.01
Cherokee (8)	49	0.13
Cheyenne (0)	2	0.01
Chickasaw (3)	6	0.02
Chippewa (0)	3	0.01
Choctaw (5)	20	0.05
Cree (1)	2	0.01
Creek (6)	7	0.02
Crow (0)	1	<0.01
Hopi (1)	3	0.01
Iroquois (5)	10	0.03
Lumbee (0)	1	<0.01
Mexican American Ind. (81)	103	0.27
Navajo (8)	13	0.03
Pima (1)	1	<0.01
Potawatomi (0)	3	0.01
Pueblo (5)	5	0.01
Seminole (2)	8	0.02
Shoshone (0)	2	0.01
Sioux (4)	9	0.02
Tohono O'Odham (0)	2	0.01
Ute (0)	1	<0.01
Yaqui (0)	7	0.02
Yuman (2)	2	0.01
Asian (8,831)	9,404	24.63
Not Hispanic (8,708)	9,119	23.88
Hispanic (123)	285	0.75
Bangladeshi (23)	23	0.06
Burmese (4)	10	0.03
Cambodian (106)	128	0.34
Chinese, ex. Taiwanese (310)	486	1.27
Filipino (1,179)	1,394	3.65
Hmong (19)	21	0.05
Indian (195)	238	0.62
Indonesian (15)	32	0.08
Japanese (205)	313	0.82
Korean (751)	800	2.10
Laotian (75)	81	0.21
Malaysian (0)	1	<0.01
Nepalese (4)	5	0.01
Pakistani (25)	31	0.08
Sri Lankan (90)	91	0.24
Taiwanese (21)	23	0.06
Thai (44)	54	0.14
Vietnamese (5,532)	5,762	15.09
Hawaii Native/Pacific Islander (217)	403	1.06
Not Hispanic (202)	313	0.82
Hispanic (15)	90	0.24
Guamanian/Chamorro (33)	60	0.16
Native Hawaiian (32)	117	0.31
Samoan (90)	141	0.37
Tongan (32)	42	0.11
White (16,991)	18,259	47.82
Not Hispanic (8,340)	8,831	23.13
Hispanic (8,651)	9,428	24.69

Stevenson Ranch

Place Type: CDP
County: Los Angeles
Population: 17,557†

Ancestry‡	Population	%
American (661)	661	3.90
Arab (116)	215	1.27
Arab (0)	87	0.51

*Notes: † The Census 2010 population figure is used to calculate the percentages in the Hispanic Origin and Race categories. Ancestry percentages are based on the 2006-2010 American Community Survey population (not shown); ‡ Numbers in parentheses indicate the number of people reporting a single ancestry; * Numbers in parentheses indicate the number of persons reporting this race alone, not in combination with any other race; Please refer to the Explanation of Data for more information.*

Lebanese (0)	12	0.07
Syrian (116)	116	0.69
Armenian (170)	201	1.19
Assyrian/Chaldean/Syriac (6)	20	0.12
Austrian (78)	89	0.53
British (20)	79	0.47
Bulgarian (0)	22	0.13
Canadian (70)	145	0.86
Czech (37)	228	1.35
Czechoslovakian (0)	11	0.06
Danish (0)	48	0.28
Dutch (30)	221	1.31
Eastern European (39)	39	0.23
English (461)	1,821	10.75
European (302)	318	1.88
Finnish (10)	10	0.06
French, ex. Basque (38)	322	1.90
French Canadian (0)	75	0.44
German (718)	2,521	14.89
Hungarian (29)	177	1.05
Iranian (22)	111	0.66
Irish (153)	1,610	9.51
Israeli (11)	18	0.11
Italian (184)	882	5.21
Lithuanian (0)	71	0.42
Northern European (9)	19	0.11
Norwegian (47)	165	0.97
Polish (112)	476	2.81
Portuguese (29)	73	0.43
Romanian (17)	17	0.10
Russian (271)	567	3.35
Scandinavian (90)	111	0.66
Scotch-Irish (105)	173	1.02
Scottish (87)	296	1.75
Slovak (0)	8	0.05
Swedish (29)	137	0.81
Swiss (0)	47	0.28
Ukrainian (0)	54	0.32
Welsh (0)	76	0.45
West Indian, ex. Hispanic (0)	184	1.09
Belizean (0)	167	0.99
Dutch West Indian (0)	17	0.10
Yugoslavian (0)	33	0.19

Hispanic Origin	Population	%
Hispanic or Latino (of any race)	2,827	16.10
Central American, ex. Mexican	238	1.36
Costa Rican	15	0.09
Guatemalan	37	0.21
Honduran	14	0.08
Nicaraguan	24	0.14
Panamanian	7	0.04
Salvadoran	136	0.77
Other Central American	5	0.03
Cuban	156	0.89
Dominican Republic	7	0.04
Mexican	1,726	9.83
Puerto Rican	87	0.50
South American	356	2.03
Argentinean	87	0.50
Bolivian	26	0.15
Chilean	33	0.19
Colombian	68	0.39
Ecuadorian	36	0.21
Peruvian	85	0.48
Uruguayan	6	0.03
Venezuelan	12	0.07
Other South American	3	0.02
Other Hispanic or Latino	257	1.46

Race*	Population	%
African-American/Black (606)	756	4.31
Not Hispanic (571)	680	3.87
Hispanic (35)	76	0.43
American Indian/Alaska Native (65)	140	0.80
Not Hispanic (52)	104	0.59
Hispanic (13)	36	0.21
Apache (0)	2	0.01
Blackfeet (0)	1	0.01
Canadian/French Am. Ind. (0)	1	0.01
Cherokee (15)	31	0.18
Chickasaw (0)	3	0.02
Chippewa (0)	5	0.03
Choctaw (1)	2	0.01
Comanche (0)	4	0.02
Creek (3)	3	0.02
Iroquois (1)	2	0.01
Lumbee (1)	3	0.02
Mexican American Ind. (8)	13	0.07
Osage (1)	1	0.01
Paiute (0)	4	0.02
Pima (1)	1	0.01
Sioux (6)	8	0.05
South American Ind. (0)	6	0.03
Asian (4,028)	4,520	25.74
Not Hispanic (3,983)	4,409	25.11
Hispanic (45)	111	0.63
Bangladeshi (14)	20	0.11
Burmese (5)	5	0.03
Cambodian (16)	16	0.09
Chinese, ex. Taiwanese (269)	427	2.43
Filipino (1,007)	1,216	6.93
Hmong (1)	4	0.02
Indian (450)	501	2.85
Indonesian (19)	32	0.18
Japanese (164)	276	1.57
Korean (1,685)	1,764	10.05
Pakistani (37)	42	0.24
Sri Lankan (20)	23	0.13
Taiwanese (46)	54	0.31
Thai (65)	78	0.44
Vietnamese (72)	98	0.56
Hawaii Native/Pacific Islander (34)	87	0.50
Not Hispanic (25)	72	0.41
Hispanic (9)	15	0.09
Fijian (1)	1	0.01
Guamanian/Chamorro (11)	17	0.10
Native Hawaiian (6)	19	0.11
White (11,271)	11,948	68.05
Not Hispanic (9,469)	9,969	56.78
Hispanic (1,802)	1,979	11.27

Stockton

Place Type: City
County: San Joaquin
Population: 291,707†

Ancestry‡	Population	%
Afghan (150)	150	0.05
African, Sub-Saharan (1,061)	1,447	0.50
African (575)	876	0.30
Ethiopian (256)	256	0.09
Liberian (81)	91	0.03
Nigerian (81)	81	0.03
Zimbabwean (68)	118	0.04
Other Sub-Saharan African (0)	25	0.01
American (4,367)	4,367	1.52
Arab (1,504)	1,750	0.61
Arab (802)	879	0.31
Egyptian (251)	251	0.09
Jordanian (22)	22	0.01
Lebanese (151)	274	0.10
Moroccan (0)	10	<0.01
Palestinian (78)	78	0.03
Syrian (100)	131	0.05
Other Arab (100)	105	0.04
Armenian (118)	136	0.05
Austrian (37)	199	0.07
Basque (135)	280	0.10
Belgian (0)	32	0.01
Brazilian (79)	142	0.05
British (203)	475	0.17
Bulgarian (0)	16	0.01
Cajun (0)	20	0.01
Canadian (217)	285	0.10
Celtic (13)	25	0.01
Croatian (73)	118	0.04
Czech (19)	197	0.07
Czechoslovakian (38)	91	0.03
Danish (251)	995	0.35
Dutch (341)	1,770	0.62
Eastern European (96)	115	0.04
English (2,649)	10,748	3.74
Estonian (8)	8	<0.01
European (1,559)	2,042	0.71
Finnish (150)	343	0.12
French, ex. Basque (606)	4,378	1.52
French Canadian (117)	443	0.15
German (4,830)	18,204	6.33
German Russian (0)	117	0.04
Greek (312)	600	0.21
Hungarian (112)	354	0.12
Iranian (336)	359	0.12
Irish (3,122)	13,023	4.53
Israeli (28)	93	0.03
Italian (4,441)	10,289	3.58
Latvian (16)	29	0.01
Lithuanian (54)	198	0.07
Luxemburger (0)	39	0.01
Maltese (27)	77	0.03
Northern European (85)	231	0.08
Norwegian (602)	1,663	0.58
Pennsylvania German (7)	41	0.01
Polish (409)	1,488	0.52
Portuguese (1,432)	3,256	1.13
Romanian (113)	149	0.05
Russian (335)	1,618	0.56
Scandinavian (22)	55	0.02
Scotch-Irish (504)	1,824	0.63
Scottish (668)	2,160	0.75
Serbian (62)	70	0.02
Slovak (16)	67	0.02
Slovene (16)	93	0.03
Swedish (386)	1,893	0.66
Swiss (68)	414	0.14
Turkish (76)	76	0.03
Ukrainian (76)	128	0.04
Welsh (159)	807	0.28
West Indian, ex. Hispanic (204)	303	0.11
Barbadian (0)	15	0.01
Belizean (73)	73	0.03
Dutch West Indian (19)	19	0.01
Haitian (15)	29	0.01
Jamaican (52)	73	0.03
West Indian (45)	73	0.03
Other West Indian (0)	21	0.01
Yugoslavian (39)	176	0.06

Hispanic Origin	Population	%
Hispanic or Latino (of any race)	117,590	40.31
Central American, ex. Mexican	3,302	1.13
Costa Rican	78	0.03
Guatemalan	793	0.27
Honduran	205	0.07
Nicaraguan	786	0.27
Panamanian	131	0.04
Salvadoran	1,296	0.44
Other Central American	13	<0.01
Cuban	245	0.08
Dominican Republic	75	0.03
Mexican	104,172	35.71
Puerto Rican	1,831	0.63
South American	962	0.33
Argentinean	72	0.02
Bolivian	37	0.01
Chilean	207	0.07
Colombian	211	0.07
Ecuadorian	86	0.03
Paraguayan	1	<0.01
Peruvian	273	0.09
Uruguayan	11	<0.01
Venezuelan	53	0.02
Other South American	11	<0.01
Other Hispanic or Latino	7,003	2.40

Race*	Population	%
African-American/Black (35,548)	41,432	14.20
Not Hispanic (33,507)	37,389	12.82
Hispanic (2,041)	4,043	1.39

*Notes: † The Census 2010 population figure is used to calculate the percentages in the Hispanic Origin and Race categories. Ancestry percentages are based on the 2006-2010 American Community Survey population (not shown); ‡ Numbers in parentheses indicate the number of people reporting a single ancestry; * Numbers in parentheses indicate the number of persons reporting this race alone, not in combination with any other race; Please refer to the Explanation of Data for more information.*

American Indian/Alaska Native (3,086)	7,284	2.50
Not Hispanic (1,237)	3,819	1.31
Hispanic (1,849)	3,465	1.19
Alaska Athabascan *(Ala. Nat.)* (6)	7	<0.01
Aleut *(Alaska Native)* (5)	17	0.01
Apache (140)	384	0.13
Arapaho (3)	9	<0.01
Blackfeet (38)	229	0.08
Canadian/French Am. Ind. (5)	17	0.01
Central American Ind. (7)	14	<0.01
Cherokee (203)	1,176	0.40
Cheyenne (5)	16	0.01
Chickasaw (11)	37	0.01
Chippewa (22)	54	0.02
Choctaw (53)	276	0.09
Colville (1)	1	<0.01
Comanche (2)	13	<0.01
Cree (2)	6	<0.01
Creek (9)	38	0.01
Crow (3)	12	<0.01
Delaware (15)	19	0.01
Hopi (8)	16	0.01
Inupiat *(Alaska Native)* (4)	4	<0.01
Iroquois (12)	25	0.01
Kiowa (1)	2	<0.01
Lumbee (2)	4	<0.01
Menominee (0)	1	<0.01
Mexican American Ind. (305)	485	0.17
Navajo (109)	233	0.08
Osage (10)	21	0.01
Ottawa (3)	4	<0.01
Paiute (8)	24	0.01
Pima (18)	31	0.01
Potawatomi (12)	35	0.01
Pueblo (26)	65	0.02
Puget Sound Salish (7)	9	<0.01
Seminole (10)	46	0.02
Shoshone (5)	17	0.01
Sioux (97)	185	0.06
South American Ind. (7)	29	0.01
Spanish American Ind. (14)	21	0.01
Tlingit-Haida *(Alaska Native)* (7)	18	0.01
Tohono O'Odham (5)	15	0.01
Tsimshian *(Alaska Native)* (0)	1	<0.01
Ute (8)	15	0.01
Yakama (1)	2	<0.01
Yaqui (60)	166	0.06
Yuman (7)	12	<0.01
Yup'ik *(Alaska Native)* (1)	4	<0.01
Asian (62,716)	71,852	24.63
Not Hispanic (60,323)	65,993	22.62
Hispanic (2,393)	5,859	2.01
Bangladeshi (5)	5	<0.01
Burmese (27)	35	0.01
Cambodian (10,170)	11,429	3.92
Chinese, ex. Taiwanese (5,067)	6,382	2.19
Filipino (21,133)	27,113	9.29
Hmong (5,819)	6,073	2.08
Indian (4,735)	5,630	1.93
Indonesian (25)	77	0.03
Japanese (1,362)	2,344	0.80
Korean (638)	912	0.31
Laotian (2,961)	3,581	1.23
Malaysian (10)	25	0.01
Pakistani (1,706)	1,904	0.65
Sri Lankan (7)	9	<0.01
Taiwanese (112)	133	0.05
Thai (148)	357	0.12
Vietnamese (6,044)	6,552	2.25
Hawaii Native/Pacific Islander (1,822)	3,566	1.22
Not Hispanic (1,622)	2,869	0.98
Hispanic (200)	697	0.24
Fijian (579)	665	0.23
Guamanian/Chamorro (250)	414	0.14
Marshallese (1)	4	<0.01
Native Hawaiian (178)	800	0.27
Samoan (424)	637	0.22
Tongan (133)	188	0.06
White (108,044)	122,069	41.85
Not Hispanic (66,836)	73,943	25.35
Hispanic (41,208)	48,126	16.50

Suisun City

Place Type: City
County: Solano
Population: 28,111†

Ancestry‡	Population	%
African, Sub-Saharan (980)	1,154	4.16
African (933)	1,089	3.93
Cape Verdean (34)	52	0.19
Nigerian (13)	13	0.05
American (502)	502	1.81
Arab (238)	296	1.07
Arab (127)	139	0.50
Lebanese (12)	18	0.06
Palestinian (99)	139	0.50
Austrian (0)	11	0.04
Belgian (0)	27	0.10
Brazilian (32)	32	0.12
British (19)	19	0.07
Canadian (0)	20	0.07
Croatian (0)	13	0.05
Czech (0)	9	0.03
Danish (182)	253	0.91
Dutch (10)	190	0.68
English (331)	1,202	4.33
European (193)	238	0.86
Finnish (136)	155	0.56
French, ex. Basque (11)	188	0.68
French Canadian (29)	71	0.26
German (502)	1,724	6.21
Greek (0)	37	0.13
Hungarian (0)	75	0.27
Irish (347)	1,328	4.79
Italian (256)	748	2.70
Latvian (0)	12	0.04
Lithuanian (37)	73	0.26
Maltese (0)	8	0.03
Northern European (10)	28	0.10
Norwegian (49)	178	0.64
Polish (99)	185	0.67
Portuguese (47)	193	0.70
Romanian (9)	21	0.08
Russian (92)	203	0.73
Scandinavian (44)	56	0.20
Scotch-Irish (39)	114	0.41
Scottish (109)	301	1.08
Slovak (11)	11	0.04
Swedish (30)	168	0.61
Swiss (0)	116	0.42
Turkish (23)	23	0.08
Ukrainian (0)	12	0.04
Welsh (11)	53	0.19
West Indian, ex. Hispanic (129)	129	0.46
Jamaican (115)	115	0.41
West Indian (14)	14	0.05
Yugoslavian (0)	54	0.19

Hispanic Origin	Population	%
Hispanic or Latino (of any race)	6,753	24.02
Central American, ex. Mexican	600	2.13
Costa Rican	16	0.06
Guatemalan	78	0.28
Honduran	17	0.06
Nicaraguan	156	0.55
Panamanian	26	0.09
Salvadoran	302	1.07
Other Central American	5	0.02
Cuban	34	0.12
Dominican Republic	12	0.04
Mexican	5,040	17.93
Puerto Rican	344	1.22
South American	132	0.47
Argentinean	5	0.02
Bolivian	6	0.02
Chilean	18	0.06
Colombian	29	0.10
Ecuadorian	14	0.05
Peruvian	38	0.14
Uruguayan	2	0.01
Venezuelan	20	0.07
Other Hispanic or Latino	591	2.10

Race*	Population	%
African-American/Black (5,713)	6,803	24.20
Not Hispanic (5,512)	6,336	22.54
Hispanic (201)	467	1.66
American Indian/Alaska Native (196)	697	2.48
Not Hispanic (96)	436	1.55
Hispanic (100)	261	0.93
Apache (4)	12	0.04
Blackfeet (2)	27	0.10
Central American Ind. (2)	2	0.01
Cherokee (5)	96	0.34
Cheyenne (0)	5	0.02
Chickasaw (4)	7	0.02
Chippewa (5)	11	0.04
Choctaw (1)	27	0.10
Comanche (0)	2	0.01
Creek (2)	13	0.05
Crow (0)	2	0.01
Inupiat *(Alaska Native)* (3)	4	0.01
Iroquois (0)	2	0.01
Mexican American Ind. (18)	41	0.15
Navajo (3)	5	0.02
Paiute (1)	1	<0.01
Potawatomi (0)	3	0.01
Pueblo (1)	2	0.01
Puget Sound Salish (0)	2	0.01
Seminole (0)	2	0.01
Shoshone (1)	1	<0.01
Sioux (3)	24	0.09
South American Ind. (2)	7	0.02
Spanish American Ind. (0)	1	<0.01
Tlingit-Haida *(Alaska Native)* (1)	4	0.01
Tohono O'Odham (0)	2	0.01
Ute (1)	4	0.01
Yaqui (3)	3	0.01
Asian (5,348)	6,702	23.84
Not Hispanic (5,226)	6,302	22.42
Hispanic (122)	400	1.42
Bangladeshi (1)	2	0.01
Cambodian (26)	35	0.12
Chinese, ex. Taiwanese (209)	429	1.53
Filipino (3,614)	4,493	15.98
Hmong (130)	133	0.47
Indian (275)	366	1.30
Indonesian (13)	22	0.08
Japanese (134)	395	1.41
Korean (56)	116	0.41
Laotian (272)	311	1.11
Malaysian (1)	7	0.02
Nepalese (2)	4	0.01
Pakistani (43)	57	0.20
Sri Lankan (3)	3	0.01
Taiwanese (3)	6	0.02
Thai (91)	133	0.47
Vietnamese (331)	376	1.34
Hawaii Native/Pacific Islander (340)	780	2.77
Not Hispanic (317)	694	2.47
Hispanic (23)	86	0.31
Fijian (64)	80	0.28
Guamanian/Chamorro (149)	321	1.14
Native Hawaiian (37)	221	0.79
Samoan (41)	91	0.32
Tongan (10)	13	0.05
White (10,805)	12,834	45.65
Not Hispanic (8,218)	9,629	34.25
Hispanic (2,587)	3,205	11.40

Sun Village

Place Type: CDP
County: Los Angeles
Population: 11,565†

Ancestry‡	Population	%
African, Sub-Saharan (14)	157	1.47

*Notes: † The Census 2010 population figure is used to calculate the percentages in the Hispanic Origin and Race categories. Ancestry percentages are based on the 2006-2010 American Community Survey population (not shown); ‡ Numbers in parentheses indicate the number of people reporting a single ancestry; * Numbers in parentheses indicate the number of persons reporting this race alone, not in combination with any other race; Please refer to the Explanation of Data for more information.*

African (14)	157	1.47
American (239)	239	2.24
Australian (0)	27	0.25
Canadian (0)	27	0.25
Czech (10)	10	0.09
Dutch (0)	140	1.31
Eastern European (70)	78	0.73
English (201)	668	6.25
European (54)	78	0.73
French, ex. Basque (12)	224	2.10
German (217)	1,030	9.63
Hungarian (22)	22	0.21
Irish (80)	672	6.29
Italian (77)	256	2.39
Norwegian (0)	55	0.51
Pennsylvania German (0)	11	0.10
Polish (64)	201	1.88
Portuguese (0)	26	0.24
Russian (0)	12	0.11
Scandinavian (11)	35	0.33
Scotch-Irish (113)	218	2.04
Scottish (93)	130	1.22
Swedish (29)	127	1.19
Swiss (0)	16	0.15
Welsh (0)	10	0.09

Hispanic Origin	Population	%
Hispanic or Latino (of any race)	7,311	63.22
Central American, ex. Mexican	769	6.65
Costa Rican	7	0.06
Guatemalan	214	1.85
Honduran	34	0.29
Nicaraguan	28	0.24
Panamanian	5	0.04
Salvadoran	478	4.13
Other Central American	3	0.03
Cuban	33	0.29
Mexican	5,919	51.18
Puerto Rican	60	0.52
South American	79	0.68
Argentinean	10	0.09
Bolivian	2	0.02
Chilean	9	0.08
Colombian	12	0.10
Ecuadorian	19	0.16
Paraguayan	1	0.01
Peruvian	25	0.22
Venezuelan	1	0.01
Other Hispanic or Latino	451	3.90

Race*	Population	%
African-American/Black (809)	928	8.02
Not Hispanic (739)	813	7.03
Hispanic (70)	115	0.99
American Indian/Alaska Native (167)	285	2.46
Not Hispanic (43)	122	1.05
Hispanic (124)	163	1.41
Apache (6)	13	0.11
Blackfeet (2)	6	0.05
Central American Ind. (1)	1	0.01
Cherokee (7)	34	0.29
Chippewa (2)	3	0.03
Choctaw (1)	3	0.03
Creek (0)	1	0.01
Delaware (0)	1	0.01
Hopi (9)	9	0.08
Iroquois (8)	21	0.18
Mexican American Ind. (15)	16	0.14
Navajo (0)	6	0.05
Paiute (4)	4	0.03
Potawatomi (1)	1	0.01
Pueblo (6)	6	0.05
Sioux (1)	7	0.06
South American Ind. (0)	2	0.02
Spanish American Ind. (0)	3	0.03
Tohono O'Odham (6)	6	0.05
Ute (0)	2	0.02
Yaqui (0)	1	0.01
Asian (129)	196	1.69
Not Hispanic (94)	138	1.19
Hispanic (35)	58	0.50
Cambodian (1)	2	0.02
Chinese, ex. Taiwanese (7)	17	0.15
Filipino (64)	90	0.78
Indian (9)	11	0.10
Indonesian (1)	1	0.01
Japanese (11)	25	0.22
Korean (20)	24	0.21
Laotian (4)	6	0.05
Taiwanese (1)	2	0.02
Thai (3)	7	0.06
Vietnamese (3)	5	0.04
Hawaii Native/Pacific Islander (24)	47	0.41
Not Hispanic (14)	23	0.20
Hispanic (10)	24	0.21
Guamanian/Chamorro (4)	12	0.10
Native Hawaiian (10)	14	0.12
Samoan (8)	9	0.08
White (6,806)	7,244	62.64
Not Hispanic (3,180)	3,326	28.76
Hispanic (3,626)	3,918	33.88

Sunnyvale

Place Type: City
County: Santa Clara
Population: 140,081†

Ancestry‡	Population	%
Afghan (82)	82	0.06
African, Sub-Saharan (138)	198	0.15
African (116)	116	0.08
Ethiopian (10)	10	0.01
Kenyan (12)	24	0.02
Other Sub-Saharan African (0)	48	0.04
Albanian (0)	12	0.01
American (1,943)	1,943	1.42
Arab (559)	832	0.61
Arab (134)	227	0.17
Egyptian (142)	165	0.12
Jordanian (7)	7	0.01
Lebanese (11)	91	0.07
Palestinian (40)	47	0.03
Syrian (0)	28	0.02
Other Arab (225)	267	0.20
Armenian (291)	419	0.31
Assyrian/Chaldean/Syriac (103)	141	0.10
Australian (35)	70	0.05
Austrian (73)	257	0.19
Basque (0)	16	0.01
Belgian (80)	177	0.13
Brazilian (19)	71	0.05
British (406)	836	0.61
Bulgarian (301)	308	0.23
Canadian (452)	738	0.54
Celtic (16)	31	0.02
Croatian (262)	388	0.28
Czech (127)	461	0.34
Czechoslovakian (67)	155	0.11
Danish (198)	851	0.62
Dutch (196)	1,131	0.83
Eastern European (111)	149	0.11
English (2,131)	8,447	6.19
Estonian (16)	36	0.03
European (1,661)	2,236	1.64
Finnish (50)	245	0.18
French, ex. Basque (815)	3,053	2.24
French Canadian (189)	492	0.36
German (2,920)	11,118	8.15
Greek (136)	383	0.28
Guyanese (69)	69	0.05
Hungarian (274)	643	0.47
Icelander (27)	40	0.03
Iranian (1,081)	1,120	0.82
Irish (1,706)	7,804	5.72
Israeli (727)	796	0.58
Italian (2,253)	4,899	3.59
Latvian (28)	46	0.03
Lithuanian (51)	95	0.07
Luxemburger (0)	34	0.02
Macedonian (0)	14	0.01
Maltese (0)	8	0.01
Northern European (260)	360	0.26
Norwegian (461)	1,476	1.08
Pennsylvania German (11)	33	0.02
Polish (600)	1,878	1.38
Portuguese (500)	1,117	0.82
Romanian (271)	594	0.44
Russian (947)	1,478	1.08
Scandinavian (131)	314	0.23
Scotch-Irish (302)	1,082	0.79
Scottish (583)	1,926	1.41
Serbian (151)	183	0.13
Slavic (145)	228	0.17
Slovak (37)	102	0.07
Slovene (19)	36	0.03
Swedish (302)	1,794	1.31
Swiss (193)	568	0.42
Turkish (88)	183	0.13
Ukrainian (228)	386	0.28
Welsh (94)	687	0.50
West Indian, ex. Hispanic (13)	13	0.01
Haitian (13)	13	0.01
Yugoslavian (153)	322	0.24

Hispanic Origin	Population	%
Hispanic or Latino (of any race)	26,517	18.93
Central American, ex. Mexican	2,609	1.86
Costa Rican	38	0.03
Guatemalan	684	0.49
Honduran	82	0.06
Nicaraguan	289	0.21
Panamanian	34	0.02
Salvadoran	1,460	1.04
Other Central American	22	0.02
Cuban	116	0.08
Dominican Republic	33	0.02
Mexican	19,939	14.23
Puerto Rican	559	0.40
South American	1,241	0.89
Argentinean	125	0.09
Bolivian	82	0.06
Chilean	83	0.06
Colombian	207	0.15
Ecuadorian	33	0.02
Paraguayan	2	<0.01
Peruvian	607	0.43
Uruguayan	19	0.01
Venezuelan	74	0.05
Other South American	9	0.01
Other Hispanic or Latino	2,020	1.44

Race*	Population	%
African-American/Black (2,735)	3,630	2.59
Not Hispanic (2,533)	3,192	2.28
Hispanic (202)	438	0.31
American Indian/Alaska Native (662)	1,438	1.03
Not Hispanic (292)	789	0.56
Hispanic (370)	649	0.46
Alaska Athabascan *(Ala. Nat.)* (3)	5	<0.01
Apache (21)	50	0.04
Blackfeet (2)	17	0.01
Canadian/French Am. Ind. (3)	8	0.01
Central American Ind. (1)	2	<0.01
Cherokee (43)	200	0.14
Chickasaw (2)	10	0.01
Chippewa (11)	17	0.01
Choctaw (17)	43	0.03
Colville (2)	2	<0.01
Comanche (0)	10	0.01
Cree (1)	3	<0.01
Creek (5)	12	0.01
Crow (0)	2	<0.01
Delaware (0)	1	<0.01
Hopi (2)	4	<0.01
Inupiat *(Alaska Native)* (4)	7	<0.01
Iroquois (4)	8	0.01
Kiowa (1)	2	<0.01
Lumbee (0)	2	<0.01
Mexican American Ind. (68)	102	0.07

*Notes: † The Census 2010 population figure is used to calculate the percentages in the Hispanic Origin and Race categories. Ancestry percentages are based on the 2006-2010 American Community Survey population (not shown); ‡ Numbers in parentheses indicate the number of people reporting a single ancestry; * Numbers in parentheses indicate the number of persons reporting this race alone, not in combination with any other race; Please refer to the Explanation of Data for more information.*

Navajo (15)	33	0.02
Osage (4)	10	0.01
Pima (5)	5	<0.01
Potawatomi (4)	6	<0.01
Pueblo (3)	6	<0.01
Seminole (0)	5	<0.01
Shoshone (3)	7	<0.01
Sioux (6)	16	0.01
South American Ind. (6)	14	0.01
Spanish American Ind. (4)	8	0.01
Tlingit-Haida *(Alaska Native)* (4)	7	<0.01
Tohono O'Odham (1)	1	<0.01
Ute (0)	4	<0.01
Yakama (0)	1	<0.01
Yaqui (13)	22	0.02
Yuman (1)	4	<0.01
Asian (57,320)	61,253	43.73
Not Hispanic (57,012)	60,435	43.14
Hispanic (308)	818	0.58
Bangladeshi (52)	61	0.04
Bhutanese (1)	1	<0.01
Burmese (110)	125	0.09
Cambodian (87)	137	0.10
Chinese, ex. Taiwanese (15,745)	17,556	12.53
Filipino (6,599)	7,847	5.60
Hmong (30)	34	0.02
Indian (21,737)	22,285	15.91
Indonesian (103)	178	0.13
Japanese (2,985)	3,950	2.82
Korean (2,996)	3,294	2.35
Laotian (34)	42	0.03
Malaysian (66)	96	0.07
Nepalese (298)	305	0.22
Pakistani (330)	398	0.28
Sri Lankan (103)	108	0.08
Taiwanese (1,527)	1,736	1.24
Thai (206)	252	0.18
Vietnamese (3,030)	3,433	2.45
Hawaii Native/Pacific Islander (638)	1,177	0.84
Not Hispanic (594)	1,022	0.73
Hispanic (44)	155	0.11
Fijian (66)	86	0.06
Guamanian/Chamorro (77)	144	0.10
Native Hawaiian (66)	288	0.21
Samoan (188)	241	0.17
Tongan (161)	186	0.13
White (60,193)	65,362	46.66
Not Hispanic (48,323)	51,946	37.08
Hispanic (11,870)	13,416	9.58

Susanville

Place Type: City
County: Lassen
Population: 17,947†

Ancestry‡	Population	%
African, Sub-Saharan (37)	53	0.30
African (37)	53	0.30
American (853)	853	4.89
Arab (0)	31	0.18
Syrian (0)	31	0.18
Armenian (8)	8	0.05
Austrian (0)	8	0.05
Basque (21)	38	0.22
British (16)	46	0.26
Canadian (42)	71	0.41
Celtic (0)	16	0.09
Czech (0)	76	0.44
Czechoslovakian (32)	32	0.18
Danish (8)	40	0.23
Dutch (86)	205	1.17
English (191)	1,494	8.56
European (231)	333	1.91
Finnish (9)	25	0.14
French, ex. Basque (108)	603	3.45
German (882)	2,824	16.17
Hungarian (21)	103	0.59
Iranian (0)	41	0.23
Irish (940)	2,446	14.01
Italian (551)	880	5.04
Northern European (47)	47	0.27
Norwegian (7)	203	1.16
Polish (120)	269	1.54
Portuguese (84)	346	1.98
Russian (21)	64	0.37
Scotch-Irish (71)	300	1.72
Scottish (330)	501	2.87
Serbian (30)	30	0.17
Slavic (0)	16	0.09
Swedish (133)	398	2.28
Swiss (0)	20	0.11
Ukrainian (36)	36	0.21
Welsh (0)	45	0.26
West Indian, ex. Hispanic (8)	64	0.37
Belizean (8)	8	0.05
Dutch West Indian (0)	48	0.27
Haitian (0)	8	0.05
Yugoslavian (26)	26	0.15

Hispanic Origin	Population	%
Hispanic or Latino (of any race)	4,259	23.73
Central American, ex. Mexican	28	0.16
Costa Rican	4	0.02
Guatemalan	1	0.01
Honduran	2	0.01
Nicaraguan	5	0.03
Panamanian	1	0.01
Salvadoran	15	0.08
Cuban	11	0.06
Dominican Republic	2	0.01
Mexican	2,737	15.25
Puerto Rican	48	0.27
South American	4	0.02
Ecuadorian	1	0.01
Peruvian	1	0.01
Venezuelan	2	0.01
Other Hispanic or Latino	1,429	7.96

Race*	Population	%
African-American/Black (2,249)	2,364	13.17
Not Hispanic (2,216)	2,309	12.87
Hispanic (33)	55	0.31
American Indian/Alaska Native (612)	849	4.73
Not Hispanic (499)	691	3.85
Hispanic (113)	158	0.88
Alaska Athabascan *(Ala. Nat.)* (0)	1	0.01
Aleut *(Alaska Native)* (3)	7	0.04
Apache (2)	4	0.02
Blackfeet (2)	9	0.05
Canadian/French Am. Ind. (1)	1	0.01
Cherokee (17)	59	0.33
Cheyenne (2)	3	0.02
Chickasaw (0)	2	0.01
Chippewa (6)	12	0.07
Choctaw (20)	33	0.18
Delaware (1)	4	0.02
Hopi (2)	2	0.01
Inupiat *(Alaska Native)* (0)	2	0.01
Iroquois (5)	10	0.06
Mexican American Ind. (16)	18	0.10
Navajo (5)	7	0.04
Osage (2)	5	0.03
Paiute (100)	156	0.87
Potawatomi (1)	1	0.01
Pueblo (2)	2	0.01
Puget Sound Salish (0)	3	0.02
Seminole (0)	1	0.01
Shoshone (3)	3	0.02
Sioux (4)	7	0.04
South American Ind. (1)	1	0.01
Tlingit-Haida *(Alaska Native)* (5)	5	0.03
Ute (0)	1	0.01
Yaqui (2)	4	0.02
Asian (198)	300	1.67
Not Hispanic (186)	263	1.47
Hispanic (12)	37	0.21
Cambodian (1)	1	0.01
Chinese, ex. Taiwanese (25)	39	0.22
Filipino (77)	117	0.65
Hmong (1)	1	0.01
Indian (25)	40	0.22
Japanese (10)	32	0.18
Korean (2)	16	0.09
Laotian (5)	5	0.03
Malaysian (1)	1	0.01
Pakistani (1)	1	0.01
Sri Lankan (0)	3	0.02
Thai (3)	5	0.03
Vietnamese (21)	28	0.16
Hawaii Native/Pacific Islander (111)	165	0.92
Not Hispanic (110)	154	0.86
Hispanic (1)	11	0.06
Fijian (4)	5	0.03
Guamanian/Chamorro (1)	4	0.02
Native Hawaiian (11)	39	0.22
Samoan (3)	5	0.03
Tongan (1)	1	0.01
White (11,269)	11,804	65.77
Not Hispanic (9,950)	10,306	57.42
Hispanic (1,319)	1,498	8.35

Taft

Place Type: City
County: Kern
Population: 9,327†

Ancestry‡	Population	%
African, Sub-Saharan (8)	8	0.09
African (8)	8	0.09
American (273)	273	2.91
Arab (8)	8	0.09
Arab (8)	8	0.09
Armenian (25)	31	0.33
Basque (41)	41	0.44
British (0)	14	0.15
Canadian (0)	12	0.13
Czech (0)	23	0.25
Danish (83)	257	2.74
Dutch (7)	64	0.68
English (342)	859	9.17
European (249)	249	2.66
French, ex. Basque (22)	190	2.03
German (338)	1,092	11.65
Greek (0)	17	0.18
Guyanese (8)	8	0.09
Irish (325)	1,211	12.92
Israeli (10)	10	0.11
Italian (58)	101	1.08
Maltese (0)	44	0.47
Northern European (45)	45	0.48
Norwegian (220)	288	3.07
Polish (14)	130	1.39
Portuguese (8)	14	0.15
Russian (0)	14	0.15
Scotch-Irish (46)	134	1.43
Scottish (20)	150	1.60
Swedish (110)	142	1.52
Swiss (7)	20	0.21
Ukrainian (0)	26	0.28
Welsh (0)	34	0.36
West Indian, ex. Hispanic (24)	24	0.26
Jamaican (24)	24	0.26
Yugoslavian (0)	8	0.09

Hispanic Origin	Population	%
Hispanic or Latino (of any race)	3,353	35.95
Central American, ex. Mexican	99	1.06
Costa Rican	6	0.06
Guatemalan	37	0.40
Honduran	7	0.08
Nicaraguan	2	0.02
Panamanian	4	0.04
Salvadoran	43	0.46
Cuban	5	0.05
Dominican Republic	9	0.10
Mexican	3,096	33.19
Puerto Rican	17	0.18
South American	24	0.26

*Notes: † The Census 2010 population figure is used to calculate the percentages in the Hispanic Origin and Race categories. Ancestry percentages are based on the 2006-2010 American Community Survey population (not shown); ‡ Numbers in parentheses indicate the number of people reporting a single ancestry; * Numbers in parentheses indicate the number of persons reporting this race alone, not in combination with any other race; Please refer to the Explanation of Data for more information.*

	Population	%
Argentinean	1	0.01
Colombian	22	0.24
Venezuelan	1	0.01
Other Hispanic or Latino	103	1.10

Race*	Population	%
African-American/Black (396)	449	4.81
Not Hispanic (361)	407	4.36
Hispanic (35)	42	0.45
American Indian/Alaska Native (118)	191	2.05
Not Hispanic (72)	138	1.48
Hispanic (46)	53	0.57
Apache (0)	1	0.01
Arapaho (0)	1	0.01
Blackfeet (1)	3	0.03
Cherokee (23)	48	0.51
Chippewa (0)	1	0.01
Choctaw (11)	16	0.17
Cree (0)	1	0.01
Creek (0)	6	0.06
Delaware (0)	3	0.03
Mexican American Ind. (25)	25	0.27
Navajo (1)	1	0.01
Paiute (1)	1	0.01
Potawatomi (2)	7	0.08
Seminole (2)	2	0.02
Sioux (0)	1	0.01
Yuman (2)	2	0.02
Asian (93)	135	1.45
Not Hispanic (92)	132	1.42
Hispanic (1)	3	0.03
Cambodian (3)	3	0.03
Chinese, ex. Taiwanese (21)	30	0.32
Filipino (17)	34	0.36
Indian (14)	14	0.15
Japanese (3)	10	0.11
Korean (6)	11	0.12
Laotian (2)	10	0.11
Pakistani (1)	4	0.04
Thai (13)	13	0.14
Vietnamese (9)	11	0.12
Hawaii Native/Pacific Islander (65)	103	1.10
Not Hispanic (62)	86	0.92
Hispanic (3)	17	0.18
Guamanian/Chamorro (1)	2	0.02
Native Hawaiian (12)	23	0.25
Samoan (46)	53	0.57
White (7,388)	7,590	81.38
Not Hispanic (5,221)	5,347	57.33
Hispanic (2,167)	2,243	24.05

Tamalpais-Homestead Valley

Place Type: CDP
County: Marin
Population: 10,735†

Ancestry‡	Population	%
American (232)	232	2.19
Arab (17)	73	0.69
Egyptian (0)	10	0.09
Lebanese (17)	50	0.47
Syrian (0)	13	0.12
Armenian (77)	102	0.96
Australian (24)	64	0.60
Austrian (51)	51	0.48
Basque (14)	28	0.26
Belgian (0)	42	0.40
Brazilian (45)	70	0.66
British (55)	118	1.11
Canadian (22)	30	0.28
Croatian (15)	81	0.76
Czech (32)	70	0.66
Czechoslovakian (13)	13	0.12
Danish (9)	118	1.11
Dutch (22)	171	1.61
Eastern European (187)	203	1.91
English (465)	1,723	16.25
Estonian (0)	11	0.10
European (572)	632	5.96
Finnish (39)	126	1.19
French, ex. Basque (87)	577	5.44
French Canadian (46)	71	0.67
German (489)	1,654	15.60
Greek (35)	115	1.08
Hungarian (0)	114	1.08
Iranian (0)	15	0.14
Irish (380)	1,604	15.13
Israeli (12)	12	0.11
Italian (273)	848	8.00
Lithuanian (23)	81	0.76
Macedonian (0)	14	0.13
Northern European (92)	92	0.87
Norwegian (46)	114	1.08
Polish (66)	364	3.43
Portuguese (37)	152	1.43
Romanian (11)	89	0.84
Russian (253)	537	5.07
Scandinavian (39)	51	0.48
Scotch-Irish (99)	202	1.91
Scottish (84)	485	4.58
Slavic (0)	36	0.34
Slovak (0)	9	0.08
Swedish (85)	302	2.85
Swiss (64)	180	1.70
Ukrainian (13)	55	0.52
Welsh (11)	79	0.75
West Indian, ex. Hispanic (0)	14	0.13
Jamaican (0)	14	0.13

Hispanic Origin	Population	%
Hispanic or Latino (of any race)	499	4.65
Central American, ex. Mexican	71	0.66
Costa Rican	4	0.04
Guatemalan	10	0.09
Nicaraguan	27	0.25
Panamanian	3	0.03
Salvadoran	26	0.24
Other Central American	1	0.01
Cuban	29	0.27
Mexican	174	1.62
Puerto Rican	34	0.32
South American	91	0.85
Argentinean	17	0.16
Bolivian	4	0.04
Chilean	4	0.04
Colombian	13	0.12
Ecuadorian	8	0.07
Paraguayan	1	0.01
Peruvian	21	0.20
Uruguayan	2	0.02
Venezuelan	16	0.15
Other South American	5	0.05
Other Hispanic or Latino	100	0.93

Race*	Population	%
African-American/Black (91)	165	1.54
Not Hispanic (85)	150	1.40
Hispanic (6)	15	0.14
American Indian/Alaska Native (24)	117	1.09
Not Hispanic (13)	95	0.88
Hispanic (11)	22	0.20
Blackfeet (0)	3	0.03
Central American Ind. (1)	1	0.01
Cherokee (1)	26	0.24
Chickasaw (1)	4	0.04
Chippewa (0)	2	0.02
Choctaw (0)	6	0.06
Creek (2)	4	0.04
Iroquois (1)	2	0.02
Lumbee (0)	1	0.01
Mexican American Ind. (2)	3	0.03
Ottawa (0)	1	0.01
Potawatomi (0)	1	0.01
Seminole (0)	3	0.03
Sioux (0)	1	0.01
South American Ind. (4)	6	0.06
Yaqui (0)	1	0.01
Asian (592)	846	7.88
Not Hispanic (587)	823	7.67
Hispanic (5)	23	0.21
Bangladeshi (1)	1	0.01
Burmese (0)	1	0.01
Chinese, ex. Taiwanese (232)	335	3.12
Filipino (52)	98	0.91
Indian (43)	61	0.57
Indonesian (3)	6	0.06
Japanese (118)	207	1.93
Korean (69)	103	0.96
Laotian (0)	1	0.01
Malaysian (0)	1	0.01
Nepalese (2)	2	0.02
Pakistani (1)	5	0.05
Sri Lankan (1)	1	0.01
Taiwanese (5)	5	0.05
Thai (15)	18	0.17
Vietnamese (19)	22	0.20
Hawaii Native/Pacific Islander (28)	45	0.42
Not Hispanic (23)	37	0.34
Hispanic (5)	8	0.07
Fijian (12)	12	0.11
Guamanian/Chamorro (2)	2	0.02
Native Hawaiian (11)	21	0.20
Samoan (1)	3	0.03
White (9,449)	9,863	91.88
Not Hispanic (9,123)	9,477	88.28
Hispanic (326)	386	3.60

Tehachapi

Place Type: City
County: Kern
Population: 14,414†

Ancestry‡	Population	%
African, Sub-Saharan (45)	45	0.32
African (45)	45	0.32
American (491)	491	3.49
Arab (8)	20	0.14
Arab (8)	12	0.09
Moroccan (0)	8	0.06
Armenian (5)	11	0.08
Austrian (0)	22	0.16
British (15)	23	0.16
Canadian (13)	51	0.36
Croatian (0)	45	0.32
Czech (0)	31	0.22
Czechoslovakian (0)	11	0.08
Danish (12)	66	0.47
Dutch (74)	273	1.94
English (271)	965	6.85
European (27)	27	0.19
Finnish (14)	14	0.10
French, ex. Basque (65)	648	4.60
French Canadian (0)	31	0.22
German (600)	2,352	16.70
Greek (15)	23	0.16
Hungarian (4)	70	0.50
Irish (395)	2,019	14.34
Italian (158)	439	3.12
Lithuanian (0)	11	0.08
Norwegian (90)	213	1.51
Polish (9)	164	1.16
Portuguese (41)	109	0.77
Russian (24)	107	0.76
Scandinavian (0)	10	0.07
Scotch-Irish (67)	200	1.42
Scottish (31)	298	2.12
Slavic (11)	11	0.08
Swedish (0)	154	1.09
Swiss (0)	18	0.13
Welsh (0)	112	0.80
West Indian, ex. Hispanic (15)	55	0.39
Bahamian (0)	4	0.03
Jamaican (15)	51	0.36
Yugoslavian (0)	10	0.07

SECTION TWO

*Notes: † The Census 2010 population figure is used to calculate the percentages in the Hispanic Origin and Race categories. Ancestry percentages are based on the 2006-2010 American Community Survey population (not shown); ‡ Numbers in parentheses indicate the number of people reporting a single ancestry; * Numbers in parentheses indicate the number of persons reporting this race alone, not in combination with any other race; Please refer to the Explanation of Data for more information.*

Hispanic Origin	Population	%
Hispanic or Latino (of any race)	5,466	37.92
Central American, ex. Mexican	95	0.66
Costa Rican	1	0.01
Guatemalan	23	0.16
Honduran	6	0.04
Nicaraguan	16	0.11
Panamanian	1	0.01
Salvadoran	46	0.32
Other Central American	2	0.01
Cuban	17	0.12
Dominican Republic	2	0.01
Mexican	4,824	33.47
Puerto Rican	47	0.33
South American	24	0.17
Argentinean	2	0.01
Chilean	1	0.01
Colombian	14	0.10
Ecuadorian	2	0.01
Peruvian	4	0.03
Venezuelan	1	0.01
Other Hispanic or Latino	457	3.17

Race*	Population	%
African-American/Black (1,297)	1,388	9.63
Not Hispanic (1,255)	1,321	9.16
Hispanic (42)	67	0.46
American Indian/Alaska Native (206)	384	2.66
Not Hispanic (100)	212	1.47
Hispanic (106)	172	1.19
Apache (4)	14	0.10
Blackfeet (0)	1	0.01
Canadian/French Am. Ind. (0)	1	0.01
Central American Ind. (1)	1	0.01
Cherokee (10)	55	0.38
Chickasaw (5)	5	0.03
Choctaw (12)	21	0.15
Comanche (1)	1	0.01
Creek (4)	11	0.08
Crow (1)	1	0.01
Hopi (1)	1	0.01
Inupiat *(Alaska Native)* (0)	1	0.01
Iroquois (0)	5	0.03
Mexican American Ind. (24)	33	0.23
Navajo (3)	14	0.10
Osage (0)	3	0.02
Paiute (2)	10	0.07
Pueblo (2)	4	0.03
Sioux (0)	7	0.05
Spanish American Ind. (2)	2	0.01
Ute (1)	3	0.02
Yaqui (2)	5	0.03
Asian (238)	331	2.30
Not Hispanic (222)	278	1.93
Hispanic (16)	53	0.37
Cambodian (13)	13	0.09
Chinese, ex. Taiwanese (13)	21	0.15
Filipino (88)	135	0.94
Hmong (1)	1	0.01
Indian (27)	31	0.22
Indonesian (2)	3	0.02
Japanese (20)	35	0.24
Korean (23)	33	0.23
Laotian (3)	3	0.02
Nepalese (3)	3	0.02
Pakistani (1)	1	0.01
Thai (6)	6	0.04
Vietnamese (32)	33	0.23
Hawaii Native/Pacific Islander (21)	40	0.28
Not Hispanic (12)	22	0.15
Hispanic (9)	18	0.12
Guamanian/Chamorro (5)	6	0.04
Native Hawaiian (7)	14	0.10
Samoan (7)	11	0.08
Tongan (1)	1	0.01
White (9,426)	9,879	68.54
Not Hispanic (7,123)	7,329	50.85
Hispanic (2,303)	2,550	17.69

Temecula

Place Type: City
County: Riverside
Population: 100,097†

Ancestry‡	Population	%
Afghan (237)	240	0.25
African, Sub-Saharan (284)	401	0.42
African (95)	131	0.14
Cape Verdean (15)	15	0.02
Ethiopian (31)	31	0.03
Sierra Leonean (12)	12	0.01
South African (0)	13	0.01
Sudanese (55)	55	0.06
Ugandan (76)	76	0.08
Zimbabwean (0)	68	0.07
Albanian (70)	70	0.07
American (2,275)	2,275	2.37
Arab (254)	424	0.44
Arab (61)	146	0.15
Egyptian (84)	131	0.14
Jordanian (57)	62	0.06
Lebanese (19)	52	0.05
Palestinian (33)	33	0.03
Armenian (0)	108	0.11
Australian (0)	69	0.07
Austrian (66)	237	0.25
Basque (54)	54	0.06
Belgian (23)	76	0.08
Brazilian (0)	11	0.01
British (261)	480	0.50
Bulgarian (23)	23	0.02
Cajun (17)	43	0.04
Canadian (264)	608	0.63
Croatian (27)	107	0.11
Czech (169)	430	0.45
Czechoslovakian (87)	132	0.14
Danish (77)	399	0.42
Dutch (318)	1,765	1.84
Eastern European (41)	41	0.04
English (3,223)	10,374	10.83
Estonian (14)	14	0.01
European (2,627)	3,436	3.59
Finnish (24)	115	0.12
French, ex. Basque (505)	3,211	3.35
French Canadian (289)	466	0.49
German (3,673)	13,609	14.20
Greek (242)	740	0.77
Hungarian (133)	573	0.60
Iranian (154)	167	0.17
Irish (2,260)	10,882	11.36
Israeli (10)	10	0.01
Italian (2,206)	7,284	7.60
Latvian (13)	13	0.01
Lithuanian (32)	59	0.06
Macedonian (11)	20	0.02
New Zealander (0)	27	0.03
Northern European (89)	117	0.12
Norwegian (449)	1,297	1.35
Pennsylvania German (12)	12	0.01
Polish (904)	3,023	3.15
Portuguese (289)	692	0.72
Romanian (28)	123	0.13
Russian (400)	953	0.99
Scandinavian (159)	245	0.26
Scotch-Irish (463)	1,154	1.20
Scottish (572)	2,456	2.56
Serbian (7)	30	0.03
Slavic (48)	48	0.05
Slovak (46)	112	0.12
Slovene (15)	15	0.02
Swedish (480)	1,668	1.74
Swiss (19)	134	0.14
Turkish (0)	9	0.01
Ukrainian (121)	219	0.23
Welsh (204)	773	0.81
West Indian, ex. Hispanic (92)	231	0.24
British West Indian (59)	198	0.21
Trinidadian/Tobagonian (9)	9	0.01
West Indian (24)	24	0.03
Yugoslavian (75)	125	0.13

Hispanic Origin	Population	%
Hispanic or Latino (of any race)	24,727	24.70
Central American, ex. Mexican	1,027	1.03
Costa Rican	68	0.07
Guatemalan	334	0.33
Honduran	61	0.06
Nicaraguan	87	0.09
Panamanian	91	0.09
Salvadoran	368	0.37
Other Central American	18	0.02
Cuban	249	0.25
Dominican Republic	77	0.08
Mexican	19,928	19.91
Puerto Rican	970	0.97
South American	848	0.85
Argentinean	131	0.13
Bolivian	23	0.02
Chilean	70	0.07
Colombian	219	0.22
Ecuadorian	109	0.11
Paraguayan	6	0.01
Peruvian	205	0.20
Uruguayan	25	0.02
Venezuelan	38	0.04
Other South American	22	0.02
Other Hispanic or Latino	1,628	1.63

Race*	Population	%
African-American/Black (4,132)	5,496	5.49
Not Hispanic (3,794)	4,828	4.82
Hispanic (338)	668	0.67
American Indian/Alaska Native (1,079)	2,038	2.04
Not Hispanic (655)	1,244	1.24
Hispanic (424)	794	0.79
Aleut *(Alaska Native)* (5)	5	<0.01
Apache (24)	65	0.06
Arapaho (1)	1	<0.01
Blackfeet (4)	30	0.03
Canadian/French Am. Ind. (0)	7	0.01
Central American Ind. (2)	4	<0.01
Cherokee (59)	211	0.21
Cheyenne (2)	9	0.01
Chickasaw (1)	9	0.01
Chippewa (11)	29	0.03
Choctaw (11)	29	0.03
Comanche (0)	3	<0.01
Creek (5)	17	0.02
Crow (1)	2	<0.01
Delaware (5)	6	0.01
Hopi (1)	1	<0.01
Inupiat *(Alaska Native)* (0)	3	<0.01
Iroquois (8)	24	0.02
Kiowa (3)	3	<0.01
Lumbee (1)	2	<0.01
Mexican American Ind. (52)	75	0.07
Navajo (31)	75	0.07
Osage (2)	3	<0.01
Ottawa (0)	2	<0.01
Paiute (2)	2	<0.01
Pima (6)	20	0.02
Potawatomi (12)	24	0.02
Pueblo (10)	18	0.02
Seminole (7)	8	0.01
Shoshone (1)	5	<0.01
Sioux (7)	25	0.02
South American Ind. (3)	8	0.01
Spanish American Ind. (1)	2	<0.01
Tohono O'Odham (2)	2	<0.01
Ute (4)	4	<0.01
Yakama (2)	5	<0.01
Yaqui (3)	9	0.01
Yuman (6)	7	0.01
Yup'ik *(Alaska Native)* (0)	4	<0.01
Asian (9,765)	12,633	12.62
Not Hispanic (9,524)	11,786	11.77
Hispanic (241)	847	0.85

*Notes: † The Census 2010 population figure is used to calculate the percentages in the Hispanic Origin and Race categories. Ancestry percentages are based on the 2006-2010 American Community Survey population (not shown); ‡ Numbers in parentheses indicate the number of people reporting a single ancestry; * Numbers in parentheses indicate the number of persons reporting this race alone, not in combination with any other race; Please refer to the Explanation of Data for more information.*

Bangladeshi (7)	7	0.01
Burmese (6)	13	0.01
Cambodian (165)	208	0.21
Chinese, ex. Taiwanese (742)	1,184	1.18
Filipino (5,494)	6,969	6.96
Hmong (34)	46	0.05
Indian (478)	609	0.61
Indonesian (53)	116	0.12
Japanese (384)	1,005	1.00
Korean (859)	1,061	1.06
Laotian (281)	322	0.32
Malaysian (6)	10	0.01
Nepalese (22)	22	0.02
Pakistani (40)	46	0.05
Sri Lankan (5)	10	0.01
Taiwanese (50)	64	0.06
Thai (211)	303	0.30
Vietnamese (581)	777	0.78
Hawaii Native/Pacific Islander (368)	890	0.89
Not Hispanic (319)	716	0.72
Hispanic (49)	174	0.17
Fijian (5)	7	0.01
Guamanian/Chamorro (167)	303	0.30
Native Hawaiian (73)	305	0.30
Samoan (76)	155	0.15
Tongan (8)	11	0.01
White (70,880)	75,939	75.87
Not Hispanic (57,246)	60,422	60.36
Hispanic (13,634)	15,517	15.50

Temescal Valley

Place Type: CDP
County: Riverside
Population: 22,535†

Ancestry‡	Population	%
Afghan (22)	22	0.10
African, Sub-Saharan (158)	177	0.78
African (30)	49	0.22
Ethiopian (67)	67	0.30
Nigerian (61)	61	0.27
American (729)	729	3.22
Arab (156)	174	0.77
Arab (73)	91	0.40
Egyptian (83)	83	0.37
Armenian (0)	12	0.05
Austrian (0)	9	0.04
Basque (0)	12	0.05
Brazilian (0)	9	0.04
British (20)	55	0.24
Canadian (73)	157	0.69
Croatian (49)	90	0.40
Czech (66)	115	0.51
Czechoslovakian (0)	57	0.25
Danish (17)	153	0.68
Dutch (106)	310	1.37
Eastern European (30)	30	0.13
English (661)	1,725	7.62
European (427)	479	2.12
Finnish (37)	74	0.33
French, ex. Basque (48)	610	2.70
French Canadian (44)	145	0.64
German (639)	2,663	11.77
Greek (9)	9	0.04
Hungarian (50)	109	0.48
Iranian (64)	128	0.57
Irish (449)	1,843	8.14
Israeli (13)	53	0.23
Italian (549)	1,415	6.25
Lithuanian (0)	10	0.04
Northern European (20)	20	0.09
Norwegian (117)	330	1.46
Polish (348)	830	3.67
Portuguese (24)	185	0.82
Russian (27)	56	0.25
Scandinavian (0)	6	0.03
Scotch-Irish (72)	125	0.55
Scottish (47)	427	1.89
Slovak (9)	40	0.18
Swedish (174)	443	1.96
Ukrainian (25)	141	0.62
Welsh (18)	101	0.45
West Indian, ex. Hispanic (44)	78	0.34
Haitian (14)	48	0.21
Jamaican (9)	9	0.04
Trinidadian/Tobagonian (21)	21	0.09
Yugoslavian (178)	205	0.91

Hispanic Origin	Population	%
Hispanic or Latino (of any race)	6,753	29.97
Central American, ex. Mexican	358	1.59
Costa Rican	27	0.12
Guatemalan	99	0.44
Honduran	16	0.07
Nicaraguan	51	0.23
Panamanian	12	0.05
Salvadoran	148	0.66
Other Central American	5	0.02
Cuban	87	0.39
Dominican Republic	8	0.04
Mexican	5,350	23.74
Puerto Rican	179	0.79
South American	348	1.54
Argentinean	55	0.24
Bolivian	13	0.06
Chilean	18	0.08
Colombian	102	0.45
Ecuadorian	53	0.24
Paraguayan	2	0.01
Peruvian	93	0.41
Uruguayan	5	0.02
Venezuelan	2	0.01
Other South American	5	0.02
Other Hispanic or Latino	423	1.88

Race*	Population	%
African-American/Black (1,507)	1,779	7.89
Not Hispanic (1,446)	1,651	7.33
Hispanic (61)	128	0.57
American Indian/Alaska Native (131)	273	1.21
Not Hispanic (53)	151	0.67
Hispanic (78)	122	0.54
Alaska Athabascan *(Ala. Nat.)* (1)	4	0.02
Aleut *(Alaska Native)* (0)	1	<0.01
Apache (2)	9	0.04
Blackfeet (2)	10	0.04
Canadian/French Am. Ind. (2)	2	0.01
Cherokee (6)	36	0.16
Chickasaw (1)	3	0.01
Chippewa (2)	3	0.01
Choctaw (6)	10	0.04
Cree (0)	3	0.01
Creek (1)	7	0.03
Delaware (0)	3	0.01
Iroquois (1)	1	<0.01
Mexican American Ind. (3)	4	0.02
Navajo (5)	7	0.03
Potawatomi (0)	2	0.01
Pueblo (4)	7	0.03
Seminole (0)	1	<0.01
Sioux (2)	5	0.02
South American Ind. (4)	4	0.02
Spanish American Ind. (3)	3	0.01
Yaqui (1)	3	0.01
Yuman (1)	1	<0.01
Asian (2,157)	2,703	11.99
Not Hispanic (2,107)	2,534	11.24
Hispanic (50)	169	0.75
Bangladeshi (11)	12	0.05
Burmese (1)	1	<0.01
Cambodian (24)	27	0.12
Chinese, ex. Taiwanese (218)	349	1.55
Filipino (652)	883	3.92
Hmong (8)	8	0.04
Indian (198)	219	0.97
Indonesian (13)	25	0.11
Japanese (86)	213	0.95
Korean (428)	481	2.13
Laotian (4)	12	0.05
Pakistani (52)	64	0.28
Sri Lankan (12)	13	0.06
Taiwanese (24)	35	0.16
Thai (30)	48	0.21
Vietnamese (271)	347	1.54
Hawaii Native/Pacific Islander (74)	163	0.72
Not Hispanic (61)	133	0.59
Hispanic (13)	30	0.13
Fijian (2)	3	0.01
Guamanian/Chamorro (20)	37	0.16
Native Hawaiian (20)	51	0.23
Samoan (19)	38	0.17
Tongan (8)	8	0.04
White (14,785)	15,918	70.64
Not Hispanic (11,380)	12,001	53.25
Hispanic (3,405)	3,917	17.38

Temple City

Place Type: City
County: Los Angeles
Population: 35,558†

Ancestry‡	Population	%
American (296)	296	0.84
Arab (241)	248	0.70
Arab (41)	41	0.12
Egyptian (143)	143	0.41
Lebanese (10)	17	0.05
Syrian (47)	47	0.13
Armenian (25)	65	0.18
Australian (0)	6	0.02
Austrian (16)	24	0.07
Belgian (6)	6	0.02
Brazilian (39)	39	0.11
British (43)	43	0.12
Canadian (24)	70	0.20
Croatian (7)	26	0.07
Czechoslovakian (0)	12	0.03
Danish (28)	167	0.47
Dutch (24)	194	0.55
Eastern European (13)	13	0.04
English (302)	1,303	3.70
European (187)	235	0.67
French, ex. Basque (88)	319	0.91
French Canadian (0)	44	0.12
German (551)	2,107	5.98
Greek (25)	86	0.24
Hungarian (7)	94	0.27
Iranian (59)	88	0.25
Irish (370)	1,284	3.65
Italian (649)	1,240	3.52
Norwegian (47)	239	0.68
Pennsylvania German (0)	16	0.05
Polish (191)	460	1.31
Portuguese (0)	6	0.02
Romanian (9)	31	0.09
Russian (20)	59	0.17
Scotch-Irish (48)	237	0.67
Scottish (43)	140	0.40
Serbian (15)	15	0.04
Slavic (0)	12	0.03
Swedish (20)	355	1.01
Swiss (0)	24	0.07
Turkish (27)	38	0.11
Ukrainian (25)	31	0.09
Welsh (56)	94	0.27
West Indian, ex. Hispanic (34)	34	0.10
Jamaican (34)	34	0.10
Yugoslavian (16)	16	0.05

Hispanic Origin	Population	%
Hispanic or Latino (of any race)	6,853	19.27
Central American, ex. Mexican	531	1.49
Costa Rican	29	0.08
Guatemalan	134	0.38
Honduran	55	0.15
Nicaraguan	70	0.20
Panamanian	9	0.03
Salvadoran	217	0.61

*Notes: † The Census 2010 population figure is used to calculate the percentages in the Hispanic Origin and Race categories. Ancestry percentages are based on the 2006-2010 American Community Survey population (not shown); ‡ Numbers in parentheses indicate the number of people reporting a single ancestry; * Numbers in parentheses indicate the number of persons reporting this race alone, not in combination with any other race; Please refer to the Explanation of Data for more information.*

Other Central American	17	0.05
Cuban	158	0.44
Dominican Republic	6	0.02
Mexican	5,315	14.95
Puerto Rican	114	0.32
South American	330	0.93
Argentinean	64	0.18
Bolivian	12	0.03
Chilean	24	0.07
Colombian	70	0.20
Ecuadorian	57	0.16
Peruvian	89	0.25
Uruguayan	6	0.02
Venezuelan	7	0.02
Other South American	1	<0.01
Other Hispanic or Latino	399	1.12

Race*	Population	%
African-American/Black (283)	375	1.05
Not Hispanic (256)	319	0.90
Hispanic (27)	56	0.16
American Indian/Alaska Native (150)	281	0.79
Not Hispanic (35)	90	0.25
Hispanic (115)	191	0.54
Apache (2)	16	0.04
Blackfeet (1)	3	0.01
Canadian/French Am. Ind. (0)	2	0.01
Central American Ind. (1)	1	<0.01
Cherokee (7)	28	0.08
Cheyenne (1)	1	<0.01
Chickasaw (0)	1	<0.01
Choctaw (1)	3	0.01
Comanche (0)	1	<0.01
Creek (2)	2	0.01
Lumbee (1)	1	<0.01
Mexican American Ind. (8)	18	0.05
Navajo (7)	13	0.04
Osage (0)	1	<0.01
Pima (4)	5	0.01
Potawatomi (0)	1	<0.01
Pueblo (5)	11	0.03
Sioux (1)	3	0.01
South American Ind. (0)	1	<0.01
Spanish American Ind. (4)	6	0.02
Tohono O'Odham (1)	2	0.01
Yuman (1)	3	0.01
Asian (19,803)	20,412	57.40
Not Hispanic (19,682)	20,154	56.68
Hispanic (121)	258	0.73
Bangladeshi (4)	5	0.01
Burmese (118)	145	0.41
Cambodian (87)	125	0.35
Chinese, ex. Taiwanese (13,001)	13,931	39.18
Filipino (756)	932	2.62
Hmong (0)	2	0.01
Indian (256)	311	0.87
Indonesian (168)	240	0.67
Japanese (519)	700	1.97
Korean (482)	550	1.55
Laotian (47)	56	0.16
Malaysian (15)	30	0.08
Pakistani (13)	15	0.04
Sri Lankan (11)	11	0.03
Taiwanese (1,753)	1,964	5.52
Thai (195)	232	0.65
Vietnamese (1,368)	1,780	5.01
Hawaii Native/Pacific Islander (31)	134	0.38
Not Hispanic (25)	114	0.32
Hispanic (6)	20	0.06
Fijian (0)	1	<0.01
Guamanian/Chamorro (9)	15	0.04
Native Hawaiian (12)	30	0.08
Samoan (4)	7	0.02
Tongan (0)	1	<0.01
White (11,941)	12,756	35.87
Not Hispanic (8,095)	8,547	24.04
Hispanic (3,846)	4,209	11.84

Templeton

Place Type: CDP
County: San Luis Obispo
Population: 7,674†

Ancestry‡	Population	%
American (314)	314	3.92
Basque (18)	18	0.22
Belgian (0)	8	0.10
British (94)	131	1.63
Canadian (24)	24	0.30
Croatian (10)	10	0.12
Czech (0)	14	0.17
Danish (14)	61	0.76
Dutch (9)	74	0.92
Eastern European (7)	22	0.27
English (338)	1,155	14.41
European (195)	195	2.43
Finnish (11)	11	0.14
French, ex. Basque (110)	228	2.84
French Canadian (13)	31	0.39
German (552)	1,625	20.27
Greek (15)	15	0.19
Irish (242)	871	10.87
Italian (243)	565	7.05
Lithuanian (14)	14	0.17
Norwegian (99)	488	6.09
Pennsylvania German (29)	29	0.36
Polish (44)	215	2.68
Portuguese (37)	200	2.50
Russian (51)	89	1.11
Scotch-Irish (108)	175	2.18
Scottish (137)	219	2.73
Slovak (0)	30	0.37
Swedish (71)	483	6.03
Swiss (54)	104	1.30
Ukrainian (14)	14	0.17
Welsh (13)	40	0.50

Hispanic Origin	Population	%
Hispanic or Latino (of any race)	1,171	15.26
Central American, ex. Mexican	20	0.26
Costa Rican	3	0.04
Guatemalan	2	0.03
Honduran	1	0.01
Nicaraguan	3	0.04
Salvadoran	11	0.14
Cuban	8	0.10
Mexican	941	12.26
Puerto Rican	28	0.36
South American	17	0.22
Argentinean	1	0.01
Chilean	4	0.05
Colombian	4	0.05
Peruvian	8	0.10
Other Hispanic or Latino	157	2.05

Race*	Population	%
African-American/Black (59)	103	1.34
Not Hispanic (52)	89	1.16
Hispanic (7)	14	0.18
American Indian/Alaska Native (80)	166	2.16
Not Hispanic (42)	112	1.46
Hispanic (38)	54	0.70
Apache (2)	4	0.05
Blackfeet (1)	2	0.03
Canadian/French Am. Ind. (0)	1	0.01
Cherokee (0)	27	0.35
Chickasaw (3)	3	0.04
Choctaw (5)	7	0.09
Comanche (1)	5	0.07
Creek (1)	1	0.01
Inupiat *(Alaska Native)* (0)	1	0.01
Iroquois (1)	1	0.01
Mexican American Ind. (6)	9	0.12
Navajo (1)	2	0.03
Osage (1)	2	0.03
Pima (1)	1	0.01
Sioux (1)	4	0.05
Spanish American Ind. (1)	1	0.01
Tlingit-Haida *(Alaska Native)* (1)	1	0.01
Yaqui (1)	2	0.03
Asian (123)	202	2.63
Not Hispanic (119)	190	2.48
Hispanic (4)	12	0.16
Cambodian (1)	1	0.01
Chinese, ex. Taiwanese (16)	37	0.48
Filipino (31)	55	0.72
Hmong (0)	1	0.01
Indian (6)	17	0.22
Indonesian (2)	5	0.07
Japanese (22)	37	0.48
Korean (11)	13	0.17
Laotian (0)	1	0.01
Malaysian (1)	3	0.04
Nepalese (0)	3	0.04
Pakistani (6)	6	0.08
Thai (2)	5	0.07
Vietnamese (17)	24	0.31
Hawaii Native/Pacific Islander (10)	22	0.29
Not Hispanic (10)	22	0.29
Guamanian/Chamorro (0)	2	0.03
Native Hawaiian (1)	2	0.03
Samoan (3)	3	0.04
White (6,833)	7,053	91.91
Not Hispanic (6,102)	6,258	81.55
Hispanic (731)	795	10.36

Thousand Oaks

Place Type: City
County: Ventura
Population: 126,683†

Ancestry‡	Population	%
Afghan (22)	22	0.02
African, Sub-Saharan (236)	301	0.24
African (72)	112	0.09
Ghanaian (128)	128	0.10
South African (36)	61	0.05
Albanian (92)	92	0.07
Alsatian (0)	25	0.02
American (5,973)	5,973	4.79
Arab (597)	1,219	0.98
Arab (104)	154	0.12
Egyptian (110)	166	0.13
Lebanese (216)	451	0.36
Moroccan (12)	12	0.01
Palestinian (0)	10	0.01
Syrian (19)	162	0.13
Other Arab (136)	264	0.21
Armenian (352)	578	0.46
Assyrian/Chaldean/Syriac (11)	22	0.02
Australian (63)	172	0.14
Austrian (212)	836	0.67
Basque (12)	28	0.02
Belgian (32)	109	0.09
Brazilian (26)	56	0.04
British (1,019)	1,514	1.21
Bulgarian (0)	11	0.01
Cajun (0)	23	0.02
Canadian (421)	725	0.58
Celtic (13)	13	0.01
Croatian (58)	398	0.32
Czech (174)	661	0.53
Czechoslovakian (88)	189	0.15
Danish (406)	1,405	1.13
Dutch (540)	1,995	1.60
Eastern European (621)	674	0.54
English (3,710)	14,138	11.34
Estonian (8)	13	0.01
European (2,520)	2,952	2.37
Finnish (73)	238	0.19
French, ex. Basque (630)	3,983	3.19
French Canadian (186)	745	0.60
German (4,973)	18,494	14.83
Greek (532)	929	0.75
Hungarian (420)	1,124	0.90
Icelander (0)	9	0.01

*Notes: † The Census 2010 population figure is used to calculate the percentages in the Hispanic Origin and Race categories. Ancestry percentages are based on the 2006-2010 American Community Survey population (not shown); ‡ Numbers in parentheses indicate the number of people reporting a single ancestry; * Numbers in parentheses indicate the number of persons reporting this race alone, not in combination with any other race; Please refer to the Explanation of Data for more information.*

Iranian (1,111)	1,536	1.23
Irish (3,922)	15,400	12.35
Israeli (245)	384	0.31
Italian (3,917)	10,438	8.37
Latvian (0)	36	0.03
Lithuanian (153)	403	0.32
Northern European (234)	252	0.20
Norwegian (939)	2,592	2.08
Pennsylvania German (0)	10	0.01
Polish (1,457)	4,985	4.00
Portuguese (326)	647	0.52
Romanian (220)	494	0.40
Russian (1,888)	4,469	3.58
Scandinavian (158)	403	0.32
Scotch-Irish (766)	2,095	1.68
Scottish (1,076)	3,283	2.63
Serbian (38)	68	0.05
Slavic (31)	56	0.04
Slovak (81)	180	0.14
Slovene (21)	94	0.08
Swedish (737)	3,155	2.53
Swiss (59)	279	0.22
Turkish (11)	145	0.12
Ukrainian (192)	544	0.44
Welsh (205)	1,003	0.80
West Indian, ex. Hispanic (70)	184	0.15
Bahamian (0)	29	0.02
Belizean (23)	23	0.02
Dutch West Indian (0)	10	0.01
Haitian (13)	46	0.04
Jamaican (13)	55	0.04
West Indian (21)	21	0.02
Yugoslavian (75)	126	0.10

Hispanic Origin	Population	%
Hispanic or Latino (of any race)	21,341	16.85
Central American, ex. Mexican	2,441	1.93
Costa Rican	87	0.07
Guatemalan	1,173	0.93
Honduran	102	0.08
Nicaraguan	231	0.18
Panamanian	37	0.03
Salvadoran	793	0.63
Other Central American	18	0.01
Cuban	280	0.22
Dominican Republic	31	0.02
Mexican	14,671	11.58
Puerto Rican	466	0.37
South American	1,325	1.05
Argentinean	278	0.22
Bolivian	22	0.02
Chilean	112	0.09
Colombian	285	0.22
Ecuadorian	145	0.11
Paraguayan	4	<0.01
Peruvian	390	0.31
Uruguayan	23	0.02
Venezuelan	42	0.03
Other South American	24	0.02
Other Hispanic or Latino	2,127	1.68

Race*	Population	%
African-American/Black (1,674)	2,375	1.87
Not Hispanic (1,508)	2,047	1.62
Hispanic (166)	328	0.26
American Indian/Alaska Native (497)	1,385	1.09
Not Hispanic (231)	806	0.64
Hispanic (266)	579	0.46
Aleut *(Alaska Native)* (1)	1	<0.01
Apache (18)	60	0.05
Arapaho (1)	1	<0.01
Blackfeet (1)	20	0.02
Canadian/French Am. Ind. (0)	4	<0.01
Central American Ind. (5)	11	0.01
Cherokee (61)	265	0.21
Cheyenne (0)	8	0.01
Chickasaw (5)	14	0.01
Chippewa (10)	19	0.01
Choctaw (16)	76	0.06
Colville (1)	1	<0.01
Comanche (3)	9	0.01
Cree (1)	6	<0.01
Creek (0)	6	<0.01
Crow (3)	4	<0.01
Delaware (0)	1	<0.01
Hopi (1)	5	<0.01
Iroquois (2)	19	0.01
Kiowa (0)	1	<0.01
Lumbee (0)	4	<0.01
Menominee (0)	1	<0.01
Mexican American Ind. (94)	148	0.12
Navajo (8)	24	0.02
Osage (4)	6	<0.01
Paiute (0)	2	<0.01
Pima (1)	3	<0.01
Potawatomi (3)	3	<0.01
Pueblo (4)	6	<0.01
Seminole (0)	1	<0.01
Shoshone (1)	2	<0.01
Sioux (7)	38	0.03
South American Ind. (10)	21	0.02
Spanish American Ind. (1)	4	<0.01
Tlingit-Haida *(Alaska Native)* (0)	2	<0.01
Tohono O'Odham (8)	9	0.01
Ute (2)	5	<0.01
Yaqui (9)	15	0.01
Yuman (0)	1	<0.01
Asian (11,043)	13,559	10.70
Not Hispanic (10,928)	13,169	10.40
Hispanic (115)	390	0.31
Bangladeshi (23)	28	0.02
Bhutanese (4)	4	<0.01
Burmese (12)	23	0.02
Cambodian (50)	69	0.05
Chinese, ex. Taiwanese (3,460)	4,113	3.25
Filipino (1,324)	1,967	1.55
Hmong (4)	7	0.01
Indian (2,518)	2,753	2.17
Indonesian (52)	129	0.10
Japanese (916)	1,640	1.29
Korean (1,097)	1,310	1.03
Laotian (7)	10	0.01
Malaysian (13)	26	0.02
Nepalese (5)	8	0.01
Pakistani (164)	187	0.15
Sri Lankan (95)	115	0.09
Taiwanese (321)	346	0.27
Thai (117)	147	0.12
Vietnamese (514)	613	0.48
Hawaii Native/Pacific Islander (146)	488	0.39
Not Hispanic (134)	419	0.33
Hispanic (12)	69	0.05
Fijian (2)	7	0.01
Guamanian/Chamorro (14)	50	0.04
Marshallese (1)	1	<0.01
Native Hawaiian (66)	210	0.17
Samoan (22)	54	0.04
Tongan (20)	37	0.03
White (101,702)	105,955	83.64
Not Hispanic (88,970)	91,960	72.59
Hispanic (12,732)	13,995	11.05

Thousand Palms

Place Type: CDP
County: Riverside
Population: 7,715†

Ancestry‡	Population	%
American (111)	111	1.54
Belgian (0)	15	0.21
Canadian (48)	109	1.52
Czech (0)	17	0.24
Czechoslovakian (50)	50	0.70
Danish (0)	65	0.90
Dutch (12)	60	0.84
English (192)	739	10.29
European (124)	194	2.70
French, ex. Basque (54)	303	4.22
German (198)	703	9.78
Irish (77)	375	5.22
Italian (62)	138	1.92
Latvian (21)	21	0.29
Norwegian (129)	160	2.23
Polish (11)	43	0.60
Russian (48)	81	1.13
Scandinavian (18)	18	0.25
Scotch-Irish (11)	105	1.46
Scottish (93)	165	2.30
Serbian (18)	18	0.25
Slovak (0)	26	0.36
Slovene (13)	27	0.38
Swedish (63)	114	1.59
Swiss (0)	16	0.22
Welsh (0)	101	1.41
West Indian, ex. Hispanic (53)	53	0.74
Jamaican (53)	53	0.74

Hispanic Origin	Population	%
Hispanic or Latino (of any race)	4,051	52.51
Central American, ex. Mexican	132	1.71
Costa Rican	1	0.01
Guatemalan	43	0.56
Honduran	1	0.01
Nicaraguan	3	0.04
Panamanian	3	0.04
Salvadoran	81	1.05
Cuban	16	0.21
Dominican Republic	1	0.01
Mexican	3,669	47.56
Puerto Rican	17	0.22
South American	14	0.18
Argentinean	1	0.01
Chilean	1	0.01
Colombian	2	0.03
Ecuadorian	2	0.03
Paraguayan	1	0.01
Peruvian	5	0.06
Venezuelan	2	0.03
Other Hispanic or Latino	202	2.62

Race*	Population	%
African-American/Black (105)	150	1.94
Not Hispanic (81)	112	1.45
Hispanic (24)	38	0.49
American Indian/Alaska Native (75)	138	1.79
Not Hispanic (35)	83	1.08
Hispanic (40)	55	0.71
Alaska Athabascan *(Ala. Nat.)* (3)	3	0.04
Aleut *(Alaska Native)* (1)	2	0.03
Apache (4)	6	0.08
Blackfeet (0)	14	0.18
Cherokee (1)	4	0.05
Chickasaw (2)	2	0.03
Chippewa (0)	5	0.06
Choctaw (3)	3	0.04
Creek (0)	1	0.01
Delaware (0)	2	0.03
Inupiat *(Alaska Native)* (1)	1	0.01
Mexican American Ind. (6)	8	0.10
Navajo (1)	2	0.03
Potawatomi (0)	1	0.01
Seminole (1)	1	0.01
Sioux (1)	2	0.03
South American Ind. (0)	1	0.01
Tohono O'Odham (1)	5	0.06
Yaqui (6)	6	0.08
Asian (129)	172	2.23
Not Hispanic (113)	138	1.79
Hispanic (16)	34	0.44
Chinese, ex. Taiwanese (2)	5	0.06
Filipino (73)	107	1.39
Indian (13)	14	0.18
Japanese (8)	11	0.14
Korean (9)	10	0.13
Laotian (4)	5	0.06
Sri Lankan (1)	2	0.03
Taiwanese (1)	1	0.01
Thai (7)	7	0.09
Vietnamese (5)	7	0.09

*Notes: † The Census 2010 population figure is used to calculate the percentages in the Hispanic Origin and Race categories. Ancestry percentages are based on the 2006-2010 American Community Survey population (not shown); ‡ Numbers in parentheses indicate the number of people reporting a single ancestry; * Numbers in parentheses indicate the number of persons reporting this race alone, not in combination with any other race; Please refer to the Explanation of Data for more information.*

Hawaii Native/Pacific Islander (10)	14	0.18
Not Hispanic (8)	11	0.14
Hispanic (2)	3	0.04
Guamanian/Chamorro (4)	4	0.05
Native Hawaiian (5)	5	0.06
Samoan (0)	1	0.01
White (5,763)	5,947	77.08
Not Hispanic (3,326)	3,404	44.12
Hispanic (2,437)	2,543	32.96

Tiburon

Place Type: Town
County: Marin
Population: 8,962†

Ancestry‡	Population	%
African, Sub-Saharan (12)	12	0.14
South African (12)	12	0.14
American (118)	118	1.34
Arab (130)	148	1.68
Egyptian (130)	130	1.47
Lebanese (0)	8	0.09
Moroccan (0)	10	0.11
Armenian (13)	54	0.61
Assyrian/Chaldean/Syriac (0)	15	0.17
Austrian (15)	28	0.32
Basque (31)	31	0.35
British (284)	284	3.22
Bulgarian (11)	11	0.12
Canadian (0)	42	0.48
Croatian (36)	72	0.82
Czech (12)	51	0.58
Czechoslovakian (12)	12	0.14
Danish (73)	134	1.52
Dutch (50)	257	2.91
Eastern European (160)	160	1.81
English (528)	1,710	19.36
European (480)	520	5.89
French, ex. Basque (65)	311	3.52
French Canadian (12)	12	0.14
German (231)	1,330	15.06
Greek (22)	34	0.39
Hungarian (0)	28	0.32
Iranian (94)	105	1.19
Irish (396)	1,748	19.79
Israeli (0)	23	0.26
Italian (178)	570	6.45
Latvian (0)	16	0.18
Lithuanian (22)	50	0.57
Norwegian (25)	47	0.53
Polish (91)	258	2.92
Portuguese (14)	61	0.69
Romanian (0)	16	0.18
Russian (120)	347	3.93
Scandinavian (25)	56	0.63
Scotch-Irish (60)	75	0.85
Scottish (90)	412	4.67
Slovak (18)	18	0.20
Swedish (75)	238	2.70
Swiss (92)	112	1.27
Ukrainian (11)	47	0.53
Welsh (28)	140	1.59
Yugoslavian (0)	13	0.15

Hispanic Origin	Population	%
Hispanic or Latino (of any race)	410	4.57
Central American, ex. Mexican	49	0.55
Guatemalan	7	0.08
Honduran	1	0.01
Nicaraguan	9	0.10
Panamanian	11	0.12
Salvadoran	21	0.23
Cuban	25	0.28
Mexican	143	1.60
Puerto Rican	19	0.21
South American	83	0.93
Argentinean	24	0.27
Chilean	9	0.10
Colombian	25	0.28
Ecuadorian	4	0.04
Peruvian	15	0.17
Venezuelan	3	0.03
Other South American	3	0.03
Other Hispanic or Latino	91	1.02

Race*	Population	%
African-American/Black (83)	141	1.57
Not Hispanic (77)	128	1.43
Hispanic (6)	13	0.15
American Indian/Alaska Native (16)	74	0.83
Not Hispanic (13)	65	0.73
Hispanic (3)	9	0.10
Apache (0)	1	0.01
Blackfeet (0)	1	0.01
Cherokee (3)	14	0.16
Chickasaw (0)	3	0.03
Choctaw (4)	6	0.07
Iroquois (0)	1	0.01
Mexican American Ind. (2)	2	0.02
Navajo (1)	2	0.02
Seminole (0)	4	0.04
South American Ind. (1)	1	0.01
Ute (0)	2	0.02
Asian (505)	762	8.50
Not Hispanic (501)	745	8.31
Hispanic (4)	17	0.19
Burmese (1)	1	0.01
Cambodian (5)	6	0.07
Chinese, ex. Taiwanese (190)	280	3.12
Filipino (36)	66	0.74
Indian (87)	117	1.31
Indonesian (0)	1	0.01
Japanese (73)	118	1.32
Korean (49)	68	0.76
Laotian (1)	1	0.01
Malaysian (1)	1	0.01
Nepalese (1)	3	0.03
Pakistani (4)	9	0.10
Sri Lankan (1)	3	0.03
Taiwanese (7)	9	0.10
Thai (6)	12	0.13
Vietnamese (16)	24	0.27
Hawaii Native/Pacific Islander (8)	23	0.26
Not Hispanic (8)	21	0.23
Hispanic (0)	2	0.02
Fijian (4)	4	0.04
Guamanian/Chamorro (0)	5	0.06
Native Hawaiian (3)	10	0.11
Tongan (1)	1	0.01
White (7,899)	8,246	92.01
Not Hispanic (7,605)	7,916	88.33
Hispanic (294)	330	3.68

Topanga

Place Type: CDP
County: Los Angeles
Population: 8,289†

Ancestry‡	Population	%
African, Sub-Saharan (13)	13	0.15
African (13)	13	0.15
American (555)	555	6.51
Arab (0)	56	0.66
Lebanese (0)	56	0.66
Armenian (98)	154	1.81
Austrian (9)	146	1.71
Belgian (0)	38	0.45
Brazilian (16)	16	0.19
British (53)	73	0.86
Canadian (0)	68	0.80
Croatian (44)	90	1.06
Czech (9)	25	0.29
Czechoslovakian (0)	15	0.18
Danish (71)	146	1.71
Dutch (44)	203	2.38
Eastern European (42)	42	0.49
English (417)	1,332	15.63
European (410)	427	5.01
Finnish (65)	75	0.88
French, ex. Basque (61)	447	5.25
French Canadian (0)	51	0.60
German (577)	1,520	17.84
Hungarian (19)	49	0.58
Iranian (110)	110	1.29
Irish (261)	887	10.41
Italian (189)	310	3.64
Latvian (13)	13	0.15
Lithuanian (11)	43	0.50
Norwegian (54)	97	1.14
Pennsylvania German (0)	17	0.20
Polish (35)	230	2.70
Portuguese (9)	71	0.83
Romanian (9)	44	0.52
Russian (170)	506	5.94
Scotch-Irish (69)	165	1.94
Scottish (98)	461	5.41
Slavic (36)	36	0.42
Slovak (0)	24	0.28
Swedish (27)	200	2.35
Swiss (21)	97	1.14
Ukrainian (4)	13	0.15
Welsh (30)	42	0.49
Yugoslavian (0)	47	0.55

Hispanic Origin	Population	%
Hispanic or Latino (of any race)	534	6.44
Central American, ex. Mexican	49	0.59
Costa Rican	2	0.02
Guatemalan	16	0.19
Honduran	1	0.01
Nicaraguan	3	0.04
Panamanian	3	0.04
Salvadoran	22	0.27
Other Central American	2	0.02
Cuban	17	0.21
Dominican Republic	7	0.08
Mexican	278	3.35
Puerto Rican	26	0.31
South American	72	0.87
Argentinean	19	0.23
Chilean	9	0.11
Colombian	11	0.13
Ecuadorian	5	0.06
Peruvian	23	0.28
Uruguayan	3	0.04
Venezuelan	2	0.02
Other Hispanic or Latino	85	1.03

Race*	Population	%
African-American/Black (117)	210	2.53
Not Hispanic (112)	183	2.21
Hispanic (5)	27	0.33
American Indian/Alaska Native (35)	133	1.60
Not Hispanic (22)	91	1.10
Hispanic (13)	42	0.51
Apache (3)	9	0.11
Blackfeet (0)	6	0.07
Cherokee (3)	28	0.34
Cheyenne (0)	1	0.01
Chippewa (0)	1	0.01
Choctaw (0)	1	0.01
Comanche (0)	1	0.01
Delaware (0)	1	0.01
Iroquois (1)	2	0.02
Lumbee (0)	1	0.01
Mexican American Ind. (9)	13	0.16
Navajo (1)	2	0.02
Pueblo (1)	2	0.02
Sioux (2)	12	0.14
South American Ind. (1)	1	0.01
Asian (353)	489	5.90
Not Hispanic (343)	469	5.66
Hispanic (10)	20	0.24
Bangladeshi (0)	2	0.02
Chinese, ex. Taiwanese (99)	137	1.65
Filipino (26)	46	0.55
Indian (40)	55	0.66
Indonesian (1)	2	0.02

*Notes: † The Census 2010 population figure is used to calculate the percentages in the Hispanic Origin and Race categories. Ancestry percentages are based on the 2006-2010 American Community Survey population (not shown); ‡ Numbers in parentheses indicate the number of people reporting a single ancestry; * Numbers in parentheses indicate the number of persons reporting this race alone, not in combination with any other race; Please refer to the Explanation of Data for more information.*

	Population	%
Japanese (73)	115	1.39
Korean (62)	81	0.98
Nepalese (0)	1	0.01
Pakistani (1)	2	0.02
Taiwanese (2)	4	0.05
Thai (6)	8	0.10
Vietnamese (24)	33	0.40
Hawaii Native/Pacific Islander (3)	11	0.13
Not Hispanic (1)	8	0.10
Hispanic (2)	3	0.04
Native Hawaiian (1)	6	0.07
White (7,313)	7,629	92.04
Not Hispanic (7,002)	7,236	87.30
Hispanic (311)	393	4.74

Torrance

Place Type: City
County: Los Angeles
Population: 145,438†

Ancestry‡	Population	%
Afghan (273)	298	0.21
African, Sub-Saharan (748)	923	0.64
African (413)	550	0.38
Ethiopian (63)	63	0.04
Kenyan (15)	15	0.01
Liberian (23)	23	0.02
Nigerian (201)	219	0.15
South African (16)	16	0.01
Ugandan (0)	20	0.01
Other Sub-Saharan African (17)	17	0.01
Albanian (6)	6	<0.01
Alsatian (0)	15	0.01
American (5,526)	5,526	3.84
Arab (930)	1,417	0.98
Arab (86)	310	0.22
Egyptian (312)	341	0.24
Jordanian (43)	86	0.06
Lebanese (178)	246	0.17
Moroccan (174)	174	0.12
Palestinian (0)	43	0.03
Syrian (104)	153	0.11
Other Arab (33)	64	0.04
Armenian (353)	485	0.34
Australian (54)	122	0.08
Austrian (135)	316	0.22
Basque (9)	16	0.01
Belgian (28)	132	0.09
Brazilian (182)	280	0.19
British (413)	692	0.48
Bulgarian (12)	70	0.05
Canadian (393)	769	0.53
Carpatho Rusyn (0)	13	0.01
Celtic (34)	34	0.02
Croatian (117)	390	0.27
Czech (156)	657	0.46
Czechoslovakian (65)	100	0.07
Danish (278)	1,058	0.73
Dutch (516)	1,908	1.33
Eastern European (170)	175	0.12
English (2,960)	11,936	8.29
Estonian (12)	48	0.03
European (918)	1,147	0.80
Finnish (138)	367	0.25
French, ex. Basque (471)	3,284	2.28
French Canadian (240)	677	0.47
German (3,990)	15,947	11.08
Greek (562)	900	0.63
Guyanese (14)	14	0.01
Hungarian (258)	780	0.54
Icelander (0)	42	0.03
Iranian (886)	1,102	0.77
Irish (3,625)	12,483	8.67
Israeli (65)	102	0.07
Italian (2,694)	7,293	5.07
Latvian (8)	112	0.08
Lithuanian (264)	536	0.37
Luxemburger (0)	22	0.02
Maltese (9)	9	0.01
New Zealander (14)	154	0.11
Northern European (159)	172	0.12
Norwegian (516)	1,798	1.25
Pennsylvania German (29)	70	0.05
Polish (665)	2,184	1.52
Portuguese (260)	666	0.46
Romanian (148)	387	0.27
Russian (678)	1,918	1.33
Scandinavian (202)	466	0.32
Scotch-Irish (401)	1,637	1.14
Scottish (710)	2,577	1.79
Serbian (138)	151	0.10
Slovak (98)	181	0.13
Slovene (0)	108	0.08
Swedish (556)	1,859	1.29
Swiss (66)	339	0.24
Turkish (140)	459	0.32
Ukrainian (126)	270	0.19
Welsh (73)	671	0.47
West Indian, ex. Hispanic (141)	198	0.14
Belizean (48)	88	0.06
Dutch West Indian (29)	38	0.03
Jamaican (0)	8	0.01
Trinidadian/Tobagonian (29)	29	0.02
West Indian (35)	35	0.02
Yugoslavian (136)	320	0.22

Hispanic Origin	Population	%
Hispanic or Latino (of any race)	23,440	16.12
Central American, ex. Mexican	2,147	1.48
Costa Rican	218	0.15
Guatemalan	630	0.43
Honduran	168	0.12
Nicaraguan	342	0.24
Panamanian	50	0.03
Salvadoran	723	0.50
Other Central American	16	0.01
Cuban	882	0.61
Dominican Republic	71	0.05
Mexican	14,880	10.23
Puerto Rican	731	0.50
South American	2,540	1.75
Argentinean	371	0.26
Bolivian	49	0.03
Chilean	221	0.15
Colombian	498	0.34
Ecuadorian	295	0.20
Paraguayan	2	<0.01
Peruvian	955	0.66
Uruguayan	23	0.02
Venezuelan	84	0.06
Other South American	42	0.03
Other Hispanic or Latino	2,189	1.51

Race*	Population	%
African-American/Black (3,955)	5,072	3.49
Not Hispanic (3,740)	4,587	3.15
Hispanic (215)	485	0.33
American Indian/Alaska Native (554)	1,532	1.05
Not Hispanic (304)	927	0.64
Hispanic (250)	605	0.42
Alaska Athabascan *(Ala. Nat.)* (0)	1	<0.01
Aleut *(Alaska Native)* (3)	6	<0.01
Apache (17)	62	0.04
Arapaho (0)	1	<0.01
Blackfeet (13)	40	0.03
Canadian/French Am. Ind. (1)	4	<0.01
Central American Ind. (3)	6	<0.01
Cherokee (53)	297	0.20
Cheyenne (0)	16	0.01
Chickasaw (7)	22	0.02
Chippewa (11)	26	0.02
Choctaw (24)	54	0.04
Colville (1)	1	<0.01
Comanche (1)	7	<0.01
Cree (2)	7	<0.01
Creek (5)	16	0.01
Delaware (2)	5	<0.01
Hopi (0)	3	<0.01
Inupiat *(Alaska Native)* (1)	1	<0.01
Iroquois (7)	19	0.01
Kiowa (1)	1	<0.01
Lumbee (4)	4	<0.01
Menominee (2)	2	<0.01
Mexican American Ind. (39)	77	0.05
Navajo (27)	42	0.03
Osage (4)	13	0.01
Paiute (3)	4	<0.01
Pima (1)	1	<0.01
Potawatomi (7)	11	0.01
Pueblo (7)	8	0.01
Puget Sound Salish (6)	13	0.01
Seminole (1)	10	0.01
Shoshone (0)	4	<0.01
Sioux (6)	32	0.02
South American Ind. (7)	26	0.02
Spanish American Ind. (11)	13	0.01
Tlingit-Haida *(Alaska Native)* (3)	3	<0.01
Tohono O'Odham (1)	8	0.01
Tsimshian *(Alaska Native)* (1)	1	<0.01
Ute (3)	3	<0.01
Yakama (0)	1	<0.01
Yaqui (10)	26	0.02
Asian (50,240)	55,499	38.16
Not Hispanic (49,707)	54,136	37.22
Hispanic (533)	1,363	0.94
Bangladeshi (53)	58	0.04
Burmese (81)	103	0.07
Cambodian (77)	100	0.07
Chinese, ex. Taiwanese (6,373)	8,045	5.53
Filipino (4,965)	6,715	4.62
Hmong (16)	19	0.01
Indian (3,921)	4,290	2.95
Indonesian (112)	221	0.15
Japanese (15,465)	18,532	12.74
Korean (12,092)	12,779	8.79
Laotian (17)	28	0.02
Malaysian (27)	33	0.02
Nepalese (29)	33	0.02
Pakistani (943)	1,050	0.72
Sri Lankan (238)	266	0.18
Taiwanese (1,271)	1,436	0.99
Thai (389)	524	0.36
Vietnamese (2,137)	2,369	1.63
Hawaii Native/Pacific Islander (530)	1,363	0.94
Not Hispanic (473)	1,118	0.77
Hispanic (57)	245	0.17
Fijian (8)	14	0.01
Guamanian/Chamorro (59)	137	0.09
Native Hawaiian (163)	634	0.44
Samoan (219)	380	0.26
Tongan (8)	17	0.01
White (74,333)	81,103	55.76
Not Hispanic (61,591)	66,475	45.71
Hispanic (12,742)	14,628	10.06

Tracy

Place Type: City
County: San Joaquin
Population: 82,922†

Ancestry‡	Population	%
Afghan (945)	953	1.20
African, Sub-Saharan (314)	335	0.42
African (314)	324	0.41
Cape Verdean (0)	11	0.01
American (1,188)	1,188	1.50
Arab (332)	402	0.51
Arab (55)	55	0.07
Egyptian (92)	116	0.15
Lebanese (0)	46	0.06
Moroccan (9)	9	0.01
Palestinian (29)	29	0.04
Other Arab (147)	147	0.19
Armenian (0)	54	0.07
Austrian (0)	9	0.01
Basque (77)	134	0.17
Belgian (13)	88	0.11
Brazilian (28)	28	0.04

*Notes: † The Census 2010 population figure is used to calculate the percentages in the Hispanic Origin and Race categories. Ancestry percentages are based on the 2006-2010 American Community Survey population (not shown); ‡ Numbers in parentheses indicate the number of people reporting a single ancestry; * Numbers in parentheses indicate the number of persons reporting this race alone, not in combination with any other race; Please refer to the Explanation of Data for more information.*

Ancestry	Population	%
British (28)	133	0.17
Bulgarian (9)	18	0.02
Canadian (58)	194	0.24
Croatian (11)	23	0.03
Czech (55)	132	0.17
Czechoslovakian (43)	43	0.05
Danish (11)	300	0.38
Dutch (64)	536	0.67
Eastern European (10)	10	0.01
English (668)	3,870	4.87
European (501)	612	0.77
Finnish (59)	168	0.21
French, ex. Basque (112)	1,994	2.51
French Canadian (37)	59	0.07
German (1,639)	7,749	9.76
Greek (26)	417	0.53
Hungarian (142)	224	0.28
Iranian (32)	116	0.15
Irish (1,034)	5,930	7.47
Italian (1,195)	4,587	5.78
Luxemburger (0)	15	0.02
Maltese (5)	5	0.01
Northern European (17)	17	0.02
Norwegian (134)	701	0.88
Polish (185)	836	1.05
Portuguese (1,632)	3,855	4.85
Romanian (20)	52	0.07
Russian (77)	272	0.34
Scandinavian (51)	116	0.15
Scotch-Irish (266)	764	0.96
Scottish (453)	1,036	1.30
Serbian (20)	68	0.09
Slovak (41)	63	0.08
Swedish (151)	1,195	1.50
Swiss (12)	190	0.24
Ukrainian (23)	31	0.04
Welsh (13)	412	0.52
West Indian, ex. Hispanic (9)	125	0.16
Barbadian (0)	27	0.03
Belizean (9)	18	0.02
Jamaican (0)	27	0.03
West Indian (0)	53	0.07
Yugoslavian (20)	68	0.09

Hispanic Origin	Population	%
Hispanic or Latino (of any race)	30,557	36.85
Central American, ex. Mexican	1,690	2.04
Costa Rican	33	0.04
Guatemalan	260	0.31
Honduran	65	0.08
Nicaraguan	427	0.51
Panamanian	58	0.07
Salvadoran	835	1.01
Other Central American	12	0.01
Cuban	136	0.16
Dominican Republic	17	0.02
Mexican	25,099	30.27
Puerto Rican	906	1.09
South American	632	0.76
Argentinean	47	0.06
Bolivian	42	0.05
Chilean	66	0.08
Colombian	68	0.08
Ecuadorian	34	0.04
Paraguayan	3	<0.01
Peruvian	337	0.41
Uruguayan	5	0.01
Venezuelan	19	0.02
Other South American	11	0.01
Other Hispanic or Latino	2,077	2.50

Race*	Population	%
African-American/Black (5,953)	7,315	8.82
Not Hispanic (5,636)	6,639	8.01
Hispanic (317)	676	0.82
American Indian/Alaska Native (715)	1,749	2.11
Not Hispanic (297)	923	1.11
Hispanic (418)	826	1.00
Alaska Athabascan *(Ala. Nat.)* (0)	1	<0.01
Aleut *(Alaska Native)* (3)	7	0.01
Apache (23)	75	0.09
Blackfeet (4)	66	0.08
Canadian/French Am. Ind. (3)	5	0.01
Central American Ind. (3)	6	0.01
Cherokee (67)	269	0.32
Cheyenne (0)	1	<0.01
Chickasaw (1)	13	0.02
Chippewa (5)	16	0.02
Choctaw (31)	84	0.10
Comanche (9)	13	0.02
Cree (1)	3	<0.01
Creek (2)	13	0.02
Delaware (0)	2	<0.01
Hopi (1)	5	0.01
Inupiat *(Alaska Native)* (1)	6	0.01
Iroquois (2)	8	0.01
Lumbee (5)	5	0.01
Mexican American Ind. (69)	112	0.14
Navajo (30)	71	0.09
Osage (1)	1	<0.01
Paiute (17)	32	0.04
Pima (1)	3	<0.01
Potawatomi (3)	11	0.01
Pueblo (6)	32	0.04
Puget Sound Salish (4)	5	0.01
Seminole (4)	7	0.01
Shoshone (0)	7	0.01
Sioux (19)	47	0.06
South American Ind. (11)	12	0.01
Spanish American Ind. (3)	6	0.01
Tlingit-Haida *(Alaska Native)* (2)	2	<0.01
Tohono O'Odham (5)	10	0.01
Ute (0)	4	<0.01
Yakama (0)	3	<0.01
Yaqui (9)	13	0.02
Asian (12,229)	15,260	18.40
Not Hispanic (11,803)	14,196	17.12
Hispanic (426)	1,064	1.28
Bangladeshi (7)	7	0.01
Burmese (49)	62	0.07
Cambodian (237)	299	0.36
Chinese, ex. Taiwanese (1,033)	1,528	1.84
Filipino (5,319)	6,666	8.04
Hmong (12)	17	0.02
Indian (3,088)	3,395	4.09
Indonesian (48)	101	0.12
Japanese (239)	629	0.76
Korean (245)	370	0.45
Laotian (133)	167	0.20
Malaysian (5)	6	0.01
Nepalese (19)	19	0.02
Pakistani (330)	360	0.43
Sri Lankan (33)	35	0.04
Taiwanese (33)	47	0.06
Thai (60)	98	0.12
Vietnamese (889)	1,046	1.26
Hawaii Native/Pacific Islander (747)	1,466	1.77
Not Hispanic (641)	1,155	1.39
Hispanic (106)	311	0.38
Fijian (182)	222	0.27
Guamanian/Chamorro (140)	254	0.31
Marshallese (0)	2	<0.01
Native Hawaiian (113)	393	0.47
Samoan (172)	280	0.34
Tongan (70)	97	0.12
White (43,724)	48,862	58.93
Not Hispanic (30,005)	33,032	39.84
Hispanic (13,719)	15,830	19.09

Truckee

Place Type: Town
County: Nevada
Population: 16,180†

Ancestry‡	Population	%
African, Sub-Saharan (41)	41	0.26
South African (41)	41	0.26
Albanian (34)	34	0.21
American (215)	215	1.36
Armenian (142)	142	0.90
Austrian (0)	92	0.58
Basque (0)	14	0.09
Belgian (0)	28	0.18
Brazilian (8)	17	0.11
British (16)	65	0.41
Canadian (108)	248	1.56
Croatian (0)	18	0.11
Czech (35)	110	0.69
Czechoslovakian (0)	45	0.28
Danish (9)	324	2.04
Dutch (92)	198	1.25
Eastern European (15)	15	0.09
English (827)	2,717	17.13
Estonian (0)	20	0.13
European (136)	165	1.04
Finnish (19)	30	0.19
French, ex. Basque (77)	650	4.10
French Canadian (19)	126	0.79
German (584)	3,084	19.44
Greek (0)	97	0.61
Guyanese (15)	15	0.09
Hungarian (17)	66	0.42
Icelander (0)	20	0.13
Iranian (16)	16	0.10
Irish (776)	3,308	20.85
Italian (310)	1,210	7.63
Lithuanian (26)	66	0.42
New Zealander (32)	98	0.62
Northern European (67)	82	0.52
Norwegian (132)	615	3.88
Pennsylvania German (38)	38	0.24
Polish (79)	381	2.40
Portuguese (0)	73	0.46
Romanian (28)	57	0.36
Russian (109)	251	1.58
Scandinavian (17)	28	0.18
Scotch-Irish (121)	249	1.57
Scottish (224)	526	3.32
Slovak (0)	10	0.06
Swedish (155)	605	3.81
Swiss (90)	387	2.44
Ukrainian (0)	8	0.05
Welsh (61)	175	1.10
Yugoslavian (0)	48	0.30

Hispanic Origin	Population	%
Hispanic or Latino (of any race)	3,016	18.64
Central American, ex. Mexican	40	0.25
Costa Rican	1	0.01
Guatemalan	5	0.03
Nicaraguan	2	0.01
Panamanian	1	0.01
Salvadoran	31	0.19
Cuban	11	0.07
Mexican	2,736	16.91
Puerto Rican	30	0.19
South American	44	0.27
Argentinean	9	0.06
Bolivian	1	0.01
Chilean	13	0.08
Colombian	6	0.04
Peruvian	8	0.05
Uruguayan	4	0.02
Venezuelan	3	0.02
Other Hispanic or Latino	155	0.96

Race*	Population	%
African-American/Black (60)	107	0.66
Not Hispanic (53)	92	0.57
Hispanic (7)	15	0.09
American Indian/Alaska Native (95)	194	1.20
Not Hispanic (52)	122	0.75
Hispanic (43)	72	0.44
Alaska Athabascan *(Ala. Nat.)* (0)	1	0.01
Aleut *(Alaska Native)* (0)	1	0.01
Apache (1)	6	0.04
Blackfeet (2)	4	0.02
Cherokee (4)	23	0.14
Chickasaw (1)	1	0.01

*Notes: † The Census 2010 population figure is used to calculate the percentages in the Hispanic Origin and Race categories. Ancestry percentages are based on the 2006-2010 American Community Survey population (not shown); ‡ Numbers in parentheses indicate the number of people reporting a single ancestry; * Numbers in parentheses indicate the number of persons reporting this race alone, not in combination with any other race; Please refer to the Explanation of Data for more information.*

Chippewa (1)	5	0.03
Choctaw (1)	6	0.04
Creek (0)	1	0.01
Delaware (1)	2	0.01
Iroquois (2)	4	0.02
Mexican American Ind. (7)	7	0.04
Navajo (2)	5	0.03
Paiute (10)	14	0.09
Potawatomi (0)	3	0.02
Sioux (2)	4	0.02
South American Ind. (1)	2	0.01
Spanish American Ind. (1)	1	0.01
Ute (0)	3	0.02
Yakama (1)	1	0.01
Yaqui (2)	6	0.04
Asian (241)	381	2.35
Not Hispanic (225)	352	2.18
Hispanic (16)	29	0.18
Chinese, ex. Taiwanese (77)	108	0.67
Filipino (40)	71	0.44
Hmong (2)	2	0.01
Indian (5)	16	0.10
Indonesian (1)	6	0.04
Japanese (55)	105	0.65
Korean (22)	29	0.18
Laotian (5)	7	0.04
Malaysian (1)	2	0.01
Pakistani (0)	4	0.02
Thai (6)	11	0.07
Vietnamese (19)	30	0.19
Hawaii Native/Pacific Islander (15)	43	0.27
Not Hispanic (12)	36	0.22
Hispanic (3)	7	0.04
Fijian (2)	6	0.04
Guamanian/Chamorro (0)	3	0.02
Native Hawaiian (9)	16	0.10
Samoan (1)	4	0.02
White (13,992)	14,322	88.52
Not Hispanic (12,568)	12,796	79.09
Hispanic (1,424)	1,526	9.43

Tulare

Place Type: City
County: Tulare
Population: 59,278†

Ancestry‡	Population	%
African, Sub-Saharan (50)	82	0.14
African (26)	58	0.10
Ethiopian (24)	24	0.04
American (1,939)	1,939	3.41
Arab (18)	60	0.11
Egyptian (0)	5	0.01
Lebanese (8)	20	0.04
Palestinian (10)	19	0.03
Other Arab (0)	16	0.03
Armenian (44)	116	0.20
Assyrian/Chaldean/Syriac (0)	10	0.02
Australian (26)	34	0.06
Austrian (0)	24	0.04
Belgian (5)	107	0.19
Brazilian (44)	44	0.08
British (0)	19	0.03
Canadian (38)	63	0.11
Croatian (0)	46	0.08
Czech (99)	99	0.17
Danish (34)	62	0.11
Dutch (286)	856	1.50
English (1,582)	3,009	5.28
European (117)	117	0.21
French, ex. Basque (107)	434	0.76
French Canadian (24)	53	0.09
German (895)	3,096	5.44
Greek (0)	24	0.04
Hungarian (14)	39	0.07
Iranian (26)	26	0.05
Irish (786)	2,856	5.02
Israeli (140)	140	0.25
Italian (187)	629	1.10
Lithuanian (15)	25	0.04
Northern European (138)	138	0.24
Norwegian (31)	272	0.48
Polish (141)	338	0.59
Portuguese (3,625)	4,347	7.63
Romanian (7)	19	0.03
Russian (39)	95	0.17
Scandinavian (0)	7	0.01
Scotch-Irish (179)	504	0.89
Scottish (81)	253	0.44
Slavic (9)	9	0.02
Swedish (31)	290	0.51
Swiss (0)	38	0.07
Welsh (28)	221	0.39
West Indian, ex. Hispanic (36)	46	0.08
Barbadian (0)	10	0.02
Haitian (36)	36	0.06

Hispanic Origin	Population	%
Hispanic or Latino (of any race)	34,062	57.46
Central American, ex. Mexican	364	0.61
Costa Rican	8	0.01
Guatemalan	88	0.15
Honduran	21	0.04
Nicaraguan	46	0.08
Panamanian	4	0.01
Salvadoran	194	0.33
Other Central American	3	0.01
Cuban	28	0.05
Dominican Republic	6	0.01
Mexican	31,539	53.21
Puerto Rican	210	0.35
South American	78	0.13
Argentinean	11	0.02
Bolivian	8	0.01
Chilean	4	0.01
Colombian	11	0.02
Ecuadorian	2	<0.01
Peruvian	35	0.06
Uruguayan	2	<0.01
Venezuelan	5	0.01
Other Hispanic or Latino	1,837	3.10

Race*	Population	%
African-American/Black (2,328)	2,898	4.89
Not Hispanic (1,987)	2,297	3.87
Hispanic (341)	601	1.01
American Indian/Alaska Native (694)	1,374	2.32
Not Hispanic (296)	688	1.16
Hispanic (398)	686	1.16
Aleut *(Alaska Native)* (0)	1	<0.01
Apache (20)	32	0.05
Blackfeet (5)	14	0.02
Canadian/French Am. Ind. (2)	3	0.01
Central American Ind. (1)	2	<0.01
Cherokee (45)	178	0.30
Cheyenne (1)	7	0.01
Chickasaw (13)	19	0.03
Chippewa (4)	7	0.01
Choctaw (59)	106	0.18
Colville (0)	2	<0.01
Comanche (3)	8	0.01
Creek (6)	12	0.02
Crow (1)	1	<0.01
Hopi (9)	9	0.02
Inupiat *(Alaska Native)* (0)	4	0.01
Iroquois (0)	1	<0.01
Kiowa (0)	1	<0.01
Lumbee (0)	1	<0.01
Mexican American Ind. (42)	63	0.11
Navajo (2)	12	0.02
Osage (1)	1	<0.01
Ottawa (0)	13	0.02
Paiute (2)	2	<0.01
Pima (1)	5	0.01
Potawatomi (4)	11	0.02
Pueblo (2)	8	0.01
Puget Sound Salish (0)	6	0.01
Seminole (4)	15	0.03
Sioux (14)	34	0.06
South American Ind. (1)	4	0.01
Spanish American Ind. (1)	1	<0.01
Tlingit-Haida *(Alaska Native)* (0)	1	<0.01
Tohono O'Odham (2)	5	0.01
Yaqui (16)	27	0.05
Yuman (2)	4	0.01
Asian (1,276)	1,752	2.96
Not Hispanic (1,144)	1,457	2.46
Hispanic (132)	295	0.50
Cambodian (14)	21	0.04
Chinese, ex. Taiwanese (121)	203	0.34
Filipino (318)	523	0.88
Hmong (77)	79	0.13
Indian (313)	350	0.59
Indonesian (3)	5	0.01
Japanese (38)	101	0.17
Korean (26)	37	0.06
Laotian (53)	63	0.11
Pakistani (9)	9	0.02
Taiwanese (1)	1	<0.01
Thai (199)	210	0.35
Vietnamese (53)	65	0.11
Hawaii Native/Pacific Islander (80)	258	0.44
Not Hispanic (52)	168	0.28
Hispanic (28)	90	0.15
Guamanian/Chamorro (12)	30	0.05
Marshallese (1)	1	<0.01
Native Hawaiian (10)	78	0.13
Samoan (6)	22	0.04
Tongan (19)	31	0.05
White (36,347)	38,776	65.41
Not Hispanic (20,597)	21,558	36.37
Hispanic (15,750)	17,218	29.05

Turlock

Place Type: City
County: Stanislaus
Population: 68,549†

Ancestry‡	Population	%
African, Sub-Saharan (156)	194	0.29
African (127)	157	0.23
Kenyan (29)	29	0.04
Other Sub-Saharan African (0)	8	0.01
American (1,476)	1,476	2.19
Arab (175)	190	0.28
Iraqi (46)	61	0.09
Lebanese (59)	59	0.09
Syrian (4)	4	0.01
Other Arab (66)	66	0.10
Armenian (75)	219	0.33
Assyrian/Chaldean/Syriac (5,495)	5,798	8.61
Australian (10)	23	0.03
Austrian (60)	92	0.14
Basque (22)	22	0.03
Belgian (25)	37	0.05
Brazilian (12)	12	0.02
British (84)	173	0.26
Canadian (50)	72	0.11
Croatian (14)	28	0.04
Czech (10)	31	0.05
Czechoslovakian (9)	31	0.05
Danish (177)	331	0.49
Dutch (307)	1,316	1.95
Eastern European (8)	8	0.01
English (1,090)	4,549	6.75
Estonian (0)	8	0.01
European (393)	474	0.70
Finnish (14)	41	0.06
French, ex. Basque (125)	1,172	1.74
French Canadian (17)	82	0.12
German (2,022)	8,224	12.21
Greek (48)	82	0.12
Hungarian (0)	8	0.01
Iranian (578)	721	1.07
Irish (831)	5,148	7.64
Italian (677)	2,785	4.13
Lithuanian (60)	136	0.20
Northern European (137)	150	0.22

*Notes: † The Census 2010 population figure is used to calculate the percentages in the Hispanic Origin and Race categories. Ancestry percentages are based on the 2006-2010 American Community Survey population (not shown); ‡ Numbers in parentheses indicate the number of people reporting a single ancestry; * Numbers in parentheses indicate the number of persons reporting this race alone, not in combination with any other race; Please refer to the Explanation of Data for more information.*

Ancestry (continued)	Population	%
Norwegian (250)	855	1.27
Pennsylvania German (21)	30	0.04
Polish (56)	332	0.49
Portuguese (2,885)	5,184	7.69
Romanian (0)	13	0.02
Russian (97)	128	0.19
Scandinavian (137)	238	0.35
Scotch-Irish (113)	611	0.91
Scottish (255)	1,504	2.23
Slavic (11)	45	0.07
Swedish (528)	1,746	2.59
Swiss (65)	249	0.37
Ukrainian (10)	10	0.01
Welsh (38)	383	0.57
West Indian, ex. Hispanic (0)	10	0.01
Dutch West Indian (0)	10	0.01
Yugoslavian (48)	48	0.07

Hispanic Origin	Population	%
Hispanic or Latino (of any race)	24,957	36.41
Central American, ex. Mexican	482	0.70
Costa Rican	10	0.01
Guatemalan	162	0.24
Honduran	44	0.06
Nicaraguan	89	0.13
Panamanian	9	0.01
Salvadoran	164	0.24
Other Central American	4	0.01
Cuban	27	0.04
Dominican Republic	5	0.01
Mexican	22,605	32.98
Puerto Rican	324	0.47
South American	240	0.35
Argentinean	21	0.03
Bolivian	11	0.02
Chilean	30	0.04
Colombian	112	0.16
Ecuadorian	10	0.01
Peruvian	53	0.08
Venezuelan	2	<0.01
Other South American	1	<0.01
Other Hispanic or Latino	1,274	1.86

Race*	Population	%
African-American/Black (1,160)	1,595	2.33
Not Hispanic (1,018)	1,337	1.95
Hispanic (142)	258	0.38
American Indian/Alaska Native (601)	1,291	1.88
Not Hispanic (316)	767	1.12
Hispanic (285)	524	0.76
Alaska Athabascan *(Ala. Nat.)* (1)	1	<0.01
Aleut *(Alaska Native)* (2)	6	0.01
Apache (20)	48	0.07
Arapaho (1)	6	0.01
Blackfeet (8)	26	0.04
Canadian/French Am. Ind. (0)	3	<0.01
Central American Ind. (0)	2	<0.01
Cherokee (83)	304	0.44
Cheyenne (1)	3	<0.01
Chickasaw (5)	10	0.01
Chippewa (10)	21	0.03
Choctaw (23)	72	0.11
Comanche (0)	2	<0.01
Creek (15)	26	0.04
Delaware (3)	7	0.01
Hopi (7)	9	0.01
Iroquois (5)	8	0.01
Mexican American Ind. (41)	64	0.09
Navajo (11)	44	0.06
Osage (2)	6	0.01
Ottawa (1)	1	<0.01
Potawatomi (2)	3	<0.01
Pueblo (1)	3	<0.01
Puget Sound Salish (1)	1	<0.01
Seminole (3)	9	0.01
Shoshone (0)	2	<0.01
Sioux (4)	17	0.02
South American Ind. (4)	14	0.02
Spanish American Ind. (10)	11	0.02
Tlingit-Haida *(Alaska Native)* (2)	3	<0.01
Tohono O'Odham (1)	5	0.01
Ute (1)	1	<0.01
Yaqui (5)	14	0.02
Asian (3,865)	5,135	7.49
Not Hispanic (3,728)	4,810	7.02
Hispanic (137)	325	0.47
Burmese (3)	3	<0.01
Cambodian (61)	85	0.12
Chinese, ex. Taiwanese (333)	415	0.61
Filipino (501)	855	1.25
Hmong (115)	120	0.18
Indian (2,292)	2,501	3.65
Indonesian (11)	19	0.03
Japanese (140)	297	0.43
Korean (116)	149	0.22
Laotian (27)	34	0.05
Nepalese (6)	6	0.01
Pakistani (30)	32	0.05
Sri Lankan (7)	7	0.01
Taiwanese (13)	14	0.02
Thai (9)	20	0.03
Vietnamese (109)	125	0.18
Hawaii Native/Pacific Islander (313)	674	0.98
Not Hispanic (271)	557	0.81
Hispanic (42)	117	0.17
Fijian (120)	156	0.23
Guamanian/Chamorro (41)	69	0.10
Native Hawaiian (73)	183	0.27
Samoan (23)	38	0.06
Tongan (1)	1	<0.01
White (47,864)	50,830	74.15
Not Hispanic (36,220)	37,886	55.27
Hispanic (11,644)	12,944	18.88

Tustin

Place Type: City
County: Orange
Population: 75,540†

Ancestry‡	Population	%
Afghan (111)	111	0.15
African, Sub-Saharan (261)	340	0.46
African (134)	155	0.21
Ghanaian (44)	44	0.06
Nigerian (66)	66	0.09
South African (17)	75	0.10
American (2,328)	2,328	3.16
Arab (558)	669	0.91
Arab (39)	73	0.10
Egyptian (230)	230	0.31
Lebanese (67)	111	0.15
Moroccan (0)	9	0.01
Palestinian (76)	76	0.10
Syrian (43)	43	0.06
Other Arab (103)	127	0.17
Armenian (118)	170	0.23
Assyrian/Chaldean/Syriac (41)	41	0.06
Australian (14)	28	0.04
Austrian (0)	42	0.06
Basque (16)	16	0.02
Belgian (6)	45	0.06
Brazilian (78)	159	0.22
British (169)	291	0.39
Bulgarian (0)	16	0.02
Canadian (77)	119	0.16
Croatian (14)	28	0.04
Czech (63)	200	0.27
Czechoslovakian (48)	80	0.11
Danish (66)	262	0.36
Dutch (338)	865	1.17
Eastern European (87)	87	0.12
English (1,252)	4,369	5.93
European (680)	729	0.99
Finnish (0)	34	0.05
French, ex. Basque (361)	1,441	1.95
French Canadian (42)	84	0.11
German (1,586)	6,048	8.20
Greek (220)	382	0.52
Hungarian (6)	209	0.28
Iranian (619)	677	0.92
Irish (1,530)	4,813	6.53
Italian (805)	2,188	2.97
Lithuanian (0)	56	0.08
Luxemburger (11)	23	0.03
Northern European (37)	37	0.05
Norwegian (260)	643	0.87
Pennsylvania German (19)	21	0.03
Polish (373)	1,037	1.41
Portuguese (37)	192	0.26
Romanian (66)	66	0.09
Russian (415)	702	0.95
Scandinavian (99)	151	0.20
Scotch-Irish (263)	800	1.09
Scottish (411)	1,044	1.42
Serbian (45)	83	0.11
Slavic (0)	86	0.12
Slovak (0)	16	0.02
Swedish (153)	735	1.00
Swiss (25)	126	0.17
Turkish (54)	84	0.11
Ukrainian (10)	101	0.14
Welsh (15)	238	0.32
West Indian, ex. Hispanic (49)	57	0.08
Jamaican (35)	43	0.06
West Indian (14)	14	0.02
Yugoslavian (46)	161	0.22

Hispanic Origin	Population	%
Hispanic or Latino (of any race)	30,024	39.75
Central American, ex. Mexican	1,738	2.30
Costa Rican	42	0.06
Guatemalan	577	0.76
Honduran	114	0.15
Nicaraguan	100	0.13
Panamanian	27	0.04
Salvadoran	871	1.15
Other Central American	7	0.01
Cuban	169	0.22
Dominican Republic	29	0.04
Mexican	24,715	32.72
Puerto Rican	233	0.31
South American	1,443	1.91
Argentinean	150	0.20
Bolivian	285	0.38
Chilean	69	0.09
Colombian	298	0.39
Ecuadorian	113	0.15
Paraguayan	4	0.01
Peruvian	463	0.61
Uruguayan	29	0.04
Venezuelan	20	0.03
Other South American	12	0.02
Other Hispanic or Latino	1,697	2.25

Race*	Population	%
African-American/Black (1,722)	2,247	2.97
Not Hispanic (1,535)	1,873	2.48
Hispanic (187)	374	0.50
American Indian/Alaska Native (442)	887	1.17
Not Hispanic (142)	373	0.49
Hispanic (300)	514	0.68
Alaska Athabascan *(Ala. Nat.)* (0)	1	<0.01
Aleut *(Alaska Native)* (1)	3	<0.01
Apache (18)	33	0.04
Arapaho (0)	2	<0.01
Blackfeet (0)	16	0.02
Canadian/French Am. Ind. (1)	6	0.01
Central American Ind. (10)	10	0.01
Cherokee (18)	84	0.11
Chickasaw (0)	3	<0.01
Chippewa (3)	13	0.02
Choctaw (11)	29	0.04
Colville (0)	1	<0.01
Comanche (3)	3	<0.01
Cree (1)	1	<0.01
Creek (1)	4	0.01
Crow (0)	2	<0.01
Delaware (0)	2	<0.01
Hopi (0)	2	<0.01

*Notes: † The Census 2010 population figure is used to calculate the percentages in the Hispanic Origin and Race categories. Ancestry percentages are based on the 2006-2010 American Community Survey population (not shown); ‡ Numbers in parentheses indicate the number of people reporting a single ancestry; * Numbers in parentheses indicate the number of persons reporting this race alone, not in combination with any other race; Please refer to the Explanation of Data for more information.*

	Population	%
Iroquois (4)	13	0.02
Kiowa (1)	1	<0.01
Mexican American Ind. (54)	79	0.10
Navajo (21)	41	0.05
Osage (0)	2	<0.01
Ottawa (0)	1	<0.01
Paiute (0)	2	<0.01
Pima (0)	1	<0.01
Potawatomi (0)	1	<0.01
Pueblo (14)	21	0.03
Shoshone (1)	3	<0.01
Sioux (7)	18	0.02
South American Ind. (10)	15	0.02
Spanish American Ind. (3)	5	0.01
Tlingit-Haida *(Alaska Native)* (1)	1	<0.01
Tohono O'Odham (1)	1	<0.01
Yaqui (10)	22	0.03
Asian (15,299)	16,973	22.47
Not Hispanic (15,147)	16,578	21.95
Hispanic (152)	395	0.52
Bangladeshi (70)	81	0.11
Burmese (30)	36	0.05
Cambodian (284)	336	0.44
Chinese, ex. Taiwanese (2,564)	3,125	4.14
Filipino (2,364)	2,870	3.80
Hmong (18)	18	0.02
Indian (2,181)	2,332	3.09
Indonesian (65)	92	0.12
Japanese (895)	1,343	1.78
Korean (2,159)	2,422	3.21
Laotian (52)	63	0.08
Malaysian (8)	10	0.01
Nepalese (8)	10	0.01
Pakistani (198)	229	0.30
Sri Lankan (65)	73	0.10
Taiwanese (684)	741	0.98
Thai (85)	114	0.15
Vietnamese (2,907)	3,244	4.29
Hawaii Native/Pacific Islander (268)	530	0.70
Not Hispanic (244)	438	0.58
Hispanic (24)	92	0.12
Fijian (7)	8	0.01
Guamanian/Chamorro (32)	78	0.10
Marshallese (74)	77	0.10
Native Hawaiian (35)	129	0.17
Samoan (56)	85	0.11
Tongan (23)	33	0.04
White (39,729)	42,774	56.62
Not Hispanic (26,317)	27,983	37.04
Hispanic (13,412)	14,791	19.58

Twentynine Palms

Place Type: City
County: San Bernardino
Population: 25,048†

Ancestry‡	Population	%
African, Sub-Saharan (159)	207	0.79
African (132)	180	0.69
Nigerian (11)	11	0.04
Somalian (16)	16	0.06
American (778)	778	2.97
Arab (16)	43	0.16
Arab (16)	32	0.12
Syrian (0)	11	0.04
Armenian (5)	10	0.04
Austrian (0)	38	0.14
Belgian (0)	11	0.04
Brazilian (15)	19	0.07
British (10)	45	0.17
Cajun (0)	35	0.13
Canadian (123)	180	0.69
Croatian (0)	19	0.07
Czech (19)	51	0.19
Czechoslovakian (10)	24	0.09
Danish (50)	105	0.40
Dutch (115)	450	1.72
English (889)	2,511	9.58
European (543)	662	2.53
Finnish (92)	157	0.60
French, ex. Basque (160)	960	3.66
French Canadian (30)	185	0.71
German (1,241)	4,471	17.06
Greek (4)	166	0.63
Hungarian (24)	119	0.45
Icelander (18)	18	0.07
Iranian (0)	16	0.06
Irish (932)	4,144	15.81
Italian (333)	1,591	6.07
Lithuanian (2)	10	0.04
Norwegian (192)	493	1.88
Polish (105)	630	2.40
Portuguese (29)	95	0.36
Russian (0)	112	0.43
Scandinavian (91)	123	0.47
Scotch-Irish (146)	308	1.17
Scottish (279)	695	2.65
Slovak (29)	63	0.24
Swedish (56)	482	1.84
Swiss (0)	98	0.37
Ukrainian (0)	66	0.25
Welsh (0)	158	0.60
West Indian, ex. Hispanic (83)	102	0.39
Haitian (11)	30	0.11
Jamaican (54)	54	0.21
West Indian (18)	18	0.07
Yugoslavian (0)	46	0.18

Hispanic Origin	Population	%
Hispanic or Latino (of any race)	5,212	20.81
Central American, ex. Mexican	272	1.09
Costa Rican	16	0.06
Guatemalan	51	0.20
Honduran	40	0.16
Nicaraguan	31	0.12
Panamanian	41	0.16
Salvadoran	92	0.37
Other Central American	1	<0.01
Cuban	81	0.32
Dominican Republic	34	0.14
Mexican	3,803	15.18
Puerto Rican	453	1.81
South American	126	0.50
Argentinean	6	0.02
Bolivian	5	0.02
Chilean	20	0.08
Colombian	31	0.12
Ecuadorian	24	0.10
Peruvian	29	0.12
Uruguayan	2	0.01
Venezuelan	9	0.04
Other Hispanic or Latino	443	1.77

Race*	Population	%
African-American/Black (2,063)	2,703	10.79
Not Hispanic (1,921)	2,395	9.56
Hispanic (142)	308	1.23
American Indian/Alaska Native (329)	719	2.87
Not Hispanic (240)	530	2.12
Hispanic (89)	189	0.75
Alaska Athabascan *(Ala. Nat.)* (3)	4	0.02
Aleut *(Alaska Native)* (1)	1	<0.01
Apache (10)	24	0.10
Arapaho (0)	1	<0.01
Blackfeet (5)	23	0.09
Canadian/French Am. Ind. (1)	1	<0.01
Central American Ind. (0)	4	0.02
Cherokee (20)	109	0.44
Cheyenne (0)	7	0.03
Chickasaw (0)	9	0.04
Chippewa (4)	18	0.07
Choctaw (2)	12	0.05
Comanche (8)	8	0.03
Cree (1)	1	<0.01
Creek (4)	7	0.03
Crow (2)	3	0.01
Delaware (4)	7	0.03
Hopi (1)	1	<0.01
Houma (1)	1	<0.01
Inupiat *(Alaska Native)* (2)	7	0.03
Iroquois (4)	12	0.05
Kiowa (1)	1	<0.01
Lumbee (2)	2	0.01
Menominee (2)	3	0.01
Mexican American Ind. (10)	26	0.10
Navajo (45)	55	0.22
Osage (1)	3	0.01
Ottawa (1)	1	<0.01
Paiute (2)	3	0.01
Pima (2)	2	0.01
Potawatomi (0)	1	<0.01
Pueblo (4)	13	0.05
Seminole (2)	3	0.01
Shoshone (1)	2	0.01
Sioux (11)	28	0.11
South American Ind. (3)	9	0.04
Tlingit-Haida *(Alaska Native)* (1)	1	<0.01
Tohono O'Odham (5)	6	0.02
Yaqui (6)	9	0.04
Yuman (4)	5	0.02
Yup'ik *(Alaska Native)* (1)	2	0.01
Asian (979)	1,569	6.26
Not Hispanic (938)	1,427	5.70
Hispanic (41)	142	0.57
Burmese (3)	5	0.02
Cambodian (30)	40	0.16
Chinese, ex. Taiwanese (43)	118	0.47
Filipino (495)	770	3.07
Hmong (25)	30	0.12
Indian (22)	44	0.18
Indonesian (3)	6	0.02
Japanese (104)	265	1.06
Korean (89)	150	0.60
Laotian (11)	15	0.06
Malaysian (0)	1	<0.01
Nepalese (1)	2	0.01
Pakistani (1)	3	0.01
Thai (12)	26	0.10
Vietnamese (98)	126	0.50
Hawaii Native/Pacific Islander (345)	556	2.22
Not Hispanic (322)	489	1.95
Hispanic (23)	67	0.27
Guamanian/Chamorro (74)	104	0.42
Marshallese (1)	2	0.01
Native Hawaiian (27)	108	0.43
Samoan (180)	299	1.19
Tongan (4)	31	0.12
White (17,938)	19,321	77.14
Not Hispanic (15,229)	16,180	64.60
Hispanic (2,709)	3,141	12.54

Ukiah

Place Type: City
County: Mendocino
Population: 16,075†

Ancestry‡	Population	%
African, Sub-Saharan (34)	34	0.21
African (34)	34	0.21
American (724)	724	4.54
Arab (9)	27	0.17
Arab (9)	9	0.06
Egyptian (0)	18	0.11
Armenian (65)	65	0.41
Austrian (0)	111	0.70
Brazilian (12)	52	0.33
British (29)	68	0.43
Canadian (20)	37	0.23
Croatian (0)	20	0.13
Czech (19)	105	0.66
Czechoslovakian (10)	21	0.13
Danish (51)	108	0.68
Dutch (123)	382	2.40
Eastern European (66)	66	0.41
English (340)	1,573	9.87
European (336)	370	2.32
Finnish (12)	158	0.99
French, ex. Basque (36)	393	2.47

*Notes: † The Census 2010 population figure is used to calculate the percentages in the Hispanic Origin and Race categories. Ancestry percentages are based on the 2006-2010 American Community Survey population (not shown); ‡ Numbers in parentheses indicate the number of people reporting a single ancestry; * Numbers in parentheses indicate the number of persons reporting this race alone, not in combination with any other race; Please refer to the Explanation of Data for more information.*

French Canadian (29)	38	0.24
German (511)	2,391	15.00
Greek (8)	54	0.34
Icelander (0)	39	0.24
Iranian (0)	9	0.06
Irish (476)	1,960	12.29
Italian (659)	1,702	10.68
Lithuanian (11)	27	0.17
Northern European (55)	55	0.35
Norwegian (20)	151	0.95
Polish (0)	83	0.52
Portuguese (152)	481	3.02
Russian (89)	269	1.69
Scandinavian (13)	64	0.40
Scotch-Irish (106)	227	1.42
Scottish (177)	395	2.48
Serbian (0)	10	0.06
Slovak (12)	12	0.08
Swedish (51)	255	1.60
Swiss (0)	68	0.43
Welsh (0)	127	0.80
West Indian, ex. Hispanic (0)	96	0.60
Dutch West Indian (0)	10	0.06
Jamaican (0)	86	0.54
Yugoslavian (0)	25	0.16

Hispanic Origin	Population	%
Hispanic or Latino (of any race)	4,458	27.73
Central American, ex. Mexican	49	0.30
Guatemalan	16	0.10
Honduran	11	0.07
Nicaraguan	11	0.07
Panamanian	1	0.01
Salvadoran	9	0.06
Other Central American	1	0.01
Cuban	11	0.07
Dominican Republic	2	0.01
Mexican	4,076	25.36
Puerto Rican	53	0.33
South American	30	0.19
Argentinean	3	0.02
Bolivian	4	0.02
Chilean	3	0.02
Colombian	5	0.03
Ecuadorian	11	0.07
Peruvian	4	0.02
Other Hispanic or Latino	237	1.47

Race*	Population	%
African-American/Black (174)	334	2.08
Not Hispanic (158)	282	1.75
Hispanic (16)	52	0.32
American Indian/Alaska Native (601)	1,028	6.40
Not Hispanic (442)	707	4.40
Hispanic (159)	321	2.00
Alaska Athabascan *(Ala. Nat.)* (1)	2	0.01
Aleut *(Alaska Native)* (0)	2	0.01
Apache (3)	14	0.09
Arapaho (1)	2	0.01
Blackfeet (4)	8	0.05
Cherokee (10)	60	0.37
Chickasaw (2)	7	0.04
Chippewa (0)	4	0.02
Choctaw (8)	28	0.17
Comanche (0)	1	0.01
Creek (0)	3	0.02
Inupiat *(Alaska Native)* (1)	1	0.01
Iroquois (1)	3	0.02
Mexican American Ind. (41)	53	0.33
Navajo (9)	13	0.08
Osage (1)	1	0.01
Paiute (4)	5	0.03
Pima (0)	1	0.01
Potawatomi (1)	5	0.03
Pueblo (1)	1	0.01
Puget Sound Salish (1)	1	0.01
Seminole (2)	9	0.06
Shoshone (1)	1	0.01
Sioux (4)	8	0.05
Spanish American Ind. (6)	6	0.04
Tohono O'Odham (1)	1	0.01
Yakama (0)	2	0.01
Yaqui (1)	10	0.06
Yuman (1)	1	0.01
Yup'ik *(Alaska Native)* (0)	1	0.01
Asian (412)	552	3.43
Not Hispanic (396)	501	3.12
Hispanic (16)	51	0.32
Cambodian (9)	12	0.07
Chinese, ex. Taiwanese (94)	116	0.72
Filipino (160)	231	1.44
Indian (34)	58	0.36
Japanese (22)	31	0.19
Korean (8)	14	0.09
Laotian (0)	1	0.01
Nepalese (4)	7	0.04
Pakistani (14)	14	0.09
Sri Lankan (1)	2	0.01
Taiwanese (1)	1	0.01
Thai (13)	15	0.09
Vietnamese (27)	30	0.19
Hawaii Native/Pacific Islander (34)	78	0.49
Not Hispanic (26)	53	0.33
Hispanic (8)	25	0.16
Guamanian/Chamorro (2)	6	0.04
Native Hawaiian (13)	36	0.22
Samoan (6)	10	0.06
White (11,592)	12,356	76.86
Not Hispanic (10,107)	10,528	65.49
Hispanic (1,485)	1,828	11.37

Union City

Place Type: City
County: Alameda
Population: 69,516†

Ancestry‡	Population	%
Afghan (1,085)	1,085	1.59
African, Sub-Saharan (305)	377	0.55
African (154)	181	0.27
Ethiopian (77)	77	0.11
Ghanaian (5)	5	0.01
Kenyan (13)	45	0.07
Nigerian (19)	19	0.03
Somalian (37)	37	0.05
Other Sub-Saharan African (0)	13	0.02
American (591)	591	0.87
Arab (215)	284	0.42
Arab (9)	52	0.08
Jordanian (69)	69	0.10
Lebanese (49)	49	0.07
Palestinian (40)	40	0.06
Other Arab (48)	74	0.11
Austrian (6)	21	0.03
Basque (15)	15	0.02
Brazilian (14)	40	0.06
British (214)	285	0.42
Canadian (68)	83	0.12
Croatian (8)	17	0.02
Czech (5)	5	0.01
Czechoslovakian (8)	17	0.02
Danish (10)	67	0.10
Dutch (107)	217	0.32
Eastern European (0)	6	0.01
English (696)	1,884	2.77
European (213)	276	0.41
French, ex. Basque (277)	704	1.03
French Canadian (71)	91	0.13
German (736)	2,937	4.31
Greek (116)	245	0.36
Guyanese (9)	21	0.03
Hungarian (33)	64	0.09
Iranian (71)	71	0.10
Irish (349)	1,814	2.66
Israeli (26)	33	0.05
Italian (490)	1,444	2.12
Lithuanian (14)	51	0.07
Northern European (23)	23	0.03
Norwegian (22)	76	0.11
Polish (84)	282	0.41
Portuguese (694)	1,114	1.64
Romanian (28)	28	0.04
Russian (32)	210	0.31
Scotch-Irish (65)	374	0.55
Scottish (102)	294	0.43
Swedish (48)	178	0.26
Swiss (27)	53	0.08
Turkish (0)	11	0.02
Ukrainian (0)	14	0.02
Welsh (8)	102	0.15
West Indian, ex. Hispanic (114)	138	0.20
Belizean (31)	31	0.05
Bermudan (0)	12	0.02
Jamaican (71)	83	0.12
Trinidadian/Tobagonian (12)	12	0.02

Hispanic Origin	Population	%
Hispanic or Latino (of any race)	15,895	22.87
Central American, ex. Mexican	1,208	1.74
Costa Rican	25	0.04
Guatemalan	137	0.20
Honduran	83	0.12
Nicaraguan	299	0.43
Panamanian	50	0.07
Salvadoran	605	0.87
Other Central American	9	0.01
Cuban	55	0.08
Dominican Republic	10	0.01
Mexican	12,652	18.20
Puerto Rican	611	0.88
South American	372	0.54
Argentinean	24	0.03
Bolivian	36	0.05
Chilean	31	0.04
Colombian	52	0.07
Ecuadorian	13	0.02
Paraguayan	3	<0.01
Peruvian	184	0.26
Uruguayan	15	0.02
Venezuelan	12	0.02
Other South American	2	<0.01
Other Hispanic or Latino	987	1.42

Race*	Population	%
African-American/Black (4,402)	5,185	7.46
Not Hispanic (4,194)	4,770	6.86
Hispanic (208)	415	0.60
American Indian/Alaska Native (329)	830	1.19
Not Hispanic (116)	418	0.60
Hispanic (213)	412	0.59
Aleut *(Alaska Native)* (1)	1	<0.01
Apache (15)	41	0.06
Arapaho (0)	3	<0.01
Blackfeet (0)	12	0.02
Cherokee (25)	145	0.21
Cheyenne (1)	6	0.01
Chickasaw (5)	11	0.02
Chippewa (3)	9	0.01
Choctaw (2)	27	0.04
Comanche (3)	10	0.01
Cree (1)	1	<0.01
Creek (3)	5	0.01
Delaware (0)	2	<0.01
Iroquois (2)	3	<0.01
Kiowa (1)	1	<0.01
Lumbee (0)	3	<0.01
Mexican American Ind. (48)	81	0.12
Navajo (4)	7	0.01
Osage (0)	1	<0.01
Pima (1)	1	<0.01
Pueblo (0)	12	0.02
Puget Sound Salish (0)	2	<0.01
Seminole (2)	5	0.01
Shoshone (1)	2	<0.01
Sioux (4)	22	0.03
South American Ind. (5)	9	0.01
Spanish American Ind. (1)	2	<0.01
Ute (2)	9	0.01
Yaqui (8)	13	0.02

*Notes: † The Census 2010 population figure is used to calculate the percentages in the Hispanic Origin and Race categories. Ancestry percentages are based on the 2006-2010 American Community Survey population (not shown); ‡ Numbers in parentheses indicate the number of people reporting a single ancestry; * Numbers in parentheses indicate the number of persons reporting this race alone, not in combination with any other race; Please refer to the Explanation of Data for more information.*

Yuman (1)	4	0.01
Asian (35,363)	38,427	55.28
Not Hispanic (35,052)	37,720	54.26
Hispanic (311)	707	1.02
Bangladeshi (18)	27	0.04
Burmese (275)	314	0.45
Cambodian (183)	248	0.36
Chinese, ex. Taiwanese (7,186)	8,102	11.65
Filipino (13,953)	15,289	21.99
Hmong (38)	40	0.06
Indian (7,966)	8,570	12.33
Indonesian (128)	207	0.30
Japanese (385)	751	1.08
Korean (650)	758	1.09
Laotian (82)	105	0.15
Malaysian (10)	21	0.03
Nepalese (40)	42	0.06
Pakistani (403)	450	0.65
Sri Lankan (32)	45	0.06
Taiwanese (391)	441	0.63
Thai (135)	167	0.24
Vietnamese (2,559)	2,851	4.10
Hawaii Native/Pacific Islander (892)	1,563	2.25
Not Hispanic (839)	1,374	1.98
Hispanic (53)	189	0.27
Fijian (323)	403	0.58
Guamanian/Chamorro (94)	187	0.27
Native Hawaiian (104)	332	0.48
Samoan (146)	251	0.36
Tongan (137)	168	0.24
White (16,640)	19,918	28.65
Not Hispanic (10,009)	12,283	17.67
Hispanic (6,631)	7,635	10.98

Upland

Place Type: City
County: San Bernardino
Population: 73,732†

Ancestry‡	Population	%
Afghan (85)	85	0.12
African, Sub-Saharan (250)	277	0.37
African (177)	186	0.25
Ethiopian (7)	7	0.01
Ghanaian (7)	7	0.01
Other Sub-Saharan African (59)	77	0.10
Albanian (0)	22	0.03
Alsatian (0)	14	0.02
American (3,521)	3,521	4.77
Arab (574)	794	1.07
Arab (159)	217	0.29
Egyptian (86)	86	0.12
Iraqi (0)	31	0.04
Jordanian (19)	28	0.04
Lebanese (121)	121	0.16
Palestinian (20)	38	0.05
Syrian (10)	46	0.06
Other Arab (159)	227	0.31
Armenian (148)	172	0.23
Australian (17)	17	0.02
Austrian (0)	92	0.12
Basque (101)	202	0.27
Belgian (0)	21	0.03
Brazilian (62)	62	0.08
British (80)	270	0.37
Cajun (0)	16	0.02
Canadian (116)	208	0.28
Celtic (12)	25	0.03
Croatian (28)	45	0.06
Czech (13)	115	0.16
Czechoslovakian (0)	191	0.26
Danish (73)	355	0.48
Dutch (210)	744	1.01
Eastern European (18)	18	0.02
English (1,353)	5,011	6.78
European (991)	1,387	1.88
Finnish (67)	219	0.30
French, ex. Basque (191)	1,763	2.39
French Canadian (90)	279	0.38
German (2,236)	9,289	12.57
Greek (177)	298	0.40
Hungarian (91)	437	0.59
Iranian (798)	798	1.08
Irish (1,458)	6,384	8.64
Israeli (34)	34	0.05
Italian (1,596)	4,901	6.63
Lithuanian (11)	51	0.07
Macedonian (0)	10	0.01
New Zealander (0)	19	0.03
Northern European (36)	36	0.05
Norwegian (347)	1,132	1.53
Pennsylvania German (15)	15	0.02
Polish (268)	1,377	1.86
Portuguese (27)	126	0.17
Romanian (59)	168	0.23
Russian (120)	266	0.36
Scandinavian (9)	38	0.05
Scotch-Irish (448)	1,085	1.47
Scottish (290)	1,242	1.68
Serbian (27)	118	0.16
Slavic (10)	32	0.04
Slovak (30)	107	0.14
Swedish (231)	1,246	1.69
Swiss (42)	140	0.19
Ukrainian (44)	150	0.20
Welsh (64)	577	0.78
West Indian, ex. Hispanic (113)	189	0.26
Jamaican (113)	113	0.15
West Indian (0)	76	0.10
Yugoslavian (73)	122	0.17

Hispanic Origin	Population	%
Hispanic or Latino (of any race)	28,035	38.02
Central American, ex. Mexican	1,628	2.21
Costa Rican	75	0.10
Guatemalan	402	0.55
Honduran	115	0.16
Nicaraguan	250	0.34
Panamanian	45	0.06
Salvadoran	719	0.98
Other Central American	22	0.03
Cuban	363	0.49
Dominican Republic	47	0.06
Mexican	22,727	30.82
Puerto Rican	443	0.60
South American	1,040	1.41
Argentinean	222	0.30
Bolivian	32	0.04
Chilean	79	0.11
Colombian	193	0.26
Ecuadorian	161	0.22
Paraguayan	3	<0.01
Peruvian	299	0.41
Uruguayan	8	0.01
Venezuelan	33	0.04
Other South American	10	0.01
Other Hispanic or Latino	1,787	2.42

Race*	Population	%
African-American/Black (5,400)	6,234	8.45
Not Hispanic (5,031)	5,553	7.53
Hispanic (369)	681	0.92
American Indian/Alaska Native (522)	1,218	1.65
Not Hispanic (184)	535	0.73
Hispanic (338)	683	0.93
Aleut *(Alaska Native)* (3)	3	<0.01
Apache (25)	63	0.09
Blackfeet (2)	22	0.03
Central American Ind. (4)	17	0.02
Cherokee (18)	153	0.21
Chickasaw (1)	8	0.01
Chippewa (2)	6	0.01
Choctaw (12)	41	0.06
Colville (0)	1	<0.01
Comanche (5)	12	0.02
Cree (1)	3	<0.01
Creek (11)	18	0.02
Crow (1)	1	<0.01
Delaware (1)	2	<0.01
Hopi (0)	1	<0.01
Iroquois (3)	7	0.01
Lumbee (1)	1	<0.01
Mexican American Ind. (37)	91	0.12
Navajo (27)	46	0.06
Osage (1)	3	<0.01
Paiute (2)	2	<0.01
Pima (3)	7	0.01
Potawatomi (10)	15	0.02
Pueblo (16)	25	0.03
Puget Sound Salish (2)	4	0.01
Seminole (4)	4	0.01
Sioux (10)	19	0.03
South American Ind. (4)	14	0.02
Spanish American Ind. (4)	6	0.01
Tlingit-Haida *(Alaska Native)* (1)	1	<0.01
Tohono O'Odham (4)	9	0.01
Tsimshian *(Alaska Native)* (0)	2	<0.01
Yaqui (20)	30	0.04
Yuman (1)	1	<0.01
Asian (6,217)	7,410	10.05
Not Hispanic (6,057)	6,915	9.38
Hispanic (160)	495	0.67
Bangladeshi (19)	23	0.03
Burmese (75)	81	0.11
Cambodian (27)	44	0.06
Chinese, ex. Taiwanese (1,149)	1,431	1.94
Filipino (1,435)	1,882	2.55
Hmong (2)	2	<0.01
Indian (674)	772	1.05
Indonesian (285)	371	0.50
Japanese (329)	566	0.77
Korean (773)	889	1.21
Laotian (17)	26	0.04
Malaysian (13)	24	0.03
Nepalese (13)	13	0.02
Pakistani (148)	163	0.22
Sri Lankan (24)	25	0.03
Taiwanese (358)	382	0.52
Thai (107)	127	0.17
Vietnamese (542)	607	0.82
Hawaii Native/Pacific Islander (159)	415	0.56
Not Hispanic (134)	281	0.38
Hispanic (25)	134	0.18
Fijian (7)	13	0.02
Guamanian/Chamorro (24)	55	0.07
Marshallese (0)	2	<0.01
Native Hawaiian (39)	140	0.19
Samoan (26)	52	0.07
Tongan (32)	51	0.07
White (48,364)	51,343	69.63
Not Hispanic (32,564)	33,874	45.94
Hispanic (15,800)	17,469	23.69

Vacaville

Place Type: City
County: Solano
Population: 92,428†

Ancestry‡	Population	%
Afghan (85)	85	0.09
African, Sub-Saharan (1,702)	2,233	2.43
African (1,541)	2,024	2.20
Ethiopian (28)	28	0.03
Ghanaian (0)	8	0.01
Sierra Leonean (91)	91	0.10
South African (33)	65	0.07
Other Sub-Saharan African (9)	17	0.02
Alsatian (0)	17	0.02
American (2,594)	2,594	2.82
Arab (116)	197	0.21
Arab (84)	84	0.09
Egyptian (8)	8	0.01
Jordanian (11)	11	0.01
Syrian (0)	81	0.09
Other Arab (13)	13	0.01
Armenian (31)	99	0.11
Assyrian/Chaldean/Syriac (57)	57	0.06
Australian (30)	37	0.04

*Notes: † The Census 2010 population figure is used to calculate the percentages in the Hispanic Origin and Race categories. Ancestry percentages are based on the 2006-2010 American Community Survey population (not shown); ‡ Numbers in parentheses indicate the number of people reporting a single ancestry; * Numbers in parentheses indicate the number of persons reporting this race alone, not in combination with any other race; Please refer to the Explanation of Data for more information.*

Austrian (92)	200	0.22
Basque (24)	108	0.12
Belgian (0)	82	0.09
Brazilian (0)	11	0.01
British (250)	477	0.52
Cajun (9)	9	0.01
Canadian (152)	163	0.18
Celtic (23)	23	0.03
Croatian (22)	59	0.06
Czech (14)	133	0.14
Czechoslovakian (50)	78	0.08
Danish (201)	809	0.88
Dutch (374)	1,283	1.40
Eastern European (41)	58	0.06
English (2,637)	9,319	10.14
European (2,028)	2,390	2.60
Finnish (110)	277	0.30
French, ex. Basque (353)	2,425	2.64
French Canadian (169)	348	0.38
German (5,076)	14,207	15.45
German Russian (6)	6	0.01
Greek (262)	551	0.60
Hungarian (156)	414	0.45
Iranian (541)	541	0.59
Irish (3,369)	10,180	11.07
Israeli (8)	8	0.01
Italian (1,927)	5,228	5.69
Latvian (0)	143	0.16
Lithuanian (98)	195	0.21
Luxemburger (0)	15	0.02
Maltese (0)	59	0.06
Northern European (25)	25	0.03
Norwegian (446)	1,150	1.25
Pennsylvania German (0)	71	0.08
Polish (316)	1,225	1.33
Portuguese (911)	1,625	1.77
Romanian (80)	109	0.12
Russian (129)	734	0.80
Scandinavian (115)	196	0.21
Scotch-Irish (597)	1,673	1.82
Scottish (870)	2,672	2.91
Serbian (30)	30	0.03
Slavic (6)	6	0.01
Slovak (13)	27	0.03
Slovene (8)	20	0.02
Swedish (481)	1,098	1.19
Swiss (148)	591	0.64
Turkish (31)	49	0.05
Ukrainian (17)	81	0.09
Welsh (80)	373	0.41
West Indian, ex. Hispanic (72)	159	0.17
Belizean (8)	50	0.05
British West Indian (0)	15	0.02
Jamaican (47)	55	0.06
Trinidadian/Tobagonian (9)	24	0.03
West Indian (8)	15	0.02
Yugoslavian (56)	91	0.10

Hispanic Origin	Population	%
Hispanic or Latino (of any race)	21,121	22.85
Central American, ex. Mexican	1,176	1.27
Costa Rican	33	0.04
Guatemalan	229	0.25
Honduran	56	0.06
Nicaraguan	317	0.34
Panamanian	95	0.10
Salvadoran	424	0.46
Other Central American	22	0.02
Cuban	164	0.18
Dominican Republic	28	0.03
Mexican	15,753	17.04
Puerto Rican	846	0.92
South American	374	0.40
Argentinean	37	0.04
Bolivian	13	0.01
Chilean	18	0.02
Colombian	67	0.07
Ecuadorian	37	0.04
Paraguayan	13	0.01
Peruvian	175	0.19
Uruguayan	1	<0.01
Venezuelan	11	0.01
Other South American	2	<0.01
Other Hispanic or Latino	2,780	3.01

Race*	Population	%
African-American/Black (9,510)	11,312	12.24
Not Hispanic (9,187)	10,590	11.46
Hispanic (323)	722	0.78
American Indian/Alaska Native (846)	2,206	2.39
Not Hispanic (510)	1,448	1.57
Hispanic (336)	758	0.82
Alaska Athabascan *(Ala. Nat.)* (1)	1	<0.01
Aleut *(Alaska Native)* (8)	20	0.02
Apache (24)	76	0.08
Blackfeet (10)	62	0.07
Canadian/French Am. Ind. (2)	8	0.01
Central American Ind. (0)	3	<0.01
Cherokee (69)	382	0.41
Cheyenne (1)	2	<0.01
Chickasaw (10)	16	0.02
Chippewa (9)	34	0.04
Choctaw (23)	87	0.09
Colville (1)	4	<0.01
Comanche (2)	11	0.01
Cree (1)	8	0.01
Creek (20)	52	0.06
Crow (1)	4	<0.01
Delaware (6)	7	0.01
Hopi (2)	4	<0.01
Inupiat *(Alaska Native)* (4)	8	0.01
Iroquois (5)	23	0.02
Kiowa (2)	5	0.01
Mexican American Ind. (53)	104	0.11
Navajo (17)	64	0.07
Osage (2)	17	0.02
Ottawa (3)	4	<0.01
Paiute (9)	17	0.02
Pima (1)	7	0.01
Potawatomi (8)	11	0.01
Pueblo (2)	15	0.02
Seminole (2)	24	0.03
Shoshone (2)	6	0.01
Sioux (19)	49	0.05
South American Ind. (4)	14	0.02
Spanish American Ind. (6)	10	0.01
Tlingit-Haida *(Alaska Native)* (4)	6	0.01
Tohono O'Odham (2)	8	0.01
Tsimshian *(Alaska Native)* (3)	3	<0.01
Ute (3)	9	0.01
Yaqui (7)	20	0.02
Yuman (0)	4	<0.01
Yup'ik *(Alaska Native)* (1)	2	<0.01
Asian (5,606)	8,485	9.18
Not Hispanic (5,378)	7,690	8.32
Hispanic (228)	795	0.86
Bangladeshi (0)	3	<0.01
Burmese (20)	25	0.03
Cambodian (20)	28	0.03
Chinese, ex. Taiwanese (620)	1,024	1.11
Filipino (3,048)	4,581	4.96
Hmong (5)	6	0.01
Indian (521)	618	0.67
Indonesian (9)	27	0.03
Japanese (416)	1,116	1.21
Korean (239)	491	0.53
Laotian (46)	70	0.08
Malaysian (1)	5	0.01
Nepalese (3)	3	<0.01
Pakistani (28)	42	0.05
Taiwanese (25)	40	0.04
Thai (74)	187	0.20
Vietnamese (287)	400	0.43
Hawaii Native/Pacific Islander (532)	1,282	1.39
Not Hispanic (436)	1,004	1.09
Hispanic (96)	278	0.30
Fijian (9)	22	0.02
Guamanian/Chamorro (187)	372	0.40
Marshallese (1)	1	<0.01
Native Hawaiian (155)	556	0.60
Samoan (107)	173	0.19
Tongan (25)	36	0.04
White (61,301)	66,853	72.33
Not Hispanic (50,811)	54,459	58.92
Hispanic (10,490)	12,394	13.41

Valinda

Place Type: CDP
County: Los Angeles
Population: 22,822†

Ancestry‡	Population	%
African, Sub-Saharan (35)	35	0.16
African (35)	35	0.16
American (197)	197	0.89
Arab (6)	6	0.03
Other Arab (6)	6	0.03
Celtic (0)	24	0.11
Dutch (72)	100	0.45
English (14)	134	0.60
French, ex. Basque (12)	26	0.12
French Canadian (10)	10	0.05
German (124)	387	1.75
Hungarian (46)	59	0.27
Irish (245)	454	2.05
Italian (58)	274	1.24
Norwegian (18)	18	0.08
Pennsylvania German (9)	9	0.04
Polish (30)	54	0.24
Romanian (141)	141	0.64
Scotch-Irish (0)	31	0.14
Scottish (0)	64	0.29
Swedish (5)	18	0.08
Swiss (0)	29	0.13
West Indian, ex. Hispanic (0)	13	0.06
West Indian (0)	13	0.06
Yugoslavian (10)	20	0.09

Hispanic Origin	Population	%
Hispanic or Latino (of any race)	17,977	78.77
Central American, ex. Mexican	1,290	5.65
Costa Rican	26	0.11
Guatemalan	342	1.50
Honduran	90	0.39
Nicaraguan	126	0.55
Panamanian	1	<0.01
Salvadoran	692	3.03
Other Central American	13	0.06
Cuban	62	0.27
Dominican Republic	7	0.03
Mexican	15,513	67.97
Puerto Rican	110	0.48
South American	184	0.81
Argentinean	20	0.09
Bolivian	6	0.03
Chilean	15	0.07
Colombian	37	0.16
Ecuadorian	57	0.25
Paraguayan	1	<0.01
Peruvian	47	0.21
Venezuelan	1	<0.01
Other Hispanic or Latino	811	3.55

Race*	Population	%
African-American/Black (439)	529	2.32
Not Hispanic (356)	397	1.74
Hispanic (83)	132	0.58
American Indian/Alaska Native (240)	370	1.62
Not Hispanic (40)	87	0.38
Hispanic (200)	283	1.24
Aleut *(Alaska Native)* (0)	2	0.01
Apache (12)	15	0.07
Central American Ind. (0)	1	<0.01
Cherokee (7)	24	0.11
Chickasaw (1)	3	0.01
Chippewa (4)	4	0.02
Choctaw (3)	7	0.03
Comanche (1)	1	<0.01
Cree (1)	6	0.03

*Notes: † The Census 2010 population figure is used to calculate the percentages in the Hispanic Origin and Race categories. Ancestry percentages are based on the 2006-2010 American Community Survey population (not shown); ‡ Numbers in parentheses indicate the number of people reporting a single ancestry; * Numbers in parentheses indicate the number of persons reporting this race alone, not in combination with any other race; Please refer to the Explanation of Data for more information.*

Crow (0)	2	0.01
Hopi (2)	2	0.01
Inupiat *(Alaska Native)* (1)	1	<0.01
Menominee (0)	2	0.01
Mexican American Ind. (38)	57	0.25
Navajo (10)	18	0.08
Osage (1)	1	<0.01
Pima (1)	1	<0.01
Potawatomi (1)	1	<0.01
Pueblo (0)	4	0.02
South American Ind. (0)	8	0.04
Spanish American Ind. (11)	12	0.05
Tohono O'Odham (5)	7	0.03
Yaqui (0)	1	<0.01
Asian (2,718)	2,914	12.77
Not Hispanic (2,627)	2,719	11.91
Hispanic (91)	195	0.85
Cambodian (14)	17	0.07
Chinese, ex. Taiwanese (538)	645	2.83
Filipino (1,458)	1,586	6.95
Indian (18)	47	0.21
Indonesian (34)	36	0.16
Japanese (44)	85	0.37
Korean (21)	29	0.13
Laotian (18)	23	0.10
Pakistani (4)	4	0.02
Taiwanese (36)	36	0.16
Thai (18)	18	0.08
Vietnamese (401)	470	2.06
Hawaii Native/Pacific Islander (42)	92	0.40
Not Hispanic (35)	61	0.27
Hispanic (7)	31	0.14
Fijian (16)	17	0.07
Guamanian/Chamorro (5)	7	0.03
Native Hawaiian (7)	29	0.13
Samoan (14)	22	0.10
Tongan (0)	1	<0.01
White (11,058)	11,717	51.34
Not Hispanic (1,597)	1,698	7.44
Hispanic (9,461)	10,019	43.90

Valle Vista

Place Type: CDP
County: Riverside
Population: 14,578†

Ancestry‡	Population	%
American (657)	657	4.71
Arab (7)	7	0.05
Egyptian (7)	7	0.05
Austrian (11)	11	0.08
British (117)	150	1.07
Canadian (46)	62	0.44
Czech (21)	31	0.22
Czechoslovakian (43)	43	0.31
Danish (18)	45	0.32
Dutch (85)	262	1.88
English (579)	1,580	11.32
European (97)	113	0.81
Finnish (28)	38	0.27
French, ex. Basque (119)	600	4.30
French Canadian (35)	97	0.69
German (815)	2,202	15.78
Greek (0)	15	0.11
Hungarian (11)	11	0.08
Iranian (26)	26	0.19
Irish (417)	1,936	13.87
Italian (305)	865	6.20
Lithuanian (20)	49	0.35
Norwegian (104)	214	1.53
Polish (57)	145	1.04
Portuguese (38)	181	1.30
Russian (9)	49	0.35
Scandinavian (42)	42	0.30
Scotch-Irish (77)	209	1.50
Scottish (85)	394	2.82
Slovene (0)	14	0.10
Swedish (34)	355	2.54
Swiss (0)	64	0.46
Turkish (0)	10	0.07
Welsh (21)	98	0.70

Hispanic Origin	Population	%
Hispanic or Latino (of any race)	4,027	27.62
Central American, ex. Mexican	165	1.13
Costa Rican	14	0.10
Guatemalan	34	0.23
Honduran	19	0.13
Nicaraguan	27	0.19
Panamanian	8	0.05
Salvadoran	62	0.43
Other Central American	1	0.01
Cuban	29	0.20
Mexican	3,368	23.10
Puerto Rican	94	0.64
South American	49	0.34
Argentinean	4	0.03
Bolivian	4	0.03
Chilean	7	0.05
Colombian	17	0.12
Peruvian	16	0.11
Other South American	1	0.01
Other Hispanic or Latino	322	2.21

Race*	Population	%
African-American/Black (440)	569	3.90
Not Hispanic (391)	488	3.35
Hispanic (49)	81	0.56
American Indian/Alaska Native (252)	464	3.18
Not Hispanic (125)	261	1.79
Hispanic (127)	203	1.39
Alaska Athabascan *(Ala. Nat.)* (1)	1	0.01
Aleut *(Alaska Native)* (1)	2	0.01
Apache (2)	7	0.05
Blackfeet (2)	13	0.09
Central American Ind. (0)	1	0.01
Cherokee (13)	47	0.32
Chickasaw (0)	2	0.01
Chippewa (3)	5	0.03
Choctaw (9)	27	0.19
Comanche (2)	2	0.01
Cree (0)	1	0.01
Creek (3)	9	0.06
Hopi (2)	2	0.01
Inupiat *(Alaska Native)* (2)	3	0.02
Iroquois (7)	7	0.05
Menominee (0)	1	0.01
Mexican American Ind. (3)	9	0.06
Navajo (4)	8	0.05
Osage (1)	3	0.02
Pima (1)	1	0.01
Potawatomi (0)	1	0.01
Shoshone (0)	11	0.08
Sioux (7)	15	0.10
South American Ind. (0)	1	0.01
Spanish American Ind. (2)	2	0.01
Tohono O'Odham (5)	6	0.04
Yaqui (0)	2	0.01
Yuman (6)	6	0.04
Asian (283)	442	3.03
Not Hispanic (265)	384	2.63
Hispanic (18)	58	0.40
Cambodian (5)	6	0.04
Chinese, ex. Taiwanese (27)	52	0.36
Filipino (87)	167	1.15
Indian (82)	86	0.59
Indonesian (2)	2	0.01
Japanese (17)	46	0.32
Korean (11)	17	0.12
Pakistani (11)	15	0.10
Sri Lankan (6)	6	0.04
Taiwanese (5)	5	0.03
Thai (6)	7	0.05
Vietnamese (10)	16	0.11
Hawaii Native/Pacific Islander (41)	76	0.52
Not Hispanic (30)	54	0.37
Hispanic (11)	22	0.15
Guamanian/Chamorro (6)	12	0.08
Native Hawaiian (16)	34	0.23
Samoan (12)	18	0.12
Tongan (1)	3	0.02
White (11,542)	12,147	83.32
Not Hispanic (9,378)	9,695	66.50
Hispanic (2,164)	2,452	16.82

Vallejo

Place Type: City
County: Solano
Population: 115,942†

Ancestry‡	Population	%
Afghan (27)	27	0.02
African, Sub-Saharan (2,811)	3,554	3.06
African (2,389)	3,101	2.67
Cape Verdean (0)	12	0.01
Ethiopian (74)	74	0.06
Kenyan (32)	32	0.03
Liberian (39)	58	0.05
Nigerian (20)	20	0.02
Somalian (203)	203	0.17
Other Sub-Saharan African (54)	54	0.05
American (1,774)	1,774	1.53
Arab (123)	303	0.26
Arab (0)	98	0.08
Egyptian (0)	19	0.02
Iraqi (34)	34	0.03
Lebanese (23)	53	0.05
Palestinian (44)	44	0.04
Syrian (0)	33	0.03
Other Arab (22)	22	0.02
Armenian (132)	195	0.17
Australian (31)	74	0.06
Austrian (26)	63	0.05
Basque (0)	19	0.02
Belgian (9)	30	0.03
Brazilian (8)	59	0.05
British (141)	256	0.22
Bulgarian (64)	79	0.07
Canadian (79)	175	0.15
Celtic (28)	37	0.03
Croatian (54)	76	0.07
Czech (36)	123	0.11
Czechoslovakian (50)	79	0.07
Danish (69)	328	0.28
Dutch (163)	784	0.68
Eastern European (52)	52	0.04
English (1,833)	4,762	4.10
European (2,049)	2,852	2.46
Finnish (34)	163	0.14
French, ex. Basque (223)	1,427	1.23
French Canadian (103)	355	0.31
German (2,061)	6,925	5.97
Greek (209)	399	0.34
Hungarian (42)	153	0.13
Iranian (82)	96	0.08
Irish (1,291)	5,673	4.89
Italian (1,030)	2,932	2.53
Latvian (0)	16	0.01
Lithuanian (41)	168	0.14
Luxemburger (0)	14	0.01
Maltese (0)	50	0.04
Northern European (107)	107	0.09
Norwegian (524)	1,107	0.95
Pennsylvania German (53)	67	0.06
Polish (269)	898	0.77
Portuguese (370)	926	0.80
Romanian (37)	37	0.03
Russian (183)	423	0.36
Scandinavian (62)	125	0.11
Scotch-Irish (247)	1,264	1.09
Scottish (336)	1,119	0.96
Slavic (0)	9	0.01
Slovak (35)	87	0.07
Slovene (0)	12	0.01
Swedish (158)	632	0.54
Swiss (55)	265	0.23
Turkish (0)	16	0.01
Ukrainian (73)	183	0.16

SECTION TWO

*Notes: † The Census 2010 population figure is used to calculate the percentages in the Hispanic Origin and Race categories. Ancestry percentages are based on the 2006-2010 American Community Survey population (not shown); ‡ Numbers in parentheses indicate the number of people reporting a single ancestry; * Numbers in parentheses indicate the number of persons reporting this race alone, not in combination with any other race; Please refer to the Explanation of Data for more information.*

Welsh (38)	363	0.31
West Indian, ex. Hispanic (209)	443	0.38
Belizean (0)	13	0.01
British West Indian (43)	43	0.04
Haitian (14)	58	0.05
Jamaican (39)	210	0.18
Trinidadian/Tobagonian (55)	61	0.05
West Indian (58)	58	0.05
Yugoslavian (44)	131	0.11

Hispanic Origin	Population	%
Hispanic or Latino (of any race)	26,165	22.57
Central American, ex. Mexican	3,861	3.33
Costa Rican	25	0.02
Guatemalan	787	0.68
Honduran	159	0.14
Nicaraguan	629	0.54
Panamanian	97	0.08
Salvadoran	2,135	1.84
Other Central American	29	0.03
Cuban	186	0.16
Dominican Republic	33	0.03
Mexican	18,611	16.05
Puerto Rican	906	0.78
South American	507	0.44
Argentinean	29	0.03
Bolivian	18	0.02
Chilean	39	0.03
Colombian	110	0.09
Ecuadorian	29	0.03
Paraguayan	16	0.01
Peruvian	215	0.19
Uruguayan	11	0.01
Venezuelan	31	0.03
Other South American	9	0.01
Other Hispanic or Latino	2,061	1.78

Race*	Population	%
African-American/Black (25,572)	28,918	24.94
Not Hispanic (24,876)	27,466	23.69
Hispanic (696)	1,452	1.25
American Indian/Alaska Native (757)	2,467	2.13
Not Hispanic (453)	1,713	1.48
Hispanic (304)	754	0.65
Alaska Athabascan *(Ala. Nat.)* (1)	1	<0.01
Aleut *(Alaska Native)* (1)	6	0.01
Apache (23)	95	0.08
Arapaho (3)	3	<0.01
Blackfeet (7)	81	0.07
Canadian/French Am. Ind. (5)	10	0.01
Central American Ind. (3)	8	0.01
Cherokee (83)	421	0.36
Cheyenne (0)	4	<0.01
Chickasaw (5)	22	0.02
Chippewa (3)	11	0.01
Choctaw (27)	118	0.10
Colville (1)	1	<0.01
Comanche (1)	12	0.01
Cree (1)	8	0.01
Creek (3)	27	0.02
Crow (1)	1	<0.01
Delaware (0)	1	<0.01
Hopi (3)	13	0.01
Iroquois (3)	15	0.01
Kiowa (3)	3	<0.01
Lumbee (1)	1	<0.01
Mexican American Ind. (71)	144	0.12
Navajo (29)	79	0.07
Osage (0)	6	0.01
Ottawa (1)	5	<0.01
Paiute (3)	8	0.01
Pima (2)	4	<0.01
Potawatomi (2)	3	<0.01
Pueblo (9)	13	0.01
Puget Sound Salish (1)	2	<0.01
Seminole (2)	26	0.02
Shoshone (1)	5	<0.01
Sioux (21)	67	0.06
South American Ind. (1)	4	<0.01
Spanish American Ind. (5)	6	0.01
Tlingit-Haida *(Alaska Native)* (2)	8	0.01
Tohono O'Odham (1)	5	<0.01
Tsimshian *(Alaska Native)* (1)	1	<0.01
Ute (2)	2	<0.01
Yakama (1)	2	<0.01
Yaqui (1)	10	0.01
Yuman (1)	7	0.01
Asian (28,895)	32,761	28.26
Not Hispanic (28,386)	31,408	27.09
Hispanic (509)	1,353	1.17
Burmese (19)	38	0.03
Cambodian (66)	87	0.08
Chinese, ex. Taiwanese (1,078)	1,715	1.48
Filipino (24,451)	27,622	23.82
Hmong (21)	28	0.02
Indian (1,148)	1,395	1.20
Indonesian (56)	78	0.07
Japanese (286)	716	0.62
Korean (234)	365	0.31
Laotian (142)	184	0.16
Malaysian (10)	37	0.03
Nepalese (8)	9	0.01
Pakistani (112)	130	0.11
Sri Lankan (3)	4	<0.01
Taiwanese (33)	39	0.03
Thai (79)	114	0.10
Vietnamese (576)	695	0.60
Hawaii Native/Pacific Islander (1,239)	2,436	2.10
Not Hispanic (1,159)	2,103	1.81
Hispanic (80)	333	0.29
Fijian (130)	190	0.16
Guamanian/Chamorro (451)	866	0.75
Native Hawaiian (135)	523	0.45
Samoan (283)	463	0.40
Tongan (90)	133	0.11
White (38,064)	44,045	37.99
Not Hispanic (28,946)	32,800	28.29
Hispanic (9,118)	11,245	9.70

Valley Center

Place Type: CDP
County: San Diego
Population: 9,277†

Ancestry‡	Population	%
American (285)	285	3.16
Arab (20)	65	0.72
Arab (20)	20	0.22
Lebanese (0)	33	0.37
Other Arab (0)	12	0.13
Armenian (26)	138	1.53
Austrian (24)	48	0.53
Belgian (0)	13	0.14
British (20)	85	0.94
Canadian (48)	156	1.73
Croatian (0)	37	0.41
Czech (0)	113	1.25
Danish (21)	89	0.99
Dutch (213)	310	3.44
English (510)	1,106	12.26
European (205)	205	2.27
Finnish (17)	17	0.19
French, ex. Basque (11)	81	0.90
French Canadian (17)	29	0.32
German (367)	1,001	11.10
Greek (15)	15	0.17
Irish (227)	696	7.71
Italian (196)	565	6.26
Lithuanian (0)	32	0.35
Northern European (20)	20	0.22
Norwegian (148)	253	2.80
Polish (69)	187	2.07
Portuguese (23)	93	1.03
Romanian (13)	26	0.29
Russian (26)	79	0.88
Scandinavian (30)	71	0.79
Scotch-Irish (12)	56	0.62
Scottish (104)	274	3.04
Serbian (0)	25	0.28
Swedish (73)	206	2.28
Swiss (10)	32	0.35
Ukrainian (10)	10	0.11
Welsh (0)	14	0.16
West Indian, ex. Hispanic (14)	55	0.61
West Indian (14)	55	0.61
Yugoslavian (45)	45	0.50

Hispanic Origin	Population	%
Hispanic or Latino (of any race)	2,581	27.82
Central American, ex. Mexican	97	1.05
Costa Rican	1	0.01
Guatemalan	79	0.85
Salvadoran	17	0.18
Cuban	10	0.11
Dominican Republic	3	0.03
Mexican	2,280	24.58
Puerto Rican	25	0.27
South American	44	0.47
Argentinean	2	0.02
Bolivian	1	0.01
Chilean	3	0.03
Colombian	29	0.31
Ecuadorian	5	0.05
Peruvian	1	0.01
Uruguayan	2	0.02
Venezuelan	1	0.01
Other Hispanic or Latino	122	1.32

Race*	Population	%
African-American/Black (84)	134	1.44
Not Hispanic (82)	122	1.32
Hispanic (2)	12	0.13
American Indian/Alaska Native (188)	334	3.60
Not Hispanic (130)	212	2.29
Hispanic (58)	122	1.32
Apache (1)	2	0.02
Cherokee (5)	23	0.25
Cheyenne (1)	1	0.01
Chickasaw (1)	2	0.02
Choctaw (0)	4	0.04
Comanche (0)	1	0.01
Creek (3)	7	0.08
Delaware (0)	5	0.05
Hopi (3)	3	0.03
Iroquois (0)	3	0.03
Lumbee (3)	3	0.03
Mexican American Ind. (10)	16	0.17
Navajo (1)	1	0.01
Osage (1)	4	0.04
Potawatomi (1)	8	0.09
Seminole (0)	2	0.02
Shoshone (0)	1	0.01
Sioux (1)	1	0.01
South American Ind. (1)	1	0.01
Tlingit-Haida *(Alaska Native)* (5)	5	0.05
Yaqui (0)	1	0.01
Asian (295)	424	4.57
Not Hispanic (281)	380	4.10
Hispanic (14)	44	0.47
Burmese (1)	4	0.04
Cambodian (5)	5	0.05
Chinese, ex. Taiwanese (15)	39	0.42
Filipino (163)	215	2.32
Indian (8)	16	0.17
Indonesian (5)	10	0.11
Japanese (43)	72	0.78
Korean (12)	20	0.22
Laotian (4)	4	0.04
Pakistani (1)	1	0.01
Taiwanese (5)	5	0.05
Thai (5)	8	0.09
Vietnamese (12)	26	0.28
Hawaii Native/Pacific Islander (16)	51	0.55
Not Hispanic (16)	38	0.41
Hispanic (0)	13	0.14
Guamanian/Chamorro (3)	11	0.12
Native Hawaiian (2)	8	0.09
Samoan (7)	14	0.15
White (6,785)	7,174	77.33

*Notes: † The Census 2010 population figure is used to calculate the percentages in the Hispanic Origin and Race categories. Ancestry percentages are based on the 2006-2010 American Community Survey population (not shown); ‡ Numbers in parentheses indicate the number of people reporting a single ancestry; * Numbers in parentheses indicate the number of persons reporting this race alone, not in combination with any other race; Please refer to the Explanation of Data for more information.*

Not Hispanic (5,933)	6,152	66.31
Hispanic (852)	1,022	11.02

Victorville

Place Type: City
County: San Bernardino
Population: 115,903†

Ancestry‡	Population	%
Afghan (29)	29	0.03
African, Sub-Saharan (703)	968	0.90
African (508)	753	0.70
Ghanaian (90)	110	0.10
Liberian (12)	12	0.01
Nigerian (93)	93	0.09
American (2,132)	2,132	1.97
Arab (398)	486	0.45
Arab (207)	207	0.19
Egyptian (159)	159	0.15
Lebanese (8)	96	0.09
Syrian (12)	12	0.01
Other Arab (12)	12	0.01
Armenian (182)	271	0.25
Assyrian/Chaldean/Syriac (18)	18	0.02
Australian (23)	177	0.16
Austrian (14)	75	0.07
Belgian (9)	45	0.04
British (120)	227	0.21
Canadian (34)	57	0.05
Celtic (24)	24	0.02
Croatian (0)	36	0.03
Czech (32)	232	0.21
Czechoslovakian (11)	71	0.07
Danish (135)	279	0.26
Dutch (229)	1,095	1.01
English (1,947)	5,862	5.42
European (370)	464	0.43
Finnish (0)	22	0.02
French, ex. Basque (209)	1,932	1.79
French Canadian (74)	247	0.23
German (2,248)	8,964	8.29
German Russian (29)	29	0.03
Greek (50)	207	0.19
Guyanese (9)	9	0.01
Hungarian (76)	284	0.26
Iranian (138)	138	0.13
Irish (1,712)	7,408	6.85
Italian (1,303)	4,701	4.35
Lithuanian (171)	384	0.36
Northern European (39)	39	0.04
Norwegian (224)	656	0.61
Pennsylvania German (27)	54	0.05
Polish (293)	1,032	0.95
Portuguese (118)	564	0.52
Romanian (53)	53	0.05
Russian (106)	255	0.24
Scandinavian (0)	24	0.02
Scotch-Irish (307)	997	0.92
Scottish (217)	992	0.92
Slavic (13)	13	0.01
Slovak (0)	9	0.01
Slovene (0)	28	0.03
Swedish (134)	730	0.68
Swiss (0)	25	0.02
Ukrainian (153)	182	0.17
Welsh (15)	272	0.25
West Indian, ex. Hispanic (252)	432	0.40
Belizean (167)	167	0.15
Haitian (43)	162	0.15
Jamaican (15)	15	0.01
Trinidadian/Tobagonian (11)	40	0.04
West Indian (16)	48	0.04
Yugoslavian (14)	34	0.03

Hispanic Origin	Population	%
Hispanic or Latino (of any race)	55,359	47.76
Central American, ex. Mexican	3,702	3.19
Costa Rican	115	0.10
Guatemalan	1,045	0.90
Honduran	245	0.21
Nicaraguan	311	0.27
Panamanian	106	0.09
Salvadoran	1,801	1.55
Other Central American	79	0.07
Cuban	399	0.34
Dominican Republic	58	0.05
Mexican	45,246	39.04
Puerto Rican	1,218	1.05
South American	745	0.64
Argentinean	94	0.08
Bolivian	24	0.02
Chilean	74	0.06
Colombian	232	0.20
Ecuadorian	106	0.09
Paraguayan	3	<0.01
Peruvian	172	0.15
Uruguayan	1	<0.01
Venezuelan	30	0.03
Other South American	9	0.01
Other Hispanic or Latino	3,991	3.44

Race*	Population	%
African-American/Black (19,483)	22,134	19.10
Not Hispanic (18,579)	20,470	17.66
Hispanic (904)	1,664	1.44
American Indian/Alaska Native (1,665)	3,164	2.73
Not Hispanic (754)	1,682	1.45
Hispanic (911)	1,482	1.28
Alaska Athabascan *(Ala. Nat.)* (1)	2	<0.01
Aleut *(Alaska Native)* (1)	2	<0.01
Apache (97)	174	0.15
Arapaho (3)	3	<0.01
Blackfeet (10)	114	0.10
Canadian/French Am. Ind. (5)	19	0.02
Central American Ind. (1)	3	<0.01
Cherokee (87)	417	0.36
Cheyenne (4)	9	0.01
Chickasaw (3)	13	0.01
Chippewa (22)	33	0.03
Choctaw (23)	81	0.07
Colville (4)	4	<0.01
Comanche (4)	14	0.01
Cree (2)	3	<0.01
Creek (7)	26	0.02
Crow (2)	3	<0.01
Delaware (2)	6	0.01
Hopi (3)	4	<0.01
Inupiat *(Alaska Native)* (9)	11	0.01
Iroquois (3)	16	0.01
Kiowa (4)	5	<0.01
Lumbee (5)	7	0.01
Menominee (0)	1	<0.01
Mexican American Ind. (132)	221	0.19
Navajo (83)	116	0.10
Osage (3)	10	0.01
Ottawa (0)	4	<0.01
Paiute (4)	10	0.01
Pima (23)	30	0.03
Potawatomi (4)	5	<0.01
Pueblo (37)	45	0.04
Puget Sound Salish (2)	2	<0.01
Seminole (1)	21	0.02
Shoshone (7)	12	0.01
Sioux (35)	60	0.05
South American Ind. (6)	15	0.01
Spanish American Ind. (11)	19	0.02
Tlingit-Haida *(Alaska Native)* (4)	4	<0.01
Tohono O'Odham (25)	35	0.03
Ute (2)	5	<0.01
Yakama (3)	3	<0.01
Yaqui (22)	48	0.04
Yuman (24)	30	0.03
Asian (4,641)	6,401	5.52
Not Hispanic (4,341)	5,516	4.76
Hispanic (300)	885	0.76
Bangladeshi (15)	16	0.01
Burmese (2)	3	<0.01
Cambodian (164)	208	0.18
Chinese, ex. Taiwanese (366)	560	0.48
Filipino (1,939)	2,680	2.31
Hmong (2)	2	<0.01
Indian (404)	509	0.44
Indonesian (67)	110	0.09
Japanese (212)	541	0.47
Korean (495)	661	0.57
Laotian (30)	44	0.04
Malaysian (12)	19	0.02
Nepalese (10)	12	0.01
Pakistani (39)	61	0.05
Sri Lankan (13)	16	0.01
Taiwanese (49)	63	0.05
Thai (128)	224	0.19
Vietnamese (525)	603	0.52
Hawaii Native/Pacific Islander (489)	1,009	0.87
Not Hispanic (390)	711	0.61
Hispanic (99)	298	0.26
Fijian (7)	7	0.01
Guamanian/Chamorro (147)	237	0.20
Native Hawaiian (91)	254	0.22
Samoan (141)	243	0.21
Tongan (59)	80	0.07
White (56,258)	61,977	53.47
Not Hispanic (32,804)	35,431	30.57
Hispanic (23,454)	26,546	22.90

View Park-Windsor Hills

Place Type: CDP
County: Los Angeles
Population: 11,075†

Ancestry‡	Population	%
African, Sub-Saharan (594)	894	8.30
African (394)	694	6.45
Ethiopian (17)	17	0.16
Ghanaian (13)	13	0.12
Nigerian (137)	137	1.27
Other Sub-Saharan African (33)	33	0.31
American (177)	177	1.64
British (4)	4	0.04
Canadian (23)	23	0.21
English (12)	95	0.88
European (13)	13	0.12
French, ex. Basque (0)	71	0.66
French Canadian (0)	24	0.22
German (10)	88	0.82
Greek (0)	30	0.28
Irish (12)	128	1.19
Italian (30)	63	0.59
Lithuanian (0)	15	0.14
Luxemburger (0)	12	0.11
New Zealander (6)	6	0.06
Russian (14)	14	0.13
Scandinavian (14)	14	0.13
Scotch-Irish (1)	1	0.01
Swedish (0)	18	0.17
West Indian, ex. Hispanic (257)	400	3.71
Haitian (182)	207	1.92
Jamaican (60)	155	1.44
Trinidadian/Tobagonian (0)	23	0.21
West Indian (15)	15	0.14

Hispanic Origin	Population	%
Hispanic or Latino (of any race)	720	6.50
Central American, ex. Mexican	195	1.76
Costa Rican	10	0.09
Guatemalan	42	0.38
Honduran	14	0.13
Nicaraguan	6	0.05
Panamanian	39	0.35
Salvadoran	80	0.72
Other Central American	4	0.04
Cuban	18	0.16
Dominican Republic	6	0.05
Mexican	331	2.99
Puerto Rican	35	0.32
South American	31	0.28
Argentinean	7	0.06
Chilean	2	0.02

*Notes: † The Census 2010 population figure is used to calculate the percentages in the Hispanic Origin and Race categories. Ancestry percentages are based on the 2006-2010 American Community Survey population (not shown); ‡ Numbers in parentheses indicate the number of people reporting a single ancestry; * Numbers in parentheses indicate the number of persons reporting this race alone, not in combination with any other race; Please refer to the Explanation of Data for more information.*

Colombian	6	0.05
Ecuadorian	3	0.03
Peruvian	6	0.05
Uruguayan	3	0.03
Venezuelan	3	0.03
Other South American	1	0.01
Other Hispanic or Latino	104	0.94

Race*	Population	%
African-American/Black (9,392)	9,907	89.45
Not Hispanic (9,209)	9,650	87.13
Hispanic (183)	257	2.32
American Indian/Alaska Native (45)	257	2.32
Not Hispanic (18)	207	1.87
Hispanic (27)	50	0.45
Apache (2)	7	0.06
Blackfeet (2)	14	0.13
Cherokee (2)	39	0.35
Chickasaw (0)	4	0.04
Choctaw (0)	16	0.14
Comanche (1)	4	0.04
Cree (0)	1	0.01
Creek (0)	8	0.07
Hopi (0)	3	0.03
Mexican American Ind. (9)	10	0.09
Navajo (2)	9	0.08
Osage (0)	1	0.01
Potawatomi (0)	1	0.01
Seminole (3)	10	0.09
South American Ind. (4)	5	0.05
Tohono O'Odham (0)	3	0.03
Asian (147)	250	2.26
Not Hispanic (143)	233	2.10
Hispanic (4)	17	0.15
Bangladeshi (6)	6	0.05
Cambodian (2)	2	0.02
Chinese, ex. Taiwanese (15)	39	0.35
Filipino (44)	73	0.66
Indian (9)	16	0.14
Indonesian (1)	1	0.01
Japanese (45)	70	0.63
Korean (10)	24	0.22
Taiwanese (2)	2	0.02
Thai (1)	2	0.02
Vietnamese (3)	5	0.05
Hawaii Native/Pacific Islander (4)	17	0.15
Not Hispanic (4)	17	0.15
Guamanian/Chamorro (1)	6	0.05
Native Hawaiian (1)	3	0.03
Samoan (0)	1	0.01
White (669)	985	8.89
Not Hispanic (463)	726	6.56
Hispanic (206)	259	2.34

Vincent

Place Type: CDP
County: Los Angeles
Population: 15,922†

Ancestry‡	Population	%
Afghan (39)	39	0.24
African, Sub-Saharan (61)	61	0.38
African (35)	35	0.22
Kenyan (14)	14	0.09
Other Sub-Saharan African (12)	12	0.07
American (171)	171	1.06
Arab (0)	5	0.03
Arab (0)	5	0.03
Australian (0)	9	0.06
Czech (17)	17	0.10
Danish (5)	30	0.19
Dutch (75)	115	0.71
Eastern European (16)	16	0.10
English (220)	628	3.88
French, ex. Basque (26)	71	0.44
German (160)	671	4.14
Hungarian (12)	36	0.22
Icelander (0)	12	0.07
Irish (77)	495	3.05
Italian (158)	463	2.86
New Zealander (11)	11	0.07
Norwegian (12)	50	0.31
Polish (21)	90	0.56
Russian (0)	3	0.02
Scotch-Irish (33)	47	0.29
Scottish (8)	88	0.54
Serbian (0)	73	0.45
Swedish (0)	23	0.14
Swiss (0)	7	0.04
Welsh (13)	81	0.50
West Indian, ex. Hispanic (67)	67	0.41
Belizean (67)	67	0.41

Hispanic Origin	Population	%
Hispanic or Latino (of any race)	11,921	74.87
Central American, ex. Mexican	926	5.82
Costa Rican	17	0.11
Guatemalan	210	1.32
Honduran	54	0.34
Nicaraguan	151	0.95
Panamanian	5	0.03
Salvadoran	477	3.00
Other Central American	12	0.08
Cuban	63	0.40
Dominican Republic	4	0.03
Mexican	10,185	63.97
Puerto Rican	83	0.52
South American	190	1.19
Argentinean	48	0.30
Bolivian	5	0.03
Chilean	10	0.06
Colombian	43	0.27
Ecuadorian	26	0.16
Paraguayan	3	0.02
Peruvian	47	0.30
Uruguayan	3	0.02
Venezuelan	3	0.02
Other South American	2	0.01
Other Hispanic or Latino	470	2.95

Race*	Population	%
African-American/Black (312)	405	2.54
Not Hispanic (271)	311	1.95
Hispanic (41)	94	0.59
American Indian/Alaska Native (146)	281	1.76
Not Hispanic (42)	72	0.45
Hispanic (104)	209	1.31
Apache (2)	15	0.09
Arapaho (0)	1	0.01
Blackfeet (1)	2	0.01
Central American Ind. (0)	3	0.02
Cherokee (10)	25	0.16
Chickasaw (1)	2	0.01
Chippewa (6)	9	0.06
Choctaw (3)	6	0.04
Hopi (3)	3	0.02
Mexican American Ind. (10)	18	0.11
Navajo (5)	14	0.09
Ottawa (0)	2	0.01
Pima (6)	6	0.04
Potawatomi (0)	2	0.01
Pueblo (4)	6	0.04
Seminole (0)	1	0.01
Shoshone (1)	5	0.03
Sioux (1)	3	0.02
South American Ind. (1)	1	0.01
Yaqui (3)	7	0.04
Asian (1,128)	1,307	8.21
Not Hispanic (1,082)	1,175	7.38
Hispanic (46)	132	0.83
Burmese (12)	12	0.08
Cambodian (5)	5	0.03
Chinese, ex. Taiwanese (243)	322	2.02
Filipino (496)	587	3.69
Indian (37)	39	0.24
Indonesian (26)	35	0.22
Japanese (56)	94	0.59
Korean (11)	17	0.11
Laotian (10)	14	0.09
Pakistani (7)	7	0.04
Taiwanese (13)	16	0.10
Thai (19)	24	0.15
Vietnamese (118)	173	1.09
Hawaii Native/Pacific Islander (31)	75	0.47
Not Hispanic (24)	51	0.32
Hispanic (7)	24	0.15
Fijian (1)	3	0.02
Guamanian/Chamorro (8)	21	0.13
Native Hawaiian (4)	15	0.09
Samoan (7)	11	0.07
Tongan (1)	2	0.01
White (8,670)	9,311	58.48
Not Hispanic (2,391)	2,516	15.80
Hispanic (6,279)	6,795	42.68

Vineyard

Place Type: CDP
County: Sacramento
Population: 24,836†

Ancestry‡	Population	%
Afghan (102)	102	0.40
African, Sub-Saharan (278)	278	1.10
African (173)	173	0.68
Cape Verdean (10)	10	0.04
Ethiopian (95)	95	0.37
American (429)	429	1.69
Arab (156)	229	0.90
Arab (111)	111	0.44
Egyptian (0)	56	0.22
Lebanese (45)	62	0.24
Armenian (0)	15	0.06
Austrian (0)	11	0.04
British (23)	134	0.53
Canadian (0)	70	0.28
Celtic (15)	15	0.06
Croatian (0)	56	0.22
Czech (0)	178	0.70
Czechoslovakian (32)	32	0.13
Danish (0)	412	1.62
Dutch (131)	376	1.48
Eastern European (11)	11	0.04
English (360)	2,002	7.89
European (309)	324	1.28
Finnish (19)	51	0.20
French, ex. Basque (35)	360	1.42
French Canadian (12)	63	0.25
German (642)	2,439	9.61
Greek (41)	64	0.25
Hungarian (0)	23	0.09
Iranian (44)	44	0.17
Irish (337)	1,959	7.72
Italian (312)	1,136	4.47
Northern European (30)	30	0.12
Norwegian (81)	526	2.07
Pennsylvania German (0)	7	0.03
Polish (72)	153	0.60
Portuguese (91)	413	1.63
Romanian (24)	24	0.09
Russian (69)	125	0.49
Scandinavian (18)	58	0.23
Scotch-Irish (33)	229	0.90
Scottish (129)	410	1.61
Serbian (17)	17	0.07
Slavic (92)	92	0.36
Swedish (37)	293	1.15
Swiss (0)	54	0.21
Ukrainian (20)	34	0.13
Welsh (28)	77	0.30
West Indian, ex. Hispanic (22)	78	0.31
Barbadian (0)	10	0.04
Jamaican (12)	20	0.08
Trinidadian/Tobagonian (10)	39	0.15
West Indian (0)	9	0.04
Yugoslavian (0)	10	0.04

Hispanic Origin	Population	%
Hispanic or Latino (of any race)	4,414	17.77

*Notes: † The Census 2010 population figure is used to calculate the percentages in the Hispanic Origin and Race categories. Ancestry percentages are based on the 2006-2010 American Community Survey population (not shown); ‡ Numbers in parentheses indicate the number of people reporting a single ancestry; * Numbers in parentheses indicate the number of persons reporting this race alone, not in combination with any other race; Please refer to the Explanation of Data for more information.*

Central American, ex. Mexican	256	1.03
Costa Rican	10	0.04
Guatemalan	32	0.13
Honduran	1	<0.01
Nicaraguan	70	0.28
Panamanian	20	0.08
Salvadoran	123	0.50
Cuban	44	0.18
Dominican Republic	2	0.01
Mexican	3,572	14.38
Puerto Rican	128	0.52
South American	76	0.31
Argentinean	8	0.03
Bolivian	2	0.01
Chilean	8	0.03
Colombian	24	0.10
Ecuadorian	1	<0.01
Paraguayan	3	0.01
Peruvian	24	0.10
Venezuelan	6	0.02
Other Hispanic or Latino	336	1.35

Race*	Population	%
African-American/Black (2,426)	2,977	11.99
Not Hispanic (2,345)	2,792	11.24
Hispanic (81)	185	0.74
American Indian/Alaska Native (163)	486	1.96
Not Hispanic (111)	331	1.33
Hispanic (52)	155	0.62
Aleut *(Alaska Native)* (0)	3	0.01
Apache (3)	11	0.04
Blackfeet (3)	24	0.10
Canadian/French Am. Ind. (0)	2	0.01
Cherokee (9)	84	0.34
Cheyenne (0)	2	0.01
Chickasaw (0)	1	<0.01
Chippewa (5)	7	0.03
Choctaw (7)	33	0.13
Cree (0)	1	<0.01
Creek (4)	13	0.05
Iroquois (0)	2	0.01
Kiowa (11)	11	0.04
Lumbee (0)	1	<0.01
Mexican American Ind. (8)	24	0.10
Navajo (7)	8	0.03
Paiute (0)	1	<0.01
Potawatomi (0)	1	<0.01
Pueblo (4)	4	0.02
Seminole (0)	2	0.01
Shoshone (0)	1	<0.01
Sioux (2)	9	0.04
South American Ind. (0)	5	0.02
Spanish American Ind. (1)	1	<0.01
Tlingit-Haida *(Alaska Native)* (0)	1	<0.01
Tohono O'Odham (4)	5	0.02
Yaqui (2)	2	0.01
Yup'ik *(Alaska Native)* (2)	2	0.01
Asian (7,293)	8,262	33.27
Not Hispanic (7,155)	7,918	31.88
Hispanic (138)	344	1.39
Cambodian (40)	54	0.22
Chinese, ex. Taiwanese (926)	1,142	4.60
Filipino (1,361)	1,772	7.13
Hmong (328)	339	1.36
Indian (1,348)	1,508	6.07
Indonesian (3)	7	0.03
Japanese (161)	377	1.52
Korean (234)	315	1.27
Laotian (193)	232	0.93
Malaysian (2)	2	0.01
Pakistani (147)	163	0.66
Sri Lankan (6)	6	0.02
Taiwanese (14)	17	0.07
Thai (12)	33	0.13
Vietnamese (2,225)	2,380	9.58
Hawaii Native/Pacific Islander (256)	443	1.78
Not Hispanic (246)	418	1.68
Hispanic (10)	25	0.10
Fijian (138)	173	0.70
Guamanian/Chamorro (18)	40	0.16
Native Hawaiian (16)	45	0.18
Samoan (26)	41	0.17
Tongan (24)	36	0.14
White (11,306)	12,523	50.42
Not Hispanic (9,277)	10,151	40.87
Hispanic (2,029)	2,372	9.55

Visalia

Place Type: City
County: Tulare
Population: 124,442†

Ancestry‡	Population	%
African, Sub-Saharan (291)	408	0.34
African (91)	208	0.17
Ethiopian (119)	119	0.10
Nigerian (81)	81	0.07
American (4,048)	4,048	3.39
Arab (301)	365	0.31
Arab (18)	46	0.04
Egyptian (10)	10	0.01
Jordanian (34)	34	0.03
Lebanese (134)	161	0.13
Palestinian (58)	58	0.05
Syrian (35)	44	0.04
Other Arab (12)	12	0.01
Armenian (364)	492	0.41
Assyrian/Chaldean/Syriac (71)	71	0.06
Australian (14)	14	0.01
Austrian (19)	88	0.07
Basque (20)	63	0.05
Belgian (5)	20	0.02
Brazilian (6)	6	0.01
British (106)	152	0.13
Bulgarian (18)	18	0.02
Canadian (128)	264	0.22
Celtic (47)	47	0.04
Croatian (16)	35	0.03
Czech (179)	339	0.28
Czechoslovakian (50)	74	0.06
Danish (92)	569	0.48
Dutch (853)	2,016	1.69
Eastern European (43)	51	0.04
English (2,295)	6,494	5.44
European (1,008)	1,098	0.92
Finnish (38)	69	0.06
French, ex. Basque (264)	1,964	1.65
French Canadian (103)	207	0.17
German (3,292)	9,722	8.15
Greek (151)	313	0.26
Hungarian (41)	113	0.09
Iranian (108)	152	0.13
Irish (2,121)	6,968	5.84
Italian (1,199)	3,089	2.59
Latvian (0)	14	0.01
Lithuanian (10)	10	0.01
Northern European (118)	176	0.15
Norwegian (420)	877	0.74
Polish (121)	589	0.49
Portuguese (1,464)	2,411	2.02
Romanian (0)	44	0.04
Russian (119)	307	0.26
Scandinavian (67)	73	0.06
Scotch-Irish (332)	979	0.82
Scottish (414)	1,236	1.04
Serbian (0)	10	0.01
Slovak (0)	38	0.03
Swedish (406)	1,130	0.95
Swiss (46)	296	0.25
Ukrainian (5)	31	0.03
Welsh (59)	350	0.29
West Indian, ex. Hispanic (16)	70	0.06
Dutch West Indian (0)	30	0.03
Haitian (0)	24	0.02
Jamaican (16)	16	0.01
Yugoslavian (10)	85	0.07

Hispanic Origin	Population	%
Hispanic or Latino (of any race)	57,262	46.02
Central American, ex. Mexican	857	0.69
Costa Rican	39	0.03
Guatemalan	190	0.15
Honduran	63	0.05
Nicaraguan	63	0.05
Panamanian	25	0.02
Salvadoran	472	0.38
Other Central American	5	<0.01
Cuban	117	0.09
Dominican Republic	22	0.02
Mexican	52,121	41.88
Puerto Rican	542	0.44
South American	336	0.27
Argentinean	66	0.05
Bolivian	12	0.01
Chilean	30	0.02
Colombian	73	0.06
Ecuadorian	25	0.02
Peruvian	85	0.07
Venezuelan	45	0.04
Other Hispanic or Latino	3,267	2.63

Race*	Population	%
African-American/Black (2,627)	3,627	2.91
Not Hispanic (2,166)	2,764	2.22
Hispanic (461)	863	0.69
American Indian/Alaska Native (1,730)	3,192	2.57
Not Hispanic (811)	1,696	1.36
Hispanic (919)	1,496	1.20
Alaska Athabascan *(Ala. Nat.)* (0)	1	<0.01
Aleut *(Alaska Native)* (1)	1	<0.01
Apache (87)	152	0.12
Arapaho (3)	3	<0.01
Blackfeet (18)	59	0.05
Canadian/French Am. Ind. (5)	7	0.01
Central American Ind. (2)	2	<0.01
Cherokee (174)	526	0.42
Cheyenne (6)	8	0.01
Chickasaw (24)	58	0.05
Chippewa (10)	15	0.01
Choctaw (66)	168	0.14
Comanche (11)	28	0.02
Cree (1)	7	0.01
Creek (18)	33	0.03
Delaware (0)	5	<0.01
Hopi (1)	1	<0.01
Inupiat *(Alaska Native)* (0)	1	<0.01
Iroquois (6)	28	0.02
Lumbee (5)	6	<0.01
Mexican American Ind. (133)	215	0.17
Navajo (41)	76	0.06
Osage (1)	9	0.01
Paiute (25)	33	0.03
Pima (2)	6	<0.01
Potawatomi (23)	31	0.02
Pueblo (2)	4	<0.01
Puget Sound Salish (10)	10	0.01
Seminole (8)	25	0.02
Shoshone (2)	3	<0.01
Sioux (11)	53	0.04
South American Ind. (3)	6	<0.01
Spanish American Ind. (8)	13	0.01
Tlingit-Haida *(Alaska Native)* (1)	2	<0.01
Tohono O'Odham (3)	4	<0.01
Ute (3)	3	<0.01
Yakama (1)	3	<0.01
Yaqui (30)	56	0.05
Yuman (1)	4	<0.01
Yup'ik *(Alaska Native)* (0)	4	<0.01
Asian (6,768)	8,272	6.65
Not Hispanic (6,421)	7,389	5.94
Hispanic (347)	883	0.71
Bangladeshi (5)	5	<0.01
Burmese (33)	41	0.03
Cambodian (49)	70	0.06
Chinese, ex. Taiwanese (607)	812	0.65
Filipino (1,513)	2,116	1.70
Hmong (542)	594	0.48
Indian (658)	743	0.60
Indonesian (9)	21	0.02

*Notes: † The Census 2010 population figure is used to calculate the percentages in the Hispanic Origin and Race categories. Ancestry percentages are based on the 2006-2010 American Community Survey population (not shown); ‡ Numbers in parentheses indicate the number of people reporting a single ancestry; * Numbers in parentheses indicate the number of persons reporting this race alone, not in combination with any other race; Please refer to the Explanation of Data for more information.*

Japanese (317)	569	0.46
Korean (191)	293	0.24
Laotian (1,027)	1,194	0.96
Malaysian (4)	4	<0.01
Nepalese (8)	8	0.01
Pakistani (106)	115	0.09
Sri Lankan (7)	16	0.01
Taiwanese (17)	31	0.02
Thai (1,056)	1,134	0.91
Vietnamese (261)	317	0.25
Hawaii Native/Pacific Islander (164)	469	0.38
Not Hispanic (129)	304	0.24
Hispanic (35)	165	0.13
Fijian (6)	21	0.02
Guamanian/Chamorro (54)	77	0.06
Marshallese (3)	3	<0.01
Native Hawaiian (45)	169	0.14
Samoan (18)	40	0.03
Tongan (6)	7	0.01
White (80,203)	84,982	68.29
Not Hispanic (55,081)	57,171	45.94
Hispanic (25,122)	27,811	22.35

Vista

Place Type: City
County: San Diego
Population: 93,834†

Ancestry‡	Population	%
Afghan (186)	186	0.20
African, Sub-Saharan (142)	241	0.26
African (142)	235	0.25
Sudanese (0)	6	0.01
Albanian (18)	18	0.02
American (1,756)	1,756	1.90
Arab (248)	328	0.35
Arab (85)	85	0.09
Egyptian (77)	77	0.08
Jordanian (6)	6	0.01
Lebanese (32)	83	0.09
Moroccan (12)	24	0.03
Palestinian (26)	26	0.03
Syrian (0)	17	0.02
Other Arab (10)	10	0.01
Armenian (50)	60	0.06
Australian (45)	55	0.06
Austrian (60)	158	0.17
Basque (15)	32	0.03
Belgian (26)	76	0.08
Brazilian (32)	32	0.03
British (199)	402	0.43
Bulgarian (34)	34	0.04
Canadian (80)	160	0.17
Celtic (0)	11	0.01
Croatian (113)	146	0.16
Czech (57)	231	0.25
Czechoslovakian (29)	55	0.06
Danish (197)	504	0.54
Dutch (190)	1,628	1.76
Eastern European (59)	59	0.06
English (3,981)	8,982	9.71
Estonian (16)	16	0.02
European (750)	1,022	1.11
Finnish (76)	371	0.40
French, ex. Basque (385)	2,777	3.00
French Canadian (88)	522	0.56
German (3,264)	10,626	11.49
Greek (175)	493	0.53
Hungarian (70)	252	0.27
Icelander (0)	32	0.03
Iranian (69)	69	0.07
Irish (1,906)	7,670	8.29
Israeli (9)	9	0.01
Italian (1,244)	3,548	3.84
Latvian (24)	30	0.03
Lithuanian (85)	135	0.15
Macedonian (11)	11	0.01
Northern European (47)	67	0.07
Norwegian (244)	992	1.07
Pennsylvania German (0)	9	0.01
Polish (367)	1,090	1.18
Portuguese (83)	339	0.37
Romanian (76)	114	0.12
Russian (198)	388	0.42
Scandinavian (70)	164	0.18
Scotch-Irish (462)	1,235	1.34
Scottish (513)	1,642	1.78
Serbian (103)	142	0.15
Slavic (29)	29	0.03
Slovak (21)	49	0.05
Slovene (0)	13	0.01
Swedish (283)	1,353	1.46
Swiss (48)	211	0.23
Turkish (81)	81	0.09
Ukrainian (45)	96	0.10
Welsh (20)	536	0.58
West Indian, ex. Hispanic (49)	68	0.07
Barbadian (10)	10	0.01
Jamaican (39)	39	0.04
Trinidadian/Tobagonian (0)	19	0.02
Yugoslavian (112)	213	0.23

Hispanic Origin	Population	%
Hispanic or Latino (of any race)	45,380	48.36
Central American, ex. Mexican	768	0.82
Costa Rican	42	0.04
Guatemalan	269	0.29
Honduran	91	0.10
Nicaraguan	45	0.05
Panamanian	65	0.07
Salvadoran	245	0.26
Other Central American	11	0.01
Cuban	131	0.14
Dominican Republic	42	0.04
Mexican	40,799	43.48
Puerto Rican	657	0.70
South American	442	0.47
Argentinean	56	0.06
Bolivian	20	0.02
Chilean	51	0.05
Colombian	134	0.14
Ecuadorian	65	0.07
Peruvian	82	0.09
Uruguayan	4	<0.01
Venezuelan	18	0.02
Other South American	12	0.01
Other Hispanic or Latino	2,541	2.71

Race*	Population	%
African-American/Black (3,137)	4,293	4.58
Not Hispanic (2,753)	3,552	3.79
Hispanic (384)	741	0.79
American Indian/Alaska Native (1,103)	1,958	2.09
Not Hispanic (336)	799	0.85
Hispanic (767)	1,159	1.24
Alaska Athabascan *(Ala. Nat.)* (3)	6	0.01
Aleut *(Alaska Native)* (1)	1	<0.01
Apache (16)	54	0.06
Arapaho (4)	6	0.01
Blackfeet (5)	26	0.03
Central American Ind. (6)	7	0.01
Cherokee (47)	172	0.18
Cheyenne (1)	1	<0.01
Chickasaw (7)	13	0.01
Chippewa (4)	19	0.02
Choctaw (9)	45	0.05
Comanche (1)	2	<0.01
Creek (2)	9	0.01
Delaware (10)	14	0.01
Hopi (4)	7	0.01
Inupiat *(Alaska Native)* (2)	7	0.01
Iroquois (3)	9	0.01
Kiowa (0)	4	<0.01
Menominee (0)	1	<0.01
Mexican American Ind. (224)	308	0.33
Navajo (35)	56	0.06
Osage (3)	6	0.01
Ottawa (0)	1	<0.01
Paiute (0)	2	<0.01
Pima (1)	3	<0.01
Potawatomi (12)	14	0.01
Pueblo (15)	20	0.02
Puget Sound Salish (0)	1	<0.01
Seminole (1)	7	0.01
Sioux (15)	34	0.04
South American Ind. (4)	9	0.01
Spanish American Ind. (26)	32	0.03
Tlingit-Haida *(Alaska Native)* (1)	1	<0.01
Tohono O'Odham (7)	10	0.01
Ute (4)	5	0.01
Yakama (1)	2	<0.01
Yaqui (18)	26	0.03
Yuman (7)	8	0.01
Yup'ik *(Alaska Native)* (1)	2	<0.01
Asian (3,979)	5,717	6.09
Not Hispanic (3,806)	5,148	5.49
Hispanic (173)	569	0.61
Bangladeshi (8)	8	0.01
Burmese (1)	1	<0.01
Cambodian (49)	59	0.06
Chinese, ex. Taiwanese (506)	740	0.79
Filipino (1,343)	2,105	2.24
Hmong (3)	3	<0.01
Indian (289)	356	0.38
Indonesian (10)	47	0.05
Japanese (445)	973	1.04
Korean (343)	456	0.49
Laotian (43)	67	0.07
Malaysian (3)	11	0.01
Nepalese (1)	2	<0.01
Pakistani (21)	25	0.03
Sri Lankan (28)	29	0.03
Taiwanese (31)	35	0.04
Thai (56)	84	0.09
Vietnamese (609)	693	0.74
Hawaii Native/Pacific Islander (677)	1,252	1.33
Not Hispanic (615)	1,013	1.08
Hispanic (62)	239	0.25
Fijian (5)	5	0.01
Guamanian/Chamorro (110)	188	0.20
Native Hawaiian (78)	362	0.39
Samoan (390)	572	0.61
Tongan (3)	11	0.01
White (59,551)	63,675	67.86
Not Hispanic (38,287)	40,368	43.02
Hispanic (21,264)	23,307	24.84

Walnut Creek

Place Type: City
County: Contra Costa
Population: 64,173†

Ancestry‡	Population	%
Afghan (0)	77	0.12
African, Sub-Saharan (172)	208	0.33
African (44)	44	0.07
Cape Verdean (0)	12	0.02
Ethiopian (128)	152	0.24
American (1,266)	1,266	1.98
Arab (492)	713	1.12
Arab (74)	100	0.16
Egyptian (36)	52	0.08
Iraqi (12)	12	0.02
Lebanese (69)	131	0.21
Moroccan (0)	36	0.06
Syrian (43)	115	0.18
Other Arab (258)	267	0.42
Armenian (208)	291	0.46
Assyrian/Chaldean/Syriac (39)	39	0.06
Australian (90)	121	0.19
Austrian (221)	512	0.80
Belgian (59)	111	0.17
Brazilian (47)	47	0.07
British (370)	684	1.07
Bulgarian (114)	114	0.18
Canadian (84)	270	0.42
Celtic (23)	37	0.06
Croatian (60)	136	0.21

*Notes: † The Census 2010 population figure is used to calculate the percentages in the Hispanic Origin and Race categories. Ancestry percentages are based on the 2006-2010 American Community Survey population (not shown); ‡ Numbers in parentheses indicate the number of people reporting a single ancestry; * Numbers in parentheses indicate the number of persons reporting this race alone, not in combination with any other race; Please refer to the Explanation of Data for more information.*

Czech (34)	260	0.41
Czechoslovakian (45)	137	0.21
Danish (146)	613	0.96
Dutch (277)	1,152	1.81
Eastern European (171)	171	0.27
English (2,895)	10,308	16.15
Estonian (0)	33	0.05
European (1,176)	1,316	2.06
Finnish (128)	357	0.56
French, ex. Basque (262)	2,243	3.52
French Canadian (181)	247	0.39
German (2,945)	11,568	18.13
Greek (212)	372	0.58
Guyanese (19)	19	0.03
Hungarian (106)	463	0.73
Icelander (0)	17	0.03
Iranian (917)	1,013	1.59
Irish (2,437)	8,805	13.80
Israeli (67)	67	0.11
Italian (1,553)	4,697	7.36
Latvian (80)	155	0.24
Lithuanian (131)	310	0.49
Luxemburger (16)	16	0.03
Maltese (47)	54	0.08
New Zealander (0)	11	0.02
Northern European (382)	409	0.64
Norwegian (400)	1,356	2.13
Polish (660)	1,693	2.65
Portuguese (440)	1,058	1.66
Romanian (61)	144	0.23
Russian (1,356)	2,317	3.63
Scandinavian (130)	218	0.34
Scotch-Irish (492)	1,286	2.02
Scottish (461)	2,364	3.70
Serbian (68)	82	0.13
Slavic (0)	10	0.02
Slovak (30)	60	0.09
Slovene (24)	24	0.04
Swedish (488)	1,765	2.77
Swiss (98)	484	0.76
Turkish (78)	113	0.18
Ukrainian (368)	529	0.83
Welsh (24)	501	0.79
West Indian, ex. Hispanic (0)	24	0.04
Barbadian (0)	24	0.04
Yugoslavian (91)	133	0.21

Hispanic Origin	Population	%
Hispanic or Latino (of any race)	5,540	8.63
Central American, ex. Mexican	646	1.01
Costa Rican	29	0.05
Guatemalan	99	0.15
Honduran	25	0.04
Nicaraguan	155	0.24
Panamanian	43	0.07
Salvadoran	282	0.44
Other Central American	13	0.02
Cuban	98	0.15
Dominican Republic	18	0.03
Mexican	3,108	4.84
Puerto Rican	217	0.34
South American	810	1.26
Argentinean	105	0.16
Bolivian	35	0.05
Chilean	86	0.13
Colombian	159	0.25
Ecuadorian	40	0.06
Paraguayan	15	0.02
Peruvian	315	0.49
Uruguayan	19	0.03
Venezuelan	31	0.05
Other South American	5	0.01
Other Hispanic or Latino	643	1.00

Race*	Population	%
African-American/Black (1,035)	1,477	2.30
Not Hispanic (996)	1,349	2.10
Hispanic (39)	128	0.20
American Indian/Alaska Native (155)	582	0.91
Not Hispanic (99)	413	0.64
Hispanic (56)	169	0.26
Alaska Athabascan *(Ala. Nat.)* (1)	1	<0.01
Aleut *(Alaska Native)* (0)	2	<0.01
Apache (1)	12	0.02
Blackfeet (0)	6	0.01
Central American Ind. (0)	1	<0.01
Cherokee (19)	114	0.18
Cheyenne (0)	3	<0.01
Chickasaw (2)	5	0.01
Chippewa (1)	18	0.03
Choctaw (9)	24	0.04
Colville (0)	2	<0.01
Comanche (0)	6	0.01
Cree (0)	1	<0.01
Creek (4)	12	0.02
Crow (0)	4	0.01
Delaware (1)	2	<0.01
Hopi (0)	3	<0.01
Houma (1)	1	<0.01
Inupiat *(Alaska Native)* (1)	3	<0.01
Iroquois (3)	8	0.01
Lumbee (1)	1	<0.01
Mexican American Ind. (13)	28	0.04
Navajo (1)	9	0.01
Osage (0)	1	<0.01
Ottawa (1)	1	<0.01
Pima (1)	2	<0.01
Potawatomi (1)	2	<0.01
Pueblo (2)	3	<0.01
Seminole (0)	1	<0.01
Sioux (4)	17	0.03
South American Ind. (5)	12	0.02
Spanish American Ind. (2)	3	<0.01
Tlingit-Haida *(Alaska Native)* (2)	3	<0.01
Tsimshian *(Alaska Native)* (1)	1	<0.01
Yaqui (0)	3	<0.01
Asian (8,027)	9,707	15.13
Not Hispanic (7,954)	9,499	14.80
Hispanic (73)	208	0.32
Bangladeshi (10)	10	0.02
Burmese (17)	23	0.04
Cambodian (12)	21	0.03
Chinese, ex. Taiwanese (2,891)	3,426	5.34
Filipino (1,420)	1,875	2.92
Indian (1,143)	1,257	1.96
Indonesian (33)	59	0.09
Japanese (733)	1,162	1.81
Korean (835)	976	1.52
Laotian (13)	17	0.03
Malaysian (9)	11	0.02
Nepalese (6)	6	0.01
Pakistani (85)	108	0.17
Sri Lankan (21)	23	0.04
Taiwanese (210)	249	0.39
Thai (66)	86	0.13
Vietnamese (159)	212	0.33
Hawaii Native/Pacific Islander (125)	288	0.45
Not Hispanic (114)	248	0.39
Hispanic (11)	40	0.06
Fijian (13)	16	0.02
Guamanian/Chamorro (22)	47	0.07
Native Hawaiian (21)	100	0.16
Samoan (15)	19	0.03
Tongan (35)	46	0.07
White (50,487)	52,951	82.51
Not Hispanic (47,170)	49,141	76.58
Hispanic (3,317)	3,810	5.94

Walnut Park

Place Type: CDP
County: Los Angeles
Population: 15,966[†]

Ancestry[‡]	Population	%
American (382)	382	2.29
Armenian (8)	8	0.05
English (32)	85	0.51
French, ex. Basque (0)	65	0.39
German (37)	48	0.29
Greek (7)	7	0.04
Irish (7)	22	0.13
Portuguese (9)	9	0.05
Scotch-Irish (12)	12	0.07

Hispanic Origin	Population	%
Hispanic or Latino (of any race)	15,543	97.35
Central American, ex. Mexican	1,461	9.15
Costa Rican	13	0.08
Guatemalan	385	2.41
Honduran	69	0.43
Nicaraguan	103	0.65
Salvadoran	879	5.51
Other Central American	12	0.08
Cuban	108	0.68
Dominican Republic	4	0.03
Mexican	13,139	82.29
Puerto Rican	59	0.37
South American	144	0.90
Argentinean	7	0.04
Bolivian	1	0.01
Chilean	2	0.01
Colombian	54	0.34
Ecuadorian	31	0.19
Peruvian	46	0.29
Uruguayan	2	0.01
Venezuelan	1	0.01
Other Hispanic or Latino	628	3.93

Race*	Population	%
African-American/Black (70)	108	0.68
Not Hispanic (27)	29	0.18
Hispanic (43)	79	0.49
American Indian/Alaska Native (277)	333	2.09
Not Hispanic (15)	15	0.09
Hispanic (262)	318	1.99
Apache (3)	5	0.03
Canadian/French Am. Ind. (0)	3	0.02
Central American Ind. (1)	1	0.01
Cherokee (1)	1	0.01
Creek (1)	2	0.01
Kiowa (1)	1	0.01
Mexican American Ind. (116)	116	0.73
Navajo (5)	7	0.04
Seminole (0)	1	0.01
Spanish American Ind. (1)	1	0.01
Yaqui (4)	4	0.03
Asian (89)	132	0.83
Not Hispanic (74)	81	0.51
Hispanic (15)	51	0.32
Cambodian (1)	1	0.01
Chinese, ex. Taiwanese (15)	18	0.11
Filipino (59)	72	0.45
Indian (0)	1	0.01
Japanese (1)	9	0.06
Korean (2)	4	0.03
Taiwanese (1)	1	0.01
Thai (4)	4	0.03
Hawaii Native/Pacific Islander (2)	20	0.13
Not Hispanic (2)	3	0.02
Hispanic (0)	17	0.11
Guamanian/Chamorro (0)	1	0.01
Native Hawaiian (1)	7	0.04
Tongan (1)	3	0.02
White (9,046)	9,477	59.36
Not Hispanic (268)	281	1.76
Hispanic (8,778)	9,196	57.60

Walnut

Place Type: City
County: Los Angeles
Population: 29,172[†]

Ancestry[‡]	Population	%
African, Sub-Saharan (40)	40	0.14
African (35)	35	0.12
Other Sub-Saharan African (5)	5	0.02
American (331)	331	1.13
Arab (315)	371	1.27

*Notes: † The Census 2010 population figure is used to calculate the percentages in the Hispanic Origin and Race categories. Ancestry percentages are based on the 2006-2010 American Community Survey population (not shown); ‡ Numbers in parentheses indicate the number of people reporting a single ancestry; * Numbers in parentheses indicate the number of persons reporting this race alone, not in combination with any other race; Please refer to the Explanation of Data for more information.*

SECTION TWO

Ancestry (continued)	Population	%
Arab (38)	62	0.21
Egyptian (194)	194	0.66
Lebanese (31)	31	0.11
Syrian (0)	32	0.11
Other Arab (52)	52	0.18
Armenian (84)	84	0.29
Austrian (0)	20	0.07
Belgian (0)	47	0.16
British (45)	59	0.20
Canadian (24)	24	0.08
Czech (11)	36	0.12
Dutch (0)	69	0.24
Eastern European (34)	34	0.12
English (183)	634	2.16
European (21)	54	0.18
French, ex. Basque (45)	203	0.69
French Canadian (0)	42	0.14
German (319)	804	2.74
Greek (12)	12	0.04
Guyanese (6)	6	0.02
Hungarian (9)	87	0.30
Iranian (152)	152	0.52
Irish (159)	598	2.04
Israeli (12)	12	0.04
Italian (216)	347	1.18
Lithuanian (9)	20	0.07
Northern European (23)	23	0.08
Norwegian (37)	37	0.13
Polish (48)	172	0.59
Portuguese (10)	20	0.07
Romanian (12)	12	0.04
Russian (8)	66	0.23
Scandinavian (0)	11	0.04
Scotch-Irish (57)	112	0.38
Scottish (63)	149	0.51
Slavic (22)	22	0.08
Slovak (9)	9	0.03
Swedish (24)	119	0.41
Swiss (0)	23	0.08
Ukrainian (0)	12	0.04
Welsh (10)	51	0.17
West Indian, ex. Hispanic (29)	41	0.14
Belizean (6)	6	0.02
British West Indian (11)	11	0.04
West Indian (12)	12	0.04
Other West Indian (0)	12	0.04

Hispanic Origin	Population	%
Hispanic or Latino (of any race)	5,575	19.11
Central American, ex. Mexican	324	1.11
Costa Rican	32	0.11
Guatemalan	63	0.22
Honduran	16	0.05
Nicaraguan	52	0.18
Panamanian	7	0.02
Salvadoran	152	0.52
Other Central American	2	0.01
Cuban	109	0.37
Dominican Republic	3	0.01
Mexican	4,471	15.33
Puerto Rican	78	0.27
South American	309	1.06
Argentinean	35	0.12
Bolivian	11	0.04
Chilean	37	0.13
Colombian	62	0.21
Ecuadorian	60	0.21
Paraguayan	3	0.01
Peruvian	98	0.34
Uruguayan	1	<0.01
Other South American	2	0.01
Other Hispanic or Latino	281	0.96

Race*	Population	%
African-American/Black (824)	954	3.27
Not Hispanic (786)	868	2.98
Hispanic (38)	86	0.29
American Indian/Alaska Native (69)	168	0.58
Not Hispanic (29)	94	0.32
Hispanic (40)	74	0.25
Apache (5)	8	0.03
Blackfeet (0)	3	0.01
Cherokee (1)	21	0.07
Iroquois (1)	5	0.02
Mexican American Ind. (8)	11	0.04
Navajo (1)	3	0.01
Pima (1)	3	0.01
Pueblo (3)	3	0.01
Sioux (3)	10	0.03
South American Ind. (2)	2	0.01
Spanish American Ind. (1)	1	<0.01
Yaqui (8)	8	0.03
Yuman (0)	3	0.01
Asian (18,567)	19,258	66.02
Not Hispanic (18,445)	18,976	65.05
Hispanic (122)	282	0.97
Bangladeshi (13)	14	0.05
Burmese (100)	119	0.41
Cambodian (54)	77	0.26
Chinese, ex. Taiwanese (8,509)	9,242	31.68
Filipino (3,885)	4,216	14.45
Indian (547)	619	2.12
Indonesian (200)	280	0.96
Japanese (534)	709	2.43
Korean (1,105)	1,171	4.01
Laotian (45)	62	0.21
Malaysian (18)	37	0.13
Nepalese (1)	2	0.01
Pakistani (215)	229	0.78
Sri Lankan (26)	29	0.10
Taiwanese (1,803)	2,064	7.08
Thai (247)	294	1.01
Vietnamese (529)	647	2.22
Hawaii Native/Pacific Islander (28)	152	0.52
Not Hispanic (28)	142	0.49
Hispanic (0)	10	0.03
Fijian (1)	1	<0.01
Guamanian/Chamorro (1)	13	0.04
Marshallese (1)	5	0.02
Native Hawaiian (10)	33	0.11
Samoan (10)	16	0.05
Tongan (5)	6	0.02
White (6,913)	7,630	26.16
Not Hispanic (3,645)	4,067	13.94
Hispanic (3,268)	3,563	12.21

Wasco

Place Type: City
County: Kern
Population: 25,545†

Ancestry‡	Population	%
Afghan (8)	8	0.03
African, Sub-Saharan (36)	36	0.14
African (28)	28	0.11
Ethiopian (8)	8	0.03
American (291)	291	1.16
Arab (16)	25	0.10
Moroccan (8)	8	0.03
Syrian (0)	9	0.04
Other Arab (8)	8	0.03
Armenian (8)	8	0.03
Australian (0)	8	0.03
Belgian (0)	9	0.04
British (0)	10	0.04
Bulgarian (8)	8	0.03
Canadian (0)	9	0.04
Celtic (0)	7	0.03
Czech (0)	18	0.07
Danish (15)	23	0.09
Dutch (39)	116	0.46
English (223)	504	2.00
European (88)	88	0.35
French, ex. Basque (23)	149	0.59
French Canadian (0)	26	0.10
German (214)	1,056	4.20
Greek (0)	33	0.13
Guyanese (9)	9	0.04
Hungarian (0)	8	0.03
Iranian (8)	8	0.03
Irish (173)	763	3.03
Italian (101)	241	0.96
Lithuanian (0)	11	0.04
Luxemburger (8)	8	0.03
New Zealander (7)	7	0.03
Norwegian (24)	74	0.29
Polish (23)	31	0.12
Portuguese (0)	12	0.05
Russian (55)	80	0.32
Scotch-Irish (16)	56	0.22
Scottish (56)	289	1.15
Swedish (37)	53	0.21
Swiss (0)	9	0.04
Turkish (8)	8	0.03
Welsh (8)	117	0.47
West Indian, ex. Hispanic (34)	42	0.17
Belizean (16)	16	0.06
Jamaican (8)	8	0.03
West Indian (10)	18	0.07
Yugoslavian (0)	10	0.04

Hispanic Origin	Population	%
Hispanic or Latino (of any race)	19,585	76.67
Central American, ex. Mexican	285	1.12
Guatemalan	51	0.20
Honduran	23	0.09
Nicaraguan	3	0.01
Panamanian	1	<0.01
Salvadoran	206	0.81
Other Central American	1	<0.01
Cuban	9	0.04
Mexican	17,814	69.74
Puerto Rican	158	0.62
South American	12	0.05
Argentinean	2	0.01
Chilean	6	0.02
Peruvian	4	0.02
Other Hispanic or Latino	1,307	5.12

Race*	Population	%
African-American/Black (1,951)	2,072	8.11
Not Hispanic (1,802)	1,847	7.23
Hispanic (149)	225	0.88
American Indian/Alaska Native (283)	413	1.62
Not Hispanic (105)	151	0.59
Hispanic (178)	262	1.03
Aleut *(Alaska Native)* (0)	1	<0.01
Apache (3)	4	0.02
Blackfeet (1)	1	<0.01
Central American Ind. (1)	1	<0.01
Cherokee (15)	37	0.14
Chickasaw (1)	1	<0.01
Chippewa (4)	4	0.02
Choctaw (13)	27	0.11
Comanche (0)	1	<0.01
Cree (0)	4	0.02
Creek (2)	2	0.01
Mexican American Ind. (44)	60	0.23
Navajo (1)	3	0.01
Pima (0)	7	0.03
Puget Sound Salish (4)	4	0.02
Shoshone (1)	1	<0.01
South American Ind. (0)	1	<0.01
Tlingit-Haida *(Alaska Native)* (1)	3	0.01
Yaqui (3)	8	0.03
Asian (180)	257	1.01
Not Hispanic (162)	193	0.76
Hispanic (18)	64	0.25
Burmese (2)	2	0.01
Cambodian (5)	14	0.05
Chinese, ex. Taiwanese (25)	26	0.10
Filipino (42)	84	0.33
Indian (37)	46	0.18
Indonesian (0)	2	0.01
Japanese (8)	11	0.04
Korean (5)	5	0.02
Pakistani (0)	4	0.02
Taiwanese (1)	2	0.01
Thai (1)	2	0.01

*Notes: † The Census 2010 population figure is used to calculate the percentages in the Hispanic Origin and Race categories. Ancestry percentages are based on the 2006-2010 American Community Survey population (not shown); ‡ Numbers in parentheses indicate the number of people reporting a single ancestry; * Numbers in parentheses indicate the number of persons reporting this race alone, not in combination with any other race; Please refer to the Explanation of Data for more information.*

Vietnamese (12)	17	0.07
Hawaii Native/Pacific Islander (12)	31	0.12
Not Hispanic (7)	12	0.05
Hispanic (5)	19	0.07
Guamanian/Chamorro (4)	8	0.03
Native Hawaiian (0)	1	<0.01
Samoan (0)	3	0.01
Tongan (5)	6	0.02
White (12,579)	13,298	52.06
Not Hispanic (3,689)	3,792	14.84
Hispanic (8,890)	9,506	37.21

Waterford

Place Type: City
County: Stanislaus
Population: 8,456†

Ancestry‡	Population	%
African, Sub-Saharan (11)	11	0.13
Ethiopian (11)	11	0.13
American (260)	260	3.13
British (9)	9	0.11
Canadian (0)	9	0.11
Croatian (0)	8	0.10
Czech (0)	11	0.13
Czechoslovakian (0)	20	0.24
Danish (6)	46	0.55
Dutch (16)	155	1.86
English (163)	492	5.92
European (61)	79	0.95
Finnish (0)	18	0.22
French, ex. Basque (9)	125	1.50
French Canadian (7)	32	0.38
German (128)	787	9.46
Greek (0)	55	0.66
Irish (403)	1,161	13.96
Italian (321)	594	7.14
Norwegian (9)	29	0.35
Polish (0)	20	0.24
Portuguese (145)	271	3.26
Russian (0)	20	0.24
Scandinavian (8)	25	0.30
Scotch-Irish (40)	53	0.64
Scottish (46)	179	2.15
Slavic (0)	10	0.12
Swedish (30)	114	1.37
Swiss (0)	90	1.08
Welsh (8)	19	0.23
Yugoslavian (10)	60	0.72

Hispanic Origin	Population	%
Hispanic or Latino (of any race)	3,579	42.32
Central American, ex. Mexican	32	0.38
Guatemalan	8	0.09
Honduran	7	0.08
Nicaraguan	2	0.02
Salvadoran	15	0.18
Cuban	5	0.06
Dominican Republic	2	0.02
Mexican	3,245	38.38
Puerto Rican	56	0.66
South American	14	0.17
Argentinean	3	0.04
Chilean	1	0.01
Colombian	2	0.02
Peruvian	7	0.08
Uruguayan	1	0.01
Other Hispanic or Latino	225	2.66

Race*	Population	%
African-American/Black (77)	120	1.42
Not Hispanic (68)	95	1.12
Hispanic (9)	25	0.30
American Indian/Alaska Native (110)	258	3.05
Not Hispanic (56)	148	1.75
Hispanic (54)	110	1.30
Apache (4)	10	0.12
Blackfeet (0)	3	0.04
Cherokee (19)	56	0.66
Chickasaw (4)	5	0.06
Chippewa (0)	2	0.02
Choctaw (5)	11	0.13
Cree (0)	1	0.01
Iroquois (0)	2	0.02
Mexican American Ind. (3)	10	0.12
Navajo (2)	2	0.02
Osage (1)	4	0.05
Ottawa (1)	1	0.01
Paiute (4)	4	0.05
Pueblo (5)	5	0.06
Sioux (4)	8	0.09
Asian (129)	209	2.47
Not Hispanic (117)	179	2.12
Hispanic (12)	30	0.35
Cambodian (5)	5	0.06
Chinese, ex. Taiwanese (21)	30	0.35
Filipino (34)	69	0.82
Indian (24)	30	0.35
Indonesian (3)	5	0.06
Japanese (9)	19	0.22
Korean (6)	14	0.17
Laotian (3)	5	0.06
Pakistani (0)	3	0.04
Taiwanese (5)	7	0.08
Thai (1)	1	0.01
Vietnamese (4)	7	0.08
Hawaii Native/Pacific Islander (11)	37	0.44
Not Hispanic (10)	27	0.32
Hispanic (1)	10	0.12
Fijian (3)	4	0.05
Guamanian/Chamorro (1)	5	0.06
Native Hawaiian (4)	19	0.22
Samoan (3)	8	0.09
White (6,003)	6,368	75.31
Not Hispanic (4,428)	4,615	54.58
Hispanic (1,575)	1,753	20.73

Watsonville

Place Type: City
County: Santa Cruz
Population: 51,199†

Ancestry‡	Population	%
Afghan (14)	27	0.05
African, Sub-Saharan (44)	44	0.09
African (44)	44	0.09
American (302)	302	0.61
Arab (34)	54	0.11
Arab (0)	10	0.02
Lebanese (0)	10	0.02
Palestinian (34)	34	0.07
Australian (11)	11	0.02
Belgian (18)	47	0.09
Brazilian (8)	8	0.02
British (10)	76	0.15
Cajun (35)	35	0.07
Canadian (28)	28	0.06
Celtic (36)	36	0.07
Croatian (119)	185	0.37
Czech (12)	75	0.15
Czechoslovakian (29)	98	0.20
Danish (24)	77	0.16
Dutch (0)	108	0.22
English (371)	1,157	2.33
Estonian (12)	12	0.02
European (136)	252	0.51
Finnish (22)	22	0.04
French, ex. Basque (90)	512	1.03
French Canadian (68)	147	0.30
German (551)	1,843	3.72
Greek (13)	75	0.15
Hungarian (0)	16	0.03
Icelander (0)	6	0.01
Iranian (25)	47	0.09
Irish (274)	1,552	3.13
Italian (350)	956	1.93
New Zealander (45)	45	0.09
Northern European (0)	21	0.04
Norwegian (163)	214	0.43
Polish (25)	178	0.36
Portuguese (551)	730	1.47
Russian (88)	217	0.44
Scotch-Irish (74)	168	0.34
Scottish (30)	148	0.30
Slavic (35)	35	0.07
Slovak (0)	9	0.02
Swedish (62)	208	0.42
Swiss (0)	41	0.08
Welsh (35)	45	0.09

Hispanic Origin	Population	%
Hispanic or Latino (of any race)	41,656	81.36
Central American, ex. Mexican	361	0.71
Costa Rican	5	0.01
Guatemalan	50	0.10
Honduran	21	0.04
Nicaraguan	16	0.03
Panamanian	6	0.01
Salvadoran	256	0.50
Other Central American	7	0.01
Cuban	18	0.04
Dominican Republic	3	0.01
Mexican	39,083	76.34
Puerto Rican	84	0.16
South American	113	0.22
Argentinean	27	0.05
Bolivian	5	0.01
Chilean	7	0.01
Colombian	18	0.04
Ecuadorian	11	0.02
Paraguayan	1	<0.01
Peruvian	43	0.08
Venezuelan	1	<0.01
Other Hispanic or Latino	1,994	3.89

Race*	Population	%
African-American/Black (358)	607	1.19
Not Hispanic (200)	325	0.63
Hispanic (158)	282	0.55
American Indian/Alaska Native (629)	1,066	2.08
Not Hispanic (139)	330	0.64
Hispanic (490)	736	1.44
Apache (27)	42	0.08
Blackfeet (4)	15	0.03
Central American Ind. (2)	5	0.01
Cherokee (21)	71	0.14
Chickasaw (0)	1	<0.01
Chippewa (2)	6	0.01
Choctaw (6)	17	0.03
Comanche (5)	11	0.02
Cree (1)	2	<0.01
Creek (3)	7	0.01
Delaware (0)	1	<0.01
Hopi (7)	12	0.02
Inupiat *(Alaska Native)* (0)	1	<0.01
Iroquois (1)	2	<0.01
Mexican American Ind. (169)	233	0.46
Navajo (6)	18	0.04
Pima (1)	1	<0.01
Potawatomi (1)	3	0.01
Pueblo (11)	12	0.02
Seminole (0)	1	<0.01
Shoshone (1)	8	0.02
Sioux (3)	5	0.01
South American Ind. (3)	4	0.01
Spanish American Ind. (6)	13	0.03
Tlingit-Haida *(Alaska Native)* (0)	5	0.01
Tohono O'Odham (0)	1	<0.01
Yaqui (9)	16	0.03
Yuman (1)	1	<0.01
Yup'ik *(Alaska Native)* (1)	1	<0.01
Asian (1,664)	2,166	4.23
Not Hispanic (1,549)	1,769	3.46
Hispanic (115)	397	0.78
Burmese (5)	5	0.01
Cambodian (7)	8	0.02
Chinese, ex. Taiwanese (201)	247	0.48
Filipino (827)	1,140	2.23

*Notes: † The Census 2010 population figure is used to calculate the percentages in the Hispanic Origin and Race categories. Ancestry percentages are based on the 2006-2010 American Community Survey population (not shown); ‡ Numbers in parentheses indicate the number of people reporting a single ancestry; * Numbers in parentheses indicate the number of persons reporting this race alone, not in combination with any other race; Please refer to the Explanation of Data for more information.*

Hmong (1)	1	<0.01
Indian (104)	133	0.26
Indonesian (1)	4	0.01
Japanese (389)	487	0.95
Korean (45)	62	0.12
Laotian (2)	4	0.01
Pakistani (5)	6	0.01
Sri Lankan (2)	2	<0.01
Taiwanese (9)	11	0.02
Thai (5)	13	0.03
Vietnamese (22)	27	0.05
Hawaii Native/Pacific Islander (40)	155	0.30
Not Hispanic (22)	69	0.13
Hispanic (18)	86	0.17
Fijian (0)	2	<0.01
Guamanian/Chamorro (5)	10	0.02
Native Hawaiian (26)	87	0.17
Samoan (8)	17	0.03
White (22,399)	24,243	47.35
Not Hispanic (7,038)	7,468	14.59
Hispanic (15,361)	16,775	32.76

West Athens

Place Type: CDP
County: Los Angeles
Population: 8,729†

Ancestry‡	Population	%
African, Sub-Saharan (474)	499	6.01
African (426)	451	5.43
Ethiopian (16)	16	0.19
Ghanaian (32)	32	0.39
English (14)	37	0.45
German (0)	23	0.28
Irish (0)	26	0.31
Polish (56)	56	0.67

Hispanic Origin	Population	%
Hispanic or Latino (of any race)	3,843	44.03
Central American, ex. Mexican	566	6.48
Costa Rican	1	0.01
Guatemalan	235	2.69
Honduran	32	0.37
Nicaraguan	28	0.32
Panamanian	10	0.11
Salvadoran	245	2.81
Other Central American	15	0.17
Cuban	7	0.08
Dominican Republic	1	0.01
Mexican	2,968	34.00
Puerto Rican	35	0.40
South American	26	0.30
Argentinean	3	0.03
Colombian	3	0.03
Ecuadorian	15	0.17
Peruvian	5	0.06
Other Hispanic or Latino	240	2.75

Race*	Population	%
African-American/Black (4,578)	4,726	54.14
Not Hispanic (4,492)	4,588	52.56
Hispanic (86)	138	1.58
American Indian/Alaska Native (31)	91	1.04
Not Hispanic (8)	43	0.49
Hispanic (23)	48	0.55
Blackfeet (0)	2	0.02
Central American Ind. (4)	4	0.05
Cherokee (0)	4	0.05
Chickasaw (0)	3	0.03
Choctaw (0)	3	0.03
Mexican American Ind. (8)	8	0.09
Sioux (1)	1	0.01
Asian (111)	143	1.64
Not Hispanic (104)	126	1.44
Hispanic (7)	17	0.19
Chinese, ex. Taiwanese (27)	29	0.33
Filipino (41)	49	0.56
Japanese (32)	46	0.53
Korean (6)	8	0.09
Thai (4)	4	0.05
Vietnamese (1)	1	0.01
Hawaii Native/Pacific Islander (10)	18	0.21
Not Hispanic (6)	11	0.13
Hispanic (4)	7	0.08
Fijian (1)	1	0.01
Guamanian/Chamorro (3)	4	0.05
Native Hawaiian (1)	4	0.05
Samoan (5)	6	0.07
Tongan (0)	1	0.01
White (1,584)	1,773	20.31
Not Hispanic (116)	170	1.95
Hispanic (1,468)	1,603	18.36

West Carson

Place Type: CDP
County: Los Angeles
Population: 21,699†

Ancestry‡	Population	%
African, Sub-Saharan (673)	743	3.55
African (673)	743	3.55
American (456)	456	2.18
Arab (56)	115	0.55
Egyptian (36)	36	0.17
Lebanese (20)	64	0.31
Palestinian (0)	15	0.07
Armenian (12)	23	0.11
Austrian (17)	37	0.18
British (67)	125	0.60
Canadian (56)	92	0.44
Croatian (21)	28	0.13
Czech (8)	8	0.04
Danish (0)	49	0.23
Dutch (23)	157	0.75
English (156)	641	3.06
European (36)	112	0.53
French, ex. Basque (111)	308	1.47
French Canadian (9)	31	0.15
German (639)	1,437	6.86
Greek (23)	23	0.11
Hungarian (16)	41	0.20
Iranian (34)	34	0.16
Irish (245)	661	3.16
Italian (147)	351	1.68
Lithuanian (76)	99	0.47
New Zealander (0)	13	0.06
Norwegian (7)	49	0.23
Polish (58)	106	0.51
Portuguese (16)	82	0.39
Romanian (15)	15	0.07
Russian (78)	104	0.50
Scandinavian (0)	23	0.11
Scotch-Irish (23)	254	1.21
Scottish (68)	122	0.58
Slavic (4)	4	0.02
Swedish (30)	87	0.42
Welsh (7)	13	0.06
West Indian, ex. Hispanic (35)	35	0.17
West Indian (35)	35	0.17

Hispanic Origin	Population	%
Hispanic or Latino (of any race)	7,100	32.72
Central American, ex. Mexican	587	2.71
Costa Rican	17	0.08
Guatemalan	188	0.87
Honduran	41	0.19
Nicaraguan	58	0.27
Panamanian	18	0.08
Salvadoran	262	1.21
Other Central American	3	0.01
Cuban	128	0.59
Dominican Republic	6	0.03
Mexican	5,332	24.57
Puerto Rican	133	0.61
South American	313	1.44
Argentinean	53	0.24
Bolivian	5	0.02
Chilean	24	0.11
Colombian	52	0.24
Ecuadorian	65	0.30
Paraguayan	5	0.02
Peruvian	96	0.44
Uruguayan	5	0.02
Venezuelan	3	0.01
Other South American	5	0.02
Other Hispanic or Latino	601	2.77

Race*	Population	%
African-American/Black (2,330)	2,564	11.82
Not Hispanic (2,263)	2,421	11.16
Hispanic (67)	143	0.66
American Indian/Alaska Native (185)	325	1.50
Not Hispanic (79)	155	0.71
Hispanic (106)	170	0.78
Apache (15)	21	0.10
Blackfeet (3)	4	0.02
Cherokee (4)	28	0.13
Chickasaw (1)	4	0.02
Choctaw (4)	4	0.02
Creek (4)	7	0.03
Hopi (0)	2	0.01
Inupiat *(Alaska Native)* (1)	1	<0.01
Iroquois (0)	2	0.01
Mexican American Ind. (22)	26	0.12
Navajo (8)	24	0.11
Osage (0)	1	<0.01
Ottawa (1)	1	<0.01
Paiute (0)	2	0.01
Pima (0)	3	0.01
Pueblo (3)	6	0.03
Seminole (1)	5	0.02
Shoshone (2)	2	0.01
Sioux (0)	7	0.03
South American Ind. (0)	1	<0.01
Spanish American Ind. (3)	3	0.01
Tlingit-Haida *(Alaska Native)* (2)	2	0.01
Ute (1)	1	<0.01
Yakama (1)	1	<0.01
Yaqui (1)	8	0.04
Asian (6,730)	7,304	33.66
Not Hispanic (6,629)	7,083	32.64
Hispanic (101)	221	1.02
Bangladeshi (9)	9	0.04
Burmese (8)	10	0.05
Cambodian (32)	35	0.16
Chinese, ex. Taiwanese (447)	594	2.74
Filipino (3,205)	3,564	16.42
Indian (153)	186	0.86
Indonesian (22)	46	0.21
Japanese (915)	1,090	5.02
Korean (1,308)	1,350	6.22
Laotian (0)	2	0.01
Malaysian (5)	7	0.03
Nepalese (17)	17	0.08
Pakistani (27)	30	0.14
Sri Lankan (28)	32	0.15
Taiwanese (65)	76	0.35
Thai (44)	55	0.25
Vietnamese (242)	292	1.35
Hawaii Native/Pacific Islander (301)	444	2.05
Not Hispanic (288)	405	1.87
Hispanic (13)	39	0.18
Fijian (2)	5	0.02
Guamanian/Chamorro (11)	27	0.12
Native Hawaiian (34)	98	0.45
Samoan (226)	293	1.35
Tongan (3)	12	0.06
White (7,630)	8,448	38.93
Not Hispanic (4,637)	5,063	23.33
Hispanic (2,993)	3,385	15.60

West Covina

Place Type: City
County: Los Angeles
Population: 106,098†

*Notes: † The Census 2010 population figure is used to calculate the percentages in the Hispanic Origin and Race categories. Ancestry percentages are based on the 2006-2010 American Community Survey population (not shown); ‡ Numbers in parentheses indicate the number of people reporting a single ancestry; * Numbers in parentheses indicate the number of persons reporting this race alone, not in combination with any other race; Please refer to the Explanation of Data for more information.*

Ancestry‡	Population	%
African, Sub-Saharan (380)	422	0.40
African (237)	279	0.26
Ghanaian (143)	143	0.14
Albanian (8)	8	0.01
American (1,760)	1,760	1.67
Arab (891)	1,030	0.98
Arab (202)	266	0.25
Egyptian (125)	171	0.16
Jordanian (0)	20	0.02
Lebanese (292)	292	0.28
Palestinian (50)	50	0.05
Syrian (222)	231	0.22
Armenian (88)	127	0.12
Austrian (0)	144	0.14
Basque (16)	33	0.03
Belgian (0)	15	0.01
Brazilian (29)	85	0.08
British (57)	110	0.10
Bulgarian (0)	20	0.02
Canadian (119)	192	0.18
Croatian (13)	31	0.03
Czech (14)	153	0.14
Czechoslovakian (10)	10	0.01
Danish (105)	319	0.30
Dutch (251)	616	0.58
Eastern European (0)	11	0.01
English (820)	2,948	2.79
European (222)	306	0.29
Finnish (6)	60	0.06
French, ex. Basque (62)	795	0.75
French Canadian (42)	125	0.12
German (1,081)	4,587	4.35
German Russian (0)	88	0.08
Greek (45)	107	0.10
Guyanese (37)	37	0.04
Hungarian (76)	130	0.12
Iranian (141)	141	0.13
Irish (411)	2,568	2.43
Israeli (25)	25	0.02
Italian (623)	2,082	1.97
Latvian (13)	13	0.01
Lithuanian (31)	80	0.08
Norwegian (174)	622	0.59
Pennsylvania German (12)	12	0.01
Polish (119)	734	0.70
Portuguese (58)	177	0.17
Romanian (10)	20	0.02
Russian (249)	400	0.38
Scandinavian (9)	34	0.03
Scotch-Irish (184)	353	0.33
Scottish (83)	411	0.39
Serbian (7)	21	0.02
Slovene (18)	34	0.03
Swedish (96)	624	0.59
Swiss (7)	109	0.10
Turkish (33)	59	0.06
Ukrainian (4)	47	0.04
Welsh (40)	130	0.12
West Indian, ex. Hispanic (176)	176	0.17
Barbadian (24)	24	0.02
Jamaican (118)	118	0.11
West Indian (34)	34	0.03
Yugoslavian (0)	31	0.03

Hispanic Origin	Population	%
Hispanic or Latino (of any race)	56,471	53.23
Central American, ex. Mexican	4,091	3.86
Costa Rican	145	0.14
Guatemalan	946	0.89
Honduran	235	0.22
Nicaraguan	611	0.58
Panamanian	85	0.08
Salvadoran	2,019	1.90
Other Central American	50	0.05
Cuban	517	0.49
Dominican Republic	29	0.03
Mexican	46,505	43.83
Puerto Rican	615	0.58
South American	1,506	1.42
Argentinean	219	0.21
Bolivian	52	0.05
Chilean	81	0.08
Colombian	331	0.31
Ecuadorian	302	0.28
Paraguayan	6	0.01
Peruvian	437	0.41
Uruguayan	20	0.02
Venezuelan	43	0.04
Other South American	15	0.01
Other Hispanic or Latino	3,208	3.02

Race*	Population	%
African-American/Black (4,741)	5,634	5.31
Not Hispanic (4,260)	4,748	4.48
Hispanic (481)	886	0.84
American Indian/Alaska Native (1,045)	1,789	1.69
Not Hispanic (232)	532	0.50
Hispanic (813)	1,257	1.18
Alaska Athabascan *(Ala. Nat.)* (0)	1	<0.01
Apache (53)	86	0.08
Arapaho (0)	2	<0.01
Blackfeet (8)	34	0.03
Canadian/French Am. Ind. (2)	2	<0.01
Central American Ind. (5)	13	0.01
Cherokee (21)	110	0.10
Cheyenne (12)	14	0.01
Chickasaw (3)	9	0.01
Chippewa (3)	11	0.01
Choctaw (8)	24	0.02
Colville (1)	5	<0.01
Comanche (1)	1	<0.01
Cree (0)	2	<0.01
Creek (3)	7	0.01
Crow (1)	1	<0.01
Delaware (5)	5	<0.01
Hopi (10)	17	0.02
Inupiat *(Alaska Native)* (0)	1	<0.01
Iroquois (1)	8	0.01
Kiowa (1)	3	<0.01
Lumbee (3)	3	<0.01
Mexican American Ind. (156)	214	0.20
Navajo (22)	65	0.06
Osage (0)	2	<0.01
Ottawa (0)	4	<0.01
Paiute (8)	10	0.01
Pima (12)	22	0.02
Potawatomi (1)	2	<0.01
Pueblo (12)	24	0.02
Seminole (1)	1	<0.01
Sioux (12)	33	0.03
South American Ind. (0)	3	<0.01
Spanish American Ind. (8)	12	0.01
Tohono O'Odham (13)	17	0.02
Ute (0)	4	<0.01
Yakama (1)	1	<0.01
Yaqui (14)	39	0.04
Yuman (0)	2	<0.01
Asian (27,333)	29,177	27.50
Not Hispanic (26,834)	27,998	26.39
Hispanic (499)	1,179	1.11
Bangladeshi (25)	27	0.03
Burmese (152)	178	0.17
Cambodian (163)	236	0.22
Chinese, ex. Taiwanese (8,012)	9,089	8.57
Filipino (10,689)	11,726	11.05
Indian (667)	775	0.73
Indonesian (311)	427	0.40
Japanese (731)	1,100	1.04
Korean (756)	843	0.79
Laotian (168)	202	0.19
Malaysian (21)	40	0.04
Nepalese (5)	9	0.01
Pakistani (122)	133	0.13
Sri Lankan (75)	82	0.08
Taiwanese (1,199)	1,347	1.27
Thai (403)	449	0.42
Vietnamese (2,790)	3,230	3.04
Hawaii Native/Pacific Islander (198)	520	0.49
Not Hispanic (142)	363	0.34
Hispanic (56)	157	0.15
Fijian (13)	25	0.02
Guamanian/Chamorro (31)	59	0.06
Native Hawaiian (59)	146	0.14
Samoan (58)	96	0.09
Tongan (6)	17	0.02
White (45,432)	48,953	46.14
Not Hispanic (16,196)	17,497	16.49
Hispanic (29,236)	31,456	29.65

West Hollywood

Place Type: City
County: Los Angeles
Population: 34,399†

Ancestry‡	Population	%
Afghan (36)	50	0.14
African, Sub-Saharan (49)	90	0.26
African (24)	65	0.19
South African (14)	14	0.04
Other Sub-Saharan African (11)	11	0.03
Albanian (12)	12	0.03
American (779)	779	2.25
Arab (214)	335	0.97
Arab (8)	8	0.02
Egyptian (53)	100	0.29
Lebanese (37)	53	0.15
Moroccan (39)	73	0.21
Palestinian (47)	47	0.14
Syrian (30)	43	0.12
Other Arab (0)	11	0.03
Armenian (151)	165	0.48
Assyrian/Chaldean/Syriac (32)	32	0.09
Australian (46)	82	0.24
Austrian (80)	234	0.68
Basque (0)	12	0.03
Belgian (60)	60	0.17
Brazilian (35)	53	0.15
British (221)	389	1.12
Bulgarian (0)	34	0.10
Canadian (117)	203	0.59
Croatian (25)	54	0.16
Czech (0)	111	0.32
Czechoslovakian (10)	10	0.03
Danish (115)	169	0.49
Dutch (114)	379	1.09
Eastern European (309)	333	0.96
English (478)	2,449	7.07
European (565)	734	2.12
Finnish (73)	109	0.31
French, ex. Basque (265)	1,475	4.26
French Canadian (96)	172	0.50
German (969)	4,478	12.92
Greek (148)	345	1.00
Guyanese (0)	12	0.03
Hungarian (190)	621	1.79
Icelander (0)	14	0.04
Iranian (665)	674	1.94
Irish (796)	3,701	10.68
Israeli (107)	198	0.57
Italian (894)	2,670	7.70
Latvian (15)	15	0.04
Lithuanian (39)	114	0.33
Macedonian (7)	7	0.02
Maltese (16)	16	0.05
New Zealander (0)	25	0.07
Northern European (55)	55	0.16
Norwegian (75)	400	1.15
Polish (448)	1,693	4.89
Portuguese (115)	346	1.00
Romanian (191)	314	0.91
Russian (3,071)	4,501	12.99
Scandinavian (70)	130	0.38
Scotch-Irish (168)	447	1.29
Scottish (71)	535	1.54
Serbian (32)	88	0.25
Slavic (0)	13	0.04
Slovak (42)	50	0.14
Slovene (36)	76	0.22

*Notes: † The Census 2010 population figure is used to calculate the percentages in the Hispanic Origin and Race categories. Ancestry percentages are based on the 2006-2010 American Community Survey population (not shown); ‡ Numbers in parentheses indicate the number of people reporting a single ancestry; * Numbers in parentheses indicate the number of persons reporting this race alone, not in combination with any other race; Please refer to the Explanation of Data for more information.*

Swedish (178)	439	1.27
Swiss (61)	192	0.55
Turkish (31)	31	0.09
Ukrainian (854)	956	2.76
Welsh (0)	222	0.64
West Indian, ex. Hispanic (0)	17	0.05
West Indian (0)	17	0.05
Yugoslavian (15)	52	0.15

Hispanic Origin	Population	%
Hispanic or Latino (of any race)	3,613	10.50
Central American, ex. Mexican	460	1.34
Costa Rican	24	0.07
Guatemalan	121	0.35
Honduran	29	0.08
Nicaraguan	37	0.11
Panamanian	22	0.06
Salvadoran	217	0.63
Other Central American	10	0.03
Cuban	178	0.52
Dominican Republic	26	0.08
Mexican	1,793	5.21
Puerto Rican	234	0.68
South American	463	1.35
Argentinean	125	0.36
Bolivian	22	0.06
Chilean	37	0.11
Colombian	105	0.31
Ecuadorian	43	0.13
Paraguayan	2	0.01
Peruvian	89	0.26
Uruguayan	8	0.02
Venezuelan	22	0.06
Other South American	10	0.03
Other Hispanic or Latino	459	1.33

Race*	Population	%
African-American/Black (1,115)	1,473	4.28
Not Hispanic (1,052)	1,353	3.93
Hispanic (63)	120	0.35
American Indian/Alaska Native (103)	365	1.06
Not Hispanic (46)	246	0.72
Hispanic (57)	119	0.35
Apache (3)	7	0.02
Arapaho (0)	1	<0.01
Blackfeet (3)	7	0.02
Central American Ind. (3)	3	0.01
Cherokee (8)	72	0.21
Cheyenne (2)	2	0.01
Chickasaw (1)	4	0.01
Chippewa (3)	6	0.02
Choctaw (5)	20	0.06
Comanche (0)	1	<0.01
Creek (0)	3	0.01
Delaware (2)	3	0.01
Hopi (3)	5	0.01
Iroquois (2)	6	0.02
Kiowa (0)	1	<0.01
Lumbee (1)	1	<0.01
Mexican American Ind. (17)	21	0.06
Navajo (4)	7	0.02
Paiute (1)	1	<0.01
Pima (1)	1	<0.01
Potawatomi (1)	2	0.01
Pueblo (4)	11	0.03
Puget Sound Salish (0)	4	0.01
Seminole (0)	8	0.02
Shoshone (1)	2	0.01
Sioux (1)	9	0.03
South American Ind. (0)	8	0.02
Spanish American Ind. (1)	1	<0.01
Yaqui (1)	2	0.01
Asian (1,874)	2,423	7.04
Not Hispanic (1,826)	2,331	6.78
Hispanic (48)	92	0.27
Bangladeshi (1)	2	0.01
Burmese (1)	1	<0.01
Cambodian (10)	14	0.04
Chinese, ex. Taiwanese (342)	487	1.42
Filipino (410)	531	1.54
Hmong (1)	1	<0.01
Indian (222)	268	0.78
Indonesian (6)	19	0.06
Japanese (266)	384	1.12
Korean (245)	308	0.90
Laotian (14)	15	0.04
Malaysian (5)	10	0.03
Nepalese (1)	1	<0.01
Pakistani (21)	25	0.07
Sri Lankan (10)	15	0.04
Taiwanese (17)	28	0.08
Thai (70)	85	0.25
Vietnamese (103)	133	0.39
Hawaii Native/Pacific Islander (34)	107	0.31
Not Hispanic (30)	95	0.28
Hispanic (4)	12	0.03
Guamanian/Chamorro (6)	8	0.02
Native Hawaiian (17)	53	0.15
Samoan (6)	19	0.06
Tongan (1)	2	0.01
White (28,979)	30,108	87.53
Not Hispanic (26,793)	27,663	80.42
Hispanic (2,186)	2,445	7.11

West Puente Valley

Place Type: CDP
County: Los Angeles
Population: 22,636†

Ancestry‡	Population	%
African, Sub-Saharan (0)	13	0.06
African (0)	13	0.06
American (204)	204	0.89
Czech (0)	14	0.06
Dutch (0)	77	0.34
English (59)	188	0.82
European (44)	44	0.19
Finnish (0)	8	0.04
French, ex. Basque (9)	72	0.32
French Canadian (9)	9	0.04
German (67)	343	1.50
Irish (205)	405	1.77
Italian (49)	61	0.27
Norwegian (0)	10	0.04
Russian (0)	12	0.05
Scandinavian (0)	27	0.12
Scotch-Irish (0)	44	0.19
Scottish (9)	9	0.04

Hispanic Origin	Population	%
Hispanic or Latino (of any race)	19,365	85.55
Central American, ex. Mexican	1,049	4.63
Costa Rican	22	0.10
Guatemalan	304	1.34
Honduran	53	0.23
Nicaraguan	139	0.61
Panamanian	2	0.01
Salvadoran	522	2.31
Other Central American	7	0.03
Cuban	76	0.34
Dominican Republic	1	<0.01
Mexican	17,034	75.25
Puerto Rican	81	0.36
South American	151	0.67
Argentinean	6	0.03
Chilean	7	0.03
Colombian	46	0.20
Ecuadorian	36	0.16
Paraguayan	3	0.01
Peruvian	38	0.17
Uruguayan	13	0.06
Venezuelan	2	0.01
Other Hispanic or Latino	973	4.30

Race*	Population	%
African-American/Black (471)	546	2.41
Not Hispanic (381)	404	1.78
Hispanic (90)	142	0.63
American Indian/Alaska Native (256)	392	1.73
Not Hispanic (37)	69	0.30
Hispanic (219)	323	1.43
Apache (8)	8	0.04
Blackfeet (2)	2	0.01
Canadian/French Am. Ind. (1)	1	<0.01
Cherokee (4)	13	0.06
Choctaw (0)	1	<0.01
Kiowa (3)	6	0.03
Mexican American Ind. (52)	75	0.33
Navajo (8)	18	0.08
Pima (9)	9	0.04
Pueblo (1)	1	<0.01
Sioux (1)	1	<0.01
Spanish American Ind. (2)	2	0.01
Tlingit-Haida *(Alaska Native)* (4)	4	0.02
Yaqui (4)	4	0.02
Yuman (3)	3	0.01
Asian (1,650)	1,814	8.01
Not Hispanic (1,615)	1,696	7.49
Hispanic (35)	118	0.52
Burmese (22)	25	0.11
Cambodian (32)	41	0.18
Chinese, ex. Taiwanese (402)	468	2.07
Filipino (631)	695	3.07
Indian (2)	16	0.07
Indonesian (2)	8	0.04
Japanese (35)	57	0.25
Korean (5)	11	0.05
Laotian (22)	24	0.11
Sri Lankan (2)	6	0.03
Taiwanese (16)	20	0.09
Thai (26)	29	0.13
Vietnamese (390)	444	1.96
Hawaii Native/Pacific Islander (28)	61	0.27
Not Hispanic (24)	45	0.20
Hispanic (4)	16	0.07
Fijian (1)	2	0.01
Guamanian/Chamorro (7)	7	0.03
Native Hawaiian (5)	16	0.07
Samoan (14)	18	0.08
White (11,383)	12,105	53.48
Not Hispanic (1,087)	1,146	5.06
Hispanic (10,296)	10,959	48.41

West Sacramento

Place Type: City
County: Yolo
Population: 48,744†

Ancestry‡	Population	%
Afghan (155)	155	0.34
African, Sub-Saharan (483)	624	1.36
African (300)	441	0.96
Cape Verdean (26)	26	0.06
Ethiopian (96)	96	0.21
South African (61)	61	0.13
American (940)	940	2.05
Arab (22)	55	0.12
Egyptian (0)	23	0.05
Syrian (22)	22	0.05
Other Arab (0)	10	0.02
Armenian (105)	122	0.27
Australian (19)	57	0.12
Austrian (37)	59	0.13
Basque (17)	17	0.04
Brazilian (0)	6	0.01
British (60)	81	0.18
Canadian (30)	30	0.07
Croatian (14)	44	0.10
Czech (31)	94	0.20
Czechoslovakian (0)	30	0.07
Danish (13)	89	0.19
Dutch (51)	409	0.89
Eastern European (28)	37	0.08
English (784)	3,400	7.40
European (759)	1,003	2.18
Finnish (12)	12	0.03
French, ex. Basque (60)	660	1.44
French Canadian (43)	105	0.23

*Notes: † The Census 2010 population figure is used to calculate the percentages in the Hispanic Origin and Race categories. Ancestry percentages are based on the 2006-2010 American Community Survey population (not shown); ‡ Numbers in parentheses indicate the number of people reporting a single ancestry; * Numbers in parentheses indicate the number of persons reporting this race alone, not in combination with any other race; Please refer to the Explanation of Data for more information.*

German (1,325)	4,903	10.67
Greek (75)	148	0.32
Hungarian (0)	4	0.01
Iranian (24)	24	0.05
Irish (753)	4,192	9.12
Israeli (9)	9	0.02
Italian (617)	2,274	4.95
Luxemburger (0)	7	0.02
Northern European (22)	22	0.05
Norwegian (187)	763	1.66
Polish (122)	837	1.82
Portuguese (487)	1,074	2.34
Romanian (116)	127	0.28
Russian (1,969)	2,378	5.17
Scandinavian (35)	129	0.28
Scotch-Irish (245)	725	1.58
Scottish (349)	813	1.77
Slovak (0)	59	0.13
Slovene (0)	7	0.02
Swedish (120)	872	1.90
Swiss (0)	81	0.18
Ukrainian (656)	716	1.56
Welsh (52)	213	0.46
Yugoslavian (28)	28	0.06

Hispanic Origin	Population	%
Hispanic or Latino (of any race)	15,282	31.35
Central American, ex. Mexican	419	0.86
Costa Rican	23	0.05
Guatemalan	108	0.22
Honduran	20	0.04
Nicaraguan	73	0.15
Panamanian	18	0.04
Salvadoran	175	0.36
Other Central American	2	<0.01
Cuban	54	0.11
Dominican Republic	15	0.03
Mexican	13,276	27.24
Puerto Rican	257	0.53
South American	198	0.41
Argentinean	19	0.04
Bolivian	11	0.02
Chilean	11	0.02
Colombian	53	0.11
Ecuadorian	26	0.05
Paraguayan	1	<0.01
Peruvian	51	0.10
Uruguayan	5	0.01
Venezuelan	15	0.03
Other South American	6	0.01
Other Hispanic or Latino	1,063	2.18

Race*	Population	%
African-American/Black (2,344)	3,034	6.22
Not Hispanic (2,180)	2,701	5.54
Hispanic (164)	333	0.68
American Indian/Alaska Native (798)	1,626	3.34
Not Hispanic (395)	898	1.84
Hispanic (403)	728	1.49
Aleut *(Alaska Native)* (1)	1	<0.01
Apache (19)	58	0.12
Arapaho (0)	1	<0.01
Blackfeet (9)	26	0.05
Canadian/French Am. Ind. (7)	10	0.02
Central American Ind. (1)	2	<0.01
Cherokee (47)	199	0.41
Cheyenne (1)	1	<0.01
Chickasaw (5)	8	0.02
Chippewa (9)	14	0.03
Choctaw (12)	34	0.07
Comanche (1)	2	<0.01
Cree (0)	1	<0.01
Creek (3)	13	0.03
Crow (3)	10	0.02
Hopi (1)	2	<0.01
Inupiat *(Alaska Native)* (2)	2	<0.01
Iroquois (7)	16	0.03
Kiowa (2)	2	<0.01
Mexican American Ind. (86)	129	0.26
Navajo (23)	42	0.09
Osage (1)	4	0.01
Paiute (4)	4	0.01
Potawatomi (4)	7	0.01
Pueblo (4)	5	0.01
Puget Sound Salish (1)	1	<0.01
Seminole (0)	1	<0.01
Shoshone (4)	5	0.01
Sioux (20)	44	0.09
South American Ind. (0)	3	0.01
Spanish American Ind. (2)	3	0.01
Tlingit-Haida *(Alaska Native)* (0)	4	0.01
Tohono O'Odham (2)	5	0.01
Ute (0)	2	<0.01
Yaqui (11)	22	0.05
Asian (5,106)	6,616	13.57
Not Hispanic (4,961)	6,162	12.64
Hispanic (145)	454	0.93
Bangladeshi (2)	2	<0.01
Burmese (4)	5	0.01
Cambodian (176)	190	0.39
Chinese, ex. Taiwanese (934)	1,172	2.40
Filipino (1,223)	1,769	3.63
Hmong (182)	196	0.40
Indian (974)	1,213	2.49
Indonesian (6)	20	0.04
Japanese (185)	423	0.87
Korean (119)	204	0.42
Laotian (489)	557	1.14
Malaysian (2)	4	0.01
Pakistani (182)	194	0.40
Sri Lankan (16)	27	0.06
Taiwanese (26)	35	0.07
Thai (23)	49	0.10
Vietnamese (323)	398	0.82
Hawaii Native/Pacific Islander (534)	1,064	2.18
Not Hispanic (502)	907	1.86
Hispanic (32)	157	0.32
Fijian (324)	387	0.79
Guamanian/Chamorro (47)	106	0.22
Marshallese (0)	1	<0.01
Native Hawaiian (36)	139	0.29
Samoan (33)	43	0.09
Tongan (40)	46	0.09
White (29,521)	32,535	66.75
Not Hispanic (23,092)	24,886	51.05
Hispanic (6,429)	7,649	15.69

West Whittier-Los Nietos

Place Type: CDP
County: Los Angeles
Population: 25,540†

Ancestry‡	Population	%
African, Sub-Saharan (29)	29	0.12
African (16)	16	0.06
Other Sub-Saharan African (13)	13	0.05
American (306)	306	1.21
Armenian (21)	21	0.08
Basque (9)	29	0.12
Czech (0)	9	0.04
Dutch (7)	62	0.25
English (109)	340	1.35
European (11)	33	0.13
French, ex. Basque (18)	111	0.44
French Canadian (0)	12	0.05
German (81)	560	2.22
Hungarian (0)	40	0.16
Iranian (20)	20	0.08
Irish (52)	499	1.98
Italian (188)	442	1.75
Norwegian (18)	97	0.39
Polish (73)	91	0.36
Portuguese (0)	9	0.04
Romanian (8)	18	0.07
Russian (9)	75	0.30
Scandinavian (19)	19	0.08
Scotch-Irish (7)	88	0.35
Scottish (14)	120	0.48
Slovak (0)	15	0.06
Swedish (0)	17	0.07
Swiss (0)	50	0.20
Ukrainian (9)	9	0.04
Welsh (13)	24	0.10
Yugoslavian (9)	35	0.14

Hispanic Origin	Population	%
Hispanic or Latino (of any race)	22,369	87.58
Central American, ex. Mexican	1,107	4.33
Costa Rican	30	0.12
Guatemalan	224	0.88
Honduran	88	0.34
Nicaraguan	122	0.48
Panamanian	9	0.04
Salvadoran	621	2.43
Other Central American	13	0.05
Cuban	81	0.32
Dominican Republic	10	0.04
Mexican	19,824	77.62
Puerto Rican	129	0.51
South American	226	0.88
Argentinean	22	0.09
Bolivian	11	0.04
Chilean	3	0.01
Colombian	25	0.10
Ecuadorian	70	0.27
Paraguayan	5	0.02
Peruvian	79	0.31
Uruguayan	10	0.04
Other South American	1	<0.01
Other Hispanic or Latino	992	3.88

Race*	Population	%
African-American/Black (254)	328	1.28
Not Hispanic (177)	202	0.79
Hispanic (77)	126	0.49
American Indian/Alaska Native (372)	547	2.14
Not Hispanic (82)	117	0.46
Hispanic (290)	430	1.68
Apache (34)	55	0.22
Arapaho (1)	3	0.01
Blackfeet (1)	3	0.01
Central American Ind. (2)	2	0.01
Cherokee (8)	20	0.08
Cheyenne (7)	8	0.03
Chippewa (1)	3	0.01
Choctaw (2)	7	0.03
Creek (5)	6	0.02
Crow (0)	1	<0.01
Hopi (4)	4	0.02
Menominee (1)	1	<0.01
Mexican American Ind. (28)	51	0.20
Navajo (13)	18	0.07
Paiute (0)	4	0.02
Pima (6)	6	0.02
Pueblo (1)	9	0.04
Sioux (0)	1	<0.01
Spanish American Ind. (1)	1	<0.01
Ute (1)	1	<0.01
Yakama (0)	1	<0.01
Yaqui (26)	28	0.11
Yuman (2)	2	0.01
Asian (393)	544	2.13
Not Hispanic (345)	388	1.52
Hispanic (48)	156	0.61
Bangladeshi (8)	8	0.03
Burmese (0)	8	0.03
Cambodian (0)	4	0.02
Chinese, ex. Taiwanese (57)	95	0.37
Filipino (181)	231	0.90
Indian (15)	23	0.09
Indonesian (4)	7	0.03
Japanese (51)	86	0.34
Korean (13)	19	0.07
Laotian (16)	16	0.06
Pakistani (1)	1	<0.01
Sri Lankan (4)	4	0.02
Taiwanese (3)	3	0.01
Thai (8)	9	0.04
Vietnamese (17)	33	0.13

*Notes: † The Census 2010 population figure is used to calculate the percentages in the Hispanic Origin and Race categories. Ancestry percentages are based on the 2006-2010 American Community Survey population (not shown); ‡ Numbers in parentheses indicate the number of people reporting a single ancestry; * Numbers in parentheses indicate the number of persons reporting this race alone, not in combination with any other race; Please refer to the Explanation of Data for more information.*

Hawaii Native/Pacific Islander (43)	75	0.29
Not Hispanic (30)	41	0.16
Hispanic (13)	34	0.13
Guamanian/Chamorro (15)	25	0.10
Native Hawaiian (12)	31	0.12
Samoan (12)	17	0.07
White (15,170)	15,934	62.39
Not Hispanic (2,369)	2,465	9.65
Hispanic (12,801)	13,469	52.74

Westlake Village

Place Type: City
County: Los Angeles
Population: 8,270†

Ancestry‡	Population	%
African, Sub-Saharan (11)	11	0.13
African (11)	11	0.13
American (572)	572	6.91
Arab (49)	120	1.45
Iraqi (9)	9	0.11
Lebanese (28)	99	1.20
Palestinian (12)	12	0.15
Armenian (8)	8	0.10
Austrian (28)	140	1.69
British (13)	23	0.28
Croatian (0)	20	0.24
Czech (31)	206	2.49
Czechoslovakian (0)	16	0.19
Danish (0)	30	0.36
Dutch (52)	115	1.39
Eastern European (14)	14	0.17
English (277)	1,224	14.79
European (183)	249	3.01
Finnish (14)	20	0.24
French, ex. Basque (53)	226	2.73
French Canadian (0)	10	0.12
German (326)	1,422	17.19
Greek (0)	33	0.40
Hungarian (78)	139	1.68
Icelander (0)	6	0.07
Iranian (213)	232	2.80
Irish (297)	919	11.11
Israeli (0)	26	0.31
Italian (460)	729	8.81
Lithuanian (21)	42	0.51
Norwegian (91)	185	2.24
Polish (97)	346	4.18
Portuguese (0)	35	0.42
Romanian (9)	9	0.11
Russian (246)	454	5.49
Scotch-Irish (111)	274	3.31
Scottish (89)	281	3.40
Serbian (0)	20	0.24
Slovak (19)	34	0.41
Swedish (65)	178	2.15
Swiss (0)	175	2.12
Turkish (12)	24	0.29
Ukrainian (0)	8	0.10
Welsh (8)	50	0.60
West Indian, ex. Hispanic (33)	93	1.12
Belizean (33)	73	0.88
Haitian (0)	20	0.24

Hispanic Origin	Population	%
Hispanic or Latino (of any race)	533	6.44
Central American, ex. Mexican	42	0.51
Guatemalan	24	0.29
Honduran	2	0.02
Nicaraguan	3	0.04
Salvadoran	13	0.16
Cuban	19	0.23
Dominican Republic	5	0.06
Mexican	296	3.58
Puerto Rican	17	0.21
South American	103	1.25
Argentinean	23	0.28
Bolivian	8	0.10
Chilean	6	0.07
Colombian	19	0.23
Ecuadorian	15	0.18
Peruvian	27	0.33
Uruguayan	1	0.01
Venezuelan	4	0.05
Other Hispanic or Latino	51	0.62

Race*	Population	%
African-American/Black (98)	134	1.62
Not Hispanic (97)	124	1.50
Hispanic (1)	10	0.12
American Indian/Alaska Native (12)	39	0.47
Not Hispanic (9)	25	0.30
Hispanic (3)	14	0.17
Apache (0)	1	0.01
Blackfeet (0)	1	0.01
Cherokee (4)	8	0.10
Chippewa (0)	1	0.01
Choctaw (0)	2	0.02
Mexican American Ind. (1)	2	0.02
Potawatomi (0)	1	0.01
Sioux (0)	6	0.07
Asian (490)	625	7.56
Not Hispanic (485)	614	7.42
Hispanic (5)	11	0.13
Chinese, ex. Taiwanese (166)	195	2.36
Filipino (53)	72	0.87
Indian (79)	96	1.16
Indonesian (0)	2	0.02
Japanese (56)	89	1.08
Korean (70)	78	0.94
Laotian (0)	1	0.01
Malaysian (3)	3	0.04
Sri Lankan (4)	4	0.05
Taiwanese (25)	28	0.34
Thai (4)	5	0.06
Vietnamese (23)	27	0.33
Hawaii Native/Pacific Islander (13)	21	0.25
Not Hispanic (11)	18	0.22
Hispanic (2)	3	0.04
Guamanian/Chamorro (2)	2	0.02
Native Hawaiian (5)	6	0.07
Samoan (3)	5	0.06
Tongan (3)	3	0.04
White (7,326)	7,530	91.05
Not Hispanic (6,940)	7,107	85.94
Hispanic (386)	423	5.11

Westminster

Place Type: City
County: Orange
Population: 89,701†

Ancestry‡	Population	%
African, Sub-Saharan (55)	55	0.06
African (55)	55	0.06
Albanian (13)	13	0.01
American (864)	864	0.97
Arab (930)	1,012	1.14
Arab (12)	12	0.01
Egyptian (296)	306	0.34
Jordanian (192)	202	0.23
Lebanese (61)	113	0.13
Palestinian (100)	100	0.11
Syrian (42)	52	0.06
Other Arab (227)	227	0.26
Armenian (351)	419	0.47
Assyrian/Chaldean/Syriac (78)	78	0.09
Austrian (100)	184	0.21
Basque (0)	35	0.04
Belgian (26)	128	0.14
Brazilian (14)	96	0.11
British (102)	148	0.17
Canadian (139)	162	0.18
Celtic (13)	27	0.03
Croatian (6)	69	0.08
Czech (18)	185	0.21
Czechoslovakian (0)	36	0.04
Danish (42)	308	0.35
Dutch (384)	1,064	1.20
Eastern European (27)	27	0.03
English (1,027)	3,721	4.18
European (384)	509	0.57
Finnish (52)	146	0.16
French, ex. Basque (243)	1,370	1.54
French Canadian (273)	434	0.49
German (2,129)	6,040	6.79
Greek (133)	197	0.22
Hungarian (125)	219	0.25
Iranian (140)	140	0.16
Irish (978)	4,442	5.00
Italian (1,086)	2,561	2.88
Latvian (8)	8	0.01
Lithuanian (43)	107	0.12
Northern European (45)	53	0.06
Norwegian (184)	615	0.69
Pennsylvania German (0)	21	0.02
Polish (329)	1,011	1.14
Portuguese (51)	138	0.16
Romanian (46)	46	0.05
Russian (125)	257	0.29
Scandinavian (12)	66	0.07
Scotch-Irish (225)	521	0.59
Scottish (129)	513	0.58
Serbian (26)	26	0.03
Slavic (11)	55	0.06
Slovak (58)	96	0.11
Slovene (0)	10	0.01
Swedish (241)	829	0.93
Swiss (14)	81	0.09
Turkish (0)	25	0.03
Ukrainian (82)	145	0.16
Welsh (83)	264	0.30
West Indian, ex. Hispanic (14)	24	0.03
Belizean (5)	10	0.01
Jamaican (0)	5	0.01
West Indian (9)	9	0.01
Yugoslavian (121)	142	0.16

Hispanic Origin	Population	%
Hispanic or Latino (of any race)	21,176	23.61
Central American, ex. Mexican	867	0.97
Costa Rican	70	0.08
Guatemalan	249	0.28
Honduran	80	0.09
Nicaraguan	58	0.06
Panamanian	30	0.03
Salvadoran	374	0.42
Other Central American	6	0.01
Cuban	213	0.24
Dominican Republic	7	0.01
Mexican	18,037	20.11
Puerto Rican	257	0.29
South American	579	0.65
Argentinean	69	0.08
Bolivian	22	0.02
Chilean	44	0.05
Colombian	122	0.14
Ecuadorian	72	0.08
Paraguayan	2	<0.01
Peruvian	229	0.26
Uruguayan	3	<0.01
Venezuelan	10	0.01
Other South American	6	0.01
Other Hispanic or Latino	1,216	1.36

Race*	Population	%
African-American/Black (849)	1,255	1.40
Not Hispanic (700)	1,003	1.12
Hispanic (149)	252	0.28
American Indian/Alaska Native (397)	980	1.09
Not Hispanic (132)	495	0.55
Hispanic (265)	485	0.54
Apache (18)	46	0.05
Blackfeet (10)	50	0.06
Central American Ind. (1)	2	<0.01
Cherokee (26)	148	0.16
Cheyenne (0)	2	<0.01
Chickasaw (0)	11	0.01

*Notes: † The Census 2010 population figure is used to calculate the percentages in the Hispanic Origin and Race categories. Ancestry percentages are based on the 2006-2010 American Community Survey population (not shown); ‡ Numbers in parentheses indicate the number of people reporting a single ancestry; * Numbers in parentheses indicate the number of persons reporting this race alone, not in combination with any other race; Please refer to the Explanation of Data for more information.*

Chippewa (6)	17	0.02
Choctaw (7)	20	0.02
Comanche (1)	4	<0.01
Cree (3)	4	<0.01
Creek (2)	9	0.01
Hopi (0)	3	<0.01
Iroquois (7)	22	0.02
Kiowa (0)	1	<0.01
Lumbee (3)	9	0.01
Mexican American Ind. (59)	84	0.09
Navajo (13)	27	0.03
Osage (0)	3	<0.01
Pima (1)	1	<0.01
Potawatomi (1)	1	<0.01
Pueblo (4)	11	0.01
Puget Sound Salish (1)	1	<0.01
Seminole (0)	3	<0.01
Shoshone (0)	3	<0.01
Sioux (15)	20	0.02
South American Ind. (1)	3	<0.01
Tlingit-Haida *(Alaska Native)* (0)	4	<0.01
Tsimshian *(Alaska Native)* (0)	8	0.01
Ute (4)	5	0.01
Yaqui (6)	14	0.02
Yuman (5)	5	0.01
Asian (42,597)	44,192	49.27
Not Hispanic (42,414)	43,687	48.70
Hispanic (183)	505	0.56
Bangladeshi (21)	21	0.02
Burmese (15)	17	0.02
Cambodian (232)	282	0.31
Chinese, ex. Taiwanese (1,856)	2,590	2.89
Filipino (1,129)	1,578	1.76
Hmong (97)	102	0.11
Indian (331)	468	0.52
Indonesian (46)	113	0.13
Japanese (854)	1,229	1.37
Korean (613)	673	0.75
Laotian (104)	138	0.15
Malaysian (0)	2	<0.01
Pakistani (100)	116	0.13
Sri Lankan (14)	14	0.02
Taiwanese (65)	81	0.09
Thai (155)	196	0.22
Vietnamese (36,058)	37,176	41.44
Hawaii Native/Pacific Islander (361)	695	0.77
Not Hispanic (324)	589	0.66
Hispanic (37)	106	0.12
Fijian (1)	1	<0.01
Guamanian/Chamorro (65)	104	0.12
Marshallese (0)	2	<0.01
Native Hawaiian (59)	191	0.21
Samoan (210)	285	0.32
Tongan (1)	7	0.01
White (32,037)	34,753	38.74
Not Hispanic (22,972)	24,556	27.38
Hispanic (9,065)	10,197	11.37

Westmont

Place Type: CDP
County: Los Angeles
Population: 31,853†

Ancestry‡	Population	%
African, Sub-Saharan (805)	906	2.89
African (637)	738	2.36
Liberian (10)	10	0.03
Nigerian (158)	158	0.50
American (311)	311	0.99
Arab (155)	155	0.50
Moroccan (155)	155	0.50
European (10)	27	0.09
French, ex. Basque (0)	31	0.10
German (52)	62	0.20
Iranian (5)	5	0.02
Irish (0)	43	0.14
Italian (8)	8	0.03
Maltese (9)	9	0.03
Portuguese (7)	23	0.07
Russian (0)	31	0.10
West Indian, ex. Hispanic (730)	768	2.45
Belizean (536)	574	1.83
Haitian (41)	41	0.13
Jamaican (130)	130	0.42
West Indian (23)	23	0.07

Hispanic Origin	Population	%
Hispanic or Latino (of any race)	14,871	46.69
Central American, ex. Mexican	4,034	12.66
Costa Rican	11	0.03
Guatemalan	1,440	4.52
Honduran	298	0.94
Nicaraguan	135	0.42
Panamanian	36	0.11
Salvadoran	2,044	6.42
Other Central American	70	0.22
Cuban	43	0.13
Dominican Republic	7	0.02
Mexican	9,357	29.38
Puerto Rican	138	0.43
South American	69	0.22
Argentinean	1	<0.01
Bolivian	6	0.02
Colombian	7	0.02
Ecuadorian	24	0.08
Peruvian	25	0.08
Other South American	6	0.02
Other Hispanic or Latino	1,223	3.84

Race*	Population	%
African-American/Black (16,262)	16,791	52.71
Not Hispanic (15,955)	16,314	51.22
Hispanic (307)	477	1.50
American Indian/Alaska Native (188)	372	1.17
Not Hispanic (38)	168	0.53
Hispanic (150)	204	0.64
Apache (3)	5	0.02
Blackfeet (5)	11	0.03
Canadian/French Am. Ind. (2)	2	0.01
Central American Ind. (6)	19	0.06
Cherokee (4)	24	0.08
Cheyenne (0)	1	<0.01
Chippewa (1)	2	0.01
Choctaw (0)	14	0.04
Creek (0)	5	0.02
Iroquois (1)	1	<0.01
Lumbee (1)	1	<0.01
Mexican American Ind. (35)	44	0.14
Navajo (1)	1	<0.01
Potawatomi (0)	1	<0.01
Pueblo (3)	3	0.01
Spanish American Ind. (4)	5	0.02
Tlingit-Haida *(Alaska Native)* (1)	2	0.01
Tohono O'Odham (0)	3	0.01
Asian (126)	213	0.67
Not Hispanic (99)	149	0.47
Hispanic (27)	64	0.20
Bangladeshi (3)	3	0.01
Cambodian (10)	11	0.03
Chinese, ex. Taiwanese (14)	23	0.07
Filipino (51)	77	0.24
Indian (18)	30	0.09
Japanese (7)	26	0.08
Korean (9)	15	0.05
Thai (7)	8	0.03
Vietnamese (2)	3	0.01
Hawaii Native/Pacific Islander (31)	71	0.22
Not Hispanic (30)	55	0.17
Hispanic (1)	16	0.05
Guamanian/Chamorro (1)	5	0.02
Native Hawaiian (2)	11	0.03
Samoan (2)	3	0.01
Tongan (24)	24	0.08
White (5,037)	5,674	17.81
Not Hispanic (324)	498	1.56
Hispanic (4,713)	5,176	16.25

Whittier

Place Type: City
County: Los Angeles
Population: 85,331†

Ancestry‡	Population	%
African, Sub-Saharan (6)	6	0.01
African (6)	6	0.01
American (1,920)	1,920	2.26
Arab (426)	515	0.61
Arab (16)	47	0.06
Egyptian (125)	125	0.15
Lebanese (240)	284	0.33
Moroccan (45)	45	0.05
Syrian (0)	14	0.02
Armenian (547)	696	0.82
Australian (20)	48	0.06
Austrian (49)	219	0.26
Basque (42)	42	0.05
Belgian (5)	18	0.02
Brazilian (29)	44	0.05
British (211)	295	0.35
Canadian (42)	108	0.13
Celtic (24)	24	0.03
Croatian (48)	99	0.12
Czech (12)	89	0.10
Czechoslovakian (19)	54	0.06
Danish (169)	555	0.65
Dutch (170)	826	0.97
English (1,368)	5,341	6.28
European (619)	842	0.99
Finnish (10)	20	0.02
French, ex. Basque (98)	1,309	1.54
French Canadian (68)	322	0.38
German (1,339)	6,448	7.59
Greek (147)	286	0.34
Hungarian (18)	124	0.15
Iranian (12)	38	0.04
Irish (919)	5,094	5.99
Israeli (9)	62	0.07
Italian (995)	2,781	3.27
Lithuanian (0)	31	0.04
Macedonian (26)	26	0.03
Northern European (9)	9	0.01
Norwegian (150)	721	0.85
Pennsylvania German (0)	80	0.09
Polish (190)	766	0.90
Portuguese (120)	210	0.25
Romanian (47)	102	0.12
Russian (267)	612	0.72
Scandinavian (68)	105	0.12
Scotch-Irish (264)	823	0.97
Scottish (214)	1,041	1.22
Serbian (4)	47	0.06
Slovak (0)	10	0.01
Slovene (11)	23	0.03
Swedish (212)	644	0.76
Swiss (102)	153	0.18
Turkish (14)	34	0.04
Ukrainian (137)	164	0.19
Welsh (111)	366	0.43
West Indian, ex. Hispanic (27)	44	0.05
Haitian (18)	18	0.02
Jamaican (0)	17	0.02
Trinidadian/Tobagonian (9)	9	0.01
Yugoslavian (0)	45	0.05

Hispanic Origin	Population	%
Hispanic or Latino (of any race)	56,081	65.72
Central American, ex. Mexican	2,758	3.23
Costa Rican	152	0.18
Guatemalan	684	0.80
Honduran	125	0.15
Nicaraguan	313	0.37
Panamanian	40	0.05
Salvadoran	1,390	1.63
Other Central American	54	0.06
Cuban	410	0.48
Dominican Republic	30	0.04

*Notes: † The Census 2010 population figure is used to calculate the percentages in the Hispanic Origin and Race categories. Ancestry percentages are based on the 2006-2010 American Community Survey population (not shown); ‡ Numbers in parentheses indicate the number of people reporting a single ancestry; * Numbers in parentheses indicate the number of persons reporting this race alone, not in combination with any other race; Please refer to the Explanation of Data for more information.*

	Population	%
Mexican	48,567	56.92
Puerto Rican	555	0.65
South American	904	1.06
Argentinean	188	0.22
Bolivian	54	0.06
Chilean	47	0.06
Colombian	192	0.23
Ecuadorian	156	0.18
Paraguayan	15	0.02
Peruvian	191	0.22
Uruguayan	14	0.02
Venezuelan	25	0.03
Other South American	22	0.03
Other Hispanic or Latino	2,857	3.35

Race*	Population	%
African-American/Black (1,092)	1,560	1.83
Not Hispanic (780)	967	1.13
Hispanic (312)	593	0.69
American Indian/Alaska Native (1,093)	1,750	2.05
Not Hispanic (226)	411	0.48
Hispanic (867)	1,339	1.57
Apache (78)	138	0.16
Blackfeet (2)	11	0.01
Central American Ind. (6)	8	0.01
Cherokee (34)	107	0.13
Cheyenne (4)	7	0.01
Chickasaw (3)	12	0.01
Chippewa (8)	11	0.01
Choctaw (2)	22	0.03
Comanche (1)	11	0.01
Creek (12)	14	0.02
Delaware (0)	1	<0.01
Hopi (8)	11	0.01
Inupiat *(Alaska Native)* (0)	5	0.01
Iroquois (5)	6	0.01
Kiowa (8)	11	0.01
Menominee (1)	1	<0.01
Mexican American Ind. (157)	229	0.27
Navajo (58)	80	0.09
Osage (1)	2	<0.01
Paiute (0)	3	<0.01
Pima (1)	5	0.01
Potawatomi (3)	4	<0.01
Pueblo (33)	45	0.05
Seminole (2)	6	0.01
Shoshone (10)	15	0.02
Sioux (17)	26	0.03
South American Ind. (2)	6	0.01
Spanish American Ind. (6)	9	0.01
Tlingit-Haida *(Alaska Native)* (1)	1	<0.01
Tohono O'Odham (8)	13	0.02
Ute (1)	2	<0.01
Yaqui (26)	50	0.06
Yuman (4)	5	0.01
Asian (3,262)	4,266	5.00
Not Hispanic (2,996)	3,517	4.12
Hispanic (266)	749	0.88
Burmese (7)	7	0.01
Cambodian (47)	55	0.06
Chinese, ex. Taiwanese (657)	923	1.08
Filipino (879)	1,213	1.42
Hmong (1)	1	<0.01
Indian (193)	251	0.29
Indonesian (20)	45	0.05
Japanese (597)	954	1.12
Korean (361)	438	0.51
Laotian (8)	8	0.01
Malaysian (4)	8	0.01
Nepalese (12)	15	0.02
Pakistani (28)	36	0.04
Sri Lankan (9)	12	0.01
Taiwanese (85)	103	0.12
Thai (82)	103	0.12
Vietnamese (113)	149	0.17
Hawaii Native/Pacific Islander (123)	319	0.37
Not Hispanic (91)	199	0.23
Hispanic (32)	120	0.14
Guamanian/Chamorro (28)	49	0.06
Native Hawaiian (36)	138	0.16
Samoan (35)	53	0.06
Tongan (12)	15	0.02
White (55,117)	58,349	68.38
Not Hispanic (24,126)	24,902	29.18
Hispanic (30,991)	33,447	39.20

Wildomar

Place Type: City
County: Riverside
Population: 32,176†

Ancestry‡	Population	%
African, Sub-Saharan (99)	111	0.36
African (99)	111	0.36
Albanian (0)	45	0.15
American (1,044)	1,044	3.41
Arab (145)	145	0.47
Arab (25)	25	0.08
Egyptian (48)	48	0.16
Iraqi (12)	12	0.04
Jordanian (16)	16	0.05
Lebanese (44)	44	0.14
Armenian (0)	105	0.34
Austrian (16)	25	0.08
Belgian (0)	10	0.03
British (87)	94	0.31
Canadian (61)	106	0.35
Croatian (6)	36	0.12
Czech (0)	46	0.15
Czechoslovakian (0)	16	0.05
Danish (58)	163	0.53
Dutch (240)	867	2.83
English (634)	1,916	6.25
European (403)	510	1.66
Finnish (9)	80	0.26
French, ex. Basque (85)	671	2.19
French Canadian (45)	95	0.31
German (1,468)	4,792	15.64
Greek (30)	37	0.12
Hungarian (13)	38	0.12
Iranian (54)	54	0.18
Irish (790)	3,603	11.76
Israeli (0)	20	0.07
Italian (706)	1,819	5.94
Maltese (12)	12	0.04
Northern European (30)	30	0.10
Norwegian (267)	903	2.95
Polish (148)	562	1.83
Portuguese (63)	264	0.86
Romanian (14)	27	0.09
Russian (69)	186	0.61
Scandinavian (22)	31	0.10
Scotch-Irish (226)	396	1.29
Scottish (207)	665	2.17
Slovak (47)	59	0.19
Slovene (0)	28	0.09
Swedish (54)	384	1.25
Swiss (14)	126	0.41
Turkish (0)	28	0.09
Ukrainian (0)	167	0.55
Welsh (51)	93	0.30
West Indian, ex. Hispanic (93)	187	0.61
Haitian (46)	140	0.46
Jamaican (47)	47	0.15
Yugoslavian (4)	13	0.04

Hispanic Origin	Population	%
Hispanic or Latino (of any race)	11,363	35.32
Central American, ex. Mexican	500	1.55
Costa Rican	25	0.08
Guatemalan	136	0.42
Honduran	35	0.11
Nicaraguan	24	0.07
Panamanian	22	0.07
Salvadoran	250	0.78
Other Central American	8	0.02
Cuban	81	0.25
Dominican Republic	20	0.06
Mexican	9,642	29.97
Puerto Rican	249	0.77
South American	193	0.60
Argentinean	43	0.13
Bolivian	5	0.02
Chilean	11	0.03
Colombian	40	0.12
Ecuadorian	36	0.11
Peruvian	38	0.12
Uruguayan	9	0.03
Venezuelan	7	0.02
Other South American	4	0.01
Other Hispanic or Latino	678	2.11

Race*	Population	%
African-American/Black (1,065)	1,349	4.19
Not Hispanic (960)	1,190	3.70
Hispanic (105)	159	0.49
American Indian/Alaska Native (376)	773	2.40
Not Hispanic (198)	455	1.41
Hispanic (178)	318	0.99
Apache (12)	37	0.11
Blackfeet (3)	14	0.04
Canadian/French Am. Ind. (0)	1	<0.01
Cherokee (20)	102	0.32
Cheyenne (1)	2	0.01
Chippewa (6)	10	0.03
Choctaw (9)	29	0.09
Comanche (4)	6	0.02
Creek (3)	4	0.01
Iroquois (1)	1	<0.01
Mexican American Ind. (43)	76	0.24
Navajo (6)	19	0.06
Osage (1)	1	<0.01
Ottawa (0)	1	<0.01
Paiute (0)	1	<0.01
Pima (1)	1	<0.01
Potawatomi (0)	2	0.01
Pueblo (2)	5	0.02
Seminole (0)	2	0.01
Sioux (3)	17	0.05
South American Ind. (1)	2	0.01
Tohono O'Odham (1)	6	0.02
Ute (0)	1	<0.01
Yaqui (8)	17	0.05
Yup'ik *(Alaska Native)* (0)	2	0.01
Asian (1,454)	2,045	6.36
Not Hispanic (1,384)	1,832	5.69
Hispanic (70)	213	0.66
Burmese (1)	1	<0.01
Cambodian (45)	50	0.16
Chinese, ex. Taiwanese (63)	161	0.50
Filipino (805)	1,113	3.46
Hmong (7)	9	0.03
Indian (48)	73	0.23
Indonesian (6)	22	0.07
Japanese (73)	180	0.56
Korean (88)	124	0.39
Laotian (54)	62	0.19
Malaysian (2)	3	0.01
Pakistani (3)	7	0.02
Sri Lankan (5)	5	0.02
Taiwanese (8)	12	0.04
Thai (20)	30	0.09
Vietnamese (180)	197	0.61
Hawaii Native/Pacific Islander (69)	215	0.67
Not Hispanic (53)	168	0.52
Hispanic (16)	47	0.15
Fijian (0)	3	0.01
Guamanian/Chamorro (29)	43	0.13
Native Hawaiian (15)	84	0.26
Samoan (11)	33	0.10
White (22,372)	23,878	74.21
Not Hispanic (17,255)	18,066	56.15
Hispanic (5,117)	5,812	18.06

Willowbrook

Place Type: CDP
County: Los Angeles
Population: 35,983†

*Notes: † The Census 2010 population figure is used to calculate the percentages in the Hispanic Origin and Race categories. Ancestry percentages are based on the 2006-2010 American Community Survey population (not shown); ‡ Numbers in parentheses indicate the number of people reporting a single ancestry; * Numbers in parentheses indicate the number of persons reporting this race alone, not in combination with any other race; Please refer to the Explanation of Data for more information.*

Ancestry‡	Population	%
African, Sub-Saharan (1,525)	1,693	4.81
African (1,498)	1,646	4.68
Ethiopian (15)	35	0.10
Nigerian (12)	12	0.03
American (637)	637	1.81
Arab (0)	19	0.05
Other Arab (0)	19	0.05
Armenian (25)	25	0.07
Canadian (38)	38	0.11
Czech (9)	9	0.03
English (10)	38	0.11
European (0)	13	0.04
French, ex. Basque (25)	126	0.36
German (11)	89	0.25
Icelander (0)	7	0.02
Iranian (9)	9	0.03
Irish (0)	126	0.36
Italian (25)	38	0.11
Scotch-Irish (0)	8	0.02
West Indian, ex. Hispanic (16)	125	0.36
Belizean (0)	26	0.07
Jamaican (16)	99	0.28

Hispanic Origin	Population	%
Hispanic or Latino (of any race)	22,979	63.86
Central American, ex. Mexican	2,344	6.51
Costa Rican	4	0.01
Guatemalan	690	1.92
Honduran	168	0.47
Nicaraguan	92	0.26
Panamanian	21	0.06
Salvadoran	1,333	3.70
Other Central American	36	0.10
Cuban	32	0.09
Mexican	19,293	53.62
Puerto Rican	94	0.26
South American	94	0.26
Argentinean	8	0.02
Chilean	1	<0.01
Colombian	14	0.04
Ecuadorian	50	0.14
Peruvian	21	0.06
Other Hispanic or Latino	1,122	3.12

Race*	Population	%
African-American/Black (12,387)	12,749	35.43
Not Hispanic (12,172)	12,396	34.45
Hispanic (215)	353	0.98
American Indian/Alaska Native (273)	453	1.26
Not Hispanic (48)	160	0.44
Hispanic (225)	293	0.81
Apache (6)	17	0.05
Arapaho (4)	8	0.02
Blackfeet (0)	9	0.03
Central American Ind. (5)	10	0.03
Cherokee (6)	34	0.09
Chickasaw (0)	2	0.01
Chippewa (0)	2	0.01
Choctaw (0)	5	0.01
Comanche (0)	3	0.01
Creek (1)	9	0.03
Hopi (1)	1	<0.01
Mexican American Ind. (48)	65	0.18
Navajo (6)	10	0.03
Ottawa (0)	2	0.01
Pueblo (5)	6	0.02
Seminole (0)	1	<0.01
Spanish American Ind. (4)	4	0.01
Yaqui (0)	2	0.01
Asian (119)	238	0.66
Not Hispanic (87)	137	0.38
Hispanic (32)	101	0.28
Cambodian (1)	1	<0.01
Chinese, ex. Taiwanese (7)	23	0.06
Filipino (54)	88	0.24
Indian (16)	37	0.10
Indonesian (0)	3	0.01
Japanese (6)	22	0.06
Korean (14)	22	0.06
Taiwanese (1)	1	<0.01
Vietnamese (11)	15	0.04
Hawaii Native/Pacific Islander (49)	105	0.29
Not Hispanic (46)	73	0.20
Hispanic (3)	32	0.09
Guamanian/Chamorro (4)	7	0.02
Native Hawaiian (6)	18	0.05
Samoan (32)	44	0.12
White (8,245)	8,950	24.87
Not Hispanic (328)	424	1.18
Hispanic (7,917)	8,526	23.69

Windsor

Place Type: Town
County: Sonoma
Population: 26,801†

Ancestry‡	Population	%
African, Sub-Saharan (15)	38	0.15
African (15)	38	0.15
American (1,019)	1,019	3.96
Arab (38)	98	0.38
Arab (30)	30	0.12
Jordanian (8)	34	0.13
Syrian (0)	34	0.13
Armenian (9)	35	0.14
Australian (73)	105	0.41
Austrian (0)	91	0.35
Basque (8)	8	0.03
British (41)	129	0.50
Canadian (32)	68	0.26
Czech (0)	106	0.41
Czechoslovakian (0)	34	0.13
Danish (42)	242	0.94
Dutch (125)	428	1.66
English (730)	2,615	10.15
European (255)	289	1.12
Finnish (17)	40	0.16
French, ex. Basque (150)	1,127	4.38
French Canadian (18)	46	0.18
German (752)	3,716	14.43
Greek (21)	139	0.54
Hungarian (36)	93	0.36
Icelander (11)	11	0.04
Irish (959)	3,347	12.99
Israeli (7)	7	0.03
Italian (784)	2,557	9.93
Latvian (0)	11	0.04
Lithuanian (14)	90	0.35
Maltese (0)	2	0.01
Northern European (126)	143	0.56
Norwegian (196)	519	2.01
Polish (59)	324	1.26
Portuguese (163)	406	1.58
Romanian (9)	9	0.03
Russian (125)	440	1.71
Scandinavian (0)	62	0.24
Scotch-Irish (266)	535	2.08
Scottish (183)	806	3.13
Swedish (68)	535	2.08
Swiss (33)	343	1.33
Ukrainian (0)	13	0.05
Welsh (52)	174	0.68
West Indian, ex. Hispanic (94)	94	0.36
Belizean (94)	94	0.36
Yugoslavian (13)	21	0.08

Hispanic Origin	Population	%
Hispanic or Latino (of any race)	8,511	31.76
Central American, ex. Mexican	187	0.70
Costa Rican	10	0.04
Guatemalan	27	0.10
Honduran	8	0.03
Nicaraguan	53	0.20
Panamanian	1	<0.01
Salvadoran	86	0.32
Other Central American	2	0.01
Cuban	32	0.12
Dominican Republic	9	0.03
Mexican	7,646	28.53
Puerto Rican	100	0.37
South American	105	0.39
Argentinean	4	0.01
Bolivian	2	0.01
Chilean	8	0.03
Colombian	19	0.07
Ecuadorian	19	0.07
Peruvian	30	0.11
Uruguayan	3	0.01
Venezuelan	14	0.05
Other South American	6	0.02
Other Hispanic or Latino	432	1.61

Race*	Population	%
African-American/Black (227)	397	1.48
Not Hispanic (191)	314	1.17
Hispanic (36)	83	0.31
American Indian/Alaska Native (594)	992	3.70
Not Hispanic (285)	487	1.82
Hispanic (309)	505	1.88
Alaska Athabascan *(Ala. Nat.)* (1)	1	<0.01
Aleut *(Alaska Native)* (6)	11	0.04
Apache (6)	20	0.07
Arapaho (0)	1	<0.01
Blackfeet (6)	11	0.04
Central American Ind. (1)	1	<0.01
Cherokee (11)	104	0.39
Cheyenne (1)	8	0.03
Chickasaw (1)	2	0.01
Chippewa (7)	15	0.06
Choctaw (3)	23	0.09
Comanche (2)	2	0.01
Cree (1)	1	<0.01
Creek (2)	4	0.01
Delaware (2)	3	0.01
Hopi (1)	4	0.01
Inupiat *(Alaska Native)* (1)	1	<0.01
Iroquois (0)	4	0.01
Lumbee (3)	4	0.01
Mexican American Ind. (86)	108	0.40
Navajo (4)	6	0.02
Osage (0)	3	0.01
Ottawa (0)	4	0.01
Potawatomi (2)	2	0.01
Pueblo (1)	2	0.01
Sioux (11)	27	0.10
South American Ind. (1)	4	0.01
Spanish American Ind. (2)	5	0.02
Tlingit-Haida *(Alaska Native)* (1)	1	<0.01
Tsimshian *(Alaska Native)* (0)	1	<0.01
Yaqui (4)	8	0.03
Asian (810)	1,228	4.58
Not Hispanic (775)	1,124	4.19
Hispanic (35)	104	0.39
Cambodian (11)	15	0.06
Chinese, ex. Taiwanese (133)	231	0.86
Filipino (174)	351	1.31
Hmong (13)	13	0.05
Indian (114)	151	0.56
Indonesian (1)	3	0.01
Japanese (63)	169	0.63
Korean (58)	75	0.28
Laotian (32)	38	0.14
Nepalese (4)	4	0.01
Pakistani (11)	13	0.05
Taiwanese (6)	7	0.03
Thai (13)	21	0.08
Vietnamese (129)	150	0.56
Hawaii Native/Pacific Islander (51)	154	0.57
Not Hispanic (48)	140	0.52
Hispanic (3)	14	0.05
Fijian (5)	10	0.04
Guamanian/Chamorro (10)	22	0.08
Native Hawaiian (11)	56	0.21
Samoan (11)	28	0.10
Tongan (4)	7	0.03
White (19,798)	20,896	77.97
Not Hispanic (16,254)	16,876	62.97
Hispanic (3,544)	4,020	15.00

*Notes: † The Census 2010 population figure is used to calculate the percentages in the Hispanic Origin and Race categories. Ancestry percentages are based on the 2006-2010 American Community Survey population (not shown); ‡ Numbers in parentheses indicate the number of people reporting a single ancestry; * Numbers in parentheses indicate the number of persons reporting this race alone, not in combination with any other race; Please refer to the Explanation of Data for more information.*

Winter Gardens

Place Type: CDP
County: San Diego
Population: 20,631†

Ancestry‡	Population	%
African, Sub-Saharan (158)	158	0.78
African (158)	158	0.78
American (990)	990	4.90
Arab (320)	320	1.58
Iraqi (200)	200	0.99
Other Arab (120)	120	0.59
Assyrian/Chaldean/Syriac (54)	54	0.27
Austrian (7)	33	0.16
Belgian (6)	37	0.18
British (105)	249	1.23
Canadian (33)	169	0.84
Celtic (14)	14	0.07
Croatian (0)	22	0.11
Czech (18)	90	0.45
Danish (73)	121	0.60
Dutch (66)	238	1.18
English (820)	2,229	11.04
European (147)	202	1.00
Finnish (0)	31	0.15
French, ex. Basque (257)	1,180	5.84
French Canadian (36)	211	1.04
German (827)	3,894	19.28
Greek (40)	76	0.38
Hungarian (34)	117	0.58
Iranian (23)	65	0.32
Irish (991)	2,742	13.58
Israeli (0)	16	0.08
Italian (743)	1,572	7.78
Latvian (10)	10	0.05
Maltese (0)	87	0.43
Norwegian (13)	507	2.51
Polish (14)	340	1.68
Portuguese (110)	309	1.53
Romanian (0)	10	0.05
Russian (52)	81	0.40
Scandinavian (106)	106	0.52
Scotch-Irish (195)	500	2.48
Scottish (137)	648	3.21
Slavic (15)	15	0.07
Swedish (45)	382	1.89
Swiss (0)	15	0.07
Ukrainian (0)	10	0.05
Welsh (30)	220	1.09
Yugoslavian (29)	41	0.20

Hispanic Origin	Population	%
Hispanic or Latino (of any race)	4,289	20.79
Central American, ex. Mexican	73	0.35
Costa Rican	17	0.08
Guatemalan	13	0.06
Honduran	4	0.02
Nicaraguan	7	0.03
Panamanian	16	0.08
Salvadoran	16	0.08
Cuban	15	0.07
Dominican Republic	6	0.03
Mexican	3,694	17.91
Puerto Rican	121	0.59
South American	39	0.19
Argentinean	6	0.03
Bolivian	1	<0.01
Chilean	2	0.01
Colombian	8	0.04
Ecuadorian	3	0.01
Peruvian	16	0.08
Venezuelan	3	0.01
Other Hispanic or Latino	341	1.65

Race*	Population	%
African-American/Black (409)	577	2.80
Not Hispanic (372)	503	2.44
Hispanic (37)	74	0.36
American Indian/Alaska Native (234)	520	2.52
Not Hispanic (157)	369	1.79
Hispanic (77)	151	0.73
Apache (14)	25	0.12
Blackfeet (7)	18	0.09
Cherokee (17)	76	0.37
Cheyenne (0)	1	<0.01
Chickasaw (2)	3	0.01
Chippewa (3)	13	0.06
Choctaw (10)	14	0.07
Comanche (1)	2	0.01
Cree (0)	1	<0.01
Creek (7)	8	0.04
Delaware (1)	1	<0.01
Inupiat *(Alaska Native)* (0)	4	0.02
Iroquois (1)	12	0.06
Lumbee (1)	1	<0.01
Mexican American Ind. (17)	28	0.14
Navajo (1)	6	0.03
Osage (0)	3	0.01
Paiute (1)	1	<0.01
Pima (2)	4	0.02
Potawatomi (1)	1	<0.01
Pueblo (1)	1	<0.01
Shoshone (1)	3	0.01
Sioux (0)	11	0.05
South American Ind. (3)	3	0.01
Spanish American Ind. (1)	1	<0.01
Tohono O'Odham (1)	7	0.03
Ute (4)	4	0.02
Yakama (0)	1	<0.01
Yaqui (2)	9	0.04
Yuman (0)	1	<0.01
Asian (345)	706	3.42
Not Hispanic (314)	584	2.83
Hispanic (31)	122	0.59
Cambodian (13)	14	0.07
Chinese, ex. Taiwanese (29)	58	0.28
Filipino (176)	334	1.62
Hmong (7)	7	0.03
Indian (5)	7	0.03
Indonesian (2)	5	0.02
Japanese (26)	121	0.59
Korean (17)	27	0.13
Laotian (6)	6	0.03
Pakistani (0)	2	0.01
Sri Lankan (2)	2	0.01
Thai (13)	17	0.08
Vietnamese (37)	55	0.27
Hawaii Native/Pacific Islander (95)	195	0.95
Not Hispanic (84)	148	0.72
Hispanic (11)	47	0.23
Fijian (1)	4	0.02
Guamanian/Chamorro (41)	57	0.28
Native Hawaiian (19)	58	0.28
Samoan (25)	41	0.20
White (16,845)	17,844	86.49
Not Hispanic (14,782)	15,378	74.54
Hispanic (2,063)	2,466	11.95

Winton

Place Type: CDP
County: Merced
Population: 10,613†

Ancestry‡	Population	%
American (484)	484	4.36
Armenian (36)	36	0.32
Czech (14)	14	0.13
Danish (0)	12	0.11
Dutch (0)	40	0.36
English (43)	234	2.11
French, ex. Basque (0)	9	0.08
German (166)	521	4.69
Hungarian (26)	26	0.23
Irish (71)	289	2.60
Italian (0)	9	0.08
Norwegian (28)	73	0.66
Polish (0)	81	0.73
Portuguese (94)	130	1.17
Russian (0)	18	0.16
Scottish (0)	23	0.21

Hispanic Origin	Population	%
Hispanic or Latino (of any race)	7,566	71.29
Central American, ex. Mexican	53	0.50
Guatemalan	16	0.15
Nicaraguan	7	0.07
Panamanian	2	0.02
Salvadoran	28	0.26
Cuban	3	0.03
Mexican	7,261	68.42
Puerto Rican	24	0.23
South American	4	0.04
Colombian	2	0.02
Ecuadorian	2	0.02
Other Hispanic or Latino	221	2.08

Race*	Population	%
African-American/Black (175)	246	2.32
Not Hispanic (150)	181	1.71
Hispanic (25)	65	0.61
American Indian/Alaska Native (140)	238	2.24
Not Hispanic (25)	83	0.78
Hispanic (115)	155	1.46
Apache (3)	5	0.05
Blackfeet (0)	2	0.02
Cherokee (5)	28	0.26
Choctaw (2)	6	0.06
Creek (3)	5	0.05
Mexican American Ind. (17)	20	0.19
Paiute (1)	1	0.01
Potawatomi (1)	1	0.01
Pueblo (0)	5	0.05
Sioux (0)	1	0.01
Spanish American Ind. (69)	69	0.65
Yaqui (2)	6	0.06
Asian (701)	796	7.50
Not Hispanic (681)	750	7.07
Hispanic (20)	46	0.43
Cambodian (5)	7	0.07
Chinese, ex. Taiwanese (3)	3	0.03
Filipino (65)	89	0.84
Hmong (425)	453	4.27
Indian (84)	110	1.04
Japanese (8)	12	0.11
Korean (12)	22	0.21
Laotian (24)	33	0.31
Taiwanese (1)	1	0.01
Thai (14)	17	0.16
Vietnamese (9)	11	0.10
Hawaii Native/Pacific Islander (8)	35	0.33
Not Hispanic (8)	25	0.24
Hispanic (0)	10	0.09
Guamanian/Chamorro (4)	12	0.11
Native Hawaiian (3)	11	0.10
Samoan (1)	3	0.03
White (5,696)	6,026	56.78
Not Hispanic (2,028)	2,134	20.11
Hispanic (3,668)	3,892	36.67

Woodcrest

Place Type: CDP
County: Riverside
Population: 14,347†

Ancestry‡	Population	%
African, Sub-Saharan (24)	48	0.34
African (11)	35	0.24
Nigerian (13)	13	0.09
American (801)	801	5.60
Arab (17)	55	0.38
Arab (0)	38	0.27
Palestinian (17)	17	0.12
Armenian (0)	5	0.03
Austrian (0)	19	0.13
Basque (0)	12	0.08
British (47)	59	0.41
Bulgarian (10)	10	0.07

*Notes: † The Census 2010 population figure is used to calculate the percentages in the Hispanic Origin and Race categories. Ancestry percentages are based on the 2006-2010 American Community Survey population (not shown); ‡ Numbers in parentheses indicate the number of people reporting a single ancestry; * Numbers in parentheses indicate the number of persons reporting this race alone, not in combination with any other race; Please refer to the Explanation of Data for more information.*

Canadian (12)	59	0.41
Croatian (0)	13	0.09
Czech (0)	13	0.09
Czechoslovakian (0)	31	0.22
Danish (12)	36	0.25
Dutch (58)	335	2.34
English (319)	1,139	7.97
European (155)	251	1.76
Finnish (39)	39	0.27
French, ex. Basque (49)	385	2.69
French Canadian (91)	196	1.37
German (431)	1,939	13.56
Greek (11)	27	0.19
Irish (512)	1,944	13.60
Italian (255)	668	4.67
Latvian (0)	14	0.10
New Zealander (13)	39	0.27
Northern European (18)	27	0.19
Norwegian (53)	152	1.06
Polish (145)	283	1.98
Portuguese (24)	86	0.60
Romanian (98)	139	0.97
Russian (36)	92	0.64
Scandinavian (27)	53	0.37
Scotch-Irish (27)	364	2.55
Scottish (82)	219	1.53
Slovak (0)	39	0.27
Slovene (0)	12	0.08
Swedish (30)	213	1.49
Swiss (0)	27	0.19
Turkish (37)	37	0.26
Ukrainian (7)	7	0.05
Welsh (22)	228	1.59
West Indian, ex. Hispanic (0)	11	0.08
Bahamian (0)	11	0.08
Yugoslavian (12)	12	0.08

Hispanic Origin	Population	%
Hispanic or Latino (of any race)	4,113	28.67
Central American, ex. Mexican	232	1.62
Costa Rican	11	0.08
Guatemalan	92	0.64
Honduran	17	0.12
Nicaraguan	15	0.10
Panamanian	4	0.03
Salvadoran	91	0.63
Other Central American	2	0.01
Cuban	68	0.47
Dominican Republic	2	0.01
Mexican	3,453	24.07
Puerto Rican	73	0.51
South American	135	0.94
Argentinean	15	0.10
Bolivian	9	0.06
Chilean	8	0.06
Colombian	42	0.29
Ecuadorian	15	0.10
Peruvian	31	0.22
Uruguayan	2	0.01
Venezuelan	11	0.08
Other South American	2	0.01
Other Hispanic or Latino	150	1.05

Race*	Population	%
African-American/Black (716)	884	6.16
Not Hispanic (687)	813	5.67
Hispanic (29)	71	0.49
American Indian/Alaska Native (69)	233	1.62
Not Hispanic (39)	138	0.96
Hispanic (30)	95	0.66
Apache (11)	15	0.10
Blackfeet (1)	5	0.03
Canadian/French Am. Ind. (1)	1	0.01
Cherokee (8)	34	0.24
Chickasaw (1)	3	0.02
Choctaw (2)	9	0.06
Creek (0)	1	0.01
Crow (0)	1	0.01
Mexican American Ind. (10)	12	0.08
Navajo (2)	10	0.07
Paiute (0)	1	0.01
Potawatomi (1)	6	0.04
Seminole (1)	2	0.01
Sioux (0)	1	0.01
Yaqui (5)	5	0.03
Asian (715)	952	6.64
Not Hispanic (697)	886	6.18
Hispanic (18)	66	0.46
Bangladeshi (1)	1	0.01
Burmese (2)	2	0.01
Cambodian (22)	23	0.16
Chinese, ex. Taiwanese (99)	140	0.98
Filipino (197)	284	1.98
Indian (65)	84	0.59
Indonesian (3)	6	0.04
Japanese (37)	91	0.63
Korean (118)	134	0.93
Laotian (10)	11	0.08
Malaysian (1)	1	0.01
Pakistani (19)	22	0.15
Sri Lankan (0)	2	0.01
Taiwanese (10)	13	0.09
Thai (14)	23	0.16
Vietnamese (86)	103	0.72
Hawaii Native/Pacific Islander (41)	73	0.51
Not Hispanic (35)	58	0.40
Hispanic (6)	15	0.10
Fijian (6)	6	0.04
Guamanian/Chamorro (14)	19	0.13
Native Hawaiian (6)	14	0.10
Samoan (3)	7	0.05
Tongan (10)	10	0.07
White (10,418)	10,987	76.58
Not Hispanic (8,380)	8,698	60.63
Hispanic (2,038)	2,289	15.95

Woodland

Place Type: City
County: Yolo
Population: 55,468†

Ancestry‡	Population	%
Afghan (13)	13	0.02
African, Sub-Saharan (20)	48	0.09
African (20)	48	0.09
Albanian (0)	30	0.05
American (1,242)	1,242	2.27
Arab (47)	93	0.17
Arab (0)	27	0.05
Jordanian (15)	15	0.03
Lebanese (9)	28	0.05
Other Arab (23)	23	0.04
Australian (27)	41	0.07
Austrian (12)	45	0.08
Basque (44)	127	0.23
Belgian (0)	17	0.03
Brazilian (13)	13	0.02
British (27)	78	0.14
Cajun (0)	11	0.02
Canadian (18)	50	0.09
Croatian (0)	75	0.14
Czech (26)	86	0.16
Czechoslovakian (10)	23	0.04
Danish (132)	471	0.86
Dutch (139)	651	1.19
Eastern European (80)	80	0.15
English (1,641)	4,976	9.08
European (759)	930	1.70
Finnish (82)	219	0.40
French, ex. Basque (189)	991	1.81
French Canadian (35)	215	0.39
German (2,362)	7,272	13.27
Greek (107)	138	0.25
Hungarian (42)	130	0.24
Icelander (15)	15	0.03
Iranian (8)	8	0.01
Irish (1,178)	4,734	8.64
Italian (857)	2,425	4.43
Lithuanian (9)	38	0.07
Luxemburger (0)	16	0.03
New Zealander (0)	7	0.01
Northern European (36)	36	0.07
Norwegian (182)	700	1.28
Pennsylvania German (17)	17	0.03
Polish (117)	473	0.86
Portuguese (340)	616	1.12
Russian (69)	227	0.41
Scandinavian (91)	123	0.22
Scotch-Irish (199)	892	1.63
Scottish (204)	1,047	1.91
Slavic (0)	11	0.02
Slovak (15)	24	0.04
Swedish (159)	725	1.32
Swiss (44)	205	0.37
Turkish (20)	20	0.04
Ukrainian (107)	133	0.24
Welsh (12)	276	0.50
West Indian, ex. Hispanic (26)	62	0.11
Haitian (8)	16	0.03
Jamaican (18)	46	0.08
Yugoslavian (13)	13	0.02

Hispanic Origin	Population	%
Hispanic or Latino (of any race)	26,289	47.39
Central American, ex. Mexican	367	0.66
Costa Rican	10	0.02
Guatemalan	69	0.12
Honduran	109	0.20
Nicaraguan	36	0.06
Panamanian	16	0.03
Salvadoran	127	0.23
Cuban	42	0.08
Dominican Republic	15	0.03
Mexican	24,330	43.86
Puerto Rican	183	0.33
South American	157	0.28
Argentinean	31	0.06
Bolivian	2	<0.01
Chilean	12	0.02
Colombian	35	0.06
Ecuadorian	12	0.02
Peruvian	46	0.08
Uruguayan	2	<0.01
Venezuelan	14	0.03
Other South American	3	0.01
Other Hispanic or Latino	1,195	2.15

Race*	Population	%
African-American/Black (855)	1,263	2.28
Not Hispanic (708)	954	1.72
Hispanic (147)	309	0.56
American Indian/Alaska Native (726)	1,468	2.65
Not Hispanic (332)	754	1.36
Hispanic (394)	714	1.29
Alaska Athabascan *(Ala. Nat.)* (1)	4	0.01
Aleut *(Alaska Native)* (1)	2	<0.01
Apache (16)	40	0.07
Blackfeet (5)	18	0.03
Canadian/French Am. Ind. (0)	1	<0.01
Central American Ind. (0)	2	<0.01
Cherokee (66)	222	0.40
Cheyenne (1)	3	0.01
Chickasaw (2)	6	0.01
Chippewa (5)	13	0.02
Choctaw (20)	60	0.11
Comanche (0)	6	0.01
Cree (0)	2	<0.01
Creek (3)	7	0.01
Crow (6)	7	0.01
Hopi (4)	6	0.01
Houma (0)	1	<0.01
Inupiat *(Alaska Native)* (2)	5	0.01
Iroquois (3)	16	0.03
Mexican American Ind. (65)	97	0.17
Navajo (15)	35	0.06
Osage (1)	2	<0.01
Paiute (10)	18	0.03
Pima (3)	5	0.01
Potawatomi (4)	7	0.01

*Notes: † The Census 2010 population figure is used to calculate the percentages in the Hispanic Origin and Race categories. Ancestry percentages are based on the 2006-2010 American Community Survey population (not shown); ‡ Numbers in parentheses indicate the number of people reporting a single ancestry; * Numbers in parentheses indicate the number of persons reporting this race alone, not in combination with any other race; Please refer to the Explanation of Data for more information.*

Pueblo (3)	9	0.02
Shoshone (10)	14	0.03
Sioux (12)	37	0.07
South American Ind. (2)	5	0.01
Spanish American Ind. (8)	9	0.02
Tlingit-Haida *(Alaska Native)* (3)	3	0.01
Tohono O'Odham (2)	2	<0.01
Yakama (5)	5	0.01
Yaqui (12)	28	0.05
Asian (3,458)	4,220	7.61
Not Hispanic (3,385)	3,937	7.10
Hispanic (73)	283	0.51
Cambodian (31)	39	0.07
Chinese, ex. Taiwanese (533)	675	1.22
Filipino (519)	801	1.44
Hmong (36)	44	0.08
Indian (995)	1,139	2.05
Indonesian (0)	2	<0.01
Japanese (198)	346	0.62
Korean (51)	77	0.14
Laotian (12)	27	0.05
Nepalese (149)	162	0.29
Pakistani (615)	677	1.22
Sri Lankan (8)	11	0.02
Taiwanese (8)	12	0.02
Thai (26)	37	0.07
Vietnamese (123)	157	0.28
Hawaii Native/Pacific Islander (169)	386	0.70
Not Hispanic (141)	283	0.51
Hispanic (28)	103	0.19
Fijian (85)	105	0.19
Guamanian/Chamorro (19)	40	0.07
Native Hawaiian (21)	84	0.15
Samoan (7)	21	0.04
Tongan (2)	5	0.01
White (34,904)	37,319	67.28
Not Hispanic (23,368)	24,340	43.88
Hispanic (11,536)	12,979	23.40

Yorba Linda

Place Type: City
County: Orange
Population: 64,234†

Ancestry‡	Population	%
African, Sub-Saharan (66)	96	0.15
African (0)	30	0.05
Nigerian (23)	23	0.04
South African (26)	26	0.04
Sudanese (9)	9	0.01
Other Sub-Saharan African (8)	8	0.01
Albanian (6)	6	0.01
American (2,302)	2,302	3.66
Arab (694)	870	1.38
Arab (153)	153	0.24
Egyptian (70)	89	0.14
Iraqi (15)	60	0.10
Jordanian (6)	25	0.04
Lebanese (291)	374	0.59
Palestinian (25)	25	0.04
Syrian (0)	10	0.02
Other Arab (134)	134	0.21
Armenian (219)	319	0.51
Assyrian/Chaldean/Syriac (4)	69	0.11
Australian (0)	6	0.01
Austrian (74)	115	0.18
Basque (12)	21	0.03
Belgian (33)	63	0.10
Brazilian (0)	24	0.04
British (169)	296	0.47
Bulgarian (8)	8	0.01
Cajun (0)	14	0.02
Canadian (199)	388	0.62
Croatian (0)	109	0.17
Czech (118)	277	0.44
Czechoslovakian (66)	120	0.19
Danish (231)	720	1.14
Dutch (319)	1,479	2.35
Eastern European (53)	63	0.10
English (2,446)	8,660	13.76
Estonian (12)	12	0.02
European (928)	1,039	1.65
Finnish (11)	82	0.13
French, ex. Basque (251)	2,344	3.73
French Canadian (120)	343	0.55
German (2,869)	11,892	18.90
Greek (192)	309	0.49
Hungarian (107)	528	0.84
Iranian (705)	789	1.25
Irish (1,634)	7,899	12.56
Israeli (15)	25	0.04
Italian (1,737)	4,743	7.54
Latvian (8)	26	0.04
Lithuanian (43)	97	0.15
Macedonian (6)	6	0.01
Northern European (34)	34	0.05
Norwegian (340)	975	1.55
Polish (384)	1,600	2.54
Portuguese (41)	129	0.21
Romanian (105)	217	0.34
Russian (218)	691	1.10
Scandinavian (100)	245	0.39
Scotch-Irish (261)	1,121	1.78
Scottish (512)	1,413	2.25
Serbian (95)	149	0.24
Slavic (74)	86	0.14
Slovak (28)	204	0.32
Slovene (0)	66	0.10
Swedish (414)	1,571	2.50
Swiss (8)	281	0.45
Turkish (9)	9	0.01
Ukrainian (77)	267	0.42
Welsh (21)	629	1.00
West Indian, ex. Hispanic (24)	32	0.05
Belizean (0)	8	0.01
Dutch West Indian (6)	6	0.01
Jamaican (18)	18	0.03
Yugoslavian (11)	87	0.14

Hispanic Origin	Population	%
Hispanic or Latino (of any race)	9,220	14.35
Central American, ex. Mexican	331	0.52
Costa Rican	39	0.06
Guatemalan	83	0.13
Honduran	21	0.03
Nicaraguan	58	0.09
Panamanian	14	0.02
Salvadoran	115	0.18
Other Central American	1	<0.01
Cuban	255	0.40
Dominican Republic	25	0.04
Mexican	6,884	10.72
Puerto Rican	200	0.31
South American	703	1.09
Argentinean	132	0.21
Bolivian	17	0.03
Chilean	33	0.05
Colombian	153	0.24
Ecuadorian	95	0.15
Paraguayan	2	<0.01
Peruvian	239	0.37
Uruguayan	16	0.02
Venezuelan	8	0.01
Other South American	8	0.01
Other Hispanic or Latino	822	1.28

Race*	Population	%
African-American/Black (835)	1,145	1.78
Not Hispanic (789)	1,032	1.61
Hispanic (46)	113	0.18
American Indian/Alaska Native (230)	634	0.99
Not Hispanic (120)	389	0.61
Hispanic (110)	245	0.38
Alaska Athabascan *(Ala. Nat.)* (1)	3	<0.01
Aleut *(Alaska Native)* (5)	5	0.01
Apache (8)	42	0.07
Blackfeet (3)	24	0.04
Canadian/French Am. Ind. (0)	2	<0.01
Central American Ind. (1)	1	<0.01
Cherokee (23)	110	0.17
Chickasaw (4)	5	0.01
Chippewa (2)	14	0.02
Choctaw (20)	50	0.08
Comanche (1)	1	<0.01
Creek (6)	7	0.01
Hopi (1)	3	<0.01
Inupiat *(Alaska Native)* (0)	1	<0.01
Iroquois (0)	3	<0.01
Mexican American Ind. (9)	19	0.03
Navajo (6)	13	0.02
Osage (7)	7	0.01
Paiute (2)	5	0.01
Pima (7)	7	0.01
Pueblo (1)	2	<0.01
Seminole (0)	4	0.01
Shoshone (0)	2	<0.01
Sioux (3)	15	0.02
South American Ind. (7)	10	0.02
Spanish American Ind. (2)	2	<0.01
Ute (0)	2	<0.01
Yaqui (4)	13	0.02
Asian (10,030)	11,494	17.89
Not Hispanic (9,957)	11,216	17.46
Hispanic (73)	278	0.43
Bangladeshi (13)	13	0.02
Burmese (17)	21	0.03
Cambodian (61)	73	0.11
Chinese, ex. Taiwanese (1,860)	2,347	3.65
Filipino (1,273)	1,657	2.58
Indian (1,421)	1,545	2.41
Indonesian (107)	158	0.25
Japanese (711)	1,147	1.79
Korean (1,966)	2,132	3.32
Laotian (16)	20	0.03
Malaysian (3)	11	0.02
Pakistani (223)	259	0.40
Sri Lankan (21)	21	0.03
Taiwanese (517)	555	0.86
Thai (120)	143	0.22
Vietnamese (1,257)	1,456	2.27
Hawaii Native/Pacific Islander (85)	245	0.38
Not Hispanic (78)	214	0.33
Hispanic (7)	31	0.05
Fijian (4)	6	0.01
Guamanian/Chamorro (17)	28	0.04
Native Hawaiian (33)	114	0.18
Samoan (9)	29	0.05
White (48,246)	50,506	78.63
Not Hispanic (42,183)	43,720	68.06
Hispanic (6,063)	6,786	10.56

Yreka

Place Type: City
County: Siskiyou
Population: 7,765†

Ancestry‡	Population	%
African, Sub-Saharan (15)	15	0.20
African (15)	15	0.20
American (324)	324	4.22
Arab (0)	9	0.12
Lebanese (0)	9	0.12
Austrian (3)	10	0.13
Basque (0)	21	0.27
Belgian (0)	23	0.30
British (27)	27	0.35
Celtic (0)	38	0.50
Croatian (0)	6	0.08
Czech (11)	23	0.30
Danish (38)	67	0.87
Dutch (16)	141	1.84
Eastern European (17)	17	0.22
English (267)	1,003	13.07
European (46)	80	1.04
Finnish (20)	23	0.30
French, ex. Basque (19)	329	4.29
French Canadian (52)	67	0.87
German (369)	1,143	14.89

*Notes: † The Census 2010 population figure is used to calculate the percentages in the Hispanic Origin and Race categories. Ancestry percentages are based on the 2006-2010 American Community Survey population (not shown); ‡ Numbers in parentheses indicate the number of people reporting a single ancestry; * Numbers in parentheses indicate the number of persons reporting this race alone, not in combination with any other race; Please refer to the Explanation of Data for more information.*

Hungarian (0)	28	0.36
Irish (308)	1,184	15.42
Italian (152)	486	6.33
Lithuanian (0)	39	0.51
Northern European (52)	52	0.68
Norwegian (35)	197	2.57
Polish (70)	111	1.45
Portuguese (105)	242	3.15
Russian (8)	61	0.79
Scandinavian (0)	16	0.21
Scotch-Irish (72)	231	3.01
Scottish (46)	215	2.80
Slovene (28)	50	0.65
Swedish (75)	337	4.39
Welsh (50)	99	1.29
Yugoslavian (0)	22	0.29

Hispanic Origin	Population	%
Hispanic or Latino (of any race)	753	9.70
Central American, ex. Mexican	20	0.26
Costa Rican	1	0.01
Guatemalan	1	0.01
Nicaraguan	6	0.08
Panamanian	3	0.04
Salvadoran	9	0.12
Cuban	6	0.08
Mexican	612	7.88
Puerto Rican	27	0.35
South American	4	0.05
Argentinean	3	0.04
Colombian	1	0.01
Other Hispanic or Latino	84	1.08

Race*	Population	%
African-American/Black (57)	123	1.58
Not Hispanic (53)	104	1.34
Hispanic (4)	19	0.24
American Indian/Alaska Native (491)	813	10.47
Not Hispanic (413)	693	8.92
Hispanic (78)	120	1.55
Aleut *(Alaska Native)* (1)	1	0.01
Apache (5)	17	0.22
Blackfeet (1)	15	0.19
Cherokee (7)	50	0.64
Cheyenne (1)	1	0.01
Chippewa (2)	4	0.05
Choctaw (1)	7	0.09
Comanche (0)	3	0.04
Creek (2)	3	0.04
Inupiat *(Alaska Native)* (1)	1	0.01
Iroquois (2)	4	0.05
Lumbee (0)	2	0.03
Mexican American Ind. (9)	14	0.18
Navajo (2)	2	0.03
Osage (6)	7	0.09
Paiute (2)	2	0.03
Pueblo (1)	1	0.01
Shoshone (2)	6	0.08
Sioux (0)	5	0.06
Tlingit-Haida *(Alaska Native)* (1)	1	0.01
Ute (1)	1	0.01
Yaqui (0)	2	0.03
Yuman (2)	2	0.03
Yup'ik *(Alaska Native)* (0)	3	0.04
Asian (94)	160	2.06
Not Hispanic (90)	151	1.94
Hispanic (4)	9	0.12
Burmese (1)	1	0.01
Cambodian (23)	28	0.36
Chinese, ex. Taiwanese (16)	29	0.37
Filipino (7)	33	0.42
Indian (16)	22	0.28
Japanese (12)	21	0.27
Korean (4)	5	0.06
Laotian (4)	9	0.12
Malaysian (0)	1	0.01
Thai (2)	4	0.05
Vietnamese (1)	3	0.04
Hawaii Native/Pacific Islander (9)	45	0.58
Not Hispanic (8)	38	0.49
Hispanic (1)	7	0.09
Guamanian/Chamorro (3)	10	0.13
Marshallese (0)	3	0.04
Native Hawaiian (4)	21	0.27
Samoan (0)	4	0.05
White (6,495)	6,916	89.07
Not Hispanic (6,078)	6,419	82.67
Hispanic (417)	497	6.40

Yuba City

Place Type: City
County: Sutter
Population: 64,925†

Ancestry‡	Population	%
African, Sub-Saharan (22)	35	0.06
African (22)	35	0.06
American (3,200)	3,200	5.04
Arab (68)	178	0.28
Arab (66)	66	0.10
Lebanese (0)	110	0.17
Syrian (2)	2	<0.01
Armenian (158)	168	0.26
Austrian (9)	15	0.02
Basque (29)	29	0.05
Belgian (0)	16	0.03
Brazilian (37)	99	0.16
British (70)	91	0.14
Cajun (9)	9	0.01
Canadian (31)	126	0.20
Celtic (10)	22	0.03
Croatian (0)	14	0.02
Czech (122)	283	0.45
Czechoslovakian (25)	259	0.41
Danish (151)	417	0.66
Dutch (217)	1,215	1.92
Eastern European (6)	18	0.03
English (1,338)	4,674	7.37
European (549)	685	1.08
Finnish (41)	123	0.19
French, ex. Basque (259)	1,371	2.16
French Canadian (9)	110	0.17
German (2,173)	7,806	12.31
Greek (54)	211	0.33
Hungarian (10)	25	0.04
Iranian (12)	61	0.10
Irish (1,178)	5,955	9.39
Italian (941)	2,285	3.60
Lithuanian (39)	54	0.09
Luxemburger (0)	43	0.07
Maltese (14)	14	0.02
Northern European (46)	46	0.07
Norwegian (239)	688	1.08
Polish (101)	533	0.84
Portuguese (543)	1,175	1.85
Romanian (16)	16	0.03
Russian (27)	262	0.41
Scandinavian (89)	254	0.40
Scotch-Irish (379)	754	1.19
Scottish (387)	1,100	1.73
Serbian (0)	15	0.02
Slavic (0)	7	0.01
Slovak (0)	64	0.10
Swedish (70)	554	0.87
Swiss (36)	248	0.39
Turkish (33)	42	0.07
Ukrainian (11)	72	0.11
Welsh (49)	268	0.42
West Indian, ex. Hispanic (18)	76	0.12
Dutch West Indian (0)	9	0.01
Jamaican (18)	53	0.08
West Indian (0)	14	0.02
Yugoslavian (19)	148	0.23

Hispanic Origin	Population	%
Hispanic or Latino (of any race)	18,413	28.36
Central American, ex. Mexican	271	0.42
Costa Rican	22	0.03
Guatemalan	51	0.08
Honduran	24	0.04
Nicaraguan	56	0.09
Panamanian	18	0.03
Salvadoran	99	0.15
Other Central American	1	<0.01
Cuban	44	0.07
Dominican Republic	4	0.01
Mexican	16,488	25.40
Puerto Rican	262	0.40
South American	116	0.18
Argentinean	17	0.03
Bolivian	1	<0.01
Chilean	5	0.01
Colombian	27	0.04
Ecuadorian	7	0.01
Paraguayan	3	<0.01
Peruvian	51	0.08
Uruguayan	1	<0.01
Other South American	4	0.01
Other Hispanic or Latino	1,228	1.89

Race*	Population	%
African-American/Black (1,591)	2,255	3.47
Not Hispanic (1,425)	1,934	2.98
Hispanic (166)	321	0.49
American Indian/Alaska Native (909)	1,967	3.03
Not Hispanic (606)	1,363	2.10
Hispanic (303)	604	0.93
Alaska Athabascan *(Ala. Nat.)* (0)	1	<0.01
Apache (21)	51	0.08
Blackfeet (6)	53	0.08
Canadian/French Am. Ind. (3)	6	0.01
Cherokee (187)	490	0.75
Cheyenne (0)	1	<0.01
Chickasaw (5)	12	0.02
Chippewa (19)	37	0.06
Choctaw (42)	84	0.13
Comanche (1)	5	0.01
Creek (11)	18	0.03
Delaware (0)	1	<0.01
Hopi (2)	10	0.02
Iroquois (2)	9	0.01
Kiowa (0)	1	<0.01
Lumbee (1)	1	<0.01
Menominee (2)	2	<0.01
Mexican American Ind. (68)	101	0.16
Navajo (7)	44	0.07
Osage (1)	5	0.01
Ottawa (1)	1	<0.01
Paiute (2)	5	0.01
Pima (0)	2	<0.01
Potawatomi (7)	12	0.02
Pueblo (7)	15	0.02
Puget Sound Salish (1)	1	<0.01
Seminole (0)	3	<0.01
Shoshone (3)	4	0.01
Sioux (13)	26	0.04
South American Ind. (7)	10	0.02
Spanish American Ind. (5)	6	0.01
Tlingit-Haida *(Alaska Native)* (2)	11	0.02
Tohono O'Odham (2)	4	0.01
Ute (1)	1	<0.01
Yaqui (7)	19	0.03
Yuman (3)	6	0.01
Asian (11,190)	12,691	19.55
Not Hispanic (11,026)	12,264	18.89
Hispanic (164)	427	0.66
Bangladeshi (2)	5	0.01
Burmese (7)	7	0.01
Cambodian (49)	60	0.09
Chinese, ex. Taiwanese (257)	370	0.57
Filipino (607)	1,004	1.55
Hmong (227)	235	0.36
Indian (8,863)	9,352	14.40
Indonesian (15)	30	0.05
Japanese (236)	452	0.70
Korean (140)	223	0.34
Laotian (34)	48	0.07
Malaysian (2)	2	<0.01
Nepalese (9)	9	0.01

*Notes: † The Census 2010 population figure is used to calculate the percentages in the Hispanic Origin and Race categories. Ancestry percentages are based on the 2006-2010 American Community Survey population (not shown); ‡ Numbers in parentheses indicate the number of people reporting a single ancestry; * Numbers in parentheses indicate the number of persons reporting this race alone, not in combination with any other race; Please refer to the Explanation of Data for more information.*

Pakistani (363)	380	0.59
Sri Lankan (6)	11	0.02
Taiwanese (1)	6	0.01
Thai (43)	88	0.14
Vietnamese (162)	193	0.30
Hawaii Native/Pacific Islander (228)	501	0.77
Not Hispanic (206)	422	0.65
Hispanic (22)	79	0.12
Fijian (20)	33	0.05
Guamanian/Chamorro (136)	189	0.29
Native Hawaiian (34)	117	0.18
Samoan (13)	42	0.06
Tongan (1)	5	0.01
White (37,382)	40,458	62.31
Not Hispanic (30,755)	32,577	50.18
Hispanic (6,627)	7,881	12.14

Yucaipa

Place Type: City
County: San Bernardino
Population: 51,367†

Ancestry‡	Population	%
African, Sub-Saharan (117)	480	0.96
African (27)	54	0.11
Nigerian (90)	348	0.69
Other Sub-Saharan African (0)	78	0.16
Albanian (34)	51	0.10
American (1,941)	1,941	3.86
Arab (232)	240	0.48
Arab (121)	121	0.24
Egyptian (14)	14	0.03
Lebanese (0)	8	0.02
Syrian (97)	97	0.19
Armenian (28)	78	0.16
Austrian (30)	180	0.36
Belgian (16)	33	0.07
British (95)	154	0.31
Canadian (266)	438	0.87
Celtic (17)	17	0.03
Czech (13)	189	0.38
Czechoslovakian (45)	60	0.12
Danish (68)	284	0.57
Dutch (240)	1,181	2.35
English (1,519)	5,884	11.71
Estonian (17)	17	0.03
European (611)	723	1.44
Finnish (29)	83	0.17
French, ex. Basque (438)	2,075	4.13
French Canadian (152)	391	0.78
German (2,666)	9,803	19.52
Greek (117)	366	0.73
Hungarian (18)	125	0.25
Icelander (18)	484	0.96
Iranian (76)	131	0.26
Irish (1,345)	5,798	11.54
Italian (572)	2,392	4.76
Lithuanian (37)	46	0.09
Macedonian (13)	13	0.03
Northern European (21)	21	0.04
Norwegian (235)	709	1.41
Pennsylvania German (0)	12	0.02
Polish (334)	1,193	2.38
Portuguese (202)	488	0.97
Romanian (151)	160	0.32
Russian (96)	240	0.48
Scandinavian (41)	143	0.28
Scotch-Irish (710)	1,302	2.59
Scottish (485)	1,330	2.65
Slovene (15)	40	0.08
Swedish (194)	1,102	2.19
Swiss (22)	53	0.11
Ukrainian (34)	94	0.19
Welsh (107)	488	0.97
West Indian, ex. Hispanic (14)	80	0.16
Bahamian (14)	14	0.03
Belizean (0)	33	0.07
Jamaican (0)	33	0.07
Yugoslavian (120)	184	0.37

Hispanic Origin	Population	%
Hispanic or Latino (of any race)	13,943	27.14
Central American, ex. Mexican	374	0.73
Costa Rican	15	0.03
Guatemalan	151	0.29
Honduran	28	0.05
Nicaraguan	66	0.13
Panamanian	17	0.03
Salvadoran	95	0.18
Other Central American	2	<0.01
Cuban	91	0.18
Dominican Republic	19	0.04
Mexican	11,979	23.32
Puerto Rican	244	0.48
South American	184	0.36
Argentinean	53	0.10
Bolivian	6	0.01
Chilean	12	0.02
Colombian	40	0.08
Ecuadorian	25	0.05
Peruvian	35	0.07
Uruguayan	3	0.01
Venezuelan	5	0.01
Other South American	5	0.01
Other Hispanic or Latino	1,052	2.05

Race*	Population	%
African-American/Black (837)	1,230	2.39
Not Hispanic (736)	1,013	1.97
Hispanic (101)	217	0.42
American Indian/Alaska Native (485)	1,109	2.16
Not Hispanic (242)	650	1.27
Hispanic (243)	459	0.89
Alaska Athabascan *(Ala. Nat.)* (1)	1	<0.01
Aleut *(Alaska Native)* (0)	1	<0.01
Apache (13)	33	0.06
Blackfeet (2)	23	0.04
Canadian/French Am. Ind. (1)	2	<0.01
Central American Ind. (0)	2	<0.01
Cherokee (39)	201	0.39
Cheyenne (3)	9	0.02
Chickasaw (2)	7	0.01
Chippewa (8)	15	0.03
Choctaw (17)	55	0.11
Comanche (0)	4	0.01
Cree (0)	1	<0.01
Creek (0)	13	0.03
Delaware (1)	4	0.01
Hopi (1)	3	0.01
Inupiat *(Alaska Native)* (2)	3	0.01
Iroquois (5)	13	0.03
Menominee (2)	2	<0.01
Mexican American Ind. (49)	71	0.14
Navajo (15)	24	0.05
Osage (1)	5	0.01
Ottawa (4)	4	0.01
Paiute (0)	2	<0.01
Pima (4)	4	0.01
Potawatomi (1)	11	0.02
Pueblo (4)	9	0.02
Seminole (0)	4	0.01
Shoshone (0)	7	0.01
Sioux (14)	31	0.06
Spanish American Ind. (1)	2	<0.01
Tlingit-Haida *(Alaska Native)* (5)	7	0.01
Tohono O'Odham (3)	3	0.01
Ute (1)	2	<0.01
Yaqui (20)	31	0.06
Asian (1,431)	2,027	3.95
Not Hispanic (1,358)	1,786	3.48
Hispanic (73)	241	0.47
Bangladeshi (9)	15	0.03
Cambodian (17)	32	0.06
Chinese, ex. Taiwanese (193)	270	0.53
Filipino (466)	698	1.36
Indian (174)	219	0.43
Indonesian (67)	91	0.18
Japanese (59)	196	0.38
Korean (214)	267	0.52
Laotian (1)	4	0.01
Malaysian (5)	5	0.01
Pakistani (18)	20	0.04
Sri Lankan (7)	8	0.02
Taiwanese (7)	9	0.02
Thai (21)	46	0.09
Vietnamese (108)	126	0.25
Hawaii Native/Pacific Islander (74)	193	0.38
Not Hispanic (62)	151	0.29
Hispanic (12)	42	0.08
Guamanian/Chamorro (7)	25	0.05
Native Hawaiian (34)	89	0.17
Samoan (18)	32	0.06
Tongan (3)	3	0.01
White (40,824)	42,728	83.18
Not Hispanic (33,866)	34,844	67.83
Hispanic (6,958)	7,884	15.35

Yucca Valley

Place Type: Town
County: San Bernardino
Population: 20,700†

Ancestry‡	Population	%
African, Sub-Saharan (40)	130	0.64
African (40)	130	0.64
American (994)	994	4.90
Arab (17)	63	0.31
Egyptian (17)	17	0.08
Lebanese (0)	46	0.23
Armenian (0)	14	0.07
Australian (14)	74	0.36
Austrian (17)	72	0.35
Belgian (16)	16	0.08
British (64)	141	0.69
Canadian (141)	153	0.75
Czech (41)	41	0.20
Czechoslovakian (13)	13	0.06
Danish (11)	54	0.27
Dutch (236)	629	3.10
Eastern European (14)	14	0.07
English (1,014)	2,949	14.53
European (335)	485	2.39
French, ex. Basque (93)	818	4.03
French Canadian (59)	87	0.43
German (1,259)	4,047	19.95
Greek (29)	97	0.48
Hungarian (124)	261	1.29
Irish (614)	2,765	13.63
Italian (701)	1,241	6.12
Latvian (0)	12	0.06
Lithuanian (0)	12	0.06
Luxemburger (12)	12	0.06
Northern European (36)	93	0.46
Norwegian (33)	88	0.43
Pennsylvania German (9)	19	0.09
Polish (228)	603	2.97
Portuguese (53)	80	0.39
Romanian (45)	60	0.30
Russian (40)	103	0.51
Scandinavian (28)	133	0.66
Scotch-Irish (204)	464	2.29
Scottish (142)	496	2.44
Slovak (14)	23	0.11
Swedish (0)	279	1.38
Swiss (13)	61	0.30
Turkish (10)	10	0.05
Ukrainian (22)	35	0.17
Welsh (0)	153	0.75
West Indian, ex. Hispanic (20)	20	0.10
Jamaican (20)	20	0.10
Yugoslavian (54)	54	0.27

Hispanic Origin	Population	%
Hispanic or Latino (of any race)	3,679	17.77
Central American, ex. Mexican	154	0.74
Costa Rican	8	0.04
Guatemalan	44	0.21
Honduran	8	0.04
Nicaraguan	22	0.11

*Notes: † The Census 2010 population figure is used to calculate the percentages in the Hispanic Origin and Race categories. Ancestry percentages are based on the 2006-2010 American Community Survey population (not shown); ‡ Numbers in parentheses indicate the number of people reporting a single ancestry; * Numbers in parentheses indicate the number of persons reporting this race alone, not in combination with any other race; Please refer to the Explanation of Data for more information.*

Panamanian	10	0.05
Salvadoran	48	0.23
Other Central American	14	0.07
Cuban	32	0.15
Dominican Republic	9	0.04
Mexican	2,960	14.30
Puerto Rican	110	0.53
South American	61	0.29
Argentinean	12	0.06
Bolivian	6	0.03
Colombian	10	0.05
Ecuadorian	12	0.06
Paraguayan	2	0.01
Peruvian	11	0.05
Uruguayan	3	0.01
Venezuelan	4	0.02
Other South American	1	<0.01
Other Hispanic or Latino	353	1.71

Race*	Population	%
African-American/Black (666)	883	4.27
Not Hispanic (601)	761	3.68
Hispanic (65)	122	0.59
American Indian/Alaska Native (232)	532	2.57
Not Hispanic (151)	353	1.71
Hispanic (81)	179	0.86
Alaska Athabascan *(Ala. Nat.)* (1)	1	<0.01
Apache (13)	21	0.10
Blackfeet (10)	25	0.12
Canadian/French Am. Ind. (0)	1	<0.01
Cherokee (26)	98	0.47
Chickasaw (2)	4	0.02
Chippewa (2)	5	0.02
Choctaw (10)	19	0.09
Comanche (0)	1	<0.01
Cree (1)	2	0.01
Creek (2)	5	0.02
Hopi (1)	1	<0.01
Iroquois (5)	7	0.03
Kiowa (0)	2	0.01
Lumbee (1)	1	<0.01
Menominee (1)	1	<0.01
Mexican American Ind. (6)	13	0.06
Navajo (6)	24	0.12
Osage (3)	5	0.02
Ottawa (1)	1	<0.01
Paiute (0)	5	0.02
Pima (1)	1	<0.01
Potawatomi (5)	6	0.03
Pueblo (8)	9	0.04
Seminole (0)	1	<0.01
Shoshone (0)	1	<0.01
Sioux (7)	13	0.06
Tlingit-Haida *(Alaska Native)* (0)	3	0.01
Tohono O'Odham (4)	4	0.02
Yaqui (17)	23	0.11
Yuman (2)	2	0.01
Asian (469)	654	3.16
Not Hispanic (450)	592	2.86
Hispanic (19)	62	0.30
Cambodian (21)	21	0.10
Chinese, ex. Taiwanese (46)	77	0.37
Filipino (157)	260	1.26
Hmong (12)	12	0.06
Indian (103)	109	0.53
Indonesian (2)	6	0.03
Japanese (36)	79	0.38
Korean (27)	44	0.21
Laotian (0)	3	0.01
Pakistani (4)	7	0.03
Thai (12)	19	0.09
Vietnamese (23)	30	0.14
Hawaii Native/Pacific Islander (44)	125	0.60
Not Hispanic (33)	94	0.45
Hispanic (11)	31	0.15
Guamanian/Chamorro (11)	32	0.15
Native Hawaiian (12)	47	0.23
Samoan (14)	25	0.12
Tongan (0)	1	<0.01
White (17,280)	18,011	87.01
Not Hispanic (15,258)	15,705	75.87
Hispanic (2,022)	2,306	11.14

*Notes: † The Census 2010 population figure is used to calculate the percentages in the Hispanic Origin and Race categories. Ancestry percentages are based on the 2006-2010 American Community Survey population (not shown); ‡ Numbers in parentheses indicate the number of people reporting a single ancestry; * Numbers in parentheses indicate the number of persons reporting this race alone, not in combination with any other race; Please refer to the Explanation of Data for more information.*

COLORADO

Place Type: State
Population: 5,029,196[†]

Ancestry[‡]	Population	%
Afghan (1,037)	1,111	0.02
African, Sub-Saharan (22,235)	27,233	0.56
African (8,869)	12,605	0.26
Cape Verdean (0)	52	<0.01
Ethiopian (6,181)	6,547	0.13
Ghanaian (742)	830	0.02
Kenyan (132)	132	<0.01
Liberian (354)	371	0.01
Nigerian (769)	832	0.02
Senegalese (93)	108	<0.01
Sierra Leonean (14)	14	<0.01
Somalian (1,828)	1,838	0.04
South African (774)	1,094	0.02
Sudanese (1,143)	1,202	0.02
Ugandan (273)	290	0.01
Zimbabwean (56)	56	<0.01
Other Sub-Saharan African (1,007)	1,262	0.03
Albanian (396)	630	0.01
Alsatian (108)	254	0.01
American (218,038)	218,038	4.46
Arab (9,646)	16,488	0.34
Arab (1,293)	1,994	0.04
Egyptian (563)	764	0.02
Iraqi (585)	730	0.01
Jordanian (346)	411	0.01
Lebanese (2,025)	5,701	0.12
Moroccan (1,290)	1,560	0.03
Palestinian (443)	653	0.01
Syrian (349)	1,344	0.03
Other Arab (2,752)	3,331	0.07
Armenian (1,568)	2,877	0.06
Assyrian/Chaldean/Syriac (104)	130	<0.01
Australian (1,314)	2,509	0.05
Austrian (5,144)	20,532	0.42
Basque (667)	1,653	0.03
Belgian (2,036)	7,111	0.15
Brazilian (1,440)	2,229	0.05
British (13,774)	27,593	0.56
Bulgarian (1,215)	2,078	0.04
Cajun (671)	1,314	0.03
Canadian (6,192)	12,644	0.26
Carpatho Rusyn (0)	23	<0.01
Celtic (838)	1,935	0.04
Croatian (2,200)	6,570	0.13
Cypriot (36)	85	<0.01
Czech (10,444)	38,207	0.78
Czechoslovakian (3,140)	6,821	0.14
Danish (11,489)	46,668	0.95
Dutch (24,047)	96,824	1.98
Eastern European (5,717)	6,705	0.14
English (164,454)	581,842	11.91
Estonian (258)	832	0.02
European (78,801)	88,809	1.82
Finnish (3,277)	11,951	0.24
French, ex. Basque (24,288)	164,476	3.37
French Canadian (10,356)	29,127	0.60
German (363,375)	1,120,643	22.93
German Russian (370)	560	0.01
Greek (8,216)	19,656	0.40
Guyanese (73)	109	<0.01
Hungarian (6,384)	21,113	0.43
Icelander (348)	1,337	0.03
Iranian (3,214)	4,419	0.09
Irish (154,795)	628,929	12.87
Israeli (840)	1,208	0.02
Italian (84,818)	253,097	5.18
Latvian (711)	2,142	0.04
Lithuanian (3,108)	10,148	0.21
Luxemburger (238)	910	0.02
Macedonian (147)	291	0.01
Maltese (180)	430	0.01
New Zealander (454)	713	0.01
Northern European (7,916)	8,513	0.17
Norwegian (35,040)	114,313	2.34
Pennsylvania German (1,219)	2,598	0.05
Polish (35,402)	123,913	2.54
Portuguese (3,159)	10,527	0.22
Romanian (2,462)	5,560	0.11
Russian (20,923)	60,224	1.23
Scandinavian (8,760)	18,006	0.37
Scotch-Irish (39,158)	108,078	2.21
Scottish (39,159)	139,848	2.86
Serbian (891)	2,263	0.05
Slavic (1,353)	3,852	0.08
Slovak (3,018)	9,132	0.19
Slovene (2,542)	5,966	0.12
Swedish (33,525)	137,182	2.81
Swiss (5,710)	25,250	0.52
Turkish (1,155)	1,702	0.03
Ukrainian (5,887)	13,260	0.27
Welsh (9,145)	46,949	0.96
West Indian, ex. Hispanic (3,976)	6,514	0.13
Bahamian (88)	108	<0.01
Barbadian (19)	72	<0.01
Belizean (130)	340	0.01
Bermudan (25)	33	<0.01
British West Indian (182)	250	0.01
Dutch West Indian (67)	335	0.01
Haitian (560)	754	0.02
Jamaican (2,210)	3,327	0.07
Trinidadian/Tobagonian (140)	208	<0.01
U.S. Virgin Islander (21)	21	<0.01
West Indian (534)	1,049	0.02
Other West Indian (0)	17	<0.01
Yugoslavian (4,041)	8,233	0.17

Hispanic Origin	Population	%
Hispanic or Latino (of any race)	1,038,687	20.65
Central American, ex. Mexican	29,386	0.58
Costa Rican	1,104	0.02
Guatemalan	7,488	0.15
Honduran	4,356	0.09
Nicaraguan	1,364	0.03
Panamanian	2,414	0.05
Salvadoran	12,329	0.25
Other Central American	331	0.01
Cuban	6,253	0.12
Dominican Republic	1,744	0.03
Mexican	757,181	15.06
Puerto Rican	22,995	0.46
South American	19,117	0.38
Argentinean	2,165	0.04
Bolivian	775	0.02
Chilean	1,678	0.03
Colombian	4,858	0.10
Ecuadorian	1,375	0.03
Paraguayan	214	<0.01
Peruvian	5,835	0.12
Uruguayan	224	<0.01
Venezuelan	1,802	0.04
Other South American	191	<0.01
Other Hispanic or Latino	202,011	4.02

Race*	Population	%
African-American/Black (201,737)	249,812	4.97
Not Hispanic (188,778)	225,218	4.48
Hispanic (12,959)	24,594	0.49
American Indian/Alaska Native (56,010)	107,832	2.14
Not Hispanic (31,244)	63,963	1.27
Hispanic (24,766)	43,869	0.87
Alaska Athabascan *(Ala. Nat.)* (115)	175	<0.01
Aleut *(Alaska Native)* (140)	241	<0.01
Apache (2,592)	5,829	0.12
Arapaho (229)	459	0.01
Blackfeet (388)	1,969	0.04
Canadian/French Am. Ind. (91)	234	<0.01
Central American Ind. (97)	181	<0.01
Cherokee (3,860)	14,310	0.28
Cheyenne (292)	676	0.01
Chickasaw (373)	760	0.02
Chippewa (881)	1,805	0.04
Choctaw (1,097)	2,659	0.05
Colville (22)	42	<0.01
Comanche (248)	576	0.01
Cree (47)	180	<0.01
Creek (322)	813	0.02
Crow (99)	208	<0.01
Delaware (125)	281	0.01
Hopi (163)	401	0.01
Houma (16)	42	<0.01
Inupiat *(Alaska Native)* (196)	297	0.01
Iroquois (377)	999	0.02
Kiowa (101)	244	<0.01
Lumbee (87)	186	<0.01
Menominee (56)	82	<0.01
Mexican American Ind. (2,683)	4,184	0.08
Navajo (6,069)	9,235	0.18
Osage (260)	541	0.01
Ottawa (45)	104	<0.01
Paiute (71)	150	<0.01
Pima (80)	124	<0.01
Potawatomi (375)	709	0.01
Pueblo (890)	1,620	0.03
Puget Sound Salish (58)	94	<0.01
Seminole (128)	424	0.01
Shoshone (194)	362	0.01
Sioux (3,420)	6,041	0.12
South American Ind. (198)	437	0.01
Spanish American Ind. (537)	765	0.02
Tlingit-Haida *(Alaska Native)* (168)	289	0.01
Tohono O'Odham (72)	111	<0.01
Tsimshian *(Alaska Native)* (12)	33	<0.01
Ute (2,529)	3,404	0.07
Yakama (20)	39	<0.01
Yaqui (175)	379	0.01
Yuman (49)	76	<0.01
Yup'ik *(Alaska Native)* (84)	131	<0.01
Asian (139,028)	185,589	3.69
Not Hispanic (135,564)	174,577	3.47
Hispanic (3,464)	11,012	0.22
Bangladeshi (272)	308	0.01
Bhutanese (478)	592	0.01
Burmese (1,693)	1,822	0.04
Cambodian (2,185)	2,803	0.06
Chinese, ex. Taiwanese (23,878)	31,781	0.63
Filipino (14,448)	26,242	0.52
Hmong (3,611)	3,859	0.08
Indian (20,369)	24,135	0.48
Indonesian (1,359)	2,037	0.04
Japanese (11,097)	22,714	0.45
Korean (20,433)	28,177	0.56
Laotian (2,118)	2,576	0.05
Malaysian (255)	378	0.01
Nepalese (2,484)	2,751	0.05
Pakistani (1,614)	2,021	0.04
Sri Lankan (218)	291	0.01
Taiwanese (1,250)	1,668	0.03
Thai (2,681)	4,232	0.08
Vietnamese (20,899)	23,933	0.48
Hawaii Native/Pacific Islander (6,623)	15,200	0.30
Not Hispanic (5,661)	12,023	0.24
Hispanic (962)	3,177	0.06
Fijian (78)	123	<0.01
Guamanian/Chamorro (1,784)	3,056	0.06
Marshallese (156)	167	<0.01
Native Hawaiian (1,783)	5,670	0.11
Samoan (1,091)	2,050	0.04
Tongan (266)	397	0.01
White (4,089,202)	4,240,231	84.31
Not Hispanic (3,520,793)	3,611,570	71.81
Hispanic (568,409)	628,661	12.50

*Notes: † The Census 2010 population figure is used to calculate the percentages in the Hispanic Origin and Race categories. Ancestry percentages are based on the 2006-2010 American Community Survey population (not shown); ‡ Numbers in parentheses indicate the number of people reporting a single ancestry; * Numbers in parentheses indicate the number of persons reporting this race alone, not in combination with any other race; Please refer to the Explanation of Data for more information.*

Alamosa

Place Type: City
County: Alamosa
Population: 8,780†

Ancestry‡	Population	%
African, Sub-Saharan (14)	14	0.16
Ethiopian (14)	14	0.16
Alsatian (16)	16	0.18
American (175)	175	2.01
Arab (14)	25	0.29
Iraqi (0)	11	0.13
Lebanese (14)	14	0.16
Austrian (0)	12	0.14
Basque (83)	83	0.95
Brazilian (14)	14	0.16
British (0)	12	0.14
Czech (0)	27	0.31
Czechoslovakian (14)	14	0.16
Danish (0)	205	2.36
Dutch (12)	139	1.60
English (306)	910	10.47
European (145)	163	1.88
Finnish (0)	3	0.03
French, ex. Basque (18)	181	2.08
French Canadian (0)	32	0.37
German (315)	1,434	16.50
Greek (0)	27	0.31
Hungarian (21)	49	0.56
Irish (157)	720	8.28
Italian (98)	178	2.05
Luxemburger (0)	11	0.13
Northern European (8)	8	0.09
Norwegian (0)	29	0.33
Polish (12)	172	1.98
Portuguese (0)	11	0.13
Russian (0)	27	0.31
Scandinavian (0)	30	0.35
Scotch-Irish (52)	110	1.27
Scottish (62)	136	1.56
Swedish (0)	62	0.71
Swiss (0)	31	0.36
Welsh (24)	115	1.32
West Indian, ex. Hispanic (0)	14	0.16
Trinidadian/Tobagonian (0)	14	0.16

Hispanic Origin	Population	%
Hispanic or Latino (of any race)	4,674	53.23
Central American, ex. Mexican	226	2.57
Costa Rican	4	0.05
Guatemalan	200	2.28
Honduran	1	0.01
Nicaraguan	1	0.01
Panamanian	5	0.06
Salvadoran	12	0.14
Other Central American	3	0.03
Cuban	10	0.11
Dominican Republic	2	0.02
Mexican	2,646	30.14
Puerto Rican	31	0.35
South American	27	0.31
Argentinean	7	0.08
Chilean	1	0.01
Colombian	11	0.13
Ecuadorian	1	0.01
Peruvian	7	0.08
Other Hispanic or Latino	1,732	19.73

Race*	Population	%
African-American/Black (145)	210	2.39
Not Hispanic (124)	164	1.87
Hispanic (21)	46	0.52
American Indian/Alaska Native (284)	446	5.08
Not Hispanic (77)	142	1.62
Hispanic (207)	304	3.46
Apache (10)	33	0.38
Blackfeet (1)	2	0.02
Canadian/French Am. Ind. (0)	1	0.01
Central American Ind. (4)	14	0.16
Cherokee (14)	35	0.40
Cheyenne (3)	3	0.03
Chickasaw (1)	1	0.01
Chippewa (2)	4	0.05
Choctaw (5)	7	0.08
Comanche (0)	1	0.01
Creek (1)	1	0.01
Crow (0)	1	0.01
Mexican American Ind. (61)	80	0.91
Navajo (37)	50	0.57
Pueblo (3)	9	0.10
Seminole (1)	1	0.01
Sioux (4)	9	0.10
Spanish American Ind. (4)	4	0.05
Ute (8)	17	0.19
Asian (107)	175	1.99
Not Hispanic (97)	133	1.51
Hispanic (10)	42	0.48
Bhutanese (0)	2	0.02
Chinese, ex. Taiwanese (23)	41	0.47
Filipino (22)	33	0.38
Hmong (2)	3	0.03
Indian (4)	13	0.15
Japanese (18)	41	0.47
Korean (12)	25	0.28
Laotian (2)	2	0.02
Pakistani (6)	8	0.09
Sri Lankan (1)	1	0.01
Taiwanese (1)	1	0.01
Thai (1)	1	0.01
Vietnamese (7)	10	0.11
Hawaii Native/Pacific Islander (13)	32	0.36
Not Hispanic (3)	16	0.18
Hispanic (10)	16	0.18
Guamanian/Chamorro (11)	17	0.19
Native Hawaiian (0)	7	0.08
Samoan (0)	1	0.01
Tongan (0)	1	0.01
White (6,130)	6,479	73.79
Not Hispanic (3,648)	3,771	42.95
Hispanic (2,482)	2,708	30.84

Arvada

Place Type: City
County: Jefferson
Population: 106,433†

Ancestry‡	Population	%
Afghan (47)	47	0.04
African, Sub-Saharan (43)	103	0.10
African (22)	65	0.06
Ghanaian (12)	12	0.01
South African (0)	17	0.02
Other Sub-Saharan African (9)	9	0.01
American (4,134)	4,134	3.94
Arab (119)	263	0.25
Arab (0)	33	0.03
Jordanian (96)	96	0.09
Lebanese (0)	66	0.06
Palestinian (12)	12	0.01
Syrian (0)	20	0.02
Other Arab (11)	36	0.03
Armenian (13)	52	0.05
Australian (66)	76	0.07
Austrian (76)	317	0.30
Basque (12)	12	0.01
Belgian (127)	372	0.35
Brazilian (30)	30	0.03
British (228)	540	0.51
Bulgarian (124)	136	0.13
Cajun (41)	41	0.04
Canadian (160)	320	0.31
Celtic (0)	25	0.02
Croatian (58)	131	0.12
Czech (314)	847	0.81
Czechoslovakian (78)	148	0.14
Danish (235)	1,173	1.12
Dutch (487)	1,916	1.83
Eastern European (65)	65	0.06
English (4,273)	15,551	14.83
Estonian (10)	10	0.01
European (2,071)	2,264	2.16
Finnish (99)	204	0.19
French, ex. Basque (791)	4,292	4.09
French Canadian (248)	583	0.56
German (9,992)	30,908	29.47
Greek (354)	919	0.88
Hungarian (261)	595	0.57
Iranian (45)	54	0.05
Irish (3,834)	16,814	16.03
Israeli (8)	8	0.01
Italian (2,978)	8,588	8.19
Latvian (40)	40	0.04
Lithuanian (100)	223	0.21
Luxemburger (0)	14	0.01
Northern European (82)	115	0.11
Norwegian (717)	2,964	2.83
Pennsylvania German (65)	94	0.09
Polish (721)	2,645	2.52
Portuguese (0)	138	0.13
Romanian (73)	124	0.12
Russian (858)	1,558	1.49
Scandinavian (240)	416	0.40
Scotch-Irish (1,080)	2,600	2.48
Scottish (927)	3,761	3.59
Serbian (9)	42	0.04
Slavic (18)	87	0.08
Slovak (112)	232	0.22
Slovene (11)	126	0.12
Swedish (903)	4,149	3.96
Swiss (159)	613	0.58
Ukrainian (278)	457	0.44
Welsh (79)	910	0.87
West Indian, ex. Hispanic (36)	49	0.05
Jamaican (36)	49	0.05
Yugoslavian (79)	119	0.11

Hispanic Origin	Population	%
Hispanic or Latino (of any race)	14,536	13.66
Central American, ex. Mexican	242	0.23
Costa Rican	14	0.01
Guatemalan	69	0.06
Honduran	35	0.03
Nicaraguan	11	0.01
Panamanian	26	0.02
Salvadoran	78	0.07
Other Central American	9	0.01
Cuban	110	0.10
Dominican Republic	11	0.01
Mexican	9,440	8.87
Puerto Rican	299	0.28
South American	341	0.32
Argentinean	32	0.03
Bolivian	20	0.02
Chilean	12	0.01
Colombian	86	0.08
Ecuadorian	29	0.03
Paraguayan	2	<0.01
Peruvian	111	0.10
Uruguayan	4	<0.01
Venezuelan	36	0.03
Other South American	9	0.01
Other Hispanic or Latino	4,093	3.85

Race*	Population	%
African-American/Black (962)	1,568	1.47
Not Hispanic (841)	1,275	1.20
Hispanic (121)	293	0.28
American Indian/Alaska Native (850)	1,868	1.76
Not Hispanic (437)	999	0.94
Hispanic (413)	869	0.82
Alaska Athabascan *(Ala. Nat.)* (1)	1	<0.01
Aleut *(Alaska Native)* (1)	3	<0.01
Apache (53)	131	0.12
Arapaho (5)	8	0.01
Blackfeet (4)	24	0.02
Canadian/French Am. Ind. (0)	2	<0.01
Central American Ind. (1)	1	<0.01
Cherokee (89)	289	0.27

*Notes: † The Census 2010 population figure is used to calculate the percentages in the Hispanic Origin and Race categories. Ancestry percentages are based on the 2006-2010 American Community Survey population (not shown); ‡ Numbers in parentheses indicate the number of people reporting a single ancestry; * Numbers in parentheses indicate the number of persons reporting this race alone, not in combination with any other race; Please refer to the Explanation of Data for more information.*

Cheyenne (1)	7	0.01
Chickasaw (6)	11	0.01
Chippewa (8)	32	0.03
Choctaw (16)	46	0.04
Colville (3)	6	0.01
Comanche (0)	4	<0.01
Cree (1)	4	<0.01
Creek (1)	10	0.01
Crow (2)	4	<0.01
Delaware (1)	5	<0.01
Hopi (4)	10	0.01
Houma (1)	1	<0.01
Inupiat *(Alaska Native)* (6)	6	0.01
Iroquois (4)	13	0.01
Kiowa (4)	4	<0.01
Menominee (1)	1	<0.01
Mexican American Ind. (18)	52	0.05
Navajo (88)	176	0.17
Osage (4)	10	0.01
Ottawa (1)	1	<0.01
Paiute (3)	4	<0.01
Potawatomi (14)	15	0.01
Pueblo (11)	37	0.03
Puget Sound Salish (2)	2	<0.01
Seminole (1)	4	<0.01
Shoshone (5)	6	0.01
Sioux (76)	160	0.15
South American Ind. (1)	3	<0.01
Spanish American Ind. (7)	8	0.01
Tlingit-Haida *(Alaska Native)* (1)	4	<0.01
Tohono O'Odham (1)	2	<0.01
Ute (25)	40	0.04
Yakama (2)	2	<0.01
Yaqui (4)	5	<0.01
Yup'ik *(Alaska Native)* (1)	1	<0.01
Asian (2,310)	3,135	2.95
Not Hispanic (2,225)	2,896	2.72
Hispanic (85)	239	0.22
Bangladeshi (2)	2	<0.01
Burmese (45)	45	0.04
Cambodian (34)	39	0.04
Chinese, ex. Taiwanese (328)	467	0.44
Filipino (170)	387	0.36
Hmong (153)	169	0.16
Indian (168)	230	0.22
Indonesian (13)	32	0.03
Japanese (347)	614	0.58
Korean (225)	322	0.30
Laotian (216)	237	0.22
Malaysian (3)	5	<0.01
Nepalese (20)	25	0.02
Pakistani (6)	10	0.01
Sri Lankan (2)	3	<0.01
Taiwanese (9)	19	0.02
Thai (44)	67	0.06
Vietnamese (394)	451	0.42
Hawaii Native/Pacific Islander (71)	209	0.20
Not Hispanic (58)	157	0.15
Hispanic (13)	52	0.05
Fijian (0)	1	<0.01
Guamanian/Chamorro (8)	17	0.02
Marshallese (3)	3	<0.01
Native Hawaiian (32)	99	0.09
Samoan (11)	18	0.02
Tongan (3)	5	<0.01
White (95,612)	98,295	92.35
Not Hispanic (86,556)	88,162	82.83
Hispanic (9,056)	10,133	9.52

Aurora

Place Type: City
County: Arapahoe
Population: 325,078†

Ancestry‡	Population	%
Afghan (153)	153	0.05
African, Sub-Saharan (5,980)	6,573	2.09
African (1,909)	2,285	0.73
Ethiopian (2,736)	2,877	0.92
Ghanaian (323)	323	0.10
Kenyan (33)	33	0.01
Nigerian (135)	153	0.05
Somalian (394)	394	0.13
South African (16)	16	0.01
Sudanese (15)	15	<0.01
Ugandan (206)	206	0.07
Zimbabwean (10)	10	<0.01
Other Sub-Saharan African (203)	261	0.08
Albanian (79)	110	0.04
American (16,179)	16,179	5.15
Arab (1,622)	2,042	0.65
Arab (287)	353	0.11
Egyptian (166)	238	0.08
Iraqi (81)	81	0.03
Jordanian (92)	92	0.03
Lebanese (177)	333	0.11
Moroccan (549)	590	0.19
Palestinian (91)	91	0.03
Syrian (9)	94	0.03
Other Arab (170)	170	0.05
Armenian (241)	312	0.10
Australian (0)	13	<0.01
Austrian (136)	644	0.21
Basque (12)	40	0.01
Belgian (51)	335	0.11
Brazilian (72)	72	0.02
British (614)	1,295	0.41
Bulgarian (12)	23	0.01
Canadian (199)	558	0.18
Celtic (70)	82	0.03
Croatian (62)	217	0.07
Cypriot (36)	36	0.01
Czech (578)	1,519	0.48
Czechoslovakian (149)	326	0.10
Danish (634)	1,738	0.55
Dutch (993)	3,806	1.21
Eastern European (185)	213	0.07
English (7,100)	23,298	7.42
European (3,060)	3,566	1.14
Finnish (169)	683	0.22
French, ex. Basque (1,314)	6,691	2.13
French Canadian (486)	1,129	0.36
German (15,789)	45,040	14.34
German Russian (129)	152	0.05
Greek (445)	920	0.29
Guyanese (73)	109	0.03
Hungarian (326)	1,058	0.34
Icelander (43)	78	0.02
Iranian (256)	274	0.09
Irish (7,829)	26,508	8.44
Italian (3,675)	9,968	3.17
Latvian (40)	71	0.02
Lithuanian (113)	317	0.10
Luxemburger (9)	44	0.01
Macedonian (21)	21	0.01
Maltese (0)	10	<0.01
Northern European (127)	157	0.05
Norwegian (1,571)	4,525	1.44
Pennsylvania German (72)	83	0.03
Polish (1,656)	5,489	1.75
Portuguese (129)	456	0.15
Romanian (188)	291	0.09
Russian (1,805)	3,483	1.11
Scandinavian (546)	754	0.24
Scotch-Irish (1,876)	4,343	1.38
Scottish (2,105)	6,166	1.96
Serbian (20)	28	0.01
Slavic (49)	176	0.06
Slovak (92)	434	0.14
Slovene (60)	185	0.06
Swedish (1,269)	5,208	1.66
Swiss (208)	951	0.30
Turkish (137)	158	0.05
Ukrainian (526)	968	0.31
Welsh (374)	1,675	0.53
West Indian, ex. Hispanic (704)	888	0.28
Bahamian (13)	13	<0.01
Belizean (0)	9	<0.01
Bermudan (0)	8	<0.01
British West Indian (70)	70	0.02
Dutch West Indian (16)	16	0.01
Haitian (150)	218	0.07
Jamaican (338)	359	0.11
Trinidadian/Tobagonian (21)	21	0.01
West Indian (96)	174	0.06
Yugoslavian (375)	590	0.19

Hispanic Origin	Population	%
Hispanic or Latino (of any race)	93,263	28.69
Central American, ex. Mexican	6,031	1.86
Costa Rican	95	0.03
Guatemalan	1,300	0.40
Honduran	970	0.30
Nicaraguan	142	0.04
Panamanian	321	0.10
Salvadoran	3,128	0.96
Other Central American	75	0.02
Cuban	578	0.18
Dominican Republic	284	0.09
Mexican	71,225	21.91
Puerto Rican	2,324	0.71
South American	2,277	0.70
Argentinean	154	0.05
Bolivian	82	0.03
Chilean	171	0.05
Colombian	483	0.15
Ecuadorian	133	0.04
Paraguayan	10	<0.01
Peruvian	1,058	0.33
Uruguayan	16	<0.01
Venezuelan	150	0.05
Other South American	20	0.01
Other Hispanic or Latino	10,544	3.24

Race*	Population	%
African-American/Black (51,196)	59,260	18.23
Not Hispanic (49,003)	55,188	16.98
Hispanic (2,193)	4,072	1.25
American Indian/Alaska Native (3,100)	7,040	2.17
Not Hispanic (1,487)	4,127	1.27
Hispanic (1,613)	2,913	0.90
Alaska Athabascan *(Ala. Nat.)* (0)	4	<0.01
Aleut *(Alaska Native)* (17)	20	0.01
Apache (119)	277	0.09
Arapaho (25)	37	0.01
Blackfeet (31)	210	0.06
Canadian/French Am. Ind. (0)	9	<0.01
Central American Ind. (13)	26	0.01
Cherokee (172)	969	0.30
Cheyenne (20)	44	0.01
Chickasaw (19)	32	0.01
Chippewa (53)	121	0.04
Choctaw (60)	188	0.06
Colville (2)	2	<0.01
Comanche (20)	39	0.01
Cree (1)	7	<0.01
Creek (20)	71	0.02
Crow (5)	6	<0.01
Delaware (3)	13	<0.01
Hopi (8)	28	0.01
Houma (1)	11	<0.01
Inupiat *(Alaska Native)* (5)	8	<0.01
Iroquois (27)	67	0.02
Kiowa (6)	12	<0.01
Lumbee (7)	15	<0.01
Menominee (3)	5	<0.01
Mexican American Ind. (241)	346	0.11
Navajo (192)	334	0.10
Osage (8)	25	0.01
Ottawa (1)	4	<0.01
Paiute (6)	11	<0.01
Pima (5)	6	<0.01
Potawatomi (12)	26	0.01
Pueblo (44)	82	0.03
Puget Sound Salish (1)	1	<0.01
Seminole (8)	40	0.01
Shoshone (13)	19	0.01
Sioux (200)	454	0.14
South American Ind. (38)	79	0.02

*Notes: † The Census 2010 population figure is used to calculate the percentages in the Hispanic Origin and Race categories. Ancestry percentages are based on the 2006-2010 American Community Survey population (not shown); ‡ Numbers in parentheses indicate the number of people reporting a single ancestry; * Numbers in parentheses indicate the number of persons reporting this race alone, not in combination with any other race; Please refer to the Explanation of Data for more information.*

	Population	%
Spanish American Ind. (15)	21	0.01
Tlingit-Haida *(Alaska Native)* (3)	6	<0.01
Tohono O'Odham (1)	2	<0.01
Ute (41)	75	0.02
Yaqui (11)	23	0.01
Yuman (3)	3	<0.01
Yup'ik *(Alaska Native)* (7)	16	<0.01
Asian (16,086)	20,109	6.19
Not Hispanic (15,735)	19,053	5.86
Hispanic (351)	1,056	0.32
Bangladeshi (51)	55	0.02
Bhutanese (233)	266	0.08
Burmese (436)	452	0.14
Cambodian (407)	519	0.16
Chinese, ex. Taiwanese (1,636)	2,282	0.70
Filipino (1,981)	3,119	0.96
Hmong (46)	61	0.02
Indian (1,627)	2,003	0.62
Indonesian (341)	436	0.13
Japanese (739)	1,634	0.50
Korean (3,459)	4,110	1.26
Laotian (164)	239	0.07
Malaysian (14)	24	0.01
Nepalese (362)	414	0.13
Pakistani (387)	458	0.14
Sri Lankan (24)	29	0.01
Taiwanese (81)	98	0.03
Thai (351)	513	0.16
Vietnamese (2,747)	3,110	0.96
Hawaii Native/Pacific Islander (1,002)	1,852	0.57
Not Hispanic (919)	1,510	0.46
Hispanic (83)	342	0.11
Fijian (20)	28	0.01
Guamanian/Chamorro (166)	308	0.09
Marshallese (64)	67	0.02
Native Hawaiian (152)	483	0.15
Samoan (169)	276	0.08
Tongan (129)	162	0.05
White (198,720)	212,302	65.31
Not Hispanic (153,715)	162,069	49.86
Hispanic (45,005)	50,233	15.45

Berkley

Place Type: CDP
County: Adams
Population: 11,207[†]

Ancestry[‡]	Population	%
American (668)	668	5.51
Arab (258)	258	2.13
Other Arab (258)	258	2.13
Austrian (26)	57	0.47
Basque (36)	36	0.30
Czech (0)	45	0.37
Czechoslovakian (0)	9	0.07
Danish (32)	32	0.26
Dutch (17)	61	0.50
English (161)	370	3.05
European (70)	112	0.92
French, ex. Basque (119)	557	4.60
French Canadian (15)	15	0.12
German (455)	1,327	10.96
Greek (0)	20	0.17
Hungarian (0)	28	0.23
Irish (108)	471	3.89
Italian (144)	413	3.41
Lithuanian (0)	7	0.06
Norwegian (22)	127	1.05
Polish (124)	146	1.21
Romanian (0)	16	0.13
Russian (0)	11	0.09
Scotch-Irish (53)	65	0.54
Scottish (16)	21	0.17
Slovene (7)	7	0.06
Swedish (16)	74	0.61
Swiss (0)	47	0.39
Ukrainian (16)	16	0.13

Hispanic Origin	Population	%
Hispanic or Latino (of any race)	6,240	55.68
Central American, ex. Mexican	62	0.55
Guatemalan	33	0.29
Honduran	9	0.08
Panamanian	4	0.04
Salvadoran	16	0.14
Cuban	15	0.13
Dominican Republic	3	0.03
Mexican	4,882	43.56
Puerto Rican	34	0.30
South American	36	0.32
Argentinean	3	0.03
Bolivian	4	0.04
Colombian	13	0.12
Ecuadorian	2	0.02
Peruvian	10	0.09
Venezuelan	4	0.04
Other Hispanic or Latino	1,208	10.78

Race*	Population	%
African-American/Black (174)	244	2.18
Not Hispanic (132)	173	1.54
Hispanic (42)	71	0.63
American Indian/Alaska Native (225)	378	3.37
Not Hispanic (95)	142	1.27
Hispanic (130)	236	2.11
Apache (15)	25	0.22
Arapaho (0)	1	0.01
Blackfeet (1)	10	0.09
Cherokee (7)	22	0.20
Chickasaw (1)	2	0.02
Chippewa (1)	1	0.01
Choctaw (3)	7	0.06
Comanche (2)	4	0.04
Creek (1)	1	0.01
Hopi (2)	2	0.02
Mexican American Ind. (10)	21	0.19
Navajo (15)	25	0.22
Osage (3)	4	0.04
Paiute (1)	1	0.01
Potawatomi (2)	2	0.02
Pueblo (3)	4	0.04
Seminole (2)	5	0.04
Shoshone (1)	1	0.01
Sioux (33)	40	0.36
South American Ind. (1)	1	0.01
Spanish American Ind. (4)	8	0.07
Ute (2)	5	0.04
Yaqui (0)	2	0.02
Asian (451)	538	4.80
Not Hispanic (428)	473	4.22
Hispanic (23)	65	0.58
Cambodian (6)	8	0.07
Chinese, ex. Taiwanese (27)	38	0.34
Filipino (11)	41	0.37
Hmong (79)	79	0.70
Indian (8)	20	0.18
Japanese (24)	44	0.39
Korean (23)	30	0.27
Laotian (40)	48	0.43
Malaysian (1)	1	0.01
Pakistani (7)	7	0.06
Taiwanese (0)	2	0.02
Thai (2)	6	0.05
Vietnamese (197)	203	1.81
Hawaii Native/Pacific Islander (10)	33	0.29
Not Hispanic (3)	10	0.09
Hispanic (7)	23	0.21
Guamanian/Chamorro (1)	3	0.03
Native Hawaiian (4)	6	0.05
White (7,433)	7,814	69.72
Not Hispanic (4,150)	4,274	38.14
Hispanic (3,283)	3,540	31.59

Black Forest

Place Type: CDP
County: El Paso
Population: 13,116[†]

Ancestry[‡]	Population	%
American (853)	853	6.34
Arab (0)	74	0.55
Lebanese (0)	74	0.55
Austrian (53)	81	0.60
Basque (12)	12	0.09
Belgian (0)	16	0.12
British (17)	157	1.17
Canadian (74)	118	0.88
Czech (23)	157	1.17
Danish (49)	176	1.31
Dutch (37)	276	2.05
Eastern European (11)	11	0.08
English (503)	2,290	17.02
European (742)	768	5.71
Finnish (0)	85	0.63
French, ex. Basque (27)	407	3.03
French Canadian (40)	146	1.09
German (1,440)	3,587	26.66
Greek (10)	80	0.59
Hungarian (26)	68	0.51
Iranian (18)	18	0.13
Irish (556)	1,968	14.63
Italian (282)	666	4.95
Latvian (0)	18	0.13
Lithuanian (0)	25	0.19
Luxemburger (0)	40	0.30
Norwegian (132)	441	3.28
Polish (122)	564	4.19
Portuguese (0)	44	0.33
Russian (55)	68	0.51
Scandinavian (43)	86	0.64
Scotch-Irish (245)	530	3.94
Scottish (263)	656	4.88
Slavic (11)	11	0.08
Slovak (19)	32	0.24
Slovene (0)	49	0.36
Swedish (140)	472	3.51
Swiss (0)	77	0.57
Ukrainian (13)	60	0.45
Welsh (30)	411	3.05

Hispanic Origin	Population	%
Hispanic or Latino (of any race)	646	4.93
Central American, ex. Mexican	23	0.18
Costa Rican	1	0.01
Guatemalan	11	0.08
Panamanian	11	0.08
Cuban	27	0.21
Dominican Republic	1	0.01
Mexican	397	3.03
Puerto Rican	47	0.36
South American	27	0.21
Argentinean	10	0.08
Chilean	1	0.01
Colombian	9	0.07
Peruvian	5	0.04
Venezuelan	2	0.02
Other Hispanic or Latino	124	0.95

Race*	Population	%
African-American/Black (165)	217	1.65
Not Hispanic (159)	209	1.59
Hispanic (6)	8	0.06
American Indian/Alaska Native (74)	180	1.37
Not Hispanic (59)	147	1.12
Hispanic (15)	33	0.25
Aleut *(Alaska Native)* (0)	1	0.01
Apache (3)	4	0.03
Blackfeet (1)	3	0.02
Canadian/French Am. Ind. (0)	1	0.01
Cherokee (15)	34	0.26
Chickasaw (1)	2	0.02
Chippewa (9)	17	0.13

*Notes: † The Census 2010 population figure is used to calculate the percentages in the Hispanic Origin and Race categories. Ancestry percentages are based on the 2006-2010 American Community Survey population (not shown); ‡ Numbers in parentheses indicate the number of people reporting a single ancestry; * Numbers in parentheses indicate the number of persons reporting this race alone, not in combination with any other race; Please refer to the Explanation of Data for more information.*

Choctaw (6)	13	0.10
Creek (1)	1	0.01
Hopi (0)	1	0.01
Iroquois (0)	6	0.05
Lumbee (2)	2	0.02
Navajo (4)	5	0.04
Potawatomi (0)	3	0.02
Pueblo (2)	4	0.03
Seminole (1)	3	0.02
Sioux (2)	6	0.05
South American Ind. (0)	1	0.01
Tohono O'Odham (0)	1	0.01
Ute (8)	8	0.06
Yaqui (0)	2	0.02
Yuman (0)	1	0.01
Asian (168)	278	2.12
Not Hispanic (166)	266	2.03
Hispanic (2)	12	0.09
Chinese, ex. Taiwanese (32)	53	0.40
Filipino (19)	46	0.35
Indian (20)	24	0.18
Indonesian (0)	5	0.04
Japanese (39)	85	0.65
Korean (39)	45	0.34
Pakistani (1)	4	0.03
Thai (1)	4	0.03
Vietnamese (6)	15	0.11
Hawaii Native/Pacific Islander (4)	25	0.19
Not Hispanic (3)	17	0.13
Hispanic (1)	8	0.06
Guamanian/Chamorro (1)	4	0.03
Native Hawaiian (0)	12	0.09
Samoan (2)	2	0.02
White (12,288)	12,562	95.78
Not Hispanic (11,826)	12,053	91.90
Hispanic (462)	509	3.88

Boulder

Place Type: City
County: Boulder
Population: 97,385†

Ancestry‡	Population	%
African, Sub-Saharan (88)	160	0.16
African (16)	75	0.08
Ethiopian (48)	48	0.05
Nigerian (13)	13	0.01
South African (11)	11	0.01
Sudanese (0)	13	0.01
Alsatian (0)	29	0.03
American (2,553)	2,553	2.63
Arab (290)	574	0.59
Arab (43)	92	0.09
Egyptian (75)	88	0.09
Lebanese (89)	242	0.25
Moroccan (0)	31	0.03
Palestinian (14)	14	0.01
Syrian (8)	21	0.02
Other Arab (61)	86	0.09
Armenian (51)	179	0.18
Assyrian/Chaldean/Syriac (48)	48	0.05
Australian (11)	77	0.08
Austrian (139)	612	0.63
Basque (24)	53	0.05
Belgian (65)	254	0.26
Brazilian (44)	62	0.06
British (758)	1,498	1.54
Bulgarian (16)	54	0.06
Cajun (0)	11	0.01
Canadian (75)	291	0.30
Celtic (19)	19	0.02
Croatian (39)	166	0.17
Czech (396)	1,263	1.30
Czechoslovakian (20)	146	0.15
Danish (244)	1,215	1.25
Dutch (616)	2,305	2.38
Eastern European (746)	866	0.89
English (4,551)	15,511	15.98
Estonian (22)	205	0.21
European (3,714)	4,098	4.22
Finnish (71)	341	0.35
French, ex. Basque (486)	3,851	3.97
French Canadian (237)	586	0.60
German (6,239)	22,473	23.16
Greek (286)	629	0.65
Hungarian (289)	1,103	1.14
Icelander (0)	36	0.04
Iranian (230)	270	0.28
Irish (4,174)	14,144	14.57
Israeli (122)	163	0.17
Italian (2,071)	6,579	6.78
Latvian (50)	150	0.15
Lithuanian (192)	594	0.61
Luxemburger (0)	21	0.02
New Zealander (31)	31	0.03
Northern European (491)	512	0.53
Norwegian (668)	2,677	2.76
Pennsylvania German (0)	13	0.01
Polish (1,228)	4,460	4.60
Portuguese (48)	289	0.30
Romanian (104)	234	0.24
Russian (1,204)	3,025	3.12
Scandinavian (383)	555	0.57
Scotch-Irish (996)	2,807	2.89
Scottish (972)	4,251	4.38
Serbian (34)	77	0.08
Slavic (43)	97	0.10
Slovak (71)	285	0.29
Slovene (35)	168	0.17
Swedish (813)	3,434	3.54
Swiss (98)	536	0.55
Turkish (43)	68	0.07
Ukrainian (152)	501	0.52
Welsh (206)	1,080	1.11
West Indian, ex. Hispanic (71)	183	0.19
Barbadian (0)	10	0.01
Belizean (0)	57	0.06
Jamaican (26)	54	0.06
Trinidadian/Tobagonian (13)	13	0.01
West Indian (32)	32	0.03
Other West Indian (0)	17	0.02
Yugoslavian (353)	408	0.42

Hispanic Origin	Population	%
Hispanic or Latino (of any race)	8,507	8.74
Central American, ex. Mexican	363	0.37
Costa Rican	29	0.03
Guatemalan	76	0.08
Honduran	28	0.03
Nicaraguan	24	0.02
Panamanian	23	0.02
Salvadoran	179	0.18
Other Central American	4	<0.01
Cuban	199	0.20
Dominican Republic	36	0.04
Mexican	5,902	6.06
Puerto Rican	252	0.26
South American	741	0.76
Argentinean	146	0.15
Bolivian	32	0.03
Chilean	96	0.10
Colombian	169	0.17
Ecuadorian	43	0.04
Paraguayan	13	0.01
Peruvian	125	0.13
Uruguayan	7	0.01
Venezuelan	103	0.11
Other South American	7	0.01
Other Hispanic or Latino	1,014	1.04

Race*	Population	%
African-American/Black (876)	1,355	1.39
Not Hispanic (828)	1,225	1.26
Hispanic (48)	130	0.13
American Indian/Alaska Native (431)	1,018	1.05
Not Hispanic (297)	746	0.77
Hispanic (134)	272	0.28
Aleut *(Alaska Native)* (1)	1	<0.01
Apache (19)	38	0.04
Arapaho (0)	6	0.01
Blackfeet (5)	23	0.02
Canadian/French Am. Ind. (2)	13	0.01
Central American Ind. (1)	1	<0.01
Cherokee (42)	174	0.18
Cheyenne (2)	8	0.01
Chickasaw (2)	6	0.01
Chippewa (5)	14	0.01
Choctaw (17)	49	0.05
Colville (0)	1	<0.01
Comanche (0)	7	0.01
Cree (0)	3	<0.01
Creek (4)	12	0.01
Crow (0)	1	<0.01
Delaware (1)	4	<0.01
Hopi (0)	1	<0.01
Inupiat *(Alaska Native)* (1)	4	<0.01
Iroquois (5)	19	0.02
Kiowa (2)	10	0.01
Lumbee (1)	2	<0.01
Mexican American Ind. (18)	34	0.03
Navajo (31)	45	0.05
Osage (3)	8	0.01
Ottawa (0)	2	<0.01
Potawatomi (3)	7	0.01
Pueblo (6)	19	0.02
Puget Sound Salish (1)	2	<0.01
Seminole (2)	7	0.01
Shoshone (3)	5	0.01
Sioux (36)	68	0.07
South American Ind. (1)	19	0.02
Tlingit-Haida *(Alaska Native)* (7)	12	0.01
Tsimshian *(Alaska Native)* (1)	1	<0.01
Ute (1)	1	<0.01
Yaqui (1)	1	<0.01
Yuman (1)	4	<0.01
Yup'ik *(Alaska Native)* (1)	1	<0.01
Asian (4,605)	5,978	6.14
Not Hispanic (4,558)	5,836	5.99
Hispanic (47)	142	0.15
Bangladeshi (2)	2	<0.01
Bhutanese (1)	1	<0.01
Burmese (5)	12	0.01
Cambodian (20)	28	0.03
Chinese, ex. Taiwanese (1,398)	1,795	1.84
Filipino (139)	333	0.34
Hmong (23)	24	0.02
Indian (805)	961	0.99
Indonesian (21)	35	0.04
Japanese (445)	815	0.84
Korean (667)	827	0.85
Laotian (18)	20	0.02
Malaysian (4)	13	0.01
Nepalese (343)	358	0.37
Pakistani (43)	58	0.06
Sri Lankan (10)	11	0.01
Taiwanese (122)	141	0.14
Thai (88)	129	0.13
Vietnamese (234)	279	0.29
Hawaii Native/Pacific Islander (74)	230	0.24
Not Hispanic (60)	197	0.20
Hispanic (14)	33	0.03
Fijian (0)	5	0.01
Guamanian/Chamorro (16)	25	0.03
Marshallese (1)	1	<0.01
Native Hawaiian (20)	93	0.10
Samoan (13)	35	0.04
Tongan (4)	13	0.01
White (85,702)	88,079	90.44
Not Hispanic (80,873)	82,812	85.04
Hispanic (4,829)	5,267	5.41

Brighton

Place Type: City
County: Adams
Population: 33,352†

Ancestry‡	Population	%
African, Sub-Saharan (192)	192	0.62

SECTION TWO

*Notes: † The Census 2010 population figure is used to calculate the percentages in the Hispanic Origin and Race categories. Ancestry percentages are based on the 2006-2010 American Community Survey population (not shown); ‡ Numbers in parentheses indicate the number of people reporting a single ancestry; * Numbers in parentheses indicate the number of persons reporting this race alone, not in combination with any other race; Please refer to the Explanation of Data for more information.*

African (73)	73	0.23
Ethiopian (109)	109	0.35
Other Sub-Saharan African (10)	10	0.03
American (1,049)	1,049	3.36
Arab (10)	10	0.03
Moroccan (10)	10	0.03
Austrian (11)	40	0.13
Basque (0)	21	0.07
Belgian (19)	57	0.18
Brazilian (56)	64	0.21
British (122)	158	0.51
Bulgarian (12)	21	0.07
Canadian (50)	101	0.32
Celtic (8)	8	0.03
Croatian (0)	13	0.04
Czech (52)	230	0.74
Czechoslovakian (0)	10	0.03
Danish (20)	136	0.44
Dutch (198)	605	1.94
Eastern European (21)	32	0.10
English (623)	2,477	7.94
European (265)	327	1.05
Finnish (0)	14	0.04
French, ex. Basque (138)	999	3.20
French Canadian (88)	200	0.64
German (2,540)	7,170	22.99
German Russian (11)	11	0.04
Greek (47)	70	0.22
Hungarian (9)	25	0.08
Irish (734)	2,907	9.32
Italian (478)	1,562	5.01
Latvian (0)	11	0.04
Lithuanian (14)	14	0.04
Luxemburger (5)	5	0.02
Norwegian (121)	641	2.06
Pennsylvania German (11)	11	0.04
Polish (99)	420	1.35
Portuguese (0)	68	0.22
Romanian (18)	18	0.06
Russian (19)	219	0.70
Scandinavian (27)	37	0.12
Scotch-Irish (147)	343	1.10
Scottish (174)	726	2.33
Slovene (13)	33	0.11
Swedish (140)	643	2.06
Swiss (0)	139	0.45
Turkish (0)	36	0.12
Ukrainian (22)	38	0.12
Welsh (29)	139	0.45
Yugoslavian (0)	14	0.04

Hispanic Origin	Population	%
Hispanic or Latino (of any race)	13,505	40.49
Central American, ex. Mexican	105	0.31
Costa Rican	7	0.02
Guatemalan	27	0.08
Honduran	23	0.07
Nicaraguan	9	0.03
Panamanian	3	0.01
Salvadoran	36	0.11
Cuban	25	0.07
Dominican Republic	26	0.08
Mexican	10,620	31.84
Puerto Rican	103	0.31
South American	59	0.18
Argentinean	3	0.01
Bolivian	2	0.01
Chilean	4	0.01
Colombian	19	0.06
Ecuadorian	3	0.01
Peruvian	23	0.07
Uruguayan	1	<0.01
Venezuelan	4	0.01
Other Hispanic or Latino	2,567	7.70

Race*	Population	%
African-American/Black (492)	703	2.11
Not Hispanic (378)	499	1.50
Hispanic (114)	204	0.61
American Indian/Alaska Native (473)	849	2.55
Not Hispanic (191)	381	1.14
Hispanic (282)	468	1.40
Aleut *(Alaska Native)* (0)	4	0.01
Apache (31)	67	0.20
Arapaho (2)	2	0.01
Blackfeet (3)	12	0.04
Canadian/French Am. Ind. (1)	1	<0.01
Central American Ind. (2)	2	0.01
Cherokee (42)	105	0.31
Cheyenne (5)	11	0.03
Chickasaw (7)	8	0.02
Chippewa (3)	13	0.04
Choctaw (3)	13	0.04
Comanche (0)	2	0.01
Cree (1)	6	0.02
Creek (0)	1	<0.01
Crow (3)	5	0.01
Delaware (2)	3	0.01
Inupiat *(Alaska Native)* (1)	1	<0.01
Iroquois (2)	5	0.01
Lumbee (1)	1	<0.01
Mexican American Ind. (26)	45	0.13
Navajo (18)	43	0.13
Osage (2)	6	0.02
Pima (1)	2	0.01
Potawatomi (2)	2	0.01
Pueblo (7)	9	0.03
Seminole (1)	9	0.03
Shoshone (0)	1	<0.01
Sioux (35)	68	0.20
Spanish American Ind. (2)	4	0.01
Tlingit-Haida *(Alaska Native)* (2)	3	0.01
Ute (1)	12	0.04
Yaqui (1)	2	0.01
Yup'ik *(Alaska Native)* (1)	1	<0.01
Asian (436)	667	2.00
Not Hispanic (402)	572	1.72
Hispanic (34)	95	0.28
Burmese (0)	1	<0.01
Cambodian (7)	7	0.02
Chinese, ex. Taiwanese (30)	49	0.15
Filipino (64)	129	0.39
Hmong (82)	90	0.27
Indian (24)	36	0.11
Indonesian (0)	3	0.01
Japanese (108)	179	0.54
Korean (55)	84	0.25
Laotian (8)	22	0.07
Malaysian (2)	3	0.01
Nepalese (5)	5	0.01
Pakistani (2)	3	0.01
Taiwanese (2)	5	0.01
Thai (5)	12	0.04
Vietnamese (9)	23	0.07
Hawaii Native/Pacific Islander (27)	67	0.20
Not Hispanic (22)	46	0.14
Hispanic (5)	21	0.06
Fijian (0)	1	<0.01
Guamanian/Chamorro (1)	6	0.02
Native Hawaiian (11)	19	0.06
Samoan (10)	17	0.05
White (25,823)	26,870	80.56
Not Hispanic (18,325)	18,792	56.34
Hispanic (7,498)	8,078	24.22

Broomfield

Place Type: City
County: Broomfield
Population: 55,889†

Ancestry‡	Population	%
African, Sub-Saharan (14)	28	0.05
African (14)	14	0.03
Other Sub-Saharan African (0)	14	0.03
Albanian (0)	9	0.02
Alsatian (10)	10	0.02
American (2,966)	2,966	5.61
Arab (332)	449	0.85
Arab (203)	203	0.38
Jordanian (52)	52	0.10
Lebanese (39)	105	0.20
Palestinian (21)	72	0.14
Other Arab (17)	17	0.03
Australian (0)	48	0.09
Austrian (61)	231	0.44
Basque (0)	44	0.08
Belgian (68)	249	0.47
British (221)	390	0.74
Canadian (54)	102	0.19
Celtic (12)	21	0.04
Croatian (12)	102	0.19
Czech (182)	714	1.35
Czechoslovakian (14)	44	0.08
Danish (207)	595	1.13
Dutch (254)	1,215	2.30
Eastern European (58)	58	0.11
English (1,721)	7,416	14.03
Estonian (11)	11	0.02
European (774)	1,004	1.90
Finnish (33)	193	0.37
French, ex. Basque (445)	1,920	3.63
French Canadian (109)	402	0.76
German (4,446)	13,509	25.55
Greek (38)	250	0.47
Hungarian (66)	283	0.54
Iranian (0)	21	0.04
Irish (2,001)	7,896	14.93
Israeli (0)	20	0.04
Italian (1,168)	4,518	8.55
Latvian (0)	9	0.02
Lithuanian (21)	156	0.30
Maltese (102)	102	0.19
Northern European (74)	85	0.16
Norwegian (286)	1,374	2.60
Pennsylvania German (73)	84	0.16
Polish (662)	1,729	3.27
Portuguese (27)	125	0.24
Romanian (0)	25	0.05
Russian (216)	632	1.20
Scandinavian (62)	268	0.51
Scotch-Irish (379)	1,272	2.41
Scottish (404)	1,662	3.14
Serbian (27)	49	0.09
Slavic (0)	49	0.09
Slovak (26)	74	0.14
Slovene (44)	90	0.17
Swedish (513)	1,486	2.81
Swiss (48)	233	0.44
Ukrainian (59)	234	0.44
Welsh (72)	883	1.67
West Indian, ex. Hispanic (7)	7	0.01
Jamaican (7)	7	0.01
Yugoslavian (9)	37	0.07

Hispanic Origin	Population	%
Hispanic or Latino (of any race)	6,216	11.12
Central American, ex. Mexican	207	0.37
Costa Rican	15	0.03
Guatemalan	32	0.06
Honduran	28	0.05
Nicaraguan	23	0.04
Panamanian	13	0.02
Salvadoran	96	0.17
Cuban	75	0.13
Dominican Republic	12	0.02
Mexican	4,317	7.72
Puerto Rican	191	0.34
South American	194	0.35
Argentinean	41	0.07
Bolivian	14	0.03
Chilean	23	0.04
Colombian	54	0.10
Ecuadorian	21	0.04
Paraguayan	1	<0.01
Peruvian	15	0.03
Uruguayan	2	<0.01
Venezuelan	21	0.04
Other South American	2	<0.01
Other Hispanic or Latino	1,220	2.18

*Notes: † The Census 2010 population figure is used to calculate the percentages in the Hispanic Origin and Race categories. Ancestry percentages are based on the 2006-2010 American Community Survey population (not shown); ‡ Numbers in parentheses indicate the number of people reporting a single ancestry; * Numbers in parentheses indicate the number of persons reporting this race alone, not in combination with any other race; Please refer to the Explanation of Data for more information.*

Race*	Population	%
African-American/Black (587)	861	1.54
Not Hispanic (530)	754	1.35
Hispanic (57)	107	0.19
American Indian/Alaska Native (336)	741	1.33
Not Hispanic (244)	497	0.89
Hispanic (92)	244	0.44
Aleut *(Alaska Native)* (1)	2	<0.01
Apache (13)	57	0.10
Arapaho (0)	1	<0.01
Blackfeet (7)	24	0.04
Canadian/French Am. Ind. (0)	2	<0.01
Central American Ind. (2)	2	<0.01
Cherokee (49)	140	0.25
Cheyenne (0)	2	<0.01
Chickasaw (0)	7	0.01
Chippewa (5)	12	0.02
Choctaw (10)	17	0.03
Comanche (1)	7	0.01
Cree (1)	3	0.01
Creek (0)	5	0.01
Crow (0)	2	<0.01
Delaware (1)	5	0.01
Hopi (0)	8	0.01
Inupiat *(Alaska Native)* (1)	6	0.01
Iroquois (1)	2	<0.01
Kiowa (1)	4	0.01
Lumbee (3)	4	0.01
Mexican American Ind. (7)	9	0.02
Navajo (29)	39	0.07
Osage (1)	2	<0.01
Ottawa (0)	1	<0.01
Pima (0)	1	<0.01
Potawatomi (2)	7	0.01
Pueblo (8)	9	0.02
Puget Sound Salish (2)	2	<0.01
Shoshone (2)	6	0.01
Sioux (36)	63	0.11
South American Ind. (1)	1	<0.01
Spanish American Ind. (5)	6	0.01
Tlingit-Haida *(Alaska Native)* (6)	6	0.01
Ute (2)	13	0.02
Yaqui (2)	4	0.01
Yup'ik *(Alaska Native)* (1)	1	<0.01
Asian (3,407)	4,097	7.33
Not Hispanic (3,368)	3,992	7.14
Hispanic (39)	105	0.19
Bangladeshi (7)	7	0.01
Burmese (1)	1	<0.01
Cambodian (69)	92	0.16
Chinese, ex. Taiwanese (728)	909	1.63
Filipino (203)	347	0.62
Hmong (278)	283	0.51
Indian (676)	733	1.31
Indonesian (23)	34	0.06
Japanese (225)	382	0.68
Korean (312)	433	0.77
Laotian (113)	130	0.23
Malaysian (5)	6	0.01
Nepalese (50)	50	0.09
Pakistani (54)	56	0.10
Sri Lankan (7)	7	0.01
Taiwanese (28)	30	0.05
Thai (55)	73	0.13
Vietnamese (423)	489	0.87
Hawaii Native/Pacific Islander (43)	120	0.21
Not Hispanic (43)	113	0.20
Hispanic (0)	7	0.01
Guamanian/Chamorro (9)	20	0.04
Native Hawaiian (19)	56	0.10
Samoan (4)	10	0.02
Tongan (1)	2	<0.01
White (48,099)	49,530	88.62
Not Hispanic (44,358)	45,349	81.14
Hispanic (3,741)	4,181	7.48

Castle Pines North

Place Type: City
County: Douglas
Population: 10,360†

Ancestry‡	Population	%
African, Sub-Saharan (12)	12	0.13
Ethiopian (12)	12	0.13
American (191)	191	2.03
Armenian (14)	31	0.33
Austrian (0)	29	0.31
Belgian (22)	22	0.23
British (61)	250	2.66
Bulgarian (0)	9	0.10
Canadian (9)	22	0.23
Croatian (0)	51	0.54
Czech (64)	199	2.11
Danish (48)	154	1.64
Dutch (43)	200	2.13
Eastern European (11)	11	0.12
English (566)	1,416	15.05
European (302)	329	3.50
Finnish (0)	75	0.80
French, ex. Basque (134)	377	4.01
French Canadian (32)	133	1.41
German (968)	2,852	30.31
Hungarian (13)	79	0.84
Iranian (15)	44	0.47
Irish (412)	1,539	16.36
Italian (168)	1,034	10.99
Lithuanian (12)	36	0.38
Maltese (0)	8	0.09
Northern European (25)	25	0.27
Norwegian (108)	310	3.29
Polish (131)	466	4.95
Portuguese (28)	82	0.87
Russian (17)	64	0.68
Scandinavian (37)	37	0.39
Scotch-Irish (38)	134	1.42
Scottish (244)	464	4.93
Slovak (0)	35	0.37
Swedish (15)	189	2.01
Swiss (0)	19	0.20
Welsh (65)	150	1.59
West Indian, ex. Hispanic (11)	58	0.62
Jamaican (11)	58	0.62
Yugoslavian (0)	20	0.21

Hispanic Origin	Population	%
Hispanic or Latino (of any race)	569	5.49
Central American, ex. Mexican	26	0.25
Costa Rican	4	0.04
Guatemalan	7	0.07
Honduran	8	0.08
Nicaraguan	1	0.01
Salvadoran	6	0.06
Cuban	9	0.09
Mexican	341	3.29
Puerto Rican	36	0.35
South American	35	0.34
Argentinean	6	0.06
Chilean	11	0.11
Colombian	10	0.10
Ecuadorian	1	0.01
Peruvian	6	0.06
Uruguayan	1	0.01
Other Hispanic or Latino	122	1.18

Race*	Population	%
African-American/Black (119)	163	1.57
Not Hispanic (115)	157	1.52
Hispanic (4)	6	0.06
American Indian/Alaska Native (22)	75	0.72
Not Hispanic (14)	56	0.54
Hispanic (8)	19	0.18
Central American Ind. (0)	1	0.01
Cherokee (5)	24	0.23
Chippewa (0)	1	0.01
Choctaw (6)	10	0.10
Iroquois (1)	1	0.01
Navajo (1)	3	0.03
Osage (3)	3	0.03
Sioux (2)	5	0.05
Ute (0)	1	0.01
Asian (269)	389	3.75
Not Hispanic (263)	371	3.58
Hispanic (6)	18	0.17
Bhutanese (1)	1	0.01
Chinese, ex. Taiwanese (45)	82	0.79
Filipino (13)	34	0.33
Indian (67)	78	0.75
Indonesian (2)	3	0.03
Japanese (13)	56	0.54
Korean (71)	82	0.79
Pakistani (15)	22	0.21
Taiwanese (4)	4	0.04
Thai (6)	6	0.06
Vietnamese (18)	30	0.29
Hawaii Native/Pacific Islander (12)	35	0.34
Not Hispanic (11)	32	0.31
Hispanic (1)	3	0.03
Guamanian/Chamorro (2)	4	0.04
Native Hawaiian (10)	29	0.28
White (9,593)	9,816	94.75
Not Hispanic (9,183)	9,373	90.47
Hispanic (410)	443	4.28

Castle Rock

Place Type: Town
County: Douglas
Population: 48,231†

Ancestry‡	Population	%
Afghan (32)	32	0.07
African, Sub-Saharan (61)	111	0.25
African (29)	79	0.18
Ethiopian (17)	17	0.04
South African (15)	15	0.03
American (2,141)	2,141	4.82
Arab (59)	100	0.23
Lebanese (0)	41	0.09
Moroccan (9)	9	0.02
Syrian (50)	50	0.11
Armenian (8)	8	0.02
Australian (28)	82	0.18
Austrian (24)	139	0.31
Belgian (0)	23	0.05
British (121)	304	0.68
Bulgarian (0)	20	0.05
Canadian (72)	207	0.47
Celtic (0)	7	0.02
Czech (196)	579	1.30
Czechoslovakian (54)	125	0.28
Danish (129)	504	1.14
Dutch (387)	1,485	3.34
Eastern European (7)	7	0.02
English (1,119)	6,090	13.72
European (632)	777	1.75
Finnish (22)	241	0.54
French, ex. Basque (294)	1,985	4.47
French Canadian (187)	368	0.83
German (3,366)	12,004	27.03
Greek (92)	281	0.63
Hungarian (20)	260	0.59
Iranian (0)	12	0.03
Irish (1,733)	8,091	18.22
Italian (1,018)	3,568	8.04
Latvian (30)	47	0.11
Lithuanian (22)	125	0.28
Luxemburger (9)	9	0.02
Macedonian (0)	7	0.02
Northern European (92)	99	0.22
Norwegian (356)	1,287	2.90
Pennsylvania German (20)	30	0.07
Polish (645)	2,067	4.66
Portuguese (27)	40	0.09
Romanian (14)	14	0.03
Russian (247)	916	2.06

SECTION TWO

*Notes: † The Census 2010 population figure is used to calculate the percentages in the Hispanic Origin and Race categories. Ancestry percentages are based on the 2006-2010 American Community Survey population (not shown); ‡ Numbers in parentheses indicate the number of people reporting a single ancestry; * Numbers in parentheses indicate the number of persons reporting this race alone, not in combination with any other race; Please refer to the Explanation of Data for more information.*

Scandinavian (33)	134	0.30
Scotch-Irish (298)	1,415	3.19
Scottish (341)	1,406	3.17
Serbian (0)	15	0.03
Slavic (0)	36	0.08
Slovak (21)	48	0.11
Slovene (0)	16	0.04
Swedish (283)	1,718	3.87
Swiss (9)	220	0.50
Ukrainian (0)	60	0.14
Welsh (174)	714	1.61
West Indian, ex. Hispanic (75)	208	0.47
Bahamian (0)	20	0.05
Jamaican (75)	188	0.42
Yugoslavian (26)	45	0.10

Hispanic Origin	Population	%
Hispanic or Latino (of any race)	4,819	9.99
Central American, ex. Mexican	158	0.33
Costa Rican	11	0.02
Guatemalan	23	0.05
Honduran	17	0.04
Nicaraguan	8	0.02
Panamanian	18	0.04
Salvadoran	81	0.17
Cuban	75	0.16
Dominican Republic	9	0.02
Mexican	3,160	6.55
Puerto Rican	289	0.60
South American	184	0.38
Argentinean	43	0.09
Bolivian	12	0.02
Chilean	15	0.03
Colombian	43	0.09
Ecuadorian	9	0.02
Peruvian	35	0.07
Uruguayan	2	<0.01
Venezuelan	19	0.04
Other South American	6	0.01
Other Hispanic or Latino	944	1.96

Race*	Population	%
African-American/Black (543)	894	1.85
Not Hispanic (472)	776	1.61
Hispanic (71)	118	0.24
American Indian/Alaska Native (286)	646	1.34
Not Hispanic (177)	427	0.89
Hispanic (109)	219	0.45
Aleut *(Alaska Native)* (1)	1	<0.01
Apache (9)	29	0.06
Arapaho (5)	6	0.01
Blackfeet (1)	10	0.02
Canadian/French Am. Ind. (4)	4	0.01
Central American Ind. (0)	1	<0.01
Cherokee (26)	108	0.22
Cheyenne (0)	1	<0.01
Chickasaw (5)	7	0.01
Chippewa (10)	16	0.03
Choctaw (12)	25	0.05
Comanche (0)	1	<0.01
Cree (0)	2	<0.01
Creek (5)	18	0.04
Crow (0)	3	0.01
Delaware (1)	1	<0.01
Hopi (0)	1	<0.01
Inupiat *(Alaska Native)* (2)	5	0.01
Iroquois (2)	8	0.02
Kiowa (0)	3	0.01
Mexican American Ind. (7)	15	0.03
Navajo (25)	61	0.13
Osage (7)	13	0.03
Ottawa (1)	1	<0.01
Pima (1)	1	<0.01
Potawatomi (1)	4	0.01
Pueblo (11)	20	0.04
Puget Sound Salish (0)	2	<0.01
Shoshone (2)	2	<0.01
Sioux (18)	28	0.06
Tsimshian *(Alaska Native)* (1)	1	<0.01
Ute (10)	11	0.02
Yakama (3)	3	0.01
Asian (811)	1,353	2.81
Not Hispanic (787)	1,247	2.59
Hispanic (24)	106	0.22
Bangladeshi (2)	2	<0.01
Cambodian (4)	7	0.01
Chinese, ex. Taiwanese (147)	225	0.47
Filipino (126)	285	0.59
Hmong (2)	3	0.01
Indian (125)	155	0.32
Indonesian (2)	7	0.01
Japanese (62)	187	0.39
Korean (199)	275	0.57
Laotian (7)	12	0.02
Nepalese (3)	6	0.01
Pakistani (19)	34	0.07
Taiwanese (12)	15	0.03
Thai (9)	18	0.04
Vietnamese (60)	101	0.21
Hawaii Native/Pacific Islander (49)	137	0.28
Not Hispanic (43)	115	0.24
Hispanic (6)	22	0.05
Guamanian/Chamorro (25)	32	0.07
Native Hawaiian (13)	58	0.12
Samoan (4)	5	0.01
White (43,768)	45,037	93.38
Not Hispanic (40,871)	41,781	86.63
Hispanic (2,897)	3,256	6.75

Ca±on City

Place Type: City
County: Fremont
Population: 16,400†

Ancestry‡	Population	%
American (601)	601	3.62
Arab (28)	28	0.17
Lebanese (15)	15	0.09
Other Arab (13)	13	0.08
Australian (0)	9	0.05
Austrian (3)	41	0.25
British (16)	44	0.27
Cajun (15)	32	0.19
Canadian (18)	43	0.26
Croatian (0)	9	0.05
Czech (12)	78	0.47
Danish (90)	169	1.02
Dutch (75)	250	1.51
English (435)	1,347	8.12
European (70)	70	0.42
French, ex. Basque (46)	463	2.79
French Canadian (0)	51	0.31
German (1,112)	2,900	17.48
Hungarian (23)	40	0.24
Irish (553)	2,026	12.21
Italian (364)	622	3.75
Lithuanian (19)	78	0.47
Northern European (15)	15	0.09
Norwegian (93)	243	1.46
Pennsylvania German (0)	8	0.05
Polish (62)	164	0.99
Portuguese (0)	20	0.12
Romanian (0)	23	0.14
Russian (6)	36	0.22
Scandinavian (0)	76	0.46
Scotch-Irish (67)	265	1.60
Scottish (43)	232	1.40
Slavic (24)	32	0.19
Slovene (22)	30	0.18
Swedish (74)	366	2.21
Swiss (23)	39	0.24
Welsh (7)	76	0.46
West Indian, ex. Hispanic (6)	6	0.04
Belizean (6)	6	0.04
Yugoslavian (7)	15	0.09

Hispanic Origin	Population	%
Hispanic or Latino (of any race)	1,564	9.54
Central American, ex. Mexican	13	0.08
Costa Rican	3	0.02
Guatemalan	1	0.01
Honduran	7	0.04
Panamanian	1	0.01
Salvadoran	1	0.01
Cuban	16	0.10
Dominican Republic	1	0.01
Mexican	1,091	6.65
Puerto Rican	35	0.21
South American	19	0.12
Argentinean	4	0.02
Chilean	1	0.01
Colombian	5	0.03
Peruvian	7	0.04
Venezuelan	2	0.01
Other Hispanic or Latino	389	2.37

Race*	Population	%
African-American/Black (286)	351	2.14
Not Hispanic (279)	337	2.05
Hispanic (7)	14	0.09
American Indian/Alaska Native (273)	470	2.87
Not Hispanic (210)	354	2.16
Hispanic (63)	116	0.71
Alaska Athabascan *(Ala. Nat.)* (4)	4	0.02
Apache (14)	30	0.18
Blackfeet (0)	6	0.04
Cherokee (39)	89	0.54
Cheyenne (0)	1	0.01
Chickasaw (1)	1	0.01
Chippewa (2)	6	0.04
Choctaw (11)	22	0.13
Comanche (1)	2	0.01
Cree (0)	3	0.02
Creek (0)	2	0.01
Crow (0)	1	0.01
Delaware (2)	3	0.02
Inupiat *(Alaska Native)* (3)	4	0.02
Iroquois (1)	3	0.02
Kiowa (1)	3	0.02
Mexican American Ind. (1)	4	0.02
Navajo (17)	22	0.13
Osage (0)	4	0.02
Paiute (0)	2	0.01
Potawatomi (2)	4	0.02
Pueblo (4)	5	0.03
Seminole (5)	5	0.03
Sioux (4)	8	0.05
Spanish American Ind. (3)	3	0.02
Tlingit-Haida *(Alaska Native)* (4)	7	0.04
Ute (4)	7	0.04
Asian (99)	158	0.96
Not Hispanic (97)	148	0.90
Hispanic (2)	10	0.06
Chinese, ex. Taiwanese (29)	49	0.30
Filipino (19)	36	0.22
Indian (13)	17	0.10
Japanese (12)	22	0.13
Korean (9)	22	0.13
Thai (1)	2	0.01
Vietnamese (6)	6	0.04
Hawaii Native/Pacific Islander (6)	15	0.09
Not Hispanic (4)	12	0.07
Hispanic (2)	3	0.02
Guamanian/Chamorro (1)	2	0.01
Native Hawaiian (3)	9	0.05
Samoan (1)	3	0.02
White (15,089)	15,430	94.09
Not Hispanic (13,990)	14,233	86.79
Hispanic (1,099)	1,197	7.30

Centennial

Place Type: City
County: Arapahoe
Population: 100,377†

Ancestry‡	Population	%
African, Sub-Saharan (361)	388	0.39
African (250)	277	0.28

*Notes: † The Census 2010 population figure is used to calculate the percentages in the Hispanic Origin and Race categories. Ancestry percentages are based on the 2006-2010 American Community Survey population (not shown); ‡ Numbers in parentheses indicate the number of people reporting a single ancestry; * Numbers in parentheses indicate the number of persons reporting this race alone, not in combination with any other race; Please refer to the Explanation of Data for more information.*

Ethiopian (104)	104	0.10
South African (7)	7	0.01
American (5,368)	5,368	5.37
Arab (112)	281	0.28
Arab (9)	9	0.01
Egyptian (12)	12	0.01
Lebanese (73)	187	0.19
Moroccan (10)	10	0.01
Syrian (2)	51	0.05
Other Arab (6)	12	0.01
Armenian (75)	95	0.10
Australian (168)	182	0.18
Austrian (128)	499	0.50
Basque (5)	29	0.03
Belgian (29)	144	0.14
Brazilian (13)	13	0.01
British (532)	1,082	1.08
Bulgarian (0)	22	0.02
Cajun (8)	8	0.01
Canadian (142)	233	0.23
Celtic (7)	65	0.07
Croatian (20)	112	0.11
Cypriot (0)	28	0.03
Czech (323)	1,144	1.14
Czechoslovakian (112)	184	0.18
Danish (267)	1,092	1.09
Dutch (784)	2,342	2.34
Eastern European (183)	217	0.22
English (4,627)	16,957	16.96
Estonian (10)	10	0.01
European (2,061)	2,327	2.33
Finnish (46)	234	0.23
French, ex. Basque (477)	4,123	4.12
French Canadian (125)	702	0.70
German (7,582)	25,563	25.56
German Russian (12)	12	0.01
Greek (223)	483	0.48
Hungarian (303)	828	0.83
Icelander (0)	14	0.01
Iranian (143)	210	0.21
Irish (3,352)	14,781	14.78
Israeli (59)	78	0.08
Italian (1,758)	5,626	5.63
Latvian (26)	45	0.05
Lithuanian (82)	336	0.34
Luxemburger (11)	92	0.09
New Zealander (81)	127	0.13
Northern European (197)	197	0.20
Norwegian (952)	2,930	2.93
Pennsylvania German (13)	32	0.03
Polish (812)	3,173	3.17
Portuguese (25)	113	0.11
Romanian (98)	139	0.14
Russian (668)	1,582	1.58
Scandinavian (243)	639	0.64
Scotch-Irish (1,339)	2,887	2.89
Scottish (1,054)	3,946	3.95
Serbian (0)	13	0.01
Slavic (28)	132	0.13
Slovak (101)	179	0.18
Slovene (41)	273	0.27
Swedish (1,066)	3,818	3.82
Swiss (165)	767	0.77
Turkish (200)	214	0.21
Ukrainian (192)	300	0.30
Welsh (188)	1,261	1.26
West Indian, ex. Hispanic (80)	169	0.17
Bahamian (15)	15	0.02
Bermudan (14)	14	0.01
Dutch West Indian (0)	42	0.04
Haitian (39)	39	0.04
Jamaican (2)	49	0.05
West Indian (10)	10	0.01
Yugoslavian (37)	229	0.23

Hispanic Origin	Population	%
Hispanic or Latino (of any race)	7,457	7.43
Central American, ex. Mexican	302	0.30
Costa Rican	22	0.02
Guatemalan	83	0.08
Honduran	25	0.02
Nicaraguan	41	0.04
Panamanian	39	0.04
Salvadoran	92	0.09
Cuban	188	0.19
Dominican Republic	31	0.03
Mexican	4,362	4.35
Puerto Rican	355	0.35
South American	598	0.60
Argentinean	76	0.08
Bolivian	18	0.02
Chilean	78	0.08
Colombian	142	0.14
Ecuadorian	38	0.04
Paraguayan	8	0.01
Peruvian	192	0.19
Uruguayan	1	<0.01
Venezuelan	39	0.04
Other South American	6	0.01
Other Hispanic or Latino	1,621	1.61

Race*	Population	%
African-American/Black (3,294)	4,265	4.25
Not Hispanic (3,146)	3,979	3.96
Hispanic (148)	286	0.28
American Indian/Alaska Native (411)	1,114	1.11
Not Hispanic (284)	810	0.81
Hispanic (127)	304	0.30
Alaska Athabascan *(Ala. Nat.)* (4)	7	0.01
Apache (12)	44	0.04
Arapaho (2)	5	<0.01
Blackfeet (5)	36	0.04
Canadian/French Am. Ind. (1)	1	<0.01
Cherokee (50)	188	0.19
Cheyenne (5)	7	0.01
Chickasaw (6)	15	0.01
Chippewa (8)	25	0.02
Choctaw (23)	56	0.06
Comanche (1)	6	0.01
Cree (1)	3	<0.01
Creek (6)	28	0.03
Crow (1)	1	<0.01
Delaware (0)	2	<0.01
Inupiat *(Alaska Native)* (1)	4	<0.01
Iroquois (11)	34	0.03
Kiowa (1)	1	<0.01
Menominee (0)	1	<0.01
Mexican American Ind. (6)	12	0.01
Navajo (47)	63	0.06
Osage (7)	9	0.01
Ottawa (0)	6	0.01
Pima (0)	1	<0.01
Potawatomi (4)	7	0.01
Pueblo (14)	20	0.02
Puget Sound Salish (0)	1	<0.01
Seminole (3)	7	0.01
Shoshone (3)	6	0.01
Sioux (22)	44	0.04
South American Ind. (2)	9	0.01
Spanish American Ind. (1)	2	<0.01
Tlingit-Haida *(Alaska Native)* (6)	9	0.01
Ute (12)	19	0.02
Yaqui (0)	4	<0.01
Asian (4,373)	5,523	5.50
Not Hispanic (4,340)	5,367	5.35
Hispanic (33)	156	0.16
Bangladeshi (11)	11	0.01
Burmese (4)	4	<0.01
Cambodian (20)	26	0.03
Chinese, ex. Taiwanese (925)	1,152	1.15
Filipino (273)	508	0.51
Hmong (10)	11	0.01
Indian (778)	892	0.89
Indonesian (65)	78	0.08
Japanese (323)	618	0.62
Korean (1,051)	1,262	1.26
Laotian (17)	24	0.02
Malaysian (2)	9	0.01
Nepalese (45)	49	0.05
Pakistani (111)	126	0.13
Sri Lankan (2)	2	<0.01
Taiwanese (52)	78	0.08
Thai (84)	123	0.12
Vietnamese (434)	492	0.49
Hawaii Native/Pacific Islander (97)	288	0.29
Not Hispanic (94)	257	0.26
Hispanic (3)	31	0.03
Fijian (2)	5	<0.01
Guamanian/Chamorro (25)	40	0.04
Marshallese (1)	1	<0.01
Native Hawaiian (28)	126	0.13
Samoan (5)	37	0.04
Tongan (2)	6	0.01
White (87,616)	90,310	89.97
Not Hispanic (82,664)	84,739	84.42
Hispanic (4,952)	5,571	5.55

Cherry Creek

Place Type: CDP
County: Arapahoe
Population: 11,120†

Ancestry‡	Population	%
African, Sub-Saharan (22)	86	0.80
South African (22)	86	0.80
American (726)	726	6.79
Arab (12)	42	0.39
Moroccan (0)	9	0.08
Other Arab (12)	33	0.31
Armenian (0)	69	0.65
Australian (0)	24	0.22
Austrian (19)	61	0.57
Belgian (0)	8	0.07
Brazilian (8)	8	0.07
British (14)	61	0.57
Canadian (40)	77	0.72
Czech (44)	121	1.13
Czechoslovakian (0)	9	0.08
Danish (27)	92	0.86
Dutch (60)	189	1.77
Eastern European (129)	142	1.33
English (621)	1,237	11.57
European (318)	415	3.88
Finnish (0)	33	0.31
French, ex. Basque (70)	355	3.32
French Canadian (28)	118	1.10
German (566)	1,941	18.16
Greek (69)	77	0.72
Hungarian (0)	26	0.24
Icelander (0)	3	0.03
Iranian (91)	91	0.85
Irish (407)	1,268	11.86
Israeli (53)	53	0.50
Italian (313)	740	6.92
Lithuanian (10)	65	0.61
Northern European (9)	9	0.08
Norwegian (66)	154	1.44
Polish (150)	415	3.88
Romanian (0)	40	0.37
Russian (379)	561	5.25
Scandinavian (47)	77	0.72
Scotch-Irish (51)	167	1.56
Scottish (149)	345	3.23
Slovak (14)	14	0.13
Slovene (0)	36	0.34
Swedish (76)	362	3.39
Swiss (7)	60	0.56
Turkish (0)	8	0.07
Ukrainian (0)	20	0.19
Welsh (0)	70	0.65
Yugoslavian (6)	12	0.11

Hispanic Origin	Population	%
Hispanic or Latino (of any race)	848	7.63
Central American, ex. Mexican	36	0.32
Costa Rican	1	0.01
Guatemalan	8	0.07
Honduran	5	0.04
Nicaraguan	7	0.06

*Notes: † The Census 2010 population figure is used to calculate the percentages in the Hispanic Origin and Race categories. Ancestry percentages are based on the 2006-2010 American Community Survey population (not shown); ‡ Numbers in parentheses indicate the number of people reporting a single ancestry; * Numbers in parentheses indicate the number of persons reporting this race alone, not in combination with any other race; Please refer to the Explanation of Data for more information.*

Panamanian	3	0.03
Salvadoran	12	0.11
Cuban	19	0.17
Dominican Republic	3	0.03
Mexican	538	4.84
Puerto Rican	22	0.20
South American	91	0.82
Argentinean	17	0.15
Bolivian	6	0.05
Chilean	8	0.07
Colombian	25	0.22
Ecuadorian	1	0.01
Paraguayan	1	0.01
Peruvian	21	0.19
Venezuelan	12	0.11
Other Hispanic or Latino	139	1.25

Race*	Population	%
African-American/Black (202)	255	2.29
Not Hispanic (188)	231	2.08
Hispanic (14)	24	0.22
American Indian/Alaska Native (31)	83	0.75
Not Hispanic (23)	62	0.56
Hispanic (8)	21	0.19
Apache (5)	7	0.06
Blackfeet (0)	1	0.01
Canadian/French Am. Ind. (1)	1	0.01
Central American Ind. (0)	1	0.01
Cherokee (1)	21	0.19
Chickasaw (1)	1	0.01
Chippewa (1)	2	0.02
Choctaw (3)	5	0.04
Cree (1)	1	0.01
Kiowa (1)	1	0.01
Mexican American Ind. (1)	1	0.01
Potawatomi (3)	3	0.03
Sioux (1)	1	0.01
South American Ind. (0)	2	0.02
Spanish American Ind. (1)	4	0.04
Yup'ik *(Alaska Native)* (0)	1	0.01
Asian (1,065)	1,228	11.04
Not Hispanic (1,064)	1,218	10.95
Hispanic (1)	10	0.09
Cambodian (1)	3	0.03
Chinese, ex. Taiwanese (310)	368	3.31
Filipino (36)	60	0.54
Indian (319)	331	2.98
Indonesian (11)	16	0.14
Japanese (69)	98	0.88
Korean (164)	182	1.64
Laotian (4)	4	0.04
Malaysian (4)	4	0.04
Nepalese (18)	18	0.16
Pakistani (5)	5	0.04
Sri Lankan (2)	9	0.08
Taiwanese (54)	62	0.56
Thai (14)	21	0.19
Vietnamese (30)	35	0.31
Hawaii Native/Pacific Islander (2)	25	0.22
Not Hispanic (2)	18	0.16
Hispanic (0)	7	0.06
Guamanian/Chamorro (0)	1	0.01
Native Hawaiian (2)	19	0.17
Samoan (0)	3	0.03
White (9,234)	9,491	85.35
Not Hispanic (8,758)	8,967	80.64
Hispanic (476)	524	4.71

Cimarron Hills

Place Type: CDP
County: El Paso
Population: 16,161†

Ancestry‡	Population	%
African, Sub-Saharan (14)	14	0.09
Sierra Leonean (14)	14	0.09
American (864)	864	5.54
Arab (22)	22	0.14
Lebanese (22)	22	0.14
Austrian (0)	3	0.02
British (0)	9	0.06
Cajun (0)	11	0.07
Canadian (0)	71	0.46
Czech (96)	254	1.63
Czechoslovakian (41)	132	0.85
Danish (58)	194	1.24
Dutch (91)	218	1.40
English (526)	1,851	11.87
European (175)	213	1.37
Finnish (19)	30	0.19
French, ex. Basque (34)	654	4.19
French Canadian (37)	194	1.24
German (1,308)	3,642	23.35
Greek (0)	36	0.23
Hungarian (67)	165	1.06
Irish (537)	1,968	12.62
Italian (348)	809	5.19
Lithuanian (0)	49	0.31
Northern European (44)	44	0.28
Norwegian (220)	429	2.75
Pennsylvania German (14)	14	0.09
Polish (259)	591	3.79
Portuguese (43)	58	0.37
Russian (37)	37	0.24
Scandinavian (89)	89	0.57
Scotch-Irish (130)	268	1.72
Scottish (79)	807	5.17
Serbian (0)	16	0.10
Slovak (32)	32	0.21
Slovene (0)	21	0.13
Swedish (56)	265	1.70
Swiss (0)	150	0.96
Ukrainian (27)	54	0.35
Welsh (0)	96	0.62
West Indian, ex. Hispanic (0)	19	0.12
Jamaican (0)	19	0.12

Hispanic Origin	Population	%
Hispanic or Latino (of any race)	2,927	18.11
Central American, ex. Mexican	97	0.60
Costa Rican	13	0.08
Guatemalan	8	0.05
Honduran	8	0.05
Nicaraguan	1	0.01
Panamanian	34	0.21
Salvadoran	32	0.20
Other Central American	1	0.01
Cuban	16	0.10
Dominican Republic	20	0.12
Mexican	1,923	11.90
Puerto Rican	248	1.53
South American	44	0.27
Argentinean	8	0.05
Chilean	2	0.01
Colombian	6	0.04
Ecuadorian	10	0.06
Peruvian	13	0.08
Uruguayan	2	0.01
Venezuelan	2	0.01
Other South American	1	0.01
Other Hispanic or Latino	579	3.58

Race*	Population	%
African-American/Black (1,155)	1,596	9.88
Not Hispanic (1,069)	1,417	8.77
Hispanic (86)	179	1.11
American Indian/Alaska Native (168)	507	3.14
Not Hispanic (87)	318	1.97
Hispanic (81)	189	1.17
Apache (12)	36	0.22
Arapaho (4)	5	0.03
Blackfeet (0)	15	0.09
Canadian/French Am. Ind. (1)	1	0.01
Cherokee (18)	103	0.64
Cheyenne (0)	1	0.01
Chickasaw (0)	1	0.01
Chippewa (7)	15	0.09
Choctaw (1)	8	0.05
Comanche (1)	1	0.01
Cree (2)	3	0.02
Creek (2)	10	0.06
Delaware (1)	2	0.01
Inupiat *(Alaska Native)* (1)	3	0.02
Iroquois (4)	6	0.04
Menominee (0)	1	0.01
Mexican American Ind. (3)	3	0.02
Navajo (15)	24	0.15
Osage (1)	2	0.01
Paiute (0)	4	0.02
Potawatomi (3)	7	0.04
Pueblo (5)	6	0.04
Puget Sound Salish (4)	8	0.05
Seminole (1)	2	0.01
Sioux (16)	50	0.31
Spanish American Ind. (2)	3	0.02
Tlingit-Haida *(Alaska Native)* (1)	3	0.02
Tohono O'Odham (0)	2	0.01
Ute (1)	1	0.01
Yaqui (1)	2	0.01
Yuman (1)	1	0.01
Asian (406)	741	4.59
Not Hispanic (398)	670	4.15
Hispanic (8)	71	0.44
Cambodian (1)	1	0.01
Chinese, ex. Taiwanese (22)	43	0.27
Filipino (159)	256	1.58
Indian (9)	15	0.09
Indonesian (2)	3	0.02
Japanese (44)	124	0.77
Korean (100)	215	1.33
Laotian (11)	14	0.09
Malaysian (1)	7	0.04
Pakistani (1)	1	0.01
Taiwanese (1)	2	0.01
Thai (12)	31	0.19
Vietnamese (27)	38	0.24
Hawaii Native/Pacific Islander (68)	134	0.83
Not Hispanic (57)	101	0.62
Hispanic (11)	33	0.20
Guamanian/Chamorro (23)	38	0.24
Native Hawaiian (18)	55	0.34
Samoan (26)	31	0.19
White (12,244)	13,214	81.76
Not Hispanic (10,859)	11,509	71.21
Hispanic (1,385)	1,705	10.55

Clifton

Place Type: CDP
County: Mesa
Population: 19,889†

Ancestry‡	Population	%
American (1,481)	1,481	7.41
Arab (0)	15	0.08
Other Arab (0)	15	0.08
Austrian (0)	29	0.15
Basque (0)	12	0.06
Belgian (0)	17	0.09
British (13)	29	0.15
Canadian (0)	14	0.07
Czech (7)	57	0.29
Czechoslovakian (0)	13	0.07
Danish (14)	129	0.65
Dutch (198)	444	2.22
English (646)	1,910	9.56
European (177)	261	1.31
Finnish (55)	129	0.65
French, ex. Basque (22)	428	2.14
French Canadian (42)	70	0.35
German (1,373)	3,828	19.15
Greek (0)	17	0.09
Hungarian (8)	12	0.06
Iranian (15)	15	0.08
Irish (791)	2,527	12.64
Italian (418)	926	4.63
Latvian (0)	18	0.09
Lithuanian (13)	16	0.08
Northern European (27)	27	0.14

*Notes: † The Census 2010 population figure is used to calculate the percentages in the Hispanic Origin and Race categories. Ancestry percentages are based on the 2006-2010 American Community Survey population (not shown); ‡ Numbers in parentheses indicate the number of people reporting a single ancestry; * Numbers in parentheses indicate the number of persons reporting this race alone, not in combination with any other race; Please refer to the Explanation of Data for more information.*

Norwegian (34)	193	0.97
Polish (74)	214	1.07
Portuguese (44)	44	0.22
Russian (0)	3	0.02
Scandinavian (0)	40	0.20
Scotch-Irish (96)	354	1.77
Scottish (293)	579	2.90
Slavic (0)	16	0.08
Slovak (0)	3	0.02
Slovene (0)	9	0.05
Swedish (66)	530	2.65
Swiss (0)	34	0.17
Welsh (15)	52	0.26

Hispanic Origin	Population	%
Hispanic or Latino (of any race)	4,230	21.27
Central American, ex. Mexican	84	0.42
Guatemalan	19	0.10
Honduran	32	0.16
Nicaraguan	7	0.04
Panamanian	7	0.04
Salvadoran	19	0.10
Cuban	11	0.06
Mexican	3,207	16.12
Puerto Rican	34	0.17
South American	41	0.21
Argentinean	10	0.05
Chilean	6	0.03
Colombian	6	0.03
Ecuadorian	3	0.02
Peruvian	8	0.04
Venezuelan	8	0.04
Other Hispanic or Latino	853	4.29

Race*	Population	%
African-American/Black (185)	328	1.65
Not Hispanic (130)	226	1.14
Hispanic (55)	102	0.51
American Indian/Alaska Native (275)	604	3.04
Not Hispanic (135)	346	1.74
Hispanic (140)	258	1.30
Aleut *(Alaska Native)* (1)	2	0.01
Apache (11)	29	0.15
Arapaho (2)	4	0.02
Blackfeet (1)	8	0.04
Cherokee (12)	78	0.39
Chickasaw (3)	7	0.04
Chippewa (8)	15	0.08
Choctaw (4)	13	0.07
Colville (0)	1	0.01
Comanche (4)	8	0.04
Cree (0)	3	0.02
Crow (0)	2	0.01
Delaware (1)	4	0.02
Hopi (1)	1	0.01
Iroquois (5)	10	0.05
Lumbee (5)	5	0.03
Mexican American Ind. (14)	26	0.13
Navajo (15)	37	0.19
Paiute (3)	3	0.02
Pima (3)	3	0.02
Potawatomi (3)	3	0.02
Seminole (0)	3	0.02
Shoshone (1)	1	0.01
Sioux (8)	22	0.11
South American Ind. (1)	2	0.01
Spanish American Ind. (0)	1	0.01
Tlingit-Haida *(Alaska Native)* (0)	3	0.02
Ute (9)	21	0.11
Yaqui (0)	1	0.01
Asian (101)	211	1.06
Not Hispanic (88)	177	0.89
Hispanic (13)	34	0.17
Cambodian (8)	8	0.04
Chinese, ex. Taiwanese (26)	32	0.16
Filipino (28)	71	0.36
Indian (9)	14	0.07
Indonesian (1)	3	0.02
Japanese (0)	18	0.09
Korean (8)	11	0.06
Laotian (2)	4	0.02
Pakistani (0)	1	0.01
Sri Lankan (0)	3	0.02
Thai (3)	4	0.02
Vietnamese (14)	20	0.10
Hawaii Native/Pacific Islander (15)	41	0.21
Not Hispanic (14)	35	0.18
Hispanic (1)	6	0.03
Guamanian/Chamorro (1)	12	0.06
Native Hawaiian (7)	10	0.05
Samoan (2)	4	0.02
Tongan (1)	3	0.02
White (16,784)	17,478	87.88
Not Hispanic (14,870)	15,254	76.70
Hispanic (1,914)	2,224	11.18

Colorado Springs

Place Type: City
County: El Paso
Population: 416,427†

Ancestry‡	Population	%
Afghan (12)	25	0.01
African, Sub-Saharan (1,464)	2,134	0.53
African (1,041)	1,583	0.39
Cape Verdean (0)	9	<0.01
Ethiopian (144)	144	0.04
Ghanaian (9)	19	<0.01
Kenyan (47)	47	0.01
Liberian (35)	35	0.01
Nigerian (21)	29	0.01
South African (14)	41	0.01
Other Sub-Saharan African (153)	227	0.06
Albanian (25)	126	0.03
Alsatian (8)	8	<0.01
American (17,720)	17,720	4.39
Arab (530)	1,502	0.37
Arab (77)	105	0.03
Egyptian (129)	142	0.04
Iraqi (0)	114	0.03
Jordanian (0)	33	0.01
Lebanese (134)	712	0.18
Palestinian (138)	138	0.03
Syrian (8)	70	0.02
Other Arab (44)	188	0.05
Armenian (207)	290	0.07
Assyrian/Chaldean/Syriac (18)	18	<0.01
Australian (50)	105	0.03
Austrian (518)	1,947	0.48
Basque (39)	96	0.02
Belgian (74)	380	0.09
Brazilian (119)	213	0.05
British (1,204)	2,744	0.68
Bulgarian (0)	54	0.01
Cajun (178)	381	0.09
Canadian (810)	1,389	0.34
Celtic (121)	150	0.04
Croatian (154)	422	0.10
Czech (722)	3,019	0.75
Czechoslovakian (336)	622	0.15
Danish (918)	3,493	0.86
Dutch (1,877)	7,669	1.90
Eastern European (268)	296	0.07
English (15,035)	51,939	12.86
Estonian (20)	81	0.02
European (7,292)	8,253	2.04
Finnish (356)	1,122	0.28
French, ex. Basque (2,317)	14,928	3.70
French Canadian (1,371)	3,287	0.81
German (28,395)	90,925	22.51
German Russian (26)	62	0.02
Greek (487)	1,203	0.30
Hungarian (552)	2,249	0.56
Icelander (25)	149	0.04
Iranian (235)	378	0.09
Irish (13,520)	53,519	13.25
Israeli (10)	20	<0.01
Italian (6,886)	20,646	5.11
Latvian (77)	138	0.03
Lithuanian (219)	943	0.23
Luxemburger (32)	73	0.02
Macedonian (11)	11	<0.01
Maltese (4)	26	0.01
New Zealander (37)	138	0.03
Northern European (464)	476	0.12
Norwegian (3,563)	11,336	2.81
Pennsylvania German (100)	195	0.05
Polish (2,767)	10,470	2.59
Portuguese (351)	1,039	0.26
Romanian (179)	451	0.11
Russian (799)	3,208	0.79
Scandinavian (672)	1,306	0.32
Scotch-Irish (3,677)	10,315	2.55
Scottish (3,430)	11,825	2.93
Serbian (100)	148	0.04
Slavic (100)	255	0.06
Slovak (288)	1,163	0.29
Slovene (164)	281	0.07
Swedish (2,210)	9,674	2.39
Swiss (338)	1,558	0.39
Turkish (46)	114	0.03
Ukrainian (346)	938	0.23
Welsh (1,026)	4,586	1.14
West Indian, ex. Hispanic (1,028)	1,333	0.33
Barbadian (0)	15	<0.01
Dutch West Indian (15)	36	0.01
Haitian (90)	130	0.03
Jamaican (803)	919	0.23
Trinidadian/Tobagonian (11)	11	<0.01
U.S. Virgin Islander (21)	21	0.01
West Indian (88)	201	0.05
Yugoslavian (418)	702	0.17

Hispanic Origin	Population	%
Hispanic or Latino (of any race)	66,866	16.06
Central American, ex. Mexican	2,456	0.59
Costa Rican	104	0.02
Guatemalan	565	0.14
Honduran	385	0.09
Nicaraguan	204	0.05
Panamanian	642	0.15
Salvadoran	521	0.13
Other Central American	35	0.01
Cuban	802	0.19
Dominican Republic	271	0.07
Mexican	44,135	10.60
Puerto Rican	4,759	1.14
South American	1,599	0.38
Argentinean	134	0.03
Bolivian	56	0.01
Chilean	105	0.03
Colombian	444	0.11
Ecuadorian	176	0.04
Paraguayan	17	<0.01
Peruvian	487	0.12
Uruguayan	18	<0.01
Venezuelan	146	0.04
Other South American	16	<0.01
Other Hispanic or Latino	12,844	3.08

Race*	Population	%
African-American/Black (26,253)	34,114	8.19
Not Hispanic (24,391)	30,514	7.33
Hispanic (1,862)	3,600	0.86
American Indian/Alaska Native (4,025)	9,632	2.31
Not Hispanic (2,403)	6,248	1.50
Hispanic (1,622)	3,384	0.81
Alaska Athabascan *(Ala. Nat.)* (14)	19	<0.01
Aleut *(Alaska Native)* (15)	23	0.01
Apache (190)	444	0.11
Arapaho (16)	33	0.01
Blackfeet (32)	229	0.05
Canadian/French Am. Ind. (13)	33	0.01
Central American Ind. (4)	14	<0.01
Cherokee (365)	1,484	0.36
Cheyenne (28)	66	0.02
Chickasaw (41)	87	0.02
Chippewa (88)	199	0.05
Choctaw (90)	277	0.07

*Notes: † The Census 2010 population figure is used to calculate the percentages in the Hispanic Origin and Race categories. Ancestry percentages are based on the 2006-2010 American Community Survey population (not shown); ‡ Numbers in parentheses indicate the number of people reporting a single ancestry; * Numbers in parentheses indicate the number of persons reporting this race alone, not in combination with any other race; Please refer to the Explanation of Data for more information.*

Colville (3)	5	<0.01
Comanche (20)	61	0.01
Cree (3)	20	<0.01
Creek (29)	80	0.02
Crow (5)	18	<0.01
Delaware (7)	21	0.01
Hopi (5)	20	<0.01
Houma (1)	2	<0.01
Inupiat *(Alaska Native)* (23)	34	0.01
Iroquois (38)	103	0.02
Kiowa (14)	33	0.01
Lumbee (17)	33	0.01
Menominee (3)	3	<0.01
Mexican American Ind. (151)	273	0.07
Navajo (427)	674	0.16
Osage (27)	67	0.02
Ottawa (8)	17	<0.01
Paiute (5)	18	<0.01
Pima (13)	22	0.01
Potawatomi (26)	57	0.01
Pueblo (70)	126	0.03
Puget Sound Salish (5)	7	<0.01
Seminole (10)	38	0.01
Shoshone (18)	44	0.01
Sioux (152)	330	0.08
South American Ind. (19)	38	0.01
Spanish American Ind. (47)	71	0.02
Tlingit-Haida *(Alaska Native)* (17)	36	0.01
Tohono O'Odham (22)	28	0.01
Tsimshian *(Alaska Native)* (3)	8	<0.01
Ute (57)	102	0.02
Yakama (2)	4	<0.01
Yaqui (8)	31	0.01
Yuman (5)	10	<0.01
Yup'ik *(Alaska Native)* (5)	13	<0.01
Asian (12,601)	19,260	4.63
Not Hispanic (12,206)	17,806	4.28
Hispanic (395)	1,454	0.35
Bangladeshi (7)	11	<0.01
Bhutanese (12)	12	<0.01
Burmese (25)	29	0.01
Cambodian (74)	112	0.03
Chinese, ex. Taiwanese (1,508)	2,269	0.54
Filipino (2,635)	4,655	1.12
Hmong (34)	37	0.01
Indian (1,791)	2,200	0.53
Indonesian (63)	135	0.03
Japanese (918)	2,354	0.57
Korean (3,316)	5,103	1.23
Laotian (75)	95	0.02
Malaysian (12)	17	<0.01
Nepalese (103)	113	0.03
Pakistani (65)	79	0.02
Sri Lankan (9)	13	<0.01
Taiwanese (50)	90	0.02
Thai (306)	557	0.13
Vietnamese (1,084)	1,352	0.32
Hawaii Native/Pacific Islander (1,290)	2,701	0.65
Not Hispanic (1,092)	2,185	0.52
Hispanic (198)	516	0.12
Fijian (10)	17	<0.01
Guamanian/Chamorro (474)	779	0.19
Marshallese (16)	17	<0.01
Native Hawaiian (288)	884	0.21
Samoan (305)	551	0.13
Tongan (9)	25	0.01
White (328,326)	346,511	83.21
Not Hispanic (294,598)	307,046	73.73
Hispanic (33,728)	39,465	9.48

Columbine

Place Type: CDP
County: Jefferson
Population: 24,280†

Ancestry‡	Population	%
African, Sub-Saharan (0)	14	0.06
African (0)	14	0.06
American (1,112)	1,112	4.64
Arab (21)	30	0.13
Lebanese (21)	21	0.09
Syrian (0)	9	0.04
Armenian (49)	94	0.39
Australian (0)	9	0.04
Austrian (46)	100	0.42
Belgian (26)	68	0.28
Brazilian (21)	21	0.09
British (55)	85	0.35
Cajun (0)	14	0.06
Canadian (34)	34	0.14
Croatian (10)	10	0.04
Czech (150)	358	1.49
Czechoslovakian (13)	40	0.17
Danish (175)	430	1.79
Dutch (127)	561	2.34
Eastern European (15)	29	0.12
English (898)	3,730	15.56
European (509)	600	2.50
Finnish (23)	34	0.14
French, ex. Basque (103)	908	3.79
French Canadian (89)	303	1.26
German (2,868)	7,875	32.85
Greek (36)	152	0.63
Hungarian (56)	121	0.50
Icelander (0)	34	0.14
Iranian (64)	64	0.27
Irish (692)	3,666	15.29
Italian (421)	1,378	5.75
Latvian (0)	30	0.13
Lithuanian (40)	53	0.22
Luxemburger (12)	34	0.14
New Zealander (42)	42	0.18
Northern European (48)	48	0.20
Norwegian (180)	639	2.67
Pennsylvania German (10)	21	0.09
Polish (214)	874	3.65
Portuguese (12)	40	0.17
Romanian (31)	40	0.17
Russian (51)	292	1.22
Scandinavian (46)	84	0.35
Scotch-Irish (245)	735	3.07
Scottish (128)	839	3.50
Serbian (12)	32	0.13
Slavic (14)	46	0.19
Slovak (58)	58	0.24
Slovene (46)	53	0.22
Swedish (199)	765	3.19
Swiss (68)	369	1.54
Turkish (58)	58	0.24
Ukrainian (37)	166	0.69
Welsh (79)	260	1.08
West Indian, ex. Hispanic (6)	6	0.03
Bahamian (6)	6	0.03
Yugoslavian (52)	118	0.49

Hispanic Origin	Population	%
Hispanic or Latino (of any race)	2,065	8.50
Central American, ex. Mexican	49	0.20
Costa Rican	5	0.02
Guatemalan	12	0.05
Honduran	6	0.02
Nicaraguan	4	0.02
Panamanian	8	0.03
Salvadoran	14	0.06
Cuban	19	0.08
Mexican	1,213	5.00
Puerto Rican	64	0.26
South American	87	0.36
Argentinean	7	0.03
Bolivian	12	0.05
Chilean	5	0.02
Colombian	18	0.07
Ecuadorian	6	0.02
Paraguayan	2	0.01
Peruvian	26	0.11
Uruguayan	5	0.02
Venezuelan	6	0.02
Other Hispanic or Latino	633	2.61

Race*	Population	%
African-American/Black (141)	246	1.01
Not Hispanic (124)	204	0.84
Hispanic (17)	42	0.17
American Indian/Alaska Native (134)	284	1.17
Not Hispanic (75)	166	0.68
Hispanic (59)	118	0.49
Apache (5)	16	0.07
Arapaho (2)	10	0.04
Blackfeet (2)	6	0.02
Canadian/French Am. Ind. (0)	1	<0.01
Central American Ind. (1)	2	0.01
Cherokee (20)	51	0.21
Chickasaw (2)	2	0.01
Chippewa (11)	14	0.06
Choctaw (6)	7	0.03
Comanche (3)	3	0.01
Creek (1)	1	<0.01
Hopi (2)	2	0.01
Iroquois (2)	4	0.02
Mexican American Ind. (1)	2	0.01
Navajo (5)	13	0.05
Osage (2)	2	0.01
Paiute (0)	1	<0.01
Pueblo (3)	9	0.04
Seminole (0)	1	<0.01
Sioux (5)	9	0.04
Spanish American Ind. (1)	1	<0.01
Ute (4)	4	0.02
Yup'ik *(Alaska Native)* (2)	2	0.01
Asian (489)	683	2.81
Not Hispanic (479)	634	2.61
Hispanic (10)	49	0.20
Cambodian (0)	3	0.01
Chinese, ex. Taiwanese (84)	130	0.54
Filipino (50)	98	0.40
Indian (40)	51	0.21
Indonesian (9)	9	0.04
Japanese (51)	108	0.44
Korean (48)	88	0.36
Laotian (4)	4	0.02
Pakistani (1)	1	<0.01
Taiwanese (6)	9	0.04
Thai (8)	15	0.06
Vietnamese (165)	180	0.74
Hawaii Native/Pacific Islander (23)	67	0.28
Not Hispanic (19)	53	0.22
Hispanic (4)	14	0.06
Fijian (3)	3	0.01
Guamanian/Chamorro (9)	9	0.04
Native Hawaiian (3)	35	0.14
Samoan (0)	7	0.03
Tongan (4)	7	0.03
White (22,466)	23,008	94.76
Not Hispanic (21,118)	21,467	88.41
Hispanic (1,348)	1,541	6.35

Commerce City

Place Type: City
County: Adams
Population: 45,913†

Ancestry‡	Population	%
African, Sub-Saharan (77)	77	0.19
African (13)	13	0.03
Ethiopian (34)	34	0.08
Liberian (30)	30	0.07
American (1,413)	1,413	3.41
Arab (0)	9	0.02
Lebanese (0)	9	0.02
Armenian (0)	14	0.03
Austrian (30)	50	0.12
Belgian (0)	36	0.09
Brazilian (14)	58	0.14
British (46)	66	0.16
Canadian (32)	32	0.08
Croatian (0)	23	0.06
Czech (47)	225	0.54

*Notes: † The Census 2010 population figure is used to calculate the percentages in the Hispanic Origin and Race categories. Ancestry percentages are based on the 2006-2010 American Community Survey population (not shown); ‡ Numbers in parentheses indicate the number of people reporting a single ancestry; * Numbers in parentheses indicate the number of persons reporting this race alone, not in combination with any other race; Please refer to the Explanation of Data for more information.*

Czechoslovakian (0)	22	0.05
Danish (43)	167	0.40
Dutch (90)	521	1.26
Eastern European (13)	13	0.03
English (746)	2,384	5.75
European (158)	178	0.43
Finnish (9)	18	0.04
French, ex. Basque (150)	788	1.90
French Canadian (73)	203	0.49
German (2,521)	7,191	17.33
Greek (106)	227	0.55
Hungarian (9)	89	0.21
Iranian (0)	16	0.04
Irish (772)	3,672	8.85
Italian (619)	1,727	4.16
Latvian (0)	20	0.05
Lithuanian (10)	57	0.14
Macedonian (8)	8	0.02
Northern European (55)	55	0.13
Norwegian (158)	544	1.31
Polish (338)	820	1.98
Portuguese (20)	77	0.19
Romanian (0)	12	0.03
Russian (121)	335	0.81
Scandinavian (68)	68	0.16
Scotch-Irish (84)	475	1.14
Scottish (171)	475	1.14
Slovene (0)	18	0.04
Swedish (119)	463	1.12
Swiss (37)	162	0.39
Ukrainian (130)	166	0.40
Welsh (17)	183	0.44
Yugoslavian (16)	23	0.06

Hispanic Origin	Population	%
Hispanic or Latino (of any race)	21,509	46.85
Central American, ex. Mexican	222	0.48
Costa Rican	3	0.01
Guatemalan	43	0.09
Honduran	34	0.07
Nicaraguan	19	0.04
Panamanian	21	0.05
Salvadoran	101	0.22
Other Central American	1	<0.01
Cuban	50	0.11
Dominican Republic	12	0.03
Mexican	17,004	37.04
Puerto Rican	221	0.48
South American	100	0.22
Argentinean	10	0.02
Bolivian	1	<0.01
Chilean	10	0.02
Colombian	41	0.09
Ecuadorian	7	0.02
Peruvian	20	0.04
Uruguayan	1	<0.01
Venezuelan	10	0.02
Other Hispanic or Latino	3,900	8.49

Race*	Population	%
African-American/Black (1,436)	1,934	4.21
Not Hispanic (1,269)	1,573	3.43
Hispanic (167)	361	0.79
American Indian/Alaska Native (673)	1,350	2.94
Not Hispanic (224)	489	1.07
Hispanic (449)	861	1.88
Alaska Athabascan *(Ala. Nat.)* (0)	1	<0.01
Aleut *(Alaska Native)* (0)	1	<0.01
Apache (38)	85	0.19
Arapaho (1)	8	0.02
Blackfeet (13)	21	0.05
Canadian/French Am. Ind. (2)	2	<0.01
Central American Ind. (0)	1	<0.01
Cherokee (50)	139	0.30
Cheyenne (2)	6	0.01
Chickasaw (6)	9	0.02
Chippewa (16)	21	0.05
Choctaw (9)	16	0.03
Comanche (0)	2	<0.01
Cree (1)	2	<0.01
Creek (8)	13	0.03
Delaware (1)	1	<0.01
Hopi (3)	14	0.03
Inupiat *(Alaska Native)* (2)	2	<0.01
Iroquois (3)	6	0.01
Lumbee (1)	1	<0.01
Mexican American Ind. (62)	152	0.33
Navajo (51)	114	0.25
Osage (1)	2	<0.01
Pima (0)	1	<0.01
Potawatomi (2)	2	<0.01
Pueblo (8)	16	0.03
Seminole (0)	5	0.01
Shoshone (2)	2	<0.01
Sioux (47)	75	0.16
Spanish American Ind. (4)	10	0.02
Tlingit-Haida *(Alaska Native)* (1)	2	<0.01
Ute (4)	9	0.02
Yaqui (3)	9	0.02
Yup'ik *(Alaska Native)* (0)	1	<0.01
Asian (1,023)	1,425	3.10
Not Hispanic (982)	1,266	2.76
Hispanic (41)	159	0.35
Cambodian (31)	53	0.12
Chinese, ex. Taiwanese (89)	135	0.29
Filipino (114)	209	0.46
Hmong (250)	264	0.58
Indian (80)	109	0.24
Indonesian (3)	6	0.01
Japanese (67)	162	0.35
Korean (78)	147	0.32
Laotian (61)	84	0.18
Malaysian (1)	1	<0.01
Nepalese (25)	25	0.05
Pakistani (7)	7	0.02
Sri Lankan (0)	1	<0.01
Taiwanese (2)	7	0.02
Thai (10)	33	0.07
Vietnamese (134)	175	0.38
Hawaii Native/Pacific Islander (32)	107	0.23
Not Hispanic (27)	71	0.15
Hispanic (5)	36	0.08
Guamanian/Chamorro (11)	26	0.06
Native Hawaiian (9)	31	0.07
Samoan (1)	11	0.02
Tongan (2)	4	0.01
White (31,704)	33,615	73.21
Not Hispanic (21,035)	21,758	47.39
Hispanic (10,669)	11,857	25.82

Cortez

Place Type: City
County: Montezuma
Population: 8,482†

Ancestry‡	Population	%
American (677)	677	8.05
Arab (0)	168	2.00
Lebanese (0)	84	1.00
Syrian (0)	84	1.00
Austrian (15)	15	0.18
Basque (10)	21	0.25
British (0)	61	0.73
Czech (12)	47	0.56
Czechoslovakian (0)	10	0.12
Danish (0)	54	0.64
Dutch (29)	166	1.97
English (451)	1,093	12.99
European (80)	80	0.95
Finnish (18)	58	0.69
French, ex. Basque (9)	251	2.98
French Canadian (0)	8	0.10
German (330)	1,577	18.75
Greek (0)	44	0.52
Hungarian (12)	12	0.14
Irish (367)	1,017	12.09
Italian (43)	247	2.94
Lithuanian (12)	12	0.14
Norwegian (36)	124	1.47
Polish (44)	218	2.59
Romanian (11)	11	0.13
Scandinavian (0)	19	0.23
Scotch-Irish (41)	221	2.63
Scottish (69)	311	3.70
Swedish (59)	169	2.01
Swiss (14)	54	0.64
Welsh (10)	103	1.22
Yugoslavian (20)	37	0.44

Hispanic Origin	Population	%
Hispanic or Latino (of any race)	1,336	15.75
Central American, ex. Mexican	12	0.14
Guatemalan	3	0.04
Honduran	2	0.02
Nicaraguan	1	0.01
Salvadoran	6	0.07
Cuban	9	0.11
Mexican	804	9.48
Puerto Rican	23	0.27
South American	6	0.07
Colombian	5	0.06
Venezuelan	1	0.01
Other Hispanic or Latino	482	5.68

Race*	Population	%
African-American/Black (33)	59	0.70
Not Hispanic (27)	50	0.59
Hispanic (6)	9	0.11
American Indian/Alaska Native (997)	1,157	13.64
Not Hispanic (908)	1,014	11.95
Hispanic (89)	143	1.69
Alaska Athabascan *(Ala. Nat.)* (0)	3	0.04
Apache (13)	19	0.22
Blackfeet (0)	1	0.01
Cherokee (16)	35	0.41
Cheyenne (0)	4	0.05
Chickasaw (1)	1	0.01
Chippewa (3)	3	0.04
Choctaw (10)	10	0.12
Comanche (0)	1	0.01
Creek (1)	4	0.05
Crow (4)	4	0.05
Hopi (0)	5	0.06
Inupiat *(Alaska Native)* (1)	2	0.02
Iroquois (1)	5	0.06
Kiowa (1)	3	0.04
Mexican American Ind. (4)	4	0.05
Navajo (645)	718	8.46
Osage (0)	1	0.01
Paiute (0)	1	0.01
Potawatomi (2)	3	0.04
Pueblo (4)	11	0.13
Seminole (0)	2	0.02
Sioux (4)	10	0.12
South American Ind. (1)	1	0.01
Spanish American Ind. (1)	1	0.01
Tohono O'Odham (0)	4	0.05
Ute (96)	119	1.40
Asian (72)	103	1.21
Not Hispanic (72)	96	1.13
Hispanic (0)	7	0.08
Cambodian (0)	1	0.01
Chinese, ex. Taiwanese (32)	34	0.40
Filipino (15)	23	0.27
Indian (3)	3	0.04
Indonesian (1)	1	0.01
Japanese (7)	14	0.17
Korean (1)	10	0.12
Nepalese (3)	3	0.04
Taiwanese (1)	1	0.01
Vietnamese (9)	11	0.13
Hawaii Native/Pacific Islander (2)	17	0.20
Not Hispanic (2)	10	0.12
Hispanic (0)	7	0.08
Guamanian/Chamorro (2)	2	0.02
Native Hawaiian (0)	13	0.15
White (6,717)	6,971	82.19
Not Hispanic (5,985)	6,122	72.18
Hispanic (732)	849	10.01

SECTION TWO

*Notes: † The Census 2010 population figure is used to calculate the percentages in the Hispanic Origin and Race categories. Ancestry percentages are based on the 2006-2010 American Community Survey population (not shown); ‡ Numbers in parentheses indicate the number of people reporting a single ancestry; * Numbers in parentheses indicate the number of persons reporting this race alone, not in combination with any other race; Please refer to the Explanation of Data for more information.*

Craig

Place Type: City
County: Moffat
Population: 9,464†

Ancestry‡	Population	%
American (719)	719	7.72
Austrian (7)	27	0.29
British (9)	9	0.10
Canadian (9)	9	0.10
Croatian (0)	11	0.12
Czech (0)	77	0.83
Czechoslovakian (25)	42	0.45
Danish (16)	24	0.26
Dutch (47)	257	2.76
English (313)	1,367	14.69
European (265)	265	2.85
Finnish (14)	46	0.49
French, ex. Basque (13)	349	3.75
French Canadian (0)	40	0.43
German (502)	1,705	18.32
Greek (12)	47	0.50
Hungarian (0)	8	0.09
Irish (400)	1,132	12.16
Israeli (0)	6	0.06
Italian (168)	457	4.91
Lithuanian (0)	21	0.23
Norwegian (24)	278	2.99
Polish (38)	204	2.19
Portuguese (0)	13	0.14
Russian (0)	61	0.66
Scandinavian (33)	66	0.71
Scotch-Irish (40)	196	2.11
Scottish (85)	313	3.36
Slovak (0)	9	0.10
Swedish (105)	263	2.83
Welsh (24)	57	0.61
Yugoslavian (0)	10	0.11

Hispanic Origin	Population	%
Hispanic or Latino (of any race)	1,651	17.45
Central American, ex. Mexican	17	0.18
Guatemalan	4	0.04
Honduran	5	0.05
Nicaraguan	5	0.05
Salvadoran	3	0.03
Cuban	3	0.03
Mexican	1,396	14.75
Puerto Rican	12	0.13
South American	25	0.26
Chilean	6	0.06
Colombian	5	0.05
Ecuadorian	1	0.01
Peruvian	12	0.13
Venezuelan	1	0.01
Other Hispanic or Latino	198	2.09

Race*	Population	%
African-American/Black (28)	65	0.69
Not Hispanic (25)	60	0.63
Hispanic (3)	5	0.05
American Indian/Alaska Native (84)	164	1.73
Not Hispanic (66)	126	1.33
Hispanic (18)	38	0.40
Apache (3)	6	0.06
Blackfeet (1)	2	0.02
Cherokee (8)	21	0.22
Cheyenne (0)	1	0.01
Chippewa (3)	4	0.04
Choctaw (1)	4	0.04
Hopi (0)	2	0.02
Iroquois (3)	3	0.03
Mexican American Ind. (2)	2	0.02
Navajo (18)	19	0.20
Osage (1)	4	0.04
Ottawa (4)	4	0.04
Potawatomi (1)	1	0.01
Seminole (0)	2	0.02
Sioux (3)	7	0.07
Spanish American Ind. (2)	2	0.02
Ute (0)	2	0.02
Asian (55)	88	0.93
Not Hispanic (54)	82	0.87
Hispanic (1)	6	0.06
Chinese, ex. Taiwanese (9)	16	0.17
Filipino (9)	20	0.21
Indian (7)	9	0.10
Indonesian (3)	4	0.04
Japanese (8)	14	0.15
Korean (3)	6	0.06
Nepalese (1)	1	0.01
Taiwanese (0)	1	0.01
Thai (3)	10	0.11
Vietnamese (3)	8	0.08
Hawaii Native/Pacific Islander (7)	26	0.27
Not Hispanic (7)	19	0.20
Hispanic (0)	7	0.07
Fijian (0)	2	0.02
Guamanian/Chamorro (0)	1	0.01
Native Hawaiian (3)	13	0.14
Samoan (2)	3	0.03
White (8,406)	8,619	91.07
Not Hispanic (7,531)	7,649	80.82
Hispanic (875)	970	10.25

Dakota Ridge

Place Type: CDP
County: Jefferson
Population: 32,005†

Ancestry‡	Population	%
African, Sub-Saharan (17)	17	0.06
African (17)	17	0.06
American (1,268)	1,268	4.12
Arab (10)	33	0.11
Lebanese (0)	13	0.04
Syrian (10)	20	0.06
Australian (45)	45	0.15
Austrian (28)	109	0.35
Belgian (0)	60	0.19
British (50)	108	0.35
Bulgarian (0)	16	0.05
Cajun (14)	37	0.12
Canadian (39)	98	0.32
Croatian (16)	47	0.15
Czech (103)	276	0.90
Czechoslovakian (43)	43	0.14
Danish (35)	326	1.06
Dutch (184)	764	2.48
English (898)	3,885	12.62
European (697)	763	2.48
Finnish (0)	38	0.12
French, ex. Basque (137)	1,211	3.93
French Canadian (181)	295	0.96
German (3,151)	9,967	32.39
Greek (37)	89	0.29
Hungarian (74)	254	0.83
Icelander (0)	12	0.04
Irish (1,145)	4,949	16.08
Italian (878)	2,223	7.22
Latvian (0)	28	0.09
Lithuanian (0)	14	0.05
Macedonian (0)	30	0.10
Maltese (0)	27	0.09
Northern European (44)	44	0.14
Norwegian (237)	863	2.80
Pennsylvania German (39)	94	0.31
Polish (155)	1,252	4.07
Portuguese (0)	22	0.07
Romanian (0)	17	0.06
Russian (59)	318	1.03
Scandinavian (26)	36	0.12
Scotch-Irish (279)	823	2.67
Scottish (492)	1,284	4.17
Serbian (10)	21	0.07
Slavic (0)	11	0.04
Slovak (9)	97	0.32
Slovene (11)	32	0.10
Swedish (379)	1,489	4.84
Swiss (13)	128	0.42
Turkish (0)	11	0.04
Ukrainian (0)	86	0.28
Welsh (60)	345	1.12
Yugoslavian (0)	7	0.02

Hispanic Origin	Population	%
Hispanic or Latino (of any race)	3,566	11.14
Central American, ex. Mexican	62	0.19
Costa Rican	7	0.02
Guatemalan	7	0.02
Honduran	6	0.02
Nicaraguan	1	<0.01
Panamanian	4	0.01
Salvadoran	37	0.12
Cuban	34	0.11
Dominican Republic	8	0.02
Mexican	2,093	6.54
Puerto Rican	96	0.30
South American	129	0.40
Argentinean	6	0.02
Bolivian	8	0.02
Chilean	8	0.02
Colombian	49	0.15
Ecuadorian	5	0.02
Peruvian	34	0.11
Uruguayan	2	0.01
Venezuelan	17	0.05
Other Hispanic or Latino	1,144	3.57

Race*	Population	%
African-American/Black (268)	444	1.39
Not Hispanic (249)	405	1.27
Hispanic (19)	39	0.12
American Indian/Alaska Native (205)	435	1.36
Not Hispanic (135)	298	0.93
Hispanic (70)	137	0.43
Alaska Athabascan *(Ala. Nat.)* (1)	1	<0.01
Apache (5)	13	0.04
Blackfeet (1)	5	0.02
Cherokee (25)	74	0.23
Chickasaw (0)	4	0.01
Chippewa (14)	27	0.08
Choctaw (6)	12	0.04
Comanche (1)	10	0.03
Creek (2)	5	0.02
Delaware (0)	1	<0.01
Hopi (1)	1	<0.01
Iroquois (1)	2	0.01
Kiowa (0)	3	0.01
Menominee (2)	2	0.01
Mexican American Ind. (10)	16	0.05
Navajo (13)	47	0.15
Osage (1)	1	<0.01
Paiute (1)	1	<0.01
Potawatomi (0)	2	0.01
Pueblo (8)	15	0.05
Puget Sound Salish (0)	1	<0.01
Shoshone (0)	2	0.01
Sioux (20)	27	0.08
South American Ind. (2)	6	0.02
Spanish American Ind. (4)	4	0.01
Ute (1)	4	0.01
Yaqui (5)	16	0.05
Asian (850)	1,095	3.42
Not Hispanic (825)	1,040	3.25
Hispanic (25)	55	0.17
Cambodian (14)	23	0.07
Chinese, ex. Taiwanese (185)	237	0.74
Filipino (116)	173	0.54
Indian (103)	114	0.36
Indonesian (12)	16	0.05
Japanese (81)	171	0.53
Korean (80)	124	0.39
Laotian (3)	8	0.02
Malaysian (1)	1	<0.01
Nepalese (6)	6	0.02
Pakistani (8)	9	0.03
Sri Lankan (1)	1	<0.01

*Notes: † The Census 2010 population figure is used to calculate the percentages in the Hispanic Origin and Race categories. Ancestry percentages are based on the 2006-2010 American Community Survey population (not shown); ‡ Numbers in parentheses indicate the number of people reporting a single ancestry; * Numbers in parentheses indicate the number of persons reporting this race alone, not in combination with any other race; Please refer to the Explanation of Data for more information.*

Taiwanese (2)	5	0.02
Thai (14)	24	0.07
Vietnamese (176)	189	0.59
Hawaii Native/Pacific Islander (24)	66	0.21
Not Hispanic (20)	54	0.17
Hispanic (4)	12	0.04
Guamanian/Chamorro (3)	13	0.04
Native Hawaiian (16)	32	0.10
Samoan (1)	5	0.02
White (29,044)	29,811	93.14
Not Hispanic (26,621)	27,121	84.74
Hispanic (2,423)	2,690	8.40

Delta

Place Type: City
County: Delta
Population: 8,915†

Ancestry‡	Population	%
American (531)	531	6.05
Austrian (23)	44	0.50
Belgian (13)	13	0.15
British (9)	9	0.10
Canadian (0)	19	0.22
Croatian (12)	21	0.24
Danish (8)	48	0.55
Dutch (27)	106	1.21
English (342)	964	10.98
European (61)	61	0.69
Finnish (0)	11	0.13
French, ex. Basque (0)	122	1.39
German (619)	1,544	17.59
German Russian (6)	6	0.07
Hungarian (0)	8	0.09
Irish (286)	905	10.31
Italian (24)	165	1.88
Norwegian (34)	110	1.25
Polish (54)	180	2.05
Portuguese (10)	10	0.11
Russian (0)	6	0.07
Scotch-Irish (84)	143	1.63
Scottish (153)	337	3.84
Swedish (54)	229	2.61
Swiss (13)	13	0.15
Welsh (31)	71	0.81
West Indian, ex. Hispanic (0)	10	0.11
Dutch West Indian (0)	10	0.11

Hispanic Origin	Population	%
Hispanic or Latino (of any race)	2,327	26.10
Central American, ex. Mexican	7	0.08
Costa Rican	2	0.02
Guatemalan	4	0.04
Salvadoran	1	0.01
Cuban	1	0.01
Mexican	1,861	20.87
Puerto Rican	1	0.01
South American	10	0.11
Colombian	9	0.10
Peruvian	1	0.01
Other Hispanic or Latino	447	5.01

Race*	Population	%
African-American/Black (23)	48	0.54
Not Hispanic (20)	41	0.46
Hispanic (3)	7	0.08
American Indian/Alaska Native (102)	228	2.56
Not Hispanic (54)	122	1.37
Hispanic (48)	106	1.19
Alaska Athabascan *(Ala. Nat.)* (1)	1	0.01
Aleut *(Alaska Native)* (0)	2	0.02
Apache (4)	13	0.15
Arapaho (0)	2	0.02
Canadian/French Am. Ind. (1)	1	0.01
Cherokee (7)	47	0.53
Cheyenne (2)	8	0.09
Chippewa (1)	1	0.01
Choctaw (0)	3	0.03
Comanche (0)	2	0.02
Creek (1)	3	0.03
Delaware (1)	1	0.01
Hopi (1)	1	0.01
Iroquois (0)	5	0.06
Mexican American Ind. (4)	11	0.12
Navajo (8)	20	0.22
Pueblo (6)	10	0.11
Shoshone (0)	2	0.02
Sioux (6)	8	0.09
Spanish American Ind. (5)	5	0.06
Ute (7)	7	0.08
Asian (60)	95	1.07
Not Hispanic (57)	85	0.95
Hispanic (3)	10	0.11
Bangladeshi (4)	4	0.04
Cambodian (12)	12	0.13
Chinese, ex. Taiwanese (7)	12	0.13
Filipino (11)	27	0.30
Indian (6)	6	0.07
Indonesian (0)	1	0.01
Japanese (5)	9	0.10
Korean (4)	4	0.04
Thai (0)	3	0.03
Vietnamese (9)	11	0.12
Hawaii Native/Pacific Islander (2)	11	0.12
Not Hispanic (0)	9	0.10
Hispanic (2)	2	0.02
Guamanian/Chamorro (0)	1	0.01
Native Hawaiian (0)	3	0.03
Samoan (2)	3	0.03
Tongan (0)	1	0.01
White (7,330)	7,584	85.07
Not Hispanic (6,340)	6,447	72.32
Hispanic (990)	1,137	12.75

Denver

Place Type: City
County: Denver
Population: 600,158†

Ancestry‡	Population	%
Afghan (142)	188	0.03
African, Sub-Saharan (6,860)	7,805	1.35
African (2,983)	3,628	0.63
Cape Verdean (0)	13	<0.01
Ethiopian (1,654)	1,761	0.30
Ghanaian (161)	172	0.03
Liberian (81)	81	0.01
Nigerian (361)	375	0.06
Senegalese (58)	73	0.01
Somalian (550)	550	0.10
South African (193)	242	0.04
Sudanese (588)	634	0.11
Other Sub-Saharan African (231)	276	0.05
Albanian (30)	30	0.01
Alsatian (0)	8	<0.01
American (19,324)	19,324	3.34
Arab (1,754)	2,656	0.46
Arab (205)	403	0.07
Egyptian (23)	83	0.01
Iraqi (218)	218	0.04
Lebanese (289)	664	0.11
Moroccan (356)	437	0.08
Palestinian (48)	48	0.01
Syrian (33)	121	0.02
Other Arab (582)	682	0.12
Armenian (93)	233	0.04
Assyrian/Chaldean/Syriac (0)	13	<0.01
Australian (198)	301	0.05
Austrian (628)	2,416	0.42
Basque (44)	99	0.02
Belgian (236)	876	0.15
Brazilian (203)	291	0.05
British (1,804)	2,850	0.49
Bulgarian (109)	139	0.02
Cajun (127)	202	0.03
Canadian (433)	1,045	0.18
Celtic (96)	126	0.02
Croatian (276)	615	0.11
Czech (1,009)	3,635	0.63
Czechoslovakian (347)	586	0.10
Danish (851)	3,528	0.61
Dutch (2,440)	8,389	1.45
Eastern European (1,469)	1,565	0.27
English (12,836)	49,616	8.58
Estonian (54)	125	0.02
European (8,089)	8,938	1.55
Finnish (285)	828	0.14
French, ex. Basque (2,115)	15,585	2.70
French Canadian (728)	2,280	0.39
German (25,327)	86,183	14.91
German Russian (6)	55	0.01
Greek (1,117)	2,504	0.43
Hungarian (861)	2,348	0.41
Icelander (46)	135	0.02
Iranian (636)	794	0.14
Irish (14,923)	58,273	10.08
Israeli (374)	462	0.08
Italian (8,417)	24,012	4.15
Latvian (31)	191	0.03
Lithuanian (500)	1,309	0.23
Luxemburger (40)	169	0.03
Macedonian (69)	78	0.01
Maltese (9)	39	0.01
New Zealander (76)	86	0.01
Northern European (1,002)	1,069	0.18
Norwegian (2,989)	8,645	1.50
Pennsylvania German (63)	164	0.03
Polish (3,960)	12,238	2.12
Portuguese (415)	1,173	0.20
Romanian (410)	923	0.16
Russian (4,019)	8,670	1.50
Scandinavian (659)	1,543	0.27
Scotch-Irish (3,942)	10,302	1.78
Scottish (2,623)	11,109	1.92
Serbian (156)	313	0.05
Slavic (135)	269	0.05
Slovak (321)	794	0.14
Slovene (203)	453	0.08
Swedish (3,271)	11,437	1.98
Swiss (571)	3,029	0.52
Turkish (306)	384	0.07
Ukrainian (963)	1,742	0.30
Welsh (687)	4,528	0.78
West Indian, ex. Hispanic (402)	789	0.14
Bahamian (16)	16	<0.01
Barbadian (9)	9	<0.01
Belizean (59)	149	0.03
Bermudan (11)	11	<0.01
British West Indian (0)	33	0.01
Dutch West Indian (0)	9	<0.01
Haitian (27)	51	0.01
Jamaican (226)	377	0.07
Trinidadian/Tobagonian (15)	15	<0.01
West Indian (39)	119	0.02
Yugoslavian (240)	420	0.07

Hispanic Origin	Population	%
Hispanic or Latino (of any race)	190,965	31.82
Central American, ex. Mexican	5,114	0.85
Costa Rican	147	0.02
Guatemalan	1,324	0.22
Honduran	799	0.13
Nicaraguan	200	0.03
Panamanian	216	0.04
Salvadoran	2,372	0.40
Other Central American	56	0.01
Cuban	909	0.15
Dominican Republic	257	0.04
Mexican	149,366	24.89
Puerto Rican	2,561	0.43
South American	2,739	0.46
Argentinean	269	0.04
Bolivian	130	0.02
Chilean	249	0.04
Colombian	730	0.12
Ecuadorian	162	0.03
Paraguayan	27	<0.01
Peruvian	835	0.14

*Notes: † The Census 2010 population figure is used to calculate the percentages in the Hispanic Origin and Race categories. Ancestry percentages are based on the 2006-2010 American Community Survey population (not shown); ‡ Numbers in parentheses indicate the number of people reporting a single ancestry; * Numbers in parentheses indicate the number of persons reporting this race alone, not in combination with any other race; Please refer to the Explanation of Data for more information.*

Uruguayan	26	<0.01
Venezuelan	284	0.05
Other South American	27	<0.01
Other Hispanic or Latino	30,019	5.00

Race*	Population	%
African-American/Black (61,435)	69,999	11.66
Not Hispanic (58,388)	64,607	10.76
Hispanic (3,047)	5,392	0.90
American Indian/Alaska Native (8,237)	14,995	2.50
Not Hispanic (3,525)	7,399	1.23
Hispanic (4,712)	7,596	1.27
Alaska Athabascan *(Ala. Nat.)* (13)	19	<0.01
Aleut *(Alaska Native)* (17)	22	<0.01
Apache (404)	849	0.14
Arapaho (45)	67	0.01
Blackfeet (29)	282	0.05
Canadian/French Am. Ind. (15)	25	<0.01
Central American Ind. (12)	28	<0.01
Cherokee (314)	1,522	0.25
Cheyenne (38)	87	0.01
Chickasaw (25)	79	0.01
Chippewa (100)	208	0.03
Choctaw (73)	275	0.05
Colville (2)	2	<0.01
Comanche (34)	53	0.01
Cree (8)	21	<0.01
Creek (38)	139	0.02
Crow (6)	14	<0.01
Delaware (7)	21	<0.01
Hopi (35)	81	0.01
Houma (1)	3	<0.01
Inupiat *(Alaska Native)* (14)	24	<0.01
Iroquois (26)	99	0.02
Kiowa (10)	33	0.01
Lumbee (7)	23	<0.01
Menominee (1)	6	<0.01
Mexican American Ind. (497)	733	0.12
Navajo (704)	1,118	0.19
Osage (36)	62	0.01
Ottawa (4)	7	<0.01
Paiute (4)	10	<0.01
Pima (20)	23	<0.01
Potawatomi (20)	70	0.01
Pueblo (147)	257	0.04
Puget Sound Salish (3)	6	<0.01
Seminole (29)	82	0.01
Shoshone (45)	56	0.01
Sioux (844)	1,213	0.20
South American Ind. (34)	72	0.01
Spanish American Ind. (104)	148	0.02
Tlingit-Haida *(Alaska Native)* (11)	17	<0.01
Tohono O'Odham (17)	18	<0.01
Ute (82)	160	0.03
Yakama (0)	1	<0.01
Yaqui (35)	73	0.01
Yuman (6)	10	<0.01
Yup'ik *(Alaska Native)* (9)	13	<0.01
Asian (20,433)	26,139	4.36
Not Hispanic (19,925)	24,571	4.09
Hispanic (508)	1,568	0.26
Bangladeshi (34)	37	0.01
Bhutanese (198)	273	0.05
Burmese (739)	800	0.13
Cambodian (553)	679	0.11
Chinese, ex. Taiwanese (3,217)	4,333	0.72
Filipino (1,585)	2,787	0.46
Hmong (54)	75	0.01
Indian (2,794)	3,395	0.57
Indonesian (223)	322	0.05
Japanese (1,590)	2,925	0.49
Korean (1,724)	2,415	0.40
Laotian (99)	151	0.03
Malaysian (24)	42	0.01
Nepalese (413)	497	0.08
Pakistani (150)	205	0.03
Sri Lankan (30)	41	0.01
Taiwanese (187)	232	0.04
Thai (443)	649	0.11
Vietnamese (5,055)	5,528	0.92
Hawaii Native/Pacific Islander (607)	1,598	0.27
Not Hispanic (495)	1,198	0.20
Hispanic (112)	400	0.07
Fijian (18)	22	<0.01
Guamanian/Chamorro (133)	270	0.04
Marshallese (14)	14	<0.01
Native Hawaiian (140)	494	0.08
Samoan (82)	168	0.03
Tongan (34)	50	0.01
White (413,696)	433,792	72.28
Not Hispanic (313,012)	323,478	53.90
Hispanic (100,684)	110,314	18.38

Derby

Place Type: CDP
County: Adams
Population: 7,685†

Ancestry‡	Population	%
American (290)	290	3.70
Canadian (0)	13	0.17
Croatian (0)	4	0.05
Danish (0)	8	0.10
Dutch (44)	129	1.64
English (78)	295	3.76
European (44)	44	0.56
French, ex. Basque (0)	123	1.57
French Canadian (12)	18	0.23
German (130)	740	9.43
Irish (66)	461	5.88
Italian (30)	105	1.34
Polish (50)	118	1.50
Russian (17)	27	0.34
Scotch-Irish (23)	78	0.99
Scottish (52)	61	0.78
Slovene (0)	4	0.05
Swedish (81)	307	3.91
Ukrainian (12)	12	0.15
Welsh (0)	9	0.11

Hispanic Origin	Population	%
Hispanic or Latino (of any race)	4,932	64.18
Central American, ex. Mexican	45	0.59
Guatemalan	14	0.18
Honduran	5	0.07
Panamanian	2	0.03
Salvadoran	24	0.31
Cuban	12	0.16
Dominican Republic	3	0.04
Mexican	4,216	54.86
Puerto Rican	23	0.30
South American	6	0.08
Colombian	4	0.05
Venezuelan	2	0.03
Other Hispanic or Latino	627	8.16

Race*	Population	%
African-American/Black (84)	121	1.57
Not Hispanic (77)	97	1.26
Hispanic (7)	24	0.31
American Indian/Alaska Native (114)	205	2.67
Not Hispanic (33)	76	0.99
Hispanic (81)	129	1.68
Apache (5)	11	0.14
Arapaho (1)	1	0.01
Blackfeet (0)	5	0.07
Cherokee (9)	25	0.33
Chippewa (3)	4	0.05
Creek (0)	2	0.03
Mexican American Ind. (2)	2	0.03
Navajo (8)	16	0.21
Potawatomi (0)	5	0.07
Pueblo (1)	4	0.05
Shoshone (0)	1	0.01
Sioux (7)	9	0.12
Spanish American Ind. (2)	3	0.04
Tohono O'Odham (6)	6	0.08
Ute (1)	3	0.04
Asian (44)	76	0.99
Not Hispanic (32)	41	0.53
Hispanic (12)	35	0.46
Chinese, ex. Taiwanese (5)	5	0.07
Filipino (9)	21	0.27
Indian (1)	4	0.05
Japanese (14)	16	0.21
Korean (1)	4	0.05
Vietnamese (9)	14	0.18
Hawaii Native/Pacific Islander (1)	2	0.03
Not Hispanic (1)	1	0.01
Hispanic (0)	1	0.01
Native Hawaiian (1)	1	0.01
White (5,053)	5,309	69.08
Not Hispanic (2,526)	2,600	33.83
Hispanic (2,527)	2,709	35.25

Durango

Place Type: City
County: La Plata
Population: 16,887†

Ancestry‡	Population	%
African, Sub-Saharan (29)	29	0.18
African (11)	11	0.07
Ethiopian (18)	18	0.11
American (1,049)	1,049	6.36
Armenian (26)	40	0.24
Australian (6)	6	0.04
Austrian (10)	20	0.12
Belgian (9)	9	0.05
British (51)	82	0.50
Canadian (0)	20	0.12
Croatian (0)	6	0.04
Czech (96)	146	0.88
Danish (36)	68	0.41
Dutch (141)	362	2.19
Eastern European (20)	55	0.33
English (577)	2,068	12.53
European (463)	488	2.96
Finnish (19)	86	0.52
French, ex. Basque (77)	716	4.34
French Canadian (44)	71	0.43
German (1,530)	3,641	22.07
Greek (65)	75	0.45
Hungarian (24)	41	0.25
Iranian (13)	25	0.15
Irish (858)	2,522	15.28
Italian (523)	1,083	6.56
Lithuanian (21)	80	0.48
Luxemburger (0)	45	0.27
Northern European (20)	27	0.16
Norwegian (243)	578	3.50
Pennsylvania German (0)	13	0.08
Polish (71)	255	1.55
Portuguese (0)	12	0.07
Romanian (0)	13	0.08
Russian (85)	203	1.23
Scandinavian (35)	96	0.58
Scotch-Irish (146)	333	2.02
Scottish (300)	675	4.09
Slovak (17)	17	0.10
Swedish (171)	530	3.21
Swiss (56)	137	0.83
Ukrainian (0)	1	0.01
Welsh (142)	293	1.78
West Indian, ex. Hispanic (0)	18	0.11
Dutch West Indian (0)	18	0.11

Hispanic Origin	Population	%
Hispanic or Latino (of any race)	2,074	12.28
Central American, ex. Mexican	30	0.18
Costa Rican	4	0.02
Guatemalan	11	0.07
Honduran	1	0.01
Nicaraguan	8	0.05
Panamanian	3	0.02
Salvadoran	3	0.02
Cuban	16	0.09
Dominican Republic	7	0.04

*Notes: † The Census 2010 population figure is used to calculate the percentages in the Hispanic Origin and Race categories. Ancestry percentages are based on the 2006-2010 American Community Survey population (not shown); ‡ Numbers in parentheses indicate the number of people reporting a single ancestry; * Numbers in parentheses indicate the number of persons reporting this race alone, not in combination with any other race; Please refer to the Explanation of Data for more information.*

Mexican	1,150	6.81
Puerto Rican	68	0.40
South American	54	0.32
Argentinean	9	0.05
Bolivian	5	0.03
Chilean	15	0.09
Colombian	7	0.04
Ecuadorian	1	0.01
Peruvian	10	0.06
Uruguayan	1	0.01
Venezuelan	4	0.02
Other South American	2	0.01
Other Hispanic or Latino	749	4.44

Race*	Population	%
African-American/Black (100)	183	1.08
Not Hispanic (89)	146	0.86
Hispanic (11)	37	0.22
American Indian/Alaska Native (1,068)	1,324	7.84
Not Hispanic (970)	1,162	6.88
Hispanic (98)	162	0.96
Alaska Athabascan *(Ala. Nat.)* (5)	7	0.04
Aleut *(Alaska Native)* (4)	9	0.05
Apache (34)	48	0.28
Arapaho (2)	6	0.04
Blackfeet (2)	6	0.04
Central American Ind. (0)	1	0.01
Cherokee (35)	78	0.46
Cheyenne (4)	6	0.04
Chickasaw (3)	7	0.04
Chippewa (9)	14	0.08
Choctaw (9)	14	0.08
Colville (1)	1	0.01
Creek (4)	10	0.06
Crow (1)	1	0.01
Delaware (0)	2	0.01
Hopi (12)	15	0.09
Inupiat *(Alaska Native)* (10)	11	0.07
Iroquois (6)	12	0.07
Kiowa (0)	2	0.01
Menominee (1)	1	0.01
Mexican American Ind. (1)	2	0.01
Navajo (513)	561	3.32
Osage (6)	12	0.07
Ottawa (0)	1	0.01
Paiute (3)	3	0.02
Pima (2)	2	0.01
Potawatomi (2)	2	0.01
Pueblo (25)	39	0.23
Puget Sound Salish (1)	1	0.01
Seminole (1)	1	0.01
Shoshone (2)	2	0.01
Sioux (25)	31	0.18
Tlingit-Haida *(Alaska Native)* (16)	22	0.13
Tsimshian *(Alaska Native)* (2)	2	0.01
Ute (56)	72	0.43
Yakama (5)	7	0.04
Yaqui (1)	2	0.01
Yuman (0)	1	0.01
Yup'ik *(Alaska Native)* (5)	9	0.05
Asian (140)	238	1.41
Not Hispanic (132)	210	1.24
Hispanic (8)	28	0.17
Cambodian (0)	1	0.01
Chinese, ex. Taiwanese (27)	33	0.20
Filipino (16)	35	0.21
Indian (14)	24	0.14
Indonesian (1)	5	0.03
Japanese (34)	61	0.36
Korean (18)	37	0.22
Laotian (1)	1	0.01
Malaysian (1)	2	0.01
Taiwanese (1)	1	0.01
Thai (7)	10	0.06
Vietnamese (14)	18	0.11
Hawaii Native/Pacific Islander (7)	26	0.15
Not Hispanic (7)	21	0.12
Hispanic (0)	5	0.03
Guamanian/Chamorro (1)	4	0.02
Native Hawaiian (1)	9	0.05
Samoan (2)	2	0.01
Tongan (0)	1	0.01
White (14,374)	14,831	87.82
Not Hispanic (13,276)	13,565	80.33
Hispanic (1,098)	1,266	7.50

Edwards

Place Type: CDP
County: Eagle
Population: 10,266†

Ancestry‡	Population	%
American (260)	260	2.89
Arab (0)	14	0.16
Palestinian (0)	14	0.16
Austrian (0)	61	0.68
British (40)	116	1.29
Czech (58)	131	1.46
Danish (23)	108	1.20
Dutch (8)	19	0.21
Eastern European (59)	59	0.66
English (227)	733	8.16
European (464)	476	5.30
French, ex. Basque (23)	153	1.70
French Canadian (103)	174	1.94
German (424)	1,855	20.65
Greek (0)	30	0.33
Hungarian (26)	26	0.29
Irish (333)	1,232	13.72
Italian (165)	628	6.99
Lithuanian (16)	16	0.18
Norwegian (28)	163	1.81
Polish (113)	264	2.94
Romanian (13)	13	0.14
Russian (51)	182	2.03
Scandinavian (88)	88	0.98
Scotch-Irish (118)	246	2.74
Scottish (43)	214	2.38
Slovak (50)	50	0.56
Slovene (0)	24	0.27
Swedish (77)	503	5.60
Swiss (0)	80	0.89
Welsh (0)	90	1.00

Hispanic Origin	Population	%
Hispanic or Latino (of any race)	3,219	31.36
Central American, ex. Mexican	128	1.25
Costa Rican	2	0.02
Guatemalan	18	0.18
Honduran	93	0.91
Panamanian	1	0.01
Salvadoran	14	0.14
Cuban	7	0.07
Dominican Republic	1	0.01
Mexican	2,797	27.25
Puerto Rican	6	0.06
South American	66	0.64
Argentinean	20	0.19
Bolivian	6	0.06
Chilean	6	0.06
Colombian	8	0.08
Ecuadorian	11	0.11
Peruvian	13	0.13
Venezuelan	1	0.01
Other South American	1	0.01
Other Hispanic or Latino	214	2.08

Race*	Population	%
African-American/Black (55)	77	0.75
Not Hispanic (34)	46	0.45
Hispanic (21)	31	0.30
American Indian/Alaska Native (28)	61	0.59
Not Hispanic (12)	25	0.24
Hispanic (16)	36	0.35
Apache (0)	4	0.04
Blackfeet (1)	2	0.02
Cherokee (3)	8	0.08
Chickasaw (0)	1	0.01
Chippewa (1)	1	0.01
Choctaw (2)	4	0.04
Iroquois (0)	1	0.01
Mexican American Ind. (0)	1	0.01
Navajo (0)	8	0.08
Pueblo (1)	1	0.01
Spanish American Ind. (0)	2	0.02
Ute (0)	2	0.02
Asian (89)	121	1.18
Not Hispanic (86)	117	1.14
Hispanic (3)	4	0.04
Chinese, ex. Taiwanese (39)	43	0.42
Filipino (7)	23	0.22
Indian (8)	11	0.11
Indonesian (2)	2	0.02
Japanese (5)	8	0.08
Korean (2)	3	0.03
Nepalese (8)	8	0.08
Taiwanese (1)	3	0.03
Thai (0)	1	0.01
Vietnamese (13)	13	0.13
Hawaii Native/Pacific Islander (3)	6	0.06
Not Hispanic (3)	5	0.05
Hispanic (0)	1	0.01
Native Hawaiian (2)	2	0.02
Samoan (1)	1	0.01
White (8,880)	8,996	87.63
Not Hispanic (6,836)	6,893	67.14
Hispanic (2,044)	2,103	20.49

Englewood

Place Type: City
County: Arapahoe
Population: 30,255†

Ancestry‡	Population	%
African, Sub-Saharan (23)	32	0.11
African (0)	9	0.03
Nigerian (8)	8	0.03
Senegalese (15)	15	0.05
Albanian (41)	41	0.14
American (1,251)	1,251	4.12
Arab (11)	41	0.14
Lebanese (11)	33	0.11
Syrian (0)	8	0.03
Armenian (10)	18	0.06
Austrian (39)	217	0.72
Belgian (24)	126	0.42
British (68)	164	0.54
Bulgarian (0)	10	0.03
Canadian (8)	23	0.08
Celtic (7)	20	0.07
Croatian (24)	24	0.08
Czech (70)	332	1.09
Czechoslovakian (22)	52	0.17
Danish (36)	452	1.49
Dutch (162)	567	1.87
Eastern European (53)	53	0.17
English (769)	3,344	11.02
European (521)	521	1.72
Finnish (46)	118	0.39
French, ex. Basque (122)	867	2.86
French Canadian (43)	76	0.25
German (2,165)	7,396	24.38
Greek (86)	162	0.53
Hungarian (16)	45	0.15
Iranian (35)	35	0.12
Irish (1,145)	4,755	15.67
Israeli (11)	11	0.04
Italian (442)	1,657	5.46
Latvian (10)	10	0.03
Lithuanian (13)	70	0.23
Macedonian (0)	14	0.05
New Zealander (0)	40	0.13
Northern European (85)	85	0.28
Norwegian (206)	910	3.00
Polish (302)	871	2.87
Portuguese (7)	56	0.18
Romanian (16)	30	0.10
Russian (103)	298	0.98

*Notes: † The Census 2010 population figure is used to calculate the percentages in the Hispanic Origin and Race categories. Ancestry percentages are based on the 2006-2010 American Community Survey population (not shown); ‡ Numbers in parentheses indicate the number of people reporting a single ancestry; * Numbers in parentheses indicate the number of persons reporting this race alone, not in combination with any other race; Please refer to the Explanation of Data for more information.*

Scandinavian (6)	68	0.22
Scotch-Irish (246)	536	1.77
Scottish (294)	949	3.13
Serbian (16)	47	0.15
Slavic (34)	42	0.14
Slovak (39)	39	0.13
Slovene (0)	6	0.02
Swedish (220)	1,511	4.98
Swiss (29)	61	0.20
Ukrainian (30)	42	0.14
Welsh (24)	369	1.22
Yugoslavian (65)	71	0.23

Hispanic Origin	Population	%
Hispanic or Latino (of any race)	5,478	18.11
Central American, ex. Mexican	156	0.52
Costa Rican	7	0.02
Guatemalan	43	0.14
Honduran	28	0.09
Nicaraguan	1	<0.01
Panamanian	3	0.01
Salvadoran	67	0.22
Other Central American	7	0.02
Cuban	29	0.10
Dominican Republic	2	0.01
Mexican	3,887	12.85
Puerto Rican	90	0.30
South American	147	0.49
Argentinean	18	0.06
Bolivian	7	0.02
Chilean	18	0.06
Colombian	11	0.04
Ecuadorian	11	0.04
Peruvian	70	0.23
Uruguayan	3	0.01
Venezuelan	7	0.02
Other South American	2	0.01
Other Hispanic or Latino	1,167	3.86

Race*	Population	%
African-American/Black (654)	933	3.08
Not Hispanic (586)	802	2.65
Hispanic (68)	131	0.43
American Indian/Alaska Native (417)	814	2.69
Not Hispanic (228)	491	1.62
Hispanic (189)	323	1.07
Aleut *(Alaska Native)* (1)	2	0.01
Apache (21)	47	0.16
Arapaho (0)	1	<0.01
Blackfeet (3)	15	0.05
Canadian/French Am. Ind. (1)	2	0.01
Cherokee (15)	113	0.37
Cheyenne (6)	7	0.02
Chickasaw (2)	5	0.02
Chippewa (9)	16	0.05
Choctaw (7)	19	0.06
Comanche (1)	4	0.01
Creek (1)	4	0.01
Crow (1)	1	<0.01
Hopi (1)	4	0.01
Inupiat *(Alaska Native)* (1)	1	<0.01
Iroquois (2)	5	0.02
Kiowa (3)	4	0.01
Mexican American Ind. (18)	26	0.09
Navajo (51)	79	0.26
Osage (1)	3	0.01
Paiute (0)	2	0.01
Pima (1)	3	0.01
Potawatomi (2)	2	0.01
Pueblo (4)	11	0.04
Seminole (0)	9	0.03
Shoshone (2)	11	0.04
Sioux (33)	52	0.17
South American Ind. (0)	4	0.01
Spanish American Ind. (1)	1	<0.01
Tohono O'Odham (2)	2	0.01
Tsimshian *(Alaska Native)* (1)	1	<0.01
Ute (1)	2	0.01
Yaqui (0)	1	<0.01
Yuman (0)	2	0.01
Asian (580)	822	2.72
Not Hispanic (541)	746	2.47
Hispanic (39)	76	0.25
Bangladeshi (1)	4	0.01
Cambodian (10)	11	0.04
Chinese, ex. Taiwanese (75)	97	0.32
Filipino (56)	111	0.37
Indian (48)	62	0.20
Indonesian (22)	28	0.09
Japanese (67)	129	0.43
Korean (78)	104	0.34
Laotian (2)	3	0.01
Malaysian (0)	2	0.01
Nepalese (15)	15	0.05
Pakistani (2)	2	0.01
Taiwanese (2)	2	0.01
Thai (22)	25	0.08
Vietnamese (122)	140	0.46
Hawaii Native/Pacific Islander (49)	97	0.32
Not Hispanic (47)	89	0.29
Hispanic (2)	8	0.03
Guamanian/Chamorro (0)	2	0.01
Native Hawaiian (9)	36	0.12
Samoan (11)	13	0.04
Tongan (1)	1	<0.01
White (25,540)	26,479	87.52
Not Hispanic (22,679)	23,285	76.96
Hispanic (2,861)	3,194	10.56

Erie

Place Type: Town
County: Weld
Population: 18,135†

Ancestry‡	Population	%
American (795)	795	4.93
Armenian (14)	14	0.09
Australian (0)	16	0.10
Austrian (28)	167	1.04
Belgian (16)	57	0.35
British (37)	91	0.56
Canadian (37)	65	0.40
Croatian (13)	40	0.25
Czech (13)	327	2.03
Czechoslovakian (0)	9	0.06
Danish (53)	185	1.15
Dutch (90)	362	2.24
English (509)	2,362	14.64
European (342)	353	2.19
Finnish (10)	103	0.64
French, ex. Basque (66)	584	3.62
French Canadian (149)	244	1.51
German (1,300)	4,517	28.00
Greek (14)	68	0.42
Hungarian (36)	104	0.64
Iranian (31)	31	0.19
Irish (605)	2,145	13.29
Italian (439)	1,013	6.28
Lithuanian (8)	118	0.73
Maltese (10)	20	0.12
Norwegian (207)	511	3.17
Polish (274)	860	5.33
Portuguese (93)	163	1.01
Romanian (40)	66	0.41
Russian (22)	212	1.31
Scandinavian (31)	31	0.19
Scotch-Irish (101)	260	1.61
Scottish (273)	647	4.01
Slovak (0)	32	0.20
Slovene (12)	45	0.28
Swedish (113)	681	4.22
Swiss (11)	90	0.56
Ukrainian (65)	102	0.63
Welsh (32)	121	0.75
West Indian, ex. Hispanic (15)	15	0.09
Jamaican (15)	15	0.09
Yugoslavian (0)	9	0.06

Hispanic Origin	Population	%
Hispanic or Latino (of any race)	1,603	8.84
Central American, ex. Mexican	60	0.33
Costa Rican	7	0.04
Guatemalan	4	0.02
Honduran	7	0.04
Nicaraguan	3	0.02
Panamanian	9	0.05
Salvadoran	30	0.17
Cuban	12	0.07
Dominican Republic	2	0.01
Mexican	1,047	5.77
Puerto Rican	36	0.20
South American	120	0.66
Argentinean	20	0.11
Bolivian	7	0.04
Chilean	10	0.06
Colombian	27	0.15
Ecuadorian	11	0.06
Paraguayan	1	0.01
Peruvian	29	0.16
Uruguayan	1	0.01
Venezuelan	14	0.08
Other Hispanic or Latino	326	1.80

Race*	Population	%
African-American/Black (118)	232	1.28
Not Hispanic (113)	203	1.12
Hispanic (5)	29	0.16
American Indian/Alaska Native (74)	217	1.20
Not Hispanic (47)	140	0.77
Hispanic (27)	77	0.42
Aleut *(Alaska Native)* (1)	4	0.02
Apache (2)	11	0.06
Blackfeet (2)	7	0.04
Central American Ind. (1)	1	0.01
Cherokee (8)	48	0.26
Cheyenne (0)	1	0.01
Choctaw (2)	5	0.03
Comanche (0)	4	0.02
Creek (1)	1	0.01
Crow (1)	1	0.01
Delaware (0)	2	0.01
Iroquois (3)	3	0.02
Lumbee (3)	3	0.02
Mexican American Ind. (2)	4	0.02
Navajo (6)	14	0.08
Paiute (0)	1	0.01
Potawatomi (1)	1	0.01
Pueblo (1)	1	0.01
Shoshone (0)	2	0.01
Sioux (7)	12	0.07
Spanish American Ind. (4)	4	0.02
Tlingit-Haida *(Alaska Native)* (1)	1	0.01
Ute (1)	2	0.01
Yup'ik *(Alaska Native)* (0)	2	0.01
Asian (761)	1,006	5.55
Not Hispanic (759)	976	5.38
Hispanic (2)	30	0.17
Bangladeshi (3)	3	0.02
Cambodian (13)	13	0.07
Chinese, ex. Taiwanese (213)	258	1.42
Filipino (55)	94	0.52
Hmong (43)	50	0.28
Indian (166)	196	1.08
Indonesian (3)	10	0.06
Japanese (64)	115	0.63
Korean (48)	86	0.47
Laotian (11)	17	0.09
Malaysian (1)	3	0.02
Nepalese (14)	14	0.08
Pakistani (6)	8	0.04
Taiwanese (8)	11	0.06
Thai (4)	14	0.08
Vietnamese (69)	83	0.46
Hawaii Native/Pacific Islander (5)	25	0.14
Not Hispanic (5)	21	0.12
Hispanic (0)	4	0.02
Guamanian/Chamorro (2)	2	0.01
Native Hawaiian (2)	18	0.10

*Notes: † The Census 2010 population figure is used to calculate the percentages in the Hispanic Origin and Race categories. Ancestry percentages are based on the 2006-2010 American Community Survey population (not shown); ‡ Numbers in parentheses indicate the number of people reporting a single ancestry; * Numbers in parentheses indicate the number of persons reporting this race alone, not in combination with any other race; Please refer to the Explanation of Data for more information.*

Samoan (1)	1	0.01
White (16,180)	16,664	91.89
Not Hispanic (15,201)	15,553	85.76
Hispanic (979)	1,111	6.13

Evans

Place Type: City
County: Weld
Population: 18,537†

Ancestry‡	Population	%
American (572)	572	3.32
Arab (26)	58	0.34
Lebanese (17)	49	0.28
Syrian (9)	9	0.05
Austrian (0)	19	0.11
British (41)	41	0.24
Canadian (31)	31	0.18
Czech (34)	174	1.01
Danish (98)	164	0.95
Dutch (14)	180	1.05
Eastern European (15)	15	0.09
English (317)	1,114	6.47
European (72)	81	0.47
Finnish (47)	51	0.30
French, ex. Basque (41)	509	2.96
French Canadian (24)	49	0.28
German (1,508)	4,167	24.19
Greek (15)	15	0.09
Hungarian (0)	110	0.64
Iranian (0)	64	0.37
Irish (367)	1,558	9.05
Italian (311)	837	4.86
Norwegian (43)	359	2.08
Pennsylvania German (0)	28	0.16
Polish (54)	211	1.23
Portuguese (0)	34	0.20
Russian (12)	249	1.45
Scotch-Irish (30)	190	1.10
Scottish (96)	336	1.95
Slovak (0)	33	0.19
Slovene (10)	10	0.06
Swedish (121)	448	2.60
Swiss (10)	97	0.56
Ukrainian (0)	14	0.08
Welsh (88)	137	0.80

Hispanic Origin	Population	%
Hispanic or Latino (of any race)	7,997	43.14
Central American, ex. Mexican	144	0.78
Guatemalan	33	0.18
Honduran	9	0.05
Nicaraguan	3	0.02
Panamanian	12	0.06
Salvadoran	81	0.44
Other Central American	6	0.03
Cuban	22	0.12
Dominican Republic	1	0.01
Mexican	6,632	35.78
Puerto Rican	67	0.36
South American	28	0.15
Argentinean	5	0.03
Bolivian	5	0.03
Colombian	7	0.04
Ecuadorian	3	0.02
Peruvian	7	0.04
Venezuelan	1	0.01
Other Hispanic or Latino	1,103	5.95

Race*	Population	%
African-American/Black (169)	260	1.40
Not Hispanic (127)	185	1.00
Hispanic (42)	75	0.40
American Indian/Alaska Native (228)	371	2.00
Not Hispanic (85)	175	0.94
Hispanic (143)	196	1.06
Aleut *(Alaska Native)* (0)	2	0.01
Apache (4)	13	0.07
Arapaho (1)	1	0.01
Blackfeet (1)	5	0.03
Central American Ind. (0)	1	0.01
Cherokee (26)	61	0.33
Chickasaw (0)	2	0.01
Chippewa (1)	4	0.02
Choctaw (3)	10	0.05
Comanche (1)	1	0.01
Cree (1)	1	0.01
Crow (1)	2	0.01
Delaware (0)	1	0.01
Inupiat *(Alaska Native)* (0)	1	0.01
Iroquois (1)	3	0.02
Mexican American Ind. (13)	14	0.08
Navajo (5)	10	0.05
Pima (0)	3	0.02
Potawatomi (3)	3	0.02
Pueblo (7)	12	0.06
Seminole (1)	5	0.03
Sioux (29)	36	0.19
Spanish American Ind. (8)	8	0.04
Tlingit-Haida *(Alaska Native)* (0)	2	0.01
Ute (2)	2	0.01
Yaqui (1)	1	0.01
Asian (164)	273	1.47
Not Hispanic (145)	229	1.24
Hispanic (19)	44	0.24
Burmese (18)	18	0.10
Cambodian (10)	12	0.06
Chinese, ex. Taiwanese (7)	20	0.11
Filipino (20)	41	0.22
Indian (25)	27	0.15
Indonesian (7)	9	0.05
Japanese (23)	50	0.27
Korean (19)	37	0.20
Laotian (0)	1	0.01
Malaysian (6)	6	0.03
Pakistani (1)	2	0.01
Thai (4)	5	0.03
Vietnamese (12)	18	0.10
Hawaii Native/Pacific Islander (11)	44	0.24
Not Hispanic (4)	19	0.10
Hispanic (7)	25	0.13
Guamanian/Chamorro (1)	3	0.02
Native Hawaiian (6)	25	0.13
Samoan (1)	3	0.02
White (14,190)	14,682	79.20
Not Hispanic (9,901)	10,113	54.56
Hispanic (4,289)	4,569	24.65

Evergreen

Place Type: CDP
County: Jefferson
Population: 9,038†

Ancestry‡	Population	%
Albanian (13)	22	0.24
American (318)	318	3.48
Arab (45)	59	0.65
Lebanese (9)	23	0.25
Other Arab (36)	36	0.39
Austrian (10)	33	0.36
Brazilian (0)	13	0.14
British (69)	91	1.00
Canadian (7)	7	0.08
Croatian (8)	42	0.46
Czech (8)	177	1.94
Danish (40)	218	2.39
Dutch (49)	254	2.78
Eastern European (41)	41	0.45
English (423)	1,759	19.25
Estonian (8)	8	0.09
European (244)	266	2.91
Finnish (5)	10	0.11
French, ex. Basque (59)	434	4.75
French Canadian (27)	34	0.37
German (660)	2,931	32.07
Greek (13)	58	0.63
Hungarian (18)	58	0.63
Irish (565)	1,722	18.84
Italian (117)	434	4.75
Latvian (22)	22	0.24
Lithuanian (0)	64	0.70
Northern European (53)	97	1.06
Norwegian (142)	534	5.84
Pennsylvania German (10)	29	0.32
Polish (20)	264	2.89
Romanian (30)	30	0.33
Russian (9)	88	0.96
Scandinavian (38)	76	0.83
Scotch-Irish (87)	325	3.56
Scottish (149)	525	5.74
Serbian (10)	10	0.11
Slavic (10)	47	0.51
Slovak (0)	8	0.09
Swedish (120)	380	4.16
Swiss (12)	99	1.08
Ukrainian (0)	70	0.77
Welsh (14)	102	1.12
Yugoslavian (8)	26	0.28

Hispanic Origin	Population	%
Hispanic or Latino (of any race)	331	3.66
Central American, ex. Mexican	16	0.18
Costa Rican	3	0.03
Guatemalan	1	0.01
Honduran	1	0.01
Nicaraguan	2	0.02
Panamanian	4	0.04
Salvadoran	5	0.06
Cuban	5	0.06
Dominican Republic	7	0.08
Mexican	172	1.90
Puerto Rican	15	0.17
South American	21	0.23
Argentinean	2	0.02
Chilean	13	0.14
Peruvian	6	0.07
Other Hispanic or Latino	95	1.05

Race*	Population	%
African-American/Black (19)	46	0.51
Not Hispanic (18)	43	0.48
Hispanic (1)	3	0.03
American Indian/Alaska Native (30)	65	0.72
Not Hispanic (23)	52	0.58
Hispanic (7)	13	0.14
Blackfeet (0)	1	0.01
Cherokee (5)	14	0.15
Cheyenne (0)	1	0.01
Chickasaw (0)	3	0.03
Chippewa (0)	1	0.01
Choctaw (0)	1	0.01
Delaware (3)	3	0.03
Inupiat *(Alaska Native)* (1)	1	0.01
Navajo (1)	3	0.03
Ottawa (1)	1	0.01
Spanish American Ind. (1)	1	0.01
Ute (2)	2	0.02
Asian (75)	133	1.47
Not Hispanic (75)	129	1.43
Hispanic (0)	4	0.04
Chinese, ex. Taiwanese (23)	31	0.34
Filipino (2)	22	0.24
Indian (16)	23	0.25
Japanese (12)	32	0.35
Korean (16)	25	0.28
Pakistani (0)	3	0.03
Vietnamese (0)	1	0.01
Hawaii Native/Pacific Islander (4)	11	0.12
Not Hispanic (4)	10	0.11
Hispanic (0)	1	0.01
Native Hawaiian (1)	3	0.03
Samoan (1)	1	0.01
Tongan (1)	1	0.01
White (8,730)	8,840	97.81
Not Hispanic (8,476)	8,570	94.82
Hispanic (254)	270	2.99

*Notes: † The Census 2010 population figure is used to calculate the percentages in the Hispanic Origin and Race categories. Ancestry percentages are based on the 2006-2010 American Community Survey population (not shown); ‡ Numbers in parentheses indicate the number of people reporting a single ancestry; * Numbers in parentheses indicate the number of persons reporting this race alone, not in combination with any other race; Please refer to the Explanation of Data for more information.*

Fairmount

Place Type: CDP
County: Jefferson
Population: 7,559†

Ancestry‡	Population	%
African, Sub-Saharan (0)	18	0.24
South African (0)	18	0.24
American (290)	290	3.87
Arab (9)	35	0.47
Lebanese (9)	35	0.47
Armenian (0)	2	0.03
Austrian (30)	71	0.95
British (50)	50	0.67
Canadian (18)	18	0.24
Czech (139)	156	2.08
Czechoslovakian (12)	24	0.32
Danish (28)	101	1.35
Dutch (56)	171	2.28
Eastern European (9)	9	0.12
English (353)	1,090	14.54
European (110)	110	1.47
Finnish (11)	11	0.15
French, ex. Basque (28)	337	4.49
French Canadian (29)	29	0.39
German (761)	2,103	28.05
Hungarian (12)	12	0.16
Irish (389)	1,113	14.84
Italian (266)	535	7.14
Norwegian (71)	227	3.03
Pennsylvania German (0)	18	0.24
Polish (109)	290	3.87
Portuguese (14)	14	0.19
Romanian (0)	13	0.17
Russian (0)	158	2.11
Scandinavian (12)	12	0.16
Scotch-Irish (58)	220	2.93
Scottish (125)	270	3.60
Swedish (32)	271	3.61
Swiss (25)	65	0.87
Ukrainian (0)	43	0.57
Welsh (16)	94	1.25
Yugoslavian (0)	17	0.23

Hispanic Origin	Population	%
Hispanic or Latino (of any race)	432	5.72
Central American, ex. Mexican	7	0.09
Costa Rican	3	0.04
Guatemalan	3	0.04
Salvadoran	1	0.01
Cuban	4	0.05
Mexican	254	3.36
Puerto Rican	12	0.16
South American	18	0.24
Argentinean	1	0.01
Bolivian	6	0.08
Chilean	1	0.01
Colombian	6	0.08
Ecuadorian	2	0.03
Peruvian	2	0.03
Other Hispanic or Latino	137	1.81

Race*	Population	%
African-American/Black (16)	29	0.38
Not Hispanic (15)	27	0.36
Hispanic (1)	2	0.03
American Indian/Alaska Native (31)	68	0.90
Not Hispanic (21)	50	0.66
Hispanic (10)	18	0.24
Apache (0)	1	0.01
Blackfeet (0)	1	0.01
Cherokee (0)	10	0.13
Cheyenne (1)	1	0.01
Chickasaw (1)	1	0.01
Choctaw (3)	4	0.05
Comanche (0)	2	0.03
Creek (0)	3	0.04
Delaware (1)	1	0.01
Mexican American Ind. (1)	2	0.03
Navajo (7)	9	0.12
Osage (0)	1	0.01
Ottawa (1)	1	0.01
Potawatomi (0)	1	0.01
Pueblo (0)	3	0.04
Puget Sound Salish (1)	1	0.01
Sioux (1)	3	0.04
Ute (4)	4	0.05
Asian (126)	175	2.32
Not Hispanic (123)	171	2.26
Hispanic (3)	4	0.05
Bangladeshi (4)	4	0.05
Burmese (0)	3	0.04
Chinese, ex. Taiwanese (38)	52	0.69
Filipino (7)	14	0.19
Indian (2)	11	0.15
Indonesian (2)	3	0.04
Japanese (13)	25	0.33
Korean (17)	21	0.28
Laotian (4)	6	0.08
Malaysian (1)	1	0.01
Taiwanese (4)	5	0.07
Thai (3)	4	0.05
Vietnamese (22)	27	0.36
Hawaii Native/Pacific Islander (5)	6	0.08
Not Hispanic (4)	5	0.07
Hispanic (1)	1	0.01
Guamanian/Chamorro (0)	1	0.01
Native Hawaiian (4)	4	0.05
White (7,205)	7,293	96.48
Not Hispanic (6,881)	6,949	91.93
Hispanic (324)	344	4.55

Federal Heights

Place Type: City
County: Adams
Population: 11,467†

Ancestry‡	Population	%
American (680)	680	5.87
Arab (0)	17	0.15
Arab (0)	12	0.10
Syrian (0)	5	0.04
Austrian (11)	52	0.45
Basque (0)	5	0.04
British (6)	16	0.14
Canadian (10)	10	0.09
Czech (12)	44	0.38
Danish (0)	12	0.10
Dutch (67)	118	1.02
English (361)	847	7.31
European (126)	138	1.19
Finnish (0)	14	0.12
French, ex. Basque (45)	293	2.53
French Canadian (34)	44	0.38
German (710)	1,794	15.48
Greek (0)	24	0.21
Hungarian (13)	49	0.42
Irish (287)	977	8.43
Italian (90)	320	2.76
Northern European (12)	12	0.10
Norwegian (18)	134	1.16
Polish (31)	64	0.55
Romanian (12)	12	0.10
Russian (83)	175	1.51
Scandinavian (60)	60	0.52
Scotch-Irish (91)	152	1.31
Scottish (45)	153	1.32
Slavic (3)	3	0.03
Slovak (8)	8	0.07
Slovene (28)	39	0.34
Swedish (84)	202	1.74
Swiss (0)	12	0.10
Welsh (12)	52	0.45
West Indian, ex. Hispanic (10)	20	0.17
West Indian (10)	20	0.17

Hispanic Origin	Population	%
Hispanic or Latino (of any race)	5,459	47.61
Central American, ex. Mexican	113	0.99
Costa Rican	1	0.01
Guatemalan	28	0.24
Honduran	34	0.30
Nicaraguan	8	0.07
Salvadoran	42	0.37
Cuban	10	0.09
Dominican Republic	1	0.01
Mexican	4,508	39.31
Puerto Rican	71	0.62
South American	22	0.19
Argentinean	5	0.04
Bolivian	3	0.03
Chilean	1	0.01
Colombian	9	0.08
Peruvian	3	0.03
Uruguayan	1	0.01
Other Hispanic or Latino	734	6.40

Race*	Population	%
African-American/Black (144)	205	1.79
Not Hispanic (107)	149	1.30
Hispanic (37)	56	0.49
American Indian/Alaska Native (187)	307	2.68
Not Hispanic (97)	175	1.53
Hispanic (90)	132	1.15
Aleut *(Alaska Native)* (2)	2	0.02
Apache (9)	16	0.14
Blackfeet (0)	2	0.02
Cherokee (16)	41	0.36
Cheyenne (0)	4	0.03
Chippewa (2)	5	0.04
Choctaw (1)	3	0.03
Crow (2)	2	0.02
Delaware (1)	2	0.02
Inupiat *(Alaska Native)* (3)	3	0.03
Kiowa (2)	2	0.02
Mexican American Ind. (18)	18	0.16
Navajo (30)	36	0.31
Potawatomi (0)	1	0.01
Pueblo (3)	5	0.04
Shoshone (1)	2	0.02
Sioux (6)	19	0.17
South American Ind. (1)	2	0.02
Spanish American Ind. (3)	3	0.03
Tlingit-Haida *(Alaska Native)* (1)	1	0.01
Tohono O'Odham (2)	3	0.03
Ute (0)	3	0.03
Yaqui (3)	3	0.03
Asian (525)	589	5.14
Not Hispanic (507)	547	4.77
Hispanic (18)	42	0.37
Cambodian (4)	4	0.03
Chinese, ex. Taiwanese (39)	55	0.48
Filipino (18)	29	0.25
Hmong (83)	88	0.77
Indian (28)	33	0.29
Japanese (17)	40	0.35
Korean (53)	55	0.48
Laotian (32)	32	0.28
Nepalese (19)	19	0.17
Pakistani (6)	6	0.05
Thai (1)	1	0.01
Vietnamese (207)	219	1.91
Hawaii Native/Pacific Islander (10)	35	0.31
Not Hispanic (9)	20	0.17
Hispanic (1)	15	0.13
Guamanian/Chamorro (1)	8	0.07
Native Hawaiian (1)	7	0.06
Tongan (4)	6	0.05
White (8,174)	8,514	74.25
Not Hispanic (5,123)	5,265	45.91
Hispanic (3,051)	3,249	28.33

Firestone

Place Type: Town
County: Weld
Population: 10,147†

*Notes: † The Census 2010 population figure is used to calculate the percentages in the Hispanic Origin and Race categories. Ancestry percentages are based on the 2006-2010 American Community Survey population (not shown); ‡ Numbers in parentheses indicate the number of people reporting a single ancestry; * Numbers in parentheses indicate the number of persons reporting this race alone, not in combination with any other race; Please refer to the Explanation of Data for more information.*

Ancestry‡	Population	%
American (278)	278	3.14
Austrian (19)	57	0.64
Belgian (0)	14	0.16
British (12)	25	0.28
Croatian (20)	20	0.23
Czech (0)	15	0.17
Czechoslovakian (0)	14	0.16
Danish (0)	128	1.44
Dutch (29)	162	1.83
English (182)	947	10.68
European (264)	463	5.22
French, ex. Basque (58)	555	6.26
French Canadian (42)	53	0.60
German (1,007)	2,725	30.74
Greek (35)	93	1.05
Hungarian (0)	52	0.59
Irish (284)	1,312	14.80
Italian (198)	486	5.48
Latvian (0)	6	0.07
Lithuanian (0)	47	0.53
Northern European (13)	13	0.15
Norwegian (31)	239	2.70
Polish (49)	215	2.42
Portuguese (0)	10	0.11
Romanian (0)	11	0.12
Russian (26)	199	2.24
Scandinavian (48)	88	0.99
Scotch-Irish (16)	116	1.31
Scottish (75)	330	3.72
Slavic (0)	22	0.25
Slovak (0)	31	0.35
Swedish (10)	471	5.31
Swiss (0)	6	0.07
Ukrainian (25)	25	0.28
Welsh (14)	86	0.97
West Indian, ex. Hispanic (0)	34	0.38
Jamaican (0)	34	0.38
Yugoslavian (18)	58	0.65

Hispanic Origin	Population	%
Hispanic or Latino (of any race)	1,642	16.18
Central American, ex. Mexican	29	0.29
Costa Rican	6	0.06
Guatemalan	2	0.02
Honduran	3	0.03
Panamanian	1	0.01
Salvadoran	17	0.17
Cuban	1	0.01
Dominican Republic	6	0.06
Mexican	1,192	11.75
Puerto Rican	40	0.39
South American	45	0.44
Chilean	1	0.01
Colombian	9	0.09
Ecuadorian	4	0.04
Peruvian	30	0.30
Other South American	1	0.01
Other Hispanic or Latino	329	3.24

Race*	Population	%
African-American/Black (73)	121	1.19
Not Hispanic (58)	94	0.93
Hispanic (15)	27	0.27
American Indian/Alaska Native (80)	189	1.86
Not Hispanic (31)	102	1.01
Hispanic (49)	87	0.86
Apache (1)	4	0.04
Blackfeet (0)	8	0.08
Cherokee (10)	29	0.29
Chickasaw (0)	4	0.04
Chippewa (0)	1	0.01
Choctaw (0)	4	0.04
Colville (1)	1	0.01
Inupiat *(Alaska Native)* (0)	1	0.01
Kiowa (0)	2	0.02
Mexican American Ind. (6)	10	0.10
Navajo (2)	4	0.04
Osage (0)	3	0.03
Potawatomi (2)	6	0.06
Pueblo (7)	8	0.08
Shoshone (0)	5	0.05
Sioux (3)	7	0.07
Ute (1)	5	0.05
Yuman (2)	2	0.02
Asian (147)	221	2.18
Not Hispanic (140)	197	1.94
Hispanic (7)	24	0.24
Burmese (1)	1	0.01
Cambodian (23)	28	0.28
Chinese, ex. Taiwanese (20)	37	0.36
Filipino (13)	31	0.31
Hmong (18)	18	0.18
Indian (8)	14	0.14
Indonesian (0)	4	0.04
Japanese (8)	29	0.29
Korean (21)	29	0.29
Laotian (4)	4	0.04
Malaysian (1)	1	0.01
Taiwanese (0)	1	0.01
Thai (2)	3	0.03
Vietnamese (15)	17	0.17
Hawaii Native/Pacific Islander (3)	20	0.20
Not Hispanic (3)	13	0.13
Hispanic (0)	7	0.07
Guamanian/Chamorro (3)	5	0.05
Native Hawaiian (0)	6	0.06
Samoan (0)	1	0.01
White (8,913)	9,192	90.59
Not Hispanic (8,110)	8,261	81.41
Hispanic (803)	931	9.18

Fort Carson

Place Type: CDP
County: El Paso
Population: 13,813†

Ancestry‡	Population	%
African, Sub-Saharan (33)	73	0.65
African (33)	64	0.57
South African (0)	9	0.08
American (689)	689	6.13
Arab (0)	6	0.05
Lebanese (0)	6	0.05
Armenian (10)	10	0.09
Belgian (0)	15	0.13
British (49)	139	1.24
Canadian (0)	10	0.09
Czech (0)	29	0.26
Czechoslovakian (0)	11	0.10
Danish (0)	59	0.52
Dutch (64)	159	1.41
English (467)	1,017	9.05
European (10)	37	0.33
French, ex. Basque (27)	500	4.45
French Canadian (5)	28	0.25
German (646)	2,178	19.37
Greek (26)	35	0.31
Hungarian (10)	10	0.09
Irish (663)	2,017	17.94
Italian (220)	768	6.83
Norwegian (0)	87	0.77
Polish (22)	398	3.54
Portuguese (0)	6	0.05
Romanian (15)	45	0.40
Russian (0)	73	0.65
Scandinavian (5)	5	0.04
Scotch-Irish (149)	294	2.61
Scottish (54)	276	2.45
Slovak (11)	22	0.20
Swedish (130)	165	1.47
Ukrainian (0)	6	0.05
Welsh (56)	204	1.81
West Indian, ex. Hispanic (10)	24	0.21
Haitian (10)	24	0.21
Yugoslavian (23)	23	0.20

Hispanic Origin	Population	%
Hispanic or Latino (of any race)	2,124	15.38
Central American, ex. Mexican	114	0.83
Costa Rican	5	0.04
Guatemalan	3	0.02
Honduran	20	0.14
Nicaraguan	19	0.14
Panamanian	25	0.18
Salvadoran	42	0.30
Cuban	44	0.32
Dominican Republic	26	0.19
Mexican	1,175	8.51
Puerto Rican	464	3.36
South American	82	0.59
Bolivian	4	0.03
Chilean	2	0.01
Colombian	40	0.29
Ecuadorian	13	0.09
Paraguayan	1	0.01
Peruvian	14	0.10
Venezuelan	8	0.06
Other Hispanic or Latino	219	1.59

Race*	Population	%
African-American/Black (1,590)	1,925	13.94
Not Hispanic (1,513)	1,773	12.84
Hispanic (77)	152	1.10
American Indian/Alaska Native (128)	323	2.34
Not Hispanic (108)	257	1.86
Hispanic (20)	66	0.48
Alaska Athabascan *(Ala. Nat.)* (0)	1	0.01
Aleut *(Alaska Native)* (0)	1	0.01
Apache (5)	11	0.08
Arapaho (4)	8	0.06
Blackfeet (1)	9	0.07
Cherokee (15)	68	0.49
Cheyenne (4)	5	0.04
Chickasaw (1)	2	0.01
Chippewa (3)	7	0.05
Choctaw (10)	19	0.14
Cree (0)	1	0.01
Crow (1)	3	0.02
Delaware (0)	1	0.01
Hopi (0)	1	0.01
Iroquois (1)	3	0.02
Kiowa (1)	4	0.03
Lumbee (2)	2	0.01
Mexican American Ind. (0)	1	0.01
Navajo (14)	26	0.19
Ottawa (1)	5	0.04
Pueblo (7)	9	0.07
Seminole (1)	3	0.02
Sioux (4)	6	0.04
South American Ind. (0)	5	0.04
Ute (1)	1	0.01
Yakama (0)	1	0.01
Yaqui (1)	1	0.01
Yup'ik *(Alaska Native)* (1)	1	0.01
Asian (302)	534	3.87
Not Hispanic (289)	485	3.51
Hispanic (13)	49	0.35
Bangladeshi (1)	1	0.01
Cambodian (8)	9	0.07
Chinese, ex. Taiwanese (15)	54	0.39
Filipino (101)	213	1.54
Hmong (3)	6	0.04
Indian (8)	14	0.10
Indonesian (2)	2	0.01
Japanese (13)	49	0.35
Korean (67)	126	0.91
Laotian (4)	5	0.04
Nepalese (1)	1	0.01
Pakistani (0)	3	0.02
Taiwanese (0)	1	0.01
Thai (4)	24	0.17
Vietnamese (16)	27	0.20
Hawaii Native/Pacific Islander (140)	221	1.60
Not Hispanic (130)	194	1.40
Hispanic (10)	27	0.20
Fijian (4)	4	0.03
Guamanian/Chamorro (47)	75	0.54
Marshallese (11)	11	0.08

SECTION TWO

*Notes: † The Census 2010 population figure is used to calculate the percentages in the Hispanic Origin and Race categories. Ancestry percentages are based on the 2006-2010 American Community Survey population (not shown); ‡ Numbers in parentheses indicate the number of people reporting a single ancestry; * Numbers in parentheses indicate the number of persons reporting this race alone, not in combination with any other race; Please refer to the Explanation of Data for more information.*

Native Hawaiian (13)	43	0.31
Samoan (18)	19	0.14
Tongan (1)	1	0.01
White (10,281)	10,949	79.27
Not Hispanic (9,079)	9,545	69.10
Hispanic (1,202)	1,404	10.16

Fort Collins

Place Type: City
County: Larimer
Population: 143,986†

Ancestry‡	Population	%
African, Sub-Saharan (177)	526	0.38
African (81)	430	0.31
Ethiopian (27)	27	0.02
Nigerian (36)	36	0.03
Senegalese (20)	20	0.01
Other Sub-Saharan African (13)	13	0.01
Alsatian (0)	34	0.02
American (4,596)	4,596	3.28
Arab (447)	707	0.50
Arab (14)	58	0.04
Iraqi (0)	8	0.01
Jordanian (22)	37	0.03
Lebanese (94)	232	0.17
Moroccan (0)	12	0.01
Palestinian (45)	45	0.03
Syrian (12)	12	0.01
Other Arab (260)	303	0.22
Armenian (13)	82	0.06
Austrian (142)	644	0.46
Basque (10)	126	0.09
Belgian (131)	349	0.25
Brazilian (47)	108	0.08
British (282)	683	0.49
Bulgarian (82)	164	0.12
Cajun (0)	20	0.01
Canadian (97)	360	0.26
Celtic (20)	20	0.01
Croatian (113)	301	0.21
Czech (350)	1,625	1.16
Czechoslovakian (140)	468	0.33
Danish (357)	1,773	1.27
Dutch (668)	3,677	2.62
Eastern European (100)	124	0.09
English (4,551)	18,471	13.19
Estonian (0)	6	<0.01
European (4,352)	4,997	3.57
Finnish (95)	416	0.30
French, ex. Basque (521)	4,820	3.44
French Canadian (312)	995	0.71
German (13,602)	44,033	31.43
German Russian (21)	21	0.01
Greek (431)	965	0.69
Hungarian (75)	599	0.43
Icelander (50)	80	0.06
Iranian (75)	137	0.10
Irish (5,025)	20,965	14.97
Israeli (8)	102	0.07
Italian (2,159)	8,484	6.06
Latvian (19)	130	0.09
Lithuanian (103)	469	0.33
Luxemburger (12)	44	0.03
Maltese (0)	8	0.01
Northern European (876)	1,013	0.72
Norwegian (1,396)	5,465	3.90
Pennsylvania German (55)	103	0.07
Polish (896)	3,692	2.64
Portuguese (80)	241	0.17
Romanian (77)	166	0.12
Russian (345)	2,045	1.46
Scandinavian (424)	977	0.70
Scotch-Irish (1,488)	4,113	2.94
Scottish (1,179)	4,607	3.29
Serbian (122)	224	0.16
Slavic (23)	98	0.07
Slovak (33)	208	0.15
Slovene (76)	247	0.18
Swedish (1,413)	5,589	3.99
Swiss (216)	1,059	0.76
Turkish (37)	69	0.05
Ukrainian (94)	693	0.49
Welsh (352)	1,548	1.11
West Indian, ex. Hispanic (109)	206	0.15
Bahamian (27)	27	0.02
Belizean (0)	13	0.01
British West Indian (12)	12	0.01
Haitian (54)	54	0.04
Jamaican (5)	70	0.05
West Indian (11)	30	0.02
Yugoslavian (89)	354	0.25

Hispanic Origin	Population	%
Hispanic or Latino (of any race)	14,572	10.12
Central American, ex. Mexican	458	0.32
Costa Rican	67	0.05
Guatemalan	129	0.09
Honduran	92	0.06
Nicaraguan	36	0.03
Panamanian	37	0.03
Salvadoran	91	0.06
Other Central American	6	<0.01
Cuban	177	0.12
Dominican Republic	40	0.03
Mexican	9,902	6.88
Puerto Rican	446	0.31
South American	581	0.40
Argentinean	108	0.08
Bolivian	42	0.03
Chilean	48	0.03
Colombian	155	0.11
Ecuadorian	33	0.02
Paraguayan	13	0.01
Peruvian	96	0.07
Uruguayan	2	<0.01
Venezuelan	76	0.05
Other South American	8	0.01
Other Hispanic or Latino	2,968	2.06

Race*	Population	%
African-American/Black (1,740)	2,714	1.88
Not Hispanic (1,583)	2,369	1.65
Hispanic (157)	345	0.24
American Indian/Alaska Native (933)	2,219	1.54
Not Hispanic (571)	1,514	1.05
Hispanic (362)	705	0.49
Alaska Athabascan *(Ala. Nat.)* (3)	6	<0.01
Aleut *(Alaska Native)* (4)	6	<0.01
Apache (40)	91	0.06
Arapaho (4)	9	0.01
Blackfeet (3)	39	0.03
Canadian/French Am. Ind. (1)	2	<0.01
Central American Ind. (3)	7	<0.01
Cherokee (79)	377	0.26
Cheyenne (10)	16	0.01
Chickasaw (15)	24	0.02
Chippewa (22)	61	0.04
Choctaw (33)	67	0.05
Colville (3)	3	<0.01
Comanche (9)	27	0.02
Cree (0)	6	<0.01
Creek (3)	10	0.01
Crow (8)	13	0.01
Delaware (5)	14	0.01
Hopi (3)	7	<0.01
Inupiat *(Alaska Native)* (1)	4	<0.01
Iroquois (5)	24	0.02
Kiowa (2)	4	<0.01
Lumbee (0)	1	<0.01
Menominee (1)	4	<0.01
Mexican American Ind. (48)	80	0.06
Navajo (73)	134	0.09
Osage (14)	28	0.02
Ottawa (1)	1	<0.01
Paiute (1)	1	<0.01
Pima (0)	2	<0.01
Potawatomi (12)	22	0.02
Pueblo (11)	25	0.02
Puget Sound Salish (2)	3	<0.01
Seminole (1)	7	<0.01
Shoshone (4)	7	<0.01
Sioux (73)	158	0.11
South American Ind. (1)	6	<0.01
Spanish American Ind. (7)	9	0.01
Tlingit-Haida *(Alaska Native)* (2)	2	<0.01
Tsimshian *(Alaska Native)* (0)	3	<0.01
Ute (12)	23	0.02
Yakama (1)	1	<0.01
Yaqui (15)	20	0.01
Yup'ik *(Alaska Native)* (0)	1	<0.01
Asian (4,222)	5,814	4.04
Not Hispanic (4,161)	5,596	3.89
Hispanic (61)	218	0.15
Bangladeshi (7)	7	<0.01
Burmese (7)	8	0.01
Cambodian (22)	33	0.02
Chinese, ex. Taiwanese (1,097)	1,363	0.95
Filipino (290)	624	0.43
Hmong (7)	8	0.01
Indian (850)	997	0.69
Indonesian (46)	61	0.04
Japanese (401)	846	0.59
Korean (603)	849	0.59
Laotian (5)	13	0.01
Malaysian (39)	40	0.03
Nepalese (50)	56	0.04
Pakistani (67)	84	0.06
Sri Lankan (30)	37	0.03
Taiwanese (99)	127	0.09
Thai (82)	124	0.09
Vietnamese (338)	404	0.28
Hawaii Native/Pacific Islander (128)	347	0.24
Not Hispanic (110)	289	0.20
Hispanic (18)	58	0.04
Guamanian/Chamorro (31)	69	0.05
Marshallese (3)	4	<0.01
Native Hawaiian (53)	167	0.12
Samoan (13)	38	0.03
Tongan (1)	2	<0.01
White (128,211)	132,255	91.85
Not Hispanic (119,695)	122,560	85.12
Hispanic (8,516)	9,695	6.73

Fort Morgan

Place Type: City
County: Morgan
Population: 11,315†

Ancestry‡	Population	%
African, Sub-Saharan (553)	553	4.92
Ethiopian (157)	157	1.40
Somalian (396)	396	3.53
American (413)	413	3.68
Arab (16)	16	0.14
Jordanian (16)	16	0.14
Belgian (0)	10	0.09
British (32)	44	0.39
Canadian (12)	54	0.48
Czech (0)	53	0.47
Danish (26)	241	2.15
Dutch (9)	153	1.36
English (201)	815	7.26
European (5)	22	0.20
French, ex. Basque (0)	188	1.67
French Canadian (0)	24	0.21
German (1,131)	2,559	22.79
Hungarian (40)	40	0.36
Irish (141)	989	8.81
Italian (66)	187	1.67
Norwegian (60)	179	1.59
Pennsylvania German (0)	17	0.15
Polish (48)	146	1.30
Portuguese (0)	17	0.15
Russian (17)	153	1.36
Scandinavian (10)	20	0.18
Scotch-Irish (62)	142	1.26
Scottish (41)	145	1.29

*Notes: † The Census 2010 population figure is used to calculate the percentages in the Hispanic Origin and Race categories. Ancestry percentages are based on the 2006-2010 American Community Survey population (not shown); ‡ Numbers in parentheses indicate the number of people reporting a single ancestry; * Numbers in parentheses indicate the number of persons reporting this race alone, not in combination with any other race; Please refer to the Explanation of Data for more information.*

Scotch-Irish (79)	171	2.22
Scottish (35)	347	4.50
Slovak (0)	17	0.22
Swedish (93)	288	3.74
Yugoslavian (0)	37	0.48

Hispanic Origin	Population	%
Hispanic or Latino (of any race)	1,222	14.08
Central American, ex. Mexican	16	0.18
Costa Rican	3	0.03
Guatemalan	3	0.03
Honduran	5	0.06
Nicaraguan	1	0.01
Salvadoran	4	0.05
Cuban	6	0.07
Dominican Republic	3	0.03
Mexican	909	10.47
Puerto Rican	19	0.22
South American	24	0.28
Argentinean	2	0.02
Chilean	2	0.02
Colombian	5	0.06
Peruvian	11	0.13
Venezuelan	4	0.05
Other Hispanic or Latino	245	2.82

Race*	Population	%
African-American/Black (47)	88	1.01
Not Hispanic (39)	71	0.82
Hispanic (8)	17	0.20
American Indian/Alaska Native (34)	103	1.19
Not Hispanic (25)	74	0.85
Hispanic (9)	29	0.33
Apache (2)	8	0.09
Arapaho (1)	1	0.01
Blackfeet (0)	1	0.01
Cherokee (7)	25	0.29
Chickasaw (0)	1	0.01
Chippewa (1)	3	0.03
Choctaw (1)	6	0.07
Crow (0)	1	0.01
Delaware (0)	1	0.01
Iroquois (0)	2	0.02
Mexican American Ind. (0)	1	0.01
Navajo (1)	6	0.07
Potawatomi (0)	2	0.02
Puget Sound Salish (0)	1	0.01
Seminole (0)	1	0.01
Shoshone (1)	1	0.01
Sioux (6)	12	0.14
South American Ind. (1)	2	0.02
Spanish American Ind. (1)	1	0.01
Asian (181)	259	2.98
Not Hispanic (180)	245	2.82
Hispanic (1)	14	0.16
Cambodian (19)	20	0.23
Chinese, ex. Taiwanese (26)	28	0.32
Filipino (12)	38	0.44
Hmong (60)	62	0.71
Indian (10)	21	0.24
Indonesian (0)	2	0.02
Japanese (12)	30	0.35
Korean (6)	16	0.18
Laotian (4)	5	0.06
Nepalese (4)	4	0.05
Pakistani (1)	1	0.01
Sri Lankan (0)	2	0.02
Thai (3)	4	0.05
Vietnamese (9)	10	0.12
Hawaii Native/Pacific Islander (1)	12	0.14
Not Hispanic (1)	10	0.12
Hispanic (0)	2	0.02
Guamanian/Chamorro (1)	2	0.02
Native Hawaiian (0)	4	0.05
White (7,747)	7,999	92.16
Not Hispanic (7,043)	7,185	82.79
Hispanic (704)	814	9.38

Fruita

Place Type: City
County: Mesa
Population: 12,646†

Ancestry‡	Population	%
American (902)	902	7.73
Arab (0)	46	0.39
Lebanese (0)	46	0.39
British (30)	43	0.37
Canadian (12)	12	0.10
Croatian (0)	81	0.69
Czech (43)	135	1.16
Czechoslovakian (7)	7	0.06
Danish (16)	86	0.74
Dutch (47)	202	1.73
Eastern European (14)	14	0.12
English (582)	1,966	16.84
European (112)	112	0.96
French, ex. Basque (76)	510	4.37
French Canadian (9)	24	0.21
German (1,230)	2,978	25.51
Greek (13)	64	0.55
Hungarian (0)	86	0.74
Irish (412)	1,747	14.96
Italian (202)	389	3.33
Norwegian (100)	177	1.52
Pennsylvania German (10)	10	0.09
Polish (10)	104	0.89
Portuguese (0)	18	0.15
Russian (0)	144	1.23
Scandinavian (0)	44	0.38
Scotch-Irish (98)	174	1.49
Scottish (169)	277	2.37
Slavic (0)	19	0.16
Slovak (18)	43	0.37
Swedish (139)	456	3.91
Swiss (0)	22	0.19
Ukrainian (0)	57	0.49
Welsh (56)	108	0.92
Yugoslavian (42)	76	0.65

Hispanic Origin	Population	%
Hispanic or Latino (of any race)	1,512	11.96
Central American, ex. Mexican	26	0.21
Costa Rican	6	0.05
Guatemalan	5	0.04
Nicaraguan	2	0.02
Panamanian	5	0.04
Salvadoran	8	0.06
Cuban	2	0.02
Dominican Republic	4	0.03
Mexican	1,027	8.12
Puerto Rican	56	0.44
South American	25	0.20
Chilean	13	0.10
Colombian	6	0.05
Ecuadorian	1	0.01
Peruvian	3	0.02
Uruguayan	1	0.01
Venezuelan	1	0.01
Other Hispanic or Latino	372	2.94

Race*	Population	%
African-American/Black (64)	131	1.04
Not Hispanic (59)	106	0.84
Hispanic (5)	25	0.20
American Indian/Alaska Native (114)	214	1.69
Not Hispanic (76)	151	1.19
Hispanic (38)	63	0.50
Apache (14)	16	0.13
Blackfeet (2)	7	0.06
Cherokee (10)	30	0.24
Cheyenne (0)	1	0.01
Chickasaw (0)	1	0.01
Chippewa (4)	10	0.08
Choctaw (6)	9	0.07
Comanche (5)	8	0.06
Creek (2)	4	0.03
Crow (0)	1	0.01
Houma (1)	1	0.01
Iroquois (3)	7	0.06
Kiowa (1)	2	0.02
Mexican American Ind. (8)	8	0.06
Navajo (4)	13	0.10
Osage (0)	1	0.01
Potawatomi (0)	1	0.01
Pueblo (1)	4	0.03
Puget Sound Salish (0)	1	0.01
Shoshone (2)	3	0.02
Sioux (0)	1	0.01
Tlingit-Haida *(Alaska Native)* (0)	4	0.03
Ute (0)	5	0.04
Asian (83)	137	1.08
Not Hispanic (82)	128	1.01
Hispanic (1)	9	0.07
Cambodian (2)	2	0.02
Chinese, ex. Taiwanese (20)	31	0.25
Filipino (10)	24	0.19
Indian (6)	6	0.05
Japanese (17)	30	0.24
Korean (14)	25	0.20
Laotian (3)	3	0.02
Nepalese (1)	1	0.01
Thai (3)	4	0.03
Vietnamese (2)	6	0.05
Hawaii Native/Pacific Islander (24)	52	0.41
Not Hispanic (17)	40	0.32
Hispanic (7)	12	0.09
Guamanian/Chamorro (5)	5	0.04
Native Hawaiian (2)	13	0.10
Samoan (3)	6	0.05
Tongan (6)	7	0.06
White (11,451)	11,752	92.93
Not Hispanic (10,713)	10,880	86.04
Hispanic (738)	872	6.90

Fruitvale

Place Type: CDP
County: Mesa
Population: 7,675†

Ancestry‡	Population	%
American (599)	599	7.79
Armenian (0)	10	0.13
Australian (10)	10	0.13
Belgian (0)	61	0.79
British (0)	21	0.27
Croatian (20)	20	0.26
Czech (11)	11	0.14
Danish (10)	125	1.62
Dutch (24)	201	2.61
Eastern European (27)	54	0.70
English (228)	1,340	17.42
European (129)	129	1.68
French, ex. Basque (37)	319	4.15
French Canadian (91)	135	1.75
German (781)	1,931	25.10
Greek (17)	17	0.22
Hungarian (0)	12	0.16
Irish (109)	1,185	15.40
Italian (109)	411	5.34
Lithuanian (9)	9	0.12
Northern European (11)	11	0.14
Norwegian (75)	174	2.26
Polish (11)	112	1.46
Portuguese (0)	22	0.29
Romanian (67)	67	0.87
Russian (20)	50	0.65
Scandinavian (7)	50	0.65
Scotch-Irish (31)	116	1.51
Scottish (55)	184	2.39
Slavic (9)	9	0.12
Slovene (20)	29	0.38
Swedish (45)	202	2.63
Turkish (11)	11	0.14
Ukrainian (23)	52	0.68
Welsh (41)	146	1.90

*Notes: † The Census 2010 population figure is used to calculate the percentages in the Hispanic Origin and Race categories. Ancestry percentages are based on the 2006-2010 American Community Survey population (not shown); ‡ Numbers in parentheses indicate the number of people reporting a single ancestry; * Numbers in parentheses indicate the number of persons reporting this race alone, not in combination with any other race; Please refer to the Explanation of Data for more information.*

Yugoslavian (51)	51	0.66

Hispanic Origin	Population	%
Hispanic or Latino (of any race)	794	10.35
Central American, ex. Mexican	3	0.04
Panamanian	1	0.01
Salvadoran	2	0.03
Cuban	9	0.12
Mexican	575	7.49
Puerto Rican	9	0.12
South American	13	0.17
Argentinean	3	0.04
Chilean	1	0.01
Colombian	1	0.01
Ecuadorian	2	0.03
Uruguayan	1	0.01
Venezuelan	5	0.07
Other Hispanic or Latino	185	2.41

Race*	Population	%
African-American/Black (29)	65	0.85
Not Hispanic (28)	55	0.72
Hispanic (1)	10	0.13
American Indian/Alaska Native (93)	169	2.20
Not Hispanic (67)	122	1.59
Hispanic (26)	47	0.61
Alaska Athabascan *(Ala. Nat.)* (1)	1	0.01
Apache (7)	14	0.18
Arapaho (0)	1	0.01
Blackfeet (3)	3	0.04
Cherokee (16)	29	0.38
Cheyenne (0)	1	0.01
Chickasaw (2)	2	0.03
Chippewa (3)	8	0.10
Choctaw (8)	9	0.12
Comanche (2)	2	0.03
Delaware (0)	4	0.05
Inupiat *(Alaska Native)* (2)	2	0.03
Iroquois (7)	7	0.09
Lumbee (1)	1	0.01
Mexican American Ind. (1)	1	0.01
Navajo (8)	17	0.22
Osage (0)	4	0.05
Potawatomi (1)	1	0.01
Pueblo (5)	5	0.07
Sioux (2)	7	0.09
Ute (1)	2	0.03
Yaqui (0)	1	0.01
Asian (48)	74	0.96
Not Hispanic (47)	70	0.91
Hispanic (1)	4	0.05
Chinese, ex. Taiwanese (12)	15	0.20
Filipino (10)	21	0.27
Indian (2)	3	0.04
Japanese (10)	17	0.22
Korean (9)	10	0.13
Vietnamese (2)	6	0.08
Hawaii Native/Pacific Islander (3)	8	0.10
Not Hispanic (2)	7	0.09
Hispanic (1)	1	0.01
Native Hawaiian (3)	5	0.07
Samoan (0)	1	0.01
White (7,014)	7,202	93.84
Not Hispanic (6,627)	6,731	87.70
Hispanic (387)	471	6.14

Glenwood Springs

Place Type: City
County: Garfield
Population: 9,614†

Ancestry‡	Population	%
American (318)	318	3.37
Austrian (37)	63	0.67
Belgian (26)	26	0.28
British (35)	35	0.37
Canadian (0)	24	0.25
Czech (12)	28	0.30
Danish (0)	63	0.67
Dutch (81)	239	2.54
English (429)	1,379	14.63
European (16)	43	0.46
French, ex. Basque (124)	308	3.27
French Canadian (36)	135	1.43
German (672)	2,024	21.47
Hungarian (0)	58	0.62
Irish (240)	1,532	16.25
Italian (368)	692	7.34
Northern European (12)	12	0.13
Norwegian (78)	472	5.01
Polish (52)	174	1.85
Portuguese (0)	21	0.22
Russian (79)	102	1.08
Scandinavian (20)	31	0.33
Scotch-Irish (141)	286	3.03
Scottish (155)	366	3.88
Slavic (0)	66	0.70
Slovene (52)	52	0.55
Swedish (17)	251	2.66
Swiss (0)	40	0.42
Ukrainian (0)	23	0.24
Welsh (34)	164	1.74

Hispanic Origin	Population	%
Hispanic or Latino (of any race)	3,031	31.53
Central American, ex. Mexican	257	2.67
Costa Rican	1	0.01
Guatemalan	62	0.64
Honduran	51	0.53
Nicaraguan	6	0.06
Panamanian	6	0.06
Salvadoran	130	1.35
Other Central American	1	0.01
Cuban	6	0.06
Mexican	2,410	25.07
Puerto Rican	52	0.54
South American	80	0.83
Argentinean	27	0.28
Bolivian	1	0.01
Chilean	5	0.05
Colombian	13	0.14
Ecuadorian	6	0.06
Paraguayan	1	0.01
Peruvian	24	0.25
Uruguayan	1	0.01
Venezuelan	2	0.02
Other Hispanic or Latino	226	2.35

Race*	Population	%
African-American/Black (116)	144	1.50
Not Hispanic (69)	86	0.89
Hispanic (47)	58	0.60
American Indian/Alaska Native (97)	182	1.89
Not Hispanic (39)	101	1.05
Hispanic (58)	81	0.84
Apache (0)	1	0.01
Arapaho (0)	3	0.03
Blackfeet (0)	1	0.01
Canadian/French Am. Ind. (1)	1	0.01
Central American Ind. (2)	2	0.02
Cherokee (5)	20	0.21
Chickasaw (0)	1	0.01
Chippewa (1)	3	0.03
Choctaw (2)	7	0.07
Comanche (0)	1	0.01
Mexican American Ind. (18)	24	0.25
Navajo (2)	2	0.02
Osage (0)	3	0.03
Ottawa (1)	2	0.02
Pueblo (0)	3	0.03
Sioux (4)	11	0.11
Ute (0)	2	0.02
Asian (76)	112	1.16
Not Hispanic (70)	103	1.07
Hispanic (6)	9	0.09
Burmese (2)	2	0.02
Cambodian (4)	4	0.04
Chinese, ex. Taiwanese (22)	31	0.32
Filipino (5)	12	0.12
Indian (6)	7	0.07
Indonesian (0)	3	0.03
Japanese (10)	17	0.18
Korean (6)	12	0.12
Laotian (0)	1	0.01
Nepalese (6)	6	0.06
Sri Lankan (1)	1	0.01
Taiwanese (1)	3	0.03
Thai (1)	2	0.02
Vietnamese (10)	11	0.11
Hawaii Native/Pacific Islander (11)	19	0.20
Not Hispanic (1)	5	0.05
Hispanic (10)	14	0.15
Guamanian/Chamorro (6)	9	0.09
Samoan (0)	1	0.01
Tongan (1)	1	0.01
White (7,821)	8,027	83.49
Not Hispanic (6,276)	6,380	66.36
Hispanic (1,545)	1,647	17.13

Golden

Place Type: City
County: Jefferson
Population: 18,867†

Ancestry‡	Population	%
American (899)	899	4.88
Arab (267)	278	1.51
Arab (55)	55	0.30
Lebanese (40)	51	0.28
Moroccan (28)	28	0.15
Other Arab (144)	144	0.78
Austrian (15)	271	1.47
Belgian (12)	60	0.33
British (48)	123	0.67
Bulgarian (0)	16	0.09
Canadian (0)	39	0.21
Croatian (6)	81	0.44
Czech (72)	156	0.85
Czechoslovakian (13)	58	0.31
Danish (78)	143	0.78
Dutch (85)	249	1.35
Eastern European (39)	39	0.21
English (684)	2,246	12.20
European (594)	639	3.47
Finnish (48)	50	0.27
French, ex. Basque (163)	748	4.06
French Canadian (51)	88	0.48
German (1,817)	5,223	28.36
Greek (52)	143	0.78
Hungarian (18)	155	0.84
Iranian (11)	66	0.36
Irish (734)	2,777	15.08
Italian (309)	1,065	5.78
Lithuanian (69)	94	0.51
New Zealander (22)	22	0.12
Northern European (16)	16	0.09
Norwegian (120)	772	4.19
Polish (271)	799	4.34
Portuguese (14)	43	0.23
Russian (37)	199	1.08
Scandinavian (57)	82	0.45
Scotch-Irish (147)	379	2.06
Scottish (78)	449	2.44
Serbian (17)	17	0.09
Slavic (12)	12	0.07
Slovak (40)	53	0.29
Swedish (62)	590	3.20
Swiss (28)	287	1.56
Turkish (10)	20	0.11
Ukrainian (0)	31	0.17
Welsh (26)	207	1.12
West Indian, ex. Hispanic (0)	31	0.17
Jamaican (0)	31	0.17
Yugoslavian (10)	10	0.05

Hispanic Origin	Population	%
Hispanic or Latino (of any race)	1,553	8.23
Central American, ex. Mexican	27	0.14

*Notes: † The Census 2010 population figure is used to calculate the percentages in the Hispanic Origin and Race categories. Ancestry percentages are based on the 2006-2010 American Community Survey population (not shown); ‡ Numbers in parentheses indicate the number of people reporting a single ancestry; * Numbers in parentheses indicate the number of persons reporting this race alone, not in combination with any other race; Please refer to the Explanation of Data for more information.*

Costa Rican	1	0.01
Guatemalan	13	0.07
Nicaraguan	2	0.01
Panamanian	4	0.02
Salvadoran	3	0.02
Other Central American	4	0.02
Cuban	19	0.10
Dominican Republic	2	0.01
Mexican	1,088	5.77
Puerto Rican	52	0.28
South American	101	0.54
Argentinean	15	0.08
Bolivian	9	0.05
Chilean	6	0.03
Colombian	13	0.07
Ecuadorian	8	0.04
Peruvian	16	0.08
Uruguayan	3	0.02
Venezuelan	31	0.16
Other Hispanic or Latino	264	1.40

Race*	Population	%
African-American/Black (233)	288	1.53
Not Hispanic (213)	260	1.38
Hispanic (20)	28	0.15
American Indian/Alaska Native (120)	229	1.21
Not Hispanic (90)	171	0.91
Hispanic (30)	58	0.31
Apache (2)	7	0.04
Blackfeet (3)	4	0.02
Central American Ind. (3)	3	0.02
Cherokee (10)	36	0.19
Cheyenne (0)	3	0.02
Chickasaw (0)	3	0.02
Chippewa (4)	7	0.04
Choctaw (1)	5	0.03
Comanche (0)	1	0.01
Cree (1)	1	0.01
Creek (3)	3	0.02
Crow (2)	2	0.01
Delaware (1)	1	0.01
Hopi (3)	3	0.02
Iroquois (0)	2	0.01
Mexican American Ind. (1)	1	0.01
Navajo (4)	15	0.08
Ottawa (1)	1	0.01
Pima (0)	1	0.01
Pueblo (2)	5	0.03
Shoshone (2)	2	0.01
Sioux (24)	30	0.16
South American Ind. (3)	3	0.02
Spanish American Ind. (1)	1	0.01
Ute (0)	1	0.01
Yup'ik *(Alaska Native)* (2)	2	0.01
Asian (717)	933	4.95
Not Hispanic (714)	920	4.88
Hispanic (3)	13	0.07
Bangladeshi (3)	3	0.02
Burmese (0)	2	0.01
Cambodian (7)	8	0.04
Chinese, ex. Taiwanese (173)	213	1.13
Filipino (22)	81	0.43
Hmong (6)	6	0.03
Indian (126)	135	0.72
Indonesian (19)	23	0.12
Japanese (57)	110	0.58
Korean (103)	141	0.75
Laotian (2)	3	0.02
Malaysian (30)	31	0.16
Nepalese (25)	27	0.14
Pakistani (1)	2	0.01
Sri Lankan (4)	4	0.02
Taiwanese (18)	20	0.11
Thai (30)	31	0.16
Vietnamese (52)	55	0.29
Hawaii Native/Pacific Islander (10)	35	0.19
Not Hispanic (10)	29	0.15
Hispanic (0)	6	0.03
Fijian (1)	1	0.01
Guamanian/Chamorro (1)	4	0.02
Native Hawaiian (3)	19	0.10
Samoan (1)	3	0.02
Tongan (1)	1	0.01
White (17,101)	17,507	92.79
Not Hispanic (15,924)	16,247	86.11
Hispanic (1,177)	1,260	6.68

Grand Junction

Place Type: City
County: Mesa
Population: 58,566†

Ancestry‡	Population	%
African, Sub-Saharan (49)	84	0.15
African (15)	21	0.04
Ethiopian (23)	52	0.09
Other Sub-Saharan African (11)	11	0.02
American (2,968)	2,968	5.27
Arab (89)	192	0.34
Arab (0)	36	0.06
Iraqi (66)	66	0.12
Lebanese (23)	23	0.04
Other Arab (0)	67	0.12
Armenian (10)	26	0.05
Australian (0)	54	0.10
Austrian (29)	201	0.36
Basque (0)	27	0.05
Belgian (26)	73	0.13
British (178)	314	0.56
Canadian (76)	116	0.21
Celtic (24)	34	0.06
Croatian (50)	95	0.17
Czech (118)	395	0.70
Czechoslovakian (69)	69	0.12
Danish (113)	739	1.31
Dutch (173)	1,345	2.39
English (2,360)	7,957	14.13
European (728)	794	1.41
Finnish (29)	112	0.20
French, ex. Basque (343)	2,337	4.15
French Canadian (68)	353	0.63
German (5,079)	14,569	25.88
Greek (98)	228	0.41
Hungarian (68)	130	0.23
Icelander (0)	35	0.06
Irish (2,158)	7,785	13.83
Italian (868)	3,006	5.34
Lithuanian (21)	63	0.11
Macedonian (0)	9	0.02
Northern European (183)	189	0.34
Norwegian (375)	1,116	1.98
Pennsylvania German (15)	15	0.03
Polish (295)	1,085	1.93
Portuguese (23)	56	0.10
Romanian (37)	102	0.18
Russian (61)	305	0.54
Scandinavian (57)	206	0.37
Scotch-Irish (662)	1,619	2.88
Scottish (674)	2,102	3.73
Serbian (0)	17	0.03
Slavic (9)	18	0.03
Slovak (65)	144	0.26
Slovene (14)	30	0.05
Swedish (540)	1,978	3.51
Swiss (77)	191	0.34
Turkish (9)	18	0.03
Ukrainian (76)	197	0.35
Welsh (272)	670	1.19
West Indian, ex. Hispanic (13)	13	0.02
Belizean (13)	13	0.02
Yugoslavian (32)	105	0.19

Hispanic Origin	Population	%
Hispanic or Latino (of any race)	8,133	13.89
Central American, ex. Mexican	129	0.22
Costa Rican	6	0.01
Guatemalan	28	0.05
Honduran	39	0.07
Nicaraguan	13	0.02
Panamanian	14	0.02
Salvadoran	28	0.05
Other Central American	1	<0.01
Cuban	46	0.08
Dominican Republic	11	0.02
Mexican	6,001	10.25
Puerto Rican	89	0.15
South American	120	0.20
Argentinean	9	0.02
Bolivian	3	0.01
Chilean	10	0.02
Colombian	34	0.06
Ecuadorian	21	0.04
Peruvian	19	0.03
Venezuelan	23	0.04
Other South American	1	<0.01
Other Hispanic or Latino	1,737	2.97

Race*	Population	%
African-American/Black (465)	770	1.31
Not Hispanic (409)	650	1.11
Hispanic (56)	120	0.20
American Indian/Alaska Native (595)	1,162	1.98
Not Hispanic (338)	714	1.22
Hispanic (257)	448	0.76
Alaska Athabascan *(Ala. Nat.)* (2)	6	0.01
Aleut *(Alaska Native)* (3)	4	0.01
Apache (26)	78	0.13
Arapaho (3)	5	0.01
Blackfeet (1)	22	0.04
Canadian/French Am. Ind. (0)	7	0.01
Central American Ind. (0)	1	<0.01
Cherokee (48)	153	0.26
Cheyenne (3)	3	0.01
Chickasaw (6)	8	0.01
Chippewa (11)	19	0.03
Choctaw (19)	40	0.07
Colville (1)	1	<0.01
Comanche (0)	1	<0.01
Cree (0)	2	<0.01
Creek (4)	7	0.01
Crow (0)	3	0.01
Delaware (3)	7	0.01
Hopi (2)	3	0.01
Inupiat *(Alaska Native)* (0)	1	<0.01
Iroquois (5)	11	0.02
Kiowa (0)	7	0.01
Lumbee (0)	2	<0.01
Menominee (1)	1	<0.01
Mexican American Ind. (17)	31	0.05
Navajo (86)	132	0.23
Osage (2)	3	0.01
Paiute (0)	1	<0.01
Potawatomi (6)	13	0.02
Pueblo (6)	11	0.02
Puget Sound Salish (1)	1	<0.01
Seminole (0)	3	0.01
Shoshone (0)	5	0.01
Sioux (18)	35	0.06
South American Ind. (0)	4	0.01
Spanish American Ind. (8)	11	0.02
Tlingit-Haida *(Alaska Native)* (0)	2	<0.01
Ute (19)	32	0.05
Yaqui (4)	5	0.01
Yup'ik *(Alaska Native)* (1)	1	<0.01
Asian (645)	1,031	1.76
Not Hispanic (622)	933	1.59
Hispanic (23)	98	0.17
Bangladeshi (4)	4	0.01
Burmese (2)	2	<0.01
Cambodian (25)	31	0.05
Chinese, ex. Taiwanese (126)	191	0.33
Filipino (119)	244	0.42
Hmong (11)	11	0.02
Indian (44)	65	0.11
Indonesian (5)	5	0.01
Japanese (84)	227	0.39
Korean (71)	110	0.19
Laotian (5)	6	0.01
Malaysian (1)	1	<0.01

*Notes: † The Census 2010 population figure is used to calculate the percentages in the Hispanic Origin and Race categories. Ancestry percentages are based on the 2006-2010 American Community Survey population (not shown); ‡ Numbers in parentheses indicate the number of people reporting a single ancestry; * Numbers in parentheses indicate the number of persons reporting this race alone, not in combination with any other race; Please refer to the Explanation of Data for more information.*

Nepalese (16)	16	0.03
Pakistani (7)	8	0.01
Sri Lankan (0)	1	<0.01
Taiwanese (4)	6	0.01
Thai (11)	14	0.02
Vietnamese (83)	93	0.16
Hawaii Native/Pacific Islander (68)	171	0.29
Not Hispanic (66)	138	0.24
Hispanic (2)	33	0.06
Guamanian/Chamorro (12)	17	0.03
Native Hawaiian (38)	96	0.16
Samoan (14)	28	0.05
Tongan (0)	1	<0.01
White (51,936)	53,414	91.20
Not Hispanic (48,008)	48,906	83.51
Hispanic (3,928)	4,508	7.70

Greeley

Place Type: City
County: Weld
Population: 92,889†

Ancestry‡	Population	%
African, Sub-Saharan (349)	438	0.48
African (83)	166	0.18
Somalian (118)	118	0.13
Sudanese (15)	15	0.02
Other Sub-Saharan African (133)	139	0.15
American (3,977)	3,977	4.36
Arab (120)	185	0.20
Arab (36)	52	0.06
Lebanese (13)	62	0.07
Moroccan (14)	14	0.02
Syrian (40)	40	0.04
Other Arab (17)	17	0.02
Australian (35)	35	0.04
Austrian (44)	300	0.33
Basque (27)	61	0.07
Belgian (13)	44	0.05
British (151)	337	0.37
Bulgarian (7)	31	0.03
Cajun (0)	17	0.02
Canadian (45)	152	0.17
Croatian (31)	101	0.11
Czech (66)	592	0.65
Czechoslovakian (68)	118	0.13
Danish (233)	721	0.79
Dutch (168)	1,538	1.69
Eastern European (39)	39	0.04
English (2,021)	8,319	9.13
European (361)	417	0.46
Finnish (59)	228	0.25
French, ex. Basque (344)	2,362	2.59
French Canadian (167)	507	0.56
German (9,335)	23,262	25.53
German Russian (21)	41	0.04
Greek (138)	138	0.15
Hungarian (56)	259	0.28
Icelander (0)	8	0.01
Iranian (14)	14	0.02
Irish (1,962)	9,564	10.50
Italian (848)	2,669	2.93
Latvian (9)	27	0.03
Lithuanian (68)	182	0.20
Northern European (140)	140	0.15
Norwegian (602)	1,975	2.17
Pennsylvania German (38)	81	0.09
Polish (319)	1,611	1.77
Portuguese (12)	69	0.08
Romanian (37)	37	0.04
Russian (98)	970	1.06
Scandinavian (65)	101	0.11
Scotch-Irish (421)	1,592	1.75
Scottish (494)	1,990	2.18
Serbian (0)	9	0.01
Slavic (7)	45	0.05
Slovak (19)	80	0.09
Slovene (0)	19	0.02
Swedish (747)	2,269	2.49
Swiss (33)	331	0.36
Turkish (0)	18	0.02
Ukrainian (76)	87	0.10
Welsh (181)	605	0.66
West Indian, ex. Hispanic (0)	22	0.02
West Indian (0)	22	0.02
Yugoslavian (35)	94	0.10

Hispanic Origin	Population	%
Hispanic or Latino (of any race)	33,440	36.00
Central American, ex. Mexican	969	1.04
Costa Rican	7	0.01
Guatemalan	479	0.52
Honduran	93	0.10
Nicaraguan	17	0.02
Panamanian	11	0.01
Salvadoran	358	0.39
Other Central American	4	<0.01
Cuban	103	0.11
Dominican Republic	26	0.03
Mexican	27,171	29.25
Puerto Rican	265	0.29
South American	191	0.21
Argentinean	20	0.02
Bolivian	9	0.01
Chilean	7	0.01
Colombian	61	0.07
Ecuadorian	6	0.01
Paraguayan	9	0.01
Peruvian	62	0.07
Venezuelan	13	0.01
Other South American	4	<0.01
Other Hispanic or Latino	4,715	5.08

Race*	Population	%
African-American/Black (1,543)	2,051	2.21
Not Hispanic (1,295)	1,616	1.74
Hispanic (248)	435	0.47
American Indian/Alaska Native (1,096)	1,995	2.15
Not Hispanic (408)	872	0.94
Hispanic (688)	1,123	1.21
Alaska Athabascan *(Ala. Nat.)* (1)	1	<0.01
Aleut *(Alaska Native)* (2)	9	0.01
Apache (59)	120	0.13
Arapaho (2)	2	<0.01
Blackfeet (5)	25	0.03
Canadian/French Am. Ind. (2)	6	0.01
Central American Ind. (4)	8	0.01
Cherokee (88)	235	0.25
Cheyenne (4)	8	0.01
Chickasaw (1)	6	0.01
Chippewa (9)	21	0.02
Choctaw (13)	28	0.03
Comanche (8)	11	0.01
Cree (3)	4	<0.01
Creek (7)	9	0.01
Crow (3)	4	<0.01
Delaware (0)	2	<0.01
Hopi (2)	9	0.01
Houma (3)	3	<0.01
Inupiat *(Alaska Native)* (5)	7	0.01
Iroquois (3)	12	0.01
Kiowa (0)	8	0.01
Lumbee (1)	2	<0.01
Menominee (1)	1	<0.01
Mexican American Ind. (77)	140	0.15
Navajo (49)	87	0.09
Osage (1)	12	0.01
Ottawa (0)	1	<0.01
Paiute (3)	4	<0.01
Pima (3)	3	<0.01
Potawatomi (11)	15	0.02
Pueblo (22)	38	0.04
Seminole (3)	4	<0.01
Shoshone (2)	2	<0.01
Sioux (74)	140	0.15
Spanish American Ind. (11)	16	0.02
Tlingit-Haida *(Alaska Native)* (1)	1	<0.01
Tohono O'Odham (6)	8	0.01
Ute (6)	12	0.01
Yaqui (5)	10	0.01
Yup'ik *(Alaska Native)* (1)	1	<0.01
Asian (1,245)	1,807	1.95
Not Hispanic (1,176)	1,618	1.74
Hispanic (69)	189	0.20
Burmese (240)	248	0.27
Cambodian (4)	5	0.01
Chinese, ex. Taiwanese (193)	258	0.28
Filipino (132)	288	0.31
Hmong (2)	2	<0.01
Indian (95)	133	0.14
Indonesian (8)	9	0.01
Japanese (174)	349	0.38
Korean (131)	193	0.21
Laotian (6)	8	0.01
Malaysian (5)	7	0.01
Nepalese (2)	4	<0.01
Pakistani (6)	11	0.01
Sri Lankan (4)	5	0.01
Taiwanese (44)	47	0.05
Thai (59)	85	0.09
Vietnamese (75)	103	0.11
Hawaii Native/Pacific Islander (111)	235	0.25
Not Hispanic (90)	169	0.18
Hispanic (21)	66	0.07
Guamanian/Chamorro (35)	50	0.05
Native Hawaiian (38)	93	0.10
Samoan (12)	23	0.02
Tongan (3)	6	0.01
White (73,485)	76,319	82.16
Not Hispanic (55,090)	56,250	60.56
Hispanic (18,395)	20,069	21.61

Greenwood Village

Place Type: City
County: Arapahoe
Population: 13,925†

Ancestry‡	Population	%
African, Sub-Saharan (0)	17	0.13
African (0)	17	0.13
American (763)	763	5.71
Arab (62)	109	0.82
Iraqi (18)	18	0.13
Lebanese (44)	77	0.58
Palestinian (0)	14	0.10
Armenian (0)	11	0.08
Austrian (6)	106	0.79
Brazilian (60)	60	0.45
British (23)	87	0.65
Canadian (143)	168	1.26
Croatian (0)	11	0.08
Czech (0)	71	0.53
Czechoslovakian (0)	13	0.10
Danish (29)	128	0.96
Dutch (39)	366	2.74
Eastern European (95)	120	0.90
English (888)	2,570	19.23
European (277)	277	2.07
Finnish (0)	15	0.11
French, ex. Basque (69)	630	4.71
French Canadian (40)	67	0.50
German (660)	3,156	23.61
Greek (130)	154	1.15
Hungarian (40)	174	1.30
Iranian (64)	64	0.48
Irish (506)	2,105	15.75
Italian (398)	753	5.63
Latvian (0)	36	0.27
Lithuanian (71)	124	0.93
Maltese (0)	10	0.07
Northern European (28)	28	0.21
Norwegian (239)	375	2.81
Polish (231)	572	4.28
Portuguese (0)	11	0.08
Romanian (0)	13	0.10
Russian (473)	837	6.26
Scotch-Irish (121)	401	3.00
Scottish (63)	412	3.08

SECTION TWO

*Notes: † The Census 2010 population figure is used to calculate the percentages in the Hispanic Origin and Race categories. Ancestry percentages are based on the 2006-2010 American Community Survey population (not shown); ‡ Numbers in parentheses indicate the number of people reporting a single ancestry; * Numbers in parentheses indicate the number of persons reporting this race alone, not in combination with any other race; Please refer to the Explanation of Data for more information.*

Serbian (0)	69	0.52
Slovak (8)	17	0.13
Slovene (12)	12	0.09
Swedish (72)	347	2.60
Swiss (0)	122	0.91
Ukrainian (111)	154	1.15
Welsh (116)	204	1.53
Yugoslavian (0)	14	0.10

Hispanic Origin	Population	%
Hispanic or Latino (of any race)	626	4.50
Central American, ex. Mexican	27	0.19
Guatemalan	9	0.06
Honduran	2	0.01
Nicaraguan	1	0.01
Panamanian	9	0.06
Salvadoran	3	0.02
Other Central American	3	0.02
Cuban	33	0.24
Dominican Republic	4	0.03
Mexican	310	2.23
Puerto Rican	34	0.24
South American	83	0.60
Argentinean	12	0.09
Bolivian	6	0.04
Chilean	8	0.06
Colombian	15	0.11
Ecuadorian	7	0.05
Paraguayan	2	0.01
Peruvian	15	0.11
Uruguayan	1	0.01
Venezuelan	17	0.12
Other Hispanic or Latino	135	0.97

Race*	Population	%
African-American/Black (221)	304	2.18
Not Hispanic (207)	275	1.97
Hispanic (14)	29	0.21
American Indian/Alaska Native (52)	116	0.83
Not Hispanic (35)	84	0.60
Hispanic (17)	32	0.23
Apache (3)	3	0.02
Cherokee (10)	31	0.22
Cheyenne (1)	1	0.01
Chickasaw (0)	1	0.01
Chippewa (1)	4	0.03
Choctaw (1)	6	0.04
Creek (3)	6	0.04
Crow (1)	1	0.01
Iroquois (0)	4	0.03
Kiowa (1)	1	0.01
Mexican American Ind. (1)	2	0.01
Navajo (4)	7	0.05
Osage (0)	1	0.01
Potawatomi (0)	1	0.01
Shoshone (1)	3	0.02
Sioux (2)	6	0.04
South American Ind. (5)	5	0.04
Tohono O'Odham (2)	2	0.01
Ute (2)	2	0.01
Asian (1,006)	1,158	8.32
Not Hispanic (1,000)	1,136	8.16
Hispanic (6)	22	0.16
Chinese, ex. Taiwanese (254)	309	2.22
Filipino (32)	49	0.35
Indian (248)	262	1.88
Indonesian (7)	13	0.09
Japanese (66)	109	0.78
Korean (284)	319	2.29
Laotian (3)	3	0.02
Nepalese (8)	8	0.06
Pakistani (12)	14	0.10
Taiwanese (14)	19	0.14
Thai (6)	10	0.07
Vietnamese (18)	26	0.19
Hawaii Native/Pacific Islander (6)	31	0.22
Not Hispanic (3)	24	0.17
Hispanic (3)	7	0.05
Guamanian/Chamorro (1)	1	0.01
Native Hawaiian (5)	23	0.17
Samoan (0)	2	0.01
White (12,216)	12,481	89.63
Not Hispanic (11,795)	12,015	86.28
Hispanic (421)	466	3.35

Gunbarrel

Place Type: CDP
County: Boulder
Population: 9,263†

Ancestry‡	Population	%
African, Sub-Saharan (0)	54	0.57
African (0)	27	0.29
Other Sub-Saharan African (0)	27	0.29
American (285)	285	3.01
Arab (17)	114	1.20
Arab (0)	12	0.13
Lebanese (0)	51	0.54
Syrian (17)	34	0.36
Other Arab (0)	17	0.18
Armenian (0)	43	0.45
Austrian (16)	163	1.72
Belgian (9)	9	0.10
British (29)	73	0.77
Canadian (0)	51	0.54
Celtic (0)	8	0.08
Czech (22)	81	0.86
Czechoslovakian (0)	35	0.37
Danish (34)	92	0.97
Dutch (34)	297	3.14
Eastern European (25)	25	0.26
English (343)	1,618	17.08
European (410)	422	4.45
Finnish (29)	36	0.38
French, ex. Basque (21)	269	2.84
French Canadian (0)	41	0.43
German (664)	2,497	26.36
Greek (16)	88	0.93
Hungarian (35)	60	0.63
Icelander (16)	24	0.25
Iranian (83)	83	0.88
Irish (471)	1,493	15.76
Italian (124)	354	3.74
Lithuanian (14)	36	0.38
Northern European (12)	12	0.13
Norwegian (74)	401	4.23
Polish (127)	410	4.33
Russian (53)	283	2.99
Scandinavian (22)	60	0.63
Scotch-Irish (102)	299	3.16
Scottish (183)	532	5.62
Slovak (0)	28	0.30
Swedish (91)	414	4.37
Swiss (0)	93	0.98
Ukrainian (8)	8	0.08
Welsh (21)	100	1.06

Hispanic Origin	Population	%
Hispanic or Latino (of any race)	392	4.23
Central American, ex. Mexican	21	0.23
Costa Rican	3	0.03
Guatemalan	6	0.06
Nicaraguan	1	0.01
Panamanian	3	0.03
Salvadoran	8	0.09
Cuban	11	0.12
Mexican	209	2.26
Puerto Rican	22	0.24
South American	54	0.58
Argentinean	15	0.16
Chilean	9	0.10
Colombian	14	0.15
Ecuadorian	3	0.03
Peruvian	9	0.10
Venezuelan	4	0.04
Other Hispanic or Latino	75	0.81

Race*	Population	%
African-American/Black (102)	146	1.58
Not Hispanic (98)	133	1.44
Hispanic (4)	13	0.14
American Indian/Alaska Native (39)	103	1.11
Not Hispanic (29)	70	0.76
Hispanic (10)	33	0.36
Apache (4)	4	0.04
Arapaho (0)	3	0.03
Blackfeet (1)	2	0.02
Cherokee (2)	15	0.16
Chickasaw (0)	1	0.01
Chippewa (2)	2	0.02
Inupiat *(Alaska Native)* (1)	1	0.01
Iroquois (1)	1	0.01
Mexican American Ind. (1)	5	0.05
Navajo (0)	2	0.02
Pueblo (2)	2	0.02
Sioux (1)	5	0.05
Asian (326)	439	4.74
Not Hispanic (321)	430	4.64
Hispanic (5)	9	0.10
Cambodian (6)	6	0.06
Chinese, ex. Taiwanese (67)	109	1.18
Filipino (10)	25	0.27
Indian (110)	121	1.31
Indonesian (10)	15	0.16
Japanese (43)	75	0.81
Korean (27)	35	0.38
Nepalese (11)	17	0.18
Pakistani (1)	2	0.02
Sri Lankan (1)	1	0.01
Taiwanese (1)	3	0.03
Thai (6)	10	0.11
Vietnamese (7)	13	0.14
Hawaii Native/Pacific Islander (4)	12	0.13
Not Hispanic (3)	11	0.12
Hispanic (1)	1	0.01
Marshallese (1)	1	0.01
Native Hawaiian (2)	3	0.03
Tongan (0)	3	0.03
White (8,491)	8,705	93.98
Not Hispanic (8,227)	8,394	90.62
Hispanic (264)	311	3.36

Highlands Ranch

Place Type: CDP
County: Douglas
Population: 96,713†

Ancestry‡	Population	%
Afghan (61)	61	0.06
African, Sub-Saharan (270)	417	0.44
African (0)	78	0.08
Ethiopian (57)	57	0.06
Ghanaian (58)	58	0.06
South African (113)	182	0.19
Zimbabwean (18)	18	0.02
Other Sub-Saharan African (24)	24	0.03
American (4,606)	4,606	4.84
Arab (228)	410	0.43
Arab (10)	10	0.01
Lebanese (185)	277	0.29
Moroccan (11)	11	0.01
Syrian (12)	43	0.05
Other Arab (10)	69	0.07
Armenian (26)	26	0.03
Australian (24)	84	0.09
Austrian (90)	623	0.66
Basque (17)	52	0.05
Belgian (48)	175	0.18
Brazilian (30)	60	0.06
British (254)	725	0.76
Bulgarian (0)	75	0.08
Canadian (393)	644	0.68
Celtic (56)	56	0.06
Croatian (33)	290	0.30
Czech (202)	934	0.98
Czechoslovakian (65)	111	0.12
Danish (371)	1,332	1.40
Dutch (1,102)	2,762	2.90

*Notes: † The Census 2010 population figure is used to calculate the percentages in the Hispanic Origin and Race categories. Ancestry percentages are based on the 2006-2010 American Community Survey population (not shown); ‡ Numbers in parentheses indicate the number of people reporting a single ancestry; * Numbers in parentheses indicate the number of persons reporting this race alone, not in combination with any other race; Please refer to the Explanation of Data for more information.*

Eastern European (143)	175	0.18
English (4,017)	14,728	15.49
European (1,881)	2,121	2.23
Finnish (107)	500	0.53
French, ex. Basque (390)	3,636	3.82
French Canadian (297)	862	0.91
German (7,288)	24,806	26.08
Greek (181)	579	0.61
Hungarian (225)	731	0.77
Icelander (0)	49	0.05
Iranian (112)	244	0.26
Irish (3,479)	14,937	15.71
Israeli (62)	62	0.07
Italian (1,685)	6,755	7.10
Latvian (18)	27	0.03
Lithuanian (65)	177	0.19
Northern European (72)	83	0.09
Norwegian (664)	2,756	2.90
Pennsylvania German (17)	17	0.02
Polish (831)	3,190	3.35
Portuguese (60)	262	0.28
Romanian (28)	96	0.10
Russian (730)	1,658	1.74
Scandinavian (274)	454	0.48
Scotch-Irish (911)	2,108	2.22
Scottish (1,152)	3,704	3.89
Serbian (24)	55	0.06
Slavic (30)	103	0.11
Slovak (15)	258	0.27
Slovene (25)	46	0.05
Swedish (687)	3,199	3.36
Swiss (320)	862	0.91
Ukrainian (128)	282	0.30
Welsh (234)	1,282	1.35
West Indian, ex. Hispanic (42)	87	0.09
Jamaican (42)	67	0.07
Trinidadian/Tobagonian (0)	20	0.02
Yugoslavian (12)	206	0.22

Hispanic Origin	Population	%
Hispanic or Latino (of any race)	6,929	7.16
Central American, ex. Mexican	239	0.25
Costa Rican	31	0.03
Guatemalan	57	0.06
Honduran	27	0.03
Nicaraguan	31	0.03
Panamanian	23	0.02
Salvadoran	70	0.07
Cuban	116	0.12
Dominican Republic	27	0.03
Mexican	4,013	4.15
Puerto Rican	371	0.38
South American	589	0.61
Argentinean	53	0.05
Bolivian	7	0.01
Chilean	28	0.03
Colombian	191	0.20
Ecuadorian	31	0.03
Paraguayan	5	0.01
Peruvian	168	0.17
Uruguayan	15	0.02
Venezuelan	81	0.08
Other South American	10	0.01
Other Hispanic or Latino	1,574	1.63

Race*	Population	%
African-American/Black (1,164)	1,689	1.75
Not Hispanic (1,103)	1,536	1.59
Hispanic (61)	153	0.16
American Indian/Alaska Native (350)	874	0.90
Not Hispanic (243)	628	0.65
Hispanic (107)	246	0.25
Alaska Athabascan *(Ala. Nat.)* (2)	3	<0.01
Aleut *(Alaska Native)* (1)	1	<0.01
Apache (4)	20	0.02
Arapaho (1)	6	0.01
Blackfeet (7)	19	0.02
Canadian/French Am. Ind. (0)	1	<0.01
Central American Ind. (8)	11	0.01
Cherokee (42)	170	0.18
Cheyenne (1)	1	<0.01
Chickasaw (6)	19	0.02
Chippewa (4)	12	0.01
Choctaw (9)	33	0.03
Comanche (7)	8	0.01
Cree (1)	2	<0.01
Creek (14)	20	0.02
Crow (1)	7	0.01
Delaware (1)	2	<0.01
Hopi (0)	7	0.01
Inupiat *(Alaska Native)* (2)	2	<0.01
Iroquois (1)	11	0.01
Lumbee (0)	1	<0.01
Menominee (5)	5	0.01
Mexican American Ind. (5)	8	0.01
Navajo (22)	39	0.04
Osage (4)	6	0.01
Ottawa (1)	1	<0.01
Potawatomi (8)	12	0.01
Pueblo (4)	5	0.01
Seminole (1)	1	<0.01
Shoshone (3)	6	0.01
Sioux (22)	47	0.05
South American Ind. (3)	7	0.01
Ute (2)	6	0.01
Yaqui (0)	1	<0.01
Asian (5,396)	6,697	6.92
Not Hispanic (5,328)	6,513	6.73
Hispanic (68)	184	0.19
Bangladeshi (20)	25	0.03
Burmese (5)	7	0.01
Cambodian (33)	46	0.05
Chinese, ex. Taiwanese (1,356)	1,645	1.70
Filipino (333)	632	0.65
Hmong (14)	14	0.01
Indian (1,476)	1,631	1.69
Indonesian (36)	55	0.06
Japanese (311)	661	0.68
Korean (697)	887	0.92
Laotian (9)	21	0.02
Malaysian (9)	9	0.01
Nepalese (37)	37	0.04
Pakistani (46)	59	0.06
Sri Lankan (16)	18	0.02
Taiwanese (93)	109	0.11
Thai (79)	116	0.12
Vietnamese (605)	714	0.74
Hawaii Native/Pacific Islander (48)	201	0.21
Not Hispanic (44)	173	0.18
Hispanic (4)	28	0.03
Fijian (2)	2	<0.01
Guamanian/Chamorro (4)	29	0.03
Native Hawaiian (27)	108	0.11
Samoan (1)	11	0.01
Tongan (5)	5	0.01
White (85,797)	88,149	91.14
Not Hispanic (80,994)	82,797	85.61
Hispanic (4,803)	5,352	5.53

Johns

Place Type: Town
County: Weld
Population: 9,887†

Ancestry‡	Population	%
American (264)	264	3.05
Australian (0)	9	0.10
Austrian (0)	21	0.24
Belgian (0)	17	0.20
British (34)	53	0.61
Bulgarian (0)	87	1.01
Canadian (0)	9	0.10
Czech (0)	44	0.51
Danish (40)	64	0.74
Dutch (40)	163	1.88
English (266)	933	10.78
European (23)	23	0.27
French, ex. Basque (25)	567	6.55
French Canadian (15)	15	0.17
German (1,203)	2,547	29.42
Irish (349)	1,459	16.86
Italian (245)	616	7.12
Lithuanian (0)	19	0.22
Norwegian (42)	213	2.46
Polish (69)	247	2.85
Portuguese (0)	27	0.31
Russian (119)	241	2.78
Scotch-Irish (134)	212	2.45
Scottish (174)	267	3.08
Swedish (51)	296	3.42
Swiss (13)	21	0.24
Ukrainian (45)	60	0.69
Welsh (20)	112	1.29
Yugoslavian (53)	53	0.61

Hispanic Origin	Population	%
Hispanic or Latino (of any race)	1,659	16.78
Central American, ex. Mexican	11	0.11
Guatemalan	4	0.04
Honduran	3	0.03
Salvadoran	4	0.04
Cuban	7	0.07
Dominican Republic	1	0.01
Mexican	1,333	13.48
Puerto Rican	18	0.18
South American	23	0.23
Argentinean	1	0.01
Chilean	2	0.02
Colombian	12	0.12
Ecuadorian	1	0.01
Peruvian	5	0.05
Venezuelan	2	0.02
Other Hispanic or Latino	266	2.69

Race*	Population	%
African-American/Black (41)	84	0.85
Not Hispanic (36)	77	0.78
Hispanic (5)	7	0.07
American Indian/Alaska Native (62)	139	1.41
Not Hispanic (47)	104	1.05
Hispanic (15)	35	0.35
Alaska Athabascan *(Ala. Nat.)* (1)	1	0.01
Apache (4)	6	0.06
Blackfeet (0)	1	0.01
Cherokee (7)	36	0.36
Cheyenne (0)	2	0.02
Chippewa (4)	9	0.09
Choctaw (2)	3	0.03
Comanche (0)	1	0.01
Cree (0)	1	0.01
Hopi (4)	4	0.04
Inupiat *(Alaska Native)* (1)	1	0.01
Mexican American Ind. (7)	7	0.07
Navajo (9)	13	0.13
Paiute (0)	1	0.01
Sioux (1)	3	0.03
Spanish American Ind. (0)	1	0.01
Tlingit-Haida *(Alaska Native)* (0)	2	0.02
Ute (2)	3	0.03
Asian (77)	137	1.39
Not Hispanic (76)	117	1.18
Hispanic (1)	20	0.20
Cambodian (5)	5	0.05
Chinese, ex. Taiwanese (24)	31	0.31
Filipino (13)	34	0.34
Indian (3)	4	0.04
Indonesian (0)	2	0.02
Japanese (1)	21	0.21
Korean (8)	11	0.11
Taiwanese (2)	2	0.02
Thai (1)	4	0.04
Vietnamese (18)	19	0.19
Hawaii Native/Pacific Islander (4)	10	0.10
Not Hispanic (4)	7	0.07
Hispanic (0)	3	0.03
Native Hawaiian (1)	3	0.03
White (8,839)	9,066	91.70
Not Hispanic (7,920)	8,046	81.38
Hispanic (919)	1,020	10.32

*Notes: † The Census 2010 population figure is used to calculate the percentages in the Hispanic Origin and Race categories. Ancestry percentages are based on the 2006-2010 American Community Survey population (not shown); ‡ Numbers in parentheses indicate the number of people reporting a single ancestry; * Numbers in parentheses indicate the number of persons reporting this race alone, not in combination with any other race; Please refer to the Explanation of Data for more information.*

Ken Caryl

Place Type: CDP
County: Jefferson
Population: 32,438†

Ancestry‡	Population	%
American (1,229)	1,229	3.65
Arab (45)	68	0.20
Egyptian (18)	18	0.05
Lebanese (0)	23	0.07
Syrian (10)	10	0.03
Other Arab (17)	17	0.05
Armenian (15)	40	0.12
Austrian (82)	182	0.54
Basque (11)	11	0.03
Belgian (0)	93	0.28
Brazilian (150)	150	0.45
British (37)	139	0.41
Bulgarian (0)	11	0.03
Cajun (0)	47	0.14
Canadian (23)	108	0.32
Croatian (0)	79	0.23
Czech (116)	273	0.81
Czechoslovakian (11)	66	0.20
Danish (122)	502	1.49
Dutch (183)	696	2.07
Eastern European (57)	85	0.25
English (1,383)	4,758	14.14
Estonian (18)	31	0.09
European (863)	910	2.70
Finnish (0)	190	0.56
French, ex. Basque (189)	1,264	3.76
French Canadian (113)	339	1.01
German (2,662)	9,008	26.76
German Russian (5)	5	0.01
Greek (10)	43	0.13
Hungarian (115)	207	0.62
Iranian (68)	68	0.20
Irish (1,490)	5,894	17.51
Italian (887)	2,537	7.54
Latvian (0)	23	0.07
Lithuanian (14)	63	0.19
Northern European (9)	9	0.03
Norwegian (467)	1,410	4.19
Polish (310)	1,183	3.51
Portuguese (26)	26	0.08
Romanian (103)	113	0.34
Russian (77)	278	0.83
Scandinavian (91)	158	0.47
Scotch-Irish (279)	940	2.79
Scottish (450)	1,498	4.45
Serbian (5)	16	0.05
Slavic (0)	34	0.10
Slovak (26)	26	0.08
Slovene (11)	26	0.08
Swedish (312)	1,094	3.25
Swiss (12)	40	0.12
Ukrainian (21)	52	0.15
Welsh (51)	414	1.23
West Indian, ex. Hispanic (10)	25	0.07
Haitian (0)	15	0.04
Jamaican (10)	10	0.03

Hispanic Origin	Population	%
Hispanic or Latino (of any race)	3,099	9.55
Central American, ex. Mexican	55	0.17
Costa Rican	2	0.01
Guatemalan	23	0.07
Honduran	9	0.03
Nicaraguan	8	0.02
Panamanian	3	0.01
Salvadoran	10	0.03
Cuban	23	0.07
Dominican Republic	4	0.01
Mexican	1,849	5.70
Puerto Rican	76	0.23
South American	134	0.41
Argentinean	6	0.02
Bolivian	17	0.05
Chilean	11	0.03
Colombian	35	0.11
Ecuadorian	4	0.01
Paraguayan	1	<0.01
Peruvian	40	0.12
Venezuelan	15	0.05
Other South American	5	0.02
Other Hispanic or Latino	958	2.95

Race*	Population	%
African-American/Black (261)	457	1.41
Not Hispanic (238)	396	1.22
Hispanic (23)	61	0.19
American Indian/Alaska Native (156)	418	1.29
Not Hispanic (105)	250	0.77
Hispanic (51)	168	0.52
Aleut *(Alaska Native)* (0)	2	0.01
Apache (15)	44	0.14
Arapaho (2)	5	0.02
Blackfeet (0)	2	0.01
Canadian/French Am. Ind. (0)	2	0.01
Cherokee (11)	46	0.14
Cheyenne (1)	1	<0.01
Chickasaw (4)	5	0.02
Chippewa (3)	10	0.03
Choctaw (4)	10	0.03
Cree (1)	1	<0.01
Creek (4)	4	0.01
Delaware (1)	4	0.01
Hopi (2)	2	0.01
Houma (2)	5	0.02
Iroquois (3)	5	0.02
Kiowa (0)	1	<0.01
Lumbee (3)	6	0.02
Menominee (6)	6	0.02
Mexican American Ind. (8)	10	0.03
Navajo (10)	25	0.08
Osage (2)	3	0.01
Potawatomi (2)	7	0.02
Pueblo (3)	5	0.02
Sioux (10)	15	0.05
South American Ind. (0)	4	0.01
Spanish American Ind. (1)	1	<0.01
Tlingit-Haida *(Alaska Native)* (2)	2	0.01
Tohono O'Odham (0)	1	<0.01
Ute (1)	2	0.01
Yaqui (0)	5	0.02
Yuman (1)	2	0.01
Asian (699)	1,002	3.09
Not Hispanic (690)	961	2.96
Hispanic (9)	41	0.13
Burmese (2)	2	0.01
Cambodian (3)	4	0.01
Chinese, ex. Taiwanese (131)	188	0.58
Filipino (78)	141	0.43
Hmong (7)	7	0.02
Indian (74)	95	0.29
Indonesian (4)	6	0.02
Japanese (84)	170	0.52
Korean (98)	146	0.45
Laotian (5)	5	0.02
Malaysian (2)	2	0.01
Nepalese (5)	5	0.02
Pakistani (7)	8	0.02
Sri Lankan (1)	1	<0.01
Taiwanese (1)	1	<0.01
Thai (12)	35	0.11
Vietnamese (154)	180	0.55
Hawaii Native/Pacific Islander (16)	44	0.14
Not Hispanic (13)	41	0.13
Hispanic (3)	3	0.01
Guamanian/Chamorro (2)	6	0.02
Native Hawaiian (9)	24	0.07
Samoan (2)	2	0.01
Tongan (1)	1	<0.01
White (29,772)	30,565	94.23
Not Hispanic (27,710)	28,224	87.01
Hispanic (2,062)	2,341	7.22

Lafayette

Place Type: City
County: Boulder
Population: 24,453†

Ancestry‡	Population	%
African, Sub-Saharan (18)	18	0.07
South African (18)	18	0.07
Alsatian (0)	8	0.03
American (841)	841	3.48
Arab (37)	53	0.22
Lebanese (24)	40	0.17
Syrian (13)	13	0.05
Armenian (0)	29	0.12
Australian (0)	10	0.04
Austrian (5)	33	0.14
Belgian (0)	26	0.11
Brazilian (13)	36	0.15
British (157)	268	1.11
Bulgarian (46)	60	0.25
Canadian (25)	104	0.43
Celtic (16)	16	0.07
Croatian (36)	49	0.20
Czech (13)	174	0.72
Czechoslovakian (0)	47	0.19
Danish (25)	269	1.11
Dutch (98)	566	2.34
Eastern European (22)	58	0.24
English (743)	3,023	12.50
Estonian (0)	31	0.13
European (325)	346	1.43
Finnish (12)	75	0.31
French, ex. Basque (130)	746	3.08
French Canadian (18)	73	0.30
German (1,399)	5,329	22.03
Greek (57)	91	0.38
Hungarian (12)	102	0.42
Iranian (16)	16	0.07
Irish (620)	3,625	14.99
Italian (652)	1,775	7.34
Latvian (9)	9	0.04
Lithuanian (22)	98	0.41
Northern European (40)	40	0.17
Norwegian (192)	602	2.49
Pennsylvania German (0)	7	0.03
Polish (250)	950	3.93
Portuguese (0)	14	0.06
Romanian (0)	16	0.07
Russian (40)	372	1.54
Scandinavian (34)	58	0.24
Scotch-Irish (172)	555	2.29
Scottish (555)	1,307	5.40
Serbian (62)	70	0.29
Slovak (0)	24	0.10
Slovene (0)	24	0.10
Swedish (95)	482	1.99
Swiss (23)	125	0.52
Ukrainian (93)	142	0.59
Welsh (24)	233	0.96
West Indian, ex. Hispanic (12)	12	0.05
Dutch West Indian (12)	12	0.05
Yugoslavian (0)	12	0.05

Hispanic Origin	Population	%
Hispanic or Latino (of any race)	4,454	18.21
Central American, ex. Mexican	198	0.81
Costa Rican	21	0.09
Guatemalan	38	0.16
Honduran	41	0.17
Nicaraguan	5	0.02
Panamanian	9	0.04
Salvadoran	84	0.34
Cuban	32	0.13
Dominican Republic	15	0.06
Mexican	3,493	14.28
Puerto Rican	68	0.28
South American	117	0.48
Argentinean	14	0.06
Bolivian	2	0.01

*Notes: † The Census 2010 population figure is used to calculate the percentages in the Hispanic Origin and Race categories. Ancestry percentages are based on the 2006-2010 American Community Survey population (not shown); ‡ Numbers in parentheses indicate the number of people reporting a single ancestry; * Numbers in parentheses indicate the number of persons reporting this race alone, not in combination with any other race; Please refer to the Explanation of Data for more information.*

Chilean	16	0.07
Colombian	28	0.11
Ecuadorian	3	0.01
Paraguayan	6	0.02
Peruvian	37	0.15
Uruguayan	1	<0.01
Venezuelan	7	0.03
Other South American	3	0.01
Other Hispanic or Latino	531	2.17

Race*	Population	%
African-American/Black (270)	431	1.76
Not Hispanic (240)	357	1.46
Hispanic (30)	74	0.30
American Indian/Alaska Native (210)	441	1.80
Not Hispanic (108)	234	0.96
Hispanic (102)	207	0.85
Apache (8)	31	0.13
Blackfeet (2)	13	0.05
Canadian/French Am. Ind. (1)	2	0.01
Central American Ind. (4)	4	0.02
Cherokee (16)	55	0.22
Cheyenne (0)	3	0.01
Chickasaw (0)	3	0.01
Chippewa (4)	7	0.03
Choctaw (5)	6	0.02
Comanche (1)	4	0.02
Creek (2)	2	0.01
Crow (1)	1	<0.01
Delaware (3)	3	0.01
Hopi (2)	5	0.02
Iroquois (1)	4	0.02
Mexican American Ind. (18)	26	0.11
Navajo (20)	34	0.14
Osage (0)	2	0.01
Pima (6)	6	0.02
Potawatomi (1)	5	0.02
Pueblo (8)	9	0.04
Seminole (1)	3	0.01
Shoshone (1)	1	<0.01
Sioux (14)	25	0.10
South American Ind. (0)	2	0.01
Spanish American Ind. (2)	3	0.01
Tlingit-Haida *(Alaska Native)* (0)	1	<0.01
Tohono O'Odham (1)	2	0.01
Ute (3)	7	0.03
Yaqui (6)	7	0.03
Yuman (1)	1	<0.01
Yup'ik *(Alaska Native)* (0)	1	<0.01
Asian (926)	1,220	4.99
Not Hispanic (914)	1,175	4.81
Hispanic (12)	45	0.18
Bhutanese (1)	1	<0.01
Burmese (15)	15	0.06
Cambodian (5)	6	0.02
Chinese, ex. Taiwanese (282)	348	1.42
Filipino (73)	136	0.56
Hmong (52)	59	0.24
Indian (158)	184	0.75
Indonesian (13)	17	0.07
Japanese (82)	181	0.74
Korean (69)	112	0.46
Laotian (9)	9	0.04
Malaysian (1)	4	0.02
Nepalese (17)	18	0.07
Pakistani (7)	9	0.04
Sri Lankan (10)	13	0.05
Taiwanese (10)	13	0.05
Thai (21)	29	0.12
Vietnamese (54)	69	0.28
Hawaii Native/Pacific Islander (12)	42	0.17
Not Hispanic (12)	37	0.15
Hispanic (0)	5	0.02
Guamanian/Chamorro (0)	2	0.01
Native Hawaiian (2)	24	0.10
Samoan (3)	5	0.02
White (20,932)	21,677	88.65
Not Hispanic (18,186)	18,664	76.33
Hispanic (2,746)	3,013	12.32

Lakewood

Place Type: City
County: Jefferson
Population: 142,980†

Ancestry‡	Population	%
African, Sub-Saharan (419)	556	0.39
African (325)	386	0.27
Ethiopian (19)	83	0.06
Nigerian (0)	12	0.01
South African (75)	75	0.05
Albanian (78)	78	0.05
American (5,074)	5,074	3.57
Arab (549)	662	0.47
Arab (238)	238	0.17
Iraqi (47)	47	0.03
Lebanese (0)	73	0.05
Moroccan (147)	147	0.10
Syrian (0)	40	0.03
Other Arab (117)	117	0.08
Armenian (108)	144	0.10
Australian (48)	57	0.04
Austrian (86)	530	0.37
Basque (98)	98	0.07
Belgian (133)	340	0.24
Brazilian (80)	127	0.09
British (358)	795	0.56
Bulgarian (62)	62	0.04
Cajun (11)	11	0.01
Canadian (153)	326	0.23
Celtic (84)	94	0.07
Croatian (165)	351	0.25
Czech (297)	931	0.66
Czechoslovakian (92)	187	0.13
Danish (440)	1,798	1.27
Dutch (746)	2,767	1.95
Eastern European (94)	116	0.08
English (5,093)	18,422	12.97
Estonian (25)	57	0.04
European (2,091)	2,264	1.59
Finnish (137)	335	0.24
French, ex. Basque (679)	5,382	3.79
French Canadian (209)	705	0.50
German (11,107)	34,745	24.46
German Russian (0)	11	0.01
Greek (115)	340	0.24
Hungarian (157)	476	0.34
Icelander (4)	4	<0.01
Iranian (120)	120	0.08
Irish (5,156)	21,132	14.88
Israeli (12)	12	0.01
Italian (2,693)	7,668	5.40
Latvian (7)	47	0.03
Lithuanian (77)	248	0.17
Luxemburger (28)	39	0.03
Maltese (0)	9	0.01
Northern European (253)	311	0.22
Norwegian (1,166)	3,582	2.52
Pennsylvania German (31)	40	0.03
Polish (937)	3,319	2.34
Portuguese (54)	242	0.17
Romanian (209)	333	0.23
Russian (369)	1,229	0.87
Scandinavian (125)	258	0.18
Scotch-Irish (1,008)	3,460	2.44
Scottish (1,080)	4,273	3.01
Serbian (12)	91	0.06
Slavic (11)	65	0.05
Slovak (95)	226	0.16
Slovene (55)	172	0.12
Swedish (979)	4,401	3.10
Swiss (181)	769	0.54
Turkish (14)	54	0.04
Ukrainian (120)	301	0.21
Welsh (304)	1,424	1.00
West Indian, ex. Hispanic (20)	68	0.05
British West Indian (9)	9	0.01
Dutch West Indian (0)	48	0.03
Jamaican (11)	11	0.01
Yugoslavian (348)	444	0.31

Hispanic Origin	Population	%
Hispanic or Latino (of any race)	31,467	22.01
Central American, ex. Mexican	649	0.45
Costa Rican	43	0.03
Guatemalan	186	0.13
Honduran	45	0.03
Nicaraguan	32	0.02
Panamanian	34	0.02
Salvadoran	299	0.21
Other Central American	10	0.01
Cuban	163	0.11
Dominican Republic	40	0.03
Mexican	22,026	15.40
Puerto Rican	522	0.37
South American	609	0.43
Argentinean	41	0.03
Bolivian	43	0.03
Chilean	79	0.06
Colombian	146	0.10
Ecuadorian	41	0.03
Paraguayan	8	0.01
Peruvian	207	0.14
Uruguayan	8	0.01
Venezuelan	36	0.03
Other Hispanic or Latino	7,458	5.22

Race*	Population	%
African-American/Black (2,231)	3,239	2.27
Not Hispanic (1,924)	2,634	1.84
Hispanic (307)	605	0.42
American Indian/Alaska Native (1,974)	3,523	2.46
Not Hispanic (987)	1,841	1.29
Hispanic (987)	1,682	1.18
Alaska Athabascan *(Ala. Nat.)* (5)	6	<0.01
Aleut *(Alaska Native)* (3)	5	<0.01
Apache (116)	240	0.17
Arapaho (7)	14	0.01
Blackfeet (21)	62	0.04
Central American Ind. (1)	4	<0.01
Cherokee (108)	391	0.27
Cheyenne (8)	20	0.01
Chickasaw (17)	28	0.02
Chippewa (46)	73	0.05
Choctaw (31)	64	0.04
Colville (2)	4	<0.01
Comanche (7)	15	0.01
Cree (1)	8	0.01
Creek (13)	23	0.02
Crow (5)	10	0.01
Delaware (3)	9	0.01
Hopi (15)	21	0.01
Inupiat *(Alaska Native)* (8)	10	0.01
Iroquois (8)	23	0.02
Kiowa (2)	2	<0.01
Lumbee (1)	3	<0.01
Menominee (1)	2	<0.01
Mexican American Ind. (94)	160	0.11
Navajo (215)	315	0.22
Osage (3)	11	0.01
Ottawa (0)	1	<0.01
Paiute (6)	6	<0.01
Potawatomi (22)	30	0.02
Pueblo (42)	75	0.05
Puget Sound Salish (9)	13	0.01
Seminole (7)	21	0.01
Shoshone (8)	15	0.01
Sioux (190)	312	0.22
South American Ind. (7)	15	0.01
Spanish American Ind. (29)	40	0.03
Tlingit-Haida *(Alaska Native)* (11)	13	0.01
Tohono O'Odham (1)	2	<0.01
Ute (32)	46	0.03
Yakama (0)	1	<0.01
Yaqui (5)	16	0.01
Yuman (7)	8	0.01
Yup'ik *(Alaska Native)* (0)	1	<0.01
Asian (4,493)	5,634	3.94

SECTION TWO

*Notes: † The Census 2010 population figure is used to calculate the percentages in the Hispanic Origin and Race categories. Ancestry percentages are based on the 2006-2010 American Community Survey population (not shown); ‡ Numbers in parentheses indicate the number of people reporting a single ancestry; * Numbers in parentheses indicate the number of persons reporting this race alone, not in combination with any other race; Please refer to the Explanation of Data for more information.*

Not Hispanic (4,347)	5,244	3.67
Hispanic (146)	390	0.27
Bangladeshi (23)	24	0.02
Burmese (13)	15	0.01
Cambodian (45)	62	0.04
Chinese, ex. Taiwanese (702)	915	0.64
Filipino (364)	665	0.47
Hmong (17)	28	0.02
Indian (459)	556	0.39
Indonesian (42)	68	0.05
Japanese (421)	713	0.50
Korean (501)	645	0.45
Laotian (19)	25	0.02
Malaysian (1)	3	<0.01
Nepalese (45)	48	0.03
Pakistani (37)	53	0.04
Sri Lankan (7)	11	0.01
Taiwanese (26)	33	0.02
Thai (45)	78	0.05
Vietnamese (1,513)	1,636	1.14
Hawaii Native/Pacific Islander (164)	354	0.25
Not Hispanic (144)	284	0.20
Hispanic (20)	70	0.05
Guamanian/Chamorro (31)	51	0.04
Marshallese (1)	3	<0.01
Native Hawaiian (58)	134	0.09
Samoan (20)	44	0.03
Tongan (5)	5	<0.01
White (118,487)	122,636	85.77
Not Hispanic (101,504)	103,725	72.55
Hispanic (16,983)	18,911	13.23

Lamar

Place Type: City
County: Prowers
Population: 7,804†

Ancestry‡	Population	%
American (275)	275	3.48
Arab (9)	9	0.11
Syrian (9)	9	0.11
Austrian (12)	21	0.27
Basque (0)	23	0.29
British (12)	12	0.15
Canadian (0)	9	0.11
Croatian (13)	13	0.16
Czech (0)	43	0.54
Czechoslovakian (0)	20	0.25
Danish (0)	15	0.19
Dutch (42)	167	2.11
English (204)	604	7.64
European (28)	28	0.35
French, ex. Basque (0)	196	2.48
German (661)	1,836	23.24
Greek (11)	22	0.28
Irish (250)	890	11.26
Italian (64)	267	3.38
Northern European (62)	62	0.78
Norwegian (61)	111	1.40
Polish (0)	11	0.14
Russian (0)	6	0.08
Scotch-Irish (30)	165	2.09
Scottish (42)	92	1.16
Serbian (8)	8	0.10
Slavic (0)	36	0.46
Swedish (21)	132	1.67
Swiss (12)	12	0.15
Welsh (13)	61	0.77

Hispanic Origin	Population	%
Hispanic or Latino (of any race)	3,100	39.72
Central American, ex. Mexican	4	0.05
Nicaraguan	1	0.01
Salvadoran	3	0.04
Cuban	2	0.03
Mexican	2,620	33.57
Puerto Rican	16	0.21
South American	5	0.06
Colombian	1	0.01
Paraguayan	1	0.01
Other South American	3	0.04
Other Hispanic or Latino	453	5.80

Race*	Population	%
African-American/Black (54)	82	1.05
Not Hispanic (47)	64	0.82
Hispanic (7)	18	0.23
American Indian/Alaska Native (79)	148	1.90
Not Hispanic (43)	87	1.11
Hispanic (36)	61	0.78
Apache (4)	5	0.06
Arapaho (0)	2	0.03
Blackfeet (2)	2	0.03
Cherokee (10)	29	0.37
Cheyenne (0)	1	0.01
Chippewa (0)	5	0.06
Choctaw (0)	1	0.01
Creek (5)	8	0.10
Mexican American Ind. (2)	5	0.06
Navajo (7)	11	0.14
Potawatomi (2)	2	0.03
Sioux (3)	4	0.05
Spanish American Ind. (3)	3	0.04
Yaqui (1)	1	0.01
Asian (28)	38	0.49
Not Hispanic (28)	34	0.44
Hispanic (0)	4	0.05
Chinese, ex. Taiwanese (4)	5	0.06
Filipino (1)	6	0.08
Indian (12)	13	0.17
Indonesian (1)	1	0.01
Japanese (1)	3	0.04
Korean (1)	2	0.03
Taiwanese (2)	2	0.03
Vietnamese (1)	1	0.01
Hawaii Native/Pacific Islander (1)	4	0.05
Not Hispanic (1)	4	0.05
Native Hawaiian (1)	4	0.05
White (6,137)	6,359	81.48
Not Hispanic (4,503)	4,574	58.61
Hispanic (1,634)	1,785	22.87

Littleton

Place Type: City
County: Arapahoe
Population: 41,737†

Ancestry‡	Population	%
Afghan (25)	25	0.06
African, Sub-Saharan (129)	142	0.34
African (28)	41	0.10
Liberian (77)	77	0.19
South African (24)	24	0.06
Albanian (34)	34	0.08
American (1,960)	1,960	4.74
Arab (16)	56	0.14
Egyptian (16)	16	0.04
Lebanese (0)	40	0.10
Armenian (10)	19	0.05
Australian (33)	107	0.26
Austrian (50)	100	0.24
Belgian (26)	37	0.09
Brazilian (30)	30	0.07
British (184)	376	0.91
Bulgarian (27)	27	0.07
Canadian (79)	186	0.45
Celtic (0)	23	0.06
Croatian (10)	73	0.18
Czech (74)	433	1.05
Czechoslovakian (8)	11	0.03
Danish (232)	599	1.45
Dutch (287)	1,063	2.57
Eastern European (43)	46	0.11
English (1,941)	6,364	15.39
European (866)	940	2.27
Finnish (0)	39	0.09
French, ex. Basque (220)	1,620	3.92
French Canadian (133)	339	0.82
German (3,258)	10,064	24.34
Greek (70)	171	0.41
Hungarian (32)	175	0.42
Icelander (52)	52	0.13
Iranian (32)	32	0.08
Irish (1,546)	6,029	14.58
Israeli (0)	11	0.03
Italian (761)	1,987	4.81
Latvian (8)	18	0.04
Lithuanian (27)	143	0.35
Luxemburger (7)	23	0.06
Macedonian (9)	9	0.02
New Zealander (10)	10	0.02
Northern European (67)	67	0.16
Norwegian (313)	858	2.07
Pennsylvania German (20)	23	0.06
Polish (523)	1,504	3.64
Portuguese (21)	101	0.24
Romanian (16)	42	0.10
Russian (75)	523	1.26
Scandinavian (109)	134	0.32
Scotch-Irish (336)	1,165	2.82
Scottish (399)	1,294	3.13
Serbian (9)	28	0.07
Slavic (0)	37	0.09
Slovak (41)	127	0.31
Slovene (27)	37	0.09
Swedish (435)	1,373	3.32
Swiss (79)	231	0.56
Turkish (0)	16	0.04
Ukrainian (19)	75	0.18
Welsh (126)	473	1.14
West Indian, ex. Hispanic (19)	50	0.12
Belizean (10)	10	0.02
Jamaican (9)	9	0.02
West Indian (0)	31	0.07
Yugoslavian (26)	103	0.25

Hispanic Origin	Population	%
Hispanic or Latino (of any race)	5,187	12.43
Central American, ex. Mexican	166	0.40
Costa Rican	8	0.02
Guatemalan	43	0.10
Honduran	36	0.09
Nicaraguan	18	0.04
Panamanian	9	0.02
Salvadoran	52	0.12
Cuban	58	0.14
Dominican Republic	5	0.01
Mexican	3,506	8.40
Puerto Rican	120	0.29
South American	147	0.35
Argentinean	12	0.03
Bolivian	3	0.01
Chilean	5	0.01
Colombian	26	0.06
Ecuadorian	5	0.01
Paraguayan	1	<0.01
Peruvian	78	0.19
Venezuelan	16	0.04
Other South American	1	<0.01
Other Hispanic or Latino	1,185	2.84

Race*	Population	%
African-American/Black (586)	848	2.03
Not Hispanic (543)	758	1.82
Hispanic (43)	90	0.22
American Indian/Alaska Native (347)	718	1.72
Not Hispanic (193)	449	1.08
Hispanic (154)	269	0.64
Alaska Athabascan *(Ala. Nat.)* (0)	1	<0.01
Apache (15)	30	0.07
Arapaho (1)	8	0.02
Blackfeet (1)	4	0.01
Canadian/French Am. Ind. (0)	1	<0.01
Cherokee (29)	99	0.24
Cheyenne (1)	2	<0.01
Chickasaw (8)	13	0.03
Chippewa (7)	11	0.03
Choctaw (5)	9	0.02

*Notes: † The Census 2010 population figure is used to calculate the percentages in the Hispanic Origin and Race categories. Ancestry percentages are based on the 2006-2010 American Community Survey population (not shown); ‡ Numbers in parentheses indicate the number of people reporting a single ancestry; * Numbers in parentheses indicate the number of persons reporting this race alone, not in combination with any other race; Please refer to the Explanation of Data for more information.*

Comanche (3)	7	0.02
Creek (0)	1	<0.01
Crow (1)	2	<0.01
Delaware (3)	3	0.01
Hopi (4)	4	0.01
Iroquois (0)	3	0.01
Menominee (0)	2	<0.01
Mexican American Ind. (17)	22	0.05
Navajo (18)	40	0.10
Osage (8)	9	0.02
Pima (0)	2	<0.01
Potawatomi (2)	3	0.01
Pueblo (14)	24	0.06
Seminole (1)	3	0.01
Shoshone (2)	4	0.01
Sioux (25)	43	0.10
South American Ind. (0)	2	<0.01
Spanish American Ind. (0)	1	<0.01
Ute (2)	5	0.01
Yaqui (1)	2	<0.01
Asian (909)	1,224	2.93
Not Hispanic (885)	1,162	2.78
Hispanic (24)	62	0.15
Bangladeshi (3)	3	0.01
Burmese (13)	13	0.03
Cambodian (4)	4	0.01
Chinese, ex. Taiwanese (232)	302	0.72
Filipino (87)	165	0.40
Hmong (2)	7	0.02
Indian (85)	118	0.28
Indonesian (22)	24	0.06
Japanese (96)	185	0.44
Korean (132)	160	0.38
Laotian (3)	3	0.01
Malaysian (0)	6	0.01
Nepalese (4)	5	0.01
Pakistani (7)	10	0.02
Sri Lankan (1)	1	<0.01
Taiwanese (10)	28	0.07
Thai (12)	20	0.05
Vietnamese (156)	173	0.41
Hawaii Native/Pacific Islander (26)	78	0.19
Not Hispanic (21)	62	0.15
Hispanic (5)	16	0.04
Guamanian/Chamorro (6)	12	0.03
Native Hawaiian (5)	30	0.07
Samoan (2)	2	<0.01
White (37,149)	38,148	91.40
Not Hispanic (34,138)	34,826	83.44
Hispanic (3,011)	3,322	7.96

Lone Tree

Place Type: City
County: Douglas
Population: 10,218†

Ancestry‡	Population	%
Afghan (40)	40	0.40
African, Sub-Saharan (48)	48	0.49
South African (48)	48	0.49
American (893)	893	9.03
Arab (32)	53	0.54
Lebanese (21)	21	0.21
Syrian (0)	10	0.10
Other Arab (11)	22	0.22
Armenian (38)	79	0.80
Austrian (0)	37	0.37
Brazilian (39)	39	0.39
British (31)	51	0.52
Bulgarian (0)	10	0.10
Canadian (114)	153	1.55
Czech (24)	118	1.19
Czechoslovakian (0)	13	0.13
Danish (18)	44	0.44
Dutch (44)	224	2.26
Eastern European (9)	9	0.09
English (452)	1,495	15.12
European (182)	193	1.95
Finnish (0)	10	0.10
French, ex. Basque (84)	389	3.93
French Canadian (93)	103	1.04
German (766)	2,554	25.82
Greek (30)	68	0.69
Hungarian (15)	45	0.46
Iranian (139)	139	1.41
Irish (338)	1,342	13.57
Israeli (49)	49	0.50
Italian (169)	740	7.48
Norwegian (134)	317	3.21
Pennsylvania German (14)	14	0.14
Polish (128)	294	2.97
Russian (62)	191	1.93
Scandinavian (10)	18	0.18
Scotch-Irish (44)	156	1.58
Scottish (42)	173	1.75
Serbian (0)	10	0.10
Slovak (0)	9	0.09
Swedish (63)	200	2.02
Swiss (0)	49	0.50
Ukrainian (49)	70	0.71
Welsh (0)	80	0.81
West Indian, ex. Hispanic (0)	10	0.10
Trinidadian/Tobagonian (0)	10	0.10
Yugoslavian (9)	9	0.09

Hispanic Origin	Population	%
Hispanic or Latino (of any race)	630	6.17
Central American, ex. Mexican	13	0.13
Costa Rican	1	0.01
Guatemalan	6	0.06
Panamanian	2	0.02
Salvadoran	4	0.04
Cuban	26	0.25
Dominican Republic	8	0.08
Mexican	382	3.74
Puerto Rican	22	0.22
South American	63	0.62
Argentinean	11	0.11
Chilean	6	0.06
Colombian	15	0.15
Ecuadorian	6	0.06
Peruvian	19	0.19
Uruguayan	1	0.01
Venezuelan	5	0.05
Other Hispanic or Latino	116	1.14

Race*	Population	%
African-American/Black (166)	214	2.09
Not Hispanic (158)	202	1.98
Hispanic (8)	12	0.12
American Indian/Alaska Native (32)	59	0.58
Not Hispanic (22)	43	0.42
Hispanic (10)	16	0.16
Aleut *(Alaska Native)* (3)	3	0.03
Apache (1)	1	0.01
Arapaho (0)	1	0.01
Blackfeet (0)	2	0.02
Cherokee (3)	10	0.10
Chickasaw (3)	4	0.04
Chippewa (1)	1	0.01
Choctaw (3)	3	0.03
Creek (1)	1	0.01
Crow (1)	1	0.01
Iroquois (0)	2	0.02
Mexican American Ind. (6)	6	0.06
Navajo (1)	1	0.01
Pueblo (1)	1	0.01
Sioux (2)	3	0.03
Spanish American Ind. (0)	1	0.01
Asian (735)	865	8.47
Not Hispanic (730)	855	8.37
Hispanic (5)	10	0.10
Cambodian (1)	3	0.03
Chinese, ex. Taiwanese (204)	235	2.30
Filipino (50)	77	0.75
Indian (218)	230	2.25
Indonesian (13)	13	0.13
Japanese (44)	87	0.85
Korean (113)	123	1.20
Nepalese (3)	3	0.03
Pakistani (3)	4	0.04
Sri Lankan (2)	2	0.02
Taiwanese (10)	11	0.11
Thai (2)	6	0.06
Vietnamese (49)	56	0.55
Hawaii Native/Pacific Islander (9)	29	0.28
Not Hispanic (8)	28	0.27
Hispanic (1)	1	0.01
Native Hawaiian (4)	22	0.22
Samoan (1)	1	0.01
White (8,913)	9,118	89.23
Not Hispanic (8,471)	8,641	84.57
Hispanic (442)	477	4.67

Longmont

Place Type: City
County: Boulder
Population: 86,270†

Ancestry‡	Population	%
Afghan (42)	57	0.07
African, Sub-Saharan (71)	326	0.39
African (31)	233	0.28
Ghanaian (33)	33	0.04
South African (0)	30	0.04
Other Sub-Saharan African (7)	30	0.04
Albanian (0)	41	0.05
American (2,636)	2,636	3.15
Arab (82)	192	0.23
Arab (0)	21	0.03
Egyptian (12)	12	0.01
Lebanese (0)	25	0.03
Syrian (0)	64	0.08
Other Arab (70)	70	0.08
Armenian (12)	24	0.03
Australian (0)	11	0.01
Austrian (90)	354	0.42
Basque (20)	36	0.04
Belgian (46)	126	0.15
Brazilian (10)	103	0.12
British (366)	507	0.61
Bulgarian (0)	22	0.03
Cajun (145)	145	0.17
Canadian (78)	173	0.21
Celtic (9)	21	0.03
Croatian (93)	242	0.29
Czech (193)	641	0.77
Czechoslovakian (55)	148	0.18
Danish (175)	624	0.75
Dutch (409)	1,901	2.27
Eastern European (70)	269	0.32
English (2,649)	9,969	11.92
Estonian (0)	9	0.01
European (2,128)	2,652	3.17
Finnish (43)	159	0.19
French, ex. Basque (401)	3,017	3.61
French Canadian (210)	627	0.75
German (5,463)	19,500	23.32
Greek (301)	566	0.68
Hungarian (45)	306	0.37
Iranian (21)	32	0.04
Irish (2,012)	9,933	11.88
Israeli (0)	11	0.01
Italian (983)	3,895	4.66
Latvian (28)	128	0.15
Lithuanian (56)	101	0.12
Luxemburger (0)	30	0.04
Macedonian (0)	3	<0.01
Maltese (13)	13	0.02
New Zealander (20)	20	0.02
Northern European (109)	116	0.14
Norwegian (570)	2,498	2.99
Pennsylvania German (99)	132	0.16
Polish (561)	2,054	2.46
Portuguese (21)	146	0.17
Romanian (0)	30	0.04
Russian (208)	919	1.10
Scandinavian (140)	293	0.35

SECTION TWO

*Notes: † The Census 2010 population figure is used to calculate the percentages in the Hispanic Origin and Race categories. Ancestry percentages are based on the 2006-2010 American Community Survey population (not shown); ‡ Numbers in parentheses indicate the number of people reporting a single ancestry; * Numbers in parentheses indicate the number of persons reporting this race alone, not in combination with any other race; Please refer to the Explanation of Data for more information.*

Scotch-Irish (837)	2,200	2.63
Scottish (622)	2,645	3.16
Slavic (19)	70	0.08
Slovak (42)	200	0.24
Slovene (32)	55	0.07
Swedish (606)	2,706	3.24
Swiss (126)	450	0.54
Turkish (48)	48	0.06
Ukrainian (39)	215	0.26
Welsh (140)	970	1.16
West Indian, ex. Hispanic (28)	41	0.05
Dutch West Indian (11)	11	0.01
Jamaican (17)	17	0.02
West Indian (0)	13	0.02
Yugoslavian (84)	190	0.23

Hispanic Origin	Population	%
Hispanic or Latino (of any race)	21,191	24.56
Central American, ex. Mexican	522	0.61
Costa Rican	12	0.01
Guatemalan	209	0.24
Honduran	58	0.07
Nicaraguan	12	0.01
Panamanian	22	0.03
Salvadoran	207	0.24
Other Central American	2	<0.01
Cuban	88	0.10
Dominican Republic	28	0.03
Mexican	17,630	20.44
Puerto Rican	288	0.33
South American	361	0.42
Argentinean	45	0.05
Bolivian	10	0.01
Chilean	22	0.03
Colombian	81	0.09
Ecuadorian	28	0.03
Paraguayan	5	0.01
Peruvian	145	0.17
Uruguayan	2	<0.01
Venezuelan	20	0.02
Other South American	3	<0.01
Other Hispanic or Latino	2,274	2.64

Race*	Population	%
African-American/Black (815)	1,263	1.46
Not Hispanic (661)	1,001	1.16
Hispanic (154)	262	0.30
American Indian/Alaska Native (859)	1,642	1.90
Not Hispanic (413)	867	1.00
Hispanic (446)	775	0.90
Alaska Athabascan *(Ala. Nat.)* (5)	5	0.01
Aleut *(Alaska Native)* (3)	8	0.01
Apache (31)	88	0.10
Arapaho (2)	4	<0.01
Blackfeet (6)	25	0.03
Canadian/French Am. Ind. (4)	4	<0.01
Central American Ind. (1)	2	<0.01
Cherokee (57)	205	0.24
Cheyenne (0)	7	0.01
Chickasaw (6)	6	0.01
Chippewa (18)	31	0.04
Choctaw (12)	40	0.05
Comanche (1)	4	<0.01
Cree (0)	2	<0.01
Creek (3)	9	0.01
Crow (0)	1	<0.01
Delaware (4)	8	0.01
Hopi (2)	5	0.01
Houma (1)	4	<0.01
Inupiat *(Alaska Native)* (13)	18	0.02
Iroquois (12)	21	0.02
Kiowa (0)	4	<0.01
Menominee (2)	2	<0.01
Mexican American Ind. (52)	85	0.10
Navajo (86)	132	0.15
Osage (3)	6	0.01
Ottawa (0)	1	<0.01
Paiute (1)	2	<0.01
Pima (4)	7	0.01
Potawatomi (1)	6	0.01
Pueblo (3)	5	0.01
Seminole (2)	8	0.01
Shoshone (3)	4	<0.01
Sioux (71)	109	0.13
South American Ind. (6)	9	0.01
Spanish American Ind. (1)	1	<0.01
Tlingit-Haida *(Alaska Native)* (4)	5	0.01
Ute (10)	31	0.04
Yakama (1)	3	<0.01
Yaqui (0)	7	0.01
Asian (2,758)	3,496	4.05
Not Hispanic (2,696)	3,324	3.85
Hispanic (62)	172	0.20
Bangladeshi (19)	21	0.02
Bhutanese (2)	4	<0.01
Burmese (1)	1	<0.01
Cambodian (193)	211	0.24
Chinese, ex. Taiwanese (612)	723	0.84
Filipino (208)	412	0.48
Hmong (4)	8	0.01
Indian (758)	807	0.94
Indonesian (6)	17	0.02
Japanese (167)	315	0.37
Korean (196)	293	0.34
Laotian (20)	22	0.03
Malaysian (29)	42	0.05
Nepalese (128)	136	0.16
Pakistani (4)	12	0.01
Sri Lankan (1)	1	<0.01
Taiwanese (24)	28	0.03
Thai (53)	73	0.08
Vietnamese (239)	269	0.31
Hawaii Native/Pacific Islander (44)	159	0.18
Not Hispanic (40)	122	0.14
Hispanic (4)	37	0.04
Fijian (0)	1	<0.01
Guamanian/Chamorro (3)	14	0.02
Marshallese (2)	2	<0.01
Native Hawaiian (12)	53	0.06
Samoan (9)	19	0.02
Tongan (3)	3	<0.01
White (71,877)	74,156	85.96
Not Hispanic (59,772)	61,071	70.79
Hispanic (12,105)	13,085	15.17

Louisville

Place Type: City
County: Boulder
Population: 18,376†

Ancestry‡	Population	%
African, Sub-Saharan (70)	79	0.43
African (9)	18	0.10
Ethiopian (61)	61	0.33
American (703)	703	3.81
Arab (23)	23	0.12
Arab (11)	11	0.06
Syrian (12)	12	0.06
Armenian (6)	6	0.03
Australian (10)	23	0.12
Austrian (9)	112	0.61
Belgian (0)	31	0.17
Brazilian (0)	11	0.06
British (161)	338	1.83
Cajun (0)	17	0.09
Canadian (0)	8	0.04
Celtic (0)	10	0.05
Croatian (26)	48	0.26
Czech (104)	335	1.81
Czechoslovakian (12)	12	0.06
Danish (26)	185	1.00
Dutch (104)	427	2.31
Eastern European (34)	34	0.18
English (820)	2,980	16.13
European (696)	758	4.10
Finnish (8)	37	0.20
French, ex. Basque (227)	1,076	5.83
French Canadian (23)	104	0.56
German (1,293)	4,975	26.94
Greek (45)	98	0.53
Hungarian (0)	123	0.67
Iranian (78)	120	0.65
Irish (669)	2,932	15.87
Italian (461)	1,367	7.40
Lithuanian (19)	78	0.42
Northern European (94)	102	0.55
Norwegian (205)	643	3.48
Pennsylvania German (7)	19	0.10
Polish (184)	825	4.47
Portuguese (0)	115	0.62
Romanian (10)	18	0.10
Russian (131)	542	2.93
Scandinavian (40)	159	0.86
Scotch-Irish (130)	429	2.32
Scottish (123)	1,009	5.46
Slavic (47)	94	0.51
Slovak (10)	41	0.22
Swedish (151)	785	4.25
Swiss (18)	140	0.76
Ukrainian (21)	81	0.44
Welsh (32)	287	1.55
West Indian, ex. Hispanic (13)	13	0.07
Haitian (13)	13	0.07
Yugoslavian (24)	32	0.17

Hispanic Origin	Population	%
Hispanic or Latino (of any race)	1,318	7.17
Central American, ex. Mexican	81	0.44
Costa Rican	4	0.02
Guatemalan	15	0.08
Honduran	4	0.02
Nicaraguan	2	0.01
Salvadoran	54	0.29
Other Central American	2	0.01
Cuban	27	0.15
Dominican Republic	12	0.07
Mexican	809	4.40
Puerto Rican	50	0.27
South American	121	0.66
Argentinean	11	0.06
Bolivian	7	0.04
Chilean	16	0.09
Colombian	43	0.23
Ecuadorian	9	0.05
Peruvian	26	0.14
Uruguayan	2	0.01
Venezuelan	7	0.04
Other Hispanic or Latino	218	1.19

Race*	Population	%
African-American/Black (112)	188	1.02
Not Hispanic (104)	166	0.90
Hispanic (8)	22	0.12
American Indian/Alaska Native (79)	200	1.09
Not Hispanic (55)	147	0.80
Hispanic (24)	53	0.29
Aleut *(Alaska Native)* (0)	1	0.01
Apache (6)	10	0.05
Blackfeet (1)	6	0.03
Canadian/French Am. Ind. (0)	2	0.01
Cherokee (4)	20	0.11
Cheyenne (1)	2	0.01
Chickasaw (0)	3	0.02
Chippewa (3)	5	0.03
Choctaw (2)	7	0.04
Comanche (2)	3	0.02
Cree (0)	2	0.01
Creek (0)	1	0.01
Delaware (0)	1	0.01
Hopi (0)	4	0.02
Iroquois (3)	8	0.04
Kiowa (1)	1	0.01
Mexican American Ind. (1)	7	0.04
Navajo (3)	4	0.02
Pima (1)	1	0.01
Potawatomi (3)	3	0.02
Pueblo (8)	8	0.04
Seminole (0)	3	0.02
Shoshone (0)	1	0.01

*Notes: † The Census 2010 population figure is used to calculate the percentages in the Hispanic Origin and Race categories. Ancestry percentages are based on the 2006-2010 American Community Survey population (not shown); ‡ Numbers in parentheses indicate the number of people reporting a single ancestry; * Numbers in parentheses indicate the number of persons reporting this race alone, not in combination with any other race; Please refer to the Explanation of Data for more information.*

Sioux (5)	14	0.08
Spanish American Ind. (2)	3	0.02
Yuman (0)	2	0.01
Asian (729)	946	5.15
Not Hispanic (723)	926	5.04
Hispanic (6)	20	0.11
Bangladeshi (9)	9	0.05
Cambodian (16)	16	0.09
Chinese, ex. Taiwanese (206)	264	1.44
Filipino (38)	73	0.40
Hmong (15)	15	0.08
Indian (145)	168	0.91
Indonesian (1)	9	0.05
Japanese (98)	161	0.88
Korean (66)	97	0.53
Laotian (4)	6	0.03
Malaysian (1)	2	0.01
Nepalese (6)	6	0.03
Pakistani (2)	2	0.01
Sri Lankan (5)	8	0.04
Taiwanese (15)	18	0.10
Thai (16)	21	0.11
Vietnamese (52)	59	0.32
Hawaii Native/Pacific Islander (7)	17	0.09
Not Hispanic (7)	17	0.09
Native Hawaiian (6)	13	0.07
Samoan (1)	1	0.01
White (16,682)	17,105	93.08
Not Hispanic (15,782)	16,121	87.73
Hispanic (900)	984	5.35

Loveland

Place Type: City
County: Larimer
Population: 66,859†

Ancestry‡	Population	%
African, Sub-Saharan (56)	56	0.09
South African (56)	56	0.09
American (2,941)	2,941	4.59
Arab (43)	172	0.27
Lebanese (9)	39	0.06
Syrian (34)	133	0.21
Armenian (0)	19	0.03
Australian (12)	74	0.12
Austrian (99)	378	0.59
Belgian (13)	106	0.17
British (242)	396	0.62
Bulgarian (24)	24	0.04
Canadian (76)	124	0.19
Celtic (0)	38	0.06
Croatian (56)	118	0.18
Czech (198)	591	0.92
Czechoslovakian (23)	41	0.06
Danish (342)	1,488	2.32
Dutch (500)	1,415	2.21
Eastern European (19)	49	0.08
English (2,407)	8,424	13.14
European (1,454)	1,896	2.96
Finnish (0)	93	0.15
French, ex. Basque (341)	2,389	3.73
French Canadian (102)	342	0.53
German (7,244)	20,892	32.59
Greek (8)	97	0.15
Hungarian (51)	253	0.39
Icelander (0)	31	0.05
Irish (1,828)	8,969	13.99
Italian (631)	2,502	3.90
Latvian (0)	16	0.02
Lithuanian (41)	177	0.28
Northern European (183)	183	0.29
Norwegian (753)	2,375	3.70
Pennsylvania German (41)	57	0.09
Polish (407)	1,829	2.85
Portuguese (63)	273	0.43
Romanian (9)	26	0.04
Russian (162)	911	1.42
Scandinavian (166)	302	0.47
Scotch-Irish (463)	1,518	2.37
Scottish (464)	2,228	3.48
Serbian (0)	68	0.11
Slavic (11)	34	0.05
Slovak (23)	128	0.20
Slovene (11)	22	0.03
Swedish (489)	2,211	3.45
Swiss (77)	500	0.78
Turkish (0)	68	0.11
Ukrainian (37)	148	0.23
Welsh (91)	655	1.02
West Indian, ex. Hispanic (82)	127	0.20
Barbadian (0)	13	0.02
Belizean (0)	32	0.05
Jamaican (51)	51	0.08
West Indian (31)	31	0.05
Yugoslavian (16)	16	0.02

Hispanic Origin	Population	%
Hispanic or Latino (of any race)	7,816	11.69
Central American, ex. Mexican	117	0.17
Costa Rican	21	0.03
Guatemalan	28	0.04
Honduran	20	0.03
Nicaraguan	5	0.01
Panamanian	7	0.01
Salvadoran	34	0.05
Other Central American	2	<0.01
Cuban	44	0.07
Dominican Republic	15	0.02
Mexican	5,979	8.94
Puerto Rican	156	0.23
South American	101	0.15
Argentinean	17	0.03
Bolivian	1	<0.01
Chilean	4	0.01
Colombian	27	0.04
Ecuadorian	2	<0.01
Paraguayan	3	<0.01
Peruvian	36	0.05
Uruguayan	3	<0.01
Venezuelan	7	0.01
Other South American	1	<0.01
Other Hispanic or Latino	1,404	2.10

Race*	Population	%
African-American/Black (375)	670	1.00
Not Hispanic (335)	572	0.86
Hispanic (40)	98	0.15
American Indian/Alaska Native (568)	1,108	1.66
Not Hispanic (310)	684	1.02
Hispanic (258)	424	0.63
Alaska Athabascan *(Ala. Nat.)* (2)	2	<0.01
Aleut *(Alaska Native)* (1)	3	<0.01
Apache (37)	67	0.10
Arapaho (4)	13	0.02
Blackfeet (1)	14	0.02
Canadian/French Am. Ind. (0)	3	<0.01
Central American Ind. (1)	1	<0.01
Cherokee (40)	175	0.26
Cheyenne (1)	2	<0.01
Chickasaw (3)	9	0.01
Chippewa (25)	32	0.05
Choctaw (13)	24	0.04
Comanche (12)	14	0.02
Cree (1)	2	<0.01
Creek (6)	11	0.02
Crow (0)	2	<0.01
Delaware (2)	3	<0.01
Hopi (1)	6	0.01
Inupiat *(Alaska Native)* (0)	3	<0.01
Iroquois (8)	14	0.02
Kiowa (2)	2	<0.01
Lumbee (1)	1	<0.01
Menominee (1)	2	<0.01
Mexican American Ind. (23)	31	0.05
Navajo (34)	63	0.09
Osage (4)	6	0.01
Paiute (3)	8	0.01
Pima (1)	1	<0.01
Potawatomi (2)	12	0.02
Pueblo (4)	17	0.03
Puget Sound Salish (2)	5	0.01
Seminole (0)	1	<0.01
Shoshone (0)	2	<0.01
Sioux (59)	95	0.14
South American Ind. (3)	7	0.01
Spanish American Ind. (4)	5	0.01
Ute (4)	4	0.01
Yaqui (0)	5	0.01
Yuman (1)	1	<0.01
Asian (669)	1,030	1.54
Not Hispanic (640)	961	1.44
Hispanic (29)	69	0.10
Cambodian (5)	9	0.01
Chinese, ex. Taiwanese (146)	206	0.31
Filipino (93)	203	0.30
Indian (60)	79	0.12
Indonesian (2)	7	0.01
Japanese (77)	184	0.28
Korean (91)	132	0.20
Laotian (2)	3	<0.01
Malaysian (1)	1	<0.01
Nepalese (1)	1	<0.01
Pakistani (4)	6	0.01
Sri Lankan (1)	2	<0.01
Taiwanese (1)	4	0.01
Thai (16)	29	0.04
Vietnamese (128)	156	0.23
Hawaii Native/Pacific Islander (37)	114	0.17
Not Hispanic (34)	96	0.14
Hispanic (3)	18	0.03
Guamanian/Chamorro (4)	11	0.02
Marshallese (2)	5	0.01
Native Hawaiian (25)	71	0.11
Samoan (1)	6	0.01
Tongan (1)	4	0.01
White (61,153)	62,702	93.78
Not Hispanic (56,727)	57,650	86.23
Hispanic (4,426)	5,052	7.56

Montrose

Place Type: City
County: Montrose
Population: 19,132†

Ancestry‡	Population	%
African, Sub-Saharan (16)	16	0.09
Ethiopian (16)	16	0.09
American (1,043)	1,043	5.72
Arab (18)	18	0.10
Iraqi (10)	10	0.05
Lebanese (8)	8	0.04
Austrian (23)	52	0.29
Belgian (13)	13	0.07
British (0)	55	0.30
Canadian (33)	33	0.18
Czech (7)	43	0.24
Czechoslovakian (13)	13	0.07
Danish (8)	99	0.54
Dutch (66)	328	1.80
English (771)	2,478	13.59
European (115)	129	0.71
Finnish (26)	26	0.14
French, ex. Basque (98)	549	3.01
French Canadian (50)	196	1.07
German (1,164)	3,332	18.27
Greek (22)	22	0.12
Irish (580)	2,341	12.84
Italian (318)	1,023	5.61
Lithuanian (0)	9	0.05
Northern European (39)	39	0.21
Norwegian (37)	190	1.04
Polish (89)	288	1.58
Portuguese (22)	51	0.28
Russian (0)	18	0.10
Scandinavian (43)	62	0.34
Scotch-Irish (113)	263	1.44
Scottish (123)	558	3.06
Slovak (0)	52	0.29

*Notes: † The Census 2010 population figure is used to calculate the percentages in the Hispanic Origin and Race categories. Ancestry percentages are based on the 2006-2010 American Community Survey population (not shown); ‡ Numbers in parentheses indicate the number of people reporting a single ancestry; * Numbers in parentheses indicate the number of persons reporting this race alone, not in combination with any other race; Please refer to the Explanation of Data for more information.*

Swedish (68)	319	1.75
Swiss (20)	137	0.75
Ukrainian (12)	12	0.07
Welsh (45)	174	0.95
West Indian, ex. Hispanic (22)	22	0.12
West Indian (22)	22	0.12

Hispanic Origin	Population	%
Hispanic or Latino (of any race)	4,137	21.62
Central American, ex. Mexican	68	0.36
Costa Rican	5	0.03
Guatemalan	15	0.08
Honduran	5	0.03
Nicaraguan	11	0.06
Panamanian	4	0.02
Salvadoran	28	0.15
Cuban	7	0.04
Dominican Republic	1	0.01
Mexican	3,151	16.47
Puerto Rican	22	0.11
South American	25	0.13
Argentinean	2	0.01
Chilean	1	0.01
Colombian	5	0.03
Ecuadorian	4	0.02
Paraguayan	8	0.04
Peruvian	4	0.02
Venezuelan	1	0.01
Other Hispanic or Latino	863	4.51

Race*	Population	%
African-American/Black (90)	145	0.76
Not Hispanic (69)	110	0.57
Hispanic (21)	35	0.18
American Indian/Alaska Native (238)	458	2.39
Not Hispanic (93)	232	1.21
Hispanic (145)	226	1.18
Aleut *(Alaska Native)* (1)	3	0.02
Apache (7)	18	0.09
Arapaho (1)	1	0.01
Blackfeet (0)	4	0.02
Cherokee (11)	62	0.32
Chickasaw (1)	1	0.01
Chippewa (3)	5	0.03
Choctaw (5)	8	0.04
Comanche (0)	2	0.01
Cree (0)	1	0.01
Creek (0)	3	0.02
Delaware (0)	4	0.02
Iroquois (4)	5	0.03
Kiowa (0)	1	0.01
Mexican American Ind. (37)	39	0.20
Navajo (20)	32	0.17
Osage (0)	1	0.01
Ottawa (1)	1	0.01
Potawatomi (2)	2	0.01
Pueblo (5)	6	0.03
Sioux (7)	14	0.07
Spanish American Ind. (0)	2	0.01
Ute (13)	16	0.08
Yaqui (3)	3	0.02
Asian (137)	214	1.12
Not Hispanic (133)	195	1.02
Hispanic (4)	19	0.10
Cambodian (0)	2	0.01
Chinese, ex. Taiwanese (22)	29	0.15
Filipino (38)	62	0.32
Indian (8)	21	0.11
Indonesian (1)	1	0.01
Japanese (14)	23	0.12
Korean (14)	26	0.14
Nepalese (7)	7	0.04
Taiwanese (3)	3	0.02
Thai (5)	10	0.05
Vietnamese (12)	19	0.10
Hawaii Native/Pacific Islander (15)	30	0.16
Not Hispanic (14)	22	0.11
Hispanic (1)	8	0.04
Guamanian/Chamorro (3)	3	0.02
Native Hawaiian (7)	9	0.05
Samoan (0)	3	0.02
White (16,507)	16,992	88.81
Not Hispanic (14,380)	14,635	76.49
Hispanic (2,127)	2,357	12.32

Northglenn

Place Type: City
County: Adams
Population: 35,789[†]

Ancestry[‡]	Population	%
African, Sub-Saharan (134)	134	0.38
African (93)	93	0.26
Ethiopian (9)	9	0.03
Kenyan (18)	18	0.05
Other Sub-Saharan African (14)	14	0.04
American (2,767)	2,767	7.88
Assyrian/Chaldean/Syriac (11)	11	0.03
Australian (11)	11	0.03
Austrian (24)	81	0.23
Basque (14)	14	0.04
British (43)	70	0.20
Bulgarian (142)	142	0.40
Cajun (0)	17	0.05
Canadian (51)	89	0.25
Celtic (23)	23	0.07
Croatian (55)	65	0.19
Czech (71)	321	0.91
Czechoslovakian (0)	17	0.05
Danish (36)	260	0.74
Dutch (95)	536	1.53
Eastern European (15)	28	0.08
English (799)	2,932	8.35
European (281)	370	1.05
Finnish (13)	64	0.18
French, ex. Basque (31)	826	2.35
French Canadian (18)	65	0.19
German (2,028)	7,046	20.06
Hungarian (87)	222	0.63
Irish (724)	3,917	11.15
Italian (286)	1,041	2.96
Lithuanian (32)	62	0.18
Northern European (15)	15	0.04
Norwegian (131)	460	1.31
Polish (459)	804	2.29
Portuguese (0)	28	0.08
Russian (53)	281	0.80
Scandinavian (40)	165	0.47
Scotch-Irish (167)	797	2.27
Scottish (152)	595	1.69
Serbian (0)	29	0.08
Slovak (32)	55	0.16
Swedish (162)	525	1.49
Swiss (10)	41	0.12
Ukrainian (31)	50	0.14
Welsh (28)	209	0.59

Hispanic Origin	Population	%
Hispanic or Latino (of any race)	10,957	30.62
Central American, ex. Mexican	216	0.60
Costa Rican	11	0.03
Guatemalan	56	0.16
Honduran	45	0.13
Nicaraguan	4	0.01
Panamanian	17	0.05
Salvadoran	81	0.23
Other Central American	2	0.01
Cuban	31	0.09
Dominican Republic	16	0.04
Mexican	7,820	21.85
Puerto Rican	139	0.39
South American	139	0.39
Argentinean	2	0.01
Bolivian	3	0.01
Chilean	8	0.02
Colombian	45	0.13
Ecuadorian	11	0.03
Peruvian	58	0.16
Uruguayan	4	0.01
Venezuelan	7	0.02
Other South American	1	<0.01
Other Hispanic or Latino	2,596	7.25

Race*	Population	%
African-American/Black (810)	1,116	3.12
Not Hispanic (710)	943	2.63
Hispanic (100)	173	0.48
American Indian/Alaska Native (473)	913	2.55
Not Hispanic (252)	461	1.29
Hispanic (221)	452	1.26
Alaska Athabascan *(Ala. Nat.)* (1)	1	<0.01
Aleut *(Alaska Native)* (2)	2	0.01
Apache (23)	55	0.15
Arapaho (0)	1	<0.01
Blackfeet (8)	21	0.06
Canadian/French Am. Ind. (3)	5	0.01
Cherokee (28)	97	0.27
Cheyenne (2)	3	0.01
Chickasaw (3)	6	0.02
Chippewa (3)	16	0.04
Choctaw (8)	19	0.05
Comanche (5)	7	0.02
Cree (0)	1	<0.01
Creek (4)	5	0.01
Crow (0)	1	<0.01
Delaware (0)	1	<0.01
Hopi (0)	2	0.01
Houma (1)	3	0.01
Iroquois (1)	4	0.01
Kiowa (4)	5	0.01
Lumbee (0)	1	<0.01
Mexican American Ind. (17)	37	0.10
Navajo (61)	95	0.27
Osage (6)	7	0.02
Ottawa (0)	2	0.01
Paiute (0)	1	<0.01
Potawatomi (2)	5	0.01
Pueblo (13)	20	0.06
Puget Sound Salish (2)	2	0.01
Seminole (0)	3	0.01
Shoshone (2)	4	0.01
Sioux (27)	52	0.15
South American Ind. (2)	3	0.01
Spanish American Ind. (12)	20	0.06
Ute (8)	15	0.04
Yaqui (5)	7	0.02
Yup'ik *(Alaska Native)* (1)	1	<0.01
Asian (1,333)	1,631	4.56
Not Hispanic (1,288)	1,504	4.20
Hispanic (45)	127	0.35
Bhutanese (9)	9	0.03
Burmese (10)	10	0.03
Cambodian (29)	35	0.10
Chinese, ex. Taiwanese (129)	178	0.50
Filipino (111)	190	0.53
Hmong (226)	236	0.66
Indian (112)	142	0.40
Indonesian (1)	4	0.01
Japanese (83)	161	0.45
Korean (70)	111	0.31
Laotian (37)	44	0.12
Nepalese (53)	57	0.16
Pakistani (46)	55	0.15
Taiwanese (3)	10	0.03
Thai (15)	21	0.06
Vietnamese (323)	352	0.98
Hawaii Native/Pacific Islander (49)	108	0.30
Not Hispanic (42)	88	0.25
Hispanic (7)	20	0.06
Guamanian/Chamorro (3)	7	0.02
Marshallese (10)	10	0.03
Native Hawaiian (15)	50	0.14
Samoan (0)	6	0.02
White (27,430)	28,820	80.53
Not Hispanic (21,817)	22,437	62.69
Hispanic (5,613)	6,383	17.84

*Notes: † The Census 2010 population figure is used to calculate the percentages in the Hispanic Origin and Race categories. Ancestry percentages are based on the 2006-2010 American Community Survey population (not shown); ‡ Numbers in parentheses indicate the number of people reporting a single ancestry; * Numbers in parentheses indicate the number of persons reporting this race alone, not in combination with any other race; Please refer to the Explanation of Data for more information.*

Parker

Place Type: Town
County: Douglas
Population: 45,297†

Ancestry‡	Population	%
African, Sub-Saharan (71)	71	0.17
African (19)	19	0.04
South African (52)	52	0.12
American (1,782)	1,782	4.19
Arab (65)	192	0.45
Arab (10)	23	0.05
Egyptian (7)	7	0.02
Lebanese (27)	119	0.28
Moroccan (12)	25	0.06
Palestinian (9)	18	0.04
Armenian (0)	12	0.03
Austrian (38)	133	0.31
Belgian (0)	11	0.03
British (151)	339	0.80
Cajun (0)	3	0.01
Canadian (86)	135	0.32
Carpatho Rusyn (0)	20	0.05
Croatian (0)	109	0.26
Czech (37)	225	0.53
Czechoslovakian (37)	82	0.19
Danish (131)	566	1.33
Dutch (213)	602	1.41
Eastern European (50)	59	0.14
English (1,774)	5,786	13.60
European (914)	1,021	2.40
Finnish (25)	151	0.35
French, ex. Basque (295)	1,918	4.51
French Canadian (108)	376	0.88
German (3,831)	12,645	29.72
Greek (16)	124	0.29
Hungarian (34)	136	0.32
Icelander (0)	31	0.07
Iranian (0)	29	0.07
Irish (1,482)	7,761	18.24
Italian (1,069)	3,159	7.42
Lithuanian (11)	68	0.16
Northern European (102)	102	0.24
Norwegian (594)	1,455	3.42
Pennsylvania German (0)	21	0.05
Polish (204)	1,188	2.79
Portuguese (77)	217	0.51
Romanian (12)	12	0.03
Russian (150)	716	1.68
Scandinavian (104)	229	0.54
Scotch-Irish (233)	1,075	2.53
Scottish (380)	1,275	3.00
Serbian (0)	31	0.07
Slovak (0)	88	0.21
Slovene (11)	21	0.05
Swedish (464)	1,663	3.91
Swiss (162)	242	0.57
Turkish (0)	13	0.03
Ukrainian (50)	109	0.26
Welsh (58)	559	1.31
West Indian, ex. Hispanic (44)	44	0.10
British West Indian (4)	4	0.01
Trinidadian/Tobagonian (5)	5	0.01
West Indian (35)	35	0.08
Yugoslavian (133)	156	0.37

Hispanic Origin	Population	%
Hispanic or Latino (of any race)	3,712	8.19
Central American, ex. Mexican	148	0.33
Costa Rican	12	0.03
Guatemalan	34	0.08
Honduran	15	0.03
Nicaraguan	10	0.02
Panamanian	43	0.09
Salvadoran	32	0.07
Other Central American	2	<0.01
Cuban	75	0.17
Dominican Republic	31	0.07
Mexican	2,229	4.92
Puerto Rican	229	0.51
South American	256	0.57
Argentinean	23	0.05
Bolivian	5	0.01
Chilean	27	0.06
Colombian	77	0.17
Ecuadorian	17	0.04
Peruvian	70	0.15
Uruguayan	2	<0.01
Venezuelan	33	0.07
Other South American	2	<0.01
Other Hispanic or Latino	744	1.64

Race*	Population	%
African-American/Black (691)	1,004	2.22
Not Hispanic (645)	908	2.00
Hispanic (46)	96	0.21
American Indian/Alaska Native (210)	476	1.05
Not Hispanic (142)	357	0.79
Hispanic (68)	119	0.26
Alaska Athabascan *(Ala. Nat.)* (3)	3	0.01
Aleut *(Alaska Native)* (2)	3	0.01
Apache (16)	26	0.06
Arapaho (0)	1	<0.01
Blackfeet (0)	14	0.03
Canadian/French Am. Ind. (0)	1	<0.01
Central American Ind. (4)	6	0.01
Cherokee (21)	76	0.17
Chickasaw (6)	10	0.02
Chippewa (4)	9	0.02
Choctaw (1)	16	0.04
Comanche (0)	1	<0.01
Creek (5)	6	0.01
Crow (3)	4	0.01
Hopi (4)	4	0.01
Iroquois (7)	14	0.03
Lumbee (2)	6	0.01
Mexican American Ind. (6)	10	0.02
Navajo (22)	33	0.07
Osage (5)	6	0.01
Paiute (1)	1	<0.01
Potawatomi (6)	6	0.01
Pueblo (4)	10	0.02
Seminole (0)	2	<0.01
Shoshone (1)	2	<0.01
Sioux (12)	22	0.05
South American Ind. (0)	2	<0.01
Tlingit-Haida *(Alaska Native)* (2)	4	0.01
Ute (0)	4	0.01
Yup'ik *(Alaska Native)* (3)	4	0.01
Asian (1,463)	2,046	4.52
Not Hispanic (1,444)	1,968	4.34
Hispanic (19)	78	0.17
Bangladeshi (12)	14	0.03
Burmese (1)	2	<0.01
Cambodian (1)	10	0.02
Chinese, ex. Taiwanese (173)	273	0.60
Filipino (161)	302	0.67
Hmong (4)	4	0.01
Indian (438)	507	1.12
Indonesian (8)	22	0.05
Japanese (87)	234	0.52
Korean (292)	388	0.86
Laotian (7)	10	0.02
Malaysian (0)	2	<0.01
Nepalese (12)	13	0.03
Pakistani (40)	50	0.11
Sri Lankan (4)	4	0.01
Taiwanese (11)	11	0.02
Thai (19)	37	0.08
Vietnamese (111)	152	0.34
Hawaii Native/Pacific Islander (45)	133	0.29
Not Hispanic (41)	111	0.25
Hispanic (4)	22	0.05
Guamanian/Chamorro (9)	20	0.04
Marshallese (2)	2	<0.01
Native Hawaiian (11)	50	0.11
Samoan (11)	26	0.06
Tongan (0)	3	0.01
White (40,797)	41,984	92.69
Not Hispanic (38,287)	39,194	86.53
Hispanic (2,510)	2,790	6.16

Pueblo West

Place Type: CDP
County: Pueblo
Population: 29,637†

Ancestry‡	Population	%
African, Sub-Saharan (24)	24	0.09
African (24)	24	0.09
Albanian (16)	16	0.06
American (1,098)	1,098	3.94
Arab (59)	59	0.21
Arab (10)	10	0.04
Other Arab (49)	49	0.18
Austrian (64)	136	0.49
Basque (0)	8	0.03
Belgian (92)	118	0.42
British (80)	120	0.43
Canadian (8)	31	0.11
Croatian (0)	17	0.06
Czech (60)	199	0.71
Czechoslovakian (18)	32	0.11
Danish (96)	346	1.24
Dutch (116)	398	1.43
Eastern European (24)	24	0.09
English (1,282)	3,677	13.20
European (173)	201	0.72
Finnish (16)	97	0.35
French, ex. Basque (135)	955	3.43
French Canadian (31)	122	0.44
German (2,270)	6,323	22.70
Greek (9)	115	0.41
Hungarian (56)	86	0.31
Iranian (47)	47	0.17
Irish (732)	3,070	11.02
Italian (875)	2,491	8.94
Lithuanian (13)	28	0.10
Northern European (133)	148	0.53
Norwegian (203)	558	2.00
Pennsylvania German (35)	57	0.20
Polish (296)	772	2.77
Portuguese (14)	45	0.16
Romanian (0)	1	<0.01
Russian (75)	197	0.71
Scandinavian (0)	19	0.07
Scotch-Irish (70)	311	1.12
Scottish (247)	668	2.40
Serbian (0)	56	0.20
Slavic (2)	17	0.06
Slovak (68)	123	0.44
Slovene (48)	164	0.59
Swedish (162)	772	2.77
Swiss (12)	254	0.91
Welsh (96)	269	0.97
Yugoslavian (165)	522	1.87

Hispanic Origin	Population	%
Hispanic or Latino (of any race)	6,787	22.90
Central American, ex. Mexican	71	0.24
Guatemalan	18	0.06
Honduran	8	0.03
Nicaraguan	15	0.05
Panamanian	8	0.03
Salvadoran	22	0.07
Cuban	34	0.11
Dominican Republic	1	<0.01
Mexican	4,218	14.23
Puerto Rican	107	0.36
South American	76	0.26
Argentinean	7	0.02
Bolivian	5	0.02
Chilean	8	0.03
Colombian	16	0.05
Ecuadorian	5	0.02
Peruvian	22	0.07
Uruguayan	1	<0.01
Venezuelan	12	0.04

*Notes: † The Census 2010 population figure is used to calculate the percentages in the Hispanic Origin and Race categories. Ancestry percentages are based on the 2006-2010 American Community Survey population (not shown); ‡ Numbers in parentheses indicate the number of people reporting a single ancestry; * Numbers in parentheses indicate the number of persons reporting this race alone, not in combination with any other race; Please refer to the Explanation of Data for more information.*

Other Hispanic or Latino	2,280	7.69

Race*	Population	%
African-American/Black (387)	579	1.95
Not Hispanic (322)	455	1.54
Hispanic (65)	124	0.42
American Indian/Alaska Native (364)	683	2.30
Not Hispanic (175)	378	1.28
Hispanic (189)	305	1.03
Aleut *(Alaska Native)* (1)	1	<0.01
Apache (27)	50	0.17
Arapaho (1)	1	<0.01
Blackfeet (4)	10	0.03
Cherokee (27)	108	0.36
Cheyenne (1)	9	0.03
Chickasaw (4)	4	0.01
Chippewa (4)	12	0.04
Choctaw (16)	32	0.11
Comanche (3)	11	0.04
Creek (0)	3	0.01
Crow (3)	3	0.01
Delaware (0)	2	0.01
Houma (1)	1	<0.01
Iroquois (1)	6	0.02
Lumbee (1)	2	0.01
Mexican American Ind. (16)	22	0.07
Navajo (43)	63	0.21
Osage (0)	1	<0.01
Ottawa (4)	4	0.01
Paiute (2)	2	0.01
Potawatomi (1)	1	<0.01
Pueblo (6)	7	0.02
Seminole (1)	4	0.01
Shoshone (1)	1	<0.01
Sioux (13)	21	0.07
South American Ind. (0)	1	<0.01
Spanish American Ind. (3)	5	0.02
Tlingit-Haida *(Alaska Native)* (1)	2	0.01
Tohono O'Odham (0)	2	0.01
Ute (3)	9	0.03
Yaqui (1)	1	<0.01
Asian (284)	468	1.58
Not Hispanic (256)	393	1.33
Hispanic (28)	75	0.25
Cambodian (17)	21	0.07
Chinese, ex. Taiwanese (47)	69	0.23
Filipino (71)	117	0.39
Indian (29)	34	0.11
Indonesian (2)	2	0.01
Japanese (32)	82	0.28
Korean (32)	60	0.20
Laotian (2)	2	0.01
Nepalese (1)	1	<0.01
Pakistani (0)	1	<0.01
Taiwanese (1)	2	0.01
Thai (8)	15	0.05
Vietnamese (11)	22	0.07
Hawaii Native/Pacific Islander (32)	58	0.20
Not Hispanic (20)	37	0.12
Hispanic (12)	21	0.07
Guamanian/Chamorro (10)	13	0.04
Native Hawaiian (18)	36	0.12
Samoan (0)	4	0.01
White (25,860)	26,698	90.08
Not Hispanic (21,552)	22,031	74.34
Hispanic (4,308)	4,667	15.75

Pueblo

Place Type: City
County: Pueblo
Population: 106,595†

Ancestry‡	Population	%
Afghan (13)	13	0.01
African, Sub-Saharan (32)	129	0.12
African (32)	120	0.11
South African (0)	9	0.01
Albanian (8)	8	0.01
American (2,762)	2,762	2.61
Arab (30)	85	0.08
Arab (0)	12	0.01
Lebanese (30)	73	0.07
Armenian (4)	4	<0.01
Austrian (162)	487	0.46
Basque (0)	12	0.01
Belgian (73)	143	0.13
Brazilian (16)	26	0.02
British (65)	165	0.16
Cajun (28)	28	0.03
Canadian (62)	137	0.13
Celtic (0)	22	0.02
Croatian (115)	268	0.25
Czech (93)	496	0.47
Czechoslovakian (41)	107	0.10
Danish (96)	313	0.30
Dutch (246)	1,227	1.16
Eastern European (17)	17	0.02
English (2,759)	8,348	7.88
European (384)	397	0.37
Finnish (34)	80	0.08
French, ex. Basque (235)	2,024	1.91
French Canadian (51)	299	0.28
German (4,618)	15,094	14.25
German Russian (10)	10	0.01
Greek (49)	236	0.22
Hungarian (96)	228	0.22
Iranian (11)	45	0.04
Irish (2,237)	9,917	9.36
Italian (3,092)	7,475	7.05
Latvian (15)	58	0.05
Lithuanian (28)	41	0.04
Luxemburger (0)	14	0.01
Macedonian (0)	8	0.01
Northern European (10)	10	0.01
Norwegian (257)	836	0.79
Pennsylvania German (10)	10	0.01
Polish (458)	1,539	1.45
Portuguese (25)	168	0.16
Romanian (86)	133	0.13
Russian (206)	568	0.54
Scandinavian (88)	129	0.12
Scotch-Irish (485)	1,652	1.56
Scottish (474)	1,613	1.52
Serbian (51)	89	0.08
Slavic (61)	153	0.14
Slovak (187)	345	0.33
Slovene (588)	1,107	1.04
Swedish (412)	1,400	1.32
Swiss (0)	135	0.13
Turkish (0)	9	0.01
Ukrainian (24)	95	0.09
Welsh (123)	587	0.55
West Indian, ex. Hispanic (146)	159	0.15
Jamaican (118)	131	0.12
Trinidadian/Tobagonian (3)	3	<0.01
West Indian (25)	25	0.02
Yugoslavian (109)	284	0.27

Hispanic Origin	Population	%
Hispanic or Latino (of any race)	53,098	49.81
Central American, ex. Mexican	198	0.19
Costa Rican	26	0.02
Guatemalan	32	0.03
Honduran	42	0.04
Nicaraguan	5	<0.01
Panamanian	41	0.04
Salvadoran	49	0.05
Other Central American	3	<0.01
Cuban	63	0.06
Dominican Republic	24	0.02
Mexican	32,847	30.81
Puerto Rican	614	0.58
South American	124	0.12
Argentinean	19	0.02
Bolivian	2	<0.01
Chilean	11	0.01
Colombian	32	0.03
Ecuadorian	12	0.01
Paraguayan	2	<0.01
Peruvian	30	0.03
Uruguayan	5	<0.01
Venezuelan	11	0.01
Other Hispanic or Latino	19,228	18.04

Race*	Population	%
African-American/Black (2,686)	3,532	3.31
Not Hispanic (2,221)	2,660	2.50
Hispanic (465)	872	0.82
American Indian/Alaska Native (2,381)	4,012	3.76
Not Hispanic (682)	1,311	1.23
Hispanic (1,699)	2,701	2.53
Alaska Athabascan *(Ala. Nat.)* (1)	1	<0.01
Aleut *(Alaska Native)* (3)	5	<0.01
Apache (203)	440	0.41
Arapaho (11)	26	0.02
Blackfeet (24)	83	0.08
Canadian/French Am. Ind. (1)	9	0.01
Central American Ind. (0)	1	<0.01
Cherokee (139)	452	0.42
Cheyenne (21)	37	0.03
Chickasaw (4)	7	0.01
Chippewa (20)	39	0.04
Choctaw (23)	54	0.05
Colville (0)	2	<0.01
Comanche (12)	25	0.02
Cree (1)	2	<0.01
Creek (4)	13	0.01
Crow (6)	6	0.01
Delaware (0)	2	<0.01
Hopi (1)	3	<0.01
Houma (1)	1	<0.01
Inupiat *(Alaska Native)* (4)	7	0.01
Iroquois (1)	7	0.01
Kiowa (0)	3	<0.01
Lumbee (0)	1	<0.01
Menominee (1)	1	<0.01
Mexican American Ind. (144)	188	0.18
Navajo (177)	340	0.32
Osage (3)	3	<0.01
Ottawa (0)	1	<0.01
Paiute (5)	14	0.01
Pima (6)	6	0.01
Potawatomi (15)	22	0.02
Pueblo (29)	62	0.06
Seminole (7)	13	0.01
Shoshone (3)	9	0.01
Sioux (91)	147	0.14
South American Ind. (7)	8	0.01
Spanish American Ind. (46)	63	0.06
Tlingit-Haida *(Alaska Native)* (2)	3	<0.01
Ute (29)	55	0.05
Yaqui (4)	5	<0.01
Yuman (2)	3	<0.01
Asian (890)	1,408	1.32
Not Hispanic (792)	1,085	1.02
Hispanic (98)	323	0.30
Bangladeshi (5)	5	<0.01
Burmese (1)	1	<0.01
Cambodian (3)	8	0.01
Chinese, ex. Taiwanese (170)	225	0.21
Filipino (169)	307	0.29
Hmong (8)	8	0.01
Indian (127)	177	0.17
Indonesian (3)	4	<0.01
Japanese (95)	224	0.21
Korean (120)	200	0.19
Laotian (16)	19	0.02
Malaysian (0)	1	<0.01
Nepalese (11)	11	0.01
Pakistani (18)	21	0.02
Taiwanese (5)	12	0.01
Thai (18)	37	0.03
Vietnamese (71)	88	0.08
Hawaii Native/Pacific Islander (112)	269	0.25
Not Hispanic (79)	146	0.14
Hispanic (33)	123	0.12
Guamanian/Chamorro (29)	42	0.04
Native Hawaiian (46)	136	0.13
Samoan (21)	45	0.04

*Notes: † The Census 2010 population figure is used to calculate the percentages in the Hispanic Origin and Race categories. Ancestry percentages are based on the 2006-2010 American Community Survey population (not shown); ‡ Numbers in parentheses indicate the number of people reporting a single ancestry; * Numbers in parentheses indicate the number of persons reporting this race alone, not in combination with any other race; Please refer to the Explanation of Data for more information.*

Tongan (3)	3	<0.01
White (80,159)	83,844	78.66
Not Hispanic (48,195)	49,391	46.34
Hispanic (31,964)	34,453	32.32

Redlands

Place Type: CDP
County: Mesa
Population: 8,685†

Ancestry‡	Population	%
Albanian (0)	11	0.14
American (407)	407	5.21
Australian (0)	30	0.38
Austrian (18)	25	0.32
Basque (0)	46	0.59
Belgian (60)	73	0.94
British (15)	29	0.37
Czech (14)	29	0.37
Czechoslovakian (0)	22	0.28
Danish (0)	29	0.37
Dutch (72)	229	2.93
English (444)	1,519	19.46
Estonian (18)	18	0.23
European (241)	241	3.09
Finnish (0)	27	0.35
French, ex. Basque (11)	263	3.37
French Canadian (9)	27	0.35
German (779)	2,327	29.81
German Russian (11)	11	0.14
Hungarian (11)	56	0.72
Irish (377)	1,346	17.24
Italian (188)	453	5.80
Lithuanian (0)	15	0.19
Norwegian (31)	128	1.64
Pennsylvania German (0)	10	0.13
Polish (35)	93	1.19
Portuguese (0)	24	0.31
Russian (14)	49	0.63
Scandinavian (0)	12	0.15
Scotch-Irish (85)	256	3.28
Scottish (113)	309	3.96
Slavic (17)	17	0.22
Slovak (0)	22	0.28
Slovene (0)	28	0.36
Swedish (113)	335	4.29
Swiss (41)	80	1.02
Ukrainian (0)	11	0.14
Welsh (13)	170	2.18
Yugoslavian (30)	38	0.49

Hispanic Origin	Population	%
Hispanic or Latino (of any race)	552	6.36
Central American, ex. Mexican	6	0.07
Costa Rican	2	0.02
Panamanian	3	0.03
Salvadoran	1	0.01
Cuban	8	0.09
Mexican	352	4.05
Puerto Rican	16	0.18
South American	18	0.21
Argentinean	8	0.09
Chilean	3	0.03
Colombian	3	0.03
Peruvian	4	0.05
Other Hispanic or Latino	152	1.75

Race*	Population	%
African-American/Black (11)	34	0.39
Not Hispanic (9)	31	0.36
Hispanic (2)	3	0.03
American Indian/Alaska Native (32)	95	1.09
Not Hispanic (23)	70	0.81
Hispanic (9)	25	0.29
Alaska Athabascan *(Ala. Nat.)* (1)	1	0.01
Apache (3)	7	0.08
Blackfeet (1)	3	0.03
Cherokee (4)	20	0.23
Choctaw (0)	2	0.02
Iroquois (3)	6	0.07
Kiowa (3)	3	0.03
Mexican American Ind. (1)	1	0.01
Navajo (0)	1	0.01
Osage (0)	1	0.01
Potawatomi (1)	1	0.01
Shoshone (3)	3	0.03
Sioux (4)	5	0.06
South American Ind. (2)	2	0.02
Ute (1)	3	0.03
Asian (67)	103	1.19
Not Hispanic (66)	97	1.12
Hispanic (1)	6	0.07
Chinese, ex. Taiwanese (12)	17	0.20
Filipino (14)	21	0.24
Indian (7)	8	0.09
Indonesian (0)	1	0.01
Japanese (17)	20	0.23
Korean (5)	14	0.16
Laotian (1)	1	0.01
Pakistani (1)	4	0.05
Taiwanese (0)	1	0.01
Thai (6)	13	0.15
Vietnamese (2)	2	0.02
Hawaii Native/Pacific Islander (8)	12	0.14
Not Hispanic (8)	9	0.10
Hispanic (0)	3	0.03
Native Hawaiian (1)	4	0.05
Samoan (2)	2	0.02
White (8,257)	8,389	96.59
Not Hispanic (7,926)	8,017	92.31
Hispanic (331)	372	4.28

Rifle

Place Type: City
County: Garfield
Population: 9,172†

Ancestry‡	Population	%
American (368)	368	4.14
Arab (0)	16	0.18
Arab (0)	16	0.18
Austrian (0)	12	0.14
British (13)	110	1.24
Canadian (38)	38	0.43
Czech (0)	60	0.68
Danish (0)	158	1.78
Dutch (72)	378	4.26
English (243)	1,113	12.53
European (110)	110	1.24
Finnish (0)	84	0.95
French, ex. Basque (36)	396	4.46
French Canadian (11)	48	0.54
German (386)	1,679	18.91
Greek (34)	34	0.38
Hungarian (0)	15	0.17
Irish (181)	1,402	15.79
Italian (197)	542	6.10
Norwegian (95)	200	2.25
Polish (40)	123	1.39
Scandinavian (11)	11	0.12
Scotch-Irish (120)	131	1.48
Scottish (12)	132	1.49
Slavic (9)	22	0.25
Swedish (77)	304	3.42
Swiss (0)	77	0.87
Ukrainian (15)	15	0.17
Welsh (0)	56	0.63
Yugoslavian (0)	15	0.17

Hispanic Origin	Population	%
Hispanic or Latino (of any race)	2,791	30.43
Central American, ex. Mexican	154	1.68
Guatemalan	51	0.56
Honduran	14	0.15
Nicaraguan	5	0.05
Salvadoran	84	0.92
Cuban	3	0.03
Mexican	2,267	24.72
Puerto Rican	20	0.22
South American	12	0.13
Argentinean	4	0.04
Ecuadorian	1	0.01
Paraguayan	2	0.02
Peruvian	2	0.02
Uruguayan	2	0.02
Venezuelan	1	0.01
Other Hispanic or Latino	335	3.65

Race*	Population	%
African-American/Black (47)	93	1.01
Not Hispanic (46)	72	0.78
Hispanic (1)	21	0.23
American Indian/Alaska Native (120)	226	2.46
Not Hispanic (67)	133	1.45
Hispanic (53)	93	1.01
Apache (5)	11	0.12
Arapaho (1)	2	0.02
Blackfeet (1)	6	0.07
Cherokee (11)	32	0.35
Cheyenne (0)	5	0.05
Chickasaw (1)	4	0.04
Chippewa (3)	4	0.04
Choctaw (5)	7	0.08
Creek (0)	1	0.01
Delaware (0)	1	0.01
Inupiat *(Alaska Native)* (1)	1	0.01
Mexican American Ind. (16)	20	0.22
Navajo (7)	16	0.17
Osage (1)	1	0.01
Ottawa (1)	1	0.01
Potawatomi (1)	2	0.02
Pueblo (0)	2	0.02
Sioux (3)	13	0.14
South American Ind. (1)	1	0.01
Spanish American Ind. (1)	2	0.02
Tlingit-Haida *(Alaska Native)* (0)	1	0.01
Ute (1)	1	0.01
Asian (52)	87	0.95
Not Hispanic (47)	79	0.86
Hispanic (5)	8	0.09
Cambodian (1)	1	0.01
Chinese, ex. Taiwanese (23)	31	0.34
Filipino (4)	14	0.15
Indian (1)	2	0.02
Indonesian (3)	4	0.04
Japanese (8)	20	0.22
Korean (5)	8	0.09
Vietnamese (2)	6	0.07
Hawaii Native/Pacific Islander (9)	16	0.17
Not Hispanic (9)	14	0.15
Hispanic (0)	2	0.02
Guamanian/Chamorro (4)	4	0.04
Native Hawaiian (5)	10	0.11
White (7,430)	7,707	84.03
Not Hispanic (6,078)	6,196	67.55
Hispanic (1,352)	1,511	16.47

Roxborough Park

Place Type: CDP
County: Douglas
Population: 9,099†

Ancestry‡	Population	%
African, Sub-Saharan (25)	25	0.27
South African (25)	25	0.27
American (445)	445	4.87
Arab (8)	8	0.09
Other Arab (8)	8	0.09
Armenian (29)	29	0.32
Austrian (0)	29	0.32
Basque (0)	18	0.20
Brazilian (14)	14	0.15
British (28)	45	0.49
Canadian (26)	40	0.44
Croatian (0)	16	0.18
Czech (10)	65	0.71
Czechoslovakian (0)	11	0.12

*Notes: † The Census 2010 population figure is used to calculate the percentages in the Hispanic Origin and Race categories. Ancestry percentages are based on the 2006-2010 American Community Survey population (not shown); ‡ Numbers in parentheses indicate the number of people reporting a single ancestry; * Numbers in parentheses indicate the number of persons reporting this race alone, not in combination with any other race; Please refer to the Explanation of Data for more information.*

Danish (16)	85	0.93
Dutch (169)	423	4.63
English (296)	1,039	11.38
European (121)	153	1.68
French, ex. Basque (31)	255	2.79
French Canadian (26)	40	0.44
German (907)	2,687	29.42
Greek (61)	61	0.67
Hungarian (36)	69	0.76
Irish (445)	1,796	19.66
Italian (169)	449	4.92
Lithuanian (16)	16	0.18
Northern European (12)	12	0.13
Norwegian (15)	151	1.65
Pennsylvania German (16)	16	0.18
Polish (118)	308	3.37
Romanian (16)	29	0.32
Russian (122)	135	1.48
Scandinavian (9)	9	0.10
Scotch-Irish (29)	98	1.07
Scottish (32)	205	2.24
Slavic (0)	8	0.09
Slovak (0)	47	0.51
Slovene (0)	15	0.16
Swedish (161)	258	2.82
Swiss (0)	13	0.14
Ukrainian (0)	17	0.19
Welsh (0)	73	0.80

Hispanic Origin	Population	%
Hispanic or Latino (of any race)	749	8.23
Central American, ex. Mexican	28	0.31
Guatemalan	3	0.03
Honduran	2	0.02
Nicaraguan	3	0.03
Panamanian	4	0.04
Salvadoran	16	0.18
Cuban	21	0.23
Dominican Republic	2	0.02
Mexican	458	5.03
Puerto Rican	25	0.27
South American	34	0.37
Argentinean	4	0.04
Chilean	8	0.09
Colombian	15	0.16
Peruvian	5	0.05
Other South American	2	0.02
Other Hispanic or Latino	181	1.99

Race*	Population	%
African-American/Black (55)	103	1.13
Not Hispanic (49)	88	0.97
Hispanic (6)	15	0.16
American Indian/Alaska Native (55)	142	1.56
Not Hispanic (31)	89	0.98
Hispanic (24)	53	0.58
Alaska Athabascan *(Ala. Nat.)* (1)	1	0.01
Apache (3)	5	0.05
Blackfeet (0)	3	0.03
Cherokee (1)	16	0.18
Cheyenne (1)	1	0.01
Chickasaw (0)	5	0.05
Chippewa (1)	2	0.02
Choctaw (5)	13	0.14
Creek (1)	1	0.01
Menominee (1)	1	0.01
Mexican American Ind. (1)	2	0.02
Navajo (2)	5	0.05
Pueblo (0)	3	0.03
Sioux (3)	6	0.07
South American Ind. (0)	3	0.03
Ute (0)	1	0.01
Yaqui (0)	2	0.02
Asian (158)	253	2.78
Not Hispanic (152)	243	2.67
Hispanic (6)	10	0.11
Chinese, ex. Taiwanese (33)	43	0.47
Filipino (18)	44	0.48
Indian (24)	31	0.34
Indonesian (3)	5	0.05
Japanese (16)	34	0.37
Korean (26)	37	0.41
Pakistani (2)	2	0.02
Taiwanese (1)	1	0.01
Thai (9)	14	0.15
Vietnamese (15)	29	0.32
Hawaii Native/Pacific Islander (5)	20	0.22
Not Hispanic (5)	17	0.19
Hispanic (0)	3	0.03
Marshallese (1)	1	0.01
Native Hawaiian (3)	11	0.12
White (8,460)	8,678	95.37
Not Hispanic (7,918)	8,083	88.83
Hispanic (542)	595	6.54

Security-Widefield

Place Type: CDP
County: El Paso
Population: 32,882†

Ancestry‡	Population	%
African, Sub-Saharan (358)	391	1.23
African (348)	381	1.19
Kenyan (10)	10	0.03
American (1,483)	1,483	4.65
Arab (0)	29	0.09
Lebanese (0)	8	0.03
Syrian (0)	21	0.07
Armenian (15)	45	0.14
Austrian (19)	141	0.44
Belgian (0)	44	0.14
British (88)	180	0.56
Canadian (28)	95	0.30
Celtic (0)	14	0.04
Croatian (19)	19	0.06
Czech (9)	152	0.48
Danish (38)	77	0.24
Dutch (77)	428	1.34
English (893)	2,762	8.66
European (447)	471	1.48
Finnish (7)	41	0.13
French, ex. Basque (91)	954	2.99
French Canadian (56)	175	0.55
German (2,598)	6,456	20.25
Greek (21)	46	0.14
Hungarian (83)	174	0.55
Icelander (0)	13	0.04
Irish (845)	3,823	11.99
Italian (444)	1,288	4.04
Lithuanian (19)	37	0.12
Norwegian (272)	617	1.93
Pennsylvania German (20)	28	0.09
Polish (132)	702	2.20
Portuguese (9)	56	0.18
Romanian (32)	57	0.18
Russian (30)	107	0.34
Scandinavian (59)	101	0.32
Scotch-Irish (107)	299	0.94
Scottish (263)	680	2.13
Slavic (11)	11	0.03
Slovak (24)	33	0.10
Slovene (0)	23	0.07
Swedish (179)	644	2.02
Swiss (40)	61	0.19
Ukrainian (0)	13	0.04
Welsh (42)	183	0.57
West Indian, ex. Hispanic (18)	213	0.67
Barbadian (10)	10	0.03
Jamaican (8)	114	0.36
West Indian (0)	89	0.28

Hispanic Origin	Population	%
Hispanic or Latino (of any race)	5,890	17.91
Central American, ex. Mexican	257	0.78
Costa Rican	6	0.02
Guatemalan	31	0.09
Honduran	21	0.06
Nicaraguan	13	0.04
Panamanian	123	0.37
Salvadoran	59	0.18
Other Central American	4	0.01
Cuban	24	0.07
Dominican Republic	32	0.10
Mexican	3,497	10.63
Puerto Rican	688	2.09
South American	73	0.22
Argentinean	2	0.01
Bolivian	3	0.01
Chilean	7	0.02
Colombian	19	0.06
Ecuadorian	21	0.06
Peruvian	20	0.06
Other South American	1	<0.01
Other Hispanic or Latino	1,319	4.01

Race*	Population	%
African-American/Black (3,314)	4,198	12.77
Not Hispanic (3,051)	3,753	11.41
Hispanic (263)	445	1.35
American Indian/Alaska Native (342)	846	2.57
Not Hispanic (205)	552	1.68
Hispanic (137)	294	0.89
Alaska Athabascan *(Ala. Nat.)* (5)	13	0.04
Aleut *(Alaska Native)* (1)	1	<0.01
Apache (23)	58	0.18
Blackfeet (5)	17	0.05
Cherokee (23)	131	0.40
Cheyenne (0)	2	0.01
Chickasaw (1)	8	0.02
Chippewa (3)	8	0.02
Choctaw (4)	14	0.04
Colville (0)	3	0.01
Comanche (3)	6	0.02
Cree (1)	3	0.01
Creek (3)	12	0.04
Crow (0)	5	0.02
Hopi (0)	2	0.01
Houma (0)	3	0.01
Inupiat *(Alaska Native)* (2)	2	0.01
Iroquois (8)	13	0.04
Kiowa (0)	1	<0.01
Lumbee (8)	13	0.04
Menominee (1)	2	0.01
Mexican American Ind. (9)	20	0.06
Navajo (48)	75	0.23
Osage (0)	1	<0.01
Ottawa (0)	1	<0.01
Pima (2)	2	0.01
Potawatomi (2)	3	0.01
Pueblo (6)	7	0.02
Puget Sound Salish (5)	8	0.02
Seminole (3)	4	0.01
Sioux (15)	33	0.10
South American Ind. (5)	5	0.02
Tohono O'Odham (3)	3	0.01
Ute (8)	16	0.05
Yakama (0)	1	<0.01
Yaqui (5)	10	0.03
Asian (968)	1,705	5.19
Not Hispanic (930)	1,548	4.71
Hispanic (38)	157	0.48
Burmese (0)	1	<0.01
Cambodian (0)	9	0.03
Chinese, ex. Taiwanese (62)	138	0.42
Filipino (362)	579	1.76
Indian (16)	39	0.12
Indonesian (3)	10	0.03
Japanese (135)	303	0.92
Korean (270)	499	1.52
Laotian (4)	8	0.02
Malaysian (0)	3	0.01
Pakistani (0)	1	<0.01
Sri Lankan (4)	4	0.01
Taiwanese (7)	15	0.05
Thai (22)	61	0.19
Vietnamese (38)	73	0.22
Hawaii Native/Pacific Islander (255)	488	1.48
Not Hispanic (246)	423	1.29
Hispanic (9)	65	0.20

*Notes: † The Census 2010 population figure is used to calculate the percentages in the Hispanic Origin and Race categories. Ancestry percentages are based on the 2006-2010 American Community Survey population (not shown); ‡ Numbers in parentheses indicate the number of people reporting a single ancestry; * Numbers in parentheses indicate the number of persons reporting this race alone, not in combination with any other race; Please refer to the Explanation of Data for more information.*

Fijian (1)	1	<0.01
Guamanian/Chamorro (125)	202	0.61
Native Hawaiian (44)	163	0.50
Samoan (56)	80	0.24
Tongan (7)	10	0.03
White (23,944)	25,867	78.67
Not Hispanic (21,001)	22,338	67.93
Hispanic (2,943)	3,529	10.73

Sherrelwood

Place Type: CDP
County: Adams
Population: 18,287†

Ancestry‡	Population	%
American (874)	874	4.95
Arab (2)	32	0.18
Arab (2)	4	0.02
Lebanese (0)	22	0.12
Moroccan (0)	6	0.03
British (18)	18	0.10
Bulgarian (0)	10	0.06
Canadian (0)	68	0.39
Croatian (0)	31	0.18
Czech (11)	53	0.30
Czechoslovakian (15)	15	0.09
Danish (11)	50	0.28
Dutch (29)	151	0.86
English (136)	637	3.61
European (188)	188	1.07
Finnish (11)	28	0.16
French, ex. Basque (95)	281	1.59
French Canadian (22)	43	0.24
German (1,048)	2,521	14.29
Greek (9)	18	0.10
Hungarian (30)	30	0.17
Irish (206)	1,194	6.77
Italian (223)	507	2.87
Norwegian (55)	122	0.69
Polish (59)	218	1.24
Russian (9)	121	0.69
Scandinavian (8)	33	0.19
Scotch-Irish (32)	137	0.78
Scottish (45)	234	1.33
Slavic (0)	12	0.07
Slovene (0)	11	0.06
Swedish (77)	221	1.25
Swiss (8)	176	1.00
Ukrainian (0)	11	0.06
Welsh (27)	36	0.20

Hispanic Origin	Population	%
Hispanic or Latino (of any race)	10,773	58.91
Central American, ex. Mexican	185	1.01
Costa Rican	2	0.01
Guatemalan	81	0.44
Honduran	28	0.15
Nicaraguan	4	0.02
Panamanian	1	0.01
Salvadoran	64	0.35
Other Central American	5	0.03
Cuban	12	0.07
Dominican Republic	4	0.02
Mexican	8,676	47.44
Puerto Rican	39	0.21
South American	48	0.26
Argentinean	3	0.02
Bolivian	3	0.02
Chilean	2	0.01
Colombian	8	0.04
Ecuadorian	5	0.03
Peruvian	19	0.10
Venezuelan	8	0.04
Other Hispanic or Latino	1,809	9.89

Race*	Population	%
African-American/Black (247)	390	2.13
Not Hispanic (207)	277	1.51
Hispanic (40)	113	0.62
American Indian/Alaska Native (377)	598	3.27
Not Hispanic (134)	228	1.25
Hispanic (243)	370	2.02
Apache (39)	58	0.32
Arapaho (0)	1	0.01
Blackfeet (1)	2	0.01
Cherokee (21)	60	0.33
Cheyenne (5)	7	0.04
Chickasaw (2)	2	0.01
Chippewa (2)	6	0.03
Choctaw (6)	7	0.04
Comanche (1)	3	0.02
Creek (1)	1	0.01
Crow (1)	1	0.01
Delaware (3)	3	0.02
Inupiat *(Alaska Native)* (1)	1	0.01
Iroquois (1)	4	0.02
Kiowa (5)	5	0.03
Mexican American Ind. (32)	51	0.28
Navajo (32)	68	0.37
Pima (0)	2	0.01
Pueblo (3)	7	0.04
Seminole (5)	5	0.03
Shoshone (0)	4	0.02
Sioux (42)	48	0.26
Spanish American Ind. (7)	8	0.04
Tlingit-Haida *(Alaska Native)* (0)	1	0.01
Tohono O'Odham (0)	2	0.01
Ute (5)	8	0.04
Asian (429)	529	2.89
Not Hispanic (409)	471	2.58
Hispanic (20)	58	0.32
Cambodian (7)	9	0.05
Chinese, ex. Taiwanese (33)	45	0.25
Filipino (31)	53	0.29
Hmong (52)	54	0.30
Indian (6)	13	0.07
Indonesian (3)	4	0.02
Japanese (71)	109	0.60
Korean (8)	25	0.14
Laotian (50)	57	0.31
Nepalese (3)	3	0.02
Pakistani (2)	2	0.01
Taiwanese (1)	3	0.02
Thai (10)	15	0.08
Vietnamese (122)	126	0.69
Hawaii Native/Pacific Islander (37)	52	0.28
Not Hispanic (33)	39	0.21
Hispanic (4)	13	0.07
Guamanian/Chamorro (13)	20	0.11
Native Hawaiian (3)	6	0.03
Samoan (10)	10	0.05
White (12,292)	12,950	70.82
Not Hispanic (6,490)	6,697	36.62
Hispanic (5,802)	6,253	34.19

Steamboat Springs

Place Type: City
County: Routt
Population: 12,088†

Ancestry‡	Population	%
American (198)	198	1.68
Arab (66)	80	0.68
Lebanese (55)	69	0.58
Other Arab (11)	11	0.09
Australian (57)	57	0.48
Austrian (14)	14	0.12
Belgian (17)	35	0.30
Canadian (36)	70	0.59
Croatian (11)	23	0.19
Czech (123)	182	1.54
Czechoslovakian (0)	11	0.09
Danish (19)	78	0.66
Dutch (172)	293	2.48
Eastern European (0)	18	0.15
English (705)	1,821	15.44
European (355)	355	3.01
Finnish (0)	51	0.43
French, ex. Basque (46)	408	3.46
French Canadian (12)	41	0.35
German (1,020)	2,489	21.10
Greek (51)	128	1.09
Hungarian (6)	40	0.34
Irish (430)	1,985	16.83
Italian (234)	579	4.91
Lithuanian (12)	12	0.10
Northern European (92)	101	0.86
Norwegian (25)	358	3.03
Polish (262)	511	4.33
Portuguese (0)	69	0.58
Romanian (35)	35	0.30
Russian (89)	307	2.60
Scandinavian (22)	103	0.87
Scotch-Irish (227)	346	2.93
Scottish (185)	558	4.73
Slovak (33)	47	0.40
Swedish (35)	326	2.76
Swiss (0)	280	2.37
Ukrainian (10)	24	0.20
Welsh (19)	146	1.24
West Indian, ex. Hispanic (11)	11	0.09
Bahamian (11)	11	0.09

Hispanic Origin	Population	%
Hispanic or Latino (of any race)	1,025	8.48
Central American, ex. Mexican	35	0.29
Costa Rican	6	0.05
Honduran	19	0.16
Nicaraguan	7	0.06
Panamanian	1	0.01
Salvadoran	2	0.02
Cuban	13	0.11
Mexican	777	6.43
Puerto Rican	38	0.31
South American	83	0.69
Argentinean	6	0.05
Bolivian	3	0.02
Chilean	2	0.02
Colombian	24	0.20
Ecuadorian	8	0.07
Peruvian	40	0.33
Other Hispanic or Latino	79	0.65

Race*	Population	%
African-American/Black (78)	108	0.89
Not Hispanic (77)	103	0.85
Hispanic (1)	5	0.04
American Indian/Alaska Native (49)	112	0.93
Not Hispanic (33)	78	0.65
Hispanic (16)	34	0.28
Apache (0)	3	0.02
Blackfeet (1)	3	0.02
Cherokee (8)	24	0.20
Chippewa (0)	3	0.02
Choctaw (1)	2	0.02
Creek (0)	1	0.01
Mexican American Ind. (1)	4	0.03
Navajo (2)	5	0.04
Osage (1)	3	0.02
Paiute (2)	2	0.02
Pueblo (1)	1	0.01
Shoshone (0)	1	0.01
Tlingit-Haida *(Alaska Native)* (0)	1	0.01
Tohono O'Odham (0)	1	0.01
Tsimshian *(Alaska Native)* (0)	1	0.01
Ute (1)	2	0.02
Asian (96)	167	1.38
Not Hispanic (91)	150	1.24
Hispanic (5)	17	0.14
Cambodian (1)	1	0.01
Chinese, ex. Taiwanese (40)	48	0.40
Filipino (11)	25	0.21
Hmong (1)	1	0.01
Indian (13)	21	0.17
Indonesian (3)	5	0.04
Japanese (10)	38	0.31
Korean (13)	19	0.16
Nepalese (3)	3	0.02

SECTION TWO

*Notes: † The Census 2010 population figure is used to calculate the percentages in the Hispanic Origin and Race categories. Ancestry percentages are based on the 2006-2010 American Community Survey population (not shown); ‡ Numbers in parentheses indicate the number of people reporting a single ancestry; * Numbers in parentheses indicate the number of persons reporting this race alone, not in combination with any other race; Please refer to the Explanation of Data for more information.*

Thai (1)	3	0.02
Hawaii Native/Pacific Islander (5)	20	0.17
Not Hispanic (4)	18	0.15
Hispanic (1)	2	0.02
Guamanian/Chamorro (1)	1	0.01
Native Hawaiian (0)	8	0.07
Samoan (0)	2	0.02
White (11,367)	11,539	95.46
Not Hispanic (10,720)	10,846	89.73
Hispanic (647)	693	5.73

Sterling

Place Type: City
County: Logan
Population: 14,777†

Ancestry‡	Population	%
American (630)	630	4.38
Arab (0)	32	0.22
Lebanese (0)	32	0.22
Australian (0)	16	0.11
Belgian (0)	13	0.09
British (0)	81	0.56
Canadian (17)	156	1.08
Czech (26)	179	1.24
Czechoslovakian (10)	16	0.11
Danish (30)	256	1.78
Dutch (26)	168	1.17
English (386)	1,284	8.92
European (126)	126	0.88
French, ex. Basque (45)	383	2.66
French Canadian (113)	145	1.01
German (2,288)	5,082	35.31
German Russian (33)	33	0.23
Irish (143)	1,446	10.05
Italian (105)	394	2.74
Norwegian (252)	423	2.94
Pennsylvania German (11)	15	0.10
Polish (104)	135	0.94
Russian (24)	101	0.70
Scotch-Irish (137)	308	2.14
Scottish (61)	278	1.93
Swedish (126)	376	2.61
Swiss (0)	14	0.10
Welsh (8)	223	1.55
Yugoslavian (0)	6	0.04

Hispanic Origin	Population	%
Hispanic or Latino (of any race)	3,084	20.87
Central American, ex. Mexican	18	0.12
Guatemalan	1	0.01
Honduran	10	0.07
Nicaraguan	1	0.01
Panamanian	4	0.03
Salvadoran	2	0.01
Cuban	1	0.01
Dominican Republic	1	0.01
Mexican	2,168	14.67
Puerto Rican	8	0.05
South American	6	0.04
Argentinean	3	0.02
Chilean	1	0.01
Colombian	2	0.01
Other Hispanic or Latino	882	5.97

Race*	Population	%
African-American/Black (873)	940	6.36
Not Hispanic (856)	909	6.15
Hispanic (17)	31	0.21
American Indian/Alaska Native (238)	343	2.32
Not Hispanic (164)	239	1.62
Hispanic (74)	104	0.70
Apache (3)	11	0.07
Arapaho (1)	1	0.01
Blackfeet (1)	7	0.05
Cherokee (5)	32	0.22
Cheyenne (1)	1	0.01
Chippewa (4)	5	0.03
Choctaw (4)	9	0.06
Comanche (1)	1	0.01
Iroquois (0)	1	0.01
Mexican American Ind. (4)	5	0.03
Navajo (7)	12	0.08
Pueblo (5)	7	0.05
Seminole (1)	1	0.01
Shoshone (1)	1	0.01
Sioux (21)	28	0.19
Spanish American Ind. (4)	5	0.03
Tlingit-Haida *(Alaska Native)* (0)	1	0.01
Ute (5)	8	0.05
Yaqui (1)	1	0.01
Asian (107)	130	0.88
Not Hispanic (99)	113	0.76
Hispanic (8)	17	0.12
Bangladeshi (2)	2	0.01
Chinese, ex. Taiwanese (17)	18	0.12
Filipino (15)	18	0.12
Hmong (2)	2	0.01
Indian (11)	12	0.08
Indonesian (4)	4	0.03
Japanese (10)	20	0.14
Korean (5)	8	0.05
Thai (2)	2	0.01
Vietnamese (1)	1	0.01
Hawaii Native/Pacific Islander (10)	24	0.16
Not Hispanic (9)	16	0.11
Hispanic (1)	8	0.05
Fijian (2)	3	0.02
Guamanian/Chamorro (1)	1	0.01
Native Hawaiian (1)	5	0.03
Samoan (1)	2	0.01
White (12,567)	12,785	86.52
Not Hispanic (10,413)	10,544	71.35
Hispanic (2,154)	2,241	15.17

Stonegate

Place Type: CDP
County: Douglas
Population: 8,962†

Ancestry‡	Population	%
American (526)	526	6.01
Arab (6)	6	0.07
Arab (6)	6	0.07
Armenian (19)	19	0.22
Austrian (8)	51	0.58
Belgian (0)	38	0.43
British (27)	105	1.20
Celtic (0)	46	0.53
Czech (0)	36	0.41
Czechoslovakian (11)	24	0.27
Danish (0)	59	0.67
Dutch (13)	102	1.17
English (490)	1,417	16.19
European (60)	71	0.81
French, ex. Basque (52)	300	3.43
German (882)	2,722	31.09
Greek (48)	92	1.05
Hungarian (22)	35	0.40
Irish (354)	1,376	15.72
Italian (180)	727	8.30
Lithuanian (0)	8	0.09
Norwegian (100)	432	4.93
Polish (86)	197	2.25
Portuguese (0)	30	0.34
Russian (23)	91	1.04
Scandinavian (13)	25	0.29
Scotch-Irish (111)	329	3.76
Scottish (95)	312	3.56
Serbian (0)	18	0.21
Slovak (80)	233	2.66
Swedish (102)	379	4.33
Swiss (31)	46	0.53
Welsh (7)	19	0.22

Hispanic Origin	Population	%
Hispanic or Latino (of any race)	676	7.54
Central American, ex. Mexican	23	0.26
Costa Rican	3	0.03
Guatemalan	7	0.08
Honduran	4	0.04
Salvadoran	9	0.10
Cuban	8	0.09
Dominican Republic	4	0.04
Mexican	389	4.34
Puerto Rican	56	0.62
South American	50	0.56
Argentinean	6	0.07
Chilean	5	0.06
Colombian	5	0.06
Ecuadorian	9	0.10
Peruvian	11	0.12
Venezuelan	14	0.16
Other Hispanic or Latino	146	1.63

Race*	Population	%
African-American/Black (72)	109	1.22
Not Hispanic (66)	102	1.14
Hispanic (6)	7	0.08
American Indian/Alaska Native (29)	60	0.67
Not Hispanic (16)	42	0.47
Hispanic (13)	18	0.20
Apache (0)	1	0.01
Blackfeet (0)	1	0.01
Canadian/French Am. Ind. (1)	1	0.01
Cherokee (5)	11	0.12
Chickasaw (3)	4	0.04
Chippewa (0)	2	0.02
Choctaw (4)	5	0.06
Creek (0)	1	0.01
Iroquois (0)	3	0.03
Mexican American Ind. (0)	1	0.01
Navajo (0)	2	0.02
Potawatomi (2)	2	0.02
Puget Sound Salish (1)	1	0.01
Sioux (0)	5	0.06
Spanish American Ind. (1)	2	0.02
Asian (270)	382	4.26
Not Hispanic (263)	362	4.04
Hispanic (7)	20	0.22
Cambodian (1)	1	0.01
Chinese, ex. Taiwanese (72)	92	1.03
Filipino (27)	47	0.52
Indian (39)	49	0.55
Indonesian (6)	8	0.09
Japanese (26)	57	0.64
Korean (54)	82	0.91
Laotian (1)	2	0.02
Malaysian (1)	1	0.01
Pakistani (0)	4	0.04
Taiwanese (4)	9	0.10
Thai (10)	14	0.16
Vietnamese (16)	23	0.26
Hawaii Native/Pacific Islander (3)	10	0.11
Not Hispanic (3)	9	0.10
Hispanic (0)	1	0.01
Native Hawaiian (1)	8	0.09
White (8,266)	8,460	94.40
Not Hispanic (7,772)	7,921	88.38
Hispanic (494)	539	6.01

Superior

Place Type: Town
County: Boulder
Population: 12,483†

Ancestry‡	Population	%
African, Sub-Saharan (12)	12	0.10
South African (12)	12	0.10
American (515)	515	4.35
Arab (80)	104	0.88
Lebanese (80)	91	0.77
Moroccan (0)	13	0.11
Armenian (0)	51	0.43
Australian (36)	36	0.30
Austrian (39)	151	1.27
Belgian (0)	17	0.14

*Notes: † The Census 2010 population figure is used to calculate the percentages in the Hispanic Origin and Race categories. Ancestry percentages are based on the 2006-2010 American Community Survey population (not shown); ‡ Numbers in parentheses indicate the number of people reporting a single ancestry; * Numbers in parentheses indicate the number of persons reporting this race alone, not in combination with any other race; Please refer to the Explanation of Data for more information.*

Ancestry	Population	%
British (98)	218	1.84
Canadian (0)	11	0.09
Czech (22)	175	1.48
Czechoslovakian (13)	26	0.22
Danish (76)	140	1.18
Dutch (44)	302	2.55
English (341)	1,585	13.37
Estonian (0)	14	0.12
European (258)	294	2.48
Finnish (0)	140	1.18
French, ex. Basque (104)	359	3.03
French Canadian (49)	130	1.10
German (499)	2,600	21.94
Greek (21)	85	0.72
Hungarian (0)	81	0.68
Irish (450)	1,610	13.58
Italian (372)	1,067	9.00
Lithuanian (37)	37	0.31
Northern European (70)	70	0.59
Norwegian (50)	268	2.26
Polish (57)	570	4.81
Russian (174)	384	3.24
Scandinavian (95)	109	0.92
Scotch-Irish (39)	163	1.38
Scottish (126)	547	4.62
Slovak (16)	90	0.76
Swedish (64)	362	3.05
Swiss (0)	39	0.33
Turkish (21)	21	0.18
Ukrainian (0)	14	0.12
Welsh (21)	144	1.21
Yugoslavian (0)	31	0.26

Hispanic Origin	Population	%
Hispanic or Latino (of any race)	827	6.63
Central American, ex. Mexican	37	0.30
Costa Rican	10	0.08
Guatemalan	13	0.10
Honduran	3	0.02
Nicaraguan	1	0.01
Panamanian	6	0.05
Salvadoran	4	0.03
Cuban	25	0.20
Dominican Republic	1	0.01
Mexican	421	3.37
Puerto Rican	57	0.46
South American	137	1.10
Argentinean	16	0.13
Bolivian	1	0.01
Chilean	16	0.13
Colombian	33	0.26
Ecuadorian	9	0.07
Paraguayan	1	0.01
Peruvian	31	0.25
Venezuelan	30	0.24
Other Hispanic or Latino	149	1.19

Race*	Population	%
African-American/Black (111)	210	1.68
Not Hispanic (103)	185	1.48
Hispanic (8)	25	0.20
American Indian/Alaska Native (24)	106	0.85
Not Hispanic (16)	75	0.60
Hispanic (8)	31	0.25
Apache (2)	2	0.02
Blackfeet (1)	5	0.04
Central American Ind. (1)	2	0.02
Cherokee (1)	11	0.09
Chickasaw (1)	2	0.02
Chippewa (2)	5	0.04
Choctaw (0)	2	0.02
Colville (0)	1	0.01
Creek (0)	1	0.01
Crow (0)	1	0.01
Hopi (0)	1	0.01
Mexican American Ind. (2)	6	0.05
Navajo (1)	2	0.02
Osage (0)	1	0.01
Pueblo (0)	1	0.01
Puget Sound Salish (1)	1	0.01
Sioux (4)	12	0.10
South American Ind. (1)	7	0.06
Tlingit-Haida *(Alaska Native)* (0)	1	0.01
Ute (0)	2	0.02
Yakama (0)	1	0.01
Asian (1,726)	2,005	16.06
Not Hispanic (1,724)	1,988	15.93
Hispanic (2)	17	0.14
Bangladeshi (0)	3	0.02
Burmese (5)	10	0.08
Cambodian (1)	1	0.01
Chinese, ex. Taiwanese (575)	652	5.22
Filipino (41)	95	0.76
Hmong (23)	23	0.18
Indian (583)	620	4.97
Indonesian (2)	6	0.05
Japanese (70)	127	1.02
Korean (199)	225	1.80
Laotian (10)	10	0.08
Malaysian (3)	3	0.02
Nepalese (27)	29	0.23
Pakistani (23)	27	0.22
Sri Lankan (1)	5	0.04
Taiwanese (23)	28	0.22
Thai (13)	22	0.18
Vietnamese (89)	106	0.85
Hawaii Native/Pacific Islander (5)	25	0.20
Not Hispanic (4)	21	0.17
Hispanic (1)	4	0.03
Guamanian/Chamorro (1)	2	0.02
Native Hawaiian (2)	17	0.14
Samoan (1)	1	0.01
White (10,032)	10,454	83.75
Not Hispanic (9,404)	9,751	78.11
Hispanic (628)	703	5.63

The Pinery

Place Type: CDP
County: Douglas
Population: 10,517†

Ancestry‡	Population	%
American (352)	352	3.46
Arab (17)	50	0.49
Lebanese (17)	50	0.49
Armenian (51)	60	0.59
Austrian (0)	41	0.40
British (16)	42	0.41
Cajun (17)	17	0.17
Canadian (17)	17	0.17
Croatian (0)	15	0.15
Czech (74)	141	1.38
Czechoslovakian (0)	17	0.17
Danish (76)	227	2.23
Dutch (96)	213	2.09
Eastern European (44)	44	0.43
English (521)	1,913	18.79
European (235)	276	2.71
Finnish (0)	16	0.16
French, ex. Basque (66)	503	4.94
French Canadian (22)	60	0.59
German (837)	3,002	29.48
Greek (26)	26	0.26
Hungarian (9)	36	0.35
Irish (490)	1,782	17.50
Italian (157)	555	5.45
Lithuanian (0)	14	0.14
Northern European (11)	21	0.21
Norwegian (52)	252	2.47
Pennsylvania German (9)	9	0.09
Polish (84)	393	3.86
Russian (49)	111	1.09
Scandinavian (32)	69	0.68
Scotch-Irish (96)	266	2.61
Scottish (146)	487	4.78
Serbian (14)	24	0.24
Slovak (53)	98	0.96
Slovene (14)	29	0.28
Swedish (216)	638	6.27
Swiss (0)	37	0.36
Ukrainian (17)	46	0.45
Welsh (33)	83	0.82
West Indian, ex. Hispanic (0)	16	0.16
Haitian (0)	16	0.16
Yugoslavian (0)	10	0.10

Hispanic Origin	Population	%
Hispanic or Latino (of any race)	545	5.18
Central American, ex. Mexican	22	0.21
Costa Rican	3	0.03
Guatemalan	12	0.11
Nicaraguan	2	0.02
Panamanian	3	0.03
Salvadoran	2	0.02
Cuban	10	0.10
Mexican	353	3.36
Puerto Rican	31	0.29
South American	35	0.33
Argentinean	5	0.05
Bolivian	1	0.01
Chilean	9	0.09
Colombian	11	0.10
Ecuadorian	3	0.03
Peruvian	3	0.03
Uruguayan	2	0.02
Venezuelan	1	0.01
Other Hispanic or Latino	94	0.89

Race*	Population	%
African-American/Black (148)	213	2.03
Not Hispanic (143)	199	1.89
Hispanic (5)	14	0.13
American Indian/Alaska Native (34)	135	1.28
Not Hispanic (30)	109	1.04
Hispanic (4)	26	0.25
Apache (0)	12	0.11
Blackfeet (1)	4	0.04
Cherokee (5)	26	0.25
Chippewa (2)	3	0.03
Choctaw (1)	7	0.07
Iroquois (0)	3	0.03
Mexican American Ind. (1)	1	0.01
Navajo (1)	9	0.09
Ottawa (0)	1	0.01
Potawatomi (0)	3	0.03
Sioux (0)	4	0.04
Ute (0)	2	0.02
Asian (190)	278	2.64
Not Hispanic (187)	268	2.55
Hispanic (3)	10	0.10
Burmese (0)	1	0.01
Chinese, ex. Taiwanese (34)	55	0.52
Filipino (37)	55	0.52
Hmong (5)	5	0.05
Indian (23)	24	0.23
Japanese (31)	70	0.67
Korean (42)	50	0.48
Taiwanese (0)	1	0.01
Thai (3)	10	0.10
Vietnamese (9)	9	0.09
Hawaii Native/Pacific Islander (5)	23	0.22
Not Hispanic (4)	20	0.19
Hispanic (1)	3	0.03
Guamanian/Chamorro (3)	3	0.03
Native Hawaiian (0)	12	0.11
Samoan (1)	6	0.06
White (9,755)	9,993	95.02
Not Hispanic (9,380)	9,572	91.01
Hispanic (375)	421	4.00

Thornton

Place Type: City
County: Adams
Population: 118,772†

Ancestry‡	Population	%
Afghan (135)	135	0.12
African, Sub-Saharan (246)	316	0.28

SECTION TWO

*Notes: † The Census 2010 population figure is used to calculate the percentages in the Hispanic Origin and Race categories. Ancestry percentages are based on the 2006-2010 American Community Survey population (not shown); ‡ Numbers in parentheses indicate the number of people reporting a single ancestry; * Numbers in parentheses indicate the number of persons reporting this race alone, not in combination with any other race; Please refer to the Explanation of Data for more information.*

African (156)	226	0.20
Ethiopian (20)	20	0.02
Nigerian (70)	70	0.06
American (7,889)	7,889	7.02
Arab (276)	395	0.35
Egyptian (12)	12	0.01
Iraqi (123)	123	0.11
Jordanian (31)	31	0.03
Lebanese (60)	151	0.13
Moroccan (9)	9	0.01
Palestinian (0)	23	0.02
Syrian (0)	5	<0.01
Other Arab (41)	41	0.04
Assyrian/Chaldean/Syriac (15)	15	0.01
Australian (16)	16	0.01
Austrian (100)	313	0.28
Belgian (0)	10	0.01
Brazilian (41)	81	0.07
British (213)	366	0.33
Bulgarian (180)	362	0.32
Canadian (107)	237	0.21
Celtic (12)	87	0.08
Croatian (39)	108	0.10
Czech (159)	826	0.74
Czechoslovakian (100)	230	0.20
Danish (73)	580	0.52
Dutch (316)	1,810	1.61
Eastern European (37)	37	0.03
English (2,558)	10,031	8.93
European (983)	1,076	0.96
Finnish (86)	334	0.30
French, ex. Basque (382)	2,927	2.60
French Canadian (275)	670	0.60
German (6,964)	23,898	21.27
Greek (159)	348	0.31
Hungarian (131)	432	0.38
Iranian (38)	65	0.06
Irish (2,650)	12,458	11.09
Italian (1,745)	5,830	5.19
Latvian (18)	31	0.03
Lithuanian (19)	123	0.11
Maltese (0)	21	0.02
Northern European (58)	76	0.07
Norwegian (603)	2,365	2.10
Pennsylvania German (18)	55	0.05
Polish (795)	2,755	2.45
Portuguese (97)	282	0.25
Romanian (32)	69	0.06
Russian (215)	892	0.79
Scandinavian (66)	92	0.08
Scotch-Irish (738)	2,056	1.83
Scottish (703)	2,687	2.39
Serbian (0)	8	0.01
Slavic (55)	157	0.14
Slovak (41)	133	0.12
Slovene (15)	38	0.03
Swedish (499)	2,664	2.37
Swiss (59)	326	0.29
Turkish (4)	4	<0.01
Ukrainian (49)	200	0.18
Welsh (141)	864	0.77
West Indian, ex. Hispanic (112)	112	0.10
Haitian (32)	32	0.03
Jamaican (25)	25	0.02
West Indian (55)	55	0.05
Yugoslavian (21)	144	0.13

Hispanic Origin	Population	%
Hispanic or Latino (of any race)	37,602	31.66
Central American, ex. Mexican	588	0.50
Costa Rican	23	0.02
Guatemalan	150	0.13
Honduran	56	0.05
Nicaraguan	48	0.04
Panamanian	26	0.02
Salvadoran	281	0.24
Other Central American	4	<0.01
Cuban	157	0.13
Dominican Republic	42	0.04
Mexican	28,054	23.62
Puerto Rican	449	0.38
South American	464	0.39
Argentinean	33	0.03
Bolivian	15	0.01
Chilean	30	0.03
Colombian	114	0.10
Ecuadorian	49	0.04
Paraguayan	11	0.01
Peruvian	157	0.13
Uruguayan	6	0.01
Venezuelan	47	0.04
Other South American	2	<0.01
Other Hispanic or Latino	7,848	6.61

Race*	Population	%
African-American/Black (2,185)	3,205	2.70
Not Hispanic (1,903)	2,589	2.18
Hispanic (282)	616	0.52
American Indian/Alaska Native (1,317)	2,565	2.16
Not Hispanic (566)	1,184	1.00
Hispanic (751)	1,381	1.16
Alaska Athabascan *(Ala. Nat.)* (2)	2	<0.01
Aleut *(Alaska Native)* (6)	10	0.01
Apache (66)	184	0.15
Arapaho (13)	24	0.02
Blackfeet (6)	24	0.02
Canadian/French Am. Ind. (2)	6	0.01
Central American Ind. (1)	1	<0.01
Cherokee (94)	287	0.24
Cheyenne (8)	13	0.01
Chickasaw (8)	18	0.02
Chippewa (16)	27	0.02
Choctaw (22)	35	0.03
Colville (1)	1	<0.01
Comanche (14)	21	0.02
Cree (4)	4	<0.01
Creek (3)	9	0.01
Crow (2)	6	0.01
Delaware (0)	2	<0.01
Hopi (4)	17	0.01
Inupiat *(Alaska Native)* (0)	3	<0.01
Iroquois (0)	10	0.01
Kiowa (5)	11	0.01
Lumbee (0)	5	<0.01
Menominee (2)	2	<0.01
Mexican American Ind. (84)	146	0.12
Navajo (105)	195	0.16
Osage (4)	10	0.01
Ottawa (1)	6	0.01
Paiute (5)	7	0.01
Pima (4)	5	<0.01
Potawatomi (10)	16	0.01
Pueblo (29)	47	0.04
Puget Sound Salish (4)	6	0.01
Seminole (2)	5	<0.01
Shoshone (10)	12	0.01
Sioux (119)	188	0.16
South American Ind. (9)	20	0.02
Spanish American Ind. (14)	27	0.02
Tlingit-Haida *(Alaska Native)* (5)	9	0.01
Tsimshian *(Alaska Native)* (0)	7	0.01
Ute (9)	20	0.02
Yakama (0)	2	<0.01
Yaqui (7)	7	0.01
Yuman (1)	1	<0.01
Asian (5,212)	6,497	5.47
Not Hispanic (5,058)	6,103	5.14
Hispanic (154)	394	0.33
Bangladeshi (1)	1	<0.01
Burmese (1)	2	<0.01
Cambodian (99)	132	0.11
Chinese, ex. Taiwanese (723)	906	0.76
Filipino (376)	667	0.56
Hmong (709)	760	0.64
Indian (607)	713	0.60
Indonesian (23)	32	0.03
Japanese (268)	589	0.50
Korean (280)	458	0.39
Laotian (321)	358	0.30
Malaysian (3)	9	0.01
Nepalese (112)	123	0.10
Pakistani (63)	92	0.08
Sri Lankan (4)	5	<0.01
Taiwanese (29)	39	0.03
Thai (54)	93	0.08
Vietnamese (1,227)	1,378	1.16
Hawaii Native/Pacific Islander (135)	336	0.28
Not Hispanic (97)	225	0.19
Hispanic (38)	111	0.09
Guamanian/Chamorro (35)	56	0.05
Native Hawaiian (40)	143	0.12
Samoan (24)	48	0.04
Tongan (1)	3	<0.01
White (91,876)	95,861	80.71
Not Hispanic (71,147)	73,164	61.60
Hispanic (20,729)	22,697	19.11

Trinidad

Place Type: City
County: Las Animas
Population: 9,096†

Ancestry‡	Population	%
American (199)	199	2.15
Arab (4)	16	0.17
Lebanese (4)	16	0.17
Australian (10)	10	0.11
Austrian (11)	34	0.37
Basque (14)	41	0.44
Belgian (13)	38	0.41
British (0)	11	0.12
Croatian (55)	75	0.81
Czech (0)	55	0.60
Danish (3)	3	0.03
Dutch (0)	86	0.93
English (199)	638	6.91
European (9)	9	0.10
Finnish (0)	68	0.74
French, ex. Basque (90)	258	2.79
French Canadian (0)	12	0.13
German (392)	1,264	13.69
Greek (0)	32	0.35
Irish (158)	689	7.46
Italian (755)	1,501	16.25
Latvian (0)	10	0.11
Norwegian (3)	84	0.91
Polish (11)	138	1.49
Russian (22)	62	0.67
Scandinavian (20)	20	0.22
Scotch-Irish (46)	157	1.70
Scottish (72)	125	1.35
Slavic (0)	22	0.24
Slovene (0)	9	0.10
Swedish (3)	62	0.67
Ukrainian (0)	16	0.17
Welsh (7)	28	0.30

Hispanic Origin	Population	%
Hispanic or Latino (of any race)	4,547	49.99
Central American, ex. Mexican	12	0.13
Honduran	1	0.01
Nicaraguan	5	0.05
Salvadoran	6	0.07
Cuban	8	0.09
Dominican Republic	1	0.01
Mexican	2,094	23.02
Puerto Rican	14	0.15
South American	8	0.09
Chilean	1	0.01
Colombian	1	0.01
Peruvian	6	0.07
Other Hispanic or Latino	2,410	26.50

Race*	Population	%
African-American/Black (86)	131	1.44
Not Hispanic (69)	96	1.06
Hispanic (17)	35	0.38
American Indian/Alaska Native (239)	394	4.33
Not Hispanic (88)	139	1.53

*Notes: † The Census 2010 population figure is used to calculate the percentages in the Hispanic Origin and Race categories. Ancestry percentages are based on the 2006-2010 American Community Survey population (not shown); ‡ Numbers in parentheses indicate the number of people reporting a single ancestry; * Numbers in parentheses indicate the number of persons reporting this race alone, not in combination with any other race; Please refer to the Explanation of Data for more information.*

Hispanic (151)	255	2.80
Apache (18)	44	0.48
Blackfeet (1)	2	0.02
Cherokee (15)	36	0.40
Cheyenne (1)	14	0.15
Chippewa (3)	6	0.07
Choctaw (3)	4	0.04
Comanche (1)	2	0.02
Hopi (1)	1	0.01
Inupiat *(Alaska Native)* (0)	1	0.01
Iroquois (0)	3	0.03
Mexican American Ind. (5)	11	0.12
Navajo (24)	43	0.47
Osage (3)	5	0.05
Paiute (1)	1	0.01
Potawatomi (6)	6	0.07
Pueblo (11)	12	0.13
Sioux (7)	7	0.08
Spanish American Ind. (10)	12	0.13
Ute (0)	5	0.05
Yaqui (1)	1	0.01
Asian (78)	104	1.14
Not Hispanic (68)	87	0.96
Hispanic (10)	17	0.19
Chinese, ex. Taiwanese (20)	21	0.23
Filipino (31)	34	0.37
Indonesian (2)	2	0.02
Japanese (6)	11	0.12
Korean (2)	4	0.04
Malaysian (2)	3	0.03
Taiwanese (2)	3	0.03
Thai (5)	5	0.05
Vietnamese (6)	7	0.08
Hawaii Native/Pacific Islander (7)	22	0.24
Not Hispanic (4)	14	0.15
Hispanic (3)	8	0.09
Guamanian/Chamorro (1)	2	0.02
Native Hawaiian (4)	9	0.10
Samoan (1)	4	0.04
White (7,415)	7,701	84.66
Not Hispanic (4,201)	4,297	47.24
Hispanic (3,214)	3,404	37.42

Welby

Place Type: CDP
County: Adams
Population: 14,846†

Ancestry‡	Population	%
African, Sub-Saharan (103)	297	2.13
African (103)	297	2.13
American (1,216)	1,216	8.71
Austrian (15)	31	0.22
Belgian (0)	29	0.21
British (0)	25	0.18
Canadian (14)	14	0.10
Czech (10)	84	0.60
Czechoslovakian (0)	9	0.06
Danish (11)	53	0.38
Dutch (21)	104	0.74
English (163)	702	5.03
European (38)	38	0.27
Finnish (0)	22	0.16
French, ex. Basque (28)	371	2.66
French Canadian (20)	48	0.34
German (593)	1,930	13.82
Greek (0)	8	0.06
Hungarian (0)	19	0.14
Irish (179)	1,307	9.36
Italian (227)	795	5.69
Lithuanian (0)	22	0.16
Northern European (4)	4	0.03
Norwegian (31)	191	1.37
Pennsylvania German (11)	11	0.08
Polish (165)	258	1.85
Portuguese (144)	158	1.13
Russian (110)	135	0.97
Scotch-Irish (24)	84	0.60
Scottish (34)	176	1.26
Swedish (23)	214	1.53
Swiss (0)	12	0.09
Welsh (48)	111	0.79

Hispanic Origin	Population	%
Hispanic or Latino (of any race)	8,117	54.67
Central American, ex. Mexican	101	0.68
Guatemalan	17	0.11
Honduran	13	0.09
Nicaraguan	7	0.05
Panamanian	10	0.07
Salvadoran	51	0.34
Other Central American	3	0.02
Cuban	16	0.11
Mexican	6,559	44.18
Puerto Rican	72	0.48
South American	56	0.38
Argentinean	2	0.01
Bolivian	3	0.02
Chilean	8	0.05
Colombian	20	0.13
Ecuadorian	7	0.05
Peruvian	11	0.07
Venezuelan	5	0.03
Other Hispanic or Latino	1,313	8.84

Race*	Population	%
African-American/Black (248)	352	2.37
Not Hispanic (193)	254	1.71
Hispanic (55)	98	0.66
American Indian/Alaska Native (344)	535	3.60
Not Hispanic (115)	182	1.23
Hispanic (229)	353	2.38
Aleut *(Alaska Native)* (1)	1	0.01
Apache (32)	52	0.35
Arapaho (4)	5	0.03
Blackfeet (3)	4	0.03
Canadian/French Am. Ind. (2)	5	0.03
Cherokee (14)	33	0.22
Chickasaw (5)	6	0.04
Chippewa (3)	6	0.04
Choctaw (0)	4	0.03
Comanche (0)	4	0.03
Cree (0)	3	0.02
Creek (1)	1	0.01
Crow (4)	6	0.04
Delaware (2)	3	0.02
Hopi (2)	2	0.01
Iroquois (5)	6	0.04
Kiowa (0)	1	0.01
Mexican American Ind. (38)	58	0.39
Navajo (39)	58	0.39
Potawatomi (1)	1	0.01
Pueblo (1)	2	0.01
Shoshone (6)	6	0.04
Sioux (34)	48	0.32
Spanish American Ind. (9)	10	0.07
Ute (3)	4	0.03
Yuman (0)	1	0.01
Asian (193)	288	1.94
Not Hispanic (184)	241	1.62
Hispanic (9)	47	0.32
Cambodian (3)	4	0.03
Chinese, ex. Taiwanese (29)	35	0.24
Filipino (34)	64	0.43
Hmong (9)	9	0.06
Indian (6)	20	0.13
Indonesian (2)	2	0.01
Japanese (20)	55	0.37
Korean (11)	21	0.14
Laotian (4)	5	0.03
Nepalese (4)	4	0.03
Pakistani (1)	1	0.01
Thai (10)	10	0.07
Vietnamese (49)	57	0.38
Hawaii Native/Pacific Islander (25)	45	0.30
Not Hispanic (17)	25	0.17
Hispanic (8)	20	0.13
Guamanian/Chamorro (0)	2	0.01
Native Hawaiian (2)	18	0.12
Samoan (11)	12	0.08
White (10,397)	10,945	73.72
Not Hispanic (6,006)	6,176	41.60
Hispanic (4,391)	4,769	32.12

Westminster

Place Type: City
County: Adams
Population: 106,114†

Ancestry‡	Population	%
African, Sub-Saharan (54)	226	0.22
African (24)	159	0.15
Ghanaian (0)	37	0.04
Nigerian (22)	22	0.02
South African (8)	8	0.01
Albanian (35)	48	0.05
American (5,072)	5,072	4.84
Arab (245)	357	0.34
Arab (10)	10	0.01
Egyptian (0)	12	0.01
Jordanian (37)	54	0.05
Lebanese (8)	79	0.08
Palestinian (0)	12	0.01
Other Arab (190)	190	0.18
Armenian (105)	139	0.13
Australian (34)	59	0.06
Austrian (117)	433	0.41
Basque (0)	48	0.05
Belgian (0)	57	0.05
British (250)	478	0.46
Bulgarian (34)	49	0.05
Cajun (0)	20	0.02
Canadian (94)	180	0.17
Celtic (28)	184	0.18
Croatian (27)	87	0.08
Czech (211)	799	0.76
Czechoslovakian (111)	239	0.23
Danish (162)	747	0.71
Dutch (628)	2,247	2.14
Eastern European (38)	48	0.05
English (3,377)	11,797	11.25
Estonian (0)	16	0.02
European (1,619)	1,728	1.65
Finnish (58)	358	0.34
French, ex. Basque (696)	4,338	4.14
French Canadian (173)	605	0.58
German (6,976)	24,320	23.19
German Russian (10)	10	0.01
Greek (164)	319	0.30
Hungarian (182)	426	0.41
Iranian (36)	45	0.04
Irish (3,076)	13,997	13.35
Italian (2,254)	7,055	6.73
Latvian (0)	28	0.03
Lithuanian (36)	257	0.25
Luxemburger (22)	22	0.02
Macedonian (20)	20	0.02
Maltese (8)	59	0.06
Northern European (85)	85	0.08
Norwegian (841)	2,810	2.68
Pennsylvania German (9)	32	0.03
Polish (805)	3,339	3.18
Portuguese (60)	252	0.24
Romanian (28)	95	0.09
Russian (766)	1,879	1.79
Scandinavian (100)	226	0.22
Scotch-Irish (719)	2,035	1.94
Scottish (565)	2,342	2.23
Slavic (13)	61	0.06
Slovak (87)	282	0.27
Slovene (43)	91	0.09
Swedish (795)	3,446	3.29
Swiss (106)	547	0.52
Turkish (44)	84	0.08
Ukrainian (68)	217	0.21
Welsh (90)	694	0.66
West Indian, ex. Hispanic (163)	191	0.18
Dutch West Indian (0)	9	0.01

*Notes: † The Census 2010 population figure is used to calculate the percentages in the Hispanic Origin and Race categories. Ancestry percentages are based on the 2006-2010 American Community Survey population (not shown); ‡ Numbers in parentheses indicate the number of people reporting a single ancestry; * Numbers in parentheses indicate the number of persons reporting this race alone, not in combination with any other race; Please refer to the Explanation of Data for more information.*

Haitian (52)	52	0.05
Jamaican (80)	80	0.08
West Indian (31)	50	0.05
Yugoslavian (134)	282	0.27

Hispanic Origin	Population	%
Hispanic or Latino (of any race)	22,006	20.74
Central American, ex. Mexican	450	0.42
Costa Rican	14	0.01
Guatemalan	175	0.16
Honduran	34	0.03
Nicaraguan	21	0.02
Panamanian	25	0.02
Salvadoran	177	0.17
Other Central American	4	<0.01
Cuban	139	0.13
Dominican Republic	20	0.02
Mexican	15,374	14.49
Puerto Rican	380	0.36
South American	436	0.41
Argentinean	59	0.06
Bolivian	14	0.01
Chilean	22	0.02
Colombian	99	0.09
Ecuadorian	32	0.03
Paraguayan	17	0.02
Peruvian	127	0.12
Uruguayan	5	<0.01
Venezuelan	56	0.05
Other South American	5	<0.01
Other Hispanic or Latino	5,207	4.91

Race*	Population	%
African-American/Black (1,505)	2,221	2.09
Not Hispanic (1,360)	1,863	1.76
Hispanic (145)	358	0.34
American Indian/Alaska Native (1,003)	2,087	1.97
Not Hispanic (470)	1,087	1.02
Hispanic (533)	1,000	0.94
Alaska Athabascan *(Ala. Nat.)* (1)	2	<0.01
Aleut *(Alaska Native)* (3)	8	0.01
Apache (45)	119	0.11
Arapaho (3)	7	0.01
Blackfeet (8)	26	0.02
Canadian/French Am. Ind. (6)	11	0.01
Cherokee (63)	254	0.24
Cheyenne (1)	10	0.01
Chickasaw (8)	22	0.02
Chippewa (24)	48	0.05
Choctaw (27)	73	0.07
Colville (0)	1	<0.01
Comanche (3)	12	0.01
Cree (1)	1	<0.01
Creek (7)	14	0.01
Crow (1)	7	0.01
Delaware (0)	2	<0.01
Hopi (3)	5	<0.01
Houma (1)	1	<0.01
Inupiat *(Alaska Native)* (1)	8	0.01
Iroquois (4)	17	0.02
Kiowa (3)	4	<0.01
Menominee (0)	3	<0.01
Mexican American Ind. (52)	76	0.07
Navajo (70)	132	0.12
Osage (2)	3	<0.01
Ottawa (1)	4	<0.01
Pima (1)	1	<0.01
Potawatomi (7)	21	0.02
Pueblo (21)	36	0.03
Puget Sound Salish (1)	1	<0.01
Seminole (3)	16	0.02
Shoshone (4)	4	<0.01
Sioux (79)	156	0.15
South American Ind. (0)	1	<0.01
Spanish American Ind. (9)	14	0.01
Tlingit-Haida *(Alaska Native)* (1)	10	0.01
Tsimshian *(Alaska Native)* (0)	4	<0.01
Ute (18)	28	0.03
Yaqui (0)	2	<0.01
Asian (5,746)	6,827	6.43
Not Hispanic (5,650)	6,511	6.14
Hispanic (96)	316	0.30
Bangladeshi (5)	8	0.01
Burmese (10)	11	0.01
Cambodian (98)	117	0.11
Chinese, ex. Taiwanese (740)	959	0.90
Filipino (364)	626	0.59
Hmong (865)	895	0.84
Indian (538)	616	0.58
Indonesian (13)	27	0.03
Japanese (333)	624	0.59
Korean (445)	593	0.56
Laotian (447)	511	0.48
Malaysian (1)	1	<0.01
Nepalese (58)	65	0.06
Pakistani (25)	26	0.02
Sri Lankan (4)	7	0.01
Taiwanese (22)	29	0.03
Thai (68)	98	0.09
Vietnamese (1,388)	1,538	1.45
Hawaii Native/Pacific Islander (114)	255	0.24
Not Hispanic (82)	182	0.17
Hispanic (32)	73	0.07
Fijian (2)	6	0.01
Guamanian/Chamorro (25)	41	0.04
Marshallese (2)	2	<0.01
Native Hawaiian (55)	123	0.12
Samoan (2)	18	0.02
White (87,045)	90,272	85.07
Not Hispanic (74,447)	76,246	71.85
Hispanic (12,598)	14,026	13.22

Wheat Ridge

Place Type: City
County: Jefferson
Population: 30,166†

Ancestry‡	Population	%
African, Sub-Saharan (0)	22	0.07
African (0)	22	0.07
American (1,057)	1,057	3.48
Australian (15)	15	0.05
Austrian (82)	204	0.67
Belgian (12)	133	0.44
Brazilian (0)	9	0.03
British (51)	225	0.74
Bulgarian (20)	20	0.07
Canadian (13)	26	0.09
Croatian (15)	15	0.05
Czech (81)	213	0.70
Czechoslovakian (0)	30	0.10
Danish (24)	346	1.14
Dutch (84)	649	2.14
English (1,354)	4,020	13.23
European (287)	306	1.01
Finnish (0)	56	0.18
French, ex. Basque (103)	1,128	3.71
French Canadian (38)	150	0.49
German (2,870)	7,494	24.67
Greek (80)	175	0.58
Hungarian (34)	61	0.20
Irish (1,007)	3,885	12.79
Italian (1,056)	2,153	7.09
Lithuanian (0)	60	0.20
Luxemburger (0)	25	0.08
Northern European (11)	11	0.04
Norwegian (184)	481	1.58
Pennsylvania German (0)	16	0.05
Polish (266)	936	3.08
Portuguese (12)	12	0.04
Russian (66)	141	0.46
Scandinavian (43)	43	0.14
Scotch-Irish (189)	699	2.30
Scottish (471)	1,199	3.95
Serbian (3)	12	0.04
Slavic (58)	58	0.19
Slovak (21)	90	0.30
Slovene (27)	27	0.09
Swedish (276)	762	2.51
Swiss (36)	100	0.33
Ukrainian (130)	218	0.72
Welsh (35)	446	1.47
Yugoslavian (37)	165	0.54

Hispanic Origin	Population	%
Hispanic or Latino (of any race)	6,309	20.91
Central American, ex. Mexican	95	0.31
Costa Rican	6	0.02
Guatemalan	32	0.11
Honduran	20	0.07
Nicaraguan	8	0.03
Panamanian	7	0.02
Salvadoran	22	0.07
Cuban	23	0.08
Dominican Republic	6	0.02
Mexican	4,435	14.70
Puerto Rican	89	0.30
South American	85	0.28
Argentinean	7	0.02
Bolivian	17	0.06
Chilean	7	0.02
Colombian	20	0.07
Ecuadorian	4	0.01
Peruvian	30	0.10
Other Hispanic or Latino	1,576	5.22

Race*	Population	%
African-American/Black (353)	531	1.76
Not Hispanic (309)	436	1.45
Hispanic (44)	95	0.31
American Indian/Alaska Native (369)	764	2.53
Not Hispanic (214)	430	1.43
Hispanic (155)	334	1.11
Alaska Athabascan *(Ala. Nat.)* (2)	2	0.01
Apache (19)	39	0.13
Arapaho (2)	4	0.01
Blackfeet (1)	15	0.05
Canadian/French Am. Ind. (0)	1	<0.01
Cherokee (16)	80	0.27
Cheyenne (4)	5	0.02
Chippewa (6)	12	0.04
Choctaw (4)	15	0.05
Colville (1)	1	<0.01
Comanche (0)	6	0.02
Cree (0)	2	0.01
Creek (3)	5	0.02
Crow (1)	8	0.03
Hopi (2)	4	0.01
Inupiat *(Alaska Native)* (2)	2	0.01
Iroquois (7)	9	0.03
Menominee (2)	2	0.01
Mexican American Ind. (16)	28	0.09
Navajo (46)	76	0.25
Osage (0)	2	0.01
Potawatomi (1)	9	0.03
Pueblo (8)	22	0.07
Puget Sound Salish (2)	2	0.01
Seminole (0)	1	<0.01
Shoshone (2)	2	0.01
Sioux (28)	54	0.18
South American Ind. (4)	5	0.02
Spanish American Ind. (2)	3	0.01
Tlingit-Haida *(Alaska Native)* (3)	3	0.01
Ute (5)	10	0.03
Yaqui (1)	1	<0.01
Yuman (2)	2	0.01
Asian (471)	691	2.29
Not Hispanic (449)	618	2.05
Hispanic (22)	73	0.24
Burmese (1)	1	<0.01
Cambodian (1)	1	<0.01
Chinese, ex. Taiwanese (78)	102	0.34
Filipino (52)	117	0.39
Hmong (6)	6	0.02
Indian (20)	42	0.14
Indonesian (5)	13	0.04
Japanese (97)	165	0.55
Korean (56)	78	0.26
Laotian (23)	23	0.08

*Notes: † The Census 2010 population figure is used to calculate the percentages in the Hispanic Origin and Race categories. Ancestry percentages are based on the 2006-2010 American Community Survey population (not shown); ‡ Numbers in parentheses indicate the number of people reporting a single ancestry; * Numbers in parentheses indicate the number of persons reporting this race alone, not in combination with any other race; Please refer to the Explanation of Data for more information.*

Malaysian (1)	1	<0.01
Nepalese (17)	24	0.08
Pakistani (2)	2	0.01
Taiwanese (1)	1	<0.01
Thai (6)	10	0.03
Vietnamese (88)	94	0.31
Hawaii Native/Pacific Islander (35)	88	0.29
Not Hispanic (31)	67	0.22
Hispanic (4)	21	0.07
Guamanian/Chamorro (11)	13	0.04
Native Hawaiian (6)	37	0.12
Samoan (3)	12	0.04
Tongan (1)	1	<0.01
White (25,814)	26,766	88.73
Not Hispanic (22,320)	22,795	75.57
Hispanic (3,494)	3,971	13.16

Windsor

Place Type: Town
County: Weld
Population: 18,644†

Ancestry‡	Population	%
African, Sub-Saharan (0)	12	0.07
African (0)	12	0.07
American (860)	860	4.97
Armenian (0)	11	0.06
Austrian (0)	60	0.35
Belgian (0)	10	0.06
British (62)	91	0.53
Canadian (286)	286	1.65
Czech (84)	363	2.10
Czechoslovakian (8)	48	0.28
Danish (65)	375	2.17
Dutch (64)	455	2.63
Eastern European (42)	47	0.27
English (584)	2,234	12.91
European (287)	316	1.83
Finnish (8)	39	0.23
French, ex. Basque (89)	755	4.36
French Canadian (82)	311	1.80
German (2,131)	5,804	33.54
Greek (22)	186	1.07
Hungarian (0)	106	0.61
Iranian (8)	22	0.13
Irish (468)	2,659	15.36
Italian (208)	1,191	6.88
Lithuanian (22)	72	0.42
Norwegian (151)	547	3.16
Pennsylvania German (0)	22	0.13
Polish (126)	401	2.32
Portuguese (14)	82	0.47
Russian (99)	327	1.89
Scandinavian (14)	71	0.41
Scotch-Irish (127)	474	2.74
Scottish (119)	540	3.12
Slavic (0)	22	0.13
Slovak (0)	14	0.08
Swedish (110)	575	3.32
Swiss (9)	68	0.39
Welsh (100)	296	1.71
Yugoslavian (46)	97	0.56

Hispanic Origin	Population	%
Hispanic or Latino (of any race)	1,676	8.99
Central American, ex. Mexican	31	0.17
Guatemalan	7	0.04
Honduran	4	0.02
Nicaraguan	3	0.02
Panamanian	2	0.01
Salvadoran	12	0.06
Other Central American	3	0.02
Cuban	6	0.03
Dominican Republic	5	0.03
Mexican	1,205	6.46
Puerto Rican	39	0.21
South American	34	0.18
Argentinean	6	0.03
Bolivian	1	0.01
Chilean	1	0.01
Colombian	10	0.05
Peruvian	13	0.07
Venezuelan	3	0.02
Other Hispanic or Latino	356	1.91

Race*	Population	%
African-American/Black (96)	157	0.84
Not Hispanic (82)	134	0.72
Hispanic (14)	23	0.12
American Indian/Alaska Native (98)	230	1.23
Not Hispanic (60)	144	0.77
Hispanic (38)	86	0.46
Apache (2)	15	0.08
Blackfeet (0)	1	0.01
Cherokee (16)	44	0.24
Chickasaw (5)	8	0.04
Chippewa (2)	8	0.04
Choctaw (1)	2	0.01
Comanche (3)	3	0.02
Creek (2)	2	0.01
Inupiat *(Alaska Native)* (0)	3	0.02
Iroquois (4)	4	0.02
Mexican American Ind. (3)	7	0.04
Navajo (2)	27	0.14
Potawatomi (2)	2	0.01
Pueblo (0)	6	0.03
Puget Sound Salish (1)	1	0.01
Seminole (1)	1	0.01
Sioux (6)	10	0.05
Spanish American Ind. (3)	3	0.02
Ute (0)	3	0.02
Yaqui (1)	1	0.01
Asian (225)	338	1.81
Not Hispanic (222)	327	1.75
Hispanic (3)	11	0.06
Cambodian (2)	4	0.02
Chinese, ex. Taiwanese (65)	87	0.47
Filipino (17)	36	0.19
Indian (26)	39	0.21
Japanese (42)	74	0.40
Korean (39)	60	0.32
Malaysian (0)	1	0.01
Pakistani (1)	4	0.02
Sri Lankan (0)	2	0.01
Taiwanese (6)	6	0.03
Thai (2)	2	0.01
Vietnamese (15)	16	0.09
Hawaii Native/Pacific Islander (5)	19	0.10
Not Hispanic (5)	16	0.09
Hispanic (0)	3	0.02
Guamanian/Chamorro (4)	4	0.02
Native Hawaiian (0)	11	0.06
Samoan (1)	1	0.01
White (17,448)	17,812	95.54
Not Hispanic (16,351)	16,582	88.94
Hispanic (1,097)	1,230	6.60

Woodmoor

Place Type: CDP
County: El Paso
Population: 8,741†

Ancestry‡	Population	%
American (331)	331	3.71
Arab (14)	28	0.31
Lebanese (14)	28	0.31
Austrian (0)	32	0.36
Basque (17)	17	0.19
British (61)	106	1.19
Canadian (19)	19	0.21
Croatian (0)	14	0.16
Czech (31)	190	2.13
Czechoslovakian (44)	79	0.89
Danish (94)	221	2.48
Dutch (86)	205	2.30
Eastern European (10)	10	0.11
English (356)	1,562	17.52
European (195)	195	2.19
Finnish (10)	26	0.29
French, ex. Basque (31)	562	6.30
French Canadian (0)	11	0.12
German (888)	2,220	24.89
Greek (33)	33	0.37
Hungarian (13)	36	0.40
Icelander (26)	26	0.29
Irish (394)	1,661	18.63
Italian (69)	319	3.58
Lithuanian (0)	10	0.11
Luxemburger (0)	12	0.13
Northern European (55)	55	0.62
Norwegian (59)	239	2.68
Polish (100)	294	3.30
Romanian (12)	38	0.43
Russian (13)	94	1.05
Scandinavian (32)	46	0.52
Scotch-Irish (105)	238	2.67
Scottish (101)	450	5.05
Serbian (0)	14	0.16
Slovene (0)	42	0.47
Swedish (95)	402	4.51
Swiss (0)	28	0.31
Turkish (21)	21	0.24
Ukrainian (0)	25	0.28
Welsh (15)	87	0.98
Yugoslavian (10)	10	0.11

Hispanic Origin	Population	%
Hispanic or Latino (of any race)	369	4.22
Central American, ex. Mexican	22	0.25
Costa Rican	1	0.01
Guatemalan	10	0.11
Panamanian	4	0.05
Salvadoran	7	0.08
Cuban	13	0.15
Mexican	211	2.41
Puerto Rican	23	0.26
South American	20	0.23
Argentinean	1	0.01
Chilean	1	0.01
Colombian	7	0.08
Peruvian	8	0.09
Venezuelan	3	0.03
Other Hispanic or Latino	80	0.92

Race*	Population	%
African-American/Black (103)	152	1.74
Not Hispanic (101)	148	1.69
Hispanic (2)	4	0.05
American Indian/Alaska Native (40)	93	1.06
Not Hispanic (32)	78	0.89
Hispanic (8)	15	0.17
Aleut *(Alaska Native)* (1)	1	0.01
Apache (1)	4	0.05
Blackfeet (0)	4	0.05
Central American Ind. (2)	2	0.02
Cherokee (6)	22	0.25
Chickasaw (1)	1	0.01
Choctaw (4)	4	0.05
Comanche (3)	3	0.03
Houma (0)	1	0.01
Iroquois (3)	5	0.06
Navajo (2)	4	0.05
Osage (0)	2	0.02
Pueblo (1)	3	0.03
Puget Sound Salish (1)	1	0.01
Sioux (3)	6	0.07
South American Ind. (1)	3	0.03
Ute (2)	3	0.03
Asian (187)	300	3.43
Not Hispanic (186)	298	3.41
Hispanic (1)	2	0.02
Burmese (0)	1	0.01
Cambodian (2)	2	0.02
Chinese, ex. Taiwanese (43)	92	1.05
Filipino (23)	55	0.63
Indian (20)	25	0.29
Japanese (23)	43	0.49
Korean (39)	65	0.74

*Notes: † The Census 2010 population figure is used to calculate the percentages in the Hispanic Origin and Race categories. Ancestry percentages are based on the 2006-2010 American Community Survey population (not shown); ‡ Numbers in parentheses indicate the number of people reporting a single ancestry; * Numbers in parentheses indicate the number of persons reporting this race alone, not in combination with any other race; Please refer to the Explanation of Data for more information.*

Laotian (0)	1	0.01
Malaysian (1)	2	0.02
Nepalese (0)	2	0.02
Thai (4)	5	0.06
Vietnamese (24)	30	0.34
Hawaii Native/Pacific Islander (2)	30	0.34
Not Hispanic (1)	29	0.33
Hispanic (1)	1	0.01
Guamanian/Chamorro (1)	1	0.01
Native Hawaiian (1)	25	0.29
White (8,141)	8,333	95.33
Not Hispanic (7,852)	8,023	91.79
Hispanic (289)	310	3.55

*Notes: † The Census 2010 population figure is used to calculate the percentages in the Hispanic Origin and Race categories. Ancestry percentages are based on the 2006-2010 American Community Survey population (not shown); ‡ Numbers in parentheses indicate the number of people reporting a single ancestry; * Numbers in parentheses indicate the number of persons reporting this race alone, not in combination with any other race; Please refer to the Explanation of Data for more information.*

CONNECTICUT

Place Type: State
Population: 3,574,097†

Ancestry‡	Population	%
Afghan (397)	478	0.01
African, Sub-Saharan (22,074)	28,542	0.80
African (11,886)	15,637	0.44
Cape Verdean (2,762)	4,381	0.12
Ethiopian (378)	481	0.01
Ghanaian (1,462)	1,522	0.04
Kenyan (309)	396	0.01
Liberian (654)	662	0.02
Nigerian (1,794)	2,078	0.06
Senegalese (19)	19	<0.01
Sierra Leonean (31)	31	<0.01
Somalian (535)	579	0.02
South African (563)	943	0.03
Sudanese (272)	292	0.01
Ugandan (73)	73	<0.01
Zimbabwean (27)	27	<0.01
Other Sub-Saharan African (1,309)	1,421	0.04
Albanian (7,744)	9,401	0.27
Alsatian (26)	104	<0.01
American (94,674)	94,674	2.67
Arab (9,596)	18,013	0.51
Arab (925)	1,375	0.04
Egyptian (1,166)	1,396	0.04
Iraqi (365)	437	0.01
Jordanian (194)	248	0.01
Lebanese (3,757)	9,293	0.26
Moroccan (1,029)	1,264	0.04
Palestinian (280)	379	0.01
Syrian (833)	2,249	0.06
Other Arab (1,047)	1,372	0.04
Armenian (2,595)	5,875	0.17
Assyrian/Chaldean/Syriac (347)	703	0.02
Australian (569)	1,433	0.04
Austrian (3,201)	15,059	0.42
Basque (42)	85	<0.01
Belgian (582)	3,118	0.09
Brazilian (15,025)	17,330	0.49
British (9,960)	16,877	0.48
Bulgarian (741)	932	0.03
Cajun (152)	273	0.01
Canadian (9,211)	18,069	0.51
Carpatho Rusyn (80)	149	<0.01
Celtic (319)	617	0.02
Croatian (1,372)	3,218	0.09
Cypriot (68)	110	<0.01
Czech (3,832)	15,840	0.45
Czechoslovakian (2,293)	6,136	0.17
Danish (3,148)	13,331	0.38
Dutch (6,396)	30,302	0.85
Eastern European (9,325)	11,000	0.31
English (87,375)	363,910	10.26
Estonian (453)	779	0.02
European (21,819)	24,255	0.68
Finnish (1,894)	6,699	0.19
French, ex. Basque (49,804)	225,310	6.35
French Canadian (47,720)	104,750	2.95
German (70,602)	361,307	10.19
German Russian (50)	67	<0.01
Greek (16,526)	31,649	0.89
Guyanese (2,795)	3,650	0.10
Hungarian (11,639)	40,489	1.14
Icelander (103)	445	0.01
Iranian (1,643)	2,460	0.07
Irish (164,317)	614,767	17.34
Israeli (808)	1,210	0.03
Italian (295,670)	675,399	19.05
Latvian (1,090)	1,876	0.05
Lithuanian (10,538)	32,136	0.91
Luxemburger (74)	246	0.01
Macedonian (653)	910	0.03
Maltese (137)	463	0.01
New Zealander (68)	176	<0.01
Northern European (2,397)	2,619	0.07
Norwegian (4,893)	19,891	0.56
Pennsylvania German (300)	874	0.02
Polish (112,302)	297,615	8.39
Portuguese (31,701)	54,496	1.54
Romanian (3,259)	6,264	0.18
Russian (26,099)	71,159	2.01
Scandinavian (1,565)	3,916	0.11
Scotch-Irish (15,356)	48,840	1.38
Scottish (16,975)	72,788	2.05
Serbian (700)	1,053	0.03
Slavic (742)	2,028	0.06
Slovak (8,079)	22,283	0.63
Slovene (585)	1,374	0.04
Soviet Union (23)	23	<0.01
Swedish (13,973)	66,693	1.88
Swiss (2,361)	10,239	0.29
Turkish (2,552)	3,256	0.09
Ukrainian (9,611)	22,353	0.63
Welsh (2,239)	14,946	0.42
West Indian, ex. Hispanic (67,997)	80,311	2.26
Bahamian (239)	365	0.01
Barbadian (906)	1,210	0.03
Belizean (68)	172	<0.01
Bermudan (98)	117	<0.01
British West Indian (1,198)	1,702	0.05
Dutch West Indian (155)	207	0.01
Haitian (16,802)	18,345	0.52
Jamaican (42,179)	48,937	1.38
Trinidadian/Tobagonian (1,932)	2,823	0.08
U.S. Virgin Islander (213)	213	0.01
West Indian (4,136)	6,104	0.17
Other West Indian (71)	116	<0.01
Yugoslavian (4,287)	5,494	0.15

Hispanic Origin	Population	%
Hispanic or Latino (of any race)	479,087	13.40
Central American, ex. Mexican	35,023	0.98
Costa Rican	2,767	0.08
Guatemalan	16,715	0.47
Honduran	6,242	0.17
Nicaraguan	1,538	0.04
Panamanian	1,304	0.04
Salvadoran	6,223	0.17
Other Central American	234	0.01
Cuban	9,490	0.27
Dominican Republic	26,093	0.73
Mexican	50,658	1.42
Puerto Rican	252,972	7.08
South American	71,355	2.00
Argentinean	3,609	0.10
Bolivian	781	0.02
Chilean	2,356	0.07
Colombian	20,048	0.56
Ecuadorian	23,677	0.66
Paraguayan	494	0.01
Peruvian	16,424	0.46
Uruguayan	1,294	0.04
Venezuelan	2,129	0.06
Other South American	543	0.02
Other Hispanic or Latino	33,496	0.94

Race*	Population	%
African-American/Black (362,296)	405,600	11.35
Not Hispanic (335,119)	365,707	10.23
Hispanic (27,177)	39,893	1.12
American Indian/Alaska Native (11,256)	31,140	0.87
Not Hispanic (6,885)	22,203	0.62
Hispanic (4,371)	8,937	0.25
Alaska Athabascan *(Ala. Nat.)* (16)	39	<0.01
Aleut *(Alaska Native)* (4)	14	<0.01
Apache (63)	194	0.01
Arapaho (3)	13	<0.01
Blackfeet (126)	1,071	0.03
Canadian/French Am. Ind. (81)	250	0.01
Central American Ind. (127)	241	0.01
Cherokee (519)	3,168	0.09
Cheyenne (18)	42	<0.01
Chickasaw (20)	72	<0.01
Chippewa (108)	281	0.01
Choctaw (48)	245	0.01
Colville (5)	5	<0.01
Comanche (13)	32	<0.01
Cree (15)	73	<0.01
Creek (35)	111	<0.01
Crow (10)	35	<0.01
Delaware (20)	84	<0.01
Hopi (11)	36	<0.01
Houma (7)	12	<0.01
Inupiat *(Alaska Native)* (15)	29	<0.01
Iroquois (206)	870	0.02
Kiowa (3)	7	<0.01
Lumbee (48)	112	<0.01
Menominee (3)	7	<0.01
Mexican American Ind. (441)	699	0.02
Navajo (73)	164	<0.01
Osage (5)	16	<0.01
Ottawa (7)	16	<0.01
Paiute (5)	10	<0.01
Pima (3)	10	<0.01
Potawatomi (17)	41	<0.01
Pueblo (62)	98	<0.01
Puget Sound Salish (6)	14	<0.01
Seminole (9)	116	<0.01
Shoshone (9)	33	<0.01
Sioux (104)	400	0.01
South American Ind. (720)	1,666	0.05
Spanish American Ind. (117)	201	0.01
Tlingit-Haida *(Alaska Native)* (15)	43	<0.01
Tohono O'Odham (12)	15	<0.01
Tsimshian *(Alaska Native)* (3)	4	<0.01
Ute (2)	12	<0.01
Yakama (1)	1	<0.01
Yaqui (9)	26	<0.01
Yuman (6)	8	<0.01
Yup'ik *(Alaska Native)* (0)	2	<0.01
Asian (135,565)	157,088	4.40
Not Hispanic (134,091)	153,269	4.29
Hispanic (1,474)	3,819	0.11
Bangladeshi (1,968)	2,287	0.06
Bhutanese (26)	30	<0.01
Burmese (701)	763	0.02
Cambodian (2,772)	3,308	0.09
Chinese, ex. Taiwanese (30,348)	35,350	0.99
Filipino (11,998)	16,402	0.46
Hmong (194)	225	0.01
Indian (46,415)	50,806	1.42
Indonesian (435)	636	0.02
Japanese (3,574)	6,203	0.17
Korean (9,619)	11,760	0.33
Laotian (3,328)	3,964	0.11
Malaysian (229)	324	0.01
Nepalese (898)	944	0.03
Pakistani (5,866)	6,640	0.19
Sri Lankan (564)	669	0.02
Taiwanese (980)	1,215	0.03
Thai (1,159)	1,705	0.05
Vietnamese (9,341)	10,804	0.30
Hawaii Native/Pacific Islander (1,428)	5,397	0.15
Not Hispanic (958)	3,528	0.10
Hispanic (470)	1,869	0.05
Fijian (14)	30	<0.01
Guamanian/Chamorro (455)	770	0.02
Marshallese (14)	15	<0.01
Native Hawaiian (322)	1,017	0.03
Samoan (155)	357	0.01
Tongan (6)	12	<0.01
White (2,772,410)	2,846,192	79.63
Not Hispanic (2,546,262)	2,595,143	72.61
Hispanic (226,148)	251,049	7.02

*Notes: † The Census 2010 population figure is used to calculate the percentages in the Hispanic Origin and Race categories. Ancestry percentages are based on the 2006-2010 American Community Survey population (not shown); ‡ Numbers in parentheses indicate the number of people reporting a single ancestry; * Numbers in parentheses indicate the number of persons reporting this race alone, not in combination with any other race; Please refer to the Explanation of Data for more information.*

Ansonia

Place Type: City/Town
County: New Haven
Population: 19,249†

Ancestry‡	Population	%
African, Sub-Saharan (175)	227	1.18
African (34)	55	0.29
Cape Verdean (113)	136	0.71
Liberian (0)	8	0.04
Other Sub-Saharan African (28)	28	0.15
Albanian (78)	78	0.41
American (386)	386	2.01
Arab (72)	87	0.45
Moroccan (72)	72	0.38
Syrian (0)	15	0.08
Austrian (89)	210	1.10
British (16)	16	0.08
Canadian (13)	13	0.07
Celtic (0)	17	0.09
Cypriot (13)	13	0.07
Czech (33)	133	0.69
Czechoslovakian (12)	47	0.25
Danish (38)	57	0.30
Dutch (8)	66	0.34
English (217)	1,234	6.44
European (171)	171	0.89
Finnish (21)	21	0.11
French, ex. Basque (119)	905	4.72
French Canadian (151)	404	2.11
German (92)	1,485	7.75
Greek (116)	131	0.68
Hungarian (75)	238	1.24
Iranian (0)	80	0.42
Irish (742)	2,733	14.26
Italian (2,644)	5,313	27.73
Lithuanian (122)	226	1.18
Norwegian (0)	72	0.38
Polish (1,066)	2,507	13.08
Portuguese (245)	334	1.74
Romanian (0)	16	0.08
Russian (180)	605	3.16
Scotch-Irish (15)	253	1.32
Scottish (57)	145	0.76
Slovak (11)	106	0.55
Swedish (27)	200	1.04
Swiss (0)	12	0.06
Ukrainian (168)	459	2.40
Welsh (23)	75	0.39
West Indian, ex. Hispanic (418)	459	2.40
Haitian (307)	307	1.60
Jamaican (79)	79	0.41
Trinidadian/Tobagonian (32)	32	0.17
West Indian (0)	41	0.21
Yugoslavian (18)	18	0.09

Hispanic Origin	Population	%
Hispanic or Latino (of any race)	3,212	16.69
Central American, ex. Mexican	174	0.90
Costa Rican	27	0.14
Guatemalan	74	0.38
Honduran	18	0.09
Nicaraguan	14	0.07
Panamanian	6	0.03
Salvadoran	35	0.18
Cuban	46	0.24
Dominican Republic	126	0.65
Mexican	174	0.90
Puerto Rican	1,871	9.72
South American	609	3.16
Argentinean	28	0.15
Bolivian	2	0.01
Chilean	25	0.13
Colombian	126	0.65
Ecuadorian	376	1.95
Peruvian	42	0.22
Uruguayan	1	0.01
Venezuelan	2	0.01
Other South American	7	0.04
Other Hispanic or Latino	212	1.10

Race*	Population	%
African-American/Black (2,230)	2,593	13.47
Not Hispanic (2,040)	2,313	12.02
Hispanic (190)	280	1.45
American Indian/Alaska Native (50)	173	0.90
Not Hispanic (41)	140	0.73
Hispanic (9)	33	0.17
Apache (0)	1	0.01
Blackfeet (0)	8	0.04
Canadian/French Am. Ind. (5)	5	0.03
Cherokee (7)	27	0.14
Iroquois (0)	5	0.03
Mexican American Ind. (3)	3	0.02
Navajo (1)	1	0.01
Sioux (0)	1	0.01
South American Ind. (1)	1	0.01
Spanish American Ind. (1)	1	0.01
Asian (371)	443	2.30
Not Hispanic (365)	426	2.21
Hispanic (6)	17	0.09
Bangladeshi (7)	7	0.04
Bhutanese (5)	5	0.03
Burmese (2)	2	0.01
Cambodian (7)	10	0.05
Chinese, ex. Taiwanese (57)	59	0.31
Filipino (50)	67	0.35
Indian (66)	75	0.39
Indonesian (1)	2	0.01
Japanese (2)	9	0.05
Korean (17)	22	0.11
Laotian (44)	49	0.25
Malaysian (1)	1	0.01
Nepalese (11)	11	0.06
Pakistani (31)	33	0.17
Thai (6)	8	0.04
Vietnamese (41)	54	0.28
Hawaii Native/Pacific Islander (6)	40	0.21
Not Hispanic (2)	21	0.11
Hispanic (4)	19	0.10
Guamanian/Chamorro (3)	4	0.02
Native Hawaiian (3)	5	0.03
White (14,942)	15,428	80.15
Not Hispanic (13,163)	13,469	69.97
Hispanic (1,779)	1,959	10.18

Avon

Place Type: Town
County: Hartford
Population: 18,098†

Ancestry‡	Population	%
African, Sub-Saharan (47)	47	0.27
South African (47)	47	0.27
Albanian (0)	36	0.20
American (654)	654	3.70
Arab (0)	58	0.33
Lebanese (0)	58	0.33
Armenian (0)	48	0.27
Austrian (78)	297	1.68
Belgian (9)	19	0.11
Brazilian (0)	58	0.33
British (39)	39	0.22
Canadian (102)	177	1.00
Croatian (0)	31	0.18
Czech (17)	118	0.67
Danish (9)	71	0.40
Dutch (59)	275	1.56
Eastern European (143)	143	0.81
English (645)	2,526	14.29
European (184)	193	1.09
Finnish (9)	16	0.09
French, ex. Basque (171)	1,153	6.52
French Canadian (130)	491	2.78
German (556)	2,695	15.24
Greek (92)	134	0.76
Hungarian (48)	181	1.02
Iranian (47)	47	0.27
Irish (890)	3,779	21.38
Israeli (0)	28	0.16
Italian (1,168)	3,158	17.86
Lithuanian (117)	164	0.93
Macedonian (11)	21	0.12
Northern European (8)	8	0.05
Norwegian (44)	143	0.81
Polish (501)	1,730	9.79
Portuguese (125)	332	1.88
Romanian (0)	34	0.19
Russian (330)	813	4.60
Scandinavian (0)	28	0.16
Scotch-Irish (129)	347	1.96
Scottish (47)	411	2.32
Slavic (0)	14	0.08
Slovak (0)	50	0.28
Slovene (7)	13	0.07
Swedish (67)	498	2.82
Swiss (10)	27	0.15
Turkish (6)	6	0.03
Ukrainian (43)	58	0.33
Welsh (9)	92	0.52
West Indian, ex. Hispanic (58)	106	0.60
Jamaican (43)	91	0.51
Trinidadian/Tobagonian (15)	15	0.08
Yugoslavian (13)	13	0.07

Hispanic Origin	Population	%
Hispanic or Latino (of any race)	613	3.39
Central American, ex. Mexican	19	0.10
Costa Rican	1	0.01
Guatemalan	6	0.03
Honduran	4	0.02
Panamanian	7	0.04
Salvadoran	1	0.01
Cuban	71	0.39
Dominican Republic	19	0.10
Mexican	115	0.64
Puerto Rican	184	1.02
South American	136	0.75
Argentinean	31	0.17
Bolivian	2	0.01
Chilean	2	0.01
Colombian	37	0.20
Ecuadorian	15	0.08
Peruvian	42	0.23
Uruguayan	3	0.02
Venezuelan	4	0.02
Other Hispanic or Latino	69	0.38

Race*	Population	%
African-American/Black (268)	351	1.94
Not Hispanic (258)	330	1.82
Hispanic (10)	21	0.12
American Indian/Alaska Native (15)	76	0.42
Not Hispanic (7)	59	0.33
Hispanic (8)	17	0.09
Blackfeet (0)	1	0.01
Canadian/French Am. Ind. (0)	3	0.02
Cherokee (0)	6	0.03
Chippewa (2)	4	0.02
Choctaw (0)	2	0.01
Delaware (0)	2	0.01
Iroquois (0)	1	0.01
Mexican American Ind. (3)	6	0.03
Seminole (0)	1	0.01
Sioux (0)	5	0.03
Asian (1,145)	1,309	7.23
Not Hispanic (1,141)	1,288	7.12
Hispanic (4)	21	0.12
Bangladeshi (2)	2	0.01
Burmese (1)	3	0.02
Cambodian (4)	4	0.02
Chinese, ex. Taiwanese (316)	384	2.12
Filipino (41)	78	0.43
Indian (468)	482	2.66
Indonesian (3)	5	0.03
Japanese (23)	45	0.25
Korean (157)	180	0.99
Laotian (2)	2	0.01

*Notes: † The Census 2010 population figure is used to calculate the percentages in the Hispanic Origin and Race categories. Ancestry percentages are based on the 2006-2010 American Community Survey population (not shown); ‡ Numbers in parentheses indicate the number of people reporting a single ancestry; * Numbers in parentheses indicate the number of persons reporting this race alone, not in combination with any other race; Please refer to the Explanation of Data for more information.*

Nepalese (1)	1	0.01
Pakistani (46)	52	0.29
Sri Lankan (15)	19	0.10
Taiwanese (5)	5	0.03
Thai (7)	7	0.04
Vietnamese (21)	28	0.15
Hawaii Native/Pacific Islander (1)	14	0.08
Not Hispanic (1)	8	0.04
Hispanic (0)	6	0.03
Native Hawaiian (0)	6	0.03
White (16,250)	16,535	91.36
Not Hispanic (15,790)	16,033	88.59
Hispanic (460)	502	2.77

Berlin

Place Type: Town
County: Hartford
Population: 19,866†

Ancestry‡	Population	%
Albanian (14)	14	0.07
American (765)	765	3.90
Arab (12)	19	0.10
Lebanese (12)	19	0.10
Armenian (153)	153	0.78
Assyrian/Chaldean/Syriac (11)	50	0.26
Austrian (31)	101	0.52
British (9)	37	0.19
Cajun (0)	16	0.08
Canadian (229)	299	1.53
Czech (10)	25	0.13
Czechoslovakian (0)	58	0.30
Danish (0)	87	0.44
Dutch (26)	158	0.81
English (250)	1,749	8.93
European (161)	177	0.90
French, ex. Basque (501)	1,778	9.08
French Canadian (247)	582	2.97
German (444)	2,470	12.61
Greek (48)	68	0.35
Hungarian (0)	134	0.68
Irish (793)	3,775	19.27
Italian (2,732)	6,520	33.28
Lithuanian (308)	434	2.22
Norwegian (9)	18	0.09
Polish (1,653)	3,945	20.14
Portuguese (120)	198	1.01
Russian (75)	259	1.32
Scandinavian (21)	21	0.11
Scotch-Irish (83)	189	0.96
Scottish (86)	316	1.61
Slavic (0)	19	0.10
Slovak (9)	58	0.30
Swedish (137)	724	3.70
Swiss (0)	25	0.13
Ukrainian (33)	218	1.11
Welsh (0)	10	0.05
West Indian, ex. Hispanic (20)	30	0.15
Jamaican (0)	10	0.05
Trinidadian/Tobagonian (20)	20	0.10
Yugoslavian (71)	71	0.36

Hispanic Origin	Population	%
Hispanic or Latino (of any race)	645	3.25
Central American, ex. Mexican	21	0.11
Guatemalan	6	0.03
Honduran	3	0.02
Salvadoran	12	0.06
Cuban	56	0.28
Dominican Republic	4	0.02
Mexican	72	0.36
Puerto Rican	275	1.38
South American	96	0.48
Argentinean	18	0.09
Bolivian	2	0.01
Chilean	1	0.01
Colombian	27	0.14
Ecuadorian	14	0.07
Paraguayan	5	0.03
Peruvian	21	0.11
Uruguayan	3	0.02
Venezuelan	3	0.02
Other South American	2	0.01
Other Hispanic or Latino	121	0.61

Race*	Population	%
African-American/Black (141)	196	0.99
Not Hispanic (128)	168	0.85
Hispanic (13)	28	0.14
American Indian/Alaska Native (25)	78	0.39
Not Hispanic (21)	69	0.35
Hispanic (4)	9	0.05
Blackfeet (0)	2	0.01
Canadian/French Am. Ind. (1)	4	0.02
Cherokee (1)	4	0.02
Cheyenne (6)	6	0.03
Choctaw (1)	1	0.01
Iroquois (0)	1	0.01
Sioux (1)	3	0.02
South American Ind. (2)	2	0.01
Asian (530)	583	2.93
Not Hispanic (527)	579	2.91
Hispanic (3)	4	0.02
Cambodian (2)	3	0.02
Chinese, ex. Taiwanese (69)	76	0.38
Filipino (53)	61	0.31
Indian (220)	225	1.13
Indonesian (2)	3	0.02
Japanese (8)	11	0.06
Korean (32)	49	0.25
Laotian (6)	6	0.03
Pakistani (29)	30	0.15
Taiwanese (4)	5	0.03
Thai (10)	17	0.09
Vietnamese (81)	87	0.44
Hawaii Native/Pacific Islander (2)	11	0.06
Not Hispanic (2)	8	0.04
Hispanic (0)	3	0.02
Guamanian/Chamorro (0)	2	0.01
Native Hawaiian (0)	3	0.02
White (18,860)	19,044	95.86
Not Hispanic (18,381)	18,520	93.22
Hispanic (479)	524	2.64

Bethel

Place Type: CDP
County: Fairfield
Population: 9,549†

Ancestry‡	Population	%
American (479)	479	5.44
Arab (74)	122	1.39
Arab (74)	74	0.84
Lebanese (0)	42	0.48
Other Arab (0)	6	0.07
Armenian (0)	28	0.32
Austrian (9)	9	0.10
Belgian (0)	28	0.32
Brazilian (83)	92	1.05
Canadian (5)	5	0.06
Celtic (26)	35	0.40
Czech (0)	52	0.59
Danish (28)	56	0.64
Dutch (73)	171	1.94
Eastern European (39)	57	0.65
English (133)	886	10.07
European (98)	111	1.26
Finnish (0)	5	0.06
French, ex. Basque (48)	305	3.47
French Canadian (35)	66	0.75
German (315)	916	10.41
Greek (19)	19	0.22
Hungarian (22)	175	1.99
Irish (716)	2,053	23.33
Italian (1,059)	2,277	25.88
Lithuanian (42)	79	0.90
Norwegian (2)	36	0.41
Polish (63)	481	5.47
Portuguese (200)	229	2.60
Romanian (36)	49	0.56
Russian (8)	117	1.33
Scandinavian (0)	7	0.08
Scotch-Irish (16)	146	1.66
Scottish (18)	80	0.91
Slovak (21)	70	0.80
Swedish (68)	309	3.51
Swiss (19)	19	0.22
Ukrainian (17)	56	0.64
Welsh (0)	30	0.34
West Indian, ex. Hispanic (132)	132	1.50
Jamaican (119)	119	1.35
West Indian (13)	13	0.15

Hispanic Origin	Population	%
Hispanic or Latino (of any race)	989	10.36
Central American, ex. Mexican	88	0.92
Costa Rican	30	0.31
Guatemalan	28	0.29
Honduran	3	0.03
Nicaraguan	2	0.02
Panamanian	2	0.02
Salvadoran	23	0.24
Cuban	10	0.10
Dominican Republic	105	1.10
Mexican	101	1.06
Puerto Rican	196	2.05
South American	392	4.11
Argentinean	12	0.13
Bolivian	3	0.03
Chilean	11	0.12
Colombian	92	0.96
Ecuadorian	226	2.37
Paraguayan	3	0.03
Peruvian	38	0.40
Uruguayan	2	0.02
Venezuelan	2	0.02
Other South American	3	0.03
Other Hispanic or Latino	97	1.02

Race*	Population	%
African-American/Black (246)	317	3.32
Not Hispanic (229)	292	3.06
Hispanic (17)	25	0.26
American Indian/Alaska Native (12)	47	0.49
Not Hispanic (10)	38	0.40
Hispanic (2)	9	0.09
Blackfeet (1)	1	0.01
Cherokee (0)	7	0.07
Cheyenne (1)	1	0.01
Mexican American Ind. (0)	1	0.01
Sioux (0)	1	0.01
South American Ind. (1)	6	0.06
Asian (554)	624	6.53
Not Hispanic (548)	614	6.43
Hispanic (6)	10	0.10
Bangladeshi (20)	20	0.21
Cambodian (49)	60	0.63
Chinese, ex. Taiwanese (44)	64	0.67
Filipino (37)	51	0.53
Hmong (1)	1	0.01
Indian (151)	171	1.79
Japanese (9)	13	0.14
Korean (42)	49	0.51
Laotian (9)	10	0.10
Malaysian (4)	5	0.05
Pakistani (44)	44	0.46
Sri Lankan (3)	3	0.03
Taiwanese (3)	3	0.03
Thai (13)	22	0.23
Vietnamese (109)	112	1.17
Hawaii Native/Pacific Islander (1)	2	0.02
Hispanic (1)	2	0.02
Samoan (1)	1	0.01
White (8,100)	8,289	86.80
Not Hispanic (7,490)	7,632	79.92
Hispanic (610)	657	6.88

*Notes: † The Census 2010 population figure is used to calculate the percentages in the Hispanic Origin and Race categories. Ancestry percentages are based on the 2006-2010 American Community Survey population (not shown); ‡ Numbers in parentheses indicate the number of people reporting a single ancestry; * Numbers in parentheses indicate the number of persons reporting this race alone, not in combination with any other race; Please refer to the Explanation of Data for more information.*

Bethel

Place Type: Town
County: Fairfield
Population: 18,584†

Ancestry‡	Population	%
Albanian (105)	115	0.63
American (915)	915	4.98
Arab (92)	178	0.97
Arab (74)	74	0.40
Lebanese (18)	98	0.53
Other Arab (0)	6	0.03
Armenian (34)	62	0.34
Austrian (9)	41	0.22
Belgian (0)	41	0.22
Brazilian (115)	135	0.73
British (55)	69	0.38
Canadian (75)	83	0.45
Celtic (26)	35	0.19
Czech (59)	196	1.07
Czechoslovakian (8)	46	0.25
Danish (34)	86	0.47
Dutch (130)	352	1.92
Eastern European (56)	74	0.40
English (571)	2,092	11.38
European (216)	243	1.32
Finnish (52)	68	0.37
French, ex. Basque (109)	580	3.16
French Canadian (116)	233	1.27
German (611)	2,305	12.54
Greek (48)	96	0.52
Hungarian (56)	285	1.55
Irish (1,348)	4,225	22.99
Italian (1,870)	4,584	24.94
Lithuanian (42)	99	0.54
Luxemburger (0)	10	0.05
Norwegian (38)	197	1.07
Polish (223)	1,173	6.38
Portuguese (341)	377	2.05
Romanian (36)	63	0.34
Russian (138)	457	2.49
Scandinavian (0)	21	0.11
Scotch-Irish (63)	345	1.88
Scottish (36)	256	1.39
Slovak (41)	163	0.89
Swedish (110)	492	2.68
Swiss (52)	65	0.35
Ukrainian (32)	186	1.01
Welsh (0)	76	0.41
West Indian, ex. Hispanic (141)	182	0.99
Jamaican (128)	169	0.92
West Indian (13)	13	0.07

Hispanic Origin	Population	%
Hispanic or Latino (of any race)	1,419	7.64
Central American, ex. Mexican	116	0.62
Costa Rican	40	0.22
Guatemalan	37	0.20
Honduran	10	0.05
Nicaraguan	4	0.02
Panamanian	2	0.01
Salvadoran	23	0.12
Cuban	14	0.08
Dominican Republic	146	0.79
Mexican	183	0.98
Puerto Rican	307	1.65
South American	505	2.72
Argentinean	35	0.19
Bolivian	3	0.02
Chilean	18	0.10
Colombian	120	0.65
Ecuadorian	253	1.36
Paraguayan	3	0.02
Peruvian	60	0.32
Uruguayan	2	0.01
Venezuelan	8	0.04
Other South American	3	0.02
Other Hispanic or Latino	148	0.80

Race*	Population	%
African-American/Black (343)	456	2.45
Not Hispanic (315)	412	2.22
Hispanic (28)	44	0.24
American Indian/Alaska Native (18)	77	0.41
Not Hispanic (15)	60	0.32
Hispanic (3)	17	0.09
Blackfeet (1)	1	0.01
Cherokee (0)	10	0.05
Cheyenne (1)	1	0.01
Creek (3)	3	0.02
Iroquois (1)	2	0.01
Mexican American Ind. (0)	2	0.01
Sioux (0)	1	0.01
South American Ind. (2)	8	0.04
Asian (833)	946	5.09
Not Hispanic (820)	926	4.98
Hispanic (13)	20	0.11
Bangladeshi (21)	21	0.11
Cambodian (69)	81	0.44
Chinese, ex. Taiwanese (136)	168	0.90
Filipino (54)	71	0.38
Hmong (1)	1	0.01
Indian (233)	254	1.37
Indonesian (0)	1	0.01
Japanese (12)	19	0.10
Korean (64)	77	0.41
Laotian (11)	14	0.08
Malaysian (4)	5	0.03
Nepalese (1)	1	0.01
Pakistani (52)	52	0.28
Sri Lankan (3)	3	0.02
Taiwanese (8)	8	0.04
Thai (19)	33	0.18
Vietnamese (125)	137	0.74
Hawaii Native/Pacific Islander (6)	9	0.05
Not Hispanic (5)	7	0.04
Hispanic (1)	2	0.01
Guamanian/Chamorro (1)	1	0.01
Native Hawaiian (0)	2	0.01
Samoan (5)	5	0.03
White (16,504)	16,815	90.48
Not Hispanic (15,598)	15,838	85.22
Hispanic (906)	977	5.26

Bloomfield

Place Type: Town
County: Hartford
Population: 20,486†

Ancestry‡	Population	%
African, Sub-Saharan (380)	455	2.24
African (239)	297	1.46
Cape Verdean (0)	17	0.08
Ghanaian (100)	100	0.49
Nigerian (13)	13	0.06
Ugandan (28)	28	0.14
American (408)	408	2.01
Arab (62)	129	0.63
Egyptian (0)	10	0.05
Iraqi (38)	38	0.19
Lebanese (0)	10	0.05
Moroccan (24)	24	0.12
Syrian (0)	47	0.23
Armenian (0)	42	0.21
Austrian (19)	33	0.16
Brazilian (21)	71	0.35
British (45)	103	0.51
Canadian (47)	47	0.23
Celtic (25)	25	0.12
Czech (29)	29	0.14
Danish (10)	69	0.34
Dutch (14)	39	0.19
Eastern European (33)	33	0.16
English (314)	1,170	5.75
European (102)	114	0.56
Finnish (0)	47	0.23
French, ex. Basque (110)	670	3.29
French Canadian (216)	334	1.64
German (181)	1,076	5.29
Greek (13)	13	0.06
Guyanese (23)	41	0.20
Hungarian (14)	39	0.19
Irish (461)	1,453	7.15
Italian (595)	1,232	6.06
Latvian (11)	17	0.08
Lithuanian (110)	168	0.83
Norwegian (62)	62	0.30
Polish (369)	621	3.05
Portuguese (26)	100	0.49
Romanian (19)	52	0.26
Russian (250)	416	2.05
Scotch-Irish (34)	128	0.63
Scottish (59)	226	1.11
Slavic (0)	11	0.05
Slovak (0)	25	0.12
Swedish (26)	107	0.53
Swiss (0)	89	0.44
Turkish (24)	24	0.12
Ukrainian (51)	110	0.54
Welsh (9)	47	0.23
West Indian, ex. Hispanic (3,772)	3,968	19.51
Barbadian (29)	61	0.30
British West Indian (20)	20	0.10
Haitian (69)	69	0.34
Jamaican (3,017)	3,181	15.64
Trinidadian/Tobagonian (213)	213	1.05
West Indian (424)	424	2.09

Hispanic Origin	Population	%
Hispanic or Latino (of any race)	1,149	5.61
Central American, ex. Mexican	50	0.24
Costa Rican	10	0.05
Guatemalan	8	0.04
Honduran	4	0.02
Nicaraguan	4	0.02
Panamanian	21	0.10
Salvadoran	3	0.01
Cuban	44	0.21
Dominican Republic	53	0.26
Mexican	32	0.16
Puerto Rican	830	4.05
South American	74	0.36
Argentinean	6	0.03
Chilean	5	0.02
Colombian	17	0.08
Ecuadorian	3	0.01
Peruvian	28	0.14
Venezuelan	11	0.05
Other South American	4	0.02
Other Hispanic or Latino	66	0.32

Race*	Population	%
African-American/Black (11,781)	12,253	59.81
Not Hispanic (11,518)	11,909	58.13
Hispanic (263)	344	1.68
American Indian/Alaska Native (52)	245	1.20
Not Hispanic (38)	195	0.95
Hispanic (14)	50	0.24
Apache (0)	1	<0.01
Blackfeet (1)	7	0.03
Canadian/French Am. Ind. (1)	3	0.01
Central American Ind. (4)	6	0.03
Cherokee (1)	34	0.17
Cheyenne (0)	2	0.01
Chippewa (0)	1	<0.01
Choctaw (0)	1	<0.01
Cree (1)	3	0.01
Creek (0)	2	0.01
Crow (0)	1	<0.01
Iroquois (1)	7	0.03
Mexican American Ind. (1)	5	0.02
Seminole (0)	3	0.01
Shoshone (1)	1	<0.01
Sioux (0)	1	<0.01
South American Ind. (4)	22	0.11
Asian (385)	507	2.47
Not Hispanic (382)	501	2.45

*Notes: † The Census 2010 population figure is used to calculate the percentages in the Hispanic Origin and Race categories. Ancestry percentages are based on the 2006-2010 American Community Survey population (not shown); ‡ Numbers in parentheses indicate the number of people reporting a single ancestry; * Numbers in parentheses indicate the number of persons reporting this race alone, not in combination with any other race; Please refer to the Explanation of Data for more information.*

Hispanic (3)	6	0.03
Bangladeshi (16)	17	0.08
Cambodian (1)	1	<0.01
Chinese, ex. Taiwanese (69)	106	0.52
Filipino (40)	59	0.29
Indian (157)	187	0.91
Indonesian (3)	3	0.01
Japanese (8)	11	0.05
Korean (17)	18	0.09
Laotian (2)	3	0.01
Malaysian (1)	1	<0.01
Pakistani (25)	31	0.15
Sri Lankan (6)	6	0.03
Taiwanese (5)	6	0.03
Thai (2)	2	0.01
Vietnamese (26)	37	0.18
Hawaii Native/Pacific Islander (8)	35	0.17
Not Hispanic (8)	30	0.15
Hispanic (0)	5	0.02
Guamanian/Chamorro (0)	2	0.01
Native Hawaiian (5)	8	0.04
Samoan (2)	2	0.01
White (7,304)	7,654	37.36
Not Hispanic (6,863)	7,139	34.85
Hispanic (441)	515	2.51

Branford

Place Type: Town
County: New Haven
Population: 28,026†

Ancestry‡	Population	%
African, Sub-Saharan (0)	46	0.16
African (0)	27	0.10
Cape Verdean (0)	8	0.03
South African (0)	11	0.04
American (841)	841	2.98
Arab (50)	58	0.21
Arab (37)	37	0.13
Lebanese (13)	13	0.05
Syrian (0)	8	0.03
Armenian (0)	42	0.15
Australian (0)	51	0.18
Austrian (13)	105	0.37
Belgian (0)	51	0.18
Brazilian (75)	75	0.27
British (48)	107	0.38
Canadian (98)	125	0.44
Croatian (28)	64	0.23
Czech (46)	65	0.23
Czechoslovakian (0)	14	0.05
Danish (11)	86	0.31
Dutch (69)	295	1.05
Eastern European (125)	139	0.49
English (759)	3,591	12.74
European (139)	149	0.53
Finnish (41)	66	0.23
French, ex. Basque (134)	938	3.33
French Canadian (104)	391	1.39
German (761)	3,757	13.33
Greek (167)	388	1.38
Hungarian (188)	591	2.10
Iranian (9)	9	0.03
Irish (2,214)	6,730	23.87
Israeli (14)	14	0.05
Italian (4,385)	8,509	30.18
Latvian (0)	11	0.04
Lithuanian (23)	242	0.86
Maltese (0)	12	0.04
Norwegian (37)	158	0.56
Polish (712)	2,347	8.32
Portuguese (96)	163	0.58
Romanian (10)	68	0.24
Russian (149)	525	1.86
Scandinavian (9)	41	0.15
Scotch-Irish (374)	521	1.85
Scottish (191)	734	2.60
Serbian (44)	110	0.39
Slovak (25)	142	0.50
Swedish (199)	1,295	4.59
Swiss (24)	220	0.78
Turkish (9)	9	0.03
Ukrainian (78)	206	0.73
Welsh (6)	186	0.66
West Indian, ex. Hispanic (0)	218	0.77
Jamaican (0)	196	0.70
Trinidadian/Tobagonian (0)	22	0.08
Yugoslavian (202)	248	0.88

Hispanic Origin	Population	%
Hispanic or Latino (of any race)	1,149	4.10
Central American, ex. Mexican	44	0.16
Costa Rican	4	0.01
Guatemalan	14	0.05
Honduran	3	0.01
Nicaraguan	4	0.01
Panamanian	4	0.01
Salvadoran	15	0.05
Cuban	35	0.12
Dominican Republic	31	0.11
Mexican	160	0.57
Puerto Rican	395	1.41
South American	389	1.39
Argentinean	24	0.09
Bolivian	5	0.02
Chilean	24	0.09
Colombian	93	0.33
Ecuadorian	200	0.71
Paraguayan	2	0.01
Peruvian	23	0.08
Uruguayan	1	<0.01
Venezuelan	10	0.04
Other South American	7	0.02
Other Hispanic or Latino	95	0.34

Race*	Population	%
African-American/Black (540)	679	2.42
Not Hispanic (507)	630	2.25
Hispanic (33)	49	0.17
American Indian/Alaska Native (63)	164	0.59
Not Hispanic (51)	142	0.51
Hispanic (12)	22	0.08
Apache (1)	1	<0.01
Blackfeet (3)	7	0.02
Cherokee (5)	17	0.06
Choctaw (1)	2	0.01
Cree (1)	1	<0.01
Creek (0)	4	0.01
Houma (0)	1	<0.01
Iroquois (2)	7	0.02
Lumbee (0)	1	<0.01
Mexican American Ind. (1)	3	0.01
Potawatomi (1)	1	<0.01
Sioux (1)	4	0.01
South American Ind. (6)	7	0.02
Tlingit-Haida *(Alaska Native)* (0)	1	<0.01
Asian (1,025)	1,137	4.06
Not Hispanic (1,020)	1,121	4.00
Hispanic (5)	16	0.06
Bangladeshi (9)	9	0.03
Burmese (1)	1	<0.01
Cambodian (17)	19	0.07
Chinese, ex. Taiwanese (256)	274	0.98
Filipino (57)	76	0.27
Indian (222)	237	0.85
Indonesian (1)	1	<0.01
Japanese (31)	50	0.18
Korean (125)	150	0.54
Laotian (1)	1	<0.01
Nepalese (85)	87	0.31
Pakistani (54)	56	0.20
Sri Lankan (2)	5	0.02
Taiwanese (3)	5	0.02
Thai (19)	26	0.09
Vietnamese (114)	124	0.44
Hawaii Native/Pacific Islander (4)	17	0.06
Not Hispanic (2)	10	0.04
Hispanic (2)	7	0.02
Guamanian/Chamorro (1)	1	<0.01
Native Hawaiian (0)	4	0.01
Samoan (1)	1	<0.01
White (25,748)	26,091	93.10
Not Hispanic (24,955)	25,223	90.00
Hispanic (793)	868	3.10

Bridgeport

Place Type: City/Town
County: Fairfield
Population: 144,229†

Ancestry‡	Population	%
Afghan (19)	19	0.01
African, Sub-Saharan (2,716)	3,053	2.14
African (696)	874	0.61
Cape Verdean (977)	1,080	0.76
Ethiopian (0)	42	0.03
Ghanaian (124)	124	0.09
Nigerian (189)	189	0.13
Somalian (180)	188	0.13
South African (28)	34	0.02
Sudanese (106)	106	0.07
Other Sub-Saharan African (416)	416	0.29
Albanian (203)	292	0.20
American (1,392)	1,392	0.98
Arab (1,027)	1,070	0.75
Arab (47)	47	0.03
Egyptian (198)	198	0.14
Iraqi (178)	178	0.12
Lebanese (215)	258	0.18
Moroccan (168)	168	0.12
Palestinian (44)	44	0.03
Syrian (81)	81	0.06
Other Arab (96)	96	0.07
Armenian (46)	102	0.07
Austrian (51)	170	0.12
Basque (7)	10	0.01
Belgian (0)	67	0.05
Brazilian (3,879)	3,942	2.76
British (80)	107	0.08
Bulgarian (50)	50	0.04
Canadian (235)	395	0.28
Croatian (13)	13	0.01
Czech (164)	315	0.22
Czechoslovakian (95)	108	0.08
Danish (0)	40	0.03
Dutch (99)	401	0.28
Eastern European (104)	104	0.07
English (638)	2,807	1.97
Estonian (13)	13	0.01
European (140)	140	0.10
Finnish (15)	59	0.04
French, ex. Basque (237)	1,611	1.13
French Canadian (177)	380	0.27
German (717)	3,628	2.54
Greek (303)	505	0.35
Guyanese (284)	284	0.20
Hungarian (635)	1,551	1.09
Iranian (37)	37	0.03
Irish (2,037)	7,322	5.14
Israeli (0)	11	0.01
Italian (4,841)	9,580	6.72
Lithuanian (60)	158	0.11
Northern European (29)	38	0.03
Norwegian (22)	165	0.12
Pennsylvania German (0)	18	0.01
Polish (1,291)	2,862	2.01
Portuguese (2,902)	3,709	2.60
Romanian (63)	99	0.07
Russian (283)	978	0.69
Scotch-Irish (151)	296	0.21
Scottish (84)	491	0.34
Serbian (115)	115	0.08
Slavic (32)	87	0.06
Slovak (416)	1,376	0.97
Swedish (86)	513	0.36
Swiss (0)	52	0.04
Turkish (45)	67	0.05
Ukrainian (179)	281	0.20

*Notes: † The Census 2010 population figure is used to calculate the percentages in the Hispanic Origin and Race categories. Ancestry percentages are based on the 2006-2010 American Community Survey population (not shown); ‡ Numbers in parentheses indicate the number of people reporting a single ancestry; * Numbers in parentheses indicate the number of persons reporting this race alone, not in combination with any other race; Please refer to the Explanation of Data for more information.*

Welsh (0)	80	0.06
West Indian, ex. Hispanic (12,948)	13,990	9.81
Bahamian (0)	8	0.01
Barbadian (117)	117	0.08
British West Indian (406)	453	0.32
Dutch West Indian (58)	58	0.04
Haitian (3,792)	4,076	2.86
Jamaican (7,806)	8,429	5.91
Trinidadian/Tobagonian (215)	233	0.16
U.S. Virgin Islander (116)	116	0.08
West Indian (438)	500	0.35
Yugoslavian (59)	122	0.09

Hispanic Origin	Population	%
Hispanic or Latino (of any race)	55,100	38.20
Central American, ex. Mexican	4,451	3.09
Costa Rican	478	0.33
Guatemalan	1,310	0.91
Honduran	999	0.69
Nicaraguan	305	0.21
Panamanian	84	0.06
Salvadoran	1,230	0.85
Other Central American	45	0.03
Cuban	935	0.65
Dominican Republic	2,429	1.68
Mexican	7,205	5.00
Puerto Rican	31,881	22.10
South American	5,531	3.83
Argentinean	117	0.08
Bolivian	33	0.02
Chilean	107	0.07
Colombian	1,948	1.35
Ecuadorian	1,950	1.35
Paraguayan	54	0.04
Peruvian	1,017	0.71
Uruguayan	110	0.08
Venezuelan	172	0.12
Other South American	23	0.02
Other Hispanic or Latino	2,668	1.85

Race*	Population	%
African-American/Black (49,842)	53,115	36.83
Not Hispanic (46,472)	48,372	33.54
Hispanic (3,370)	4,743	3.29
American Indian/Alaska Native (789)	1,817	1.26
Not Hispanic (286)	891	0.62
Hispanic (503)	926	0.64
Aleut *(Alaska Native)* (0)	4	<0.01
Apache (0)	2	<0.01
Blackfeet (5)	62	0.04
Canadian/French Am. Ind. (4)	10	0.01
Central American Ind. (6)	18	0.01
Cherokee (45)	189	0.13
Chippewa (0)	8	0.01
Choctaw (0)	3	<0.01
Cree (1)	1	<0.01
Creek (2)	3	<0.01
Crow (1)	1	<0.01
Iroquois (6)	20	0.01
Lumbee (2)	2	<0.01
Mexican American Ind. (79)	111	0.08
Navajo (2)	4	<0.01
Paiute (2)	3	<0.01
Pueblo (6)	16	0.01
Seminole (1)	5	<0.01
Shoshone (0)	6	<0.01
Sioux (4)	12	0.01
South American Ind. (87)	146	0.10
Spanish American Ind. (21)	26	0.02
Tohono O'Odham (3)	3	<0.01
Ute (0)	1	<0.01
Yaqui (0)	1	<0.01
Asian (4,918)	5,671	3.93
Not Hispanic (4,781)	5,348	3.71
Hispanic (137)	323	0.22
Bangladeshi (122)	163	0.11
Burmese (9)	11	0.01
Cambodian (359)	402	0.28
Chinese, ex. Taiwanese (801)	925	0.64
Filipino (216)	307	0.21
Hmong (1)	1	<0.01
Indian (1,136)	1,342	0.93
Indonesian (18)	25	0.02
Japanese (84)	170	0.12
Korean (196)	248	0.17
Laotian (416)	474	0.33
Malaysian (17)	18	0.01
Nepalese (62)	63	0.04
Pakistani (150)	171	0.12
Sri Lankan (2)	4	<0.01
Taiwanese (12)	15	0.01
Thai (73)	95	0.07
Vietnamese (990)	1,058	0.73
Hawaii Native/Pacific Islander (151)	622	0.43
Not Hispanic (66)	355	0.25
Hispanic (85)	267	0.19
Fijian (1)	1	<0.01
Guamanian/Chamorro (40)	70	0.05
Marshallese (2)	2	<0.01
Native Hawaiian (37)	65	0.05
Samoan (28)	76	0.05
White (57,070)	61,014	42.30
Not Hispanic (32,794)	34,434	23.87
Hispanic (24,276)	26,580	18.43

Bristol

Place Type: City/Town
County: Hartford
Population: 60,477†

Ancestry‡	Population	%
African, Sub-Saharan (24)	55	0.09
African (0)	31	0.05
Ghanaian (12)	12	0.02
Nigerian (12)	12	0.02
Albanian (175)	210	0.35
American (1,861)	1,861	3.08
Arab (104)	165	0.27
Egyptian (84)	95	0.16
Jordanian (0)	10	0.02
Lebanese (0)	13	0.02
Moroccan (20)	20	0.03
Syrian (0)	27	0.04
Armenian (31)	60	0.10
Assyrian/Chaldean/Syriac (64)	73	0.12
Austrian (18)	178	0.29
Belgian (0)	36	0.06
Brazilian (0)	29	0.05
British (28)	164	0.27
Canadian (645)	905	1.50
Celtic (10)	10	0.02
Croatian (0)	15	0.02
Czech (50)	313	0.52
Czechoslovakian (35)	50	0.08
Danish (18)	118	0.20
Dutch (43)	341	0.56
English (1,030)	5,321	8.80
European (99)	170	0.28
Finnish (0)	46	0.08
French, ex. Basque (3,659)	11,084	18.33
French Canadian (2,293)	3,692	6.11
German (1,241)	6,564	10.86
Greek (205)	341	0.56
Guyanese (0)	18	0.03
Hungarian (60)	400	0.66
Iranian (34)	34	0.06
Irish (2,141)	10,816	17.89
Italian (5,108)	12,861	21.27
Lithuanian (178)	607	1.00
New Zealander (0)	36	0.06
Northern European (8)	8	0.01
Norwegian (12)	174	0.29
Pennsylvania German (0)	26	0.04
Polish (3,373)	8,846	14.63
Portuguese (145)	432	0.71
Romanian (0)	81	0.13
Russian (183)	551	0.91
Scandinavian (42)	131	0.22
Scotch-Irish (192)	666	1.10
Scottish (145)	996	1.65
Slavic (0)	39	0.06
Slovak (36)	194	0.32
Slovene (22)	51	0.08
Swedish (198)	1,160	1.92
Swiss (28)	133	0.22
Turkish (148)	160	0.26
Ukrainian (159)	391	0.65
Welsh (0)	142	0.23
West Indian, ex. Hispanic (224)	370	0.61
Barbadian (25)	25	0.04
Dutch West Indian (8)	8	0.01
Jamaican (152)	277	0.46
West Indian (39)	60	0.10

Hispanic Origin	Population	%
Hispanic or Latino (of any race)	5,829	9.64
Central American, ex. Mexican	166	0.27
Costa Rican	8	0.01
Guatemalan	68	0.11
Honduran	43	0.07
Nicaraguan	16	0.03
Panamanian	11	0.02
Salvadoran	20	0.03
Cuban	82	0.14
Dominican Republic	246	0.41
Mexican	539	0.89
Puerto Rican	3,771	6.24
South American	697	1.15
Argentinean	36	0.06
Bolivian	3	<0.01
Chilean	19	0.03
Colombian	173	0.29
Ecuadorian	307	0.51
Paraguayan	1	<0.01
Peruvian	115	0.19
Uruguayan	2	<0.01
Venezuelan	36	0.06
Other South American	5	0.01
Other Hispanic or Latino	328	0.54

Race*	Population	%
African-American/Black (2,323)	3,197	5.29
Not Hispanic (2,035)	2,714	4.49
Hispanic (288)	483	0.80
American Indian/Alaska Native (117)	442	0.73
Not Hispanic (75)	364	0.60
Hispanic (42)	78	0.13
Apache (3)	7	0.01
Blackfeet (1)	22	0.04
Canadian/French Am. Ind. (3)	6	0.01
Cherokee (10)	62	0.10
Chickasaw (0)	2	<0.01
Chippewa (7)	8	0.01
Comanche (0)	1	<0.01
Cree (0)	1	<0.01
Creek (0)	1	<0.01
Iroquois (7)	21	0.03
Mexican American Ind. (3)	8	0.01
Navajo (0)	2	<0.01
Pueblo (4)	4	0.01
Shoshone (1)	1	<0.01
Sioux (1)	8	0.01
South American Ind. (5)	10	0.02
Spanish American Ind. (1)	1	<0.01
Yaqui (0)	2	<0.01
Asian (1,173)	1,414	2.34
Not Hispanic (1,155)	1,364	2.26
Hispanic (18)	50	0.08
Bangladeshi (35)	35	0.06
Burmese (1)	3	<0.01
Cambodian (111)	123	0.20
Chinese, ex. Taiwanese (169)	243	0.40
Filipino (148)	223	0.37
Indian (239)	266	0.44
Indonesian (6)	7	0.01
Japanese (23)	58	0.10
Korean (69)	103	0.17
Laotian (78)	96	0.16
Malaysian (6)	10	0.02

*Notes: † The Census 2010 population figure is used to calculate the percentages in the Hispanic Origin and Race categories. Ancestry percentages are based on the 2006-2010 American Community Survey population (not shown); ‡ Numbers in parentheses indicate the number of people reporting a single ancestry; * Numbers in parentheses indicate the number of persons reporting this race alone, not in combination with any other race; Please refer to the Explanation of Data for more information.*

Nepalese (6)	7	0.01
Pakistani (83)	94	0.16
Sri Lankan (3)	3	<0.01
Thai (17)	25	0.04
Vietnamese (112)	138	0.23
Hawaii Native/Pacific Islander (10)	74	0.12
Not Hispanic (10)	42	0.07
Hispanic (0)	32	0.05
Guamanian/Chamorro (1)	1	<0.01
Native Hawaiian (4)	19	0.03
Samoan (3)	13	0.02
White (53,065)	54,413	89.97
Not Hispanic (50,194)	51,199	84.66
Hispanic (2,871)	3,214	5.31

Brookfield

Place Type: Town
County: Fairfield
Population: 16,452†

Ancestry‡	Population	%
Albanian (25)	101	0.62
American (808)	808	4.98
Arab (44)	208	1.28
Arab (16)	16	0.10
Lebanese (28)	153	0.94
Syrian (0)	39	0.24
Armenian (6)	37	0.23
Austrian (11)	45	0.28
Belgian (19)	76	0.47
Brazilian (30)	30	0.19
British (79)	110	0.68
Bulgarian (33)	33	0.20
Canadian (28)	153	0.94
Czech (55)	128	0.79
Czechoslovakian (13)	121	0.75
Danish (0)	96	0.59
Dutch (35)	106	0.65
Eastern European (27)	27	0.17
English (374)	1,779	10.97
European (279)	295	1.82
Finnish (84)	134	0.83
French, ex. Basque (29)	597	3.68
French Canadian (142)	287	1.77
German (441)	2,394	14.77
Greek (63)	108	0.67
Guyanese (12)	66	0.41
Hungarian (12)	70	0.43
Irish (1,099)	3,392	20.92
Italian (1,863)	4,174	25.74
Lithuanian (42)	88	0.54
Macedonian (0)	76	0.47
Northern European (22)	22	0.14
Norwegian (29)	113	0.70
Polish (277)	871	5.37
Portuguese (220)	414	2.55
Russian (230)	502	3.10
Scandinavian (15)	15	0.09
Scotch-Irish (57)	255	1.57
Scottish (68)	367	2.26
Slovak (47)	169	1.04
Swedish (109)	669	4.13
Swiss (34)	66	0.41
Ukrainian (10)	25	0.15
Welsh (11)	98	0.60
West Indian, ex. Hispanic (49)	70	0.43
Barbadian (12)	12	0.07
Haitian (23)	23	0.14
Jamaican (14)	35	0.22
Yugoslavian (0)	10	0.06

Hispanic Origin	Population	%
Hispanic or Latino (of any race)	710	4.32
Central American, ex. Mexican	29	0.18
Costa Rican	7	0.04
Guatemalan	12	0.07
Honduran	1	0.01
Nicaraguan	2	0.01
Panamanian	2	0.01
Salvadoran	5	0.03
Cuban	41	0.25
Dominican Republic	62	0.38
Mexican	95	0.58
Puerto Rican	213	1.29
South American	179	1.09
Argentinean	18	0.11
Chilean	8	0.05
Colombian	45	0.27
Ecuadorian	75	0.46
Paraguayan	2	0.01
Peruvian	21	0.13
Uruguayan	1	0.01
Venezuelan	5	0.03
Other South American	4	0.02
Other Hispanic or Latino	91	0.55

Race*	Population	%
African-American/Black (177)	222	1.35
Not Hispanic (161)	195	1.19
Hispanic (16)	27	0.16
American Indian/Alaska Native (7)	47	0.29
Not Hispanic (6)	42	0.26
Hispanic (1)	5	0.03
Blackfeet (0)	8	0.05
Cherokee (1)	3	0.02
Iroquois (0)	2	0.01
Lumbee (1)	1	0.01
Mexican American Ind. (0)	2	0.01
Asian (598)	679	4.13
Not Hispanic (595)	669	4.07
Hispanic (3)	10	0.06
Bangladeshi (5)	6	0.04
Cambodian (10)	17	0.10
Chinese, ex. Taiwanese (150)	181	1.10
Filipino (61)	87	0.53
Indian (230)	244	1.48
Indonesian (1)	2	0.01
Japanese (10)	20	0.12
Korean (46)	58	0.35
Laotian (0)	3	0.02
Nepalese (3)	3	0.02
Pakistani (16)	20	0.12
Sri Lankan (4)	8	0.05
Taiwanese (7)	7	0.04
Thai (5)	14	0.09
Vietnamese (20)	25	0.15
Hawaii Native/Pacific Islander (0)	8	0.05
Not Hispanic (0)	8	0.05
Native Hawaiian (0)	5	0.03
White (15,285)	15,453	93.93
Not Hispanic (14,766)	14,899	90.56
Hispanic (519)	554	3.37

Brooklyn

Place Type: Town
County: Windham
Population: 8,210†

Ancestry‡	Population	%
Afghan (18)	18	0.22
African, Sub-Saharan (9)	9	0.11
Cape Verdean (9)	9	0.11
Albanian (51)	51	0.63
American (165)	165	2.04
Arab (0)	9	0.11
Syrian (0)	9	0.11
Austrian (0)	9	0.11
Belgian (0)	6	0.07
British (19)	28	0.35
Canadian (63)	116	1.43
Croatian (12)	41	0.51
Danish (7)	7	0.09
Dutch (34)	133	1.64
English (301)	1,142	14.11
European (71)	112	1.38
Finnish (62)	139	1.72
French, ex. Basque (470)	1,806	22.32
French Canadian (418)	843	10.42
German (84)	451	5.57
Greek (49)	74	0.91
Hungarian (0)	26	0.32
Irish (397)	1,367	16.89
Italian (436)	1,042	12.88
Latvian (0)	9	0.11
Lithuanian (10)	118	1.46
Norwegian (0)	12	0.15
Polish (142)	457	5.65
Portuguese (35)	60	0.74
Russian (0)	103	1.27
Scotch-Irish (54)	164	2.03
Scottish (32)	141	1.74
Serbian (8)	8	0.10
Slovak (11)	11	0.14
Swedish (87)	352	4.35
Swiss (0)	15	0.19
Ukrainian (12)	12	0.15
Welsh (0)	64	0.79
West Indian, ex. Hispanic (0)	8	0.10
British West Indian (0)	8	0.10

Hispanic Origin	Population	%
Hispanic or Latino (of any race)	325	3.96
Central American, ex. Mexican	4	0.05
Guatemalan	1	0.01
Honduran	1	0.01
Salvadoran	2	0.02
Cuban	19	0.23
Dominican Republic	1	0.01
Mexican	43	0.52
Puerto Rican	113	1.38
South American	14	0.17
Colombian	7	0.09
Ecuadorian	4	0.05
Peruvian	2	0.02
Venezuelan	1	0.01
Other Hispanic or Latino	131	1.60

Race*	Population	%
African-American/Black (241)	289	3.52
Not Hispanic (226)	272	3.31
Hispanic (15)	17	0.21
American Indian/Alaska Native (24)	70	0.85
Not Hispanic (22)	65	0.79
Hispanic (2)	5	0.06
Blackfeet (0)	3	0.04
Cherokee (0)	6	0.07
Chippewa (1)	2	0.02
Choctaw (0)	2	0.02
Creek (0)	2	0.02
Delaware (0)	2	0.02
Iroquois (0)	1	0.01
South American Ind. (1)	1	0.01
Asian (88)	112	1.36
Not Hispanic (86)	107	1.30
Hispanic (2)	5	0.06
Cambodian (5)	5	0.06
Chinese, ex. Taiwanese (19)	22	0.27
Filipino (2)	8	0.10
Indian (17)	20	0.24
Indonesian (1)	1	0.01
Japanese (1)	2	0.02
Korean (4)	10	0.12
Laotian (29)	31	0.38
Nepalese (0)	1	0.01
Thai (2)	3	0.04
Vietnamese (1)	1	0.01
Hawaii Native/Pacific Islander (2)	2	0.02
Not Hispanic (2)	2	0.02
Native Hawaiian (2)	2	0.02
White (7,605)	7,698	93.76
Not Hispanic (7,450)	7,534	91.77
Hispanic (155)	164	2.00

Burlington

Place Type: Town
County: Hartford
Population: 9,301†

*Notes: † The Census 2010 population figure is used to calculate the percentages in the Hispanic Origin and Race categories. Ancestry percentages are based on the 2006-2010 American Community Survey population (not shown); ‡ Numbers in parentheses indicate the number of people reporting a single ancestry; * Numbers in parentheses indicate the number of persons reporting this race alone, not in combination with any other race; Please refer to the Explanation of Data for more information.*

Ancestry‡	Population	%
African, Sub-Saharan (11)	27	0.30
African (11)	11	0.12
South African (0)	16	0.18
American (316)	316	3.47
Arab (0)	43	0.47
Syrian (0)	43	0.47
Armenian (0)	11	0.12
Austrian (13)	44	0.48
Belgian (0)	50	0.55
Brazilian (15)	24	0.26
Canadian (54)	126	1.38
Croatian (10)	10	0.11
Czech (0)	82	0.90
Czechoslovakian (27)	37	0.41
Danish (0)	34	0.37
Dutch (26)	103	1.13
Eastern European (10)	10	0.11
English (194)	1,268	13.93
European (45)	45	0.49
Finnish (24)	24	0.26
French, ex. Basque (229)	967	10.62
French Canadian (219)	405	4.45
German (211)	1,460	16.04
Greek (9)	68	0.75
Hungarian (0)	19	0.21
Irish (369)	1,894	20.81
Italian (808)	2,151	23.63
Lithuanian (74)	264	2.90
Norwegian (37)	46	0.51
Pennsylvania German (0)	12	0.13
Polish (435)	1,444	15.86
Portuguese (64)	128	1.41
Russian (17)	196	2.15
Scotch-Irish (9)	93	1.02
Scottish (44)	294	3.23
Slovene (0)	9	0.10
Swedish (113)	339	3.72
Swiss (0)	80	0.88
Ukrainian (0)	56	0.62
Welsh (0)	104	1.14

Hispanic Origin	Population	%
Hispanic or Latino (of any race)	246	2.64
Central American, ex. Mexican	7	0.08
Guatemalan	3	0.03
Honduran	1	0.01
Nicaraguan	1	0.01
Panamanian	2	0.02
Cuban	15	0.16
Dominican Republic	11	0.12
Mexican	28	0.30
Puerto Rican	87	0.94
South American	48	0.52
Argentinean	4	0.04
Bolivian	1	0.01
Chilean	3	0.03
Colombian	29	0.31
Ecuadorian	2	0.02
Peruvian	6	0.06
Uruguayan	3	0.03
Other Hispanic or Latino	50	0.54

Race*	Population	%
African-American/Black (60)	80	0.86
Not Hispanic (55)	72	0.77
Hispanic (5)	8	0.09
American Indian/Alaska Native (1)	15	0.16
Not Hispanic (1)	14	0.15
Hispanic (0)	1	0.01
Cherokee (0)	3	0.03
Iroquois (0)	2	0.02
South American Ind. (0)	1	0.01
Asian (138)	185	1.99
Not Hispanic (136)	180	1.94
Hispanic (2)	5	0.05
Cambodian (18)	21	0.23
Chinese, ex. Taiwanese (33)	43	0.46
Filipino (7)	13	0.14
Hmong (1)	1	0.01
Indian (33)	50	0.54
Indonesian (1)	1	0.01
Japanese (5)	7	0.08
Korean (12)	14	0.15
Pakistani (1)	1	0.01
Sri Lankan (3)	3	0.03
Vietnamese (8)	13	0.14
Hawaii Native/Pacific Islander (3)	6	0.06
Not Hispanic (3)	6	0.06
Native Hawaiian (0)	2	0.02
White (8,974)	9,047	97.27
Not Hispanic (8,784)	8,850	95.15
Hispanic (190)	197	2.12

Canton

Place Type: Town
County: Hartford
Population: 10,292†

Ancestry‡	Population	%
American (386)	386	3.85
Arab (9)	17	0.17
Lebanese (9)	17	0.17
Austrian (35)	56	0.56
British (80)	112	1.12
Canadian (84)	101	1.01
Croatian (0)	11	0.11
Czech (0)	9	0.09
Czechoslovakian (0)	12	0.12
Danish (0)	45	0.45
Dutch (36)	292	2.91
Eastern European (39)	54	0.54
English (467)	1,640	16.34
European (137)	180	1.79
Finnish (11)	32	0.32
French, ex. Basque (93)	623	6.21
French Canadian (159)	356	3.55
German (312)	1,847	18.40
Greek (19)	19	0.19
Guyanese (20)	20	0.20
Hungarian (26)	111	1.11
Irish (421)	2,004	19.97
Israeli (9)	9	0.09
Italian (700)	1,802	17.95
Lithuanian (78)	195	1.94
Northern European (28)	43	0.43
Norwegian (9)	24	0.24
Pennsylvania German (15)	44	0.44
Polish (376)	1,489	14.84
Portuguese (75)	171	1.70
Russian (60)	259	2.58
Scandinavian (9)	30	0.30
Scotch-Irish (52)	251	2.50
Scottish (53)	427	4.25
Slavic (11)	11	0.11
Slovak (29)	50	0.50
Swedish (64)	542	5.40
Swiss (33)	58	0.58
Ukrainian (18)	134	1.34
Welsh (0)	71	0.71
West Indian, ex. Hispanic (0)	11	0.11
Jamaican (0)	11	0.11
Yugoslavian (0)	42	0.42

Hispanic Origin	Population	%
Hispanic or Latino (of any race)	265	2.57
Central American, ex. Mexican	25	0.24
Costa Rican	9	0.09
Guatemalan	4	0.04
Panamanian	3	0.03
Salvadoran	9	0.09
Cuban	25	0.24
Dominican Republic	9	0.09
Mexican	51	0.50
Puerto Rican	83	0.81
South American	52	0.51
Argentinean	15	0.15
Bolivian	2	0.02
Chilean	3	0.03
Colombian	16	0.16
Ecuadorian	2	0.02
Peruvian	9	0.09
Uruguayan	5	0.05
Other Hispanic or Latino	20	0.19

Race*	Population	%
African-American/Black (94)	141	1.37
Not Hispanic (82)	121	1.18
Hispanic (12)	20	0.19
American Indian/Alaska Native (26)	63	0.61
Not Hispanic (19)	52	0.51
Hispanic (7)	11	0.11
Canadian/French Am. Ind. (0)	1	0.01
Cherokee (2)	6	0.06
Chippewa (1)	1	0.01
Hopi (0)	4	0.04
Iroquois (2)	3	0.03
South American Ind. (1)	2	0.02
Yaqui (0)	3	0.03
Asian (155)	187	1.82
Not Hispanic (151)	178	1.73
Hispanic (4)	9	0.09
Cambodian (3)	3	0.03
Chinese, ex. Taiwanese (58)	72	0.70
Filipino (14)	23	0.22
Indian (21)	24	0.23
Japanese (5)	8	0.08
Korean (23)	27	0.26
Pakistani (4)	4	0.04
Thai (1)	1	0.01
Vietnamese (22)	24	0.23
Hawaii Native/Pacific Islander (2)	7	0.07
Not Hispanic (1)	6	0.06
Hispanic (1)	1	0.01
Guamanian/Chamorro (1)	1	0.01
Native Hawaiian (0)	2	0.02
White (9,851)	9,966	96.83
Not Hispanic (9,671)	9,766	94.89
Hispanic (180)	200	1.94

Cheshire

Place Type: Town
County: New Haven
Population: 29,261†

Ancestry‡	Population	%
Afghan (57)	57	0.20
African, Sub-Saharan (115)	141	0.48
African (98)	115	0.39
Cape Verdean (0)	9	0.03
Nigerian (17)	17	0.06
Albanian (7)	35	0.12
American (587)	587	2.01
Arab (39)	80	0.27
Lebanese (0)	33	0.11
Moroccan (39)	39	0.13
Syrian (0)	8	0.03
Armenian (11)	52	0.18
Austrian (29)	78	0.27
Belgian (0)	28	0.10
Brazilian (71)	71	0.24
British (54)	134	0.46
Bulgarian (0)	25	0.09
Canadian (8)	80	0.27
Croatian (14)	53	0.18
Czech (11)	122	0.42
Czechoslovakian (0)	53	0.18
Danish (55)	163	0.56
Dutch (10)	243	0.83
Eastern European (148)	148	0.51
English (735)	3,534	12.11
European (244)	244	0.84
French, ex. Basque (221)	1,461	5.01
French Canadian (136)	542	1.86
German (540)	3,353	11.49
Greek (282)	496	1.70
Hungarian (45)	397	1.36
Irish (1,551)	6,979	23.91

*Notes: † The Census 2010 population figure is used to calculate the percentages in the Hispanic Origin and Race categories. Ancestry percentages are based on the 2006-2010 American Community Survey population (not shown); ‡ Numbers in parentheses indicate the number of people reporting a single ancestry; * Numbers in parentheses indicate the number of persons reporting this race alone, not in combination with any other race; Please refer to the Explanation of Data for more information.*

Italian (2,875)	7,555	25.89
Latvian (15)	44	0.15
Lithuanian (120)	239	0.82
Maltese (0)	4	0.01
Norwegian (73)	200	0.69
Polish (671)	2,545	8.72
Portuguese (309)	535	1.83
Romanian (70)	136	0.47
Russian (198)	760	2.60
Scandinavian (36)	66	0.23
Scotch-Irish (241)	637	2.18
Scottish (262)	626	2.15
Slavic (0)	25	0.09
Slovak (16)	161	0.55
Slovene (16)	16	0.05
Swedish (297)	981	3.36
Swiss (10)	95	0.33
Turkish (17)	17	0.06
Ukrainian (84)	215	0.74
Welsh (9)	131	0.45
West Indian, ex. Hispanic (67)	105	0.36
Haitian (18)	18	0.06
Jamaican (41)	79	0.27
West Indian (8)	8	0.03

Hispanic Origin	Population	%
Hispanic or Latino (of any race)	1,375	4.70
Central American, ex. Mexican	58	0.20
Costa Rican	22	0.08
Guatemalan	14	0.05
Honduran	3	0.01
Nicaraguan	5	0.02
Panamanian	6	0.02
Salvadoran	7	0.02
Other Central American	1	<0.01
Cuban	76	0.26
Dominican Republic	50	0.17
Mexican	164	0.56
Puerto Rican	693	2.37
South American	217	0.74
Argentinean	31	0.11
Bolivian	4	0.01
Chilean	20	0.07
Colombian	84	0.29
Ecuadorian	25	0.09
Peruvian	27	0.09
Uruguayan	1	<0.01
Venezuelan	25	0.09
Other Hispanic or Latino	117	0.40

Race*	Population	%
African-American/Black (1,461)	1,570	5.37
Not Hispanic (1,374)	1,463	5.00
Hispanic (87)	107	0.37
American Indian/Alaska Native (30)	110	0.38
Not Hispanic (15)	91	0.31
Hispanic (15)	19	0.06
Apache (0)	1	<0.01
Blackfeet (0)	1	<0.01
Cherokee (1)	13	0.04
Chippewa (1)	1	<0.01
Iroquois (4)	12	0.04
Navajo (1)	1	<0.01
Seminole (0)	1	<0.01
Sioux (2)	13	0.04
South American Ind. (5)	6	0.02
Asian (1,489)	1,691	5.78
Not Hispanic (1,477)	1,663	5.68
Hispanic (12)	28	0.10
Bangladeshi (38)	42	0.14
Cambodian (10)	16	0.05
Chinese, ex. Taiwanese (657)	703	2.40
Filipino (90)	136	0.46
Indian (386)	434	1.48
Japanese (25)	54	0.18
Korean (97)	122	0.42
Pakistani (96)	100	0.34
Sri Lankan (10)	12	0.04
Taiwanese (9)	12	0.04
Thai (3)	4	0.01
Vietnamese (32)	41	0.14
Hawaii Native/Pacific Islander (12)	17	0.06
Not Hispanic (12)	15	0.05
Hispanic (0)	2	0.01
Native Hawaiian (7)	8	0.03
Samoan (3)	3	0.01
White (25,503)	25,870	88.41
Not Hispanic (24,637)	24,945	85.25
Hispanic (866)	925	3.16

Clinton

Place Type: Town
County: Middlesex
Population: 13,260†

Ancestry‡	Population	%
Afghan (33)	33	0.25
African, Sub-Saharan (0)	7	0.05
South African (0)	7	0.05
American (423)	423	3.18
Australian (10)	23	0.17
Austrian (9)	59	0.44
Brazilian (122)	122	0.92
British (111)	219	1.64
Canadian (13)	75	0.56
Celtic (50)	50	0.38
Czech (23)	119	0.89
Czechoslovakian (0)	8	0.06
Danish (9)	113	0.85
Dutch (41)	121	0.91
Eastern European (9)	9	0.07
English (671)	2,122	15.94
Estonian (0)	11	0.08
European (67)	67	0.50
Finnish (0)	19	0.14
French, ex. Basque (109)	834	6.26
French Canadian (283)	654	4.91
German (364)	2,245	16.86
Greek (69)	105	0.79
Hungarian (38)	245	1.84
Icelander (0)	9	0.07
Iranian (7)	7	0.05
Irish (766)	3,581	26.89
Italian (1,339)	3,292	24.72
Latvian (0)	17	0.13
Lithuanian (48)	138	1.04
Northern European (0)	9	0.07
Norwegian (0)	108	0.81
Pennsylvania German (9)	9	0.07
Polish (205)	1,052	7.90
Portuguese (250)	287	2.16
Russian (94)	307	2.31
Scandinavian (12)	24	0.18
Scotch-Irish (63)	98	0.74
Scottish (129)	377	2.83
Slavic (0)	10	0.08
Slovak (25)	25	0.19
Slovene (0)	11	0.08
Swedish (83)	381	2.86
Swiss (0)	8	0.06
Turkish (6)	6	0.05
Ukrainian (10)	55	0.41
Welsh (27)	102	0.77
Yugoslavian (31)	31	0.23

Hispanic Origin	Population	%
Hispanic or Latino (of any race)	661	4.98
Central American, ex. Mexican	34	0.26
Costa Rican	5	0.04
Guatemalan	16	0.12
Honduran	3	0.02
Panamanian	2	0.02
Salvadoran	8	0.06
Cuban	12	0.09
Dominican Republic	15	0.11
Mexican	53	0.40
Puerto Rican	258	1.95
South American	189	1.43
Argentinean	11	0.08
Bolivian	1	0.01
Chilean	10	0.08
Colombian	26	0.20
Ecuadorian	130	0.98
Peruvian	6	0.05
Uruguayan	2	0.02
Venezuelan	2	0.02
Other South American	1	0.01
Other Hispanic or Latino	100	0.75

Race*	Population	%
African-American/Black (85)	124	0.94
Not Hispanic (85)	120	0.90
Hispanic (0)	4	0.03
American Indian/Alaska Native (20)	62	0.47
Not Hispanic (16)	52	0.39
Hispanic (4)	10	0.08
Apache (0)	1	0.01
Blackfeet (0)	4	0.03
Canadian/French Am. Ind. (0)	2	0.02
Cherokee (4)	10	0.08
Chickasaw (0)	1	0.01
Cree (0)	1	0.01
Delaware (1)	1	0.01
Iroquois (2)	4	0.03
South American Ind. (2)	2	0.02
Asian (238)	295	2.22
Not Hispanic (236)	292	2.20
Hispanic (2)	3	0.02
Bangladeshi (1)	1	0.01
Cambodian (7)	9	0.07
Chinese, ex. Taiwanese (48)	63	0.48
Filipino (15)	24	0.18
Indian (48)	60	0.45
Japanese (3)	8	0.06
Korean (25)	28	0.21
Laotian (3)	3	0.02
Nepalese (1)	3	0.02
Pakistani (2)	2	0.02
Sri Lankan (2)	2	0.02
Taiwanese (1)	1	0.01
Thai (1)	1	0.01
Vietnamese (69)	80	0.60
Hawaii Native/Pacific Islander (7)	9	0.07
Not Hispanic (7)	9	0.07
Guamanian/Chamorro (7)	8	0.06
White (12,555)	12,723	95.95
Not Hispanic (12,101)	12,218	92.14
Hispanic (454)	505	3.81

Colchester

Place Type: Town
County: New London
Population: 16,068†

Ancestry‡	Population	%
African, Sub-Saharan (0)	10	0.06
African (0)	10	0.06
American (703)	703	4.44
Arab (0)	157	0.99
Lebanese (0)	157	0.99
Armenian (0)	19	0.12
Austrian (61)	153	0.97
British (10)	25	0.16
Canadian (85)	190	1.20
Czech (11)	129	0.81
Czechoslovakian (0)	18	0.11
Danish (29)	54	0.34
Dutch (11)	143	0.90
English (457)	2,079	13.12
European (94)	94	0.59
French, ex. Basque (376)	2,001	12.63
French Canadian (608)	1,308	8.25
German (297)	1,710	10.79
Greek (79)	247	1.56
Guyanese (16)	27	0.17
Hungarian (12)	119	0.75
Irish (743)	3,581	22.59
Israeli (9)	9	0.06

*Notes: † The Census 2010 population figure is used to calculate the percentages in the Hispanic Origin and Race categories. Ancestry percentages are based on the 2006-2010 American Community Survey population (not shown); ‡ Numbers in parentheses indicate the number of people reporting a single ancestry; * Numbers in parentheses indicate the number of persons reporting this race alone, not in combination with any other race; Please refer to the Explanation of Data for more information.*

Italian (1,031)	3,119	19.68
Lithuanian (18)	155	0.98
Norwegian (25)	235	1.48
Polish (481)	2,333	14.72
Portuguese (119)	229	1.44
Russian (110)	395	2.49
Scandinavian (9)	71	0.45
Scotch-Irish (102)	490	3.09
Scottish (148)	595	3.75
Slavic (27)	27	0.17
Slovak (0)	85	0.54
Swedish (42)	455	2.87
Swiss (0)	57	0.36
Ukrainian (175)	201	1.27
Welsh (39)	83	0.52
West Indian, ex. Hispanic (73)	103	0.65
Jamaican (73)	103	0.65
Yugoslavian (0)	18	0.11

Hispanic Origin	Population	%
Hispanic or Latino (of any race)	524	3.26
Central American, ex. Mexican	28	0.17
Costa Rican	3	0.02
Guatemalan	10	0.06
Honduran	5	0.03
Salvadoran	10	0.06
Cuban	25	0.16
Dominican Republic	13	0.08
Mexican	66	0.41
Puerto Rican	279	1.74
South American	67	0.42
Argentinean	4	0.02
Bolivian	1	0.01
Chilean	6	0.04
Colombian	14	0.09
Ecuadorian	11	0.07
Peruvian	27	0.17
Uruguayan	2	0.01
Other South American	2	0.01
Other Hispanic or Latino	46	0.29

Race*	Population	%
African-American/Black (265)	374	2.33
Not Hispanic (240)	334	2.08
Hispanic (25)	40	0.25
American Indian/Alaska Native (82)	182	1.13
Not Hispanic (63)	155	0.96
Hispanic (19)	27	0.17
Alaska Athabascan *(Ala. Nat.)* (5)	9	0.06
Aleut *(Alaska Native)* (0)	3	0.02
Apache (1)	2	0.01
Blackfeet (0)	5	0.03
Cherokee (4)	16	0.10
Chippewa (4)	5	0.03
Choctaw (1)	2	0.01
Cree (0)	2	0.01
Creek (0)	1	0.01
Iroquois (1)	2	0.01
Lumbee (1)	1	0.01
Navajo (0)	2	0.01
Sioux (0)	2	0.01
South American Ind. (9)	15	0.09
Asian (220)	302	1.88
Not Hispanic (219)	299	1.86
Hispanic (1)	3	0.02
Bangladeshi (2)	11	0.07
Cambodian (7)	7	0.04
Chinese, ex. Taiwanese (45)	56	0.35
Filipino (22)	41	0.26
Indian (86)	101	0.63
Indonesian (1)	1	0.01
Japanese (7)	19	0.12
Korean (14)	27	0.17
Laotian (2)	2	0.01
Malaysian (1)	1	0.01
Pakistani (2)	2	0.01
Taiwanese (1)	1	0.01
Thai (0)	4	0.02
Vietnamese (20)	22	0.14
Hawaii Native/Pacific Islander (1)	11	0.07
Not Hispanic (1)	10	0.06
Hispanic (0)	1	0.01
Guamanian/Chamorro (0)	2	0.01
Native Hawaiian (1)	4	0.02
White (15,081)	15,325	95.38
Not Hispanic (14,778)	14,985	93.26
Hispanic (303)	340	2.12

Conning Towers Nautilus Park

Place Type: CDP
County: New London
Population: 8,834†

Ancestry‡	Population	%
Albanian (105)	105	1.14
American (413)	413	4.47
Austrian (0)	92	0.99
British (0)	63	0.68
Cajun (0)	11	0.12
Canadian (0)	28	0.30
Celtic (0)	6	0.06
Czechoslovakian (10)	28	0.30
Danish (0)	58	0.63
Dutch (99)	252	2.73
English (438)	1,141	12.34
European (71)	71	0.77
Finnish (0)	28	0.30
French, ex. Basque (57)	435	4.70
French Canadian (58)	174	1.88
German (481)	1,877	20.30
Greek (0)	8	0.09
Hungarian (0)	30	0.32
Irish (457)	1,525	16.49
Italian (178)	678	7.33
Lithuanian (0)	30	0.32
Northern European (25)	25	0.27
Norwegian (34)	120	1.30
Pennsylvania German (13)	13	0.14
Polish (135)	472	5.10
Portuguese (0)	11	0.12
Romanian (0)	25	0.27
Russian (9)	43	0.47
Scotch-Irish (42)	280	3.03
Scottish (51)	265	2.87
Slovak (0)	35	0.38
Slovene (9)	9	0.10
Swedish (13)	201	2.17
Swiss (0)	8	0.09
Ukrainian (12)	24	0.26
Welsh (61)	169	1.83
West Indian, ex. Hispanic (19)	41	0.44
Jamaican (19)	41	0.44

Hispanic Origin	Population	%
Hispanic or Latino (of any race)	916	10.37
Central American, ex. Mexican	40	0.45
Costa Rican	2	0.02
Guatemalan	5	0.06
Honduran	7	0.08
Nicaraguan	5	0.06
Panamanian	12	0.14
Salvadoran	9	0.10
Cuban	27	0.31
Dominican Republic	44	0.50
Mexican	318	3.60
Puerto Rican	314	3.55
South American	82	0.93
Argentinean	2	0.02
Bolivian	6	0.07
Chilean	1	0.01
Colombian	34	0.38
Ecuadorian	12	0.14
Peruvian	16	0.18
Venezuelan	9	0.10
Other South American	2	0.02
Other Hispanic or Latino	91	1.03

Race*	Population	%
African-American/Black (785)	1,020	11.55
Not Hispanic (723)	927	10.49
Hispanic (62)	93	1.05
American Indian/Alaska Native (73)	272	3.08
Not Hispanic (63)	224	2.54
Hispanic (10)	48	0.54
Aleut *(Alaska Native)* (0)	1	0.01
Apache (1)	3	0.03
Arapaho (0)	4	0.05
Blackfeet (0)	6	0.07
Cherokee (13)	63	0.71
Chippewa (2)	2	0.02
Choctaw (2)	10	0.11
Cree (0)	4	0.05
Crow (0)	1	0.01
Delaware (0)	5	0.06
Inupiat *(Alaska Native)* (2)	2	0.02
Iroquois (2)	3	0.03
Kiowa (0)	1	0.01
Mexican American Ind. (1)	1	0.01
Navajo (4)	4	0.05
Pima (0)	1	0.01
Sioux (0)	6	0.07
South American Ind. (3)	11	0.12
Tlingit-Haida *(Alaska Native)* (0)	2	0.02
Asian (326)	506	5.73
Not Hispanic (304)	463	5.24
Hispanic (22)	43	0.49
Cambodian (1)	3	0.03
Chinese, ex. Taiwanese (43)	71	0.80
Filipino (137)	232	2.63
Hmong (1)	1	0.01
Indian (37)	39	0.44
Indonesian (1)	2	0.02
Japanese (28)	60	0.68
Korean (25)	55	0.62
Laotian (8)	9	0.10
Pakistani (6)	6	0.07
Sri Lankan (1)	2	0.02
Taiwanese (0)	3	0.03
Thai (3)	9	0.10
Vietnamese (22)	31	0.35
Hawaii Native/Pacific Islander (11)	62	0.70
Not Hispanic (11)	52	0.59
Hispanic (0)	10	0.11
Fijian (0)	1	0.01
Guamanian/Chamorro (3)	14	0.16
Native Hawaiian (2)	16	0.18
Samoan (3)	12	0.14
Tongan (0)	1	0.01
White (6,923)	7,417	83.96
Not Hispanic (6,359)	6,768	76.61
Hispanic (564)	649	7.35

Coventry

Place Type: Town
County: Tolland
Population: 12,435†

Ancestry‡	Population	%
African, Sub-Saharan (8)	52	0.42
Ghanaian (8)	8	0.06
South African (0)	44	0.36
American (137)	137	1.11
Arab (19)	69	0.56
Lebanese (19)	69	0.56
Armenian (14)	32	0.26
Austrian (14)	86	0.70
British (14)	58	0.47
Canadian (34)	34	0.28
Czech (0)	11	0.09
Czechoslovakian (0)	21	0.17
Danish (0)	15	0.12
Dutch (26)	63	0.51
Eastern European (10)	10	0.08
English (356)	2,227	18.03
European (0)	10	0.08

*Notes: † The Census 2010 population figure is used to calculate the percentages in the Hispanic Origin and Race categories. Ancestry percentages are based on the 2006-2010 American Community Survey population (not shown); ‡ Numbers in parentheses indicate the number of people reporting a single ancestry; * Numbers in parentheses indicate the number of persons reporting this race alone, not in combination with any other race; Please refer to the Explanation of Data for more information.*

Finnish (0)	24	0.19
French, ex. Basque (559)	2,178	17.63
French Canadian (340)	731	5.92
German (366)	1,938	15.69
Greek (0)	41	0.33
Hungarian (10)	73	0.59
Irish (587)	3,072	24.87
Italian (713)	2,272	18.39
Lithuanian (43)	93	0.75
Norwegian (0)	110	0.89
Polish (412)	1,378	11.15
Portuguese (99)	257	2.08
Russian (39)	149	1.21
Scotch-Irish (191)	430	3.48
Scottish (86)	548	4.44
Slavic (0)	38	0.31
Slovak (0)	11	0.09
Swedish (43)	347	2.81
Swiss (0)	72	0.58
Turkish (123)	123	1.00
Ukrainian (29)	217	1.76
Welsh (0)	82	0.66
West Indian, ex. Hispanic (0)	60	0.49
Dutch West Indian (0)	26	0.21
Jamaican (0)	34	0.28
Yugoslavian (0)	13	0.11

Hispanic Origin	Population	%
Hispanic or Latino (of any race)	325	2.61
Central American, ex. Mexican	18	0.14
Guatemalan	13	0.10
Nicaraguan	3	0.02
Panamanian	2	0.02
Cuban	12	0.10
Dominican Republic	6	0.05
Mexican	60	0.48
Puerto Rican	154	1.24
South American	48	0.39
Argentinean	5	0.04
Bolivian	2	0.02
Chilean	1	0.01
Colombian	20	0.16
Ecuadorian	2	0.02
Peruvian	17	0.14
Venezuelan	1	0.01
Other Hispanic or Latino	27	0.22

Race*	Population	%
African-American/Black (128)	192	1.54
Not Hispanic (118)	176	1.42
Hispanic (10)	16	0.13
American Indian/Alaska Native (30)	97	0.78
Not Hispanic (25)	87	0.70
Hispanic (5)	10	0.08
Apache (0)	1	0.01
Blackfeet (2)	9	0.07
Cherokee (4)	11	0.09
Chippewa (2)	2	0.02
Creek (1)	2	0.02
Iroquois (3)	5	0.04
Kiowa (0)	1	0.01
Lumbee (1)	2	0.02
Mexican American Ind. (1)	1	0.01
Pueblo (1)	1	0.01
South American Ind. (1)	3	0.02
Asian (107)	158	1.27
Not Hispanic (103)	154	1.24
Hispanic (4)	4	0.03
Bangladeshi (6)	6	0.05
Burmese (1)	2	0.02
Chinese, ex. Taiwanese (23)	32	0.26
Filipino (11)	18	0.14
Indian (15)	18	0.14
Japanese (3)	12	0.10
Korean (19)	31	0.25
Pakistani (16)	17	0.14
Thai (0)	2	0.02
Vietnamese (5)	5	0.04
Hawaii Native/Pacific Islander (1)	8	0.06
Not Hispanic (0)	6	0.05
Hispanic (1)	2	0.02
Native Hawaiian (1)	3	0.02
White (11,910)	12,088	97.21
Not Hispanic (11,683)	11,842	95.23
Hispanic (227)	246	1.98

Cromwell

Place Type: Town
County: Middlesex
Population: 14,005†

Ancestry‡	Population	%
African, Sub-Saharan (11)	11	0.08
Ghanaian (11)	11	0.08
Albanian (23)	23	0.17
American (593)	593	4.27
Arab (18)	49	0.35
Arab (2)	2	0.01
Lebanese (16)	47	0.34
Austrian (0)	100	0.72
Belgian (0)	10	0.07
Brazilian (13)	13	0.09
British (24)	35	0.25
Canadian (21)	46	0.33
Croatian (58)	67	0.48
Czech (0)	28	0.20
Czechoslovakian (12)	24	0.17
Danish (9)	73	0.53
Dutch (43)	171	1.23
English (300)	1,469	10.58
European (47)	67	0.48
Finnish (10)	19	0.14
French, ex. Basque (125)	913	6.57
French Canadian (249)	544	3.92
German (403)	1,679	12.09
Greek (68)	113	0.81
Hungarian (47)	98	0.71
Irish (542)	2,426	17.47
Israeli (26)	26	0.19
Italian (2,099)	4,247	30.58
Lithuanian (9)	52	0.37
Norwegian (21)	87	0.63
Polish (815)	1,598	11.51
Portuguese (107)	249	1.79
Russian (59)	166	1.20
Scotch-Irish (53)	239	1.72
Scottish (36)	145	1.04
Serbian (25)	34	0.24
Slovak (12)	24	0.17
Swedish (181)	593	4.27
Swiss (0)	44	0.32
Ukrainian (48)	107	0.77
Welsh (21)	21	0.15
West Indian, ex. Hispanic (75)	90	0.65
Haitian (15)	15	0.11
Jamaican (60)	75	0.54
Yugoslavian (190)	200	1.44

Hispanic Origin	Population	%
Hispanic or Latino (of any race)	633	4.52
Central American, ex. Mexican	26	0.19
Costa Rican	2	0.01
Guatemalan	1	0.01
Honduran	10	0.07
Nicaraguan	2	0.01
Panamanian	3	0.02
Salvadoran	8	0.06
Cuban	49	0.35
Dominican Republic	31	0.22
Mexican	65	0.46
Puerto Rican	310	2.21
South American	113	0.81
Argentinean	16	0.11
Chilean	3	0.02
Colombian	18	0.13
Ecuadorian	5	0.04
Paraguayan	5	0.04
Peruvian	58	0.41
Venezuelan	8	0.06
Other Hispanic or Latino	39	0.28

Race*	Population	%
African-American/Black (593)	727	5.19
Not Hispanic (552)	667	4.76
Hispanic (41)	60	0.43
American Indian/Alaska Native (13)	55	0.39
Not Hispanic (12)	51	0.36
Hispanic (1)	4	0.03
Blackfeet (0)	6	0.04
Canadian/French Am. Ind. (2)	4	0.03
Cherokee (2)	13	0.09
Chickasaw (1)	1	0.01
Iroquois (3)	4	0.03
Navajo (0)	1	0.01
Tlingit-Haida *(Alaska Native)* (0)	1	0.01
Asian (465)	539	3.85
Not Hispanic (462)	531	3.79
Hispanic (3)	8	0.06
Bangladeshi (30)	34	0.24
Chinese, ex. Taiwanese (50)	55	0.39
Filipino (51)	67	0.48
Indian (208)	225	1.61
Japanese (9)	20	0.14
Korean (15)	18	0.13
Laotian (8)	12	0.09
Pakistani (40)	49	0.35
Sri Lankan (5)	5	0.04
Taiwanese (3)	3	0.02
Thai (1)	2	0.01
Vietnamese (38)	43	0.31
Hawaii Native/Pacific Islander (3)	10	0.07
Not Hispanic (1)	8	0.06
Hispanic (2)	2	0.01
Native Hawaiian (3)	7	0.05
Samoan (0)	1	0.01
White (12,534)	12,772	91.20
Not Hispanic (12,132)	12,323	87.99
Hispanic (402)	449	3.21

Danbury

Place Type: City/Town
County: Fairfield
Population: 80,893†

Ancestry‡	Population	%
African, Sub-Saharan (442)	618	0.78
African (231)	255	0.32
Cape Verdean (41)	158	0.20
Nigerian (137)	137	0.17
South African (22)	57	0.07
Other Sub-Saharan African (11)	11	0.01
Albanian (69)	135	0.17
Alsatian (0)	9	0.01
American (2,041)	2,041	2.57
Arab (674)	1,217	1.53
Arab (0)	12	0.02
Egyptian (30)	30	0.04
Jordanian (36)	36	0.05
Lebanese (381)	809	1.02
Palestinian (11)	11	0.01
Syrian (190)	293	0.37
Other Arab (26)	26	0.03
Armenian (53)	91	0.11
Australian (0)	49	0.06
Austrian (10)	203	0.26
Belgian (0)	10	0.01
Brazilian (4,067)	4,363	5.50
British (188)	249	0.31
Canadian (117)	208	0.26
Carpatho Rusyn (17)	17	0.02
Celtic (15)	29	0.04
Croatian (16)	44	0.06
Czech (82)	255	0.32
Czechoslovakian (48)	227	0.29
Danish (32)	161	0.20
Dutch (91)	491	0.62
Eastern European (147)	147	0.19
English (1,233)	4,725	5.95

*Notes: † The Census 2010 population figure is used to calculate the percentages in the Hispanic Origin and Race categories. Ancestry percentages are based on the 2006-2010 American Community Survey population (not shown); ‡ Numbers in parentheses indicate the number of people reporting a single ancestry; * Numbers in parentheses indicate the number of persons reporting this race alone, not in combination with any other race; Please refer to the Explanation of Data for more information.*

European (257)	339	0.43
Finnish (49)	49	0.06
French, ex. Basque (321)	1,544	1.95
French Canadian (502)	805	1.01
German (1,733)	7,023	8.85
Greek (242)	383	0.48
Guyanese (13)	13	0.02
Hungarian (193)	611	0.77
Iranian (19)	30	0.04
Irish (3,797)	10,990	13.85
Italian (5,751)	11,954	15.06
Latvian (27)	27	0.03
Lithuanian (37)	254	0.32
Maltese (0)	25	0.03
Northern European (13)	39	0.05
Norwegian (132)	384	0.48
Pennsylvania German (6)	20	0.03
Polish (1,326)	3,427	4.32
Portuguese (3,500)	4,065	5.12
Romanian (40)	51	0.06
Russian (430)	917	1.16
Scandinavian (40)	154	0.19
Scotch-Irish (260)	563	0.71
Scottish (382)	1,136	1.43
Slavic (21)	37	0.05
Slovak (303)	606	0.76
Swedish (152)	729	0.92
Swiss (58)	160	0.20
Turkish (12)	12	0.02
Ukrainian (54)	154	0.19
Welsh (52)	200	0.25
West Indian, ex. Hispanic (807)	1,049	1.32
Barbadian (12)	23	0.03
Bermudan (8)	8	0.01
Haitian (119)	210	0.26
Jamaican (540)	668	0.84
Trinidadian/Tobagonian (0)	12	0.02
West Indian (128)	128	0.16
Yugoslavian (9)	37	0.05

Hispanic Origin	Population	%
Hispanic or Latino (of any race)	20,185	24.95
Central American, ex. Mexican	1,840	2.27
Costa Rican	88	0.11
Guatemalan	1,036	1.28
Honduran	168	0.21
Nicaraguan	239	0.30
Panamanian	40	0.05
Salvadoran	259	0.32
Other Central American	10	0.01
Cuban	167	0.21
Dominican Republic	3,852	4.76
Mexican	2,102	2.60
Puerto Rican	2,513	3.11
South American	7,674	9.49
Argentinean	93	0.11
Bolivian	23	0.03
Chilean	33	0.04
Colombian	736	0.91
Ecuadorian	6,125	7.57
Paraguayan	17	0.02
Peruvian	510	0.63
Uruguayan	28	0.03
Venezuelan	51	0.06
Other South American	58	0.07
Other Hispanic or Latino	2,037	2.52

Race*	Population	%
African-American/Black (5,803)	6,961	8.61
Not Hispanic (5,030)	5,824	7.20
Hispanic (773)	1,137	1.41
American Indian/Alaska Native (326)	773	0.96
Not Hispanic (106)	366	0.45
Hispanic (220)	407	0.50
Alaska Athabascan *(Ala. Nat.)* (1)	1	<0.01
Apache (0)	1	<0.01
Blackfeet (2)	12	0.01
Canadian/French Am. Ind. (2)	5	0.01
Central American Ind. (8)	9	0.01
Cherokee (18)	69	0.09
Cheyenne (0)	1	<0.01
Chippewa (3)	12	0.01
Choctaw (0)	1	<0.01
Creek (2)	4	<0.01
Crow (0)	1	<0.01
Iroquois (7)	22	0.03
Lumbee (0)	1	<0.01
Menominee (1)	1	<0.01
Mexican American Ind. (16)	31	0.04
Navajo (3)	4	<0.01
Pima (2)	4	<0.01
Pueblo (6)	11	0.01
Sioux (3)	10	0.01
South American Ind. (15)	44	0.05
Spanish American Ind. (2)	11	0.01
Tlingit-Haida *(Alaska Native)* (2)	3	<0.01
Tohono O'Odham (2)	2	<0.01
Ute (0)	1	<0.01
Yakama (1)	1	<0.01
Asian (5,474)	6,004	7.42
Not Hispanic (5,399)	5,835	7.21
Hispanic (75)	169	0.21
Bangladeshi (118)	132	0.16
Burmese (4)	10	0.01
Cambodian (606)	744	0.92
Chinese, ex. Taiwanese (700)	815	1.01
Filipino (427)	523	0.65
Hmong (1)	1	<0.01
Indian (2,243)	2,423	3.00
Indonesian (3)	7	0.01
Japanese (45)	88	0.11
Korean (133)	152	0.19
Laotian (145)	190	0.23
Malaysian (3)	4	<0.01
Nepalese (3)	6	0.01
Pakistani (304)	322	0.40
Sri Lankan (12)	13	0.02
Taiwanese (17)	23	0.03
Thai (47)	101	0.12
Vietnamese (356)	412	0.51
Hawaii Native/Pacific Islander (30)	161	0.20
Not Hispanic (21)	87	0.11
Hispanic (9)	74	0.09
Fijian (0)	3	<0.01
Guamanian/Chamorro (2)	5	0.01
Native Hawaiian (12)	29	0.04
Samoan (2)	3	<0.01
White (55,202)	58,240	72.00
Not Hispanic (46,309)	48,008	59.35
Hispanic (8,893)	10,232	12.65

Darien

Place Type: CDP/Town
County: Fairfield
Population: 20,732[†]

Ancestry[‡]	Population	%
African, Sub-Saharan (0)	12	0.06
South African (0)	12	0.06
American (999)	999	4.89
Arab (0)	84	0.41
Lebanese (0)	74	0.36
Syrian (0)	10	0.05
Armenian (26)	26	0.13
Australian (21)	21	0.10
Austrian (80)	262	1.28
Belgian (34)	99	0.48
Brazilian (31)	31	0.15
British (236)	375	1.84
Bulgarian (30)	30	0.15
Canadian (33)	128	0.63
Croatian (0)	106	0.52
Czech (0)	57	0.28
Czechoslovakian (0)	27	0.13
Danish (46)	138	0.68
Dutch (94)	389	1.91
Eastern European (92)	104	0.51
English (1,104)	4,264	20.89
Estonian (11)	18	0.09
European (399)	399	1.95
Finnish (0)	28	0.14
French, ex. Basque (120)	737	3.61
French Canadian (14)	106	0.52
German (440)	3,504	17.16
Greek (81)	274	1.34
Hungarian (14)	131	0.64
Icelander (0)	12	0.06
Irish (1,797)	5,536	27.12
Israeli (12)	12	0.06
Italian (1,503)	3,844	18.83
Lithuanian (11)	11	0.05
Luxemburger (0)	41	0.20
New Zealander (0)	10	0.05
Northern European (143)	143	0.70
Norwegian (75)	440	2.16
Polish (104)	655	3.21
Portuguese (65)	116	0.57
Romanian (0)	10	0.05
Russian (53)	269	1.32
Scandinavian (82)	122	0.60
Scotch-Irish (199)	666	3.26
Scottish (240)	1,236	6.05
Slovak (17)	106	0.52
Slovene (5)	29	0.14
Swedish (36)	506	2.48
Swiss (49)	151	0.74
Turkish (5)	5	0.02
Ukrainian (50)	85	0.42
Welsh (11)	86	0.42
Yugoslavian (10)	70	0.34

Hispanic Origin	Population	%
Hispanic or Latino (of any race)	743	3.58
Central American, ex. Mexican	58	0.28
Costa Rican	2	0.01
Guatemalan	28	0.14
Honduran	15	0.07
Nicaraguan	2	0.01
Panamanian	3	0.01
Salvadoran	8	0.04
Cuban	33	0.16
Dominican Republic	27	0.13
Mexican	129	0.62
Puerto Rican	102	0.49
South American	269	1.30
Argentinean	45	0.22
Bolivian	2	0.01
Chilean	21	0.10
Colombian	68	0.33
Ecuadorian	46	0.22
Peruvian	53	0.26
Uruguayan	9	0.04
Venezuelan	22	0.11
Other South American	3	0.01
Other Hispanic or Latino	125	0.60

Race*	Population	%
African-American/Black (104)	138	0.67
Not Hispanic (98)	126	0.61
Hispanic (6)	12	0.06
American Indian/Alaska Native (20)	54	0.26
Not Hispanic (17)	45	0.22
Hispanic (3)	9	0.04
Apache (1)	1	<0.01
Central American Ind. (0)	1	<0.01
Cherokee (6)	10	0.05
Chippewa (0)	1	<0.01
Choctaw (1)	2	0.01
Iroquois (1)	2	0.01
Mexican American Ind. (1)	1	<0.01
Navajo (3)	3	0.01
Osage (0)	1	<0.01
Asian (744)	889	4.29
Not Hispanic (744)	887	4.28
Hispanic (0)	2	0.01
Burmese (1)	1	<0.01
Chinese, ex. Taiwanese (252)	313	1.51
Filipino (49)	76	0.37
Indian (196)	225	1.09

*Notes: † The Census 2010 population figure is used to calculate the percentages in the Hispanic Origin and Race categories. Ancestry percentages are based on the 2006-2010 American Community Survey population (not shown); ‡ Numbers in parentheses indicate the number of people reporting a single ancestry; * Numbers in parentheses indicate the number of persons reporting this race alone, not in combination with any other race; Please refer to the Explanation of Data for more information.*

Japanese (72)	96	0.46
Korean (97)	129	0.62
Laotian (1)	5	0.02
Pakistani (14)	15	0.07
Sri Lankan (1)	1	<0.01
Taiwanese (7)	7	0.03
Thai (7)	13	0.06
Vietnamese (17)	18	0.09
Hawaii Native/Pacific Islander (5)	10	0.05
Not Hispanic (5)	9	0.04
Hispanic (0)	1	<0.01
Fijian (0)	3	0.01
Guamanian/Chamorro (1)	1	<0.01
Native Hawaiian (1)	4	0.02
White (19,508)	19,729	95.16
Not Hispanic (18,898)	19,091	92.08
Hispanic (610)	638	3.08

Derby

Place Type: City/Town
County: New Haven
Population: 12,902†

Ancestry‡	Population	%
African, Sub-Saharan (97)	97	0.76
African (97)	97	0.76
American (328)	328	2.56
Arab (0)	13	0.10
Lebanese (0)	13	0.10
Austrian (0)	12	0.09
Brazilian (20)	20	0.16
British (28)	28	0.22
Canadian (0)	31	0.24
Carpatho Rusyn (0)	20	0.16
Czech (0)	16	0.12
Czechoslovakian (0)	12	0.09
Dutch (55)	130	1.01
English (399)	1,152	8.98
French, ex. Basque (109)	568	4.43
French Canadian (30)	101	0.79
German (347)	1,206	9.40
Greek (27)	72	0.56
Hungarian (32)	396	3.09
Irish (497)	1,868	14.56
Italian (1,777)	3,459	26.97
Lithuanian (10)	52	0.41
Maltese (0)	35	0.27
Polish (654)	1,411	11.00
Portuguese (148)	163	1.27
Romanian (81)	81	0.63
Russian (53)	296	2.31
Scotch-Irish (23)	79	0.62
Scottish (60)	252	1.96
Serbian (40)	78	0.61
Slovak (25)	78	0.61
Swedish (0)	164	1.28
Swiss (0)	110	0.86
Ukrainian (35)	192	1.50
Welsh (16)	164	1.28
West Indian, ex. Hispanic (130)	216	1.68
Haitian (99)	114	0.89
Jamaican (31)	86	0.67
West Indian (0)	16	0.12
Yugoslavian (93)	144	1.12

Hispanic Origin	Population	%
Hispanic or Latino (of any race)	1,830	14.18
Central American, ex. Mexican	176	1.36
Costa Rican	16	0.12
Guatemalan	108	0.84
Honduran	26	0.20
Nicaraguan	5	0.04
Panamanian	3	0.02
Salvadoran	12	0.09
Other Central American	6	0.05
Cuban	43	0.33
Dominican Republic	56	0.43
Mexican	152	1.18
Puerto Rican	940	7.29
South American	348	2.70
Argentinean	17	0.13
Bolivian	1	0.01
Chilean	22	0.17
Colombian	52	0.40
Ecuadorian	221	1.71
Peruvian	22	0.17
Uruguayan	4	0.03
Venezuelan	2	0.02
Other South American	7	0.05
Other Hispanic or Latino	115	0.89

Race*	Population	%
African-American/Black (980)	1,168	9.05
Not Hispanic (891)	1,021	7.91
Hispanic (89)	147	1.14
American Indian/Alaska Native (22)	87	0.67
Not Hispanic (21)	67	0.52
Hispanic (1)	20	0.16
Blackfeet (2)	5	0.04
Canadian/French Am. Ind. (0)	3	0.02
Cherokee (0)	8	0.06
Chippewa (1)	1	0.01
Iroquois (2)	6	0.05
South American Ind. (0)	1	0.01
Asian (332)	369	2.86
Not Hispanic (323)	353	2.74
Hispanic (9)	16	0.12
Bangladeshi (13)	13	0.10
Cambodian (1)	1	0.01
Chinese, ex. Taiwanese (36)	39	0.30
Filipino (32)	41	0.32
Hmong (7)	7	0.05
Indian (106)	109	0.84
Indonesian (0)	2	0.02
Japanese (2)	5	0.04
Korean (24)	28	0.22
Laotian (34)	37	0.29
Pakistani (28)	29	0.22
Sri Lankan (2)	2	0.02
Thai (8)	9	0.07
Vietnamese (28)	28	0.22
Hawaii Native/Pacific Islander (1)	15	0.12
Not Hispanic (1)	10	0.08
Hispanic (0)	5	0.04
Guamanian/Chamorro (0)	2	0.02
Native Hawaiian (1)	3	0.02
White (10,681)	10,956	84.92
Not Hispanic (9,599)	9,770	75.72
Hispanic (1,082)	1,186	9.19

East Haddam

Place Type: Town
County: Middlesex
Population: 9,126†

Ancestry‡	Population	%
American (740)	740	8.19
Arab (0)	87	0.96
Arab (0)	81	0.90
Syrian (0)	6	0.07
Armenian (0)	12	0.13
Austrian (0)	7	0.08
British (72)	103	1.14
Canadian (65)	93	1.03
Czech (16)	139	1.54
Danish (46)	121	1.34
Dutch (47)	182	2.01
English (356)	1,545	17.09
European (30)	30	0.33
Finnish (0)	19	0.21
French, ex. Basque (132)	778	8.61
French Canadian (222)	413	4.57
German (271)	1,160	12.83
Greek (0)	37	0.41
Hungarian (22)	77	0.85
Irish (540)	2,533	28.03
Italian (545)	1,913	21.17
Latvian (23)	23	0.25
Lithuanian (11)	83	0.92
Northern European (35)	35	0.39
Norwegian (0)	115	1.27
Polish (304)	1,107	12.25
Portuguese (0)	79	0.87
Russian (0)	47	0.52
Scandinavian (11)	34	0.38
Scotch-Irish (44)	156	1.73
Scottish (89)	409	4.53
Swedish (167)	623	6.89
Swiss (0)	25	0.28
Ukrainian (13)	129	1.43
Welsh (0)	12	0.13

Hispanic Origin	Population	%
Hispanic or Latino (of any race)	210	2.30
Central American, ex. Mexican	10	0.11
Guatemalan	3	0.03
Honduran	1	0.01
Nicaraguan	3	0.03
Panamanian	1	0.01
Salvadoran	2	0.02
Cuban	21	0.23
Mexican	26	0.28
Puerto Rican	102	1.12
South American	30	0.33
Argentinean	5	0.05
Chilean	2	0.02
Ecuadorian	19	0.21
Uruguayan	3	0.03
Venezuelan	1	0.01
Other Hispanic or Latino	21	0.23

Race*	Population	%
African-American/Black (64)	104	1.14
Not Hispanic (50)	86	0.94
Hispanic (14)	18	0.20
American Indian/Alaska Native (21)	52	0.57
Not Hispanic (20)	49	0.54
Hispanic (1)	3	0.03
Blackfeet (0)	3	0.03
Canadian/French Am. Ind. (1)	1	0.01
Cherokee (1)	8	0.09
Iroquois (1)	3	0.03
South American Ind. (0)	1	0.01
Asian (63)	83	0.91
Not Hispanic (61)	80	0.88
Hispanic (2)	3	0.03
Cambodian (1)	5	0.05
Chinese, ex. Taiwanese (13)	23	0.25
Filipino (9)	9	0.10
Indian (3)	8	0.09
Indonesian (1)	2	0.02
Japanese (4)	11	0.12
Korean (14)	15	0.16
Pakistani (9)	9	0.10
Thai (1)	1	0.01
Hawaii Native/Pacific Islander (4)	6	0.07
Not Hispanic (4)	5	0.05
Hispanic (0)	1	0.01
Guamanian/Chamorro (1)	1	0.01
Native Hawaiian (0)	1	0.01
Samoan (3)	3	0.03
White (8,832)	8,925	97.80
Not Hispanic (8,696)	8,777	96.18
Hispanic (136)	148	1.62

East Hampton

Place Type: Town
County: Middlesex
Population: 12,959†

Ancestry‡	Population	%
African, Sub-Saharan (14)	14	0.11
Kenyan (14)	14	0.11
American (235)	235	1.82
Arab (29)	85	0.66
Lebanese (14)	14	0.11
Syrian (15)	71	0.55

*Notes: † The Census 2010 population figure is used to calculate the percentages in the Hispanic Origin and Race categories. Ancestry percentages are based on the 2006-2010 American Community Survey population (not shown); ‡ Numbers in parentheses indicate the number of people reporting a single ancestry; * Numbers in parentheses indicate the number of persons reporting this race alone, not in combination with any other race; Please refer to the Explanation of Data for more information.*

Armenian (5)	15	0.12
Austrian (48)	59	0.46
Brazilian (0)	27	0.21
British (20)	40	0.31
Canadian (44)	111	0.86
Czech (0)	52	0.40
Danish (56)	56	0.43
Dutch (13)	100	0.78
Eastern European (75)	75	0.58
English (328)	1,930	14.97
European (36)	36	0.28
Finnish (0)	6	0.05
French, ex. Basque (168)	1,499	11.63
French Canadian (201)	480	3.72
German (391)	1,797	13.94
Greek (24)	106	0.82
Hungarian (35)	59	0.46
Irish (952)	3,060	23.74
Italian (1,173)	2,989	23.19
Lithuanian (0)	90	0.70
Northern European (25)	25	0.19
Norwegian (12)	54	0.42
Polish (692)	1,406	10.91
Portuguese (101)	201	1.56
Romanian (0)	29	0.22
Russian (62)	331	2.57
Scandinavian (29)	36	0.28
Scotch-Irish (110)	406	3.15
Scottish (60)	306	2.37
Slovak (0)	35	0.27
Swedish (117)	569	4.41
Swiss (0)	24	0.19
Ukrainian (6)	107	0.83
Welsh (0)	50	0.39
West Indian, ex. Hispanic (54)	76	0.59
Jamaican (40)	49	0.38
U.S. Virgin Islander (14)	14	0.11
West Indian (0)	13	0.10

Hispanic Origin	Population	%
Hispanic or Latino (of any race)	344	2.65
Central American, ex. Mexican	14	0.11
Guatemalan	2	0.02
Honduran	3	0.02
Nicaraguan	1	0.01
Panamanian	1	0.01
Salvadoran	5	0.04
Other Central American	2	0.02
Cuban	25	0.19
Dominican Republic	4	0.03
Mexican	42	0.32
Puerto Rican	164	1.27
South American	57	0.44
Argentinean	2	0.02
Colombian	29	0.22
Ecuadorian	20	0.15
Peruvian	3	0.02
Venezuelan	3	0.02
Other Hispanic or Latino	38	0.29

Race*	Population	%
African-American/Black (137)	187	1.44
Not Hispanic (136)	176	1.36
Hispanic (1)	11	0.08
American Indian/Alaska Native (10)	62	0.48
Not Hispanic (10)	53	0.41
Hispanic (0)	9	0.07
Aleut *(Alaska Native)* (1)	1	0.01
Apache (0)	1	0.01
Blackfeet (0)	3	0.02
Canadian/French Am. Ind. (1)	1	0.01
Cherokee (1)	12	0.09
Chippewa (1)	1	0.01
Iroquois (1)	7	0.05
Kiowa (0)	1	0.01
Sioux (0)	1	0.01
Asian (201)	275	2.12
Not Hispanic (197)	266	2.05
Hispanic (4)	9	0.07
Bangladeshi (6)	6	0.05
Burmese (3)	3	0.02
Cambodian (7)	7	0.05
Chinese, ex. Taiwanese (32)	43	0.33
Filipino (35)	50	0.39
Indian (63)	77	0.59
Indonesian (1)	3	0.02
Japanese (8)	18	0.14
Korean (32)	37	0.29
Laotian (1)	3	0.02
Pakistani (9)	9	0.07
Thai (1)	1	0.01
Vietnamese (2)	6	0.05
Hawaii Native/Pacific Islander (2)	4	0.03
Not Hispanic (2)	4	0.03
Marshallese (1)	1	0.01
Native Hawaiian (1)	2	0.02
White (12,361)	12,528	96.67
Not Hispanic (12,117)	12,253	94.55
Hispanic (244)	275	2.12

East Hartford

Place Type: CDP/Town
County: Hartford
Population: 51,252†

Ancestry‡	Population	%
African, Sub-Saharan (1,436)	1,498	2.94
African (1,047)	1,104	2.17
Cape Verdean (22)	27	0.05
Ethiopian (16)	16	0.03
Ghanaian (249)	249	0.49
Nigerian (102)	102	0.20
Albanian (89)	89	0.17
American (873)	873	1.71
Arab (212)	304	0.60
Lebanese (178)	253	0.50
Moroccan (26)	26	0.05
Syrian (0)	9	0.02
Other Arab (8)	16	0.03
Armenian (68)	93	0.18
Austrian (0)	44	0.09
Belgian (0)	7	0.01
Brazilian (0)	29	0.06
British (31)	60	0.12
Cajun (0)	17	0.03
Canadian (75)	121	0.24
Croatian (9)	21	0.04
Czech (6)	49	0.10
Czechoslovakian (39)	53	0.10
Danish (102)	200	0.39
Dutch (51)	144	0.28
English (635)	3,725	7.31
European (97)	97	0.19
Finnish (0)	29	0.06
French, ex. Basque (1,029)	3,347	6.57
French Canadian (883)	1,409	2.76
German (433)	2,324	4.56
Greek (172)	218	0.43
Guyanese (51)	100	0.20
Hungarian (62)	299	0.59
Icelander (0)	104	0.20
Iranian (12)	12	0.02
Irish (1,440)	5,343	10.48
Israeli (25)	25	0.05
Italian (2,394)	4,917	9.65
Lithuanian (110)	329	0.65
Northern European (0)	24	0.05
Norwegian (40)	85	0.17
Polish (1,354)	2,735	5.37
Portuguese (461)	804	1.58
Russian (100)	170	0.33
Scandinavian (12)	12	0.02
Scotch-Irish (164)	613	1.20
Scottish (166)	692	1.36
Slavic (10)	28	0.05
Slovak (8)	25	0.05
Swedish (205)	576	1.13
Swiss (62)	75	0.15
Ukrainian (149)	222	0.44
Welsh (12)	112	0.22
West Indian, ex. Hispanic (2,485)	2,797	5.49
Barbadian (79)	79	0.15
Bermudan (20)	20	0.04
British West Indian (74)	84	0.16
Haitian (103)	168	0.33
Jamaican (1,970)	2,176	4.27
Trinidadian/Tobagonian (42)	73	0.14
West Indian (197)	197	0.39

Hispanic Origin	Population	%
Hispanic or Latino (of any race)	13,232	25.82
Central American, ex. Mexican	809	1.58
Costa Rican	13	0.03
Guatemalan	52	0.10
Honduran	185	0.36
Nicaraguan	13	0.03
Panamanian	32	0.06
Salvadoran	504	0.98
Other Central American	10	0.02
Cuban	156	0.30
Dominican Republic	418	0.82
Mexican	568	1.11
Puerto Rican	8,903	17.37
South American	1,675	3.27
Argentinean	33	0.06
Bolivian	90	0.18
Chilean	26	0.05
Colombian	410	0.80
Ecuadorian	89	0.17
Paraguayan	2	<0.01
Peruvian	962	1.88
Uruguayan	20	0.04
Venezuelan	29	0.06
Other South American	14	0.03
Other Hispanic or Latino	703	1.37

Race*	Population	%
African-American/Black (13,342)	14,399	28.09
Not Hispanic (12,393)	13,054	25.47
Hispanic (949)	1,345	2.62
American Indian/Alaska Native (212)	547	1.07
Not Hispanic (101)	338	0.66
Hispanic (111)	209	0.41
Apache (3)	5	0.01
Blackfeet (0)	30	0.06
Canadian/French Am. Ind. (0)	3	0.01
Central American Ind. (6)	11	0.02
Cherokee (10)	36	0.07
Chippewa (1)	2	<0.01
Choctaw (0)	1	<0.01
Cree (3)	3	0.01
Iroquois (5)	17	0.03
Lumbee (0)	1	<0.01
Mexican American Ind. (6)	7	0.01
Navajo (0)	1	<0.01
Potawatomi (1)	5	0.01
Seminole (0)	7	0.01
Sioux (2)	5	0.01
South American Ind. (11)	25	0.05
Spanish American Ind. (3)	3	0.01
Asian (2,943)	3,255	6.35
Not Hispanic (2,899)	3,145	6.14
Hispanic (44)	110	0.21
Bangladeshi (21)	27	0.05
Cambodian (35)	45	0.09
Chinese, ex. Taiwanese (104)	153	0.30
Filipino (175)	212	0.41
Hmong (1)	5	0.01
Indian (1,198)	1,303	2.54
Indonesian (4)	12	0.02
Japanese (23)	43	0.08
Korean (44)	46	0.09
Laotian (312)	336	0.66
Malaysian (2)	2	<0.01
Nepalese (13)	15	0.03
Pakistani (62)	73	0.14
Sri Lankan (1)	2	<0.01
Thai (13)	26	0.05
Vietnamese (826)	876	1.71

*Notes: † The Census 2010 population figure is used to calculate the percentages in the Hispanic Origin and Race categories. Ancestry percentages are based on the 2006-2010 American Community Survey population (not shown); ‡ Numbers in parentheses indicate the number of people reporting a single ancestry; * Numbers in parentheses indicate the number of persons reporting this race alone, not in combination with any other race; Please refer to the Explanation of Data for more information.*

Hawaii Native/Pacific Islander (35)	132	0.26
Not Hispanic (6)	47	0.09
Hispanic (29)	85	0.17
Guamanian/Chamorro (11)	11	0.02
Native Hawaiian (9)	29	0.06
Samoan (9)	9	0.02
White (26,284)	27,602	53.86
Not Hispanic (21,452)	22,168	43.25
Hispanic (4,832)	5,434	10.60

East Haven

Place Type: CDP/Town
County: New Haven
Population: 29,257†

Ancestry‡	Population	%
African, Sub-Saharan (0)	21	0.07
Cape Verdean (0)	21	0.07
Albanian (133)	133	0.46
American (404)	404	1.39
Arab (96)	136	0.47
Iraqi (58)	58	0.20
Lebanese (0)	30	0.10
Syrian (0)	10	0.03
Other Arab (38)	38	0.13
Armenian (0)	97	0.33
Austrian (29)	69	0.24
Belgian (0)	13	0.04
Brazilian (23)	38	0.13
British (65)	101	0.35
Canadian (10)	90	0.31
Czech (16)	102	0.35
Danish (9)	19	0.07
Dutch (15)	226	0.78
English (464)	2,366	8.14
European (78)	96	0.33
Finnish (11)	72	0.25
French, ex. Basque (197)	1,262	4.34
French Canadian (245)	674	2.32
German (380)	2,119	7.29
Greek (15)	224	0.77
Guyanese (81)	81	0.28
Hungarian (47)	190	0.65
Irish (1,429)	5,491	18.89
Israeli (12)	12	0.04
Italian (9,029)	14,372	49.43
Latvian (10)	10	0.03
Lithuanian (62)	176	0.61
Norwegian (25)	143	0.49
Pennsylvania German (0)	12	0.04
Polish (823)	2,301	7.91
Portuguese (191)	295	1.01
Russian (27)	334	1.15
Scandinavian (15)	15	0.05
Scotch-Irish (163)	341	1.17
Scottish (88)	296	1.02
Slavic (0)	157	0.54
Slovak (12)	40	0.14
Swedish (261)	526	1.81
Ukrainian (25)	59	0.20
Welsh (48)	133	0.46
West Indian, ex. Hispanic (124)	177	0.61
Jamaican (124)	166	0.57
West Indian (0)	11	0.04
Yugoslavian (36)	36	0.12

Hispanic Origin	Population	%
Hispanic or Latino (of any race)	3,012	10.29
Central American, ex. Mexican	141	0.48
Costa Rican	4	0.01
Guatemalan	84	0.29
Honduran	7	0.02
Nicaraguan	10	0.03
Panamanian	5	0.02
Salvadoran	31	0.11
Cuban	74	0.25
Dominican Republic	83	0.28
Mexican	365	1.25
Puerto Rican	1,347	4.60
South American	809	2.77
Argentinean	35	0.12
Chilean	29	0.10
Colombian	157	0.54
Ecuadorian	518	1.77
Paraguayan	1	<0.01
Peruvian	39	0.13
Uruguayan	1	<0.01
Venezuelan	27	0.09
Other South American	2	0.01
Other Hispanic or Latino	193	0.66

Race*	Population	%
African-American/Black (841)	1,008	3.45
Not Hispanic (771)	919	3.14
Hispanic (70)	89	0.30
American Indian/Alaska Native (50)	166	0.57
Not Hispanic (32)	133	0.45
Hispanic (18)	33	0.11
Blackfeet (0)	8	0.03
Canadian/French Am. Ind. (0)	1	<0.01
Central American Ind. (1)	1	<0.01
Cherokee (5)	17	0.06
Cheyenne (0)	1	<0.01
Chippewa (4)	5	0.02
Choctaw (1)	7	0.02
Cree (0)	1	<0.01
Delaware (1)	1	<0.01
Inupiat *(Alaska Native)* (0)	1	<0.01
Iroquois (0)	1	<0.01
Mexican American Ind. (4)	4	0.01
Navajo (1)	1	<0.01
Sioux (0)	5	0.02
South American Ind. (2)	3	0.01
Spanish American Ind. (1)	3	0.01
Asian (966)	1,057	3.61
Not Hispanic (954)	1,038	3.55
Hispanic (12)	19	0.06
Bangladeshi (4)	4	0.01
Burmese (2)	2	0.01
Cambodian (103)	112	0.38
Chinese, ex. Taiwanese (97)	116	0.40
Filipino (114)	145	0.50
Indian (276)	296	1.01
Indonesian (3)	3	0.01
Japanese (9)	18	0.06
Korean (31)	34	0.12
Laotian (37)	45	0.15
Malaysian (2)	2	0.01
Nepalese (3)	3	0.01
Pakistani (44)	49	0.17
Sri Lankan (1)	1	<0.01
Taiwanese (2)	3	0.01
Thai (22)	26	0.09
Vietnamese (185)	188	0.64
Hawaii Native/Pacific Islander (2)	4	0.01
Not Hispanic (2)	4	0.01
Native Hawaiian (1)	2	0.01
White (25,887)	26,298	89.89
Not Hispanic (24,154)	24,418	83.46
Hispanic (1,733)	1,880	6.43

East Lyme

Place Type: Town
County: New London
Population: 19,159†

Ancestry‡	Population	%
African, Sub-Saharan (27)	51	0.27
Nigerian (27)	27	0.14
South African (0)	24	0.13
Albanian (9)	9	0.05
American (897)	897	4.70
Arab (78)	125	0.66
Lebanese (78)	125	0.66
Armenian (26)	26	0.14
Australian (32)	49	0.26
Austrian (26)	115	0.60
Brazilian (50)	73	0.38
British (44)	44	0.23
Canadian (19)	64	0.34
Croatian (0)	42	0.22
Czech (0)	39	0.20
Czechoslovakian (27)	30	0.16
Danish (24)	67	0.35
Dutch (38)	175	0.92
Eastern European (29)	29	0.15
English (963)	3,032	15.90
European (91)	135	0.71
Finnish (21)	81	0.42
French, ex. Basque (140)	1,015	5.32
French Canadian (245)	566	2.97
German (488)	2,238	11.74
Greek (129)	206	1.08
Hungarian (77)	231	1.21
Irish (1,054)	4,085	21.42
Italian (1,389)	3,616	18.96
Lithuanian (106)	301	1.58
Luxemburger (25)	25	0.13
Northern European (36)	36	0.19
Norwegian (24)	82	0.43
Pennsylvania German (0)	7	0.04
Polish (485)	1,647	8.64
Portuguese (25)	157	0.82
Romanian (10)	32	0.17
Russian (89)	486	2.55
Scandinavian (0)	9	0.05
Scotch-Irish (32)	366	1.92
Scottish (225)	837	4.39
Serbian (11)	11	0.06
Slovak (0)	33	0.17
Swedish (63)	398	2.09
Swiss (11)	32	0.17
Ukrainian (314)	454	2.38
Welsh (26)	77	0.40
West Indian, ex. Hispanic (16)	95	0.50
Bahamian (0)	31	0.16
Haitian (11)	11	0.06
Jamaican (5)	12	0.06
Trinidadian/Tobagonian (0)	9	0.05
West Indian (0)	32	0.17
Yugoslavian (9)	9	0.05

Hispanic Origin	Population	%
Hispanic or Latino (of any race)	1,015	5.30
Central American, ex. Mexican	33	0.17
Costa Rican	7	0.04
Guatemalan	6	0.03
Honduran	1	0.01
Panamanian	6	0.03
Salvadoran	13	0.07
Cuban	25	0.13
Dominican Republic	20	0.10
Mexican	85	0.44
Puerto Rican	242	1.26
South American	138	0.72
Argentinean	10	0.05
Bolivian	2	0.01
Chilean	13	0.07
Colombian	51	0.27
Ecuadorian	38	0.20
Peruvian	16	0.08
Uruguayan	4	0.02
Venezuelan	4	0.02
Other Hispanic or Latino	472	2.46

Race*	Population	%
African-American/Black (1,008)	1,112	5.80
Not Hispanic (970)	1,061	5.54
Hispanic (38)	51	0.27
American Indian/Alaska Native (55)	141	0.74
Not Hispanic (44)	117	0.61
Hispanic (11)	24	0.13
Blackfeet (0)	2	0.01
Canadian/French Am. Ind. (0)	3	0.02
Cherokee (9)	21	0.11
Chippewa (5)	5	0.03
Choctaw (0)	4	0.02
Iroquois (5)	9	0.05

*Notes: † The Census 2010 population figure is used to calculate the percentages in the Hispanic Origin and Race categories. Ancestry percentages are based on the 2006-2010 American Community Survey population (not shown); ‡ Numbers in parentheses indicate the number of people reporting a single ancestry; * Numbers in parentheses indicate the number of persons reporting this race alone, not in combination with any other race; Please refer to the Explanation of Data for more information.*

Navajo (2)	2	0.01
Seminole (0)	1	0.01
Sioux (1)	2	0.01
South American Ind. (2)	5	0.03
Asian (1,036)	1,194	6.23
Not Hispanic (1,029)	1,177	6.14
Hispanic (7)	17	0.09
Bangladeshi (20)	21	0.11
Cambodian (6)	8	0.04
Chinese, ex. Taiwanese (470)	511	2.67
Filipino (46)	90	0.47
Indian (291)	311	1.62
Indonesian (0)	2	0.01
Japanese (21)	45	0.23
Korean (46)	59	0.31
Laotian (13)	14	0.07
Malaysian (0)	1	0.01
Nepalese (11)	11	0.06
Pakistani (39)	39	0.20
Sri Lankan (21)	21	0.11
Taiwanese (12)	13	0.07
Thai (0)	2	0.01
Vietnamese (17)	28	0.15
Hawaii Native/Pacific Islander (6)	23	0.12
Not Hispanic (5)	20	0.10
Hispanic (1)	3	0.02
Guamanian/Chamorro (2)	4	0.02
Native Hawaiian (0)	10	0.05
Samoan (0)	1	0.01
White (16,183)	16,495	86.10
Not Hispanic (15,792)	16,047	83.76
Hispanic (391)	448	2.34

East Windsor

Place Type: Town
County: Hartford
Population: 11,162†

Ancestry‡	Population	%
African, Sub-Saharan (19)	19	0.17
Nigerian (19)	19	0.17
American (411)	411	3.76
Armenian (0)	10	0.09
Austrian (15)	50	0.46
British (30)	41	0.38
Canadian (37)	64	0.59
Dutch (0)	73	0.67
English (239)	1,280	11.72
Estonian (18)	18	0.16
European (50)	50	0.46
Finnish (13)	35	0.32
French, ex. Basque (394)	1,675	15.34
French Canadian (171)	396	3.63
German (206)	1,085	9.93
Greek (0)	96	0.88
Guyanese (39)	39	0.36
Hungarian (0)	46	0.42
Irish (549)	1,894	17.34
Italian (503)	1,485	13.60
Lithuanian (124)	301	2.76
Norwegian (9)	26	0.24
Pennsylvania German (0)	23	0.21
Polish (603)	1,182	10.82
Portuguese (43)	88	0.81
Russian (66)	130	1.19
Scandinavian (0)	12	0.11
Scotch-Irish (44)	141	1.29
Scottish (141)	487	4.46
Slavic (35)	35	0.32
Slovak (30)	51	0.47
Swedish (40)	107	0.98
Swiss (0)	14	0.13
Ukrainian (0)	15	0.14
Welsh (0)	36	0.33
West Indian, ex. Hispanic (184)	386	3.53
Haitian (0)	36	0.33
Jamaican (169)	335	3.07
West Indian (15)	15	0.14

Hispanic Origin	Population	%
Hispanic or Latino (of any race)	641	5.74
Central American, ex. Mexican	44	0.39
Costa Rican	6	0.05
Guatemalan	12	0.11
Honduran	3	0.03
Panamanian	1	0.01
Salvadoran	17	0.15
Other Central American	5	0.04
Cuban	11	0.10
Dominican Republic	18	0.16
Mexican	66	0.59
Puerto Rican	405	3.63
South American	57	0.51
Argentinean	7	0.06
Chilean	2	0.02
Colombian	13	0.12
Ecuadorian	5	0.04
Peruvian	29	0.26
Venezuelan	1	0.01
Other Hispanic or Latino	40	0.36

Race*	Population	%
African-American/Black (774)	894	8.01
Not Hispanic (742)	835	7.48
Hispanic (32)	59	0.53
American Indian/Alaska Native (15)	79	0.71
Not Hispanic (12)	63	0.56
Hispanic (3)	16	0.14
Cherokee (0)	5	0.04
Choctaw (0)	1	0.01
Iroquois (0)	6	0.05
Mexican American Ind. (0)	1	0.01
Seminole (0)	2	0.02
Sioux (0)	1	0.01
South American Ind. (0)	1	0.01
Asian (520)	560	5.02
Not Hispanic (518)	558	5.00
Hispanic (2)	2	0.02
Cambodian (6)	6	0.05
Chinese, ex. Taiwanese (33)	35	0.31
Filipino (26)	35	0.31
Indian (345)	350	3.14
Japanese (8)	9	0.08
Korean (18)	23	0.21
Laotian (15)	22	0.20
Pakistani (31)	33	0.30
Taiwanese (3)	3	0.03
Thai (0)	1	0.01
Vietnamese (31)	36	0.32
Hawaii Native/Pacific Islander (5)	15	0.13
Not Hispanic (0)	6	0.05
Hispanic (5)	9	0.08
Guamanian/Chamorro (5)	5	0.04
Native Hawaiian (0)	1	0.01
White (9,360)	9,549	85.55
Not Hispanic (9,068)	9,202	82.44
Hispanic (292)	347	3.11

Ellington

Place Type: Town
County: Tolland
Population: 15,602†

Ancestry‡	Population	%
African, Sub-Saharan (59)	59	0.39
African (59)	59	0.39
Albanian (0)	39	0.26
American (521)	521	3.42
Arab (12)	12	0.08
Egyptian (12)	12	0.08
Austrian (26)	63	0.41
Brazilian (17)	17	0.11
British (37)	126	0.83
Bulgarian (9)	9	0.06
Cajun (17)	17	0.11
Canadian (124)	190	1.25
Croatian (0)	10	0.07
Czech (0)	17	0.11
Czechoslovakian (0)	119	0.78
Danish (39)	159	1.04
Dutch (55)	143	0.94
Eastern European (10)	10	0.07
English (505)	1,988	13.05
European (68)	68	0.45
Finnish (12)	37	0.24
French, ex. Basque (335)	1,684	11.06
French Canadian (345)	962	6.32
German (425)	2,453	16.11
Greek (10)	70	0.46
Hungarian (13)	37	0.24
Irish (676)	3,391	22.27
Italian (942)	3,053	20.05
Lithuanian (93)	237	1.56
Norwegian (44)	98	0.64
Pennsylvania German (13)	13	0.09
Polish (586)	1,869	12.27
Portuguese (307)	407	2.67
Russian (77)	135	0.89
Scandinavian (24)	50	0.33
Scotch-Irish (60)	202	1.33
Scottish (162)	451	2.96
Serbian (15)	15	0.10
Slavic (50)	50	0.33
Slovak (33)	49	0.32
Swedish (25)	358	2.35
Swiss (303)	692	4.54
Ukrainian (14)	108	0.71
Welsh (11)	37	0.24
West Indian, ex. Hispanic (34)	34	0.22
Barbadian (8)	8	0.05
Jamaican (26)	26	0.17

Hispanic Origin	Population	%
Hispanic or Latino (of any race)	406	2.60
Central American, ex. Mexican	17	0.11
Costa Rican	6	0.04
Guatemalan	5	0.03
Honduran	1	0.01
Nicaraguan	1	0.01
Panamanian	4	0.03
Cuban	25	0.16
Dominican Republic	5	0.03
Mexican	77	0.49
Puerto Rican	197	1.26
South American	59	0.38
Argentinean	6	0.04
Colombian	24	0.15
Ecuadorian	4	0.03
Peruvian	23	0.15
Uruguayan	1	0.01
Venezuelan	1	0.01
Other Hispanic or Latino	26	0.17

Race*	Population	%
African-American/Black (301)	420	2.69
Not Hispanic (283)	390	2.50
Hispanic (18)	30	0.19
American Indian/Alaska Native (29)	93	0.60
Not Hispanic (25)	84	0.54
Hispanic (4)	9	0.06
Blackfeet (0)	9	0.06
Canadian/French Am. Ind. (1)	4	0.03
Central American Ind. (1)	1	0.01
Cherokee (2)	6	0.04
Chippewa (1)	2	0.01
Choctaw (0)	1	0.01
Iroquois (0)	10	0.06
Osage (0)	1	0.01
Ottawa (0)	1	0.01
South American Ind. (0)	1	0.01
Asian (517)	599	3.84
Not Hispanic (516)	594	3.81
Hispanic (1)	5	0.03
Cambodian (2)	2	0.01
Chinese, ex. Taiwanese (114)	122	0.78
Filipino (19)	45	0.29
Hmong (3)	5	0.03
Indian (256)	265	1.70

*Notes: † The Census 2010 population figure is used to calculate the percentages in the Hispanic Origin and Race categories. Ancestry percentages are based on the 2006-2010 American Community Survey population (not shown); ‡ Numbers in parentheses indicate the number of people reporting a single ancestry; * Numbers in parentheses indicate the number of persons reporting this race alone, not in combination with any other race; Please refer to the Explanation of Data for more information.*

Indonesian (1)	1	0.01
Japanese (10)	17	0.11
Korean (38)	50	0.32
Laotian (4)	7	0.04
Pakistani (20)	27	0.17
Taiwanese (2)	2	0.01
Vietnamese (37)	42	0.27
Hawaii Native/Pacific Islander (3)	8	0.05
Not Hispanic (2)	7	0.04
Hispanic (1)	1	0.01
Guamanian/Chamorro (2)	4	0.03
Native Hawaiian (0)	1	0.01
Samoan (1)	3	0.02
White (14,369)	14,615	93.67
Not Hispanic (14,104)	14,321	91.79
Hispanic (265)	294	1.88

Enfield

Place Type: Town
County: Hartford
Population: 44,654†

Ancestry‡	Population	%
African, Sub-Saharan (353)	414	0.92
African (328)	389	0.87
Cape Verdean (17)	17	0.04
Other Sub-Saharan African (8)	8	0.02
American (1,177)	1,177	2.63
Arab (204)	278	0.62
Lebanese (187)	250	0.56
Moroccan (9)	9	0.02
Syrian (0)	11	0.02
Other Arab (8)	8	0.02
Armenian (50)	198	0.44
Australian (9)	9	0.02
Austrian (0)	183	0.41
Belgian (8)	111	0.25
Brazilian (39)	39	0.09
British (52)	148	0.33
Canadian (176)	345	0.77
Carpatho Rusyn (8)	8	0.02
Croatian (30)	62	0.14
Czech (31)	230	0.51
Czechoslovakian (0)	48	0.11
Danish (39)	278	0.62
Dutch (21)	339	0.76
English (1,379)	5,579	12.45
European (268)	328	0.73
Finnish (35)	214	0.48
French, ex. Basque (1,374)	6,826	15.24
French Canadian (1,393)	2,971	6.63
German (690)	4,683	10.45
German Russian (18)	18	0.04
Greek (104)	331	0.74
Guyanese (77)	81	0.18
Hungarian (143)	342	0.76
Iranian (63)	63	0.14
Irish (2,451)	10,690	23.86
Italian (2,820)	8,173	18.25
Lithuanian (195)	429	0.96
Norwegian (126)	462	1.03
Polish (2,199)	5,936	13.25
Portuguese (87)	421	0.94
Russian (74)	423	0.94
Scandinavian (26)	36	0.08
Scotch-Irish (229)	850	1.90
Scottish (212)	996	2.22
Slavic (0)	28	0.06
Slovak (73)	99	0.22
Swedish (118)	684	1.53
Swiss (14)	20	0.04
Turkish (16)	31	0.07
Ukrainian (165)	277	0.62
Welsh (22)	218	0.49
West Indian, ex. Hispanic (187)	356	0.79
Haitian (2)	37	0.08
Jamaican (160)	243	0.54
Trinidadian/Tobagonian (9)	9	0.02
West Indian (16)	67	0.15
Yugoslavian (0)	31	0.07

Hispanic Origin	Population	%
Hispanic or Latino (of any race)	3,006	6.73
Central American, ex. Mexican	74	0.17
Costa Rican	4	0.01
Guatemalan	21	0.05
Honduran	11	0.02
Nicaraguan	2	<0.01
Panamanian	17	0.04
Salvadoran	19	0.04
Cuban	73	0.16
Dominican Republic	48	0.11
Mexican	407	0.91
Puerto Rican	1,145	2.56
South American	195	0.44
Argentinean	10	0.02
Chilean	1	<0.01
Colombian	88	0.20
Ecuadorian	25	0.06
Paraguayan	2	<0.01
Peruvian	57	0.13
Venezuelan	11	0.02
Other South American	1	<0.01
Other Hispanic or Latino	1,064	2.38

Race*	Population	%
African-American/Black (2,755)	3,188	7.14
Not Hispanic (2,611)	2,994	6.70
Hispanic (144)	194	0.43
American Indian/Alaska Native (75)	309	0.69
Not Hispanic (58)	266	0.60
Hispanic (17)	43	0.10
Apache (0)	2	<0.01
Blackfeet (1)	20	0.04
Canadian/French Am. Ind. (0)	5	0.01
Cherokee (3)	51	0.11
Cheyenne (0)	1	<0.01
Chickasaw (0)	1	<0.01
Chippewa (0)	2	<0.01
Choctaw (1)	1	<0.01
Cree (1)	3	0.01
Creek (0)	2	<0.01
Delaware (0)	3	0.01
Iroquois (3)	19	0.04
Lumbee (0)	1	<0.01
Mexican American Ind. (3)	3	0.01
Navajo (0)	6	0.01
Potawatomi (0)	1	<0.01
Seminole (0)	3	0.01
Sioux (0)	6	0.01
South American Ind. (8)	14	0.03
Asian (869)	1,057	2.37
Not Hispanic (864)	1,034	2.32
Hispanic (5)	23	0.05
Cambodian (29)	32	0.07
Chinese, ex. Taiwanese (97)	127	0.28
Filipino (102)	155	0.35
Hmong (94)	96	0.21
Indian (289)	328	0.73
Indonesian (4)	6	0.01
Japanese (15)	30	0.07
Korean (49)	54	0.12
Laotian (24)	34	0.08
Pakistani (26)	30	0.07
Taiwanese (1)	3	0.01
Thai (10)	14	0.03
Vietnamese (91)	107	0.24
Hawaii Native/Pacific Islander (18)	53	0.12
Not Hispanic (15)	45	0.10
Hispanic (3)	8	0.02
Guamanian/Chamorro (1)	3	0.01
Marshallese (1)	1	<0.01
Native Hawaiian (7)	17	0.04
Samoan (1)	4	0.01
White (38,497)	39,252	87.90
Not Hispanic (37,336)	37,951	84.99
Hispanic (1,161)	1,301	2.91

Fairfield

Place Type: Town
County: Fairfield
Population: 59,404†

Ancestry‡	Population	%
African, Sub-Saharan (50)	94	0.16
African (32)	32	0.05
Cape Verdean (0)	15	0.03
South African (18)	47	0.08
Albanian (145)	226	0.38
Alsatian (0)	10	0.02
American (1,617)	1,617	2.75
Arab (122)	305	0.52
Egyptian (15)	15	0.03
Lebanese (50)	175	0.30
Moroccan (15)	15	0.03
Palestinian (16)	16	0.03
Syrian (14)	35	0.06
Other Arab (12)	49	0.08
Armenian (89)	192	0.33
Australian (18)	26	0.04
Austrian (101)	492	0.84
Belgian (7)	39	0.07
Brazilian (66)	101	0.17
British (545)	699	1.19
Canadian (108)	333	0.57
Celtic (11)	11	0.02
Croatian (48)	63	0.11
Czech (129)	425	0.72
Czechoslovakian (38)	78	0.13
Danish (118)	227	0.39
Dutch (136)	590	1.00
Eastern European (220)	350	0.60
English (1,433)	7,034	11.98
Estonian (7)	7	0.01
European (564)	606	1.03
Finnish (75)	229	0.39
French, ex. Basque (326)	1,573	2.68
French Canadian (430)	1,097	1.87
German (1,147)	7,197	12.26
Greek (393)	870	1.48
Hungarian (1,194)	3,015	5.13
Iranian (36)	36	0.06
Irish (4,720)	15,091	25.70
Israeli (42)	52	0.09
Italian (4,644)	12,403	21.12
Latvian (0)	45	0.08
Lithuanian (116)	457	0.78
Macedonian (7)	7	0.01
Northern European (37)	37	0.06
Norwegian (121)	450	0.77
Pennsylvania German (0)	13	0.02
Polish (1,150)	3,830	6.52
Portuguese (591)	950	1.62
Romanian (75)	159	0.27
Russian (714)	2,225	3.79
Scandinavian (86)	233	0.40
Scotch-Irish (439)	1,005	1.71
Scottish (370)	1,607	2.74
Slavic (0)	20	0.03
Slovak (256)	658	1.12
Slovene (110)	190	0.32
Swedish (261)	1,319	2.25
Swiss (55)	164	0.28
Turkish (72)	96	0.16
Ukrainian (109)	236	0.40
Welsh (39)	268	0.46
West Indian, ex. Hispanic (171)	173	0.29
Haitian (86)	86	0.15
Jamaican (48)	49	0.08
West Indian (37)	38	0.06
Yugoslavian (53)	69	0.12

Hispanic Origin	Population	%
Hispanic or Latino (of any race)	2,999	5.05
Central American, ex. Mexican	222	0.37
Costa Rican	19	0.03
Guatemalan	101	0.17

SECTION TWO

*Notes: † The Census 2010 population figure is used to calculate the percentages in the Hispanic Origin and Race categories. Ancestry percentages are based on the 2006-2010 American Community Survey population (not shown); ‡ Numbers in parentheses indicate the number of people reporting a single ancestry; * Numbers in parentheses indicate the number of persons reporting this race alone, not in combination with any other race; Please refer to the Explanation of Data for more information.*

Honduran	15	0.03
Nicaraguan	18	0.03
Panamanian	14	0.02
Salvadoran	51	0.09
Other Central American	4	0.01
Cuban	218	0.37
Dominican Republic	132	0.22
Mexican	467	0.79
Puerto Rican	848	1.43
South American	814	1.37
Argentinean	61	0.10
Bolivian	10	0.02
Chilean	30	0.05
Colombian	292	0.49
Ecuadorian	148	0.25
Paraguayan	34	0.06
Peruvian	177	0.30
Uruguayan	22	0.04
Venezuelan	34	0.06
Other South American	6	0.01
Other Hispanic or Latino	298	0.50

Race*	Population	%
African-American/Black (1,089)	1,330	2.24
Not Hispanic (1,015)	1,203	2.03
Hispanic (74)	127	0.21
American Indian/Alaska Native (35)	202	0.34
Not Hispanic (18)	137	0.23
Hispanic (17)	65	0.11
Apache (2)	5	0.01
Blackfeet (0)	5	0.01
Central American Ind. (3)	6	0.01
Cherokee (1)	19	0.03
Chickasaw (0)	1	<0.01
Chippewa (1)	1	<0.01
Choctaw (3)	3	0.01
Comanche (0)	1	<0.01
Delaware (0)	1	<0.01
Lumbee (0)	4	0.01
Mexican American Ind. (3)	11	0.02
Puget Sound Salish (0)	1	<0.01
Sioux (0)	3	0.01
South American Ind. (6)	19	0.03
Tlingit-Haida *(Alaska Native)* (0)	1	<0.01
Tohono O'Odham (1)	1	<0.01
Yaqui (1)	1	<0.01
Asian (2,203)	2,649	4.46
Not Hispanic (2,177)	2,595	4.37
Hispanic (26)	54	0.09
Bangladeshi (40)	51	0.09
Burmese (4)	7	0.01
Cambodian (43)	59	0.10
Chinese, ex. Taiwanese (615)	747	1.26
Filipino (152)	232	0.39
Indian (632)	713	1.20
Indonesian (0)	3	0.01
Japanese (63)	113	0.19
Korean (270)	316	0.53
Laotian (13)	20	0.03
Malaysian (1)	3	0.01
Nepalese (18)	18	0.03
Pakistani (142)	155	0.26
Sri Lankan (7)	8	0.01
Taiwanese (10)	13	0.02
Thai (25)	36	0.06
Vietnamese (65)	85	0.14
Hawaii Native/Pacific Islander (9)	25	0.04
Not Hispanic (7)	20	0.03
Hispanic (2)	5	0.01
Fijian (2)	2	<0.01
Guamanian/Chamorro (2)	3	0.01
Native Hawaiian (2)	12	0.02
Samoan (1)	2	<0.01
White (54,409)	55,261	93.03
Not Hispanic (52,278)	52,950	89.14
Hispanic (2,131)	2,311	3.89

Farmington

Place Type: Town
County: Hartford
Population: 25,340†

Ancestry‡	Population	%
African, Sub-Saharan (109)	360	1.44
African (109)	360	1.44
Albanian (32)	32	0.13
American (977)	977	3.90
Arab (58)	125	0.50
Iraqi (0)	46	0.18
Lebanese (47)	68	0.27
Moroccan (11)	11	0.04
Armenian (52)	185	0.74
Australian (0)	25	0.10
Austrian (48)	189	0.75
Belgian (34)	34	0.14
Brazilian (12)	30	0.12
British (66)	124	0.49
Bulgarian (41)	41	0.16
Canadian (91)	103	0.41
Croatian (0)	25	0.10
Czech (9)	118	0.47
Czechoslovakian (32)	32	0.13
Danish (33)	123	0.49
Dutch (141)	448	1.79
Eastern European (55)	80	0.32
English (1,158)	3,606	14.39
European (181)	189	0.75
Finnish (8)	70	0.28
French, ex. Basque (376)	1,834	7.32
French Canadian (483)	1,011	4.03
German (625)	2,818	11.24
Greek (77)	195	0.78
Hungarian (21)	135	0.54
Icelander (7)	7	0.03
Iranian (45)	123	0.49
Irish (1,528)	4,655	18.57
Italian (1,679)	4,135	16.50
Latvian (62)	62	0.25
Lithuanian (148)	413	1.65
Luxemburger (11)	11	0.04
Northern European (0)	14	0.06
Norwegian (80)	224	0.89
Polish (1,638)	2,885	11.51
Portuguese (100)	134	0.53
Romanian (19)	50	0.20
Russian (289)	574	2.29
Scandinavian (16)	42	0.17
Scotch-Irish (117)	312	1.24
Scottish (130)	740	2.95
Slovak (82)	155	0.62
Slovene (0)	24	0.10
Swedish (287)	909	3.63
Swiss (30)	103	0.41
Turkish (148)	148	0.59
Ukrainian (267)	440	1.76
Welsh (19)	92	0.37
West Indian, ex. Hispanic (80)	160	0.64
Barbadian (33)	81	0.32
Jamaican (11)	20	0.08
Trinidadian/Tobagonian (36)	45	0.18
West Indian (0)	14	0.06
Yugoslavian (15)	32	0.13

Hispanic Origin	Population	%
Hispanic or Latino (of any race)	966	3.81
Central American, ex. Mexican	45	0.18
Costa Rican	5	0.02
Guatemalan	19	0.07
Honduran	6	0.02
Nicaraguan	5	0.02
Panamanian	4	0.02
Salvadoran	6	0.02
Cuban	41	0.16
Dominican Republic	27	0.11
Mexican	111	0.44
Puerto Rican	386	1.52
South American	233	0.92
Argentinean	23	0.09
Bolivian	1	<0.01
Chilean	10	0.04
Colombian	81	0.32
Ecuadorian	18	0.07
Paraguayan	4	0.02
Peruvian	71	0.28
Uruguayan	5	0.02
Venezuelan	20	0.08
Other Hispanic or Latino	123	0.49

Race*	Population	%
African-American/Black (619)	754	2.98
Not Hispanic (573)	689	2.72
Hispanic (46)	65	0.26
American Indian/Alaska Native (26)	88	0.35
Not Hispanic (16)	61	0.24
Hispanic (10)	27	0.11
Blackfeet (3)	4	0.02
Canadian/French Am. Ind. (1)	4	0.02
Cherokee (5)	12	0.05
Chickasaw (0)	1	<0.01
Iroquois (0)	4	0.02
Lumbee (0)	3	0.01
Mexican American Ind. (4)	4	0.02
Pueblo (1)	1	<0.01
Sioux (0)	1	<0.01
South American Ind. (0)	3	0.01
Asian (2,045)	2,260	8.92
Not Hispanic (2,037)	2,238	8.83
Hispanic (8)	22	0.09
Bangladeshi (9)	9	0.04
Cambodian (9)	9	0.04
Chinese, ex. Taiwanese (527)	600	2.37
Filipino (75)	99	0.39
Hmong (2)	2	0.01
Indian (876)	921	3.63
Indonesian (10)	15	0.06
Japanese (52)	77	0.30
Korean (214)	239	0.94
Laotian (17)	23	0.09
Pakistani (104)	120	0.47
Sri Lankan (4)	6	0.02
Taiwanese (23)	25	0.10
Thai (5)	6	0.02
Vietnamese (71)	78	0.31
Hawaii Native/Pacific Islander (5)	21	0.08
Not Hispanic (5)	20	0.08
Hispanic (0)	1	<0.01
Native Hawaiian (0)	7	0.03
White (22,021)	22,401	88.40
Not Hispanic (21,356)	21,671	85.52
Hispanic (665)	730	2.88

Glastonbury

Place Type: Town
County: Hartford
Population: 34,427†

Ancestry‡	Population	%
African, Sub-Saharan (58)	79	0.23
African (25)	25	0.07
Cape Verdean (21)	42	0.12
Ethiopian (7)	7	0.02
Liberian (5)	5	0.01
Albanian (49)	71	0.21
American (766)	766	2.25
Arab (133)	322	0.95
Iraqi (29)	29	0.09
Lebanese (64)	203	0.60
Syrian (16)	66	0.19
Other Arab (24)	24	0.07
Armenian (11)	20	0.06
Austrian (27)	129	0.38
Belgian (0)	31	0.09
Brazilian (45)	64	0.19
British (210)	296	0.87
Bulgarian (0)	52	0.15

*Notes: † The Census 2010 population figure is used to calculate the percentages in the Hispanic Origin and Race categories. Ancestry percentages are based on the 2006-2010 American Community Survey population (not shown); ‡ Numbers in parentheses indicate the number of people reporting a single ancestry; * Numbers in parentheses indicate the number of persons reporting this race alone, not in combination with any other race; Please refer to the Explanation of Data for more information.*

Canadian (121)	360	1.06
Czech (39)	263	0.77
Czechoslovakian (27)	65	0.19
Danish (0)	195	0.57
Dutch (58)	341	1.00
Eastern European (382)	440	1.29
English (1,169)	4,986	14.67
Estonian (19)	19	0.06
European (126)	134	0.39
Finnish (0)	44	0.13
French, ex. Basque (414)	2,520	7.42
French Canadian (508)	1,109	3.26
German (1,303)	4,974	14.64
Greek (228)	470	1.38
Guyanese (11)	11	0.03
Hungarian (48)	354	1.04
Icelander (0)	15	0.04
Iranian (22)	22	0.06
Irish (1,867)	7,708	22.68
Italian (2,185)	6,709	19.74
Lithuanian (130)	588	1.73
Luxemburger (0)	11	0.03
Northern European (57)	57	0.17
Norwegian (35)	110	0.32
Pennsylvania German (17)	17	0.05
Polish (986)	3,485	10.25
Portuguese (314)	551	1.62
Romanian (0)	110	0.32
Russian (357)	838	2.47
Scandinavian (22)	22	0.06
Scotch-Irish (210)	529	1.56
Scottish (325)	833	2.45
Slavic (29)	68	0.20
Slovak (44)	110	0.32
Slovene (11)	34	0.10
Swedish (157)	1,041	3.06
Swiss (9)	134	0.39
Turkish (21)	21	0.06
Ukrainian (89)	221	0.65
Welsh (18)	139	0.41
West Indian, ex. Hispanic (77)	124	0.36
Barbadian (0)	33	0.10
Jamaican (77)	91	0.27
Yugoslavian (0)	5	0.01

Hispanic Origin	Population	%
Hispanic or Latino (of any race)	1,468	4.26
Central American, ex. Mexican	67	0.19
Costa Rican	11	0.03
Guatemalan	17	0.05
Honduran	17	0.05
Nicaraguan	12	0.03
Panamanian	7	0.02
Salvadoran	3	0.01
Cuban	91	0.26
Dominican Republic	53	0.15
Mexican	148	0.43
Puerto Rican	574	1.67
South American	417	1.21
Argentinean	28	0.08
Bolivian	5	0.01
Chilean	14	0.04
Colombian	147	0.43
Ecuadorian	16	0.05
Paraguayan	1	<0.01
Peruvian	189	0.55
Uruguayan	1	<0.01
Venezuelan	15	0.04
Other South American	1	<0.01
Other Hispanic or Latino	118	0.34

Race*	Population	%
African-American/Black (700)	889	2.58
Not Hispanic (641)	793	2.30
Hispanic (59)	96	0.28
American Indian/Alaska Native (62)	190	0.55
Not Hispanic (41)	151	0.44
Hispanic (21)	39	0.11
Blackfeet (1)	3	0.01
Canadian/French Am. Ind. (0)	3	0.01
Cherokee (6)	17	0.05
Creek (0)	1	<0.01
Iroquois (1)	12	0.03
Mexican American Ind. (1)	1	<0.01
Navajo (3)	3	0.01
Potawatomi (1)	2	0.01
Sioux (2)	3	0.01
South American Ind. (3)	8	0.02
Tlingit-Haida *(Alaska Native)* (1)	1	<0.01
Asian (2,334)	2,606	7.57
Not Hispanic (2,329)	2,582	7.50
Hispanic (5)	24	0.07
Bangladeshi (34)	37	0.11
Burmese (2)	3	0.01
Cambodian (5)	9	0.03
Chinese, ex. Taiwanese (515)	573	1.66
Filipino (111)	168	0.49
Indian (969)	1,035	3.01
Indonesian (1)	2	0.01
Japanese (60)	96	0.28
Korean (299)	337	0.98
Laotian (14)	16	0.05
Nepalese (10)	12	0.03
Pakistani (102)	109	0.32
Sri Lankan (17)	18	0.05
Taiwanese (34)	36	0.10
Thai (5)	9	0.03
Vietnamese (101)	117	0.34
Hawaii Native/Pacific Islander (0)	16	0.05
Not Hispanic (0)	14	0.04
Hispanic (0)	2	0.01
Guamanian/Chamorro (0)	1	<0.01
Native Hawaiian (0)	5	0.01
Samoan (0)	1	<0.01
White (30,403)	30,916	89.80
Not Hispanic (29,428)	29,861	86.74
Hispanic (975)	1,055	3.06

Granby

Place Type: Town
County: Hartford
Population: 11,282†

Ancestry‡	Population	%
Alsatian (0)	16	0.14
American (632)	632	5.68
Austrian (35)	112	1.01
British (47)	74	0.67
Canadian (32)	64	0.58
Czech (0)	30	0.27
Danish (11)	73	0.66
Dutch (22)	92	0.83
Eastern European (14)	46	0.41
English (570)	2,468	22.19
European (60)	60	0.54
Finnish (0)	10	0.09
French, ex. Basque (172)	1,033	9.29
French Canadian (134)	661	5.94
German (236)	1,817	16.33
Greek (33)	46	0.41
Hungarian (18)	30	0.27
Irish (548)	2,912	26.18
Italian (436)	1,781	16.01
Latvian (9)	25	0.22
Lithuanian (17)	126	1.13
Norwegian (37)	93	0.84
Polish (396)	1,315	11.82
Portuguese (25)	25	0.22
Romanian (9)	19	0.17
Russian (122)	262	2.36
Scandinavian (7)	58	0.52
Scotch-Irish (14)	174	1.56
Scottish (124)	421	3.78
Slavic (17)	17	0.15
Slovak (0)	61	0.55
Swedish (112)	527	4.74
Swiss (0)	41	0.37
Ukrainian (35)	75	0.67
Welsh (0)	163	1.47
West Indian, ex. Hispanic (94)	94	0.85
Jamaican (19)	19	0.17
West Indian (75)	75	0.67

Hispanic Origin	Population	%
Hispanic or Latino (of any race)	196	1.74
Central American, ex. Mexican	11	0.10
Costa Rican	2	0.02
Guatemalan	2	0.02
Honduran	1	0.01
Nicaraguan	1	0.01
Panamanian	5	0.04
Cuban	11	0.10
Dominican Republic	9	0.08
Mexican	33	0.29
Puerto Rican	76	0.67
South American	36	0.32
Argentinean	6	0.05
Chilean	3	0.03
Colombian	9	0.08
Ecuadorian	5	0.04
Peruvian	7	0.06
Uruguayan	4	0.04
Venezuelan	2	0.02
Other Hispanic or Latino	20	0.18

Race*	Population	%
African-American/Black (122)	172	1.52
Not Hispanic (116)	160	1.42
Hispanic (6)	12	0.11
American Indian/Alaska Native (17)	58	0.51
Not Hispanic (16)	55	0.49
Hispanic (1)	3	0.03
Apache (1)	1	0.01
Canadian/French Am. Ind. (1)	1	0.01
Central American Ind. (0)	3	0.03
Cherokee (0)	6	0.05
Chippewa (1)	2	0.02
Choctaw (1)	1	0.01
Creek (1)	1	0.01
Iroquois (0)	2	0.02
Lumbee (1)	1	0.01
Sioux (1)	2	0.02
Asian (100)	143	1.27
Not Hispanic (100)	143	1.27
Cambodian (3)	5	0.04
Chinese, ex. Taiwanese (35)	45	0.40
Filipino (6)	19	0.17
Indian (10)	11	0.10
Japanese (3)	5	0.04
Korean (15)	19	0.17
Nepalese (1)	3	0.03
Taiwanese (1)	4	0.04
Thai (1)	1	0.01
Vietnamese (16)	23	0.20
Hawaii Native/Pacific Islander (6)	13	0.12
Not Hispanic (6)	12	0.11
Hispanic (0)	1	0.01
Native Hawaiian (2)	7	0.06
White (10,871)	10,994	97.45
Not Hispanic (10,723)	10,835	96.04
Hispanic (148)	159	1.41

Greenwich

Place Type: CDP
County: Fairfield
Population: 12,942†

Ancestry‡	Population	%
African, Sub-Saharan (20)	20	0.15
Nigerian (20)	20	0.15
Albanian (86)	86	0.65
American (656)	656	4.94
Arab (28)	62	0.47
Lebanese (17)	51	0.38
Other Arab (11)	11	0.08
Armenian (16)	46	0.35
Austrian (13)	47	0.35
Belgian (23)	23	0.17

*Notes: † The Census 2010 population figure is used to calculate the percentages in the Hispanic Origin and Race categories. Ancestry percentages are based on the 2006-2010 American Community Survey population (not shown); ‡ Numbers in parentheses indicate the number of people reporting a single ancestry; * Numbers in parentheses indicate the number of persons reporting this race alone, not in combination with any other race; Please refer to the Explanation of Data for more information.*

Ancestry (cont.)	Population	%
Brazilian (432)	494	3.72
British (173)	208	1.57
Canadian (103)	135	1.02
Celtic (9)	9	0.07
Croatian (28)	28	0.21
Czech (13)	79	0.60
Danish (6)	87	0.66
Dutch (96)	197	1.48
Eastern European (59)	59	0.44
English (323)	1,428	10.76
European (241)	241	1.82
French, ex. Basque (58)	260	1.96
French Canadian (33)	80	0.60
German (684)	1,472	11.09
Greek (102)	120	0.90
Hungarian (33)	71	0.54
Irish (739)	2,096	15.79
Israeli (8)	8	0.06
Italian (1,088)	1,921	14.48
Lithuanian (9)	73	0.55
New Zealander (13)	13	0.10
Norwegian (0)	134	1.01
Polish (380)	732	5.52
Portuguese (88)	163	1.23
Romanian (122)	122	0.92
Russian (226)	311	2.34
Scandinavian (9)	20	0.15
Scotch-Irish (48)	307	2.31
Scottish (115)	330	2.49
Slovak (9)	79	0.60
Slovene (96)	96	0.72
Swedish (140)	307	2.31
Swiss (22)	31	0.23
Ukrainian (0)	73	0.55
Welsh (50)	112	0.84
West Indian, ex. Hispanic (230)	254	1.91
Bahamian (135)	135	1.02
British West Indian (10)	10	0.08
Haitian (0)	7	0.05
Jamaican (65)	82	0.62
West Indian (20)	20	0.15

Hispanic Origin	Population	%
Hispanic or Latino (of any race)	1,803	13.93
Central American, ex. Mexican	177	1.37
Costa Rican	2	0.02
Guatemalan	89	0.69
Honduran	26	0.20
Nicaraguan	6	0.05
Panamanian	4	0.03
Salvadoran	50	0.39
Cuban	42	0.32
Dominican Republic	64	0.49
Mexican	188	1.45
Puerto Rican	145	1.12
South American	954	7.37
Argentinean	32	0.25
Bolivian	25	0.19
Chilean	35	0.27
Colombian	464	3.59
Ecuadorian	166	1.28
Paraguayan	17	0.13
Peruvian	142	1.10
Uruguayan	58	0.45
Venezuelan	11	0.08
Other South American	4	0.03
Other Hispanic or Latino	233	1.80

Race*	Population	%
African-American/Black (640)	752	5.81
Not Hispanic (609)	702	5.42
Hispanic (31)	50	0.39
American Indian/Alaska Native (17)	54	0.42
Not Hispanic (6)	28	0.22
Hispanic (11)	26	0.20
Apache (0)	1	0.01
Blackfeet (0)	3	0.02
Canadian/French Am. Ind. (0)	1	0.01
Cree (0)	1	0.01
Iroquois (0)	2	0.02
Mexican American Ind. (3)	7	0.05
Osage (0)	1	0.01
South American Ind. (5)	9	0.07
Ute (0)	1	0.01
Asian (1,010)	1,126	8.70
Not Hispanic (1,001)	1,105	8.54
Hispanic (9)	21	0.16
Cambodian (3)	4	0.03
Chinese, ex. Taiwanese (211)	228	1.76
Filipino (329)	361	2.79
Indian (156)	180	1.39
Indonesian (3)	3	0.02
Japanese (180)	202	1.56
Korean (65)	84	0.65
Laotian (2)	2	0.02
Malaysian (1)	5	0.04
Nepalese (0)	4	0.03
Pakistani (6)	15	0.12
Taiwanese (4)	4	0.03
Thai (5)	5	0.04
Vietnamese (19)	23	0.18
Hawaii Native/Pacific Islander (6)	18	0.14
Not Hispanic (2)	11	0.08
Hispanic (4)	7	0.05
Guamanian/Chamorro (4)	5	0.04
Native Hawaiian (0)	3	0.02
White (10,466)	10,755	83.10
Not Hispanic (9,227)	9,416	72.76
Hispanic (1,239)	1,339	10.35

Greenwich

Place Type: Town
County: Fairfield
Population: 61,171†

Ancestry‡	Population	%
Afghan (84)	84	0.14
African, Sub-Saharan (57)	68	0.11
Ethiopian (10)	21	0.03
Nigerian (20)	20	0.03
South African (27)	27	0.04
Albanian (86)	86	0.14
Alsatian (10)	10	0.02
American (2,866)	2,866	4.71
Arab (245)	348	0.57
Arab (29)	29	0.05
Lebanese (86)	179	0.29
Moroccan (119)	119	0.20
Syrian (0)	10	0.02
Other Arab (11)	11	0.02
Armenian (51)	87	0.14
Australian (77)	196	0.32
Austrian (88)	391	0.64
Basque (0)	11	0.02
Belgian (30)	72	0.12
Brazilian (650)	760	1.25
British (1,029)	1,236	2.03
Bulgarian (11)	11	0.02
Canadian (227)	439	0.72
Celtic (9)	19	0.03
Croatian (53)	109	0.18
Czech (96)	284	0.47
Czechoslovakian (59)	173	0.28
Danish (122)	326	0.54
Dutch (494)	1,306	2.15
Eastern European (383)	434	0.71
English (2,022)	8,179	13.45
European (1,168)	1,296	2.13
Finnish (57)	129	0.21
French, ex. Basque (276)	1,779	2.93
French Canadian (227)	566	0.93
German (2,024)	7,535	12.39
Greek (596)	1,047	1.72
Hungarian (229)	670	1.10
Iranian (91)	91	0.15
Irish (3,508)	10,437	17.16
Israeli (19)	19	0.03
Italian (5,833)	10,944	18.00
Latvian (0)	26	0.04
Lithuanian (77)	244	0.40
Maltese (13)	27	0.04
New Zealander (13)	22	0.04
Northern European (81)	108	0.18
Norwegian (109)	549	0.90
Polish (1,106)	3,113	5.12
Portuguese (201)	369	0.61
Romanian (152)	234	0.38
Russian (947)	2,143	3.52
Scandinavian (69)	80	0.13
Scotch-Irish (408)	1,313	2.16
Scottish (601)	2,337	3.84
Slavic (50)	50	0.08
Slovak (82)	453	0.74
Slovene (112)	120	0.20
Swedish (328)	1,097	1.80
Swiss (156)	289	0.48
Turkish (6)	23	0.04
Ukrainian (43)	181	0.30
Welsh (89)	393	0.65
West Indian, ex. Hispanic (327)	351	0.58
Bahamian (135)	135	0.22
British West Indian (10)	10	0.02
Haitian (0)	7	0.01
Jamaican (132)	149	0.25
West Indian (50)	50	0.08

Hispanic Origin	Population	%
Hispanic or Latino (of any race)	5,964	9.75
Central American, ex. Mexican	511	0.84
Costa Rican	17	0.03
Guatemalan	290	0.47
Honduran	50	0.08
Nicaraguan	14	0.02
Panamanian	16	0.03
Salvadoran	124	0.20
Cuban	187	0.31
Dominican Republic	149	0.24
Mexican	797	1.30
Puerto Rican	539	0.88
South American	3,008	4.92
Argentinean	426	0.70
Bolivian	65	0.11
Chilean	196	0.32
Colombian	1,038	1.70
Ecuadorian	389	0.64
Paraguayan	71	0.12
Peruvian	549	0.90
Uruguayan	146	0.24
Venezuelan	113	0.18
Other South American	15	0.02
Other Hispanic or Latino	773	1.26

Race*	Population	%
African-American/Black (1,314)	1,578	2.58
Not Hispanic (1,232)	1,428	2.33
Hispanic (82)	150	0.25
American Indian/Alaska Native (84)	234	0.38
Not Hispanic (35)	134	0.22
Hispanic (49)	100	0.16
Alaska Athabascan *(Ala. Nat.)* (0)	2	<0.01
Apache (1)	2	<0.01
Blackfeet (0)	4	0.01
Canadian/French Am. Ind. (0)	2	<0.01
Central American Ind. (1)	3	<0.01
Cherokee (2)	19	0.03
Chippewa (2)	2	<0.01
Cree (0)	1	<0.01
Creek (0)	2	<0.01
Delaware (1)	7	0.01
Iroquois (3)	11	0.02
Mexican American Ind. (4)	9	0.01
Osage (0)	1	<0.01
Puget Sound Salish (1)	1	<0.01
Sioux (0)	1	<0.01
South American Ind. (22)	45	0.07
Ute (0)	1	<0.01
Asian (4,039)	4,641	7.59
Not Hispanic (4,017)	4,577	7.48
Hispanic (22)	64	0.10

*Notes: † The Census 2010 population figure is used to calculate the percentages in the Hispanic Origin and Race categories. Ancestry percentages are based on the 2006-2010 American Community Survey population (not shown); ‡ Numbers in parentheses indicate the number of people reporting a single ancestry; * Numbers in parentheses indicate the number of persons reporting this race alone, not in combination with any other race; Please refer to the Explanation of Data for more information.*

Bangladeshi (2)	8	0.01
Burmese (1)	2	<0.01
Cambodian (4)	5	0.01
Chinese, ex. Taiwanese (1,007)	1,188	1.94
Filipino (688)	773	1.26
Hmong (2)	2	<0.01
Indian (628)	750	1.23
Indonesian (9)	14	0.02
Japanese (1,055)	1,177	1.92
Korean (384)	506	0.83
Laotian (6)	6	0.01
Malaysian (3)	7	0.01
Nepalese (5)	9	0.01
Pakistani (19)	36	0.06
Sri Lankan (2)	3	<0.01
Taiwanese (24)	36	0.06
Thai (14)	19	0.03
Vietnamese (59)	72	0.12
Hawaii Native/Pacific Islander (14)	50	0.08
Not Hispanic (8)	38	0.06
Hispanic (6)	12	0.02
Fijian (2)	2	<0.01
Guamanian/Chamorro (6)	8	0.01
Native Hawaiian (2)	16	0.03
White (53,054)	54,167	88.55
Not Hispanic (48,807)	49,617	81.11
Hispanic (4,247)	4,550	7.44

Griswold

Place Type: Town
County: New London
Population: 11,951†

Ancestry‡	Population	%
African, Sub-Saharan (17)	17	0.14
South African (17)	17	0.14
Albanian (0)	16	0.14
American (307)	307	2.61
Arab (71)	103	0.87
Arab (16)	16	0.14
Lebanese (40)	72	0.61
Syrian (15)	15	0.13
Austrian (0)	32	0.27
Brazilian (18)	18	0.15
Canadian (35)	42	0.36
Czech (0)	30	0.25
Czechoslovakian (18)	33	0.28
Danish (11)	28	0.24
Dutch (102)	205	1.74
English (462)	1,439	12.22
European (50)	50	0.42
Finnish (75)	134	1.14
French, ex. Basque (692)	2,259	19.19
French Canadian (660)	1,183	10.05
German (137)	1,151	9.78
Greek (48)	86	0.73
Hungarian (0)	108	0.92
Irish (406)	1,954	16.60
Italian (439)	1,430	12.15
Lithuanian (43)	74	0.63
Norwegian (0)	18	0.15
Polish (670)	1,743	14.80
Portuguese (32)	169	1.44
Russian (0)	173	1.47
Scandinavian (14)	14	0.12
Scotch-Irish (79)	95	0.81
Scottish (96)	466	3.96
Slovak (0)	39	0.33
Swedish (0)	117	0.99
Ukrainian (28)	62	0.53
Welsh (0)	153	1.30

Hispanic Origin	Population	%
Hispanic or Latino (of any race)	396	3.31
Central American, ex. Mexican	18	0.15
Guatemalan	8	0.07
Honduran	4	0.03
Panamanian	1	0.01
Salvadoran	2	0.02
Other Central American	3	0.03
Cuban	5	0.04
Dominican Republic	9	0.08
Mexican	88	0.74
Puerto Rican	213	1.78
South American	38	0.32
Argentinean	1	0.01
Bolivian	3	0.03
Colombian	3	0.03
Ecuadorian	12	0.10
Peruvian	17	0.14
Venezuelan	1	0.01
Other South American	1	0.01
Other Hispanic or Latino	25	0.21

Race*	Population	%
African-American/Black (210)	359	3.00
Not Hispanic (190)	328	2.74
Hispanic (20)	31	0.26
American Indian/Alaska Native (110)	257	2.15
Not Hispanic (101)	239	2.00
Hispanic (9)	18	0.15
Blackfeet (1)	3	0.03
Cherokee (5)	29	0.24
Chickasaw (0)	1	0.01
Choctaw (1)	1	0.01
Delaware (0)	1	0.01
Iroquois (0)	3	0.03
Ottawa (0)	1	0.01
Sioux (6)	7	0.06
South American Ind. (1)	1	0.01
Asian (267)	326	2.73
Not Hispanic (265)	322	2.69
Hispanic (2)	4	0.03
Chinese, ex. Taiwanese (78)	92	0.77
Filipino (33)	62	0.52
Indian (94)	101	0.85
Japanese (6)	16	0.13
Korean (15)	19	0.16
Laotian (13)	15	0.13
Pakistani (4)	4	0.03
Sri Lankan (0)	1	0.01
Taiwanese (2)	5	0.04
Thai (2)	2	0.02
Vietnamese (10)	16	0.13
Hawaii Native/Pacific Islander (3)	18	0.15
Not Hispanic (3)	11	0.09
Hispanic (0)	7	0.06
Guamanian/Chamorro (1)	5	0.04
Native Hawaiian (2)	4	0.03
White (10,952)	11,255	94.18
Not Hispanic (10,698)	10,962	91.72
Hispanic (254)	293	2.45

Groton

Place Type: City
County: New London
Population: 10,389†

Ancestry‡	Population	%
African, Sub-Saharan (23)	52	0.51
African (0)	29	0.28
Cape Verdean (23)	23	0.22
American (278)	278	2.72
Arab (0)	45	0.44
Lebanese (0)	45	0.44
Austrian (0)	13	0.13
British (33)	33	0.32
Canadian (22)	34	0.33
Croatian (12)	12	0.12
Czech (21)	52	0.51
Czechoslovakian (0)	15	0.15
Dutch (55)	217	2.12
English (313)	1,864	18.23
European (115)	124	1.21
French, ex. Basque (110)	680	6.65
French Canadian (167)	591	5.78
German (100)	1,157	11.32
Greek (36)	81	0.79
Guyanese (0)	16	0.16
Hungarian (0)	10	0.10
Irish (266)	1,725	16.87
Italian (503)	1,584	15.49
Lithuanian (8)	46	0.45
Norwegian (0)	27	0.26
Polish (143)	741	7.25
Portuguese (50)	206	2.01
Romanian (152)	152	1.49
Russian (0)	69	0.67
Scandinavian (20)	32	0.31
Scotch-Irish (51)	205	2.00
Scottish (61)	349	3.41
Slovak (0)	31	0.30
Swedish (12)	321	3.14
Swiss (0)	41	0.40
Ukrainian (0)	33	0.32
Welsh (0)	111	1.09
West Indian, ex. Hispanic (61)	140	1.37
Bahamian (0)	27	0.26
British West Indian (14)	22	0.22
Haitian (36)	62	0.61
Jamaican (11)	29	0.28

Hispanic Origin	Population	%
Hispanic or Latino (of any race)	1,520	14.63
Central American, ex. Mexican	70	0.67
Costa Rican	1	0.01
Guatemalan	7	0.07
Honduran	8	0.08
Panamanian	20	0.19
Salvadoran	27	0.26
Other Central American	7	0.07
Cuban	17	0.16
Dominican Republic	163	1.57
Mexican	139	1.34
Puerto Rican	905	8.71
South American	118	1.14
Argentinean	11	0.11
Chilean	3	0.03
Colombian	24	0.23
Ecuadorian	28	0.27
Peruvian	48	0.46
Uruguayan	2	0.02
Venezuelan	2	0.02
Other Hispanic or Latino	108	1.04

Race*	Population	%
African-American/Black (1,064)	1,504	14.48
Not Hispanic (915)	1,258	12.11
Hispanic (149)	246	2.37
American Indian/Alaska Native (90)	265	2.55
Not Hispanic (68)	200	1.93
Hispanic (22)	65	0.63
Apache (0)	2	0.02
Blackfeet (0)	4	0.04
Central American Ind. (3)	3	0.03
Cherokee (8)	40	0.39
Chickasaw (0)	1	0.01
Chippewa (2)	4	0.04
Choctaw (0)	2	0.02
Cree (1)	1	0.01
Creek (2)	2	0.02
Inupiat *(Alaska Native)* (1)	2	0.02
Iroquois (1)	3	0.03
Potawatomi (1)	1	0.01
Seminole (0)	2	0.02
Sioux (0)	2	0.02
South American Ind. (6)	20	0.19
Tlingit-Haida *(Alaska Native)* (0)	1	0.01
Asian (807)	927	8.92
Not Hispanic (790)	892	8.59
Hispanic (17)	35	0.34
Bangladeshi (3)	4	0.04
Burmese (1)	1	0.01
Cambodian (2)	4	0.04
Chinese, ex. Taiwanese (106)	128	1.23
Filipino (148)	216	2.08
Hmong (1)	1	0.01
Indian (431)	441	4.24

*Notes: † The Census 2010 population figure is used to calculate the percentages in the Hispanic Origin and Race categories. Ancestry percentages are based on the 2006-2010 American Community Survey population (not shown); ‡ Numbers in parentheses indicate the number of people reporting a single ancestry; * Numbers in parentheses indicate the number of persons reporting this race alone, not in combination with any other race; Please refer to the Explanation of Data for more information.*

Japanese (8)	22	0.21
Korean (28)	35	0.34
Laotian (10)	14	0.13
Nepalese (8)	8	0.08
Pakistani (22)	24	0.23
Sri Lankan (1)	1	0.01
Taiwanese (1)	1	0.01
Thai (3)	4	0.04
Vietnamese (23)	28	0.27
Hawaii Native/Pacific Islander (5)	31	0.30
Not Hispanic (3)	22	0.21
Hispanic (2)	9	0.09
Guamanian/Chamorro (1)	5	0.05
Native Hawaiian (1)	7	0.07
Samoan (0)	2	0.02
White (7,324)	7,832	75.39
Not Hispanic (6,593)	6,969	67.08
Hispanic (731)	863	8.31

Groton

Place Type: Town
County: New London
Population: 40,115†

Ancestry‡	Population	%
African, Sub-Saharan (35)	97	0.24
African (10)	72	0.18
Cape Verdean (25)	25	0.06
Albanian (105)	108	0.27
American (1,400)	1,400	3.48
Arab (71)	153	0.38
Egyptian (62)	62	0.15
Lebanese (0)	82	0.20
Other Arab (9)	9	0.02
Armenian (11)	70	0.17
Austrian (20)	224	0.56
Belgian (34)	102	0.25
Brazilian (9)	26	0.06
British (111)	229	0.57
Cajun (0)	11	0.03
Canadian (73)	165	0.41
Celtic (8)	44	0.11
Croatian (22)	22	0.05
Czech (45)	117	0.29
Czechoslovakian (21)	63	0.16
Danish (41)	169	0.42
Dutch (230)	673	1.67
Eastern European (7)	7	0.02
English (1,745)	6,424	15.96
Estonian (0)	3	0.01
European (354)	363	0.90
Finnish (0)	28	0.07
French, ex. Basque (403)	2,284	5.67
French Canadian (497)	1,479	3.67
German (1,092)	6,127	15.22
Greek (97)	254	0.63
Guyanese (0)	16	0.04
Hungarian (94)	254	0.63
Irish (1,836)	7,560	18.78
Italian (1,534)	5,143	12.78
Lithuanian (57)	176	0.44
Northern European (74)	74	0.18
Norwegian (125)	577	1.43
Pennsylvania German (26)	26	0.06
Polish (745)	2,731	6.78
Portuguese (178)	663	1.65
Romanian (152)	177	0.44
Russian (75)	436	1.08
Scandinavian (30)	45	0.11
Scotch-Irish (282)	1,049	2.61
Scottish (204)	1,172	2.91
Serbian (0)	12	0.03
Slavic (8)	8	0.02
Slovak (28)	117	0.29
Slovene (9)	9	0.02
Swedish (162)	997	2.48
Swiss (9)	135	0.34
Ukrainian (20)	84	0.21
Welsh (81)	409	1.02
West Indian, ex. Hispanic (100)	222	0.55
Bahamian (0)	27	0.07
British West Indian (14)	22	0.05
Haitian (36)	62	0.15
Jamaican (38)	99	0.25
Trinidadian/Tobagonian (12)	12	0.03
Yugoslavian (0)	12	0.03

Hispanic Origin	Population	%
Hispanic or Latino (of any race)	3,575	8.91
Central American, ex. Mexican	234	0.58
Costa Rican	6	0.01
Guatemalan	50	0.12
Honduran	18	0.04
Nicaraguan	9	0.02
Panamanian	60	0.15
Salvadoran	84	0.21
Other Central American	7	0.02
Cuban	50	0.12
Dominican Republic	264	0.66
Mexican	668	1.67
Puerto Rican	1,729	4.31
South American	345	0.86
Argentinean	24	0.06
Bolivian	8	0.02
Chilean	6	0.01
Colombian	109	0.27
Ecuadorian	76	0.19
Paraguayan	2	<0.01
Peruvian	95	0.24
Uruguayan	2	<0.01
Venezuelan	21	0.05
Other South American	2	<0.01
Other Hispanic or Latino	285	0.71

Race*	Population	%
African-American/Black (2,761)	3,843	9.58
Not Hispanic (2,471)	3,373	8.41
Hispanic (290)	470	1.17
American Indian/Alaska Native (311)	951	2.37
Not Hispanic (259)	786	1.96
Hispanic (52)	165	0.41
Aleut *(Alaska Native)* (0)	1	<0.01
Apache (6)	10	0.02
Arapaho (0)	4	0.01
Blackfeet (0)	15	0.04
Canadian/French Am. Ind. (4)	4	0.01
Central American Ind. (4)	4	0.01
Cherokee (28)	140	0.35
Chickasaw (0)	2	<0.01
Chippewa (6)	12	0.03
Choctaw (2)	12	0.03
Cree (1)	6	0.01
Creek (2)	2	<0.01
Crow (0)	1	<0.01
Delaware (1)	6	0.01
Inupiat *(Alaska Native)* (3)	4	0.01
Iroquois (4)	7	0.02
Kiowa (0)	1	<0.01
Mexican American Ind. (4)	4	0.01
Navajo (6)	7	0.02
Pima (0)	1	<0.01
Potawatomi (1)	1	<0.01
Seminole (0)	3	0.01
Sioux (3)	16	0.04
South American Ind. (16)	43	0.11
Tlingit-Haida *(Alaska Native)* (0)	4	0.01
Asian (2,502)	3,084	7.69
Not Hispanic (2,450)	2,959	7.38
Hispanic (52)	125	0.31
Bangladeshi (6)	8	0.02
Burmese (4)	4	0.01
Cambodian (8)	15	0.04
Chinese, ex. Taiwanese (327)	417	1.04
Filipino (772)	1,075	2.68
Hmong (3)	3	0.01
Indian (980)	1,043	2.60
Indonesian (6)	7	0.02
Japanese (63)	148	0.37
Korean (101)	155	0.39
Laotian (32)	41	0.10
Malaysian (1)	6	0.01
Nepalese (8)	8	0.02
Pakistani (55)	65	0.16
Sri Lankan (3)	5	0.01
Taiwanese (5)	11	0.03
Thai (19)	30	0.07
Vietnamese (58)	80	0.20
Hawaii Native/Pacific Islander (34)	142	0.35
Not Hispanic (31)	114	0.28
Hispanic (3)	28	0.07
Fijian (0)	1	<0.01
Guamanian/Chamorro (18)	49	0.12
Native Hawaiian (4)	33	0.08
Samoan (3)	17	0.04
Tongan (0)	1	<0.01
White (31,607)	33,268	82.93
Not Hispanic (29,653)	30,985	77.24
Hispanic (1,954)	2,283	5.69

Guilford

Place Type: Town
County: New Haven
Population: 22,375†

Ancestry‡	Population	%
African, Sub-Saharan (29)	81	0.36
African (12)	48	0.22
Other Sub-Saharan African (17)	33	0.15
American (678)	678	3.05
Arab (27)	69	0.31
Arab (0)	22	0.10
Egyptian (17)	17	0.08
Lebanese (10)	30	0.14
Armenian (21)	32	0.14
Australian (17)	17	0.08
Austrian (21)	100	0.45
Belgian (21)	21	0.09
British (134)	156	0.70
Canadian (16)	65	0.29
Croatian (26)	62	0.28
Czech (21)	81	0.36
Czechoslovakian (62)	107	0.48
Danish (8)	109	0.49
Dutch (73)	183	0.82
Eastern European (64)	64	0.29
English (1,343)	3,887	17.49
European (153)	163	0.73
Finnish (0)	60	0.27
French, ex. Basque (152)	899	4.05
French Canadian (330)	587	2.64
German (704)	3,558	16.01
Greek (45)	190	0.86
Hungarian (36)	238	1.07
Iranian (16)	16	0.07
Irish (1,432)	5,653	25.44
Italian (2,788)	6,231	28.04
Latvian (11)	22	0.10
Lithuanian (98)	227	1.02
Macedonian (0)	20	0.09
Northern European (19)	19	0.09
Norwegian (26)	289	1.30
Pennsylvania German (27)	27	0.12
Polish (402)	1,628	7.33
Portuguese (15)	163	0.73
Romanian (0)	27	0.12
Russian (231)	684	3.08
Scandinavian (40)	40	0.18
Scotch-Irish (111)	480	2.16
Scottish (69)	452	2.03
Slovak (9)	67	0.30
Swedish (101)	642	2.89
Swiss (10)	80	0.36
Ukrainian (61)	199	0.90
Welsh (7)	54	0.24
Yugoslavian (65)	85	0.38

Hispanic Origin	Population	%
Hispanic or Latino (of any race)	779	3.48

*Notes: † The Census 2010 population figure is used to calculate the percentages in the Hispanic Origin and Race categories. Ancestry percentages are based on the 2006-2010 American Community Survey population (not shown); ‡ Numbers in parentheses indicate the number of people reporting a single ancestry; * Numbers in parentheses indicate the number of persons reporting this race alone, not in combination with any other race; Please refer to the Explanation of Data for more information.*

Central American, ex. Mexican	38	0.17
Costa Rican	6	0.03
Guatemalan	18	0.08
Honduran	4	0.02
Nicaraguan	2	0.01
Panamanian	4	0.02
Salvadoran	4	0.02
Cuban	32	0.14
Dominican Republic	23	0.10
Mexican	99	0.44
Puerto Rican	260	1.16
South American	266	1.19
Argentinean	25	0.11
Chilean	48	0.21
Colombian	89	0.40
Ecuadorian	64	0.29
Paraguayan	1	<0.01
Peruvian	24	0.11
Venezuelan	9	0.04
Other South American	6	0.03
Other Hispanic or Latino	61	0.27

Race*	Population	%
African-American/Black (178)	246	1.10
Not Hispanic (160)	214	0.96
Hispanic (18)	32	0.14
American Indian/Alaska Native (14)	92	0.41
Not Hispanic (14)	87	0.39
Hispanic (0)	5	0.02
Blackfeet (0)	3	0.01
Cherokee (3)	18	0.08
Chippewa (0)	3	0.01
Choctaw (0)	2	0.01
Creek (3)	7	0.03
Iroquois (0)	2	0.01
Mexican American Ind. (0)	2	0.01
Potawatomi (0)	1	<0.01
South American Ind. (0)	1	<0.01
Asian (542)	649	2.90
Not Hispanic (535)	641	2.86
Hispanic (7)	8	0.04
Cambodian (9)	10	0.04
Chinese, ex. Taiwanese (260)	294	1.31
Filipino (26)	35	0.16
Indian (107)	120	0.54
Indonesian (1)	1	<0.01
Japanese (18)	30	0.13
Korean (70)	95	0.42
Pakistani (3)	5	0.02
Taiwanese (7)	9	0.04
Thai (5)	7	0.03
Vietnamese (15)	19	0.08
Hawaii Native/Pacific Islander (2)	5	0.02
Not Hispanic (1)	4	0.02
Hispanic (1)	1	<0.01
Guamanian/Chamorro (1)	2	0.01
Native Hawaiian (0)	2	0.01
White (21,191)	21,448	95.86
Not Hispanic (20,640)	20,859	93.22
Hispanic (551)	589	2.63

Haddam

Place Type: Town
County: Middlesex
Population: 8,346†

Ancestry‡	Population	%
Albanian (10)	10	0.12
American (321)	321	3.92
Armenian (0)	117	1.43
Assyrian/Chaldean/Syriac (0)	40	0.49
Austrian (0)	36	0.44
British (39)	101	1.23
Canadian (7)	47	0.57
Czech (27)	68	0.83
Czechoslovakian (10)	18	0.22
Danish (0)	13	0.16
Dutch (11)	120	1.47
English (245)	1,247	15.24
European (75)	101	1.23
Finnish (21)	27	0.33
French, ex. Basque (80)	620	7.57
French Canadian (52)	267	3.26
German (233)	1,102	13.46
Greek (30)	147	1.80
Hungarian (19)	87	1.06
Irish (276)	1,974	24.12
Italian (637)	2,240	27.37
Lithuanian (12)	133	1.62
Norwegian (11)	11	0.13
Polish (169)	918	11.22
Portuguese (131)	203	2.48
Russian (13)	25	0.31
Scotch-Irish (21)	199	2.43
Scottish (100)	313	3.82
Slavic (10)	10	0.12
Slovak (0)	55	0.67
Swedish (81)	326	3.98
Swiss (0)	25	0.31
Ukrainian (0)	52	0.64
Welsh (41)	113	1.38

Hispanic Origin	Population	%
Hispanic or Latino (of any race)	139	1.67
Central American, ex. Mexican	13	0.16
Guatemalan	2	0.02
Honduran	11	0.13
Cuban	9	0.11
Dominican Republic	2	0.02
Mexican	12	0.14
Puerto Rican	49	0.59
South American	27	0.32
Argentinean	3	0.04
Chilean	2	0.02
Colombian	16	0.19
Ecuadorian	2	0.02
Paraguayan	1	0.01
Peruvian	3	0.04
Other Hispanic or Latino	27	0.32

Race*	Population	%
African-American/Black (89)	126	1.51
Not Hispanic (85)	113	1.35
Hispanic (4)	13	0.16
American Indian/Alaska Native (12)	67	0.80
Not Hispanic (10)	63	0.75
Hispanic (2)	4	0.05
Apache (0)	2	0.02
Blackfeet (0)	5	0.06
Canadian/French Am. Ind. (0)	1	0.01
Cherokee (0)	6	0.07
Choctaw (0)	2	0.02
Iroquois (0)	12	0.14
Mexican American Ind. (1)	1	0.01
Sioux (0)	2	0.02
Tlingit-Haida *(Alaska Native)* (1)	1	0.01
Asian (121)	147	1.76
Not Hispanic (121)	147	1.76
Cambodian (12)	12	0.14
Chinese, ex. Taiwanese (14)	15	0.18
Filipino (13)	23	0.28
Indian (31)	34	0.41
Japanese (6)	10	0.12
Korean (10)	17	0.20
Laotian (5)	5	0.06
Pakistani (13)	13	0.16
Taiwanese (1)	1	0.01
Thai (1)	1	0.01
Vietnamese (10)	10	0.12
Hawaii Native/Pacific Islander (2)	2	0.02
Not Hispanic (2)	2	0.02
White (7,985)	8,097	97.02
Not Hispanic (7,872)	7,973	95.53
Hispanic (113)	124	1.49

Hamden

Place Type: Town
County: New Haven
Population: 60,960†

Ancestry‡	Population	%
African, Sub-Saharan (311)	429	0.71
African (275)	348	0.58
Cape Verdean (15)	23	0.04
Nigerian (9)	46	0.08
Other Sub-Saharan African (12)	12	0.02
Albanian (63)	63	0.10
American (1,398)	1,398	2.32
Arab (171)	266	0.44
Arab (67)	67	0.11
Egyptian (34)	34	0.06
Lebanese (60)	112	0.19
Syrian (0)	43	0.07
Other Arab (10)	10	0.02
Armenian (7)	27	0.04
Assyrian/Chaldean/Syriac (10)	10	0.02
Australian (2)	2	<0.01
Austrian (56)	167	0.28
Belgian (0)	92	0.15
Brazilian (14)	14	0.02
British (143)	240	0.40
Canadian (47)	226	0.37
Celtic (0)	13	0.02
Croatian (0)	10	0.02
Cypriot (0)	17	0.03
Czech (20)	177	0.29
Czechoslovakian (12)	46	0.08
Danish (33)	301	0.50
Dutch (14)	345	0.57
Eastern European (347)	466	0.77
English (1,100)	4,443	7.37
European (414)	501	0.83
Finnish (37)	128	0.21
French, ex. Basque (303)	2,117	3.51
French Canadian (282)	912	1.51
German (833)	4,613	7.65
Greek (336)	778	1.29
Hungarian (56)	407	0.68
Iranian (32)	71	0.12
Irish (3,298)	10,825	17.95
Israeli (15)	15	0.02
Italian (8,106)	15,740	26.11
Latvian (10)	22	0.04
Lithuanian (154)	558	0.93
Northern European (4)	4	0.01
Norwegian (96)	249	0.41
Polish (1,098)	3,405	5.65
Portuguese (247)	512	0.85
Romanian (40)	97	0.16
Russian (606)	1,266	2.10
Scandinavian (12)	88	0.15
Scotch-Irish (339)	675	1.12
Scottish (207)	941	1.56
Slavic (0)	135	0.22
Slovak (70)	249	0.41
Swedish (182)	814	1.35
Swiss (11)	90	0.15
Turkish (123)	123	0.20
Ukrainian (117)	378	0.63
Welsh (0)	168	0.28
West Indian, ex. Hispanic (1,132)	1,364	2.26
British West Indian (30)	30	0.05
Haitian (54)	55	0.09
Jamaican (899)	979	1.62
Trinidadian/Tobagonian (93)	123	0.20
West Indian (56)	177	0.29
Yugoslavian (77)	77	0.13

Hispanic Origin	Population	%
Hispanic or Latino (of any race)	5,327	8.74
Central American, ex. Mexican	178	0.29
Costa Rican	14	0.02
Guatemalan	68	0.11
Honduran	20	0.03

*Notes: † The Census 2010 population figure is used to calculate the percentages in the Hispanic Origin and Race categories. Ancestry percentages are based on the 2006-2010 American Community Survey population (not shown); ‡ Numbers in parentheses indicate the number of people reporting a single ancestry; * Numbers in parentheses indicate the number of persons reporting this race alone, not in combination with any other race; Please refer to the Explanation of Data for more information.*

Nicaraguan	14	0.02
Panamanian	21	0.03
Salvadoran	40	0.07
Other Central American	1	<0.01
Cuban	152	0.25
Dominican Republic	228	0.37
Mexican	783	1.28
Puerto Rican	2,575	4.22
South American	1,045	1.71
Argentinean	107	0.18
Bolivian	5	0.01
Chilean	140	0.23
Colombian	294	0.48
Ecuadorian	252	0.41
Paraguayan	12	0.02
Peruvian	150	0.25
Uruguayan	7	0.01
Venezuelan	60	0.10
Other South American	18	0.03
Other Hispanic or Latino	366	0.60

Race*	Population	%
African-American/Black (12,307)	13,291	21.80
Not Hispanic (11,869)	12,623	20.71
Hispanic (438)	668	1.10
American Indian/Alaska Native (91)	432	0.71
Not Hispanic (54)	321	0.53
Hispanic (37)	111	0.18
Blackfeet (1)	27	0.04
Canadian/French Am. Ind. (1)	2	<0.01
Central American Ind. (2)	3	<0.01
Cherokee (3)	51	0.08
Cheyenne (1)	1	<0.01
Chickasaw (0)	1	<0.01
Chippewa (0)	4	0.01
Choctaw (0)	6	0.01
Comanche (0)	1	<0.01
Creek (0)	1	<0.01
Iroquois (2)	13	0.02
Lumbee (1)	4	0.01
Mexican American Ind. (8)	12	0.02
Ottawa (1)	1	<0.01
Pueblo (0)	1	<0.01
Seminole (0)	2	<0.01
Shoshone (3)	3	<0.01
Sioux (0)	3	<0.01
South American Ind. (4)	23	0.04
Spanish American Ind. (5)	5	0.01
Asian (3,332)	3,780	6.20
Not Hispanic (3,304)	3,719	6.10
Hispanic (28)	61	0.10
Bangladeshi (64)	70	0.11
Burmese (2)	2	<0.01
Cambodian (46)	59	0.10
Chinese, ex. Taiwanese (631)	752	1.23
Filipino (427)	539	0.88
Indian (1,028)	1,144	1.88
Indonesian (15)	20	0.03
Japanese (82)	116	0.19
Korean (434)	486	0.80
Laotian (14)	17	0.03
Malaysian (2)	6	0.01
Nepalese (14)	14	0.02
Pakistani (210)	242	0.40
Sri Lankan (23)	23	0.04
Taiwanese (29)	33	0.05
Thai (37)	42	0.07
Vietnamese (116)	145	0.24
Hawaii Native/Pacific Islander (17)	60	0.10
Not Hispanic (12)	45	0.07
Hispanic (5)	15	0.02
Fijian (1)	2	<0.01
Guamanian/Chamorro (9)	15	0.02
Marshallese (1)	1	<0.01
Native Hawaiian (2)	4	0.01
Samoan (2)	5	0.01
White (41,728)	42,996	70.53
Not Hispanic (39,086)	40,031	65.67
Hispanic (2,642)	2,965	4.86

Hartford

Place Type: City/Town
County: Hartford
Population: 124,775†

Ancestry‡	Population	%
Afghan (35)	35	0.03
African, Sub-Saharan (2,541)	3,267	2.62
African (1,933)	2,605	2.09
Cape Verdean (31)	65	0.05
Ethiopian (7)	7	0.01
Ghanaian (24)	24	0.02
Kenyan (66)	66	0.05
Liberian (45)	45	0.04
Nigerian (33)	33	0.03
Somalian (295)	315	0.25
Other Sub-Saharan African (107)	107	0.09
Albanian (211)	250	0.20
American (1,360)	1,360	1.09
Arab (164)	316	0.25
Arab (68)	68	0.05
Egyptian (19)	19	0.02
Jordanian (11)	11	0.01
Lebanese (35)	109	0.09
Palestinian (0)	13	0.01
Syrian (0)	40	0.03
Other Arab (31)	56	0.04
Armenian (54)	62	0.05
Australian (0)	7	0.01
Austrian (0)	78	0.06
Belgian (0)	12	0.01
Brazilian (691)	756	0.61
British (173)	295	0.24
Bulgarian (2)	10	0.01
Canadian (52)	108	0.09
Croatian (78)	111	0.09
Czech (31)	94	0.08
Czechoslovakian (12)	62	0.05
Danish (45)	126	0.10
Dutch (0)	178	0.14
Eastern European (89)	103	0.08
English (782)	2,726	2.18
Estonian (0)	12	0.01
European (139)	193	0.15
Finnish (13)	41	0.03
French, ex. Basque (500)	2,279	1.83
French Canadian (237)	572	0.46
German (471)	2,251	1.80
Greek (169)	280	0.22
Guyanese (1,063)	1,086	0.87
Hungarian (18)	151	0.12
Irish (1,426)	4,428	3.55
Israeli (15)	15	0.01
Italian (2,349)	5,204	4.17
Latvian (11)	11	0.01
Lithuanian (140)	285	0.23
Macedonian (22)	22	0.02
Maltese (0)	12	0.01
Northern European (24)	24	0.02
Norwegian (41)	207	0.17
Polish (1,494)	2,658	2.13
Portuguese (651)	978	0.78
Romanian (125)	172	0.14
Russian (211)	685	0.55
Scandinavian (0)	10	0.01
Scotch-Irish (105)	315	0.25
Scottish (85)	548	0.44
Serbian (13)	33	0.03
Slovak (13)	13	0.01
Swedish (127)	645	0.52
Swiss (0)	40	0.03
Turkish (154)	200	0.16
Ukrainian (94)	169	0.14
Welsh (16)	129	0.10
West Indian, ex. Hispanic (11,665)	13,498	10.82
Barbadian (157)	208	0.17
Belizean (10)	10	0.01
British West Indian (137)	209	0.17
Haitian (332)	332	0.27
Jamaican (9,875)	11,200	8.98
Trinidadian/Tobagonian (135)	244	0.20
U.S. Virgin Islander (39)	39	0.03
West Indian (949)	1,211	0.97
Other West Indian (31)	45	0.04
Yugoslavian (1,157)	1,163	0.93

Hispanic Origin	Population	%
Hispanic or Latino (of any race)	54,185	43.43
Central American, ex. Mexican	1,124	0.90
Costa Rican	23	0.02
Guatemalan	354	0.28
Honduran	307	0.25
Nicaraguan	48	0.04
Panamanian	68	0.05
Salvadoran	315	0.25
Other Central American	9	0.01
Cuban	661	0.53
Dominican Republic	2,191	1.76
Mexican	2,272	1.82
Puerto Rican	41,995	33.66
South American	3,773	3.02
Argentinean	80	0.06
Bolivian	25	0.02
Chilean	31	0.02
Colombian	1,074	0.86
Ecuadorian	287	0.23
Paraguayan	6	<0.01
Peruvian	2,119	1.70
Uruguayan	17	0.01
Venezuelan	69	0.06
Other South American	65	0.05
Other Hispanic or Latino	2,169	1.74

Race*	Population	%
African-American/Black (48,331)	51,253	41.08
Not Hispanic (44,223)	45,704	36.63
Hispanic (4,108)	5,549	4.45
American Indian/Alaska Native (777)	1,759	1.41
Not Hispanic (309)	917	0.73
Hispanic (468)	842	0.67
Alaska Athabascan *(Ala. Nat.)* (0)	1	<0.01
Aleut *(Alaska Native)* (0)	2	<0.01
Apache (0)	2	<0.01
Arapaho (1)	1	<0.01
Blackfeet (4)	46	0.04
Canadian/French Am. Ind. (2)	3	<0.01
Central American Ind. (8)	24	0.02
Cherokee (31)	135	0.11
Cheyenne (0)	1	<0.01
Chickasaw (1)	1	<0.01
Chippewa (6)	7	0.01
Choctaw (0)	9	0.01
Comanche (2)	6	<0.01
Creek (0)	1	<0.01
Crow (0)	4	<0.01
Hopi (0)	1	<0.01
Inupiat *(Alaska Native)* (2)	2	<0.01
Iroquois (1)	23	0.02
Mexican American Ind. (10)	19	0.02
Navajo (1)	16	0.01
Pueblo (3)	4	<0.01
Seminole (1)	15	0.01
Shoshone (1)	3	<0.01
Sioux (2)	10	0.01
South American Ind. (80)	194	0.16
Spanish American Ind. (6)	12	0.01
Tlingit-Haida *(Alaska Native)* (1)	1	<0.01
Tohono O'Odham (1)	1	<0.01
Ute (0)	1	<0.01
Yaqui (1)	1	<0.01
Asian (3,437)	4,074	3.27
Not Hispanic (3,347)	3,808	3.05
Hispanic (90)	266	0.21
Bangladeshi (40)	49	0.04
Bhutanese (17)	17	0.01
Burmese (537)	553	0.44
Cambodian (5)	15	0.01
Chinese, ex. Taiwanese (298)	419	0.34

*Notes: † The Census 2010 population figure is used to calculate the percentages in the Hispanic Origin and Race categories. Ancestry percentages are based on the 2006-2010 American Community Survey population (not shown); ‡ Numbers in parentheses indicate the number of people reporting a single ancestry; * Numbers in parentheses indicate the number of persons reporting this race alone, not in combination with any other race; Please refer to the Explanation of Data for more information.*

Filipino (136)	189	0.15
Indian (1,461)	1,635	1.31
Indonesian (23)	24	0.02
Japanese (30)	71	0.06
Korean (145)	175	0.14
Laotian (36)	48	0.04
Malaysian (2)	3	<0.01
Nepalese (28)	28	0.02
Pakistani (102)	125	0.10
Sri Lankan (16)	16	0.01
Taiwanese (31)	34	0.03
Thai (24)	40	0.03
Vietnamese (374)	406	0.33
Hawaii Native/Pacific Islander (62)	447	0.36
Not Hispanic (27)	229	0.18
Hispanic (35)	218	0.17
Fijian (1)	1	<0.01
Guamanian/Chamorro (8)	19	0.02
Native Hawaiian (17)	38	0.03
Samoan (5)	18	0.01
White (37,205)	40,483	32.44
Not Hispanic (19,765)	20,917	16.76
Hispanic (17,440)	19,566	15.68

Hebron

Place Type: Town
County: Tolland
Population: 9,686†

Ancestry‡	Population	%
American (250)	250	2.61
Armenian (21)	84	0.88
Austrian (0)	58	0.61
Belgian (0)	14	0.15
Brazilian (0)	16	0.17
British (38)	71	0.74
Canadian (20)	38	0.40
Croatian (0)	8	0.08
Czech (10)	16	0.17
Czechoslovakian (17)	55	0.57
Danish (20)	84	0.88
Dutch (15)	68	0.71
English (365)	1,738	18.16
European (67)	67	0.70
French, ex. Basque (188)	963	10.06
French Canadian (168)	721	7.53
German (146)	1,285	13.43
Greek (0)	55	0.57
Hungarian (9)	61	0.64
Irish (599)	2,381	24.88
Italian (680)	2,284	23.86
Lithuanian (25)	213	2.23
Norwegian (0)	15	0.16
Polish (389)	1,151	12.03
Portuguese (41)	88	0.92
Romanian (0)	20	0.21
Russian (50)	240	2.51
Scotch-Irish (75)	253	2.64
Scottish (65)	395	4.13
Slovak (52)	67	0.70
Slovene (0)	8	0.08
Swedish (0)	242	2.53
Swiss (0)	42	0.44
Ukrainian (34)	195	2.04
Welsh (0)	85	0.89

Hispanic Origin	Population	%
Hispanic or Latino (of any race)	224	2.31
Central American, ex. Mexican	19	0.20
Guatemalan	5	0.05
Panamanian	1	0.01
Salvadoran	13	0.13
Cuban	14	0.14
Dominican Republic	4	0.04
Mexican	33	0.34
Puerto Rican	86	0.89
South American	34	0.35
Argentinean	5	0.05
Chilean	6	0.06
Colombian	10	0.10
Paraguayan	1	0.01
Peruvian	11	0.11
Venezuelan	1	0.01
Other Hispanic or Latino	34	0.35

Race*	Population	%
African-American/Black (48)	83	0.86
Not Hispanic (47)	79	0.82
Hispanic (1)	4	0.04
American Indian/Alaska Native (17)	68	0.70
Not Hispanic (16)	61	0.63
Hispanic (1)	7	0.07
Apache (1)	1	0.01
Blackfeet (0)	2	0.02
Cherokee (1)	7	0.07
Mexican American Ind. (0)	1	0.01
Navajo (0)	1	0.01
Potawatomi (1)	1	0.01
Pueblo (1)	1	0.01
Tlingit-Haida *(Alaska Native)* (0)	3	0.03
Asian (95)	139	1.44
Not Hispanic (94)	136	1.40
Hispanic (1)	3	0.03
Cambodian (1)	1	0.01
Chinese, ex. Taiwanese (25)	32	0.33
Filipino (14)	29	0.30
Indian (11)	13	0.13
Japanese (3)	11	0.11
Korean (18)	24	0.25
Pakistani (6)	6	0.06
Taiwanese (5)	6	0.06
Thai (1)	1	0.01
Vietnamese (4)	4	0.04
Hawaii Native/Pacific Islander (4)	13	0.13
Not Hispanic (4)	12	0.12
Hispanic (0)	1	0.01
Guamanian/Chamorro (1)	1	0.01
Native Hawaiian (3)	5	0.05
Samoan (0)	4	0.04
White (9,367)	9,489	97.97
Not Hispanic (9,184)	9,288	95.89
Hispanic (183)	201	2.08

Kensington

Place Type: CDP
County: Hartford
Population: 8,459†

Ancestry‡	Population	%
Albanian (14)	14	0.16
American (347)	347	3.96
Armenian (153)	153	1.75
Assyrian/Chaldean/Syriac (0)	39	0.45
Austrian (12)	36	0.41
Canadian (65)	117	1.34
Czech (0)	15	0.17
Czechoslovakian (0)	39	0.45
Dutch (0)	57	0.65
English (57)	755	8.62
European (161)	177	2.02
French, ex. Basque (244)	877	10.01
French Canadian (132)	235	2.68
German (67)	1,024	11.69
Greek (12)	25	0.29
Hungarian (0)	109	1.24
Irish (430)	2,055	23.46
Italian (1,396)	3,226	36.82
Lithuanian (28)	98	1.12
Polish (598)	1,535	17.52
Russian (54)	194	2.21
Scandinavian (21)	21	0.24
Scotch-Irish (0)	25	0.29
Scottish (48)	157	1.79
Slovak (0)	13	0.15
Swedish (76)	456	5.20
Ukrainian (13)	76	0.87

Hispanic Origin	Population	%
Hispanic or Latino (of any race)	290	3.43
Central American, ex. Mexican	6	0.07
Honduran	2	0.02
Salvadoran	4	0.05
Cuban	19	0.22
Dominican Republic	3	0.04
Mexican	35	0.41
Puerto Rican	125	1.48
South American	46	0.54
Argentinean	14	0.17
Bolivian	2	0.02
Colombian	17	0.20
Ecuadorian	4	0.05
Paraguayan	4	0.05
Peruvian	2	0.02
Uruguayan	3	0.04
Other Hispanic or Latino	56	0.66

Race*	Population	%
African-American/Black (56)	84	0.99
Not Hispanic (51)	71	0.84
Hispanic (5)	13	0.15
American Indian/Alaska Native (7)	37	0.44
Not Hispanic (4)	30	0.35
Hispanic (3)	7	0.08
Canadian/French Am. Ind. (0)	3	0.04
Cherokee (1)	2	0.02
Choctaw (1)	1	0.01
Iroquois (0)	1	0.01
Sioux (0)	1	0.01
South American Ind. (2)	2	0.02
Asian (226)	243	2.87
Not Hispanic (226)	243	2.87
Cambodian (1)	1	0.01
Chinese, ex. Taiwanese (36)	37	0.44
Filipino (21)	23	0.27
Indian (104)	104	1.23
Indonesian (1)	2	0.02
Japanese (4)	7	0.08
Korean (15)	21	0.25
Pakistani (5)	5	0.06
Taiwanese (1)	1	0.01
Thai (1)	4	0.05
Vietnamese (37)	38	0.45
Hawaii Native/Pacific Islander (2)	7	0.08
Not Hispanic (2)	5	0.06
Hispanic (0)	2	0.02
Native Hawaiian (0)	3	0.04
White (8,043)	8,124	96.04
Not Hispanic (7,811)	7,876	93.11
Hispanic (232)	248	2.93

Killingly

Place Type: Town
County: Windham
Population: 17,370†

Ancestry‡	Population	%
African, Sub-Saharan (18)	18	0.10
Cape Verdean (18)	18	0.10
American (366)	366	2.11
Arab (31)	114	0.66
Arab (12)	12	0.07
Lebanese (12)	59	0.34
Syrian (7)	43	0.25
Armenian (0)	13	0.07
Austrian (15)	56	0.32
Belgian (0)	19	0.11
British (26)	40	0.23
Canadian (108)	170	0.98
Czech (0)	45	0.26
Czechoslovakian (0)	9	0.05
Dutch (43)	145	0.84
English (496)	2,291	13.21
Estonian (0)	15	0.09
European (64)	64	0.37
Finnish (29)	69	0.40
French, ex. Basque (1,458)	4,805	27.70

*Notes: † The Census 2010 population figure is used to calculate the percentages in the Hispanic Origin and Race categories. Ancestry percentages are based on the 2006-2010 American Community Survey population (not shown); ‡ Numbers in parentheses indicate the number of people reporting a single ancestry; * Numbers in parentheses indicate the number of persons reporting this race alone, not in combination with any other race; Please refer to the Explanation of Data for more information.*

Ancestry	Population	%
French Canadian (1,190)	2,541	14.65
German (271)	1,512	8.72
Greek (14)	71	0.41
Hungarian (0)	29	0.17
Iranian (0)	20	0.12
Irish (677)	3,321	19.14
Italian (705)	2,287	13.18
Latvian (0)	17	0.10
Lithuanian (13)	72	0.42
Norwegian (7)	44	0.25
Pennsylvania German (0)	31	0.18
Polish (396)	1,858	10.71
Portuguese (210)	530	3.06
Russian (19)	121	0.70
Scandinavian (22)	22	0.13
Scotch-Irish (78)	319	1.84
Scottish (111)	503	2.90
Slovak (11)	25	0.14
Swedish (89)	355	2.05
Swiss (0)	26	0.15
Ukrainian (0)	25	0.14
Welsh (44)	196	1.13
West Indian, ex. Hispanic (64)	64	0.37
Jamaican (64)	64	0.37

Hispanic Origin	Population	%
Hispanic or Latino (of any race)	516	2.97
Central American, ex. Mexican	10	0.06
Guatemalan	3	0.02
Panamanian	2	0.01
Salvadoran	5	0.03
Cuban	10	0.06
Dominican Republic	12	0.07
Mexican	105	0.60
Puerto Rican	285	1.64
South American	23	0.13
Argentinean	1	0.01
Colombian	12	0.07
Ecuadorian	2	0.01
Peruvian	6	0.03
Uruguayan	1	0.01
Other South American	1	0.01
Other Hispanic or Latino	71	0.41

Race*	Population	%
African-American/Black (263)	427	2.46
Not Hispanic (244)	383	2.20
Hispanic (19)	44	0.25
American Indian/Alaska Native (73)	252	1.45
Not Hispanic (65)	228	1.31
Hispanic (8)	24	0.14
Blackfeet (1)	8	0.05
Canadian/French Am. Ind. (1)	2	0.01
Cherokee (3)	22	0.13
Cheyenne (1)	1	0.01
Comanche (1)	1	0.01
Cree (1)	1	0.01
Crow (0)	2	0.01
Inupiat *(Alaska Native)* (0)	4	0.02
Iroquois (1)	2	0.01
Mexican American Ind. (1)	3	0.02
Navajo (0)	6	0.03
Seminole (0)	1	0.01
Sioux (0)	6	0.03
South American Ind. (2)	3	0.02
Tlingit-Haida *(Alaska Native)* (0)	2	0.01
Asian (312)	375	2.16
Not Hispanic (312)	372	2.14
Hispanic (0)	3	0.02
Cambodian (5)	5	0.03
Chinese, ex. Taiwanese (53)	55	0.32
Filipino (18)	33	0.19
Indian (29)	34	0.20
Japanese (3)	11	0.06
Korean (6)	12	0.07
Laotian (166)	183	1.05
Thai (2)	10	0.06
Vietnamese (10)	12	0.07
Hawaii Native/Pacific Islander (2)	8	0.05
Not Hispanic (2)	8	0.05
Guamanian/Chamorro (0)	2	0.01
Native Hawaiian (2)	4	0.02
Samoan (0)	1	0.01
White (16,173)	16,557	95.32
Not Hispanic (15,865)	16,196	93.24
Hispanic (308)	361	2.08

Ledyard

Place Type: Town
County: New London
Population: 15,051[†]

Ancestry[‡]	Population	%
African, Sub-Saharan (124)	156	1.04
African (0)	3	0.02
Cape Verdean (124)	153	1.02
Albanian (12)	48	0.32
American (464)	464	3.09
Arab (48)	178	1.18
Lebanese (48)	178	1.18
Austrian (0)	33	0.22
Belgian (13)	13	0.09
British (45)	59	0.39
Bulgarian (0)	42	0.28
Canadian (32)	47	0.31
Celtic (13)	26	0.17
Croatian (16)	16	0.11
Czech (0)	32	0.21
Czechoslovakian (4)	4	0.03
Danish (15)	29	0.19
Dutch (28)	210	1.40
Eastern European (11)	25	0.17
English (924)	2,969	19.76
Estonian (12)	12	0.08
European (365)	365	2.43
Finnish (0)	12	0.08
French, ex. Basque (230)	1,058	7.04
French Canadian (353)	604	4.02
German (387)	2,036	13.55
Greek (0)	44	0.29
Hungarian (43)	135	0.90
Iranian (12)	12	0.08
Irish (673)	2,943	19.59
Italian (713)	2,556	17.01
Latvian (0)	16	0.11
Lithuanian (18)	122	0.81
Northern European (17)	17	0.11
Norwegian (11)	54	0.36
Polish (214)	1,201	7.99
Portuguese (101)	492	3.27
Russian (0)	56	0.37
Scandinavian (0)	12	0.08
Scotch-Irish (83)	399	2.66
Scottish (94)	568	3.78
Slovak (12)	73	0.49
Slovene (0)	11	0.07
Swedish (31)	189	1.26
Swiss (25)	184	1.22
Turkish (0)	42	0.28
Ukrainian (68)	127	0.85
Welsh (0)	181	1.20
West Indian, ex. Hispanic (21)	46	0.31
Jamaican (6)	6	0.04
Trinidadian/Tobagonian (15)	40	0.27

Hispanic Origin	Population	%
Hispanic or Latino (of any race)	835	5.55
Central American, ex. Mexican	60	0.40
Costa Rican	7	0.05
Guatemalan	12	0.08
Nicaraguan	1	0.01
Panamanian	18	0.12
Salvadoran	22	0.15
Cuban	20	0.13
Dominican Republic	29	0.19
Mexican	140	0.93
Puerto Rican	371	2.46
South American	134	0.89
Argentinean	4	0.03
Bolivian	4	0.03
Chilean	2	0.01
Colombian	24	0.16
Ecuadorian	12	0.08
Peruvian	87	0.58
Venezuelan	1	0.01
Other Hispanic or Latino	81	0.54

Race*	Population	%
African-American/Black (493)	814	5.41
Not Hispanic (456)	718	4.77
Hispanic (37)	96	0.64
American Indian/Alaska Native (375)	694	4.61
Not Hispanic (335)	611	4.06
Hispanic (40)	83	0.55
Aleut *(Alaska Native)* (1)	1	0.01
Apache (1)	7	0.05
Blackfeet (1)	3	0.02
Central American Ind. (1)	1	0.01
Cherokee (8)	28	0.19
Chickasaw (4)	4	0.03
Chippewa (3)	4	0.03
Choctaw (1)	11	0.07
Comanche (3)	3	0.02
Delaware (1)	5	0.03
Hopi (0)	4	0.03
Houma (3)	5	0.03
Iroquois (0)	6	0.04
Kiowa (1)	1	0.01
Lumbee (4)	4	0.03
Mexican American Ind. (3)	3	0.02
Pueblo (1)	1	0.01
Sioux (3)	6	0.04
South American Ind. (2)	8	0.05
Spanish American Ind. (4)	8	0.05
Tlingit-Haida *(Alaska Native)* (0)	1	0.01
Asian (530)	663	4.41
Not Hispanic (526)	647	4.30
Hispanic (4)	16	0.11
Cambodian (7)	7	0.05
Chinese, ex. Taiwanese (197)	220	1.46
Filipino (155)	227	1.51
Indian (59)	65	0.43
Indonesian (2)	3	0.02
Japanese (25)	56	0.37
Korean (13)	16	0.11
Laotian (20)	23	0.15
Malaysian (0)	3	0.02
Nepalese (5)	5	0.03
Sri Lankan (3)	4	0.03
Thai (8)	10	0.07
Vietnamese (19)	27	0.18
Hawaii Native/Pacific Islander (10)	38	0.25
Not Hispanic (10)	37	0.25
Hispanic (0)	1	0.01
Guamanian/Chamorro (5)	21	0.14
Native Hawaiian (5)	10	0.07
White (12,849)	13,290	88.30
Not Hispanic (12,362)	12,735	84.61
Hispanic (487)	555	3.69

Litchfield

Place Type: Town
County: Litchfield
Population: 8,466[†]

Ancestry[‡]	Population	%
American (248)	248	2.91
Arab (24)	51	0.60
Arab (17)	17	0.20
Lebanese (4)	16	0.19
Palestinian (3)	3	0.04
Syrian (0)	15	0.18
Austrian (23)	69	0.81
British (18)	24	0.28
Canadian (3)	3	0.04
Czech (38)	67	0.79
Czechoslovakian (6)	6	0.07
Danish (20)	36	0.42

*Notes: † The Census 2010 population figure is used to calculate the percentages in the Hispanic Origin and Race categories. Ancestry percentages are based on the 2006-2010 American Community Survey population (not shown); ‡ Numbers in parentheses indicate the number of people reporting a single ancestry; * Numbers in parentheses indicate the number of persons reporting this race alone, not in combination with any other race; Please refer to the Explanation of Data for more information.*

Dutch (16)	39	0.46
Eastern European (0)	7	0.08
English (368)	1,638	19.24
European (126)	174	2.04
Finnish (16)	40	0.47
French, ex. Basque (177)	924	10.86
French Canadian (77)	300	3.52
German (347)	1,242	14.59
Greek (50)	70	0.82
Hungarian (37)	243	2.85
Irish (585)	1,745	20.50
Italian (894)	2,008	23.59
Lithuanian (44)	145	1.70
Norwegian (16)	56	0.66
Pennsylvania German (3)	3	0.04
Polish (118)	412	4.84
Portuguese (22)	83	0.98
Russian (63)	189	2.22
Scandinavian (0)	10	0.12
Scotch-Irish (34)	206	2.42
Scottish (43)	330	3.88
Slovak (10)	48	0.56
Swedish (14)	161	1.89
Swiss (3)	10	0.12
Turkish (8)	8	0.09
Ukrainian (10)	52	0.61
Welsh (10)	39	0.46
West Indian, ex. Hispanic (0)	7	0.08
Bermudan (0)	7	0.08
Yugoslavian (3)	3	0.04

Hispanic Origin	Population	%
Hispanic or Latino (of any race)	173	2.04
Central American, ex. Mexican	2	0.02
Guatemalan	1	0.01
Other Central American	1	0.01
Cuban	13	0.15
Dominican Republic	10	0.12
Mexican	45	0.53
Puerto Rican	51	0.60
South American	14	0.17
Chilean	2	0.02
Colombian	5	0.06
Ecuadorian	2	0.02
Peruvian	1	0.01
Other South American	4	0.05
Other Hispanic or Latino	38	0.45

Race*	Population	%
African-American/Black (52)	81	0.96
Not Hispanic (49)	75	0.89
Hispanic (3)	6	0.07
American Indian/Alaska Native (13)	59	0.70
Not Hispanic (10)	52	0.61
Hispanic (3)	7	0.08
Blackfeet (0)	10	0.12
Cherokee (1)	8	0.09
Chippewa (0)	4	0.05
Creek (2)	2	0.02
Iroquois (0)	1	0.01
South American Ind. (1)	1	0.01
Asian (77)	121	1.43
Not Hispanic (76)	117	1.38
Hispanic (1)	4	0.05
Bangladeshi (3)	3	0.04
Burmese (0)	1	0.01
Chinese, ex. Taiwanese (16)	39	0.46
Filipino (16)	27	0.32
Indian (17)	17	0.20
Indonesian (1)	1	0.01
Japanese (0)	9	0.11
Korean (10)	12	0.14
Thai (1)	1	0.01
Vietnamese (8)	9	0.11
Hawaii Native/Pacific Islander (12)	15	0.18
Not Hispanic (12)	15	0.18
Native Hawaiian (3)	5	0.06
White (8,149)	8,266	97.64
Not Hispanic (8,025)	8,130	96.03
Hispanic (124)	136	1.61

Madison

Place Type: Town
County: New Haven
Population: 18,269†

Ancestry‡	Population	%
African, Sub-Saharan (11)	24	0.13
African (11)	24	0.13
American (351)	351	1.93
Arab (30)	42	0.23
Arab (0)	12	0.07
Lebanese (30)	30	0.16
Armenian (63)	92	0.50
Australian (17)	49	0.27
Austrian (58)	336	1.84
Belgian (12)	12	0.07
British (91)	192	1.05
Canadian (22)	91	0.50
Croatian (76)	89	0.49
Czech (48)	101	0.55
Czechoslovakian (16)	43	0.24
Danish (42)	226	1.24
Dutch (65)	326	1.79
Eastern European (47)	98	0.54
English (692)	3,164	17.36
European (187)	187	1.03
Finnish (0)	23	0.13
French, ex. Basque (66)	1,006	5.52
French Canadian (74)	563	3.09
German (487)	3,638	19.96
Greek (15)	51	0.28
Hungarian (104)	310	1.70
Iranian (39)	56	0.31
Irish (1,629)	5,417	29.72
Italian (1,510)	4,081	22.39
Lithuanian (60)	241	1.32
Maltese (12)	26	0.14
Norwegian (38)	175	0.96
Polish (374)	1,288	7.07
Portuguese (57)	98	0.54
Romanian (20)	58	0.32
Russian (216)	662	3.63
Scotch-Irish (91)	347	1.90
Scottish (328)	1,211	6.64
Serbian (0)	15	0.08
Slavic (0)	13	0.07
Slovak (8)	99	0.54
Swedish (121)	673	3.69
Swiss (10)	92	0.50
Turkish (11)	11	0.06
Ukrainian (11)	65	0.36
Welsh (22)	83	0.46
West Indian, ex. Hispanic (77)	77	0.42
Jamaican (77)	77	0.42

Hispanic Origin	Population	%
Hispanic or Latino (of any race)	375	2.05
Central American, ex. Mexican	30	0.16
Costa Rican	5	0.03
Guatemalan	18	0.10
Honduran	1	0.01
Panamanian	4	0.02
Salvadoran	2	0.01
Cuban	20	0.11
Dominican Republic	16	0.09
Mexican	81	0.44
Puerto Rican	82	0.45
South American	88	0.48
Argentinean	14	0.08
Bolivian	1	0.01
Chilean	7	0.04
Colombian	31	0.17
Ecuadorian	14	0.08
Paraguayan	4	0.02
Peruvian	11	0.06
Venezuelan	2	0.01
Other South American	4	0.02
Other Hispanic or Latino	58	0.32

Race*	Population	%
African-American/Black (110)	163	0.89
Not Hispanic (100)	147	0.80
Hispanic (10)	16	0.09
American Indian/Alaska Native (25)	84	0.46
Not Hispanic (11)	62	0.34
Hispanic (14)	22	0.12
Blackfeet (0)	3	0.02
Canadian/French Am. Ind. (0)	1	0.01
Cherokee (2)	19	0.10
Choctaw (0)	1	0.01
Iroquois (1)	2	0.01
Mexican American Ind. (4)	5	0.03
Sioux (3)	7	0.04
South American Ind. (4)	8	0.04
Asian (408)	517	2.83
Not Hispanic (405)	512	2.80
Hispanic (3)	5	0.03
Bangladeshi (1)	3	0.02
Chinese, ex. Taiwanese (184)	208	1.14
Filipino (21)	37	0.20
Indian (106)	140	0.77
Indonesian (1)	4	0.02
Japanese (7)	25	0.14
Korean (30)	47	0.26
Laotian (1)	1	0.01
Pakistani (7)	10	0.05
Taiwanese (5)	10	0.05
Thai (6)	10	0.05
Vietnamese (19)	27	0.15
Hawaii Native/Pacific Islander (2)	5	0.03
Not Hispanic (2)	5	0.03
Native Hawaiian (2)	4	0.02
White (17,403)	17,619	96.44
Not Hispanic (17,152)	17,349	94.96
Hispanic (251)	270	1.48

Manchester

Place Type: CDP
County: Hartford
Population: 30,577†

Ancestry‡	Population	%
African, Sub-Saharan (293)	348	1.16
African (258)	313	1.05
Ethiopian (26)	26	0.09
Ghanaian (9)	9	0.03
American (1,346)	1,346	4.50
Arab (0)	20	0.07
Lebanese (0)	20	0.07
Armenian (48)	62	0.21
Austrian (17)	122	0.41
Belgian (47)	109	0.36
Brazilian (64)	77	0.26
British (21)	177	0.59
Canadian (94)	201	0.67
Croatian (0)	11	0.04
Czech (20)	95	0.32
Czechoslovakian (0)	27	0.09
Danish (104)	147	0.49
Dutch (48)	202	0.68
Eastern European (39)	39	0.13
English (902)	3,948	13.20
European (140)	208	0.70
Finnish (15)	61	0.20
French, ex. Basque (485)	2,209	7.38
French Canadian (523)	1,188	3.97
German (577)	3,269	10.93
Greek (84)	250	0.84
Guyanese (12)	12	0.04
Hungarian (13)	217	0.73
Iranian (11)	11	0.04
Irish (1,321)	5,544	18.53
Italian (1,475)	4,358	14.57
Latvian (34)	44	0.15
Lithuanian (138)	397	1.33
Northern European (14)	14	0.05
Norwegian (23)	157	0.52

SECTION TWO

*Notes: † The Census 2010 population figure is used to calculate the percentages in the Hispanic Origin and Race categories. Ancestry percentages are based on the 2006-2010 American Community Survey population (not shown); ‡ Numbers in parentheses indicate the number of people reporting a single ancestry; * Numbers in parentheses indicate the number of persons reporting this race alone, not in combination with any other race; Please refer to the Explanation of Data for more information.*

Polish (665)	2,502	8.36
Portuguese (124)	335	1.12
Romanian (100)	152	0.51
Russian (145)	344	1.15
Scandinavian (8)	23	0.08
Scotch-Irish (67)	306	1.02
Scottish (189)	820	2.74
Slavic (0)	6	0.02
Slovak (0)	39	0.13
Slovene (0)	61	0.20
Swedish (222)	541	1.81
Swiss (0)	66	0.22
Ukrainian (30)	111	0.37
Welsh (32)	143	0.48
West Indian, ex. Hispanic (595)	789	2.64
Barbadian (17)	17	0.06
British West Indian (56)	64	0.21
Haitian (11)	45	0.15
Jamaican (285)	384	1.28
Trinidadian/Tobagonian (12)	12	0.04
West Indian (214)	267	0.89

Hispanic Origin	Population	%
Hispanic or Latino (of any race)	4,480	14.65
Central American, ex. Mexican	151	0.49
Costa Rican	6	0.02
Guatemalan	17	0.06
Honduran	15	0.05
Nicaraguan	10	0.03
Panamanian	15	0.05
Salvadoran	87	0.28
Other Central American	1	<0.01
Cuban	75	0.25
Dominican Republic	107	0.35
Mexican	208	0.68
Puerto Rican	3,146	10.29
South American	570	1.86
Argentinean	27	0.09
Bolivian	4	0.01
Chilean	9	0.03
Colombian	196	0.64
Ecuadorian	72	0.24
Peruvian	236	0.77
Uruguayan	7	0.02
Venezuelan	16	0.05
Other South American	3	0.01
Other Hispanic or Latino	223	0.73

Race*	Population	%
African-American/Black (4,172)	4,855	15.88
Not Hispanic (3,802)	4,291	14.03
Hispanic (370)	564	1.84
American Indian/Alaska Native (109)	339	1.11
Not Hispanic (60)	244	0.80
Hispanic (49)	95	0.31
Apache (0)	2	0.01
Blackfeet (8)	33	0.11
Canadian/French Am. Ind. (0)	2	0.01
Central American Ind. (4)	4	0.01
Cherokee (4)	24	0.08
Chippewa (0)	6	0.02
Choctaw (0)	1	<0.01
Comanche (0)	1	<0.01
Cree (1)	2	0.01
Iroquois (5)	17	0.06
Lumbee (0)	4	0.01
Mexican American Ind. (2)	5	0.02
Seminole (0)	2	0.01
Sioux (0)	7	0.02
South American Ind. (15)	25	0.08
Asian (1,270)	1,493	4.88
Not Hispanic (1,250)	1,441	4.71
Hispanic (20)	52	0.17
Bangladeshi (163)	194	0.63
Burmese (1)	2	0.01
Cambodian (23)	27	0.09
Chinese, ex. Taiwanese (156)	197	0.64
Filipino (90)	144	0.47
Hmong (6)	7	0.02
Indian (336)	402	1.31
Indonesian (0)	4	0.01
Japanese (18)	30	0.10
Korean (41)	62	0.20
Laotian (83)	114	0.37
Malaysian (7)	7	0.02
Nepalese (3)	4	0.01
Pakistani (124)	139	0.45
Sri Lankan (5)	5	0.02
Taiwanese (7)	9	0.03
Thai (7)	13	0.04
Vietnamese (91)	120	0.39
Hawaii Native/Pacific Islander (8)	41	0.13
Not Hispanic (6)	23	0.08
Hispanic (2)	18	0.06
Fijian (0)	1	<0.01
Guamanian/Chamorro (1)	1	<0.01
Native Hawaiian (5)	9	0.03
Samoan (0)	4	0.01
White (22,122)	23,092	75.52
Not Hispanic (20,151)	20,811	68.06
Hispanic (1,971)	2,281	7.46

Manchester

Place Type: Town
County: Hartford
Population: 58,241†

Ancestry‡	Population	%
African, Sub-Saharan (367)	439	0.76
African (263)	335	0.58
Ethiopian (26)	26	0.05
Ghanaian (78)	78	0.14
American (1,962)	1,962	3.40
Arab (35)	122	0.21
Jordanian (7)	20	0.03
Lebanese (12)	66	0.11
Syrian (16)	36	0.06
Armenian (60)	88	0.15
Assyrian/Chaldean/Syriac (0)	24	0.04
Austrian (41)	279	0.48
Belgian (47)	109	0.19
Brazilian (183)	196	0.34
British (32)	290	0.50
Canadian (251)	435	0.75
Celtic (9)	9	0.02
Croatian (12)	54	0.09
Czech (35)	163	0.28
Czechoslovakian (25)	89	0.15
Danish (166)	284	0.49
Dutch (61)	418	0.73
Eastern European (39)	50	0.09
English (1,646)	7,092	12.30
European (363)	431	0.75
Finnish (15)	71	0.12
French, ex. Basque (1,081)	4,986	8.65
French Canadian (897)	2,168	3.76
German (1,097)	6,166	10.70
Greek (133)	371	0.64
Guyanese (25)	58	0.10
Hungarian (43)	482	0.84
Iranian (18)	31	0.05
Irish (2,589)	10,305	17.88
Italian (3,250)	8,083	14.02
Latvian (48)	93	0.16
Lithuanian (223)	708	1.23
New Zealander (1)	1	<0.01
Northern European (14)	14	0.02
Norwegian (68)	269	0.47
Pennsylvania German (11)	11	0.02
Polish (1,494)	4,548	7.89
Portuguese (175)	583	1.01
Romanian (123)	205	0.36
Russian (241)	838	1.45
Scandinavian (8)	23	0.04
Scotch-Irish (235)	721	1.25
Scottish (349)	1,372	2.38
Slavic (0)	20	0.03
Slovak (41)	238	0.41
Slovene (0)	61	0.11
Swedish (350)	1,188	2.06
Swiss (26)	157	0.27
Turkish (0)	15	0.03
Ukrainian (131)	283	0.49
Welsh (32)	298	0.52
West Indian, ex. Hispanic (860)	1,242	2.15
Bahamian (0)	29	0.05
Barbadian (33)	64	0.11
British West Indian (56)	64	0.11
Haitian (45)	79	0.14
Jamaican (500)	685	1.19
Trinidadian/Tobagonian (12)	12	0.02
West Indian (214)	309	0.54
Yugoslavian (17)	28	0.05

Hispanic Origin	Population	%
Hispanic or Latino (of any race)	6,988	12.00
Central American, ex. Mexican	227	0.39
Costa Rican	13	0.02
Guatemalan	34	0.06
Honduran	29	0.05
Nicaraguan	11	0.02
Panamanian	32	0.05
Salvadoran	107	0.18
Other Central American	1	<0.01
Cuban	145	0.25
Dominican Republic	202	0.35
Mexican	344	0.59
Puerto Rican	4,782	8.21
South American	907	1.56
Argentinean	50	0.09
Bolivian	8	0.01
Chilean	34	0.06
Colombian	326	0.56
Ecuadorian	98	0.17
Peruvian	350	0.60
Uruguayan	9	0.02
Venezuelan	27	0.05
Other South American	5	0.01
Other Hispanic or Latino	381	0.65

Race*	Population	%
African-American/Black (7,152)	8,243	14.15
Not Hispanic (6,602)	7,368	12.65
Hispanic (550)	875	1.50
American Indian/Alaska Native (183)	538	0.92
Not Hispanic (103)	390	0.67
Hispanic (80)	148	0.25
Apache (0)	2	<0.01
Blackfeet (8)	39	0.07
Canadian/French Am. Ind. (2)	6	0.01
Central American Ind. (4)	5	0.01
Cherokee (8)	42	0.07
Chippewa (3)	12	0.02
Choctaw (0)	3	0.01
Comanche (0)	1	<0.01
Cree (1)	2	<0.01
Creek (0)	1	<0.01
Delaware (0)	1	<0.01
Iroquois (8)	22	0.04
Lumbee (0)	4	0.01
Mexican American Ind. (2)	5	0.01
Ottawa (1)	1	<0.01
Potawatomi (1)	1	<0.01
Seminole (0)	2	<0.01
Sioux (1)	11	0.02
South American Ind. (16)	37	0.06
Spanish American Ind. (0)	2	<0.01
Asian (4,627)	5,122	8.79
Not Hispanic (4,591)	5,028	8.63
Hispanic (36)	94	0.16
Bangladeshi (257)	305	0.52
Burmese (3)	4	0.01
Cambodian (35)	42	0.07
Chinese, ex. Taiwanese (324)	414	0.71
Filipino (202)	316	0.54
Hmong (8)	12	0.02
Indian (2,734)	2,902	4.98
Indonesian (5)	9	0.02
Japanese (30)	50	0.09

*Notes: † The Census 2010 population figure is used to calculate the percentages in the Hispanic Origin and Race categories. Ancestry percentages are based on the 2006-2010 American Community Survey population (not shown); ‡ Numbers in parentheses indicate the number of people reporting a single ancestry; * Numbers in parentheses indicate the number of persons reporting this race alone, not in combination with any other race; Please refer to the Explanation of Data for more information.*

Korean (214)	261	0.45
Laotian (117)	152	0.26
Malaysian (7)	10	0.02
Nepalese (6)	9	0.02
Pakistani (240)	279	0.48
Sri Lankan (14)	14	0.02
Taiwanese (14)	17	0.03
Thai (16)	23	0.04
Vietnamese (184)	235	0.40
Hawaii Native/Pacific Islander (21)	82	0.14
Not Hispanic (19)	52	0.09
Hispanic (2)	30	0.05
Fijian (1)	2	<0.01
Guamanian/Chamorro (8)	10	0.02
Native Hawaiian (6)	15	0.03
Samoan (1)	5	0.01
White (41,585)	43,174	74.13
Not Hispanic (38,457)	39,551	67.91
Hispanic (3,128)	3,623	6.22

Mansfield

Place Type: Town
County: Tolland
Population: 26,543†

Ancestry‡	Population	%
Afghan (0)	10	0.04
African, Sub-Saharan (142)	307	1.19
African (0)	60	0.23
Ethiopian (5)	5	0.02
Ghanaian (105)	105	0.41
Kenyan (12)	55	0.21
Nigerian (13)	27	0.10
South African (7)	44	0.17
Other Sub-Saharan African (0)	11	0.04
Albanian (24)	24	0.09
American (305)	305	1.18
Arab (143)	378	1.46
Arab (122)	182	0.70
Lebanese (16)	166	0.64
Syrian (0)	12	0.05
Other Arab (5)	18	0.07
Armenian (0)	13	0.05
Australian (0)	13	0.05
Austrian (0)	117	0.45
Belgian (0)	7	0.03
Brazilian (8)	20	0.08
British (89)	257	0.99
Canadian (72)	176	0.68
Cypriot (14)	14	0.05
Czech (0)	138	0.53
Czechoslovakian (33)	46	0.18
Danish (13)	153	0.59
Dutch (72)	263	1.02
Eastern European (113)	113	0.44
English (762)	2,708	10.47
European (265)	365	1.41
Finnish (18)	138	0.53
French, ex. Basque (421)	1,746	6.75
French Canadian (430)	1,122	4.34
German (473)	3,208	12.41
Greek (93)	248	0.96
Guyanese (10)	10	0.04
Hungarian (69)	263	1.02
Iranian (15)	15	0.06
Irish (667)	4,317	16.70
Israeli (0)	25	0.10
Italian (1,012)	3,645	14.10
Latvian (27)	76	0.29
Lithuanian (58)	255	0.99
Northern European (128)	140	0.54
Norwegian (66)	294	1.14
Pennsylvania German (0)	36	0.14
Polish (612)	2,017	7.80
Portuguese (57)	227	0.88
Romanian (10)	36	0.14
Russian (241)	725	2.80
Scandinavian (11)	11	0.04
Scotch-Irish (105)	533	2.06
Scottish (76)	701	2.71
Slovak (64)	119	0.46
Swedish (105)	718	2.78
Swiss (11)	58	0.22
Turkish (0)	49	0.19
Ukrainian (58)	266	1.03
Welsh (0)	240	0.93
West Indian, ex. Hispanic (167)	221	0.85
British West Indian (0)	9	0.03
Haitian (36)	45	0.17
Jamaican (94)	130	0.50
West Indian (37)	37	0.14

Hispanic Origin	Population	%
Hispanic or Latino (of any race)	1,606	6.05
Central American, ex. Mexican	62	0.23
Costa Rican	4	0.02
Guatemalan	23	0.09
Honduran	5	0.02
Nicaraguan	13	0.05
Panamanian	8	0.03
Salvadoran	9	0.03
Cuban	84	0.32
Dominican Republic	69	0.26
Mexican	133	0.50
Puerto Rican	621	2.34
South American	276	1.04
Argentinean	31	0.12
Bolivian	5	0.02
Chilean	26	0.10
Colombian	98	0.37
Ecuadorian	31	0.12
Paraguayan	1	<0.01
Peruvian	57	0.21
Uruguayan	7	0.03
Venezuelan	18	0.07
Other South American	2	0.01
Other Hispanic or Latino	361	1.36

Race*	Population	%
African-American/Black (1,409)	1,636	6.16
Not Hispanic (1,330)	1,511	5.69
Hispanic (79)	125	0.47
American Indian/Alaska Native (33)	170	0.64
Not Hispanic (21)	118	0.44
Hispanic (12)	52	0.20
Apache (0)	1	<0.01
Blackfeet (4)	17	0.06
Canadian/French Am. Ind. (1)	3	0.01
Cherokee (0)	19	0.07
Chickasaw (1)	1	<0.01
Chippewa (1)	1	<0.01
Choctaw (0)	1	<0.01
Comanche (0)	1	<0.01
Creek (1)	1	<0.01
Hopi (0)	3	0.01
Inupiat *(Alaska Native)* (0)	1	<0.01
Iroquois (1)	7	0.03
Lumbee (1)	1	<0.01
Mexican American Ind. (3)	9	0.03
Navajo (0)	1	<0.01
Potawatomi (1)	3	0.01
Sioux (1)	2	0.01
South American Ind. (4)	7	0.03
Asian (2,227)	2,549	9.60
Not Hispanic (2,213)	2,505	9.44
Hispanic (14)	44	0.17
Bangladeshi (24)	27	0.10
Cambodian (22)	32	0.12
Chinese, ex. Taiwanese (815)	905	3.41
Filipino (98)	157	0.59
Indian (602)	660	2.49
Indonesian (7)	10	0.04
Japanese (34)	83	0.31
Korean (224)	253	0.95
Laotian (17)	18	0.07
Malaysian (4)	9	0.03
Nepalese (36)	37	0.14
Pakistani (72)	87	0.33
Sri Lankan (21)	21	0.08
Taiwanese (57)	66	0.25
Thai (7)	13	0.05
Vietnamese (119)	143	0.54
Hawaii Native/Pacific Islander (9)	34	0.13
Not Hispanic (7)	29	0.11
Hispanic (2)	5	0.02
Fijian (1)	1	<0.01
Guamanian/Chamorro (0)	3	0.01
Native Hawaiian (6)	14	0.05
Samoan (1)	4	0.02
White (21,590)	22,164	83.50
Not Hispanic (20,775)	21,245	80.04
Hispanic (815)	919	3.46

Meriden

Place Type: City/Town
County: New Haven
Population: 60,868†

Ancestry‡	Population	%
African, Sub-Saharan (121)	156	0.26
African (61)	86	0.14
Cape Verdean (52)	62	0.10
Ghanaian (8)	8	0.01
Albanian (119)	119	0.20
American (1,436)	1,436	2.37
Arab (221)	274	0.45
Lebanese (39)	39	0.06
Moroccan (106)	140	0.23
Palestinian (76)	95	0.16
Armenian (9)	21	0.03
Austrian (66)	179	0.30
Brazilian (34)	60	0.10
British (59)	99	0.16
Canadian (186)	259	0.43
Celtic (15)	30	0.05
Croatian (73)	95	0.16
Czech (0)	131	0.22
Czechoslovakian (67)	162	0.27
Danish (7)	78	0.13
Dutch (67)	531	0.88
Eastern European (58)	58	0.10
English (931)	5,217	8.63
European (136)	136	0.22
Finnish (0)	34	0.06
French, ex. Basque (1,011)	4,463	7.38
French Canadian (1,010)	1,681	2.78
German (1,188)	6,177	10.21
Greek (76)	230	0.38
Guyanese (106)	106	0.18
Hungarian (83)	543	0.90
Iranian (10)	10	0.02
Irish (1,930)	9,018	14.91
Italian (3,674)	9,585	15.85
Latvian (13)	13	0.02
Lithuanian (116)	319	0.53
Luxemburger (0)	18	0.03
Norwegian (81)	142	0.23
Polish (3,260)	7,331	12.12
Portuguese (133)	430	0.71
Romanian (20)	26	0.04
Russian (122)	559	0.92
Scandinavian (0)	12	0.02
Scotch-Irish (126)	531	0.88
Scottish (201)	676	1.12
Slavic (55)	64	0.11
Slovak (42)	81	0.13
Slovene (0)	13	0.02
Swedish (25)	525	0.87
Swiss (32)	124	0.21
Ukrainian (101)	213	0.35
Welsh (34)	152	0.25
West Indian, ex. Hispanic (248)	365	0.60
British West Indian (16)	16	0.03
Haitian (23)	23	0.04
Jamaican (165)	213	0.35
Trinidadian/Tobagonian (44)	85	0.14
West Indian (0)	28	0.05
Yugoslavian (39)	39	0.06

*Notes: † The Census 2010 population figure is used to calculate the percentages in the Hispanic Origin and Race categories. Ancestry percentages are based on the 2006-2010 American Community Survey population (not shown); ‡ Numbers in parentheses indicate the number of people reporting a single ancestry; * Numbers in parentheses indicate the number of persons reporting this race alone, not in combination with any other race; Please refer to the Explanation of Data for more information.*

Hispanic Origin	Population	%
Hispanic or Latino (of any race)	17,590	28.90
Central American, ex. Mexican	303	0.50
Costa Rican	10	0.02
Guatemalan	93	0.15
Honduran	48	0.08
Nicaraguan	72	0.12
Panamanian	34	0.06
Salvadoran	41	0.07
Other Central American	5	0.01
Cuban	190	0.31
Dominican Republic	562	0.92
Mexican	2,385	3.92
Puerto Rican	12,572	20.65
South American	858	1.41
Argentinean	61	0.10
Bolivian	6	0.01
Chilean	17	0.03
Colombian	191	0.31
Ecuadorian	470	0.77
Paraguayan	4	0.01
Peruvian	88	0.14
Uruguayan	11	0.02
Venezuelan	9	0.01
Other South American	1	<0.01
Other Hispanic or Latino	720	1.18

Race*	Population	%
African-American/Black (5,876)	7,062	11.60
Not Hispanic (4,980)	5,696	9.36
Hispanic (896)	1,366	2.24
American Indian/Alaska Native (302)	755	1.24
Not Hispanic (118)	402	0.66
Hispanic (184)	353	0.58
Aleut *(Alaska Native)* (1)	1	<0.01
Apache (2)	4	0.01
Blackfeet (6)	34	0.06
Canadian/French Am. Ind. (0)	4	0.01
Central American Ind. (1)	3	<0.01
Cherokee (21)	91	0.15
Chickasaw (0)	4	0.01
Chippewa (2)	2	<0.01
Choctaw (0)	3	<0.01
Cree (0)	3	<0.01
Hopi (0)	5	0.01
Iroquois (4)	21	0.03
Lumbee (0)	1	<0.01
Mexican American Ind. (24)	26	0.04
Navajo (2)	3	<0.01
Seminole (1)	2	<0.01
Sioux (2)	7	0.01
South American Ind. (3)	33	0.05
Spanish American Ind. (5)	6	0.01
Asian (1,277)	1,523	2.50
Not Hispanic (1,250)	1,444	2.37
Hispanic (27)	79	0.13
Bangladeshi (42)	51	0.08
Cambodian (28)	32	0.05
Chinese, ex. Taiwanese (155)	199	0.33
Filipino (205)	258	0.42
Indian (395)	459	0.75
Indonesian (8)	9	0.01
Japanese (13)	44	0.07
Korean (48)	66	0.11
Laotian (109)	122	0.20
Malaysian (2)	2	<0.01
Nepalese (5)	5	0.01
Pakistani (75)	100	0.16
Sri Lankan (1)	1	<0.01
Taiwanese (0)	1	<0.01
Thai (3)	12	0.02
Vietnamese (124)	149	0.24
Hawaii Native/Pacific Islander (34)	101	0.17
Not Hispanic (9)	36	0.06
Hispanic (25)	65	0.11
Guamanian/Chamorro (7)	10	0.02
Native Hawaiian (12)	22	0.04
Samoan (1)	5	0.01
White (44,727)	46,477	76.36
Not Hispanic (35,809)	36,699	60.29
Hispanic (8,918)	9,778	16.06

Middlebury

Place Type: Town
County: New Haven
Population: 7,575†

Ancestry‡	Population	%
Albanian (17)	17	0.23
American (185)	185	2.50
Arab (10)	59	0.80
Lebanese (10)	59	0.80
Armenian (15)	15	0.20
Austrian (0)	78	1.06
Belgian (0)	30	0.41
British (15)	15	0.20
Canadian (0)	22	0.30
Czech (0)	88	1.19
Danish (0)	23	0.31
Dutch (14)	116	1.57
Eastern European (0)	8	0.11
English (148)	1,151	15.58
Estonian (0)	7	0.09
European (37)	37	0.50
Finnish (0)	38	0.51
French, ex. Basque (60)	460	6.22
French Canadian (167)	339	4.59
German (208)	964	13.04
Greek (78)	136	1.84
Hungarian (8)	59	0.80
Irish (678)	1,985	26.86
Italian (826)	2,027	27.43
Latvian (0)	40	0.54
Lithuanian (85)	158	2.14
Norwegian (0)	11	0.15
Polish (119)	505	6.83
Portuguese (86)	153	2.07
Russian (33)	195	2.64
Scandinavian (0)	8	0.11
Scotch-Irish (41)	146	1.98
Scottish (80)	194	2.63
Slovak (0)	83	1.12
Swedish (7)	241	3.26
Welsh (0)	8	0.11
Yugoslavian (0)	7	0.09

Hispanic Origin	Population	%
Hispanic or Latino (of any race)	208	2.75
Central American, ex. Mexican	7	0.09
Costa Rican	2	0.03
Guatemalan	1	0.01
Nicaraguan	2	0.03
Panamanian	1	0.01
Salvadoran	1	0.01
Cuban	14	0.18
Dominican Republic	8	0.11
Mexican	9	0.12
Puerto Rican	101	1.33
South American	49	0.65
Argentinean	1	0.01
Chilean	7	0.09
Colombian	11	0.15
Ecuadorian	22	0.29
Peruvian	7	0.09
Venezuelan	1	0.01
Other Hispanic or Latino	20	0.26

Race*	Population	%
African-American/Black (73)	89	1.17
Not Hispanic (67)	80	1.06
Hispanic (6)	9	0.12
American Indian/Alaska Native (4)	20	0.26
Not Hispanic (4)	19	0.25
Hispanic (0)	1	0.01
Blackfeet (1)	1	0.01
Cherokee (0)	1	0.01
Chippewa (1)	1	0.01
Iroquois (0)	4	0.05
Mexican American Ind. (0)	1	0.01
Sioux (1)	1	0.01
Asian (287)	328	4.33
Not Hispanic (286)	323	4.26
Hispanic (1)	5	0.07
Bangladeshi (6)	6	0.08
Cambodian (5)	7	0.09
Chinese, ex. Taiwanese (79)	82	1.08
Filipino (29)	42	0.55
Indian (110)	110	1.45
Japanese (3)	4	0.05
Korean (9)	14	0.18
Laotian (1)	1	0.01
Pakistani (18)	18	0.24
Sri Lankan (7)	7	0.09
Taiwanese (3)	3	0.04
Thai (1)	2	0.03
Vietnamese (11)	13	0.17
Hawaii Native/Pacific Islander (2)	4	0.05
Not Hispanic (2)	4	0.05
Native Hawaiian (2)	4	0.05
White (7,096)	7,167	94.61
Not Hispanic (6,925)	6,986	92.22
Hispanic (171)	181	2.39

Middletown

Place Type: City/Town
County: Middlesex
Population: 47,648†

Ancestry‡	Population	%
African, Sub-Saharan (246)	349	0.74
African (100)	203	0.43
Cape Verdean (28)	28	0.06
Ghanaian (105)	105	0.22
Nigerian (13)	13	0.03
Albanian (0)	33	0.07
Alsatian (8)	8	0.02
American (1,204)	1,204	2.54
Arab (228)	360	0.76
Arab (9)	12	0.03
Iraqi (20)	20	0.04
Lebanese (36)	135	0.29
Moroccan (58)	58	0.12
Syrian (50)	56	0.12
Other Arab (55)	79	0.17
Armenian (0)	39	0.08
Australian (23)	63	0.13
Austrian (17)	137	0.29
Belgian (12)	17	0.04
Brazilian (37)	37	0.08
British (42)	134	0.28
Bulgarian (63)	63	0.13
Cajun (10)	20	0.04
Canadian (50)	69	0.15
Croatian (22)	80	0.17
Czech (41)	234	0.49
Czechoslovakian (33)	102	0.22
Danish (14)	82	0.17
Dutch (81)	404	0.85
Eastern European (138)	138	0.29
English (1,003)	4,427	9.35
European (253)	264	0.56
Finnish (8)	38	0.08
French, ex. Basque (414)	2,783	5.88
French Canadian (681)	1,363	2.88
German (1,106)	5,118	10.81
Greek (146)	268	0.57
Hungarian (17)	271	0.57
Iranian (22)	30	0.06
Irish (1,714)	7,127	15.05
Italian (5,111)	11,016	23.27
Latvian (26)	26	0.05
Lithuanian (86)	387	0.82
Macedonian (65)	65	0.14
Northern European (17)	17	0.04
Norwegian (50)	147	0.31
Polish (2,201)	5,522	11.66
Portuguese (173)	383	0.81
Romanian (43)	77	0.16

*Notes: † The Census 2010 population figure is used to calculate the percentages in the Hispanic Origin and Race categories. Ancestry percentages are based on the 2006-2010 American Community Survey population (not shown); ‡ Numbers in parentheses indicate the number of people reporting a single ancestry; * Numbers in parentheses indicate the number of persons reporting this race alone, not in combination with any other race; Please refer to the Explanation of Data for more information.*

Ancestry (cont.)	Population	%
Russian (229)	643	1.36
Scandinavian (119)	205	0.43
Scotch-Irish (147)	382	0.81
Scottish (179)	872	1.84
Slavic (6)	6	0.01
Slovak (72)	159	0.34
Slovene (0)	14	0.03
Swedish (154)	959	2.03
Swiss (15)	140	0.30
Turkish (61)	61	0.13
Ukrainian (93)	279	0.59
Welsh (96)	364	0.77
West Indian, ex. Hispanic (582)	779	1.65
Barbadian (116)	116	0.24
British West Indian (5)	5	0.01
Jamaican (450)	534	1.13
Trinidadian/Tobagonian (11)	11	0.02
West Indian (0)	102	0.22
Other West Indian (0)	11	0.02
Yugoslavian (111)	125	0.26

Hispanic Origin	Population	%
Hispanic or Latino (of any race)	3,949	8.29
Central American, ex. Mexican	166	0.35
Costa Rican	19	0.04
Guatemalan	40	0.08
Honduran	41	0.09
Nicaraguan	12	0.03
Panamanian	23	0.05
Salvadoran	31	0.07
Cuban	129	0.27
Dominican Republic	195	0.41
Mexican	356	0.75
Puerto Rican	2,398	5.03
South American	371	0.78
Argentinean	20	0.04
Bolivian	4	0.01
Chilean	29	0.06
Colombian	110	0.23
Ecuadorian	118	0.25
Paraguayan	6	0.01
Peruvian	63	0.13
Uruguayan	5	0.01
Venezuelan	15	0.03
Other South American	1	<0.01
Other Hispanic or Latino	334	0.70

Race*	Population	%
African-American/Black (6,110)	7,194	15.10
Not Hispanic (5,734)	6,605	13.86
Hispanic (376)	589	1.24
American Indian/Alaska Native (104)	455	0.95
Not Hispanic (77)	359	0.75
Hispanic (27)	96	0.20
Alaska Athabascan *(Ala. Nat.)* (2)	9	0.02
Apache (2)	8	0.02
Arapaho (0)	1	<0.01
Blackfeet (3)	23	0.05
Canadian/French Am. Ind. (2)	8	0.02
Central American Ind. (2)	3	0.01
Cherokee (8)	71	0.15
Cheyenne (2)	2	<0.01
Chippewa (1)	4	0.01
Choctaw (1)	4	0.01
Cree (0)	1	<0.01
Creek (0)	2	<0.01
Delaware (1)	1	<0.01
Inupiat *(Alaska Native)* (2)	3	0.01
Iroquois (1)	12	0.03
Lumbee (0)	2	<0.01
Mexican American Ind. (2)	2	<0.01
Navajo (1)	7	0.01
Ottawa (0)	2	<0.01
Seminole (1)	1	<0.01
Sioux (3)	18	0.04
South American Ind. (2)	11	0.02
Ute (0)	1	<0.01
Yaqui (0)	1	<0.01
Asian (2,319)	2,735	5.74
Not Hispanic (2,297)	2,679	5.62
Hispanic (22)	56	0.12
Bangladeshi (58)	60	0.13
Burmese (5)	5	0.01
Cambodian (77)	98	0.21
Chinese, ex. Taiwanese (379)	505	1.06
Filipino (212)	286	0.60
Hmong (6)	7	0.01
Indian (971)	1,062	2.23
Indonesian (17)	20	0.04
Japanese (50)	113	0.24
Korean (140)	163	0.34
Laotian (40)	56	0.12
Malaysian (7)	8	0.02
Nepalese (28)	30	0.06
Pakistani (83)	90	0.19
Sri Lankan (31)	46	0.10
Taiwanese (28)	33	0.07
Thai (36)	48	0.10
Vietnamese (55)	85	0.18
Hawaii Native/Pacific Islander (27)	79	0.17
Not Hispanic (26)	65	0.14
Hispanic (1)	14	0.03
Fijian (0)	1	<0.01
Guamanian/Chamorro (6)	9	0.02
Native Hawaiian (4)	17	0.04
Samoan (2)	6	0.01
White (36,138)	37,571	78.85
Not Hispanic (34,116)	35,263	74.01
Hispanic (2,022)	2,308	4.84

Milford

Place Type: City
County: New Haven
Population: 51,271†

Ancestry‡	Population	%
African, Sub-Saharan (153)	308	0.60
African (21)	21	0.04
Cape Verdean (99)	212	0.42
Nigerian (21)	63	0.12
Other Sub-Saharan African (12)	12	0.02
Albanian (105)	112	0.22
American (1,054)	1,054	2.07
Arab (180)	318	0.62
Arab (0)	14	0.03
Egyptian (55)	55	0.11
Jordanian (28)	28	0.05
Lebanese (35)	139	0.27
Moroccan (12)	12	0.02
Palestinian (15)	15	0.03
Syrian (8)	28	0.05
Other Arab (27)	27	0.05
Armenian (14)	92	0.18
Australian (17)	25	0.05
Austrian (44)	188	0.37
Belgian (0)	71	0.14
Brazilian (346)	346	0.68
British (115)	307	0.60
Bulgarian (29)	29	0.06
Canadian (84)	167	0.33
Celtic (8)	8	0.02
Croatian (7)	224	0.44
Czech (92)	265	0.52
Czechoslovakian (132)	266	0.52
Danish (45)	225	0.44
Dutch (56)	406	0.80
Eastern European (85)	85	0.17
English (1,013)	5,812	11.39
Estonian (10)	20	0.04
European (242)	242	0.47
Finnish (9)	97	0.19
French, ex. Basque (413)	2,547	4.99
French Canadian (342)	1,439	2.82
German (1,075)	6,556	12.85
Greek (426)	594	1.16
Hungarian (437)	1,533	3.00
Irish (3,257)	13,332	26.13
Israeli (8)	8	0.02
Italian (5,274)	13,306	26.08
Latvian (18)	51	0.10
Lithuanian (142)	593	1.16
Northern European (51)	51	0.10
Norwegian (92)	180	0.35
Pennsylvania German (0)	10	0.02
Polish (1,553)	5,097	9.99
Portuguese (237)	693	1.36
Romanian (42)	93	0.18
Russian (409)	1,212	2.38
Scandinavian (6)	6	0.01
Scotch-Irish (252)	751	1.47
Scottish (326)	1,627	3.19
Serbian (8)	8	0.02
Slavic (0)	19	0.04
Slovak (425)	1,397	2.74
Slovene (0)	42	0.08
Swedish (207)	1,137	2.23
Swiss (8)	74	0.15
Turkish (25)	25	0.05
Ukrainian (163)	457	0.90
Welsh (21)	242	0.47
West Indian, ex. Hispanic (190)	303	0.59
Barbadian (10)	50	0.10
Bermudan (8)	8	0.02
British West Indian (21)	21	0.04
Haitian (67)	92	0.18
Jamaican (84)	132	0.26
Yugoslavian (79)	104	0.20

Hispanic Origin	Population	%
Hispanic or Latino (of any race)	2,669	5.21
Central American, ex. Mexican	139	0.27
Costa Rican	29	0.06
Guatemalan	43	0.08
Honduran	23	0.04
Nicaraguan	7	0.01
Panamanian	7	0.01
Salvadoran	28	0.05
Other Central American	2	<0.01
Cuban	178	0.35
Dominican Republic	109	0.21
Mexican	191	0.37
Puerto Rican	1,331	2.60
South American	501	0.98
Argentinean	46	0.09
Bolivian	5	0.01
Chilean	37	0.07
Colombian	206	0.40
Ecuadorian	106	0.21
Paraguayan	5	0.01
Peruvian	75	0.15
Uruguayan	8	0.02
Venezuelan	12	0.02
Other South American	1	<0.01
Other Hispanic or Latino	220	0.43

Race*	Population	%
African-American/Black (1,314)	1,603	3.13
Not Hispanic (1,226)	1,467	2.86
Hispanic (88)	136	0.27
American Indian/Alaska Native (73)	229	0.45
Not Hispanic (57)	192	0.37
Hispanic (16)	37	0.07
Apache (1)	1	<0.01
Blackfeet (1)	5	0.01
Canadian/French Am. Ind. (0)	1	<0.01
Central American Ind. (0)	2	<0.01
Cherokee (3)	17	0.03
Cheyenne (1)	2	<0.01
Chippewa (0)	11	0.02
Choctaw (1)	2	<0.01
Colville (1)	1	<0.01
Crow (0)	1	<0.01
Delaware (0)	1	<0.01
Iroquois (4)	10	0.02
Mexican American Ind. (4)	6	0.01
Seminole (0)	1	<0.01
Sioux (0)	2	<0.01
South American Ind. (2)	7	0.01
Spanish American Ind. (1)	1	<0.01

*Notes: † The Census 2010 population figure is used to calculate the percentages in the Hispanic Origin and Race categories. Ancestry percentages are based on the 2006-2010 American Community Survey population (not shown); ‡ Numbers in parentheses indicate the number of people reporting a single ancestry; * Numbers in parentheses indicate the number of persons reporting this race alone, not in combination with any other race; Please refer to the Explanation of Data for more information.*

Race*	Population	%
Yaqui (0)	1	<0.01
Asian (2,805)	3,128	6.10
Not Hispanic (2,785)	3,073	5.99
Hispanic (20)	55	0.11
Bangladeshi (16)	16	0.03
Burmese (7)	9	0.02
Cambodian (51)	59	0.12
Chinese, ex. Taiwanese (473)	563	1.10
Filipino (367)	438	0.85
Indian (1,280)	1,353	2.64
Indonesian (14)	19	0.04
Japanese (28)	56	0.11
Korean (141)	177	0.35
Laotian (53)	64	0.12
Malaysian (1)	7	0.01
Nepalese (8)	11	0.02
Pakistani (112)	128	0.25
Sri Lankan (5)	8	0.02
Taiwanese (13)	14	0.03
Thai (17)	35	0.07
Vietnamese (118)	148	0.29
Hawaii Native/Pacific Islander (19)	48	0.09
Not Hispanic (18)	41	0.08
Hispanic (1)	7	0.01
Guamanian/Chamorro (0)	2	<0.01
Native Hawaiian (5)	10	0.02
Samoan (5)	8	0.02
White (45,549)	46,265	90.24
Not Hispanic (43,770)	44,310	86.42
Hispanic (1,779)	1,955	3.81

Milford

Place Type: Town
County: New Haven
Population: 52,759†

Ancestry‡	Population	%
African, Sub-Saharan (172)	327	0.62
African (40)	40	0.08
Cape Verdean (99)	212	0.40
Nigerian (21)	63	0.12
Other Sub-Saharan African (12)	12	0.02
Albanian (112)	119	0.23
American (1,122)	1,122	2.13
Arab (190)	328	0.62
Arab (0)	14	0.03
Egyptian (55)	55	0.10
Jordanian (28)	28	0.05
Lebanese (39)	143	0.27
Moroccan (12)	12	0.02
Palestinian (15)	15	0.03
Syrian (8)	28	0.05
Other Arab (33)	33	0.06
Armenian (20)	109	0.21
Australian (17)	25	0.05
Austrian (47)	204	0.39
Belgian (0)	71	0.13
Brazilian (346)	353	0.67
British (115)	310	0.59
Bulgarian (29)	29	0.05
Canadian (84)	167	0.32
Celtic (8)	8	0.02
Croatian (7)	224	0.42
Czech (92)	271	0.51
Czechoslovakian (132)	269	0.51
Danish (45)	236	0.45
Dutch (56)	428	0.81
Eastern European (94)	94	0.18
English (1,060)	6,050	11.47
Estonian (10)	20	0.04
European (254)	254	0.48
Finnish (9)	100	0.19
French, ex. Basque (413)	2,595	4.92
French Canadian (349)	1,482	2.81
German (1,104)	6,786	12.86
Greek (429)	609	1.15
Hungarian (454)	1,573	2.98
Irish (3,409)	13,876	26.30
Israeli (8)	8	0.02
Italian (5,443)	13,786	26.13
Latvian (18)	51	0.10
Lithuanian (145)	609	1.15
Northern European (51)	51	0.10
Norwegian (92)	199	0.38
Pennsylvania German (0)	10	0.02
Polish (1,583)	5,258	9.97
Portuguese (237)	723	1.37
Romanian (42)	97	0.18
Russian (460)	1,302	2.47
Scandinavian (6)	9	0.02
Scotch-Irish (257)	780	1.48
Scottish (341)	1,657	3.14
Serbian (8)	8	0.02
Slavic (0)	19	0.04
Slovak (428)	1,428	2.71
Slovene (0)	42	0.08
Swedish (207)	1,152	2.18
Swiss (8)	74	0.14
Turkish (25)	25	0.05
Ukrainian (170)	473	0.90
Welsh (25)	254	0.48
West Indian, ex. Hispanic (190)	303	0.57
Barbadian (10)	50	0.09
Bermudan (8)	8	0.02
British West Indian (21)	21	0.04
Haitian (67)	92	0.17
Jamaican (84)	132	0.25
Yugoslavian (79)	104	0.20

Hispanic Origin	Population	%
Hispanic or Latino (of any race)	2,756	5.22
Central American, ex. Mexican	141	0.27
Costa Rican	29	0.05
Guatemalan	45	0.09
Honduran	23	0.04
Nicaraguan	7	0.01
Panamanian	7	0.01
Salvadoran	28	0.05
Other Central American	2	<0.01
Cuban	184	0.35
Dominican Republic	110	0.21
Mexican	198	0.38
Puerto Rican	1,375	2.61
South American	511	0.97
Argentinean	47	0.09
Bolivian	5	0.01
Chilean	37	0.07
Colombian	212	0.40
Ecuadorian	108	0.20
Paraguayan	5	0.01
Peruvian	76	0.14
Uruguayan	8	0.02
Venezuelan	12	0.02
Other South American	1	<0.01
Other Hispanic or Latino	237	0.45

Race*	Population	%
African-American/Black (1,328)	1,620	3.07
Not Hispanic (1,238)	1,482	2.81
Hispanic (90)	138	0.26
American Indian/Alaska Native (73)	231	0.44
Not Hispanic (57)	194	0.37
Hispanic (16)	37	0.07
Apache (1)	1	<0.01
Blackfeet (1)	5	0.01
Canadian/French Am. Ind. (0)	1	<0.01
Central American Ind. (0)	2	<0.01
Cherokee (3)	17	0.03
Cheyenne (1)	2	<0.01
Chippewa (0)	11	0.02
Choctaw (1)	2	<0.01
Colville (1)	1	<0.01
Cree (0)	1	<0.01
Crow (0)	1	<0.01
Delaware (0)	1	<0.01
Iroquois (4)	11	0.02
Mexican American Ind. (4)	6	0.01
Seminole (0)	1	<0.01
Sioux (0)	2	<0.01
South American Ind. (2)	7	0.01
Spanish American Ind. (1)	1	<0.01
Yaqui (0)	1	<0.01
Asian (2,821)	3,147	5.96
Not Hispanic (2,801)	3,092	5.86
Hispanic (20)	55	0.10
Bangladeshi (16)	16	0.03
Burmese (7)	9	0.02
Cambodian (51)	59	0.11
Chinese, ex. Taiwanese (480)	570	1.08
Filipino (368)	439	0.83
Indian (1,284)	1,357	2.57
Indonesian (17)	22	0.04
Japanese (28)	57	0.11
Korean (141)	177	0.34
Laotian (53)	64	0.12
Malaysian (1)	7	0.01
Nepalese (8)	11	0.02
Pakistani (112)	128	0.24
Sri Lankan (5)	8	0.02
Taiwanese (13)	14	0.03
Thai (17)	35	0.07
Vietnamese (119)	151	0.29
Hawaii Native/Pacific Islander (19)	48	0.09
Not Hispanic (18)	41	0.08
Hispanic (1)	7	0.01
Guamanian/Chamorro (0)	2	<0.01
Native Hawaiian (5)	10	0.02
Samoan (5)	8	0.02
White (46,989)	47,715	90.44
Not Hispanic (45,135)	45,683	86.59
Hispanic (1,854)	2,032	3.85

Monroe

Place Type: Town
County: Fairfield
Population: 19,479†

Ancestry‡	Population	%
African, Sub-Saharan (65)	65	0.34
African (65)	65	0.34
American (467)	467	2.42
Arab (40)	92	0.48
Lebanese (40)	66	0.34
Syrian (0)	26	0.13
Armenian (0)	46	0.24
Austrian (12)	69	0.36
Brazilian (59)	59	0.31
British (6)	20	0.10
Bulgarian (31)	31	0.16
Canadian (11)	65	0.34
Croatian (0)	13	0.07
Czech (28)	174	0.90
Czechoslovakian (40)	50	0.26
Dutch (15)	323	1.67
Eastern European (132)	132	0.68
English (231)	2,295	11.88
European (188)	201	1.04
Finnish (17)	31	0.16
French, ex. Basque (74)	518	2.68
French Canadian (41)	119	0.62
German (680)	2,375	12.30
Greek (127)	256	1.33
Hungarian (194)	641	3.32
Icelander (0)	60	0.31
Irish (926)	4,190	21.69
Israeli (0)	30	0.16
Italian (2,980)	6,078	31.47
Latvian (13)	13	0.07
Lithuanian (39)	98	0.51
Norwegian (85)	277	1.43
Polish (559)	1,646	8.52
Portuguese (387)	487	2.52
Romanian (36)	82	0.42
Russian (157)	563	2.91
Scandinavian (14)	14	0.07
Scotch-Irish (126)	390	2.02
Scottish (61)	485	2.51
Slavic (12)	24	0.12

*Notes: † The Census 2010 population figure is used to calculate the percentages in the Hispanic Origin and Race categories. Ancestry percentages are based on the 2006-2010 American Community Survey population (not shown); ‡ Numbers in parentheses indicate the number of people reporting a single ancestry; * Numbers in parentheses indicate the number of persons reporting this race alone, not in combination with any other race; Please refer to the Explanation of Data for more information.*

Ancestry	Population	%
Slovak (69)	428	2.22
Slovene (17)	37	0.19
Swedish (166)	521	2.70
Swiss (13)	24	0.12
Turkish (28)	98	0.51
Ukrainian (51)	321	1.66
Welsh (46)	100	0.52
Yugoslavian (10)	23	0.12

Hispanic Origin	Population	%
Hispanic or Latino (of any race)	919	4.72
Central American, ex. Mexican	73	0.37
Costa Rican	12	0.06
Guatemalan	11	0.06
Honduran	24	0.12
Nicaraguan	11	0.06
Panamanian	6	0.03
Salvadoran	9	0.05
Cuban	89	0.46
Dominican Republic	36	0.18
Mexican	81	0.42
Puerto Rican	343	1.76
South American	208	1.07
Argentinean	18	0.09
Chilean	17	0.09
Colombian	70	0.36
Ecuadorian	51	0.26
Paraguayan	2	0.01
Peruvian	37	0.19
Uruguayan	2	0.01
Venezuelan	10	0.05
Other South American	1	0.01
Other Hispanic or Latino	89	0.46

Race*	Population	%
African-American/Black (274)	368	1.89
Not Hispanic (259)	324	1.66
Hispanic (15)	44	0.23
American Indian/Alaska Native (13)	84	0.43
Not Hispanic (11)	66	0.34
Hispanic (2)	18	0.09
Blackfeet (0)	1	0.01
Canadian/French Am. Ind. (0)	7	0.04
Cherokee (0)	7	0.04
Cheyenne (0)	1	0.01
Choctaw (0)	2	0.01
Creek (0)	4	0.02
Crow (1)	1	0.01
Iroquois (3)	6	0.03
Mexican American Ind. (1)	2	0.01
Sioux (0)	4	0.02
South American Ind. (0)	8	0.04
Ute (0)	1	0.01
Asian (408)	526	2.70
Not Hispanic (402)	510	2.62
Hispanic (6)	16	0.08
Bangladeshi (1)	1	0.01
Cambodian (9)	9	0.05
Chinese, ex. Taiwanese (71)	107	0.55
Filipino (26)	39	0.20
Indian (199)	221	1.13
Indonesian (1)	2	0.01
Japanese (16)	30	0.15
Korean (35)	48	0.25
Pakistani (32)	35	0.18
Thai (3)	6	0.03
Vietnamese (12)	14	0.07
Hawaii Native/Pacific Islander (2)	15	0.08
Not Hispanic (2)	13	0.07
Hispanic (0)	2	0.01
Native Hawaiian (1)	8	0.04
Samoan (1)	1	0.01
White (18,331)	18,613	95.55
Not Hispanic (17,645)	17,856	91.67
Hispanic (686)	757	3.89

Montville

Place Type: Town
County: New London
Population: 19,571†

Ancestry‡	Population	%
African, Sub-Saharan (58)	93	0.48
Cape Verdean (44)	44	0.23
Ghanaian (14)	49	0.25
American (556)	556	2.86
Arab (13)	28	0.14
Lebanese (4)	19	0.10
Palestinian (9)	9	0.05
Belgian (0)	15	0.08
British (4)	4	0.02
Canadian (34)	34	0.17
Croatian (12)	12	0.06
Czech (19)	19	0.10
Czechoslovakian (0)	16	0.08
Danish (43)	159	0.82
Dutch (7)	90	0.46
Eastern European (25)	37	0.19
English (432)	1,995	10.25
European (13)	30	0.15
Finnish (11)	24	0.12
French, ex. Basque (441)	1,769	9.09
French Canadian (282)	814	4.18
German (550)	1,776	9.12
Greek (63)	129	0.66
Hungarian (21)	74	0.38
Irish (1,252)	4,055	20.83
Italian (888)	3,396	17.44
Latvian (13)	13	0.07
Lithuanian (16)	79	0.41
Luxemburger (0)	11	0.06
Maltese (4)	4	0.02
Northern European (15)	15	0.08
Norwegian (27)	194	1.00
Pennsylvania German (0)	13	0.07
Polish (749)	2,631	13.51
Portuguese (217)	619	3.18
Romanian (0)	11	0.06
Russian (56)	325	1.67
Scandinavian (0)	10	0.05
Scotch-Irish (102)	250	1.28
Scottish (129)	323	1.66
Slovak (32)	79	0.41
Swedish (69)	295	1.52
Swiss (0)	38	0.20
Ukrainian (19)	171	0.88
Welsh (14)	81	0.42
West Indian, ex. Hispanic (87)	123	0.63
Haitian (64)	100	0.51
Jamaican (15)	15	0.08
West Indian (8)	8	0.04

Hispanic Origin	Population	%
Hispanic or Latino (of any race)	1,440	7.36
Central American, ex. Mexican	51	0.26
Costa Rican	7	0.04
Guatemalan	11	0.06
Honduran	9	0.05
Nicaraguan	1	0.01
Panamanian	7	0.04
Salvadoran	16	0.08
Cuban	23	0.12
Dominican Republic	45	0.23
Mexican	121	0.62
Puerto Rican	574	2.93
South American	129	0.66
Argentinean	2	0.01
Bolivian	3	0.02
Chilean	4	0.02
Colombian	43	0.22
Ecuadorian	8	0.04
Peruvian	64	0.33
Uruguayan	2	0.01
Venezuelan	1	0.01
Other South American	2	0.01
Other Hispanic or Latino	497	2.54

Race*	Population	%
African-American/Black (1,126)	1,459	7.45
Not Hispanic (1,066)	1,341	6.85
Hispanic (60)	118	0.60
American Indian/Alaska Native (360)	639	3.27
Not Hispanic (308)	558	2.85
Hispanic (52)	81	0.41
Apache (4)	5	0.03
Blackfeet (0)	7	0.04
Canadian/French Am. Ind. (1)	3	0.02
Cherokee (2)	31	0.16
Cheyenne (0)	1	0.01
Chippewa (4)	7	0.04
Choctaw (0)	2	0.01
Cree (0)	1	0.01
Creek (0)	1	0.01
Crow (1)	3	0.02
Delaware (0)	2	0.01
Iroquois (0)	5	0.03
Mexican American Ind. (4)	5	0.03
Navajo (1)	3	0.02
Sioux (2)	2	0.01
South American Ind. (11)	18	0.09
Spanish American Ind. (0)	1	0.01
Tsimshian *(Alaska Native)* (1)	1	0.01
Yuman (1)	1	0.01
Asian (1,248)	1,438	7.35
Not Hispanic (1,245)	1,416	7.24
Hispanic (3)	22	0.11
Bangladeshi (6)	6	0.03
Burmese (4)	5	0.03
Cambodian (15)	17	0.09
Chinese, ex. Taiwanese (944)	985	5.03
Filipino (101)	211	1.08
Indian (67)	78	0.40
Indonesian (3)	5	0.03
Japanese (14)	38	0.19
Korean (30)	39	0.20
Laotian (1)	1	0.01
Malaysian (2)	2	0.01
Nepalese (4)	4	0.02
Pakistani (5)	5	0.03
Sri Lankan (3)	3	0.02
Taiwanese (1)	5	0.03
Thai (1)	1	0.01
Vietnamese (10)	12	0.06
Hawaii Native/Pacific Islander (8)	37	0.19
Not Hispanic (8)	33	0.17
Hispanic (0)	4	0.02
Guamanian/Chamorro (2)	13	0.07
Native Hawaiian (5)	11	0.06
Samoan (0)	1	0.01
White (15,409)	16,028	81.90
Not Hispanic (14,867)	15,386	78.62
Hispanic (542)	642	3.28

Naugatuck

Place Type: Borough/Town
County: New Haven
Population: 31,862†

Ancestry‡	Population	%
African, Sub-Saharan (110)	130	0.41
Cape Verdean (110)	110	0.35
Other Sub-Saharan African (0)	20	0.06
Albanian (6)	24	0.08
American (607)	607	1.91
Arab (198)	290	0.91
Arab (48)	82	0.26
Lebanese (35)	82	0.26
Palestinian (0)	11	0.03
Syrian (32)	32	0.10
Other Arab (83)	83	0.26
Australian (0)	12	0.04
Austrian (13)	134	0.42
Brazilian (191)	267	0.84
British (25)	104	0.33

*Notes: † The Census 2010 population figure is used to calculate the percentages in the Hispanic Origin and Race categories. Ancestry percentages are based on the 2006-2010 American Community Survey population (not shown); ‡ Numbers in parentheses indicate the number of people reporting a single ancestry; * Numbers in parentheses indicate the number of persons reporting this race alone, not in combination with any other race; Please refer to the Explanation of Data for more information.*

Canadian (14)	93	0.29
Czech (12)	147	0.46
Czechoslovakian (54)	89	0.28
Danish (0)	8	0.03
Dutch (0)	241	0.76
Eastern European (7)	7	0.02
English (568)	2,788	8.78
Finnish (0)	17	0.05
French, ex. Basque (244)	1,765	5.56
French Canadian (437)	1,065	3.35
German (550)	3,671	11.56
Greek (68)	68	0.21
Hungarian (266)	648	2.04
Icelander (0)	28	0.09
Iranian (29)	57	0.18
Irish (1,543)	6,279	19.78
Italian (3,172)	7,931	24.98
Latvian (14)	14	0.04
Lithuanian (142)	610	1.92
Norwegian (18)	99	0.31
Polish (1,515)	4,155	13.09
Portuguese (1,863)	2,253	7.10
Romanian (0)	86	0.27
Russian (180)	473	1.49
Scandinavian (54)	54	0.17
Scotch-Irish (185)	646	2.03
Scottish (169)	582	1.83
Slavic (0)	14	0.04
Slovak (64)	135	0.43
Swedish (66)	700	2.21
Swiss (0)	21	0.07
Ukrainian (22)	92	0.29
Welsh (0)	201	0.63
West Indian, ex. Hispanic (134)	212	0.67
Barbadian (0)	17	0.05
Haitian (0)	12	0.04
Jamaican (111)	111	0.35
Trinidadian/Tobagonian (23)	72	0.23

Hispanic Origin	Population	%
Hispanic or Latino (of any race)	2,929	9.19
Central American, ex. Mexican	100	0.31
Costa Rican	16	0.05
Guatemalan	35	0.11
Honduran	9	0.03
Nicaraguan	13	0.04
Panamanian	15	0.05
Salvadoran	12	0.04
Cuban	89	0.28
Dominican Republic	149	0.47
Mexican	191	0.60
Puerto Rican	1,705	5.35
South American	475	1.49
Argentinean	14	0.04
Bolivian	1	<0.01
Chilean	19	0.06
Colombian	117	0.37
Ecuadorian	235	0.74
Paraguayan	1	<0.01
Peruvian	34	0.11
Uruguayan	27	0.08
Venezuelan	20	0.06
Other South American	7	0.02
Other Hispanic or Latino	220	0.69

Race*	Population	%
African-American/Black (1,575)	1,949	6.12
Not Hispanic (1,427)	1,719	5.40
Hispanic (148)	230	0.72
American Indian/Alaska Native (62)	185	0.58
Not Hispanic (49)	169	0.53
Hispanic (13)	16	0.05
Blackfeet (0)	3	0.01
Cherokee (0)	19	0.06
Chippewa (3)	6	0.02
Choctaw (1)	2	0.01
Cree (1)	2	0.01
Creek (2)	2	0.01
Hopi (1)	2	0.01
Iroquois (0)	6	0.02
Lumbee (1)	1	<0.01
Seminole (0)	1	<0.01
Sioux (1)	3	0.01
South American Ind. (4)	6	0.02
Asian (969)	1,091	3.42
Not Hispanic (962)	1,067	3.35
Hispanic (7)	24	0.08
Bangladeshi (9)	12	0.04
Burmese (7)	7	0.02
Cambodian (38)	41	0.13
Chinese, ex. Taiwanese (104)	120	0.38
Filipino (69)	83	0.26
Indian (487)	512	1.61
Indonesian (1)	2	0.01
Japanese (2)	16	0.05
Korean (34)	56	0.18
Laotian (35)	43	0.13
Pakistani (50)	57	0.18
Sri Lankan (0)	3	0.01
Taiwanese (1)	2	0.01
Thai (8)	11	0.03
Vietnamese (77)	87	0.27
Hawaii Native/Pacific Islander (3)	31	0.10
Not Hispanic (2)	27	0.08
Hispanic (1)	4	0.01
Guamanian/Chamorro (0)	1	<0.01
Native Hawaiian (3)	8	0.03
White (27,700)	28,339	88.94
Not Hispanic (25,767)	26,236	82.34
Hispanic (1,933)	2,103	6.60

New Britain

Place Type: City/Town
County: Hartford
Population: 73,206†

Ancestry‡	Population	%
African, Sub-Saharan (606)	756	1.04
African (374)	404	0.55
Cape Verdean (13)	133	0.18
Ghanaian (103)	103	0.14
Liberian (6)	6	0.01
Nigerian (11)	11	0.02
Sierra Leonean (13)	13	0.02
Other Sub-Saharan African (86)	86	0.12
Albanian (34)	34	0.05
American (913)	913	1.25
Arab (131)	161	0.22
Arab (47)	47	0.06
Lebanese (13)	43	0.06
Palestinian (19)	19	0.03
Other Arab (52)	52	0.07
Armenian (105)	123	0.17
Assyrian/Chaldean/Syriac (166)	213	0.29
Austrian (53)	229	0.31
Brazilian (159)	171	0.23
British (11)	82	0.11
Canadian (69)	144	0.20
Croatian (0)	11	0.02
Czech (25)	85	0.12
Czechoslovakian (8)	17	0.02
Danish (5)	157	0.22
Dutch (74)	156	0.21
English (662)	2,924	4.01
European (114)	145	0.20
Finnish (4)	93	0.13
French, ex. Basque (1,015)	3,339	4.58
French Canadian (733)	1,297	1.78
German (887)	3,351	4.59
Greek (141)	221	0.30
Guyanese (23)	34	0.05
Hungarian (116)	214	0.29
Iranian (40)	66	0.09
Irish (1,502)	6,340	8.69
Italian (3,747)	7,772	10.65
Latvian (10)	22	0.03
Lithuanian (240)	572	0.78
Norwegian (21)	138	0.19
Polish (11,966)	14,770	20.25
Portuguese (244)	426	0.58
Romanian (45)	45	0.06
Russian (260)	637	0.87
Scotch-Irish (137)	415	0.57
Scottish (278)	580	0.80
Slavic (30)	30	0.04
Slovak (98)	173	0.24
Swedish (230)	1,178	1.61
Swiss (0)	10	0.01
Turkish (16)	16	0.02
Ukrainian (453)	633	0.87
Welsh (0)	84	0.12
West Indian, ex. Hispanic (1,048)	1,437	1.97
British West Indian (76)	228	0.31
Haitian (331)	352	0.48
Jamaican (602)	687	0.94
Trinidadian/Tobagonian (0)	63	0.09
West Indian (39)	107	0.15
Yugoslavian (522)	522	0.72

Hispanic Origin	Population	%
Hispanic or Latino (of any race)	26,934	36.79
Central American, ex. Mexican	388	0.53
Costa Rican	22	0.03
Guatemalan	116	0.16
Honduran	82	0.11
Nicaraguan	43	0.06
Panamanian	30	0.04
Salvadoran	92	0.13
Other Central American	3	<0.01
Cuban	233	0.32
Dominican Republic	1,055	1.44
Mexican	1,257	1.72
Puerto Rican	21,914	29.93
South American	1,199	1.64
Argentinean	83	0.11
Bolivian	10	0.01
Chilean	36	0.05
Colombian	333	0.45
Ecuadorian	285	0.39
Paraguayan	2	<0.01
Peruvian	409	0.56
Uruguayan	3	<0.01
Venezuelan	32	0.04
Other South American	6	0.01
Other Hispanic or Latino	888	1.21

Race*	Population	%
African-American/Black (9,527)	11,207	15.31
Not Hispanic (7,982)	8,873	12.12
Hispanic (1,545)	2,334	3.19
American Indian/Alaska Native (271)	722	0.99
Not Hispanic (99)	376	0.51
Hispanic (172)	346	0.47
Alaska Athabascan *(Ala. Nat.)* (1)	2	<0.01
Apache (2)	17	0.02
Arapaho (1)	1	<0.01
Blackfeet (2)	18	0.02
Canadian/French Am. Ind. (7)	13	0.02
Central American Ind. (1)	1	<0.01
Cherokee (2)	64	0.09
Chippewa (0)	2	<0.01
Choctaw (0)	3	<0.01
Creek (0)	1	<0.01
Delaware (1)	3	<0.01
Iroquois (5)	13	0.02
Mexican American Ind. (11)	19	0.03
Navajo (0)	2	<0.01
Osage (0)	4	0.01
Paiute (1)	1	<0.01
Pueblo (28)	30	0.04
Seminole (0)	1	<0.01
Sioux (9)	16	0.02
South American Ind. (28)	67	0.09
Spanish American Ind. (4)	4	0.01
Tlingit-Haida *(Alaska Native)* (0)	1	<0.01
Yuman (0)	1	<0.01
Asian (1,729)	2,194	3.00
Not Hispanic (1,672)	2,042	2.79
Hispanic (57)	152	0.21

*Notes: † The Census 2010 population figure is used to calculate the percentages in the Hispanic Origin and Race categories. Ancestry percentages are based on the 2006-2010 American Community Survey population (not shown); ‡ Numbers in parentheses indicate the number of people reporting a single ancestry; * Numbers in parentheses indicate the number of persons reporting this race alone, not in combination with any other race; Please refer to the Explanation of Data for more information.*

	Population	%
Bangladeshi (29)	37	0.05
Cambodian (61)	82	0.11
Chinese, ex. Taiwanese (215)	285	0.39
Filipino (72)	126	0.17
Indian (535)	592	0.81
Indonesian (6)	6	0.01
Japanese (17)	47	0.06
Korean (96)	110	0.15
Laotian (284)	341	0.47
Malaysian (3)	3	<0.01
Nepalese (1)	1	<0.01
Pakistani (75)	86	0.12
Sri Lankan (8)	8	0.01
Taiwanese (10)	13	0.02
Thai (23)	36	0.05
Vietnamese (161)	190	0.26
Hawaii Native/Pacific Islander (27)	143	0.20
Not Hispanic (16)	69	0.09
Hispanic (11)	74	0.10
Fijian (0)	1	<0.01
Guamanian/Chamorro (5)	13	0.02
Marshallese (1)	1	<0.01
Native Hawaiian (5)	22	0.03
Samoan (2)	7	0.01
White (46,579)	48,964	66.89
Not Hispanic (34,919)	36,133	49.36
Hispanic (11,660)	12,831	17.53

New Canaan

Place Type: Town
County: Fairfield
Population: 19,738†

Ancestry‡	Population	%
Afghan (0)	33	0.17
American (1,240)	1,240	6.34
Arab (20)	61	0.31
Egyptian (12)	12	0.06
Lebanese (8)	49	0.25
Armenian (54)	168	0.86
Australian (0)	20	0.10
Austrian (82)	130	0.66
Belgian (0)	28	0.14
Brazilian (0)	30	0.15
British (181)	279	1.43
Bulgarian (29)	41	0.21
Canadian (50)	133	0.68
Celtic (9)	18	0.09
Croatian (3)	3	0.02
Czech (67)	241	1.23
Czechoslovakian (37)	51	0.26
Danish (54)	210	1.07
Dutch (107)	263	1.34
Eastern European (117)	168	0.86
English (1,239)	3,550	18.15
European (361)	394	2.01
Finnish (32)	39	0.20
French, ex. Basque (205)	784	4.01
French Canadian (29)	153	0.78
German (571)	3,038	15.53
Greek (122)	289	1.48
Hungarian (88)	224	1.14
Iranian (53)	53	0.27
Irish (1,977)	4,745	24.25
Italian (1,357)	3,250	16.61
Lithuanian (23)	134	0.68
Maltese (13)	13	0.07
Norwegian (79)	358	1.83
Polish (53)	576	2.94
Portuguese (50)	94	0.48
Romanian (22)	62	0.32
Russian (259)	510	2.61
Scotch-Irish (208)	399	2.04
Scottish (212)	794	4.06
Serbian (17)	17	0.09
Slavic (0)	33	0.17
Slovak (22)	68	0.35
Swedish (19)	227	1.16
Swiss (132)	185	0.95
Ukrainian (42)	128	0.65
Welsh (15)	81	0.41
West Indian, ex. Hispanic (0)	15	0.08
Haitian (0)	15	0.08
Yugoslavian (31)	45	0.23

Hispanic Origin	Population	%
Hispanic or Latino (of any race)	570	2.89
Central American, ex. Mexican	42	0.21
Costa Rican	1	0.01
Guatemalan	23	0.12
Honduran	5	0.03
Nicaraguan	3	0.02
Salvadoran	10	0.05
Cuban	38	0.19
Dominican Republic	32	0.16
Mexican	116	0.59
Puerto Rican	64	0.32
South American	203	1.03
Argentinean	19	0.10
Bolivian	4	0.02
Chilean	5	0.03
Colombian	73	0.37
Ecuadorian	21	0.11
Paraguayan	10	0.05
Peruvian	28	0.14
Uruguayan	13	0.07
Venezuelan	30	0.15
Other Hispanic or Latino	75	0.38

Race*	Population	%
African-American/Black (197)	244	1.24
Not Hispanic (194)	238	1.21
Hispanic (3)	6	0.03
American Indian/Alaska Native (30)	61	0.31
Not Hispanic (22)	50	0.25
Hispanic (8)	11	0.06
Blackfeet (1)	1	0.01
Cherokee (0)	7	0.04
Chippewa (0)	1	0.01
Delaware (4)	4	0.02
Mexican American Ind. (6)	6	0.03
South American Ind. (0)	1	0.01
Spanish American Ind. (0)	1	0.01
Tlingit-Haida *(Alaska Native)* (1)	3	0.02
Ute (0)	1	0.01
Asian (663)	828	4.19
Not Hispanic (662)	818	4.14
Hispanic (1)	10	0.05
Chinese, ex. Taiwanese (229)	298	1.51
Filipino (61)	86	0.44
Indian (173)	213	1.08
Indonesian (3)	3	0.02
Japanese (21)	34	0.17
Korean (95)	127	0.64
Malaysian (1)	4	0.02
Pakistani (16)	23	0.12
Taiwanese (7)	11	0.06
Thai (5)	6	0.03
Vietnamese (15)	22	0.11
Hawaii Native/Pacific Islander (3)	11	0.06
Not Hispanic (3)	10	0.05
Hispanic (0)	1	0.01
Guamanian/Chamorro (3)	4	0.02
Native Hawaiian (0)	1	0.01
White (18,481)	18,731	94.90
Not Hispanic (18,032)	18,247	92.45
Hispanic (449)	484	2.45

New Fairfield

Place Type: Town
County: Fairfield
Population: 13,881†

Ancestry‡	Population	%
African, Sub-Saharan (57)	82	0.59
African (13)	38	0.28
South African (44)	44	0.32
American (454)	454	3.29
Arab (11)	19	0.14
Lebanese (0)	8	0.06
Syrian (11)	11	0.08
Australian (11)	21	0.15
Austrian (49)	133	0.96
Brazilian (74)	74	0.54
British (38)	98	0.71
Canadian (10)	29	0.21
Croatian (10)	32	0.23
Czech (0)	189	1.37
Czechoslovakian (0)	40	0.29
Danish (23)	46	0.33
Dutch (0)	109	0.79
Eastern European (16)	16	0.12
English (340)	1,576	11.42
European (86)	144	1.04
Finnish (0)	42	0.30
French, ex. Basque (38)	512	3.71
French Canadian (46)	125	0.91
German (605)	2,170	15.72
Greek (14)	37	0.27
Hungarian (82)	278	2.01
Iranian (10)	10	0.07
Irish (1,431)	3,695	26.78
Israeli (44)	44	0.32
Italian (1,626)	3,865	28.01
Lithuanian (38)	46	0.33
Macedonian (35)	35	0.25
Northern European (12)	12	0.09
Norwegian (43)	241	1.75
Polish (179)	819	5.93
Portuguese (117)	208	1.51
Romanian (13)	13	0.09
Russian (61)	270	1.96
Scandinavian (0)	50	0.36
Scotch-Irish (75)	211	1.53
Scottish (19)	176	1.28
Serbian (32)	32	0.23
Slavic (10)	10	0.07
Slovak (109)	151	1.09
Slovene (0)	8	0.06
Swedish (161)	459	3.33
Swiss (58)	119	0.86
Ukrainian (37)	60	0.43
Welsh (18)	157	1.14
West Indian, ex. Hispanic (0)	12	0.09
Jamaican (0)	12	0.09
Yugoslavian (10)	55	0.40

Hispanic Origin	Population	%
Hispanic or Latino (of any race)	611	4.40
Central American, ex. Mexican	32	0.23
Guatemalan	16	0.12
Honduran	4	0.03
Nicaraguan	1	0.01
Salvadoran	11	0.08
Cuban	40	0.29
Dominican Republic	45	0.32
Mexican	68	0.49
Puerto Rican	213	1.53
South American	162	1.17
Argentinean	13	0.09
Chilean	9	0.06
Colombian	59	0.43
Ecuadorian	45	0.32
Paraguayan	2	0.01
Peruvian	24	0.17
Uruguayan	5	0.04
Venezuelan	1	0.01
Other South American	4	0.03
Other Hispanic or Latino	51	0.37

Race*	Population	%
African-American/Black (149)	196	1.41
Not Hispanic (142)	177	1.28
Hispanic (7)	19	0.14
American Indian/Alaska Native (18)	61	0.44
Not Hispanic (15)	50	0.36
Hispanic (3)	11	0.08
Blackfeet (0)	4	0.03

*Notes: † The Census 2010 population figure is used to calculate the percentages in the Hispanic Origin and Race categories. Ancestry percentages are based on the 2006-2010 American Community Survey population (not shown); ‡ Numbers in parentheses indicate the number of people reporting a single ancestry; * Numbers in parentheses indicate the number of persons reporting this race alone, not in combination with any other race; Please refer to the Explanation of Data for more information.*

Central American Ind. (0)	1	0.01
Cherokee (6)	13	0.09
Choctaw (0)	1	0.01
Creek (2)	2	0.01
Iroquois (0)	11	0.08
Lumbee (1)	1	0.01
South American Ind. (1)	2	0.01
Spanish American Ind. (0)	4	0.03
Asian (232)	309	2.23
Not Hispanic (232)	302	2.18
Hispanic (0)	7	0.05
Bangladeshi (2)	2	0.01
Cambodian (3)	5	0.04
Chinese, ex. Taiwanese (46)	67	0.48
Filipino (45)	61	0.44
Indian (89)	99	0.71
Indonesian (1)	2	0.01
Japanese (9)	18	0.13
Korean (19)	26	0.19
Pakistani (7)	8	0.06
Sri Lankan (4)	4	0.03
Thai (2)	10	0.07
Vietnamese (1)	3	0.02
Hawaii Native/Pacific Islander (8)	13	0.09
Not Hispanic (8)	9	0.06
Hispanic (0)	4	0.03
Guamanian/Chamorro (2)	2	0.01
Native Hawaiian (0)	1	0.01
White (13,161)	13,341	96.11
Not Hispanic (12,694)	12,829	92.42
Hispanic (467)	512	3.69

New Haven

Place Type: City/Town
County: New Haven
Population: 129,779†

Ancestry‡	Population	%
Afghan (12)	12	0.01
African, Sub-Saharan (2,101)	2,581	2.00
African (1,153)	1,563	1.21
Cape Verdean (67)	117	0.09
Ethiopian (67)	77	0.06
Ghanaian (87)	97	0.08
Kenyan (26)	26	0.02
Nigerian (456)	456	0.35
Sierra Leonean (18)	18	0.01
South African (57)	57	0.04
Other Sub-Saharan African (170)	170	0.13
Albanian (72)	72	0.06
American (977)	977	0.76
Arab (329)	542	0.42
Arab (129)	129	0.10
Egyptian (74)	123	0.10
Jordanian (12)	12	0.01
Lebanese (48)	69	0.05
Moroccan (20)	20	0.02
Palestinian (20)	20	0.02
Syrian (0)	73	0.06
Other Arab (26)	96	0.07
Armenian (49)	67	0.05
Australian (51)	86	0.07
Austrian (81)	305	0.24
Belgian (0)	60	0.05
Brazilian (24)	103	0.08
British (183)	457	0.35
Bulgarian (54)	54	0.04
Cajun (15)	15	0.01
Canadian (197)	378	0.29
Croatian (6)	17	0.01
Czech (21)	199	0.15
Czechoslovakian (20)	85	0.07
Danish (185)	499	0.39
Dutch (168)	739	0.57
Eastern European (375)	505	0.39
English (922)	4,883	3.79
Estonian (0)	9	0.01
European (1,137)	1,416	1.10
Finnish (21)	61	0.05
French, ex. Basque (308)	2,209	1.71
French Canadian (257)	711	0.55
German (1,398)	6,181	4.80
German Russian (17)	34	0.03
Greek (272)	551	0.43
Guyanese (285)	305	0.24
Hungarian (99)	340	0.26
Icelander (0)	11	0.01
Iranian (23)	58	0.05
Irish (2,706)	8,987	6.97
Israeli (167)	236	0.18
Italian (6,492)	12,171	9.44
Latvian (62)	87	0.07
Lithuanian (66)	313	0.24
Luxemburger (0)	11	0.01
Macedonian (0)	11	0.01
Northern European (168)	196	0.15
Norwegian (91)	390	0.30
Pennsylvania German (0)	17	0.01
Polish (1,019)	3,277	2.54
Portuguese (126)	510	0.40
Romanian (160)	239	0.19
Russian (855)	2,240	1.74
Scandinavian (10)	56	0.04
Scotch-Irish (249)	758	0.59
Scottish (209)	911	0.71
Serbian (24)	67	0.05
Slavic (9)	36	0.03
Slovak (27)	105	0.08
Slovene (0)	17	0.01
Soviet Union (23)	23	0.02
Swedish (318)	1,026	0.80
Swiss (22)	158	0.12
Turkish (115)	152	0.12
Ukrainian (247)	465	0.36
Welsh (32)	338	0.26
West Indian, ex. Hispanic (2,724)	3,422	2.66
Barbadian (26)	67	0.05
Bermudan (24)	24	0.02
British West Indian (78)	101	0.08
Haitian (440)	558	0.43
Jamaican (1,589)	1,979	1.54
Trinidadian/Tobagonian (189)	203	0.16
West Indian (378)	490	0.38
Yugoslavian (0)	10	0.01

Hispanic Origin	Population	%
Hispanic or Latino (of any race)	35,591	27.42
Central American, ex. Mexican	1,373	1.06
Costa Rican	56	0.04
Guatemalan	728	0.56
Honduran	209	0.16
Nicaraguan	54	0.04
Panamanian	77	0.06
Salvadoran	243	0.19
Other Central American	6	<0.01
Cuban	485	0.37
Dominican Republic	1,097	0.85
Mexican	6,907	5.32
Puerto Rican	20,505	15.80
South American	3,426	2.64
Argentinean	182	0.14
Bolivian	25	0.02
Chilean	164	0.13
Colombian	469	0.36
Ecuadorian	1,978	1.52
Paraguayan	8	0.01
Peruvian	448	0.35
Uruguayan	14	0.01
Venezuelan	127	0.10
Other South American	11	0.01
Other Hispanic or Latino	1,798	1.39

Race*	Population	%
African-American/Black (45,938)	48,799	37.60
Not Hispanic (43,332)	45,302	34.91
Hispanic (2,606)	3,497	2.69
American Indian/Alaska Native (660)	1,781	1.37
Not Hispanic (379)	1,221	0.94
Hispanic (281)	560	0.43
Alaska Athabascan *(Ala. Nat.)* (0)	1	<0.01
Apache (2)	6	<0.01
Blackfeet (14)	72	0.06
Canadian/French Am. Ind. (2)	4	<0.01
Central American Ind. (14)	18	0.01
Cherokee (36)	229	0.18
Cheyenne (2)	2	<0.01
Chickasaw (1)	6	<0.01
Chippewa (4)	9	0.01
Choctaw (1)	16	0.01
Comanche (1)	4	<0.01
Cree (0)	2	<0.01
Creek (1)	4	<0.01
Crow (1)	1	<0.01
Delaware (3)	11	0.01
Hopi (1)	3	<0.01
Houma (0)	1	<0.01
Inupiat *(Alaska Native)* (1)	1	<0.01
Iroquois (5)	20	0.02
Kiowa (0)	1	<0.01
Lumbee (2)	13	0.01
Mexican American Ind. (25)	47	0.04
Navajo (9)	13	0.01
Osage (0)	1	<0.01
Ottawa (3)	5	<0.01
Potawatomi (1)	2	<0.01
Pueblo (3)	4	<0.01
Puget Sound Salish (2)	3	<0.01
Seminole (1)	10	0.01
Shoshone (0)	5	<0.01
Sioux (1)	21	0.02
South American Ind. (41)	108	0.08
Spanish American Ind. (0)	7	0.01
Tohono O'Odham (2)	4	<0.01
Tsimshian *(Alaska Native)* (0)	1	<0.01
Asian (5,945)	6,926	5.34
Not Hispanic (5,864)	6,715	5.17
Hispanic (81)	211	0.16
Bangladeshi (47)	55	0.04
Bhutanese (1)	1	<0.01
Burmese (9)	13	0.01
Cambodian (96)	112	0.09
Chinese, ex. Taiwanese (2,389)	2,710	2.09
Filipino (341)	457	0.35
Hmong (1)	2	<0.01
Indian (1,186)	1,372	1.06
Indonesian (11)	25	0.02
Japanese (232)	392	0.30
Korean (660)	763	0.59
Laotian (166)	186	0.14
Malaysian (18)	25	0.02
Nepalese (70)	73	0.06
Pakistani (128)	154	0.12
Sri Lankan (28)	37	0.03
Taiwanese (121)	139	0.11
Thai (62)	75	0.06
Vietnamese (173)	220	0.17
Hawaii Native/Pacific Islander (71)	237	0.18
Not Hispanic (34)	130	0.10
Hispanic (37)	107	0.08
Fijian (0)	2	<0.01
Guamanian/Chamorro (28)	35	0.03
Native Hawaiian (8)	41	0.03
Samoan (14)	16	0.01
Tongan (0)	2	<0.01
White (55,228)	58,880	45.37
Not Hispanic (41,230)	43,390	33.43
Hispanic (13,998)	15,490	11.94

New London

Place Type: City/Town
County: New London
Population: 27,620†

Ancestry‡	Population	%
African, Sub-Saharan (114)	264	0.96
African (51)	69	0.25
Cape Verdean (46)	163	0.59
Ghanaian (0)	15	0.05

*Notes: † The Census 2010 population figure is used to calculate the percentages in the Hispanic Origin and Race categories. Ancestry percentages are based on the 2006-2010 American Community Survey population (not shown); ‡ Numbers in parentheses indicate the number of people reporting a single ancestry; * Numbers in parentheses indicate the number of persons reporting this race alone, not in combination with any other race; Please refer to the Explanation of Data for more information.*

Senegalese (5)	5	0.02
Other Sub-Saharan African (12)	12	0.04
Albanian (40)	53	0.19
American (789)	789	2.87
Arab (50)	134	0.49
Egyptian (14)	14	0.05
Lebanese (36)	76	0.28
Palestinian (0)	8	0.03
Syrian (0)	36	0.13
Armenian (9)	24	0.09
Australian (0)	21	0.08
Austrian (35)	35	0.13
Belgian (0)	16	0.06
British (21)	121	0.44
Bulgarian (13)	13	0.05
Canadian (12)	39	0.14
Celtic (0)	24	0.09
Czech (90)	214	0.78
Czechoslovakian (0)	83	0.30
Danish (0)	78	0.28
Dutch (44)	160	0.58
Eastern European (48)	48	0.17
English (474)	1,746	6.35
European (93)	93	0.34
Finnish (35)	46	0.17
French, ex. Basque (116)	797	2.90
French Canadian (131)	410	1.49
German (366)	2,334	8.49
Greek (84)	252	0.92
Hungarian (14)	58	0.21
Icelander (0)	12	0.04
Irish (917)	3,332	12.12
Israeli (10)	10	0.04
Italian (1,099)	2,862	10.41
Lithuanian (9)	102	0.37
Norwegian (57)	287	1.04
Polish (427)	1,506	5.48
Portuguese (192)	542	1.97
Romanian (59)	115	0.42
Russian (283)	490	1.78
Scandinavian (0)	11	0.04
Scotch-Irish (16)	362	1.32
Scottish (172)	558	2.03
Serbian (0)	9	0.03
Slavic (0)	10	0.04
Slovene (12)	23	0.08
Swedish (55)	353	1.28
Swiss (0)	58	0.21
Turkish (13)	13	0.05
Ukrainian (0)	14	0.05
Welsh (0)	45	0.16
West Indian, ex. Hispanic (673)	847	3.08
Belizean (0)	10	0.04
British West Indian (20)	20	0.07
Haitian (449)	515	1.87
Jamaican (161)	223	0.81
West Indian (40)	76	0.28
Other West Indian (3)	3	0.01
Yugoslavian (0)	28	0.10

Hispanic Origin	Population	%
Hispanic or Latino (of any race)	7,815	28.29
Central American, ex. Mexican	533	1.93
Costa Rican	28	0.10
Guatemalan	77	0.28
Honduran	108	0.39
Nicaraguan	6	0.02
Panamanian	76	0.28
Salvadoran	234	0.85
Other Central American	4	0.01
Cuban	74	0.27
Dominican Republic	1,230	4.45
Mexican	366	1.33
Puerto Rican	4,264	15.44
South American	975	3.53
Argentinean	16	0.06
Bolivian	3	0.01
Chilean	18	0.07
Colombian	134	0.49
Ecuadorian	241	0.87
Paraguayan	7	0.03
Peruvian	513	1.86
Uruguayan	13	0.05
Venezuelan	16	0.06
Other South American	14	0.05
Other Hispanic or Latino	373	1.35

Race*	Population	%
African-American/Black (4,818)	5,917	21.42
Not Hispanic (4,214)	4,985	18.05
Hispanic (604)	932	3.37
American Indian/Alaska Native (266)	767	2.78
Not Hispanic (159)	531	1.92
Hispanic (107)	236	0.85
Apache (0)	8	0.03
Blackfeet (4)	21	0.08
Canadian/French Am. Ind. (0)	3	0.01
Central American Ind. (2)	4	0.01
Cherokee (10)	87	0.31
Cheyenne (0)	1	<0.01
Chickasaw (0)	1	<0.01
Chippewa (2)	9	0.03
Choctaw (0)	6	0.02
Creek (0)	3	0.01
Delaware (1)	2	0.01
Inupiat *(Alaska Native)* (1)	1	<0.01
Iroquois (8)	23	0.08
Lumbee (7)	7	0.03
Mexican American Ind. (8)	14	0.05
Navajo (8)	10	0.04
Osage (0)	1	<0.01
Ottawa (1)	1	<0.01
Pueblo (0)	1	<0.01
Seminole (1)	4	0.01
Shoshone (0)	4	0.01
Sioux (0)	3	0.01
South American Ind. (39)	58	0.21
Spanish American Ind. (0)	1	<0.01
Tlingit-Haida *(Alaska Native)* (0)	2	0.01
Tohono O'Odham (2)	2	0.01
Yaqui (4)	4	0.01
Asian (722)	1,023	3.70
Not Hispanic (695)	946	3.43
Hispanic (27)	77	0.28
Bangladeshi (9)	9	0.03
Burmese (1)	1	<0.01
Cambodian (13)	23	0.08
Chinese, ex. Taiwanese (147)	205	0.74
Filipino (163)	286	1.04
Hmong (2)	3	0.01
Indian (176)	206	0.75
Indonesian (4)	4	0.01
Japanese (20)	78	0.28
Korean (39)	64	0.23
Laotian (8)	12	0.04
Malaysian (1)	1	<0.01
Nepalese (16)	16	0.06
Pakistani (35)	40	0.14
Sri Lankan (1)	2	0.01
Taiwanese (3)	3	0.01
Thai (15)	21	0.08
Vietnamese (34)	53	0.19
Hawaii Native/Pacific Islander (44)	164	0.59
Not Hispanic (34)	107	0.39
Hispanic (10)	57	0.21
Guamanian/Chamorro (7)	21	0.08
Marshallese (3)	3	0.01
Native Hawaiian (9)	41	0.15
Samoan (7)	11	0.04
White (16,678)	18,053	65.36
Not Hispanic (13,490)	14,343	51.93
Hispanic (3,188)	3,710	13.43

New Milford

Place Type: Town
County: Litchfield
Population: 28,142†

Ancestry‡	Population	%
Albanian (54)	54	0.19
American (656)	656	2.33
Arab (52)	200	0.71
Egyptian (18)	74	0.26
Lebanese (14)	69	0.25
Syrian (20)	57	0.20
Armenian (0)	91	0.32
Australian (0)	11	0.04
Austrian (23)	158	0.56
Belgian (0)	42	0.15
Brazilian (463)	474	1.68
British (103)	123	0.44
Bulgarian (28)	28	0.10
Canadian (7)	102	0.36
Croatian (0)	23	0.08
Czech (24)	201	0.71
Czechoslovakian (36)	51	0.18
Danish (32)	123	0.44
Dutch (84)	363	1.29
Eastern European (58)	58	0.21
English (792)	3,788	13.45
Estonian (9)	9	0.03
European (169)	169	0.60
Finnish (8)	34	0.12
French, ex. Basque (98)	1,107	3.93
French Canadian (454)	857	3.04
German (1,501)	5,481	19.46
Greek (94)	280	0.99
Hungarian (135)	488	1.73
Icelander (0)	9	0.03
Iranian (20)	20	0.07
Irish (2,214)	6,647	23.61
Italian (2,208)	5,680	20.17
Lithuanian (50)	216	0.77
Maltese (0)	27	0.10
Northern European (42)	42	0.15
Norwegian (81)	193	0.69
Polish (593)	1,928	6.85
Portuguese (366)	561	1.99
Romanian (35)	35	0.12
Russian (151)	568	2.02
Scandinavian (10)	23	0.08
Scotch-Irish (127)	435	1.54
Scottish (156)	610	2.17
Slavic (12)	12	0.04
Slovak (70)	166	0.59
Slovene (0)	17	0.06
Swedish (120)	542	1.92
Swiss (19)	121	0.43
Turkish (0)	8	0.03
Ukrainian (31)	79	0.28
Welsh (40)	196	0.70
West Indian, ex. Hispanic (103)	165	0.59
Barbadian (23)	23	0.08
Dutch West Indian (40)	40	0.14
Jamaican (9)	22	0.08
West Indian (31)	60	0.21
Other West Indian (0)	20	0.07

Hispanic Origin	Population	%
Hispanic or Latino (of any race)	1,693	6.02
Central American, ex. Mexican	108	0.38
Costa Rican	21	0.07
Guatemalan	67	0.24
Honduran	5	0.02
Nicaraguan	3	0.01
Salvadoran	12	0.04
Cuban	69	0.25
Dominican Republic	141	0.50
Mexican	232	0.82
Puerto Rican	446	1.58
South American	546	1.94
Argentinean	26	0.09
Bolivian	8	0.03
Chilean	22	0.08
Colombian	90	0.32
Ecuadorian	265	0.94
Peruvian	111	0.39
Uruguayan	9	0.03

*Notes: † The Census 2010 population figure is used to calculate the percentages in the Hispanic Origin and Race categories. Ancestry percentages are based on the 2006-2010 American Community Survey population (not shown); ‡ Numbers in parentheses indicate the number of people reporting a single ancestry; * Numbers in parentheses indicate the number of persons reporting this race alone, not in combination with any other race; Please refer to the Explanation of Data for more information.*

	Population	%
Venezuelan	10	0.04
Other South American	5	0.02
Other Hispanic or Latino	151	0.54

Race*	Population	%
African-American/Black (484)	650	2.31
Not Hispanic (452)	591	2.10
Hispanic (32)	59	0.21
American Indian/Alaska Native (68)	206	0.73
Not Hispanic (46)	141	0.50
Hispanic (22)	65	0.23
Apache (3)	4	0.01
Blackfeet (2)	9	0.03
Cherokee (1)	26	0.09
Cheyenne (1)	1	<0.01
Chippewa (0)	1	<0.01
Hopi (1)	2	0.01
Iroquois (4)	19	0.07
Mexican American Ind. (4)	7	0.02
Osage (1)	1	<0.01
Potawatomi (0)	3	0.01
Seminole (0)	3	0.01
South American Ind. (5)	16	0.06
Tohono O'Odham (1)	1	<0.01
Yuman (0)	1	<0.01
Asian (779)	955	3.39
Not Hispanic (772)	933	3.32
Hispanic (7)	22	0.08
Bangladeshi (34)	34	0.12
Burmese (1)	1	<0.01
Cambodian (52)	62	0.22
Chinese, ex. Taiwanese (198)	236	0.84
Filipino (102)	149	0.53
Indian (229)	257	0.91
Indonesian (1)	3	0.01
Japanese (16)	30	0.11
Korean (51)	66	0.23
Laotian (25)	38	0.14
Pakistani (1)	1	<0.01
Sri Lankan (7)	7	0.02
Taiwanese (0)	1	<0.01
Thai (12)	21	0.07
Vietnamese (24)	30	0.11
Hawaii Native/Pacific Islander (11)	22	0.08
Not Hispanic (7)	13	0.05
Hispanic (4)	9	0.03
Guamanian/Chamorro (3)	3	0.01
Native Hawaiian (5)	9	0.03
Samoan (2)	2	0.01
White (25,809)	26,267	93.34
Not Hispanic (24,709)	25,057	89.04
Hispanic (1,100)	1,210	4.30

Newington

Place Type: CDP/Town
County: Hartford
Population: 30,562†

Ancestry‡	Population	%
Afghan (0)	23	0.08
African, Sub-Saharan (434)	491	1.62
African (412)	453	1.49
Cape Verdean (5)	5	0.02
Nigerian (6)	6	0.02
Somalian (0)	16	0.05
Other Sub-Saharan African (11)	11	0.04
Albanian (187)	187	0.62
American (779)	779	2.57
Arab (90)	144	0.47
Arab (0)	15	0.05
Jordanian (60)	60	0.20
Lebanese (30)	69	0.23
Armenian (202)	297	0.98
Assyrian/Chaldean/Syriac (52)	52	0.17
Austrian (58)	185	0.61
Belgian (0)	26	0.09
Brazilian (148)	148	0.49
British (23)	23	0.08
Canadian (67)	181	0.60
Croatian (14)	29	0.10
Cypriot (23)	23	0.08
Czech (10)	34	0.11
Czechoslovakian (23)	31	0.10
Danish (0)	144	0.47
Dutch (32)	127	0.42
Eastern European (55)	55	0.18
English (547)	2,673	8.80
European (84)	84	0.28
Finnish (13)	13	0.04
French, ex. Basque (673)	2,337	7.70
French Canadian (534)	1,169	3.85
German (581)	2,220	7.31
Greek (118)	304	1.00
Guyanese (48)	48	0.16
Hungarian (64)	124	0.41
Irish (1,316)	5,165	17.01
Italian (3,098)	6,772	22.30
Lithuanian (143)	344	1.13
Northern European (26)	26	0.09
Norwegian (29)	137	0.45
Polish (2,848)	4,954	16.32
Portuguese (950)	1,283	4.23
Romanian (116)	125	0.41
Russian (177)	541	1.78
Scandinavian (11)	41	0.14
Scotch-Irish (78)	216	0.71
Scottish (157)	593	1.95
Slavic (8)	31	0.10
Slovak (23)	34	0.11
Swedish (146)	697	2.30
Swiss (0)	32	0.11
Ukrainian (165)	317	1.04
Welsh (9)	109	0.36
West Indian, ex. Hispanic (71)	71	0.23
Haitian (12)	12	0.04
Jamaican (59)	59	0.19
Yugoslavian (68)	79	0.26

Hispanic Origin	Population	%
Hispanic or Latino (of any race)	2,308	7.55
Central American, ex. Mexican	65	0.21
Costa Rican	2	0.01
Guatemalan	11	0.04
Honduran	6	0.02
Nicaraguan	12	0.04
Panamanian	6	0.02
Salvadoran	22	0.07
Other Central American	6	0.02
Cuban	125	0.41
Dominican Republic	79	0.26
Mexican	114	0.37
Puerto Rican	1,308	4.28
South American	473	1.55
Argentinean	47	0.15
Bolivian	7	0.02
Chilean	8	0.03
Colombian	151	0.49
Ecuadorian	30	0.10
Peruvian	213	0.70
Uruguayan	5	0.02
Venezuelan	6	0.02
Other South American	6	0.02
Other Hispanic or Latino	144	0.47

Race*	Population	%
African-American/Black (1,075)	1,346	4.40
Not Hispanic (996)	1,193	3.90
Hispanic (79)	153	0.50
American Indian/Alaska Native (48)	172	0.56
Not Hispanic (24)	111	0.36
Hispanic (24)	61	0.20
Blackfeet (1)	5	0.02
Central American Ind. (2)	2	0.01
Cherokee (3)	11	0.04
Choctaw (0)	6	0.02
Cree (0)	1	<0.01
Iroquois (1)	8	0.03
Mexican American Ind. (1)	1	<0.01
Navajo (0)	1	<0.01
Sioux (0)	2	0.01
South American Ind. (11)	22	0.07
Spanish American Ind. (0)	1	<0.01
Tlingit-Haida *(Alaska Native)* (0)	2	0.01
Yuman (1)	1	<0.01
Asian (1,736)	1,941	6.35
Not Hispanic (1,727)	1,917	6.27
Hispanic (9)	24	0.08
Bangladeshi (17)	19	0.06
Burmese (1)	1	<0.01
Cambodian (7)	7	0.02
Chinese, ex. Taiwanese (225)	262	0.86
Filipino (177)	202	0.66
Indian (774)	817	2.67
Indonesian (4)	6	0.02
Japanese (15)	33	0.11
Korean (79)	96	0.31
Laotian (19)	27	0.09
Pakistani (131)	137	0.45
Sri Lankan (5)	5	0.02
Taiwanese (1)	1	<0.01
Thai (4)	5	0.02
Vietnamese (236)	262	0.86
Hawaii Native/Pacific Islander (4)	24	0.08
Not Hispanic (2)	17	0.06
Hispanic (2)	7	0.02
Guamanian/Chamorro (1)	2	0.01
Native Hawaiian (0)	2	0.01
Samoan (2)	3	0.01
White (26,436)	26,926	88.10
Not Hispanic (25,021)	25,365	83.00
Hispanic (1,415)	1,561	5.11

Newtown

Place Type: Town
County: Fairfield
Population: 27,560†

Ancestry‡	Population	%
African, Sub-Saharan (60)	96	0.36
African (29)	65	0.24
Nigerian (31)	31	0.11
Albanian (64)	77	0.29
American (667)	667	2.47
Arab (55)	273	1.01
Egyptian (8)	8	0.03
Lebanese (24)	150	0.56
Syrian (23)	104	0.39
Other Arab (0)	11	0.04
Armenian (31)	94	0.35
Austrian (40)	209	0.78
Brazilian (45)	99	0.37
British (132)	267	0.99
Bulgarian (0)	3	0.01
Canadian (83)	146	0.54
Celtic (13)	13	0.05
Croatian (23)	62	0.23
Czech (155)	388	1.44
Czechoslovakian (22)	58	0.22
Danish (14)	100	0.37
Dutch (59)	392	1.45
Eastern European (170)	213	0.79
English (603)	3,209	11.90
Estonian (24)	50	0.19
European (399)	429	1.59
Finnish (8)	13	0.05
French, ex. Basque (185)	1,300	4.82
French Canadian (293)	555	2.06
German (1,221)	4,664	17.30
Greek (131)	348	1.29
Hungarian (150)	709	2.63
Irish (1,425)	6,082	22.56
Italian (2,510)	6,383	23.68
Lithuanian (22)	188	0.70
Northern European (4)	4	0.01
Norwegian (39)	178	0.66
Polish (569)	2,143	7.95
Portuguese (207)	331	1.23
Romanian (13)	35	0.13

*Notes: † The Census 2010 population figure is used to calculate the percentages in the Hispanic Origin and Race categories. Ancestry percentages are based on the 2006-2010 American Community Survey population (not shown); ‡ Numbers in parentheses indicate the number of people reporting a single ancestry; * Numbers in parentheses indicate the number of persons reporting this race alone, not in combination with any other race; Please refer to the Explanation of Data for more information.*

Russian (402)	893	3.31
Scandinavian (19)	57	0.21
Scotch-Irish (230)	450	1.67
Scottish (192)	678	2.52
Slavic (13)	13	0.05
Slovak (85)	261	0.97
Slovene (15)	73	0.27
Swedish (72)	606	2.25
Swiss (35)	112	0.42
Turkish (57)	74	0.27
Ukrainian (19)	86	0.32
Welsh (47)	226	0.84
West Indian, ex. Hispanic (27)	27	0.10
Haitian (14)	14	0.05
Trinidadian/Tobagonian (13)	13	0.05

Hispanic Origin	Population	%
Hispanic or Latino (of any race)	1,033	3.75
Central American, ex. Mexican	85	0.31
Costa Rican	7	0.03
Guatemalan	21	0.08
Honduran	13	0.05
Nicaraguan	12	0.04
Panamanian	2	0.01
Salvadoran	30	0.11
Cuban	71	0.26
Dominican Republic	34	0.12
Mexican	138	0.50
Puerto Rican	279	1.01
South American	282	1.02
Argentinean	27	0.10
Bolivian	5	0.02
Chilean	14	0.05
Colombian	93	0.34
Ecuadorian	83	0.30
Peruvian	40	0.15
Uruguayan	5	0.02
Venezuelan	12	0.04
Other South American	3	0.01
Other Hispanic or Latino	144	0.52

Race*	Population	%
African-American/Black (444)	523	1.90
Not Hispanic (433)	502	1.82
Hispanic (11)	21	0.08
American Indian/Alaska Native (33)	89	0.32
Not Hispanic (27)	76	0.28
Hispanic (6)	13	0.05
Blackfeet (1)	5	0.02
Canadian/French Am. Ind. (0)	1	<0.01
Central American Ind. (5)	7	0.03
Cherokee (1)	7	0.03
Chickasaw (0)	2	0.01
Chippewa (1)	1	<0.01
Cree (0)	3	0.01
Iroquois (3)	6	0.02
Kiowa (1)	1	<0.01
Mexican American Ind. (1)	1	<0.01
Seminole (0)	1	<0.01
Sioux (1)	3	0.01
South American Ind. (2)	4	0.01
Asian (648)	797	2.89
Not Hispanic (645)	777	2.82
Hispanic (3)	20	0.07
Bangladeshi (14)	18	0.07
Cambodian (12)	13	0.05
Chinese, ex. Taiwanese (194)	217	0.79
Filipino (47)	67	0.24
Indian (210)	234	0.85
Indonesian (1)	4	0.01
Japanese (17)	47	0.17
Korean (83)	104	0.38
Laotian (1)	2	0.01
Malaysian (1)	5	0.02
Pakistani (2)	11	0.04
Sri Lankan (6)	10	0.04
Taiwanese (5)	8	0.03
Thai (8)	12	0.04
Vietnamese (22)	28	0.10
Hawaii Native/Pacific Islander (8)	23	0.08
Not Hispanic (7)	21	0.08
Hispanic (1)	2	0.01
Fijian (1)	1	<0.01
Guamanian/Chamorro (1)	1	<0.01
Native Hawaiian (5)	10	0.04
Samoan (1)	5	0.02
White (25,914)	26,213	95.11
Not Hispanic (25,133)	25,380	92.09
Hispanic (781)	833	3.02

North Branford

Place Type: Town
County: New Haven
Population: 14,407†

Ancestry‡	Population	%
African, Sub-Saharan (0)	14	0.10
African (0)	14	0.10
American (356)	356	2.48
Australian (0)	30	0.21
Austrian (0)	56	0.39
Belgian (0)	17	0.12
Brazilian (0)	13	0.09
British (11)	48	0.33
Canadian (14)	26	0.18
Czech (0)	13	0.09
Czechoslovakian (0)	13	0.09
Dutch (0)	63	0.44
Eastern European (18)	18	0.13
English (538)	1,509	10.53
European (0)	43	0.30
Finnish (0)	9	0.06
French, ex. Basque (107)	956	6.67
French Canadian (42)	303	2.11
German (428)	2,058	14.36
Greek (36)	212	1.48
Hungarian (33)	145	1.01
Irish (870)	3,894	27.17
Italian (2,927)	5,710	39.84
Latvian (13)	13	0.09
Lithuanian (0)	173	1.21
Norwegian (0)	16	0.11
Polish (501)	1,535	10.71
Portuguese (44)	138	0.96
Russian (120)	244	1.70
Scandinavian (15)	34	0.24
Scotch-Irish (94)	151	1.05
Scottish (26)	191	1.33
Slovak (17)	26	0.18
Swedish (74)	293	2.04
Swiss (12)	34	0.24
Ukrainian (12)	36	0.25
Welsh (0)	44	0.31
West Indian, ex. Hispanic (0)	19	0.13
Trinidadian/Tobagonian (0)	19	0.13

Hispanic Origin	Population	%
Hispanic or Latino (of any race)	421	2.92
Central American, ex. Mexican	21	0.15
Costa Rican	6	0.04
Guatemalan	8	0.06
Panamanian	3	0.02
Salvadoran	4	0.03
Cuban	24	0.17
Dominican Republic	10	0.07
Mexican	45	0.31
Puerto Rican	212	1.47
South American	55	0.38
Argentinean	7	0.05
Bolivian	3	0.02
Chilean	3	0.02
Colombian	15	0.10
Ecuadorian	22	0.15
Paraguayan	1	0.01
Peruvian	2	0.01
Uruguayan	2	0.01
Other Hispanic or Latino	54	0.37

Race*	Population	%
African-American/Black (191)	237	1.65
Not Hispanic (187)	230	1.60
Hispanic (4)	7	0.05
American Indian/Alaska Native (14)	62	0.43
Not Hispanic (8)	55	0.38
Hispanic (6)	7	0.05
Cherokee (1)	9	0.06
Chippewa (0)	1	0.01
Choctaw (0)	2	0.01
Delaware (0)	3	0.02
Iroquois (0)	4	0.03
Mexican American Ind. (5)	5	0.03
Potawatomi (1)	1	0.01
Seminole (0)	1	0.01
Yuman (1)	1	0.01
Asian (227)	260	1.80
Not Hispanic (225)	256	1.78
Hispanic (2)	4	0.03
Cambodian (8)	10	0.07
Chinese, ex. Taiwanese (70)	81	0.56
Filipino (32)	41	0.28
Indian (53)	54	0.37
Japanese (6)	8	0.06
Korean (16)	21	0.15
Laotian (9)	9	0.06
Pakistani (10)	10	0.07
Sri Lankan (1)	2	0.01
Thai (2)	4	0.03
Vietnamese (9)	16	0.11
Hawaii Native/Pacific Islander (5)	9	0.06
Not Hispanic (5)	9	0.06
Native Hawaiian (1)	5	0.03
White (13,758)	13,892	96.43
Not Hispanic (13,430)	13,545	94.02
Hispanic (328)	347	2.41

North Haven

Place Type: CDP/Town
County: New Haven
Population: 24,093†

Ancestry‡	Population	%
African, Sub-Saharan (43)	55	0.23
African (36)	36	0.15
Cape Verdean (7)	19	0.08
American (380)	380	1.59
Arab (9)	9	0.04
Lebanese (9)	9	0.04
Austrian (11)	56	0.23
Belgian (0)	19	0.08
Brazilian (20)	55	0.23
British (30)	30	0.13
Canadian (50)	97	0.41
Czech (39)	80	0.33
Czechoslovakian (9)	30	0.13
Danish (0)	36	0.15
Dutch (9)	119	0.50
Eastern European (98)	98	0.41
English (422)	2,509	10.49
Estonian (0)	17	0.07
European (153)	183	0.76
Finnish (0)	13	0.05
French, ex. Basque (163)	891	3.72
French Canadian (158)	449	1.88
German (441)	2,101	8.78
Greek (74)	117	0.49
Hungarian (33)	175	0.73
Icelander (0)	10	0.04
Irish (1,142)	4,564	19.07
Italian (6,293)	10,432	43.60
Latvian (0)	16	0.07
Lithuanian (63)	200	0.84
Northern European (35)	35	0.15
Norwegian (18)	104	0.43
Polish (1,024)	2,562	10.71
Portuguese (99)	224	0.94
Romanian (55)	55	0.23

*Notes: † The Census 2010 population figure is used to calculate the percentages in the Hispanic Origin and Race categories. Ancestry percentages are based on the 2006-2010 American Community Survey population (not shown); ‡ Numbers in parentheses indicate the number of people reporting a single ancestry; * Numbers in parentheses indicate the number of persons reporting this race alone, not in combination with any other race; Please refer to the Explanation of Data for more information.*

Ancestry (continued)	Population	%
Russian (194)	469	1.96
Scandinavian (0)	46	0.19
Scotch-Irish (101)	288	1.20
Scottish (69)	468	1.96
Serbian (0)	16	0.07
Slavic (0)	14	0.06
Slovak (0)	21	0.09
Swedish (26)	261	1.09
Swiss (0)	89	0.37
Ukrainian (47)	218	0.91
Welsh (18)	96	0.40
West Indian, ex. Hispanic (101)	113	0.47
Bahamian (34)	34	0.14
Haitian (31)	31	0.13
Jamaican (18)	18	0.08
West Indian (18)	30	0.13

Hispanic Origin	Population	%
Hispanic or Latino (of any race)	929	3.86
Central American, ex. Mexican	52	0.22
Costa Rican	2	0.01
Guatemalan	21	0.09
Honduran	7	0.03
Nicaraguan	3	0.01
Panamanian	4	0.02
Salvadoran	13	0.05
Other Central American	2	0.01
Cuban	47	0.20
Dominican Republic	24	0.10
Mexican	105	0.44
Puerto Rican	447	1.86
South American	138	0.57
Argentinean	18	0.07
Chilean	7	0.03
Colombian	47	0.20
Ecuadorian	34	0.14
Paraguayan	3	0.01
Peruvian	23	0.10
Venezuelan	6	0.02
Other Hispanic or Latino	116	0.48

Race*	Population	%
African-American/Black (725)	848	3.52
Not Hispanic (693)	791	3.28
Hispanic (32)	57	0.24
American Indian/Alaska Native (28)	99	0.41
Not Hispanic (23)	80	0.33
Hispanic (5)	19	0.08
Alaska Athabascan *(Ala. Nat.)* (0)	1	<0.01
Blackfeet (4)	5	0.02
Canadian/French Am. Ind. (0)	4	0.02
Cherokee (0)	10	0.04
Chickasaw (0)	5	0.02
Chippewa (0)	1	<0.01
Hopi (3)	3	0.01
Iroquois (0)	3	0.01
Lumbee (1)	1	<0.01
Mexican American Ind. (1)	6	0.02
South American Ind. (2)	3	0.01
Asian (1,132)	1,253	5.20
Not Hispanic (1,121)	1,236	5.13
Hispanic (11)	17	0.07
Bangladeshi (3)	3	0.01
Bhutanese (1)	3	0.01
Cambodian (32)	37	0.15
Chinese, ex. Taiwanese (356)	387	1.61
Filipino (93)	108	0.45
Indian (239)	266	1.10
Indonesian (0)	3	0.01
Japanese (15)	33	0.14
Korean (120)	148	0.61
Laotian (35)	36	0.15
Pakistani (66)	80	0.33
Sri Lankan (1)	1	<0.01
Taiwanese (19)	21	0.09
Thai (15)	18	0.07
Vietnamese (81)	98	0.41
Hawaii Native/Pacific Islander (7)	21	0.09
Not Hispanic (7)	21	0.09
Guamanian/Chamorro (0)	2	0.01
Native Hawaiian (6)	10	0.04
White (21,663)	21,932	91.03
Not Hispanic (21,056)	21,258	88.23
Hispanic (607)	674	2.80

Norwalk

Place Type: City/Town
County: Fairfield
Population: 85,603†

Ancestry‡	Population	%
African, Sub-Saharan (332)	442	0.52
African (300)	385	0.46
Cape Verdean (32)	45	0.05
South African (0)	12	0.01
Albanian (42)	84	0.10
American (2,392)	2,392	2.83
Arab (145)	221	0.26
Egyptian (29)	45	0.05
Lebanese (61)	108	0.13
Moroccan (15)	15	0.02
Palestinian (8)	8	0.01
Syrian (0)	13	0.02
Other Arab (32)	32	0.04
Armenian (56)	56	0.07
Austrian (56)	436	0.52
Basque (10)	10	0.01
Belgian (35)	245	0.29
Brazilian (198)	216	0.26
British (268)	380	0.45
Bulgarian (13)	13	0.02
Canadian (43)	188	0.22
Celtic (28)	37	0.04
Croatian (75)	141	0.17
Czech (153)	449	0.53
Czechoslovakian (68)	91	0.11
Danish (77)	217	0.26
Dutch (181)	654	0.77
Eastern European (311)	333	0.39
English (2,158)	6,493	7.67
European (570)	590	0.70
Finnish (47)	94	0.11
French, ex. Basque (320)	1,632	1.93
French Canadian (432)	742	0.88
German (1,387)	6,215	7.35
Greek (2,118)	2,483	2.93
Hungarian (872)	1,736	2.05
Iranian (90)	90	0.11
Irish (4,053)	11,681	13.81
Israeli (12)	25	0.03
Italian (8,545)	16,929	20.01
Latvian (59)	80	0.09
Lithuanian (243)	513	0.61
Maltese (29)	64	0.08
New Zealander (39)	39	0.05
Northern European (65)	80	0.09
Norwegian (142)	540	0.64
Pennsylvania German (0)	8	0.01
Polish (1,560)	3,781	4.47
Portuguese (177)	282	0.33
Romanian (93)	168	0.20
Russian (770)	1,439	1.70
Scandinavian (54)	54	0.06
Scotch-Irish (434)	1,139	1.35
Scottish (317)	1,348	1.59
Serbian (0)	10	0.01
Slavic (13)	13	0.02
Slovak (180)	349	0.41
Slovene (67)	87	0.10
Swedish (256)	1,134	1.34
Swiss (50)	289	0.34
Turkish (23)	23	0.03
Ukrainian (84)	292	0.35
Welsh (45)	315	0.37
West Indian, ex. Hispanic (2,613)	2,966	3.51
Bahamian (60)	60	0.07
Barbadian (47)	47	0.06
Belizean (13)	13	0.02
Dutch West Indian (28)	28	0.03
Haitian (1,268)	1,377	1.63
Jamaican (1,071)	1,207	1.43
Trinidadian/Tobagonian (88)	169	0.20
West Indian (38)	65	0.08
Yugoslavian (14)	24	0.03

Hispanic Origin	Population	%
Hispanic or Latino (of any race)	20,770	24.26
Central American, ex. Mexican	5,186	6.06
Costa Rican	1,024	1.20
Guatemalan	1,619	1.89
Honduran	1,506	1.76
Nicaraguan	231	0.27
Panamanian	32	0.04
Salvadoran	754	0.88
Other Central American	20	0.02
Cuban	244	0.29
Dominican Republic	824	0.96
Mexican	3,962	4.63
Puerto Rican	3,190	3.73
South American	5,799	6.77
Argentinean	126	0.15
Bolivian	69	0.08
Chilean	128	0.15
Colombian	3,084	3.60
Ecuadorian	1,027	1.20
Paraguayan	41	0.05
Peruvian	859	1.00
Uruguayan	128	0.15
Venezuelan	319	0.37
Other South American	18	0.02
Other Hispanic or Latino	1,565	1.83

Race*	Population	%
African-American/Black (12,187)	13,208	15.43
Not Hispanic (11,472)	12,188	14.24
Hispanic (715)	1,020	1.19
American Indian/Alaska Native (328)	722	0.84
Not Hispanic (94)	363	0.42
Hispanic (234)	359	0.42
Alaska Athabascan *(Ala. Nat.)* (0)	1	<0.01
Apache (0)	2	<0.01
Arapaho (0)	1	<0.01
Blackfeet (1)	11	0.01
Canadian/French Am. Ind. (0)	1	<0.01
Central American Ind. (5)	17	0.02
Cherokee (5)	67	0.08
Chippewa (0)	1	<0.01
Choctaw (3)	6	0.01
Cree (1)	1	<0.01
Creek (3)	8	0.01
Crow (0)	1	<0.01
Delaware (1)	2	<0.01
Houma (1)	1	<0.01
Iroquois (10)	14	0.02
Lumbee (1)	1	<0.01
Mexican American Ind. (27)	37	0.04
Navajo (1)	5	0.01
Osage (0)	1	<0.01
Ottawa (0)	1	<0.01
Potawatomi (1)	1	<0.01
Pueblo (1)	2	<0.01
Seminole (0)	3	<0.01
Sioux (2)	7	0.01
South American Ind. (10)	28	0.03
Spanish American Ind. (12)	17	0.02
Tlingit-Haida *(Alaska Native)* (2)	2	<0.01
Ute (0)	1	<0.01
Yaqui (0)	1	<0.01
Asian (4,098)	4,608	5.38
Not Hispanic (4,045)	4,488	5.24
Hispanic (53)	120	0.14
Bangladeshi (104)	124	0.14
Burmese (4)	5	0.01
Cambodian (1)	4	<0.01
Chinese, ex. Taiwanese (748)	870	1.02
Filipino (603)	688	0.80
Indian (1,860)	1,983	2.32
Indonesian (22)	33	0.04
Japanese (91)	145	0.17

*Notes: † The Census 2010 population figure is used to calculate the percentages in the Hispanic Origin and Race categories. Ancestry percentages are based on the 2006-2010 American Community Survey population (not shown); ‡ Numbers in parentheses indicate the number of people reporting a single ancestry; * Numbers in parentheses indicate the number of persons reporting this race alone, not in combination with any other race; Please refer to the Explanation of Data for more information.*

Korean (217)	259	0.30
Laotian (8)	11	0.01
Malaysian (7)	11	0.01
Nepalese (26)	27	0.03
Pakistani (133)	148	0.17
Sri Lankan (14)	17	0.02
Taiwanese (27)	31	0.04
Thai (60)	78	0.09
Vietnamese (60)	90	0.11
Hawaii Native/Pacific Islander (55)	145	0.17
Not Hispanic (25)	70	0.08
Hispanic (30)	75	0.09
Guamanian/Chamorro (20)	27	0.03
Native Hawaiian (10)	14	0.02
Samoan (10)	14	0.02
Tongan (0)	2	<0.01
White (58,826)	60,711	70.92
Not Hispanic (47,718)	48,680	56.87
Hispanic (11,108)	12,031	14.05

Norwich

Place Type: City/Town
County: New London
Population: 40,493†

Ancestry‡	Population	%
African, Sub-Saharan (452)	857	2.15
African (89)	186	0.47
Cape Verdean (245)	519	1.30
Ethiopian (12)	26	0.07
Ghanaian (36)	36	0.09
Nigerian (34)	34	0.09
Sudanese (0)	20	0.05
Other Sub-Saharan African (36)	36	0.09
Albanian (10)	10	0.03
American (1,358)	1,358	3.41
Arab (76)	110	0.28
Arab (23)	23	0.06
Lebanese (35)	69	0.17
Syrian (18)	18	0.05
Austrian (0)	120	0.30
Belgian (0)	107	0.27
Brazilian (116)	142	0.36
British (116)	242	0.61
Canadian (50)	102	0.26
Czech (9)	106	0.27
Czechoslovakian (20)	20	0.05
Danish (14)	147	0.37
Dutch (44)	236	0.59
Eastern European (39)	70	0.18
English (1,607)	4,560	11.44
European (328)	347	0.87
Finnish (23)	105	0.26
French, ex. Basque (1,350)	4,350	10.92
French Canadian (970)	1,892	4.75
German (604)	3,405	8.55
Greek (107)	291	0.73
Hungarian (0)	227	0.57
Iranian (0)	10	0.03
Irish (1,753)	6,090	15.28
Italian (1,546)	4,360	10.94
Latvian (0)	12	0.03
Lithuanian (99)	194	0.49
Northern European (62)	62	0.16
Norwegian (38)	174	0.44
Pennsylvania German (0)	47	0.12
Polish (1,581)	4,360	10.94
Portuguese (137)	404	1.01
Romanian (11)	11	0.03
Russian (99)	336	0.84
Scotch-Irish (357)	882	2.21
Scottish (96)	768	1.93
Slavic (0)	8	0.02
Slovak (55)	127	0.32
Swedish (38)	609	1.53
Swiss (0)	18	0.05
Ukrainian (71)	147	0.37
Welsh (0)	67	0.17
West Indian, ex. Hispanic (1,909)	2,123	5.33
British West Indian (16)	16	0.04
Haitian (1,843)	1,976	4.96
Jamaican (0)	72	0.18
Trinidadian/Tobagonian (50)	59	0.15
Yugoslavian (0)	13	0.03

Hispanic Origin	Population	%
Hispanic or Latino (of any race)	5,083	12.55
Central American, ex. Mexican	177	0.44
Costa Rican	16	0.04
Guatemalan	75	0.19
Honduran	21	0.05
Nicaraguan	3	0.01
Panamanian	22	0.05
Salvadoran	40	0.10
Cuban	79	0.20
Dominican Republic	455	1.12
Mexican	568	1.40
Puerto Rican	2,798	6.91
South American	654	1.62
Argentinean	23	0.06
Bolivian	5	0.01
Chilean	2	<0.01
Colombian	71	0.18
Ecuadorian	29	0.07
Paraguayan	2	<0.01
Peruvian	507	1.25
Uruguayan	6	0.01
Venezuelan	6	0.01
Other South American	3	0.01
Other Hispanic or Latino	352	0.87

Race*	Population	%
African-American/Black (4,218)	5,497	13.58
Not Hispanic (3,862)	4,906	12.12
Hispanic (356)	591	1.46
American Indian/Alaska Native (476)	1,133	2.80
Not Hispanic (390)	939	2.32
Hispanic (86)	194	0.48
Alaska Athabascan *(Ala. Nat.)* (1)	1	<0.01
Apache (3)	6	0.01
Blackfeet (6)	21	0.05
Canadian/French Am. Ind. (0)	1	<0.01
Central American Ind. (1)	1	<0.01
Cherokee (17)	100	0.25
Cheyenne (1)	3	0.01
Chickasaw (1)	1	<0.01
Chippewa (1)	7	0.02
Choctaw (3)	8	0.02
Comanche (2)	2	<0.01
Creek (1)	7	0.02
Delaware (2)	2	<0.01
Iroquois (3)	18	0.04
Lumbee (0)	4	0.01
Mexican American Ind. (2)	5	0.01
Navajo (1)	6	0.01
Potawatomi (2)	4	0.01
Pueblo (2)	2	<0.01
Seminole (0)	4	0.01
Sioux (7)	15	0.04
South American Ind. (14)	35	0.09
Spanish American Ind. (4)	4	0.01
Tlingit-Haida *(Alaska Native)* (2)	4	0.01
Yaqui (0)	1	<0.01
Asian (3,113)	3,442	8.50
Not Hispanic (3,087)	3,373	8.33
Hispanic (26)	69	0.17
Bangladeshi (75)	86	0.21
Burmese (3)	3	0.01
Cambodian (42)	47	0.12
Chinese, ex. Taiwanese (1,955)	2,036	5.03
Filipino (200)	306	0.76
Indian (366)	438	1.08
Indonesian (8)	14	0.03
Japanese (16)	50	0.12
Korean (69)	88	0.22
Laotian (54)	70	0.17
Malaysian (4)	7	0.02
Nepalese (4)	4	0.01
Pakistani (49)	58	0.14
Taiwanese (3)	6	0.01
Thai (32)	36	0.09
Vietnamese (142)	169	0.42
Hawaii Native/Pacific Islander (53)	165	0.41
Not Hispanic (48)	141	0.35
Hispanic (5)	24	0.06
Guamanian/Chamorro (11)	24	0.06
Native Hawaiian (5)	16	0.04
Samoan (12)	17	0.04
White (28,155)	29,710	73.37
Not Hispanic (26,179)	27,343	67.53
Hispanic (1,976)	2,367	5.85

Oakville

Place Type: CDP
County: Litchfield
Population: 9,047†

Ancestry‡	Population	%
Albanian (339)	339	3.61
American (195)	195	2.08
Arab (0)	30	0.32
Lebanese (0)	30	0.32
Austrian (0)	15	0.16
Brazilian (30)	41	0.44
British (0)	33	0.35
Bulgarian (25)	25	0.27
Canadian (22)	22	0.23
Czech (0)	50	0.53
Czechoslovakian (8)	17	0.18
Danish (0)	58	0.62
Dutch (11)	11	0.12
English (174)	935	9.97
Finnish (11)	11	0.12
French, ex. Basque (195)	1,249	13.31
French Canadian (120)	357	3.81
German (159)	489	5.21
Greek (42)	42	0.45
Hungarian (14)	39	0.42
Irish (503)	1,687	17.98
Italian (1,644)	2,998	31.96
Lithuanian (139)	305	3.25
Northern European (21)	21	0.22
Pennsylvania German (11)	23	0.25
Polish (180)	803	8.56
Portuguese (124)	169	1.80
Russian (152)	254	2.71
Scotch-Irish (7)	49	0.52
Scottish (20)	179	1.91
Slavic (19)	19	0.20
Slovak (0)	14	0.15
Swedish (32)	89	0.95
Ukrainian (79)	127	1.35
Welsh (0)	21	0.22
West Indian, ex. Hispanic (45)	45	0.48
British West Indian (45)	45	0.48

Hispanic Origin	Population	%
Hispanic or Latino (of any race)	447	4.94
Central American, ex. Mexican	10	0.11
Guatemalan	2	0.02
Honduran	2	0.02
Nicaraguan	1	0.01
Panamanian	1	0.01
Salvadoran	4	0.04
Cuban	10	0.11
Dominican Republic	16	0.18
Mexican	38	0.42
Puerto Rican	296	3.27
South American	51	0.56
Argentinean	11	0.12
Chilean	1	0.01
Colombian	16	0.18
Ecuadorian	14	0.15
Peruvian	2	0.02
Uruguayan	3	0.03
Venezuelan	3	0.03
Other South American	1	0.01
Other Hispanic or Latino	26	0.29

*Notes: † The Census 2010 population figure is used to calculate the percentages in the Hispanic Origin and Race categories. Ancestry percentages are based on the 2006-2010 American Community Survey population (not shown); ‡ Numbers in parentheses indicate the number of people reporting a single ancestry; * Numbers in parentheses indicate the number of persons reporting this race alone, not in combination with any other race; Please refer to the Explanation of Data for more information.*

Race*	Population	%
African-American/Black (169)	228	2.52
Not Hispanic (156)	203	2.24
Hispanic (13)	25	0.28
American Indian/Alaska Native (27)	70	0.77
Not Hispanic (26)	64	0.71
Hispanic (1)	6	0.07
Blackfeet (0)	3	0.03
Canadian/French Am. Ind. (2)	2	0.02
Cherokee (6)	10	0.11
Choctaw (0)	2	0.02
Iroquois (1)	4	0.04
South American Ind. (0)	2	0.02
Asian (161)	195	2.16
Not Hispanic (161)	195	2.16
Bangladeshi (7)	7	0.08
Cambodian (4)	5	0.06
Chinese, ex. Taiwanese (25)	28	0.31
Filipino (52)	64	0.71
Indian (15)	21	0.23
Indonesian (1)	1	0.01
Korean (10)	13	0.14
Pakistani (8)	12	0.13
Vietnamese (34)	39	0.43
Hawaii Native/Pacific Islander (0)	4	0.04
Not Hispanic (0)	4	0.04
Native Hawaiian (0)	2	0.02
White (8,422)	8,539	94.38
Not Hispanic (8,134)	8,236	91.04
Hispanic (288)	303	3.35

Old Lyme

Place Type: Town
County: New London
Population: 7,603†

Ancestry‡	Population	%
African, Sub-Saharan (20)	20	0.26
African (11)	11	0.14
Ghanaian (9)	9	0.12
American (323)	323	4.26
Arab (38)	99	1.30
Lebanese (38)	99	1.30
Armenian (0)	34	0.45
Austrian (0)	17	0.22
Belgian (0)	10	0.13
British (98)	180	2.37
Canadian (83)	146	1.92
Czech (22)	36	0.47
Czechoslovakian (0)	20	0.26
Danish (26)	44	0.58
Dutch (39)	107	1.41
English (467)	1,712	22.56
European (61)	61	0.80
French, ex. Basque (110)	618	8.14
French Canadian (74)	300	3.95
German (311)	1,213	15.98
Greek (60)	111	1.46
Hungarian (9)	89	1.17
Irish (613)	1,836	24.19
Italian (652)	1,352	17.82
Lithuanian (5)	75	0.99
Northern European (9)	9	0.12
Norwegian (19)	79	1.04
Polish (188)	760	10.01
Portuguese (60)	116	1.53
Russian (40)	131	1.73
Scandinavian (12)	62	0.82
Scotch-Irish (72)	185	2.44
Scottish (14)	168	2.21
Swedish (64)	250	3.29
Swiss (24)	85	1.12
Ukrainian (29)	86	1.13
Welsh (18)	35	0.46
West Indian, ex. Hispanic (10)	10	0.13
West Indian (10)	10	0.13

Hispanic Origin	Population	%
Hispanic or Latino (of any race)	184	2.42
Central American, ex. Mexican	6	0.08
Guatemalan	1	0.01
Honduran	1	0.01
Nicaraguan	3	0.04
Salvadoran	1	0.01
Cuban	3	0.04
Dominican Republic	5	0.07
Mexican	31	0.41
Puerto Rican	68	0.89
South American	42	0.55
Argentinean	8	0.11
Colombian	3	0.04
Ecuadorian	27	0.36
Peruvian	2	0.03
Venezuelan	2	0.03
Other Hispanic or Latino	29	0.38

Race*	Population	%
African-American/Black (35)	46	0.61
Not Hispanic (35)	44	0.58
Hispanic (0)	2	0.03
American Indian/Alaska Native (14)	38	0.50
Not Hispanic (9)	27	0.36
Hispanic (5)	11	0.14
Cherokee (1)	3	0.04
Chippewa (2)	4	0.05
Choctaw (2)	2	0.03
Iroquois (0)	1	0.01
Mexican American Ind. (0)	3	0.04
Navajo (0)	3	0.04
Sioux (1)	2	0.03
South American Ind. (2)	2	0.03
Asian (155)	193	2.54
Not Hispanic (154)	192	2.53
Hispanic (1)	1	0.01
Chinese, ex. Taiwanese (71)	84	1.10
Filipino (8)	15	0.20
Indian (23)	33	0.43
Japanese (5)	7	0.09
Korean (17)	20	0.26
Laotian (7)	10	0.13
Pakistani (4)	4	0.05
Sri Lankan (1)	1	0.01
Taiwanese (2)	3	0.04
Thai (3)	5	0.07
Vietnamese (5)	7	0.09
Hawaii Native/Pacific Islander (0)	2	0.03
Not Hispanic (0)	1	0.01
Hispanic (0)	1	0.01
Native Hawaiian (0)	1	0.01
Samoan (0)	1	0.01
White (7,277)	7,355	96.74
Not Hispanic (7,142)	7,204	94.75
Hispanic (135)	151	1.99

Old Saybrook

Place Type: Town
County: Middlesex
Population: 10,242†

Ancestry‡	Population	%
African, Sub-Saharan (42)	42	0.41
African (42)	42	0.41
American (260)	260	2.52
Austrian (9)	32	0.31
British (24)	24	0.23
Canadian (58)	58	0.56
Croatian (0)	11	0.11
Czech (0)	31	0.30
Czechoslovakian (0)	12	0.12
Danish (0)	8	0.08
Dutch (17)	81	0.78
English (564)	1,989	19.26
European (53)	91	0.88
Finnish (0)	17	0.16
French, ex. Basque (217)	632	6.12
French Canadian (162)	363	3.52
German (323)	1,546	14.97
Greek (120)	148	1.43
Hungarian (17)	116	1.12
Icelander (0)	3	0.03
Irish (724)	2,683	25.98
Italian (1,294)	2,676	25.92
Latvian (23)	23	0.22
Lithuanian (72)	117	1.13
Maltese (0)	13	0.13
Northern European (25)	25	0.24
Norwegian (0)	57	0.55
Pennsylvania German (15)	15	0.15
Polish (312)	856	8.29
Portuguese (55)	55	0.53
Romanian (0)	16	0.15
Russian (82)	123	1.19
Scotch-Irish (49)	167	1.62
Scottish (33)	389	3.77
Slovak (9)	25	0.24
Swedish (102)	394	3.82
Swiss (6)	6	0.06
Ukrainian (40)	55	0.53
Welsh (0)	98	0.95

Hispanic Origin	Population	%
Hispanic or Latino (of any race)	342	3.34
Central American, ex. Mexican	55	0.54
Costa Rican	2	0.02
Guatemalan	15	0.15
Honduran	7	0.07
Nicaraguan	2	0.02
Salvadoran	26	0.25
Other Central American	3	0.03
Cuban	12	0.12
Dominican Republic	2	0.02
Mexican	43	0.42
Puerto Rican	53	0.52
South American	128	1.25
Argentinean	8	0.08
Chilean	3	0.03
Colombian	13	0.13
Ecuadorian	100	0.98
Paraguayan	1	0.01
Peruvian	2	0.02
Venezuelan	1	0.01
Other Hispanic or Latino	49	0.48

Race*	Population	%
African-American/Black (97)	136	1.33
Not Hispanic (96)	126	1.23
Hispanic (1)	10	0.10
American Indian/Alaska Native (7)	36	0.35
Not Hispanic (6)	31	0.30
Hispanic (1)	5	0.05
Cherokee (4)	6	0.06
Choctaw (0)	1	0.01
Inupiat *(Alaska Native)* (0)	1	0.01
Iroquois (1)	4	0.04
Asian (243)	299	2.92
Not Hispanic (243)	297	2.90
Hispanic (0)	2	0.02
Bangladeshi (4)	4	0.04
Burmese (2)	2	0.02
Chinese, ex. Taiwanese (115)	135	1.32
Filipino (18)	28	0.27
Indian (18)	31	0.30
Japanese (4)	5	0.05
Korean (28)	31	0.30
Laotian (27)	29	0.28
Nepalese (4)	4	0.04
Thai (9)	11	0.11
Vietnamese (5)	6	0.06
Hawaii Native/Pacific Islander (3)	8	0.08
Not Hispanic (2)	6	0.06
Hispanic (1)	2	0.02
Native Hawaiian (1)	3	0.03
White (9,617)	9,749	95.19
Not Hispanic (9,404)	9,504	92.79
Hispanic (213)	245	2.39

*Notes: † The Census 2010 population figure is used to calculate the percentages in the Hispanic Origin and Race categories. Ancestry percentages are based on the 2006-2010 American Community Survey population (not shown); ‡ Numbers in parentheses indicate the number of people reporting a single ancestry; * Numbers in parentheses indicate the number of persons reporting this race alone, not in combination with any other race; Please refer to the Explanation of Data for more information.*

Orange

Place Type: CDP/Town
County: New Haven
Population: 13,956†

Ancestry‡	Population	%
African, Sub-Saharan (43)	43	0.31
African (14)	14	0.10
Liberian (29)	29	0.21
American (289)	289	2.09
Armenian (31)	74	0.54
Austrian (14)	62	0.45
Belgian (0)	13	0.09
Brazilian (8)	60	0.43
British (0)	7	0.05
Bulgarian (0)	7	0.05
Canadian (9)	16	0.12
Czech (19)	46	0.33
Czechoslovakian (24)	33	0.24
Danish (37)	83	0.60
Dutch (43)	186	1.34
Eastern European (86)	86	0.62
English (381)	1,569	11.34
European (210)	210	1.52
Finnish (0)	13	0.09
French, ex. Basque (98)	413	2.99
French Canadian (101)	221	1.60
German (209)	1,289	9.32
Greek (78)	189	1.37
Hungarian (56)	157	1.14
Iranian (41)	77	0.56
Irish (852)	2,798	20.23
Italian (2,289)	4,137	29.91
Latvian (0)	7	0.05
Lithuanian (43)	126	0.91
Norwegian (29)	79	0.57
Polish (566)	1,477	10.68
Portuguese (65)	159	1.15
Romanian (10)	22	0.16
Russian (223)	569	4.11
Scotch-Irish (79)	238	1.72
Scottish (77)	210	1.52
Slavic (0)	13	0.09
Slovak (69)	102	0.74
Swedish (25)	328	2.37
Turkish (19)	46	0.33
Ukrainian (16)	115	0.83
Welsh (9)	25	0.18
West Indian, ex. Hispanic (179)	218	1.58
Jamaican (179)	218	1.58
Yugoslavian (0)	10	0.07

Hispanic Origin	Population	%
Hispanic or Latino (of any race)	398	2.85
Central American, ex. Mexican	24	0.17
Costa Rican	4	0.03
Guatemalan	12	0.09
Honduran	3	0.02
Salvadoran	5	0.04
Cuban	35	0.25
Dominican Republic	31	0.22
Mexican	34	0.24
Puerto Rican	126	0.90
South American	112	0.80
Argentinean	17	0.12
Chilean	11	0.08
Colombian	49	0.35
Ecuadorian	19	0.14
Peruvian	5	0.04
Uruguayan	2	0.01
Venezuelan	6	0.04
Other South American	3	0.02
Other Hispanic or Latino	36	0.26

Race*	Population	%
African-American/Black (202)	250	1.79
Not Hispanic (198)	245	1.76
Hispanic (4)	5	0.04
American Indian/Alaska Native (17)	47	0.34
Not Hispanic (13)	41	0.29
Hispanic (4)	6	0.04
Apache (2)	2	0.01
Blackfeet (0)	3	0.02
Cherokee (2)	3	0.02
Cree (0)	1	0.01
Iroquois (1)	3	0.02
Potawatomi (2)	2	0.01
Asian (1,047)	1,131	8.10
Not Hispanic (1,045)	1,124	8.05
Hispanic (2)	7	0.05
Bangladeshi (11)	11	0.08
Cambodian (2)	2	0.01
Chinese, ex. Taiwanese (374)	404	2.89
Filipino (48)	61	0.44
Indian (266)	276	1.98
Japanese (15)	26	0.19
Korean (175)	193	1.38
Laotian (9)	9	0.06
Nepalese (3)	3	0.02
Pakistani (72)	77	0.55
Sri Lankan (14)	14	0.10
Taiwanese (28)	32	0.23
Thai (6)	6	0.04
Vietnamese (7)	7	0.05
Hawaii Native/Pacific Islander (0)	10	0.07
Not Hispanic (0)	10	0.07
Native Hawaiian (0)	2	0.01
White (12,418)	12,584	90.17
Not Hispanic (12,120)	12,261	87.85
Hispanic (298)	323	2.31

Oxford

Place Type: Town
County: New Haven
Population: 12,683†

Ancestry‡	Population	%
Albanian (109)	109	0.89
American (562)	562	4.61
Arab (8)	30	0.25
Lebanese (0)	22	0.18
Other Arab (8)	8	0.07
Armenian (0)	40	0.33
Austrian (34)	97	0.80
Belgian (0)	58	0.48
British (8)	41	0.34
Canadian (36)	93	0.76
Celtic (0)	9	0.07
Czech (21)	216	1.77
Czechoslovakian (7)	16	0.13
Danish (0)	27	0.22
Dutch (31)	113	0.93
Eastern European (29)	29	0.24
English (521)	1,523	12.49
European (93)	104	0.85
French, ex. Basque (81)	677	5.55
French Canadian (131)	305	2.50
German (343)	1,916	15.72
Greek (19)	96	0.79
Hungarian (60)	274	2.25
Irish (715)	2,575	21.12
Italian (1,416)	3,292	27.00
Latvian (0)	16	0.13
Lithuanian (123)	312	2.56
Norwegian (30)	92	0.75
Polish (394)	1,335	10.95
Portuguese (156)	288	2.36
Russian (52)	353	2.90
Scandinavian (23)	23	0.19
Scotch-Irish (14)	135	1.11
Scottish (27)	194	1.59
Slovak (97)	241	1.98
Swedish (0)	163	1.34
Swiss (11)	11	0.09
Ukrainian (60)	188	1.54
Welsh (0)	20	0.16
West Indian, ex. Hispanic (61)	61	0.50
Dutch West Indian (11)	11	0.09
Jamaican (50)	50	0.41

Hispanic Origin	Population	%
Hispanic or Latino (of any race)	468	3.69
Central American, ex. Mexican	19	0.15
Costa Rican	14	0.11
Guatemalan	4	0.03
Panamanian	1	0.01
Cuban	32	0.25
Dominican Republic	6	0.05
Mexican	38	0.30
Puerto Rican	221	1.74
South American	95	0.75
Argentinean	12	0.09
Bolivian	4	0.03
Chilean	11	0.09
Colombian	27	0.21
Ecuadorian	23	0.18
Peruvian	11	0.09
Uruguayan	3	0.02
Venezuelan	4	0.03
Other Hispanic or Latino	57	0.45

Race*	Population	%
African-American/Black (145)	193	1.52
Not Hispanic (134)	172	1.36
Hispanic (11)	21	0.17
American Indian/Alaska Native (13)	51	0.40
Not Hispanic (13)	42	0.33
Hispanic (0)	9	0.07
Blackfeet (0)	1	0.01
Cherokee (2)	4	0.03
Chickasaw (2)	2	0.02
Iroquois (1)	6	0.05
Mexican American Ind. (0)	6	0.05
Shoshone (0)	2	0.02
Asian (195)	240	1.89
Not Hispanic (195)	239	1.88
Hispanic (0)	1	0.01
Burmese (0)	2	0.02
Cambodian (3)	3	0.02
Chinese, ex. Taiwanese (54)	57	0.45
Filipino (15)	25	0.20
Indian (41)	53	0.42
Japanese (5)	8	0.06
Korean (37)	43	0.34
Laotian (4)	6	0.05
Pakistani (13)	13	0.10
Sri Lankan (6)	8	0.06
Taiwanese (1)	1	0.01
Thai (5)	7	0.06
Vietnamese (8)	10	0.08
Hawaii Native/Pacific Islander (3)	13	0.10
Not Hispanic (3)	9	0.07
Hispanic (0)	4	0.03
Guamanian/Chamorro (0)	4	0.03
Native Hawaiian (3)	7	0.06
Samoan (0)	1	0.01
White (12,106)	12,235	96.47
Not Hispanic (11,745)	11,844	93.38
Hispanic (361)	391	3.08

Plainfield

Place Type: Town
County: Windham
Population: 15,405†

Ancestry‡	Population	%
Albanian (44)	44	0.29
American (517)	517	3.36
Arab (34)	80	0.52
Arab (0)	13	0.08
Egyptian (10)	10	0.07
Lebanese (15)	15	0.10
Syrian (0)	33	0.21
Other Arab (9)	9	0.06
Armenian (11)	11	0.07
Austrian (0)	16	0.10
Belgian (0)	19	0.12

*Notes: † The Census 2010 population figure is used to calculate the percentages in the Hispanic Origin and Race categories. Ancestry percentages are based on the 2006-2010 American Community Survey population (not shown); ‡ Numbers in parentheses indicate the number of people reporting a single ancestry; * Numbers in parentheses indicate the number of persons reporting this race alone, not in combination with any other race; Please refer to the Explanation of Data for more information.*

Brazilian (14)	27	0.18
British (35)	56	0.36
Canadian (81)	179	1.16
Czech (32)	96	0.62
Danish (11)	26	0.17
Dutch (23)	60	0.39
English (394)	1,909	12.41
Estonian (16)	16	0.10
European (23)	36	0.23
Finnish (77)	255	1.66
French, ex. Basque (1,467)	4,019	26.12
French Canadian (1,564)	2,392	15.55
German (305)	2,002	13.01
Greek (78)	133	0.86
Hungarian (0)	42	0.27
Irish (493)	3,111	20.22
Italian (336)	1,805	11.73
Lithuanian (22)	158	1.03
Northern European (31)	31	0.20
Norwegian (11)	63	0.41
Polish (348)	1,236	8.03
Portuguese (45)	240	1.56
Russian (18)	128	0.83
Scandinavian (0)	10	0.07
Scotch-Irish (128)	244	1.59
Scottish (40)	163	1.06
Slovak (0)	13	0.08
Slovene (17)	17	0.11
Swedish (0)	137	0.89
Swiss (9)	25	0.16
Ukrainian (7)	7	0.05
Welsh (40)	135	0.88
Yugoslavian (0)	13	0.08

Hispanic Origin	Population	%
Hispanic or Latino (of any race)	651	4.23
Central American, ex. Mexican	38	0.25
Costa Rican	3	0.02
Guatemalan	16	0.10
Honduran	7	0.05
Nicaraguan	1	0.01
Salvadoran	11	0.07
Cuban	23	0.15
Dominican Republic	30	0.19
Mexican	105	0.68
Puerto Rican	367	2.38
South American	41	0.27
Argentinean	4	0.03
Chilean	1	0.01
Colombian	16	0.10
Ecuadorian	13	0.08
Peruvian	6	0.04
Venezuelan	1	0.01
Other Hispanic or Latino	47	0.31

Race*	Population	%
African-American/Black (177)	326	2.12
Not Hispanic (160)	286	1.86
Hispanic (17)	40	0.26
American Indian/Alaska Native (88)	251	1.63
Not Hispanic (85)	229	1.49
Hispanic (3)	22	0.14
Blackfeet (0)	4	0.03
Canadian/French Am. Ind. (1)	3	0.02
Central American Ind. (2)	2	0.01
Cherokee (0)	12	0.08
Chippewa (0)	2	0.01
Choctaw (3)	6	0.04
Creek (1)	1	0.01
Inupiat *(Alaska Native)* (0)	1	0.01
Iroquois (3)	8	0.05
Lumbee (1)	1	0.01
Potawatomi (1)	1	0.01
Sioux (1)	4	0.03
South American Ind. (0)	4	0.03
Yaqui (1)	1	0.01
Asian (159)	230	1.49
Not Hispanic (157)	218	1.42
Hispanic (2)	12	0.08
Cambodian (2)	3	0.02
Chinese, ex. Taiwanese (15)	28	0.18
Filipino (37)	69	0.45
Indian (33)	34	0.22
Indonesian (1)	2	0.01
Japanese (1)	7	0.05
Korean (8)	14	0.09
Laotian (13)	20	0.13
Nepalese (1)	3	0.02
Pakistani (29)	30	0.19
Thai (1)	1	0.01
Vietnamese (11)	14	0.09
Hawaii Native/Pacific Islander (12)	34	0.22
Not Hispanic (12)	29	0.19
Hispanic (0)	5	0.03
Guamanian/Chamorro (7)	14	0.09
Native Hawaiian (0)	8	0.05
White (14,416)	14,774	95.90
Not Hispanic (13,989)	14,290	92.76
Hispanic (427)	484	3.14

Plainville

Place Type: Town
County: Hartford
Population: 17,716†

Ancestry‡	Population	%
African, Sub-Saharan (9)	23	0.13
African (9)	23	0.13
American (684)	684	3.88
Arab (73)	169	0.96
Lebanese (55)	151	0.86
Other Arab (18)	18	0.10
Armenian (20)	46	0.26
Australian (37)	37	0.21
Austrian (15)	43	0.24
Brazilian (15)	15	0.09
British (0)	19	0.11
Cajun (14)	14	0.08
Canadian (170)	254	1.44
Czech (0)	32	0.18
Danish (0)	53	0.30
Dutch (25)	46	0.26
English (356)	1,598	9.07
European (8)	8	0.05
Finnish (24)	24	0.14
French, ex. Basque (791)	2,719	15.43
French Canadian (680)	977	5.54
German (284)	1,777	10.08
Greek (108)	134	0.76
Hungarian (14)	93	0.53
Irish (791)	2,827	16.04
Italian (2,068)	4,547	25.80
Lithuanian (36)	129	0.73
Norwegian (10)	31	0.18
Pennsylvania German (12)	12	0.07
Polish (1,524)	3,325	18.87
Portuguese (61)	142	0.81
Russian (45)	117	0.66
Scandinavian (14)	14	0.08
Scotch-Irish (43)	210	1.19
Scottish (120)	315	1.79
Slovak (22)	59	0.33
Slovene (0)	10	0.06
Swedish (41)	467	2.65
Swiss (0)	95	0.54
Turkish (53)	53	0.30
Ukrainian (108)	201	1.14
Welsh (7)	38	0.22
West Indian, ex. Hispanic (19)	34	0.19
Jamaican (19)	34	0.19
Yugoslavian (53)	67	0.38

Hispanic Origin	Population	%
Hispanic or Latino (of any race)	1,095	6.18
Central American, ex. Mexican	34	0.19
Guatemalan	15	0.08
Honduran	1	0.01
Nicaraguan	2	0.01
Panamanian	10	0.06
Salvadoran	6	0.03
Cuban	27	0.15
Dominican Republic	24	0.14
Mexican	215	1.21
Puerto Rican	566	3.19
South American	95	0.54
Argentinean	16	0.09
Bolivian	1	0.01
Chilean	3	0.02
Colombian	37	0.21
Ecuadorian	5	0.03
Peruvian	27	0.15
Venezuelan	6	0.03
Other Hispanic or Latino	134	0.76

Race*	Population	%
African-American/Black (533)	670	3.78
Not Hispanic (506)	625	3.53
Hispanic (27)	45	0.25
American Indian/Alaska Native (24)	96	0.54
Not Hispanic (21)	88	0.50
Hispanic (3)	8	0.05
Blackfeet (0)	4	0.02
Canadian/French Am. Ind. (2)	2	0.01
Cherokee (1)	3	0.02
Chippewa (0)	5	0.03
Choctaw (0)	1	0.01
Iroquois (0)	8	0.05
Mexican American Ind. (0)	1	0.01
South American Ind. (0)	2	0.01
Asian (382)	436	2.46
Not Hispanic (380)	427	2.41
Hispanic (2)	9	0.05
Cambodian (13)	16	0.09
Chinese, ex. Taiwanese (65)	72	0.41
Filipino (46)	59	0.33
Indian (86)	88	0.50
Indonesian (4)	4	0.02
Japanese (4)	16	0.09
Korean (21)	29	0.16
Laotian (57)	59	0.33
Malaysian (2)	2	0.01
Pakistani (20)	24	0.14
Taiwanese (2)	2	0.01
Thai (10)	10	0.06
Vietnamese (34)	39	0.22
Hawaii Native/Pacific Islander (6)	12	0.07
Not Hispanic (6)	8	0.05
Hispanic (0)	4	0.02
Guamanian/Chamorro (1)	2	0.01
Samoan (2)	2	0.01
White (16,094)	16,383	92.48
Not Hispanic (15,472)	15,681	88.51
Hispanic (622)	702	3.96

Plymouth

Place Type: Town
County: Litchfield
Population: 12,243†

Ancestry‡	Population	%
Albanian (11)	26	0.21
American (517)	517	4.23
Arab (29)	107	0.88
Egyptian (0)	24	0.20
Lebanese (29)	71	0.58
Other Arab (0)	12	0.10
Australian (0)	10	0.08
Austrian (20)	29	0.24
British (45)	45	0.37
Cajun (0)	19	0.16
Canadian (52)	73	0.60
Czech (10)	64	0.52
Danish (13)	105	0.86
Dutch (0)	150	1.23
Eastern European (11)	21	0.17
English (320)	1,175	9.62
Estonian (11)	11	0.09
European (43)	61	0.50

*Notes: † The Census 2010 population figure is used to calculate the percentages in the Hispanic Origin and Race categories. Ancestry percentages are based on the 2006-2010 American Community Survey population (not shown); ‡ Numbers in parentheses indicate the number of people reporting a single ancestry; * Numbers in parentheses indicate the number of persons reporting this race alone, not in combination with any other race; Please refer to the Explanation of Data for more information.*

Ancestry	Population	%
French, ex. Basque (634)	1,861	15.24
French Canadian (285)	724	5.93
German (378)	1,772	14.51
Greek (29)	65	0.53
Hungarian (21)	127	1.04
Iranian (10)	10	0.08
Irish (724)	2,876	23.55
Italian (693)	2,474	20.26
Lithuanian (58)	272	2.23
Northern European (23)	23	0.19
Norwegian (22)	72	0.59
Pennsylvania German (0)	25	0.20
Polish (748)	1,949	15.96
Portuguese (11)	84	0.69
Russian (44)	189	1.55
Scandinavian (0)	113	0.93
Scotch-Irish (107)	182	1.49
Scottish (34)	219	1.79
Slovak (15)	15	0.12
Swedish (30)	303	2.48
Swiss (0)	10	0.08
Ukrainian (84)	153	1.25
Welsh (9)	39	0.32

Hispanic Origin	Population	%
Hispanic or Latino (of any race)	370	3.02
Central American, ex. Mexican	7	0.06
Guatemalan	4	0.03
Honduran	1	0.01
Nicaraguan	2	0.02
Cuban	8	0.07
Dominican Republic	21	0.17
Mexican	32	0.26
Puerto Rican	205	1.67
South American	48	0.39
Argentinean	6	0.05
Colombian	17	0.14
Ecuadorian	6	0.05
Paraguayan	2	0.02
Peruvian	11	0.09
Uruguayan	1	0.01
Venezuelan	5	0.04
Other Hispanic or Latino	49	0.40

Race*	Population	%
African-American/Black (102)	183	1.49
Not Hispanic (94)	162	1.32
Hispanic (8)	21	0.17
American Indian/Alaska Native (22)	107	0.87
Not Hispanic (14)	92	0.75
Hispanic (8)	15	0.12
Alaska Athabascan *(Ala. Nat.)* (1)	4	0.03
Blackfeet (0)	8	0.07
Canadian/French Am. Ind. (0)	1	0.01
Cherokee (1)	11	0.09
Iroquois (1)	2	0.02
Sioux (0)	3	0.02
Asian (100)	129	1.05
Not Hispanic (98)	124	1.01
Hispanic (2)	5	0.04
Cambodian (1)	3	0.02
Chinese, ex. Taiwanese (19)	26	0.21
Filipino (12)	18	0.15
Indian (21)	29	0.24
Indonesian (1)	1	0.01
Japanese (11)	12	0.10
Korean (5)	10	0.08
Laotian (4)	6	0.05
Malaysian (3)	3	0.02
Pakistani (3)	3	0.02
Thai (1)	2	0.02
Vietnamese (7)	14	0.11
Hawaii Native/Pacific Islander (2)	6	0.05
Not Hispanic (2)	4	0.03
Hispanic (0)	2	0.02
Samoan (2)	3	0.02
White (11,748)	11,932	97.46
Not Hispanic (11,494)	11,654	95.19
Hispanic (254)	278	2.27

Portland

Place Type: Town
County: Middlesex
Population: 9,508†

Ancestry‡	Population	%
African, Sub-Saharan (0)	12	0.13
Cape Verdean (0)	12	0.13
American (218)	218	2.31
Arab (0)	26	0.28
Lebanese (0)	26	0.28
Armenian (132)	148	1.57
Belgian (0)	43	0.46
British (21)	43	0.46
Cajun (8)	8	0.08
Canadian (30)	70	0.74
Czech (8)	22	0.23
Czechoslovakian (0)	11	0.12
Danish (9)	25	0.27
Dutch (21)	98	1.04
Eastern European (17)	17	0.18
English (323)	1,234	13.10
European (96)	96	1.02
French, ex. Basque (49)	729	7.74
French Canadian (277)	563	5.98
German (228)	1,287	13.66
Greek (9)	40	0.42
Hungarian (24)	154	1.63
Irish (381)	2,297	24.38
Italian (851)	2,479	26.31
Lithuanian (18)	83	0.88
Norwegian (9)	9	0.10
Pennsylvania German (11)	11	0.12
Polish (427)	1,556	16.51
Portuguese (14)	76	0.81
Russian (39)	96	1.02
Scotch-Irish (26)	160	1.70
Scottish (66)	199	2.11
Slavic (0)	9	0.10
Slovak (12)	28	0.30
Swedish (121)	538	5.71
Swiss (0)	6	0.06
Ukrainian (10)	171	1.81
Welsh (9)	109	1.16
West Indian, ex. Hispanic (36)	99	1.05
Haitian (19)	39	0.41
Jamaican (17)	60	0.64

Hispanic Origin	Population	%
Hispanic or Latino (of any race)	310	3.26
Central American, ex. Mexican	18	0.19
Guatemalan	2	0.02
Honduran	1	0.01
Panamanian	10	0.11
Salvadoran	5	0.05
Cuban	14	0.15
Dominican Republic	10	0.11
Mexican	36	0.38
Puerto Rican	144	1.51
South American	42	0.44
Argentinean	5	0.05
Chilean	2	0.02
Colombian	12	0.13
Ecuadorian	3	0.03
Peruvian	16	0.17
Other South American	4	0.04
Other Hispanic or Latino	46	0.48

Race*	Population	%
African-American/Black (207)	288	3.03
Not Hispanic (195)	267	2.81
Hispanic (12)	21	0.22
American Indian/Alaska Native (7)	57	0.60
Not Hispanic (6)	46	0.48
Hispanic (1)	11	0.12
Blackfeet (0)	3	0.03
Central American Ind. (1)	1	0.01
Cherokee (1)	4	0.04
Chickasaw (0)	1	0.01
Iroquois (0)	4	0.04
Navajo (0)	1	0.01
Seminole (0)	1	0.01
Sioux (0)	1	0.01
South American Ind. (0)	3	0.03
Yaqui (0)	3	0.03
Asian (92)	125	1.31
Not Hispanic (92)	124	1.30
Hispanic (0)	1	0.01
Cambodian (1)	4	0.04
Chinese, ex. Taiwanese (30)	32	0.34
Filipino (12)	20	0.21
Indian (11)	16	0.17
Japanese (4)	12	0.13
Korean (9)	17	0.18
Laotian (2)	2	0.02
Pakistani (8)	8	0.08
Taiwanese (3)	3	0.03
Thai (3)	6	0.06
Vietnamese (5)	6	0.06
Hawaii Native/Pacific Islander (1)	10	0.11
Not Hispanic (1)	10	0.11
Native Hawaiian (1)	10	0.11
White (8,957)	9,106	95.77
Not Hispanic (8,757)	8,883	93.43
Hispanic (200)	223	2.35

Prospect

Place Type: Town
County: New Haven
Population: 9,405†

Ancestry‡	Population	%
Albanian (162)	238	2.56
American (341)	341	3.67
Arab (8)	36	0.39
Lebanese (8)	36	0.39
British (11)	32	0.34
Canadian (19)	27	0.29
Croatian (8)	8	0.09
Czech (0)	7	0.08
Danish (12)	23	0.25
Dutch (0)	26	0.28
English (86)	910	9.80
French, ex. Basque (186)	841	9.06
French Canadian (192)	416	4.48
German (200)	1,241	13.37
Greek (53)	81	0.87
Hungarian (12)	121	1.30
Irish (507)	2,158	23.25
Italian (1,412)	2,853	30.74
Latvian (0)	10	0.11
Lithuanian (125)	258	2.78
Norwegian (0)	32	0.34
Polish (369)	1,325	14.27
Portuguese (189)	220	2.37
Romanian (95)	95	1.02
Russian (136)	469	5.05
Scotch-Irish (10)	46	0.50
Scottish (16)	80	0.86
Slovak (34)	62	0.67
Swedish (0)	60	0.65
Swiss (0)	13	0.14
Turkish (12)	12	0.13
Ukrainian (20)	29	0.31
Welsh (0)	11	0.12
Yugoslavian (0)	14	0.15

Hispanic Origin	Population	%
Hispanic or Latino (of any race)	312	3.32
Central American, ex. Mexican	5	0.05
Costa Rican	1	0.01
Guatemalan	3	0.03
Nicaraguan	1	0.01
Cuban	16	0.17
Dominican Republic	11	0.12
Mexican	33	0.35
Puerto Rican	184	1.96
South American	36	0.38

SECTION TWO

*Notes: † The Census 2010 population figure is used to calculate the percentages in the Hispanic Origin and Race categories. Ancestry percentages are based on the 2006-2010 American Community Survey population (not shown); ‡ Numbers in parentheses indicate the number of people reporting a single ancestry; * Numbers in parentheses indicate the number of persons reporting this race alone, not in combination with any other race; Please refer to the Explanation of Data for more information.*

Argentinean	2	0.02
Chilean	5	0.05
Colombian	21	0.22
Ecuadorian	4	0.04
Venezuelan	4	0.04
Other Hispanic or Latino	27	0.29

Race*	Population	%
African-American/Black (177)	213	2.26
Not Hispanic (175)	209	2.22
Hispanic (2)	4	0.04
American Indian/Alaska Native (12)	56	0.60
Not Hispanic (11)	45	0.48
Hispanic (1)	11	0.12
Canadian/French Am. Ind. (1)	2	0.02
Cherokee (0)	5	0.05
Choctaw (0)	1	0.01
Hopi (1)	1	0.01
Iroquois (2)	4	0.04
Mexican American Ind. (0)	4	0.04
South American Ind. (0)	3	0.03
Asian (73)	85	0.90
Not Hispanic (73)	83	0.88
Hispanic (0)	2	0.02
Chinese, ex. Taiwanese (11)	11	0.12
Filipino (6)	8	0.09
Indian (31)	34	0.36
Japanese (0)	1	0.01
Korean (17)	20	0.21
Pakistani (1)	1	0.01
Taiwanese (2)	2	0.02
Thai (5)	5	0.05
Hawaii Native/Pacific Islander (0)	8	0.09
Not Hispanic (0)	5	0.05
Hispanic (0)	3	0.03
White (8,964)	9,060	96.33
Not Hispanic (8,740)	8,818	93.76
Hispanic (224)	242	2.57

Putnam

Place Type: Town
County: Windham
Population: 9,584†

Ancestry‡	Population	%
African, Sub-Saharan (14)	14	0.15
Cape Verdean (14)	14	0.15
Albanian (0)	10	0.10
American (226)	226	2.36
Arab (0)	17	0.18
Lebanese (0)	17	0.18
Armenian (0)	70	0.73
Austrian (0)	11	0.12
Brazilian (86)	86	0.90
British (11)	19	0.20
Canadian (254)	263	2.75
Danish (17)	17	0.18
Dutch (69)	137	1.43
English (274)	1,585	16.57
European (11)	11	0.12
Finnish (10)	62	0.65
French, ex. Basque (411)	1,860	19.45
French Canadian (878)	1,599	16.72
German (103)	1,030	10.77
Greek (52)	71	0.74
Hungarian (11)	84	0.88
Irish (596)	2,004	20.95
Italian (263)	1,043	10.91
Lithuanian (16)	24	0.25
Norwegian (17)	17	0.18
Polish (287)	849	8.88
Portuguese (18)	114	1.19
Russian (0)	38	0.40
Scotch-Irish (8)	152	1.59
Scottish (10)	168	1.76
Slovene (15)	15	0.16
Swedish (14)	250	2.61
Ukrainian (0)	18	0.19
Welsh (0)	20	0.21
West Indian, ex. Hispanic (0)	17	0.18
Jamaican (0)	17	0.18
Yugoslavian (19)	74	0.77

Hispanic Origin	Population	%
Hispanic or Latino (of any race)	282	2.94
Central American, ex. Mexican	5	0.05
Guatemalan	3	0.03
Honduran	1	0.01
Salvadoran	1	0.01
Cuban	4	0.04
Dominican Republic	25	0.26
Mexican	61	0.64
Puerto Rican	135	1.41
South American	22	0.23
Chilean	1	0.01
Colombian	12	0.13
Ecuadorian	3	0.03
Paraguayan	2	0.02
Peruvian	2	0.02
Uruguayan	1	0.01
Venezuelan	1	0.01
Other Hispanic or Latino	30	0.31

Race*	Population	%
African-American/Black (126)	219	2.29
Not Hispanic (115)	193	2.01
Hispanic (11)	26	0.27
American Indian/Alaska Native (60)	147	1.53
Not Hispanic (59)	141	1.47
Hispanic (1)	6	0.06
Apache (0)	5	0.05
Blackfeet (2)	5	0.05
Cherokee (0)	9	0.09
Delaware (0)	1	0.01
Iroquois (1)	2	0.02
Navajo (1)	1	0.01
Sioux (0)	3	0.03
Asian (97)	115	1.20
Not Hispanic (94)	112	1.17
Hispanic (3)	3	0.03
Chinese, ex. Taiwanese (21)	23	0.24
Filipino (13)	18	0.19
Indian (16)	18	0.19
Japanese (1)	2	0.02
Korean (5)	5	0.05
Laotian (22)	23	0.24
Nepalese (1)	1	0.01
Pakistani (2)	2	0.02
Sri Lankan (1)	1	0.01
Thai (2)	5	0.05
Vietnamese (4)	5	0.05
Hawaii Native/Pacific Islander (3)	21	0.22
Not Hispanic (3)	20	0.21
Hispanic (0)	1	0.01
Guamanian/Chamorro (0)	1	0.01
Native Hawaiian (1)	10	0.10
Samoan (2)	2	0.02
White (9,018)	9,222	96.22
Not Hispanic (8,833)	9,001	93.92
Hispanic (185)	221	2.31

Redding

Place Type: Town
County: Fairfield
Population: 9,158†

Ancestry‡	Population	%
American (412)	412	4.61
Arab (95)	163	1.82
Lebanese (74)	108	1.21
Syrian (0)	34	0.38
Other Arab (21)	21	0.23
Australian (0)	64	0.72
Austrian (7)	124	1.39
Belgian (0)	8	0.09
Brazilian (89)	162	1.81
British (80)	91	1.02
Canadian (23)	23	0.26
Czech (44)	65	0.73
Czechoslovakian (11)	18	0.20
Danish (0)	29	0.32
Dutch (51)	108	1.21
Eastern European (34)	34	0.38
English (344)	1,464	16.37
European (87)	116	1.30
Finnish (0)	53	0.59
French, ex. Basque (21)	412	4.61
French Canadian (49)	71	0.79
German (493)	1,739	19.44
Greek (101)	214	2.39
Hungarian (49)	187	2.09
Irish (576)	1,743	19.49
Italian (464)	1,199	13.40
Latvian (6)	6	0.07
Lithuanian (39)	78	0.87
Northern European (8)	8	0.09
Norwegian (41)	175	1.96
Pennsylvania German (8)	8	0.09
Polish (237)	703	7.86
Portuguese (28)	59	0.66
Romanian (106)	115	1.29
Russian (165)	377	4.21
Scandinavian (34)	70	0.78
Scotch-Irish (30)	119	1.33
Scottish (140)	407	4.55
Swedish (81)	221	2.47
Swiss (10)	86	0.96
Ukrainian (8)	47	0.53
Welsh (0)	105	1.17
West Indian, ex. Hispanic (9)	28	0.31
Bahamian (0)	19	0.21
Jamaican (9)	9	0.10

Hispanic Origin	Population	%
Hispanic or Latino (of any race)	237	2.59
Central American, ex. Mexican	19	0.21
Costa Rican	9	0.10
Guatemalan	6	0.07
Honduran	2	0.02
Salvadoran	2	0.02
Cuban	20	0.22
Dominican Republic	12	0.13
Mexican	30	0.33
Puerto Rican	50	0.55
South American	73	0.80
Argentinean	3	0.03
Bolivian	12	0.13
Chilean	4	0.04
Colombian	21	0.23
Ecuadorian	3	0.03
Paraguayan	1	0.01
Peruvian	15	0.16
Uruguayan	9	0.10
Venezuelan	5	0.05
Other Hispanic or Latino	33	0.36

Race*	Population	%
African-American/Black (63)	103	1.12
Not Hispanic (60)	97	1.06
Hispanic (3)	6	0.07
American Indian/Alaska Native (13)	37	0.40
Not Hispanic (8)	32	0.35
Hispanic (5)	5	0.05
Apache (0)	4	0.04
Blackfeet (0)	1	0.01
Cherokee (0)	2	0.02
Cheyenne (0)	1	0.01
Choctaw (3)	4	0.04
Cree (0)	1	0.01
Mexican American Ind. (1)	1	0.01
Paiute (1)	1	0.01
Pueblo (0)	1	0.01
South American Ind. (1)	1	0.01
Yuman (3)	3	0.03
Asian (200)	285	3.11
Not Hispanic (195)	277	3.02
Hispanic (5)	8	0.09
Burmese (3)	3	0.03

*Notes: † The Census 2010 population figure is used to calculate the percentages in the Hispanic Origin and Race categories. Ancestry percentages are based on the 2006-2010 American Community Survey population (not shown); ‡ Numbers in parentheses indicate the number of people reporting a single ancestry; * Numbers in parentheses indicate the number of persons reporting this race alone, not in combination with any other race; Please refer to the Explanation of Data for more information.*

Cambodian (0)	4	0.04
Chinese, ex. Taiwanese (69)	90	0.98
Filipino (9)	36	0.39
Indian (54)	58	0.63
Indonesian (2)	4	0.04
Japanese (16)	38	0.41
Korean (23)	33	0.36
Nepalese (1)	1	0.01
Pakistani (6)	6	0.07
Taiwanese (2)	2	0.02
Thai (3)	9	0.10
Vietnamese (1)	4	0.04
Hawaii Native/Pacific Islander (6)	14	0.15
Not Hispanic (5)	13	0.14
Hispanic (1)	1	0.01
Guamanian/Chamorro (1)	1	0.01
Native Hawaiian (1)	3	0.03
White (8,693)	8,833	96.45
Not Hispanic (8,500)	8,632	94.26
Hispanic (193)	201	2.19

Ridgefield

Place Type: CDP
County: Fairfield
Population: 7,645†

Ancestry‡	Population	%
African, Sub-Saharan (9)	9	0.12
Nigerian (9)	9	0.12
American (220)	220	2.85
Arab (0)	114	1.48
Arab (0)	68	0.88
Lebanese (0)	23	0.30
Syrian (0)	23	0.30
Armenian (14)	93	1.20
Australian (13)	19	0.25
Austrian (7)	125	1.62
Brazilian (19)	19	0.25
British (40)	54	0.70
Canadian (13)	13	0.17
Czech (15)	56	0.73
Danish (0)	47	0.61
Dutch (24)	149	1.93
Eastern European (18)	18	0.23
English (295)	953	12.34
European (90)	90	1.17
Finnish (0)	9	0.12
French, ex. Basque (48)	234	3.03
French Canadian (0)	84	1.09
German (209)	1,238	16.03
Greek (18)	73	0.95
Hungarian (30)	132	1.71
Irish (851)	2,317	30.01
Italian (621)	1,856	24.04
Lithuanian (0)	29	0.38
Maltese (14)	14	0.18
Northern European (22)	22	0.28
Norwegian (22)	108	1.40
Polish (88)	441	5.71
Portuguese (0)	52	0.67
Romanian (0)	61	0.79
Russian (27)	374	4.84
Scotch-Irish (72)	166	2.15
Scottish (15)	196	2.54
Serbian (13)	13	0.17
Slovak (12)	85	1.10
Swedish (34)	45	0.58
Swiss (0)	39	0.51
Turkish (0)	18	0.23
Ukrainian (0)	47	0.61
Welsh (0)	14	0.18

Hispanic Origin	Population	%
Hispanic or Latino (of any race)	320	4.19
Central American, ex. Mexican	18	0.24
Costa Rican	4	0.05
Guatemalan	7	0.09
Salvadoran	7	0.09
Cuban	25	0.33
Dominican Republic	15	0.20
Mexican	71	0.93
Puerto Rican	62	0.81
South American	80	1.05
Argentinean	12	0.16
Chilean	4	0.05
Colombian	30	0.39
Ecuadorian	13	0.17
Paraguayan	6	0.08
Peruvian	8	0.10
Uruguayan	1	0.01
Venezuelan	3	0.04
Other South American	3	0.04
Other Hispanic or Latino	49	0.64

Race*	Population	%
African-American/Black (79)	98	1.28
Not Hispanic (75)	91	1.19
Hispanic (4)	7	0.09
American Indian/Alaska Native (4)	22	0.29
Not Hispanic (4)	19	0.25
Hispanic (0)	3	0.04
Canadian/French Am. Ind. (0)	1	0.01
Cherokee (0)	1	0.01
Navajo (0)	1	0.01
Yaqui (0)	1	0.01
Asian (228)	294	3.85
Not Hispanic (228)	289	3.78
Hispanic (0)	5	0.07
Bangladeshi (5)	5	0.07
Chinese, ex. Taiwanese (77)	98	1.28
Filipino (16)	27	0.35
Indian (49)	58	0.76
Indonesian (1)	1	0.01
Japanese (8)	19	0.25
Korean (48)	57	0.75
Nepalese (4)	4	0.05
Pakistani (2)	2	0.03
Sri Lankan (6)	8	0.10
Thai (1)	3	0.04
Vietnamese (3)	9	0.12
Hawaii Native/Pacific Islander (2)	7	0.09
Not Hispanic (2)	7	0.09
Guamanian/Chamorro (0)	1	0.01
Native Hawaiian (1)	1	0.01
Samoan (0)	1	0.01
White (7,153)	7,256	94.91
Not Hispanic (6,915)	6,994	91.48
Hispanic (238)	262	3.43

Ridgefield

Place Type: Town
County: Fairfield
Population: 24,638†

Ancestry‡	Population	%
African, Sub-Saharan (49)	69	0.28
Nigerian (9)	9	0.04
South African (40)	60	0.25
Albanian (0)	46	0.19
American (975)	975	4.01
Arab (83)	206	0.85
Arab (0)	68	0.28
Lebanese (49)	72	0.30
Palestinian (34)	34	0.14
Syrian (0)	23	0.09
Other Arab (0)	9	0.04
Armenian (22)	148	0.61
Australian (19)	25	0.10
Austrian (34)	310	1.28
Basque (11)	11	0.05
Belgian (0)	12	0.05
Brazilian (19)	19	0.08
British (221)	312	1.28
Canadian (115)	144	0.59
Croatian (29)	142	0.58
Czech (49)	217	0.89
Czechoslovakian (11)	11	0.05
Danish (19)	140	0.58
Dutch (59)	306	1.26
Eastern European (82)	98	0.40
English (931)	3,559	14.65
Estonian (0)	29	0.12
European (337)	361	1.49
Finnish (11)	31	0.13
French, ex. Basque (95)	848	3.49
French Canadian (71)	332	1.37
German (904)	4,123	16.97
Greek (76)	158	0.65
Guyanese (14)	65	0.27
Hungarian (78)	506	2.08
Iranian (14)	14	0.06
Irish (1,800)	6,340	26.09
Israeli (0)	46	0.19
Italian (2,268)	5,710	23.50
Latvian (9)	29	0.12
Lithuanian (33)	78	0.32
Maltese (30)	58	0.24
Northern European (37)	37	0.15
Norwegian (106)	409	1.68
Polish (563)	1,617	6.65
Portuguese (0)	113	0.47
Romanian (17)	86	0.35
Russian (264)	983	4.05
Scotch-Irish (125)	505	2.08
Scottish (189)	789	3.25
Serbian (13)	13	0.05
Slavic (0)	30	0.12
Slovak (12)	138	0.57
Slovene (10)	10	0.04
Swedish (74)	314	1.29
Swiss (45)	145	0.60
Turkish (0)	34	0.14
Ukrainian (52)	156	0.64
Welsh (0)	122	0.50
West Indian, ex. Hispanic (45)	45	0.19
Barbadian (15)	15	0.06
Jamaican (30)	30	0.12
Yugoslavian (0)	8	0.03

Hispanic Origin	Population	%
Hispanic or Latino (of any race)	941	3.82
Central American, ex. Mexican	56	0.23
Costa Rican	13	0.05
Guatemalan	29	0.12
Honduran	2	0.01
Nicaraguan	3	0.01
Panamanian	1	<0.01
Salvadoran	8	0.03
Cuban	91	0.37
Dominican Republic	40	0.16
Mexican	145	0.59
Puerto Rican	198	0.80
South American	286	1.16
Argentinean	30	0.12
Bolivian	6	0.02
Chilean	26	0.11
Colombian	106	0.43
Ecuadorian	55	0.22
Paraguayan	13	0.05
Peruvian	35	0.14
Uruguayan	5	0.02
Venezuelan	7	0.03
Other South American	3	0.01
Other Hispanic or Latino	125	0.51

Race*	Population	%
African-American/Black (179)	229	0.93
Not Hispanic (174)	214	0.87
Hispanic (5)	15	0.06
American Indian/Alaska Native (23)	76	0.31
Not Hispanic (19)	54	0.22
Hispanic (4)	22	0.09
Arapaho (0)	3	0.01
Canadian/French Am. Ind. (0)	1	<0.01
Cherokee (0)	3	0.01
Cheyenne (0)	1	<0.01
Chickasaw (0)	1	<0.01
Choctaw (3)	5	0.02

SECTION TWO

*Notes: † The Census 2010 population figure is used to calculate the percentages in the Hispanic Origin and Race categories. Ancestry percentages are based on the 2006-2010 American Community Survey population (not shown); ‡ Numbers in parentheses indicate the number of people reporting a single ancestry; * Numbers in parentheses indicate the number of persons reporting this race alone, not in combination with any other race; Please refer to the Explanation of Data for more information.*

Iroquois (3)	3	0.01
Mexican American Ind. (1)	4	0.02
Navajo (0)	1	<0.01
South American Ind. (1)	5	0.02
Ute (0)	1	<0.01
Yaqui (0)	1	<0.01
Asian (788)	1,003	4.07
Not Hispanic (780)	985	4.00
Hispanic (8)	18	0.07
Bangladeshi (5)	5	0.02
Cambodian (2)	2	0.01
Chinese, ex. Taiwanese (279)	350	1.42
Filipino (50)	94	0.38
Indian (239)	270	1.10
Indonesian (1)	4	0.02
Japanese (35)	65	0.26
Korean (112)	125	0.51
Nepalese (4)	4	0.02
Pakistani (7)	7	0.03
Sri Lankan (12)	17	0.07
Taiwanese (2)	6	0.02
Thai (4)	8	0.03
Vietnamese (16)	28	0.11
Hawaii Native/Pacific Islander (12)	26	0.11
Not Hispanic (12)	26	0.11
Guamanian/Chamorro (0)	3	0.01
Native Hawaiian (2)	3	0.01
Samoan (2)	3	0.01
White (23,147)	23,473	95.27
Not Hispanic (22,404)	22,660	91.97
Hispanic (743)	813	3.30

Riverside

Place Type: CDP
County: Fairfield
Population: 8,416†

Ancestry‡	Population	%
American (253)	253	3.01
Arab (23)	23	0.27
Arab (5)	5	0.06
Lebanese (18)	18	0.21
Armenian (25)	25	0.30
Australian (29)	87	1.03
Austrian (17)	28	0.33
Belgian (7)	28	0.33
Brazilian (0)	16	0.19
British (50)	84	1.00
Canadian (52)	71	0.84
Celtic (0)	10	0.12
Czech (8)	8	0.10
Czechoslovakian (0)	11	0.13
Danish (33)	52	0.62
Dutch (49)	145	1.72
Eastern European (24)	24	0.29
English (459)	1,348	16.02
European (57)	76	0.90
Finnish (57)	57	0.68
French, ex. Basque (21)	164	1.95
French Canadian (116)	240	2.85
German (246)	1,195	14.20
Greek (190)	369	4.39
Hungarian (8)	54	0.64
Irish (737)	1,714	20.37
Italian (936)	1,890	22.47
Latvian (0)	18	0.21
Lithuanian (27)	86	1.02
Maltese (0)	14	0.17
Norwegian (11)	81	0.96
Polish (104)	318	3.78
Portuguese (12)	12	0.14
Romanian (0)	11	0.13
Russian (58)	202	2.40
Scotch-Irish (81)	102	1.21
Scottish (107)	396	4.71
Slovak (12)	24	0.29
Slovene (9)	9	0.11
Swedish (17)	167	1.99
Swiss (79)	108	1.28
Ukrainian (0)	10	0.12
Welsh (0)	66	0.78

Hispanic Origin	Population	%
Hispanic or Latino (of any race)	667	7.93
Central American, ex. Mexican	27	0.32
Guatemalan	14	0.17
Honduran	1	0.01
Nicaraguan	2	0.02
Salvadoran	10	0.12
Cuban	26	0.31
Dominican Republic	19	0.23
Mexican	90	1.07
Puerto Rican	79	0.94
South American	344	4.09
Argentinean	164	1.95
Chilean	35	0.42
Colombian	68	0.81
Ecuadorian	28	0.33
Paraguayan	4	0.05
Peruvian	29	0.34
Uruguayan	5	0.06
Venezuelan	8	0.10
Other South American	3	0.04
Other Hispanic or Latino	82	0.97

Race*	Population	%
African-American/Black (121)	142	1.69
Not Hispanic (109)	123	1.46
Hispanic (12)	19	0.23
American Indian/Alaska Native (8)	25	0.30
Not Hispanic (4)	15	0.18
Hispanic (4)	10	0.12
Apache (1)	1	0.01
Canadian/French Am. Ind. (0)	1	0.01
Cherokee (1)	4	0.05
Delaware (0)	3	0.04
South American Ind. (4)	7	0.08
Asian (639)	722	8.58
Not Hispanic (637)	720	8.56
Hispanic (2)	2	0.02
Bangladeshi (1)	3	0.04
Chinese, ex. Taiwanese (217)	247	2.93
Filipino (40)	50	0.59
Indian (69)	85	1.01
Indonesian (1)	1	0.01
Japanese (222)	233	2.77
Korean (57)	68	0.81
Pakistani (3)	5	0.06
Taiwanese (4)	4	0.05
Thai (2)	2	0.02
Vietnamese (10)	17	0.20
Hawaii Native/Pacific Islander (3)	5	0.06
Not Hispanic (1)	2	0.02
Hispanic (2)	3	0.04
Guamanian/Chamorro (2)	2	0.02
White (7,392)	7,512	89.26
Not Hispanic (6,866)	6,970	82.82
Hispanic (526)	542	6.44

Rocky Hill

Place Type: Town
County: Hartford
Population: 19,709†

Ancestry‡	Population	%
Afghan (54)	54	0.28
African, Sub-Saharan (139)	153	0.79
African (104)	118	0.61
Nigerian (35)	35	0.18
American (316)	316	1.63
Arab (23)	23	0.12
Lebanese (23)	23	0.12
Armenian (24)	132	0.68
Assyrian/Chaldean/Syriac (4)	12	0.06
Austrian (0)	73	0.38
British (20)	34	0.18
Canadian (0)	82	0.42
Czech (0)	101	0.52
Czechoslovakian (16)	16	0.08
Danish (69)	102	0.53
Dutch (24)	146	0.75
English (520)	1,672	8.61
Estonian (13)	13	0.07
European (265)	286	1.47
Finnish (24)	24	0.12
French, ex. Basque (115)	1,141	5.88
French Canadian (343)	586	3.02
German (210)	1,272	6.55
Greek (146)	274	1.41
Guyanese (74)	74	0.38
Hungarian (21)	65	0.33
Irish (658)	2,807	14.46
Italian (3,096)	5,382	27.72
Lithuanian (59)	336	1.73
Norwegian (0)	57	0.29
Polish (1,060)	2,173	11.19
Portuguese (138)	279	1.44
Romanian (11)	11	0.06
Russian (103)	232	1.19
Scotch-Irish (45)	141	0.73
Scottish (85)	292	1.50
Slovak (11)	45	0.23
Swedish (66)	346	1.78
Swiss (22)	33	0.17
Turkish (0)	12	0.06
Ukrainian (137)	174	0.90
Welsh (0)	50	0.26
West Indian, ex. Hispanic (177)	261	1.34
British West Indian (0)	9	0.05
Haitian (101)	112	0.58
Jamaican (0)	55	0.28
West Indian (76)	85	0.44
Yugoslavian (85)	85	0.44

Hispanic Origin	Population	%
Hispanic or Latino (of any race)	1,061	5.38
Central American, ex. Mexican	43	0.22
Guatemalan	7	0.04
Honduran	14	0.07
Nicaraguan	3	0.02
Panamanian	5	0.03
Salvadoran	14	0.07
Cuban	75	0.38
Dominican Republic	47	0.24
Mexican	56	0.28
Puerto Rican	533	2.70
South American	230	1.17
Argentinean	18	0.09
Chilean	5	0.03
Colombian	61	0.31
Ecuadorian	24	0.12
Paraguayan	6	0.03
Peruvian	91	0.46
Uruguayan	13	0.07
Venezuelan	11	0.06
Other South American	1	0.01
Other Hispanic or Latino	77	0.39

Race*	Population	%
African-American/Black (740)	854	4.33
Not Hispanic (715)	793	4.02
Hispanic (25)	61	0.31
American Indian/Alaska Native (43)	111	0.56
Not Hispanic (29)	84	0.43
Hispanic (14)	27	0.14
Blackfeet (0)	1	0.01
Cherokee (4)	15	0.08
Chickasaw (1)	1	0.01
Chippewa (1)	2	0.01
Choctaw (0)	1	0.01
Houma (0)	1	0.01
Iroquois (1)	2	0.01
Kiowa (1)	1	0.01
Mexican American Ind. (2)	3	0.02
Seminole (0)	2	0.01
Sioux (3)	4	0.02
South American Ind. (2)	9	0.05
Spanish American Ind. (1)	1	0.01

*Notes: † The Census 2010 population figure is used to calculate the percentages in the Hispanic Origin and Race categories. Ancestry percentages are based on the 2006-2010 American Community Survey population (not shown); ‡ Numbers in parentheses indicate the number of people reporting a single ancestry; * Numbers in parentheses indicate the number of persons reporting this race alone, not in combination with any other race; Please refer to the Explanation of Data for more information.*

Asian (1,943)	2,068	10.49
Not Hispanic (1,936)	2,051	10.41
Hispanic (7)	17	0.09
Bangladeshi (9)	9	0.05
Cambodian (9)	9	0.05
Chinese, ex. Taiwanese (123)	144	0.73
Filipino (70)	82	0.42
Indian (1,493)	1,558	7.91
Indonesian (2)	3	0.02
Japanese (4)	12	0.06
Korean (48)	55	0.28
Laotian (10)	16	0.08
Nepalese (1)	1	0.01
Pakistani (72)	102	0.52
Sri Lankan (7)	8	0.04
Taiwanese (8)	8	0.04
Thai (2)	4	0.02
Vietnamese (36)	47	0.24
Hawaii Native/Pacific Islander (1)	11	0.06
Not Hispanic (1)	8	0.04
Hispanic (0)	3	0.02
Guamanian/Chamorro (0)	1	0.01
Native Hawaiian (0)	5	0.03
White (16,380)	16,640	84.43
Not Hispanic (15,719)	15,903	80.69
Hispanic (661)	737	3.74

Seymour

Place Type: Town
County: New Haven
Population: 16,540†

Ancestry‡	Population	%
African, Sub-Saharan (45)	45	0.27
Cape Verdean (45)	45	0.27
American (97)	97	0.59
Austrian (39)	163	1.00
Brazilian (10)	10	0.06
British (18)	42	0.26
Canadian (14)	53	0.32
Czech (166)	240	1.47
Czechoslovakian (17)	50	0.31
Danish (20)	58	0.35
Dutch (51)	177	1.08
Eastern European (19)	19	0.12
English (470)	1,623	9.92
European (48)	48	0.29
Finnish (0)	27	0.16
French, ex. Basque (240)	873	5.33
French Canadian (133)	401	2.45
German (217)	1,784	10.90
Greek (281)	376	2.30
Hungarian (107)	396	2.42
Iranian (0)	13	0.08
Irish (735)	3,222	19.69
Israeli (0)	22	0.13
Italian (1,799)	4,857	29.68
Lithuanian (63)	250	1.53
Norwegian (17)	125	0.76
Polish (1,341)	3,003	18.35
Portuguese (331)	415	2.54
Russian (54)	708	4.33
Scotch-Irish (60)	147	0.90
Scottish (76)	284	1.74
Slovak (43)	251	1.53
Slovene (0)	13	0.08
Swedish (10)	206	1.26
Swiss (0)	19	0.12
Turkish (7)	21	0.13
Ukrainian (133)	389	2.38
Welsh (9)	20	0.12
West Indian, ex. Hispanic (23)	99	0.60
Jamaican (23)	99	0.60

Hispanic Origin	Population	%
Hispanic or Latino (of any race)	1,064	6.43
Central American, ex. Mexican	52	0.31
Costa Rican	10	0.06
Guatemalan	29	0.18
Honduran	1	0.01
Panamanian	4	0.02
Salvadoran	8	0.05
Cuban	43	0.26
Dominican Republic	24	0.15
Mexican	58	0.35
Puerto Rican	611	3.69
South American	195	1.18
Argentinean	3	0.02
Chilean	42	0.25
Colombian	44	0.27
Ecuadorian	90	0.54
Peruvian	6	0.04
Uruguayan	3	0.02
Other South American	7	0.04
Other Hispanic or Latino	81	0.49

Race*	Population	%
African-American/Black (427)	522	3.16
Not Hispanic (395)	467	2.82
Hispanic (32)	55	0.33
American Indian/Alaska Native (26)	110	0.67
Not Hispanic (18)	80	0.48
Hispanic (8)	30	0.18
Blackfeet (3)	19	0.11
Canadian/French Am. Ind. (0)	2	0.01
Cherokee (0)	10	0.06
Chippewa (1)	2	0.01
Choctaw (0)	1	0.01
Comanche (1)	1	0.01
Creek (0)	3	0.02
Iroquois (2)	10	0.06
Mexican American Ind. (1)	1	0.01
Seminole (0)	3	0.02
Sioux (0)	1	0.01
South American Ind. (2)	9	0.05
Asian (365)	430	2.60
Not Hispanic (359)	417	2.52
Hispanic (6)	13	0.08
Bangladeshi (16)	17	0.10
Cambodian (2)	2	0.01
Chinese, ex. Taiwanese (53)	72	0.44
Filipino (44)	57	0.34
Indian (168)	179	1.08
Indonesian (1)	3	0.02
Japanese (3)	7	0.04
Korean (33)	39	0.24
Laotian (10)	14	0.08
Malaysian (0)	4	0.02
Nepalese (2)	2	0.01
Pakistani (14)	16	0.10
Thai (0)	1	0.01
Vietnamese (4)	6	0.04
Hawaii Native/Pacific Islander (1)	11	0.07
Not Hispanic (0)	7	0.04
Hispanic (1)	4	0.02
Guamanian/Chamorro (1)	2	0.01
White (15,287)	15,487	93.63
Not Hispanic (14,516)	14,669	88.69
Hispanic (771)	818	4.95

Shelton

Place Type: City/Town
County: Fairfield
Population: 39,559†

Ancestry‡	Population	%
African, Sub-Saharan (119)	153	0.39
Cape Verdean (22)	50	0.13
Ghanaian (52)	52	0.13
Liberian (45)	45	0.12
Other Sub-Saharan African (0)	6	0.02
Albanian (125)	177	0.45
Alsatian (0)	27	0.07
American (825)	825	2.11
Arab (54)	146	0.37
Lebanese (0)	69	0.18
Palestinian (8)	8	0.02
Syrian (16)	39	0.10
Other Arab (30)	30	0.08
Armenian (79)	104	0.27
Australian (0)	18	0.05
Austrian (95)	264	0.68
Belgian (18)	40	0.10
Brazilian (124)	228	0.58
British (92)	194	0.50
Cajun (7)	7	0.02
Canadian (25)	70	0.18
Celtic (0)	9	0.02
Croatian (17)	30	0.08
Czech (149)	508	1.30
Czechoslovakian (116)	158	0.40
Danish (29)	220	0.56
Dutch (129)	464	1.19
Eastern European (9)	20	0.05
English (759)	3,814	9.76
European (168)	168	0.43
Finnish (0)	15	0.04
French, ex. Basque (173)	1,543	3.95
French Canadian (234)	938	2.40
German (840)	4,320	11.06
Greek (193)	220	0.56
Hungarian (430)	1,299	3.33
Icelander (44)	44	0.11
Irish (1,641)	6,926	17.73
Italian (5,452)	10,482	26.83
Lithuanian (132)	396	1.01
Macedonian (0)	38	0.10
Maltese (0)	12	0.03
Norwegian (23)	53	0.14
Polish (1,803)	4,375	11.20
Portuguese (1,330)	1,827	4.68
Romanian (26)	71	0.18
Russian (584)	1,440	3.69
Scandinavian (27)	37	0.09
Scotch-Irish (77)	387	0.99
Scottish (171)	711	1.82
Serbian (0)	14	0.04
Slavic (20)	20	0.05
Slovak (567)	1,351	3.46
Slovene (0)	28	0.07
Swedish (178)	673	1.72
Swiss (0)	38	0.10
Turkish (93)	107	0.27
Ukrainian (245)	454	1.16
Welsh (20)	61	0.16
West Indian, ex. Hispanic (510)	529	1.35
Haitian (73)	73	0.19
Jamaican (437)	456	1.17
Yugoslavian (22)	54	0.14

Hispanic Origin	Population	%
Hispanic or Latino (of any race)	2,353	5.95
Central American, ex. Mexican	121	0.31
Costa Rican	23	0.06
Guatemalan	42	0.11
Honduran	21	0.05
Nicaraguan	3	0.01
Panamanian	5	0.01
Salvadoran	24	0.06
Other Central American	3	0.01
Cuban	107	0.27
Dominican Republic	73	0.18
Mexican	171	0.43
Puerto Rican	1,166	2.95
South American	469	1.19
Argentinean	22	0.06
Bolivian	3	0.01
Chilean	15	0.04
Colombian	109	0.28
Ecuadorian	211	0.53
Paraguayan	1	<0.01
Peruvian	82	0.21
Uruguayan	9	0.02
Venezuelan	16	0.04
Other South American	1	<0.01
Other Hispanic or Latino	246	0.62

*Notes: † The Census 2010 population figure is used to calculate the percentages in the Hispanic Origin and Race categories. Ancestry percentages are based on the 2006-2010 American Community Survey population (not shown); ‡ Numbers in parentheses indicate the number of people reporting a single ancestry; * Numbers in parentheses indicate the number of persons reporting this race alone, not in combination with any other race; Please refer to the Explanation of Data for more information.*

Race*	Population	%
African-American/Black (935)	1,148	2.90
Not Hispanic (865)	1,016	2.57
Hispanic (70)	132	0.33
American Indian/Alaska Native (57)	167	0.42
Not Hispanic (45)	140	0.35
Hispanic (12)	27	0.07
Blackfeet (0)	3	0.01
Cherokee (0)	10	0.03
Chippewa (2)	4	0.01
Choctaw (0)	2	0.01
Colville (2)	2	0.01
Creek (0)	3	0.01
Iroquois (2)	9	0.02
Lumbee (3)	4	0.01
Mexican American Ind. (2)	2	0.01
Seminole (1)	1	<0.01
Sioux (0)	1	<0.01
South American Ind. (0)	6	0.02
Spanish American Ind. (1)	1	<0.01
Asian (1,529)	1,654	4.18
Not Hispanic (1,522)	1,632	4.13
Hispanic (7)	22	0.06
Bangladeshi (11)	11	0.03
Burmese (1)	2	0.01
Cambodian (21)	25	0.06
Chinese, ex. Taiwanese (267)	298	0.75
Filipino (194)	209	0.53
Indian (587)	620	1.57
Indonesian (4)	8	0.02
Japanese (9)	24	0.06
Korean (146)	158	0.40
Laotian (45)	60	0.15
Nepalese (6)	6	0.02
Pakistani (49)	53	0.13
Sri Lankan (17)	17	0.04
Taiwanese (12)	17	0.04
Thai (10)	11	0.03
Vietnamese (103)	113	0.29
Hawaii Native/Pacific Islander (3)	29	0.07
Not Hispanic (0)	18	0.05
Hispanic (3)	11	0.03
Guamanian/Chamorro (3)	9	0.02
Native Hawaiian (0)	3	0.01
Samoan (0)	1	<0.01
White (35,904)	36,390	91.99
Not Hispanic (34,333)	34,656	87.61
Hispanic (1,571)	1,734	4.38

Simsbury

Place Type: Town
County: Hartford
Population: 23,511†

Ancestry‡	Population	%
African, Sub-Saharan (55)	63	0.27
African (25)	33	0.14
Ugandan (30)	30	0.13
Albanian (44)	44	0.19
American (860)	860	3.66
Arab (32)	51	0.22
Lebanese (8)	16	0.07
Syrian (0)	11	0.05
Other Arab (24)	24	0.10
Armenian (33)	133	0.57
Australian (22)	34	0.14
Austrian (0)	106	0.45
Belgian (0)	90	0.38
Brazilian (11)	54	0.23
British (107)	167	0.71
Cajun (12)	12	0.05
Canadian (98)	218	0.93
Czech (7)	151	0.64
Czechoslovakian (8)	43	0.18
Danish (38)	287	1.22
Dutch (88)	308	1.31
Eastern European (132)	137	0.58
English (918)	4,076	17.36
Estonian (9)	18	0.08
European (408)	428	1.82
Finnish (0)	17	0.07
French, ex. Basque (270)	1,168	4.98
French Canadian (375)	740	3.15
German (598)	3,476	14.81
Greek (36)	174	0.74
Hungarian (56)	319	1.36
Iranian (42)	42	0.18
Irish (1,736)	6,030	25.68
Israeli (9)	15	0.06
Italian (1,272)	3,726	15.87
Latvian (21)	21	0.09
Lithuanian (55)	292	1.24
Northern European (24)	24	0.10
Norwegian (44)	175	0.75
Polish (695)	2,331	9.93
Portuguese (125)	225	0.96
Romanian (13)	29	0.12
Russian (282)	939	4.00
Scandinavian (39)	71	0.30
Scotch-Irish (77)	477	2.03
Scottish (166)	964	4.11
Serbian (8)	8	0.03
Slavic (9)	9	0.04
Slovak (16)	65	0.28
Swedish (248)	759	3.23
Swiss (0)	112	0.48
Ukrainian (152)	216	0.92
Welsh (22)	123	0.52
West Indian, ex. Hispanic (41)	88	0.37
Haitian (0)	8	0.03
Jamaican (41)	80	0.34
Yugoslavian (0)	10	0.04

Hispanic Origin	Population	%
Hispanic or Latino (of any race)	737	3.13
Central American, ex. Mexican	51	0.22
Costa Rican	4	0.02
Guatemalan	28	0.12
Honduran	8	0.03
Nicaraguan	5	0.02
Panamanian	3	0.01
Salvadoran	3	0.01
Cuban	73	0.31
Dominican Republic	29	0.12
Mexican	113	0.48
Puerto Rican	216	0.92
South American	165	0.70
Argentinean	23	0.10
Bolivian	6	0.03
Chilean	18	0.08
Colombian	44	0.19
Ecuadorian	11	0.05
Paraguayan	1	<0.01
Peruvian	46	0.20
Venezuelan	9	0.04
Other South American	7	0.03
Other Hispanic or Latino	90	0.38

Race*	Population	%
African-American/Black (405)	515	2.19
Not Hispanic (369)	456	1.94
Hispanic (36)	59	0.25
American Indian/Alaska Native (21)	99	0.42
Not Hispanic (15)	85	0.36
Hispanic (6)	14	0.06
Apache (0)	2	0.01
Blackfeet (0)	2	0.01
Canadian/French Am. Ind. (1)	1	<0.01
Cherokee (1)	12	0.05
Cheyenne (1)	1	<0.01
Chippewa (1)	2	0.01
Choctaw (0)	4	0.02
Comanche (1)	1	<0.01
Creek (0)	1	<0.01
Iroquois (0)	1	<0.01
Mexican American Ind. (1)	1	<0.01
Sioux (1)	4	0.02
South American Ind. (1)	4	0.02
Asian (889)	1,094	4.65
Not Hispanic (888)	1,082	4.60
Hispanic (1)	12	0.05
Burmese (3)	3	0.01
Cambodian (2)	2	0.01
Chinese, ex. Taiwanese (233)	285	1.21
Filipino (50)	93	0.40
Hmong (4)	5	0.02
Indian (269)	301	1.28
Indonesian (3)	4	0.02
Japanese (32)	60	0.26
Korean (183)	207	0.88
Laotian (4)	4	0.02
Pakistani (16)	19	0.08
Sri Lankan (4)	5	0.02
Taiwanese (14)	18	0.08
Thai (13)	18	0.08
Vietnamese (31)	38	0.16
Hawaii Native/Pacific Islander (4)	13	0.06
Not Hispanic (4)	13	0.06
Guamanian/Chamorro (3)	5	0.02
Native Hawaiian (1)	6	0.03
White (21,642)	22,025	93.68
Not Hispanic (21,118)	21,437	91.18
Hispanic (524)	588	2.50

Somers

Place Type: Town
County: Tolland
Population: 11,444†

Ancestry‡	Population	%
African, Sub-Saharan (43)	67	0.59
African (43)	59	0.52
Cape Verdean (0)	8	0.07
American (312)	312	2.74
Arab (0)	8	0.07
Lebanese (0)	8	0.07
Armenian (0)	8	0.07
Austrian (0)	12	0.11
Canadian (160)	188	1.65
Croatian (5)	5	0.04
Czech (19)	48	0.42
Czechoslovakian (15)	15	0.13
Danish (9)	40	0.35
Dutch (5)	81	0.71
Eastern European (31)	31	0.27
English (529)	2,115	18.59
European (41)	41	0.36
French, ex. Basque (496)	1,629	14.32
French Canadian (312)	525	4.61
German (223)	1,115	9.80
Greek (0)	56	0.49
Guyanese (0)	4	0.04
Hungarian (0)	32	0.28
Icelander (9)	9	0.08
Iranian (13)	36	0.32
Irish (663)	2,896	25.45
Italian (534)	1,949	17.13
Lithuanian (71)	141	1.24
Northern European (0)	8	0.07
Norwegian (11)	41	0.36
Polish (531)	1,184	10.41
Portuguese (97)	299	2.63
Russian (8)	44	0.39
Scandinavian (8)	8	0.07
Scotch-Irish (85)	171	1.50
Scottish (80)	328	2.88
Slavic (0)	15	0.13
Slovak (9)	9	0.08
Swedish (13)	113	0.99
Welsh (0)	37	0.33
West Indian, ex. Hispanic (60)	93	0.82
Haitian (12)	12	0.11
Jamaican (31)	39	0.34
West Indian (17)	42	0.37

Hispanic Origin	Population	%
Hispanic or Latino (of any race)	850	7.43

*Notes: † The Census 2010 population figure is used to calculate the percentages in the Hispanic Origin and Race categories. Ancestry percentages are based on the 2006-2010 American Community Survey population (not shown); ‡ Numbers in parentheses indicate the number of people reporting a single ancestry; * Numbers in parentheses indicate the number of persons reporting this race alone, not in combination with any other race; Please refer to the Explanation of Data for more information.*

Central American, ex. Mexican	22	0.19
Costa Rican	1	0.01
Guatemalan	10	0.09
Panamanian	5	0.04
Salvadoran	6	0.05
Cuban	6	0.05
Dominican Republic	10	0.09
Mexican	34	0.30
Puerto Rican	82	0.72
South American	39	0.34
Argentinean	5	0.04
Chilean	3	0.03
Colombian	10	0.09
Ecuadorian	7	0.06
Paraguayan	1	0.01
Peruvian	13	0.11
Other Hispanic or Latino	657	5.74

Race*	Population	%
African-American/Black (994)	1,021	8.92
Not Hispanic (973)	990	8.65
Hispanic (21)	31	0.27
American Indian/Alaska Native (17)	47	0.41
Not Hispanic (14)	42	0.37
Hispanic (3)	5	0.04
Blackfeet (0)	1	0.01
Canadian/French Am. Ind. (0)	5	0.04
Cherokee (0)	1	0.01
Comanche (0)	1	0.01
Lumbee (1)	3	0.03
Sioux (2)	3	0.03
South American Ind. (1)	1	0.01
Asian (90)	142	1.24
Not Hispanic (90)	140	1.22
Hispanic (0)	2	0.02
Chinese, ex. Taiwanese (21)	38	0.33
Filipino (6)	20	0.17
Indian (31)	39	0.34
Indonesian (0)	3	0.03
Japanese (1)	4	0.03
Korean (7)	9	0.08
Laotian (1)	3	0.03
Pakistani (1)	1	0.01
Taiwanese (3)	6	0.05
Vietnamese (9)	11	0.10
Hawaii Native/Pacific Islander (3)	8	0.07
Not Hispanic (3)	8	0.07
Guamanian/Chamorro (1)	2	0.02
Native Hawaiian (0)	1	0.01
Samoan (0)	1	0.01
White (9,565)	9,669	84.49
Not Hispanic (9,410)	9,500	83.01
Hispanic (155)	169	1.48

South Windsor

Place Type: Town
County: Hartford
Population: 25,709†

Ancestry‡	Population	%
African, Sub-Saharan (228)	228	0.89
African (125)	125	0.49
Ghanaian (11)	11	0.04
Nigerian (69)	69	0.27
Other Sub-Saharan African (23)	23	0.09
American (662)	662	2.60
Arab (36)	93	0.37
Arab (0)	23	0.09
Syrian (36)	70	0.27
Australian (0)	17	0.07
Austrian (46)	277	1.09
Belgian (0)	13	0.05
Brazilian (11)	28	0.11
British (0)	20	0.08
Canadian (123)	319	1.25
Croatian (0)	19	0.07
Czech (17)	70	0.27
Czechoslovakian (0)	14	0.05
Danish (37)	159	0.62
Dutch (31)	231	0.91
Eastern European (98)	98	0.38
English (596)	3,086	12.11
Estonian (13)	13	0.05
European (98)	98	0.38
Finnish (28)	298	1.17
French, ex. Basque (527)	2,356	9.25
French Canadian (620)	1,555	6.10
German (439)	2,837	11.14
Greek (203)	318	1.25
Hungarian (94)	361	1.42
Iranian (58)	58	0.23
Irish (1,010)	4,896	19.22
Italian (1,745)	5,167	20.28
Latvian (135)	135	0.53
Lithuanian (110)	363	1.42
Norwegian (0)	231	0.91
Polish (1,160)	2,918	11.45
Portuguese (228)	543	2.13
Russian (148)	469	1.84
Scandinavian (38)	112	0.44
Scotch-Irish (129)	482	1.89
Scottish (108)	695	2.73
Serbian (0)	27	0.11
Slavic (11)	11	0.04
Slovak (33)	153	0.60
Swedish (135)	598	2.35
Swiss (9)	75	0.29
Turkish (63)	63	0.25
Ukrainian (109)	278	1.09
Welsh (0)	77	0.30
West Indian, ex. Hispanic (170)	326	1.28
British West Indian (14)	29	0.11
Jamaican (156)	263	1.03
West Indian (0)	34	0.13

Hispanic Origin	Population	%
Hispanic or Latino (of any race)	1,100	4.28
Central American, ex. Mexican	60	0.23
Costa Rican	6	0.02
Guatemalan	6	0.02
Honduran	3	0.01
Nicaraguan	7	0.03
Panamanian	7	0.03
Salvadoran	31	0.12
Cuban	34	0.13
Dominican Republic	31	0.12
Mexican	108	0.42
Puerto Rican	543	2.11
South American	246	0.96
Argentinean	22	0.09
Chilean	12	0.05
Colombian	73	0.28
Ecuadorian	10	0.04
Peruvian	112	0.44
Uruguayan	4	0.02
Venezuelan	12	0.05
Other South American	1	<0.01
Other Hispanic or Latino	78	0.30

Race*	Population	%
African-American/Black (987)	1,191	4.63
Not Hispanic (941)	1,113	4.33
Hispanic (46)	78	0.30
American Indian/Alaska Native (46)	126	0.49
Not Hispanic (33)	101	0.39
Hispanic (13)	25	0.10
Blackfeet (0)	3	0.01
Canadian/French Am. Ind. (0)	1	<0.01
Cherokee (4)	18	0.07
Chippewa (0)	1	<0.01
Iroquois (0)	4	0.02
Mexican American Ind. (1)	1	<0.01
Pima (1)	1	<0.01
Seminole (0)	1	<0.01
Shoshone (1)	1	<0.01
South American Ind. (8)	10	0.04
Yaqui (0)	1	<0.01
Asian (2,082)	2,307	8.97
Not Hispanic (2,075)	2,272	8.84
Hispanic (7)	35	0.14
Bangladeshi (25)	32	0.12
Bhutanese (1)	3	0.01
Cambodian (7)	7	0.03
Chinese, ex. Taiwanese (302)	337	1.31
Filipino (95)	156	0.61
Indian (928)	978	3.80
Indonesian (0)	3	0.01
Japanese (9)	26	0.10
Korean (186)	199	0.77
Laotian (22)	25	0.10
Malaysian (1)	2	0.01
Nepalese (3)	3	0.01
Pakistani (227)	239	0.93
Sri Lankan (8)	8	0.03
Taiwanese (12)	12	0.05
Thai (10)	11	0.04
Vietnamese (188)	207	0.81
Hawaii Native/Pacific Islander (13)	27	0.11
Not Hispanic (13)	27	0.11
Guamanian/Chamorro (7)	10	0.04
Native Hawaiian (3)	3	0.01
Samoan (0)	1	<0.01
White (21,745)	22,152	86.16
Not Hispanic (21,114)	21,438	83.39
Hispanic (631)	714	2.78

Southbury

Place Type: Town
County: New Haven
Population: 19,904†

Ancestry‡	Population	%
African, Sub-Saharan (110)	123	0.62
African (110)	110	0.56
South African (0)	13	0.07
Albanian (0)	28	0.14
American (601)	601	3.05
Arab (5)	60	0.30
Lebanese (5)	33	0.17
Syrian (0)	27	0.14
Austrian (22)	147	0.75
Belgian (18)	47	0.24
Brazilian (36)	36	0.18
British (107)	121	0.61
Canadian (160)	301	1.53
Celtic (6)	6	0.03
Czech (14)	199	1.01
Czechoslovakian (0)	34	0.17
Danish (13)	117	0.59
Dutch (64)	410	2.08
Eastern European (264)	264	1.34
English (589)	2,573	13.07
European (108)	127	0.64
Finnish (0)	7	0.04
French, ex. Basque (71)	740	3.76
French Canadian (116)	394	2.00
German (920)	3,417	17.35
Greek (259)	304	1.54
Hungarian (168)	312	1.58
Iranian (116)	116	0.59
Irish (1,106)	3,920	19.91
Israeli (16)	47	0.24
Italian (1,829)	3,969	20.16
Lithuanian (92)	260	1.32
Norwegian (86)	184	0.93
Pennsylvania German (0)	55	0.28
Polish (384)	1,405	7.14
Portuguese (94)	261	1.33
Romanian (26)	41	0.21
Russian (177)	480	2.44
Scandinavian (39)	94	0.48
Scotch-Irish (103)	284	1.44
Scottish (133)	461	2.34
Slavic (0)	18	0.09
Slovak (123)	254	1.29
Swedish (89)	506	2.57
Swiss (0)	104	0.53
Turkish (12)	12	0.06

*Notes: † The Census 2010 population figure is used to calculate the percentages in the Hispanic Origin and Race categories. Ancestry percentages are based on the 2006-2010 American Community Survey population (not shown); ‡ Numbers in parentheses indicate the number of people reporting a single ancestry; * Numbers in parentheses indicate the number of persons reporting this race alone, not in combination with any other race; Please refer to the Explanation of Data for more information.*

Ukrainian (118)	159	0.81
Welsh (0)	36	0.18

Hispanic Origin	Population	%
Hispanic or Latino (of any race)	523	2.63
Central American, ex. Mexican	30	0.15
Costa Rican	7	0.04
Guatemalan	14	0.07
Honduran	2	0.01
Nicaraguan	6	0.03
Panamanian	1	0.01
Cuban	43	0.22
Dominican Republic	32	0.16
Mexican	62	0.31
Puerto Rican	159	0.80
South American	108	0.54
Argentinean	9	0.05
Bolivian	1	0.01
Chilean	8	0.04
Colombian	32	0.16
Ecuadorian	50	0.25
Paraguayan	1	0.01
Peruvian	3	0.02
Uruguayan	2	0.01
Venezuelan	1	0.01
Other South American	1	0.01
Other Hispanic or Latino	89	0.45

Race*	Population	%
African-American/Black (166)	208	1.05
Not Hispanic (156)	188	0.94
Hispanic (10)	20	0.10
American Indian/Alaska Native (21)	85	0.43
Not Hispanic (15)	67	0.34
Hispanic (6)	18	0.09
Blackfeet (0)	3	0.02
Canadian/French Am. Ind. (4)	4	0.02
Cherokee (0)	6	0.03
Chippewa (1)	1	0.01
Choctaw (0)	1	0.01
Iroquois (0)	1	0.01
Asian (531)	636	3.20
Not Hispanic (531)	633	3.18
Hispanic (0)	3	0.02
Cambodian (3)	5	0.03
Chinese, ex. Taiwanese (196)	235	1.18
Filipino (41)	68	0.34
Indian (158)	169	0.85
Indonesian (0)	2	0.01
Japanese (11)	29	0.15
Korean (53)	63	0.32
Laotian (0)	3	0.02
Malaysian (0)	5	0.03
Nepalese (4)	4	0.02
Pakistani (7)	8	0.04
Sri Lankan (4)	4	0.02
Taiwanese (7)	7	0.04
Thai (8)	10	0.05
Vietnamese (19)	24	0.12
Hawaii Native/Pacific Islander (4)	10	0.05
Not Hispanic (4)	10	0.05
Guamanian/Chamorro (0)	1	0.01
Marshallese (1)	1	0.01
Native Hawaiian (1)	1	0.01
Samoan (0)	1	0.01
White (18,871)	19,090	95.91
Not Hispanic (18,462)	18,640	93.65
Hispanic (409)	450	2.26

Southington

Place Type: Town
County: Hartford
Population: 43,069†

Ancestry‡	Population	%
African, Sub-Saharan (79)	79	0.19
African (65)	65	0.15
Cape Verdean (14)	14	0.03
Albanian (108)	135	0.32
American (1,519)	1,519	3.57
Arab (29)	156	0.37
Arab (0)	8	0.02
Lebanese (20)	87	0.20
Moroccan (0)	43	0.10
Syrian (9)	18	0.04
Armenian (24)	60	0.14
Assyrian/Chaldean/Syriac (9)	171	0.40
Australian (0)	19	0.04
Austrian (80)	268	0.63
Belgian (8)	59	0.14
Brazilian (69)	69	0.16
British (69)	154	0.36
Cajun (11)	11	0.03
Canadian (203)	370	0.87
Carpatho Rusyn (0)	21	0.05
Croatian (13)	58	0.14
Czech (13)	112	0.26
Czechoslovakian (40)	58	0.14
Danish (61)	121	0.28
Dutch (77)	278	0.65
Eastern European (9)	9	0.02
English (875)	4,940	11.63
Estonian (11)	11	0.03
European (241)	241	0.57
Finnish (11)	36	0.08
French, ex. Basque (1,173)	5,006	11.78
French Canadian (945)	1,953	4.60
German (1,019)	5,390	12.69
Greek (136)	440	1.04
Hungarian (156)	484	1.14
Irish (1,836)	7,965	18.75
Italian (5,643)	13,107	30.85
Latvian (0)	13	0.03
Lithuanian (245)	586	1.38
Luxemburger (0)	10	0.02
Macedonian (0)	13	0.03
Norwegian (25)	217	0.51
Pennsylvania German (14)	14	0.03
Polish (2,649)	6,969	16.40
Portuguese (217)	511	1.20
Romanian (10)	22	0.05
Russian (115)	433	1.02
Scandinavian (18)	26	0.06
Scotch-Irish (140)	718	1.69
Scottish (164)	811	1.91
Serbian (0)	38	0.09
Slavic (26)	63	0.15
Slovak (85)	291	0.68
Slovene (0)	12	0.03
Swedish (187)	1,120	2.64
Swiss (14)	50	0.12
Ukrainian (42)	170	0.40
Welsh (14)	167	0.39
Yugoslavian (47)	93	0.22

Hispanic Origin	Population	%
Hispanic or Latino (of any race)	1,474	3.42
Central American, ex. Mexican	35	0.08
Costa Rican	3	0.01
Guatemalan	19	0.04
Honduran	6	0.01
Panamanian	5	0.01
Salvadoran	2	<0.01
Cuban	66	0.15
Dominican Republic	35	0.08
Mexican	134	0.31
Puerto Rican	900	2.09
South American	182	0.42
Argentinean	22	0.05
Bolivian	2	<0.01
Chilean	17	0.04
Colombian	44	0.10
Ecuadorian	35	0.08
Paraguayan	1	<0.01
Peruvian	54	0.13
Uruguayan	4	0.01
Venezuelan	3	0.01
Other Hispanic or Latino	122	0.28

Race*	Population	%
African-American/Black (637)	828	1.92
Not Hispanic (567)	729	1.69
Hispanic (70)	99	0.23
American Indian/Alaska Native (66)	180	0.42
Not Hispanic (53)	157	0.36
Hispanic (13)	23	0.05
Apache (1)	1	<0.01
Blackfeet (1)	6	0.01
Canadian/French Am. Ind. (1)	1	<0.01
Cherokee (6)	27	0.06
Chickasaw (0)	1	<0.01
Chippewa (4)	4	0.01
Comanche (1)	1	<0.01
Iroquois (1)	7	0.02
Mexican American Ind. (1)	1	<0.01
Navajo (6)	6	0.01
Sioux (0)	3	0.01
South American Ind. (0)	2	<0.01
Asian (942)	1,086	2.52
Not Hispanic (941)	1,074	2.49
Hispanic (1)	12	0.03
Bangladeshi (4)	4	0.01
Burmese (3)	3	0.01
Cambodian (35)	39	0.09
Chinese, ex. Taiwanese (147)	187	0.43
Filipino (78)	109	0.25
Indian (365)	392	0.91
Indonesian (1)	2	<0.01
Japanese (14)	24	0.06
Korean (76)	96	0.22
Laotian (4)	6	0.01
Pakistani (91)	99	0.23
Sri Lankan (2)	2	<0.01
Taiwanese (6)	6	0.01
Thai (6)	12	0.03
Vietnamese (69)	82	0.19
Hawaii Native/Pacific Islander (11)	28	0.07
Not Hispanic (6)	22	0.05
Hispanic (5)	6	0.01
Fijian (0)	1	<0.01
Guamanian/Chamorro (8)	8	0.02
Native Hawaiian (1)	9	0.02
Samoan (1)	1	<0.01
White (40,611)	41,074	95.37
Not Hispanic (39,617)	39,978	92.82
Hispanic (994)	1,096	2.54

Southwood Acres

Place Type: CDP
County: Hartford
Population: 7,657†

Ancestry‡	Population	%
American (84)	84	1.07
Arab (40)	86	1.09
Lebanese (31)	77	0.98
Moroccan (9)	9	0.11
Armenian (0)	119	1.51
Austrian (0)	35	0.44
British (0)	20	0.25
Carpatho Rusyn (8)	8	0.10
Czech (11)	78	0.99
Czechoslovakian (0)	9	0.11
Danish (0)	63	0.80
Dutch (0)	50	0.64
English (429)	1,444	18.34
European (22)	22	0.28
French, ex. Basque (346)	1,386	17.61
French Canadian (303)	450	5.72
German (144)	979	12.44
Greek (18)	88	1.12
Hungarian (8)	50	0.64
Irish (611)	2,127	27.02
Italian (423)	1,628	20.68
Lithuanian (73)	154	1.96
Norwegian (9)	18	0.23
Polish (389)	1,112	14.13

*Notes: † The Census 2010 population figure is used to calculate the percentages in the Hispanic Origin and Race categories. Ancestry percentages are based on the 2006-2010 American Community Survey population (not shown); ‡ Numbers in parentheses indicate the number of people reporting a single ancestry; * Numbers in parentheses indicate the number of persons reporting this race alone, not in combination with any other race; Please refer to the Explanation of Data for more information.*

Portuguese (11)	53	0.67
Russian (0)	11	0.14
Scandinavian (0)	10	0.13
Scotch-Irish (93)	224	2.85
Scottish (35)	205	2.60
Slavic (0)	17	0.22
Slovak (45)	55	0.70
Swedish (18)	115	1.46
Ukrainian (118)	132	1.68

Hispanic Origin	Population	%
Hispanic or Latino (of any race)	199	2.60
Central American, ex. Mexican	12	0.16
Costa Rican	2	0.03
Guatemalan	4	0.05
Panamanian	6	0.08
Cuban	11	0.14
Dominican Republic	3	0.04
Mexican	26	0.34
Puerto Rican	122	1.59
South American	18	0.24
Argentinean	2	0.03
Colombian	7	0.09
Ecuadorian	2	0.03
Peruvian	7	0.09
Other Hispanic or Latino	7	0.09

Race*	Population	%
African-American/Black (107)	144	1.88
Not Hispanic (100)	131	1.71
Hispanic (7)	13	0.17
American Indian/Alaska Native (11)	36	0.47
Not Hispanic (8)	30	0.39
Hispanic (3)	6	0.08
Blackfeet (0)	1	0.01
Cherokee (1)	5	0.07
Chippewa (0)	1	0.01
Cree (0)	1	0.01
Creek (0)	2	0.03
Lumbee (0)	1	0.01
Mexican American Ind. (2)	2	0.03
Navajo (0)	1	0.01
Sioux (0)	1	0.01
South American Ind. (3)	3	0.04
Asian (92)	121	1.58
Not Hispanic (90)	116	1.51
Hispanic (2)	5	0.07
Cambodian (6)	6	0.08
Chinese, ex. Taiwanese (11)	17	0.22
Filipino (12)	20	0.26
Hmong (24)	24	0.31
Indian (11)	18	0.24
Japanese (2)	6	0.08
Korean (10)	14	0.18
Laotian (0)	3	0.04
Pakistani (4)	4	0.05
Taiwanese (1)	1	0.01
Vietnamese (6)	8	0.10
Hawaii Native/Pacific Islander (2)	9	0.12
Not Hispanic (2)	9	0.12
Guamanian/Chamorro (0)	2	0.03
Native Hawaiian (1)	1	0.01
White (7,279)	7,368	96.23
Not Hispanic (7,164)	7,241	94.57
Hispanic (115)	127	1.66

Stafford

Place Type: Town
County: Tolland
Population: 12,087†

Ancestry‡	Population	%
American (716)	716	5.94
Arab (0)	79	0.66
Lebanese (0)	79	0.66
Armenian (0)	42	0.35
Austrian (0)	35	0.29
British (86)	103	0.86
Canadian (65)	150	1.25
Czech (43)	150	1.25
Danish (11)	19	0.16
Dutch (35)	131	1.09
English (332)	1,614	13.40
European (123)	137	1.14
Finnish (64)	70	0.58
French, ex. Basque (551)	1,727	14.34
French Canadian (326)	707	5.87
German (188)	1,442	11.97
Greek (19)	85	0.71
Hungarian (0)	49	0.41
Irish (453)	2,700	22.41
Italian (758)	2,219	18.42
Lithuanian (54)	149	1.24
Norwegian (27)	78	0.65
Polish (475)	1,253	10.40
Portuguese (25)	35	0.29
Russian (81)	154	1.28
Scandinavian (23)	23	0.19
Scotch-Irish (64)	266	2.21
Scottish (67)	399	3.31
Slovak (73)	169	1.40
Swedish (47)	187	1.55
Swiss (13)	13	0.11
Ukrainian (126)	170	1.41
Welsh (69)	83	0.69
West Indian, ex. Hispanic (6)	6	0.05
Jamaican (6)	6	0.05

Hispanic Origin	Population	%
Hispanic or Latino (of any race)	347	2.87
Central American, ex. Mexican	9	0.07
Honduran	6	0.05
Nicaraguan	3	0.02
Cuban	4	0.03
Dominican Republic	9	0.07
Mexican	98	0.81
Puerto Rican	167	1.38
South American	35	0.29
Argentinean	7	0.06
Chilean	2	0.02
Colombian	2	0.02
Ecuadorian	1	0.01
Peruvian	17	0.14
Uruguayan	4	0.03
Other South American	2	0.02
Other Hispanic or Latino	25	0.21

Race*	Population	%
African-American/Black (84)	159	1.32
Not Hispanic (74)	145	1.20
Hispanic (10)	14	0.12
American Indian/Alaska Native (19)	100	0.83
Not Hispanic (17)	98	0.81
Hispanic (2)	2	0.02
Blackfeet (1)	5	0.04
Canadian/French Am. Ind. (0)	3	0.02
Cherokee (0)	6	0.05
Delaware (1)	1	0.01
Iroquois (0)	7	0.06
Lumbee (1)	1	0.01
Mexican American Ind. (0)	1	0.01
Navajo (1)	1	0.01
Shoshone (0)	1	0.01
Sioux (0)	2	0.02
South American Ind. (1)	1	0.01
Asian (133)	188	1.56
Not Hispanic (131)	184	1.52
Hispanic (2)	4	0.03
Burmese (2)	2	0.02
Cambodian (0)	3	0.02
Chinese, ex. Taiwanese (13)	23	0.19
Filipino (10)	18	0.15
Hmong (33)	37	0.31
Indian (29)	36	0.30
Indonesian (0)	5	0.04
Japanese (6)	20	0.17
Korean (7)	7	0.06
Laotian (18)	22	0.18
Thai (1)	8	0.07
Vietnamese (9)	18	0.15
Hawaii Native/Pacific Islander (1)	15	0.12
Not Hispanic (0)	11	0.09
Hispanic (1)	4	0.03
Native Hawaiian (1)	3	0.02
Samoan (0)	1	0.01
White (11,546)	11,748	97.20
Not Hispanic (11,325)	11,504	95.18
Hispanic (221)	244	2.02

Stamford

Place Type: City/Town
County: Fairfield
Population: 122,643†

Ancestry‡	Population	%
African, Sub-Saharan (487)	637	0.53
African (158)	223	0.18
Cape Verdean (0)	33	0.03
Ethiopian (143)	143	0.12
Ghanaian (9)	9	0.01
Nigerian (57)	57	0.05
South African (88)	128	0.11
Other Sub-Saharan African (32)	44	0.04
Albanian (641)	747	0.62
Alsatian (8)	8	0.01
American (2,220)	2,220	1.84
Arab (380)	490	0.41
Arab (66)	66	0.05
Egyptian (52)	81	0.07
Iraqi (11)	11	0.01
Jordanian (8)	8	0.01
Lebanese (97)	136	0.11
Moroccan (131)	131	0.11
Syrian (0)	21	0.02
Other Arab (15)	36	0.03
Armenian (65)	98	0.08
Assyrian/Chaldean/Syriac (0)	11	0.01
Australian (77)	86	0.07
Austrian (40)	343	0.28
Basque (0)	11	0.01
Belgian (26)	106	0.09
Brazilian (496)	692	0.57
British (353)	458	0.38
Bulgarian (85)	100	0.08
Cajun (16)	16	0.01
Canadian (185)	489	0.40
Carpatho Rusyn (0)	12	0.01
Celtic (38)	38	0.03
Croatian (144)	247	0.20
Czech (212)	529	0.44
Czechoslovakian (177)	254	0.21
Danish (115)	374	0.31
Dutch (178)	605	0.50
Eastern European (745)	1,022	0.85
English (1,686)	5,884	4.87
Estonian (19)	19	0.02
European (671)	742	0.61
Finnish (12)	38	0.03
French, ex. Basque (342)	2,231	1.85
French Canadian (132)	514	0.43
German (1,639)	7,927	6.56
Greek (1,528)	2,296	1.90
Guyanese (0)	27	0.02
Hungarian (337)	1,005	0.83
Iranian (143)	193	0.16
Irish (3,940)	12,128	10.03
Israeli (61)	61	0.05
Italian (10,735)	18,300	15.14
Latvian (15)	30	0.02
Lithuanian (193)	499	0.41
Luxemburger (0)	19	0.02
Macedonian (15)	15	0.01
Maltese (0)	24	0.02
Northern European (73)	91	0.08
Norwegian (97)	414	0.34
Pennsylvania German (28)	28	0.02
Polish (3,533)	6,643	5.49
Portuguese (331)	500	0.41

SECTION TWO

*Notes: † The Census 2010 population figure is used to calculate the percentages in the Hispanic Origin and Race categories. Ancestry percentages are based on the 2006-2010 American Community Survey population (not shown); ‡ Numbers in parentheses indicate the number of people reporting a single ancestry; * Numbers in parentheses indicate the number of persons reporting this race alone, not in combination with any other race; Please refer to the Explanation of Data for more information.*

Romanian (299)	506	0.42
Russian (2,545)	4,722	3.91
Scandinavian (11)	92	0.08
Scotch-Irish (253)	959	0.79
Scottish (411)	1,626	1.34
Serbian (46)	46	0.04
Slavic (16)	52	0.04
Slovak (456)	836	0.69
Slovene (39)	39	0.03
Swedish (146)	599	0.50
Swiss (65)	286	0.24
Turkish (135)	166	0.14
Ukrainian (509)	1,004	0.83
Welsh (67)	329	0.27
West Indian, ex. Hispanic (7,829)	8,540	7.06
British West Indian (38)	38	0.03
Haitian (4,929)	5,112	4.23
Jamaican (2,576)	2,945	2.44
Trinidadian/Tobagonian (158)	158	0.13
West Indian (128)	287	0.24
Yugoslavian (128)	141	0.12

Hispanic Origin	Population	%
Hispanic or Latino (of any race)	29,188	23.80
Central American, ex. Mexican	9,866	8.04
Costa Rican	133	0.11
Guatemalan	7,707	6.28
Honduran	1,279	1.04
Nicaraguan	53	0.04
Panamanian	61	0.05
Salvadoran	584	0.48
Other Central American	49	0.04
Cuban	403	0.33
Dominican Republic	1,476	1.20
Mexican	2,478	2.02
Puerto Rican	3,458	2.82
South American	8,807	7.18
Argentinean	278	0.23
Bolivian	112	0.09
Chilean	282	0.23
Colombian	2,679	2.18
Ecuadorian	2,313	1.89
Paraguayan	37	0.03
Peruvian	2,560	2.09
Uruguayan	371	0.30
Venezuelan	142	0.12
Other South American	33	0.03
Other Hispanic or Latino	2,700	2.20

Race*	Population	%
African-American/Black (17,061)	18,512	15.09
Not Hispanic (16,106)	16,872	13.76
Hispanic (955)	1,640	1.34
American Indian/Alaska Native (393)	914	0.75
Not Hispanic (124)	402	0.33
Hispanic (269)	512	0.42
Apache (0)	2	<0.01
Blackfeet (2)	13	0.01
Canadian/French Am. Ind. (3)	5	<0.01
Central American Ind. (12)	15	0.01
Cherokee (17)	62	0.05
Chickasaw (0)	1	<0.01
Chippewa (3)	4	<0.01
Choctaw (1)	8	0.01
Cree (0)	8	0.01
Creek (1)	3	<0.01
Hopi (0)	2	<0.01
Inupiat *(Alaska Native)* (2)	2	<0.01
Iroquois (1)	7	0.01
Lumbee (0)	7	0.01
Mexican American Ind. (42)	67	0.05
Navajo (1)	1	<0.01
Pueblo (1)	3	<0.01
Sioux (1)	10	0.01
South American Ind. (44)	78	0.06
Spanish American Ind. (6)	8	0.01
Tohono O'Odham (0)	1	<0.01
Asian (9,675)	10,607	8.65
Not Hispanic (9,604)	10,418	8.49
Hispanic (71)	189	0.15
Bangladeshi (208)	249	0.20
Burmese (9)	11	0.01
Cambodian (4)	5	<0.01
Chinese, ex. Taiwanese (1,916)	2,181	1.78
Filipino (991)	1,161	0.95
Hmong (0)	1	<0.01
Indian (5,133)	5,404	4.41
Indonesian (30)	39	0.03
Japanese (187)	273	0.22
Korean (348)	422	0.34
Laotian (16)	17	0.01
Malaysian (9)	10	0.01
Nepalese (40)	40	0.03
Pakistani (223)	265	0.22
Sri Lankan (25)	29	0.02
Taiwanese (62)	76	0.06
Thai (41)	49	0.04
Vietnamese (154)	207	0.17
Hawaii Native/Pacific Islander (86)	222	0.18
Not Hispanic (43)	130	0.11
Hispanic (43)	92	0.08
Fijian (1)	1	<0.01
Guamanian/Chamorro (68)	91	0.07
Native Hawaiian (2)	8	0.01
Samoan (0)	1	<0.01
White (79,663)	82,716	67.44
Not Hispanic (65,406)	66,663	54.36
Hispanic (14,257)	16,053	13.09

Stonington

Place Type: Town
County: New London
Population: 18,545†

Ancestry‡	Population	%
African, Sub-Saharan (47)	64	0.35
African (8)	11	0.06
Cape Verdean (0)	14	0.08
South African (25)	25	0.14
Zimbabwean (14)	14	0.08
American (494)	494	2.67
Arab (84)	136	0.74
Lebanese (3)	46	0.25
Syrian (81)	90	0.49
Armenian (7)	7	0.04
Austrian (8)	52	0.28
Belgian (16)	25	0.14
Brazilian (3)	3	0.02
British (172)	230	1.24
Canadian (51)	67	0.36
Croatian (0)	4	0.02
Czech (3)	41	0.22
Czechoslovakian (0)	54	0.29
Danish (3)	20	0.11
Dutch (36)	321	1.74
Eastern European (72)	72	0.39
English (1,289)	3,657	19.77
Estonian (72)	72	0.39
European (153)	188	1.02
Finnish (23)	61	0.33
French, ex. Basque (250)	1,189	6.43
French Canadian (362)	940	5.08
German (496)	2,254	12.19
Greek (143)	219	1.18
Hungarian (0)	37	0.20
Iranian (28)	28	0.15
Irish (1,157)	4,043	21.86
Italian (1,278)	3,319	17.94
Latvian (15)	15	0.08
Lithuanian (10)	69	0.37
Northern European (35)	35	0.19
Norwegian (41)	244	1.32
Polish (299)	1,321	7.14
Portuguese (671)	1,295	7.00
Romanian (0)	11	0.06
Russian (99)	408	2.21
Scandinavian (0)	37	0.20
Scotch-Irish (213)	587	3.17
Scottish (298)	781	4.22
Serbian (0)	23	0.12
Slovak (0)	67	0.36
Slovene (0)	4	0.02
Swedish (31)	499	2.70
Swiss (10)	57	0.31
Ukrainian (32)	108	0.58
Welsh (37)	189	1.02
West Indian, ex. Hispanic (16)	25	0.14
Jamaican (16)	16	0.09
West Indian (0)	9	0.05
Yugoslavian (0)	40	0.22

Hispanic Origin	Population	%
Hispanic or Latino (of any race)	436	2.35
Central American, ex. Mexican	16	0.09
Costa Rican	4	0.02
Guatemalan	5	0.03
Honduran	5	0.03
Nicaraguan	1	0.01
Panamanian	1	0.01
Cuban	21	0.11
Dominican Republic	11	0.06
Mexican	90	0.49
Puerto Rican	154	0.83
South American	76	0.41
Argentinean	12	0.06
Chilean	2	0.01
Colombian	11	0.06
Ecuadorian	35	0.19
Peruvian	15	0.08
Venezuelan	1	0.01
Other Hispanic or Latino	68	0.37

Race*	Population	%
African-American/Black (176)	313	1.69
Not Hispanic (156)	281	1.52
Hispanic (20)	32	0.17
American Indian/Alaska Native (77)	185	1.00
Not Hispanic (71)	170	0.92
Hispanic (6)	15	0.08
Blackfeet (0)	2	0.01
Canadian/French Am. Ind. (0)	2	0.01
Central American Ind. (1)	1	0.01
Cherokee (0)	12	0.06
Chippewa (1)	1	0.01
Choctaw (1)	6	0.03
Creek (1)	1	0.01
Iroquois (0)	3	0.02
Lumbee (2)	2	0.01
Mexican American Ind. (0)	1	0.01
Navajo (1)	2	0.01
Ottawa (0)	2	0.01
Sioux (0)	3	0.02
South American Ind. (1)	4	0.02
Asian (344)	469	2.53
Not Hispanic (341)	463	2.50
Hispanic (3)	6	0.03
Burmese (1)	1	0.01
Cambodian (0)	3	0.02
Chinese, ex. Taiwanese (140)	161	0.87
Filipino (29)	72	0.39
Indian (77)	91	0.49
Indonesian (0)	1	0.01
Japanese (16)	38	0.20
Korean (22)	27	0.15
Laotian (6)	9	0.05
Pakistani (16)	17	0.09
Taiwanese (6)	6	0.03
Thai (4)	14	0.08
Vietnamese (15)	20	0.11
Hawaii Native/Pacific Islander (6)	11	0.06
Not Hispanic (6)	11	0.06
Guamanian/Chamorro (1)	3	0.02
Native Hawaiian (2)	4	0.02
White (17,473)	17,788	95.92
Not Hispanic (17,210)	17,487	94.29
Hispanic (263)	301	1.62

*Notes: † The Census 2010 population figure is used to calculate the percentages in the Hispanic Origin and Race categories. Ancestry percentages are based on the 2006-2010 American Community Survey population (not shown); ‡ Numbers in parentheses indicate the number of people reporting a single ancestry; * Numbers in parentheses indicate the number of persons reporting this race alone, not in combination with any other race; Please refer to the Explanation of Data for more information.*

Storrs

Place Type: CDP
County: Tolland
Population: 15,344†

Ancestry‡	Population	%
African, Sub-Saharan (43)	95	0.67
Ethiopian (5)	5	0.04
Ghanaian (25)	25	0.18
Nigerian (13)	27	0.19
South African (0)	27	0.19
Other Sub-Saharan African (0)	11	0.08
Albanian (24)	24	0.17
American (146)	146	1.03
Arab (57)	132	0.93
Arab (52)	52	0.37
Lebanese (0)	50	0.35
Syrian (0)	12	0.08
Other Arab (5)	18	0.13
Armenian (0)	13	0.09
Australian (0)	13	0.09
Austrian (0)	22	0.16
Brazilian (8)	20	0.14
British (61)	170	1.20
Canadian (0)	80	0.57
Cypriot (14)	14	0.10
Czech (0)	54	0.38
Czechoslovakian (0)	13	0.09
Danish (13)	115	0.81
Dutch (52)	148	1.05
Eastern European (61)	61	0.43
English (206)	1,205	8.53
European (126)	166	1.17
Finnish (0)	13	0.09
French, ex. Basque (100)	466	3.30
French Canadian (76)	426	3.01
German (184)	1,530	10.82
Greek (86)	211	1.49
Guyanese (10)	10	0.07
Hungarian (12)	60	0.42
Irish (429)	2,545	18.01
Israeli (0)	25	0.18
Italian (748)	2,505	17.72
Latvian (0)	35	0.25
Lithuanian (10)	120	0.85
Northern European (25)	37	0.26
Norwegian (23)	186	1.32
Pennsylvania German (0)	36	0.25
Polish (301)	1,092	7.73
Portuguese (23)	117	0.83
Romanian (0)	26	0.18
Russian (104)	533	3.77
Scotch-Irish (13)	194	1.37
Scottish (25)	287	2.03
Slovak (0)	13	0.09
Swedish (25)	381	2.70
Swiss (0)	36	0.25
Turkish (0)	49	0.35
Ukrainian (23)	153	1.08
Welsh (0)	125	0.88
West Indian, ex. Hispanic (127)	152	1.08
Haitian (36)	36	0.25
Jamaican (79)	104	0.74
West Indian (12)	12	0.08

Hispanic Origin	Population	%
Hispanic or Latino (of any race)	850	5.54
Central American, ex. Mexican	44	0.29
Costa Rican	4	0.03
Guatemalan	12	0.08
Honduran	3	0.02
Nicaraguan	9	0.06
Panamanian	7	0.05
Salvadoran	9	0.06
Cuban	63	0.41
Dominican Republic	54	0.35
Mexican	70	0.46
Puerto Rican	327	2.13
South American	201	1.31
Argentinean	19	0.12
Bolivian	4	0.03
Chilean	16	0.10
Colombian	72	0.47
Ecuadorian	28	0.18
Paraguayan	1	0.01
Peruvian	42	0.27
Uruguayan	3	0.02
Venezuelan	14	0.09
Other South American	2	0.01
Other Hispanic or Latino	91	0.59

Race*	Population	%
African-American/Black (796)	927	6.04
Not Hispanic (740)	840	5.47
Hispanic (56)	87	0.57
American Indian/Alaska Native (17)	74	0.48
Not Hispanic (12)	54	0.35
Hispanic (5)	20	0.13
Blackfeet (1)	3	0.02
Canadian/French Am. Ind. (0)	2	0.01
Cherokee (0)	11	0.07
Chickasaw (1)	1	0.01
Chippewa (1)	1	0.01
Comanche (0)	1	0.01
Hopi (0)	1	0.01
Inupiat *(Alaska Native)* (0)	1	0.01
Iroquois (1)	5	0.03
Mexican American Ind. (1)	5	0.03
Navajo (0)	1	0.01
Sioux (1)	2	0.01
South American Ind. (0)	1	0.01
Asian (1,509)	1,721	11.22
Not Hispanic (1,499)	1,697	11.06
Hispanic (10)	24	0.16
Bangladeshi (18)	21	0.14
Cambodian (21)	30	0.20
Chinese, ex. Taiwanese (497)	564	3.68
Filipino (74)	114	0.74
Indian (431)	467	3.04
Indonesian (7)	10	0.07
Japanese (19)	45	0.29
Korean (158)	175	1.14
Laotian (14)	15	0.10
Malaysian (1)	3	0.02
Nepalese (19)	19	0.12
Pakistani (48)	56	0.36
Sri Lankan (6)	6	0.04
Taiwanese (36)	41	0.27
Thai (5)	11	0.07
Vietnamese (103)	122	0.80
Hawaii Native/Pacific Islander (7)	28	0.18
Not Hispanic (5)	23	0.15
Hispanic (2)	5	0.03
Fijian (1)	1	0.01
Guamanian/Chamorro (0)	3	0.02
Native Hawaiian (4)	9	0.06
Samoan (1)	4	0.03
White (12,370)	12,690	82.70
Not Hispanic (11,884)	12,156	79.22
Hispanic (486)	534	3.48

Stratford

Place Type: CDP/Town
County: Fairfield
Population: 51,384†

Ancestry‡	Population	%
African, Sub-Saharan (306)	335	0.66
African (38)	67	0.13
Cape Verdean (103)	103	0.20
Ghanaian (41)	41	0.08
Kenyan (28)	28	0.06
Nigerian (58)	58	0.11
Somalian (20)	20	0.04
Other Sub-Saharan African (18)	18	0.04
Albanian (83)	131	0.26
American (1,173)	1,173	2.31
Arab (98)	221	0.43
Jordanian (15)	46	0.09
Lebanese (50)	94	0.18
Palestinian (0)	48	0.09
Syrian (33)	33	0.06
Armenian (68)	127	0.25
Austrian (56)	138	0.27
Basque (14)	14	0.03
Belgian (9)	17	0.03
Brazilian (152)	222	0.44
British (50)	115	0.23
Canadian (63)	207	0.41
Carpatho Rusyn (47)	47	0.09
Celtic (12)	12	0.02
Croatian (25)	25	0.05
Czech (78)	198	0.39
Czechoslovakian (117)	189	0.37
Danish (9)	157	0.31
Dutch (58)	327	0.64
Eastern European (59)	59	0.12
English (999)	4,238	8.34
Estonian (44)	44	0.09
European (144)	144	0.28
Finnish (16)	46	0.09
French, ex. Basque (229)	1,799	3.54
French Canadian (323)	897	1.77
German (817)	4,474	8.80
Greek (249)	490	0.96
Hungarian (480)	1,477	2.91
Icelander (9)	34	0.07
Iranian (20)	39	0.08
Irish (2,025)	8,252	16.24
Israeli (9)	9	0.02
Italian (4,353)	10,381	20.43
Latvian (41)	41	0.08
Lithuanian (56)	215	0.42
Macedonian (18)	18	0.04
Maltese (0)	17	0.03
Northern European (92)	92	0.18
Norwegian (101)	323	0.64
Pennsylvania German (0)	8	0.02
Polish (1,845)	4,602	9.06
Portuguese (402)	822	1.62
Romanian (81)	112	0.22
Russian (326)	899	1.77
Scandinavian (9)	9	0.02
Scotch-Irish (167)	643	1.27
Scottish (209)	577	1.14
Serbian (225)	225	0.44
Slavic (11)	11	0.02
Slovak (1,217)	2,753	5.42
Slovene (20)	33	0.06
Swedish (120)	785	1.54
Swiss (0)	26	0.05
Turkish (154)	189	0.37
Ukrainian (127)	237	0.47
Welsh (12)	84	0.17
West Indian, ex. Hispanic (1,999)	2,155	4.24
Bahamian (0)	12	0.02
Haitian (1,253)	1,328	2.61
Jamaican (746)	815	1.60
Yugoslavian (101)	132	0.26

Hispanic Origin	Population	%
Hispanic or Latino (of any race)	7,114	13.84
Central American, ex. Mexican	703	1.37
Costa Rican	71	0.14
Guatemalan	330	0.64
Honduran	81	0.16
Nicaraguan	27	0.05
Panamanian	16	0.03
Salvadoran	177	0.34
Other Central American	1	<0.01
Cuban	224	0.44
Dominican Republic	276	0.54
Mexican	465	0.90
Puerto Rican	3,974	7.73
South American	1,044	2.03
Argentinean	41	0.08
Bolivian	35	0.07
Chilean	15	0.03

*Notes: † The Census 2010 population figure is used to calculate the percentages in the Hispanic Origin and Race categories. Ancestry percentages are based on the 2006-2010 American Community Survey population (not shown); ‡ Numbers in parentheses indicate the number of people reporting a single ancestry; * Numbers in parentheses indicate the number of persons reporting this race alone, not in combination with any other race; Please refer to the Explanation of Data for more information.*

Colombian	433	0.84
Ecuadorian	323	0.63
Paraguayan	13	0.03
Peruvian	119	0.23
Uruguayan	26	0.05
Venezuelan	26	0.05
Other South American	13	0.03
Other Hispanic or Latino	428	0.83

Race*	Population	%
African-American/Black (7,347)	8,062	15.69
Not Hispanic (6,963)	7,492	14.58
Hispanic (384)	570	1.11
American Indian/Alaska Native (128)	335	0.65
Not Hispanic (75)	259	0.50
Hispanic (53)	76	0.15
Apache (0)	2	<0.01
Arapaho (1)	1	<0.01
Blackfeet (1)	22	0.04
Central American Ind. (1)	1	<0.01
Cherokee (11)	51	0.10
Cheyenne (0)	1	<0.01
Chickasaw (1)	1	<0.01
Chippewa (2)	5	0.01
Choctaw (3)	4	0.01
Colville (1)	1	<0.01
Creek (1)	1	<0.01
Hopi (1)	1	<0.01
Iroquois (1)	13	0.03
Lumbee (4)	4	0.01
Menominee (0)	1	<0.01
Mexican American Ind. (4)	5	0.01
Navajo (3)	3	0.01
Seminole (0)	6	0.01
Sioux (4)	4	0.01
South American Ind. (4)	6	0.01
Spanish American Ind. (4)	8	0.02
Asian (1,214)	1,453	2.83
Not Hispanic (1,199)	1,407	2.74
Hispanic (15)	46	0.09
Bangladeshi (11)	11	0.02
Cambodian (50)	57	0.11
Chinese, ex. Taiwanese (197)	233	0.45
Filipino (178)	210	0.41
Indian (293)	346	0.67
Indonesian (7)	7	0.01
Japanese (16)	44	0.09
Korean (95)	116	0.23
Laotian (66)	85	0.17
Nepalese (5)	6	0.01
Pakistani (95)	110	0.21
Sri Lankan (10)	10	0.02
Taiwanese (8)	8	0.02
Thai (15)	24	0.05
Vietnamese (116)	147	0.29
Hawaii Native/Pacific Islander (27)	95	0.18
Not Hispanic (25)	70	0.14
Hispanic (2)	25	0.05
Guamanian/Chamorro (3)	8	0.02
Native Hawaiian (6)	15	0.03
Samoan (3)	3	0.01
White (39,249)	40,259	78.35
Not Hispanic (35,040)	35,691	69.46
Hispanic (4,209)	4,568	8.89

Suffield

Place Type: Town
County: Hartford
Population: 15,735†

Ancestry‡	Population	%
African, Sub-Saharan (76)	92	0.60
African (76)	92	0.60
Albanian (9)	9	0.06
American (398)	398	2.59
Arab (30)	39	0.25
Lebanese (30)	39	0.25
Armenian (0)	23	0.15
Assyrian/Chaldean/Syriac (9)	9	0.06
Austrian (16)	125	0.81
Belgian (0)	20	0.13
Brazilian (8)	8	0.05
British (38)	178	1.16
Bulgarian (71)	71	0.46
Canadian (85)	155	1.01
Croatian (0)	9	0.06
Czech (0)	80	0.52
Czechoslovakian (19)	56	0.36
Danish (17)	139	0.91
Dutch (11)	123	0.80
English (383)	2,237	14.57
European (19)	33	0.21
Finnish (9)	53	0.35
French, ex. Basque (436)	1,495	9.73
French Canadian (527)	1,065	6.93
German (156)	1,470	9.57
Greek (141)	186	1.21
Guyanese (9)	9	0.06
Hungarian (40)	147	0.96
Irish (804)	3,619	23.57
Italian (1,130)	2,848	18.55
Lithuanian (56)	113	0.74
Northern European (21)	21	0.14
Norwegian (9)	37	0.24
Polish (768)	2,045	13.32
Portuguese (24)	50	0.33
Romanian (0)	9	0.06
Russian (83)	235	1.53
Scotch-Irish (122)	297	1.93
Scottish (84)	613	3.99
Slovak (20)	107	0.70
Swedish (55)	268	1.75
Swiss (18)	62	0.40
Ukrainian (7)	25	0.16
Welsh (0)	69	0.45
West Indian, ex. Hispanic (177)	201	1.31
Jamaican (143)	167	1.09
West Indian (34)	34	0.22
Yugoslavian (8)	8	0.05

Hispanic Origin	Population	%
Hispanic or Latino (of any race)	886	5.63
Central American, ex. Mexican	16	0.10
Guatemalan	6	0.04
Nicaraguan	2	0.01
Panamanian	1	0.01
Salvadoran	7	0.04
Cuban	14	0.09
Dominican Republic	11	0.07
Mexican	63	0.40
Puerto Rican	147	0.93
South American	45	0.29
Argentinean	2	0.01
Bolivian	4	0.03
Chilean	1	0.01
Colombian	16	0.10
Paraguayan	1	0.01
Peruvian	10	0.06
Venezuelan	9	0.06
Other South American	2	0.01
Other Hispanic or Latino	590	3.75

Race*	Population	%
African-American/Black (1,229)	1,286	8.17
Not Hispanic (1,180)	1,230	7.82
Hispanic (49)	56	0.36
American Indian/Alaska Native (24)	81	0.51
Not Hispanic (20)	75	0.48
Hispanic (4)	6	0.04
Blackfeet (0)	8	0.05
Cherokee (0)	10	0.06
Chickasaw (0)	3	0.02
Creek (0)	1	0.01
Iroquois (2)	7	0.04
Sioux (0)	1	0.01
South American Ind. (2)	2	0.01
Asian (204)	271	1.72
Not Hispanic (201)	264	1.68
Hispanic (3)	7	0.04
Bangladeshi (1)	2	0.01
Cambodian (1)	1	0.01
Chinese, ex. Taiwanese (47)	63	0.40
Filipino (14)	21	0.13
Indian (53)	61	0.39
Japanese (9)	32	0.20
Korean (31)	31	0.20
Laotian (5)	7	0.04
Malaysian (1)	1	0.01
Nepalese (1)	1	0.01
Pakistani (3)	5	0.03
Taiwanese (1)	3	0.02
Thai (1)	5	0.03
Vietnamese (17)	18	0.11
Hawaii Native/Pacific Islander (6)	11	0.07
Not Hispanic (6)	11	0.07
Guamanian/Chamorro (1)	1	0.01
Marshallese (2)	2	0.01
Native Hawaiian (1)	5	0.03
Samoan (0)	2	0.01
White (13,499)	13,662	86.83
Not Hispanic (13,270)	13,411	85.23
Hispanic (229)	251	1.60

Thomaston

Place Type: Town
County: Litchfield
Population: 7,887†

Ancestry‡	Population	%
Albanian (77)	77	0.98
American (237)	237	3.01
Arab (0)	30	0.38
Arab (0)	30	0.38
Armenian (0)	35	0.44
Austrian (7)	17	0.22
British (0)	32	0.41
Canadian (26)	45	0.57
Czech (0)	43	0.55
Czechoslovakian (35)	175	2.22
Danish (0)	22	0.28
Dutch (0)	22	0.28
Eastern European (20)	20	0.25
English (268)	1,299	16.50
European (80)	80	1.02
Finnish (0)	7	0.09
French, ex. Basque (133)	972	12.35
French Canadian (159)	466	5.92
German (62)	912	11.58
Greek (0)	11	0.14
Hungarian (0)	45	0.57
Irish (372)	1,866	23.70
Italian (520)	1,833	23.28
Lithuanian (63)	289	3.67
Norwegian (21)	21	0.27
Polish (382)	1,102	14.00
Portuguese (62)	88	1.12
Romanian (0)	30	0.38
Russian (7)	109	1.38
Scandinavian (10)	10	0.13
Scotch-Irish (58)	327	4.15
Scottish (18)	364	4.62
Slovak (0)	32	0.41
Swedish (38)	331	4.20
Swiss (0)	10	0.13
Ukrainian (10)	52	0.66
West Indian, ex. Hispanic (9)	9	0.11
Jamaican (9)	9	0.11

Hispanic Origin	Population	%
Hispanic or Latino (of any race)	202	2.56
Central American, ex. Mexican	1	0.01
Salvadoran	1	0.01
Cuban	3	0.04
Dominican Republic	7	0.09
Mexican	20	0.25
Puerto Rican	127	1.61
South American	15	0.19
Argentinean	1	0.01

*Notes: † The Census 2010 population figure is used to calculate the percentages in the Hispanic Origin and Race categories. Ancestry percentages are based on the 2006-2010 American Community Survey population (not shown); ‡ Numbers in parentheses indicate the number of people reporting a single ancestry; * Numbers in parentheses indicate the number of persons reporting this race alone, not in combination with any other race; Please refer to the Explanation of Data for more information.*

	Population	%
Colombian	7	0.09
Ecuadorian	6	0.08
Peruvian	1	0.01
Other Hispanic or Latino	29	0.37

Race*	Population	%
African-American/Black (34)	63	0.80
Not Hispanic (27)	52	0.66
Hispanic (7)	11	0.14
American Indian/Alaska Native (26)	62	0.79
Not Hispanic (19)	49	0.62
Hispanic (7)	13	0.16
Blackfeet (0)	1	0.01
Canadian/French Am. Ind. (0)	3	0.04
Cherokee (0)	2	0.03
Chippewa (0)	1	0.01
Iroquois (1)	6	0.08
Mexican American Ind. (1)	2	0.03
Navajo (1)	1	0.01
Sioux (1)	2	0.03
Spanish American Ind. (3)	3	0.04
Asian (60)	75	0.95
Not Hispanic (58)	72	0.91
Hispanic (2)	3	0.04
Bangladeshi (1)	2	0.03
Chinese, ex. Taiwanese (14)	16	0.20
Filipino (25)	27	0.34
Indian (6)	8	0.10
Japanese (0)	4	0.05
Korean (4)	5	0.06
Laotian (4)	4	0.05
Malaysian (4)	4	0.05
Thai (2)	2	0.03
Hawaii Native/Pacific Islander (0)	1	0.01
Not Hispanic (0)	1	0.01
Native Hawaiian (0)	1	0.01
White (7,631)	7,711	97.77
Not Hispanic (7,511)	7,574	96.03
Hispanic (120)	137	1.74

Thompson

Place Type: Town
County: Windham
Population: 9,458†

Ancestry‡	Population	%
Albanian (37)	56	0.59
American (381)	381	4.04
Arab (0)	10	0.11
Egyptian (0)	10	0.11
Austrian (31)	59	0.63
British (8)	18	0.19
Canadian (58)	95	1.01
Czech (0)	43	0.46
Dutch (0)	43	0.46
English (163)	1,215	12.88
European (13)	27	0.29
Finnish (0)	46	0.49
French, ex. Basque (655)	2,872	30.44
French Canadian (748)	1,463	15.51
German (205)	880	9.33
Greek (57)	97	1.03
Hungarian (11)	19	0.20
Irish (174)	1,840	19.50
Italian (138)	871	9.23
Lithuanian (46)	111	1.18
Norwegian (16)	42	0.45
Polish (335)	1,729	18.33
Portuguese (19)	115	1.22
Romanian (34)	34	0.36
Russian (13)	51	0.54
Scandinavian (6)	26	0.28
Scotch-Irish (17)	109	1.16
Scottish (51)	228	2.42
Slovak (14)	71	0.75
Swedish (80)	279	2.96
Ukrainian (21)	29	0.31
Welsh (0)	44	0.47
West Indian, ex. Hispanic (0)	12	0.13
Bermudan (0)	12	0.13

Hispanic Origin	Population	%
Hispanic or Latino (of any race)	166	1.76
Central American, ex. Mexican	12	0.13
Costa Rican	5	0.05
Guatemalan	4	0.04
Panamanian	3	0.03
Cuban	3	0.03
Dominican Republic	6	0.06
Mexican	13	0.14
Puerto Rican	104	1.10
South American	13	0.14
Argentinean	1	0.01
Colombian	10	0.11
Peruvian	1	0.01
Venezuelan	1	0.01
Other Hispanic or Latino	15	0.16

Race*	Population	%
African-American/Black (57)	100	1.06
Not Hispanic (51)	84	0.89
Hispanic (6)	16	0.17
American Indian/Alaska Native (38)	106	1.12
Not Hispanic (32)	96	1.02
Hispanic (6)	10	0.11
Apache (0)	3	0.03
Blackfeet (1)	3	0.03
Canadian/French Am. Ind. (1)	4	0.04
Cherokee (3)	13	0.14
Cree (0)	1	0.01
Creek (0)	1	0.01
Iroquois (2)	7	0.07
Mexican American Ind. (3)	3	0.03
Shoshone (1)	1	0.01
Sioux (0)	3	0.03
Tsimshian *(Alaska Native)* (2)	2	0.02
Asian (65)	93	0.98
Not Hispanic (64)	92	0.97
Hispanic (1)	1	0.01
Cambodian (1)	1	0.01
Chinese, ex. Taiwanese (12)	17	0.18
Filipino (21)	32	0.34
Hmong (0)	1	0.01
Indian (10)	11	0.12
Japanese (0)	5	0.05
Korean (2)	2	0.02
Laotian (3)	3	0.03
Nepalese (4)	4	0.04
Pakistani (4)	4	0.04
Thai (2)	2	0.02
Vietnamese (3)	9	0.10
Hawaii Native/Pacific Islander (4)	7	0.07
Not Hispanic (4)	7	0.07
Native Hawaiian (3)	5	0.05
Samoan (1)	1	0.01
White (9,074)	9,230	97.59
Not Hispanic (8,992)	9,120	96.43
Hispanic (82)	110	1.16

Thompsonville

Place Type: CDP
County: Hartford
Population: 8,577†

Ancestry‡	Population	%
African, Sub-Saharan (235)	264	2.99
African (235)	264	2.99
American (137)	137	1.55
Armenian (0)	8	0.09
Austrian (0)	11	0.12
Belgian (0)	79	0.89
Brazilian (15)	15	0.17
Canadian (42)	108	1.22
Czech (12)	58	0.66
Danish (0)	59	0.67
Dutch (0)	135	1.53
English (119)	823	9.31
European (59)	89	1.01
French, ex. Basque (160)	1,119	12.66
French Canadian (112)	337	3.81
German (19)	835	9.45
German Russian (10)	10	0.11
Greek (54)	54	0.61
Guyanese (69)	69	0.78
Irish (323)	2,403	27.19
Italian (765)	1,710	19.35
Lithuanian (19)	44	0.50
Norwegian (53)	263	2.98
Polish (596)	1,437	16.26
Portuguese (36)	113	1.28
Russian (13)	40	0.45
Scotch-Irish (28)	141	1.60
Scottish (11)	62	0.70
Swedish (26)	98	1.11
Ukrainian (0)	7	0.08
Welsh (0)	53	0.60
West Indian, ex. Hispanic (104)	104	1.18
Jamaican (104)	104	1.18

Hispanic Origin	Population	%
Hispanic or Latino (of any race)	978	11.40
Central American, ex. Mexican	29	0.34
Costa Rican	1	0.01
Guatemalan	8	0.09
Honduran	3	0.03
Nicaraguan	1	0.01
Panamanian	2	0.02
Salvadoran	14	0.16
Cuban	14	0.16
Dominican Republic	19	0.22
Mexican	268	3.12
Puerto Rican	555	6.47
South American	61	0.71
Argentinean	4	0.05
Colombian	29	0.34
Ecuadorian	4	0.05
Paraguayan	2	0.02
Peruvian	12	0.14
Venezuelan	9	0.10
Other South American	1	0.01
Other Hispanic or Latino	32	0.37

Race*	Population	%
African-American/Black (626)	823	9.60
Not Hispanic (553)	724	8.44
Hispanic (73)	99	1.15
American Indian/Alaska Native (28)	111	1.29
Not Hispanic (22)	92	1.07
Hispanic (6)	19	0.22
Blackfeet (1)	15	0.17
Canadian/French Am. Ind. (0)	1	0.01
Cherokee (1)	29	0.34
Iroquois (1)	8	0.09
Navajo (0)	5	0.06
Sioux (0)	5	0.06
Asian (227)	295	3.44
Not Hispanic (226)	291	3.39
Hispanic (1)	4	0.05
Cambodian (8)	8	0.09
Chinese, ex. Taiwanese (20)	29	0.34
Filipino (8)	30	0.35
Hmong (22)	24	0.28
Indian (107)	119	1.39
Indonesian (1)	3	0.03
Japanese (4)	7	0.08
Korean (14)	15	0.17
Laotian (8)	8	0.09
Pakistani (10)	14	0.16
Thai (2)	2	0.02
Vietnamese (17)	23	0.27
Hawaii Native/Pacific Islander (6)	21	0.24
Not Hispanic (3)	18	0.21
Hispanic (3)	3	0.03
Guamanian/Chamorro (1)	1	0.01
Native Hawaiian (0)	3	0.03
Samoan (1)	4	0.05
White (6,992)	7,289	84.98
Not Hispanic (6,503)	6,732	78.49

*Notes: † The Census 2010 population figure is used to calculate the percentages in the Hispanic Origin and Race categories. Ancestry percentages are based on the 2006-2010 American Community Survey population (not shown); ‡ Numbers in parentheses indicate the number of people reporting a single ancestry; * Numbers in parentheses indicate the number of persons reporting this race alone, not in combination with any other race; Please refer to the Explanation of Data for more information.*

SECTION TWO

Hispanic (489)	557	6.49

Tolland

Place Type: Town
County: Tolland
Population: 15,052†

Ancestry‡	Population	%
African, Sub-Saharan (0)	102	0.69
African (0)	102	0.69
American (916)	916	6.19
Arab (23)	84	0.57
Lebanese (23)	84	0.57
Armenian (40)	106	0.72
Australian (0)	11	0.07
Austrian (0)	15	0.10
Belgian (0)	12	0.08
British (38)	116	0.78
Cajun (12)	12	0.08
Canadian (10)	184	1.24
Croatian (37)	37	0.25
Czech (29)	114	0.77
Czechoslovakian (30)	121	0.82
Danish (13)	102	0.69
Dutch (57)	220	1.49
Eastern European (14)	14	0.09
English (750)	2,596	17.53
European (40)	68	0.46
Finnish (12)	77	0.52
French, ex. Basque (317)	1,572	10.62
French Canadian (371)	962	6.50
German (415)	2,502	16.90
Greek (23)	158	1.07
Hungarian (0)	91	0.61
Iranian (11)	11	0.07
Irish (548)	3,510	23.70
Italian (646)	2,374	16.03
Lithuanian (58)	264	1.78
Northern European (49)	49	0.33
Norwegian (15)	75	0.51
Polish (461)	1,892	12.78
Portuguese (60)	88	0.59
Romanian (12)	12	0.08
Russian (62)	289	1.95
Scotch-Irish (88)	302	2.04
Scottish (45)	347	2.34
Slavic (0)	14	0.09
Slovak (0)	31	0.21
Swedish (86)	409	2.76
Swiss (27)	106	0.72
Ukrainian (31)	39	0.26
Welsh (12)	113	0.76
West Indian, ex. Hispanic (13)	92	0.62
Haitian (13)	13	0.09
West Indian (0)	79	0.53

Hispanic Origin	Population	%
Hispanic or Latino (of any race)	336	2.23
Central American, ex. Mexican	12	0.08
Guatemalan	5	0.03
Honduran	2	0.01
Nicaraguan	2	0.01
Salvadoran	1	0.01
Other Central American	2	0.01
Cuban	30	0.20
Dominican Republic	6	0.04
Mexican	47	0.31
Puerto Rican	166	1.10
South American	44	0.29
Argentinean	4	0.03
Chilean	6	0.04
Colombian	15	0.10
Ecuadorian	6	0.04
Paraguayan	1	0.01
Peruvian	9	0.06
Uruguayan	2	0.01
Venezuelan	1	0.01
Other Hispanic or Latino	31	0.21

Race*	Population	%
African-American/Black (173)	216	1.44
Not Hispanic (161)	200	1.33
Hispanic (12)	16	0.11
American Indian/Alaska Native (12)	53	0.35
Not Hispanic (10)	47	0.31
Hispanic (2)	6	0.04
Canadian/French Am. Ind. (0)	1	0.01
Cherokee (0)	5	0.03
Chickasaw (0)	1	0.01
Iroquois (0)	1	0.01
Menominee (0)	1	0.01
Mexican American Ind. (1)	5	0.03
Sioux (0)	1	0.01
Asian (353)	422	2.80
Not Hispanic (346)	415	2.76
Hispanic (7)	7	0.05
Bangladeshi (4)	4	0.03
Chinese, ex. Taiwanese (65)	83	0.55
Filipino (7)	15	0.10
Hmong (14)	14	0.09
Indian (111)	141	0.94
Indonesian (1)	1	0.01
Japanese (7)	14	0.09
Korean (44)	49	0.33
Laotian (8)	18	0.12
Pakistani (36)	37	0.25
Taiwanese (11)	11	0.07
Thai (1)	1	0.01
Vietnamese (14)	23	0.15
Hawaii Native/Pacific Islander (4)	7	0.05
Not Hispanic (3)	6	0.04
Hispanic (1)	1	0.01
Guamanian/Chamorro (1)	1	0.01
Native Hawaiian (1)	2	0.01
Tongan (2)	2	0.01
White (14,249)	14,395	95.64
Not Hispanic (14,025)	14,154	94.03
Hispanic (224)	241	1.60

Torrington

Place Type: City/Town
County: Litchfield
Population: 36,383†

Ancestry‡	Population	%
African, Sub-Saharan (19)	19	0.05
African (13)	13	0.04
Other Sub-Saharan African (6)	6	0.02
Albanian (0)	26	0.07
American (1,075)	1,075	2.95
Arab (129)	267	0.73
Egyptian (15)	15	0.04
Iraqi (0)	13	0.04
Lebanese (114)	239	0.66
Armenian (0)	34	0.09
Australian (0)	41	0.11
Austrian (27)	111	0.30
Belgian (0)	9	0.02
Brazilian (77)	77	0.21
British (58)	178	0.49
Canadian (21)	37	0.10
Czech (77)	126	0.35
Czechoslovakian (15)	111	0.30
Danish (18)	217	0.60
Dutch (61)	341	0.94
Eastern European (24)	24	0.07
English (1,427)	4,019	11.03
Estonian (0)	57	0.16
European (104)	104	0.29
Finnish (14)	35	0.10
French, ex. Basque (762)	4,091	11.23
French Canadian (769)	1,357	3.73
German (643)	4,240	11.64
Greek (9)	140	0.38
Hungarian (179)	693	1.90
Irish (1,847)	6,087	16.71
Italian (3,828)	9,345	25.66
Latvian (51)	51	0.14
Lithuanian (228)	560	1.54
Norwegian (23)	308	0.85
Pennsylvania German (10)	10	0.03
Polish (1,148)	3,119	8.56
Portuguese (117)	348	0.96
Romanian (22)	22	0.06
Russian (132)	492	1.35
Scandinavian (0)	24	0.07
Scotch-Irish (115)	347	0.95
Scottish (90)	622	1.71
Slavic (0)	69	0.19
Slovak (337)	805	2.21
Slovene (11)	11	0.03
Swedish (147)	777	2.13
Swiss (38)	196	0.54
Turkish (8)	8	0.02
Ukrainian (60)	122	0.33
Welsh (11)	93	0.26
West Indian, ex. Hispanic (102)	174	0.48
Jamaican (22)	22	0.06
Trinidadian/Tobagonian (10)	26	0.07
West Indian (48)	104	0.29
Other West Indian (22)	22	0.06
Yugoslavian (15)	32	0.09

Hispanic Origin	Population	%
Hispanic or Latino (of any race)	3,193	8.78
Central American, ex. Mexican	83	0.23
Costa Rican	14	0.04
Guatemalan	30	0.08
Honduran	9	0.02
Nicaraguan	5	0.01
Panamanian	12	0.03
Salvadoran	13	0.04
Cuban	76	0.21
Dominican Republic	707	1.94
Mexican	216	0.59
Puerto Rican	981	2.70
South American	730	2.01
Argentinean	9	0.02
Bolivian	4	0.01
Chilean	14	0.04
Colombian	25	0.07
Ecuadorian	633	1.74
Paraguayan	1	<0.01
Peruvian	25	0.07
Uruguayan	4	0.01
Venezuelan	12	0.03
Other South American	3	0.01
Other Hispanic or Latino	400	1.10

Race*	Population	%
African-American/Black (974)	1,453	3.99
Not Hispanic (776)	1,150	3.16
Hispanic (198)	303	0.83
American Indian/Alaska Native (90)	338	0.93
Not Hispanic (50)	241	0.66
Hispanic (40)	97	0.27
Apache (6)	10	0.03
Blackfeet (2)	11	0.03
Canadian/French Am. Ind. (0)	3	0.01
Central American Ind. (2)	3	0.01
Cherokee (1)	37	0.10
Cheyenne (0)	4	0.01
Chickasaw (0)	6	0.02
Chippewa (1)	6	0.02
Choctaw (0)	1	<0.01
Comanche (1)	2	0.01
Cree (0)	1	<0.01
Delaware (0)	3	0.01
Iroquois (4)	13	0.04
Mexican American Ind. (4)	8	0.02
Navajo (1)	3	0.01
Pueblo (0)	3	0.01
Sioux (2)	2	0.01
South American Ind. (8)	9	0.02
Spanish American Ind. (0)	1	<0.01
Asian (785)	914	2.51
Not Hispanic (777)	885	2.43

*Notes: † The Census 2010 population figure is used to calculate the percentages in the Hispanic Origin and Race categories. Ancestry percentages are based on the 2006-2010 American Community Survey population (not shown); ‡ Numbers in parentheses indicate the number of people reporting a single ancestry; * Numbers in parentheses indicate the number of persons reporting this race alone, not in combination with any other race; Please refer to the Explanation of Data for more information.*

Hispanic (8)	29	0.08
Bangladeshi (24)	24	0.07
Cambodian (34)	37	0.10
Chinese, ex. Taiwanese (101)	119	0.33
Filipino (91)	126	0.35
Indian (124)	143	0.39
Indonesian (16)	22	0.06
Japanese (7)	20	0.05
Korean (94)	116	0.32
Laotian (82)	96	0.26
Nepalese (1)	1	<0.01
Pakistani (26)	31	0.09
Sri Lankan (4)	4	0.01
Taiwanese (2)	3	0.01
Thai (4)	9	0.02
Vietnamese (145)	157	0.43
Hawaii Native/Pacific Islander (9)	52	0.14
Not Hispanic (9)	28	0.08
Hispanic (0)	24	0.07
Guamanian/Chamorro (4)	5	0.01
Native Hawaiian (1)	12	0.03
Samoan (1)	3	0.01
White (32,278)	33,092	90.95
Not Hispanic (30,898)	31,485	86.54
Hispanic (1,380)	1,607	4.42

Trumbull

Place Type: CDP/Town
County: Fairfield
Population: 36,018†

Ancestry‡	Population	%
African, Sub-Saharan (243)	343	0.97
African (59)	142	0.40
Cape Verdean (43)	60	0.17
Kenyan (141)	141	0.40
Albanian (31)	79	0.22
American (610)	610	1.72
Arab (169)	365	1.03
Egyptian (48)	73	0.21
Lebanese (10)	89	0.25
Moroccan (21)	72	0.20
Syrian (90)	131	0.37
Armenian (76)	114	0.32
Australian (0)	34	0.10
Austrian (23)	163	0.46
Belgian (12)	37	0.10
Brazilian (119)	153	0.43
British (51)	91	0.26
Canadian (44)	102	0.29
Carpatho Rusyn (8)	8	0.02
Croatian (0)	6	0.02
Czech (18)	238	0.67
Czechoslovakian (42)	109	0.31
Danish (82)	257	0.72
Dutch (68)	225	0.63
Eastern European (69)	69	0.19
English (730)	2,642	7.44
Estonian (20)	80	0.23
European (299)	319	0.90
Finnish (10)	21	0.06
French, ex. Basque (184)	969	2.73
French Canadian (146)	443	1.25
German (772)	4,277	12.05
Greek (397)	694	1.96
Guyanese (93)	93	0.26
Hungarian (385)	1,193	3.36
Iranian (70)	70	0.20
Irish (2,269)	8,060	22.71
Israeli (0)	33	0.09
Italian (5,526)	10,988	30.96
Latvian (29)	61	0.17
Lithuanian (222)	564	1.59
Macedonian (0)	65	0.18
Northern European (91)	91	0.26
Norwegian (40)	201	0.57
Polish (862)	2,582	7.27
Portuguese (690)	836	2.36
Romanian (137)	231	0.65
Russian (640)	1,433	4.04
Scandinavian (0)	36	0.10
Scotch-Irish (156)	479	1.35
Scottish (127)	569	1.60
Slavic (8)	8	0.02
Slovak (356)	919	2.59
Slovene (0)	48	0.14
Swedish (174)	495	1.39
Swiss (12)	127	0.36
Turkish (40)	40	0.11
Ukrainian (39)	136	0.38
Welsh (9)	148	0.42
West Indian, ex. Hispanic (71)	139	0.39
Haitian (29)	61	0.17
Jamaican (27)	27	0.08
Trinidadian/Tobagonian (15)	51	0.14
Yugoslavian (107)	116	0.33

Hispanic Origin	Population	%
Hispanic or Latino (of any race)	2,068	5.74
Central American, ex. Mexican	161	0.45
Costa Rican	33	0.09
Guatemalan	76	0.21
Honduran	14	0.04
Nicaraguan	3	0.01
Panamanian	3	0.01
Salvadoran	32	0.09
Cuban	137	0.38
Dominican Republic	89	0.25
Mexican	143	0.40
Puerto Rican	792	2.20
South American	501	1.39
Argentinean	50	0.14
Bolivian	8	0.02
Chilean	8	0.02
Colombian	131	0.36
Ecuadorian	116	0.32
Paraguayan	18	0.05
Peruvian	101	0.28
Uruguayan	27	0.07
Venezuelan	26	0.07
Other South American	16	0.04
Other Hispanic or Latino	245	0.68

Race*	Population	%
African-American/Black (1,126)	1,281	3.56
Not Hispanic (1,070)	1,192	3.31
Hispanic (56)	89	0.25
American Indian/Alaska Native (21)	100	0.28
Not Hispanic (19)	80	0.22
Hispanic (2)	20	0.06
Apache (0)	2	0.01
Blackfeet (0)	3	0.01
Canadian/French Am. Ind. (2)	3	0.01
Cherokee (0)	12	0.03
Chickasaw (0)	2	0.01
Chippewa (3)	9	0.02
Choctaw (0)	2	0.01
Iroquois (0)	11	0.03
South American Ind. (0)	5	0.01
Asian (1,573)	1,775	4.93
Not Hispanic (1,559)	1,750	4.86
Hispanic (14)	25	0.07
Bangladeshi (12)	13	0.04
Burmese (2)	2	0.01
Cambodian (48)	50	0.14
Chinese, ex. Taiwanese (321)	370	1.03
Filipino (83)	107	0.30
Indian (654)	705	1.96
Indonesian (3)	3	0.01
Japanese (21)	43	0.12
Korean (188)	220	0.61
Laotian (6)	7	0.02
Malaysian (1)	1	<0.01
Nepalese (8)	8	0.02
Pakistani (27)	31	0.09
Sri Lankan (19)	29	0.08
Taiwanese (7)	14	0.04
Thai (6)	14	0.04
Vietnamese (118)	133	0.37
Hawaii Native/Pacific Islander (3)	16	0.04
Not Hispanic (2)	11	0.03
Hispanic (1)	5	0.01
Guamanian/Chamorro (1)	4	0.01
Native Hawaiian (2)	4	0.01
Samoan (0)	2	0.01
White (32,424)	32,822	91.13
Not Hispanic (30,872)	31,178	86.56
Hispanic (1,552)	1,644	4.56

Vernon

Place Type: Town
County: Tolland
Population: 29,179†

Ancestry‡	Population	%
African, Sub-Saharan (68)	68	0.23
African (55)	55	0.19
Zimbabwean (13)	13	0.04
American (1,148)	1,148	3.93
Arab (56)	56	0.19
Other Arab (56)	56	0.19
Austrian (9)	30	0.10
Belgian (13)	21	0.07
Brazilian (169)	169	0.58
British (105)	166	0.57
Bulgarian (0)	13	0.04
Canadian (116)	306	1.05
Czech (23)	196	0.67
Czechoslovakian (0)	53	0.18
Danish (30)	268	0.92
Dutch (56)	247	0.85
Eastern European (29)	72	0.25
English (962)	3,321	11.37
European (122)	133	0.46
Finnish (0)	58	0.20
French, ex. Basque (814)	2,783	9.53
French Canadian (666)	1,463	5.01
German (943)	4,255	14.57
Greek (188)	279	0.96
Guyanese (18)	32	0.11
Hungarian (26)	203	0.70
Icelander (0)	10	0.03
Iranian (10)	49	0.17
Irish (1,498)	5,379	18.42
Italian (1,601)	4,178	14.31
Latvian (54)	54	0.18
Lithuanian (115)	460	1.58
Norwegian (72)	272	0.93
Pennsylvania German (0)	42	0.14
Polish (1,310)	2,955	10.12
Portuguese (154)	269	0.92
Romanian (0)	14	0.05
Russian (107)	338	1.16
Scotch-Irish (140)	670	2.29
Scottish (226)	991	3.39
Slavic (14)	21	0.07
Slovak (63)	159	0.54
Swedish (290)	882	3.02
Swiss (15)	219	0.75
Turkish (15)	15	0.05
Ukrainian (111)	215	0.74
Welsh (58)	254	0.87
West Indian, ex. Hispanic (488)	701	2.40
Jamaican (426)	476	1.63
Trinidadian/Tobagonian (62)	211	0.72
West Indian (0)	14	0.05

Hispanic Origin	Population	%
Hispanic or Latino (of any race)	1,907	6.54
Central American, ex. Mexican	86	0.29
Costa Rican	4	0.01
Guatemalan	21	0.07
Honduran	4	0.01
Nicaraguan	15	0.05
Panamanian	14	0.05
Salvadoran	28	0.10
Cuban	43	0.15
Dominican Republic	53	0.18

*Notes: † The Census 2010 population figure is used to calculate the percentages in the Hispanic Origin and Race categories. Ancestry percentages are based on the 2006-2010 American Community Survey population (not shown); ‡ Numbers in parentheses indicate the number of people reporting a single ancestry; * Numbers in parentheses indicate the number of persons reporting this race alone, not in combination with any other race; Please refer to the Explanation of Data for more information.*

Mexican	89	0.31
Puerto Rican	1,342	4.60
South American	172	0.59
Argentinean	13	0.04
Bolivian	1	<0.01
Chilean	7	0.02
Colombian	38	0.13
Ecuadorian	36	0.12
Peruvian	56	0.19
Uruguayan	9	0.03
Venezuelan	12	0.04
Other Hispanic or Latino	122	0.42

Race*	Population	%
African-American/Black (1,697)	2,088	7.16
Not Hispanic (1,554)	1,879	6.44
Hispanic (143)	209	0.72
American Indian/Alaska Native (68)	249	0.85
Not Hispanic (59)	200	0.69
Hispanic (9)	49	0.17
Apache (0)	2	0.01
Blackfeet (1)	14	0.05
Canadian/French Am. Ind. (0)	3	0.01
Cherokee (8)	35	0.12
Chickasaw (0)	1	<0.01
Chippewa (0)	1	<0.01
Crow (5)	5	0.02
Delaware (1)	3	0.01
Inupiat *(Alaska Native)* (1)	2	0.01
Iroquois (0)	2	0.01
Lumbee (1)	5	0.02
Menominee (1)	1	<0.01
Mexican American Ind. (1)	1	<0.01
Ottawa (1)	1	<0.01
Potawatomi (0)	1	<0.01
Seminole (0)	2	0.01
Sioux (1)	5	0.02
South American Ind. (1)	2	0.01
Spanish American Ind. (1)	1	<0.01
Asian (1,263)	1,411	4.84
Not Hispanic (1,245)	1,381	4.73
Hispanic (18)	30	0.10
Bangladeshi (4)	4	0.01
Burmese (2)	2	0.01
Cambodian (0)	1	<0.01
Chinese, ex. Taiwanese (171)	198	0.68
Filipino (36)	57	0.20
Hmong (7)	8	0.03
Indian (369)	399	1.37
Indonesian (1)	2	0.01
Japanese (25)	42	0.14
Korean (121)	142	0.49
Laotian (14)	17	0.06
Malaysian (5)	7	0.02
Pakistani (285)	318	1.09
Sri Lankan (4)	4	0.01
Taiwanese (4)	4	0.01
Thai (13)	17	0.06
Vietnamese (145)	161	0.55
Hawaii Native/Pacific Islander (10)	33	0.11
Not Hispanic (9)	29	0.10
Hispanic (1)	4	0.01
Fijian (1)	1	<0.01
Guamanian/Chamorro (4)	11	0.04
Native Hawaiian (2)	7	0.02
White (24,825)	25,468	87.28
Not Hispanic (23,804)	24,311	83.32
Hispanic (1,021)	1,157	3.97

Wallingford Center

Place Type: CDP
County: New Haven
Population: 18,209†

Ancestry‡	Population	%
African, Sub-Saharan (57)	57	0.32
Ghanaian (57)	57	0.32
Albanian (13)	13	0.07
American (450)	450	2.51
Arab (18)	18	0.10
Other Arab (18)	18	0.10
Armenian (0)	25	0.14
Australian (17)	47	0.26
Austrian (0)	19	0.11
British (42)	42	0.23
Canadian (27)	39	0.22
Czech (0)	97	0.54
Czechoslovakian (15)	55	0.31
Danish (0)	37	0.21
Dutch (13)	136	0.76
Eastern European (7)	32	0.18
English (470)	1,962	10.93
European (74)	74	0.41
Finnish (0)	121	0.67
French, ex. Basque (244)	1,266	7.05
French Canadian (203)	420	2.34
German (324)	1,967	10.96
Greek (0)	73	0.41
Hungarian (120)	389	2.17
Icelander (9)	9	0.05
Iranian (19)	19	0.11
Irish (952)	4,213	23.47
Israeli (13)	13	0.07
Italian (1,974)	4,585	25.55
Lithuanian (43)	272	1.52
Maltese (17)	17	0.09
Northern European (0)	7	0.04
Norwegian (0)	18	0.10
Polish (853)	2,058	11.47
Portuguese (190)	374	2.08
Romanian (0)	9	0.05
Russian (47)	227	1.26
Scandinavian (0)	13	0.07
Scotch-Irish (26)	234	1.30
Scottish (61)	232	1.29
Slavic (0)	21	0.12
Slovak (48)	64	0.36
Swedish (94)	398	2.22
Swiss (0)	63	0.35
Turkish (137)	144	0.80
Ukrainian (27)	82	0.46
Welsh (0)	32	0.18
West Indian, ex. Hispanic (42)	63	0.35
British West Indian (30)	30	0.17
West Indian (12)	33	0.18

Hispanic Origin	Population	%
Hispanic or Latino (of any race)	2,610	14.33
Central American, ex. Mexican	56	0.31
Costa Rican	7	0.04
Guatemalan	19	0.10
Honduran	17	0.09
Nicaraguan	4	0.02
Panamanian	1	0.01
Salvadoran	8	0.04
Cuban	55	0.30
Dominican Republic	43	0.24
Mexican	1,068	5.87
Puerto Rican	812	4.46
South American	395	2.17
Argentinean	18	0.10
Bolivian	3	0.02
Chilean	15	0.08
Colombian	56	0.31
Ecuadorian	270	1.48
Paraguayan	2	0.01
Peruvian	23	0.13
Uruguayan	3	0.02
Venezuelan	5	0.03
Other Hispanic or Latino	181	0.99

Race*	Population	%
African-American/Black (348)	466	2.56
Not Hispanic (296)	391	2.15
Hispanic (52)	75	0.41
American Indian/Alaska Native (44)	130	0.71
Not Hispanic (19)	86	0.47
Hispanic (25)	44	0.24
Blackfeet (0)	3	0.02
Canadian/French Am. Ind. (1)	2	0.01
Central American Ind. (1)	1	0.01
Cherokee (3)	20	0.11
Choctaw (0)	1	0.01
Comanche (0)	1	0.01
Creek (0)	2	0.01
Crow (0)	1	0.01
Iroquois (2)	2	0.01
Osage (2)	2	0.01
Pueblo (0)	4	0.02
South American Ind. (3)	6	0.03
Asian (612)	697	3.83
Not Hispanic (609)	684	3.76
Hispanic (3)	13	0.07
Bangladeshi (20)	25	0.14
Cambodian (4)	5	0.03
Chinese, ex. Taiwanese (134)	159	0.87
Filipino (80)	96	0.53
Indian (156)	182	1.00
Indonesian (1)	1	0.01
Japanese (7)	17	0.09
Korean (27)	37	0.20
Laotian (1)	6	0.03
Nepalese (8)	9	0.05
Pakistani (71)	81	0.44
Taiwanese (5)	8	0.04
Thai (3)	5	0.03
Vietnamese (42)	60	0.33
Hawaii Native/Pacific Islander (3)	8	0.04
Not Hispanic (2)	5	0.03
Hispanic (1)	3	0.02
Guamanian/Chamorro (1)	2	0.01
White (15,924)	16,232	89.14
Not Hispanic (14,417)	14,611	80.24
Hispanic (1,507)	1,621	8.90

Wallingford

Place Type: Town
County: New Haven
Population: 45,135†

Ancestry‡	Population	%
African, Sub-Saharan (70)	70	0.16
Cape Verdean (13)	13	0.03
Ghanaian (57)	57	0.13
Albanian (73)	83	0.19
American (1,180)	1,180	2.63
Arab (137)	221	0.49
Egyptian (37)	37	0.08
Lebanese (61)	145	0.32
Moroccan (21)	21	0.05
Other Arab (18)	18	0.04
Armenian (10)	35	0.08
Australian (17)	47	0.10
Austrian (14)	88	0.20
Belgian (21)	64	0.14
Brazilian (0)	27	0.06
British (52)	92	0.21
Canadian (65)	116	0.26
Croatian (0)	8	0.02
Czech (75)	316	0.71
Czechoslovakian (23)	72	0.16
Danish (14)	92	0.21
Dutch (39)	287	0.64
Eastern European (27)	52	0.12
English (1,355)	5,343	11.93
Estonian (0)	10	0.02
European (236)	256	0.57
Finnish (0)	164	0.37
French, ex. Basque (445)	2,729	6.09
French Canadian (533)	1,176	2.63
German (777)	6,046	13.50
Greek (119)	540	1.21
Hungarian (383)	1,067	2.38
Icelander (9)	9	0.02
Iranian (79)	142	0.32
Irish (2,206)	10,185	22.74
Israeli (22)	38	0.08
Italian (5,822)	13,926	31.09

*Notes: † The Census 2010 population figure is used to calculate the percentages in the Hispanic Origin and Race categories. Ancestry percentages are based on the 2006-2010 American Community Survey population (not shown); ‡ Numbers in parentheses indicate the number of people reporting a single ancestry; * Numbers in parentheses indicate the number of persons reporting this race alone, not in combination with any other race; Please refer to the Explanation of Data for more information.*

Latvian (0)	31	0.07
Lithuanian (83)	613	1.37
Maltese (36)	73	0.16
Northern European (13)	20	0.04
Norwegian (63)	222	0.50
Pennsylvania German (8)	8	0.02
Polish (1,820)	4,733	10.57
Portuguese (323)	581	1.30
Romanian (9)	61	0.14
Russian (207)	645	1.44
Scandinavian (0)	13	0.03
Scotch-Irish (97)	756	1.69
Scottish (148)	825	1.84
Slavic (0)	38	0.08
Slovak (62)	78	0.17
Swedish (125)	940	2.10
Swiss (0)	72	0.16
Turkish (137)	144	0.32
Ukrainian (151)	312	0.70
Welsh (9)	146	0.33
West Indian, ex. Hispanic (42)	63	0.14
British West Indian (30)	30	0.07
West Indian (12)	33	0.07

Hispanic Origin	Population	%
Hispanic or Latino (of any race)	3,562	7.89
Central American, ex. Mexican	74	0.16
Costa Rican	7	0.02
Guatemalan	32	0.07
Honduran	18	0.04
Nicaraguan	7	0.02
Panamanian	1	<0.01
Salvadoran	9	0.02
Cuban	126	0.28
Dominican Republic	71	0.16
Mexican	1,199	2.66
Puerto Rican	1,261	2.79
South American	554	1.23
Argentinean	32	0.07
Bolivian	3	0.01
Chilean	23	0.05
Colombian	129	0.29
Ecuadorian	309	0.68
Paraguayan	2	<0.01
Peruvian	39	0.09
Uruguayan	5	0.01
Venezuelan	11	0.02
Other South American	1	<0.01
Other Hispanic or Latino	277	0.61

Race*	Population	%
African-American/Black (652)	860	1.91
Not Hispanic (587)	766	1.70
Hispanic (65)	94	0.21
American Indian/Alaska Native (76)	242	0.54
Not Hispanic (42)	184	0.41
Hispanic (34)	58	0.13
Blackfeet (1)	5	0.01
Canadian/French Am. Ind. (1)	5	0.01
Central American Ind. (1)	1	<0.01
Cherokee (5)	33	0.07
Chippewa (0)	4	0.01
Choctaw (0)	1	<0.01
Colville (1)	1	<0.01
Comanche (0)	2	<0.01
Creek (0)	2	<0.01
Crow (0)	1	<0.01
Iroquois (4)	4	0.01
Osage (2)	2	<0.01
Pueblo (0)	4	0.01
Puget Sound Salish (1)	1	<0.01
Seminole (0)	1	<0.01
Sioux (0)	8	0.02
South American Ind. (7)	10	0.02
Spanish American Ind. (1)	1	<0.01
Asian (1,531)	1,739	3.85
Not Hispanic (1,526)	1,719	3.81
Hispanic (5)	20	0.04
Bangladeshi (37)	50	0.11
Cambodian (9)	10	0.02
Chinese, ex. Taiwanese (320)	376	0.83
Filipino (179)	234	0.52
Indian (498)	550	1.22
Indonesian (1)	2	<0.01
Japanese (19)	46	0.10
Korean (105)	125	0.28
Laotian (24)	33	0.07
Malaysian (1)	1	<0.01
Nepalese (8)	9	0.02
Pakistani (111)	124	0.27
Sri Lankan (15)	15	0.03
Taiwanese (9)	13	0.03
Thai (8)	16	0.04
Vietnamese (100)	128	0.28
Hawaii Native/Pacific Islander (5)	23	0.05
Not Hispanic (4)	18	0.04
Hispanic (1)	5	0.01
Guamanian/Chamorro (1)	2	<0.01
Native Hawaiian (1)	6	0.01
White (41,077)	41,656	92.29
Not Hispanic (38,879)	39,300	87.07
Hispanic (2,198)	2,356	5.22

Waterbury

Place Type: City/Town
County: New Haven
Population: 110,366†

Ancestry‡	Population	%
African, Sub-Saharan (1,625)	2,194	2.00
African (1,284)	1,693	1.54
Cape Verdean (208)	353	0.32
Ethiopian (10)	10	0.01
Ghanaian (11)	11	0.01
Nigerian (28)	43	0.04
Ugandan (15)	15	0.01
Other Sub-Saharan African (69)	69	0.06
Albanian (2,378)	2,423	2.20
American (1,433)	1,433	1.30
Arab (505)	741	0.67
Arab (31)	31	0.03
Egyptian (121)	121	0.11
Iraqi (31)	31	0.03
Lebanese (171)	268	0.24
Moroccan (48)	155	0.14
Syrian (9)	9	0.01
Other Arab (94)	126	0.11
Armenian (13)	13	0.01
Austrian (46)	111	0.10
Belgian (26)	26	0.02
Brazilian (698)	725	0.66
British (48)	69	0.06
Canadian (244)	301	0.27
Croatian (46)	55	0.05
Czech (0)	80	0.07
Czechoslovakian (0)	25	0.02
Danish (0)	130	0.12
Dutch (52)	651	0.59
Eastern European (23)	23	0.02
English (753)	4,691	4.27
European (164)	178	0.16
Finnish (7)	7	0.01
French, ex. Basque (1,540)	5,775	5.25
French Canadian (855)	1,796	1.63
German (836)	4,230	3.85
Greek (265)	509	0.46
Guyanese (168)	468	0.43
Hungarian (149)	690	0.63
Irish (3,939)	13,152	11.96
Israeli (65)	65	0.06
Italian (11,003)	20,320	18.48
Lithuanian (630)	1,489	1.35
Macedonian (403)	403	0.37
Northern European (14)	14	0.01
Norwegian (0)	96	0.09
Polish (1,116)	3,849	3.50
Portuguese (2,064)	2,996	2.73
Romanian (84)	92	0.08
Russian (170)	942	0.86
Scandinavian (38)	38	0.03
Scotch-Irish (313)	722	0.66
Scottish (120)	483	0.44
Slavic (15)	15	0.01
Slovak (95)	244	0.22
Slovene (0)	32	0.03
Swedish (133)	666	0.61
Swiss (0)	9	0.01
Turkish (203)	203	0.18
Ukrainian (90)	229	0.21
Welsh (10)	144	0.13
West Indian, ex. Hispanic (2,715)	3,170	2.88
Barbadian (118)	118	0.11
British West Indian (56)	56	0.05
Dutch West Indian (0)	26	0.02
Haitian (361)	419	0.38
Jamaican (1,980)	2,171	1.97
Trinidadian/Tobagonian (106)	210	0.19
U.S. Virgin Islander (44)	44	0.04
West Indian (44)	120	0.11
Other West Indian (6)	6	0.01
Yugoslavian (12)	38	0.03

Hispanic Origin	Population	%
Hispanic or Latino (of any race)	34,446	31.21
Central American, ex. Mexican	824	0.75
Costa Rican	49	0.04
Guatemalan	166	0.15
Honduran	346	0.31
Nicaraguan	46	0.04
Panamanian	64	0.06
Salvadoran	139	0.13
Other Central American	14	0.01
Cuban	277	0.25
Dominican Republic	3,743	3.39
Mexican	1,572	1.42
Puerto Rican	24,947	22.60
South American	1,823	1.65
Argentinean	76	0.07
Bolivian	6	0.01
Chilean	22	0.02
Colombian	458	0.41
Ecuadorian	972	0.88
Paraguayan	3	<0.01
Peruvian	162	0.15
Uruguayan	22	0.02
Venezuelan	73	0.07
Other South American	29	0.03
Other Hispanic or Latino	1,260	1.14

Race*	Population	%
African-American/Black (22,138)	25,279	22.90
Not Hispanic (19,654)	21,686	19.65
Hispanic (2,484)	3,593	3.26
American Indian/Alaska Native (626)	1,407	1.27
Not Hispanic (313)	845	0.77
Hispanic (313)	562	0.51
Apache (4)	11	0.01
Blackfeet (8)	44	0.04
Canadian/French Am. Ind. (1)	5	<0.01
Central American Ind. (18)	30	0.03
Cherokee (12)	95	0.09
Chickasaw (3)	3	<0.01
Chippewa (0)	7	0.01
Choctaw (0)	8	0.01
Creek (2)	3	<0.01
Crow (0)	4	<0.01
Delaware (0)	2	<0.01
Inupiat *(Alaska Native)* (1)	1	<0.01
Iroquois (4)	22	0.02
Lumbee (0)	1	<0.01
Mexican American Ind. (19)	24	0.02
Navajo (1)	7	0.01
Paiute (1)	1	<0.01
Potawatomi (0)	1	<0.01
Pueblo (1)	4	<0.01
Puget Sound Salish (0)	5	<0.01
Seminole (0)	5	<0.01
Sioux (2)	11	0.01
South American Ind. (34)	88	0.08

*Notes: † The Census 2010 population figure is used to calculate the percentages in the Hispanic Origin and Race categories. Ancestry percentages are based on the 2006-2010 American Community Survey population (not shown); ‡ Numbers in parentheses indicate the number of people reporting a single ancestry; * Numbers in parentheses indicate the number of persons reporting this race alone, not in combination with any other race; Please refer to the Explanation of Data for more information.*

Spanish American Ind. (12)	26	0.02
Yaqui (1)	1	<0.01
Asian (1,989)	2,499	2.26
Not Hispanic (1,933)	2,339	2.12
Hispanic (56)	160	0.14
Bangladeshi (41)	43	0.04
Burmese (28)	31	0.03
Cambodian (67)	84	0.08
Chinese, ex. Taiwanese (197)	262	0.24
Filipino (159)	234	0.21
Indian (847)	984	0.89
Indonesian (5)	8	0.01
Japanese (34)	90	0.08
Korean (43)	72	0.07
Laotian (34)	46	0.04
Malaysian (1)	3	<0.01
Nepalese (9)	9	0.01
Pakistani (177)	211	0.19
Sri Lankan (8)	8	0.01
Taiwanese (11)	14	0.01
Thai (13)	20	0.02
Vietnamese (205)	229	0.21
Hawaii Native/Pacific Islander (38)	316	0.29
Not Hispanic (26)	173	0.16
Hispanic (12)	143	0.13
Guamanian/Chamorro (7)	9	0.01
Marshallese (1)	1	<0.01
Native Hawaiian (5)	24	0.02
Samoan (0)	3	<0.01
Tongan (1)	1	<0.01
White (64,864)	68,542	62.10
Not Hispanic (50,081)	52,069	47.18
Hispanic (14,783)	16,473	14.93

Waterford

Place Type: Town
County: New London
Population: 19,517†

Ancestry‡	Population	%
African, Sub-Saharan (42)	54	0.28
African (0)	12	0.06
Ghanaian (42)	42	0.22
Albanian (22)	46	0.24
American (1,037)	1,037	5.34
Arab (130)	200	1.03
Lebanese (115)	178	0.92
Syrian (15)	22	0.11
Armenian (0)	7	0.04
Austrian (0)	73	0.38
Belgian (8)	8	0.04
British (203)	230	1.18
Canadian (36)	65	0.33
Celtic (6)	12	0.06
Croatian (10)	52	0.27
Czech (0)	70	0.36
Czechoslovakian (0)	53	0.27
Danish (14)	31	0.16
Dutch (49)	166	0.85
Eastern European (47)	47	0.24
English (761)	3,098	15.94
Estonian (14)	14	0.07
European (202)	224	1.15
Finnish (0)	8	0.04
French, ex. Basque (249)	1,577	8.12
French Canadian (259)	629	3.24
German (457)	2,264	11.65
Greek (301)	366	1.88
Hungarian (34)	219	1.13
Icelander (7)	7	0.04
Iranian (0)	8	0.04
Irish (1,140)	3,922	20.19
Italian (1,538)	4,691	24.14
Latvian (10)	58	0.30
Lithuanian (42)	163	0.84
Northern European (11)	11	0.06
Norwegian (19)	196	1.01
Polish (453)	1,655	8.52
Portuguese (140)	480	2.47
Romanian (0)	29	0.15
Russian (166)	426	2.19
Scandinavian (21)	33	0.17
Scotch-Irish (218)	451	2.32
Scottish (227)	884	4.55
Slovak (0)	20	0.10
Swedish (86)	360	1.85
Swiss (0)	21	0.11
Ukrainian (21)	99	0.51
Welsh (71)	188	0.97
West Indian, ex. Hispanic (10)	30	0.15
West Indian (10)	30	0.15
Yugoslavian (23)	23	0.12

Hispanic Origin	Population	%
Hispanic or Latino (of any race)	922	4.72
Central American, ex. Mexican	62	0.32
Costa Rican	7	0.04
Guatemalan	9	0.05
Honduran	8	0.04
Nicaraguan	4	0.02
Panamanian	6	0.03
Salvadoran	28	0.14
Cuban	36	0.18
Dominican Republic	81	0.42
Mexican	84	0.43
Puerto Rican	424	2.17
South American	137	0.70
Argentinean	5	0.03
Bolivian	9	0.05
Chilean	3	0.02
Colombian	28	0.14
Ecuadorian	8	0.04
Paraguayan	3	0.02
Peruvian	76	0.39
Venezuelan	5	0.03
Other Hispanic or Latino	98	0.50

Race*	Population	%
African-American/Black (487)	695	3.56
Not Hispanic (443)	619	3.17
Hispanic (44)	76	0.39
American Indian/Alaska Native (105)	245	1.26
Not Hispanic (92)	208	1.07
Hispanic (13)	37	0.19
Apache (0)	3	0.02
Blackfeet (0)	10	0.05
Canadian/French Am. Ind. (0)	1	0.01
Cherokee (6)	22	0.11
Choctaw (0)	2	0.01
Cree (0)	5	0.03
Creek (0)	1	0.01
Iroquois (1)	4	0.02
Lumbee (3)	5	0.03
Mexican American Ind. (1)	1	0.01
Navajo (2)	3	0.02
Potawatomi (2)	2	0.01
Sioux (2)	7	0.04
South American Ind. (0)	9	0.05
Spanish American Ind. (1)	1	0.01
Asian (728)	880	4.51
Not Hispanic (726)	869	4.45
Hispanic (2)	11	0.06
Burmese (5)	5	0.03
Cambodian (48)	48	0.25
Chinese, ex. Taiwanese (290)	314	1.61
Filipino (115)	207	1.06
Indian (124)	136	0.70
Indonesian (1)	4	0.02
Japanese (12)	26	0.13
Korean (33)	39	0.20
Laotian (5)	7	0.04
Pakistani (43)	43	0.22
Taiwanese (4)	5	0.03
Thai (3)	5	0.03
Vietnamese (23)	24	0.12
Hawaii Native/Pacific Islander (2)	22	0.11
Not Hispanic (2)	21	0.11
Hispanic (0)	1	0.01
Guamanian/Chamorro (0)	7	0.04
Native Hawaiian (1)	8	0.04
White (17,453)	17,907	91.75
Not Hispanic (16,912)	17,276	88.52
Hispanic (541)	631	3.23

Watertown

Place Type: Town
County: Litchfield
Population: 22,514†

Ancestry‡	Population	%
Afghan (55)	55	0.24
Albanian (367)	443	1.97
American (464)	464	2.06
Arab (20)	103	0.46
Lebanese (20)	103	0.46
Austrian (17)	56	0.25
Brazilian (51)	62	0.28
British (43)	91	0.40
Bulgarian (25)	25	0.11
Cajun (9)	9	0.04
Canadian (33)	112	0.50
Czech (0)	65	0.29
Czechoslovakian (8)	17	0.08
Danish (0)	58	0.26
Dutch (63)	236	1.05
English (416)	2,317	10.29
European (50)	50	0.22
Finnish (11)	51	0.23
French, ex. Basque (406)	2,518	11.18
French Canadian (357)	959	4.26
German (324)	2,232	9.91
Greek (68)	107	0.48
Hungarian (51)	149	0.66
Irish (1,359)	4,810	21.36
Italian (3,630)	7,992	35.49
Latvian (8)	8	0.04
Lithuanian (359)	892	3.96
Northern European (32)	32	0.14
Norwegian (0)	12	0.05
Pennsylvania German (11)	23	0.10
Polish (407)	1,767	7.85
Portuguese (403)	578	2.57
Romanian (0)	64	0.28
Russian (195)	441	1.96
Scandinavian (16)	35	0.16
Scotch-Irish (55)	192	0.85
Scottish (63)	455	2.02
Slavic (34)	34	0.15
Slovak (14)	38	0.17
Slovene (29)	29	0.13
Swedish (72)	367	1.63
Swiss (16)	32	0.14
Turkish (0)	14	0.06
Ukrainian (79)	160	0.71
Welsh (0)	66	0.29
West Indian, ex. Hispanic (84)	84	0.37
British West Indian (45)	45	0.20
Jamaican (39)	39	0.17
Yugoslavian (15)	31	0.14

Hispanic Origin	Population	%
Hispanic or Latino (of any race)	838	3.72
Central American, ex. Mexican	20	0.09
Costa Rican	2	0.01
Guatemalan	7	0.03
Honduran	4	0.02
Nicaraguan	1	<0.01
Panamanian	1	<0.01
Salvadoran	5	0.02
Cuban	31	0.14
Dominican Republic	36	0.16
Mexican	77	0.34
Puerto Rican	500	2.22
South American	96	0.43
Argentinean	14	0.06
Chilean	5	0.02
Colombian	25	0.11
Ecuadorian	35	0.16

*Notes: † The Census 2010 population figure is used to calculate the percentages in the Hispanic Origin and Race categories. Ancestry percentages are based on the 2006-2010 American Community Survey population (not shown); ‡ Numbers in parentheses indicate the number of people reporting a single ancestry; * Numbers in parentheses indicate the number of persons reporting this race alone, not in combination with any other race; Please refer to the Explanation of Data for more information.*

Peruvian	3	0.01
Uruguayan	3	0.01
Venezuelan	10	0.04
Other South American	1	<0.01
Other Hispanic or Latino	78	0.35

Race*	Population	%
African-American/Black (315)	440	1.95
Not Hispanic (292)	390	1.73
Hispanic (23)	50	0.22
American Indian/Alaska Native (58)	148	0.66
Not Hispanic (51)	130	0.58
Hispanic (7)	18	0.08
Apache (2)	2	0.01
Blackfeet (3)	11	0.05
Canadian/French Am. Ind. (3)	3	0.01
Central American Ind. (0)	1	<0.01
Cherokee (8)	19	0.08
Choctaw (0)	2	0.01
Iroquois (1)	4	0.02
Lumbee (0)	2	0.01
Sioux (2)	2	0.01
South American Ind. (0)	2	0.01
Tlingit-Haida *(Alaska Native)* (0)	1	<0.01
Asian (376)	443	1.97
Not Hispanic (376)	438	1.95
Hispanic (0)	5	0.02
Bangladeshi (7)	7	0.03
Burmese (5)	5	0.02
Cambodian (10)	11	0.05
Chinese, ex. Taiwanese (67)	72	0.32
Filipino (105)	129	0.57
Indian (71)	81	0.36
Indonesian (1)	1	<0.01
Japanese (3)	5	0.02
Korean (27)	35	0.16
Pakistani (14)	18	0.08
Taiwanese (4)	7	0.03
Thai (1)	1	<0.01
Vietnamese (46)	52	0.23
Hawaii Native/Pacific Islander (1)	20	0.09
Not Hispanic (1)	10	0.04
Hispanic (0)	10	0.04
Native Hawaiian (1)	4	0.02
Samoan (0)	1	<0.01
White (21,249)	21,510	95.54
Not Hispanic (20,707)	20,921	92.92
Hispanic (542)	589	2.62

West Hartford

Place Type: CDP/Town
County: Hartford
Population: 63,268†

Ancestry‡	Population	%
African, Sub-Saharan (437)	459	0.73
African (101)	101	0.16
Nigerian (90)	90	0.14
Somalian (40)	40	0.06
South African (45)	67	0.11
Sudanese (115)	115	0.18
Other Sub-Saharan African (46)	46	0.07
Albanian (41)	41	0.07
American (2,007)	2,007	3.19
Arab (232)	393	0.62
Lebanese (133)	275	0.44
Moroccan (11)	11	0.02
Syrian (6)	6	0.01
Other Arab (82)	101	0.16
Armenian (224)	279	0.44
Assyrian/Chaldean/Syriac (22)	35	0.06
Australian (0)	8	0.01
Austrian (63)	404	0.64
Brazilian (101)	323	0.51
British (174)	345	0.55
Bulgarian (57)	57	0.09
Canadian (153)	448	0.71
Celtic (0)	37	0.06
Croatian (0)	70	0.11
Cypriot (18)	43	0.07
Czech (118)	215	0.34
Czechoslovakian (65)	113	0.18
Danish (50)	214	0.34
Dutch (119)	351	0.56
Eastern European (731)	894	1.42
English (1,178)	6,314	10.04
Estonian (8)	16	0.03
European (742)	806	1.28
Finnish (48)	141	0.22
French, ex. Basque (759)	2,783	4.42
French Canadian (705)	1,401	2.23
German (1,492)	6,749	10.73
German Russian (15)	15	0.02
Greek (248)	501	0.80
Guyanese (21)	21	0.03
Hungarian (168)	642	1.02
Iranian (30)	47	0.07
Irish (4,152)	11,653	18.53
Israeli (101)	109	0.17
Italian (2,952)	7,850	12.48
Latvian (32)	56	0.09
Lithuanian (194)	563	0.90
New Zealander (10)	10	0.02
Northern European (16)	16	0.03
Norwegian (77)	284	0.45
Pennsylvania German (11)	11	0.02
Polish (1,320)	4,382	6.97
Portuguese (1,085)	1,473	2.34
Romanian (99)	273	0.43
Russian (1,708)	3,388	5.39
Scandinavian (0)	8	0.01
Scotch-Irish (331)	915	1.45
Scottish (268)	1,284	2.04
Slavic (0)	25	0.04
Slovak (86)	252	0.40
Swedish (336)	1,522	2.42
Swiss (69)	134	0.21
Turkish (0)	7	0.01
Ukrainian (587)	837	1.33
Welsh (92)	375	0.60
West Indian, ex. Hispanic (962)	1,210	1.92
Barbadian (18)	18	0.03
Bermudan (26)	26	0.04
British West Indian (0)	18	0.03
Haitian (31)	38	0.06
Jamaican (593)	765	1.22
Trinidadian/Tobagonian (61)	80	0.13
West Indian (224)	256	0.41
Other West Indian (9)	9	0.01
Yugoslavian (41)	58	0.09

Hispanic Origin	Population	%
Hispanic or Latino (of any race)	6,192	9.79
Central American, ex. Mexican	226	0.36
Costa Rican	10	0.02
Guatemalan	65	0.10
Honduran	34	0.05
Nicaraguan	17	0.03
Panamanian	16	0.03
Salvadoran	84	0.13
Cuban	208	0.33
Dominican Republic	300	0.47
Mexican	394	0.62
Puerto Rican	2,864	4.53
South American	1,758	2.78
Argentinean	129	0.20
Bolivian	17	0.03
Chilean	68	0.11
Colombian	423	0.67
Ecuadorian	68	0.11
Paraguayan	10	0.02
Peruvian	964	1.52
Uruguayan	22	0.03
Venezuelan	49	0.08
Other South American	8	0.01
Other Hispanic or Latino	442	0.70

Race*	Population	%
African-American/Black (3,982)	4,686	7.41
Not Hispanic (3,624)	4,131	6.53
Hispanic (358)	555	0.88
American Indian/Alaska Native (113)	427	0.67
Not Hispanic (58)	265	0.42
Hispanic (55)	162	0.26
Blackfeet (2)	24	0.04
Canadian/French Am. Ind. (0)	7	0.01
Central American Ind. (3)	8	0.01
Cherokee (2)	30	0.05
Chickasaw (1)	4	0.01
Choctaw (0)	5	0.01
Cree (1)	4	0.01
Creek (0)	3	<0.01
Crow (0)	1	<0.01
Delaware (0)	1	<0.01
Inupiat *(Alaska Native)* (0)	1	<0.01
Iroquois (2)	4	0.01
Mexican American Ind. (4)	9	0.01
Navajo (1)	1	<0.01
Sioux (0)	1	<0.01
South American Ind. (19)	67	0.11
Tlingit-Haida *(Alaska Native)* (1)	1	<0.01
Asian (4,666)	5,271	8.33
Not Hispanic (4,623)	5,176	8.18
Hispanic (43)	95	0.15
Bangladeshi (12)	17	0.03
Burmese (7)	10	0.02
Cambodian (84)	90	0.14
Chinese, ex. Taiwanese (1,136)	1,305	2.06
Filipino (171)	229	0.36
Indian (1,126)	1,258	1.99
Indonesian (6)	13	0.02
Japanese (81)	173	0.27
Korean (216)	262	0.41
Laotian (59)	65	0.10
Malaysian (6)	7	0.01
Nepalese (240)	245	0.39
Pakistani (234)	262	0.41
Sri Lankan (10)	11	0.02
Taiwanese (50)	72	0.11
Thai (36)	42	0.07
Vietnamese (1,013)	1,116	1.76
Hawaii Native/Pacific Islander (24)	89	0.14
Not Hispanic (15)	56	0.09
Hispanic (9)	33	0.05
Guamanian/Chamorro (3)	4	0.01
Native Hawaiian (1)	12	0.02
Samoan (1)	1	<0.01
Tongan (2)	2	<0.01
White (50,349)	51,696	81.71
Not Hispanic (47,307)	48,267	76.29
Hispanic (3,042)	3,429	5.42

West Haven

Place Type: City/Town
County: New Haven
Population: 55,564†

Ancestry‡	Population	%
African, Sub-Saharan (1,763)	2,153	3.91
African (596)	682	1.24
Cape Verdean (59)	214	0.39
Ethiopian (24)	24	0.04
Ghanaian (122)	122	0.22
Liberian (524)	524	0.95
Nigerian (263)	412	0.75
Senegalese (14)	14	0.03
Sudanese (51)	51	0.09
Other Sub-Saharan African (110)	110	0.20
Albanian (136)	238	0.43
American (1,130)	1,130	2.05
Arab (250)	597	1.08
Arab (43)	43	0.08
Egyptian (95)	95	0.17
Lebanese (93)	440	0.80
Moroccan (19)	19	0.03
Armenian (10)	91	0.17
Austrian (15)	102	0.19
Belgian (22)	34	0.06

SECTION TWO

*Notes: † The Census 2010 population figure is used to calculate the percentages in the Hispanic Origin and Race categories. Ancestry percentages are based on the 2006-2010 American Community Survey population (not shown); ‡ Numbers in parentheses indicate the number of people reporting a single ancestry; * Numbers in parentheses indicate the number of persons reporting this race alone, not in combination with any other race; Please refer to the Explanation of Data for more information.*

Brazilian (137)	137	0.25
British (25)	67	0.12
Canadian (0)	32	0.06
Croatian (22)	38	0.07
Czech (17)	342	0.62
Czechoslovakian (0)	89	0.16
Danish (22)	120	0.22
Dutch (12)	205	0.37
Eastern European (61)	61	0.11
English (667)	3,357	6.10
European (87)	87	0.16
Finnish (32)	60	0.11
French, ex. Basque (331)	1,890	3.43
French Canadian (224)	796	1.45
German (623)	4,233	7.69
Greek (194)	464	0.84
Guyanese (60)	224	0.41
Hungarian (68)	255	0.46
Iranian (0)	91	0.17
Irish (2,706)	9,580	17.40
Italian (7,922)	14,769	26.82
Lithuanian (68)	148	0.27
Macedonian (0)	16	0.03
Norwegian (47)	117	0.21
Polish (552)	2,488	4.52
Portuguese (320)	450	0.82
Romanian (14)	14	0.03
Russian (402)	848	1.54
Scotch-Irish (166)	706	1.28
Scottish (170)	508	0.92
Serbian (46)	46	0.08
Slovak (109)	412	0.75
Swedish (35)	556	1.01
Swiss (0)	14	0.03
Turkish (276)	276	0.50
Ukrainian (31)	334	0.61
Welsh (0)	111	0.20
West Indian, ex. Hispanic (1,465)	1,714	3.11
Barbadian (28)	28	0.05
British West Indian (36)	100	0.18
Haitian (156)	156	0.28
Jamaican (1,056)	1,150	2.09
Trinidadian/Tobagonian (146)	162	0.29
West Indian (43)	118	0.21
Yugoslavian (122)	135	0.25

Hispanic Origin	**Population**	**%**
Hispanic or Latino (of any race)	10,155	18.28
Central American, ex. Mexican	904	1.63
Costa Rican	43	0.08
Guatemalan	584	1.05
Honduran	72	0.13
Nicaraguan	14	0.03
Panamanian	50	0.09
Salvadoran	138	0.25
Other Central American	3	0.01
Cuban	143	0.26
Dominican Republic	404	0.73
Mexican	2,029	3.65
Puerto Rican	4,282	7.71
South American	1,800	3.24
Argentinean	117	0.21
Bolivian	13	0.02
Chilean	50	0.09
Colombian	587	1.06
Ecuadorian	621	1.12
Paraguayan	3	0.01
Peruvian	348	0.63
Uruguayan	20	0.04
Venezuelan	38	0.07
Other South American	3	0.01
Other Hispanic or Latino	593	1.07

Race*	**Population**	**%**
African-American/Black (10,917)	12,015	21.62
Not Hispanic (10,205)	11,025	19.84
Hispanic (712)	990	1.78
American Indian/Alaska Native (178)	544	0.98
Not Hispanic (89)	323	0.58
Hispanic (89)	221	0.40
Apache (1)	1	<0.01
Blackfeet (2)	17	0.03
Canadian/French Am. Ind. (0)	2	<0.01
Central American Ind. (3)	8	0.01
Cherokee (4)	71	0.13
Chickasaw (0)	1	<0.01
Chippewa (2)	4	0.01
Cree (0)	1	<0.01
Crow (0)	1	<0.01
Delaware (0)	1	<0.01
Iroquois (1)	5	0.01
Lumbee (3)	3	0.01
Mexican American Ind. (17)	20	0.04
Paiute (0)	2	<0.01
Pima (0)	4	0.01
Puget Sound Salish (2)	2	<0.01
Seminole (0)	1	<0.01
Sioux (1)	1	<0.01
South American Ind. (21)	39	0.07
Spanish American Ind. (0)	1	<0.01
Yaqui (1)	1	<0.01
Yup'ik *(Alaska Native)* (0)	2	<0.01
Asian (2,077)	2,441	4.39
Not Hispanic (2,056)	2,372	4.27
Hispanic (21)	69	0.12
Bangladeshi (16)	19	0.03
Cambodian (63)	68	0.12
Chinese, ex. Taiwanese (362)	395	0.71
Filipino (345)	403	0.73
Indian (563)	641	1.15
Indonesian (61)	66	0.12
Japanese (24)	63	0.11
Korean (81)	109	0.20
Laotian (31)	40	0.07
Malaysian (70)	81	0.15
Nepalese (21)	22	0.04
Pakistani (188)	212	0.38
Sri Lankan (2)	4	0.01
Taiwanese (12)	16	0.03
Thai (39)	48	0.09
Vietnamese (114)	128	0.23
Hawaii Native/Pacific Islander (90)	183	0.33
Not Hispanic (43)	108	0.19
Hispanic (47)	75	0.13
Fijian (0)	1	<0.01
Guamanian/Chamorro (72)	82	0.15
Native Hawaiian (12)	24	0.04
Samoan (3)	11	0.02
Tongan (0)	1	<0.01
White (36,498)	37,980	68.35
Not Hispanic (31,635)	32,595	58.66
Hispanic (4,863)	5,385	9.69

Weston

Place Type: Town
County: Fairfield
Population: 10,179†

Ancestry‡	**Population**	**%**
African, Sub-Saharan (41)	71	0.70
African (19)	49	0.49
South African (22)	22	0.22
American (432)	432	4.28
Arab (0)	39	0.39
Iraqi (0)	13	0.13
Other Arab (0)	26	0.26
Armenian (32)	32	0.32
Austrian (111)	235	2.33
Brazilian (8)	8	0.08
British (34)	55	0.55
Canadian (0)	9	0.09
Croatian (0)	19	0.19
Czech (27)	118	1.17
Danish (0)	139	1.38
Dutch (18)	57	0.57
Eastern European (373)	395	3.92
English (209)	1,113	11.03
European (272)	290	2.87
French, ex. Basque (13)	242	2.40
French Canadian (17)	57	0.57
German (347)	1,493	14.80
Greek (17)	75	0.74
Hungarian (70)	152	1.51
Iranian (10)	23	0.23
Irish (428)	1,766	17.51
Israeli (7)	7	0.07
Italian (863)	2,062	20.44
Lithuanian (0)	17	0.17
Maltese (0)	17	0.17
Northern European (70)	70	0.69
Norwegian (25)	65	0.64
Polish (155)	665	6.59
Romanian (18)	50	0.50
Russian (520)	1,356	13.44
Scandinavian (0)	42	0.42
Scotch-Irish (33)	145	1.44
Scottish (20)	155	1.54
Slavic (0)	19	0.19
Slovene (0)	10	0.10
Swedish (74)	234	2.32
Swiss (19)	157	1.56
Ukrainian (21)	127	1.26
Welsh (0)	55	0.55
West Indian, ex. Hispanic (0)	40	0.40
British West Indian (0)	32	0.32
West Indian (0)	8	0.08

Hispanic Origin	**Population**	**%**
Hispanic or Latino (of any race)	336	3.30
Central American, ex. Mexican	22	0.22
Costa Rican	9	0.09
Guatemalan	5	0.05
Honduran	1	0.01
Panamanian	4	0.04
Salvadoran	3	0.03
Cuban	37	0.36
Dominican Republic	12	0.12
Mexican	55	0.54
Puerto Rican	47	0.46
South American	93	0.91
Argentinean	22	0.22
Chilean	7	0.07
Colombian	24	0.24
Ecuadorian	23	0.23
Paraguayan	4	0.04
Peruvian	3	0.03
Uruguayan	4	0.04
Venezuelan	6	0.06
Other Hispanic or Latino	70	0.69

Race*	**Population**	**%**
African-American/Black (131)	178	1.75
Not Hispanic (130)	173	1.70
Hispanic (1)	5	0.05
American Indian/Alaska Native (12)	26	0.26
Not Hispanic (10)	22	0.22
Hispanic (2)	4	0.04
Cherokee (7)	9	0.09
Choctaw (0)	3	0.03
Hopi (0)	1	0.01
Mexican American Ind. (1)	1	0.01
Asian (295)	426	4.19
Not Hispanic (293)	417	4.10
Hispanic (2)	9	0.09
Bangladeshi (0)	2	0.02
Cambodian (1)	1	0.01
Chinese, ex. Taiwanese (105)	141	1.39
Filipino (10)	18	0.18
Indian (59)	84	0.83
Japanese (23)	53	0.52
Korean (48)	72	0.71
Malaysian (2)	2	0.02
Pakistani (17)	17	0.17
Sri Lankan (5)	5	0.05
Taiwanese (1)	4	0.04
Thai (9)	10	0.10
Vietnamese (9)	9	0.09
Hawaii Native/Pacific Islander (2)	9	0.09
Not Hispanic (2)	9	0.09

*Notes: † The Census 2010 population figure is used to calculate the percentages in the Hispanic Origin and Race categories. Ancestry percentages are based on the 2006-2010 American Community Survey population (not shown); ‡ Numbers in parentheses indicate the number of people reporting a single ancestry; * Numbers in parentheses indicate the number of persons reporting this race alone, not in combination with any other race; Please refer to the Explanation of Data for more information.*

Marshallese (1)	1	0.01
Native Hawaiian (0)	4	0.04
Samoan (1)	1	0.01
White (9,463)	9,638	94.69
Not Hispanic (9,212)	9,373	92.08
Hispanic (251)	265	2.60

Westport

Place Type: CDP/Town
County: Fairfield
Population: 26,391†

Ancestry‡	Population	%
African, Sub-Saharan (38)	38	0.15
African (12)	12	0.05
South African (26)	26	0.10
Albanian (0)	30	0.11
American (1,211)	1,211	4.64
Arab (76)	113	0.43
Lebanese (44)	71	0.27
Palestinian (8)	8	0.03
Syrian (0)	10	0.04
Other Arab (24)	24	0.09
Armenian (9)	9	0.03
Austrian (75)	315	1.21
Belgian (14)	26	0.10
Brazilian (0)	18	0.07
British (231)	383	1.47
Bulgarian (10)	10	0.04
Canadian (86)	130	0.50
Croatian (143)	214	0.82
Czech (8)	216	0.83
Czechoslovakian (22)	72	0.28
Danish (10)	32	0.12
Dutch (30)	389	1.49
Eastern European (878)	982	3.76
English (790)	3,215	12.31
Estonian (0)	30	0.11
European (750)	760	2.91
Finnish (21)	28	0.11
French, ex. Basque (137)	698	2.67
French Canadian (99)	512	1.96
German (812)	3,521	13.49
Greek (246)	530	2.03
Hungarian (164)	519	1.99
Icelander (0)	11	0.04
Iranian (35)	35	0.13
Irish (1,165)	4,337	16.61
Israeli (52)	100	0.38
Italian (1,943)	4,446	17.03
Latvian (41)	41	0.16
Lithuanian (74)	155	0.59
Macedonian (0)	8	0.03
Northern European (80)	80	0.31
Norwegian (51)	335	1.28
Polish (414)	2,206	8.45
Portuguese (13)	43	0.16
Romanian (90)	248	0.95
Russian (1,017)	2,494	9.55
Scotch-Irish (165)	452	1.73
Scottish (156)	837	3.21
Slovak (32)	161	0.62
Swedish (115)	315	1.21
Swiss (147)	209	0.80
Turkish (0)	82	0.31
Ukrainian (46)	140	0.54
Welsh (58)	200	0.77
West Indian, ex. Hispanic (55)	55	0.21
Jamaican (55)	55	0.21
Yugoslavian (10)	32	0.12

Hispanic Origin	Population	%
Hispanic or Latino (of any race)	932	3.53
Central American, ex. Mexican	79	0.30
Costa Rican	11	0.04
Guatemalan	26	0.10
Honduran	18	0.07
Nicaraguan	6	0.02
Panamanian	8	0.03
Salvadoran	10	0.04
Cuban	83	0.31
Dominican Republic	43	0.16
Mexican	169	0.64
Puerto Rican	147	0.56
South American	273	1.03
Argentinean	40	0.15
Bolivian	10	0.04
Chilean	26	0.10
Colombian	86	0.33
Ecuadorian	35	0.13
Paraguayan	7	0.03
Peruvian	44	0.17
Venezuelan	25	0.09
Other Hispanic or Latino	138	0.52

Race*	Population	%
African-American/Black (305)	392	1.49
Not Hispanic (292)	362	1.37
Hispanic (13)	30	0.11
American Indian/Alaska Native (16)	63	0.24
Not Hispanic (5)	39	0.15
Hispanic (11)	24	0.09
Apache (1)	3	0.01
Blackfeet (1)	1	<0.01
Cherokee (0)	6	0.02
Chippewa (0)	4	0.02
Choctaw (0)	1	<0.01
Hopi (3)	3	0.01
Iroquois (2)	7	0.03
Mexican American Ind. (0)	3	0.01
Navajo (0)	1	<0.01
Seminole (0)	1	<0.01
Sioux (1)	1	<0.01
South American Ind. (4)	8	0.03
Asian (1,047)	1,302	4.93
Not Hispanic (1,038)	1,280	4.85
Hispanic (9)	22	0.08
Bhutanese (1)	1	<0.01
Burmese (3)	4	0.02
Cambodian (0)	1	<0.01
Chinese, ex. Taiwanese (366)	480	1.82
Filipino (62)	90	0.34
Indian (261)	310	1.17
Indonesian (2)	3	0.01
Japanese (52)	100	0.38
Korean (139)	207	0.78
Laotian (1)	1	<0.01
Malaysian (1)	2	0.01
Pakistani (32)	33	0.13
Sri Lankan (5)	11	0.04
Taiwanese (23)	32	0.12
Thai (19)	28	0.11
Vietnamese (15)	29	0.11
Hawaii Native/Pacific Islander (9)	33	0.13
Not Hispanic (8)	28	0.11
Hispanic (1)	5	0.02
Guamanian/Chamorro (1)	10	0.04
Native Hawaiian (6)	11	0.04
Samoan (0)	5	0.02
White (24,429)	24,815	94.03
Not Hispanic (23,715)	24,020	91.02
Hispanic (714)	795	3.01

Wethersfield

Place Type: CDP/Town
County: Hartford
Population: 26,668†

Ancestry‡	Population	%
African, Sub-Saharan (0)	18	0.07
Nigerian (0)	18	0.07
Albanian (287)	287	1.08
American (522)	522	1.96
Arab (11)	48	0.18
Arab (0)	12	0.05
Lebanese (11)	36	0.14
Armenian (44)	74	0.28
Austrian (10)	81	0.30
Belgian (0)	20	0.08
Brazilian (0)	13	0.05
British (0)	109	0.41
Canadian (22)	47	0.18
Croatian (22)	55	0.21
Czech (18)	67	0.25
Czechoslovakian (0)	32	0.12
Danish (0)	87	0.33
Dutch (24)	102	0.38
Eastern European (53)	53	0.20
English (339)	2,579	9.69
European (130)	130	0.49
Finnish (0)	66	0.25
French, ex. Basque (437)	1,959	7.36
French Canadian (260)	619	2.33
German (426)	1,975	7.42
Greek (262)	502	1.89
Guyanese (0)	24	0.09
Hungarian (96)	239	0.90
Icelander (7)	7	0.03
Irish (1,716)	5,942	22.33
Italian (4,444)	8,241	30.97
Latvian (12)	12	0.05
Lithuanian (103)	348	1.31
Norwegian (43)	261	0.98
Pennsylvania German (0)	9	0.03
Polish (1,614)	3,392	12.75
Portuguese (367)	597	2.24
Romanian (10)	36	0.14
Russian (108)	328	1.23
Scandinavian (9)	9	0.03
Scotch-Irish (79)	386	1.45
Scottish (62)	497	1.87
Slavic (22)	22	0.08
Slovak (38)	66	0.25
Slovene (11)	11	0.04
Swedish (220)	488	1.83
Swiss (0)	47	0.18
Ukrainian (157)	211	0.79
Welsh (48)	272	1.02
West Indian, ex. Hispanic (56)	73	0.27
Jamaican (56)	73	0.27
Yugoslavian (346)	346	1.30

Hispanic Origin	Population	%
Hispanic or Latino (of any race)	2,185	8.19
Central American, ex. Mexican	45	0.17
Costa Rican	6	0.02
Guatemalan	4	0.01
Honduran	4	0.01
Nicaraguan	3	0.01
Panamanian	3	0.01
Salvadoran	23	0.09
Other Central American	2	0.01
Cuban	58	0.22
Dominican Republic	122	0.46
Mexican	113	0.42
Puerto Rican	1,329	4.98
South American	396	1.48
Argentinean	58	0.22
Bolivian	2	0.01
Chilean	11	0.04
Colombian	81	0.30
Ecuadorian	11	0.04
Paraguayan	3	0.01
Peruvian	201	0.75
Uruguayan	1	<0.01
Venezuelan	23	0.09
Other South American	5	0.02
Other Hispanic or Latino	122	0.46

Race*	Population	%
African-American/Black (840)	1,011	3.79
Not Hispanic (738)	872	3.27
Hispanic (102)	139	0.52
American Indian/Alaska Native (31)	116	0.43
Not Hispanic (21)	74	0.28
Hispanic (10)	42	0.16
Blackfeet (0)	3	0.01
Canadian/French Am. Ind. (1)	1	<0.01

*Notes: † The Census 2010 population figure is used to calculate the percentages in the Hispanic Origin and Race categories. Ancestry percentages are based on the 2006-2010 American Community Survey population (not shown); ‡ Numbers in parentheses indicate the number of people reporting a single ancestry; * Numbers in parentheses indicate the number of persons reporting this race alone, not in combination with any other race; Please refer to the Explanation of Data for more information.*

Cherokee (1)	19	0.07
Chippewa (0)	1	<0.01
Choctaw (0)	2	0.01
Houma (2)	2	0.01
Iroquois (1)	4	0.01
Navajo (0)	3	0.01
Sioux (0)	4	0.01
South American Ind. (9)	20	0.07
Spanish American Ind. (0)	1	<0.01
Asian (765)	899	3.37
Not Hispanic (757)	883	3.31
Hispanic (8)	16	0.06
Bangladeshi (13)	16	0.06
Burmese (1)	1	<0.01
Cambodian (1)	1	<0.01
Chinese, ex. Taiwanese (149)	178	0.67
Filipino (70)	87	0.33
Indian (229)	264	0.99
Japanese (10)	13	0.05
Korean (50)	66	0.25
Laotian (9)	9	0.03
Nepalese (6)	7	0.03
Pakistani (46)	53	0.20
Sri Lankan (1)	1	<0.01
Taiwanese (6)	7	0.03
Thai (12)	12	0.04
Vietnamese (104)	123	0.46
Hawaii Native/Pacific Islander (4)	27	0.10
Not Hispanic (4)	19	0.07
Hispanic (0)	8	0.03
Guamanian/Chamorro (3)	3	0.01
Native Hawaiian (0)	4	0.01
Samoan (1)	1	<0.01
White (23,876)	24,257	90.96
Not Hispanic (22,600)	22,874	85.77
Hispanic (1,276)	1,383	5.19

Willimantic

Place Type: CDP
County: Windham
Population: 17,737†

Ancestry‡	Population	%
African, Sub-Saharan (80)	105	0.60
African (29)	54	0.31
Cape Verdean (12)	12	0.07
Ghanaian (17)	17	0.10
Kenyan (22)	22	0.13
Albanian (11)	11	0.06
American (241)	241	1.38
Arab (103)	136	0.78
Arab (7)	19	0.11
Egyptian (96)	96	0.55
Lebanese (0)	10	0.06
Syrian (0)	11	0.06
Armenian (0)	26	0.15
Austrian (19)	56	0.32
Belgian (0)	13	0.07
British (30)	90	0.51
Canadian (130)	167	0.96
Czech (12)	107	0.61
Czechoslovakian (10)	33	0.19
Danish (0)	54	0.31
Dutch (17)	62	0.35
English (208)	935	5.35
Estonian (5)	11	0.06
European (19)	30	0.17
Finnish (52)	74	0.42
French, ex. Basque (259)	1,106	6.33
French Canadian (558)	1,259	7.20
German (141)	1,248	7.14
Greek (29)	92	0.53
Guyanese (29)	29	0.17
Hungarian (0)	47	0.27
Irish (515)	2,414	13.81
Italian (459)	1,840	10.52
Latvian (27)	27	0.15
Lithuanian (0)	77	0.44
Macedonian (9)	9	0.05
Northern European (17)	17	0.10
Norwegian (12)	25	0.14
Polish (233)	1,026	5.87
Portuguese (5)	84	0.48
Russian (75)	163	0.93
Scotch-Irish (44)	147	0.84
Scottish (59)	218	1.25
Slavic (0)	17	0.10
Slovak (22)	35	0.20
Slovene (0)	12	0.07
Swedish (44)	179	1.02
Turkish (11)	11	0.06
Ukrainian (85)	346	1.98
Welsh (18)	42	0.24
West Indian, ex. Hispanic (145)	198	1.13
Haitian (12)	12	0.07
Jamaican (95)	95	0.54
Trinidadian/Tobagonian (38)	48	0.27
West Indian (0)	43	0.25

Hispanic Origin	Population	%
Hispanic or Latino (of any race)	7,060	39.80
Central American, ex. Mexican	238	1.34
Costa Rican	5	0.03
Guatemalan	175	0.99
Honduran	3	0.02
Nicaraguan	2	0.01
Panamanian	39	0.22
Salvadoran	14	0.08
Cuban	32	0.18
Dominican Republic	176	0.99
Mexican	1,605	9.05
Puerto Rican	4,686	26.42
South American	175	0.99
Argentinean	6	0.03
Bolivian	1	0.01
Chilean	13	0.07
Colombian	62	0.35
Ecuadorian	28	0.16
Paraguayan	2	0.01
Peruvian	44	0.25
Uruguayan	6	0.03
Venezuelan	8	0.05
Other South American	5	0.03
Other Hispanic or Latino	148	0.83

Race*	Population	%
African-American/Black (1,324)	1,622	9.14
Not Hispanic (869)	1,047	5.90
Hispanic (455)	575	3.24
American Indian/Alaska Native (106)	237	1.34
Not Hispanic (43)	122	0.69
Hispanic (63)	115	0.65
Blackfeet (0)	14	0.08
Canadian/French Am. Ind. (6)	6	0.03
Central American Ind. (0)	1	0.01
Cherokee (1)	17	0.10
Chickasaw (1)	1	0.01
Chippewa (1)	1	0.01
Choctaw (0)	1	0.01
Inupiat *(Alaska Native)* (0)	1	0.01
Iroquois (9)	10	0.06
Lumbee (1)	1	0.01
Mexican American Ind. (18)	27	0.15
Navajo (1)	1	0.01
Pueblo (2)	2	0.01
Seminole (0)	1	0.01
Sioux (1)	3	0.02
South American Ind. (14)	26	0.15
Spanish American Ind. (9)	9	0.05
Asian (330)	410	2.31
Not Hispanic (319)	390	2.20
Hispanic (11)	20	0.11
Bangladeshi (1)	1	0.01
Burmese (0)	3	0.02
Cambodian (1)	2	0.01
Chinese, ex. Taiwanese (139)	156	0.88
Filipino (15)	32	0.18
Hmong (2)	2	0.01
Indian (59)	63	0.36
Japanese (7)	15	0.08
Korean (30)	37	0.21
Laotian (7)	9	0.05
Malaysian (3)	3	0.02
Nepalese (5)	5	0.03
Pakistani (11)	12	0.07
Sri Lankan (9)	9	0.05
Taiwanese (3)	3	0.02
Thai (1)	2	0.01
Vietnamese (28)	29	0.16
Hawaii Native/Pacific Islander (15)	38	0.21
Not Hispanic (11)	18	0.10
Hispanic (4)	20	0.11
Guamanian/Chamorro (6)	10	0.06
Native Hawaiian (0)	3	0.02
Samoan (0)	1	0.01
White (11,704)	12,266	69.15
Not Hispanic (9,113)	9,384	52.91
Hispanic (2,591)	2,882	16.25

Wilton

Place Type: Town
County: Fairfield
Population: 18,062†

Ancestry‡	Population	%
African, Sub-Saharan (19)	19	0.11
Ethiopian (7)	7	0.04
South African (12)	12	0.07
Albanian (0)	16	0.09
American (487)	487	2.72
Arab (11)	56	0.31
Syrian (11)	56	0.31
Armenian (65)	94	0.53
Austrian (43)	128	0.72
Belgian (0)	50	0.28
Brazilian (14)	14	0.08
British (326)	382	2.14
Bulgarian (0)	14	0.08
Cajun (0)	11	0.06
Canadian (78)	118	0.66
Croatian (9)	33	0.18
Czech (62)	124	0.69
Czechoslovakian (10)	33	0.18
Danish (85)	226	1.26
Dutch (54)	199	1.11
Eastern European (61)	89	0.50
English (943)	2,940	16.45
Estonian (65)	65	0.36
European (154)	160	0.90
Finnish (11)	27	0.15
French, ex. Basque (78)	498	2.79
French Canadian (60)	233	1.30
German (480)	2,738	15.32
Greek (68)	170	0.95
Hungarian (80)	172	0.96
Icelander (11)	11	0.06
Iranian (40)	40	0.22
Irish (1,571)	4,463	24.97
Israeli (6)	12	0.07
Italian (1,525)	3,256	18.22
Latvian (29)	51	0.29
Lithuanian (31)	56	0.31
Luxemburger (28)	57	0.32
New Zealander (5)	5	0.03
Northern European (114)	114	0.64
Norwegian (10)	86	0.48
Polish (356)	1,007	5.63
Portuguese (13)	67	0.37
Romanian (0)	22	0.12
Russian (259)	607	3.40
Scandinavian (9)	28	0.16
Scotch-Irish (137)	363	2.03
Scottish (97)	524	2.93
Slovak (26)	69	0.39
Swedish (118)	450	2.52
Swiss (60)	390	2.18
Ukrainian (65)	74	0.41
Welsh (33)	111	0.62

*Notes: † The Census 2010 population figure is used to calculate the percentages in the Hispanic Origin and Race categories. Ancestry percentages are based on the 2006-2010 American Community Survey population (not shown); ‡ Numbers in parentheses indicate the number of people reporting a single ancestry; * Numbers in parentheses indicate the number of persons reporting this race alone, not in combination with any other race; Please refer to the Explanation of Data for more information.*

West Indian, ex. Hispanic (0)	25	0.14
West Indian (0)	25	0.14

Hispanic Origin	Population	%
Hispanic or Latino (of any race)	537	2.97
Central American, ex. Mexican	57	0.32
Costa Rican	20	0.11
Guatemalan	14	0.08
Honduran	9	0.05
Nicaraguan	2	0.01
Panamanian	6	0.03
Salvadoran	3	0.02
Other Central American	3	0.02
Cuban	66	0.37
Dominican Republic	8	0.04
Mexican	56	0.31
Puerto Rican	99	0.55
South American	171	0.95
Argentinean	18	0.10
Bolivian	1	0.01
Chilean	18	0.10
Colombian	55	0.30
Ecuadorian	27	0.15
Paraguayan	1	0.01
Peruvian	22	0.12
Uruguayan	1	0.01
Venezuelan	24	0.13
Other South American	4	0.02
Other Hispanic or Latino	80	0.44

Race*	Population	%
African-American/Black (180)	241	1.33
Not Hispanic (164)	210	1.16
Hispanic (16)	31	0.17
American Indian/Alaska Native (10)	50	0.28
Not Hispanic (6)	41	0.23
Hispanic (4)	9	0.05
Central American Ind. (0)	3	0.02
Cherokee (0)	16	0.09
Iroquois (0)	1	0.01
Mexican American Ind. (3)	3	0.02
Potawatomi (0)	1	0.01
Sioux (0)	1	0.01
South American Ind. (0)	1	0.01
Asian (827)	1,018	5.64
Not Hispanic (821)	1,004	5.56
Hispanic (6)	14	0.08
Bangladeshi (4)	4	0.02
Cambodian (2)	3	0.02
Chinese, ex. Taiwanese (292)	361	2.00
Filipino (49)	72	0.40
Indian (238)	267	1.48
Indonesian (0)	1	0.01
Japanese (48)	84	0.47
Korean (135)	164	0.91
Laotian (2)	2	0.01
Pakistani (8)	10	0.06
Sri Lankan (8)	8	0.04
Taiwanese (6)	8	0.04
Thai (7)	12	0.07
Vietnamese (10)	13	0.07
Hawaii Native/Pacific Islander (0)	5	0.03
Not Hispanic (0)	5	0.03
Native Hawaiian (0)	2	0.01
White (16,666)	16,931	93.74
Not Hispanic (16,255)	16,483	91.26
Hispanic (411)	448	2.48

Winchester

Place Type: Town
County: Litchfield
Population: 11,242†

Ancestry‡	Population	%
American (428)	428	3.81
Arab (44)	62	0.55
Arab (0)	6	0.05
Lebanese (44)	56	0.50
Austrian (12)	12	0.11
British (53)	66	0.59
Canadian (46)	121	1.08
Celtic (0)	33	0.29
Czech (0)	28	0.25
Czechoslovakian (0)	33	0.29
Danish (0)	65	0.58
Dutch (31)	184	1.64
Eastern European (20)	40	0.36
English (406)	1,413	12.59
European (71)	71	0.63
Finnish (0)	96	0.86
French, ex. Basque (323)	1,251	11.15
French Canadian (231)	770	6.86
German (373)	1,594	14.21
Greek (0)	45	0.40
Hungarian (17)	153	1.36
Irish (349)	2,173	19.37
Italian (820)	2,590	23.08
Lithuanian (28)	192	1.71
Norwegian (235)	288	2.57
Polish (213)	727	6.48
Portuguese (38)	129	1.15
Russian (26)	141	1.26
Scandinavian (0)	15	0.13
Scotch-Irish (44)	261	2.33
Scottish (55)	198	1.76
Slovak (65)	166	1.48
Swedish (33)	260	2.32
Swiss (0)	62	0.55
Ukrainian (8)	8	0.07
Welsh (10)	45	0.40
West Indian, ex. Hispanic (27)	52	0.46
West Indian (27)	52	0.46

Hispanic Origin	Population	%
Hispanic or Latino (of any race)	583	5.19
Central American, ex. Mexican	5	0.04
Costa Rican	1	0.01
Guatemalan	3	0.03
Salvadoran	1	0.01
Cuban	10	0.09
Dominican Republic	233	2.07
Mexican	45	0.40
Puerto Rican	198	1.76
South American	41	0.36
Argentinean	4	0.04
Bolivian	4	0.04
Chilean	5	0.04
Colombian	11	0.10
Ecuadorian	13	0.12
Paraguayan	3	0.03
Peruvian	1	0.01
Other Hispanic or Latino	51	0.45

Race*	Population	%
African-American/Black (201)	285	2.54
Not Hispanic (136)	202	1.80
Hispanic (65)	83	0.74
American Indian/Alaska Native (26)	102	0.91
Not Hispanic (15)	83	0.74
Hispanic (11)	19	0.17
Apache (1)	1	0.01
Canadian/French Am. Ind. (1)	4	0.04
Cherokee (5)	15	0.13
Cheyenne (1)	1	0.01
Chickasaw (0)	1	0.01
Iroquois (0)	3	0.03
Lumbee (0)	1	0.01
Navajo (2)	2	0.02
Pueblo (1)	1	0.01
Seminole (1)	1	0.01
Sioux (1)	2	0.02
South American Ind. (3)	8	0.07
Asian (109)	150	1.33
Not Hispanic (102)	141	1.25
Hispanic (7)	9	0.08
Cambodian (1)	1	0.01
Chinese, ex. Taiwanese (26)	36	0.32
Filipino (18)	30	0.27
Indian (13)	15	0.13
Japanese (4)	9	0.08
Korean (3)	5	0.04
Laotian (5)	6	0.05
Pakistani (3)	3	0.03
Vietnamese (34)	41	0.36
Hawaii Native/Pacific Islander (1)	12	0.11
Not Hispanic (1)	9	0.08
Hispanic (0)	3	0.03
Native Hawaiian (1)	9	0.08
White (10,468)	10,670	94.91
Not Hispanic (10,230)	10,392	92.44
Hispanic (238)	278	2.47

Windham

Place Type: Town
County: Windham
Population: 25,268†

Ancestry‡	Population	%
African, Sub-Saharan (80)	105	0.42
African (29)	54	0.22
Cape Verdean (12)	12	0.05
Ghanaian (17)	17	0.07
Kenyan (22)	22	0.09
Albanian (11)	11	0.04
American (611)	611	2.44
Arab (103)	159	0.64
Arab (7)	19	0.08
Egyptian (96)	96	0.38
Lebanese (0)	33	0.13
Syrian (0)	11	0.04
Armenian (0)	26	0.10
Austrian (34)	124	0.50
Belgian (0)	13	0.05
British (45)	105	0.42
Canadian (210)	247	0.99
Czech (12)	129	0.52
Czechoslovakian (17)	64	0.26
Danish (0)	54	0.22
Dutch (30)	147	0.59
English (564)	2,083	8.32
Estonian (5)	11	0.04
European (50)	61	0.24
Finnish (52)	103	0.41
French, ex. Basque (742)	2,152	8.60
French Canadian (881)	1,873	7.48
German (247)	2,037	8.14
Greek (29)	92	0.37
Guyanese (29)	29	0.12
Hungarian (0)	63	0.25
Irish (814)	3,795	15.16
Italian (725)	2,560	10.23
Latvian (27)	27	0.11
Lithuanian (28)	105	0.42
Macedonian (9)	9	0.04
Northern European (17)	17	0.07
Norwegian (38)	121	0.48
Polish (392)	1,419	5.67
Portuguese (33)	183	0.73
Russian (128)	291	1.16
Scotch-Irish (130)	317	1.27
Scottish (116)	353	1.41
Slavic (7)	24	0.10
Slovak (22)	35	0.14
Slovene (0)	12	0.05
Swedish (272)	586	2.34
Swiss (18)	18	0.07
Turkish (11)	11	0.04
Ukrainian (151)	452	1.81
Welsh (23)	71	0.28
West Indian, ex. Hispanic (145)	198	0.79
Haitian (12)	12	0.05
Jamaican (95)	95	0.38
Trinidadian/Tobagonian (38)	48	0.19
West Indian (0)	43	0.17

Hispanic Origin	Population	%
Hispanic or Latino (of any race)	8,653	34.24
Central American, ex. Mexican	249	0.99

SECTION TWO

*Notes: † The Census 2010 population figure is used to calculate the percentages in the Hispanic Origin and Race categories. Ancestry percentages are based on the 2006-2010 American Community Survey population (not shown); ‡ Numbers in parentheses indicate the number of people reporting a single ancestry; * Numbers in parentheses indicate the number of persons reporting this race alone, not in combination with any other race; Please refer to the Explanation of Data for more information.*

Costa Rican	8	0.03
Guatemalan	178	0.70
Honduran	3	0.01
Nicaraguan	2	0.01
Panamanian	41	0.16
Salvadoran	17	0.07
Cuban	35	0.14
Dominican Republic	196	0.78
Mexican	1,704	6.74
Puerto Rican	6,061	23.99
South American	216	0.85
Argentinean	8	0.03
Bolivian	2	0.01
Chilean	13	0.05
Colombian	75	0.30
Ecuadorian	35	0.14
Paraguayan	3	0.01
Peruvian	59	0.23
Uruguayan	8	0.03
Venezuelan	8	0.03
Other South American	5	0.02
Other Hispanic or Latino	192	0.76

Race*	Population	%
African-American/Black (1,535)	1,937	7.67
Not Hispanic (990)	1,236	4.89
Hispanic (545)	701	2.77
American Indian/Alaska Native (155)	369	1.46
Not Hispanic (65)	213	0.84
Hispanic (90)	156	0.62
Blackfeet (1)	29	0.11
Canadian/French Am. Ind. (6)	6	0.02
Central American Ind. (0)	1	<0.01
Cherokee (4)	30	0.12
Chickasaw (1)	1	<0.01
Chippewa (1)	1	<0.01
Choctaw (0)	1	<0.01
Crow (0)	4	0.02
Inupiat *(Alaska Native)* (0)	2	0.01
Iroquois (9)	10	0.04
Lumbee (1)	2	0.01
Mexican American Ind. (18)	27	0.11
Navajo (1)	1	<0.01
Pueblo (2)	2	0.01
Seminole (0)	1	<0.01
Shoshone (0)	1	<0.01
Sioux (1)	4	0.02
South American Ind. (21)	33	0.13
Spanish American Ind. (9)	9	0.04
Asian (371)	485	1.92
Not Hispanic (356)	452	1.79
Hispanic (15)	33	0.13
Bangladeshi (1)	1	<0.01
Burmese (0)	3	0.01
Cambodian (1)	3	0.01
Chinese, ex. Taiwanese (146)	165	0.65
Filipino (23)	47	0.19
Hmong (2)	2	0.01
Indian (62)	70	0.28
Indonesian (4)	5	0.02
Japanese (10)	27	0.11
Korean (34)	43	0.17
Laotian (9)	11	0.04
Malaysian (3)	3	0.01
Nepalese (5)	5	0.02
Pakistani (14)	17	0.07
Sri Lankan (9)	9	0.04
Taiwanese (3)	3	0.01
Thai (3)	4	0.02
Vietnamese (31)	34	0.13
Hawaii Native/Pacific Islander (18)	53	0.21
Not Hispanic (12)	26	0.10
Hispanic (6)	27	0.11
Fijian (0)	1	<0.01
Guamanian/Chamorro (8)	12	0.05
Native Hawaiian (1)	9	0.04
Samoan (0)	2	0.01
White (18,029)	18,787	74.35
Not Hispanic (14,719)	15,118	59.83
Hispanic (3,310)	3,669	14.52

Windsor Locks

Place Type: CDP/Town
County: Hartford
Population: 12,498†

Ancestry‡	Population	%
African, Sub-Saharan (73)	73	0.59
African (73)	73	0.59
Albanian (12)	48	0.39
American (267)	267	2.15
Arab (17)	17	0.14
Jordanian (17)	17	0.14
Austrian (0)	23	0.19
Belgian (12)	29	0.23
Brazilian (0)	15	0.12
British (14)	14	0.11
Canadian (32)	48	0.39
Celtic (0)	11	0.09
Croatian (11)	11	0.09
Czech (32)	73	0.59
Czechoslovakian (7)	30	0.24
Danish (103)	115	0.93
Dutch (0)	36	0.29
Eastern European (19)	19	0.15
English (275)	1,367	11.01
European (28)	28	0.23
Finnish (33)	43	0.35
French, ex. Basque (579)	1,995	16.06
French Canadian (381)	654	5.27
German (187)	1,264	10.18
Greek (79)	109	0.88
Guyanese (10)	10	0.08
Hungarian (0)	42	0.34
Irish (813)	3,020	24.32
Italian (956)	2,719	21.89
Lithuanian (17)	117	0.94
Norwegian (0)	10	0.08
Polish (516)	1,199	9.65
Portuguese (118)	298	2.40
Romanian (33)	33	0.27
Russian (28)	97	0.78
Scandinavian (0)	35	0.28
Scotch-Irish (47)	136	1.10
Scottish (18)	203	1.63
Slovak (0)	14	0.11
Swedish (53)	370	2.98
Ukrainian (36)	64	0.52
Welsh (0)	10	0.08
West Indian, ex. Hispanic (11)	11	0.09
Jamaican (11)	11	0.09
Yugoslavian (46)	46	0.37

Hispanic Origin	Population	%
Hispanic or Latino (of any race)	576	4.61
Central American, ex. Mexican	21	0.17
Guatemalan	11	0.09
Honduran	2	0.02
Nicaraguan	1	0.01
Panamanian	3	0.02
Salvadoran	4	0.03
Cuban	13	0.10
Dominican Republic	8	0.06
Mexican	61	0.49
Puerto Rican	376	3.01
South American	63	0.50
Chilean	1	0.01
Colombian	20	0.16
Ecuadorian	12	0.10
Peruvian	28	0.22
Venezuelan	1	0.01
Other South American	1	0.01
Other Hispanic or Latino	34	0.27

Race*	Population	%
African-American/Black (605)	762	6.10
Not Hispanic (575)	708	5.66
Hispanic (30)	54	0.43
American Indian/Alaska Native (15)	97	0.78
Not Hispanic (13)	89	0.71
Hispanic (2)	8	0.06
Blackfeet (0)	7	0.06
Central American Ind. (0)	1	0.01
Cherokee (1)	11	0.09
Chickasaw (0)	1	0.01
Chippewa (0)	1	0.01
Iroquois (1)	3	0.02
Mexican American Ind. (1)	1	0.01
Seminole (0)	3	0.02
Sioux (2)	4	0.03
South American Ind. (1)	2	0.02
Asian (667)	754	6.03
Not Hispanic (665)	747	5.98
Hispanic (2)	7	0.06
Cambodian (11)	11	0.09
Chinese, ex. Taiwanese (53)	58	0.46
Filipino (41)	53	0.42
Indian (298)	336	2.69
Indonesian (6)	7	0.06
Japanese (3)	8	0.06
Korean (31)	36	0.29
Laotian (42)	42	0.34
Nepalese (9)	9	0.07
Pakistani (73)	78	0.62
Sri Lankan (9)	9	0.07
Thai (1)	3	0.02
Vietnamese (62)	70	0.56
Hawaii Native/Pacific Islander (0)	9	0.07
Not Hispanic (0)	7	0.06
Hispanic (0)	2	0.02
White (10,728)	11,003	88.04
Not Hispanic (10,390)	10,607	84.87
Hispanic (338)	396	3.17

Windsor

Place Type: Town
County: Hartford
Population: 29,044†

Ancestry‡	Population	%
Afghan (22)	22	0.08
African, Sub-Saharan (562)	824	2.85
African (494)	695	2.40
South African (23)	64	0.22
Other Sub-Saharan African (45)	65	0.22
Albanian (42)	42	0.15
Alsatian (0)	9	0.03
American (730)	730	2.52
Arab (124)	255	0.88
Lebanese (73)	148	0.51
Moroccan (51)	51	0.18
Syrian (0)	56	0.19
Armenian (0)	31	0.11
Austrian (9)	93	0.32
Belgian (7)	7	0.02
British (87)	164	0.57
Canadian (60)	137	0.47
Croatian (0)	21	0.07
Czech (28)	56	0.19
Czechoslovakian (24)	50	0.17
Danish (43)	126	0.44
Dutch (35)	321	1.11
Eastern European (36)	36	0.12
English (710)	2,886	9.97
European (158)	216	0.75
Finnish (10)	57	0.20
French, ex. Basque (345)	1,489	5.14
French Canadian (286)	761	2.63
German (507)	2,221	7.67
Greek (0)	19	0.07
Hungarian (51)	143	0.49
Iranian (0)	14	0.05
Irish (1,026)	3,617	12.50
Italian (1,018)	2,857	9.87
Latvian (8)	8	0.03
Lithuanian (87)	270	0.93
Norwegian (11)	211	0.73
Polish (709)	2,175	7.51
Portuguese (288)	490	1.69

*Notes: † The Census 2010 population figure is used to calculate the percentages in the Hispanic Origin and Race categories. Ancestry percentages are based on the 2006-2010 American Community Survey population (not shown); ‡ Numbers in parentheses indicate the number of people reporting a single ancestry; * Numbers in parentheses indicate the number of persons reporting this race alone, not in combination with any other race; Please refer to the Explanation of Data for more information.*

Romanian (13)	35	0.12
Russian (82)	408	1.41
Scandinavian (0)	55	0.19
Scotch-Irish (99)	263	0.91
Scottish (148)	636	2.20
Slovak (11)	55	0.19
Swedish (103)	406	1.40
Swiss (21)	31	0.11
Ukrainian (27)	92	0.32
Welsh (33)	131	0.45
West Indian, ex. Hispanic (2,663)	3,451	11.92
Belizean (45)	139	0.48
British West Indian (0)	29	0.10
Haitian (52)	63	0.22
Jamaican (2,351)	2,923	10.10
West Indian (215)	297	1.03

Hispanic Origin	Population	%
Hispanic or Latino (of any race)	2,442	8.41
Central American, ex. Mexican	81	0.28
Costa Rican	5	0.02
Guatemalan	10	0.03
Honduran	13	0.04
Nicaraguan	2	0.01
Panamanian	14	0.05
Salvadoran	37	0.13
Cuban	80	0.28
Dominican Republic	97	0.33
Mexican	121	0.42
Puerto Rican	1,616	5.56
South American	259	0.89
Argentinean	6	0.02
Bolivian	4	0.01
Chilean	3	0.01
Colombian	110	0.38
Ecuadorian	23	0.08
Paraguayan	4	0.01
Peruvian	90	0.31
Venezuelan	11	0.04
Other South American	8	0.03
Other Hispanic or Latino	188	0.65

Race*	Population	%
African-American/Black (9,967)	10,607	36.52
Not Hispanic (9,648)	10,120	34.84
Hispanic (319)	487	1.68
American Indian/Alaska Native (61)	257	0.88
Not Hispanic (49)	214	0.74
Hispanic (12)	43	0.15
Apache (1)	4	0.01
Blackfeet (1)	17	0.06
Central American Ind. (0)	1	<0.01
Cherokee (5)	46	0.16
Chickasaw (1)	3	0.01
Cree (1)	2	0.01
Creek (0)	4	0.01
Iroquois (1)	6	0.02
Seminole (0)	1	<0.01
Sioux (1)	1	<0.01
South American Ind. (3)	16	0.06
Spanish American Ind. (3)	5	0.02
Tlingit-Haida *(Alaska Native)* (0)	1	<0.01
Asian (1,300)	1,496	5.15
Not Hispanic (1,289)	1,469	5.06
Hispanic (11)	27	0.09
Bangladeshi (38)	39	0.13
Cambodian (10)	12	0.04
Chinese, ex. Taiwanese (182)	229	0.79
Filipino (93)	109	0.38
Hmong (0)	7	0.02
Indian (532)	577	1.99
Indonesian (11)	12	0.04
Japanese (13)	28	0.10
Korean (27)	46	0.16
Laotian (42)	46	0.16
Malaysian (1)	3	0.01
Nepalese (9)	10	0.03
Pakistani (96)	100	0.34
Sri Lankan (8)	8	0.03
Taiwanese (5)	6	0.02
Thai (4)	8	0.03
Vietnamese (197)	210	0.72
Hawaii Native/Pacific Islander (2)	35	0.12
Not Hispanic (2)	29	0.10
Hispanic (0)	6	0.02
Native Hawaiian (1)	2	0.01
Samoan (1)	5	0.02
White (15,892)	16,571	57.05
Not Hispanic (14,858)	15,367	52.91
Hispanic (1,034)	1,204	4.15

Winsted

Place Type: CDP
County: Litchfield
Population: 7,712†

Ancestry‡	Population	%
American (298)	298	4.07
Arab (32)	44	0.60
Lebanese (32)	44	0.60
British (0)	13	0.18
Canadian (36)	59	0.81
Celtic (0)	33	0.45
Danish (0)	36	0.49
Dutch (31)	128	1.75
Eastern European (20)	40	0.55
English (285)	817	11.16
European (71)	71	0.97
Finnish (0)	28	0.38
French, ex. Basque (230)	971	13.27
French Canadian (87)	404	5.52
German (138)	842	11.51
Greek (0)	12	0.16
Hungarian (17)	86	1.18
Irish (243)	1,538	21.02
Italian (632)	1,798	24.57
Lithuanian (0)	63	0.86
Norwegian (24)	52	0.71
Polish (103)	457	6.24
Portuguese (38)	120	1.64
Russian (0)	43	0.59
Scandinavian (0)	15	0.20
Scotch-Irish (0)	104	1.42
Scottish (55)	156	2.13
Slovak (18)	46	0.63
Swedish (13)	194	2.65
Ukrainian (8)	8	0.11
Welsh (0)	12	0.16
West Indian, ex. Hispanic (27)	52	0.71
West Indian (27)	52	0.71

Hispanic Origin	Population	%
Hispanic or Latino (of any race)	503	6.52
Central American, ex. Mexican	2	0.03
Costa Rican	1	0.01
Guatemalan	1	0.01
Cuban	4	0.05
Dominican Republic	217	2.81
Mexican	35	0.45
Puerto Rican	171	2.22
South American	30	0.39
Argentinean	4	0.05
Bolivian	4	0.05
Chilean	2	0.03
Colombian	11	0.14
Ecuadorian	7	0.09
Paraguayan	1	0.01
Peruvian	1	0.01
Other Hispanic or Latino	44	0.57

Race*	Population	%
African-American/Black (167)	227	2.94
Not Hispanic (105)	148	1.92
Hispanic (62)	79	1.02
American Indian/Alaska Native (22)	80	1.04
Not Hispanic (11)	66	0.86
Hispanic (11)	14	0.18
Apache (1)	1	0.01
Canadian/French Am. Ind. (0)	2	0.03
Cherokee (4)	13	0.17
Chickasaw (0)	1	0.01
Iroquois (0)	2	0.03
Lumbee (0)	1	0.01
Navajo (2)	2	0.03
Pueblo (1)	1	0.01
Seminole (1)	1	0.01
Sioux (1)	1	0.01
South American Ind. (3)	6	0.08
Asian (98)	125	1.62
Not Hispanic (91)	116	1.50
Hispanic (7)	9	0.12
Chinese, ex. Taiwanese (22)	28	0.36
Filipino (17)	28	0.36
Indian (13)	15	0.19
Japanese (4)	5	0.06
Korean (3)	5	0.06
Laotian (5)	6	0.08
Pakistani (3)	3	0.04
Vietnamese (29)	32	0.41
Hawaii Native/Pacific Islander (0)	7	0.09
Not Hispanic (0)	4	0.05
Hispanic (0)	3	0.04
Native Hawaiian (0)	4	0.05
White (7,065)	7,211	93.50
Not Hispanic (6,876)	6,991	90.65
Hispanic (189)	220	2.85

Wolcott

Place Type: Town
County: New Haven
Population: 16,680†

Ancestry‡	Population	%
African, Sub-Saharan (10)	10	0.06
Ghanaian (10)	10	0.06
Albanian (123)	165	1.00
American (614)	614	3.73
Arab (40)	70	0.43
Lebanese (40)	70	0.43
Armenian (0)	14	0.09
Austrian (14)	14	0.09
Belgian (9)	24	0.15
Brazilian (12)	25	0.15
British (0)	13	0.08
Canadian (86)	160	0.97
Croatian (0)	12	0.07
Czech (117)	147	0.89
Danish (0)	9	0.05
Dutch (41)	183	1.11
English (240)	1,171	7.12
European (78)	78	0.47
French, ex. Basque (689)	1,946	11.83
French Canadian (579)	891	5.42
German (172)	1,474	8.96
Greek (12)	44	0.27
Guyanese (27)	27	0.16
Hungarian (122)	215	1.31
Icelander (0)	12	0.07
Iranian (0)	47	0.29
Irish (981)	3,358	20.42
Italian (2,808)	5,587	33.97
Lithuanian (132)	319	1.94
Macedonian (40)	40	0.24
Norwegian (0)	12	0.07
Polish (308)	1,248	7.59
Portuguese (239)	319	1.94
Romanian (69)	69	0.42
Russian (96)	327	1.99
Scotch-Irish (41)	162	0.99
Scottish (91)	358	2.18
Slavic (0)	13	0.08
Slovak (51)	85	0.52
Swedish (58)	218	1.33
Swiss (10)	10	0.06
Turkish (15)	31	0.19
Ukrainian (17)	115	0.70
Welsh (0)	13	0.08
West Indian, ex. Hispanic (71)	115	0.70

SECTION TWO

*Notes: † The Census 2010 population figure is used to calculate the percentages in the Hispanic Origin and Race categories. Ancestry percentages are based on the 2006-2010 American Community Survey population (not shown); ‡ Numbers in parentheses indicate the number of people reporting a single ancestry; * Numbers in parentheses indicate the number of persons reporting this race alone, not in combination with any other race; Please refer to the Explanation of Data for more information.*

Jamaican (52)	81	0.49
Trinidadian/Tobagonian (19)	19	0.12
West Indian (0)	15	0.09
Yugoslavian (43)	43	0.26

Hispanic Origin	Population	%
Hispanic or Latino (of any race)	611	3.66
Central American, ex. Mexican	8	0.05
Costa Rican	2	0.01
Guatemalan	3	0.02
Panamanian	3	0.02
Cuban	16	0.10
Dominican Republic	24	0.14
Mexican	51	0.31
Puerto Rican	411	2.46
South American	45	0.27
Argentinean	7	0.04
Chilean	4	0.02
Colombian	14	0.08
Ecuadorian	9	0.05
Paraguayan	1	0.01
Peruvian	9	0.05
Uruguayan	1	0.01
Other Hispanic or Latino	56	0.34

Race*	Population	%
African-American/Black (293)	410	2.46
Not Hispanic (261)	357	2.14
Hispanic (32)	53	0.32
American Indian/Alaska Native (26)	81	0.49
Not Hispanic (17)	59	0.35
Hispanic (9)	22	0.13
Alaska Athabascan *(Ala. Nat.)* (4)	4	0.02
Apache (1)	1	0.01
Blackfeet (0)	1	0.01
Cherokee (1)	6	0.04
Choctaw (0)	1	0.01
Delaware (0)	1	0.01
Iroquois (0)	2	0.01
Mexican American Ind. (2)	3	0.02
South American Ind. (0)	8	0.05
Asian (210)	258	1.55
Not Hispanic (205)	252	1.51
Hispanic (5)	6	0.04
Bangladeshi (7)	7	0.04
Chinese, ex. Taiwanese (56)	64	0.38
Filipino (13)	17	0.10
Indian (71)	89	0.53
Japanese (3)	8	0.05
Korean (22)	29	0.17
Laotian (7)	7	0.04
Malaysian (1)	1	0.01
Pakistani (4)	5	0.03
Sri Lankan (6)	10	0.06
Taiwanese (2)	2	0.01
Thai (1)	1	0.01
Vietnamese (15)	16	0.10
Hawaii Native/Pacific Islander (3)	6	0.04
Not Hispanic (3)	6	0.04
Native Hawaiian (2)	4	0.02
White (15,758)	15,974	95.77
Not Hispanic (15,360)	15,533	93.12
Hispanic (398)	441	2.64

Woodbridge

Place Type: Town
County: New Haven
Population: 8,990†

Ancestry‡	Population	%
American (292)	292	3.24
Arab (0)	28	0.31
Lebanese (0)	14	0.16
Syrian (0)	14	0.16
Armenian (19)	19	0.21
Austrian (0)	85	0.94
Belgian (0)	34	0.38
Canadian (0)	12	0.13
Czech (0)	46	0.51
Dutch (0)	40	0.44
Eastern European (188)	208	2.31
English (216)	1,224	13.59
European (219)	219	2.43
French, ex. Basque (23)	285	3.16
French Canadian (22)	153	1.70
German (128)	800	8.88
Greek (130)	206	2.29
Hungarian (105)	550	6.11
Iranian (0)	17	0.19
Irish (479)	1,368	15.19
Italian (1,116)	2,210	24.54
Lithuanian (46)	126	1.40
Norwegian (48)	144	1.60
Pennsylvania German (0)	11	0.12
Polish (164)	781	8.67
Portuguese (46)	75	0.83
Romanian (0)	16	0.18
Russian (462)	836	9.28
Scotch-Irish (45)	120	1.33
Scottish (17)	135	1.50
Slovak (5)	5	0.06
Swedish (25)	189	2.10
Ukrainian (21)	53	0.59
Welsh (0)	75	0.83

Hispanic Origin	Population	%
Hispanic or Latino (of any race)	284	3.16
Central American, ex. Mexican	17	0.19
Costa Rican	2	0.02
Guatemalan	4	0.04
Honduran	6	0.07
Nicaraguan	1	0.01
Panamanian	1	0.01
Salvadoran	3	0.03
Cuban	22	0.24
Dominican Republic	9	0.10
Mexican	33	0.37
Puerto Rican	73	0.81
South American	99	1.10
Argentinean	27	0.30
Bolivian	2	0.02
Chilean	6	0.07
Colombian	27	0.30
Ecuadorian	12	0.13
Paraguayan	1	0.01
Peruvian	8	0.09
Uruguayan	4	0.04
Venezuelan	8	0.09
Other South American	4	0.04
Other Hispanic or Latino	31	0.34

Race*	Population	%
African-American/Black (179)	214	2.38
Not Hispanic (173)	201	2.24
Hispanic (6)	13	0.14
American Indian/Alaska Native (5)	35	0.39
Not Hispanic (4)	31	0.34
Hispanic (1)	4	0.04
Cherokee (1)	6	0.07
Iroquois (0)	1	0.01
South American Ind. (2)	3	0.03
Asian (784)	861	9.58
Not Hispanic (780)	853	9.49
Hispanic (4)	8	0.09
Burmese (0)	3	0.03
Cambodian (4)	4	0.04
Chinese, ex. Taiwanese (373)	394	4.38
Filipino (31)	41	0.46
Indian (159)	174	1.94
Indonesian (2)	6	0.07
Japanese (14)	24	0.27
Korean (132)	140	1.56
Pakistani (16)	16	0.18
Sri Lankan (4)	4	0.04
Taiwanese (15)	17	0.19
Thai (5)	5	0.06
Vietnamese (8)	8	0.09
Hawaii Native/Pacific Islander (1)	6	0.07
Not Hispanic (1)	5	0.06
Hispanic (0)	1	0.01
Native Hawaiian (1)	4	0.04
White (7,822)	7,963	88.58
Not Hispanic (7,605)	7,724	85.92
Hispanic (217)	239	2.66

Woodbury

Place Type: Town
County: Litchfield
Population: 9,975†

Ancestry‡	Population	%
Afghan (8)	23	0.23
African, Sub-Saharan (44)	86	0.87
Ethiopian (44)	70	0.71
Other Sub-Saharan African (0)	16	0.16
Albanian (0)	11	0.11
American (403)	403	4.07
Arab (11)	52	0.52
Arab (0)	13	0.13
Egyptian (11)	11	0.11
Lebanese (0)	28	0.28
Austrian (47)	194	1.96
Belgian (0)	11	0.11
Brazilian (0)	22	0.22
British (35)	35	0.35
Bulgarian (19)	19	0.19
Canadian (40)	104	1.05
Czech (0)	94	0.95
Czechoslovakian (0)	17	0.17
Danish (11)	71	0.72
Dutch (0)	255	2.57
Eastern European (55)	55	0.56
English (545)	2,181	22.01
European (30)	98	0.99
Finnish (0)	14	0.14
French, ex. Basque (100)	935	9.44
French Canadian (47)	187	1.89
German (458)	1,753	17.69
Greek (35)	52	0.52
Hungarian (13)	84	0.85
Irish (539)	2,214	22.34
Italian (865)	2,317	23.38
Latvian (0)	11	0.11
Lithuanian (64)	124	1.25
Norwegian (12)	164	1.66
Pennsylvania German (0)	16	0.16
Polish (125)	438	4.42
Portuguese (29)	267	2.69
Romanian (27)	27	0.27
Russian (81)	299	3.02
Scandinavian (10)	10	0.10
Scotch-Irish (98)	203	2.05
Scottish (41)	296	2.99
Serbian (10)	10	0.10
Slavic (0)	12	0.12
Slovak (36)	80	0.81
Swedish (59)	255	2.57
Swiss (0)	21	0.21
Ukrainian (36)	104	1.05
Welsh (12)	12	0.12
West Indian, ex. Hispanic (170)	170	1.72
Jamaican (120)	120	1.21
Trinidadian/Tobagonian (50)	50	0.50

Hispanic Origin	Population	%
Hispanic or Latino (of any race)	245	2.46
Central American, ex. Mexican	8	0.08
Guatemalan	8	0.08
Cuban	20	0.20
Dominican Republic	15	0.15
Mexican	42	0.42
Puerto Rican	74	0.74
South American	57	0.57
Argentinean	13	0.13
Bolivian	1	0.01
Chilean	7	0.07
Colombian	10	0.10
Ecuadorian	15	0.15

*Notes: † The Census 2010 population figure is used to calculate the percentages in the Hispanic Origin and Race categories. Ancestry percentages are based on the 2006-2010 American Community Survey population (not shown); ‡ Numbers in parentheses indicate the number of people reporting a single ancestry; * Numbers in parentheses indicate the number of persons reporting this race alone, not in combination with any other race; Please refer to the Explanation of Data for more information.*

Peruvian	4	0.04
Uruguayan	1	0.01
Venezuelan	5	0.05
Other South American	1	0.01
Other Hispanic or Latino	29	0.29

Race*	Population	%
African-American/Black (57)	92	0.92
Not Hispanic (55)	86	0.86
Hispanic (2)	6	0.06
American Indian/Alaska Native (33)	79	0.79
Not Hispanic (24)	67	0.67
Hispanic (9)	12	0.12
Blackfeet (0)	5	0.05
Central American Ind. (1)	1	0.01
Cherokee (0)	15	0.15
Choctaw (0)	1	0.01
Iroquois (0)	1	0.01
Mexican American Ind. (1)	1	0.01
Sioux (0)	1	0.01
South American Ind. (1)	3	0.03
Asian (168)	224	2.25
Not Hispanic (167)	217	2.18
Hispanic (1)	7	0.07
Chinese, ex. Taiwanese (35)	50	0.50
Filipino (24)	34	0.34
Indian (63)	73	0.73
Japanese (8)	11	0.11
Korean (11)	22	0.22
Pakistani (1)	2	0.02
Sri Lankan (3)	3	0.03
Taiwanese (1)	1	0.01
Thai (7)	7	0.07
Vietnamese (8)	11	0.11
Hawaii Native/Pacific Islander (0)	3	0.03
Hispanic (0)	3	0.03
Native Hawaiian (0)	2	0.02
White (9,547)	9,672	96.96
Not Hispanic (9,366)	9,473	94.97
Hispanic (181)	199	1.99

Woodstock

Place Type: Town
County: Windham
Population: 7,964†

Ancestry‡	Population	%
African, Sub-Saharan (0)	101	1.28
Cape Verdean (0)	57	0.72
Kenyan (0)	44	0.56
American (327)	327	4.14
Arab (15)	15	0.19
Arab (15)	15	0.19
Australian (47)	47	0.60
Austrian (7)	17	0.22
British (29)	61	0.77
Canadian (22)	37	0.47
Czech (15)	15	0.19
Danish (14)	81	1.03
Dutch (83)	305	3.86
English (535)	1,347	17.07
European (64)	64	0.81
Finnish (13)	111	1.41
French, ex. Basque (265)	1,672	21.19
French Canadian (329)	614	7.78
German (138)	1,026	13.00
Greek (0)	37	0.47
Hungarian (0)	70	0.89
Irish (357)	1,629	20.64
Italian (266)	669	8.48
Lithuanian (0)	132	1.67
Norwegian (0)	30	0.38
Pennsylvania German (9)	9	0.11
Polish (278)	919	11.64
Portuguese (18)	117	1.48
Romanian (0)	17	0.22
Russian (0)	277	3.51
Scotch-Irish (74)	237	3.00
Scottish (24)	164	2.08
Slovak (0)	14	0.18
Swedish (102)	501	6.35
Swiss (0)	9	0.11
Turkish (2)	2	0.03
Ukrainian (0)	36	0.46
West Indian, ex. Hispanic (0)	11	0.14
Jamaican (0)	11	0.14

Hispanic Origin	Population	%
Hispanic or Latino (of any race)	119	1.49
Central American, ex. Mexican	14	0.18
Guatemalan	13	0.16
Panamanian	1	0.01
Cuban	5	0.06
Dominican Republic	5	0.06
Mexican	28	0.35
Puerto Rican	36	0.45
South American	12	0.15
Bolivian	1	0.01
Chilean	1	0.01
Colombian	1	0.01
Ecuadorian	3	0.04
Paraguayan	2	0.03
Peruvian	3	0.04
Other South American	1	0.01
Other Hispanic or Latino	19	0.24

Race*	Population	%
African-American/Black (30)	48	0.60
Not Hispanic (30)	47	0.59
Hispanic (0)	1	0.01
American Indian/Alaska Native (25)	56	0.70
Not Hispanic (19)	49	0.62
Hispanic (6)	7	0.09
Blackfeet (0)	2	0.03
Cherokee (0)	7	0.09
Cheyenne (0)	2	0.03
Chippewa (1)	1	0.01
Choctaw (2)	2	0.03
Cree (0)	2	0.03
Inupiat *(Alaska Native)* (1)	1	0.01
Iroquois (0)	2	0.03
Mexican American Ind. (0)	1	0.01
Seminole (1)	3	0.04
Shoshone (0)	1	0.01
Sioux (0)	1	0.01
Spanish American Ind. (4)	4	0.05
Asian (59)	79	0.99
Not Hispanic (59)	79	0.99
Chinese, ex. Taiwanese (18)	22	0.28
Filipino (7)	12	0.15
Indian (11)	16	0.20
Japanese (8)	11	0.14
Korean (6)	10	0.13
Pakistani (5)	7	0.09
Thai (2)	3	0.04
Hawaii Native/Pacific Islander (1)	4	0.05
Not Hispanic (1)	4	0.05
Native Hawaiian (1)	4	0.05
White (7,743)	7,817	98.15
Not Hispanic (7,662)	7,725	97.00
Hispanic (81)	92	1.16

*Notes: † The Census 2010 population figure is used to calculate the percentages in the Hispanic Origin and Race categories. Ancestry percentages are based on the 2006-2010 American Community Survey population (not shown); ‡ Numbers in parentheses indicate the number of people reporting a single ancestry; * Numbers in parentheses indicate the number of persons reporting this race alone, not in combination with any other race; Please refer to the Explanation of Data for more information.*

DELAWARE

Place Type: State
Population: 897,934[†]

Ancestry[‡]	Population	%
Afghan (50)	86	0.01
African, Sub-Saharan (8,711)	10,135	1.15
African (5,140)	6,305	0.72
Cape Verdean (39)	47	0.01
Ethiopian (218)	218	0.02
Ghanaian (530)	544	0.06
Kenyan (811)	811	0.09
Liberian (483)	504	0.06
Nigerian (1,021)	1,100	0.12
Senegalese (4)	4	<0.01
Sierra Leonean (61)	63	0.01
Somalian (12)	12	<0.01
South African (132)	132	0.01
Sudanese (42)	70	0.01
Ugandan (12)	12	<0.01
Other Sub-Saharan African (206)	313	0.04
Albanian (197)	269	0.03
Alsatian (0)	30	<0.01
American (37,428)	37,428	4.25
Arab (1,997)	2,836	0.32
Arab (280)	483	0.05
Egyptian (151)	209	0.02
Iraqi (0)	1	<0.01
Jordanian (93)	122	0.01
Lebanese (327)	654	0.07
Moroccan (155)	218	0.02
Palestinian (84)	125	0.01
Syrian (39)	119	0.01
Other Arab (868)	905	0.10
Armenian (178)	448	0.05
Assyrian/Chaldean/Syriac (0)	6	<0.01
Australian (47)	50	0.01
Austrian (560)	2,016	0.23
Basque (24)	81	0.01
Belgian (76)	303	0.03
Brazilian (145)	221	0.03
British (2,635)	4,508	0.51
Bulgarian (211)	230	0.03
Cajun (0)	86	0.01
Canadian (1,074)	1,825	0.21
Carpatho Rusyn (8)	8	<0.01
Celtic (73)	107	0.01
Croatian (232)	487	0.06
Czech (697)	2,392	0.27
Czechoslovakian (381)	966	0.11
Danish (530)	1,776	0.20
Dutch (2,907)	14,189	1.61
Eastern European (986)	1,108	0.13
English (37,156)	108,450	12.31
Estonian (97)	348	0.04
European (4,818)	5,354	0.61
Finnish (186)	475	0.05
French, ex. Basque (3,775)	19,289	2.19
French Canadian (1,227)	3,283	0.37
German (38,828)	141,172	16.02
Greek (2,280)	4,820	0.55
Guyanese (377)	506	0.06
Hungarian (1,176)	4,921	0.56
Icelander (12)	52	0.01
Iranian (428)	599	0.07
Irish (50,649)	160,416	18.20
Israeli (99)	117	0.01
Italian (33,868)	86,944	9.87
Latvian (58)	180	0.02
Lithuanian (930)	2,741	0.31
Luxemburger (21)	41	<0.01
Macedonian (13)	13	<0.01
Maltese (39)	63	0.01
New Zealander (19)	22	<0.01
Northern European (241)	286	0.03
Norwegian (1,492)	4,636	0.53
Pennsylvania German (2,092)	3,020	0.34
Polish (15,562)	45,593	5.17
Portuguese (970)	1,897	0.22
Romanian (620)	1,323	0.15
Russian (2,286)	7,508	0.85
Scandinavian (191)	720	0.08
Scotch-Irish (6,147)	15,385	1.75
Scottish (5,132)	16,995	1.93
Serbian (86)	223	0.03
Slavic (162)	583	0.07
Slovak (711)	1,961	0.22
Slovene (41)	183	0.02
Swedish (2,066)	7,281	0.83
Swiss (381)	2,262	0.26
Turkish (523)	652	0.07
Ukrainian (2,186)	5,892	0.67
Welsh (1,958)	9,396	1.07
West Indian, ex. Hispanic (7,099)	8,678	0.98
Barbadian (75)	136	0.02
Belizean (14)	28	<0.01
Bermudan (0)	31	<0.01
British West Indian (153)	204	0.02
Dutch West Indian (0)	100	0.01
Haitian (2,357)	2,555	0.29
Jamaican (3,459)	4,136	0.47
Trinidadian/Tobagonian (357)	541	0.06
U.S. Virgin Islander (42)	42	<0.01
West Indian (629)	878	0.10
Other West Indian (13)	27	<0.01
Yugoslavian (199)	323	0.04

Hispanic Origin	Population	%
Hispanic or Latino (of any race)	73,221	8.15
Central American, ex. Mexican	8,112	0.90
Costa Rican	243	0.03
Guatemalan	5,202	0.58
Honduran	675	0.08
Nicaraguan	225	0.03
Panamanian	501	0.06
Salvadoran	1,231	0.14
Other Central American	35	<0.01
Cuban	1,443	0.16
Dominican Republic	2,035	0.23
Mexican	30,283	3.37
Puerto Rican	22,533	2.51
South American	3,849	0.43
Argentinean	360	0.04
Bolivian	112	0.01
Chilean	335	0.04
Colombian	1,248	0.14
Ecuadorian	545	0.06
Paraguayan	48	0.01
Peruvian	704	0.08
Uruguayan	50	0.01
Venezuelan	389	0.04
Other South American	58	0.01
Other Hispanic or Latino	4,966	0.55

Race*	Population	%
African-American/Black (191,814)	205,923	22.93
Not Hispanic (186,782)	198,589	22.12
Hispanic (5,032)	7,334	0.82
American Indian/Alaska Native (4,181)	9,899	1.10
Not Hispanic (2,824)	7,679	0.86
Hispanic (1,357)	2,220	0.25
Alaska Athabascan *(Ala. Nat.)* (2)	5	<0.01
Aleut *(Alaska Native)* (2)	3	<0.01
Apache (25)	76	0.01
Arapaho (1)	2	<0.01
Blackfeet (31)	336	0.04
Canadian/French Am. Ind. (8)	28	<0.01
Central American Ind. (35)	64	0.01
Cherokee (392)	1,669	0.19
Cheyenne (1)	8	<0.01
Chickasaw (3)	10	<0.01
Chippewa (34)	61	0.01
Choctaw (26)	63	0.01
Comanche (1)	7	<0.01
Cree (1)	5	<0.01
Creek (14)	29	<0.01
Crow (0)	8	<0.01
Delaware (206)	360	0.04
Hopi (0)	14	<0.01
Houma (5)	5	<0.01
Inupiat *(Alaska Native)* (3)	12	<0.01
Iroquois (41)	104	0.01
Kiowa (2)	5	<0.01
Lumbee (32)	54	0.01
Menominee (3)	5	<0.01
Mexican American Ind. (267)	368	0.04
Navajo (27)	46	0.01
Osage (1)	4	<0.01
Ottawa (5)	16	<0.01
Paiute (2)	2	<0.01
Pima (6)	6	<0.01
Potawatomi (26)	34	<0.01
Pueblo (4)	10	<0.01
Puget Sound Salish (1)	1	<0.01
Seminole (5)	49	0.01
Shoshone (1)	8	<0.01
Sioux (33)	131	0.01
South American Ind. (77)	162	0.02
Spanish American Ind. (19)	38	<0.01
Tlingit-Haida *(Alaska Native)* (2)	4	<0.01
Tohono O'Odham (2)	2	<0.01
Yakama (1)	2	<0.01
Yaqui (0)	1	<0.01
Yuman (1)	1	<0.01
Yup'ik *(Alaska Native)* (0)	1	<0.01
Asian (28,549)	33,701	3.75
Not Hispanic (28,308)	33,042	3.68
Hispanic (241)	659	0.07
Bangladeshi (342)	383	0.04
Bhutanese (1)	1	<0.01
Burmese (43)	51	0.01
Cambodian (77)	113	0.01
Chinese, ex. Taiwanese (5,923)	6,761	0.75
Filipino (3,276)	4,637	0.52
Hmong (3)	3	<0.01
Indian (11,424)	12,344	1.37
Indonesian (82)	123	0.01
Japanese (540)	1,196	0.13
Korean (2,540)	3,099	0.35
Laotian (167)	208	0.02
Malaysian (32)	48	0.01
Nepalese (58)	61	0.01
Pakistani (1,090)	1,198	0.13
Sri Lankan (61)	69	0.01
Taiwanese (241)	283	0.03
Thai (293)	544	0.06
Vietnamese (1,438)	1,688	0.19
Hawaii Native/Pacific Islander (400)	1,216	0.14
Not Hispanic (238)	842	0.09
Hispanic (162)	374	0.04
Fijian (0)	10	<0.01
Guamanian/Chamorro (215)	319	0.04
Marshallese (2)	3	<0.01
Native Hawaiian (74)	266	0.03
Samoan (34)	82	0.01
Tongan (3)	12	<0.01
White (618,617)	637,392	70.98
Not Hispanic (586,752)	601,625	67.00
Hispanic (31,865)	35,767	3.98

*Notes: † The Census 2010 population figure is used to calculate the percentages in the Hispanic Origin and Race categories. Ancestry percentages are based on the 2006-2010 American Community Survey population (not shown); ‡ Numbers in parentheses indicate the number of people reporting a single ancestry; * Numbers in parentheses indicate the number of persons reporting this race alone, not in combination with any other race; Please refer to the Explanation of Data for more information.*

Bear

Place Type: CDP
County: New Castle
Population: 19,371†

Ancestry‡	Population	%
African, Sub-Saharan (531)	531	2.83
African (445)	445	2.37
Nigerian (76)	76	0.41
South African (10)	10	0.05
American (567)	567	3.02
Arab (27)	35	0.19
Lebanese (27)	27	0.14
Syrian (0)	8	0.04
Austrian (13)	13	0.07
Czechoslovakian (0)	26	0.14
Danish (0)	16	0.09
Dutch (0)	29	0.15
English (509)	1,178	6.28
European (43)	43	0.23
French, ex. Basque (103)	387	2.06
French Canadian (11)	11	0.06
German (410)	1,613	8.60
Greek (0)	91	0.49
Hungarian (0)	22	0.12
Irish (856)	2,323	12.39
Italian (686)	1,622	8.65
Lithuanian (26)	26	0.14
Luxemburger (7)	7	0.04
Norwegian (71)	71	0.38
Pennsylvania German (9)	20	0.11
Polish (552)	945	5.04
Portuguese (7)	7	0.04
Romanian (15)	32	0.17
Russian (26)	144	0.77
Scandinavian (8)	27	0.14
Scotch-Irish (116)	174	0.93
Scottish (108)	209	1.11
Slovak (10)	10	0.05
Swedish (0)	147	0.78
Swiss (0)	12	0.06
Turkish (116)	116	0.62
Ukrainian (8)	72	0.38
Welsh (71)	131	0.70
West Indian, ex. Hispanic (126)	145	0.77
Haitian (64)	64	0.34
Jamaican (48)	67	0.36
West Indian (14)	14	0.07

Hispanic Origin	Population	%
Hispanic or Latino (of any race)	2,750	14.20
Central American, ex. Mexican	83	0.43
Costa Rican	18	0.09
Guatemalan	9	0.05
Honduran	13	0.07
Nicaraguan	5	0.03
Panamanian	16	0.08
Salvadoran	22	0.11
Cuban	26	0.13
Dominican Republic	87	0.45
Mexican	1,673	8.64
Puerto Rican	658	3.40
South American	135	0.70
Argentinean	5	0.03
Chilean	10	0.05
Colombian	62	0.32
Ecuadorian	15	0.08
Peruvian	28	0.14
Uruguayan	3	0.02
Venezuelan	12	0.06
Other Hispanic or Latino	88	0.45

Race*	Population	%
African-American/Black (6,682)	7,129	36.80
Not Hispanic (6,507)	6,866	35.44
Hispanic (175)	263	1.36
American Indian/Alaska Native (62)	211	1.09
Not Hispanic (33)	151	0.78
Hispanic (29)	60	0.31
Arapaho (1)	2	0.01
Blackfeet (1)	9	0.05
Canadian/French Am. Ind. (0)	4	0.02
Central American Ind. (0)	1	0.01
Cherokee (5)	36	0.19
Delaware (0)	1	0.01
Iroquois (1)	3	0.02
Lumbee (0)	1	0.01
Mexican American Ind. (4)	7	0.04
Sioux (1)	3	0.02
South American Ind. (1)	4	0.02
Spanish American Ind. (7)	9	0.05
Asian (812)	944	4.87
Not Hispanic (811)	935	4.83
Hispanic (1)	9	0.05
Bangladeshi (4)	9	0.05
Burmese (3)	3	0.02
Cambodian (1)	3	0.02
Chinese, ex. Taiwanese (89)	100	0.52
Filipino (100)	129	0.67
Indian (365)	400	2.06
Indonesian (9)	9	0.05
Japanese (10)	20	0.10
Korean (29)	35	0.18
Laotian (9)	15	0.08
Malaysian (3)	3	0.02
Pakistani (29)	38	0.20
Sri Lankan (4)	4	0.02
Thai (6)	18	0.09
Vietnamese (112)	116	0.60
Hawaii Native/Pacific Islander (5)	16	0.08
Not Hispanic (5)	13	0.07
Hispanic (0)	3	0.02
Guamanian/Chamorro (3)	3	0.02
Native Hawaiian (2)	4	0.02
White (9,776)	10,298	53.16
Not Hispanic (8,741)	9,103	46.99
Hispanic (1,035)	1,195	6.17

Brookside

Place Type: CDP
County: New Castle
Population: 14,353†

Ancestry‡	Population	%
African, Sub-Saharan (59)	59	0.41
African (25)	25	0.17
Kenyan (34)	34	0.24
American (466)	466	3.24
Arab (598)	598	4.16
Other Arab (598)	598	4.16
Austrian (0)	24	0.17
British (0)	93	0.65
Celtic (8)	8	0.06
Czech (0)	23	0.16
Czechoslovakian (8)	21	0.15
Danish (7)	82	0.57
Dutch (0)	127	0.88
English (480)	1,780	12.39
European (72)	110	0.77
French, ex. Basque (35)	389	2.71
French Canadian (27)	48	0.33
German (1,031)	3,008	20.94
Greek (0)	20	0.14
Hungarian (7)	185	1.29
Irish (746)	2,757	19.19
Italian (487)	1,149	8.00
Norwegian (50)	64	0.45
Pennsylvania German (69)	69	0.48
Polish (65)	580	4.04
Portuguese (0)	13	0.09
Russian (0)	93	0.65
Scotch-Irish (164)	313	2.18
Scottish (65)	179	1.25
Slavic (0)	19	0.13
Slovak (9)	29	0.20
Swedish (15)	43	0.30
Swiss (0)	35	0.24
Turkish (13)	13	0.09
Ukrainian (15)	44	0.31
Welsh (48)	257	1.79
West Indian, ex. Hispanic (68)	83	0.58
Jamaican (68)	83	0.58
Yugoslavian (48)	48	0.33

Hispanic Origin	Population	%
Hispanic or Latino (of any race)	1,601	11.15
Central American, ex. Mexican	50	0.35
Costa Rican	3	0.02
Guatemalan	10	0.07
Honduran	17	0.12
Nicaraguan	8	0.06
Panamanian	8	0.06
Salvadoran	4	0.03
Cuban	14	0.10
Dominican Republic	65	0.45
Mexican	806	5.62
Puerto Rican	472	3.29
South American	112	0.78
Argentinean	10	0.07
Bolivian	9	0.06
Chilean	2	0.01
Colombian	31	0.22
Ecuadorian	13	0.09
Peruvian	27	0.19
Uruguayan	5	0.03
Venezuelan	9	0.06
Other South American	6	0.04
Other Hispanic or Latino	82	0.57

Race*	Population	%
African-American/Black (2,745)	3,070	21.39
Not Hispanic (2,657)	2,948	20.54
Hispanic (88)	122	0.85
American Indian/Alaska Native (54)	172	1.20
Not Hispanic (37)	150	1.05
Hispanic (17)	22	0.15
Blackfeet (1)	4	0.03
Canadian/French Am. Ind. (1)	2	0.01
Cherokee (13)	35	0.24
Choctaw (0)	2	0.01
Delaware (1)	4	0.03
Inupiat *(Alaska Native)* (0)	3	0.02
Iroquois (0)	1	0.01
Mexican American Ind. (10)	10	0.07
Navajo (0)	1	0.01
Potawatomi (2)	2	0.01
Seminole (0)	1	0.01
Sioux (0)	5	0.03
South American Ind. (0)	2	0.01
Asian (449)	529	3.69
Not Hispanic (442)	520	3.62
Hispanic (7)	9	0.06
Bangladeshi (5)	7	0.05
Chinese, ex. Taiwanese (66)	81	0.56
Filipino (49)	63	0.44
Indian (190)	214	1.49
Japanese (5)	9	0.06
Korean (28)	39	0.27
Laotian (16)	16	0.11
Pakistani (58)	58	0.40
Thai (4)	10	0.07
Vietnamese (14)	16	0.11
Hawaii Native/Pacific Islander (2)	37	0.26
Not Hispanic (0)	28	0.20
Hispanic (2)	9	0.06
Guamanian/Chamorro (0)	3	0.02
Native Hawaiian (0)	12	0.08
White (9,773)	10,218	71.19
Not Hispanic (9,156)	9,525	66.36
Hispanic (617)	693	4.83

Claymont

Place Type: CDP
County: New Castle
Population: 8,253†

*Notes: † The Census 2010 population figure is used to calculate the percentages in the Hispanic Origin and Race categories. Ancestry percentages are based on the 2006-2010 American Community Survey population (not shown); ‡ Numbers in parentheses indicate the number of people reporting a single ancestry; * Numbers in parentheses indicate the number of persons reporting this race alone, not in combination with any other race; Please refer to the Explanation of Data for more information.*

Ancestry‡	Population	%
African, Sub-Saharan (42)	42	0.56
African (33)	33	0.44
Ghanaian (9)	9	0.12
American (165)	165	2.20
Arab (0)	18	0.24
Arab (0)	9	0.12
Lebanese (0)	9	0.12
Austrian (32)	41	0.55
Belgian (0)	9	0.12
British (29)	45	0.60
Czechoslovakian (9)	9	0.12
Dutch (12)	40	0.53
English (245)	954	12.70
French, ex. Basque (10)	296	3.94
French Canadian (0)	50	0.67
German (292)	969	12.90
Greek (15)	66	0.88
Irish (704)	1,862	24.79
Italian (339)	929	12.37
Lithuanian (11)	52	0.69
Norwegian (0)	21	0.28
Pennsylvania German (17)	55	0.73
Polish (146)	392	5.22
Portuguese (0)	20	0.27
Romanian (0)	37	0.49
Russian (0)	8	0.11
Scandinavian (0)	10	0.13
Scotch-Irish (0)	233	3.10
Scottish (47)	173	2.30
Slavic (9)	19	0.25
Slovak (0)	8	0.11
Swedish (10)	20	0.27
Ukrainian (115)	134	1.78
Welsh (15)	77	1.03
West Indian, ex. Hispanic (0)	9	0.12
Jamaican (0)	9	0.12

Hispanic Origin	Population	%
Hispanic or Latino (of any race)	584	7.08
Central American, ex. Mexican	19	0.23
Costa Rican	4	0.05
Guatemalan	2	0.02
Panamanian	5	0.06
Salvadoran	8	0.10
Cuban	11	0.13
Dominican Republic	10	0.12
Mexican	325	3.94
Puerto Rican	174	2.11
South American	25	0.30
Argentinean	8	0.10
Bolivian	1	0.01
Chilean	1	0.01
Colombian	4	0.05
Ecuadorian	1	0.01
Peruvian	8	0.10
Venezuelan	2	0.02
Other Hispanic or Latino	20	0.24

Race*	Population	%
African-American/Black (2,232)	2,344	28.40
Not Hispanic (2,176)	2,270	27.51
Hispanic (56)	74	0.90
American Indian/Alaska Native (28)	62	0.75
Not Hispanic (15)	46	0.56
Hispanic (13)	16	0.19
Central American Ind. (0)	1	0.01
Cherokee (1)	9	0.11
Creek (0)	1	0.01
Iroquois (0)	1	0.01
Mexican American Ind. (1)	1	0.01
Navajo (1)	1	0.01
Ottawa (1)	1	0.01
Sioux (0)	3	0.04
Asian (315)	347	4.20
Not Hispanic (305)	336	4.07
Hispanic (10)	11	0.13
Bangladeshi (59)	63	0.76
Cambodian (7)	7	0.08
Chinese, ex. Taiwanese (45)	52	0.63
Filipino (26)	28	0.34
Indian (128)	137	1.66
Indonesian (5)	6	0.07
Japanese (3)	9	0.11
Korean (11)	16	0.19
Malaysian (4)	4	0.05
Pakistani (11)	11	0.13
Thai (0)	2	0.02
Vietnamese (10)	10	0.12
Hawaii Native/Pacific Islander (9)	14	0.17
Not Hispanic (2)	6	0.07
Hispanic (7)	8	0.10
Native Hawaiian (7)	8	0.10
Samoan (2)	2	0.02
White (5,286)	5,435	65.85
Not Hispanic (5,028)	5,151	62.41
Hispanic (258)	284	3.44

Dover

Place Type: City
County: Kent
Population: 36,047†

Ancestry‡	Population	%
African, Sub-Saharan (764)	922	2.60
African (407)	546	1.54
Ghanaian (16)	16	0.05
Liberian (40)	47	0.13
Nigerian (301)	313	0.88
American (1,115)	1,115	3.14
Arab (104)	104	0.29
Arab (26)	26	0.07
Jordanian (66)	66	0.19
Syrian (12)	12	0.03
Armenian (0)	16	0.05
Australian (9)	9	0.03
Austrian (37)	118	0.33
Brazilian (0)	12	0.03
British (27)	66	0.19
Canadian (39)	65	0.18
Czech (10)	60	0.17
Czechoslovakian (7)	7	0.02
Danish (68)	145	0.41
Dutch (64)	511	1.44
English (1,102)	3,004	8.47
European (201)	201	0.57
Finnish (0)	33	0.09
French, ex. Basque (113)	738	2.08
French Canadian (80)	234	0.66
German (1,146)	4,756	13.41
Greek (13)	100	0.28
Hungarian (39)	254	0.72
Irish (1,136)	4,401	12.41
Italian (656)	1,907	5.38
Lithuanian (21)	67	0.19
Norwegian (39)	136	0.38
Pennsylvania German (29)	59	0.17
Polish (323)	941	2.65
Portuguese (13)	98	0.28
Romanian (0)	12	0.03
Russian (0)	146	0.41
Scandinavian (11)	11	0.03
Scotch-Irish (199)	547	1.54
Scottish (159)	499	1.41
Slovak (0)	22	0.06
Slovene (0)	38	0.11
Swedish (122)	373	1.05
Swiss (10)	32	0.09
Turkish (18)	18	0.05
Ukrainian (35)	158	0.45
Welsh (21)	232	0.65
West Indian, ex. Hispanic (618)	787	2.22
Barbadian (0)	25	0.07
Belizean (14)	14	0.04
British West Indian (25)	32	0.09
Haitian (185)	263	0.74
Jamaican (394)	439	1.24
Trinidadian/Tobagonian (0)	14	0.04
Yugoslavian (4)	11	0.03

Hispanic Origin	Population	%
Hispanic or Latino (of any race)	2,362	6.55
Central American, ex. Mexican	190	0.53
Costa Rican	7	0.02
Guatemalan	65	0.18
Honduran	27	0.07
Nicaraguan	7	0.02
Panamanian	47	0.13
Salvadoran	37	0.10
Cuban	83	0.23
Dominican Republic	87	0.24
Mexican	584	1.62
Puerto Rican	1,091	3.03
South American	126	0.35
Argentinean	3	0.01
Bolivian	12	0.03
Chilean	8	0.02
Colombian	45	0.12
Ecuadorian	14	0.04
Paraguayan	1	<0.01
Peruvian	20	0.06
Uruguayan	2	0.01
Venezuelan	17	0.05
Other South American	4	0.01
Other Hispanic or Latino	201	0.56

Race*	Population	%
African-American/Black (15,215)	16,312	45.25
Not Hispanic (14,798)	15,726	43.63
Hispanic (417)	586	1.63
American Indian/Alaska Native (196)	571	1.58
Not Hispanic (164)	487	1.35
Hispanic (32)	84	0.23
Apache (0)	2	0.01
Blackfeet (3)	27	0.07
Canadian/French Am. Ind. (1)	1	<0.01
Central American Ind. (1)	1	<0.01
Cherokee (21)	118	0.33
Chickasaw (1)	1	<0.01
Chippewa (1)	1	<0.01
Choctaw (2)	8	0.02
Creek (1)	3	0.01
Delaware (26)	34	0.09
Iroquois (2)	4	0.01
Kiowa (0)	1	<0.01
Lumbee (0)	2	0.01
Mexican American Ind. (1)	3	0.01
Navajo (4)	7	0.02
Pueblo (1)	1	<0.01
Seminole (0)	9	0.02
Shoshone (0)	2	0.01
Sioux (1)	6	0.02
South American Ind. (8)	13	0.04
Spanish American Ind. (0)	2	0.01
Asian (982)	1,310	3.63
Not Hispanic (975)	1,257	3.49
Hispanic (7)	53	0.15
Burmese (2)	2	0.01
Cambodian (1)	2	0.01
Chinese, ex. Taiwanese (145)	198	0.55
Filipino (292)	403	1.12
Hmong (1)	1	<0.01
Indian (269)	304	0.84
Indonesian (4)	4	0.01
Japanese (32)	75	0.21
Korean (87)	129	0.36
Pakistani (34)	39	0.11
Sri Lankan (1)	1	<0.01
Taiwanese (4)	9	0.02
Thai (38)	66	0.18
Vietnamese (32)	48	0.13
Hawaii Native/Pacific Islander (23)	75	0.21
Not Hispanic (16)	62	0.17
Hispanic (7)	13	0.04
Guamanian/Chamorro (10)	15	0.04
Native Hawaiian (6)	25	0.07
Samoan (0)	3	0.01
Tongan (0)	1	<0.01
White (17,393)	18,446	51.17
Not Hispanic (16,443)	17,338	48.10

*Notes: † The Census 2010 population figure is used to calculate the percentages in the Hispanic Origin and Race categories. Ancestry percentages are based on the 2006-2010 American Community Survey population (not shown); ‡ Numbers in parentheses indicate the number of people reporting a single ancestry; * Numbers in parentheses indicate the number of persons reporting this race alone, not in combination with any other race; Please refer to the Explanation of Data for more information.*

Hispanic (950)	1,108	3.07

Glasgow

Place Type: CDP
County: New Castle
Population: 14,303†

Ancestry‡	Population	%
African, Sub-Saharan (691)	779	4.98
African (209)	295	1.89
Ghanaian (105)	105	0.67
Kenyan (98)	98	0.63
Nigerian (135)	135	0.86
Sierra Leonean (3)	5	0.03
South African (38)	38	0.24
Other Sub-Saharan African (103)	103	0.66
American (546)	546	3.49
Arab (13)	46	0.29
Syrian (13)	46	0.29
Austrian (22)	149	0.95
British (65)	65	0.42
Canadian (51)	51	0.33
Celtic (13)	13	0.08
Croatian (11)	11	0.07
Czech (38)	95	0.61
Czechoslovakian (0)	96	0.61
Danish (0)	18	0.12
Dutch (26)	109	0.70
English (300)	1,069	6.83
European (63)	63	0.40
Finnish (16)	16	0.10
French, ex. Basque (13)	122	0.78
French Canadian (14)	14	0.09
German (361)	1,920	12.27
Greek (0)	55	0.35
Guyanese (36)	36	0.23
Hungarian (13)	54	0.35
Irish (797)	2,654	16.96
Italian (758)	1,787	11.42
Lithuanian (27)	43	0.27
Maltese (25)	25	0.16
Norwegian (0)	32	0.20
Polish (338)	1,230	7.86
Portuguese (17)	43	0.27
Russian (95)	228	1.46
Scotch-Irish (116)	246	1.57
Scottish (92)	211	1.35
Slovak (57)	110	0.70
Swedish (0)	50	0.32
Swiss (0)	14	0.09
Ukrainian (18)	107	0.68
Welsh (0)	50	0.32
West Indian, ex. Hispanic (250)	337	2.15
Barbadian (0)	7	0.04
British West Indian (17)	17	0.11
Jamaican (160)	182	1.16
Trinidadian/Tobagonian (48)	99	0.63
West Indian (25)	32	0.20

Hispanic Origin	Population	%
Hispanic or Latino (of any race)	716	5.01
Central American, ex. Mexican	46	0.32
Costa Rican	2	0.01
Guatemalan	6	0.04
Honduran	15	0.10
Nicaraguan	1	0.01
Panamanian	9	0.06
Salvadoran	13	0.09
Cuban	18	0.13
Dominican Republic	33	0.23
Mexican	218	1.52
Puerto Rican	278	1.94
South American	87	0.61
Argentinean	2	0.01
Bolivian	3	0.02
Colombian	35	0.24
Ecuadorian	7	0.05
Peruvian	30	0.21
Uruguayan	1	0.01
Venezuelan	9	0.06
Other Hispanic or Latino	36	0.25

Race*	Population	%
African-American/Black (3,586)	3,862	27.00
Not Hispanic (3,491)	3,724	26.04
Hispanic (95)	138	0.96
American Indian/Alaska Native (48)	119	0.83
Not Hispanic (41)	103	0.72
Hispanic (7)	16	0.11
Blackfeet (0)	7	0.05
Central American Ind. (2)	2	0.01
Cherokee (4)	12	0.08
Chippewa (1)	1	0.01
Choctaw (3)	5	0.03
Creek (0)	1	0.01
Delaware (0)	2	0.01
Inupiat *(Alaska Native)* (1)	2	0.01
Iroquois (1)	1	0.01
Lumbee (4)	5	0.03
Mexican American Ind. (2)	3	0.02
Navajo (1)	1	0.01
Ottawa (1)	2	0.01
Sioux (0)	1	0.01
Spanish American Ind. (1)	2	0.01
Tohono O'Odham (2)	2	0.01
Yakama (0)	1	0.01
Asian (816)	937	6.55
Not Hispanic (815)	932	6.52
Hispanic (1)	5	0.03
Bangladeshi (3)	3	0.02
Burmese (6)	6	0.04
Cambodian (4)	4	0.03
Chinese, ex. Taiwanese (135)	165	1.15
Filipino (66)	104	0.73
Hmong (2)	2	0.01
Indian (413)	436	3.05
Japanese (4)	14	0.10
Korean (45)	58	0.41
Laotian (21)	21	0.15
Malaysian (2)	2	0.01
Nepalese (6)	6	0.04
Pakistani (30)	36	0.25
Sri Lankan (9)	9	0.06
Taiwanese (7)	7	0.05
Thai (3)	3	0.02
Vietnamese (38)	51	0.36
Hawaii Native/Pacific Islander (4)	10	0.07
Not Hispanic (4)	8	0.06
Hispanic (0)	2	0.01
Native Hawaiian (3)	3	0.02
White (9,193)	9,505	66.45
Not Hispanic (8,860)	9,136	63.87
Hispanic (333)	369	2.58

Hockessin

Place Type: CDP
County: New Castle
Population: 13,527†

Ancestry‡	Population	%
African, Sub-Saharan (19)	19	0.15
African (19)	19	0.15
Albanian (0)	14	0.11
American (326)	326	2.52
Arab (15)	15	0.12
Egyptian (15)	15	0.12
Armenian (11)	11	0.09
Austrian (0)	25	0.19
British (51)	71	0.55
Bulgarian (0)	12	0.09
Canadian (18)	30	0.23
Croatian (0)	13	0.10
Czech (0)	39	0.30
Czechoslovakian (0)	25	0.19
Danish (0)	11	0.09
Dutch (79)	372	2.88
Eastern European (28)	28	0.22
English (619)	1,886	14.60
European (141)	141	1.09
French, ex. Basque (67)	422	3.27
French Canadian (14)	37	0.29
German (709)	2,422	18.75
Greek (125)	281	2.18
Hungarian (19)	93	0.72
Irish (1,111)	3,517	27.22
Italian (709)	2,179	16.87
Latvian (0)	14	0.11
Lithuanian (149)	171	1.32
Northern European (23)	39	0.30
Norwegian (17)	121	0.94
Pennsylvania German (80)	94	0.73
Polish (250)	1,247	9.65
Portuguese (0)	34	0.26
Romanian (0)	12	0.09
Scotch-Irish (51)	196	1.52
Scottish (88)	360	2.79
Slovene (0)	12	0.09
Swedish (21)	94	0.73
Swiss (11)	85	0.66
Ukrainian (62)	129	1.00
Welsh (72)	280	2.17

Hispanic Origin	Population	%
Hispanic or Latino (of any race)	400	2.96
Central American, ex. Mexican	24	0.18
Costa Rican	1	0.01
Guatemalan	10	0.07
Honduran	8	0.06
Panamanian	4	0.03
Salvadoran	1	0.01
Cuban	45	0.33
Dominican Republic	7	0.05
Mexican	121	0.89
Puerto Rican	64	0.47
South American	71	0.52
Argentinean	21	0.16
Bolivian	3	0.02
Chilean	3	0.02
Colombian	28	0.21
Ecuadorian	6	0.04
Peruvian	7	0.05
Venezuelan	3	0.02
Other Hispanic or Latino	68	0.50

Race*	Population	%
African-American/Black (396)	434	3.21
Not Hispanic (388)	415	3.07
Hispanic (8)	19	0.14
American Indian/Alaska Native (21)	59	0.44
Not Hispanic (18)	50	0.37
Hispanic (3)	9	0.07
Apache (1)	1	0.01
Blackfeet (0)	3	0.02
Cherokee (5)	14	0.10
Choctaw (0)	5	0.04
Delaware (5)	5	0.04
Mexican American Ind. (1)	1	0.01
Ottawa (0)	3	0.02
Potawatomi (0)	1	0.01
Sioux (0)	4	0.03
South American Ind. (0)	1	0.01
Asian (1,297)	1,429	10.56
Not Hispanic (1,289)	1,416	10.47
Hispanic (8)	13	0.10
Bangladeshi (3)	3	0.02
Chinese, ex. Taiwanese (499)	548	4.05
Filipino (79)	100	0.74
Indian (443)	465	3.44
Indonesian (1)	8	0.06
Japanese (19)	31	0.23
Korean (155)	163	1.20
Pakistani (37)	37	0.27
Taiwanese (22)	22	0.16
Thai (5)	13	0.10
Vietnamese (16)	19	0.14
Hawaii Native/Pacific Islander (9)	17	0.13
Not Hispanic (9)	17	0.13
Guamanian/Chamorro (4)	4	0.03

*Notes: † The Census 2010 population figure is used to calculate the percentages in the Hispanic Origin and Race categories. Ancestry percentages are based on the 2006-2010 American Community Survey population (not shown); ‡ Numbers in parentheses indicate the number of people reporting a single ancestry; * Numbers in parentheses indicate the number of persons reporting this race alone, not in combination with any other race; Please refer to the Explanation of Data for more information.*

Native Hawaiian (0)	1	0.01
Samoan (0)	3	0.02
White (11,524)	11,712	86.58
Not Hispanic (11,232)	11,391	84.21
Hispanic (292)	321	2.37

Middle

Place Type: Town
County: New Castle
Population: 18,871†

Ancestry‡	Population	%
African, Sub-Saharan (388)	440	2.64
African (293)	317	1.90
Ghanaian (19)	19	0.11
Kenyan (21)	21	0.13
Liberian (34)	34	0.20
Nigerian (9)	9	0.05
Sudanese (12)	40	0.24
American (846)	846	5.08
Arab (0)	9	0.05
Egyptian (0)	9	0.05
Australian (16)	16	0.10
Austrian (8)	24	0.14
Belgian (0)	9	0.05
Canadian (0)	7	0.04
Czech (12)	69	0.41
Czechoslovakian (0)	31	0.19
Danish (0)	18	0.11
Dutch (0)	340	2.04
English (413)	1,857	11.15
European (51)	79	0.47
French, ex. Basque (27)	414	2.49
French Canadian (42)	64	0.38
German (427)	2,765	16.61
Greek (75)	89	0.53
Hungarian (11)	266	1.60
Irish (1,047)	3,219	19.34
Italian (610)	1,816	10.91
Lithuanian (0)	10	0.06
Pennsylvania German (0)	30	0.18
Polish (164)	579	3.48
Romanian (17)	25	0.15
Russian (39)	142	0.85
Scandinavian (0)	48	0.29
Scotch-Irish (19)	134	0.80
Scottish (14)	274	1.65
Slavic (0)	59	0.35
Slovak (9)	18	0.11
Swedish (65)	185	1.11
Swiss (20)	59	0.35
Turkish (0)	9	0.05
Ukrainian (15)	130	0.78
Welsh (9)	82	0.49
West Indian, ex. Hispanic (232)	301	1.81
British West Indian (15)	15	0.09
Haitian (0)	29	0.17
Jamaican (59)	75	0.45
Trinidadian/Tobagonian (8)	24	0.14
West Indian (150)	158	0.95
Yugoslavian (19)	19	0.11

Hispanic Origin	Population	%
Hispanic or Latino (of any race)	1,396	7.40
Central American, ex. Mexican	108	0.57
Costa Rican	21	0.11
Guatemalan	34	0.18
Honduran	6	0.03
Nicaraguan	5	0.03
Panamanian	18	0.10
Salvadoran	24	0.13
Cuban	54	0.29
Dominican Republic	30	0.16
Mexican	487	2.58
Puerto Rican	513	2.72
South American	93	0.49
Argentinean	4	0.02
Chilean	6	0.03
Colombian	45	0.24
Ecuadorian	12	0.06
Peruvian	19	0.10
Venezuelan	7	0.04
Other Hispanic or Latino	111	0.59

Race*	Population	%
African-American/Black (5,367)	5,772	30.59
Not Hispanic (5,247)	5,572	29.53
Hispanic (120)	200	1.06
American Indian/Alaska Native (36)	143	0.76
Not Hispanic (23)	104	0.55
Hispanic (13)	39	0.21
Blackfeet (1)	17	0.09
Cherokee (2)	24	0.13
Choctaw (0)	1	0.01
Iroquois (0)	1	0.01
Lumbee (0)	1	0.01
Mexican American Ind. (7)	8	0.04
Seminole (1)	3	0.02
Sioux (0)	1	0.01
South American Ind. (0)	3	0.02
Spanish American Ind. (1)	1	0.01
Asian (709)	841	4.46
Not Hispanic (706)	826	4.38
Hispanic (3)	15	0.08
Cambodian (3)	10	0.05
Chinese, ex. Taiwanese (100)	115	0.61
Filipino (114)	151	0.80
Indian (302)	317	1.68
Indonesian (0)	5	0.03
Japanese (5)	22	0.12
Korean (54)	72	0.38
Laotian (2)	8	0.04
Pakistani (33)	33	0.17
Taiwanese (4)	6	0.03
Thai (5)	17	0.09
Vietnamese (68)	77	0.41
Hawaii Native/Pacific Islander (8)	27	0.14
Not Hispanic (8)	22	0.12
Hispanic (0)	5	0.03
Fijian (0)	3	0.02
Guamanian/Chamorro (0)	1	0.01
Native Hawaiian (6)	10	0.05
Samoan (2)	2	0.01
White (11,688)	12,145	64.36
Not Hispanic (10,978)	11,346	60.12
Hispanic (710)	799	4.23

Milford

Place Type: City
County: Sussex
Population: 9,559†

Ancestry‡	Population	%
African, Sub-Saharan (13)	13	0.14
African (13)	13	0.14
American (357)	357	3.89
Arab (22)	22	0.24
Egyptian (22)	22	0.24
British (11)	40	0.44
Canadian (29)	52	0.57
Croatian (0)	47	0.51
Czechoslovakian (11)	11	0.12
Danish (9)	19	0.21
Dutch (13)	75	0.82
Eastern European (38)	38	0.41
English (334)	1,136	12.37
European (22)	22	0.24
Finnish (11)	11	0.12
French, ex. Basque (129)	212	2.31
French Canadian (0)	12	0.13
German (520)	1,385	15.09
Greek (30)	46	0.50
Hungarian (0)	13	0.14
Irish (545)	1,482	16.14
Italian (286)	530	5.77
Lithuanian (10)	10	0.11
Luxemburger (0)	12	0.13
Norwegian (30)	43	0.47
Pennsylvania German (0)	36	0.39
Polish (62)	210	2.29
Portuguese (12)	12	0.13
Russian (24)	48	0.52
Scandinavian (0)	46	0.50
Scotch-Irish (36)	151	1.64
Scottish (47)	185	2.02
Swedish (0)	22	0.24
Swiss (0)	24	0.26
Welsh (141)	200	2.18
West Indian, ex. Hispanic (111)	121	1.32
Haitian (95)	95	1.03
Jamaican (16)	16	0.17
West Indian (0)	10	0.11
Yugoslavian (0)	8	0.09

Hispanic Origin	Population	%
Hispanic or Latino (of any race)	1,510	15.80
Central American, ex. Mexican	339	3.55
Guatemalan	273	2.86
Honduran	25	0.26
Nicaraguan	4	0.04
Panamanian	6	0.06
Salvadoran	31	0.32
Cuban	7	0.07
Dominican Republic	41	0.43
Mexican	632	6.61
Puerto Rican	302	3.16
South American	52	0.54
Argentinean	4	0.04
Bolivian	8	0.08
Chilean	1	0.01
Colombian	12	0.13
Ecuadorian	6	0.06
Peruvian	19	0.20
Venezuelan	2	0.02
Other Hispanic or Latino	137	1.43

Race*	Population	%
African-American/Black (2,128)	2,304	24.10
Not Hispanic (2,054)	2,195	22.96
Hispanic (74)	109	1.14
American Indian/Alaska Native (50)	115	1.20
Not Hispanic (31)	83	0.87
Hispanic (19)	32	0.33
Blackfeet (0)	3	0.03
Central American Ind. (6)	6	0.06
Cherokee (4)	17	0.18
Comanche (0)	1	0.01
Inupiat *(Alaska Native)* (1)	1	0.01
Mexican American Ind. (2)	3	0.03
Ottawa (1)	1	0.01
Sioux (2)	3	0.03
South American Ind. (1)	1	0.01
Asian (110)	137	1.43
Not Hispanic (100)	120	1.26
Hispanic (10)	17	0.18
Cambodian (0)	2	0.02
Chinese, ex. Taiwanese (16)	20	0.21
Filipino (25)	33	0.35
Indian (33)	40	0.42
Japanese (4)	7	0.07
Korean (1)	3	0.03
Laotian (0)	3	0.03
Pakistani (9)	10	0.10
Thai (6)	10	0.10
Vietnamese (6)	10	0.10
Hawaii Native/Pacific Islander (22)	45	0.47
Not Hispanic (6)	24	0.25
Hispanic (16)	21	0.22
Fijian (0)	1	0.01
Guamanian/Chamorro (21)	22	0.23
Native Hawaiian (0)	2	0.02
Samoan (1)	2	0.02
White (6,215)	6,404	66.99
Not Hispanic (5,654)	5,803	60.71
Hispanic (561)	601	6.29

*Notes: † The Census 2010 population figure is used to calculate the percentages in the Hispanic Origin and Race categories. Ancestry percentages are based on the 2006-2010 American Community Survey population (not shown); ‡ Numbers in parentheses indicate the number of people reporting a single ancestry; * Numbers in parentheses indicate the number of persons reporting this race alone, not in combination with any other race; Please refer to the Explanation of Data for more information.*

Newark

Place Type: City
County: New Castle
Population: 31,454†

Ancestry‡	Population	%
African, Sub-Saharan (150)	172	0.55
African (77)	77	0.25
Ethiopian (22)	22	0.07
Ghanaian (11)	25	0.08
Nigerian (8)	16	0.05
South African (32)	32	0.10
Albanian (15)	15	0.05
American (730)	730	2.35
Arab (89)	159	0.51
Arab (0)	11	0.04
Egyptian (13)	13	0.04
Iraqi (0)	1	<0.01
Jordanian (0)	29	0.09
Palestinian (0)	29	0.09
Other Arab (76)	76	0.24
Armenian (9)	31	0.10
Assyrian/Chaldean/Syriac (0)	6	0.02
Austrian (46)	161	0.52
Belgian (0)	10	0.03
Brazilian (21)	21	0.07
British (146)	302	0.97
Bulgarian (50)	50	0.16
Canadian (108)	119	0.38
Croatian (0)	12	0.04
Czech (86)	296	0.95
Czechoslovakian (0)	92	0.30
Danish (21)	65	0.21
Dutch (81)	417	1.34
Eastern European (51)	51	0.16
English (1,512)	4,410	14.18
European (484)	519	1.67
Finnish (11)	40	0.13
French, ex. Basque (183)	651	2.09
French Canadian (32)	51	0.16
German (1,260)	5,570	17.90
Greek (63)	200	0.64
Guyanese (21)	21	0.07
Hungarian (32)	238	0.77
Iranian (20)	20	0.06
Irish (2,341)	6,480	20.83
Israeli (0)	14	0.05
Italian (1,622)	4,246	13.65
Latvian (10)	23	0.07
Lithuanian (96)	221	0.71
Macedonian (13)	13	0.04
Northern European (45)	45	0.14
Norwegian (23)	184	0.59
Pennsylvania German (50)	70	0.23
Polish (572)	1,870	6.01
Portuguese (44)	51	0.16
Romanian (97)	145	0.47
Russian (113)	425	1.37
Scandinavian (22)	22	0.07
Scotch-Irish (425)	757	2.43
Scottish (236)	825	2.65
Serbian (32)	32	0.10
Slavic (11)	40	0.13
Slovak (7)	120	0.39
Swedish (211)	461	1.48
Swiss (19)	119	0.38
Turkish (47)	54	0.17
Ukrainian (98)	264	0.85
Welsh (36)	326	1.05
West Indian, ex. Hispanic (71)	81	0.26
Haitian (12)	12	0.04
Jamaican (59)	59	0.19
West Indian (0)	10	0.03
Yugoslavian (24)	31	0.10

Hispanic Origin	Population	%
Hispanic or Latino (of any race)	1,503	4.78
Central American, ex. Mexican	92	0.29
Costa Rican	6	0.02
Guatemalan	12	0.04
Honduran	22	0.07
Nicaraguan	14	0.04
Panamanian	22	0.07
Salvadoran	16	0.05
Cuban	138	0.44
Dominican Republic	46	0.15
Mexican	356	1.13
Puerto Rican	416	1.32
South American	305	0.97
Argentinean	34	0.11
Bolivian	3	0.01
Chilean	28	0.09
Colombian	119	0.38
Ecuadorian	54	0.17
Paraguayan	5	0.02
Peruvian	42	0.13
Uruguayan	7	0.02
Venezuelan	13	0.04
Other Hispanic or Latino	150	0.48

Race*	Population	%
African-American/Black (2,094)	2,412	7.67
Not Hispanic (2,027)	2,287	7.27
Hispanic (67)	125	0.40
American Indian/Alaska Native (53)	194	0.62
Not Hispanic (42)	160	0.51
Hispanic (11)	34	0.11
Alaska Athabascan *(Ala. Nat.)* (0)	1	<0.01
Apache (1)	4	0.01
Blackfeet (1)	10	0.03
Canadian/French Am. Ind. (0)	1	<0.01
Central American Ind. (0)	1	<0.01
Cherokee (8)	39	0.12
Chickasaw (0)	1	<0.01
Cree (0)	1	<0.01
Creek (0)	1	<0.01
Crow (0)	1	<0.01
Delaware (1)	2	0.01
Iroquois (0)	3	0.01
Lumbee (0)	1	<0.01
Menominee (1)	1	<0.01
Mexican American Ind. (2)	2	0.01
Pueblo (0)	1	<0.01
Seminole (1)	1	<0.01
Sioux (1)	3	0.01
South American Ind. (7)	10	0.03
Asian (2,245)	2,570	8.17
Not Hispanic (2,237)	2,548	8.10
Hispanic (8)	22	0.07
Bangladeshi (5)	6	0.02
Chinese, ex. Taiwanese (1,057)	1,153	3.67
Filipino (82)	157	0.50
Indian (591)	624	1.98
Indonesian (3)	9	0.03
Japanese (59)	100	0.32
Korean (233)	261	0.83
Laotian (2)	2	0.01
Malaysian (3)	5	0.02
Nepalese (5)	6	0.02
Pakistani (38)	43	0.14
Sri Lankan (4)	4	0.01
Taiwanese (41)	52	0.17
Thai (22)	29	0.09
Vietnamese (45)	64	0.20
Hawaii Native/Pacific Islander (10)	41	0.13
Not Hispanic (5)	29	0.09
Hispanic (5)	12	0.04
Guamanian/Chamorro (4)	7	0.02
Native Hawaiian (2)	8	0.03
Samoan (1)	1	<0.01
White (25,906)	26,532	84.35
Not Hispanic (24,965)	25,494	81.05
Hispanic (941)	1,038	3.30

North Star

Place Type: CDP
County: New Castle
Population: 7,980†

Ancestry‡	Population	%
African, Sub-Saharan (37)	37	0.47
Other Sub-Saharan African (37)	37	0.47
Albanian (0)	33	0.42
American (279)	279	3.52
Arab (0)	19	0.24
Lebanese (0)	19	0.24
Austrian (13)	113	1.43
British (48)	48	0.61
Cajun (0)	22	0.28
Canadian (0)	14	0.18
Czech (0)	47	0.59
Czechoslovakian (0)	3	0.04
Danish (0)	15	0.19
Dutch (19)	88	1.11
Eastern European (75)	86	1.08
English (536)	1,334	16.82
European (70)	89	1.12
French, ex. Basque (35)	276	3.48
French Canadian (30)	30	0.38
German (222)	1,477	18.63
Greek (107)	139	1.75
Hungarian (0)	58	0.73
Irish (540)	1,969	24.83
Italian (447)	1,395	17.59
Latvian (32)	32	0.40
Lithuanian (0)	40	0.50
Norwegian (65)	93	1.17
Polish (228)	804	10.14
Portuguese (0)	11	0.14
Romanian (0)	12	0.15
Russian (58)	222	2.80
Scandinavian (0)	23	0.29
Scotch-Irish (65)	129	1.63
Scottish (6)	99	1.25
Slavic (13)	33	0.42
Swedish (33)	102	1.29
Swiss (0)	75	0.95
Turkish (0)	11	0.14
Ukrainian (28)	97	1.22
Welsh (56)	166	2.09

Hispanic Origin	Population	%
Hispanic or Latino (of any race)	134	1.68
Central American, ex. Mexican	8	0.10
Guatemalan	3	0.04
Nicaraguan	1	0.01
Panamanian	1	0.01
Salvadoran	3	0.04
Cuban	12	0.15
Dominican Republic	4	0.05
Mexican	22	0.28
Puerto Rican	46	0.58
South American	27	0.34
Argentinean	3	0.04
Bolivian	1	0.01
Chilean	1	0.01
Colombian	7	0.09
Ecuadorian	4	0.05
Paraguayan	1	0.01
Peruvian	8	0.10
Venezuelan	2	0.03
Other Hispanic or Latino	15	0.19

Race*	Population	%
African-American/Black (250)	270	3.38
Not Hispanic (249)	269	3.37
Hispanic (1)	1	0.01
American Indian/Alaska Native (3)	11	0.14
Not Hispanic (3)	11	0.14
Cherokee (0)	4	0.05
Choctaw (1)	1	0.01
Delaware (1)	1	0.01
Asian (626)	687	8.61
Not Hispanic (626)	684	8.57
Hispanic (0)	3	0.04
Chinese, ex. Taiwanese (236)	245	3.07
Filipino (44)	54	0.68
Indian (196)	218	2.73
Japanese (11)	15	0.19

*Notes: † The Census 2010 population figure is used to calculate the percentages in the Hispanic Origin and Race categories. Ancestry percentages are based on the 2006-2010 American Community Survey population (not shown); ‡ Numbers in parentheses indicate the number of people reporting a single ancestry; * Numbers in parentheses indicate the number of persons reporting this race alone, not in combination with any other race; Please refer to the Explanation of Data for more information.*

Korean (70)	74	0.93
Laotian (1)	3	0.04
Nepalese (2)	2	0.03
Pakistani (23)	25	0.31
Sri Lankan (3)	3	0.04
Taiwanese (17)	19	0.24
Thai (3)	7	0.09
Vietnamese (16)	16	0.20
White (6,983)	7,066	88.55
Not Hispanic (6,871)	6,942	86.99
Hispanic (112)	124	1.55

Pike Creek

Place Type: CDP
County: New Castle
Population: 7,898†

Ancestry‡	Population	%
African, Sub-Saharan (13)	13	0.16
African (13)	13	0.16
American (57)	57	0.71
Arab (68)	68	0.85
Egyptian (44)	44	0.55
Palestinian (24)	24	0.30
Armenian (0)	10	0.12
Austrian (18)	41	0.51
Belgian (0)	15	0.19
Brazilian (0)	9	0.11
British (88)	164	2.04
Czech (13)	73	0.91
Czechoslovakian (14)	14	0.17
Danish (0)	68	0.85
Dutch (12)	106	1.32
Eastern European (12)	12	0.15
English (221)	873	10.88
Estonian (12)	12	0.15
European (114)	114	1.42
French, ex. Basque (13)	201	2.50
French Canadian (0)	11	0.14
German (364)	1,505	18.75
Greek (47)	62	0.77
Hungarian (26)	155	1.93
Iranian (104)	104	1.30
Irish (967)	2,638	32.87
Italian (412)	1,329	16.56
Lithuanian (0)	48	0.60
Norwegian (0)	69	0.86
Polish (221)	704	8.77
Portuguese (0)	12	0.15
Russian (24)	85	1.06
Scandinavian (12)	12	0.15
Scotch-Irish (97)	178	2.22
Scottish (56)	153	1.91
Slovak (12)	38	0.47
Swedish (0)	43	0.54
Swiss (12)	41	0.51
Ukrainian (0)	144	1.79
Welsh (0)	27	0.34
Yugoslavian (0)	34	0.42

Hispanic Origin	Population	%
Hispanic or Latino (of any race)	219	2.77
Central American, ex. Mexican	17	0.22
Costa Rican	6	0.08
Guatemalan	5	0.06
Honduran	1	0.01
Nicaraguan	1	0.01
Panamanian	1	0.01
Salvadoran	3	0.04
Cuban	12	0.15
Dominican Republic	4	0.05
Mexican	39	0.49
Puerto Rican	73	0.92
South American	60	0.76
Argentinean	9	0.11
Bolivian	4	0.05
Chilean	3	0.04
Colombian	23	0.29
Ecuadorian	5	0.06
Peruvian	5	0.06
Venezuelan	10	0.13
Other South American	1	0.01
Other Hispanic or Latino	14	0.18

Race*	Population	%
African-American/Black (294)	332	4.20
Not Hispanic (289)	323	4.09
Hispanic (5)	9	0.11
American Indian/Alaska Native (12)	19	0.24
Not Hispanic (11)	18	0.23
Hispanic (1)	1	0.01
Cherokee (1)	5	0.06
Chippewa (0)	1	0.01
Potawatomi (3)	3	0.04
Puget Sound Salish (1)	1	0.01
Asian (836)	905	11.46
Not Hispanic (836)	904	11.45
Hispanic (0)	1	0.01
Bangladeshi (3)	3	0.04
Chinese, ex. Taiwanese (277)	284	3.60
Filipino (32)	44	0.56
Indian (302)	314	3.98
Indonesian (1)	1	0.01
Japanese (9)	17	0.22
Korean (148)	156	1.98
Nepalese (2)	2	0.03
Pakistani (33)	33	0.42
Taiwanese (11)	12	0.15
Thai (1)	1	0.01
Vietnamese (10)	12	0.15
Hawaii Native/Pacific Islander (0)	3	0.04
Not Hispanic (0)	3	0.04
Native Hawaiian (0)	1	0.01
White (6,601)	6,702	84.86
Not Hispanic (6,423)	6,512	82.45
Hispanic (178)	190	2.41

Pike Creek Valley

Place Type: CDP
County: New Castle
Population: 11,217†

Ancestry‡	Population	%
African, Sub-Saharan (78)	78	0.68
African (52)	52	0.46
Other Sub-Saharan African (26)	26	0.23
American (526)	526	4.61
Arab (5)	5	0.04
Moroccan (5)	5	0.04
Armenian (18)	55	0.48
Austrian (0)	45	0.39
Belgian (0)	5	0.04
British (27)	84	0.74
Bulgarian (51)	51	0.45
Czech (0)	65	0.57
Czechoslovakian (0)	19	0.17
Danish (21)	71	0.62
Dutch (55)	113	0.99
English (299)	1,486	13.04
Estonian (49)	79	0.69
European (83)	102	0.89
French, ex. Basque (39)	174	1.53
French Canadian (55)	72	0.63
German (502)	2,398	21.04
Greek (9)	85	0.75
Hungarian (22)	63	0.55
Iranian (10)	10	0.09
Irish (812)	2,674	23.46
Israeli (5)	5	0.04
Italian (653)	1,665	14.61
Lithuanian (37)	55	0.48
Norwegian (0)	33	0.29
Polish (212)	674	5.91
Portuguese (151)	165	1.45
Russian (27)	139	1.22
Scandinavian (0)	81	0.71
Scotch-Irish (125)	324	2.84
Scottish (122)	275	2.41
Serbian (0)	38	0.33
Swedish (11)	223	1.96
Swiss (13)	101	0.89
Ukrainian (35)	91	0.80
Welsh (17)	142	1.25
West Indian, ex. Hispanic (0)	57	0.50
British West Indian (0)	26	0.23
Jamaican (0)	31	0.27
Yugoslavian (49)	49	0.43

Hispanic Origin	Population	%
Hispanic or Latino (of any race)	677	6.04
Central American, ex. Mexican	47	0.42
Costa Rican	3	0.03
Guatemalan	7	0.06
Honduran	29	0.26
Panamanian	6	0.05
Salvadoran	2	0.02
Cuban	34	0.30
Dominican Republic	8	0.07
Mexican	203	1.81
Puerto Rican	206	1.84
South American	122	1.09
Argentinean	4	0.04
Bolivian	2	0.02
Chilean	7	0.06
Colombian	34	0.30
Ecuadorian	29	0.26
Paraguayan	1	0.01
Peruvian	11	0.10
Venezuelan	33	0.29
Other South American	1	0.01
Other Hispanic or Latino	57	0.51

Race*	Population	%
African-American/Black (936)	1,067	9.51
Not Hispanic (906)	1,014	9.04
Hispanic (30)	53	0.47
American Indian/Alaska Native (19)	77	0.69
Not Hispanic (9)	66	0.59
Hispanic (10)	11	0.10
Blackfeet (0)	3	0.03
Central American Ind. (1)	1	0.01
Cherokee (2)	17	0.15
Choctaw (1)	1	0.01
Creek (0)	1	0.01
Potawatomi (1)	1	0.01
Asian (880)	977	8.71
Not Hispanic (876)	962	8.58
Hispanic (4)	15	0.13
Bangladeshi (13)	17	0.15
Burmese (2)	2	0.02
Cambodian (0)	1	0.01
Chinese, ex. Taiwanese (152)	166	1.48
Filipino (40)	49	0.44
Indian (352)	381	3.40
Indonesian (1)	3	0.03
Japanese (16)	21	0.19
Korean (228)	241	2.15
Laotian (1)	1	0.01
Nepalese (2)	2	0.02
Pakistani (20)	22	0.20
Sri Lankan (13)	14	0.12
Taiwanese (9)	9	0.08
Vietnamese (12)	19	0.17
Hawaii Native/Pacific Islander (0)	8	0.07
Not Hispanic (0)	7	0.06
Hispanic (0)	1	0.01
Guamanian/Chamorro (0)	1	0.01
Native Hawaiian (0)	2	0.02
Samoan (0)	3	0.03
White (8,892)	9,112	81.23
Not Hispanic (8,510)	8,693	77.50
Hispanic (382)	419	3.74

Smyrna

Place Type: Town
County: Kent
Population: 10,023†

SECTION TWO

*Notes: † The Census 2010 population figure is used to calculate the percentages in the Hispanic Origin and Race categories. Ancestry percentages are based on the 2006-2010 American Community Survey population (not shown); ‡ Numbers in parentheses indicate the number of people reporting a single ancestry; * Numbers in parentheses indicate the number of persons reporting this race alone, not in combination with any other race; Please refer to the Explanation of Data for more information.*

Ancestry‡	Population	%
Afghan (16)	52	0.56
African, Sub-Saharan (90)	121	1.30
African (86)	117	1.25
Liberian (4)	4	0.04
American (386)	386	4.14
Austrian (0)	12	0.13
Canadian (10)	27	0.29
Czech (49)	63	0.68
Czechoslovakian (12)	12	0.13
Danish (0)	9	0.10
Dutch (8)	290	3.11
English (219)	799	8.56
French, ex. Basque (0)	223	2.39
French Canadian (16)	35	0.38
German (757)	2,011	21.55
Greek (17)	17	0.18
Hungarian (0)	25	0.27
Iranian (5)	5	0.05
Irish (432)	1,405	15.06
Italian (208)	990	10.61
Norwegian (22)	72	0.77
Pennsylvania German (53)	53	0.57
Polish (83)	281	3.01
Romanian (0)	17	0.18
Russian (0)	50	0.54
Scotch-Irish (68)	115	1.23
Scottish (9)	53	0.57
Slavic (0)	36	0.39
Swedish (0)	57	0.61
Swiss (15)	15	0.16
Ukrainian (38)	50	0.54
Welsh (25)	91	0.98
West Indian, ex. Hispanic (28)	28	0.30
Haitian (16)	16	0.17
Jamaican (12)	12	0.13

Hispanic Origin	Population	%
Hispanic or Latino (of any race)	592	5.91
Central American, ex. Mexican	47	0.47
Guatemalan	1	0.01
Honduran	7	0.07
Nicaraguan	3	0.03
Panamanian	9	0.09
Salvadoran	27	0.27
Cuban	7	0.07
Dominican Republic	15	0.15
Mexican	155	1.55
Puerto Rican	286	2.85
South American	36	0.36
Argentinean	3	0.03
Chilean	5	0.05
Colombian	11	0.11
Peruvian	16	0.16
Venezuelan	1	0.01
Other Hispanic or Latino	46	0.46

Race*	Population	%
African-American/Black (2,918)	3,156	31.49
Not Hispanic (2,860)	3,060	30.53
Hispanic (58)	96	0.96
American Indian/Alaska Native (32)	117	1.17
Not Hispanic (24)	103	1.03
Hispanic (8)	14	0.14
Alaska Athabascan *(Ala. Nat.)* (1)	2	0.02
Blackfeet (0)	3	0.03
Canadian/French Am. Ind. (1)	1	0.01
Cherokee (1)	18	0.18
Delaware (3)	5	0.05
Hopi (0)	3	0.03
Lumbee (0)	3	0.03
Mexican American Ind. (3)	3	0.03
Potawatomi (2)	2	0.02
Seminole (0)	1	0.01
Sioux (0)	2	0.02
Spanish American Ind. (3)	3	0.03
Asian (153)	211	2.11
Not Hispanic (152)	207	2.07
Hispanic (1)	4	0.04
Cambodian (1)	1	0.01
Chinese, ex. Taiwanese (15)	22	0.22
Filipino (41)	57	0.57
Indian (19)	25	0.25
Indonesian (1)	1	0.01
Japanese (3)	7	0.07
Korean (14)	16	0.16
Laotian (3)	5	0.05
Pakistani (1)	1	0.01
Thai (2)	11	0.11
Vietnamese (24)	30	0.30
Hawaii Native/Pacific Islander (5)	16	0.16
Not Hispanic (2)	13	0.13
Hispanic (3)	3	0.03
Guamanian/Chamorro (3)	9	0.09
Native Hawaiian (1)	2	0.02
Samoan (0)	1	0.01
White (6,324)	6,647	66.32
Not Hispanic (6,061)	6,321	63.06
Hispanic (263)	326	3.25

Wilmington Manor

Place Type: CDP
County: New Castle
Population: 7,889†

Ancestry‡	Population	%
African, Sub-Saharan (162)	199	2.53
African (162)	199	2.53
American (455)	455	5.79
British (10)	10	0.13
Canadian (17)	33	0.42
Czech (0)	13	0.17
Dutch (0)	89	1.13
English (295)	838	10.65
European (28)	28	0.36
French, ex. Basque (9)	170	2.16
French Canadian (0)	48	0.61
German (237)	1,199	15.24
Hungarian (0)	9	0.11
Irish (516)	1,410	17.93
Italian (294)	861	10.95
Norwegian (0)	9	0.11
Pennsylvania German (0)	15	0.19
Polish (145)	437	5.56
Portuguese (0)	46	0.58
Russian (0)	9	0.11
Scotch-Irish (86)	197	2.50
Scottish (23)	85	1.08
Slavic (8)	8	0.10
Slovak (13)	26	0.33
Swedish (31)	95	1.21
Swiss (9)	9	0.11
Ukrainian (24)	93	1.18
Welsh (0)	9	0.11

Hispanic Origin	Population	%
Hispanic or Latino (of any race)	1,553	19.69
Central American, ex. Mexican	35	0.44
Costa Rican	3	0.04
Guatemalan	4	0.05
Honduran	2	0.03
Nicaraguan	3	0.04
Panamanian	2	0.03
Salvadoran	21	0.27
Cuban	9	0.11
Dominican Republic	20	0.25
Mexican	925	11.73
Puerto Rican	482	6.11
South American	25	0.32
Chilean	7	0.09
Colombian	8	0.10
Ecuadorian	4	0.05
Peruvian	3	0.04
Venezuelan	3	0.04
Other Hispanic or Latino	57	0.72

Race*	Population	%
African-American/Black (1,221)	1,337	16.95
Not Hispanic (1,173)	1,259	15.96
Hispanic (48)	78	0.99
American Indian/Alaska Native (41)	93	1.18
Not Hispanic (28)	69	0.87
Hispanic (13)	24	0.30
Apache (0)	6	0.08
Cherokee (2)	21	0.27
Choctaw (1)	1	0.01
Creek (5)	5	0.06
Hopi (0)	4	0.05
Mexican American Ind. (1)	1	0.01
Potawatomi (1)	1	0.01
Asian (84)	133	1.69
Not Hispanic (84)	130	1.65
Hispanic (0)	3	0.04
Bangladeshi (1)	1	0.01
Cambodian (1)	3	0.04
Chinese, ex. Taiwanese (1)	1	0.01
Filipino (49)	68	0.86
Indian (10)	17	0.22
Japanese (3)	5	0.06
Korean (6)	15	0.19
Pakistani (6)	6	0.08
Thai (2)	9	0.11
Vietnamese (3)	7	0.09
Hawaii Native/Pacific Islander (1)	7	0.09
Not Hispanic (1)	7	0.09
Guamanian/Chamorro (1)	1	0.01
Native Hawaiian (0)	1	0.01
White (5,413)	5,602	71.01
Not Hispanic (4,855)	4,988	63.23
Hispanic (558)	614	7.78

Wilmington

Place Type: City
County: New Castle
Population: 70,851†

Ancestry‡	Population	%
African, Sub-Saharan (415)	596	0.83
African (324)	472	0.66
Liberian (69)	69	0.10
Nigerian (22)	37	0.05
Other Sub-Saharan African (0)	18	0.03
American (977)	977	1.37
Arab (94)	94	0.13
Arab (23)	23	0.03
Moroccan (44)	44	0.06
Other Arab (27)	27	0.04
Armenian (7)	11	0.02
Austrian (23)	97	0.14
Belgian (0)	24	0.03
Brazilian (8)	8	0.01
British (185)	251	0.35
Canadian (174)	234	0.33
Croatian (38)	61	0.09
Czech (54)	143	0.20
Czechoslovakian (18)	31	0.04
Danish (113)	127	0.18
Dutch (67)	397	0.56
Eastern European (165)	165	0.23
English (1,073)	4,423	6.19
European (114)	160	0.22
French, ex. Basque (159)	678	0.95
French Canadian (61)	153	0.21
German (1,044)	5,169	7.24
Greek (75)	134	0.19
Guyanese (0)	46	0.06
Hungarian (44)	232	0.32
Iranian (10)	10	0.01
Irish (2,468)	7,378	10.33
Italian (2,043)	4,486	6.28
Lithuanian (5)	72	0.10
Northern European (16)	16	0.02
Norwegian (78)	120	0.17
Pennsylvania German (30)	62	0.09
Polish (855)	2,117	2.96
Portuguese (20)	43	0.06
Romanian (25)	70	0.10
Russian (169)	413	0.58

*Notes: † The Census 2010 population figure is used to calculate the percentages in the Hispanic Origin and Race categories. Ancestry percentages are based on the 2006-2010 American Community Survey population (not shown); ‡ Numbers in parentheses indicate the number of people reporting a single ancestry; * Numbers in parentheses indicate the number of persons reporting this race alone, not in combination with any other race; Please refer to the Explanation of Data for more information.*

Ancestry	Population	%
Scotch-Irish (175)	995	1.39
Scottish (130)	711	1.00
Slavic (15)	26	0.04
Slovak (0)	37	0.05
Slovene (0)	24	0.03
Swedish (56)	297	0.42
Swiss (22)	93	0.13
Ukrainian (89)	286	0.40
Welsh (71)	281	0.39
West Indian, ex. Hispanic (795)	999	1.40
Barbadian (0)	11	0.02
Haitian (142)	144	0.20
Jamaican (611)	687	0.96
Trinidadian/Tobagonian (24)	41	0.06
West Indian (18)	102	0.14
Other West Indian (0)	14	0.02
Yugoslavian (5)	5	0.01

Hispanic Origin	Population	%
Hispanic or Latino (of any race)	8,788	12.40
Central American, ex. Mexican	217	0.31
Costa Rican	10	0.01
Guatemalan	68	0.10
Honduran	31	0.04
Nicaraguan	9	0.01
Panamanian	46	0.06
Salvadoran	50	0.07
Other Central American	3	<0.01
Cuban	116	0.16
Dominican Republic	371	0.52
Mexican	3,060	4.32
Puerto Rican	4,404	6.22
South American	224	0.32
Argentinean	27	0.04
Bolivian	1	<0.01
Chilean	18	0.03
Colombian	75	0.11
Ecuadorian	34	0.05
Paraguayan	2	<0.01
Peruvian	29	0.04
Uruguayan	1	<0.01
Venezuelan	34	0.05
Other South American	3	<0.01
Other Hispanic or Latino	396	0.56

Race*	Population	%
African-American/Black (41,127)	42,426	59.88
Not Hispanic (40,170)	41,144	58.07
Hispanic (957)	1,282	1.81
American Indian/Alaska Native (312)	808	1.14
Not Hispanic (158)	556	0.78
Hispanic (154)	252	0.36
Apache (1)	3	<0.01
Blackfeet (1)	29	0.04
Canadian/French Am. Ind. (0)	1	<0.01
Central American Ind. (1)	2	<0.01
Cherokee (30)	125	0.18
Chippewa (0)	3	<0.01
Choctaw (1)	1	<0.01
Comanche (0)	2	<0.01
Cree (1)	1	<0.01
Crow (0)	1	<0.01
Delaware (4)	17	0.02
Iroquois (1)	8	0.01
Lumbee (2)	3	<0.01
Mexican American Ind. (55)	65	0.09
Navajo (2)	2	<0.01
Seminole (0)	5	0.01
South American Ind. (19)	34	0.05
Spanish American Ind. (1)	4	0.01
Tlingit-Haida *(Alaska Native)* (0)	1	<0.01
Asian (685)	886	1.25
Not Hispanic (648)	833	1.18
Hispanic (37)	53	0.07
Bangladeshi (13)	13	0.02
Bhutanese (1)	1	<0.01
Cambodian (2)	3	<0.01
Chinese, ex. Taiwanese (118)	161	0.23
Filipino (82)	116	0.16
Indian (215)	258	0.36
Indonesian (1)	2	<0.01
Japanese (24)	62	0.09
Korean (106)	130	0.18
Laotian (0)	1	<0.01
Pakistani (31)	32	0.05
Taiwanese (6)	6	0.01
Thai (11)	13	0.02
Vietnamese (28)	36	0.05
Hawaii Native/Pacific Islander (10)	87	0.12
Not Hispanic (4)	43	0.06
Hispanic (6)	44	0.06
Guamanian/Chamorro (1)	4	0.01
Marshallese (1)	2	<0.01
Native Hawaiian (2)	12	0.02
Samoan (5)	9	0.01
Tongan (0)	2	<0.01
White (23,079)	24,233	34.20
Not Hispanic (19,770)	20,532	28.98
Hispanic (3,309)	3,701	5.22

*Notes: † The Census 2010 population figure is used to calculate the percentages in the Hispanic Origin and Race categories. Ancestry percentages are based on the 2006-2010 American Community Survey population (not shown); ‡ Numbers in parentheses indicate the number of people reporting a single ancestry; * Numbers in parentheses indicate the number of persons reporting this race alone, not in combination with any other race; Please refer to the Explanation of Data for more information.*

DISTRICT OF COLUMBIA

Place Type: State
Population: 601,723†

Ancestry‡	Population	%
Afghan (55)	121	0.02
African, Sub-Saharan (13,712)	15,795	2.70
African (7,524)	9,069	1.55
Cape Verdean (60)	93	0.02
Ethiopian (2,521)	2,601	0.45
Ghanaian (347)	385	0.07
Kenyan (211)	211	0.04
Liberian (73)	91	0.02
Nigerian (1,546)	1,682	0.29
Senegalese (125)	163	0.03
Sierra Leonean (172)	172	0.03
Somalian (0)	13	<0.01
South African (144)	182	0.03
Sudanese (51)	51	0.01
Ugandan (74)	74	0.01
Zimbabwean (13)	13	<0.01
Other Sub-Saharan African (851)	995	0.17
Albanian (138)	183	0.03
Alsatian (0)	39	0.01
American (8,279)	8,279	1.42
Arab (2,125)	3,776	0.65
Arab (490)	627	0.11
Egyptian (189)	315	0.05
Iraqi (34)	114	0.02
Jordanian (28)	28	<0.01
Lebanese (604)	1,243	0.21
Moroccan (259)	362	0.06
Palestinian (139)	261	0.04
Syrian (44)	251	0.04
Other Arab (338)	575	0.10
Armenian (299)	574	0.10
Assyrian/Chaldean/Syriac (14)	14	<0.01
Australian (140)	295	0.05
Austrian (480)	2,131	0.36
Basque (139)	222	0.04
Belgian (186)	496	0.08
Brazilian (287)	616	0.11
British (2,236)	4,625	0.79
Bulgarian (225)	309	0.05
Cajun (41)	73	0.01
Canadian (478)	972	0.17
Carpatho Rusyn (0)	40	0.01
Celtic (27)	48	0.01
Croatian (261)	611	0.10
Cypriot (11)	11	<0.01
Czech (397)	1,392	0.24
Czechoslovakian (138)	278	0.05
Danish (517)	1,495	0.26
Dutch (985)	3,668	0.63
Eastern European (3,666)	3,934	0.67
English (8,700)	30,309	5.19
Estonian (125)	177	0.03
European (6,695)	7,573	1.30
Finnish (360)	778	0.13
French, ex. Basque (2,177)	9,561	1.64
French Canadian (781)	1,916	0.33
German (9,588)	38,822	6.64
Greek (1,128)	2,120	0.36
Guyanese (261)	355	0.06
Hungarian (508)	2,196	0.38
Icelander (10)	59	0.01
Iranian (879)	1,262	0.22
Irish (12,531)	39,622	6.78
Israeli (152)	279	0.05
Italian (5,746)	17,817	3.05
Latvian (94)	297	0.05
Lithuanian (492)	1,441	0.25
Luxemburger (16)	127	0.02
Macedonian (114)	125	0.02
Maltese (0)	24	<0.01
New Zealander (148)	174	0.03
Northern European (533)	610	0.10
Norwegian (923)	3,821	0.65
Pennsylvania German (42)	67	0.01
Polish (3,094)	11,744	2.01
Portuguese (494)	1,209	0.21
Romanian (491)	1,068	0.18
Russian (3,683)	9,585	1.64
Scandinavian (311)	895	0.15
Scotch-Irish (2,286)	5,907	1.01
Scottish (1,889)	7,961	1.36
Serbian (166)	330	0.06
Slavic (92)	134	0.02
Slovak (258)	930	0.16
Slovene (132)	334	0.06
Swedish (894)	4,055	0.69
Swiss (288)	1,732	0.30
Turkish (416)	511	0.09
Ukrainian (677)	1,967	0.34
Welsh (305)	2,671	0.46
West Indian, ex. Hispanic (6,080)	8,198	1.40
Bahamian (70)	120	0.02
Barbadian (134)	267	0.05
Belizean (58)	101	0.02
Bermudan (34)	41	0.01
British West Indian (221)	296	0.05
Dutch West Indian (15)	26	<0.01
Haitian (878)	1,095	0.19
Jamaican (2,674)	3,576	0.61
Trinidadian/Tobagonian (1,071)	1,288	0.22
U.S. Virgin Islander (128)	171	0.03
West Indian (797)	1,217	0.21
Yugoslavian (154)	243	0.04

Hispanic Origin	Population	%
Hispanic or Latino (of any race)	54,749	9.10
Central American, ex. Mexican	23,354	3.88
Costa Rican	258	0.04
Guatemalan	2,635	0.44
Honduran	2,139	0.36
Nicaraguan	859	0.14
Panamanian	742	0.12
Salvadoran	16,611	2.76
Other Central American	110	0.02
Cuban	1,789	0.30
Dominican Republic	2,508	0.42
Mexican	8,507	1.41
Puerto Rican	3,129	0.52
South American	7,639	1.27
Argentinean	1,134	0.19
Bolivian	591	0.10
Chilean	697	0.12
Colombian	1,982	0.33
Ecuadorian	707	0.12
Paraguayan	161	0.03
Peruvian	1,482	0.25
Uruguayan	216	0.04
Venezuelan	596	0.10
Other South American	73	0.01
Other Hispanic or Latino	7,823	1.30

Race*	Population	%
African-American/Black (305,125)	314,352	52.24
Not Hispanic (301,053)	308,617	51.29
Hispanic (4,072)	5,735	0.95
American Indian/Alaska Native (2,079)	6,521	1.08
Not Hispanic (1,322)	4,932	0.82
Hispanic (757)	1,589	0.26
Alaska Athabascan *(Ala. Nat.)* (2)	9	<0.01
Aleut *(Alaska Native)* (3)	3	<0.01
Apache (20)	51	0.01
Arapaho (1)	1	<0.01
Blackfeet (19)	236	0.04
Canadian/French Am. Ind. (8)	13	<0.01
Central American Ind. (53)	96	0.02
Cherokee (149)	1,036	0.17
Cheyenne (1)	4	<0.01
Chickasaw (13)	36	0.01
Chippewa (9)	35	0.01
Choctaw (17)	105	0.02
Colville (3)	4	<0.01
Comanche (5)	15	<0.01
Cree (1)	10	<0.01
Creek (18)	62	0.01
Crow (1)	9	<0.01
Delaware (3)	12	<0.01
Hopi (1)	2	<0.01
Houma (2)	2	<0.01
Inupiat *(Alaska Native)* (3)	6	<0.01
Iroquois (13)	82	0.01
Kiowa (2)	2	<0.01
Lumbee (13)	35	0.01
Menominee (1)	1	<0.01
Mexican American Ind. (120)	220	0.04
Navajo (32)	62	0.01
Osage (2)	17	<0.01
Ottawa (0)	2	<0.01
Paiute (3)	3	<0.01
Pima (1)	1	<0.01
Potawatomi (7)	15	<0.01
Pueblo (23)	29	<0.01
Seminole (16)	40	0.01
Shoshone (1)	4	<0.01
Sioux (29)	83	0.01
South American Ind. (49)	154	0.03
Spanish American Ind. (35)	51	0.01
Tlingit-Haida *(Alaska Native)* (3)	10	<0.01
Tohono O'Odham (1)	3	<0.01
Ute (1)	1	<0.01
Yakama (1)	2	<0.01
Yaqui (9)	15	<0.01
Yuman (1)	5	<0.01
Yup'ik *(Alaska Native)* (0)	3	<0.01
Asian (21,056)	26,857	4.46
Not Hispanic (20,818)	26,126	4.34
Hispanic (238)	731	0.12
Bangladeshi (226)	266	0.04
Bhutanese (3)	3	<0.01
Burmese (110)	134	0.02
Cambodian (70)	97	0.02
Chinese, ex. Taiwanese (4,887)	6,204	1.03
Filipino (2,690)	3,670	0.61
Hmong (22)	26	<0.01
Indian (5,214)	6,417	1.07
Indonesian (146)	226	0.04
Japanese (1,172)	2,010	0.33
Korean (2,290)	2,990	0.50
Laotian (58)	69	0.01
Malaysian (41)	66	0.01
Nepalese (139)	161	0.03
Pakistani (558)	688	0.11
Sri Lankan (176)	221	0.04
Taiwanese (328)	402	0.07
Thai (375)	497	0.08
Vietnamese (1,567)	1,856	0.31
Hawaii Native/Pacific Islander (302)	1,320	0.22
Not Hispanic (216)	821	0.14
Hispanic (86)	499	0.08
Fijian (18)	23	<0.01
Guamanian/Chamorro (111)	187	0.03
Marshallese (4)	5	<0.01
Native Hawaiian (75)	264	0.04
Samoan (29)	82	0.01
Tongan (2)	5	<0.01
White (231,471)	243,650	40.49
Not Hispanic (209,464)	218,422	36.30
Hispanic (22,007)	25,228	4.19

*Notes: † The Census 2010 population figure is used to calculate the percentages in the Hispanic Origin and Race categories. Ancestry percentages are based on the 2006-2010 American Community Survey population (not shown); ‡ Numbers in parentheses indicate the number of people reporting a single ancestry; * Numbers in parentheses indicate the number of persons reporting this race alone, not in combination with any other race; Please refer to the Explanation of Data for more information.*

FLORIDA

Place Type: State
Population: 18,801,310†

Ancestry‡	Population	%
Afghan (1,013)	1,078	0.01
African, Sub-Saharan (117,119)	145,105	0.78
African (93,310)	116,581	0.63
Cape Verdean (1,904)	2,983	0.02
Ethiopian (3,408)	3,615	0.02
Ghanaian (1,079)	1,187	0.01
Kenyan (582)	925	<0.01
Liberian (1,035)	1,287	0.01
Nigerian (7,217)	8,180	0.04
Senegalese (130)	147	<0.01
Sierra Leonean (239)	339	<0.01
South African (4,580)	5,723	0.03
Sudanese (936)	943	0.01
Ugandan (59)	59	<0.01
Zimbabwean (430)	442	<0.01
Other Sub-Saharan African (2,210)	2,694	0.01
Albanian (9,609)	11,060	0.06
Alsatian (199)	444	<0.01
American (1,269,765)	1,269,765	6.86
Arab (61,241)	95,752	0.52
Arab (10,665)	15,315	0.08
Egyptian (8,722)	10,623	0.06
Iraqi (1,043)	1,718	0.01
Jordanian (2,241)	2,907	0.02
Lebanese (16,275)	32,346	0.17
Moroccan (6,840)	8,858	0.05
Palestinian (4,213)	5,557	0.03
Syrian (5,535)	10,081	0.05
Other Arab (5,707)	8,347	0.05
Armenian (7,605)	13,446	0.07
Assyrian/Chaldean/Syriac (661)	996	0.01
Australian (2,593)	5,111	0.03
Austrian (18,311)	57,024	0.31
Basque (1,005)	1,998	0.01
Belgian (5,960)	15,450	0.08
Brazilian (61,316)	73,827	0.40
British (53,330)	89,770	0.48
Bulgarian (4,854)	6,029	0.03
Cajun (1,684)	3,242	0.02
Canadian (45,111)	71,240	0.38
Carpatho Rusyn (197)	320	<0.01
Celtic (1,225)	2,843	0.02
Croatian (7,340)	16,360	0.09
Cypriot (84)	135	<0.01
Czech (20,960)	60,744	0.33
Czechoslovakian (8,534)	17,795	0.10
Danish (14,614)	47,700	0.26
Dutch (57,477)	232,801	1.26
Eastern European (20,547)	22,944	0.12
English (614,884)	1,629,852	8.80
Estonian (1,263)	1,990	0.01
European (143,570)	167,285	0.90
Finnish (11,262)	28,029	0.15
French, ex. Basque (117,715)	504,650	2.73
French Canadian (64,924)	119,700	0.65
German (715,019)	2,212,580	11.95
German Russian (226)	462	<0.01
Greek (50,033)	94,742	0.51
Guyanese (16,075)	21,902	0.12
Hungarian (43,295)	106,462	0.58
Icelander (1,251)	2,368	0.01
Iranian (10,281)	12,999	0.07
Irish (618,272)	1,979,058	10.69
Israeli (12,693)	16,091	0.09
Italian (576,365)	1,215,631	6.57
Latvian (2,449)	4,921	0.03
Lithuanian (18,150)	43,399	0.23
Luxemburger (377)	1,222	0.01
Macedonian (1,607)	2,426	0.01
Maltese (1,487)	2,930	0.02
New Zealander (587)	990	0.01
Northern European (6,220)	7,003	0.04
Norwegian (42,288)	118,894	0.64
Pennsylvania German (5,905)	10,545	0.06
Polish (199,740)	511,229	2.76
Portuguese (34,131)	69,509	0.38
Romanian (19,029)	35,837	0.19
Russian (114,599)	239,314	1.29
Scandinavian (10,096)	20,098	0.11
Scotch-Irish (127,786)	289,491	1.56
Scottish (116,155)	335,948	1.81
Serbian (5,267)	8,922	0.05
Slavic (2,601)	6,656	0.04
Slovak (14,287)	33,763	0.18
Slovene (2,650)	5,739	0.03
Soviet Union (65)	134	<0.01
Swedish (47,025)	164,461	0.89
Swiss (11,108)	38,285	0.21
Turkish (9,634)	15,289	0.08
Ukrainian (24,365)	48,668	0.26
Welsh (22,409)	101,857	0.55
West Indian, ex. Hispanic (666,011)	750,598	4.05
Bahamian (18,491)	24,810	0.13
Barbadian (4,309)	5,629	0.03
Belizean (2,912)	4,237	0.02
Bermudan (683)	1,077	0.01
British West Indian (9,865)	12,326	0.07
Dutch West Indian (1,056)	2,022	0.01
Haitian (359,952)	380,005	2.05
Jamaican (212,242)	246,902	1.33
Trinidadian/Tobagonian (22,570)	29,267	0.16
U.S. Virgin Islander (3,322)	4,333	0.02
West Indian (30,065)	38,779	0.21
Other West Indian (544)	1,211	0.01
Yugoslavian (14,240)	20,414	0.11

Hispanic Origin	Population	%
Hispanic or Latino (of any race)	4,223,806	22.47
Central American, ex. Mexican	432,665	2.30
Costa Rican	20,761	0.11
Guatemalan	83,882	0.45
Honduran	107,302	0.57
Nicaraguan	135,143	0.72
Panamanian	28,741	0.15
Salvadoran	55,144	0.29
Other Central American	1,692	0.01
Cuban	1,213,438	6.45
Dominican Republic	172,451	0.92
Mexican	629,718	3.35
Puerto Rican	847,550	4.51
South American	674,542	3.59
Argentinean	56,260	0.30
Bolivian	10,938	0.06
Chilean	23,549	0.13
Colombian	300,414	1.60
Ecuadorian	60,574	0.32
Paraguayan	2,222	0.01
Peruvian	100,965	0.54
Uruguayan	14,542	0.08
Venezuelan	102,116	0.54
Other South American	2,962	0.02
Other Hispanic or Latino	253,442	1.35

Race*	Population	%
African-American/Black (2,999,862)	3,200,663	17.02
Not Hispanic (2,851,100)	2,997,371	15.94
Hispanic (148,762)	203,292	1.08
American Indian/Alaska Native (71,458)	162,562	0.86
Not Hispanic (47,265)	118,469	0.63
Hispanic (24,193)	44,093	0.23
Alaska Athabascan *(Ala. Nat.)* (132)	195	<0.01
Aleut *(Alaska Native)* (83)	154	<0.01
Apache (725)	1,912	0.01
Arapaho (30)	96	<0.01
Blackfeet (778)	4,377	0.02
Canadian/French Am. Ind. (331)	684	<0.01
Central American Ind. (1,440)	2,454	0.01
Cherokee (8,943)	32,342	0.17
Cheyenne (103)	263	<0.01
Chickasaw (330)	685	<0.01
Chippewa (1,470)	2,689	0.01
Choctaw (1,200)	2,829	0.02
Colville (10)	19	<0.01
Comanche (169)	385	<0.01
Cree (121)	433	<0.01
Creek (3,682)	6,779	0.04
Crow (77)	228	<0.01
Delaware (279)	647	<0.01
Hopi (25)	99	<0.01
Houma (123)	175	<0.01
Inupiat *(Alaska Native)* (151)	289	<0.01
Iroquois (1,425)	3,312	0.02
Kiowa (83)	137	<0.01
Lumbee (997)	1,459	0.01
Menominee (61)	121	<0.01
Mexican American Ind. (6,089)	7,967	0.04
Navajo (519)	1,043	0.01
Osage (135)	308	<0.01
Ottawa (141)	264	<0.01
Paiute (50)	86	<0.01
Pima (22)	53	<0.01
Potawatomi (333)	565	<0.01
Pueblo (187)	375	<0.01
Puget Sound Salish (47)	71	<0.01
Seminole (2,865)	4,816	0.03
Shoshone (70)	165	<0.01
Sioux (1,000)	2,480	0.01
South American Ind. (2,278)	5,238	0.03
Spanish American Ind. (886)	1,358	0.01
Tlingit-Haida *(Alaska Native)* (153)	374	<0.01
Tohono O'Odham (28)	71	<0.01
Tsimshian *(Alaska Native)* (12)	24	<0.01
Ute (34)	83	<0.01
Yakama (15)	34	<0.01
Yaqui (75)	157	<0.01
Yuman (26)	35	<0.01
Yup'ik *(Alaska Native)* (39)	86	<0.01
Asian (454,821)	573,083	3.05
Not Hispanic (445,216)	546,075	2.90
Hispanic (9,605)	27,008	0.14
Bangladeshi (5,114)	6,115	0.03
Bhutanese (201)	232	<0.01
Burmese (2,322)	2,578	0.01
Cambodian (5,283)	6,267	0.03
Chinese, ex. Taiwanese (68,680)	90,381	0.48
Filipino (90,223)	122,691	0.65
Hmong (1,093)	1,208	0.01
Indian (128,735)	151,438	0.81
Indonesian (1,747)	2,874	0.02
Japanese (13,224)	25,747	0.14
Korean (26,205)	35,629	0.19
Laotian (4,896)	6,152	0.03
Malaysian (455)	769	<0.01
Nepalese (850)	945	0.01
Pakistani (13,568)	16,035	0.09
Sri Lankan (1,232)	1,517	0.01
Taiwanese (3,265)	4,218	0.02
Thai (10,801)	15,333	0.08
Vietnamese (58,470)	65,772	0.35
Hawaii Native/Pacific Islander (12,286)	39,914	0.21
Not Hispanic (9,725)	31,138	0.17
Hispanic (2,561)	8,776	0.05
Fijian (155)	255	<0.01
Guamanian/Chamorro (3,747)	5,904	0.03
Marshallese (220)	290	<0.01
Native Hawaiian (2,809)	8,023	0.04
Samoan (1,153)	2,493	0.01
Tongan (445)	683	<0.01
White (14,109,162)	14,488,435	77.06
Not Hispanic (10,884,722)	11,115,250	59.12
Hispanic (3,224,440)	3,373,185	17.94

*Notes: † The Census 2010 population figure is used to calculate the percentages in the Hispanic Origin and Race categories. Ancestry percentages are based on the 2006-2010 American Community Survey population (not shown); ‡ Numbers in parentheses indicate the number of people reporting a single ancestry; * Numbers in parentheses indicate the number of persons reporting this race alone, not in combination with any other race; Please refer to the Explanation of Data for more information.*

Alachua

Place Type: City
County: Alachua
Population: 9,059†

Ancestry‡	Population	%
African, Sub-Saharan (0)	20	0.23
African (0)	20	0.23
Albanian (0)	12	0.14
American (712)	712	8.18
Austrian (20)	34	0.39
Belgian (0)	6	0.07
British (36)	78	0.90
Cajun (16)	16	0.18
Canadian (12)	12	0.14
Croatian (13)	28	0.32
Dutch (57)	105	1.21
Eastern European (4)	4	0.05
English (385)	835	9.59
European (124)	136	1.56
French, ex. Basque (89)	452	5.19
French Canadian (22)	33	0.38
German (514)	1,456	16.72
Hungarian (0)	22	0.25
Irish (375)	1,011	11.61
Italian (102)	427	4.90
Norwegian (60)	74	0.85
Polish (30)	77	0.88
Portuguese (0)	10	0.11
Russian (37)	46	0.53
Scotch-Irish (155)	396	4.55
Scottish (46)	222	2.55
Slavic (9)	9	0.10
Swedish (37)	71	0.82
Swiss (13)	25	0.29
Ukrainian (0)	9	0.10
Welsh (6)	71	0.82
West Indian, ex. Hispanic (192)	196	2.25
Haitian (35)	35	0.40
Jamaican (0)	4	0.05
West Indian (157)	157	1.80

Hispanic Origin	Population	%
Hispanic or Latino (of any race)	628	6.93
Central American, ex. Mexican	79	0.87
Costa Rican	2	0.02
Guatemalan	32	0.35
Honduran	13	0.14
Nicaraguan	12	0.13
Panamanian	10	0.11
Salvadoran	10	0.11
Cuban	82	0.91
Dominican Republic	17	0.19
Mexican	99	1.09
Puerto Rican	179	1.98
South American	124	1.37
Argentinean	7	0.08
Bolivian	2	0.02
Chilean	1	0.01
Colombian	53	0.59
Ecuadorian	10	0.11
Paraguayan	3	0.03
Peruvian	28	0.31
Uruguayan	2	0.02
Venezuelan	18	0.20
Other Hispanic or Latino	48	0.53

Race*	Population	%
African-American/Black (1,939)	2,023	22.33
Not Hispanic (1,919)	1,997	22.04
Hispanic (20)	26	0.29
American Indian/Alaska Native (33)	96	1.06
Not Hispanic (30)	86	0.95
Hispanic (3)	10	0.11
Apache (3)	4	0.04
Blackfeet (0)	6	0.07
Central American Ind. (0)	1	0.01
Cherokee (6)	30	0.33
Chickasaw (0)	2	0.02
Chippewa (0)	1	0.01
Choctaw (0)	1	0.01
Creek (5)	5	0.06
Crow (0)	2	0.02
Iroquois (1)	4	0.04
Mexican American Ind. (0)	1	0.01
Sioux (2)	2	0.02
Asian (199)	241	2.66
Not Hispanic (198)	233	2.57
Hispanic (1)	8	0.09
Bangladeshi (4)	4	0.04
Cambodian (5)	6	0.07
Chinese, ex. Taiwanese (22)	29	0.32
Filipino (20)	28	0.31
Indian (104)	118	1.30
Indonesian (1)	3	0.03
Japanese (9)	13	0.14
Korean (14)	15	0.17
Laotian (1)	2	0.02
Thai (2)	4	0.04
Vietnamese (8)	8	0.09
Hawaii Native/Pacific Islander (3)	12	0.13
Not Hispanic (3)	11	0.12
Hispanic (0)	1	0.01
Native Hawaiian (1)	2	0.02
Samoan (2)	2	0.02
White (6,524)	6,697	73.93
Not Hispanic (6,098)	6,239	68.87
Hispanic (426)	458	5.06

Alafaya

Place Type: CDP
County: Orange
Population: 78,113†

Ancestry‡	Population	%
Afghan (120)	120	0.16
African, Sub-Saharan (96)	155	0.20
African (96)	141	0.18
South African (0)	14	0.02
Albanian (47)	47	0.06
American (4,245)	4,245	5.50
Arab (779)	854	1.11
Arab (201)	201	0.26
Egyptian (168)	168	0.22
Jordanian (13)	54	0.07
Lebanese (48)	52	0.07
Moroccan (65)	95	0.12
Palestinian (32)	32	0.04
Syrian (16)	16	0.02
Other Arab (236)	236	0.31
Armenian (30)	78	0.10
Assyrian/Chaldean/Syriac (50)	50	0.06
Australian (11)	29	0.04
Austrian (47)	163	0.21
Belgian (28)	28	0.04
Brazilian (162)	231	0.30
British (72)	185	0.24
Cajun (0)	13	0.02
Canadian (96)	152	0.20
Croatian (0)	22	0.03
Czech (35)	59	0.08
Czechoslovakian (22)	103	0.13
Danish (49)	169	0.22
Dutch (335)	1,017	1.32
Eastern European (20)	31	0.04
English (1,317)	4,892	6.33
Estonian (14)	14	0.02
European (662)	719	0.93
Finnish (125)	221	0.29
French, ex. Basque (306)	1,462	1.89
French Canadian (53)	328	0.42
German (2,630)	9,070	11.74
Greek (180)	325	0.42
Guyanese (214)	291	0.38
Hungarian (48)	169	0.22
Iranian (160)	160	0.21
Irish (1,767)	6,207	8.04
Israeli (145)	145	0.19
Italian (2,181)	5,541	7.17
Latvian (0)	14	0.02
Lithuanian (21)	84	0.11
Luxemburger (12)	12	0.02
Norwegian (145)	394	0.51
Pennsylvania German (59)	85	0.11
Polish (503)	1,536	1.99
Portuguese (159)	392	0.51
Romanian (50)	50	0.06
Russian (245)	713	0.92
Scandinavian (17)	125	0.16
Scotch-Irish (187)	569	0.74
Scottish (447)	1,191	1.54
Serbian (13)	35	0.05
Slavic (45)	139	0.18
Slovak (0)	28	0.04
Swedish (121)	652	0.84
Swiss (11)	127	0.16
Turkish (108)	142	0.18
Ukrainian (52)	90	0.12
Welsh (38)	463	0.60
West Indian, ex. Hispanic (1,706)	1,991	2.58
Bahamian (15)	15	0.02
Barbadian (0)	14	0.02
Haitian (111)	134	0.17
Jamaican (1,046)	1,252	1.62
Trinidadian/Tobagonian (286)	286	0.37
U.S. Virgin Islander (33)	33	0.04
West Indian (215)	257	0.33
Yugoslavian (9)	41	0.05

Hispanic Origin	Population	%
Hispanic or Latino (of any race)	25,448	32.58
Central American, ex. Mexican	1,089	1.39
Costa Rican	136	0.17
Guatemalan	156	0.20
Honduran	232	0.30
Nicaraguan	124	0.16
Panamanian	230	0.29
Salvadoran	205	0.26
Other Central American	6	0.01
Cuban	1,861	2.38
Dominican Republic	1,878	2.40
Mexican	1,280	1.64
Puerto Rican	14,044	17.98
South American	4,114	5.27
Argentinean	130	0.17
Bolivian	42	0.05
Chilean	83	0.11
Colombian	2,251	2.88
Ecuadorian	489	0.63
Paraguayan	15	0.02
Peruvian	413	0.53
Uruguayan	33	0.04
Venezuelan	653	0.84
Other South American	5	0.01
Other Hispanic or Latino	1,182	1.51

Race*	Population	%
African-American/Black (8,126)	9,428	12.07
Not Hispanic (7,035)	7,855	10.06
Hispanic (1,091)	1,573	2.01
American Indian/Alaska Native (241)	602	0.77
Not Hispanic (107)	328	0.42
Hispanic (134)	274	0.35
Apache (2)	3	<0.01
Blackfeet (0)	7	0.01
Central American Ind. (5)	13	0.02
Cherokee (22)	80	0.10
Chickasaw (1)	3	<0.01
Chippewa (4)	4	0.01
Choctaw (3)	5	0.01
Comanche (0)	2	<0.01
Creek (3)	12	0.02
Crow (0)	3	<0.01
Delaware (0)	1	<0.01
Hopi (0)	1	<0.01
Iroquois (1)	4	0.01
Lumbee (2)	4	0.01
Mexican American Ind. (5)	6	0.01

*Notes: † The Census 2010 population figure is used to calculate the percentages in the Hispanic Origin and Race categories. Ancestry percentages are based on the 2006-2010 American Community Survey population (not shown); ‡ Numbers in parentheses indicate the number of people reporting a single ancestry; * Numbers in parentheses indicate the number of persons reporting this race alone, not in combination with any other race; Please refer to the Explanation of Data for more information.*

Navajo (8)	13	0.02
Osage (1)	4	0.01
Potawatomi (1)	2	<0.01
Pueblo (6)	6	0.01
Seminole (8)	14	0.02
Sioux (1)	4	0.01
South American Ind. (22)	63	0.08
Spanish American Ind. (3)	5	0.01
Tlingit-Haida *(Alaska Native)* (1)	1	<0.01
Asian (5,305)	6,411	8.21
Not Hispanic (5,198)	6,143	7.86
Hispanic (107)	268	0.34
Bangladeshi (14)	19	0.02
Burmese (14)	17	0.02
Cambodian (37)	45	0.06
Chinese, ex. Taiwanese (772)	1,005	1.29
Filipino (1,351)	1,710	2.19
Hmong (1)	1	<0.01
Indian (1,170)	1,357	1.74
Indonesian (6)	24	0.03
Japanese (92)	219	0.28
Korean (237)	330	0.42
Laotian (22)	36	0.05
Malaysian (3)	6	0.01
Nepalese (9)	9	0.01
Pakistani (137)	145	0.19
Sri Lankan (3)	3	<0.01
Taiwanese (66)	80	0.10
Thai (76)	102	0.13
Vietnamese (1,105)	1,195	1.53
Hawaii Native/Pacific Islander (55)	254	0.33
Not Hispanic (48)	191	0.24
Hispanic (7)	63	0.08
Guamanian/Chamorro (13)	25	0.03
Marshallese (0)	4	0.01
Native Hawaiian (15)	70	0.09
Samoan (4)	12	0.02
Tongan (4)	8	0.01
White (55,852)	58,340	74.69
Not Hispanic (38,220)	39,634	50.74
Hispanic (17,632)	18,706	23.95

Altamonte Springs

Place Type: City
County: Seminole
Population: 41,496†

Ancestry‡	Population	%
African, Sub-Saharan (126)	126	0.30
African (95)	95	0.23
Kenyan (9)	9	0.02
Other Sub-Saharan African (22)	22	0.05
Albanian (24)	24	0.06
American (2,009)	2,009	4.77
Arab (72)	149	0.35
Arab (32)	37	0.09
Egyptian (17)	17	0.04
Iraqi (0)	14	0.03
Lebanese (0)	29	0.07
Syrian (23)	38	0.09
Other Arab (0)	14	0.03
Armenian (30)	113	0.27
Australian (0)	18	0.04
Austrian (111)	202	0.48
Brazilian (95)	141	0.33
British (83)	239	0.57
Bulgarian (17)	17	0.04
Canadian (54)	96	0.23
Czech (100)	192	0.46
Czechoslovakian (24)	58	0.14
Danish (31)	67	0.16
Dutch (91)	408	0.97
Eastern European (27)	27	0.06
English (1,566)	4,065	9.65
European (1,753)	2,147	5.10
Finnish (23)	57	0.14
French, ex. Basque (179)	1,519	3.61
French Canadian (113)	325	0.77
German (1,776)	6,063	14.39
Greek (31)	168	0.40
Hungarian (38)	434	1.03
Iranian (37)	37	0.09
Irish (1,441)	4,694	11.14
Israeli (10)	10	0.02
Italian (1,275)	2,698	6.40
Latvian (44)	71	0.17
Lithuanian (44)	132	0.31
Northern European (15)	15	0.04
Norwegian (40)	238	0.56
Polish (648)	1,461	3.47
Portuguese (286)	345	0.82
Romanian (42)	183	0.43
Russian (424)	914	2.17
Scandinavian (48)	137	0.33
Scotch-Irish (297)	859	2.04
Scottish (204)	798	1.89
Serbian (0)	37	0.09
Slovak (0)	45	0.11
Slovene (7)	7	0.02
Swedish (31)	342	0.81
Swiss (14)	146	0.35
Turkish (35)	63	0.15
Ukrainian (69)	95	0.23
Welsh (128)	426	1.01
West Indian, ex. Hispanic (793)	1,144	2.72
British West Indian (0)	50	0.12
Haitian (121)	221	0.52
Jamaican (385)	491	1.17
Trinidadian/Tobagonian (129)	153	0.36
West Indian (158)	229	0.54

Hispanic Origin	Population	%
Hispanic or Latino (of any race)	10,067	24.26
Central American, ex. Mexican	602	1.45
Costa Rican	80	0.19
Guatemalan	58	0.14
Honduran	103	0.25
Nicaraguan	142	0.34
Panamanian	114	0.27
Salvadoran	99	0.24
Other Central American	6	0.01
Cuban	786	1.89
Dominican Republic	616	1.48
Mexican	932	2.25
Puerto Rican	4,738	11.42
South American	1,860	4.48
Argentinean	134	0.32
Bolivian	16	0.04
Chilean	27	0.07
Colombian	908	2.19
Ecuadorian	203	0.49
Paraguayan	4	0.01
Peruvian	262	0.63
Uruguayan	25	0.06
Venezuelan	269	0.65
Other South American	12	0.03
Other Hispanic or Latino	533	1.28

Race*	Population	%
African-American/Black (5,721)	6,500	15.66
Not Hispanic (5,288)	5,786	13.94
Hispanic (433)	714	1.72
American Indian/Alaska Native (141)	422	1.02
Not Hispanic (94)	299	0.72
Hispanic (47)	123	0.30
Apache (3)	8	0.02
Blackfeet (1)	12	0.03
Canadian/French Am. Ind. (1)	5	0.01
Central American Ind. (2)	9	0.02
Cherokee (24)	84	0.20
Cheyenne (2)	3	0.01
Chickasaw (3)	6	0.01
Chippewa (5)	9	0.02
Choctaw (6)	19	0.05
Comanche (1)	1	<0.01
Cree (0)	2	<0.01
Creek (5)	8	0.02
Crow (0)	3	0.01
Delaware (0)	1	<0.01
Houma (0)	1	<0.01
Iroquois (2)	9	0.02
Lumbee (1)	2	<0.01
Mexican American Ind. (5)	9	0.02
Navajo (0)	2	<0.01
Osage (1)	1	<0.01
Ottawa (0)	1	<0.01
Pima (0)	1	<0.01
Pueblo (1)	3	0.01
Seminole (1)	5	0.01
Sioux (3)	12	0.03
South American Ind. (16)	47	0.11
Spanish American Ind. (3)	3	0.01
Yakama (0)	1	<0.01
Yaqui (1)	1	<0.01
Asian (1,391)	1,727	4.16
Not Hispanic (1,356)	1,625	3.92
Hispanic (35)	102	0.25
Bangladeshi (7)	8	0.02
Burmese (2)	2	<0.01
Cambodian (17)	17	0.04
Chinese, ex. Taiwanese (159)	206	0.50
Filipino (288)	388	0.94
Hmong (1)	2	<0.01
Indian (529)	591	1.42
Indonesian (20)	21	0.05
Japanese (30)	68	0.16
Korean (165)	195	0.47
Laotian (21)	27	0.07
Malaysian (1)	3	0.01
Pakistani (12)	18	0.04
Sri Lankan (2)	3	0.01
Taiwanese (6)	10	0.02
Thai (10)	16	0.04
Vietnamese (73)	95	0.23
Hawaii Native/Pacific Islander (22)	83	0.20
Not Hispanic (21)	65	0.16
Hispanic (1)	18	0.04
Guamanian/Chamorro (2)	6	0.01
Native Hawaiian (9)	26	0.06
Samoan (2)	5	0.01
White (30,068)	31,311	75.46
Not Hispanic (23,678)	24,395	58.79
Hispanic (6,390)	6,916	16.67

Apollo Beach

Place Type: CDP
County: Hillsborough
Population: 14,055†

Ancestry‡	Population	%
African, Sub-Saharan (14)	14	0.10
African (14)	14	0.10
Albanian (0)	7	0.05
American (970)	970	7.20
Arab (15)	35	0.26
Syrian (15)	35	0.26
Austrian (59)	117	0.87
Basque (0)	21	0.16
British (60)	60	0.45
Cajun (31)	31	0.23
Canadian (85)	95	0.70
Czech (37)	113	0.84
Czechoslovakian (0)	20	0.15
Danish (14)	64	0.47
Dutch (52)	141	1.05
English (919)	1,710	12.68
European (64)	64	0.47
Finnish (0)	31	0.23
French, ex. Basque (97)	650	4.82
French Canadian (150)	165	1.22
German (791)	2,723	20.20
Greek (34)	62	0.46
Hungarian (56)	172	1.28
Irish (647)	1,933	14.34
Israeli (20)	20	0.15
Italian (507)	1,012	7.51
Lithuanian (0)	16	0.12
Norwegian (32)	139	1.03

SECTION TWO

*Notes: † The Census 2010 population figure is used to calculate the percentages in the Hispanic Origin and Race categories. Ancestry percentages are based on the 2006-2010 American Community Survey population (not shown); ‡ Numbers in parentheses indicate the number of people reporting a single ancestry; * Numbers in parentheses indicate the number of persons reporting this race alone, not in combination with any other race; Please refer to the Explanation of Data for more information.*

Polish (229)	524	3.89
Portuguese (0)	20	0.15
Romanian (0)	40	0.30
Russian (56)	172	1.28
Scotch-Irish (129)	256	1.90
Scottish (29)	274	2.03
Serbian (0)	15	0.11
Slovak (28)	44	0.33
Swedish (63)	132	0.98
Swiss (13)	44	0.33
Ukrainian (33)	66	0.49
Welsh (16)	165	1.22
West Indian, ex. Hispanic (37)	57	0.42
British West Indian (19)	39	0.29
Trinidadian/Tobagonian (18)	18	0.13

Hispanic Origin	Population	%
Hispanic or Latino (of any race)	1,780	12.66
Central American, ex. Mexican	80	0.57
Costa Rican	13	0.09
Guatemalan	12	0.09
Honduran	7	0.05
Nicaraguan	16	0.11
Panamanian	16	0.11
Salvadoran	16	0.11
Cuban	209	1.49
Dominican Republic	77	0.55
Mexican	533	3.79
Puerto Rican	567	4.03
South American	153	1.09
Argentinean	9	0.06
Bolivian	3	0.02
Chilean	3	0.02
Colombian	65	0.46
Ecuadorian	15	0.11
Peruvian	38	0.27
Venezuelan	20	0.14
Other Hispanic or Latino	161	1.15

Race*	Population	%
African-American/Black (836)	924	6.57
Not Hispanic (786)	855	6.08
Hispanic (50)	69	0.49
American Indian/Alaska Native (52)	137	0.97
Not Hispanic (33)	93	0.66
Hispanic (19)	44	0.31
Alaska Athabascan *(Ala. Nat.)* (2)	2	0.01
Apache (0)	1	0.01
Blackfeet (1)	7	0.05
Canadian/French Am. Ind. (1)	1	0.01
Cherokee (10)	39	0.28
Chickasaw (1)	1	0.01
Chippewa (0)	1	0.01
Choctaw (1)	1	0.01
Creek (1)	5	0.04
Iroquois (2)	5	0.04
Lumbee (0)	1	0.01
Mexican American Ind. (1)	2	0.01
Potawatomi (0)	1	0.01
Seminole (1)	4	0.03
Sioux (1)	1	0.01
South American Ind. (1)	6	0.04
Tlingit-Haida *(Alaska Native)* (1)	1	0.01
Asian (355)	443	3.15
Not Hispanic (354)	438	3.12
Hispanic (1)	5	0.04
Bangladeshi (3)	5	0.04
Burmese (4)	4	0.03
Cambodian (16)	16	0.11
Chinese, ex. Taiwanese (47)	63	0.45
Filipino (79)	113	0.80
Hmong (4)	4	0.03
Indian (76)	91	0.65
Indonesian (0)	1	0.01
Japanese (10)	22	0.16
Korean (20)	26	0.18
Laotian (9)	9	0.06
Pakistani (18)	18	0.13
Taiwanese (0)	2	0.01
Thai (11)	12	0.09
Vietnamese (53)	60	0.43
Hawaii Native/Pacific Islander (5)	26	0.18
Not Hispanic (5)	15	0.11
Hispanic (0)	11	0.08
Guamanian/Chamorro (1)	4	0.03
Native Hawaiian (1)	8	0.06
White (12,141)	12,406	88.27
Not Hispanic (10,869)	11,052	78.63
Hispanic (1,272)	1,354	9.63

Apopka

Place Type: City
County: Orange
Population: 41,542†

Ancestry‡	Population	%
African, Sub-Saharan (54)	318	0.81
African (8)	180	0.46
Cape Verdean (0)	56	0.14
South African (46)	82	0.21
American (2,959)	2,959	7.49
Arab (24)	63	0.16
Lebanese (24)	63	0.16
Armenian (14)	79	0.20
Austrian (8)	62	0.16
Belgian (10)	44	0.11
Brazilian (57)	78	0.20
British (45)	102	0.26
Canadian (66)	89	0.23
Croatian (0)	13	0.03
Czech (0)	54	0.14
Danish (25)	69	0.17
Dutch (72)	319	0.81
Eastern European (60)	60	0.15
English (1,931)	4,186	10.60
European (166)	268	0.68
French, ex. Basque (200)	1,118	2.83
French Canadian (79)	274	0.69
German (1,458)	4,715	11.94
Greek (13)	203	0.51
Guyanese (0)	20	0.05
Hungarian (102)	163	0.41
Iranian (39)	39	0.10
Irish (1,066)	3,577	9.06
Italian (1,115)	2,502	6.34
Lithuanian (43)	113	0.29
Norwegian (264)	358	0.91
Pennsylvania German (35)	35	0.09
Polish (259)	695	1.76
Portuguese (62)	140	0.35
Romanian (11)	27	0.07
Russian (30)	183	0.46
Scandinavian (0)	12	0.03
Scotch-Irish (121)	444	1.12
Scottish (222)	583	1.48
Slovak (33)	72	0.18
Slovene (0)	37	0.09
Swedish (14)	238	0.60
Swiss (16)	27	0.07
Turkish (0)	14	0.04
Ukrainian (40)	64	0.16
Welsh (47)	161	0.41
West Indian, ex. Hispanic (1,165)	1,401	3.55
Haitian (471)	491	1.24
Jamaican (520)	631	1.60
Trinidadian/Tobagonian (38)	106	0.27
West Indian (136)	173	0.44

Hispanic Origin	Population	%
Hispanic or Latino (of any race)	10,548	25.39
Central American, ex. Mexican	901	2.17
Costa Rican	35	0.08
Guatemalan	346	0.83
Honduran	224	0.54
Nicaraguan	105	0.25
Panamanian	77	0.19
Salvadoran	113	0.27
Other Central American	1	<0.01
Cuban	625	1.50
Dominican Republic	528	1.27
Mexican	3,695	8.89
Puerto Rican	3,400	8.18
South American	888	2.14
Argentinean	48	0.12
Bolivian	14	0.03
Chilean	21	0.05
Colombian	412	0.99
Ecuadorian	109	0.26
Peruvian	124	0.30
Uruguayan	3	0.01
Venezuelan	144	0.35
Other South American	13	0.03
Other Hispanic or Latino	511	1.23

Race*	Population	%
African-American/Black (8,586)	9,178	22.09
Not Hispanic (8,147)	8,571	20.63
Hispanic (439)	607	1.46
American Indian/Alaska Native (125)	332	0.80
Not Hispanic (69)	212	0.51
Hispanic (56)	120	0.29
Alaska Athabascan *(Ala. Nat.)* (2)	2	<0.01
Apache (4)	8	0.02
Blackfeet (1)	13	0.03
Central American Ind. (1)	3	0.01
Cherokee (15)	68	0.16
Choctaw (2)	3	0.01
Cree (0)	3	0.01
Creek (1)	5	0.01
Iroquois (7)	10	0.02
Lumbee (0)	1	<0.01
Mexican American Ind. (13)	26	0.06
Navajo (2)	4	0.01
Osage (0)	1	<0.01
Ottawa (1)	4	0.01
Potawatomi (1)	2	<0.01
Puget Sound Salish (1)	1	<0.01
Seminole (2)	4	0.01
Sioux (0)	1	<0.01
South American Ind. (8)	19	0.05
Spanish American Ind. (3)	3	0.01
Tlingit-Haida *(Alaska Native)* (2)	2	<0.01
Asian (1,331)	1,655	3.98
Not Hispanic (1,309)	1,561	3.76
Hispanic (22)	94	0.23
Bangladeshi (4)	10	0.02
Burmese (0)	3	0.01
Cambodian (20)	22	0.05
Chinese, ex. Taiwanese (154)	223	0.54
Filipino (234)	317	0.76
Hmong (0)	1	<0.01
Indian (318)	408	0.98
Indonesian (14)	14	0.03
Japanese (12)	45	0.11
Korean (180)	196	0.47
Laotian (52)	53	0.13
Malaysian (4)	4	0.01
Pakistani (14)	18	0.04
Sri Lankan (7)	9	0.02
Taiwanese (4)	4	0.01
Thai (7)	18	0.04
Vietnamese (271)	311	0.75
Hawaii Native/Pacific Islander (37)	117	0.28
Not Hispanic (19)	64	0.15
Hispanic (18)	53	0.13
Guamanian/Chamorro (20)	28	0.07
Native Hawaiian (7)	28	0.07
Samoan (3)	3	0.01
White (26,701)	27,751	66.80
Not Hispanic (20,553)	21,128	50.86
Hispanic (6,148)	6,623	15.94

Arcadia

Place Type: City
County: DeSoto
Population: 7,637†

*Notes: † The Census 2010 population figure is used to calculate the percentages in the Hispanic Origin and Race categories. Ancestry percentages are based on the 2006-2010 American Community Survey population (not shown); ‡ Numbers in parentheses indicate the number of people reporting a single ancestry; * Numbers in parentheses indicate the number of persons reporting this race alone, not in combination with any other race; Please refer to the Explanation of Data for more information.*

Ancestry‡	Population	%
African, Sub-Saharan (29)	29	0.39
African (29)	29	0.39
American (555)	555	7.40
Brazilian (29)	29	0.39
British (14)	44	0.59
Canadian (13)	34	0.45
Czech (0)	23	0.31
Danish (0)	9	0.12
Dutch (0)	61	0.81
English (115)	326	4.35
European (25)	25	0.33
French, ex. Basque (21)	78	1.04
French Canadian (0)	12	0.16
German (146)	430	5.74
Irish (334)	723	9.64
Italian (35)	256	3.41
Lithuanian (0)	13	0.17
Polish (36)	117	1.56
Scotch-Irish (33)	107	1.43
Scottish (68)	167	2.23
Swedish (41)	71	0.95
West Indian, ex. Hispanic (160)	160	2.13
Haitian (70)	70	0.93
Jamaican (90)	90	1.20

Hispanic Origin	Population	%
Hispanic or Latino (of any race)	2,534	33.18
Central American, ex. Mexican	95	1.24
Costa Rican	5	0.07
Guatemalan	47	0.62
Honduran	15	0.20
Nicaraguan	10	0.13
Panamanian	1	0.01
Salvadoran	17	0.22
Cuban	77	1.01
Dominican Republic	19	0.25
Mexican	2,139	28.01
Puerto Rican	119	1.56
South American	7	0.09
Colombian	5	0.07
Peruvian	2	0.03
Other Hispanic or Latino	78	1.02

Race*	Population	%
African-American/Black (1,922)	1,997	26.15
Not Hispanic (1,876)	1,930	25.27
Hispanic (46)	67	0.88
American Indian/Alaska Native (40)	83	1.09
Not Hispanic (10)	42	0.55
Hispanic (30)	41	0.54
Apache (5)	5	0.07
Blackfeet (0)	2	0.03
Central American Ind. (7)	8	0.10
Cherokee (6)	21	0.27
Iroquois (0)	2	0.03
Mexican American Ind. (1)	5	0.07
Seminole (0)	2	0.03
Sioux (1)	2	0.03
South American Ind. (0)	1	0.01
Asian (57)	68	0.89
Not Hispanic (51)	60	0.79
Hispanic (6)	8	0.10
Bangladeshi (0)	4	0.05
Chinese, ex. Taiwanese (4)	6	0.08
Filipino (17)	22	0.29
Indian (19)	27	0.35
Japanese (3)	3	0.04
Pakistani (1)	1	0.01
Thai (0)	1	0.01
Vietnamese (9)	9	0.12
Hawaii Native/Pacific Islander (6)	14	0.18
Not Hispanic (0)	3	0.04
Hispanic (6)	11	0.14
Guamanian/Chamorro (6)	9	0.12
Native Hawaiian (0)	1	0.01
Samoan (0)	2	0.03
White (4,038)	4,209	55.11
Not Hispanic (3,062)	3,151	41.26
Hispanic (976)	1,058	13.85

Asbury Lake

Place Type: CDP
County: Clay
Population: 8,700†

Ancestry‡	Population	%
American (831)	831	9.57
Arab (18)	47	0.54
Arab (18)	47	0.54
Armenian (0)	11	0.13
Belgian (16)	51	0.59
Canadian (0)	13	0.15
Czech (9)	93	1.07
Dutch (12)	31	0.36
Eastern European (13)	13	0.15
English (549)	1,109	12.77
European (15)	71	0.82
Finnish (11)	45	0.52
French, ex. Basque (50)	145	1.67
French Canadian (27)	85	0.98
German (565)	1,345	15.49
Greek (0)	13	0.15
Hungarian (8)	27	0.31
Irish (409)	1,403	16.16
Italian (311)	690	7.95
Lithuanian (26)	26	0.30
Norwegian (15)	153	1.76
Polish (79)	271	3.12
Portuguese (10)	95	1.09
Russian (9)	92	1.06
Scandinavian (36)	36	0.41
Scotch-Irish (125)	141	1.62
Scottish (115)	313	3.60
Swedish (47)	194	2.23
Yugoslavian (0)	73	0.84

Hispanic Origin	Population	%
Hispanic or Latino (of any race)	580	6.67
Central American, ex. Mexican	48	0.55
Costa Rican	3	0.03
Honduran	1	0.01
Nicaraguan	11	0.13
Panamanian	23	0.26
Salvadoran	10	0.11
Cuban	39	0.45
Dominican Republic	31	0.36
Mexican	139	1.60
Puerto Rican	232	2.67
South American	54	0.62
Argentinean	5	0.06
Bolivian	4	0.05
Chilean	2	0.02
Colombian	16	0.18
Ecuadorian	7	0.08
Peruvian	10	0.11
Venezuelan	7	0.08
Other South American	3	0.03
Other Hispanic or Latino	37	0.43

Race*	Population	%
African-American/Black (495)	554	6.37
Not Hispanic (464)	517	5.94
Hispanic (31)	37	0.43
American Indian/Alaska Native (44)	92	1.06
Not Hispanic (41)	87	1.00
Hispanic (3)	5	0.06
Apache (1)	1	0.01
Blackfeet (2)	5	0.06
Cherokee (8)	25	0.29
Chickasaw (5)	5	0.06
Chippewa (0)	1	0.01
Choctaw (1)	3	0.03
Creek (3)	4	0.05
Iroquois (2)	2	0.02
Lumbee (0)	1	0.01
Navajo (2)	2	0.02
Osage (0)	1	0.01
Potawatomi (0)	1	0.01
Seminole (1)	3	0.03
Sioux (0)	1	0.01
South American Ind. (1)	1	0.01
Asian (116)	186	2.14
Not Hispanic (114)	180	2.07
Hispanic (2)	6	0.07
Cambodian (4)	4	0.05
Chinese, ex. Taiwanese (10)	15	0.17
Filipino (46)	87	1.00
Indian (15)	16	0.18
Japanese (11)	18	0.21
Korean (13)	27	0.31
Malaysian (0)	1	0.01
Thai (3)	10	0.11
Vietnamese (3)	13	0.15
Hawaii Native/Pacific Islander (13)	28	0.32
Not Hispanic (10)	18	0.21
Hispanic (3)	10	0.11
Guamanian/Chamorro (10)	21	0.24
Samoan (0)	2	0.02
White (7,727)	7,914	90.97
Not Hispanic (7,338)	7,476	85.93
Hispanic (389)	438	5.03

Atlantic Beach

Place Type: City
County: Duval
Population: 12,655†

Ancestry‡	Population	%
African, Sub-Saharan (21)	21	0.16
African (21)	21	0.16
American (867)	867	6.69
Arab (0)	48	0.37
Lebanese (0)	48	0.37
Armenian (0)	56	0.43
Austrian (12)	12	0.09
Brazilian (0)	14	0.11
British (60)	112	0.86
Canadian (21)	21	0.16
Celtic (33)	33	0.25
Czech (13)	67	0.52
Czechoslovakian (0)	16	0.12
Danish (28)	81	0.62
Dutch (29)	248	1.91
English (675)	1,843	14.21
European (159)	168	1.30
Finnish (0)	42	0.32
French, ex. Basque (104)	358	2.76
French Canadian (7)	77	0.59
German (455)	1,725	13.30
Greek (32)	32	0.25
Hungarian (13)	13	0.10
Iranian (13)	13	0.10
Irish (727)	2,234	17.23
Italian (228)	786	6.06
Lithuanian (15)	57	0.44
Norwegian (68)	113	0.87
Polish (69)	267	2.06
Portuguese (0)	14	0.11
Romanian (13)	13	0.10
Russian (24)	76	0.59
Scotch-Irish (295)	510	3.93
Scottish (98)	525	4.05
Serbian (0)	10	0.08
Slovak (0)	34	0.26
Swedish (14)	70	0.54
Swiss (0)	87	0.67
Ukrainian (30)	72	0.56
Welsh (27)	57	0.44
West Indian, ex. Hispanic (12)	12	0.09
Jamaican (12)	12	0.09
Yugoslavian (19)	19	0.15

Hispanic Origin	Population	%
Hispanic or Latino (of any race)	680	5.37
Central American, ex. Mexican	36	0.28
Costa Rican	4	0.03
Guatemalan	3	0.02
Honduran	6	0.05

SECTION TWO

*Notes: † The Census 2010 population figure is used to calculate the percentages in the Hispanic Origin and Race categories. Ancestry percentages are based on the 2006-2010 American Community Survey population (not shown); ‡ Numbers in parentheses indicate the number of people reporting a single ancestry; * Numbers in parentheses indicate the number of persons reporting this race alone, not in combination with any other race; Please refer to the Explanation of Data for more information.*

Nicaraguan	3	0.02
Panamanian	10	0.08
Salvadoran	10	0.08
Cuban	57	0.45
Dominican Republic	5	0.04
Mexican	208	1.64
Puerto Rican	215	1.70
South American	84	0.66
Argentinean	2	0.02
Bolivian	1	0.01
Chilean	4	0.03
Colombian	43	0.34
Ecuadorian	7	0.06
Peruvian	18	0.14
Uruguayan	1	0.01
Venezuelan	6	0.05
Other South American	2	0.02
Other Hispanic or Latino	75	0.59

Race*	Population	%
African-American/Black (1,368)	1,488	11.76
Not Hispanic (1,345)	1,459	11.53
Hispanic (23)	29	0.23
American Indian/Alaska Native (64)	143	1.13
Not Hispanic (54)	119	0.94
Hispanic (10)	24	0.19
Blackfeet (1)	6	0.05
Cherokee (11)	30	0.24
Chickasaw (0)	1	0.01
Chippewa (4)	4	0.03
Choctaw (1)	2	0.02
Comanche (0)	1	0.01
Houma (1)	2	0.02
Iroquois (0)	3	0.02
Lumbee (0)	1	0.01
Mexican American Ind. (1)	10	0.08
Navajo (1)	1	0.01
Osage (0)	1	0.01
Paiute (3)	3	0.02
Pueblo (0)	1	0.01
Sioux (6)	6	0.05
South American Ind. (5)	6	0.05
Asian (238)	370	2.92
Not Hispanic (230)	356	2.81
Hispanic (8)	14	0.11
Bangladeshi (1)	1	0.01
Chinese, ex. Taiwanese (21)	36	0.28
Filipino (164)	250	1.98
Indian (8)	15	0.12
Indonesian (0)	1	0.01
Japanese (4)	26	0.21
Korean (10)	13	0.10
Nepalese (6)	6	0.05
Pakistani (1)	1	0.01
Sri Lankan (5)	5	0.04
Thai (1)	3	0.02
Vietnamese (8)	17	0.13
Hawaii Native/Pacific Islander (17)	42	0.33
Not Hispanic (10)	30	0.24
Hispanic (7)	12	0.09
Guamanian/Chamorro (10)	14	0.11
Native Hawaiian (2)	10	0.08
Samoan (3)	3	0.02
White (10,438)	10,748	84.93
Not Hispanic (10,023)	10,280	81.23
Hispanic (415)	468	3.70

Auburndale

Place Type: City
County: Polk
Population: 13,507†

Ancestry‡	Population	%
African, Sub-Saharan (163)	171	1.28
Nigerian (163)	163	1.22
South African (0)	8	0.06
American (867)	867	6.47
Austrian (8)	37	0.28
British (10)	40	0.30
Canadian (9)	21	0.16
Celtic (11)	11	0.08
Croatian (15)	15	0.11
Danish (0)	12	0.09
Dutch (21)	254	1.90
English (557)	1,233	9.21
European (46)	63	0.47
Finnish (0)	64	0.48
French, ex. Basque (74)	326	2.43
French Canadian (96)	104	0.78
German (546)	1,844	13.77
Greek (63)	119	0.89
Hungarian (0)	29	0.22
Irish (442)	1,548	11.56
Italian (186)	935	6.98
Lithuanian (0)	9	0.07
Northern European (8)	8	0.06
Norwegian (36)	103	0.77
Pennsylvania German (9)	9	0.07
Polish (165)	308	2.30
Portuguese (23)	83	0.62
Russian (0)	8	0.06
Scandinavian (8)	8	0.06
Scotch-Irish (65)	132	0.99
Scottish (106)	247	1.84
Serbian (0)	8	0.06
Slovene (0)	9	0.07
Swedish (14)	68	0.51
Swiss (7)	7	0.05
Ukrainian (0)	37	0.28
Welsh (39)	47	0.35
West Indian, ex. Hispanic (609)	609	4.55
Barbadian (29)	29	0.22
Haitian (459)	459	3.43
Jamaican (112)	112	0.84
Trinidadian/Tobagonian (9)	9	0.07
Yugoslavian (7)	15	0.11

Hispanic Origin	Population	%
Hispanic or Latino (of any race)	1,771	13.11
Central American, ex. Mexican	59	0.44
Costa Rican	8	0.06
Guatemalan	26	0.19
Honduran	11	0.08
Nicaraguan	4	0.03
Panamanian	4	0.03
Salvadoran	6	0.04
Cuban	99	0.73
Dominican Republic	37	0.27
Mexican	960	7.11
Puerto Rican	434	3.21
South American	82	0.61
Argentinean	4	0.03
Chilean	6	0.04
Colombian	25	0.19
Ecuadorian	18	0.13
Peruvian	8	0.06
Uruguayan	2	0.01
Venezuelan	19	0.14
Other Hispanic or Latino	100	0.74

Race*	Population	%
African-American/Black (1,724)	1,861	13.78
Not Hispanic (1,677)	1,781	13.19
Hispanic (47)	80	0.59
American Indian/Alaska Native (48)	117	0.87
Not Hispanic (24)	85	0.63
Hispanic (24)	32	0.24
Aleut *(Alaska Native)* (1)	3	0.02
Apache (0)	1	0.01
Blackfeet (1)	6	0.04
Cherokee (7)	26	0.19
Chickasaw (0)	1	0.01
Choctaw (0)	1	0.01
Iroquois (4)	5	0.04
Lumbee (2)	2	0.01
Menominee (0)	3	0.02
Mexican American Ind. (4)	4	0.03
Sioux (0)	1	0.01
South American Ind. (1)	1	0.01
Asian (158)	196	1.45
Not Hispanic (154)	184	1.36
Hispanic (4)	12	0.09
Bangladeshi (4)	4	0.03
Chinese, ex. Taiwanese (27)	34	0.25
Filipino (24)	31	0.23
Indian (50)	58	0.43
Japanese (10)	18	0.13
Korean (15)	19	0.14
Thai (2)	2	0.01
Vietnamese (16)	24	0.18
Hawaii Native/Pacific Islander (3)	21	0.16
Not Hispanic (0)	15	0.11
Hispanic (3)	6	0.04
Guamanian/Chamorro (0)	1	0.01
Native Hawaiian (2)	5	0.04
Samoan (1)	1	0.01
White (10,803)	11,062	81.90
Not Hispanic (9,679)	9,838	72.84
Hispanic (1,124)	1,224	9.06

Aventura

Place Type: City
County: Miami-Dade
Population: 35,762†

Ancestry‡	Population	%
African, Sub-Saharan (74)	174	0.52
African (58)	120	0.36
Nigerian (16)	37	0.11
South African (0)	17	0.05
American (1,563)	1,563	4.63
Arab (582)	702	2.08
Egyptian (53)	53	0.16
Lebanese (116)	116	0.34
Moroccan (227)	256	0.76
Syrian (170)	245	0.73
Other Arab (16)	32	0.09
Armenian (74)	74	0.22
Australian (32)	44	0.13
Austrian (165)	507	1.50
Belgian (174)	174	0.52
Brazilian (243)	257	0.76
British (156)	181	0.54
Bulgarian (0)	15	0.04
Canadian (124)	150	0.44
Czech (0)	31	0.09
Czechoslovakian (29)	35	0.10
Danish (20)	35	0.10
Dutch (59)	191	0.57
Eastern European (544)	544	1.61
English (523)	950	2.81
Estonian (25)	25	0.07
European (553)	608	1.80
Finnish (0)	8	0.02
French, ex. Basque (258)	578	1.71
French Canadian (27)	89	0.26
German (500)	1,274	3.77
Greek (132)	155	0.46
Hungarian (262)	538	1.59
Iranian (85)	93	0.28
Irish (226)	769	2.28
Israeli (1,316)	1,402	4.15
Italian (907)	1,606	4.76
Lithuanian (119)	232	0.69
Norwegian (28)	103	0.30
Polish (1,530)	2,612	7.73
Portuguese (129)	236	0.70
Romanian (129)	439	1.30
Russian (2,382)	3,483	10.31
Scotch-Irish (0)	11	0.03
Scottish (46)	122	0.36
Slovak (74)	74	0.22
Soviet Union (0)	30	0.09
Swedish (51)	198	0.59
Swiss (0)	31	0.09
Turkish (155)	263	0.78
Ukrainian (231)	365	1.08
Welsh (14)	14	0.04

*Notes: † The Census 2010 population figure is used to calculate the percentages in the Hispanic Origin and Race categories. Ancestry percentages are based on the 2006-2010 American Community Survey population (not shown); ‡ Numbers in parentheses indicate the number of people reporting a single ancestry; * Numbers in parentheses indicate the number of persons reporting this race alone, not in combination with any other race; Please refer to the Explanation of Data for more information.*

West Indian, ex. Hispanic (200)	269	0.80
Belizean (93)	93	0.28
Haitian (58)	58	0.17
Jamaican (49)	118	0.35
Yugoslavian (42)	69	0.20

Hispanic Origin	Population	%
Hispanic or Latino (of any race)	12,798	35.79
Central American, ex. Mexican	531	1.48
Costa Rican	65	0.18
Guatemalan	78	0.22
Honduran	94	0.26
Nicaraguan	153	0.43
Panamanian	82	0.23
Salvadoran	59	0.16
Cuban	1,408	3.94
Dominican Republic	374	1.05
Mexican	831	2.32
Puerto Rican	695	1.94
South American	8,112	22.68
Argentinean	1,579	4.42
Bolivian	85	0.24
Chilean	176	0.49
Colombian	3,285	9.19
Ecuadorian	330	0.92
Paraguayan	22	0.06
Peruvian	713	1.99
Uruguayan	148	0.41
Venezuelan	1,765	4.94
Other South American	9	0.03
Other Hispanic or Latino	847	2.37

Race*	Population	%
African-American/Black (1,382)	1,578	4.41
Not Hispanic (1,211)	1,334	3.73
Hispanic (171)	244	0.68
American Indian/Alaska Native (41)	85	0.24
Not Hispanic (31)	52	0.15
Hispanic (10)	33	0.09
Blackfeet (2)	3	0.01
Canadian/French Am. Ind. (3)	3	0.01
Central American Ind. (0)	1	<0.01
Cherokee (4)	6	0.02
Chippewa (1)	1	<0.01
Hopi (0)	1	<0.01
Iroquois (0)	1	<0.01
Mexican American Ind. (1)	2	0.01
Seminole (0)	1	<0.01
South American Ind. (5)	12	0.03
Asian (648)	798	2.23
Not Hispanic (619)	746	2.09
Hispanic (29)	52	0.15
Bangladeshi (7)	7	0.02
Burmese (2)	2	0.01
Cambodian (1)	1	<0.01
Chinese, ex. Taiwanese (181)	207	0.58
Filipino (86)	101	0.28
Indian (158)	190	0.53
Indonesian (4)	5	0.01
Japanese (35)	52	0.15
Korean (62)	65	0.18
Laotian (0)	2	0.01
Nepalese (1)	1	<0.01
Pakistani (19)	22	0.06
Sri Lankan (1)	1	<0.01
Taiwanese (19)	23	0.06
Thai (11)	19	0.05
Vietnamese (35)	41	0.11
Hawaii Native/Pacific Islander (6)	29	0.08
Not Hispanic (6)	23	0.06
Hispanic (0)	6	0.02
Guamanian/Chamorro (2)	3	0.01
Native Hawaiian (1)	3	0.01
Samoan (0)	3	0.01
White (32,345)	32,877	91.93
Not Hispanic (20,711)	20,970	58.64
Hispanic (11,634)	11,907	33.30

Avon Park

Place Type: City
County: Highlands
Population: 8,836†

Ancestry‡	Population	%
African, Sub-Saharan (87)	272	3.03
African (87)	272	3.03
American (618)	618	6.89
Austrian (0)	13	0.15
Brazilian (12)	12	0.13
Canadian (118)	184	2.05
Czechoslovakian (9)	9	0.10
Dutch (72)	114	1.27
English (236)	469	5.23
French, ex. Basque (24)	54	0.60
French Canadian (11)	11	0.12
German (324)	585	6.53
Greek (70)	104	1.16
Hungarian (10)	10	0.11
Irish (25)	425	4.74
Italian (103)	237	2.64
Norwegian (0)	20	0.22
Polish (20)	29	0.32
Russian (0)	46	0.51
Scotch-Irish (46)	101	1.13
Scottish (16)	52	0.58
Slovak (0)	26	0.29
Swedish (0)	58	0.65
Swiss (0)	9	0.10
Ukrainian (0)	11	0.12
Welsh (0)	17	0.19
West Indian, ex. Hispanic (249)	504	5.62
Bahamian (27)	27	0.30
Haitian (112)	112	1.25
Jamaican (110)	365	4.07

Hispanic Origin	Population	%
Hispanic or Latino (of any race)	2,576	29.15
Central American, ex. Mexican	71	0.80
Costa Rican	2	0.02
Guatemalan	12	0.14
Honduran	36	0.41
Nicaraguan	8	0.09
Panamanian	4	0.05
Salvadoran	9	0.10
Cuban	90	1.02
Dominican Republic	28	0.32
Mexican	1,481	16.76
Puerto Rican	795	9.00
South American	37	0.42
Argentinean	1	0.01
Colombian	13	0.15
Ecuadorian	8	0.09
Peruvian	9	0.10
Uruguayan	1	0.01
Venezuelan	5	0.06
Other Hispanic or Latino	74	0.84

Race*	Population	%
African-American/Black (2,481)	2,613	29.57
Not Hispanic (2,363)	2,460	27.84
Hispanic (118)	153	1.73
American Indian/Alaska Native (30)	90	1.02
Not Hispanic (20)	53	0.60
Hispanic (10)	37	0.42
Blackfeet (0)	1	0.01
Central American Ind. (1)	3	0.03
Cherokee (3)	11	0.12
Chippewa (0)	1	0.01
Creek (2)	2	0.02
Crow (1)	2	0.02
Lumbee (3)	3	0.03
Sioux (0)	1	0.01
South American Ind. (0)	9	0.10
Asian (74)	101	1.14
Not Hispanic (70)	92	1.04
Hispanic (4)	9	0.10
Bangladeshi (6)	10	0.11
Cambodian (0)	2	0.02
Chinese, ex. Taiwanese (2)	6	0.07
Filipino (22)	29	0.33
Indian (21)	32	0.36
Indonesian (2)	3	0.03
Japanese (1)	1	0.01
Korean (5)	5	0.06
Pakistani (0)	1	0.01
Thai (1)	1	0.01
Hawaii Native/Pacific Islander (1)	14	0.16
Not Hispanic (1)	11	0.12
Hispanic (0)	3	0.03
Guamanian/Chamorro (1)	3	0.03
Samoan (0)	1	0.01
White (4,901)	5,239	59.29
Not Hispanic (3,647)	3,763	42.59
Hispanic (1,254)	1,476	16.70

Azalea Park

Place Type: CDP
County: Orange
Population: 12,556†

Ancestry‡	Population	%
African, Sub-Saharan (45)	45	0.34
African (45)	45	0.34
American (718)	718	5.47
Arab (147)	147	1.12
Moroccan (147)	147	1.12
Austrian (0)	10	0.08
Brazilian (78)	78	0.59
British (28)	80	0.61
Canadian (6)	27	0.21
Dutch (26)	41	0.31
English (103)	382	2.91
European (26)	38	0.29
French, ex. Basque (60)	103	0.78
French Canadian (0)	27	0.21
German (357)	1,027	7.83
Guyanese (24)	46	0.35
Hungarian (0)	10	0.08
Icelander (0)	11	0.08
Irish (24)	612	4.66
Italian (111)	280	2.13
Polish (24)	59	0.45
Portuguese (40)	40	0.30
Romanian (9)	9	0.07
Russian (17)	66	0.50
Scandinavian (0)	25	0.19
Scotch-Irish (37)	80	0.61
Scottish (51)	83	0.63
Slovak (0)	18	0.14
Swedish (21)	60	0.46
Ukrainian (12)	12	0.09
Welsh (0)	12	0.09
West Indian, ex. Hispanic (196)	298	2.27
Barbadian (25)	25	0.19
British West Indian (11)	11	0.08
Jamaican (92)	111	0.85
Trinidadian/Tobagonian (0)	83	0.63
U.S. Virgin Islander (31)	31	0.24
West Indian (37)	37	0.28

Hispanic Origin	Population	%
Hispanic or Latino (of any race)	7,413	59.04
Central American, ex. Mexican	452	3.60
Costa Rican	21	0.17
Guatemalan	76	0.61
Honduran	179	1.43
Nicaraguan	40	0.32
Panamanian	36	0.29
Salvadoran	100	0.80
Cuban	716	5.70
Dominican Republic	408	3.25
Mexican	387	3.08
Puerto Rican	4,583	36.50
South American	528	4.21
Argentinean	16	0.13
Bolivian	8	0.06

*Notes: † The Census 2010 population figure is used to calculate the percentages in the Hispanic Origin and Race categories. Ancestry percentages are based on the 2006-2010 American Community Survey population (not shown); ‡ Numbers in parentheses indicate the number of people reporting a single ancestry; * Numbers in parentheses indicate the number of persons reporting this race alone, not in combination with any other race; Please refer to the Explanation of Data for more information.*

Chilean	13	0.10
Colombian	308	2.45
Ecuadorian	64	0.51
Peruvian	53	0.42
Uruguayan	3	0.02
Venezuelan	62	0.49
Other South American	1	0.01
Other Hispanic or Latino	339	2.70

Race*	Population	%
African-American/Black (1,294)	1,498	11.93
Not Hispanic (915)	988	7.87
Hispanic (379)	510	4.06
American Indian/Alaska Native (48)	111	0.88
Not Hispanic (18)	45	0.36
Hispanic (30)	66	0.53
Blackfeet (0)	4	0.03
Central American Ind. (1)	1	0.01
Cherokee (3)	13	0.10
Chippewa (1)	3	0.02
Iroquois (0)	1	0.01
Kiowa (1)	2	0.02
Mexican American Ind. (1)	1	0.01
Ottawa (0)	1	0.01
Pueblo (0)	1	0.01
Seminole (0)	1	0.01
Sioux (1)	1	0.01
South American Ind. (3)	5	0.04
Asian (467)	539	4.29
Not Hispanic (447)	499	3.97
Hispanic (20)	40	0.32
Bangladeshi (0)	3	0.02
Cambodian (1)	3	0.02
Chinese, ex. Taiwanese (48)	69	0.55
Filipino (58)	72	0.57
Indian (48)	65	0.52
Japanese (8)	14	0.11
Korean (19)	24	0.19
Laotian (2)	2	0.02
Pakistani (23)	26	0.21
Thai (8)	10	0.08
Vietnamese (237)	243	1.94
Hawaii Native/Pacific Islander (10)	37	0.29
Not Hispanic (7)	23	0.18
Hispanic (3)	14	0.11
Guamanian/Chamorro (6)	10	0.08
Native Hawaiian (3)	7	0.06
White (8,462)	8,869	70.64
Not Hispanic (3,577)	3,680	29.31
Hispanic (4,885)	5,189	41.33

Bardmoor

Place Type: CDP
County: Pinellas
Population: 9,732†

Ancestry‡	Population	%
African, Sub-Saharan (6)	6	0.06
African (6)	6	0.06
American (1,118)	1,118	10.84
Arab (249)	249	2.41
Egyptian (249)	249	2.41
Austrian (0)	38	0.37
Brazilian (0)	49	0.48
Canadian (67)	80	0.78
Czech (15)	15	0.15
Czechoslovakian (22)	41	0.40
Danish (0)	25	0.24
Dutch (0)	96	0.93
English (437)	1,214	11.77
European (76)	94	0.91
French, ex. Basque (148)	573	5.56
French Canadian (37)	169	1.64
German (1,088)	2,393	23.21
Greek (56)	68	0.66
Hungarian (69)	116	1.12
Irish (420)	1,746	16.93
Italian (329)	942	9.13
Latvian (0)	29	0.28
Lithuanian (0)	16	0.16
Maltese (26)	26	0.25
Norwegian (115)	249	2.41
Polish (88)	361	3.50
Portuguese (0)	29	0.28
Romanian (19)	19	0.18
Russian (28)	57	0.55
Scotch-Irish (78)	108	1.05
Scottish (79)	151	1.46
Slavic (10)	10	0.10
Slovak (7)	30	0.29
Swedish (53)	161	1.56
Swiss (15)	75	0.73
Ukrainian (0)	51	0.49
Welsh (6)	55	0.53
West Indian, ex. Hispanic (13)	13	0.13
Jamaican (13)	13	0.13
Yugoslavian (0)	22	0.21

Hispanic Origin	Population	%
Hispanic or Latino (of any race)	701	7.20
Central American, ex. Mexican	59	0.61
Costa Rican	10	0.10
Guatemalan	8	0.08
Honduran	15	0.15
Nicaraguan	5	0.05
Panamanian	6	0.06
Salvadoran	15	0.15
Cuban	51	0.52
Dominican Republic	23	0.24
Mexican	115	1.18
Puerto Rican	319	3.28
South American	79	0.81
Chilean	3	0.03
Colombian	42	0.43
Ecuadorian	8	0.08
Paraguayan	4	0.04
Peruvian	9	0.09
Uruguayan	1	0.01
Venezuelan	12	0.12
Other Hispanic or Latino	55	0.57

Race*	Population	%
African-American/Black (249)	329	3.38
Not Hispanic (232)	291	2.99
Hispanic (17)	38	0.39
American Indian/Alaska Native (55)	87	0.89
Not Hispanic (31)	55	0.57
Hispanic (24)	32	0.33
Alaska Athabascan *(Ala. Nat.)* (0)	1	0.01
Apache (1)	1	0.01
Blackfeet (1)	7	0.07
Cherokee (9)	22	0.23
Chippewa (1)	2	0.02
Choctaw (1)	3	0.03
Iroquois (0)	1	0.01
Osage (0)	1	0.01
Pima (1)	1	0.01
Potawatomi (1)	1	0.01
Pueblo (0)	1	0.01
Seminole (0)	1	0.01
Shoshone (0)	2	0.02
Spanish American Ind. (1)	5	0.05
Asian (418)	492	5.06
Not Hispanic (415)	486	4.99
Hispanic (3)	6	0.06
Bangladeshi (1)	1	0.01
Cambodian (6)	9	0.09
Chinese, ex. Taiwanese (34)	42	0.43
Filipino (44)	68	0.70
Hmong (4)	4	0.04
Indian (142)	150	1.54
Indonesian (2)	2	0.02
Japanese (7)	11	0.11
Korean (21)	27	0.28
Laotian (24)	25	0.26
Taiwanese (0)	1	0.01
Thai (12)	13	0.13
Vietnamese (109)	125	1.28
Hawaii Native/Pacific Islander (4)	15	0.15
Not Hispanic (4)	15	0.15
Native Hawaiian (2)	6	0.06
Tongan (1)	6	0.06
White (8,637)	8,813	90.56
Not Hispanic (8,184)	8,326	85.55
Hispanic (453)	487	5.00

Bartow

Place Type: City
County: Polk
Population: 17,298†

Ancestry‡	Population	%
African, Sub-Saharan (253)	280	1.63
African (253)	253	1.47
Nigerian (0)	6	0.03
South African (0)	21	0.12
American (1,168)	1,168	6.78
Arab (27)	38	0.22
Egyptian (10)	21	0.12
Lebanese (17)	17	0.10
Australian (0)	6	0.03
Belgian (0)	12	0.07
British (44)	72	0.42
Cajun (0)	10	0.06
Canadian (28)	61	0.35
Croatian (19)	19	0.11
Czech (0)	22	0.13
Danish (0)	25	0.15
Dutch (75)	159	0.92
English (749)	1,618	9.39
European (428)	428	2.48
Finnish (14)	14	0.08
French, ex. Basque (136)	359	2.08
French Canadian (0)	74	0.43
German (572)	1,464	8.50
Greek (45)	56	0.33
Hungarian (11)	71	0.41
Irish (297)	1,235	7.17
Italian (263)	455	2.64
Lithuanian (7)	27	0.16
Norwegian (0)	38	0.22
Pennsylvania German (14)	14	0.08
Polish (185)	245	1.42
Portuguese (32)	115	0.67
Russian (0)	34	0.20
Scotch-Irish (257)	434	2.52
Scottish (276)	411	2.39
Slovak (0)	7	0.04
Swedish (0)	28	0.16
Swiss (13)	53	0.31
Welsh (7)	95	0.55
West Indian, ex. Hispanic (116)	141	0.82
Belizean (8)	8	0.05
Haitian (72)	79	0.46
Jamaican (14)	32	0.19
U.S. Virgin Islander (22)	22	0.13

Hispanic Origin	Population	%
Hispanic or Latino (of any race)	2,546	14.72
Central American, ex. Mexican	53	0.31
Costa Rican	2	0.01
Guatemalan	15	0.09
Honduran	17	0.10
Nicaraguan	3	0.02
Panamanian	13	0.08
Salvadoran	3	0.02
Cuban	136	0.79
Dominican Republic	30	0.17
Mexican	1,636	9.46
Puerto Rican	409	2.36
South American	57	0.33
Argentinean	4	0.02
Bolivian	1	0.01
Chilean	5	0.03
Colombian	21	0.12
Ecuadorian	5	0.03
Peruvian	18	0.10
Venezuelan	3	0.02

*Notes: † The Census 2010 population figure is used to calculate the percentages in the Hispanic Origin and Race categories. Ancestry percentages are based on the 2006-2010 American Community Survey population (not shown); ‡ Numbers in parentheses indicate the number of people reporting a single ancestry; * Numbers in parentheses indicate the number of persons reporting this race alone, not in combination with any other race; Please refer to the Explanation of Data for more information.*

Other Hispanic or Latino	225	1.30

Race*	Population	%
African-American/Black (4,101)	4,302	24.87
Not Hispanic (4,023)	4,181	24.17
Hispanic (78)	121	0.70
American Indian/Alaska Native (50)	129	0.75
Not Hispanic (36)	103	0.60
Hispanic (14)	26	0.15
Apache (0)	1	0.01
Blackfeet (0)	4	0.02
Cherokee (11)	38	0.22
Chippewa (3)	5	0.03
Choctaw (0)	1	0.01
Cree (0)	1	0.01
Creek (4)	7	0.04
Iroquois (3)	4	0.02
Lumbee (1)	1	0.01
Mexican American Ind. (0)	1	0.01
Osage (1)	1	0.01
Ottawa (1)	1	0.01
Seminole (2)	3	0.02
Sioux (2)	3	0.02
Asian (187)	263	1.52
Not Hispanic (187)	258	1.49
Hispanic (0)	5	0.03
Bangladeshi (6)	6	0.03
Cambodian (1)	1	0.01
Chinese, ex. Taiwanese (8)	13	0.08
Filipino (21)	29	0.17
Hmong (2)	2	0.01
Indian (111)	137	0.79
Indonesian (1)	2	0.01
Japanese (6)	12	0.07
Korean (2)	16	0.09
Laotian (17)	17	0.10
Nepalese (2)	3	0.02
Sri Lankan (1)	4	0.02
Thai (3)	10	0.06
Vietnamese (5)	6	0.03
Hawaii Native/Pacific Islander (10)	22	0.13
Not Hispanic (10)	20	0.12
Hispanic (0)	2	0.01
Guamanian/Chamorro (6)	7	0.04
Native Hawaiian (0)	1	0.01
Samoan (1)	2	0.01
White (11,699)	12,052	69.67
Not Hispanic (10,216)	10,425	60.27
Hispanic (1,483)	1,627	9.41

Bayonet Point

Place Type: CDP
County: Pasco
Population: 23,467†

Ancestry‡	Population	%
African, Sub-Saharan (359)	359	1.52
Other Sub-Saharan African (359)	359	1.52
Albanian (15)	38	0.16
American (1,329)	1,329	5.63
Arab (65)	75	0.32
Egyptian (0)	10	0.04
Lebanese (16)	16	0.07
Syrian (49)	49	0.21
Armenian (12)	12	0.05
Australian (0)	28	0.12
Austrian (10)	108	0.46
Belgian (151)	160	0.68
British (47)	54	0.23
Canadian (87)	199	0.84
Croatian (14)	26	0.11
Czech (35)	85	0.36
Czechoslovakian (18)	18	0.08
Danish (0)	11	0.05
Dutch (141)	563	2.39
Eastern European (10)	10	0.04
English (956)	2,427	10.29
European (105)	105	0.45
Finnish (24)	59	0.25
French, ex. Basque (489)	1,539	6.53
French Canadian (228)	429	1.82
German (1,437)	4,339	18.40
Greek (143)	226	0.96
Hungarian (59)	227	0.96
Irish (1,019)	3,921	16.62
Italian (2,280)	4,140	17.55
Lithuanian (39)	47	0.20
Macedonian (0)	11	0.05
Maltese (44)	60	0.25
Norwegian (50)	114	0.48
Pennsylvania German (33)	33	0.14
Polish (538)	1,190	5.05
Portuguese (109)	141	0.60
Russian (72)	134	0.57
Scandinavian (41)	41	0.17
Scotch-Irish (268)	437	1.85
Scottish (320)	512	2.17
Serbian (31)	31	0.13
Slovak (43)	89	0.38
Swedish (53)	339	1.44
Swiss (11)	32	0.14
Turkish (15)	15	0.06
Ukrainian (16)	43	0.18
Welsh (51)	132	0.56
West Indian, ex. Hispanic (20)	29	0.12
Dutch West Indian (0)	9	0.04
Haitian (14)	14	0.06
Jamaican (6)	6	0.03
Yugoslavian (84)	84	0.36

Hispanic Origin	Population	%
Hispanic or Latino (of any race)	2,107	8.98
Central American, ex. Mexican	138	0.59
Costa Rican	20	0.09
Guatemalan	17	0.07
Honduran	38	0.16
Nicaraguan	18	0.08
Panamanian	13	0.06
Salvadoran	31	0.13
Other Central American	1	<0.01
Cuban	237	1.01
Dominican Republic	75	0.32
Mexican	225	0.96
Puerto Rican	1,084	4.62
South American	177	0.75
Argentinean	5	0.02
Bolivian	4	0.02
Chilean	7	0.03
Colombian	72	0.31
Ecuadorian	24	0.10
Peruvian	38	0.16
Uruguayan	10	0.04
Venezuelan	17	0.07
Other Hispanic or Latino	171	0.73

Race*	Population	%
African-American/Black (449)	641	2.73
Not Hispanic (392)	552	2.35
Hispanic (57)	89	0.38
American Indian/Alaska Native (81)	240	1.02
Not Hispanic (58)	201	0.86
Hispanic (23)	39	0.17
Apache (0)	5	0.02
Blackfeet (3)	10	0.04
Central American Ind. (1)	1	<0.01
Cherokee (10)	61	0.26
Cheyenne (0)	3	0.01
Chippewa (1)	5	0.02
Choctaw (0)	1	<0.01
Cree (0)	2	0.01
Creek (1)	3	0.01
Iroquois (2)	12	0.05
Mexican American Ind. (2)	3	0.01
Navajo (1)	1	<0.01
Potawatomi (3)	3	0.01
Seminole (3)	7	0.03
Shoshone (0)	3	0.01
Sioux (5)	8	0.03
South American Ind. (3)	3	0.01
Asian (271)	399	1.70
Not Hispanic (268)	383	1.63
Hispanic (3)	16	0.07
Burmese (1)	1	<0.01
Chinese, ex. Taiwanese (53)	58	0.25
Filipino (68)	125	0.53
Hmong (6)	6	0.03
Indian (65)	82	0.35
Indonesian (2)	6	0.03
Japanese (8)	26	0.11
Korean (13)	25	0.11
Laotian (1)	1	<0.01
Pakistani (10)	11	0.05
Taiwanese (1)	1	<0.01
Thai (5)	10	0.04
Vietnamese (34)	44	0.19
Hawaii Native/Pacific Islander (12)	41	0.17
Not Hispanic (10)	24	0.10
Hispanic (2)	17	0.07
Fijian (2)	2	0.01
Marshallese (0)	6	0.03
Native Hawaiian (1)	7	0.03
Samoan (0)	4	0.02
White (21,671)	22,150	94.39
Not Hispanic (20,218)	20,579	87.69
Hispanic (1,453)	1,571	6.69

Bayshore Gardens

Place Type: CDP
County: Manatee
Population: 16,323†

Ancestry‡	Population	%
African, Sub-Saharan (266)	266	1.59
African (266)	266	1.59
American (1,016)	1,016	6.08
Arab (9)	19	0.11
Lebanese (9)	9	0.05
Syrian (0)	10	0.06
Armenian (13)	13	0.08
Australian (0)	15	0.09
Austrian (0)	96	0.57
Belgian (0)	13	0.08
British (44)	111	0.66
Canadian (13)	87	0.52
Croatian (9)	9	0.05
Czech (27)	73	0.44
Czechoslovakian (12)	46	0.28
Danish (53)	162	0.97
Dutch (51)	366	2.19
English (1,075)	2,707	16.19
European (15)	25	0.15
French, ex. Basque (168)	596	3.57
French Canadian (134)	134	0.80
German (804)	2,949	17.64
Greek (28)	28	0.17
Hungarian (219)	230	1.38
Irish (632)	2,362	14.13
Italian (585)	913	5.46
Lithuanian (45)	45	0.27
Norwegian (106)	185	1.11
Pennsylvania German (14)	14	0.08
Polish (160)	503	3.01
Portuguese (35)	35	0.21
Romanian (13)	13	0.08
Russian (0)	65	0.39
Scandinavian (39)	85	0.51
Scotch-Irish (114)	309	1.85
Scottish (46)	225	1.35
Slavic (27)	43	0.26
Slovak (52)	79	0.47
Swedish (36)	163	0.97
Swiss (14)	98	0.59
Ukrainian (43)	52	0.31
Welsh (28)	132	0.79
West Indian, ex. Hispanic (574)	574	3.43
Bahamian (26)	26	0.16
Haitian (548)	548	3.28

*Notes: † The Census 2010 population figure is used to calculate the percentages in the Hispanic Origin and Race categories. Ancestry percentages are based on the 2006-2010 American Community Survey population (not shown); ‡ Numbers in parentheses indicate the number of people reporting a single ancestry; * Numbers in parentheses indicate the number of persons reporting this race alone, not in combination with any other race; Please refer to the Explanation of Data for more information.*

Hispanic Origin	Population	%
Hispanic or Latino (of any race)	3,105	19.02
Central American, ex. Mexican	519	3.18
Costa Rican	10	0.06
Guatemalan	192	1.18
Honduran	204	1.25
Nicaraguan	42	0.26
Panamanian	11	0.07
Salvadoran	60	0.37
Cuban	201	1.23
Dominican Republic	47	0.29
Mexican	1,360	8.33
Puerto Rican	509	3.12
South American	223	1.37
Argentinean	21	0.13
Chilean	3	0.02
Colombian	104	0.64
Ecuadorian	50	0.31
Peruvian	17	0.10
Uruguayan	5	0.03
Venezuelan	21	0.13
Other South American	2	0.01
Other Hispanic or Latino	246	1.51

Race*	Population	%
African-American/Black (1,200)	1,406	8.61
Not Hispanic (1,130)	1,287	7.88
Hispanic (70)	119	0.73
American Indian/Alaska Native (86)	185	1.13
Not Hispanic (38)	115	0.70
Hispanic (48)	70	0.43
Apache (1)	2	0.01
Blackfeet (0)	5	0.03
Canadian/French Am. Ind. (1)	1	0.01
Cherokee (10)	33	0.20
Cheyenne (2)	4	0.02
Chippewa (3)	5	0.03
Cree (0)	2	0.01
Iroquois (0)	4	0.02
Menominee (1)	1	0.01
Mexican American Ind. (8)	8	0.05
Navajo (1)	1	0.01
Pueblo (0)	1	0.01
Seminole (0)	4	0.02
Sioux (0)	5	0.03
South American Ind. (0)	6	0.04
Asian (174)	214	1.31
Not Hispanic (169)	204	1.25
Hispanic (5)	10	0.06
Cambodian (13)	21	0.13
Chinese, ex. Taiwanese (6)	13	0.08
Filipino (30)	37	0.23
Indian (32)	35	0.21
Indonesian (1)	1	0.01
Japanese (3)	11	0.07
Korean (11)	12	0.07
Laotian (5)	5	0.03
Malaysian (1)	1	0.01
Pakistani (0)	3	0.02
Thai (30)	33	0.20
Vietnamese (35)	42	0.26
Hawaii Native/Pacific Islander (11)	22	0.13
Not Hispanic (10)	20	0.12
Hispanic (1)	2	0.01
Guamanian/Chamorro (2)	3	0.02
Native Hawaiian (1)	2	0.01
Samoan (2)	4	0.02
Tongan (6)	6	0.04
White (13,216)	13,623	83.46
Not Hispanic (11,583)	11,812	72.36
Hispanic (1,633)	1,811	11.09

Bee Ridge

Place Type: CDP
County: Sarasota
Population: 9,598†

Ancestry‡	Population	%
African, Sub-Saharan (16)	16	0.16
South African (16)	16	0.16
American (554)	554	5.54
Arab (13)	68	0.68
Moroccan (0)	55	0.55
Syrian (13)	13	0.13
Armenian (138)	186	1.86
Austrian (0)	32	0.32
Belgian (7)	30	0.30
British (41)	113	1.13
Canadian (49)	138	1.38
Czech (165)	193	1.93
Czechoslovakian (42)	52	0.52
Danish (12)	67	0.67
Dutch (38)	96	0.96
English (696)	1,806	18.07
European (142)	142	1.42
Finnish (0)	19	0.19
French, ex. Basque (180)	671	6.71
French Canadian (62)	87	0.87
German (747)	2,040	20.41
Greek (15)	15	0.15
Hungarian (66)	136	1.36
Irish (569)	1,643	16.44
Italian (645)	1,222	12.22
Latvian (0)	14	0.14
Lithuanian (13)	34	0.34
Norwegian (69)	69	0.69
Pennsylvania German (13)	26	0.26
Polish (165)	388	3.88
Portuguese (10)	52	0.52
Russian (61)	182	1.82
Scotch-Irish (17)	142	1.42
Scottish (107)	272	2.72
Swedish (50)	294	2.94
Swiss (13)	72	0.72
Ukrainian (72)	82	0.82
Welsh (0)	103	1.03
Yugoslavian (0)	37	0.37

Hispanic Origin	Population	%
Hispanic or Latino (of any race)	522	5.44
Central American, ex. Mexican	34	0.35
Costa Rican	6	0.06
Guatemalan	5	0.05
Honduran	10	0.10
Nicaraguan	11	0.11
Salvadoran	2	0.02
Cuban	74	0.77
Dominican Republic	8	0.08
Mexican	150	1.56
Puerto Rican	113	1.18
South American	99	1.03
Argentinean	6	0.06
Chilean	3	0.03
Colombian	47	0.49
Ecuadorian	7	0.07
Paraguayan	4	0.04
Peruvian	22	0.23
Uruguayan	1	0.01
Venezuelan	9	0.09
Other Hispanic or Latino	44	0.46

Race*	Population	%
African-American/Black (120)	160	1.67
Not Hispanic (116)	152	1.58
Hispanic (4)	8	0.08
American Indian/Alaska Native (29)	66	0.69
Not Hispanic (23)	51	0.53
Hispanic (6)	15	0.16
Blackfeet (0)	2	0.02
Canadian/French Am. Ind. (0)	1	0.01
Central American Ind. (4)	4	0.04
Cherokee (3)	12	0.13
Chippewa (2)	3	0.03
Choctaw (1)	1	0.01
Creek (1)	1	0.01
Iroquois (7)	7	0.07
Lumbee (0)	1	0.01
Mexican American Ind. (2)	2	0.02
Potawatomi (1)	1	0.01
Seminole (0)	1	0.01
Asian (173)	205	2.14
Not Hispanic (173)	203	2.12
Hispanic (0)	2	0.02
Bangladeshi (4)	4	0.04
Burmese (2)	6	0.06
Chinese, ex. Taiwanese (35)	38	0.40
Filipino (22)	31	0.32
Indian (31)	38	0.40
Japanese (4)	10	0.10
Korean (12)	12	0.13
Laotian (6)	7	0.07
Taiwanese (1)	3	0.03
Thai (6)	9	0.09
Vietnamese (46)	49	0.51
Hawaii Native/Pacific Islander (0)	5	0.05
Not Hispanic (0)	3	0.03
Hispanic (0)	2	0.02
White (9,071)	9,171	95.55
Not Hispanic (8,673)	8,754	91.21
Hispanic (398)	417	4.34

Bellair-Meadowbrook Terrace

Place Type: CDP
County: Clay
Population: 13,343†

Ancestry‡	Population	%
African, Sub-Saharan (102)	125	0.96
African (102)	125	0.96
American (975)	975	7.48
Arab (0)	17	0.13
Lebanese (0)	17	0.13
Austrian (8)	8	0.06
Brazilian (8)	8	0.06
British (14)	31	0.24
Canadian (38)	48	0.37
Celtic (0)	16	0.12
Czech (0)	12	0.09
Czechoslovakian (0)	44	0.34
Danish (16)	16	0.12
Dutch (10)	148	1.14
English (511)	1,114	8.55
European (140)	175	1.34
Finnish (12)	34	0.26
French, ex. Basque (164)	294	2.26
French Canadian (62)	85	0.65
German (771)	2,181	16.74
Greek (12)	49	0.38
Guyanese (19)	19	0.15
Hungarian (7)	33	0.25
Irish (517)	1,675	12.86
Italian (292)	628	4.82
Lithuanian (0)	20	0.15
Norwegian (18)	103	0.79
Polish (76)	318	2.44
Portuguese (47)	47	0.36
Russian (0)	12	0.09
Scandinavian (0)	46	0.35
Scotch-Irish (139)	301	2.31
Scottish (47)	132	1.01
Slavic (18)	18	0.14
Slovene (0)	12	0.09
Swedish (0)	124	0.95
Swiss (0)	12	0.09
Welsh (24)	71	0.55
West Indian, ex. Hispanic (180)	180	1.38
Haitian (149)	149	1.14
Jamaican (15)	15	0.12
Trinidadian/Tobagonian (16)	16	0.12
Yugoslavian (25)	25	0.19

Hispanic Origin	Population	%
Hispanic or Latino (of any race)	1,677	12.57
Central American, ex. Mexican	141	1.06
Costa Rican	9	0.07
Guatemalan	7	0.05

*Notes: † The Census 2010 population figure is used to calculate the percentages in the Hispanic Origin and Race categories. Ancestry percentages are based on the 2006-2010 American Community Survey population (not shown); ‡ Numbers in parentheses indicate the number of people reporting a single ancestry; * Numbers in parentheses indicate the number of persons reporting this race alone, not in combination with any other race; Please refer to the Explanation of Data for more information.*

Honduran	35	0.26
Nicaraguan	15	0.11
Panamanian	43	0.32
Salvadoran	32	0.24
Cuban	120	0.90
Dominican Republic	74	0.55
Mexican	400	3.00
Puerto Rican	674	5.05
South American	158	1.18
Argentinean	23	0.17
Bolivian	6	0.04
Chilean	6	0.04
Colombian	90	0.67
Ecuadorian	14	0.10
Peruvian	13	0.10
Uruguayan	4	0.03
Venezuelan	2	0.01
Other Hispanic or Latino	110	0.82

Race*	Population	%
African-American/Black (2,393)	2,627	19.69
Not Hispanic (2,305)	2,491	18.67
Hispanic (88)	136	1.02
American Indian/Alaska Native (61)	166	1.24
Not Hispanic (46)	138	1.03
Hispanic (15)	28	0.21
Blackfeet (1)	6	0.04
Canadian/French Am. Ind. (0)	1	0.01
Cherokee (11)	50	0.37
Cheyenne (0)	1	0.01
Chickasaw (0)	1	0.01
Chippewa (3)	4	0.03
Comanche (1)	1	0.01
Creek (1)	1	0.01
Hopi (0)	1	0.01
Iroquois (6)	7	0.05
Lumbee (1)	1	0.01
Mexican American Ind. (0)	4	0.03
Navajo (1)	2	0.01
Paiute (1)	1	0.01
Shoshone (1)	1	0.01
Sioux (0)	3	0.02
South American Ind. (1)	1	0.01
Asian (366)	485	3.63
Not Hispanic (352)	458	3.43
Hispanic (14)	27	0.20
Burmese (2)	2	0.01
Cambodian (6)	6	0.04
Chinese, ex. Taiwanese (19)	30	0.22
Filipino (213)	284	2.13
Indian (26)	37	0.28
Japanese (18)	30	0.22
Korean (33)	47	0.35
Laotian (1)	3	0.02
Malaysian (1)	1	0.01
Nepalese (4)	4	0.03
Pakistani (3)	7	0.05
Taiwanese (2)	2	0.01
Thai (3)	9	0.07
Vietnamese (19)	28	0.21
Hawaii Native/Pacific Islander (23)	48	0.36
Not Hispanic (19)	42	0.31
Hispanic (4)	6	0.04
Guamanian/Chamorro (13)	17	0.13
Native Hawaiian (6)	10	0.07
Samoan (3)	5	0.04
White (9,454)	9,860	73.90
Not Hispanic (8,574)	8,889	66.62
Hispanic (880)	971	7.28

Belle Glade

Place Type: City
County: Palm Beach
Population: 17,467†

Ancestry‡	Population	%
African, Sub-Saharan (747)	863	4.89
African (709)	825	4.67
Nigerian (38)	38	0.22
American (437)	437	2.47
Arab (169)	251	1.42
Arab (19)	19	0.11
Jordanian (11)	52	0.29
Palestinian (139)	180	1.02
Austrian (0)	22	0.12
British (232)	232	1.31
Canadian (2)	8	0.05
Czech (30)	30	0.17
Czechoslovakian (12)	12	0.07
Dutch (73)	92	0.52
English (297)	469	2.66
European (53)	88	0.50
French, ex. Basque (0)	10	0.06
German (20)	381	2.16
Hungarian (11)	51	0.29
Irish (86)	252	1.43
Israeli (10)	32	0.18
Italian (90)	90	0.51
Polish (12)	32	0.18
Scotch-Irish (23)	62	0.35
Scottish (0)	13	0.07
West Indian, ex. Hispanic (2,226)	2,549	14.43
Bahamian (51)	68	0.39
Barbadian (18)	18	0.10
Haitian (1,682)	1,829	10.36
Jamaican (467)	626	3.54
West Indian (8)	8	0.05

Hispanic Origin	Population	%
Hispanic or Latino (of any race)	5,979	34.23
Central American, ex. Mexican	488	2.79
Costa Rican	33	0.19
Guatemalan	117	0.67
Honduran	79	0.45
Nicaraguan	132	0.76
Panamanian	4	0.02
Salvadoran	123	0.70
Cuban	1,042	5.97
Dominican Republic	104	0.60
Mexican	3,806	21.79
Puerto Rican	277	1.59
South American	43	0.25
Argentinean	5	0.03
Chilean	1	0.01
Colombian	27	0.15
Ecuadorian	2	0.01
Peruvian	1	0.01
Uruguayan	5	0.03
Venezuelan	2	0.01
Other Hispanic or Latino	219	1.25

Race*	Population	%
African-American/Black (9,831)	9,979	57.13
Not Hispanic (9,716)	9,819	56.21
Hispanic (115)	160	0.92
American Indian/Alaska Native (29)	46	0.26
Not Hispanic (9)	22	0.13
Hispanic (20)	24	0.14
Canadian/French Am. Ind. (0)	2	0.01
Cherokee (1)	1	0.01
Inupiat *(Alaska Native)* (1)	1	0.01
Mexican American Ind. (4)	4	0.02
Sioux (0)	1	0.01
Tlingit-Haida *(Alaska Native)* (0)	2	0.01
Asian (82)	130	0.74
Not Hispanic (79)	124	0.71
Hispanic (3)	6	0.03
Bangladeshi (28)	35	0.20
Chinese, ex. Taiwanese (16)	22	0.13
Filipino (2)	3	0.02
Indian (17)	31	0.18
Korean (2)	2	0.01
Vietnamese (13)	14	0.08
Hawaii Native/Pacific Islander (27)	73	0.42
Not Hispanic (1)	41	0.23
Hispanic (26)	32	0.18
Guamanian/Chamorro (17)	17	0.10
Native Hawaiian (2)	3	0.02
Samoan (6)	6	0.03
White (5,438)	5,674	32.48
Not Hispanic (1,540)	1,604	9.18
Hispanic (3,898)	4,070	23.30

Bellview

Place Type: CDP
County: Escambia
Population: 23,355†

Ancestry‡	Population	%
African, Sub-Saharan (100)	173	0.71
African (100)	100	0.41
Cape Verdean (0)	73	0.30
Albanian (0)	32	0.13
American (2,569)	2,569	10.47
Arab (37)	46	0.19
Lebanese (0)	9	0.04
Other Arab (37)	37	0.15
Australian (14)	14	0.06
Austrian (19)	72	0.29
British (82)	150	0.61
Canadian (34)	34	0.14
Czech (11)	55	0.22
Czechoslovakian (14)	29	0.12
Danish (0)	13	0.05
Dutch (55)	275	1.12
Eastern European (14)	14	0.06
English (1,114)	2,935	11.96
European (105)	135	0.55
French, ex. Basque (196)	829	3.38
French Canadian (98)	127	0.52
German (740)	2,685	10.94
German Russian (9)	9	0.04
Greek (55)	86	0.35
Hungarian (8)	8	0.03
Irish (834)	2,504	10.21
Italian (446)	861	3.51
Maltese (12)	12	0.05
Northern European (18)	18	0.07
Norwegian (67)	226	0.92
Polish (33)	228	0.93
Portuguese (74)	205	0.84
Romanian (0)	12	0.05
Russian (0)	56	0.23
Scandinavian (9)	9	0.04
Scotch-Irish (259)	484	1.97
Scottish (135)	441	1.80
Slavic (16)	16	0.07
Slovak (28)	60	0.24
Slovene (0)	11	0.04
Swedish (241)	417	1.70
Swiss (20)	67	0.27
Ukrainian (0)	16	0.07
Welsh (19)	38	0.15
West Indian, ex. Hispanic (291)	291	1.19
Bahamian (49)	49	0.20
Haitian (54)	54	0.22
Jamaican (188)	188	0.77

Hispanic Origin	Population	%
Hispanic or Latino (of any race)	1,033	4.42
Central American, ex. Mexican	95	0.41
Costa Rican	4	0.02
Guatemalan	3	0.01
Honduran	40	0.17
Nicaraguan	4	0.02
Panamanian	26	0.11
Salvadoran	18	0.08
Cuban	69	0.30
Dominican Republic	11	0.05
Mexican	405	1.73
Puerto Rican	233	1.00
South American	72	0.31
Argentinean	4	0.02
Bolivian	3	0.01
Chilean	3	0.01
Colombian	32	0.14
Ecuadorian	7	0.03
Peruvian	15	0.06

*Notes: † The Census 2010 population figure is used to calculate the percentages in the Hispanic Origin and Race categories. Ancestry percentages are based on the 2006-2010 American Community Survey population (not shown); ‡ Numbers in parentheses indicate the number of people reporting a single ancestry; * Numbers in parentheses indicate the number of persons reporting this race alone, not in combination with any other race; Please refer to the Explanation of Data for more information.*

Uruguayan	2	0.01
Venezuelan	1	<0.01
Other South American	5	0.02
Other Hispanic or Latino	148	0.63

Race*	Population	%
African-American/Black (4,280)	4,660	19.95
Not Hispanic (4,240)	4,557	19.51
Hispanic (40)	103	0.44
American Indian/Alaska Native (182)	483	2.07
Not Hispanic (172)	443	1.90
Hispanic (10)	40	0.17
Aleut *(Alaska Native)* (2)	2	0.01
Apache (2)	7	0.03
Blackfeet (6)	10	0.04
Canadian/French Am. Ind. (0)	1	<0.01
Cherokee (14)	82	0.35
Chickasaw (0)	1	<0.01
Chippewa (2)	2	0.01
Choctaw (6)	19	0.08
Colville (0)	1	<0.01
Comanche (1)	6	0.03
Creek (67)	129	0.55
Delaware (1)	1	<0.01
Houma (6)	7	0.03
Iroquois (0)	4	0.02
Lumbee (1)	5	0.02
Mexican American Ind. (1)	2	0.01
Navajo (1)	1	<0.01
Osage (1)	1	<0.01
Ottawa (4)	6	0.03
Paiute (0)	2	0.01
Potawatomi (2)	2	0.01
Seminole (1)	4	0.02
Sioux (1)	8	0.03
South American Ind. (3)	3	0.01
Asian (1,023)	1,380	5.91
Not Hispanic (998)	1,329	5.69
Hispanic (25)	51	0.22
Burmese (11)	11	0.05
Cambodian (7)	12	0.05
Chinese, ex. Taiwanese (20)	39	0.17
Filipino (582)	845	3.62
Indian (77)	82	0.35
Indonesian (0)	1	<0.01
Japanese (42)	95	0.41
Korean (21)	53	0.23
Laotian (3)	4	0.02
Pakistani (1)	2	0.01
Taiwanese (2)	2	0.01
Thai (6)	17	0.07
Vietnamese (221)	234	1.00
Hawaii Native/Pacific Islander (52)	119	0.51
Not Hispanic (49)	100	0.43
Hispanic (3)	19	0.08
Fijian (1)	2	0.01
Guamanian/Chamorro (23)	35	0.15
Native Hawaiian (16)	38	0.16
Samoan (3)	13	0.06
Tongan (8)	8	0.03
White (16,592)	17,440	74.67
Not Hispanic (16,009)	16,744	71.69
Hispanic (583)	696	2.98

Beverly Hills

Place Type: CDP
County: Citrus
Population: 8,445†

Ancestry‡	Population	%
African, Sub-Saharan (51)	51	0.60
African (51)	51	0.60
Albanian (90)	90	1.06
American (1,317)	1,317	15.46
Arab (14)	36	0.42
Other Arab (14)	36	0.42
Armenian (13)	28	0.33
Australian (0)	14	0.16
Austrian (48)	78	0.92
British (0)	17	0.20
Canadian (25)	89	1.04
Czech (24)	24	0.28
Czechoslovakian (0)	15	0.18
Danish (64)	83	0.97
Dutch (0)	99	1.16
English (280)	793	9.31
European (22)	22	0.26
French, ex. Basque (29)	188	2.21
French Canadian (46)	75	0.88
German (433)	1,211	14.21
Greek (0)	11	0.13
Hungarian (72)	99	1.16
Irish (440)	1,201	14.10
Italian (549)	1,127	13.23
Lithuanian (0)	10	0.12
Norwegian (33)	69	0.81
Polish (241)	415	4.87
Portuguese (64)	79	0.93
Romanian (11)	11	0.13
Russian (0)	36	0.42
Scandinavian (0)	15	0.18
Scotch-Irish (159)	234	2.75
Scottish (183)	239	2.81
Slovak (16)	26	0.31
Swedish (14)	89	1.04
Swiss (36)	63	0.74
Ukrainian (28)	38	0.45
Welsh (0)	28	0.33
West Indian, ex. Hispanic (15)	15	0.18
Jamaican (15)	15	0.18

Hispanic Origin	Population	%
Hispanic or Latino (of any race)	673	7.97
Central American, ex. Mexican	71	0.84
Costa Rican	10	0.12
Guatemalan	4	0.05
Honduran	26	0.31
Nicaraguan	15	0.18
Panamanian	11	0.13
Salvadoran	5	0.06
Cuban	66	0.78
Dominican Republic	22	0.26
Mexican	134	1.59
Puerto Rican	280	3.32
South American	65	0.77
Argentinean	4	0.05
Colombian	33	0.39
Ecuadorian	6	0.07
Paraguayan	1	0.01
Peruvian	1	0.01
Venezuelan	20	0.24
Other Hispanic or Latino	35	0.41

Race*	Population	%
African-American/Black (299)	385	4.56
Not Hispanic (273)	342	4.05
Hispanic (26)	43	0.51
American Indian/Alaska Native (34)	85	1.01
Not Hispanic (22)	66	0.78
Hispanic (12)	19	0.22
Apache (3)	4	0.05
Blackfeet (0)	2	0.02
Cherokee (4)	17	0.20
Chippewa (3)	3	0.04
Comanche (0)	1	0.01
Creek (2)	2	0.02
Delaware (1)	1	0.01
Sioux (7)	8	0.09
South American Ind. (3)	3	0.04
Asian (102)	151	1.79
Not Hispanic (102)	144	1.71
Hispanic (0)	7	0.08
Chinese, ex. Taiwanese (5)	12	0.14
Filipino (34)	60	0.71
Indian (37)	44	0.52
Japanese (5)	9	0.11
Korean (4)	4	0.05
Pakistani (5)	10	0.12
Sri Lankan (1)	1	0.01
Thai (7)	12	0.14
Vietnamese (1)	4	0.05
Hawaii Native/Pacific Islander (4)	24	0.28
Not Hispanic (3)	19	0.22
Hispanic (1)	5	0.06
Native Hawaiian (3)	13	0.15
White (7,662)	7,841	92.85
Not Hispanic (7,204)	7,334	86.84
Hispanic (458)	507	6.00

Bithlo

Place Type: CDP
County: Orange
Population: 8,268†

Ancestry‡	Population	%
American (1,122)	1,122	14.66
Arab (29)	29	0.38
Egyptian (13)	13	0.17
Lebanese (16)	16	0.21
Austrian (0)	51	0.67
Danish (38)	55	0.72
Dutch (0)	65	0.85
English (102)	491	6.42
European (226)	226	2.95
Finnish (13)	13	0.17
French, ex. Basque (31)	124	1.62
French Canadian (11)	48	0.63
German (259)	903	11.80
Guyanese (29)	29	0.38
Hungarian (0)	13	0.17
Irish (138)	841	10.99
Italian (140)	537	7.02
Norwegian (0)	27	0.35
Polish (55)	100	1.31
Russian (41)	41	0.54
Scotch-Irish (0)	6	0.08
Scottish (47)	201	2.63
Serbian (0)	40	0.52
Swedish (0)	51	0.67
Welsh (21)	91	1.19
West Indian, ex. Hispanic (287)	303	3.96
Jamaican (266)	282	3.69
Trinidadian/Tobagonian (21)	21	0.27

Hispanic Origin	Population	%
Hispanic or Latino (of any race)	1,805	21.83
Central American, ex. Mexican	70	0.85
Costa Rican	7	0.08
Guatemalan	16	0.19
Honduran	14	0.17
Nicaraguan	7	0.08
Panamanian	9	0.11
Salvadoran	17	0.21
Cuban	137	1.66
Dominican Republic	99	1.20
Mexican	186	2.25
Puerto Rican	1,035	12.52
South American	215	2.60
Argentinean	9	0.11
Bolivian	1	0.01
Chilean	4	0.05
Colombian	114	1.38
Ecuadorian	42	0.51
Paraguayan	1	0.01
Peruvian	25	0.30
Uruguayan	3	0.04
Venezuelan	11	0.13
Other South American	5	0.06
Other Hispanic or Latino	63	0.76

Race*	Population	%
African-American/Black (592)	671	8.12
Not Hispanic (514)	576	6.97
Hispanic (78)	95	1.15
American Indian/Alaska Native (53)	143	1.73
Not Hispanic (37)	111	1.34
Hispanic (16)	32	0.39
Apache (0)	7	0.08

*Notes: † The Census 2010 population figure is used to calculate the percentages in the Hispanic Origin and Race categories. Ancestry percentages are based on the 2006-2010 American Community Survey population (not shown); ‡ Numbers in parentheses indicate the number of people reporting a single ancestry; * Numbers in parentheses indicate the number of persons reporting this race alone, not in combination with any other race; Please refer to the Explanation of Data for more information.*

Arapaho (0)	1	0.01
Blackfeet (1)	4	0.05
Cherokee (6)	34	0.41
Chippewa (2)	3	0.04
Choctaw (0)	6	0.07
Colville (1)	1	0.01
Creek (1)	1	0.01
Delaware (0)	5	0.06
Hopi (1)	1	0.01
Iroquois (4)	4	0.05
Mexican American Ind. (0)	1	0.01
Navajo (1)	1	0.01
Seminole (1)	2	0.02
Sioux (3)	3	0.04
South American Ind. (1)	7	0.08
Asian (301)	389	4.70
Not Hispanic (297)	381	4.61
Hispanic (4)	8	0.10
Bangladeshi (4)	4	0.05
Cambodian (11)	11	0.13
Chinese, ex. Taiwanese (26)	42	0.51
Filipino (43)	80	0.97
Indian (80)	87	1.05
Indonesian (1)	1	0.01
Japanese (5)	13	0.16
Korean (5)	15	0.18
Laotian (3)	3	0.04
Pakistani (17)	18	0.22
Taiwanese (1)	1	0.01
Thai (3)	6	0.07
Vietnamese (82)	94	1.14
Hawaii Native/Pacific Islander (15)	22	0.27
Not Hispanic (13)	19	0.23
Hispanic (2)	3	0.04
Guamanian/Chamorro (8)	9	0.11
Native Hawaiian (6)	11	0.13
White (6,683)	6,929	83.81
Not Hispanic (5,382)	5,549	67.11
Hispanic (1,301)	1,380	16.69

Bloomingdale

Place Type: CDP
County: Hillsborough
Population: 22,711†

Ancestry‡	Population	%
African, Sub-Saharan (21)	160	0.73
African (0)	13	0.06
Ghanaian (0)	17	0.08
South African (21)	113	0.52
Other Sub-Saharan African (0)	17	0.08
American (1,583)	1,583	7.27
Arab (16)	49	0.22
Egyptian (16)	16	0.07
Syrian (0)	33	0.15
Austrian (0)	70	0.32
Basque (0)	18	0.08
Belgian (17)	17	0.08
British (137)	224	1.03
Canadian (37)	194	0.89
Carpatho Rusyn (31)	31	0.14
Croatian (0)	77	0.35
Czech (45)	133	0.61
Czechoslovakian (11)	29	0.13
Danish (16)	92	0.42
Dutch (28)	198	0.91
Eastern European (16)	63	0.29
English (1,024)	3,179	14.59
Estonian (42)	128	0.59
European (155)	254	1.17
Finnish (75)	75	0.34
French, ex. Basque (246)	839	3.85
French Canadian (55)	151	0.69
German (1,010)	3,626	16.64
Greek (37)	288	1.32
Hungarian (319)	422	1.94
Irish (1,003)	3,517	16.14
Italian (724)	1,981	9.09
Latvian (20)	20	0.09
Lithuanian (66)	235	1.08
Norwegian (130)	333	1.53
Polish (319)	987	4.53
Portuguese (27)	84	0.39
Romanian (37)	70	0.32
Russian (129)	243	1.12
Scotch-Irish (256)	682	3.13
Scottish (227)	642	2.95
Serbian (0)	63	0.29
Slovak (25)	91	0.42
Swedish (122)	347	1.59
Swiss (0)	12	0.06
Ukrainian (17)	65	0.30
Welsh (23)	156	0.72
West Indian, ex. Hispanic (125)	174	0.80
Bahamian (45)	45	0.21
Haitian (41)	59	0.27
Jamaican (11)	28	0.13
Trinidadian/Tobagonian (28)	42	0.19
Yugoslavian (0)	11	0.05

Hispanic Origin	Population	%
Hispanic or Latino (of any race)	2,708	11.92
Central American, ex. Mexican	160	0.70
Costa Rican	27	0.12
Guatemalan	20	0.09
Honduran	30	0.13
Nicaraguan	14	0.06
Panamanian	46	0.20
Salvadoran	23	0.10
Cuban	481	2.12
Dominican Republic	145	0.64
Mexican	327	1.44
Puerto Rican	1,001	4.41
South American	308	1.36
Argentinean	33	0.15
Bolivian	6	0.03
Chilean	25	0.11
Colombian	133	0.59
Ecuadorian	29	0.13
Paraguayan	4	0.02
Peruvian	58	0.26
Uruguayan	2	0.01
Venezuelan	15	0.07
Other South American	3	0.01
Other Hispanic or Latino	286	1.26

Race*	Population	%
African-American/Black (1,907)	2,165	9.53
Not Hispanic (1,788)	1,974	8.69
Hispanic (119)	191	0.84
American Indian/Alaska Native (83)	204	0.90
Not Hispanic (72)	181	0.80
Hispanic (11)	23	0.10
Alaska Athabascan *(Ala. Nat.)* (0)	1	<0.01
Apache (1)	1	<0.01
Blackfeet (2)	11	0.05
Cherokee (22)	69	0.30
Cheyenne (1)	1	<0.01
Chickasaw (0)	2	0.01
Chippewa (3)	9	0.04
Choctaw (5)	6	0.03
Creek (5)	8	0.04
Inupiat *(Alaska Native)* (2)	3	0.01
Iroquois (0)	4	0.02
Lumbee (2)	2	0.01
Menominee (0)	2	0.01
Mexican American Ind. (2)	2	0.01
Potawatomi (3)	3	0.01
Seminole (0)	2	0.01
Sioux (1)	3	0.01
South American Ind. (1)	1	<0.01
Spanish American Ind. (1)	1	<0.01
Asian (564)	812	3.58
Not Hispanic (554)	774	3.41
Hispanic (10)	38	0.17
Cambodian (6)	9	0.04
Chinese, ex. Taiwanese (68)	104	0.46
Filipino (103)	177	0.78
Hmong (6)	6	0.03
Indian (191)	219	0.96
Indonesian (0)	1	<0.01
Japanese (30)	91	0.40
Korean (43)	69	0.30
Malaysian (1)	5	0.02
Nepalese (1)	3	0.01
Pakistani (2)	2	0.01
Sri Lankan (3)	3	0.01
Taiwanese (1)	2	0.01
Thai (28)	34	0.15
Vietnamese (54)	74	0.33
Hawaii Native/Pacific Islander (32)	69	0.30
Not Hispanic (29)	58	0.26
Hispanic (3)	11	0.05
Fijian (7)	7	0.03
Guamanian/Chamorro (9)	10	0.04
Marshallese (1)	2	0.01
Native Hawaiian (11)	24	0.11
Samoan (2)	8	0.04
White (19,131)	19,714	86.80
Not Hispanic (17,011)	17,456	76.86
Hispanic (2,120)	2,258	9.94

Boca Raton

Place Type: City
County: Palm Beach
Population: 84,392†

Ancestry‡	Population	%
Afghan (204)	204	0.24
African, Sub-Saharan (461)	653	0.77
African (282)	464	0.55
South African (169)	179	0.21
Zimbabwean (10)	10	0.01
Albanian (14)	14	0.02
American (3,628)	3,628	4.26
Arab (430)	618	0.73
Arab (34)	34	0.04
Egyptian (136)	154	0.18
Lebanese (74)	187	0.22
Moroccan (144)	154	0.18
Syrian (34)	63	0.07
Other Arab (8)	26	0.03
Armenian (279)	379	0.45
Australian (49)	60	0.07
Austrian (392)	1,141	1.34
Belgian (48)	82	0.10
Brazilian (1,349)	1,485	1.75
British (417)	696	0.82
Bulgarian (97)	97	0.11
Cajun (0)	10	0.01
Canadian (456)	542	0.64
Carpatho Rusyn (0)	10	0.01
Croatian (53)	100	0.12
Czech (246)	533	0.63
Czechoslovakian (28)	130	0.15
Danish (162)	344	0.40
Dutch (136)	1,081	1.27
Eastern European (819)	840	0.99
English (2,448)	8,030	9.44
Estonian (9)	9	0.01
European (1,872)	2,015	2.37
Finnish (58)	174	0.20
French, ex. Basque (640)	2,655	3.12
French Canadian (225)	421	0.49
German (3,849)	12,835	15.09
Greek (593)	916	1.08
Guyanese (0)	24	0.03
Hungarian (512)	1,294	1.52
Icelander (8)	26	0.03
Iranian (193)	193	0.23
Irish (3,520)	11,003	12.93
Israeli (176)	229	0.27
Italian (5,599)	10,571	12.42
Latvian (15)	79	0.09
Lithuanian (429)	662	0.78
Maltese (16)	57	0.07
Northern European (14)	14	0.02
Norwegian (390)	1,039	1.22

SECTION TWO

*Notes: † The Census 2010 population figure is used to calculate the percentages in the Hispanic Origin and Race categories. Ancestry percentages are based on the 2006-2010 American Community Survey population (not shown); ‡ Numbers in parentheses indicate the number of people reporting a single ancestry; * Numbers in parentheses indicate the number of persons reporting this race alone, not in combination with any other race; Please refer to the Explanation of Data for more information.*

Pennsylvania German (0)	12	0.01
Polish (2,005)	5,073	5.96
Portuguese (372)	516	0.61
Romanian (364)	689	0.81
Russian (2,971)	6,136	7.21
Scandinavian (0)	101	0.12
Scotch-Irish (622)	1,311	1.54
Scottish (761)	1,928	2.27
Serbian (0)	16	0.02
Slovak (44)	202	0.24
Slovene (101)	101	0.12
Soviet Union (10)	10	0.01
Swedish (386)	959	1.13
Swiss (124)	517	0.61
Turkish (177)	277	0.33
Ukrainian (146)	467	0.55
Welsh (75)	258	0.30
West Indian, ex. Hispanic (1,735)	1,959	2.30
Bahamian (0)	11	0.01
Barbadian (19)	19	0.02
British West Indian (117)	117	0.14
Haitian (1,210)	1,265	1.49
Jamaican (330)	417	0.49
Trinidadian/Tobagonian (36)	36	0.04
U.S. Virgin Islander (0)	55	0.06
West Indian (23)	39	0.05
Yugoslavian (2)	74	0.09

Hispanic Origin	Population	%
Hispanic or Latino (of any race)	10,021	11.87
Central American, ex. Mexican	840	1.00
Costa Rican	75	0.09
Guatemalan	297	0.35
Honduran	147	0.17
Nicaraguan	118	0.14
Panamanian	79	0.09
Salvadoran	123	0.15
Other Central American	1	<0.01
Cuban	1,538	1.82
Dominican Republic	328	0.39
Mexican	1,494	1.77
Puerto Rican	1,089	1.29
South American	3,543	4.20
Argentinean	345	0.41
Bolivian	114	0.14
Chilean	145	0.17
Colombian	1,412	1.67
Ecuadorian	262	0.31
Paraguayan	18	0.02
Peruvian	587	0.70
Uruguayan	88	0.10
Venezuelan	554	0.66
Other South American	18	0.02
Other Hispanic or Latino	1,189	1.41

Race*	Population	%
African-American/Black (4,411)	4,831	5.72
Not Hispanic (4,204)	4,534	5.37
Hispanic (207)	297	0.35
American Indian/Alaska Native (157)	356	0.42
Not Hispanic (108)	251	0.30
Hispanic (49)	105	0.12
Alaska Athabascan *(Ala. Nat.)* (2)	2	<0.01
Apache (2)	7	0.01
Blackfeet (0)	11	0.01
Central American Ind. (1)	1	<0.01
Cherokee (19)	64	0.08
Chickasaw (2)	4	<0.01
Chippewa (2)	6	0.01
Choctaw (5)	9	0.01
Comanche (1)	1	<0.01
Creek (0)	5	0.01
Iroquois (3)	8	0.01
Lumbee (3)	3	<0.01
Mexican American Ind. (11)	13	0.02
Navajo (0)	3	<0.01
Osage (0)	2	<0.01
Pima (0)	1	<0.01
Potawatomi (6)	7	0.01
Seminole (2)	8	0.01
Shoshone (5)	6	0.01
Sioux (4)	5	0.01
South American Ind. (3)	21	0.02
Spanish American Ind. (6)	6	0.01
Tlingit-Haida *(Alaska Native)* (0)	1	<0.01
Asian (2,045)	2,542	3.01
Not Hispanic (2,025)	2,469	2.93
Hispanic (20)	73	0.09
Bangladeshi (70)	87	0.10
Burmese (9)	27	0.03
Cambodian (7)	12	0.01
Chinese, ex. Taiwanese (432)	542	0.64
Filipino (192)	297	0.35
Indian (601)	734	0.87
Indonesian (4)	7	0.01
Japanese (91)	151	0.18
Korean (123)	160	0.19
Laotian (4)	6	0.01
Malaysian (1)	1	<0.01
Nepalese (22)	22	0.03
Pakistani (111)	118	0.14
Sri Lankan (9)	10	0.01
Taiwanese (21)	26	0.03
Thai (56)	74	0.09
Vietnamese (139)	166	0.20
Hawaii Native/Pacific Islander (43)	101	0.12
Not Hispanic (27)	80	0.09
Hispanic (16)	21	0.02
Fijian (2)	2	<0.01
Guamanian/Chamorro (23)	29	0.03
Native Hawaiian (7)	20	0.02
Samoan (1)	5	0.01
White (74,674)	75,899	89.94
Not Hispanic (66,787)	67,608	80.11
Hispanic (7,887)	8,291	9.82

Bonita Springs

Place Type: City
County: Lee
Population: 43,914†

Ancestry‡	Population	%
African, Sub-Saharan (15)	15	0.03
African (15)	15	0.03
Albanian (62)	76	0.18
American (3,519)	3,519	8.12
Arab (245)	260	0.60
Arab (28)	28	0.06
Egyptian (162)	162	0.37
Lebanese (45)	60	0.14
Syrian (10)	10	0.02
Armenian (57)	67	0.15
Assyrian/Chaldean/Syriac (14)	14	0.03
Austrian (27)	192	0.44
Belgian (90)	153	0.35
British (306)	370	0.85
Bulgarian (0)	15	0.03
Canadian (354)	406	0.94
Croatian (17)	112	0.26
Czech (126)	293	0.68
Czechoslovakian (47)	55	0.13
Danish (70)	226	0.52
Dutch (216)	583	1.34
Eastern European (51)	51	0.12
English (2,196)	5,720	13.19
European (297)	349	0.81
Finnish (44)	67	0.15
French, ex. Basque (329)	1,456	3.36
French Canadian (230)	289	0.67
German (2,942)	7,537	17.39
Greek (100)	180	0.42
Guyanese (14)	14	0.03
Hungarian (237)	394	0.91
Icelander (0)	10	0.02
Iranian (11)	11	0.03
Irish (2,191)	5,703	13.15
Italian (1,799)	3,480	8.03
Latvian (12)	12	0.03
Lithuanian (151)	224	0.52
Luxemburger (0)	9	0.02
Macedonian (22)	22	0.05
Norwegian (186)	514	1.19
Pennsylvania German (103)	115	0.27
Polish (734)	1,819	4.20
Portuguese (208)	271	0.63
Romanian (0)	26	0.06
Russian (140)	266	0.61
Scandinavian (132)	132	0.30
Scotch-Irish (458)	975	2.25
Scottish (511)	1,631	3.76
Serbian (22)	55	0.13
Slavic (13)	26	0.06
Slovak (99)	171	0.39
Slovene (35)	79	0.18
Swedish (296)	693	1.60
Swiss (58)	138	0.32
Turkish (12)	45	0.10
Ukrainian (65)	178	0.41
Welsh (35)	373	0.86
West Indian, ex. Hispanic (11)	18	0.04
Haitian (11)	18	0.04
Yugoslavian (13)	23	0.05

Hispanic Origin	Population	%
Hispanic or Latino (of any race)	9,877	22.49
Central American, ex. Mexican	2,152	4.90
Costa Rican	47	0.11
Guatemalan	1,539	3.50
Honduran	198	0.45
Nicaraguan	94	0.21
Panamanian	1	<0.01
Salvadoran	266	0.61
Other Central American	7	0.02
Cuban	371	0.84
Dominican Republic	68	0.15
Mexican	5,846	13.31
Puerto Rican	389	0.89
South American	561	1.28
Argentinean	74	0.17
Bolivian	71	0.16
Chilean	14	0.03
Colombian	237	0.54
Ecuadorian	34	0.08
Paraguayan	2	<0.01
Peruvian	62	0.14
Uruguayan	26	0.06
Venezuelan	40	0.09
Other South American	1	<0.01
Other Hispanic or Latino	490	1.12

Race*	Population	%
African-American/Black (352)	482	1.10
Not Hispanic (289)	368	0.84
Hispanic (63)	114	0.26
American Indian/Alaska Native (227)	326	0.74
Not Hispanic (58)	118	0.27
Hispanic (169)	208	0.47
Apache (3)	3	0.01
Blackfeet (1)	4	0.01
Canadian/French Am. Ind. (0)	1	<0.01
Central American Ind. (12)	14	0.03
Cherokee (9)	29	0.07
Chippewa (3)	8	0.02
Choctaw (1)	3	0.01
Comanche (3)	5	0.01
Cree (0)	1	<0.01
Creek (11)	11	0.03
Crow (0)	1	<0.01
Delaware (0)	2	<0.01
Inupiat *(Alaska Native)* (1)	1	<0.01
Iroquois (3)	6	0.01
Lumbee (1)	1	<0.01
Mexican American Ind. (63)	69	0.16
Navajo (4)	4	0.01
Ottawa (2)	2	<0.01
Pueblo (0)	3	0.01
Seminole (2)	3	0.01
Sioux (1)	1	<0.01
South American Ind. (2)	2	<0.01

*Notes: † The Census 2010 population figure is used to calculate the percentages in the Hispanic Origin and Race categories. Ancestry percentages are based on the 2006-2010 American Community Survey population (not shown); ‡ Numbers in parentheses indicate the number of people reporting a single ancestry; * Numbers in parentheses indicate the number of persons reporting this race alone, not in combination with any other race; Please refer to the Explanation of Data for more information.*

Spanish American Ind. (2)	10	0.02
Asian (449)	548	1.25
Not Hispanic (433)	512	1.17
Hispanic (16)	36	0.08
Bangladeshi (4)	6	0.01
Burmese (3)	3	0.01
Cambodian (2)	2	<0.01
Chinese, ex. Taiwanese (87)	96	0.22
Filipino (71)	95	0.22
Indian (98)	130	0.30
Indonesian (2)	2	<0.01
Japanese (11)	18	0.04
Korean (17)	23	0.05
Malaysian (1)	1	<0.01
Pakistani (16)	19	0.04
Taiwanese (1)	1	<0.01
Thai (12)	13	0.03
Vietnamese (110)	117	0.27
Hawaii Native/Pacific Islander (62)	91	0.21
Not Hispanic (14)	29	0.07
Hispanic (48)	62	0.14
Guamanian/Chamorro (49)	52	0.12
Native Hawaiian (2)	11	0.03
Samoan (1)	2	<0.01
White (38,995)	39,524	90.00
Not Hispanic (32,980)	33,182	75.56
Hispanic (6,015)	6,342	14.44

Boynton Beach

Place Type: City
County: Palm Beach
Population: 68,217†

Ancestry‡	Population	%
African, Sub-Saharan (209)	276	0.41
African (143)	210	0.31
Ethiopian (10)	10	0.01
South African (56)	56	0.08
American (3,218)	3,218	4.76
Arab (20)	44	0.07
Lebanese (20)	44	0.07
Armenian (9)	29	0.04
Australian (52)	87	0.13
Austrian (219)	497	0.74
Belgian (36)	58	0.09
Brazilian (175)	276	0.41
British (32)	110	0.16
Bulgarian (0)	12	0.02
Canadian (233)	312	0.46
Celtic (0)	12	0.02
Croatian (45)	114	0.17
Czech (183)	364	0.54
Czechoslovakian (41)	41	0.06
Danish (114)	177	0.26
Dutch (353)	862	1.28
Eastern European (160)	175	0.26
English (1,676)	4,780	7.07
Estonian (18)	18	0.03
European (319)	351	0.52
Finnish (22)	91	0.13
French, ex. Basque (285)	1,547	2.29
French Canadian (211)	381	0.56
German (1,998)	6,022	8.91
Greek (311)	426	0.63
Guyanese (0)	11	0.02
Hungarian (299)	521	0.77
Irish (2,732)	6,531	9.66
Israeli (0)	23	0.03
Italian (3,622)	6,465	9.57
Latvian (26)	26	0.04
Lithuanian (135)	197	0.29
Macedonian (44)	44	0.07
New Zealander (0)	9	0.01
Norwegian (196)	363	0.54
Pennsylvania German (71)	101	0.15
Polish (1,190)	2,869	4.25
Portuguese (147)	260	0.38
Romanian (101)	166	0.25
Russian (1,198)	2,162	3.20
Scandinavian (75)	85	0.13
Scotch-Irish (270)	725	1.07
Scottish (275)	950	1.41
Serbian (85)	146	0.22
Slovak (0)	39	0.06
Slovene (8)	8	0.01
Swedish (148)	553	0.82
Swiss (19)	87	0.13
Turkish (20)	30	0.04
Ukrainian (127)	177	0.26
Welsh (109)	400	0.59
West Indian, ex. Hispanic (10,668)	10,890	16.11
Bahamian (228)	228	0.34
Barbadian (102)	102	0.15
British West Indian (35)	35	0.05
Haitian (8,873)	8,900	13.17
Jamaican (1,202)	1,347	1.99
Trinidadian/Tobagonian (120)	153	0.23
U.S. Virgin Islander (8)	8	0.01
West Indian (100)	117	0.17
Yugoslavian (0)	26	0.04

Hispanic Origin	Population	%
Hispanic or Latino (of any race)	8,702	12.76
Central American, ex. Mexican	1,208	1.77
Costa Rican	92	0.13
Guatemalan	408	0.60
Honduran	168	0.25
Nicaraguan	133	0.19
Panamanian	43	0.06
Salvadoran	359	0.53
Other Central American	5	0.01
Cuban	899	1.32
Dominican Republic	425	0.62
Mexican	1,555	2.28
Puerto Rican	2,137	3.13
South American	1,852	2.71
Argentinean	142	0.21
Bolivian	33	0.05
Chilean	65	0.10
Colombian	773	1.13
Ecuadorian	201	0.29
Paraguayan	16	0.02
Peruvian	312	0.46
Uruguayan	93	0.14
Venezuelan	208	0.30
Other South American	9	0.01
Other Hispanic or Latino	626	0.92

Race*	Population	%
African-American/Black (20,646)	21,424	31.41
Not Hispanic (20,218)	20,865	30.59
Hispanic (428)	559	0.82
American Indian/Alaska Native (196)	412	0.60
Not Hispanic (100)	264	0.39
Hispanic (96)	148	0.22
Apache (3)	4	0.01
Blackfeet (0)	6	0.01
Canadian/French Am. Ind. (0)	1	<0.01
Central American Ind. (4)	6	0.01
Cherokee (13)	63	0.09
Chippewa (5)	5	0.01
Choctaw (0)	3	<0.01
Creek (2)	6	0.01
Iroquois (4)	10	0.01
Kiowa (1)	1	<0.01
Lumbee (1)	1	<0.01
Menominee (1)	1	<0.01
Mexican American Ind. (61)	74	0.11
Navajo (2)	5	0.01
Pima (1)	1	<0.01
Potawatomi (1)	1	<0.01
Pueblo (1)	1	<0.01
Sioux (1)	3	<0.01
South American Ind. (12)	20	0.03
Spanish American Ind. (0)	5	0.01
Tlingit-Haida *(Alaska Native)* (0)	2	<0.01
Yuman (3)	3	<0.01
Yup'ik *(Alaska Native)* (1)	1	<0.01
Asian (1,473)	1,851	2.71
Not Hispanic (1,438)	1,773	2.60
Hispanic (35)	78	0.11
Bangladeshi (93)	107	0.16
Burmese (7)	9	0.01
Cambodian (6)	6	0.01
Chinese, ex. Taiwanese (239)	317	0.46
Filipino (222)	293	0.43
Indian (488)	595	0.87
Indonesian (18)	19	0.03
Japanese (30)	47	0.07
Korean (57)	77	0.11
Laotian (8)	9	0.01
Malaysian (2)	3	<0.01
Nepalese (7)	7	0.01
Pakistani (19)	22	0.03
Sri Lankan (2)	2	<0.01
Taiwanese (13)	14	0.02
Thai (54)	78	0.11
Vietnamese (147)	168	0.25
Hawaii Native/Pacific Islander (26)	182	0.27
Not Hispanic (21)	162	0.24
Hispanic (5)	20	0.03
Guamanian/Chamorro (7)	13	0.02
Native Hawaiian (3)	18	0.03
Samoan (6)	7	0.01
White (42,599)	43,662	64.00
Not Hispanic (36,534)	37,229	54.57
Hispanic (6,065)	6,433	9.43

Bradenton

Place Type: City
County: Manatee
Population: 49,546†

Ancestry‡	Population	%
African, Sub-Saharan (67)	111	0.22
African (20)	64	0.13
Ghanaian (37)	37	0.07
Kenyan (10)	10	0.02
American (2,188)	2,188	4.33
Arab (12)	53	0.10
Lebanese (12)	24	0.05
Syrian (0)	21	0.04
Other Arab (0)	8	0.02
Armenian (14)	14	0.03
Austrian (33)	173	0.34
Belgian (40)	121	0.24
Brazilian (11)	23	0.05
British (134)	232	0.46
Canadian (158)	232	0.46
Celtic (9)	25	0.05
Croatian (56)	182	0.36
Czech (14)	111	0.22
Czechoslovakian (0)	77	0.15
Danish (46)	177	0.35
Dutch (558)	1,444	2.86
Eastern European (11)	23	0.05
English (2,302)	6,430	12.72
Estonian (33)	33	0.07
European (125)	188	0.37
Finnish (16)	96	0.19
French, ex. Basque (412)	1,918	3.80
French Canadian (296)	463	0.92
German (3,313)	8,771	17.36
Greek (67)	108	0.21
Hungarian (106)	224	0.44
Icelander (0)	29	0.06
Iranian (11)	11	0.02
Irish (1,822)	6,045	11.96
Italian (1,902)	3,512	6.95
Lithuanian (59)	214	0.42
Macedonian (32)	32	0.06
Maltese (13)	13	0.03
Northern European (3)	3	0.01
Norwegian (39)	267	0.53
Pennsylvania German (13)	42	0.08
Polish (486)	1,315	2.60
Portuguese (61)	61	0.12
Romanian (16)	26	0.05

*Notes: † The Census 2010 population figure is used to calculate the percentages in the Hispanic Origin and Race categories. Ancestry percentages are based on the 2006-2010 American Community Survey population (not shown); ‡ Numbers in parentheses indicate the number of people reporting a single ancestry; * Numbers in parentheses indicate the number of persons reporting this race alone, not in combination with any other race; Please refer to the Explanation of Data for more information.*

Russian (204)	397	0.79
Scandinavian (68)	93	0.18
Scotch-Irish (343)	745	1.47
Scottish (343)	1,115	2.21
Serbian (12)	12	0.02
Slavic (12)	12	0.02
Slovak (95)	129	0.26
Swedish (82)	627	1.24
Swiss (60)	164	0.32
Ukrainian (80)	151	0.30
Welsh (241)	660	1.31
West Indian, ex. Hispanic (855)	1,111	2.20
Bahamian (53)	53	0.10
Barbadian (21)	71	0.14
British West Indian (66)	159	0.31
Dutch West Indian (24)	24	0.05
Haitian (393)	401	0.79
Jamaican (130)	142	0.28
Trinidadian/Tobagonian (25)	118	0.23
West Indian (143)	143	0.28
Yugoslavian (71)	71	0.14

Hispanic Origin	Population	%
Hispanic or Latino (of any race)	8,424	17.00
Central American, ex. Mexican	703	1.42
Costa Rican	22	0.04
Guatemalan	165	0.33
Honduran	320	0.65
Nicaraguan	56	0.11
Panamanian	21	0.04
Salvadoran	116	0.23
Other Central American	3	0.01
Cuban	346	0.70
Dominican Republic	85	0.17
Mexican	5,148	10.39
Puerto Rican	1,085	2.19
South American	526	1.06
Argentinean	40	0.08
Bolivian	14	0.03
Chilean	20	0.04
Colombian	209	0.42
Ecuadorian	57	0.12
Paraguayan	4	0.01
Peruvian	96	0.19
Uruguayan	20	0.04
Venezuelan	65	0.13
Other South American	1	<0.01
Other Hispanic or Latino	531	1.07

Race*	Population	%
African-American/Black (7,888)	8,490	17.14
Not Hispanic (7,693)	8,167	16.48
Hispanic (195)	323	0.65
American Indian/Alaska Native (161)	428	0.86
Not Hispanic (84)	292	0.59
Hispanic (77)	136	0.27
Apache (7)	7	0.01
Blackfeet (3)	13	0.03
Canadian/French Am. Ind. (0)	1	<0.01
Central American Ind. (9)	13	0.03
Cherokee (11)	78	0.16
Cheyenne (1)	3	0.01
Chippewa (1)	3	0.01
Choctaw (1)	10	0.02
Comanche (1)	1	<0.01
Cree (0)	3	0.01
Creek (0)	9	0.02
Delaware (1)	1	<0.01
Iroquois (4)	11	0.02
Kiowa (2)	2	<0.01
Lumbee (2)	2	<0.01
Mexican American Ind. (21)	24	0.05
Navajo (3)	5	0.01
Ottawa (0)	1	<0.01
Potawatomi (2)	2	<0.01
Pueblo (3)	3	0.01
Seminole (1)	14	0.03
Shoshone (1)	1	<0.01
Sioux (3)	7	0.01
South American Ind. (1)	3	0.01
Spanish American Ind. (1)	2	<0.01
Asian (539)	714	1.44
Not Hispanic (523)	667	1.35
Hispanic (16)	47	0.09
Bangladeshi (3)	7	0.01
Burmese (4)	6	0.01
Cambodian (18)	26	0.05
Chinese, ex. Taiwanese (122)	148	0.30
Filipino (111)	162	0.33
Indian (94)	116	0.23
Indonesian (0)	2	<0.01
Japanese (22)	45	0.09
Korean (31)	56	0.11
Laotian (9)	11	0.02
Nepalese (4)	4	0.01
Pakistani (5)	6	0.01
Taiwanese (1)	2	<0.01
Thai (20)	26	0.05
Vietnamese (60)	70	0.14
Hawaii Native/Pacific Islander (34)	71	0.14
Not Hispanic (30)	56	0.11
Hispanic (4)	15	0.03
Guamanian/Chamorro (11)	17	0.03
Native Hawaiian (0)	5	0.01
Samoan (3)	3	0.01
Tongan (18)	25	0.05
White (36,297)	37,328	75.34
Not Hispanic (31,918)	32,615	65.83
Hispanic (4,379)	4,713	9.51

Brandon

Place Type: CDP
County: Hillsborough
Population: 103,483[†]

Ancestry[‡]	Population	%
African, Sub-Saharan (956)	1,247	1.25
African (482)	729	0.73
Cape Verdean (11)	11	0.01
Ethiopian (191)	191	0.19
Ghanaian (37)	37	0.04
Liberian (0)	34	0.03
Nigerian (214)	214	0.21
South African (21)	31	0.03
American (6,980)	6,980	7.01
Arab (152)	291	0.29
Arab (53)	69	0.07
Egyptian (15)	15	0.02
Lebanese (53)	137	0.14
Syrian (0)	39	0.04
Other Arab (31)	31	0.03
Armenian (22)	22	0.02
Austrian (30)	264	0.27
Basque (29)	29	0.03
Belgian (22)	68	0.07
Brazilian (337)	337	0.34
British (286)	516	0.52
Cajun (65)	65	0.07
Canadian (177)	267	0.27
Croatian (9)	76	0.08
Czech (83)	433	0.43
Czechoslovakian (0)	18	0.02
Danish (85)	207	0.21
Dutch (187)	1,140	1.14
English (3,053)	9,544	9.58
European (807)	1,082	1.09
Finnish (27)	57	0.06
French, ex. Basque (587)	2,836	2.85
French Canadian (451)	865	0.87
German (4,061)	14,003	14.06
Greek (512)	912	0.92
Guyanese (124)	186	0.19
Hungarian (268)	624	0.63
Icelander (0)	104	0.10
Iranian (24)	24	0.02
Irish (3,389)	12,080	12.13
Israeli (10)	25	0.03
Italian (2,830)	8,022	8.05
Latvian (25)	25	0.03
Lithuanian (148)	247	0.25
Northern European (14)	21	0.02
Norwegian (158)	528	0.53
Pennsylvania German (27)	27	0.03
Polish (811)	2,432	2.44
Portuguese (164)	744	0.75
Romanian (15)	49	0.05
Russian (220)	657	0.66
Scandinavian (21)	56	0.06
Scotch-Irish (877)	2,069	2.08
Scottish (838)	2,493	2.50
Serbian (17)	22	0.02
Slavic (19)	38	0.04
Slovak (139)	198	0.20
Slovene (28)	50	0.05
Swedish (100)	909	0.91
Swiss (32)	204	0.20
Turkish (74)	113	0.11
Ukrainian (150)	361	0.36
Welsh (94)	504	0.51
West Indian, ex. Hispanic (1,892)	2,144	2.15
Bahamian (37)	70	0.07
Barbadian (8)	8	0.01
Bermudan (0)	16	0.02
British West Indian (60)	89	0.09
Dutch West Indian (12)	12	0.01
Haitian (331)	331	0.33
Jamaican (1,064)	1,222	1.23
Trinidadian/Tobagonian (48)	64	0.06
U.S. Virgin Islander (188)	188	0.19
West Indian (133)	133	0.13
Other West Indian (11)	11	0.01
Yugoslavian (12)	103	0.10

Hispanic Origin	Population	%
Hispanic or Latino (of any race)	21,687	20.96
Central American, ex. Mexican	1,388	1.34
Costa Rican	128	0.12
Guatemalan	227	0.22
Honduran	352	0.34
Nicaraguan	185	0.18
Panamanian	294	0.28
Salvadoran	187	0.18
Other Central American	15	0.01
Cuban	2,690	2.60
Dominican Republic	1,335	1.29
Mexican	2,413	2.33
Puerto Rican	9,574	9.25
South American	2,194	2.12
Argentinean	105	0.10
Bolivian	18	0.02
Chilean	73	0.07
Colombian	1,139	1.10
Ecuadorian	233	0.23
Paraguayan	3	<0.01
Peruvian	357	0.34
Uruguayan	63	0.06
Venezuelan	191	0.18
Other South American	12	0.01
Other Hispanic or Latino	2,093	2.02

Race*	Population	%
African-American/Black (16,648)	18,420	17.80
Not Hispanic (15,515)	16,736	16.17
Hispanic (1,133)	1,684	1.63
American Indian/Alaska Native (412)	1,051	1.02
Not Hispanic (294)	752	0.73
Hispanic (118)	299	0.29
Alaska Athabascan *(Ala. Nat.)* (2)	2	<0.01
Apache (3)	14	0.01
Arapaho (0)	2	<0.01
Blackfeet (1)	23	0.02
Canadian/French Am. Ind. (1)	2	<0.01
Central American Ind. (7)	15	0.01
Cherokee (63)	230	0.22
Cheyenne (0)	2	<0.01
Chickasaw (2)	3	<0.01
Chippewa (10)	12	0.01
Choctaw (19)	24	0.02
Comanche (0)	1	<0.01

*Notes: † The Census 2010 population figure is used to calculate the percentages in the Hispanic Origin and Race categories. Ancestry percentages are based on the 2006-2010 American Community Survey population (not shown); ‡ Numbers in parentheses indicate the number of people reporting a single ancestry; * Numbers in parentheses indicate the number of persons reporting this race alone, not in combination with any other race; Please refer to the Explanation of Data for more information.*

Cree (0)	2	<0.01
Creek (11)	32	0.03
Delaware (5)	6	0.01
Inupiat *(Alaska Native)* (5)	6	0.01
Iroquois (13)	16	0.02
Kiowa (1)	1	<0.01
Lumbee (11)	14	0.01
Menominee (1)	1	<0.01
Mexican American Ind. (5)	14	0.01
Navajo (4)	9	0.01
Osage (2)	2	<0.01
Potawatomi (6)	9	0.01
Pueblo (2)	2	<0.01
Seminole (42)	57	0.06
Shoshone (1)	1	<0.01
Sioux (3)	9	0.01
South American Ind. (12)	46	0.04
Spanish American Ind. (8)	10	0.01
Yup'ik *(Alaska Native)* (0)	1	<0.01
Asian (3,585)	4,584	4.43
Not Hispanic (3,502)	4,338	4.19
Hispanic (83)	246	0.24
Bangladeshi (10)	11	0.01
Burmese (4)	4	<0.01
Cambodian (11)	17	0.02
Chinese, ex. Taiwanese (299)	409	0.40
Filipino (663)	934	0.90
Hmong (12)	12	0.01
Indian (1,535)	1,692	1.64
Indonesian (33)	44	0.04
Japanese (89)	246	0.24
Korean (277)	407	0.39
Laotian (11)	25	0.02
Malaysian (7)	7	0.01
Nepalese (1)	1	<0.01
Pakistani (41)	45	0.04
Sri Lankan (8)	8	0.01
Taiwanese (18)	21	0.02
Thai (137)	211	0.20
Vietnamese (320)	396	0.38
Hawaii Native/Pacific Islander (99)	263	0.25
Not Hispanic (86)	209	0.20
Hispanic (13)	54	0.05
Fijian (1)	4	<0.01
Guamanian/Chamorro (21)	34	0.03
Native Hawaiian (35)	75	0.07
Samoan (13)	21	0.02
Tongan (0)	1	<0.01
White (74,504)	77,459	74.85
Not Hispanic (59,871)	61,711	59.63
Hispanic (14,633)	15,748	15.22

Brent

Place Type: CDP
County: Escambia
Population: 21,804†

Ancestry‡	Population	%
African, Sub-Saharan (189)	203	0.86
African (189)	203	0.86
American (1,131)	1,131	4.79
Arab (9)	31	0.13
Arab (9)	22	0.09
Lebanese (0)	9	0.04
British (72)	165	0.70
Canadian (51)	91	0.39
Celtic (0)	23	0.10
Czech (24)	120	0.51
Danish (0)	15	0.06
Dutch (71)	318	1.35
English (473)	1,507	6.38
European (102)	148	0.63
Finnish (0)	26	0.11
French, ex. Basque (155)	522	2.21
French Canadian (13)	109	0.46
German (921)	2,563	10.85
Greek (74)	103	0.44
Guyanese (0)	14	0.06
Hungarian (15)	15	0.06
Irish (508)	1,902	8.05
Italian (232)	558	2.36
Norwegian (34)	78	0.33
Polish (161)	443	1.88
Portuguese (7)	7	0.03
Russian (15)	42	0.18
Scandinavian (14)	37	0.16
Scotch-Irish (314)	522	2.21
Scottish (217)	520	2.20
Slovak (0)	20	0.08
Slovene (0)	27	0.11
Swedish (27)	56	0.24
Swiss (9)	22	0.09
Ukrainian (9)	53	0.22
Welsh (11)	116	0.49
West Indian, ex. Hispanic (477)	614	2.60
Bahamian (77)	118	0.50
Barbadian (30)	30	0.13
Haitian (320)	320	1.35
Jamaican (50)	146	0.62
Yugoslavian (0)	27	0.11

Hispanic Origin	Population	%
Hispanic or Latino (of any race)	910	4.17
Central American, ex. Mexican	125	0.57
Costa Rican	4	0.02
Guatemalan	24	0.11
Honduran	58	0.27
Nicaraguan	10	0.05
Panamanian	20	0.09
Salvadoran	9	0.04
Cuban	36	0.17
Dominican Republic	9	0.04
Mexican	351	1.61
Puerto Rican	191	0.88
South American	74	0.34
Argentinean	1	<0.01
Chilean	6	0.03
Colombian	13	0.06
Ecuadorian	10	0.05
Paraguayan	1	<0.01
Peruvian	35	0.16
Uruguayan	4	0.02
Venezuelan	4	0.02
Other Hispanic or Latino	124	0.57

Race*	Population	%
African-American/Black (8,523)	8,878	40.72
Not Hispanic (8,440)	8,747	40.12
Hispanic (83)	131	0.60
American Indian/Alaska Native (171)	413	1.89
Not Hispanic (144)	372	1.71
Hispanic (27)	41	0.19
Alaska Athabascan *(Ala. Nat.)* (2)	4	0.02
Apache (1)	5	0.02
Blackfeet (1)	3	0.01
Canadian/French Am. Ind. (0)	3	0.01
Cherokee (30)	88	0.40
Cheyenne (0)	1	<0.01
Chippewa (1)	2	0.01
Choctaw (2)	6	0.03
Colville (1)	1	<0.01
Creek (42)	63	0.29
Houma (1)	1	<0.01
Inupiat *(Alaska Native)* (1)	5	0.02
Iroquois (5)	5	0.02
Mexican American Ind. (6)	12	0.06
Navajo (7)	8	0.04
Pima (0)	2	0.01
Potawatomi (0)	2	0.01
Pueblo (0)	2	0.01
Puget Sound Salish (0)	1	<0.01
Seminole (0)	1	<0.01
Sioux (6)	11	0.05
South American Ind. (1)	2	0.01
Yup'ik *(Alaska Native)* (0)	1	<0.01
Asian (823)	1,038	4.76
Not Hispanic (810)	999	4.58
Hispanic (13)	39	0.18
Bangladeshi (6)	7	0.03
Cambodian (18)	24	0.11
Chinese, ex. Taiwanese (78)	131	0.60
Filipino (221)	315	1.44
Hmong (4)	5	0.02
Indian (41)	58	0.27
Indonesian (84)	101	0.46
Japanese (27)	49	0.22
Korean (105)	131	0.60
Laotian (7)	9	0.04
Malaysian (1)	2	0.01
Nepalese (1)	1	<0.01
Pakistani (11)	11	0.05
Sri Lankan (0)	1	<0.01
Thai (7)	13	0.06
Vietnamese (174)	196	0.90
Hawaii Native/Pacific Islander (60)	112	0.51
Not Hispanic (60)	110	0.50
Hispanic (0)	2	0.01
Guamanian/Chamorro (10)	22	0.10
Marshallese (1)	1	<0.01
Native Hawaiian (6)	16	0.07
Samoan (7)	9	0.04
Tongan (13)	15	0.07
White (11,272)	11,803	54.13
Not Hispanic (10,810)	11,271	51.69
Hispanic (462)	532	2.44

Brooksville

Place Type: City
County: Hernando
Population: 7,719†

Ancestry‡	Population	%
African, Sub-Saharan (23)	23	0.29
African (23)	23	0.29
American (300)	300	3.81
Arab (20)	59	0.75
Arab (20)	20	0.25
Other Arab (0)	39	0.49
Austrian (0)	50	0.63
Brazilian (99)	99	1.26
British (0)	6	0.08
Canadian (7)	17	0.22
Czech (12)	21	0.27
Czechoslovakian (6)	6	0.08
Danish (8)	33	0.42
Dutch (0)	86	1.09
English (299)	943	11.96
European (8)	8	0.10
Finnish (7)	7	0.09
French, ex. Basque (97)	433	5.49
French Canadian (61)	78	0.99
German (262)	1,068	13.55
Greek (37)	37	0.47
Hungarian (7)	24	0.30
Irish (527)	1,436	18.21
Italian (251)	612	7.76
Lithuanian (0)	72	0.91
Maltese (0)	11	0.14
Norwegian (17)	23	0.29
Pennsylvania German (0)	32	0.41
Polish (128)	379	4.81
Portuguese (20)	59	0.75
Russian (0)	7	0.09
Scandinavian (0)	8	0.10
Scotch-Irish (67)	109	1.38
Scottish (42)	190	2.41
Slovak (0)	9	0.11
Swedish (8)	76	0.96
Ukrainian (25)	83	1.05
Welsh (29)	70	0.89
West Indian, ex. Hispanic (35)	35	0.44
Haitian (10)	10	0.13
Jamaican (25)	25	0.32

Hispanic Origin	Population	%
Hispanic or Latino (of any race)	509	6.59
Central American, ex. Mexican	28	0.36
Guatemalan	12	0.16

*Notes: † The Census 2010 population figure is used to calculate the percentages in the Hispanic Origin and Race categories. Ancestry percentages are based on the 2006-2010 American Community Survey population (not shown); ‡ Numbers in parentheses indicate the number of people reporting a single ancestry; * Numbers in parentheses indicate the number of persons reporting this race alone, not in combination with any other race; Please refer to the Explanation of Data for more information.*

SECTION TWO

Honduran	6	0.08
Panamanian	4	0.05
Salvadoran	6	0.08
Cuban	55	0.71
Dominican Republic	5	0.06
Mexican	123	1.59
Puerto Rican	226	2.93
South American	12	0.16
Argentinean	1	0.01
Colombian	6	0.08
Ecuadorian	2	0.03
Peruvian	3	0.04
Other Hispanic or Latino	60	0.78

Race*	Population	%
African-American/Black (1,386)	1,477	19.13
Not Hispanic (1,374)	1,444	18.71
Hispanic (12)	33	0.43
American Indian/Alaska Native (30)	75	0.97
Not Hispanic (28)	69	0.89
Hispanic (2)	6	0.08
Canadian/French Am. Ind. (3)	4	0.05
Cherokee (5)	14	0.18
Chickasaw (0)	4	0.05
Iroquois (0)	1	0.01
Yakama (0)	1	0.01
Asian (71)	90	1.17
Not Hispanic (71)	87	1.13
Hispanic (0)	3	0.04
Bangladeshi (12)	13	0.17
Chinese, ex. Taiwanese (11)	15	0.19
Filipino (10)	14	0.18
Indian (21)	23	0.30
Japanese (4)	10	0.13
Korean (2)	5	0.06
Laotian (1)	2	0.03
Pakistani (6)	6	0.08
Vietnamese (0)	2	0.03
Hawaii Native/Pacific Islander (6)	14	0.18
Not Hispanic (5)	7	0.09
Hispanic (1)	7	0.09
Native Hawaiian (2)	3	0.04
White (5,939)	6,075	78.70
Not Hispanic (5,609)	5,713	74.01
Hispanic (330)	362	4.69

Brownsville

Place Type: CDP
County: Miami-Dade
Population: 15,313†

Ancestry‡	Population	%
African, Sub-Saharan (175)	175	1.34
African (158)	158	1.21
Ghanaian (17)	17	0.13
American (237)	237	1.82
Dutch (0)	9	0.07
English (8)	46	0.35
French, ex. Basque (0)	74	0.57
German (0)	9	0.07
Guyanese (0)	9	0.07
Scotch-Irish (0)	9	0.07
Scottish (13)	13	0.10
Ukrainian (0)	9	0.07
Welsh (0)	27	0.21
West Indian, ex. Hispanic (566)	601	4.61
Bahamian (32)	47	0.36
British West Indian (38)	58	0.44
Haitian (356)	356	2.73
Jamaican (140)	140	1.07

Hispanic Origin	Population	%
Hispanic or Latino (of any race)	3,939	25.72
Central American, ex. Mexican	1,465	9.57
Costa Rican	12	0.08
Guatemalan	57	0.37
Honduran	423	2.76
Nicaraguan	867	5.66
Panamanian	30	0.20
Salvadoran	68	0.44
Other Central American	8	0.05
Cuban	1,268	8.28
Dominican Republic	278	1.82
Mexican	75	0.49
Puerto Rican	313	2.04
South American	200	1.31
Argentinean	29	0.19
Chilean	8	0.05
Colombian	75	0.49
Ecuadorian	19	0.12
Peruvian	36	0.24
Uruguayan	4	0.03
Venezuelan	29	0.19
Other Hispanic or Latino	340	2.22

Race*	Population	%
African-American/Black (11,445)	11,601	75.76
Not Hispanic (11,081)	11,156	72.85
Hispanic (364)	445	2.91
American Indian/Alaska Native (45)	107	0.70
Not Hispanic (13)	42	0.27
Hispanic (32)	65	0.42
Alaska Athabascan *(Ala. Nat.)* (1)	1	0.01
Blackfeet (1)	2	0.01
Central American Ind. (3)	3	0.02
Cherokee (0)	10	0.07
Creek (0)	1	0.01
Pueblo (0)	1	0.01
South American Ind. (7)	8	0.05
Spanish American Ind. (0)	1	0.01
Asian (7)	37	0.24
Not Hispanic (7)	31	0.20
Hispanic (0)	6	0.04
Chinese, ex. Taiwanese (0)	2	0.01
Indian (4)	18	0.12
Japanese (0)	2	0.01
Korean (0)	1	0.01
Vietnamese (0)	1	0.01
Hawaii Native/Pacific Islander (0)	17	0.11
Not Hispanic (0)	11	0.07
Hispanic (0)	6	0.04
Guamanian/Chamorro (0)	1	0.01
Native Hawaiian (0)	2	0.01
Samoan (0)	2	0.01
White (3,038)	3,203	20.92
Not Hispanic (181)	203	1.33
Hispanic (2,857)	3,000	19.59

Buenaventura Lakes

Place Type: CDP
County: Osceola
Population: 26,079†

Ancestry‡	Population	%
African, Sub-Saharan (87)	129	0.48
African (87)	105	0.39
Cape Verdean (0)	24	0.09
American (1,025)	1,025	3.82
Arab (210)	238	0.89
Moroccan (210)	238	0.89
Armenian (0)	12	0.04
Brazilian (166)	166	0.62
Canadian (0)	12	0.04
Czech (0)	12	0.04
Czechoslovakian (15)	15	0.06
Dutch (0)	84	0.31
English (248)	523	1.95
European (42)	60	0.22
French, ex. Basque (12)	231	0.86
French Canadian (35)	35	0.13
German (686)	972	3.62
Greek (35)	48	0.18
Guyanese (19)	42	0.16
Hungarian (0)	18	0.07
Irish (102)	354	1.32
Italian (186)	362	1.35
Lithuanian (11)	35	0.13
Norwegian (13)	63	0.23
Polish (24)	98	0.37
Portuguese (19)	99	0.37
Russian (0)	67	0.25
Scotch-Irish (60)	74	0.28
Scottish (56)	95	0.35
Slovak (0)	16	0.06
Slovene (0)	10	0.04
Swedish (273)	315	1.17
Turkish (67)	67	0.25
Ukrainian (10)	10	0.04
Welsh (0)	13	0.05
West Indian, ex. Hispanic (1,129)	1,219	4.54
British West Indian (85)	97	0.36
Haitian (361)	416	1.55
Jamaican (622)	622	2.32
Trinidadian/Tobagonian (61)	84	0.31

Hispanic Origin	Population	%
Hispanic or Latino (of any race)	18,160	69.63
Central American, ex. Mexican	731	2.80
Costa Rican	45	0.17
Guatemalan	90	0.35
Honduran	143	0.55
Nicaraguan	143	0.55
Panamanian	66	0.25
Salvadoran	239	0.92
Other Central American	5	0.02
Cuban	799	3.06
Dominican Republic	1,687	6.47
Mexican	585	2.24
Puerto Rican	11,618	44.55
South American	2,108	8.08
Argentinean	154	0.59
Bolivian	18	0.07
Chilean	29	0.11
Colombian	1,198	4.59
Ecuadorian	246	0.94
Paraguayan	2	0.01
Peruvian	234	0.90
Uruguayan	33	0.13
Venezuelan	177	0.68
Other South American	17	0.07
Other Hispanic or Latino	632	2.42

Race*	Population	%
African-American/Black (3,697)	4,255	16.32
Not Hispanic (2,750)	2,983	11.44
Hispanic (947)	1,272	4.88
American Indian/Alaska Native (145)	258	0.99
Not Hispanic (27)	76	0.29
Hispanic (118)	182	0.70
Apache (1)	1	<0.01
Blackfeet (2)	8	0.03
Canadian/French Am. Ind. (16)	16	0.06
Central American Ind. (7)	17	0.07
Cherokee (4)	18	0.07
Creek (0)	4	0.02
Iroquois (1)	2	0.01
Mexican American Ind. (13)	13	0.05
South American Ind. (6)	13	0.05
Spanish American Ind. (3)	4	0.02
Asian (670)	863	3.31
Not Hispanic (632)	758	2.91
Hispanic (38)	105	0.40
Bangladeshi (4)	4	0.02
Burmese (3)	3	0.01
Cambodian (0)	2	0.01
Chinese, ex. Taiwanese (45)	79	0.30
Filipino (255)	303	1.16
Indian (265)	318	1.22
Indonesian (2)	3	0.01
Japanese (18)	31	0.12
Korean (4)	6	0.02
Laotian (4)	4	0.02
Malaysian (0)	2	0.01
Pakistani (16)	22	0.08
Taiwanese (3)	5	0.02
Thai (11)	11	0.04
Vietnamese (21)	30	0.12
Hawaii Native/Pacific Islander (31)	119	0.46

*Notes: † The Census 2010 population figure is used to calculate the percentages in the Hispanic Origin and Race categories. Ancestry percentages are based on the 2006-2010 American Community Survey population (not shown); ‡ Numbers in parentheses indicate the number of people reporting a single ancestry; * Numbers in parentheses indicate the number of persons reporting this race alone, not in combination with any other race; Please refer to the Explanation of Data for more information.*

Not Hispanic (25)	61	0.23
Hispanic (6)	58	0.22
Guamanian/Chamorro (7)	7	0.03
Marshallese (2)	4	0.02
Native Hawaiian (6)	24	0.09
Samoan (3)	5	0.02
Tongan (6)	6	0.02
White (15,948)	16,888	64.76
Not Hispanic (3,947)	4,174	16.01
Hispanic (12,001)	12,714	48.75

Callaway

Place Type: City
County: Bay
Population: 14,405†

Ancestry‡	Population	%
African, Sub-Saharan (96)	96	0.66
African (96)	96	0.66
American (2,110)	2,110	14.50
Arab (12)	12	0.08
Egyptian (12)	12	0.08
Austrian (0)	17	0.12
British (59)	140	0.96
Czech (17)	26	0.18
Czechoslovakian (0)	27	0.19
Danish (0)	5	0.03
Dutch (0)	193	1.33
English (552)	1,428	9.81
European (69)	69	0.47
Finnish (8)	33	0.23
French, ex. Basque (121)	469	3.22
French Canadian (95)	176	1.21
German (666)	1,787	12.28
Hungarian (46)	55	0.38
Iranian (15)	15	0.10
Irish (517)	1,402	9.63
Italian (205)	324	2.23
Lithuanian (0)	45	0.31
Norwegian (158)	318	2.19
Polish (41)	105	0.72
Portuguese (0)	38	0.26
Russian (43)	101	0.69
Scandinavian (30)	30	0.21
Scotch-Irish (241)	437	3.00
Scottish (182)	450	3.09
Slovak (0)	18	0.12
Swedish (41)	82	0.56
Ukrainian (36)	53	0.36
Welsh (12)	66	0.45
West Indian, ex. Hispanic (40)	40	0.27
Haitian (29)	29	0.20
Jamaican (11)	11	0.08
Yugoslavian (0)	17	0.12

Hispanic Origin	Population	%
Hispanic or Latino (of any race)	849	5.89
Central American, ex. Mexican	66	0.46
Guatemalan	14	0.10
Honduran	14	0.10
Nicaraguan	2	0.01
Panamanian	33	0.23
Salvadoran	3	0.02
Cuban	40	0.28
Dominican Republic	9	0.06
Mexican	325	2.26
Puerto Rican	255	1.77
South American	46	0.32
Bolivian	3	0.02
Chilean	6	0.04
Colombian	15	0.10
Ecuadorian	6	0.04
Peruvian	15	0.10
Venezuelan	1	0.01
Other Hispanic or Latino	108	0.75

Race*	Population	%
African-American/Black (2,619)	2,912	20.22
Not Hispanic (2,563)	2,833	19.67
Hispanic (56)	79	0.55
American Indian/Alaska Native (95)	215	1.49
Not Hispanic (82)	187	1.30
Hispanic (13)	28	0.19
Apache (1)	5	0.03
Blackfeet (3)	9	0.06
Cherokee (23)	60	0.42
Chippewa (1)	1	0.01
Choctaw (3)	4	0.03
Creek (7)	19	0.13
Houma (2)	2	0.01
Inupiat *(Alaska Native)* (0)	1	0.01
Iroquois (0)	1	0.01
Lumbee (2)	2	0.01
Mexican American Ind. (1)	1	0.01
Ottawa (1)	1	0.01
Potawatomi (3)	3	0.02
Seminole (0)	9	0.06
Shoshone (0)	1	0.01
Sioux (8)	8	0.06
South American Ind. (1)	1	0.01
Yuman (1)	1	0.01
Asian (592)	886	6.15
Not Hispanic (584)	850	5.90
Hispanic (8)	36	0.25
Bangladeshi (0)	1	0.01
Chinese, ex. Taiwanese (29)	41	0.28
Filipino (213)	334	2.32
Indian (29)	46	0.32
Indonesian (1)	4	0.03
Japanese (23)	63	0.44
Korean (93)	143	0.99
Laotian (5)	5	0.03
Malaysian (0)	2	0.01
Taiwanese (8)	11	0.08
Thai (64)	106	0.74
Vietnamese (101)	119	0.83
Hawaii Native/Pacific Islander (13)	38	0.26
Not Hispanic (11)	33	0.23
Hispanic (2)	5	0.03
Guamanian/Chamorro (5)	9	0.06
Native Hawaiian (6)	14	0.10
Samoan (1)	6	0.04
White (10,239)	10,804	75.00
Not Hispanic (9,730)	10,221	70.95
Hispanic (509)	583	4.05

Cape Canaveral

Place Type: City
County: Brevard
Population: 9,912†

Ancestry‡	Population	%
African, Sub-Saharan (0)	62	0.63
African (0)	62	0.63
American (869)	869	8.77
Arab (40)	61	0.62
Lebanese (40)	61	0.62
Australian (16)	26	0.26
Austrian (31)	31	0.31
British (35)	35	0.35
Cajun (0)	13	0.13
Canadian (41)	41	0.41
Celtic (0)	22	0.22
Czech (15)	36	0.36
Czechoslovakian (0)	33	0.33
Danish (13)	13	0.13
Dutch (64)	234	2.36
English (558)	1,315	13.28
European (130)	130	1.31
French, ex. Basque (140)	495	5.00
French Canadian (182)	205	2.07
German (493)	1,940	19.59
Hungarian (16)	52	0.53
Irish (298)	1,222	12.34
Italian (441)	1,147	11.58
Lithuanian (7)	7	0.07
Luxemburger (0)	11	0.11
Norwegian (15)	75	0.76
Polish (180)	374	3.78
Portuguese (90)	120	1.21
Romanian (15)	28	0.28
Russian (229)	325	3.28
Scandinavian (16)	31	0.31
Scotch-Irish (151)	301	3.04
Scottish (66)	280	2.83
Slavic (29)	29	0.29
Slovak (9)	39	0.39
Swedish (26)	42	0.42
Swiss (14)	66	0.67
Ukrainian (0)	23	0.23
Welsh (26)	119	1.20

Hispanic Origin	Population	%
Hispanic or Latino (of any race)	562	5.67
Central American, ex. Mexican	39	0.39
Costa Rican	6	0.06
Guatemalan	7	0.07
Honduran	5	0.05
Nicaraguan	5	0.05
Panamanian	13	0.13
Salvadoran	3	0.03
Cuban	69	0.70
Dominican Republic	25	0.25
Mexican	97	0.98
Puerto Rican	164	1.65
South American	99	1.00
Argentinean	16	0.16
Bolivian	2	0.02
Chilean	4	0.04
Colombian	45	0.45
Ecuadorian	5	0.05
Paraguayan	1	0.01
Peruvian	12	0.12
Uruguayan	1	0.01
Venezuelan	12	0.12
Other South American	1	0.01
Other Hispanic or Latino	69	0.70

Race*	Population	%
African-American/Black (237)	301	3.04
Not Hispanic (221)	274	2.76
Hispanic (16)	27	0.27
American Indian/Alaska Native (33)	85	0.86
Not Hispanic (27)	74	0.75
Hispanic (6)	11	0.11
Aleut *(Alaska Native)* (2)	2	0.02
Apache (2)	6	0.06
Blackfeet (1)	1	0.01
Canadian/French Am. Ind. (0)	1	0.01
Central American Ind. (0)	2	0.02
Cherokee (5)	23	0.23
Chippewa (0)	1	0.01
Choctaw (1)	4	0.04
Cree (0)	1	0.01
Delaware (1)	2	0.02
Iroquois (1)	3	0.03
Mexican American Ind. (1)	1	0.01
Navajo (1)	3	0.03
Osage (1)	1	0.01
Shoshone (1)	1	0.01
Sioux (0)	6	0.06
South American Ind. (0)	3	0.03
Tlingit-Haida *(Alaska Native)* (1)	2	0.02
Yuman (1)	1	0.01
Asian (180)	222	2.24
Not Hispanic (179)	218	2.20
Hispanic (1)	4	0.04
Burmese (3)	3	0.03
Cambodian (1)	1	0.01
Chinese, ex. Taiwanese (31)	36	0.36
Filipino (46)	59	0.60
Indian (44)	52	0.52
Japanese (10)	15	0.15
Korean (10)	13	0.13
Pakistani (5)	5	0.05
Thai (6)	12	0.12
Vietnamese (17)	22	0.22
Hawaii Native/Pacific Islander (11)	15	0.15

*Notes: † The Census 2010 population figure is used to calculate the percentages in the Hispanic Origin and Race categories. Ancestry percentages are based on the 2006-2010 American Community Survey population (not shown); ‡ Numbers in parentheses indicate the number of people reporting a single ancestry; * Numbers in parentheses indicate the number of persons reporting this race alone, not in combination with any other race; Please refer to the Explanation of Data for more information.*

Not Hispanic (7)	11	0.11
Hispanic (4)	4	0.04
Guamanian/Chamorro (8)	8	0.08
Native Hawaiian (2)	5	0.05
Samoan (0)	2	0.02
White (9,208)	9,367	94.50
Not Hispanic (8,766)	8,893	89.72
Hispanic (442)	474	4.78

Cape Coral

Place Type: City
County: Lee
Population: 154,305†

Ancestry‡	Population	%
African, Sub-Saharan (166)	259	0.17
African (42)	111	0.07
Ghanaian (49)	49	0.03
Liberian (8)	8	0.01
Nigerian (0)	14	0.01
South African (49)	59	0.04
Other Sub-Saharan African (18)	18	0.01
Alsatian (20)	20	0.01
American (17,041)	17,041	11.38
Arab (320)	495	0.33
Arab (59)	71	0.05
Lebanese (115)	203	0.14
Moroccan (0)	7	<0.01
Palestinian (0)	15	0.01
Syrian (89)	124	0.08
Other Arab (57)	75	0.05
Armenian (156)	229	0.15
Australian (0)	18	0.01
Austrian (35)	242	0.16
Basque (0)	17	0.01
Belgian (45)	99	0.07
Brazilian (391)	654	0.44
British (324)	427	0.29
Bulgarian (37)	45	0.03
Canadian (305)	522	0.35
Croatian (91)	243	0.16
Czech (254)	834	0.56
Czechoslovakian (125)	271	0.18
Danish (76)	448	0.30
Dutch (467)	2,248	1.50
English (4,398)	14,168	9.46
European (652)	771	0.51
Finnish (100)	309	0.21
French, ex. Basque (992)	5,201	3.47
French Canadian (528)	1,155	0.77
German (8,916)	26,747	17.86
Greek (376)	1,037	0.69
Guyanese (26)	87	0.06
Hungarian (398)	1,031	0.69
Iranian (0)	46	0.03
Irish (6,138)	21,849	14.59
Israeli (20)	20	0.01
Italian (8,721)	17,100	11.42
Latvian (33)	59	0.04
Lithuanian (177)	439	0.29
Luxemburger (7)	7	<0.01
Macedonian (19)	19	0.01
Maltese (13)	13	0.01
Northern European (10)	10	0.01
Norwegian (571)	1,505	1.00
Pennsylvania German (98)	185	0.12
Polish (2,269)	6,408	4.28
Portuguese (483)	980	0.65
Romanian (53)	112	0.07
Russian (525)	1,154	0.77
Scandinavian (45)	296	0.20
Scotch-Irish (720)	2,177	1.45
Scottish (947)	2,874	1.92
Serbian (25)	73	0.05
Slavic (0)	97	0.06
Slovak (191)	407	0.27
Slovene (38)	93	0.06
Swedish (395)	1,761	1.18
Swiss (112)	328	0.22
Turkish (20)	32	0.02
Ukrainian (76)	303	0.20
Welsh (136)	878	0.59
West Indian, ex. Hispanic (2,337)	2,621	1.75
Belizean (145)	161	0.11
Haitian (1,123)	1,244	0.83
Jamaican (748)	817	0.55
Trinidadian/Tobagonian (308)	339	0.23
West Indian (13)	60	0.04
Yugoslavian (150)	164	0.11

Hispanic Origin	Population	%
Hispanic or Latino (of any race)	30,017	19.45
Central American, ex. Mexican	2,127	1.38
Costa Rican	207	0.13
Guatemalan	322	0.21
Honduran	625	0.41
Nicaraguan	410	0.27
Panamanian	119	0.08
Salvadoran	440	0.29
Other Central American	4	<0.01
Cuban	9,843	6.38
Dominican Republic	1,631	1.06
Mexican	2,710	1.76
Puerto Rican	7,261	4.71
South American	4,657	3.02
Argentinean	313	0.20
Bolivian	78	0.05
Chilean	80	0.05
Colombian	2,313	1.50
Ecuadorian	540	0.35
Paraguayan	16	0.01
Peruvian	749	0.49
Uruguayan	121	0.08
Venezuelan	411	0.27
Other South American	36	0.02
Other Hispanic or Latino	1,788	1.16

Race*	Population	%
African-American/Black (6,594)	8,026	5.20
Not Hispanic (5,679)	6,734	4.36
Hispanic (915)	1,292	0.84
American Indian/Alaska Native (474)	1,083	0.70
Not Hispanic (356)	840	0.54
Hispanic (118)	243	0.16
Alaska Athabascan *(Ala. Nat.)* (2)	3	<0.01
Apache (4)	8	0.01
Blackfeet (5)	36	0.02
Canadian/French Am. Ind. (8)	12	0.01
Central American Ind. (2)	3	<0.01
Cherokee (51)	205	0.13
Cheyenne (1)	1	<0.01
Chickasaw (1)	6	<0.01
Chippewa (23)	55	0.04
Choctaw (13)	16	0.01
Comanche (1)	4	<0.01
Cree (0)	4	<0.01
Creek (3)	7	<0.01
Delaware (3)	4	<0.01
Inupiat *(Alaska Native)* (1)	2	<0.01
Iroquois (17)	27	0.02
Lumbee (12)	13	0.01
Mexican American Ind. (6)	13	0.01
Navajo (4)	8	0.01
Osage (6)	7	<0.01
Ottawa (1)	1	<0.01
Paiute (2)	2	<0.01
Pima (0)	1	<0.01
Potawatomi (10)	10	0.01
Pueblo (1)	1	<0.01
Puget Sound Salish (1)	1	<0.01
Seminole (0)	2	<0.01
Shoshone (1)	2	<0.01
Sioux (19)	28	0.02
South American Ind. (26)	52	0.03
Spanish American Ind. (4)	5	<0.01
Ute (0)	1	<0.01
Yaqui (1)	2	<0.01
Yuman (1)	1	<0.01
Yup'ik *(Alaska Native)* (0)	2	<0.01
Asian (2,339)	3,150	2.04
Not Hispanic (2,272)	2,937	1.90
Hispanic (67)	213	0.14
Bangladeshi (20)	26	0.02
Burmese (3)	4	<0.01
Cambodian (10)	14	0.01
Chinese, ex. Taiwanese (301)	410	0.27
Filipino (679)	949	0.62
Indian (368)	448	0.29
Indonesian (11)	21	0.01
Japanese (69)	180	0.12
Korean (155)	253	0.16
Laotian (57)	75	0.05
Malaysian (6)	10	0.01
Pakistani (53)	58	0.04
Sri Lankan (3)	4	<0.01
Taiwanese (6)	11	0.01
Thai (58)	94	0.06
Vietnamese (434)	493	0.32
Hawaii Native/Pacific Islander (82)	231	0.15
Not Hispanic (60)	158	0.10
Hispanic (22)	73	0.05
Guamanian/Chamorro (17)	33	0.02
Native Hawaiian (34)	89	0.06
Samoan (5)	11	0.01
Tongan (4)	4	<0.01
White (136,030)	139,231	90.23
Not Hispanic (113,476)	115,414	74.80
Hispanic (22,554)	23,817	15.44

Carrollwood

Place Type: CDP
County: Hillsborough
Population: 33,365†

Ancestry‡	Population	%
African, Sub-Saharan (252)	270	0.79
African (179)	197	0.57
Ethiopian (73)	73	0.21
Albanian (0)	11	0.03
American (1,965)	1,965	5.72
Arab (384)	556	1.62
Arab (12)	145	0.42
Iraqi (8)	8	0.02
Jordanian (208)	208	0.61
Lebanese (0)	15	0.04
Moroccan (156)	173	0.50
Palestinian (0)	7	0.02
Armenian (0)	30	0.09
Australian (12)	28	0.08
Austrian (8)	56	0.16
Belgian (10)	50	0.15
Brazilian (105)	118	0.34
British (151)	238	0.69
Bulgarian (119)	184	0.54
Cajun (13)	13	0.04
Canadian (320)	368	1.07
Croatian (21)	48	0.14
Czech (12)	66	0.19
Czechoslovakian (0)	21	0.06
Danish (11)	38	0.11
Dutch (219)	589	1.72
Eastern European (37)	37	0.11
English (1,493)	3,990	11.62
European (289)	345	1.00
Finnish (31)	51	0.15
French, ex. Basque (113)	766	2.23
French Canadian (112)	290	0.84
German (1,255)	4,428	12.90
Greek (60)	140	0.41
Hungarian (65)	135	0.39
Iranian (52)	80	0.23
Irish (1,222)	3,389	9.87
Israeli (24)	32	0.09
Italian (1,669)	3,477	10.13
Lithuanian (18)	52	0.15
Northern European (46)	46	0.13
Norwegian (23)	176	0.51
Pennsylvania German (18)	26	0.08

*Notes: † The Census 2010 population figure is used to calculate the percentages in the Hispanic Origin and Race categories. Ancestry percentages are based on the 2006-2010 American Community Survey population (not shown); ‡ Numbers in parentheses indicate the number of people reporting a single ancestry; * Numbers in parentheses indicate the number of persons reporting this race alone, not in combination with any other race; Please refer to the Explanation of Data for more information.*

Ancestry	Population	%
Polish (436)	1,438	4.19
Portuguese (44)	223	0.65
Romanian (0)	49	0.14
Russian (144)	590	1.72
Scandinavian (20)	33	0.10
Scotch-Irish (161)	531	1.55
Scottish (302)	727	2.12
Serbian (51)	72	0.21
Slovak (24)	34	0.10
Swedish (60)	327	0.95
Swiss (57)	165	0.48
Ukrainian (14)	80	0.23
Welsh (17)	225	0.66
West Indian, ex. Hispanic (240)	282	0.82
Haitian (0)	10	0.03
Jamaican (97)	129	0.38
Trinidadian/Tobagonian (41)	41	0.12
West Indian (102)	102	0.30
Yugoslavian (45)	45	0.13

Hispanic Origin	Population	%
Hispanic or Latino (of any race)	9,155	27.44
Central American, ex. Mexican	461	1.38
Costa Rican	60	0.18
Guatemalan	65	0.19
Honduran	128	0.38
Nicaraguan	42	0.13
Panamanian	85	0.25
Salvadoran	70	0.21
Other Central American	11	0.03
Cuban	2,108	6.32
Dominican Republic	359	1.08
Mexican	469	1.41
Puerto Rican	2,782	8.34
South American	1,820	5.45
Argentinean	51	0.15
Bolivian	11	0.03
Chilean	32	0.10
Colombian	1,090	3.27
Ecuadorian	188	0.56
Paraguayan	7	0.02
Peruvian	212	0.64
Uruguayan	25	0.07
Venezuelan	197	0.59
Other South American	7	0.02
Other Hispanic or Latino	1,156	3.46

Race*	Population	%
African-American/Black (2,594)	3,063	9.18
Not Hispanic (2,296)	2,579	7.73
Hispanic (298)	484	1.45
American Indian/Alaska Native (74)	286	0.86
Not Hispanic (45)	180	0.54
Hispanic (29)	106	0.32
Apache (2)	6	0.02
Arapaho (0)	5	0.01
Blackfeet (1)	6	0.02
Canadian/French Am. Ind. (0)	4	0.01
Central American Ind. (2)	6	0.02
Cherokee (11)	53	0.16
Cheyenne (1)	1	<0.01
Chickasaw (0)	3	0.01
Chippewa (3)	7	0.02
Choctaw (3)	6	0.02
Cree (0)	6	0.02
Creek (2)	3	0.01
Crow (0)	1	<0.01
Delaware (0)	1	<0.01
Iroquois (4)	13	0.04
Mexican American Ind. (1)	2	0.01
Navajo (1)	3	0.01
Potawatomi (3)	3	0.01
Puget Sound Salish (1)	1	<0.01
Seminole (2)	7	0.02
Sioux (3)	9	0.03
South American Ind. (6)	23	0.07
Tlingit-Haida *(Alaska Native)* (1)	1	<0.01
Asian (1,279)	1,562	4.68
Not Hispanic (1,257)	1,491	4.47
Hispanic (22)	71	0.21
Bangladeshi (10)	11	0.03
Burmese (3)	3	0.01
Cambodian (5)	9	0.03
Chinese, ex. Taiwanese (140)	192	0.58
Filipino (207)	289	0.87
Indian (371)	423	1.27
Indonesian (6)	7	0.02
Japanese (32)	57	0.17
Korean (63)	92	0.28
Laotian (3)	4	0.01
Malaysian (1)	2	0.01
Nepalese (9)	9	0.03
Pakistani (11)	18	0.05
Sri Lankan (3)	3	0.01
Taiwanese (9)	15	0.04
Thai (32)	43	0.13
Vietnamese (335)	365	1.09
Hawaii Native/Pacific Islander (16)	68	0.20
Not Hispanic (12)	48	0.14
Hispanic (4)	20	0.06
Guamanian/Chamorro (5)	10	0.03
Marshallese (0)	1	<0.01
Native Hawaiian (6)	15	0.04
Samoan (2)	4	0.01
White (26,963)	27,853	83.48
Not Hispanic (19,934)	20,407	61.16
Hispanic (7,029)	7,446	22.32

Casselberry

Place Type: City
County: Seminole
Population: 26,241†

Ancestry‡	Population	%
African, Sub-Saharan (81)	81	0.31
African (81)	81	0.31
American (1,044)	1,044	3.98
Arab (30)	40	0.15
Iraqi (15)	15	0.06
Lebanese (15)	15	0.06
Syrian (0)	10	0.04
Armenian (10)	21	0.08
Austrian (32)	117	0.45
Belgian (38)	54	0.21
British (122)	233	0.89
Bulgarian (11)	11	0.04
Canadian (182)	341	1.30
Celtic (0)	14	0.05
Croatian (0)	11	0.04
Czech (22)	35	0.13
Czechoslovakian (17)	26	0.10
Danish (0)	5	0.02
Dutch (151)	482	1.84
Eastern European (21)	21	0.08
English (791)	2,339	8.91
European (495)	739	2.82
Finnish (41)	54	0.21
French, ex. Basque (271)	907	3.46
French Canadian (90)	117	0.45
German (1,616)	4,675	17.82
Greek (81)	222	0.85
Guyanese (19)	19	0.07
Hungarian (5)	74	0.28
Iranian (9)	9	0.03
Irish (1,196)	3,840	14.63
Italian (1,131)	2,280	8.69
Lithuanian (0)	18	0.07
Norwegian (103)	297	1.13
Pennsylvania German (9)	25	0.10
Polish (225)	882	3.36
Portuguese (39)	159	0.61
Russian (102)	198	0.75
Scotch-Irish (204)	503	1.92
Scottish (112)	394	1.50
Serbian (127)	127	0.48
Slavic (0)	40	0.15
Slovak (30)	44	0.17
Swedish (71)	196	0.75
Swiss (0)	84	0.32
Turkish (0)	54	0.21
Ukrainian (22)	51	0.19
Welsh (143)	279	1.06
West Indian, ex. Hispanic (358)	428	1.63
Haitian (182)	209	0.80
Jamaican (64)	64	0.24
Trinidadian/Tobagonian (42)	42	0.16
West Indian (70)	113	0.43

Hispanic Origin	Population	%
Hispanic or Latino (of any race)	5,923	22.57
Central American, ex. Mexican	273	1.04
Costa Rican	29	0.11
Guatemalan	49	0.19
Honduran	58	0.22
Nicaraguan	42	0.16
Panamanian	46	0.18
Salvadoran	49	0.19
Cuban	479	1.83
Dominican Republic	322	1.23
Mexican	438	1.67
Puerto Rican	3,159	12.04
South American	949	3.62
Argentinean	76	0.29
Bolivian	4	0.02
Chilean	21	0.08
Colombian	533	2.03
Ecuadorian	111	0.42
Peruvian	102	0.39
Uruguayan	2	0.01
Venezuelan	94	0.36
Other South American	6	0.02
Other Hispanic or Latino	303	1.15

Race*	Population	%
African-American/Black (2,109)	2,530	9.64
Not Hispanic (1,843)	2,109	8.04
Hispanic (266)	421	1.60
American Indian/Alaska Native (102)	297	1.13
Not Hispanic (78)	210	0.80
Hispanic (24)	87	0.33
Apache (0)	1	<0.01
Blackfeet (0)	7	0.03
Canadian/French Am. Ind. (1)	2	0.01
Central American Ind. (0)	1	<0.01
Cherokee (34)	91	0.35
Cheyenne (0)	1	<0.01
Chickasaw (0)	1	<0.01
Chippewa (3)	4	0.02
Choctaw (2)	6	0.02
Cree (0)	4	0.02
Creek (8)	11	0.04
Delaware (0)	2	0.01
Houma (1)	1	<0.01
Inupiat *(Alaska Native)* (0)	1	<0.01
Iroquois (2)	3	0.01
Lumbee (1)	1	<0.01
Mexican American Ind. (2)	2	0.01
Navajo (1)	1	<0.01
Osage (1)	1	<0.01
Potawatomi (0)	1	<0.01
Pueblo (0)	1	<0.01
Seminole (3)	4	0.02
Sioux (1)	6	0.02
South American Ind. (2)	33	0.13
Asian (773)	987	3.76
Not Hispanic (758)	944	3.60
Hispanic (15)	43	0.16
Bangladeshi (1)	1	<0.01
Burmese (8)	8	0.03
Chinese, ex. Taiwanese (156)	214	0.82
Filipino (166)	222	0.85
Indian (206)	232	0.88
Indonesian (6)	7	0.03
Japanese (16)	37	0.14
Korean (36)	48	0.18
Laotian (6)	13	0.05
Nepalese (2)	2	0.01
Pakistani (17)	19	0.07
Taiwanese (9)	14	0.05

*Notes: † The Census 2010 population figure is used to calculate the percentages in the Hispanic Origin and Race categories. Ancestry percentages are based on the 2006-2010 American Community Survey population (not shown); ‡ Numbers in parentheses indicate the number of people reporting a single ancestry; * Numbers in parentheses indicate the number of persons reporting this race alone, not in combination with any other race; Please refer to the Explanation of Data for more information.*

Thai (8)	22	0.08
Vietnamese (107)	129	0.49
Hawaii Native/Pacific Islander (23)	60	0.23
Not Hispanic (21)	45	0.17
Hispanic (2)	15	0.06
Guamanian/Chamorro (5)	11	0.04
Native Hawaiian (10)	22	0.08
Samoan (0)	2	0.01
White (21,009)	21,787	83.03
Not Hispanic (17,023)	17,463	66.55
Hispanic (3,986)	4,324	16.48

Cheval

Place Type: CDP
County: Hillsborough
Population: 10,702†

Ancestry‡	Population	%
African, Sub-Saharan (163)	163	1.58
African (60)	60	0.58
South African (103)	103	1.00
American (487)	487	4.73
Arab (70)	70	0.68
Arab (53)	53	0.51
Jordanian (17)	17	0.17
Armenian (24)	24	0.23
Austrian (23)	36	0.35
Belgian (16)	26	0.25
British (42)	89	0.86
Cajun (0)	25	0.24
Canadian (37)	52	0.50
Czech (0)	17	0.17
Danish (0)	26	0.25
Dutch (30)	75	0.73
English (252)	699	6.79
European (108)	119	1.16
French, ex. Basque (7)	166	1.61
French Canadian (20)	30	0.29
German (543)	1,886	18.31
Greek (0)	12	0.12
Hungarian (0)	30	0.29
Iranian (73)	73	0.71
Irish (520)	1,434	13.92
Italian (298)	1,164	11.30
Lithuanian (0)	28	0.27
Macedonian (0)	41	0.40
Norwegian (30)	139	1.35
Pennsylvania German (14)	14	0.14
Polish (112)	579	5.62
Portuguese (15)	31	0.30
Romanian (25)	37	0.36
Russian (25)	93	0.90
Scandinavian (17)	35	0.34
Scotch-Irish (70)	220	2.14
Scottish (84)	226	2.19
Serbian (0)	46	0.45
Slovak (28)	28	0.27
Swedish (0)	89	0.86
Turkish (148)	164	1.59
Ukrainian (0)	15	0.15
Welsh (0)	77	0.75
West Indian, ex. Hispanic (10)	10	0.10
Haitian (10)	10	0.10
Yugoslavian (0)	28	0.27

Hispanic Origin	Population	%
Hispanic or Latino (of any race)	2,009	18.77
Central American, ex. Mexican	112	1.05
Costa Rican	21	0.20
Guatemalan	13	0.12
Honduran	19	0.18
Nicaraguan	16	0.15
Panamanian	31	0.29
Salvadoran	12	0.11
Cuban	339	3.17
Dominican Republic	104	0.97
Mexican	102	0.95
Puerto Rican	710	6.63
South American	410	3.83
Argentinean	12	0.11
Bolivian	5	0.05
Chilean	11	0.10
Colombian	189	1.77
Ecuadorian	27	0.25
Paraguayan	5	0.05
Peruvian	70	0.65
Uruguayan	2	0.02
Venezuelan	82	0.77
Other South American	7	0.07
Other Hispanic or Latino	232	2.17

Race*	Population	%
African-American/Black (809)	929	8.68
Not Hispanic (744)	835	7.80
Hispanic (65)	94	0.88
American Indian/Alaska Native (31)	83	0.78
Not Hispanic (18)	54	0.50
Hispanic (13)	29	0.27
Apache (0)	3	0.03
Blackfeet (0)	1	0.01
Central American Ind. (1)	1	0.01
Cherokee (3)	16	0.15
Creek (0)	3	0.03
Iroquois (3)	3	0.03
Lumbee (1)	1	0.01
Mexican American Ind. (2)	2	0.02
Sioux (0)	1	0.01
South American Ind. (4)	8	0.07
Asian (653)	738	6.90
Not Hispanic (640)	719	6.72
Hispanic (13)	19	0.18
Chinese, ex. Taiwanese (100)	118	1.10
Filipino (62)	75	0.70
Indian (303)	319	2.98
Indonesian (2)	2	0.02
Japanese (12)	25	0.23
Korean (58)	64	0.60
Laotian (1)	1	0.01
Malaysian (6)	6	0.06
Pakistani (16)	17	0.16
Taiwanese (6)	6	0.06
Thai (8)	16	0.15
Vietnamese (70)	81	0.76
Hawaii Native/Pacific Islander (6)	25	0.23
Not Hispanic (5)	21	0.20
Hispanic (1)	4	0.04
Native Hawaiian (4)	15	0.14
Samoan (1)	2	0.02
Tongan (0)	1	0.01
White (8,592)	8,878	82.96
Not Hispanic (7,065)	7,247	67.72
Hispanic (1,527)	1,631	15.24

Citrus Park

Place Type: CDP
County: Hillsborough
Population: 24,252†

Ancestry‡	Population	%
African, Sub-Saharan (151)	222	0.91
African (73)	100	0.41
Ethiopian (20)	42	0.17
South African (38)	38	0.16
Other Sub-Saharan African (20)	42	0.17
American (1,194)	1,194	4.89
Arab (73)	73	0.30
Lebanese (28)	28	0.11
Palestinian (9)	9	0.04
Other Arab (36)	36	0.15
Austrian (0)	28	0.11
Belgian (0)	22	0.09
Brazilian (61)	61	0.25
British (56)	101	0.41
Canadian (133)	158	0.65
Carpatho Rusyn (0)	11	0.05
Celtic (0)	27	0.11
Croatian (0)	22	0.09
Czech (0)	51	0.21
Czechoslovakian (0)	42	0.17
Danish (7)	24	0.10
Dutch (20)	189	0.77
Eastern European (64)	74	0.30
English (1,232)	2,793	11.44
European (85)	110	0.45
Finnish (0)	39	0.16
French, ex. Basque (126)	702	2.88
French Canadian (26)	69	0.28
German (957)	3,039	12.45
Greek (0)	27	0.11
Guyanese (63)	63	0.26
Hungarian (30)	193	0.79
Irish (711)	2,967	12.16
Italian (876)	2,126	8.71
Lithuanian (0)	11	0.05
Luxemburger (0)	12	0.05
Norwegian (11)	140	0.57
Polish (100)	646	2.65
Portuguese (7)	29	0.12
Romanian (0)	12	0.05
Russian (55)	159	0.65
Scandinavian (19)	19	0.08
Scotch-Irish (68)	281	1.15
Scottish (143)	294	1.20
Slovak (16)	74	0.30
Swedish (59)	208	0.85
Swiss (0)	6	0.02
Ukrainian (28)	127	0.52
Welsh (21)	157	0.64
West Indian, ex. Hispanic (249)	379	1.55
Bahamian (27)	27	0.11
Barbadian (14)	14	0.06
British West Indian (6)	6	0.02
Dutch West Indian (8)	8	0.03
Haitian (94)	94	0.39
Jamaican (78)	121	0.50
Trinidadian/Tobagonian (22)	54	0.22
West Indian (0)	42	0.17
Other West Indian (0)	13	0.05

Hispanic Origin	Population	%
Hispanic or Latino (of any race)	8,148	33.60
Central American, ex. Mexican	368	1.52
Costa Rican	25	0.10
Guatemalan	40	0.16
Honduran	85	0.35
Nicaraguan	51	0.21
Panamanian	96	0.40
Salvadoran	71	0.29
Cuban	2,069	8.53
Dominican Republic	428	1.76
Mexican	419	1.73
Puerto Rican	2,712	11.18
South American	1,501	6.19
Argentinean	29	0.12
Bolivian	11	0.05
Chilean	17	0.07
Colombian	848	3.50
Ecuadorian	129	0.53
Paraguayan	3	0.01
Peruvian	242	1.00
Uruguayan	14	0.06
Venezuelan	200	0.82
Other South American	8	0.03
Other Hispanic or Latino	651	2.68

Race*	Population	%
African-American/Black (2,111)	2,498	10.30
Not Hispanic (1,811)	2,049	8.45
Hispanic (300)	449	1.85
American Indian/Alaska Native (100)	238	0.98
Not Hispanic (45)	127	0.52
Hispanic (55)	111	0.46
Apache (4)	4	0.02
Blackfeet (1)	2	0.01
Central American Ind. (0)	3	0.01
Cherokee (15)	54	0.22
Chippewa (1)	1	<0.01
Creek (5)	9	0.04

*Notes: † The Census 2010 population figure is used to calculate the percentages in the Hispanic Origin and Race categories. Ancestry percentages are based on the 2006-2010 American Community Survey population (not shown); ‡ Numbers in parentheses indicate the number of people reporting a single ancestry; * Numbers in parentheses indicate the number of persons reporting this race alone, not in combination with any other race; Please refer to the Explanation of Data for more information.*

Race*	Population	%
Delaware (1)	1	<0.01
Iroquois (1)	6	0.02
Lumbee (6)	6	0.02
Mexican American Ind. (2)	2	0.01
Navajo (0)	3	0.01
Osage (1)	1	<0.01
Seminole (2)	4	0.02
Sioux (1)	6	0.02
South American Ind. (11)	27	0.11
Spanish American Ind. (9)	15	0.06
Yaqui (0)	1	<0.01
Asian (1,147)	1,376	5.67
Not Hispanic (1,122)	1,308	5.39
Hispanic (25)	68	0.28
Bangladeshi (2)	2	0.01
Burmese (2)	2	0.01
Cambodian (6)	7	0.03
Chinese, ex. Taiwanese (131)	172	0.71
Filipino (112)	143	0.59
Hmong (2)	2	0.01
Indian (319)	373	1.54
Indonesian (3)	8	0.03
Japanese (24)	34	0.14
Korean (95)	116	0.48
Laotian (11)	13	0.05
Nepalese (2)	2	0.01
Pakistani (16)	23	0.09
Taiwanese (7)	10	0.04
Thai (22)	42	0.17
Vietnamese (360)	382	1.58
Hawaii Native/Pacific Islander (19)	45	0.19
Not Hispanic (8)	28	0.12
Hispanic (11)	17	0.07
Guamanian/Chamorro (10)	12	0.05
Native Hawaiian (4)	8	0.03
White (19,004)	19,685	81.17
Not Hispanic (12,590)	12,958	53.43
Hispanic (6,414)	6,727	27.74

Citrus Springs

Place Type: CDP
County: Citrus
Population: 8,622†

Ancestry‡	Population	%
African, Sub-Saharan (14)	14	0.18
Cape Verdean (14)	14	0.18
American (1,496)	1,496	19.60
Arab (9)	18	0.24
Egyptian (9)	18	0.24
British (12)	25	0.33
Canadian (198)	198	2.59
Czech (13)	110	1.44
Czechoslovakian (0)	11	0.14
Danish (0)	8	0.10
Dutch (0)	216	2.83
English (454)	1,064	13.94
European (18)	27	0.35
Finnish (13)	13	0.17
French, ex. Basque (17)	212	2.78
French Canadian (57)	156	2.04
German (358)	1,380	18.08
Greek (18)	114	1.49
Hungarian (0)	42	0.55
Irish (463)	1,398	18.32
Italian (275)	522	6.84
Northern European (26)	26	0.34
Norwegian (11)	20	0.26
Polish (31)	144	1.89
Portuguese (0)	28	0.37
Scotch-Irish (147)	227	2.97
Scottish (33)	142	1.86
Slovak (52)	52	0.68
Swedish (60)	148	1.94
Ukrainian (0)	34	0.45
Welsh (24)	39	0.51
West Indian, ex. Hispanic (31)	31	0.41
Jamaican (31)	31	0.41

Hispanic Origin	Population	%
Hispanic or Latino (of any race)	799	9.27
Central American, ex. Mexican	49	0.57
Costa Rican	7	0.08
Guatemalan	5	0.06
Honduran	1	0.01
Nicaraguan	7	0.08
Panamanian	19	0.22
Salvadoran	10	0.12
Cuban	75	0.87
Dominican Republic	42	0.49
Mexican	87	1.01
Puerto Rican	427	4.95
South American	59	0.68
Argentinean	8	0.09
Bolivian	2	0.02
Chilean	3	0.03
Colombian	19	0.22
Ecuadorian	18	0.21
Peruvian	2	0.02
Venezuelan	6	0.07
Other South American	1	0.01
Other Hispanic or Latino	60	0.70

Race*	Population	%
African-American/Black (443)	549	6.37
Not Hispanic (409)	488	5.66
Hispanic (34)	61	0.71
American Indian/Alaska Native (33)	80	0.93
Not Hispanic (29)	69	0.80
Hispanic (4)	11	0.13
Blackfeet (0)	3	0.03
Cherokee (9)	25	0.29
Chippewa (0)	1	0.01
Creek (0)	1	0.01
Iroquois (1)	2	0.02
Lumbee (4)	4	0.05
Mexican American Ind. (2)	5	0.06
Seminole (3)	3	0.03
Sioux (3)	4	0.05
Spanish American Ind. (2)	2	0.02
Asian (127)	164	1.90
Not Hispanic (125)	157	1.82
Hispanic (2)	7	0.08
Cambodian (1)	3	0.03
Chinese, ex. Taiwanese (17)	25	0.29
Filipino (53)	68	0.79
Indian (20)	31	0.36
Indonesian (1)	1	0.01
Japanese (0)	2	0.02
Korean (6)	7	0.08
Laotian (0)	3	0.03
Taiwanese (4)	4	0.05
Thai (4)	7	0.08
Vietnamese (12)	12	0.14
Hawaii Native/Pacific Islander (4)	25	0.29
Not Hispanic (4)	24	0.28
Hispanic (0)	1	0.01
Guamanian/Chamorro (1)	3	0.03
Native Hawaiian (3)	15	0.17
White (7,665)	7,850	91.05
Not Hispanic (7,100)	7,225	83.80
Hispanic (565)	625	7.25

Clearwater

Place Type: City
County: Pinellas
Population: 107,685†

Ancestry‡	Population	%
African, Sub-Saharan (479)	558	0.52
African (320)	377	0.35
Cape Verdean (46)	46	0.04
Nigerian (42)	42	0.04
South African (57)	69	0.06
Other Sub-Saharan African (14)	24	0.02
Albanian (796)	796	0.74
American (13,526)	13,526	12.52
Arab (286)	348	0.32
Arab (15)	15	0.01
Egyptian (131)	131	0.12
Lebanese (55)	102	0.09
Moroccan (56)	56	0.05
Syrian (19)	34	0.03
Other Arab (10)	10	0.01
Armenian (38)	76	0.07
Australian (53)	97	0.09
Austrian (96)	592	0.55
Belgian (77)	113	0.10
Brazilian (146)	199	0.18
British (543)	855	0.79
Bulgarian (239)	239	0.22
Canadian (450)	671	0.62
Celtic (0)	19	0.02
Croatian (37)	110	0.10
Cypriot (4)	4	<0.01
Czech (242)	493	0.46
Czechoslovakian (82)	118	0.11
Danish (138)	536	0.50
Dutch (396)	1,663	1.54
Eastern European (109)	109	0.10
English (4,084)	11,955	11.06
Estonian (25)	40	0.04
European (454)	544	0.50
Finnish (173)	322	0.30
French, ex. Basque (829)	3,307	3.06
French Canadian (495)	980	0.91
German (5,184)	16,465	15.24
Greek (1,511)	2,266	2.10
Guyanese (22)	78	0.07
Hungarian (341)	692	0.64
Icelander (19)	29	0.03
Iranian (30)	30	0.03
Irish (4,554)	15,052	13.93
Israeli (15)	29	0.03
Italian (3,750)	8,650	8.01
Latvian (0)	25	0.02
Lithuanian (187)	401	0.37
Macedonian (38)	38	0.04
Maltese (0)	12	0.01
New Zealander (53)	53	0.05
Northern European (106)	106	0.10
Norwegian (326)	1,028	0.95
Pennsylvania German (49)	49	0.05
Polish (1,586)	4,257	3.94
Portuguese (152)	446	0.41
Romanian (139)	200	0.19
Russian (370)	1,006	0.93
Scandinavian (74)	128	0.12
Scotch-Irish (681)	1,614	1.49
Scottish (831)	2,647	2.45
Serbian (103)	123	0.11
Slavic (30)	63	0.06
Slovak (224)	350	0.32
Slovene (19)	19	0.02
Swedish (388)	1,438	1.33
Swiss (138)	325	0.30
Turkish (95)	254	0.24
Ukrainian (421)	608	0.56
Welsh (209)	743	0.69
West Indian, ex. Hispanic (394)	551	0.51
Bermudan (0)	41	0.04
British West Indian (0)	14	0.01
Dutch West Indian (5)	5	<0.01
Haitian (106)	152	0.14
Jamaican (234)	290	0.27
Trinidadian/Tobagonian (26)	26	0.02
West Indian (23)	23	0.02
Yugoslavian (350)	363	0.34

Hispanic Origin	Population	%
Hispanic or Latino (of any race)	15,245	14.16
Central American, ex. Mexican	702	0.65
Costa Rican	113	0.10
Guatemalan	106	0.10
Honduran	199	0.18
Nicaraguan	51	0.05
Panamanian	83	0.08
Salvadoran	146	0.14

*Notes: † The Census 2010 population figure is used to calculate the percentages in the Hispanic Origin and Race categories. Ancestry percentages are based on the 2006-2010 American Community Survey population (not shown); ‡ Numbers in parentheses indicate the number of people reporting a single ancestry; * Numbers in parentheses indicate the number of persons reporting this race alone, not in combination with any other race; Please refer to the Explanation of Data for more information.*

Other Central American	4	<0.01
Cuban	703	0.65
Dominican Republic	340	0.32
Mexican	7,830	7.27
Puerto Rican	3,002	2.79
South American	1,609	1.49
Argentinean	108	0.10
Bolivian	41	0.04
Chilean	46	0.04
Colombian	686	0.64
Ecuadorian	169	0.16
Paraguayan	4	<0.01
Peruvian	312	0.29
Uruguayan	39	0.04
Venezuelan	193	0.18
Other South American	11	0.01
Other Hispanic or Latino	1,059	0.98

Race*	Population	%
African-American/Black (11,752)	12,935	12.01
Not Hispanic (11,267)	12,238	11.36
Hispanic (485)	697	0.65
American Indian/Alaska Native (494)	1,060	0.98
Not Hispanic (234)	689	0.64
Hispanic (260)	371	0.34
Apache (6)	9	0.01
Arapaho (1)	2	<0.01
Blackfeet (3)	27	0.03
Canadian/French Am. Ind. (3)	3	<0.01
Cherokee (38)	177	0.16
Chickasaw (1)	3	<0.01
Chippewa (8)	27	0.03
Choctaw (4)	11	0.01
Comanche (0)	2	<0.01
Cree (1)	3	<0.01
Creek (4)	12	0.01
Crow (0)	1	<0.01
Delaware (0)	2	<0.01
Inupiat *(Alaska Native)* (1)	1	<0.01
Iroquois (14)	29	0.03
Lumbee (6)	12	0.01
Menominee (2)	2	<0.01
Mexican American Ind. (81)	87	0.08
Navajo (4)	4	<0.01
Osage (2)	2	<0.01
Ottawa (0)	3	<0.01
Potawatomi (1)	1	<0.01
Pueblo (0)	3	<0.01
Puget Sound Salish (1)	1	<0.01
Seminole (3)	13	0.01
Sioux (5)	16	0.01
South American Ind. (5)	18	0.02
Tlingit-Haida *(Alaska Native)* (0)	1	<0.01
Tohono O'Odham (2)	5	<0.01
Yaqui (1)	1	<0.01
Asian (2,311)	2,894	2.69
Not Hispanic (2,255)	2,772	2.57
Hispanic (56)	122	0.11
Bangladeshi (4)	5	<0.01
Burmese (6)	6	0.01
Cambodian (20)	24	0.02
Chinese, ex. Taiwanese (321)	443	0.41
Filipino (610)	788	0.73
Hmong (26)	35	0.03
Indian (500)	595	0.55
Indonesian (8)	15	0.01
Japanese (72)	170	0.16
Korean (104)	158	0.15
Laotian (32)	43	0.04
Malaysian (1)	1	<0.01
Nepalese (5)	6	0.01
Pakistani (20)	25	0.02
Sri Lankan (6)	6	0.01
Taiwanese (17)	23	0.02
Thai (98)	128	0.12
Vietnamese (319)	369	0.34
Hawaii Native/Pacific Islander (145)	253	0.23
Not Hispanic (124)	190	0.18
Hispanic (21)	63	0.06
Fijian (1)	1	<0.01
Guamanian/Chamorro (24)	33	0.03
Native Hawaiian (19)	40	0.04
Samoan (5)	11	0.01
Tongan (14)	15	0.01
White (85,936)	88,189	81.90
Not Hispanic (76,536)	78,119	72.54
Hispanic (9,400)	10,070	9.35

Clermont

Place Type: City
County: Lake
Population: 28,742†

Ancestry‡	Population	%
African, Sub-Saharan (45)	165	0.63
African (30)	85	0.33
South African (15)	80	0.31
American (1,410)	1,410	5.39
Arab (26)	95	0.36
Arab (0)	18	0.07
Egyptian (18)	18	0.07
Lebanese (0)	13	0.05
Moroccan (8)	37	0.14
Syrian (0)	9	0.03
Austrian (24)	79	0.30
Belgian (6)	14	0.05
Brazilian (0)	18	0.07
British (58)	105	0.40
Canadian (65)	137	0.52
Croatian (9)	9	0.03
Czech (73)	155	0.59
Czechoslovakian (12)	20	0.08
Danish (16)	92	0.35
Dutch (178)	514	1.97
Eastern European (54)	73	0.28
English (1,201)	2,785	10.65
Estonian (0)	12	0.05
European (94)	123	0.47
Finnish (12)	12	0.05
French, ex. Basque (170)	729	2.79
French Canadian (102)	196	0.75
German (1,328)	3,756	14.37
Greek (37)	77	0.29
Guyanese (626)	775	2.96
Hungarian (31)	119	0.46
Irish (872)	3,050	11.67
Italian (1,217)	2,609	9.98
Latvian (36)	36	0.14
Lithuanian (7)	21	0.08
Macedonian (60)	60	0.23
Maltese (6)	26	0.10
Norwegian (112)	276	1.06
Pennsylvania German (13)	26	0.10
Polish (459)	915	3.50
Portuguese (53)	94	0.36
Romanian (0)	44	0.17
Russian (29)	173	0.66
Scotch-Irish (107)	272	1.04
Scottish (126)	499	1.91
Slavic (0)	29	0.11
Slovak (51)	51	0.20
Swedish (88)	192	0.73
Swiss (0)	39	0.15
Turkish (12)	12	0.05
Ukrainian (16)	115	0.44
Welsh (27)	161	0.62
West Indian, ex. Hispanic (1,222)	1,385	5.30
Barbadian (0)	25	0.10
British West Indian (9)	9	0.03
Haitian (440)	440	1.68
Jamaican (386)	441	1.69
Trinidadian/Tobagonian (252)	297	1.14
West Indian (135)	173	0.66

Hispanic Origin	Population	%
Hispanic or Latino (of any race)	5,102	17.75
Central American, ex. Mexican	268	0.93
Costa Rican	25	0.09
Guatemalan	56	0.19
Honduran	64	0.22
Nicaraguan	45	0.16
Panamanian	44	0.15
Salvadoran	31	0.11
Other Central American	3	0.01
Cuban	390	1.36
Dominican Republic	357	1.24
Mexican	474	1.65
Puerto Rican	2,517	8.76
South American	733	2.55
Argentinean	27	0.09
Bolivian	2	0.01
Chilean	17	0.06
Colombian	292	1.02
Ecuadorian	111	0.39
Paraguayan	2	0.01
Peruvian	84	0.29
Uruguayan	14	0.05
Venezuelan	152	0.53
Other South American	32	0.11
Other Hispanic or Latino	363	1.26

Race*	Population	%
African-American/Black (4,141)	4,597	15.99
Not Hispanic (3,852)	4,181	14.55
Hispanic (289)	416	1.45
American Indian/Alaska Native (120)	342	1.19
Not Hispanic (87)	227	0.79
Hispanic (33)	115	0.40
Apache (0)	1	<0.01
Arapaho (0)	4	0.01
Blackfeet (1)	8	0.03
Central American Ind. (0)	2	0.01
Cherokee (9)	49	0.17
Chippewa (5)	6	0.02
Choctaw (1)	5	0.02
Creek (6)	14	0.05
Inupiat *(Alaska Native)* (0)	1	<0.01
Iroquois (0)	1	<0.01
Kiowa (1)	1	<0.01
Mexican American Ind. (4)	15	0.05
Navajo (3)	7	0.02
Paiute (0)	1	<0.01
Potawatomi (2)	2	0.01
Pueblo (0)	2	0.01
Seminole (3)	10	0.03
Shoshone (1)	1	<0.01
Sioux (0)	3	0.01
South American Ind. (1)	21	0.07
Spanish American Ind. (4)	4	0.01
Yaqui (1)	1	<0.01
Asian (1,203)	1,615	5.62
Not Hispanic (1,185)	1,562	5.43
Hispanic (18)	53	0.18
Bangladeshi (4)	4	0.01
Cambodian (1)	2	0.01
Chinese, ex. Taiwanese (89)	138	0.48
Filipino (207)	294	1.02
Hmong (6)	6	0.02
Indian (622)	776	2.70
Indonesian (2)	5	0.02
Japanese (24)	39	0.14
Korean (55)	77	0.27
Laotian (3)	3	0.01
Nepalese (4)	4	0.01
Pakistani (32)	49	0.17
Sri Lankan (4)	4	0.01
Taiwanese (8)	8	0.03
Thai (7)	8	0.03
Vietnamese (63)	75	0.26
Hawaii Native/Pacific Islander (27)	101	0.35
Not Hispanic (18)	82	0.29
Hispanic (9)	19	0.07
Guamanian/Chamorro (3)	5	0.02
Native Hawaiian (5)	15	0.05
Samoan (2)	12	0.04
White (20,606)	21,322	74.18
Not Hispanic (17,377)	17,833	62.05
Hispanic (3,229)	3,489	12.14

*Notes: † The Census 2010 population figure is used to calculate the percentages in the Hispanic Origin and Race categories. Ancestry percentages are based on the 2006-2010 American Community Survey population (not shown); ‡ Numbers in parentheses indicate the number of people reporting a single ancestry; * Numbers in parentheses indicate the number of persons reporting this race alone, not in combination with any other race; Please refer to the Explanation of Data for more information.*

Cocoa Beach

Place Type: City
County: Brevard
Population: 11,231†

Ancestry‡	Population	%
African, Sub-Saharan (0)	14	0.12
African (0)	14	0.12
American (978)	978	8.37
Arab (78)	107	0.92
Egyptian (10)	10	0.09
Lebanese (27)	44	0.38
Syrian (41)	53	0.45
Armenian (15)	15	0.13
Austrian (45)	92	0.79
Belgian (0)	25	0.21
Brazilian (34)	96	0.82
British (114)	140	1.20
Canadian (38)	88	0.75
Croatian (19)	19	0.16
Czech (61)	132	1.13
Czechoslovakian (0)	12	0.10
Danish (10)	101	0.86
Dutch (96)	232	1.99
Eastern European (8)	8	0.07
English (649)	1,821	15.59
European (37)	52	0.45
French, ex. Basque (102)	509	4.36
French Canadian (13)	26	0.22
German (890)	2,800	23.98
Greek (68)	109	0.93
Hungarian (9)	69	0.59
Irish (809)	2,696	23.09
Italian (512)	1,011	8.66
Lithuanian (77)	110	0.94
Norwegian (44)	109	0.93
Pennsylvania German (12)	12	0.10
Polish (130)	619	5.30
Portuguese (32)	76	0.65
Romanian (7)	7	0.06
Russian (39)	130	1.11
Scandinavian (21)	21	0.18
Scotch-Irish (257)	325	2.78
Scottish (135)	487	4.17
Slovak (25)	25	0.21
Swedish (51)	119	1.02
Swiss (14)	60	0.51
Ukrainian (13)	25	0.21
Welsh (55)	127	1.09
West Indian, ex. Hispanic (79)	104	0.89
Bahamian (19)	19	0.16
Jamaican (60)	85	0.73

Hispanic Origin	Population	%
Hispanic or Latino (of any race)	354	3.15
Central American, ex. Mexican	22	0.20
Costa Rican	3	0.03
Guatemalan	7	0.06
Honduran	5	0.04
Nicaraguan	2	0.02
Panamanian	4	0.04
Salvadoran	1	0.01
Cuban	73	0.65
Dominican Republic	8	0.07
Mexican	77	0.69
Puerto Rican	71	0.63
South American	66	0.59
Argentinean	17	0.15
Chilean	4	0.04
Colombian	21	0.19
Ecuadorian	6	0.05
Paraguayan	2	0.02
Peruvian	5	0.04
Venezuelan	11	0.10
Other Hispanic or Latino	37	0.33

Race*	Population	%
African-American/Black (86)	115	1.02
Not Hispanic (83)	109	0.97
Hispanic (3)	6	0.05
American Indian/Alaska Native (40)	87	0.77
Not Hispanic (33)	75	0.67
Hispanic (7)	12	0.11
Aleut *(Alaska Native)* (1)	1	0.01
Apache (0)	4	0.04
Blackfeet (1)	1	0.01
Central American Ind. (0)	1	0.01
Cherokee (6)	23	0.20
Cheyenne (0)	1	0.01
Choctaw (1)	2	0.02
Inupiat *(Alaska Native)* (1)	1	0.01
Iroquois (0)	1	0.01
Lumbee (1)	1	0.01
Mexican American Ind. (1)	1	0.01
Navajo (1)	1	0.01
Osage (2)	2	0.02
Ottawa (0)	1	0.01
Pueblo (2)	2	0.02
Sioux (0)	1	0.01
South American Ind. (2)	2	0.02
Asian (173)	223	1.99
Not Hispanic (169)	216	1.92
Hispanic (4)	7	0.06
Bangladeshi (2)	2	0.02
Burmese (1)	1	0.01
Chinese, ex. Taiwanese (43)	54	0.48
Filipino (25)	44	0.39
Indian (42)	44	0.39
Indonesian (0)	1	0.01
Japanese (15)	21	0.19
Korean (18)	24	0.21
Taiwanese (2)	5	0.04
Thai (16)	19	0.17
Vietnamese (7)	12	0.11
Hawaii Native/Pacific Islander (2)	10	0.09
Not Hispanic (1)	9	0.08
Hispanic (1)	1	0.01
Native Hawaiian (1)	5	0.04
Samoan (1)	2	0.02
White (10,741)	10,866	96.75
Not Hispanic (10,457)	10,563	94.05
Hispanic (284)	303	2.70

Cocoa

Place Type: City
County: Brevard
Population: 17,140†

Ancestry‡	Population	%
African, Sub-Saharan (134)	134	0.77
African (134)	134	0.77
American (1,112)	1,112	6.37
Arab (49)	49	0.28
Lebanese (49)	49	0.28
Austrian (0)	71	0.41
Belgian (0)	8	0.05
British (118)	175	1.00
Canadian (0)	25	0.14
Czech (12)	51	0.29
Danish (0)	23	0.13
Dutch (65)	100	0.57
English (613)	1,359	7.79
European (46)	46	0.26
French, ex. Basque (147)	366	2.10
French Canadian (81)	117	0.67
German (527)	1,705	9.77
Greek (23)	73	0.42
Hungarian (53)	107	0.61
Irish (700)	1,833	10.50
Italian (350)	890	5.10
Northern European (27)	27	0.15
Norwegian (16)	42	0.24
Polish (104)	668	3.83
Portuguese (18)	29	0.17
Russian (22)	33	0.19
Scotch-Irish (68)	114	0.65
Scottish (93)	363	2.08
Slavic (8)	8	0.05
Slovene (0)	32	0.18
Swedish (27)	140	0.80
Swiss (20)	48	0.28
Ukrainian (16)	16	0.09
Welsh (14)	87	0.50
West Indian, ex. Hispanic (126)	140	0.80
Bahamian (43)	43	0.25
Haitian (55)	69	0.40
Jamaican (28)	28	0.16
Yugoslavian (0)	8	0.05

Hispanic Origin	Population	%
Hispanic or Latino (of any race)	1,931	11.27
Central American, ex. Mexican	628	3.66
Costa Rican	3	0.02
Guatemalan	514	3.00
Honduran	67	0.39
Nicaraguan	8	0.05
Panamanian	17	0.10
Salvadoran	19	0.11
Cuban	104	0.61
Dominican Republic	39	0.23
Mexican	519	3.03
Puerto Rican	359	2.09
South American	75	0.44
Argentinean	7	0.04
Bolivian	1	0.01
Chilean	2	0.01
Colombian	20	0.12
Ecuadorian	6	0.04
Peruvian	12	0.07
Uruguayan	2	0.01
Venezuelan	19	0.11
Other South American	6	0.04
Other Hispanic or Latino	207	1.21

Race*	Population	%
African-American/Black (5,369)	5,671	33.09
Not Hispanic (5,253)	5,510	32.15
Hispanic (116)	161	0.94
American Indian/Alaska Native (94)	217	1.27
Not Hispanic (75)	185	1.08
Hispanic (19)	32	0.19
Apache (5)	7	0.04
Blackfeet (1)	7	0.04
Canadian/French Am. Ind. (0)	1	0.01
Cherokee (17)	59	0.34
Chickasaw (2)	3	0.02
Chippewa (2)	4	0.02
Choctaw (3)	4	0.02
Creek (2)	4	0.02
Iroquois (3)	5	0.03
Lumbee (5)	8	0.05
Mexican American Ind. (8)	13	0.08
Ottawa (0)	1	0.01
Potawatomi (1)	4	0.02
Seminole (0)	3	0.02
Sioux (0)	1	0.01
South American Ind. (2)	2	0.01
Spanish American Ind. (2)	2	0.01
Asian (182)	267	1.56
Not Hispanic (175)	244	1.42
Hispanic (7)	23	0.13
Bangladeshi (1)	1	0.01
Cambodian (4)	4	0.02
Chinese, ex. Taiwanese (9)	16	0.09
Filipino (52)	74	0.43
Indian (36)	39	0.23
Japanese (20)	36	0.21
Korean (9)	23	0.13
Laotian (3)	3	0.02
Thai (9)	15	0.09
Vietnamese (31)	35	0.20
Hawaii Native/Pacific Islander (46)	67	0.39
Not Hispanic (10)	24	0.14
Hispanic (36)	43	0.25
Guamanian/Chamorro (38)	45	0.26
Marshallese (0)	1	0.01
Native Hawaiian (4)	12	0.07
Samoan (0)	2	0.01

*Notes: † The Census 2010 population figure is used to calculate the percentages in the Hispanic Origin and Race categories. Ancestry percentages are based on the 2006-2010 American Community Survey population (not shown); ‡ Numbers in parentheses indicate the number of people reporting a single ancestry; * Numbers in parentheses indicate the number of persons reporting this race alone, not in combination with any other race; Please refer to the Explanation of Data for more information.*

White (10,141)	10,534	61.46
Not Hispanic (9,285)	9,599	56.00
Hispanic (856)	935	5.46

Coconut Creek

Place Type: City
County: Broward
Population: 52,909†

Ancestry‡	Population	%
African, Sub-Saharan (57)	106	0.21
African (45)	94	0.18
South African (12)	12	0.02
Albanian (22)	22	0.04
American (1,839)	1,839	3.57
Arab (574)	838	1.63
Arab (40)	79	0.15
Egyptian (326)	332	0.64
Iraqi (17)	71	0.14
Jordanian (18)	18	0.03
Lebanese (42)	113	0.22
Moroccan (83)	83	0.16
Syrian (24)	49	0.10
Other Arab (24)	93	0.18
Armenian (9)	9	0.02
Australian (57)	191	0.37
Austrian (206)	564	1.09
Belgian (52)	52	0.10
Brazilian (2,261)	2,476	4.80
British (241)	333	0.65
Canadian (240)	322	0.62
Czech (63)	173	0.34
Czechoslovakian (0)	12	0.02
Danish (72)	232	0.45
Dutch (140)	485	0.94
Eastern European (248)	248	0.48
English (1,069)	2,825	5.48
European (371)	386	0.75
French, ex. Basque (162)	1,251	2.43
French Canadian (85)	122	0.24
German (1,476)	5,116	9.93
Greek (111)	268	0.52
Guyanese (261)	317	0.62
Hungarian (203)	452	0.88
Iranian (66)	66	0.13
Irish (1,118)	4,057	7.87
Israeli (207)	244	0.47
Italian (3,814)	6,836	13.26
Latvian (41)	56	0.11
Lithuanian (96)	226	0.44
Luxemburger (37)	78	0.15
Norwegian (90)	165	0.32
Polish (1,219)	2,746	5.33
Portuguese (338)	539	1.05
Romanian (83)	284	0.55
Russian (1,299)	2,576	5.00
Scotch-Irish (89)	420	0.81
Scottish (201)	682	1.32
Slovak (40)	120	0.23
Swedish (56)	300	0.58
Swiss (78)	102	0.20
Turkish (125)	197	0.38
Ukrainian (80)	145	0.28
Welsh (37)	252	0.49
West Indian, ex. Hispanic (3,548)	3,889	7.55
Bahamian (13)	13	0.03
Barbadian (165)	165	0.32
British West Indian (34)	34	0.07
Dutch West Indian (25)	25	0.05
Haitian (1,451)	1,620	3.14
Jamaican (1,644)	1,685	3.27
Trinidadian/Tobagonian (136)	171	0.33
West Indian (80)	176	0.34
Yugoslavian (0)	27	0.05

Hispanic Origin	Population	%
Hispanic or Latino (of any race)	10,800	20.41
Central American, ex. Mexican	821	1.55
Costa Rican	78	0.15
Guatemalan	170	0.32
Honduran	190	0.36
Nicaraguan	169	0.32
Panamanian	85	0.16
Salvadoran	124	0.23
Other Central American	5	0.01
Cuban	979	1.85
Dominican Republic	736	1.39
Mexican	1,120	2.12
Puerto Rican	2,196	4.15
South American	4,166	7.87
Argentinean	309	0.58
Bolivian	46	0.09
Chilean	80	0.15
Colombian	1,857	3.51
Ecuadorian	380	0.72
Paraguayan	8	0.02
Peruvian	859	1.62
Uruguayan	57	0.11
Venezuelan	531	1.00
Other South American	39	0.07
Other Hispanic or Latino	782	1.48

Race*	Population	%
African-American/Black (7,256)	7,925	14.98
Not Hispanic (6,882)	7,389	13.97
Hispanic (374)	536	1.01
American Indian/Alaska Native (72)	224	0.42
Not Hispanic (47)	148	0.28
Hispanic (25)	76	0.14
Apache (0)	2	<0.01
Arapaho (1)	1	<0.01
Blackfeet (0)	2	<0.01
Canadian/French Am. Ind. (4)	4	0.01
Central American Ind. (1)	6	0.01
Cherokee (4)	28	0.05
Chippewa (3)	4	0.01
Comanche (1)	1	<0.01
Creek (0)	4	0.01
Delaware (0)	4	0.01
Houma (4)	4	0.01
Iroquois (2)	6	0.01
Lumbee (1)	1	<0.01
Mexican American Ind. (5)	8	0.02
Navajo (1)	1	<0.01
Osage (0)	3	0.01
Ottawa (0)	3	0.01
Seminole (1)	2	<0.01
Sioux (0)	2	<0.01
South American Ind. (2)	17	0.03
Asian (2,018)	2,486	4.70
Not Hispanic (1,992)	2,389	4.52
Hispanic (26)	97	0.18
Bangladeshi (52)	61	0.12
Burmese (21)	21	0.04
Cambodian (2)	4	0.01
Chinese, ex. Taiwanese (348)	454	0.86
Filipino (175)	255	0.48
Indian (726)	873	1.65
Indonesian (3)	4	0.01
Japanese (29)	61	0.12
Korean (57)	73	0.14
Laotian (5)	5	0.01
Malaysian (4)	9	0.02
Nepalese (5)	5	0.01
Pakistani (153)	164	0.31
Sri Lankan (5)	5	0.01
Taiwanese (13)	17	0.03
Thai (56)	66	0.12
Vietnamese (310)	345	0.65
Hawaii Native/Pacific Islander (17)	127	0.24
Not Hispanic (17)	101	0.19
Hispanic (0)	26	0.05
Fijian (1)	3	0.01
Guamanian/Chamorro (0)	1	<0.01
Native Hawaiian (9)	28	0.05
Samoan (2)	5	0.01
Tongan (1)	3	0.01
White (39,830)	41,033	77.55
Not Hispanic (31,570)	32,314	61.07
Hispanic (8,260)	8,719	16.48

Conway

Place Type: CDP
County: Orange
Population: 13,467†

Ancestry‡	Population	%
African, Sub-Saharan (0)	16	0.11
African (0)	16	0.11
American (1,351)	1,351	9.45
Arab (35)	130	0.91
Arab (22)	77	0.54
Lebanese (13)	44	0.31
Syrian (0)	9	0.06
Austrian (18)	56	0.39
Belgian (30)	88	0.62
British (56)	111	0.78
Croatian (0)	10	0.07
Czech (20)	54	0.38
Danish (0)	10	0.07
Dutch (67)	195	1.36
English (522)	2,034	14.23
European (161)	194	1.36
Finnish (0)	14	0.10
French, ex. Basque (40)	553	3.87
French Canadian (28)	88	0.62
German (639)	2,506	17.53
Greek (14)	29	0.20
Guyanese (15)	15	0.10
Hungarian (23)	90	0.63
Irish (486)	2,157	15.09
Italian (288)	1,127	7.88
Lithuanian (0)	30	0.21
Northern European (14)	14	0.10
Norwegian (20)	85	0.59
Polish (96)	298	2.08
Portuguese (30)	65	0.45
Russian (15)	15	0.10
Scandinavian (20)	57	0.40
Scotch-Irish (145)	448	3.13
Scottish (151)	465	3.25
Slovak (11)	21	0.15
Swedish (25)	151	1.06
Swiss (0)	17	0.12
Welsh (46)	234	1.64
West Indian, ex. Hispanic (317)	333	2.33
Trinidadian/Tobagonian (290)	290	2.03
U.S. Virgin Islander (27)	27	0.19
West Indian (0)	16	0.11

Hispanic Origin	Population	%
Hispanic or Latino (of any race)	2,222	16.50
Central American, ex. Mexican	110	0.82
Costa Rican	14	0.10
Guatemalan	16	0.12
Honduran	37	0.27
Nicaraguan	20	0.15
Panamanian	13	0.10
Salvadoran	10	0.07
Cuban	284	2.11
Dominican Republic	118	0.88
Mexican	149	1.11
Puerto Rican	1,094	8.12
South American	335	2.49
Argentinean	15	0.11
Bolivian	1	0.01
Chilean	14	0.10
Colombian	172	1.28
Ecuadorian	37	0.27
Peruvian	38	0.28
Uruguayan	10	0.07
Venezuelan	48	0.36
Other Hispanic or Latino	132	0.98

Race*	Population	%
African-American/Black (503)	590	4.38
Not Hispanic (411)	461	3.42
Hispanic (92)	129	0.96

*Notes: † The Census 2010 population figure is used to calculate the percentages in the Hispanic Origin and Race categories. Ancestry percentages are based on the 2006-2010 American Community Survey population (not shown); ‡ Numbers in parentheses indicate the number of people reporting a single ancestry; * Numbers in parentheses indicate the number of persons reporting this race alone, not in combination with any other race; Please refer to the Explanation of Data for more information.*

American Indian/Alaska Native (37)	111	0.82
Not Hispanic (22)	64	0.48
Hispanic (15)	47	0.35
Apache (4)	5	0.04
Blackfeet (0)	1	0.01
Central American Ind. (0)	1	0.01
Cherokee (7)	16	0.12
Chippewa (1)	1	0.01
Choctaw (0)	1	0.01
Creek (3)	3	0.02
Iroquois (0)	5	0.04
Mexican American Ind. (1)	2	0.01
Pima (0)	1	0.01
Pueblo (0)	1	0.01
Seminole (1)	3	0.02
Sioux (0)	1	0.01
South American Ind. (3)	7	0.05
Yaqui (0)	1	0.01
Asian (297)	396	2.94
Not Hispanic (292)	377	2.80
Hispanic (5)	19	0.14
Cambodian (2)	2	0.01
Chinese, ex. Taiwanese (23)	33	0.25
Filipino (105)	141	1.05
Indian (62)	68	0.50
Indonesian (1)	1	0.01
Japanese (25)	50	0.37
Korean (6)	12	0.09
Laotian (1)	1	0.01
Pakistani (8)	10	0.07
Taiwanese (3)	3	0.02
Thai (3)	3	0.02
Vietnamese (35)	44	0.33
Hawaii Native/Pacific Islander (13)	24	0.18
Not Hispanic (13)	22	0.16
Hispanic (0)	2	0.01
Guamanian/Chamorro (5)	7	0.05
Native Hawaiian (0)	2	0.01
Samoan (0)	2	0.01
White (11,935)	12,187	90.50
Not Hispanic (10,315)	10,466	77.72
Hispanic (1,620)	1,721	12.78

Cooper City

Place Type: City
County: Broward
Population: 28,547†

Ancestry‡	Population	%
African, Sub-Saharan (47)	90	0.31
African (12)	25	0.09
Nigerian (17)	32	0.11
South African (18)	18	0.06
Other Sub-Saharan African (0)	15	0.05
American (1,244)	1,244	4.34
Arab (91)	171	0.60
Arab (17)	17	0.06
Egyptian (21)	21	0.07
Lebanese (44)	73	0.25
Moroccan (9)	9	0.03
Syrian (0)	31	0.11
Other Arab (0)	20	0.07
Armenian (15)	37	0.13
Austrian (100)	194	0.68
Belgian (0)	17	0.06
Brazilian (10)	19	0.07
British (102)	207	0.72
Bulgarian (74)	74	0.26
Canadian (63)	96	0.33
Croatian (0)	17	0.06
Czech (9)	40	0.14
Czechoslovakian (0)	12	0.04
Danish (0)	20	0.07
Dutch (106)	227	0.79
Eastern European (302)	339	1.18
English (596)	2,211	7.72
European (286)	306	1.07
Finnish (9)	22	0.08
French, ex. Basque (211)	761	2.66
French Canadian (82)	166	0.58
German (717)	3,574	12.47
Greek (73)	196	0.68
Guyanese (43)	52	0.18
Hungarian (102)	311	1.09
Iranian (20)	20	0.07
Irish (955)	3,543	12.36
Israeli (270)	425	1.48
Italian (1,993)	4,090	14.27
Lithuanian (47)	71	0.25
Maltese (12)	12	0.04
Northern European (11)	11	0.04
Norwegian (38)	137	0.48
Pennsylvania German (0)	11	0.04
Polish (473)	1,461	5.10
Portuguese (38)	65	0.23
Romanian (33)	140	0.49
Russian (780)	1,533	5.35
Scandinavian (9)	9	0.03
Scotch-Irish (41)	231	0.81
Scottish (157)	481	1.68
Slavic (0)	10	0.03
Slovak (19)	19	0.07
Swedish (57)	299	1.04
Swiss (13)	68	0.24
Turkish (46)	77	0.27
Ukrainian (11)	15	0.05
Welsh (0)	60	0.21
West Indian, ex. Hispanic (778)	973	3.40
Bahamian (10)	10	0.03
Haitian (266)	320	1.12
Jamaican (428)	515	1.80
Trinidadian/Tobagonian (18)	59	0.21
West Indian (56)	69	0.24
Yugoslavian (0)	11	0.04

Hispanic Origin	Population	%
Hispanic or Latino (of any race)	6,520	22.84
Central American, ex. Mexican	452	1.58
Costa Rican	69	0.24
Guatemalan	71	0.25
Honduran	73	0.26
Nicaraguan	115	0.40
Panamanian	65	0.23
Salvadoran	59	0.21
Cuban	2,246	7.87
Dominican Republic	315	1.10
Mexican	212	0.74
Puerto Rican	1,040	3.64
South American	1,881	6.59
Argentinean	145	0.51
Bolivian	17	0.06
Chilean	74	0.26
Colombian	923	3.23
Ecuadorian	190	0.67
Paraguayan	1	<0.01
Peruvian	303	1.06
Uruguayan	38	0.13
Venezuelan	185	0.65
Other South American	5	0.02
Other Hispanic or Latino	374	1.31

Race*	Population	%
African-American/Black (1,412)	1,670	5.85
Not Hispanic (1,290)	1,479	5.18
Hispanic (122)	191	0.67
American Indian/Alaska Native (81)	155	0.54
Not Hispanic (60)	108	0.38
Hispanic (21)	47	0.16
Aleut *(Alaska Native)* (0)	1	<0.01
Apache (1)	2	0.01
Central American Ind. (1)	3	0.01
Cherokee (6)	32	0.11
Cheyenne (1)	1	<0.01
Chippewa (0)	2	0.01
Choctaw (2)	5	0.02
Creek (4)	4	0.01
Delaware (0)	1	<0.01
Iroquois (8)	11	0.04
Lumbee (0)	3	0.01
Menominee (1)	1	<0.01
Mexican American Ind. (1)	2	0.01
Potawatomi (4)	4	0.01
Seminole (13)	15	0.05
Sioux (2)	3	0.01
South American Ind. (2)	8	0.03
Spanish American Ind. (7)	7	0.02
Asian (1,575)	1,874	6.56
Not Hispanic (1,556)	1,813	6.35
Hispanic (19)	61	0.21
Bangladeshi (47)	49	0.17
Cambodian (1)	2	0.01
Chinese, ex. Taiwanese (307)	392	1.37
Filipino (118)	162	0.57
Indian (676)	774	2.71
Indonesian (1)	2	0.01
Japanese (13)	34	0.12
Korean (107)	125	0.44
Laotian (2)	2	0.01
Malaysian (1)	7	0.02
Nepalese (3)	3	0.01
Pakistani (117)	139	0.49
Sri Lankan (5)	6	0.02
Taiwanese (27)	27	0.09
Thai (46)	48	0.17
Vietnamese (70)	73	0.26
Hawaii Native/Pacific Islander (9)	41	0.14
Not Hispanic (7)	34	0.12
Hispanic (2)	7	0.02
Native Hawaiian (2)	15	0.05
Samoan (2)	2	0.01
White (24,291)	24,809	86.91
Not Hispanic (18,577)	18,885	66.15
Hispanic (5,714)	5,924	20.75

Coral Gables

Place Type: City
County: Miami-Dade
Population: 46,780†

Ancestry‡	Population	%
African, Sub-Saharan (43)	59	0.13
African (0)	16	0.03
Liberian (33)	33	0.07
South African (10)	10	0.02
American (1,601)	1,601	3.48
Arab (261)	609	1.33
Arab (71)	109	0.24
Lebanese (69)	337	0.73
Moroccan (10)	26	0.06
Palestinian (5)	18	0.04
Syrian (106)	119	0.26
Armenian (0)	32	0.07
Australian (16)	16	0.03
Austrian (155)	323	0.70
Basque (32)	72	0.16
Belgian (77)	105	0.23
Brazilian (344)	377	0.82
British (363)	664	1.44
Bulgarian (22)	40	0.09
Canadian (23)	129	0.28
Croatian (36)	46	0.10
Cypriot (12)	24	0.05
Czech (75)	122	0.27
Danish (37)	88	0.19
Dutch (114)	284	0.62
Eastern European (108)	108	0.24
English (731)	2,525	5.49
Estonian (11)	11	0.02
European (423)	511	1.11
Finnish (0)	12	0.03
French, ex. Basque (88)	1,010	2.20
French Canadian (54)	107	0.23
German (588)	3,016	6.56
Greek (332)	438	0.95
Guyanese (16)	16	0.03
Hungarian (89)	242	0.53
Irish (913)	2,924	6.36
Israeli (37)	37	0.08

SECTION TWO

*Notes: † The Census 2010 population figure is used to calculate the percentages in the Hispanic Origin and Race categories. Ancestry percentages are based on the 2006-2010 American Community Survey population (not shown); ‡ Numbers in parentheses indicate the number of people reporting a single ancestry; * Numbers in parentheses indicate the number of persons reporting this race alone, not in combination with any other race; Please refer to the Explanation of Data for more information.*

Italian (1,132)	2,606	5.67
Latvian (13)	15	0.03
Lithuanian (0)	97	0.21
Luxemburger (0)	14	0.03
New Zealander (0)	23	0.05
Norwegian (94)	311	0.68
Polish (494)	1,224	2.66
Portuguese (20)	109	0.24
Romanian (13)	49	0.11
Russian (506)	1,286	2.80
Scandinavian (13)	57	0.12
Scotch-Irish (198)	426	0.93
Scottish (125)	758	1.65
Serbian (8)	21	0.05
Slavic (9)	9	0.02
Slovene (0)	18	0.04
Swedish (120)	476	1.04
Swiss (41)	141	0.31
Turkish (57)	73	0.16
Ukrainian (60)	177	0.39
Welsh (43)	164	0.36
West Indian, ex. Hispanic (279)	493	1.07
Bahamian (28)	46	0.10
Belizean (18)	18	0.04
British West Indian (0)	70	0.15
Haitian (55)	71	0.15
Jamaican (120)	230	0.50
Trinidadian/Tobagonian (42)	42	0.09
Other West Indian (16)	16	0.03
Yugoslavian (0)	49	0.11

Hispanic Origin	Population	%
Hispanic or Latino (of any race)	25,062	53.57
Central American, ex. Mexican	1,489	3.18
Costa Rican	99	0.21
Guatemalan	122	0.26
Honduran	291	0.62
Nicaraguan	651	1.39
Panamanian	151	0.32
Salvadoran	169	0.36
Other Central American	6	0.01
Cuban	14,657	31.33
Dominican Republic	480	1.03
Mexican	829	1.77
Puerto Rican	1,144	2.45
South American	4,941	10.56
Argentinean	557	1.19
Bolivian	85	0.18
Chilean	230	0.49
Colombian	1,678	3.59
Ecuadorian	351	0.75
Paraguayan	36	0.08
Peruvian	651	1.39
Uruguayan	147	0.31
Venezuelan	1,201	2.57
Other South American	5	0.01
Other Hispanic or Latino	1,522	3.25

Race*	Population	%
African-American/Black (1,400)	1,655	3.54
Not Hispanic (1,175)	1,321	2.82
Hispanic (225)	334	0.71
American Indian/Alaska Native (47)	113	0.24
Not Hispanic (19)	58	0.12
Hispanic (28)	55	0.12
Blackfeet (0)	1	<0.01
Canadian/French Am. Ind. (0)	1	<0.01
Central American Ind. (2)	2	<0.01
Cherokee (5)	19	0.04
Choctaw (0)	2	<0.01
Iroquois (4)	6	0.01
Mexican American Ind. (2)	6	0.01
Navajo (1)	1	<0.01
Pueblo (1)	1	<0.01
South American Ind. (5)	13	0.03
Spanish American Ind. (1)	2	<0.01
Asian (1,286)	1,616	3.45
Not Hispanic (1,250)	1,509	3.23
Hispanic (36)	107	0.23
Bangladeshi (5)	7	0.01
Burmese (2)	4	0.01
Chinese, ex. Taiwanese (480)	588	1.26
Filipino (105)	154	0.33
Indian (362)	427	0.91
Indonesian (1)	4	0.01
Japanese (86)	140	0.30
Korean (65)	102	0.22
Laotian (1)	2	<0.01
Malaysian (5)	7	0.01
Pakistani (41)	52	0.11
Sri Lankan (5)	7	0.01
Taiwanese (32)	33	0.07
Thai (22)	24	0.05
Vietnamese (25)	43	0.09
Hawaii Native/Pacific Islander (10)	32	0.07
Not Hispanic (8)	23	0.05
Hispanic (2)	9	0.02
Fijian (2)	2	<0.01
Guamanian/Chamorro (2)	4	0.01
Native Hawaiian (3)	11	0.02
Samoan (2)	2	<0.01
White (42,568)	43,292	92.54
Not Hispanic (18,764)	19,123	40.88
Hispanic (23,804)	24,169	51.67

Coral Springs

Place Type: City
County: Broward
Population: 121,096†

Ancestry‡	Population	%
African, Sub-Saharan (323)	737	0.61
African (178)	558	0.46
Cape Verdean (41)	41	0.03
Nigerian (10)	10	0.01
South African (82)	116	0.10
Zimbabwean (12)	12	0.01
Albanian (8)	8	0.01
American (6,886)	6,886	5.69
Arab (459)	698	0.58
Arab (48)	48	0.04
Egyptian (93)	113	0.09
Iraqi (13)	13	0.01
Lebanese (159)	245	0.20
Moroccan (0)	38	0.03
Syrian (64)	140	0.12
Other Arab (82)	101	0.08
Armenian (98)	152	0.13
Australian (13)	42	0.03
Austrian (276)	692	0.57
Belgian (11)	87	0.07
Brazilian (1,147)	1,206	1.00
British (225)	395	0.33
Canadian (425)	849	0.70
Croatian (37)	189	0.16
Czech (79)	433	0.36
Czechoslovakian (30)	97	0.08
Danish (52)	183	0.15
Dutch (241)	870	0.72
Eastern European (712)	762	0.63
English (2,247)	7,251	5.99
Estonian (0)	8	0.01
European (1,219)	1,289	1.06
Finnish (0)	52	0.04
French, ex. Basque (642)	2,876	2.37
French Canadian (276)	630	0.52
German (3,234)	11,926	9.85
Greek (340)	799	0.66
Guyanese (265)	367	0.30
Hungarian (309)	1,126	0.93
Icelander (30)	55	0.05
Iranian (133)	140	0.12
Irish (3,259)	10,893	8.99
Israeli (334)	481	0.40
Italian (5,987)	12,634	10.43
Latvian (123)	158	0.13
Lithuanian (148)	309	0.26
Macedonian (0)	13	0.01
Norwegian (254)	466	0.38
Pennsylvania German (26)	26	0.02
Polish (2,079)	5,871	4.85
Portuguese (141)	363	0.30
Romanian (111)	382	0.32
Russian (2,546)	5,962	4.92
Scandinavian (134)	168	0.14
Scotch-Irish (390)	876	0.72
Scottish (433)	1,377	1.14
Serbian (92)	160	0.13
Slavic (23)	158	0.13
Slovak (40)	141	0.12
Slovene (0)	13	0.01
Swedish (234)	533	0.44
Swiss (46)	270	0.22
Turkish (149)	149	0.12
Ukrainian (155)	296	0.24
Welsh (60)	587	0.48
West Indian, ex. Hispanic (9,781)	11,510	9.50
Bahamian (73)	98	0.08
Barbadian (17)	17	0.01
British West Indian (30)	121	0.10
Dutch West Indian (128)	157	0.13
Haitian (4,171)	4,916	4.06
Jamaican (4,255)	4,883	4.03
Trinidadian/Tobagonian (410)	486	0.40
West Indian (697)	832	0.69
Yugoslavian (36)	93	0.08

Hispanic Origin	Population	%
Hispanic or Latino (of any race)	28,442	23.49
Central American, ex. Mexican	1,865	1.54
Costa Rican	165	0.14
Guatemalan	324	0.27
Honduran	395	0.33
Nicaraguan	341	0.28
Panamanian	290	0.24
Salvadoran	337	0.28
Other Central American	13	0.01
Cuban	2,853	2.36
Dominican Republic	1,938	1.60
Mexican	2,199	1.82
Puerto Rican	5,910	4.88
South American	11,749	9.70
Argentinean	832	0.69
Bolivian	146	0.12
Chilean	342	0.28
Colombian	5,521	4.56
Ecuadorian	956	0.79
Paraguayan	35	0.03
Peruvian	2,226	1.84
Uruguayan	224	0.18
Venezuelan	1,414	1.17
Other South American	53	0.04
Other Hispanic or Latino	1,928	1.59

Race*	Population	%
African-American/Black (21,730)	23,675	19.55
Not Hispanic (20,713)	22,177	18.31
Hispanic (1,017)	1,498	1.24
American Indian/Alaska Native (288)	679	0.56
Not Hispanic (167)	429	0.35
Hispanic (121)	250	0.21
Aleut *(Alaska Native)* (1)	1	<0.01
Apache (1)	10	0.01
Arapaho (0)	1	<0.01
Blackfeet (3)	15	0.01
Canadian/French Am. Ind. (2)	4	<0.01
Central American Ind. (12)	20	0.02
Cherokee (22)	98	0.08
Chickasaw (4)	7	0.01
Chippewa (5)	7	0.01
Choctaw (7)	14	0.01
Cree (0)	1	<0.01
Creek (4)	6	<0.01
Delaware (2)	4	<0.01
Iroquois (8)	17	0.01
Lumbee (3)	8	0.01
Mexican American Ind. (15)	36	0.03
Navajo (3)	3	<0.01
Pueblo (0)	1	<0.01

*Notes: † The Census 2010 population figure is used to calculate the percentages in the Hispanic Origin and Race categories. Ancestry percentages are based on the 2006-2010 American Community Survey population (not shown); ‡ Numbers in parentheses indicate the number of people reporting a single ancestry; * Numbers in parentheses indicate the number of persons reporting this race alone, not in combination with any other race; Please refer to the Explanation of Data for more information.*

Seminole (4)	4	<0.01
Sioux (1)	9	0.01
South American Ind. (17)	44	0.04
Spanish American Ind. (8)	9	0.01
Tlingit-Haida *(Alaska Native)* (0)	1	<0.01
Asian (6,170)	7,429	6.13
Not Hispanic (6,091)	7,145	5.90
Hispanic (79)	284	0.23
Bangladeshi (66)	78	0.06
Burmese (37)	39	0.03
Cambodian (10)	11	0.01
Chinese, ex. Taiwanese (1,264)	1,613	1.33
Filipino (486)	684	0.56
Hmong (5)	6	<0.01
Indian (2,722)	3,141	2.59
Indonesian (24)	41	0.03
Japanese (83)	157	0.13
Korean (236)	278	0.23
Laotian (4)	14	0.01
Malaysian (6)	8	0.01
Nepalese (3)	3	<0.01
Pakistani (466)	508	0.42
Sri Lankan (54)	71	0.06
Taiwanese (32)	43	0.04
Thai (49)	71	0.06
Vietnamese (421)	464	0.38
Hawaii Native/Pacific Islander (67)	318	0.26
Not Hispanic (54)	263	0.22
Hispanic (13)	55	0.05
Guamanian/Chamorro (18)	22	0.02
Native Hawaiian (8)	28	0.02
Samoan (4)	11	0.01
White (83,757)	86,668	71.57
Not Hispanic (62,496)	64,125	52.95
Hispanic (21,261)	22,543	18.62

Coral Terrace

Place Type: CDP
County: Miami-Dade
Population: 24,376†

Ancestry‡	Population	%
American (239)	239	1.04
Arab (0)	30	0.13
Lebanese (0)	19	0.08
Moroccan (0)	11	0.05
Austrian (0)	11	0.05
Brazilian (83)	83	0.36
British (21)	21	0.09
Canadian (37)	57	0.25
Czech (0)	11	0.05
Czechoslovakian (0)	15	0.07
Dutch (20)	105	0.46
Eastern European (17)	17	0.07
English (134)	474	2.07
European (0)	17	0.07
French, ex. Basque (0)	93	0.41
German (111)	339	1.48
Greek (8)	16	0.07
Irish (77)	385	1.68
Italian (199)	301	1.31
Lithuanian (10)	10	0.04
Northern European (11)	11	0.05
Polish (35)	65	0.28
Portuguese (7)	7	0.03
Romanian (39)	56	0.24
Russian (0)	32	0.14
Scotch-Irish (44)	54	0.24
Scottish (18)	61	0.27
West Indian, ex. Hispanic (18)	27	0.12
Haitian (18)	18	0.08
Jamaican (0)	9	0.04
Yugoslavian (26)	46	0.20

Hispanic Origin	Population	%
Hispanic or Latino (of any race)	21,595	88.59
Central American, ex. Mexican	1,672	6.86
Costa Rican	92	0.38
Guatemalan	95	0.39
Honduran	388	1.59
Nicaraguan	861	3.53
Panamanian	64	0.26
Salvadoran	169	0.69
Other Central American	3	0.01
Cuban	16,780	68.84
Dominican Republic	219	0.90
Mexican	189	0.78
Puerto Rican	453	1.86
South American	1,533	6.29
Argentinean	137	0.56
Bolivian	50	0.21
Chilean	119	0.49
Colombian	528	2.17
Ecuadorian	104	0.43
Paraguayan	14	0.06
Peruvian	286	1.17
Uruguayan	37	0.15
Venezuelan	258	1.06
Other Hispanic or Latino	749	3.07

Race*	Population	%
African-American/Black (383)	457	1.87
Not Hispanic (83)	101	0.41
Hispanic (300)	356	1.46
American Indian/Alaska Native (28)	50	0.21
Not Hispanic (10)	13	0.05
Hispanic (18)	37	0.15
Alaska Athabascan *(Ala. Nat.)* (1)	1	<0.01
Apache (0)	3	0.01
Cherokee (0)	2	0.01
Chippewa (2)	2	0.01
Lumbee (3)	3	0.01
Mexican American Ind. (6)	7	0.03
Paiute (1)	1	<0.01
South American Ind. (0)	2	0.01
Spanish American Ind. (0)	1	<0.01
Asian (140)	199	0.82
Not Hispanic (126)	152	0.62
Hispanic (14)	47	0.19
Bangladeshi (7)	8	0.03
Chinese, ex. Taiwanese (45)	80	0.33
Filipino (35)	40	0.16
Indian (7)	14	0.06
Japanese (5)	8	0.03
Korean (4)	10	0.04
Pakistani (4)	7	0.03
Sri Lankan (2)	2	0.01
Taiwanese (7)	8	0.03
Thai (0)	3	0.01
Vietnamese (13)	18	0.07
Hawaii Native/Pacific Islander (0)	12	0.05
Not Hispanic (0)	4	0.02
Hispanic (0)	8	0.03
Native Hawaiian (0)	3	0.01
Samoan (0)	1	<0.01
White (23,123)	23,403	96.01
Not Hispanic (2,502)	2,545	10.44
Hispanic (20,621)	20,858	85.57

Country Club

Place Type: CDP
County: Miami-Dade
Population: 47,105†

Ancestry‡	Population	%
African, Sub-Saharan (110)	172	0.43
African (110)	172	0.43
American (1,447)	1,447	3.64
Arab (86)	116	0.29
Arab (23)	23	0.06
Egyptian (14)	14	0.04
Lebanese (32)	32	0.08
Moroccan (0)	5	0.01
Palestinian (17)	42	0.11
Austrian (0)	95	0.24
Brazilian (12)	17	0.04
British (10)	10	0.03
Canadian (15)	51	0.13
Czech (0)	12	0.03
Danish (4)	4	0.01
Eastern European (0)	5	0.01
English (102)	329	0.83
European (95)	122	0.31
French, ex. Basque (48)	176	0.44
French Canadian (33)	33	0.08
German (127)	493	1.24
Greek (13)	34	0.09
Guyanese (0)	14	0.04
Hungarian (0)	16	0.04
Irish (144)	347	0.87
Israeli (16)	32	0.08
Italian (245)	592	1.49
Norwegian (0)	13	0.03
Polish (53)	93	0.23
Romanian (0)	19	0.05
Russian (28)	106	0.27
Scotch-Irish (5)	13	0.03
Scottish (0)	32	0.08
Slovak (0)	5	0.01
Swedish (16)	16	0.04
West Indian, ex. Hispanic (1,759)	2,093	5.27
Bahamian (93)	93	0.23
Barbadian (0)	36	0.09
British West Indian (25)	25	0.06
Haitian (708)	741	1.87
Jamaican (846)	1,053	2.65
Trinidadian/Tobagonian (71)	122	0.31
U.S. Virgin Islander (0)	7	0.02
Other West Indian (16)	16	0.04

Hispanic Origin	Population	%
Hispanic or Latino (of any race)	37,133	78.83
Central American, ex. Mexican	3,509	7.45
Costa Rican	206	0.44
Guatemalan	294	0.62
Honduran	748	1.59
Nicaraguan	1,772	3.76
Panamanian	249	0.53
Salvadoran	240	0.51
Cuban	15,509	32.92
Dominican Republic	2,999	6.37
Mexican	466	0.99
Puerto Rican	2,786	5.91
South American	10,161	21.57
Argentinean	366	0.78
Bolivian	46	0.10
Chilean	233	0.49
Colombian	6,439	13.67
Ecuadorian	768	1.63
Paraguayan	9	0.02
Peruvian	1,033	2.19
Uruguayan	100	0.21
Venezuelan	1,161	2.46
Other South American	6	0.01
Other Hispanic or Latino	1,703	3.62

Race*	Population	%
African-American/Black (6,242)	6,697	14.22
Not Hispanic (4,946)	5,103	10.83
Hispanic (1,296)	1,594	3.38
American Indian/Alaska Native (60)	121	0.26
Not Hispanic (19)	48	0.10
Hispanic (41)	73	0.15
Central American Ind. (6)	8	0.02
Cherokee (1)	5	0.01
Chickasaw (0)	1	<0.01
Chippewa (1)	1	<0.01
Creek (1)	1	<0.01
Mexican American Ind. (2)	5	0.01
Seminole (1)	3	0.01
South American Ind. (2)	6	0.01
Spanish American Ind. (11)	14	0.03
Asian (908)	1,086	2.31
Not Hispanic (868)	983	2.09
Hispanic (40)	103	0.22
Bangladeshi (4)	5	0.01
Chinese, ex. Taiwanese (209)	248	0.53
Filipino (153)	188	0.40

*Notes: † The Census 2010 population figure is used to calculate the percentages in the Hispanic Origin and Race categories. Ancestry percentages are based on the 2006-2010 American Community Survey population (not shown); ‡ Numbers in parentheses indicate the number of people reporting a single ancestry; * Numbers in parentheses indicate the number of persons reporting this race alone, not in combination with any other race; Please refer to the Explanation of Data for more information.*

SECTION TWO

Hmong (1)	1	<0.01
Indian (263)	321	0.68
Indonesian (1)	1	<0.01
Japanese (34)	55	0.12
Korean (26)	29	0.06
Malaysian (1)	1	<0.01
Nepalese (3)	3	0.01
Pakistani (107)	134	0.28
Sri Lankan (3)	3	0.01
Thai (8)	13	0.03
Vietnamese (56)	60	0.13
Hawaii Native/Pacific Islander (10)	56	0.12
Not Hispanic (2)	23	0.05
Hispanic (8)	33	0.07
Fijian (2)	2	<0.01
Guamanian/Chamorro (1)	2	<0.01
Native Hawaiian (1)	3	0.01
Samoan (0)	1	<0.01
White (36,446)	37,300	79.18
Not Hispanic (3,783)	3,961	8.41
Hispanic (32,663)	33,339	70.78

Country Walk

Place Type: CDP
County: Miami-Dade
Population: 15,997†

Ancestry‡	Population	%
African, Sub-Saharan (23)	23	0.14
Nigerian (23)	23	0.14
American (420)	420	2.64
Arab (15)	196	1.23
Arab (15)	185	1.16
Syrian (0)	11	0.07
Belgian (0)	22	0.14
Brazilian (57)	89	0.56
British (0)	110	0.69
Celtic (24)	24	0.15
Dutch (0)	29	0.18
English (14)	159	1.00
European (43)	43	0.27
French, ex. Basque (28)	218	1.37
French Canadian (73)	107	0.67
German (374)	833	5.24
Greek (13)	13	0.08
Hungarian (25)	55	0.35
Iranian (0)	29	0.18
Irish (62)	285	1.79
Italian (143)	477	3.00
Norwegian (15)	15	0.09
Polish (75)	171	1.07
Portuguese (0)	28	0.18
Romanian (13)	13	0.08
Russian (41)	91	0.57
Scotch-Irish (12)	12	0.08
Scottish (22)	108	0.68
Swedish (0)	16	0.10
Welsh (14)	14	0.09
West Indian, ex. Hispanic (1,472)	1,913	12.03
Barbadian (116)	116	0.73
Haitian (688)	858	5.39
Jamaican (662)	914	5.75
Trinidadian/Tobagonian (6)	19	0.12
West Indian (0)	6	0.04

Hispanic Origin	Population	%
Hispanic or Latino (of any race)	11,234	70.23
Central American, ex. Mexican	1,093	6.83
Costa Rican	40	0.25
Guatemalan	74	0.46
Honduran	190	1.19
Nicaraguan	624	3.90
Panamanian	73	0.46
Salvadoran	88	0.55
Other Central American	4	0.03
Cuban	5,230	32.69
Dominican Republic	506	3.16
Mexican	171	1.07
Puerto Rican	961	6.01
South American	2,721	17.01
Argentinean	151	0.94
Bolivian	46	0.29
Chilean	115	0.72
Colombian	1,322	8.26
Ecuadorian	208	1.30
Paraguayan	4	0.03
Peruvian	467	2.92
Uruguayan	50	0.31
Venezuelan	353	2.21
Other South American	5	0.03
Other Hispanic or Latino	552	3.45

Race*	Population	%
African-American/Black (1,595)	1,809	11.31
Not Hispanic (1,416)	1,563	9.77
Hispanic (179)	246	1.54
American Indian/Alaska Native (13)	38	0.24
Not Hispanic (3)	13	0.08
Hispanic (10)	25	0.16
Cree (0)	3	0.02
Iroquois (0)	1	0.01
Mexican American Ind. (7)	8	0.05
South American Ind. (2)	17	0.11
Asian (427)	581	3.63
Not Hispanic (412)	526	3.29
Hispanic (15)	55	0.34
Bangladeshi (5)	5	0.03
Chinese, ex. Taiwanese (104)	172	1.08
Filipino (76)	88	0.55
Indian (106)	173	1.08
Japanese (8)	15	0.09
Korean (14)	15	0.09
Malaysian (2)	2	0.01
Pakistani (34)	46	0.29
Taiwanese (1)	1	0.01
Thai (4)	9	0.06
Vietnamese (53)	55	0.34
Hawaii Native/Pacific Islander (8)	18	0.11
Not Hispanic (8)	18	0.11
Native Hawaiian (4)	5	0.03
Samoan (1)	3	0.02
White (13,123)	13,424	83.92
Not Hispanic (2,657)	2,778	17.37
Hispanic (10,466)	10,646	66.55

Crestview

Place Type: City
County: Okaloosa
Population: 20,978†

Ancestry‡	Population	%
African, Sub-Saharan (103)	103	0.51
African (103)	103	0.51
American (3,123)	3,123	15.48
Arab (52)	86	0.43
Arab (9)	9	0.04
Lebanese (20)	20	0.10
Other Arab (23)	57	0.28
Austrian (0)	12	0.06
British (90)	142	0.70
Canadian (95)	106	0.53
Croatian (16)	23	0.11
Czech (36)	64	0.32
Danish (0)	14	0.07
Dutch (14)	189	0.94
Eastern European (17)	17	0.08
English (833)	1,649	8.17
European (152)	238	1.18
Finnish (9)	9	0.04
French, ex. Basque (192)	564	2.80
French Canadian (25)	25	0.12
German (895)	2,609	12.93
Greek (41)	80	0.40
Guyanese (15)	15	0.07
Hungarian (28)	45	0.22
Irish (518)	1,863	9.23
Italian (318)	835	4.14
Lithuanian (28)	28	0.14
Northern European (13)	13	0.06
Norwegian (28)	107	0.53
Polish (207)	469	2.32
Russian (14)	143	0.71
Scandinavian (0)	7	0.03
Scotch-Irish (252)	522	2.59
Scottish (140)	294	1.46
Slovak (0)	32	0.16
Swedish (40)	141	0.70
Swiss (8)	16	0.08
Ukrainian (22)	87	0.43
Welsh (272)	371	1.84
West Indian, ex. Hispanic (59)	67	0.33
Bahamian (0)	8	0.04
Jamaican (59)	59	0.29

Hispanic Origin	Population	%
Hispanic or Latino (of any race)	1,390	6.63
Central American, ex. Mexican	143	0.68
Costa Rican	8	0.04
Guatemalan	18	0.09
Honduran	26	0.12
Nicaraguan	18	0.09
Panamanian	58	0.28
Salvadoran	13	0.06
Other Central American	2	0.01
Cuban	56	0.27
Dominican Republic	42	0.20
Mexican	530	2.53
Puerto Rican	408	1.94
South American	67	0.32
Argentinean	5	0.02
Bolivian	1	<0.01
Chilean	6	0.03
Colombian	21	0.10
Ecuadorian	11	0.05
Peruvian	21	0.10
Uruguayan	1	<0.01
Venezuelan	1	<0.01
Other Hispanic or Latino	144	0.69

Race*	Population	%
African-American/Black (3,902)	4,293	20.46
Not Hispanic (3,793)	4,131	19.69
Hispanic (109)	162	0.77
American Indian/Alaska Native (112)	297	1.42
Not Hispanic (85)	244	1.16
Hispanic (27)	53	0.25
Alaska Athabascan *(Ala. Nat.)* (1)	1	<0.01
Apache (1)	9	0.04
Blackfeet (1)	15	0.07
Canadian/French Am. Ind. (0)	1	<0.01
Central American Ind. (2)	2	0.01
Cherokee (21)	87	0.41
Cheyenne (0)	1	<0.01
Chickasaw (2)	3	0.01
Chippewa (4)	7	0.03
Choctaw (4)	7	0.03
Comanche (0)	4	0.02
Creek (20)	35	0.17
Delaware (1)	1	<0.01
Lumbee (1)	4	0.02
Mexican American Ind. (8)	10	0.05
Navajo (2)	5	0.02
Ottawa (2)	4	0.02
Potawatomi (0)	4	0.02
Pueblo (3)	3	0.01
Seminole (1)	3	0.01
Shoshone (0)	1	<0.01
Sioux (3)	5	0.02
South American Ind. (6)	6	0.03
Asian (649)	1,013	4.83
Not Hispanic (636)	960	4.58
Hispanic (13)	53	0.25
Burmese (5)	5	0.02
Cambodian (2)	2	0.01
Chinese, ex. Taiwanese (51)	80	0.38
Filipino (267)	449	2.14
Indian (68)	91	0.43
Indonesian (2)	4	0.02

*Notes: † The Census 2010 population figure is used to calculate the percentages in the Hispanic Origin and Race categories. Ancestry percentages are based on the 2006-2010 American Community Survey population (not shown); ‡ Numbers in parentheses indicate the number of people reporting a single ancestry; * Numbers in parentheses indicate the number of persons reporting this race alone, not in combination with any other race; Please refer to the Explanation of Data for more information.*

Japanese (29)	92	0.44
Korean (111)	180	0.86
Laotian (2)	3	0.01
Pakistani (3)	3	0.01
Sri Lankan (1)	1	<0.01
Taiwanese (6)	9	0.04
Thai (31)	49	0.23
Vietnamese (38)	46	0.22
Hawaii Native/Pacific Islander (60)	133	0.63
Not Hispanic (55)	117	0.56
Hispanic (5)	16	0.08
Guamanian/Chamorro (27)	46	0.22
Native Hawaiian (19)	55	0.26
Samoan (0)	4	0.02
White (14,982)	15,794	75.29
Not Hispanic (14,208)	14,887	70.96
Hispanic (774)	907	4.32

Cutler Bay

Place Type: Town
County: Miami-Dade
Population: 40,286†

Ancestry‡	Population	%
African, Sub-Saharan (23)	34	0.09
African (23)	34	0.09
American (3,870)	3,870	10.08
Arab (244)	513	1.34
Arab (160)	160	0.42
Jordanian (27)	262	0.68
Lebanese (22)	22	0.06
Moroccan (0)	34	0.09
Palestinian (8)	8	0.02
Syrian (27)	27	0.07
Austrian (70)	112	0.29
Brazilian (84)	84	0.22
British (115)	147	0.38
Canadian (31)	86	0.22
Czech (49)	109	0.28
Czechoslovakian (31)	31	0.08
Danish (9)	9	0.02
Dutch (31)	321	0.84
Eastern European (11)	23	0.06
English (616)	1,757	4.57
European (466)	549	1.43
Finnish (10)	46	0.12
French, ex. Basque (254)	611	1.59
French Canadian (15)	29	0.08
German (552)	2,266	5.90
Greek (52)	102	0.27
Hungarian (39)	74	0.19
Irish (401)	1,807	4.70
Israeli (122)	122	0.32
Italian (631)	1,575	4.10
Lithuanian (20)	20	0.05
Norwegian (23)	137	0.36
Polish (192)	620	1.61
Portuguese (9)	75	0.20
Russian (27)	103	0.27
Scandinavian (47)	47	0.12
Scotch-Irish (99)	225	0.59
Scottish (113)	387	1.01
Slavic (0)	13	0.03
Slovak (22)	50	0.13
Swedish (41)	75	0.20
Swiss (0)	18	0.05
Ukrainian (8)	8	0.02
Welsh (0)	75	0.20
West Indian, ex. Hispanic (2,515)	2,932	7.63
Bahamian (35)	44	0.11
Barbadian (12)	12	0.03
Belizean (63)	173	0.45
British West Indian (55)	55	0.14
Haitian (480)	597	1.55
Jamaican (1,448)	1,608	4.19
Trinidadian/Tobagonian (340)	340	0.89
West Indian (82)	93	0.24
Other West Indian (0)	10	0.03
Yugoslavian (0)	11	0.03

Hispanic Origin	Population	%
Hispanic or Latino (of any race)	21,936	54.45
Central American, ex. Mexican	2,566	6.37
Costa Rican	122	0.30
Guatemalan	199	0.49
Honduran	528	1.31
Nicaraguan	1,266	3.14
Panamanian	187	0.46
Salvadoran	258	0.64
Other Central American	6	0.01
Cuban	9,858	24.47
Dominican Republic	1,057	2.62
Mexican	732	1.82
Puerto Rican	2,669	6.63
South American	3,989	9.90
Argentinean	343	0.85
Bolivian	81	0.20
Chilean	194	0.48
Colombian	1,731	4.30
Ecuadorian	290	0.72
Paraguayan	30	0.07
Peruvian	643	1.60
Uruguayan	59	0.15
Venezuelan	597	1.48
Other South American	21	0.05
Other Hispanic or Latino	1,065	2.64

Race*	Population	%
African-American/Black (5,725)	6,383	15.84
Not Hispanic (5,137)	5,543	13.76
Hispanic (588)	840	2.09
American Indian/Alaska Native (97)	211	0.52
Not Hispanic (31)	102	0.25
Hispanic (66)	109	0.27
Blackfeet (0)	9	0.02
Central American Ind. (9)	14	0.03
Cherokee (5)	22	0.05
Cheyenne (0)	1	<0.01
Chippewa (0)	3	0.01
Choctaw (0)	2	<0.01
Colville (1)	1	<0.01
Creek (1)	2	<0.01
Iroquois (0)	1	<0.01
Mexican American Ind. (3)	5	0.01
Navajo (0)	3	0.01
Paiute (1)	1	<0.01
Seminole (0)	2	<0.01
Sioux (5)	5	0.01
South American Ind. (8)	22	0.05
Spanish American Ind. (3)	4	0.01
Yup'ik *(Alaska Native)* (0)	2	<0.01
Asian (916)	1,295	3.21
Not Hispanic (881)	1,196	2.97
Hispanic (35)	99	0.25
Bangladeshi (9)	12	0.03
Burmese (1)	2	<0.01
Cambodian (1)	1	<0.01
Chinese, ex. Taiwanese (179)	293	0.73
Filipino (117)	162	0.40
Indian (320)	439	1.09
Indonesian (2)	4	0.01
Japanese (27)	56	0.14
Korean (33)	51	0.13
Malaysian (1)	2	<0.01
Pakistani (31)	42	0.10
Taiwanese (3)	3	0.01
Thai (37)	46	0.11
Vietnamese (126)	147	0.36
Hawaii Native/Pacific Islander (28)	104	0.26
Not Hispanic (26)	82	0.20
Hispanic (2)	22	0.05
Fijian (0)	1	<0.01
Guamanian/Chamorro (4)	10	0.02
Native Hawaiian (3)	17	0.04
Samoan (3)	4	0.01
White (31,137)	32,106	79.70
Not Hispanic (11,468)	11,890	29.51
Hispanic (19,669)	20,216	50.18

Cypress Gardens

Place Type: CDP
County: Polk
Population: 8,917†

Ancestry‡	Population	%
American (2,293)	2,293	23.90
Austrian (0)	8	0.08
British (27)	45	0.47
Canadian (0)	7	0.07
Czech (15)	15	0.16
Danish (7)	18	0.19
Dutch (21)	101	1.05
English (656)	1,772	18.47
European (63)	108	1.13
French, ex. Basque (62)	385	4.01
German (435)	1,696	17.68
Greek (113)	136	1.42
Guyanese (17)	17	0.18
Hungarian (19)	115	1.20
Icelander (0)	12	0.13
Irish (323)	1,312	13.68
Italian (152)	544	5.67
Maltese (12)	12	0.13
Norwegian (36)	36	0.38
Pennsylvania German (0)	26	0.27
Polish (104)	291	3.03
Romanian (0)	45	0.47
Russian (0)	38	0.40
Scandinavian (14)	14	0.15
Scotch-Irish (241)	416	4.34
Scottish (42)	388	4.04
Slovak (13)	65	0.68
Swedish (45)	53	0.55
Swiss (11)	30	0.31
Ukrainian (26)	51	0.53
Welsh (0)	21	0.22
West Indian, ex. Hispanic (34)	34	0.35
West Indian (34)	34	0.35
Yugoslavian (0)	9	0.09

Hispanic Origin	Population	%
Hispanic or Latino (of any race)	552	6.19
Central American, ex. Mexican	21	0.24
Costa Rican	1	0.01
Guatemalan	2	0.02
Honduran	2	0.02
Nicaraguan	6	0.07
Panamanian	7	0.08
Salvadoran	3	0.03
Cuban	88	0.99
Dominican Republic	14	0.16
Mexican	187	2.10
Puerto Rican	173	1.94
South American	33	0.37
Argentinean	7	0.08
Bolivian	3	0.03
Chilean	3	0.03
Colombian	7	0.08
Ecuadorian	3	0.03
Peruvian	4	0.04
Uruguayan	2	0.02
Venezuelan	4	0.04
Other Hispanic or Latino	36	0.40

Race*	Population	%
African-American/Black (401)	452	5.07
Not Hispanic (390)	436	4.89
Hispanic (11)	16	0.18
American Indian/Alaska Native (32)	61	0.68
Not Hispanic (24)	52	0.58
Hispanic (8)	9	0.10
Cherokee (8)	20	0.22
Chippewa (1)	2	0.02
Choctaw (1)	1	0.01
Comanche (0)	1	0.01
Creek (1)	2	0.02
Delaware (3)	3	0.03
Ottawa (0)	1	0.01

SECTION TWO

*Notes: † The Census 2010 population figure is used to calculate the percentages in the Hispanic Origin and Race categories. Ancestry percentages are based on the 2006-2010 American Community Survey population (not shown); ‡ Numbers in parentheses indicate the number of people reporting a single ancestry; * Numbers in parentheses indicate the number of persons reporting this race alone, not in combination with any other race; Please refer to the Explanation of Data for more information.*

Seminole (1)	1	0.01
South American Ind. (7)	7	0.08
Asian (170)	206	2.31
Not Hispanic (170)	205	2.30
Hispanic (0)	1	0.01
Bangladeshi (7)	8	0.09
Burmese (2)	3	0.03
Chinese, ex. Taiwanese (28)	36	0.40
Filipino (32)	39	0.44
Indian (38)	42	0.47
Japanese (4)	7	0.08
Korean (12)	13	0.15
Pakistani (1)	3	0.03
Sri Lankan (2)	2	0.02
Taiwanese (4)	4	0.04
Vietnamese (28)	34	0.38
Hawaii Native/Pacific Islander (7)	13	0.15
Not Hispanic (7)	12	0.13
Hispanic (0)	1	0.01
Guamanian/Chamorro (1)	3	0.03
White (8,100)	8,203	91.99
Not Hispanic (7,671)	7,758	87.00
Hispanic (429)	445	4.99

Cypress Lake

Place Type: CDP
County: Lee
Population: 11,846†

Ancestry‡	Population	%
American (1,044)	1,044	8.66
Arab (12)	130	1.08
Iraqi (12)	12	0.10
Lebanese (0)	118	0.98
Austrian (26)	53	0.44
Belgian (16)	16	0.13
British (20)	30	0.25
Bulgarian (25)	25	0.21
Canadian (64)	86	0.71
Carpatho Rusyn (9)	18	0.15
Croatian (25)	25	0.21
Czech (23)	63	0.52
Czechoslovakian (50)	50	0.41
Danish (11)	41	0.34
Dutch (104)	332	2.75
English (1,057)	2,344	19.44
European (40)	40	0.33
Finnish (43)	43	0.36
French, ex. Basque (150)	439	3.64
French Canadian (171)	171	1.42
German (912)	2,299	19.06
Greek (29)	45	0.37
Hungarian (45)	109	0.90
Irish (757)	1,948	16.15
Italian (751)	1,213	10.06
Latvian (84)	84	0.70
Lithuanian (31)	58	0.48
Northern European (17)	56	0.46
Norwegian (69)	200	1.66
Polish (200)	504	4.18
Portuguese (0)	10	0.08
Romanian (12)	12	0.10
Russian (48)	77	0.64
Scandinavian (11)	11	0.09
Scotch-Irish (140)	328	2.72
Scottish (147)	400	3.32
Serbian (0)	30	0.25
Slavic (0)	16	0.13
Slovak (26)	26	0.22
Swedish (95)	234	1.94
Swiss (9)	46	0.38
Ukrainian (27)	67	0.56
Welsh (64)	164	1.36
West Indian, ex. Hispanic (14)	14	0.12
Jamaican (14)	14	0.12
Yugoslavian (40)	49	0.41

Hispanic Origin	Population	%
Hispanic or Latino (of any race)	971	8.20
Central American, ex. Mexican	66	0.56
Costa Rican	23	0.19
Guatemalan	17	0.14
Honduran	12	0.10
Nicaraguan	4	0.03
Panamanian	8	0.07
Salvadoran	1	0.01
Other Central American	1	0.01
Cuban	91	0.77
Dominican Republic	44	0.37
Mexican	311	2.63
Puerto Rican	223	1.88
South American	176	1.49
Argentinean	17	0.14
Chilean	8	0.07
Colombian	62	0.52
Ecuadorian	19	0.16
Peruvian	31	0.26
Venezuelan	34	0.29
Other South American	5	0.04
Other Hispanic or Latino	60	0.51

Race*	Population	%
African-American/Black (255)	310	2.62
Not Hispanic (201)	244	2.06
Hispanic (54)	66	0.56
American Indian/Alaska Native (25)	51	0.43
Not Hispanic (18)	39	0.33
Hispanic (7)	12	0.10
Canadian/French Am. Ind. (1)	2	0.02
Cherokee (3)	9	0.08
Creek (0)	1	0.01
Iroquois (2)	2	0.02
Lumbee (2)	2	0.02
Mexican American Ind. (1)	2	0.02
Pima (0)	1	0.01
Sioux (0)	1	0.01
South American Ind. (1)	2	0.02
Tlingit-Haida *(Alaska Native)* (0)	1	0.01
Asian (100)	140	1.18
Not Hispanic (99)	137	1.16
Hispanic (1)	3	0.03
Chinese, ex. Taiwanese (18)	22	0.19
Filipino (25)	42	0.35
Indian (20)	24	0.20
Japanese (6)	20	0.17
Korean (8)	12	0.10
Malaysian (1)	1	0.01
Thai (3)	4	0.03
Vietnamese (8)	10	0.08
Hawaii Native/Pacific Islander (2)	4	0.03
Not Hispanic (2)	2	0.02
Hispanic (0)	2	0.02
White (11,126)	11,258	95.04
Not Hispanic (10,429)	10,525	88.85
Hispanic (697)	733	6.19

Dania Beach

Place Type: City
County: Broward
Population: 29,639†

Ancestry‡	Population	%
African, Sub-Saharan (37)	81	0.28
African (14)	58	0.20
Other Sub-Saharan African (23)	23	0.08
Albanian (137)	137	0.47
American (2,608)	2,608	8.87
Arab (98)	154	0.52
Egyptian (14)	14	0.05
Iraqi (0)	28	0.10
Lebanese (14)	22	0.07
Moroccan (30)	30	0.10
Syrian (9)	29	0.10
Other Arab (31)	31	0.11
Armenian (11)	11	0.04
Austrian (14)	112	0.38
Belgian (53)	53	0.18
Brazilian (118)	145	0.49
British (117)	159	0.54
Canadian (362)	449	1.53
Celtic (9)	9	0.03
Croatian (5)	13	0.04
Czech (12)	117	0.40
Czechoslovakian (24)	24	0.08
Danish (9)	96	0.33
Dutch (22)	299	1.02
Eastern European (58)	58	0.20
English (536)	1,942	6.60
European (107)	167	0.57
Finnish (54)	54	0.18
French, ex. Basque (101)	598	2.03
French Canadian (382)	434	1.48
German (845)	2,326	7.91
Greek (62)	185	0.63
Guyanese (17)	17	0.06
Hungarian (117)	129	0.44
Irish (830)	3,050	10.37
Israeli (165)	165	0.56
Italian (2,282)	3,335	11.34
Norwegian (14)	44	0.15
Polish (352)	796	2.71
Portuguese (60)	288	0.98
Romanian (69)	98	0.33
Russian (227)	596	2.03
Scandinavian (0)	11	0.04
Scotch-Irish (175)	285	0.97
Scottish (137)	395	1.34
Serbian (28)	28	0.10
Soviet Union (11)	11	0.04
Swedish (53)	311	1.06
Swiss (31)	56	0.19
Ukrainian (59)	150	0.51
Welsh (0)	83	0.28
West Indian, ex. Hispanic (2,091)	2,429	8.26
Bahamian (81)	204	0.69
Haitian (754)	754	2.56
Jamaican (970)	1,093	3.72
Trinidadian/Tobagonian (241)	298	1.01
West Indian (45)	80	0.27
Yugoslavian (16)	16	0.05

Hispanic Origin	Population	%
Hispanic or Latino (of any race)	6,652	22.44
Central American, ex. Mexican	599	2.02
Costa Rican	31	0.10
Guatemalan	89	0.30
Honduran	163	0.55
Nicaraguan	133	0.45
Panamanian	58	0.20
Salvadoran	118	0.40
Other Central American	7	0.02
Cuban	1,160	3.91
Dominican Republic	422	1.42
Mexican	324	1.09
Puerto Rican	1,433	4.83
South American	2,135	7.20
Argentinean	266	0.90
Bolivian	29	0.10
Chilean	56	0.19
Colombian	877	2.96
Ecuadorian	189	0.64
Paraguayan	4	0.01
Peruvian	411	1.39
Uruguayan	43	0.15
Venezuelan	255	0.86
Other South American	5	0.02
Other Hispanic or Latino	579	1.95

Race*	Population	%
African-American/Black (6,461)	6,810	22.98
Not Hispanic (6,205)	6,457	21.79
Hispanic (256)	353	1.19
American Indian/Alaska Native (97)	203	0.68
Not Hispanic (69)	149	0.50
Hispanic (28)	54	0.18
Aleut *(Alaska Native)* (1)	1	<0.01
Apache (1)	5	0.02
Arapaho (0)	1	<0.01

*Notes: † The Census 2010 population figure is used to calculate the percentages in the Hispanic Origin and Race categories. Ancestry percentages are based on the 2006-2010 American Community Survey population (not shown); ‡ Numbers in parentheses indicate the number of people reporting a single ancestry; * Numbers in parentheses indicate the number of persons reporting this race alone, not in combination with any other race; Please refer to the Explanation of Data for more information.*

Blackfeet (0)	3	0.01
Canadian/French Am. Ind. (0)	3	0.01
Central American Ind. (3)	6	0.02
Cherokee (18)	34	0.11
Chickasaw (1)	1	<0.01
Choctaw (2)	2	0.01
Creek (1)	3	0.01
Iroquois (2)	4	0.01
Lumbee (0)	1	<0.01
Mexican American Ind. (3)	4	0.01
Navajo (0)	1	<0.01
Potawatomi (1)	1	<0.01
Pueblo (0)	1	<0.01
Seminole (8)	10	0.03
Sioux (4)	4	0.01
South American Ind. (5)	7	0.02
Spanish American Ind. (1)	4	0.01
Asian (622)	792	2.67
Not Hispanic (606)	745	2.51
Hispanic (16)	47	0.16
Bangladeshi (35)	38	0.13
Burmese (1)	5	0.02
Chinese, ex. Taiwanese (126)	162	0.55
Filipino (103)	138	0.47
Hmong (2)	2	0.01
Indian (172)	219	0.74
Indonesian (5)	5	0.02
Japanese (30)	45	0.15
Korean (36)	44	0.15
Laotian (5)	6	0.02
Pakistani (26)	34	0.11
Sri Lankan (1)	2	0.01
Taiwanese (3)	3	0.01
Thai (29)	32	0.11
Vietnamese (19)	28	0.09
Hawaii Native/Pacific Islander (15)	42	0.14
Not Hispanic (14)	33	0.11
Hispanic (1)	9	0.03
Guamanian/Chamorro (2)	6	0.02
Native Hawaiian (7)	14	0.05
Samoan (0)	2	0.01
White (20,624)	21,243	71.67
Not Hispanic (15,580)	15,905	53.66
Hispanic (5,044)	5,338	18.01

Davie

Place Type: Town
County: Broward
Population: 91,992†

Ancestry‡	Population	%
African, Sub-Saharan (557)	665	0.73
African (436)	498	0.55
Cape Verdean (0)	34	0.04
Ethiopian (22)	22	0.02
Nigerian (39)	39	0.04
South African (44)	56	0.06
Other Sub-Saharan African (16)	16	0.02
American (4,503)	4,503	4.97
Arab (758)	1,027	1.13
Arab (0)	10	0.01
Egyptian (134)	157	0.17
Iraqi (8)	8	0.01
Jordanian (163)	235	0.26
Lebanese (153)	252	0.28
Moroccan (103)	103	0.11
Syrian (82)	140	0.15
Other Arab (115)	122	0.13
Armenian (44)	63	0.07
Australian (39)	39	0.04
Austrian (51)	295	0.33
Basque (17)	17	0.02
Belgian (52)	59	0.07
Brazilian (361)	383	0.42
British (158)	375	0.41
Bulgarian (33)	65	0.07
Canadian (324)	463	0.51
Croatian (16)	133	0.15
Czech (12)	268	0.30
Czechoslovakian (48)	103	0.11
Danish (43)	167	0.18
Dutch (228)	984	1.09
Eastern European (284)	334	0.37
English (1,882)	5,994	6.61
Estonian (0)	11	0.01
European (991)	1,236	1.36
Finnish (36)	129	0.14
French, ex. Basque (624)	2,465	2.72
French Canadian (441)	841	0.93
German (3,257)	11,400	12.58
Greek (369)	767	0.85
Guyanese (54)	79	0.09
Hungarian (125)	564	0.62
Iranian (311)	354	0.39
Irish (2,583)	10,339	11.41
Israeli (205)	230	0.25
Italian (4,661)	10,482	11.56
Latvian (0)	14	0.02
Lithuanian (94)	327	0.36
New Zealander (0)	18	0.02
Norwegian (167)	583	0.64
Pennsylvania German (30)	80	0.09
Polish (1,174)	3,355	3.70
Portuguese (185)	370	0.41
Romanian (408)	546	0.60
Russian (810)	2,404	2.65
Scandinavian (70)	209	0.23
Scotch-Irish (277)	1,191	1.31
Scottish (455)	1,249	1.38
Serbian (20)	20	0.02
Slavic (0)	12	0.01
Slovak (75)	121	0.13
Slovene (0)	25	0.03
Swedish (207)	501	0.55
Swiss (56)	114	0.13
Turkish (51)	51	0.06
Ukrainian (277)	488	0.54
Welsh (11)	345	0.38
West Indian, ex. Hispanic (2,292)	3,019	3.33
Bahamian (124)	124	0.14
Barbadian (13)	13	0.01
Belizean (11)	11	0.01
Bermudan (0)	11	0.01
British West Indian (13)	13	0.01
Haitian (835)	1,054	1.16
Jamaican (991)	1,431	1.58
Trinidadian/Tobagonian (45)	60	0.07
West Indian (260)	302	0.33
Yugoslavian (14)	25	0.03

Hispanic Origin	Population	%
Hispanic or Latino (of any race)	26,809	29.14
Central American, ex. Mexican	2,693	2.93
Costa Rican	203	0.22
Guatemalan	552	0.60
Honduran	612	0.67
Nicaraguan	542	0.59
Panamanian	231	0.25
Salvadoran	547	0.59
Other Central American	6	0.01
Cuban	6,071	6.60
Dominican Republic	1,479	1.61
Mexican	1,600	1.74
Puerto Rican	5,006	5.44
South American	8,321	9.05
Argentinean	566	0.62
Bolivian	74	0.08
Chilean	268	0.29
Colombian	3,715	4.04
Ecuadorian	774	0.84
Paraguayan	15	0.02
Peruvian	1,533	1.67
Uruguayan	121	0.13
Venezuelan	1,231	1.34
Other South American	24	0.03
Other Hispanic or Latino	1,639	1.78

Race*	Population	%
African-American/Black (7,401)	8,509	9.25
Not Hispanic (6,671)	7,435	8.08
Hispanic (730)	1,074	1.17
American Indian/Alaska Native (321)	655	0.71
Not Hispanic (223)	437	0.48
Hispanic (98)	218	0.24
Alaska Athabascan *(Ala. Nat.)* (1)	1	<0.01
Apache (4)	6	0.01
Blackfeet (2)	20	0.02
Canadian/French Am. Ind. (1)	1	<0.01
Central American Ind. (12)	27	0.03
Cherokee (13)	81	0.09
Chickasaw (4)	6	0.01
Chippewa (0)	2	<0.01
Choctaw (4)	5	0.01
Cree (0)	1	<0.01
Creek (4)	7	0.01
Delaware (0)	2	<0.01
Inupiat *(Alaska Native)* (3)	3	<0.01
Iroquois (5)	12	0.01
Lumbee (3)	5	0.01
Menominee (1)	1	<0.01
Mexican American Ind. (6)	12	0.01
Navajo (2)	8	0.01
Osage (0)	2	<0.01
Pueblo (1)	1	<0.01
Seminole (80)	84	0.09
Sioux (3)	9	0.01
South American Ind. (22)	47	0.05
Spanish American Ind. (5)	5	0.01
Tlingit-Haida *(Alaska Native)* (1)	1	<0.01
Asian (4,201)	5,142	5.59
Not Hispanic (4,135)	4,911	5.34
Hispanic (66)	231	0.25
Bangladeshi (94)	112	0.12
Burmese (21)	29	0.03
Cambodian (9)	10	0.01
Chinese, ex. Taiwanese (828)	1,124	1.22
Filipino (407)	522	0.57
Hmong (3)	3	<0.01
Indian (1,492)	1,746	1.90
Indonesian (6)	12	0.01
Japanese (60)	141	0.15
Korean (270)	325	0.35
Laotian (13)	19	0.02
Malaysian (6)	10	0.01
Nepalese (7)	10	0.01
Pakistani (355)	407	0.44
Sri Lankan (9)	20	0.02
Taiwanese (69)	87	0.09
Thai (63)	90	0.10
Vietnamese (269)	300	0.33
Hawaii Native/Pacific Islander (57)	195	0.21
Not Hispanic (44)	154	0.17
Hispanic (13)	41	0.04
Guamanian/Chamorro (24)	36	0.04
Native Hawaiian (10)	39	0.04
Samoan (6)	13	0.01
White (73,673)	75,949	82.56
Not Hispanic (52,212)	53,372	58.02
Hispanic (21,461)	22,577	24.54

Daytona Beach

Place Type: City
County: Volusia
Population: 61,005†

Ancestry‡	Population	%
African, Sub-Saharan (763)	768	1.22
African (569)	569	0.90
Cape Verdean (0)	5	0.01
Ghanaian (49)	49	0.08
Nigerian (130)	130	0.21
Other Sub-Saharan African (15)	15	0.02
Albanian (13)	13	0.02
American (3,472)	3,472	5.52
Arab (388)	537	0.85
Arab (130)	138	0.22
Egyptian (117)	117	0.19
Lebanese (29)	93	0.15

*Notes: † The Census 2010 population figure is used to calculate the percentages in the Hispanic Origin and Race categories. Ancestry percentages are based on the 2006-2010 American Community Survey population (not shown); ‡ Numbers in parentheses indicate the number of people reporting a single ancestry; * Numbers in parentheses indicate the number of persons reporting this race alone, not in combination with any other race; Please refer to the Explanation of Data for more information.*

Ancestry	Population	%
Moroccan (51)	51	0.08
Palestinian (14)	45	0.07
Syrian (0)	46	0.07
Other Arab (47)	47	0.07
Armenian (85)	103	0.16
Austrian (40)	77	0.12
Basque (0)	11	0.02
Belgian (0)	18	0.03
Brazilian (46)	80	0.13
British (259)	430	0.68
Bulgarian (0)	19	0.03
Canadian (215)	255	0.41
Celtic (12)	12	0.02
Croatian (36)	80	0.13
Czech (28)	104	0.17
Czechoslovakian (34)	71	0.11
Danish (9)	93	0.15
Dutch (188)	660	1.05
Eastern European (82)	82	0.13
English (1,985)	4,808	7.64
European (228)	263	0.42
Finnish (88)	88	0.14
French, ex. Basque (548)	1,492	2.37
French Canadian (258)	405	0.64
German (2,873)	6,797	10.81
Greek (329)	449	0.71
Guyanese (61)	61	0.10
Hungarian (263)	368	0.59
Iranian (49)	49	0.08
Irish (2,603)	6,059	9.63
Israeli (257)	257	0.41
Italian (1,726)	3,472	5.52
Latvian (0)	13	0.02
Lithuanian (28)	141	0.22
Maltese (17)	17	0.03
Northern European (15)	15	0.02
Norwegian (118)	572	0.91
Pennsylvania German (7)	7	0.01
Polish (753)	1,704	2.71
Portuguese (192)	278	0.44
Romanian (11)	11	0.02
Russian (111)	274	0.44
Scandinavian (0)	83	0.13
Scotch-Irish (219)	752	1.20
Scottish (382)	1,109	1.76
Serbian (10)	24	0.04
Slavic (14)	26	0.04
Slovak (34)	46	0.07
Slovene (0)	28	0.04
Swedish (85)	372	0.59
Swiss (32)	158	0.25
Ukrainian (92)	281	0.45
Welsh (56)	358	0.57
West Indian, ex. Hispanic (1,969)	2,253	3.58
Bahamian (35)	128	0.20
Barbadian (35)	46	0.07
Belizean (18)	18	0.03
British West Indian (51)	51	0.08
Haitian (777)	872	1.39
Jamaican (918)	984	1.56
Trinidadian/Tobagonian (107)	107	0.17
West Indian (14)	33	0.05
Other West Indian (14)	14	0.02
Yugoslavian (120)	120	0.19

Hispanic Origin	Population	%
Hispanic or Latino (of any race)	3,755	6.16
Central American, ex. Mexican	326	0.53
Costa Rican	31	0.05
Guatemalan	74	0.12
Honduran	117	0.19
Nicaraguan	24	0.04
Panamanian	36	0.06
Salvadoran	36	0.06
Other Central American	8	0.01
Cuban	303	0.50
Dominican Republic	90	0.15
Mexican	759	1.24
Puerto Rican	1,449	2.38
South American	474	0.78
Argentinean	49	0.08
Bolivian	5	0.01
Chilean	27	0.04
Colombian	168	0.28
Ecuadorian	79	0.13
Paraguayan	2	<0.01
Peruvian	72	0.12
Uruguayan	19	0.03
Venezuelan	48	0.08
Other South American	5	0.01
Other Hispanic or Latino	354	0.58

Race*	Population	%
African-American/Black (21,585)	22,409	36.73
Not Hispanic (21,254)	21,955	35.99
Hispanic (331)	454	0.74
American Indian/Alaska Native (216)	599	0.98
Not Hispanic (185)	503	0.82
Hispanic (31)	96	0.16
Alaska Athabascan *(Ala. Nat.)* (1)	1	<0.01
Aleut *(Alaska Native)* (1)	1	<0.01
Apache (5)	10	0.02
Blackfeet (6)	37	0.06
Canadian/French Am. Ind. (0)	2	<0.01
Central American Ind. (2)	3	<0.01
Cherokee (32)	141	0.23
Chickasaw (2)	2	<0.01
Chippewa (8)	16	0.03
Choctaw (1)	6	0.01
Comanche (0)	1	<0.01
Creek (3)	5	0.01
Delaware (5)	8	0.01
Iroquois (8)	21	0.03
Lumbee (1)	4	0.01
Menominee (0)	1	<0.01
Mexican American Ind. (1)	5	0.01
Navajo (3)	3	<0.01
Osage (1)	1	<0.01
Ottawa (1)	1	<0.01
Pima (0)	1	<0.01
Potawatomi (1)	1	<0.01
Pueblo (1)	1	<0.01
Seminole (2)	8	0.01
Shoshone (0)	1	<0.01
Sioux (4)	6	0.01
South American Ind. (2)	9	0.01
Spanish American Ind. (2)	3	<0.01
Ute (1)	3	<0.01
Yup'ik *(Alaska Native)* (1)	1	<0.01
Asian (1,374)	1,653	2.71
Not Hispanic (1,354)	1,606	2.63
Hispanic (20)	47	0.08
Bangladeshi (1)	2	<0.01
Burmese (5)	5	0.01
Cambodian (12)	15	0.02
Chinese, ex. Taiwanese (172)	222	0.36
Filipino (149)	212	0.35
Hmong (1)	1	<0.01
Indian (517)	573	0.94
Indonesian (19)	24	0.04
Japanese (44)	68	0.11
Korean (161)	192	0.31
Laotian (6)	7	0.01
Malaysian (14)	17	0.03
Nepalese (3)	3	<0.01
Pakistani (21)	24	0.04
Sri Lankan (25)	29	0.05
Taiwanese (9)	10	0.02
Thai (31)	35	0.06
Vietnamese (128)	141	0.23
Hawaii Native/Pacific Islander (27)	93	0.15
Not Hispanic (21)	80	0.13
Hispanic (6)	13	0.02
Guamanian/Chamorro (2)	17	0.03
Native Hawaiian (5)	16	0.03
Samoan (2)	6	0.01
Tongan (6)	7	0.01
White (35,265)	36,411	59.69
Not Hispanic (33,179)	34,077	55.86
Hispanic (2,086)	2,334	3.83

DeBary

Place Type: City
County: Volusia
Population: 19,320†

Ancestry‡	Population	%
American (1,065)	1,065	5.59
Arab (27)	39	0.20
Palestinian (13)	13	0.07
Syrian (0)	12	0.06
Other Arab (14)	14	0.07
Austrian (0)	81	0.42
Belgian (38)	38	0.20
Brazilian (0)	45	0.24
British (83)	209	1.10
Canadian (164)	349	1.83
Croatian (12)	40	0.21
Czech (25)	84	0.44
Czechoslovakian (8)	63	0.33
Danish (17)	116	0.61
Dutch (54)	208	1.09
Eastern European (14)	52	0.27
English (927)	2,388	12.52
European (91)	138	0.72
Finnish (13)	13	0.07
French, ex. Basque (288)	1,170	6.14
French Canadian (83)	131	0.69
German (1,096)	4,295	22.52
Greek (8)	91	0.48
Hungarian (14)	90	0.47
Irish (920)	3,335	17.49
Italian (936)	2,063	10.82
Lithuanian (16)	36	0.19
Maltese (18)	18	0.09
Northern European (17)	17	0.09
Norwegian (14)	204	1.07
Pennsylvania German (15)	15	0.08
Polish (335)	841	4.41
Portuguese (31)	97	0.51
Romanian (11)	22	0.12
Russian (14)	170	0.89
Scandinavian (38)	95	0.50
Scotch-Irish (364)	520	2.73
Scottish (172)	450	2.36
Slavic (0)	25	0.13
Slovak (11)	24	0.13
Slovene (12)	12	0.06
Swedish (94)	316	1.66
Swiss (0)	72	0.38
Ukrainian (14)	52	0.27
Welsh (0)	81	0.42
West Indian, ex. Hispanic (135)	179	0.94
Barbadian (27)	49	0.26
Haitian (18)	18	0.09
Jamaican (75)	97	0.51
Trinidadian/Tobagonian (15)	15	0.08

Hispanic Origin	Population	%
Hispanic or Latino (of any race)	1,756	9.09
Central American, ex. Mexican	86	0.45
Costa Rican	15	0.08
Guatemalan	13	0.07
Honduran	20	0.10
Nicaraguan	12	0.06
Panamanian	14	0.07
Salvadoran	12	0.06
Cuban	152	0.79
Dominican Republic	37	0.19
Mexican	146	0.76
Puerto Rican	1,009	5.22
South American	215	1.11
Argentinean	18	0.09
Bolivian	2	0.01
Chilean	8	0.04
Colombian	111	0.57
Ecuadorian	28	0.14
Peruvian	27	0.14
Uruguayan	3	0.02
Venezuelan	18	0.09

*Notes: † The Census 2010 population figure is used to calculate the percentages in the Hispanic Origin and Race categories. Ancestry percentages are based on the 2006-2010 American Community Survey population (not shown); ‡ Numbers in parentheses indicate the number of people reporting a single ancestry; * Numbers in parentheses indicate the number of persons reporting this race alone, not in combination with any other race; Please refer to the Explanation of Data for more information.*

Other Hispanic or Latino	111	0.57

Race*	Population	%
African-American/Black (769)	891	4.61
Not Hispanic (721)	809	4.19
Hispanic (48)	82	0.42
American Indian/Alaska Native (62)	150	0.78
Not Hispanic (47)	119	0.62
Hispanic (15)	31	0.16
Apache (0)	2	0.01
Blackfeet (1)	4	0.02
Central American Ind. (0)	2	0.01
Cherokee (10)	42	0.22
Chickasaw (0)	1	0.01
Chippewa (7)	8	0.04
Choctaw (0)	2	0.01
Cree (1)	1	0.01
Creek (8)	8	0.04
Delaware (1)	5	0.03
Iroquois (4)	7	0.04
Kiowa (0)	1	0.01
Mexican American Ind. (3)	8	0.04
Navajo (0)	1	0.01
Osage (1)	1	0.01
Paiute (1)	1	0.01
Potawatomi (0)	2	0.01
Seminole (0)	5	0.03
Sioux (1)	2	0.01
South American Ind. (10)	13	0.07
Spanish American Ind. (0)	1	0.01
Ute (0)	1	0.01
Asian (362)	465	2.41
Not Hispanic (358)	444	2.30
Hispanic (4)	21	0.11
Cambodian (1)	3	0.02
Chinese, ex. Taiwanese (52)	66	0.34
Filipino (80)	107	0.55
Hmong (1)	2	0.01
Indian (82)	96	0.50
Indonesian (5)	5	0.03
Japanese (14)	30	0.16
Korean (20)	31	0.16
Laotian (7)	7	0.04
Malaysian (0)	1	0.01
Pakistani (20)	28	0.14
Taiwanese (1)	1	0.01
Thai (3)	7	0.04
Vietnamese (55)	60	0.31
Hawaii Native/Pacific Islander (2)	17	0.09
Not Hispanic (2)	12	0.06
Hispanic (0)	5	0.03
Guamanian/Chamorro (0)	2	0.01
Native Hawaiian (2)	2	0.01
White (17,484)	17,790	92.08
Not Hispanic (16,164)	16,378	84.77
Hispanic (1,320)	1,412	7.31

DeLand

Place Type: City
County: Volusia
Population: 27,031†

Ancestry‡	Population	%
African, Sub-Saharan (55)	79	0.30
African (55)	79	0.30
Albanian (29)	29	0.11
American (1,359)	1,359	5.14
Arab (19)	136	0.51
Arab (8)	39	0.15
Iraqi (4)	4	0.02
Lebanese (0)	71	0.27
Palestinian (7)	7	0.03
Other Arab (0)	15	0.06
Australian (40)	40	0.15
Austrian (20)	139	0.53
Brazilian (13)	26	0.10
British (98)	175	0.66
Canadian (40)	47	0.18
Croatian (40)	81	0.31
Czech (21)	37	0.14
Czechoslovakian (25)	67	0.25
Danish (17)	61	0.23
Dutch (70)	286	1.08
Eastern European (12)	12	0.05
English (923)	3,121	11.80
European (268)	287	1.09
Finnish (53)	79	0.30
French, ex. Basque (205)	806	3.05
French Canadian (79)	180	0.68
German (1,359)	4,179	15.80
Greek (152)	204	0.77
Hungarian (102)	290	1.10
Iranian (12)	12	0.05
Irish (1,179)	3,690	13.95
Italian (942)	1,806	6.83
Latvian (0)	9	0.03
Lithuanian (71)	130	0.49
Northern European (19)	19	0.07
Norwegian (81)	169	0.64
Pennsylvania German (8)	19	0.07
Polish (219)	649	2.45
Portuguese (32)	51	0.19
Romanian (11)	11	0.04
Russian (155)	189	0.71
Scandinavian (73)	73	0.28
Scotch-Irish (200)	571	2.16
Scottish (201)	579	2.19
Slavic (8)	8	0.03
Slovak (17)	30	0.11
Slovene (20)	20	0.08
Swedish (124)	276	1.04
Swiss (7)	75	0.28
Turkish (10)	10	0.04
Ukrainian (0)	13	0.05
Welsh (78)	152	0.57
West Indian, ex. Hispanic (278)	433	1.64
Haitian (27)	45	0.17
Jamaican (172)	278	1.05
West Indian (79)	110	0.42
Yugoslavian (8)	39	0.15

Hispanic Origin	Population	%
Hispanic or Latino (of any race)	3,422	12.66
Central American, ex. Mexican	133	0.49
Costa Rican	11	0.04
Guatemalan	13	0.05
Honduran	28	0.10
Nicaraguan	18	0.07
Panamanian	26	0.10
Salvadoran	37	0.14
Cuban	181	0.67
Dominican Republic	75	0.28
Mexican	1,517	5.61
Puerto Rican	1,086	4.02
South American	258	0.95
Argentinean	11	0.04
Bolivian	4	0.01
Chilean	11	0.04
Colombian	120	0.44
Ecuadorian	31	0.11
Peruvian	28	0.10
Uruguayan	6	0.02
Venezuelan	45	0.17
Other South American	2	0.01
Other Hispanic or Latino	172	0.64

Race*	Population	%
African-American/Black (4,610)	4,951	18.32
Not Hispanic (4,465)	4,717	17.45
Hispanic (145)	234	0.87
American Indian/Alaska Native (71)	252	0.93
Not Hispanic (56)	212	0.78
Hispanic (15)	40	0.15
Alaska Athabascan *(Ala. Nat.)* (2)	2	0.01
Apache (1)	4	0.01
Arapaho (0)	1	<0.01
Blackfeet (1)	11	0.04
Cherokee (6)	71	0.26
Cheyenne (2)	2	0.01
Chickasaw (1)	6	0.02
Chippewa (2)	12	0.04
Choctaw (2)	8	0.03
Comanche (3)	3	0.01
Creek (6)	7	0.03
Inupiat *(Alaska Native)* (2)	2	0.01
Iroquois (4)	11	0.04
Lumbee (0)	1	<0.01
Ottawa (1)	1	<0.01
Potawatomi (1)	1	<0.01
Seminole (0)	4	0.01
Sioux (0)	1	<0.01
South American Ind. (1)	3	0.01
Asian (501)	602	2.23
Not Hispanic (484)	576	2.13
Hispanic (17)	26	0.10
Bangladeshi (56)	60	0.22
Cambodian (1)	1	<0.01
Chinese, ex. Taiwanese (78)	93	0.34
Filipino (144)	165	0.61
Hmong (1)	1	<0.01
Indian (131)	154	0.57
Indonesian (2)	5	0.02
Japanese (8)	23	0.09
Korean (9)	21	0.08
Laotian (8)	9	0.03
Malaysian (1)	1	<0.01
Pakistani (4)	4	0.01
Sri Lankan (1)	3	0.01
Thai (10)	13	0.05
Vietnamese (26)	40	0.15
Hawaii Native/Pacific Islander (20)	36	0.13
Not Hispanic (14)	25	0.09
Hispanic (6)	11	0.04
Guamanian/Chamorro (6)	6	0.02
Native Hawaiian (2)	10	0.04
Samoan (5)	5	0.02
White (20,142)	20,677	76.49
Not Hispanic (18,122)	18,497	68.43
Hispanic (2,020)	2,180	8.06

Deerfield Beach

Place Type: City
County: Broward
Population: 75,018†

Ancestry‡	Population	%
African, Sub-Saharan (244)	303	0.40
African (159)	169	0.22
Cape Verdean (0)	49	0.07
Nigerian (24)	24	0.03
South African (61)	61	0.08
Albanian (100)	143	0.19
American (2,489)	2,489	3.31
Arab (350)	467	0.62
Arab (104)	104	0.14
Egyptian (60)	98	0.13
Lebanese (63)	87	0.12
Palestinian (13)	13	0.02
Syrian (76)	97	0.13
Other Arab (34)	68	0.09
Armenian (57)	57	0.08
Australian (0)	17	0.02
Austrian (357)	740	0.98
Belgian (51)	64	0.09
Brazilian (6,685)	7,233	9.61
British (99)	115	0.15
Cajun (13)	62	0.08
Canadian (577)	759	1.01
Carpatho Rusyn (12)	12	0.02
Celtic (7)	7	0.01
Croatian (30)	30	0.04
Czech (167)	669	0.89
Czechoslovakian (31)	31	0.04
Danish (17)	181	0.24
Dutch (175)	563	0.75
Eastern European (58)	58	0.08
English (1,520)	4,889	6.49
European (515)	531	0.71

*Notes: † The Census 2010 population figure is used to calculate the percentages in the Hispanic Origin and Race categories. Ancestry percentages are based on the 2006-2010 American Community Survey population (not shown); ‡ Numbers in parentheses indicate the number of people reporting a single ancestry; * Numbers in parentheses indicate the number of persons reporting this race alone, not in combination with any other race; Please refer to the Explanation of Data for more information.*

Ancestry	Population	%
Finnish (0)	102	0.14
French, ex. Basque (339)	1,470	1.95
French Canadian (369)	540	0.72
German (2,070)	7,652	10.17
Greek (364)	642	0.85
Guyanese (269)	269	0.36
Hungarian (427)	828	1.10
Icelander (0)	31	0.04
Iranian (0)	12	0.02
Irish (1,761)	7,531	10.00
Israeli (54)	80	0.11
Italian (3,759)	7,354	9.77
Latvian (12)	28	0.04
Lithuanian (156)	251	0.33
Macedonian (59)	59	0.08
Maltese (23)	138	0.18
Northern European (17)	31	0.04
Norwegian (132)	521	0.69
Pennsylvania German (34)	49	0.07
Polish (1,272)	2,922	3.88
Portuguese (231)	470	0.62
Romanian (297)	381	0.51
Russian (974)	2,117	2.81
Scandinavian (89)	187	0.25
Scotch-Irish (266)	640	0.85
Scottish (245)	771	1.02
Serbian (73)	99	0.13
Slovak (96)	154	0.20
Slovene (21)	26	0.03
Swedish (119)	512	0.68
Swiss (25)	124	0.16
Turkish (146)	176	0.23
Ukrainian (153)	304	0.40
Welsh (59)	211	0.28
West Indian, ex. Hispanic (8,441)	8,681	11.53
Bahamian (144)	158	0.21
Barbadian (140)	140	0.19
British West Indian (230)	242	0.32
Haitian (6,920)	6,931	9.21
Jamaican (843)	960	1.28
Trinidadian/Tobagonian (9)	49	0.07
U.S. Virgin Islander (3)	3	<0.01
West Indian (99)	145	0.19
Other West Indian (53)	53	0.07
Yugoslavian (30)	46	0.06

Hispanic Origin	Population	%
Hispanic or Latino (of any race)	10,620	14.16
Central American, ex. Mexican	1,221	1.63
Costa Rican	124	0.17
Guatemalan	163	0.22
Honduran	577	0.77
Nicaraguan	152	0.20
Panamanian	56	0.07
Salvadoran	144	0.19
Other Central American	5	0.01
Cuban	1,073	1.43
Dominican Republic	653	0.87
Mexican	1,481	1.97
Puerto Rican	2,153	2.87
South American	3,070	4.09
Argentinean	282	0.38
Bolivian	49	0.07
Chilean	96	0.13
Colombian	1,196	1.59
Ecuadorian	270	0.36
Paraguayan	18	0.02
Peruvian	615	0.82
Uruguayan	195	0.26
Venezuelan	328	0.44
Other South American	21	0.03
Other Hispanic or Latino	969	1.29

Race*	Population	%
African-American/Black (19,223)	20,039	26.71
Not Hispanic (18,724)	19,388	25.84
Hispanic (499)	651	0.87
American Indian/Alaska Native (159)	411	0.55
Not Hispanic (105)	280	0.37
Hispanic (54)	131	0.17
Apache (0)	7	0.01
Blackfeet (1)	7	0.01
Canadian/French Am. Ind. (1)	2	<0.01
Central American Ind. (2)	7	0.01
Cherokee (17)	51	0.07
Chippewa (1)	5	0.01
Choctaw (2)	18	0.02
Cree (1)	3	<0.01
Creek (2)	4	0.01
Delaware (1)	1	<0.01
Iroquois (5)	7	0.01
Lumbee (9)	9	0.01
Mexican American Ind. (8)	18	0.02
Navajo (1)	1	<0.01
Ottawa (1)	2	<0.01
Paiute (2)	2	<0.01
Seminole (1)	6	0.01
Sioux (1)	8	0.01
South American Ind. (6)	23	0.03
Spanish American Ind. (0)	4	0.01
Tlingit-Haida *(Alaska Native)* (0)	2	<0.01
Yakama (0)	1	<0.01
Yaqui (1)	3	<0.01
Asian (1,145)	1,502	2.00
Not Hispanic (1,102)	1,405	1.87
Hispanic (43)	97	0.13
Bangladeshi (67)	75	0.10
Burmese (4)	4	0.01
Cambodian (15)	22	0.03
Chinese, ex. Taiwanese (188)	261	0.35
Filipino (125)	173	0.23
Indian (280)	363	0.48
Indonesian (8)	14	0.02
Japanese (46)	86	0.11
Korean (42)	57	0.08
Laotian (7)	7	0.01
Pakistani (40)	48	0.06
Sri Lankan (7)	8	0.01
Taiwanese (6)	8	0.01
Thai (71)	83	0.11
Vietnamese (175)	193	0.26
Hawaii Native/Pacific Islander (25)	146	0.19
Not Hispanic (19)	120	0.16
Hispanic (6)	26	0.03
Guamanian/Chamorro (5)	11	0.01
Native Hawaiian (12)	29	0.04
Samoan (0)	6	0.01
White (49,339)	50,919	67.88
Not Hispanic (41,991)	43,032	57.36
Hispanic (7,348)	7,887	10.51

Delray Beach

Place Type: City
County: Palm Beach
Population: 60,522†

Ancestry‡	Population	%
African, Sub-Saharan (738)	842	1.38
African (431)	535	0.88
Cape Verdean (144)	144	0.24
South African (53)	53	0.09
Sudanese (26)	26	0.04
Other Sub-Saharan African (84)	84	0.14
Albanian (147)	147	0.24
American (2,029)	2,029	3.32
Arab (129)	254	0.42
Egyptian (10)	10	0.02
Lebanese (94)	143	0.23
Palestinian (18)	46	0.08
Syrian (7)	55	0.09
Armenian (73)	73	0.12
Australian (0)	21	0.03
Austrian (188)	431	0.71
Basque (0)	8	0.01
Belgian (0)	169	0.28
Brazilian (331)	348	0.57
British (263)	439	0.72
Canadian (180)	257	0.42
Croatian (12)	32	0.05
Czech (77)	201	0.33
Czechoslovakian (57)	57	0.09
Danish (83)	131	0.21
Dutch (268)	564	0.92
Eastern European (427)	427	0.70
English (1,635)	4,470	7.32
Estonian (28)	28	0.05
European (748)	786	1.29
Finnish (94)	214	0.35
French, ex. Basque (456)	1,478	2.42
French Canadian (261)	468	0.77
German (2,122)	6,024	9.86
German Russian (38)	38	0.06
Greek (116)	223	0.37
Guyanese (0)	32	0.05
Hungarian (230)	598	0.98
Irish (2,498)	7,038	11.52
Israeli (55)	92	0.15
Italian (3,643)	6,022	9.86
Latvian (60)	121	0.20
Lithuanian (158)	249	0.41
Luxemburger (14)	14	0.02
Northern European (17)	17	0.03
Norwegian (139)	573	0.94
Polish (1,035)	2,346	3.84
Portuguese (162)	220	0.36
Romanian (263)	402	0.66
Russian (1,225)	2,265	3.71
Scotch-Irish (362)	746	1.22
Scottish (361)	1,237	2.02
Serbian (20)	30	0.05
Slovak (91)	155	0.25
Slovene (10)	22	0.04
Swedish (204)	530	0.87
Swiss (25)	140	0.23
Turkish (23)	23	0.04
Ukrainian (75)	134	0.22
Welsh (92)	335	0.55
West Indian, ex. Hispanic (7,862)	8,076	13.22
Bahamian (326)	346	0.57
Barbadian (26)	39	0.06
British West Indian (79)	93	0.15
Haitian (7,053)	7,178	11.75
Jamaican (345)	387	0.63
Trinidadian/Tobagonian (12)	12	0.02
U.S. Virgin Islander (13)	13	0.02
West Indian (8)	8	0.01
Yugoslavian (0)	9	0.01

Hispanic Origin	Population	%
Hispanic or Latino (of any race)	5,769	9.53
Central American, ex. Mexican	697	1.15
Costa Rican	55	0.09
Guatemalan	357	0.59
Honduran	103	0.17
Nicaraguan	54	0.09
Panamanian	20	0.03
Salvadoran	103	0.17
Other Central American	5	0.01
Cuban	553	0.91
Dominican Republic	207	0.34
Mexican	1,697	2.80
Puerto Rican	942	1.56
South American	1,270	2.10
Argentinean	127	0.21
Bolivian	30	0.05
Chilean	52	0.09
Colombian	512	0.85
Ecuadorian	139	0.23
Paraguayan	11	0.02
Peruvian	203	0.34
Uruguayan	32	0.05
Venezuelan	150	0.25
Other South American	14	0.02
Other Hispanic or Latino	403	0.67

Race*	Population	%
African-American/Black (16,961)	17,516	28.94
Not Hispanic (16,759)	17,213	28.44
Hispanic (202)	303	0.50

*Notes: † The Census 2010 population figure is used to calculate the percentages in the Hispanic Origin and Race categories. Ancestry percentages are based on the 2006-2010 American Community Survey population (not shown); ‡ Numbers in parentheses indicate the number of people reporting a single ancestry; * Numbers in parentheses indicate the number of persons reporting this race alone, not in combination with any other race; Please refer to the Explanation of Data for more information.*

American Indian/Alaska Native (122)	321	0.53
Not Hispanic (87)	249	0.41
Hispanic (35)	72	0.12
Arapaho (0)	1	<0.01
Blackfeet (3)	5	0.01
Canadian/French Am. Ind. (2)	2	<0.01
Central American Ind. (3)	9	0.01
Cherokee (8)	38	0.06
Cheyenne (1)	1	<0.01
Chickasaw (0)	1	<0.01
Chippewa (4)	7	0.01
Choctaw (4)	7	0.01
Comanche (1)	5	0.01
Creek (1)	1	<0.01
Delaware (0)	1	<0.01
Iroquois (7)	13	0.02
Lumbee (2)	2	<0.01
Mexican American Ind. (9)	13	0.02
Navajo (3)	3	<0.01
Osage (0)	1	<0.01
Potawatomi (1)	1	<0.01
Puget Sound Salish (1)	1	<0.01
Seminole (2)	4	0.01
Sioux (2)	3	<0.01
South American Ind. (11)	19	0.03
Spanish American Ind. (1)	1	<0.01
Tlingit-Haida *(Alaska Native)* (1)	2	<0.01
Asian (1,107)	1,394	2.30
Not Hispanic (1,088)	1,339	2.21
Hispanic (19)	55	0.09
Bangladeshi (61)	67	0.11
Burmese (5)	6	0.01
Cambodian (1)	3	<0.01
Chinese, ex. Taiwanese (160)	229	0.38
Filipino (155)	203	0.34
Hmong (1)	1	<0.01
Indian (432)	497	0.82
Indonesian (8)	13	0.02
Japanese (30)	59	0.10
Korean (34)	47	0.08
Laotian (1)	1	<0.01
Malaysian (0)	1	<0.01
Nepalese (1)	3	<0.01
Pakistani (16)	23	0.04
Sri Lankan (2)	4	0.01
Taiwanese (4)	10	0.02
Thai (61)	71	0.12
Vietnamese (76)	82	0.14
Hawaii Native/Pacific Islander (35)	175	0.29
Not Hispanic (27)	160	0.26
Hispanic (8)	15	0.02
Fijian (1)	1	<0.01
Guamanian/Chamorro (8)	11	0.02
Native Hawaiian (4)	13	0.02
White (39,768)	40,470	66.87
Not Hispanic (35,844)	36,313	60.00
Hispanic (3,924)	4,157	6.87

Deltona

Place Type: City
County: Volusia
Population: 85,182†

Ancestry‡	Population	%
African, Sub-Saharan (174)	519	0.62
African (174)	450	0.53
Cape Verdean (0)	57	0.07
Other Sub-Saharan African (0)	12	0.01
American (3,348)	3,348	3.98
Arab (143)	393	0.47
Arab (43)	71	0.08
Lebanese (53)	259	0.31
Moroccan (25)	41	0.05
Other Arab (22)	22	0.03
Armenian (7)	7	0.01
Austrian (15)	101	0.12
Basque (51)	51	0.06
Belgian (0)	98	0.12
Brazilian (7)	7	0.01
British (86)	209	0.25
Bulgarian (39)	39	0.05
Canadian (213)	325	0.39
Carpatho Rusyn (13)	13	0.02
Croatian (55)	68	0.08
Czech (56)	209	0.25
Czechoslovakian (36)	130	0.15
Danish (42)	85	0.10
Dutch (91)	797	0.95
Eastern European (41)	41	0.05
English (2,050)	6,896	8.19
European (292)	398	0.47
Finnish (16)	131	0.16
French, ex. Basque (591)	2,802	3.33
French Canadian (364)	495	0.59
German (4,001)	12,314	14.63
Greek (172)	516	0.61
Guyanese (149)	168	0.20
Hungarian (189)	718	0.85
Irish (3,114)	10,225	12.15
Italian (3,444)	7,207	8.56
Lithuanian (10)	87	0.10
New Zealander (0)	5	0.01
Northern European (0)	29	0.03
Norwegian (187)	591	0.70
Pennsylvania German (27)	42	0.05
Polish (588)	2,096	2.49
Portuguese (269)	535	0.64
Romanian (212)	280	0.33
Russian (237)	573	0.68
Scandinavian (10)	22	0.03
Scotch-Irish (455)	1,334	1.58
Scottish (637)	1,617	1.92
Slovak (50)	118	0.14
Slovene (0)	16	0.02
Swedish (127)	630	0.75
Swiss (81)	185	0.22
Ukrainian (14)	131	0.16
Welsh (119)	423	0.50
West Indian, ex. Hispanic (1,798)	2,054	2.44
Bahamian (18)	18	0.02
Barbadian (0)	18	0.02
Bermudan (5)	5	0.01
British West Indian (42)	42	0.05
Dutch West Indian (23)	23	0.03
Haitian (920)	920	1.09
Jamaican (509)	652	0.77
U.S. Virgin Islander (0)	20	0.02
West Indian (281)	329	0.39
Other West Indian (0)	27	0.03
Yugoslavian (29)	55	0.07

Hispanic Origin	Population	%
Hispanic or Latino (of any race)	25,734	30.21
Central American, ex. Mexican	1,173	1.38
Costa Rican	89	0.10
Guatemalan	160	0.19
Honduran	267	0.31
Nicaraguan	150	0.18
Panamanian	213	0.25
Salvadoran	288	0.34
Other Central American	6	0.01
Cuban	1,548	1.82
Dominican Republic	1,240	1.46
Mexican	1,340	1.57
Puerto Rican	17,661	20.73
South American	1,755	2.06
Argentinean	128	0.15
Bolivian	22	0.03
Chilean	61	0.07
Colombian	776	0.91
Ecuadorian	391	0.46
Paraguayan	7	0.01
Peruvian	212	0.25
Uruguayan	32	0.04
Venezuelan	119	0.14
Other South American	7	0.01
Other Hispanic or Latino	1,017	1.19

Race*	Population	%
African-American/Black (9,271)	10,744	12.61
Not Hispanic (8,058)	8,838	10.38
Hispanic (1,213)	1,906	2.24
American Indian/Alaska Native (414)	1,044	1.23
Not Hispanic (236)	686	0.81
Hispanic (178)	358	0.42
Alaska Athabascan *(Ala. Nat.)* (2)	2	<0.01
Apache (3)	7	0.01
Blackfeet (5)	54	0.06
Canadian/French Am. Ind. (4)	4	<0.01
Central American Ind. (2)	3	<0.01
Cherokee (66)	242	0.28
Chippewa (14)	17	0.02
Choctaw (7)	15	0.02
Comanche (0)	2	<0.01
Cree (0)	4	<0.01
Creek (11)	24	0.03
Crow (0)	3	<0.01
Delaware (4)	12	0.01
Hopi (0)	1	<0.01
Houma (0)	1	<0.01
Iroquois (16)	33	0.04
Kiowa (3)	3	<0.01
Lumbee (5)	5	0.01
Mexican American Ind. (6)	10	0.01
Navajo (1)	2	<0.01
Osage (0)	2	<0.01
Ottawa (2)	2	<0.01
Paiute (0)	1	<0.01
Potawatomi (1)	1	<0.01
Pueblo (1)	1	<0.01
Seminole (1)	8	0.01
Sioux (6)	10	0.01
South American Ind. (37)	75	0.09
Spanish American Ind. (1)	2	<0.01
Tohono O'Odham (2)	12	0.01
Asian (1,074)	1,586	1.86
Not Hispanic (988)	1,353	1.59
Hispanic (86)	233	0.27
Bangladeshi (8)	8	0.01
Burmese (5)	5	0.01
Cambodian (19)	24	0.03
Chinese, ex. Taiwanese (147)	235	0.28
Filipino (295)	454	0.53
Hmong (2)	2	<0.01
Indian (202)	277	0.33
Indonesian (2)	8	0.01
Japanese (33)	80	0.09
Korean (46)	110	0.13
Laotian (98)	115	0.14
Malaysian (0)	7	0.01
Nepalese (1)	1	<0.01
Pakistani (18)	21	0.02
Sri Lankan (2)	2	<0.01
Taiwanese (1)	2	<0.01
Thai (26)	42	0.05
Vietnamese (111)	138	0.16
Hawaii Native/Pacific Islander (49)	163	0.19
Not Hispanic (29)	81	0.10
Hispanic (20)	82	0.10
Guamanian/Chamorro (15)	29	0.03
Native Hawaiian (6)	29	0.03
Samoan (5)	10	0.01
Tongan (6)	6	0.01
White (65,348)	67,871	79.68
Not Hispanic (48,502)	49,736	58.39
Hispanic (16,846)	18,135	21.29

Destin

Place Type: City
County: Okaloosa
Population: 12,305†

Ancestry‡	Population	%
American (1,297)	1,297	10.54
Arab (0)	18	0.15
Lebanese (0)	12	0.10

SECTION TWO

*Notes: † The Census 2010 population figure is used to calculate the percentages in the Hispanic Origin and Race categories. Ancestry percentages are based on the 2006-2010 American Community Survey population (not shown); ‡ Numbers in parentheses indicate the number of people reporting a single ancestry; * Numbers in parentheses indicate the number of persons reporting this race alone, not in combination with any other race; Please refer to the Explanation of Data for more information.*

Ancestry	Population	%
Syrian (0)	6	0.05
Armenian (10)	24	0.20
Australian (14)	27	0.22
Austrian (0)	8	0.07
Belgian (9)	23	0.19
Brazilian (75)	75	0.61
British (57)	66	0.54
Czech (26)	47	0.38
Czechoslovakian (17)	17	0.14
Danish (15)	39	0.32
Dutch (95)	336	2.73
English (642)	1,648	13.39
European (92)	96	0.78
French, ex. Basque (157)	435	3.53
French Canadian (58)	107	0.87
German (836)	1,983	16.11
Greek (31)	102	0.83
Hungarian (8)	58	0.47
Irish (815)	1,780	14.46
Israeli (22)	22	0.18
Italian (189)	469	3.81
Lithuanian (16)	16	0.13
Northern European (12)	12	0.10
Norwegian (44)	123	1.00
Pennsylvania German (18)	18	0.15
Polish (154)	261	2.12
Romanian (53)	53	0.43
Russian (11)	11	0.09
Scandinavian (0)	1	0.01
Scotch-Irish (153)	297	2.41
Scottish (122)	343	2.79
Slovak (0)	19	0.15
Swedish (42)	208	1.69
Swiss (10)	10	0.08
Turkish (32)	32	0.26
Ukrainian (8)	8	0.07
Welsh (0)	10	0.08
Yugoslavian (0)	4	0.03

Hispanic Origin	Population	%
Hispanic or Latino (of any race)	796	6.47
Central American, ex. Mexican	52	0.42
Costa Rican	13	0.11
Guatemalan	7	0.06
Honduran	15	0.12
Nicaraguan	2	0.02
Panamanian	9	0.07
Salvadoran	6	0.05
Cuban	42	0.34
Dominican Republic	10	0.08
Mexican	428	3.48
Puerto Rican	99	0.80
South American	48	0.39
Argentinean	1	0.01
Chilean	4	0.03
Colombian	8	0.07
Ecuadorian	9	0.07
Peruvian	19	0.15
Venezuelan	6	0.05
Other South American	1	0.01
Other Hispanic or Latino	117	0.95

Race*	Population	%
African-American/Black (183)	259	2.10
Not Hispanic (180)	249	2.02
Hispanic (3)	10	0.08
American Indian/Alaska Native (36)	171	1.39
Not Hispanic (31)	156	1.27
Hispanic (5)	15	0.12
Apache (1)	4	0.03
Blackfeet (0)	1	0.01
Cherokee (4)	51	0.41
Chippewa (1)	2	0.02
Choctaw (0)	7	0.06
Cree (0)	1	0.01
Creek (3)	13	0.11
Iroquois (1)	1	0.01
Kiowa (0)	1	0.01
Lumbee (1)	1	0.01
Menominee (1)	1	0.01
Puget Sound Salish (1)	1	0.01
Seminole (1)	2	0.02
Sioux (0)	1	0.01
Asian (256)	399	3.24
Not Hispanic (248)	378	3.07
Hispanic (8)	21	0.17
Cambodian (3)	3	0.02
Chinese, ex. Taiwanese (36)	46	0.37
Filipino (75)	133	1.08
Indian (14)	16	0.13
Indonesian (1)	3	0.02
Japanese (14)	31	0.25
Korean (27)	58	0.47
Laotian (1)	1	0.01
Nepalese (1)	1	0.01
Taiwanese (1)	1	0.01
Thai (43)	78	0.63
Vietnamese (26)	33	0.27
Hawaii Native/Pacific Islander (13)	24	0.20
Not Hispanic (13)	24	0.20
Guamanian/Chamorro (0)	1	0.01
Native Hawaiian (9)	15	0.12
Samoan (0)	2	0.02
White (11,088)	11,423	92.83
Not Hispanic (10,645)	10,933	88.85
Hispanic (443)	490	3.98

Doctor Phillips

Place Type: CDP
County: Orange
Population: 10,981†

Ancestry‡	Population	%
African, Sub-Saharan (24)	50	0.45
African (10)	36	0.32
South African (14)	14	0.12
Albanian (13)	25	0.22
American (740)	740	6.59
Arab (316)	342	3.05
Arab (209)	209	1.86
Lebanese (14)	40	0.36
Palestinian (93)	93	0.83
Armenian (0)	9	0.08
Assyrian/Chaldean/Syriac (11)	11	0.10
Australian (0)	8	0.07
Austrian (14)	20	0.18
Brazilian (131)	131	1.17
British (60)	80	0.71
Canadian (52)	64	0.57
Croatian (0)	23	0.20
Czech (25)	85	0.76
Danish (10)	42	0.37
Dutch (7)	83	0.74
Eastern European (23)	34	0.30
English (287)	1,011	9.01
European (148)	182	1.62
Finnish (19)	19	0.17
French, ex. Basque (119)	421	3.75
French Canadian (9)	71	0.63
German (521)	1,628	14.50
Greek (105)	141	1.26
Hungarian (30)	80	0.71
Iranian (45)	45	0.40
Irish (256)	970	8.64
Italian (752)	1,163	10.36
Lithuanian (33)	41	0.37
Maltese (13)	27	0.24
Northern European (70)	70	0.62
Norwegian (8)	83	0.74
Pennsylvania German (16)	27	0.24
Polish (128)	375	3.34
Portuguese (14)	25	0.22
Romanian (0)	18	0.16
Russian (174)	237	2.11
Scandinavian (0)	32	0.29
Scotch-Irish (76)	191	1.70
Scottish (40)	277	2.47
Slovak (0)	21	0.19
Slovene (12)	12	0.11
Swedish (54)	140	1.25
Swiss (0)	10	0.09
Ukrainian (0)	8	0.07
West Indian, ex. Hispanic (144)	153	1.36
Haitian (0)	9	0.08
Jamaican (144)	144	1.28

Hispanic Origin	Population	%
Hispanic or Latino (of any race)	1,413	12.87
Central American, ex. Mexican	87	0.79
Costa Rican	11	0.10
Guatemalan	10	0.09
Honduran	20	0.18
Nicaraguan	17	0.15
Panamanian	22	0.20
Salvadoran	6	0.05
Other Central American	1	0.01
Cuban	122	1.11
Dominican Republic	85	0.77
Mexican	111	1.01
Puerto Rican	476	4.33
South American	405	3.69
Argentinean	56	0.51
Bolivian	6	0.05
Chilean	17	0.15
Colombian	143	1.30
Ecuadorian	28	0.25
Peruvian	40	0.36
Uruguayan	8	0.07
Venezuelan	106	0.97
Other South American	1	0.01
Other Hispanic or Latino	127	1.16

Race*	Population	%
African-American/Black (451)	551	5.02
Not Hispanic (403)	483	4.40
Hispanic (48)	68	0.62
American Indian/Alaska Native (22)	64	0.58
Not Hispanic (12)	47	0.43
Hispanic (10)	17	0.15
Blackfeet (0)	3	0.03
Cherokee (2)	6	0.05
Iroquois (0)	3	0.03
Seminole (3)	6	0.05
South American Ind. (0)	1	0.01
Asian (1,531)	1,721	15.67
Not Hispanic (1,528)	1,714	15.61
Hispanic (3)	7	0.06
Bangladeshi (11)	11	0.10
Cambodian (4)	4	0.04
Chinese, ex. Taiwanese (262)	287	2.61
Filipino (106)	135	1.23
Indian (577)	633	5.76
Indonesian (8)	9	0.08
Japanese (58)	66	0.60
Korean (135)	150	1.37
Pakistani (198)	215	1.96
Sri Lankan (8)	8	0.07
Taiwanese (14)	17	0.15
Thai (18)	25	0.23
Vietnamese (70)	88	0.80
Hawaii Native/Pacific Islander (3)	33	0.30
Not Hispanic (3)	22	0.20
Hispanic (0)	11	0.10
Guamanian/Chamorro (1)	1	0.01
Native Hawaiian (0)	11	0.10
Tongan (0)	3	0.03
White (8,245)	8,551	77.87
Not Hispanic (7,237)	7,475	68.07
Hispanic (1,008)	1,076	9.80

Doral

Place Type: City
County: Miami-Dade
Population: 45,704†

Ancestry‡	Population	%
Albanian (35)	35	0.09
American (921)	921	2.24

*Notes: † The Census 2010 population figure is used to calculate the percentages in the Hispanic Origin and Race categories. Ancestry percentages are based on the 2006-2010 American Community Survey population (not shown); ‡ Numbers in parentheses indicate the number of people reporting a single ancestry; * Numbers in parentheses indicate the number of persons reporting this race alone, not in combination with any other race; Please refer to the Explanation of Data for more information.*

Ancestry	Population	%
Arab (181)	370	0.90
Arab (7)	28	0.07
Lebanese (146)	280	0.68
Palestinian (13)	32	0.08
Syrian (15)	30	0.07
Armenian (20)	68	0.17
Australian (23)	23	0.06
Austrian (30)	39	0.09
Basque (43)	62	0.15
Belgian (0)	9	0.02
Brazilian (1,045)	1,174	2.85
British (20)	60	0.15
Croatian (11)	11	0.03
Danish (9)	9	0.02
Dutch (0)	54	0.13
English (136)	389	0.95
European (114)	178	0.43
Finnish (0)	73	0.18
French, ex. Basque (253)	546	1.33
French Canadian (0)	15	0.04
German (516)	875	2.13
Greek (35)	45	0.11
Guyanese (9)	9	0.02
Hungarian (19)	28	0.07
Iranian (187)	187	0.45
Irish (102)	400	0.97
Israeli (13)	13	0.03
Italian (747)	1,449	3.52
Latvian (14)	14	0.03
Norwegian (6)	6	0.01
Polish (51)	248	0.60
Portuguese (137)	195	0.47
Romanian (69)	77	0.19
Russian (111)	161	0.39
Scotch-Irish (15)	33	0.08
Scottish (28)	68	0.17
Serbian (0)	19	0.05
Slavic (0)	8	0.02
Swedish (15)	76	0.18
Swiss (17)	17	0.04
Turkish (122)	147	0.36
Ukrainian (0)	13	0.03
Welsh (0)	14	0.03
West Indian, ex. Hispanic (457)	545	1.32
Bahamian (14)	14	0.03
Barbadian (9)	33	0.08
British West Indian (62)	62	0.15
Dutch West Indian (41)	41	0.10
Haitian (146)	191	0.46
Jamaican (104)	118	0.29
Trinidadian/Tobagonian (11)	11	0.03
West Indian (70)	75	0.18

Hispanic Origin	Population	%
Hispanic or Latino (of any race)	36,344	79.52
Central American, ex. Mexican	2,402	5.26
Costa Rican	184	0.40
Guatemalan	263	0.58
Honduran	462	1.01
Nicaraguan	871	1.91
Panamanian	387	0.85
Salvadoran	234	0.51
Other Central American	1	<0.01
Cuban	5,806	12.70
Dominican Republic	1,751	3.83
Mexican	1,152	2.52
Puerto Rican	2,238	4.90
South American	21,078	46.12
Argentinean	1,082	2.37
Bolivian	192	0.42
Chilean	622	1.36
Colombian	6,731	14.73
Ecuadorian	1,248	2.73
Paraguayan	59	0.13
Peruvian	1,535	3.36
Uruguayan	180	0.39
Venezuelan	9,423	20.62
Other South American	6	0.01
Other Hispanic or Latino	1,917	4.19

Race*	Population	%
African-American/Black (1,139)	1,375	3.01
Not Hispanic (745)	822	1.80
Hispanic (394)	553	1.21
American Indian/Alaska Native (57)	112	0.25
Not Hispanic (17)	33	0.07
Hispanic (40)	79	0.17
Blackfeet (0)	3	0.01
Central American Ind. (1)	4	0.01
Cherokee (7)	10	0.02
Choctaw (0)	1	<0.01
Mexican American Ind. (2)	4	0.01
Navajo (1)	1	<0.01
Potawatomi (4)	4	0.01
Sioux (0)	1	<0.01
South American Ind. (15)	22	0.05
Spanish American Ind. (4)	6	0.01
Ute (1)	1	<0.01
Asian (1,633)	1,838	4.02
Not Hispanic (1,566)	1,705	3.73
Hispanic (67)	133	0.29
Bangladeshi (3)	6	0.01
Burmese (9)	9	0.02
Cambodian (5)	6	0.01
Chinese, ex. Taiwanese (400)	478	1.05
Filipino (101)	112	0.25
Hmong (0)	2	<0.01
Indian (514)	553	1.21
Indonesian (2)	2	<0.01
Japanese (166)	182	0.40
Korean (256)	271	0.59
Malaysian (3)	4	0.01
Pakistani (36)	49	0.11
Taiwanese (52)	65	0.14
Thai (13)	19	0.04
Vietnamese (25)	29	0.06
Hawaii Native/Pacific Islander (7)	19	0.04
Not Hispanic (3)	9	0.02
Hispanic (4)	10	0.02
Fijian (1)	1	<0.01
Guamanian/Chamorro (1)	1	<0.01
Native Hawaiian (2)	3	0.01
Samoan (0)	1	<0.01
White (40,552)	41,401	90.59
Not Hispanic (6,659)	6,875	15.04
Hispanic (33,893)	34,526	75.54

Dunedin

Place Type: City
County: Pinellas
Population: 35,321†

Ancestry‡	Population	%
African, Sub-Saharan (42)	42	0.12
African (42)	42	0.12
American (3,024)	3,024	8.54
Arab (8)	82	0.23
Lebanese (0)	20	0.06
Palestinian (0)	13	0.04
Syrian (0)	19	0.05
Other Arab (8)	30	0.08
Armenian (51)	73	0.21
Austrian (49)	120	0.34
Belgian (17)	50	0.14
Brazilian (90)	221	0.62
British (313)	360	1.02
Canadian (197)	298	0.84
Croatian (15)	63	0.18
Czech (42)	86	0.24
Czechoslovakian (12)	27	0.08
Danish (121)	306	0.86
Dutch (243)	727	2.05
Eastern European (23)	23	0.06
English (1,894)	5,899	16.66
European (372)	401	1.13
Finnish (57)	76	0.21
French, ex. Basque (242)	1,742	4.92
French Canadian (192)	544	1.54
German (2,536)	7,268	20.53
German Russian (15)	15	0.04
Greek (561)	847	2.39
Hungarian (102)	204	0.58
Iranian (26)	26	0.07
Irish (1,755)	6,308	17.82
Italian (1,372)	3,542	10.00
Latvian (7)	7	0.02
Lithuanian (104)	237	0.67
Northern European (12)	21	0.06
Norwegian (103)	353	1.00
Pennsylvania German (21)	55	0.16
Polish (494)	1,498	4.23
Portuguese (92)	319	0.90
Romanian (32)	80	0.23
Russian (132)	409	1.16
Scandinavian (36)	48	0.14
Scotch-Irish (415)	966	2.73
Scottish (529)	1,207	3.41
Slavic (21)	21	0.06
Slovak (163)	240	0.68
Slovene (52)	80	0.23
Swedish (116)	561	1.58
Swiss (40)	174	0.49
Turkish (0)	207	0.58
Ukrainian (90)	191	0.54
Welsh (42)	238	0.67
West Indian, ex. Hispanic (43)	63	0.18
Haitian (10)	30	0.08
Jamaican (11)	11	0.03
West Indian (22)	22	0.06
Yugoslavian (41)	98	0.28

Hispanic Origin	Population	%
Hispanic or Latino (of any race)	2,093	5.93
Central American, ex. Mexican	106	0.30
Costa Rican	10	0.03
Guatemalan	33	0.09
Honduran	12	0.03
Nicaraguan	5	0.01
Panamanian	22	0.06
Salvadoran	24	0.07
Cuban	201	0.57
Dominican Republic	52	0.15
Mexican	593	1.68
Puerto Rican	558	1.58
South American	396	1.12
Argentinean	23	0.07
Bolivian	17	0.05
Chilean	27	0.08
Colombian	162	0.46
Ecuadorian	39	0.11
Peruvian	70	0.20
Uruguayan	10	0.03
Venezuelan	45	0.13
Other South American	3	0.01
Other Hispanic or Latino	187	0.53

Race*	Population	%
African-American/Black (1,150)	1,407	3.98
Not Hispanic (1,096)	1,314	3.72
Hispanic (54)	93	0.26
American Indian/Alaska Native (104)	285	0.81
Not Hispanic (74)	218	0.62
Hispanic (30)	67	0.19
Aleut *(Alaska Native)* (1)	1	<0.01
Apache (1)	4	0.01
Blackfeet (1)	5	0.01
Canadian/French Am. Ind. (1)	1	<0.01
Cherokee (28)	91	0.26
Chickasaw (1)	1	<0.01
Chippewa (3)	6	0.02
Choctaw (5)	7	0.02
Comanche (1)	1	<0.01
Creek (0)	2	0.01
Delaware (1)	4	0.01
Iroquois (6)	13	0.04
Lumbee (2)	3	0.01
Mexican American Ind. (2)	3	0.01
Navajo (0)	2	0.01

*Notes: † The Census 2010 population figure is used to calculate the percentages in the Hispanic Origin and Race categories. Ancestry percentages are based on the 2006-2010 American Community Survey population (not shown); ‡ Numbers in parentheses indicate the number of people reporting a single ancestry; * Numbers in parentheses indicate the number of persons reporting this race alone, not in combination with any other race; Please refer to the Explanation of Data for more information.*

Ottawa (1)	1	<0.01
Paiute (2)	2	0.01
Potawatomi (0)	2	0.01
Seminole (2)	5	0.01
Shoshone (0)	1	<0.01
Sioux (3)	9	0.03
South American Ind. (1)	3	0.01
Spanish American Ind. (1)	1	<0.01
Asian (569)	738	2.09
Not Hispanic (568)	716	2.03
Hispanic (1)	22	0.06
Bangladeshi (1)	1	<0.01
Cambodian (7)	7	0.02
Chinese, ex. Taiwanese (100)	129	0.37
Filipino (168)	221	0.63
Hmong (11)	11	0.03
Indian (135)	167	0.47
Indonesian (1)	3	0.01
Japanese (15)	28	0.08
Korean (32)	47	0.13
Laotian (1)	2	0.01
Malaysian (0)	7	0.02
Nepalese (1)	1	<0.01
Pakistani (3)	3	0.01
Sri Lankan (1)	2	0.01
Taiwanese (1)	1	<0.01
Thai (5)	9	0.03
Vietnamese (58)	64	0.18
Hawaii Native/Pacific Islander (52)	86	0.24
Not Hispanic (50)	82	0.23
Hispanic (2)	4	0.01
Guamanian/Chamorro (7)	13	0.04
Native Hawaiian (3)	7	0.02
Samoan (2)	4	0.01
Tongan (0)	5	0.01
White (32,338)	32,912	93.18
Not Hispanic (30,874)	31,311	88.65
Hispanic (1,464)	1,601	4.53

East Lake

Place Type: CDP
County: Pinellas
Population: 30,962†

Ancestry‡	Population	%
African, Sub-Saharan (47)	53	0.17
African (47)	53	0.17
Albanian (15)	31	0.10
American (1,420)	1,420	4.54
Arab (171)	338	1.08
Arab (12)	35	0.11
Egyptian (82)	107	0.34
Lebanese (29)	122	0.39
Moroccan (12)	38	0.12
Syrian (36)	36	0.12
Armenian (13)	36	0.12
Austrian (135)	221	0.71
Belgian (13)	38	0.12
Brazilian (26)	26	0.08
British (337)	463	1.48
Bulgarian (76)	76	0.24
Canadian (164)	286	0.91
Croatian (15)	38	0.12
Czech (143)	230	0.73
Danish (60)	136	0.43
Dutch (133)	736	2.35
Eastern European (142)	142	0.45
English (1,293)	4,956	15.84
European (514)	554	1.77
Finnish (15)	59	0.19
French, ex. Basque (156)	1,025	3.28
French Canadian (108)	282	0.90
German (1,739)	6,637	21.21
Greek (536)	750	2.40
Guyanese (28)	28	0.09
Hungarian (50)	211	0.67
Iranian (15)	15	0.05
Irish (1,565)	5,746	18.36
Italian (2,022)	5,077	16.22
Latvian (40)	52	0.17
Lithuanian (74)	236	0.75
Luxemburger (0)	13	0.04
Macedonian (0)	15	0.05
Maltese (14)	14	0.04
New Zealander (29)	29	0.09
Northern European (91)	91	0.29
Norwegian (170)	458	1.46
Pennsylvania German (8)	32	0.10
Polish (601)	1,727	5.52
Portuguese (14)	53	0.17
Romanian (55)	68	0.22
Russian (175)	621	1.98
Scandinavian (0)	48	0.15
Scotch-Irish (195)	591	1.89
Scottish (194)	681	2.18
Serbian (23)	23	0.07
Slavic (13)	42	0.13
Slovak (84)	170	0.54
Slovene (0)	12	0.04
Swedish (104)	430	1.37
Swiss (38)	94	0.30
Ukrainian (78)	213	0.68
Welsh (0)	364	1.16
West Indian, ex. Hispanic (30)	105	0.34
Jamaican (0)	75	0.24
Trinidadian/Tobagonian (30)	30	0.10
Yugoslavian (318)	403	1.29

Hispanic Origin	Population	%
Hispanic or Latino (of any race)	1,842	5.95
Central American, ex. Mexican	105	0.34
Costa Rican	13	0.04
Guatemalan	28	0.09
Honduran	20	0.06
Nicaraguan	17	0.05
Panamanian	20	0.06
Salvadoran	7	0.02
Cuban	199	0.64
Dominican Republic	50	0.16
Mexican	218	0.70
Puerto Rican	625	2.02
South American	455	1.47
Argentinean	31	0.10
Bolivian	19	0.06
Chilean	22	0.07
Colombian	196	0.63
Ecuadorian	39	0.13
Paraguayan	4	0.01
Peruvian	68	0.22
Uruguayan	4	0.01
Venezuelan	60	0.19
Other South American	12	0.04
Other Hispanic or Latino	190	0.61

Race*	Population	%
African-American/Black (499)	646	2.09
Not Hispanic (455)	570	1.84
Hispanic (44)	76	0.25
American Indian/Alaska Native (44)	136	0.44
Not Hispanic (37)	119	0.38
Hispanic (7)	17	0.05
Blackfeet (1)	4	0.01
Central American Ind. (5)	8	0.03
Cherokee (6)	22	0.07
Chickasaw (1)	1	<0.01
Chippewa (3)	3	0.01
Choctaw (2)	8	0.03
Cree (1)	1	<0.01
Creek (3)	3	0.01
Delaware (0)	1	<0.01
Hopi (0)	2	0.01
Iroquois (3)	4	0.01
Lumbee (1)	1	<0.01
Navajo (1)	1	<0.01
Seminole (0)	4	0.01
Sioux (0)	3	0.01
South American Ind. (1)	1	<0.01
Spanish American Ind. (1)	1	<0.01
Asian (1,076)	1,332	4.30
Not Hispanic (1,058)	1,305	4.21
Hispanic (18)	27	0.09
Bangladeshi (3)	3	0.01
Cambodian (5)	7	0.02
Chinese, ex. Taiwanese (125)	151	0.49
Filipino (143)	208	0.67
Indian (532)	584	1.89
Indonesian (2)	2	0.01
Japanese (32)	62	0.20
Korean (66)	81	0.26
Laotian (3)	3	0.01
Pakistani (34)	40	0.13
Sri Lankan (10)	10	0.03
Taiwanese (14)	19	0.06
Thai (17)	22	0.07
Vietnamese (49)	61	0.20
Hawaii Native/Pacific Islander (6)	30	0.10
Not Hispanic (6)	28	0.09
Hispanic (0)	2	0.01
Guamanian/Chamorro (1)	2	0.01
Native Hawaiian (3)	14	0.05
Samoan (2)	3	0.01
White (28,593)	29,057	93.85
Not Hispanic (27,107)	27,483	88.76
Hispanic (1,486)	1,574	5.08

East Lake-Orient Park

Place Type: CDP
County: Hillsborough
Population: 22,753†

Ancestry‡	Population	%
Afghan (229)	229	0.96
African, Sub-Saharan (164)	233	0.97
African (164)	180	0.75
Nigerian (0)	53	0.22
American (1,155)	1,155	4.82
Arab (20)	33	0.14
Lebanese (0)	13	0.05
Moroccan (13)	13	0.05
Syrian (7)	7	0.03
Australian (0)	12	0.05
Austrian (10)	32	0.13
British (0)	65	0.27
Canadian (8)	19	0.08
Croatian (0)	9	0.04
Czech (0)	11	0.05
Czechoslovakian (0)	10	0.04
Danish (0)	30	0.13
Dutch (22)	264	1.10
English (919)	1,776	7.41
European (42)	42	0.18
Finnish (0)	32	0.13
French, ex. Basque (131)	449	1.87
French Canadian (26)	63	0.26
German (438)	1,851	7.72
Greek (14)	14	0.06
Guyanese (34)	34	0.14
Iranian (45)	45	0.19
Irish (231)	1,531	6.39
Italian (333)	617	2.57
Macedonian (9)	9	0.04
Norwegian (0)	92	0.38
Polish (38)	217	0.91
Portuguese (12)	22	0.09
Russian (75)	111	0.46
Scotch-Irish (61)	179	0.75
Scottish (53)	195	0.81
Serbian (20)	20	0.08
Slovak (0)	41	0.17
Swedish (109)	244	1.02
Swiss (0)	29	0.12
Ukrainian (0)	19	0.08
Welsh (48)	65	0.27
West Indian, ex. Hispanic (1,396)	1,734	7.23
Barbadian (0)	14	0.06
Belizean (0)	24	0.10
British West Indian (191)	275	1.15
Haitian (634)	649	2.71

*Notes: † The Census 2010 population figure is used to calculate the percentages in the Hispanic Origin and Race categories. Ancestry percentages are based on the 2006-2010 American Community Survey population (not shown); ‡ Numbers in parentheses indicate the number of people reporting a single ancestry; * Numbers in parentheses indicate the number of persons reporting this race alone, not in combination with any other race; Please refer to the Explanation of Data for more information.*

Jamaican (356)	427	1.78
Trinidadian/Tobagonian (103)	140	0.58
U.S. Virgin Islander (8)	8	0.03
West Indian (104)	197	0.82
Yugoslavian (111)	111	0.46

Hispanic Origin	Population	%
Hispanic or Latino (of any race)	3,916	17.21
Central American, ex. Mexican	303	1.33
Costa Rican	17	0.07
Guatemalan	34	0.15
Honduran	100	0.44
Nicaraguan	20	0.09
Panamanian	39	0.17
Salvadoran	85	0.37
Other Central American	8	0.04
Cuban	619	2.72
Dominican Republic	216	0.95
Mexican	456	2.00
Puerto Rican	1,702	7.48
South American	349	1.53
Argentinean	9	0.04
Bolivian	7	0.03
Chilean	5	0.02
Colombian	142	0.62
Ecuadorian	65	0.29
Peruvian	73	0.32
Uruguayan	11	0.05
Venezuelan	37	0.16
Other Hispanic or Latino	271	1.19

Race*	Population	%
African-American/Black (9,965)	10,465	45.99
Not Hispanic (9,573)	9,917	43.59
Hispanic (392)	548	2.41
American Indian/Alaska Native (113)	285	1.25
Not Hispanic (85)	224	0.98
Hispanic (28)	61	0.27
Apache (0)	5	0.02
Blackfeet (0)	3	0.01
Central American Ind. (8)	11	0.05
Cherokee (23)	77	0.34
Chippewa (3)	3	0.01
Choctaw (0)	2	0.01
Comanche (0)	2	0.01
Cree (0)	1	<0.01
Creek (4)	7	0.03
Iroquois (4)	8	0.04
Lumbee (1)	2	0.01
Mexican American Ind. (3)	9	0.04
Navajo (1)	3	0.01
Osage (1)	1	<0.01
Seminole (1)	2	0.01
Sioux (2)	4	0.02
South American Ind. (1)	6	0.03
Spanish American Ind. (0)	3	0.01
Tlingit-Haida *(Alaska Native)* (2)	3	0.01
Asian (639)	784	3.45
Not Hispanic (635)	758	3.33
Hispanic (4)	26	0.11
Bangladeshi (25)	28	0.12
Burmese (10)	10	0.04
Chinese, ex. Taiwanese (38)	54	0.24
Filipino (83)	123	0.54
Hmong (5)	5	0.02
Indian (331)	359	1.58
Indonesian (1)	2	0.01
Japanese (6)	22	0.10
Korean (33)	39	0.17
Laotian (2)	2	0.01
Malaysian (1)	1	<0.01
Pakistani (36)	45	0.20
Sri Lankan (1)	1	<0.01
Taiwanese (1)	3	0.01
Thai (14)	17	0.07
Vietnamese (27)	38	0.17
Hawaii Native/Pacific Islander (20)	68	0.30
Not Hispanic (5)	43	0.19
Hispanic (15)	25	0.11
Guamanian/Chamorro (0)	1	<0.01
Native Hawaiian (11)	17	0.07
Samoan (0)	2	0.01
Tongan (1)	2	0.01
White (10,274)	10,907	47.94
Not Hispanic (7,948)	8,367	36.77
Hispanic (2,326)	2,540	11.16

East Milton

Place Type: CDP
County: Santa Rosa
Population: 11,074†

Ancestry‡	Population	%
African, Sub-Saharan (61)	61	0.67
African (61)	61	0.67
American (1,004)	1,004	11.02
Arab (78)	78	0.86
Arab (39)	39	0.43
Jordanian (39)	39	0.43
Austrian (0)	77	0.85
Brazilian (8)	16	0.18
Canadian (0)	72	0.79
Croatian (0)	60	0.66
Czech (0)	15	0.16
Czechoslovakian (14)	35	0.38
Danish (0)	77	0.85
Dutch (0)	25	0.27
English (408)	595	6.53
European (0)	117	1.28
French, ex. Basque (54)	279	3.06
French Canadian (68)	68	0.75
German (239)	1,418	15.57
Greek (0)	29	0.32
Hungarian (20)	59	0.65
Irish (297)	1,395	15.31
Italian (124)	317	3.48
Norwegian (14)	68	0.75
Polish (0)	12	0.13
Portuguese (0)	12	0.13
Russian (0)	37	0.41
Scotch-Irish (85)	95	1.04
Scottish (29)	78	0.86
Swedish (0)	15	0.16
Swiss (29)	29	0.32
Welsh (0)	58	0.64
West Indian, ex. Hispanic (49)	63	0.69
Haitian (9)	9	0.10
Jamaican (23)	30	0.33
Trinidadian/Tobagonian (6)	6	0.07
West Indian (11)	18	0.20

Hispanic Origin	Population	%
Hispanic or Latino (of any race)	450	4.06
Central American, ex. Mexican	44	0.40
Costa Rican	2	0.02
Guatemalan	15	0.14
Honduran	6	0.05
Nicaraguan	5	0.05
Panamanian	8	0.07
Salvadoran	8	0.07
Cuban	62	0.56
Dominican Republic	8	0.07
Mexican	152	1.37
Puerto Rican	89	0.80
South American	14	0.13
Colombian	11	0.10
Peruvian	1	0.01
Uruguayan	1	0.01
Venezuelan	1	0.01
Other Hispanic or Latino	81	0.73

Race*	Population	%
African-American/Black (2,164)	2,221	20.06
Not Hispanic (2,139)	2,194	19.81
Hispanic (25)	27	0.24
American Indian/Alaska Native (105)	247	2.23
Not Hispanic (97)	233	2.10
Hispanic (8)	14	0.13
Apache (3)	4	0.04
Blackfeet (1)	4	0.04
Cherokee (23)	77	0.70
Chickasaw (3)	3	0.03
Chippewa (2)	2	0.02
Choctaw (3)	4	0.04
Creek (30)	55	0.50
Crow (1)	1	0.01
Delaware (1)	1	0.01
Houma (1)	1	0.01
Iroquois (2)	3	0.03
Mexican American Ind. (4)	5	0.05
Navajo (0)	4	0.04
Potawatomi (2)	2	0.02
Seminole (1)	2	0.02
Sioux (1)	1	0.01
Ute (1)	1	0.01
Yaqui (0)	1	0.01
Asian (54)	113	1.02
Not Hispanic (52)	110	0.99
Hispanic (2)	3	0.03
Cambodian (2)	2	0.02
Chinese, ex. Taiwanese (0)	3	0.03
Filipino (22)	52	0.47
Indian (8)	11	0.10
Japanese (3)	20	0.18
Korean (4)	9	0.08
Thai (5)	11	0.10
Vietnamese (5)	6	0.05
Hawaii Native/Pacific Islander (13)	22	0.20
Not Hispanic (13)	18	0.16
Hispanic (0)	4	0.04
Guamanian/Chamorro (7)	11	0.10
Native Hawaiian (1)	4	0.04
Samoan (0)	1	0.01
White (8,425)	8,661	78.21
Not Hispanic (8,076)	8,294	74.90
Hispanic (349)	367	3.31

Edgewater

Place Type: City
County: Volusia
Population: 20,750†

Ancestry‡	Population	%
African, Sub-Saharan (11)	11	0.05
African (11)	11	0.05
Albanian (0)	7	0.03
American (1,198)	1,198	5.74
Arab (42)	87	0.42
Egyptian (42)	42	0.20
Lebanese (0)	45	0.22
Armenian (36)	67	0.32
Austrian (31)	83	0.40
British (38)	67	0.32
Canadian (50)	64	0.31
Celtic (13)	38	0.18
Croatian (10)	31	0.15
Czech (17)	90	0.43
Czechoslovakian (0)	13	0.06
Danish (31)	109	0.52
Dutch (95)	293	1.40
English (882)	2,835	13.59
European (197)	197	0.94
Finnish (41)	105	0.50
French, ex. Basque (226)	1,010	4.84
French Canadian (153)	367	1.76
German (923)	3,348	16.05
Greek (51)	73	0.35
Hungarian (32)	82	0.39
Irish (1,383)	3,769	18.06
Italian (1,149)	2,168	10.39
Lithuanian (91)	130	0.62
Northern European (34)	34	0.16
Norwegian (177)	350	1.68
Pennsylvania German (31)	31	0.15
Polish (292)	794	3.81
Portuguese (78)	199	0.95
Romanian (9)	9	0.04
Russian (31)	96	0.46

SECTION TWO

*Notes: † The Census 2010 population figure is used to calculate the percentages in the Hispanic Origin and Race categories. Ancestry percentages are based on the 2006-2010 American Community Survey population (not shown); ‡ Numbers in parentheses indicate the number of people reporting a single ancestry; * Numbers in parentheses indicate the number of persons reporting this race alone, not in combination with any other race; Please refer to the Explanation of Data for more information.*

Scotch-Irish (173)	303	1.45
Scottish (221)	545	2.61
Slovak (0)	24	0.12
Slovene (39)	39	0.19
Swedish (58)	301	1.44
Ukrainian (0)	145	0.69
Welsh (91)	445	2.13
West Indian, ex. Hispanic (71)	71	0.34
British West Indian (25)	25	0.12
West Indian (46)	46	0.22

Hispanic Origin	Population	%
Hispanic or Latino (of any race)	713	3.44
Central American, ex. Mexican	35	0.17
Costa Rican	1	<0.01
Guatemalan	1	<0.01
Honduran	6	0.03
Nicaraguan	6	0.03
Panamanian	11	0.05
Salvadoran	9	0.04
Other Central American	1	<0.01
Cuban	86	0.41
Dominican Republic	19	0.09
Mexican	153	0.74
Puerto Rican	272	1.31
South American	79	0.38
Argentinean	7	0.03
Bolivian	4	0.02
Chilean	3	0.01
Colombian	19	0.09
Ecuadorian	8	0.04
Paraguayan	1	<0.01
Peruvian	13	0.06
Uruguayan	2	0.01
Venezuelan	19	0.09
Other South American	3	0.01
Other Hispanic or Latino	69	0.33

Race*	Population	%
African-American/Black (542)	682	3.29
Not Hispanic (522)	650	3.13
Hispanic (20)	32	0.15
American Indian/Alaska Native (62)	176	0.85
Not Hispanic (53)	159	0.77
Hispanic (9)	17	0.08
Apache (2)	3	0.01
Blackfeet (1)	9	0.04
Canadian/French Am. Ind. (1)	8	0.04
Cherokee (7)	44	0.21
Chickasaw (3)	3	0.01
Chippewa (7)	8	0.04
Choctaw (2)	7	0.03
Cree (0)	2	0.01
Creek (1)	2	0.01
Crow (0)	1	<0.01
Delaware (2)	3	0.01
Iroquois (2)	4	0.02
Kiowa (0)	2	0.01
Lumbee (1)	1	<0.01
Menominee (0)	1	<0.01
Mexican American Ind. (1)	1	<0.01
Navajo (1)	3	0.01
Osage (0)	1	<0.01
Ottawa (1)	1	<0.01
Potawatomi (1)	1	<0.01
Seminole (0)	1	<0.01
Sioux (1)	4	0.02
South American Ind. (2)	4	0.02
Ute (1)	1	<0.01
Asian (187)	234	1.13
Not Hispanic (182)	226	1.09
Hispanic (5)	8	0.04
Cambodian (3)	3	0.01
Chinese, ex. Taiwanese (20)	26	0.13
Filipino (44)	63	0.30
Indian (53)	57	0.27
Indonesian (2)	4	0.02
Japanese (18)	31	0.15
Korean (13)	16	0.08
Laotian (2)	2	0.01
Pakistani (1)	1	<0.01
Thai (7)	9	0.04
Vietnamese (13)	14	0.07
Hawaii Native/Pacific Islander (2)	12	0.06
Not Hispanic (1)	11	0.05
Hispanic (1)	1	<0.01
Native Hawaiian (2)	10	0.05
White (19,524)	19,834	95.59
Not Hispanic (18,972)	19,248	92.76
Hispanic (552)	586	2.82

Egypt Lake-Leto

Place Type: CDP
County: Hillsborough
Population: 35,282†

Ancestry‡	Population	%
African, Sub-Saharan (149)	258	0.74
African (46)	108	0.31
Ethiopian (73)	73	0.21
Nigerian (0)	23	0.07
Sierra Leonean (0)	24	0.07
South African (30)	30	0.09
American (1,243)	1,243	3.55
Arab (164)	193	0.55
Arab (101)	101	0.29
Egyptian (24)	24	0.07
Lebanese (0)	29	0.08
Moroccan (30)	30	0.09
Syrian (9)	9	0.03
Austrian (0)	11	0.03
Belgian (0)	25	0.07
Brazilian (77)	77	0.22
British (14)	35	0.10
Bulgarian (30)	30	0.09
Canadian (0)	11	0.03
Czech (0)	65	0.19
Danish (23)	23	0.07
Dutch (0)	198	0.57
Eastern European (54)	54	0.15
English (440)	1,605	4.58
European (93)	101	0.29
French, ex. Basque (90)	491	1.40
French Canadian (0)	32	0.09
German (755)	2,187	6.24
Greek (91)	299	0.85
Guyanese (14)	14	0.04
Hungarian (26)	61	0.17
Iranian (0)	19	0.05
Irish (517)	1,412	4.03
Italian (709)	1,603	4.58
Lithuanian (10)	10	0.03
Norwegian (32)	96	0.27
Polish (94)	299	0.85
Portuguese (136)	185	0.53
Romanian (0)	26	0.07
Russian (23)	136	0.39
Scotch-Irish (82)	279	0.80
Scottish (41)	285	0.81
Serbian (0)	24	0.07
Slavic (0)	10	0.03
Slovene (0)	13	0.04
Swedish (26)	163	0.47
Turkish (0)	41	0.12
Ukrainian (14)	14	0.04
Welsh (25)	83	0.24
West Indian, ex. Hispanic (985)	1,113	3.18
Barbadian (0)	17	0.05
Haitian (135)	183	0.52
Jamaican (201)	264	0.75
West Indian (634)	634	1.81
Other West Indian (15)	15	0.04

Hispanic Origin	Population	%
Hispanic or Latino (of any race)	21,157	59.97
Central American, ex. Mexican	943	2.67
Costa Rican	90	0.26
Guatemalan	173	0.49
Honduran	335	0.95
Nicaraguan	115	0.33
Panamanian	86	0.24
Salvadoran	144	0.41
Cuban	9,697	27.48
Dominican Republic	1,042	2.95
Mexican	1,288	3.65
Puerto Rican	4,902	13.89
South American	1,910	5.41
Argentinean	79	0.22
Bolivian	35	0.10
Chilean	30	0.09
Colombian	1,027	2.91
Ecuadorian	170	0.48
Paraguayan	1	<0.01
Peruvian	254	0.72
Uruguayan	75	0.21
Venezuelan	236	0.67
Other South American	3	0.01
Other Hispanic or Latino	1,375	3.90

Race*	Population	%
African-American/Black (3,809)	4,306	12.20
Not Hispanic (2,939)	3,150	8.93
Hispanic (870)	1,156	3.28
American Indian/Alaska Native (115)	274	0.78
Not Hispanic (46)	130	0.37
Hispanic (69)	144	0.41
Apache (0)	1	<0.01
Blackfeet (3)	15	0.04
Canadian/French Am. Ind. (5)	5	0.01
Central American Ind. (6)	8	0.02
Cherokee (11)	50	0.14
Chippewa (2)	3	0.01
Choctaw (1)	9	0.03
Creek (1)	3	0.01
Inupiat *(Alaska Native)* (2)	2	0.01
Iroquois (0)	2	0.01
Lumbee (2)	2	0.01
Mexican American Ind. (1)	5	0.01
Osage (0)	3	0.01
Seminole (5)	6	0.02
Sioux (1)	5	0.01
South American Ind. (3)	22	0.06
Spanish American Ind. (0)	6	0.02
Yup'ik *(Alaska Native)* (1)	1	<0.01
Asian (1,296)	1,479	4.19
Not Hispanic (1,258)	1,391	3.94
Hispanic (38)	88	0.25
Bangladeshi (5)	5	0.01
Burmese (1)	1	<0.01
Cambodian (3)	7	0.02
Chinese, ex. Taiwanese (90)	125	0.35
Filipino (89)	132	0.37
Indian (266)	290	0.82
Indonesian (1)	1	<0.01
Japanese (9)	16	0.05
Korean (54)	67	0.19
Laotian (5)	6	0.02
Nepalese (1)	1	<0.01
Pakistani (11)	13	0.04
Sri Lankan (2)	2	0.01
Taiwanese (1)	1	<0.01
Thai (18)	30	0.09
Vietnamese (700)	738	2.09
Hawaii Native/Pacific Islander (17)	60	0.17
Not Hispanic (8)	22	0.06
Hispanic (9)	38	0.11
Guamanian/Chamorro (3)	6	0.02
Native Hawaiian (5)	12	0.03
Samoan (0)	2	0.01
White (26,578)	27,543	78.07
Not Hispanic (9,417)	9,740	27.61
Hispanic (17,161)	17,803	50.46

Elfers

Place Type: CDP
County: Pasco
Population: 13,986†

*Notes: † The Census 2010 population figure is used to calculate the percentages in the Hispanic Origin and Race categories. Ancestry percentages are based on the 2006-2010 American Community Survey population (not shown); ‡ Numbers in parentheses indicate the number of people reporting a single ancestry; * Numbers in parentheses indicate the number of persons reporting this race alone, not in combination with any other race; Please refer to the Explanation of Data for more information.*

Ancestry‡	Population	%
African, Sub-Saharan (183)	183	1.38
Liberian (183)	183	1.38
Albanian (31)	112	0.85
American (976)	976	7.38
Arab (0)	9	0.07
Syrian (0)	9	0.07
Armenian (0)	5	0.04
Austrian (0)	9	0.07
Belgian (6)	16	0.12
British (25)	62	0.47
Bulgarian (0)	24	0.18
Canadian (40)	117	0.88
Celtic (0)	11	0.08
Croatian (12)	22	0.17
Czech (12)	75	0.57
Czechoslovakian (17)	17	0.13
Danish (0)	54	0.41
Dutch (42)	320	2.42
Eastern European (20)	20	0.15
English (287)	1,285	9.72
European (54)	66	0.50
Finnish (0)	13	0.10
French, ex. Basque (218)	826	6.25
French Canadian (98)	136	1.03
German (876)	3,062	23.16
Greek (198)	331	2.50
Hungarian (35)	80	0.61
Iranian (0)	20	0.15
Irish (571)	2,223	16.81
Italian (732)	1,611	12.18
Norwegian (18)	63	0.48
Polish (196)	547	4.14
Portuguese (33)	43	0.33
Russian (40)	84	0.64
Scotch-Irish (113)	272	2.06
Scottish (127)	355	2.68
Serbian (57)	67	0.51
Slovak (17)	36	0.27
Swedish (71)	227	1.72
Swiss (6)	38	0.29
Ukrainian (0)	7	0.05
Welsh (32)	185	1.40
West Indian, ex. Hispanic (166)	166	1.26
Bahamian (5)	5	0.04
Jamaican (161)	161	1.22
Yugoslavian (60)	60	0.45

Hispanic Origin	Population	%
Hispanic or Latino (of any race)	1,562	11.17
Central American, ex. Mexican	101	0.72
Costa Rican	12	0.09
Guatemalan	10	0.07
Honduran	36	0.26
Nicaraguan	8	0.06
Panamanian	6	0.04
Salvadoran	29	0.21
Cuban	137	0.98
Dominican Republic	69	0.49
Mexican	370	2.65
Puerto Rican	664	4.75
South American	132	0.94
Argentinean	4	0.03
Bolivian	9	0.06
Chilean	3	0.02
Colombian	67	0.48
Ecuadorian	16	0.11
Peruvian	14	0.10
Uruguayan	1	0.01
Venezuelan	12	0.09
Other South American	6	0.04
Other Hispanic or Latino	89	0.64

Race*	Population	%
African-American/Black (436)	576	4.12
Not Hispanic (375)	479	3.42
Hispanic (61)	97	0.69
American Indian/Alaska Native (53)	136	0.97
Not Hispanic (36)	112	0.80
Hispanic (17)	24	0.17
Apache (0)	2	0.01
Blackfeet (0)	3	0.02
Central American Ind. (0)	1	0.01
Cherokee (5)	33	0.24
Chippewa (1)	2	0.01
Creek (1)	2	0.01
Iroquois (4)	11	0.08
Navajo (0)	1	0.01
Potawatomi (0)	1	0.01
Seminole (0)	1	0.01
Sioux (1)	1	0.01
South American Ind. (3)	3	0.02
Spanish American Ind. (1)	1	0.01
Asian (283)	343	2.45
Not Hispanic (281)	335	2.40
Hispanic (2)	8	0.06
Cambodian (0)	1	0.01
Chinese, ex. Taiwanese (11)	16	0.11
Filipino (64)	90	0.64
Indian (51)	57	0.41
Indonesian (2)	2	0.01
Japanese (3)	7	0.05
Korean (7)	13	0.09
Laotian (2)	3	0.02
Pakistani (0)	1	0.01
Thai (5)	6	0.04
Vietnamese (132)	141	1.01
Hawaii Native/Pacific Islander (12)	23	0.16
Not Hispanic (12)	20	0.14
Hispanic (0)	3	0.02
Guamanian/Chamorro (0)	1	0.01
Native Hawaiian (1)	2	0.01
Samoan (7)	11	0.08
Tongan (4)	6	0.04
White (12,485)	12,811	91.60
Not Hispanic (11,476)	11,704	83.68
Hispanic (1,009)	1,107	7.92

Englewood

Place Type: CDP
County: Sarasota
Population: 14,863†

Ancestry‡	Population	%
American (1,050)	1,050	6.61
Arab (0)	26	0.16
Lebanese (0)	13	0.08
Moroccan (0)	13	0.08
Armenian (50)	67	0.42
Australian (21)	21	0.13
Austrian (11)	36	0.23
Belgian (0)	39	0.25
Brazilian (82)	82	0.52
British (106)	134	0.84
Canadian (51)	205	1.29
Celtic (0)	114	0.72
Croatian (77)	88	0.55
Czech (71)	127	0.80
Czechoslovakian (25)	25	0.16
Danish (37)	100	0.63
Dutch (85)	337	2.12
English (1,016)	3,086	19.42
Estonian (6)	6	0.04
European (71)	82	0.52
Finnish (113)	132	0.83
French, ex. Basque (203)	810	5.10
French Canadian (170)	263	1.66
German (1,493)	3,741	23.54
Greek (32)	45	0.28
Hungarian (35)	59	0.37
Irish (808)	2,619	16.48
Italian (485)	887	5.58
Lithuanian (42)	104	0.65
Luxemburger (13)	13	0.08
Norwegian (196)	333	2.10
Pennsylvania German (0)	28	0.18
Polish (208)	542	3.41
Portuguese (21)	144	0.91
Romanian (33)	33	0.21
Russian (91)	199	1.25
Scandinavian (11)	24	0.15
Scotch-Irish (133)	417	2.62
Scottish (189)	654	4.12
Serbian (14)	23	0.14
Slavic (0)	7	0.04
Slovak (56)	68	0.43
Slovene (21)	21	0.13
Swedish (138)	359	2.26
Swiss (0)	33	0.21
Ukrainian (12)	45	0.28
Welsh (101)	310	1.95
West Indian, ex. Hispanic (0)	28	0.18
Jamaican (0)	28	0.18
Yugoslavian (14)	14	0.09

Hispanic Origin	Population	%
Hispanic or Latino (of any race)	374	2.52
Central American, ex. Mexican	13	0.09
Costa Rican	2	0.01
Guatemalan	3	0.02
Honduran	2	0.01
Nicaraguan	3	0.02
Salvadoran	3	0.02
Cuban	23	0.15
Dominican Republic	1	0.01
Mexican	189	1.27
Puerto Rican	76	0.51
South American	36	0.24
Argentinean	4	0.03
Chilean	2	0.01
Colombian	11	0.07
Ecuadorian	8	0.05
Peruvian	4	0.03
Venezuelan	7	0.05
Other Hispanic or Latino	36	0.24

Race*	Population	%
African-American/Black (45)	76	0.51
Not Hispanic (42)	70	0.47
Hispanic (3)	6	0.04
American Indian/Alaska Native (36)	94	0.63
Not Hispanic (31)	88	0.59
Hispanic (5)	6	0.04
Apache (2)	2	0.01
Blackfeet (0)	6	0.04
Canadian/French Am. Ind. (0)	3	0.02
Cherokee (4)	20	0.13
Chickasaw (1)	1	0.01
Chippewa (6)	7	0.05
Iroquois (1)	5	0.03
Kiowa (0)	1	0.01
Mexican American Ind. (4)	4	0.03
Navajo (1)	1	0.01
Osage (1)	1	0.01
Seminole (1)	2	0.01
Sioux (0)	2	0.01
Spanish American Ind. (0)	1	0.01
Asian (106)	139	0.94
Not Hispanic (105)	137	0.92
Hispanic (1)	2	0.01
Cambodian (12)	13	0.09
Chinese, ex. Taiwanese (13)	15	0.10
Filipino (34)	44	0.30
Indian (18)	22	0.15
Japanese (5)	8	0.05
Korean (6)	14	0.09
Taiwanese (1)	1	0.01
Thai (6)	8	0.05
Vietnamese (8)	11	0.07
Hawaii Native/Pacific Islander (5)	16	0.11
Not Hispanic (5)	15	0.10
Hispanic (0)	1	0.01
Native Hawaiian (2)	6	0.04
Samoan (3)	8	0.05
White (14,436)	14,582	98.11
Not Hispanic (14,171)	14,296	96.19
Hispanic (265)	286	1.92

*Notes: † The Census 2010 population figure is used to calculate the percentages in the Hispanic Origin and Race categories. Ancestry percentages are based on the 2006-2010 American Community Survey population (not shown); ‡ Numbers in parentheses indicate the number of people reporting a single ancestry; * Numbers in parentheses indicate the number of persons reporting this race alone, not in combination with any other race; Please refer to the Explanation of Data for more information.*

Ensley

Place Type: CDP
County: Escambia
Population: 20,602†

Ancestry‡	Population	%
Afghan (0)	17	0.09
African, Sub-Saharan (133)	147	0.81
African (105)	119	0.65
Ethiopian (28)	28	0.15
American (1,355)	1,355	7.43
Austrian (12)	12	0.07
Belgian (0)	31	0.17
Brazilian (11)	22	0.12
British (75)	98	0.54
Canadian (14)	14	0.08
Czech (36)	48	0.26
Danish (24)	44	0.24
Dutch (71)	173	0.95
English (740)	1,355	7.43
European (352)	407	2.23
Finnish (0)	11	0.06
French, ex. Basque (141)	540	2.96
French Canadian (65)	116	0.64
German (879)	1,954	10.71
Greek (9)	48	0.26
Hungarian (20)	96	0.53
Irish (811)	2,303	12.63
Italian (265)	699	3.83
Lithuanian (13)	30	0.16
Northern European (16)	31	0.17
Norwegian (56)	218	1.20
Pennsylvania German (0)	18	0.10
Polish (9)	101	0.55
Portuguese (28)	49	0.27
Russian (20)	20	0.11
Scandinavian (31)	31	0.17
Scotch-Irish (237)	412	2.26
Scottish (105)	304	1.67
Slavic (15)	15	0.08
Swedish (63)	127	0.70
Swiss (0)	13	0.07
Welsh (12)	111	0.61
West Indian, ex. Hispanic (250)	298	1.63
British West Indian (136)	136	0.75
Dutch West Indian (0)	45	0.25
Haitian (48)	51	0.28
Jamaican (31)	31	0.17
Trinidadian/Tobagonian (35)	35	0.19
Yugoslavian (23)	23	0.13

Hispanic Origin	Population	%
Hispanic or Latino (of any race)	1,010	4.90
Central American, ex. Mexican	84	0.41
Costa Rican	5	0.02
Guatemalan	9	0.04
Honduran	29	0.14
Nicaraguan	7	0.03
Panamanian	17	0.08
Salvadoran	17	0.08
Cuban	54	0.26
Dominican Republic	9	0.04
Mexican	533	2.59
Puerto Rican	160	0.78
South American	55	0.27
Argentinean	6	0.03
Chilean	2	0.01
Colombian	27	0.13
Ecuadorian	7	0.03
Peruvian	8	0.04
Venezuelan	5	0.02
Other Hispanic or Latino	115	0.56

Race*	Population	%
African-American/Black (6,139)	6,403	31.08
Not Hispanic (6,063)	6,293	30.55
Hispanic (76)	110	0.53
American Indian/Alaska Native (217)	442	2.15
Not Hispanic (201)	396	1.92
Hispanic (16)	46	0.22
Apache (0)	1	<0.01
Blackfeet (9)	21	0.10
Canadian/French Am. Ind. (0)	1	<0.01
Central American Ind. (2)	2	0.01
Cherokee (19)	83	0.40
Cheyenne (1)	1	<0.01
Chickasaw (2)	6	0.03
Chippewa (3)	4	0.02
Choctaw (3)	14	0.07
Creek (78)	116	0.56
Crow (1)	1	<0.01
Houma (6)	12	0.06
Iroquois (3)	3	0.01
Lumbee (4)	4	0.02
Mexican American Ind. (4)	6	0.03
Navajo (3)	5	0.02
Ottawa (1)	1	<0.01
Potawatomi (1)	1	<0.01
Seminole (0)	2	0.01
Shoshone (0)	1	<0.01
Sioux (3)	4	0.02
South American Ind. (1)	3	0.01
Ute (1)	2	0.01
Asian (448)	600	2.91
Not Hispanic (446)	587	2.85
Hispanic (2)	13	0.06
Cambodian (4)	5	0.02
Chinese, ex. Taiwanese (70)	88	0.43
Filipino (117)	178	0.86
Indian (47)	52	0.25
Indonesian (0)	5	0.02
Japanese (25)	47	0.23
Korean (24)	48	0.23
Laotian (1)	2	0.01
Pakistani (2)	2	0.01
Thai (6)	11	0.05
Vietnamese (138)	151	0.73
Hawaii Native/Pacific Islander (7)	41	0.20
Not Hispanic (7)	40	0.19
Hispanic (0)	1	<0.01
Guamanian/Chamorro (4)	6	0.03
Native Hawaiian (0)	11	0.05
Samoan (0)	1	<0.01
White (12,800)	13,365	64.87
Not Hispanic (12,311)	12,789	62.08
Hispanic (489)	576	2.80

Estero

Place Type: CDP
County: Lee
Population: 22,612†

Ancestry‡	Population	%
African, Sub-Saharan (42)	42	0.20
African (29)	29	0.14
South African (13)	13	0.06
Albanian (0)	27	0.13
American (1,986)	1,986	9.28
Arab (34)	46	0.22
Lebanese (25)	37	0.17
Syrian (9)	9	0.04
Armenian (23)	23	0.11
Austrian (17)	98	0.46
Belgian (59)	73	0.34
Brazilian (10)	10	0.05
British (101)	166	0.78
Canadian (168)	283	1.32
Croatian (7)	81	0.38
Czech (16)	101	0.47
Czechoslovakian (38)	49	0.23
Danish (18)	46	0.22
Dutch (88)	345	1.61
Eastern European (21)	28	0.13
English (1,167)	3,246	15.17
Estonian (8)	8	0.04
European (144)	179	0.84
Finnish (0)	32	0.15
French, ex. Basque (267)	964	4.51
French Canadian (241)	302	1.41
German (2,069)	4,618	21.59
Greek (46)	69	0.32
Hungarian (95)	212	0.99
Irish (1,342)	3,477	16.25
Italian (1,226)	2,026	9.47
Latvian (8)	8	0.04
Lithuanian (83)	107	0.50
Luxemburger (0)	12	0.06
New Zealander (50)	50	0.23
Northern European (21)	36	0.17
Norwegian (186)	394	1.84
Pennsylvania German (11)	40	0.19
Polish (553)	1,005	4.70
Portuguese (199)	230	1.08
Romanian (93)	93	0.43
Russian (189)	257	1.20
Scandinavian (19)	33	0.15
Scotch-Irish (147)	544	2.54
Scottish (380)	706	3.30
Serbian (10)	25	0.12
Slavic (45)	91	0.43
Slovak (43)	63	0.29
Slovene (24)	45	0.21
Swedish (212)	532	2.49
Swiss (26)	87	0.41
Ukrainian (50)	66	0.31
Welsh (47)	232	1.08
Yugoslavian (10)	10	0.05

Hispanic Origin	Population	%
Hispanic or Latino (of any race)	1,327	5.87
Central American, ex. Mexican	106	0.47
Costa Rican	13	0.06
Guatemalan	26	0.11
Honduran	29	0.13
Nicaraguan	16	0.07
Panamanian	9	0.04
Salvadoran	13	0.06
Cuban	136	0.60
Dominican Republic	14	0.06
Mexican	601	2.66
Puerto Rican	165	0.73
South American	220	0.97
Argentinean	29	0.13
Bolivian	5	0.02
Chilean	17	0.08
Colombian	92	0.41
Ecuadorian	19	0.08
Paraguayan	2	0.01
Peruvian	26	0.11
Uruguayan	8	0.04
Venezuelan	22	0.10
Other Hispanic or Latino	85	0.38

Race*	Population	%
African-American/Black (234)	303	1.34
Not Hispanic (215)	278	1.23
Hispanic (19)	25	0.11
American Indian/Alaska Native (28)	68	0.30
Not Hispanic (18)	58	0.26
Hispanic (10)	10	0.04
Blackfeet (0)	5	0.02
Cherokee (7)	14	0.06
Chickasaw (1)	3	0.01
Chippewa (2)	3	0.01
Crow (0)	2	0.01
Hopi (0)	1	<0.01
Mexican American Ind. (3)	3	0.01
Potawatomi (0)	1	<0.01
South American Ind. (1)	1	<0.01
Tohono O'Odham (1)	1	<0.01
Asian (304)	361	1.60
Not Hispanic (291)	341	1.51
Hispanic (13)	20	0.09
Bangladeshi (3)	3	0.01
Chinese, ex. Taiwanese (50)	65	0.29
Filipino (58)	74	0.33
Indian (50)	58	0.26
Japanese (17)	24	0.11

*Notes: † The Census 2010 population figure is used to calculate the percentages in the Hispanic Origin and Race categories. Ancestry percentages are based on the 2006-2010 American Community Survey population (not shown); ‡ Numbers in parentheses indicate the number of people reporting a single ancestry; * Numbers in parentheses indicate the number of persons reporting this race alone, not in combination with any other race; Please refer to the Explanation of Data for more information.*

Korean (14)	17	0.08
Laotian (2)	2	0.01
Malaysian (1)	1	<0.01
Pakistani (2)	3	0.01
Thai (1)	1	<0.01
Vietnamese (85)	92	0.41
Hawaii Native/Pacific Islander (8)	20	0.09
Not Hispanic (5)	13	0.06
Hispanic (3)	7	0.03
Guamanian/Chamorro (4)	5	0.02
Marshallese (1)	1	<0.01
Native Hawaiian (1)	6	0.03
White (21,530)	21,713	96.02
Not Hispanic (20,596)	20,722	91.64
Hispanic (934)	991	4.38

Eustis

Place Type: City
County: Lake
Population: 18,558†

Ancestry‡	Population	%
African, Sub-Saharan (55)	55	0.29
African (55)	55	0.29
American (3,864)	3,864	20.68
Arab (22)	22	0.12
Lebanese (22)	22	0.12
Armenian (13)	32	0.17
Australian (13)	13	0.07
Austrian (0)	47	0.25
Belgian (0)	66	0.35
British (96)	203	1.09
Canadian (41)	76	0.41
Czech (24)	43	0.23
Czechoslovakian (21)	21	0.11
Danish (14)	138	0.74
Dutch (112)	367	1.96
Eastern European (20)	59	0.32
English (1,007)	2,298	12.30
European (47)	55	0.29
Finnish (0)	8	0.04
French, ex. Basque (206)	618	3.31
French Canadian (109)	166	0.89
German (981)	2,442	13.07
Greek (10)	39	0.21
Hungarian (18)	28	0.15
Icelander (5)	18	0.10
Irish (468)	1,810	9.68
Italian (298)	743	3.98
Lithuanian (0)	47	0.25
Norwegian (20)	122	0.65
Polish (35)	291	1.56
Portuguese (0)	13	0.07
Romanian (0)	16	0.09
Russian (12)	118	0.63
Scandinavian (12)	33	0.18
Scotch-Irish (105)	267	1.43
Scottish (179)	419	2.24
Serbian (0)	53	0.28
Slovak (20)	102	0.55
Swedish (34)	132	0.71
Swiss (0)	23	0.12
Welsh (68)	120	0.64
West Indian, ex. Hispanic (196)	206	1.10
Haitian (28)	28	0.15
Jamaican (83)	83	0.44
Trinidadian/Tobagonian (85)	95	0.51

Hispanic Origin	Population	%
Hispanic or Latino (of any race)	2,202	11.87
Central American, ex. Mexican	87	0.47
Costa Rican	9	0.05
Guatemalan	10	0.05
Honduran	17	0.09
Nicaraguan	12	0.06
Panamanian	9	0.05
Salvadoran	29	0.16
Other Central American	1	0.01
Cuban	128	0.69
Dominican Republic	36	0.19
Mexican	1,093	5.89
Puerto Rican	527	2.84
South American	180	0.97
Argentinean	17	0.09
Chilean	3	0.02
Colombian	59	0.32
Ecuadorian	32	0.17
Paraguayan	1	0.01
Peruvian	46	0.25
Uruguayan	2	0.01
Venezuelan	20	0.11
Other Hispanic or Latino	151	0.81

Race*	Population	%
African-American/Black (3,229)	3,451	18.60
Not Hispanic (3,152)	3,335	17.97
Hispanic (77)	116	0.63
American Indian/Alaska Native (78)	209	1.13
Not Hispanic (62)	181	0.98
Hispanic (16)	28	0.15
Aleut *(Alaska Native)* (0)	3	0.02
Apache (3)	6	0.03
Arapaho (3)	3	0.02
Blackfeet (0)	8	0.04
Central American Ind. (4)	6	0.03
Cherokee (14)	42	0.23
Choctaw (2)	4	0.02
Comanche (1)	1	0.01
Cree (1)	1	0.01
Creek (4)	9	0.05
Delaware (1)	1	0.01
Iroquois (2)	11	0.06
Lumbee (1)	1	0.01
Mexican American Ind. (2)	2	0.01
Ottawa (0)	1	0.01
Potawatomi (1)	3	0.02
Seminole (0)	2	0.01
Shoshone (1)	1	0.01
Sioux (1)	4	0.02
South American Ind. (2)	2	0.01
Asian (215)	273	1.47
Not Hispanic (205)	247	1.33
Hispanic (10)	26	0.14
Bangladeshi (3)	3	0.02
Chinese, ex. Taiwanese (34)	54	0.29
Filipino (46)	70	0.38
Indian (53)	67	0.36
Japanese (12)	16	0.09
Korean (12)	19	0.10
Laotian (0)	1	0.01
Pakistani (0)	4	0.02
Thai (8)	12	0.06
Vietnamese (20)	35	0.19
Hawaii Native/Pacific Islander (1)	14	0.08
Not Hispanic (1)	12	0.06
Hispanic (0)	2	0.01
Native Hawaiian (1)	8	0.04
White (13,893)	14,249	76.78
Not Hispanic (12,606)	12,866	69.33
Hispanic (1,287)	1,383	7.45

Fairview Shores

Place Type: CDP
County: Orange
Population: 10,239†

Ancestry‡	Population	%
African, Sub-Saharan (19)	19	0.18
Ethiopian (19)	19	0.18
American (764)	764	7.41
Armenian (8)	8	0.08
Austrian (53)	53	0.51
Belgian (0)	11	0.11
British (40)	98	0.95
Czech (0)	37	0.36
Danish (9)	19	0.18
Dutch (17)	44	0.43
English (494)	997	9.67
European (29)	29	0.28
French, ex. Basque (13)	224	2.17
French Canadian (0)	70	0.68
German (456)	1,389	13.48
Greek (0)	17	0.16
Hungarian (43)	92	0.89
Irish (567)	1,686	16.36
Italian (227)	750	7.28
Norwegian (7)	39	0.38
Polish (54)	297	2.88
Russian (22)	68	0.66
Scotch-Irish (26)	76	0.74
Scottish (143)	221	2.14
Slovak (11)	11	0.11
Slovene (11)	11	0.11
Swedish (29)	150	1.46
Swiss (15)	66	0.64
Turkish (19)	19	0.18
Ukrainian (23)	23	0.22
Welsh (0)	55	0.53
West Indian, ex. Hispanic (461)	461	4.47
Haitian (168)	168	1.63
Jamaican (281)	281	2.73
West Indian (12)	12	0.12
Yugoslavian (0)	11	0.11

Hispanic Origin	Population	%
Hispanic or Latino (of any race)	1,438	14.04
Central American, ex. Mexican	71	0.69
Costa Rican	10	0.10
Guatemalan	14	0.14
Honduran	8	0.08
Nicaraguan	13	0.13
Panamanian	15	0.15
Salvadoran	11	0.11
Cuban	156	1.52
Dominican Republic	85	0.83
Mexican	243	2.37
Puerto Rican	661	6.46
South American	106	1.04
Argentinean	11	0.11
Chilean	6	0.06
Colombian	51	0.50
Ecuadorian	11	0.11
Peruvian	11	0.11
Uruguayan	4	0.04
Venezuelan	9	0.09
Other South American	3	0.03
Other Hispanic or Latino	116	1.13

Race*	Population	%
African-American/Black (1,850)	2,015	19.68
Not Hispanic (1,759)	1,881	18.37
Hispanic (91)	134	1.31
American Indian/Alaska Native (44)	128	1.25
Not Hispanic (31)	101	0.99
Hispanic (13)	27	0.26
Alaska Athabascan *(Ala. Nat.)* (1)	1	0.01
Blackfeet (1)	4	0.04
Canadian/French Am. Ind. (0)	1	0.01
Central American Ind. (1)	1	0.01
Cherokee (11)	32	0.31
Chippewa (1)	6	0.06
Cree (0)	1	0.01
Delaware (0)	1	0.01
Iroquois (1)	10	0.10
Lumbee (0)	1	0.01
Menominee (1)	1	0.01
Mexican American Ind. (4)	4	0.04
Navajo (1)	4	0.04
Osage (0)	1	0.01
Seminole (1)	5	0.05
South American Ind. (1)	5	0.05
Asian (383)	469	4.58
Not Hispanic (378)	456	4.45
Hispanic (5)	13	0.13
Burmese (3)	3	0.03
Chinese, ex. Taiwanese (28)	30	0.29
Filipino (76)	100	0.98
Indian (18)	30	0.29

*Notes: † The Census 2010 population figure is used to calculate the percentages in the Hispanic Origin and Race categories. Ancestry percentages are based on the 2006-2010 American Community Survey population (not shown); ‡ Numbers in parentheses indicate the number of people reporting a single ancestry; * Numbers in parentheses indicate the number of persons reporting this race alone, not in combination with any other race; Please refer to the Explanation of Data for more information.*

	Population	%
Indonesian (1)	3	0.03
Japanese (6)	16	0.16
Korean (32)	48	0.47
Laotian (6)	11	0.11
Taiwanese (1)	4	0.04
Thai (11)	21	0.21
Vietnamese (182)	197	1.92
Hawaii Native/Pacific Islander (7)	27	0.26
Not Hispanic (6)	25	0.24
Hispanic (1)	2	0.02
Guamanian/Chamorro (0)	1	0.01
Native Hawaiian (4)	10	0.10
Samoan (1)	2	0.02
White (7,158)	7,467	72.93
Not Hispanic (6,334)	6,550	63.97
Hispanic (824)	917	8.96

Fern Park

Place Type: CDP
County: Seminole
Population: 7,704†

Ancestry‡	Population	%
American (485)	485	6.58
Arab (17)	23	0.31
Arab (6)	12	0.16
Lebanese (11)	11	0.15
Austrian (17)	17	0.23
British (14)	52	0.71
Canadian (0)	18	0.24
Czech (29)	68	0.92
Dutch (71)	146	1.98
Eastern European (12)	26	0.35
English (602)	1,166	15.83
European (324)	324	4.40
Finnish (17)	17	0.23
French, ex. Basque (39)	341	4.63
French Canadian (0)	92	1.25
German (513)	1,308	17.75
Greek (0)	35	0.48
Hungarian (10)	10	0.14
Irish (277)	1,219	16.55
Italian (266)	812	11.02
Lithuanian (0)	35	0.48
Norwegian (0)	26	0.35
Pennsylvania German (12)	12	0.16
Polish (88)	309	4.19
Portuguese (11)	11	0.15
Russian (83)	246	3.34
Scotch-Irish (22)	40	0.54
Scottish (51)	134	1.82
Swedish (0)	39	0.53
Swiss (0)	12	0.16
Ukrainian (30)	30	0.41
Welsh (0)	98	1.33
West Indian, ex. Hispanic (40)	40	0.54
Bermudan (16)	16	0.22
Jamaican (24)	24	0.33

Hispanic Origin	Population	%
Hispanic or Latino (of any race)	1,231	15.98
Central American, ex. Mexican	53	0.69
Costa Rican	9	0.12
Guatemalan	13	0.17
Honduran	5	0.06
Nicaraguan	5	0.06
Panamanian	9	0.12
Salvadoran	12	0.16
Cuban	119	1.54
Dominican Republic	74	0.96
Mexican	127	1.65
Puerto Rican	611	7.93
South American	159	2.06
Argentinean	11	0.14
Bolivian	7	0.09
Chilean	4	0.05
Colombian	60	0.78
Ecuadorian	23	0.30
Paraguayan	1	0.01
Peruvian	29	0.38
Uruguayan	4	0.05
Venezuelan	16	0.21
Other South American	4	0.05
Other Hispanic or Latino	88	1.14

Race*	Population	%
African-American/Black (629)	701	9.10
Not Hispanic (587)	637	8.27
Hispanic (42)	64	0.83
American Indian/Alaska Native (42)	70	0.91
Not Hispanic (30)	53	0.69
Hispanic (12)	17	0.22
Blackfeet (0)	1	0.01
Canadian/French Am. Ind. (3)	3	0.04
Cherokee (5)	15	0.19
Chickasaw (0)	4	0.05
Choctaw (1)	2	0.03
Creek (1)	1	0.01
Delaware (1)	1	0.01
Menominee (0)	2	0.03
Mexican American Ind. (4)	6	0.08
Potawatomi (1)	1	0.01
Seminole (1)	1	0.01
South American Ind. (4)	4	0.05
Tlingit-Haida *(Alaska Native)* (1)	1	0.01
Asian (141)	194	2.52
Not Hispanic (138)	183	2.38
Hispanic (3)	11	0.14
Chinese, ex. Taiwanese (52)	61	0.79
Filipino (24)	40	0.52
Indian (19)	32	0.42
Indonesian (1)	1	0.01
Japanese (6)	9	0.12
Korean (5)	13	0.17
Laotian (1)	1	0.01
Nepalese (2)	2	0.03
Pakistani (2)	2	0.03
Taiwanese (2)	2	0.03
Thai (0)	6	0.08
Vietnamese (25)	31	0.40
Hawaii Native/Pacific Islander (1)	12	0.16
Not Hispanic (1)	11	0.14
Hispanic (0)	1	0.01
Fijian (1)	2	0.03
Native Hawaiian (0)	3	0.04
White (6,410)	6,574	85.33
Not Hispanic (5,577)	5,682	73.75
Hispanic (833)	892	11.58

Fernandina Beach

Place Type: City
County: Nassau
Population: 11,487†

Ancestry‡	Population	%
American (1,210)	1,210	10.57
Armenian (23)	23	0.20
Austrian (0)	32	0.28
British (96)	109	0.95
Canadian (0)	14	0.12
Croatian (41)	41	0.36
Czech (0)	11	0.10
Czechoslovakian (0)	23	0.20
Danish (14)	47	0.41
Dutch (18)	100	0.87
English (557)	1,426	12.46
European (198)	198	1.73
Finnish (32)	32	0.28
French, ex. Basque (66)	339	2.96
French Canadian (36)	68	0.59
German (281)	1,333	11.65
Greek (26)	42	0.37
Hungarian (0)	15	0.13
Irish (620)	1,697	14.83
Italian (179)	545	4.76
Lithuanian (0)	16	0.14
Northern European (15)	15	0.13
Norwegian (0)	70	0.61
Polish (127)	332	2.90
Portuguese (71)	112	0.98
Romanian (14)	14	0.12
Russian (0)	94	0.82
Scandinavian (7)	7	0.06
Scotch-Irish (96)	414	3.62
Scottish (180)	418	3.65
Slovak (55)	114	1.00
Swedish (12)	82	0.72
Swiss (0)	66	0.58
Turkish (0)	27	0.24
Welsh (0)	39	0.34
West Indian, ex. Hispanic (25)	25	0.22
Haitian (25)	25	0.22

Hispanic Origin	Population	%
Hispanic or Latino (of any race)	610	5.31
Central American, ex. Mexican	68	0.59
Costa Rican	6	0.05
Guatemalan	20	0.17
Honduran	22	0.19
Nicaraguan	11	0.10
Panamanian	3	0.03
Salvadoran	6	0.05
Cuban	29	0.25
Dominican Republic	8	0.07
Mexican	312	2.72
Puerto Rican	71	0.62
South American	72	0.63
Argentinean	10	0.09
Chilean	9	0.08
Colombian	21	0.18
Ecuadorian	6	0.05
Peruvian	7	0.06
Uruguayan	18	0.16
Venezuelan	1	0.01
Other Hispanic or Latino	50	0.44

Race*	Population	%
African-American/Black (1,339)	1,406	12.24
Not Hispanic (1,320)	1,382	12.03
Hispanic (19)	24	0.21
American Indian/Alaska Native (50)	98	0.85
Not Hispanic (38)	85	0.74
Hispanic (12)	13	0.11
Apache (2)	4	0.03
Blackfeet (0)	1	0.01
Cherokee (9)	20	0.17
Chippewa (3)	3	0.03
Choctaw (2)	3	0.03
Creek (0)	1	0.01
Crow (1)	1	0.01
Inupiat *(Alaska Native)* (2)	2	0.02
Iroquois (0)	2	0.02
Mexican American Ind. (2)	3	0.03
Potawatomi (1)	1	0.01
Seminole (2)	2	0.02
Asian (132)	185	1.61
Not Hispanic (131)	182	1.58
Hispanic (1)	3	0.03
Chinese, ex. Taiwanese (31)	37	0.32
Filipino (31)	48	0.42
Indian (24)	29	0.25
Indonesian (0)	1	0.01
Japanese (14)	31	0.27
Korean (14)	20	0.17
Laotian (1)	1	0.01
Thai (3)	5	0.04
Vietnamese (4)	6	0.05
Hawaii Native/Pacific Islander (9)	18	0.16
Not Hispanic (9)	16	0.14
Hispanic (0)	2	0.02
Guamanian/Chamorro (3)	6	0.05
Native Hawaiian (6)	7	0.06
White (9,582)	9,744	84.83
Not Hispanic (9,216)	9,347	81.37
Hispanic (366)	397	3.46

*Notes: † The Census 2010 population figure is used to calculate the percentages in the Hispanic Origin and Race categories. Ancestry percentages are based on the 2006-2010 American Community Survey population (not shown); ‡ Numbers in parentheses indicate the number of people reporting a single ancestry; * Numbers in parentheses indicate the number of persons reporting this race alone, not in combination with any other race; Please refer to the Explanation of Data for more information.*

Ferry Pass

Place Type: CDP
County: Escambia
Population: 28,921†

Ancestry‡	Population	%
African, Sub-Saharan (87)	153	0.56
African (76)	87	0.32
Cape Verdean (11)	66	0.24
American (2,014)	2,014	7.38
Arab (102)	130	0.48
Egyptian (70)	84	0.31
Jordanian (19)	19	0.07
Syrian (0)	14	0.05
Other Arab (13)	13	0.05
Armenian (15)	30	0.11
Australian (0)	30	0.11
Austrian (0)	46	0.17
Basque (15)	27	0.10
Brazilian (47)	47	0.17
British (90)	233	0.85
Cajun (12)	12	0.04
Canadian (91)	109	0.40
Celtic (0)	14	0.05
Croatian (0)	13	0.05
Czech (86)	116	0.43
Danish (72)	145	0.53
Dutch (101)	471	1.73
English (1,489)	3,447	12.63
European (339)	372	1.36
Finnish (15)	58	0.21
French, ex. Basque (266)	1,088	3.99
French Canadian (93)	128	0.47
German (1,748)	4,398	16.12
Greek (93)	148	0.54
Guyanese (15)	15	0.05
Hungarian (68)	140	0.51
Icelander (36)	53	0.19
Irish (1,365)	3,938	14.43
Italian (503)	1,439	5.27
Lithuanian (47)	47	0.17
Luxemburger (0)	28	0.10
Norwegian (73)	169	0.62
Polish (180)	642	2.35
Portuguese (26)	68	0.25
Romanian (12)	12	0.04
Russian (111)	190	0.70
Scandinavian (30)	42	0.15
Scotch-Irish (697)	1,309	4.80
Scottish (229)	742	2.72
Swedish (73)	294	1.08
Swiss (12)	12	0.04
Turkish (0)	10	0.04
Ukrainian (0)	11	0.04
Welsh (96)	237	0.87
West Indian, ex. Hispanic (479)	499	1.83
Bahamian (13)	13	0.05
Dutch West Indian (0)	11	0.04
Haitian (59)	59	0.22
Jamaican (212)	221	0.81
West Indian (195)	195	0.71
Yugoslavian (16)	16	0.06

Hispanic Origin	Population	%
Hispanic or Latino (of any race)	1,700	5.88
Central American, ex. Mexican	210	0.73
Costa Rican	17	0.06
Guatemalan	28	0.10
Honduran	47	0.16
Nicaraguan	22	0.08
Panamanian	39	0.13
Salvadoran	57	0.20
Cuban	133	0.46
Dominican Republic	27	0.09
Mexican	607	2.10
Puerto Rican	378	1.31
South American	138	0.48
Argentinean	15	0.05
Chilean	6	0.02
Colombian	59	0.20
Ecuadorian	7	0.02
Paraguayan	3	0.01
Peruvian	20	0.07
Uruguayan	5	0.02
Venezuelan	22	0.08
Other South American	1	<0.01
Other Hispanic or Latino	207	0.72

Race*	Population	%
African-American/Black (4,434)	4,820	16.67
Not Hispanic (4,340)	4,680	16.18
Hispanic (94)	140	0.48
American Indian/Alaska Native (193)	454	1.57
Not Hispanic (169)	398	1.38
Hispanic (24)	56	0.19
Aleut *(Alaska Native)* (1)	1	<0.01
Apache (1)	6	0.02
Blackfeet (1)	5	0.02
Cherokee (26)	88	0.30
Chickasaw (0)	1	<0.01
Chippewa (4)	6	0.02
Choctaw (2)	12	0.04
Comanche (1)	2	0.01
Creek (60)	96	0.33
Delaware (2)	4	0.01
Houma (2)	2	0.01
Iroquois (2)	3	0.01
Lumbee (0)	1	<0.01
Menominee (2)	2	0.01
Mexican American Ind. (9)	14	0.05
Navajo (0)	4	0.01
Osage (2)	2	0.01
Ottawa (1)	1	<0.01
Pima (1)	1	<0.01
Potawatomi (0)	2	0.01
Pueblo (1)	1	<0.01
Seminole (2)	7	0.02
Shoshone (0)	2	0.01
Sioux (4)	5	0.02
South American Ind. (1)	1	<0.01
Tlingit-Haida *(Alaska Native)* (1)	1	<0.01
Asian (634)	963	3.33
Not Hispanic (614)	914	3.16
Hispanic (20)	49	0.17
Bangladeshi (9)	9	0.03
Cambodian (4)	8	0.03
Chinese, ex. Taiwanese (88)	112	0.39
Filipino (187)	343	1.19
Indian (88)	97	0.34
Indonesian (6)	10	0.03
Japanese (41)	103	0.36
Korean (49)	93	0.32
Malaysian (4)	4	0.01
Pakistani (11)	13	0.04
Sri Lankan (1)	1	<0.01
Taiwanese (14)	14	0.05
Thai (15)	24	0.08
Vietnamese (101)	119	0.41
Hawaii Native/Pacific Islander (13)	60	0.21
Not Hispanic (13)	54	0.19
Hispanic (0)	6	0.02
Guamanian/Chamorro (3)	17	0.06
Native Hawaiian (6)	20	0.07
Samoan (2)	4	0.01
Tongan (1)	1	<0.01
White (22,225)	23,081	79.81
Not Hispanic (21,205)	21,935	75.84
Hispanic (1,020)	1,146	3.96

Fish Hawk

Place Type: CDP
County: Hillsborough
Population: 14,087†

Ancestry‡	Population	%
African, Sub-Saharan (99)	175	1.35
African (95)	158	1.22
Ghanaian (4)	4	0.03
South African (0)	13	0.10
American (1,341)	1,341	10.38
Armenian (7)	14	0.11
Australian (0)	15	0.12
Austrian (30)	66	0.51
Brazilian (59)	59	0.46
British (85)	157	1.21
Canadian (200)	200	1.55
Croatian (0)	33	0.26
Czech (22)	110	0.85
Danish (14)	14	0.11
Dutch (80)	153	1.18
Eastern European (88)	88	0.68
English (378)	1,504	11.64
European (57)	141	1.09
French, ex. Basque (79)	442	3.42
French Canadian (25)	53	0.41
German (643)	2,018	15.62
Greek (25)	93	0.72
Guyanese (6)	12	0.09
Hungarian (0)	57	0.44
Irish (802)	2,615	20.24
Italian (371)	1,350	10.45
Lithuanian (0)	17	0.13
Norwegian (19)	26	0.20
Polish (284)	633	4.90
Portuguese (48)	101	0.78
Russian (180)	393	3.04
Scotch-Irish (176)	240	1.86
Scottish (188)	310	2.40
Slavic (10)	10	0.08
Slovak (0)	66	0.51
Swedish (25)	103	0.80
Turkish (0)	39	0.30
Ukrainian (29)	29	0.22
Welsh (37)	147	1.14
West Indian, ex. Hispanic (143)	191	1.48
British West Indian (85)	85	0.66
Jamaican (54)	69	0.53
Trinidadian/Tobagonian (4)	4	0.03
West Indian (0)	33	0.26
Yugoslavian (0)	8	0.06

Hispanic Origin	Population	%
Hispanic or Latino (of any race)	1,645	11.68
Central American, ex. Mexican	125	0.89
Costa Rican	12	0.09
Guatemalan	16	0.11
Honduran	26	0.18
Nicaraguan	16	0.11
Panamanian	34	0.24
Salvadoran	21	0.15
Cuban	268	1.90
Dominican Republic	77	0.55
Mexican	233	1.65
Puerto Rican	526	3.73
South American	279	1.98
Argentinean	16	0.11
Bolivian	2	0.01
Chilean	13	0.09
Colombian	159	1.13
Ecuadorian	17	0.12
Peruvian	46	0.33
Uruguayan	2	0.01
Venezuelan	24	0.17
Other Hispanic or Latino	137	0.97

Race*	Population	%
African-American/Black (586)	711	5.05
Not Hispanic (547)	652	4.63
Hispanic (39)	59	0.42
American Indian/Alaska Native (18)	91	0.65
Not Hispanic (13)	69	0.49
Hispanic (5)	22	0.16
Apache (0)	4	0.03
Cherokee (3)	27	0.19
Chickasaw (1)	1	0.01
Chippewa (0)	2	0.01
Creek (1)	6	0.04
Iroquois (1)	1	0.01

*Notes: † The Census 2010 population figure is used to calculate the percentages in the Hispanic Origin and Race categories. Ancestry percentages are based on the 2006-2010 American Community Survey population (not shown); ‡ Numbers in parentheses indicate the number of people reporting a single ancestry; * Numbers in parentheses indicate the number of persons reporting this race alone, not in combination with any other race; Please refer to the Explanation of Data for more information.*

Lumbee (1)	2	0.01
Mexican American Ind. (0)	3	0.02
Navajo (0)	4	0.03
Pueblo (1)	3	0.02
Seminole (0)	2	0.01
South American Ind. (0)	1	0.01
Ute (2)	2	0.01
Asian (498)	667	4.73
Not Hispanic (491)	633	4.49
Hispanic (7)	34	0.24
Burmese (2)	2	0.01
Cambodian (1)	3	0.02
Chinese, ex. Taiwanese (81)	107	0.76
Filipino (109)	149	1.06
Hmong (2)	2	0.01
Indian (162)	190	1.35
Indonesian (0)	1	0.01
Japanese (17)	39	0.28
Korean (46)	84	0.60
Laotian (1)	2	0.01
Pakistani (22)	24	0.17
Taiwanese (7)	8	0.06
Thai (10)	18	0.13
Vietnamese (13)	16	0.11
Hawaii Native/Pacific Islander (8)	31	0.22
Not Hispanic (7)	27	0.19
Hispanic (1)	4	0.03
Guamanian/Chamorro (6)	11	0.08
Native Hawaiian (1)	18	0.13
Samoan (0)	4	0.03
White (12,406)	12,719	90.29
Not Hispanic (11,078)	11,315	80.32
Hispanic (1,328)	1,404	9.97

Fleming Island

Place Type: CDP
County: Clay
Population: 27,126†

Ancestry‡	Population	%
African, Sub-Saharan (165)	197	0.71
African (122)	154	0.55
South African (43)	43	0.15
American (2,220)	2,220	7.95
Arab (13)	74	0.27
Arab (0)	17	0.06
Lebanese (0)	8	0.03
Palestinian (13)	49	0.18
Austrian (0)	40	0.14
British (90)	102	0.37
Cajun (10)	26	0.09
Canadian (60)	82	0.29
Croatian (16)	32	0.11
Czech (53)	105	0.38
Czechoslovakian (33)	78	0.28
Danish (27)	50	0.18
Dutch (64)	506	1.81
English (1,699)	4,509	16.16
European (141)	190	0.68
Finnish (44)	70	0.25
French, ex. Basque (335)	1,011	3.62
French Canadian (117)	241	0.86
German (1,822)	5,702	20.43
Greek (79)	189	0.68
Hungarian (97)	187	0.67
Irish (1,142)	4,168	14.93
Italian (1,010)	2,103	7.54
Latvian (0)	14	0.05
Lithuanian (0)	73	0.26
Macedonian (7)	27	0.10
Norwegian (109)	289	1.04
Pennsylvania German (17)	35	0.13
Polish (351)	1,046	3.75
Portuguese (8)	50	0.18
Romanian (23)	58	0.21
Russian (75)	232	0.83
Scandinavian (41)	57	0.20
Scotch-Irish (243)	591	2.12
Scottish (209)	982	3.52
Slavic (0)	30	0.11
Slovak (9)	244	0.87
Slovene (18)	66	0.24
Swedish (88)	366	1.31
Swiss (12)	47	0.17
Ukrainian (7)	40	0.14
Welsh (16)	209	0.75
West Indian, ex. Hispanic (153)	153	0.55
British West Indian (18)	18	0.06
Haitian (120)	120	0.43
Jamaican (15)	15	0.05
Yugoslavian (24)	102	0.37

Hispanic Origin	Population	%
Hispanic or Latino (of any race)	1,742	6.42
Central American, ex. Mexican	117	0.43
Costa Rican	21	0.08
Guatemalan	15	0.06
Honduran	11	0.04
Nicaraguan	14	0.05
Panamanian	42	0.15
Salvadoran	14	0.05
Cuban	204	0.75
Dominican Republic	54	0.20
Mexican	332	1.22
Puerto Rican	625	2.30
South American	229	0.84
Argentinean	10	0.04
Bolivian	5	0.02
Chilean	20	0.07
Colombian	99	0.36
Ecuadorian	40	0.15
Paraguayan	6	0.02
Peruvian	26	0.10
Uruguayan	3	0.01
Venezuelan	12	0.04
Other South American	8	0.03
Other Hispanic or Latino	181	0.67

Race*	Population	%
African-American/Black (1,401)	1,632	6.02
Not Hispanic (1,331)	1,516	5.59
Hispanic (70)	116	0.43
American Indian/Alaska Native (80)	216	0.80
Not Hispanic (69)	182	0.67
Hispanic (11)	34	0.13
Apache (1)	4	0.01
Blackfeet (1)	5	0.02
Canadian/French Am. Ind. (1)	1	<0.01
Central American Ind. (0)	3	0.01
Cherokee (14)	50	0.18
Chickasaw (5)	5	0.02
Chippewa (1)	1	<0.01
Choctaw (2)	3	0.01
Colville (1)	1	<0.01
Creek (5)	12	0.04
Crow (0)	1	<0.01
Iroquois (1)	4	0.01
Lumbee (2)	6	0.02
Seminole (1)	10	0.04
Sioux (3)	4	0.01
South American Ind. (0)	2	0.01
Asian (1,122)	1,468	5.41
Not Hispanic (1,099)	1,400	5.16
Hispanic (23)	68	0.25
Bangladeshi (0)	3	0.01
Burmese (1)	4	0.01
Cambodian (37)	40	0.15
Chinese, ex. Taiwanese (111)	149	0.55
Filipino (488)	637	2.35
Hmong (0)	1	<0.01
Indian (188)	212	0.78
Japanese (38)	100	0.37
Korean (79)	114	0.42
Laotian (0)	1	<0.01
Malaysian (3)	3	0.01
Pakistani (12)	13	0.05
Sri Lankan (5)	5	0.02
Taiwanese (6)	11	0.04
Thai (15)	25	0.09
Vietnamese (90)	107	0.39
Hawaii Native/Pacific Islander (23)	56	0.21
Not Hispanic (23)	55	0.20
Hispanic (0)	1	<0.01
Guamanian/Chamorro (5)	11	0.04
Native Hawaiian (5)	19	0.07
Samoan (6)	13	0.05
White (23,387)	24,042	88.63
Not Hispanic (22,232)	22,737	83.82
Hispanic (1,155)	1,305	4.81

Florida City

Place Type: City
County: Miami-Dade
Population: 11,245†

Ancestry‡	Population	%
African, Sub-Saharan (19)	19	0.18
African (19)	19	0.18
American (901)	901	8.50
Australian (32)	32	0.30
Brazilian (25)	52	0.49
Dutch (0)	27	0.25
German (0)	109	1.03
Irish (0)	87	0.82
Italian (0)	58	0.55
Swiss (0)	11	0.10
West Indian, ex. Hispanic (1,028)	1,194	11.26
Bahamian (15)	26	0.25
British West Indian (26)	26	0.25
Haitian (930)	1,052	9.92
Jamaican (57)	90	0.85

Hispanic Origin	Population	%
Hispanic or Latino (of any race)	4,763	42.36
Central American, ex. Mexican	637	5.66
Costa Rican	14	0.12
Guatemalan	102	0.91
Honduran	113	1.00
Nicaraguan	113	1.00
Panamanian	27	0.24
Salvadoran	268	2.38
Cuban	911	8.10
Dominican Republic	141	1.25
Mexican	2,025	18.01
Puerto Rican	613	5.45
South American	178	1.58
Argentinean	6	0.05
Bolivian	11	0.10
Chilean	5	0.04
Colombian	84	0.75
Ecuadorian	15	0.13
Peruvian	17	0.15
Uruguayan	5	0.04
Venezuelan	35	0.31
Other Hispanic or Latino	258	2.29

Race*	Population	%
African-American/Black (5,890)	6,030	53.62
Not Hispanic (5,674)	5,775	51.36
Hispanic (216)	255	2.27
American Indian/Alaska Native (28)	51	0.45
Not Hispanic (6)	23	0.20
Hispanic (22)	28	0.25
Apache (0)	1	0.01
Blackfeet (0)	1	0.01
Central American Ind. (1)	2	0.02
Cherokee (1)	5	0.04
Choctaw (0)	2	0.02
Mexican American Ind. (1)	1	0.01
Tlingit-Haida *(Alaska Native)* (0)	5	0.04
Asian (39)	74	0.66
Not Hispanic (36)	58	0.52
Hispanic (3)	16	0.14
Chinese, ex. Taiwanese (8)	16	0.14
Filipino (2)	15	0.13
Indian (16)	19	0.17
Indonesian (1)	1	0.01
Japanese (2)	5	0.04

*Notes: † The Census 2010 population figure is used to calculate the percentages in the Hispanic Origin and Race categories. Ancestry percentages are based on the 2006-2010 American Community Survey population (not shown); ‡ Numbers in parentheses indicate the number of people reporting a single ancestry; * Numbers in parentheses indicate the number of persons reporting this race alone, not in combination with any other race; Please refer to the Explanation of Data for more information.*

Korean (2)	3	0.03
Vietnamese (3)	4	0.04
Hawaii Native/Pacific Islander (4)	42	0.37
Not Hispanic (4)	34	0.30
Hispanic (0)	8	0.07
Guamanian/Chamorro (1)	3	0.03
Native Hawaiian (1)	1	0.01
Samoan (1)	5	0.04
White (4,398)	4,603	40.93
Not Hispanic (625)	676	6.01
Hispanic (3,773)	3,927	34.92

Florida Ridge

Place Type: CDP
County: Indian River
Population: 18,164†

Ancestry‡	Population	%
American (1,114)	1,114	6.58
Arab (77)	77	0.45
Egyptian (36)	36	0.21
Lebanese (14)	14	0.08
Syrian (27)	27	0.16
Armenian (11)	27	0.16
Assyrian/Chaldean/Syriac (0)	8	0.05
Australian (0)	12	0.07
Austrian (17)	54	0.32
Brazilian (228)	228	1.35
British (26)	26	0.15
Bulgarian (0)	10	0.06
Cajun (17)	17	0.10
Canadian (14)	25	0.15
Czech (0)	31	0.18
Danish (12)	117	0.69
Dutch (29)	316	1.87
Eastern European (27)	27	0.16
English (575)	2,224	13.14
European (99)	106	0.63
French, ex. Basque (106)	644	3.80
French Canadian (142)	166	0.98
German (1,019)	3,219	19.01
Greek (73)	121	0.71
Hungarian (12)	46	0.27
Irish (819)	2,916	17.22
Italian (600)	1,436	8.48
Lithuanian (0)	11	0.06
Luxemburger (11)	11	0.06
Northern European (27)	27	0.16
Norwegian (43)	83	0.49
Polish (109)	397	2.34
Portuguese (53)	190	1.12
Romanian (13)	53	0.31
Russian (43)	126	0.74
Scandinavian (14)	44	0.26
Scotch-Irish (157)	355	2.10
Scottish (126)	413	2.44
Slovak (18)	29	0.17
Swedish (99)	236	1.39
Swiss (0)	11	0.06
Ukrainian (11)	22	0.13
Welsh (8)	87	0.51
West Indian, ex. Hispanic (388)	510	3.01
Bahamian (15)	57	0.34
Haitian (268)	284	1.68
Jamaican (93)	157	0.93
West Indian (12)	12	0.07
Yugoslavian (13)	13	0.08

Hispanic Origin	Population	%
Hispanic or Latino (of any race)	1,933	10.64
Central American, ex. Mexican	153	0.84
Costa Rican	4	0.02
Guatemalan	17	0.09
Honduran	64	0.35
Nicaraguan	26	0.14
Panamanian	13	0.07
Salvadoran	29	0.16
Cuban	232	1.28
Dominican Republic	33	0.18
Mexican	808	4.45
Puerto Rican	298	1.64
South American	295	1.62
Argentinean	11	0.06
Bolivian	3	0.02
Chilean	11	0.06
Colombian	137	0.75
Ecuadorian	40	0.22
Paraguayan	3	0.02
Peruvian	54	0.30
Uruguayan	4	0.02
Venezuelan	29	0.16
Other South American	3	0.02
Other Hispanic or Latino	114	0.63

Race*	Population	%
African-American/Black (2,838)	3,018	16.62
Not Hispanic (2,791)	2,941	16.19
Hispanic (47)	77	0.42
American Indian/Alaska Native (60)	157	0.86
Not Hispanic (46)	129	0.71
Hispanic (14)	28	0.15
Apache (0)	1	0.01
Blackfeet (4)	8	0.04
Canadian/French Am. Ind. (0)	3	0.02
Cherokee (16)	40	0.22
Cree (0)	1	0.01
Creek (3)	3	0.02
Iroquois (3)	4	0.02
Lumbee (2)	4	0.02
Mexican American Ind. (9)	10	0.06
Navajo (2)	4	0.02
Sioux (4)	5	0.03
South American Ind. (1)	5	0.03
Spanish American Ind. (0)	1	0.01
Tlingit-Haida *(Alaska Native)* (0)	2	0.01
Asian (224)	304	1.67
Not Hispanic (220)	294	1.62
Hispanic (4)	10	0.06
Bangladeshi (1)	1	0.01
Burmese (2)	2	0.01
Cambodian (6)	8	0.04
Chinese, ex. Taiwanese (16)	29	0.16
Filipino (33)	56	0.31
Indian (35)	44	0.24
Indonesian (1)	3	0.02
Japanese (3)	11	0.06
Korean (17)	22	0.12
Laotian (2)	2	0.01
Malaysian (0)	1	0.01
Nepalese (1)	1	0.01
Pakistani (12)	20	0.11
Taiwanese (0)	1	0.01
Thai (30)	34	0.19
Vietnamese (60)	63	0.35
Hawaii Native/Pacific Islander (9)	45	0.25
Not Hispanic (9)	33	0.18
Hispanic (0)	12	0.07
Guamanian/Chamorro (2)	5	0.03
Native Hawaiian (1)	5	0.03
White (14,139)	14,487	79.76
Not Hispanic (12,845)	13,109	72.17
Hispanic (1,294)	1,378	7.59

Forest City

Place Type: CDP
County: Seminole
Population: 13,854†

Ancestry‡	Population	%
African, Sub-Saharan (67)	67	0.48
African (67)	67	0.48
American (737)	737	5.30
Arab (85)	130	0.93
Lebanese (41)	76	0.55
Moroccan (29)	39	0.28
Syrian (15)	15	0.11
Austrian (11)	31	0.22
Belgian (0)	37	0.27
British (103)	103	0.74
Bulgarian (34)	34	0.24
Canadian (13)	13	0.09
Czechoslovakian (0)	24	0.17
Danish (0)	17	0.12
Dutch (37)	296	2.13
English (291)	1,038	7.46
European (738)	808	5.81
Finnish (0)	9	0.06
French, ex. Basque (98)	386	2.77
French Canadian (0)	34	0.24
German (522)	1,892	13.59
Greek (19)	31	0.22
Hungarian (0)	23	0.17
Irish (721)	2,116	15.20
Israeli (0)	99	0.71
Italian (300)	815	5.86
Norwegian (89)	119	0.86
Polish (111)	213	1.53
Portuguese (49)	49	0.35
Romanian (11)	11	0.08
Russian (84)	108	0.78
Scandinavian (13)	13	0.09
Scotch-Irish (163)	239	1.72
Scottish (206)	330	2.37
Slovak (16)	41	0.29
Swedish (24)	96	0.69
Swiss (0)	8	0.06
Ukrainian (0)	41	0.29
Welsh (15)	130	0.93
West Indian, ex. Hispanic (325)	357	2.57
Bahamian (107)	107	0.77
Haitian (72)	91	0.65
Jamaican (110)	123	0.88
West Indian (36)	36	0.26

Hispanic Origin	Population	%
Hispanic or Latino (of any race)	3,374	24.35
Central American, ex. Mexican	183	1.32
Costa Rican	14	0.10
Guatemalan	37	0.27
Honduran	42	0.30
Nicaraguan	28	0.20
Panamanian	22	0.16
Salvadoran	38	0.27
Other Central American	2	0.01
Cuban	680	4.91
Dominican Republic	228	1.65
Mexican	265	1.91
Puerto Rican	1,299	9.38
South American	534	3.85
Argentinean	27	0.19
Bolivian	6	0.04
Chilean	26	0.19
Colombian	232	1.67
Ecuadorian	66	0.48
Peruvian	99	0.71
Uruguayan	2	0.01
Venezuelan	72	0.52
Other South American	4	0.03
Other Hispanic or Latino	185	1.34

Race*	Population	%
African-American/Black (1,115)	1,284	9.27
Not Hispanic (984)	1,078	7.78
Hispanic (131)	206	1.49
American Indian/Alaska Native (34)	80	0.58
Not Hispanic (27)	67	0.48
Hispanic (7)	13	0.09
Apache (0)	1	0.01
Blackfeet (1)	4	0.03
Cherokee (6)	23	0.17
Chippewa (3)	3	0.02
Comanche (0)	1	0.01
Creek (0)	3	0.02
Iroquois (0)	1	0.01
Lumbee (1)	1	0.01
Mexican American Ind. (1)	1	0.01
Seminole (1)	2	0.01
Spanish American Ind. (0)	2	0.01

SECTION TWO

*Notes: † The Census 2010 population figure is used to calculate the percentages in the Hispanic Origin and Race categories. Ancestry percentages are based on the 2006-2010 American Community Survey population (not shown); ‡ Numbers in parentheses indicate the number of people reporting a single ancestry; * Numbers in parentheses indicate the number of persons reporting this race alone, not in combination with any other race; Please refer to the Explanation of Data for more information.*

Asian (590)	698	5.04
Not Hispanic (577)	669	4.83
Hispanic (13)	29	0.21
Bangladeshi (4)	6	0.04
Burmese (7)	7	0.05
Cambodian (8)	8	0.06
Chinese, ex. Taiwanese (97)	118	0.85
Filipino (55)	84	0.61
Hmong (2)	3	0.02
Indian (154)	180	1.30
Japanese (8)	18	0.13
Korean (160)	172	1.24
Pakistani (11)	11	0.08
Thai (9)	13	0.09
Vietnamese (60)	65	0.47
Hawaii Native/Pacific Islander (1)	21	0.15
Not Hispanic (1)	11	0.08
Hispanic (0)	10	0.07
White (10,972)	11,312	81.65
Not Hispanic (8,633)	8,803	63.54
Hispanic (2,339)	2,509	18.11

Fort Lauderdale

Place Type: City
County: Broward
Population: 165,521†

Ancestry‡	Population	%
Afghan (34)	34	0.02
African, Sub-Saharan (736)	914	0.55
African (500)	596	0.36
Nigerian (37)	37	0.02
Senegalese (62)	62	0.04
South African (137)	187	0.11
Other Sub-Saharan African (0)	32	0.02
Albanian (99)	99	0.06
American (11,911)	11,911	7.12
Arab (697)	932	0.56
Arab (103)	138	0.08
Egyptian (92)	120	0.07
Iraqi (13)	13	0.01
Jordanian (136)	136	0.08
Lebanese (202)	301	0.18
Moroccan (32)	32	0.02
Syrian (50)	94	0.06
Other Arab (69)	98	0.06
Armenian (162)	217	0.13
Australian (70)	139	0.08
Austrian (158)	748	0.45
Basque (31)	31	0.02
Belgian (87)	374	0.22
Brazilian (695)	816	0.49
British (591)	976	0.58
Bulgarian (82)	92	0.05
Cajun (14)	14	0.01
Canadian (626)	952	0.57
Celtic (25)	25	0.01
Croatian (111)	173	0.10
Czech (127)	451	0.27
Czechoslovakian (77)	183	0.11
Danish (203)	452	0.27
Dutch (508)	1,657	0.99
Eastern European (330)	376	0.22
English (4,441)	11,809	7.06
Estonian (0)	14	0.01
European (941)	1,030	0.62
Finnish (103)	347	0.21
French, ex. Basque (1,008)	3,584	2.14
French Canadian (382)	814	0.49
German (5,341)	16,849	10.07
Greek (677)	1,067	0.64
Guyanese (29)	40	0.02
Hungarian (425)	970	0.58
Icelander (61)	97	0.06
Iranian (224)	236	0.14
Irish (5,788)	17,238	10.31
Israeli (165)	195	0.12
Italian (6,856)	13,550	8.10
Latvian (108)	147	0.09
Lithuanian (93)	335	0.20
Macedonian (11)	11	0.01
Maltese (0)	9	0.01
New Zealander (15)	15	0.01
Northern European (17)	35	0.02
Norwegian (286)	845	0.51
Pennsylvania German (44)	59	0.04
Polish (2,134)	5,027	3.01
Portuguese (315)	572	0.34
Romanian (170)	272	0.16
Russian (1,492)	3,176	1.90
Scandinavian (121)	284	0.17
Scotch-Irish (867)	1,962	1.17
Scottish (870)	2,904	1.74
Serbian (29)	29	0.02
Slavic (10)	67	0.04
Slovak (141)	500	0.30
Slovene (31)	58	0.03
Swedish (584)	1,657	0.99
Swiss (82)	284	0.17
Turkish (230)	309	0.18
Ukrainian (278)	619	0.37
Welsh (91)	598	0.36
West Indian, ex. Hispanic (15,809)	16,929	10.12
Bahamian (481)	644	0.38
Barbadian (119)	157	0.09
Belizean (27)	64	0.04
British West Indian (292)	318	0.19
Dutch West Indian (25)	25	0.01
Haitian (10,463)	10,769	6.44
Jamaican (3,828)	4,265	2.55
Trinidadian/Tobagonian (194)	251	0.15
U.S. Virgin Islander (12)	12	0.01
West Indian (368)	424	0.25
Yugoslavian (34)	140	0.08

Hispanic Origin	Population	%
Hispanic or Latino (of any race)	22,752	13.75
Central American, ex. Mexican	4,424	2.67
Costa Rican	143	0.09
Guatemalan	1,413	0.85
Honduran	1,002	0.61
Nicaraguan	354	0.21
Panamanian	198	0.12
Salvadoran	1,284	0.78
Other Central American	30	0.02
Cuban	4,093	2.47
Dominican Republic	692	0.42
Mexican	2,742	1.66
Puerto Rican	3,821	2.31
South American	4,939	2.98
Argentinean	616	0.37
Bolivian	93	0.06
Chilean	180	0.11
Colombian	1,768	1.07
Ecuadorian	380	0.23
Paraguayan	18	0.01
Peruvian	962	0.58
Uruguayan	218	0.13
Venezuelan	661	0.40
Other South American	43	0.03
Other Hispanic or Latino	2,041	1.23

Race*	Population	%
African-American/Black (51,240)	53,024	32.03
Not Hispanic (50,258)	51,645	31.20
Hispanic (982)	1,379	0.83
American Indian/Alaska Native (439)	1,044	0.63
Not Hispanic (329)	822	0.50
Hispanic (110)	222	0.13
Apache (4)	10	0.01
Blackfeet (2)	31	0.02
Canadian/French Am. Ind. (4)	10	0.01
Central American Ind. (3)	12	0.01
Cherokee (63)	192	0.12
Cheyenne (0)	1	<0.01
Chickasaw (2)	4	<0.01
Chippewa (8)	15	0.01
Choctaw (8)	25	0.02
Comanche (1)	1	<0.01
Creek (7)	11	0.01
Delaware (0)	2	<0.01
Hopi (0)	2	<0.01
Houma (2)	2	<0.01
Inupiat *(Alaska Native)* (1)	2	<0.01
Iroquois (13)	24	0.01
Lumbee (3)	3	<0.01
Menominee (1)	1	<0.01
Mexican American Ind. (9)	23	0.01
Navajo (3)	5	<0.01
Osage (3)	3	<0.01
Ottawa (3)	3	<0.01
Potawatomi (1)	1	<0.01
Pueblo (1)	2	<0.01
Puget Sound Salish (0)	1	<0.01
Seminole (14)	24	0.01
Shoshone (0)	2	<0.01
Sioux (7)	22	0.01
South American Ind. (21)	35	0.02
Spanish American Ind. (10)	11	0.01
Tlingit-Haida *(Alaska Native)* (3)	8	<0.01
Tohono O'Odham (0)	1	<0.01
Yakama (1)	1	<0.01
Asian (2,444)	3,238	1.96
Not Hispanic (2,406)	3,097	1.87
Hispanic (38)	141	0.09
Bangladeshi (79)	95	0.06
Burmese (17)	22	0.01
Cambodian (7)	8	<0.01
Chinese, ex. Taiwanese (355)	546	0.33
Filipino (458)	591	0.36
Indian (718)	936	0.57
Indonesian (16)	28	0.02
Japanese (126)	218	0.13
Korean (108)	151	0.09
Laotian (6)	10	0.01
Malaysian (4)	5	<0.01
Nepalese (4)	4	<0.01
Pakistani (44)	62	0.04
Sri Lankan (3)	3	<0.01
Taiwanese (24)	28	0.02
Thai (104)	122	0.07
Vietnamese (227)	264	0.16
Hawaii Native/Pacific Islander (85)	447	0.27
Not Hispanic (71)	381	0.23
Hispanic (14)	66	0.04
Fijian (1)	4	<0.01
Guamanian/Chamorro (19)	27	0.02
Marshallese (8)	8	<0.01
Native Hawaiian (30)	63	0.04
Samoan (6)	21	0.01
Tongan (0)	1	<0.01
White (103,675)	106,175	64.15
Not Hispanic (86,903)	88,415	53.42
Hispanic (16,772)	17,760	10.73

Fort Myers

Place Type: City
County: Lee
Population: 62,298†

Ancestry‡	Population	%
African, Sub-Saharan (791)	859	1.38
African (489)	557	0.89
Nigerian (283)	283	0.45
South African (19)	19	0.03
American (7,858)	7,858	12.60
Arab (45)	239	0.38
Arab (0)	12	0.02
Egyptian (0)	67	0.11
Lebanese (35)	129	0.21
Palestinian (0)	21	0.03
Other Arab (10)	10	0.02
Austrian (32)	190	0.30
Belgian (11)	26	0.04
Brazilian (466)	667	1.07
British (228)	357	0.57
Bulgarian (13)	22	0.04
Cajun (10)	10	0.02

*Notes: † The Census 2010 population figure is used to calculate the percentages in the Hispanic Origin and Race categories. Ancestry percentages are based on the 2006-2010 American Community Survey population (not shown); ‡ Numbers in parentheses indicate the number of people reporting a single ancestry; * Numbers in parentheses indicate the number of persons reporting this race alone, not in combination with any other race; Please refer to the Explanation of Data for more information.*

Canadian (79)	159	0.25
Croatian (0)	33	0.05
Czech (15)	71	0.11
Czechoslovakian (21)	35	0.06
Danish (62)	133	0.21
Dutch (54)	584	0.94
Eastern European (8)	8	0.01
English (1,821)	4,237	6.79
European (182)	189	0.30
Finnish (0)	55	0.09
French, ex. Basque (266)	940	1.51
French Canadian (122)	253	0.41
German (2,164)	5,580	8.95
Greek (8)	86	0.14
Hungarian (62)	236	0.38
Irish (1,554)	4,391	7.04
Israeli (50)	50	0.08
Italian (1,455)	2,910	4.67
Lithuanian (64)	269	0.43
Maltese (14)	14	0.02
Norwegian (95)	294	0.47
Pennsylvania German (10)	10	0.02
Polish (499)	1,286	2.06
Portuguese (125)	298	0.48
Romanian (35)	91	0.15
Russian (34)	133	0.21
Scandinavian (73)	103	0.17
Scotch-Irish (472)	877	1.41
Scottish (311)	804	1.29
Serbian (45)	104	0.17
Slavic (10)	24	0.04
Slovak (89)	174	0.28
Swedish (147)	470	0.75
Swiss (42)	134	0.21
Turkish (69)	69	0.11
Ukrainian (25)	84	0.13
Welsh (95)	141	0.23
West Indian, ex. Hispanic (3,832)	3,917	6.28
Bahamian (11)	22	0.04
British West Indian (50)	50	0.08
Haitian (3,478)	3,519	5.64
Jamaican (239)	272	0.44
West Indian (54)	54	0.09

Hispanic Origin	Population	%
Hispanic or Latino (of any race)	12,438	19.97
Central American, ex. Mexican	2,446	3.93
Costa Rican	48	0.08
Guatemalan	1,757	2.82
Honduran	308	0.49
Nicaraguan	105	0.17
Panamanian	58	0.09
Salvadoran	144	0.23
Other Central American	26	0.04
Cuban	880	1.41
Dominican Republic	466	0.75
Mexican	3,701	5.94
Puerto Rican	2,976	4.78
South American	1,044	1.68
Argentinean	86	0.14
Bolivian	29	0.05
Chilean	29	0.05
Colombian	449	0.72
Ecuadorian	136	0.22
Paraguayan	10	0.02
Peruvian	138	0.22
Uruguayan	16	0.03
Venezuelan	139	0.22
Other South American	12	0.02
Other Hispanic or Latino	925	1.48

Race*	Population	%
African-American/Black (20,138)	20,932	33.60
Not Hispanic (19,495)	20,108	32.28
Hispanic (643)	824	1.32
American Indian/Alaska Native (394)	655	1.05
Not Hispanic (142)	337	0.54
Hispanic (252)	318	0.51
Apache (1)	2	<0.01
Arapaho (0)	1	<0.01
Blackfeet (5)	10	0.02
Central American Ind. (19)	36	0.06
Cherokee (20)	75	0.12
Chickasaw (2)	2	<0.01
Chippewa (4)	8	0.01
Choctaw (2)	8	0.01
Comanche (0)	2	<0.01
Cree (0)	1	<0.01
Creek (1)	5	0.01
Crow (0)	1	<0.01
Inupiat *(Alaska Native)* (1)	1	<0.01
Iroquois (3)	8	0.01
Lumbee (3)	9	0.01
Menominee (1)	1	<0.01
Mexican American Ind. (149)	159	0.26
Navajo (1)	3	<0.01
Ottawa (0)	1	<0.01
Seminole (10)	11	0.02
Sioux (3)	8	0.01
South American Ind. (4)	8	0.01
Spanish American Ind. (4)	5	0.01
Tlingit-Haida *(Alaska Native)* (0)	5	0.01
Yaqui (9)	9	0.01
Yup'ik *(Alaska Native)* (2)	2	<0.01
Asian (975)	1,268	2.04
Not Hispanic (946)	1,189	1.91
Hispanic (29)	79	0.13
Bangladeshi (32)	39	0.06
Burmese (1)	1	<0.01
Cambodian (3)	3	<0.01
Chinese, ex. Taiwanese (142)	179	0.29
Filipino (147)	213	0.34
Hmong (1)	1	<0.01
Indian (343)	404	0.65
Indonesian (6)	6	0.01
Japanese (20)	48	0.08
Korean (61)	84	0.13
Laotian (18)	26	0.04
Nepalese (4)	4	0.01
Pakistani (15)	22	0.04
Sri Lankan (6)	6	0.01
Taiwanese (2)	4	0.01
Thai (14)	25	0.04
Vietnamese (129)	133	0.21
Hawaii Native/Pacific Islander (51)	159	0.26
Not Hispanic (30)	104	0.17
Hispanic (21)	55	0.09
Guamanian/Chamorro (34)	42	0.07
Marshallese (1)	1	<0.01
Native Hawaiian (5)	19	0.03
Samoan (2)	2	<0.01
White (34,022)	35,372	56.78
Not Hispanic (27,786)	28,541	45.81
Hispanic (6,236)	6,831	10.97

Fort Pierce

Place Type: City
County: St. Lucie
Population: 41,590†

Ancestry‡	Population	%
African, Sub-Saharan (2,399)	2,399	5.65
African (2,399)	2,399	5.65
American (1,846)	1,846	4.35
Arab (46)	55	0.13
Lebanese (9)	9	0.02
Moroccan (0)	9	0.02
Syrian (37)	37	0.09
Austrian (0)	108	0.25
Belgian (11)	33	0.08
Brazilian (32)	32	0.08
British (42)	62	0.15
Canadian (0)	46	0.11
Celtic (0)	26	0.06
Croatian (10)	21	0.05
Czech (72)	100	0.24
Czechoslovakian (0)	14	0.03
Danish (49)	49	0.12
Dutch (108)	309	0.73
English (1,157)	2,511	5.91
European (1,409)	1,432	3.37
Finnish (0)	20	0.05
French, ex. Basque (160)	531	1.25
French Canadian (219)	264	0.62
German (831)	2,943	6.93
Greek (44)	44	0.10
Hungarian (22)	100	0.24
Irish (1,131)	2,567	6.04
Italian (767)	1,553	3.66
Lithuanian (26)	26	0.06
Maltese (9)	9	0.02
Norwegian (110)	110	0.26
Pennsylvania German (40)	56	0.13
Polish (257)	547	1.29
Portuguese (14)	14	0.03
Romanian (20)	20	0.05
Russian (19)	218	0.51
Scotch-Irish (27)	248	0.58
Scottish (226)	568	1.34
Serbian (0)	11	0.03
Slavic (33)	33	0.08
Slovak (41)	55	0.13
Slovene (13)	13	0.03
Swedish (23)	142	0.33
Swiss (88)	99	0.23
Ukrainian (9)	9	0.02
Welsh (0)	76	0.18
West Indian, ex. Hispanic (2,700)	2,869	6.75
Bahamian (70)	112	0.26
Barbadian (71)	71	0.17
Haitian (2,112)	2,187	5.15
Jamaican (347)	384	0.90
Trinidadian/Tobagonian (25)	25	0.06
West Indian (75)	90	0.21

Hispanic Origin	Population	%
Hispanic or Latino (of any race)	9,004	21.65
Central American, ex. Mexican	963	2.32
Costa Rican	7	0.02
Guatemalan	444	1.07
Honduran	335	0.81
Nicaraguan	34	0.08
Panamanian	11	0.03
Salvadoran	131	0.31
Other Central American	1	<0.01
Cuban	233	0.56
Dominican Republic	58	0.14
Mexican	6,431	15.46
Puerto Rican	670	1.61
South American	216	0.52
Argentinean	18	0.04
Bolivian	7	0.02
Chilean	5	0.01
Colombian	96	0.23
Ecuadorian	35	0.08
Paraguayan	2	<0.01
Peruvian	14	0.03
Uruguayan	4	0.01
Venezuelan	28	0.07
Other South American	7	0.02
Other Hispanic or Latino	433	1.04

Race*	Population	%
African-American/Black (16,998)	17,540	42.17
Not Hispanic (16,787)	17,224	41.41
Hispanic (211)	316	0.76
American Indian/Alaska Native (253)	483	1.16
Not Hispanic (107)	279	0.67
Hispanic (146)	204	0.49
Apache (2)	7	0.02
Blackfeet (1)	15	0.04
Cherokee (11)	73	0.18
Chippewa (3)	5	0.01
Choctaw (4)	10	0.02
Comanche (1)	3	0.01
Cree (0)	1	<0.01
Creek (11)	12	0.03
Delaware (4)	5	0.01
Iroquois (0)	4	0.01

*Notes: † The Census 2010 population figure is used to calculate the percentages in the Hispanic Origin and Race categories. Ancestry percentages are based on the 2006-2010 American Community Survey population (not shown); ‡ Numbers in parentheses indicate the number of people reporting a single ancestry; * Numbers in parentheses indicate the number of persons reporting this race alone, not in combination with any other race; Please refer to the Explanation of Data for more information.*

Race*	Population	%
Lumbee (0)	1	<0.01
Mexican American Ind. (34)	35	0.08
Navajo (2)	2	<0.01
Potawatomi (0)	1	<0.01
Pueblo (1)	1	<0.01
Seminole (4)	13	0.03
Sioux (1)	1	<0.01
South American Ind. (7)	8	0.02
Yaqui (0)	1	<0.01
Asian (354)	493	1.19
Not Hispanic (337)	445	1.07
Hispanic (17)	48	0.12
Bangladeshi (22)	31	0.07
Cambodian (8)	10	0.02
Chinese, ex. Taiwanese (59)	84	0.20
Filipino (61)	83	0.20
Indian (107)	147	0.35
Indonesian (3)	5	0.01
Japanese (7)	16	0.04
Korean (22)	41	0.10
Pakistani (20)	31	0.07
Thai (7)	7	0.02
Vietnamese (16)	17	0.04
Hawaii Native/Pacific Islander (23)	107	0.26
Not Hispanic (20)	94	0.23
Hispanic (3)	13	0.03
Guamanian/Chamorro (8)	12	0.03
Native Hawaiian (5)	21	0.05
Samoan (5)	8	0.02
White (18,857)	19,676	47.31
Not Hispanic (14,639)	15,043	36.17
Hispanic (4,218)	4,633	11.14

Fort Walton Beach

Place Type: City
County: Okaloosa
Population: 19,507†

Ancestry‡	Population	%
African, Sub-Saharan (47)	66	0.33
African (20)	39	0.20
Ethiopian (27)	27	0.14
American (2,962)	2,962	14.82
Arab (25)	40	0.20
Lebanese (25)	25	0.13
Syrian (0)	15	0.08
Armenian (9)	9	0.05
Australian (0)	10	0.05
Belgian (10)	10	0.05
Brazilian (62)	62	0.31
British (66)	115	0.58
Canadian (36)	58	0.29
Croatian (33)	89	0.45
Czech (32)	74	0.37
Danish (59)	92	0.46
Dutch (35)	254	1.27
English (664)	1,819	9.10
European (204)	204	1.02
Finnish (22)	45	0.23
French, ex. Basque (74)	565	2.83
French Canadian (8)	119	0.60
German (863)	2,623	13.12
Greek (33)	67	0.34
Hungarian (9)	16	0.08
Irish (767)	2,388	11.95
Italian (270)	642	3.21
Northern European (29)	29	0.15
Norwegian (16)	66	0.33
Polish (110)	566	2.83
Portuguese (25)	69	0.35
Romanian (20)	27	0.14
Russian (139)	179	0.90
Scandinavian (5)	31	0.16
Scotch-Irish (225)	467	2.34
Scottish (138)	554	2.77
Slavic (26)	43	0.22
Slovak (0)	37	0.19
Swedish (65)	166	0.83
Swiss (20)	20	0.10
Ukrainian (15)	28	0.14
Welsh (22)	78	0.39
West Indian, ex. Hispanic (91)	127	0.64
Jamaican (70)	70	0.35
West Indian (21)	57	0.29
Yugoslavian (0)	16	0.08

Hispanic Origin	Population	%
Hispanic or Latino (of any race)	1,538	7.88
Central American, ex. Mexican	249	1.28
Costa Rican	5	0.03
Guatemalan	32	0.16
Honduran	119	0.61
Nicaraguan	21	0.11
Panamanian	56	0.29
Salvadoran	16	0.08
Cuban	70	0.36
Dominican Republic	42	0.22
Mexican	589	3.02
Puerto Rican	337	1.73
South American	82	0.42
Argentinean	17	0.09
Chilean	4	0.02
Colombian	34	0.17
Ecuadorian	3	0.02
Peruvian	14	0.07
Venezuelan	10	0.05
Other Hispanic or Latino	169	0.87

Race*	Population	%
African-American/Black (2,406)	2,714	13.91
Not Hispanic (2,331)	2,592	13.29
Hispanic (75)	122	0.63
American Indian/Alaska Native (127)	293	1.50
Not Hispanic (104)	240	1.23
Hispanic (23)	53	0.27
Aleut *(Alaska Native)* (1)	1	0.01
Apache (0)	2	0.01
Blackfeet (1)	3	0.02
Central American Ind. (2)	2	0.01
Cherokee (24)	65	0.33
Chippewa (2)	11	0.06
Choctaw (7)	17	0.09
Cree (1)	1	0.01
Creek (18)	23	0.12
Inupiat *(Alaska Native)* (1)	1	0.01
Iroquois (6)	7	0.04
Lumbee (3)	3	0.02
Mexican American Ind. (1)	2	0.01
Navajo (0)	1	0.01
Potawatomi (1)	4	0.02
Pueblo (3)	5	0.03
Seminole (4)	6	0.03
Sioux (3)	7	0.04
South American Ind. (2)	2	0.01
Yaqui (1)	1	0.01
Asian (632)	923	4.73
Not Hispanic (618)	862	4.42
Hispanic (14)	61	0.31
Bangladeshi (8)	8	0.04
Burmese (4)	7	0.04
Cambodian (0)	1	0.01
Chinese, ex. Taiwanese (40)	72	0.37
Filipino (224)	361	1.85
Hmong (2)	2	0.01
Indian (20)	43	0.22
Japanese (44)	85	0.44
Korean (63)	98	0.50
Laotian (4)	4	0.02
Pakistani (2)	4	0.02
Taiwanese (1)	5	0.03
Thai (140)	190	0.97
Vietnamese (36)	38	0.19
Hawaii Native/Pacific Islander (58)	104	0.53
Not Hispanic (54)	93	0.48
Hispanic (4)	11	0.06
Fijian (2)	2	0.01
Guamanian/Chamorro (36)	43	0.22
Native Hawaiian (9)	17	0.09
Samoan (4)	12	0.06
White (15,165)	15,793	80.96
Not Hispanic (14,245)	14,769	75.71
Hispanic (920)	1,024	5.25

Fountainebleau

Place Type: CDP
County: Miami-Dade
Population: 59,764†

Ancestry‡	Population	%
African, Sub-Saharan (11)	28	0.05
African (0)	17	0.03
Nigerian (11)	11	0.02
American (400)	400	0.68
Arab (118)	255	0.43
Arab (23)	112	0.19
Lebanese (13)	61	0.10
Other Arab (82)	82	0.14
Austrian (0)	16	0.03
Basque (27)	60	0.10
Brazilian (575)	642	1.09
British (25)	25	0.04
Czech (0)	7	0.01
Danish (0)	19	0.03
Dutch (11)	80	0.14
Eastern European (13)	13	0.02
English (46)	150	0.25
European (33)	54	0.09
French, ex. Basque (31)	202	0.34
German (102)	311	0.53
Greek (13)	24	0.04
Hungarian (14)	23	0.04
Irish (37)	367	0.62
Israeli (35)	124	0.21
Italian (311)	697	1.18
Lithuanian (0)	11	0.02
Norwegian (0)	9	0.02
Polish (43)	93	0.16
Portuguese (36)	56	0.09
Russian (89)	103	0.17
Scotch-Irish (0)	40	0.07
Scottish (0)	14	0.02
Serbian (37)	37	0.06
Swiss (0)	9	0.02
Turkish (0)	12	0.02
Ukrainian (36)	36	0.06
West Indian, ex. Hispanic (302)	364	0.62
Barbadian (0)	8	0.01
British West Indian (63)	63	0.11
Dutch West Indian (16)	16	0.03
Haitian (23)	61	0.10
Jamaican (54)	62	0.11
Trinidadian/Tobagonian (146)	154	0.26

Hispanic Origin	Population	%
Hispanic or Latino (of any race)	54,727	91.57
Central American, ex. Mexican	9,106	15.24
Costa Rican	255	0.43
Guatemalan	338	0.57
Honduran	1,117	1.87
Nicaraguan	6,738	11.27
Panamanian	272	0.46
Salvadoran	383	0.64
Other Central American	3	0.01
Cuban	27,798	46.51
Dominican Republic	2,063	3.45
Mexican	557	0.93
Puerto Rican	1,837	3.07
South American	11,183	18.71
Argentinean	780	1.31
Bolivian	215	0.36
Chilean	549	0.92
Colombian	4,714	7.89
Ecuadorian	914	1.53
Paraguayan	56	0.09
Peruvian	1,408	2.36
Uruguayan	209	0.35
Venezuelan	2,334	3.91
Other South American	4	0.01

*Notes: † The Census 2010 population figure is used to calculate the percentages in the Hispanic Origin and Race categories. Ancestry percentages are based on the 2006-2010 American Community Survey population (not shown); ‡ Numbers in parentheses indicate the number of people reporting a single ancestry; * Numbers in parentheses indicate the number of persons reporting this race alone, not in combination with any other race; Please refer to the Explanation of Data for more information.*

Other Hispanic or Latino	2,183	3.65

Race*	Population	%
African-American/Black (1,302)	1,606	2.69
Not Hispanic (415)	469	0.78
Hispanic (887)	1,137	1.90
American Indian/Alaska Native (62)	98	0.16
Not Hispanic (19)	26	0.04
Hispanic (43)	72	0.12
Blackfeet (0)	1	<0.01
Canadian/French Am. Ind. (0)	1	<0.01
Central American Ind. (2)	4	0.01
Cherokee (3)	5	0.01
Chippewa (1)	2	<0.01
Iroquois (1)	1	<0.01
Mexican American Ind. (1)	3	0.01
Seminole (1)	1	<0.01
Sioux (0)	1	<0.01
South American Ind. (4)	9	0.02
Spanish American Ind. (4)	5	0.01
Tlingit-Haida *(Alaska Native)* (1)	1	<0.01
Asian (870)	1,011	1.69
Not Hispanic (824)	904	1.51
Hispanic (46)	107	0.18
Bangladeshi (4)	4	0.01
Chinese, ex. Taiwanese (254)	302	0.51
Filipino (70)	84	0.14
Indian (354)	371	0.62
Indonesian (3)	3	0.01
Japanese (25)	38	0.06
Korean (38)	47	0.08
Malaysian (5)	5	0.01
Nepalese (23)	23	0.04
Pakistani (45)	48	0.08
Taiwanese (8)	8	0.01
Thai (9)	10	0.02
Vietnamese (15)	17	0.03
Hawaii Native/Pacific Islander (0)	26	0.04
Not Hispanic (0)	9	0.02
Hispanic (0)	17	0.03
Guamanian/Chamorro (0)	2	<0.01
Native Hawaiian (0)	7	0.01
Samoan (0)	1	<0.01
White (54,529)	55,583	93.00
Not Hispanic (3,558)	3,677	6.15
Hispanic (50,971)	51,906	86.85

Four Corners

Place Type: CDP
County: Lake
Population: 26,116†

Ancestry‡	Population	%
African, Sub-Saharan (93)	125	0.49
African (36)	68	0.27
South African (57)	57	0.22
Albanian (37)	37	0.14
American (899)	899	3.52
Arab (134)	242	0.95
Arab (13)	13	0.05
Lebanese (15)	15	0.06
Moroccan (106)	117	0.46
Other Arab (0)	97	0.38
Armenian (24)	24	0.09
Austrian (10)	38	0.15
Belgian (22)	33	0.13
Brazilian (34)	34	0.13
British (337)	413	1.62
Canadian (40)	89	0.35
Czech (14)	126	0.49
Danish (42)	42	0.16
Dutch (66)	259	1.01
Eastern European (30)	30	0.12
English (1,080)	2,240	8.78
European (148)	222	0.87
Finnish (47)	224	0.88
French, ex. Basque (106)	614	2.41
French Canadian (134)	280	1.10
German (1,113)	3,478	13.63
Greek (47)	58	0.23
Guyanese (68)	68	0.27
Hungarian (0)	152	0.60
Irish (880)	2,786	10.92
Italian (585)	1,700	6.66
Lithuanian (58)	165	0.65
Norwegian (153)	401	1.57
Pennsylvania German (28)	28	0.11
Polish (197)	819	3.21
Portuguese (109)	170	0.67
Romanian (0)	15	0.06
Russian (125)	293	1.15
Scandinavian (0)	30	0.12
Scotch-Irish (151)	353	1.38
Scottish (176)	495	1.94
Serbian (0)	11	0.04
Slovak (47)	128	0.50
Slovene (9)	9	0.04
Swedish (70)	143	0.56
Swiss (0)	50	0.20
Turkish (0)	14	0.05
Ukrainian (0)	102	0.40
Welsh (9)	79	0.31
West Indian, ex. Hispanic (492)	701	2.75
British West Indian (12)	12	0.05
Haitian (257)	257	1.01
Jamaican (100)	217	0.85
Trinidadian/Tobagonian (65)	65	0.25
West Indian (58)	150	0.59
Yugoslavian (14)	14	0.05

Hispanic Origin	Population	%
Hispanic or Latino (of any race)	7,859	30.09
Central American, ex. Mexican	353	1.35
Costa Rican	39	0.15
Guatemalan	66	0.25
Honduran	52	0.20
Nicaraguan	58	0.22
Panamanian	50	0.19
Salvadoran	87	0.33
Other Central American	1	<0.01
Cuban	438	1.68
Dominican Republic	490	1.88
Mexican	534	2.04
Puerto Rican	4,375	16.75
South American	1,230	4.71
Argentinean	53	0.20
Bolivian	4	0.02
Chilean	21	0.08
Colombian	540	2.07
Ecuadorian	210	0.80
Paraguayan	2	0.01
Peruvian	191	0.73
Uruguayan	11	0.04
Venezuelan	176	0.67
Other South American	22	0.08
Other Hispanic or Latino	439	1.68

Race*	Population	%
African-American/Black (2,092)	2,454	9.40
Not Hispanic (1,769)	1,998	7.65
Hispanic (323)	456	1.75
American Indian/Alaska Native (142)	308	1.18
Not Hispanic (81)	215	0.82
Hispanic (61)	93	0.36
Apache (0)	2	0.01
Blackfeet (2)	11	0.04
Central American Ind. (7)	8	0.03
Cherokee (20)	68	0.26
Cheyenne (1)	2	0.01
Chickasaw (2)	2	0.01
Chippewa (4)	9	0.03
Choctaw (7)	7	0.03
Creek (0)	3	0.01
Hopi (0)	2	0.01
Iroquois (1)	6	0.02
Mexican American Ind. (11)	14	0.05
Navajo (1)	1	<0.01
Seminole (0)	12	0.05
Sioux (0)	3	0.01
South American Ind. (5)	13	0.05
Spanish American Ind. (4)	4	0.02
Yaqui (1)	1	<0.01
Asian (648)	844	3.23
Not Hispanic (621)	783	3.00
Hispanic (27)	61	0.23
Burmese (4)	4	0.02
Cambodian (2)	2	0.01
Chinese, ex. Taiwanese (103)	131	0.50
Filipino (140)	189	0.72
Hmong (2)	2	0.01
Indian (201)	237	0.91
Indonesian (6)	10	0.04
Japanese (30)	66	0.25
Korean (31)	53	0.20
Laotian (8)	8	0.03
Malaysian (0)	2	0.01
Pakistani (27)	28	0.11
Sri Lankan (3)	3	0.01
Taiwanese (6)	7	0.03
Thai (9)	15	0.06
Vietnamese (55)	66	0.25
Hawaii Native/Pacific Islander (36)	89	0.34
Not Hispanic (29)	57	0.22
Hispanic (7)	32	0.12
Guamanian/Chamorro (4)	6	0.02
Native Hawaiian (15)	26	0.10
Samoan (1)	3	0.01
Tongan (5)	5	0.02
White (19,870)	20,615	78.94
Not Hispanic (15,167)	15,573	59.63
Hispanic (4,703)	5,042	19.31

Fruit Cove

Place Type: CDP
County: St. Johns
Population: 29,362†

Ancestry‡	Population	%
Albanian (213)	213	0.72
American (3,417)	3,417	11.55
Arab (6)	6	0.02
Egyptian (6)	6	0.02
Armenian (43)	73	0.25
Assyrian/Chaldean/Syriac (14)	14	0.05
Australian (0)	14	0.05
Austrian (49)	158	0.53
Brazilian (8)	34	0.11
British (95)	135	0.46
Canadian (0)	72	0.24
Croatian (13)	38	0.13
Czech (19)	121	0.41
Czechoslovakian (17)	17	0.06
Danish (23)	69	0.23
Dutch (87)	360	1.22
Eastern European (56)	56	0.19
English (1,529)	4,287	14.49
Estonian (9)	9	0.03
European (588)	625	2.11
Finnish (0)	24	0.08
French, ex. Basque (210)	854	2.89
French Canadian (242)	363	1.23
German (1,668)	5,413	18.29
Greek (120)	173	0.58
Hungarian (18)	91	0.31
Iranian (140)	140	0.47
Irish (2,146)	5,039	17.03
Italian (1,112)	2,638	8.92
Lithuanian (76)	109	0.37
Maltese (0)	21	0.07
Northern European (6)	6	0.02
Norwegian (29)	266	0.90
Polish (513)	1,218	4.12
Portuguese (63)	107	0.36
Romanian (42)	99	0.33
Russian (130)	304	1.03
Scandinavian (26)	40	0.14
Scotch-Irish (576)	1,111	3.75
Scottish (279)	727	2.46

*Notes: † The Census 2010 population figure is used to calculate the percentages in the Hispanic Origin and Race categories. Ancestry percentages are based on the 2006-2010 American Community Survey population (not shown); ‡ Numbers in parentheses indicate the number of people reporting a single ancestry; * Numbers in parentheses indicate the number of persons reporting this race alone, not in combination with any other race; Please refer to the Explanation of Data for more information.*

Ancestry	Population	%
Slovak (45)	229	0.77
Slovene (0)	4	0.01
Swedish (78)	282	0.95
Swiss (11)	108	0.37
Turkish (0)	17	0.06
Ukrainian (86)	107	0.36
Welsh (52)	228	0.77
West Indian, ex. Hispanic (9)	37	0.13
Jamaican (9)	21	0.07
West Indian (0)	16	0.05

Hispanic Origin	Population	%
Hispanic or Latino (of any race)	1,691	5.76
Central American, ex. Mexican	103	0.35
Costa Rican	20	0.07
Guatemalan	15	0.05
Honduran	25	0.09
Nicaraguan	18	0.06
Panamanian	12	0.04
Salvadoran	9	0.03
Other Central American	4	0.01
Cuban	243	0.83
Dominican Republic	57	0.19
Mexican	277	0.94
Puerto Rican	558	1.90
South American	304	1.04
Argentinean	29	0.10
Bolivian	14	0.05
Chilean	20	0.07
Colombian	128	0.44
Ecuadorian	30	0.10
Paraguayan	1	<0.01
Peruvian	30	0.10
Uruguayan	1	<0.01
Venezuelan	47	0.16
Other South American	4	0.01
Other Hispanic or Latino	149	0.51

Race*	Population	%
African-American/Black (1,004)	1,176	4.01
Not Hispanic (950)	1,089	3.71
Hispanic (54)	87	0.30
American Indian/Alaska Native (65)	190	0.65
Not Hispanic (58)	159	0.54
Hispanic (7)	31	0.11
Alaska Athabascan *(Ala. Nat.)* (1)	2	0.01
Aleut *(Alaska Native)* (0)	3	0.01
Apache (1)	2	0.01
Blackfeet (0)	3	0.01
Cherokee (16)	45	0.15
Chippewa (1)	1	<0.01
Choctaw (4)	4	0.01
Comanche (1)	1	<0.01
Cree (0)	3	0.01
Creek (2)	3	0.01
Iroquois (2)	4	0.01
Lumbee (4)	6	0.02
Mexican American Ind. (1)	1	<0.01
Potawatomi (0)	4	0.01
Pueblo (0)	5	0.02
Seminole (0)	2	0.01
Sioux (1)	4	0.01
South American Ind. (0)	4	0.01
Yaqui (0)	1	<0.01
Asian (782)	1,045	3.56
Not Hispanic (766)	1,005	3.42
Hispanic (16)	40	0.14
Bangladeshi (1)	1	<0.01
Burmese (3)	3	0.01
Cambodian (13)	20	0.07
Chinese, ex. Taiwanese (138)	168	0.57
Filipino (210)	307	1.05
Indian (197)	228	0.78
Indonesian (4)	5	0.02
Japanese (27)	62	0.21
Korean (42)	72	0.25
Laotian (1)	3	0.01
Malaysian (3)	3	0.01
Nepalese (4)	4	0.01
Pakistani (27)	30	0.10
Sri Lankan (3)	4	0.01
Taiwanese (8)	10	0.03
Thai (6)	12	0.04
Vietnamese (62)	74	0.25
Hawaii Native/Pacific Islander (8)	32	0.11
Not Hispanic (7)	30	0.10
Hispanic (1)	2	0.01
Guamanian/Chamorro (2)	11	0.04
Native Hawaiian (1)	8	0.03
Samoan (1)	5	0.02
White (26,649)	27,205	92.65
Not Hispanic (25,368)	25,813	87.91
Hispanic (1,281)	1,392	4.74

Fruitville

Place Type: CDP
County: Sarasota
Population: 13,224†

Ancestry‡	Population	%
African, Sub-Saharan (29)	38	0.27
African (0)	9	0.06
South African (29)	29	0.21
Albanian (23)	23	0.17
American (762)	762	5.49
Arab (39)	46	0.33
Lebanese (39)	46	0.33
Austrian (19)	32	0.23
Brazilian (59)	59	0.42
British (61)	89	0.64
Bulgarian (265)	265	1.91
Canadian (49)	60	0.43
Croatian (55)	95	0.68
Czech (0)	41	0.30
Danish (14)	59	0.42
Dutch (50)	228	1.64
Eastern European (12)	12	0.09
English (525)	1,725	12.42
European (29)	29	0.21
Finnish (13)	22	0.16
French, ex. Basque (119)	631	4.54
French Canadian (54)	54	0.39
German (904)	3,099	22.31
Greek (79)	160	1.15
Hungarian (73)	252	1.81
Icelander (13)	13	0.09
Irish (577)	2,350	16.92
Italian (628)	1,475	10.62
Lithuanian (22)	68	0.49
Northern European (8)	8	0.06
Norwegian (22)	95	0.68
Pennsylvania German (21)	42	0.30
Polish (134)	552	3.97
Portuguese (81)	123	0.89
Russian (48)	370	2.66
Scandinavian (20)	73	0.53
Scotch-Irish (118)	280	2.02
Scottish (53)	327	2.35
Serbian (32)	46	0.33
Slavic (0)	29	0.21
Slovak (17)	76	0.55
Swedish (78)	346	2.49
Swiss (23)	173	1.25
Turkish (7)	7	0.05
Ukrainian (83)	127	0.91
Welsh (40)	257	1.85
West Indian, ex. Hispanic (36)	58	0.42
Dutch West Indian (25)	25	0.18
Trinidadian/Tobagonian (11)	22	0.16
West Indian (0)	11	0.08
Yugoslavian (9)	23	0.17

Hispanic Origin	Population	%
Hispanic or Latino (of any race)	1,151	8.70
Central American, ex. Mexican	63	0.48
Costa Rican	5	0.04
Guatemalan	14	0.11
Honduran	20	0.15
Nicaraguan	6	0.05
Panamanian	11	0.08
Salvadoran	7	0.05
Cuban	179	1.35
Dominican Republic	18	0.14
Mexican	407	3.08
Puerto Rican	186	1.41
South American	232	1.75
Argentinean	20	0.15
Bolivian	2	0.02
Chilean	14	0.11
Colombian	95	0.72
Ecuadorian	13	0.10
Peruvian	55	0.42
Uruguayan	1	0.01
Venezuelan	32	0.24
Other Hispanic or Latino	66	0.50

Race*	Population	%
African-American/Black (326)	421	3.18
Not Hispanic (300)	378	2.86
Hispanic (26)	43	0.33
American Indian/Alaska Native (30)	70	0.53
Not Hispanic (15)	47	0.36
Hispanic (15)	23	0.17
Apache (0)	3	0.02
Blackfeet (0)	4	0.03
Cherokee (6)	11	0.08
Cree (0)	1	0.01
Iroquois (1)	3	0.02
Mexican American Ind. (2)	2	0.02
Navajo (1)	1	0.01
Pueblo (1)	2	0.02
Spanish American Ind. (0)	4	0.03
Asian (255)	297	2.25
Not Hispanic (251)	290	2.19
Hispanic (4)	7	0.05
Burmese (5)	6	0.05
Cambodian (3)	5	0.04
Chinese, ex. Taiwanese (54)	57	0.43
Filipino (29)	41	0.31
Indian (20)	28	0.21
Indonesian (0)	3	0.02
Japanese (12)	17	0.13
Korean (9)	14	0.11
Laotian (1)	1	0.01
Pakistani (10)	10	0.08
Taiwanese (3)	4	0.03
Thai (9)	11	0.08
Vietnamese (81)	89	0.67
Hawaii Native/Pacific Islander (3)	9	0.07
Not Hispanic (1)	3	0.02
Hispanic (2)	6	0.05
Native Hawaiian (0)	1	0.01
Tongan (1)	2	0.02
White (12,145)	12,329	93.23
Not Hispanic (11,350)	11,485	86.85
Hispanic (795)	844	6.38

Fuller Heights

Place Type: CDP
County: Polk
Population: 8,758†

Ancestry‡	Population	%
African, Sub-Saharan (11)	11	0.14
Other Sub-Saharan African (11)	11	0.14
American (678)	678	8.70
Arab (0)	105	1.35
Lebanese (0)	105	1.35
Australian (12)	12	0.15
Austrian (16)	56	0.72
British (26)	26	0.33
Croatian (11)	22	0.28
Czech (11)	11	0.14
Dutch (0)	36	0.46
English (183)	517	6.64
European (14)	14	0.18
Finnish (29)	29	0.37
French, ex. Basque (11)	141	1.81

*Notes: † The Census 2010 population figure is used to calculate the percentages in the Hispanic Origin and Race categories. Ancestry percentages are based on the 2006-2010 American Community Survey population (not shown); ‡ Numbers in parentheses indicate the number of people reporting a single ancestry; * Numbers in parentheses indicate the number of persons reporting this race alone, not in combination with any other race; Please refer to the Explanation of Data for more information.*

French Canadian (0)	38	0.49
German (472)	1,140	14.63
Greek (16)	16	0.21
Hungarian (10)	32	0.41
Icelander (0)	30	0.39
Irish (438)	789	10.13
Italian (138)	337	4.32
Norwegian (13)	70	0.90
Polish (84)	133	1.71
Portuguese (13)	68	0.87
Scotch-Irish (41)	130	1.67
Scottish (101)	251	3.22
Slovak (13)	27	0.35
Swedish (10)	54	0.69
Swiss (21)	50	0.64
Welsh (16)	26	0.33
West Indian, ex. Hispanic (34)	47	0.60
Barbadian (18)	18	0.23
Jamaican (16)	16	0.21
Trinidadian/Tobagonian (0)	13	0.17

Hispanic Origin	Population	%
Hispanic or Latino (of any race)	1,758	20.07
Central American, ex. Mexican	99	1.13
Costa Rican	14	0.16
Guatemalan	12	0.14
Honduran	14	0.16
Nicaraguan	32	0.37
Panamanian	10	0.11
Salvadoran	15	0.17
Other Central American	2	0.02
Cuban	205	2.34
Dominican Republic	53	0.61
Mexican	774	8.84
Puerto Rican	391	4.46
South American	160	1.83
Argentinean	1	0.01
Bolivian	2	0.02
Chilean	8	0.09
Colombian	67	0.77
Ecuadorian	33	0.38
Peruvian	11	0.13
Uruguayan	4	0.05
Venezuelan	33	0.38
Other South American	1	0.01
Other Hispanic or Latino	76	0.87

Race*	Population	%
African-American/Black (756)	849	9.69
Not Hispanic (727)	809	9.24
Hispanic (29)	40	0.46
American Indian/Alaska Native (19)	60	0.69
Not Hispanic (15)	47	0.54
Hispanic (4)	13	0.15
Central American Ind. (1)	1	0.01
Cherokee (4)	17	0.19
Chippewa (4)	4	0.05
Choctaw (2)	3	0.03
Creek (0)	2	0.02
Iroquois (2)	2	0.02
Mexican American Ind. (3)	5	0.06
Seminole (0)	3	0.03
Sioux (0)	1	0.01
Asian (158)	215	2.45
Not Hispanic (157)	207	2.36
Hispanic (1)	8	0.09
Cambodian (4)	4	0.05
Chinese, ex. Taiwanese (28)	33	0.38
Filipino (13)	26	0.30
Indian (58)	73	0.83
Japanese (5)	8	0.09
Korean (9)	22	0.25
Laotian (4)	8	0.09
Pakistani (8)	8	0.09
Thai (1)	3	0.03
Vietnamese (21)	23	0.26
Hawaii Native/Pacific Islander (4)	10	0.11
Not Hispanic (0)	5	0.06
Hispanic (4)	5	0.06
Guamanian/Chamorro (4)	4	0.05
Native Hawaiian (0)	1	0.01
White (7,180)	7,404	84.54
Not Hispanic (5,942)	6,074	69.35
Hispanic (1,238)	1,330	15.19

Gainesville

Place Type: City
County: Alachua
Population: 124,354†

Ancestry‡	Population	%
African, Sub-Saharan (759)	834	0.67
African (588)	617	0.50
Ethiopian (17)	17	0.01
Ghanaian (28)	28	0.02
Nigerian (64)	93	0.07
South African (38)	55	0.04
Other Sub-Saharan African (24)	24	0.02
Albanian (13)	13	0.01
Alsatian (15)	15	0.01
American (3,221)	3,221	2.59
Arab (668)	1,113	0.90
Arab (266)	319	0.26
Egyptian (29)	46	0.04
Jordanian (86)	86	0.07
Lebanese (92)	359	0.29
Moroccan (18)	71	0.06
Palestinian (57)	71	0.06
Syrian (9)	24	0.02
Other Arab (111)	137	0.11
Armenian (0)	114	0.09
Australian (42)	106	0.09
Austrian (116)	471	0.38
Basque (29)	29	0.02
Belgian (20)	61	0.05
Brazilian (362)	441	0.35
British (420)	789	0.63
Bulgarian (12)	24	0.02
Cajun (23)	45	0.04
Canadian (111)	246	0.20
Celtic (37)	46	0.04
Croatian (152)	218	0.18
Cypriot (10)	10	0.01
Czech (93)	387	0.31
Czechoslovakian (0)	142	0.11
Danish (72)	190	0.15
Dutch (259)	1,135	0.91
Eastern European (302)	400	0.32
English (4,238)	13,080	10.53
European (1,426)	1,533	1.23
Finnish (59)	196	0.16
French, ex. Basque (645)	3,247	2.61
French Canadian (206)	532	0.43
German (4,350)	15,893	12.79
Greek (337)	831	0.67
Guyanese (57)	101	0.08
Hungarian (62)	392	0.32
Icelander (14)	14	0.01
Iranian (143)	155	0.12
Irish (3,937)	13,599	10.94
Israeli (80)	125	0.10
Italian (2,286)	7,203	5.80
Latvian (0)	17	0.01
Lithuanian (95)	331	0.27
Luxemburger (0)	14	0.01
Macedonian (19)	19	0.02
Maltese (13)	13	0.01
New Zealander (31)	31	0.02
Northern European (42)	70	0.06
Norwegian (239)	960	0.77
Pennsylvania German (14)	75	0.06
Polish (1,290)	4,579	3.68
Portuguese (93)	249	0.20
Romanian (83)	458	0.37
Russian (823)	2,277	1.83
Scandinavian (64)	224	0.18
Scotch-Irish (921)	2,342	1.88
Scottish (855)	2,624	2.11
Serbian (0)	16	0.01
Slavic (0)	31	0.02
Slovak (10)	84	0.07
Slovene (25)	31	0.02
Swedish (313)	1,568	1.26
Swiss (149)	345	0.28
Turkish (179)	218	0.18
Ukrainian (196)	311	0.25
Welsh (120)	748	0.60
West Indian, ex. Hispanic (1,526)	1,943	1.56
Bahamian (45)	64	0.05
Barbadian (50)	50	0.04
British West Indian (0)	5	<0.01
Haitian (566)	653	0.53
Jamaican (564)	736	0.59
Trinidadian/Tobagonian (32)	85	0.07
U.S. Virgin Islander (74)	74	0.06
West Indian (195)	276	0.22
Yugoslavian (36)	57	0.05

Hispanic Origin	Population	%
Hispanic or Latino (of any race)	12,387	9.96
Central American, ex. Mexican	1,149	0.92
Costa Rican	125	0.10
Guatemalan	145	0.12
Honduran	241	0.19
Nicaraguan	332	0.27
Panamanian	165	0.13
Salvadoran	141	0.11
Cuban	2,886	2.32
Dominican Republic	374	0.30
Mexican	1,394	1.12
Puerto Rican	2,539	2.04
South American	2,966	2.39
Argentinean	215	0.17
Bolivian	63	0.05
Chilean	171	0.14
Colombian	1,172	0.94
Ecuadorian	228	0.18
Paraguayan	25	0.02
Peruvian	450	0.36
Uruguayan	34	0.03
Venezuelan	581	0.47
Other South American	27	0.02
Other Hispanic or Latino	1,079	0.87

Race*	Population	%
African-American/Black (28,575)	30,212	24.30
Not Hispanic (28,038)	29,358	23.61
Hispanic (537)	854	0.69
American Indian/Alaska Native (379)	1,049	0.84
Not Hispanic (279)	818	0.66
Hispanic (100)	231	0.19
Alaska Athabascan *(Ala. Nat.)* (1)	1	<0.01
Apache (7)	15	0.01
Blackfeet (2)	16	0.01
Canadian/French Am. Ind. (4)	6	<0.01
Central American Ind. (5)	8	0.01
Cherokee (47)	234	0.19
Chickasaw (1)	3	<0.01
Chippewa (3)	16	0.01
Choctaw (10)	21	0.02
Comanche (0)	3	<0.01
Cree (3)	5	<0.01
Creek (13)	26	0.02
Crow (1)	3	<0.01
Delaware (1)	3	<0.01
Hopi (0)	3	<0.01
Houma (1)	2	<0.01
Iroquois (17)	26	0.02
Kiowa (1)	1	<0.01
Lumbee (8)	13	0.01
Mexican American Ind. (8)	12	0.01
Navajo (4)	9	0.01
Osage (1)	2	<0.01
Ottawa (1)	3	<0.01
Potawatomi (2)	2	<0.01
Pueblo (4)	5	<0.01
Seminole (8)	22	0.02
Sioux (16)	25	0.02
South American Ind. (22)	46	0.04

*Notes: † The Census 2010 population figure is used to calculate the percentages in the Hispanic Origin and Race categories. Ancestry percentages are based on the 2006-2010 American Community Survey population (not shown); ‡ Numbers in parentheses indicate the number of people reporting a single ancestry; * Numbers in parentheses indicate the number of persons reporting this race alone, not in combination with any other race; Please refer to the Explanation of Data for more information.*

Spanish American Ind. (1)	1	<0.01
Yaqui (3)	4	<0.01
Asian (8,526)	9,973	8.02
Not Hispanic (8,424)	9,727	7.82
Hispanic (102)	246	0.20
Bangladeshi (104)	107	0.09
Bhutanese (0)	1	<0.01
Burmese (17)	19	0.02
Cambodian (39)	53	0.04
Chinese, ex. Taiwanese (2,240)	2,570	2.07
Filipino (1,018)	1,324	1.06
Hmong (3)	3	<0.01
Indian (2,616)	2,872	2.31
Indonesian (27)	50	0.04
Japanese (187)	363	0.29
Korean (773)	906	0.73
Laotian (6)	16	0.01
Malaysian (6)	12	0.01
Nepalese (24)	26	0.02
Pakistani (144)	170	0.14
Sri Lankan (21)	25	0.02
Taiwanese (220)	249	0.20
Thai (83)	134	0.11
Vietnamese (676)	807	0.65
Hawaii Native/Pacific Islander (65)	217	0.17
Not Hispanic (60)	193	0.16
Hispanic (5)	24	0.02
Guamanian/Chamorro (13)	27	0.02
Native Hawaiian (26)	59	0.05
Samoan (9)	26	0.02
Tongan (1)	3	<0.01
White (80,725)	83,818	67.40
Not Hispanic (71,903)	74,304	59.75
Hispanic (8,822)	9,514	7.65

Gateway

Place Type: CDP
County: Lee
Population: 8,401†

Ancestry‡	Population	%
American (733)	733	8.27
Arab (14)	47	0.53
Lebanese (14)	47	0.53
Armenian (13)	13	0.15
Australian (9)	9	0.10
Austrian (0)	10	0.11
Belgian (46)	67	0.76
British (9)	28	0.32
Canadian (0)	37	0.42
Croatian (25)	39	0.44
Czech (12)	112	1.26
Czechoslovakian (15)	15	0.17
Danish (0)	28	0.32
Dutch (21)	278	3.14
English (210)	745	8.40
European (22)	22	0.25
Finnish (31)	31	0.35
French, ex. Basque (4)	256	2.89
French Canadian (80)	130	1.47
German (519)	1,606	18.12
Greek (112)	112	1.26
Hungarian (0)	28	0.32
Irish (340)	1,495	16.87
Italian (545)	1,188	13.40
Lithuanian (91)	103	1.16
Northern European (0)	20	0.23
Norwegian (37)	133	1.50
Pennsylvania German (8)	8	0.09
Polish (195)	466	5.26
Romanian (9)	9	0.10
Russian (56)	276	3.11
Scandinavian (0)	12	0.14
Scotch-Irish (163)	229	2.58
Scottish (67)	155	1.75
Slovak (12)	31	0.35
Swedish (45)	126	1.42
Swiss (0)	16	0.18
Ukrainian (0)	47	0.53
Welsh (14)	49	0.55
West Indian, ex. Hispanic (108)	108	1.22
Haitian (41)	41	0.46
Jamaican (67)	67	0.76
Yugoslavian (0)	11	0.12

Hispanic Origin	Population	%
Hispanic or Latino (of any race)	944	11.24
Central American, ex. Mexican	56	0.67
Costa Rican	13	0.15
Guatemalan	12	0.14
Honduran	15	0.18
Nicaraguan	5	0.06
Panamanian	5	0.06
Salvadoran	4	0.05
Other Central American	2	0.02
Cuban	124	1.48
Dominican Republic	56	0.67
Mexican	114	1.36
Puerto Rican	229	2.73
South American	279	3.32
Argentinean	15	0.18
Bolivian	9	0.11
Chilean	12	0.14
Colombian	127	1.51
Ecuadorian	46	0.55
Peruvian	41	0.49
Venezuelan	29	0.35
Other Hispanic or Latino	86	1.02

Race*	Population	%
African-American/Black (420)	507	6.03
Not Hispanic (391)	458	5.45
Hispanic (29)	49	0.58
American Indian/Alaska Native (15)	42	0.50
Not Hispanic (11)	30	0.36
Hispanic (4)	12	0.14
Cherokee (2)	12	0.14
Chickasaw (0)	1	0.01
Chippewa (3)	3	0.04
Choctaw (0)	1	0.01
Delaware (1)	1	0.01
Mexican American Ind. (2)	2	0.02
Potawatomi (1)	1	0.01
South American Ind. (0)	7	0.08
Ute (0)	1	0.01
Asian (259)	336	4.00
Not Hispanic (256)	328	3.90
Hispanic (3)	8	0.10
Bangladeshi (10)	10	0.12
Burmese (2)	2	0.02
Chinese, ex. Taiwanese (30)	45	0.54
Filipino (64)	84	1.00
Indian (55)	62	0.74
Indonesian (3)	6	0.07
Japanese (0)	1	0.01
Korean (24)	34	0.40
Laotian (1)	1	0.01
Sri Lankan (6)	10	0.12
Taiwanese (0)	1	0.01
Thai (4)	4	0.05
Vietnamese (47)	56	0.67
Hawaii Native/Pacific Islander (1)	12	0.14
Not Hispanic (1)	12	0.14
Native Hawaiian (0)	1	0.01
White (7,382)	7,536	89.70
Not Hispanic (6,647)	6,761	80.48
Hispanic (735)	775	9.23

Gibsonton

Place Type: CDP
County: Hillsborough
Population: 14,234†

Ancestry‡	Population	%
African, Sub-Saharan (197)	230	1.76
African (197)	230	1.76
American (1,000)	1,000	7.63
Arab (25)	25	0.19
Egyptian (25)	25	0.19
Australian (9)	9	0.07
Belgian (7)	7	0.05
Brazilian (47)	47	0.36
British (23)	88	0.67
Canadian (21)	47	0.36
Czech (9)	104	0.79
Czechoslovakian (11)	11	0.08
Dutch (58)	374	2.85
English (394)	785	5.99
European (9)	38	0.29
Finnish (7)	7	0.05
French, ex. Basque (45)	111	0.85
French Canadian (0)	37	0.28
German (387)	1,437	10.97
Greek (32)	32	0.24
Hungarian (0)	45	0.34
Irish (460)	1,253	9.56
Italian (250)	454	3.46
Macedonian (22)	22	0.17
Norwegian (21)	61	0.47
Pennsylvania German (49)	49	0.37
Polish (53)	149	1.14
Portuguese (18)	68	0.52
Russian (56)	134	1.02
Scotch-Irish (53)	205	1.56
Scottish (56)	192	1.47
Slovak (21)	21	0.16
Swedish (12)	12	0.09
Swiss (5)	20	0.15
Turkish (0)	94	0.72
Ukrainian (0)	10	0.08
Welsh (0)	38	0.29
West Indian, ex. Hispanic (316)	364	2.78
British West Indian (0)	11	0.08
Haitian (154)	154	1.18
Jamaican (155)	192	1.47
West Indian (7)	7	0.05
Yugoslavian (0)	10	0.08

Hispanic Origin	Population	%
Hispanic or Latino (of any race)	3,969	27.88
Central American, ex. Mexican	208	1.46
Costa Rican	27	0.19
Guatemalan	44	0.31
Honduran	54	0.38
Nicaraguan	22	0.15
Panamanian	17	0.12
Salvadoran	37	0.26
Other Central American	7	0.05
Cuban	202	1.42
Dominican Republic	89	0.63
Mexican	2,314	16.26
Puerto Rican	764	5.37
South American	175	1.23
Argentinean	4	0.03
Bolivian	7	0.05
Colombian	90	0.63
Ecuadorian	25	0.18
Peruvian	25	0.18
Venezuelan	24	0.17
Other Hispanic or Latino	217	1.52

Race*	Population	%
African-American/Black (1,805)	1,981	13.92
Not Hispanic (1,704)	1,837	12.91
Hispanic (101)	144	1.01
American Indian/Alaska Native (83)	153	1.07
Not Hispanic (74)	129	0.91
Hispanic (9)	24	0.17
Aleut *(Alaska Native)* (0)	1	0.01
Apache (0)	1	0.01
Blackfeet (4)	4	0.03
Central American Ind. (0)	1	0.01
Cherokee (11)	29	0.20
Cheyenne (1)	1	0.01
Chippewa (9)	9	0.06
Choctaw (0)	1	0.01
Creek (6)	6	0.04
Hopi (0)	6	0.04

*Notes: † The Census 2010 population figure is used to calculate the percentages in the Hispanic Origin and Race categories. Ancestry percentages are based on the 2006-2010 American Community Survey population (not shown); ‡ Numbers in parentheses indicate the number of people reporting a single ancestry; * Numbers in parentheses indicate the number of persons reporting this race alone, not in combination with any other race; Please refer to the Explanation of Data for more information.*

Race* (continued)	Population	%
Inupiat *(Alaska Native)* (1)	2	0.01
Iroquois (1)	2	0.01
Lumbee (2)	3	0.02
Navajo (0)	1	0.01
Osage (0)	1	0.01
Paiute (0)	1	0.01
Pueblo (1)	2	0.01
Seminole (1)	6	0.04
Sioux (1)	5	0.04
South American Ind. (1)	1	0.01
Asian (253)	366	2.57
Not Hispanic (245)	339	2.38
Hispanic (8)	27	0.19
Bangladeshi (5)	5	0.04
Cambodian (2)	6	0.04
Chinese, ex. Taiwanese (28)	39	0.27
Filipino (48)	90	0.63
Indian (52)	66	0.46
Japanese (5)	13	0.09
Korean (13)	21	0.15
Laotian (2)	6	0.04
Pakistani (14)	14	0.10
Taiwanese (1)	1	0.01
Thai (16)	20	0.14
Vietnamese (55)	76	0.53
Hawaii Native/Pacific Islander (16)	36	0.25
Not Hispanic (10)	24	0.17
Hispanic (6)	12	0.08
Guamanian/Chamorro (6)	9	0.06
Native Hawaiian (10)	14	0.10
White (10,362)	10,753	75.54
Not Hispanic (7,948)	8,188	57.52
Hispanic (2,414)	2,565	18.02

Gifford

Place Type: CDP
County: Indian River
Population: 9,590†

Ancestry‡	Population	%
African, Sub-Saharan (64)	64	0.61
African (64)	64	0.61
American (945)	945	9.08
Arab (13)	13	0.12
Egyptian (13)	13	0.12
Austrian (7)	16	0.15
Belgian (0)	12	0.12
British (17)	17	0.16
Canadian (71)	79	0.76
Czech (27)	37	0.36
Czechoslovakian (0)	13	0.12
Danish (9)	15	0.14
Dutch (8)	129	1.24
Eastern European (9)	9	0.09
English (274)	950	9.12
European (36)	36	0.35
French, ex. Basque (34)	211	2.03
French Canadian (0)	12	0.12
German (206)	703	6.75
Hungarian (0)	8	0.08
Irish (207)	1,034	9.93
Italian (183)	343	3.29
Latvian (5)	5	0.05
Lithuanian (24)	38	0.36
Northern European (12)	12	0.12
Norwegian (33)	44	0.42
Polish (98)	319	3.06
Russian (7)	25	0.24
Scotch-Irish (32)	136	1.31
Scottish (56)	136	1.31
Swedish (18)	87	0.84
Swiss (5)	20	0.19
Welsh (8)	49	0.47
West Indian, ex. Hispanic (414)	462	4.44
Bahamian (66)	83	0.80
British West Indian (16)	16	0.15
Haitian (230)	252	2.42
Jamaican (102)	111	1.07

Hispanic Origin	Population	%
Hispanic or Latino (of any race)	811	8.46
Central American, ex. Mexican	48	0.50
Costa Rican	2	0.02
Guatemalan	17	0.18
Honduran	4	0.04
Nicaraguan	9	0.09
Panamanian	6	0.06
Salvadoran	10	0.10
Cuban	34	0.35
Dominican Republic	11	0.11
Mexican	532	5.55
Puerto Rican	78	0.81
South American	64	0.67
Argentinean	4	0.04
Bolivian	1	0.01
Chilean	1	0.01
Colombian	31	0.32
Ecuadorian	7	0.07
Peruvian	11	0.11
Venezuelan	9	0.09
Other Hispanic or Latino	44	0.46

Race*	Population	%
African-American/Black (4,188)	4,291	44.74
Not Hispanic (4,170)	4,261	44.43
Hispanic (18)	30	0.31
American Indian/Alaska Native (30)	61	0.64
Not Hispanic (16)	41	0.43
Hispanic (14)	20	0.21
Apache (1)	1	0.01
Blackfeet (1)	2	0.02
Cherokee (3)	17	0.18
Creek (0)	2	0.02
Lumbee (0)	2	0.02
Mexican American Ind. (11)	11	0.11
Navajo (0)	1	0.01
Seminole (0)	2	0.02
South American Ind. (1)	1	0.01
Asian (58)	88	0.92
Not Hispanic (58)	88	0.92
Chinese, ex. Taiwanese (14)	17	0.18
Filipino (11)	13	0.14
Indian (9)	14	0.15
Japanese (3)	9	0.09
Korean (5)	7	0.07
Laotian (1)	1	0.01
Pakistani (2)	2	0.02
Sri Lankan (2)	2	0.02
Thai (1)	4	0.04
Vietnamese (5)	5	0.05
Hawaii Native/Pacific Islander (1)	3	0.03
Not Hispanic (1)	3	0.03
Guamanian/Chamorro (0)	1	0.01
Native Hawaiian (1)	1	0.01
White (4,767)	4,879	50.88
Not Hispanic (4,399)	4,493	46.85
Hispanic (368)	386	4.03

Gladeview

Place Type: CDP
County: Miami-Dade
Population: 11,535†

Ancestry‡	Population	%
African, Sub-Saharan (21)	35	0.32
African (15)	15	0.14
Cape Verdean (0)	14	0.13
Other Sub-Saharan African (6)	6	0.05
American (523)	523	4.73
British (20)	20	0.18
French, ex. Basque (5)	5	0.05
German (13)	13	0.12
Irish (0)	45	0.41
Italian (0)	39	0.35
Russian (36)	36	0.33
West Indian, ex. Hispanic (183)	205	1.85
Bahamian (0)	10	0.09
British West Indian (22)	22	0.20
Haitian (55)	67	0.61
Jamaican (99)	99	0.90
Trinidadian/Tobagonian (7)	7	0.06

Hispanic Origin	Population	%
Hispanic or Latino (of any race)	2,786	24.15
Central American, ex. Mexican	1,085	9.41
Costa Rican	12	0.10
Guatemalan	58	0.50
Honduran	397	3.44
Nicaraguan	557	4.83
Panamanian	16	0.14
Salvadoran	44	0.38
Other Central American	1	0.01
Cuban	749	6.49
Dominican Republic	181	1.57
Mexican	97	0.84
Puerto Rican	296	2.57
South American	121	1.05
Argentinean	14	0.12
Bolivian	10	0.09
Chilean	5	0.04
Colombian	55	0.48
Ecuadorian	5	0.04
Peruvian	13	0.11
Uruguayan	3	0.03
Venezuelan	12	0.10
Other South American	4	0.03
Other Hispanic or Latino	257	2.23

Race*	Population	%
African-American/Black (8,674)	8,821	76.47
Not Hispanic (8,429)	8,534	73.98
Hispanic (245)	287	2.49
American Indian/Alaska Native (16)	60	0.52
Not Hispanic (10)	43	0.37
Hispanic (6)	17	0.15
Apache (1)	5	0.04
Central American Ind. (1)	1	0.01
Cherokee (0)	12	0.10
Creek (0)	1	0.01
Seminole (0)	1	0.01
Spanish American Ind. (1)	1	0.01
Asian (25)	56	0.49
Not Hispanic (23)	40	0.35
Hispanic (2)	16	0.14
Chinese, ex. Taiwanese (3)	9	0.08
Filipino (6)	12	0.10
Indian (9)	10	0.09
Japanese (0)	1	0.01
Thai (4)	5	0.04
Hawaii Native/Pacific Islander (0)	15	0.13
Not Hispanic (0)	11	0.10
Hispanic (0)	4	0.03
Guamanian/Chamorro (0)	1	0.01
Native Hawaiian (0)	3	0.03
White (2,008)	2,189	18.98
Not Hispanic (159)	208	1.80
Hispanic (1,849)	1,981	17.17

Glenvar Heights

Place Type: CDP
County: Miami-Dade
Population: 16,898†

Ancestry‡	Population	%
African, Sub-Saharan (22)	57	0.37
African (22)	57	0.37
American (446)	446	2.93
Arab (48)	288	1.89
Arab (25)	163	1.07
Egyptian (12)	12	0.08
Lebanese (0)	102	0.67
Syrian (11)	11	0.07
Austrian (11)	24	0.16
Basque (16)	16	0.11
Belgian (15)	15	0.10
Brazilian (120)	120	0.79
British (67)	67	0.44

SECTION TWO

*Notes: † The Census 2010 population figure is used to calculate the percentages in the Hispanic Origin and Race categories. Ancestry percentages are based on the 2006-2010 American Community Survey population (not shown); ‡ Numbers in parentheses indicate the number of people reporting a single ancestry; * Numbers in parentheses indicate the number of persons reporting this race alone, not in combination with any other race; Please refer to the Explanation of Data for more information.*

Canadian (26)	92	0.60
Czechoslovakian (13)	13	0.09
Danish (0)	11	0.07
Dutch (12)	33	0.22
English (155)	574	3.77
European (98)	121	0.79
French, ex. Basque (46)	181	1.19
German (387)	930	6.11
Greek (34)	76	0.50
Hungarian (29)	58	0.38
Iranian (64)	64	0.42
Irish (178)	703	4.62
Italian (168)	511	3.36
Latvian (0)	21	0.14
Lithuanian (12)	62	0.41
New Zealander (14)	14	0.09
Norwegian (7)	31	0.20
Polish (65)	213	1.40
Portuguese (0)	13	0.09
Russian (44)	120	0.79
Scotch-Irish (38)	88	0.58
Scottish (27)	58	0.38
Slovak (0)	11	0.07
Swedish (14)	74	0.49
Swiss (11)	41	0.27
Welsh (0)	66	0.43
West Indian, ex. Hispanic (211)	211	1.39
British West Indian (27)	27	0.18
Haitian (13)	13	0.09
Jamaican (44)	44	0.29
West Indian (127)	127	0.83

Hispanic Origin	Population	%
Hispanic or Latino (of any race)	11,241	66.52
Central American, ex. Mexican	1,023	6.05
Costa Rican	45	0.27
Guatemalan	99	0.59
Honduran	233	1.38
Nicaraguan	454	2.69
Panamanian	90	0.53
Salvadoran	98	0.58
Other Central American	4	0.02
Cuban	6,488	38.40
Dominican Republic	235	1.39
Mexican	220	1.30
Puerto Rican	524	3.10
South American	2,154	12.75
Argentinean	140	0.83
Bolivian	49	0.29
Chilean	111	0.66
Colombian	850	5.03
Ecuadorian	146	0.86
Paraguayan	15	0.09
Peruvian	426	2.52
Uruguayan	24	0.14
Venezuelan	391	2.31
Other South American	2	0.01
Other Hispanic or Latino	597	3.53

Race*	Population	%
African-American/Black (538)	663	3.92
Not Hispanic (425)	498	2.95
Hispanic (113)	165	0.98
American Indian/Alaska Native (23)	52	0.31
Not Hispanic (8)	22	0.13
Hispanic (15)	30	0.18
Apache (0)	1	0.01
Blackfeet (0)	1	0.01
Central American Ind. (1)	3	0.02
Cherokee (0)	6	0.04
Comanche (0)	3	0.02
Creek (0)	1	0.01
Mexican American Ind. (4)	4	0.02
South American Ind. (2)	5	0.03
Spanish American Ind. (1)	1	0.01
Asian (481)	587	3.47
Not Hispanic (454)	539	3.19
Hispanic (27)	48	0.28
Cambodian (1)	2	0.01
Chinese, ex. Taiwanese (191)	223	1.32
Filipino (61)	72	0.43
Indian (104)	125	0.74
Indonesian (1)	2	0.01
Japanese (22)	27	0.16
Korean (13)	18	0.11
Malaysian (0)	4	0.02
Pakistani (9)	15	0.09
Sri Lankan (9)	10	0.06
Taiwanese (15)	19	0.11
Thai (17)	19	0.11
Vietnamese (23)	28	0.17
Hawaii Native/Pacific Islander (6)	14	0.08
Not Hispanic (4)	8	0.05
Hispanic (2)	6	0.04
Native Hawaiian (3)	6	0.04
Samoan (1)	1	0.01
White (15,013)	15,306	90.58
Not Hispanic (4,558)	4,667	27.62
Hispanic (10,455)	10,639	62.96

Golden Gate

Place Type: CDP
County: Collier
Population: 23,961†

Ancestry‡	Population	%
African, Sub-Saharan (272)	298	1.23
African (272)	298	1.23
American (604)	604	2.50
Arab (25)	25	0.10
Lebanese (13)	13	0.05
Syrian (12)	12	0.05
Armenian (0)	20	0.08
Canadian (44)	67	0.28
Czechoslovakian (0)	14	0.06
Dutch (23)	141	0.58
English (216)	936	3.88
Estonian (12)	12	0.05
European (69)	106	0.44
French, ex. Basque (287)	430	1.78
French Canadian (82)	86	0.36
German (270)	1,814	7.52
Greek (12)	30	0.12
Hungarian (13)	27	0.11
Irish (386)	1,087	4.50
Italian (222)	345	1.43
Northern European (31)	31	0.13
Norwegian (30)	96	0.40
Polish (43)	228	0.94
Portuguese (13)	47	0.19
Romanian (0)	16	0.07
Russian (0)	44	0.18
Scotch-Irish (163)	458	1.90
Scottish (30)	56	0.23
Slavic (0)	25	0.10
Slovak (109)	109	0.45
Swedish (12)	80	0.33
Welsh (44)	140	0.58
West Indian, ex. Hispanic (1,809)	1,914	7.93
Bahamian (179)	179	0.74
Haitian (1,398)	1,469	6.09
Jamaican (46)	80	0.33
Trinidadian/Tobagonian (58)	58	0.24
West Indian (128)	128	0.53
Yugoslavian (0)	13	0.05

Hispanic Origin	Population	%
Hispanic or Latino (of any race)	14,023	58.52
Central American, ex. Mexican	1,831	7.64
Costa Rican	55	0.23
Guatemalan	631	2.63
Honduran	741	3.09
Nicaraguan	130	0.54
Panamanian	22	0.09
Salvadoran	241	1.01
Other Central American	11	0.05
Cuban	3,941	16.45
Dominican Republic	207	0.86
Mexican	5,470	22.83
Puerto Rican	815	3.40
South American	1,170	4.88
Argentinean	93	0.39
Bolivian	290	1.21
Chilean	12	0.05
Colombian	405	1.69
Ecuadorian	51	0.21
Paraguayan	2	0.01
Peruvian	207	0.86
Uruguayan	47	0.20
Venezuelan	61	0.25
Other South American	2	0.01
Other Hispanic or Latino	589	2.46

Race*	Population	%
African-American/Black (3,876)	4,125	17.22
Not Hispanic (3,633)	3,821	15.95
Hispanic (243)	304	1.27
American Indian/Alaska Native (166)	227	0.95
Not Hispanic (61)	93	0.39
Hispanic (105)	134	0.56
Alaska Athabascan *(Ala. Nat.)* (0)	1	<0.01
Apache (3)	5	0.02
Blackfeet (0)	2	0.01
Canadian/French Am. Ind. (4)	4	0.02
Central American Ind. (0)	9	0.04
Cherokee (14)	24	0.10
Chickasaw (6)	6	0.03
Chippewa (2)	2	0.01
Creek (0)	1	<0.01
Delaware (0)	1	<0.01
Iroquois (2)	3	0.01
Mexican American Ind. (44)	51	0.21
Navajo (0)	2	0.01
Seminole (5)	5	0.02
Spanish American Ind. (2)	4	0.02
Tlingit-Haida *(Alaska Native)* (1)	1	<0.01
Asian (159)	300	1.25
Not Hispanic (151)	201	0.84
Hispanic (8)	99	0.41
Cambodian (1)	1	<0.01
Chinese, ex. Taiwanese (29)	44	0.18
Filipino (19)	42	0.18
Indian (39)	51	0.21
Japanese (3)	12	0.05
Korean (5)	5	0.02
Laotian (3)	4	0.02
Pakistani (2)	2	0.01
Thai (3)	4	0.02
Vietnamese (41)	52	0.22
Hawaii Native/Pacific Islander (0)	61	0.25
Not Hispanic (0)	45	0.19
Hispanic (0)	16	0.07
Guamanian/Chamorro (0)	9	0.04
Native Hawaiian (0)	2	0.01
White (15,821)	16,559	69.11
Not Hispanic (5,797)	5,958	24.87
Hispanic (10,024)	10,601	44.24

Golden Glades

Place Type: CDP
County: Miami-Dade
Population: 33,145†

Ancestry‡	Population	%
African, Sub-Saharan (334)	390	1.18
African (334)	390	1.18
American (729)	729	2.21
Arab (29)	29	0.09
Moroccan (29)	29	0.09
Brazilian (16)	16	0.05
British (8)	28	0.08
Czech (0)	10	0.03
Danish (0)	15	0.05
Dutch (0)	46	0.14
English (159)	347	1.05
Finnish (10)	10	0.03
French, ex. Basque (136)	260	0.79
French Canadian (11)	19	0.06

*Notes: † The Census 2010 population figure is used to calculate the percentages in the Hispanic Origin and Race categories. Ancestry percentages are based on the 2006-2010 American Community Survey population (not shown); ‡ Numbers in parentheses indicate the number of people reporting a single ancestry; * Numbers in parentheses indicate the number of persons reporting this race alone, not in combination with any other race; Please refer to the Explanation of Data for more information.*

German (235)	515	1.56
Greek (8)	28	0.08
Hungarian (30)	56	0.17
Irish (146)	448	1.36
Israeli (0)	39	0.12
Italian (128)	235	0.71
Lithuanian (0)	6	0.02
Norwegian (21)	25	0.08
Polish (40)	99	0.30
Portuguese (14)	34	0.10
Romanian (24)	24	0.07
Russian (15)	39	0.12
Scandinavian (0)	20	0.06
Scotch-Irish (21)	51	0.15
Scottish (15)	46	0.14
Swedish (0)	28	0.08
Swiss (0)	18	0.05
Turkish (0)	8	0.02
West Indian, ex. Hispanic (14,191)	14,555	44.15
Bahamian (298)	317	0.96
Barbadian (24)	24	0.07
Belizean (49)	49	0.15
British West Indian (230)	230	0.70
Haitian (12,801)	13,085	39.69
Jamaican (712)	759	2.30
Trinidadian/Tobagonian (44)	44	0.13
U.S. Virgin Islander (14)	14	0.04
West Indian (19)	33	0.10

Hispanic Origin	Population	%
Hispanic or Latino (of any race)	6,134	18.51
Central American, ex. Mexican	1,325	4.00
Costa Rican	34	0.10
Guatemalan	109	0.33
Honduran	489	1.48
Nicaraguan	528	1.59
Panamanian	55	0.17
Salvadoran	99	0.30
Other Central American	11	0.03
Cuban	1,428	4.31
Dominican Republic	703	2.12
Mexican	177	0.53
Puerto Rican	1,114	3.36
South American	821	2.48
Argentinean	98	0.30
Bolivian	13	0.04
Chilean	24	0.07
Colombian	311	0.94
Ecuadorian	74	0.22
Paraguayan	2	0.01
Peruvian	200	0.60
Uruguayan	16	0.05
Venezuelan	73	0.22
Other South American	10	0.03
Other Hispanic or Latino	566	1.71

Race*	Population	%
African-American/Black (24,141)	24,852	74.98
Not Hispanic (23,358)	23,917	72.16
Hispanic (783)	935	2.82
American Indian/Alaska Native (86)	196	0.59
Not Hispanic (46)	125	0.38
Hispanic (40)	71	0.21
Blackfeet (0)	1	<0.01
Central American Ind. (7)	9	0.03
Cherokee (5)	17	0.05
Chippewa (4)	4	0.01
Iroquois (1)	1	<0.01
Seminole (1)	1	<0.01
Sioux (1)	3	0.01
South American Ind. (6)	12	0.04
Tlingit-Haida *(Alaska Native)* (1)	5	0.02
Asian (538)	745	2.25
Not Hispanic (520)	691	2.08
Hispanic (18)	54	0.16
Bangladeshi (1)	1	<0.01
Burmese (5)	5	0.02
Cambodian (5)	5	0.02
Chinese, ex. Taiwanese (77)	111	0.33
Filipino (177)	204	0.62
Indian (139)	200	0.60
Indonesian (9)	9	0.03
Japanese (9)	14	0.04
Korean (3)	5	0.02
Laotian (8)	10	0.03
Pakistani (13)	25	0.08
Taiwanese (1)	1	<0.01
Thai (3)	6	0.02
Vietnamese (49)	52	0.16
Hawaii Native/Pacific Islander (18)	249	0.75
Not Hispanic (15)	215	0.65
Hispanic (3)	34	0.10
Guamanian/Chamorro (2)	6	0.02
Native Hawaiian (1)	9	0.03
Samoan (0)	1	<0.01
White (6,418)	6,841	20.64
Not Hispanic (2,334)	2,505	7.56
Hispanic (4,084)	4,336	13.08

Goldenrod

Place Type: CDP
County: Orange
Population: 12,039†

Ancestry‡	Population	%
African, Sub-Saharan (16)	16	0.11
African (16)	16	0.11
American (499)	499	3.48
Arab (9)	9	0.06
Lebanese (9)	9	0.06
Austrian (0)	39	0.27
British (6)	46	0.32
Canadian (12)	18	0.13
Celtic (15)	15	0.10
Czech (9)	21	0.15
Czechoslovakian (13)	31	0.22
Danish (14)	68	0.47
Dutch (39)	486	3.39
English (522)	1,195	8.34
European (107)	107	0.75
Finnish (10)	92	0.64
French, ex. Basque (35)	305	2.13
French Canadian (56)	88	0.61
German (565)	2,641	18.44
Greek (12)	48	0.34
Guyanese (23)	23	0.16
Hungarian (140)	154	1.08
Icelander (20)	20	0.14
Iranian (17)	17	0.12
Irish (632)	1,826	12.75
Israeli (9)	9	0.06
Italian (561)	1,160	8.10
Northern European (8)	8	0.06
Norwegian (32)	134	0.94
Polish (103)	368	2.57
Portuguese (10)	18	0.13
Romanian (0)	12	0.08
Russian (44)	102	0.71
Scotch-Irish (69)	227	1.58
Scottish (71)	149	1.04
Swedish (33)	109	0.76
Swiss (42)	54	0.38
Ukrainian (35)	59	0.41
Welsh (23)	33	0.23
West Indian, ex. Hispanic (170)	331	2.31
Bermudan (0)	18	0.13
Haitian (0)	12	0.08
Jamaican (87)	102	0.71
Trinidadian/Tobagonian (45)	45	0.31
U.S. Virgin Islander (0)	116	0.81
West Indian (38)	38	0.27

Hispanic Origin	Population	%
Hispanic or Latino (of any race)	2,671	22.19
Central American, ex. Mexican	165	1.37
Costa Rican	12	0.10
Guatemalan	23	0.19
Honduran	42	0.35
Nicaraguan	24	0.20
Panamanian	24	0.20
Salvadoran	39	0.32
Other Central American	1	0.01
Cuban	202	1.68
Dominican Republic	124	1.03
Mexican	339	2.82
Puerto Rican	1,401	11.64
South American	309	2.57
Argentinean	10	0.08
Bolivian	2	0.02
Chilean	11	0.09
Colombian	155	1.29
Ecuadorian	37	0.31
Paraguayan	1	0.01
Peruvian	44	0.37
Uruguayan	7	0.06
Venezuelan	42	0.35
Other Hispanic or Latino	131	1.09

Race*	Population	%
African-American/Black (1,104)	1,268	10.53
Not Hispanic (982)	1,082	8.99
Hispanic (122)	186	1.54
American Indian/Alaska Native (48)	118	0.98
Not Hispanic (25)	80	0.66
Hispanic (23)	38	0.32
Blackfeet (0)	6	0.05
Cherokee (4)	30	0.25
Chickasaw (1)	1	0.01
Chippewa (1)	1	0.01
Hopi (0)	2	0.02
Iroquois (1)	1	0.01
Mexican American Ind. (6)	8	0.07
Navajo (0)	5	0.04
Seminole (1)	2	0.02
Sioux (0)	3	0.02
South American Ind. (4)	4	0.03
Tohono O'Odham (0)	1	0.01
Asian (366)	460	3.82
Not Hispanic (354)	430	3.57
Hispanic (12)	30	0.25
Bangladeshi (4)	4	0.03
Cambodian (3)	3	0.02
Chinese, ex. Taiwanese (71)	92	0.76
Filipino (83)	110	0.91
Indian (62)	81	0.67
Indonesian (1)	2	0.02
Japanese (18)	28	0.23
Korean (25)	38	0.32
Laotian (0)	1	0.01
Pakistani (3)	7	0.06
Taiwanese (12)	12	0.10
Thai (17)	23	0.19
Vietnamese (59)	63	0.52
Hawaii Native/Pacific Islander (11)	27	0.22
Not Hispanic (5)	15	0.12
Hispanic (6)	12	0.10
Guamanian/Chamorro (2)	6	0.05
Marshallese (1)	1	0.01
Native Hawaiian (5)	15	0.12
White (9,340)	9,670	80.32
Not Hispanic (7,743)	7,933	65.89
Hispanic (1,597)	1,737	14.43

Gonzalez

Place Type: CDP
County: Escambia
Population: 13,273†

Ancestry‡	Population	%
African, Sub-Saharan (22)	22	0.18
African (22)	22	0.18
Albanian (8)	8	0.06
American (1,647)	1,647	13.34
Arab (62)	73	0.59
Lebanese (40)	51	0.41
Other Arab (22)	22	0.18
Austrian (14)	70	0.57
British (27)	40	0.32

*Notes: † The Census 2010 population figure is used to calculate the percentages in the Hispanic Origin and Race categories. Ancestry percentages are based on the 2006-2010 American Community Survey population (not shown); ‡ Numbers in parentheses indicate the number of people reporting a single ancestry; * Numbers in parentheses indicate the number of persons reporting this race alone, not in combination with any other race; Please refer to the Explanation of Data for more information.*

Ancestry	Population	%
Cajun (19)	19	0.15
Canadian (74)	103	0.83
Czech (15)	36	0.29
Dutch (0)	96	0.78
Eastern European (8)	8	0.06
English (658)	1,439	11.65
European (255)	255	2.07
French, ex. Basque (116)	405	3.28
French Canadian (28)	142	1.15
German (544)	1,504	12.18
Greek (0)	87	0.70
Irish (366)	1,561	12.64
Italian (434)	798	6.46
Lithuanian (0)	19	0.15
Norwegian (8)	78	0.63
Polish (75)	102	0.83
Portuguese (15)	34	0.28
Romanian (13)	13	0.11
Russian (26)	69	0.56
Scandinavian (60)	60	0.49
Scotch-Irish (113)	230	1.86
Scottish (70)	564	4.57
Slavic (14)	33	0.27
Swedish (114)	344	2.79
Swiss (36)	36	0.29
Turkish (73)	73	0.59
Ukrainian (68)	68	0.55
Welsh (0)	86	0.70
West Indian, ex. Hispanic (146)	146	1.18
Jamaican (146)	146	1.18

Hispanic Origin	Population	%
Hispanic or Latino (of any race)	380	2.86
Central American, ex. Mexican	27	0.20
Costa Rican	4	0.03
Guatemalan	2	0.02
Honduran	7	0.05
Nicaraguan	2	0.02
Panamanian	6	0.05
Salvadoran	6	0.05
Cuban	37	0.28
Dominican Republic	8	0.06
Mexican	144	1.08
Puerto Rican	87	0.66
South American	24	0.18
Argentinean	3	0.02
Colombian	12	0.09
Ecuadorian	6	0.05
Uruguayan	2	0.02
Venezuelan	1	0.01
Other Hispanic or Latino	53	0.40

Race*	Population	%
African-American/Black (1,412)	1,507	11.35
Not Hispanic (1,397)	1,490	11.23
Hispanic (15)	17	0.13
American Indian/Alaska Native (118)	239	1.80
Not Hispanic (109)	224	1.69
Hispanic (9)	15	0.11
Blackfeet (2)	8	0.06
Central American Ind. (1)	2	0.02
Cherokee (15)	52	0.39
Cheyenne (1)	2	0.02
Chippewa (0)	2	0.02
Choctaw (3)	5	0.04
Comanche (1)	1	0.01
Creek (46)	77	0.58
Delaware (0)	1	0.01
Iroquois (1)	1	0.01
Mexican American Ind. (3)	3	0.02
Navajo (1)	1	0.01
Potawatomi (2)	2	0.02
Seminole (1)	1	0.01
Shoshone (0)	1	0.01
Yaqui (1)	3	0.02
Asian (231)	342	2.58
Not Hispanic (219)	324	2.44
Hispanic (12)	18	0.14
Cambodian (4)	6	0.05
Chinese, ex. Taiwanese (37)	49	0.37
Filipino (73)	132	0.99
Indian (6)	7	0.05
Indonesian (1)	2	0.02
Japanese (16)	32	0.24
Korean (14)	26	0.20
Malaysian (2)	2	0.02
Taiwanese (3)	3	0.02
Thai (2)	3	0.02
Vietnamese (67)	80	0.60
Hawaii Native/Pacific Islander (5)	16	0.12
Not Hispanic (4)	12	0.09
Hispanic (1)	4	0.03
Guamanian/Chamorro (2)	6	0.05
Native Hawaiian (2)	6	0.05
Samoan (0)	2	0.02
White (11,133)	11,426	86.08
Not Hispanic (10,852)	11,123	83.80
Hispanic (281)	303	2.28

Goulds

Place Type: CDP
County: Miami-Dade
Population: 10,103†

Ancestry‡	Population	%
African, Sub-Saharan (3)	3	0.03
African (3)	3	0.03
American (2,438)	2,438	26.49
Canadian (46)	130	1.41
English (81)	112	1.22
French, ex. Basque (0)	9	0.10
German (49)	49	0.53
Irish (16)	16	0.17
Italian (4)	104	1.13
Polish (18)	18	0.20
Scottish (0)	7	0.08
Swiss (0)	37	0.40
West Indian, ex. Hispanic (449)	521	5.66
Bahamian (299)	299	3.25
Haitian (76)	91	0.99
Jamaican (74)	131	1.42

Hispanic Origin	Population	%
Hispanic or Latino (of any race)	4,144	41.02
Central American, ex. Mexican	659	6.52
Costa Rican	16	0.16
Guatemalan	60	0.59
Honduran	142	1.41
Nicaraguan	323	3.20
Panamanian	35	0.35
Salvadoran	83	0.82
Cuban	2,014	19.93
Dominican Republic	165	1.63
Mexican	277	2.74
Puerto Rican	439	4.35
South American	367	3.63
Argentinean	16	0.16
Bolivian	1	0.01
Chilean	16	0.16
Colombian	145	1.44
Ecuadorian	39	0.39
Paraguayan	1	0.01
Peruvian	84	0.83
Uruguayan	8	0.08
Venezuelan	57	0.56
Other Hispanic or Latino	223	2.21

Race*	Population	%
African-American/Black (5,578)	5,728	56.70
Not Hispanic (5,330)	5,431	53.76
Hispanic (248)	297	2.94
American Indian/Alaska Native (17)	37	0.37
Not Hispanic (4)	18	0.18
Hispanic (13)	19	0.19
Alaska Athabascan *(Ala. Nat.)* (1)	1	0.01
Central American Ind. (1)	1	0.01
Cherokee (1)	9	0.09
Mexican American Ind. (1)	1	0.01
Sioux (0)	1	0.01
South American Ind. (2)	2	0.02
Spanish American Ind. (1)	1	0.01
Asian (65)	101	1.00
Not Hispanic (60)	92	0.91
Hispanic (5)	9	0.09
Chinese, ex. Taiwanese (7)	27	0.27
Filipino (7)	10	0.10
Indian (20)	24	0.24
Japanese (2)	8	0.08
Pakistani (0)	2	0.02
Sri Lankan (3)	3	0.03
Thai (2)	3	0.03
Vietnamese (9)	12	0.12
Hawaii Native/Pacific Islander (0)	22	0.22
Not Hispanic (0)	18	0.18
Hispanic (0)	4	0.04
Guamanian/Chamorro (0)	2	0.02
Native Hawaiian (0)	3	0.03
Samoan (0)	1	0.01
White (3,949)	4,108	40.66
Not Hispanic (429)	495	4.90
Hispanic (3,520)	3,613	35.76

Greenacres

Place Type: City
County: Palm Beach
Population: 37,573†

Ancestry‡	Population	%
African, Sub-Saharan (300)	343	0.95
African (243)	286	0.79
Nigerian (57)	57	0.16
Albanian (9)	32	0.09
American (1,245)	1,245	3.43
Arab (3)	41	0.11
Egyptian (3)	32	0.09
Lebanese (0)	9	0.02
Armenian (15)	30	0.08
Austrian (59)	171	0.47
Belgian (0)	20	0.06
Brazilian (151)	151	0.42
British (108)	133	0.37
Cajun (9)	40	0.11
Canadian (33)	63	0.17
Croatian (27)	42	0.12
Czech (19)	149	0.41
Czechoslovakian (0)	12	0.03
Danish (46)	186	0.51
Dutch (244)	497	1.37
Eastern European (12)	12	0.03
English (618)	2,258	6.23
European (224)	269	0.74
Finnish (85)	194	0.54
French, ex. Basque (82)	942	2.60
French Canadian (70)	122	0.34
German (551)	3,018	8.32
Greek (168)	750	2.07
Guyanese (16)	16	0.04
Hungarian (295)	471	1.30
Irish (718)	2,529	6.97
Israeli (0)	13	0.04
Italian (1,486)	2,557	7.05
Latvian (0)	51	0.14
Lithuanian (25)	25	0.07
Norwegian (67)	231	0.64
Polish (229)	753	2.08
Portuguese (46)	76	0.21
Romanian (42)	78	0.22
Russian (423)	644	1.78
Scandinavian (0)	23	0.06
Scotch-Irish (178)	496	1.37
Scottish (114)	412	1.14
Slovak (17)	25	0.07
Swedish (27)	271	0.75
Swiss (0)	57	0.16
Turkish (0)	6	0.02
Ukrainian (60)	116	0.32
Welsh (0)	238	0.66
West Indian, ex. Hispanic (2,676)	2,775	7.65

*Notes: † The Census 2010 population figure is used to calculate the percentages in the Hispanic Origin and Race categories. Ancestry percentages are based on the 2006-2010 American Community Survey population (not shown); ‡ Numbers in parentheses indicate the number of people reporting a single ancestry; * Numbers in parentheses indicate the number of persons reporting this race alone, not in combination with any other race; Please refer to the Explanation of Data for more information.*

Barbadian (40)	40	0.11
Haitian (1,896)	1,896	5.23
Jamaican (647)	688	1.90
Trinidadian/Tobagonian (57)	57	0.16
U.S. Virgin Islander (36)	36	0.10
West Indian (0)	58	0.16
Yugoslavian (12)	12	0.03

Hispanic Origin	Population	%
Hispanic or Latino (of any race)	14,390	38.30
Central American, ex. Mexican	2,244	5.97
Costa Rican	86	0.23
Guatemalan	624	1.66
Honduran	836	2.23
Nicaraguan	294	0.78
Panamanian	60	0.16
Salvadoran	342	0.91
Other Central American	2	0.01
Cuban	1,593	4.24
Dominican Republic	757	2.01
Mexican	3,360	8.94
Puerto Rican	2,475	6.59
South American	3,241	8.63
Argentinean	246	0.65
Bolivian	68	0.18
Chilean	101	0.27
Colombian	1,707	4.54
Ecuadorian	271	0.72
Paraguayan	13	0.03
Peruvian	435	1.16
Uruguayan	130	0.35
Venezuelan	266	0.71
Other South American	4	0.01
Other Hispanic or Latino	720	1.92

Race*	Population	%
African-American/Black (6,370)	6,853	18.24
Not Hispanic (6,008)	6,338	16.87
Hispanic (362)	515	1.37
American Indian/Alaska Native (253)	399	1.06
Not Hispanic (57)	131	0.35
Hispanic (196)	268	0.71
Apache (0)	2	0.01
Blackfeet (0)	5	0.01
Canadian/French Am. Ind. (0)	1	<0.01
Central American Ind. (9)	20	0.05
Cherokee (6)	27	0.07
Chippewa (1)	3	0.01
Choctaw (1)	2	0.01
Delaware (0)	5	0.01
Iroquois (1)	3	0.01
Mexican American Ind. (90)	95	0.25
Navajo (1)	3	0.01
Potawatomi (4)	4	0.01
Seminole (0)	5	0.01
Sioux (6)	6	0.02
South American Ind. (8)	17	0.05
Spanish American Ind. (1)	1	<0.01
Tlingit-Haida *(Alaska Native)* (1)	4	0.01
Asian (1,137)	1,368	3.64
Not Hispanic (1,104)	1,288	3.43
Hispanic (33)	80	0.21
Bangladeshi (94)	114	0.30
Burmese (12)	12	0.03
Cambodian (1)	1	<0.01
Chinese, ex. Taiwanese (139)	184	0.49
Filipino (189)	221	0.59
Indian (370)	439	1.17
Indonesian (10)	15	0.04
Japanese (7)	26	0.07
Korean (21)	25	0.07
Laotian (1)	1	<0.01
Malaysian (2)	4	0.01
Nepalese (14)	14	0.04
Pakistani (85)	95	0.25
Sri Lankan (4)	4	0.01
Taiwanese (3)	4	0.01
Thai (24)	31	0.08
Vietnamese (100)	110	0.29
Hawaii Native/Pacific Islander (34)	120	0.32
Not Hispanic (25)	92	0.24
Hispanic (9)	28	0.07
Guamanian/Chamorro (5)	11	0.03
Native Hawaiian (6)	13	0.03
Samoan (2)	7	0.02
White (25,166)	26,104	69.48
Not Hispanic (15,347)	15,707	41.80
Hispanic (9,819)	10,397	27.67

Groveland

Place Type: City
County: Lake
Population: 8,729†

Ancestry‡	Population	%
African, Sub-Saharan (162)	197	2.48
African (162)	186	2.34
Liberian (0)	11	0.14
American (321)	321	4.05
Brazilian (0)	51	0.64
British (99)	125	1.58
Canadian (17)	36	0.45
Danish (0)	7	0.09
Dutch (80)	136	1.71
English (142)	393	4.95
European (59)	97	1.22
French, ex. Basque (53)	187	2.36
French Canadian (17)	39	0.49
German (629)	1,192	15.02
Greek (0)	10	0.13
Guyanese (113)	125	1.58
Hungarian (0)	13	0.16
Irish (126)	569	7.17
Italian (221)	573	7.22
Lithuanian (57)	57	0.72
Norwegian (13)	96	1.21
Pennsylvania German (8)	8	0.10
Polish (67)	124	1.56
Portuguese (9)	19	0.24
Russian (0)	15	0.19
Scotch-Irish (70)	136	1.71
Scottish (9)	39	0.49
Serbian (20)	20	0.25
Slovak (0)	14	0.18
Swedish (24)	74	0.93
Ukrainian (0)	10	0.13
West Indian, ex. Hispanic (74)	83	1.05
British West Indian (9)	9	0.11
Jamaican (18)	27	0.34
West Indian (47)	47	0.59

Hispanic Origin	Population	%
Hispanic or Latino (of any race)	2,263	25.93
Central American, ex. Mexican	136	1.56
Costa Rican	7	0.08
Guatemalan	14	0.16
Honduran	57	0.65
Nicaraguan	17	0.19
Panamanian	23	0.26
Salvadoran	18	0.21
Cuban	134	1.54
Dominican Republic	98	1.12
Mexican	790	9.05
Puerto Rican	759	8.70
South American	239	2.74
Argentinean	17	0.19
Bolivian	6	0.07
Chilean	3	0.03
Colombian	104	1.19
Ecuadorian	50	0.57
Peruvian	25	0.29
Uruguayan	2	0.02
Venezuelan	25	0.29
Other South American	7	0.08
Other Hispanic or Latino	107	1.23

Race*	Population	%
African-American/Black (1,486)	1,645	18.85
Not Hispanic (1,385)	1,514	17.34
Hispanic (101)	131	1.50
American Indian/Alaska Native (91)	171	1.96
Not Hispanic (69)	135	1.55
Hispanic (22)	36	0.41
Apache (0)	3	0.03
Blackfeet (0)	4	0.05
Cherokee (9)	21	0.24
Chippewa (2)	4	0.05
Choctaw (1)	1	0.01
Creek (2)	2	0.02
Crow (0)	2	0.02
Delaware (0)	1	0.01
Kiowa (1)	1	0.01
Lumbee (2)	2	0.02
Mexican American Ind. (1)	1	0.01
Ottawa (4)	6	0.07
Seminole (1)	2	0.02
Sioux (1)	1	0.01
South American Ind. (2)	3	0.03
Asian (221)	329	3.77
Not Hispanic (211)	303	3.47
Hispanic (10)	26	0.30
Bangladeshi (1)	1	0.01
Burmese (1)	2	0.02
Chinese, ex. Taiwanese (14)	40	0.46
Filipino (43)	62	0.71
Hmong (14)	15	0.17
Indian (121)	141	1.62
Japanese (3)	15	0.17
Korean (8)	16	0.18
Laotian (1)	2	0.02
Thai (3)	3	0.03
Vietnamese (8)	18	0.21
Hawaii Native/Pacific Islander (8)	41	0.47
Not Hispanic (8)	39	0.45
Hispanic (0)	2	0.02
Guamanian/Chamorro (0)	1	0.01
Native Hawaiian (3)	7	0.08
Samoan (3)	3	0.03
White (5,730)	6,004	68.78
Not Hispanic (4,445)	4,606	52.77
Hispanic (1,285)	1,398	16.02

Gulf Gate Estates

Place Type: CDP
County: Sarasota
Population: 10,911†

Ancestry‡	Population	%
African, Sub-Saharan (202)	215	1.97
African (202)	202	1.85
South African (0)	13	0.12
Albanian (0)	12	0.11
American (711)	711	6.52
Arab (0)	7	0.06
Other Arab (0)	7	0.06
Austrian (14)	39	0.36
British (12)	12	0.11
Bulgarian (25)	25	0.23
Canadian (27)	27	0.25
Croatian (22)	36	0.33
Czech (104)	129	1.18
Czechoslovakian (21)	34	0.31
Danish (14)	118	1.08
Dutch (70)	293	2.69
English (460)	1,613	14.80
European (0)	16	0.15
Finnish (13)	13	0.12
French, ex. Basque (46)	503	4.61
French Canadian (94)	131	1.20
German (839)	2,383	21.86
Greek (81)	108	0.99
Hungarian (46)	46	0.42
Irish (450)	1,582	14.51
Israeli (111)	111	1.02
Italian (442)	833	7.64
Latvian (0)	19	0.17
Lithuanian (52)	69	0.63
Norwegian (27)	120	1.10

*Notes: † The Census 2010 population figure is used to calculate the percentages in the Hispanic Origin and Race categories. Ancestry percentages are based on the 2006-2010 American Community Survey population (not shown); ‡ Numbers in parentheses indicate the number of people reporting a single ancestry; * Numbers in parentheses indicate the number of persons reporting this race alone, not in combination with any other race; Please refer to the Explanation of Data for more information.*

Polish (269)	544	4.99
Portuguese (53)	123	1.13
Romanian (24)	36	0.33
Russian (31)	140	1.28
Scotch-Irish (107)	187	1.72
Scottish (46)	233	2.14
Serbian (119)	131	1.20
Slavic (14)	14	0.13
Slovak (0)	45	0.41
Slovene (0)	13	0.12
Swedish (72)	212	1.94
Swiss (0)	15	0.14
Ukrainian (14)	37	0.34
Welsh (13)	83	0.76
West Indian, ex. Hispanic (23)	23	0.21
Haitian (23)	23	0.21
Yugoslavian (0)	5	0.05

Hispanic Origin	Population	%
Hispanic or Latino (of any race)	862	7.90
Central American, ex. Mexican	47	0.43
Costa Rican	8	0.07
Guatemalan	12	0.11
Honduran	8	0.07
Nicaraguan	8	0.07
Panamanian	3	0.03
Salvadoran	8	0.07
Cuban	68	0.62
Dominican Republic	19	0.17
Mexican	337	3.09
Puerto Rican	124	1.14
South American	157	1.44
Argentinean	35	0.32
Bolivian	2	0.02
Chilean	5	0.05
Colombian	45	0.41
Ecuadorian	13	0.12
Peruvian	40	0.37
Uruguayan	1	0.01
Venezuelan	11	0.10
Other South American	5	0.05
Other Hispanic or Latino	110	1.01

Race*	Population	%
African-American/Black (175)	243	2.23
Not Hispanic (158)	219	2.01
Hispanic (17)	24	0.22
American Indian/Alaska Native (30)	76	0.70
Not Hispanic (29)	66	0.60
Hispanic (1)	10	0.09
Blackfeet (0)	6	0.05
Central American Ind. (1)	1	0.01
Cherokee (8)	18	0.16
Choctaw (0)	2	0.02
Creek (0)	1	0.01
Delaware (1)	2	0.02
Iroquois (2)	3	0.03
Seminole (3)	3	0.03
Sioux (2)	2	0.02
South American Ind. (0)	5	0.05
Asian (125)	165	1.51
Not Hispanic (123)	158	1.45
Hispanic (2)	7	0.06
Chinese, ex. Taiwanese (27)	37	0.34
Filipino (19)	32	0.29
Indian (20)	22	0.20
Indonesian (2)	4	0.04
Japanese (11)	17	0.16
Korean (12)	13	0.12
Laotian (1)	1	0.01
Thai (4)	5	0.05
Vietnamese (21)	27	0.25
Hawaii Native/Pacific Islander (2)	11	0.10
Not Hispanic (1)	8	0.07
Hispanic (1)	3	0.03
Guamanian/Chamorro (0)	1	0.01
Native Hawaiian (0)	2	0.02
Samoan (0)	2	0.02
White (10,172)	10,346	94.82
Not Hispanic (9,587)	9,715	89.04
Hispanic (585)	631	5.78

Gulfport

Place Type: City
County: Pinellas
Population: 12,029†

Ancestry‡	Population	%
African, Sub-Saharan (10)	27	0.22
African (10)	27	0.22
American (348)	348	2.86
Arab (8)	57	0.47
Arab (8)	8	0.07
Lebanese (0)	49	0.40
Austrian (5)	19	0.16
Belgian (13)	20	0.16
British (41)	79	0.65
Bulgarian (34)	42	0.35
Cajun (8)	8	0.07
Canadian (55)	55	0.45
Croatian (0)	44	0.36
Czech (91)	98	0.81
Czechoslovakian (0)	11	0.09
Danish (24)	56	0.46
Dutch (38)	188	1.55
Eastern European (14)	14	0.12
English (460)	1,662	13.67
European (107)	156	1.28
Finnish (89)	110	0.90
French, ex. Basque (247)	1,002	8.24
French Canadian (87)	154	1.27
German (698)	2,415	19.86
Greek (52)	104	0.86
Hungarian (43)	193	1.59
Irish (871)	2,102	17.29
Israeli (8)	8	0.07
Italian (523)	1,099	9.04
Lithuanian (31)	49	0.40
Norwegian (0)	68	0.56
Polish (192)	578	4.75
Portuguese (14)	88	0.72
Russian (180)	231	1.90
Scandinavian (0)	21	0.17
Scotch-Irish (68)	227	1.87
Scottish (27)	367	3.02
Serbian (11)	11	0.09
Slavic (8)	37	0.30
Slovak (13)	21	0.17
Slovene (11)	11	0.09
Soviet Union (7)	7	0.06
Swedish (36)	322	2.65
Swiss (52)	202	1.66
Ukrainian (37)	81	0.67
Welsh (23)	106	0.87
West Indian, ex. Hispanic (91)	160	1.32
Bahamian (0)	17	0.14
Haitian (37)	89	0.73
Jamaican (39)	39	0.32
Trinidadian/Tobagonian (15)	15	0.12
Yugoslavian (13)	13	0.11

Hispanic Origin	Population	%
Hispanic or Latino (of any race)	593	4.93
Central American, ex. Mexican	20	0.17
Costa Rican	3	0.02
Honduran	1	0.01
Panamanian	12	0.10
Salvadoran	3	0.02
Other Central American	1	0.01
Cuban	91	0.76
Dominican Republic	9	0.07
Mexican	93	0.77
Puerto Rican	235	1.95
South American	77	0.64
Argentinean	13	0.11
Chilean	2	0.02
Colombian	38	0.32
Ecuadorian	3	0.02
Peruvian	11	0.09
Uruguayan	4	0.03
Venezuelan	6	0.05
Other Hispanic or Latino	68	0.57

Race*	Population	%
African-American/Black (1,106)	1,214	10.09
Not Hispanic (1,086)	1,179	9.80
Hispanic (20)	35	0.29
American Indian/Alaska Native (51)	118	0.98
Not Hispanic (46)	107	0.89
Hispanic (5)	11	0.09
Apache (1)	3	0.02
Blackfeet (0)	2	0.02
Cherokee (7)	14	0.12
Cheyenne (1)	1	0.01
Chickasaw (1)	1	0.01
Choctaw (3)	3	0.02
Comanche (1)	1	0.01
Creek (0)	1	0.01
Delaware (1)	1	0.01
Inupiat *(Alaska Native)* (1)	1	0.01
Iroquois (3)	4	0.03
Kiowa (1)	1	0.01
Lumbee (3)	3	0.02
Mexican American Ind. (0)	4	0.03
Navajo (1)	3	0.02
Sioux (1)	4	0.03
South American Ind. (2)	2	0.02
Spanish American Ind. (0)	1	0.01
Asian (148)	197	1.64
Not Hispanic (146)	191	1.59
Hispanic (2)	6	0.05
Cambodian (1)	3	0.02
Chinese, ex. Taiwanese (22)	31	0.26
Filipino (36)	47	0.39
Indian (46)	49	0.41
Indonesian (1)	2	0.02
Japanese (5)	16	0.13
Korean (4)	10	0.08
Laotian (5)	8	0.07
Pakistani (1)	1	0.01
Sri Lankan (1)	1	0.01
Thai (6)	8	0.07
Vietnamese (12)	14	0.12
Hawaii Native/Pacific Islander (13)	29	0.24
Not Hispanic (12)	26	0.22
Hispanic (1)	3	0.02
Fijian (2)	2	0.02
Guamanian/Chamorro (2)	5	0.04
Native Hawaiian (1)	6	0.05
Samoan (0)	3	0.02
Tongan (4)	4	0.03
White (10,356)	10,566	87.84
Not Hispanic (9,929)	10,104	84.00
Hispanic (427)	462	3.84

Haines City

Place Type: City
County: Polk
Population: 20,535†

Ancestry‡	Population	%
African, Sub-Saharan (109)	146	0.74
African (109)	146	0.74
American (2,348)	2,348	11.86
Arab (90)	162	0.82
Egyptian (0)	59	0.30
Moroccan (24)	24	0.12
Syrian (6)	19	0.10
Other Arab (60)	60	0.30
Brazilian (27)	27	0.14
British (7)	17	0.09
Czech (8)	46	0.23
Czechoslovakian (0)	11	0.06
Dutch (23)	116	0.59
English (550)	909	4.59
European (30)	30	0.15
Finnish (20)	20	0.10
French, ex. Basque (139)	398	2.01

*Notes: † The Census 2010 population figure is used to calculate the percentages in the Hispanic Origin and Race categories. Ancestry percentages are based on the 2006-2010 American Community Survey population (not shown); ‡ Numbers in parentheses indicate the number of people reporting a single ancestry; * Numbers in parentheses indicate the number of persons reporting this race alone, not in combination with any other race; Please refer to the Explanation of Data for more information.*

French Canadian (26)	75	0.38
German (497)	1,233	6.23
Greek (0)	8	0.04
Guyanese (23)	110	0.56
Hungarian (17)	90	0.45
Irish (249)	765	3.86
Italian (146)	323	1.63
Northern European (14)	14	0.07
Norwegian (0)	37	0.19
Polish (112)	197	1.00
Portuguese (37)	49	0.25
Romanian (0)	13	0.07
Scotch-Irish (53)	167	0.84
Scottish (26)	109	0.55
Swedish (82)	159	0.80
Welsh (14)	26	0.13
West Indian, ex. Hispanic (1,067)	1,146	5.79
Bahamian (58)	91	0.46
Haitian (650)	650	3.28
Jamaican (359)	405	2.05

Hispanic Origin	Population	%
Hispanic or Latino (of any race)	7,980	38.86
Central American, ex. Mexican	338	1.65
Costa Rican	23	0.11
Guatemalan	43	0.21
Honduran	85	0.41
Nicaraguan	121	0.59
Panamanian	11	0.05
Salvadoran	54	0.26
Other Central American	1	<0.01
Cuban	119	0.58
Dominican Republic	174	0.85
Mexican	4,817	23.46
Puerto Rican	1,951	9.50
South American	292	1.42
Argentinean	19	0.09
Bolivian	6	0.03
Chilean	2	0.01
Colombian	115	0.56
Ecuadorian	56	0.27
Peruvian	39	0.19
Uruguayan	12	0.06
Venezuelan	43	0.21
Other Hispanic or Latino	289	1.41

Race*	Population	%
African-American/Black (5,644)	5,861	28.54
Not Hispanic (5,425)	5,574	27.14
Hispanic (219)	287	1.40
American Indian/Alaska Native (108)	173	0.84
Not Hispanic (36)	80	0.39
Hispanic (72)	93	0.45
Blackfeet (0)	9	0.04
Central American Ind. (1)	2	0.01
Cherokee (10)	23	0.11
Chippewa (1)	5	0.02
Choctaw (2)	6	0.03
Creek (3)	4	0.02
Iroquois (2)	2	0.01
Mexican American Ind. (13)	17	0.08
Paiute (0)	1	<0.01
Potawatomi (1)	1	<0.01
Seminole (1)	1	<0.01
South American Ind. (7)	9	0.04
Spanish American Ind. (3)	4	0.02
Asian (293)	366	1.78
Not Hispanic (280)	336	1.64
Hispanic (13)	30	0.15
Bangladeshi (4)	4	0.02
Burmese (0)	1	<0.01
Cambodian (1)	3	0.01
Chinese, ex. Taiwanese (58)	68	0.33
Filipino (81)	102	0.50
Indian (84)	112	0.55
Indonesian (1)	1	<0.01
Japanese (6)	17	0.08
Korean (6)	6	0.03
Laotian (2)	4	0.02
Pakistani (3)	3	0.01
Vietnamese (37)	38	0.19
Hawaii Native/Pacific Islander (4)	59	0.29
Not Hispanic (4)	40	0.19
Hispanic (0)	19	0.09
Guamanian/Chamorro (3)	11	0.05
Native Hawaiian (0)	11	0.05
Samoan (0)	5	0.02
White (10,969)	11,411	55.57
Not Hispanic (6,540)	6,705	32.65
Hispanic (4,429)	4,706	22.92

Hallandale Beach

Place Type: City
County: Broward
Population: 37,113†

Ancestry‡	Population	%
African, Sub-Saharan (328)	394	1.07
African (291)	357	0.97
Ghanaian (17)	17	0.05
Sudanese (20)	20	0.05
Albanian (13)	13	0.04
American (1,501)	1,501	4.08
Arab (246)	400	1.09
Arab (20)	29	0.08
Egyptian (74)	74	0.20
Lebanese (0)	133	0.36
Palestinian (29)	41	0.11
Syrian (39)	39	0.11
Other Arab (84)	84	0.23
Armenian (30)	30	0.08
Australian (0)	45	0.12
Austrian (69)	100	0.27
Basque (0)	26	0.07
Belgian (0)	19	0.05
Brazilian (25)	25	0.07
British (86)	113	0.31
Bulgarian (54)	54	0.15
Canadian (298)	304	0.83
Czech (22)	49	0.13
Czechoslovakian (13)	25	0.07
Dutch (26)	26	0.07
Eastern European (44)	44	0.12
English (458)	1,077	2.93
Estonian (26)	26	0.07
European (59)	95	0.26
Finnish (0)	26	0.07
French, ex. Basque (142)	446	1.21
French Canadian (442)	454	1.24
German (654)	1,674	4.55
Greek (213)	333	0.91
Guyanese (7)	18	0.05
Hungarian (354)	505	1.37
Iranian (41)	41	0.11
Irish (578)	1,307	3.56
Israeli (177)	177	0.48
Italian (2,200)	3,323	9.04
Latvian (19)	19	0.05
Lithuanian (57)	73	0.20
Macedonian (12)	12	0.03
Norwegian (81)	161	0.44
Polish (865)	1,229	3.34
Portuguese (129)	202	0.55
Romanian (746)	797	2.17
Russian (1,437)	1,827	4.97
Scandinavian (27)	46	0.13
Scotch-Irish (13)	112	0.30
Scottish (86)	247	0.67
Serbian (27)	27	0.07
Slavic (0)	40	0.11
Slovak (13)	40	0.11
Slovene (13)	13	0.04
Soviet Union (0)	16	0.04
Swedish (0)	114	0.31
Swiss (26)	68	0.19
Turkish (19)	36	0.10
Ukrainian (292)	367	1.00
Welsh (57)	76	0.21
West Indian, ex. Hispanic (1,778)	2,278	6.20
Bahamian (125)	125	0.34
British West Indian (35)	71	0.19
Haitian (853)	1,069	2.91
Jamaican (678)	862	2.35
Trinidadian/Tobagonian (48)	98	0.27
West Indian (39)	53	0.14

Hispanic Origin	Population	%
Hispanic or Latino (of any race)	11,809	31.82
Central American, ex. Mexican	1,171	3.16
Costa Rican	112	0.30
Guatemalan	122	0.33
Honduran	460	1.24
Nicaraguan	265	0.71
Panamanian	86	0.23
Salvadoran	120	0.32
Other Central American	6	0.02
Cuban	2,251	6.07
Dominican Republic	583	1.57
Mexican	603	1.62
Puerto Rican	1,416	3.82
South American	4,912	13.24
Argentinean	724	1.95
Bolivian	43	0.12
Chilean	140	0.38
Colombian	1,874	5.05
Ecuadorian	346	0.93
Paraguayan	10	0.03
Peruvian	1,053	2.84
Uruguayan	213	0.57
Venezuelan	500	1.35
Other South American	9	0.02
Other Hispanic or Latino	873	2.35

Race*	Population	%
African-American/Black (6,948)	7,308	19.69
Not Hispanic (6,548)	6,756	18.20
Hispanic (400)	552	1.49
American Indian/Alaska Native (78)	194	0.52
Not Hispanic (37)	97	0.26
Hispanic (41)	97	0.26
Apache (0)	1	<0.01
Blackfeet (0)	2	0.01
Canadian/French Am. Ind. (3)	5	0.01
Central American Ind. (3)	6	0.02
Cherokee (4)	17	0.05
Chickasaw (0)	2	0.01
Chippewa (1)	3	0.01
Choctaw (0)	3	0.01
Creek (1)	1	<0.01
Delaware (3)	5	0.01
Hopi (1)	1	<0.01
Inupiat *(Alaska Native)* (1)	1	<0.01
Mexican American Ind. (7)	13	0.04
Navajo (2)	2	0.01
Osage (0)	1	<0.01
Potawatomi (1)	2	0.01
Pueblo (0)	1	<0.01
Seminole (1)	1	<0.01
South American Ind. (4)	20	0.05
Spanish American Ind. (2)	4	0.01
Yaqui (3)	3	0.01
Asian (532)	732	1.97
Not Hispanic (520)	680	1.83
Hispanic (12)	52	0.14
Bangladeshi (17)	25	0.07
Cambodian (5)	6	0.02
Chinese, ex. Taiwanese (96)	119	0.32
Filipino (66)	99	0.27
Hmong (0)	1	<0.01
Indian (182)	245	0.66
Indonesian (15)	19	0.05
Japanese (31)	48	0.13
Korean (15)	22	0.06
Laotian (1)	3	0.01
Pakistani (24)	29	0.08
Sri Lankan (1)	1	<0.01
Taiwanese (2)	2	0.01
Thai (28)	35	0.09
Vietnamese (9)	23	0.06

*Notes: † The Census 2010 population figure is used to calculate the percentages in the Hispanic Origin and Race categories. Ancestry percentages are based on the 2006-2010 American Community Survey population (not shown); ‡ Numbers in parentheses indicate the number of people reporting a single ancestry; * Numbers in parentheses indicate the number of persons reporting this race alone, not in combination with any other race; Please refer to the Explanation of Data for more information.*

Race*	Population	%
Hawaii Native/Pacific Islander (12)	61	0.16
Not Hispanic (9)	44	0.12
Hispanic (3)	17	0.05
Fijian (0)	1	<0.01
Guamanian/Chamorro (0)	1	<0.01
Native Hawaiian (4)	10	0.03
Samoan (6)	9	0.02
Tongan (0)	1	<0.01
White (27,343)	28,096	75.70
Not Hispanic (17,695)	17,979	48.44
Hispanic (9,648)	10,117	27.26

Hernando

Place Type: CDP
County: Citrus
Population: 9,054†

Ancestry‡	Population	%
American (2,626)	2,626	29.17
Arab (0)	12	0.13
Lebanese (0)	12	0.13
Armenian (0)	6	0.07
Austrian (14)	14	0.16
British (12)	26	0.29
Croatian (16)	16	0.18
Czechoslovakian (13)	13	0.14
Danish (0)	36	0.40
Dutch (55)	156	1.73
English (569)	1,272	14.13
European (36)	47	0.52
Finnish (0)	47	0.52
French, ex. Basque (124)	495	5.50
French Canadian (17)	31	0.34
German (533)	1,452	16.13
Hungarian (35)	35	0.39
Icelander (0)	15	0.17
Irish (388)	1,233	13.70
Italian (104)	430	4.78
Lithuanian (0)	12	0.13
Norwegian (53)	102	1.13
Pennsylvania German (24)	24	0.27
Polish (176)	410	4.56
Portuguese (10)	22	0.24
Romanian (24)	33	0.37
Russian (0)	15	0.17
Scotch-Irish (85)	222	2.47
Scottish (46)	157	1.74
Slovak (46)	46	0.51
Swedish (0)	120	1.33
Ukrainian (61)	74	0.82
Welsh (0)	54	0.60

Hispanic Origin	Population	%
Hispanic or Latino (of any race)	313	3.46
Central American, ex. Mexican	22	0.24
Guatemalan	1	0.01
Honduran	15	0.17
Nicaraguan	1	0.01
Panamanian	5	0.06
Cuban	44	0.49
Dominican Republic	4	0.04
Mexican	69	0.76
Puerto Rican	119	1.31
South American	19	0.21
Argentinean	1	0.01
Chilean	1	0.01
Colombian	16	0.18
Uruguayan	1	0.01
Other Hispanic or Latino	36	0.40

Race*	Population	%
African-American/Black (203)	243	2.68
Not Hispanic (185)	218	2.41
Hispanic (18)	25	0.28
American Indian/Alaska Native (39)	92	1.02
Not Hispanic (31)	83	0.92
Hispanic (8)	9	0.10
Blackfeet (0)	2	0.02
Canadian/French Am. Ind. (1)	1	0.01
Cherokee (6)	29	0.32
Chippewa (2)	4	0.04
Choctaw (0)	2	0.02
Cree (1)	1	0.01
Iroquois (3)	7	0.08
Lumbee (2)	2	0.02
Ottawa (1)	1	0.01
Potawatomi (0)	1	0.01
Asian (47)	64	0.71
Not Hispanic (46)	63	0.70
Hispanic (1)	1	0.01
Chinese, ex. Taiwanese (4)	5	0.06
Filipino (27)	30	0.33
Indian (2)	6	0.07
Japanese (3)	6	0.07
Korean (4)	8	0.09
Thai (2)	2	0.02
Vietnamese (4)	5	0.06
Hawaii Native/Pacific Islander (2)	5	0.06
Not Hispanic (2)	5	0.06
Native Hawaiian (1)	2	0.02
White (8,583)	8,704	96.13
Not Hispanic (8,371)	8,472	93.57
Hispanic (212)	232	2.56

Hialeah Gardens

Place Type: City
County: Miami-Dade
Population: 21,744†

Ancestry‡	Population	%
American (185)	185	0.87
Canadian (0)	10	0.05
English (0)	54	0.25
European (23)	65	0.31
French, ex. Basque (0)	29	0.14
German (0)	12	0.06
Irish (2)	88	0.41
Italian (35)	65	0.31
Portuguese (49)	49	0.23
West Indian, ex. Hispanic (37)	37	0.17
Haitian (21)	21	0.10
West Indian (16)	16	0.08

Hispanic Origin	Population	%
Hispanic or Latino (of any race)	20,630	94.88
Central American, ex. Mexican	2,048	9.42
Costa Rican	44	0.20
Guatemalan	119	0.55
Honduran	402	1.85
Nicaraguan	1,321	6.08
Panamanian	52	0.24
Salvadoran	110	0.51
Cuban	14,314	65.83
Dominican Republic	724	3.33
Mexican	158	0.73
Puerto Rican	633	2.91
South American	2,070	9.52
Argentinean	112	0.52
Bolivian	19	0.09
Chilean	59	0.27
Colombian	1,142	5.25
Ecuadorian	207	0.95
Peruvian	258	1.19
Uruguayan	37	0.17
Venezuelan	235	1.08
Other South American	1	<0.01
Other Hispanic or Latino	683	3.14

Race*	Population	%
African-American/Black (489)	570	2.62
Not Hispanic (69)	70	0.32
Hispanic (420)	500	2.30
American Indian/Alaska Native (18)	29	0.13
Not Hispanic (3)	3	0.01
Hispanic (15)	26	0.12
Central American Ind. (4)	4	0.02
Cherokee (1)	2	0.01
Navajo (1)	1	<0.01
Seminole (1)	1	<0.01
Sioux (1)	1	<0.01
Spanish American Ind. (0)	1	<0.01
Asian (146)	167	0.77
Not Hispanic (134)	141	0.65
Hispanic (12)	26	0.12
Bangladeshi (1)	5	0.02
Chinese, ex. Taiwanese (81)	90	0.41
Filipino (5)	10	0.05
Indian (24)	33	0.15
Japanese (0)	2	0.01
Korean (0)	2	0.01
Pakistani (9)	14	0.06
Vietnamese (17)	20	0.09
Hawaii Native/Pacific Islander (1)	3	0.01
Hispanic (1)	3	0.01
White (20,195)	20,451	94.05
Not Hispanic (883)	899	4.13
Hispanic (19,312)	19,552	89.92

Hialeah

Place Type: City
County: Miami-Dade
Population: 224,669†

Ancestry‡	Population	%
African, Sub-Saharan (224)	1,014	0.45
African (184)	974	0.43
Nigerian (40)	40	0.02
Albanian (0)	11	<0.01
American (2,297)	2,297	1.02
Arab (176)	418	0.19
Arab (0)	132	0.06
Lebanese (144)	226	0.10
Palestinian (23)	51	0.02
Other Arab (9)	9	<0.01
Assyrian/Chaldean/Syriac (0)	10	<0.01
Austrian (11)	32	0.01
Basque (10)	10	<0.01
Belgian (31)	31	0.01
Brazilian (190)	266	0.12
British (21)	96	0.04
Bulgarian (15)	15	0.01
Czech (0)	31	0.01
Danish (0)	30	0.01
Dutch (31)	62	0.03
Eastern European (8)	8	<0.01
English (253)	551	0.25
European (9)	71	0.03
French, ex. Basque (115)	555	0.25
French Canadian (0)	12	0.01
German (456)	1,208	0.54
Greek (12)	25	0.01
Hungarian (14)	105	0.05
Iranian (0)	46	0.02
Irish (290)	621	0.28
Italian (611)	1,498	0.67
Latvian (17)	45	0.02
Norwegian (25)	58	0.03
Polish (46)	186	0.08
Portuguese (118)	145	0.06
Romanian (16)	24	0.01
Russian (44)	73	0.03
Scotch-Irish (52)	196	0.09
Scottish (25)	97	0.04
Swedish (31)	49	0.02
Swiss (0)	38	0.02
Turkish (21)	21	0.01
West Indian, ex. Hispanic (338)	375	0.17
Bahamian (47)	47	0.02
Belizean (0)	37	0.02
British West Indian (18)	18	0.01
Haitian (25)	25	0.01
Jamaican (70)	70	0.03
Trinidadian/Tobagonian (167)	167	0.07
U.S. Virgin Islander (11)	11	<0.01

Hispanic Origin	Population	%
Hispanic or Latino (of any race)	212,805	94.72

*Notes: † The Census 2010 population figure is used to calculate the percentages in the Hispanic Origin and Race categories. Ancestry percentages are based on the 2006-2010 American Community Survey population (not shown); ‡ Numbers in parentheses indicate the number of people reporting a single ancestry; * Numbers in parentheses indicate the number of persons reporting this race alone, not in combination with any other race; Please refer to the Explanation of Data for more information.*

Central American, ex. Mexican	17,305	7.70
Costa Rican	476	0.21
Guatemalan	1,120	0.50
Honduran	3,744	1.67
Nicaraguan	10,410	4.63
Panamanian	391	0.17
Salvadoran	1,151	0.51
Other Central American	13	0.01
Cuban	164,717	73.32
Dominican Republic	4,206	1.87
Mexican	1,825	0.81
Puerto Rican	5,027	2.24
South American	13,835	6.16
Argentinean	1,087	0.48
Bolivian	96	0.04
Chilean	602	0.27
Colombian	6,800	3.03
Ecuadorian	1,606	0.71
Paraguayan	24	0.01
Peruvian	1,920	0.85
Uruguayan	291	0.13
Venezuelan	1,405	0.63
Other South American	4	<0.01
Other Hispanic or Latino	5,890	2.62

Race*	Population	%
African-American/Black (6,051)	6,750	3.00
Not Hispanic (1,209)	1,271	0.57
Hispanic (4,842)	5,479	2.44
American Indian/Alaska Native (251)	415	0.18
Not Hispanic (73)	114	0.05
Hispanic (178)	301	0.13
Alaska Athabascan *(Ala. Nat.)* (2)	3	<0.01
Central American Ind. (13)	24	0.01
Cherokee (10)	31	0.01
Chickasaw (3)	3	<0.01
Chippewa (2)	2	<0.01
Choctaw (3)	3	<0.01
Cree (1)	1	<0.01
Inupiat *(Alaska Native)* (2)	2	<0.01
Iroquois (2)	2	<0.01
Mexican American Ind. (14)	23	0.01
Osage (1)	1	<0.01
Seminole (3)	4	<0.01
Sioux (2)	4	<0.01
South American Ind. (28)	48	0.02
Spanish American Ind. (29)	35	0.02
Asian (791)	1,108	0.49
Not Hispanic (697)	837	0.37
Hispanic (94)	271	0.12
Bangladeshi (11)	12	0.01
Chinese, ex. Taiwanese (345)	449	0.20
Filipino (100)	132	0.06
Indian (130)	192	0.09
Indonesian (0)	3	<0.01
Japanese (17)	42	0.02
Korean (8)	24	0.01
Laotian (3)	3	<0.01
Pakistani (93)	138	0.06
Taiwanese (3)	3	<0.01
Thai (3)	7	<0.01
Vietnamese (38)	43	0.02
Hawaii Native/Pacific Islander (10)	128	0.06
Not Hispanic (2)	24	0.01
Hispanic (8)	104	0.05
Guamanian/Chamorro (1)	2	<0.01
Native Hawaiian (1)	8	<0.01
Samoan (1)	7	<0.01
White (208,050)	211,188	94.00
Not Hispanic (9,511)	9,703	4.32
Hispanic (198,539)	201,485	89.68

Highland City

Place Type: CDP
County: Polk
Population: 10,834†

Ancestry‡	Population	%
American (905)	905	8.87
Arab (12)	12	0.12
Lebanese (12)	12	0.12
Armenian (84)	84	0.82
Austrian (0)	58	0.57
British (12)	12	0.12
Canadian (49)	49	0.48
Celtic (12)	12	0.12
Czech (0)	10	0.10
Czechoslovakian (0)	33	0.32
Danish (0)	18	0.18
Dutch (44)	247	2.42
English (461)	1,269	12.43
European (65)	75	0.73
French, ex. Basque (100)	344	3.37
French Canadian (0)	17	0.17
German (628)	1,716	16.81
Greek (58)	146	1.43
Hungarian (0)	39	0.38
Irish (199)	1,206	11.81
Italian (198)	500	4.90
Lithuanian (0)	15	0.15
Norwegian (30)	150	1.47
Polish (123)	237	2.32
Portuguese (0)	9	0.09
Romanian (0)	13	0.13
Scotch-Irish (188)	300	2.94
Scottish (49)	128	1.25
Serbian (0)	17	0.17
Slovak (12)	46	0.45
Swedish (39)	95	0.93
Swiss (54)	54	0.53
Ukrainian (12)	12	0.12
Welsh (28)	64	0.63
West Indian, ex. Hispanic (83)	83	0.81
Haitian (83)	83	0.81

Hispanic Origin	Population	%
Hispanic or Latino (of any race)	1,377	12.71
Central American, ex. Mexican	59	0.54
Costa Rican	2	0.02
Guatemalan	8	0.07
Honduran	24	0.22
Nicaraguan	8	0.07
Panamanian	7	0.06
Salvadoran	10	0.09
Cuban	253	2.34
Dominican Republic	47	0.43
Mexican	281	2.59
Puerto Rican	533	4.92
South American	148	1.37
Argentinean	8	0.07
Bolivian	1	0.01
Chilean	3	0.03
Colombian	65	0.60
Ecuadorian	30	0.28
Peruvian	17	0.16
Uruguayan	2	0.02
Venezuelan	20	0.18
Other South American	2	0.02
Other Hispanic or Latino	56	0.52

Race*	Population	%
African-American/Black (1,024)	1,097	10.13
Not Hispanic (973)	1,027	9.48
Hispanic (51)	70	0.65
American Indian/Alaska Native (46)	90	0.83
Not Hispanic (26)	66	0.61
Hispanic (20)	24	0.22
Blackfeet (2)	2	0.02
Central American Ind. (3)	3	0.03
Cherokee (8)	24	0.22
Chippewa (1)	1	0.01
Choctaw (2)	2	0.02
Comanche (0)	1	0.01
Iroquois (1)	1	0.01
Kiowa (0)	1	0.01
Lumbee (5)	5	0.05
Potawatomi (2)	2	0.02
Pueblo (1)	1	0.01
Seminole (0)	1	0.01
Sioux (1)	2	0.02
South American Ind. (7)	10	0.09
Asian (457)	525	4.85
Not Hispanic (457)	513	4.74
Hispanic (0)	12	0.11
Cambodian (3)	4	0.04
Chinese, ex. Taiwanese (45)	57	0.53
Filipino (49)	61	0.56
Indian (270)	293	2.70
Indonesian (7)	9	0.08
Japanese (5)	9	0.08
Korean (10)	17	0.16
Laotian (11)	16	0.15
Pakistani (1)	2	0.02
Sri Lankan (2)	2	0.02
Taiwanese (1)	3	0.03
Thai (1)	3	0.03
Vietnamese (31)	36	0.33
Hawaii Native/Pacific Islander (4)	17	0.16
Not Hispanic (4)	16	0.15
Hispanic (0)	1	0.01
Guamanian/Chamorro (1)	3	0.03
Native Hawaiian (2)	7	0.06
Tongan (1)	1	0.01
White (8,778)	8,966	82.76
Not Hispanic (7,828)	7,946	73.34
Hispanic (950)	1,020	9.41

Hobe Sound

Place Type: CDP
County: Martin
Population: 11,521†

Ancestry‡	Population	%
African, Sub-Saharan (46)	61	0.52
African (46)	46	0.39
Cape Verdean (0)	15	0.13
American (379)	379	3.21
Arab (7)	7	0.06
Lebanese (7)	7	0.06
Armenian (15)	31	0.26
Austrian (0)	32	0.27
Belgian (8)	16	0.14
British (52)	76	0.64
Canadian (57)	84	0.71
Czech (0)	32	0.27
Czechoslovakian (0)	10	0.08
Danish (37)	81	0.69
Dutch (53)	235	1.99
Eastern European (20)	20	0.17
English (616)	1,801	15.25
European (60)	76	0.64
Finnish (42)	55	0.47
French, ex. Basque (117)	610	5.16
French Canadian (62)	94	0.80
German (1,079)	2,911	24.64
Greek (44)	101	0.85
Hungarian (0)	32	0.27
Iranian (0)	9	0.08
Irish (772)	2,085	17.65
Italian (764)	1,516	12.83
Latvian (6)	6	0.05
Lithuanian (31)	219	1.85
Norwegian (92)	156	1.32
Polish (160)	584	4.94
Portuguese (19)	52	0.44
Romanian (10)	33	0.28
Russian (66)	170	1.44
Scandinavian (8)	16	0.14
Scotch-Irish (125)	495	4.19
Scottish (138)	365	3.09
Slovak (0)	23	0.19
Swedish (22)	83	0.70
Swiss (37)	37	0.31
Ukrainian (15)	15	0.13
Welsh (35)	48	0.41
West Indian, ex. Hispanic (28)	28	0.24
Jamaican (28)	28	0.24

*Notes: † The Census 2010 population figure is used to calculate the percentages in the Hispanic Origin and Race categories. Ancestry percentages are based on the 2006-2010 American Community Survey population (not shown); ‡ Numbers in parentheses indicate the number of people reporting a single ancestry; * Numbers in parentheses indicate the number of persons reporting this race alone, not in combination with any other race; Please refer to the Explanation of Data for more information.*

Hispanic Origin	Population	%
Hispanic or Latino (of any race)	603	5.23
Central American, ex. Mexican	63	0.55
Costa Rican	6	0.05
Guatemalan	24	0.21
Honduran	20	0.17
Salvadoran	13	0.11
Cuban	61	0.53
Dominican Republic	11	0.10
Mexican	235	2.04
Puerto Rican	90	0.78
South American	78	0.68
Argentinean	7	0.06
Chilean	15	0.13
Colombian	22	0.19
Ecuadorian	10	0.09
Paraguayan	7	0.06
Peruvian	14	0.12
Venezuelan	3	0.03
Other Hispanic or Latino	65	0.56

Race*	Population	%
African-American/Black (806)	857	7.44
Not Hispanic (796)	842	7.31
Hispanic (10)	15	0.13
American Indian/Alaska Native (31)	82	0.71
Not Hispanic (28)	75	0.65
Hispanic (3)	7	0.06
Apache (4)	5	0.04
Blackfeet (0)	1	0.01
Cherokee (6)	19	0.16
Chickasaw (3)	3	0.03
Chippewa (0)	6	0.05
Creek (1)	4	0.03
Iroquois (4)	5	0.04
Lumbee (1)	1	0.01
Mexican American Ind. (0)	1	0.01
Potawatomi (0)	1	0.01
Sioux (0)	1	0.01
Asian (92)	119	1.03
Not Hispanic (89)	116	1.01
Hispanic (3)	3	0.03
Bangladeshi (3)	3	0.03
Burmese (1)	1	0.01
Chinese, ex. Taiwanese (29)	32	0.28
Filipino (22)	28	0.24
Indian (17)	26	0.23
Japanese (4)	5	0.04
Korean (7)	11	0.10
Taiwanese (4)	4	0.03
Thai (2)	2	0.02
Vietnamese (2)	2	0.02
Hawaii Native/Pacific Islander (7)	17	0.15
Not Hispanic (6)	16	0.14
Hispanic (1)	1	0.01
Guamanian/Chamorro (5)	5	0.04
Native Hawaiian (1)	2	0.02
White (10,290)	10,409	90.35
Not Hispanic (9,871)	9,972	86.55
Hispanic (419)	437	3.79

Holiday

Place Type: CDP
County: Pasco
Population: 22,403†

Ancestry‡	Population	%
Albanian (67)	67	0.30
American (1,449)	1,449	6.50
Arab (12)	12	0.05
Egyptian (12)	12	0.05
Armenian (33)	52	0.23
Australian (87)	87	0.39
Austrian (32)	79	0.35
Brazilian (24)	24	0.11
British (83)	154	0.69
Canadian (77)	111	0.50
Croatian (0)	40	0.18
Czech (16)	144	0.65
Czechoslovakian (8)	8	0.04
Danish (34)	63	0.28
Dutch (120)	457	2.05
English (1,045)	2,853	12.79
European (105)	105	0.47
French, ex. Basque (236)	1,282	5.75
French Canadian (155)	181	0.81
German (1,602)	4,433	19.88
Greek (690)	728	3.26
Hungarian (110)	228	1.02
Irish (891)	3,685	16.52
Israeli (0)	16	0.07
Italian (1,408)	2,745	12.31
Lithuanian (16)	120	0.54
Norwegian (129)	313	1.40
Pennsylvania German (19)	53	0.24
Polish (530)	1,180	5.29
Portuguese (8)	61	0.27
Russian (34)	310	1.39
Scotch-Irish (77)	469	2.10
Scottish (134)	497	2.23
Serbian (0)	9	0.04
Slovak (58)	161	0.72
Slovene (0)	47	0.21
Swedish (44)	269	1.21
Swiss (0)	121	0.54
Ukrainian (14)	115	0.52
Welsh (26)	154	0.69
West Indian, ex. Hispanic (97)	97	0.43
Jamaican (97)	97	0.43

Hispanic Origin	Population	%
Hispanic or Latino (of any race)	2,241	10.00
Central American, ex. Mexican	146	0.65
Costa Rican	12	0.05
Guatemalan	25	0.11
Honduran	50	0.22
Nicaraguan	12	0.05
Panamanian	9	0.04
Salvadoran	38	0.17
Cuban	158	0.71
Dominican Republic	83	0.37
Mexican	410	1.83
Puerto Rican	1,048	4.68
South American	238	1.06
Argentinean	12	0.05
Bolivian	5	0.02
Chilean	1	<0.01
Colombian	95	0.42
Ecuadorian	50	0.22
Paraguayan	1	<0.01
Peruvian	44	0.20
Uruguayan	11	0.05
Venezuelan	18	0.08
Other South American	1	<0.01
Other Hispanic or Latino	158	0.71

Race*	Population	%
African-American/Black (921)	1,154	5.15
Not Hispanic (824)	1,023	4.57
Hispanic (97)	131	0.58
American Indian/Alaska Native (114)	243	1.08
Not Hispanic (89)	207	0.92
Hispanic (25)	36	0.16
Apache (0)	1	<0.01
Blackfeet (6)	9	0.04
Central American Ind. (0)	4	0.02
Cherokee (18)	50	0.22
Chippewa (6)	15	0.07
Choctaw (3)	3	0.01
Creek (0)	1	<0.01
Crow (0)	1	<0.01
Inupiat *(Alaska Native)* (2)	2	0.01
Iroquois (1)	5	0.02
Lumbee (0)	1	<0.01
Mexican American Ind. (1)	1	<0.01
Navajo (0)	1	<0.01
Ottawa (0)	1	<0.01
Potawatomi (0)	3	0.01
Pueblo (1)	1	<0.01
Seminole (1)	2	0.01
Shoshone (0)	1	<0.01
Sioux (4)	4	0.02
South American Ind. (2)	2	0.01
Asian (310)	417	1.86
Not Hispanic (304)	396	1.77
Hispanic (6)	21	0.09
Bangladeshi (8)	11	0.05
Cambodian (15)	15	0.07
Chinese, ex. Taiwanese (27)	42	0.19
Filipino (57)	83	0.37
Hmong (1)	5	0.02
Indian (36)	43	0.19
Indonesian (1)	2	0.01
Japanese (8)	21	0.09
Korean (10)	27	0.12
Laotian (12)	14	0.06
Malaysian (1)	3	0.01
Pakistani (2)	5	0.02
Taiwanese (1)	1	<0.01
Thai (12)	16	0.07
Vietnamese (111)	119	0.53
Hawaii Native/Pacific Islander (5)	35	0.16
Not Hispanic (4)	27	0.12
Hispanic (1)	8	0.04
Native Hawaiian (2)	14	0.06
Samoan (0)	7	0.03
White (20,042)	20,517	91.58
Not Hispanic (18,523)	18,887	84.31
Hispanic (1,519)	1,630	7.28

Holly Hill

Place Type: City
County: Volusia
Population: 11,659†

Ancestry‡	Population	%
African, Sub-Saharan (85)	108	0.90
Cape Verdean (85)	108	0.90
American (1,939)	1,939	16.16
Arab (10)	10	0.08
Lebanese (10)	10	0.08
Austrian (22)	47	0.39
Belgian (59)	59	0.49
Brazilian (0)	19	0.16
British (21)	21	0.18
Czech (27)	27	0.23
Czechoslovakian (11)	11	0.09
Danish (46)	46	0.38
Dutch (51)	270	2.25
English (317)	923	7.69
European (56)	70	0.58
Finnish (12)	45	0.38
French, ex. Basque (124)	305	2.54
French Canadian (66)	136	1.13
German (1,000)	1,765	14.71
Greek (13)	82	0.68
Hungarian (22)	22	0.18
Irish (1,105)	1,806	15.06
Italian (616)	1,004	8.37
Latvian (14)	14	0.12
Norwegian (36)	111	0.93
Pennsylvania German (107)	131	1.09
Polish (174)	420	3.50
Romanian (0)	6	0.05
Russian (0)	49	0.41
Scotch-Irish (94)	159	1.33
Scottish (205)	431	3.59
Slovak (12)	21	0.18
Swedish (0)	52	0.43
Welsh (0)	23	0.19
West Indian, ex. Hispanic (117)	154	1.28
Bahamian (36)	36	0.30
Jamaican (66)	66	0.55
West Indian (15)	52	0.43

Hispanic Origin	Population	%
Hispanic or Latino (of any race)	788	6.76
Central American, ex. Mexican	111	0.95

*Notes: † The Census 2010 population figure is used to calculate the percentages in the Hispanic Origin and Race categories. Ancestry percentages are based on the 2006-2010 American Community Survey population (not shown); ‡ Numbers in parentheses indicate the number of people reporting a single ancestry; * Numbers in parentheses indicate the number of persons reporting this race alone, not in combination with any other race; Please refer to the Explanation of Data for more information.*

Costa Rican	6	0.05
Guatemalan	31	0.27
Honduran	42	0.36
Nicaraguan	11	0.09
Panamanian	7	0.06
Salvadoran	13	0.11
Other Central American	1	0.01
Cuban	63	0.54
Dominican Republic	22	0.19
Mexican	206	1.77
Puerto Rican	274	2.35
South American	56	0.48
Argentinean	2	0.02
Chilean	3	0.03
Colombian	22	0.19
Ecuadorian	9	0.08
Peruvian	4	0.03
Uruguayan	8	0.07
Venezuelan	8	0.07
Other Hispanic or Latino	56	0.48

Race*	Population	%
African-American/Black (1,771)	1,936	16.61
Not Hispanic (1,711)	1,850	15.87
Hispanic (60)	86	0.74
American Indian/Alaska Native (62)	154	1.32
Not Hispanic (58)	138	1.18
Hispanic (4)	16	0.14
Apache (0)	1	0.01
Blackfeet (1)	8	0.07
Cherokee (14)	35	0.30
Chippewa (6)	15	0.13
Choctaw (1)	1	0.01
Comanche (0)	1	0.01
Cree (1)	3	0.03
Creek (2)	2	0.02
Iroquois (0)	5	0.04
Menominee (1)	1	0.01
Mexican American Ind. (1)	6	0.05
Navajo (0)	1	0.01
Pima (1)	1	0.01
Seminole (0)	4	0.03
Sioux (0)	1	0.01
Asian (109)	152	1.30
Not Hispanic (108)	146	1.25
Hispanic (1)	6	0.05
Chinese, ex. Taiwanese (8)	12	0.10
Filipino (20)	29	0.25
Indian (53)	65	0.56
Indonesian (3)	3	0.03
Japanese (2)	4	0.03
Korean (6)	9	0.08
Thai (1)	2	0.02
Vietnamese (14)	21	0.18
Hawaii Native/Pacific Islander (3)	5	0.04
Not Hispanic (3)	5	0.04
Guamanian/Chamorro (2)	2	0.02
Native Hawaiian (1)	1	0.01
White (9,153)	9,426	80.85
Not Hispanic (8,727)	8,935	76.64
Hispanic (426)	491	4.21

Hollywood

Place Type: City
County: Broward
Population: 140,768†

Ancestry‡	Population	%
African, Sub-Saharan (481)	757	0.54
African (262)	516	0.37
Cape Verdean (0)	6	<0.01
Ghanaian (18)	18	0.01
Nigerian (28)	28	0.02
South African (149)	165	0.12
Other Sub-Saharan African (24)	24	0.02
Albanian (15)	15	0.01
American (8,678)	8,678	6.14
Arab (814)	1,374	0.97
Arab (166)	217	0.15
Egyptian (47)	134	0.09
Iraqi (22)	22	0.02
Lebanese (287)	448	0.32
Moroccan (67)	102	0.07
Palestinian (13)	52	0.04
Syrian (88)	217	0.15
Other Arab (124)	182	0.13
Armenian (155)	199	0.14
Australian (44)	91	0.06
Austrian (261)	675	0.48
Belgian (16)	59	0.04
Brazilian (455)	805	0.57
British (418)	655	0.46
Bulgarian (111)	119	0.08
Cajun (32)	50	0.04
Canadian (1,092)	1,525	1.08
Croatian (22)	59	0.04
Czech (196)	429	0.30
Czechoslovakian (63)	108	0.08
Danish (53)	168	0.12
Dutch (336)	1,140	0.81
Eastern European (279)	391	0.28
English (2,804)	7,231	5.12
European (1,063)	1,142	0.81
Finnish (55)	127	0.09
French, ex. Basque (1,028)	3,544	2.51
French Canadian (542)	801	0.57
German (2,985)	10,802	7.65
Greek (529)	883	0.63
Guyanese (106)	184	0.13
Hungarian (803)	1,601	1.13
Icelander (73)	73	0.05
Iranian (190)	217	0.15
Irish (2,896)	10,634	7.53
Israeli (1,381)	1,625	1.15
Italian (6,066)	12,552	8.89
Latvian (14)	30	0.02
Lithuanian (96)	313	0.22
Macedonian (63)	63	0.04
New Zealander (0)	6	<0.01
Northern European (18)	18	0.01
Norwegian (140)	385	0.27
Pennsylvania German (46)	73	0.05
Polish (2,195)	4,507	3.19
Portuguese (225)	462	0.33
Romanian (1,454)	1,788	1.27
Russian (1,598)	3,407	2.41
Scandinavian (0)	12	0.01
Scotch-Irish (337)	946	0.67
Scottish (482)	1,205	0.85
Serbian (103)	132	0.09
Slavic (19)	50	0.04
Slovak (102)	249	0.18
Slovene (30)	30	0.02
Swedish (180)	746	0.53
Swiss (32)	165	0.12
Turkish (153)	217	0.15
Ukrainian (662)	1,005	0.71
Welsh (90)	426	0.30
West Indian, ex. Hispanic (9,030)	11,302	8.00
Bahamian (552)	922	0.65
Barbadian (61)	78	0.06
Belizean (137)	267	0.19
Bermudan (6)	6	<0.01
British West Indian (143)	329	0.23
Dutch West Indian (0)	19	0.01
Haitian (4,101)	4,542	3.22
Jamaican (3,508)	4,072	2.88
Trinidadian/Tobagonian (282)	664	0.47
U.S. Virgin Islander (93)	93	0.07
West Indian (147)	310	0.22
Yugoslavian (72)	124	0.09

Hispanic Origin	Population	%
Hispanic or Latino (of any race)	45,825	32.55
Central American, ex. Mexican	4,896	3.48
Costa Rican	349	0.25
Guatemalan	712	0.51
Honduran	1,283	0.91
Nicaraguan	1,321	0.94
Panamanian	398	0.28
Salvadoran	822	0.58
Other Central American	11	0.01
Cuban	9,258	6.58
Dominican Republic	3,481	2.47
Mexican	1,970	1.40
Puerto Rican	8,818	6.26
South American	14,020	9.96
Argentinean	1,626	1.16
Bolivian	130	0.09
Chilean	542	0.39
Colombian	5,583	3.97
Ecuadorian	1,203	0.85
Paraguayan	38	0.03
Peruvian	2,995	2.13
Uruguayan	498	0.35
Venezuelan	1,334	0.95
Other South American	71	0.05
Other Hispanic or Latino	3,382	2.40

Race*	Population	%
African-American/Black (23,572)	25,608	18.19
Not Hispanic (21,663)	22,868	16.25
Hispanic (1,909)	2,740	1.95
American Indian/Alaska Native (519)	1,071	0.76
Not Hispanic (281)	628	0.45
Hispanic (238)	443	0.31
Alaska Athabascan *(Ala. Nat.)* (1)	1	<0.01
Aleut *(Alaska Native)* (3)	3	<0.01
Apache (0)	1	<0.01
Blackfeet (7)	25	0.02
Canadian/French Am. Ind. (2)	3	<0.01
Central American Ind. (9)	15	0.01
Cherokee (43)	129	0.09
Chickasaw (2)	4	<0.01
Chippewa (2)	10	0.01
Choctaw (11)	20	0.01
Comanche (1)	5	<0.01
Cree (1)	1	<0.01
Creek (8)	15	0.01
Crow (0)	1	<0.01
Delaware (0)	4	<0.01
Inupiat *(Alaska Native)* (0)	1	<0.01
Iroquois (10)	23	0.02
Lumbee (6)	9	0.01
Mexican American Ind. (33)	43	0.03
Navajo (3)	8	0.01
Osage (1)	1	<0.01
Ottawa (1)	1	<0.01
Paiute (1)	1	<0.01
Potawatomi (3)	3	<0.01
Puget Sound Salish (1)	1	<0.01
Seminole (40)	60	0.04
Shoshone (1)	1	<0.01
Sioux (3)	5	<0.01
South American Ind. (40)	75	0.05
Spanish American Ind. (15)	19	0.01
Tlingit-Haida *(Alaska Native)* (0)	2	<0.01
Tohono O'Odham (1)	1	<0.01
Yuman (0)	1	<0.01
Asian (3,396)	4,426	3.14
Not Hispanic (3,282)	4,119	2.93
Hispanic (114)	307	0.22
Bangladeshi (80)	99	0.07
Burmese (62)	66	0.05
Cambodian (8)	12	0.01
Chinese, ex. Taiwanese (590)	849	0.60
Filipino (381)	526	0.37
Indian (1,281)	1,580	1.12
Indonesian (10)	26	0.02
Japanese (81)	147	0.10
Korean (92)	134	0.10
Laotian (5)	11	0.01
Malaysian (8)	11	0.01
Nepalese (1)	1	<0.01
Pakistani (257)	294	0.21
Sri Lankan (1)	6	<0.01
Taiwanese (20)	21	0.01
Thai (87)	106	0.08
Vietnamese (244)	275	0.20

*Notes: † The Census 2010 population figure is used to calculate the percentages in the Hispanic Origin and Race categories. Ancestry percentages are based on the 2006-2010 American Community Survey population (not shown); ‡ Numbers in parentheses indicate the number of people reporting a single ancestry; * Numbers in parentheses indicate the number of persons reporting this race alone, not in combination with any other race; Please refer to the Explanation of Data for more information.*

Hawaii Native/Pacific Islander (123)	411	0.29
Not Hispanic (109)	336	0.24
Hispanic (14)	75	0.05
Guamanian/Chamorro (15)	24	0.02
Marshallese (1)	1	<0.01
Native Hawaiian (25)	61	0.04
Samoan (6)	16	0.01
Tongan (31)	39	0.03
White (102,293)	105,711	75.10
Not Hispanic (66,934)	68,340	48.55
Hispanic (35,359)	37,371	26.55

Homestead

Place Type: City
County: Miami-Dade
Population: 60,512†

Ancestry‡	Population	%
African, Sub-Saharan (71)	114	0.21
African (71)	114	0.21
American (2,061)	2,061	3.74
Arab (11)	25	0.05
Lebanese (0)	14	0.03
Syrian (11)	11	0.02
Armenian (23)	80	0.15
Austrian (13)	13	0.02
Basque (24)	24	0.04
Brazilian (204)	251	0.46
British (31)	83	0.15
Canadian (0)	124	0.23
Czech (28)	59	0.11
Czechoslovakian (16)	16	0.03
Danish (25)	34	0.06
Dutch (22)	225	0.41
English (434)	1,278	2.32
European (177)	342	0.62
French, ex. Basque (70)	280	0.51
French Canadian (11)	32	0.06
German (542)	2,060	3.74
Greek (32)	32	0.06
Guyanese (18)	18	0.03
Hungarian (48)	81	0.15
Iranian (12)	43	0.08
Irish (634)	1,949	3.54
Italian (451)	941	1.71
Norwegian (9)	69	0.13
Pennsylvania German (7)	7	0.01
Polish (74)	298	0.54
Portuguese (95)	138	0.25
Russian (81)	176	0.32
Scandinavian (30)	72	0.13
Scotch-Irish (132)	215	0.39
Scottish (9)	94	0.17
Slavic (14)	14	0.03
Slovak (0)	12	0.02
Swedish (58)	167	0.30
Swiss (0)	13	0.02
Turkish (0)	6	0.01
Ukrainian (0)	25	0.05
Welsh (6)	114	0.21
West Indian, ex. Hispanic (1,862)	2,508	4.55
Barbadian (24)	24	0.04
Belizean (19)	19	0.03
British West Indian (12)	12	0.02
Haitian (1,176)	1,236	2.24
Jamaican (344)	689	1.25
Trinidadian/Tobagonian (79)	320	0.58
U.S. Virgin Islander (40)	40	0.07
West Indian (168)	168	0.30
Yugoslavian (8)	8	0.01

Hispanic Origin	Population	%
Hispanic or Latino (of any race)	38,078	62.93
Central American, ex. Mexican	7,477	12.36
Costa Rican	181	0.30
Guatemalan	3,275	5.41
Honduran	936	1.55
Nicaraguan	1,354	2.24
Panamanian	200	0.33
Salvadoran	1,507	2.49
Other Central American	24	0.04
Cuban	9,524	15.74
Dominican Republic	1,259	2.08
Mexican	9,311	15.39
Puerto Rican	5,186	8.57
South American	3,564	5.89
Argentinean	210	0.35
Bolivian	39	0.06
Chilean	131	0.22
Colombian	1,540	2.54
Ecuadorian	338	0.56
Paraguayan	5	0.01
Peruvian	560	0.93
Uruguayan	57	0.09
Venezuelan	667	1.10
Other South American	17	0.03
Other Hispanic or Latino	1,757	2.90

Race*	Population	%
African-American/Black (12,316)	13,096	21.64
Not Hispanic (11,132)	11,554	19.09
Hispanic (1,184)	1,542	2.55
American Indian/Alaska Native (245)	466	0.77
Not Hispanic (77)	168	0.28
Hispanic (168)	298	0.49
Apache (3)	4	0.01
Blackfeet (2)	3	<0.01
Canadian/French Am. Ind. (0)	1	<0.01
Central American Ind. (17)	28	0.05
Cherokee (15)	47	0.08
Chickasaw (1)	2	<0.01
Chippewa (1)	9	0.01
Choctaw (4)	14	0.02
Creek (1)	1	<0.01
Iroquois (4)	6	0.01
Kiowa (1)	1	<0.01
Lumbee (6)	8	0.01
Mexican American Ind. (52)	83	0.14
Navajo (0)	9	0.01
Ottawa (0)	1	<0.01
Potawatomi (0)	1	<0.01
Pueblo (1)	1	<0.01
Puget Sound Salish (1)	1	<0.01
Seminole (0)	1	<0.01
Sioux (0)	2	<0.01
South American Ind. (20)	34	0.06
Spanish American Ind. (1)	3	<0.01
Tlingit-Haida *(Alaska Native)* (1)	1	<0.01
Yakama (2)	2	<0.01
Asian (724)	1,038	1.72
Not Hispanic (684)	913	1.51
Hispanic (40)	125	0.21
Bangladeshi (30)	31	0.05
Burmese (8)	9	0.01
Cambodian (22)	27	0.04
Chinese, ex. Taiwanese (81)	171	0.28
Filipino (142)	217	0.36
Indian (223)	277	0.46
Indonesian (6)	7	0.01
Japanese (24)	45	0.07
Korean (32)	48	0.08
Laotian (2)	6	0.01
Malaysian (1)	4	0.01
Nepalese (5)	5	0.01
Pakistani (13)	14	0.02
Sri Lankan (1)	2	<0.01
Taiwanese (6)	11	0.02
Thai (18)	42	0.07
Vietnamese (85)	102	0.17
Hawaii Native/Pacific Islander (74)	200	0.33
Not Hispanic (64)	157	0.26
Hispanic (10)	43	0.07
Fijian (2)	2	<0.01
Guamanian/Chamorro (54)	67	0.11
Native Hawaiian (5)	23	0.04
Samoan (7)	15	0.02
Tongan (0)	1	<0.01
White (40,467)	42,327	69.95
Not Hispanic (9,684)	10,120	16.72
Hispanic (30,783)	32,207	53.22

Homosassa Springs

Place Type: CDP
County: Citrus
Population: 13,791†

Ancestry‡	Population	%
Albanian (15)	30	0.20
American (2,190)	2,190	14.71
Arab (90)	90	0.60
Lebanese (78)	78	0.52
Syrian (12)	12	0.08
Austrian (55)	55	0.37
Canadian (116)	127	0.85
Croatian (0)	50	0.34
Czech (16)	105	0.71
Danish (0)	27	0.18
Dutch (52)	433	2.91
English (644)	1,332	8.95
European (31)	31	0.21
Finnish (15)	15	0.10
French, ex. Basque (136)	751	5.04
French Canadian (160)	174	1.17
German (979)	2,623	17.62
Greek (46)	112	0.75
Hungarian (16)	78	0.52
Irish (948)	2,422	16.27
Italian (524)	1,081	7.26
Lithuanian (0)	46	0.31
Norwegian (67)	141	0.95
Pennsylvania German (14)	23	0.15
Polish (155)	634	4.26
Portuguese (101)	125	0.84
Russian (27)	156	1.05
Scandinavian (13)	32	0.21
Scotch-Irish (125)	272	1.83
Scottish (224)	350	2.35
Slovak (15)	15	0.10
Slovene (0)	13	0.09
Swedish (134)	287	1.93
Swiss (24)	39	0.26
Ukrainian (0)	42	0.28
Welsh (15)	42	0.28
West Indian, ex. Hispanic (18)	36	0.24
Jamaican (18)	18	0.12
West Indian (0)	18	0.12

Hispanic Origin	Population	%
Hispanic or Latino (of any race)	497	3.60
Central American, ex. Mexican	21	0.15
Costa Rican	2	0.01
Guatemalan	4	0.03
Honduran	6	0.04
Nicaraguan	2	0.01
Panamanian	6	0.04
Salvadoran	1	0.01
Cuban	72	0.52
Dominican Republic	11	0.08
Mexican	90	0.65
Puerto Rican	195	1.41
South American	37	0.27
Argentinean	1	0.01
Colombian	15	0.11
Ecuadorian	8	0.06
Peruvian	3	0.02
Uruguayan	3	0.02
Venezuelan	7	0.05
Other Hispanic or Latino	71	0.51

Race*	Population	%
African-American/Black (129)	214	1.55
Not Hispanic (124)	193	1.40
Hispanic (5)	21	0.15
American Indian/Alaska Native (59)	178	1.29
Not Hispanic (56)	152	1.10
Hispanic (3)	26	0.19
Apache (2)	7	0.05
Blackfeet (1)	8	0.06

*Notes: † The Census 2010 population figure is used to calculate the percentages in the Hispanic Origin and Race categories. Ancestry percentages are based on the 2006-2010 American Community Survey population (not shown); ‡ Numbers in parentheses indicate the number of people reporting a single ancestry; * Numbers in parentheses indicate the number of persons reporting this race alone, not in combination with any other race; Please refer to the Explanation of Data for more information.*

Cherokee (15)	56	0.41
Chippewa (4)	10	0.07
Choctaw (0)	1	0.01
Creek (3)	8	0.06
Crow (0)	1	0.01
Delaware (0)	1	0.01
Iroquois (2)	6	0.04
Lumbee (1)	1	0.01
Mexican American Ind. (2)	2	0.01
Navajo (2)	4	0.03
Ottawa (1)	2	0.01
Potawatomi (3)	4	0.03
Seminole (0)	8	0.06
Sioux (0)	6	0.04
Asian (101)	150	1.09
Not Hispanic (100)	137	0.99
Hispanic (1)	13	0.09
Chinese, ex. Taiwanese (17)	20	0.15
Filipino (29)	44	0.32
Indian (33)	52	0.38
Japanese (3)	8	0.06
Korean (8)	10	0.07
Thai (0)	2	0.01
Vietnamese (7)	14	0.10
Hawaii Native/Pacific Islander (4)	14	0.10
Not Hispanic (4)	11	0.08
Hispanic (0)	3	0.02
Guamanian/Chamorro (2)	5	0.04
Native Hawaiian (1)	4	0.03
Samoan (1)	4	0.03
White (13,187)	13,422	97.32
Not Hispanic (12,805)	12,985	94.16
Hispanic (382)	437	3.17

Horizon West

Place Type: CDP
County: Orange
Population: 14,000†

Ancestry‡	Population	%
African, Sub-Saharan (14)	35	0.35
African (0)	21	0.21
South African (14)	14	0.14
American (820)	820	8.12
Arab (66)	110	1.09
Egyptian (13)	13	0.13
Iraqi (7)	7	0.07
Lebanese (33)	52	0.52
Moroccan (0)	18	0.18
Syrian (6)	6	0.06
Other Arab (7)	14	0.14
Austrian (0)	56	0.55
Brazilian (204)	216	2.14
British (75)	146	1.45
Canadian (30)	30	0.30
Croatian (0)	28	0.28
Danish (0)	26	0.26
Dutch (33)	93	0.92
English (391)	935	9.26
European (128)	133	1.32
French, ex. Basque (52)	203	2.01
French Canadian (81)	81	0.80
German (471)	1,116	11.06
Greek (39)	108	1.07
Hungarian (16)	86	0.85
Iranian (38)	38	0.38
Irish (142)	801	7.94
Italian (383)	966	9.57
Lithuanian (6)	35	0.35
New Zealander (0)	11	0.11
Norwegian (63)	146	1.45
Polish (68)	257	2.55
Portuguese (12)	24	0.24
Russian (33)	46	0.46
Scandinavian (0)	28	0.28
Scotch-Irish (94)	237	2.35
Scottish (80)	197	1.95
Serbian (8)	8	0.08
Slovak (0)	16	0.16
Swedish (21)	76	0.75
Swiss (10)	34	0.34
Turkish (7)	7	0.07
Ukrainian (23)	23	0.23
Welsh (49)	181	1.79
West Indian, ex. Hispanic (119)	139	1.38
Bermudan (0)	9	0.09
British West Indian (20)	20	0.20
Haitian (13)	13	0.13
Jamaican (86)	86	0.85
West Indian (0)	11	0.11
Yugoslavian (0)	16	0.16

Hispanic Origin	Population	%
Hispanic or Latino (of any race)	2,766	19.76
Central American, ex. Mexican	129	0.92
Costa Rican	11	0.08
Guatemalan	33	0.24
Honduran	21	0.15
Nicaraguan	19	0.14
Panamanian	15	0.11
Salvadoran	30	0.21
Cuban	183	1.31
Dominican Republic	151	1.08
Mexican	256	1.83
Puerto Rican	1,005	7.18
South American	834	5.96
Argentinean	21	0.15
Bolivian	13	0.09
Chilean	17	0.12
Colombian	400	2.86
Ecuadorian	45	0.32
Peruvian	91	0.65
Uruguayan	1	0.01
Venezuelan	237	1.69
Other South American	9	0.06
Other Hispanic or Latino	208	1.49

Race*	Population	%
African-American/Black (893)	1,038	7.41
Not Hispanic (839)	941	6.72
Hispanic (54)	97	0.69
American Indian/Alaska Native (47)	106	0.76
Not Hispanic (22)	68	0.49
Hispanic (25)	38	0.27
Alaska Athabascan *(Ala. Nat.)* (4)	4	0.03
Apache (1)	3	0.02
Blackfeet (0)	3	0.02
Cherokee (3)	14	0.10
Chippewa (1)	1	0.01
Creek (1)	1	0.01
Delaware (2)	2	0.01
Iroquois (2)	2	0.01
Lumbee (3)	3	0.02
Mexican American Ind. (1)	1	0.01
Potawatomi (0)	1	0.01
South American Ind. (3)	4	0.03
Tsimshian *(Alaska Native)* (1)	1	0.01
Asian (1,146)	1,363	9.74
Not Hispanic (1,129)	1,321	9.44
Hispanic (17)	42	0.30
Bangladeshi (9)	9	0.06
Burmese (1)	1	0.01
Cambodian (9)	11	0.08
Chinese, ex. Taiwanese (240)	272	1.94
Filipino (138)	183	1.31
Indian (356)	416	2.97
Indonesian (5)	7	0.05
Japanese (28)	56	0.40
Korean (83)	95	0.68
Laotian (4)	8	0.06
Nepalese (1)	1	0.01
Pakistani (96)	127	0.91
Sri Lankan (3)	4	0.03
Taiwanese (5)	6	0.04
Thai (14)	16	0.11
Vietnamese (117)	130	0.93
Hawaii Native/Pacific Islander (21)	37	0.26
Not Hispanic (10)	24	0.17
Hispanic (11)	13	0.09
Guamanian/Chamorro (7)	7	0.05
Native Hawaiian (10)	16	0.11
Tongan (1)	1	0.01
White (10,913)	11,284	80.60
Not Hispanic (8,856)	9,104	65.03
Hispanic (2,057)	2,180	15.57

Hudson

Place Type: CDP
County: Pasco
Population: 12,158†

Ancestry‡	Population	%
African, Sub-Saharan (17)	17	0.13
African (17)	17	0.13
American (771)	771	5.81
Arab (27)	39	0.29
Arab (15)	27	0.20
Lebanese (12)	12	0.09
Armenian (0)	14	0.11
Austrian (38)	56	0.42
British (41)	86	0.65
Bulgarian (25)	25	0.19
Canadian (28)	79	0.59
Croatian (23)	23	0.17
Czech (32)	49	0.37
Danish (13)	44	0.33
Dutch (136)	404	3.04
Eastern European (9)	9	0.07
English (643)	1,235	9.30
European (64)	64	0.48
Finnish (73)	135	1.02
French, ex. Basque (161)	680	5.12
French Canadian (48)	76	0.57
German (873)	2,579	19.42
Greek (23)	47	0.35
Hungarian (24)	79	0.59
Irish (739)	2,398	18.06
Italian (1,035)	1,836	13.83
Lithuanian (0)	9	0.07
Maltese (13)	23	0.17
Norwegian (23)	47	0.35
Pennsylvania German (61)	61	0.46
Polish (406)	948	7.14
Portuguese (25)	62	0.47
Romanian (21)	21	0.16
Russian (41)	118	0.89
Scandinavian (8)	8	0.06
Scotch-Irish (90)	238	1.79
Scottish (199)	456	3.43
Slavic (20)	40	0.30
Slovak (0)	85	0.64
Swedish (151)	420	3.16
Swiss (0)	12	0.09
Turkish (53)	53	0.40
Ukrainian (32)	32	0.24
Welsh (54)	93	0.70
West Indian, ex. Hispanic (9)	9	0.07
Jamaican (9)	9	0.07

Hispanic Origin	Population	%
Hispanic or Latino (of any race)	603	4.96
Central American, ex. Mexican	25	0.21
Costa Rican	4	0.03
Guatemalan	2	0.02
Honduran	8	0.07
Nicaraguan	3	0.02
Panamanian	1	0.01
Salvadoran	7	0.06
Cuban	85	0.70
Dominican Republic	7	0.06
Mexican	105	0.86
Puerto Rican	269	2.21
South American	47	0.39
Argentinean	10	0.08
Chilean	4	0.03
Colombian	16	0.13
Ecuadorian	6	0.05
Peruvian	7	0.06

*Notes: † The Census 2010 population figure is used to calculate the percentages in the Hispanic Origin and Race categories. Ancestry percentages are based on the 2006-2010 American Community Survey population (not shown); ‡ Numbers in parentheses indicate the number of people reporting a single ancestry; * Numbers in parentheses indicate the number of persons reporting this race alone, not in combination with any other race; Please refer to the Explanation of Data for more information.*

Venezuelan	4	0.03
Other Hispanic or Latino	65	0.53

Race*	Population	%
African-American/Black (91)	153	1.26
Not Hispanic (85)	135	1.11
Hispanic (6)	18	0.15
American Indian/Alaska Native (45)	113	0.93
Not Hispanic (42)	102	0.84
Hispanic (3)	11	0.09
Apache (0)	2	0.02
Blackfeet (1)	4	0.03
Cherokee (12)	26	0.21
Cheyenne (1)	2	0.02
Chippewa (2)	4	0.03
Choctaw (1)	1	0.01
Comanche (0)	2	0.02
Creek (0)	1	0.01
Crow (0)	1	0.01
Inupiat *(Alaska Native)* (1)	1	0.01
Iroquois (2)	4	0.03
Lumbee (1)	1	0.01
Mexican American Ind. (1)	1	0.01
Navajo (1)	1	0.01
Seminole (0)	1	0.01
Sioux (1)	3	0.02
Tlingit-Haida *(Alaska Native)* (1)	1	0.01
Asian (149)	196	1.61
Not Hispanic (145)	187	1.54
Hispanic (4)	9	0.07
Bangladeshi (3)	3	0.02
Chinese, ex. Taiwanese (35)	44	0.36
Filipino (41)	57	0.47
Indian (33)	35	0.29
Japanese (5)	12	0.10
Korean (9)	17	0.14
Malaysian (1)	3	0.02
Thai (6)	6	0.05
Vietnamese (10)	13	0.11
Hawaii Native/Pacific Islander (6)	18	0.15
Not Hispanic (6)	17	0.14
Hispanic (0)	1	0.01
Guamanian/Chamorro (2)	4	0.03
Native Hawaiian (1)	2	0.02
Tongan (1)	4	0.03
White (11,591)	11,742	96.58
Not Hispanic (11,131)	11,249	92.52
Hispanic (460)	493	4.05

Hunters Creek

Place Type: CDP
County: Orange
Population: 14,321†

Ancestry‡	Population	%
African, Sub-Saharan (25)	25	0.18
Cape Verdean (11)	11	0.08
Ghanaian (14)	14	0.10
American (887)	887	6.21
Arab (106)	158	1.11
Egyptian (61)	61	0.43
Lebanese (9)	37	0.26
Moroccan (13)	13	0.09
Palestinian (23)	47	0.33
Austrian (0)	95	0.67
Belgian (29)	47	0.33
Brazilian (59)	87	0.61
British (11)	11	0.08
Canadian (14)	49	0.34
Croatian (0)	15	0.11
Czech (13)	86	0.60
Danish (22)	36	0.25
Dutch (47)	89	0.62
English (245)	750	5.25
European (48)	102	0.71
Finnish (0)	61	0.43
French, ex. Basque (66)	271	1.90
French Canadian (33)	55	0.39
German (383)	1,835	12.85
Greek (0)	182	1.27
Guyanese (0)	13	0.09
Hungarian (40)	68	0.48
Irish (318)	1,570	11.00
Italian (542)	1,408	9.86
Lithuanian (14)	23	0.16
Macedonian (0)	46	0.32
Norwegian (24)	37	0.26
Polish (167)	533	3.73
Portuguese (16)	16	0.11
Romanian (32)	44	0.31
Russian (52)	116	0.81
Scandinavian (0)	31	0.22
Scotch-Irish (45)	110	0.77
Scottish (130)	365	2.56
Slovak (8)	8	0.06
Slovene (0)	11	0.08
Swedish (130)	355	2.49
Swiss (0)	16	0.11
Turkish (0)	31	0.22
West Indian, ex. Hispanic (229)	311	2.18
Jamaican (212)	253	1.77
West Indian (17)	58	0.41
Yugoslavian (28)	69	0.48

Hispanic Origin	Population	%
Hispanic or Latino (of any race)	5,094	35.57
Central American, ex. Mexican	224	1.56
Costa Rican	19	0.13
Guatemalan	39	0.27
Honduran	44	0.31
Nicaraguan	42	0.29
Panamanian	43	0.30
Salvadoran	36	0.25
Other Central American	1	0.01
Cuban	281	1.96
Dominican Republic	422	2.95
Mexican	273	1.91
Puerto Rican	2,099	14.66
South American	1,569	10.96
Argentinean	62	0.43
Bolivian	19	0.13
Chilean	25	0.17
Colombian	830	5.80
Ecuadorian	63	0.44
Paraguayan	1	0.01
Peruvian	152	1.06
Uruguayan	5	0.03
Venezuelan	412	2.88
Other Hispanic or Latino	226	1.58

Race*	Population	%
African-American/Black (1,089)	1,263	8.82
Not Hispanic (891)	999	6.98
Hispanic (198)	264	1.84
American Indian/Alaska Native (43)	114	0.80
Not Hispanic (22)	68	0.47
Hispanic (21)	46	0.32
Blackfeet (0)	4	0.03
Central American Ind. (0)	1	0.01
Cherokee (5)	16	0.11
Choctaw (3)	3	0.02
Creek (0)	1	0.01
Crow (0)	1	0.01
Delaware (3)	3	0.02
Iroquois (2)	2	0.01
Mexican American Ind. (1)	1	0.01
Navajo (1)	1	0.01
Potawatomi (1)	1	0.01
Seminole (0)	3	0.02
South American Ind. (1)	8	0.06
Tohono O'Odham (0)	2	0.01
Asian (971)	1,141	7.97
Not Hispanic (936)	1,069	7.46
Hispanic (35)	72	0.50
Bangladeshi (4)	9	0.06
Burmese (3)	3	0.02
Cambodian (0)	1	0.01
Chinese, ex. Taiwanese (119)	148	1.03
Filipino (225)	261	1.82
Indian (292)	328	2.29
Indonesian (3)	7	0.05
Japanese (40)	74	0.52
Korean (19)	29	0.20
Laotian (3)	3	0.02
Nepalese (3)	3	0.02
Pakistani (87)	106	0.74
Sri Lankan (20)	20	0.14
Taiwanese (15)	23	0.16
Thai (26)	32	0.22
Vietnamese (61)	67	0.47
Hawaii Native/Pacific Islander (44)	71	0.50
Not Hispanic (43)	57	0.40
Hispanic (1)	14	0.10
Guamanian/Chamorro (14)	21	0.15
Native Hawaiian (8)	13	0.09
Samoan (3)	10	0.07
White (10,446)	10,869	75.90
Not Hispanic (6,947)	7,187	50.19
Hispanic (3,499)	3,682	25.71

Immokalee

Place Type: CDP
County: Collier
Population: 24,154†

Ancestry‡	Population	%
African, Sub-Saharan (0)	36	0.19
African (0)	36	0.19
American (178)	178	0.94
English (51)	83	0.44
French, ex. Basque (0)	14	0.07
German (42)	121	0.64
Irish (20)	84	0.44
Italian (10)	21	0.11
Scotch-Irish (0)	8	0.04
West Indian, ex. Hispanic (2,558)	2,594	13.70
Haitian (2,558)	2,594	13.70

Hispanic Origin	Population	%
Hispanic or Latino (of any race)	18,267	75.63
Central American, ex. Mexican	1,573	6.51
Costa Rican	7	0.03
Guatemalan	1,436	5.95
Honduran	57	0.24
Nicaraguan	22	0.09
Salvadoran	51	0.21
Cuban	82	0.34
Dominican Republic	33	0.14
Mexican	15,714	65.06
Puerto Rican	354	1.47
South American	24	0.10
Bolivian	1	<0.01
Colombian	7	0.03
Ecuadorian	2	0.01
Paraguayan	4	0.02
Peruvian	9	0.04
Venezuelan	1	<0.01
Other Hispanic or Latino	487	2.02

Race*	Population	%
African-American/Black (4,563)	4,910	20.33
Not Hispanic (4,447)	4,732	19.59
Hispanic (116)	178	0.74
American Indian/Alaska Native (243)	303	1.25
Not Hispanic (96)	115	0.48
Hispanic (147)	188	0.78
Apache (8)	8	0.03
Blackfeet (2)	2	0.01
Canadian/French Am. Ind. (8)	8	0.03
Central American Ind. (3)	5	0.02
Cherokee (2)	4	0.02
Chickasaw (3)	3	0.01
Chippewa (5)	5	0.02
Creek (4)	4	0.02
Iroquois (0)	1	<0.01
Mexican American Ind. (30)	38	0.16
Pueblo (3)	3	0.01
Seminole (110)	119	0.49

*Notes: † The Census 2010 population figure is used to calculate the percentages in the Hispanic Origin and Race categories. Ancestry percentages are based on the 2006-2010 American Community Survey population (not shown); ‡ Numbers in parentheses indicate the number of people reporting a single ancestry; * Numbers in parentheses indicate the number of persons reporting this race alone, not in combination with any other race; Please refer to the Explanation of Data for more information.*

South American Ind. (7)	7	0.03
Spanish American Ind. (3)	3	0.01
Tlingit-Haida *(Alaska Native)* (0)	3	0.01
Yup'ik *(Alaska Native)* (0)	1	<0.01
Asian (40)	127	0.53
Not Hispanic (23)	78	0.32
Hispanic (17)	49	0.20
Bangladeshi (5)	5	0.02
Chinese, ex. Taiwanese (3)	3	0.01
Filipino (2)	4	0.02
Indian (9)	22	0.09
Japanese (3)	8	0.03
Korean (0)	1	<0.01
Laotian (3)	3	0.01
Thai (0)	5	0.02
Vietnamese (0)	1	<0.01
Hawaii Native/Pacific Islander (41)	267	1.11
Not Hispanic (1)	146	0.60
Hispanic (40)	121	0.50
Guamanian/Chamorro (37)	37	0.15
Native Hawaiian (1)	2	0.01
White (10,423)	11,005	45.56
Not Hispanic (997)	1,034	4.28
Hispanic (9,426)	9,971	41.28

Indian Harbour Beach

Place Type: City
County: Brevard
Population: 8,225†

Ancestry‡	Population	%
American (779)	779	9.31
Arab (70)	124	1.48
Egyptian (33)	56	0.67
Iraqi (37)	37	0.44
Lebanese (0)	31	0.37
Austrian (48)	63	0.75
Belgian (0)	15	0.18
British (109)	140	1.67
Canadian (20)	29	0.35
Czech (0)	17	0.20
Czechoslovakian (0)	5	0.06
Danish (10)	29	0.35
Dutch (15)	181	2.16
English (444)	1,155	13.81
European (38)	80	0.96
Finnish (0)	15	0.18
French, ex. Basque (139)	487	5.82
French Canadian (89)	134	1.60
German (665)	1,910	22.84
Greek (31)	49	0.59
Hungarian (104)	163	1.95
Irish (431)	1,730	20.69
Italian (503)	927	11.08
Latvian (22)	22	0.26
Lithuanian (9)	14	0.17
Norwegian (11)	76	0.91
Polish (142)	302	3.61
Romanian (9)	57	0.68
Russian (0)	115	1.38
Scandinavian (15)	22	0.26
Scotch-Irish (79)	351	4.20
Scottish (165)	247	2.95
Slavic (0)	5	0.06
Slovak (16)	16	0.19
Swedish (36)	92	1.10
Swiss (42)	48	0.57
Welsh (0)	76	0.91
Yugoslavian (0)	10	0.12

Hispanic Origin	Population	%
Hispanic or Latino (of any race)	395	4.80
Central American, ex. Mexican	24	0.29
Costa Rican	4	0.05
Guatemalan	3	0.04
Honduran	9	0.11
Nicaraguan	2	0.02
Panamanian	5	0.06
Salvadoran	1	0.01
Cuban	53	0.64
Dominican Republic	11	0.13
Mexican	90	1.09
Puerto Rican	85	1.03
South American	67	0.81
Argentinean	5	0.06
Chilean	10	0.12
Colombian	17	0.21
Ecuadorian	4	0.05
Paraguayan	1	0.01
Peruvian	20	0.24
Venezuelan	10	0.12
Other Hispanic or Latino	65	0.79

Race*	Population	%
African-American/Black (72)	110	1.34
Not Hispanic (66)	99	1.20
Hispanic (6)	11	0.13
American Indian/Alaska Native (17)	50	0.61
Not Hispanic (16)	45	0.55
Hispanic (1)	5	0.06
Central American Ind. (0)	1	0.01
Cherokee (7)	13	0.16
Chickasaw (0)	4	0.05
Choctaw (0)	1	0.01
Creek (0)	4	0.05
Inupiat *(Alaska Native)* (1)	1	0.01
Iroquois (1)	1	0.01
Seminole (0)	1	0.01
South American Ind. (0)	2	0.02
Asian (137)	200	2.43
Not Hispanic (132)	189	2.30
Hispanic (5)	11	0.13
Burmese (2)	2	0.02
Cambodian (2)	2	0.02
Chinese, ex. Taiwanese (11)	18	0.22
Filipino (24)	46	0.56
Indian (43)	55	0.67
Indonesian (1)	2	0.02
Japanese (9)	28	0.34
Korean (13)	21	0.26
Sri Lankan (1)	1	0.01
Taiwanese (2)	2	0.02
Thai (10)	15	0.18
Vietnamese (7)	12	0.15
Hawaii Native/Pacific Islander (3)	11	0.13
Not Hispanic (3)	11	0.13
Native Hawaiian (1)	5	0.06
Samoan (2)	4	0.05
White (7,787)	7,923	96.33
Not Hispanic (7,463)	7,578	92.13
Hispanic (324)	345	4.19

Iona

Place Type: CDP
County: Lee
Population: 15,369†

Ancestry‡	Population	%
American (1,011)	1,011	6.82
Arab (32)	100	0.67
Lebanese (32)	100	0.67
Armenian (10)	10	0.07
Australian (18)	18	0.12
Austrian (30)	153	1.03
British (18)	62	0.42
Canadian (151)	173	1.17
Croatian (11)	11	0.07
Czech (39)	114	0.77
Czechoslovakian (16)	16	0.11
Danish (75)	137	0.92
Dutch (43)	260	1.75
English (927)	2,392	16.14
Estonian (12)	12	0.08
European (23)	30	0.20
Finnish (24)	55	0.37
French, ex. Basque (201)	820	5.53
French Canadian (101)	145	0.98
German (1,356)	3,275	22.10
Greek (15)	34	0.23
Hungarian (10)	209	1.41
Irish (962)	2,484	16.76
Italian (820)	1,526	10.30
Lithuanian (24)	61	0.41
Northern European (9)	9	0.06
Norwegian (118)	346	2.33
Pennsylvania German (16)	16	0.11
Polish (275)	628	4.24
Portuguese (68)	113	0.76
Russian (61)	179	1.21
Scandinavian (45)	45	0.30
Scotch-Irish (252)	524	3.54
Scottish (140)	355	2.40
Serbian (19)	19	0.13
Slavic (16)	16	0.11
Slovak (49)	144	0.97
Slovene (0)	12	0.08
Swedish (65)	231	1.56
Swiss (18)	101	0.68
Ukrainian (29)	29	0.20
Welsh (13)	88	0.59
West Indian, ex. Hispanic (12)	12	0.08
Jamaican (12)	12	0.08

Hispanic Origin	Population	%
Hispanic or Latino (of any race)	859	5.59
Central American, ex. Mexican	74	0.48
Guatemalan	40	0.26
Honduran	10	0.07
Nicaraguan	13	0.08
Panamanian	5	0.03
Salvadoran	5	0.03
Other Central American	1	0.01
Cuban	61	0.40
Dominican Republic	28	0.18
Mexican	395	2.57
Puerto Rican	158	1.03
South American	63	0.41
Argentinean	7	0.05
Bolivian	3	0.02
Chilean	8	0.05
Colombian	22	0.14
Ecuadorian	5	0.03
Paraguayan	1	0.01
Peruvian	5	0.03
Uruguayan	3	0.02
Venezuelan	8	0.05
Other South American	1	0.01
Other Hispanic or Latino	80	0.52

Race*	Population	%
African-American/Black (163)	210	1.37
Not Hispanic (133)	177	1.15
Hispanic (30)	33	0.21
American Indian/Alaska Native (28)	68	0.44
Not Hispanic (24)	62	0.40
Hispanic (4)	6	0.04
Blackfeet (2)	3	0.02
Canadian/French Am. Ind. (1)	2	0.01
Cherokee (3)	20	0.13
Chippewa (3)	7	0.05
Choctaw (1)	1	0.01
Cree (0)	1	0.01
Creek (1)	4	0.03
Iroquois (1)	3	0.02
Potawatomi (1)	2	0.01
Seminole (0)	1	0.01
Sioux (0)	5	0.03
Spanish American Ind. (2)	3	0.02
Tlingit-Haida *(Alaska Native)* (2)	2	0.01
Asian (153)	218	1.42
Not Hispanic (151)	210	1.37
Hispanic (2)	8	0.05
Bangladeshi (15)	16	0.10
Cambodian (1)	1	0.01
Chinese, ex. Taiwanese (32)	36	0.23
Filipino (16)	31	0.20
Indian (47)	64	0.42
Japanese (8)	14	0.09

SECTION TWO

*Notes: † The Census 2010 population figure is used to calculate the percentages in the Hispanic Origin and Race categories. Ancestry percentages are based on the 2006-2010 American Community Survey population (not shown); ‡ Numbers in parentheses indicate the number of people reporting a single ancestry; * Numbers in parentheses indicate the number of persons reporting this race alone, not in combination with any other race; Please refer to the Explanation of Data for more information.*

Korean (9)	10	0.07
Laotian (0)	1	0.01
Pakistani (1)	5	0.03
Thai (11)	14	0.09
Vietnamese (6)	11	0.07
Hawaii Native/Pacific Islander (5)	11	0.07
Not Hispanic (5)	9	0.06
Hispanic (0)	2	0.01
Guamanian/Chamorro (3)	4	0.03
Native Hawaiian (1)	3	0.02
Samoan (0)	2	0.01
White (14,580)	14,760	96.04
Not Hispanic (14,049)	14,193	92.35
Hispanic (531)	567	3.69

Ives Estates

Place Type: CDP
County: Miami-Dade
Population: 19,525†

Ancestry‡	Population	%
African, Sub-Saharan (14)	78	0.44
African (14)	78	0.44
American (421)	421	2.39
Arab (112)	214	1.22
Arab (0)	11	0.06
Egyptian (76)	76	0.43
Lebanese (0)	28	0.16
Palestinian (25)	25	0.14
Syrian (11)	22	0.13
Other Arab (0)	52	0.30
Austrian (17)	62	0.35
Belgian (0)	7	0.04
Brazilian (180)	180	1.02
British (135)	147	0.84
Canadian (41)	54	0.31
Czech (21)	21	0.12
Dutch (13)	13	0.07
Eastern European (11)	11	0.06
English (84)	272	1.55
European (39)	47	0.27
French, ex. Basque (58)	152	0.86
French Canadian (35)	61	0.35
German (202)	339	1.93
Greek (11)	11	0.06
Guyanese (11)	11	0.06
Hungarian (19)	19	0.11
Icelander (51)	51	0.29
Iranian (25)	25	0.14
Irish (221)	444	2.52
Israeli (22)	22	0.13
Italian (228)	393	2.23
Lithuanian (9)	9	0.05
Macedonian (34)	34	0.19
Polish (71)	146	0.83
Romanian (57)	183	1.04
Russian (406)	646	3.67
Scotch-Irish (0)	6	0.03
Scottish (7)	50	0.28
Slovak (0)	9	0.05
Turkish (14)	14	0.08
Ukrainian (0)	70	0.40
Welsh (0)	6	0.03
West Indian, ex. Hispanic (5,104)	5,425	30.82
Bahamian (191)	250	1.42
Belizean (67)	67	0.38
British West Indian (2)	2	0.01
Haitian (3,334)	3,433	19.51
Jamaican (1,203)	1,347	7.65
Trinidadian/Tobagonian (307)	307	1.74
West Indian (0)	19	0.11
Yugoslavian (12)	12	0.07

Hispanic Origin	Population	%
Hispanic or Latino (of any race)	5,402	27.67
Central American, ex. Mexican	796	4.08
Costa Rican	73	0.37
Guatemalan	84	0.43
Honduran	252	1.29
Nicaraguan	266	1.36
Panamanian	53	0.27
Salvadoran	62	0.32
Other Central American	6	0.03
Cuban	752	3.85
Dominican Republic	460	2.36
Mexican	139	0.71
Puerto Rican	729	3.73
South American	2,104	10.78
Argentinean	422	2.16
Bolivian	37	0.19
Chilean	75	0.38
Colombian	797	4.08
Ecuadorian	114	0.58
Paraguayan	5	0.03
Peruvian	429	2.20
Uruguayan	34	0.17
Venezuelan	186	0.95
Other South American	5	0.03
Other Hispanic or Latino	422	2.16

Race*	Population	%
African-American/Black (9,755)	10,140	51.93
Not Hispanic (9,348)	9,643	49.39
Hispanic (407)	497	2.55
American Indian/Alaska Native (49)	104	0.53
Not Hispanic (30)	63	0.32
Hispanic (19)	41	0.21
Apache (3)	3	0.02
Blackfeet (3)	5	0.03
Central American Ind. (1)	4	0.02
Cherokee (1)	4	0.02
Cheyenne (1)	1	0.01
Chippewa (5)	5	0.03
Inupiat *(Alaska Native)* (1)	1	0.01
Mexican American Ind. (5)	9	0.05
Sioux (0)	1	0.01
South American Ind. (5)	11	0.06
Spanish American Ind. (3)	3	0.02
Asian (579)	771	3.95
Not Hispanic (569)	730	3.74
Hispanic (10)	41	0.21
Bangladeshi (23)	36	0.18
Burmese (1)	1	0.01
Cambodian (3)	3	0.02
Chinese, ex. Taiwanese (111)	147	0.75
Filipino (101)	126	0.65
Indian (160)	239	1.22
Indonesian (4)	6	0.03
Japanese (16)	27	0.14
Korean (17)	17	0.09
Laotian (1)	1	0.01
Malaysian (1)	1	0.01
Pakistani (47)	62	0.32
Thai (32)	35	0.18
Vietnamese (8)	17	0.09
Hawaii Native/Pacific Islander (7)	83	0.43
Not Hispanic (6)	72	0.37
Hispanic (1)	11	0.06
Native Hawaiian (2)	2	0.01
Samoan (0)	6	0.03
White (7,868)	8,314	42.58
Not Hispanic (3,639)	3,868	19.81
Hispanic (4,229)	4,446	22.77

Jacksonville Beach

Place Type: City
County: Duval
Population: 21,362†

Ancestry‡	Population	%
American (1,538)	1,538	7.18
Arab (109)	184	0.86
Arab (16)	26	0.12
Lebanese (16)	50	0.23
Moroccan (0)	16	0.07
Palestinian (51)	51	0.24
Syrian (26)	26	0.12
Other Arab (0)	15	0.07
Armenian (34)	34	0.16
Australian (0)	11	0.05
Austrian (19)	30	0.14
Belgian (6)	15	0.07
Brazilian (0)	18	0.08
British (101)	188	0.88
Canadian (16)	29	0.14
Czech (17)	81	0.38
Czechoslovakian (13)	13	0.06
Danish (64)	64	0.30
Dutch (75)	449	2.09
English (1,522)	3,599	16.79
European (127)	230	1.07
Finnish (15)	34	0.16
French, ex. Basque (218)	1,295	6.04
French Canadian (32)	94	0.44
German (830)	3,340	15.58
Greek (13)	48	0.22
Hungarian (49)	66	0.31
Irish (1,103)	3,404	15.88
Israeli (0)	12	0.06
Italian (595)	1,838	8.58
Latvian (0)	42	0.20
Lithuanian (16)	97	0.45
Maltese (21)	21	0.10
Norwegian (70)	181	0.84
Pennsylvania German (13)	13	0.06
Polish (253)	943	4.40
Portuguese (0)	82	0.38
Romanian (80)	90	0.42
Russian (74)	241	1.12
Scandinavian (0)	29	0.14
Scotch-Irish (380)	761	3.55
Scottish (204)	651	3.04
Slovak (0)	12	0.06
Slovene (16)	16	0.07
Swedish (58)	353	1.65
Swiss (0)	34	0.16
Turkish (0)	43	0.20
Ukrainian (96)	147	0.69
Welsh (30)	227	1.06
West Indian, ex. Hispanic (12)	12	0.06
West Indian (12)	12	0.06
Yugoslavian (0)	61	0.28

Hispanic Origin	Population	%
Hispanic or Latino (of any race)	923	4.32
Central American, ex. Mexican	62	0.29
Costa Rican	12	0.06
Guatemalan	4	0.02
Honduran	4	0.02
Nicaraguan	6	0.03
Panamanian	28	0.13
Salvadoran	8	0.04
Cuban	115	0.54
Dominican Republic	14	0.07
Mexican	278	1.30
Puerto Rican	215	1.01
South American	131	0.61
Argentinean	12	0.06
Chilean	17	0.08
Colombian	37	0.17
Ecuadorian	4	0.02
Paraguayan	2	0.01
Peruvian	38	0.18
Uruguayan	5	0.02
Venezuelan	16	0.07
Other Hispanic or Latino	108	0.51

Race*	Population	%
African-American/Black (832)	983	4.60
Not Hispanic (811)	939	4.40
Hispanic (21)	44	0.21
American Indian/Alaska Native (51)	165	0.77
Not Hispanic (49)	154	0.72
Hispanic (2)	11	0.05
Apache (2)	5	0.02
Arapaho (0)	1	<0.01
Canadian/French Am. Ind. (0)	2	0.01
Central American Ind. (0)	3	0.01

*Notes: † The Census 2010 population figure is used to calculate the percentages in the Hispanic Origin and Race categories. Ancestry percentages are based on the 2006-2010 American Community Survey population (not shown); ‡ Numbers in parentheses indicate the number of people reporting a single ancestry; * Numbers in parentheses indicate the number of persons reporting this race alone, not in combination with any other race; Please refer to the Explanation of Data for more information.*

Cherokee (8)	53	0.25
Chickasaw (0)	2	0.01
Chippewa (0)	1	<0.01
Choctaw (9)	13	0.06
Delaware (3)	3	0.01
Iroquois (1)	6	0.03
Lumbee (3)	3	0.01
Mexican American Ind. (0)	3	0.01
Seminole (0)	1	<0.01
South American Ind. (0)	3	0.01
Asian (369)	595	2.79
Not Hispanic (358)	561	2.63
Hispanic (11)	34	0.16
Cambodian (8)	9	0.04
Chinese, ex. Taiwanese (31)	54	0.25
Filipino (185)	297	1.39
Indian (46)	60	0.28
Japanese (22)	50	0.23
Korean (23)	54	0.25
Laotian (2)	7	0.03
Malaysian (0)	1	<0.01
Pakistani (1)	2	0.01
Sri Lankan (0)	1	<0.01
Taiwanese (5)	5	0.02
Thai (12)	23	0.11
Vietnamese (17)	30	0.14
Hawaii Native/Pacific Islander (10)	38	0.18
Not Hispanic (9)	35	0.16
Hispanic (1)	3	0.01
Guamanian/Chamorro (2)	6	0.03
Native Hawaiian (5)	16	0.07
Samoan (0)	1	<0.01
White (19,427)	19,852	92.93
Not Hispanic (18,784)	19,153	89.66
Hispanic (643)	699	3.27

Jacksonville

Place Type: City
County: Duval
Population: 821,784†

Ancestry‡	Population	%
Afghan (169)	178	0.02
African, Sub-Saharan (11,645)	14,490	1.78
African (8,890)	11,387	1.40
Cape Verdean (12)	34	<0.01
Ethiopian (1,185)	1,185	0.15
Ghanaian (27)	27	<0.01
Kenyan (0)	50	0.01
Liberian (337)	369	0.05
Nigerian (605)	787	0.10
Senegalese (14)	14	<0.01
Sierra Leonean (42)	87	0.01
South African (53)	70	0.01
Sudanese (425)	425	0.05
Other Sub-Saharan African (55)	55	0.01
Albanian (2,478)	2,515	0.31
American (54,229)	54,229	6.68
Arab (5,179)	7,436	0.92
Arab (1,432)	2,036	0.25
Egyptian (227)	398	0.05
Iraqi (311)	363	0.04
Jordanian (59)	81	0.01
Lebanese (964)	1,636	0.20
Moroccan (13)	13	<0.01
Palestinian (463)	616	0.08
Syrian (1,143)	1,637	0.20
Other Arab (567)	656	0.08
Armenian (50)	113	0.01
Australian (120)	179	0.02
Austrian (274)	1,515	0.19
Belgian (120)	548	0.07
Brazilian (1,033)	1,313	0.16
British (1,641)	3,347	0.41
Bulgarian (46)	58	0.01
Cajun (150)	305	0.04
Canadian (523)	1,013	0.12
Celtic (0)	69	0.01
Croatian (631)	974	0.12
Czech (521)	2,003	0.25
Czechoslovakian (208)	596	0.07
Danish (417)	1,631	0.20
Dutch (2,030)	9,104	1.12
Eastern European (385)	401	0.05
English (28,578)	71,352	8.79
Estonian (9)	9	<0.01
European (5,242)	6,325	0.78
Finnish (271)	886	0.11
French, ex. Basque (4,065)	17,794	2.19
French Canadian (1,864)	3,992	0.49
German (25,061)	84,470	10.40
German Russian (13)	19	<0.01
Greek (1,123)	2,672	0.33
Guyanese (432)	578	0.07
Hungarian (984)	3,540	0.44
Icelander (40)	169	0.02
Iranian (486)	620	0.08
Irish (24,783)	83,146	10.24
Israeli (50)	50	0.01
Italian (12,309)	31,420	3.87
Latvian (11)	40	<0.01
Lithuanian (408)	912	0.11
Luxemburger (15)	51	0.01
Macedonian (10)	34	<0.01
Maltese (60)	127	0.02
New Zealander (31)	52	0.01
Northern European (395)	395	0.05
Norwegian (1,502)	4,449	0.55
Pennsylvania German (109)	211	0.03
Polish (4,410)	13,924	1.72
Portuguese (848)	1,985	0.24
Romanian (446)	765	0.09
Russian (2,533)	5,097	0.63
Scandinavian (426)	993	0.12
Scotch-Irish (7,245)	16,183	1.99
Scottish (6,031)	16,504	2.03
Serbian (402)	525	0.06
Slavic (25)	448	0.06
Slovak (242)	847	0.10
Slovene (88)	238	0.03
Swedish (1,089)	4,315	0.53
Swiss (350)	1,260	0.16
Turkish (357)	432	0.05
Ukrainian (787)	1,510	0.19
Welsh (1,050)	4,080	0.50
West Indian, ex. Hispanic (8,591)	11,629	1.43
Bahamian (409)	631	0.08
Barbadian (233)	399	0.05
Belizean (107)	211	0.03
Bermudan (28)	101	0.01
British West Indian (177)	300	0.04
Dutch West Indian (41)	43	0.01
Haitian (3,990)	4,568	0.56
Jamaican (2,521)	3,825	0.47
Trinidadian/Tobagonian (301)	381	0.05
U.S. Virgin Islander (88)	103	0.01
West Indian (696)	1,067	0.13
Yugoslavian (3,423)	3,786	0.47

Hispanic Origin	Population	%
Hispanic or Latino (of any race)	63,485	7.73
Central American, ex. Mexican	6,594	0.80
Costa Rican	542	0.07
Guatemalan	914	0.11
Honduran	1,983	0.24
Nicaraguan	902	0.11
Panamanian	1,165	0.14
Salvadoran	1,039	0.13
Other Central American	49	0.01
Cuban	7,006	0.85
Dominican Republic	2,172	0.26
Mexican	13,838	1.68
Puerto Rican	21,128	2.57
South American	7,152	0.87
Argentinean	387	0.05
Bolivian	231	0.03
Chilean	287	0.03
Colombian	3,197	0.39
Ecuadorian	808	0.10
Paraguayan	16	<0.01
Peruvian	1,282	0.16
Uruguayan	129	0.02
Venezuelan	751	0.09
Other South American	64	0.01
Other Hispanic or Latino	5,595	0.68

Race*	Population	%
African-American/Black (252,421)	263,662	32.08
Not Hispanic (247,516)	256,648	31.23
Hispanic (4,905)	7,014	0.85
American Indian/Alaska Native (3,270)	8,319	1.01
Not Hispanic (2,687)	7,014	0.85
Hispanic (583)	1,305	0.16
Alaska Athabascan *(Ala. Nat.)* (9)	10	<0.01
Aleut *(Alaska Native)* (6)	6	<0.01
Apache (31)	110	0.01
Arapaho (2)	5	<0.01
Blackfeet (58)	263	0.03
Canadian/French Am. Ind. (9)	22	<0.01
Central American Ind. (37)	65	0.01
Cherokee (564)	2,004	0.24
Cheyenne (3)	8	<0.01
Chickasaw (11)	21	<0.01
Chippewa (57)	91	0.01
Choctaw (72)	178	0.02
Colville (0)	4	<0.01
Comanche (7)	19	<0.01
Cree (10)	25	<0.01
Creek (121)	241	0.03
Crow (7)	11	<0.01
Delaware (15)	39	<0.01
Hopi (0)	6	<0.01
Houma (24)	27	<0.01
Inupiat *(Alaska Native)* (3)	10	<0.01
Iroquois (66)	139	0.02
Kiowa (5)	8	<0.01
Lumbee (86)	127	0.02
Menominee (2)	3	<0.01
Mexican American Ind. (68)	109	0.01
Navajo (40)	88	0.01
Osage (9)	21	<0.01
Ottawa (2)	5	<0.01
Paiute (2)	3	<0.01
Potawatomi (19)	25	<0.01
Pueblo (6)	18	<0.01
Puget Sound Salish (1)	1	<0.01
Seminole (47)	165	0.02
Shoshone (7)	16	<0.01
Sioux (82)	146	0.02
South American Ind. (69)	144	0.02
Spanish American Ind. (17)	26	<0.01
Tlingit-Haida *(Alaska Native)* (5)	12	<0.01
Tohono O'Odham (3)	3	<0.01
Tsimshian *(Alaska Native)* (1)	1	<0.01
Ute (3)	4	<0.01
Yakama (1)	4	<0.01
Yaqui (6)	10	<0.01
Yuman (0)	1	<0.01
Yup'ik *(Alaska Native)* (1)	4	<0.01
Asian (35,222)	43,100	5.24
Not Hispanic (34,731)	41,726	5.08
Hispanic (491)	1,374	0.17
Bangladeshi (64)	71	0.01
Bhutanese (201)	231	0.03
Burmese (841)	910	0.11
Cambodian (1,512)	1,683	0.20
Chinese, ex. Taiwanese (2,356)	3,152	0.38
Filipino (14,458)	18,513	2.25
Hmong (21)	22	<0.01
Indian (7,108)	7,900	0.96
Indonesian (67)	123	0.01
Japanese (678)	1,514	0.18
Korean (1,514)	2,087	0.25
Laotian (311)	391	0.05
Malaysian (23)	46	0.01
Nepalese (104)	127	0.02
Pakistani (366)	423	0.05
Sri Lankan (37)	40	<0.01
Taiwanese (138)	189	0.02

*Notes: † The Census 2010 population figure is used to calculate the percentages in the Hispanic Origin and Race categories. Ancestry percentages are based on the 2006-2010 American Community Survey population (not shown); ‡ Numbers in parentheses indicate the number of people reporting a single ancestry; * Numbers in parentheses indicate the number of persons reporting this race alone, not in combination with any other race; Please refer to the Explanation of Data for more information.*

Thai (336)	557	0.07
Vietnamese (3,779)	4,210	0.51
Hawaii Native/Pacific Islander (765)	2,152	0.26
Not Hispanic (668)	1,791	0.22
Hispanic (97)	361	0.04
Fijian (5)	10	<0.01
Guamanian/Chamorro (294)	522	0.06
Marshallese (1)	1	<0.01
Native Hawaiian (188)	548	0.07
Samoan (74)	176	0.02
Tongan (8)	18	<0.01
White (488,473)	507,456	61.75
Not Hispanic (452,525)	467,544	56.89
Hispanic (35,948)	39,912	4.86

Jasmine Estates

Place Type: CDP
County: Pasco
Population: 18,989†

Ancestry‡	Population	%
African, Sub-Saharan (48)	48	0.25
Sierra Leonean (13)	13	0.07
South African (35)	35	0.18
American (1,171)	1,171	6.16
Arab (25)	25	0.13
Lebanese (25)	25	0.13
Austrian (0)	75	0.39
Belgian (0)	15	0.08
British (106)	116	0.61
Canadian (45)	84	0.44
Croatian (14)	81	0.43
Czech (34)	70	0.37
Czechoslovakian (13)	13	0.07
Danish (0)	121	0.64
Dutch (81)	209	1.10
English (654)	2,008	10.56
European (33)	42	0.22
Finnish (55)	65	0.34
French, ex. Basque (104)	455	2.39
French Canadian (64)	184	0.97
German (889)	3,703	19.47
Greek (207)	357	1.88
Hungarian (139)	317	1.67
Irish (803)	3,673	19.32
Italian (1,523)	3,214	16.90
Lithuanian (12)	100	0.53
Norwegian (16)	69	0.36
Pennsylvania German (41)	58	0.31
Polish (483)	966	5.08
Portuguese (90)	133	0.70
Romanian (0)	116	0.61
Russian (123)	198	1.04
Scandinavian (26)	26	0.14
Scotch-Irish (91)	279	1.47
Scottish (100)	411	2.16
Serbian (77)	88	0.46
Slovak (70)	102	0.54
Slovene (9)	9	0.05
Swedish (11)	141	0.74
Swiss (7)	40	0.21
Ukrainian (35)	103	0.54
Welsh (0)	275	1.45
West Indian, ex. Hispanic (213)	281	1.48
Haitian (136)	160	0.84
Jamaican (32)	76	0.40
West Indian (45)	45	0.24
Yugoslavian (111)	122	0.64

Hispanic Origin	Population	%
Hispanic or Latino (of any race)	2,698	14.21
Central American, ex. Mexican	171	0.90
Costa Rican	13	0.07
Guatemalan	19	0.10
Honduran	74	0.39
Nicaraguan	15	0.08
Panamanian	10	0.05
Salvadoran	39	0.21
Other Central American	1	0.01
Cuban	393	2.07
Dominican Republic	89	0.47
Mexican	278	1.46
Puerto Rican	1,388	7.31
South American	236	1.24
Argentinean	14	0.07
Bolivian	1	0.01
Chilean	5	0.03
Colombian	104	0.55
Ecuadorian	41	0.22
Peruvian	45	0.24
Uruguayan	14	0.07
Venezuelan	12	0.06
Other Hispanic or Latino	143	0.75

Race*	Population	%
African-American/Black (668)	882	4.64
Not Hispanic (598)	760	4.00
Hispanic (70)	122	0.64
American Indian/Alaska Native (93)	216	1.14
Not Hispanic (62)	156	0.82
Hispanic (31)	60	0.32
Aleut *(Alaska Native)* (1)	1	0.01
Apache (0)	1	0.01
Blackfeet (0)	18	0.09
Cherokee (16)	46	0.24
Chippewa (6)	7	0.04
Choctaw (4)	5	0.03
Creek (2)	3	0.02
Crow (0)	3	0.02
Iroquois (3)	10	0.05
Lumbee (1)	1	0.01
Mexican American Ind. (2)	2	0.01
Pima (1)	4	0.02
Seminole (2)	6	0.03
Sioux (2)	9	0.05
South American Ind. (2)	6	0.03
Asian (221)	336	1.77
Not Hispanic (212)	298	1.57
Hispanic (9)	38	0.20
Bangladeshi (0)	7	0.04
Chinese, ex. Taiwanese (47)	64	0.34
Filipino (75)	121	0.64
Indian (26)	39	0.21
Indonesian (7)	9	0.05
Japanese (4)	11	0.06
Korean (6)	22	0.12
Laotian (4)	4	0.02
Pakistani (0)	1	0.01
Thai (2)	5	0.03
Vietnamese (38)	44	0.23
Hawaii Native/Pacific Islander (5)	21	0.11
Not Hispanic (3)	16	0.08
Hispanic (2)	5	0.03
Guamanian/Chamorro (2)	4	0.02
Native Hawaiian (2)	7	0.04
Samoan (0)	2	0.01
White (16,768)	17,200	90.58
Not Hispanic (15,063)	15,352	80.85
Hispanic (1,705)	1,848	9.73

Jensen Beach

Place Type: CDP
County: Martin
Population: 11,707†

Ancestry‡	Population	%
Albanian (0)	19	0.15
American (548)	548	4.39
Armenian (0)	11	0.09
Brazilian (27)	27	0.22
British (52)	60	0.48
Canadian (44)	114	0.91
Croatian (0)	37	0.30
Czech (15)	63	0.50
Czechoslovakian (0)	12	0.10
Danish (26)	122	0.98
Dutch (120)	218	1.75
Eastern European (11)	11	0.09
English (590)	1,876	15.03
European (227)	227	1.82
Finnish (24)	57	0.46
French, ex. Basque (56)	406	3.25
French Canadian (63)	99	0.79
German (818)	2,463	19.73
Greek (72)	124	0.99
Hungarian (7)	78	0.62
Irish (501)	2,276	18.23
Italian (938)	2,080	16.66
Latvian (0)	33	0.26
Lithuanian (8)	8	0.06
Norwegian (73)	106	0.85
Polish (296)	550	4.41
Portuguese (8)	8	0.06
Russian (0)	109	0.87
Scandinavian (19)	29	0.23
Scotch-Irish (166)	379	3.04
Scottish (149)	364	2.92
Slovak (16)	25	0.20
Swedish (52)	115	0.92
Swiss (7)	43	0.34
Turkish (0)	14	0.11
Ukrainian (8)	8	0.06
Welsh (14)	86	0.69
West Indian, ex. Hispanic (33)	33	0.26
Barbadian (27)	27	0.22
Jamaican (6)	6	0.05

Hispanic Origin	Population	%
Hispanic or Latino (of any race)	567	4.84
Central American, ex. Mexican	52	0.44
Costa Rican	9	0.08
Guatemalan	24	0.21
Honduran	7	0.06
Nicaraguan	5	0.04
Panamanian	6	0.05
Other Central American	1	0.01
Cuban	85	0.73
Dominican Republic	3	0.03
Mexican	185	1.58
Puerto Rican	130	1.11
South American	60	0.51
Argentinean	6	0.05
Chilean	7	0.06
Colombian	27	0.23
Ecuadorian	8	0.07
Peruvian	5	0.04
Venezuelan	7	0.06
Other Hispanic or Latino	52	0.44

Race*	Population	%
African-American/Black (290)	339	2.90
Not Hispanic (277)	317	2.71
Hispanic (13)	22	0.19
American Indian/Alaska Native (23)	81	0.69
Not Hispanic (20)	73	0.62
Hispanic (3)	8	0.07
Blackfeet (0)	1	0.01
Canadian/French Am. Ind. (1)	2	0.02
Cherokee (5)	31	0.26
Chickasaw (1)	4	0.03
Delaware (0)	1	0.01
Iroquois (1)	3	0.03
Mexican American Ind. (1)	2	0.02
Pueblo (0)	1	0.01
Seminole (1)	1	0.01
Sioux (1)	1	0.01
Ute (0)	1	0.01
Asian (78)	115	0.98
Not Hispanic (78)	113	0.97
Hispanic (0)	2	0.02
Chinese, ex. Taiwanese (24)	30	0.26
Filipino (15)	28	0.24
Indian (15)	20	0.17
Indonesian (1)	1	0.01
Japanese (2)	5	0.04
Korean (4)	6	0.05
Thai (1)	2	0.02
Vietnamese (13)	21	0.18

*Notes: † The Census 2010 population figure is used to calculate the percentages in the Hispanic Origin and Race categories. Ancestry percentages are based on the 2006-2010 American Community Survey population (not shown); ‡ Numbers in parentheses indicate the number of people reporting a single ancestry; * Numbers in parentheses indicate the number of persons reporting this race alone, not in combination with any other race; Please refer to the Explanation of Data for more information.*

Hawaii Native/Pacific Islander (3)	11	0.09
Not Hispanic (2)	8	0.07
Hispanic (1)	3	0.03
Guamanian/Chamorro (1)	4	0.03
Native Hawaiian (1)	1	0.01
White (11,067)	11,200	95.67
Not Hispanic (10,629)	10,747	91.80
Hispanic (438)	453	3.87

Jupiter Farms

Place Type: CDP
County: Palm Beach
Population: 11,994†

Ancestry‡	Population	%
American (695)	695	5.79
Arab (59)	199	1.66
Egyptian (31)	31	0.26
Lebanese (0)	30	0.25
Syrian (28)	138	1.15
Armenian (0)	6	0.05
Austrian (12)	36	0.30
Belgian (0)	8	0.07
Brazilian (27)	151	1.26
British (58)	98	0.82
Bulgarian (0)	13	0.11
Canadian (72)	76	0.63
Celtic (36)	36	0.30
Czech (0)	90	0.75
Czechoslovakian (0)	11	0.09
Danish (19)	38	0.32
Dutch (0)	136	1.13
Eastern European (12)	23	0.19
English (352)	1,266	10.55
European (34)	59	0.49
Finnish (0)	40	0.33
French, ex. Basque (93)	538	4.48
French Canadian (61)	103	0.86
German (388)	2,142	17.86
Greek (22)	47	0.39
Guyanese (50)	50	0.42
Hungarian (0)	126	1.05
Iranian (0)	4	0.03
Irish (705)	2,111	17.60
Israeli (42)	42	0.35
Italian (479)	1,500	12.50
Latvian (7)	7	0.06
Lithuanian (50)	60	0.50
Luxemburger (10)	10	0.08
Norwegian (42)	259	2.16
Polish (193)	663	5.53
Portuguese (9)	9	0.08
Romanian (0)	13	0.11
Russian (30)	231	1.93
Scotch-Irish (112)	323	2.69
Scottish (103)	278	2.32
Slovak (0)	13	0.11
Swedish (53)	174	1.45
Swiss (0)	34	0.28
Ukrainian (8)	20	0.17
Welsh (8)	116	0.97
West Indian, ex. Hispanic (138)	276	2.30
Bahamian (40)	40	0.33
Jamaican (98)	236	1.97
Yugoslavian (0)	16	0.13

Hispanic Origin	Population	%
Hispanic or Latino (of any race)	1,036	8.64
Central American, ex. Mexican	82	0.68
Costa Rican	22	0.18
Guatemalan	37	0.31
Honduran	4	0.03
Nicaraguan	4	0.03
Panamanian	2	0.02
Salvadoran	13	0.11
Cuban	322	2.68
Dominican Republic	23	0.19
Mexican	137	1.14
Puerto Rican	213	1.78
South American	197	1.64
Argentinean	11	0.09
Bolivian	3	0.03
Chilean	6	0.05
Colombian	89	0.74
Ecuadorian	25	0.21
Paraguayan	1	0.01
Peruvian	34	0.28
Uruguayan	13	0.11
Venezuelan	6	0.05
Other South American	9	0.08
Other Hispanic or Latino	62	0.52

Race*	Population	%
African-American/Black (142)	200	1.67
Not Hispanic (128)	176	1.47
Hispanic (14)	24	0.20
American Indian/Alaska Native (27)	65	0.54
Not Hispanic (25)	54	0.45
Hispanic (2)	11	0.09
Apache (1)	1	0.01
Blackfeet (0)	2	0.02
Cherokee (4)	16	0.13
Chippewa (0)	4	0.03
Choctaw (1)	1	0.01
Creek (7)	7	0.06
Iroquois (2)	5	0.04
Potawatomi (1)	1	0.01
Sioux (0)	1	0.01
South American Ind. (1)	3	0.03
Asian (119)	190	1.58
Not Hispanic (117)	185	1.54
Hispanic (2)	5	0.04
Chinese, ex. Taiwanese (19)	32	0.27
Filipino (30)	46	0.38
Indian (29)	38	0.32
Indonesian (2)	2	0.02
Japanese (5)	15	0.13
Korean (9)	15	0.13
Pakistani (4)	6	0.05
Sri Lankan (4)	5	0.04
Thai (3)	4	0.03
Vietnamese (9)	10	0.08
Hawaii Native/Pacific Islander (3)	8	0.07
Not Hispanic (3)	8	0.07
White (11,365)	11,551	96.31
Not Hispanic (10,517)	10,653	88.82
Hispanic (848)	898	7.49

Jupiter

Place Type: Town
County: Palm Beach
Population: 55,156†

Ancestry‡	Population	%
African, Sub-Saharan (42)	64	0.12
African (0)	22	0.04
South African (42)	42	0.08
American (2,153)	2,153	4.07
Arab (86)	175	0.33
Lebanese (75)	149	0.28
Syrian (11)	11	0.02
Other Arab (0)	15	0.03
Armenian (43)	53	0.10
Austrian (144)	439	0.83
Belgian (40)	94	0.18
Brazilian (23)	74	0.14
British (121)	287	0.54
Cajun (0)	10	0.02
Canadian (224)	393	0.74
Croatian (23)	33	0.06
Czech (24)	304	0.58
Czechoslovakian (78)	113	0.21
Danish (56)	246	0.47
Dutch (221)	771	1.46
Eastern European (21)	38	0.07
English (1,993)	6,343	12.00
Estonian (0)	98	0.19
European (653)	775	1.47
Finnish (125)	233	0.44
French, ex. Basque (252)	1,808	3.42
French Canadian (276)	588	1.11
German (2,794)	9,479	17.93
Greek (297)	498	0.94
Hungarian (120)	303	0.57
Icelander (34)	34	0.06
Iranian (40)	40	0.08
Irish (2,990)	9,149	17.31
Israeli (18)	18	0.03
Italian (3,626)	7,051	13.34
Latvian (20)	54	0.10
Lithuanian (169)	328	0.62
Luxemburger (0)	9	0.02
Northern European (17)	222	0.42
Norwegian (119)	664	1.26
Polish (925)	2,545	4.82
Portuguese (44)	419	0.79
Romanian (44)	104	0.20
Russian (522)	1,129	2.14
Scandinavian (9)	18	0.03
Scotch-Irish (479)	1,128	2.13
Scottish (506)	1,455	2.75
Serbian (66)	186	0.35
Slovak (28)	145	0.27
Slovene (0)	10	0.02
Swedish (176)	940	1.78
Swiss (62)	122	0.23
Turkish (10)	10	0.02
Ukrainian (45)	197	0.37
Welsh (27)	317	0.60
West Indian, ex. Hispanic (151)	252	0.48
Bahamian (17)	17	0.03
British West Indian (9)	9	0.02
Dutch West Indian (0)	15	0.03
Haitian (12)	17	0.03
Jamaican (93)	153	0.29
Trinidadian/Tobagonian (20)	32	0.06
West Indian (0)	9	0.02
Yugoslavian (0)	22	0.04

Hispanic Origin	Population	%
Hispanic or Latino (of any race)	6,994	12.68
Central American, ex. Mexican	2,241	4.06
Costa Rican	22	0.04
Guatemalan	1,987	3.60
Honduran	58	0.11
Nicaraguan	44	0.08
Panamanian	17	0.03
Salvadoran	93	0.17
Other Central American	20	0.04
Cuban	725	1.31
Dominican Republic	109	0.20
Mexican	1,658	3.01
Puerto Rican	750	1.36
South American	1,042	1.89
Argentinean	119	0.22
Bolivian	20	0.04
Chilean	38	0.07
Colombian	456	0.83
Ecuadorian	112	0.20
Paraguayan	9	0.02
Peruvian	134	0.24
Uruguayan	28	0.05
Venezuelan	114	0.21
Other South American	12	0.02
Other Hispanic or Latino	469	0.85

Race*	Population	%
African-American/Black (849)	1,038	1.88
Not Hispanic (774)	934	1.69
Hispanic (75)	104	0.19
American Indian/Alaska Native (289)	516	0.94
Not Hispanic (77)	203	0.37
Hispanic (212)	313	0.57
Apache (4)	4	0.01
Blackfeet (1)	5	0.01
Canadian/French Am. Ind. (2)	3	0.01
Central American Ind. (32)	56	0.10
Cherokee (5)	63	0.11

SECTION TWO

*Notes: † The Census 2010 population figure is used to calculate the percentages in the Hispanic Origin and Race categories. Ancestry percentages are based on the 2006-2010 American Community Survey population (not shown); ‡ Numbers in parentheses indicate the number of people reporting a single ancestry; * Numbers in parentheses indicate the number of persons reporting this race alone, not in combination with any other race; Please refer to the Explanation of Data for more information.*

Chippewa (6)	12	0.02
Choctaw (2)	7	0.01
Comanche (0)	1	<0.01
Creek (3)	3	0.01
Crow (1)	1	<0.01
Delaware (1)	3	0.01
Hopi (0)	4	0.01
Iroquois (3)	6	0.01
Lumbee (7)	9	0.02
Mexican American Ind. (140)	175	0.32
Potawatomi (5)	5	0.01
Seminole (0)	3	0.01
Sioux (2)	4	0.01
South American Ind. (4)	13	0.02
Spanish American Ind. (0)	1	<0.01
Ute (0)	1	<0.01
Yaqui (1)	1	<0.01
Asian (1,105)	1,432	2.60
Not Hispanic (1,076)	1,372	2.49
Hispanic (29)	60	0.11
Bangladeshi (4)	6	0.01
Burmese (11)	13	0.02
Cambodian (1)	1	<0.01
Chinese, ex. Taiwanese (244)	319	0.58
Filipino (121)	191	0.35
Indian (376)	424	0.77
Indonesian (0)	1	<0.01
Japanese (38)	84	0.15
Korean (67)	102	0.18
Malaysian (4)	4	0.01
Nepalese (3)	5	0.01
Pakistani (3)	6	0.01
Taiwanese (4)	8	0.01
Thai (11)	22	0.04
Vietnamese (160)	176	0.32
Hawaii Native/Pacific Islander (26)	74	0.13
Not Hispanic (25)	52	0.09
Hispanic (1)	22	0.04
Guamanian/Chamorro (12)	14	0.03
Native Hawaiian (6)	16	0.03
Samoan (2)	7	0.01
White (49,973)	50,786	92.08
Not Hispanic (45,569)	46,085	83.55
Hispanic (4,404)	4,701	8.52

Kendale Lakes

Place Type: CDP
County: Miami-Dade
Population: 56,148†

Ancestry‡	Population	%
African, Sub-Saharan (0)	21	0.04
African (0)	21	0.04
American (1,705)	1,705	3.06
Arab (181)	474	0.85
Arab (32)	32	0.06
Egyptian (19)	19	0.03
Lebanese (52)	262	0.47
Palestinian (49)	58	0.10
Syrian (29)	29	0.05
Other Arab (0)	74	0.13
Austrian (7)	35	0.06
Belgian (17)	17	0.03
Brazilian (102)	174	0.31
British (18)	28	0.05
Canadian (11)	42	0.08
Czech (15)	29	0.05
Czechoslovakian (0)	24	0.04
Danish (13)	13	0.02
Dutch (24)	71	0.13
Eastern European (15)	15	0.03
English (132)	663	1.19
Estonian (0)	19	0.03
European (72)	122	0.22
French, ex. Basque (78)	304	0.55
French Canadian (0)	12	0.02
German (358)	818	1.47
Greek (29)	43	0.08
Guyanese (114)	166	0.30
Hungarian (26)	136	0.24
Iranian (15)	15	0.03
Irish (259)	751	1.35
Israeli (11)	42	0.08
Italian (454)	1,088	1.95
Lithuanian (0)	12	0.02
Norwegian (7)	47	0.08
Pennsylvania German (0)	9	0.02
Polish (85)	284	0.51
Portuguese (43)	83	0.15
Romanian (9)	32	0.06
Russian (120)	231	0.41
Scotch-Irish (25)	93	0.17
Scottish (0)	166	0.30
Serbian (15)	15	0.03
Slovak (31)	52	0.09
Swedish (21)	36	0.06
Swiss (0)	15	0.03
Turkish (5)	5	0.01
Ukrainian (0)	13	0.02
Welsh (24)	63	0.11
West Indian, ex. Hispanic (420)	558	1.00
Barbadian (27)	27	0.05
Belizean (13)	13	0.02
Haitian (135)	135	0.24
Jamaican (245)	255	0.46
West Indian (0)	128	0.23

Hispanic Origin	Population	%
Hispanic or Latino (of any race)	48,584	86.53
Central American, ex. Mexican	5,076	9.04
Costa Rican	153	0.27
Guatemalan	238	0.42
Honduran	569	1.01
Nicaraguan	3,560	6.34
Panamanian	201	0.36
Salvadoran	349	0.62
Other Central American	6	0.01
Cuban	29,095	51.82
Dominican Republic	1,197	2.13
Mexican	765	1.36
Puerto Rican	1,805	3.21
South American	8,687	15.47
Argentinean	509	0.91
Bolivian	167	0.30
Chilean	469	0.84
Colombian	4,281	7.62
Ecuadorian	527	0.94
Paraguayan	17	0.03
Peruvian	1,473	2.62
Uruguayan	161	0.29
Venezuelan	1,082	1.93
Other South American	1	<0.01
Other Hispanic or Latino	1,959	3.49

Race*	Population	%
African-American/Black (1,257)	1,505	2.68
Not Hispanic (631)	716	1.28
Hispanic (626)	789	1.41
American Indian/Alaska Native (45)	98	0.17
Not Hispanic (14)	30	0.05
Hispanic (31)	68	0.12
Apache (2)	2	<0.01
Blackfeet (0)	2	<0.01
Central American Ind. (4)	5	0.01
Cherokee (0)	2	<0.01
Comanche (1)	2	<0.01
Iroquois (2)	4	0.01
Kiowa (1)	2	<0.01
Mexican American Ind. (3)	3	0.01
Navajo (3)	4	0.01
Osage (0)	1	<0.01
Sioux (0)	2	<0.01
South American Ind. (9)	19	0.03
Spanish American Ind. (3)	4	0.01
Asian (786)	1,007	1.79
Not Hispanic (721)	848	1.51
Hispanic (65)	159	0.28
Bangladeshi (0)	2	<0.01
Burmese (2)	3	0.01
Chinese, ex. Taiwanese (330)	419	0.75
Filipino (96)	121	0.22
Indian (139)	170	0.30
Japanese (35)	60	0.11
Korean (8)	14	0.02
Pakistani (85)	116	0.21
Taiwanese (7)	9	0.02
Thai (8)	10	0.02
Vietnamese (52)	62	0.11
Hawaii Native/Pacific Islander (5)	34	0.06
Not Hispanic (1)	10	0.02
Hispanic (4)	24	0.04
Guamanian/Chamorro (0)	3	0.01
Native Hawaiian (0)	4	0.01
Samoan (4)	5	0.01
White (51,721)	52,598	93.68
Not Hispanic (5,937)	6,102	10.87
Hispanic (45,784)	46,496	82.81

Kendall

Place Type: CDP
County: Miami-Dade
Population: 75,371†

Ancestry‡	Population	%
African, Sub-Saharan (25)	25	0.03
African (25)	25	0.03
Albanian (55)	55	0.07
American (3,706)	3,706	4.83
Arab (425)	1,079	1.41
Arab (28)	115	0.15
Jordanian (60)	60	0.08
Lebanese (199)	627	0.82
Moroccan (43)	43	0.06
Palestinian (55)	92	0.12
Syrian (40)	110	0.14
Other Arab (0)	32	0.04
Armenian (0)	37	0.05
Assyrian/Chaldean/Syriac (24)	24	0.03
Australian (13)	13	0.02
Austrian (38)	261	0.34
Basque (77)	226	0.29
Belgian (17)	78	0.10
Brazilian (223)	303	0.40
British (158)	326	0.43
Bulgarian (13)	28	0.04
Cajun (12)	44	0.06
Canadian (102)	234	0.31
Croatian (31)	45	0.06
Czech (26)	101	0.13
Czechoslovakian (33)	33	0.04
Danish (39)	94	0.12
Dutch (201)	454	0.59
Eastern European (194)	229	0.30
English (724)	2,146	2.80
European (196)	271	0.35
Finnish (10)	52	0.07
French, ex. Basque (522)	1,216	1.59
French Canadian (27)	54	0.07
German (855)	3,004	3.92
Greek (164)	263	0.34
Guyanese (14)	14	0.02
Hungarian (94)	306	0.40
Iranian (125)	125	0.16
Irish (880)	2,630	3.43
Israeli (131)	205	0.27
Italian (1,036)	2,353	3.07
Latvian (16)	54	0.07
Lithuanian (47)	119	0.16
Norwegian (60)	293	0.38
Pennsylvania German (16)	16	0.02
Polish (577)	1,292	1.69
Portuguese (103)	237	0.31
Romanian (52)	298	0.39
Russian (788)	1,859	2.42
Scandinavian (0)	9	0.01
Scotch-Irish (70)	380	0.50
Scottish (185)	466	0.61
Serbian (0)	36	0.05

*Notes: † The Census 2010 population figure is used to calculate the percentages in the Hispanic Origin and Race categories. Ancestry percentages are based on the 2006-2010 American Community Survey population (not shown); ‡ Numbers in parentheses indicate the number of people reporting a single ancestry; * Numbers in parentheses indicate the number of persons reporting this race alone, not in combination with any other race; Please refer to the Explanation of Data for more information.*

Slovak (35)	35	0.05
Swedish (93)	296	0.39
Swiss (113)	232	0.30
Turkish (68)	167	0.22
Ukrainian (193)	280	0.37
Welsh (0)	64	0.08
West Indian, ex. Hispanic (1,391)	2,243	2.93
Bahamian (25)	44	0.06
Barbadian (0)	20	0.03
British West Indian (9)	9	0.01
Haitian (572)	718	0.94
Jamaican (473)	978	1.28
Trinidadian/Tobagonian (154)	221	0.29
U.S. Virgin Islander (9)	9	0.01
West Indian (149)	244	0.32
Yugoslavian (22)	33	0.04

Hispanic Origin	Population	%
Hispanic or Latino (of any race)	48,038	63.74
Central American, ex. Mexican	4,668	6.19
Costa Rican	260	0.34
Guatemalan	289	0.38
Honduran	705	0.94
Nicaraguan	2,629	3.49
Panamanian	336	0.45
Salvadoran	426	0.57
Other Central American	23	0.03
Cuban	24,533	32.55
Dominican Republic	1,383	1.83
Mexican	796	1.06
Puerto Rican	2,461	3.27
South American	11,514	15.28
Argentinean	840	1.11
Bolivian	274	0.36
Chilean	613	0.81
Colombian	4,870	6.46
Ecuadorian	766	1.02
Paraguayan	22	0.03
Peruvian	2,280	3.03
Uruguayan	188	0.25
Venezuelan	1,611	2.14
Other South American	50	0.07
Other Hispanic or Latino	2,683	3.56

Race*	Population	%
African-American/Black (3,302)	3,918	5.20
Not Hispanic (2,680)	3,018	4.00
Hispanic (622)	900	1.19
American Indian/Alaska Native (103)	220	0.29
Not Hispanic (37)	81	0.11
Hispanic (66)	139	0.18
Alaska Athabascan *(Ala. Nat.)* (0)	1	<0.01
Apache (2)	2	<0.01
Blackfeet (0)	1	<0.01
Central American Ind. (10)	14	0.02
Cherokee (5)	18	0.02
Chippewa (0)	2	<0.01
Creek (2)	2	<0.01
Lumbee (1)	1	<0.01
Mexican American Ind. (14)	18	0.02
Paiute (0)	2	<0.01
Pueblo (0)	2	<0.01
South American Ind. (10)	37	0.05
Tlingit-Haida *(Alaska Native)* (2)	2	<0.01
Asian (2,267)	2,833	3.76
Not Hispanic (2,190)	2,617	3.47
Hispanic (77)	216	0.29
Bangladeshi (5)	6	0.01
Burmese (22)	23	0.03
Chinese, ex. Taiwanese (756)	1,005	1.33
Filipino (266)	335	0.44
Indian (535)	622	0.83
Indonesian (5)	5	0.01
Japanese (104)	158	0.21
Korean (104)	125	0.17
Laotian (4)	12	0.02
Malaysian (4)	5	0.01
Nepalese (7)	7	0.01
Pakistani (143)	178	0.24
Sri Lankan (8)	9	0.01
Taiwanese (18)	23	0.03
Thai (54)	68	0.09
Vietnamese (149)	173	0.23
Hawaii Native/Pacific Islander (29)	86	0.11
Not Hispanic (24)	66	0.09
Hispanic (5)	20	0.03
Guamanian/Chamorro (6)	9	0.01
Native Hawaiian (3)	12	0.02
Samoan (1)	3	<0.01
White (66,281)	67,658	89.77
Not Hispanic (21,432)	21,981	29.16
Hispanic (44,849)	45,677	60.60

Kendall West

Place Type: CDP
County: Miami-Dade
Population: 36,154†

Ancestry‡	Population	%
African, Sub-Saharan (25)	25	0.07
Nigerian (25)	25	0.07
American (584)	584	1.65
Arab (9)	49	0.14
Arab (0)	9	0.03
Lebanese (0)	31	0.09
Palestinian (9)	9	0.03
Australian (17)	17	0.05
Austrian (0)	12	0.03
Basque (26)	26	0.07
Brazilian (668)	681	1.93
Bulgarian (0)	19	0.05
Canadian (94)	120	0.34
Dutch (19)	97	0.27
Eastern European (9)	9	0.03
English (110)	236	0.67
European (59)	83	0.24
French, ex. Basque (0)	149	0.42
German (65)	396	1.12
Greek (0)	40	0.11
Hungarian (54)	81	0.23
Iranian (47)	47	0.13
Irish (48)	228	0.65
Israeli (14)	31	0.09
Italian (155)	493	1.40
Lithuanian (0)	13	0.04
Polish (0)	18	0.05
Portuguese (42)	51	0.14
Russian (68)	89	0.25
Scandinavian (11)	11	0.03
Scotch-Irish (56)	86	0.24
Scottish (0)	42	0.12
Slavic (0)	76	0.22
Swiss (0)	6	0.02
Welsh (0)	87	0.25
West Indian, ex. Hispanic (548)	591	1.67
British West Indian (21)	21	0.06
Haitian (216)	216	0.61
Jamaican (288)	331	0.94
West Indian (23)	23	0.07
Yugoslavian (13)	13	0.04

Hispanic Origin	Population	%
Hispanic or Latino (of any race)	31,912	88.27
Central American, ex. Mexican	3,435	9.50
Costa Rican	100	0.28
Guatemalan	167	0.46
Honduran	469	1.30
Nicaraguan	2,265	6.26
Panamanian	162	0.45
Salvadoran	253	0.70
Other Central American	19	0.05
Cuban	16,109	44.56
Dominican Republic	1,064	2.94
Mexican	392	1.08
Puerto Rican	1,621	4.48
South American	7,715	21.34
Argentinean	432	1.19
Bolivian	100	0.28
Chilean	276	0.76
Colombian	3,772	10.43
Ecuadorian	487	1.35
Paraguayan	9	0.02
Peruvian	1,369	3.79
Uruguayan	145	0.40
Venezuelan	1,118	3.09
Other South American	7	0.02
Other Hispanic or Latino	1,576	4.36

Race*	Population	%
African-American/Black (1,163)	1,387	3.84
Not Hispanic (626)	708	1.96
Hispanic (537)	679	1.88
American Indian/Alaska Native (59)	113	0.31
Not Hispanic (12)	17	0.05
Hispanic (47)	96	0.27
Blackfeet (1)	1	<0.01
Central American Ind. (0)	1	<0.01
Cherokee (0)	2	0.01
Mexican American Ind. (3)	13	0.04
Navajo (3)	3	0.01
Potawatomi (2)	2	0.01
South American Ind. (12)	24	0.07
Asian (426)	561	1.55
Not Hispanic (389)	479	1.32
Hispanic (37)	82	0.23
Bangladeshi (4)	4	0.01
Chinese, ex. Taiwanese (158)	213	0.59
Filipino (66)	81	0.22
Hmong (0)	1	<0.01
Indian (99)	116	0.32
Indonesian (0)	1	<0.01
Japanese (6)	9	0.02
Korean (12)	14	0.04
Laotian (0)	1	<0.01
Malaysian (0)	1	<0.01
Pakistani (41)	59	0.16
Taiwanese (1)	1	<0.01
Thai (3)	6	0.02
Vietnamese (17)	17	0.05
Hawaii Native/Pacific Islander (11)	39	0.11
Not Hispanic (2)	8	0.02
Hispanic (9)	31	0.09
Native Hawaiian (1)	7	0.02
White (32,461)	33,161	91.72
Not Hispanic (2,982)	3,123	8.64
Hispanic (29,479)	30,038	83.08

Key Biscayne

Place Type: Village
County: Miami-Dade
Population: 12,344†

Ancestry‡	Population	%
African, Sub-Saharan (30)	30	0.25
South African (30)	30	0.25
American (229)	229	1.91
Arab (34)	76	0.63
Egyptian (34)	34	0.28
Lebanese (0)	34	0.28
Syrian (0)	8	0.07
Austrian (61)	72	0.60
Basque (16)	16	0.13
Belgian (0)	6	0.05
Brazilian (517)	555	4.63
British (344)	344	2.87
Canadian (54)	124	1.03
Croatian (22)	35	0.29
Danish (27)	27	0.23
Dutch (0)	15	0.13
Eastern European (32)	32	0.27
English (35)	176	1.47
European (200)	231	1.93
Finnish (20)	20	0.17
French, ex. Basque (75)	268	2.24
French Canadian (0)	12	0.10
German (197)	853	7.12
Greek (27)	27	0.23
Hungarian (53)	94	0.78

*Notes: † The Census 2010 population figure is used to calculate the percentages in the Hispanic Origin and Race categories. Ancestry percentages are based on the 2006-2010 American Community Survey population (not shown); ‡ Numbers in parentheses indicate the number of people reporting a single ancestry; * Numbers in parentheses indicate the number of persons reporting this race alone, not in combination with any other race; Please refer to the Explanation of Data for more information.*

Icelander (8)	8	0.07
Irish (314)	591	4.93
Israeli (14)	14	0.12
Italian (224)	865	7.22
Lithuanian (0)	8	0.07
Norwegian (13)	13	0.11
Polish (77)	246	2.05
Portuguese (0)	22	0.18
Romanian (32)	87	0.73
Russian (97)	290	2.42
Scotch-Irish (57)	115	0.96
Scottish (11)	104	0.87
Swedish (86)	117	0.98
Swiss (26)	37	0.31
Turkish (31)	37	0.31
Welsh (15)	25	0.21
West Indian, ex. Hispanic (0)	12	0.10
Jamaican (0)	12	0.10
Yugoslavian (20)	31	0.26

Hispanic Origin	Population	%
Hispanic or Latino (of any race)	7,602	61.58
Central American, ex. Mexican	533	4.32
Costa Rican	40	0.32
Guatemalan	78	0.63
Honduran	56	0.45
Nicaraguan	251	2.03
Panamanian	26	0.21
Salvadoran	82	0.66
Cuban	2,051	16.62
Dominican Republic	36	0.29
Mexican	510	4.13
Puerto Rican	192	1.56
South American	3,413	27.65
Argentinean	708	5.74
Bolivian	55	0.45
Chilean	185	1.50
Colombian	1,083	8.77
Ecuadorian	134	1.09
Paraguayan	50	0.41
Peruvian	397	3.22
Uruguayan	93	0.75
Venezuelan	706	5.72
Other South American	2	0.02
Other Hispanic or Latino	867	7.02

Race*	Population	%
African-American/Black (50)	77	0.62
Not Hispanic (33)	48	0.39
Hispanic (17)	29	0.23
American Indian/Alaska Native (15)	19	0.15
Not Hispanic (4)	5	0.04
Hispanic (11)	14	0.11
Apache (2)	2	0.02
Blackfeet (2)	2	0.02
Chickasaw (1)	1	0.01
Mexican American Ind. (1)	1	0.01
Sioux (0)	1	0.01
Asian (135)	192	1.56
Not Hispanic (127)	156	1.26
Hispanic (8)	36	0.29
Chinese, ex. Taiwanese (36)	60	0.49
Filipino (21)	34	0.28
Indian (38)	42	0.34
Indonesian (1)	1	0.01
Japanese (18)	25	0.20
Korean (15)	21	0.17
Pakistani (0)	1	0.01
Sri Lankan (0)	1	0.01
Taiwanese (1)	2	0.02
Thai (2)	2	0.02
Vietnamese (1)	3	0.02
Hawaii Native/Pacific Islander (0)	7	0.06
Not Hispanic (0)	1	0.01
Hispanic (0)	6	0.05
Guamanian/Chamorro (0)	1	0.01
Native Hawaiian (0)	5	0.04
White (11,872)	12,010	97.29
Not Hispanic (4,503)	4,555	36.90
Hispanic (7,369)	7,455	60.39

Key Largo

Place Type: CDP
County: Monroe
Population: 10,433†

Ancestry‡	Population	%
African, Sub-Saharan (0)	10	0.09
African (0)	10	0.09
American (1,257)	1,257	10.89
Arab (25)	47	0.41
Egyptian (11)	11	0.10
Lebanese (0)	22	0.19
Syrian (14)	14	0.12
Australian (0)	9	0.08
Austrian (8)	40	0.35
Belgian (0)	11	0.10
Brazilian (0)	9	0.08
British (52)	129	1.12
Bulgarian (9)	9	0.08
Cajun (0)	17	0.15
Canadian (10)	10	0.09
Czech (19)	38	0.33
Czechoslovakian (19)	19	0.16
Danish (20)	20	0.17
Dutch (85)	225	1.95
Eastern European (10)	10	0.09
English (607)	1,493	12.94
Estonian (13)	13	0.11
European (100)	153	1.33
Finnish (0)	11	0.10
French, ex. Basque (119)	347	3.01
French Canadian (69)	117	1.01
German (415)	1,652	14.32
Greek (14)	31	0.27
Hungarian (10)	71	0.62
Irish (201)	1,312	11.37
Italian (233)	763	6.61
Lithuanian (0)	51	0.44
Norwegian (60)	150	1.30
Polish (157)	408	3.54
Portuguese (0)	8	0.07
Romanian (7)	29	0.25
Russian (49)	162	1.40
Scotch-Irish (60)	136	1.18
Scottish (97)	304	2.63
Slovak (32)	57	0.49
Swedish (56)	297	2.57
Swiss (20)	20	0.17
Ukrainian (0)	20	0.17
Welsh (0)	58	0.50

Hispanic Origin	Population	%
Hispanic or Latino (of any race)	2,471	23.68
Central American, ex. Mexican	154	1.48
Costa Rican	8	0.08
Guatemalan	38	0.36
Honduran	45	0.43
Nicaraguan	31	0.30
Panamanian	5	0.05
Salvadoran	27	0.26
Cuban	1,380	13.23
Dominican Republic	19	0.18
Mexican	524	5.02
Puerto Rican	123	1.18
South American	141	1.35
Argentinean	9	0.09
Chilean	12	0.12
Colombian	68	0.65
Ecuadorian	2	0.02
Peruvian	34	0.33
Uruguayan	2	0.02
Venezuelan	9	0.09
Other South American	5	0.05
Other Hispanic or Latino	130	1.25

Race*	Population	%
African-American/Black (244)	289	2.77
Not Hispanic (237)	261	2.50
Hispanic (7)	28	0.27
American Indian/Alaska Native (57)	146	1.40
Not Hispanic (53)	139	1.33
Hispanic (4)	7	0.07
Apache (0)	1	0.01
Blackfeet (1)	4	0.04
Cherokee (10)	48	0.46
Cheyenne (1)	3	0.03
Chickasaw (0)	1	0.01
Chippewa (0)	5	0.05
Choctaw (3)	4	0.04
Creek (0)	3	0.03
Iroquois (3)	5	0.05
Mexican American Ind. (5)	5	0.05
Navajo (0)	1	0.01
Seminole (0)	1	0.01
Sioux (0)	1	0.01
Asian (81)	108	1.04
Not Hispanic (76)	101	0.97
Hispanic (5)	7	0.07
Chinese, ex. Taiwanese (15)	24	0.23
Filipino (11)	13	0.12
Indian (22)	29	0.28
Indonesian (4)	6	0.06
Japanese (4)	5	0.05
Korean (2)	7	0.07
Pakistani (1)	3	0.03
Thai (15)	15	0.14
Vietnamese (3)	3	0.03
Hawaii Native/Pacific Islander (11)	17	0.16
Not Hispanic (9)	14	0.13
Hispanic (2)	3	0.03
Guamanian/Chamorro (3)	5	0.05
Native Hawaiian (7)	9	0.09
White (9,703)	9,887	94.77
Not Hispanic (7,436)	7,570	72.56
Hispanic (2,267)	2,317	22.21

Key West

Place Type: City
County: Monroe
Population: 24,649†

Ancestry‡	Population	%
African, Sub-Saharan (1,021)	1,043	4.27
African (1,013)	1,035	4.24
South African (8)	8	0.03
American (743)	743	3.04
Arab (9)	49	0.20
Lebanese (9)	39	0.16
Syrian (0)	10	0.04
Australian (36)	45	0.18
Austrian (46)	113	0.46
Belgian (21)	21	0.09
Brazilian (13)	22	0.09
British (147)	163	0.67
Bulgarian (102)	102	0.42
Cajun (0)	41	0.17
Canadian (82)	96	0.39
Celtic (0)	48	0.20
Czech (124)	183	0.75
Danish (31)	61	0.25
Dutch (38)	187	0.77
Eastern European (45)	45	0.18
English (2,476)	3,850	15.77
European (173)	203	0.83
Finnish (10)	61	0.25
French, ex. Basque (580)	907	3.72
French Canadian (67)	204	0.84
German (1,433)	2,812	11.52
Greek (38)	73	0.30
Hungarian (47)	91	0.37
Irish (1,585)	3,035	12.43
Israeli (22)	22	0.09
Italian (685)	1,435	5.88
Lithuanian (9)	96	0.39
Luxemburger (0)	12	0.05
Northern European (17)	17	0.07
Norwegian (55)	208	0.85
Polish (505)	836	3.42

*Notes: † The Census 2010 population figure is used to calculate the percentages in the Hispanic Origin and Race categories. Ancestry percentages are based on the 2006-2010 American Community Survey population (not shown); ‡ Numbers in parentheses indicate the number of people reporting a single ancestry; * Numbers in parentheses indicate the number of persons reporting this race alone, not in combination with any other race; Please refer to the Explanation of Data for more information.*

Ancestry	Population	%
Portuguese (52)	80	0.33
Romanian (64)	64	0.26
Russian (221)	363	1.49
Scandinavian (9)	9	0.04
Scotch-Irish (69)	214	0.88
Scottish (213)	508	2.08
Serbian (0)	17	0.07
Slovak (50)	78	0.32
Slovene (27)	27	0.11
Swedish (114)	283	1.16
Swiss (0)	13	0.05
Ukrainian (77)	87	0.36
Welsh (0)	114	0.47
West Indian, ex. Hispanic (405)	475	1.95
Bahamian (0)	11	0.05
Dutch West Indian (0)	28	0.11
Haitian (355)	355	1.45
Jamaican (50)	81	0.33

Hispanic Origin	Population	%
Hispanic or Latino (of any race)	5,228	21.21
Central American, ex. Mexican	902	3.66
Costa Rican	25	0.10
Guatemalan	147	0.60
Honduran	69	0.28
Nicaraguan	585	2.37
Panamanian	21	0.09
Salvadoran	39	0.16
Other Central American	16	0.06
Cuban	2,422	9.83
Dominican Republic	49	0.20
Mexican	606	2.46
Puerto Rican	405	1.64
South American	410	1.66
Argentinean	52	0.21
Bolivian	15	0.06
Chilean	25	0.10
Colombian	119	0.48
Ecuadorian	39	0.16
Paraguayan	4	0.02
Peruvian	102	0.41
Uruguayan	3	0.01
Venezuelan	46	0.19
Other South American	5	0.02
Other Hispanic or Latino	434	1.76

Race*	Population	%
African-American/Black (2,403)	2,606	10.57
Not Hispanic (2,215)	2,372	9.62
Hispanic (188)	234	0.95
American Indian/Alaska Native (105)	203	0.82
Not Hispanic (84)	170	0.69
Hispanic (21)	33	0.13
Alaska Athabascan *(Ala. Nat.)* (2)	2	0.01
Apache (0)	2	0.01
Blackfeet (0)	2	0.01
Canadian/French Am. Ind. (1)	2	0.01
Central American Ind. (0)	1	<0.01
Cherokee (24)	54	0.22
Cheyenne (0)	3	0.01
Chippewa (1)	1	<0.01
Choctaw (1)	6	0.02
Creek (1)	2	0.01
Crow (0)	1	<0.01
Delaware (0)	4	0.02
Inupiat *(Alaska Native)* (1)	2	0.01
Iroquois (2)	2	0.01
Lumbee (1)	1	<0.01
Mexican American Ind. (6)	7	0.03
Navajo (1)	1	<0.01
Puget Sound Salish (0)	1	<0.01
Sioux (2)	6	0.02
South American Ind. (3)	3	0.01
Tsimshian *(Alaska Native)* (0)	1	<0.01
Yaqui (0)	2	0.01
Asian (402)	596	2.42
Not Hispanic (386)	557	2.26
Hispanic (16)	39	0.16
Bangladeshi (8)	8	0.03
Burmese (3)	3	0.01
Cambodian (5)	6	0.02
Chinese, ex. Taiwanese (65)	87	0.35
Filipino (100)	139	0.56
Hmong (5)	5	0.02
Indian (92)	112	0.45
Japanese (36)	61	0.25
Korean (17)	32	0.13
Malaysian (0)	1	<0.01
Pakistani (1)	2	0.01
Taiwanese (2)	5	0.02
Thai (12)	12	0.05
Vietnamese (22)	26	0.11
Hawaii Native/Pacific Islander (39)	75	0.30
Not Hispanic (34)	62	0.25
Hispanic (5)	13	0.05
Guamanian/Chamorro (18)	27	0.11
Marshallese (3)	3	0.01
Native Hawaiian (9)	22	0.09
Samoan (4)	8	0.03
White (20,649)	21,080	85.52
Not Hispanic (16,286)	16,597	67.33
Hispanic (4,363)	4,483	18.19

Keystone

Place Type: CDP
County: Hillsborough
Population: 24,039†

Ancestry‡	Population	%
African, Sub-Saharan (17)	17	0.08
African (17)	17	0.08
American (1,331)	1,331	6.17
Arab (24)	24	0.11
Egyptian (11)	11	0.05
Lebanese (13)	13	0.06
Armenian (24)	24	0.11
Australian (0)	13	0.06
Austrian (22)	116	0.54
Basque (19)	19	0.09
Brazilian (9)	9	0.04
British (55)	115	0.53
Canadian (13)	46	0.21
Croatian (0)	19	0.09
Czech (30)	149	0.69
Czechoslovakian (91)	112	0.52
Danish (16)	32	0.15
Dutch (49)	133	0.62
Eastern European (49)	49	0.23
English (888)	3,008	13.95
European (276)	337	1.56
Finnish (21)	32	0.15
French, ex. Basque (57)	760	3.52
French Canadian (122)	260	1.21
German (1,609)	5,368	24.89
Greek (51)	173	0.80
Hungarian (101)	248	1.15
Iranian (64)	80	0.37
Irish (697)	3,536	16.39
Israeli (13)	13	0.06
Italian (943)	2,571	11.92
Lithuanian (56)	130	0.60
Northern European (23)	23	0.11
Norwegian (159)	322	1.49
Pennsylvania German (0)	7	0.03
Polish (490)	1,026	4.76
Portuguese (0)	27	0.13
Russian (72)	209	0.97
Scotch-Irish (152)	347	1.61
Scottish (165)	500	2.32
Slovak (118)	221	1.02
Slovene (0)	38	0.18
Swedish (105)	235	1.09
Swiss (0)	35	0.16
Ukrainian (0)	36	0.17
Welsh (25)	171	0.79
West Indian, ex. Hispanic (244)	309	1.43
Haitian (25)	71	0.33
Jamaican (219)	238	1.10

Hispanic Origin	Population	%
Hispanic or Latino (of any race)	2,611	10.86
Central American, ex. Mexican	119	0.50
Costa Rican	10	0.04
Guatemalan	24	0.10
Honduran	24	0.10
Nicaraguan	9	0.04
Panamanian	27	0.11
Salvadoran	25	0.10
Cuban	671	2.79
Dominican Republic	120	0.50
Mexican	170	0.71
Puerto Rican	670	2.79
South American	450	1.87
Argentinean	30	0.12
Bolivian	11	0.05
Chilean	6	0.02
Colombian	275	1.14
Ecuadorian	35	0.15
Peruvian	39	0.16
Uruguayan	1	<0.01
Venezuelan	52	0.22
Other South American	1	<0.01
Other Hispanic or Latino	411	1.71

Race*	Population	%
African-American/Black (938)	1,112	4.63
Not Hispanic (901)	1,043	4.34
Hispanic (37)	69	0.29
American Indian/Alaska Native (56)	157	0.65
Not Hispanic (46)	130	0.54
Hispanic (10)	27	0.11
Blackfeet (1)	1	<0.01
Canadian/French Am. Ind. (0)	1	<0.01
Central American Ind. (1)	1	<0.01
Cherokee (9)	38	0.16
Chickasaw (3)	3	0.01
Chippewa (1)	3	0.01
Choctaw (0)	8	0.03
Creek (2)	5	0.02
Delaware (1)	1	<0.01
Iroquois (2)	5	0.02
Mexican American Ind. (5)	5	0.02
Osage (2)	2	0.01
Pueblo (4)	4	0.02
Seminole (1)	5	0.02
South American Ind. (0)	1	<0.01
Spanish American Ind. (1)	1	<0.01
Asian (1,338)	1,619	6.73
Not Hispanic (1,322)	1,573	6.54
Hispanic (16)	46	0.19
Burmese (3)	3	0.01
Cambodian (1)	1	<0.01
Chinese, ex. Taiwanese (134)	204	0.85
Filipino (114)	181	0.75
Indian (588)	622	2.59
Indonesian (2)	7	0.03
Japanese (10)	53	0.22
Korean (203)	226	0.94
Laotian (1)	1	<0.01
Malaysian (2)	2	0.01
Pakistani (52)	57	0.24
Sri Lankan (7)	7	0.03
Taiwanese (16)	17	0.07
Thai (17)	22	0.09
Vietnamese (145)	175	0.73
Hawaii Native/Pacific Islander (15)	38	0.16
Not Hispanic (9)	29	0.12
Hispanic (6)	9	0.04
Guamanian/Chamorro (6)	8	0.03
Native Hawaiian (2)	11	0.05
Samoan (2)	3	0.01
Tongan (1)	3	0.01
White (20,821)	21,329	88.73
Not Hispanic (18,627)	19,013	79.09
Hispanic (2,194)	2,316	9.63

*Notes: † The Census 2010 population figure is used to calculate the percentages in the Hispanic Origin and Race categories. Ancestry percentages are based on the 2006-2010 American Community Survey population (not shown); ‡ Numbers in parentheses indicate the number of people reporting a single ancestry; * Numbers in parentheses indicate the number of persons reporting this race alone, not in combination with any other race; Please refer to the Explanation of Data for more information.*

Kissimmee

Place Type: City
County: Osceola
Population: 59,682†

Ancestry‡	Population	%
African, Sub-Saharan (228)	265	0.45
African (156)	193	0.33
Cape Verdean (44)	44	0.07
Nigerian (28)	28	0.05
American (1,841)	1,841	3.10
Arab (469)	542	0.91
Arab (51)	80	0.13
Iraqi (9)	9	0.02
Lebanese (52)	67	0.11
Moroccan (312)	312	0.53
Syrian (0)	29	0.05
Other Arab (45)	45	0.08
Armenian (0)	32	0.05
Belgian (10)	38	0.06
Brazilian (531)	746	1.26
British (153)	259	0.44
Bulgarian (63)	63	0.11
Cajun (22)	48	0.08
Canadian (18)	96	0.16
Croatian (15)	15	0.03
Czech (26)	87	0.15
Czechoslovakian (0)	7	0.01
Danish (0)	16	0.03
Dutch (89)	319	0.54
English (901)	2,761	4.65
European (152)	228	0.38
Finnish (0)	61	0.10
French, ex. Basque (327)	1,086	1.83
French Canadian (144)	279	0.47
German (1,149)	3,796	6.40
Greek (13)	217	0.37
Guyanese (116)	153	0.26
Hungarian (110)	165	0.28
Iranian (0)	14	0.02
Irish (823)	3,225	5.43
Israeli (30)	30	0.05
Italian (1,399)	3,045	5.13
Lithuanian (22)	136	0.23
Norwegian (92)	153	0.26
Polish (207)	817	1.38
Portuguese (98)	173	0.29
Romanian (14)	50	0.08
Russian (120)	237	0.40
Scotch-Irish (132)	384	0.65
Scottish (77)	669	1.13
Slavic (10)	21	0.04
Slovak (20)	20	0.03
Swedish (104)	332	0.56
Swiss (14)	39	0.07
Ukrainian (0)	63	0.11
Welsh (11)	154	0.26
West Indian, ex. Hispanic (1,220)	1,470	2.48
Barbadian (36)	36	0.06
British West Indian (78)	78	0.13
Haitian (388)	388	0.65
Jamaican (475)	662	1.12
Trinidadian/Tobagonian (144)	175	0.29
West Indian (99)	131	0.22

Hispanic Origin	Population	%
Hispanic or Latino (of any race)	35,170	58.93
Central American, ex. Mexican	2,036	3.41
Costa Rican	115	0.19
Guatemalan	274	0.46
Honduran	387	0.65
Nicaraguan	339	0.57
Panamanian	167	0.28
Salvadoran	753	1.26
Other Central American	1	<0.01
Cuban	1,524	2.55
Dominican Republic	3,061	5.13
Mexican	2,351	3.94
Puerto Rican	19,728	33.06
South American	5,135	8.60
Argentinean	283	0.47
Bolivian	35	0.06
Chilean	127	0.21
Colombian	2,370	3.97
Ecuadorian	533	0.89
Paraguayan	5	0.01
Peruvian	750	1.26
Uruguayan	164	0.27
Venezuelan	848	1.42
Other South American	20	0.03
Other Hispanic or Latino	1,335	2.24

Race*	Population	%
African-American/Black (7,386)	8,515	14.27
Not Hispanic (5,725)	6,167	10.33
Hispanic (1,661)	2,348	3.93
American Indian/Alaska Native (349)	671	1.12
Not Hispanic (125)	262	0.44
Hispanic (224)	409	0.69
Aleut *(Alaska Native)* (0)	3	0.01
Apache (3)	10	0.02
Blackfeet (3)	7	0.01
Central American Ind. (2)	9	0.02
Cherokee (23)	61	0.10
Cheyenne (0)	2	<0.01
Chippewa (4)	5	0.01
Choctaw (3)	6	0.01
Comanche (0)	1	<0.01
Cree (0)	4	0.01
Creek (0)	8	0.01
Delaware (1)	1	<0.01
Iroquois (3)	13	0.02
Kiowa (0)	1	<0.01
Menominee (1)	1	<0.01
Mexican American Ind. (20)	31	0.05
Pima (3)	3	0.01
Potawatomi (2)	2	<0.01
Pueblo (1)	3	0.01
Seminole (2)	7	0.01
Shoshone (1)	1	<0.01
Sioux (3)	8	0.01
South American Ind. (47)	76	0.13
Spanish American Ind. (10)	19	0.03
Yup'ik *(Alaska Native)* (0)	1	<0.01
Asian (2,005)	2,417	4.05
Not Hispanic (1,925)	2,230	3.74
Hispanic (80)	187	0.31
Bangladeshi (134)	155	0.26
Burmese (1)	1	<0.01
Cambodian (7)	7	0.01
Chinese, ex. Taiwanese (201)	243	0.41
Filipino (461)	551	0.92
Hmong (5)	5	0.01
Indian (630)	767	1.29
Indonesian (5)	6	0.01
Japanese (32)	55	0.09
Korean (25)	40	0.07
Laotian (2)	11	0.02
Malaysian (1)	2	<0.01
Nepalese (1)	1	<0.01
Pakistani (252)	269	0.45
Sri Lankan (12)	13	0.02
Taiwanese (3)	4	0.01
Thai (26)	35	0.06
Vietnamese (97)	126	0.21
Hawaii Native/Pacific Islander (50)	200	0.34
Not Hispanic (44)	128	0.21
Hispanic (6)	72	0.12
Fijian (3)	6	0.01
Guamanian/Chamorro (11)	13	0.02
Marshallese (6)	9	0.02
Native Hawaiian (19)	36	0.06
Samoan (1)	3	0.01
White (39,431)	41,597	69.70
Not Hispanic (15,633)	16,238	27.21
Hispanic (23,798)	25,359	42.49

Lady Lake

Place Type: Town
County: Lake
Population: 13,926†

Ancestry‡	Population	%
Albanian (14)	14	0.10
American (2,022)	2,022	14.37
Arab (51)	51	0.36
Lebanese (51)	51	0.36
Belgian (37)	64	0.45
British (15)	15	0.11
Canadian (80)	80	0.57
Croatian (33)	33	0.23
Czech (0)	65	0.46
Czechoslovakian (0)	20	0.14
Danish (23)	50	0.36
Dutch (79)	339	2.41
Eastern European (15)	15	0.11
English (709)	2,019	14.35
European (16)	16	0.11
Finnish (14)	47	0.33
French, ex. Basque (220)	772	5.49
French Canadian (275)	336	2.39
German (1,200)	2,877	20.44
Greek (31)	31	0.22
Guyanese (0)	131	0.93
Hungarian (56)	136	0.97
Irish (766)	2,141	15.21
Italian (638)	997	7.08
Lithuanian (28)	28	0.20
Macedonian (15)	15	0.11
Norwegian (59)	154	1.09
Pennsylvania German (52)	52	0.37
Polish (225)	628	4.46
Portuguese (46)	61	0.43
Romanian (0)	10	0.07
Russian (36)	69	0.49
Scandinavian (0)	20	0.14
Scotch-Irish (100)	374	2.66
Scottish (194)	371	2.64
Slovak (26)	42	0.30
Swedish (98)	271	1.93
Swiss (0)	20	0.14
Ukrainian (14)	28	0.20
Welsh (0)	157	1.12
West Indian, ex. Hispanic (0)	89	0.63
Jamaican (0)	89	0.63
Yugoslavian (0)	16	0.11

Hispanic Origin	Population	%
Hispanic or Latino (of any race)	595	4.27
Central American, ex. Mexican	34	0.24
Costa Rican	10	0.07
Guatemalan	6	0.04
Honduran	10	0.07
Nicaraguan	2	0.01
Panamanian	3	0.02
Salvadoran	3	0.02
Cuban	46	0.33
Dominican Republic	12	0.09
Mexican	248	1.78
Puerto Rican	172	1.24
South American	39	0.28
Bolivian	2	0.01
Chilean	2	0.01
Colombian	19	0.14
Ecuadorian	3	0.02
Paraguayan	1	0.01
Peruvian	6	0.04
Venezuelan	6	0.04
Other Hispanic or Latino	44	0.32

Race*	Population	%
African-American/Black (709)	790	5.67
Not Hispanic (685)	753	5.41
Hispanic (24)	37	0.27
American Indian/Alaska Native (49)	95	0.68
Not Hispanic (42)	83	0.60

*Notes: † The Census 2010 population figure is used to calculate the percentages in the Hispanic Origin and Race categories. Ancestry percentages are based on the 2006-2010 American Community Survey population (not shown); ‡ Numbers in parentheses indicate the number of people reporting a single ancestry; * Numbers in parentheses indicate the number of persons reporting this race alone, not in combination with any other race; Please refer to the Explanation of Data for more information.*

Hispanic (7)	12	0.09
Apache (2)	2	0.01
Blackfeet (1)	2	0.01
Canadian/French Am. Ind. (1)	1	0.01
Cherokee (16)	28	0.20
Chippewa (0)	3	0.02
Choctaw (0)	1	0.01
Comanche (1)	1	0.01
Creek (1)	1	0.01
Inupiat *(Alaska Native)* (0)	2	0.01
Iroquois (5)	9	0.06
Navajo (0)	1	0.01
Puget Sound Salish (0)	2	0.01
Seminole (1)	1	0.01
Sioux (3)	6	0.04
Tlingit-Haida *(Alaska Native)* (0)	2	0.01
Asian (150)	180	1.29
Not Hispanic (150)	179	1.29
Hispanic (0)	1	0.01
Burmese (5)	5	0.04
Chinese, ex. Taiwanese (23)	25	0.18
Filipino (38)	47	0.34
Indian (26)	35	0.25
Indonesian (1)	2	0.01
Japanese (9)	12	0.09
Korean (8)	10	0.07
Laotian (0)	1	0.01
Pakistani (2)	2	0.01
Vietnamese (35)	38	0.27
Hawaii Native/Pacific Islander (13)	17	0.12
Not Hispanic (13)	17	0.12
Guamanian/Chamorro (2)	3	0.02
Marshallese (9)	9	0.06
Native Hawaiian (1)	3	0.02
Samoan (1)	1	0.01
White (12,647)	12,800	91.91
Not Hispanic (12,279)	12,412	89.13
Hispanic (368)	388	2.79

Lake Butler

Place Type: CDP
County: Orange
Population: 15,400†

Ancestry‡	Population	%
African, Sub-Saharan (108)	138	0.88
African (9)	9	0.06
Kenyan (85)	85	0.54
South African (14)	44	0.28
American (1,321)	1,321	8.43
Arab (39)	121	0.77
Arab (9)	9	0.06
Egyptian (0)	18	0.11
Lebanese (30)	85	0.54
Syrian (0)	9	0.06
Armenian (51)	51	0.33
Australian (9)	9	0.06
Austrian (76)	158	1.01
Belgian (12)	12	0.08
Brazilian (61)	104	0.66
British (85)	196	1.25
Canadian (19)	33	0.21
Croatian (0)	33	0.21
Czech (0)	72	0.46
Czechoslovakian (19)	30	0.19
Danish (58)	93	0.59
Dutch (35)	200	1.28
English (723)	1,894	12.09
European (369)	369	2.36
Finnish (43)	154	0.98
French, ex. Basque (65)	490	3.13
French Canadian (29)	139	0.89
German (559)	2,032	12.97
Greek (167)	337	2.15
Hungarian (16)	78	0.50
Iranian (208)	208	1.33
Irish (700)	1,865	11.90
Italian (487)	1,157	7.39
Maltese (0)	11	0.07
Norwegian (166)	302	1.93
Pennsylvania German (14)	14	0.09
Polish (76)	482	3.08
Portuguese (65)	221	1.41
Romanian (0)	42	0.27
Russian (131)	471	3.01
Scandinavian (24)	39	0.25
Scotch-Irish (148)	272	1.74
Scottish (185)	402	2.57
Slavic (0)	13	0.08
Slovak (40)	77	0.49
Swedish (47)	153	0.98
Swiss (0)	93	0.59
Turkish (84)	224	1.43
Ukrainian (45)	92	0.59
Welsh (44)	150	0.96
West Indian, ex. Hispanic (97)	143	0.91
Haitian (19)	42	0.27
Jamaican (78)	101	0.64

Hispanic Origin	Population	%
Hispanic or Latino (of any race)	1,721	11.18
Central American, ex. Mexican	102	0.66
Costa Rican	8	0.05
Guatemalan	29	0.19
Honduran	19	0.12
Nicaraguan	25	0.16
Panamanian	16	0.10
Salvadoran	5	0.03
Cuban	279	1.81
Dominican Republic	82	0.53
Mexican	110	0.71
Puerto Rican	481	3.12
South American	521	3.38
Argentinean	37	0.24
Bolivian	4	0.03
Chilean	18	0.12
Colombian	213	1.38
Ecuadorian	51	0.33
Peruvian	37	0.24
Uruguayan	3	0.02
Venezuelan	157	1.02
Other South American	1	0.01
Other Hispanic or Latino	146	0.95

Race*	Population	%
African-American/Black (1,018)	1,123	7.29
Not Hispanic (962)	1,037	6.73
Hispanic (56)	86	0.56
American Indian/Alaska Native (24)	51	0.33
Not Hispanic (21)	47	0.31
Hispanic (3)	4	0.03
Blackfeet (0)	3	0.02
Central American Ind. (1)	1	0.01
Cherokee (0)	8	0.05
Chickasaw (1)	3	0.02
Chippewa (2)	2	0.01
Comanche (1)	1	0.01
Iroquois (1)	3	0.02
Mexican American Ind. (1)	1	0.01
Potawatomi (1)	2	0.01
Spanish American Ind. (4)	5	0.03
Asian (1,441)	1,648	10.70
Not Hispanic (1,423)	1,614	10.48
Hispanic (18)	34	0.22
Bangladeshi (3)	6	0.04
Burmese (2)	2	0.01
Cambodian (12)	14	0.09
Chinese, ex. Taiwanese (177)	210	1.36
Filipino (137)	174	1.13
Indian (639)	684	4.44
Indonesian (8)	9	0.06
Japanese (23)	55	0.36
Korean (166)	198	1.29
Malaysian (1)	2	0.01
Pakistani (111)	128	0.83
Sri Lankan (4)	4	0.03
Taiwanese (17)	23	0.15
Thai (10)	14	0.09
Vietnamese (87)	102	0.66
Hawaii Native/Pacific Islander (6)	22	0.14
Not Hispanic (5)	20	0.13
Hispanic (1)	2	0.01
Guamanian/Chamorro (1)	4	0.03
Native Hawaiian (1)	4	0.03
Samoan (3)	3	0.02
White (12,312)	12,571	81.63
Not Hispanic (10,922)	11,134	72.30
Hispanic (1,390)	1,437	9.33

Lake City

Place Type: City
County: Columbia
Population: 12,046†

Ancestry‡	Population	%
African, Sub-Saharan (1,549)	1,604	13.03
African (1,549)	1,604	13.03
American (490)	490	3.98
Arab (20)	59	0.48
Arab (0)	33	0.27
Lebanese (0)	6	0.05
Palestinian (20)	20	0.16
Belgian (0)	14	0.11
British (9)	41	0.33
Canadian (8)	78	0.63
Celtic (9)	9	0.07
Dutch (33)	80	0.65
Eastern European (15)	15	0.12
English (670)	1,121	9.11
European (6)	176	1.43
French, ex. Basque (142)	311	2.53
French Canadian (17)	90	0.73
German (446)	1,069	8.68
Greek (17)	17	0.14
Hungarian (3)	19	0.15
Irish (373)	880	7.15
Italian (109)	286	2.32
Lithuanian (7)	7	0.06
Norwegian (35)	35	0.28
Polish (53)	180	1.46
Portuguese (21)	21	0.17
Russian (14)	85	0.69
Scandinavian (0)	8	0.06
Scotch-Irish (99)	195	1.58
Scottish (112)	254	2.06
Swedish (12)	46	0.37
Ukrainian (0)	24	0.19
Welsh (0)	30	0.24
West Indian, ex. Hispanic (29)	174	1.41
Jamaican (29)	72	0.58
West Indian (0)	102	0.83

Hispanic Origin	Population	%
Hispanic or Latino (of any race)	650	5.40
Central American, ex. Mexican	44	0.37
Costa Rican	4	0.03
Guatemalan	4	0.03
Honduran	6	0.05
Nicaraguan	13	0.11
Panamanian	5	0.04
Salvadoran	11	0.09
Other Central American	1	0.01
Cuban	81	0.67
Dominican Republic	36	0.30
Mexican	158	1.31
Puerto Rican	184	1.53
South American	67	0.56
Argentinean	1	0.01
Bolivian	4	0.03
Colombian	30	0.25
Ecuadorian	2	0.02
Peruvian	18	0.15
Venezuelan	10	0.08
Other South American	2	0.02
Other Hispanic or Latino	80	0.66

Race*	Population	%
African-American/Black (4,488)	4,698	39.00

*Notes: † The Census 2010 population figure is used to calculate the percentages in the Hispanic Origin and Race categories. Ancestry percentages are based on the 2006-2010 American Community Survey population (not shown); ‡ Numbers in parentheses indicate the number of people reporting a single ancestry; * Numbers in parentheses indicate the number of persons reporting this race alone, not in combination with any other race; Please refer to the Explanation of Data for more information.*

Not Hispanic (4,432)	4,596	38.15
Hispanic (56)	102	0.85
American Indian/Alaska Native (51)	137	1.14
Not Hispanic (47)	128	1.06
Hispanic (4)	9	0.07
Aleut *(Alaska Native)* (2)	2	0.02
Apache (1)	2	0.02
Blackfeet (1)	6	0.05
Cherokee (12)	45	0.37
Chippewa (2)	3	0.02
Choctaw (1)	3	0.02
Comanche (0)	1	0.01
Creek (3)	3	0.02
Inupiat *(Alaska Native)* (1)	2	0.02
Kiowa (2)	2	0.02
Seminole (1)	7	0.06
Sioux (0)	4	0.03
Tohono O'Odham (0)	5	0.04
Asian (195)	233	1.93
Not Hispanic (192)	227	1.88
Hispanic (3)	6	0.05
Burmese (2)	2	0.02
Chinese, ex. Taiwanese (26)	33	0.27
Filipino (36)	44	0.37
Indian (92)	97	0.81
Indonesian (3)	4	0.03
Japanese (2)	5	0.04
Korean (3)	12	0.10
Nepalese (1)	1	0.01
Pakistani (1)	1	0.01
Sri Lankan (0)	1	0.01
Taiwanese (4)	4	0.03
Vietnamese (15)	17	0.14
Hawaii Native/Pacific Islander (0)	14	0.12
Not Hispanic (0)	11	0.09
Hispanic (0)	3	0.02
Guamanian/Chamorro (0)	1	0.01
Native Hawaiian (0)	5	0.04
Samoan (0)	3	0.02
White (6,816)	7,088	58.84
Not Hispanic (6,453)	6,669	55.36
Hispanic (363)	419	3.48

Lake Magdalene

Place Type: CDP
County: Hillsborough
Population: 28,509†

Ancestry‡	Population	%
African, Sub-Saharan (171)	230	0.78
African (157)	157	0.53
Kenyan (0)	48	0.16
South African (14)	25	0.08
American (2,111)	2,111	7.13
Arab (137)	234	0.79
Egyptian (97)	97	0.33
Lebanese (0)	79	0.27
Syrian (0)	18	0.06
Other Arab (40)	40	0.14
Armenian (0)	11	0.04
Austrian (31)	55	0.19
Brazilian (0)	13	0.04
British (78)	140	0.47
Canadian (0)	54	0.18
Celtic (0)	15	0.05
Croatian (0)	24	0.08
Czech (30)	71	0.24
Czechoslovakian (9)	9	0.03
Danish (69)	99	0.33
Dutch (44)	255	0.86
Eastern European (53)	53	0.18
English (1,409)	3,617	12.22
Estonian (12)	12	0.04
European (284)	363	1.23
Finnish (0)	15	0.05
French, ex. Basque (276)	1,121	3.79
French Canadian (79)	213	0.72
German (1,136)	3,928	13.27
Greek (70)	170	0.57
Guyanese (0)	21	0.07
Hungarian (423)	499	1.69
Iranian (21)	21	0.07
Irish (1,147)	3,870	13.08
Italian (812)	1,938	6.55
Lithuanian (28)	86	0.29
Luxemburger (0)	16	0.05
Northern European (10)	10	0.03
Norwegian (94)	152	0.51
Pennsylvania German (0)	10	0.03
Polish (312)	751	2.54
Portuguese (64)	99	0.33
Romanian (0)	18	0.06
Russian (152)	576	1.95
Scandinavian (70)	106	0.36
Scotch-Irish (233)	439	1.48
Scottish (290)	794	2.68
Serbian (37)	55	0.19
Slavic (10)	10	0.03
Slovak (45)	72	0.24
Swedish (26)	291	0.98
Swiss (8)	17	0.06
Ukrainian (68)	96	0.32
Welsh (72)	505	1.71
West Indian, ex. Hispanic (416)	494	1.67
Bahamian (20)	41	0.14
Belizean (55)	55	0.19
British West Indian (28)	28	0.09
Haitian (304)	304	1.03
Trinidadian/Tobagonian (9)	56	0.19
Other West Indian (0)	10	0.03

Hispanic Origin	Population	%
Hispanic or Latino (of any race)	6,019	21.11
Central American, ex. Mexican	377	1.32
Costa Rican	42	0.15
Guatemalan	22	0.08
Honduran	144	0.51
Nicaraguan	42	0.15
Panamanian	48	0.17
Salvadoran	77	0.27
Other Central American	2	0.01
Cuban	1,344	4.71
Dominican Republic	216	0.76
Mexican	490	1.72
Puerto Rican	2,003	7.03
South American	830	2.91
Argentinean	26	0.09
Bolivian	18	0.06
Chilean	2	0.01
Colombian	402	1.41
Ecuadorian	87	0.31
Paraguayan	1	<0.01
Peruvian	156	0.55
Uruguayan	8	0.03
Venezuelan	116	0.41
Other South American	14	0.05
Other Hispanic or Latino	759	2.66

Race*	Population	%
African-American/Black (2,192)	2,526	8.86
Not Hispanic (1,974)	2,199	7.71
Hispanic (218)	327	1.15
American Indian/Alaska Native (82)	257	0.90
Not Hispanic (55)	180	0.63
Hispanic (27)	77	0.27
Apache (1)	5	0.02
Blackfeet (0)	5	0.02
Central American Ind. (0)	4	0.01
Cherokee (18)	58	0.20
Chickasaw (0)	1	<0.01
Chippewa (3)	3	0.01
Choctaw (0)	3	0.01
Colville (0)	1	<0.01
Comanche (0)	3	0.01
Cree (0)	3	0.01
Creek (1)	2	0.01
Crow (1)	1	<0.01
Inupiat *(Alaska Native)* (0)	3	0.01
Iroquois (2)	5	0.02
Lumbee (5)	7	0.02
Menominee (1)	1	<0.01
Navajo (0)	2	0.01
Potawatomi (2)	2	0.01
Sioux (5)	5	0.02
South American Ind. (1)	6	0.02
Spanish American Ind. (0)	1	<0.01
Tohono O'Odham (1)	1	<0.01
Asian (786)	1,041	3.65
Not Hispanic (774)	983	3.45
Hispanic (12)	58	0.20
Bangladeshi (1)	2	0.01
Burmese (6)	6	0.02
Chinese, ex. Taiwanese (109)	135	0.47
Filipino (144)	186	0.65
Indian (259)	305	1.07
Indonesian (8)	12	0.04
Japanese (31)	74	0.26
Korean (53)	93	0.33
Laotian (6)	6	0.02
Malaysian (1)	1	<0.01
Pakistani (16)	26	0.09
Sri Lankan (1)	1	<0.01
Taiwanese (7)	7	0.02
Thai (20)	24	0.08
Vietnamese (103)	123	0.43
Hawaii Native/Pacific Islander (16)	44	0.15
Not Hispanic (16)	36	0.13
Hispanic (0)	8	0.03
Guamanian/Chamorro (8)	10	0.04
Native Hawaiian (1)	14	0.05
Samoan (0)	1	<0.01
White (23,597)	24,330	85.34
Not Hispanic (19,076)	19,527	68.49
Hispanic (4,521)	4,803	16.85

Lake Mary

Place Type: City
County: Seminole
Population: 13,822†

Ancestry‡	Population	%
African, Sub-Saharan (67)	79	0.58
African (0)	12	0.09
South African (67)	67	0.49
Albanian (72)	72	0.53
American (572)	572	4.22
Arab (0)	73	0.54
Arab (0)	19	0.14
Lebanese (0)	54	0.40
Australian (8)	45	0.33
Austrian (0)	21	0.15
British (27)	37	0.27
Canadian (14)	14	0.10
Croatian (0)	17	0.13
Czech (33)	58	0.43
Czechoslovakian (49)	100	0.74
Danish (0)	32	0.24
Dutch (55)	326	2.41
English (734)	1,870	13.80
European (739)	767	5.66
Finnish (10)	32	0.24
French, ex. Basque (57)	543	4.01
French Canadian (166)	237	1.75
German (540)	2,033	15.00
Greek (20)	20	0.15
Iranian (127)	127	0.94
Irish (537)	2,030	14.98
Italian (672)	1,447	10.68
Lithuanian (13)	35	0.26
Maltese (14)	29	0.21
Norwegian (35)	157	1.16
Pennsylvania German (0)	21	0.15
Polish (89)	525	3.87
Portuguese (55)	91	0.67
Russian (49)	68	0.50
Scandinavian (27)	27	0.20
Scotch-Irish (344)	483	3.56
Scottish (248)	514	3.79

*Notes: † The Census 2010 population figure is used to calculate the percentages in the Hispanic Origin and Race categories. Ancestry percentages are based on the 2006-2010 American Community Survey population (not shown); ‡ Numbers in parentheses indicate the number of people reporting a single ancestry; * Numbers in parentheses indicate the number of persons reporting this race alone, not in combination with any other race; Please refer to the Explanation of Data for more information.*

	Population	%
Serbian (0)	29	0.21
Slavic (0)	37	0.27
Slovak (10)	21	0.15
Swedish (8)	157	1.16
Turkish (14)	14	0.10
Ukrainian (0)	2	0.01
Welsh (5)	180	1.33
West Indian, ex. Hispanic (71)	83	0.61
Jamaican (71)	71	0.52
West Indian (0)	12	0.09

Hispanic Origin	Population	%
Hispanic or Latino (of any race)	1,408	10.19
Central American, ex. Mexican	68	0.49
Costa Rican	11	0.08
Guatemalan	14	0.10
Honduran	8	0.06
Nicaraguan	9	0.07
Panamanian	15	0.11
Salvadoran	10	0.07
Other Central American	1	0.01
Cuban	130	0.94
Dominican Republic	77	0.56
Mexican	130	0.94
Puerto Rican	615	4.45
South American	314	2.27
Argentinean	18	0.13
Bolivian	1	0.01
Chilean	9	0.07
Colombian	158	1.14
Ecuadorian	18	0.13
Peruvian	47	0.34
Uruguayan	4	0.03
Venezuelan	52	0.38
Other South American	7	0.05
Other Hispanic or Latino	74	0.54

Race*	Population	%
African-American/Black (688)	821	5.94
Not Hispanic (642)	744	5.38
Hispanic (46)	77	0.56
American Indian/Alaska Native (35)	87	0.63
Not Hispanic (32)	69	0.50
Hispanic (3)	18	0.13
Blackfeet (0)	6	0.04
Central American Ind. (2)	2	0.01
Cherokee (8)	18	0.13
Choctaw (6)	6	0.04
Creek (0)	3	0.02
Lumbee (1)	1	0.01
South American Ind. (1)	13	0.09
Asian (828)	975	7.05
Not Hispanic (822)	956	6.92
Hispanic (6)	19	0.14
Bangladeshi (15)	15	0.11
Burmese (1)	1	0.01
Cambodian (9)	10	0.07
Chinese, ex. Taiwanese (134)	166	1.20
Filipino (130)	160	1.16
Indian (303)	335	2.42
Indonesian (2)	5	0.04
Japanese (15)	33	0.24
Korean (52)	69	0.50
Laotian (30)	33	0.24
Malaysian (1)	1	0.01
Pakistani (17)	17	0.12
Sri Lankan (4)	4	0.03
Taiwanese (5)	5	0.04
Thai (10)	15	0.11
Vietnamese (61)	78	0.56
Hawaii Native/Pacific Islander (4)	8	0.06
Not Hispanic (4)	8	0.06
Native Hawaiian (1)	3	0.02
White (11,684)	11,963	86.55
Not Hispanic (10,641)	10,843	78.45
Hispanic (1,043)	1,120	8.10

Lake Park

Place Type: Town
County: Palm Beach
Population: 8,155†

Ancestry‡	Population	%
African, Sub-Saharan (125)	171	2.08
African (125)	171	2.08
American (264)	264	3.22
Arab (25)	25	0.30
Egyptian (25)	25	0.30
Brazilian (37)	37	0.45
British (55)	55	0.67
Canadian (43)	64	0.78
Croatian (0)	11	0.13
Danish (0)	15	0.18
Dutch (14)	24	0.29
English (92)	495	6.03
European (48)	48	0.58
French, ex. Basque (45)	170	2.07
French Canadian (22)	48	0.58
German (174)	638	7.77
Greek (0)	81	0.99
Guyanese (25)	25	0.30
Hungarian (34)	34	0.41
Irish (250)	549	6.69
Italian (100)	283	3.45
Norwegian (20)	33	0.40
Polish (21)	149	1.82
Portuguese (0)	5	0.06
Scotch-Irish (0)	20	0.24
Scottish (10)	27	0.33
Serbian (0)	21	0.26
Slovak (0)	21	0.26
Swedish (23)	41	0.50
Swiss (16)	25	0.30
Ukrainian (0)	33	0.40
West Indian, ex. Hispanic (2,410)	2,448	29.82
Bahamian (7)	7	0.09
Barbadian (45)	45	0.55
British West Indian (12)	12	0.15
Haitian (2,150)	2,150	26.19
Jamaican (196)	234	2.85

Hispanic Origin	Population	%
Hispanic or Latino (of any race)	653	8.01
Central American, ex. Mexican	155	1.90
Costa Rican	17	0.21
Guatemalan	33	0.40
Honduran	53	0.65
Nicaraguan	31	0.38
Panamanian	10	0.12
Salvadoran	11	0.13
Cuban	52	0.64
Dominican Republic	25	0.31
Mexican	71	0.87
Puerto Rican	196	2.40
South American	86	1.05
Argentinean	13	0.16
Bolivian	1	0.01
Colombian	45	0.55
Ecuadorian	1	0.01
Peruvian	15	0.18
Uruguayan	1	0.01
Venezuelan	10	0.12
Other Hispanic or Latino	68	0.83

Race*	Population	%
African-American/Black (4,485)	4,661	57.16
Not Hispanic (4,378)	4,523	55.46
Hispanic (107)	138	1.69
American Indian/Alaska Native (15)	59	0.72
Not Hispanic (11)	48	0.59
Hispanic (4)	11	0.13
Alaska Athabascan *(Ala. Nat.)* (0)	1	0.01
Blackfeet (1)	4	0.05
Cherokee (4)	17	0.21
Choctaw (0)	2	0.02
Iroquois (0)	6	0.07
Seminole (0)	1	0.01
Asian (198)	246	3.02
Not Hispanic (197)	241	2.96
Hispanic (1)	5	0.06
Bangladeshi (8)	8	0.10
Cambodian (1)	3	0.04
Chinese, ex. Taiwanese (19)	31	0.38
Filipino (11)	18	0.22
Indian (27)	41	0.50
Japanese (3)	5	0.06
Korean (3)	4	0.05
Laotian (38)	41	0.50
Malaysian (2)	2	0.02
Pakistani (1)	1	0.01
Thai (11)	11	0.13
Vietnamese (53)	61	0.75
Hawaii Native/Pacific Islander (6)	50	0.61
Not Hispanic (6)	46	0.56
Hispanic (0)	4	0.05
Guamanian/Chamorro (6)	6	0.07
White (3,054)	3,171	38.88
Not Hispanic (2,710)	2,808	34.43
Hispanic (344)	363	4.45

Lake Wales

Place Type: City
County: Polk
Population: 14,225†

Ancestry‡	Population	%
African, Sub-Saharan (30)	115	0.83
African (30)	115	0.83
American (1,118)	1,118	8.05
Assyrian/Chaldean/Syriac (0)	19	0.14
Australian (17)	17	0.12
Belgian (0)	10	0.07
British (16)	33	0.24
Canadian (53)	180	1.30
Croatian (17)	24	0.17
Czech (17)	26	0.19
Danish (0)	23	0.17
Dutch (76)	280	2.02
English (549)	1,229	8.85
European (16)	16	0.12
Finnish (13)	13	0.09
French, ex. Basque (31)	237	1.71
French Canadian (39)	71	0.51
German (610)	1,684	12.13
Greek (0)	42	0.30
Hungarian (25)	54	0.39
Irish (585)	1,569	11.30
Israeli (57)	57	0.41
Italian (310)	474	3.41
Lithuanian (12)	44	0.32
Macedonian (0)	13	0.09
Norwegian (98)	171	1.23
Pennsylvania German (9)	9	0.06
Polish (146)	294	2.12
Russian (41)	59	0.42
Scandinavian (13)	13	0.09
Scotch-Irish (51)	132	0.95
Scottish (22)	124	0.89
Slavic (0)	26	0.19
Slovak (20)	61	0.44
Swedish (21)	91	0.66
Ukrainian (0)	28	0.20
Welsh (12)	74	0.53
West Indian, ex. Hispanic (219)	219	1.58
Bahamian (42)	42	0.30
Haitian (49)	49	0.35
Jamaican (128)	128	0.92
Yugoslavian (13)	22	0.16

Hispanic Origin	Population	%
Hispanic or Latino (of any race)	2,222	15.62
Central American, ex. Mexican	94	0.66
Costa Rican	2	0.01
Guatemalan	50	0.35
Honduran	23	0.16

*Notes: † The Census 2010 population figure is used to calculate the percentages in the Hispanic Origin and Race categories. Ancestry percentages are based on the 2006-2010 American Community Survey population (not shown); ‡ Numbers in parentheses indicate the number of people reporting a single ancestry; * Numbers in parentheses indicate the number of persons reporting this race alone, not in combination with any other race; Please refer to the Explanation of Data for more information.*

Nicaraguan	5	0.04
Panamanian	8	0.06
Salvadoran	6	0.04
Cuban	110	0.77
Dominican Republic	35	0.25
Mexican	1,158	8.14
Puerto Rican	617	4.34
South American	83	0.58
Argentinean	2	0.01
Colombian	13	0.09
Ecuadorian	28	0.20
Peruvian	24	0.17
Uruguayan	7	0.05
Venezuelan	9	0.06
Other Hispanic or Latino	125	0.88

Race*	Population	%
African-American/Black (3,905)	4,072	28.63
Not Hispanic (3,784)	3,923	27.58
Hispanic (121)	149	1.05
American Indian/Alaska Native (69)	141	0.99
Not Hispanic (46)	107	0.75
Hispanic (23)	34	0.24
Apache (0)	2	0.01
Blackfeet (0)	3	0.02
Central American Ind. (2)	2	0.01
Cherokee (12)	52	0.37
Cheyenne (0)	2	0.01
Creek (1)	2	0.01
Iroquois (3)	3	0.02
Lumbee (3)	3	0.02
Mexican American Ind. (7)	9	0.06
Navajo (0)	1	0.01
Potawatomi (2)	2	0.01
Seminole (4)	6	0.04
Sioux (0)	5	0.04
South American Ind. (0)	1	0.01
Asian (119)	154	1.08
Not Hispanic (117)	149	1.05
Hispanic (2)	5	0.04
Bangladeshi (0)	2	0.01
Cambodian (0)	1	0.01
Chinese, ex. Taiwanese (25)	28	0.20
Filipino (39)	49	0.34
Indian (31)	33	0.23
Indonesian (1)	3	0.02
Japanese (7)	10	0.07
Korean (1)	3	0.02
Laotian (1)	2	0.01
Pakistani (0)	1	0.01
Taiwanese (0)	1	0.01
Thai (4)	5	0.04
Vietnamese (1)	1	0.01
Hawaii Native/Pacific Islander (12)	32	0.22
Not Hispanic (3)	14	0.10
Hispanic (9)	18	0.13
Guamanian/Chamorro (7)	9	0.06
Native Hawaiian (2)	4	0.03
Samoan (0)	1	0.01
Tongan (1)	1	0.01
White (9,250)	9,515	66.89
Not Hispanic (7,820)	7,981	56.11
Hispanic (1,430)	1,534	10.78

Lake Worth

Place Type: City
County: Palm Beach
Population: 34,910†

Ancestry‡	Population	%
African, Sub-Saharan (109)	175	0.49
African (76)	142	0.40
South African (33)	33	0.09
American (481)	481	1.36
Arab (198)	246	0.69
Egyptian (145)	145	0.41
Lebanese (53)	84	0.24
Other Arab (0)	17	0.05
Armenian (0)	57	0.16
Australian (0)	100	0.28
Austrian (27)	64	0.18
Belgian (12)	12	0.03
Brazilian (70)	82	0.23
British (93)	172	0.49
Canadian (97)	127	0.36
Celtic (0)	10	0.03
Croatian (10)	21	0.06
Czech (108)	160	0.45
Czechoslovakian (30)	30	0.08
Danish (32)	110	0.31
Dutch (83)	310	0.88
English (421)	2,335	6.59
European (123)	123	0.35
Finnish (475)	542	1.53
French, ex. Basque (92)	821	2.32
French Canadian (204)	345	0.97
German (555)	2,825	7.98
Greek (71)	137	0.39
Guyanese (21)	21	0.06
Hungarian (77)	83	0.23
Iranian (32)	32	0.09
Irish (852)	3,092	8.73
Italian (460)	1,263	3.57
Latvian (14)	14	0.04
Lithuanian (57)	88	0.25
Northern European (14)	14	0.04
Norwegian (46)	226	0.64
Polish (224)	664	1.88
Portuguese (60)	174	0.49
Romanian (10)	56	0.16
Russian (115)	255	0.72
Scandinavian (24)	45	0.13
Scotch-Irish (113)	304	0.86
Scottish (177)	686	1.94
Slavic (0)	11	0.03
Slovak (25)	47	0.13
Swedish (34)	186	0.53
Swiss (0)	13	0.04
Ukrainian (0)	15	0.04
Welsh (23)	137	0.39
West Indian, ex. Hispanic (4,075)	4,230	11.95
Bahamian (51)	106	0.30
Belizean (0)	10	0.03
Haitian (3,592)	3,598	10.16
Jamaican (359)	392	1.11
Trinidadian/Tobagonian (73)	82	0.23
U.S. Virgin Islander (0)	42	0.12

Hispanic Origin	Population	%
Hispanic or Latino (of any race)	13,834	39.63
Central American, ex. Mexican	6,320	18.10
Costa Rican	51	0.15
Guatemalan	4,432	12.70
Honduran	906	2.60
Nicaraguan	180	0.52
Panamanian	22	0.06
Salvadoran	687	1.97
Other Central American	42	0.12
Cuban	1,438	4.12
Dominican Republic	314	0.90
Mexican	2,765	7.92
Puerto Rican	1,413	4.05
South American	726	2.08
Argentinean	69	0.20
Bolivian	33	0.09
Chilean	27	0.08
Colombian	285	0.82
Ecuadorian	68	0.19
Paraguayan	12	0.03
Peruvian	100	0.29
Uruguayan	62	0.18
Venezuelan	65	0.19
Other South American	5	0.01
Other Hispanic or Latino	858	2.46

Race*	Population	%
African-American/Black (6,917)	7,331	21.00
Not Hispanic (6,603)	6,911	19.80
Hispanic (314)	420	1.20
American Indian/Alaska Native (1,962)	2,346	6.72
Not Hispanic (322)	420	1.20
Hispanic (1,640)	1,926	5.52
Apache (7)	7	0.02
Central American Ind. (233)	255	0.73
Cherokee (12)	42	0.12
Chickasaw (1)	2	0.01
Chippewa (1)	2	0.01
Choctaw (5)	9	0.03
Comanche (0)	4	0.01
Creek (0)	1	<0.01
Delaware (0)	1	<0.01
Hopi (3)	7	0.02
Iroquois (4)	4	0.01
Kiowa (2)	2	0.01
Lumbee (1)	1	<0.01
Menominee (0)	2	0.01
Mexican American Ind. (1,405)	1,624	4.65
Navajo (3)	4	0.01
Ottawa (1)	1	<0.01
Pueblo (1)	1	<0.01
Seminole (8)	9	0.03
Sioux (2)	2	0.01
South American Ind. (10)	19	0.05
Spanish American Ind. (16)	18	0.05
Tlingit-Haida *(Alaska Native)* (2)	4	0.01
Asian (335)	486	1.39
Not Hispanic (308)	404	1.16
Hispanic (27)	82	0.23
Bangladeshi (17)	18	0.05
Burmese (9)	9	0.03
Cambodian (0)	1	<0.01
Chinese, ex. Taiwanese (30)	49	0.14
Filipino (91)	107	0.31
Indian (91)	112	0.32
Indonesian (5)	6	0.02
Japanese (11)	22	0.06
Korean (21)	32	0.09
Laotian (0)	1	<0.01
Nepalese (1)	1	<0.01
Pakistani (3)	3	0.01
Sri Lankan (2)	2	0.01
Thai (8)	12	0.03
Vietnamese (27)	32	0.09
Hawaii Native/Pacific Islander (31)	139	0.40
Not Hispanic (22)	82	0.23
Hispanic (9)	57	0.16
Fijian (3)	6	0.02
Guamanian/Chamorro (14)	39	0.11
Native Hawaiian (5)	12	0.03
Samoan (1)	4	0.01
White (20,959)	22,216	63.64
Not Hispanic (13,291)	13,602	38.96
Hispanic (7,668)	8,614	24.67

Lakeland Highlands

Place Type: CDP
County: Polk
Population: 11,056†

Ancestry‡	Population	%
African, Sub-Saharan (50)	50	0.43
African (50)	50	0.43
American (715)	715	6.20
Arab (0)	30	0.26
Iraqi (0)	12	0.10
Lebanese (0)	9	0.08
Syrian (0)	9	0.08
Austrian (24)	47	0.41
Belgian (10)	15	0.13
Brazilian (0)	7	0.06
British (15)	87	0.75
Bulgarian (0)	12	0.10
Canadian (95)	95	0.82
Croatian (9)	20	0.17
Czech (11)	27	0.23
Danish (0)	21	0.18
Dutch (17)	114	0.99
Eastern European (39)	100	0.87

*Notes: † The Census 2010 population figure is used to calculate the percentages in the Hispanic Origin and Race categories. Ancestry percentages are based on the 2006-2010 American Community Survey population (not shown); ‡ Numbers in parentheses indicate the number of people reporting a single ancestry; * Numbers in parentheses indicate the number of persons reporting this race alone, not in combination with any other race; Please refer to the Explanation of Data for more information.*

English (934)	2,519	21.85
European (200)	218	1.89
Finnish (0)	31	0.27
French, ex. Basque (81)	496	4.30
French Canadian (83)	223	1.93
German (842)	2,186	18.96
Greek (0)	129	1.12
Hungarian (0)	74	0.64
Irish (516)	1,639	14.22
Italian (259)	750	6.51
Latvian (0)	14	0.12
Lithuanian (0)	15	0.13
Norwegian (36)	133	1.15
Polish (203)	306	2.65
Portuguese (0)	8	0.07
Russian (51)	108	0.94
Scandinavian (11)	27	0.23
Scotch-Irish (220)	546	4.74
Scottish (107)	323	2.80
Serbian (8)	8	0.07
Slovak (8)	8	0.07
Slovene (12)	38	0.33
Swedish (46)	237	2.06
Swiss (7)	104	0.90
Ukrainian (21)	93	0.81
Welsh (34)	149	1.29

Hispanic Origin	Population	%
Hispanic or Latino (of any race)	871	7.88
Central American, ex. Mexican	64	0.58
Costa Rican	7	0.06
Guatemalan	11	0.10
Honduran	6	0.05
Nicaraguan	9	0.08
Panamanian	16	0.14
Salvadoran	15	0.14
Cuban	242	2.19
Dominican Republic	35	0.32
Mexican	134	1.21
Puerto Rican	210	1.90
South American	118	1.07
Argentinean	11	0.10
Bolivian	1	0.01
Chilean	2	0.02
Colombian	50	0.45
Ecuadorian	12	0.11
Paraguayan	1	0.01
Peruvian	23	0.21
Venezuelan	17	0.15
Other South American	1	0.01
Other Hispanic or Latino	68	0.62

Race*	Population	%
African-American/Black (374)	428	3.87
Not Hispanic (355)	396	3.58
Hispanic (19)	32	0.29
American Indian/Alaska Native (21)	66	0.60
Not Hispanic (19)	63	0.57
Hispanic (2)	3	0.03
Apache (0)	1	0.01
Blackfeet (0)	1	0.01
Cherokee (4)	21	0.19
Choctaw (1)	3	0.03
Creek (2)	4	0.04
Crow (0)	1	0.01
Ottawa (1)	1	0.01
Tlingit-Haida *(Alaska Native)* (0)	1	0.01
Asian (237)	316	2.86
Not Hispanic (235)	307	2.78
Hispanic (2)	9	0.08
Bangladeshi (3)	3	0.03
Chinese, ex. Taiwanese (27)	43	0.39
Filipino (52)	76	0.69
Indian (93)	105	0.95
Indonesian (3)	4	0.04
Japanese (5)	13	0.12
Korean (24)	30	0.27
Laotian (1)	1	0.01
Pakistani (6)	6	0.05
Sri Lankan (2)	2	0.02
Taiwanese (1)	1	0.01
Thai (6)	14	0.13
Vietnamese (8)	10	0.09
Hawaii Native/Pacific Islander (4)	15	0.14
Not Hispanic (4)	14	0.13
Hispanic (0)	1	0.01
Fijian (2)	2	0.02
Guamanian/Chamorro (0)	2	0.02
Native Hawaiian (2)	7	0.06
White (10,122)	10,295	93.12
Not Hispanic (9,402)	9,541	86.30
Hispanic (720)	754	6.82

Lakeland

Place Type: City
County: Polk
Population: 97,422†

Ancestry‡	Population	%
African, Sub-Saharan (383)	694	0.72
African (271)	475	0.49
Kenyan (57)	57	0.06
Liberian (42)	94	0.10
Nigerian (0)	38	0.04
Senegalese (0)	17	0.02
South African (13)	13	0.01
American (7,617)	7,617	7.88
Arab (109)	628	0.65
Arab (14)	46	0.05
Egyptian (66)	105	0.11
Lebanese (0)	38	0.04
Moroccan (0)	160	0.17
Syrian (0)	45	0.05
Other Arab (29)	234	0.24
Armenian (42)	42	0.04
Australian (14)	110	0.11
Austrian (29)	112	0.12
Belgian (34)	93	0.10
Brazilian (53)	69	0.07
British (246)	387	0.40
Cajun (17)	33	0.03
Canadian (117)	296	0.31
Celtic (7)	7	0.01
Croatian (0)	123	0.13
Czech (94)	457	0.47
Czechoslovakian (23)	99	0.10
Danish (99)	163	0.17
Dutch (261)	1,491	1.54
Eastern European (25)	25	0.03
English (5,639)	12,932	13.38
European (436)	548	0.57
Finnish (153)	168	0.17
French, ex. Basque (799)	2,540	2.63
French Canadian (483)	700	0.72
German (3,930)	13,640	14.12
Greek (231)	351	0.36
Guyanese (38)	38	0.04
Hungarian (95)	397	0.41
Icelander (10)	10	0.01
Iranian (14)	39	0.04
Irish (3,204)	11,116	11.50
Israeli (15)	45	0.05
Italian (2,008)	4,102	4.25
Lithuanian (41)	83	0.09
New Zealander (0)	14	0.01
Norwegian (195)	483	0.50
Pennsylvania German (36)	43	0.04
Polish (776)	2,025	2.10
Portuguese (94)	270	0.28
Romanian (0)	55	0.06
Russian (191)	554	0.57
Scandinavian (0)	7	0.01
Scotch-Irish (1,005)	2,747	2.84
Scottish (641)	2,024	2.09
Serbian (21)	36	0.04
Slavic (40)	40	0.04
Slovak (22)	90	0.09
Slovene (30)	53	0.05
Swedish (226)	857	0.89
Swiss (23)	149	0.15
Turkish (85)	128	0.13
Ukrainian (44)	56	0.06
Welsh (127)	819	0.85
West Indian, ex. Hispanic (1,216)	1,712	1.77
Bahamian (7)	7	0.01
Barbadian (40)	40	0.04
Belizean (14)	14	0.01
British West Indian (31)	31	0.03
Haitian (272)	332	0.34
Jamaican (728)	1,016	1.05
Trinidadian/Tobagonian (58)	90	0.09
West Indian (66)	85	0.09
Other West Indian (0)	97	0.10
Yugoslavian (101)	258	0.27

Hispanic Origin	Population	%
Hispanic or Latino (of any race)	12,271	12.60
Central American, ex. Mexican	833	0.86
Costa Rican	58	0.06
Guatemalan	213	0.22
Honduran	241	0.25
Nicaraguan	150	0.15
Panamanian	87	0.09
Salvadoran	72	0.07
Other Central American	12	0.01
Cuban	1,563	1.60
Dominican Republic	385	0.40
Mexican	3,036	3.12
Puerto Rican	4,857	4.99
South American	841	0.86
Argentinean	44	0.05
Bolivian	16	0.02
Chilean	25	0.03
Colombian	356	0.37
Ecuadorian	97	0.10
Paraguayan	1	<0.01
Peruvian	158	0.16
Uruguayan	15	0.02
Venezuelan	111	0.11
Other South American	18	0.02
Other Hispanic or Latino	756	0.78

Race*	Population	%
African-American/Black (20,351)	21,747	22.32
Not Hispanic (19,788)	20,829	21.38
Hispanic (563)	918	0.94
American Indian/Alaska Native (311)	886	0.91
Not Hispanic (253)	712	0.73
Hispanic (58)	174	0.18
Aleut *(Alaska Native)* (1)	1	<0.01
Apache (0)	3	<0.01
Blackfeet (6)	24	0.02
Central American Ind. (4)	5	0.01
Cherokee (62)	229	0.24
Chickasaw (1)	7	0.01
Chippewa (10)	14	0.01
Choctaw (7)	20	0.02
Comanche (1)	1	<0.01
Creek (6)	28	0.03
Crow (1)	1	<0.01
Delaware (1)	3	<0.01
Inupiat *(Alaska Native)* (1)	1	<0.01
Iroquois (7)	15	0.02
Kiowa (1)	1	<0.01
Lumbee (12)	16	0.02
Menominee (1)	1	<0.01
Mexican American Ind. (3)	16	0.02
Navajo (9)	13	0.01
Ottawa (2)	2	<0.01
Paiute (2)	2	<0.01
Pima (0)	1	<0.01
Seminole (0)	14	0.01
Sioux (3)	11	0.01
South American Ind. (7)	15	0.02
Spanish American Ind. (1)	1	<0.01
Tohono O'Odham (0)	3	<0.01
Asian (1,758)	2,179	2.24
Not Hispanic (1,717)	2,081	2.14
Hispanic (41)	98	0.10

*Notes: † The Census 2010 population figure is used to calculate the percentages in the Hispanic Origin and Race categories. Ancestry percentages are based on the 2006-2010 American Community Survey population (not shown); ‡ Numbers in parentheses indicate the number of people reporting a single ancestry; * Numbers in parentheses indicate the number of persons reporting this race alone, not in combination with any other race; Please refer to the Explanation of Data for more information.*

Bangladeshi (27)	31	0.03
Burmese (14)	15	0.02
Cambodian (40)	49	0.05
Chinese, ex. Taiwanese (157)	221	0.23
Filipino (345)	457	0.47
Hmong (22)	26	0.03
Indian (653)	743	0.76
Indonesian (8)	11	0.01
Japanese (42)	80	0.08
Korean (100)	143	0.15
Laotian (56)	69	0.07
Malaysian (1)	2	<0.01
Nepalese (5)	5	0.01
Pakistani (23)	27	0.03
Sri Lankan (7)	7	0.01
Taiwanese (11)	17	0.02
Thai (47)	75	0.08
Vietnamese (108)	133	0.14
Hawaii Native/Pacific Islander (87)	212	0.22
Not Hispanic (62)	157	0.16
Hispanic (25)	55	0.06
Fijian (0)	3	<0.01
Guamanian/Chamorro (26)	42	0.04
Marshallese (12)	12	0.01
Native Hawaiian (15)	44	0.05
Samoan (11)	23	0.02
White (69,011)	71,133	73.02
Not Hispanic (61,468)	62,871	64.53
Hispanic (7,543)	8,262	8.48

Lakeside

Place Type: CDP
County: Clay
Population: 30,943†

Ancestry‡	Population	%
African, Sub-Saharan (74)	74	0.24
African (41)	41	0.13
Other Sub-Saharan African (33)	33	0.11
Alsatian (11)	11	0.04
American (2,568)	2,568	8.18
Arab (61)	105	0.33
Arab (43)	87	0.28
Palestinian (18)	18	0.06
Australian (0)	18	0.06
Austrian (17)	31	0.10
Belgian (13)	13	0.04
Brazilian (16)	96	0.31
British (60)	141	0.45
Canadian (39)	73	0.23
Croatian (14)	41	0.13
Czech (10)	77	0.25
Czechoslovakian (0)	12	0.04
Danish (0)	50	0.16
Dutch (221)	740	2.36
Eastern European (11)	11	0.04
English (1,677)	4,051	12.90
European (254)	267	0.85
Finnish (0)	19	0.06
French, ex. Basque (97)	1,063	3.39
French Canadian (107)	277	0.88
German (1,656)	4,631	14.75
Greek (16)	16	0.05
Hungarian (111)	180	0.57
Iranian (15)	78	0.25
Irish (1,051)	4,343	13.83
Israeli (7)	15	0.05
Italian (678)	1,985	6.32
Northern European (15)	15	0.05
Norwegian (168)	405	1.29
Pennsylvania German (23)	23	0.07
Polish (525)	1,111	3.54
Portuguese (16)	91	0.29
Romanian (34)	34	0.11
Russian (78)	130	0.41
Scotch-Irish (297)	593	1.89
Scottish (387)	865	2.76
Slovak (0)	38	0.12
Swedish (51)	122	0.39
Swiss (0)	90	0.29
Ukrainian (79)	167	0.53
Welsh (26)	250	0.80
West Indian, ex. Hispanic (273)	314	1.00
Haitian (136)	166	0.53
Jamaican (116)	127	0.40
West Indian (21)	21	0.07
Yugoslavian (0)	25	0.08

Hispanic Origin	Population	%
Hispanic or Latino (of any race)	2,513	8.12
Central American, ex. Mexican	224	0.72
Costa Rican	23	0.07
Guatemalan	23	0.07
Honduran	37	0.12
Nicaraguan	63	0.20
Panamanian	41	0.13
Salvadoran	32	0.10
Other Central American	5	0.02
Cuban	194	0.63
Dominican Republic	122	0.39
Mexican	561	1.81
Puerto Rican	874	2.82
South American	262	0.85
Argentinean	28	0.09
Bolivian	3	0.01
Chilean	2	0.01
Colombian	140	0.45
Ecuadorian	32	0.10
Peruvian	44	0.14
Uruguayan	1	<0.01
Venezuelan	12	0.04
Other Hispanic or Latino	276	0.89

Race*	Population	%
African-American/Black (3,100)	3,603	11.64
Not Hispanic (2,962)	3,353	10.84
Hispanic (138)	250	0.81
American Indian/Alaska Native (162)	424	1.37
Not Hispanic (126)	361	1.17
Hispanic (36)	63	0.20
Apache (4)	6	0.02
Blackfeet (2)	19	0.06
Central American Ind. (4)	10	0.03
Cherokee (24)	108	0.35
Chippewa (1)	2	0.01
Choctaw (7)	17	0.05
Comanche (5)	5	0.02
Creek (3)	4	0.01
Delaware (0)	2	0.01
Inupiat *(Alaska Native)* (4)	4	0.01
Iroquois (7)	15	0.05
Kiowa (1)	1	<0.01
Lumbee (8)	8	0.03
Mexican American Ind. (6)	7	0.02
Navajo (7)	11	0.04
Osage (0)	2	0.01
Potawatomi (2)	4	0.01
Seminole (2)	12	0.04
Sioux (3)	10	0.03
South American Ind. (3)	3	0.01
Spanish American Ind. (3)	3	0.01
Yaqui (1)	1	<0.01
Asian (918)	1,296	4.19
Not Hispanic (889)	1,221	3.95
Hispanic (29)	75	0.24
Bangladeshi (4)	4	0.01
Burmese (3)	3	0.01
Cambodian (22)	24	0.08
Chinese, ex. Taiwanese (75)	124	0.40
Filipino (531)	791	2.56
Indian (75)	86	0.28
Japanese (31)	91	0.29
Korean (26)	38	0.12
Laotian (6)	12	0.04
Malaysian (0)	1	<0.01
Pakistani (20)	21	0.07
Sri Lankan (2)	7	0.02
Taiwanese (1)	1	<0.01
Thai (12)	22	0.07
Vietnamese (74)	86	0.28
Hawaii Native/Pacific Islander (41)	112	0.36
Not Hispanic (34)	89	0.29
Hispanic (7)	23	0.07
Guamanian/Chamorro (16)	41	0.13
Native Hawaiian (13)	44	0.14
Samoan (6)	7	0.02
White (25,022)	26,002	84.03
Not Hispanic (23,476)	24,249	78.37
Hispanic (1,546)	1,753	5.67

Lakewood Park

Place Type: CDP
County: St. Lucie
Population: 11,323†

Ancestry‡	Population	%
African, Sub-Saharan (0)	25	0.21
Nigerian (0)	25	0.21
American (1,024)	1,024	8.64
Australian (0)	25	0.21
Belgian (0)	14	0.12
Brazilian (0)	6	0.05
British (106)	106	0.89
Canadian (76)	264	2.23
Croatian (18)	18	0.15
Czech (14)	14	0.12
Danish (0)	36	0.30
Dutch (0)	124	1.05
English (531)	1,469	12.39
European (429)	460	3.88
Finnish (0)	70	0.59
French, ex. Basque (217)	588	4.96
French Canadian (92)	172	1.45
German (706)	2,262	19.08
Greek (17)	79	0.67
Hungarian (12)	27	0.23
Irish (695)	2,206	18.61
Italian (558)	1,061	8.95
Latvian (0)	15	0.13
Lithuanian (16)	32	0.27
Norwegian (53)	98	0.83
Polish (210)	521	4.39
Portuguese (30)	36	0.30
Russian (0)	52	0.44
Scandinavian (0)	6	0.05
Scotch-Irish (87)	183	1.54
Scottish (87)	262	2.21
Slovak (0)	15	0.13
Swedish (22)	102	0.86
Swiss (0)	25	0.21
Ukrainian (0)	13	0.11
Welsh (20)	40	0.34
West Indian, ex. Hispanic (122)	278	2.34
Bahamian (0)	15	0.13
Belizean (14)	14	0.12
Haitian (96)	237	2.00
Jamaican (12)	12	0.10
Yugoslavian (9)	9	0.08

Hispanic Origin	Population	%
Hispanic or Latino (of any race)	741	6.54
Central American, ex. Mexican	45	0.40
Costa Rican	2	0.02
Guatemalan	12	0.11
Honduran	19	0.17
Nicaraguan	5	0.04
Panamanian	3	0.03
Salvadoran	2	0.02
Other Central American	2	0.02
Cuban	105	0.93
Dominican Republic	9	0.08
Mexican	289	2.55
Puerto Rican	170	1.50
South American	78	0.69
Argentinean	8	0.07
Bolivian	3	0.03
Chilean	3	0.03
Colombian	35	0.31

*Notes: † The Census 2010 population figure is used to calculate the percentages in the Hispanic Origin and Race categories. Ancestry percentages are based on the 2006-2010 American Community Survey population (not shown); ‡ Numbers in parentheses indicate the number of people reporting a single ancestry; * Numbers in parentheses indicate the number of persons reporting this race alone, not in combination with any other race; Please refer to the Explanation of Data for more information.*

Ecuadorian	14	0.12
Peruvian	9	0.08
Venezuelan	6	0.05
Other Hispanic or Latino	45	0.40

Race*	Population	%
African-American/Black (1,124)	1,214	10.72
Not Hispanic (1,106)	1,187	10.48
Hispanic (18)	27	0.24
American Indian/Alaska Native (32)	85	0.75
Not Hispanic (28)	78	0.69
Hispanic (4)	7	0.06
Alaska Athabascan *(Ala. Nat.)* (1)	1	0.01
Apache (0)	1	0.01
Blackfeet (0)	3	0.03
Canadian/French Am. Ind. (4)	5	0.04
Cherokee (5)	22	0.19
Cheyenne (1)	1	0.01
Chippewa (0)	1	0.01
Choctaw (0)	4	0.04
Iroquois (0)	2	0.02
Mexican American Ind. (0)	2	0.02
Navajo (1)	1	0.01
Ottawa (0)	1	0.01
Seminole (0)	2	0.02
Sioux (2)	3	0.03
Spanish American Ind. (0)	1	0.01
Tlingit-Haida *(Alaska Native)* (1)	1	0.01
Asian (174)	232	2.05
Not Hispanic (172)	222	1.96
Hispanic (2)	10	0.09
Bangladeshi (2)	2	0.02
Cambodian (2)	2	0.02
Chinese, ex. Taiwanese (18)	31	0.27
Filipino (22)	39	0.34
Indian (48)	50	0.44
Japanese (6)	15	0.13
Korean (4)	10	0.09
Pakistani (6)	7	0.06
Thai (13)	19	0.17
Vietnamese (48)	49	0.43
Hawaii Native/Pacific Islander (3)	17	0.15
Not Hispanic (2)	11	0.10
Hispanic (1)	6	0.05
Native Hawaiian (3)	7	0.06
Samoan (0)	1	0.01
White (9,616)	9,803	86.58
Not Hispanic (9,075)	9,226	81.48
Hispanic (541)	577	5.10

Land O' Lakes

Place Type: CDP
County: Pasco
Population: 31,996†

Ancestry‡	Population	%
African, Sub-Saharan (129)	129	0.40
African (29)	29	0.09
Cape Verdean (58)	58	0.18
Other Sub-Saharan African (42)	42	0.13
American (2,307)	2,307	7.16
Arab (190)	284	0.88
Arab (86)	105	0.33
Egyptian (69)	69	0.21
Lebanese (23)	98	0.30
Moroccan (12)	12	0.04
Armenian (10)	10	0.03
Austrian (49)	187	0.58
Belgian (0)	11	0.03
Brazilian (65)	84	0.26
British (59)	360	1.12
Canadian (127)	178	0.55
Celtic (0)	30	0.09
Croatian (6)	12	0.04
Czech (7)	91	0.28
Czechoslovakian (73)	112	0.35
Danish (23)	106	0.33
Dutch (102)	345	1.07
Eastern European (16)	34	0.11
English (1,636)	4,864	15.10
European (256)	302	0.94
Finnish (10)	36	0.11
French, ex. Basque (465)	1,544	4.79
French Canadian (65)	202	0.63
German (1,737)	6,371	19.78
Greek (84)	268	0.83
Guyanese (58)	86	0.27
Hungarian (185)	500	1.55
Irish (1,396)	4,753	14.76
Italian (965)	2,207	6.85
Lithuanian (30)	68	0.21
Northern European (50)	50	0.16
Norwegian (167)	503	1.56
Pennsylvania German (16)	16	0.05
Polish (426)	1,521	4.72
Portuguese (191)	277	0.86
Romanian (0)	60	0.19
Russian (145)	287	0.89
Scandinavian (13)	66	0.20
Scotch-Irish (152)	475	1.47
Scottish (203)	995	3.09
Slavic (18)	127	0.39
Slovak (0)	117	0.36
Slovene (0)	6	0.02
Swedish (127)	405	1.26
Swiss (80)	118	0.37
Ukrainian (32)	96	0.30
Welsh (54)	257	0.80
West Indian, ex. Hispanic (586)	744	2.31
Barbadian (0)	28	0.09
Haitian (110)	110	0.34
Jamaican (245)	245	0.76
Trinidadian/Tobagonian (23)	38	0.12
West Indian (208)	323	1.00
Yugoslavian (41)	66	0.20

Hispanic Origin	Population	%
Hispanic or Latino (of any race)	4,860	15.19
Central American, ex. Mexican	237	0.74
Costa Rican	16	0.05
Guatemalan	37	0.12
Honduran	55	0.17
Nicaraguan	14	0.04
Panamanian	59	0.18
Salvadoran	53	0.17
Other Central American	3	0.01
Cuban	933	2.92
Dominican Republic	191	0.60
Mexican	362	1.13
Puerto Rican	1,953	6.10
South American	665	2.08
Argentinean	10	0.03
Bolivian	12	0.04
Chilean	5	0.02
Colombian	415	1.30
Ecuadorian	76	0.24
Peruvian	60	0.19
Uruguayan	12	0.04
Venezuelan	67	0.21
Other South American	8	0.03
Other Hispanic or Latino	519	1.62

Race*	Population	%
African-American/Black (1,613)	1,910	5.97
Not Hispanic (1,469)	1,675	5.24
Hispanic (144)	235	0.73
American Indian/Alaska Native (90)	272	0.85
Not Hispanic (70)	206	0.64
Hispanic (20)	66	0.21
Apache (5)	6	0.02
Blackfeet (2)	9	0.03
Canadian/French Am. Ind. (1)	2	0.01
Central American Ind. (0)	1	<0.01
Cherokee (15)	55	0.17
Cheyenne (1)	1	<0.01
Chickasaw (1)	2	0.01
Chippewa (3)	7	0.02
Choctaw (4)	4	0.01
Comanche (0)	1	<0.01
Cree (1)	5	0.02
Creek (1)	1	<0.01
Crow (0)	1	<0.01
Delaware (0)	1	<0.01
Houma (0)	3	0.01
Inupiat *(Alaska Native)* (1)	1	<0.01
Iroquois (4)	12	0.04
Menominee (0)	3	0.01
Mexican American Ind. (6)	7	0.02
Navajo (1)	1	<0.01
Potawatomi (1)	1	<0.01
Seminole (2)	5	0.02
Sioux (1)	6	0.02
South American Ind. (2)	18	0.06
Spanish American Ind. (1)	1	<0.01
Tlingit-Haida *(Alaska Native)* (2)	2	0.01
Asian (927)	1,180	3.69
Not Hispanic (913)	1,138	3.56
Hispanic (14)	42	0.13
Bangladeshi (4)	7	0.02
Burmese (9)	9	0.03
Cambodian (3)	3	0.01
Chinese, ex. Taiwanese (133)	188	0.59
Filipino (180)	245	0.77
Indian (264)	293	0.92
Indonesian (6)	14	0.04
Japanese (14)	57	0.18
Korean (67)	99	0.31
Laotian (2)	9	0.03
Malaysian (4)	4	0.01
Nepalese (4)	4	0.01
Pakistani (20)	21	0.07
Sri Lankan (6)	7	0.02
Taiwanese (2)	5	0.02
Thai (16)	36	0.11
Vietnamese (165)	187	0.58
Hawaii Native/Pacific Islander (28)	57	0.18
Not Hispanic (22)	44	0.14
Hispanic (6)	13	0.04
Guamanian/Chamorro (8)	13	0.04
Native Hawaiian (14)	23	0.07
Samoan (1)	2	0.01
White (27,786)	28,523	89.15
Not Hispanic (24,058)	24,533	76.68
Hispanic (3,728)	3,990	12.47

Lantana

Place Type: Town
County: Palm Beach
Population: 10,423†

Ancestry‡	Population	%
African, Sub-Saharan (52)	52	0.50
African (17)	17	0.16
Kenyan (35)	35	0.34
American (299)	299	2.89
Arab (16)	16	0.15
Egyptian (16)	16	0.15
Australian (8)	8	0.08
Austrian (20)	35	0.34
British (65)	69	0.67
Canadian (84)	92	0.89
Celtic (31)	31	0.30
Czech (0)	21	0.20
Dutch (9)	99	0.96
English (162)	648	6.26
European (202)	202	1.95
Finnish (204)	278	2.69
French, ex. Basque (64)	370	3.58
French Canadian (13)	68	0.66
German (223)	848	8.19
Greek (54)	54	0.52
Guyanese (14)	48	0.46
Hungarian (36)	36	0.35
Irish (213)	701	6.77
Italian (403)	696	6.73
Latvian (17)	17	0.16
Lithuanian (36)	46	0.44
Norwegian (54)	54	0.52

*Notes: † The Census 2010 population figure is used to calculate the percentages in the Hispanic Origin and Race categories. Ancestry percentages are based on the 2006-2010 American Community Survey population (not shown); ‡ Numbers in parentheses indicate the number of people reporting a single ancestry; * Numbers in parentheses indicate the number of persons reporting this race alone, not in combination with any other race; Please refer to the Explanation of Data for more information.*

SECTION TWO

Polish (246)	481	4.65
Portuguese (28)	92	0.89
Russian (50)	201	1.94
Scotch-Irish (63)	102	0.99
Scottish (6)	59	0.57
Serbian (32)	32	0.31
Slavic (0)	18	0.17
Slovak (11)	11	0.11
Swedish (37)	221	2.14
Ukrainian (12)	35	0.34
Welsh (20)	31	0.30
West Indian, ex. Hispanic (1,413)	1,581	15.28
Bahamian (87)	87	0.84
Bermudan (0)	27	0.26
British West Indian (0)	7	0.07
Haitian (1,243)	1,270	12.27
Jamaican (59)	111	1.07
West Indian (24)	79	0.76
Yugoslavian (64)	64	0.62

Hispanic Origin	Population	%
Hispanic or Latino (of any race)	1,935	18.56
Central American, ex. Mexican	470	4.51
Costa Rican	13	0.12
Guatemalan	118	1.13
Honduran	50	0.48
Nicaraguan	20	0.19
Panamanian	3	0.03
Salvadoran	265	2.54
Other Central American	1	0.01
Cuban	146	1.40
Dominican Republic	64	0.61
Mexican	413	3.96
Puerto Rican	468	4.49
South American	242	2.32
Argentinean	16	0.15
Bolivian	2	0.02
Chilean	11	0.11
Colombian	122	1.17
Ecuadorian	23	0.22
Paraguayan	1	0.01
Peruvian	31	0.30
Uruguayan	15	0.14
Venezuelan	21	0.20
Other Hispanic or Latino	132	1.27

Race*	Population	%
African-American/Black (2,290)	2,413	23.15
Not Hispanic (2,227)	2,330	22.35
Hispanic (63)	83	0.80
American Indian/Alaska Native (45)	129	1.24
Not Hispanic (20)	60	0.58
Hispanic (25)	69	0.66
Apache (0)	1	0.01
Blackfeet (0)	1	0.01
Central American Ind. (1)	1	0.01
Cherokee (7)	21	0.20
Choctaw (1)	1	0.01
Creek (0)	6	0.06
Iroquois (0)	2	0.02
Mexican American Ind. (11)	20	0.19
Pueblo (1)	1	0.01
Sioux (0)	1	0.01
South American Ind. (0)	1	0.01
Asian (160)	207	1.99
Not Hispanic (157)	195	1.87
Hispanic (3)	12	0.12
Bangladeshi (8)	15	0.14
Burmese (4)	4	0.04
Cambodian (0)	1	0.01
Chinese, ex. Taiwanese (19)	30	0.29
Filipino (24)	30	0.29
Indian (40)	51	0.49
Indonesian (2)	5	0.05
Japanese (3)	5	0.05
Korean (12)	16	0.15
Laotian (1)	1	0.01
Thai (11)	19	0.18
Vietnamese (14)	17	0.16
Hawaii Native/Pacific Islander (13)	53	0.51
Not Hispanic (13)	51	0.49
Hispanic (0)	2	0.02
Guamanian/Chamorro (1)	1	0.01
Native Hawaiian (2)	2	0.02
Samoan (0)	5	0.05
White (7,220)	7,410	71.09
Not Hispanic (5,867)	5,972	57.30
Hispanic (1,353)	1,438	13.80

Largo

Place Type: City
County: Pinellas
Population: 77,648†

Ancestry‡	Population	%
African, Sub-Saharan (11)	30	0.04
African (11)	19	0.02
Ghanaian (0)	11	0.01
Albanian (464)	475	0.62
American (5,778)	5,778	7.49
Arab (155)	317	0.41
Arab (25)	78	0.10
Egyptian (62)	62	0.08
Jordanian (39)	39	0.05
Lebanese (19)	76	0.10
Syrian (0)	52	0.07
Other Arab (10)	10	0.01
Armenian (45)	45	0.06
Australian (0)	14	0.02
Austrian (120)	305	0.40
Belgian (26)	93	0.12
Brazilian (229)	229	0.30
British (334)	420	0.54
Bulgarian (24)	88	0.11
Cajun (57)	57	0.07
Canadian (870)	1,037	1.34
Celtic (13)	13	0.02
Croatian (86)	110	0.14
Czech (132)	290	0.38
Czechoslovakian (72)	136	0.18
Danish (66)	411	0.53
Dutch (428)	1,470	1.91
Eastern European (11)	11	0.01
English (4,172)	9,787	12.69
European (602)	662	0.86
Finnish (73)	187	0.24
French, ex. Basque (695)	3,025	3.92
French Canadian (475)	668	0.87
German (5,551)	14,099	18.28
Greek (378)	743	0.96
Guyanese (35)	45	0.06
Hungarian (287)	544	0.71
Iranian (20)	53	0.07
Irish (4,306)	12,367	16.04
Italian (2,783)	6,122	7.94
Lithuanian (121)	180	0.23
Northern European (70)	70	0.09
Norwegian (194)	665	0.86
Pennsylvania German (64)	100	0.13
Polish (1,967)	3,868	5.02
Portuguese (164)	356	0.46
Romanian (20)	43	0.06
Russian (286)	761	0.99
Scandinavian (22)	50	0.06
Scotch-Irish (551)	1,185	1.54
Scottish (770)	1,840	2.39
Serbian (52)	70	0.09
Slavic (9)	9	0.01
Slovak (51)	285	0.37
Slovene (69)	104	0.13
Swedish (560)	1,248	1.62
Swiss (101)	229	0.30
Turkish (54)	79	0.10
Ukrainian (306)	476	0.62
Welsh (190)	787	1.02
West Indian, ex. Hispanic (237)	265	0.34
Bermudan (14)	14	0.02
Haitian (32)	32	0.04
Jamaican (93)	105	0.14
Trinidadian/Tobagonian (60)	60	0.08
West Indian (38)	54	0.07
Yugoslavian (375)	387	0.50

Hispanic Origin	Population	%
Hispanic or Latino (of any race)	6,982	8.99
Central American, ex. Mexican	372	0.48
Costa Rican	47	0.06
Guatemalan	72	0.09
Honduran	80	0.10
Nicaraguan	23	0.03
Panamanian	50	0.06
Salvadoran	100	0.13
Cuban	447	0.58
Dominican Republic	162	0.21
Mexican	2,440	3.14
Puerto Rican	2,277	2.93
South American	772	0.99
Argentinean	80	0.10
Bolivian	19	0.02
Chilean	33	0.04
Colombian	346	0.45
Ecuadorian	77	0.10
Paraguayan	2	<0.01
Peruvian	107	0.14
Uruguayan	10	0.01
Venezuelan	90	0.12
Other South American	8	0.01
Other Hispanic or Latino	512	0.66

Race*	Population	%
African-American/Black (4,312)	5,112	6.58
Not Hispanic (4,083)	4,736	6.10
Hispanic (229)	376	0.48
American Indian/Alaska Native (259)	700	0.90
Not Hispanic (190)	573	0.74
Hispanic (69)	127	0.16
Apache (0)	8	0.01
Blackfeet (5)	23	0.03
Canadian/French Am. Ind. (1)	2	<0.01
Cherokee (33)	174	0.22
Cheyenne (1)	1	<0.01
Chickasaw (0)	3	<0.01
Chippewa (6)	13	0.02
Choctaw (6)	17	0.02
Comanche (0)	5	0.01
Creek (1)	4	0.01
Crow (2)	3	<0.01
Delaware (2)	5	0.01
Inupiat *(Alaska Native)* (1)	1	<0.01
Iroquois (10)	32	0.04
Lumbee (7)	11	0.01
Mexican American Ind. (12)	15	0.02
Navajo (13)	15	0.02
Osage (0)	1	<0.01
Potawatomi (1)	1	<0.01
Pueblo (2)	2	<0.01
Seminole (3)	7	0.01
Shoshone (0)	1	<0.01
Sioux (2)	10	0.01
South American Ind. (6)	9	0.01
Spanish American Ind. (2)	2	<0.01
Tlingit-Haida *(Alaska Native)* (2)	2	<0.01
Tsimshian *(Alaska Native)* (1)	1	<0.01
Ute (0)	1	<0.01
Yaqui (1)	2	<0.01
Yup'ik *(Alaska Native)* (1)	1	<0.01
Asian (2,083)	2,491	3.21
Not Hispanic (2,043)	2,426	3.12
Hispanic (40)	65	0.08
Bangladeshi (12)	15	0.02
Burmese (0)	1	<0.01
Cambodian (16)	28	0.04
Chinese, ex. Taiwanese (269)	309	0.40
Filipino (451)	598	0.77
Hmong (30)	30	0.04
Indian (530)	583	0.75
Indonesian (9)	14	0.02
Japanese (55)	96	0.12
Korean (69)	93	0.12

*Notes: † The Census 2010 population figure is used to calculate the percentages in the Hispanic Origin and Race categories. Ancestry percentages are based on the 2006-2010 American Community Survey population (not shown); ‡ Numbers in parentheses indicate the number of people reporting a single ancestry; * Numbers in parentheses indicate the number of persons reporting this race alone, not in combination with any other race; Please refer to the Explanation of Data for more information.*

	Population	%
Laotian (65)	69	0.09
Nepalese (8)	12	0.02
Pakistani (16)	18	0.02
Sri Lankan (1)	2	<0.01
Taiwanese (13)	13	0.02
Thai (40)	57	0.07
Vietnamese (417)	477	0.61
Hawaii Native/Pacific Islander (125)	243	0.31
Not Hispanic (116)	206	0.27
Hispanic (9)	37	0.05
Fijian (1)	6	0.01
Guamanian/Chamorro (5)	8	0.01
Marshallese (6)	6	0.01
Native Hawaiian (7)	34	0.04
Samoan (4)	14	0.02
Tongan (22)	31	0.04
White (66,973)	68,586	88.33
Not Hispanic (62,703)	63,901	82.30
Hispanic (4,270)	4,685	6.03

Lauderdale Lakes

Place Type: City
County: Broward
Population: 32,593†

Ancestry‡	Population	%
African, Sub-Saharan (499)	669	2.06
African (350)	520	1.60
Ghanaian (59)	59	0.18
Nigerian (90)	90	0.28
American (1,220)	1,220	3.75
Arab (14)	14	0.04
Lebanese (14)	14	0.04
Austrian (25)	25	0.08
Brazilian (45)	45	0.14
British (33)	61	0.19
Canadian (184)	199	0.61
Czech (14)	40	0.12
Danish (0)	11	0.03
Dutch (0)	3	0.01
English (211)	401	1.23
European (75)	75	0.23
French, ex. Basque (137)	285	0.88
French Canadian (333)	333	1.02
German (201)	650	2.00
Greek (8)	8	0.02
Guyanese (71)	117	0.36
Hungarian (20)	47	0.14
Irish (145)	593	1.82
Italian (672)	950	2.92
Latvian (13)	13	0.04
Lithuanian (0)	12	0.04
Polish (84)	135	0.41
Portuguese (30)	30	0.09
Romanian (13)	13	0.04
Russian (126)	133	0.41
Scotch-Irish (65)	65	0.20
Scottish (12)	22	0.07
Slovak (13)	25	0.08
Swedish (9)	74	0.23
Swiss (7)	7	0.02
Ukrainian (0)	30	0.09
West Indian, ex. Hispanic (13,955)	14,867	45.68
Bahamian (301)	393	1.21
Barbadian (34)	52	0.16
Bermudan (131)	131	0.40
British West Indian (33)	55	0.17
Haitian (6,108)	6,503	19.98
Jamaican (6,875)	7,173	22.04
Trinidadian/Tobagonian (179)	226	0.69
West Indian (294)	334	1.03

Hispanic Origin	Population	%
Hispanic or Latino (of any race)	1,763	5.41
Central American, ex. Mexican	195	0.60
Costa Rican	13	0.04
Guatemalan	8	0.02
Honduran	76	0.23
Nicaraguan	31	0.10
Panamanian	29	0.09
Salvadoran	35	0.11
Other Central American	3	0.01
Cuban	208	0.64
Dominican Republic	160	0.49
Mexican	161	0.49
Puerto Rican	447	1.37
South American	389	1.19
Argentinean	43	0.13
Bolivian	5	0.02
Chilean	8	0.02
Colombian	195	0.60
Ecuadorian	24	0.07
Paraguayan	4	0.01
Peruvian	48	0.15
Uruguayan	17	0.05
Venezuelan	40	0.12
Other South American	5	0.02
Other Hispanic or Latino	203	0.62

Race*	Population	%
African-American/Black (26,278)	26,966	82.74
Not Hispanic (25,887)	26,511	81.34
Hispanic (391)	455	1.40
American Indian/Alaska Native (75)	186	0.57
Not Hispanic (58)	156	0.48
Hispanic (17)	30	0.09
Blackfeet (0)	8	0.02
Canadian/French Am. Ind. (2)	2	0.01
Central American Ind. (7)	12	0.04
Cherokee (4)	12	0.04
Cheyenne (1)	2	0.01
Chickasaw (0)	2	0.01
Chippewa (2)	2	0.01
Choctaw (0)	1	<0.01
Inupiat *(Alaska Native)* (0)	1	<0.01
Sioux (3)	4	0.01
South American Ind. (0)	2	0.01
Spanish American Ind. (0)	1	<0.01
Tlingit-Haida *(Alaska Native)* (0)	3	0.01
Asian (399)	581	1.78
Not Hispanic (395)	562	1.72
Hispanic (4)	19	0.06
Bangladeshi (5)	5	0.02
Chinese, ex. Taiwanese (63)	113	0.35
Filipino (32)	47	0.14
Indian (154)	231	0.71
Indonesian (1)	2	0.01
Japanese (4)	16	0.05
Korean (6)	9	0.03
Laotian (4)	7	0.02
Pakistani (18)	19	0.06
Thai (4)	4	0.01
Vietnamese (79)	81	0.25
Hawaii Native/Pacific Islander (7)	219	0.67
Not Hispanic (7)	209	0.64
Hispanic (0)	10	0.03
Native Hawaiian (2)	3	0.01
White (4,623)	4,915	15.08
Not Hispanic (3,682)	3,914	12.01
Hispanic (941)	1,001	3.07

Lauderhill

Place Type: City
County: Broward
Population: 66,887†

Ancestry‡	Population	%
African, Sub-Saharan (577)	759	1.13
African (546)	728	1.08
Nigerian (31)	31	0.05
American (2,224)	2,224	3.31
Arab (82)	102	0.15
Arab (13)	23	0.03
Egyptian (44)	44	0.07
Moroccan (0)	10	0.01
Other Arab (25)	25	0.04
Armenian (0)	47	0.07
Austrian (35)	207	0.31
Brazilian (55)	74	0.11
British (148)	174	0.26
Bulgarian (17)	64	0.10
Canadian (96)	149	0.22
Croatian (24)	24	0.04
Czech (11)	38	0.06
Czechoslovakian (6)	6	0.01
Danish (8)	29	0.04
Dutch (104)	183	0.27
Eastern European (88)	88	0.13
English (563)	1,304	1.94
Estonian (32)	32	0.05
European (188)	220	0.33
Finnish (0)	20	0.03
French, ex. Basque (142)	396	0.59
French Canadian (338)	361	0.54
German (536)	1,350	2.01
Greek (45)	179	0.27
Guyanese (81)	112	0.17
Hungarian (88)	234	0.35
Irish (398)	1,143	1.70
Israeli (40)	56	0.08
Italian (838)	1,302	1.94
Lithuanian (14)	38	0.06
Norwegian (0)	84	0.13
Pennsylvania German (7)	7	0.01
Polish (129)	440	0.66
Portuguese (0)	63	0.09
Romanian (159)	159	0.24
Russian (711)	990	1.47
Scotch-Irish (14)	76	0.11
Scottish (39)	196	0.29
Serbian (0)	16	0.02
Slovak (0)	18	0.03
Swedish (9)	59	0.09
Swiss (8)	8	0.01
Turkish (36)	36	0.05
Ukrainian (66)	259	0.39
West Indian, ex. Hispanic (23,218)	24,371	36.31
Bahamian (270)	410	0.61
Barbadian (96)	122	0.18
Belizean (54)	54	0.08
British West Indian (185)	185	0.28
Haitian (8,371)	8,629	12.85
Jamaican (12,902)	13,451	20.04
Trinidadian/Tobagonian (614)	643	0.96
U.S. Virgin Islander (13)	47	0.07
West Indian (713)	830	1.24
Yugoslavian (0)	8	0.01

Hispanic Origin	Population	%
Hispanic or Latino (of any race)	4,930	7.37
Central American, ex. Mexican	612	0.91
Costa Rican	65	0.10
Guatemalan	66	0.10
Honduran	174	0.26
Nicaraguan	93	0.14
Panamanian	111	0.17
Salvadoran	100	0.15
Other Central American	3	<0.01
Cuban	526	0.79
Dominican Republic	383	0.57
Mexican	243	0.36
Puerto Rican	1,138	1.70
South American	1,610	2.41
Argentinean	129	0.19
Bolivian	21	0.03
Chilean	50	0.07
Colombian	768	1.15
Ecuadorian	156	0.23
Peruvian	271	0.41
Uruguayan	32	0.05
Venezuelan	175	0.26
Other South American	8	0.01
Other Hispanic or Latino	418	0.62

Race*	Population	%
African-American/Black (50,751)	52,065	77.84
Not Hispanic (49,969)	51,107	76.41
Hispanic (782)	958	1.43

*Notes: † The Census 2010 population figure is used to calculate the percentages in the Hispanic Origin and Race categories. Ancestry percentages are based on the 2006-2010 American Community Survey population (not shown); ‡ Numbers in parentheses indicate the number of people reporting a single ancestry; * Numbers in parentheses indicate the number of persons reporting this race alone, not in combination with any other race; Please refer to the Explanation of Data for more information.*

American Indian/Alaska Native (178)	368	0.55
Not Hispanic (136)	287	0.43
Hispanic (42)	81	0.12
Apache (2)	5	0.01
Blackfeet (0)	12	0.02
Canadian/French Am. Ind. (4)	4	0.01
Central American Ind. (2)	7	0.01
Cherokee (12)	45	0.07
Chickasaw (0)	2	<0.01
Chippewa (1)	1	<0.01
Choctaw (0)	1	<0.01
Cree (1)	1	<0.01
Houma (5)	5	0.01
Iroquois (1)	1	<0.01
Lumbee (1)	1	<0.01
Mexican American Ind. (1)	3	<0.01
Navajo (0)	8	0.01
Pueblo (2)	3	<0.01
Seminole (4)	10	0.01
Shoshone (0)	1	<0.01
Sioux (2)	7	0.01
South American Ind. (4)	10	0.01
Spanish American Ind. (3)	3	<0.01
Tlingit-Haida *(Alaska Native)* (0)	2	<0.01
Asian (1,062)	1,530	2.29
Not Hispanic (1,051)	1,480	2.21
Hispanic (11)	50	0.07
Bangladeshi (50)	51	0.08
Burmese (1)	1	<0.01
Cambodian (0)	1	<0.01
Chinese, ex. Taiwanese (227)	354	0.53
Filipino (128)	171	0.26
Indian (404)	590	0.88
Indonesian (3)	4	0.01
Japanese (19)	38	0.06
Korean (22)	44	0.07
Laotian (0)	2	<0.01
Malaysian (4)	4	0.01
Pakistani (30)	35	0.05
Sri Lankan (4)	5	0.01
Taiwanese (3)	4	0.01
Thai (17)	18	0.03
Vietnamese (86)	93	0.14
Hawaii Native/Pacific Islander (24)	300	0.45
Not Hispanic (21)	278	0.42
Hispanic (3)	22	0.03
Guamanian/Chamorro (9)	16	0.02
Native Hawaiian (2)	9	0.01
Samoan (1)	4	0.01
Tongan (0)	1	<0.01
White (12,182)	12,947	19.36
Not Hispanic (9,148)	9,703	14.51
Hispanic (3,034)	3,244	4.85

Laurel

Place Type: CDP
County: Sarasota
Population: 8,171†

Ancestry‡	Population	%
African, Sub-Saharan (147)	147	1.83
Zimbabwean (147)	147	1.83
American (567)	567	7.06
Arab (8)	50	0.62
Iraqi (8)	8	0.10
Lebanese (0)	42	0.52
Armenian (56)	69	0.86
Austrian (15)	15	0.19
Brazilian (17)	17	0.21
British (49)	49	0.61
Canadian (59)	127	1.58
Croatian (0)	14	0.17
Czech (15)	121	1.51
Danish (18)	78	0.97
Dutch (127)	172	2.14
Eastern European (11)	11	0.14
English (411)	1,202	14.97
European (142)	142	1.77
Finnish (15)	15	0.19
French, ex. Basque (97)	260	3.24
French Canadian (11)	22	0.27
German (638)	1,637	20.39
Greek (15)	34	0.42
Hungarian (67)	109	1.36
Irish (551)	1,663	20.72
Israeli (0)	24	0.30
Italian (570)	878	10.94
Norwegian (25)	98	1.22
Pennsylvania German (19)	19	0.24
Polish (149)	307	3.82
Portuguese (0)	26	0.32
Romanian (19)	38	0.47
Russian (57)	130	1.62
Scotch-Irish (84)	248	3.09
Scottish (84)	314	3.91
Slovak (38)	120	1.49
Swedish (37)	165	2.06
Swiss (0)	27	0.34
Ukrainian (0)	5	0.06
Welsh (18)	71	0.88
West Indian, ex. Hispanic (0)	22	0.27
Jamaican (0)	22	0.27
Yugoslavian (0)	7	0.09

Hispanic Origin	Population	%
Hispanic or Latino (of any race)	195	2.39
Central American, ex. Mexican	17	0.21
Costa Rican	2	0.02
Guatemalan	5	0.06
Honduran	1	0.01
Nicaraguan	2	0.02
Panamanian	1	0.01
Salvadoran	6	0.07
Cuban	19	0.23
Dominican Republic	1	0.01
Mexican	67	0.82
Puerto Rican	34	0.42
South American	27	0.33
Argentinean	4	0.05
Bolivian	1	0.01
Chilean	1	0.01
Colombian	10	0.12
Paraguayan	1	0.01
Peruvian	3	0.04
Uruguayan	1	0.01
Venezuelan	6	0.07
Other Hispanic or Latino	30	0.37

Race*	Population	%
African-American/Black (177)	214	2.62
Not Hispanic (173)	204	2.50
Hispanic (4)	10	0.12
American Indian/Alaska Native (20)	78	0.95
Not Hispanic (13)	63	0.77
Hispanic (7)	15	0.18
Blackfeet (0)	3	0.04
Cherokee (5)	19	0.23
Chippewa (1)	2	0.02
Choctaw (0)	4	0.05
Cree (0)	2	0.02
Creek (2)	2	0.02
Iroquois (0)	1	0.01
Mexican American Ind. (1)	1	0.01
Osage (0)	1	0.01
Sioux (0)	5	0.06
Ute (0)	1	0.01
Asian (88)	119	1.46
Not Hispanic (87)	117	1.43
Hispanic (1)	2	0.02
Chinese, ex. Taiwanese (19)	26	0.32
Filipino (29)	36	0.44
Indian (14)	20	0.24
Indonesian (2)	2	0.02
Japanese (1)	6	0.07
Korean (2)	4	0.05
Nepalese (1)	1	0.01
Thai (4)	4	0.05
Vietnamese (15)	19	0.23
Hawaii Native/Pacific Islander (3)	8	0.10
Not Hispanic (3)	7	0.09
Hispanic (0)	1	0.01
Native Hawaiian (1)	5	0.06
White (7,708)	7,833	95.86
Not Hispanic (7,586)	7,689	94.10
Hispanic (122)	144	1.76

Lealman

Place Type: CDP
County: Pinellas
Population: 19,879†

Ancestry‡	Population	%
African, Sub-Saharan (30)	52	0.25
African (30)	52	0.25
American (1,520)	1,520	7.41
Arab (77)	167	0.81
Egyptian (22)	22	0.11
Lebanese (11)	101	0.49
Palestinian (44)	44	0.21
Austrian (0)	12	0.06
Belgian (0)	26	0.13
Brazilian (9)	9	0.04
British (26)	94	0.46
Bulgarian (58)	58	0.28
Cajun (11)	11	0.05
Canadian (143)	155	0.76
Celtic (10)	19	0.09
Croatian (109)	144	0.70
Czech (21)	138	0.67
Czechoslovakian (30)	63	0.31
Danish (15)	82	0.40
Dutch (41)	351	1.71
English (947)	2,149	10.47
Estonian (12)	12	0.06
European (175)	194	0.95
Finnish (0)	22	0.11
French, ex. Basque (316)	910	4.44
French Canadian (175)	434	2.12
German (1,362)	3,572	17.41
Greek (0)	11	0.05
Hungarian (36)	122	0.59
Iranian (0)	15	0.07
Irish (1,117)	3,059	14.91
Israeli (0)	10	0.05
Italian (809)	1,983	9.66
Lithuanian (21)	101	0.49
Maltese (0)	22	0.11
Norwegian (26)	144	0.70
Pennsylvania German (12)	12	0.06
Polish (306)	734	3.58
Portuguese (45)	225	1.10
Romanian (10)	20	0.10
Russian (65)	125	0.61
Scandinavian (34)	34	0.17
Scotch-Irish (82)	286	1.39
Scottish (57)	470	2.29
Slovak (0)	11	0.05
Swedish (40)	144	0.70
Swiss (24)	68	0.33
Welsh (18)	198	0.97
West Indian, ex. Hispanic (93)	116	0.57
Jamaican (3)	26	0.13
Trinidadian/Tobagonian (90)	90	0.44
Yugoslavian (118)	118	0.58

Hispanic Origin	Population	%
Hispanic or Latino (of any race)	1,897	9.54
Central American, ex. Mexican	105	0.53
Costa Rican	11	0.06
Guatemalan	6	0.03
Honduran	49	0.25
Nicaraguan	9	0.05
Panamanian	9	0.05
Salvadoran	21	0.11
Cuban	416	2.09
Dominican Republic	44	0.22
Mexican	387	1.95
Puerto Rican	682	3.43

*Notes: † The Census 2010 population figure is used to calculate the percentages in the Hispanic Origin and Race categories. Ancestry percentages are based on the 2006-2010 American Community Survey population (not shown); ‡ Numbers in parentheses indicate the number of people reporting a single ancestry; * Numbers in parentheses indicate the number of persons reporting this race alone, not in combination with any other race; Please refer to the Explanation of Data for more information.*

South American	154	0.77
Argentinean	7	0.04
Bolivian	10	0.05
Chilean	6	0.03
Colombian	67	0.34
Ecuadorian	12	0.06
Peruvian	23	0.12
Uruguayan	4	0.02
Venezuelan	20	0.10
Other South American	5	0.03
Other Hispanic or Latino	109	0.55

Race*	Population	%
African-American/Black (1,684)	1,896	9.54
Not Hispanic (1,593)	1,759	8.85
Hispanic (91)	137	0.69
American Indian/Alaska Native (105)	258	1.30
Not Hispanic (71)	207	1.04
Hispanic (34)	51	0.26
Aleut *(Alaska Native)* (1)	1	0.01
Apache (2)	6	0.03
Blackfeet (2)	14	0.07
Canadian/French Am. Ind. (0)	1	0.01
Cherokee (18)	64	0.32
Cheyenne (1)	1	0.01
Chickasaw (3)	3	0.02
Chippewa (13)	18	0.09
Choctaw (0)	4	0.02
Cree (2)	2	0.01
Creek (5)	6	0.03
Inupiat *(Alaska Native)* (3)	5	0.03
Iroquois (4)	13	0.07
Mexican American Ind. (7)	7	0.04
Osage (0)	1	0.01
Seminole (0)	4	0.02
Shoshone (1)	1	0.01
Sioux (1)	4	0.02
South American Ind. (3)	5	0.03
Asian (1,378)	1,534	7.72
Not Hispanic (1,367)	1,515	7.62
Hispanic (11)	19	0.10
Cambodian (123)	138	0.69
Chinese, ex. Taiwanese (46)	68	0.34
Filipino (66)	103	0.52
Indian (65)	104	0.52
Indonesian (2)	7	0.04
Japanese (10)	20	0.10
Korean (7)	18	0.09
Laotian (207)	238	1.20
Malaysian (1)	1	0.01
Nepalese (0)	1	0.01
Sri Lankan (1)	1	0.01
Taiwanese (1)	1	0.01
Thai (30)	40	0.20
Vietnamese (735)	807	4.06
Hawaii Native/Pacific Islander (17)	53	0.27
Not Hispanic (14)	35	0.18
Hispanic (3)	18	0.09
Guamanian/Chamorro (1)	6	0.03
Native Hawaiian (2)	13	0.07
Samoan (2)	4	0.02
Tongan (8)	11	0.06
White (15,616)	16,121	81.10
Not Hispanic (14,489)	14,861	74.76
Hispanic (1,127)	1,260	6.34

Leesburg

Place Type: City
County: Lake
Population: 20,117†

Ancestry‡	Population	%
African, Sub-Saharan (0)	9	0.04
African (0)	9	0.04
American (825)	825	4.10
Arab (11)	11	0.05
Lebanese (11)	11	0.05
Austrian (23)	33	0.16
Belgian (34)	34	0.17
Brazilian (59)	59	0.29
British (50)	86	0.43
Canadian (25)	48	0.24
Celtic (0)	29	0.14
Croatian (18)	18	0.09
Czech (0)	13	0.06
Czechoslovakian (8)	8	0.04
Danish (13)	99	0.49
Dutch (97)	443	2.20
English (673)	1,883	9.35
European (71)	84	0.42
Finnish (0)	45	0.22
French, ex. Basque (98)	726	3.61
French Canadian (103)	140	0.70
German (730)	2,363	11.73
Greek (114)	114	0.57
Guyanese (0)	113	0.56
Hungarian (23)	80	0.40
Irish (678)	2,393	11.88
Italian (427)	980	4.87
Lithuanian (23)	54	0.27
Northern European (15)	15	0.07
Norwegian (62)	135	0.67
Polish (157)	412	2.05
Portuguese (29)	29	0.14
Romanian (17)	45	0.22
Russian (20)	52	0.26
Scotch-Irish (333)	576	2.86
Scottish (155)	419	2.08
Slovak (0)	5	0.02
Swedish (74)	165	0.82
Swiss (45)	75	0.37
Ukrainian (0)	35	0.17
Welsh (37)	103	0.51
West Indian, ex. Hispanic (334)	415	2.06
Bahamian (39)	39	0.19
Haitian (36)	36	0.18
Jamaican (259)	327	1.62
Trinidadian/Tobagonian (0)	13	0.06
Yugoslavian (0)	28	0.14

Hispanic Origin	Population	%
Hispanic or Latino (of any race)	1,805	8.97
Central American, ex. Mexican	145	0.72
Costa Rican	7	0.03
Guatemalan	34	0.17
Honduran	18	0.09
Nicaraguan	8	0.04
Panamanian	69	0.34
Salvadoran	9	0.04
Cuban	113	0.56
Dominican Republic	31	0.15
Mexican	842	4.19
Puerto Rican	495	2.46
South American	82	0.41
Argentinean	15	0.07
Chilean	3	0.01
Colombian	32	0.16
Ecuadorian	2	0.01
Peruvian	27	0.13
Uruguayan	1	<0.01
Venezuelan	2	0.01
Other Hispanic or Latino	97	0.48

Race*	Population	%
African-American/Black (5,666)	5,983	29.74
Not Hispanic (5,560)	5,826	28.96
Hispanic (106)	157	0.78
American Indian/Alaska Native (70)	192	0.95
Not Hispanic (55)	160	0.80
Hispanic (15)	32	0.16
Alaska Athabascan *(Ala. Nat.)* (1)	1	<0.01
Apache (2)	3	0.01
Blackfeet (1)	9	0.04
Canadian/French Am. Ind. (0)	2	0.01
Cherokee (8)	49	0.24
Chippewa (3)	6	0.03
Choctaw (3)	7	0.03
Creek (2)	2	0.01
Iroquois (3)	6	0.03
Lumbee (2)	4	0.02
Mexican American Ind. (1)	1	<0.01
Seminole (0)	4	0.02
Sioux (0)	1	<0.01
South American Ind. (1)	2	0.01
Yup'ik *(Alaska Native)* (0)	1	<0.01
Asian (342)	404	2.01
Not Hispanic (340)	391	1.94
Hispanic (2)	13	0.06
Bangladeshi (17)	17	0.08
Cambodian (1)	2	0.01
Chinese, ex. Taiwanese (61)	68	0.34
Filipino (76)	87	0.43
Indian (108)	129	0.64
Japanese (5)	18	0.09
Korean (7)	12	0.06
Laotian (2)	2	0.01
Pakistani (10)	10	0.05
Thai (7)	12	0.06
Vietnamese (37)	38	0.19
Hawaii Native/Pacific Islander (45)	71	0.35
Not Hispanic (43)	57	0.28
Hispanic (2)	14	0.07
Guamanian/Chamorro (2)	2	0.01
Marshallese (26)	26	0.13
Native Hawaiian (2)	5	0.02
Samoan (2)	2	0.01
White (12,774)	13,208	65.66
Not Hispanic (11,917)	12,242	60.85
Hispanic (857)	966	4.80

Lehigh Acres

Place Type: CDP
County: Lee
Population: 86,784†

Ancestry‡	Population	%
African, Sub-Saharan (95)	174	0.21
African (93)	172	0.20
Liberian (2)	2	<0.01
American (10,490)	10,490	12.42
Arab (14)	54	0.06
Lebanese (0)	40	0.05
Syrian (14)	14	0.02
Austrian (52)	133	0.16
Belgian (27)	50	0.06
Brazilian (420)	558	0.66
British (248)	356	0.42
Bulgarian (22)	22	0.03
Cajun (18)	18	0.02
Canadian (126)	189	0.22
Croatian (30)	38	0.05
Czech (109)	339	0.40
Czechoslovakian (10)	73	0.09
Danish (32)	91	0.11
Dutch (239)	1,285	1.52
English (1,763)	4,966	5.88
European (361)	566	0.67
Finnish (11)	39	0.05
French, ex. Basque (585)	2,362	2.80
French Canadian (272)	727	0.86
German (3,270)	10,456	12.38
Greek (100)	259	0.31
Guyanese (333)	333	0.39
Hungarian (34)	336	0.40
Irish (1,870)	7,343	8.70
Israeli (0)	30	0.04
Italian (1,835)	4,700	5.57
Latvian (31)	78	0.09
Lithuanian (57)	196	0.23
Maltese (0)	17	0.02
Northern European (12)	12	0.01
Norwegian (196)	429	0.51
Pennsylvania German (0)	23	0.03
Polish (525)	1,963	2.32
Portuguese (293)	394	0.47
Romanian (15)	30	0.04
Russian (257)	495	0.59
Scandinavian (16)	16	0.02

*Notes: † The Census 2010 population figure is used to calculate the percentages in the Hispanic Origin and Race categories. Ancestry percentages are based on the 2006-2010 American Community Survey population (not shown); ‡ Numbers in parentheses indicate the number of people reporting a single ancestry; * Numbers in parentheses indicate the number of persons reporting this race alone, not in combination with any other race; Please refer to the Explanation of Data for more information.*

Scotch-Irish (262)	543	0.64
Scottish (273)	821	0.97
Serbian (71)	71	0.08
Slavic (0)	33	0.04
Slovak (46)	137	0.16
Slovene (0)	21	0.02
Swedish (135)	724	0.86
Swiss (17)	88	0.10
Ukrainian (53)	101	0.12
Welsh (51)	385	0.46
West Indian, ex. Hispanic (6,658)	7,052	8.35
Bahamian (41)	89	0.11
Barbadian (41)	41	0.05
British West Indian (24)	24	0.03
Haitian (3,302)	3,428	4.06
Jamaican (3,084)	3,168	3.75
Trinidadian/Tobagonian (76)	100	0.12
West Indian (70)	141	0.17
Other West Indian (20)	61	0.07
Yugoslavian (4)	4	<0.01

Hispanic Origin	Population	%
Hispanic or Latino (of any race)	29,797	34.33
Central American, ex. Mexican	2,598	2.99
Costa Rican	122	0.14
Guatemalan	652	0.75
Honduran	901	1.04
Nicaraguan	424	0.49
Panamanian	88	0.10
Salvadoran	393	0.45
Other Central American	18	0.02
Cuban	6,506	7.50
Dominican Republic	861	0.99
Mexican	9,005	10.38
Puerto Rican	7,864	9.06
South American	1,653	1.90
Argentinean	127	0.15
Bolivian	67	0.08
Chilean	35	0.04
Colombian	743	0.86
Ecuadorian	172	0.20
Paraguayan	10	0.01
Peruvian	273	0.31
Uruguayan	55	0.06
Venezuelan	152	0.18
Other South American	19	0.02
Other Hispanic or Latino	1,310	1.51

Race*	Population	%
African-American/Black (16,707)	18,002	20.74
Not Hispanic (15,652)	16,530	19.05
Hispanic (1,055)	1,472	1.70
American Indian/Alaska Native (364)	777	0.90
Not Hispanic (234)	518	0.60
Hispanic (130)	259	0.30
Alaska Athabascan *(Ala. Nat.)* (2)	2	<0.01
Apache (3)	10	0.01
Blackfeet (1)	22	0.03
Canadian/French Am. Ind. (1)	5	0.01
Central American Ind. (1)	7	0.01
Cherokee (37)	146	0.17
Chickasaw (2)	6	0.01
Chippewa (7)	13	0.01
Choctaw (7)	12	0.01
Comanche (1)	1	<0.01
Creek (10)	17	0.02
Delaware (0)	3	<0.01
Inupiat *(Alaska Native)* (2)	2	<0.01
Iroquois (6)	12	0.01
Lumbee (5)	8	0.01
Mexican American Ind. (12)	20	0.02
Navajo (2)	3	<0.01
Osage (4)	4	<0.01
Ottawa (1)	2	<0.01
Potawatomi (1)	5	0.01
Seminole (27)	44	0.05
Sioux (3)	11	0.01
South American Ind. (17)	41	0.05
Spanish American Ind. (5)	7	0.01
Tlingit-Haida *(Alaska Native)* (2)	2	<0.01
Asian (1,060)	1,418	1.63
Not Hispanic (1,019)	1,315	1.52
Hispanic (41)	103	0.12
Bangladeshi (18)	18	0.02
Burmese (4)	6	0.01
Cambodian (8)	9	0.01
Chinese, ex. Taiwanese (133)	205	0.24
Filipino (214)	298	0.34
Indian (333)	399	0.46
Indonesian (1)	4	<0.01
Japanese (24)	58	0.07
Korean (39)	64	0.07
Laotian (89)	116	0.13
Pakistani (6)	13	0.01
Sri Lankan (1)	1	<0.01
Thai (31)	40	0.05
Vietnamese (121)	129	0.15
Hawaii Native/Pacific Islander (65)	259	0.30
Not Hispanic (25)	170	0.20
Hispanic (40)	89	0.10
Fijian (1)	2	<0.01
Guamanian/Chamorro (27)	38	0.04
Native Hawaiian (9)	43	0.05
Samoan (5)	11	0.01
Tongan (1)	1	<0.01
White (58,545)	60,871	70.14
Not Hispanic (38,364)	39,450	45.46
Hispanic (20,181)	21,421	24.68

Leisure City

Place Type: CDP
County: Miami-Dade
Population: 22,655†

Ancestry‡	Population	%
African, Sub-Saharan (51)	51	0.24
African (30)	30	0.14
Nigerian (21)	21	0.10
American (472)	472	2.18
Austrian (12)	12	0.06
Brazilian (13)	13	0.06
British (6)	6	0.03
Danish (0)	5	0.02
Dutch (0)	11	0.05
English (31)	141	0.65
French, ex. Basque (9)	46	0.21
French Canadian (0)	36	0.17
German (104)	311	1.44
Irish (108)	384	1.78
Italian (61)	107	0.50
Polish (11)	132	0.61
Portuguese (14)	44	0.20
Romanian (0)	12	0.06
Russian (0)	26	0.12
Scottish (0)	26	0.12
Slavic (28)	28	0.13
Swedish (0)	33	0.15
Welsh (0)	15	0.07
West Indian, ex. Hispanic (1,348)	1,442	6.67
Barbadian (11)	11	0.05
Haitian (1,119)	1,177	5.45
Jamaican (218)	254	1.18

Hispanic Origin	Population	%
Hispanic or Latino (of any race)	16,978	74.94
Central American, ex. Mexican	2,351	10.38
Costa Rican	51	0.23
Guatemalan	501	2.21
Honduran	489	2.16
Nicaraguan	547	2.41
Panamanian	43	0.19
Salvadoran	712	3.14
Other Central American	8	0.04
Cuban	5,934	26.19
Dominican Republic	303	1.34
Mexican	5,084	22.44
Puerto Rican	2,050	9.05
South American	682	3.01
Argentinean	44	0.19
Bolivian	15	0.07
Chilean	54	0.24
Colombian	276	1.22
Ecuadorian	80	0.35
Paraguayan	2	0.01
Peruvian	116	0.51
Uruguayan	19	0.08
Venezuelan	76	0.34
Other Hispanic or Latino	574	2.53

Race*	Population	%
African-American/Black (3,962)	4,131	18.23
Not Hispanic (3,473)	3,551	15.67
Hispanic (489)	580	2.56
American Indian/Alaska Native (56)	107	0.47
Not Hispanic (17)	45	0.20
Hispanic (39)	62	0.27
Apache (0)	2	0.01
Blackfeet (0)	1	<0.01
Central American Ind. (7)	11	0.05
Cherokee (1)	9	0.04
Chickasaw (0)	1	<0.01
Choctaw (4)	4	0.02
Creek (0)	1	<0.01
Delaware (3)	3	0.01
Lumbee (1)	1	<0.01
Mexican American Ind. (8)	8	0.04
Sioux (0)	1	<0.01
South American Ind. (2)	2	0.01
Tlingit-Haida *(Alaska Native)* (1)	2	0.01
Yup'ik *(Alaska Native)* (1)	2	0.01
Asian (203)	290	1.28
Not Hispanic (186)	244	1.08
Hispanic (17)	46	0.20
Bangladeshi (33)	39	0.17
Cambodian (8)	8	0.04
Chinese, ex. Taiwanese (10)	20	0.09
Filipino (16)	36	0.16
Indian (44)	61	0.27
Indonesian (1)	3	0.01
Japanese (5)	10	0.04
Korean (13)	23	0.10
Laotian (9)	10	0.04
Pakistani (3)	3	0.01
Sri Lankan (1)	1	<0.01
Taiwanese (5)	6	0.03
Thai (28)	39	0.17
Vietnamese (10)	15	0.07
Hawaii Native/Pacific Islander (4)	32	0.14
Not Hispanic (0)	10	0.04
Hispanic (4)	22	0.10
Guamanian/Chamorro (1)	2	0.01
Native Hawaiian (3)	4	0.02
White (16,528)	17,030	75.17
Not Hispanic (1,809)	1,900	8.39
Hispanic (14,719)	15,130	66.78

Lighthouse Point

Place Type: City
County: Broward
Population: 10,344†

Ancestry‡	Population	%
African, Sub-Saharan (48)	57	0.55
African (11)	20	0.19
South African (37)	37	0.35
American (336)	336	3.21
Arab (36)	87	0.83
Arab (19)	19	0.18
Lebanese (0)	51	0.49
Syrian (17)	17	0.16
Armenian (14)	158	1.51
Austrian (28)	74	0.71
Belgian (0)	7	0.07
Brazilian (61)	75	0.72
British (68)	103	0.98
Canadian (0)	56	0.54
Croatian (13)	20	0.19
Czech (44)	66	0.63

*Notes: † The Census 2010 population figure is used to calculate the percentages in the Hispanic Origin and Race categories. Ancestry percentages are based on the 2006-2010 American Community Survey population (not shown); ‡ Numbers in parentheses indicate the number of people reporting a single ancestry; * Numbers in parentheses indicate the number of persons reporting this race alone, not in combination with any other race; Please refer to the Explanation of Data for more information.*

Czechoslovakian (0)	5	0.05
Danish (19)	58	0.55
Dutch (22)	149	1.42
Eastern European (29)	29	0.28
English (366)	1,233	11.79
European (132)	132	1.26
French, ex. Basque (129)	477	4.56
French Canadian (75)	126	1.20
German (719)	2,622	25.07
Greek (47)	81	0.77
Guyanese (35)	156	1.49
Hungarian (57)	207	1.98
Irish (1,263)	2,898	27.71
Italian (668)	1,257	12.02
Lithuanian (16)	16	0.15
Northern European (17)	17	0.16
Norwegian (44)	160	1.53
Polish (140)	339	3.24
Portuguese (12)	23	0.22
Russian (66)	282	2.70
Scotch-Irish (309)	468	4.48
Scottish (104)	290	2.77
Slovak (0)	15	0.14
Slovene (17)	30	0.29
Swedish (52)	198	1.89
Swiss (0)	49	0.47
Ukrainian (34)	58	0.55
Welsh (33)	71	0.68
West Indian, ex. Hispanic (134)	155	1.48
Bahamian (0)	12	0.11
Dutch West Indian (55)	55	0.53
Haitian (79)	79	0.76
West Indian (0)	9	0.09
Yugoslavian (11)	11	0.11

Hispanic Origin	Population	%
Hispanic or Latino (of any race)	779	7.53
Central American, ex. Mexican	57	0.55
Costa Rican	10	0.10
Guatemalan	9	0.09
Honduran	18	0.17
Nicaraguan	8	0.08
Panamanian	4	0.04
Salvadoran	8	0.08
Cuban	209	2.02
Dominican Republic	17	0.16
Mexican	39	0.38
Puerto Rican	126	1.22
South American	224	2.17
Argentinean	26	0.25
Bolivian	5	0.05
Chilean	12	0.12
Colombian	78	0.75
Ecuadorian	20	0.19
Paraguayan	2	0.02
Peruvian	32	0.31
Uruguayan	18	0.17
Venezuelan	30	0.29
Other South American	1	0.01
Other Hispanic or Latino	107	1.03

Race*	Population	%
African-American/Black (171)	209	2.02
Not Hispanic (156)	187	1.81
Hispanic (15)	22	0.21
American Indian/Alaska Native (27)	60	0.58
Not Hispanic (25)	56	0.54
Hispanic (2)	4	0.04
Blackfeet (0)	1	0.01
Cherokee (5)	13	0.13
Chippewa (1)	2	0.02
Choctaw (1)	1	0.01
Creek (5)	6	0.06
Iroquois (0)	2	0.02
Mexican American Ind. (2)	2	0.02
Navajo (0)	1	0.01
Ottawa (2)	2	0.02
Potawatomi (1)	1	0.01
Seminole (2)	2	0.02
Shoshone (1)	1	0.01
Tlingit-Haida *(Alaska Native)* (0)	1	0.01
Asian (161)	227	2.19
Not Hispanic (159)	217	2.10
Hispanic (2)	10	0.10
Bangladeshi (8)	8	0.08
Chinese, ex. Taiwanese (38)	53	0.51
Filipino (31)	46	0.44
Indian (30)	42	0.41
Japanese (6)	9	0.09
Korean (13)	18	0.17
Laotian (1)	3	0.03
Taiwanese (4)	4	0.04
Thai (16)	18	0.17
Vietnamese (9)	15	0.15
Hawaii Native/Pacific Islander (3)	9	0.09
Not Hispanic (3)	9	0.09
Native Hawaiian (0)	3	0.03
White (9,727)	9,873	95.45
Not Hispanic (9,067)	9,182	88.77
Hispanic (660)	691	6.68

Lockhart

Place Type: CDP
County: Orange
Population: 13,060†

Ancestry‡	Population	%
African, Sub-Saharan (44)	64	0.50
African (0)	20	0.16
Nigerian (44)	44	0.34
American (785)	785	6.15
Arab (0)	14	0.11
Syrian (0)	14	0.11
Austrian (0)	39	0.31
British (48)	48	0.38
Cajun (0)	16	0.13
Canadian (43)	56	0.44
Croatian (60)	60	0.47
Czech (0)	11	0.09
Czechoslovakian (0)	25	0.20
Danish (0)	8	0.06
Dutch (59)	245	1.92
Eastern European (0)	28	0.22
English (254)	1,003	7.86
European (62)	62	0.49
Finnish (16)	26	0.20
French, ex. Basque (54)	137	1.07
French Canadian (38)	49	0.38
German (377)	1,395	10.93
Greek (0)	16	0.13
Hungarian (48)	48	0.38
Irish (348)	1,065	8.34
Italian (180)	601	4.71
Northern European (13)	13	0.10
Norwegian (15)	40	0.31
Polish (70)	146	1.14
Portuguese (0)	25	0.20
Romanian (14)	14	0.11
Russian (43)	176	1.38
Scotch-Irish (57)	245	1.92
Scottish (50)	151	1.18
Serbian (0)	13	0.10
Slovak (13)	48	0.38
Slovene (0)	11	0.09
Swedish (29)	40	0.31
Turkish (0)	12	0.09
Ukrainian (0)	30	0.24
Welsh (0)	117	0.92
West Indian, ex. Hispanic (270)	293	2.30
Bahamian (15)	15	0.12
Haitian (0)	12	0.09
Jamaican (157)	157	1.23
Trinidadian/Tobagonian (20)	31	0.24
West Indian (78)	78	0.61
Yugoslavian (11)	11	0.09

Hispanic Origin	Population	%
Hispanic or Latino (of any race)	2,757	21.11
Central American, ex. Mexican	175	1.34
Costa Rican	17	0.13
Guatemalan	28	0.21
Honduran	58	0.44
Nicaraguan	25	0.19
Panamanian	19	0.15
Salvadoran	27	0.21
Other Central American	1	0.01
Cuban	288	2.21
Dominican Republic	183	1.40
Mexican	356	2.73
Puerto Rican	1,316	10.08
South American	274	2.10
Argentinean	8	0.06
Bolivian	2	0.02
Chilean	10	0.08
Colombian	135	1.03
Ecuadorian	44	0.34
Peruvian	32	0.25
Uruguayan	3	0.02
Venezuelan	37	0.28
Other South American	3	0.02
Other Hispanic or Latino	165	1.26

Race*	Population	%
African-American/Black (2,960)	3,264	24.99
Not Hispanic (2,797)	3,010	23.05
Hispanic (163)	254	1.94
American Indian/Alaska Native (61)	140	1.07
Not Hispanic (44)	107	0.82
Hispanic (17)	33	0.25
Aleut *(Alaska Native)* (0)	3	0.02
Apache (1)	1	0.01
Blackfeet (3)	5	0.04
Central American Ind. (0)	1	0.01
Cherokee (8)	34	0.26
Chippewa (1)	1	0.01
Choctaw (3)	3	0.02
Comanche (0)	2	0.02
Creek (2)	3	0.02
Iroquois (2)	3	0.02
Lumbee (3)	3	0.02
Mexican American Ind. (3)	3	0.02
Osage (0)	1	0.01
Seminole (1)	2	0.02
Sioux (1)	1	0.01
South American Ind. (5)	5	0.04
Spanish American Ind. (3)	3	0.02
Yaqui (2)	2	0.02
Asian (486)	598	4.58
Not Hispanic (484)	565	4.33
Hispanic (2)	33	0.25
Bangladeshi (10)	12	0.09
Chinese, ex. Taiwanese (31)	47	0.36
Filipino (158)	189	1.45
Indian (76)	106	0.81
Indonesian (7)	7	0.05
Japanese (1)	11	0.08
Korean (29)	42	0.32
Laotian (3)	3	0.02
Pakistani (9)	9	0.07
Sri Lankan (1)	1	0.01
Taiwanese (2)	2	0.02
Thai (5)	6	0.05
Vietnamese (142)	157	1.20
Hawaii Native/Pacific Islander (1)	12	0.09
Not Hispanic (1)	11	0.08
Hispanic (0)	1	0.01
Native Hawaiian (0)	1	0.01
Samoan (0)	2	0.02
White (8,342)	8,775	67.19
Not Hispanic (6,627)	6,881	52.69
Hispanic (1,715)	1,894	14.50

Longwood

Place Type: City
County: Seminole
Population: 13,657†

SECTION TWO

*Notes: † The Census 2010 population figure is used to calculate the percentages in the Hispanic Origin and Race categories. Ancestry percentages are based on the 2006-2010 American Community Survey population (not shown); ‡ Numbers in parentheses indicate the number of people reporting a single ancestry; * Numbers in parentheses indicate the number of persons reporting this race alone, not in combination with any other race; Please refer to the Explanation of Data for more information.*

Ancestry‡	Population	%
American (858)	858	6.11
Arab (49)	101	0.72
Egyptian (18)	18	0.13
Lebanese (22)	74	0.53
Palestinian (9)	9	0.06
Armenian (6)	6	0.04
Austrian (21)	30	0.21
Basque (10)	10	0.07
Belgian (0)	8	0.06
British (105)	112	0.80
Bulgarian (0)	13	0.09
Canadian (11)	18	0.13
Celtic (9)	9	0.06
Czech (48)	99	0.71
Czechoslovakian (0)	14	0.10
Danish (0)	11	0.08
Dutch (81)	145	1.03
English (787)	1,886	13.43
European (925)	1,010	7.19
Finnish (14)	57	0.41
French, ex. Basque (43)	314	2.24
French Canadian (71)	126	0.90
German (837)	2,431	17.32
Greek (15)	72	0.51
Hungarian (21)	51	0.36
Irish (324)	1,909	13.60
Italian (603)	1,052	7.49
Lithuanian (20)	20	0.14
Maltese (10)	10	0.07
Norwegian (22)	108	0.77
Pennsylvania German (23)	23	0.16
Polish (63)	565	4.02
Portuguese (0)	9	0.06
Russian (36)	191	1.36
Scandinavian (9)	9	0.06
Scotch-Irish (125)	242	1.72
Scottish (90)	307	2.19
Serbian (0)	45	0.32
Slovak (28)	64	0.46
Swedish (16)	168	1.20
Swiss (0)	25	0.18
Turkish (8)	8	0.06
Ukrainian (8)	20	0.14
Welsh (36)	106	0.76
West Indian, ex. Hispanic (253)	308	2.19
Barbadian (0)	19	0.14
Belizean (51)	70	0.50
British West Indian (13)	13	0.09
Haitian (19)	19	0.14
Jamaican (60)	60	0.43
Trinidadian/Tobagonian (8)	8	0.06
U.S. Virgin Islander (9)	9	0.06
West Indian (93)	110	0.78
Yugoslavian (48)	48	0.34

Hispanic Origin	Population	%
Hispanic or Latino (of any race)	2,152	15.76
Central American, ex. Mexican	106	0.78
Costa Rican	10	0.07
Guatemalan	17	0.12
Honduran	18	0.13
Nicaraguan	21	0.15
Panamanian	12	0.09
Salvadoran	28	0.21
Cuban	194	1.42
Dominican Republic	90	0.66
Mexican	238	1.74
Puerto Rican	1,057	7.74
South American	332	2.43
Argentinean	35	0.26
Bolivian	1	0.01
Chilean	5	0.04
Colombian	193	1.41
Ecuadorian	41	0.30
Peruvian	18	0.13
Uruguayan	4	0.03
Venezuelan	34	0.25
Other South American	1	0.01
Other Hispanic or Latino	135	0.99

Race*	Population	%
African-American/Black (702)	816	5.97
Not Hispanic (612)	690	5.05
Hispanic (90)	126	0.92
American Indian/Alaska Native (62)	137	1.00
Not Hispanic (47)	110	0.81
Hispanic (15)	27	0.20
Blackfeet (2)	8	0.06
Canadian/French Am. Ind. (1)	2	0.01
Central American Ind. (0)	1	0.01
Cherokee (17)	46	0.34
Choctaw (0)	3	0.02
Creek (6)	7	0.05
Iroquois (1)	2	0.01
Lumbee (1)	1	0.01
Mexican American Ind. (7)	7	0.05
Ottawa (1)	1	0.01
Seminole (0)	1	0.01
Sioux (4)	6	0.04
South American Ind. (3)	3	0.02
Spanish American Ind. (1)	1	0.01
Asian (460)	562	4.12
Not Hispanic (448)	543	3.98
Hispanic (12)	19	0.14
Bangladeshi (8)	9	0.07
Chinese, ex. Taiwanese (63)	85	0.62
Filipino (52)	83	0.61
Hmong (7)	7	0.05
Indian (177)	187	1.37
Indonesian (3)	3	0.02
Japanese (7)	21	0.15
Korean (26)	33	0.24
Laotian (13)	19	0.14
Pakistani (8)	8	0.06
Taiwanese (1)	7	0.05
Thai (2)	10	0.07
Vietnamese (65)	69	0.51
Hawaii Native/Pacific Islander (9)	17	0.12
Not Hispanic (9)	17	0.12
Guamanian/Chamorro (4)	4	0.03
Native Hawaiian (1)	3	0.02
Samoan (4)	4	0.03
White (11,672)	11,980	87.72
Not Hispanic (10,123)	10,315	75.53
Hispanic (1,549)	1,665	12.19

Lutz

Place Type: CDP
County: Hillsborough
Population: 19,344†

Ancestry‡	Population	%
African, Sub-Saharan (7)	7	0.04
African (7)	7	0.04
Albanian (12)	51	0.26
American (1,828)	1,828	9.28
Arab (0)	35	0.18
Arab (0)	20	0.10
Lebanese (0)	9	0.05
Syrian (0)	6	0.03
Armenian (12)	12	0.06
Australian (9)	9	0.05
Austrian (0)	81	0.41
Brazilian (29)	64	0.33
British (118)	191	0.97
Canadian (8)	80	0.41
Croatian (0)	20	0.10
Czech (55)	75	0.38
Danish (12)	71	0.36
Dutch (114)	554	2.81
Eastern European (0)	23	0.12
English (1,000)	2,757	14.00
European (206)	236	1.20
Finnish (24)	24	0.12
French, ex. Basque (129)	641	3.26
French Canadian (107)	184	0.93
German (850)	3,035	15.41
Greek (84)	88	0.45
Hungarian (23)	131	0.67
Iranian (39)	39	0.20
Irish (768)	2,677	13.60
Italian (815)	2,109	10.71
Lithuanian (57)	68	0.35
Norwegian (86)	205	1.04
Pennsylvania German (11)	11	0.06
Polish (130)	402	2.04
Portuguese (29)	47	0.24
Romanian (11)	11	0.06
Russian (35)	132	0.67
Scandinavian (16)	16	0.08
Scotch-Irish (124)	406	2.06
Scottish (179)	542	2.75
Serbian (12)	12	0.06
Slovak (65)	112	0.57
Swedish (98)	240	1.22
Swiss (0)	29	0.15
Turkish (149)	180	0.91
Ukrainian (11)	50	0.25
Welsh (11)	139	0.71
West Indian, ex. Hispanic (446)	507	2.57
Barbadian (6)	6	0.03
Bermudan (27)	27	0.14
Haitian (163)	163	0.83
Jamaican (150)	173	0.88
U.S. Virgin Islander (51)	51	0.26
West Indian (49)	87	0.44
Yugoslavian (10)	10	0.05

Hispanic Origin	Population	%
Hispanic or Latino (of any race)	2,468	12.76
Central American, ex. Mexican	135	0.70
Costa Rican	19	0.10
Guatemalan	5	0.03
Honduran	64	0.33
Nicaraguan	13	0.07
Panamanian	25	0.13
Salvadoran	9	0.05
Cuban	665	3.44
Dominican Republic	60	0.31
Mexican	225	1.16
Puerto Rican	697	3.60
South American	236	1.22
Argentinean	14	0.07
Bolivian	3	0.02
Chilean	8	0.04
Colombian	112	0.58
Ecuadorian	20	0.10
Paraguayan	2	0.01
Peruvian	36	0.19
Uruguayan	8	0.04
Venezuelan	31	0.16
Other South American	2	0.01
Other Hispanic or Latino	450	2.33

Race*	Population	%
African-American/Black (930)	1,071	5.54
Not Hispanic (877)	969	5.01
Hispanic (53)	102	0.53
American Indian/Alaska Native (68)	186	0.96
Not Hispanic (54)	138	0.71
Hispanic (14)	48	0.25
Alaska Athabascan *(Ala. Nat.)* (0)	1	0.01
Apache (0)	3	0.02
Blackfeet (1)	6	0.03
Canadian/French Am. Ind. (0)	1	0.01
Cherokee (9)	50	0.26
Cheyenne (1)	2	0.01
Chippewa (0)	4	0.02
Choctaw (1)	8	0.04
Cree (1)	3	0.02
Creek (0)	3	0.02
Inupiat *(Alaska Native)* (1)	1	0.01
Iroquois (2)	4	0.02
Lumbee (3)	3	0.02
Menominee (1)	2	0.01
Mexican American Ind. (1)	1	0.01
Osage (3)	6	0.03
Potawatomi (1)	2	0.01

*Notes: † The Census 2010 population figure is used to calculate the percentages in the Hispanic Origin and Race categories. Ancestry percentages are based on the 2006-2010 American Community Survey population (not shown); ‡ Numbers in parentheses indicate the number of people reporting a single ancestry; * Numbers in parentheses indicate the number of persons reporting this race alone, not in combination with any other race; Please refer to the Explanation of Data for more information.*

Pueblo (0)	1	0.01
Seminole (0)	2	0.01
Sioux (5)	6	0.03
South American Ind. (3)	7	0.04
Asian (480)	610	3.15
Not Hispanic (467)	567	2.93
Hispanic (13)	43	0.22
Bangladeshi (8)	8	0.04
Cambodian (2)	2	0.01
Chinese, ex. Taiwanese (55)	85	0.44
Filipino (90)	122	0.63
Hmong (1)	2	0.01
Indian (148)	169	0.87
Indonesian (2)	2	0.01
Japanese (6)	20	0.10
Korean (55)	63	0.33
Pakistani (8)	10	0.05
Sri Lankan (5)	8	0.04
Taiwanese (4)	5	0.03
Thai (9)	11	0.06
Vietnamese (76)	87	0.45
Hawaii Native/Pacific Islander (21)	43	0.22
Not Hispanic (9)	29	0.15
Hispanic (12)	14	0.07
Guamanian/Chamorro (13)	14	0.07
Native Hawaiian (7)	14	0.07
Samoan (1)	6	0.03
White (17,172)	17,517	90.56
Not Hispanic (15,169)	15,404	79.63
Hispanic (2,003)	2,113	10.92

Lynn Haven

Place Type: City
County: Bay
Population: 18,493†

Ancestry‡	Population	%
African, Sub-Saharan (50)	50	0.28
African (50)	50	0.28
American (2,244)	2,244	12.67
Arab (121)	164	0.93
Iraqi (121)	121	0.68
Lebanese (0)	43	0.24
Austrian (7)	7	0.04
Belgian (0)	34	0.19
British (54)	115	0.65
Cajun (10)	10	0.06
Croatian (0)	14	0.08
Czech (16)	30	0.17
Czechoslovakian (91)	91	0.51
Dutch (33)	233	1.32
English (1,081)	2,357	13.31
European (190)	303	1.71
Finnish (11)	11	0.06
French, ex. Basque (112)	703	3.97
French Canadian (61)	67	0.38
German (931)	2,656	15.00
Greek (37)	37	0.21
Hungarian (57)	78	0.44
Irish (631)	2,586	14.60
Italian (566)	1,233	6.96
Lithuanian (43)	58	0.33
Norwegian (19)	101	0.57
Polish (40)	245	1.38
Portuguese (0)	34	0.19
Russian (65)	120	0.68
Scandinavian (68)	79	0.45
Scotch-Irish (254)	452	2.55
Scottish (205)	587	3.31
Slovak (0)	21	0.12
Swedish (0)	98	0.55
Ukrainian (0)	18	0.10
Welsh (30)	59	0.33
West Indian, ex. Hispanic (17)	64	0.36
Trinidadian/Tobagonian (17)	64	0.36

Hispanic Origin	Population	%
Hispanic or Latino (of any race)	759	4.10
Central American, ex. Mexican	83	0.45
Costa Rican	3	0.02
Guatemalan	11	0.06
Honduran	21	0.11
Nicaraguan	11	0.06
Panamanian	19	0.10
Salvadoran	17	0.09
Other Central American	1	0.01
Cuban	47	0.25
Dominican Republic	15	0.08
Mexican	251	1.36
Puerto Rican	220	1.19
South American	52	0.28
Argentinean	4	0.02
Bolivian	4	0.02
Chilean	1	0.01
Colombian	21	0.11
Ecuadorian	3	0.02
Peruvian	12	0.06
Venezuelan	7	0.04
Other Hispanic or Latino	91	0.49

Race*	Population	%
African-American/Black (1,856)	2,073	11.21
Not Hispanic (1,831)	2,017	10.91
Hispanic (25)	56	0.30
American Indian/Alaska Native (104)	211	1.14
Not Hispanic (90)	186	1.01
Hispanic (14)	25	0.14
Aleut *(Alaska Native)* (0)	5	0.03
Apache (1)	2	0.01
Blackfeet (0)	2	0.01
Central American Ind. (2)	2	0.01
Cherokee (14)	52	0.28
Choctaw (9)	11	0.06
Cree (1)	1	0.01
Creek (25)	35	0.19
Hopi (1)	1	0.01
Houma (1)	1	0.01
Iroquois (4)	5	0.03
Lumbee (4)	5	0.03
Mexican American Ind. (2)	3	0.02
Navajo (0)	3	0.02
Puget Sound Salish (1)	1	0.01
Seminole (4)	7	0.04
Sioux (2)	2	0.01
Tlingit-Haida *(Alaska Native)* (2)	3	0.02
Asian (442)	648	3.50
Not Hispanic (433)	620	3.35
Hispanic (9)	28	0.15
Bangladeshi (4)	4	0.02
Cambodian (3)	3	0.02
Chinese, ex. Taiwanese (39)	55	0.30
Filipino (92)	178	0.96
Indian (95)	103	0.56
Indonesian (1)	2	0.01
Japanese (17)	47	0.25
Korean (47)	90	0.49
Pakistani (57)	57	0.31
Thai (9)	20	0.11
Vietnamese (63)	81	0.44
Hawaii Native/Pacific Islander (23)	67	0.36
Not Hispanic (21)	62	0.34
Hispanic (2)	5	0.03
Guamanian/Chamorro (1)	9	0.05
Native Hawaiian (11)	34	0.18
Samoan (0)	2	0.01
White (15,379)	15,863	85.78
Not Hispanic (14,891)	15,307	82.77
Hispanic (488)	556	3.01

Maitland

Place Type: City
County: Orange
Population: 15,751†

Ancestry‡	Population	%
African, Sub-Saharan (119)	119	0.76
African (96)	96	0.61
South African (23)	23	0.15
Albanian (0)	36	0.23
American (848)	848	5.39
Arab (13)	41	0.26
Lebanese (13)	41	0.26
Austrian (0)	39	0.25
Belgian (54)	54	0.34
Brazilian (18)	32	0.20
British (10)	39	0.25
Canadian (32)	32	0.20
Croatian (38)	66	0.42
Cypriot (12)	12	0.08
Czech (10)	54	0.34
Danish (0)	43	0.27
Dutch (172)	252	1.60
Eastern European (128)	128	0.81
English (1,078)	2,475	15.72
Estonian (26)	26	0.17
European (496)	661	4.20
French, ex. Basque (61)	530	3.37
French Canadian (20)	84	0.53
German (818)	2,532	16.08
Greek (86)	119	0.76
Hungarian (64)	144	0.91
Iranian (78)	90	0.57
Irish (563)	2,120	13.47
Italian (552)	1,166	7.41
Latvian (0)	14	0.09
Lithuanian (29)	29	0.18
Luxemburger (9)	9	0.06
Norwegian (0)	98	0.62
Polish (216)	532	3.38
Portuguese (0)	29	0.18
Russian (276)	556	3.53
Scandinavian (18)	44	0.28
Scotch-Irish (132)	394	2.50
Scottish (86)	377	2.39
Slovak (11)	34	0.22
Slovene (0)	30	0.19
Swedish (26)	166	1.05
Swiss (26)	89	0.57
Turkish (24)	24	0.15
Ukrainian (0)	20	0.13
Welsh (20)	78	0.50
West Indian, ex. Hispanic (76)	356	2.26
British West Indian (0)	140	0.89
Jamaican (76)	76	0.48
Trinidadian/Tobagonian (0)	140	0.89
Yugoslavian (29)	29	0.18

Hispanic Origin	Population	%
Hispanic or Latino (of any race)	1,642	10.42
Central American, ex. Mexican	82	0.52
Costa Rican	12	0.08
Guatemalan	18	0.11
Honduran	9	0.06
Nicaraguan	16	0.10
Panamanian	18	0.11
Salvadoran	9	0.06
Cuban	136	0.86
Dominican Republic	81	0.51
Mexican	150	0.95
Puerto Rican	716	4.55
South American	358	2.27
Argentinean	21	0.13
Bolivian	7	0.04
Chilean	22	0.14
Colombian	155	0.98
Ecuadorian	30	0.19
Peruvian	30	0.19
Uruguayan	1	0.01
Venezuelan	90	0.57
Other South American	2	0.01
Other Hispanic or Latino	119	0.76

Race*	Population	%
African-American/Black (1,742)	1,922	12.20
Not Hispanic (1,657)	1,780	11.30
Hispanic (85)	142	0.90
American Indian/Alaska Native (25)	98	0.62
Not Hispanic (17)	80	0.51

*Notes: † The Census 2010 population figure is used to calculate the percentages in the Hispanic Origin and Race categories. Ancestry percentages are based on the 2006-2010 American Community Survey population (not shown); ‡ Numbers in parentheses indicate the number of people reporting a single ancestry; * Numbers in parentheses indicate the number of persons reporting this race alone, not in combination with any other race; Please refer to the Explanation of Data for more information.*

Hispanic (8)	18	0.11
Alaska Athabascan *(Ala. Nat.)* (1)	4	0.03
Aleut *(Alaska Native)* (1)	2	0.01
Apache (0)	3	0.02
Blackfeet (0)	4	0.03
Central American Ind. (1)	2	0.01
Cherokee (7)	28	0.18
Chippewa (0)	1	0.01
Choctaw (1)	2	0.01
Iroquois (0)	3	0.02
Lumbee (2)	2	0.01
Menominee (0)	3	0.02
Ottawa (1)	1	0.01
Seminole (1)	3	0.02
Shoshone (1)	1	0.01
Sioux (1)	5	0.03
Asian (544)	683	4.34
Not Hispanic (538)	657	4.17
Hispanic (6)	26	0.17
Burmese (0)	1	0.01
Chinese, ex. Taiwanese (63)	92	0.58
Filipino (79)	104	0.66
Indian (231)	248	1.57
Japanese (12)	26	0.17
Korean (49)	63	0.40
Laotian (3)	3	0.02
Malaysian (1)	3	0.02
Pakistani (18)	22	0.14
Taiwanese (3)	4	0.03
Thai (7)	17	0.11
Vietnamese (61)	76	0.48
Hawaii Native/Pacific Islander (5)	18	0.11
Not Hispanic (5)	16	0.10
Hispanic (0)	2	0.01
Guamanian/Chamorro (2)	3	0.02
Native Hawaiian (3)	4	0.03
White (12,693)	13,007	82.58
Not Hispanic (11,595)	11,817	75.02
Hispanic (1,098)	1,190	7.56

Mango

Place Type: CDP
County: Hillsborough
Population: 11,313†

Ancestry‡	Population	%
African, Sub-Saharan (7)	7	0.06
African (7)	7	0.06
American (1,442)	1,442	13.37
Arab (0)	14	0.13
Lebanese (0)	14	0.13
Austrian (20)	15	0.14
Brazilian (48)	48	0.44
British (0)	50	0.46
Canadian (16)	16	0.15
Czech (14)	49	0.45
Dutch (34)	218	2.02
English (246)	790	7.32
European (24)	24	0.22
French, ex. Basque (37)	105	0.97
French Canadian (43)	54	0.50
German (326)	1,351	12.52
Greek (0)	25	0.23
Hungarian (21)	43	0.40
Irish (737)	1,440	13.35
Italian (95)	521	4.83
Lithuanian (23)	23	0.21
Norwegian (55)	79	0.73
Polish (54)	271	2.51
Portuguese (0)	12	0.11
Russian (20)	66	0.61
Scotch-Irish (159)	330	3.06
Scottish (0)	173	1.60
Slovak (22)	38	0.35
Swedish (0)	102	0.95
Swiss (0)	12	0.11
Ukrainian (0)	20	0.19
Welsh (12)	24	0.22
West Indian, ex. Hispanic (265)	302	2.80
Haitian (97)	107	0.99
Jamaican (121)	148	1.37
West Indian (47)	47	0.44

Hispanic Origin	Population	%
Hispanic or Latino (of any race)	2,798	24.73
Central American, ex. Mexican	209	1.85
Costa Rican	8	0.07
Guatemalan	96	0.85
Honduran	42	0.37
Nicaraguan	10	0.09
Panamanian	11	0.10
Salvadoran	42	0.37
Cuban	249	2.20
Dominican Republic	76	0.67
Mexican	1,032	9.12
Puerto Rican	912	8.06
South American	142	1.26
Argentinean	2	0.02
Chilean	2	0.02
Colombian	92	0.81
Ecuadorian	9	0.08
Paraguayan	1	0.01
Peruvian	20	0.18
Uruguayan	1	0.01
Venezuelan	15	0.13
Other Hispanic or Latino	178	1.57

Race*	Population	%
African-American/Black (1,744)	1,867	16.50
Not Hispanic (1,614)	1,702	15.04
Hispanic (130)	165	1.46
American Indian/Alaska Native (85)	180	1.59
Not Hispanic (52)	131	1.16
Hispanic (33)	49	0.43
Apache (6)	10	0.09
Blackfeet (3)	14	0.12
Canadian/French Am. Ind. (2)	4	0.04
Central American Ind. (4)	4	0.04
Cherokee (8)	32	0.28
Chickasaw (0)	2	0.02
Chippewa (1)	1	0.01
Choctaw (1)	3	0.03
Creek (0)	4	0.04
Iroquois (1)	3	0.03
Menominee (1)	1	0.01
Navajo (3)	3	0.03
Seminole (3)	6	0.05
Sioux (2)	5	0.04
South American Ind. (0)	2	0.02
Asian (173)	237	2.09
Not Hispanic (171)	227	2.01
Hispanic (2)	10	0.09
Cambodian (0)	1	0.01
Chinese, ex. Taiwanese (10)	15	0.13
Filipino (31)	50	0.44
Hmong (7)	7	0.06
Indian (37)	45	0.40
Indonesian (1)	2	0.02
Japanese (3)	17	0.15
Korean (8)	10	0.09
Laotian (2)	4	0.04
Pakistani (1)	1	0.01
Thai (34)	38	0.34
Vietnamese (31)	38	0.34
Hawaii Native/Pacific Islander (18)	28	0.25
Not Hispanic (13)	17	0.15
Hispanic (5)	11	0.10
Guamanian/Chamorro (13)	16	0.14
Native Hawaiian (4)	6	0.05
Tongan (0)	1	0.01
White (8,066)	8,363	73.92
Not Hispanic (6,440)	6,625	58.56
Hispanic (1,626)	1,738	15.36

Marathon

Place Type: City
County: Monroe
Population: 8,297†

Ancestry‡	Population	%
African, Sub-Saharan (19)	19	0.22
African (19)	19	0.22
American (268)	268	3.15
Arab (144)	155	1.82
Lebanese (144)	155	1.82
Austrian (35)	49	0.58
Basque (0)	11	0.13
Belgian (95)	95	1.12
British (43)	55	0.65
Canadian (35)	35	0.41
Celtic (0)	10	0.12
Croatian (0)	9	0.11
Czech (11)	24	0.28
Czechoslovakian (0)	14	0.16
Dutch (14)	55	0.65
English (645)	1,265	14.89
European (41)	75	0.88
Finnish (0)	13	0.15
French, ex. Basque (40)	217	2.55
French Canadian (30)	52	0.61
German (671)	1,460	17.18
Greek (24)	24	0.28
Hungarian (53)	81	0.95
Irish (569)	1,057	12.44
Italian (275)	606	7.13
Lithuanian (33)	43	0.51
Northern European (19)	19	0.22
Norwegian (36)	103	1.21
Polish (196)	416	4.90
Portuguese (34)	74	0.87
Romanian (0)	9	0.11
Russian (26)	73	0.86
Scotch-Irish (129)	215	2.53
Scottish (29)	102	1.20
Slovene (0)	52	0.61
Swedish (25)	77	0.91
Swiss (0)	27	0.32
Welsh (11)	44	0.52
West Indian, ex. Hispanic (0)	28	0.33
Other West Indian (0)	28	0.33
Yugoslavian (0)	25	0.29

Hispanic Origin	Population	%
Hispanic or Latino (of any race)	2,224	26.80
Central American, ex. Mexican	342	4.12
Costa Rican	14	0.17
Guatemalan	143	1.72
Honduran	47	0.57
Nicaraguan	125	1.51
Panamanian	6	0.07
Salvadoran	7	0.08
Cuban	1,256	15.14
Dominican Republic	50	0.60
Mexican	299	3.60
Puerto Rican	88	1.06
South American	72	0.87
Argentinean	7	0.08
Chilean	1	0.01
Colombian	18	0.22
Ecuadorian	4	0.05
Peruvian	12	0.14
Venezuelan	30	0.36
Other Hispanic or Latino	117	1.41

Race*	Population	%
African-American/Black (395)	453	5.46
Not Hispanic (357)	401	4.83
Hispanic (38)	52	0.63
American Indian/Alaska Native (26)	69	0.83
Not Hispanic (25)	64	0.77
Hispanic (1)	5	0.06
Apache (1)	1	0.01
Blackfeet (0)	7	0.08
Central American Ind. (0)	1	0.01
Cherokee (4)	13	0.16
Chippewa (0)	1	0.01
Lumbee (0)	1	0.01
Menominee (0)	1	0.01
Mexican American Ind. (1)	1	0.01

*Notes: † The Census 2010 population figure is used to calculate the percentages in the Hispanic Origin and Race categories. Ancestry percentages are based on the 2006-2010 American Community Survey population (not shown); ‡ Numbers in parentheses indicate the number of people reporting a single ancestry; * Numbers in parentheses indicate the number of persons reporting this race alone, not in combination with any other race; Please refer to the Explanation of Data for more information.*

Seminole (1)	2	0.02
Sioux (1)	2	0.02
Yuman (1)	1	0.01
Asian (90)	103	1.24
Not Hispanic (90)	101	1.22
Hispanic (0)	2	0.02
Bangladeshi (2)	2	0.02
Burmese (4)	4	0.05
Cambodian (2)	3	0.04
Chinese, ex. Taiwanese (13)	15	0.18
Filipino (15)	22	0.27
Indian (16)	17	0.20
Japanese (2)	3	0.04
Korean (8)	9	0.11
Thai (9)	10	0.12
Vietnamese (7)	7	0.08
Hawaii Native/Pacific Islander (2)	6	0.07
Not Hispanic (2)	6	0.07
Guamanian/Chamorro (1)	1	0.01
Native Hawaiian (1)	3	0.04
White (7,505)	7,637	92.05
Not Hispanic (5,508)	5,581	67.27
Hispanic (1,997)	2,056	24.78

Marco Island

Place Type: City
County: Collier
Population: 16,413†

Ancestry‡	Population	%
Albanian (0)	67	0.40
American (903)	903	5.45
Arab (53)	53	0.32
Arab (37)	37	0.22
Lebanese (16)	16	0.10
Armenian (15)	15	0.09
Australian (17)	32	0.19
Austrian (66)	106	0.64
Belgian (16)	16	0.10
British (26)	26	0.16
Bulgarian (5)	5	0.03
Canadian (114)	131	0.79
Celtic (0)	13	0.08
Croatian (10)	45	0.27
Czech (46)	109	0.66
Czechoslovakian (14)	26	0.16
Danish (8)	53	0.32
Dutch (26)	219	1.32
Eastern European (10)	10	0.06
English (709)	2,125	12.81
European (118)	118	0.71
Finnish (54)	65	0.39
French, ex. Basque (180)	600	3.62
French Canadian (183)	222	1.34
German (1,487)	3,475	20.95
Greek (128)	203	1.22
Hungarian (82)	153	0.92
Irish (913)	2,819	17.00
Italian (1,086)	1,858	11.20
Lithuanian (28)	60	0.36
Norwegian (167)	345	2.08
Pennsylvania German (15)	15	0.09
Polish (423)	893	5.38
Portuguese (52)	107	0.65
Romanian (180)	192	1.16
Russian (74)	175	1.06
Scandinavian (22)	38	0.23
Scotch-Irish (232)	452	2.73
Scottish (114)	416	2.51
Slovak (154)	170	1.03
Slovene (13)	23	0.14
Swedish (129)	349	2.10
Swiss (47)	86	0.52
Turkish (15)	15	0.09
Ukrainian (90)	119	0.72
Welsh (24)	237	1.43

Hispanic Origin	Population	%
Hispanic or Latino (of any race)	1,162	7.08
Central American, ex. Mexican	159	0.97
Costa Rican	13	0.08
Guatemalan	87	0.53
Honduran	8	0.05
Nicaraguan	4	0.02
Panamanian	5	0.03
Salvadoran	39	0.24
Other Central American	3	0.02
Cuban	234	1.43
Dominican Republic	13	0.08
Mexican	445	2.71
Puerto Rican	70	0.43
South American	148	0.90
Argentinean	15	0.09
Bolivian	1	0.01
Chilean	7	0.04
Colombian	61	0.37
Ecuadorian	10	0.06
Paraguayan	1	0.01
Peruvian	15	0.09
Uruguayan	12	0.07
Venezuelan	26	0.16
Other Hispanic or Latino	93	0.57

Race*	Population	%
African-American/Black (88)	114	0.69
Not Hispanic (83)	104	0.63
Hispanic (5)	10	0.06
American Indian/Alaska Native (16)	48	0.29
Not Hispanic (13)	44	0.27
Hispanic (3)	4	0.02
Blackfeet (0)	2	0.01
Cherokee (3)	17	0.10
Cree (0)	1	0.01
Iroquois (0)	1	0.01
Navajo (1)	1	0.01
Osage (0)	2	0.01
Seminole (1)	1	0.01
Sioux (1)	1	0.01
South American Ind. (0)	1	0.01
Asian (181)	222	1.35
Not Hispanic (178)	214	1.30
Hispanic (3)	8	0.05
Bangladeshi (4)	5	0.03
Chinese, ex. Taiwanese (13)	20	0.12
Filipino (34)	43	0.26
Indian (40)	48	0.29
Indonesian (3)	5	0.03
Japanese (7)	8	0.05
Korean (11)	11	0.07
Pakistani (4)	4	0.02
Sri Lankan (2)	2	0.01
Taiwanese (2)	2	0.01
Thai (5)	5	0.03
Vietnamese (52)	60	0.37
Hawaii Native/Pacific Islander (6)	8	0.05
Not Hispanic (5)	6	0.04
Hispanic (1)	2	0.01
Guamanian/Chamorro (2)	2	0.01
Native Hawaiian (0)	1	0.01
White (15,736)	15,841	96.51
Not Hispanic (14,866)	14,943	91.04
Hispanic (870)	898	5.47

Margate

Place Type: City
County: Broward
Population: 53,284†

Ancestry‡	Population	%
African, Sub-Saharan (996)	1,187	2.21
African (996)	1,102	2.06
South African (0)	85	0.16
American (1,717)	1,717	3.20
Arab (109)	180	0.34
Arab (69)	69	0.13
Jordanian (0)	14	0.03
Lebanese (0)	10	0.02
Palestinian (30)	44	0.08
Syrian (10)	29	0.05
Other Arab (0)	14	0.03
Armenian (52)	52	0.10
Austrian (41)	132	0.25
Basque (0)	14	0.03
Belgian (17)	29	0.05
Brazilian (405)	438	0.82
British (38)	113	0.21
Bulgarian (53)	83	0.15
Canadian (227)	304	0.57
Croatian (51)	67	0.13
Czech (99)	208	0.39
Danish (8)	146	0.27
Dutch (108)	928	1.73
Eastern European (74)	74	0.14
English (815)	2,939	5.48
European (118)	204	0.38
Finnish (34)	117	0.22
French, ex. Basque (99)	997	1.86
French Canadian (229)	311	0.58
German (1,143)	4,571	8.53
Greek (97)	133	0.25
Guyanese (128)	128	0.24
Hungarian (148)	467	0.87
Iranian (55)	68	0.13
Irish (1,369)	4,783	8.92
Israeli (47)	47	0.09
Italian (3,828)	5,752	10.73
Lithuanian (20)	181	0.34
Maltese (171)	171	0.32
Norwegian (81)	229	0.43
Pennsylvania German (0)	89	0.17
Polish (738)	1,545	2.88
Portuguese (278)	374	0.70
Romanian (242)	417	0.78
Russian (482)	1,135	2.12
Scotch-Irish (240)	474	0.88
Scottish (103)	442	0.82
Serbian (0)	15	0.03
Slavic (66)	80	0.15
Slovak (14)	115	0.21
Swedish (168)	564	1.05
Swiss (0)	13	0.02
Turkish (291)	291	0.54
Ukrainian (42)	125	0.23
Welsh (0)	263	0.49
West Indian, ex. Hispanic (5,972)	6,566	12.25
Bahamian (179)	179	0.33
British West Indian (170)	170	0.32
Dutch West Indian (0)	14	0.03
Haitian (3,066)	3,141	5.86
Jamaican (2,092)	2,558	4.77
Trinidadian/Tobagonian (268)	293	0.55
U.S. Virgin Islander (0)	14	0.03
West Indian (197)	197	0.37
Yugoslavian (198)	214	0.40

Hispanic Origin	Population	%
Hispanic or Latino (of any race)	11,846	22.23
Central American, ex. Mexican	1,451	2.72
Costa Rican	108	0.20
Guatemalan	257	0.48
Honduran	384	0.72
Nicaraguan	151	0.28
Panamanian	90	0.17
Salvadoran	458	0.86
Other Central American	3	0.01
Cuban	970	1.82
Dominican Republic	615	1.15
Mexican	1,033	1.94
Puerto Rican	2,841	5.33
South American	4,158	7.80
Argentinean	263	0.49
Bolivian	28	0.05
Chilean	68	0.13
Colombian	2,220	4.17
Ecuadorian	365	0.69
Paraguayan	7	0.01
Peruvian	772	1.45
Uruguayan	80	0.15

SECTION TWO

*Notes: † The Census 2010 population figure is used to calculate the percentages in the Hispanic Origin and Race categories. Ancestry percentages are based on the 2006-2010 American Community Survey population (not shown); ‡ Numbers in parentheses indicate the number of people reporting a single ancestry; * Numbers in parentheses indicate the number of persons reporting this race alone, not in combination with any other race; Please refer to the Explanation of Data for more information.*

Venezuelan	341	0.64
Other South American	14	0.03
Other Hispanic or Latino	778	1.46

Race*	Population	%
African-American/Black (13,726)	14,578	27.36
Not Hispanic (13,222)	13,903	26.09
Hispanic (504)	675	1.27
American Indian/Alaska Native (198)	387	0.73
Not Hispanic (96)	234	0.44
Hispanic (102)	153	0.29
Apache (2)	2	<0.01
Blackfeet (1)	11	0.02
Central American Ind. (3)	6	0.01
Cherokee (12)	54	0.10
Chippewa (4)	4	0.01
Creek (0)	5	0.01
Delaware (3)	4	0.01
Iroquois (4)	8	0.02
Lumbee (1)	1	<0.01
Mexican American Ind. (44)	47	0.09
Navajo (2)	2	<0.01
Potawatomi (1)	1	<0.01
Seminole (1)	5	0.01
Shoshone (2)	2	<0.01
Sioux (2)	2	<0.01
South American Ind. (10)	12	0.02
Tlingit-Haida *(Alaska Native)* (0)	5	0.01
Asian (2,150)	2,577	4.84
Not Hispanic (2,107)	2,485	4.66
Hispanic (43)	92	0.17
Bangladeshi (24)	31	0.06
Cambodian (3)	3	0.01
Chinese, ex. Taiwanese (311)	445	0.84
Filipino (206)	252	0.47
Indian (847)	1,022	1.92
Japanese (31)	54	0.10
Korean (24)	34	0.06
Laotian (4)	5	0.01
Malaysian (1)	2	<0.01
Nepalese (2)	2	<0.01
Pakistani (50)	60	0.11
Taiwanese (0)	2	<0.01
Thai (36)	56	0.11
Vietnamese (514)	547	1.03
Hawaii Native/Pacific Islander (33)	204	0.38
Not Hispanic (29)	174	0.33
Hispanic (4)	30	0.06
Fijian (0)	1	<0.01
Guamanian/Chamorro (6)	14	0.03
Native Hawaiian (3)	15	0.03
Samoan (2)	6	0.01
White (33,037)	34,181	64.15
Not Hispanic (24,521)	25,133	47.17
Hispanic (8,516)	9,048	16.98

Meadow Woods

Place Type: CDP
County: Orange
Population: 25,558†

Ancestry‡	Population	%
African, Sub-Saharan (23)	23	0.10
African (23)	23	0.10
American (369)	369	1.55
Arab (34)	46	0.19
Lebanese (22)	22	0.09
Moroccan (12)	24	0.10
Armenian (0)	8	0.03
Brazilian (28)	54	0.23
British (29)	29	0.12
Celtic (0)	12	0.05
Croatian (24)	24	0.10
Czech (10)	10	0.04
Dutch (0)	105	0.44
Eastern European (17)	17	0.07
English (124)	306	1.29
European (156)	163	0.69
French, ex. Basque (70)	180	0.76
French Canadian (0)	98	0.41
German (117)	682	2.87
Greek (0)	18	0.08
Guyanese (39)	79	0.33
Hungarian (37)	45	0.19
Iranian (42)	42	0.18
Irish (164)	580	2.44
Italian (280)	726	3.06
Northern European (18)	18	0.08
Norwegian (38)	73	0.31
Polish (85)	227	0.96
Romanian (43)	86	0.36
Russian (155)	168	0.71
Scotch-Irish (79)	114	0.48
Scottish (18)	29	0.12
Slovak (12)	12	0.05
Swedish (0)	21	0.09
Swiss (0)	11	0.05
Welsh (0)	121	0.51
West Indian, ex. Hispanic (1,191)	1,191	5.01
Barbadian (9)	9	0.04
British West Indian (30)	30	0.13
Haitian (372)	372	1.57
Jamaican (390)	390	1.64
Trinidadian/Tobagonian (151)	151	0.64
West Indian (239)	239	1.01
Yugoslavian (140)	140	0.59

Hispanic Origin	Population	%
Hispanic or Latino (of any race)	17,185	67.24
Central American, ex. Mexican	696	2.72
Costa Rican	69	0.27
Guatemalan	98	0.38
Honduran	129	0.50
Nicaraguan	118	0.46
Panamanian	100	0.39
Salvadoran	179	0.70
Other Central American	3	0.01
Cuban	657	2.57
Dominican Republic	1,651	6.46
Mexican	469	1.84
Puerto Rican	8,974	35.11
South American	3,989	15.61
Argentinean	122	0.48
Bolivian	32	0.13
Chilean	37	0.14
Colombian	2,226	8.71
Ecuadorian	526	2.06
Paraguayan	3	0.01
Peruvian	351	1.37
Uruguayan	22	0.09
Venezuelan	660	2.58
Other South American	10	0.04
Other Hispanic or Latino	749	2.93

Race*	Population	%
African-American/Black (3,527)	3,964	15.51
Not Hispanic (2,784)	2,993	11.71
Hispanic (743)	971	3.80
American Indian/Alaska Native (98)	206	0.81
Not Hispanic (30)	71	0.28
Hispanic (68)	135	0.53
Blackfeet (0)	2	0.01
Central American Ind. (3)	6	0.02
Cherokee (3)	15	0.06
Chippewa (3)	4	0.02
Choctaw (0)	3	0.01
Cree (0)	1	<0.01
Houma (0)	1	<0.01
Iroquois (1)	1	<0.01
Lumbee (0)	1	<0.01
Mexican American Ind. (0)	1	<0.01
Osage (0)	1	<0.01
Sioux (1)	1	<0.01
South American Ind. (7)	29	0.11
Spanish American Ind. (7)	8	0.03
Asian (1,171)	1,388	5.43
Not Hispanic (1,127)	1,297	5.07
Hispanic (44)	91	0.36
Burmese (3)	3	0.01
Cambodian (13)	14	0.05
Chinese, ex. Taiwanese (134)	166	0.65
Filipino (337)	385	1.51
Hmong (3)	3	0.01
Indian (340)	412	1.61
Indonesian (0)	1	<0.01
Japanese (30)	47	0.18
Korean (33)	54	0.21
Laotian (2)	2	0.01
Nepalese (2)	3	0.01
Pakistani (85)	92	0.36
Sri Lankan (2)	7	0.03
Taiwanese (8)	10	0.04
Thai (9)	12	0.05
Vietnamese (135)	138	0.54
Hawaii Native/Pacific Islander (54)	125	0.49
Not Hispanic (46)	98	0.38
Hispanic (8)	27	0.11
Fijian (1)	1	<0.01
Guamanian/Chamorro (8)	13	0.05
Native Hawaiian (9)	24	0.09
Samoan (13)	26	0.10
Tongan (7)	12	0.05
White (15,644)	16,529	64.67
Not Hispanic (3,762)	4,014	15.71
Hispanic (11,882)	12,515	48.97

Medulla

Place Type: CDP
County: Polk
Population: 8,892†

Ancestry‡	Population	%
African, Sub-Saharan (90)	90	1.10
African (90)	90	1.10
American (499)	499	6.08
Austrian (0)	10	0.12
British (9)	79	0.96
Canadian (0)	8	0.10
Croatian (0)	22	0.27
Danish (0)	11	0.13
Dutch (56)	141	1.72
English (771)	1,118	13.62
European (37)	37	0.45
French, ex. Basque (62)	444	5.41
French Canadian (18)	18	0.22
German (432)	1,625	19.79
Greek (79)	117	1.43
Hungarian (0)	10	0.12
Irish (332)	1,364	16.61
Italian (139)	322	3.92
Lithuanian (9)	19	0.23
Norwegian (0)	24	0.29
Polish (146)	224	2.73
Portuguese (9)	9	0.11
Romanian (16)	16	0.19
Scotch-Irish (47)	79	0.96
Scottish (42)	137	1.67
Swedish (0)	45	0.55
Ukrainian (45)	45	0.55
Welsh (0)	41	0.50
West Indian, ex. Hispanic (49)	49	0.60
Barbadian (38)	38	0.46
Jamaican (11)	11	0.13

Hispanic Origin	Population	%
Hispanic or Latino (of any race)	1,190	13.38
Central American, ex. Mexican	99	1.11
Costa Rican	4	0.04
Guatemalan	41	0.46
Honduran	20	0.22
Nicaraguan	10	0.11
Panamanian	3	0.03
Salvadoran	21	0.24
Cuban	153	1.72
Dominican Republic	35	0.39
Mexican	318	3.58
Puerto Rican	416	4.68
South American	95	1.07

*Notes: † The Census 2010 population figure is used to calculate the percentages in the Hispanic Origin and Race categories. Ancestry percentages are based on the 2006-2010 American Community Survey population (not shown); ‡ Numbers in parentheses indicate the number of people reporting a single ancestry; * Numbers in parentheses indicate the number of persons reporting this race alone, not in combination with any other race; Please refer to the Explanation of Data for more information.*

Argentinean	5	0.06
Chilean	5	0.06
Colombian	23	0.26
Ecuadorian	29	0.33
Peruvian	19	0.21
Uruguayan	2	0.02
Venezuelan	10	0.11
Other South American	2	0.02
Other Hispanic or Latino	74	0.83

Race*	Population	%
African-American/Black (1,220)	1,344	15.11
Not Hispanic (1,180)	1,259	14.16
Hispanic (40)	85	0.96
American Indian/Alaska Native (32)	90	1.01
Not Hispanic (25)	72	0.81
Hispanic (7)	18	0.20
Cherokee (8)	29	0.33
Chippewa (0)	4	0.04
Choctaw (1)	6	0.07
Cree (1)	1	0.01
Mexican American Ind. (0)	1	0.01
South American Ind. (2)	11	0.12
Asian (110)	146	1.64
Not Hispanic (110)	141	1.59
Hispanic (0)	5	0.06
Cambodian (1)	1	0.01
Chinese, ex. Taiwanese (13)	17	0.19
Filipino (43)	57	0.64
Hmong (1)	1	0.01
Indian (17)	20	0.22
Japanese (2)	9	0.10
Korean (9)	10	0.11
Pakistani (5)	5	0.06
Taiwanese (0)	1	0.01
Thai (6)	8	0.09
Vietnamese (13)	13	0.15
Hawaii Native/Pacific Islander (2)	8	0.09
Not Hispanic (2)	7	0.08
Hispanic (0)	1	0.01
Native Hawaiian (2)	2	0.02
White (7,015)	7,226	81.26
Not Hispanic (6,217)	6,348	71.39
Hispanic (798)	878	9.87

Melbourne

Place Type: City
County: Brevard
Population: 76,068†

Ancestry‡	Population	%
African, Sub-Saharan (155)	224	0.29
African (65)	134	0.17
Nigerian (45)	45	0.06
South African (3)	3	<0.01
Zimbabwean (42)	42	0.05
American (6,523)	6,523	8.50
Arab (284)	366	0.48
Arab (121)	126	0.16
Egyptian (9)	9	0.01
Lebanese (110)	174	0.23
Moroccan (31)	39	0.05
Other Arab (13)	18	0.02
Armenian (34)	80	0.10
Assyrian/Chaldean/Syriac (10)	10	0.01
Austrian (117)	320	0.42
Basque (0)	11	0.01
Belgian (23)	52	0.07
Brazilian (23)	23	0.03
British (324)	707	0.92
Bulgarian (0)	10	0.01
Cajun (0)	66	0.09
Canadian (218)	382	0.50
Carpatho Rusyn (13)	13	0.02
Celtic (0)	77	0.10
Croatian (16)	96	0.13
Czech (113)	264	0.34
Czechoslovakian (80)	165	0.22
Danish (38)	233	0.30
Dutch (329)	1,343	1.75
Eastern European (23)	23	0.03
English (3,130)	8,748	11.40
European (984)	1,015	1.32
Finnish (57)	254	0.33
French, ex. Basque (660)	3,448	4.49
French Canadian (482)	713	0.93
German (3,776)	13,015	16.96
Greek (264)	533	0.69
Guyanese (13)	53	0.07
Hungarian (154)	391	0.51
Iranian (20)	20	0.03
Irish (3,084)	11,755	15.32
Israeli (13)	13	0.02
Italian (3,167)	6,678	8.70
Latvian (15)	15	0.02
Lithuanian (49)	170	0.22
Macedonian (59)	59	0.08
Maltese (0)	33	0.04
Northern European (83)	83	0.11
Norwegian (166)	732	0.95
Pennsylvania German (51)	79	0.10
Polish (1,026)	2,939	3.83
Portuguese (245)	442	0.58
Romanian (15)	41	0.05
Russian (94)	461	0.60
Scandinavian (9)	46	0.06
Scotch-Irish (844)	1,880	2.45
Scottish (554)	1,719	2.24
Serbian (39)	103	0.13
Slavic (15)	15	0.02
Slovak (125)	282	0.37
Slovene (14)	37	0.05
Swedish (286)	1,172	1.53
Swiss (41)	180	0.23
Turkish (14)	29	0.04
Ukrainian (66)	195	0.25
Welsh (130)	614	0.80
West Indian, ex. Hispanic (808)	1,115	1.45
Bahamian (51)	51	0.07
Barbadian (18)	18	0.02
British West Indian (21)	59	0.08
Dutch West Indian (6)	6	0.01
Haitian (90)	90	0.12
Jamaican (419)	631	0.82
Trinidadian/Tobagonian (153)	166	0.22
West Indian (31)	75	0.10
Other West Indian (19)	19	0.02
Yugoslavian (32)	60	0.08

Hispanic Origin	Population	%
Hispanic or Latino (of any race)	6,794	8.93
Central American, ex. Mexican	507	0.67
Costa Rican	74	0.10
Guatemalan	119	0.16
Honduran	88	0.12
Nicaraguan	56	0.07
Panamanian	136	0.18
Salvadoran	33	0.04
Other Central American	1	<0.01
Cuban	648	0.85
Dominican Republic	281	0.37
Mexican	1,418	1.86
Puerto Rican	2,604	3.42
South American	729	0.96
Argentinean	56	0.07
Bolivian	12	0.02
Chilean	33	0.04
Colombian	309	0.41
Ecuadorian	100	0.13
Peruvian	104	0.14
Uruguayan	8	0.01
Venezuelan	98	0.13
Other South American	9	0.01
Other Hispanic or Latino	607	0.80

Race*	Population	%
African-American/Black (7,836)	8,872	11.66
Not Hispanic (7,553)	8,395	11.04
Hispanic (283)	477	0.63
American Indian/Alaska Native (245)	831	1.09
Not Hispanic (184)	658	0.87
Hispanic (61)	173	0.23
Alaska Athabascan *(Ala. Nat.)* (6)	6	0.01
Aleut *(Alaska Native)* (1)	2	<0.01
Apache (3)	5	0.01
Blackfeet (4)	46	0.06
Canadian/French Am. Ind. (1)	3	<0.01
Central American Ind. (1)	10	0.01
Cherokee (45)	221	0.29
Cheyenne (0)	1	<0.01
Chickasaw (0)	3	<0.01
Chippewa (7)	13	0.02
Choctaw (5)	20	0.03
Comanche (0)	1	<0.01
Cree (0)	4	0.01
Creek (1)	3	<0.01
Crow (0)	1	<0.01
Delaware (0)	1	<0.01
Hopi (0)	3	<0.01
Houma (1)	1	<0.01
Inupiat *(Alaska Native)* (2)	2	<0.01
Iroquois (11)	20	0.03
Kiowa (1)	1	<0.01
Lumbee (2)	7	0.01
Menominee (1)	1	<0.01
Mexican American Ind. (12)	17	0.02
Ottawa (0)	1	<0.01
Potawatomi (0)	1	<0.01
Pueblo (2)	4	0.01
Puget Sound Salish (3)	3	<0.01
Seminole (1)	5	0.01
Shoshone (1)	1	<0.01
Sioux (6)	22	0.03
South American Ind. (5)	26	0.03
Spanish American Ind. (1)	1	<0.01
Tsimshian *(Alaska Native)* (0)	1	<0.01
Ute (1)	1	<0.01
Asian (2,370)	3,168	4.16
Not Hispanic (2,331)	3,034	3.99
Hispanic (39)	134	0.18
Bangladeshi (9)	10	0.01
Burmese (13)	13	0.02
Cambodian (19)	25	0.03
Chinese, ex. Taiwanese (359)	471	0.62
Filipino (434)	695	0.91
Indian (684)	754	0.99
Indonesian (6)	15	0.02
Japanese (115)	233	0.31
Korean (143)	202	0.27
Laotian (9)	9	0.01
Malaysian (5)	6	0.01
Nepalese (6)	6	0.01
Pakistani (22)	27	0.04
Sri Lankan (7)	7	0.01
Taiwanese (54)	58	0.08
Thai (161)	226	0.30
Vietnamese (240)	269	0.35
Hawaii Native/Pacific Islander (71)	190	0.25
Not Hispanic (53)	143	0.19
Hispanic (18)	47	0.06
Fijian (2)	2	<0.01
Guamanian/Chamorro (22)	34	0.04
Marshallese (0)	4	0.01
Native Hawaiian (27)	66	0.09
Samoan (4)	19	0.02
Tongan (0)	2	<0.01
White (61,562)	63,658	83.69
Not Hispanic (57,149)	58,788	77.28
Hispanic (4,413)	4,870	6.40

Memphis

Place Type: CDP
County: Manatee
Population: 7,848†

Ancestry‡	Population	%
African, Sub-Saharan (207)	274	3.21
African (207)	274	3.21

*Notes: † The Census 2010 population figure is used to calculate the percentages in the Hispanic Origin and Race categories. Ancestry percentages are based on the 2006-2010 American Community Survey population (not shown); ‡ Numbers in parentheses indicate the number of people reporting a single ancestry; * Numbers in parentheses indicate the number of persons reporting this race alone, not in combination with any other race; Please refer to the Explanation of Data for more information.*

American (931)	931	10.90
British (0)	17	0.20
Cajun (0)	13	0.15
Canadian (14)	14	0.16
Czech (0)	19	0.22
Dutch (66)	151	1.77
English (77)	394	4.61
French, ex. Basque (56)	79	0.92
French Canadian (39)	55	0.64
German (225)	736	8.61
Greek (0)	34	0.40
Irish (37)	428	5.01
Italian (185)	455	5.33
Lithuanian (15)	37	0.43
Polish (23)	79	0.92
Scotch-Irish (15)	64	0.75
Scottish (39)	272	3.18
Slovak (18)	18	0.21
Swedish (26)	45	0.53
Swiss (0)	32	0.37
Ukrainian (41)	41	0.48
West Indian, ex. Hispanic (0)	28	0.33
Jamaican (0)	28	0.33

Hispanic Origin	Population	%
Hispanic or Latino (of any race)	2,237	28.50
Central American, ex. Mexican	69	0.88
Guatemalan	20	0.25
Honduran	13	0.17
Nicaraguan	5	0.06
Salvadoran	31	0.40
Cuban	47	0.60
Dominican Republic	20	0.25
Mexican	1,929	24.58
Puerto Rican	88	1.12
South American	29	0.37
Argentinean	2	0.03
Colombian	10	0.13
Paraguayan	3	0.04
Peruvian	4	0.05
Uruguayan	1	0.01
Venezuelan	9	0.11
Other Hispanic or Latino	55	0.70

Race*	Population	%
African-American/Black (2,852)	2,920	37.21
Not Hispanic (2,806)	2,858	36.42
Hispanic (46)	62	0.79
American Indian/Alaska Native (44)	61	0.78
Not Hispanic (13)	30	0.38
Hispanic (31)	31	0.40
Aleut *(Alaska Native)* (1)	1	0.01
Canadian/French Am. Ind. (0)	2	0.03
Cherokee (1)	4	0.05
Chippewa (2)	2	0.03
Creek (3)	3	0.04
Iroquois (0)	1	0.01
Mexican American Ind. (5)	5	0.06
Seminole (0)	1	0.01
South American Ind. (5)	5	0.06
Spanish American Ind. (1)	1	0.01
Yaqui (1)	1	0.01
Asian (25)	33	0.42
Not Hispanic (23)	31	0.40
Hispanic (2)	2	0.03
Cambodian (1)	1	0.01
Chinese, ex. Taiwanese (5)	8	0.10
Filipino (8)	10	0.13
Indian (6)	7	0.09
Japanese (3)	3	0.04
Korean (0)	2	0.03
Vietnamese (1)	1	0.01
Hawaii Native/Pacific Islander (17)	22	0.28
Not Hispanic (7)	11	0.14
Hispanic (10)	11	0.14
Guamanian/Chamorro (15)	15	0.19
Native Hawaiian (0)	1	0.01
White (3,511)	3,611	46.01
Not Hispanic (2,678)	2,734	34.84
Hispanic (833)	877	11.17

Merritt Island

Place Type: CDP
County: Brevard
Population: 34,743†

Ancestry‡	Population	%
African, Sub-Saharan (294)	294	0.86
African (158)	158	0.46
Ethiopian (136)	136	0.40
American (3,122)	3,122	9.13
Arab (61)	111	0.32
Arab (12)	12	0.04
Lebanese (5)	45	0.13
Syrian (44)	54	0.16
Armenian (103)	112	0.33
Austrian (65)	111	0.32
Belgian (49)	138	0.40
Brazilian (5)	5	0.01
British (204)	224	0.65
Canadian (112)	176	0.51
Croatian (12)	27	0.08
Czech (45)	201	0.59
Czechoslovakian (49)	68	0.20
Danish (41)	201	0.59
Dutch (155)	720	2.10
Eastern European (21)	21	0.06
English (1,935)	5,227	15.28
Estonian (7)	7	0.02
European (322)	381	1.11
Finnish (0)	52	0.15
French, ex. Basque (203)	1,342	3.92
French Canadian (103)	253	0.74
German (2,160)	6,468	18.91
Greek (30)	42	0.12
Hungarian (171)	412	1.20
Icelander (0)	11	0.03
Irish (1,797)	5,736	16.77
Italian (1,413)	2,939	8.59
Lithuanian (29)	79	0.23
Northern European (26)	26	0.08
Norwegian (92)	288	0.84
Pennsylvania German (9)	9	0.03
Polish (445)	1,215	3.55
Portuguese (68)	140	0.41
Romanian (9)	9	0.03
Russian (25)	210	0.61
Scotch-Irish (515)	915	2.68
Scottish (464)	1,109	3.24
Serbian (0)	9	0.03
Slovak (10)	10	0.03
Slovene (14)	25	0.07
Swedish (111)	452	1.32
Swiss (11)	76	0.22
Ukrainian (50)	93	0.27
Welsh (23)	212	0.62
West Indian, ex. Hispanic (436)	486	1.42
Barbadian (9)	25	0.07
Belizean (9)	9	0.03
Haitian (387)	387	1.13
Jamaican (23)	33	0.10
Trinidadian/Tobagonian (8)	32	0.09
Yugoslavian (0)	41	0.12

Hispanic Origin	Population	%
Hispanic or Latino (of any race)	2,129	6.13
Central American, ex. Mexican	188	0.54
Costa Rican	29	0.08
Guatemalan	64	0.18
Honduran	24	0.07
Nicaraguan	14	0.04
Panamanian	41	0.12
Salvadoran	16	0.05
Cuban	360	1.04
Dominican Republic	66	0.19
Mexican	427	1.23
Puerto Rican	651	1.87
South American	249	0.72
Argentinean	30	0.09
Bolivian	4	0.01
Chilean	11	0.03
Colombian	94	0.27
Ecuadorian	32	0.09
Peruvian	36	0.10
Uruguayan	11	0.03
Venezuelan	26	0.07
Other South American	5	0.01
Other Hispanic or Latino	188	0.54

Race*	Population	%
African-American/Black (1,696)	2,051	5.90
Not Hispanic (1,625)	1,931	5.56
Hispanic (71)	120	0.35
American Indian/Alaska Native (169)	381	1.10
Not Hispanic (137)	327	0.94
Hispanic (32)	54	0.16
Apache (1)	3	0.01
Blackfeet (0)	6	0.02
Canadian/French Am. Ind. (2)	2	0.01
Central American Ind. (1)	1	<0.01
Cherokee (28)	99	0.28
Cheyenne (1)	1	<0.01
Chickasaw (1)	2	0.01
Chippewa (3)	3	0.01
Choctaw (4)	5	0.01
Comanche (5)	5	0.01
Cree (3)	3	0.01
Creek (4)	5	0.01
Crow (0)	1	<0.01
Delaware (0)	3	0.01
Iroquois (9)	12	0.03
Lumbee (4)	5	0.01
Mexican American Ind. (4)	4	0.01
Navajo (5)	5	0.01
Paiute (2)	2	0.01
Potawatomi (0)	1	<0.01
Pueblo (2)	4	0.01
Seminole (0)	3	0.01
Shoshone (0)	2	0.01
Sioux (3)	13	0.04
South American Ind. (5)	8	0.02
Spanish American Ind. (1)	1	<0.01
Tohono O'Odham (1)	2	0.01
Ute (2)	2	0.01
Asian (781)	1,068	3.07
Not Hispanic (772)	1,033	2.97
Hispanic (9)	35	0.10
Burmese (5)	5	0.01
Cambodian (16)	19	0.05
Chinese, ex. Taiwanese (117)	177	0.51
Filipino (132)	204	0.59
Hmong (1)	1	<0.01
Indian (198)	240	0.69
Indonesian (6)	7	0.02
Japanese (35)	71	0.20
Korean (38)	64	0.18
Laotian (3)	7	0.02
Pakistani (1)	9	0.03
Sri Lankan (1)	3	0.01
Taiwanese (22)	31	0.09
Thai (37)	52	0.15
Vietnamese (126)	170	0.49
Hawaii Native/Pacific Islander (40)	80	0.23
Not Hispanic (37)	68	0.20
Hispanic (3)	12	0.03
Guamanian/Chamorro (6)	8	0.02
Marshallese (16)	19	0.05
Native Hawaiian (3)	21	0.06
Samoan (5)	9	0.03
White (30,832)	31,642	91.07
Not Hispanic (29,241)	29,925	86.13
Hispanic (1,591)	1,717	4.94

Miami Beach

Place Type: City
County: Miami-Dade
Population: 87,779†

*Notes: † The Census 2010 population figure is used to calculate the percentages in the Hispanic Origin and Race categories. Ancestry percentages are based on the 2006-2010 American Community Survey population (not shown); ‡ Numbers in parentheses indicate the number of people reporting a single ancestry; * Numbers in parentheses indicate the number of persons reporting this race alone, not in combination with any other race; Please refer to the Explanation of Data for more information.*

Ancestry‡	Population	%
African, Sub-Saharan (244)	729	0.83
African (160)	635	0.73
South African (84)	94	0.11
Albanian (25)	25	0.03
American (2,466)	2,466	2.82
Arab (756)	1,358	1.55
Arab (231)	522	0.60
Egyptian (102)	102	0.12
Iraqi (56)	56	0.06
Jordanian (0)	18	0.02
Lebanese (119)	295	0.34
Moroccan (131)	189	0.22
Palestinian (60)	78	0.09
Syrian (33)	63	0.07
Other Arab (24)	35	0.04
Armenian (23)	54	0.06
Assyrian/Chaldean/Syriac (9)	9	0.01
Australian (0)	15	0.02
Austrian (174)	452	0.52
Basque (34)	95	0.11
Belgian (0)	48	0.05
Brazilian (606)	886	1.01
British (283)	522	0.60
Bulgarian (123)	123	0.14
Canadian (188)	294	0.34
Carpatho Rusyn (17)	17	0.02
Celtic (49)	49	0.06
Croatian (63)	109	0.12
Czech (82)	208	0.24
Czechoslovakian (88)	256	0.29
Danish (34)	56	0.06
Dutch (216)	464	0.53
Eastern European (525)	525	0.60
English (715)	2,664	3.04
Estonian (11)	11	0.01
European (935)	1,083	1.24
Finnish (33)	33	0.04
French, ex. Basque (568)	3,229	3.69
French Canadian (79)	172	0.20
German (1,432)	5,223	5.96
Greek (180)	381	0.44
Hungarian (672)	1,011	1.15
Iranian (162)	255	0.29
Irish (937)	3,364	3.84
Israeli (476)	565	0.65
Italian (3,444)	7,839	8.95
Latvian (100)	131	0.15
Lithuanian (88)	229	0.26
Macedonian (13)	13	0.01
Maltese (10)	31	0.04
New Zealander (0)	44	0.05
Northern European (26)	26	0.03
Norwegian (125)	412	0.47
Pennsylvania German (16)	28	0.03
Polish (1,394)	2,988	3.41
Portuguese (152)	480	0.55
Romanian (403)	617	0.70
Russian (2,196)	3,331	3.80
Scandinavian (70)	100	0.11
Scotch-Irish (249)	458	0.52
Scottish (212)	539	0.62
Serbian (58)	77	0.09
Slavic (19)	47	0.05
Slovak (122)	254	0.29
Slovene (30)	46	0.05
Swedish (183)	590	0.67
Swiss (201)	271	0.31
Turkish (313)	584	0.67
Ukrainian (265)	386	0.44
Welsh (7)	98	0.11
West Indian, ex. Hispanic (443)	736	0.84
British West Indian (0)	38	0.04
Haitian (190)	279	0.32
Jamaican (164)	244	0.28
Trinidadian/Tobagonian (0)	86	0.10
West Indian (89)	89	0.10
Yugoslavian (237)	254	0.29

Hispanic Origin	Population	%
Hispanic or Latino (of any race)	46,564	53.05
Central American, ex. Mexican	4,661	5.31
Costa Rican	298	0.34
Guatemalan	1,432	1.63
Honduran	1,483	1.69
Nicaraguan	912	1.04
Panamanian	240	0.27
Salvadoran	274	0.31
Other Central American	22	0.03
Cuban	17,599	20.05
Dominican Republic	1,212	1.38
Mexican	1,548	1.76
Puerto Rican	3,242	3.69
South American	15,106	17.21
Argentinean	4,030	4.59
Bolivian	211	0.24
Chilean	739	0.84
Colombian	4,327	4.93
Ecuadorian	830	0.95
Paraguayan	87	0.10
Peruvian	2,091	2.38
Uruguayan	958	1.09
Venezuelan	1,802	2.05
Other South American	31	0.04
Other Hispanic or Latino	3,196	3.64

Race*	Population	%
African-American/Black (3,825)	4,553	5.19
Not Hispanic (2,710)	3,105	3.54
Hispanic (1,115)	1,448	1.65
American Indian/Alaska Native (256)	565	0.64
Not Hispanic (95)	273	0.31
Hispanic (161)	292	0.33
Aleut *(Alaska Native)* (0)	1	<0.01
Apache (2)	4	<0.01
Blackfeet (1)	12	0.01
Canadian/French Am. Ind. (1)	1	<0.01
Central American Ind. (23)	35	0.04
Cherokee (12)	64	0.07
Chippewa (0)	5	0.01
Choctaw (3)	6	0.01
Creek (0)	1	<0.01
Delaware (0)	4	<0.01
Hopi (1)	1	<0.01
Houma (1)	1	<0.01
Inupiat *(Alaska Native)* (0)	1	<0.01
Iroquois (3)	7	0.01
Mexican American Ind. (30)	42	0.05
Pueblo (1)	5	0.01
Seminole (5)	6	0.01
Sioux (8)	11	0.01
South American Ind. (37)	62	0.07
Spanish American Ind. (15)	22	0.03
Yaqui (0)	1	<0.01
Asian (1,635)	2,169	2.47
Not Hispanic (1,564)	1,953	2.22
Hispanic (71)	216	0.25
Bangladeshi (62)	78	0.09
Cambodian (1)	5	0.01
Chinese, ex. Taiwanese (225)	364	0.41
Filipino (384)	456	0.52
Indian (510)	641	0.73
Indonesian (41)	49	0.06
Japanese (108)	164	0.19
Korean (90)	122	0.14
Laotian (7)	8	0.01
Malaysian (2)	2	<0.01
Nepalese (3)	3	<0.01
Pakistani (21)	25	0.03
Sri Lankan (4)	4	<0.01
Taiwanese (6)	9	0.01
Thai (49)	64	0.07
Vietnamese (52)	68	0.08
Hawaii Native/Pacific Islander (45)	129	0.15
Not Hispanic (28)	81	0.09
Hispanic (17)	48	0.05
Fijian (0)	1	<0.01
Guamanian/Chamorro (7)	8	0.01
Native Hawaiian (20)	40	0.05
Samoan (3)	6	0.01
Tongan (0)	3	<0.01
White (76,677)	78,687	89.64
Not Hispanic (35,530)	36,316	41.37
Hispanic (41,147)	42,371	48.27

Miami Gardens

Place Type: City
County: Miami-Dade
Population: 107,167†

Ancestry‡	Population	%
African, Sub-Saharan (1,320)	1,535	1.45
African (977)	1,192	1.13
Ethiopian (15)	15	0.01
Nigerian (207)	207	0.20
Other Sub-Saharan African (121)	121	0.11
American (7,958)	7,958	7.53
Arab (126)	139	0.13
Egyptian (16)	16	0.02
Lebanese (0)	13	0.01
Moroccan (17)	17	0.02
Palestinian (93)	93	0.09
Brazilian (165)	165	0.16
British (159)	159	0.15
Canadian (92)	98	0.09
Croatian (0)	30	0.03
Czech (119)	141	0.13
Danish (0)	8	0.01
Dutch (18)	32	0.03
Eastern European (15)	15	0.01
English (206)	394	0.37
European (2)	2	<0.01
French, ex. Basque (67)	209	0.20
French Canadian (28)	54	0.05
German (118)	458	0.43
Greek (14)	23	0.02
Guyanese (260)	322	0.30
Hungarian (12)	72	0.07
Irish (160)	493	0.47
Israeli (13)	13	0.01
Italian (431)	657	0.62
Lithuanian (12)	12	0.01
Pennsylvania German (0)	65	0.06
Polish (87)	122	0.12
Portuguese (0)	18	0.02
Romanian (26)	54	0.05
Russian (0)	29	0.03
Scotch-Irish (26)	98	0.09
Scottish (102)	137	0.13
Slovak (11)	11	0.01
Swiss (0)	12	0.01
Ukrainian (6)	15	0.01
Welsh (29)	29	0.03
West Indian, ex. Hispanic (20,648)	22,012	20.84
Bahamian (1,510)	1,706	1.61
Barbadian (20)	55	0.05
Belizean (40)	112	0.11
British West Indian (411)	438	0.41
Haitian (8,838)	9,122	8.63
Jamaican (8,998)	9,447	8.94
Trinidadian/Tobagonian (247)	247	0.23
U.S. Virgin Islander (137)	252	0.24
West Indian (447)	633	0.60
Yugoslavian (0)	18	0.02

Hispanic Origin	Population	%
Hispanic or Latino (of any race)	23,606	22.03
Central American, ex. Mexican	4,338	4.05
Costa Rican	140	0.13
Guatemalan	315	0.29
Honduran	1,068	1.00
Nicaraguan	2,134	1.99
Panamanian	361	0.34
Salvadoran	292	0.27
Other Central American	28	0.03
Cuban	9,587	8.95
Dominican Republic	2,521	2.35
Mexican	474	0.44

*Notes: † The Census 2010 population figure is used to calculate the percentages in the Hispanic Origin and Race categories. Ancestry percentages are based on the 2006-2010 American Community Survey population (not shown); ‡ Numbers in parentheses indicate the number of people reporting a single ancestry; * Numbers in parentheses indicate the number of persons reporting this race alone, not in combination with any other race; Please refer to the Explanation of Data for more information.*

Puerto Rican	2,745	2.56
South American	2,291	2.14
Argentinean	136	0.13
Bolivian	18	0.02
Chilean	74	0.07
Colombian	1,127	1.05
Ecuadorian	300	0.28
Paraguayan	7	0.01
Peruvian	371	0.35
Uruguayan	11	0.01
Venezuelan	240	0.22
Other South American	7	0.01
Other Hispanic or Latino	1,650	1.54

Race*	Population	%
African-American/Black (81,776)	83,474	77.89
Not Hispanic (78,629)	79,681	74.35
Hispanic (3,147)	3,793	3.54
American Indian/Alaska Native (264)	581	0.54
Not Hispanic (154)	370	0.35
Hispanic (110)	211	0.20
Apache (1)	1	<0.01
Blackfeet (1)	9	0.01
Canadian/French Am. Ind. (0)	1	<0.01
Central American Ind. (2)	20	0.02
Cherokee (14)	67	0.06
Chippewa (1)	2	<0.01
Choctaw (0)	1	<0.01
Cree (0)	1	<0.01
Creek (0)	2	<0.01
Iroquois (1)	2	<0.01
Mexican American Ind. (15)	17	0.02
Osage (1)	2	<0.01
Potawatomi (3)	4	<0.01
Pueblo (1)	2	<0.01
Seminole (8)	12	0.01
Sioux (6)	6	0.01
South American Ind. (13)	29	0.03
Spanish American Ind. (8)	10	0.01
Tlingit-Haida *(Alaska Native)* (1)	6	0.01
Asian (643)	964	0.90
Not Hispanic (611)	870	0.81
Hispanic (32)	94	0.09
Bangladeshi (3)	4	<0.01
Burmese (25)	25	0.02
Chinese, ex. Taiwanese (100)	199	0.19
Filipino (82)	98	0.09
Indian (188)	285	0.27
Japanese (7)	21	0.02
Korean (12)	18	0.02
Laotian (2)	2	<0.01
Pakistani (33)	43	0.04
Thai (2)	3	<0.01
Vietnamese (160)	163	0.15
Hawaii Native/Pacific Islander (30)	376	0.35
Not Hispanic (27)	321	0.30
Hispanic (3)	55	0.05
Guamanian/Chamorro (5)	10	0.01
Native Hawaiian (2)	8	0.01
Samoan (0)	3	<0.01
White (19,625)	20,866	19.47
Not Hispanic (2,806)	3,162	2.95
Hispanic (16,819)	17,704	16.52

Miami Lakes

Place Type: Town
County: Miami-Dade
Population: 29,361†

Ancestry‡	Population	%
African, Sub-Saharan (140)	184	0.66
African (30)	30	0.11
Cape Verdean (11)	11	0.04
Nigerian (99)	143	0.51
American (540)	540	1.92
Arab (36)	87	0.31
Lebanese (36)	87	0.31
Armenian (13)	13	0.05
Austrian (26)	48	0.17
Brazilian (105)	157	0.56
British (14)	14	0.05
Czech (0)	19	0.07
Czechoslovakian (0)	52	0.19
Danish (0)	94	0.33
Dutch (5)	34	0.12
English (242)	662	2.36
European (66)	88	0.31
French, ex. Basque (80)	122	0.43
German (228)	835	2.97
Greek (37)	60	0.21
Hungarian (22)	22	0.08
Iranian (95)	95	0.34
Irish (294)	509	1.81
Italian (323)	795	2.83
Norwegian (0)	6	0.02
Polish (157)	336	1.20
Portuguese (35)	83	0.30
Russian (39)	134	0.48
Scotch-Irish (31)	64	0.23
Scottish (27)	79	0.28
Swedish (20)	53	0.19
Swiss (0)	8	0.03
Turkish (10)	37	0.13
Ukrainian (0)	12	0.04
West Indian, ex. Hispanic (149)	159	0.57
Barbadian (0)	10	0.04
Belizean (13)	13	0.05
Haitian (136)	136	0.48
Yugoslavian (0)	11	0.04

Hispanic Origin	Population	%
Hispanic or Latino (of any race)	23,826	81.15
Central American, ex. Mexican	1,165	3.97
Costa Rican	96	0.33
Guatemalan	81	0.28
Honduran	230	0.78
Nicaraguan	574	1.95
Panamanian	115	0.39
Salvadoran	67	0.23
Other Central American	2	0.01
Cuban	16,752	57.06
Dominican Republic	691	2.35
Mexican	232	0.79
Puerto Rican	1,176	4.01
South American	2,968	10.11
Argentinean	220	0.75
Bolivian	33	0.11
Chilean	120	0.41
Colombian	1,548	5.27
Ecuadorian	280	0.95
Paraguayan	8	0.03
Peruvian	371	1.26
Uruguayan	50	0.17
Venezuelan	337	1.15
Other South American	1	<0.01
Other Hispanic or Latino	842	2.87

Race*	Population	%
African-American/Black (963)	1,073	3.65
Not Hispanic (718)	763	2.60
Hispanic (245)	310	1.06
American Indian/Alaska Native (25)	76	0.26
Not Hispanic (4)	24	0.08
Hispanic (21)	52	0.18
Central American Ind. (4)	4	0.01
Cherokee (0)	8	0.03
Cree (0)	4	0.01
Creek (0)	1	<0.01
Mexican American Ind. (1)	3	0.01
South American Ind. (1)	11	0.04
Spanish American Ind. (0)	1	<0.01
Asian (429)	545	1.86
Not Hispanic (407)	482	1.64
Hispanic (22)	63	0.21
Bangladeshi (5)	5	0.02
Chinese, ex. Taiwanese (137)	179	0.61
Filipino (64)	78	0.27
Indian (81)	95	0.32
Indonesian (2)	3	0.01
Japanese (12)	15	0.05
Korean (28)	44	0.15
Laotian (1)	3	0.01
Nepalese (1)	1	<0.01
Pakistani (33)	40	0.14
Sri Lankan (4)	4	0.01
Taiwanese (16)	18	0.06
Thai (3)	3	0.01
Vietnamese (25)	28	0.10
Hawaii Native/Pacific Islander (2)	21	0.07
Not Hispanic (2)	10	0.03
Hispanic (0)	11	0.04
Native Hawaiian (2)	5	0.02
White (26,938)	27,361	93.19
Not Hispanic (4,227)	4,352	14.82
Hispanic (22,711)	23,009	78.37

Miami Shores

Place Type: Village
County: Miami-Dade
Population: 10,493†

Ancestry‡	Population	%
African, Sub-Saharan (19)	35	0.33
African (19)	35	0.33
American (775)	775	7.37
Arab (103)	144	1.37
Egyptian (0)	17	0.16
Lebanese (35)	35	0.33
Moroccan (11)	11	0.10
Syrian (29)	29	0.28
Other Arab (28)	52	0.49
Armenian (11)	11	0.10
Austrian (12)	79	0.75
Belgian (9)	9	0.09
Brazilian (0)	53	0.50
Canadian (0)	18	0.17
Croatian (26)	32	0.30
Czech (13)	27	0.26
Czechoslovakian (11)	11	0.10
Danish (0)	11	0.10
Dutch (26)	63	0.60
Eastern European (29)	29	0.28
English (209)	794	7.55
European (119)	141	1.34
Finnish (0)	16	0.15
French, ex. Basque (93)	236	2.24
German (341)	864	8.22
Greek (10)	100	0.95
Hungarian (34)	60	0.57
Irish (406)	1,146	10.90
Italian (353)	956	9.09
Lithuanian (25)	25	0.24
New Zealander (0)	18	0.17
Norwegian (72)	114	1.08
Polish (92)	360	3.42
Portuguese (11)	11	0.10
Romanian (0)	47	0.45
Russian (72)	207	1.97
Scotch-Irish (13)	131	1.25
Scottish (46)	298	2.83
Slovak (25)	83	0.79
Swedish (10)	35	0.33
Swiss (25)	25	0.24
Ukrainian (8)	8	0.08
Welsh (0)	33	0.31
West Indian, ex. Hispanic (1,161)	1,286	12.23
Bahamian (37)	64	0.61
Barbadian (8)	8	0.08
British West Indian (86)	86	0.82
Haitian (711)	751	7.14
Jamaican (177)	235	2.24
Trinidadian/Tobagonian (15)	15	0.14
U.S. Virgin Islander (34)	34	0.32
West Indian (86)	86	0.82
Other West Indian (7)	7	0.07
Yugoslavian (0)	8	0.08

*Notes: † The Census 2010 population figure is used to calculate the percentages in the Hispanic Origin and Race categories. Ancestry percentages are based on the 2006-2010 American Community Survey population (not shown); ‡ Numbers in parentheses indicate the number of people reporting a single ancestry; * Numbers in parentheses indicate the number of persons reporting this race alone, not in combination with any other race; Please refer to the Explanation of Data for more information.*

Hispanic Origin	Population	%
Hispanic or Latino (of any race)	3,215	30.64
Central American, ex. Mexican	344	3.28
Costa Rican	17	0.16
Guatemalan	57	0.54
Honduran	69	0.66
Nicaraguan	161	1.53
Panamanian	22	0.21
Salvadoran	14	0.13
Other Central American	4	0.04
Cuban	1,074	10.24
Dominican Republic	150	1.43
Mexican	95	0.91
Puerto Rican	369	3.52
South American	835	7.96
Argentinean	172	1.64
Bolivian	13	0.12
Chilean	32	0.30
Colombian	270	2.57
Ecuadorian	43	0.41
Paraguayan	1	0.01
Peruvian	161	1.53
Uruguayan	14	0.13
Venezuelan	128	1.22
Other South American	1	0.01
Other Hispanic or Latino	348	3.32

Race*	Population	%
African-American/Black (2,499)	2,665	25.40
Not Hispanic (2,352)	2,473	23.57
Hispanic (147)	192	1.83
American Indian/Alaska Native (32)	63	0.60
Not Hispanic (22)	45	0.43
Hispanic (10)	18	0.17
Apache (0)	1	0.01
Central American Ind. (1)	1	0.01
Cherokee (2)	6	0.06
Chippewa (0)	1	0.01
Choctaw (1)	1	0.01
Mexican American Ind. (0)	1	0.01
South American Ind. (2)	3	0.03
Spanish American Ind. (0)	1	0.01
Tlingit-Haida *(Alaska Native)* (7)	9	0.09
Asian (270)	365	3.48
Not Hispanic (262)	335	3.19
Hispanic (8)	30	0.29
Bangladeshi (4)	8	0.08
Cambodian (4)	4	0.04
Chinese, ex. Taiwanese (31)	59	0.56
Filipino (126)	153	1.46
Indian (35)	55	0.52
Indonesian (1)	4	0.04
Japanese (13)	21	0.20
Korean (9)	13	0.12
Pakistani (9)	12	0.11
Sri Lankan (0)	3	0.03
Taiwanese (2)	2	0.02
Thai (4)	7	0.07
Vietnamese (7)	8	0.08
Hawaii Native/Pacific Islander (9)	32	0.30
Not Hispanic (9)	29	0.28
Hispanic (0)	3	0.03
Native Hawaiian (1)	1	0.01
Samoan (0)	1	0.01
Tongan (1)	3	0.03
White (7,147)	7,350	70.05
Not Hispanic (4,420)	4,551	43.37
Hispanic (2,727)	2,799	26.67

Miami Springs

Place Type: City
County: Miami-Dade
Population: 13,809†

Ancestry‡	Population	%
American (1,000)	1,000	7.27
Armenian (0)	9	0.07
British (24)	98	0.71
Canadian (13)	25	0.18
Czech (41)	59	0.43
Czechoslovakian (13)	13	0.09
Dutch (10)	138	1.00
English (213)	559	4.07
European (0)	50	0.36
French, ex. Basque (83)	210	1.53
French Canadian (9)	9	0.07
German (211)	703	5.11
Greek (58)	89	0.65
Guyanese (0)	74	0.54
Hungarian (11)	23	0.17
Irish (231)	650	4.73
Israeli (6)	6	0.04
Italian (230)	366	2.66
Lithuanian (12)	38	0.28
Luxemburger (0)	12	0.09
Polish (37)	122	0.89
Russian (28)	55	0.40
Scandinavian (8)	33	0.24
Scotch-Irish (22)	127	0.92
Scottish (23)	71	0.52
Slovak (13)	51	0.37
Swedish (0)	25	0.18
Swiss (19)	19	0.14
Ukrainian (10)	10	0.07
Welsh (0)	8	0.06
West Indian, ex. Hispanic (37)	105	0.76
Belizean (9)	33	0.24
Dutch West Indian (10)	32	0.23
Jamaican (18)	40	0.29
Yugoslavian (14)	52	0.38

Hispanic Origin	Population	%
Hispanic or Latino (of any race)	9,826	71.16
Central American, ex. Mexican	838	6.07
Costa Rican	91	0.66
Guatemalan	79	0.57
Honduran	183	1.33
Nicaraguan	395	2.86
Panamanian	41	0.30
Salvadoran	43	0.31
Other Central American	6	0.04
Cuban	6,185	44.79
Dominican Republic	258	1.87
Mexican	136	0.98
Puerto Rican	453	3.28
South American	1,565	11.33
Argentinean	138	1.00
Bolivian	41	0.30
Chilean	72	0.52
Colombian	568	4.11
Ecuadorian	149	1.08
Paraguayan	1	0.01
Peruvian	344	2.49
Uruguayan	15	0.11
Venezuelan	230	1.67
Other South American	7	0.05
Other Hispanic or Latino	391	2.83

Race*	Population	%
African-American/Black (220)	266	1.93
Not Hispanic (114)	130	0.94
Hispanic (106)	136	0.98
American Indian/Alaska Native (27)	54	0.39
Not Hispanic (10)	23	0.17
Hispanic (17)	31	0.22
Central American Ind. (1)	2	0.01
Cherokee (1)	4	0.03
Chickasaw (1)	1	0.01
Chippewa (3)	3	0.02
Iroquois (0)	2	0.01
Lumbee (1)	1	0.01
Mexican American Ind. (2)	3	0.02
Navajo (1)	1	0.01
South American Ind. (4)	9	0.07
Spanish American Ind. (1)	2	0.01
Asian (170)	230	1.67
Not Hispanic (159)	185	1.34
Hispanic (11)	45	0.33
Chinese, ex. Taiwanese (31)	55	0.40
Filipino (16)	23	0.17
Indian (69)	75	0.54
Indonesian (2)	2	0.01
Japanese (3)	10	0.07
Korean (5)	9	0.07
Nepalese (1)	1	0.01
Pakistani (24)	32	0.23
Taiwanese (2)	2	0.01
Thai (6)	6	0.04
Vietnamese (5)	5	0.04
Hawaii Native/Pacific Islander (0)	8	0.06
Not Hispanic (0)	4	0.03
Hispanic (0)	4	0.03
Native Hawaiian (0)	3	0.02
White (12,895)	13,098	94.85
Not Hispanic (3,630)	3,677	26.63
Hispanic (9,265)	9,421	68.22

Miami

Place Type: City
County: Miami-Dade
Population: 399,457†

Ancestry‡	Population	%
African, Sub-Saharan (1,285)	1,522	0.39
African (932)	1,113	0.28
Cape Verdean (16)	16	<0.01
Ethiopian (174)	174	0.04
Nigerian (144)	200	0.05
Other Sub-Saharan African (19)	19	<0.01
Alsatian (0)	9	<0.01
American (7,482)	7,482	1.91
Arab (1,310)	1,934	0.49
Arab (184)	276	0.07
Egyptian (158)	178	0.05
Iraqi (0)	15	<0.01
Jordanian (122)	122	0.03
Lebanese (453)	856	0.22
Moroccan (127)	153	0.04
Palestinian (83)	95	0.02
Syrian (105)	105	0.03
Other Arab (78)	134	0.03
Armenian (23)	53	0.01
Assyrian/Chaldean/Syriac (10)	10	<0.01
Australian (10)	10	<0.01
Austrian (180)	404	0.10
Basque (34)	51	0.01
Belgian (17)	58	0.01
Brazilian (1,889)	2,185	0.56
British (1,055)	1,572	0.40
Bulgarian (36)	36	0.01
Canadian (96)	210	0.05
Celtic (0)	57	0.01
Croatian (24)	54	0.01
Czech (185)	345	0.09
Czechoslovakian (24)	161	0.04
Danish (68)	285	0.07
Dutch (271)	887	0.23
Eastern European (308)	308	0.08
English (1,243)	3,892	0.99
European (628)	835	0.21
Finnish (21)	100	0.03
French, ex. Basque (773)	3,160	0.81
French Canadian (171)	267	0.07
German (1,750)	6,635	1.69
Greek (275)	546	0.14
Guyanese (32)	42	0.01
Hungarian (178)	386	0.10
Icelander (60)	60	0.02
Iranian (188)	264	0.07
Irish (1,603)	5,392	1.38
Israeli (119)	165	0.04
Italian (2,857)	6,144	1.57
Latvian (29)	89	0.02
Lithuanian (91)	188	0.05
Luxemburger (5)	5	<0.01
Macedonian (50)	82	0.02
Maltese (146)	146	0.04
New Zealander (0)	10	<0.01

*Notes: † The Census 2010 population figure is used to calculate the percentages in the Hispanic Origin and Race categories. Ancestry percentages are based on the 2006-2010 American Community Survey population (not shown); ‡ Numbers in parentheses indicate the number of people reporting a single ancestry; * Numbers in parentheses indicate the number of persons reporting this race alone, not in combination with any other race; Please refer to the Explanation of Data for more information.*

Northern European (39)	39	0.01
Norwegian (52)	205	0.05
Pennsylvania German (22)	30	0.01
Polish (676)	1,980	0.51
Portuguese (362)	701	0.18
Romanian (216)	423	0.11
Russian (1,027)	2,188	0.56
Scandinavian (15)	48	0.01
Scotch-Irish (257)	696	0.18
Scottish (199)	732	0.19
Serbian (35)	35	0.01
Slavic (30)	44	0.01
Slovak (58)	125	0.03
Slovene (50)	50	0.01
Swedish (260)	916	0.23
Swiss (47)	216	0.06
Turkish (95)	152	0.04
Ukrainian (35)	151	0.04
Welsh (105)	315	0.08
West Indian, ex. Hispanic (20,403)	22,133	5.65
Bahamian (1,140)	1,673	0.43
Belizean (22)	22	0.01
Bermudan (52)	52	0.01
British West Indian (318)	338	0.09
Dutch West Indian (55)	55	0.01
Haitian (17,045)	17,451	4.46
Jamaican (1,239)	1,770	0.45
Trinidadian/Tobagonian (240)	352	0.09
U.S. Virgin Islander (26)	40	0.01
West Indian (266)	372	0.10
Other West Indian (0)	8	<0.01
Yugoslavian (73)	157	0.04

Hispanic Origin	Population	%
Hispanic or Latino (of any race)	279,456	69.96
Central American, ex. Mexican	62,995	15.77
Costa Rican	1,197	0.30
Guatemalan	4,135	1.04
Honduran	23,209	5.81
Nicaraguan	28,618	7.16
Panamanian	1,113	0.28
Salvadoran	4,610	1.15
Other Central American	113	0.03
Cuban	137,301	34.37
Dominican Republic	9,668	2.42
Mexican	5,830	1.46
Puerto Rican	12,789	3.20
South American	34,718	8.69
Argentinean	4,891	1.22
Bolivian	709	0.18
Chilean	1,427	0.36
Colombian	12,966	3.25
Ecuadorian	2,777	0.70
Paraguayan	131	0.03
Peruvian	4,946	1.24
Uruguayan	1,040	0.26
Venezuelan	5,770	1.44
Other South American	61	0.02
Other Hispanic or Latino	16,155	4.04

Race*	Population	%
African-American/Black (76,880)	80,625	20.18
Not Hispanic (64,993)	66,636	16.68
Hispanic (11,887)	13,989	3.50
American Indian/Alaska Native (1,195)	2,240	0.56
Not Hispanic (361)	810	0.20
Hispanic (834)	1,430	0.36
Alaska Athabascan *(Ala. Nat.)* (1)	2	<0.01
Aleut *(Alaska Native)* (0)	1	<0.01
Apache (3)	11	<0.01
Blackfeet (7)	22	0.01
Canadian/French Am. Ind. (2)	2	<0.01
Central American Ind. (127)	222	0.06
Cherokee (53)	152	0.04
Cheyenne (0)	1	<0.01
Chippewa (2)	5	<0.01
Choctaw (2)	5	<0.01
Cree (2)	2	<0.01
Creek (3)	6	<0.01
Crow (0)	1	<0.01
Iroquois (11)	15	<0.01
Lumbee (5)	6	<0.01
Mexican American Ind. (76)	125	0.03
Navajo (1)	10	<0.01
Paiute (0)	2	<0.01
Pueblo (1)	5	<0.01
Seminole (1)	6	<0.01
Sioux (5)	8	<0.01
South American Ind. (86)	147	0.04
Spanish American Ind. (48)	105	0.03
Tlingit-Haida *(Alaska Native)* (2)	8	<0.01
Ute (0)	2	<0.01
Yaqui (0)	1	<0.01
Asian (3,953)	5,395	1.35
Not Hispanic (3,649)	4,641	1.16
Hispanic (304)	754	0.19
Bangladeshi (20)	25	0.01
Burmese (20)	20	0.01
Cambodian (7)	15	<0.01
Chinese, ex. Taiwanese (1,031)	1,389	0.35
Filipino (647)	787	0.20
Indian (1,206)	1,523	0.38
Indonesian (55)	69	0.02
Japanese (245)	373	0.09
Korean (213)	287	0.07
Laotian (7)	15	<0.01
Malaysian (3)	11	<0.01
Nepalese (3)	4	<0.01
Pakistani (80)	111	0.03
Sri Lankan (26)	34	0.01
Taiwanese (49)	57	0.01
Thai (55)	81	0.02
Vietnamese (125)	173	0.04
Hawaii Native/Pacific Islander (85)	705	0.18
Not Hispanic (58)	460	0.12
Hispanic (27)	245	0.06
Fijian (1)	1	<0.01
Guamanian/Chamorro (13)	37	0.01
Native Hawaiian (23)	80	0.02
Samoan (8)	24	0.01
White (289,920)	298,092	74.62
Not Hispanic (47,622)	49,161	12.31
Hispanic (242,298)	248,931	62.32

Micco

Place Type: CDP
County: Brevard
Population: 9,052†

Ancestry‡	Population	%
American (828)	828	8.90
Arab (0)	15	0.16
Lebanese (0)	15	0.16
Armenian (0)	15	0.16
Austrian (44)	44	0.47
British (30)	30	0.32
Canadian (59)	94	1.01
Croatian (34)	66	0.71
Czech (0)	177	1.90
Czechoslovakian (25)	36	0.39
Danish (12)	20	0.22
Dutch (62)	308	3.31
English (495)	1,631	17.54
European (102)	118	1.27
French, ex. Basque (215)	761	8.18
French Canadian (113)	123	1.32
German (811)	2,265	24.35
Greek (77)	91	0.98
Hungarian (42)	101	1.09
Irish (795)	2,370	25.48
Italian (531)	785	8.44
Lithuanian (15)	37	0.40
Norwegian (66)	78	0.84
Pennsylvania German (14)	24	0.26
Polish (198)	348	3.74
Portuguese (41)	88	0.95
Russian (12)	33	0.35
Scandinavian (0)	18	0.19
Scotch-Irish (149)	221	2.38
Scottish (67)	376	4.04
Slovak (0)	13	0.14
Swedish (10)	61	0.66
Swiss (0)	43	0.46
Ukrainian (30)	30	0.32
Welsh (26)	94	1.01

Hispanic Origin	Population	%
Hispanic or Latino (of any race)	158	1.75
Central American, ex. Mexican	10	0.11
Costa Rican	1	0.01
Honduran	1	0.01
Nicaraguan	2	0.02
Panamanian	3	0.03
Salvadoran	3	0.03
Cuban	13	0.14
Dominican Republic	2	0.02
Mexican	31	0.34
Puerto Rican	71	0.78
South American	13	0.14
Argentinean	1	0.01
Bolivian	1	0.01
Colombian	8	0.09
Ecuadorian	1	0.01
Peruvian	1	0.01
Venezuelan	1	0.01
Other Hispanic or Latino	18	0.20

Race*	Population	%
African-American/Black (39)	69	0.76
Not Hispanic (36)	60	0.66
Hispanic (3)	9	0.10
American Indian/Alaska Native (31)	68	0.75
Not Hispanic (29)	65	0.72
Hispanic (2)	3	0.03
Blackfeet (1)	2	0.02
Central American Ind. (1)	1	0.01
Cherokee (6)	24	0.27
Cheyenne (1)	1	0.01
Chippewa (4)	5	0.06
Creek (0)	3	0.03
Iroquois (2)	6	0.07
Navajo (1)	1	0.01
Ottawa (0)	1	0.01
Seminole (0)	1	0.01
Sioux (0)	2	0.02
Asian (24)	44	0.49
Not Hispanic (21)	38	0.42
Hispanic (3)	6	0.07
Chinese, ex. Taiwanese (1)	7	0.08
Filipino (13)	17	0.19
Indian (1)	5	0.06
Japanese (0)	3	0.03
Korean (5)	7	0.08
Vietnamese (1)	1	0.01
Hawaii Native/Pacific Islander (0)	8	0.09
Not Hispanic (0)	8	0.09
Native Hawaiian (0)	5	0.06
White (8,825)	8,913	98.46
Not Hispanic (8,728)	8,798	97.19
Hispanic (97)	115	1.27

Middleburg

Place Type: CDP
County: Clay
Population: 13,008†

Ancestry‡	Population	%
African, Sub-Saharan (31)	31	0.24
African (31)	31	0.24
American (1,911)	1,911	14.83
Arab (7)	7	0.05
Other Arab (7)	7	0.05
Austrian (13)	34	0.26
Belgian (0)	13	0.10
British (45)	65	0.50
Canadian (69)	90	0.70
Croatian (19)	19	0.15
Czech (83)	111	0.86

*Notes: † The Census 2010 population figure is used to calculate the percentages in the Hispanic Origin and Race categories. Ancestry percentages are based on the 2006-2010 American Community Survey population (not shown); ‡ Numbers in parentheses indicate the number of people reporting a single ancestry; * Numbers in parentheses indicate the number of persons reporting this race alone, not in combination with any other race; Please refer to the Explanation of Data for more information.*

Czechoslovakian (38)	57	0.44
Danish (41)	127	0.99
Dutch (13)	76	0.59
English (478)	1,100	8.54
French, ex. Basque (109)	784	6.08
French Canadian (70)	106	0.82
German (658)	2,478	19.23
Greek (0)	7	0.05
Hungarian (0)	42	0.33
Irish (531)	1,855	14.39
Italian (183)	1,158	8.99
Lithuanian (24)	74	0.57
Northern European (54)	54	0.42
Norwegian (18)	49	0.38
Polish (48)	230	1.78
Portuguese (0)	10	0.08
Romanian (8)	8	0.06
Russian (27)	63	0.49
Scotch-Irish (395)	512	3.97
Scottish (80)	203	1.58
Swedish (11)	158	1.23
Swiss (0)	32	0.25
Turkish (0)	16	0.12
Ukrainian (0)	19	0.15
Welsh (15)	29	0.23

Hispanic Origin	Population	%
Hispanic or Latino (of any race)	537	4.13
Central American, ex. Mexican	41	0.32
Costa Rican	3	0.02
Guatemalan	12	0.09
Honduran	1	0.01
Nicaraguan	12	0.09
Panamanian	3	0.02
Salvadoran	9	0.07
Other Central American	1	0.01
Cuban	55	0.42
Dominican Republic	14	0.11
Mexican	149	1.15
Puerto Rican	189	1.45
South American	29	0.22
Argentinean	3	0.02
Chilean	7	0.05
Colombian	8	0.06
Ecuadorian	5	0.04
Peruvian	6	0.05
Other Hispanic or Latino	60	0.46

Race*	Population	%
African-American/Black (398)	448	3.44
Not Hispanic (370)	414	3.18
Hispanic (28)	34	0.26
American Indian/Alaska Native (76)	185	1.42
Not Hispanic (70)	165	1.27
Hispanic (6)	20	0.15
Blackfeet (1)	3	0.02
Canadian/French Am. Ind. (9)	9	0.07
Cherokee (19)	48	0.37
Chippewa (2)	6	0.05
Choctaw (2)	3	0.02
Creek (3)	8	0.06
Iroquois (3)	3	0.02
Menominee (0)	1	0.01
Mexican American Ind. (0)	3	0.02
Navajo (1)	3	0.02
Seminole (3)	4	0.03
Sioux (3)	3	0.02
South American Ind. (2)	2	0.02
Yuman (1)	1	0.01
Asian (88)	135	1.04
Not Hispanic (84)	128	0.98
Hispanic (4)	7	0.05
Cambodian (3)	9	0.07
Chinese, ex. Taiwanese (5)	5	0.04
Filipino (43)	71	0.55
Indian (15)	18	0.14
Japanese (11)	12	0.09
Korean (3)	5	0.04
Thai (2)	3	0.02
Vietnamese (4)	7	0.05
Hawaii Native/Pacific Islander (5)	29	0.22
Not Hispanic (5)	26	0.20
Hispanic (0)	3	0.02
Guamanian/Chamorro (3)	7	0.05
Native Hawaiian (1)	13	0.10
Samoan (0)	2	0.02
White (12,090)	12,310	94.63
Not Hispanic (11,736)	11,926	91.68
Hispanic (354)	384	2.95

Midway

Place Type: CDP
County: Santa Rosa
Population: 16,115†

Ancestry‡	Population	%
African, Sub-Saharan (8)	8	0.05
South African (8)	8	0.05
American (1,847)	1,847	11.85
Austrian (0)	45	0.29
Belgian (20)	20	0.13
Brazilian (51)	51	0.33
British (55)	80	0.51
Cajun (51)	51	0.33
Canadian (24)	46	0.30
Croatian (14)	33	0.21
Czech (0)	39	0.25
Czechoslovakian (40)	40	0.26
Danish (13)	59	0.38
Dutch (105)	432	2.77
Eastern European (22)	22	0.14
English (816)	2,116	13.58
European (286)	352	2.26
Finnish (38)	38	0.24
French, ex. Basque (193)	905	5.81
French Canadian (29)	29	0.19
German (849)	2,696	17.30
Greek (39)	50	0.32
Hungarian (11)	86	0.55
Irish (909)	2,782	17.85
Italian (318)	1,016	6.52
Lithuanian (26)	40	0.26
Northern European (10)	10	0.06
Norwegian (37)	99	0.64
Polish (152)	401	2.57
Portuguese (9)	23	0.15
Romanian (0)	16	0.10
Russian (25)	25	0.16
Scandinavian (0)	12	0.08
Scotch-Irish (327)	627	4.02
Scottish (96)	224	1.44
Slovak (9)	18	0.12
Swedish (0)	194	1.24
Swiss (0)	61	0.39
Welsh (28)	84	0.54
West Indian, ex. Hispanic (21)	21	0.13
West Indian (21)	21	0.13

Hispanic Origin	Population	%
Hispanic or Latino (of any race)	740	4.59
Central American, ex. Mexican	74	0.46
Costa Rican	6	0.04
Guatemalan	11	0.07
Honduran	23	0.14
Nicaraguan	6	0.04
Panamanian	17	0.11
Salvadoran	7	0.04
Other Central American	4	0.02
Cuban	47	0.29
Dominican Republic	9	0.06
Mexican	271	1.68
Puerto Rican	164	1.02
South American	73	0.45
Argentinean	5	0.03
Bolivian	1	0.01
Chilean	6	0.04
Colombian	34	0.21
Ecuadorian	5	0.03
Paraguayan	2	0.01
Peruvian	10	0.06
Uruguayan	3	0.02
Venezuelan	4	0.02
Other South American	3	0.02
Other Hispanic or Latino	102	0.63

Race*	Population	%
African-American/Black (322)	429	2.66
Not Hispanic (293)	381	2.36
Hispanic (29)	48	0.30
American Indian/Alaska Native (118)	252	1.56
Not Hispanic (105)	216	1.34
Hispanic (13)	36	0.22
Aleut *(Alaska Native)* (1)	1	0.01
Apache (0)	4	0.02
Blackfeet (4)	10	0.06
Canadian/French Am. Ind. (0)	1	0.01
Central American Ind. (4)	4	0.02
Cherokee (32)	72	0.45
Chickasaw (0)	1	0.01
Chippewa (2)	4	0.02
Choctaw (5)	8	0.05
Cree (0)	1	0.01
Creek (10)	26	0.16
Houma (2)	3	0.02
Iroquois (0)	1	0.01
Menominee (2)	2	0.01
Mexican American Ind. (2)	2	0.01
Navajo (1)	1	0.01
Potawatomi (1)	1	0.01
Pueblo (1)	1	0.01
Sioux (3)	5	0.03
South American Ind. (0)	1	0.01
Yaqui (1)	1	0.01
Asian (301)	436	2.71
Not Hispanic (297)	418	2.59
Hispanic (4)	18	0.11
Bangladeshi (9)	9	0.06
Cambodian (4)	4	0.02
Chinese, ex. Taiwanese (18)	30	0.19
Filipino (73)	132	0.82
Indian (47)	52	0.32
Indonesian (1)	5	0.03
Japanese (14)	33	0.20
Korean (28)	44	0.27
Laotian (1)	3	0.02
Pakistani (4)	4	0.02
Sri Lankan (1)	1	0.01
Taiwanese (2)	6	0.04
Thai (9)	19	0.12
Vietnamese (81)	88	0.55
Hawaii Native/Pacific Islander (16)	40	0.25
Not Hispanic (13)	35	0.22
Hispanic (3)	5	0.03
Guamanian/Chamorro (11)	24	0.15
Native Hawaiian (2)	10	0.06
Samoan (3)	5	0.03
White (14,819)	15,179	94.19
Not Hispanic (14,329)	14,622	90.74
Hispanic (490)	557	3.46

Milton

Place Type: City
County: Santa Rosa
Population: 8,826†

Ancestry‡	Population	%
African, Sub-Saharan (0)	70	0.80
African (0)	70	0.80
American (771)	771	8.86
Arab (0)	14	0.16
Lebanese (0)	14	0.16
Australian (70)	103	1.18
Canadian (10)	10	0.11
Croatian (6)	6	0.07
Czech (0)	232	2.67
Danish (23)	64	0.74
Dutch (0)	33	0.38
English (347)	885	10.17

*Notes: † The Census 2010 population figure is used to calculate the percentages in the Hispanic Origin and Race categories. Ancestry percentages are based on the 2006-2010 American Community Survey population (not shown); ‡ Numbers in parentheses indicate the number of people reporting a single ancestry; * Numbers in parentheses indicate the number of persons reporting this race alone, not in combination with any other race; Please refer to the Explanation of Data for more information.*

SECTION TWO

Ancestry‡	Population	%
European (50)	63	0.72
French, ex. Basque (11)	258	2.97
French Canadian (32)	51	0.59
German (269)	1,053	12.10
Guyanese (69)	69	0.79
Hungarian (17)	43	0.49
Irish (227)	1,033	11.87
Italian (164)	330	3.79
Latvian (12)	12	0.14
Norwegian (0)	13	0.15
Pennsylvania German (55)	55	0.63
Polish (44)	78	0.90
Russian (14)	16	0.18
Scandinavian (0)	9	0.10
Scotch-Irish (158)	324	3.72
Scottish (52)	284	3.26
Swedish (19)	74	0.85
Welsh (34)	185	2.13
West Indian, ex. Hispanic (40)	56	0.64
Dutch West Indian (9)	9	0.10
Haitian (13)	13	0.15
West Indian (18)	34	0.39
Yugoslavian (6)	6	0.07

Hispanic Origin	Population	%
Hispanic or Latino (of any race)	426	4.83
Central American, ex. Mexican	33	0.37
Guatemalan	5	0.06
Honduran	8	0.09
Nicaraguan	3	0.03
Panamanian	7	0.08
Salvadoran	10	0.11
Cuban	19	0.22
Dominican Republic	5	0.06
Mexican	209	2.37
Puerto Rican	97	1.10
South American	21	0.24
Argentinean	2	0.02
Bolivian	1	0.01
Colombian	12	0.14
Ecuadorian	3	0.03
Peruvian	2	0.02
Venezuelan	1	0.01
Other Hispanic or Latino	42	0.48

Race*	Population	%
African-American/Black (1,227)	1,375	15.58
Not Hispanic (1,200)	1,343	15.22
Hispanic (27)	32	0.36
American Indian/Alaska Native (64)	165	1.87
Not Hispanic (62)	155	1.76
Hispanic (2)	10	0.11
Blackfeet (1)	6	0.07
Central American Ind. (1)	1	0.01
Cherokee (19)	51	0.58
Chickasaw (1)	1	0.01
Chippewa (1)	2	0.02
Choctaw (1)	3	0.03
Creek (11)	24	0.27
Delaware (0)	4	0.05
Houma (0)	1	0.01
Iroquois (1)	1	0.01
Ottawa (1)	2	0.02
Seminole (0)	2	0.02
Sioux (0)	1	0.01
Yaqui (0)	2	0.02
Asian (197)	321	3.64
Not Hispanic (188)	308	3.49
Hispanic (9)	13	0.15
Chinese, ex. Taiwanese (21)	27	0.31
Filipino (126)	197	2.23
Indian (13)	20	0.23
Indonesian (2)	8	0.09
Japanese (15)	32	0.36
Korean (4)	10	0.11
Pakistani (1)	6	0.07
Thai (3)	3	0.03
Vietnamese (9)	14	0.16
Hawaii Native/Pacific Islander (23)	30	0.34
Not Hispanic (19)	26	0.29
Hispanic (4)	4	0.05
Guamanian/Chamorro (12)	18	0.20
Native Hawaiian (3)	3	0.03
Samoan (2)	2	0.02
White (6,828)	7,153	81.04
Not Hispanic (6,594)	6,880	77.95
Hispanic (234)	273	3.09

Minneola

Place Type: City
County: Lake
Population: 9,403†

Ancestry‡	Population	%
African, Sub-Saharan (53)	119	1.32
African (53)	119	1.32
American (473)	473	5.25
Austrian (0)	30	0.33
British (46)	164	1.82
Czech (0)	10	0.11
Dutch (52)	211	2.34
English (292)	712	7.91
European (108)	108	1.20
Finnish (0)	37	0.41
French, ex. Basque (15)	176	1.95
French Canadian (11)	28	0.31
German (300)	952	10.57
Greek (18)	60	0.67
Hungarian (0)	15	0.17
Irish (275)	995	11.05
Italian (419)	888	9.86
Lithuanian (0)	16	0.18
Norwegian (53)	263	2.92
Polish (74)	295	3.28
Portuguese (8)	34	0.38
Russian (84)	84	0.93
Scandinavian (8)	8	0.09
Scotch-Irish (37)	63	0.70
Scottish (68)	153	1.70
Serbian (7)	21	0.23
Slovak (0)	27	0.30
Slovene (0)	14	0.16
Swedish (7)	31	0.34
Swiss (10)	37	0.41
Ukrainian (0)	8	0.09
Welsh (0)	60	0.67
West Indian, ex. Hispanic (526)	772	8.57
Bahamian (7)	7	0.08
Haitian (74)	74	0.82
Jamaican (217)	463	5.14
Trinidadian/Tobagonian (59)	59	0.66
West Indian (169)	169	1.88

Hispanic Origin	Population	%
Hispanic or Latino (of any race)	1,908	20.29
Central American, ex. Mexican	106	1.13
Costa Rican	4	0.04
Guatemalan	10	0.11
Honduran	35	0.37
Nicaraguan	26	0.28
Panamanian	6	0.06
Salvadoran	25	0.27
Cuban	134	1.43
Dominican Republic	85	0.90
Mexican	307	3.26
Puerto Rican	994	10.57
South American	175	1.86
Argentinean	6	0.06
Chilean	9	0.10
Colombian	61	0.65
Ecuadorian	33	0.35
Peruvian	41	0.44
Uruguayan	3	0.03
Venezuelan	16	0.17
Other South American	6	0.06
Other Hispanic or Latino	107	1.14

Race*	Population	%
African-American/Black (1,061)	1,179	12.54
Not Hispanic (970)	1,063	11.30
Hispanic (91)	116	1.23
American Indian/Alaska Native (60)	130	1.38
Not Hispanic (32)	91	0.97
Hispanic (28)	39	0.41
Apache (0)	1	0.01
Blackfeet (1)	3	0.03
Cherokee (8)	26	0.28
Chickasaw (1)	1	0.01
Chippewa (1)	2	0.02
Choctaw (1)	1	0.01
Creek (1)	5	0.05
Crow (0)	3	0.03
Iroquois (0)	1	0.01
Lumbee (0)	1	0.01
Navajo (2)	2	0.02
Potawatomi (3)	3	0.03
Pueblo (1)	1	0.01
Sioux (0)	3	0.03
South American Ind. (7)	7	0.07
Yaqui (0)	1	0.01
Asian (231)	329	3.50
Not Hispanic (228)	313	3.33
Hispanic (3)	16	0.17
Bangladeshi (1)	1	0.01
Chinese, ex. Taiwanese (19)	25	0.27
Filipino (33)	53	0.56
Indian (147)	180	1.91
Indonesian (1)	1	0.01
Japanese (9)	12	0.13
Korean (9)	30	0.32
Malaysian (1)	1	0.01
Pakistani (0)	1	0.01
Taiwanese (3)	3	0.03
Thai (2)	2	0.02
Vietnamese (2)	3	0.03
Hawaii Native/Pacific Islander (5)	38	0.40
Not Hispanic (2)	28	0.30
Hispanic (3)	10	0.11
Native Hawaiian (0)	9	0.10
Samoan (2)	3	0.03
White (7,197)	7,420	78.91
Not Hispanic (5,944)	6,085	64.71
Hispanic (1,253)	1,335	14.20

Miramar

Place Type: City
County: Broward
Population: 122,041†

Ancestry‡	Population	%
Afghan (0)	31	0.03
African, Sub-Saharan (1,248)	1,606	1.41
African (763)	1,121	0.99
Nigerian (446)	446	0.39
Other Sub-Saharan African (39)	39	0.03
Alsatian (0)	10	0.01
American (4,221)	4,221	3.71
Arab (684)	865	0.76
Arab (97)	97	0.09
Egyptian (142)	142	0.12
Jordanian (248)	248	0.22
Lebanese (35)	144	0.13
Moroccan (0)	11	0.01
Palestinian (85)	117	0.10
Syrian (21)	36	0.03
Other Arab (56)	70	0.06
Armenian (13)	13	0.01
Austrian (42)	89	0.08
Brazilian (434)	657	0.58
British (34)	110	0.10
Bulgarian (9)	29	0.03
Canadian (126)	281	0.25
Croatian (0)	36	0.03
Czech (69)	222	0.20
Czechoslovakian (0)	16	0.01
Danish (0)	8	0.01
Dutch (153)	292	0.26
Eastern European (14)	14	0.01

*Notes: † The Census 2010 population figure is used to calculate the percentages in the Hispanic Origin and Race categories. Ancestry percentages are based on the 2006-2010 American Community Survey population (not shown); ‡ Numbers in parentheses indicate the number of people reporting a single ancestry; * Numbers in parentheses indicate the number of persons reporting this race alone, not in combination with any other race; Please refer to the Explanation of Data for more information.*

Ancestry	Population	%
English (522)	1,748	1.54
European (166)	325	0.29
Finnish (12)	22	0.02
French, ex. Basque (76)	753	0.66
French Canadian (108)	247	0.22
German (581)	2,721	2.39
German Russian (13)	13	0.01
Greek (259)	276	0.24
Guyanese (347)	609	0.54
Hungarian (30)	145	0.13
Icelander (12)	12	0.01
Iranian (69)	69	0.06
Irish (571)	2,516	2.21
Italian (1,026)	2,732	2.40
Lithuanian (7)	29	0.03
Norwegian (21)	46	0.04
Pennsylvania German (37)	37	0.03
Polish (148)	541	0.48
Portuguese (192)	313	0.28
Romanian (0)	28	0.02
Russian (71)	345	0.30
Scotch-Irish (100)	287	0.25
Scottish (138)	289	0.25
Serbian (0)	10	0.01
Slavic (15)	15	0.01
Slovak (32)	73	0.06
Slovene (16)	16	0.01
Swedish (59)	148	0.13
Swiss (0)	84	0.07
Ukrainian (42)	98	0.09
Welsh (24)	122	0.11
West Indian, ex. Hispanic (24,187)	27,767	24.42
Bahamian (290)	414	0.36
Barbadian (261)	261	0.23
Belizean (221)	324	0.28
British West Indian (292)	292	0.26
Dutch West Indian (0)	24	0.02
Haitian (9,355)	10,494	9.23
Jamaican (12,450)	14,117	12.42
Trinidadian/Tobagonian (757)	1,024	0.90
U.S. Virgin Islander (71)	105	0.09
West Indian (490)	712	0.63
Yugoslavian (10)	21	0.02

Hispanic Origin	Population	%
Hispanic or Latino (of any race)	45,039	36.90
Central American, ex. Mexican	4,460	3.65
Costa Rican	315	0.26
Guatemalan	409	0.34
Honduran	1,011	0.83
Nicaraguan	1,691	1.39
Panamanian	700	0.57
Salvadoran	314	0.26
Other Central American	20	0.02
Cuban	12,924	10.59
Dominican Republic	4,529	3.71
Mexican	1,230	1.01
Puerto Rican	6,658	5.46
South American	12,551	10.28
Argentinean	558	0.46
Bolivian	116	0.10
Chilean	340	0.28
Colombian	6,230	5.10
Ecuadorian	1,132	0.93
Paraguayan	20	0.02
Peruvian	1,401	1.15
Uruguayan	142	0.12
Venezuelan	2,594	2.13
Other South American	18	0.01
Other Hispanic or Latino	2,687	2.20

Race*	Population	%
African-American/Black (55,781)	58,514	47.95
Not Hispanic (53,036)	54,974	45.05
Hispanic (2,745)	3,540	2.90
American Indian/Alaska Native (288)	691	0.57
Not Hispanic (173)	426	0.35
Hispanic (115)	265	0.22
Aleut *(Alaska Native)* (0)	1	<0.01
Apache (0)	2	<0.01
Arapaho (0)	5	<0.01
Blackfeet (0)	10	0.01
Central American Ind. (3)	16	0.01
Cherokee (6)	57	0.05
Chickasaw (0)	2	<0.01
Chippewa (4)	5	<0.01
Choctaw (2)	7	0.01
Creek (4)	19	0.02
Inupiat *(Alaska Native)* (1)	4	<0.01
Iroquois (1)	3	<0.01
Lumbee (2)	2	<0.01
Mexican American Ind. (7)	11	0.01
Navajo (1)	1	<0.01
Seminole (15)	23	0.02
Sioux (2)	6	<0.01
South American Ind. (33)	58	0.05
Spanish American Ind. (3)	8	0.01
Asian (6,383)	7,680	6.29
Not Hispanic (6,244)	7,313	5.99
Hispanic (139)	367	0.30
Bangladeshi (70)	76	0.06
Burmese (6)	6	<0.01
Cambodian (13)	17	0.01
Chinese, ex. Taiwanese (1,286)	1,751	1.43
Filipino (1,087)	1,261	1.03
Indian (2,256)	2,697	2.21
Indonesian (4)	6	<0.01
Japanese (58)	113	0.09
Korean (163)	197	0.16
Laotian (7)	8	0.01
Malaysian (8)	10	0.01
Nepalese (6)	6	<0.01
Pakistani (501)	587	0.48
Sri Lankan (8)	10	0.01
Taiwanese (22)	26	0.02
Thai (37)	53	0.04
Vietnamese (667)	690	0.57
Hawaii Native/Pacific Islander (55)	454	0.37
Not Hispanic (54)	407	0.33
Hispanic (1)	47	0.04
Guamanian/Chamorro (16)	20	0.02
Native Hawaiian (4)	19	0.02
Samoan (3)	5	<0.01
Tongan (1)	2	<0.01
White (49,979)	52,713	43.19
Not Hispanic (14,152)	15,366	12.59
Hispanic (35,827)	37,347	30.60

Mount Dora

Place Type: City
County: Lake
Population: 12,370†

Ancestry‡	Population	%
American (1,176)	1,176	9.51
Arab (46)	46	0.37
Syrian (46)	46	0.37
Austrian (12)	21	0.17
Belgian (0)	10	0.08
British (29)	76	0.61
Canadian (96)	178	1.44
Croatian (18)	106	0.86
Czech (22)	22	0.18
Danish (12)	24	0.19
Dutch (15)	118	0.95
Eastern European (0)	13	0.11
English (582)	1,447	11.70
European (186)	241	1.95
French, ex. Basque (86)	366	2.96
French Canadian (48)	92	0.74
German (762)	1,518	12.27
German Russian (75)	75	0.61
Guyanese (10)	10	0.08
Hungarian (16)	49	0.40
Irish (412)	1,400	11.32
Italian (364)	690	5.58
Lithuanian (11)	91	0.74
Norwegian (62)	139	1.12
Pennsylvania German (15)	15	0.12
Polish (105)	213	1.72
Portuguese (0)	17	0.14
Romanian (0)	11	0.09
Russian (66)	151	1.22
Scotch-Irish (30)	143	1.16
Scottish (116)	184	1.49
Slavic (0)	23	0.19
Slovak (28)	47	0.38
Swedish (130)	188	1.52
Swiss (159)	201	1.63
Ukrainian (26)	38	0.31
Welsh (49)	65	0.53
West Indian, ex. Hispanic (123)	211	1.71
Haitian (66)	66	0.53
Jamaican (41)	41	0.33
Trinidadian/Tobagonian (16)	16	0.13
West Indian (0)	88	0.71

Hispanic Origin	Population	%
Hispanic or Latino (of any race)	1,448	11.71
Central American, ex. Mexican	44	0.36
Costa Rican	4	0.03
Guatemalan	4	0.03
Honduran	14	0.11
Nicaraguan	4	0.03
Panamanian	8	0.06
Salvadoran	10	0.08
Cuban	90	0.73
Dominican Republic	25	0.20
Mexican	697	5.63
Puerto Rican	376	3.04
South American	125	1.01
Argentinean	11	0.09
Chilean	1	0.01
Colombian	41	0.33
Ecuadorian	12	0.10
Paraguayan	4	0.03
Peruvian	34	0.27
Uruguayan	8	0.06
Venezuelan	14	0.11
Other Hispanic or Latino	91	0.74

Race*	Population	%
African-American/Black (1,930)	2,025	16.37
Not Hispanic (1,899)	1,967	15.90
Hispanic (31)	58	0.47
American Indian/Alaska Native (50)	110	0.89
Not Hispanic (42)	95	0.77
Hispanic (8)	15	0.12
Apache (3)	3	0.02
Blackfeet (0)	1	0.01
Canadian/French Am. Ind. (1)	4	0.03
Cherokee (5)	23	0.19
Cheyenne (1)	1	0.01
Chippewa (2)	5	0.04
Choctaw (2)	2	0.02
Creek (0)	3	0.02
Delaware (0)	2	0.02
Inupiat *(Alaska Native)* (3)	3	0.02
Lumbee (0)	2	0.02
Mexican American Ind. (0)	3	0.02
Osage (0)	1	0.01
Sioux (0)	1	0.01
South American Ind. (3)	4	0.03
Tlingit-Haida *(Alaska Native)* (2)	2	0.02
Asian (228)	276	2.23
Not Hispanic (214)	254	2.05
Hispanic (14)	22	0.18
Bangladeshi (19)	20	0.16
Cambodian (6)	6	0.05
Chinese, ex. Taiwanese (11)	21	0.17
Filipino (27)	33	0.27
Indian (102)	108	0.87
Japanese (12)	17	0.14
Korean (19)	23	0.19
Nepalese (2)	3	0.02
Pakistani (2)	2	0.02
Thai (7)	8	0.06
Vietnamese (15)	22	0.18
Hawaii Native/Pacific Islander (10)	23	0.19

*Notes: † The Census 2010 population figure is used to calculate the percentages in the Hispanic Origin and Race categories. Ancestry percentages are based on the 2006-2010 American Community Survey population (not shown); ‡ Numbers in parentheses indicate the number of people reporting a single ancestry; * Numbers in parentheses indicate the number of persons reporting this race alone, not in combination with any other race; Please refer to the Explanation of Data for more information.*

	Population	%
Not Hispanic (9)	20	0.16
Hispanic (1)	3	0.02
Marshallese (4)	4	0.03
Native Hawaiian (1)	2	0.02
Samoan (1)	1	0.01
White (9,584)	9,767	78.96
Not Hispanic (8,602)	8,719	70.49
Hispanic (982)	1,048	8.47

Myrtle Grove

Place Type: CDP
County: Escambia
Population: 15,870†

Ancestry‡	Population	%
African, Sub-Saharan (94)	150	0.93
African (27)	51	0.32
Cape Verdean (14)	14	0.09
Nigerian (38)	38	0.24
Other Sub-Saharan African (15)	47	0.29
American (1,454)	1,454	9.05
Arab (10)	10	0.06
Arab (10)	10	0.06
Austrian (15)	15	0.09
Belgian (0)	16	0.10
British (80)	95	0.59
Czech (0)	21	0.13
Danish (30)	74	0.46
Dutch (15)	238	1.48
English (495)	1,487	9.25
European (51)	91	0.57
Finnish (21)	39	0.24
French, ex. Basque (197)	582	3.62
French Canadian (90)	125	0.78
German (559)	2,242	13.95
Greek (110)	168	1.05
Guyanese (18)	18	0.11
Hungarian (57)	107	0.67
Irish (389)	2,016	12.54
Italian (227)	783	4.87
Lithuanian (14)	14	0.09
Northern European (12)	12	0.07
Norwegian (34)	216	1.34
Polish (90)	386	2.40
Portuguese (53)	117	0.73
Russian (16)	44	0.27
Scandinavian (0)	3	0.02
Scotch-Irish (109)	418	2.60
Scottish (118)	358	2.23
Slovene (8)	8	0.05
Swedish (62)	120	0.75
Swiss (10)	14	0.09
Welsh (10)	134	0.83
West Indian, ex. Hispanic (183)	223	1.39
Belizean (62)	62	0.39
Dutch West Indian (11)	27	0.17
Haitian (8)	8	0.05
Jamaican (102)	126	0.78

Hispanic Origin	Population	%
Hispanic or Latino (of any race)	1,010	6.36
Central American, ex. Mexican	116	0.73
Costa Rican	13	0.08
Guatemalan	7	0.04
Honduran	38	0.24
Nicaraguan	8	0.05
Panamanian	29	0.18
Salvadoran	21	0.13
Cuban	60	0.38
Dominican Republic	14	0.09
Mexican	467	2.94
Puerto Rican	182	1.15
South American	66	0.42
Argentinean	2	0.01
Bolivian	12	0.08
Chilean	1	0.01
Colombian	21	0.13
Ecuadorian	18	0.11
Paraguayan	4	0.03
Peruvian	5	0.03
Venezuelan	3	0.02
Other Hispanic or Latino	105	0.66

Race*	Population	%
African-American/Black (2,925)	3,203	20.18
Not Hispanic (2,881)	3,128	19.71
Hispanic (44)	75	0.47
American Indian/Alaska Native (100)	300	1.89
Not Hispanic (85)	268	1.69
Hispanic (15)	32	0.20
Alaska Athabascan *(Ala. Nat.)* (1)	1	0.01
Apache (2)	5	0.03
Blackfeet (0)	11	0.07
Cherokee (28)	79	0.50
Chickasaw (1)	3	0.02
Chippewa (1)	1	0.01
Choctaw (1)	9	0.06
Comanche (2)	2	0.01
Cree (0)	1	0.01
Creek (27)	59	0.37
Delaware (1)	1	0.01
Inupiat *(Alaska Native)* (1)	1	0.01
Iroquois (0)	4	0.03
Lumbee (1)	2	0.01
Navajo (2)	2	0.01
Seminole (1)	1	0.01
Shoshone (1)	1	0.01
Sioux (0)	5	0.03
South American Ind. (0)	2	0.01
Tlingit-Haida *(Alaska Native)* (1)	4	0.03
Tohono O'Odham (1)	1	0.01
Yup'ik *(Alaska Native)* (1)	1	0.01
Asian (817)	1,099	6.93
Not Hispanic (801)	1,052	6.63
Hispanic (16)	47	0.30
Cambodian (5)	8	0.05
Chinese, ex. Taiwanese (27)	62	0.39
Filipino (539)	715	4.51
Hmong (5)	5	0.03
Indian (38)	51	0.32
Japanese (33)	69	0.43
Korean (21)	33	0.21
Laotian (2)	7	0.04
Malaysian (0)	1	0.01
Taiwanese (1)	1	0.01
Thai (3)	7	0.04
Vietnamese (134)	150	0.95
Hawaii Native/Pacific Islander (30)	104	0.66
Not Hispanic (28)	99	0.62
Hispanic (2)	5	0.03
Guamanian/Chamorro (11)	26	0.16
Native Hawaiian (3)	28	0.18
Samoan (7)	12	0.08
White (10,954)	11,563	72.86
Not Hispanic (10,436)	10,955	69.03
Hispanic (518)	608	3.83

Naples

Place Type: City
County: Collier
Population: 19,537†

Ancestry‡	Population	%
African, Sub-Saharan (23)	23	0.11
African (23)	23	0.11
Alsatian (18)	18	0.09
American (1,310)	1,310	6.42
Arab (48)	93	0.46
Egyptian (13)	44	0.22
Iraqi (14)	14	0.07
Lebanese (0)	14	0.07
Palestinian (20)	20	0.10
Other Arab (1)	1	<0.01
Armenian (39)	87	0.43
Assyrian/Chaldean/Syriac (9)	9	0.04
Australian (15)	15	0.07
Austrian (35)	66	0.32
Belgian (8)	125	0.61
British (277)	377	1.85
Canadian (111)	173	0.85
Croatian (0)	13	0.06
Czech (87)	141	0.69
Czechoslovakian (35)	74	0.36
Danish (36)	102	0.50
Dutch (253)	458	2.24
Eastern European (116)	116	0.57
English (1,448)	3,919	19.21
European (176)	176	0.86
Finnish (42)	52	0.25
French, ex. Basque (174)	870	4.26
French Canadian (44)	77	0.38
German (1,487)	4,083	20.01
Greek (168)	180	0.88
Hungarian (84)	207	1.01
Irish (1,099)	3,642	17.85
Italian (1,229)	1,884	9.23
Latvian (17)	17	0.08
Lithuanian (47)	87	0.43
Northern European (9)	9	0.04
Norwegian (82)	304	1.49
Pennsylvania German (40)	40	0.20
Polish (506)	933	4.57
Portuguese (50)	104	0.51
Romanian (16)	31	0.15
Russian (237)	343	1.68
Scandinavian (37)	58	0.28
Scotch-Irish (312)	646	3.17
Scottish (338)	869	4.26
Slavic (0)	10	0.05
Slovak (23)	46	0.23
Slovene (24)	53	0.26
Swedish (123)	428	2.10
Swiss (37)	170	0.83
Turkish (9)	30	0.15
Ukrainian (41)	80	0.39
Welsh (55)	225	1.10
West Indian, ex. Hispanic (308)	323	1.58
Bahamian (31)	31	0.15
Haitian (145)	160	0.78
Jamaican (108)	108	0.53
Trinidadian/Tobagonian (16)	16	0.08
West Indian (8)	8	0.04

Hispanic Origin	Population	%
Hispanic or Latino (of any race)	881	4.51
Central American, ex. Mexican	66	0.34
Costa Rican	5	0.03
Guatemalan	11	0.06
Honduran	20	0.10
Nicaraguan	5	0.03
Panamanian	7	0.04
Salvadoran	18	0.09
Cuban	310	1.59
Dominican Republic	33	0.17
Mexican	146	0.75
Puerto Rican	110	0.56
South American	121	0.62
Argentinean	11	0.06
Bolivian	3	0.02
Chilean	2	0.01
Colombian	57	0.29
Ecuadorian	7	0.04
Paraguayan	5	0.03
Peruvian	22	0.11
Uruguayan	6	0.03
Venezuelan	8	0.04
Other Hispanic or Latino	95	0.49

Race*	Population	%
African-American/Black (812)	885	4.53
Not Hispanic (779)	838	4.29
Hispanic (33)	47	0.24
American Indian/Alaska Native (27)	79	0.40
Not Hispanic (22)	64	0.33
Hispanic (5)	15	0.08
Blackfeet (0)	8	0.04
Cherokee (4)	10	0.05
Chippewa (1)	3	0.02

*Notes: † The Census 2010 population figure is used to calculate the percentages in the Hispanic Origin and Race categories. Ancestry percentages are based on the 2006-2010 American Community Survey population (not shown); ‡ Numbers in parentheses indicate the number of people reporting a single ancestry; * Numbers in parentheses indicate the number of persons reporting this race alone, not in combination with any other race; Please refer to the Explanation of Data for more information.*

	Population	%
Choctaw (0)	1	0.01
Iroquois (1)	3	0.02
Navajo (0)	1	0.01
Potawatomi (0)	2	0.01
Seminole (4)	5	0.03
Tlingit-Haida *(Alaska Native)* (0)	1	0.01
Asian (120)	189	0.97
Not Hispanic (118)	174	0.89
Hispanic (2)	15	0.08
Burmese (1)	1	0.01
Chinese, ex. Taiwanese (38)	57	0.29
Filipino (13)	27	0.14
Indian (30)	42	0.21
Indonesian (2)	3	0.02
Japanese (11)	16	0.08
Korean (11)	16	0.08
Taiwanese (0)	1	0.01
Thai (4)	5	0.03
Vietnamese (9)	10	0.05
Hawaii Native/Pacific Islander (3)	41	0.21
Not Hispanic (3)	40	0.20
Hispanic (0)	1	0.01
Guamanian/Chamorro (0)	4	0.02
Native Hawaiian (1)	9	0.05
Tongan (0)	1	0.01
White (18,235)	18,391	94.13
Not Hispanic (17,566)	17,683	90.51
Hispanic (669)	708	3.62

Naranja

Place Type: CDP
County: Miami-Dade
Population: 8,303†

Ancestry‡	Population	%
American (235)	235	3.68
Arab (29)	29	0.45
Other Arab (29)	29	0.45
Belgian (0)	12	0.19
Brazilian (102)	102	1.60
British (0)	5	0.08
French, ex. Basque (0)	26	0.41
German (32)	61	0.96
Irish (11)	56	0.88
Italian (0)	18	0.28
Polish (40)	83	1.30
Portuguese (0)	12	0.19
Scotch-Irish (11)	11	0.17
Swedish (15)	50	0.78
West Indian, ex. Hispanic (740)	775	12.14
Haitian (244)	279	4.37
Jamaican (318)	318	4.98
West Indian (178)	178	2.79

Hispanic Origin	Population	%
Hispanic or Latino (of any race)	4,285	51.61
Central American, ex. Mexican	617	7.43
Costa Rican	16	0.19
Guatemalan	51	0.61
Honduran	123	1.48
Nicaraguan	296	3.56
Panamanian	58	0.70
Salvadoran	70	0.84
Other Central American	3	0.04
Cuban	1,458	17.56
Dominican Republic	204	2.46
Mexican	437	5.26
Puerto Rican	687	8.27
South American	619	7.46
Argentinean	57	0.69
Bolivian	8	0.10
Chilean	18	0.22
Colombian	276	3.32
Ecuadorian	71	0.86
Peruvian	94	1.13
Uruguayan	4	0.05
Venezuelan	91	1.10
Other Hispanic or Latino	263	3.17

Race*	Population	%
African-American/Black (3,429)	3,569	42.98
Not Hispanic (3,172)	3,248	39.12
Hispanic (257)	321	3.87
American Indian/Alaska Native (24)	56	0.67
Not Hispanic (11)	33	0.40
Hispanic (13)	23	0.28
Canadian/French Am. Ind. (0)	1	0.01
Cherokee (2)	3	0.04
Iroquois (0)	1	0.01
Navajo (1)	2	0.02
South American Ind. (0)	2	0.02
Spanish American Ind. (0)	1	0.01
Tlingit-Haida *(Alaska Native)* (0)	1	0.01
Asian (194)	232	2.79
Not Hispanic (193)	219	2.64
Hispanic (1)	13	0.16
Bangladeshi (3)	3	0.04
Cambodian (6)	8	0.10
Chinese, ex. Taiwanese (26)	40	0.48
Filipino (60)	65	0.78
Hmong (4)	4	0.05
Indian (38)	49	0.59
Japanese (1)	3	0.04
Korean (0)	1	0.01
Pakistani (5)	5	0.06
Thai (11)	13	0.16
Vietnamese (37)	38	0.46
Hawaii Native/Pacific Islander (1)	9	0.11
Not Hispanic (1)	8	0.10
Hispanic (0)	1	0.01
Native Hawaiian (1)	1	0.01
White (3,978)	4,151	49.99
Not Hispanic (519)	569	6.85
Hispanic (3,459)	3,582	43.14

Navarre

Place Type: CDP
County: Santa Rosa
Population: 31,378†

Ancestry‡	Population	%
African, Sub-Saharan (127)	127	0.43
African (48)	48	0.16
Kenyan (79)	79	0.27
American (3,675)	3,675	12.36
Arab (73)	110	0.37
Egyptian (22)	22	0.07
Lebanese (51)	88	0.30
Austrian (11)	11	0.04
Belgian (11)	17	0.06
Brazilian (0)	13	0.04
British (40)	142	0.48
Cajun (0)	28	0.09
Canadian (0)	16	0.05
Croatian (0)	16	0.05
Czech (89)	185	0.62
Czechoslovakian (9)	9	0.03
Danish (12)	68	0.23
Dutch (50)	272	0.91
English (1,211)	3,316	11.15
European (287)	323	1.09
Finnish (14)	106	0.36
French, ex. Basque (255)	1,606	5.40
French Canadian (68)	92	0.31
German (1,601)	4,873	16.38
Greek (14)	52	0.17
Hungarian (67)	157	0.53
Irish (1,106)	4,416	14.85
Italian (782)	1,588	5.34
Lithuanian (10)	71	0.24
Northern European (14)	14	0.05
Norwegian (65)	196	0.66
Polish (213)	778	2.62
Portuguese (21)	84	0.28
Romanian (0)	15	0.05
Russian (65)	100	0.34
Scandinavian (34)	49	0.16
Scotch-Irish (358)	726	2.44
Scottish (252)	670	2.25
Slovak (0)	50	0.17
Slovene (19)	19	0.06
Swedish (55)	193	0.65
Swiss (0)	13	0.04
Turkish (49)	49	0.16
Welsh (64)	269	0.90
West Indian, ex. Hispanic (141)	153	0.51
British West Indian (10)	10	0.03
Haitian (81)	81	0.27
Jamaican (45)	45	0.15
West Indian (5)	5	0.02
Other West Indian (0)	12	0.04
Yugoslavian (12)	12	0.04

Hispanic Origin	Population	%
Hispanic or Latino (of any race)	2,200	7.01
Central American, ex. Mexican	196	0.62
Costa Rican	10	0.03
Guatemalan	16	0.05
Honduran	69	0.22
Nicaraguan	17	0.05
Panamanian	69	0.22
Salvadoran	13	0.04
Other Central American	2	0.01
Cuban	92	0.29
Dominican Republic	37	0.12
Mexican	851	2.71
Puerto Rican	588	1.87
South American	167	0.53
Argentinean	9	0.03
Bolivian	2	0.01
Chilean	9	0.03
Colombian	87	0.28
Ecuadorian	32	0.10
Peruvian	21	0.07
Uruguayan	1	<0.01
Venezuelan	6	0.02
Other Hispanic or Latino	269	0.86

Race*	Population	%
African-American/Black (2,043)	2,479	7.90
Not Hispanic (1,942)	2,316	7.38
Hispanic (101)	163	0.52
American Indian/Alaska Native (169)	443	1.41
Not Hispanic (142)	382	1.22
Hispanic (27)	61	0.19
Apache (4)	11	0.04
Blackfeet (1)	5	0.02
Cherokee (27)	115	0.37
Chickasaw (0)	2	0.01
Chippewa (6)	9	0.03
Choctaw (7)	11	0.04
Colville (0)	1	<0.01
Cree (0)	1	<0.01
Creek (15)	29	0.09
Delaware (6)	9	0.03
Inupiat *(Alaska Native)* (2)	5	0.02
Iroquois (2)	4	0.01
Kiowa (1)	1	<0.01
Lumbee (14)	22	0.07
Mexican American Ind. (3)	9	0.03
Navajo (2)	4	0.01
Osage (0)	1	<0.01
Potawatomi (5)	8	0.03
Pueblo (2)	2	0.01
Seminole (2)	6	0.02
Sioux (2)	10	0.03
South American Ind. (8)	10	0.03
Tlingit-Haida *(Alaska Native)* (0)	3	0.01
Tohono O'Odham (0)	3	0.01
Yaqui (0)	1	<0.01
Asian (1,050)	1,723	5.49
Not Hispanic (1,020)	1,642	5.23
Hispanic (30)	81	0.26
Burmese (0)	2	0.01
Cambodian (12)	12	0.04
Chinese, ex. Taiwanese (54)	94	0.30
Filipino (480)	828	2.64

SECTION TWO

*Notes: † The Census 2010 population figure is used to calculate the percentages in the Hispanic Origin and Race categories. Ancestry percentages are based on the 2006-2010 American Community Survey population (not shown); ‡ Numbers in parentheses indicate the number of people reporting a single ancestry; * Numbers in parentheses indicate the number of persons reporting this race alone, not in combination with any other race; Please refer to the Explanation of Data for more information.*

Indian (41)	64	0.20
Indonesian (0)	1	<0.01
Japanese (62)	164	0.52
Korean (131)	241	0.77
Laotian (9)	12	0.04
Pakistani (8)	9	0.03
Taiwanese (2)	5	0.02
Thai (93)	175	0.56
Vietnamese (130)	142	0.45
Hawaii Native/Pacific Islander (60)	159	0.51
Not Hispanic (55)	139	0.44
Hispanic (5)	20	0.06
Fijian (2)	4	0.01
Guamanian/Chamorro (27)	56	0.18
Native Hawaiian (20)	59	0.19
Samoan (0)	1	<0.01
Tongan (2)	2	0.01
White (26,109)	27,324	87.08
Not Hispanic (24,809)	25,817	82.28
Hispanic (1,300)	1,507	4.80

New Port Richey East

Place Type: CDP
County: Pasco
Population: 10,036†

Ancestry‡	Population	%
American (444)	444	4.67
Austrian (0)	16	0.17
Belgian (0)	20	0.21
Brazilian (56)	56	0.59
British (0)	27	0.28
Canadian (76)	83	0.87
Czech (31)	82	0.86
Czechoslovakian (0)	4	0.04
Danish (51)	127	1.33
Dutch (43)	280	2.94
English (399)	1,139	11.97
European (30)	30	0.32
Finnish (22)	32	0.34
French, ex. Basque (78)	530	5.57
French Canadian (0)	44	0.46
German (662)	2,015	21.18
Greek (119)	187	1.97
Hungarian (51)	148	1.56
Irish (522)	1,137	11.95
Italian (929)	1,650	17.34
Lithuanian (0)	58	0.61
Norwegian (7)	26	0.27
Pennsylvania German (12)	12	0.13
Polish (96)	306	3.22
Portuguese (23)	41	0.43
Romanian (29)	29	0.30
Russian (0)	95	1.00
Scotch-Irish (17)	220	2.31
Scottish (57)	172	1.81
Slovak (0)	26	0.27
Swedish (44)	217	2.28
Swiss (0)	12	0.13
Ukrainian (34)	84	0.88
Welsh (32)	72	0.76
West Indian, ex. Hispanic (39)	59	0.62
Haitian (0)	20	0.21
Jamaican (39)	39	0.41
Yugoslavian (27)	64	0.67

Hispanic Origin	Population	%
Hispanic or Latino (of any race)	1,026	10.22
Central American, ex. Mexican	49	0.49
Costa Rican	9	0.09
Guatemalan	3	0.03
Honduran	15	0.15
Nicaraguan	4	0.04
Panamanian	9	0.09
Salvadoran	8	0.08
Other Central American	1	0.01
Cuban	45	0.45
Dominican Republic	26	0.26
Mexican	197	1.96
Puerto Rican	511	5.09
South American	108	1.08
Argentinean	6	0.06
Chilean	5	0.05
Colombian	44	0.44
Ecuadorian	18	0.18
Peruvian	27	0.27
Uruguayan	2	0.02
Venezuelan	5	0.05
Other South American	1	0.01
Other Hispanic or Latino	90	0.90

Race*	Population	%
African-American/Black (240)	322	3.21
Not Hispanic (193)	254	2.53
Hispanic (47)	68	0.68
American Indian/Alaska Native (32)	86	0.86
Not Hispanic (19)	70	0.70
Hispanic (13)	16	0.16
Blackfeet (0)	8	0.08
Cherokee (7)	27	0.27
Chippewa (1)	1	0.01
Choctaw (0)	3	0.03
Comanche (2)	2	0.02
Cree (0)	3	0.03
Creek (1)	2	0.02
Crow (1)	1	0.01
Iroquois (0)	3	0.03
Seminole (1)	1	0.01
Sioux (0)	4	0.04
South American Ind. (4)	5	0.05
Asian (162)	200	1.99
Not Hispanic (156)	189	1.88
Hispanic (6)	11	0.11
Bangladeshi (1)	1	0.01
Chinese, ex. Taiwanese (23)	31	0.31
Filipino (40)	64	0.64
Indian (15)	21	0.21
Indonesian (3)	4	0.04
Japanese (14)	17	0.17
Korean (7)	10	0.10
Laotian (12)	14	0.14
Thai (6)	6	0.06
Vietnamese (30)	32	0.32
Hawaii Native/Pacific Islander (2)	7	0.07
Not Hispanic (2)	5	0.05
Hispanic (0)	2	0.02
Native Hawaiian (2)	3	0.03
White (9,184)	9,361	93.27
Not Hispanic (8,481)	8,615	85.84
Hispanic (703)	746	7.43

New Port Richey

Place Type: City
County: Pasco
Population: 14,911†

Ancestry‡	Population	%
American (1,036)	1,036	6.66
Arab (0)	43	0.28
Arab (0)	43	0.28
Australian (8)	8	0.05
Belgian (8)	8	0.05
British (123)	123	0.79
Canadian (47)	56	0.36
Carpatho Rusyn (7)	17	0.11
Croatian (14)	14	0.09
Czech (0)	59	0.38
Czechoslovakian (19)	34	0.22
Danish (9)	32	0.21
Dutch (45)	365	2.35
English (657)	1,812	11.65
European (95)	115	0.74
Finnish (14)	45	0.29
French, ex. Basque (318)	915	5.88
French Canadian (131)	166	1.07
German (814)	2,361	15.18
Greek (99)	352	2.26
Guyanese (28)	28	0.18
Hungarian (17)	105	0.68
Icelander (15)	35	0.23
Irish (1,011)	2,734	17.58
Italian (1,036)	2,081	13.38
Latvian (8)	8	0.05
Lithuanian (0)	97	0.62
New Zealander (16)	16	0.10
Norwegian (41)	179	1.15
Pennsylvania German (13)	13	0.08
Polish (482)	893	5.74
Portuguese (10)	51	0.33
Romanian (44)	44	0.28
Russian (53)	186	1.20
Scotch-Irish (176)	319	2.05
Scottish (147)	387	2.49
Slavic (14)	14	0.09
Slovak (21)	89	0.57
Slovene (15)	15	0.10
Swedish (119)	321	2.06
Swiss (0)	61	0.39
Welsh (9)	161	1.04
Yugoslavian (177)	191	1.23

Hispanic Origin	Population	%
Hispanic or Latino (of any race)	1,671	11.21
Central American, ex. Mexican	60	0.40
Costa Rican	3	0.02
Guatemalan	21	0.14
Honduran	15	0.10
Nicaraguan	5	0.03
Panamanian	4	0.03
Salvadoran	5	0.03
Other Central American	7	0.05
Cuban	110	0.74
Dominican Republic	33	0.22
Mexican	539	3.61
Puerto Rican	703	4.71
South American	77	0.52
Argentinean	5	0.03
Bolivian	1	0.01
Colombian	31	0.21
Ecuadorian	18	0.12
Peruvian	14	0.09
Uruguayan	3	0.02
Venezuelan	1	0.01
Other South American	4	0.03
Other Hispanic or Latino	149	1.00

Race*	Population	%
African-American/Black (448)	619	4.15
Not Hispanic (387)	512	3.43
Hispanic (61)	107	0.72
American Indian/Alaska Native (74)	208	1.39
Not Hispanic (54)	172	1.15
Hispanic (20)	36	0.24
Apache (2)	4	0.03
Blackfeet (1)	9	0.06
Cherokee (8)	55	0.37
Chickasaw (1)	1	0.01
Chippewa (0)	6	0.04
Choctaw (2)	6	0.04
Creek (0)	2	0.01
Delaware (0)	2	0.01
Iroquois (5)	15	0.10
Lumbee (3)	6	0.04
Mexican American Ind. (7)	7	0.05
Navajo (1)	3	0.02
Osage (1)	1	0.01
Ottawa (1)	1	0.01
Paiute (1)	1	0.01
Potawatomi (0)	2	0.01
Seminole (0)	2	0.01
Sioux (2)	7	0.05
South American Ind. (0)	4	0.03
Asian (211)	275	1.84
Not Hispanic (211)	262	1.76
Hispanic (0)	13	0.09
Cambodian (4)	4	0.03
Chinese, ex. Taiwanese (25)	26	0.17
Filipino (40)	70	0.47

*Notes: † The Census 2010 population figure is used to calculate the percentages in the Hispanic Origin and Race categories. Ancestry percentages are based on the 2006-2010 American Community Survey population (not shown); ‡ Numbers in parentheses indicate the number of people reporting a single ancestry; * Numbers in parentheses indicate the number of persons reporting this race alone, not in combination with any other race; Please refer to the Explanation of Data for more information.*

Indian (58)	73	0.49
Japanese (4)	6	0.04
Korean (9)	18	0.12
Laotian (1)	1	0.01
Pakistani (5)	5	0.03
Taiwanese (1)	1	0.01
Thai (8)	15	0.10
Vietnamese (49)	52	0.35
Hawaii Native/Pacific Islander (6)	36	0.24
Not Hispanic (3)	25	0.17
Hispanic (3)	11	0.07
Guamanian/Chamorro (3)	3	0.02
Native Hawaiian (1)	15	0.10
Samoan (0)	1	0.01
Tongan (1)	3	0.02
White (13,258)	13,614	91.30
Not Hispanic (12,289)	12,545	84.13
Hispanic (969)	1,069	7.17

New Smyrna Beach

Place Type: City
County: Volusia
Population: 22,464†

Ancestry‡	Population	%
American (1,170)	1,170	5.19
Arab (46)	46	0.20
Lebanese (19)	19	0.08
Moroccan (27)	27	0.12
Armenian (0)	26	0.12
Australian (15)	15	0.07
Austrian (10)	10	0.04
Belgian (5)	41	0.18
British (172)	217	0.96
Bulgarian (0)	15	0.07
Canadian (55)	130	0.58
Croatian (17)	76	0.34
Czech (66)	125	0.55
Danish (16)	63	0.28
Dutch (37)	181	0.80
English (1,214)	3,626	16.09
Estonian (10)	10	0.04
European (188)	224	0.99
Finnish (42)	53	0.24
French, ex. Basque (323)	1,110	4.92
French Canadian (204)	290	1.29
German (1,136)	3,787	16.80
Greek (66)	134	0.59
Hungarian (16)	161	0.71
Irish (1,540)	4,474	19.85
Italian (838)	1,842	8.17
Latvian (0)	16	0.07
Lithuanian (27)	98	0.43
Northern European (14)	14	0.06
Norwegian (212)	482	2.14
Pennsylvania German (8)	108	0.48
Polish (414)	1,115	4.95
Portuguese (118)	221	0.98
Romanian (34)	34	0.15
Russian (24)	99	0.44
Scandinavian (29)	181	0.80
Scotch-Irish (285)	667	2.96
Scottish (204)	658	2.92
Serbian (231)	231	1.02
Slavic (0)	25	0.11
Slovak (13)	13	0.06
Slovene (0)	78	0.35
Swedish (106)	469	2.08
Swiss (15)	37	0.16
Ukrainian (13)	13	0.06
Welsh (26)	198	0.88
West Indian, ex. Hispanic (79)	89	0.39
Bahamian (40)	40	0.18
Haitian (15)	15	0.07
Jamaican (24)	24	0.11
West Indian (0)	10	0.04
Yugoslavian (0)	22	0.10

Hispanic Origin	Population	%
Hispanic or Latino (of any race)	632	2.81
Central American, ex. Mexican	39	0.17
Costa Rican	10	0.04
Guatemalan	1	<0.01
Honduran	10	0.04
Nicaraguan	6	0.03
Panamanian	4	0.02
Salvadoran	8	0.04
Cuban	59	0.26
Dominican Republic	6	0.03
Mexican	123	0.55
Puerto Rican	248	1.10
South American	79	0.35
Argentinean	6	0.03
Bolivian	1	<0.01
Chilean	4	0.02
Colombian	37	0.16
Ecuadorian	3	0.01
Peruvian	7	0.03
Uruguayan	3	0.01
Venezuelan	16	0.07
Other South American	2	0.01
Other Hispanic or Latino	78	0.35

Race*	Population	%
African-American/Black (1,324)	1,450	6.45
Not Hispanic (1,307)	1,422	6.33
Hispanic (17)	28	0.12
American Indian/Alaska Native (66)	163	0.73
Not Hispanic (57)	145	0.65
Hispanic (9)	18	0.08
Apache (1)	1	<0.01
Blackfeet (0)	1	<0.01
Canadian/French Am. Ind. (0)	2	0.01
Cherokee (13)	44	0.20
Cheyenne (0)	1	<0.01
Chickasaw (1)	2	0.01
Chippewa (8)	13	0.06
Choctaw (0)	1	<0.01
Cree (0)	2	0.01
Iroquois (0)	2	0.01
Kiowa (1)	1	<0.01
Lumbee (3)	4	0.02
Mexican American Ind. (1)	2	0.01
Navajo (1)	2	0.01
Seminole (1)	2	0.01
Sioux (0)	10	0.04
South American Ind. (0)	1	<0.01
Ute (2)	2	0.01
Asian (251)	330	1.47
Not Hispanic (244)	314	1.40
Hispanic (7)	16	0.07
Bangladeshi (4)	5	0.02
Burmese (2)	2	0.01
Chinese, ex. Taiwanese (42)	50	0.22
Filipino (45)	68	0.30
Hmong (0)	1	<0.01
Indian (60)	71	0.32
Indonesian (0)	2	0.01
Japanese (12)	31	0.14
Korean (13)	18	0.08
Thai (9)	15	0.07
Vietnamese (47)	51	0.23
Hawaii Native/Pacific Islander (1)	9	0.04
Not Hispanic (1)	8	0.04
Hispanic (0)	1	<0.01
Native Hawaiian (0)	1	<0.01
Samoan (1)	5	0.02
White (20,406)	20,689	92.10
Not Hispanic (19,951)	20,195	89.90
Hispanic (455)	494	2.20

Niceville

Place Type: City
County: Okaloosa
Population: 12,749†

Ancestry‡	Population	%
American (1,988)	1,988	15.52
Arab (0)	27	0.21
Moroccan (0)	18	0.14
Other Arab (0)	9	0.07
Austrian (0)	14	0.11
Brazilian (71)	71	0.55
British (57)	94	0.73
Canadian (31)	47	0.37
Czech (40)	52	0.41
Czechoslovakian (19)	19	0.15
Danish (24)	69	0.54
Dutch (80)	362	2.83
English (468)	1,690	13.19
European (227)	236	1.84
French, ex. Basque (137)	529	4.13
French Canadian (153)	336	2.62
German (525)	2,022	15.79
German Russian (37)	37	0.29
Greek (24)	24	0.19
Hungarian (0)	82	0.64
Irish (787)	1,895	14.79
Italian (131)	476	3.72
Lithuanian (0)	12	0.09
Norwegian (37)	108	0.84
Polish (121)	476	3.72
Portuguese (31)	31	0.24
Russian (26)	63	0.49
Scandinavian (0)	18	0.14
Scotch-Irish (55)	277	2.16
Scottish (174)	453	3.54
Serbian (0)	11	0.09
Slovak (0)	11	0.09
Swedish (39)	84	0.66
Turkish (17)	17	0.13
Welsh (20)	111	0.87
West Indian, ex. Hispanic (28)	85	0.66
Haitian (13)	47	0.37
Jamaican (15)	38	0.30
Yugoslavian (0)	9	0.07

Hispanic Origin	Population	%
Hispanic or Latino (of any race)	600	4.71
Central American, ex. Mexican	45	0.35
Guatemalan	4	0.03
Honduran	14	0.11
Nicaraguan	2	0.02
Panamanian	18	0.14
Salvadoran	7	0.05
Cuban	34	0.27
Dominican Republic	13	0.10
Mexican	250	1.96
Puerto Rican	140	1.10
South American	31	0.24
Argentinean	5	0.04
Bolivian	1	0.01
Chilean	2	0.02
Colombian	8	0.06
Ecuadorian	1	0.01
Peruvian	6	0.05
Uruguayan	2	0.02
Venezuelan	6	0.05
Other Hispanic or Latino	87	0.68

Race*	Population	%
African-American/Black (531)	692	5.43
Not Hispanic (519)	656	5.15
Hispanic (12)	36	0.28
American Indian/Alaska Native (77)	212	1.66
Not Hispanic (65)	182	1.43
Hispanic (12)	30	0.24
Alaska Athabascan *(Ala. Nat.)* (0)	1	0.01
Apache (5)	7	0.05
Blackfeet (0)	3	0.02
Canadian/French Am. Ind. (0)	1	0.01
Central American Ind. (2)	3	0.02
Cherokee (22)	59	0.46
Chickasaw (1)	1	0.01
Chippewa (6)	9	0.07
Choctaw (1)	7	0.05

*Notes: † The Census 2010 population figure is used to calculate the percentages in the Hispanic Origin and Race categories. Ancestry percentages are based on the 2006-2010 American Community Survey population (not shown); ‡ Numbers in parentheses indicate the number of people reporting a single ancestry; * Numbers in parentheses indicate the number of persons reporting this race alone, not in combination with any other race; Please refer to the Explanation of Data for more information.*

Creek (10)	18	0.14
Delaware (0)	3	0.02
Iroquois (0)	1	0.01
Mexican American Ind. (2)	6	0.05
Osage (4)	6	0.05
Ottawa (0)	1	0.01
Potawatomi (0)	1	0.01
Pueblo (0)	2	0.02
Puget Sound Salish (1)	1	0.01
Seminole (1)	3	0.02
Shoshone (0)	1	0.01
Sioux (1)	9	0.07
South American Ind. (0)	2	0.02
Asian (406)	647	5.07
Not Hispanic (400)	626	4.91
Hispanic (6)	21	0.16
Cambodian (1)	1	0.01
Chinese, ex. Taiwanese (30)	59	0.46
Filipino (162)	270	2.12
Indian (13)	25	0.20
Indonesian (5)	5	0.04
Japanese (28)	66	0.52
Korean (70)	102	0.80
Laotian (1)	2	0.02
Taiwanese (3)	5	0.04
Thai (48)	72	0.56
Vietnamese (34)	38	0.30
Hawaii Native/Pacific Islander (12)	32	0.25
Not Hispanic (11)	30	0.24
Hispanic (1)	2	0.02
Guamanian/Chamorro (8)	11	0.09
Native Hawaiian (1)	8	0.06
Samoan (0)	4	0.03
White (11,123)	11,574	90.78
Not Hispanic (10,704)	11,090	86.99
Hispanic (419)	484	3.80

North Fort Myers

Place Type: CDP
County: Lee
Population: 39,407†

Ancestry‡	Population	%
African, Sub-Saharan (0)	7	0.02
African (0)	7	0.02
Albanian (10)	10	0.02
American (5,575)	5,575	13.54
Arab (31)	84	0.20
Egyptian (0)	26	0.06
Lebanese (31)	51	0.12
Syrian (0)	7	0.02
Armenian (21)	21	0.05
Assyrian/Chaldean/Syriac (0)	14	0.03
Austrian (84)	267	0.65
Belgian (27)	79	0.19
British (188)	262	0.64
Bulgarian (13)	13	0.03
Canadian (410)	480	1.17
Croatian (20)	65	0.16
Czech (79)	138	0.34
Czechoslovakian (80)	96	0.23
Danish (84)	146	0.35
Dutch (299)	814	1.98
Eastern European (21)	21	0.05
English (2,640)	6,631	16.10
Estonian (53)	53	0.13
European (257)	289	0.70
Finnish (64)	171	0.42
French, ex. Basque (551)	2,142	5.20
French Canadian (344)	475	1.15
German (3,213)	8,935	21.69
Greek (78)	239	0.58
Hungarian (101)	332	0.81
Irish (2,375)	7,054	17.13
Israeli (15)	15	0.04
Italian (1,637)	2,849	6.92
Latvian (18)	18	0.04
Lithuanian (46)	117	0.28
Northern European (69)	69	0.17
Norwegian (328)	581	1.41
Pennsylvania German (66)	80	0.19
Polish (705)	1,566	3.80
Portuguese (54)	65	0.16
Romanian (15)	55	0.13
Russian (82)	252	0.61
Scandinavian (29)	59	0.14
Scotch-Irish (403)	818	1.99
Scottish (564)	1,200	2.91
Serbian (0)	11	0.03
Slavic (0)	36	0.09
Slovak (83)	120	0.29
Slovene (0)	25	0.06
Swedish (219)	621	1.51
Swiss (97)	258	0.63
Turkish (0)	45	0.11
Ukrainian (154)	213	0.52
Welsh (134)	553	1.34
West Indian, ex. Hispanic (125)	214	0.52
British West Indian (99)	123	0.30
Haitian (26)	26	0.06
Jamaican (0)	31	0.08
U.S. Virgin Islander (0)	10	0.02
West Indian (0)	24	0.06
Yugoslavian (18)	38	0.09

Hispanic Origin	Population	%
Hispanic or Latino (of any race)	2,438	6.19
Central American, ex. Mexican	211	0.54
Costa Rican	19	0.05
Guatemalan	62	0.16
Honduran	55	0.14
Nicaraguan	31	0.08
Panamanian	2	0.01
Salvadoran	38	0.10
Other Central American	4	0.01
Cuban	446	1.13
Dominican Republic	56	0.14
Mexican	732	1.86
Puerto Rican	628	1.59
South American	214	0.54
Argentinean	59	0.15
Bolivian	6	0.02
Chilean	3	0.01
Colombian	83	0.21
Ecuadorian	19	0.05
Paraguayan	2	0.01
Peruvian	17	0.04
Uruguayan	1	<0.01
Venezuelan	23	0.06
Other South American	1	<0.01
Other Hispanic or Latino	151	0.38

Race*	Population	%
African-American/Black (574)	703	1.78
Not Hispanic (508)	622	1.58
Hispanic (66)	81	0.21
American Indian/Alaska Native (141)	304	0.77
Not Hispanic (108)	255	0.65
Hispanic (33)	49	0.12
Apache (1)	5	0.01
Blackfeet (2)	9	0.02
Canadian/French Am. Ind. (1)	1	<0.01
Cherokee (18)	74	0.19
Chickasaw (0)	1	<0.01
Chippewa (9)	12	0.03
Choctaw (5)	12	0.03
Comanche (1)	1	<0.01
Creek (3)	6	0.02
Delaware (1)	2	0.01
Houma (1)	1	<0.01
Iroquois (3)	9	0.02
Lumbee (1)	1	<0.01
Mexican American Ind. (13)	13	0.03
Navajo (1)	1	<0.01
Osage (0)	2	0.01
Ottawa (1)	1	<0.01
Seminole (4)	4	0.01
Sioux (4)	6	0.02
South American Ind. (4)	4	0.01
Spanish American Ind. (0)	2	0.01
Asian (254)	326	0.83
Not Hispanic (254)	318	0.81
Hispanic (0)	8	0.02
Bangladeshi (2)	2	0.01
Cambodian (4)	5	0.01
Chinese, ex. Taiwanese (35)	41	0.10
Filipino (64)	81	0.21
Indian (32)	48	0.12
Indonesian (2)	2	0.01
Japanese (11)	19	0.05
Korean (11)	27	0.07
Laotian (55)	56	0.14
Taiwanese (3)	7	0.02
Thai (15)	17	0.04
Vietnamese (1)	9	0.02
Hawaii Native/Pacific Islander (20)	44	0.11
Not Hispanic (18)	28	0.07
Hispanic (2)	16	0.04
Guamanian/Chamorro (5)	7	0.02
Marshallese (6)	6	0.02
Native Hawaiian (2)	5	0.01
Samoan (2)	4	0.01
White (37,319)	37,734	95.75
Not Hispanic (35,742)	36,045	91.47
Hispanic (1,577)	1,689	4.29

North Lauderdale

Place Type: City
County: Broward
Population: 41,023†

Ancestry‡	Population	%
African, Sub-Saharan (258)	359	0.88
African (200)	301	0.74
Cape Verdean (38)	38	0.09
Sudanese (10)	10	0.02
Other Sub-Saharan African (10)	10	0.02
Albanian (6)	6	0.01
American (855)	855	2.09
Arab (32)	41	0.10
Egyptian (0)	9	0.02
Lebanese (32)	32	0.08
Armenian (24)	33	0.08
Assyrian/Chaldean/Syriac (42)	42	0.10
Australian (0)	10	0.02
Austrian (0)	27	0.07
Brazilian (151)	151	0.37
British (27)	27	0.07
Canadian (35)	100	0.24
Croatian (4)	19	0.05
Czech (21)	28	0.07
Czechoslovakian (21)	21	0.05
Danish (30)	43	0.11
Dutch (36)	75	0.18
Eastern European (13)	32	0.08
English (510)	1,036	2.54
European (12)	12	0.03
Finnish (21)	31	0.08
French, ex. Basque (52)	159	0.39
French Canadian (85)	92	0.23
German (361)	995	2.44
Greek (11)	63	0.15
Guyanese (136)	136	0.33
Hungarian (88)	164	0.40
Irish (519)	1,286	3.15
Italian (623)	1,004	2.46
Lithuanian (23)	23	0.06
Norwegian (0)	32	0.08
Polish (203)	462	1.13
Portuguese (33)	88	0.22
Romanian (108)	129	0.32
Russian (267)	433	1.06
Scandinavian (0)	11	0.03
Scotch-Irish (13)	34	0.08
Scottish (56)	93	0.23
Serbian (0)	29	0.07
Slavic (42)	42	0.10
Slovak (0)	17	0.04

*Notes: † The Census 2010 population figure is used to calculate the percentages in the Hispanic Origin and Race categories. Ancestry percentages are based on the 2006-2010 American Community Survey population (not shown); ‡ Numbers in parentheses indicate the number of people reporting a single ancestry; * Numbers in parentheses indicate the number of persons reporting this race alone, not in combination with any other race; Please refer to the Explanation of Data for more information.*

Swedish (6)	28	0.07
Ukrainian (41)	58	0.14
West Indian, ex. Hispanic (13,777)	14,218	34.83
Bahamian (523)	539	1.32
Barbadian (57)	57	0.14
British West Indian (240)	265	0.65
Haitian (7,491)	7,642	18.72
Jamaican (4,532)	4,709	11.54
Trinidadian/Tobagonian (344)	377	0.92
U.S. Virgin Islander (161)	161	0.39
West Indian (429)	468	1.15
Yugoslavian (0)	12	0.03

Hispanic Origin	Population	%
Hispanic or Latino (of any race)	10,578	25.79
Central American, ex. Mexican	2,104	5.13
Costa Rican	38	0.09
Guatemalan	149	0.36
Honduran	560	1.37
Nicaraguan	236	0.58
Panamanian	76	0.19
Salvadoran	1,037	2.53
Other Central American	8	0.02
Cuban	602	1.47
Dominican Republic	660	1.61
Mexican	2,043	4.98
Puerto Rican	1,948	4.75
South American	2,572	6.27
Argentinean	127	0.31
Bolivian	9	0.02
Chilean	38	0.09
Colombian	1,481	3.61
Ecuadorian	219	0.53
Paraguayan	5	0.01
Peruvian	444	1.08
Uruguayan	74	0.18
Venezuelan	158	0.39
Other South American	17	0.04
Other Hispanic or Latino	649	1.58

Race*	Population	%
African-American/Black (21,916)	22,881	55.78
Not Hispanic (21,334)	22,085	53.84
Hispanic (582)	796	1.94
American Indian/Alaska Native (135)	296	0.72
Not Hispanic (72)	179	0.44
Hispanic (63)	117	0.29
Apache (0)	1	<0.01
Blackfeet (1)	2	<0.01
Central American Ind. (10)	26	0.06
Cherokee (6)	32	0.08
Iroquois (3)	12	0.03
Mexican American Ind. (16)	17	0.04
Puget Sound Salish (3)	4	0.01
Sioux (1)	4	0.01
South American Ind. (8)	16	0.04
Spanish American Ind. (3)	4	0.01
Tlingit-Haida *(Alaska Native)* (0)	2	<0.01
Yaqui (0)	1	<0.01
Asian (1,209)	1,571	3.83
Not Hispanic (1,184)	1,502	3.66
Hispanic (25)	69	0.17
Bangladeshi (20)	26	0.06
Cambodian (4)	4	0.01
Chinese, ex. Taiwanese (106)	165	0.40
Filipino (90)	123	0.30
Indian (480)	635	1.55
Japanese (10)	23	0.06
Korean (9)	19	0.05
Laotian (1)	4	0.01
Pakistani (5)	15	0.04
Sri Lankan (2)	2	<0.01
Taiwanese (3)	3	0.01
Thai (21)	22	0.05
Vietnamese (415)	445	1.08
Hawaii Native/Pacific Islander (25)	201	0.49
Not Hispanic (25)	184	0.45
Hispanic (0)	17	0.04
Fijian (2)	2	<0.01
Guamanian/Chamorro (2)	2	<0.01
Native Hawaiian (1)	8	0.02
White (13,576)	14,476	35.29
Not Hispanic (6,603)	7,058	17.20
Hispanic (6,973)	7,418	18.08

North Miami Beach

Place Type: City
County: Miami-Dade
Population: 41,523†

Ancestry‡	Population	%
African, Sub-Saharan (247)	517	1.25
African (141)	333	0.81
Nigerian (29)	29	0.07
Sudanese (77)	77	0.19
Other Sub-Saharan African (0)	78	0.19
American (1,358)	1,358	3.28
Arab (279)	440	1.06
Arab (88)	88	0.21
Egyptian (46)	46	0.11
Lebanese (48)	111	0.27
Moroccan (97)	158	0.38
Syrian (0)	17	0.04
Other Arab (0)	20	0.05
Australian (77)	77	0.19
Austrian (47)	100	0.24
Basque (8)	8	0.02
Belgian (0)	78	0.19
Brazilian (257)	312	0.75
British (5)	50	0.12
Bulgarian (11)	11	0.03
Canadian (0)	9	0.02
Czech (11)	11	0.03
Czechoslovakian (15)	15	0.04
Dutch (24)	108	0.26
Eastern European (55)	55	0.13
English (147)	417	1.01
European (173)	173	0.42
French, ex. Basque (108)	325	0.79
French Canadian (23)	23	0.06
German (194)	712	1.72
Greek (104)	130	0.31
Guyanese (72)	86	0.21
Hungarian (46)	46	0.11
Iranian (35)	52	0.13
Irish (401)	821	1.99
Israeli (154)	154	0.37
Italian (824)	1,181	2.86
Latvian (0)	7	0.02
Lithuanian (35)	35	0.08
Norwegian (57)	57	0.14
Polish (257)	576	1.39
Portuguese (19)	61	0.15
Romanian (62)	85	0.21
Russian (880)	1,367	3.31
Scandinavian (14)	14	0.03
Scotch-Irish (54)	69	0.17
Scottish (14)	94	0.23
Slavic (0)	29	0.07
Slovak (11)	11	0.03
Swedish (72)	72	0.17
Swiss (0)	10	0.02
Turkish (14)	14	0.03
Ukrainian (117)	140	0.34
Welsh (8)	21	0.05
West Indian, ex. Hispanic (11,918)	12,390	29.96
Bahamian (221)	251	0.61
Barbadian (13)	13	0.03
Belizean (35)	125	0.30
British West Indian (23)	23	0.06
Dutch West Indian (33)	57	0.14
Haitian (9,647)	9,807	23.71
Jamaican (1,820)	1,880	4.55
Trinidadian/Tobagonian (106)	167	0.40
West Indian (20)	43	0.10
Other West Indian (0)	24	0.06

Hispanic Origin	Population	%
Hispanic or Latino (of any race)	15,213	36.64
Central American, ex. Mexican	2,569	6.19
Costa Rican	115	0.28
Guatemalan	391	0.94
Honduran	1,088	2.62
Nicaraguan	699	1.68
Panamanian	101	0.24
Salvadoran	167	0.40
Other Central American	8	0.02
Cuban	2,909	7.01
Dominican Republic	1,336	3.22
Mexican	411	0.99
Puerto Rican	1,844	4.44
South American	4,830	11.63
Argentinean	704	1.70
Bolivian	76	0.18
Chilean	160	0.39
Colombian	1,687	4.06
Ecuadorian	278	0.67
Paraguayan	16	0.04
Peruvian	1,325	3.19
Uruguayan	186	0.45
Venezuelan	377	0.91
Other South American	21	0.05
Other Hispanic or Latino	1,314	3.16

Race*	Population	%
African-American/Black (17,177)	18,011	43.38
Not Hispanic (16,251)	16,857	40.60
Hispanic (926)	1,154	2.78
American Indian/Alaska Native (102)	275	0.66
Not Hispanic (58)	165	0.40
Hispanic (44)	110	0.26
Blackfeet (3)	9	0.02
Central American Ind. (3)	4	0.01
Cherokee (7)	20	0.05
Creek (1)	1	<0.01
Delaware (1)	1	<0.01
Iroquois (0)	3	0.01
Mexican American Ind. (7)	9	0.02
Seminole (1)	1	<0.01
Shoshone (1)	1	<0.01
South American Ind. (3)	12	0.03
Spanish American Ind. (0)	1	<0.01
Tlingit-Haida *(Alaska Native)* (0)	8	0.02
Ute (0)	1	<0.01
Yaqui (0)	1	<0.01
Asian (1,416)	1,697	4.09
Not Hispanic (1,373)	1,620	3.90
Hispanic (43)	77	0.19
Bangladeshi (91)	100	0.24
Burmese (10)	13	0.03
Cambodian (2)	2	<0.01
Chinese, ex. Taiwanese (535)	584	1.41
Filipino (315)	360	0.87
Hmong (1)	1	<0.01
Indian (170)	259	0.62
Indonesian (7)	14	0.03
Japanese (32)	41	0.10
Korean (12)	14	0.03
Laotian (4)	7	0.02
Pakistani (50)	65	0.16
Sri Lankan (0)	1	<0.01
Taiwanese (5)	7	0.02
Thai (46)	49	0.12
Vietnamese (54)	67	0.16
Hawaii Native/Pacific Islander (23)	262	0.63
Not Hispanic (16)	244	0.59
Hispanic (7)	18	0.04
Guamanian/Chamorro (6)	6	0.01
Native Hawaiian (3)	6	0.01
Samoan (0)	1	<0.01
White (19,569)	20,476	49.31
Not Hispanic (7,630)	7,937	19.11
Hispanic (11,939)	12,539	30.20

North Miami

Place Type: City
County: Miami-Dade
Population: 58,786†

*Notes: † The Census 2010 population figure is used to calculate the percentages in the Hispanic Origin and Race categories. Ancestry percentages are based on the 2006-2010 American Community Survey population (not shown); ‡ Numbers in parentheses indicate the number of people reporting a single ancestry; * Numbers in parentheses indicate the number of persons reporting this race alone, not in combination with any other race; Please refer to the Explanation of Data for more information.*

Ancestry‡	Population	%
African, Sub-Saharan (516)	761	1.29
African (411)	617	1.05
Ethiopian (14)	14	0.02
Kenyan (35)	35	0.06
Nigerian (56)	95	0.16
American (987)	987	1.68
Arab (47)	108	0.18
Arab (34)	34	0.06
Jordanian (0)	47	0.08
Lebanese (13)	27	0.05
Armenian (22)	22	0.04
Austrian (0)	84	0.14
Belgian (0)	12	0.02
Brazilian (347)	484	0.82
British (9)	49	0.08
Bulgarian (49)	63	0.11
Canadian (13)	87	0.15
Carpatho Rusyn (18)	18	0.03
Croatian (11)	11	0.02
Czech (45)	139	0.24
Danish (14)	58	0.10
Dutch (33)	117	0.20
Eastern European (9)	9	0.02
English (203)	729	1.24
European (178)	272	0.46
Finnish (21)	43	0.07
French, ex. Basque (228)	539	0.92
French Canadian (12)	53	0.09
German (296)	943	1.60
Greek (29)	96	0.16
Guyanese (57)	57	0.10
Hungarian (52)	117	0.20
Irish (351)	898	1.53
Israeli (15)	15	0.03
Italian (489)	1,125	1.91
Lithuanian (26)	39	0.07
Northern European (57)	57	0.10
Norwegian (0)	41	0.07
Polish (149)	344	0.58
Portuguese (39)	79	0.13
Romanian (0)	43	0.07
Russian (112)	370	0.63
Scotch-Irish (125)	160	0.27
Scottish (20)	198	0.34
Slavic (7)	7	0.01
Slovene (0)	28	0.05
Swedish (0)	128	0.22
Swiss (15)	28	0.05
Turkish (14)	48	0.08
Ukrainian (13)	35	0.06
Welsh (0)	22	0.04
West Indian, ex. Hispanic (25,585)	26,808	45.58
Bahamian (506)	512	0.87
Barbadian (0)	44	0.07
British West Indian (56)	88	0.15
Haitian (22,391)	22,944	39.01
Jamaican (2,480)	2,862	4.87
Trinidadian/Tobagonian (76)	76	0.13
U.S. Virgin Islander (23)	55	0.09
West Indian (5)	140	0.24
Other West Indian (48)	87	0.15
Yugoslavian (0)	12	0.02

Hispanic Origin	Population	%
Hispanic or Latino (of any race)	15,959	27.15
Central American, ex. Mexican	3,137	5.34
Costa Rican	99	0.17
Guatemalan	349	0.59
Honduran	1,342	2.28
Nicaraguan	999	1.70
Panamanian	154	0.26
Salvadoran	187	0.32
Other Central American	7	0.01
Cuban	3,762	6.40
Dominican Republic	1,391	2.37
Mexican	441	0.75
Puerto Rican	2,274	3.87
South American	3,560	6.06
Argentinean	627	1.07
Bolivian	48	0.08
Chilean	150	0.26
Colombian	1,363	2.32
Ecuadorian	257	0.44
Paraguayan	15	0.03
Peruvian	565	0.96
Uruguayan	122	0.21
Venezuelan	390	0.66
Other South American	23	0.04
Other Hispanic or Latino	1,394	2.37

Race*	Population	%
African-American/Black (34,634)	35,824	60.94
Not Hispanic (33,243)	34,105	58.02
Hispanic (1,391)	1,719	2.92
American Indian/Alaska Native (212)	457	0.78
Not Hispanic (123)	281	0.48
Hispanic (89)	176	0.30
Alaska Athabascan *(Ala. Nat.)* (2)	3	0.01
Blackfeet (3)	9	0.02
Canadian/French Am. Ind. (0)	6	0.01
Central American Ind. (21)	33	0.06
Cherokee (7)	17	0.03
Chickasaw (0)	1	<0.01
Delaware (0)	1	<0.01
Inupiat *(Alaska Native)* (0)	3	0.01
Iroquois (5)	7	0.01
Mexican American Ind. (4)	6	0.01
Navajo (1)	3	0.01
Ottawa (1)	2	<0.01
Potawatomi (1)	1	<0.01
Pueblo (1)	2	<0.01
Seminole (0)	1	<0.01
Sioux (1)	2	<0.01
South American Ind. (4)	11	0.02
Spanish American Ind. (1)	5	0.01
Tlingit-Haida *(Alaska Native)* (7)	21	0.04
Asian (972)	1,293	2.20
Not Hispanic (950)	1,218	2.07
Hispanic (22)	75	0.13
Bangladeshi (24)	26	0.04
Burmese (1)	1	<0.01
Cambodian (0)	1	<0.01
Chinese, ex. Taiwanese (147)	205	0.35
Filipino (279)	320	0.54
Hmong (1)	1	<0.01
Indian (269)	372	0.63
Indonesian (3)	5	0.01
Japanese (39)	53	0.09
Korean (46)	55	0.09
Laotian (11)	12	0.02
Pakistani (19)	29	0.05
Taiwanese (8)	11	0.02
Thai (21)	29	0.05
Vietnamese (39)	44	0.07
Hawaii Native/Pacific Islander (31)	330	0.56
Not Hispanic (22)	299	0.51
Hispanic (9)	31	0.05
Guamanian/Chamorro (7)	10	0.02
Native Hawaiian (6)	15	0.03
Samoan (0)	1	<0.01
White (19,160)	20,091	34.18
Not Hispanic (7,287)	7,603	12.93
Hispanic (11,873)	12,488	21.24

North Palm Beach

Place Type: Village
County: Palm Beach
Population: 12,015†

Ancestry‡	Population	%
African, Sub-Saharan (52)	52	0.43
Nigerian (42)	42	0.35
South African (10)	10	0.08
American (389)	389	3.20
Arab (0)	10	0.08
Lebanese (0)	10	0.08
Armenian (11)	11	0.09
Australian (0)	29	0.24
Austrian (13)	118	0.97
Belgian (32)	81	0.67
Brazilian (96)	96	0.79
British (16)	43	0.35
Bulgarian (13)	13	0.11
Canadian (64)	74	0.61
Croatian (0)	29	0.24
Czech (15)	92	0.76
Danish (14)	55	0.45
Dutch (114)	254	2.09
English (508)	1,975	16.25
European (84)	84	0.69
Finnish (14)	34	0.28
French, ex. Basque (77)	489	4.02
French Canadian (58)	102	0.84
German (625)	2,644	21.76
Greek (0)	115	0.95
Hungarian (41)	80	0.66
Irish (654)	2,461	20.25
Italian (1,126)	1,854	15.26
Lithuanian (12)	41	0.34
Northern European (12)	12	0.10
Norwegian (45)	81	0.67
Pennsylvania German (0)	7	0.06
Polish (161)	819	6.74
Portuguese (47)	62	0.51
Romanian (0)	34	0.28
Russian (93)	470	3.87
Scotch-Irish (72)	282	2.32
Scottish (41)	308	2.53
Serbian (24)	24	0.20
Slavic (18)	18	0.15
Slovak (0)	46	0.38
Slovene (0)	27	0.22
Swedish (0)	158	1.30
Swiss (0)	76	0.63
Turkish (59)	59	0.49
Ukrainian (20)	39	0.32
Welsh (26)	105	0.86
Yugoslavian (36)	49	0.40

Hispanic Origin	Population	%
Hispanic or Latino (of any race)	826	6.87
Central American, ex. Mexican	55	0.46
Costa Rican	5	0.04
Guatemalan	17	0.14
Honduran	6	0.05
Nicaraguan	9	0.07
Panamanian	11	0.09
Salvadoran	5	0.04
Other Central American	2	0.02
Cuban	222	1.85
Dominican Republic	10	0.08
Mexican	71	0.59
Puerto Rican	179	1.49
South American	215	1.79
Argentinean	19	0.16
Chilean	12	0.10
Colombian	83	0.69
Ecuadorian	35	0.29
Paraguayan	2	0.02
Peruvian	33	0.27
Uruguayan	5	0.04
Venezuelan	26	0.22
Other Hispanic or Latino	74	0.62

Race*	Population	%
African-American/Black (320)	361	3.00
Not Hispanic (303)	336	2.80
Hispanic (17)	25	0.21
American Indian/Alaska Native (10)	30	0.25
Not Hispanic (8)	24	0.20
Hispanic (2)	6	0.05
Apache (0)	1	0.01
Cherokee (2)	4	0.03
Iroquois (2)	2	0.02
Lumbee (1)	1	0.01
Navajo (0)	1	0.01
Osage (0)	1	0.01
Seminole (3)	3	0.02

*Notes: † The Census 2010 population figure is used to calculate the percentages in the Hispanic Origin and Race categories. Ancestry percentages are based on the 2006-2010 American Community Survey population (not shown); ‡ Numbers in parentheses indicate the number of people reporting a single ancestry; * Numbers in parentheses indicate the number of persons reporting this race alone, not in combination with any other race; Please refer to the Explanation of Data for more information.*

Sioux (0)	1	0.01
South American Ind. (0)	2	0.02
Asian (204)	270	2.25
Not Hispanic (201)	266	2.21
Hispanic (3)	4	0.03
Bangladeshi (3)	6	0.05
Burmese (6)	10	0.08
Chinese, ex. Taiwanese (42)	47	0.39
Filipino (30)	43	0.36
Indian (41)	58	0.48
Indonesian (1)	3	0.02
Japanese (11)	15	0.12
Korean (7)	10	0.08
Laotian (6)	6	0.05
Nepalese (6)	6	0.05
Sri Lankan (1)	1	0.01
Taiwanese (2)	5	0.04
Thai (6)	12	0.10
Vietnamese (34)	41	0.34
Hawaii Native/Pacific Islander (1)	4	0.03
Not Hispanic (0)	3	0.02
Hispanic (1)	1	0.01
Guamanian/Chamorro (1)	1	0.01
Native Hawaiian (0)	1	0.01
Samoan (0)	1	0.01
White (11,215)	11,351	94.47
Not Hispanic (10,547)	10,646	88.61
Hispanic (668)	705	5.87

North Port

Place Type: City
County: Sarasota
Population: 57,357†

Ancestry‡	Population	%
African, Sub-Saharan (20)	47	0.09
African (14)	41	0.08
Nigerian (6)	6	0.01
American (3,686)	3,686	7.09
Arab (24)	78	0.15
Arab (24)	24	0.05
Lebanese (0)	38	0.07
Syrian (0)	8	0.02
Other Arab (0)	8	0.02
Armenian (0)	83	0.16
Australian (0)	9	0.02
Austrian (22)	90	0.17
Belgian (10)	28	0.05
Brazilian (10)	10	0.02
British (93)	139	0.27
Bulgarian (7)	14	0.03
Canadian (212)	349	0.67
Carpatho Rusyn (0)	11	0.02
Celtic (0)	47	0.09
Croatian (14)	91	0.18
Czech (54)	192	0.37
Czechoslovakian (8)	46	0.09
Danish (93)	308	0.59
Dutch (265)	966	1.86
Eastern European (14)	14	0.03
English (1,633)	4,954	9.53
European (418)	484	0.93
Finnish (87)	93	0.18
French, ex. Basque (590)	2,524	4.86
French Canadian (405)	724	1.39
German (2,924)	9,911	19.07
Greek (64)	225	0.43
Hungarian (395)	745	1.43
Irish (2,328)	7,949	15.29
Italian (2,163)	4,974	9.57
Lithuanian (32)	188	0.36
Maltese (17)	26	0.05
Northern European (15)	15	0.03
Norwegian (83)	416	0.80
Pennsylvania German (14)	51	0.10
Polish (993)	2,665	5.13
Portuguese (175)	562	1.08
Romanian (39)	65	0.13
Russian (441)	826	1.59
Scandinavian (28)	28	0.05
Scotch-Irish (303)	753	1.45
Scottish (318)	1,119	2.15
Serbian (49)	49	0.09
Slavic (0)	35	0.07
Slovak (90)	225	0.43
Slovene (0)	40	0.08
Swedish (217)	1,042	2.00
Swiss (0)	64	0.12
Ukrainian (732)	905	1.74
Welsh (47)	338	0.65
West Indian, ex. Hispanic (1,238)	1,456	2.80
Barbadian (3)	3	0.01
Belizean (58)	58	0.11
British West Indian (55)	82	0.16
Haitian (648)	701	1.35
Jamaican (393)	519	1.00
West Indian (81)	93	0.18
Yugoslavian (112)	141	0.27

Hispanic Origin	Population	%
Hispanic or Latino (of any race)	5,004	8.72
Central American, ex. Mexican	361	0.63
Costa Rican	31	0.05
Guatemalan	73	0.13
Honduran	103	0.18
Nicaraguan	58	0.10
Panamanian	45	0.08
Salvadoran	43	0.07
Other Central American	8	0.01
Cuban	711	1.24
Dominican Republic	230	0.40
Mexican	944	1.65
Puerto Rican	1,639	2.86
South American	750	1.31
Argentinean	37	0.06
Bolivian	9	0.02
Chilean	32	0.06
Colombian	292	0.51
Ecuadorian	87	0.15
Paraguayan	2	<0.01
Peruvian	183	0.32
Uruguayan	33	0.06
Venezuelan	69	0.12
Other South American	6	0.01
Other Hispanic or Latino	369	0.64

Race*	Population	%
African-American/Black (4,020)	4,657	8.12
Not Hispanic (3,824)	4,340	7.57
Hispanic (196)	317	0.55
American Indian/Alaska Native (152)	417	0.73
Not Hispanic (109)	323	0.56
Hispanic (43)	94	0.16
Apache (2)	9	0.02
Arapaho (0)	4	0.01
Blackfeet (4)	13	0.02
Canadian/French Am. Ind. (0)	1	<0.01
Cherokee (20)	92	0.16
Chickasaw (3)	3	0.01
Chippewa (5)	15	0.03
Choctaw (3)	10	0.02
Comanche (0)	1	<0.01
Creek (2)	2	<0.01
Inupiat *(Alaska Native)* (2)	2	<0.01
Iroquois (7)	16	0.03
Lumbee (5)	6	0.01
Mexican American Ind. (11)	20	0.03
Navajo (2)	4	0.01
Ottawa (3)	4	0.01
Pima (0)	1	<0.01
Seminole (2)	3	0.01
Shoshone (0)	1	<0.01
Sioux (9)	24	0.04
South American Ind. (2)	7	0.01
Spanish American Ind. (0)	1	<0.01
Yup'ik *(Alaska Native)* (0)	3	0.01
Asian (665)	881	1.54
Not Hispanic (648)	829	1.45
Hispanic (17)	52	0.09
Bangladeshi (1)	1	<0.01
Burmese (6)	6	0.01
Cambodian (4)	6	0.01
Chinese, ex. Taiwanese (88)	114	0.20
Filipino (161)	246	0.43
Hmong (8)	8	0.01
Indian (186)	212	0.37
Indonesian (0)	4	0.01
Japanese (17)	42	0.07
Korean (31)	52	0.09
Laotian (3)	7	0.01
Pakistani (16)	16	0.03
Sri Lankan (1)	1	<0.01
Taiwanese (4)	5	0.01
Thai (21)	34	0.06
Vietnamese (98)	107	0.19
Hawaii Native/Pacific Islander (33)	83	0.14
Not Hispanic (23)	68	0.12
Hispanic (10)	15	0.03
Fijian (2)	2	<0.01
Guamanian/Chamorro (4)	7	0.01
Native Hawaiian (16)	32	0.06
White (50,246)	51,332	89.50
Not Hispanic (46,752)	47,546	82.89
Hispanic (3,494)	3,786	6.60

North Weeki Wachee

Place Type: CDP
County: Hernando
Population: 8,524†

Ancestry‡	Population	%
American (702)	702	8.36
Arab (54)	54	0.64
Arab (54)	54	0.64
Austrian (0)	32	0.38
Belgian (21)	34	0.40
British (12)	28	0.33
Canadian (17)	96	1.14
Celtic (18)	18	0.21
Croatian (15)	26	0.31
Czech (15)	92	1.10
Czechoslovakian (0)	14	0.17
Danish (0)	28	0.33
Dutch (14)	93	1.11
English (332)	977	11.63
European (87)	100	1.19
French, ex. Basque (35)	469	5.58
French Canadian (28)	67	0.80
German (534)	1,807	21.52
Greek (14)	104	1.24
Irish (477)	2,036	24.24
Italian (674)	1,029	12.25
Lithuanian (9)	20	0.24
Maltese (13)	13	0.15
Norwegian (19)	54	0.64
Polish (180)	469	5.58
Portuguese (92)	158	1.88
Russian (55)	121	1.44
Scotch-Irish (43)	184	2.19
Scottish (39)	145	1.73
Slavic (0)	15	0.18
Slovak (14)	14	0.17
Slovene (10)	10	0.12
Swedish (28)	145	1.73
Swiss (16)	30	0.36
Ukrainian (14)	28	0.33

Hispanic Origin	Population	%
Hispanic or Latino (of any race)	707	8.29
Central American, ex. Mexican	30	0.35
Guatemalan	8	0.09
Honduran	11	0.13
Nicaraguan	2	0.02
Panamanian	4	0.05
Salvadoran	5	0.06
Cuban	64	0.75
Dominican Republic	18	0.21
Mexican	65	0.76

SECTION TWO

*Notes: † The Census 2010 population figure is used to calculate the percentages in the Hispanic Origin and Race categories. Ancestry percentages are based on the 2006-2010 American Community Survey population (not shown); ‡ Numbers in parentheses indicate the number of people reporting a single ancestry; * Numbers in parentheses indicate the number of persons reporting this race alone, not in combination with any other race; Please refer to the Explanation of Data for more information.*

Puerto Rican	414	4.86
South American	49	0.57
Argentinean	1	0.01
Chilean	1	0.01
Colombian	23	0.27
Ecuadorian	9	0.11
Peruvian	2	0.02
Uruguayan	4	0.05
Venezuelan	9	0.11
Other Hispanic or Latino	67	0.79

Race*	Population	%
African-American/Black (196)	236	2.77
Not Hispanic (177)	204	2.39
Hispanic (19)	32	0.38
American Indian/Alaska Native (25)	64	0.75
Not Hispanic (24)	56	0.66
Hispanic (1)	8	0.09
Blackfeet (1)	8	0.09
Canadian/French Am. Ind. (1)	1	0.01
Cherokee (6)	18	0.21
Chippewa (4)	5	0.06
Cree (0)	1	0.01
Creek (0)	1	0.01
Hopi (0)	1	0.01
Iroquois (0)	1	0.01
Lumbee (3)	3	0.04
Ottawa (1)	2	0.02
Sioux (1)	1	0.01
South American Ind. (0)	1	0.01
Asian (71)	96	1.13
Not Hispanic (69)	93	1.09
Hispanic (2)	3	0.04
Chinese, ex. Taiwanese (14)	16	0.19
Filipino (19)	24	0.28
Hmong (1)	1	0.01
Indian (17)	26	0.31
Indonesian (1)	1	0.01
Japanese (7)	11	0.13
Korean (1)	4	0.05
Taiwanese (2)	2	0.02
Thai (5)	6	0.07
Vietnamese (2)	3	0.04
Hawaii Native/Pacific Islander (2)	9	0.11
Not Hispanic (2)	8	0.09
Hispanic (0)	1	0.01
Native Hawaiian (2)	7	0.08
White (8,018)	8,126	95.33
Not Hispanic (7,458)	7,535	88.40
Hispanic (560)	591	6.93

Northdale

Place Type: CDP
County: Hillsborough
Population: 22,079†

Ancestry‡	Population	%
African, Sub-Saharan (193)	199	0.86
African (52)	58	0.25
Nigerian (141)	141	0.61
American (1,377)	1,377	5.94
Arab (117)	134	0.58
Egyptian (39)	39	0.17
Lebanese (67)	84	0.36
Palestinian (11)	11	0.05
Armenian (8)	8	0.03
Australian (30)	30	0.13
Austrian (17)	29	0.13
Basque (12)	20	0.09
Brazilian (119)	141	0.61
British (50)	117	0.51
Canadian (45)	52	0.22
Croatian (0)	27	0.12
Czech (33)	88	0.38
Danish (20)	20	0.09
Dutch (143)	582	2.51
Eastern European (27)	62	0.27
English (786)	2,796	12.07
European (149)	171	0.74
Finnish (0)	29	0.13
French, ex. Basque (138)	651	2.81
French Canadian (41)	160	0.69
German (925)	3,139	13.55
Greek (30)	44	0.19
Hungarian (67)	109	0.47
Irish (860)	3,273	14.13
Israeli (33)	48	0.21
Italian (730)	1,785	7.71
Lithuanian (13)	107	0.46
Luxemburger (0)	14	0.06
Macedonian (18)	18	0.08
Norwegian (109)	340	1.47
Polish (339)	866	3.74
Portuguese (13)	26	0.11
Romanian (14)	23	0.10
Russian (116)	198	0.85
Scandinavian (31)	179	0.77
Scotch-Irish (188)	423	1.83
Scottish (76)	440	1.90
Serbian (0)	13	0.06
Slovak (31)	68	0.29
Swedish (188)	235	1.01
Swiss (0)	18	0.08
Turkish (258)	258	1.11
Ukrainian (42)	69	0.30
Welsh (7)	150	0.65
West Indian, ex. Hispanic (156)	247	1.07
Bahamian (10)	40	0.17
British West Indian (19)	19	0.08
Haitian (57)	87	0.38
Jamaican (8)	27	0.12
Trinidadian/Tobagonian (31)	43	0.19
West Indian (31)	31	0.13
Yugoslavian (0)	9	0.04

Hispanic Origin	Population	%
Hispanic or Latino (of any race)	5,191	23.51
Central American, ex. Mexican	306	1.39
Costa Rican	34	0.15
Guatemalan	22	0.10
Honduran	68	0.31
Nicaraguan	36	0.16
Panamanian	73	0.33
Salvadoran	73	0.33
Cuban	1,477	6.69
Dominican Republic	252	1.14
Mexican	313	1.42
Puerto Rican	1,461	6.62
South American	909	4.12
Argentinean	19	0.09
Bolivian	5	0.02
Chilean	12	0.05
Colombian	452	2.05
Ecuadorian	94	0.43
Peruvian	178	0.81
Uruguayan	9	0.04
Venezuelan	124	0.56
Other South American	16	0.07
Other Hispanic or Latino	473	2.14

Race*	Population	%
African-American/Black (1,514)	1,776	8.04
Not Hispanic (1,380)	1,569	7.11
Hispanic (134)	207	0.94
American Indian/Alaska Native (47)	159	0.72
Not Hispanic (30)	108	0.49
Hispanic (17)	51	0.23
Alaska Athabascan *(Ala. Nat.)* (0)	1	<0.01
Apache (0)	1	<0.01
Blackfeet (0)	6	0.03
Central American Ind. (1)	1	<0.01
Cherokee (6)	22	0.10
Chippewa (1)	1	<0.01
Choctaw (3)	7	0.03
Delaware (1)	2	0.01
Iroquois (1)	1	<0.01
Lumbee (2)	5	0.02
Mexican American Ind. (3)	3	0.01
Navajo (1)	2	0.01
Osage (1)	6	0.03
Ottawa (0)	1	<0.01
Seminole (1)	3	0.01
Sioux (4)	7	0.03
South American Ind. (4)	8	0.04
Asian (1,029)	1,261	5.71
Not Hispanic (1,006)	1,209	5.48
Hispanic (23)	52	0.24
Cambodian (3)	4	0.02
Chinese, ex. Taiwanese (130)	186	0.84
Filipino (162)	233	1.06
Hmong (11)	11	0.05
Indian (321)	360	1.63
Indonesian (7)	7	0.03
Japanese (9)	46	0.21
Korean (121)	146	0.66
Laotian (4)	5	0.02
Nepalese (3)	3	0.01
Pakistani (2)	2	0.01
Sri Lankan (8)	8	0.04
Taiwanese (9)	14	0.06
Thai (33)	38	0.17
Vietnamese (179)	192	0.87
Hawaii Native/Pacific Islander (10)	45	0.20
Not Hispanic (5)	36	0.16
Hispanic (5)	9	0.04
Guamanian/Chamorro (4)	4	0.02
Native Hawaiian (5)	13	0.06
Samoan (0)	4	0.02
White (18,236)	18,740	84.88
Not Hispanic (13,984)	14,304	64.79
Hispanic (4,252)	4,436	20.09

Oak Ridge

Place Type: CDP
County: Orange
Population: 22,685†

Ancestry‡	Population	%
African, Sub-Saharan (293)	376	1.87
African (283)	366	1.82
Other Sub-Saharan African (10)	10	0.05
American (694)	694	3.46
Arab (176)	248	1.24
Arab (0)	26	0.13
Jordanian (0)	10	0.05
Lebanese (102)	102	0.51
Moroccan (0)	12	0.06
Palestinian (52)	66	0.33
Other Arab (22)	32	0.16
Austrian (0)	9	0.04
Brazilian (115)	115	0.57
British (15)	23	0.11
Bulgarian (0)	33	0.16
Canadian (0)	54	0.27
Czech (6)	6	0.03
Danish (0)	14	0.07
Dutch (11)	11	0.05
English (82)	394	1.96
European (22)	22	0.11
French, ex. Basque (41)	97	0.48
French Canadian (37)	70	0.35
German (87)	504	2.51
Greek (43)	43	0.21
Irish (118)	387	1.93
Italian (64)	201	1.00
Norwegian (0)	11	0.05
Polish (66)	191	0.95
Portuguese (56)	56	0.28
Romanian (71)	71	0.35
Scotch-Irish (7)	15	0.07
Scottish (32)	97	0.48
Slovak (7)	40	0.20
Swedish (0)	8	0.04
Swiss (7)	36	0.18
Turkish (22)	22	0.11
West Indian, ex. Hispanic (3,095)	3,240	16.15
British West Indian (28)	28	0.14
Haitian (2,580)	2,725	13.59

*Notes: † The Census 2010 population figure is used to calculate the percentages in the Hispanic Origin and Race categories. Ancestry percentages are based on the 2006-2010 American Community Survey population (not shown); ‡ Numbers in parentheses indicate the number of people reporting a single ancestry; * Numbers in parentheses indicate the number of persons reporting this race alone, not in combination with any other race; Please refer to the Explanation of Data for more information.*

Jamaican (408)	408	2.03
Trinidadian/Tobagonian (31)	31	0.15
West Indian (48)	48	0.24

Hispanic Origin	Population	%
Hispanic or Latino (of any race)	9,990	44.04
Central American, ex. Mexican	1,026	4.52
Costa Rican	14	0.06
Guatemalan	241	1.06
Honduran	443	1.95
Nicaraguan	78	0.34
Panamanian	41	0.18
Salvadoran	208	0.92
Other Central American	1	<0.01
Cuban	724	3.19
Dominican Republic	960	4.23
Mexican	2,252	9.93
Puerto Rican	3,704	16.33
South American	928	4.09
Argentinean	45	0.20
Bolivian	6	0.03
Chilean	7	0.03
Colombian	402	1.77
Ecuadorian	121	0.53
Peruvian	192	0.85
Uruguayan	42	0.19
Venezuelan	107	0.47
Other South American	6	0.03
Other Hispanic or Latino	396	1.75

Race*	Population	%
African-American/Black (9,072)	9,589	42.27
Not Hispanic (8,373)	8,705	38.37
Hispanic (699)	884	3.90
American Indian/Alaska Native (126)	238	1.05
Not Hispanic (50)	110	0.48
Hispanic (76)	128	0.56
Apache (3)	5	0.02
Blackfeet (3)	15	0.07
Central American Ind. (7)	7	0.03
Cherokee (3)	21	0.09
Chippewa (1)	1	<0.01
Choctaw (0)	1	<0.01
Iroquois (3)	4	0.02
Mexican American Ind. (9)	12	0.05
Seminole (0)	3	0.01
Sioux (0)	2	0.01
South American Ind. (8)	17	0.07
Spanish American Ind. (2)	4	0.02
Asian (986)	1,161	5.12
Not Hispanic (965)	1,107	4.88
Hispanic (21)	54	0.24
Bangladeshi (5)	5	0.02
Burmese (1)	1	<0.01
Cambodian (31)	53	0.23
Chinese, ex. Taiwanese (71)	86	0.38
Filipino (108)	133	0.59
Indian (132)	175	0.77
Indonesian (1)	1	<0.01
Japanese (8)	14	0.06
Korean (6)	14	0.06
Laotian (22)	29	0.13
Malaysian (0)	1	<0.01
Pakistani (9)	9	0.04
Taiwanese (4)	4	0.02
Thai (6)	18	0.08
Vietnamese (546)	578	2.55
Hawaii Native/Pacific Islander (69)	226	1.00
Not Hispanic (69)	190	0.84
Hispanic (0)	36	0.16
Fijian (2)	2	0.01
Guamanian/Chamorro (3)	5	0.02
Native Hawaiian (4)	9	0.04
Samoan (1)	3	0.01
Tongan (8)	11	0.05
White (8,813)	9,475	41.77
Not Hispanic (2,685)	2,874	12.67
Hispanic (6,128)	6,601	29.10

Oakland Park

Place Type: City
County: Broward
Population: 41,363†

Ancestry‡	Population	%
African, Sub-Saharan (167)	181	0.43
African (128)	142	0.34
Nigerian (39)	39	0.09
Alsatian (23)	23	0.06
American (1,823)	1,823	4.37
Arab (158)	226	0.54
Lebanese (71)	139	0.33
Moroccan (11)	11	0.03
Syrian (5)	5	0.01
Other Arab (71)	71	0.17
Armenian (0)	16	0.04
Australian (0)	11	0.03
Austrian (45)	78	0.19
Belgian (15)	32	0.08
Brazilian (508)	695	1.67
British (59)	111	0.27
Bulgarian (46)	46	0.11
Canadian (98)	146	0.35
Celtic (29)	29	0.07
Croatian (0)	16	0.04
Czech (102)	249	0.60
Czechoslovakian (0)	16	0.04
Danish (14)	63	0.15
Dutch (84)	490	1.17
Eastern European (31)	31	0.07
English (1,101)	3,181	7.62
European (159)	174	0.42
Finnish (0)	36	0.09
French, ex. Basque (187)	971	2.33
French Canadian (186)	369	0.88
German (1,242)	4,004	9.59
Greek (58)	121	0.29
Guyanese (0)	14	0.03
Hungarian (129)	260	0.62
Irish (1,580)	5,064	12.13
Israeli (51)	51	0.12
Italian (1,927)	3,646	8.74
Lithuanian (89)	149	0.36
Norwegian (25)	59	0.14
Pennsylvania German (30)	30	0.07
Polish (366)	1,018	2.44
Portuguese (450)	679	1.63
Romanian (112)	182	0.44
Russian (172)	408	0.98
Scandinavian (0)	49	0.12
Scotch-Irish (275)	525	1.26
Scottish (257)	584	1.40
Slovak (34)	61	0.15
Swedish (63)	224	0.54
Swiss (0)	84	0.20
Turkish (26)	50	0.12
Ukrainian (26)	68	0.16
Welsh (20)	177	0.42
West Indian, ex. Hispanic (4,517)	4,977	11.93
Bahamian (290)	290	0.69
Barbadian (24)	24	0.06
Bermudan (0)	34	0.08
Haitian (3,525)	3,572	8.56
Jamaican (542)	760	1.82
Trinidadian/Tobagonian (60)	202	0.48
West Indian (76)	95	0.23
Yugoslavian (28)	28	0.07

Hispanic Origin	Population	%
Hispanic or Latino (of any race)	10,584	25.59
Central American, ex. Mexican	2,915	7.05
Costa Rican	64	0.15
Guatemalan	649	1.57
Honduran	491	1.19
Nicaraguan	169	0.41
Panamanian	62	0.15
Salvadoran	1,460	3.53
Other Central American	20	0.05
Cuban	1,319	3.19
Dominican Republic	354	0.86
Mexican	1,430	3.46
Puerto Rican	1,496	3.62
South American	2,195	5.31
Argentinean	191	0.46
Bolivian	47	0.11
Chilean	94	0.23
Colombian	660	1.60
Ecuadorian	186	0.45
Paraguayan	11	0.03
Peruvian	514	1.24
Uruguayan	218	0.53
Venezuelan	260	0.63
Other South American	14	0.03
Other Hispanic or Latino	875	2.12

Race*	Population	%
African-American/Black (10,608)	11,264	27.23
Not Hispanic (10,306)	10,798	26.11
Hispanic (302)	466	1.13
American Indian/Alaska Native (115)	305	0.74
Not Hispanic (74)	209	0.51
Hispanic (41)	96	0.23
Apache (1)	3	0.01
Blackfeet (0)	11	0.03
Canadian/French Am. Ind. (3)	5	0.01
Central American Ind. (8)	9	0.02
Cherokee (12)	56	0.14
Chickasaw (2)	2	<0.01
Chippewa (2)	2	<0.01
Choctaw (1)	2	<0.01
Cree (0)	2	<0.01
Inupiat *(Alaska Native)* (0)	1	<0.01
Iroquois (3)	9	0.02
Lumbee (1)	1	<0.01
Mexican American Ind. (2)	5	0.01
Navajo (1)	2	<0.01
Osage (1)	1	<0.01
Paiute (0)	1	<0.01
Seminole (7)	11	0.03
Sioux (2)	4	0.01
South American Ind. (5)	20	0.05
Spanish American Ind. (1)	2	<0.01
Tlingit-Haida *(Alaska Native)* (0)	2	<0.01
Asian (815)	1,122	2.71
Not Hispanic (796)	1,043	2.52
Hispanic (19)	79	0.19
Bangladeshi (32)	34	0.08
Burmese (13)	14	0.03
Cambodian (1)	3	0.01
Chinese, ex. Taiwanese (106)	164	0.40
Filipino (106)	163	0.39
Indian (247)	327	0.79
Indonesian (9)	12	0.03
Japanese (40)	69	0.17
Korean (37)	49	0.12
Laotian (11)	13	0.03
Nepalese (2)	3	0.01
Pakistani (27)	28	0.07
Sri Lankan (0)	1	<0.01
Taiwanese (6)	7	0.02
Thai (66)	81	0.20
Vietnamese (69)	85	0.21
Hawaii Native/Pacific Islander (35)	174	0.42
Not Hispanic (29)	137	0.33
Hispanic (6)	37	0.09
Guamanian/Chamorro (5)	11	0.03
Native Hawaiian (3)	18	0.04
Samoan (4)	13	0.03
Tongan (0)	1	<0.01
White (25,906)	26,953	65.16
Not Hispanic (18,650)	19,144	46.28
Hispanic (7,256)	7,809	18.88

Oakleaf Plantation

Place Type: CDP
County: Clay
Population: 20,315†

*Notes: † The Census 2010 population figure is used to calculate the percentages in the Hispanic Origin and Race categories. Ancestry percentages are based on the 2006-2010 American Community Survey population (not shown); ‡ Numbers in parentheses indicate the number of people reporting a single ancestry; * Numbers in parentheses indicate the number of persons reporting this race alone, not in combination with any other race; Please refer to the Explanation of Data for more information.*

Ancestry‡	Population	%
African, Sub-Saharan (197)	197	1.09
African (187)	187	1.04
Nigerian (10)	10	0.06
American (756)	756	4.19
Arab (37)	78	0.43
Arab (28)	60	0.33
Lebanese (9)	18	0.10
Armenian (0)	14	0.08
Austrian (14)	36	0.20
Belgian (0)	27	0.15
Brazilian (10)	10	0.06
British (26)	176	0.98
Canadian (97)	97	0.54
Czech (35)	105	0.58
Danish (40)	90	0.50
Dutch (19)	116	0.64
English (366)	1,468	8.13
European (78)	78	0.43
Finnish (11)	55	0.30
French, ex. Basque (21)	337	1.87
French Canadian (79)	182	1.01
German (651)	2,230	12.36
Greek (37)	104	0.58
Guyanese (0)	9	0.05
Hungarian (21)	148	0.82
Iranian (64)	64	0.35
Irish (649)	2,364	13.10
Italian (468)	1,154	6.39
Lithuanian (29)	90	0.50
Norwegian (78)	87	0.48
Pennsylvania German (0)	17	0.09
Polish (64)	235	1.30
Portuguese (17)	67	0.37
Romanian (44)	44	0.24
Russian (69)	69	0.38
Scandinavian (0)	36	0.20
Scotch-Irish (126)	346	1.92
Scottish (209)	387	2.14
Serbian (0)	33	0.18
Slovak (17)	69	0.38
Swedish (0)	88	0.49
Turkish (0)	8	0.04
Ukrainian (9)	9	0.05
Welsh (45)	104	0.58
West Indian, ex. Hispanic (358)	392	2.17
Belizean (0)	17	0.09
Haitian (105)	122	0.68
Jamaican (234)	234	1.30
Trinidadian/Tobagonian (19)	19	0.11
Yugoslavian (17)	17	0.09

Hispanic Origin	Population	%
Hispanic or Latino (of any race)	2,637	12.98
Central American, ex. Mexican	231	1.14
Costa Rican	19	0.09
Guatemalan	15	0.07
Honduran	31	0.15
Nicaraguan	36	0.18
Panamanian	71	0.35
Salvadoran	59	0.29
Cuban	167	0.82
Dominican Republic	173	0.85
Mexican	448	2.21
Puerto Rican	1,067	5.25
South American	370	1.82
Argentinean	6	0.03
Bolivian	2	0.01
Chilean	5	0.02
Colombian	159	0.78
Ecuadorian	88	0.43
Paraguayan	5	0.02
Peruvian	54	0.27
Venezuelan	50	0.25
Other South American	1	<0.01
Other Hispanic or Latino	181	0.89

Race*	Population	%
African-American/Black (5,136)	5,565	27.39
Not Hispanic (4,937)	5,263	25.91
Hispanic (199)	302	1.49
American Indian/Alaska Native (65)	217	1.07
Not Hispanic (46)	168	0.83
Hispanic (19)	49	0.24
Blackfeet (0)	3	0.01
Central American Ind. (1)	1	<0.01
Cherokee (5)	59	0.29
Chippewa (0)	7	0.03
Choctaw (1)	4	0.02
Comanche (1)	1	<0.01
Cree (3)	3	0.01
Creek (1)	1	<0.01
Iroquois (5)	5	0.02
Lumbee (0)	3	0.01
Navajo (8)	8	0.04
Osage (0)	5	0.02
Ottawa (1)	1	<0.01
Seminole (3)	7	0.03
Sioux (1)	1	<0.01
South American Ind. (1)	6	0.03
Asian (1,600)	1,972	9.71
Not Hispanic (1,557)	1,875	9.23
Hispanic (43)	97	0.48
Bangladeshi (5)	7	0.03
Cambodian (56)	60	0.30
Chinese, ex. Taiwanese (84)	112	0.55
Filipino (1,011)	1,259	6.20
Hmong (1)	2	0.01
Indian (154)	179	0.88
Indonesian (0)	4	0.02
Japanese (34)	86	0.42
Korean (95)	113	0.56
Laotian (4)	8	0.04
Malaysian (1)	1	<0.01
Pakistani (20)	26	0.13
Taiwanese (12)	13	0.06
Thai (7)	12	0.06
Vietnamese (66)	97	0.48
Hawaii Native/Pacific Islander (26)	67	0.33
Not Hispanic (24)	58	0.29
Hispanic (2)	9	0.04
Guamanian/Chamorro (16)	22	0.11
Native Hawaiian (8)	16	0.08
Samoan (0)	1	<0.01
White (11,941)	12,676	62.40
Not Hispanic (10,410)	10,952	53.91
Hispanic (1,531)	1,724	8.49

Ocala

Place Type: City
County: Marion
Population: 56,315†

Ancestry‡	Population	%
African, Sub-Saharan (1,965)	2,248	4.01
African (1,867)	2,150	3.84
Nigerian (15)	15	0.03
South African (49)	49	0.09
Other Sub-Saharan African (34)	34	0.06
Alsatian (0)	10	0.02
American (2,413)	2,413	4.31
Arab (53)	110	0.20
Lebanese (53)	110	0.20
Armenian (49)	63	0.11
Austrian (38)	99	0.18
Basque (9)	9	0.02
Belgian (3)	11	0.02
Brazilian (21)	29	0.05
British (49)	215	0.38
Canadian (125)	177	0.32
Croatian (0)	28	0.05
Czech (40)	201	0.36
Czechoslovakian (106)	194	0.35
Danish (49)	72	0.13
Dutch (221)	865	1.54
Eastern European (0)	17	0.03
English (2,216)	5,293	9.44
Estonian (9)	9	0.02
European (201)	303	0.54
Finnish (29)	112	0.20
French, ex. Basque (518)	1,440	2.57
French Canadian (101)	248	0.44
German (2,889)	7,428	13.25
Greek (20)	86	0.15
Hungarian (47)	191	0.34
Irish (2,416)	6,685	11.93
Italian (1,371)	3,113	5.55
Lithuanian (37)	49	0.09
Macedonian (23)	23	0.04
Norwegian (116)	281	0.50
Pennsylvania German (8)	8	0.01
Polish (334)	944	1.68
Portuguese (34)	140	0.25
Romanian (36)	100	0.18
Russian (126)	323	0.58
Scandinavian (31)	146	0.26
Scotch-Irish (496)	1,146	2.04
Scottish (481)	1,100	1.96
Serbian (0)	18	0.03
Slavic (0)	10	0.02
Slovak (0)	41	0.07
Slovene (13)	13	0.02
Swedish (52)	253	0.45
Swiss (46)	113	0.20
Ukrainian (81)	121	0.22
Welsh (183)	320	0.57
West Indian, ex. Hispanic (415)	679	1.21
Bahamian (10)	72	0.13
Barbadian (17)	17	0.03
Belizean (0)	9	0.02
Haitian (56)	56	0.10
Jamaican (286)	417	0.74
Trinidadian/Tobagonian (6)	15	0.03
U.S. Virgin Islander (6)	6	0.01
West Indian (34)	87	0.16

Hispanic Origin	Population	%
Hispanic or Latino (of any race)	6,586	11.69
Central American, ex. Mexican	509	0.90
Costa Rican	26	0.05
Guatemalan	127	0.23
Honduran	142	0.25
Nicaraguan	79	0.14
Panamanian	71	0.13
Salvadoran	64	0.11
Cuban	578	1.03
Dominican Republic	228	0.40
Mexican	1,294	2.30
Puerto Rican	2,740	4.87
South American	857	1.52
Argentinean	22	0.04
Bolivian	7	0.01
Chilean	14	0.02
Colombian	412	0.73
Ecuadorian	147	0.26
Peruvian	87	0.15
Uruguayan	5	0.01
Venezuelan	154	0.27
Other South American	9	0.02
Other Hispanic or Latino	380	0.67

Race*	Population	%
African-American/Black (11,795)	12,427	22.07
Not Hispanic (11,497)	12,006	21.32
Hispanic (298)	421	0.75
American Indian/Alaska Native (188)	529	0.94
Not Hispanic (117)	370	0.66
Hispanic (71)	159	0.28
Apache (2)	7	0.01
Blackfeet (1)	11	0.02
Central American Ind. (1)	6	0.01
Cherokee (27)	121	0.21
Chippewa (3)	5	0.01
Choctaw (4)	5	0.01
Comanche (1)	1	<0.01
Creek (7)	15	0.03
Crow (0)	1	<0.01
Delaware (4)	4	0.01
Iroquois (3)	12	0.02

*Notes: † The Census 2010 population figure is used to calculate the percentages in the Hispanic Origin and Race categories. Ancestry percentages are based on the 2006-2010 American Community Survey population (not shown); ‡ Numbers in parentheses indicate the number of people reporting a single ancestry; * Numbers in parentheses indicate the number of persons reporting this race alone, not in combination with any other race; Please refer to the Explanation of Data for more information.*

Kiowa (1)	1	<0.01
Lumbee (3)	16	0.03
Menominee (1)	4	0.01
Mexican American Ind. (31)	57	0.10
Seminole (1)	7	0.01
Sioux (1)	6	0.01
South American Ind. (3)	6	0.01
Spanish American Ind. (0)	1	<0.01
Tlingit-Haida *(Alaska Native)* (1)	1	<0.01
Tohono O'Odham (0)	1	<0.01
Asian (1,464)	1,707	3.03
Not Hispanic (1,455)	1,675	2.97
Hispanic (9)	32	0.06
Bangladeshi (19)	19	0.03
Burmese (2)	2	<0.01
Cambodian (5)	9	0.02
Chinese, ex. Taiwanese (210)	266	0.47
Filipino (300)	354	0.63
Indian (593)	657	1.17
Indonesian (1)	11	0.02
Japanese (21)	52	0.09
Korean (69)	85	0.15
Malaysian (3)	3	0.01
Nepalese (1)	1	<0.01
Pakistani (34)	37	0.07
Taiwanese (7)	10	0.02
Thai (25)	32	0.06
Vietnamese (111)	131	0.23
Hawaii Native/Pacific Islander (17)	89	0.16
Not Hispanic (9)	59	0.10
Hispanic (8)	30	0.05
Guamanian/Chamorro (4)	11	0.02
Native Hawaiian (11)	33	0.06
Samoan (0)	4	0.01
White (39,822)	40,987	72.78
Not Hispanic (35,623)	36,401	64.64
Hispanic (4,199)	4,586	8.14

Ocoee

Place Type: City
County: Orange
Population: 35,579†

Ancestry‡	Population	%
African, Sub-Saharan (86)	128	0.37
African (67)	109	0.32
Ethiopian (19)	19	0.06
Albanian (0)	19	0.06
American (2,779)	2,779	8.14
Arab (119)	255	0.75
Arab (12)	47	0.14
Egyptian (19)	57	0.17
Lebanese (36)	44	0.13
Moroccan (35)	35	0.10
Syrian (0)	17	0.05
Other Arab (17)	55	0.16
Armenian (0)	46	0.13
Austrian (0)	20	0.06
Brazilian (89)	89	0.26
British (182)	273	0.80
Bulgarian (17)	17	0.05
Canadian (28)	68	0.20
Croatian (0)	15	0.04
Czech (11)	59	0.17
Czechoslovakian (6)	37	0.11
Danish (45)	102	0.30
Dutch (89)	359	1.05
Eastern European (18)	18	0.05
English (1,025)	3,012	8.82
European (239)	239	0.70
Finnish (45)	103	0.30
French, ex. Basque (228)	936	2.74
French Canadian (37)	81	0.24
German (1,409)	4,039	11.83
Greek (133)	202	0.59
Guyanese (241)	255	0.75
Hungarian (15)	149	0.44
Irish (752)	3,238	9.49
Italian (590)	1,554	4.55
Lithuanian (0)	35	0.10
Macedonian (12)	12	0.04
New Zealander (0)	8	0.02
Northern European (16)	16	0.05
Norwegian (94)	324	0.95
Polish (378)	703	2.06
Portuguese (182)	278	0.81
Romanian (0)	18	0.05
Russian (102)	200	0.59
Scandinavian (17)	17	0.05
Scotch-Irish (361)	692	2.03
Scottish (286)	621	1.82
Serbian (0)	15	0.04
Slavic (3)	24	0.07
Slovak (17)	48	0.14
Swedish (27)	135	0.40
Swiss (11)	143	0.42
Ukrainian (10)	25	0.07
Welsh (37)	136	0.40
West Indian, ex. Hispanic (939)	980	2.87
Bahamian (14)	14	0.04
Barbadian (9)	9	0.03
British West Indian (0)	16	0.05
Dutch West Indian (0)	16	0.05
Haitian (313)	313	0.92
Jamaican (393)	393	1.15
West Indian (210)	219	0.64

Hispanic Origin	Population	%
Hispanic or Latino (of any race)	7,394	20.78
Central American, ex. Mexican	729	2.05
Costa Rican	44	0.12
Guatemalan	487	1.37
Honduran	58	0.16
Nicaraguan	39	0.11
Panamanian	52	0.15
Salvadoran	44	0.12
Other Central American	5	0.01
Cuban	367	1.03
Dominican Republic	256	0.72
Mexican	3,040	8.54
Puerto Rican	2,051	5.76
South American	608	1.71
Argentinean	31	0.09
Bolivian	3	0.01
Chilean	13	0.04
Colombian	290	0.82
Ecuadorian	93	0.26
Paraguayan	5	0.01
Peruvian	57	0.16
Uruguayan	3	0.01
Venezuelan	105	0.30
Other South American	8	0.02
Other Hispanic or Latino	343	0.96

Race*	Population	%
African-American/Black (6,238)	6,702	18.84
Not Hispanic (5,968)	6,325	17.78
Hispanic (270)	377	1.06
American Indian/Alaska Native (141)	310	0.87
Not Hispanic (91)	207	0.58
Hispanic (50)	103	0.29
Apache (2)	3	0.01
Blackfeet (0)	4	0.01
Canadian/French Am. Ind. (2)	2	0.01
Central American Ind. (3)	3	0.01
Cherokee (11)	35	0.10
Chickasaw (0)	1	<0.01
Chippewa (2)	6	0.02
Choctaw (1)	5	0.01
Comanche (1)	1	<0.01
Creek (4)	11	0.03
Iroquois (2)	4	0.01
Lumbee (1)	1	<0.01
Mexican American Ind. (11)	14	0.04
Navajo (0)	1	<0.01
Ottawa (3)	5	0.01
Seminole (5)	9	0.03
Shoshone (0)	1	<0.01
Sioux (1)	1	<0.01
South American Ind. (6)	20	0.06
Spanish American Ind. (3)	4	0.01
Yaqui (1)	3	0.01
Asian (1,972)	2,395	6.73
Not Hispanic (1,945)	2,324	6.53
Hispanic (27)	71	0.20
Bangladeshi (20)	24	0.07
Cambodian (12)	19	0.05
Chinese, ex. Taiwanese (120)	181	0.51
Filipino (211)	274	0.77
Indian (793)	935	2.63
Indonesian (1)	2	0.01
Japanese (29)	61	0.17
Korean (76)	100	0.28
Laotian (16)	23	0.06
Pakistani (30)	34	0.10
Sri Lankan (12)	12	0.03
Taiwanese (6)	9	0.03
Thai (8)	12	0.03
Vietnamese (556)	577	1.62
Hawaii Native/Pacific Islander (27)	158	0.44
Not Hispanic (19)	124	0.35
Hispanic (8)	34	0.10
Guamanian/Chamorro (9)	11	0.03
Marshallese (0)	1	<0.01
Native Hawaiian (4)	18	0.05
Samoan (3)	8	0.02
White (23,752)	24,512	68.89
Not Hispanic (19,086)	19,534	54.90
Hispanic (4,666)	4,978	13.99

Ojus

Place Type: CDP
County: Miami-Dade
Population: 18,036†

Ancestry‡	Population	%
African, Sub-Saharan (24)	36	0.21
African (24)	36	0.21
American (987)	987	5.81
Arab (148)	195	1.15
Arab (0)	15	0.09
Egyptian (71)	71	0.42
Iraqi (28)	35	0.21
Lebanese (39)	49	0.29
Moroccan (10)	10	0.06
Other Arab (0)	15	0.09
Armenian (7)	7	0.04
Austrian (80)	184	1.08
Belgian (10)	10	0.06
Brazilian (360)	413	2.43
British (19)	37	0.22
Canadian (0)	25	0.15
Czech (22)	22	0.13
Czechoslovakian (0)	10	0.06
Danish (5)	15	0.09
Dutch (77)	77	0.45
Eastern European (74)	175	1.03
English (180)	385	2.27
European (232)	244	1.44
French, ex. Basque (63)	146	0.86
German (117)	591	3.48
Greek (153)	153	0.90
Guyanese (17)	17	0.10
Hungarian (123)	191	1.12
Irish (118)	329	1.94
Israeli (337)	447	2.63
Italian (344)	689	4.06
Latvian (0)	8	0.05
Lithuanian (8)	19	0.11
Polish (369)	697	4.10
Portuguese (0)	15	0.09
Romanian (9)	36	0.21
Russian (958)	1,499	8.83
Scotch-Irish (0)	26	0.15
Scottish (0)	32	0.19
Swedish (14)	24	0.14
Swiss (22)	53	0.31
Turkish (44)	71	0.42

*Notes: † The Census 2010 population figure is used to calculate the percentages in the Hispanic Origin and Race categories. Ancestry percentages are based on the 2006-2010 American Community Survey population (not shown); ‡ Numbers in parentheses indicate the number of people reporting a single ancestry; * Numbers in parentheses indicate the number of persons reporting this race alone, not in combination with any other race; Please refer to the Explanation of Data for more information.*

Ukrainian (24)	46	0.27
Welsh (0)	43	0.25
West Indian, ex. Hispanic (673)	834	4.91
Bahamian (13)	13	0.08
British West Indian (0)	13	0.08
Haitian (551)	595	3.50
Jamaican (57)	139	0.82
Trinidadian/Tobagonian (52)	74	0.44

Hispanic Origin	Population	%
Hispanic or Latino (of any race)	7,979	44.24
Central American, ex. Mexican	698	3.87
Costa Rican	53	0.29
Guatemalan	106	0.59
Honduran	200	1.11
Nicaraguan	215	1.19
Panamanian	72	0.40
Salvadoran	47	0.26
Other Central American	5	0.03
Cuban	1,439	7.98
Dominican Republic	476	2.64
Mexican	223	1.24
Puerto Rican	567	3.14
South American	4,059	22.50
Argentinean	720	3.99
Bolivian	71	0.39
Chilean	134	0.74
Colombian	1,415	7.85
Ecuadorian	198	1.10
Paraguayan	9	0.05
Peruvian	897	4.97
Uruguayan	114	0.63
Venezuelan	491	2.72
Other South American	10	0.06
Other Hispanic or Latino	517	2.87

Race*	Population	%
African-American/Black (1,822)	1,995	11.06
Not Hispanic (1,611)	1,709	9.48
Hispanic (211)	286	1.59
American Indian/Alaska Native (23)	70	0.39
Not Hispanic (4)	25	0.14
Hispanic (19)	45	0.25
Canadian/French Am. Ind. (1)	1	0.01
Central American Ind. (9)	10	0.06
Cherokee (0)	4	0.02
Mexican American Ind. (1)	3	0.02
South American Ind. (1)	3	0.02
Spanish American Ind. (1)	2	0.01
Asian (374)	501	2.78
Not Hispanic (364)	464	2.57
Hispanic (10)	37	0.21
Bangladeshi (7)	14	0.08
Cambodian (1)	5	0.03
Chinese, ex. Taiwanese (138)	153	0.85
Filipino (62)	81	0.45
Indian (78)	108	0.60
Indonesian (0)	1	0.01
Japanese (7)	11	0.06
Korean (7)	13	0.07
Laotian (1)	3	0.02
Pakistani (13)	20	0.11
Taiwanese (7)	7	0.04
Thai (14)	17	0.09
Vietnamese (16)	23	0.13
Hawaii Native/Pacific Islander (9)	26	0.14
Not Hispanic (9)	18	0.10
Hispanic (0)	8	0.04
Guamanian/Chamorro (2)	2	0.01
Native Hawaiian (2)	3	0.02
Samoan (0)	1	0.01
White (14,649)	15,067	83.54
Not Hispanic (7,772)	7,945	44.05
Hispanic (6,877)	7,122	39.49

Oldsmar

Place Type: City
County: Pinellas
Population: 13,591†

Ancestry‡	Population	%
African, Sub-Saharan (12)	24	0.18
Nigerian (12)	24	0.18
Albanian (10)	10	0.07
American (779)	779	5.83
Arab (69)	102	0.76
Arab (0)	10	0.07
Egyptian (65)	65	0.49
Syrian (4)	27	0.20
Australian (18)	18	0.13
Belgian (0)	30	0.22
British (48)	106	0.79
Canadian (34)	46	0.34
Croatian (10)	10	0.07
Czech (0)	7	0.05
Danish (0)	6	0.04
Dutch (24)	254	1.90
English (475)	1,466	10.98
European (31)	31	0.23
Finnish (64)	95	0.71
French, ex. Basque (30)	552	4.13
French Canadian (69)	95	0.71
German (779)	2,304	17.25
Greek (292)	350	2.62
Guyanese (17)	34	0.25
Hungarian (121)	129	0.97
Irish (402)	2,018	15.11
Israeli (4)	4	0.03
Italian (543)	1,853	13.87
Lithuanian (6)	6	0.04
Norwegian (38)	138	1.03
Pennsylvania German (15)	15	0.11
Polish (237)	682	5.11
Portuguese (35)	54	0.40
Russian (13)	39	0.29
Scandinavian (28)	64	0.48
Scotch-Irish (143)	285	2.13
Scottish (150)	249	1.86
Slovak (19)	59	0.44
Swedish (85)	286	2.14
Swiss (0)	55	0.41
Welsh (57)	286	2.14
West Indian, ex. Hispanic (74)	130	0.97
Haitian (61)	61	0.46
Jamaican (13)	32	0.24
Trinidadian/Tobagonian (0)	37	0.28

Hispanic Origin	Population	%
Hispanic or Latino (of any race)	1,543	11.35
Central American, ex. Mexican	90	0.66
Costa Rican	5	0.04
Guatemalan	18	0.13
Honduran	32	0.24
Nicaraguan	9	0.07
Panamanian	18	0.13
Salvadoran	8	0.06
Cuban	174	1.28
Dominican Republic	38	0.28
Mexican	219	1.61
Puerto Rican	577	4.25
South American	298	2.19
Argentinean	12	0.09
Bolivian	7	0.05
Chilean	8	0.06
Colombian	117	0.86
Ecuadorian	48	0.35
Paraguayan	1	0.01
Peruvian	62	0.46
Uruguayan	3	0.02
Venezuelan	35	0.26
Other South American	5	0.04
Other Hispanic or Latino	147	1.08

Race*	Population	%
African-American/Black (739)	871	6.41
Not Hispanic (678)	788	5.80
Hispanic (61)	83	0.61
American Indian/Alaska Native (27)	96	0.71
Not Hispanic (24)	86	0.63
Hispanic (3)	10	0.07
Apache (1)	1	0.01
Blackfeet (0)	5	0.04
Cherokee (2)	20	0.15
Chickasaw (1)	1	0.01
Chippewa (2)	2	0.01
Cree (1)	2	0.01
Delaware (1)	3	0.02
Hopi (2)	2	0.01
Iroquois (1)	1	0.01
Lumbee (1)	1	0.01
Navajo (0)	1	0.01
Pima (0)	1	0.01
Sioux (0)	2	0.01
South American Ind. (0)	1	0.01
Asian (800)	899	6.61
Not Hispanic (792)	876	6.45
Hispanic (8)	23	0.17
Cambodian (2)	5	0.04
Chinese, ex. Taiwanese (93)	108	0.79
Filipino (138)	170	1.25
Hmong (21)	21	0.15
Indian (368)	380	2.80
Japanese (15)	35	0.26
Korean (19)	28	0.21
Laotian (15)	19	0.14
Malaysian (1)	2	0.01
Pakistani (25)	27	0.20
Sri Lankan (5)	5	0.04
Taiwanese (3)	4	0.03
Thai (4)	10	0.07
Vietnamese (64)	71	0.52
Hawaii Native/Pacific Islander (11)	20	0.15
Not Hispanic (10)	17	0.13
Hispanic (1)	3	0.02
Guamanian/Chamorro (2)	3	0.02
Native Hawaiian (0)	1	0.01
Samoan (5)	6	0.04
White (11,411)	11,697	86.06
Not Hispanic (10,259)	10,486	77.15
Hispanic (1,152)	1,211	8.91

Olympia Heights

Place Type: CDP
County: Miami-Dade
Population: 13,488†

Ancestry‡	Population	%
American (155)	155	1.34
Arab (14)	78	0.67
Arab (14)	63	0.55
Iraqi (0)	15	0.13
Austrian (8)	14	0.12
Belgian (0)	15	0.13
Canadian (0)	27	0.23
Celtic (10)	10	0.09
Czech (33)	38	0.33
Danish (28)	45	0.39
Dutch (7)	7	0.06
Eastern European (19)	19	0.16
English (89)	155	1.34
French, ex. Basque (0)	49	0.42
French Canadian (10)	10	0.09
German (88)	301	2.60
Guyanese (14)	14	0.12
Hungarian (23)	56	0.48
Irish (92)	203	1.76
Israeli (0)	15	0.13
Italian (76)	174	1.51
Lithuanian (21)	21	0.18
Luxemburger (0)	18	0.16
Polish (66)	162	1.40
Russian (27)	43	0.37
Scotch-Irish (21)	51	0.44
Scottish (0)	12	0.10
Swedish (0)	21	0.18
Swiss (0)	13	0.11
Turkish (38)	38	0.33
Ukrainian (15)	42	0.36
Welsh (0)	15	0.13

*Notes: † The Census 2010 population figure is used to calculate the percentages in the Hispanic Origin and Race categories. Ancestry percentages are based on the 2006-2010 American Community Survey population (not shown); ‡ Numbers in parentheses indicate the number of people reporting a single ancestry; * Numbers in parentheses indicate the number of persons reporting this race alone, not in combination with any other race; Please refer to the Explanation of Data for more information.*

Hispanic Origin	Population	%
Hispanic or Latino (of any race)	11,573	85.80
Central American, ex. Mexican	751	5.57
Costa Rican	27	0.20
Guatemalan	121	0.90
Honduran	138	1.02
Nicaraguan	372	2.76
Panamanian	25	0.19
Salvadoran	68	0.50
Cuban	9,103	67.49
Dominican Republic	106	0.79
Mexican	200	1.48
Puerto Rican	304	2.25
South American	768	5.69
Argentinean	68	0.50
Bolivian	21	0.16
Chilean	49	0.36
Colombian	331	2.45
Ecuadorian	53	0.39
Paraguayan	2	0.01
Peruvian	124	0.92
Uruguayan	14	0.10
Venezuelan	106	0.79
Other Hispanic or Latino	341	2.53

Race*	Population	%
African-American/Black (161)	195	1.45
Not Hispanic (25)	29	0.22
Hispanic (136)	166	1.23
American Indian/Alaska Native (34)	41	0.30
Not Hispanic (6)	8	0.06
Hispanic (28)	33	0.24
Blackfeet (1)	1	0.01
Central American Ind. (4)	4	0.03
Cherokee (3)	4	0.03
Mexican American Ind. (14)	16	0.12
Navajo (1)	1	0.01
Sioux (0)	1	0.01
Asian (87)	111	0.82
Not Hispanic (73)	84	0.62
Hispanic (14)	27	0.20
Burmese (3)	3	0.02
Chinese, ex. Taiwanese (36)	40	0.30
Filipino (6)	14	0.10
Indian (15)	18	0.13
Japanese (4)	4	0.03
Pakistani (15)	15	0.11
Thai (0)	1	0.01
Vietnamese (7)	8	0.06
Hawaii Native/Pacific Islander (11)	13	0.10
Not Hispanic (0)	1	0.01
Hispanic (11)	12	0.09
Guamanian/Chamorro (8)	9	0.07
Native Hawaiian (3)	4	0.03
White (12,838)	12,971	96.17
Not Hispanic (1,781)	1,798	13.33
Hispanic (11,057)	11,173	82.84

Opa-locka

Place Type: City
County: Miami-Dade
Population: 15,219†

Ancestry‡	Population	%
African, Sub-Saharan (174)	213	1.41
African (50)	89	0.59
Nigerian (124)	124	0.82
American (1,119)	1,119	7.40
Basque (35)	35	0.23
Czech (11)	11	0.07
Danish (1)	1	0.01
Dutch (0)	14	0.09
English (0)	14	0.09
European (1)	1	0.01
German (69)	230	1.52
Irish (24)	56	0.37
Italian (0)	12	0.08
Norwegian (0)	1	0.01
Pennsylvania German (17)	17	0.11
Polish (17)	17	0.11
Scotch-Irish (20)	20	0.13
West Indian, ex. Hispanic (1,226)	1,307	8.65
Bahamian (397)	435	2.88
British West Indian (99)	99	0.66
Haitian (533)	547	3.62
Jamaican (173)	202	1.34
Trinidadian/Tobagonian (11)	11	0.07
West Indian (13)	13	0.09

Hispanic Origin	Population	%
Hispanic or Latino (of any race)	5,378	35.34
Central American, ex. Mexican	1,138	7.48
Costa Rican	9	0.06
Guatemalan	98	0.64
Honduran	413	2.71
Nicaraguan	532	3.50
Panamanian	16	0.11
Salvadoran	68	0.45
Other Central American	2	0.01
Cuban	2,248	14.77
Dominican Republic	605	3.98
Mexican	142	0.93
Puerto Rican	613	4.03
South American	267	1.75
Argentinean	29	0.19
Bolivian	2	0.01
Chilean	4	0.03
Colombian	93	0.61
Ecuadorian	48	0.32
Paraguayan	9	0.06
Peruvian	59	0.39
Uruguayan	6	0.04
Venezuelan	15	0.10
Other South American	2	0.01
Other Hispanic or Latino	365	2.40

Race*	Population	%
African-American/Black (10,011)	10,184	66.92
Not Hispanic (9,366)	9,438	62.01
Hispanic (645)	746	4.90
American Indian/Alaska Native (31)	66	0.43
Not Hispanic (21)	42	0.28
Hispanic (10)	24	0.16
Alaska Athabascan *(Ala. Nat.)* (2)	2	0.01
Central American Ind. (1)	2	0.01
Cherokee (4)	12	0.08
Delaware (0)	1	0.01
Mexican American Ind. (1)	1	0.01
Pueblo (0)	1	0.01
South American Ind. (2)	2	0.01
Asian (35)	53	0.35
Not Hispanic (27)	40	0.26
Hispanic (8)	13	0.09
Chinese, ex. Taiwanese (0)	3	0.02
Filipino (5)	5	0.03
Indian (5)	8	0.05
Japanese (0)	2	0.01
Korean (0)	1	0.01
Laotian (8)	9	0.06
Thai (1)	1	0.01
Vietnamese (14)	14	0.09
Hawaii Native/Pacific Islander (31)	54	0.35
Not Hispanic (1)	18	0.12
Hispanic (30)	36	0.24
Guamanian/Chamorro (28)	29	0.19
Native Hawaiian (0)	2	0.01
White (4,220)	4,404	28.94
Not Hispanic (323)	355	2.33
Hispanic (3,897)	4,049	26.60

Orange City

Place Type: City
County: Volusia
Population: 10,599†

Ancestry‡	Population	%
American (756)	756	7.33
Arab (0)	23	0.22
Lebanese (0)	23	0.22
Austrian (0)	11	0.11
British (14)	114	1.11
Canadian (90)	90	0.87
Czech (8)	18	0.17
Danish (14)	25	0.24
Dutch (29)	86	0.83
English (366)	1,238	12.00
European (14)	14	0.14
French, ex. Basque (58)	471	4.57
French Canadian (135)	144	1.40
German (426)	1,792	17.37
Greek (0)	5	0.05
Hungarian (15)	58	0.56
Irish (472)	1,750	16.96
Israeli (33)	33	0.32
Italian (358)	965	9.35
Lithuanian (9)	27	0.26
Norwegian (0)	87	0.84
Pennsylvania German (16)	16	0.16
Polish (176)	348	3.37
Portuguese (0)	58	0.56
Russian (16)	28	0.27
Scandinavian (0)	100	0.97
Scotch-Irish (94)	139	1.35
Scottish (124)	325	3.15
Swedish (44)	163	1.58
Swiss (0)	12	0.12
Welsh (11)	67	0.65
West Indian, ex. Hispanic (37)	102	0.99
Jamaican (35)	100	0.97
Trinidadian/Tobagonian (2)	2	0.02
Yugoslavian (10)	10	0.10

Hispanic Origin	Population	%
Hispanic or Latino (of any race)	1,794	16.93
Central American, ex. Mexican	77	0.73
Costa Rican	6	0.06
Guatemalan	9	0.08
Honduran	14	0.13
Nicaraguan	12	0.11
Panamanian	23	0.22
Salvadoran	13	0.12
Cuban	76	0.72
Dominican Republic	56	0.53
Mexican	135	1.27
Puerto Rican	1,246	11.76
South American	117	1.10
Argentinean	5	0.05
Bolivian	1	0.01
Chilean	11	0.10
Colombian	48	0.45
Ecuadorian	26	0.25
Peruvian	10	0.09
Uruguayan	6	0.06
Venezuelan	10	0.09
Other Hispanic or Latino	87	0.82

Race*	Population	%
African-American/Black (688)	778	7.34
Not Hispanic (609)	669	6.31
Hispanic (79)	109	1.03
American Indian/Alaska Native (41)	106	1.00
Not Hispanic (34)	88	0.83
Hispanic (7)	18	0.17
Blackfeet (1)	2	0.02
Cherokee (8)	31	0.29
Cheyenne (0)	1	0.01
Chickasaw (1)	2	0.02
Chippewa (3)	3	0.03
Choctaw (1)	1	0.01
Creek (1)	1	0.01
Iroquois (6)	6	0.06
Mexican American Ind. (1)	1	0.01
Osage (0)	1	0.01
Sioux (0)	2	0.02
South American Ind. (3)	7	0.07
Asian (157)	200	1.89
Not Hispanic (149)	189	1.78
Hispanic (8)	11	0.10

*Notes: † The Census 2010 population figure is used to calculate the percentages in the Hispanic Origin and Race categories. Ancestry percentages are based on the 2006-2010 American Community Survey population (not shown); ‡ Numbers in parentheses indicate the number of people reporting a single ancestry; * Numbers in parentheses indicate the number of persons reporting this race alone, not in combination with any other race; Please refer to the Explanation of Data for more information.*

Bangladeshi (6)	6	0.06
Burmese (1)	1	0.01
Cambodian (0)	3	0.03
Chinese, ex. Taiwanese (36)	44	0.42
Filipino (36)	52	0.49
Indian (54)	56	0.53
Indonesian (2)	3	0.03
Japanese (4)	5	0.05
Korean (3)	6	0.06
Laotian (2)	5	0.05
Pakistani (3)	6	0.06
Sri Lankan (0)	3	0.03
Thai (2)	3	0.03
Vietnamese (4)	7	0.07
Hawaii Native/Pacific Islander (2)	4	0.04
Not Hispanic (2)	4	0.04
Guamanian/Chamorro (1)	1	0.01
Native Hawaiian (0)	1	0.01
Samoan (1)	2	0.02
White (9,087)	9,312	87.86
Not Hispanic (7,852)	7,993	75.41
Hispanic (1,235)	1,319	12.44

Orange Park

Place Type: Town
County: Clay
Population: 8,412†

Ancestry‡	Population	%
American (637)	637	7.31
Arab (0)	86	0.99
Arab (0)	43	0.49
Syrian (0)	43	0.49
Armenian (0)	45	0.52
British (49)	49	0.56
Bulgarian (18)	57	0.65
Canadian (0)	15	0.17
Czech (0)	56	0.64
Czechoslovakian (15)	15	0.17
Danish (0)	31	0.36
Dutch (46)	173	1.98
English (563)	1,235	14.17
European (65)	65	0.75
Finnish (7)	24	0.28
French, ex. Basque (0)	244	2.80
French Canadian (0)	24	0.28
German (472)	1,264	14.50
Greek (25)	46	0.53
Hungarian (23)	23	0.26
Irish (141)	692	7.94
Italian (212)	335	3.84
Norwegian (30)	30	0.34
Polish (36)	164	1.88
Portuguese (0)	11	0.13
Russian (12)	12	0.14
Scotch-Irish (292)	520	5.97
Scottish (110)	218	2.50
Slovak (0)	25	0.29
Swedish (27)	96	1.10
Swiss (0)	26	0.30
Ukrainian (0)	9	0.10
Welsh (33)	116	1.33
West Indian, ex. Hispanic (186)	186	2.13
British West Indian (28)	28	0.32
Haitian (158)	158	1.81

Hispanic Origin	Population	%
Hispanic or Latino (of any race)	740	8.80
Central American, ex. Mexican	61	0.73
Costa Rican	1	0.01
Guatemalan	12	0.14
Honduran	10	0.12
Nicaraguan	5	0.06
Panamanian	13	0.15
Salvadoran	16	0.19
Other Central American	4	0.05
Cuban	54	0.64
Dominican Republic	35	0.42
Mexican	192	2.28
Puerto Rican	241	2.86
South American	61	0.73
Argentinean	8	0.10
Chilean	6	0.07
Colombian	25	0.30
Ecuadorian	4	0.05
Peruvian	8	0.10
Venezuelan	10	0.12
Other Hispanic or Latino	96	1.14

Race*	Population	%
African-American/Black (1,242)	1,351	16.06
Not Hispanic (1,199)	1,284	15.26
Hispanic (43)	67	0.80
American Indian/Alaska Native (29)	112	1.33
Not Hispanic (26)	97	1.15
Hispanic (3)	15	0.18
Alaska Athabascan *(Ala. Nat.)* (2)	2	0.02
Aleut *(Alaska Native)* (0)	2	0.02
Apache (0)	4	0.05
Cherokee (6)	36	0.43
Chickasaw (0)	3	0.04
Chippewa (0)	1	0.01
Choctaw (1)	3	0.04
Cree (0)	2	0.02
Creek (7)	9	0.11
Crow (0)	4	0.05
Iroquois (2)	2	0.02
Lumbee (0)	1	0.01
Seminole (0)	4	0.05
Sioux (2)	2	0.02
Asian (269)	361	4.29
Not Hispanic (263)	340	4.04
Hispanic (6)	21	0.25
Cambodian (4)	4	0.05
Chinese, ex. Taiwanese (15)	22	0.26
Filipino (141)	207	2.46
Hmong (1)	1	0.01
Indian (20)	23	0.27
Japanese (16)	23	0.27
Korean (10)	19	0.23
Taiwanese (1)	1	0.01
Thai (2)	5	0.06
Vietnamese (40)	40	0.48
Hawaii Native/Pacific Islander (11)	22	0.26
Not Hispanic (5)	14	0.17
Hispanic (6)	8	0.10
Guamanian/Chamorro (7)	9	0.11
Native Hawaiian (4)	6	0.07
Samoan (0)	3	0.04
White (6,383)	6,626	78.77
Not Hispanic (5,968)	6,145	73.05
Hispanic (415)	481	5.72

Orlando

Place Type: City
County: Orange
Population: 238,300†

Ancestry‡	Population	%
African, Sub-Saharan (1,306)	1,863	0.80
African (882)	1,271	0.54
Cape Verdean (10)	23	0.01
Ethiopian (55)	55	0.02
Ghanaian (23)	67	0.03
Kenyan (0)	33	0.01
Liberian (0)	78	0.03
Nigerian (226)	226	0.10
South African (66)	66	0.03
Zimbabwean (7)	7	<0.01
Other Sub-Saharan African (37)	37	0.02
Albanian (87)	87	0.04
American (9,820)	9,820	4.20
Arab (1,509)	1,823	0.78
Arab (94)	120	0.05
Egyptian (50)	72	0.03
Iraqi (10)	10	<0.01
Lebanese (270)	434	0.19
Moroccan (765)	792	0.34
Palestinian (45)	45	0.02
Syrian (60)	107	0.05
Other Arab (215)	243	0.10
Armenian (65)	130	0.06
Assyrian/Chaldean/Syriac (23)	23	0.01
Australian (55)	79	0.03
Austrian (270)	522	0.22
Basque (37)	47	0.02
Belgian (0)	88	0.04
Brazilian (5,174)	5,755	2.46
British (586)	1,113	0.48
Bulgarian (83)	83	0.04
Cajun (30)	129	0.06
Canadian (338)	702	0.30
Celtic (24)	24	0.01
Croatian (57)	147	0.06
Czech (99)	398	0.17
Czechoslovakian (16)	213	0.09
Danish (98)	349	0.15
Dutch (709)	2,146	0.92
Eastern European (161)	189	0.08
English (5,311)	15,676	6.71
Estonian (97)	109	0.05
European (1,342)	1,508	0.65
Finnish (32)	226	0.10
French, ex. Basque (1,077)	4,658	1.99
French Canadian (449)	1,146	0.49
German (6,745)	21,835	9.34
Greek (460)	777	0.33
Guyanese (183)	324	0.14
Hungarian (193)	620	0.27
Icelander (10)	28	0.01
Iranian (92)	189	0.08
Irish (5,995)	19,764	8.46
Israeli (7)	55	0.02
Italian (4,862)	12,187	5.21
Lithuanian (128)	307	0.13
Luxemburger (24)	24	0.01
Maltese (14)	14	0.01
Northern European (84)	84	0.04
Norwegian (587)	1,695	0.73
Pennsylvania German (80)	122	0.05
Polish (1,313)	4,082	1.75
Portuguese (745)	1,169	0.50
Romanian (100)	271	0.12
Russian (554)	1,352	0.58
Scandinavian (148)	215	0.09
Scotch-Irish (1,345)	3,361	1.44
Scottish (1,283)	3,660	1.57
Serbian (10)	36	0.02
Slavic (25)	58	0.02
Slovak (160)	371	0.16
Slovene (11)	11	<0.01
Swedish (611)	2,100	0.90
Swiss (57)	351	0.15
Turkish (279)	321	0.14
Ukrainian (343)	575	0.25
Welsh (273)	1,309	0.56
West Indian, ex. Hispanic (11,214)	12,816	5.48
Bahamian (163)	224	0.10
Barbadian (37)	47	0.02
Belizean (41)	41	0.02
British West Indian (311)	342	0.15
Dutch West Indian (13)	13	0.01
Haitian (6,651)	7,164	3.07
Jamaican (2,337)	3,028	1.30
Trinidadian/Tobagonian (465)	613	0.26
U.S. Virgin Islander (77)	105	0.04
West Indian (1,119)	1,216	0.52
Other West Indian (0)	23	0.01
Yugoslavian (90)	214	0.09

Hispanic Origin	Population	%
Hispanic or Latino (of any race)	60,483	25.38
Central American, ex. Mexican	3,306	1.39
Costa Rican	245	0.10
Guatemalan	597	0.25
Honduran	956	0.40
Nicaraguan	377	0.16
Panamanian	596	0.25

*Notes: † The Census 2010 population figure is used to calculate the percentages in the Hispanic Origin and Race categories. Ancestry percentages are based on the 2006-2010 American Community Survey population (not shown); ‡ Numbers in parentheses indicate the number of people reporting a single ancestry; * Numbers in parentheses indicate the number of persons reporting this race alone, not in combination with any other race; Please refer to the Explanation of Data for more information.*

Salvadoran	521	0.22
Other Central American	14	0.01
Cuban	4,299	1.80
Dominican Republic	4,278	1.80
Mexican	4,262	1.79
Puerto Rican	31,201	13.09
South American	9,977	4.19
Argentinean	421	0.18
Bolivian	108	0.05
Chilean	290	0.12
Colombian	4,688	1.97
Ecuadorian	1,039	0.44
Paraguayan	15	0.01
Peruvian	1,144	0.48
Uruguayan	129	0.05
Venezuelan	2,076	0.87
Other South American	67	0.03
Other Hispanic or Latino	3,160	1.33

Race*	Population	%
African-American/Black (66,876)	70,758	29.69
Not Hispanic (63,584)	66,175	27.77
Hispanic (3,292)	4,583	1.92
American Indian/Alaska Native (902)	2,170	0.91
Not Hispanic (483)	1,354	0.57
Hispanic (419)	816	0.34
Alaska Athabascan *(Ala. Nat.)* (4)	6	<0.01
Aleut *(Alaska Native)* (1)	3	<0.01
Apache (8)	29	0.01
Arapaho (0)	1	<0.01
Blackfeet (5)	37	0.02
Canadian/French Am. Ind. (1)	2	<0.01
Central American Ind. (10)	28	0.01
Cherokee (88)	331	0.14
Cheyenne (0)	1	<0.01
Chickasaw (0)	3	<0.01
Chippewa (17)	23	0.01
Choctaw (13)	30	0.01
Colville (1)	1	<0.01
Comanche (3)	5	<0.01
Cree (0)	3	<0.01
Creek (11)	26	0.01
Crow (0)	1	<0.01
Delaware (3)	8	<0.01
Hopi (1)	2	<0.01
Inupiat *(Alaska Native)* (4)	4	<0.01
Iroquois (5)	19	0.01
Lumbee (10)	12	0.01
Mexican American Ind. (49)	73	0.03
Navajo (9)	11	<0.01
Osage (2)	4	<0.01
Ottawa (2)	3	<0.01
Paiute (0)	1	<0.01
Potawatomi (0)	3	<0.01
Pueblo (3)	6	<0.01
Puget Sound Salish (4)	4	<0.01
Seminole (11)	23	0.01
Shoshone (3)	4	<0.01
Sioux (12)	29	0.01
South American Ind. (57)	166	0.07
Spanish American Ind. (23)	33	0.01
Tlingit-Haida *(Alaska Native)* (3)	10	<0.01
Tohono O'Odham (1)	1	<0.01
Asian (8,944)	10,873	4.56
Not Hispanic (8,756)	10,384	4.36
Hispanic (188)	489	0.21
Bangladeshi (17)	26	0.01
Burmese (39)	44	0.02
Cambodian (43)	55	0.02
Chinese, ex. Taiwanese (1,372)	1,760	0.74
Filipino (1,595)	2,066	0.87
Hmong (8)	8	<0.01
Indian (2,245)	2,588	1.09
Indonesian (38)	49	0.02
Japanese (330)	554	0.23
Korean (718)	905	0.38
Laotian (46)	57	0.02
Malaysian (21)	36	0.02
Nepalese (22)	22	0.01
Pakistani (297)	338	0.14
Sri Lankan (23)	36	0.02
Taiwanese (115)	135	0.06
Thai (124)	201	0.08
Vietnamese (1,567)	1,734	0.73
Hawaii Native/Pacific Islander (183)	715	0.30
Not Hispanic (130)	505	0.21
Hispanic (53)	210	0.09
Guamanian/Chamorro (26)	49	0.02
Marshallese (0)	5	<0.01
Native Hawaiian (65)	161	0.07
Samoan (20)	51	0.02
Tongan (11)	24	0.01
White (137,159)	143,262	60.12
Not Hispanic (98,533)	102,017	42.81
Hispanic (38,626)	41,245	17.31

Ormond Beach

Place Type: City
County: Volusia
Population: 38,137†

Ancestry‡	Population	%
African, Sub-Saharan (40)	57	0.15
African (40)	57	0.15
Albanian (0)	21	0.05
American (3,208)	3,208	8.30
Arab (281)	313	0.81
Arab (48)	48	0.12
Egyptian (159)	159	0.41
Lebanese (38)	70	0.18
Moroccan (22)	22	0.06
Syrian (14)	14	0.04
Armenian (38)	38	0.10
Australian (9)	9	0.02
Austrian (69)	91	0.24
Belgian (11)	61	0.16
Brazilian (12)	30	0.08
British (123)	356	0.92
Canadian (74)	150	0.39
Croatian (16)	30	0.08
Czech (56)	218	0.56
Czechoslovakian (58)	74	0.19
Danish (54)	223	0.58
Dutch (213)	884	2.29
Eastern European (0)	49	0.13
English (2,137)	5,207	13.47
European (303)	325	0.84
Finnish (51)	98	0.25
French, ex. Basque (609)	2,276	5.89
French Canadian (182)	416	1.08
German (2,543)	6,680	17.28
Greek (230)	376	0.97
Hungarian (153)	439	1.14
Icelander (38)	145	0.38
Iranian (130)	154	0.40
Irish (2,553)	6,427	16.63
Israeli (78)	78	0.20
Italian (2,224)	4,459	11.54
Latvian (16)	16	0.04
Lithuanian (55)	93	0.24
Macedonian (9)	9	0.02
Northern European (10)	10	0.03
Norwegian (49)	231	0.60
Pennsylvania German (0)	134	0.35
Polish (583)	1,324	3.43
Portuguese (35)	236	0.61
Romanian (32)	68	0.18
Russian (393)	613	1.59
Scandinavian (0)	32	0.08
Scotch-Irish (259)	962	2.49
Scottish (316)	1,036	2.68
Serbian (13)	43	0.11
Slavic (0)	15	0.04
Slovak (78)	78	0.20
Slovene (12)	26	0.07
Swedish (159)	567	1.47
Swiss (130)	160	0.41
Ukrainian (190)	276	0.71
Welsh (113)	324	0.84
West Indian, ex. Hispanic (54)	67	0.17
Jamaican (27)	40	0.10
West Indian (20)	20	0.05
Other West Indian (7)	7	0.02
Yugoslavian (63)	75	0.19

Hispanic Origin	Population	%
Hispanic or Latino (of any race)	1,579	4.14
Central American, ex. Mexican	106	0.28
Costa Rican	29	0.08
Guatemalan	31	0.08
Honduran	12	0.03
Nicaraguan	12	0.03
Panamanian	5	0.01
Salvadoran	14	0.04
Other Central American	3	0.01
Cuban	172	0.45
Dominican Republic	23	0.06
Mexican	276	0.72
Puerto Rican	481	1.26
South American	355	0.93
Argentinean	44	0.12
Bolivian	16	0.04
Chilean	31	0.08
Colombian	103	0.27
Ecuadorian	61	0.16
Paraguayan	3	0.01
Peruvian	43	0.11
Uruguayan	23	0.06
Venezuelan	29	0.08
Other South American	2	0.01
Other Hispanic or Latino	166	0.44

Race*	Population	%
African-American/Black (1,229)	1,414	3.71
Not Hispanic (1,196)	1,361	3.57
Hispanic (33)	53	0.14
American Indian/Alaska Native (64)	254	0.67
Not Hispanic (56)	225	0.59
Hispanic (8)	29	0.08
Aleut *(Alaska Native)* (1)	1	<0.01
Blackfeet (2)	14	0.04
Canadian/French Am. Ind. (1)	1	<0.01
Central American Ind. (0)	4	0.01
Cherokee (7)	81	0.21
Chickasaw (1)	1	<0.01
Chippewa (3)	10	0.03
Choctaw (2)	3	0.01
Comanche (1)	1	<0.01
Creek (2)	11	0.03
Houma (1)	1	<0.01
Inupiat *(Alaska Native)* (1)	1	<0.01
Iroquois (1)	9	0.02
Kiowa (2)	2	0.01
Lumbee (1)	1	<0.01
Mexican American Ind. (0)	4	0.01
Ottawa (2)	2	0.01
Seminole (0)	5	0.01
Sioux (0)	1	<0.01
Tlingit-Haida *(Alaska Native)* (0)	3	0.01
Asian (864)	1,031	2.70
Not Hispanic (856)	1,012	2.65
Hispanic (8)	19	0.05
Burmese (3)	3	0.01
Cambodian (10)	10	0.03
Chinese, ex. Taiwanese (100)	115	0.30
Filipino (160)	209	0.55
Hmong (1)	2	0.01
Indian (341)	382	1.00
Indonesian (3)	3	0.01
Japanese (23)	46	0.12
Korean (52)	58	0.15
Laotian (2)	2	0.01
Malaysian (1)	3	0.01
Pakistani (42)	54	0.14
Sri Lankan (1)	2	0.01
Taiwanese (3)	3	0.01
Thai (13)	20	0.05
Vietnamese (82)	88	0.23
Hawaii Native/Pacific Islander (13)	36	0.09

*Notes: † The Census 2010 population figure is used to calculate the percentages in the Hispanic Origin and Race categories. Ancestry percentages are based on the 2006-2010 American Community Survey population (not shown); ‡ Numbers in parentheses indicate the number of people reporting a single ancestry; * Numbers in parentheses indicate the number of persons reporting this race alone, not in combination with any other race; Please refer to the Explanation of Data for more information.*

Not Hispanic (13)	30	0.08
Hispanic (0)	6	0.02
Fijian (3)	3	0.01
Guamanian/Chamorro (1)	10	0.03
Native Hawaiian (2)	4	0.01
Samoan (6)	10	0.03
White (35,157)	35,658	93.50
Not Hispanic (33,920)	34,339	90.04
Hispanic (1,237)	1,319	3.46

Oviedo

Place Type: City
County: Seminole
Population: 33,342†

Ancestry‡	Population	%
African, Sub-Saharan (120)	149	0.46
African (114)	143	0.44
Zimbabwean (6)	6	0.02
Albanian (48)	48	0.15
American (1,180)	1,180	3.64
Arab (254)	317	0.98
Arab (140)	149	0.46
Egyptian (34)	34	0.10
Lebanese (37)	91	0.28
Moroccan (30)	30	0.09
Other Arab (13)	13	0.04
Armenian (16)	61	0.19
Austrian (22)	82	0.25
Belgian (0)	19	0.06
Brazilian (0)	12	0.04
British (135)	271	0.84
Cajun (0)	15	0.05
Canadian (43)	75	0.23
Celtic (9)	21	0.06
Czech (25)	121	0.37
Czechoslovakian (0)	9	0.03
Danish (44)	258	0.80
Dutch (74)	474	1.46
Eastern European (11)	22	0.07
English (1,186)	3,576	11.02
Estonian (0)	11	0.03
European (2,057)	2,222	6.85
Finnish (58)	66	0.20
French, ex. Basque (341)	1,298	4.00
French Canadian (72)	216	0.67
German (923)	4,713	14.53
Greek (17)	47	0.14
Guyanese (9)	32	0.10
Hungarian (67)	91	0.28
Iranian (44)	64	0.20
Irish (1,185)	5,104	15.73
Italian (1,275)	3,254	10.03
Lithuanian (30)	103	0.32
Macedonian (12)	12	0.04
Northern European (39)	39	0.12
Norwegian (79)	287	0.88
Polish (403)	1,365	4.21
Portuguese (35)	149	0.46
Romanian (105)	105	0.32
Russian (282)	432	1.33
Scandinavian (15)	56	0.17
Scotch-Irish (232)	687	2.12
Scottish (222)	858	2.64
Serbian (12)	65	0.20
Slavic (0)	19	0.06
Slovak (39)	79	0.24
Slovene (0)	16	0.05
Swedish (27)	305	0.94
Swiss (0)	35	0.11
Turkish (0)	26	0.08
Ukrainian (0)	44	0.14
Welsh (86)	361	1.11
West Indian, ex. Hispanic (383)	509	1.57
Bahamian (61)	122	0.38
British West Indian (8)	8	0.02
Dutch West Indian (0)	5	0.02
Haitian (47)	47	0.14
Jamaican (216)	226	0.70
Trinidadian/Tobagonian (39)	52	0.16
West Indian (12)	49	0.15

Hispanic Origin	Population	%
Hispanic or Latino (of any race)	5,441	16.32
Central American, ex. Mexican	249	0.75
Costa Rican	33	0.10
Guatemalan	37	0.11
Honduran	27	0.08
Nicaraguan	33	0.10
Panamanian	67	0.20
Salvadoran	47	0.14
Other Central American	5	0.01
Cuban	439	1.32
Dominican Republic	243	0.73
Mexican	516	1.55
Puerto Rican	2,668	8.00
South American	1,016	3.05
Argentinean	33	0.10
Bolivian	10	0.03
Chilean	16	0.05
Colombian	474	1.42
Ecuadorian	176	0.53
Peruvian	138	0.41
Uruguayan	12	0.04
Venezuelan	150	0.45
Other South American	7	0.02
Other Hispanic or Latino	310	0.93

Race*	Population	%
African-American/Black (2,873)	3,183	9.55
Not Hispanic (2,695)	2,915	8.74
Hispanic (178)	268	0.80
American Indian/Alaska Native (67)	258	0.77
Not Hispanic (52)	177	0.53
Hispanic (15)	81	0.24
Apache (0)	2	0.01
Blackfeet (1)	6	0.02
Cherokee (12)	65	0.19
Chickasaw (3)	3	0.01
Chippewa (5)	7	0.02
Choctaw (1)	2	0.01
Iroquois (0)	9	0.03
Lumbee (0)	2	0.01
Mexican American Ind. (2)	5	0.01
Potawatomi (3)	3	0.01
Seminole (1)	13	0.04
Sioux (3)	4	0.01
South American Ind. (2)	26	0.08
Tlingit-Haida *(Alaska Native)* (0)	1	<0.01
Tohono O'Odham (1)	2	0.01
Asian (1,261)	1,636	4.91
Not Hispanic (1,241)	1,564	4.69
Hispanic (20)	72	0.22
Bangladeshi (12)	13	0.04
Cambodian (4)	4	0.01
Chinese, ex. Taiwanese (274)	361	1.08
Filipino (194)	290	0.87
Indian (424)	482	1.45
Indonesian (4)	4	0.01
Japanese (36)	93	0.28
Korean (108)	144	0.43
Laotian (1)	1	<0.01
Pakistani (41)	46	0.14
Sri Lankan (6)	7	0.02
Taiwanese (15)	17	0.05
Thai (15)	28	0.08
Vietnamese (78)	94	0.28
Hawaii Native/Pacific Islander (10)	34	0.10
Not Hispanic (9)	26	0.08
Hispanic (1)	8	0.02
Fijian (1)	1	<0.01
Guamanian/Chamorro (2)	4	0.01
Native Hawaiian (2)	10	0.03
Samoan (2)	3	0.01
White (27,293)	28,080	84.22
Not Hispanic (23,178)	23,700	71.08
Hispanic (4,115)	4,380	13.14

Pace

Place Type: CDP
County: Santa Rosa
Population: 20,039†

Ancestry‡	Population	%
African, Sub-Saharan (168)	183	0.94
African (168)	183	0.94
American (2,403)	2,403	12.32
Arab (15)	15	0.08
Arab (15)	15	0.08
Austrian (0)	23	0.12
Brazilian (23)	33	0.17
British (8)	30	0.15
Bulgarian (11)	11	0.06
Cajun (7)	7	0.04
Canadian (18)	34	0.17
Czech (14)	31	0.16
Danish (13)	55	0.28
Dutch (123)	560	2.87
Eastern European (30)	30	0.15
English (983)	2,418	12.40
European (154)	215	1.10
Finnish (11)	11	0.06
French, ex. Basque (67)	627	3.22
French Canadian (44)	97	0.50
German (953)	3,235	16.59
Greek (7)	75	0.38
Hungarian (46)	288	1.48
Iranian (26)	26	0.13
Irish (811)	2,939	15.07
Italian (292)	1,064	5.46
Macedonian (0)	15	0.08
Northern European (14)	14	0.07
Norwegian (8)	84	0.43
Pennsylvania German (20)	20	0.10
Polish (111)	445	2.28
Portuguese (59)	105	0.54
Romanian (0)	34	0.17
Russian (27)	49	0.25
Scandinavian (9)	31	0.16
Scotch-Irish (473)	858	4.40
Scottish (174)	640	3.28
Slovak (10)	42	0.22
Swedish (38)	111	0.57
Swiss (29)	48	0.25
Ukrainian (54)	65	0.33
Welsh (15)	150	0.77
West Indian, ex. Hispanic (168)	429	2.20
Dutch West Indian (43)	235	1.21
Haitian (23)	38	0.19
Jamaican (19)	34	0.17
West Indian (40)	40	0.21
Other West Indian (43)	82	0.42

Hispanic Origin	Population	%
Hispanic or Latino (of any race)	727	3.63
Central American, ex. Mexican	46	0.23
Costa Rican	4	0.02
Guatemalan	4	0.02
Honduran	15	0.07
Nicaraguan	3	0.01
Panamanian	14	0.07
Salvadoran	6	0.03
Cuban	62	0.31
Dominican Republic	14	0.07
Mexican	332	1.66
Puerto Rican	128	0.64
South American	48	0.24
Argentinean	2	0.01
Chilean	2	0.01
Colombian	13	0.06
Ecuadorian	19	0.09
Peruvian	5	0.02
Venezuelan	7	0.03
Other Hispanic or Latino	97	0.48

Race*	Population	%
African-American/Black (378)	528	2.63

*Notes: † The Census 2010 population figure is used to calculate the percentages in the Hispanic Origin and Race categories. Ancestry percentages are based on the 2006-2010 American Community Survey population (not shown); ‡ Numbers in parentheses indicate the number of people reporting a single ancestry; * Numbers in parentheses indicate the number of persons reporting this race alone, not in combination with any other race; Please refer to the Explanation of Data for more information.*

Not Hispanic (356)	498	2.49
Hispanic (22)	30	0.15
American Indian/Alaska Native (195)	400	2.00
Not Hispanic (186)	377	1.88
Hispanic (9)	23	0.11
Alaska Athabascan *(Ala. Nat.)* (1)	1	<0.01
Apache (0)	1	<0.01
Blackfeet (3)	13	0.06
Cherokee (34)	110	0.55
Chickasaw (2)	2	0.01
Chippewa (0)	1	<0.01
Choctaw (3)	14	0.07
Comanche (2)	2	0.01
Creek (57)	109	0.54
Houma (1)	3	0.01
Iroquois (1)	3	0.01
Lumbee (0)	1	<0.01
Menominee (1)	1	<0.01
Mexican American Ind. (1)	6	0.03
Navajo (2)	2	0.01
Paiute (2)	2	0.01
Potawatomi (0)	1	<0.01
Seminole (3)	11	0.05
Sioux (4)	4	0.02
Asian (292)	447	2.23
Not Hispanic (288)	431	2.15
Hispanic (4)	16	0.08
Chinese, ex. Taiwanese (27)	40	0.20
Filipino (127)	209	1.04
Indian (13)	26	0.13
Indonesian (6)	9	0.04
Japanese (24)	34	0.17
Korean (28)	55	0.27
Malaysian (0)	1	<0.01
Pakistani (6)	6	0.03
Sri Lankan (4)	4	0.02
Taiwanese (2)	2	0.01
Thai (9)	12	0.06
Vietnamese (38)	51	0.25
Hawaii Native/Pacific Islander (26)	63	0.31
Not Hispanic (24)	57	0.28
Hispanic (2)	6	0.03
Guamanian/Chamorro (6)	20	0.10
Marshallese (1)	1	<0.01
Native Hawaiian (5)	14	0.07
Samoan (8)	10	0.05
White (18,457)	18,971	94.67
Not Hispanic (17,966)	18,424	91.94
Hispanic (491)	547	2.73

Palatka

Place Type: City
County: Putnam
Population: 10,558†

Ancestry‡	Population	%
African, Sub-Saharan (253)	312	2.93
African (253)	312	2.93
American (1,262)	1,262	11.83
British (8)	22	0.21
Canadian (33)	33	0.31
Czech (0)	9	0.08
Danish (0)	52	0.49
Dutch (6)	41	0.38
English (377)	660	6.19
European (10)	10	0.09
Finnish (0)	41	0.38
French, ex. Basque (43)	145	1.36
French Canadian (83)	118	1.11
German (328)	678	6.36
Greek (0)	20	0.19
Hungarian (0)	11	0.10
Irish (177)	538	5.05
Italian (83)	219	2.05
Lithuanian (47)	47	0.44
Northern European (0)	14	0.13
Norwegian (0)	9	0.08
Scotch-Irish (34)	153	1.43
Scottish (70)	115	1.08
Swedish (20)	145	1.36
Swiss (14)	14	0.13
Welsh (10)	42	0.39
West Indian, ex. Hispanic (93)	121	1.13
Haitian (67)	67	0.63
Jamaican (15)	43	0.40
U.S. Virgin Islander (11)	11	0.10

Hispanic Origin	Population	%
Hispanic or Latino (of any race)	483	4.57
Central American, ex. Mexican	6	0.06
Guatemalan	4	0.04
Nicaraguan	1	0.01
Panamanian	1	0.01
Cuban	36	0.34
Dominican Republic	6	0.06
Mexican	114	1.08
Puerto Rican	274	2.60
South American	9	0.09
Bolivian	1	0.01
Colombian	2	0.02
Peruvian	6	0.06
Other Hispanic or Latino	38	0.36

Race*	Population	%
African-American/Black (5,255)	5,374	50.90
Not Hispanic (5,200)	5,302	50.22
Hispanic (55)	72	0.68
American Indian/Alaska Native (32)	65	0.62
Not Hispanic (30)	61	0.58
Hispanic (2)	4	0.04
Blackfeet (2)	5	0.05
Cherokee (5)	22	0.21
Chippewa (1)	1	0.01
Creek (1)	3	0.03
Iroquois (2)	2	0.02
Lumbee (1)	1	0.01
Seminole (0)	3	0.03
Sioux (1)	1	0.01
Asian (60)	81	0.77
Not Hispanic (60)	80	0.76
Hispanic (0)	1	0.01
Bangladeshi (2)	3	0.03
Chinese, ex. Taiwanese (18)	19	0.18
Filipino (7)	16	0.15
Indian (18)	19	0.18
Japanese (1)	1	0.01
Korean (2)	3	0.03
Pakistani (1)	1	0.01
Thai (0)	1	0.01
Vietnamese (7)	7	0.07
Hawaii Native/Pacific Islander (2)	14	0.13
Not Hispanic (2)	12	0.11
Hispanic (0)	2	0.02
Guamanian/Chamorro (2)	2	0.02
Native Hawaiian (0)	7	0.07
White (4,884)	5,029	47.63
Not Hispanic (4,622)	4,752	45.01
Hispanic (262)	277	2.62

Palm Bay

Place Type: City
County: Brevard
Population: 103,190†

Ancestry‡	Population	%
African, Sub-Saharan (579)	990	0.98
African (508)	836	0.83
Cape Verdean (0)	26	0.03
Liberian (36)	36	0.04
Sudanese (10)	10	0.01
Other Sub-Saharan African (25)	82	0.08
Albanian (27)	27	0.03
American (8,953)	8,953	8.90
Arab (286)	436	0.43
Arab (47)	47	0.05
Jordanian (11)	11	0.01
Lebanese (137)	196	0.19
Moroccan (0)	51	0.05
Syrian (0)	40	0.04
Other Arab (91)	91	0.09
Armenian (17)	33	0.03
Australian (15)	15	0.01
Austrian (45)	183	0.18
Belgian (29)	59	0.06
Brazilian (67)	92	0.09
British (365)	674	0.67
Cajun (0)	13	0.01
Canadian (161)	248	0.25
Croatian (19)	81	0.08
Czech (113)	284	0.28
Czechoslovakian (32)	85	0.08
Danish (27)	277	0.28
Dutch (240)	1,389	1.38
Eastern European (10)	62	0.06
English (3,386)	9,448	9.39
Estonian (16)	16	0.02
European (535)	625	0.62
Finnish (104)	287	0.29
French, ex. Basque (765)	3,795	3.77
French Canadian (616)	1,152	1.14
German (4,423)	15,206	15.11
German Russian (0)	12	0.01
Greek (181)	308	0.31
Guyanese (185)	244	0.24
Hungarian (253)	602	0.60
Icelander (12)	12	0.01
Iranian (46)	46	0.05
Irish (4,482)	14,026	13.94
Italian (3,938)	8,834	8.78
Latvian (0)	8	0.01
Lithuanian (102)	263	0.26
Maltese (15)	24	0.02
New Zealander (0)	14	0.01
Norwegian (286)	752	0.75
Pennsylvania German (13)	32	0.03
Polish (1,153)	3,281	3.26
Portuguese (121)	645	0.64
Romanian (192)	237	0.24
Russian (243)	763	0.76
Scandinavian (25)	38	0.04
Scotch-Irish (555)	1,584	1.57
Scottish (630)	1,722	1.71
Serbian (49)	49	0.05
Slavic (24)	24	0.02
Slovak (28)	149	0.15
Swedish (198)	964	0.96
Swiss (25)	94	0.09
Turkish (20)	36	0.04
Ukrainian (68)	169	0.17
Welsh (142)	644	0.64
West Indian, ex. Hispanic (7,112)	7,918	7.87
Bahamian (19)	19	0.02
Barbadian (150)	166	0.16
Belizean (37)	37	0.04
British West Indian (97)	97	0.10
Dutch West Indian (15)	33	0.03
Haitian (2,612)	2,670	2.65
Jamaican (3,582)	3,984	3.96
Trinidadian/Tobagonian (249)	475	0.47
West Indian (351)	437	0.43
Yugoslavian (0)	17	0.02

Hispanic Origin	Population	%
Hispanic or Latino (of any race)	14,572	14.12
Central American, ex. Mexican	1,080	1.05
Costa Rican	87	0.08
Guatemalan	132	0.13
Honduran	246	0.24
Nicaraguan	140	0.14
Panamanian	237	0.23
Salvadoran	233	0.23
Other Central American	5	<0.01
Cuban	1,373	1.33
Dominican Republic	896	0.87
Mexican	1,369	1.33
Puerto Rican	7,463	7.23
South American	1,439	1.39
Argentinean	52	0.05

*Notes: † The Census 2010 population figure is used to calculate the percentages in the Hispanic Origin and Race categories. Ancestry percentages are based on the 2006-2010 American Community Survey population (not shown); ‡ Numbers in parentheses indicate the number of people reporting a single ancestry; * Numbers in parentheses indicate the number of persons reporting this race alone, not in combination with any other race; Please refer to the Explanation of Data for more information.*

Bolivian	31	0.03
Chilean	38	0.04
Colombian	697	0.68
Ecuadorian	246	0.24
Paraguayan	14	0.01
Peruvian	210	0.20
Uruguayan	17	0.02
Venezuelan	105	0.10
Other South American	29	0.03
Other Hispanic or Latino	952	0.92

Race*	Population	%
African-American/Black (18,475)	20,429	19.80
Not Hispanic (17,590)	19,087	18.50
Hispanic (885)	1,342	1.30
American Indian/Alaska Native (474)	1,151	1.12
Not Hispanic (349)	858	0.83
Hispanic (125)	293	0.28
Alaska Athabascan *(Ala. Nat.)* (4)	4	<0.01
Aleut *(Alaska Native)* (2)	2	<0.01
Apache (6)	13	0.01
Arapaho (1)	2	<0.01
Blackfeet (10)	37	0.04
Canadian/French Am. Ind. (9)	18	0.02
Central American Ind. (9)	11	0.01
Cherokee (68)	229	0.22
Cheyenne (1)	6	0.01
Chickasaw (0)	11	0.01
Chippewa (15)	16	0.02
Choctaw (4)	15	0.01
Comanche (3)	6	0.01
Cree (0)	3	<0.01
Creek (9)	16	0.02
Hopi (0)	3	<0.01
Inupiat *(Alaska Native)* (4)	4	<0.01
Iroquois (8)	20	0.02
Kiowa (2)	2	<0.01
Lumbee (3)	4	<0.01
Menominee (1)	1	<0.01
Mexican American Ind. (12)	24	0.02
Navajo (9)	13	0.01
Osage (0)	1	<0.01
Potawatomi (4)	6	0.01
Pueblo (2)	5	<0.01
Seminole (7)	23	0.02
Shoshone (0)	1	<0.01
Sioux (6)	28	0.03
South American Ind. (11)	44	0.04
Spanish American Ind. (2)	3	<0.01
Tlingit-Haida *(Alaska Native)* (1)	1	<0.01
Yakama (0)	1	<0.01
Yaqui (0)	1	<0.01
Yuman (0)	1	<0.01
Yup'ik *(Alaska Native)* (3)	3	<0.01
Asian (1,848)	2,833	2.75
Not Hispanic (1,789)	2,617	2.54
Hispanic (59)	216	0.21
Bangladeshi (1)	5	<0.01
Burmese (2)	2	<0.01
Cambodian (25)	36	0.03
Chinese, ex. Taiwanese (199)	356	0.34
Filipino (515)	837	0.81
Hmong (1)	3	<0.01
Indian (369)	521	0.50
Indonesian (10)	22	0.02
Japanese (69)	195	0.19
Korean (151)	235	0.23
Laotian (9)	16	0.02
Malaysian (1)	4	<0.01
Pakistani (28)	31	0.03
Taiwanese (12)	17	0.02
Thai (87)	121	0.12
Vietnamese (294)	355	0.34
Hawaii Native/Pacific Islander (59)	262	0.25
Not Hispanic (50)	204	0.20
Hispanic (9)	58	0.06
Fijian (1)	2	<0.01
Guamanian/Chamorro (17)	29	0.03
Native Hawaiian (12)	48	0.05
Samoan (9)	18	0.02
Tongan (1)	3	<0.01
White (75,265)	78,274	75.85
Not Hispanic (65,967)	68,060	65.96
Hispanic (9,298)	10,214	9.90

Palm Beach Gardens

Place Type: City
County: Palm Beach
Population: 48,452†

Ancestry‡	Population	%
African, Sub-Saharan (218)	292	0.63
African (204)	255	0.55
Ethiopian (0)	23	0.05
South African (14)	14	0.03
Albanian (11)	11	0.02
American (2,867)	2,867	6.14
Arab (470)	618	1.32
Arab (66)	66	0.14
Egyptian (15)	37	0.08
Jordanian (118)	118	0.25
Lebanese (209)	335	0.72
Moroccan (37)	37	0.08
Syrian (14)	14	0.03
Other Arab (11)	11	0.02
Armenian (20)	31	0.07
Australian (15)	15	0.03
Austrian (107)	440	0.94
Belgian (11)	59	0.13
Brazilian (217)	243	0.52
British (52)	214	0.46
Canadian (140)	182	0.39
Croatian (0)	35	0.07
Czech (103)	266	0.57
Czechoslovakian (63)	92	0.20
Danish (37)	162	0.35
Dutch (187)	612	1.31
Eastern European (181)	181	0.39
English (1,590)	5,683	12.17
European (483)	528	1.13
Finnish (80)	146	0.31
French, ex. Basque (449)	1,656	3.55
French Canadian (227)	489	1.05
German (1,754)	7,148	15.30
Greek (280)	730	1.56
Hungarian (180)	512	1.10
Iranian (20)	66	0.14
Irish (2,193)	7,185	15.38
Israeli (145)	199	0.43
Italian (2,814)	5,780	12.37
Latvian (19)	19	0.04
Lithuanian (135)	246	0.53
Luxemburger (0)	29	0.06
Norwegian (136)	244	0.52
Pennsylvania German (13)	13	0.03
Polish (1,140)	2,614	5.60
Portuguese (143)	199	0.43
Romanian (142)	217	0.46
Russian (1,397)	2,484	5.32
Scandinavian (44)	112	0.24
Scotch-Irish (314)	895	1.92
Scottish (292)	1,132	2.42
Serbian (5)	5	0.01
Slavic (8)	70	0.15
Slovak (81)	117	0.25
Slovene (15)	15	0.03
Swedish (164)	611	1.31
Swiss (24)	72	0.15
Turkish (24)	39	0.08
Ukrainian (307)	383	0.82
Welsh (119)	532	1.14
West Indian, ex. Hispanic (1,045)	1,269	2.72
Bahamian (140)	163	0.35
Belizean (13)	28	0.06
Haitian (468)	654	1.40
Jamaican (405)	405	0.87
West Indian (19)	19	0.04
Yugoslavian (82)	158	0.34

Hispanic Origin	Population	%
Hispanic or Latino (of any race)	4,314	8.90
Central American, ex. Mexican	383	0.79
Costa Rican	33	0.07
Guatemalan	173	0.36
Honduran	72	0.15
Nicaraguan	47	0.10
Panamanian	27	0.06
Salvadoran	31	0.06
Cuban	795	1.64
Dominican Republic	97	0.20
Mexican	441	0.91
Puerto Rican	761	1.57
South American	1,475	3.04
Argentinean	155	0.32
Bolivian	18	0.04
Chilean	77	0.16
Colombian	607	1.25
Ecuadorian	161	0.33
Paraguayan	5	0.01
Peruvian	253	0.52
Uruguayan	38	0.08
Venezuelan	146	0.30
Other South American	15	0.03
Other Hispanic or Latino	362	0.75

Race*	Population	%
African-American/Black (2,133)	2,457	5.07
Not Hispanic (2,050)	2,318	4.78
Hispanic (83)	139	0.29
American Indian/Alaska Native (79)	236	0.49
Not Hispanic (58)	169	0.35
Hispanic (21)	67	0.14
Apache (0)	4	0.01
Blackfeet (0)	1	<0.01
Central American Ind. (1)	2	<0.01
Cherokee (6)	27	0.06
Cheyenne (0)	1	<0.01
Chickasaw (0)	1	<0.01
Chippewa (2)	7	0.01
Choctaw (0)	7	0.01
Comanche (2)	4	0.01
Cree (1)	4	0.01
Creek (3)	6	0.01
Delaware (3)	3	0.01
Inupiat *(Alaska Native)* (1)	1	<0.01
Iroquois (2)	8	0.02
Lumbee (3)	3	0.01
Mexican American Ind. (8)	14	0.03
Pima (0)	1	<0.01
Potawatomi (0)	4	0.01
Seminole (2)	2	<0.01
Sioux (1)	3	0.01
South American Ind. (3)	6	0.01
Spanish American Ind. (0)	1	<0.01
Asian (1,506)	1,788	3.69
Not Hispanic (1,481)	1,723	3.56
Hispanic (25)	65	0.13
Bangladeshi (45)	48	0.10
Burmese (11)	11	0.02
Cambodian (4)	6	0.01
Chinese, ex. Taiwanese (316)	390	0.80
Filipino (147)	219	0.45
Indian (465)	531	1.10
Indonesian (8)	14	0.03
Japanese (37)	53	0.11
Korean (105)	136	0.28
Laotian (4)	8	0.02
Malaysian (1)	1	<0.01
Pakistani (42)	48	0.10
Sri Lankan (4)	9	0.02
Taiwanese (10)	11	0.02
Thai (30)	48	0.10
Vietnamese (219)	238	0.49
Hawaii Native/Pacific Islander (18)	61	0.13
Not Hispanic (17)	55	0.11
Hispanic (1)	6	0.01
Guamanian/Chamorro (5)	13	0.03
Native Hawaiian (7)	17	0.04
Samoan (0)	3	0.01

*Notes: † The Census 2010 population figure is used to calculate the percentages in the Hispanic Origin and Race categories. Ancestry percentages are based on the 2006-2010 American Community Survey population (not shown); ‡ Numbers in parentheses indicate the number of people reporting a single ancestry; * Numbers in parentheses indicate the number of persons reporting this race alone, not in combination with any other race; Please refer to the Explanation of Data for more information.*

	Population	%
Tongan (1)	1	<0.01
White (43,267)	43,909	90.62
Not Hispanic (39,861)	40,333	83.24
Hispanic (3,406)	3,576	7.38

Palm Beach

Place Type: Town
County: Palm Beach
Population: 8,348†

Ancestry‡	Population	%
Alsatian (10)	10	0.12
American (559)	559	6.44
Arab (43)	83	0.96
Egyptian (19)	31	0.36
Lebanese (0)	18	0.21
Moroccan (0)	10	0.12
Syrian (24)	24	0.28
Armenian (33)	33	0.38
Australian (0)	15	0.17
Austrian (24)	142	1.64
British (319)	369	4.25
Bulgarian (0)	9	0.10
Canadian (66)	66	0.76
Celtic (25)	25	0.29
Czech (0)	22	0.25
Czechoslovakian (0)	9	0.10
Danish (0)	27	0.31
Dutch (54)	209	2.41
Eastern European (62)	98	1.13
English (514)	1,339	15.44
European (78)	78	0.90
Finnish (34)	34	0.39
French, ex. Basque (187)	438	5.05
French Canadian (33)	33	0.38
German (485)	1,502	17.31
Greek (80)	110	1.27
Hungarian (20)	116	1.34
Icelander (10)	10	0.12
Iranian (24)	36	0.41
Irish (414)	1,032	11.90
Italian (311)	557	6.42
Latvian (0)	12	0.14
Lithuanian (45)	120	1.38
Northern European (32)	32	0.37
Norwegian (162)	212	2.44
Polish (261)	475	5.48
Portuguese (0)	20	0.23
Romanian (177)	177	2.04
Russian (428)	825	9.51
Scandinavian (14)	14	0.16
Scotch-Irish (57)	118	1.36
Scottish (80)	301	3.47
Slovak (15)	38	0.44
Swedish (28)	28	0.32
Swiss (29)	50	0.58
Ukrainian (21)	56	0.65
Welsh (23)	45	0.52

Hispanic Origin	Population	%
Hispanic or Latino (of any race)	327	3.92
Central American, ex. Mexican	29	0.35
Costa Rican	5	0.06
Guatemalan	2	0.02
Honduran	5	0.06
Nicaraguan	9	0.11
Panamanian	4	0.05
Salvadoran	4	0.05
Cuban	98	1.17
Dominican Republic	13	0.16
Mexican	31	0.37
Puerto Rican	24	0.29
South American	96	1.15
Argentinean	19	0.23
Bolivian	2	0.02
Chilean	5	0.06
Colombian	31	0.37
Ecuadorian	5	0.06
Paraguayan	2	0.02
Peruvian	24	0.29
Uruguayan	4	0.05
Venezuelan	4	0.05
Other Hispanic or Latino	36	0.43

Race*	Population	%
African-American/Black (53)	70	0.84
Not Hispanic (39)	53	0.63
Hispanic (14)	17	0.20
American Indian/Alaska Native (2)	8	0.10
Not Hispanic (2)	7	0.08
Hispanic (0)	1	0.01
Cherokee (1)	3	0.04
Asian (87)	98	1.17
Not Hispanic (87)	96	1.15
Hispanic (0)	2	0.02
Cambodian (1)	1	0.01
Chinese, ex. Taiwanese (24)	26	0.31
Filipino (22)	27	0.32
Indian (15)	20	0.24
Indonesian (0)	1	0.01
Japanese (5)	6	0.07
Korean (7)	7	0.08
Malaysian (0)	1	0.01
Pakistani (1)	1	0.01
Taiwanese (1)	1	0.01
Thai (6)	7	0.08
Vietnamese (1)	1	0.01
Hawaii Native/Pacific Islander (0)	2	0.02
Not Hispanic (0)	2	0.02
Samoan (0)	1	0.01
Tongan (0)	1	0.01
White (8,134)	8,170	97.87
Not Hispanic (7,854)	7,878	94.37
Hispanic (280)	292	3.50

Palm City

Place Type: CDP
County: Martin
Population: 23,120†

Ancestry‡	Population	%
American (968)	968	4.19
Arab (16)	59	0.26
Arab (0)	11	0.05
Lebanese (0)	14	0.06
Moroccan (0)	18	0.08
Syrian (16)	16	0.07
Armenian (0)	109	0.47
Austrian (23)	90	0.39
Belgian (24)	33	0.14
Brazilian (111)	189	0.82
British (122)	312	1.35
Canadian (71)	71	0.31
Celtic (12)	12	0.05
Croatian (0)	30	0.13
Czech (35)	165	0.71
Czechoslovakian (63)	63	0.27
Danish (26)	207	0.90
Dutch (165)	474	2.05
Eastern European (46)	46	0.20
English (1,428)	3,677	15.92
European (170)	240	1.04
Finnish (27)	87	0.38
French, ex. Basque (72)	774	3.35
French Canadian (115)	259	1.12
German (1,456)	4,653	20.15
Greek (149)	434	1.88
Hungarian (65)	239	1.03
Icelander (0)	15	0.06
Irish (1,464)	4,111	17.80
Israeli (0)	27	0.12
Italian (1,776)	3,406	14.75
Latvian (28)	61	0.26
Lithuanian (79)	171	0.74
Macedonian (42)	42	0.18
Maltese (0)	13	0.06
Norwegian (79)	277	1.20
Pennsylvania German (35)	35	0.15
Polish (539)	1,227	5.31
Portuguese (0)	89	0.39
Romanian (50)	98	0.42
Russian (175)	747	3.23
Scandinavian (0)	22	0.10
Scotch-Irish (197)	568	2.46
Scottish (107)	938	4.06
Slavic (0)	7	0.03
Slovak (26)	202	0.87
Swedish (110)	330	1.43
Swiss (49)	154	0.67
Turkish (58)	84	0.36
Ukrainian (95)	216	0.94
Welsh (43)	107	0.46
West Indian, ex. Hispanic (14)	14	0.06
Haitian (14)	14	0.06
Yugoslavian (0)	51	0.22

Hispanic Origin	Population	%
Hispanic or Latino (of any race)	1,241	5.37
Central American, ex. Mexican	103	0.45
Costa Rican	6	0.03
Guatemalan	31	0.13
Honduran	8	0.03
Nicaraguan	24	0.10
Panamanian	10	0.04
Salvadoran	18	0.08
Other Central American	6	0.03
Cuban	242	1.05
Dominican Republic	20	0.09
Mexican	190	0.82
Puerto Rican	325	1.41
South American	266	1.15
Argentinean	34	0.15
Bolivian	4	0.02
Chilean	14	0.06
Colombian	99	0.43
Ecuadorian	39	0.17
Paraguayan	4	0.02
Peruvian	32	0.14
Uruguayan	2	0.01
Venezuelan	38	0.16
Other Hispanic or Latino	95	0.41

Race*	Population	%
African-American/Black (248)	318	1.38
Not Hispanic (239)	288	1.25
Hispanic (9)	30	0.13
American Indian/Alaska Native (29)	98	0.42
Not Hispanic (16)	74	0.32
Hispanic (13)	24	0.10
Aleut *(Alaska Native)* (1)	2	0.01
Blackfeet (1)	1	<0.01
Canadian/French Am. Ind. (2)	2	0.01
Central American Ind. (1)	1	<0.01
Cherokee (3)	30	0.13
Chickasaw (0)	1	<0.01
Iroquois (4)	5	0.02
Mexican American Ind. (5)	6	0.03
Seminole (1)	3	0.01
Sioux (0)	1	<0.01
South American Ind. (2)	5	0.02
Asian (365)	487	2.11
Not Hispanic (360)	466	2.02
Hispanic (5)	21	0.09
Bangladeshi (4)	4	0.02
Burmese (7)	7	0.03
Cambodian (0)	1	<0.01
Chinese, ex. Taiwanese (94)	117	0.51
Filipino (28)	53	0.23
Indian (161)	189	0.82
Indonesian (0)	1	<0.01
Japanese (6)	19	0.08
Korean (18)	24	0.10
Malaysian (1)	2	0.01
Pakistani (0)	1	<0.01
Thai (23)	32	0.14
Vietnamese (7)	15	0.06
Hawaii Native/Pacific Islander (7)	18	0.08
Not Hispanic (7)	13	0.06

*Notes: † The Census 2010 population figure is used to calculate the percentages in the Hispanic Origin and Race categories. Ancestry percentages are based on the 2006-2010 American Community Survey population (not shown); ‡ Numbers in parentheses indicate the number of people reporting a single ancestry; * Numbers in parentheses indicate the number of persons reporting this race alone, not in combination with any other race; Please refer to the Explanation of Data for more information.*

SECTION TWO

Hispanic (0)	5	0.02
Guamanian/Chamorro (2)	9	0.04
Native Hawaiian (3)	4	0.02
Samoan (0)	1	<0.01
White (22,049)	22,315	96.52
Not Hispanic (21,024)	21,222	91.79
Hispanic (1,025)	1,093	4.73

Palm Coast

Place Type: City
County: Flagler
Population: 75,180†

Ancestry‡	Population	%
African, Sub-Saharan (631)	686	0.97
African (308)	363	0.51
Nigerian (323)	323	0.46
Albanian (0)	24	0.03
American (5,736)	5,736	8.09
Arab (111)	205	0.29
Arab (0)	22	0.03
Egyptian (18)	18	0.03
Lebanese (34)	65	0.09
Moroccan (36)	69	0.10
Palestinian (23)	23	0.03
Syrian (0)	8	0.01
Armenian (0)	16	0.02
Australian (20)	28	0.04
Austrian (80)	319	0.45
Belgian (148)	166	0.23
Brazilian (38)	38	0.05
British (121)	273	0.38
Bulgarian (217)	217	0.31
Cajun (71)	71	0.10
Canadian (91)	236	0.33
Croatian (23)	98	0.14
Czech (201)	439	0.62
Czechoslovakian (34)	65	0.09
Danish (61)	198	0.28
Dutch (163)	803	1.13
Eastern European (63)	63	0.09
English (2,218)	6,499	9.16
Estonian (34)	34	0.05
European (397)	461	0.65
Finnish (6)	41	0.06
French, ex. Basque (585)	2,004	2.83
French Canadian (220)	379	0.53
German (3,692)	10,494	14.80
Greek (64)	331	0.47
Guyanese (138)	138	0.19
Hungarian (212)	692	0.98
Irish (3,636)	9,616	13.56
Italian (5,099)	9,274	13.08
Latvian (46)	46	0.06
Lithuanian (39)	164	0.23
Macedonian (55)	70	0.10
Maltese (24)	43	0.06
Northern European (43)	43	0.06
Norwegian (285)	453	0.64
Pennsylvania German (13)	68	0.10
Polish (1,232)	2,922	4.12
Portuguese (1,422)	1,613	2.27
Romanian (12)	38	0.05
Russian (1,038)	1,482	2.09
Scandinavian (14)	30	0.04
Scotch-Irish (361)	977	1.38
Scottish (658)	1,549	2.18
Serbian (23)	23	0.03
Slovak (152)	238	0.34
Slovene (29)	29	0.04
Swedish (263)	542	0.76
Swiss (29)	126	0.18
Turkish (26)	26	0.04
Ukrainian (642)	723	1.02
Welsh (112)	383	0.54
West Indian, ex. Hispanic (2,072)	2,571	3.63
Barbadian (44)	70	0.10
British West Indian (0)	76	0.11
Haitian (562)	562	0.79
Jamaican (1,069)	1,285	1.81
Trinidadian/Tobagonian (223)	381	0.54
West Indian (160)	183	0.26
Other West Indian (14)	14	0.02
Yugoslavian (17)	51	0.07

Hispanic Origin	Population	%
Hispanic or Latino (of any race)	7,552	10.05
Central American, ex. Mexican	507	0.67
Costa Rican	66	0.09
Guatemalan	85	0.11
Honduran	85	0.11
Nicaraguan	39	0.05
Panamanian	93	0.12
Salvadoran	134	0.18
Other Central American	5	0.01
Cuban	987	1.31
Dominican Republic	200	0.27
Mexican	763	1.01
Puerto Rican	3,177	4.23
South American	1,246	1.66
Argentinean	101	0.13
Bolivian	20	0.03
Chilean	71	0.09
Colombian	491	0.65
Ecuadorian	129	0.17
Paraguayan	10	0.01
Peruvian	215	0.29
Uruguayan	92	0.12
Venezuelan	111	0.15
Other South American	6	0.01
Other Hispanic or Latino	672	0.89

Race*	Population	%
African-American/Black (9,585)	10,558	14.04
Not Hispanic (9,191)	9,930	13.21
Hispanic (394)	628	0.84
American Indian/Alaska Native (191)	573	0.76
Not Hispanic (155)	462	0.61
Hispanic (36)	111	0.15
Aleut *(Alaska Native)* (2)	2	<0.01
Apache (1)	6	0.01
Blackfeet (5)	32	0.04
Central American Ind. (0)	2	<0.01
Cherokee (35)	151	0.20
Chickasaw (1)	8	0.01
Chippewa (9)	14	0.02
Choctaw (5)	15	0.02
Comanche (3)	5	0.01
Cree (0)	1	<0.01
Creek (14)	27	0.04
Crow (0)	1	<0.01
Delaware (1)	9	0.01
Hopi (0)	1	<0.01
Iroquois (3)	33	0.04
Lumbee (1)	5	0.01
Mexican American Ind. (13)	14	0.02
Navajo (11)	16	0.02
Ottawa (1)	3	<0.01
Potawatomi (3)	3	<0.01
Seminole (5)	6	0.01
Sioux (9)	16	0.02
South American Ind. (3)	10	0.01
Spanish American Ind. (0)	1	<0.01
Asian (1,902)	2,332	3.10
Not Hispanic (1,878)	2,235	2.97
Hispanic (24)	97	0.13
Bangladeshi (1)	5	0.01
Burmese (8)	11	0.01
Cambodian (350)	370	0.49
Chinese, ex. Taiwanese (221)	318	0.42
Filipino (664)	830	1.10
Indian (249)	313	0.42
Indonesian (1)	6	0.01
Japanese (33)	67	0.09
Korean (47)	84	0.11
Laotian (10)	18	0.02
Malaysian (1)	4	0.01
Nepalese (4)	4	0.01
Pakistani (24)	31	0.04
Taiwanese (3)	7	0.01
Thai (29)	47	0.06
Vietnamese (154)	178	0.24
Hawaii Native/Pacific Islander (56)	153	0.20
Not Hispanic (44)	119	0.16
Hispanic (12)	34	0.05
Guamanian/Chamorro (13)	16	0.02
Native Hawaiian (12)	38	0.05
Samoan (6)	23	0.03
Tongan (7)	7	0.01
White (60,063)	61,631	81.98
Not Hispanic (54,762)	55,885	74.33
Hispanic (5,301)	5,746	7.64

Palm Harbor

Place Type: CDP
County: Pinellas
Population: 57,439†

Ancestry‡	Population	%
African, Sub-Saharan (59)	92	0.16
African (45)	62	0.11
Nigerian (14)	14	0.02
South African (0)	16	0.03
Albanian (142)	176	0.30
American (2,549)	2,549	4.38
Arab (196)	387	0.66
Egyptian (131)	150	0.26
Lebanese (53)	182	0.31
Syrian (12)	55	0.09
Armenian (98)	138	0.24
Australian (0)	14	0.02
Austrian (62)	308	0.53
Basque (12)	12	0.02
Belgian (13)	50	0.09
Brazilian (58)	58	0.10
British (305)	476	0.82
Bulgarian (57)	57	0.10
Canadian (295)	351	0.60
Croatian (103)	222	0.38
Cypriot (12)	12	0.02
Czech (165)	421	0.72
Czechoslovakian (92)	145	0.25
Danish (40)	307	0.53
Dutch (202)	1,088	1.87
Eastern European (44)	44	0.08
English (2,939)	8,521	14.64
European (419)	460	0.79
Finnish (44)	130	0.22
French, ex. Basque (613)	2,729	4.69
French Canadian (441)	887	1.52
German (3,722)	13,069	22.45
Greek (842)	1,194	2.05
Hungarian (201)	611	1.05
Iranian (57)	160	0.27
Irish (2,888)	11,825	20.31
Italian (3,445)	8,145	13.99
Latvian (0)	57	0.10
Lithuanian (22)	155	0.27
Luxemburger (10)	28	0.05
Macedonian (26)	26	0.04
Maltese (18)	18	0.03
New Zealander (0)	20	0.03
Northern European (25)	25	0.04
Norwegian (179)	506	0.87
Pennsylvania German (77)	144	0.25
Polish (1,440)	3,796	6.52
Portuguese (206)	367	0.63
Romanian (130)	231	0.40
Russian (320)	925	1.59
Scandinavian (66)	146	0.25
Scotch-Irish (524)	1,477	2.54
Scottish (533)	1,875	3.22
Serbian (17)	78	0.13
Slavic (23)	37	0.06
Slovak (114)	259	0.44
Slovene (9)	9	0.02
Swedish (216)	858	1.47
Swiss (79)	163	0.28

*Notes: † The Census 2010 population figure is used to calculate the percentages in the Hispanic Origin and Race categories. Ancestry percentages are based on the 2006-2010 American Community Survey population (not shown); ‡ Numbers in parentheses indicate the number of people reporting a single ancestry; * Numbers in parentheses indicate the number of persons reporting this race alone, not in combination with any other race; Please refer to the Explanation of Data for more information.*

Turkish (11)	42	0.07
Ukrainian (145)	415	0.71
Welsh (96)	656	1.13
West Indian, ex. Hispanic (30)	76	0.13
Bahamian (0)	32	0.05
Jamaican (30)	30	0.05
West Indian (0)	14	0.02
Yugoslavian (59)	59	0.10

Hispanic Origin	Population	%
Hispanic or Latino (of any race)	3,407	5.93
Central American, ex. Mexican	179	0.31
Costa Rican	26	0.05
Guatemalan	38	0.07
Honduran	34	0.06
Nicaraguan	15	0.03
Panamanian	37	0.06
Salvadoran	29	0.05
Cuban	376	0.65
Dominican Republic	89	0.15
Mexican	502	0.87
Puerto Rican	1,109	1.93
South American	810	1.41
Argentinean	48	0.08
Bolivian	17	0.03
Chilean	34	0.06
Colombian	387	0.67
Ecuadorian	71	0.12
Paraguayan	2	<0.01
Peruvian	143	0.25
Uruguayan	10	0.02
Venezuelan	98	0.17
Other Hispanic or Latino	342	0.60

Race*	Population	%
African-American/Black (1,157)	1,505	2.62
Not Hispanic (1,044)	1,332	2.32
Hispanic (113)	173	0.30
American Indian/Alaska Native (117)	347	0.60
Not Hispanic (103)	290	0.50
Hispanic (14)	57	0.10
Apache (0)	6	0.01
Blackfeet (0)	7	0.01
Canadian/French Am. Ind. (1)	2	<0.01
Cherokee (23)	65	0.11
Chickasaw (3)	3	0.01
Chippewa (9)	16	0.03
Choctaw (2)	8	0.01
Creek (3)	8	0.01
Crow (1)	1	<0.01
Delaware (2)	7	0.01
Iroquois (6)	20	0.03
Lumbee (5)	10	0.02
Mexican American Ind. (2)	8	0.01
Navajo (1)	2	<0.01
Osage (2)	2	<0.01
Ottawa (1)	2	<0.01
Paiute (1)	1	<0.01
Potawatomi (2)	2	<0.01
Pueblo (0)	2	<0.01
Puget Sound Salish (0)	1	<0.01
Seminole (2)	8	0.01
Sioux (5)	11	0.02
South American Ind. (0)	11	0.02
Tlingit-Haida *(Alaska Native)* (1)	1	<0.01
Asian (922)	1,291	2.25
Not Hispanic (906)	1,246	2.17
Hispanic (16)	45	0.08
Bangladeshi (7)	7	0.01
Burmese (2)	2	<0.01
Cambodian (14)	18	0.03
Chinese, ex. Taiwanese (160)	204	0.36
Filipino (196)	305	0.53
Indian (190)	231	0.40
Indonesian (10)	15	0.03
Japanese (32)	85	0.15
Korean (53)	83	0.14
Laotian (16)	19	0.03
Malaysian (1)	2	<0.01
Nepalese (5)	5	0.01
Pakistani (22)	27	0.05
Sri Lankan (4)	4	0.01
Taiwanese (7)	7	0.01
Thai (44)	60	0.10
Vietnamese (131)	146	0.25
Hawaii Native/Pacific Islander (21)	52	0.09
Not Hispanic (20)	48	0.08
Hispanic (1)	4	0.01
Guamanian/Chamorro (2)	4	0.01
Native Hawaiian (11)	25	0.04
Samoan (6)	7	0.01
Tongan (1)	1	<0.01
White (53,710)	54,648	95.14
Not Hispanic (51,091)	51,810	90.20
Hispanic (2,619)	2,838	4.94

Palm River-Clair Mel

Place Type: CDP
County: Hillsborough
Population: 21,024†

Ancestry‡	Population	%
African, Sub-Saharan (108)	441	2.10
African (61)	385	1.84
Cape Verdean (0)	9	0.04
Nigerian (47)	47	0.22
American (711)	711	3.39
Belgian (16)	16	0.08
British (45)	161	0.77
Cajun (8)	8	0.04
Canadian (10)	21	0.10
Czech (9)	9	0.04
Czechoslovakian (31)	94	0.45
Dutch (9)	164	0.78
English (316)	725	3.46
European (30)	39	0.19
French, ex. Basque (139)	315	1.50
French Canadian (27)	89	0.42
German (496)	1,190	5.67
Greek (0)	23	0.11
Hungarian (0)	82	0.39
Irish (433)	1,103	5.26
Italian (221)	1,156	5.51
Lithuanian (0)	26	0.12
Norwegian (0)	11	0.05
Pennsylvania German (8)	15	0.07
Polish (71)	225	1.07
Portuguese (115)	189	0.90
Russian (19)	60	0.29
Scandinavian (239)	239	1.14
Scotch-Irish (174)	226	1.08
Scottish (23)	151	0.72
Swedish (0)	21	0.10
Ukrainian (11)	26	0.12
Welsh (0)	53	0.25
West Indian, ex. Hispanic (933)	1,101	5.25
Bahamian (77)	77	0.37
Belizean (11)	11	0.05
Haitian (232)	249	1.19
Jamaican (137)	137	0.65
Trinidadian/Tobagonian (76)	119	0.57
U.S. Virgin Islander (97)	97	0.46
West Indian (303)	411	1.96

Hispanic Origin	Population	%
Hispanic or Latino (of any race)	8,214	39.07
Central American, ex. Mexican	511	2.43
Costa Rican	67	0.32
Guatemalan	105	0.50
Honduran	99	0.47
Nicaraguan	72	0.34
Panamanian	56	0.27
Salvadoran	111	0.53
Other Central American	1	<0.01
Cuban	2,497	11.88
Dominican Republic	395	1.88
Mexican	1,144	5.44
Puerto Rican	2,886	13.73
South American	351	1.67
Argentinean	17	0.08
Bolivian	3	0.01
Chilean	8	0.04
Colombian	169	0.80
Ecuadorian	50	0.24
Peruvian	38	0.18
Uruguayan	7	0.03
Venezuelan	53	0.25
Other South American	6	0.03
Other Hispanic or Latino	430	2.05

Race*	Population	%
African-American/Black (6,336)	6,697	31.85
Not Hispanic (5,891)	6,126	29.14
Hispanic (445)	571	2.72
American Indian/Alaska Native (89)	206	0.98
Not Hispanic (58)	144	0.68
Hispanic (31)	62	0.29
Apache (3)	7	0.03
Blackfeet (0)	9	0.04
Central American Ind. (8)	11	0.05
Cherokee (17)	60	0.29
Cheyenne (0)	1	<0.01
Chippewa (3)	3	0.01
Choctaw (0)	1	<0.01
Iroquois (0)	2	0.01
Mexican American Ind. (1)	5	0.02
Paiute (2)	2	0.01
Seminole (5)	11	0.05
Sioux (1)	2	0.01
South American Ind. (5)	7	0.03
Spanish American Ind. (0)	1	<0.01
Asian (461)	575	2.73
Not Hispanic (452)	540	2.57
Hispanic (9)	35	0.17
Bangladeshi (2)	2	0.01
Cambodian (2)	8	0.04
Chinese, ex. Taiwanese (34)	43	0.20
Filipino (88)	116	0.55
Hmong (17)	17	0.08
Indian (106)	121	0.58
Indonesian (3)	4	0.02
Japanese (15)	35	0.17
Korean (25)	42	0.20
Laotian (1)	1	<0.01
Pakistani (7)	7	0.03
Sri Lankan (2)	2	0.01
Taiwanese (2)	2	0.01
Thai (40)	64	0.30
Vietnamese (96)	109	0.52
Hawaii Native/Pacific Islander (11)	67	0.32
Not Hispanic (6)	38	0.18
Hispanic (5)	29	0.14
Fijian (1)	2	0.01
Guamanian/Chamorro (3)	3	0.01
Native Hawaiian (1)	7	0.03
Samoan (3)	5	0.02
White (11,471)	12,069	57.41
Not Hispanic (6,006)	6,276	29.85
Hispanic (5,465)	5,793	27.55

Palm Springs

Place Type: Village
County: Palm Beach
Population: 18,928†

Ancestry‡	Population	%
African, Sub-Saharan (65)	65	0.35
African (30)	30	0.16
Kenyan (35)	35	0.19
Albanian (123)	123	0.66
American (437)	437	2.34
Arab (44)	44	0.24
Egyptian (16)	16	0.09
Lebanese (28)	28	0.15
Armenian (22)	22	0.12
British (9)	46	0.25
Cajun (0)	23	0.12
Canadian (8)	40	0.21

*Notes: † The Census 2010 population figure is used to calculate the percentages in the Hispanic Origin and Race categories. Ancestry percentages are based on the 2006-2010 American Community Survey population (not shown); ‡ Numbers in parentheses indicate the number of people reporting a single ancestry; * Numbers in parentheses indicate the number of persons reporting this race alone, not in combination with any other race; Please refer to the Explanation of Data for more information.*

Czechoslovakian (0)	39	0.21
Danish (12)	20	0.11
Dutch (16)	115	0.62
English (268)	985	5.28
European (13)	13	0.07
Finnish (57)	71	0.38
French, ex. Basque (57)	540	2.89
French Canadian (81)	147	0.79
German (212)	1,261	6.75
Greek (23)	48	0.26
Hungarian (29)	55	0.29
Irish (375)	1,248	6.69
Italian (617)	1,080	5.79
Latvian (0)	6	0.03
Lithuanian (7)	13	0.07
Luxemburger (0)	7	0.04
Northern European (49)	49	0.26
Norwegian (24)	87	0.47
Pennsylvania German (13)	13	0.07
Polish (291)	626	3.35
Portuguese (9)	37	0.20
Russian (9)	209	1.12
Scandinavian (10)	10	0.05
Scotch-Irish (46)	102	0.55
Scottish (65)	375	2.01
Slovak (12)	54	0.29
Swedish (40)	86	0.46
Swiss (0)	21	0.11
Turkish (13)	13	0.07
Ukrainian (0)	22	0.12
Welsh (30)	131	0.70
West Indian, ex. Hispanic (1,103)	1,376	7.37
Bahamian (158)	158	0.85
Barbadian (0)	9	0.05
Haitian (650)	678	3.63
Jamaican (295)	495	2.65
West Indian (0)	36	0.19

Hispanic Origin	Population	%
Hispanic or Latino (of any race)	9,585	50.64
Central American, ex. Mexican	1,172	6.19
Costa Rican	63	0.33
Guatemalan	322	1.70
Honduran	405	2.14
Nicaraguan	171	0.90
Panamanian	13	0.07
Salvadoran	186	0.98
Other Central American	12	0.06
Cuban	3,249	17.17
Dominican Republic	427	2.26
Mexican	1,258	6.65
Puerto Rican	1,383	7.31
South American	1,509	7.97
Argentinean	114	0.60
Bolivian	51	0.27
Chilean	21	0.11
Colombian	704	3.72
Ecuadorian	193	1.02
Paraguayan	11	0.06
Peruvian	208	1.10
Uruguayan	104	0.55
Venezuelan	93	0.49
Other South American	10	0.05
Other Hispanic or Latino	587	3.10

Race*	Population	%
African-American/Black (2,290)	2,561	13.53
Not Hispanic (1,987)	2,164	11.43
Hispanic (303)	397	2.10
American Indian/Alaska Native (97)	197	1.04
Not Hispanic (23)	69	0.36
Hispanic (74)	128	0.68
Apache (0)	2	0.01
Blackfeet (0)	4	0.02
Central American Ind. (4)	8	0.04
Cherokee (3)	20	0.11
Chippewa (0)	4	0.02
Delaware (0)	1	0.01
Inupiat *(Alaska Native)* (4)	4	0.02
Mexican American Ind. (31)	45	0.24
Navajo (3)	3	0.02
Osage (0)	1	0.01
Ottawa (0)	1	0.01
Potawatomi (6)	14	0.07
Pueblo (1)	3	0.02
Sioux (2)	2	0.01
South American Ind. (1)	3	0.02
Spanish American Ind. (1)	1	0.01
Tsimshian *(Alaska Native)* (1)	1	0.01
Asian (325)	415	2.19
Not Hispanic (314)	391	2.07
Hispanic (11)	24	0.13
Bangladeshi (55)	79	0.42
Chinese, ex. Taiwanese (39)	47	0.25
Filipino (42)	61	0.32
Indian (74)	111	0.59
Indonesian (1)	4	0.02
Japanese (3)	6	0.03
Korean (11)	18	0.10
Laotian (1)	1	0.01
Nepalese (12)	14	0.07
Pakistani (1)	6	0.03
Sri Lankan (4)	6	0.03
Thai (28)	30	0.16
Vietnamese (25)	30	0.16
Hawaii Native/Pacific Islander (27)	72	0.38
Not Hispanic (4)	27	0.14
Hispanic (23)	45	0.24
Guamanian/Chamorro (17)	21	0.11
Native Hawaiian (7)	11	0.06
Samoan (3)	3	0.02
White (13,760)	14,351	75.82
Not Hispanic (6,698)	6,902	36.46
Hispanic (7,062)	7,449	39.35

Palm Valley

Place Type: CDP
County: St. Johns
Population: 20,019†

Ancestry‡	Population	%
African, Sub-Saharan (0)	19	0.10
African (0)	19	0.10
American (1,911)	1,911	9.58
Arab (92)	126	0.63
Arab (63)	63	0.32
Iraqi (16)	16	0.08
Lebanese (13)	47	0.24
Armenian (98)	185	0.93
Austrian (13)	42	0.21
British (107)	146	0.73
Bulgarian (26)	26	0.13
Canadian (51)	141	0.71
Croatian (12)	25	0.13
Czech (65)	202	1.01
Danish (38)	157	0.79
Dutch (86)	218	1.09
Eastern European (82)	82	0.41
English (1,072)	3,299	16.53
European (427)	451	2.26
Finnish (0)	63	0.32
French, ex. Basque (110)	770	3.86
French Canadian (55)	129	0.65
German (1,132)	3,601	18.05
Greek (58)	175	0.88
Hungarian (23)	74	0.37
Iranian (0)	14	0.07
Irish (1,365)	3,533	17.71
Italian (618)	1,791	8.98
Lithuanian (0)	46	0.23
Luxemburger (0)	11	0.06
Northern European (31)	43	0.22
Norwegian (99)	174	0.87
Polish (243)	889	4.46
Portuguese (125)	125	0.63
Romanian (12)	12	0.06
Russian (229)	394	1.97
Scandinavian (58)	71	0.36
Scotch-Irish (104)	508	2.55
Scottish (422)	860	4.31
Slovak (23)	62	0.31
Slovene (10)	23	0.12
Swedish (182)	361	1.81
Swiss (49)	150	0.75
Turkish (11)	11	0.06
Ukrainian (72)	152	0.76
Welsh (47)	183	0.92
West Indian, ex. Hispanic (0)	37	0.19
Trinidadian/Tobagonian (0)	37	0.19
Yugoslavian (0)	9	0.05

Hispanic Origin	Population	%
Hispanic or Latino (of any race)	756	3.78
Central American, ex. Mexican	53	0.26
Costa Rican	2	0.01
Guatemalan	16	0.08
Honduran	8	0.04
Nicaraguan	5	0.02
Panamanian	11	0.05
Salvadoran	11	0.05
Cuban	138	0.69
Dominican Republic	14	0.07
Mexican	121	0.60
Puerto Rican	172	0.86
South American	158	0.79
Argentinean	12	0.06
Bolivian	7	0.03
Chilean	9	0.04
Colombian	64	0.32
Ecuadorian	16	0.08
Peruvian	34	0.17
Uruguayan	7	0.03
Venezuelan	9	0.04
Other Hispanic or Latino	100	0.50

Race*	Population	%
African-American/Black (252)	326	1.63
Not Hispanic (240)	300	1.50
Hispanic (12)	26	0.13
American Indian/Alaska Native (32)	78	0.39
Not Hispanic (19)	59	0.29
Hispanic (13)	19	0.09
Apache (1)	1	<0.01
Blackfeet (1)	1	<0.01
Canadian/French Am. Ind. (1)	1	<0.01
Cherokee (6)	23	0.11
Chickasaw (0)	2	0.01
Chippewa (1)	1	<0.01
Choctaw (0)	3	0.01
Cree (0)	1	<0.01
Delaware (0)	3	0.01
Lumbee (1)	1	<0.01
Mexican American Ind. (2)	2	0.01
Osage (0)	1	<0.01
Sioux (4)	6	0.03
South American Ind. (1)	1	<0.01
Asian (353)	503	2.51
Not Hispanic (350)	494	2.47
Hispanic (3)	9	0.04
Burmese (2)	2	0.01
Chinese, ex. Taiwanese (68)	101	0.50
Filipino (72)	125	0.62
Indian (109)	125	0.62
Indonesian (6)	8	0.04
Japanese (14)	28	0.14
Korean (33)	48	0.24
Laotian (0)	1	<0.01
Malaysian (0)	1	<0.01
Nepalese (4)	4	0.02
Pakistani (1)	1	<0.01
Taiwanese (7)	8	0.04
Thai (9)	12	0.06
Vietnamese (15)	18	0.09
Hawaii Native/Pacific Islander (10)	18	0.09
Not Hispanic (8)	16	0.08
Hispanic (2)	2	0.01
Guamanian/Chamorro (1)	4	0.02
Native Hawaiian (5)	7	0.03
Samoan (0)	1	<0.01

*Notes: † The Census 2010 population figure is used to calculate the percentages in the Hispanic Origin and Race categories. Ancestry percentages are based on the 2006-2010 American Community Survey population (not shown); ‡ Numbers in parentheses indicate the number of people reporting a single ancestry; * Numbers in parentheses indicate the number of persons reporting this race alone, not in combination with any other race; Please refer to the Explanation of Data for more information.*

White (18,977)	19,223	96.02
Not Hispanic (18,378)	18,592	92.87
Hispanic (599)	631	3.15

Palmetto Bay

Place Type: Village
County: Miami-Dade
Population: 23,410†

Ancestry‡	Population	%
African, Sub-Saharan (105)	105	0.45
African (20)	20	0.09
Nigerian (78)	78	0.33
South African (7)	7	0.03
American (1,741)	1,741	7.44
Arab (131)	318	1.36
Arab (25)	25	0.11
Egyptian (38)	54	0.23
Iraqi (8)	35	0.15
Lebanese (40)	142	0.61
Moroccan (20)	62	0.26
Armenian (0)	24	0.10
Assyrian/Chaldean/Syriac (0)	10	0.04
Australian (0)	15	0.06
Austrian (27)	44	0.19
Belgian (30)	41	0.18
Brazilian (145)	230	0.98
British (101)	238	1.02
Canadian (56)	67	0.29
Czech (0)	75	0.32
Czechoslovakian (20)	20	0.09
Danish (65)	104	0.44
Dutch (34)	184	0.79
Eastern European (197)	212	0.91
English (473)	1,436	6.13
European (484)	530	2.26
Finnish (12)	40	0.17
French, ex. Basque (299)	940	4.02
French Canadian (23)	150	0.64
German (615)	1,920	8.20
Greek (65)	129	0.55
Guyanese (51)	51	0.22
Hungarian (87)	171	0.73
Iranian (140)	140	0.60
Irish (707)	1,955	8.35
Israeli (0)	45	0.19
Italian (419)	1,231	5.26
Lithuanian (39)	110	0.47
Norwegian (19)	67	0.29
Polish (190)	636	2.72
Portuguese (57)	117	0.50
Romanian (26)	73	0.31
Russian (354)	719	3.07
Scandinavian (17)	58	0.25
Scotch-Irish (40)	198	0.85
Scottish (84)	339	1.45
Slavic (13)	13	0.06
Slovak (16)	16	0.07
Swedish (26)	152	0.65
Swiss (25)	45	0.19
Turkish (0)	16	0.07
Ukrainian (0)	68	0.29
Welsh (17)	17	0.07
West Indian, ex. Hispanic (796)	911	3.89
Bahamian (41)	41	0.18
British West Indian (9)	9	0.04
Haitian (94)	126	0.54
Jamaican (632)	707	3.02
Trinidadian/Tobagonian (20)	28	0.12
Yugoslavian (12)	43	0.18

Hispanic Origin	Population	%
Hispanic or Latino (of any race)	9,025	38.55
Central American, ex. Mexican	894	3.82
Costa Rican	63	0.27
Guatemalan	117	0.50
Honduran	139	0.59
Nicaraguan	341	1.46
Panamanian	66	0.28
Salvadoran	168	0.72
Cuban	4,206	17.97
Dominican Republic	300	1.28
Mexican	283	1.21
Puerto Rican	679	2.90
South American	2,114	9.03
Argentinean	265	1.13
Bolivian	74	0.32
Chilean	183	0.78
Colombian	661	2.82
Ecuadorian	163	0.70
Paraguayan	10	0.04
Peruvian	379	1.62
Uruguayan	25	0.11
Venezuelan	345	1.47
Other South American	9	0.04
Other Hispanic or Latino	549	2.35

Race*	Population	%
African-American/Black (1,461)	1,676	7.16
Not Hispanic (1,313)	1,463	6.25
Hispanic (148)	213	0.91
American Indian/Alaska Native (19)	59	0.25
Not Hispanic (8)	32	0.14
Hispanic (11)	27	0.12
Blackfeet (0)	1	<0.01
Cherokee (2)	13	0.06
Creek (4)	6	0.03
Paiute (0)	2	0.01
South American Ind. (4)	10	0.04
Spanish American Ind. (3)	4	0.02
Asian (1,051)	1,283	5.48
Not Hispanic (1,032)	1,238	5.29
Hispanic (19)	45	0.19
Burmese (2)	2	0.01
Cambodian (1)	1	<0.01
Chinese, ex. Taiwanese (521)	591	2.52
Filipino (80)	101	0.43
Hmong (3)	3	0.01
Indian (225)	278	1.19
Indonesian (0)	3	0.01
Japanese (25)	41	0.18
Korean (51)	61	0.26
Malaysian (0)	1	<0.01
Pakistani (7)	11	0.05
Sri Lankan (2)	4	0.02
Taiwanese (19)	20	0.09
Thai (31)	32	0.14
Vietnamese (48)	60	0.26
Hawaii Native/Pacific Islander (10)	27	0.12
Not Hispanic (10)	18	0.08
Hispanic (0)	9	0.04
Fijian (0)	1	<0.01
Guamanian/Chamorro (3)	3	0.01
Native Hawaiian (3)	6	0.03
Samoan (2)	3	0.01
White (19,886)	20,292	86.68
Not Hispanic (11,593)	11,859	50.66
Hispanic (8,293)	8,433	36.02

Palmetto Estates

Place Type: CDP
County: Miami-Dade
Population: 13,535†

Ancestry‡	Population	%
African, Sub-Saharan (12)	39	0.29
African (12)	12	0.09
Ghanaian (0)	10	0.07
Nigerian (0)	17	0.12
American (879)	879	6.45
Arab (0)	40	0.29
Arab (0)	40	0.29
British (13)	13	0.10
Bulgarian (12)	24	0.18
Croatian (22)	22	0.16
Dutch (33)	85	0.62
English (77)	262	1.92
European (0)	60	0.44
French, ex. Basque (71)	93	0.68
German (35)	272	2.00
Greek (8)	81	0.59
Guyanese (36)	62	0.46
Hungarian (0)	8	0.06
Irish (43)	153	1.12
Italian (96)	132	0.97
Lithuanian (0)	6	0.04
Polish (19)	56	0.41
Portuguese (28)	59	0.43
Russian (0)	34	0.25
Scotch-Irish (11)	113	0.83
Scottish (0)	19	0.14
Welsh (5)	5	0.04
West Indian, ex. Hispanic (1,895)	2,124	15.59
Bahamian (135)	135	0.99
Barbadian (54)	54	0.40
British West Indian (26)	26	0.19
Haitian (844)	898	6.59
Jamaican (509)	576	4.23
Trinidadian/Tobagonian (327)	421	3.09
West Indian (0)	14	0.10

Hispanic Origin	Population	%
Hispanic or Latino (of any race)	5,840	43.15
Central American, ex. Mexican	1,209	8.93
Costa Rican	45	0.33
Guatemalan	83	0.61
Honduran	288	2.13
Nicaraguan	559	4.13
Panamanian	74	0.55
Salvadoran	160	1.18
Cuban	2,404	17.76
Dominican Republic	270	1.99
Mexican	112	0.83
Puerto Rican	515	3.80
South American	972	7.18
Argentinean	44	0.33
Bolivian	10	0.07
Chilean	49	0.36
Colombian	426	3.15
Ecuadorian	61	0.45
Paraguayan	2	0.01
Peruvian	285	2.11
Uruguayan	11	0.08
Venezuelan	84	0.62
Other Hispanic or Latino	358	2.64

Race*	Population	%
African-American/Black (5,660)	6,000	44.33
Not Hispanic (5,308)	5,532	40.87
Hispanic (352)	468	3.46
American Indian/Alaska Native (20)	74	0.55
Not Hispanic (10)	49	0.36
Hispanic (10)	25	0.18
Blackfeet (1)	1	0.01
Canadian/French Am. Ind. (0)	1	0.01
Central American Ind. (1)	10	0.07
Cherokee (2)	20	0.15
Pueblo (0)	2	0.01
Seminole (1)	1	0.01
South American Ind. (5)	5	0.04
Spanish American Ind. (5)	5	0.04
Asian (450)	605	4.47
Not Hispanic (444)	577	4.26
Hispanic (6)	28	0.21
Chinese, ex. Taiwanese (81)	141	1.04
Filipino (68)	87	0.64
Indian (188)	243	1.80
Indonesian (1)	1	0.01
Japanese (5)	9	0.07
Korean (11)	15	0.11
Laotian (6)	6	0.04
Pakistani (15)	20	0.15
Thai (5)	10	0.07
Vietnamese (55)	60	0.44
Hawaii Native/Pacific Islander (7)	45	0.33
Not Hispanic (7)	41	0.30
Hispanic (0)	4	0.03
White (6,409)	6,742	49.81

SECTION TWO

*Notes: † The Census 2010 population figure is used to calculate the percentages in the Hispanic Origin and Race categories. Ancestry percentages are based on the 2006-2010 American Community Survey population (not shown); ‡ Numbers in parentheses indicate the number of people reporting a single ancestry; * Numbers in parentheses indicate the number of persons reporting this race alone, not in combination with any other race; Please refer to the Explanation of Data for more information.*

Not Hispanic (1,546)	1,696	12.53
Hispanic (4,863)	5,046	37.28

Palmetto

Place Type: City
County: Manatee
Population: 12,606†

Ancestry‡	Population	%
American (966)	966	7.52
Arab (11)	36	0.28
Lebanese (11)	11	0.09
Palestinian (0)	25	0.19
Austrian (68)	92	0.72
Belgian (12)	12	0.09
British (0)	24	0.19
Cajun (0)	15	0.12
Croatian (0)	14	0.11
Czech (18)	87	0.68
Czechoslovakian (15)	42	0.33
Danish (12)	12	0.09
Dutch (46)	292	2.27
English (666)	1,704	13.26
European (74)	74	0.58
French, ex. Basque (69)	321	2.50
French Canadian (110)	151	1.17
German (744)	1,813	14.11
Greek (0)	44	0.34
Hungarian (0)	38	0.30
Irish (268)	1,236	9.62
Italian (446)	644	5.01
Lithuanian (0)	38	0.30
Northern European (8)	8	0.06
Norwegian (22)	49	0.38
Pennsylvania German (34)	34	0.26
Polish (146)	199	1.55
Portuguese (29)	29	0.23
Russian (32)	78	0.61
Scotch-Irish (169)	269	2.09
Scottish (136)	592	4.61
Slavic (0)	10	0.08
Slovak (10)	44	0.34
Swedish (17)	84	0.65
Swiss (10)	58	0.45
Ukrainian (0)	16	0.12
Welsh (0)	49	0.38
West Indian, ex. Hispanic (161)	197	1.53
Haitian (161)	197	1.53

Hispanic Origin	Population	%
Hispanic or Latino (of any race)	3,571	28.33
Central American, ex. Mexican	190	1.51
Costa Rican	2	0.02
Guatemalan	93	0.74
Honduran	29	0.23
Nicaraguan	11	0.09
Panamanian	2	0.02
Salvadoran	44	0.35
Other Central American	9	0.07
Cuban	48	0.38
Dominican Republic	6	0.05
Mexican	2,925	23.20
Puerto Rican	209	1.66
South American	35	0.28
Argentinean	3	0.02
Chilean	2	0.02
Colombian	20	0.16
Ecuadorian	3	0.02
Paraguayan	2	0.02
Peruvian	4	0.03
Venezuelan	1	0.01
Other Hispanic or Latino	158	1.25

Race*	Population	%
African-American/Black (1,325)	1,426	11.31
Not Hispanic (1,293)	1,381	10.96
Hispanic (32)	45	0.36
American Indian/Alaska Native (50)	130	1.03
Not Hispanic (29)	88	0.70
Hispanic (21)	42	0.33
Blackfeet (0)	11	0.09
Cherokee (8)	25	0.20
Cheyenne (0)	2	0.02
Chippewa (3)	4	0.03
Choctaw (1)	2	0.02
Delaware (0)	1	0.01
Iroquois (0)	1	0.01
Lumbee (1)	1	0.01
Menominee (1)	2	0.02
Navajo (0)	3	0.02
Ottawa (1)	1	0.01
Seminole (1)	4	0.03
Asian (76)	111	0.88
Not Hispanic (71)	100	0.79
Hispanic (5)	11	0.09
Cambodian (1)	1	0.01
Chinese, ex. Taiwanese (14)	26	0.21
Filipino (18)	22	0.17
Indian (17)	28	0.22
Japanese (2)	10	0.08
Korean (8)	9	0.07
Pakistani (1)	1	0.01
Taiwanese (1)	4	0.03
Thai (6)	8	0.06
Vietnamese (5)	6	0.05
Hawaii Native/Pacific Islander (1)	13	0.10
Not Hispanic (1)	12	0.10
Hispanic (0)	1	0.01
Guamanian/Chamorro (1)	1	0.01
Native Hawaiian (0)	5	0.04
Samoan (0)	1	0.01
White (9,091)	9,331	74.02
Not Hispanic (7,456)	7,601	60.30
Hispanic (1,635)	1,730	13.72

Panama City Beach

Place Type: City
County: Bay
Population: 12,018†

Ancestry‡	Population	%
American (991)	991	8.72
Austrian (0)	27	0.24
British (56)	56	0.49
Canadian (152)	163	1.43
Czech (89)	116	1.02
Danish (78)	78	0.69
Dutch (51)	238	2.09
Eastern European (43)	43	0.38
English (773)	1,798	15.82
European (49)	49	0.43
Finnish (10)	27	0.24
French, ex. Basque (118)	331	2.91
French Canadian (95)	95	0.84
German (896)	2,129	18.73
Greek (48)	131	1.15
Hungarian (53)	64	0.56
Irish (575)	1,592	14.01
Italian (264)	599	5.27
Northern European (38)	38	0.33
Norwegian (26)	279	2.46
Pennsylvania German (0)	14	0.12
Polish (191)	333	2.93
Portuguese (0)	11	0.10
Romanian (13)	13	0.11
Russian (15)	30	0.26
Scotch-Irish (145)	274	2.41
Scottish (185)	500	4.40
Serbian (14)	14	0.12
Slovak (14)	46	0.40
Slovene (15)	15	0.13
Swedish (14)	28	0.25
Swiss (0)	34	0.30
Ukrainian (8)	8	0.07
Welsh (0)	105	0.92

Hispanic Origin	Population	%
Hispanic or Latino (of any race)	697	5.80
Central American, ex. Mexican	64	0.53
Guatemalan	7	0.06
Honduran	30	0.25
Nicaraguan	3	0.02
Panamanian	10	0.08
Salvadoran	14	0.12
Cuban	45	0.37
Dominican Republic	2	0.02
Mexican	282	2.35
Puerto Rican	120	1.00
South American	67	0.56
Argentinean	5	0.04
Bolivian	1	0.01
Chilean	14	0.12
Colombian	15	0.12
Ecuadorian	10	0.08
Paraguayan	3	0.02
Peruvian	13	0.11
Venezuelan	3	0.02
Other South American	3	0.02
Other Hispanic or Latino	117	0.97

Race*	Population	%
African-American/Black (273)	352	2.93
Not Hispanic (268)	346	2.88
Hispanic (5)	6	0.05
American Indian/Alaska Native (70)	211	1.76
Not Hispanic (64)	199	1.66
Hispanic (6)	12	0.10
Blackfeet (1)	2	0.02
Cherokee (17)	74	0.62
Chickasaw (0)	3	0.02
Chippewa (8)	13	0.11
Choctaw (1)	5	0.04
Creek (0)	9	0.07
Delaware (2)	2	0.02
Houma (1)	1	0.01
Mexican American Ind. (4)	4	0.03
Seminole (1)	2	0.02
Sioux (5)	6	0.05
Tlingit-Haida *(Alaska Native)* (0)	1	0.01
Asian (328)	436	3.63
Not Hispanic (326)	421	3.50
Hispanic (2)	15	0.12
Burmese (2)	2	0.02
Cambodian (1)	1	0.01
Chinese, ex. Taiwanese (21)	28	0.23
Filipino (73)	122	1.02
Indian (80)	84	0.70
Japanese (13)	29	0.24
Korean (8)	19	0.16
Laotian (1)	3	0.02
Pakistani (7)	13	0.11
Thai (59)	71	0.59
Vietnamese (45)	52	0.43
Hawaii Native/Pacific Islander (6)	27	0.22
Not Hispanic (6)	24	0.20
Hispanic (0)	3	0.02
Guamanian/Chamorro (1)	6	0.05
Native Hawaiian (5)	16	0.13
Samoan (0)	2	0.02
White (10,759)	11,111	92.45
Not Hispanic (10,334)	10,623	88.39
Hispanic (425)	488	4.06

Panama City

Place Type: City
County: Bay
Population: 36,484†

Ancestry‡	Population	%
African, Sub-Saharan (32)	84	0.23
African (32)	61	0.17
Ethiopian (0)	23	0.06
American (3,774)	3,774	10.26
Arab (427)	493	1.34
Arab (139)	152	0.41
Egyptian (114)	114	0.31
Lebanese (83)	83	0.23

*Notes: † The Census 2010 population figure is used to calculate the percentages in the Hispanic Origin and Race categories. Ancestry percentages are based on the 2006-2010 American Community Survey population (not shown); ‡ Numbers in parentheses indicate the number of people reporting a single ancestry; * Numbers in parentheses indicate the number of persons reporting this race alone, not in combination with any other race; Please refer to the Explanation of Data for more information.*

Moroccan (0)	17	0.05
Palestinian (91)	91	0.25
Other Arab (0)	36	0.10
Austrian (26)	45	0.12
Belgian (0)	29	0.08
British (112)	239	0.65
Cajun (17)	17	0.05
Canadian (159)	186	0.51
Croatian (34)	34	0.09
Czech (36)	41	0.11
Czechoslovakian (0)	9	0.02
Danish (128)	199	0.54
Dutch (38)	442	1.20
Eastern European (54)	86	0.23
English (2,424)	4,708	12.80
European (194)	239	0.65
Finnish (34)	34	0.09
French, ex. Basque (240)	1,197	3.25
French Canadian (72)	123	0.33
German (1,326)	4,091	11.12
German Russian (0)	29	0.08
Greek (76)	184	0.50
Hungarian (10)	61	0.17
Icelander (15)	15	0.04
Iranian (39)	48	0.13
Irish (1,346)	4,275	11.62
Italian (712)	1,507	4.10
Lithuanian (11)	22	0.06
Northern European (40)	40	0.11
Norwegian (150)	435	1.18
Pennsylvania German (19)	19	0.05
Polish (140)	455	1.24
Portuguese (181)	213	0.58
Romanian (0)	9	0.02
Russian (37)	109	0.30
Scandinavian (24)	24	0.07
Scotch-Irish (343)	724	1.97
Scottish (261)	657	1.79
Slovak (13)	13	0.04
Swedish (64)	261	0.71
Swiss (10)	47	0.13
Turkish (21)	30	0.08
Ukrainian (27)	55	0.15
Welsh (48)	271	0.74
West Indian, ex. Hispanic (101)	184	0.50
Bahamian (24)	24	0.07
Dutch West Indian (0)	22	0.06
Haitian (22)	48	0.13
Jamaican (55)	90	0.24
Yugoslavian (42)	42	0.11

Hispanic Origin	Population	%
Hispanic or Latino (of any race)	1,844	5.05
Central American, ex. Mexican	176	0.48
Costa Rican	21	0.06
Guatemalan	38	0.10
Honduran	65	0.18
Nicaraguan	9	0.02
Panamanian	32	0.09
Salvadoran	10	0.03
Other Central American	1	<0.01
Cuban	133	0.36
Dominican Republic	10	0.03
Mexican	724	1.98
Puerto Rican	528	1.45
South American	84	0.23
Argentinean	11	0.03
Bolivian	1	<0.01
Chilean	6	0.02
Colombian	31	0.08
Ecuadorian	3	0.01
Peruvian	27	0.07
Venezuelan	4	0.01
Other South American	1	<0.01
Other Hispanic or Latino	189	0.52

Race*	Population	%
African-American/Black (8,026)	8,517	23.34
Not Hispanic (7,921)	8,361	22.92
Hispanic (105)	156	0.43
American Indian/Alaska Native (190)	513	1.41
Not Hispanic (163)	453	1.24
Hispanic (27)	60	0.16
Alaska Athabascan *(Ala. Nat.)* (1)	2	0.01
Apache (2)	3	0.01
Blackfeet (4)	13	0.04
Canadian/French Am. Ind. (1)	2	0.01
Cherokee (36)	128	0.35
Chickasaw (0)	1	<0.01
Chippewa (1)	1	<0.01
Choctaw (0)	5	0.01
Comanche (1)	1	<0.01
Creek (26)	54	0.15
Delaware (1)	1	<0.01
Houma (0)	1	<0.01
Inupiat *(Alaska Native)* (0)	4	0.01
Iroquois (1)	5	0.01
Kiowa (0)	1	<0.01
Lumbee (7)	12	0.03
Mexican American Ind. (5)	6	0.02
Navajo (2)	7	0.02
Osage (0)	2	0.01
Pueblo (0)	4	0.01
Seminole (5)	11	0.03
Sioux (5)	14	0.04
South American Ind. (0)	5	0.01
Tlingit-Haida *(Alaska Native)* (2)	6	0.02
Asian (596)	848	2.32
Not Hispanic (587)	826	2.26
Hispanic (9)	22	0.06
Bangladeshi (1)	1	<0.01
Burmese (0)	1	<0.01
Cambodian (2)	2	0.01
Chinese, ex. Taiwanese (59)	83	0.23
Filipino (90)	167	0.46
Indian (104)	118	0.32
Indonesian (3)	3	0.01
Japanese (23)	59	0.16
Korean (38)	63	0.17
Pakistani (18)	32	0.09
Sri Lankan (5)	6	0.02
Taiwanese (0)	1	<0.01
Thai (21)	41	0.11
Vietnamese (188)	239	0.66
Hawaii Native/Pacific Islander (33)	84	0.23
Not Hispanic (22)	69	0.19
Hispanic (11)	15	0.04
Guamanian/Chamorro (11)	14	0.04
Native Hawaiian (12)	41	0.11
Samoan (5)	7	0.02
White (26,138)	27,032	74.09
Not Hispanic (25,021)	25,768	70.63
Hispanic (1,117)	1,264	3.46

Parkland

Place Type: City
County: Broward
Population: 23,962†

Ancestry‡	Population	%
African, Sub-Saharan (114)	192	0.86
African (52)	79	0.35
Cape Verdean (0)	51	0.23
South African (54)	54	0.24
Sudanese (8)	8	0.04
American (1,346)	1,346	6.00
Arab (70)	81	0.36
Egyptian (32)	43	0.19
Other Arab (38)	38	0.17
Armenian (33)	33	0.15
Austrian (15)	166	0.74
Belgian (14)	14	0.06
Brazilian (258)	258	1.15
British (25)	47	0.21
Canadian (129)	129	0.57
Croatian (13)	81	0.36
Czech (43)	68	0.30
Czechoslovakian (0)	29	0.13
Danish (56)	102	0.45
Dutch (96)	158	0.70
Eastern European (117)	117	0.52
English (339)	1,576	7.02
European (109)	109	0.49
French, ex. Basque (56)	569	2.54
French Canadian (46)	143	0.64
German (624)	2,655	11.83
Greek (7)	38	0.17
Guyanese (64)	64	0.29
Hungarian (165)	385	1.72
Iranian (0)	25	0.11
Irish (703)	2,566	11.43
Israeli (0)	21	0.09
Italian (1,285)	3,232	14.40
Latvian (0)	58	0.26
Lithuanian (26)	215	0.96
Macedonian (56)	56	0.25
New Zealander (28)	28	0.12
Norwegian (29)	111	0.49
Pennsylvania German (0)	12	0.05
Polish (453)	1,545	6.88
Portuguese (5)	5	0.02
Romanian (27)	201	0.90
Russian (898)	1,951	8.69
Scandinavian (7)	7	0.03
Scotch-Irish (56)	96	0.43
Scottish (99)	265	1.18
Swedish (0)	151	0.67
Swiss (0)	169	0.75
Turkish (13)	135	0.60
Ukrainian (24)	63	0.28
Welsh (14)	53	0.24
West Indian, ex. Hispanic (502)	549	2.45
Belizean (11)	11	0.05
Haitian (52)	52	0.23
Jamaican (439)	474	2.11
Trinidadian/Tobagonian (0)	12	0.05

Hispanic Origin	Population	%
Hispanic or Latino (of any race)	3,113	12.99
Central American, ex. Mexican	202	0.84
Costa Rican	31	0.13
Guatemalan	33	0.14
Honduran	21	0.09
Nicaraguan	50	0.21
Panamanian	45	0.19
Salvadoran	22	0.09
Cuban	501	2.09
Dominican Republic	141	0.59
Mexican	329	1.37
Puerto Rican	527	2.20
South American	1,186	4.95
Argentinean	90	0.38
Bolivian	20	0.08
Chilean	50	0.21
Colombian	492	2.05
Ecuadorian	95	0.40
Paraguayan	2	0.01
Peruvian	166	0.69
Uruguayan	14	0.06
Venezuelan	253	1.06
Other South American	4	0.02
Other Hispanic or Latino	227	0.95

Race*	Population	%
African-American/Black (1,563)	1,719	7.17
Not Hispanic (1,504)	1,626	6.79
Hispanic (59)	93	0.39
American Indian/Alaska Native (32)	82	0.34
Not Hispanic (16)	47	0.20
Hispanic (16)	35	0.15
Central American Ind. (1)	1	<0.01
Cherokee (2)	14	0.06
Chippewa (0)	2	0.01
Lumbee (0)	1	<0.01
Mexican American Ind. (1)	1	<0.01
Navajo (0)	2	0.01
Potawatomi (0)	1	<0.01
Seminole (1)	3	0.01
South American Ind. (7)	10	0.04

*Notes: † The Census 2010 population figure is used to calculate the percentages in the Hispanic Origin and Race categories. Ancestry percentages are based on the 2006-2010 American Community Survey population (not shown); ‡ Numbers in parentheses indicate the number of people reporting a single ancestry; * Numbers in parentheses indicate the number of persons reporting this race alone, not in combination with any other race; Please refer to the Explanation of Data for more information.*

Tlingit-Haida *(Alaska Native)* (2)	4	0.02
Asian (1,405)	1,638	6.84
Not Hispanic (1,396)	1,608	6.71
Hispanic (9)	30	0.13
Bangladeshi (16)	16	0.07
Chinese, ex. Taiwanese (396)	450	1.88
Filipino (86)	119	0.50
Hmong (1)	1	<0.01
Indian (539)	597	2.49
Indonesian (3)	4	0.02
Japanese (11)	21	0.09
Korean (81)	95	0.40
Laotian (0)	1	<0.01
Pakistani (99)	115	0.48
Sri Lankan (2)	5	0.02
Taiwanese (28)	28	0.12
Thai (9)	13	0.05
Vietnamese (100)	103	0.43
Hawaii Native/Pacific Islander (5)	13	0.05
Not Hispanic (3)	11	0.05
Hispanic (2)	2	0.01
Fijian (1)	1	<0.01
Guamanian/Chamorro (2)	2	0.01
Native Hawaiian (2)	5	0.02
White (20,136)	20,480	85.47
Not Hispanic (17,506)	17,742	74.04
Hispanic (2,630)	2,738	11.43

Pasadena Hills

Place Type: CDP
County: Pasco
Population: 7,570†

Ancestry‡	Population	%
African, Sub-Saharan (78)	78	1.12
African (78)	78	1.12
American (345)	345	4.96
Arab (0)	11	0.16
Lebanese (0)	11	0.16
British (0)	15	0.22
Canadian (13)	13	0.19
Czechoslovakian (15)	15	0.22
Danish (38)	48	0.69
Dutch (17)	166	2.39
English (392)	806	11.60
European (118)	118	1.70
French, ex. Basque (44)	250	3.60
French Canadian (48)	83	1.19
German (545)	1,232	17.73
Greek (30)	62	0.89
Hungarian (35)	68	0.98
Irish (440)	1,098	15.80
Italian (114)	462	6.65
Lithuanian (19)	19	0.27
Polish (34)	215	3.09
Portuguese (23)	100	1.44
Romanian (96)	96	1.38
Russian (15)	70	1.01
Scandinavian (0)	79	1.14
Scotch-Irish (29)	176	2.53
Scottish (86)	218	3.14
Swedish (15)	37	0.53
Swiss (49)	49	0.71
Welsh (0)	106	1.53
West Indian, ex. Hispanic (41)	41	0.59
Haitian (41)	41	0.59
Yugoslavian (16)	16	0.23

Hispanic Origin	Population	%
Hispanic or Latino (of any race)	801	10.58
Central American, ex. Mexican	37	0.49
Costa Rican	9	0.12
Guatemalan	5	0.07
Honduran	9	0.12
Nicaraguan	6	0.08
Panamanian	6	0.08
Salvadoran	2	0.03
Cuban	84	1.11
Dominican Republic	39	0.52
Mexican	224	2.96
Puerto Rican	267	3.53
South American	75	0.99
Chilean	2	0.03
Colombian	31	0.41
Ecuadorian	10	0.13
Peruvian	9	0.12
Venezuelan	23	0.30
Other Hispanic or Latino	75	0.99

Race*	Population	%
African-American/Black (385)	457	6.04
Not Hispanic (356)	401	5.30
Hispanic (29)	56	0.74
American Indian/Alaska Native (30)	67	0.89
Not Hispanic (25)	57	0.75
Hispanic (5)	10	0.13
Apache (0)	2	0.03
Blackfeet (0)	4	0.05
Cherokee (11)	29	0.38
Chippewa (4)	4	0.05
Creek (0)	1	0.01
Iroquois (0)	1	0.01
Kiowa (1)	1	0.01
Lumbee (4)	7	0.09
Potawatomi (1)	2	0.03
Seminole (0)	2	0.03
Sioux (1)	2	0.03
Spanish American Ind. (2)	2	0.03
Yakama (1)	2	0.03
Asian (166)	203	2.68
Not Hispanic (166)	199	2.63
Hispanic (0)	4	0.05
Cambodian (0)	2	0.03
Chinese, ex. Taiwanese (17)	21	0.28
Filipino (36)	47	0.62
Indian (67)	72	0.95
Indonesian (1)	1	0.01
Japanese (3)	6	0.08
Korean (18)	19	0.25
Laotian (1)	1	0.01
Pakistani (5)	6	0.08
Sri Lankan (2)	2	0.03
Thai (2)	2	0.03
Vietnamese (7)	8	0.11
Hawaii Native/Pacific Islander (0)	5	0.07
Hispanic (0)	5	0.07
White (6,674)	6,818	90.07
Not Hispanic (6,108)	6,203	81.94
Hispanic (566)	615	8.12

Pebble Creek

Place Type: CDP
County: Hillsborough
Population: 7,622†

Ancestry‡	Population	%
African, Sub-Saharan (60)	72	0.95
African (14)	26	0.34
South African (46)	46	0.61
American (670)	670	8.86
Arab (31)	54	0.71
Arab (31)	31	0.41
Syrian (0)	9	0.12
Other Arab (0)	14	0.19
Armenian (0)	9	0.12
Austrian (0)	10	0.13
Belgian (0)	11	0.15
British (51)	51	0.67
Czech (0)	42	0.56
Czechoslovakian (88)	145	1.92
Danish (0)	38	0.50
Dutch (21)	75	0.99
English (183)	527	6.97
European (72)	93	1.23
French, ex. Basque (64)	208	2.75
German (274)	910	12.04
Hungarian (10)	42	0.56
Iranian (10)	10	0.13
Irish (247)	958	12.67
Italian (165)	626	8.28
Northern European (0)	20	0.26
Norwegian (22)	33	0.44
Polish (24)	131	1.73
Portuguese (19)	30	0.40
Russian (0)	14	0.19
Scandinavian (12)	26	0.34
Scotch-Irish (27)	48	0.63
Scottish (12)	82	1.08
Serbian (21)	21	0.28
Slovak (15)	15	0.20
Swedish (0)	20	0.26
Swiss (29)	84	1.11
Turkish (16)	16	0.21
Ukrainian (34)	43	0.57
Welsh (13)	13	0.17
West Indian, ex. Hispanic (394)	510	6.75
Bahamian (172)	223	2.95
Bermudan (20)	20	0.26
Jamaican (108)	173	2.29
Trinidadian/Tobagonian (94)	94	1.24
Yugoslavian (7)	7	0.09

Hispanic Origin	Population	%
Hispanic or Latino (of any race)	1,370	17.97
Central American, ex. Mexican	83	1.09
Costa Rican	12	0.16
Guatemalan	6	0.08
Honduran	9	0.12
Nicaraguan	13	0.17
Panamanian	29	0.38
Salvadoran	13	0.17
Other Central American	1	0.01
Cuban	213	2.79
Dominican Republic	94	1.23
Mexican	86	1.13
Puerto Rican	475	6.23
South American	288	3.78
Argentinean	9	0.12
Bolivian	2	0.03
Chilean	10	0.13
Colombian	140	1.84
Ecuadorian	30	0.39
Peruvian	41	0.54
Venezuelan	55	0.72
Other South American	1	0.01
Other Hispanic or Latino	131	1.72

Race*	Population	%
African-American/Black (916)	1,026	13.46
Not Hispanic (860)	932	12.23
Hispanic (56)	94	1.23
American Indian/Alaska Native (11)	41	0.54
Not Hispanic (1)	24	0.31
Hispanic (10)	17	0.22
Central American Ind. (1)	1	0.01
Cherokee (0)	6	0.08
Choctaw (0)	1	0.01
Navajo (0)	1	0.01
Seminole (0)	1	0.01
Sioux (1)	1	0.01
South American Ind. (4)	7	0.09
Asian (975)	1,138	14.93
Not Hispanic (960)	1,105	14.50
Hispanic (15)	33	0.43
Bangladeshi (1)	1	0.01
Chinese, ex. Taiwanese (130)	149	1.95
Filipino (121)	149	1.95
Indian (497)	536	7.03
Indonesian (1)	1	0.01
Japanese (8)	19	0.25
Korean (84)	98	1.29
Laotian (2)	2	0.03
Malaysian (1)	2	0.03
Nepalese (2)	2	0.03
Pakistani (21)	21	0.28
Taiwanese (9)	11	0.14
Thai (5)	8	0.10
Vietnamese (55)	70	0.92

*Notes: † The Census 2010 population figure is used to calculate the percentages in the Hispanic Origin and Race categories. Ancestry percentages are based on the 2006-2010 American Community Survey population (not shown); ‡ Numbers in parentheses indicate the number of people reporting a single ancestry; * Numbers in parentheses indicate the number of persons reporting this race alone, not in combination with any other race; Please refer to the Explanation of Data for more information.*

Hawaii Native/Pacific Islander (2)	10	0.13
Not Hispanic (2)	10	0.13
Guamanian/Chamorro (1)	4	0.05
Native Hawaiian (0)	2	0.03
White (5,165)	5,404	70.90
Not Hispanic (4,180)	4,350	57.07
Hispanic (985)	1,054	13.83

Pembroke Pines

Place Type: City
County: Broward
Population: 154,750†

Ancestry‡	Population	%
African, Sub-Saharan (1,113)	1,344	0.88
African (388)	582	0.38
Cape Verdean (61)	87	0.06
Ghanaian (34)	34	0.02
Nigerian (416)	416	0.27
South African (214)	214	0.14
Other Sub-Saharan African (0)	11	0.01
Albanian (0)	8	0.01
American (6,852)	6,852	4.50
Arab (870)	1,356	0.89
Arab (75)	96	0.06
Egyptian (45)	45	0.03
Iraqi (0)	73	0.05
Jordanian (14)	30	0.02
Lebanese (183)	331	0.22
Moroccan (10)	21	0.01
Palestinian (378)	404	0.27
Syrian (95)	192	0.13
Other Arab (70)	164	0.11
Armenian (58)	105	0.07
Australian (50)	103	0.07
Austrian (242)	484	0.32
Basque (10)	19	0.01
Belgian (0)	26	0.02
Brazilian (852)	1,118	0.73
British (336)	496	0.33
Canadian (391)	602	0.40
Celtic (0)	10	0.01
Croatian (28)	66	0.04
Czech (99)	151	0.10
Czechoslovakian (29)	29	0.02
Danish (82)	399	0.26
Dutch (456)	1,181	0.78
Eastern European (282)	337	0.22
English (1,228)	4,650	3.05
European (1,051)	1,308	0.86
Finnish (51)	79	0.05
French, ex. Basque (444)	2,190	1.44
French Canadian (325)	566	0.37
German (2,552)	8,660	5.68
Greek (226)	453	0.30
Guyanese (210)	557	0.37
Hungarian (233)	714	0.47
Iranian (151)	168	0.11
Irish (2,609)	8,542	5.61
Israeli (254)	443	0.29
Italian (5,603)	10,601	6.96
Latvian (9)	21	0.01
Lithuanian (83)	261	0.17
Luxemburger (13)	13	0.01
Macedonian (11)	11	0.01
Maltese (0)	6	<0.01
Northern European (36)	36	0.02
Norwegian (112)	373	0.24
Pennsylvania German (37)	128	0.08
Polish (1,528)	3,956	2.60
Portuguese (250)	421	0.28
Romanian (364)	756	0.50
Russian (1,414)	2,834	1.86
Scandinavian (12)	30	0.02
Scotch-Irish (205)	626	0.41
Scottish (307)	936	0.61
Serbian (13)	65	0.04
Slavic (9)	41	0.03
Slovak (0)	81	0.05
Slovene (59)	169	0.11
Swedish (201)	844	0.55
Swiss (44)	127	0.08
Turkish (232)	289	0.19
Ukrainian (92)	257	0.17
Welsh (38)	324	0.21
West Indian, ex. Hispanic (15,387)	17,733	11.64
Bahamian (420)	499	0.33
Barbadian (122)	320	0.21
Belizean (31)	31	0.02
Bermudan (22)	67	0.04
British West Indian (239)	246	0.16
Dutch West Indian (16)	16	0.01
Haitian (6,182)	6,591	4.33
Jamaican (6,970)	8,136	5.34
Trinidadian/Tobagonian (740)	836	0.55
U.S. Virgin Islander (18)	18	0.01
West Indian (627)	953	0.63
Other West Indian (0)	20	0.01
Yugoslavian (43)	43	0.03

Hispanic Origin	Population	%
Hispanic or Latino (of any race)	64,061	41.40
Central American, ex. Mexican	4,614	2.98
Costa Rican	407	0.26
Guatemalan	529	0.34
Honduran	996	0.64
Nicaraguan	1,423	0.92
Panamanian	676	0.44
Salvadoran	575	0.37
Other Central American	8	0.01
Cuban	19,826	12.81
Dominican Republic	4,804	3.10
Mexican	1,658	1.07
Puerto Rican	10,490	6.78
South American	19,424	12.55
Argentinean	1,147	0.74
Bolivian	153	0.10
Chilean	558	0.36
Colombian	9,937	6.42
Ecuadorian	1,732	1.12
Paraguayan	33	0.02
Peruvian	2,638	1.70
Uruguayan	243	0.16
Venezuelan	2,937	1.90
Other South American	46	0.03
Other Hispanic or Latino	3,245	2.10

Race*	Population	%
African-American/Black (30,644)	33,182	21.44
Not Hispanic (28,435)	30,139	19.48
Hispanic (2,209)	3,043	1.97
American Indian/Alaska Native (392)	837	0.54
Not Hispanic (260)	522	0.34
Hispanic (132)	315	0.20
Alaska Athabascan *(Ala. Nat.)* (4)	5	<0.01
Apache (4)	6	<0.01
Arapaho (1)	1	<0.01
Blackfeet (1)	9	0.01
Canadian/French Am. Ind. (2)	2	<0.01
Central American Ind. (8)	19	0.01
Cherokee (32)	79	0.05
Chickasaw (0)	1	<0.01
Chippewa (2)	9	0.01
Choctaw (4)	13	0.01
Comanche (1)	1	<0.01
Creek (7)	16	0.01
Hopi (1)	1	<0.01
Houma (6)	6	<0.01
Iroquois (4)	4	<0.01
Lumbee (1)	1	<0.01
Mexican American Ind. (16)	25	0.02
Navajo (1)	5	<0.01
Osage (0)	1	<0.01
Seminole (56)	65	0.04
Sioux (2)	6	<0.01
South American Ind. (32)	75	0.05
Spanish American Ind. (2)	10	0.01
Tlingit-Haida *(Alaska Native)* (0)	3	<0.01
Yakama (1)	1	<0.01
Yaqui (0)	1	<0.01
Asian (7,627)	9,278	6.00
Not Hispanic (7,469)	8,804	5.69
Hispanic (158)	474	0.31
Bangladeshi (70)	88	0.06
Burmese (20)	22	0.01
Cambodian (11)	12	0.01
Chinese, ex. Taiwanese (1,377)	1,951	1.26
Filipino (1,171)	1,398	0.90
Hmong (6)	6	<0.01
Indian (2,879)	3,466	2.24
Indonesian (18)	34	0.02
Japanese (129)	266	0.17
Korean (340)	395	0.26
Laotian (14)	18	0.01
Malaysian (14)	18	0.01
Nepalese (0)	2	<0.01
Pakistani (681)	782	0.51
Sri Lankan (19)	20	0.01
Taiwanese (63)	82	0.05
Thai (76)	100	0.06
Vietnamese (428)	472	0.31
Hawaii Native/Pacific Islander (73)	318	0.21
Not Hispanic (55)	239	0.15
Hispanic (18)	79	0.05
Fijian (1)	4	<0.01
Guamanian/Chamorro (24)	30	0.02
Native Hawaiian (8)	38	0.02
Samoan (5)	11	0.01
Tongan (1)	1	<0.01
White (104,139)	107,718	69.61
Not Hispanic (50,964)	52,589	33.98
Hispanic (53,175)	55,129	35.62

Pensacola

Place Type: City
County: Escambia
Population: 51,923†

Ancestry‡	Population	%
African, Sub-Saharan (400)	466	0.88
African (387)	453	0.86
Nigerian (13)	13	0.02
American (3,314)	3,314	6.26
Arab (15)	87	0.16
Egyptian (15)	15	0.03
Lebanese (0)	15	0.03
Moroccan (0)	28	0.05
Syrian (0)	29	0.05
Armenian (53)	79	0.15
Australian (0)	23	0.04
Austrian (27)	115	0.22
Belgian (25)	177	0.33
Brazilian (134)	134	0.25
British (88)	239	0.45
Cajun (22)	52	0.10
Canadian (92)	122	0.23
Celtic (0)	9	0.02
Croatian (0)	6	0.01
Czech (25)	117	0.22
Czechoslovakian (0)	60	0.11
Danish (12)	89	0.17
Dutch (175)	995	1.88
Eastern European (60)	71	0.13
English (2,267)	5,844	11.05
European (646)	768	1.45
Finnish (0)	38	0.07
French, ex. Basque (421)	2,208	4.17
French Canadian (128)	264	0.50
German (1,844)	7,030	13.29
Greek (154)	333	0.63
Guyanese (29)	29	0.05
Hungarian (0)	131	0.25
Icelander (0)	15	0.03
Iranian (0)	6	0.01
Irish (1,980)	6,692	12.65
Italian (1,118)	2,478	4.68
Lithuanian (30)	98	0.19
Luxemburger (0)	7	0.01

*Notes: † The Census 2010 population figure is used to calculate the percentages in the Hispanic Origin and Race categories. Ancestry percentages are based on the 2006-2010 American Community Survey population (not shown); ‡ Numbers in parentheses indicate the number of people reporting a single ancestry; * Numbers in parentheses indicate the number of persons reporting this race alone, not in combination with any other race; Please refer to the Explanation of Data for more information.*

Ancestry	Population	%
Northern European (43)	57	0.11
Norwegian (189)	756	1.43
Pennsylvania German (68)	68	0.13
Polish (336)	1,263	2.39
Portuguese (106)	198	0.37
Russian (179)	411	0.78
Scandinavian (50)	116	0.22
Scotch-Irish (883)	1,641	3.10
Scottish (629)	1,616	3.05
Slovak (12)	12	0.02
Slovene (23)	46	0.09
Swedish (91)	465	0.88
Swiss (0)	49	0.09
Ukrainian (59)	113	0.21
Welsh (38)	313	0.59
West Indian, ex. Hispanic (810)	873	1.65
British West Indian (66)	66	0.12
Dutch West Indian (34)	34	0.06
Haitian (212)	223	0.42
Jamaican (215)	254	0.48
Trinidadian/Tobagonian (264)	264	0.50
West Indian (19)	32	0.06
Yugoslavian (0)	10	0.02

Hispanic Origin	Population	%
Hispanic or Latino (of any race)	1,711	3.30
Central American, ex. Mexican	161	0.31
Costa Rican	22	0.04
Guatemalan	17	0.03
Honduran	35	0.07
Nicaraguan	18	0.03
Panamanian	33	0.06
Salvadoran	27	0.05
Other Central American	9	0.02
Cuban	148	0.29
Dominican Republic	36	0.07
Mexican	574	1.11
Puerto Rican	368	0.71
South American	178	0.34
Argentinean	17	0.03
Bolivian	7	0.01
Chilean	17	0.03
Colombian	53	0.10
Ecuadorian	14	0.03
Peruvian	45	0.09
Uruguayan	4	0.01
Venezuelan	15	0.03
Other South American	6	0.01
Other Hispanic or Latino	246	0.47

Race*	Population	%
African-American/Black (14,530)	15,070	29.02
Not Hispanic (14,420)	14,875	28.65
Hispanic (110)	195	0.38
American Indian/Alaska Native (291)	677	1.30
Not Hispanic (269)	611	1.18
Hispanic (22)	66	0.13
Apache (2)	5	0.01
Blackfeet (3)	19	0.04
Canadian/French Am. Ind. (1)	1	<0.01
Central American Ind. (1)	1	<0.01
Cherokee (52)	171	0.33
Cheyenne (1)	4	0.01
Chickasaw (5)	6	0.01
Chippewa (3)	5	0.01
Choctaw (5)	15	0.03
Cree (1)	1	<0.01
Creek (91)	138	0.27
Delaware (0)	3	0.01
Hopi (1)	1	<0.01
Houma (2)	3	0.01
Iroquois (1)	3	0.01
Lumbee (0)	1	<0.01
Mexican American Ind. (1)	11	0.02
Navajo (7)	9	0.02
Osage (0)	2	<0.01
Ottawa (1)	1	<0.01
Paiute (0)	1	<0.01
Pima (1)	1	<0.01
Potawatomi (1)	2	<0.01
Pueblo (0)	7	0.01
Puget Sound Salish (0)	1	<0.01
Seminole (0)	3	0.01
Shoshone (1)	1	<0.01
Sioux (7)	12	0.02
South American Ind. (7)	8	0.02
Asian (1,037)	1,390	2.68
Not Hispanic (1,024)	1,345	2.59
Hispanic (13)	45	0.09
Bangladeshi (3)	3	0.01
Burmese (7)	7	0.01
Cambodian (12)	16	0.03
Chinese, ex. Taiwanese (159)	214	0.41
Filipino (250)	421	0.81
Hmong (2)	2	<0.01
Indian (109)	140	0.27
Indonesian (2)	5	0.01
Japanese (53)	100	0.19
Korean (80)	119	0.23
Laotian (1)	2	<0.01
Nepalese (7)	7	0.01
Pakistani (11)	14	0.03
Sri Lankan (0)	3	0.01
Taiwanese (5)	9	0.02
Thai (22)	29	0.06
Vietnamese (275)	299	0.58
Hawaii Native/Pacific Islander (62)	136	0.26
Not Hispanic (62)	128	0.25
Hispanic (0)	8	0.02
Guamanian/Chamorro (24)	41	0.08
Native Hawaiian (12)	37	0.07
Samoan (10)	21	0.04
Tongan (10)	10	0.02
White (34,446)	35,449	68.27
Not Hispanic (33,383)	34,227	65.92
Hispanic (1,063)	1,222	2.35

Pine Castle

Place Type: CDP
County: Orange
Population: 10,805†

Ancestry‡	Population	%
American (432)	432	3.95
Arab (184)	184	1.68
Egyptian (128)	128	1.17
Jordanian (27)	27	0.25
Moroccan (29)	29	0.27
Assyrian/Chaldean/Syriac (333)	333	3.05
Brazilian (52)	80	0.73
British (14)	14	0.13
Czech (0)	10	0.09
Danish (34)	73	0.67
Dutch (8)	86	0.79
English (204)	512	4.69
European (29)	29	0.27
French, ex. Basque (48)	89	0.81
French Canadian (18)	18	0.16
German (202)	537	4.92
Guyanese (33)	33	0.30
Hungarian (8)	15	0.14
Irish (132)	481	4.40
Italian (49)	209	1.91
Latvian (0)	63	0.58
Norwegian (14)	87	0.80
Polish (228)	258	2.36
Portuguese (14)	86	0.79
Russian (12)	28	0.26
Scotch-Irish (35)	66	0.60
Scottish (11)	39	0.36
Swedish (10)	24	0.22
Swiss (0)	16	0.15
Ukrainian (0)	18	0.16
Welsh (0)	23	0.21
West Indian, ex. Hispanic (994)	994	9.10
Haitian (886)	886	8.11
Trinidadian/Tobagonian (31)	31	0.28
West Indian (77)	77	0.70
Yugoslavian (59)	59	0.54

Hispanic Origin	Population	%
Hispanic or Latino (of any race)	5,252	48.61
Central American, ex. Mexican	329	3.04
Costa Rican	14	0.13
Guatemalan	72	0.67
Honduran	97	0.90
Nicaraguan	36	0.33
Panamanian	25	0.23
Salvadoran	85	0.79
Cuban	646	5.98
Dominican Republic	300	2.78
Mexican	1,103	10.21
Puerto Rican	2,349	21.74
South American	366	3.39
Argentinean	35	0.32
Bolivian	5	0.05
Chilean	6	0.06
Colombian	130	1.20
Ecuadorian	68	0.63
Peruvian	50	0.46
Uruguayan	12	0.11
Venezuelan	52	0.48
Other South American	8	0.07
Other Hispanic or Latino	159	1.47

Race*	Population	%
African-American/Black (1,831)	1,977	18.30
Not Hispanic (1,592)	1,659	15.35
Hispanic (239)	318	2.94
American Indian/Alaska Native (83)	136	1.26
Not Hispanic (29)	54	0.50
Hispanic (54)	82	0.76
Apache (1)	2	0.02
Blackfeet (0)	4	0.04
Central American Ind. (2)	2	0.02
Cherokee (1)	9	0.08
Chickasaw (1)	3	0.03
Chippewa (3)	3	0.03
Choctaw (0)	1	0.01
Comanche (1)	1	0.01
Creek (0)	1	0.01
Lumbee (0)	3	0.03
Mexican American Ind. (9)	13	0.12
Potawatomi (1)	2	0.02
Seminole (3)	3	0.03
South American Ind. (4)	6	0.06
Spanish American Ind. (1)	3	0.03
Asian (522)	609	5.64
Not Hispanic (510)	575	5.32
Hispanic (12)	34	0.31
Bangladeshi (27)	27	0.25
Burmese (52)	56	0.52
Cambodian (3)	3	0.03
Chinese, ex. Taiwanese (34)	45	0.42
Filipino (74)	99	0.92
Indian (65)	86	0.80
Japanese (3)	11	0.10
Korean (20)	29	0.27
Pakistani (21)	21	0.19
Sri Lankan (0)	1	0.01
Thai (7)	10	0.09
Vietnamese (188)	199	1.84
Hawaii Native/Pacific Islander (17)	52	0.48
Not Hispanic (15)	34	0.31
Hispanic (2)	18	0.17
Fijian (4)	4	0.04
Native Hawaiian (5)	11	0.10
Samoan (0)	2	0.02
Tongan (1)	1	0.01
White (6,673)	6,983	64.63
Not Hispanic (3,198)	3,294	30.49
Hispanic (3,475)	3,689	34.14

Pine Hills

Place Type: CDP
County: Orange
Population: 60,076†

*Notes: † The Census 2010 population figure is used to calculate the percentages in the Hispanic Origin and Race categories. Ancestry percentages are based on the 2006-2010 American Community Survey population (not shown); ‡ Numbers in parentheses indicate the number of people reporting a single ancestry; * Numbers in parentheses indicate the number of persons reporting this race alone, not in combination with any other race; Please refer to the Explanation of Data for more information.*

Ancestry‡	Population	%
Afghan (28)	28	0.04
African, Sub-Saharan (371)	549	0.83
African (324)	451	0.68
Ethiopian (0)	34	0.05
Ghanaian (36)	36	0.05
Nigerian (11)	28	0.04
American (1,639)	1,639	2.48
Arab (41)	163	0.25
Lebanese (19)	66	0.10
Syrian (22)	97	0.15
Austrian (0)	7	0.01
Basque (14)	14	0.02
Belgian (0)	46	0.07
British (35)	101	0.15
Canadian (58)	58	0.09
Croatian (0)	5	0.01
Czech (10)	47	0.07
Danish (44)	156	0.24
Dutch (54)	387	0.58
English (660)	2,058	3.11
European (51)	70	0.11
Finnish (0)	11	0.02
French, ex. Basque (168)	584	0.88
French Canadian (53)	67	0.10
German (580)	1,895	2.86
Greek (20)	51	0.08
Guyanese (605)	881	1.33
Hungarian (14)	54	0.08
Irish (491)	1,880	2.84
Italian (319)	846	1.28
Lithuanian (5)	11	0.02
Norwegian (12)	62	0.09
Polish (82)	247	0.37
Portuguese (15)	55	0.08
Russian (12)	76	0.11
Scandinavian (0)	14	0.02
Scotch-Irish (82)	307	0.46
Scottish (57)	290	0.44
Slovak (25)	52	0.08
Swedish (134)	197	0.30
Swiss (0)	46	0.07
Ukrainian (0)	15	0.02
Welsh (0)	77	0.12
West Indian, ex. Hispanic (16,724)	18,274	27.60
Bahamian (91)	201	0.30
Barbadian (26)	36	0.05
Belizean (0)	27	0.04
British West Indian (388)	425	0.64
Haitian (9,902)	10,217	15.43
Jamaican (4,615)	5,236	7.91
Trinidadian/Tobagonian (599)	720	1.09
U.S. Virgin Islander (405)	435	0.66
West Indian (698)	977	1.48
Yugoslavian (17)	17	0.03

Hispanic Origin	Population	%
Hispanic or Latino (of any race)	8,324	13.86
Central American, ex. Mexican	808	1.34
Costa Rican	31	0.05
Guatemalan	162	0.27
Honduran	242	0.40
Nicaraguan	90	0.15
Panamanian	113	0.19
Salvadoran	166	0.28
Other Central American	4	0.01
Cuban	343	0.57
Dominican Republic	662	1.10
Mexican	1,477	2.46
Puerto Rican	4,115	6.85
South American	417	0.69
Argentinean	14	0.02
Bolivian	4	0.01
Chilean	9	0.01
Colombian	157	0.26
Ecuadorian	65	0.11
Paraguayan	1	<0.01
Peruvian	42	0.07
Uruguayan	9	0.01
Venezuelan	81	0.13
Other South American	35	0.06
Other Hispanic or Latino	502	0.84

Race*	Population	%
African-American/Black (40,611)	41,922	69.78
Not Hispanic (39,642)	40,711	67.77
Hispanic (969)	1,211	2.02
American Indian/Alaska Native (280)	627	1.04
Not Hispanic (167)	444	0.74
Hispanic (113)	183	0.30
Apache (1)	4	0.01
Arapaho (1)	1	<0.01
Blackfeet (0)	14	0.02
Canadian/French Am. Ind. (1)	2	<0.01
Central American Ind. (1)	1	<0.01
Cherokee (22)	67	0.11
Cheyenne (1)	3	<0.01
Chippewa (1)	6	0.01
Choctaw (3)	8	0.01
Comanche (1)	1	<0.01
Creek (3)	8	0.01
Delaware (4)	4	0.01
Inupiat *(Alaska Native)* (1)	1	<0.01
Iroquois (0)	2	<0.01
Lumbee (0)	1	<0.01
Mexican American Ind. (3)	3	<0.01
Navajo (0)	5	0.01
Potawatomi (0)	1	<0.01
Puget Sound Salish (0)	4	0.01
Seminole (1)	10	0.02
Sioux (2)	9	0.01
South American Ind. (16)	25	0.04
Spanish American Ind. (5)	6	0.01
Tlingit-Haida *(Alaska Native)* (3)	7	0.01
Asian (2,259)	2,751	4.58
Not Hispanic (2,225)	2,657	4.42
Hispanic (34)	94	0.16
Bangladeshi (6)	7	0.01
Burmese (1)	1	<0.01
Cambodian (0)	1	<0.01
Chinese, ex. Taiwanese (106)	189	0.31
Filipino (102)	147	0.24
Hmong (0)	1	<0.01
Indian (764)	984	1.64
Indonesian (2)	7	0.01
Japanese (19)	41	0.07
Korean (21)	32	0.05
Laotian (19)	20	0.03
Pakistani (18)	25	0.04
Sri Lankan (1)	6	0.01
Thai (24)	30	0.05
Vietnamese (1,104)	1,152	1.92
Hawaii Native/Pacific Islander (51)	353	0.59
Not Hispanic (41)	306	0.51
Hispanic (10)	47	0.08
Guamanian/Chamorro (13)	22	0.04
Native Hawaiian (1)	10	0.02
Samoan (7)	12	0.02
Tongan (0)	4	0.01
White (11,783)	12,743	21.21
Not Hispanic (7,793)	8,370	13.93
Hispanic (3,990)	4,373	7.28

Pine Ridge

Place Type: CDP
County: Citrus
Population: 9,598†

Ancestry‡	Population	%
African, Sub-Saharan (0)	10	0.11
Nigerian (0)	10	0.11
American (1,412)	1,412	15.85
Armenian (0)	13	0.15
Austrian (0)	47	0.53
Belgian (23)	23	0.26
British (33)	46	0.52
Canadian (7)	21	0.24
Czech (0)	30	0.34
Danish (11)	22	0.25
Dutch (118)	286	3.21
English (353)	1,162	13.04
European (73)	73	0.82
Finnish (0)	13	0.15
French, ex. Basque (176)	411	4.61
French Canadian (54)	77	0.86
German (746)	1,895	21.27
Greek (63)	104	1.17
Hungarian (10)	75	0.84
Irish (335)	1,361	15.27
Italian (665)	915	10.27
Lithuanian (9)	32	0.36
Norwegian (8)	45	0.51
Polish (169)	346	3.88
Portuguese (21)	34	0.38
Russian (56)	109	1.22
Scandinavian (12)	27	0.30
Scotch-Irish (61)	123	1.38
Scottish (47)	174	1.95
Serbian (14)	14	0.16
Slovak (38)	57	0.64
Swedish (19)	133	1.49
Turkish (0)	10	0.11
Ukrainian (17)	17	0.19
Welsh (23)	65	0.73
West Indian, ex. Hispanic (24)	50	0.56
Barbadian (24)	24	0.27
Dutch West Indian (0)	26	0.29
Yugoslavian (0)	16	0.18

Hispanic Origin	Population	%
Hispanic or Latino (of any race)	544	5.67
Central American, ex. Mexican	66	0.69
Costa Rican	8	0.08
Guatemalan	4	0.04
Honduran	26	0.27
Nicaraguan	1	0.01
Panamanian	21	0.22
Salvadoran	6	0.06
Cuban	73	0.76
Dominican Republic	4	0.04
Mexican	62	0.65
Puerto Rican	252	2.63
South American	37	0.39
Argentinean	7	0.07
Bolivian	1	0.01
Chilean	2	0.02
Colombian	15	0.16
Ecuadorian	3	0.03
Peruvian	2	0.02
Venezuelan	7	0.07
Other Hispanic or Latino	50	0.52

Race*	Population	%
African-American/Black (402)	451	4.70
Not Hispanic (378)	419	4.37
Hispanic (24)	32	0.33
American Indian/Alaska Native (19)	69	0.72
Not Hispanic (13)	56	0.58
Hispanic (6)	13	0.14
Blackfeet (0)	1	0.01
Canadian/French Am. Ind. (1)	3	0.03
Central American Ind. (1)	1	0.01
Cherokee (0)	9	0.09
Choctaw (0)	1	0.01
Houma (1)	2	0.02
Osage (1)	1	0.01
Seminole (0)	1	0.01
Sioux (5)	5	0.05
South American Ind. (0)	1	0.01
Asian (218)	270	2.81
Not Hispanic (216)	262	2.73
Hispanic (2)	8	0.08
Burmese (1)	1	0.01
Cambodian (5)	6	0.06
Chinese, ex. Taiwanese (19)	28	0.29
Filipino (114)	141	1.47
Indian (36)	38	0.40
Indonesian (0)	2	0.02
Japanese (5)	9	0.09

*Notes: † The Census 2010 population figure is used to calculate the percentages in the Hispanic Origin and Race categories. Ancestry percentages are based on the 2006-2010 American Community Survey population (not shown); ‡ Numbers in parentheses indicate the number of people reporting a single ancestry; * Numbers in parentheses indicate the number of persons reporting this race alone, not in combination with any other race; Please refer to the Explanation of Data for more information.*

Korean (16)	23	0.24
Laotian (1)	3	0.03
Malaysian (2)	2	0.02
Taiwanese (2)	2	0.02
Thai (3)	4	0.04
Vietnamese (10)	10	0.10
Hawaii Native/Pacific Islander (3)	7	0.07
Not Hispanic (3)	7	0.07
Native Hawaiian (1)	1	0.01
Tongan (1)	1	0.01
White (8,740)	8,846	92.17
Not Hispanic (8,315)	8,402	87.54
Hispanic (425)	444	4.63

Pinecrest

Place Type: Village
County: Miami-Dade
Population: 18,223†

Ancestry‡	Population	%
American (996)	996	5.43
Arab (96)	194	1.06
Arab (0)	58	0.32
Lebanese (24)	64	0.35
Palestinian (72)	72	0.39
Austrian (29)	104	0.57
Belgian (14)	30	0.16
British (114)	234	1.28
Canadian (30)	30	0.16
Croatian (0)	13	0.07
Czech (29)	61	0.33
Czechoslovakian (27)	27	0.15
Danish (97)	106	0.58
Dutch (103)	310	1.69
Eastern European (86)	135	0.74
English (396)	1,519	8.28
European (256)	271	1.48
Finnish (0)	62	0.34
French, ex. Basque (60)	523	2.85
French Canadian (13)	13	0.07
German (559)	1,911	10.42
Greek (84)	131	0.71
Hungarian (15)	48	0.26
Iranian (0)	16	0.09
Irish (333)	1,188	6.48
Israeli (15)	15	0.08
Italian (273)	986	5.38
Lithuanian (62)	116	0.63
Macedonian (0)	16	0.09
Northern European (59)	59	0.32
Norwegian (0)	83	0.45
Polish (130)	711	3.88
Portuguese (15)	58	0.32
Russian (439)	1,255	6.84
Scandinavian (0)	78	0.43
Scotch-Irish (23)	74	0.40
Scottish (170)	395	2.15
Slavic (20)	47	0.26
Slovak (0)	109	0.59
Swedish (25)	247	1.35
Swiss (25)	77	0.42
Ukrainian (122)	137	0.75
Welsh (11)	99	0.54
West Indian, ex. Hispanic (140)	201	1.10
Bahamian (17)	17	0.09
Haitian (85)	131	0.71
Jamaican (38)	53	0.29

Hispanic Origin	Population	%
Hispanic or Latino (of any race)	7,528	41.31
Central American, ex. Mexican	653	3.58
Costa Rican	40	0.22
Guatemalan	38	0.21
Honduran	74	0.41
Nicaraguan	368	2.02
Panamanian	57	0.31
Salvadoran	73	0.40
Other Central American	3	0.02
Cuban	3,923	21.53
Dominican Republic	187	1.03
Mexican	295	1.62
Puerto Rican	366	2.01
South American	1,675	9.19
Argentinean	192	1.05
Bolivian	54	0.30
Chilean	146	0.80
Colombian	545	2.99
Ecuadorian	98	0.54
Paraguayan	7	0.04
Peruvian	247	1.36
Uruguayan	36	0.20
Venezuelan	348	1.91
Other South American	2	0.01
Other Hispanic or Latino	429	2.35

Race*	Population	%
African-American/Black (364)	434	2.38
Not Hispanic (321)	373	2.05
Hispanic (43)	61	0.33
American Indian/Alaska Native (26)	52	0.29
Not Hispanic (12)	30	0.16
Hispanic (14)	22	0.12
Canadian/French Am. Ind. (0)	4	0.02
Cherokee (1)	3	0.02
Lumbee (2)	2	0.01
Mexican American Ind. (1)	1	0.01
Paiute (1)	1	0.01
Seminole (1)	1	0.01
Sioux (3)	3	0.02
South American Ind. (3)	9	0.05
Spanish American Ind. (6)	7	0.04
Asian (965)	1,118	6.14
Not Hispanic (945)	1,064	5.84
Hispanic (20)	54	0.30
Burmese (9)	13	0.07
Cambodian (0)	1	0.01
Chinese, ex. Taiwanese (463)	524	2.88
Filipino (36)	50	0.27
Indian (211)	230	1.26
Indonesian (8)	9	0.05
Japanese (49)	69	0.38
Korean (82)	91	0.50
Laotian (1)	1	0.01
Pakistani (21)	23	0.13
Sri Lankan (1)	1	0.01
Taiwanese (30)	38	0.21
Thai (27)	31	0.17
Vietnamese (3)	16	0.09
Hawaii Native/Pacific Islander (0)	9	0.05
Not Hispanic (0)	7	0.04
Hispanic (0)	2	0.01
Native Hawaiian (0)	5	0.03
Samoan (0)	1	0.01
White (16,410)	16,670	91.48
Not Hispanic (9,193)	9,345	51.28
Hispanic (7,217)	7,325	40.20

Pinellas Park

Place Type: City
County: Pinellas
Population: 49,079†

Ancestry‡	Population	%
African, Sub-Saharan (131)	131	0.27
African (99)	99	0.20
Cape Verdean (32)	32	0.07
Albanian (223)	223	0.46
American (1,979)	1,979	4.06
Arab (75)	115	0.24
Arab (23)	23	0.05
Egyptian (20)	20	0.04
Lebanese (32)	54	0.11
Syrian (0)	18	0.04
Armenian (17)	17	0.03
Australian (0)	22	0.05
Austrian (33)	119	0.24
Belgian (97)	126	0.26
Brazilian (48)	56	0.11
British (67)	183	0.38
Bulgarian (36)	36	0.07
Canadian (316)	392	0.80
Croatian (23)	116	0.24
Czech (80)	121	0.25
Czechoslovakian (81)	109	0.22
Danish (17)	80	0.16
Dutch (131)	680	1.39
Eastern European (15)	15	0.03
English (2,785)	6,088	12.48
Estonian (62)	62	0.13
European (371)	435	0.89
Finnish (16)	33	0.07
French, ex. Basque (561)	2,218	4.55
French Canadian (616)	778	1.60
German (3,602)	8,659	17.75
Greek (313)	384	0.79
Guyanese (222)	222	0.46
Hungarian (157)	390	0.80
Irish (2,078)	5,897	12.09
Italian (2,152)	3,845	7.88
Latvian (0)	46	0.09
Lithuanian (99)	250	0.51
Macedonian (13)	13	0.03
Norwegian (98)	295	0.60
Pennsylvania German (11)	36	0.07
Polish (886)	1,637	3.36
Portuguese (111)	173	0.35
Romanian (9)	9	0.02
Russian (163)	417	0.85
Scandinavian (23)	54	0.11
Scotch-Irish (517)	920	1.89
Scottish (578)	1,135	2.33
Serbian (0)	8	0.02
Slovak (26)	61	0.13
Swedish (210)	668	1.37
Swiss (89)	147	0.30
Ukrainian (148)	302	0.62
Welsh (84)	250	0.51
West Indian, ex. Hispanic (105)	169	0.35
Belizean (67)	67	0.14
Haitian (8)	8	0.02
Jamaican (0)	64	0.13
Trinidadian/Tobagonian (22)	22	0.05
West Indian (8)	8	0.02
Yugoslavian (499)	524	1.07

Hispanic Origin	Population	%
Hispanic or Latino (of any race)	5,266	10.73
Central American, ex. Mexican	339	0.69
Costa Rican	43	0.09
Guatemalan	71	0.14
Honduran	84	0.17
Nicaraguan	39	0.08
Panamanian	44	0.09
Salvadoran	53	0.11
Other Central American	5	0.01
Cuban	491	1.00
Dominican Republic	189	0.39
Mexican	1,285	2.62
Puerto Rican	2,056	4.19
South American	552	1.12
Argentinean	26	0.05
Bolivian	12	0.02
Chilean	13	0.03
Colombian	253	0.52
Ecuadorian	54	0.11
Peruvian	70	0.14
Uruguayan	5	0.01
Venezuelan	116	0.24
Other South American	3	0.01
Other Hispanic or Latino	354	0.72

Race*	Population	%
African-American/Black (2,310)	2,801	5.71
Not Hispanic (2,133)	2,508	5.11
Hispanic (177)	293	0.60
American Indian/Alaska Native (166)	472	0.96
Not Hispanic (119)	379	0.77
Hispanic (47)	93	0.19

*Notes: † The Census 2010 population figure is used to calculate the percentages in the Hispanic Origin and Race categories. Ancestry percentages are based on the 2006-2010 American Community Survey population (not shown); ‡ Numbers in parentheses indicate the number of people reporting a single ancestry; * Numbers in parentheses indicate the number of persons reporting this race alone, not in combination with any other race; Please refer to the Explanation of Data for more information.*

Apache (2)	9	0.02
Blackfeet (1)	27	0.06
Canadian/French Am. Ind. (0)	1	<0.01
Central American Ind. (1)	4	0.01
Cherokee (25)	109	0.22
Chickasaw (1)	2	<0.01
Chippewa (7)	14	0.03
Choctaw (2)	7	0.01
Cree (0)	1	<0.01
Creek (2)	5	0.01
Delaware (1)	1	<0.01
Inupiat *(Alaska Native)* (3)	3	0.01
Iroquois (3)	14	0.03
Lumbee (2)	3	0.01
Mexican American Ind. (6)	8	0.02
Navajo (0)	1	<0.01
Ottawa (0)	1	<0.01
Potawatomi (0)	1	<0.01
Seminole (0)	5	0.01
Shoshone (1)	2	<0.01
Sioux (3)	11	0.02
South American Ind. (4)	14	0.03
Tsimshian *(Alaska Native)* (1)	1	<0.01
Asian (3,578)	3,971	8.09
Not Hispanic (3,535)	3,900	7.95
Hispanic (43)	71	0.14
Bangladeshi (7)	7	0.01
Burmese (8)	8	0.02
Cambodian (179)	200	0.41
Chinese, ex. Taiwanese (206)	267	0.54
Filipino (531)	665	1.35
Hmong (24)	24	0.05
Indian (317)	377	0.77
Indonesian (2)	2	<0.01
Japanese (34)	68	0.14
Korean (63)	98	0.20
Laotian (311)	359	0.73
Malaysian (5)	6	0.01
Pakistani (12)	12	0.02
Sri Lankan (3)	3	0.01
Taiwanese (3)	5	0.01
Thai (56)	88	0.18
Vietnamese (1,660)	1,763	3.59
Hawaii Native/Pacific Islander (67)	127	0.26
Not Hispanic (55)	99	0.20
Hispanic (12)	28	0.06
Fijian (1)	3	0.01
Guamanian/Chamorro (11)	16	0.03
Marshallese (22)	25	0.05
Native Hawaiian (2)	20	0.04
Samoan (7)	8	0.02
Tongan (14)	16	0.03
White (40,076)	41,240	84.03
Not Hispanic (36,851)	37,737	76.89
Hispanic (3,225)	3,503	7.14

Pinewood

Place Type: CDP
County: Miami-Dade
Population: 16,520†

Ancestry‡	Population	%
African, Sub-Saharan (156)	174	1.09
African (156)	166	1.04
Cape Verdean (0)	8	0.05
American (494)	494	3.10
Arab (15)	15	0.09
Arab (15)	15	0.09
British (9)	9	0.06
Czech (22)	34	0.21
English (41)	41	0.26
German (0)	12	0.08
Greek (11)	11	0.07
Guyanese (18)	18	0.11
Irish (0)	25	0.16
Italian (1)	2	0.01
Pennsylvania German (0)	19	0.12
Polish (8)	27	0.17
West Indian, ex. Hispanic (4,248)	4,875	30.55
Bahamian (242)	558	3.50
Belizean (13)	13	0.08
Haitian (3,642)	3,655	22.90
Jamaican (225)	446	2.79
Trinidadian/Tobagonian (15)	25	0.16
West Indian (111)	178	1.12

Hispanic Origin	Population	%
Hispanic or Latino (of any race)	3,761	22.77
Central American, ex. Mexican	1,128	6.83
Costa Rican	12	0.07
Guatemalan	68	0.41
Honduran	477	2.89
Nicaraguan	510	3.09
Panamanian	25	0.15
Salvadoran	35	0.21
Other Central American	1	0.01
Cuban	995	6.02
Dominican Republic	431	2.61
Mexican	77	0.47
Puerto Rican	592	3.58
South American	192	1.16
Argentinean	11	0.07
Bolivian	4	0.02
Chilean	5	0.03
Colombian	85	0.51
Ecuadorian	34	0.21
Peruvian	35	0.21
Uruguayan	3	0.02
Venezuelan	15	0.09
Other Hispanic or Latino	346	2.09

Race*	Population	%
African-American/Black (12,444)	12,744	77.14
Not Hispanic (11,995)	12,210	73.91
Hispanic (449)	534	3.23
American Indian/Alaska Native (40)	107	0.65
Not Hispanic (27)	78	0.47
Hispanic (13)	29	0.18
Blackfeet (1)	3	0.02
Central American Ind. (3)	7	0.04
Cherokee (0)	6	0.04
Creek (0)	1	0.01
Delaware (1)	1	0.01
Iroquois (0)	1	0.01
Mexican American Ind. (1)	1	0.01
Pueblo (0)	2	0.01
Seminole (0)	2	0.01
South American Ind. (1)	2	0.01
Tlingit-Haida *(Alaska Native)* (0)	6	0.04
Asian (79)	130	0.79
Not Hispanic (77)	120	0.73
Hispanic (2)	10	0.06
Burmese (1)	1	0.01
Chinese, ex. Taiwanese (1)	8	0.05
Filipino (20)	27	0.16
Indian (52)	60	0.36
Japanese (1)	2	0.01
Pakistani (2)	2	0.01
Hawaii Native/Pacific Islander (8)	113	0.68
Not Hispanic (7)	104	0.63
Hispanic (1)	9	0.05
Native Hawaiian (1)	1	0.01
Samoan (2)	3	0.02
White (2,885)	3,068	18.57
Not Hispanic (368)	400	2.42
Hispanic (2,517)	2,668	16.15

Plant City

Place Type: City
County: Hillsborough
Population: 34,721†

Ancestry‡	Population	%
African, Sub-Saharan (25)	25	0.07
African (25)	25	0.07
American (3,941)	3,941	11.52
Arab (195)	440	1.29
Egyptian (38)	38	0.11
Jordanian (50)	154	0.45
Lebanese (34)	34	0.10
Palestinian (43)	147	0.43
Syrian (0)	37	0.11
Other Arab (30)	30	0.09
Armenian (12)	12	0.04
Australian (0)	9	0.03
Austrian (20)	58	0.17
Belgian (0)	8	0.02
Brazilian (53)	53	0.15
British (128)	156	0.46
Canadian (53)	83	0.24
Croatian (0)	36	0.11
Czech (23)	70	0.20
Czechoslovakian (20)	20	0.06
Dutch (45)	257	0.75
English (1,081)	2,733	7.99
European (199)	199	0.58
Finnish (0)	78	0.23
French, ex. Basque (139)	627	1.83
French Canadian (62)	214	0.63
German (1,031)	3,345	9.78
Greek (23)	53	0.15
Hungarian (113)	230	0.67
Irish (830)	3,204	9.36
Italian (529)	974	2.85
Lithuanian (34)	78	0.23
Northern European (25)	25	0.07
Norwegian (105)	248	0.72
Pennsylvania German (13)	62	0.18
Polish (180)	511	1.49
Portuguese (31)	63	0.18
Romanian (37)	37	0.11
Russian (150)	173	0.51
Scandinavian (17)	43	0.13
Scotch-Irish (361)	486	1.42
Scottish (251)	628	1.84
Serbian (0)	21	0.06
Slavic (0)	6	0.02
Slovak (0)	30	0.09
Swedish (76)	178	0.52
Swiss (0)	69	0.20
Turkish (26)	26	0.08
Welsh (163)	374	1.09
West Indian, ex. Hispanic (131)	173	0.51
British West Indian (52)	52	0.15
Jamaican (61)	103	0.30
Trinidadian/Tobagonian (18)	18	0.05

Hispanic Origin	Population	%
Hispanic or Latino (of any race)	9,984	28.75
Central American, ex. Mexican	403	1.16
Costa Rican	25	0.07
Guatemalan	128	0.37
Honduran	97	0.28
Nicaraguan	38	0.11
Panamanian	20	0.06
Salvadoran	83	0.24
Other Central American	12	0.03
Cuban	419	1.21
Dominican Republic	113	0.33
Mexican	6,861	19.76
Puerto Rican	1,569	4.52
South American	258	0.74
Argentinean	18	0.05
Bolivian	2	0.01
Chilean	7	0.02
Colombian	91	0.26
Ecuadorian	36	0.10
Paraguayan	3	0.01
Peruvian	87	0.25
Uruguayan	1	<0.01
Venezuelan	11	0.03
Other South American	2	0.01
Other Hispanic or Latino	361	1.04

Race*	Population	%
African-American/Black (5,247)	5,573	16.05
Not Hispanic (5,051)	5,285	15.22
Hispanic (196)	288	0.83

*Notes: † The Census 2010 population figure is used to calculate the percentages in the Hispanic Origin and Race categories. Ancestry percentages are based on the 2006-2010 American Community Survey population (not shown); ‡ Numbers in parentheses indicate the number of people reporting a single ancestry; * Numbers in parentheses indicate the number of persons reporting this race alone, not in combination with any other race; Please refer to the Explanation of Data for more information.*

American Indian/Alaska Native (219)	384	1.11
Not Hispanic (128)	246	0.71
Hispanic (91)	138	0.40
Apache (1)	3	0.01
Blackfeet (7)	11	0.03
Canadian/French Am. Ind. (1)	1	<0.01
Central American Ind. (2)	6	0.02
Cherokee (22)	72	0.21
Cheyenne (0)	1	<0.01
Chickasaw (1)	1	<0.01
Chippewa (5)	5	0.01
Choctaw (5)	8	0.02
Comanche (1)	2	0.01
Cree (1)	1	<0.01
Creek (8)	11	0.03
Delaware (1)	1	<0.01
Iroquois (1)	18	0.05
Lumbee (1)	4	0.01
Mexican American Ind. (37)	40	0.12
Potawatomi (0)	1	<0.01
Seminole (6)	9	0.03
Sioux (3)	3	0.01
South American Ind. (5)	12	0.03
Spanish American Ind. (3)	3	0.01
Ute (0)	1	<0.01
Yup'ik *(Alaska Native)* (0)	3	0.01
Asian (496)	659	1.90
Not Hispanic (487)	634	1.83
Hispanic (9)	25	0.07
Cambodian (16)	17	0.05
Chinese, ex. Taiwanese (46)	67	0.19
Filipino (59)	98	0.28
Hmong (15)	15	0.04
Indian (174)	202	0.58
Indonesian (0)	2	0.01
Japanese (15)	41	0.12
Korean (17)	40	0.12
Nepalese (3)	3	0.01
Pakistani (22)	30	0.09
Taiwanese (3)	3	0.01
Thai (41)	46	0.13
Vietnamese (70)	79	0.23
Hawaii Native/Pacific Islander (11)	51	0.15
Not Hispanic (11)	39	0.11
Hispanic (0)	12	0.03
Guamanian/Chamorro (4)	9	0.03
Native Hawaiian (2)	13	0.04
Samoan (4)	4	0.01
White (24,140)	24,892	71.69
Not Hispanic (18,555)	18,948	54.57
Hispanic (5,585)	5,944	17.12

Plantation

Place Type: City
County: Broward
Population: 84,955†

Ancestry‡	Population	%
Afghan (56)	56	0.07
African, Sub-Saharan (1,493)	1,647	1.94
African (1,286)	1,406	1.65
Liberian (122)	137	0.16
South African (85)	99	0.12
Other Sub-Saharan African (0)	5	0.01
Albanian (18)	18	0.02
Alsatian (14)	14	0.02
American (4,024)	4,024	4.73
Arab (486)	977	1.15
Arab (60)	74	0.09
Egyptian (74)	90	0.11
Iraqi (14)	14	0.02
Jordanian (41)	41	0.05
Lebanese (207)	462	0.54
Moroccan (37)	191	0.22
Palestinian (0)	10	0.01
Syrian (29)	55	0.06
Other Arab (24)	40	0.05
Armenian (18)	83	0.10
Austrian (276)	501	0.59
Basque (9)	9	0.01
Belgian (12)	24	0.03
Brazilian (268)	300	0.35
British (378)	604	0.71
Bulgarian (10)	25	0.03
Canadian (69)	294	0.35
Croatian (137)	240	0.28
Czech (95)	273	0.32
Czechoslovakian (0)	7	0.01
Danish (148)	270	0.32
Dutch (234)	679	0.80
Eastern European (426)	468	0.55
English (1,852)	5,510	6.48
European (1,166)	1,323	1.55
Finnish (22)	87	0.10
French, ex. Basque (310)	1,624	1.91
French Canadian (128)	298	0.35
German (2,356)	8,599	10.11
Greek (99)	254	0.30
Guyanese (93)	93	0.11
Hungarian (297)	820	0.96
Iranian (40)	40	0.05
Irish (2,072)	7,946	9.34
Israeli (742)	939	1.10
Italian (3,896)	8,338	9.80
Lithuanian (43)	270	0.32
Maltese (16)	63	0.07
Northern European (0)	14	0.02
Norwegian (92)	497	0.58
Pennsylvania German (5)	5	0.01
Polish (1,643)	4,038	4.75
Portuguese (101)	206	0.24
Romanian (325)	499	0.59
Russian (1,538)	3,102	3.65
Scandinavian (0)	29	0.03
Scotch-Irish (410)	981	1.15
Scottish (277)	1,061	1.25
Serbian (20)	36	0.04
Slovak (47)	166	0.20
Slovene (0)	9	0.01
Swedish (207)	584	0.69
Swiss (44)	216	0.25
Turkish (260)	294	0.35
Ukrainian (114)	238	0.28
Welsh (103)	322	0.38
West Indian, ex. Hispanic (9,073)	9,883	11.61
Bahamian (58)	75	0.09
Barbadian (38)	38	0.04
British West Indian (192)	250	0.29
Haitian (3,031)	3,353	3.94
Jamaican (5,221)	5,589	6.57
Trinidadian/Tobagonian (219)	226	0.27
West Indian (314)	352	0.41
Yugoslavian (0)	39	0.05

Hispanic Origin	Population	%
Hispanic or Latino (of any race)	17,372	20.45
Central American, ex. Mexican	1,325	1.56
Costa Rican	139	0.16
Guatemalan	197	0.23
Honduran	307	0.36
Nicaraguan	291	0.34
Panamanian	176	0.21
Salvadoran	213	0.25
Other Central American	2	<0.01
Cuban	3,398	4.00
Dominican Republic	1,016	1.20
Mexican	817	0.96
Puerto Rican	3,221	3.79
South American	6,394	7.53
Argentinean	458	0.54
Bolivian	77	0.09
Chilean	212	0.25
Colombian	2,947	3.47
Ecuadorian	624	0.73
Paraguayan	23	0.03
Peruvian	1,071	1.26
Uruguayan	115	0.14
Venezuelan	836	0.98
Other South American	31	0.04
Other Hispanic or Latino	1,201	1.41

Race*	Population	%
African-American/Black (17,217)	18,512	21.79
Not Hispanic (16,470)	17,492	20.59
Hispanic (747)	1,020	1.20
American Indian/Alaska Native (199)	433	0.51
Not Hispanic (146)	300	0.35
Hispanic (53)	133	0.16
Alaska Athabascan *(Ala. Nat.)* (1)	1	<0.01
Aleut *(Alaska Native)* (1)	1	<0.01
Apache (0)	3	<0.01
Blackfeet (0)	6	0.01
Central American Ind. (3)	10	0.01
Cherokee (19)	63	0.07
Chickasaw (1)	2	<0.01
Chippewa (2)	3	<0.01
Choctaw (4)	11	0.01
Comanche (2)	2	<0.01
Creek (2)	3	<0.01
Delaware (1)	3	<0.01
Iroquois (7)	13	0.02
Lumbee (1)	1	<0.01
Mexican American Ind. (12)	15	0.02
Navajo (2)	2	<0.01
Pima (1)	1	<0.01
Potawatomi (2)	2	<0.01
Pueblo (0)	5	0.01
Seminole (22)	30	0.04
Sioux (2)	4	<0.01
South American Ind. (17)	35	0.04
Spanish American Ind. (0)	3	<0.01
Tlingit-Haida *(Alaska Native)* (0)	2	<0.01
Yaqui (0)	2	<0.01
Asian (3,297)	4,230	4.98
Not Hispanic (3,221)	4,045	4.76
Hispanic (76)	185	0.22
Bangladeshi (48)	50	0.06
Burmese (39)	41	0.05
Cambodian (2)	5	0.01
Chinese, ex. Taiwanese (538)	806	0.95
Filipino (315)	435	0.51
Indian (1,585)	1,866	2.20
Indonesian (10)	15	0.02
Japanese (87)	168	0.20
Korean (113)	149	0.18
Laotian (13)	14	0.02
Malaysian (5)	5	0.01
Nepalese (2)	2	<0.01
Pakistani (122)	139	0.16
Sri Lankan (9)	12	0.01
Taiwanese (37)	44	0.05
Thai (61)	76	0.09
Vietnamese (190)	217	0.26
Hawaii Native/Pacific Islander (57)	219	0.26
Not Hispanic (46)	190	0.22
Hispanic (11)	29	0.03
Guamanian/Chamorro (6)	11	0.01
Native Hawaiian (13)	35	0.04
Samoan (6)	8	0.01
Tongan (2)	8	0.01
White (59,398)	61,131	71.96
Not Hispanic (45,599)	46,717	54.99
Hispanic (13,799)	14,414	16.97

Poinciana

Place Type: CDP
County: Osceola
Population: 53,193†

Ancestry‡	Population	%
African, Sub-Saharan (1,025)	1,419	2.83
African (770)	1,126	2.25
Cape Verdean (183)	202	0.40
Ghanaian (14)	14	0.03
Nigerian (58)	58	0.12
Other Sub-Saharan African (0)	19	0.04
Alsatian (0)	16	0.03
American (1,196)	1,196	2.39

*Notes: † The Census 2010 population figure is used to calculate the percentages in the Hispanic Origin and Race categories. Ancestry percentages are based on the 2006-2010 American Community Survey population (not shown); ‡ Numbers in parentheses indicate the number of people reporting a single ancestry; * Numbers in parentheses indicate the number of persons reporting this race alone, not in combination with any other race; Please refer to the Explanation of Data for more information.*

Arab (98)	135	0.27
Arab (74)	74	0.15
Egyptian (11)	11	0.02
Lebanese (0)	7	0.01
Moroccan (13)	13	0.03
Syrian (0)	30	0.06
Armenian (10)	10	0.02
Austrian (11)	11	0.02
Belgian (0)	8	0.02
Brazilian (83)	83	0.17
British (73)	138	0.28
Canadian (61)	126	0.25
Croatian (0)	13	0.03
Czech (52)	73	0.15
Czechoslovakian (10)	10	0.02
Danish (12)	92	0.18
Dutch (75)	296	0.59
Eastern European (25)	25	0.05
English (660)	1,689	3.37
European (169)	178	0.36
Finnish (8)	27	0.05
French, ex. Basque (184)	989	1.98
French Canadian (39)	129	0.26
German (981)	2,346	4.69
German Russian (0)	13	0.03
Guyanese (72)	87	0.17
Hungarian (40)	99	0.20
Iranian (0)	5	0.01
Irish (599)	1,969	3.93
Italian (1,216)	2,084	4.16
Lithuanian (21)	46	0.09
Maltese (0)	26	0.05
Norwegian (61)	155	0.31
Pennsylvania German (0)	11	0.02
Polish (373)	683	1.36
Portuguese (83)	116	0.23
Romanian (40)	145	0.29
Russian (163)	276	0.55
Scandinavian (13)	13	0.03
Scotch-Irish (85)	241	0.48
Scottish (60)	308	0.62
Serbian (0)	19	0.04
Slavic (0)	16	0.03
Slovak (0)	9	0.02
Swedish (52)	149	0.30
Turkish (47)	47	0.09
Ukrainian (8)	23	0.05
Welsh (24)	75	0.15
West Indian, ex. Hispanic (5,330)	6,118	12.22
Bahamian (32)	79	0.16
Barbadian (23)	23	0.05
Belizean (17)	17	0.03
British West Indian (69)	69	0.14
Haitian (2,455)	2,520	5.03
Jamaican (2,036)	2,471	4.94
Trinidadian/Tobagonian (234)	376	0.75
U.S. Virgin Islander (0)	9	0.02
West Indian (464)	510	1.02
Other West Indian (0)	44	0.09
Yugoslavian (0)	29	0.06

Hispanic Origin	Population	%
Hispanic or Latino (of any race)	27,234	51.20
Central American, ex. Mexican	1,389	2.61
Costa Rican	96	0.18
Guatemalan	176	0.33
Honduran	315	0.59
Nicaraguan	236	0.44
Panamanian	208	0.39
Salvadoran	349	0.66
Other Central American	9	0.02
Cuban	1,150	2.16
Dominican Republic	1,833	3.45
Mexican	927	1.74
Puerto Rican	19,055	35.82
South American	1,791	3.37
Argentinean	117	0.22
Bolivian	5	0.01
Chilean	68	0.13
Colombian	828	1.56
Ecuadorian	285	0.54
Paraguayan	5	0.01
Peruvian	280	0.53
Uruguayan	29	0.05
Venezuelan	155	0.29
Other South American	19	0.04
Other Hispanic or Latino	1,089	2.05

Race*	Population	%
African-American/Black (13,016)	14,444	27.15
Not Hispanic (11,321)	12,138	22.82
Hispanic (1,695)	2,306	4.34
American Indian/Alaska Native (387)	730	1.37
Not Hispanic (124)	310	0.58
Hispanic (263)	420	0.79
Apache (3)	5	0.01
Blackfeet (0)	6	0.01
Central American Ind. (6)	12	0.02
Cherokee (16)	71	0.13
Chickasaw (0)	1	<0.01
Chippewa (4)	10	0.02
Choctaw (0)	5	0.01
Comanche (3)	3	0.01
Cree (0)	1	<0.01
Creek (0)	6	0.01
Hopi (0)	1	<0.01
Inupiat *(Alaska Native)* (0)	2	<0.01
Iroquois (12)	35	0.07
Kiowa (1)	1	<0.01
Lumbee (2)	2	<0.01
Mexican American Ind. (18)	33	0.06
Navajo (3)	4	0.01
Potawatomi (1)	2	<0.01
Pueblo (0)	1	<0.01
Seminole (2)	5	0.01
Sioux (3)	4	0.01
South American Ind. (56)	94	0.18
Spanish American Ind. (10)	15	0.03
Tlingit-Haida *(Alaska Native)* (0)	1	<0.01
Ute (1)	1	<0.01
Yaqui (1)	1	<0.01
Asian (960)	1,401	2.63
Not Hispanic (910)	1,251	2.35
Hispanic (50)	150	0.28
Bangladeshi (13)	22	0.04
Cambodian (23)	24	0.05
Chinese, ex. Taiwanese (77)	155	0.29
Filipino (225)	323	0.61
Indian (438)	571	1.07
Indonesian (2)	5	0.01
Japanese (17)	32	0.06
Korean (32)	37	0.07
Laotian (0)	2	<0.01
Malaysian (2)	3	0.01
Pakistani (6)	12	0.02
Sri Lankan (2)	2	<0.01
Taiwanese (4)	4	0.01
Thai (8)	22	0.04
Vietnamese (75)	112	0.21
Hawaii Native/Pacific Islander (108)	321	0.60
Not Hispanic (82)	248	0.47
Hispanic (26)	73	0.14
Guamanian/Chamorro (24)	28	0.05
Native Hawaiian (4)	22	0.04
Samoan (9)	14	0.03
Tongan (8)	9	0.02
White (30,022)	31,862	59.90
Not Hispanic (12,015)	12,646	23.77
Hispanic (18,007)	19,216	36.13

Pompano Beach

Place Type: City
County: Broward
Population: 99,845†

Ancestry‡	Population	%
African, Sub-Saharan (287)	336	0.33
African (250)	299	0.30
Nigerian (37)	37	0.04
Albanian (60)	60	0.06
American (2,865)	2,865	2.85
Arab (395)	546	0.54
Egyptian (61)	61	0.06
Jordanian (17)	17	0.02
Lebanese (142)	257	0.26
Moroccan (103)	103	0.10
Syrian (0)	29	0.03
Other Arab (72)	79	0.08
Armenian (71)	92	0.09
Austrian (137)	379	0.38
Belgian (30)	76	0.08
Brazilian (2,820)	2,923	2.91
British (229)	366	0.36
Bulgarian (143)	143	0.14
Canadian (498)	651	0.65
Carpatho Rusyn (14)	14	0.01
Croatian (23)	60	0.06
Czech (90)	231	0.23
Czechoslovakian (54)	120	0.12
Danish (147)	271	0.27
Dutch (331)	1,311	1.31
Eastern European (82)	110	0.11
English (2,248)	6,651	6.62
Estonian (32)	32	0.03
European (370)	415	0.41
Finnish (26)	63	0.06
French, ex. Basque (690)	2,442	2.43
French Canadian (439)	660	0.66
German (2,974)	10,363	10.32
Greek (385)	490	0.49
Guyanese (44)	44	0.04
Hungarian (305)	628	0.63
Iranian (10)	10	0.01
Irish (3,583)	10,279	10.24
Israeli (8)	8	0.01
Italian (5,265)	8,487	8.45
Latvian (14)	27	0.03
Lithuanian (152)	308	0.31
Macedonian (63)	63	0.06
Northern European (36)	36	0.04
Norwegian (88)	419	0.42
Polish (1,193)	2,936	2.92
Portuguese (396)	638	0.64
Romanian (233)	344	0.34
Russian (1,407)	2,603	2.59
Scandinavian (34)	61	0.06
Scotch-Irish (360)	1,266	1.26
Scottish (334)	1,367	1.36
Serbian (121)	155	0.15
Slavic (16)	24	0.02
Slovak (63)	131	0.13
Slovene (25)	42	0.04
Swedish (281)	606	0.60
Swiss (54)	160	0.16
Turkish (62)	75	0.07
Ukrainian (234)	455	0.45
Welsh (14)	395	0.39
West Indian, ex. Hispanic (10,429)	10,664	10.62
Bahamian (140)	147	0.15
Barbadian (10)	10	0.01
Belizean (0)	29	0.03
British West Indian (22)	22	0.02
Dutch West Indian (9)	9	0.01
Haitian (9,196)	9,316	9.28
Jamaican (788)	827	0.82
Trinidadian/Tobagonian (115)	146	0.15
West Indian (149)	158	0.16
Yugoslavian (65)	81	0.08

Hispanic Origin	Population	%
Hispanic or Latino (of any race)	17,509	17.54
Central American, ex. Mexican	2,330	2.33
Costa Rican	92	0.09
Guatemalan	582	0.58
Honduran	1,036	1.04
Nicaraguan	204	0.20
Panamanian	84	0.08
Salvadoran	319	0.32
Other Central American	13	0.01

SECTION TWO

*Notes: † The Census 2010 population figure is used to calculate the percentages in the Hispanic Origin and Race categories. Ancestry percentages are based on the 2006-2010 American Community Survey population (not shown); ‡ Numbers in parentheses indicate the number of people reporting a single ancestry; * Numbers in parentheses indicate the number of persons reporting this race alone, not in combination with any other race; Please refer to the Explanation of Data for more information.*

Cuban	1,601	1.60
Dominican Republic	619	0.62
Mexican	4,907	4.91
Puerto Rican	2,976	2.98
South American	3,572	3.58
Argentinean	292	0.29
Bolivian	58	0.06
Chilean	108	0.11
Colombian	1,209	1.21
Ecuadorian	300	0.30
Paraguayan	8	0.01
Peruvian	651	0.65
Uruguayan	195	0.20
Venezuelan	719	0.72
Other South American	32	0.03
Other Hispanic or Latino	1,504	1.51

Race*	Population	%
African-American/Black (28,849)	29,888	29.93
Not Hispanic (28,177)	28,958	29.00
Hispanic (672)	930	0.93
American Indian/Alaska Native (285)	605	0.61
Not Hispanic (188)	438	0.44
Hispanic (97)	167	0.17
Aleut *(Alaska Native)* (2)	6	0.01
Apache (1)	6	0.01
Blackfeet (1)	14	0.01
Canadian/French Am. Ind. (1)	5	0.01
Central American Ind. (8)	11	0.01
Cherokee (37)	114	0.11
Chickasaw (1)	2	<0.01
Chippewa (10)	16	0.02
Choctaw (4)	9	0.01
Comanche (0)	2	<0.01
Creek (4)	7	0.01
Houma (1)	1	<0.01
Inupiat *(Alaska Native)* (0)	1	<0.01
Iroquois (4)	10	0.01
Lumbee (4)	6	0.01
Mexican American Ind. (20)	30	0.03
Navajo (1)	2	<0.01
Potawatomi (1)	1	<0.01
Pueblo (1)	1	<0.01
Seminole (4)	7	0.01
Shoshone (0)	1	<0.01
Sioux (4)	9	0.01
South American Ind. (6)	16	0.02
Spanish American Ind. (7)	11	0.01
Tlingit-Haida *(Alaska Native)* (1)	4	<0.01
Tsimshian *(Alaska Native)* (0)	1	<0.01
Asian (1,302)	1,694	1.70
Not Hispanic (1,259)	1,591	1.59
Hispanic (43)	103	0.10
Bangladeshi (55)	71	0.07
Burmese (1)	1	<0.01
Cambodian (6)	6	0.01
Chinese, ex. Taiwanese (226)	296	0.30
Filipino (159)	218	0.22
Hmong (1)	1	<0.01
Indian (370)	473	0.47
Indonesian (2)	15	0.02
Japanese (48)	99	0.10
Korean (53)	77	0.08
Laotian (6)	11	0.01
Malaysian (1)	2	<0.01
Nepalese (2)	2	<0.01
Pakistani (57)	60	0.06
Sri Lankan (2)	2	<0.01
Taiwanese (12)	14	0.01
Thai (94)	99	0.10
Vietnamese (151)	163	0.16
Hawaii Native/Pacific Islander (49)	231	0.23
Not Hispanic (30)	187	0.19
Hispanic (19)	44	0.04
Fijian (1)	3	<0.01
Guamanian/Chamorro (14)	18	0.02
Marshallese (0)	1	<0.01
Native Hawaiian (11)	31	0.03
Samoan (7)	16	0.02
White (62,515)	64,333	64.43
Not Hispanic (50,522)	51,574	51.65
Hispanic (11,993)	12,759	12.78

Port Charlotte

Place Type: CDP
County: Charlotte
Population: 54,392†

Ancestry‡	Population	%
African, Sub-Saharan (210)	437	0.77
African (133)	320	0.57
Cape Verdean (0)	40	0.07
Ghanaian (16)	16	0.03
Nigerian (61)	61	0.11
American (6,970)	6,970	12.33
Arab (127)	181	0.32
Egyptian (57)	57	0.10
Lebanese (10)	64	0.11
Moroccan (12)	12	0.02
Palestinian (48)	48	0.08
Assyrian/Chaldean/Syriac (11)	11	0.02
Austrian (90)	261	0.46
Basque (17)	17	0.03
Belgian (11)	65	0.11
Brazilian (14)	26	0.05
British (57)	207	0.37
Canadian (293)	394	0.70
Croatian (144)	202	0.36
Czech (197)	374	0.66
Czechoslovakian (26)	61	0.11
Danish (29)	205	0.36
Dutch (300)	1,172	2.07
English (2,043)	6,375	11.28
European (373)	390	0.69
Finnish (41)	57	0.10
French, ex. Basque (532)	2,914	5.16
French Canadian (242)	382	0.68
German (3,047)	9,415	16.66
Greek (195)	444	0.79
Guyanese (83)	83	0.15
Hungarian (267)	460	0.81
Irish (1,938)	7,270	12.86
Italian (2,502)	5,307	9.39
Lithuanian (105)	256	0.45
Maltese (10)	10	0.02
Norwegian (144)	574	1.02
Pennsylvania German (17)	73	0.13
Polish (928)	2,115	3.74
Portuguese (329)	660	1.17
Romanian (34)	142	0.25
Russian (251)	721	1.28
Scandinavian (14)	46	0.08
Scotch-Irish (412)	945	1.67
Scottish (341)	1,290	2.28
Serbian (0)	14	0.02
Slavic (37)	37	0.07
Slovak (197)	364	0.64
Slovene (0)	13	0.02
Swedish (137)	640	1.13
Swiss (55)	241	0.43
Ukrainian (57)	194	0.34
Welsh (29)	398	0.70
West Indian, ex. Hispanic (2,551)	3,012	5.33
Barbadian (47)	71	0.13
Belizean (41)	49	0.09
British West Indian (7)	7	0.01
Dutch West Indian (9)	9	0.02
Haitian (798)	834	1.48
Jamaican (1,252)	1,575	2.79
Trinidadian/Tobagonian (28)	88	0.16
West Indian (369)	379	0.67
Yugoslavian (44)	117	0.21

Hispanic Origin	Population	%
Hispanic or Latino (of any race)	4,713	8.66
Central American, ex. Mexican	304	0.56
Costa Rican	29	0.05
Guatemalan	57	0.10
Honduran	63	0.12
Nicaraguan	26	0.05
Panamanian	100	0.18
Salvadoran	29	0.05
Cuban	881	1.62
Dominican Republic	317	0.58
Mexican	940	1.73
Puerto Rican	1,470	2.70
South American	472	0.87
Argentinean	36	0.07
Bolivian	7	0.01
Chilean	17	0.03
Colombian	204	0.38
Ecuadorian	70	0.13
Peruvian	88	0.16
Uruguayan	13	0.02
Venezuelan	33	0.06
Other South American	4	0.01
Other Hispanic or Latino	329	0.60

Race*	Population	%
African-American/Black (5,046)	5,665	10.42
Not Hispanic (4,753)	5,250	9.65
Hispanic (293)	415	0.76
American Indian/Alaska Native (163)	446	0.82
Not Hispanic (130)	384	0.71
Hispanic (33)	62	0.11
Aleut *(Alaska Native)* (0)	1	<0.01
Apache (2)	4	0.01
Blackfeet (4)	18	0.03
Canadian/French Am. Ind. (2)	4	0.01
Central American Ind. (0)	3	0.01
Cherokee (26)	124	0.23
Cheyenne (1)	1	<0.01
Chickasaw (1)	1	<0.01
Chippewa (15)	19	0.03
Choctaw (1)	3	0.01
Cree (1)	1	<0.01
Creek (5)	7	0.01
Crow (0)	1	<0.01
Delaware (12)	14	0.03
Hopi (0)	1	<0.01
Houma (0)	1	<0.01
Inupiat *(Alaska Native)* (0)	1	<0.01
Iroquois (6)	8	0.01
Lumbee (0)	2	<0.01
Mexican American Ind. (6)	7	0.01
Navajo (3)	5	0.01
Ottawa (0)	4	0.01
Paiute (0)	2	<0.01
Potawatomi (2)	2	<0.01
Pueblo (1)	1	<0.01
Seminole (1)	4	0.01
Shoshone (1)	1	<0.01
Sioux (3)	12	0.02
South American Ind. (10)	20	0.04
Spanish American Ind. (1)	1	<0.01
Yaqui (3)	3	0.01
Asian (855)	1,138	2.09
Not Hispanic (838)	1,097	2.02
Hispanic (17)	41	0.08
Burmese (1)	4	0.01
Cambodian (3)	3	0.01
Chinese, ex. Taiwanese (133)	172	0.32
Filipino (294)	386	0.71
Indian (173)	206	0.38
Indonesian (4)	7	0.01
Japanese (31)	75	0.14
Korean (25)	45	0.08
Laotian (2)	6	0.01
Malaysian (1)	7	0.01
Nepalese (2)	2	<0.01
Pakistani (43)	55	0.10
Taiwanese (4)	6	0.01
Thai (33)	54	0.10
Vietnamese (75)	79	0.15
Hawaii Native/Pacific Islander (34)	127	0.23
Not Hispanic (26)	96	0.18
Hispanic (8)	31	0.06
Guamanian/Chamorro (12)	19	0.03
Marshallese (0)	2	<0.01

*Notes: † The Census 2010 population figure is used to calculate the percentages in the Hispanic Origin and Race categories. Ancestry percentages are based on the 2006-2010 American Community Survey population (not shown); ‡ Numbers in parentheses indicate the number of people reporting a single ancestry; * Numbers in parentheses indicate the number of persons reporting this race alone, not in combination with any other race; Please refer to the Explanation of Data for more information.*

	Population	%
Native Hawaiian (12)	32	0.06
Samoan (4)	9	0.02
White (46,136)	47,152	86.69
Not Hispanic (42,903)	43,697	80.34
Hispanic (3,233)	3,455	6.35

Port Orange

Place Type: City
County: Volusia
Population: 56,048†

Ancestry‡	Population	%
African, Sub-Saharan (18)	98	0.18
African (0)	30	0.05
Cape Verdean (0)	25	0.05
Nigerian (18)	43	0.08
Albanian (29)	43	0.08
American (3,866)	3,866	6.97
Arab (542)	629	1.13
Egyptian (177)	177	0.32
Lebanese (307)	332	0.60
Syrian (45)	57	0.10
Other Arab (13)	63	0.11
Armenian (14)	56	0.10
Austrian (93)	245	0.44
Belgian (11)	78	0.14
Brazilian (14)	14	0.03
British (219)	392	0.71
Canadian (89)	222	0.40
Croatian (15)	31	0.06
Czech (67)	173	0.31
Czechoslovakian (26)	71	0.13
Danish (76)	261	0.47
Dutch (282)	1,041	1.88
English (2,688)	7,552	13.61
Estonian (62)	62	0.11
European (575)	631	1.14
Finnish (0)	12	0.02
French, ex. Basque (581)	2,612	4.71
French Canadian (492)	731	1.32
German (3,370)	9,730	17.53
Greek (130)	430	0.77
Hungarian (178)	291	0.52
Iranian (108)	108	0.19
Irish (3,497)	9,717	17.51
Italian (3,474)	7,480	13.48
Latvian (0)	20	0.04
Lithuanian (103)	178	0.32
Norwegian (124)	517	0.93
Pennsylvania German (51)	84	0.15
Polish (1,164)	2,987	5.38
Portuguese (214)	297	0.54
Romanian (14)	109	0.20
Russian (264)	598	1.08
Scandinavian (13)	45	0.08
Scotch-Irish (415)	1,175	2.12
Scottish (432)	1,544	2.78
Serbian (0)	11	0.02
Slavic (24)	24	0.04
Slovak (79)	152	0.27
Slovene (35)	47	0.08
Swedish (119)	697	1.26
Swiss (40)	125	0.23
Ukrainian (94)	251	0.45
Welsh (27)	217	0.39
West Indian, ex. Hispanic (302)	302	0.54
Bahamian (37)	37	0.07
Haitian (69)	69	0.12
Jamaican (122)	122	0.22
Trinidadian/Tobagonian (74)	74	0.13
Yugoslavian (11)	30	0.05

Hispanic Origin	Population	%
Hispanic or Latino (of any race)	2,535	4.52
Central American, ex. Mexican	150	0.27
Costa Rican	10	0.02
Guatemalan	24	0.04
Honduran	27	0.05
Nicaraguan	27	0.05
Panamanian	36	0.06
Salvadoran	24	0.04
Other Central American	2	<0.01
Cuban	213	0.38
Dominican Republic	73	0.13
Mexican	471	0.84
Puerto Rican	949	1.69
South American	442	0.79
Argentinean	43	0.08
Bolivian	10	0.02
Chilean	31	0.06
Colombian	160	0.29
Ecuadorian	72	0.13
Paraguayan	3	0.01
Peruvian	39	0.07
Uruguayan	27	0.05
Venezuelan	53	0.09
Other South American	4	0.01
Other Hispanic or Latino	237	0.42

Race*	Population	%
African-American/Black (1,855)	2,183	3.89
Not Hispanic (1,790)	2,076	3.70
Hispanic (65)	107	0.19
American Indian/Alaska Native (170)	438	0.78
Not Hispanic (147)	378	0.67
Hispanic (23)	60	0.11
Apache (2)	7	0.01
Blackfeet (5)	32	0.06
Canadian/French Am. Ind. (1)	1	<0.01
Central American Ind. (2)	3	0.01
Cherokee (20)	109	0.19
Chippewa (8)	19	0.03
Choctaw (7)	9	0.02
Cree (3)	6	0.01
Creek (9)	20	0.04
Delaware (1)	6	0.01
Iroquois (9)	21	0.04
Kiowa (2)	2	<0.01
Lumbee (5)	10	0.02
Mexican American Ind. (1)	6	0.01
Navajo (3)	6	0.01
Osage (1)	3	0.01
Paiute (1)	1	<0.01
Pima (1)	1	<0.01
Potawatomi (3)	4	0.01
Pueblo (1)	1	<0.01
Seminole (8)	13	0.02
Shoshone (0)	1	<0.01
Sioux (5)	14	0.02
South American Ind. (1)	6	0.01
Spanish American Ind. (3)	5	0.01
Tlingit-Haida *(Alaska Native)* (1)	1	<0.01
Yuman (1)	1	<0.01
Asian (1,261)	1,605	2.86
Not Hispanic (1,250)	1,557	2.78
Hispanic (11)	48	0.09
Bangladeshi (22)	22	0.04
Burmese (6)	7	0.01
Cambodian (7)	8	0.01
Chinese, ex. Taiwanese (220)	262	0.47
Filipino (173)	279	0.50
Indian (362)	402	0.72
Indonesian (7)	17	0.03
Japanese (30)	83	0.15
Korean (119)	159	0.28
Laotian (4)	8	0.01
Malaysian (0)	1	<0.01
Pakistani (18)	19	0.03
Sri Lankan (5)	5	0.01
Taiwanese (16)	18	0.03
Thai (37)	52	0.09
Vietnamese (179)	201	0.36
Hawaii Native/Pacific Islander (21)	82	0.15
Not Hispanic (21)	76	0.14
Hispanic (0)	6	0.01
Guamanian/Chamorro (4)	8	0.01
Native Hawaiian (9)	25	0.04
Samoan (4)	11	0.02
White (51,176)	52,090	92.94
Not Hispanic (49,392)	50,138	89.46
Hispanic (1,784)	1,952	3.48

Port Salerno

Place Type: CDP
County: Martin
Population: 10,091†

Ancestry‡	Population	%
African, Sub-Saharan (25)	25	0.25
African (13)	13	0.13
South African (12)	12	0.12
American (267)	267	2.67
British (60)	60	0.60
Canadian (0)	22	0.22
Celtic (11)	11	0.11
Croatian (11)	24	0.24
Czech (22)	74	0.74
Czechoslovakian (0)	42	0.42
Danish (22)	84	0.84
Dutch (0)	156	1.56
English (441)	1,256	12.57
European (13)	13	0.13
Finnish (0)	26	0.26
French, ex. Basque (62)	364	3.64
French Canadian (47)	110	1.10
German (846)	2,258	22.60
Greek (0)	43	0.43
Hungarian (65)	107	1.07
Irish (661)	1,690	16.92
Italian (415)	869	8.70
Lithuanian (13)	171	1.71
Northern European (14)	14	0.14
Norwegian (37)	110	1.10
Polish (105)	438	4.38
Portuguese (0)	10	0.10
Russian (46)	61	0.61
Scandinavian (0)	87	0.87
Scotch-Irish (47)	146	1.46
Scottish (28)	202	2.02
Slavic (0)	13	0.13
Slovak (15)	30	0.30
Swedish (31)	183	1.83
Swiss (8)	8	0.08
Ukrainian (11)	21	0.21
Welsh (6)	106	1.06
West Indian, ex. Hispanic (154)	154	1.54
Haitian (110)	110	1.10
Trinidadian/Tobagonian (44)	44	0.44

Hispanic Origin	Population	%
Hispanic or Latino (of any race)	1,488	14.75
Central American, ex. Mexican	364	3.61
Costa Rican	1	0.01
Guatemalan	295	2.92
Honduran	45	0.45
Nicaraguan	2	0.02
Panamanian	3	0.03
Salvadoran	18	0.18
Cuban	75	0.74
Dominican Republic	22	0.22
Mexican	631	6.25
Puerto Rican	230	2.28
South American	76	0.75
Argentinean	8	0.08
Chilean	7	0.07
Colombian	20	0.20
Ecuadorian	8	0.08
Peruvian	16	0.16
Uruguayan	2	0.02
Venezuelan	15	0.15
Other Hispanic or Latino	90	0.89

Race*	Population	%
African-American/Black (920)	1,008	9.99
Not Hispanic (872)	934	9.26
Hispanic (48)	74	0.73
American Indian/Alaska Native (62)	100	0.99
Not Hispanic (38)	71	0.70

*Notes: † The Census 2010 population figure is used to calculate the percentages in the Hispanic Origin and Race categories. Ancestry percentages are based on the 2006-2010 American Community Survey population (not shown); ‡ Numbers in parentheses indicate the number of people reporting a single ancestry; * Numbers in parentheses indicate the number of persons reporting this race alone, not in combination with any other race; Please refer to the Explanation of Data for more information.*

Hispanic (24)	29	0.29
Apache (0)	1	0.01
Blackfeet (0)	1	0.01
Canadian/French Am. Ind. (0)	1	0.01
Central American Ind. (5)	5	0.05
Cherokee (6)	14	0.14
Chippewa (2)	2	0.02
Choctaw (1)	1	0.01
Delaware (0)	2	0.02
Iroquois (1)	4	0.04
Menominee (1)	1	0.01
Mexican American Ind. (17)	17	0.17
Navajo (0)	4	0.04
Potawatomi (0)	1	0.01
Pueblo (1)	1	0.01
Seminole (0)	2	0.02
Sioux (1)	1	0.01
Spanish American Ind. (0)	1	0.01
Tlingit-Haida *(Alaska Native)* (1)	1	0.01
Asian (68)	106	1.05
Not Hispanic (65)	93	0.92
Hispanic (3)	13	0.13
Bangladeshi (2)	2	0.02
Chinese, ex. Taiwanese (10)	22	0.22
Filipino (16)	30	0.30
Indian (10)	12	0.12
Indonesian (0)	3	0.03
Japanese (4)	13	0.13
Korean (0)	4	0.04
Pakistani (1)	1	0.01
Sri Lankan (6)	6	0.06
Thai (6)	7	0.07
Vietnamese (9)	10	0.10
Hawaii Native/Pacific Islander (7)	22	0.22
Not Hispanic (4)	17	0.17
Hispanic (3)	5	0.05
Fijian (3)	3	0.03
Guamanian/Chamorro (3)	3	0.03
Native Hawaiian (0)	4	0.04
White (8,299)	8,482	84.06
Not Hispanic (7,499)	7,600	75.31
Hispanic (800)	882	8.74

Port St. John

Place Type: CDP
County: Brevard
Population: 12,267†

Ancestry‡	Population	%
African, Sub-Saharan (34)	59	0.46
African (34)	59	0.46
American (1,007)	1,007	7.93
Arab (33)	33	0.26
Syrian (33)	33	0.26
Austrian (23)	65	0.51
Belgian (0)	15	0.12
British (44)	54	0.43
Canadian (0)	35	0.28
Croatian (0)	16	0.13
Czech (0)	12	0.09
Czechoslovakian (12)	12	0.09
Danish (0)	25	0.20
Dutch (149)	438	3.45
English (284)	1,463	11.52
European (43)	73	0.57
Finnish (0)	16	0.13
French, ex. Basque (134)	909	7.15
French Canadian (177)	311	2.45
German (290)	1,771	13.94
Greek (25)	25	0.20
Hungarian (0)	84	0.66
Irish (537)	2,331	18.35
Italian (297)	899	7.08
Norwegian (16)	46	0.36
Pennsylvania German (49)	49	0.39
Polish (52)	259	2.04
Portuguese (14)	28	0.22
Russian (0)	19	0.15
Scandinavian (12)	24	0.19
Scotch-Irish (68)	116	0.91
Scottish (87)	609	4.79
Serbian (43)	55	0.43
Slovak (10)	37	0.29
Swedish (29)	95	0.75
Swiss (15)	31	0.24
Welsh (14)	98	0.77
Yugoslavian (0)	11	0.09

Hispanic Origin	Population	%
Hispanic or Latino (of any race)	737	6.01
Central American, ex. Mexican	49	0.40
Costa Rican	8	0.07
Guatemalan	11	0.09
Honduran	6	0.05
Nicaraguan	11	0.09
Panamanian	11	0.09
Salvadoran	2	0.02
Cuban	137	1.12
Dominican Republic	23	0.19
Mexican	118	0.96
Puerto Rican	252	2.05
South American	64	0.52
Argentinean	8	0.07
Chilean	2	0.02
Colombian	26	0.21
Peruvian	10	0.08
Venezuelan	18	0.15
Other Hispanic or Latino	94	0.77

Race*	Population	%
African-American/Black (674)	762	6.21
Not Hispanic (642)	723	5.89
Hispanic (32)	39	0.32
American Indian/Alaska Native (64)	151	1.23
Not Hispanic (58)	138	1.12
Hispanic (6)	13	0.11
Aleut *(Alaska Native)* (1)	1	0.01
Apache (0)	2	0.02
Blackfeet (2)	11	0.09
Cherokee (11)	38	0.31
Cheyenne (0)	2	0.02
Chickasaw (2)	3	0.02
Chippewa (1)	1	0.01
Choctaw (4)	4	0.03
Comanche (0)	1	0.01
Creek (1)	3	0.02
Crow (1)	3	0.02
Hopi (0)	1	0.01
Inupiat *(Alaska Native)* (1)	1	0.01
Iroquois (0)	1	0.01
Kiowa (1)	1	0.01
Lumbee (4)	4	0.03
Mexican American Ind. (0)	1	0.01
Pueblo (0)	1	0.01
Seminole (0)	1	0.01
Sioux (1)	5	0.04
South American Ind. (4)	5	0.04
Spanish American Ind. (0)	1	0.01
Asian (121)	214	1.74
Not Hispanic (116)	202	1.65
Hispanic (5)	12	0.10
Cambodian (2)	2	0.02
Chinese, ex. Taiwanese (12)	23	0.19
Filipino (52)	92	0.75
Indian (6)	16	0.13
Indonesian (1)	6	0.05
Japanese (10)	34	0.28
Korean (6)	10	0.08
Malaysian (2)	6	0.05
Thai (7)	13	0.11
Vietnamese (16)	18	0.15
Hawaii Native/Pacific Islander (37)	72	0.59
Not Hispanic (36)	69	0.56
Hispanic (1)	3	0.02
Guamanian/Chamorro (23)	29	0.24
Marshallese (1)	3	0.02
Native Hawaiian (4)	15	0.12
Samoan (3)	7	0.06
White (10,977)	11,246	91.68
Not Hispanic (10,420)	10,643	86.76
Hispanic (557)	603	4.92

Port St. Lucie

Place Type: City
County: St. Lucie
Population: 164,603†

Ancestry‡	Population	%
African, Sub-Saharan (1,489)	1,603	1.03
African (1,270)	1,329	0.86
Cape Verdean (20)	20	0.01
Kenyan (15)	15	0.01
Sierra Leonean (0)	9	0.01
South African (0)	46	0.03
Other Sub-Saharan African (184)	184	0.12
American (7,734)	7,734	4.99
Arab (402)	640	0.41
Arab (156)	156	0.10
Lebanese (110)	247	0.16
Moroccan (77)	86	0.06
Palestinian (31)	31	0.02
Syrian (0)	43	0.03
Other Arab (28)	77	0.05
Armenian (81)	131	0.08
Assyrian/Chaldean/Syriac (0)	49	0.03
Australian (14)	68	0.04
Austrian (150)	328	0.21
Basque (0)	18	0.01
Belgian (60)	126	0.08
Brazilian (942)	1,029	0.66
British (290)	657	0.42
Bulgarian (59)	59	0.04
Canadian (476)	751	0.48
Celtic (30)	30	0.02
Croatian (39)	138	0.09
Czech (200)	500	0.32
Czechoslovakian (188)	242	0.16
Danish (70)	167	0.11
Dutch (299)	1,414	0.91
Eastern European (75)	75	0.05
English (3,778)	12,034	7.76
European (1,280)	1,402	0.90
Finnish (37)	168	0.11
French, ex. Basque (1,377)	5,074	3.27
French Canadian (559)	1,566	1.01
German (5,991)	21,105	13.62
Greek (439)	800	0.52
Guyanese (83)	281	0.18
Hungarian (354)	1,349	0.87
Iranian (6)	57	0.04
Irish (6,054)	20,714	13.36
Israeli (38)	38	0.02
Italian (10,432)	20,962	13.52
Latvian (28)	28	0.02
Lithuanian (106)	316	0.20
Macedonian (34)	34	0.02
Maltese (10)	10	0.01
New Zealander (0)	20	0.01
Norwegian (494)	1,380	0.89
Pennsylvania German (26)	57	0.04
Polish (1,795)	5,248	3.39
Portuguese (672)	1,500	0.97
Romanian (70)	227	0.15
Russian (605)	1,340	0.86
Scandinavian (149)	225	0.15
Scotch-Irish (985)	2,209	1.43
Scottish (715)	2,322	1.50
Serbian (0)	37	0.02
Slavic (40)	78	0.05
Slovak (109)	288	0.19
Slovene (9)	9	0.01
Swedish (396)	1,794	1.16
Swiss (35)	142	0.09
Turkish (33)	80	0.05
Ukrainian (133)	349	0.23
Welsh (165)	736	0.47
West Indian, ex. Hispanic (9,958)	11,418	7.37
Bahamian (334)	398	0.26

*Notes: † The Census 2010 population figure is used to calculate the percentages in the Hispanic Origin and Race categories. Ancestry percentages are based on the 2006-2010 American Community Survey population (not shown); ‡ Numbers in parentheses indicate the number of people reporting a single ancestry; * Numbers in parentheses indicate the number of persons reporting this race alone, not in combination with any other race; Please refer to the Explanation of Data for more information.*

Barbadian (24)	24	0.02
Belizean (22)	22	0.01
British West Indian (25)	42	0.03
Haitian (4,594)	4,942	3.19
Jamaican (3,890)	4,629	2.99
Trinidadian/Tobagonian (819)	1,013	0.65
U.S. Virgin Islander (81)	81	0.05
West Indian (169)	267	0.17
Yugoslavian (13)	70	0.05

Hispanic Origin	Population	%
Hispanic or Latino (of any race)	30,250	18.38
Central American, ex. Mexican	3,241	1.97
Costa Rican	170	0.10
Guatemalan	712	0.43
Honduran	967	0.59
Nicaraguan	537	0.33
Panamanian	263	0.16
Salvadoran	565	0.34
Other Central American	27	0.02
Cuban	4,120	2.50
Dominican Republic	1,686	1.02
Mexican	4,335	2.63
Puerto Rican	9,737	5.92
South American	5,157	3.13
Argentinean	369	0.22
Bolivian	66	0.04
Chilean	193	0.12
Colombian	2,518	1.53
Ecuadorian	718	0.44
Paraguayan	14	0.01
Peruvian	701	0.43
Uruguayan	102	0.06
Venezuelan	441	0.27
Other South American	35	0.02
Other Hispanic or Latino	1,974	1.20

Race*	Population	%
African-American/Black (26,898)	29,398	17.86
Not Hispanic (25,612)	27,494	16.70
Hispanic (1,286)	1,904	1.16
American Indian/Alaska Native (627)	1,491	0.91
Not Hispanic (371)	1,020	0.62
Hispanic (256)	471	0.29
Alaska Athabascan *(Ala. Nat.)* (1)	1	<0.01
Aleut *(Alaska Native)* (2)	2	<0.01
Apache (6)	17	0.01
Arapaho (0)	1	<0.01
Blackfeet (6)	49	0.03
Canadian/French Am. Ind. (5)	5	<0.01
Central American Ind. (14)	27	0.02
Cherokee (73)	255	0.15
Cheyenne (2)	5	<0.01
Chickasaw (7)	11	0.01
Chippewa (31)	41	0.02
Choctaw (8)	15	0.01
Comanche (0)	3	<0.01
Cree (0)	3	<0.01
Creek (7)	20	0.01
Crow (0)	2	<0.01
Delaware (4)	5	<0.01
Hopi (1)	1	<0.01
Houma (4)	4	<0.01
Inupiat *(Alaska Native)* (1)	2	<0.01
Iroquois (13)	38	0.02
Kiowa (0)	1	<0.01
Lumbee (1)	1	<0.01
Menominee (0)	1	<0.01
Mexican American Ind. (40)	59	0.04
Navajo (7)	10	0.01
Osage (1)	2	<0.01
Ottawa (0)	1	<0.01
Paiute (0)	1	<0.01
Potawatomi (2)	3	<0.01
Seminole (23)	60	0.04
Shoshone (2)	3	<0.01
Sioux (2)	9	0.01
South American Ind. (18)	69	0.04
Spanish American Ind. (8)	14	0.01
Tlingit-Haida *(Alaska Native)* (3)	4	<0.01
Ute (1)	5	<0.01
Asian (3,267)	4,281	2.60
Not Hispanic (3,194)	4,047	2.46
Hispanic (73)	234	0.14
Bangladeshi (32)	36	0.02
Burmese (12)	12	0.01
Cambodian (91)	102	0.06
Chinese, ex. Taiwanese (421)	613	0.37
Filipino (809)	1,079	0.66
Hmong (0)	1	<0.01
Indian (873)	1,101	0.67
Indonesian (24)	43	0.03
Japanese (63)	149	0.09
Korean (126)	191	0.12
Laotian (14)	19	0.01
Malaysian (6)	6	<0.01
Pakistani (78)	101	0.06
Sri Lankan (11)	11	0.01
Taiwanese (5)	14	0.01
Thai (72)	101	0.06
Vietnamese (495)	546	0.33
Hawaii Native/Pacific Islander (114)	427	0.26
Not Hispanic (86)	333	0.20
Hispanic (28)	94	0.06
Fijian (4)	4	<0.01
Guamanian/Chamorro (41)	53	0.03
Marshallese (8)	10	0.01
Native Hawaiian (30)	62	0.04
Samoan (6)	19	0.01
White (122,289)	126,189	76.66
Not Hispanic (101,329)	103,666	62.98
Hispanic (20,960)	22,523	13.68

Princeton

Place Type: CDP
County: Miami-Dade
Population: 22,038†

Ancestry‡	Population	%
African, Sub-Saharan (52)	52	0.25
African (52)	52	0.25
American (944)	944	4.58
Arab (49)	49	0.24
Arab (49)	49	0.24
Brazilian (8)	8	0.04
British (7)	7	0.03
Canadian (31)	51	0.25
Danish (0)	12	0.06
Dutch (6)	31	0.15
English (0)	156	0.76
European (18)	18	0.09
French, ex. Basque (10)	241	1.17
French Canadian (8)	8	0.04
German (59)	331	1.61
Guyanese (100)	100	0.48
Irish (163)	306	1.48
Italian (23)	292	1.42
Lithuanian (15)	15	0.07
Norwegian (0)	15	0.07
Polish (13)	13	0.06
Russian (8)	20	0.10
Scotch-Irish (0)	23	0.11
Scottish (0)	19	0.09
Welsh (6)	6	0.03
West Indian, ex. Hispanic (969)	1,091	5.29
Bahamian (146)	146	0.71
Bermudan (6)	6	0.03
Haitian (68)	86	0.42
Jamaican (683)	787	3.82
Trinidadian/Tobagonian (37)	37	0.18
West Indian (17)	17	0.08
Other West Indian (12)	12	0.06

Hispanic Origin	Population	%
Hispanic or Latino (of any race)	13,416	60.88
Central American, ex. Mexican	2,158	9.79
Costa Rican	59	0.27
Guatemalan	190	0.86
Honduran	415	1.88
Nicaraguan	1,077	4.89
Panamanian	130	0.59
Salvadoran	282	1.28
Other Central American	5	0.02
Cuban	5,294	24.02
Dominican Republic	667	3.03
Mexican	1,262	5.73
Puerto Rican	1,797	8.15
South American	1,589	7.21
Argentinean	84	0.38
Bolivian	27	0.12
Chilean	56	0.25
Colombian	711	3.23
Ecuadorian	166	0.75
Paraguayan	2	0.01
Peruvian	224	1.02
Uruguayan	34	0.15
Venezuelan	283	1.28
Other South American	2	0.01
Other Hispanic or Latino	649	2.94

Race*	Population	%
African-American/Black (6,775)	7,076	32.11
Not Hispanic (6,165)	6,330	28.72
Hispanic (610)	746	3.39
American Indian/Alaska Native (44)	80	0.36
Not Hispanic (26)	46	0.21
Hispanic (18)	34	0.15
Apache (6)	6	0.03
Blackfeet (2)	4	0.02
Central American Ind. (3)	6	0.03
Cherokee (0)	5	0.02
Choctaw (2)	3	0.01
Creek (2)	2	0.01
Inupiat *(Alaska Native)* (1)	1	<0.01
Mexican American Ind. (4)	4	0.02
Sioux (0)	1	<0.01
South American Ind. (7)	12	0.05
Asian (306)	431	1.96
Not Hispanic (297)	385	1.75
Hispanic (9)	46	0.21
Bangladeshi (5)	8	0.04
Chinese, ex. Taiwanese (36)	91	0.41
Filipino (61)	71	0.32
Indian (60)	99	0.45
Japanese (9)	18	0.08
Korean (11)	14	0.06
Laotian (8)	11	0.05
Pakistani (16)	18	0.08
Taiwanese (0)	1	<0.01
Thai (21)	27	0.12
Vietnamese (65)	69	0.31
Hawaii Native/Pacific Islander (11)	54	0.25
Not Hispanic (10)	40	0.18
Hispanic (1)	14	0.06
Guamanian/Chamorro (3)	3	0.01
Native Hawaiian (1)	2	0.01
Samoan (2)	3	0.01
White (13,322)	13,803	62.63
Not Hispanic (1,857)	1,982	8.99
Hispanic (11,465)	11,821	53.64

Punta Gorda

Place Type: City
County: Charlotte
Population: 16,641†

Ancestry‡	Population	%
African, Sub-Saharan (0)	109	0.66
African (0)	109	0.66
Albanian (0)	12	0.07
American (1,998)	1,998	12.06
Arab (78)	97	0.59
Lebanese (18)	37	0.22
Palestinian (60)	60	0.36
Armenian (12)	12	0.07
Austrian (28)	65	0.39
Belgian (0)	15	0.09
Brazilian (15)	15	0.09

*Notes: † The Census 2010 population figure is used to calculate the percentages in the Hispanic Origin and Race categories. Ancestry percentages are based on the 2006-2010 American Community Survey population (not shown); ‡ Numbers in parentheses indicate the number of people reporting a single ancestry; * Numbers in parentheses indicate the number of persons reporting this race alone, not in combination with any other race; Please refer to the Explanation of Data for more information.*

British (103)	160	0.97
Canadian (53)	77	0.46
Croatian (44)	44	0.27
Czech (0)	56	0.34
Czechoslovakian (9)	18	0.11
Danish (25)	89	0.54
Dutch (249)	554	3.34
Eastern European (19)	35	0.21
English (1,007)	2,782	16.79
European (225)	270	1.63
Finnish (31)	63	0.38
French, ex. Basque (232)	468	2.82
French Canadian (108)	158	0.95
German (1,251)	3,216	19.41
Greek (35)	35	0.21
Hungarian (0)	76	0.46
Icelander (23)	23	0.14
Irish (858)	2,629	15.87
Italian (727)	1,298	7.83
Latvian (12)	12	0.07
Lithuanian (121)	203	1.23
Norwegian (13)	228	1.38
Pennsylvania German (25)	25	0.15
Polish (497)	676	4.08
Portuguese (14)	22	0.13
Russian (32)	72	0.43
Scandinavian (13)	13	0.08
Scotch-Irish (104)	493	2.98
Scottish (253)	640	3.86
Serbian (0)	15	0.09
Slavic (12)	55	0.33
Slovak (44)	44	0.27
Swedish (200)	460	2.78
Swiss (96)	142	0.86
Ukrainian (52)	256	1.54
Welsh (29)	174	1.05
West Indian, ex. Hispanic (92)	247	1.49
Bahamian (44)	44	0.27
Jamaican (48)	157	0.95
West Indian (0)	46	0.28
Yugoslavian (0)	50	0.30

Hispanic Origin	**Population**	**%**
Hispanic or Latino (of any race)	746	4.48
Central American, ex. Mexican	29	0.17
Costa Rican	4	0.02
Guatemalan	2	0.01
Honduran	10	0.06
Panamanian	7	0.04
Salvadoran	6	0.04
Cuban	148	0.89
Dominican Republic	33	0.20
Mexican	109	0.66
Puerto Rican	267	1.60
South American	103	0.62
Argentinean	8	0.05
Bolivian	5	0.03
Chilean	16	0.10
Colombian	32	0.19
Ecuadorian	11	0.07
Paraguayan	1	0.01
Peruvian	21	0.13
Uruguayan	4	0.02
Venezuelan	5	0.03
Other Hispanic or Latino	57	0.34

Race*	**Population**	**%**
African-American/Black (553)	654	3.93
Not Hispanic (523)	604	3.63
Hispanic (30)	50	0.30
American Indian/Alaska Native (34)	110	0.66
Not Hispanic (22)	86	0.52
Hispanic (12)	24	0.14
Apache (1)	2	0.01
Blackfeet (1)	2	0.01
Cherokee (4)	31	0.19
Chippewa (2)	5	0.03
Choctaw (0)	1	0.01
Cree (1)	1	0.01
Creek (0)	1	0.01
Crow (1)	1	0.01
Delaware (0)	1	0.01
Iroquois (0)	1	0.01
Mexican American Ind. (1)	1	0.01
Navajo (0)	1	0.01
Paiute (1)	1	0.01
Sioux (1)	5	0.03
South American Ind. (0)	3	0.02
Asian (191)	225	1.35
Not Hispanic (190)	218	1.31
Hispanic (1)	7	0.04
Bangladeshi (3)	3	0.02
Cambodian (1)	1	0.01
Chinese, ex. Taiwanese (20)	24	0.14
Filipino (42)	54	0.32
Indian (44)	57	0.34
Indonesian (0)	1	0.01
Japanese (10)	13	0.08
Korean (8)	8	0.05
Laotian (2)	2	0.01
Pakistani (2)	2	0.01
Taiwanese (4)	4	0.02
Thai (7)	7	0.04
Vietnamese (42)	42	0.25
Hawaii Native/Pacific Islander (2)	3	0.02
Not Hispanic (2)	3	0.02
Guamanian/Chamorro (1)	1	0.01
Native Hawaiian (0)	1	0.01
White (15,533)	15,727	94.51
Not Hispanic (14,972)	15,132	90.93
Hispanic (561)	595	3.58

Quincy

Place Type: City
County: Gadsden
Population: 7,972†

Ancestry‡	**Population**	**%**
African, Sub-Saharan (18)	18	0.23
African (18)	18	0.23
American (340)	340	4.35
Belgian (0)	15	0.19
British (0)	37	0.47
Dutch (17)	53	0.68
English (65)	362	4.63
European (55)	55	0.70
French, ex. Basque (14)	69	0.88
French Canadian (18)	18	0.23
German (48)	184	2.36
Irish (147)	456	5.84
Norwegian (17)	17	0.22
Scotch-Irish (54)	69	0.88
Scottish (0)	51	0.65
Welsh (19)	36	0.46
West Indian, ex. Hispanic (80)	80	1.02
Bahamian (48)	48	0.61
Jamaican (32)	32	0.41

Hispanic Origin	**Population**	**%**
Hispanic or Latino (of any race)	1,108	13.90
Central American, ex. Mexican	312	3.91
Costa Rican	3	0.04
Guatemalan	27	0.34
Honduran	10	0.13
Nicaraguan	1	0.01
Salvadoran	271	3.40
Cuban	15	0.19
Dominican Republic	14	0.18
Mexican	649	8.14
Puerto Rican	32	0.40
South American	3	0.04
Colombian	3	0.04
Other Hispanic or Latino	83	1.04

Race*	**Population**	**%**
African-American/Black (5,134)	5,187	65.07
Not Hispanic (5,111)	5,158	64.70
Hispanic (23)	29	0.36
American Indian/Alaska Native (45)	73	0.92
Not Hispanic (24)	47	0.59
Hispanic (21)	26	0.33
Blackfeet (0)	2	0.03
Cherokee (3)	7	0.09
Chippewa (3)	7	0.09
Creek (2)	4	0.05
Mexican American Ind. (3)	3	0.04
Seminole (2)	4	0.05
Asian (56)	67	0.84
Not Hispanic (52)	63	0.79
Hispanic (4)	4	0.05
Chinese, ex. Taiwanese (9)	13	0.16
Filipino (32)	38	0.48
Indian (11)	11	0.14
Japanese (0)	3	0.04
Thai (2)	2	0.03
Hawaii Native/Pacific Islander (4)	22	0.28
Not Hispanic (0)	7	0.09
Hispanic (4)	15	0.19
Native Hawaiian (0)	7	0.09
White (1,866)	1,947	24.42
Not Hispanic (1,594)	1,646	20.65
Hispanic (272)	301	3.78

Richmond Heights

Place Type: CDP
County: Miami-Dade
Population: 8,541†

Ancestry‡	**Population**	**%**
African, Sub-Saharan (0)	6	0.07
Ghanaian (0)	6	0.07
American (336)	336	3.71
Czech (8)	45	0.50
English (10)	39	0.43
Guyanese (60)	60	0.66
Italian (3)	3	0.03
Polish (13)	45	0.50
Portuguese (17)	17	0.19
Russian (0)	12	0.13
Scottish (9)	9	0.10
West Indian, ex. Hispanic (600)	682	7.53
Bahamian (252)	308	3.40
British West Indian (11)	11	0.12
Haitian (169)	169	1.87
Jamaican (94)	120	1.33
Trinidadian/Tobagonian (65)	65	0.72
West Indian (9)	9	0.10

Hispanic Origin	**Population**	**%**
Hispanic or Latino (of any race)	2,136	25.01
Central American, ex. Mexican	498	5.83
Costa Rican	12	0.14
Guatemalan	56	0.66
Honduran	85	1.00
Nicaraguan	283	3.31
Panamanian	26	0.30
Salvadoran	32	0.37
Other Central American	4	0.05
Cuban	788	9.23
Dominican Republic	109	1.28
Mexican	50	0.59
Puerto Rican	244	2.86
South American	330	3.86
Argentinean	19	0.22
Bolivian	4	0.05
Chilean	15	0.18
Colombian	118	1.38
Ecuadorian	27	0.32
Peruvian	90	1.05
Uruguayan	7	0.08
Venezuelan	50	0.59
Other Hispanic or Latino	117	1.37

Race*	**Population**	**%**
African-American/Black (6,160)	6,308	73.86
Not Hispanic (5,961)	6,057	70.92
Hispanic (199)	251	2.94
American Indian/Alaska Native (22)	55	0.64

*Notes: † The Census 2010 population figure is used to calculate the percentages in the Hispanic Origin and Race categories. Ancestry percentages are based on the 2006-2010 American Community Survey population (not shown); ‡ Numbers in parentheses indicate the number of people reporting a single ancestry; * Numbers in parentheses indicate the number of persons reporting this race alone, not in combination with any other race; Please refer to the Explanation of Data for more information.*

Not Hispanic (16)	41	0.48
Hispanic (6)	14	0.16
Blackfeet (0)	10	0.12
Cherokee (1)	5	0.06
Choctaw (0)	1	0.01
Creek (0)	1	0.01
Lumbee (1)	2	0.02
Mexican American Ind. (1)	1	0.01
South American Ind. (1)	1	0.01
Spanish American Ind. (3)	3	0.04
Asian (37)	83	0.97
Not Hispanic (36)	76	0.89
Hispanic (1)	7	0.08
Chinese, ex. Taiwanese (15)	28	0.33
Filipino (3)	6	0.07
Indian (6)	30	0.35
Japanese (3)	3	0.04
Laotian (1)	2	0.02
Thai (2)	4	0.05
Vietnamese (1)	1	0.01
Hawaii Native/Pacific Islander (1)	19	0.22
Not Hispanic (1)	15	0.18
Hispanic (0)	4	0.05
Guamanian/Chamorro (0)	1	0.01
Native Hawaiian (1)	5	0.06
White (1,946)	2,087	24.44
Not Hispanic (251)	303	3.55
Hispanic (1,695)	1,784	20.89

Richmond West

Place Type: CDP
County: Miami-Dade
Population: 31,973†

Ancestry‡	Population	%
African, Sub-Saharan (28)	39	0.12
Cape Verdean (10)	21	0.06
South African (18)	18	0.06
American (852)	852	2.62
Arab (245)	378	1.16
Arab (212)	255	0.78
Lebanese (0)	78	0.24
Moroccan (33)	33	0.10
Syrian (0)	12	0.04
Brazilian (129)	158	0.49
British (17)	31	0.10
Czech (0)	14	0.04
Czechoslovakian (0)	10	0.03
Danish (0)	5	0.02
Dutch (38)	75	0.23
English (143)	338	1.04
European (191)	191	0.59
French, ex. Basque (13)	114	0.35
French Canadian (0)	27	0.08
German (138)	531	1.63
Greek (0)	12	0.04
Guyanese (24)	38	0.12
Hungarian (13)	22	0.07
Irish (80)	300	0.92
Italian (260)	563	1.73
Polish (56)	95	0.29
Romanian (19)	49	0.15
Russian (57)	88	0.27
Scotch-Irish (0)	34	0.10
Scottish (0)	12	0.04
Serbian (0)	27	0.08
Turkish (38)	38	0.12
Ukrainian (15)	42	0.13
Welsh (8)	8	0.02
West Indian, ex. Hispanic (874)	1,244	3.83
Bahamian (28)	91	0.28
Barbadian (56)	56	0.17
Belizean (11)	63	0.19
British West Indian (30)	30	0.09
Haitian (410)	509	1.57
Jamaican (193)	318	0.98
Trinidadian/Tobagonian (113)	124	0.38
U.S. Virgin Islander (33)	33	0.10
West Indian (0)	20	0.06

Hispanic Origin	Population	%
Hispanic or Latino (of any race)	25,110	78.54
Central American, ex. Mexican	3,300	10.32
Costa Rican	105	0.33
Guatemalan	172	0.54
Honduran	540	1.69
Nicaraguan	2,039	6.38
Panamanian	207	0.65
Salvadoran	235	0.73
Other Central American	2	0.01
Cuban	12,818	40.09
Dominican Republic	1,112	3.48
Mexican	363	1.14
Puerto Rican	1,924	6.02
South American	4,392	13.74
Argentinean	223	0.70
Bolivian	69	0.22
Chilean	165	0.52
Colombian	2,117	6.62
Ecuadorian	284	0.89
Paraguayan	12	0.04
Peruvian	954	2.98
Uruguayan	27	0.08
Venezuelan	537	1.68
Other South American	4	0.01
Other Hispanic or Latino	1,201	3.76

Race*	Population	%
African-American/Black (2,480)	2,855	8.93
Not Hispanic (2,008)	2,223	6.95
Hispanic (472)	632	1.98
American Indian/Alaska Native (57)	105	0.33
Not Hispanic (36)	48	0.15
Hispanic (21)	57	0.18
Apache (0)	1	<0.01
Blackfeet (0)	2	0.01
Central American Ind. (2)	6	0.02
Cherokee (4)	5	0.02
Comanche (0)	2	0.01
Iroquois (1)	2	0.01
Mexican American Ind. (0)	4	0.01
Pueblo (0)	4	0.01
South American Ind. (15)	18	0.06
Spanish American Ind. (0)	1	<0.01
Asian (634)	923	2.89
Not Hispanic (598)	806	2.52
Hispanic (36)	117	0.37
Bangladeshi (10)	11	0.03
Burmese (6)	6	0.02
Chinese, ex. Taiwanese (164)	290	0.91
Filipino (130)	164	0.51
Indian (193)	240	0.75
Indonesian (4)	6	0.02
Japanese (12)	21	0.07
Korean (6)	20	0.06
Laotian (0)	2	0.01
Pakistani (47)	58	0.18
Thai (7)	9	0.03
Vietnamese (31)	42	0.13
Hawaii Native/Pacific Islander (5)	47	0.15
Not Hispanic (2)	28	0.09
Hispanic (3)	19	0.06
Guamanian/Chamorro (2)	5	0.02
Native Hawaiian (0)	8	0.03
White (26,321)	27,051	84.61
Not Hispanic (3,764)	3,966	12.40
Hispanic (22,557)	23,085	72.20

Riverview

Place Type: CDP
County: Hillsborough
Population: 71,050†

Ancestry‡	Population	%
African, Sub-Saharan (203)	254	0.39
African (22)	33	0.05
Cape Verdean (84)	124	0.19
Ethiopian (83)	83	0.13
South African (14)	14	0.02
American (4,848)	4,848	7.42
Arab (264)	399	0.61
Arab (52)	52	0.08
Egyptian (31)	101	0.15
Lebanese (5)	54	0.08
Moroccan (83)	83	0.13
Palestinian (93)	93	0.14
Syrian (0)	16	0.02
Armenian (20)	44	0.07
Australian (9)	19	0.03
Austrian (24)	177	0.27
Belgian (59)	150	0.23
Brazilian (125)	125	0.19
British (307)	451	0.69
Cajun (33)	57	0.09
Canadian (20)	125	0.19
Croatian (11)	28	0.04
Czech (96)	239	0.37
Czechoslovakian (0)	22	0.03
Danish (37)	206	0.32
Dutch (335)	1,254	1.92
Eastern European (76)	76	0.12
English (2,606)	6,090	9.32
European (936)	1,091	1.67
Finnish (48)	98	0.15
French, ex. Basque (314)	1,513	2.32
French Canadian (237)	403	0.62
German (2,251)	7,974	12.21
Greek (36)	217	0.33
Guyanese (77)	146	0.22
Hungarian (100)	271	0.41
Irish (3,000)	9,208	14.10
Italian (1,758)	4,209	6.44
Lithuanian (31)	160	0.24
New Zealander (18)	18	0.03
Norwegian (62)	428	0.66
Pennsylvania German (0)	17	0.03
Polish (817)	2,064	3.16
Portuguese (32)	77	0.12
Romanian (31)	53	0.08
Russian (94)	185	0.28
Scandinavian (0)	11	0.02
Scotch-Irish (625)	1,267	1.94
Scottish (452)	1,323	2.03
Serbian (8)	20	0.03
Slavic (17)	17	0.03
Slovak (14)	14	0.02
Swedish (178)	564	0.86
Swiss (41)	210	0.32
Ukrainian (43)	99	0.15
Welsh (274)	658	1.01
West Indian, ex. Hispanic (1,559)	1,844	2.82
Dutch West Indian (0)	7	0.01
Haitian (307)	341	0.52
Jamaican (755)	910	1.39
Trinidadian/Tobagonian (127)	173	0.26
West Indian (342)	385	0.59
Other West Indian (28)	28	0.04
Yugoslavian (209)	220	0.34

Hispanic Origin	Population	%
Hispanic or Latino (of any race)	14,946	21.04
Central American, ex. Mexican	1,013	1.43
Costa Rican	78	0.11
Guatemalan	143	0.20
Honduran	231	0.33
Nicaraguan	110	0.15
Panamanian	264	0.37
Salvadoran	178	0.25
Other Central American	9	0.01
Cuban	1,450	2.04
Dominican Republic	1,004	1.41
Mexican	2,904	4.09
Puerto Rican	5,992	8.43
South American	1,700	2.39
Argentinean	59	0.08
Bolivian	10	0.01
Chilean	41	0.06
Colombian	899	1.27
Ecuadorian	193	0.27

*Notes: † The Census 2010 population figure is used to calculate the percentages in the Hispanic Origin and Race categories. Ancestry percentages are based on the 2006-2010 American Community Survey population (not shown); ‡ Numbers in parentheses indicate the number of people reporting a single ancestry; * Numbers in parentheses indicate the number of persons reporting this race alone, not in combination with any other race; Please refer to the Explanation of Data for more information.*

	Population	%
Paraguayan	2	<0.01
Peruvian	224	0.32
Uruguayan	29	0.04
Venezuelan	228	0.32
Other South American	15	0.02
Other Hispanic or Latino	883	1.24

Race*	Population	%
African-American/Black (12,064)	13,492	18.99
Not Hispanic (11,216)	12,179	17.14
Hispanic (848)	1,313	1.85
American Indian/Alaska Native (294)	764	1.08
Not Hispanic (200)	555	0.78
Hispanic (94)	209	0.29
Alaska Athabascan *(Ala. Nat.)* (3)	4	0.01
Aleut *(Alaska Native)* (1)	4	0.01
Apache (1)	8	0.01
Blackfeet (2)	16	0.02
Canadian/French Am. Ind. (2)	3	<0.01
Central American Ind. (1)	7	0.01
Cherokee (40)	149	0.21
Chickasaw (2)	3	<0.01
Chippewa (5)	10	0.01
Choctaw (4)	11	0.02
Creek (13)	25	0.04
Crow (0)	1	<0.01
Delaware (0)	3	<0.01
Hopi (1)	1	<0.01
Iroquois (2)	4	0.01
Lumbee (4)	13	0.02
Menominee (8)	8	0.01
Mexican American Ind. (17)	29	0.04
Navajo (6)	6	0.01
Ottawa (6)	6	0.01
Pima (0)	1	<0.01
Potawatomi (0)	2	<0.01
Seminole (6)	14	0.02
Sioux (4)	23	0.03
South American Ind. (5)	23	0.03
Spanish American Ind. (0)	1	<0.01
Yaqui (0)	1	<0.01
Asian (2,203)	3,049	4.29
Not Hispanic (2,163)	2,905	4.09
Hispanic (40)	144	0.20
Bangladeshi (12)	12	0.02
Burmese (10)	10	0.01
Cambodian (12)	12	0.02
Chinese, ex. Taiwanese (184)	274	0.39
Filipino (550)	803	1.13
Hmong (17)	17	0.02
Indian (654)	794	1.12
Indonesian (6)	15	0.02
Japanese (50)	174	0.24
Korean (138)	212	0.30
Laotian (22)	35	0.05
Malaysian (1)	1	<0.01
Nepalese (2)	2	<0.01
Pakistani (32)	41	0.06
Sri Lankan (14)	17	0.02
Taiwanese (10)	22	0.03
Thai (54)	114	0.16
Vietnamese (362)	433	0.61
Hawaii Native/Pacific Islander (68)	212	0.30
Not Hispanic (62)	182	0.26
Hispanic (6)	30	0.04
Fijian (1)	1	<0.01
Guamanian/Chamorro (20)	39	0.05
Marshallese (1)	3	<0.01
Native Hawaiian (24)	55	0.08
Samoan (1)	8	0.01
Tongan (0)	3	<0.01
White (49,896)	52,204	73.48
Not Hispanic (40,332)	41,798	58.83
Hispanic (9,564)	10,406	14.65

Riviera Beach

Place Type: City
County: Palm Beach
Population: 32,488†

Ancestry‡	Population	%
African, Sub-Saharan (231)	274	0.84
African (231)	274	0.84
American (656)	656	2.02
Arab (77)	77	0.24
Egyptian (41)	41	0.13
Lebanese (36)	36	0.11
Armenian (14)	14	0.04
Austrian (21)	46	0.14
British (36)	70	0.22
Bulgarian (11)	53	0.16
Canadian (59)	59	0.18
Croatian (0)	9	0.03
Czech (51)	77	0.24
Czechoslovakian (10)	30	0.09
Danish (12)	46	0.14
Dutch (24)	114	0.35
Eastern European (19)	19	0.06
English (331)	1,141	3.51
Estonian (9)	9	0.03
European (115)	125	0.38
Finnish (21)	55	0.17
French, ex. Basque (124)	355	1.09
French Canadian (100)	107	0.33
German (316)	1,364	4.20
Greek (68)	92	0.28
Guyanese (0)	40	0.12
Hungarian (11)	21	0.06
Icelander (0)	14	0.04
Iranian (54)	54	0.17
Irish (376)	1,176	3.62
Italian (571)	1,209	3.72
Lithuanian (59)	109	0.34
Luxemburger (0)	9	0.03
Norwegian (26)	76	0.23
Pennsylvania German (0)	33	0.10
Polish (100)	290	0.89
Portuguese (26)	26	0.08
Romanian (0)	69	0.21
Russian (159)	326	1.00
Scandinavian (0)	12	0.04
Scotch-Irish (104)	186	0.57
Scottish (34)	371	1.14
Slovak (48)	57	0.18
Slovene (7)	16	0.05
Swedish (20)	181	0.56
Swiss (8)	27	0.08
Turkish (10)	10	0.03
Ukrainian (5)	24	0.07
Welsh (0)	19	0.06
West Indian, ex. Hispanic (3,497)	3,715	11.44
Bahamian (177)	200	0.62
Belizean (0)	8	0.02
British West Indian (23)	23	0.07
Haitian (1,776)	1,785	5.49
Jamaican (1,474)	1,645	5.06
Trinidadian/Tobagonian (11)	11	0.03
West Indian (36)	43	0.13

Hispanic Origin	Population	%
Hispanic or Latino (of any race)	2,418	7.44
Central American, ex. Mexican	594	1.83
Costa Rican	12	0.04
Guatemalan	324	1.00
Honduran	105	0.32
Nicaraguan	77	0.24
Panamanian	28	0.09
Salvadoran	46	0.14
Other Central American	2	0.01
Cuban	241	0.74
Dominican Republic	94	0.29
Mexican	340	1.05
Puerto Rican	518	1.59
South American	415	1.28
Argentinean	24	0.07
Bolivian	1	<0.01
Chilean	6	0.02
Colombian	212	0.65
Ecuadorian	52	0.16
Peruvian	73	0.22
Uruguayan	12	0.04
Venezuelan	32	0.10
Other South American	3	0.01
Other Hispanic or Latino	216	0.66

Race*	Population	%
African-American/Black (21,401)	21,921	67.47
Not Hispanic (21,126)	21,549	66.33
Hispanic (275)	372	1.15
American Indian/Alaska Native (114)	270	0.83
Not Hispanic (76)	192	0.59
Hispanic (38)	78	0.24
Apache (0)	3	0.01
Arapaho (0)	1	<0.01
Blackfeet (0)	2	0.01
Canadian/French Am. Ind. (0)	1	<0.01
Central American Ind. (6)	6	0.02
Cherokee (7)	45	0.14
Choctaw (1)	1	<0.01
Delaware (0)	1	<0.01
Iroquois (1)	3	0.01
Mexican American Ind. (7)	14	0.04
Seminole (0)	8	0.02
Sioux (2)	3	0.01
South American Ind. (0)	3	0.01
Spanish American Ind. (1)	1	<0.01
Tlingit-Haida *(Alaska Native)* (1)	2	0.01
Asian (769)	901	2.77
Not Hispanic (765)	883	2.72
Hispanic (4)	18	0.06
Bangladeshi (40)	45	0.14
Chinese, ex. Taiwanese (79)	105	0.32
Filipino (128)	149	0.46
Indian (212)	251	0.77
Indonesian (2)	3	0.01
Japanese (8)	8	0.02
Korean (32)	43	0.13
Laotian (15)	15	0.05
Malaysian (1)	2	0.01
Nepalese (1)	1	<0.01
Pakistani (9)	12	0.04
Sri Lankan (5)	6	0.02
Taiwanese (3)	4	0.01
Thai (37)	42	0.13
Vietnamese (171)	181	0.56
Hawaii Native/Pacific Islander (25)	124	0.38
Not Hispanic (18)	109	0.34
Hispanic (7)	15	0.05
Fijian (1)	1	<0.01
Guamanian/Chamorro (7)	12	0.04
Native Hawaiian (0)	2	0.01
Samoan (0)	1	<0.01
Tongan (2)	7	0.02
White (8,782)	9,222	28.39
Not Hispanic (7,440)	7,738	23.82
Hispanic (1,342)	1,484	4.57

Rockledge

Place Type: City
County: Brevard
Population: 24,926†

Ancestry‡	Population	%
African, Sub-Saharan (69)	93	0.38
African (69)	93	0.38
Albanian (6)	12	0.05
American (2,311)	2,311	9.43
Arab (77)	77	0.31
Lebanese (25)	25	0.10
Moroccan (42)	42	0.17
Syrian (10)	10	0.04
Austrian (29)	109	0.44
Basque (13)	13	0.05
Belgian (0)	20	0.08
Brazilian (0)	46	0.19
British (31)	86	0.35
Canadian (97)	136	0.56
Carpatho Rusyn (0)	12	0.05
Croatian (0)	12	0.05

*Notes: † The Census 2010 population figure is used to calculate the percentages in the Hispanic Origin and Race categories. Ancestry percentages are based on the 2006-2010 American Community Survey population (not shown); ‡ Numbers in parentheses indicate the number of people reporting a single ancestry; * Numbers in parentheses indicate the number of persons reporting this race alone, not in combination with any other race; Please refer to the Explanation of Data for more information.*

Ancestry (continued)	Population	%
Czech (52)	131	0.53
Czechoslovakian (18)	18	0.07
Danish (51)	87	0.36
Dutch (73)	570	2.33
Eastern European (0)	12	0.05
English (1,185)	3,126	12.76
European (149)	201	0.82
Finnish (20)	31	0.13
French, ex. Basque (232)	962	3.93
French Canadian (168)	317	1.29
German (1,484)	4,292	17.52
Greek (10)	41	0.17
Hungarian (90)	184	0.75
Icelander (0)	6	0.02
Iranian (114)	114	0.47
Irish (1,377)	4,086	16.68
Italian (898)	2,205	9.00
Lithuanian (38)	141	0.58
Northern European (16)	16	0.07
Norwegian (32)	163	0.67
Polish (225)	900	3.67
Portuguese (12)	95	0.39
Romanian (0)	12	0.05
Russian (117)	241	0.98
Scandinavian (63)	70	0.29
Scotch-Irish (221)	475	1.94
Scottish (80)	609	2.49
Slavic (23)	23	0.09
Slovak (21)	25	0.10
Slovene (12)	27	0.11
Swedish (73)	464	1.89
Swiss (40)	67	0.27
Ukrainian (79)	133	0.54
Welsh (26)	180	0.73
West Indian, ex. Hispanic (133)	167	0.68
Bahamian (61)	61	0.25
Haitian (21)	21	0.09
Jamaican (51)	51	0.21
Trinidadian/Tobagonian (0)	34	0.14

Hispanic Origin	Population	%
Hispanic or Latino (of any race)	1,590	6.38
Central American, ex. Mexican	165	0.66
Costa Rican	10	0.04
Guatemalan	63	0.25
Honduran	14	0.06
Nicaraguan	16	0.06
Panamanian	53	0.21
Salvadoran	9	0.04
Cuban	183	0.73
Dominican Republic	25	0.10
Mexican	403	1.62
Puerto Rican	526	2.11
South American	160	0.64
Argentinean	30	0.12
Bolivian	3	0.01
Chilean	7	0.03
Colombian	77	0.31
Ecuadorian	9	0.04
Peruvian	13	0.05
Uruguayan	6	0.02
Venezuelan	14	0.06
Other South American	1	<0.01
Other Hispanic or Latino	128	0.51

Race*	Population	%
African-American/Black (3,608)	3,917	15.71
Not Hispanic (3,506)	3,783	15.18
Hispanic (102)	134	0.54
American Indian/Alaska Native (84)	198	0.79
Not Hispanic (66)	164	0.66
Hispanic (18)	34	0.14
Aleut *(Alaska Native)* (0)	7	0.03
Apache (1)	3	0.01
Blackfeet (0)	2	0.01
Canadian/French Am. Ind. (0)	1	<0.01
Cherokee (12)	41	0.16
Cheyenne (1)	2	0.01
Chickasaw (2)	2	0.01
Chippewa (6)	6	0.02
Choctaw (1)	2	0.01
Comanche (1)	1	<0.01
Cree (2)	2	0.01
Creek (0)	2	0.01
Iroquois (4)	8	0.03
Lumbee (3)	3	0.01
Menominee (0)	4	0.02
Mexican American Ind. (1)	1	<0.01
Sioux (3)	7	0.03
South American Ind. (1)	1	<0.01
Asian (604)	825	3.31
Not Hispanic (586)	789	3.17
Hispanic (18)	36	0.14
Bangladeshi (0)	1	<0.01
Cambodian (5)	9	0.04
Chinese, ex. Taiwanese (89)	115	0.46
Filipino (118)	203	0.81
Indian (164)	183	0.73
Indonesian (2)	8	0.03
Japanese (38)	82	0.33
Korean (42)	66	0.26
Laotian (3)	6	0.02
Malaysian (1)	2	0.01
Pakistani (1)	2	0.01
Taiwanese (2)	9	0.04
Thai (22)	29	0.12
Vietnamese (96)	110	0.44
Hawaii Native/Pacific Islander (29)	68	0.27
Not Hispanic (25)	60	0.24
Hispanic (4)	8	0.03
Fijian (1)	1	<0.01
Guamanian/Chamorro (5)	18	0.07
Marshallese (9)	12	0.05
Native Hawaiian (10)	18	0.07
Samoan (2)	6	0.02
White (19,614)	20,177	80.95
Not Hispanic (18,569)	19,035	76.37
Hispanic (1,045)	1,142	4.58

Rotonda

Place Type: CDP
County: Charlotte
Population: 8,759†

Ancestry‡	Population	%
American (1,218)	1,218	12.77
Arab (27)	41	0.43
Lebanese (14)	28	0.29
Syrian (13)	13	0.14
Armenian (14)	14	0.15
Australian (0)	32	0.34
Austrian (59)	99	1.04
Belgian (26)	26	0.27
British (172)	184	1.93
Canadian (13)	24	0.25
Croatian (25)	57	0.60
Czech (56)	105	1.10
Danish (14)	28	0.29
Dutch (32)	276	2.89
English (759)	1,670	17.51
European (40)	40	0.42
Finnish (29)	38	0.40
French, ex. Basque (103)	409	4.29
French Canadian (73)	142	1.49
German (753)	1,859	19.49
Greek (0)	34	0.36
Hungarian (36)	50	0.52
Irish (631)	1,587	16.64
Italian (464)	975	10.22
Lithuanian (0)	23	0.24
Norwegian (32)	115	1.21
Polish (309)	618	6.48
Portuguese (74)	74	0.78
Russian (38)	108	1.13
Scotch-Irish (185)	231	2.42
Scottish (129)	356	3.73
Slovak (56)	56	0.59
Swedish (34)	103	1.08
Swiss (0)	42	0.44
Ukrainian (11)	49	0.51
Welsh (12)	76	0.80

Hispanic Origin	Population	%
Hispanic or Latino (of any race)	168	1.92
Central American, ex. Mexican	7	0.08
Costa Rican	1	0.01
Guatemalan	1	0.01
Honduran	2	0.02
Panamanian	3	0.03
Cuban	17	0.19
Dominican Republic	2	0.02
Mexican	44	0.50
Puerto Rican	52	0.59
South American	29	0.33
Argentinean	4	0.05
Colombian	16	0.18
Ecuadorian	5	0.06
Peruvian	2	0.02
Uruguayan	1	0.01
Venezuelan	1	0.01
Other Hispanic or Latino	17	0.19

Race*	Population	%
African-American/Black (89)	106	1.21
Not Hispanic (86)	102	1.16
Hispanic (3)	4	0.05
American Indian/Alaska Native (9)	28	0.32
Not Hispanic (9)	27	0.31
Hispanic (0)	1	0.01
Cherokee (2)	8	0.09
Chippewa (1)	1	0.01
Delaware (1)	2	0.02
Iroquois (1)	1	0.01
Lumbee (1)	1	0.01
Tlingit-Haida *(Alaska Native)* (1)	1	0.01
Asian (62)	73	0.83
Not Hispanic (61)	72	0.82
Hispanic (1)	1	0.01
Chinese, ex. Taiwanese (17)	22	0.25
Filipino (7)	10	0.11
Indian (12)	13	0.15
Indonesian (2)	2	0.02
Japanese (8)	10	0.11
Korean (6)	6	0.07
Thai (0)	1	0.01
Vietnamese (10)	10	0.11
Hawaii Native/Pacific Islander (0)	2	0.02
Not Hispanic (0)	1	0.01
Hispanic (0)	1	0.01
Native Hawaiian (0)	2	0.02
White (8,526)	8,569	97.83
Not Hispanic (8,391)	8,429	96.23
Hispanic (135)	140	1.60

Royal Palm Beach

Place Type: Village
County: Palm Beach
Population: 34,140†

Ancestry‡	Population	%
African, Sub-Saharan (816)	882	2.74
African (776)	798	2.48
Cape Verdean (0)	20	0.06
Nigerian (29)	29	0.09
South African (11)	35	0.11
American (1,685)	1,685	5.23
Arab (155)	209	0.65
Arab (117)	126	0.39
Jordanian (38)	38	0.12
Lebanese (0)	27	0.08
Syrian (0)	18	0.06
Armenian (7)	7	0.02
Austrian (12)	233	0.72
Belgian (0)	15	0.05
Brazilian (74)	79	0.25
British (95)	124	0.38
Bulgarian (25)	44	0.14
Canadian (18)	79	0.25

*Notes: † The Census 2010 population figure is used to calculate the percentages in the Hispanic Origin and Race categories. Ancestry percentages are based on the 2006-2010 American Community Survey population (not shown); ‡ Numbers in parentheses indicate the number of people reporting a single ancestry; * Numbers in parentheses indicate the number of persons reporting this race alone, not in combination with any other race; Please refer to the Explanation of Data for more information.*

Celtic (0)	10	0.03
Croatian (42)	42	0.13
Czech (39)	366	1.14
Czechoslovakian (0)	11	0.03
Danish (39)	56	0.17
Dutch (39)	295	0.92
Eastern European (103)	131	0.41
English (410)	1,705	5.29
European (258)	319	0.99
Finnish (13)	33	0.10
French, ex. Basque (206)	792	2.46
French Canadian (61)	129	0.40
German (1,065)	3,695	11.47
Greek (24)	185	0.57
Guyanese (32)	40	0.12
Hungarian (39)	358	1.11
Irish (747)	3,616	11.23
Israeli (11)	11	0.03
Italian (1,619)	3,484	10.82
Lithuanian (17)	30	0.09
Norwegian (22)	125	0.39
Pennsylvania German (13)	24	0.07
Polish (604)	1,627	5.05
Portuguese (166)	243	0.75
Romanian (26)	127	0.39
Russian (248)	801	2.49
Scandinavian (0)	21	0.07
Scotch-Irish (48)	237	0.74
Scottish (110)	482	1.50
Serbian (0)	16	0.05
Slavic (0)	19	0.06
Slovak (30)	101	0.31
Slovene (37)	47	0.15
Swedish (39)	160	0.50
Swiss (0)	16	0.05
Ukrainian (17)	32	0.10
Welsh (0)	145	0.45
West Indian, ex. Hispanic (2,652)	2,831	8.79
Bahamian (96)	154	0.48
Barbadian (34)	34	0.11
Haitian (903)	961	2.98
Jamaican (1,526)	1,589	4.93
Trinidadian/Tobagonian (6)	6	0.02
West Indian (87)	87	0.27

Hispanic Origin	Population	%
Hispanic or Latino (of any race)	6,950	20.36
Central American, ex. Mexican	522	1.53
Costa Rican	59	0.17
Guatemalan	92	0.27
Honduran	111	0.33
Nicaraguan	131	0.38
Panamanian	61	0.18
Salvadoran	68	0.20
Cuban	1,521	4.46
Dominican Republic	471	1.38
Mexican	654	1.92
Puerto Rican	1,646	4.82
South American	1,764	5.17
Argentinean	68	0.20
Bolivian	20	0.06
Chilean	27	0.08
Colombian	917	2.69
Ecuadorian	198	0.58
Paraguayan	11	0.03
Peruvian	262	0.77
Uruguayan	56	0.16
Venezuelan	195	0.57
Other South American	10	0.03
Other Hispanic or Latino	372	1.09

Race*	Population	%
African-American/Black (7,738)	8,240	24.14
Not Hispanic (7,452)	7,824	22.92
Hispanic (286)	416	1.22
American Indian/Alaska Native (68)	188	0.55
Not Hispanic (42)	123	0.36
Hispanic (26)	65	0.19
Apache (1)	1	<0.01
Blackfeet (0)	2	0.01
Cherokee (10)	33	0.10
Chippewa (2)	3	0.01
Choctaw (1)	6	0.02
Creek (1)	1	<0.01
Crow (1)	1	<0.01
Houma (4)	4	0.01
Inupiat *(Alaska Native)* (0)	1	<0.01
Iroquois (1)	1	<0.01
Mexican American Ind. (10)	15	0.04
Navajo (0)	3	0.01
Osage (1)	1	<0.01
Pueblo (1)	1	<0.01
Seminole (1)	1	<0.01
Sioux (0)	1	<0.01
South American Ind. (8)	11	0.03
Spanish American Ind. (0)	1	<0.01
Tlingit-Haida *(Alaska Native)* (1)	1	<0.01
Asian (1,435)	1,763	5.16
Not Hispanic (1,418)	1,701	4.98
Hispanic (17)	62	0.18
Bangladeshi (26)	35	0.10
Chinese, ex. Taiwanese (187)	255	0.75
Filipino (340)	414	1.21
Indian (484)	571	1.67
Indonesian (7)	22	0.06
Japanese (22)	47	0.14
Korean (41)	53	0.16
Malaysian (7)	7	0.02
Nepalese (11)	11	0.03
Pakistani (37)	38	0.11
Sri Lankan (4)	4	0.01
Taiwanese (1)	2	0.01
Thai (34)	39	0.11
Vietnamese (173)	206	0.60
Hawaii Native/Pacific Islander (15)	97	0.28
Not Hispanic (14)	63	0.18
Hispanic (1)	34	0.10
Guamanian/Chamorro (0)	1	<0.01
Native Hawaiian (6)	21	0.06
Samoan (6)	7	0.02
Tongan (0)	1	<0.01
White (22,741)	23,493	68.81
Not Hispanic (17,445)	17,932	52.52
Hispanic (5,296)	5,561	16.29

Ruskin

Place Type: CDP
County: Hillsborough
Population: 17,208†

Ancestry‡	Population	%
African, Sub-Saharan (23)	23	0.16
African (23)	23	0.16
American (1,535)	1,535	10.60
Arab (7)	7	0.05
Lebanese (7)	7	0.05
Austrian (0)	12	0.08
Carpatho Rusyn (30)	30	0.21
Croatian (49)	49	0.34
Czechoslovakian (10)	10	0.07
Dutch (95)	318	2.20
English (483)	924	6.38
European (23)	44	0.30
Finnish (20)	36	0.25
French, ex. Basque (61)	429	2.96
French Canadian (31)	38	0.26
German (453)	1,386	9.57
Greek (0)	11	0.08
Hungarian (11)	16	0.11
Iranian (32)	32	0.22
Irish (651)	1,713	11.83
Italian (655)	844	5.83
Latvian (0)	9	0.06
Lithuanian (18)	58	0.40
Norwegian (0)	82	0.57
Polish (40)	156	1.08
Portuguese (0)	45	0.31
Romanian (15)	15	0.10
Russian (0)	14	0.10
Scotch-Irish (14)	127	0.88
Scottish (29)	70	0.48
Serbian (10)	10	0.07
Slovak (11)	11	0.08
Swedish (58)	165	1.14
Swiss (0)	43	0.30
Turkish (10)	10	0.07
Welsh (36)	48	0.33
West Indian, ex. Hispanic (131)	173	1.19
British West Indian (0)	21	0.15
Haitian (110)	110	0.76
West Indian (21)	42	0.29

Hispanic Origin	Population	%
Hispanic or Latino (of any race)	7,377	42.87
Central American, ex. Mexican	357	2.07
Costa Rican	17	0.10
Guatemalan	172	1.00
Honduran	61	0.35
Nicaraguan	30	0.17
Panamanian	30	0.17
Salvadoran	47	0.27
Cuban	232	1.35
Dominican Republic	109	0.63
Mexican	5,303	30.82
Puerto Rican	940	5.46
South American	197	1.14
Argentinean	4	0.02
Bolivian	1	0.01
Chilean	8	0.05
Colombian	94	0.55
Ecuadorian	36	0.21
Peruvian	30	0.17
Venezuelan	22	0.13
Other South American	2	0.01
Other Hispanic or Latino	239	1.39

Race*	Population	%
African-American/Black (1,570)	1,704	9.90
Not Hispanic (1,470)	1,560	9.07
Hispanic (100)	144	0.84
American Indian/Alaska Native (56)	123	0.71
Not Hispanic (42)	98	0.57
Hispanic (14)	25	0.15
Alaska Athabascan *(Ala. Nat.)* (1)	1	0.01
Apache (1)	1	0.01
Blackfeet (1)	1	0.01
Canadian/French Am. Ind. (1)	1	0.01
Central American Ind. (1)	1	0.01
Cherokee (6)	27	0.16
Chickasaw (1)	1	0.01
Chippewa (2)	3	0.02
Comanche (0)	3	0.02
Lumbee (1)	1	0.01
Mexican American Ind. (2)	2	0.01
Potawatomi (1)	1	0.01
Pueblo (0)	1	0.01
Seminole (1)	4	0.02
Sioux (6)	7	0.04
South American Ind. (2)	9	0.05
Asian (229)	301	1.75
Not Hispanic (212)	255	1.48
Hispanic (17)	46	0.27
Bangladeshi (1)	1	0.01
Cambodian (0)	3	0.02
Chinese, ex. Taiwanese (32)	51	0.30
Filipino (54)	78	0.45
Hmong (4)	4	0.02
Indian (51)	63	0.37
Japanese (1)	6	0.03
Korean (5)	11	0.06
Laotian (6)	13	0.08
Nepalese (1)	1	0.01
Pakistani (1)	1	0.01
Taiwanese (0)	3	0.02
Thai (6)	13	0.08
Vietnamese (48)	61	0.35
Hawaii Native/Pacific Islander (10)	31	0.18
Not Hispanic (9)	24	0.14
Hispanic (1)	7	0.04

*Notes: † The Census 2010 population figure is used to calculate the percentages in the Hispanic Origin and Race categories. Ancestry percentages are based on the 2006-2010 American Community Survey population (not shown); ‡ Numbers in parentheses indicate the number of people reporting a single ancestry; * Numbers in parentheses indicate the number of persons reporting this race alone, not in combination with any other race; Please refer to the Explanation of Data for more information.*

Guamanian/Chamorro (6)	7	0.04
Native Hawaiian (2)	12	0.07
Samoan (2)	4	0.02
White (12,340)	12,660	73.57
Not Hispanic (7,884)	8,038	46.71
Hispanic (4,456)	4,622	26.86

Safety Harbor

Place Type: City
County: Pinellas
Population: 16,884†

Ancestry‡	Population	%
African, Sub-Saharan (60)	60	0.35
African (60)	60	0.35
American (882)	882	5.21
Arab (41)	109	0.64
Arab (16)	16	0.09
Egyptian (17)	45	0.27
Lebanese (0)	33	0.19
Syrian (0)	7	0.04
Other Arab (8)	8	0.05
Austrian (29)	81	0.48
Belgian (15)	15	0.09
Brazilian (0)	37	0.22
British (64)	75	0.44
Canadian (84)	148	0.87
Croatian (20)	20	0.12
Czech (11)	134	0.79
Danish (28)	54	0.32
Dutch (93)	721	4.26
Eastern European (22)	22	0.13
English (800)	2,022	11.94
European (235)	259	1.53
Finnish (0)	34	0.20
French, ex. Basque (65)	700	4.13
French Canadian (121)	241	1.42
German (1,254)	3,510	20.73
Greek (87)	132	0.78
Hungarian (11)	182	1.07
Iranian (6)	43	0.25
Irish (771)	2,919	17.24
Israeli (24)	24	0.14
Italian (914)	1,659	9.80
Lithuanian (55)	95	0.56
New Zealander (12)	12	0.07
Northern European (74)	74	0.44
Norwegian (113)	335	1.98
Pennsylvania German (9)	9	0.05
Polish (351)	701	4.14
Portuguese (23)	74	0.44
Russian (111)	169	1.00
Scotch-Irish (279)	488	2.88
Scottish (228)	513	3.03
Serbian (11)	33	0.19
Slavic (12)	12	0.07
Slovak (8)	80	0.47
Slovene (0)	13	0.08
Swedish (149)	366	2.16
Swiss (15)	15	0.09
Ukrainian (0)	51	0.30
Welsh (66)	254	1.50
West Indian, ex. Hispanic (70)	87	0.51
Bahamian (0)	17	0.10
Jamaican (70)	70	0.41
Yugoslavian (76)	93	0.55

Hispanic Origin	Population	%
Hispanic or Latino (of any race)	974	5.77
Central American, ex. Mexican	60	0.36
Costa Rican	5	0.03
Guatemalan	19	0.11
Honduran	17	0.10
Nicaraguan	2	0.01
Panamanian	7	0.04
Salvadoran	10	0.06
Cuban	124	0.73
Dominican Republic	25	0.15
Mexican	250	1.48
Puerto Rican	288	1.71
South American	142	0.84
Argentinean	4	0.02
Bolivian	5	0.03
Chilean	1	0.01
Colombian	72	0.43
Ecuadorian	13	0.08
Peruvian	24	0.14
Uruguayan	3	0.02
Venezuelan	18	0.11
Other South American	2	0.01
Other Hispanic or Latino	85	0.50

Race*	Population	%
African-American/Black (760)	869	5.15
Not Hispanic (742)	829	4.91
Hispanic (18)	40	0.24
American Indian/Alaska Native (30)	122	0.72
Not Hispanic (22)	100	0.59
Hispanic (8)	22	0.13
Apache (0)	1	0.01
Blackfeet (0)	5	0.03
Central American Ind. (1)	1	0.01
Cherokee (4)	37	0.22
Chippewa (1)	5	0.03
Choctaw (1)	6	0.04
Creek (2)	2	0.01
Delaware (1)	2	0.01
Iroquois (1)	9	0.05
Mexican American Ind. (1)	1	0.01
Seminole (0)	3	0.02
Sioux (0)	2	0.01
South American Ind. (1)	8	0.05
Yaqui (0)	3	0.02
Asian (440)	555	3.29
Not Hispanic (435)	541	3.20
Hispanic (5)	14	0.08
Cambodian (6)	6	0.04
Chinese, ex. Taiwanese (101)	128	0.76
Filipino (67)	87	0.52
Hmong (1)	4	0.02
Indian (112)	126	0.75
Indonesian (4)	6	0.04
Japanese (17)	35	0.21
Korean (31)	32	0.19
Laotian (4)	6	0.04
Malaysian (3)	4	0.02
Pakistani (5)	5	0.03
Sri Lankan (2)	4	0.02
Taiwanese (12)	16	0.09
Thai (19)	21	0.12
Vietnamese (40)	44	0.26
Hawaii Native/Pacific Islander (6)	26	0.15
Not Hispanic (6)	24	0.14
Hispanic (0)	2	0.01
Fijian (2)	2	0.01
Guamanian/Chamorro (0)	1	0.01
Native Hawaiian (0)	8	0.05
Samoan (1)	1	0.01
White (15,137)	15,448	91.49
Not Hispanic (14,406)	14,651	86.77
Hispanic (731)	797	4.72

San Carlos Park

Place Type: CDP
County: Lee
Population: 16,824†

Ancestry‡	Population	%
African, Sub-Saharan (17)	75	0.42
African (17)	75	0.42
American (1,730)	1,730	9.75
Arab (0)	122	0.69
Arab (0)	47	0.27
Lebanese (0)	75	0.42
Austrian (43)	43	0.24
Belgian (9)	49	0.28
Brazilian (73)	73	0.41
British (21)	48	0.27
Canadian (17)	35	0.20
Croatian (32)	45	0.25
Czech (14)	26	0.15
Danish (0)	36	0.20
Dutch (90)	291	1.64
English (592)	1,696	9.56
Estonian (7)	7	0.04
Finnish (29)	71	0.40
French, ex. Basque (200)	554	3.12
French Canadian (93)	148	0.83
German (1,065)	2,972	16.76
Greek (19)	42	0.24
Hungarian (73)	158	0.89
Irish (744)	2,349	13.24
Italian (333)	1,085	6.12
Lithuanian (0)	11	0.06
Norwegian (64)	91	0.51
Pennsylvania German (32)	32	0.18
Polish (192)	568	3.20
Portuguese (13)	13	0.07
Romanian (130)	153	0.86
Russian (0)	13	0.07
Scandinavian (0)	25	0.14
Scotch-Irish (34)	194	1.09
Scottish (117)	325	1.83
Slavic (14)	14	0.08
Swedish (140)	278	1.57
Swiss (16)	63	0.36
Ukrainian (65)	72	0.41
Welsh (0)	228	1.29
West Indian, ex. Hispanic (414)	535	3.02
British West Indian (36)	51	0.29
Haitian (358)	358	2.02
Jamaican (0)	34	0.19
West Indian (20)	92	0.52
Yugoslavian (0)	14	0.08

Hispanic Origin	Population	%
Hispanic or Latino (of any race)	4,041	24.02
Central American, ex. Mexican	537	3.19
Costa Rican	26	0.15
Guatemalan	150	0.89
Honduran	155	0.92
Nicaraguan	62	0.37
Panamanian	11	0.07
Salvadoran	131	0.78
Other Central American	2	0.01
Cuban	361	2.15
Dominican Republic	57	0.34
Mexican	1,987	11.81
Puerto Rican	503	2.99
South American	396	2.35
Argentinean	66	0.39
Bolivian	38	0.23
Chilean	6	0.04
Colombian	122	0.73
Ecuadorian	32	0.19
Paraguayan	1	0.01
Peruvian	71	0.42
Uruguayan	22	0.13
Venezuelan	38	0.23
Other Hispanic or Latino	200	1.19

Race*	Population	%
African-American/Black (483)	586	3.48
Not Hispanic (452)	534	3.17
Hispanic (31)	52	0.31
American Indian/Alaska Native (66)	143	0.85
Not Hispanic (56)	109	0.65
Hispanic (10)	34	0.20
Blackfeet (1)	3	0.02
Central American Ind. (5)	6	0.04
Cherokee (16)	28	0.17
Chippewa (1)	3	0.02
Creek (0)	1	0.01
Hopi (0)	1	0.01
Iroquois (2)	3	0.02
Kiowa (0)	2	0.01
Mexican American Ind. (5)	6	0.04
Potawatomi (1)	1	0.01

*Notes: † The Census 2010 population figure is used to calculate the percentages in the Hispanic Origin and Race categories. Ancestry percentages are based on the 2006-2010 American Community Survey population (not shown); ‡ Numbers in parentheses indicate the number of people reporting a single ancestry; * Numbers in parentheses indicate the number of persons reporting this race alone, not in combination with any other race; Please refer to the Explanation of Data for more information.*

Seminole (0)	2	0.01
Sioux (4)	4	0.02
South American Ind. (0)	3	0.02
Asian (230)	274	1.63
Not Hispanic (224)	262	1.56
Hispanic (6)	12	0.07
Bangladeshi (9)	9	0.05
Cambodian (1)	1	0.01
Chinese, ex. Taiwanese (58)	65	0.39
Filipino (46)	65	0.39
Indian (21)	22	0.13
Indonesian (1)	1	0.01
Japanese (6)	12	0.07
Korean (16)	20	0.12
Laotian (3)	3	0.02
Malaysian (4)	4	0.02
Nepalese (1)	1	0.01
Pakistani (5)	5	0.03
Taiwanese (1)	3	0.02
Thai (7)	10	0.06
Vietnamese (38)	38	0.23
Hawaii Native/Pacific Islander (4)	21	0.12
Not Hispanic (1)	14	0.08
Hispanic (3)	7	0.04
Guamanian/Chamorro (4)	6	0.04
Native Hawaiian (0)	3	0.02
White (14,531)	14,807	88.01
Not Hispanic (11,830)	11,985	71.24
Hispanic (2,701)	2,822	16.77

Sanford

Place Type: City
County: Seminole
Population: 53,570†

Ancestry‡	Population	%
African, Sub-Saharan (743)	1,097	2.13
African (584)	928	1.80
Kenyan (30)	30	0.06
Liberian (20)	22	0.04
Nigerian (92)	92	0.18
Sierra Leonean (0)	8	0.02
Other Sub-Saharan African (17)	17	0.03
American (1,895)	1,895	3.68
Arab (309)	385	0.75
Arab (5)	17	0.03
Egyptian (26)	26	0.05
Lebanese (39)	103	0.20
Syrian (47)	47	0.09
Other Arab (192)	192	0.37
Australian (14)	14	0.03
Austrian (84)	202	0.39
Brazilian (9)	60	0.12
British (53)	126	0.24
Canadian (9)	9	0.02
Croatian (10)	22	0.04
Czech (104)	170	0.33
Czechoslovakian (22)	117	0.23
Danish (21)	42	0.08
Dutch (105)	703	1.37
Eastern European (13)	13	0.03
English (1,696)	3,909	7.60
European (1,448)	1,953	3.80
Finnish (85)	296	0.58
French, ex. Basque (233)	1,063	2.07
French Canadian (133)	375	0.73
German (1,314)	4,640	9.02
Greek (81)	222	0.43
Guyanese (30)	47	0.09
Hungarian (74)	124	0.24
Icelander (0)	12	0.02
Iranian (13)	13	0.03
Irish (1,249)	4,272	8.30
Italian (1,342)	2,884	5.61
Lithuanian (10)	148	0.29
Norwegian (63)	180	0.35
Pennsylvania German (14)	14	0.03
Polish (417)	1,161	2.26
Portuguese (25)	110	0.21
Romanian (0)	14	0.03
Russian (212)	502	0.98
Scandinavian (70)	70	0.14
Scotch-Irish (675)	1,057	2.05
Scottish (56)	501	0.97
Serbian (28)	35	0.07
Slavic (12)	21	0.04
Slovak (14)	28	0.05
Slovene (8)	8	0.02
Swedish (162)	326	0.63
Swiss (0)	36	0.07
Ukrainian (35)	131	0.25
Welsh (53)	175	0.34
West Indian, ex. Hispanic (714)	949	1.84
Barbadian (34)	34	0.07
Bermudan (67)	67	0.13
British West Indian (13)	25	0.05
Haitian (148)	250	0.49
Jamaican (290)	376	0.73
Trinidadian/Tobagonian (43)	60	0.12
West Indian (119)	137	0.27

Hispanic Origin	Population	%
Hispanic or Latino (of any race)	10,844	20.24
Central American, ex. Mexican	848	1.58
Costa Rican	39	0.07
Guatemalan	274	0.51
Honduran	115	0.21
Nicaraguan	95	0.18
Panamanian	154	0.29
Salvadoran	171	0.32
Cuban	396	0.74
Dominican Republic	444	0.83
Mexican	1,776	3.32
Puerto Rican	5,538	10.34
South American	1,246	2.33
Argentinean	113	0.21
Bolivian	25	0.05
Chilean	27	0.05
Colombian	563	1.05
Ecuadorian	205	0.38
Peruvian	129	0.24
Uruguayan	25	0.05
Venezuelan	155	0.29
Other South American	4	0.01
Other Hispanic or Latino	596	1.11

Race*	Population	%
African-American/Black (16,332)	17,310	32.31
Not Hispanic (15,660)	16,361	30.54
Hispanic (672)	949	1.77
American Indian/Alaska Native (291)	639	1.19
Not Hispanic (204)	479	0.89
Hispanic (87)	160	0.30
Aleut *(Alaska Native)* (1)	1	<0.01
Apache (5)	9	0.02
Blackfeet (7)	17	0.03
Canadian/French Am. Ind. (0)	3	0.01
Central American Ind. (4)	5	0.01
Cherokee (49)	146	0.27
Chickasaw (0)	2	<0.01
Chippewa (14)	27	0.05
Choctaw (16)	23	0.04
Comanche (5)	6	0.01
Creek (3)	19	0.04
Delaware (0)	2	<0.01
Hopi (1)	1	<0.01
Houma (1)	1	<0.01
Inupiat *(Alaska Native)* (5)	8	0.01
Iroquois (4)	11	0.02
Lumbee (1)	4	0.01
Menominee (1)	1	<0.01
Mexican American Ind. (9)	18	0.03
Navajo (4)	4	0.01
Potawatomi (2)	2	<0.01
Pueblo (1)	1	<0.01
Seminole (4)	14	0.03
Sioux (1)	2	<0.01
South American Ind. (10)	15	0.03
Spanish American Ind. (1)	3	0.01
Yup'ik *(Alaska Native)* (0)	3	0.01
Asian (1,504)	1,851	3.46
Not Hispanic (1,473)	1,770	3.30
Hispanic (31)	81	0.15
Bangladeshi (44)	50	0.09
Burmese (4)	4	0.01
Cambodian (2)	3	0.01
Chinese, ex. Taiwanese (144)	204	0.38
Filipino (208)	282	0.53
Indian (631)	719	1.34
Indonesian (5)	11	0.02
Japanese (33)	58	0.11
Korean (71)	96	0.18
Laotian (62)	66	0.12
Malaysian (3)	6	0.01
Pakistani (75)	77	0.14
Sri Lankan (15)	17	0.03
Taiwanese (8)	11	0.02
Thai (15)	36	0.07
Vietnamese (125)	144	0.27
Hawaii Native/Pacific Islander (44)	152	0.28
Not Hispanic (22)	91	0.17
Hispanic (22)	61	0.11
Fijian (0)	1	<0.01
Guamanian/Chamorro (21)	28	0.05
Native Hawaiian (9)	26	0.05
Samoan (3)	16	0.03
Tongan (1)	5	0.01
White (30,714)	32,074	59.87
Not Hispanic (24,096)	24,918	46.51
Hispanic (6,618)	7,156	13.36

Sarasota Springs

Place Type: CDP
County: Sarasota
Population: 14,395†

Ancestry‡	Population	%
African, Sub-Saharan (45)	153	1.06
South African (45)	153	1.06
American (1,030)	1,030	7.12
Arab (51)	212	1.46
Arab (0)	22	0.15
Egyptian (0)	8	0.06
Jordanian (12)	12	0.08
Lebanese (39)	132	0.91
Syrian (0)	32	0.22
Other Arab (0)	6	0.04
Armenian (0)	16	0.11
Australian (12)	12	0.08
Austrian (0)	43	0.30
Belgian (0)	27	0.19
Brazilian (13)	13	0.09
British (10)	10	0.07
Bulgarian (5)	5	0.03
Canadian (15)	71	0.49
Celtic (11)	11	0.08
Czech (23)	86	0.59
Czechoslovakian (8)	29	0.20
Dutch (44)	409	2.83
Eastern European (29)	38	0.26
English (1,036)	2,118	14.63
European (111)	170	1.17
Finnish (12)	23	0.16
French, ex. Basque (147)	740	5.11
French Canadian (11)	80	0.55
German (1,067)	3,324	22.96
Greek (10)	10	0.07
Hungarian (48)	113	0.78
Irish (773)	2,684	18.54
Italian (741)	1,583	10.94
Lithuanian (0)	35	0.24
Norwegian (6)	129	0.89
Pennsylvania German (28)	28	0.19
Polish (264)	760	5.25
Portuguese (165)	176	1.22
Romanian (34)	34	0.23
Russian (62)	194	1.34
Scandinavian (102)	114	0.79

*Notes: † The Census 2010 population figure is used to calculate the percentages in the Hispanic Origin and Race categories. Ancestry percentages are based on the 2006-2010 American Community Survey population (not shown); ‡ Numbers in parentheses indicate the number of people reporting a single ancestry; * Numbers in parentheses indicate the number of persons reporting this race alone, not in combination with any other race; Please refer to the Explanation of Data for more information.*

Ancestry	Population	%
Scotch-Irish (150)	397	2.74
Scottish (104)	433	2.99
Serbian (0)	46	0.32
Slovak (15)	123	0.85
Slovene (0)	11	0.08
Swedish (53)	222	1.53
Swiss (111)	222	1.53
Turkish (49)	157	1.08
Ukrainian (10)	10	0.07
Welsh (50)	232	1.60
West Indian, ex. Hispanic (123)	123	0.85
Haitian (123)	123	0.85
Yugoslavian (0)	19	0.13

Hispanic Origin	Population	%
Hispanic or Latino (of any race)	1,562	10.85
Central American, ex. Mexican	100	0.69
Costa Rican	6	0.04
Guatemalan	21	0.15
Honduran	32	0.22
Nicaraguan	24	0.17
Panamanian	8	0.06
Salvadoran	9	0.06
Cuban	275	1.91
Dominican Republic	55	0.38
Mexican	476	3.31
Puerto Rican	211	1.47
South American	326	2.26
Argentinean	23	0.16
Bolivian	9	0.06
Chilean	22	0.15
Colombian	128	0.89
Ecuadorian	15	0.10
Paraguayan	6	0.04
Peruvian	94	0.65
Venezuelan	28	0.19
Other South American	1	0.01
Other Hispanic or Latino	119	0.83

Race*	Population	%
African-American/Black (270)	389	2.70
Not Hispanic (249)	344	2.39
Hispanic (21)	45	0.31
American Indian/Alaska Native (40)	129	0.90
Not Hispanic (25)	101	0.70
Hispanic (15)	28	0.19
Apache (0)	1	0.01
Blackfeet (1)	1	0.01
Cherokee (5)	29	0.20
Chippewa (0)	4	0.03
Choctaw (1)	4	0.03
Comanche (1)	1	0.01
Creek (2)	2	0.01
Inupiat *(Alaska Native)* (0)	1	0.01
Iroquois (1)	3	0.02
Mexican American Ind. (0)	6	0.04
Seminole (2)	5	0.03
Shoshone (0)	1	0.01
South American Ind. (0)	4	0.03
Spanish American Ind. (1)	3	0.02
Asian (139)	205	1.42
Not Hispanic (135)	196	1.36
Hispanic (4)	9	0.06
Cambodian (1)	1	0.01
Chinese, ex. Taiwanese (37)	42	0.29
Filipino (30)	44	0.31
Indian (12)	17	0.12
Indonesian (0)	3	0.02
Japanese (12)	27	0.19
Korean (5)	7	0.05
Taiwanese (1)	1	0.01
Thai (9)	18	0.13
Vietnamese (25)	27	0.19
Hawaii Native/Pacific Islander (1)	23	0.16
Not Hispanic (1)	22	0.15
Hispanic (0)	1	0.01
Guamanian/Chamorro (0)	2	0.01
Native Hawaiian (0)	2	0.01
Samoan (0)	3	0.02
Tongan (1)	1	0.01
White (13,338)	13,622	94.63
Not Hispanic (12,182)	12,381	86.01
Hispanic (1,156)	1,241	8.62

Sarasota

Place Type: City
County: Sarasota
Population: 51,917†

Ancestry‡	Population	%
African, Sub-Saharan (146)	255	0.48
African (102)	184	0.35
South African (44)	71	0.13
Alsatian (11)	11	0.02
American (1,892)	1,892	3.58
Arab (147)	195	0.37
Arab (0)	9	0.02
Egyptian (26)	26	0.05
Jordanian (52)	61	0.12
Lebanese (28)	37	0.07
Syrian (0)	21	0.04
Other Arab (41)	41	0.08
Armenian (26)	26	0.05
Australian (62)	77	0.15
Austrian (72)	222	0.42
Belgian (47)	103	0.19
Brazilian (173)	240	0.45
British (279)	532	1.01
Bulgarian (101)	101	0.19
Canadian (91)	162	0.31
Celtic (11)	27	0.05
Croatian (24)	34	0.06
Czech (91)	302	0.57
Czechoslovakian (30)	92	0.17
Danish (36)	174	0.33
Dutch (172)	927	1.75
Eastern European (68)	136	0.26
English (2,257)	5,973	11.30
European (412)	423	0.80
Finnish (67)	109	0.21
French, ex. Basque (662)	2,309	4.37
French Canadian (146)	315	0.60
German (2,419)	7,864	14.87
German Russian (0)	15	0.03
Greek (178)	383	0.72
Hungarian (97)	492	0.93
Irish (1,924)	7,139	13.50
Israeli (44)	44	0.08
Italian (1,595)	3,855	7.29
Latvian (10)	24	0.05
Lithuanian (93)	173	0.33
Northern European (36)	36	0.07
Norwegian (86)	500	0.95
Pennsylvania German (0)	27	0.05
Polish (628)	1,341	2.54
Portuguese (23)	84	0.16
Romanian (12)	171	0.32
Russian (548)	954	1.80
Scandinavian (25)	40	0.08
Scotch-Irish (337)	1,128	2.13
Scottish (343)	1,149	2.17
Serbian (12)	12	0.02
Slovak (51)	73	0.14
Slovene (10)	10	0.02
Swedish (350)	984	1.86
Swiss (89)	243	0.46
Ukrainian (87)	143	0.27
Welsh (65)	288	0.54
West Indian, ex. Hispanic (504)	585	1.11
Barbadian (16)	16	0.03
Belizean (55)	55	0.10
Haitian (218)	255	0.48
Jamaican (215)	243	0.46
West Indian (0)	16	0.03
Yugoslavian (16)	32	0.06

Hispanic Origin	Population	%
Hispanic or Latino (of any race)	8,634	16.63
Central American, ex. Mexican	522	1.01
Costa Rican	22	0.04
Guatemalan	205	0.39
Honduran	131	0.25
Nicaraguan	87	0.17
Panamanian	43	0.08
Salvadoran	24	0.05
Other Central American	10	0.02
Cuban	1,082	2.08
Dominican Republic	168	0.32
Mexican	4,616	8.89
Puerto Rican	926	1.78
South American	871	1.68
Argentinean	112	0.22
Bolivian	10	0.02
Chilean	37	0.07
Colombian	304	0.59
Ecuadorian	47	0.09
Paraguayan	8	0.02
Peruvian	269	0.52
Uruguayan	10	0.02
Venezuelan	68	0.13
Other South American	6	0.01
Other Hispanic or Latino	449	0.86

Race*	Population	%
African-American/Black (7,844)	8,420	16.22
Not Hispanic (7,558)	7,987	15.38
Hispanic (286)	433	0.83
American Indian/Alaska Native (221)	512	0.99
Not Hispanic (118)	332	0.64
Hispanic (103)	180	0.35
Apache (0)	4	0.01
Blackfeet (2)	8	0.02
Canadian/French Am. Ind. (0)	5	0.01
Central American Ind. (6)	11	0.02
Cherokee (16)	78	0.15
Cheyenne (1)	2	<0.01
Chippewa (11)	12	0.02
Choctaw (7)	23	0.04
Cree (0)	7	0.01
Creek (5)	6	0.01
Crow (1)	2	<0.01
Inupiat *(Alaska Native)* (0)	1	<0.01
Iroquois (3)	14	0.03
Lumbee (5)	5	0.01
Mexican American Ind. (40)	49	0.09
Navajo (1)	2	<0.01
Ottawa (1)	1	<0.01
Pueblo (0)	2	<0.01
Seminole (3)	9	0.02
Shoshone (1)	2	<0.01
Sioux (1)	8	0.02
South American Ind. (9)	16	0.03
Spanish American Ind. (0)	1	<0.01
Asian (691)	910	1.75
Not Hispanic (676)	859	1.65
Hispanic (15)	51	0.10
Bangladeshi (6)	6	0.01
Burmese (5)	5	0.01
Cambodian (2)	4	0.01
Chinese, ex. Taiwanese (113)	141	0.27
Filipino (114)	170	0.33
Hmong (0)	1	<0.01
Indian (154)	199	0.38
Indonesian (4)	7	0.01
Japanese (23)	62	0.12
Korean (70)	88	0.17
Laotian (9)	10	0.02
Malaysian (1)	2	<0.01
Nepalese (0)	4	0.01
Pakistani (3)	6	0.01
Sri Lankan (3)	3	0.01
Taiwanese (5)	5	0.01
Thai (19)	21	0.04
Vietnamese (124)	130	0.25
Hawaii Native/Pacific Islander (22)	80	0.15
Not Hispanic (15)	60	0.12
Hispanic (7)	20	0.04
Guamanian/Chamorro (8)	11	0.02
Native Hawaiian (5)	35	0.07

*Notes: † The Census 2010 population figure is used to calculate the percentages in the Hispanic Origin and Race categories. Ancestry percentages are based on the 2006-2010 American Community Survey population (not shown); ‡ Numbers in parentheses indicate the number of people reporting a single ancestry; * Numbers in parentheses indicate the number of persons reporting this race alone, not in combination with any other race; Please refer to the Explanation of Data for more information.*

Samoan (2)	3	0.01
White (39,152)	40,194	77.42
Not Hispanic (34,052)	34,720	66.88
Hispanic (5,100)	5,474	10.54

Satellite Beach

Place Type: City
County: Brevard
Population: 10,109†

Ancestry‡	Population	%
American (632)	632	5.97
Arab (48)	103	0.97
Lebanese (48)	103	0.97
Armenian (10)	21	0.20
Austrian (26)	69	0.65
Basque (0)	10	0.09
British (81)	147	1.39
Cajun (25)	25	0.24
Canadian (22)	22	0.21
Croatian (0)	13	0.12
Czech (0)	77	0.73
Dutch (61)	207	1.96
Eastern European (19)	19	0.18
English (680)	1,999	18.89
European (150)	150	1.42
Finnish (8)	8	0.08
French, ex. Basque (72)	347	3.28
French Canadian (34)	73	0.69
German (801)	2,667	25.20
Greek (59)	68	0.64
Hungarian (30)	59	0.56
Iranian (0)	9	0.09
Irish (630)	2,203	20.82
Italian (671)	1,315	12.43
Lithuanian (10)	22	0.21
New Zealander (10)	28	0.26
Norwegian (0)	64	0.60
Pennsylvania German (18)	25	0.24
Polish (179)	484	4.57
Portuguese (0)	47	0.44
Russian (36)	114	1.08
Scandinavian (0)	9	0.09
Scotch-Irish (235)	351	3.32
Scottish (106)	391	3.69
Slavic (0)	28	0.26
Slovak (18)	18	0.17
Slovene (0)	2	0.02
Swedish (93)	239	2.26
Swiss (0)	32	0.30
Ukrainian (9)	9	0.09
Welsh (9)	154	1.46
West Indian, ex. Hispanic (53)	118	1.11
Jamaican (0)	65	0.61
Trinidadian/Tobagonian (11)	11	0.10
U.S. Virgin Islander (42)	42	0.40

Hispanic Origin	Population	%
Hispanic or Latino (of any race)	587	5.81
Central American, ex. Mexican	41	0.41
Costa Rican	9	0.09
Guatemalan	4	0.04
Honduran	5	0.05
Nicaraguan	14	0.14
Panamanian	7	0.07
Salvadoran	2	0.02
Cuban	88	0.87
Dominican Republic	7	0.07
Mexican	129	1.28
Puerto Rican	153	1.51
South American	77	0.76
Argentinean	11	0.11
Chilean	2	0.02
Colombian	25	0.25
Ecuadorian	17	0.17
Peruvian	18	0.18
Venezuelan	4	0.04
Other Hispanic or Latino	92	0.91

Race*	Population	%
African-American/Black (199)	276	2.73
Not Hispanic (187)	249	2.46
Hispanic (12)	27	0.27
American Indian/Alaska Native (27)	88	0.87
Not Hispanic (21)	70	0.69
Hispanic (6)	18	0.18
Apache (0)	2	0.02
Blackfeet (4)	8	0.08
Cherokee (4)	19	0.19
Chickasaw (0)	2	0.02
Chippewa (0)	1	0.01
Creek (3)	4	0.04
Iroquois (1)	9	0.09
Lumbee (0)	1	0.01
Mexican American Ind. (0)	1	0.01
Navajo (2)	4	0.04
Sioux (1)	1	0.01
South American Ind. (2)	3	0.03
Spanish American Ind. (1)	1	0.01
Asian (177)	253	2.50
Not Hispanic (173)	232	2.29
Hispanic (4)	21	0.21
Burmese (3)	3	0.03
Cambodian (0)	1	0.01
Chinese, ex. Taiwanese (40)	68	0.67
Filipino (30)	54	0.53
Indian (29)	39	0.39
Indonesian (1)	1	0.01
Japanese (15)	20	0.20
Korean (14)	25	0.25
Malaysian (0)	2	0.02
Taiwanese (3)	3	0.03
Thai (11)	15	0.15
Vietnamese (19)	21	0.21
Hawaii Native/Pacific Islander (5)	15	0.15
Not Hispanic (5)	13	0.13
Hispanic (0)	2	0.02
Guamanian/Chamorro (0)	2	0.02
Native Hawaiian (4)	9	0.09
White (9,396)	9,605	95.01
Not Hispanic (8,943)	9,105	90.07
Hispanic (453)	500	4.95

Sebastian

Place Type: City
County: Indian River
Population: 21,929†

Ancestry‡	Population	%
African, Sub-Saharan (0)	8	0.04
South African (0)	8	0.04
American (1,478)	1,478	6.96
Arab (31)	120	0.57
Arab (0)	22	0.10
Lebanese (0)	28	0.13
Palestinian (31)	47	0.22
Other Arab (0)	23	0.11
Armenian (32)	84	0.40
Austrian (0)	180	0.85
Belgian (0)	17	0.08
British (126)	209	0.98
Canadian (68)	128	0.60
Czech (71)	159	0.75
Danish (14)	28	0.13
Dutch (183)	492	2.32
Eastern European (61)	61	0.29
English (619)	2,773	13.06
Estonian (10)	69	0.32
European (48)	79	0.37
Finnish (13)	13	0.06
French, ex. Basque (166)	859	4.04
French Canadian (115)	196	0.92
German (1,458)	4,459	21.00
Greek (55)	67	0.32
Hungarian (38)	119	0.56
Irish (1,512)	4,552	21.43
Italian (1,120)	2,662	12.53
Lithuanian (44)	116	0.55
Maltese (21)	51	0.24
Norwegian (80)	207	0.97
Pennsylvania German (0)	17	0.08
Polish (454)	1,019	4.80
Portuguese (25)	54	0.25
Romanian (19)	72	0.34
Russian (107)	496	2.34
Scandinavian (49)	72	0.34
Scotch-Irish (367)	685	3.23
Scottish (136)	525	2.47
Serbian (11)	11	0.05
Slovak (0)	12	0.06
Swedish (105)	242	1.14
Swiss (0)	21	0.10
Ukrainian (22)	68	0.32
Welsh (9)	140	0.66
West Indian, ex. Hispanic (91)	116	0.55
Jamaican (91)	116	0.55

Hispanic Origin	Population	%
Hispanic or Latino (of any race)	1,525	6.95
Central American, ex. Mexican	56	0.26
Costa Rican	2	0.01
Guatemalan	6	0.03
Honduran	17	0.08
Nicaraguan	8	0.04
Panamanian	4	0.02
Salvadoran	19	0.09
Cuban	259	1.18
Dominican Republic	36	0.16
Mexican	389	1.77
Puerto Rican	413	1.88
South American	287	1.31
Argentinean	5	0.02
Chilean	8	0.04
Colombian	175	0.80
Ecuadorian	26	0.12
Peruvian	44	0.20
Uruguayan	1	<0.01
Venezuelan	27	0.12
Other South American	1	<0.01
Other Hispanic or Latino	85	0.39

Race*	Population	%
African-American/Black (1,155)	1,311	5.98
Not Hispanic (1,120)	1,255	5.72
Hispanic (35)	56	0.26
American Indian/Alaska Native (46)	153	0.70
Not Hispanic (42)	136	0.62
Hispanic (4)	17	0.08
Apache (1)	4	0.02
Arapaho (1)	1	<0.01
Blackfeet (2)	11	0.05
Canadian/French Am. Ind. (1)	1	<0.01
Cherokee (7)	35	0.16
Chickasaw (1)	1	<0.01
Chippewa (1)	5	0.02
Choctaw (4)	6	0.03
Creek (4)	5	0.02
Iroquois (2)	2	0.01
Mexican American Ind. (1)	2	0.01
Navajo (0)	4	0.02
Seminole (0)	1	<0.01
Sioux (0)	3	0.01
South American Ind. (1)	2	0.01
Asian (252)	316	1.44
Not Hispanic (252)	310	1.41
Hispanic (0)	6	0.03
Burmese (4)	7	0.03
Cambodian (7)	7	0.03
Chinese, ex. Taiwanese (22)	30	0.14
Filipino (58)	71	0.32
Indian (43)	57	0.26
Indonesian (11)	12	0.05
Japanese (12)	24	0.11
Korean (20)	28	0.13
Pakistani (13)	13	0.06
Sri Lankan (1)	3	0.01
Taiwanese (1)	1	<0.01

*Notes: † The Census 2010 population figure is used to calculate the percentages in the Hispanic Origin and Race categories. Ancestry percentages are based on the 2006-2010 American Community Survey population (not shown); ‡ Numbers in parentheses indicate the number of people reporting a single ancestry; * Numbers in parentheses indicate the number of persons reporting this race alone, not in combination with any other race; Please refer to the Explanation of Data for more information.*

Thai (4)	9	0.04
Vietnamese (40)	43	0.20
Hawaii Native/Pacific Islander (7)	28	0.13
Not Hispanic (5)	15	0.07
Hispanic (2)	13	0.06
Guamanian/Chamorro (2)	2	0.01
Native Hawaiian (1)	11	0.05
White (19,845)	20,152	91.90
Not Hispanic (18,695)	18,925	86.30
Hispanic (1,150)	1,227	5.60

Sebring

Place Type: City
County: Highlands
Population: 10,491†

Ancestry‡	Population	%
African, Sub-Saharan (45)	45	0.43
African (45)	45	0.43
American (1,262)	1,262	11.95
Arab (22)	22	0.21
Lebanese (22)	22	0.21
Austrian (0)	35	0.33
British (32)	32	0.30
Bulgarian (0)	15	0.14
Canadian (0)	54	0.51
Czech (0)	17	0.16
Danish (0)	21	0.20
Dutch (44)	287	2.72
English (286)	791	7.49
European (27)	46	0.44
Finnish (0)	15	0.14
French, ex. Basque (70)	351	3.32
French Canadian (78)	120	1.14
German (576)	1,326	12.56
Greek (0)	15	0.14
Hungarian (15)	56	0.53
Irish (397)	1,163	11.01
Italian (257)	618	5.85
Lithuanian (0)	22	0.21
Pennsylvania German (15)	15	0.14
Polish (61)	89	0.84
Russian (9)	16	0.15
Scotch-Irish (141)	178	1.69
Scottish (56)	141	1.34
Slovak (0)	12	0.11
Swedish (57)	93	0.88
Swiss (0)	14	0.13
Welsh (0)	11	0.10
West Indian, ex. Hispanic (10)	10	0.09
Jamaican (10)	10	0.09

Hispanic Origin	Population	%
Hispanic or Latino (of any race)	1,845	17.59
Central American, ex. Mexican	69	0.66
Costa Rican	13	0.12
Guatemalan	10	0.10
Honduran	7	0.07
Nicaraguan	21	0.20
Panamanian	7	0.07
Salvadoran	11	0.10
Cuban	179	1.71
Dominican Republic	19	0.18
Mexican	693	6.61
Puerto Rican	660	6.29
South American	67	0.64
Argentinean	3	0.03
Bolivian	2	0.02
Chilean	1	0.01
Colombian	31	0.30
Ecuadorian	12	0.11
Peruvian	12	0.11
Venezuelan	5	0.05
Other South American	1	0.01
Other Hispanic or Latino	158	1.51

Race*	Population	%
African-American/Black (1,544)	1,686	16.07
Not Hispanic (1,466)	1,572	14.98
Hispanic (78)	114	1.09
American Indian/Alaska Native (78)	145	1.38
Not Hispanic (57)	113	1.08
Hispanic (21)	32	0.31
Apache (3)	6	0.06
Blackfeet (0)	2	0.02
Central American Ind. (0)	1	0.01
Cherokee (5)	18	0.17
Chippewa (1)	3	0.03
Choctaw (0)	1	0.01
Comanche (1)	1	0.01
Cree (1)	1	0.01
Creek (3)	3	0.03
Delaware (3)	3	0.03
Lumbee (16)	17	0.16
Mexican American Ind. (6)	6	0.06
Potawatomi (1)	1	0.01
Seminole (0)	1	0.01
Sioux (0)	1	0.01
South American Ind. (0)	3	0.03
Spanish American Ind. (0)	1	0.01
Asian (143)	170	1.62
Not Hispanic (141)	165	1.57
Hispanic (2)	5	0.05
Bangladeshi (3)	4	0.04
Burmese (6)	6	0.06
Chinese, ex. Taiwanese (2)	7	0.07
Filipino (70)	77	0.73
Indian (32)	39	0.37
Japanese (10)	13	0.12
Korean (6)	8	0.08
Pakistani (0)	3	0.03
Thai (2)	3	0.03
Vietnamese (5)	7	0.07
Hawaii Native/Pacific Islander (4)	24	0.23
Not Hispanic (2)	13	0.12
Hispanic (2)	11	0.10
Guamanian/Chamorro (1)	5	0.05
Native Hawaiian (1)	5	0.05
White (7,973)	8,203	78.19
Not Hispanic (6,802)	6,949	66.24
Hispanic (1,171)	1,254	11.95

Seffner

Place Type: CDP
County: Hillsborough
Population: 7,579†

Ancestry‡	Population	%
African, Sub-Saharan (58)	58	0.78
African (30)	30	0.40
South African (28)	28	0.37
American (768)	768	10.27
Belgian (10)	10	0.13
British (15)	37	0.49
Cajun (21)	21	0.28
Canadian (54)	181	2.42
Czech (7)	35	0.47
Danish (29)	49	0.66
Dutch (0)	95	1.27
English (226)	603	8.06
Finnish (0)	20	0.27
French, ex. Basque (34)	234	3.13
French Canadian (38)	38	0.51
German (360)	1,307	17.47
Greek (73)	108	1.44
Hungarian (0)	22	0.29
Irish (294)	725	9.69
Italian (264)	653	8.73
Lithuanian (0)	12	0.16
Norwegian (0)	42	0.56
Polish (78)	275	3.68
Portuguese (29)	29	0.39
Russian (31)	31	0.41
Scandinavian (7)	7	0.09
Scotch-Irish (80)	227	3.03
Scottish (72)	205	2.74
Slovak (9)	26	0.35
Swedish (27)	235	3.14
Swiss (0)	11	0.15
Ukrainian (40)	40	0.53
Welsh (13)	13	0.17
West Indian, ex. Hispanic (42)	42	0.56
Bahamian (26)	26	0.35
Haitian (16)	16	0.21

Hispanic Origin	Population	%
Hispanic or Latino (of any race)	1,203	15.87
Central American, ex. Mexican	36	0.47
Costa Rican	4	0.05
Guatemalan	8	0.11
Honduran	9	0.12
Nicaraguan	1	0.01
Panamanian	7	0.09
Salvadoran	7	0.09
Cuban	179	2.36
Dominican Republic	38	0.50
Mexican	254	3.35
Puerto Rican	541	7.14
South American	69	0.91
Argentinean	1	0.01
Bolivian	4	0.05
Colombian	37	0.49
Ecuadorian	4	0.05
Peruvian	7	0.09
Uruguayan	2	0.03
Venezuelan	14	0.18
Other Hispanic or Latino	86	1.13

Race*	Population	%
African-American/Black (1,003)	1,114	14.70
Not Hispanic (951)	1,031	13.60
Hispanic (52)	83	1.10
American Indian/Alaska Native (36)	67	0.88
Not Hispanic (21)	51	0.67
Hispanic (15)	16	0.21
Apache (7)	9	0.12
Cherokee (11)	21	0.28
Cree (1)	1	0.01
Creek (0)	3	0.04
Iroquois (0)	2	0.03
Lumbee (1)	1	0.01
Mexican American Ind. (2)	2	0.03
Navajo (0)	1	0.01
Potawatomi (0)	1	0.01
Seminole (2)	3	0.04
Asian (289)	339	4.47
Not Hispanic (286)	329	4.34
Hispanic (3)	10	0.13
Bangladeshi (5)	5	0.07
Cambodian (2)	2	0.03
Chinese, ex. Taiwanese (15)	23	0.30
Filipino (45)	54	0.71
Hmong (6)	6	0.08
Indian (99)	105	1.39
Japanese (14)	19	0.25
Korean (15)	24	0.32
Pakistani (12)	12	0.16
Taiwanese (2)	2	0.03
Thai (17)	23	0.30
Vietnamese (47)	52	0.69
Hawaii Native/Pacific Islander (2)	7	0.09
Not Hispanic (2)	7	0.09
Native Hawaiian (2)	3	0.04
White (5,798)	5,982	78.93
Not Hispanic (4,949)	5,078	67.00
Hispanic (849)	904	11.93

Seminole

Place Type: City
County: Pinellas
Population: 17,233†

Ancestry‡	Population	%
American (1,552)	1,552	8.97
Arab (219)	259	1.50
Arab (116)	116	0.67
Lebanese (74)	95	0.55

*Notes: † The Census 2010 population figure is used to calculate the percentages in the Hispanic Origin and Race categories. Ancestry percentages are based on the 2006-2010 American Community Survey population (not shown); ‡ Numbers in parentheses indicate the number of people reporting a single ancestry; * Numbers in parentheses indicate the number of persons reporting this race alone, not in combination with any other race; Please refer to the Explanation of Data for more information.*

Ancestry (cont.)	Population	%
Moroccan (12)	12	0.07
Syrian (17)	36	0.21
Austrian (57)	90	0.52
Belgian (0)	37	0.21
Brazilian (51)	51	0.29
British (72)	294	1.70
Canadian (86)	134	0.77
Celtic (0)	11	0.06
Czech (19)	105	0.61
Czechoslovakian (0)	52	0.30
Danish (17)	47	0.27
Dutch (71)	436	2.52
Eastern European (21)	21	0.12
English (1,047)	2,555	14.77
European (22)	48	0.28
Finnish (24)	60	0.35
French, ex. Basque (161)	631	3.65
French Canadian (68)	161	0.93
German (1,804)	3,837	22.19
Greek (34)	131	0.76
Guyanese (18)	18	0.10
Hungarian (37)	78	0.45
Iranian (20)	20	0.12
Irish (489)	2,570	14.86
Israeli (9)	18	0.10
Italian (733)	1,466	8.48
Lithuanian (49)	161	0.93
Maltese (15)	32	0.19
Norwegian (51)	202	1.17
Polish (295)	755	4.37
Portuguese (78)	132	0.76
Romanian (12)	27	0.16
Russian (115)	329	1.90
Scotch-Irish (129)	204	1.18
Scottish (152)	515	2.98
Slovak (61)	101	0.58
Swedish (28)	228	1.32
Swiss (15)	54	0.31
Ukrainian (0)	24	0.14
Welsh (83)	264	1.53
West Indian, ex. Hispanic (0)	66	0.38
Haitian (0)	19	0.11
U.S. Virgin Islander (0)	47	0.27
Yugoslavian (68)	111	0.64

Hispanic Origin	Population	%
Hispanic or Latino (of any race)	750	4.35
Central American, ex. Mexican	43	0.25
Costa Rican	4	0.02
Guatemalan	9	0.05
Honduran	9	0.05
Nicaraguan	5	0.03
Panamanian	10	0.06
Salvadoran	4	0.02
Other Central American	2	0.01
Cuban	89	0.52
Dominican Republic	18	0.10
Mexican	135	0.78
Puerto Rican	265	1.54
South American	112	0.65
Argentinean	6	0.03
Bolivian	2	0.01
Chilean	9	0.05
Colombian	60	0.35
Ecuadorian	6	0.03
Peruvian	18	0.10
Venezuelan	10	0.06
Other South American	1	0.01
Other Hispanic or Latino	88	0.51

Race*	Population	%
African-American/Black (243)	311	1.80
Not Hispanic (229)	289	1.68
Hispanic (14)	22	0.13
American Indian/Alaska Native (59)	100	0.58
Not Hispanic (56)	96	0.56
Hispanic (3)	4	0.02
Apache (1)	2	0.01
Canadian/French Am. Ind. (2)	2	0.01
Cherokee (6)	21	0.12
Chickasaw (2)	2	0.01
Chippewa (4)	4	0.02
Choctaw (3)	4	0.02
Comanche (0)	3	0.02
Cree (2)	3	0.02
Creek (2)	2	0.01
Delaware (1)	4	0.02
Iroquois (8)	10	0.06
Potawatomi (1)	1	0.01
Shoshone (0)	1	0.01
Sioux (2)	2	0.01
South American Ind. (0)	2	0.01
Yaqui (0)	1	0.01
Asian (402)	489	2.84
Not Hispanic (395)	476	2.76
Hispanic (7)	13	0.08
Bangladeshi (6)	6	0.03
Cambodian (4)	5	0.03
Chinese, ex. Taiwanese (64)	76	0.44
Filipino (82)	110	0.64
Indian (135)	140	0.81
Indonesian (2)	2	0.01
Japanese (13)	26	0.15
Korean (20)	28	0.16
Laotian (3)	3	0.02
Nepalese (0)	1	0.01
Pakistani (7)	7	0.04
Taiwanese (3)	7	0.04
Thai (10)	16	0.09
Vietnamese (42)	44	0.26
Hawaii Native/Pacific Islander (8)	15	0.09
Not Hispanic (8)	15	0.09
Native Hawaiian (4)	8	0.05
Samoan (0)	1	0.01
Tongan (3)	4	0.02
White (16,187)	16,390	95.11
Not Hispanic (15,600)	15,763	91.47
Hispanic (587)	627	3.64

Shady Hills

Place Type: CDP
County: Pasco
Population: 11,523†

Ancestry‡	Population	%
Albanian (0)	29	0.25
American (974)	974	8.48
Arab (0)	11	0.10
Lebanese (0)	11	0.10
Austrian (30)	60	0.52
British (61)	84	0.73
Canadian (0)	89	0.78
Croatian (0)	10	0.09
Czech (72)	147	1.28
Dutch (60)	256	2.23
English (496)	1,744	15.19
European (14)	14	0.12
Finnish (0)	37	0.32
French, ex. Basque (109)	815	7.10
French Canadian (165)	240	2.09
German (967)	2,767	24.10
Greek (31)	51	0.44
Hungarian (91)	194	1.69
Irish (410)	2,389	20.81
Italian (666)	1,062	9.25
Lithuanian (21)	154	1.34
Norwegian (40)	52	0.45
Polish (148)	638	5.56
Portuguese (21)	160	1.39
Romanian (0)	14	0.12
Russian (0)	60	0.52
Scotch-Irish (100)	250	2.18
Scottish (49)	185	1.61
Slovak (12)	12	0.10
Swedish (44)	102	0.89
Swiss (0)	16	0.14
Welsh (0)	140	1.22
Yugoslavian (0)	20	0.17

Hispanic Origin	Population	%
Hispanic or Latino (of any race)	748	6.49
Central American, ex. Mexican	40	0.35
Costa Rican	3	0.03
Guatemalan	12	0.10
Honduran	17	0.15
Nicaraguan	1	0.01
Panamanian	4	0.03
Salvadoran	3	0.03
Cuban	168	1.46
Dominican Republic	6	0.05
Mexican	129	1.12
Puerto Rican	293	2.54
South American	30	0.26
Argentinean	1	0.01
Chilean	1	0.01
Colombian	13	0.11
Peruvian	5	0.04
Uruguayan	6	0.05
Venezuelan	3	0.03
Other South American	1	0.01
Other Hispanic or Latino	82	0.71

Race*	Population	%
African-American/Black (83)	128	1.11
Not Hispanic (75)	115	1.00
Hispanic (8)	13	0.11
American Indian/Alaska Native (61)	138	1.20
Not Hispanic (53)	123	1.07
Hispanic (8)	15	0.13
Apache (1)	2	0.02
Blackfeet (0)	1	0.01
Cherokee (30)	44	0.38
Cheyenne (1)	1	0.01
Chickasaw (0)	1	0.01
Chippewa (3)	5	0.04
Creek (4)	5	0.04
Iroquois (1)	1	0.01
Lumbee (1)	1	0.01
Mexican American Ind. (1)	1	0.01
Seminole (1)	3	0.03
Sioux (0)	1	0.01
South American Ind. (1)	1	0.01
Asian (57)	85	0.74
Not Hispanic (49)	71	0.62
Hispanic (8)	14	0.12
Chinese, ex. Taiwanese (11)	13	0.11
Filipino (24)	31	0.27
Indonesian (0)	3	0.03
Japanese (1)	8	0.07
Korean (5)	7	0.06
Nepalese (1)	1	0.01
Taiwanese (1)	2	0.02
Thai (3)	7	0.06
Vietnamese (5)	5	0.04
Hawaii Native/Pacific Islander (4)	12	0.10
Not Hispanic (4)	9	0.08
Hispanic (0)	3	0.03
Guamanian/Chamorro (0)	1	0.01
Native Hawaiian (2)	6	0.05
White (11,019)	11,190	97.11
Not Hispanic (10,447)	10,583	91.84
Hispanic (572)	607	5.27

South Bradenton

Place Type: CDP
County: Manatee
Population: 22,178†

Ancestry‡	Population	%
African, Sub-Saharan (48)	48	0.22
African (48)	48	0.22
American (619)	619	2.84
Arab (0)	153	0.70
Lebanese (0)	43	0.20
Moroccan (0)	110	0.50
Belgian (0)	17	0.08
Brazilian (89)	89	0.41
British (94)	150	0.69

*Notes: † The Census 2010 population figure is used to calculate the percentages in the Hispanic Origin and Race categories. Ancestry percentages are based on the 2006-2010 American Community Survey population (not shown); ‡ Numbers in parentheses indicate the number of people reporting a single ancestry; * Numbers in parentheses indicate the number of persons reporting this race alone, not in combination with any other race; Please refer to the Explanation of Data for more information.*

Canadian (53)	62	0.28
Czech (12)	45	0.21
Danish (12)	12	0.06
Dutch (105)	520	2.39
Eastern European (13)	13	0.06
English (936)	2,746	12.60
European (122)	129	0.59
Finnish (55)	64	0.29
French, ex. Basque (157)	1,119	5.14
French Canadian (66)	97	0.45
German (1,111)	3,352	15.38
Greek (182)	219	1.01
Hungarian (66)	80	0.37
Irish (982)	3,104	14.25
Italian (433)	1,030	4.73
Latvian (0)	11	0.05
Lithuanian (21)	66	0.30
Northern European (0)	8	0.04
Norwegian (36)	89	0.41
Pennsylvania German (13)	26	0.12
Polish (213)	814	3.74
Portuguese (61)	173	0.79
Romanian (53)	89	0.41
Russian (190)	402	1.84
Scandinavian (0)	13	0.06
Scotch-Irish (109)	406	1.86
Scottish (132)	581	2.67
Serbian (21)	45	0.21
Slovak (13)	40	0.18
Swedish (108)	229	1.05
Swiss (28)	38	0.17
Ukrainian (64)	101	0.46
Welsh (118)	178	0.82
West Indian, ex. Hispanic (277)	400	1.84
Bahamian (25)	25	0.11
Barbadian (19)	19	0.09
Haitian (150)	150	0.69
Jamaican (40)	53	0.24
West Indian (43)	153	0.70

Hispanic Origin	Population	%
Hispanic or Latino (of any race)	4,622	20.84
Central American, ex. Mexican	632	2.85
Costa Rican	6	0.03
Guatemalan	192	0.87
Honduran	257	1.16
Nicaraguan	51	0.23
Panamanian	7	0.03
Salvadoran	119	0.54
Cuban	254	1.15
Dominican Republic	68	0.31
Mexican	2,427	10.94
Puerto Rican	722	3.26
South American	304	1.37
Argentinean	28	0.13
Chilean	12	0.05
Colombian	124	0.56
Ecuadorian	42	0.19
Peruvian	60	0.27
Uruguayan	4	0.02
Venezuelan	34	0.15
Other Hispanic or Latino	215	0.97

Race*	Population	%
African-American/Black (2,036)	2,366	10.67
Not Hispanic (1,932)	2,176	9.81
Hispanic (104)	190	0.86
American Indian/Alaska Native (123)	249	1.12
Not Hispanic (56)	142	0.64
Hispanic (67)	107	0.48
Apache (1)	1	<0.01
Blackfeet (4)	8	0.04
Canadian/French Am. Ind. (0)	1	<0.01
Cherokee (9)	36	0.16
Chippewa (4)	4	0.02
Iroquois (5)	6	0.03
Mexican American Ind. (1)	7	0.03
Navajo (2)	3	0.01
Osage (0)	1	<0.01
Ottawa (1)	2	0.01
Potawatomi (1)	4	0.02
Seminole (4)	7	0.03
Shoshone (0)	1	<0.01
Sioux (2)	4	0.02
South American Ind. (0)	1	<0.01
Spanish American Ind. (8)	9	0.04
Yup'ik *(Alaska Native)* (0)	1	<0.01
Asian (339)	411	1.85
Not Hispanic (338)	405	1.83
Hispanic (1)	6	0.03
Cambodian (17)	24	0.11
Chinese, ex. Taiwanese (62)	82	0.37
Filipino (57)	76	0.34
Indian (106)	123	0.55
Japanese (15)	27	0.12
Korean (4)	6	0.03
Laotian (0)	2	0.01
Pakistani (9)	9	0.04
Taiwanese (1)	6	0.03
Thai (4)	5	0.02
Vietnamese (38)	45	0.20
Hawaii Native/Pacific Islander (26)	60	0.27
Not Hispanic (17)	42	0.19
Hispanic (9)	18	0.08
Fijian (2)	2	0.01
Guamanian/Chamorro (10)	14	0.06
Native Hawaiian (7)	9	0.04
Samoan (1)	2	0.01
Tongan (2)	5	0.02
White (17,266)	17,818	80.34
Not Hispanic (14,778)	15,119	68.17
Hispanic (2,488)	2,699	12.17

South Daytona

Place Type: City
County: Volusia
Population: 12,252†

Ancestry‡	Population	%
American (1,450)	1,450	11.35
Arab (171)	171	1.34
Egyptian (68)	68	0.53
Lebanese (103)	103	0.81
Armenian (27)	44	0.34
Austrian (0)	22	0.17
British (75)	133	1.04
Canadian (0)	37	0.29
Croatian (13)	13	0.10
Czech (19)	19	0.15
Czechoslovakian (10)	21	0.16
Dutch (39)	228	1.79
English (803)	1,835	14.37
European (9)	34	0.27
Finnish (20)	20	0.16
French, ex. Basque (61)	341	2.67
French Canadian (168)	244	1.91
German (931)	2,296	17.98
Greek (76)	127	0.99
Hungarian (145)	295	2.31
Irish (530)	2,035	15.93
Italian (581)	1,014	7.94
Lithuanian (12)	12	0.09
Macedonian (0)	2	0.02
Maltese (0)	36	0.28
Norwegian (56)	101	0.79
Polish (71)	263	2.06
Portuguese (23)	54	0.42
Romanian (11)	17	0.13
Russian (29)	35	0.27
Scotch-Irish (63)	158	1.24
Scottish (35)	366	2.87
Serbian (0)	17	0.13
Slovak (8)	34	0.27
Swedish (30)	88	0.69
Swiss (0)	12	0.09
Turkish (11)	11	0.09
Ukrainian (11)	20	0.16
Welsh (21)	85	0.67
West Indian, ex. Hispanic (35)	35	0.27
Barbadian (12)	12	0.09
Jamaican (23)	23	0.18
Yugoslavian (34)	34	0.27

Hispanic Origin	Population	%
Hispanic or Latino (of any race)	672	5.48
Central American, ex. Mexican	54	0.44
Costa Rican	3	0.02
Guatemalan	6	0.05
Honduran	15	0.12
Nicaraguan	8	0.07
Panamanian	10	0.08
Salvadoran	12	0.10
Cuban	48	0.39
Dominican Republic	25	0.20
Mexican	124	1.01
Puerto Rican	263	2.15
South American	82	0.67
Argentinean	16	0.13
Bolivian	1	0.01
Chilean	3	0.02
Colombian	26	0.21
Ecuadorian	12	0.10
Peruvian	3	0.02
Uruguayan	11	0.09
Venezuelan	10	0.08
Other Hispanic or Latino	76	0.62

Race*	Population	%
African-American/Black (1,336)	1,466	11.97
Not Hispanic (1,315)	1,434	11.70
Hispanic (21)	32	0.26
American Indian/Alaska Native (35)	96	0.78
Not Hispanic (31)	87	0.71
Hispanic (4)	9	0.07
Alaska Athabascan *(Ala. Nat.)* (1)	1	0.01
Apache (1)	1	0.01
Blackfeet (1)	3	0.02
Cherokee (9)	28	0.23
Chippewa (1)	2	0.02
Choctaw (0)	1	0.01
Creek (0)	3	0.02
Iroquois (3)	4	0.03
Mexican American Ind. (1)	1	0.01
Navajo (0)	3	0.02
Puget Sound Salish (3)	3	0.02
Seminole (4)	6	0.05
South American Ind. (2)	2	0.02
Asian (135)	186	1.52
Not Hispanic (133)	180	1.47
Hispanic (2)	6	0.05
Bangladeshi (3)	3	0.02
Chinese, ex. Taiwanese (13)	21	0.17
Filipino (43)	61	0.50
Indian (41)	48	0.39
Japanese (2)	11	0.09
Korean (13)	15	0.12
Pakistani (1)	1	0.01
Thai (6)	10	0.08
Vietnamese (12)	12	0.10
Hawaii Native/Pacific Islander (7)	14	0.11
Not Hispanic (7)	14	0.11
Guamanian/Chamorro (1)	1	0.01
Native Hawaiian (1)	6	0.05
White (10,327)	10,568	86.26
Not Hispanic (9,862)	10,054	82.06
Hispanic (465)	514	4.20

South Miami Heights

Place Type: CDP
County: Miami-Dade
Population: 35,696†

Ancestry‡	Population	%
African, Sub-Saharan (43)	109	0.30
African (43)	109	0.30
American (2,365)	2,365	6.46
Arab (38)	197	0.54
Arab (0)	43	0.12

SECTION TWO

*Notes: † The Census 2010 population figure is used to calculate the percentages in the Hispanic Origin and Race categories. Ancestry percentages are based on the 2006-2010 American Community Survey population (not shown); ‡ Numbers in parentheses indicate the number of people reporting a single ancestry; * Numbers in parentheses indicate the number of persons reporting this race alone, not in combination with any other race; Please refer to the Explanation of Data for more information.*

Egyptian (38)	90	0.25
Palestinian (0)	64	0.17
Austrian (32)	125	0.34
Brazilian (32)	72	0.20
British (51)	58	0.16
Czech (0)	13	0.04
Czechoslovakian (15)	15	0.04
Dutch (8)	133	0.36
English (133)	246	0.67
European (14)	14	0.04
French, ex. Basque (17)	218	0.60
French Canadian (9)	24	0.07
German (97)	437	1.19
Guyanese (465)	611	1.67
Irish (154)	412	1.12
Italian (33)	135	0.37
Norwegian (10)	32	0.09
Polish (50)	153	0.42
Portuguese (24)	67	0.18
Russian (13)	29	0.08
Scotch-Irish (8)	108	0.29
Scottish (3)	3	0.01
Swedish (0)	21	0.06
West Indian, ex. Hispanic (2,578)	3,633	9.92
Bahamian (77)	121	0.33
British West Indian (95)	180	0.49
Haitian (944)	1,272	3.47
Jamaican (1,030)	1,488	4.06
Trinidadian/Tobagonian (287)	419	1.14
West Indian (145)	153	0.42

Hispanic Origin	Population	%
Hispanic or Latino (of any race)	24,258	67.96
Central American, ex. Mexican	3,456	9.68
Costa Rican	106	0.30
Guatemalan	243	0.68
Honduran	839	2.35
Nicaraguan	1,585	4.44
Panamanian	158	0.44
Salvadoran	511	1.43
Other Central American	14	0.04
Cuban	13,466	37.72
Dominican Republic	988	2.77
Mexican	1,107	3.10
Puerto Rican	2,065	5.78
South American	2,066	5.79
Argentinean	115	0.32
Bolivian	29	0.08
Chilean	84	0.24
Colombian	1,007	2.82
Ecuadorian	205	0.57
Paraguayan	7	0.02
Peruvian	398	1.11
Uruguayan	41	0.11
Venezuelan	170	0.48
Other South American	10	0.03
Other Hispanic or Latino	1,110	3.11

Race*	Population	%
African-American/Black (8,671)	9,114	25.53
Not Hispanic (7,792)	8,032	22.50
Hispanic (879)	1,082	3.03
American Indian/Alaska Native (73)	173	0.48
Not Hispanic (47)	99	0.28
Hispanic (26)	74	0.21
Blackfeet (0)	5	0.01
Canadian/French Am. Ind. (1)	1	<0.01
Central American Ind. (2)	4	0.01
Cherokee (7)	30	0.08
Chippewa (0)	1	<0.01
Choctaw (0)	2	0.01
Creek (1)	1	<0.01
Mexican American Ind. (0)	4	0.01
Osage (1)	2	0.01
Seminole (0)	2	0.01
Sioux (1)	1	<0.01
South American Ind. (5)	23	0.06
Spanish American Ind. (0)	1	<0.01
Tlingit-Haida *(Alaska Native)* (1)	2	0.01
Asian (532)	748	2.10
Not Hispanic (514)	683	1.91
Hispanic (18)	65	0.18
Bangladeshi (6)	6	0.02
Cambodian (0)	1	<0.01
Chinese, ex. Taiwanese (38)	83	0.23
Filipino (60)	83	0.23
Indian (326)	417	1.17
Japanese (4)	7	0.02
Korean (2)	4	0.01
Laotian (0)	3	0.01
Pakistani (26)	31	0.09
Sri Lankan (6)	6	0.02
Thai (2)	3	0.01
Vietnamese (45)	47	0.13
Hawaii Native/Pacific Islander (5)	87	0.24
Not Hispanic (4)	73	0.20
Hispanic (1)	14	0.04
Native Hawaiian (2)	3	0.01
Samoan (0)	1	<0.01
White (23,980)	24,697	69.19
Not Hispanic (2,561)	2,689	7.53
Hispanic (21,419)	22,008	61.65

South Miami

Place Type: City
County: Miami-Dade
Population: 11,657†

Ancestry‡	Population	%
African, Sub-Saharan (104)	104	0.91
African (73)	73	0.64
Other Sub-Saharan African (31)	31	0.27
American (686)	686	6.00
Arab (87)	214	1.87
Arab (18)	30	0.26
Egyptian (15)	15	0.13
Lebanese (17)	103	0.90
Syrian (14)	24	0.21
Other Arab (23)	42	0.37
Brazilian (29)	77	0.67
British (44)	58	0.51
Bulgarian (0)	14	0.12
Canadian (64)	64	0.56
Croatian (0)	7	0.06
Czech (0)	15	0.13
Dutch (0)	46	0.40
English (335)	744	6.51
European (61)	61	0.53
Finnish (0)	14	0.12
French, ex. Basque (7)	42	0.37
French Canadian (13)	71	0.62
German (234)	885	7.74
Greek (15)	83	0.73
Hungarian (0)	14	0.12
Irish (111)	568	4.97
Italian (307)	524	4.59
Lithuanian (0)	22	0.19
Northern European (0)	50	0.44
Norwegian (0)	68	0.60
Polish (18)	167	1.46
Romanian (0)	27	0.24
Russian (39)	107	0.94
Scotch-Irish (89)	171	1.50
Scottish (16)	133	1.16
Serbian (0)	14	0.12
Slavic (0)	14	0.12
Slovak (15)	15	0.13
Swedish (10)	96	0.84
Swiss (0)	49	0.43
Welsh (14)	14	0.12
West Indian, ex. Hispanic (252)	309	2.70
Bahamian (0)	30	0.26
Haitian (105)	105	0.92
Jamaican (103)	130	1.14
Trinidadian/Tobagonian (13)	13	0.11
West Indian (31)	31	0.27

Hispanic Origin	Population	%
Hispanic or Latino (of any race)	5,025	43.11
Central American, ex. Mexican	406	3.48
Costa Rican	31	0.27
Guatemalan	33	0.28
Honduran	67	0.57
Nicaraguan	191	1.64
Panamanian	42	0.36
Salvadoran	40	0.34
Other Central American	2	0.02
Cuban	3,012	25.84
Dominican Republic	108	0.93
Mexican	95	0.81
Puerto Rican	246	2.11
South American	837	7.18
Argentinean	100	0.86
Bolivian	17	0.15
Chilean	45	0.39
Colombian	283	2.43
Ecuadorian	59	0.51
Paraguayan	14	0.12
Peruvian	113	0.97
Uruguayan	18	0.15
Venezuelan	188	1.61
Other Hispanic or Latino	321	2.75

Race*	Population	%
African-American/Black (1,985)	2,072	17.77
Not Hispanic (1,906)	1,958	16.80
Hispanic (79)	114	0.98
American Indian/Alaska Native (31)	70	0.60
Not Hispanic (14)	38	0.33
Hispanic (17)	32	0.27
Central American Ind. (2)	2	0.02
Cherokee (1)	9	0.08
Choctaw (4)	4	0.03
Menominee (0)	1	0.01
Mexican American Ind. (2)	2	0.02
Seminole (1)	1	0.01
South American Ind. (1)	2	0.02
Spanish American Ind. (1)	1	0.01
Asian (459)	555	4.76
Not Hispanic (440)	504	4.32
Hispanic (19)	51	0.44
Burmese (2)	2	0.02
Cambodian (7)	7	0.06
Chinese, ex. Taiwanese (113)	144	1.24
Filipino (89)	107	0.92
Indian (131)	138	1.18
Indonesian (0)	2	0.02
Japanese (14)	30	0.26
Korean (25)	30	0.26
Malaysian (0)	1	0.01
Pakistani (9)	15	0.13
Sri Lankan (9)	9	0.08
Taiwanese (9)	9	0.08
Thai (27)	32	0.27
Vietnamese (11)	23	0.20
Hawaii Native/Pacific Islander (5)	16	0.14
Not Hispanic (4)	13	0.11
Hispanic (1)	3	0.03
Fijian (0)	1	0.01
Guamanian/Chamorro (1)	1	0.01
Native Hawaiian (1)	5	0.04
Samoan (0)	1	0.01
White (8,749)	8,940	76.69
Not Hispanic (4,123)	4,225	36.24
Hispanic (4,626)	4,715	40.45

South Venice

Place Type: CDP
County: Sarasota
Population: 13,949†

Ancestry‡	Population	%
American (1,017)	1,017	7.30
Arab (0)	35	0.25
Iraqi (0)	35	0.25
Armenian (0)	21	0.15
Austrian (0)	61	0.44
Belgian (0)	15	0.11

*Notes: † The Census 2010 population figure is used to calculate the percentages in the Hispanic Origin and Race categories. Ancestry percentages are based on the 2006-2010 American Community Survey population (not shown); ‡ Numbers in parentheses indicate the number of people reporting a single ancestry; * Numbers in parentheses indicate the number of persons reporting this race alone, not in combination with any other race; Please refer to the Explanation of Data for more information.*

British (12)	38	0.27
Canadian (0)	47	0.34
Croatian (18)	18	0.13
Czech (13)	39	0.28
Czechoslovakian (45)	57	0.41
Dutch (177)	291	2.09
English (693)	2,349	16.85
European (106)	106	0.76
Finnish (7)	40	0.29
French, ex. Basque (172)	731	5.24
French Canadian (107)	186	1.33
German (978)	2,940	21.09
Greek (56)	101	0.72
Guyanese (13)	13	0.09
Hungarian (73)	174	1.25
Irish (617)	1,962	14.08
Israeli (16)	16	0.11
Italian (630)	1,349	9.68
Lithuanian (28)	38	0.27
Norwegian (30)	291	2.09
Pennsylvania German (53)	65	0.47
Polish (287)	815	5.85
Portuguese (61)	61	0.44
Romanian (14)	29	0.21
Russian (119)	212	1.52
Scandinavian (23)	36	0.26
Scotch-Irish (113)	383	2.75
Scottish (133)	493	3.54
Slavic (0)	19	0.14
Slovak (18)	80	0.57
Swedish (12)	399	2.86
Swiss (17)	190	1.36
Ukrainian (128)	286	2.05
Welsh (26)	137	0.98

Hispanic Origin	Population	%
Hispanic or Latino (of any race)	503	3.61
Central American, ex. Mexican	75	0.54
Costa Rican	11	0.08
Guatemalan	7	0.05
Honduran	10	0.07
Nicaraguan	3	0.02
Panamanian	1	0.01
Salvadoran	43	0.31
Cuban	44	0.32
Dominican Republic	11	0.08
Mexican	150	1.08
Puerto Rican	117	0.84
South American	77	0.55
Argentinean	15	0.11
Bolivian	1	0.01
Chilean	3	0.02
Colombian	26	0.19
Ecuadorian	2	0.01
Paraguayan	1	0.01
Peruvian	20	0.14
Venezuelan	9	0.06
Other Hispanic or Latino	29	0.21

Race*	Population	%
African-American/Black (90)	149	1.07
Not Hispanic (88)	138	0.99
Hispanic (2)	11	0.08
American Indian/Alaska Native (30)	82	0.59
Not Hispanic (28)	74	0.53
Hispanic (2)	8	0.06
Apache (1)	3	0.02
Blackfeet (0)	2	0.01
Cherokee (8)	14	0.10
Chippewa (3)	3	0.02
Creek (1)	2	0.01
Iroquois (0)	1	0.01
Lumbee (2)	2	0.01
Mexican American Ind. (2)	2	0.01
Navajo (1)	1	0.01
Seminole (1)	5	0.04
Asian (140)	184	1.32
Not Hispanic (139)	180	1.29
Hispanic (1)	4	0.03
Cambodian (11)	14	0.10
Chinese, ex. Taiwanese (22)	32	0.23
Filipino (55)	74	0.53
Indian (17)	29	0.21
Indonesian (1)	1	0.01
Japanese (1)	3	0.02
Korean (7)	9	0.06
Pakistani (1)	1	0.01
Thai (5)	5	0.04
Vietnamese (9)	9	0.06
Hawaii Native/Pacific Islander (6)	16	0.11
Not Hispanic (6)	14	0.10
Hispanic (0)	2	0.01
Guamanian/Chamorro (0)	1	0.01
Native Hawaiian (3)	5	0.04
Samoan (0)	1	0.01
White (13,352)	13,534	97.02
Not Hispanic (13,029)	13,164	94.37
Hispanic (323)	370	2.65

Southchase

Place Type: CDP
County: Orange
Population: 15,921†

Ancestry‡	Population	%
African, Sub-Saharan (144)	160	0.97
African (17)	33	0.20
Ethiopian (58)	58	0.35
South African (59)	59	0.36
Other Sub-Saharan African (10)	10	0.06
American (689)	689	4.18
Arab (397)	411	2.49
Arab (21)	21	0.13
Egyptian (65)	65	0.39
Lebanese (108)	108	0.66
Moroccan (117)	117	0.71
Syrian (86)	100	0.61
Brazilian (662)	662	4.02
British (29)	40	0.24
Bulgarian (15)	15	0.09
Canadian (124)	202	1.23
Danish (0)	12	0.07
Dutch (64)	188	1.14
English (192)	331	2.01
European (41)	41	0.25
Finnish (0)	16	0.10
French, ex. Basque (62)	241	1.46
German (443)	944	5.73
Greek (20)	64	0.39
Guyanese (102)	102	0.62
Hungarian (0)	11	0.07
Irish (348)	683	4.14
Italian (168)	369	2.24
Latvian (0)	17	0.10
Lithuanian (4)	4	0.02
Maltese (25)	25	0.15
Norwegian (22)	60	0.36
Polish (37)	115	0.70
Portuguese (23)	64	0.39
Romanian (0)	10	0.06
Russian (24)	132	0.80
Scotch-Irish (1)	31	0.19
Scottish (61)	128	0.78
Slovak (0)	30	0.18
Swedish (0)	50	0.30
Swiss (20)	20	0.12
Turkish (33)	48	0.29
Ukrainian (34)	79	0.48
Welsh (0)	11	0.07
West Indian, ex. Hispanic (1,026)	1,114	6.76
Haitian (669)	715	4.34
Jamaican (299)	327	1.98
Trinidadian/Tobagonian (24)	38	0.23
West Indian (34)	34	0.21
Yugoslavian (144)	144	0.87

Hispanic Origin	Population	%
Hispanic or Latino (of any race)	7,755	48.71
Central American, ex. Mexican	327	2.05
Costa Rican	41	0.26
Guatemalan	45	0.28
Honduran	49	0.31
Nicaraguan	38	0.24
Panamanian	61	0.38
Salvadoran	92	0.58
Other Central American	1	0.01
Cuban	423	2.66
Dominican Republic	798	5.01
Mexican	219	1.38
Puerto Rican	3,497	21.96
South American	2,073	13.02
Argentinean	46	0.29
Bolivian	13	0.08
Chilean	46	0.29
Colombian	1,184	7.44
Ecuadorian	242	1.52
Paraguayan	4	0.03
Peruvian	186	1.17
Uruguayan	24	0.15
Venezuelan	317	1.99
Other South American	11	0.07
Other Hispanic or Latino	418	2.63

Race*	Population	%
African-American/Black (2,234)	2,522	15.84
Not Hispanic (1,920)	2,084	13.09
Hispanic (314)	438	2.75
American Indian/Alaska Native (52)	128	0.80
Not Hispanic (16)	55	0.35
Hispanic (36)	73	0.46
Central American Ind. (1)	3	0.02
Cherokee (3)	7	0.04
Chickasaw (2)	2	0.01
Choctaw (0)	2	0.01
Lumbee (4)	8	0.05
Mexican American Ind. (3)	4	0.03
Shoshone (1)	1	0.01
South American Ind. (9)	19	0.12
Spanish American Ind. (7)	7	0.04
Asian (1,751)	1,969	12.37
Not Hispanic (1,722)	1,896	11.91
Hispanic (29)	73	0.46
Bangladeshi (51)	51	0.32
Burmese (1)	1	0.01
Cambodian (13)	17	0.11
Chinese, ex. Taiwanese (230)	265	1.66
Filipino (303)	337	2.12
Indian (532)	612	3.84
Indonesian (4)	4	0.03
Japanese (28)	44	0.28
Korean (19)	30	0.19
Malaysian (1)	1	0.01
Pakistani (153)	166	1.04
Sri Lankan (3)	3	0.02
Taiwanese (21)	23	0.14
Thai (20)	29	0.18
Vietnamese (311)	336	2.11
Hawaii Native/Pacific Islander (25)	92	0.58
Not Hispanic (24)	69	0.43
Hispanic (1)	23	0.14
Fijian (4)	4	0.03
Guamanian/Chamorro (1)	1	0.01
Native Hawaiian (3)	15	0.09
Samoan (5)	9	0.06
White (8,875)	9,403	59.06
Not Hispanic (3,897)	4,125	25.91
Hispanic (4,978)	5,278	33.15

Spring Hill

Place Type: CDP
County: Hernando
Population: 98,621†

Ancestry‡	Population	%
African, Sub-Saharan (684)	687	0.71
African (653)	653	0.68
Ethiopian (23)	23	0.02
South African (8)	11	0.01

*Notes: † The Census 2010 population figure is used to calculate the percentages in the Hispanic Origin and Race categories. Ancestry percentages are based on the 2006-2010 American Community Survey population (not shown); ‡ Numbers in parentheses indicate the number of people reporting a single ancestry; * Numbers in parentheses indicate the number of persons reporting this race alone, not in combination with any other race; Please refer to the Explanation of Data for more information.*

Albanian (132)	153	0.16
American (4,976)	4,976	5.15
Arab (127)	307	0.32
Lebanese (10)	76	0.08
Syrian (117)	231	0.24
Armenian (0)	14	0.01
Austrian (88)	344	0.36
Basque (0)	26	0.03
Belgian (9)	73	0.08
Brazilian (60)	111	0.11
British (156)	344	0.36
Cajun (15)	53	0.05
Canadian (84)	134	0.14
Celtic (0)	6	0.01
Croatian (17)	49	0.05
Czech (153)	640	0.66
Czechoslovakian (40)	275	0.28
Danish (21)	230	0.24
Dutch (288)	1,443	1.49
Eastern European (10)	10	0.01
English (2,761)	9,178	9.49
Estonian (39)	39	0.04
European (220)	345	0.36
Finnish (52)	177	0.18
French, ex. Basque (641)	4,231	4.38
French Canadian (761)	1,262	1.31
German (5,217)	17,278	17.87
Greek (541)	894	0.92
Guyanese (75)	75	0.08
Hungarian (720)	1,198	1.24
Iranian (0)	13	0.01
Irish (4,609)	18,343	18.97
Israeli (76)	76	0.08
Italian (8,321)	16,923	17.50
Latvian (0)	13	0.01
Lithuanian (150)	286	0.30
Luxemburger (0)	14	0.01
Maltese (29)	100	0.10
New Zealander (14)	27	0.03
Norwegian (358)	1,029	1.06
Pennsylvania German (14)	120	0.12
Polish (2,060)	5,645	5.84
Portuguese (369)	587	0.61
Romanian (56)	86	0.09
Russian (393)	876	0.91
Scandinavian (69)	195	0.20
Scotch-Irish (732)	1,603	1.66
Scottish (616)	2,091	2.16
Serbian (14)	59	0.06
Slavic (44)	71	0.07
Slovak (143)	239	0.25
Slovene (31)	31	0.03
Swedish (197)	1,233	1.28
Swiss (0)	141	0.15
Turkish (47)	63	0.07
Ukrainian (161)	310	0.32
Welsh (171)	553	0.57
West Indian, ex. Hispanic (742)	858	0.89
Bahamian (25)	42	0.04
Barbadian (24)	24	0.02
Belizean (22)	46	0.05
British West Indian (21)	21	0.02
Haitian (346)	373	0.39
Jamaican (254)	263	0.27
Trinidadian/Tobagonian (20)	20	0.02
U.S. Virgin Islander (0)	20	0.02
West Indian (30)	49	0.05
Yugoslavian (14)	30	0.03

Hispanic Origin	Population	%
Hispanic or Latino (of any race)	13,379	13.57
Central American, ex. Mexican	608	0.62
Costa Rican	53	0.05
Guatemalan	104	0.11
Honduran	147	0.15
Nicaraguan	42	0.04
Panamanian	139	0.14
Salvadoran	114	0.12
Other Central American	9	0.01
Cuban	1,332	1.35
Dominican Republic	560	0.57
Mexican	960	0.97
Puerto Rican	8,072	8.18
South American	970	0.98
Argentinean	62	0.06
Bolivian	10	0.01
Chilean	27	0.03
Colombian	486	0.49
Ecuadorian	163	0.17
Paraguayan	3	<0.01
Peruvian	115	0.12
Uruguayan	24	0.02
Venezuelan	74	0.08
Other South American	6	0.01
Other Hispanic or Latino	877	0.89

Race*	Population	%
African-American/Black (5,036)	6,106	6.19
Not Hispanic (4,485)	5,230	5.30
Hispanic (551)	876	0.89
American Indian/Alaska Native (354)	916	0.93
Not Hispanic (259)	709	0.72
Hispanic (95)	207	0.21
Apache (6)	9	0.01
Blackfeet (8)	50	0.05
Canadian/French Am. Ind. (2)	6	0.01
Central American Ind. (3)	6	0.01
Cherokee (52)	222	0.23
Chickasaw (3)	6	0.01
Chippewa (7)	23	0.02
Choctaw (9)	18	0.02
Comanche (1)	2	<0.01
Cree (0)	1	<0.01
Creek (4)	14	0.01
Delaware (6)	7	0.01
Hopi (0)	2	<0.01
Iroquois (22)	46	0.05
Kiowa (2)	2	<0.01
Lumbee (8)	9	0.01
Mexican American Ind. (16)	21	0.02
Navajo (2)	8	0.01
Ottawa (1)	5	0.01
Pima (0)	4	<0.01
Potawatomi (1)	3	<0.01
Seminole (4)	9	0.01
Sioux (5)	16	0.02
South American Ind. (11)	30	0.03
Spanish American Ind. (5)	8	0.01
Tlingit-Haida *(Alaska Native)* (2)	4	<0.01
Asian (1,385)	1,892	1.92
Not Hispanic (1,349)	1,783	1.81
Hispanic (36)	109	0.11
Burmese (6)	6	0.01
Cambodian (7)	11	0.01
Chinese, ex. Taiwanese (231)	322	0.33
Filipino (388)	593	0.60
Hmong (1)	1	<0.01
Indian (313)	392	0.40
Indonesian (9)	16	0.02
Japanese (36)	75	0.08
Korean (79)	116	0.12
Laotian (4)	4	<0.01
Malaysian (0)	3	<0.01
Pakistani (20)	23	0.02
Sri Lankan (8)	8	0.01
Taiwanese (4)	11	0.01
Thai (37)	49	0.05
Vietnamese (193)	218	0.22
Hawaii Native/Pacific Islander (43)	142	0.14
Not Hispanic (38)	104	0.11
Hispanic (5)	38	0.04
Guamanian/Chamorro (10)	13	0.01
Marshallese (1)	1	<0.01
Native Hawaiian (14)	39	0.04
Samoan (5)	12	0.01
Tongan (1)	1	<0.01
White (86,887)	88,939	90.18
Not Hispanic (77,399)	78,761	79.86
Hispanic (9,488)	10,178	10.32

Springfield

Place Type: City
County: Bay
Population: 8,903†

Ancestry‡	Population	%
American (1,304)	1,304	14.51
Austrian (13)	13	0.14
Bulgarian (20)	20	0.22
Canadian (16)	16	0.18
Czech (0)	17	0.19
Danish (10)	10	0.11
Dutch (0)	124	1.38
English (492)	684	7.61
European (40)	71	0.79
Finnish (0)	24	0.27
French, ex. Basque (202)	348	3.87
French Canadian (62)	80	0.89
German (325)	788	8.77
Greek (0)	15	0.17
Hungarian (10)	10	0.11
Irish (382)	836	9.30
Italian (63)	107	1.19
Lithuanian (0)	26	0.29
Norwegian (17)	17	0.19
Polish (0)	33	0.37
Portuguese (8)	8	0.09
Scandinavian (10)	10	0.11
Scotch-Irish (70)	162	1.80
Scottish (25)	104	1.16
Slovak (0)	15	0.17
Swedish (12)	49	0.55
Welsh (50)	62	0.69
West Indian, ex. Hispanic (135)	135	1.50
Haitian (72)	72	0.80
Jamaican (63)	63	0.70

Hispanic Origin	Population	%
Hispanic or Latino (of any race)	518	5.82
Central American, ex. Mexican	28	0.31
Costa Rican	3	0.03
Guatemalan	1	0.01
Honduran	8	0.09
Nicaraguan	1	0.01
Panamanian	11	0.12
Salvadoran	4	0.04
Cuban	20	0.22
Dominican Republic	7	0.08
Mexican	230	2.58
Puerto Rican	167	1.88
South American	20	0.22
Colombian	3	0.03
Ecuadorian	4	0.04
Peruvian	12	0.13
Venezuelan	1	0.01
Other Hispanic or Latino	46	0.52

Race*	Population	%
African-American/Black (2,116)	2,296	25.79
Not Hispanic (2,074)	2,238	25.14
Hispanic (42)	58	0.65
American Indian/Alaska Native (64)	163	1.83
Not Hispanic (59)	150	1.68
Hispanic (5)	13	0.15
Blackfeet (4)	13	0.15
Canadian/French Am. Ind. (5)	5	0.06
Cherokee (13)	44	0.49
Chippewa (0)	1	0.01
Choctaw (2)	6	0.07
Cree (0)	1	0.01
Creek (9)	20	0.22
Iroquois (0)	3	0.03
Lumbee (1)	2	0.02
Mexican American Ind. (4)	6	0.07
Seminole (0)	1	0.01
South American Ind. (0)	1	0.01
Asian (335)	437	4.91
Not Hispanic (332)	424	4.76
Hispanic (3)	13	0.15

*Notes: † The Census 2010 population figure is used to calculate the percentages in the Hispanic Origin and Race categories. Ancestry percentages are based on the 2006-2010 American Community Survey population (not shown); ‡ Numbers in parentheses indicate the number of people reporting a single ancestry; * Numbers in parentheses indicate the number of persons reporting this race alone, not in combination with any other race; Please refer to the Explanation of Data for more information.*

Cambodian (1)	1	0.01
Chinese, ex. Taiwanese (5)	11	0.12
Filipino (61)	96	1.08
Indian (6)	15	0.17
Indonesian (0)	1	0.01
Japanese (10)	33	0.37
Korean (14)	27	0.30
Laotian (0)	1	0.01
Pakistani (4)	4	0.04
Sri Lankan (0)	1	0.01
Thai (25)	43	0.48
Vietnamese (193)	218	2.45
Hawaii Native/Pacific Islander (8)	15	0.17
Not Hispanic (7)	14	0.16
Hispanic (1)	1	0.01
Guamanian/Chamorro (2)	2	0.02
Native Hawaiian (2)	3	0.03
Samoan (0)	1	0.01
White (5,872)	6,158	69.17
Not Hispanic (5,612)	5,861	65.83
Hispanic (260)	297	3.34

St. Augustine

Place Type: City
County: St. Johns
Population: 12,975†

Ancestry‡	Population	%
African, Sub-Saharan (23)	23	0.18
African (23)	23	0.18
American (1,133)	1,133	8.78
Arab (0)	35	0.27
Lebanese (0)	26	0.20
Other Arab (0)	9	0.07
Armenian (0)	47	0.36
Austrian (38)	38	0.29
Belgian (0)	15	0.12
Brazilian (0)	17	0.13
British (69)	91	0.71
Cajun (0)	14	0.11
Canadian (11)	62	0.48
Czech (63)	119	0.92
Danish (6)	52	0.40
Dutch (49)	208	1.61
Eastern European (12)	12	0.09
English (616)	1,464	11.35
European (171)	225	1.74
Finnish (0)	14	0.11
French, ex. Basque (185)	463	3.59
French Canadian (232)	280	2.17
German (465)	1,465	11.36
Greek (167)	223	1.73
Hungarian (87)	113	0.88
Irish (944)	1,788	13.86
Italian (784)	1,378	10.68
Lithuanian (6)	6	0.05
Northern European (29)	29	0.22
Norwegian (25)	57	0.44
Polish (83)	300	2.33
Portuguese (24)	32	0.25
Russian (28)	115	0.89
Scandinavian (0)	23	0.18
Scotch-Irish (102)	286	2.22
Scottish (307)	422	3.27
Slovak (0)	14	0.11
Slovene (0)	9	0.07
Swedish (103)	245	1.90
Swiss (16)	35	0.27
Turkish (24)	24	0.19
Ukrainian (26)	33	0.26
Welsh (14)	86	0.67
West Indian, ex. Hispanic (49)	49	0.38
Dutch West Indian (14)	14	0.11
Haitian (20)	20	0.16
Jamaican (15)	15	0.12
Yugoslavian (0)	6	0.05

Hispanic Origin	Population	%
Hispanic or Latino (of any race)	656	5.06
Central American, ex. Mexican	38	0.29
Costa Rican	5	0.04
Guatemalan	11	0.08
Nicaraguan	1	0.01
Panamanian	8	0.06
Salvadoran	13	0.10
Cuban	81	0.62
Dominican Republic	9	0.07
Mexican	134	1.03
Puerto Rican	188	1.45
South American	72	0.55
Argentinean	10	0.08
Chilean	1	0.01
Colombian	30	0.23
Ecuadorian	12	0.09
Peruvian	4	0.03
Venezuelan	15	0.12
Other Hispanic or Latino	134	1.03

Race*	Population	%
African-American/Black (1,506)	1,595	12.29
Not Hispanic (1,460)	1,543	11.89
Hispanic (46)	52	0.40
American Indian/Alaska Native (52)	128	0.99
Not Hispanic (46)	118	0.91
Hispanic (6)	10	0.08
Aleut *(Alaska Native)* (0)	1	0.01
Canadian/French Am. Ind. (0)	1	0.01
Cherokee (9)	38	0.29
Chickasaw (1)	2	0.02
Chippewa (2)	2	0.02
Choctaw (1)	2	0.02
Creek (0)	2	0.02
Crow (0)	1	0.01
Iroquois (2)	4	0.03
Lumbee (1)	4	0.03
Mexican American Ind. (2)	2	0.02
Navajo (0)	1	0.01
Ottawa (2)	2	0.02
Paiute (0)	1	0.01
South American Ind. (1)	2	0.02
Asian (162)	206	1.59
Not Hispanic (155)	196	1.51
Hispanic (7)	10	0.08
Cambodian (9)	10	0.08
Chinese, ex. Taiwanese (22)	29	0.22
Filipino (26)	37	0.29
Hmong (0)	1	0.01
Indian (68)	76	0.59
Japanese (7)	16	0.12
Korean (3)	9	0.07
Laotian (0)	1	0.01
Malaysian (0)	1	0.01
Nepalese (1)	1	0.01
Pakistani (4)	6	0.05
Thai (4)	7	0.05
Vietnamese (12)	13	0.10
Hawaii Native/Pacific Islander (12)	20	0.15
Not Hispanic (10)	17	0.13
Hispanic (2)	3	0.02
Guamanian/Chamorro (3)	3	0.02
Native Hawaiian (0)	2	0.02
Samoan (5)	5	0.04
White (10,923)	11,110	85.63
Not Hispanic (10,443)	10,609	81.76
Hispanic (480)	501	3.86

St. Cloud

Place Type: City
County: Osceola
Population: 35,183†

Ancestry‡	Population	%
African, Sub-Saharan (86)	111	0.33
African (38)	63	0.19
Zimbabwean (48)	48	0.14
American (4,998)	4,998	14.81
Arab (13)	13	0.04
Other Arab (13)	13	0.04
Armenian (0)	13	0.04
Australian (11)	46	0.14
Austrian (11)	23	0.07
Belgian (45)	74	0.22
Brazilian (30)	59	0.17
British (46)	132	0.39
Canadian (8)	19	0.06
Croatian (9)	40	0.12
Czech (50)	95	0.28
Czechoslovakian (90)	90	0.27
Danish (42)	134	0.40
Dutch (175)	535	1.59
English (1,036)	2,550	7.56
European (170)	191	0.57
Finnish (0)	15	0.04
French, ex. Basque (170)	844	2.50
French Canadian (117)	165	0.49
German (1,366)	4,243	12.57
Greek (18)	74	0.22
Guyanese (13)	13	0.04
Hungarian (62)	96	0.28
Iranian (12)	12	0.04
Irish (1,499)	4,621	13.70
Italian (1,331)	2,730	8.09
Lithuanian (0)	71	0.21
Norwegian (0)	96	0.28
Pennsylvania German (49)	49	0.15
Polish (296)	1,165	3.45
Portuguese (137)	402	1.19
Romanian (0)	24	0.07
Russian (67)	139	0.41
Scandinavian (0)	97	0.29
Scotch-Irish (227)	435	1.29
Scottish (184)	332	0.98
Slavic (0)	35	0.10
Swedish (38)	236	0.70
Swiss (12)	38	0.11
Ukrainian (25)	108	0.32
Welsh (0)	161	0.48
West Indian, ex. Hispanic (409)	474	1.40
Jamaican (386)	409	1.21
Trinidadian/Tobagonian (23)	23	0.07
West Indian (0)	42	0.12

Hispanic Origin	Population	%
Hispanic or Latino (of any race)	10,280	29.22
Central American, ex. Mexican	428	1.22
Costa Rican	45	0.13
Guatemalan	61	0.17
Honduran	99	0.28
Nicaraguan	59	0.17
Panamanian	67	0.19
Salvadoran	95	0.27
Other Central American	2	0.01
Cuban	536	1.52
Dominican Republic	693	1.97
Mexican	671	1.91
Puerto Rican	6,574	18.69
South American	1,056	3.00
Argentinean	44	0.13
Bolivian	16	0.05
Chilean	33	0.09
Colombian	507	1.44
Ecuadorian	175	0.50
Paraguayan	1	<0.01
Peruvian	89	0.25
Uruguayan	12	0.03
Venezuelan	161	0.46
Other South American	18	0.05
Other Hispanic or Latino	322	0.92

Race*	Population	%
African-American/Black (2,052)	2,540	7.22
Not Hispanic (1,633)	1,909	5.43
Hispanic (419)	631	1.79
American Indian/Alaska Native (132)	357	1.01
Not Hispanic (79)	223	0.63
Hispanic (53)	134	0.38
Apache (0)	5	0.01
Blackfeet (3)	16	0.05

*Notes: † The Census 2010 population figure is used to calculate the percentages in the Hispanic Origin and Race categories. Ancestry percentages are based on the 2006-2010 American Community Survey population (not shown); ‡ Numbers in parentheses indicate the number of people reporting a single ancestry; * Numbers in parentheses indicate the number of persons reporting this race alone, not in combination with any other race; Please refer to the Explanation of Data for more information.*

Canadian/French Am. Ind. (1)	1	<0.01
Central American Ind. (6)	9	0.03
Cherokee (19)	61	0.17
Chippewa (2)	4	0.01
Choctaw (3)	4	0.01
Creek (3)	3	0.01
Iroquois (3)	6	0.02
Lumbee (3)	3	0.01
Navajo (2)	2	0.01
Pueblo (1)	1	<0.01
Seminole (1)	2	0.01
Shoshone (0)	5	0.01
Sioux (0)	3	0.01
South American Ind. (10)	33	0.09
Spanish American Ind. (1)	3	0.01
Tlingit-Haida *(Alaska Native)* (1)	1	<0.01
Tohono O'Odham (0)	4	0.01
Asian (613)	881	2.50
Not Hispanic (580)	797	2.27
Hispanic (33)	84	0.24
Bangladeshi (1)	1	<0.01
Burmese (0)	1	<0.01
Cambodian (16)	16	0.05
Chinese, ex. Taiwanese (89)	127	0.36
Filipino (156)	240	0.68
Indian (225)	292	0.83
Indonesian (2)	16	0.05
Japanese (11)	38	0.11
Korean (23)	46	0.13
Laotian (5)	11	0.03
Pakistani (20)	23	0.07
Taiwanese (3)	6	0.02
Thai (17)	33	0.09
Vietnamese (14)	26	0.07
Hawaii Native/Pacific Islander (26)	107	0.30
Not Hispanic (21)	73	0.21
Hispanic (5)	34	0.10
Fijian (1)	1	<0.01
Guamanian/Chamorro (9)	12	0.03
Native Hawaiian (10)	18	0.05
Samoan (0)	1	<0.01
Tongan (1)	4	0.01
White (29,000)	29,995	85.25
Not Hispanic (21,851)	22,349	63.52
Hispanic (7,149)	7,646	21.73

St. Pete Beach

Place Type: City
County: Pinellas
Population: 9,346†

Ancestry‡	Population	%
African, Sub-Saharan (10)	10	0.11
South African (10)	10	0.11
American (438)	438	4.61
Arab (0)	29	0.31
Syrian (0)	29	0.31
Austrian (68)	95	1.00
Belgian (0)	17	0.18
British (0)	8	0.08
Canadian (53)	79	0.83
Croatian (0)	23	0.24
Czech (31)	47	0.50
Czechoslovakian (12)	12	0.13
Danish (28)	98	1.03
Dutch (60)	103	1.08
English (542)	1,750	18.43
European (68)	68	0.72
Finnish (29)	49	0.52
French, ex. Basque (62)	426	4.49
French Canadian (24)	50	0.53
German (593)	1,837	19.35
Greek (51)	97	1.02
Hungarian (10)	92	0.97
Iranian (38)	38	0.40
Irish (906)	2,062	21.72
Italian (474)	1,166	12.28
Latvian (0)	11	0.12
Lithuanian (282)	306	3.22
Norwegian (14)	65	0.68
Polish (156)	399	4.20
Portuguese (40)	40	0.42
Romanian (50)	50	0.53
Russian (157)	157	1.65
Scandinavian (17)	17	0.18
Scotch-Irish (113)	248	2.61
Scottish (73)	210	2.21
Serbian (88)	88	0.93
Slavic (40)	40	0.42
Slovak (46)	61	0.64
Swedish (34)	230	2.42
Swiss (0)	62	0.65
Ukrainian (31)	31	0.33
Welsh (16)	111	1.17

Hispanic Origin	Population	%
Hispanic or Latino (of any race)	412	4.41
Central American, ex. Mexican	29	0.31
Costa Rican	9	0.10
Guatemalan	5	0.05
Honduran	3	0.03
Nicaraguan	1	0.01
Salvadoran	11	0.12
Cuban	76	0.81
Dominican Republic	7	0.07
Mexican	137	1.47
Puerto Rican	45	0.48
South American	59	0.63
Argentinean	8	0.09
Bolivian	1	0.01
Chilean	6	0.06
Colombian	23	0.25
Ecuadorian	5	0.05
Peruvian	10	0.11
Venezuelan	5	0.05
Other South American	1	0.01
Other Hispanic or Latino	59	0.63

Race*	Population	%
African-American/Black (67)	93	1.00
Not Hispanic (64)	87	0.93
Hispanic (3)	6	0.06
American Indian/Alaska Native (24)	48	0.51
Not Hispanic (23)	45	0.48
Hispanic (1)	3	0.03
Arapaho (0)	1	0.01
Blackfeet (1)	2	0.02
Cherokee (4)	10	0.11
Chickasaw (0)	1	0.01
Chippewa (1)	3	0.03
Creek (2)	3	0.03
Inupiat *(Alaska Native)* (3)	3	0.03
Kiowa (0)	1	0.01
Navajo (1)	1	0.01
Sioux (1)	2	0.02
Asian (106)	140	1.50
Not Hispanic (106)	138	1.48
Hispanic (0)	2	0.02
Chinese, ex. Taiwanese (19)	25	0.27
Filipino (15)	26	0.28
Indian (30)	38	0.41
Indonesian (1)	1	0.01
Japanese (4)	7	0.07
Korean (12)	13	0.14
Taiwanese (1)	1	0.01
Thai (9)	10	0.11
Vietnamese (9)	10	0.11
Hawaii Native/Pacific Islander (3)	8	0.09
Not Hispanic (3)	8	0.09
Native Hawaiian (2)	3	0.03
Samoan (1)	2	0.02
White (8,969)	9,060	96.94
Not Hispanic (8,643)	8,720	93.30
Hispanic (326)	340	3.64

St. Petersburg

Place Type: City
County: Pinellas
Population: 244,769†

Ancestry‡	Population	%
African, Sub-Saharan (3,327)	3,479	1.42
African (3,009)	3,161	1.29
Cape Verdean (9)	9	<0.01
Ethiopian (105)	105	0.04
Ghanaian (20)	20	0.01
Kenyan (29)	29	0.01
Liberian (104)	104	0.04
South African (32)	32	0.01
Sudanese (19)	19	0.01
Albanian (348)	365	0.15
Alsatian (0)	46	0.02
American (9,124)	9,124	3.71
Arab (1,263)	1,890	0.77
Arab (162)	162	0.07
Egyptian (45)	67	0.03
Iraqi (5)	49	0.02
Jordanian (176)	176	0.07
Lebanese (198)	582	0.24
Moroccan (458)	458	0.19
Palestinian (25)	97	0.04
Syrian (12)	117	0.05
Other Arab (182)	182	0.07
Armenian (150)	177	0.07
Australian (37)	47	0.02
Austrian (223)	1,012	0.41
Basque (13)	13	0.01
Belgian (80)	195	0.08
Brazilian (234)	285	0.12
British (917)	1,467	0.60
Bulgarian (531)	584	0.24
Cajun (89)	184	0.07
Canadian (570)	968	0.39
Celtic (7)	20	0.01
Croatian (160)	342	0.14
Czech (299)	1,213	0.49
Czechoslovakian (94)	224	0.09
Danish (290)	805	0.33
Dutch (904)	3,222	1.31
Eastern European (249)	249	0.10
English (9,708)	25,968	10.57
European (2,931)	3,434	1.40
Finnish (177)	544	0.22
French, ex. Basque (2,062)	8,590	3.50
French Canadian (843)	1,651	0.67
German (11,674)	35,808	14.57
Greek (526)	1,228	0.50
Guyanese (158)	178	0.07
Hungarian (469)	1,123	0.46
Icelander (34)	41	0.02
Iranian (257)	266	0.11
Irish (10,818)	32,964	13.42
Israeli (26)	26	0.01
Italian (8,007)	16,213	6.60
Latvian (53)	53	0.02
Lithuanian (428)	1,041	0.42
Macedonian (29)	37	0.02
Maltese (10)	20	0.01
Northern European (195)	221	0.09
Norwegian (593)	1,597	0.65
Pennsylvania German (86)	230	0.09
Polish (3,477)	8,031	3.27
Portuguese (474)	863	0.35
Romanian (115)	315	0.13
Russian (876)	1,987	0.81
Scandinavian (193)	279	0.11
Scotch-Irish (2,116)	4,877	1.98
Scottish (2,110)	6,164	2.51
Serbian (361)	572	0.23
Slavic (16)	92	0.04
Slovak (174)	630	0.26
Slovene (45)	91	0.04
Swedish (894)	3,112	1.27

*Notes: † The Census 2010 population figure is used to calculate the percentages in the Hispanic Origin and Race categories. Ancestry percentages are based on the 2006-2010 American Community Survey population (not shown); ‡ Numbers in parentheses indicate the number of people reporting a single ancestry; * Numbers in parentheses indicate the number of persons reporting this race alone, not in combination with any other race; Please refer to the Explanation of Data for more information.*

Swiss (217)	789	0.32
Turkish (69)	87	0.04
Ukrainian (587)	965	0.39
Welsh (313)	1,382	0.56
West Indian, ex. Hispanic (1,787)	2,176	0.89
Bahamian (132)	152	0.06
Barbadian (14)	29	0.01
British West Indian (15)	115	0.05
Haitian (334)	422	0.17
Jamaican (864)	976	0.40
Trinidadian/Tobagonian (180)	180	0.07
West Indian (190)	244	0.10
Other West Indian (58)	58	0.02
Yugoslavian (1,889)	2,058	0.84

Hispanic Origin	Population	%
Hispanic or Latino (of any race)	16,214	6.62
Central American, ex. Mexican	921	0.38
Costa Rican	152	0.06
Guatemalan	142	0.06
Honduran	198	0.08
Nicaraguan	108	0.04
Panamanian	221	0.09
Salvadoran	86	0.04
Other Central American	14	0.01
Cuban	2,835	1.16
Dominican Republic	485	0.20
Mexican	2,855	1.17
Puerto Rican	5,272	2.15
South American	2,209	0.90
Argentinean	166	0.07
Bolivian	63	0.03
Chilean	95	0.04
Colombian	844	0.34
Ecuadorian	229	0.09
Paraguayan	8	<0.01
Peruvian	321	0.13
Uruguayan	27	0.01
Venezuelan	413	0.17
Other South American	43	0.02
Other Hispanic or Latino	1,637	0.67

Race*	Population	%
African-American/Black (58,577)	61,640	25.18
Not Hispanic (57,489)	60,020	24.52
Hispanic (1,088)	1,620	0.66
American Indian/Alaska Native (723)	2,148	0.88
Not Hispanic (567)	1,834	0.75
Hispanic (156)	314	0.13
Alaska Athabascan *(Ala. Nat.)* (1)	1	<0.01
Aleut *(Alaska Native)* (1)	1	<0.01
Apache (10)	37	0.02
Arapaho (0)	1	<0.01
Blackfeet (6)	89	0.04
Canadian/French Am. Ind. (4)	9	<0.01
Central American Ind. (5)	8	<0.01
Cherokee (119)	494	0.20
Cheyenne (0)	3	<0.01
Chickasaw (6)	9	<0.01
Chippewa (16)	32	0.01
Choctaw (18)	45	0.02
Comanche (6)	14	0.01
Cree (0)	6	<0.01
Creek (13)	39	0.02
Crow (1)	11	<0.01
Delaware (6)	13	0.01
Hopi (1)	2	<0.01
Inupiat *(Alaska Native)* (4)	6	<0.01
Iroquois (30)	77	0.03
Kiowa (0)	2	<0.01
Lumbee (12)	19	0.01
Mexican American Ind. (38)	59	0.02
Navajo (12)	20	0.01
Osage (1)	9	<0.01
Ottawa (3)	4	<0.01
Paiute (1)	1	<0.01
Pima (1)	1	<0.01
Potawatomi (4)	5	<0.01
Pueblo (2)	10	<0.01
Seminole (6)	39	0.02
Sioux (9)	41	0.02
South American Ind. (17)	31	0.01
Spanish American Ind. (2)	3	<0.01
Tlingit-Haida *(Alaska Native)* (0)	3	<0.01
Tohono O'Odham (1)	2	<0.01
Ute (1)	8	<0.01
Yakama (1)	1	<0.01
Yaqui (1)	2	<0.01
Asian (7,779)	9,555	3.90
Not Hispanic (7,672)	9,239	3.77
Hispanic (107)	316	0.13
Bangladeshi (87)	105	0.04
Burmese (16)	17	0.01
Cambodian (505)	628	0.26
Chinese, ex. Taiwanese (636)	925	0.38
Filipino (1,163)	1,597	0.65
Hmong (15)	15	0.01
Indian (1,147)	1,444	0.59
Indonesian (16)	40	0.02
Japanese (163)	338	0.14
Korean (303)	441	0.18
Laotian (1,040)	1,235	0.50
Malaysian (4)	7	<0.01
Nepalese (9)	9	<0.01
Pakistani (50)	61	0.02
Sri Lankan (6)	6	<0.01
Taiwanese (35)	48	0.02
Thai (220)	311	0.13
Vietnamese (1,893)	2,159	0.88
Hawaii Native/Pacific Islander (135)	420	0.17
Not Hispanic (106)	341	0.14
Hispanic (29)	79	0.03
Fijian (6)	8	<0.01
Guamanian/Chamorro (31)	43	0.02
Native Hawaiian (31)	94	0.04
Samoan (7)	18	0.01
Tongan (23)	28	0.01
White (168,036)	172,891	70.63
Not Hispanic (157,409)	161,333	65.91
Hispanic (10,627)	11,558	4.72

Stuart

Place Type: City
County: Martin
Population: 15,593†

Ancestry‡	Population	%
African, Sub-Saharan (7)	34	0.22
African (0)	27	0.17
South African (7)	7	0.04
Albanian (0)	8	0.05
American (858)	858	5.50
Arab (33)	74	0.47
Egyptian (16)	16	0.10
Palestinian (17)	58	0.37
Australian (0)	11	0.07
Austrian (25)	25	0.16
Belgian (15)	29	0.19
British (28)	67	0.43
Bulgarian (5)	5	0.03
Canadian (16)	16	0.10
Czech (55)	98	0.63
Czechoslovakian (31)	31	0.20
Danish (5)	25	0.16
Dutch (71)	210	1.35
Eastern European (12)	12	0.08
English (787)	1,947	12.49
European (104)	104	0.67
Finnish (9)	9	0.06
French, ex. Basque (98)	455	2.92
French Canadian (248)	380	2.44
German (1,142)	2,963	19.01
Greek (98)	147	0.94
Hungarian (102)	200	1.28
Irish (919)	2,369	15.20
Italian (758)	1,622	10.40
Lithuanian (16)	42	0.27
Maltese (47)	47	0.30
Northern European (15)	15	0.10
Norwegian (46)	110	0.71
Pennsylvania German (27)	27	0.17
Polish (201)	355	2.28
Portuguese (0)	10	0.06
Romanian (0)	27	0.17
Russian (40)	95	0.61
Scandinavian (25)	63	0.40
Scotch-Irish (142)	426	2.73
Scottish (170)	396	2.54
Slovak (0)	9	0.06
Swedish (93)	352	2.26
Swiss (14)	29	0.19
Ukrainian (28)	28	0.18
Welsh (24)	254	1.63
West Indian, ex. Hispanic (244)	244	1.57
Haitian (35)	35	0.22
Jamaican (184)	184	1.18
Trinidadian/Tobagonian (16)	16	0.10
West Indian (9)	9	0.06
Yugoslavian (0)	44	0.28

Hispanic Origin	Population	%
Hispanic or Latino (of any race)	1,923	12.33
Central American, ex. Mexican	487	3.12
Costa Rican	6	0.04
Guatemalan	360	2.31
Honduran	67	0.43
Nicaraguan	22	0.14
Panamanian	7	0.04
Salvadoran	21	0.13
Other Central American	4	0.03
Cuban	131	0.84
Dominican Republic	24	0.15
Mexican	509	3.26
Puerto Rican	433	2.78
South American	201	1.29
Argentinean	29	0.19
Bolivian	3	0.02
Chilean	3	0.02
Colombian	80	0.51
Ecuadorian	27	0.17
Peruvian	22	0.14
Uruguayan	3	0.02
Venezuelan	34	0.22
Other Hispanic or Latino	138	0.89

Race*	Population	%
African-American/Black (1,872)	2,045	13.11
Not Hispanic (1,815)	1,940	12.44
Hispanic (57)	105	0.67
American Indian/Alaska Native (45)	124	0.80
Not Hispanic (28)	87	0.56
Hispanic (17)	37	0.24
Apache (1)	4	0.03
Blackfeet (1)	6	0.04
Canadian/French Am. Ind. (1)	2	0.01
Central American Ind. (3)	3	0.02
Cherokee (3)	14	0.09
Cheyenne (1)	1	0.01
Chippewa (0)	1	0.01
Choctaw (4)	7	0.04
Cree (1)	5	0.03
Creek (0)	2	0.01
Delaware (0)	2	0.01
Iroquois (2)	4	0.03
Mexican American Ind. (12)	18	0.12
Navajo (3)	6	0.04
Osage (0)	1	0.01
Sioux (1)	1	0.01
South American Ind. (1)	7	0.04
Asian (171)	233	1.49
Not Hispanic (171)	230	1.48
Hispanic (0)	3	0.02
Bangladeshi (13)	13	0.08
Burmese (3)	3	0.02
Chinese, ex. Taiwanese (41)	60	0.38
Filipino (26)	40	0.26
Indian (35)	41	0.26
Japanese (16)	30	0.19
Korean (2)	9	0.06

SECTION TWO

*Notes: † The Census 2010 population figure is used to calculate the percentages in the Hispanic Origin and Race categories. Ancestry percentages are based on the 2006-2010 American Community Survey population (not shown); ‡ Numbers in parentheses indicate the number of people reporting a single ancestry; * Numbers in parentheses indicate the number of persons reporting this race alone, not in combination with any other race; Please refer to the Explanation of Data for more information.*

Laotian (0)	4	0.03
Malaysian (2)	2	0.01
Pakistani (5)	5	0.03
Taiwanese (2)	2	0.01
Thai (6)	6	0.04
Vietnamese (15)	19	0.12
Hawaii Native/Pacific Islander (12)	28	0.18
Not Hispanic (10)	26	0.17
Hispanic (2)	2	0.01
Guamanian/Chamorro (0)	2	0.01
Native Hawaiian (6)	14	0.09
Samoan (1)	1	0.01
White (12,467)	12,764	81.86
Not Hispanic (11,392)	11,577	74.24
Hispanic (1,075)	1,187	7.61

Sugarmill Woods

Place Type: CDP
County: Citrus
Population: 8,287†

Ancestry‡	Population	%
American (508)	508	7.00
Arab (22)	22	0.30
Egyptian (22)	22	0.30
Austrian (29)	42	0.58
Basque (45)	45	0.62
Belgian (14)	27	0.37
British (0)	13	0.18
Canadian (85)	98	1.35
Czech (11)	70	0.96
Czechoslovakian (15)	15	0.21
Danish (0)	37	0.51
Dutch (52)	199	2.74
English (394)	1,253	17.27
European (76)	76	1.05
Finnish (0)	14	0.19
French, ex. Basque (63)	435	6.00
French Canadian (38)	93	1.28
German (581)	1,569	21.63
Greek (94)	169	2.33
Hungarian (28)	45	0.62
Irish (528)	1,175	16.20
Italian (261)	636	8.77
Latvian (14)	45	0.62
Lithuanian (17)	26	0.36
Norwegian (16)	41	0.57
Polish (199)	443	6.11
Portuguese (0)	16	0.22
Russian (13)	43	0.59
Scandinavian (0)	27	0.37
Scotch-Irish (95)	156	2.15
Scottish (96)	292	4.02
Swedish (107)	194	2.67
Swiss (13)	47	0.65
Ukrainian (8)	8	0.11
Welsh (26)	127	1.75

Hispanic Origin	Population	%
Hispanic or Latino (of any race)	297	3.58
Central American, ex. Mexican	18	0.22
Guatemalan	3	0.04
Honduran	6	0.07
Nicaraguan	3	0.04
Panamanian	4	0.05
Salvadoran	2	0.02
Cuban	39	0.47
Dominican Republic	15	0.18
Mexican	49	0.59
Puerto Rican	123	1.48
South American	24	0.29
Argentinean	7	0.08
Bolivian	2	0.02
Chilean	2	0.02
Colombian	1	0.01
Ecuadorian	6	0.07
Peruvian	4	0.05
Venezuelan	1	0.01
Other South American	1	0.01
Other Hispanic or Latino	29	0.35

Race*	Population	%
African-American/Black (153)	175	2.11
Not Hispanic (146)	159	1.92
Hispanic (7)	16	0.19
American Indian/Alaska Native (13)	43	0.52
Not Hispanic (12)	41	0.49
Hispanic (1)	2	0.02
Cherokee (1)	11	0.13
Chippewa (1)	5	0.06
Cree (0)	2	0.02
Creek (0)	1	0.01
Ottawa (1)	1	0.01
Seminole (1)	1	0.01
Sioux (3)	6	0.07
Spanish American Ind. (1)	2	0.02
Asian (112)	135	1.63
Not Hispanic (110)	130	1.57
Hispanic (2)	5	0.06
Cambodian (1)	1	0.01
Chinese, ex. Taiwanese (14)	27	0.33
Filipino (53)	54	0.65
Indian (2)	5	0.06
Japanese (8)	12	0.14
Korean (1)	1	0.01
Pakistani (12)	12	0.14
Taiwanese (2)	2	0.02
Thai (4)	4	0.05
Vietnamese (14)	15	0.18
Hawaii Native/Pacific Islander (1)	3	0.04
Not Hispanic (1)	3	0.04
Native Hawaiian (1)	1	0.01
Samoan (0)	1	0.01
White (7,875)	7,958	96.03
Not Hispanic (7,652)	7,714	93.09
Hispanic (223)	244	2.94

Sun City Center

Place Type: CDP
County: Hillsborough
Population: 19,258†

Ancestry‡	Population	%
African, Sub-Saharan (13)	27	0.14
African (13)	27	0.14
American (1,598)	1,598	8.38
Arab (15)	41	0.22
Lebanese (15)	28	0.15
Syrian (0)	13	0.07
Armenian (0)	14	0.07
Assyrian/Chaldean/Syriac (0)	14	0.07
Australian (12)	12	0.06
Austrian (41)	86	0.45
Belgian (13)	74	0.39
British (44)	59	0.31
Bulgarian (12)	12	0.06
Canadian (79)	103	0.54
Croatian (42)	52	0.27
Czech (92)	125	0.66
Czechoslovakian (46)	46	0.24
Danish (78)	185	0.97
Dutch (232)	516	2.71
Eastern European (52)	52	0.27
English (1,766)	3,925	20.59
European (190)	190	1.00
Finnish (13)	26	0.14
French, ex. Basque (206)	696	3.65
French Canadian (266)	334	1.75
German (2,277)	4,605	24.16
German Russian (0)	20	0.10
Greek (60)	66	0.35
Hungarian (76)	112	0.59
Irish (1,341)	3,162	16.59
Italian (1,103)	1,480	7.76
Latvian (0)	8	0.04
Lithuanian (30)	54	0.28
Norwegian (162)	271	1.42
Pennsylvania German (13)	26	0.14
Polish (510)	912	4.78
Portuguese (58)	58	0.30
Romanian (8)	8	0.04
Russian (140)	213	1.12
Scandinavian (10)	36	0.19
Scotch-Irish (371)	657	3.45
Scottish (210)	718	3.77
Slavic (0)	12	0.06
Slovak (13)	13	0.07
Slovene (13)	19	0.10
Swedish (113)	355	1.86
Swiss (24)	133	0.70
Turkish (0)	14	0.07
Ukrainian (0)	13	0.07
Welsh (94)	287	1.51
West Indian, ex. Hispanic (0)	20	0.10
Other West Indian (0)	20	0.10
Yugoslavian (34)	34	0.18

Hispanic Origin	Population	%
Hispanic or Latino (of any race)	614	3.19
Central American, ex. Mexican	34	0.18
Costa Rican	8	0.04
Guatemalan	2	0.01
Honduran	6	0.03
Nicaraguan	3	0.02
Panamanian	14	0.07
Salvadoran	1	0.01
Cuban	70	0.36
Dominican Republic	26	0.14
Mexican	114	0.59
Puerto Rican	244	1.27
South American	64	0.33
Argentinean	4	0.02
Bolivian	3	0.02
Chilean	2	0.01
Colombian	37	0.19
Ecuadorian	11	0.06
Peruvian	1	0.01
Venezuelan	6	0.03
Other Hispanic or Latino	62	0.32

Race*	Population	%
African-American/Black (394)	429	2.23
Not Hispanic (378)	409	2.12
Hispanic (16)	20	0.10
American Indian/Alaska Native (23)	65	0.34
Not Hispanic (16)	56	0.29
Hispanic (7)	9	0.05
Cherokee (6)	19	0.10
Chippewa (0)	1	0.01
Choctaw (1)	1	0.01
Creek (1)	1	0.01
Iroquois (0)	1	0.01
Lumbee (1)	1	0.01
Mexican American Ind. (1)	1	0.01
Navajo (1)	1	0.01
Osage (0)	1	0.01
Seminole (2)	2	0.01
South American Ind. (1)	2	0.01
Asian (170)	205	1.06
Not Hispanic (169)	200	1.04
Hispanic (1)	5	0.03
Chinese, ex. Taiwanese (22)	30	0.16
Filipino (35)	52	0.27
Hmong (1)	2	0.01
Indian (39)	41	0.21
Indonesian (1)	1	0.01
Japanese (28)	32	0.17
Korean (16)	22	0.11
Laotian (1)	1	0.01
Pakistani (2)	2	0.01
Taiwanese (3)	3	0.02
Thai (7)	7	0.04
Vietnamese (13)	14	0.07
Hawaii Native/Pacific Islander (8)	21	0.11
Not Hispanic (7)	16	0.08
Hispanic (1)	5	0.03
Guamanian/Chamorro (2)	2	0.01
Native Hawaiian (1)	6	0.03

*Notes: † The Census 2010 population figure is used to calculate the percentages in the Hispanic Origin and Race categories. Ancestry percentages are based on the 2006-2010 American Community Survey population (not shown); ‡ Numbers in parentheses indicate the number of people reporting a single ancestry; * Numbers in parentheses indicate the number of persons reporting this race alone, not in combination with any other race; Please refer to the Explanation of Data for more information.*

White (18,446)	18,561	96.38
Not Hispanic (17,968)	18,063	93.79
Hispanic (478)	498	2.59

Sunny Isles Beach

Place Type: City
County: Miami-Dade
Population: 20,832†

Ancestry‡	Population	%
African, Sub-Saharan (84)	84	0.42
African (64)	64	0.32
Nigerian (20)	20	0.10
American (1,228)	1,228	6.21
Arab (100)	173	0.87
Egyptian (40)	40	0.20
Lebanese (15)	73	0.37
Moroccan (0)	15	0.08
Syrian (23)	23	0.12
Other Arab (22)	22	0.11
Armenian (36)	36	0.18
Austrian (4)	95	0.48
Belgian (0)	15	0.08
Brazilian (138)	156	0.79
British (86)	113	0.57
Bulgarian (19)	19	0.10
Canadian (108)	123	0.62
Croatian (0)	35	0.18
Czech (21)	51	0.26
Czechoslovakian (0)	19	0.10
Danish (0)	39	0.20
Dutch (32)	94	0.48
Eastern European (55)	55	0.28
English (173)	313	1.58
European (119)	119	0.60
French, ex. Basque (209)	393	1.99
French Canadian (106)	152	0.77
German (424)	877	4.43
Greek (47)	96	0.49
Hungarian (118)	191	0.97
Iranian (72)	72	0.36
Irish (174)	477	2.41
Israeli (420)	432	2.18
Italian (705)	1,199	6.06
Lithuanian (22)	22	0.11
Norwegian (92)	177	0.89
Polish (731)	1,032	5.22
Portuguese (42)	79	0.40
Romanian (21)	79	0.40
Russian (1,469)	1,839	9.30
Scotch-Irish (0)	20	0.10
Scottish (26)	75	0.38
Serbian (13)	13	0.07
Swedish (0)	25	0.13
Swiss (14)	14	0.07
Turkish (92)	126	0.64
Ukrainian (249)	265	1.34
Welsh (14)	42	0.21
West Indian, ex. Hispanic (35)	65	0.33
Dutch West Indian (0)	30	0.15
Haitian (16)	16	0.08
Jamaican (19)	19	0.10
Yugoslavian (40)	40	0.20

Hispanic Origin	Population	%
Hispanic or Latino (of any race)	9,247	44.39
Central American, ex. Mexican	398	1.91
Costa Rican	70	0.34
Guatemalan	55	0.26
Honduran	99	0.48
Nicaraguan	82	0.39
Panamanian	43	0.21
Salvadoran	47	0.23
Other Central American	2	0.01
Cuban	1,990	9.55
Dominican Republic	285	1.37
Mexican	286	1.37
Puerto Rican	490	2.35
South American	5,237	25.14
Argentinean	1,032	4.95
Bolivian	50	0.24
Chilean	146	0.70
Colombian	2,175	10.44
Ecuadorian	246	1.18
Paraguayan	17	0.08
Peruvian	653	3.13
Uruguayan	170	0.82
Venezuelan	734	3.52
Other South American	14	0.07
Other Hispanic or Latino	561	2.69

Race*	Population	%
African-American/Black (662)	797	3.83
Not Hispanic (552)	608	2.92
Hispanic (110)	189	0.91
American Indian/Alaska Native (34)	72	0.35
Not Hispanic (22)	42	0.20
Hispanic (12)	30	0.14
Canadian/French Am. Ind. (0)	1	<0.01
Central American Ind. (0)	1	<0.01
Cherokee (2)	2	0.01
Chippewa (5)	5	0.02
Creek (1)	1	<0.01
Mexican American Ind. (2)	2	0.01
Seminole (1)	1	<0.01
Sioux (1)	1	<0.01
South American Ind. (4)	14	0.07
Tlingit-Haida *(Alaska Native)* (1)	2	0.01
Asian (292)	431	2.07
Not Hispanic (287)	398	1.91
Hispanic (5)	33	0.16
Bangladeshi (2)	6	0.03
Cambodian (1)	2	0.01
Chinese, ex. Taiwanese (53)	75	0.36
Filipino (28)	33	0.16
Hmong (2)	2	0.01
Indian (90)	121	0.58
Indonesian (4)	4	0.02
Japanese (35)	47	0.23
Korean (29)	40	0.19
Pakistani (9)	20	0.10
Sri Lankan (1)	2	0.01
Taiwanese (5)	5	0.02
Thai (7)	9	0.04
Vietnamese (6)	9	0.04
Hawaii Native/Pacific Islander (2)	12	0.06
Not Hispanic (2)	9	0.04
Hispanic (0)	3	0.01
Guamanian/Chamorro (0)	1	<0.01
Native Hawaiian (0)	1	<0.01
White (18,883)	19,287	92.58
Not Hispanic (10,457)	10,645	51.10
Hispanic (8,426)	8,642	41.48

Sunrise

Place Type: City
County: Broward
Population: 84,439†

Ancestry‡	Population	%
African, Sub-Saharan (527)	684	0.80
African (433)	542	0.64
Nigerian (94)	118	0.14
Zimbabwean (0)	12	0.01
Other Sub-Saharan African (0)	12	0.01
Albanian (24)	24	0.03
American (2,809)	2,809	3.30
Arab (427)	533	0.63
Arab (44)	100	0.12
Egyptian (55)	55	0.06
Jordanian (68)	68	0.08
Lebanese (180)	210	0.25
Moroccan (0)	12	0.01
Palestinian (23)	31	0.04
Other Arab (57)	57	0.07
Armenian (151)	151	0.18
Austrian (98)	305	0.36
Brazilian (544)	582	0.68
British (225)	246	0.29
Canadian (245)	319	0.37
Croatian (19)	50	0.06
Czech (80)	199	0.23
Czechoslovakian (25)	35	0.04
Danish (72)	163	0.19
Dutch (162)	584	0.69
Eastern European (24)	39	0.05
English (687)	2,562	3.01
European (479)	522	0.61
Finnish (0)	23	0.03
French, ex. Basque (468)	1,282	1.51
French Canadian (254)	268	0.32
German (1,789)	5,341	6.28
Greek (323)	377	0.44
Guyanese (122)	170	0.20
Hungarian (454)	738	0.87
Iranian (132)	143	0.17
Irish (1,564)	4,872	5.73
Israeli (225)	238	0.28
Italian (3,871)	6,702	7.88
Latvian (31)	45	0.05
Lithuanian (10)	81	0.10
Luxemburger (0)	12	0.01
Maltese (42)	42	0.05
New Zealander (0)	7	0.01
Norwegian (80)	210	0.25
Pennsylvania German (15)	53	0.06
Polish (899)	2,451	2.88
Portuguese (88)	221	0.26
Romanian (238)	378	0.44
Russian (1,212)	2,230	2.62
Scandinavian (0)	10	0.01
Scotch-Irish (167)	484	0.57
Scottish (238)	658	0.77
Serbian (10)	10	0.01
Slavic (11)	18	0.02
Slovak (13)	44	0.05
Slovene (15)	15	0.02
Swedish (22)	197	0.23
Swiss (10)	50	0.06
Turkish (21)	64	0.08
Ukrainian (97)	189	0.22
Welsh (13)	71	0.08
West Indian, ex. Hispanic (16,066)	18,263	21.47
Bahamian (356)	576	0.68
Barbadian (59)	59	0.07
Belizean (24)	24	0.03
British West Indian (91)	108	0.13
Dutch West Indian (49)	49	0.06
Haitian (4,725)	5,128	6.03
Jamaican (9,740)	10,844	12.75
Trinidadian/Tobagonian (637)	828	0.97
U.S. Virgin Islander (120)	141	0.17
West Indian (265)	506	0.59
Yugoslavian (10)	26	0.03

Hispanic Origin	Population	%
Hispanic or Latino (of any race)	21,621	25.61
Central American, ex. Mexican	1,785	2.11
Costa Rican	166	0.20
Guatemalan	280	0.33
Honduran	401	0.47
Nicaraguan	338	0.40
Panamanian	244	0.29
Salvadoran	346	0.41
Other Central American	10	0.01
Cuban	2,956	3.50
Dominican Republic	1,387	1.64
Mexican	722	0.86
Puerto Rican	4,210	4.99
South American	9,204	10.90
Argentinean	451	0.53
Bolivian	64	0.08
Chilean	171	0.20
Colombian	4,592	5.44
Ecuadorian	995	1.18
Paraguayan	15	0.02
Peruvian	1,503	1.78
Uruguayan	135	0.16

*Notes: † The Census 2010 population figure is used to calculate the percentages in the Hispanic Origin and Race categories. Ancestry percentages are based on the 2006-2010 American Community Survey population (not shown); ‡ Numbers in parentheses indicate the number of people reporting a single ancestry; * Numbers in parentheses indicate the number of persons reporting this race alone, not in combination with any other race; Please refer to the Explanation of Data for more information.*

Venezuelan	1,241	1.47
Other South American	37	0.04
Other Hispanic or Latino	1,357	1.61

Race*	Population	%
African-American/Black (26,863)	28,432	33.67
Not Hispanic (25,950)	27,127	32.13
Hispanic (913)	1,305	1.55
American Indian/Alaska Native (256)	504	0.60
Not Hispanic (159)	324	0.38
Hispanic (97)	180	0.21
Alaska Athabascan *(Ala. Nat.)* (2)	2	<0.01
Apache (0)	1	<0.01
Blackfeet (1)	9	0.01
Canadian/French Am. Ind. (2)	3	<0.01
Central American Ind. (8)	13	0.02
Cherokee (9)	46	0.05
Cheyenne (3)	3	<0.01
Chickasaw (0)	3	<0.01
Chippewa (4)	8	0.01
Choctaw (0)	2	<0.01
Creek (0)	1	<0.01
Delaware (1)	4	<0.01
Iroquois (9)	17	0.02
Lumbee (0)	3	<0.01
Menominee (0)	1	<0.01
Mexican American Ind. (11)	16	0.02
Navajo (1)	1	<0.01
Osage (1)	1	<0.01
Pima (1)	2	<0.01
Potawatomi (0)	1	<0.01
Pueblo (1)	2	<0.01
Seminole (13)	16	0.02
Sioux (7)	15	0.02
South American Ind. (28)	59	0.07
Spanish American Ind. (5)	10	0.01
Tlingit-Haida *(Alaska Native)* (0)	7	0.01
Tsimshian *(Alaska Native)* (1)	1	<0.01
Asian (3,439)	4,279	5.07
Not Hispanic (3,374)	4,072	4.82
Hispanic (65)	207	0.25
Bangladeshi (31)	51	0.06
Burmese (7)	7	0.01
Cambodian (1)	1	<0.01
Chinese, ex. Taiwanese (750)	974	1.15
Filipino (313)	421	0.50
Hmong (1)	1	<0.01
Indian (1,385)	1,645	1.95
Indonesian (8)	16	0.02
Japanese (46)	96	0.11
Korean (125)	155	0.18
Laotian (21)	27	0.03
Malaysian (2)	6	0.01
Nepalese (6)	8	0.01
Pakistani (265)	304	0.36
Sri Lankan (9)	10	0.01
Taiwanese (13)	16	0.02
Thai (33)	47	0.06
Vietnamese (270)	292	0.35
Hawaii Native/Pacific Islander (71)	286	0.34
Not Hispanic (65)	255	0.30
Hispanic (6)	31	0.04
Fijian (4)	5	0.01
Guamanian/Chamorro (5)	9	0.01
Native Hawaiian (9)	28	0.03
Samoan (9)	14	0.02
Tongan (1)	3	<0.01
White (47,622)	49,461	58.58
Not Hispanic (31,016)	31,985	37.88
Hispanic (16,606)	17,476	20.70

Sunset

Place Type: CDP
County: Miami-Dade
Population: 16,389†

Ancestry‡	Population	%
American (595)	595	3.65
Arab (34)	117	0.72
Arab (12)	12	0.07
Lebanese (22)	85	0.52
Other Arab (0)	20	0.12
Austrian (53)	71	0.44
Belgian (0)	9	0.06
British (19)	46	0.28
Bulgarian (0)	23	0.14
Canadian (29)	41	0.25
Czech (0)	9	0.06
Dutch (12)	12	0.07
English (60)	236	1.45
French, ex. Basque (0)	53	0.33
German (34)	465	2.85
Hungarian (12)	89	0.55
Irish (11)	260	1.60
Italian (135)	626	3.84
Lithuanian (12)	12	0.07
Norwegian (39)	48	0.29
Polish (11)	147	0.90
Portuguese (7)	41	0.25
Russian (0)	82	0.50
Scotch-Irish (12)	112	0.69
Scottish (0)	84	0.52
Slavic (12)	12	0.07
Slovak (0)	12	0.07
Swiss (0)	14	0.09
Ukrainian (0)	53	0.33
West Indian, ex. Hispanic (35)	41	0.25
Belizean (35)	35	0.21
Jamaican (0)	6	0.04

Hispanic Origin	Population	%
Hispanic or Latino (of any race)	13,164	80.32
Central American, ex. Mexican	920	5.61
Costa Rican	36	0.22
Guatemalan	77	0.47
Honduran	125	0.76
Nicaraguan	549	3.35
Panamanian	37	0.23
Salvadoran	96	0.59
Cuban	9,552	58.28
Dominican Republic	150	0.92
Mexican	171	1.04
Puerto Rican	416	2.54
South American	1,414	8.63
Argentinean	131	0.80
Bolivian	42	0.26
Chilean	94	0.57
Colombian	572	3.49
Ecuadorian	110	0.67
Paraguayan	3	0.02
Peruvian	236	1.44
Uruguayan	25	0.15
Venezuelan	200	1.22
Other South American	1	0.01
Other Hispanic or Latino	541	3.30

Race*	Population	%
African-American/Black (210)	280	1.71
Not Hispanic (109)	147	0.90
Hispanic (101)	133	0.81
American Indian/Alaska Native (10)	29	0.18
Not Hispanic (2)	16	0.10
Hispanic (8)	13	0.08
Cherokee (0)	4	0.02
Creek (1)	1	0.01
Iroquois (0)	2	0.01
Mexican American Ind. (1)	1	0.01
Potawatomi (0)	2	0.01
Sioux (0)	1	0.01
South American Ind. (1)	2	0.01
Asian (334)	420	2.56
Not Hispanic (315)	368	2.25
Hispanic (19)	52	0.32
Bangladeshi (0)	1	0.01
Chinese, ex. Taiwanese (125)	175	1.07
Filipino (52)	57	0.35
Indian (74)	87	0.53
Japanese (9)	15	0.09
Korean (9)	13	0.08
Pakistani (10)	18	0.11
Sri Lankan (2)	2	0.01
Thai (11)	15	0.09
Vietnamese (20)	28	0.17
Hawaii Native/Pacific Islander (0)	7	0.04
Not Hispanic (0)	6	0.04
Hispanic (0)	1	0.01
Guamanian/Chamorro (0)	1	0.01
White (15,313)	15,505	94.61
Not Hispanic (2,666)	2,742	16.73
Hispanic (12,647)	12,763	77.88

Sweetwater

Place Type: City
County: Miami-Dade
Population: 13,499†

Ancestry‡	Population	%
American (65)	65	0.48
German (0)	6	0.04
Hungarian (0)	6	0.04
Irish (14)	14	0.10
Italian (75)	89	0.65

Hispanic Origin	Population	%
Hispanic or Latino (of any race)	12,894	95.52
Central American, ex. Mexican	3,538	26.21
Costa Rican	35	0.26
Guatemalan	42	0.31
Honduran	247	1.83
Nicaraguan	3,102	22.98
Panamanian	24	0.18
Salvadoran	78	0.58
Other Central American	10	0.07
Cuban	7,672	56.83
Dominican Republic	120	0.89
Mexican	118	0.87
Puerto Rican	164	1.21
South American	804	5.96
Argentinean	62	0.46
Bolivian	13	0.10
Chilean	50	0.37
Colombian	354	2.62
Ecuadorian	63	0.47
Paraguayan	4	0.03
Peruvian	125	0.93
Uruguayan	13	0.10
Venezuelan	119	0.88
Other South American	1	0.01
Other Hispanic or Latino	478	3.54

Race*	Population	%
African-American/Black (240)	293	2.17
Not Hispanic (44)	48	0.36
Hispanic (196)	245	1.81
American Indian/Alaska Native (33)	43	0.32
Not Hispanic (3)	5	0.04
Hispanic (30)	38	0.28
Central American Ind. (4)	5	0.04
Mexican American Ind. (3)	4	0.03
Pueblo (1)	1	0.01
Spanish American Ind. (3)	3	0.02
Asian (72)	90	0.67
Not Hispanic (66)	72	0.53
Hispanic (6)	18	0.13
Chinese, ex. Taiwanese (46)	55	0.41
Filipino (2)	6	0.04
Indian (13)	15	0.11
Indonesian (1)	2	0.01
Japanese (0)	1	0.01
Korean (1)	1	0.01
Malaysian (1)	1	0.01
Pakistani (1)	2	0.01
Taiwanese (2)	2	0.01
Vietnamese (5)	5	0.04
Hawaii Native/Pacific Islander (0)	3	0.02
Hispanic (0)	3	0.02
Native Hawaiian (0)	2	0.01
White (12,471)	12,729	94.30

*Notes: † The Census 2010 population figure is used to calculate the percentages in the Hispanic Origin and Race categories. Ancestry percentages are based on the 2006-2010 American Community Survey population (not shown); ‡ Numbers in parentheses indicate the number of people reporting a single ancestry; * Numbers in parentheses indicate the number of persons reporting this race alone, not in combination with any other race; Please refer to the Explanation of Data for more information.*

Not Hispanic (475)	486	3.60
Hispanic (11,996)	12,243	90.70

Tallahassee

Place Type: City
County: Leon
Population: 181,376†

Ancestry‡	Population	%
African, Sub-Saharan (9,225)	9,997	5.65
African (8,550)	9,217	5.21
Cape Verdean (0)	60	0.03
Ethiopian (38)	59	0.03
Ghanaian (78)	78	0.04
Kenyan (17)	17	0.01
Nigerian (303)	303	0.17
Senegalese (38)	38	0.02
South African (25)	25	0.01
Ugandan (11)	11	0.01
Other Sub-Saharan African (165)	189	0.11
Albanian (68)	68	0.04
American (7,126)	7,126	4.03
Arab (539)	868	0.49
Arab (61)	90	0.05
Egyptian (158)	185	0.10
Lebanese (137)	312	0.18
Moroccan (45)	45	0.03
Palestinian (113)	142	0.08
Syrian (15)	84	0.05
Other Arab (10)	10	0.01
Armenian (59)	226	0.13
Australian (6)	24	0.01
Austrian (88)	438	0.25
Basque (0)	52	0.03
Belgian (34)	148	0.08
Brazilian (19)	127	0.07
British (556)	1,112	0.63
Bulgarian (9)	9	0.01
Cajun (0)	40	0.02
Canadian (162)	524	0.30
Celtic (16)	32	0.02
Croatian (11)	93	0.05
Czech (157)	904	0.51
Czechoslovakian (86)	212	0.12
Danish (150)	449	0.25
Dutch (546)	1,745	0.99
Eastern European (158)	199	0.11
English (6,302)	16,491	9.33
European (1,409)	1,665	0.94
Finnish (163)	258	0.15
French, ex. Basque (813)	4,527	2.56
French Canadian (197)	648	0.37
German (5,091)	19,225	10.87
Greek (299)	917	0.52
Guyanese (107)	178	0.10
Hungarian (252)	827	0.47
Iranian (209)	334	0.19
Irish (5,533)	19,003	10.75
Israeli (81)	81	0.05
Italian (3,034)	8,891	5.03
Latvian (6)	25	0.01
Lithuanian (74)	311	0.18
Macedonian (7)	29	0.02
Maltese (0)	16	0.01
Northern European (175)	187	0.11
Norwegian (430)	1,307	0.74
Pennsylvania German (32)	82	0.05
Polish (1,092)	3,950	2.23
Portuguese (84)	312	0.18
Romanian (24)	215	0.12
Russian (456)	1,423	0.80
Scandinavian (0)	76	0.04
Scotch-Irish (2,060)	4,512	2.55
Scottish (1,445)	4,424	2.50
Serbian (81)	172	0.10
Slavic (29)	94	0.05
Slovak (51)	277	0.16
Slovene (54)	72	0.04
Swedish (352)	1,442	0.82
Swiss (29)	296	0.17
Turkish (143)	211	0.12
Ukrainian (72)	273	0.15
Welsh (331)	1,611	0.91
West Indian, ex. Hispanic (3,080)	4,789	2.71
Bahamian (146)	349	0.20
Barbadian (29)	29	0.02
Belizean (0)	49	0.03
Bermudan (32)	47	0.03
British West Indian (54)	54	0.03
Dutch West Indian (30)	45	0.03
Haitian (1,281)	1,735	0.98
Jamaican (1,103)	1,644	0.93
Trinidadian/Tobagonian (144)	196	0.11
U.S. Virgin Islander (59)	203	0.11
West Indian (202)	420	0.24
Other West Indian (0)	18	0.01
Yugoslavian (58)	169	0.10

Hispanic Origin	Population	%
Hispanic or Latino (of any race)	11,346	6.26
Central American, ex. Mexican	1,170	0.65
Costa Rican	79	0.04
Guatemalan	160	0.09
Honduran	231	0.13
Nicaraguan	221	0.12
Panamanian	255	0.14
Salvadoran	218	0.12
Other Central American	6	<0.01
Cuban	2,302	1.27
Dominican Republic	372	0.21
Mexican	2,354	1.30
Puerto Rican	2,275	1.25
South American	1,701	0.94
Argentinean	121	0.07
Bolivian	56	0.03
Chilean	75	0.04
Colombian	800	0.44
Ecuadorian	106	0.06
Paraguayan	21	0.01
Peruvian	244	0.13
Uruguayan	21	0.01
Venezuelan	245	0.14
Other South American	12	0.01
Other Hispanic or Latino	1,172	0.65

Race*	Population	%
African-American/Black (63,475)	65,685	36.21
Not Hispanic (62,538)	64,409	35.51
Hispanic (937)	1,276	0.70
American Indian/Alaska Native (443)	1,421	0.78
Not Hispanic (381)	1,237	0.68
Hispanic (62)	184	0.10
Apache (7)	21	0.01
Blackfeet (5)	34	0.02
Canadian/French Am. Ind. (0)	3	<0.01
Central American Ind. (1)	4	<0.01
Cherokee (65)	335	0.18
Cheyenne (1)	7	<0.01
Chickasaw (3)	7	<0.01
Chippewa (4)	16	0.01
Choctaw (7)	29	0.02
Comanche (1)	6	<0.01
Cree (0)	2	<0.01
Creek (41)	83	0.05
Crow (0)	5	<0.01
Delaware (5)	13	0.01
Inupiat *(Alaska Native)* (2)	6	<0.01
Iroquois (5)	22	0.01
Kiowa (3)	5	<0.01
Lumbee (5)	9	<0.01
Mexican American Ind. (3)	21	0.01
Navajo (0)	7	<0.01
Osage (2)	4	<0.01
Ottawa (2)	6	<0.01
Pima (1)	1	<0.01
Potawatomi (1)	6	<0.01
Pueblo (3)	3	<0.01
Seminole (6)	38	0.02
Sioux (9)	22	0.01
South American Ind. (7)	13	0.01
Spanish American Ind. (1)	2	<0.01
Tohono O'Odham (2)	3	<0.01
Tsimshian *(Alaska Native)* (0)	4	<0.01
Ute (1)	1	<0.01
Yakama (0)	1	<0.01
Asian (6,653)	7,926	4.37
Not Hispanic (6,566)	7,697	4.24
Hispanic (87)	229	0.13
Bangladeshi (32)	38	0.02
Burmese (20)	20	0.01
Cambodian (24)	30	0.02
Chinese, ex. Taiwanese (1,638)	1,866	1.03
Filipino (585)	914	0.50
Hmong (3)	4	<0.01
Indian (2,219)	2,415	1.33
Indonesian (48)	56	0.03
Japanese (154)	337	0.19
Korean (768)	899	0.50
Laotian (10)	14	0.01
Malaysian (11)	18	0.01
Nepalese (28)	31	0.02
Pakistani (171)	195	0.11
Sri Lankan (21)	22	0.01
Taiwanese (112)	133	0.07
Thai (59)	106	0.06
Vietnamese (523)	602	0.33
Hawaii Native/Pacific Islander (100)	273	0.15
Not Hispanic (88)	235	0.13
Hispanic (12)	38	0.02
Guamanian/Chamorro (18)	47	0.03
Native Hawaiian (37)	93	0.05
Samoan (16)	31	0.02
Tongan (5)	8	<0.01
White (104,171)	107,544	59.29
Not Hispanic (96,753)	99,500	54.86
Hispanic (7,418)	8,044	4.43

Tamarac

Place Type: City
County: Broward
Population: 60,427†

Ancestry‡	Population	%
African, Sub-Saharan (233)	282	0.47
African (143)	192	0.32
Kenyan (33)	33	0.06
Nigerian (46)	46	0.08
South African (11)	11	0.02
American (2,598)	2,598	4.34
Arab (331)	380	0.64
Arab (15)	15	0.03
Egyptian (30)	30	0.05
Lebanese (62)	62	0.10
Moroccan (0)	32	0.05
Palestinian (218)	218	0.36
Syrian (0)	17	0.03
Other Arab (6)	6	0.01
Armenian (10)	32	0.05
Austrian (215)	498	0.83
Belgian (14)	65	0.11
Brazilian (151)	169	0.28
British (48)	160	0.27
Bulgarian (20)	33	0.06
Canadian (144)	206	0.34
Celtic (30)	30	0.05
Croatian (0)	6	0.01
Czech (70)	110	0.18
Czechoslovakian (37)	37	0.06
Dutch (116)	348	0.58
Eastern European (255)	255	0.43
English (1,028)	2,353	3.94
European (424)	465	0.78
Finnish (14)	27	0.05
French, ex. Basque (254)	914	1.53
French Canadian (292)	351	0.59
German (1,590)	3,867	6.47
Greek (329)	479	0.80
Guyanese (362)	398	0.67

*Notes: † The Census 2010 population figure is used to calculate the percentages in the Hispanic Origin and Race categories. Ancestry percentages are based on the 2006-2010 American Community Survey population (not shown); ‡ Numbers in parentheses indicate the number of people reporting a single ancestry; * Numbers in parentheses indicate the number of persons reporting this race alone, not in combination with any other race; Please refer to the Explanation of Data for more information.*

Ancestry	Population	%
Hungarian (586)	958	1.60
Iranian (101)	139	0.23
Irish (1,672)	4,114	6.88
Israeli (45)	45	0.08
Italian (3,591)	5,107	8.54
Latvian (20)	20	0.03
Lithuanian (48)	131	0.22
Macedonian (13)	13	0.02
Northern European (40)	40	0.07
Norwegian (98)	231	0.39
Pennsylvania German (21)	29	0.05
Polish (1,812)	3,404	5.69
Portuguese (59)	106	0.18
Romanian (550)	706	1.18
Russian (1,847)	2,736	4.58
Scandinavian (12)	12	0.02
Scotch-Irish (133)	390	0.65
Scottish (126)	326	0.55
Slavic (0)	13	0.02
Slovak (14)	25	0.04
Slovene (0)	8	0.01
Swedish (223)	350	0.59
Swiss (33)	98	0.16
Turkish (107)	119	0.20
Ukrainian (196)	232	0.39
Welsh (36)	116	0.19
West Indian, ex. Hispanic (6,493)	6,937	11.60
Bahamian (78)	100	0.17
Belizean (82)	82	0.14
British West Indian (115)	147	0.25
Dutch West Indian (18)	18	0.03
Haitian (2,097)	2,124	3.55
Jamaican (3,546)	3,828	6.40
Trinidadian/Tobagonian (355)	422	0.71
U.S. Virgin Islander (33)	33	0.06
West Indian (169)	183	0.31
Yugoslavian (0)	24	0.04

Hispanic Origin	Population	%
Hispanic or Latino (of any race)	14,713	24.35
Central American, ex. Mexican	1,205	1.99
Costa Rican	106	0.18
Guatemalan	151	0.25
Honduran	252	0.42
Nicaraguan	183	0.30
Panamanian	186	0.31
Salvadoran	326	0.54
Other Central American	1	<0.01
Cuban	1,510	2.50
Dominican Republic	815	1.35
Mexican	617	1.02
Puerto Rican	3,029	5.01
South American	6,607	10.93
Argentinean	370	0.61
Bolivian	59	0.10
Chilean	129	0.21
Colombian	3,762	6.23
Ecuadorian	516	0.85
Paraguayan	19	0.03
Peruvian	966	1.60
Uruguayan	125	0.21
Venezuelan	643	1.06
Other South American	18	0.03
Other Hispanic or Latino	930	1.54

Race*	Population	%
African-American/Black (13,940)	14,798	24.49
Not Hispanic (13,304)	13,990	23.15
Hispanic (636)	808	1.34
American Indian/Alaska Native (109)	285	0.47
Not Hispanic (73)	187	0.31
Hispanic (36)	98	0.16
Blackfeet (1)	5	0.01
Canadian/French Am. Ind. (3)	3	<0.01
Central American Ind. (2)	2	<0.01
Cherokee (10)	28	0.05
Cheyenne (0)	2	<0.01
Chippewa (1)	3	<0.01
Choctaw (0)	1	<0.01
Creek (0)	5	0.01
Delaware (1)	1	<0.01
Iroquois (2)	6	0.01
Lumbee (1)	2	<0.01
Mexican American Ind. (1)	1	<0.01
Navajo (4)	7	0.01
Ottawa (0)	1	<0.01
Puget Sound Salish (0)	1	<0.01
Seminole (0)	1	<0.01
Sioux (4)	4	0.01
South American Ind. (3)	12	0.02
Spanish American Ind. (4)	5	0.01
Tlingit-Haida *(Alaska Native)* (0)	1	<0.01
Asian (1,524)	1,957	3.24
Not Hispanic (1,504)	1,868	3.09
Hispanic (20)	89	0.15
Bangladeshi (40)	47	0.08
Burmese (3)	3	<0.01
Cambodian (1)	1	<0.01
Chinese, ex. Taiwanese (313)	426	0.70
Filipino (137)	185	0.31
Hmong (1)	1	<0.01
Indian (635)	769	1.27
Indonesian (2)	2	<0.01
Japanese (21)	39	0.06
Korean (50)	75	0.12
Laotian (4)	5	0.01
Malaysian (1)	5	0.01
Pakistani (100)	110	0.18
Sri Lankan (1)	1	<0.01
Taiwanese (7)	12	0.02
Thai (25)	36	0.06
Vietnamese (131)	148	0.24
Hawaii Native/Pacific Islander (25)	120	0.20
Not Hispanic (18)	100	0.17
Hispanic (7)	20	0.03
Fijian (0)	3	<0.01
Guamanian/Chamorro (2)	2	<0.01
Native Hawaiian (5)	18	0.03
Samoan (1)	1	<0.01
White (40,613)	41,825	69.22
Not Hispanic (29,579)	30,173	49.93
Hispanic (11,034)	11,652	19.28

Tamiami

Place Type: CDP
County: Miami-Dade
Population: 55,271†

Ancestry‡	Population	%
African, Sub-Saharan (101)	123	0.22
African (0)	12	0.02
Nigerian (101)	101	0.18
Other Sub-Saharan African (0)	10	0.02
American (452)	452	0.83
Arab (83)	178	0.33
Arab (34)	61	0.11
Lebanese (49)	105	0.19
Syrian (0)	12	0.02
Austrian (0)	10	0.02
Brazilian (41)	72	0.13
English (7)	69	0.13
European (74)	74	0.14
French, ex. Basque (35)	128	0.23
French Canadian (8)	8	0.01
German (101)	337	0.62
Hungarian (13)	13	0.02
Iranian (30)	75	0.14
Irish (261)	538	0.98
Israeli (24)	24	0.04
Italian (261)	613	1.12
Norwegian (0)	10	0.02
Polish (13)	51	0.09
Portuguese (16)	85	0.16
Russian (29)	29	0.05
Scotch-Irish (45)	45	0.08
Scottish (22)	51	0.09
Swedish (0)	27	0.05
Turkish (57)	57	0.10
Ukrainian (0)	10	0.02
Welsh (0)	11	0.02
West Indian, ex. Hispanic (350)	350	0.64
Haitian (149)	149	0.27
Jamaican (134)	134	0.24
Trinidadian/Tobagonian (67)	67	0.12

Hispanic Origin	Population	%
Hispanic or Latino (of any race)	51,217	92.67
Central American, ex. Mexican	4,850	8.77
Costa Rican	144	0.26
Guatemalan	228	0.41
Honduran	540	0.98
Nicaraguan	3,476	6.29
Panamanian	216	0.39
Salvadoran	239	0.43
Other Central American	7	0.01
Cuban	36,180	65.46
Dominican Republic	985	1.78
Mexican	464	0.84
Puerto Rican	1,307	2.36
South American	5,642	10.21
Argentinean	356	0.64
Bolivian	99	0.18
Chilean	301	0.54
Colombian	2,594	4.69
Ecuadorian	480	0.87
Paraguayan	17	0.03
Peruvian	697	1.26
Uruguayan	79	0.14
Venezuelan	1,018	1.84
Other South American	1	<0.01
Other Hispanic or Latino	1,789	3.24

Race*	Population	%
African-American/Black (745)	926	1.68
Not Hispanic (162)	191	0.35
Hispanic (583)	735	1.33
American Indian/Alaska Native (39)	75	0.14
Not Hispanic (16)	22	0.04
Hispanic (23)	53	0.10
Central American Ind. (2)	7	0.01
Cherokee (0)	1	<0.01
Chippewa (4)	4	0.01
Lumbee (1)	1	<0.01
Mexican American Ind. (1)	4	0.01
South American Ind. (3)	6	0.01
Spanish American Ind. (2)	3	0.01
Asian (386)	516	0.93
Not Hispanic (328)	382	0.69
Hispanic (58)	134	0.24
Bangladeshi (1)	1	<0.01
Burmese (1)	3	0.01
Chinese, ex. Taiwanese (113)	162	0.29
Filipino (25)	38	0.07
Indian (91)	101	0.18
Japanese (19)	31	0.06
Korean (17)	17	0.03
Malaysian (1)	1	<0.01
Pakistani (17)	29	0.05
Taiwanese (20)	24	0.04
Thai (3)	3	0.01
Vietnamese (60)	62	0.11
Hawaii Native/Pacific Islander (1)	18	0.03
Not Hispanic (0)	1	<0.01
Hispanic (1)	17	0.03
Guamanian/Chamorro (1)	1	<0.01
Native Hawaiian (0)	3	0.01
Samoan (0)	1	<0.01
White (52,238)	52,879	95.67
Not Hispanic (3,418)	3,489	6.31
Hispanic (48,820)	49,390	89.36

Tampa

Place Type: City
County: Hillsborough
Population: 335,709†

Ancestry‡	Population	%
Afghan (17)	17	0.01

*Notes: † The Census 2010 population figure is used to calculate the percentages in the Hispanic Origin and Race categories. Ancestry percentages are based on the 2006-2010 American Community Survey population (not shown); ‡ Numbers in parentheses indicate the number of people reporting a single ancestry; * Numbers in parentheses indicate the number of persons reporting this race alone, not in combination with any other race; Please refer to the Explanation of Data for more information.*

Ancestry	Population	%
African, Sub-Saharan (4,295)	4,857	1.46
African (3,183)	3,637	1.09
Cape Verdean (16)	67	0.02
Ethiopian (93)	93	0.03
Ghanaian (49)	49	0.01
Nigerian (503)	552	0.17
Senegalese (16)	16	<0.01
South African (221)	229	0.07
Zimbabwean (86)	86	0.03
Other Sub-Saharan African (128)	128	0.04
Albanian (0)	66	0.02
American (12,011)	12,011	3.60
Arab (2,071)	2,508	0.75
Arab (560)	631	0.19
Egyptian (236)	236	0.07
Jordanian (62)	62	0.02
Lebanese (467)	774	0.23
Moroccan (222)	222	0.07
Palestinian (97)	97	0.03
Syrian (159)	171	0.05
Other Arab (268)	315	0.09
Armenian (96)	297	0.09
Australian (104)	118	0.04
Austrian (319)	1,167	0.35
Basque (19)	40	0.01
Belgian (60)	174	0.05
Brazilian (262)	537	0.16
British (1,122)	1,784	0.54
Bulgarian (80)	106	0.03
Cajun (22)	22	0.01
Canadian (556)	1,176	0.35
Celtic (8)	63	0.02
Croatian (175)	274	0.08
Czech (152)	774	0.23
Czechoslovakian (113)	326	0.10
Danish (262)	1,010	0.30
Dutch (880)	3,201	0.96
Eastern European (300)	315	0.09
English (9,328)	24,468	7.34
Estonian (0)	12	<0.01
European (2,510)	2,706	0.81
Finnish (100)	234	0.07
French, ex. Basque (1,249)	7,410	2.22
French Canadian (764)	1,567	0.47
German (9,767)	34,654	10.40
Greek (919)	1,723	0.52
Guyanese (200)	240	0.07
Hungarian (597)	1,529	0.46
Icelander (84)	132	0.04
Iranian (168)	294	0.09
Irish (8,891)	30,312	9.09
Israeli (57)	68	0.02
Italian (8,740)	21,394	6.42
Latvian (31)	94	0.03
Lithuanian (203)	542	0.16
Luxemburger (9)	55	0.02
Macedonian (0)	12	<0.01
Maltese (12)	21	0.01
New Zealander (19)	19	0.01
Northern European (148)	181	0.05
Norwegian (553)	1,286	0.39
Pennsylvania German (10)	19	0.01
Polish (1,827)	6,411	1.92
Portuguese (282)	863	0.26
Romanian (82)	360	0.11
Russian (1,561)	3,488	1.05
Scandinavian (145)	258	0.08
Scotch-Irish (1,932)	4,470	1.34
Scottish (1,843)	5,811	1.74
Serbian (68)	99	0.03
Slavic (22)	68	0.02
Slovak (81)	419	0.13
Slovene (15)	53	0.02
Swedish (480)	2,227	0.67
Swiss (57)	398	0.12
Turkish (253)	478	0.14
Ukrainian (326)	741	0.22
Welsh (408)	1,777	0.53
West Indian, ex. Hispanic (8,450)	9,430	2.83
Bahamian (105)	105	0.03
Barbadian (31)	44	0.01
Belizean (61)	61	0.02
British West Indian (92)	131	0.04
Haitian (2,592)	2,943	0.88
Jamaican (1,816)	2,151	0.65
Trinidadian/Tobagonian (413)	437	0.13
U.S. Virgin Islander (194)	209	0.06
West Indian (3,146)	3,326	1.00
Other West Indian (0)	23	0.01
Yugoslavian (313)	438	0.13

Hispanic Origin	Population	%
Hispanic or Latino (of any race)	77,472	23.08
Central American, ex. Mexican	5,234	1.56
Costa Rican	374	0.11
Guatemalan	842	0.25
Honduran	2,004	0.60
Nicaraguan	537	0.16
Panamanian	656	0.20
Salvadoran	787	0.23
Other Central American	34	0.01
Cuban	21,295	6.34
Dominican Republic	3,110	0.93
Mexican	9,583	2.85
Puerto Rican	24,057	7.17
South American	6,102	1.82
Argentinean	386	0.11
Bolivian	164	0.05
Chilean	165	0.05
Colombian	2,846	0.85
Ecuadorian	814	0.24
Paraguayan	17	0.01
Peruvian	800	0.24
Uruguayan	91	0.03
Venezuelan	785	0.23
Other South American	34	0.01
Other Hispanic or Latino	8,091	2.41

Race*	Population	%
African-American/Black (87,872)	93,054	27.72
Not Hispanic (83,032)	86,662	25.81
Hispanic (4,840)	6,392	1.90
American Indian/Alaska Native (1,248)	3,161	0.94
Not Hispanic (755)	2,121	0.63
Hispanic (493)	1,040	0.31
Apache (10)	37	0.01
Arapaho (0)	3	<0.01
Blackfeet (10)	97	0.03
Canadian/French Am. Ind. (6)	10	<0.01
Central American Ind. (31)	54	0.02
Cherokee (157)	669	0.20
Cheyenne (0)	2	<0.01
Chickasaw (4)	8	<0.01
Chippewa (29)	43	0.01
Choctaw (27)	57	0.02
Comanche (6)	15	<0.01
Cree (4)	14	<0.01
Creek (22)	54	0.02
Crow (0)	4	<0.01
Delaware (2)	6	<0.01
Hopi (1)	1	<0.01
Houma (1)	3	<0.01
Inupiat *(Alaska Native)* (2)	2	<0.01
Iroquois (41)	68	0.02
Lumbee (31)	57	0.02
Mexican American Ind. (81)	125	0.04
Navajo (14)	20	0.01
Osage (2)	8	<0.01
Ottawa (2)	4	<0.01
Paiute (1)	1	<0.01
Potawatomi (2)	4	<0.01
Pueblo (4)	6	<0.01
Puget Sound Salish (4)	8	<0.01
Seminole (17)	66	0.02
Shoshone (3)	6	<0.01
Sioux (17)	36	0.01
South American Ind. (74)	166	0.05
Spanish American Ind. (10)	12	<0.01
Tlingit-Haida *(Alaska Native)* (1)	3	<0.01
Tohono O'Odham (0)	1	<0.01
Ute (0)	2	<0.01
Yakama (2)	3	<0.01
Yaqui (1)	5	<0.01
Yuman (1)	2	<0.01
Yup'ik *(Alaska Native)* (3)	3	<0.01
Asian (11,560)	14,358	4.28
Not Hispanic (11,362)	13,757	4.10
Hispanic (198)	601	0.18
Bangladeshi (71)	97	0.03
Burmese (111)	114	0.03
Cambodian (31)	43	0.01
Chinese, ex. Taiwanese (1,587)	2,021	0.60
Filipino (1,592)	2,365	0.70
Hmong (21)	24	0.01
Indian (3,933)	4,425	1.32
Indonesian (35)	56	0.02
Japanese (245)	519	0.15
Korean (878)	1,173	0.35
Laotian (61)	76	0.02
Malaysian (9)	19	0.01
Nepalese (36)	38	0.01
Pakistani (377)	432	0.13
Sri Lankan (57)	66	0.02
Taiwanese (101)	134	0.04
Thai (322)	474	0.14
Vietnamese (1,661)	1,863	0.55
Hawaii Native/Pacific Islander (254)	858	0.26
Not Hispanic (207)	643	0.19
Hispanic (47)	215	0.06
Fijian (2)	4	<0.01
Guamanian/Chamorro (67)	121	0.04
Marshallese (3)	5	<0.01
Native Hawaiian (56)	158	0.05
Samoan (24)	50	0.01
Tongan (7)	10	<0.01
White (211,217)	219,680	65.44
Not Hispanic (155,552)	160,715	47.87
Hispanic (55,665)	58,965	17.56

Tarpon Springs

Place Type: City
County: Pinellas
Population: 23,484†

Ancestry‡	Population	%
African, Sub-Saharan (139)	165	0.72
African (118)	144	0.62
South African (21)	21	0.09
Albanian (79)	79	0.34
American (1,247)	1,247	5.41
Arab (143)	164	0.71
Arab (8)	8	0.03
Egyptian (20)	20	0.09
Lebanese (49)	62	0.27
Palestinian (52)	52	0.23
Syrian (0)	8	0.03
Other Arab (14)	14	0.06
Armenian (0)	51	0.22
Austrian (26)	88	0.38
Belgian (26)	36	0.16
British (39)	118	0.51
Bulgarian (0)	13	0.06
Canadian (8)	39	0.17
Croatian (10)	90	0.39
Cypriot (0)	19	0.08
Czech (45)	186	0.81
Czechoslovakian (0)	17	0.07
Danish (38)	173	0.75
Dutch (138)	569	2.47
English (791)	2,382	10.32
European (235)	374	1.62
Finnish (0)	30	0.13
French, ex. Basque (92)	889	3.85
French Canadian (114)	184	0.80
German (1,176)	4,205	18.23
Greek (2,411)	2,892	12.54
Hungarian (133)	482	2.09
Irish (1,142)	4,019	17.42
Italian (1,282)	2,798	12.13

*Notes: † The Census 2010 population figure is used to calculate the percentages in the Hispanic Origin and Race categories. Ancestry percentages are based on the 2006-2010 American Community Survey population (not shown); ‡ Numbers in parentheses indicate the number of people reporting a single ancestry; * Numbers in parentheses indicate the number of persons reporting this race alone, not in combination with any other race; Please refer to the Explanation of Data for more information.*

Ancestry	Population	%
Lithuanian (60)	73	0.32
Norwegian (69)	396	1.72
Pennsylvania German (21)	21	0.09
Polish (543)	1,013	4.39
Portuguese (80)	98	0.42
Romanian (19)	19	0.08
Russian (66)	300	1.30
Scandinavian (0)	12	0.05
Scotch-Irish (134)	331	1.43
Scottish (111)	549	2.38
Serbian (16)	16	0.07
Slavic (0)	8	0.03
Slovak (0)	42	0.18
Slovene (38)	38	0.16
Swedish (8)	423	1.83
Swiss (16)	112	0.49
Ukrainian (63)	152	0.66
Welsh (57)	177	0.77
West Indian, ex. Hispanic (30)	84	0.36
Jamaican (19)	47	0.20
West Indian (11)	37	0.16
Yugoslavian (27)	27	0.12

Hispanic Origin	Population	%
Hispanic or Latino (of any race)	1,707	7.27
Central American, ex. Mexican	59	0.25
Costa Rican	7	0.03
Guatemalan	21	0.09
Honduran	9	0.04
Nicaraguan	6	0.03
Panamanian	9	0.04
Salvadoran	7	0.03
Cuban	140	0.60
Dominican Republic	59	0.25
Mexican	433	1.84
Puerto Rican	605	2.58
South American	255	1.09
Argentinean	20	0.09
Bolivian	3	0.01
Chilean	18	0.08
Colombian	94	0.40
Ecuadorian	59	0.25
Peruvian	39	0.17
Venezuelan	21	0.09
Other South American	1	<0.01
Other Hispanic or Latino	156	0.66

Race*	Population	%
African-American/Black (1,496)	1,705	7.26
Not Hispanic (1,437)	1,589	6.77
Hispanic (59)	116	0.49
American Indian/Alaska Native (73)	177	0.75
Not Hispanic (50)	139	0.59
Hispanic (23)	38	0.16
Apache (1)	2	0.01
Blackfeet (0)	2	0.01
Canadian/French Am. Ind. (2)	9	0.04
Central American Ind. (2)	2	0.01
Cherokee (8)	54	0.23
Chippewa (4)	7	0.03
Choctaw (1)	1	<0.01
Colville (0)	1	<0.01
Cree (0)	1	<0.01
Creek (3)	3	0.01
Crow (0)	2	0.01
Iroquois (1)	5	0.02
Lumbee (6)	6	0.03
Mexican American Ind. (2)	2	0.01
Ottawa (0)	1	<0.01
Sioux (0)	2	0.01
South American Ind. (6)	6	0.03
Tlingit-Haida *(Alaska Native)* (1)	1	<0.01
Yup'ik *(Alaska Native)* (0)	1	<0.01
Asian (339)	476	2.03
Not Hispanic (331)	454	1.93
Hispanic (8)	22	0.09
Burmese (3)	3	0.01
Cambodian (4)	4	0.02
Chinese, ex. Taiwanese (53)	74	0.32
Filipino (59)	93	0.40
Hmong (2)	2	0.01
Indian (72)	94	0.40
Indonesian (7)	7	0.03
Japanese (18)	34	0.14
Korean (21)	36	0.15
Laotian (11)	19	0.08
Malaysian (1)	1	<0.01
Sri Lankan (1)	1	<0.01
Taiwanese (7)	8	0.03
Thai (18)	30	0.13
Vietnamese (45)	53	0.23
Hawaii Native/Pacific Islander (19)	36	0.15
Not Hispanic (19)	35	0.15
Hispanic (0)	1	<0.01
Fijian (2)	3	0.01
Marshallese (4)	9	0.04
Native Hawaiian (2)	3	0.01
Samoan (3)	4	0.02
Tongan (1)	1	<0.01
White (20,678)	21,121	89.94
Not Hispanic (19,531)	19,853	84.54
Hispanic (1,147)	1,268	5.40

Tavares

Place Type: City
County: Lake
Population: 13,951†

Ancestry‡	Population	%
African, Sub-Saharan (47)	71	0.52
African (20)	44	0.32
Cape Verdean (15)	15	0.11
Ethiopian (12)	12	0.09
American (2,611)	2,611	19.08
Arab (0)	24	0.18
Egyptian (0)	12	0.09
Lebanese (0)	12	0.09
Austrian (16)	60	0.44
Belgian (0)	24	0.18
Brazilian (16)	16	0.12
British (106)	137	1.00
Canadian (32)	32	0.23
Czech (15)	65	0.48
Czechoslovakian (16)	16	0.12
Danish (85)	85	0.62
Dutch (197)	411	3.00
Eastern European (14)	14	0.10
English (692)	1,956	14.30
European (123)	150	1.10
Finnish (0)	14	0.10
French, ex. Basque (195)	484	3.54
French Canadian (109)	138	1.01
German (808)	2,163	15.81
Guyanese (113)	113	0.83
Hungarian (0)	21	0.15
Irish (405)	1,678	12.26
Italian (333)	697	5.09
Lithuanian (35)	35	0.26
Norwegian (40)	93	0.68
Polish (277)	523	3.82
Romanian (0)	10	0.07
Russian (0)	60	0.44
Scandinavian (28)	28	0.20
Scotch-Irish (152)	406	2.97
Scottish (101)	291	2.13
Serbian (15)	15	0.11
Slovak (25)	46	0.34
Swedish (24)	168	1.23
Swiss (28)	54	0.39
Ukrainian (0)	68	0.50
Welsh (28)	103	0.75
West Indian, ex. Hispanic (201)	215	1.57
Jamaican (47)	47	0.34
Trinidadian/Tobagonian (142)	142	1.04
U.S. Virgin Islander (12)	12	0.09
West Indian (0)	14	0.10

Hispanic Origin	Population	%
Hispanic or Latino (of any race)	1,083	7.76
Central American, ex. Mexican	49	0.35
Costa Rican	8	0.06
Guatemalan	8	0.06
Honduran	3	0.02
Nicaraguan	5	0.04
Panamanian	16	0.11
Salvadoran	9	0.06
Cuban	67	0.48
Dominican Republic	42	0.30
Mexican	362	2.59
Puerto Rican	353	2.53
South American	133	0.95
Argentinean	10	0.07
Chilean	3	0.02
Colombian	74	0.53
Ecuadorian	13	0.09
Peruvian	16	0.11
Venezuelan	17	0.12
Other Hispanic or Latino	77	0.55

Race*	Population	%
African-American/Black (1,420)	1,530	10.97
Not Hispanic (1,349)	1,430	10.25
Hispanic (71)	100	0.72
American Indian/Alaska Native (51)	116	0.83
Not Hispanic (48)	107	0.77
Hispanic (3)	9	0.06
Apache (2)	2	0.01
Blackfeet (2)	7	0.05
Cherokee (5)	21	0.15
Chippewa (2)	4	0.03
Creek (3)	4	0.03
Delaware (0)	1	0.01
Hopi (0)	2	0.01
Iroquois (2)	3	0.02
Navajo (1)	3	0.02
Ottawa (0)	1	0.01
Sioux (0)	1	0.01
Asian (237)	286	2.05
Not Hispanic (235)	275	1.97
Hispanic (2)	11	0.08
Bangladeshi (0)	4	0.03
Chinese, ex. Taiwanese (21)	27	0.19
Filipino (42)	49	0.35
Indian (129)	148	1.06
Japanese (6)	7	0.05
Korean (4)	10	0.07
Pakistani (7)	7	0.05
Thai (3)	3	0.02
Vietnamese (10)	13	0.09
Hawaii Native/Pacific Islander (7)	14	0.10
Not Hispanic (7)	14	0.10
Marshallese (7)	7	0.05
Native Hawaiian (0)	1	0.01
White (11,766)	11,967	85.78
Not Hispanic (11,047)	11,179	80.13
Hispanic (719)	788	5.65

Temple Terrace

Place Type: City
County: Hillsborough
Population: 24,541†

Ancestry‡	Population	%
African, Sub-Saharan (167)	199	0.82
African (95)	120	0.50
Ghanaian (17)	17	0.07
South African (20)	20	0.08
Sudanese (35)	42	0.17
Albanian (342)	342	1.41
American (1,188)	1,188	4.90
Arab (456)	723	2.98
Arab (92)	92	0.38
Egyptian (23)	64	0.26
Iraqi (0)	113	0.47
Jordanian (29)	29	0.12
Palestinian (139)	139	0.57
Syrian (48)	48	0.20
Other Arab (125)	238	0.98

*Notes: † The Census 2010 population figure is used to calculate the percentages in the Hispanic Origin and Race categories. Ancestry percentages are based on the 2006-2010 American Community Survey population (not shown); ‡ Numbers in parentheses indicate the number of people reporting a single ancestry; * Numbers in parentheses indicate the number of persons reporting this race alone, not in combination with any other race; Please refer to the Explanation of Data for more information.*

Ancestry	Population	%
Australian (0)	11	0.05
Austrian (26)	47	0.19
Brazilian (33)	44	0.18
British (27)	34	0.14
Bulgarian (10)	10	0.04
Cajun (6)	6	0.02
Canadian (68)	68	0.28
Croatian (27)	27	0.11
Czech (0)	30	0.12
Danish (0)	22	0.09
Dutch (102)	282	1.16
Eastern European (10)	10	0.04
English (1,178)	2,506	10.34
European (229)	264	1.09
Finnish (36)	77	0.32
French, ex. Basque (144)	704	2.91
French Canadian (97)	208	0.86
German (1,098)	3,355	13.85
Greek (0)	27	0.11
Guyanese (53)	63	0.26
Hungarian (117)	199	0.82
Irish (689)	2,586	10.67
Italian (783)	1,607	6.63
Latvian (12)	28	0.12
Lithuanian (0)	7	0.03
Macedonian (12)	12	0.05
Northern European (34)	34	0.14
Norwegian (94)	259	1.07
Polish (193)	490	2.02
Portuguese (8)	74	0.31
Romanian (0)	38	0.16
Russian (88)	251	1.04
Scandinavian (61)	96	0.40
Scotch-Irish (186)	441	1.82
Scottish (187)	518	2.14
Slovak (0)	9	0.04
Swedish (86)	200	0.83
Swiss (43)	88	0.36
Ukrainian (13)	31	0.13
Welsh (0)	58	0.24
West Indian, ex. Hispanic (398)	525	2.17
Belizean (52)	52	0.21
British West Indian (55)	55	0.23
Haitian (126)	173	0.71
Jamaican (95)	125	0.52
Trinidadian/Tobagonian (23)	39	0.16
U.S. Virgin Islander (31)	31	0.13
West Indian (16)	50	0.21
Yugoslavian (33)	33	0.14

Hispanic Origin	Population	%
Hispanic or Latino (of any race)	3,597	14.66
Central American, ex. Mexican	240	0.98
Costa Rican	35	0.14
Guatemalan	26	0.11
Honduran	64	0.26
Nicaraguan	21	0.09
Panamanian	36	0.15
Salvadoran	55	0.22
Other Central American	3	0.01
Cuban	520	2.12
Dominican Republic	160	0.65
Mexican	479	1.95
Puerto Rican	1,245	5.07
South American	530	2.16
Argentinean	11	0.04
Bolivian	9	0.04
Chilean	12	0.05
Colombian	330	1.34
Ecuadorian	61	0.25
Peruvian	53	0.22
Uruguayan	3	0.01
Venezuelan	47	0.19
Other South American	4	0.02
Other Hispanic or Latino	423	1.72

Race*	Population	%
African-American/Black (4,793)	5,161	21.03
Not Hispanic (4,581)	4,858	19.80
Hispanic (212)	303	1.23
American Indian/Alaska Native (107)	219	0.89
Not Hispanic (84)	173	0.70
Hispanic (23)	46	0.19
Blackfeet (4)	9	0.04
Central American Ind. (1)	2	0.01
Cherokee (3)	27	0.11
Chickasaw (2)	2	0.01
Chippewa (0)	1	<0.01
Choctaw (2)	7	0.03
Creek (0)	1	<0.01
Delaware (0)	1	<0.01
Hopi (1)	1	<0.01
Iroquois (3)	6	0.02
Lumbee (3)	3	0.01
Mexican American Ind. (3)	3	0.01
Navajo (4)	4	0.02
Seminole (2)	6	0.02
South American Ind. (0)	5	0.02
Tlingit-Haida *(Alaska Native)* (0)	1	<0.01
Asian (1,338)	1,609	6.56
Not Hispanic (1,328)	1,574	6.41
Hispanic (10)	35	0.14
Bangladeshi (14)	14	0.06
Burmese (9)	10	0.04
Cambodian (5)	6	0.02
Chinese, ex. Taiwanese (106)	133	0.54
Filipino (100)	159	0.65
Indian (798)	847	3.45
Indonesian (5)	6	0.02
Japanese (26)	37	0.15
Korean (57)	87	0.35
Laotian (2)	3	0.01
Malaysian (2)	5	0.02
Pakistani (48)	80	0.33
Sri Lankan (2)	2	0.01
Taiwanese (18)	23	0.09
Thai (18)	19	0.08
Vietnamese (80)	92	0.37
Hawaii Native/Pacific Islander (17)	50	0.20
Not Hispanic (17)	49	0.20
Hispanic (0)	1	<0.01
Guamanian/Chamorro (1)	4	0.02
Native Hawaiian (4)	7	0.03
Samoan (2)	3	0.01
Tongan (0)	1	<0.01
White (16,697)	17,308	70.53
Not Hispanic (14,299)	14,737	60.05
Hispanic (2,398)	2,571	10.48

The Acreage

Place Type: CDP
County: Palm Beach
Population: 38,704†

Ancestry‡	Population	%
African, Sub-Saharan (24)	60	0.16
African (24)	60	0.16
American (1,748)	1,748	4.62
Arab (13)	66	0.17
Arab (0)	14	0.04
Lebanese (13)	40	0.11
Moroccan (0)	12	0.03
Armenian (10)	10	0.03
Australian (28)	28	0.07
Austrian (144)	187	0.49
Basque (0)	46	0.12
Belgian (0)	21	0.06
Brazilian (20)	20	0.05
British (92)	191	0.50
Bulgarian (8)	8	0.02
Canadian (63)	144	0.38
Croatian (0)	12	0.03
Czech (0)	32	0.08
Czechoslovakian (133)	191	0.50
Danish (21)	256	0.68
Dutch (111)	816	2.16
Eastern European (18)	35	0.09
English (806)	3,222	8.51
European (270)	461	1.22
Finnish (12)	109	0.29
French, ex. Basque (225)	1,275	3.37
French Canadian (135)	310	0.82
German (1,968)	7,073	18.68
Greek (53)	267	0.71
Guyanese (41)	41	0.11
Hungarian (338)	533	1.41
Iranian (9)	9	0.02
Irish (1,481)	5,993	15.83
Israeli (0)	36	0.10
Italian (2,052)	4,863	12.84
Lithuanian (17)	105	0.28
Macedonian (10)	10	0.03
Norwegian (47)	212	0.56
Pennsylvania German (0)	14	0.04
Polish (565)	1,640	4.33
Portuguese (40)	94	0.25
Romanian (18)	18	0.05
Russian (116)	376	0.99
Scandinavian (35)	35	0.09
Scotch-Irish (171)	403	1.06
Scottish (91)	425	1.12
Slovak (21)	89	0.24
Swedish (118)	298	0.79
Ukrainian (114)	223	0.59
Welsh (66)	239	0.63
West Indian, ex. Hispanic (2,554)	3,061	8.08
British West Indian (69)	84	0.22
Haitian (602)	715	1.89
Jamaican (1,565)	1,809	4.78
Trinidadian/Tobagonian (200)	283	0.75
West Indian (118)	170	0.45

Hispanic Origin	Population	%
Hispanic or Latino (of any race)	6,881	17.78
Central American, ex. Mexican	604	1.56
Costa Rican	57	0.15
Guatemalan	134	0.35
Honduran	117	0.30
Nicaraguan	140	0.36
Panamanian	57	0.15
Salvadoran	98	0.25
Other Central American	1	<0.01
Cuban	2,364	6.11
Dominican Republic	270	0.70
Mexican	783	2.02
Puerto Rican	1,266	3.27
South American	1,196	3.09
Argentinean	128	0.33
Bolivian	29	0.07
Chilean	52	0.13
Colombian	569	1.47
Ecuadorian	148	0.38
Paraguayan	3	0.01
Peruvian	150	0.39
Uruguayan	22	0.06
Venezuelan	79	0.20
Other South American	16	0.04
Other Hispanic or Latino	398	1.03

Race*	Population	%
African-American/Black (5,164)	5,620	14.52
Not Hispanic (4,972)	5,334	13.78
Hispanic (192)	286	0.74
American Indian/Alaska Native (108)	257	0.66
Not Hispanic (81)	203	0.52
Hispanic (27)	54	0.14
Aleut *(Alaska Native)* (0)	1	<0.01
Apache (2)	3	0.01
Arapaho (2)	3	0.01
Blackfeet (2)	5	0.01
Canadian/French Am. Ind. (1)	1	<0.01
Central American Ind. (7)	15	0.04
Cherokee (13)	43	0.11
Chippewa (4)	7	0.02
Choctaw (5)	7	0.02
Delaware (3)	4	0.01
Inupiat *(Alaska Native)* (0)	1	<0.01
Iroquois (1)	3	0.01
Mexican American Ind. (0)	1	<0.01

*Notes: † The Census 2010 population figure is used to calculate the percentages in the Hispanic Origin and Race categories. Ancestry percentages are based on the 2006-2010 American Community Survey population (not shown); ‡ Numbers in parentheses indicate the number of people reporting a single ancestry; * Numbers in parentheses indicate the number of persons reporting this race alone, not in combination with any other race; Please refer to the Explanation of Data for more information.*

Navajo (6)	6	0.02
Seminole (3)	5	0.01
Sioux (2)	7	0.02
South American Ind. (4)	7	0.02
Yup'ik *(Alaska Native)* (0)	1	<0.01
Asian (1,022)	1,369	3.54
Not Hispanic (989)	1,293	3.34
Hispanic (33)	76	0.20
Bangladeshi (7)	11	0.03
Burmese (3)	3	0.01
Cambodian (17)	17	0.04
Chinese, ex. Taiwanese (120)	218	0.56
Filipino (149)	204	0.53
Hmong (0)	1	<0.01
Indian (359)	456	1.18
Indonesian (2)	6	0.02
Japanese (19)	51	0.13
Korean (19)	35	0.09
Laotian (34)	36	0.09
Malaysian (3)	3	0.01
Pakistani (30)	36	0.09
Sri Lankan (1)	1	<0.01
Taiwanese (4)	6	0.02
Thai (25)	39	0.10
Vietnamese (185)	192	0.50
Hawaii Native/Pacific Islander (22)	74	0.19
Not Hispanic (21)	67	0.17
Hispanic (1)	7	0.02
Guamanian/Chamorro (2)	4	0.01
Native Hawaiian (5)	10	0.03
Samoan (8)	8	0.02
White (30,529)	31,186	80.58
Not Hispanic (24,939)	25,362	65.53
Hispanic (5,590)	5,824	15.05

The Crossings

Place Type: CDP
County: Miami-Dade
Population: 22,758†

Ancestry‡	Population	%
African, Sub-Saharan (0)	44	0.19
African (0)	44	0.19
American (946)	946	3.98
Arab (93)	153	0.64
Arab (48)	48	0.20
Lebanese (0)	60	0.25
Palestinian (30)	30	0.13
Syrian (15)	15	0.06
Australian (15)	15	0.06
Austrian (13)	90	0.38
Brazilian (135)	174	0.73
British (6)	6	0.03
Canadian (15)	15	0.06
Dutch (0)	50	0.21
Eastern European (33)	33	0.14
English (69)	197	0.83
European (131)	168	0.71
Finnish (21)	51	0.21
French, ex. Basque (26)	177	0.75
French Canadian (0)	50	0.21
German (93)	642	2.70
Greek (7)	118	0.50
Guyanese (47)	47	0.20
Hungarian (0)	39	0.16
Iranian (87)	102	0.43
Irish (307)	939	3.96
Israeli (13)	29	0.12
Italian (293)	705	2.97
Lithuanian (18)	95	0.40
Norwegian (24)	114	0.48
Polish (41)	144	0.61
Portuguese (10)	40	0.17
Russian (135)	247	1.04
Scandinavian (14)	14	0.06
Scotch-Irish (20)	56	0.24
Scottish (55)	55	0.23
Swedish (0)	44	0.19
Swiss (0)	23	0.10
West Indian, ex. Hispanic (1,312)	1,618	6.82
Bahamian (21)	78	0.33
Haitian (651)	741	3.12
Jamaican (593)	678	2.86
Trinidadian/Tobagonian (47)	121	0.51

Hispanic Origin	Population	%
Hispanic or Latino (of any race)	15,803	69.44
Central American, ex. Mexican	1,464	6.43
Costa Rican	77	0.34
Guatemalan	68	0.30
Honduran	200	0.88
Nicaraguan	885	3.89
Panamanian	99	0.44
Salvadoran	132	0.58
Other Central American	3	0.01
Cuban	7,065	31.04
Dominican Republic	446	1.96
Mexican	187	0.82
Puerto Rican	993	4.36
South American	4,756	20.90
Argentinean	374	1.64
Bolivian	69	0.30
Chilean	269	1.18
Colombian	2,106	9.25
Ecuadorian	232	1.02
Paraguayan	16	0.07
Peruvian	1,006	4.42
Uruguayan	81	0.36
Venezuelan	591	2.60
Other South American	12	0.05
Other Hispanic or Latino	892	3.92

Race*	Population	%
African-American/Black (1,059)	1,265	5.56
Not Hispanic (918)	1,063	4.67
Hispanic (141)	202	0.89
American Indian/Alaska Native (34)	69	0.30
Not Hispanic (10)	29	0.13
Hispanic (24)	40	0.18
Blackfeet (0)	1	<0.01
Central American Ind. (2)	2	0.01
Cherokee (1)	14	0.06
Chickasaw (0)	3	0.01
Chippewa (1)	1	<0.01
Iroquois (1)	2	0.01
Mexican American Ind. (1)	1	<0.01
Pueblo (0)	2	0.01
Sioux (1)	1	<0.01
South American Ind. (6)	11	0.05
Spanish American Ind. (1)	1	<0.01
Tohono O'Odham (1)	2	0.01
Asian (579)	791	3.48
Not Hispanic (559)	728	3.20
Hispanic (20)	63	0.28
Bangladeshi (7)	7	0.03
Burmese (3)	3	0.01
Cambodian (0)	1	<0.01
Chinese, ex. Taiwanese (220)	306	1.34
Filipino (19)	33	0.15
Indian (182)	228	1.00
Indonesian (1)	2	0.01
Japanese (30)	39	0.17
Korean (17)	23	0.10
Laotian (2)	3	0.01
Malaysian (0)	1	<0.01
Pakistani (36)	47	0.21
Sri Lankan (1)	1	<0.01
Taiwanese (7)	9	0.04
Thai (9)	10	0.04
Vietnamese (28)	30	0.13
Hawaii Native/Pacific Islander (1)	15	0.07
Not Hispanic (1)	11	0.05
Hispanic (0)	4	0.02
Guamanian/Chamorro (0)	1	<0.01
Native Hawaiian (0)	2	0.01
White (20,026)	20,472	89.96
Not Hispanic (5,100)	5,303	23.30
Hispanic (14,926)	15,169	66.65

The Hammocks

Place Type: CDP
County: Miami-Dade
Population: 51,003†

Ancestry‡	Population	%
Afghan (14)	14	0.03
African, Sub-Saharan (157)	234	0.47
African (82)	82	0.16
Liberian (66)	66	0.13
Nigerian (9)	86	0.17
American (1,381)	1,381	2.76
Arab (113)	298	0.60
Arab (28)	53	0.11
Lebanese (73)	175	0.35
Moroccan (12)	12	0.02
Other Arab (0)	58	0.12
Armenian (14)	14	0.03
Austrian (26)	58	0.12
Basque (10)	43	0.09
Belgian (0)	77	0.15
Brazilian (567)	764	1.53
British (0)	88	0.18
Canadian (25)	46	0.09
Croatian (8)	8	0.02
Czech (144)	182	0.36
Danish (0)	9	0.02
Dutch (31)	200	0.40
Eastern European (103)	125	0.25
English (149)	530	1.06
European (50)	73	0.15
Finnish (31)	67	0.13
French, ex. Basque (36)	354	0.71
French Canadian (13)	31	0.06
German (214)	825	1.65
Greek (42)	140	0.28
Guyanese (23)	106	0.21
Hungarian (11)	11	0.02
Irish (171)	658	1.32
Israeli (35)	35	0.07
Italian (714)	1,402	2.80
Norwegian (9)	25	0.05
Polish (72)	414	0.83
Portuguese (71)	128	0.26
Romanian (34)	82	0.16
Russian (14)	35	0.07
Scotch-Irish (27)	117	0.23
Scottish (25)	111	0.22
Swedish (15)	40	0.08
Swiss (19)	28	0.06
Ukrainian (0)	43	0.09
Welsh (0)	39	0.08
West Indian, ex. Hispanic (1,606)	1,843	3.69
Bahamian (83)	118	0.24
Barbadian (100)	112	0.22
Belizean (26)	26	0.05
Haitian (544)	639	1.28
Jamaican (704)	799	1.60
Trinidadian/Tobagonian (62)	62	0.12
West Indian (57)	57	0.11
Other West Indian (30)	30	0.06
Yugoslavian (0)	15	0.03

Hispanic Origin	Population	%
Hispanic or Latino (of any race)	39,244	76.94
Central American, ex. Mexican	4,063	7.97
Costa Rican	190	0.37
Guatemalan	215	0.42
Honduran	588	1.15
Nicaraguan	2,391	4.69
Panamanian	310	0.61
Salvadoran	357	0.70
Other Central American	12	0.02
Cuban	13,605	26.67
Dominican Republic	1,907	3.74
Mexican	579	1.14
Puerto Rican	2,934	5.75
South American	13,807	27.07
Argentinean	687	1.35

*Notes: † The Census 2010 population figure is used to calculate the percentages in the Hispanic Origin and Race categories. Ancestry percentages are based on the 2006-2010 American Community Survey population (not shown); ‡ Numbers in parentheses indicate the number of people reporting a single ancestry; * Numbers in parentheses indicate the number of persons reporting this race alone, not in combination with any other race; Please refer to the Explanation of Data for more information.*

Bolivian	156	0.31
Chilean	564	1.11
Colombian	6,896	13.52
Ecuadorian	868	1.70
Paraguayan	18	0.04
Peruvian	2,403	4.71
Uruguayan	130	0.25
Venezuelan	2,065	4.05
Other South American	20	0.04
Other Hispanic or Latino	2,349	4.61

Race*	Population	%
African-American/Black (3,118)	3,653	7.16
Not Hispanic (2,430)	2,717	5.33
Hispanic (688)	936	1.84
American Indian/Alaska Native (84)	154	0.30
Not Hispanic (40)	65	0.13
Hispanic (44)	89	0.17
Apache (0)	1	<0.01
Blackfeet (2)	2	<0.01
Canadian/French Am. Ind. (1)	4	0.01
Central American Ind. (0)	1	<0.01
Cherokee (7)	16	0.03
Chickasaw (3)	3	0.01
Chippewa (4)	5	0.01
Choctaw (2)	2	<0.01
Hopi (0)	1	<0.01
Inupiat *(Alaska Native)* (0)	1	<0.01
Iroquois (0)	1	<0.01
Mexican American Ind. (3)	8	0.02
Seminole (5)	8	0.02
Sioux (0)	2	<0.01
South American Ind. (4)	20	0.04
Spanish American Ind. (12)	12	0.02
Asian (1,569)	1,995	3.91
Not Hispanic (1,499)	1,830	3.59
Hispanic (70)	165	0.32
Bangladeshi (5)	5	0.01
Chinese, ex. Taiwanese (482)	644	1.26
Filipino (268)	323	0.63
Indian (401)	489	0.96
Indonesian (3)	3	0.01
Japanese (34)	54	0.11
Korean (24)	36	0.07
Laotian (10)	14	0.03
Malaysian (0)	1	<0.01
Pakistani (163)	186	0.36
Sri Lankan (6)	10	0.02
Taiwanese (7)	9	0.02
Thai (19)	31	0.06
Vietnamese (90)	109	0.21
Hawaii Native/Pacific Islander (9)	61	0.12
Not Hispanic (7)	40	0.08
Hispanic (2)	21	0.04
Guamanian/Chamorro (4)	4	0.01
Native Hawaiian (2)	3	0.01
Samoan (1)	1	<0.01
Tongan (1)	1	<0.01
White (43,341)	44,587	87.42
Not Hispanic (7,119)	7,488	14.68
Hispanic (36,222)	37,099	72.74

The Villages

Place Type: CDP
County: Sumter
Population: 51,442†

Ancestry‡	Population	%
American (2,363)	2,363	5.86
Arab (0)	35	0.09
Lebanese (0)	13	0.03
Syrian (0)	22	0.05
Assyrian/Chaldean/Syriac (11)	20	0.05
Austrian (130)	348	0.86
Belgian (47)	155	0.38
British (294)	399	0.99
Cajun (27)	27	0.07
Canadian (121)	169	0.42
Celtic (0)	13	0.03
Croatian (91)	118	0.29
Czech (183)	402	1.00
Czechoslovakian (13)	25	0.06
Danish (84)	347	0.86
Dutch (372)	1,066	2.64
Eastern European (37)	49	0.12
English (2,728)	7,369	18.27
European (329)	329	0.82
Finnish (95)	218	0.54
French, ex. Basque (462)	1,834	4.55
French Canadian (760)	950	2.35
German (4,314)	9,577	23.74
Greek (74)	131	0.32
Hungarian (215)	408	1.01
Irish (2,633)	6,826	16.92
Italian (3,274)	4,683	11.61
Latvian (29)	81	0.20
Lithuanian (122)	190	0.47
Luxemburger (0)	12	0.03
Macedonian (0)	14	0.03
Northern European (33)	33	0.08
Norwegian (340)	601	1.49
Pennsylvania German (17)	17	0.04
Polish (1,121)	2,357	5.84
Portuguese (127)	185	0.46
Romanian (80)	139	0.34
Russian (204)	620	1.54
Scandinavian (97)	111	0.28
Scotch-Irish (649)	1,240	3.07
Scottish (601)	1,658	4.11
Serbian (12)	12	0.03
Slavic (31)	61	0.15
Slovak (223)	365	0.90
Slovene (18)	40	0.10
Swedish (156)	762	1.89
Swiss (22)	314	0.78
Turkish (14)	14	0.03
Ukrainian (71)	155	0.38
Welsh (129)	653	1.62
West Indian, ex. Hispanic (55)	55	0.14
British West Indian (18)	18	0.04
Jamaican (37)	37	0.09
Yugoslavian (15)	37	0.09

Hispanic Origin	Population	%
Hispanic or Latino (of any race)	768	1.49
Central American, ex. Mexican	26	0.05
Costa Rican	4	0.01
Guatemalan	4	0.01
Honduran	9	0.02
Nicaraguan	4	0.01
Panamanian	3	0.01
Salvadoran	2	<0.01
Cuban	95	0.18
Dominican Republic	8	0.02
Mexican	123	0.24
Puerto Rican	309	0.60
South American	91	0.18
Argentinean	19	0.04
Bolivian	6	0.01
Chilean	3	0.01
Colombian	36	0.07
Ecuadorian	5	0.01
Paraguayan	1	<0.01
Peruvian	6	0.01
Uruguayan	5	0.01
Venezuelan	10	0.02
Other Hispanic or Latino	116	0.23

Race*	Population	%
African-American/Black (314)	331	0.64
Not Hispanic (303)	317	0.62
Hispanic (11)	14	0.03
American Indian/Alaska Native (52)	127	0.25
Not Hispanic (51)	123	0.24
Hispanic (1)	4	0.01
Blackfeet (0)	1	<0.01
Cherokee (8)	32	0.06
Chippewa (5)	9	0.02
Choctaw (2)	5	0.01
Cree (1)	1	<0.01
Creek (4)	5	0.01
Delaware (2)	2	<0.01
Iroquois (3)	9	0.02
Lumbee (2)	3	0.01
Menominee (0)	2	<0.01
Mexican American Ind. (1)	2	<0.01
Potawatomi (1)	1	<0.01
Sioux (1)	1	<0.01
Tlingit-Haida *(Alaska Native)* (0)	1	<0.01
Asian (342)	376	0.73
Not Hispanic (340)	371	0.72
Hispanic (2)	5	0.01
Burmese (1)	1	<0.01
Chinese, ex. Taiwanese (42)	59	0.11
Filipino (175)	182	0.35
Indian (19)	26	0.05
Indonesian (2)	2	<0.01
Japanese (26)	28	0.05
Korean (44)	45	0.09
Malaysian (2)	2	<0.01
Pakistani (1)	1	<0.01
Taiwanese (5)	6	0.01
Thai (13)	13	0.03
Vietnamese (7)	7	0.01
Hawaii Native/Pacific Islander (11)	28	0.05
Not Hispanic (6)	21	0.04
Hispanic (5)	7	0.01
Guamanian/Chamorro (4)	5	0.01
Native Hawaiian (3)	16	0.03
Samoan (2)	2	<0.01
White (50,511)	50,651	98.46
Not Hispanic (49,840)	49,955	97.11
Hispanic (671)	696	1.35

Thonotosassa

Place Type: CDP
County: Hillsborough
Population: 13,014†

Ancestry‡	Population	%
African, Sub-Saharan (16)	16	0.13
African (16)	16	0.13
Albanian (0)	8	0.07
American (1,222)	1,222	10.26
Arab (0)	6	0.05
Lebanese (0)	6	0.05
Austrian (0)	53	0.44
Belgian (11)	23	0.19
Brazilian (10)	20	0.17
British (63)	102	0.86
Canadian (10)	51	0.43
Czech (13)	21	0.18
Danish (0)	28	0.24
Dutch (23)	141	1.18
English (333)	1,299	10.91
European (37)	62	0.52
Finnish (0)	10	0.08
French, ex. Basque (49)	359	3.01
French Canadian (43)	95	0.80
German (541)	1,713	14.38
Greek (9)	43	0.36
Hungarian (0)	7	0.06
Irish (573)	1,624	13.63
Italian (276)	574	4.82
Norwegian (0)	9	0.08
Pennsylvania German (39)	39	0.33
Polish (55)	284	2.38
Romanian (9)	9	0.08
Russian (0)	31	0.26
Scotch-Irish (158)	268	2.25
Scottish (78)	371	3.11
Slovak (42)	42	0.35
Swedish (33)	142	1.19
Welsh (31)	136	1.14
West Indian, ex. Hispanic (55)	63	0.53
Dutch West Indian (0)	8	0.07
Jamaican (55)	55	0.46

*Notes: † The Census 2010 population figure is used to calculate the percentages in the Hispanic Origin and Race categories. Ancestry percentages are based on the 2006-2010 American Community Survey population (not shown); ‡ Numbers in parentheses indicate the number of people reporting a single ancestry; * Numbers in parentheses indicate the number of persons reporting this race alone, not in combination with any other race; Please refer to the Explanation of Data for more information.*

Hispanic Origin	Population	%
Hispanic or Latino (of any race)	1,536	11.80
Central American, ex. Mexican	84	0.65
Costa Rican	6	0.05
Guatemalan	20	0.15
Honduran	30	0.23
Nicaraguan	9	0.07
Panamanian	1	0.01
Salvadoran	18	0.14
Cuban	195	1.50
Dominican Republic	24	0.18
Mexican	581	4.46
Puerto Rican	439	3.37
South American	64	0.49
Argentinean	15	0.12
Chilean	4	0.03
Colombian	34	0.26
Ecuadorian	2	0.02
Peruvian	7	0.05
Venezuelan	2	0.02
Other Hispanic or Latino	149	1.14

Race*	Population	%
African-American/Black (2,025)	2,191	16.84
Not Hispanic (1,993)	2,133	16.39
Hispanic (32)	58	0.45
American Indian/Alaska Native (64)	185	1.42
Not Hispanic (42)	151	1.16
Hispanic (22)	34	0.26
Aleut *(Alaska Native)* (2)	2	0.02
Apache (0)	3	0.02
Blackfeet (0)	9	0.07
Canadian/French Am. Ind. (0)	1	0.01
Cherokee (7)	53	0.41
Choctaw (0)	1	0.01
Comanche (0)	1	0.01
Creek (3)	18	0.14
Iroquois (5)	8	0.06
Mexican American Ind. (7)	7	0.05
Pima (0)	1	0.01
Puget Sound Salish (0)	1	0.01
Seminole (1)	6	0.05
Sioux (2)	8	0.06
South American Ind. (5)	5	0.04
Yuman (0)	1	0.01
Asian (221)	283	2.17
Not Hispanic (218)	279	2.14
Hispanic (3)	4	0.03
Chinese, ex. Taiwanese (28)	48	0.37
Filipino (31)	54	0.41
Indian (84)	94	0.72
Japanese (0)	4	0.03
Korean (6)	9	0.07
Pakistani (22)	22	0.17
Thai (5)	6	0.05
Vietnamese (36)	42	0.32
Hawaii Native/Pacific Islander (3)	8	0.06
Not Hispanic (3)	8	0.06
Fijian (0)	2	0.02
Native Hawaiian (1)	3	0.02
White (9,978)	10,291	79.08
Not Hispanic (8,943)	9,187	70.59
Hispanic (1,035)	1,104	8.48

Three Lakes

Place Type: CDP
County: Miami-Dade
Population: 15,047†

Ancestry‡	Population	%
African, Sub-Saharan (41)	68	0.47
African (41)	68	0.47
American (946)	946	6.56
Arab (43)	43	0.30
Lebanese (43)	43	0.30
Austrian (13)	53	0.37
British (16)	25	0.17
Canadian (13)	48	0.33
Croatian (20)	20	0.14
Czech (0)	15	0.10
English (58)	264	1.83
European (15)	15	0.10
French, ex. Basque (10)	79	0.55
French Canadian (0)	120	0.83
German (53)	422	2.92
Guyanese (0)	45	0.31
Hungarian (0)	22	0.15
Iranian (51)	51	0.35
Irish (76)	339	2.35
Italian (182)	592	4.10
Lithuanian (0)	52	0.36
Norwegian (22)	107	0.74
Polish (36)	141	0.98
Portuguese (12)	34	0.24
Russian (27)	46	0.32
Scandinavian (0)	14	0.10
Scotch-Irish (10)	80	0.55
Scottish (0)	25	0.17
Swedish (15)	54	0.37
Welsh (14)	29	0.20
West Indian, ex. Hispanic (684)	919	6.37
Barbadian (20)	20	0.14
Haitian (184)	216	1.50
Jamaican (402)	507	3.51
Trinidadian/Tobagonian (35)	133	0.92
West Indian (43)	43	0.30

Hispanic Origin	Population	%
Hispanic or Latino (of any race)	9,843	65.42
Central American, ex. Mexican	1,012	6.73
Costa Rican	51	0.34
Guatemalan	65	0.43
Honduran	191	1.27
Nicaraguan	513	3.41
Panamanian	89	0.59
Salvadoran	102	0.68
Other Central American	1	0.01
Cuban	3,186	21.17
Dominican Republic	488	3.24
Mexican	178	1.18
Puerto Rican	995	6.61
South American	3,392	22.54
Argentinean	173	1.15
Bolivian	63	0.42
Chilean	116	0.77
Colombian	1,619	10.76
Ecuadorian	197	1.31
Paraguayan	7	0.05
Peruvian	538	3.58
Uruguayan	23	0.15
Venezuelan	654	4.35
Other South American	2	0.01
Other Hispanic or Latino	592	3.93

Race*	Population	%
African-American/Black (1,571)	1,795	11.93
Not Hispanic (1,388)	1,535	10.20
Hispanic (183)	260	1.73
American Indian/Alaska Native (23)	40	0.27
Not Hispanic (8)	15	0.10
Hispanic (15)	25	0.17
Canadian/French Am. Ind. (1)	1	0.01
Cherokee (1)	2	0.01
Creek (0)	1	0.01
Mexican American Ind. (1)	1	0.01
Seminole (0)	1	0.01
Sioux (1)	2	0.01
South American Ind. (0)	1	0.01
Spanish American Ind. (1)	1	0.01
Asian (694)	883	5.87
Not Hispanic (667)	822	5.46
Hispanic (27)	61	0.41
Burmese (0)	1	0.01
Chinese, ex. Taiwanese (232)	317	2.11
Filipino (84)	105	0.70
Indian (252)	299	1.99
Japanese (12)	19	0.13
Korean (16)	21	0.14
Malaysian (0)	1	0.01
Nepalese (3)	3	0.02
Pakistani (24)	31	0.21
Taiwanese (5)	6	0.04
Thai (16)	19	0.13
Vietnamese (32)	36	0.24
Hawaii Native/Pacific Islander (7)	18	0.12
Not Hispanic (7)	16	0.11
Hispanic (0)	2	0.01
Fijian (1)	1	0.01
Guamanian/Chamorro (5)	5	0.03
Native Hawaiian (0)	1	0.01
Samoan (1)	2	0.01
White (11,756)	12,108	80.47
Not Hispanic (2,805)	2,953	19.63
Hispanic (8,951)	9,155	60.84

Titusville

Place Type: City
County: Brevard
Population: 43,761†

Ancestry‡	Population	%
African, Sub-Saharan (280)	306	0.70
African (265)	291	0.66
Ethiopian (15)	15	0.03
Albanian (15)	15	0.03
American (2,780)	2,780	6.32
Arab (41)	70	0.16
Lebanese (41)	57	0.13
Syrian (0)	13	0.03
Assyrian/Chaldean/Syriac (11)	11	0.03
Austrian (13)	168	0.38
Belgian (10)	72	0.16
Brazilian (0)	12	0.03
British (45)	141	0.32
Bulgarian (0)	21	0.05
Canadian (68)	82	0.19
Celtic (14)	43	0.10
Croatian (0)	58	0.13
Czech (65)	120	0.27
Czechoslovakian (28)	95	0.22
Danish (27)	76	0.17
Dutch (119)	690	1.57
Eastern European (15)	15	0.03
English (2,160)	5,494	12.49
European (640)	710	1.61
Finnish (0)	34	0.08
French, ex. Basque (280)	1,725	3.92
French Canadian (121)	347	0.79
German (1,991)	6,283	14.28
Greek (210)	225	0.51
Hungarian (75)	246	0.56
Iranian (36)	50	0.11
Irish (1,557)	5,108	11.61
Italian (1,199)	2,581	5.87
Lithuanian (40)	119	0.27
Macedonian (0)	13	0.03
Maltese (0)	13	0.03
Northern European (22)	22	0.05
Norwegian (173)	338	0.77
Pennsylvania German (0)	12	0.03
Polish (499)	1,247	2.83
Portuguese (61)	107	0.24
Romanian (31)	31	0.07
Russian (78)	247	0.56
Scandinavian (83)	134	0.30
Scotch-Irish (733)	1,285	2.92
Scottish (378)	933	2.12
Serbian (0)	45	0.10
Slavic (14)	14	0.03
Slovak (146)	194	0.44
Swedish (96)	321	0.73
Swiss (21)	88	0.20
Ukrainian (36)	64	0.15
Welsh (60)	410	0.93
West Indian, ex. Hispanic (406)	495	1.13
Bahamian (34)	34	0.08
British West Indian (215)	215	0.49
Haitian (49)	118	0.27

*Notes: † The Census 2010 population figure is used to calculate the percentages in the Hispanic Origin and Race categories. Ancestry percentages are based on the 2006-2010 American Community Survey population (not shown); ‡ Numbers in parentheses indicate the number of people reporting a single ancestry; * Numbers in parentheses indicate the number of persons reporting this race alone, not in combination with any other race; Please refer to the Explanation of Data for more information.*

Jamaican (91)	111	0.25
West Indian (17)	17	0.04
Yugoslavian (0)	12	0.03

Hispanic Origin	Population	%
Hispanic or Latino (of any race)	2,825	6.46
Central American, ex. Mexican	166	0.38
Costa Rican	20	0.05
Guatemalan	28	0.06
Honduran	24	0.05
Nicaraguan	21	0.05
Panamanian	48	0.11
Salvadoran	24	0.05
Other Central American	1	<0.01
Cuban	321	0.73
Dominican Republic	129	0.29
Mexican	482	1.10
Puerto Rican	1,276	2.92
South American	206	0.47
Argentinean	11	0.03
Bolivian	9	0.02
Chilean	7	0.02
Colombian	84	0.19
Ecuadorian	10	0.02
Paraguayan	2	<0.01
Peruvian	45	0.10
Uruguayan	3	0.01
Venezuelan	30	0.07
Other South American	5	0.01
Other Hispanic or Latino	245	0.56

Race*	Population	%
African-American/Black (5,909)	6,448	14.73
Not Hispanic (5,727)	6,178	14.12
Hispanic (182)	270	0.62
American Indian/Alaska Native (206)	578	1.32
Not Hispanic (168)	496	1.13
Hispanic (38)	82	0.19
Aleut *(Alaska Native)* (0)	2	<0.01
Apache (4)	8	0.02
Blackfeet (9)	25	0.06
Canadian/French Am. Ind. (0)	1	<0.01
Central American Ind. (1)	2	<0.01
Cherokee (55)	183	0.42
Chickasaw (1)	9	0.02
Chippewa (4)	9	0.02
Choctaw (1)	7	0.02
Comanche (4)	5	0.01
Cree (0)	1	<0.01
Creek (5)	7	0.02
Crow (0)	1	<0.01
Iroquois (11)	29	0.07
Kiowa (0)	1	<0.01
Lumbee (6)	9	0.02
Mexican American Ind. (2)	2	<0.01
Navajo (5)	8	0.02
Pueblo (4)	4	0.01
Seminole (3)	13	0.03
Sioux (3)	10	0.02
South American Ind. (2)	9	0.02
Tlingit-Haida *(Alaska Native)* (3)	3	0.01
Asian (608)	824	1.88
Not Hispanic (596)	787	1.80
Hispanic (12)	37	0.08
Cambodian (6)	6	0.01
Chinese, ex. Taiwanese (98)	140	0.32
Filipino (142)	209	0.48
Indian (199)	234	0.53
Japanese (27)	79	0.18
Korean (18)	38	0.09
Laotian (1)	1	<0.01
Malaysian (1)	1	<0.01
Pakistani (21)	24	0.05
Taiwanese (6)	9	0.02
Thai (30)	40	0.09
Vietnamese (33)	44	0.10
Hawaii Native/Pacific Islander (41)	108	0.25
Not Hispanic (37)	92	0.21
Hispanic (4)	16	0.04
Guamanian/Chamorro (15)	25	0.06
Native Hawaiian (12)	37	0.08
Samoan (8)	12	0.03
White (35,375)	36,338	83.04
Not Hispanic (33,445)	34,238	78.24
Hispanic (1,930)	2,100	4.80

Town 'n' Country

Place Type: CDP
County: Hillsborough
Population: 78,442†

Ancestry‡	Population	%
African, Sub-Saharan (372)	506	0.66
African (269)	390	0.51
Nigerian (13)	26	0.03
Other Sub-Saharan African (90)	90	0.12
American (2,739)	2,739	3.55
Arab (370)	663	0.86
Arab (45)	136	0.18
Egyptian (143)	143	0.19
Iraqi (13)	13	0.02
Lebanese (113)	173	0.22
Moroccan (0)	90	0.12
Syrian (56)	56	0.07
Other Arab (0)	52	0.07
Armenian (14)	14	0.02
Australian (54)	54	0.07
Austrian (35)	243	0.31
Belgian (0)	10	0.01
Brazilian (391)	399	0.52
British (250)	385	0.50
Cajun (67)	67	0.09
Canadian (137)	193	0.25
Celtic (14)	14	0.02
Croatian (39)	86	0.11
Czech (90)	339	0.44
Czechoslovakian (0)	64	0.08
Danish (160)	572	0.74
Dutch (161)	792	1.03
Eastern European (13)	13	0.02
English (1,732)	5,107	6.62
European (438)	478	0.62
Finnish (12)	58	0.08
French, ex. Basque (454)	1,945	2.52
French Canadian (223)	379	0.49
German (2,256)	7,407	9.60
Greek (224)	413	0.54
Guyanese (144)	144	0.19
Hungarian (79)	238	0.31
Iranian (43)	43	0.06
Irish (2,626)	8,005	10.37
Israeli (33)	33	0.04
Italian (1,813)	4,364	5.66
Latvian (0)	14	0.02
Lithuanian (42)	117	0.15
Luxemburger (10)	10	0.01
Maltese (0)	30	0.04
Northern European (35)	35	0.05
Norwegian (52)	222	0.29
Pennsylvania German (18)	18	0.02
Polish (586)	2,002	2.59
Portuguese (260)	429	0.56
Romanian (59)	59	0.08
Russian (138)	412	0.53
Scandinavian (32)	92	0.12
Scotch-Irish (404)	915	1.19
Scottish (335)	957	1.24
Slavic (0)	9	0.01
Slovak (29)	109	0.14
Swedish (159)	543	0.70
Swiss (0)	37	0.05
Turkish (13)	13	0.02
Ukrainian (27)	85	0.11
Welsh (47)	528	0.68
West Indian, ex. Hispanic (1,862)	2,212	2.87
Barbadian (8)	8	0.01
Belizean (25)	49	0.06
British West Indian (114)	114	0.15
Dutch West Indian (0)	33	0.04
Haitian (215)	288	0.37
Jamaican (959)	1,077	1.40
Trinidadian/Tobagonian (257)	285	0.37
West Indian (284)	358	0.46
Yugoslavian (13)	25	0.03

Hispanic Origin	Population	%
Hispanic or Latino (of any race)	34,380	43.83
Central American, ex. Mexican	1,444	1.84
Costa Rican	177	0.23
Guatemalan	191	0.24
Honduran	353	0.45
Nicaraguan	229	0.29
Panamanian	214	0.27
Salvadoran	273	0.35
Other Central American	7	0.01
Cuban	11,570	14.75
Dominican Republic	2,248	2.87
Mexican	1,505	1.92
Puerto Rican	10,742	13.69
South American	4,669	5.95
Argentinean	138	0.18
Bolivian	83	0.11
Chilean	78	0.10
Colombian	2,631	3.35
Ecuadorian	454	0.58
Paraguayan	1	<0.01
Peruvian	800	1.02
Uruguayan	51	0.07
Venezuelan	397	0.51
Other South American	36	0.05
Other Hispanic or Latino	2,202	2.81

Race*	Population	%
African-American/Black (7,588)	8,818	11.24
Not Hispanic (6,169)	6,837	8.72
Hispanic (1,419)	1,981	2.53
American Indian/Alaska Native (350)	750	0.96
Not Hispanic (172)	439	0.56
Hispanic (178)	311	0.40
Alaska Athabascan *(Ala. Nat.)* (0)	3	<0.01
Aleut *(Alaska Native)* (1)	2	<0.01
Apache (1)	4	0.01
Blackfeet (4)	27	0.03
Canadian/French Am. Ind. (2)	4	0.01
Central American Ind. (4)	10	0.01
Cherokee (37)	125	0.16
Cheyenne (0)	1	<0.01
Chickasaw (2)	2	<0.01
Chippewa (6)	9	0.01
Choctaw (4)	7	0.01
Comanche (2)	3	<0.01
Cree (0)	1	<0.01
Creek (9)	17	0.02
Crow (0)	1	<0.01
Delaware (3)	5	0.01
Iroquois (8)	18	0.02
Lumbee (2)	2	<0.01
Mexican American Ind. (23)	30	0.04
Navajo (2)	3	<0.01
Ottawa (1)	1	<0.01
Potawatomi (0)	1	<0.01
Seminole (8)	12	0.02
Sioux (7)	18	0.02
South American Ind. (31)	58	0.07
Spanish American Ind. (4)	8	0.01
Tlingit-Haida *(Alaska Native)* (1)	1	<0.01
Tohono O'Odham (1)	3	<0.01
Asian (3,198)	3,787	4.83
Not Hispanic (3,139)	3,619	4.61
Hispanic (59)	168	0.21
Bangladeshi (7)	13	0.02
Burmese (16)	16	0.02
Cambodian (15)	16	0.02
Chinese, ex. Taiwanese (347)	430	0.55
Filipino (306)	443	0.56
Hmong (1)	1	<0.01
Indian (867)	963	1.23
Indonesian (7)	11	0.01
Japanese (45)	91	0.12

*Notes: † The Census 2010 population figure is used to calculate the percentages in the Hispanic Origin and Race categories. Ancestry percentages are based on the 2006-2010 American Community Survey population (not shown); ‡ Numbers in parentheses indicate the number of people reporting a single ancestry; * Numbers in parentheses indicate the number of persons reporting this race alone, not in combination with any other race; Please refer to the Explanation of Data for more information.*

Race*	Population	%
Korean (327)	412	0.53
Laotian (16)	17	0.02
Malaysian (2)	6	0.01
Nepalese (1)	1	<0.01
Pakistani (21)	31	0.04
Sri Lankan (3)	3	<0.01
Taiwanese (20)	23	0.03
Thai (93)	132	0.17
Vietnamese (1,044)	1,097	1.40
Hawaii Native/Pacific Islander (53)	207	0.26
Not Hispanic (39)	115	0.15
Hispanic (14)	92	0.12
Fijian (3)	3	<0.01
Guamanian/Chamorro (9)	19	0.02
Marshallese (1)	1	<0.01
Native Hawaiian (20)	43	0.05
Samoan (9)	14	0.02
White (59,596)	61,962	78.99
Not Hispanic (32,992)	34,030	43.38
Hispanic (26,604)	27,932	35.61

Trinity

Place Type: CDP
County: Pasco
Population: 10,907†

Ancestry‡	Population	%
American (330)	330	3.05
Arab (14)	14	0.13
Lebanese (14)	14	0.13
Armenian (13)	27	0.25
Austrian (0)	70	0.65
Belgian (0)	15	0.14
British (10)	10	0.09
Canadian (0)	10	0.09
Croatian (11)	35	0.32
Czech (40)	102	0.94
Czechoslovakian (18)	37	0.34
Dutch (8)	155	1.43
English (544)	1,548	14.31
European (0)	98	0.91
Finnish (0)	81	0.75
French, ex. Basque (71)	372	3.44
French Canadian (51)	181	1.67
German (519)	2,596	24.00
Greek (119)	219	2.02
Hungarian (43)	132	1.22
Irish (605)	2,569	23.75
Italian (965)	1,865	17.24
Lithuanian (43)	89	0.82
Norwegian (98)	233	2.15
Polish (247)	605	5.59
Portuguese (30)	50	0.46
Romanian (29)	29	0.27
Russian (14)	178	1.65
Scotch-Irish (154)	247	2.28
Scottish (48)	263	2.43
Slavic (27)	27	0.25
Slovak (11)	44	0.41
Swedish (54)	102	0.94
Swiss (0)	14	0.13
Turkish (46)	78	0.72
Ukrainian (210)	243	2.25
Welsh (10)	98	0.91
Yugoslavian (0)	15	0.14

Hispanic Origin	Population	%
Hispanic or Latino (of any race)	604	5.54
Central American, ex. Mexican	49	0.45
Costa Rican	9	0.08
Guatemalan	17	0.16
Honduran	7	0.06
Nicaraguan	2	0.02
Panamanian	7	0.06
Salvadoran	7	0.06
Cuban	59	0.54
Dominican Republic	18	0.17
Mexican	82	0.75
Puerto Rican	245	2.25
South American	91	0.83
Argentinean	9	0.08
Bolivian	1	0.01
Chilean	4	0.04
Colombian	28	0.26
Ecuadorian	26	0.24
Peruvian	10	0.09
Venezuelan	13	0.12
Other Hispanic or Latino	60	0.55

Race*	Population	%
African-American/Black (164)	209	1.92
Not Hispanic (157)	193	1.77
Hispanic (7)	16	0.15
American Indian/Alaska Native (18)	40	0.37
Not Hispanic (15)	34	0.31
Hispanic (3)	6	0.06
Central American Ind. (2)	2	0.02
Cherokee (0)	6	0.06
Chickasaw (0)	1	0.01
Chippewa (0)	3	0.03
Creek (0)	1	0.01
Iroquois (3)	9	0.08
Mexican American Ind. (1)	1	0.01
Ottawa (1)	1	0.01
Tlingit-Haida *(Alaska Native)* (0)	1	0.01
Asian (314)	383	3.51
Not Hispanic (313)	374	3.43
Hispanic (1)	9	0.08
Bangladeshi (4)	4	0.04
Chinese, ex. Taiwanese (34)	43	0.39
Filipino (64)	84	0.77
Indian (101)	113	1.04
Indonesian (1)	2	0.02
Japanese (7)	16	0.15
Korean (15)	20	0.18
Laotian (9)	14	0.13
Malaysian (1)	1	0.01
Pakistani (13)	16	0.15
Taiwanese (2)	2	0.02
Thai (3)	3	0.03
Vietnamese (58)	58	0.53
Hawaii Native/Pacific Islander (2)	11	0.10
Not Hispanic (1)	9	0.08
Hispanic (1)	2	0.02
Guamanian/Chamorro (1)	1	0.01
Native Hawaiian (1)	4	0.04
White (10,162)	10,296	94.40
Not Hispanic (9,687)	9,784	89.70
Hispanic (475)	512	4.69

Union Park

Place Type: CDP
County: Orange
Population: 9,765†

Ancestry‡	Population	%
African, Sub-Saharan (86)	86	0.85
African (76)	76	0.75
Other Sub-Saharan African (10)	10	0.10
American (487)	487	4.80
Arab (128)	139	1.37
Lebanese (109)	109	1.07
Moroccan (19)	19	0.19
Syrian (0)	11	0.11
Australian (0)	27	0.27
Belgian (0)	10	0.10
British (15)	31	0.31
Canadian (25)	76	0.75
Czechoslovakian (11)	25	0.25
Danish (0)	14	0.14
Dutch (0)	84	0.83
English (128)	533	5.25
European (44)	44	0.43
Finnish (6)	6	0.06
French, ex. Basque (22)	90	0.89
French Canadian (0)	10	0.10
German (376)	1,145	11.27
Greek (60)	101	0.99
Hungarian (30)	41	0.40
Irish (237)	759	7.47
Israeli (12)	12	0.12
Italian (102)	386	3.80
Latvian (0)	8	0.08
Lithuanian (31)	109	1.07
Norwegian (38)	127	1.25
Pennsylvania German (8)	18	0.18
Polish (65)	151	1.49
Portuguese (13)	13	0.13
Romanian (0)	11	0.11
Russian (7)	7	0.07
Scotch-Irish (54)	144	1.42
Scottish (31)	192	1.89
Slovak (0)	23	0.23
Swedish (0)	87	0.86
Ukrainian (0)	20	0.20
Welsh (8)	32	0.32
West Indian, ex. Hispanic (205)	241	2.37
Bahamian (0)	12	0.12
Haitian (29)	29	0.29
Jamaican (125)	134	1.32
West Indian (51)	66	0.65

Hispanic Origin	Population	%
Hispanic or Latino (of any race)	4,001	40.97
Central American, ex. Mexican	211	2.16
Costa Rican	27	0.28
Guatemalan	34	0.35
Honduran	25	0.26
Nicaraguan	46	0.47
Panamanian	43	0.44
Salvadoran	30	0.31
Other Central American	6	0.06
Cuban	344	3.52
Dominican Republic	237	2.43
Mexican	248	2.54
Puerto Rican	2,520	25.81
South American	329	3.37
Argentinean	6	0.06
Chilean	22	0.23
Colombian	160	1.64
Ecuadorian	37	0.38
Peruvian	56	0.57
Venezuelan	47	0.48
Other South American	1	0.01
Other Hispanic or Latino	112	1.15

Race*	Population	%
African-American/Black (834)	985	10.09
Not Hispanic (616)	699	7.16
Hispanic (218)	286	2.93
American Indian/Alaska Native (66)	132	1.35
Not Hispanic (31)	71	0.73
Hispanic (35)	61	0.62
Apache (0)	1	0.01
Blackfeet (0)	4	0.04
Central American Ind. (2)	3	0.03
Cherokee (3)	14	0.14
Chickasaw (0)	2	0.02
Chippewa (1)	3	0.03
Choctaw (0)	1	0.01
Creek (1)	3	0.03
Delaware (2)	2	0.02
Inupiat *(Alaska Native)* (1)	3	0.03
Iroquois (1)	1	0.01
Lumbee (1)	1	0.01
Mexican American Ind. (7)	9	0.09
Osage (0)	1	0.01
Pueblo (4)	4	0.04
Seminole (0)	2	0.02
Sioux (1)	1	0.01
South American Ind. (2)	8	0.08
Spanish American Ind. (2)	2	0.02
Ute (0)	2	0.02
Asian (394)	508	5.20
Not Hispanic (391)	478	4.90
Hispanic (3)	30	0.31
Bangladeshi (3)	4	0.04
Cambodian (3)	7	0.07

*Notes: † The Census 2010 population figure is used to calculate the percentages in the Hispanic Origin and Race categories. Ancestry percentages are based on the 2006-2010 American Community Survey population (not shown); ‡ Numbers in parentheses indicate the number of people reporting a single ancestry; * Numbers in parentheses indicate the number of persons reporting this race alone, not in combination with any other race; Please refer to the Explanation of Data for more information.*

Chinese, ex. Taiwanese (47)	59	0.60
Filipino (97)	126	1.29
Indian (85)	101	1.03
Indonesian (5)	5	0.05
Japanese (11)	22	0.23
Korean (18)	28	0.29
Laotian (2)	6	0.06
Pakistani (2)	2	0.02
Sri Lankan (2)	3	0.03
Taiwanese (4)	5	0.05
Thai (3)	4	0.04
Vietnamese (101)	107	1.10
Hawaii Native/Pacific Islander (31)	59	0.60
Not Hispanic (27)	50	0.51
Hispanic (4)	9	0.09
Fijian (1)	1	0.01
Guamanian/Chamorro (1)	7	0.07
Native Hawaiian (6)	9	0.09
White (7,215)	7,499	76.79
Not Hispanic (4,473)	4,602	47.13
Hispanic (2,742)	2,897	29.67

University

Place Type: CDP
County: Hillsborough
Population: 41,163†

Ancestry‡	Population	%
African, Sub-Saharan (608)	736	1.82
African (464)	592	1.46
Ghanaian (40)	40	0.10
Liberian (29)	29	0.07
Nigerian (39)	39	0.10
Sudanese (36)	36	0.09
Albanian (0)	29	0.07
American (1,385)	1,385	3.42
Arab (73)	138	0.34
Arab (33)	45	0.11
Iraqi (28)	28	0.07
Palestinian (0)	36	0.09
Syrian (0)	17	0.04
Other Arab (12)	12	0.03
Armenian (0)	31	0.08
Australian (0)	19	0.05
Austrian (10)	37	0.09
Brazilian (65)	90	0.22
British (87)	173	0.43
Bulgarian (22)	31	0.08
Canadian (69)	97	0.24
Celtic (0)	22	0.05
Croatian (0)	78	0.19
Czech (18)	38	0.09
Czechoslovakian (0)	10	0.02
Danish (12)	77	0.19
Dutch (69)	402	0.99
Eastern European (50)	50	0.12
English (845)	2,123	5.24
European (134)	152	0.38
Finnish (0)	16	0.04
French, ex. Basque (292)	950	2.35
French Canadian (83)	110	0.27
German (840)	2,931	7.24
Greek (58)	260	0.64
Hungarian (39)	146	0.36
Icelander (0)	12	0.03
Iranian (38)	80	0.20
Irish (688)	2,841	7.02
Italian (526)	1,711	4.23
Lithuanian (80)	101	0.25
Maltese (0)	11	0.03
Northern European (7)	7	0.02
Norwegian (97)	264	0.65
Pennsylvania German (0)	27	0.07
Polish (104)	464	1.15
Portuguese (38)	141	0.35
Romanian (0)	29	0.07
Russian (77)	248	0.61
Scandinavian (0)	43	0.11
Scotch-Irish (53)	224	0.55
Scottish (196)	551	1.36
Serbian (10)	24	0.06
Slovak (7)	21	0.05
Swedish (0)	89	0.22
Swiss (0)	29	0.07
Turkish (98)	98	0.24
Ukrainian (22)	61	0.15
Welsh (14)	170	0.42
West Indian, ex. Hispanic (2,317)	2,802	6.92
British West Indian (194)	194	0.48
Haitian (1,085)	1,162	2.87
Jamaican (533)	853	2.11
Trinidadian/Tobagonian (26)	26	0.06
U.S. Virgin Islander (14)	19	0.05
West Indian (465)	539	1.33
Other West Indian (0)	9	0.02

Hispanic Origin	Population	%
Hispanic or Latino (of any race)	11,983	29.11
Central American, ex. Mexican	1,342	3.26
Costa Rican	60	0.15
Guatemalan	100	0.24
Honduran	922	2.24
Nicaraguan	75	0.18
Panamanian	67	0.16
Salvadoran	111	0.27
Other Central American	7	0.02
Cuban	850	2.06
Dominican Republic	403	0.98
Mexican	3,058	7.43
Puerto Rican	4,854	11.79
South American	714	1.73
Argentinean	21	0.05
Bolivian	4	0.01
Chilean	8	0.02
Colombian	321	0.78
Ecuadorian	82	0.20
Paraguayan	3	0.01
Peruvian	154	0.37
Uruguayan	19	0.05
Venezuelan	96	0.23
Other South American	6	0.01
Other Hispanic or Latino	762	1.85

Race*	Population	%
African-American/Black (13,518)	14,416	35.02
Not Hispanic (12,699)	13,256	32.20
Hispanic (819)	1,160	2.82
American Indian/Alaska Native (250)	548	1.33
Not Hispanic (108)	308	0.75
Hispanic (142)	240	0.58
Apache (3)	14	0.03
Blackfeet (1)	24	0.06
Canadian/French Am. Ind. (1)	1	<0.01
Central American Ind. (7)	9	0.02
Cherokee (26)	104	0.25
Chippewa (5)	6	0.01
Choctaw (1)	5	0.01
Comanche (0)	1	<0.01
Cree (0)	5	0.01
Creek (3)	9	0.02
Delaware (1)	6	0.01
Iroquois (2)	7	0.02
Kiowa (0)	1	<0.01
Lumbee (1)	3	0.01
Mexican American Ind. (43)	50	0.12
Osage (0)	1	<0.01
Potawatomi (0)	1	<0.01
Seminole (2)	7	0.02
Shoshone (1)	1	<0.01
Sioux (1)	4	0.01
South American Ind. (7)	19	0.05
Spanish American Ind. (12)	13	0.03
Tlingit-Haida (Alaska Native) (1)	1	<0.01
Yaqui (1)	1	<0.01
Asian (1,547)	1,871	4.55
Not Hispanic (1,531)	1,818	4.42
Hispanic (16)	53	0.13
Bangladeshi (22)	27	0.07
Burmese (8)	8	0.02
Cambodian (6)	10	0.02
Chinese, ex. Taiwanese (388)	455	1.11
Filipino (149)	222	0.54
Hmong (1)	3	0.01
Indian (582)	640	1.55
Indonesian (6)	8	0.02
Japanese (37)	62	0.15
Korean (70)	90	0.22
Laotian (8)	10	0.02
Malaysian (8)	8	0.02
Nepalese (30)	33	0.08
Pakistani (29)	34	0.08
Sri Lankan (15)	15	0.04
Taiwanese (11)	15	0.04
Thai (11)	30	0.07
Vietnamese (126)	143	0.35
Hawaii Native/Pacific Islander (35)	125	0.30
Not Hispanic (26)	94	0.23
Hispanic (9)	31	0.08
Guamanian/Chamorro (10)	17	0.04
Native Hawaiian (9)	29	0.07
Samoan (4)	7	0.02
Tongan (0)	1	<0.01
White (20,571)	21,749	52.84
Not Hispanic (13,814)	14,458	35.12
Hispanic (6,757)	7,291	17.71

University

Place Type: CDP
County: Orange
Population: 31,084†

Ancestry‡	Population	%
African, Sub-Saharan (76)	199	0.94
African (32)	49	0.23
Ethiopian (23)	23	0.11
Ghanaian (21)	21	0.10
Nigerian (0)	106	0.50
American (1,600)	1,600	7.55
Arab (305)	402	1.90
Arab (132)	132	0.62
Egyptian (0)	37	0.17
Moroccan (16)	68	0.32
Palestinian (60)	60	0.28
Syrian (16)	24	0.11
Other Arab (81)	81	0.38
Austrian (18)	117	0.55
Belgian (14)	14	0.07
Brazilian (17)	46	0.22
British (149)	188	0.89
Bulgarian (25)	25	0.12
Canadian (26)	56	0.26
Czech (0)	87	0.41
Czechoslovakian (0)	27	0.13
Danish (22)	58	0.27
Dutch (119)	356	1.68
Eastern European (9)	26	0.12
English (506)	1,429	6.75
European (149)	174	0.82
Finnish (0)	67	0.32
French, ex. Basque (92)	478	2.26
French Canadian (31)	86	0.41
German (720)	2,345	11.07
Greek (58)	152	0.72
Hungarian (44)	72	0.34
Iranian (37)	37	0.17
Irish (597)	2,130	10.06
Israeli (14)	47	0.22
Italian (732)	1,934	9.13
Latvian (0)	18	0.08
Lithuanian (32)	126	0.59
Norwegian (51)	202	0.95
Polish (220)	572	2.70
Portuguese (44)	133	0.63
Romanian (16)	16	0.08
Russian (99)	245	1.16
Scotch-Irish (16)	308	1.45
Scottish (38)	143	0.68
Slovak (0)	15	0.07

SECTION TWO

*Notes: † The Census 2010 population figure is used to calculate the percentages in the Hispanic Origin and Race categories. Ancestry percentages are based on the 2006-2010 American Community Survey population (not shown); ‡ Numbers in parentheses indicate the number of people reporting a single ancestry; * Numbers in parentheses indicate the number of persons reporting this race alone, not in combination with any other race; Please refer to the Explanation of Data for more information.*

Swedish (42)	150	0.71
Swiss (0)	25	0.12
Turkish (42)	62	0.29
Ukrainian (28)	71	0.34
Welsh (0)	62	0.29
West Indian, ex. Hispanic (648)	751	3.55
Bahamian (128)	128	0.60
Barbadian (49)	49	0.23
British West Indian (20)	30	0.14
Haitian (66)	66	0.31
Jamaican (207)	288	1.36
West Indian (178)	190	0.90

Hispanic Origin	Population	%
Hispanic or Latino (of any race)	6,527	21.00
Central American, ex. Mexican	272	0.88
Costa Rican	25	0.08
Guatemalan	31	0.10
Honduran	67	0.22
Nicaraguan	34	0.11
Panamanian	74	0.24
Salvadoran	41	0.13
Cuban	702	2.26
Dominican Republic	228	0.73
Mexican	496	1.60
Puerto Rican	2,980	9.59
South American	758	2.44
Argentinean	41	0.13
Bolivian	9	0.03
Chilean	19	0.06
Colombian	355	1.14
Ecuadorian	114	0.37
Paraguayan	2	0.01
Peruvian	100	0.32
Uruguayan	8	0.03
Venezuelan	109	0.35
Other South American	1	<0.01
Other Hispanic or Latino	1,091	3.51

Race*	Population	%
African-American/Black (3,770)	4,070	13.09
Not Hispanic (3,497)	3,695	11.89
Hispanic (273)	375	1.21
American Indian/Alaska Native (106)	213	0.69
Not Hispanic (84)	152	0.49
Hispanic (22)	61	0.20
Apache (1)	2	0.01
Cherokee (10)	46	0.15
Chippewa (2)	3	0.01
Comanche (5)	5	0.02
Cree (0)	1	<0.01
Creek (6)	7	0.02
Inupiat *(Alaska Native)* (6)	6	0.02
Iroquois (3)	6	0.02
Lumbee (1)	1	<0.01
Mexican American Ind. (3)	7	0.02
Navajo (0)	2	0.01
Potawatomi (0)	6	0.02
Seminole (0)	4	0.01
Sioux (0)	5	0.02
South American Ind. (3)	6	0.02
Asian (1,721)	1,935	6.23
Not Hispanic (1,691)	1,877	6.04
Hispanic (30)	58	0.19
Bangladeshi (24)	24	0.08
Burmese (3)	3	0.01
Cambodian (4)	5	0.02
Chinese, ex. Taiwanese (391)	434	1.40
Filipino (192)	247	0.79
Hmong (1)	1	<0.01
Indian (453)	480	1.54
Indonesian (5)	6	0.02
Japanese (38)	53	0.17
Korean (63)	79	0.25
Laotian (0)	2	0.01
Nepalese (10)	10	0.03
Pakistani (70)	76	0.24
Sri Lankan (2)	2	0.01
Taiwanese (10)	12	0.04
Thai (31)	38	0.12
Vietnamese (178)	183	0.59
Hawaii Native/Pacific Islander (35)	82	0.26
Not Hispanic (27)	62	0.20
Hispanic (8)	20	0.06
Guamanian/Chamorro (7)	13	0.04
Native Hawaiian (12)	14	0.05
Samoan (4)	9	0.03
White (23,031)	23,604	75.94
Not Hispanic (18,759)	19,098	61.44
Hispanic (4,272)	4,506	14.50

University Park

Place Type: CDP
County: Miami-Dade
Population: 26,995†

Ancestry‡	Population	%
African, Sub-Saharan (16)	16	0.07
African (16)	16	0.07
American (286)	286	1.18
Arab (27)	27	0.11
Lebanese (13)	13	0.05
Other Arab (14)	14	0.06
Austrian (17)	31	0.13
Brazilian (10)	10	0.04
British (0)	10	0.04
Czech (9)	67	0.28
Danish (14)	42	0.17
Dutch (0)	18	0.07
English (0)	155	0.64
French, ex. Basque (14)	85	0.35
German (53)	187	0.77
Greek (0)	6	0.02
Irish (11)	81	0.33
Italian (50)	205	0.84
Lithuanian (0)	11	0.05
Polish (35)	70	0.29
Russian (33)	126	0.52
Scotch-Irish (0)	39	0.16
Scottish (0)	6	0.02
Swedish (22)	22	0.09
Swiss (0)	21	0.09
Welsh (0)	16	0.07
West Indian, ex. Hispanic (267)	316	1.30
Bahamian (16)	16	0.07
Haitian (42)	42	0.17
Jamaican (161)	210	0.86
Trinidadian/Tobagonian (30)	30	0.12
West Indian (18)	18	0.07

Hispanic Origin	Population	%
Hispanic or Latino (of any race)	22,938	84.97
Central American, ex. Mexican	1,909	7.07
Costa Rican	74	0.27
Guatemalan	174	0.64
Honduran	272	1.01
Nicaraguan	1,167	4.32
Panamanian	65	0.24
Salvadoran	156	0.58
Other Central American	1	<0.01
Cuban	17,155	63.55
Dominican Republic	317	1.17
Mexican	251	0.93
Puerto Rican	572	2.12
South American	2,104	7.79
Argentinean	183	0.68
Bolivian	80	0.30
Chilean	104	0.39
Colombian	865	3.20
Ecuadorian	144	0.53
Paraguayan	11	0.04
Peruvian	353	1.31
Uruguayan	57	0.21
Venezuelan	306	1.13
Other South American	1	<0.01
Other Hispanic or Latino	630	2.33

Race*	Population	%
African-American/Black (1,228)	1,362	5.05
Not Hispanic (865)	946	3.50
Hispanic (363)	416	1.54
American Indian/Alaska Native (27)	76	0.28
Not Hispanic (4)	21	0.08
Hispanic (23)	55	0.20
Blackfeet (0)	1	<0.01
Central American Ind. (0)	1	<0.01
Cherokee (3)	9	0.03
Choctaw (0)	1	<0.01
Cree (0)	1	<0.01
Mexican American Ind. (10)	10	0.04
Pima (1)	1	<0.01
Seminole (0)	1	<0.01
Sioux (0)	1	<0.01
South American Ind. (2)	6	0.02
Spanish American Ind. (1)	4	0.01
Asian (514)	619	2.29
Not Hispanic (502)	571	2.12
Hispanic (12)	48	0.18
Bangladeshi (5)	5	0.02
Burmese (4)	5	0.02
Cambodian (0)	1	<0.01
Chinese, ex. Taiwanese (137)	168	0.62
Filipino (66)	83	0.31
Indian (211)	229	0.85
Japanese (9)	16	0.06
Korean (9)	17	0.06
Nepalese (5)	5	0.02
Pakistani (24)	31	0.11
Sri Lankan (5)	5	0.02
Taiwanese (4)	9	0.03
Thai (6)	7	0.03
Vietnamese (15)	19	0.07
Hawaii Native/Pacific Islander (6)	17	0.06
Not Hispanic (5)	9	0.03
Hispanic (1)	8	0.03
Fijian (0)	1	<0.01
Guamanian/Chamorro (0)	1	<0.01
Native Hawaiian (3)	8	0.03
Samoan (1)	1	<0.01
White (24,345)	24,704	91.51
Not Hispanic (2,501)	2,605	9.65
Hispanic (21,844)	22,099	81.86

Upper Grand Lagoon

Place Type: CDP
County: Bay
Population: 13,963†

Ancestry‡	Population	%
American (818)	818	6.55
Austrian (0)	31	0.25
Belgian (21)	42	0.34
Brazilian (13)	13	0.10
British (10)	54	0.43
Bulgarian (0)	14	0.11
Canadian (62)	89	0.71
Czech (22)	74	0.59
Danish (12)	99	0.79
Dutch (60)	170	1.36
Eastern European (0)	12	0.10
English (1,352)	2,540	20.35
European (225)	263	2.11
Finnish (10)	10	0.08
French, ex. Basque (206)	534	4.28
French Canadian (70)	237	1.90
German (636)	2,015	16.14
Greek (65)	85	0.68
Hungarian (26)	53	0.42
Irish (526)	1,509	12.09
Israeli (0)	33	0.26
Italian (304)	1,018	8.16
Lithuanian (0)	33	0.26
New Zealander (39)	85	0.68
Northern European (46)	46	0.37
Norwegian (70)	95	0.76
Polish (34)	116	0.93
Portuguese (17)	87	0.70
Russian (15)	47	0.38

*Notes: † The Census 2010 population figure is used to calculate the percentages in the Hispanic Origin and Race categories. Ancestry percentages are based on the 2006-2010 American Community Survey population (not shown); ‡ Numbers in parentheses indicate the number of people reporting a single ancestry; * Numbers in parentheses indicate the number of persons reporting this race alone, not in combination with any other race; Please refer to the Explanation of Data for more information.*

Scandinavian (0)	34	0.27
Scotch-Irish (69)	188	1.51
Scottish (191)	356	2.85
Slovak (0)	27	0.22
Slovene (0)	12	0.10
Swedish (72)	93	0.75
Swiss (0)	12	0.10
Turkish (35)	35	0.28
Ukrainian (26)	98	0.79
Welsh (0)	31	0.25
West Indian, ex. Hispanic (24)	62	0.50
Dutch West Indian (0)	8	0.06
Trinidadian/Tobagonian (9)	9	0.07
West Indian (15)	45	0.36

Hispanic Origin	Population	%
Hispanic or Latino (of any race)	648	4.64
Central American, ex. Mexican	41	0.29
Costa Rican	8	0.06
Guatemalan	1	0.01
Honduran	12	0.09
Nicaraguan	5	0.04
Panamanian	12	0.09
Salvadoran	3	0.02
Cuban	68	0.49
Dominican Republic	5	0.04
Mexican	262	1.88
Puerto Rican	142	1.02
South American	34	0.24
Argentinean	3	0.02
Chilean	2	0.01
Colombian	12	0.09
Ecuadorian	1	0.01
Paraguayan	1	0.01
Peruvian	9	0.06
Venezuelan	5	0.04
Other South American	1	0.01
Other Hispanic or Latino	96	0.69

Race*	Population	%
African-American/Black (317)	441	3.16
Not Hispanic (310)	417	2.99
Hispanic (7)	24	0.17
American Indian/Alaska Native (68)	267	1.91
Not Hispanic (63)	248	1.78
Hispanic (5)	19	0.14
Apache (2)	3	0.02
Arapaho (0)	1	0.01
Blackfeet (1)	8	0.06
Cherokee (17)	75	0.54
Cheyenne (0)	6	0.04
Chickasaw (4)	7	0.05
Chippewa (0)	4	0.03
Choctaw (0)	7	0.05
Creek (2)	15	0.11
Crow (0)	1	0.01
Delaware (2)	2	0.01
Iroquois (1)	4	0.03
Lumbee (1)	2	0.01
Mexican American Ind. (2)	3	0.02
Navajo (0)	2	0.01
Osage (4)	4	0.03
Ottawa (1)	4	0.03
Seminole (1)	7	0.05
Sioux (1)	7	0.05
South American Ind. (1)	5	0.04
Asian (228)	359	2.57
Not Hispanic (228)	352	2.52
Hispanic (0)	7	0.05
Bangladeshi (5)	5	0.04
Chinese, ex. Taiwanese (17)	27	0.19
Filipino (44)	78	0.56
Indian (46)	53	0.38
Indonesian (1)	3	0.02
Japanese (15)	45	0.32
Korean (18)	42	0.30
Pakistani (0)	6	0.04
Taiwanese (5)	5	0.04
Thai (28)	37	0.26
Vietnamese (38)	39	0.28
Hawaii Native/Pacific Islander (17)	25	0.18
Not Hispanic (17)	23	0.16
Hispanic (0)	2	0.01
Fijian (0)	1	0.01
Guamanian/Chamorro (1)	4	0.03
Native Hawaiian (14)	14	0.10
Samoan (1)	3	0.02
White (12,728)	13,148	94.16
Not Hispanic (12,298)	12,645	90.56
Hispanic (430)	503	3.60

Valrico

Place Type: CDP
County: Hillsborough
Population: 35,545†

Ancestry‡	Population	%
African, Sub-Saharan (269)	281	0.81
African (63)	63	0.18
Cape Verdean (22)	34	0.10
Nigerian (63)	63	0.18
Sierra Leonean (121)	121	0.35
American (2,130)	2,130	6.15
Arab (139)	205	0.59
Arab (54)	54	0.16
Egyptian (43)	43	0.12
Lebanese (42)	47	0.14
Moroccan (0)	12	0.03
Syrian (0)	25	0.07
Other Arab (0)	24	0.07
Armenian (11)	20	0.06
Austrian (0)	32	0.09
Belgian (0)	10	0.03
British (91)	298	0.86
Bulgarian (31)	31	0.09
Canadian (28)	51	0.15
Croatian (12)	12	0.03
Czech (14)	145	0.42
Czechoslovakian (49)	81	0.23
Danish (68)	188	0.54
Dutch (187)	1,135	3.28
English (1,382)	4,087	11.80
European (248)	281	0.81
Finnish (0)	13	0.04
French, ex. Basque (190)	1,444	4.17
French Canadian (36)	329	0.95
German (1,223)	5,933	17.13
Greek (53)	155	0.45
Guyanese (17)	136	0.39
Hungarian (48)	194	0.56
Icelander (14)	14	0.04
Irish (1,414)	5,360	15.48
Italian (1,224)	3,459	9.99
Lithuanian (135)	317	0.92
Luxemburger (20)	20	0.06
Macedonian (13)	36	0.10
New Zealander (8)	8	0.02
Northern European (40)	40	0.12
Norwegian (120)	492	1.42
Polish (330)	1,084	3.13
Portuguese (33)	132	0.38
Russian (51)	290	0.84
Scandinavian (35)	64	0.18
Scotch-Irish (253)	975	2.82
Scottish (368)	1,278	3.69
Slavic (10)	89	0.26
Slovak (26)	74	0.21
Slovene (10)	10	0.03
Swedish (179)	277	0.80
Swiss (10)	73	0.21
Turkish (12)	27	0.08
Ukrainian (6)	47	0.14
Welsh (58)	273	0.79
West Indian, ex. Hispanic (648)	787	2.27
Bahamian (38)	38	0.11
British West Indian (186)	186	0.54
Haitian (0)	15	0.04
Jamaican (238)	331	0.96
Trinidadian/Tobagonian (29)	37	0.11
West Indian (157)	180	0.52

Hispanic Origin	Population	%
Hispanic or Latino (of any race)	5,803	16.33
Central American, ex. Mexican	295	0.83
Costa Rican	20	0.06
Guatemalan	49	0.14
Honduran	73	0.21
Nicaraguan	38	0.11
Panamanian	61	0.17
Salvadoran	54	0.15
Cuban	830	2.34
Dominican Republic	357	1.00
Mexican	916	2.58
Puerto Rican	2,349	6.61
South American	568	1.60
Argentinean	33	0.09
Bolivian	1	<0.01
Chilean	22	0.06
Colombian	285	0.80
Ecuadorian	88	0.25
Peruvian	74	0.21
Uruguayan	6	0.02
Venezuelan	54	0.15
Other South American	5	0.01
Other Hispanic or Latino	488	1.37

Race*	Population	%
African-American/Black (3,096)	3,524	9.91
Not Hispanic (2,883)	3,152	8.87
Hispanic (213)	372	1.05
American Indian/Alaska Native (99)	302	0.85
Not Hispanic (73)	223	0.63
Hispanic (26)	79	0.22
Alaska Athabascan *(Ala. Nat.)* (0)	1	<0.01
Aleut *(Alaska Native)* (0)	2	0.01
Apache (1)	8	0.02
Blackfeet (0)	2	0.01
Cherokee (9)	59	0.17
Chippewa (2)	2	0.01
Choctaw (4)	6	0.02
Creek (4)	9	0.03
Iroquois (3)	6	0.02
Lumbee (3)	3	0.01
Mexican American Ind. (2)	4	0.01
Navajo (1)	6	0.02
Puget Sound Salish (0)	4	0.01
Seminole (18)	25	0.07
Sioux (1)	5	0.01
South American Ind. (5)	23	0.06
Spanish American Ind. (2)	3	0.01
Yaqui (3)	4	0.01
Asian (1,396)	1,712	4.82
Not Hispanic (1,376)	1,654	4.65
Hispanic (20)	58	0.16
Bangladeshi (9)	9	0.03
Burmese (1)	3	0.01
Cambodian (0)	2	0.01
Chinese, ex. Taiwanese (129)	169	0.48
Filipino (279)	367	1.03
Hmong (2)	2	0.01
Indian (693)	722	2.03
Indonesian (3)	5	0.01
Japanese (31)	78	0.22
Korean (83)	113	0.32
Laotian (7)	7	0.02
Pakistani (22)	25	0.07
Taiwanese (5)	9	0.03
Thai (34)	50	0.14
Vietnamese (74)	81	0.23
Hawaii Native/Pacific Islander (21)	58	0.16
Not Hispanic (15)	38	0.11
Hispanic (6)	20	0.06
Fijian (0)	1	<0.01
Guamanian/Chamorro (6)	8	0.02
Native Hawaiian (2)	12	0.03
Samoan (1)	2	0.01
White (28,937)	29,751	83.70
Not Hispanic (24,660)	25,181	70.84
Hispanic (4,277)	4,570	12.86

*Notes: † The Census 2010 population figure is used to calculate the percentages in the Hispanic Origin and Race categories. Ancestry percentages are based on the 2006-2010 American Community Survey population (not shown); ‡ Numbers in parentheses indicate the number of people reporting a single ancestry; * Numbers in parentheses indicate the number of persons reporting this race alone, not in combination with any other race; Please refer to the Explanation of Data for more information.*

Venice

Place Type: City
County: Sarasota
Population: 20,748†

Ancestry‡	Population	%
Albanian (114)	114	0.55
Alsatian (0)	16	0.08
American (938)	938	4.53
Arab (52)	52	0.25
Lebanese (13)	13	0.06
Other Arab (39)	39	0.19
Armenian (21)	21	0.10
Austrian (14)	129	0.62
Belgian (0)	25	0.12
Brazilian (0)	15	0.07
British (199)	223	1.08
Canadian (95)	172	0.83
Croatian (16)	16	0.08
Czech (77)	203	0.98
Czechoslovakian (16)	16	0.08
Danish (23)	86	0.42
Dutch (127)	418	2.02
English (1,664)	4,054	19.60
European (107)	119	0.58
Finnish (23)	41	0.20
French, ex. Basque (294)	1,024	4.95
French Canadian (191)	285	1.38
German (1,625)	4,418	21.36
Greek (63)	87	0.42
Hungarian (122)	342	1.65
Irish (1,165)	3,222	15.57
Italian (876)	1,758	8.50
Lithuanian (89)	216	1.04
Luxemburger (0)	15	0.07
Maltese (12)	12	0.06
Northern European (20)	20	0.10
Norwegian (77)	278	1.34
Pennsylvania German (9)	22	0.11
Polish (513)	987	4.77
Portuguese (7)	77	0.37
Romanian (15)	25	0.12
Russian (296)	495	2.39
Scandinavian (0)	11	0.05
Scotch-Irish (245)	628	3.04
Scottish (153)	613	2.96
Slavic (0)	8	0.04
Slovak (36)	77	0.37
Slovene (11)	11	0.05
Swedish (146)	294	1.42
Swiss (56)	123	0.59
Ukrainian (38)	65	0.31
Welsh (32)	190	0.92
West Indian, ex. Hispanic (0)	15	0.07
Jamaican (0)	15	0.07

Hispanic Origin	Population	%
Hispanic or Latino (of any race)	551	2.66
Central American, ex. Mexican	64	0.31
Costa Rican	7	0.03
Guatemalan	17	0.08
Honduran	11	0.05
Nicaraguan	2	0.01
Panamanian	10	0.05
Salvadoran	17	0.08
Cuban	53	0.26
Dominican Republic	4	0.02
Mexican	202	0.97
Puerto Rican	95	0.46
South American	85	0.41
Argentinean	7	0.03
Bolivian	4	0.02
Chilean	18	0.09
Colombian	32	0.15
Ecuadorian	4	0.02
Paraguayan	1	<0.01
Peruvian	13	0.06
Venezuelan	6	0.03
Other Hispanic or Latino	48	0.23

Race*	Population	%
African-American/Black (125)	159	0.77
Not Hispanic (113)	144	0.69
Hispanic (12)	15	0.07
American Indian/Alaska Native (29)	93	0.45
Not Hispanic (24)	84	0.40
Hispanic (5)	9	0.04
Apache (0)	4	0.02
Blackfeet (2)	7	0.03
Cherokee (5)	21	0.10
Chickasaw (0)	1	<0.01
Chippewa (0)	2	0.01
Choctaw (0)	1	<0.01
Crow (1)	1	<0.01
Delaware (1)	1	<0.01
Iroquois (1)	4	0.02
Menominee (1)	1	<0.01
Mexican American Ind. (1)	1	<0.01
Potawatomi (1)	3	0.01
Seminole (1)	2	0.01
Sioux (0)	2	0.01
South American Ind. (3)	3	0.01
Asian (154)	191	0.92
Not Hispanic (152)	189	0.91
Hispanic (2)	2	0.01
Burmese (4)	4	0.02
Chinese, ex. Taiwanese (28)	36	0.17
Filipino (26)	36	0.17
Hmong (1)	1	<0.01
Indian (25)	31	0.15
Indonesian (2)	2	0.01
Japanese (6)	8	0.04
Korean (14)	16	0.08
Malaysian (0)	1	<0.01
Pakistani (11)	11	0.05
Taiwanese (1)	1	<0.01
Thai (7)	9	0.04
Vietnamese (22)	24	0.12
Hawaii Native/Pacific Islander (4)	13	0.06
Not Hispanic (3)	12	0.06
Hispanic (1)	1	<0.01
Marshallese (1)	1	<0.01
Native Hawaiian (0)	4	0.02
White (20,185)	20,323	97.95
Not Hispanic (19,762)	19,881	95.82
Hispanic (423)	442	2.13

Vero Beach South

Place Type: CDP
County: Indian River
Population: 23,092†

Ancestry‡	Population	%
African, Sub-Saharan (21)	31	0.13
African (21)	31	0.13
Albanian (11)	11	0.05
American (1,418)	1,418	6.14
Arab (13)	72	0.31
Lebanese (13)	72	0.31
Australian (17)	17	0.07
Austrian (18)	118	0.51
Belgian (21)	28	0.12
Brazilian (31)	31	0.13
British (57)	164	0.71
Canadian (123)	219	0.95
Croatian (0)	22	0.10
Czech (21)	110	0.48
Czechoslovakian (32)	32	0.14
Danish (26)	82	0.36
Dutch (76)	345	1.49
Eastern European (29)	29	0.13
English (1,349)	3,778	16.36
European (105)	105	0.45
Finnish (9)	9	0.04
French, ex. Basque (159)	1,168	5.06
French Canadian (117)	199	0.86
German (1,407)	5,012	21.71
Greek (71)	90	0.39
Hungarian (146)	311	1.35
Irish (1,050)	4,343	18.81
Israeli (19)	19	0.08
Italian (936)	2,332	10.10
Lithuanian (26)	26	0.11
Macedonian (19)	19	0.08
Norwegian (86)	229	0.99
Pennsylvania German (0)	17	0.07
Polish (445)	1,204	5.21
Portuguese (96)	132	0.57
Romanian (0)	9	0.04
Russian (98)	470	2.04
Scandinavian (8)	32	0.14
Scotch-Irish (246)	611	2.65
Scottish (229)	670	2.90
Slovak (9)	61	0.26
Slovene (10)	10	0.04
Swedish (134)	692	3.00
Swiss (14)	40	0.17
Ukrainian (30)	38	0.16
Welsh (45)	257	1.11
West Indian, ex. Hispanic (163)	239	1.04
Haitian (152)	218	0.94
Jamaican (11)	21	0.09
Yugoslavian (0)	43	0.19

Hispanic Origin	Population	%
Hispanic or Latino (of any race)	2,205	9.55
Central American, ex. Mexican	185	0.80
Costa Rican	14	0.06
Guatemalan	29	0.13
Honduran	54	0.23
Nicaraguan	22	0.10
Panamanian	9	0.04
Salvadoran	57	0.25
Cuban	252	1.09
Dominican Republic	28	0.12
Mexican	747	3.23
Puerto Rican	380	1.65
South American	437	1.89
Argentinean	12	0.05
Chilean	22	0.10
Colombian	265	1.15
Ecuadorian	27	0.12
Paraguayan	1	<0.01
Peruvian	67	0.29
Venezuelan	43	0.19
Other Hispanic or Latino	176	0.76

Race*	Population	%
African-American/Black (1,221)	1,372	5.94
Not Hispanic (1,159)	1,279	5.54
Hispanic (62)	93	0.40
American Indian/Alaska Native (90)	187	0.81
Not Hispanic (57)	140	0.61
Hispanic (33)	47	0.20
Alaska Athabascan *(Ala. Nat.)* (1)	1	<0.01
Apache (0)	2	0.01
Blackfeet (0)	8	0.03
Cherokee (21)	48	0.21
Chippewa (7)	7	0.03
Choctaw (0)	1	<0.01
Creek (2)	7	0.03
Crow (0)	1	<0.01
Delaware (3)	5	0.02
Iroquois (3)	5	0.02
Lumbee (0)	2	0.01
Mexican American Ind. (14)	15	0.06
Osage (0)	1	<0.01
Potawatomi (0)	3	0.01
Seminole (1)	2	0.01
Sioux (0)	1	<0.01
South American Ind. (1)	3	0.01
Spanish American Ind. (6)	6	0.03
Asian (373)	459	1.99
Not Hispanic (365)	434	1.88
Hispanic (8)	25	0.11
Bangladeshi (7)	7	0.03
Burmese (2)	2	0.01
Cambodian (9)	10	0.04

*Notes: † The Census 2010 population figure is used to calculate the percentages in the Hispanic Origin and Race categories. Ancestry percentages are based on the 2006-2010 American Community Survey population (not shown); ‡ Numbers in parentheses indicate the number of people reporting a single ancestry; * Numbers in parentheses indicate the number of persons reporting this race alone, not in combination with any other race; Please refer to the Explanation of Data for more information.*

Chinese, ex. Taiwanese (40)	49	0.21
Filipino (57)	77	0.33
Indian (126)	138	0.60
Indonesian (1)	2	0.01
Japanese (7)	31	0.13
Korean (14)	17	0.07
Laotian (1)	1	<0.01
Nepalese (0)	1	<0.01
Pakistani (27)	29	0.13
Sri Lankan (2)	2	0.01
Taiwanese (5)	7	0.03
Thai (21)	30	0.13
Vietnamese (46)	53	0.23
Hawaii Native/Pacific Islander (8)	17	0.07
Not Hispanic (8)	15	0.06
Hispanic (0)	2	0.01
Guamanian/Chamorro (3)	5	0.02
Native Hawaiian (4)	6	0.03
Tongan (1)	1	<0.01
White (20,538)	20,902	90.52
Not Hispanic (18,980)	19,237	83.31
Hispanic (1,558)	1,665	7.21

Vero Beach

Place Type: City
County: Indian River
Population: 15,220†

Ancestry‡	Population	%
American (1,225)	1,225	7.72
Arab (245)	271	1.71
Egyptian (56)	56	0.35
Lebanese (0)	26	0.16
Moroccan (11)	11	0.07
Other Arab (178)	178	1.12
Assyrian/Chaldean/Syriac (23)	23	0.14
Australian (0)	22	0.14
Austrian (37)	44	0.28
Belgian (21)	69	0.43
British (74)	94	0.59
Canadian (13)	75	0.47
Croatian (0)	14	0.09
Czech (30)	89	0.56
Danish (7)	42	0.26
Dutch (76)	320	2.02
English (733)	2,315	14.59
European (117)	136	0.86
Finnish (15)	53	0.33
French, ex. Basque (101)	690	4.35
French Canadian (103)	123	0.78
German (1,067)	3,259	20.54
Greek (26)	26	0.16
Hungarian (42)	279	1.76
Iranian (10)	10	0.06
Irish (1,124)	3,463	21.83
Israeli (24)	24	0.15
Italian (485)	1,354	8.53
Lithuanian (0)	45	0.28
Northern European (41)	41	0.26
Norwegian (52)	138	0.87
Polish (201)	526	3.32
Portuguese (26)	99	0.62
Russian (7)	43	0.27
Scandinavian (21)	121	0.76
Scotch-Irish (205)	342	2.16
Scottish (131)	453	2.86
Slovak (14)	14	0.09
Swedish (94)	312	1.97
Swiss (61)	147	0.93
Turkish (39)	178	1.12
Ukrainian (0)	73	0.46
Welsh (51)	147	0.93
West Indian, ex. Hispanic (13)	13	0.08
Haitian (13)	13	0.08

Hispanic Origin	Population	%
Hispanic or Latino (of any race)	1,634	10.74
Central American, ex. Mexican	141	0.93
Costa Rican	5	0.03
Guatemalan	32	0.21
Honduran	46	0.30
Nicaraguan	11	0.07
Panamanian	8	0.05
Salvadoran	38	0.25
Other Central American	1	0.01
Cuban	99	0.65
Dominican Republic	15	0.10
Mexican	866	5.69
Puerto Rican	199	1.31
South American	150	0.99
Argentinean	12	0.08
Bolivian	4	0.03
Chilean	18	0.12
Colombian	68	0.45
Ecuadorian	10	0.07
Peruvian	23	0.15
Uruguayan	1	0.01
Venezuelan	14	0.09
Other Hispanic or Latino	164	1.08

Race*	Population	%
African-American/Black (733)	838	5.51
Not Hispanic (676)	764	5.02
Hispanic (57)	74	0.49
American Indian/Alaska Native (44)	107	0.70
Not Hispanic (26)	83	0.55
Hispanic (18)	24	0.16
Apache (2)	2	0.01
Blackfeet (1)	7	0.05
Canadian/French Am. Ind. (1)	2	0.01
Cherokee (3)	17	0.11
Choctaw (3)	3	0.02
Cree (0)	2	0.01
Delaware (1)	1	0.01
Iroquois (0)	1	0.01
Lumbee (1)	1	0.01
Mexican American Ind. (3)	3	0.02
Navajo (1)	1	0.01
Potawatomi (0)	1	0.01
Seminole (1)	7	0.05
Shoshone (0)	1	0.01
Sioux (0)	1	0.01
South American Ind. (2)	3	0.02
Spanish American Ind. (2)	2	0.01
Asian (280)	330	2.17
Not Hispanic (279)	322	2.12
Hispanic (1)	8	0.05
Bangladeshi (3)	5	0.03
Burmese (2)	2	0.01
Cambodian (1)	1	0.01
Chinese, ex. Taiwanese (104)	108	0.71
Filipino (18)	28	0.18
Indian (49)	63	0.41
Japanese (6)	13	0.09
Korean (45)	50	0.33
Laotian (1)	1	0.01
Pakistani (0)	2	0.01
Taiwanese (2)	2	0.01
Thai (11)	11	0.07
Vietnamese (30)	40	0.26
Hawaii Native/Pacific Islander (14)	30	0.20
Not Hispanic (14)	29	0.19
Hispanic (0)	1	0.01
Guamanian/Chamorro (3)	3	0.02
Native Hawaiian (8)	11	0.07
Samoan (3)	4	0.03
White (13,316)	13,544	88.99
Not Hispanic (12,394)	12,547	82.44
Hispanic (922)	997	6.55

Viera East

Place Type: CDP
County: Brevard
Population: 10,757†

Ancestry‡	Population	%
African, Sub-Saharan (0)	11	0.09
South African (0)	11	0.09
American (898)	898	7.56
Arab (191)	191	1.61
Egyptian (177)	177	1.49
Other Arab (14)	14	0.12
Australian (0)	15	0.13
Austrian (11)	44	0.37
Belgian (0)	17	0.14
British (22)	93	0.78
Bulgarian (19)	19	0.16
Canadian (27)	38	0.32
Czech (20)	59	0.50
Danish (46)	155	1.31
Dutch (20)	254	2.14
Eastern European (12)	12	0.10
English (788)	1,764	14.85
European (132)	237	2.00
French, ex. Basque (39)	410	3.45
French Canadian (158)	158	1.33
German (766)	2,136	17.99
Greek (41)	41	0.35
Hungarian (62)	81	0.68
Irish (506)	1,619	13.63
Israeli (9)	9	0.08
Italian (557)	1,447	12.19
Lithuanian (0)	21	0.18
Norwegian (71)	203	1.71
Pennsylvania German (14)	14	0.12
Polish (40)	316	2.66
Portuguese (58)	118	0.99
Romanian (4)	4	0.03
Russian (56)	88	0.74
Scotch-Irish (148)	352	2.96
Scottish (50)	368	3.10
Serbian (0)	10	0.08
Slovak (0)	79	0.67
Slovene (0)	15	0.13
Swedish (70)	206	1.73
Swiss (0)	45	0.38
Ukrainian (31)	35	0.29
Welsh (0)	16	0.13
West Indian, ex. Hispanic (108)	127	1.07
Barbadian (6)	6	0.05
Bermudan (28)	28	0.24
Jamaican (50)	69	0.58
Trinidadian/Tobagonian (19)	19	0.16
West Indian (5)	5	0.04

Hispanic Origin	Population	%
Hispanic or Latino (of any race)	854	7.94
Central American, ex. Mexican	56	0.52
Costa Rican	7	0.07
Guatemalan	11	0.10
Honduran	13	0.12
Nicaraguan	8	0.07
Panamanian	15	0.14
Salvadoran	2	0.02
Cuban	71	0.66
Dominican Republic	26	0.24
Mexican	112	1.04
Puerto Rican	343	3.19
South American	153	1.42
Argentinean	11	0.10
Chilean	19	0.18
Colombian	41	0.38
Ecuadorian	23	0.21
Peruvian	41	0.38
Uruguayan	1	0.01
Venezuelan	16	0.15
Other South American	1	0.01
Other Hispanic or Latino	93	0.86

Race*	Population	%
African-American/Black (515)	649	6.03
Not Hispanic (490)	589	5.48
Hispanic (25)	60	0.56
American Indian/Alaska Native (19)	74	0.69
Not Hispanic (18)	53	0.49
Hispanic (1)	21	0.20
Apache (1)	1	0.01
Blackfeet (0)	6	0.06

*Notes: † The Census 2010 population figure is used to calculate the percentages in the Hispanic Origin and Race categories. Ancestry percentages are based on the 2006-2010 American Community Survey population (not shown); ‡ Numbers in parentheses indicate the number of people reporting a single ancestry; * Numbers in parentheses indicate the number of persons reporting this race alone, not in combination with any other race; Please refer to the Explanation of Data for more information.*

Central American Ind. (0)	3	0.03
Cherokee (2)	14	0.13
Cheyenne (2)	2	0.02
Chippewa (0)	2	0.02
Choctaw (3)	3	0.03
Cree (0)	1	0.01
Creek (0)	3	0.03
Iroquois (0)	4	0.04
Mexican American Ind. (0)	1	0.01
Ottawa (1)	1	0.01
South American Ind. (0)	6	0.06
Tlingit-Haida *(Alaska Native)* (1)	1	0.01
Asian (350)	472	4.39
Not Hispanic (346)	450	4.18
Hispanic (4)	22	0.20
Bangladeshi (2)	2	0.02
Chinese, ex. Taiwanese (49)	68	0.63
Filipino (106)	150	1.39
Indian (76)	90	0.84
Indonesian (1)	1	0.01
Japanese (21)	31	0.29
Korean (21)	41	0.38
Laotian (1)	1	0.01
Pakistani (1)	1	0.01
Sri Lankan (1)	2	0.02
Taiwanese (4)	6	0.06
Thai (13)	23	0.21
Vietnamese (47)	53	0.49
Hawaii Native/Pacific Islander (1)	13	0.12
Not Hispanic (0)	9	0.08
Hispanic (1)	4	0.04
Guamanian/Chamorro (1)	1	0.01
Native Hawaiian (0)	1	0.01
Tongan (0)	3	0.03
White (9,458)	9,709	90.26
Not Hispanic (8,796)	8,992	83.59
Hispanic (662)	717	6.67

Villas

Place Type: CDP
County: Lee
Population: 11,569†

Ancestry‡	Population	%
African, Sub-Saharan (0)	54	0.49
African (0)	54	0.49
Albanian (5)	5	0.05
American (778)	778	7.10
Austrian (0)	24	0.22
Belgian (22)	22	0.20
Brazilian (16)	16	0.15
British (16)	88	0.80
Canadian (38)	58	0.53
Celtic (52)	52	0.47
Croatian (12)	12	0.11
Czech (12)	34	0.31
Czechoslovakian (9)	9	0.08
Danish (14)	14	0.13
Dutch (59)	156	1.42
Eastern European (5)	5	0.05
English (601)	1,765	16.12
Estonian (0)	10	0.09
European (39)	39	0.36
Finnish (17)	67	0.61
French, ex. Basque (61)	361	3.30
French Canadian (113)	148	1.35
German (717)	2,048	18.70
Greek (84)	100	0.91
Hungarian (76)	125	1.14
Iranian (27)	27	0.25
Irish (361)	1,666	15.21
Italian (548)	933	8.52
Lithuanian (6)	16	0.15
Norwegian (62)	93	0.85
Polish (159)	372	3.40
Portuguese (0)	68	0.62
Romanian (41)	41	0.37
Russian (36)	49	0.45
Scotch-Irish (83)	154	1.41
Scottish (117)	425	3.88
Slovak (9)	33	0.30
Swedish (61)	137	1.25
Swiss (0)	37	0.34
Ukrainian (30)	61	0.56
Welsh (24)	169	1.54
West Indian, ex. Hispanic (155)	233	2.13
Belizean (60)	60	0.55
Haitian (88)	134	1.22
Jamaican (7)	39	0.36

Hispanic Origin	Population	%
Hispanic or Latino (of any race)	1,515	13.10
Central American, ex. Mexican	142	1.23
Costa Rican	24	0.21
Guatemalan	23	0.20
Honduran	42	0.36
Nicaraguan	19	0.16
Panamanian	11	0.10
Salvadoran	18	0.16
Other Central American	5	0.04
Cuban	147	1.27
Dominican Republic	61	0.53
Mexican	491	4.24
Puerto Rican	333	2.88
South American	253	2.19
Argentinean	19	0.16
Bolivian	23	0.20
Chilean	10	0.09
Colombian	98	0.85
Ecuadorian	11	0.10
Paraguayan	1	0.01
Peruvian	47	0.41
Uruguayan	7	0.06
Venezuelan	28	0.24
Other South American	9	0.08
Other Hispanic or Latino	88	0.76

Race*	Population	%
African-American/Black (482)	588	5.08
Not Hispanic (437)	522	4.51
Hispanic (45)	66	0.57
American Indian/Alaska Native (18)	58	0.50
Not Hispanic (13)	46	0.40
Hispanic (5)	12	0.10
Apache (1)	4	0.03
Blackfeet (0)	1	0.01
Cherokee (6)	15	0.13
Chippewa (2)	3	0.03
Choctaw (0)	1	0.01
Creek (1)	2	0.02
Iroquois (0)	3	0.03
Mexican American Ind. (1)	1	0.01
Potawatomi (1)	1	0.01
Sioux (1)	2	0.02
Spanish American Ind. (1)	2	0.02
Asian (169)	214	1.85
Not Hispanic (166)	209	1.81
Hispanic (3)	5	0.04
Bangladeshi (5)	5	0.04
Chinese, ex. Taiwanese (27)	30	0.26
Filipino (27)	40	0.35
Indian (36)	42	0.36
Indonesian (1)	3	0.03
Japanese (7)	10	0.09
Korean (13)	14	0.12
Laotian (1)	1	0.01
Pakistani (0)	6	0.05
Sri Lankan (3)	3	0.03
Taiwanese (8)	8	0.07
Thai (16)	16	0.14
Vietnamese (19)	23	0.20
Hawaii Native/Pacific Islander (13)	34	0.29
Not Hispanic (7)	26	0.22
Hispanic (6)	8	0.07
Native Hawaiian (10)	12	0.10
Samoan (3)	3	0.03
White (10,195)	10,394	89.84
Not Hispanic (9,250)	9,375	81.04
Hispanic (945)	1,019	8.81

Warrington

Place Type: CDP
County: Escambia
Population: 14,531†

Ancestry‡	Population	%
African, Sub-Saharan (32)	32	0.22
African (32)	32	0.22
American (1,458)	1,458	9.99
Arab (7)	7	0.05
Egyptian (7)	7	0.05
Australian (0)	8	0.05
Austrian (17)	17	0.12
Belgian (0)	24	0.16
Brazilian (9)	9	0.06
British (77)	125	0.86
Cajun (40)	40	0.27
Czech (47)	56	0.38
Dutch (14)	93	0.64
English (561)	1,737	11.90
European (70)	142	0.97
Finnish (0)	10	0.07
French, ex. Basque (132)	775	5.31
French Canadian (58)	121	0.83
German (717)	2,231	15.28
Greek (35)	48	0.33
Hungarian (28)	52	0.36
Irish (492)	1,800	12.33
Italian (272)	811	5.55
Lithuanian (17)	38	0.26
Norwegian (15)	74	0.51
Polish (146)	258	1.77
Portuguese (139)	162	1.11
Russian (0)	42	0.29
Scotch-Irish (174)	420	2.88
Scottish (107)	332	2.27
Swedish (53)	96	0.66
Ukrainian (34)	86	0.59
Welsh (34)	58	0.40
West Indian, ex. Hispanic (14)	14	0.10
Trinidadian/Tobagonian (14)	14	0.10

Hispanic Origin	Population	%
Hispanic or Latino (of any race)	775	5.33
Central American, ex. Mexican	74	0.51
Guatemalan	7	0.05
Honduran	30	0.21
Nicaraguan	2	0.01
Panamanian	19	0.13
Salvadoran	16	0.11
Cuban	45	0.31
Dominican Republic	13	0.09
Mexican	342	2.35
Puerto Rican	130	0.89
South American	25	0.17
Bolivian	6	0.04
Colombian	8	0.06
Ecuadorian	1	0.01
Peruvian	7	0.05
Uruguayan	1	0.01
Venezuelan	1	0.01
Other South American	1	0.01
Other Hispanic or Latino	146	1.00

Race*	Population	%
African-American/Black (3,167)	3,410	23.47
Not Hispanic (3,130)	3,342	23.00
Hispanic (37)	68	0.47
American Indian/Alaska Native (156)	368	2.53
Not Hispanic (136)	324	2.23
Hispanic (20)	44	0.30
Apache (1)	6	0.04
Blackfeet (0)	10	0.07
Central American Ind. (0)	2	0.01
Cherokee (18)	67	0.46
Cheyenne (0)	1	0.01
Chickasaw (1)	3	0.02
Chippewa (4)	5	0.03
Choctaw (4)	11	0.08

*Notes: † The Census 2010 population figure is used to calculate the percentages in the Hispanic Origin and Race categories. Ancestry percentages are based on the 2006-2010 American Community Survey population (not shown); ‡ Numbers in parentheses indicate the number of people reporting a single ancestry; * Numbers in parentheses indicate the number of persons reporting this race alone, not in combination with any other race; Please refer to the Explanation of Data for more information.*

Cree (2)	3	0.02
Creek (37)	71	0.49
Crow (1)	2	0.01
Delaware (0)	1	0.01
Iroquois (5)	8	0.06
Lumbee (1)	1	0.01
Mexican American Ind. (5)	5	0.03
Navajo (1)	2	0.01
Pueblo (0)	1	0.01
Seminole (3)	5	0.03
Shoshone (0)	1	0.01
Sioux (1)	5	0.03
South American Ind. (1)	4	0.03
Spanish American Ind. (5)	5	0.03
Tlingit-Haida *(Alaska Native)* (1)	1	0.01
Ute (0)	1	0.01
Asian (367)	509	3.50
Not Hispanic (365)	485	3.34
Hispanic (2)	24	0.17
Cambodian (1)	1	0.01
Chinese, ex. Taiwanese (10)	21	0.14
Filipino (212)	306	2.11
Indian (12)	22	0.15
Indonesian (0)	1	0.01
Japanese (11)	27	0.19
Korean (6)	17	0.12
Laotian (3)	3	0.02
Malaysian (1)	3	0.02
Taiwanese (0)	2	0.01
Thai (4)	4	0.03
Vietnamese (98)	110	0.76
Hawaii Native/Pacific Islander (21)	52	0.36
Not Hispanic (21)	44	0.30
Hispanic (0)	8	0.06
Guamanian/Chamorro (11)	19	0.13
Native Hawaiian (6)	19	0.13
Samoan (1)	4	0.03
White (10,010)	10,474	72.08
Not Hispanic (9,628)	10,006	68.86
Hispanic (382)	468	3.22

Wekiwa Springs

Place Type: CDP
County: Seminole
Population: 21,998†

Ancestry‡	Population	%
African, Sub-Saharan (39)	62	0.28
African (16)	16	0.07
South African (23)	46	0.20
American (1,337)	1,337	5.95
Arab (242)	302	1.34
Egyptian (16)	16	0.07
Lebanese (148)	208	0.93
Moroccan (19)	19	0.08
Other Arab (59)	59	0.26
Armenian (32)	73	0.32
Assyrian/Chaldean/Syriac (0)	14	0.06
Australian (14)	59	0.26
Austrian (18)	100	0.45
Belgian (27)	50	0.22
Brazilian (0)	30	0.13
British (89)	163	0.73
Canadian (76)	121	0.54
Croatian (18)	39	0.17
Czech (109)	218	0.97
Danish (49)	139	0.62
Dutch (118)	442	1.97
Eastern European (112)	114	0.51
English (1,390)	3,568	15.88
European (1,475)	1,586	7.06
Finnish (0)	7	0.03
French, ex. Basque (153)	782	3.48
French Canadian (47)	205	0.91
German (1,108)	4,251	18.92
Greek (73)	168	0.75
Hungarian (97)	318	1.42
Iranian (70)	70	0.31
Irish (1,063)	3,849	17.13
Israeli (59)	59	0.26
Italian (596)	1,681	7.48
Latvian (0)	10	0.04
Lithuanian (49)	211	0.94
Norwegian (34)	245	1.09
Pennsylvania German (10)	10	0.04
Polish (227)	963	4.29
Portuguese (61)	166	0.74
Romanian (0)	57	0.25
Russian (165)	429	1.91
Scotch-Irish (190)	413	1.84
Scottish (149)	511	2.27
Serbian (6)	6	0.03
Slovak (15)	99	0.44
Slovene (10)	10	0.04
Swedish (34)	202	0.90
Swiss (32)	67	0.30
Ukrainian (20)	110	0.49
Welsh (122)	286	1.27
West Indian, ex. Hispanic (215)	215	0.96
Haitian (92)	92	0.41
Jamaican (43)	43	0.19
Trinidadian/Tobagonian (80)	80	0.36
Yugoslavian (10)	10	0.04

Hispanic Origin	Population	%
Hispanic or Latino (of any race)	2,126	9.66
Central American, ex. Mexican	85	0.39
Costa Rican	21	0.10
Guatemalan	22	0.10
Honduran	9	0.04
Nicaraguan	12	0.05
Panamanian	6	0.03
Salvadoran	15	0.07
Cuban	303	1.38
Dominican Republic	96	0.44
Mexican	181	0.82
Puerto Rican	750	3.41
South American	510	2.32
Argentinean	51	0.23
Bolivian	8	0.04
Chilean	20	0.09
Colombian	221	1.00
Ecuadorian	48	0.22
Peruvian	80	0.36
Uruguayan	3	0.01
Venezuelan	71	0.32
Other South American	8	0.04
Other Hispanic or Latino	201	0.91

Race*	Population	%
African-American/Black (599)	744	3.38
Not Hispanic (574)	680	3.09
Hispanic (25)	64	0.29
American Indian/Alaska Native (31)	117	0.53
Not Hispanic (20)	94	0.43
Hispanic (11)	23	0.10
Blackfeet (0)	2	0.01
Central American Ind. (0)	2	0.01
Cherokee (3)	28	0.13
Chippewa (1)	3	0.01
Choctaw (2)	3	0.01
Cree (0)	1	<0.01
Creek (2)	4	0.02
Iroquois (0)	2	0.01
Lumbee (1)	1	<0.01
Potawatomi (4)	5	0.02
Seminole (1)	3	0.01
Sioux (1)	1	<0.01
South American Ind. (0)	7	0.03
Spanish American Ind. (1)	2	0.01
Tlingit-Haida *(Alaska Native)* (0)	3	0.01
Yup'ik *(Alaska Native)* (1)	1	<0.01
Asian (630)	822	3.74
Not Hispanic (621)	786	3.57
Hispanic (9)	36	0.16
Bangladeshi (9)	9	0.04
Burmese (4)	4	0.02
Cambodian (5)	5	0.02
Chinese, ex. Taiwanese (114)	145	0.66
Filipino (55)	97	0.44
Indian (218)	252	1.15
Indonesian (2)	2	0.01
Japanese (15)	42	0.19
Korean (109)	126	0.57
Malaysian (1)	1	<0.01
Pakistani (26)	30	0.14
Taiwanese (8)	8	0.04
Thai (7)	13	0.06
Vietnamese (45)	57	0.26
Hawaii Native/Pacific Islander (8)	24	0.11
Not Hispanic (5)	19	0.09
Hispanic (3)	5	0.02
Guamanian/Chamorro (3)	4	0.02
Native Hawaiian (2)	8	0.04
White (19,990)	20,395	92.71
Not Hispanic (18,279)	18,575	84.44
Hispanic (1,711)	1,820	8.27

Wellington

Place Type: Village
County: Palm Beach
Population: 56,508†

Ancestry‡	Population	%
Afghan (50)	50	0.09
African, Sub-Saharan (800)	909	1.69
African (709)	818	1.52
South African (91)	91	0.17
Albanian (57)	70	0.13
American (2,387)	2,387	4.44
Arab (120)	182	0.34
Egyptian (0)	30	0.06
Jordanian (24)	24	0.04
Lebanese (31)	38	0.07
Syrian (0)	25	0.05
Other Arab (65)	65	0.12
Armenian (244)	367	0.68
Austrian (99)	267	0.50
Belgian (30)	107	0.20
Brazilian (161)	220	0.41
British (176)	667	1.24
Canadian (260)	379	0.71
Croatian (67)	188	0.35
Czech (180)	229	0.43
Czechoslovakian (15)	26	0.05
Danish (54)	181	0.34
Dutch (75)	673	1.25
Eastern European (139)	143	0.27
English (1,497)	5,320	9.90
European (764)	789	1.47
Finnish (106)	237	0.44
French, ex. Basque (135)	1,242	2.31
French Canadian (137)	264	0.49
German (1,733)	7,998	14.88
Greek (170)	324	0.60
Guyanese (22)	22	0.04
Hungarian (79)	238	0.44
Iranian (144)	176	0.33
Irish (1,474)	6,582	12.25
Israeli (22)	55	0.10
Italian (3,318)	6,933	12.90
Latvian (4)	10	0.02
Lithuanian (107)	177	0.33
Macedonian (8)	8	0.01
Northern European (24)	24	0.04
Norwegian (80)	311	0.58
Pennsylvania German (9)	20	0.04
Polish (1,110)	2,782	5.18
Portuguese (52)	190	0.35
Romanian (45)	132	0.25
Russian (624)	1,563	2.91
Scandinavian (95)	174	0.32
Scotch-Irish (325)	738	1.37
Scottish (181)	640	1.19
Slavic (0)	32	0.06
Slovak (20)	106	0.20
Slovene (26)	37	0.07
Swedish (106)	451	0.84

SECTION TWO

*Notes: † The Census 2010 population figure is used to calculate the percentages in the Hispanic Origin and Race categories. Ancestry percentages are based on the 2006-2010 American Community Survey population (not shown); ‡ Numbers in parentheses indicate the number of people reporting a single ancestry; * Numbers in parentheses indicate the number of persons reporting this race alone, not in combination with any other race; Please refer to the Explanation of Data for more information.*

Swiss (11)	47	0.09
Turkish (0)	93	0.17
Ukrainian (165)	239	0.44
Welsh (13)	233	0.43
West Indian, ex. Hispanic (2,582)	3,156	5.87
Bahamian (10)	15	0.03
Belizean (16)	16	0.03
British West Indian (18)	18	0.03
Haitian (794)	858	1.60
Jamaican (1,119)	1,514	2.82
Trinidadian/Tobagonian (77)	132	0.25
West Indian (548)	603	1.12
Yugoslavian (11)	80	0.15

Hispanic Origin	Population	%
Hispanic or Latino (of any race)	10,952	19.38
Central American, ex. Mexican	809	1.43
Costa Rican	109	0.19
Guatemalan	144	0.25
Honduran	145	0.26
Nicaraguan	191	0.34
Panamanian	82	0.15
Salvadoran	131	0.23
Other Central American	7	0.01
Cuban	2,179	3.86
Dominican Republic	631	1.12
Mexican	1,235	2.19
Puerto Rican	1,950	3.45
South American	3,468	6.14
Argentinean	460	0.81
Bolivian	61	0.11
Chilean	111	0.20
Colombian	1,479	2.62
Ecuadorian	365	0.65
Paraguayan	18	0.03
Peruvian	403	0.71
Uruguayan	120	0.21
Venezuelan	439	0.78
Other South American	12	0.02
Other Hispanic or Latino	680	1.20

Race*	Population	%
African-American/Black (5,858)	6,459	11.43
Not Hispanic (5,626)	6,105	10.80
Hispanic (232)	354	0.63
American Indian/Alaska Native (103)	276	0.49
Not Hispanic (48)	172	0.30
Hispanic (55)	104	0.18
Aleut *(Alaska Native)* (0)	2	<0.01
Apache (2)	3	0.01
Blackfeet (1)	1	<0.01
Canadian/French Am. Ind. (0)	3	0.01
Central American Ind. (6)	11	0.02
Cherokee (3)	52	0.09
Chickasaw (1)	1	<0.01
Chippewa (4)	6	0.01
Choctaw (1)	1	<0.01
Comanche (0)	1	<0.01
Creek (1)	1	<0.01
Delaware (2)	2	<0.01
Houma (1)	3	0.01
Iroquois (0)	2	<0.01
Kiowa (1)	2	<0.01
Lumbee (1)	1	<0.01
Menominee (0)	3	0.01
Mexican American Ind. (15)	19	0.03
Navajo (0)	1	<0.01
Ottawa (1)	2	<0.01
Paiute (0)	1	<0.01
Potawatomi (2)	3	0.01
Pueblo (3)	3	0.01
Seminole (0)	5	0.01
South American Ind. (2)	8	0.01
Spanish American Ind. (0)	4	0.01
Asian (2,165)	2,670	4.72
Not Hispanic (2,144)	2,579	4.56
Hispanic (21)	91	0.16
Bangladeshi (47)	48	0.08
Burmese (9)	9	0.02
Cambodian (11)	16	0.03
Chinese, ex. Taiwanese (429)	561	0.99
Filipino (264)	373	0.66
Indian (845)	1,011	1.79
Indonesian (3)	3	0.01
Japanese (35)	67	0.12
Korean (97)	155	0.27
Laotian (4)	4	0.01
Malaysian (1)	7	0.01
Nepalese (15)	18	0.03
Pakistani (58)	74	0.13
Sri Lankan (16)	16	0.03
Taiwanese (8)	13	0.02
Thai (28)	36	0.06
Vietnamese (236)	246	0.44
Hawaii Native/Pacific Islander (22)	103	0.18
Not Hispanic (19)	89	0.16
Hispanic (3)	14	0.02
Fijian (1)	1	<0.01
Guamanian/Chamorro (2)	2	<0.01
Native Hawaiian (4)	13	0.02
Samoan (1)	1	<0.01
White (45,212)	46,337	82.00
Not Hispanic (36,605)	37,331	66.06
Hispanic (8,607)	9,006	15.94

Wesley Chapel

Place Type: CDP
County: Pasco
Population: 44,092†

Ancestry‡	Population	%
African, Sub-Saharan (349)	572	1.46
African (35)	258	0.66
Cape Verdean (70)	70	0.18
Nigerian (221)	221	0.56
South African (23)	23	0.06
Albanian (53)	53	0.13
American (1,967)	1,967	5.00
Arab (305)	333	0.85
Egyptian (9)	9	0.02
Lebanese (143)	143	0.36
Moroccan (34)	34	0.09
Syrian (119)	147	0.37
Australian (0)	36	0.09
Austrian (27)	65	0.17
Belgian (0)	50	0.13
Brazilian (46)	57	0.15
British (21)	77	0.20
Cajun (0)	28	0.07
Canadian (57)	108	0.27
Croatian (32)	32	0.08
Czech (32)	115	0.29
Czechoslovakian (26)	56	0.14
Danish (81)	157	0.40
Dutch (62)	531	1.35
Eastern European (34)	34	0.09
English (1,298)	4,316	10.98
European (234)	286	0.73
Finnish (14)	25	0.06
French, ex. Basque (158)	1,174	2.99
French Canadian (217)	585	1.49
German (1,930)	6,349	16.15
Greek (20)	51	0.13
Guyanese (0)	33	0.08
Hungarian (127)	324	0.82
Iranian (93)	93	0.24
Irish (1,426)	4,795	12.20
Italian (1,093)	3,120	7.94
Lithuanian (50)	241	0.61
Macedonian (20)	20	0.05
Northern European (20)	20	0.05
Norwegian (124)	486	1.24
Pennsylvania German (33)	101	0.26
Polish (384)	1,254	3.19
Portuguese (11)	61	0.16
Russian (160)	361	0.92
Scandinavian (0)	149	0.38
Scotch-Irish (260)	757	1.93
Scottish (104)	646	1.64
Serbian (30)	40	0.10
Slavic (14)	34	0.09
Slovene (14)	38	0.10
Swedish (132)	463	1.18
Swiss (9)	47	0.12
Turkish (82)	150	0.38
Ukrainian (36)	54	0.14
Welsh (45)	220	0.56
West Indian, ex. Hispanic (1,066)	1,173	2.98
Bermudan (9)	9	0.02
Haitian (127)	127	0.32
Jamaican (370)	395	1.00
Trinidadian/Tobagonian (101)	101	0.26
West Indian (459)	541	1.38
Yugoslavian (114)	148	0.38

Hispanic Origin	Population	%
Hispanic or Latino (of any race)	8,871	20.12
Central American, ex. Mexican	523	1.19
Costa Rican	49	0.11
Guatemalan	51	0.12
Honduran	150	0.34
Nicaraguan	79	0.18
Panamanian	115	0.26
Salvadoran	79	0.18
Cuban	956	2.17
Dominican Republic	499	1.13
Mexican	731	1.66
Puerto Rican	3,818	8.66
South American	1,739	3.94
Argentinean	40	0.09
Bolivian	21	0.05
Chilean	36	0.08
Colombian	869	1.97
Ecuadorian	189	0.43
Paraguayan	13	0.03
Peruvian	236	0.54
Uruguayan	16	0.04
Venezuelan	313	0.71
Other South American	6	0.01
Other Hispanic or Latino	605	1.37

Race*	Population	%
African-American/Black (5,023)	5,702	12.93
Not Hispanic (4,675)	5,194	11.78
Hispanic (348)	508	1.15
American Indian/Alaska Native (112)	360	0.82
Not Hispanic (83)	267	0.61
Hispanic (29)	93	0.21
Apache (4)	6	0.01
Arapaho (1)	2	<0.01
Blackfeet (7)	22	0.05
Canadian/French Am. Ind. (0)	3	0.01
Central American Ind. (0)	1	<0.01
Cherokee (16)	92	0.21
Cheyenne (0)	1	<0.01
Chippewa (8)	11	0.02
Choctaw (0)	7	0.02
Creek (1)	3	0.01
Delaware (0)	1	<0.01
Iroquois (1)	9	0.02
Lumbee (3)	5	0.01
Mexican American Ind. (4)	8	0.02
Navajo (1)	4	0.01
Potawatomi (5)	6	0.01
Pueblo (1)	1	<0.01
Seminole (2)	5	0.01
Sioux (2)	7	0.02
South American Ind. (5)	17	0.04
Spanish American Ind. (1)	1	<0.01
Asian (2,524)	3,078	6.98
Not Hispanic (2,488)	2,946	6.68
Hispanic (36)	132	0.30
Bangladeshi (7)	12	0.03
Burmese (18)	19	0.04
Cambodian (1)	1	<0.01
Chinese, ex. Taiwanese (266)	345	0.78
Filipino (486)	637	1.44
Hmong (4)	4	0.01
Indian (967)	1,079	2.45

*Notes: † The Census 2010 population figure is used to calculate the percentages in the Hispanic Origin and Race categories. Ancestry percentages are based on the 2006-2010 American Community Survey population (not shown); ‡ Numbers in parentheses indicate the number of people reporting a single ancestry; * Numbers in parentheses indicate the number of persons reporting this race alone, not in combination with any other race; Please refer to the Explanation of Data for more information.*

Indonesian (2)	9	0.02
Japanese (38)	92	0.21
Korean (202)	257	0.58
Laotian (5)	10	0.02
Malaysian (1)	1	<0.01
Nepalese (13)	13	0.03
Pakistani (104)	120	0.27
Sri Lankan (28)	29	0.07
Taiwanese (15)	17	0.04
Thai (35)	51	0.12
Vietnamese (242)	266	0.60
Hawaii Native/Pacific Islander (50)	113	0.26
Not Hispanic (44)	85	0.19
Hispanic (6)	28	0.06
Guamanian/Chamorro (12)	16	0.04
Native Hawaiian (7)	23	0.05
Samoan (14)	23	0.05
White (33,057)	34,353	77.91
Not Hispanic (26,741)	27,596	62.59
Hispanic (6,316)	6,757	15.32

West Lealman

Place Type: CDP
County: Pinellas
Population: 15,651†

Ancestry‡	Population	%
African, Sub-Saharan (39)	78	0.53
African (39)	47	0.32
Cape Verdean (0)	31	0.21
American (789)	789	5.41
Arab (10)	10	0.07
Lebanese (10)	10	0.07
Armenian (0)	8	0.05
Belgian (0)	43	0.29
Brazilian (12)	12	0.08
British (105)	118	0.81
Cajun (10)	10	0.07
Canadian (94)	128	0.88
Czech (153)	197	1.35
Danish (9)	31	0.21
Dutch (119)	312	2.14
English (674)	1,889	12.95
European (185)	185	1.27
Finnish (0)	31	0.21
French, ex. Basque (227)	1,108	7.59
French Canadian (205)	388	2.66
German (994)	2,502	17.15
Greek (0)	16	0.11
Hungarian (113)	169	1.16
Irish (1,055)	2,633	18.05
Italian (680)	1,066	7.31
Lithuanian (55)	55	0.38
Macedonian (10)	10	0.07
Northern European (10)	10	0.07
Norwegian (46)	142	0.97
Pennsylvania German (9)	30	0.21
Polish (252)	682	4.67
Portuguese (36)	62	0.42
Romanian (39)	39	0.27
Russian (25)	56	0.38
Scandinavian (17)	17	0.12
Scotch-Irish (162)	350	2.40
Scottish (246)	422	2.89
Serbian (0)	17	0.12
Swedish (10)	30	0.21
Swiss (12)	12	0.08
Ukrainian (19)	48	0.33
Welsh (42)	137	0.94
West Indian, ex. Hispanic (110)	110	0.75
Haitian (110)	110	0.75
Yugoslavian (24)	40	0.27

Hispanic Origin	Population	%
Hispanic or Latino (of any race)	1,303	8.33
Central American, ex. Mexican	63	0.40
Costa Rican	9	0.06
Guatemalan	9	0.06
Honduran	25	0.16
Nicaraguan	7	0.04
Panamanian	8	0.05
Salvadoran	5	0.03
Cuban	205	1.31
Dominican Republic	26	0.17
Mexican	409	2.61
Puerto Rican	442	2.82
South American	78	0.50
Argentinean	2	0.01
Bolivian	4	0.03
Chilean	1	0.01
Colombian	26	0.17
Ecuadorian	16	0.10
Peruvian	13	0.08
Uruguayan	3	0.02
Venezuelan	13	0.08
Other Hispanic or Latino	80	0.51

Race*	Population	%
African-American/Black (704)	865	5.53
Not Hispanic (661)	796	5.09
Hispanic (43)	69	0.44
American Indian/Alaska Native (58)	199	1.27
Not Hispanic (56)	184	1.18
Hispanic (2)	15	0.10
Apache (1)	2	0.01
Blackfeet (0)	4	0.03
Canadian/French Am. Ind. (0)	4	0.03
Cherokee (19)	75	0.48
Chickasaw (1)	2	0.01
Chippewa (3)	5	0.03
Choctaw (1)	4	0.03
Cree (1)	2	0.01
Creek (0)	2	0.01
Delaware (1)	2	0.01
Iroquois (6)	13	0.08
Kiowa (1)	1	0.01
Menominee (1)	1	0.01
Mexican American Ind. (1)	1	0.01
Osage (0)	1	0.01
Potawatomi (1)	1	0.01
Shoshone (2)	2	0.01
Sioux (0)	4	0.03
South American Ind. (1)	2	0.01
Asian (612)	697	4.45
Not Hispanic (610)	692	4.42
Hispanic (2)	5	0.03
Bangladeshi (7)	10	0.06
Burmese (0)	1	0.01
Cambodian (71)	73	0.47
Chinese, ex. Taiwanese (31)	42	0.27
Filipino (78)	97	0.62
Hmong (4)	4	0.03
Indian (67)	96	0.61
Indonesian (0)	2	0.01
Japanese (12)	23	0.15
Korean (10)	16	0.10
Laotian (29)	47	0.30
Malaysian (5)	5	0.03
Pakistani (4)	7	0.04
Sri Lankan (0)	2	0.01
Taiwanese (2)	3	0.02
Thai (11)	13	0.08
Vietnamese (236)	251	1.60
Hawaii Native/Pacific Islander (15)	32	0.20
Not Hispanic (15)	29	0.19
Hispanic (0)	3	0.02
Marshallese (13)	14	0.09
Native Hawaiian (0)	3	0.02
Samoan (0)	1	0.01
White (13,498)	13,849	88.49
Not Hispanic (12,665)	12,946	82.72
Hispanic (833)	903	5.77

West Little River

Place Type: CDP
County: Miami-Dade
Population: 34,699†

Ancestry‡	Population	%
African, Sub-Saharan (257)	323	0.99
African (257)	323	0.99
American (1,045)	1,045	3.21
Arab (15)	15	0.05
Arab (15)	15	0.05
Dutch (0)	6	0.02
English (0)	73	0.22
French, ex. Basque (10)	73	0.22
German (0)	65	0.20
Hungarian (12)	12	0.04
Irish (0)	29	0.09
Italian (38)	79	0.24
Lithuanian (0)	36	0.11
Norwegian (7)	7	0.02
Scottish (0)	9	0.03
Swedish (0)	12	0.04
West Indian, ex. Hispanic (3,471)	3,693	11.34
Bahamian (228)	314	0.96
Belizean (26)	31	0.10
British West Indian (27)	27	0.08
Haitian (2,650)	2,707	8.31
Jamaican (445)	488	1.50
Trinidadian/Tobagonian (16)	16	0.05
West Indian (79)	110	0.34

Hispanic Origin	Population	%
Hispanic or Latino (of any race)	17,550	50.58
Central American, ex. Mexican	5,083	14.65
Costa Rican	33	0.10
Guatemalan	695	2.00
Honduran	1,902	5.48
Nicaraguan	2,112	6.09
Panamanian	46	0.13
Salvadoran	291	0.84
Other Central American	4	0.01
Cuban	8,014	23.10
Dominican Republic	1,179	3.40
Mexican	265	0.76
Puerto Rican	1,126	3.25
South American	686	1.98
Argentinean	94	0.27
Bolivian	1	<0.01
Chilean	16	0.05
Colombian	307	0.88
Ecuadorian	61	0.18
Paraguayan	5	0.01
Peruvian	153	0.44
Uruguayan	10	0.03
Venezuelan	37	0.11
Other South American	2	0.01
Other Hispanic or Latino	1,197	3.45

Race*	Population	%
African-American/Black (17,098)	17,437	50.25
Not Hispanic (15,929)	16,096	46.39
Hispanic (1,169)	1,341	3.86
American Indian/Alaska Native (83)	182	0.52
Not Hispanic (27)	77	0.22
Hispanic (56)	105	0.30
Blackfeet (0)	8	0.02
Central American Ind. (8)	15	0.04
Cherokee (3)	10	0.03
Mexican American Ind. (2)	3	0.01
Pueblo (0)	2	0.01
Seminole (0)	2	0.01
South American Ind. (1)	1	<0.01
Spanish American Ind. (10)	16	0.05
Asian (55)	134	0.39
Not Hispanic (37)	99	0.29
Hispanic (18)	35	0.10
Chinese, ex. Taiwanese (17)	31	0.09
Filipino (13)	25	0.07
Indian (13)	46	0.13
Indonesian (2)	2	0.01
Japanese (1)	2	0.01
Korean (0)	4	0.01
Laotian (1)	1	<0.01
Malaysian (0)	1	<0.01
Pakistani (1)	1	<0.01

*Notes: † The Census 2010 population figure is used to calculate the percentages in the Hispanic Origin and Race categories. Ancestry percentages are based on the 2006-2010 American Community Survey population (not shown); ‡ Numbers in parentheses indicate the number of people reporting a single ancestry; * Numbers in parentheses indicate the number of persons reporting this race alone, not in combination with any other race; Please refer to the Explanation of Data for more information.*

Vietnamese (3)	4	0.01
Hawaii Native/Pacific Islander (9)	83	0.24
Not Hispanic (7)	61	0.18
Hispanic (2)	22	0.06
Guamanian/Chamorro (0)	2	0.01
Native Hawaiian (3)	3	0.01
Tongan (3)	3	0.01
White (14,826)	15,491	44.64
Not Hispanic (909)	974	2.81
Hispanic (13,917)	14,517	41.84

West Melbourne

Place Type: City
County: Brevard
Population: 18,355†

Ancestry‡	Population	%
African, Sub-Saharan (100)	100	0.58
African (100)	100	0.58
Albanian (12)	12	0.07
Alsatian (0)	10	0.06
American (1,683)	1,683	9.80
Arab (72)	126	0.73
Arab (47)	47	0.27
Lebanese (14)	68	0.40
Moroccan (11)	11	0.06
Armenian (0)	9	0.05
Austrian (10)	19	0.11
Brazilian (0)	9	0.05
British (36)	47	0.27
Canadian (46)	89	0.52
Croatian (8)	19	0.11
Czech (13)	57	0.33
Danish (36)	77	0.45
Dutch (84)	338	1.97
English (752)	2,237	13.03
European (293)	293	1.71
French, ex. Basque (104)	435	2.53
French Canadian (83)	141	0.82
German (1,192)	3,137	18.27
Greek (25)	121	0.70
Hungarian (0)	32	0.19
Iranian (27)	27	0.16
Irish (784)	2,890	16.83
Italian (839)	1,824	10.62
Lithuanian (9)	72	0.42
Norwegian (32)	96	0.56
Polish (282)	839	4.89
Portuguese (214)	234	1.36
Romanian (26)	26	0.15
Russian (24)	157	0.91
Scotch-Irish (166)	338	1.97
Scottish (102)	401	2.34
Serbian (0)	11	0.06
Slavic (14)	25	0.15
Slovak (10)	49	0.29
Swedish (45)	184	1.07
Swiss (13)	36	0.21
Ukrainian (38)	133	0.77
Welsh (47)	129	0.75
West Indian, ex. Hispanic (192)	192	1.12
Haitian (18)	18	0.10
Jamaican (159)	159	0.93
West Indian (15)	15	0.09
Yugoslavian (11)	11	0.06

Hispanic Origin	Population	%
Hispanic or Latino (of any race)	1,653	9.01
Central American, ex. Mexican	129	0.70
Costa Rican	6	0.03
Guatemalan	29	0.16
Honduran	38	0.21
Nicaraguan	8	0.04
Panamanian	38	0.21
Salvadoran	10	0.05
Cuban	149	0.81
Dominican Republic	115	0.63
Mexican	205	1.12
Puerto Rican	699	3.81
South American	223	1.21
Argentinean	8	0.04
Bolivian	5	0.03
Chilean	10	0.05
Colombian	113	0.62
Ecuadorian	19	0.10
Paraguayan	3	0.02
Peruvian	23	0.13
Uruguayan	3	0.02
Venezuelan	39	0.21
Other Hispanic or Latino	133	0.72

Race*	Population	%
African-American/Black (903)	1,102	6.00
Not Hispanic (805)	953	5.19
Hispanic (98)	149	0.81
American Indian/Alaska Native (47)	128	0.70
Not Hispanic (36)	101	0.55
Hispanic (11)	27	0.15
Aleut *(Alaska Native)* (4)	4	0.02
Blackfeet (0)	9	0.05
Canadian/French Am. Ind. (1)	1	0.01
Cherokee (8)	32	0.17
Chippewa (2)	4	0.02
Choctaw (0)	3	0.02
Comanche (0)	1	0.01
Creek (0)	2	0.01
Iroquois (0)	6	0.03
Navajo (0)	1	0.01
Pueblo (1)	1	0.01
Sioux (1)	4	0.02
South American Ind. (1)	1	0.01
Asian (915)	1,110	6.05
Not Hispanic (904)	1,080	5.88
Hispanic (11)	30	0.16
Bangladeshi (10)	10	0.05
Burmese (12)	12	0.07
Cambodian (1)	1	0.01
Chinese, ex. Taiwanese (114)	138	0.75
Filipino (213)	285	1.55
Indian (289)	303	1.65
Indonesian (6)	7	0.04
Japanese (24)	42	0.23
Korean (55)	75	0.41
Laotian (1)	1	0.01
Nepalese (2)	2	0.01
Pakistani (6)	6	0.03
Taiwanese (10)	12	0.07
Thai (27)	32	0.17
Vietnamese (131)	145	0.79
Hawaii Native/Pacific Islander (3)	39	0.21
Not Hispanic (3)	29	0.16
Hispanic (0)	10	0.05
Guamanian/Chamorro (1)	2	0.01
Native Hawaiian (1)	18	0.10
Samoan (1)	6	0.03
Tongan (0)	2	0.01
White (15,691)	16,129	87.87
Not Hispanic (14,547)	14,879	81.06
Hispanic (1,144)	1,250	6.81

West Palm Beach

Place Type: City
County: Palm Beach
Population: 99,919†

Ancestry‡	Population	%
Afghan (45)	45	0.05
African, Sub-Saharan (546)	1,109	1.13
African (336)	786	0.80
Ethiopian (14)	30	0.03
South African (51)	75	0.08
Ugandan (16)	16	0.02
Other Sub-Saharan African (129)	202	0.21
Albanian (27)	27	0.03
American (3,297)	3,297	3.37
Arab (159)	311	0.32
Arab (23)	52	0.05
Egyptian (11)	11	0.01
Lebanese (45)	92	0.09
Moroccan (24)	24	0.02
Syrian (0)	76	0.08
Other Arab (56)	56	0.06
Armenian (20)	20	0.02
Australian (11)	11	0.01
Austrian (93)	594	0.61
Basque (0)	50	0.05
Belgian (52)	141	0.14
Brazilian (245)	335	0.34
British (272)	543	0.56
Bulgarian (28)	28	0.03
Canadian (447)	609	0.62
Croatian (42)	180	0.18
Czech (257)	486	0.50
Czechoslovakian (55)	113	0.12
Danish (29)	79	0.08
Dutch (279)	672	0.69
Eastern European (135)	135	0.14
English (1,935)	5,888	6.02
European (358)	471	0.48
Finnish (74)	105	0.11
French, ex. Basque (623)	2,354	2.41
French Canadian (225)	456	0.47
German (3,080)	8,625	8.82
Greek (385)	698	0.71
Guyanese (91)	91	0.09
Hungarian (164)	441	0.45
Icelander (0)	24	0.02
Iranian (78)	89	0.09
Irish (2,261)	7,677	7.85
Israeli (72)	82	0.08
Italian (3,235)	5,991	6.13
Latvian (0)	25	0.03
Lithuanian (98)	261	0.27
Luxemburger (0)	48	0.05
Macedonian (11)	15	0.02
Maltese (9)	44	0.04
New Zealander (14)	14	0.01
Northern European (84)	84	0.09
Norwegian (176)	475	0.49
Polish (1,085)	2,609	2.67
Portuguese (290)	475	0.49
Romanian (121)	240	0.25
Russian (1,038)	2,017	2.06
Scandinavian (22)	22	0.02
Scotch-Irish (362)	871	0.89
Scottish (445)	1,297	1.33
Serbian (0)	19	0.02
Slovak (79)	131	0.13
Slovene (10)	41	0.04
Swedish (105)	510	0.52
Swiss (7)	146	0.15
Turkish (84)	105	0.11
Ukrainian (132)	234	0.24
Welsh (127)	405	0.41
West Indian, ex. Hispanic (7,420)	8,010	8.19
Bahamian (151)	226	0.23
Barbadian (11)	11	0.01
Belizean (49)	63	0.06
Bermudan (44)	44	0.04
British West Indian (143)	157	0.16
Haitian (3,817)	3,930	4.02
Jamaican (2,898)	3,173	3.24
Trinidadian/Tobagonian (278)	375	0.38
U.S. Virgin Islander (29)	29	0.03
West Indian (0)	2	<0.01
Yugoslavian (28)	28	0.03

Hispanic Origin	Population	%
Hispanic or Latino (of any race)	22,601	22.62
Central American, ex. Mexican	5,454	5.46
Costa Rican	169	0.17
Guatemalan	3,897	3.90
Honduran	573	0.57
Nicaraguan	501	0.50
Panamanian	109	0.11
Salvadoran	179	0.18
Other Central American	26	0.03
Cuban	5,337	5.34

*Notes: † The Census 2010 population figure is used to calculate the percentages in the Hispanic Origin and Race categories. Ancestry percentages are based on the 2006-2010 American Community Survey population (not shown); ‡ Numbers in parentheses indicate the number of people reporting a single ancestry; * Numbers in parentheses indicate the number of persons reporting this race alone, not in combination with any other race; Please refer to the Explanation of Data for more information.*

Dominican Republic	983	0.98
Mexican	2,805	2.81
Puerto Rican	3,291	3.29
South American	3,265	3.27
Argentinean	302	0.30
Bolivian	72	0.07
Chilean	115	0.12
Colombian	1,535	1.54
Ecuadorian	343	0.34
Paraguayan	20	0.02
Peruvian	432	0.43
Uruguayan	128	0.13
Venezuelan	297	0.30
Other South American	21	0.02
Other Hispanic or Latino	1,466	1.47

Race*	Population	%
African-American/Black (32,429)	33,705	33.73
Not Hispanic (31,474)	32,440	32.47
Hispanic (955)	1,265	1.27
American Indian/Alaska Native (499)	940	0.94
Not Hispanic (205)	486	0.49
Hispanic (294)	454	0.45
Alaska Athabascan *(Ala. Nat.)* (1)	1	<0.01
Apache (0)	3	<0.01
Blackfeet (2)	20	0.02
Central American Ind. (25)	41	0.04
Cherokee (32)	96	0.10
Cheyenne (0)	3	<0.01
Chickasaw (1)	1	<0.01
Chippewa (7)	10	0.01
Choctaw (3)	6	0.01
Comanche (0)	1	<0.01
Cree (0)	2	<0.01
Creek (5)	7	0.01
Crow (7)	7	0.01
Delaware (4)	6	0.01
Iroquois (5)	11	0.01
Lumbee (1)	1	<0.01
Menominee (1)	2	<0.01
Mexican American Ind. (135)	206	0.21
Navajo (0)	2	<0.01
Osage (0)	1	<0.01
Ottawa (1)	1	<0.01
Puget Sound Salish (6)	6	0.01
Seminole (1)	7	0.01
Sioux (0)	8	0.01
South American Ind. (16)	23	0.02
Spanish American Ind. (2)	6	0.01
Tlingit-Haida *(Alaska Native)* (1)	5	0.01
Yaqui (1)	1	<0.01
Asian (2,256)	2,824	2.83
Not Hispanic (2,213)	2,685	2.69
Hispanic (43)	139	0.14
Bangladeshi (54)	68	0.07
Burmese (5)	5	0.01
Cambodian (13)	17	0.02
Chinese, ex. Taiwanese (321)	442	0.44
Filipino (438)	551	0.55
Indian (684)	831	0.83
Indonesian (16)	16	0.02
Japanese (61)	117	0.12
Korean (136)	192	0.19
Laotian (8)	9	0.01
Malaysian (1)	2	<0.01
Nepalese (22)	25	0.03
Pakistani (64)	79	0.08
Sri Lankan (8)	8	0.01
Taiwanese (7)	11	0.01
Thai (65)	80	0.08
Vietnamese (219)	252	0.25
Hawaii Native/Pacific Islander (114)	324	0.32
Not Hispanic (71)	253	0.25
Hispanic (43)	71	0.07
Fijian (1)	1	<0.01
Guamanian/Chamorro (54)	67	0.07
Marshallese (1)	1	<0.01
Native Hawaiian (18)	41	0.04
Samoan (2)	18	0.02
White (56,673)	58,616	58.66
Not Hispanic (41,588)	42,568	42.60
Hispanic (15,085)	16,048	16.06

West Park

Place Type: City
County: Broward
Population: 14,156†

Ancestry‡	Population	%
African, Sub-Saharan (47)	98	0.69
African (47)	98	0.69
American (1,168)	1,168	8.19
Arab (110)	110	0.77
Other Arab (110)	110	0.77
Austrian (0)	11	0.08
British (53)	53	0.37
Dutch (23)	23	0.16
English (22)	529	3.71
European (0)	30	0.21
French, ex. Basque (0)	44	0.31
French Canadian (19)	19	0.13
German (24)	232	1.63
Greek (0)	32	0.22
Hungarian (27)	27	0.19
Irish (75)	527	3.70
Israeli (10)	10	0.07
Italian (97)	326	2.29
Lithuanian (0)	10	0.07
Norwegian (0)	12	0.08
Polish (12)	35	0.25
Portuguese (0)	14	0.10
Romanian (0)	21	0.15
Russian (31)	56	0.39
Scotch-Irish (0)	15	0.11
Scottish (0)	33	0.23
Slovak (8)	8	0.06
Welsh (0)	19	0.13
West Indian, ex. Hispanic (1,629)	2,100	14.73
Bahamian (113)	247	1.73
Barbadian (0)	13	0.09
Bermudan (0)	13	0.09
British West Indian (118)	137	0.96
Haitian (317)	513	3.60
Jamaican (951)	987	6.92
Trinidadian/Tobagonian (97)	143	1.00
West Indian (33)	47	0.33

Hispanic Origin	Population	%
Hispanic or Latino (of any race)	4,091	28.90
Central American, ex. Mexican	693	4.90
Costa Rican	20	0.14
Guatemalan	78	0.55
Honduran	265	1.87
Nicaraguan	169	1.19
Panamanian	82	0.58
Salvadoran	77	0.54
Other Central American	2	0.01
Cuban	901	6.36
Dominican Republic	528	3.73
Mexican	278	1.96
Puerto Rican	780	5.51
South American	545	3.85
Argentinean	44	0.31
Bolivian	3	0.02
Chilean	55	0.39
Colombian	215	1.52
Ecuadorian	50	0.35
Peruvian	138	0.97
Uruguayan	14	0.10
Venezuelan	26	0.18
Other Hispanic or Latino	366	2.59

Race*	Population	%
African-American/Black (8,192)	8,459	59.76
Not Hispanic (7,828)	7,984	56.40
Hispanic (364)	475	3.36
American Indian/Alaska Native (56)	96	0.68
Not Hispanic (37)	59	0.42
Hispanic (19)	37	0.26
Blackfeet (0)	1	0.01
Canadian/French Am. Ind. (5)	5	0.04
Central American Ind. (0)	1	0.01
Cherokee (3)	9	0.06
Chippewa (1)	1	0.01
Choctaw (5)	5	0.04
Creek (2)	2	0.01
Mexican American Ind. (7)	8	0.06
Sioux (2)	2	0.01
South American Ind. (1)	2	0.01
Spanish American Ind. (0)	2	0.01
Asian (148)	230	1.62
Not Hispanic (140)	205	1.45
Hispanic (8)	25	0.18
Bangladeshi (0)	2	0.01
Chinese, ex. Taiwanese (9)	20	0.14
Filipino (15)	22	0.16
Indian (67)	105	0.74
Indonesian (1)	1	0.01
Japanese (7)	10	0.07
Korean (2)	5	0.04
Laotian (2)	2	0.01
Pakistani (12)	21	0.15
Taiwanese (1)	1	0.01
Thai (15)	21	0.15
Vietnamese (4)	7	0.05
Hawaii Native/Pacific Islander (7)	37	0.26
Not Hispanic (5)	24	0.17
Hispanic (2)	13	0.09
Guamanian/Chamorro (1)	1	0.01
Native Hawaiian (1)	2	0.01
White (4,646)	4,937	34.88
Not Hispanic (1,805)	1,917	13.54
Hispanic (2,841)	3,020	21.33

West Pensacola

Place Type: CDP
County: Escambia
Population: 21,339†

Ancestry‡	Population	%
African, Sub-Saharan (225)	253	1.19
African (152)	180	0.85
Cape Verdean (53)	53	0.25
South African (20)	20	0.09
American (2,213)	2,213	10.42
Austrian (0)	34	0.16
British (7)	49	0.23
Bulgarian (13)	13	0.06
Canadian (44)	51	0.24
Croatian (8)	18	0.08
Czech (11)	36	0.17
Danish (0)	71	0.33
Dutch (77)	395	1.86
English (522)	1,238	5.83
European (18)	52	0.24
French, ex. Basque (46)	393	1.85
French Canadian (36)	82	0.39
German (344)	1,374	6.47
Greek (21)	87	0.41
Hungarian (12)	74	0.35
Irish (477)	1,796	8.46
Italian (218)	493	2.32
Lithuanian (10)	10	0.05
Norwegian (34)	123	0.58
Pennsylvania German (18)	18	0.08
Polish (54)	216	1.02
Portuguese (0)	11	0.05
Romanian (9)	20	0.09
Russian (30)	113	0.53
Scandinavian (9)	16	0.08
Scotch-Irish (102)	328	1.54
Scottish (226)	346	1.63
Swedish (9)	187	0.88
Ukrainian (0)	10	0.05
Welsh (0)	16	0.08
West Indian, ex. Hispanic (357)	535	2.52
Dutch West Indian (0)	15	0.07
Haitian (71)	130	0.61

*Notes: † The Census 2010 population figure is used to calculate the percentages in the Hispanic Origin and Race categories. Ancestry percentages are based on the 2006-2010 American Community Survey population (not shown); ‡ Numbers in parentheses indicate the number of people reporting a single ancestry; * Numbers in parentheses indicate the number of persons reporting this race alone, not in combination with any other race; Please refer to the Explanation of Data for more information.*

Jamaican (239)	296	1.39
Trinidadian/Tobagonian (11)	58	0.27
West Indian (36)	36	0.17

Hispanic Origin	Population	%
Hispanic or Latino (of any race)	1,115	5.23
Central American, ex. Mexican	157	0.74
Costa Rican	4	0.02
Guatemalan	40	0.19
Honduran	78	0.37
Nicaraguan	14	0.07
Panamanian	9	0.04
Salvadoran	11	0.05
Other Central American	1	<0.01
Cuban	61	0.29
Dominican Republic	15	0.07
Mexican	509	2.39
Puerto Rican	175	0.82
South American	37	0.17
Argentinean	2	0.01
Bolivian	10	0.05
Chilean	1	<0.01
Colombian	12	0.06
Ecuadorian	4	0.02
Peruvian	8	0.04
Other Hispanic or Latino	161	0.75

Race*	Population	%
African-American/Black (9,007)	9,379	43.95
Not Hispanic (8,926)	9,267	43.43
Hispanic (81)	112	0.52
American Indian/Alaska Native (222)	404	1.89
Not Hispanic (212)	379	1.78
Hispanic (10)	25	0.12
Apache (0)	1	<0.01
Blackfeet (4)	12	0.06
Cherokee (43)	94	0.44
Chippewa (1)	2	0.01
Choctaw (1)	4	0.02
Cree (0)	1	<0.01
Creek (68)	100	0.47
Delaware (1)	1	<0.01
Iroquois (0)	4	0.02
Lumbee (2)	2	0.01
Mexican American Ind. (1)	6	0.03
Potawatomi (2)	2	0.01
Seminole (1)	5	0.02
Sioux (2)	15	0.07
South American Ind. (1)	1	<0.01
Tsimshian *(Alaska Native)* (1)	2	0.01
Asian (711)	903	4.23
Not Hispanic (698)	878	4.11
Hispanic (13)	25	0.12
Bangladeshi (0)	2	0.01
Cambodian (8)	9	0.04
Chinese, ex. Taiwanese (7)	20	0.09
Filipino (289)	402	1.88
Indian (18)	32	0.15
Japanese (15)	42	0.20
Korean (15)	27	0.13
Laotian (4)	5	0.02
Pakistani (7)	9	0.04
Sri Lankan (0)	1	<0.01
Taiwanese (1)	1	<0.01
Thai (6)	8	0.04
Vietnamese (308)	346	1.62
Hawaii Native/Pacific Islander (56)	82	0.38
Not Hispanic (52)	75	0.35
Hispanic (4)	7	0.03
Guamanian/Chamorro (29)	32	0.15
Native Hawaiian (9)	22	0.10
Samoan (8)	13	0.06
White (10,194)	10,756	50.41
Not Hispanic (9,691)	10,163	47.63
Hispanic (503)	593	2.78

West Perrine

Place Type: CDP
County: Miami-Dade
Population: 9,460†

Ancestry‡	Population	%
African, Sub-Saharan (184)	184	1.84
African (184)	184	1.84
American (1,900)	1,900	18.98
Arab (0)	43	0.43
Egyptian (0)	43	0.43
British (12)	12	0.12
Danish (11)	11	0.11
Dutch (0)	19	0.19
English (166)	224	2.24
German (27)	54	0.54
Irish (12)	78	0.78
Italian (24)	71	0.71
Polish (12)	34	0.34
Portuguese (0)	20	0.20
Scotch-Irish (10)	25	0.25
Scottish (0)	11	0.11
West Indian, ex. Hispanic (852)	1,224	12.23
Bahamian (69)	69	0.69
British West Indian (10)	10	0.10
Haitian (188)	231	2.31
Jamaican (518)	831	8.30
Trinidadian/Tobagonian (55)	71	0.71
West Indian (12)	12	0.12

Hispanic Origin	Population	%
Hispanic or Latino (of any race)	2,998	31.69
Central American, ex. Mexican	524	5.54
Costa Rican	18	0.19
Guatemalan	45	0.48
Honduran	109	1.15
Nicaraguan	259	2.74
Panamanian	34	0.36
Salvadoran	57	0.60
Other Central American	2	0.02
Cuban	1,351	14.28
Dominican Republic	212	2.24
Mexican	120	1.27
Puerto Rican	286	3.02
South American	348	3.68
Argentinean	22	0.23
Bolivian	1	0.01
Chilean	18	0.19
Colombian	141	1.49
Ecuadorian	18	0.19
Peruvian	87	0.92
Uruguayan	5	0.05
Venezuelan	56	0.59
Other Hispanic or Latino	157	1.66

Race*	Population	%
African-American/Black (5,927)	6,074	64.21
Not Hispanic (5,702)	5,806	61.37
Hispanic (225)	268	2.83
American Indian/Alaska Native (30)	41	0.43
Not Hispanic (21)	31	0.33
Hispanic (9)	10	0.11
Cherokee (2)	2	0.02
Chippewa (1)	1	0.01
Lumbee (4)	5	0.05
Seminole (3)	3	0.03
Asian (98)	153	1.62
Not Hispanic (96)	141	1.49
Hispanic (2)	12	0.13
Chinese, ex. Taiwanese (25)	48	0.51
Filipino (4)	5	0.05
Indian (44)	63	0.67
Japanese (2)	2	0.02
Korean (3)	5	0.05
Pakistani (1)	1	0.01
Taiwanese (1)	2	0.02
Vietnamese (15)	16	0.17
Hawaii Native/Pacific Islander (0)	26	0.27
Not Hispanic (0)	23	0.24
Hispanic (0)	3	0.03
Native Hawaiian (0)	1	0.01
Samoan (0)	1	0.01
White (2,921)	3,039	32.12
Not Hispanic (490)	533	5.63
Hispanic (2,431)	2,506	26.49

Westchase

Place Type: CDP
County: Hillsborough
Population: 21,747†

Ancestry‡	Population	%
African, Sub-Saharan (23)	83	0.39
African (0)	60	0.29
South African (23)	23	0.11
Albanian (0)	26	0.12
American (1,251)	1,251	5.95
Arab (155)	177	0.84
Arab (12)	26	0.12
Egyptian (92)	92	0.44
Lebanese (51)	59	0.28
Armenian (31)	37	0.18
Austrian (32)	82	0.39
Brazilian (200)	200	0.95
British (107)	219	1.04
Canadian (9)	9	0.04
Celtic (9)	24	0.11
Croatian (0)	45	0.21
Czech (61)	250	1.19
Czechoslovakian (0)	26	0.12
Danish (32)	102	0.48
Dutch (39)	274	1.30
English (521)	1,842	8.76
European (317)	344	1.64
French, ex. Basque (156)	580	2.76
French Canadian (38)	61	0.29
German (1,086)	3,604	17.13
Greek (160)	267	1.27
Guyanese (10)	10	0.05
Hungarian (47)	155	0.74
Irish (800)	3,083	14.66
Israeli (0)	25	0.12
Italian (939)	2,366	11.25
Latvian (0)	13	0.06
Lithuanian (72)	177	0.84
Macedonian (13)	13	0.06
Norwegian (70)	303	1.44
Pennsylvania German (0)	72	0.34
Polish (257)	912	4.34
Portuguese (0)	6	0.03
Romanian (22)	70	0.33
Russian (167)	313	1.49
Scotch-Irish (240)	537	2.55
Scottish (194)	631	3.00
Serbian (11)	36	0.17
Slovak (37)	67	0.32
Swedish (84)	236	1.12
Swiss (0)	64	0.30
Turkish (67)	67	0.32
Ukrainian (27)	64	0.30
Welsh (34)	127	0.60
West Indian, ex. Hispanic (35)	43	0.20
Jamaican (27)	27	0.13
West Indian (8)	16	0.08

Hispanic Origin	Population	%
Hispanic or Latino (of any race)	3,368	15.49
Central American, ex. Mexican	188	0.86
Costa Rican	21	0.10
Guatemalan	28	0.13
Honduran	32	0.15
Nicaraguan	26	0.12
Panamanian	46	0.21
Salvadoran	35	0.16
Cuban	778	3.58
Dominican Republic	142	0.65
Mexican	206	0.95
Puerto Rican	1,006	4.63

*Notes: † The Census 2010 population figure is used to calculate the percentages in the Hispanic Origin and Race categories. Ancestry percentages are based on the 2006-2010 American Community Survey population (not shown); ‡ Numbers in parentheses indicate the number of people reporting a single ancestry; * Numbers in parentheses indicate the number of persons reporting this race alone, not in combination with any other race; Please refer to the Explanation of Data for more information.*

South American	746	3.43
Argentinean	31	0.14
Bolivian	9	0.04
Chilean	31	0.14
Colombian	361	1.66
Ecuadorian	92	0.42
Paraguayan	3	0.01
Peruvian	96	0.44
Uruguayan	6	0.03
Venezuelan	109	0.50
Other South American	8	0.04
Other Hispanic or Latino	302	1.39

Race*	Population	%
African-American/Black (1,158)	1,422	6.54
Not Hispanic (1,060)	1,231	5.66
Hispanic (98)	191	0.88
American Indian/Alaska Native (40)	105	0.48
Not Hispanic (25)	70	0.32
Hispanic (15)	35	0.16
Apache (0)	7	0.03
Blackfeet (0)	1	<0.01
Central American Ind. (0)	2	0.01
Cherokee (2)	16	0.07
Chippewa (3)	3	0.01
Choctaw (0)	3	0.01
Iroquois (0)	3	0.01
Lumbee (2)	2	0.01
Mexican American Ind. (6)	8	0.04
Ottawa (1)	1	<0.01
Potawatomi (0)	4	0.02
Seminole (3)	3	0.01
Sioux (0)	1	<0.01
South American Ind. (1)	5	0.02
Spanish American Ind. (1)	1	<0.01
Asian (1,441)	1,709	7.86
Not Hispanic (1,416)	1,663	7.65
Hispanic (25)	46	0.21
Bangladeshi (9)	9	0.04
Burmese (1)	3	0.01
Cambodian (6)	6	0.03
Chinese, ex. Taiwanese (180)	233	1.07
Filipino (145)	215	0.99
Hmong (3)	3	0.01
Indian (535)	576	2.65
Indonesian (4)	5	0.02
Japanese (57)	91	0.42
Korean (201)	230	1.06
Laotian (1)	2	0.01
Malaysian (4)	9	0.04
Pakistani (40)	48	0.22
Sri Lankan (16)	17	0.08
Taiwanese (7)	11	0.05
Thai (7)	19	0.09
Vietnamese (186)	200	0.92
Hawaii Native/Pacific Islander (13)	42	0.19
Not Hispanic (13)	40	0.18
Hispanic (0)	2	0.01
Guamanian/Chamorro (3)	10	0.05
Native Hawaiian (6)	19	0.09
White (17,952)	18,501	85.07
Not Hispanic (15,342)	15,714	72.26
Hispanic (2,610)	2,787	12.82

Westchester

Place Type: CDP
County: Miami-Dade
Population: 29,862†

Ancestry‡	Population	%
African, Sub-Saharan (0)	97	0.34
African (0)	97	0.34
American (218)	218	0.76
Arab (106)	144	0.50
Arab (74)	74	0.26
Lebanese (32)	32	0.11
Syrian (0)	38	0.13
Austrian (54)	112	0.39
Basque (32)	32	0.11
Brazilian (0)	58	0.20
British (10)	10	0.03
Czech (0)	12	0.04
Dutch (0)	23	0.08
English (161)	379	1.32
French, ex. Basque (0)	143	0.50
French Canadian (0)	17	0.06
German (112)	299	1.04
Hungarian (88)	88	0.31
Irish (134)	244	0.85
Italian (153)	359	1.25
Latvian (0)	11	0.04
Lithuanian (0)	10	0.03
Polish (16)	61	0.21
Portuguese (0)	14	0.05
Russian (36)	136	0.47
Scotch-Irish (11)	19	0.07
Scottish (0)	12	0.04
Slovak (18)	18	0.06
Swedish (0)	9	0.03
Swiss (0)	21	0.07
Ukrainian (0)	11	0.04
Welsh (0)	24	0.08
West Indian, ex. Hispanic (60)	60	0.21
Bahamian (9)	9	0.03
Haitian (35)	35	0.12
West Indian (16)	16	0.06

Hispanic Origin	Population	%
Hispanic or Latino (of any race)	27,211	91.12
Central American, ex. Mexican	1,978	6.62
Costa Rican	103	0.34
Guatemalan	287	0.96
Honduran	344	1.15
Nicaraguan	1,013	3.39
Panamanian	43	0.14
Salvadoran	186	0.62
Other Central American	2	0.01
Cuban	21,391	71.63
Dominican Republic	382	1.28
Mexican	292	0.98
Puerto Rican	504	1.69
South American	1,805	6.04
Argentinean	174	0.58
Bolivian	31	0.10
Chilean	112	0.38
Colombian	665	2.23
Ecuadorian	178	0.60
Paraguayan	4	0.01
Peruvian	317	1.06
Uruguayan	66	0.22
Venezuelan	258	0.86
Other Hispanic or Latino	859	2.88

Race*	Population	%
African-American/Black (364)	425	1.42
Not Hispanic (73)	88	0.29
Hispanic (291)	337	1.13
American Indian/Alaska Native (23)	49	0.16
Not Hispanic (9)	16	0.05
Hispanic (14)	33	0.11
Blackfeet (0)	1	<0.01
Central American Ind. (2)	6	0.02
Cherokee (1)	2	0.01
Choctaw (1)	1	<0.01
South American Ind. (2)	4	0.01
Spanish American Ind. (5)	11	0.04
Asian (134)	184	0.62
Not Hispanic (114)	137	0.46
Hispanic (20)	47	0.16
Burmese (2)	2	0.01
Chinese, ex. Taiwanese (58)	76	0.25
Filipino (5)	9	0.03
Indian (11)	14	0.05
Japanese (5)	6	0.02
Korean (10)	13	0.04
Pakistani (16)	16	0.05
Sri Lankan (1)	1	<0.01
Thai (4)	5	0.02
Vietnamese (17)	21	0.07
Hawaii Native/Pacific Islander (1)	17	0.06
Not Hispanic (0)	11	0.04
Hispanic (1)	6	0.02
Native Hawaiian (0)	3	0.01
Samoan (1)	1	<0.01
White (28,566)	28,882	96.72
Not Hispanic (2,404)	2,431	8.14
Hispanic (26,162)	26,451	88.58

Westgate

Place Type: CDP
County: Palm Beach
Population: 7,975†

Ancestry‡	Population	%
American (474)	474	6.41
Armenian (0)	8	0.11
Canadian (0)	6	0.08
Dutch (8)	60	0.81
English (56)	200	2.70
French, ex. Basque (0)	19	0.26
French Canadian (16)	55	0.74
German (76)	265	3.58
Greek (0)	11	0.15
Irish (90)	231	3.12
Italian (25)	130	1.76
Lithuanian (0)	11	0.15
Polish (21)	28	0.38
Scotch-Irish (35)	72	0.97
Scottish (0)	27	0.37
West Indian, ex. Hispanic (824)	903	12.21
Bahamian (13)	13	0.18
Haitian (754)	820	11.09
Jamaican (57)	57	0.77
West Indian (0)	13	0.18

Hispanic Origin	Population	%
Hispanic or Latino (of any race)	3,321	41.64
Central American, ex. Mexican	1,154	14.47
Costa Rican	11	0.14
Guatemalan	775	9.72
Honduran	129	1.62
Nicaraguan	96	1.20
Panamanian	5	0.06
Salvadoran	137	1.72
Other Central American	1	0.01
Cuban	350	4.39
Dominican Republic	160	2.01
Mexican	881	11.05
Puerto Rican	403	5.05
South American	163	2.04
Argentinean	6	0.08
Bolivian	4	0.05
Chilean	13	0.16
Colombian	84	1.05
Ecuadorian	15	0.19
Paraguayan	1	0.01
Peruvian	16	0.20
Uruguayan	13	0.16
Venezuelan	11	0.14
Other Hispanic or Latino	210	2.63

Race*	Population	%
African-American/Black (2,962)	3,189	39.99
Not Hispanic (2,900)	3,016	37.82
Hispanic (62)	173	2.17
American Indian/Alaska Native (70)	148	1.86
Not Hispanic (16)	52	0.65
Hispanic (54)	96	1.20
Aleut *(Alaska Native)* (1)	1	0.01
Central American Ind. (0)	3	0.04
Cherokee (3)	14	0.18
Cheyenne (0)	3	0.04
Iroquois (3)	5	0.06
Lumbee (1)	4	0.05
Mexican American Ind. (23)	48	0.60
Sioux (0)	1	0.01
South American Ind. (1)	1	0.01
Asian (138)	164	2.06

*Notes: † The Census 2010 population figure is used to calculate the percentages in the Hispanic Origin and Race categories. Ancestry percentages are based on the 2006-2010 American Community Survey population (not shown); ‡ Numbers in parentheses indicate the number of people reporting a single ancestry; * Numbers in parentheses indicate the number of persons reporting this race alone, not in combination with any other race; Please refer to the Explanation of Data for more information.*

Not Hispanic (132)	151	1.89
Hispanic (6)	13	0.16
Bangladeshi (36)	42	0.53
Cambodian (1)	1	0.01
Chinese, ex. Taiwanese (4)	9	0.11
Filipino (9)	9	0.11
Indian (67)	81	1.02
Korean (1)	3	0.04
Nepalese (0)	1	0.01
Thai (2)	2	0.03
Vietnamese (12)	18	0.23
Hawaii Native/Pacific Islander (13)	35	0.44
Not Hispanic (8)	25	0.31
Hispanic (5)	10	0.13
Guamanian/Chamorro (13)	13	0.16
White (3,282)	3,603	45.18
Not Hispanic (1,441)	1,521	19.07
Hispanic (1,841)	2,082	26.11

Weston

Place Type: City
County: Broward
Population: 65,333†

Ancestry‡	Population	%
African, Sub-Saharan (294)	350	0.56
African (218)	233	0.37
Sierra Leonean (0)	14	0.02
South African (76)	103	0.16
American (2,318)	2,318	3.69
Arab (210)	460	0.73
Arab (0)	27	0.04
Egyptian (18)	37	0.06
Iraqi (33)	99	0.16
Lebanese (97)	223	0.36
Moroccan (39)	39	0.06
Syrian (23)	35	0.06
Armenian (21)	108	0.17
Austrian (188)	520	0.83
Belgian (33)	53	0.08
Brazilian (520)	698	1.11
British (397)	549	0.87
Bulgarian (0)	11	0.02
Canadian (213)	324	0.52
Croatian (14)	24	0.04
Czech (56)	165	0.26
Czechoslovakian (13)	37	0.06
Danish (23)	93	0.15
Dutch (154)	666	1.06
Eastern European (503)	503	0.80
English (1,059)	2,811	4.48
Estonian (12)	12	0.02
European (1,258)	1,698	2.71
Finnish (0)	15	0.02
French, ex. Basque (433)	1,214	1.93
French Canadian (126)	227	0.36
German (1,225)	4,413	7.03
Greek (101)	265	0.42
Guyanese (15)	15	0.02
Hungarian (90)	366	0.58
Icelander (18)	30	0.05
Iranian (135)	213	0.34
Irish (974)	3,479	5.54
Israeli (235)	250	0.40
Italian (2,336)	4,960	7.90
Lithuanian (29)	175	0.28
Northern European (16)	16	0.03
Norwegian (21)	150	0.24
Pennsylvania German (16)	30	0.05
Polish (897)	2,181	3.48
Portuguese (419)	723	1.15
Romanian (134)	324	0.52
Russian (1,177)	2,926	4.66
Scandinavian (18)	18	0.03
Scotch-Irish (211)	429	0.68
Scottish (151)	446	0.71
Serbian (10)	10	0.02
Slavic (0)	26	0.04
Slovak (0)	84	0.13
Slovene (11)	54	0.09
Swedish (39)	396	0.63
Swiss (32)	193	0.31
Turkish (84)	272	0.43
Ukrainian (16)	115	0.18
Welsh (14)	146	0.23
West Indian, ex. Hispanic (1,452)	1,900	3.03
Barbadian (24)	24	0.04
British West Indian (25)	25	0.04
Haitian (317)	512	0.82
Jamaican (938)	1,191	1.90
Trinidadian/Tobagonian (135)	135	0.22
West Indian (13)	13	0.02
Yugoslavian (8)	27	0.04

Hispanic Origin	Population	%
Hispanic or Latino (of any race)	29,353	44.93
Central American, ex. Mexican	1,215	1.86
Costa Rican	105	0.16
Guatemalan	282	0.43
Honduran	189	0.29
Nicaraguan	288	0.44
Panamanian	137	0.21
Salvadoran	213	0.33
Other Central American	1	<0.01
Cuban	3,134	4.80
Dominican Republic	988	1.51
Mexican	1,293	1.98
Puerto Rican	2,695	4.13
South American	18,234	27.91
Argentinean	946	1.45
Bolivian	130	0.20
Chilean	306	0.47
Colombian	7,637	11.69
Ecuadorian	1,000	1.53
Paraguayan	28	0.04
Peruvian	1,677	2.57
Uruguayan	133	0.20
Venezuelan	6,360	9.73
Other South American	17	0.03
Other Hispanic or Latino	1,794	2.75

Race*	Population	%
African-American/Black (2,860)	3,358	5.14
Not Hispanic (2,592)	2,942	4.50
Hispanic (268)	416	0.64
American Indian/Alaska Native (87)	316	0.48
Not Hispanic (46)	209	0.32
Hispanic (41)	107	0.16
Apache (1)	5	0.01
Blackfeet (0)	1	<0.01
Central American Ind. (5)	13	0.02
Cherokee (6)	18	0.03
Chippewa (0)	4	0.01
Choctaw (1)	1	<0.01
Creek (0)	1	<0.01
Delaware (0)	4	0.01
Iroquois (1)	2	<0.01
Lumbee (0)	3	<0.01
Mexican American Ind. (6)	9	0.01
Navajo (0)	2	<0.01
Pima (1)	4	0.01
Potawatomi (3)	3	<0.01
Seminole (14)	15	0.02
Sioux (0)	2	<0.01
South American Ind. (16)	22	0.03
Spanish American Ind. (1)	1	<0.01
Tlingit-Haida *(Alaska Native)* (1)	2	<0.01
Asian (3,000)	3,558	5.45
Not Hispanic (2,950)	3,417	5.23
Hispanic (50)	141	0.22
Burmese (5)	5	0.01
Cambodian (1)	2	<0.01
Chinese, ex. Taiwanese (653)	822	1.26
Filipino (229)	341	0.52
Indian (1,133)	1,278	1.96
Indonesian (9)	12	0.02
Japanese (123)	185	0.28
Korean (512)	532	0.81
Laotian (3)	9	0.01
Pakistani (136)	173	0.26
Sri Lankan (6)	7	0.01
Taiwanese (42)	52	0.08
Thai (17)	24	0.04
Vietnamese (51)	69	0.11
Hawaii Native/Pacific Islander (24)	70	0.11
Not Hispanic (22)	58	0.09
Hispanic (2)	12	0.02
Guamanian/Chamorro (7)	21	0.03
Marshallese (1)	1	<0.01
Native Hawaiian (9)	16	0.02
Samoan (2)	3	<0.01
White (56,044)	57,367	87.81
Not Hispanic (29,287)	29,982	45.89
Hispanic (26,757)	27,385	41.92

Westview

Place Type: CDP
County: Miami-Dade
Population: 9,650†

Ancestry‡	Population	%
African, Sub-Saharan (62)	75	0.80
African (32)	45	0.48
Other Sub-Saharan African (30)	30	0.32
American (222)	222	2.37
Arab (33)	33	0.35
Moroccan (33)	33	0.35
British (0)	13	0.14
English (25)	25	0.27
German (0)	24	0.26
Hungarian (0)	9	0.10
Italian (0)	15	0.16
Pennsylvania German (9)	9	0.10
West Indian, ex. Hispanic (2,124)	2,276	24.34
Bahamian (137)	164	1.75
Belizean (0)	18	0.19
British West Indian (50)	63	0.67
Haitian (1,314)	1,341	14.34
Jamaican (585)	652	6.97
West Indian (38)	38	0.41

Hispanic Origin	Population	%
Hispanic or Latino (of any race)	2,859	29.63
Central American, ex. Mexican	655	6.79
Costa Rican	12	0.12
Guatemalan	49	0.51
Honduran	220	2.28
Nicaraguan	311	3.22
Panamanian	34	0.35
Salvadoran	28	0.29
Other Central American	1	0.01
Cuban	980	10.16
Dominican Republic	429	4.45
Mexican	43	0.45
Puerto Rican	418	4.33
South American	140	1.45
Argentinean	21	0.22
Bolivian	2	0.02
Chilean	1	0.01
Colombian	57	0.59
Ecuadorian	23	0.24
Peruvian	19	0.20
Venezuelan	11	0.11
Other South American	6	0.06
Other Hispanic or Latino	194	2.01

Race*	Population	%
African-American/Black (6,706)	6,874	71.23
Not Hispanic (6,414)	6,515	67.51
Hispanic (292)	359	3.72
American Indian/Alaska Native (28)	57	0.59
Not Hispanic (16)	42	0.44
Hispanic (12)	15	0.16
Central American Ind. (2)	2	0.02
Cherokee (2)	2	0.02
Chippewa (3)	3	0.03
Mexican American Ind. (2)	2	0.02
South American Ind. (1)	2	0.02

*Notes: † The Census 2010 population figure is used to calculate the percentages in the Hispanic Origin and Race categories. Ancestry percentages are based on the 2006-2010 American Community Survey population (not shown); ‡ Numbers in parentheses indicate the number of people reporting a single ancestry; * Numbers in parentheses indicate the number of persons reporting this race alone, not in combination with any other race; Please refer to the Explanation of Data for more information.*

Asian (18)	46	0.48
Not Hispanic (18)	39	0.40
Hispanic (0)	7	0.07
Bangladeshi (0)	1	0.01
Chinese, ex. Taiwanese (3)	8	0.08
Filipino (1)	1	0.01
Indian (6)	16	0.17
Japanese (0)	1	0.01
Korean (1)	1	0.01
Pakistani (0)	1	0.01
Sri Lankan (1)	1	0.01
Thai (1)	3	0.03
Vietnamese (2)	2	0.02
Hawaii Native/Pacific Islander (13)	44	0.46
Not Hispanic (5)	30	0.31
Hispanic (8)	14	0.15
Guamanian/Chamorro (13)	13	0.13
White (2,285)	2,422	25.10
Not Hispanic (226)	248	2.57
Hispanic (2,059)	2,174	22.53

Westwood Lakes

Place Type: CDP
County: Miami-Dade
Population: 11,838†

Ancestry‡	Population	%
African, Sub-Saharan (0)	65	0.59
African (0)	65	0.59
American (91)	91	0.82
Arab (11)	23	0.21
Lebanese (11)	23	0.21
Canadian (11)	11	0.10
Czech (0)	22	0.20
Dutch (13)	13	0.12
English (0)	44	0.40
European (107)	107	0.97
French, ex. Basque (0)	13	0.12
French Canadian (0)	3	0.03
German (32)	221	2.00
Hungarian (21)	34	0.31
Irish (37)	95	0.86
Italian (30)	140	1.27
Lithuanian (10)	10	0.09
Polish (11)	42	0.38
Romanian (0)	18	0.16
Russian (22)	61	0.55
Scotch-Irish (56)	56	0.51
Scottish (11)	11	0.10
Swedish (0)	3	0.03

Hispanic Origin	Population	%
Hispanic or Latino (of any race)	10,177	85.97
Central American, ex. Mexican	777	6.56
Costa Rican	22	0.19
Guatemalan	119	1.01
Honduran	96	0.81
Nicaraguan	440	3.72
Panamanian	20	0.17
Salvadoran	80	0.68
Cuban	7,539	63.68
Dominican Republic	117	0.99
Mexican	462	3.90
Puerto Rican	254	2.15
South American	753	6.36
Argentinean	31	0.26
Bolivian	18	0.15
Chilean	41	0.35
Colombian	289	2.44
Ecuadorian	76	0.64
Peruvian	196	1.66
Uruguayan	6	0.05
Venezuelan	96	0.81
Other Hispanic or Latino	275	2.32

Race*	Population	%
African-American/Black (152)	178	1.50
Not Hispanic (28)	34	0.29
Hispanic (124)	144	1.22
American Indian/Alaska Native (5)	17	0.14
Not Hispanic (3)	6	0.05
Hispanic (2)	11	0.09
Apache (0)	4	0.03
Cherokee (0)	1	0.01
Chippewa (0)	1	0.01
Choctaw (1)	1	0.01
Lumbee (1)	1	0.01
Shoshone (0)	1	0.01
Spanish American Ind. (0)	2	0.02
Asian (118)	148	1.25
Not Hispanic (115)	129	1.09
Hispanic (3)	19	0.16
Chinese, ex. Taiwanese (21)	42	0.35
Filipino (0)	5	0.04
Indian (2)	10	0.08
Japanese (2)	4	0.03
Pakistani (34)	43	0.36
Taiwanese (0)	1	0.01
Vietnamese (40)	52	0.44
Hawaii Native/Pacific Islander (0)	9	0.08
Hispanic (0)	9	0.08
Native Hawaiian (0)	3	0.03
White (11,147)	11,331	95.72
Not Hispanic (1,483)	1,505	12.71
Hispanic (9,664)	9,826	83.00

Williamsburg

Place Type: CDP
County: Orange
Population: 7,646†

Ancestry‡	Population	%
African, Sub-Saharan (69)	85	1.24
African (34)	50	0.73
Other Sub-Saharan African (35)	35	0.51
American (607)	607	8.86
Arab (117)	131	1.91
Arab (17)	24	0.35
Lebanese (16)	16	0.23
Moroccan (84)	84	1.23
Other Arab (0)	7	0.10
Austrian (0)	48	0.70
Brazilian (244)	259	3.78
British (11)	26	0.38
Canadian (46)	59	0.86
Croatian (0)	30	0.44
Czech (12)	23	0.34
Czechoslovakian (15)	15	0.22
Danish (21)	31	0.45
Dutch (31)	90	1.31
English (190)	556	8.11
European (75)	103	1.50
French, ex. Basque (56)	306	4.47
French Canadian (32)	47	0.69
German (168)	954	13.92
Greek (33)	49	0.72
Hungarian (39)	137	2.00
Irish (379)	816	11.91
Israeli (37)	37	0.54
Italian (419)	846	12.35
Lithuanian (15)	30	0.44
Norwegian (51)	141	2.06
Polish (187)	282	4.12
Portuguese (58)	182	2.66
Russian (46)	117	1.71
Scotch-Irish (52)	129	1.88
Scottish (0)	65	0.95
Slovak (27)	27	0.39
Slovene (0)	16	0.23
Swedish (0)	40	0.58
Turkish (0)	98	1.43
Ukrainian (16)	30	0.44
Welsh (27)	69	1.01
West Indian, ex. Hispanic (68)	68	0.99
Barbadian (15)	15	0.22
Haitian (16)	16	0.23
Jamaican (21)	21	0.31
Trinidadian/Tobagonian (16)	16	0.23

Hispanic Origin	Population	%
Hispanic or Latino (of any race)	1,316	17.21
Central American, ex. Mexican	68	0.89
Costa Rican	14	0.18
Guatemalan	16	0.21
Honduran	13	0.17
Nicaraguan	3	0.04
Panamanian	16	0.21
Salvadoran	6	0.08
Cuban	77	1.01
Dominican Republic	79	1.03
Mexican	107	1.40
Puerto Rican	579	7.57
South American	339	4.43
Argentinean	37	0.48
Bolivian	4	0.05
Chilean	19	0.25
Colombian	165	2.16
Ecuadorian	44	0.58
Peruvian	43	0.56
Uruguayan	1	0.01
Venezuelan	26	0.34
Other Hispanic or Latino	67	0.88

Race*	Population	%
African-American/Black (306)	390	5.10
Not Hispanic (282)	343	4.49
Hispanic (24)	47	0.61
American Indian/Alaska Native (13)	51	0.67
Not Hispanic (12)	34	0.44
Hispanic (1)	17	0.22
Apache (1)	1	0.01
Blackfeet (1)	1	0.01
Cherokee (5)	15	0.20
Iroquois (0)	1	0.01
Lumbee (5)	5	0.07
Yuman (0)	2	0.03
Asian (492)	584	7.64
Not Hispanic (482)	566	7.40
Hispanic (10)	18	0.24
Bangladeshi (5)	5	0.07
Burmese (3)	3	0.04
Cambodian (17)	18	0.24
Chinese, ex. Taiwanese (144)	165	2.16
Filipino (89)	97	1.27
Indian (98)	117	1.53
Indonesian (0)	2	0.03
Japanese (53)	62	0.81
Korean (20)	27	0.35
Pakistani (3)	3	0.04
Taiwanese (2)	3	0.04
Thai (14)	18	0.24
Vietnamese (32)	34	0.44
Hawaii Native/Pacific Islander (45)	51	0.67
Not Hispanic (44)	49	0.64
Hispanic (1)	2	0.03
Fijian (0)	8	0.10
Guamanian/Chamorro (1)	2	0.03
Samoan (12)	12	0.16
Tongan (1)	9	0.12
White (6,315)	6,496	84.96
Not Hispanic (5,316)	5,435	71.08
Hispanic (999)	1,061	13.88

Wilton Manors

Place Type: City
County: Broward
Population: 11,632†

Ancestry‡	Population	%
American (1,198)	1,198	10.09
Arab (0)	16	0.13
Lebanese (0)	16	0.13
Armenian (0)	15	0.13
Austrian (25)	56	0.47
Brazilian (39)	50	0.42
British (55)	82	0.69
Canadian (36)	36	0.30
Czech (16)	30	0.25

SECTION TWO

*Notes: † The Census 2010 population figure is used to calculate the percentages in the Hispanic Origin and Race categories. Ancestry percentages are based on the 2006-2010 American Community Survey population (not shown); ‡ Numbers in parentheses indicate the number of people reporting a single ancestry; * Numbers in parentheses indicate the number of persons reporting this race alone, not in combination with any other race; Please refer to the Explanation of Data for more information.*

Danish (16)	40	0.34
Dutch (32)	106	0.89
Eastern European (36)	36	0.30
English (456)	1,274	10.73
European (145)	184	1.55
Finnish (0)	20	0.17
French, ex. Basque (169)	474	3.99
French Canadian (75)	100	0.84
German (535)	1,474	12.41
Greek (90)	90	0.76
Guyanese (0)	30	0.25
Hungarian (0)	42	0.35
Irish (790)	1,752	14.75
Italian (491)	1,054	8.87
Lithuanian (0)	13	0.11
Norwegian (11)	75	0.63
Polish (165)	621	5.23
Portuguese (13)	13	0.11
Russian (151)	259	2.18
Scandinavian (0)	12	0.10
Scotch-Irish (16)	77	0.65
Scottish (114)	268	2.26
Slovak (0)	30	0.25
Swedish (13)	88	0.74
Swiss (0)	17	0.14
Ukrainian (39)	107	0.90
Welsh (12)	61	0.51
West Indian, ex. Hispanic (969)	969	8.16
Haitian (924)	924	7.78
Jamaican (45)	45	0.38

Hispanic Origin	Population	%
Hispanic or Latino (of any race)	1,498	12.88
Central American, ex. Mexican	192	1.65
Costa Rican	19	0.16
Guatemalan	33	0.28
Honduran	36	0.31
Nicaraguan	16	0.14
Panamanian	30	0.26
Salvadoran	58	0.50
Cuban	263	2.26
Dominican Republic	38	0.33
Mexican	224	1.93
Puerto Rican	336	2.89
South American	311	2.67
Argentinean	31	0.27
Bolivian	3	0.03
Chilean	22	0.19
Colombian	112	0.96
Ecuadorian	21	0.18
Paraguayan	1	0.01
Peruvian	44	0.38
Uruguayan	13	0.11
Venezuelan	57	0.49
Other South American	7	0.06
Other Hispanic or Latino	134	1.15

Race*	Population	%
African-American/Black (1,440)	1,552	13.34
Not Hispanic (1,399)	1,486	12.78
Hispanic (41)	66	0.57
American Indian/Alaska Native (30)	58	0.50
Not Hispanic (19)	45	0.39
Hispanic (11)	13	0.11
Apache (0)	1	0.01
Blackfeet (0)	1	0.01
Central American Ind. (2)	2	0.02
Cherokee (4)	13	0.11
Chickasaw (0)	1	0.01
Chippewa (1)	1	0.01
Choctaw (2)	2	0.02
Creek (1)	1	0.01
Delaware (1)	1	0.01
Inupiat *(Alaska Native)* (0)	1	0.01
Iroquois (1)	1	0.01
Lumbee (2)	2	0.02
Navajo (1)	1	0.01
South American Ind. (3)	3	0.03
Asian (252)	339	2.91
Not Hispanic (247)	319	2.74
Hispanic (5)	20	0.17
Bangladeshi (12)	13	0.11
Cambodian (1)	1	0.01
Chinese, ex. Taiwanese (30)	50	0.43
Filipino (40)	53	0.46
Indian (81)	112	0.96
Indonesian (10)	10	0.09
Japanese (14)	20	0.17
Korean (10)	15	0.13
Laotian (1)	1	0.01
Malaysian (2)	2	0.02
Pakistani (3)	3	0.03
Taiwanese (0)	4	0.03
Thai (27)	27	0.23
Vietnamese (16)	20	0.17
Hawaii Native/Pacific Islander (3)	12	0.10
Not Hispanic (2)	8	0.07
Hispanic (1)	4	0.03
Guamanian/Chamorro (3)	3	0.03
White (9,396)	9,561	82.20
Not Hispanic (8,283)	8,398	72.20
Hispanic (1,113)	1,163	10.00

Winter Garden

Place Type: City
County: Orange
Population: 34,568†

Ancestry‡	Population	%
African, Sub-Saharan (386)	451	1.43
African (353)	418	1.33
South African (33)	33	0.10
American (2,590)	2,590	8.23
Arab (29)	54	0.17
Lebanese (29)	29	0.09
Syrian (0)	25	0.08
Armenian (102)	164	0.52
Australian (16)	16	0.05
Austrian (0)	9	0.03
Basque (15)	15	0.05
Brazilian (91)	140	0.44
British (114)	169	0.54
Bulgarian (23)	23	0.07
Cajun (0)	34	0.11
Canadian (0)	40	0.13
Croatian (14)	14	0.04
Czech (19)	48	0.15
Czechoslovakian (0)	16	0.05
Danish (0)	32	0.10
Dutch (47)	322	1.02
English (1,027)	2,527	8.03
European (306)	415	1.32
Finnish (15)	31	0.10
French, ex. Basque (121)	723	2.30
French Canadian (123)	168	0.53
German (1,060)	3,566	11.33
Greek (52)	147	0.47
Guyanese (280)	307	0.98
Hungarian (21)	72	0.23
Icelander (12)	25	0.08
Iranian (47)	47	0.15
Irish (829)	3,073	9.76
Israeli (0)	9	0.03
Italian (695)	2,130	6.77
Lithuanian (0)	35	0.11
Norwegian (55)	220	0.70
Polish (181)	452	1.44
Portuguese (87)	177	0.56
Romanian (42)	60	0.19
Russian (24)	66	0.21
Scandinavian (50)	65	0.21
Scotch-Irish (370)	663	2.11
Scottish (364)	644	2.05
Slovak (59)	59	0.19
Swedish (43)	218	0.69
Turkish (25)	51	0.16
Ukrainian (84)	216	0.69
Welsh (60)	131	0.42
West Indian, ex. Hispanic (1,026)	1,134	3.60
Bahamian (43)	43	0.14
British West Indian (59)	59	0.19
Haitian (292)	332	1.05
Jamaican (295)	295	0.94
Trinidadian/Tobagonian (0)	34	0.11
U.S. Virgin Islander (43)	43	0.14
West Indian (294)	328	1.04
Yugoslavian (32)	48	0.15

Hispanic Origin	Population	%
Hispanic or Latino (of any race)	7,606	22.00
Central American, ex. Mexican	504	1.46
Costa Rican	23	0.07
Guatemalan	191	0.55
Honduran	110	0.32
Nicaraguan	58	0.17
Panamanian	47	0.14
Salvadoran	73	0.21
Other Central American	2	0.01
Cuban	418	1.21
Dominican Republic	429	1.24
Mexican	2,242	6.49
Puerto Rican	2,640	7.64
South American	999	2.89
Argentinean	35	0.10
Bolivian	20	0.06
Chilean	17	0.05
Colombian	461	1.33
Ecuadorian	139	0.40
Paraguayan	2	0.01
Peruvian	100	0.29
Uruguayan	5	0.01
Venezuelan	195	0.56
Other South American	25	0.07
Other Hispanic or Latino	374	1.08

Race*	Population	%
African-American/Black (5,520)	6,059	17.53
Not Hispanic (5,274)	5,665	16.39
Hispanic (246)	394	1.14
American Indian/Alaska Native (124)	319	0.92
Not Hispanic (59)	181	0.52
Hispanic (65)	138	0.40
Aleut *(Alaska Native)* (0)	1	<0.01
Apache (4)	6	0.02
Blackfeet (0)	5	0.01
Canadian/French Am. Ind. (0)	1	<0.01
Central American Ind. (0)	1	<0.01
Cherokee (9)	38	0.11
Cheyenne (0)	1	<0.01
Chippewa (1)	1	<0.01
Choctaw (0)	3	0.01
Cree (0)	1	<0.01
Creek (0)	5	0.01
Hopi (0)	5	0.01
Iroquois (1)	3	0.01
Kiowa (2)	2	0.01
Lumbee (2)	3	0.01
Mexican American Ind. (1)	1	<0.01
Navajo (1)	1	<0.01
Shoshone (0)	1	<0.01
Sioux (3)	6	0.02
South American Ind. (12)	24	0.07
Spanish American Ind. (0)	1	<0.01
Tlingit-Haida *(Alaska Native)* (1)	1	<0.01
Yaqui (1)	1	<0.01
Asian (1,761)	2,198	6.36
Not Hispanic (1,726)	2,104	6.09
Hispanic (35)	94	0.27
Bangladeshi (1)	6	0.02
Burmese (3)	3	0.01
Cambodian (15)	18	0.05
Chinese, ex. Taiwanese (182)	227	0.66
Filipino (217)	318	0.92
Indian (849)	1,002	2.90
Indonesian (3)	5	0.01
Japanese (33)	51	0.15
Korean (93)	115	0.33
Laotian (16)	24	0.07
Malaysian (2)	2	0.01

*Notes: † The Census 2010 population figure is used to calculate the percentages in the Hispanic Origin and Race categories. Ancestry percentages are based on the 2006-2010 American Community Survey population (not shown); ‡ Numbers in parentheses indicate the number of people reporting a single ancestry; * Numbers in parentheses indicate the number of persons reporting this race alone, not in combination with any other race; Please refer to the Explanation of Data for more information.*

Pakistani (22)	34	0.10
Sri Lankan (5)	7	0.02
Taiwanese (8)	9	0.03
Thai (15)	21	0.06
Vietnamese (260)	275	0.80
Hawaii Native/Pacific Islander (39)	137	0.40
Not Hispanic (33)	115	0.33
Hispanic (6)	22	0.06
Guamanian/Chamorro (6)	12	0.03
Native Hawaiian (2)	16	0.05
Samoan (4)	9	0.03
White (23,778)	24,601	71.17
Not Hispanic (18,762)	19,233	55.64
Hispanic (5,016)	5,368	15.53

Winter Haven

Place Type: City
County: Polk
Population: 33,874†

Ancestry‡	Population	%
African, Sub-Saharan (282)	441	1.33
African (252)	411	1.24
Cape Verdean (15)	15	0.05
Nigerian (15)	15	0.05
American (6,048)	6,048	18.26
Arab (0)	8	0.02
Lebanese (0)	8	0.02
Austrian (30)	77	0.23
Belgian (0)	14	0.04
Brazilian (10)	10	0.03
British (44)	95	0.29
Canadian (48)	77	0.23
Czech (82)	111	0.34
Czechoslovakian (17)	17	0.05
Danish (9)	78	0.24
Dutch (110)	281	0.85
Eastern European (11)	11	0.03
English (1,460)	2,894	8.74
European (181)	211	0.64
Finnish (0)	10	0.03
French, ex. Basque (318)	969	2.93
French Canadian (286)	328	0.99
German (1,282)	3,418	10.32
Greek (5)	97	0.29
Hungarian (47)	67	0.20
Iranian (16)	16	0.05
Irish (671)	2,187	6.60
Italian (387)	791	2.39
Latvian (12)	12	0.04
Lithuanian (44)	58	0.18
Maltese (11)	11	0.03
Northern European (15)	15	0.05
Norwegian (54)	132	0.40
Pennsylvania German (8)	8	0.02
Polish (388)	648	1.96
Portuguese (118)	189	0.57
Romanian (0)	9	0.03
Russian (18)	73	0.22
Scandinavian (15)	36	0.11
Scotch-Irish (234)	468	1.41
Scottish (97)	447	1.35
Slovak (183)	183	0.55
Slovene (0)	9	0.03
Swedish (53)	191	0.58
Swiss (44)	73	0.22
Ukrainian (18)	100	0.30
Welsh (10)	88	0.27
West Indian, ex. Hispanic (1,537)	1,744	5.26
Bahamian (0)	31	0.09
Barbadian (10)	10	0.03
British West Indian (37)	37	0.11
Haitian (1,148)	1,307	3.95
Jamaican (267)	284	0.86
West Indian (75)	75	0.23

Hispanic Origin	Population	%
Hispanic or Latino (of any race)	3,737	11.03
Central American, ex. Mexican	195	0.58
Costa Rican	12	0.04
Guatemalan	35	0.10
Honduran	56	0.17
Nicaraguan	52	0.15
Panamanian	26	0.08
Salvadoran	14	0.04
Cuban	267	0.79
Dominican Republic	178	0.53
Mexican	919	2.71
Puerto Rican	1,673	4.94
South American	278	0.82
Argentinean	23	0.07
Bolivian	3	0.01
Chilean	15	0.04
Colombian	134	0.40
Ecuadorian	31	0.09
Paraguayan	1	<0.01
Peruvian	41	0.12
Uruguayan	3	0.01
Venezuelan	24	0.07
Other South American	3	0.01
Other Hispanic or Latino	227	0.67

Race*	Population	%
African-American/Black (9,377)	9,783	28.88
Not Hispanic (9,149)	9,467	27.95
Hispanic (228)	316	0.93
American Indian/Alaska Native (106)	249	0.74
Not Hispanic (65)	182	0.54
Hispanic (41)	67	0.20
Alaska Athabascan *(Ala. Nat.)* (0)	2	0.01
Aleut *(Alaska Native)* (1)	1	<0.01
Apache (1)	5	0.01
Blackfeet (2)	14	0.04
Canadian/French Am. Ind. (0)	1	<0.01
Cherokee (20)	63	0.19
Cheyenne (1)	3	0.01
Chickasaw (1)	1	<0.01
Chippewa (1)	1	<0.01
Choctaw (3)	5	0.01
Cree (1)	1	<0.01
Creek (3)	7	0.02
Iroquois (2)	13	0.04
Lumbee (3)	3	0.01
Mexican American Ind. (10)	14	0.04
Navajo (0)	1	<0.01
Osage (0)	1	<0.01
Seminole (0)	3	0.01
Shoshone (0)	1	<0.01
Sioux (3)	7	0.02
South American Ind. (4)	11	0.03
Yaqui (0)	1	<0.01
Asian (678)	820	2.42
Not Hispanic (667)	788	2.33
Hispanic (11)	32	0.09
Bangladeshi (9)	15	0.04
Chinese, ex. Taiwanese (80)	101	0.30
Filipino (154)	183	0.54
Hmong (1)	1	<0.01
Indian (203)	239	0.71
Indonesian (2)	2	0.01
Japanese (17)	25	0.07
Korean (19)	23	0.07
Laotian (1)	1	<0.01
Nepalese (7)	7	0.02
Pakistani (4)	5	0.01
Sri Lankan (7)	7	0.02
Taiwanese (6)	8	0.02
Thai (9)	14	0.04
Vietnamese (139)	147	0.43
Hawaii Native/Pacific Islander (29)	86	0.25
Not Hispanic (28)	66	0.19
Hispanic (1)	20	0.06
Guamanian/Chamorro (9)	13	0.04
Marshallese (2)	4	0.01
Native Hawaiian (7)	11	0.03
Samoan (4)	5	0.01
White (21,909)	22,487	66.38
Not Hispanic (19,674)	20,040	59.16
Hispanic (2,235)	2,447	7.22

Winter Park

Place Type: City
County: Orange
Population: 27,852†

Ancestry‡	Population	%
African, Sub-Saharan (13)	64	0.23
African (0)	31	0.11
Ethiopian (0)	20	0.07
Other Sub-Saharan African (13)	13	0.05
American (2,169)	2,169	7.69
Arab (124)	212	0.75
Iraqi (95)	125	0.44
Lebanese (0)	13	0.05
Palestinian (15)	15	0.05
Other Arab (14)	59	0.21
Armenian (0)	26	0.09
Austrian (137)	233	0.83
Belgian (8)	39	0.14
Brazilian (14)	14	0.05
British (151)	292	1.04
Canadian (112)	134	0.47
Czech (32)	150	0.53
Czechoslovakian (0)	35	0.12
Danish (13)	261	0.93
Dutch (89)	370	1.31
Eastern European (48)	89	0.32
English (1,761)	5,068	17.96
European (323)	432	1.53
Finnish (64)	102	0.36
French, ex. Basque (180)	847	3.00
French Canadian (45)	218	0.77
German (1,647)	5,048	17.89
Greek (58)	197	0.70
Guyanese (0)	13	0.05
Hungarian (93)	211	0.75
Iranian (132)	218	0.77
Irish (1,144)	3,818	13.53
Italian (805)	2,063	7.31
Latvian (8)	8	0.03
Lithuanian (28)	155	0.55
Luxemburger (0)	10	0.04
Northern European (11)	25	0.09
Norwegian (95)	262	0.93
Pennsylvania German (14)	37	0.13
Polish (186)	765	2.71
Portuguese (52)	92	0.33
Romanian (76)	97	0.34
Russian (144)	379	1.34
Scandinavian (0)	22	0.08
Scotch-Irish (475)	948	3.36
Scottish (400)	955	3.39
Serbian (15)	15	0.05
Slavic (10)	10	0.04
Slovak (21)	51	0.18
Slovene (0)	28	0.10
Swedish (141)	358	1.27
Swiss (25)	214	0.76
Turkish (0)	74	0.26
Ukrainian (23)	73	0.26
Welsh (36)	537	1.90
West Indian, ex. Hispanic (94)	170	0.60
Bahamian (14)	14	0.05
Haitian (18)	47	0.17
Jamaican (50)	97	0.34
U.S. Virgin Islander (12)	12	0.04
Yugoslavian (29)	29	0.10

Hispanic Origin	Population	%
Hispanic or Latino (of any race)	1,943	6.98
Central American, ex. Mexican	132	0.47
Costa Rican	14	0.05
Guatemalan	25	0.09
Honduran	16	0.06
Nicaraguan	14	0.05
Panamanian	30	0.11
Salvadoran	32	0.11
Other Central American	1	<0.01
Cuban	270	0.97

*Notes: † The Census 2010 population figure is used to calculate the percentages in the Hispanic Origin and Race categories. Ancestry percentages are based on the 2006-2010 American Community Survey population (not shown); ‡ Numbers in parentheses indicate the number of people reporting a single ancestry; * Numbers in parentheses indicate the number of persons reporting this race alone, not in combination with any other race; Please refer to the Explanation of Data for more information.*

Dominican Republic	68	0.24
Mexican	218	0.78
Puerto Rican	751	2.70
South American	330	1.18
Argentinean	26	0.09
Bolivian	7	0.03
Chilean	23	0.08
Colombian	125	0.45
Ecuadorian	27	0.10
Paraguayan	8	0.03
Peruvian	51	0.18
Uruguayan	2	0.01
Venezuelan	50	0.18
Other South American	11	0.04
Other Hispanic or Latino	174	0.62

Race*	Population	%
African-American/Black (2,105)	2,304	8.27
Not Hispanic (2,034)	2,188	7.86
Hispanic (71)	116	0.42
American Indian/Alaska Native (50)	182	0.65
Not Hispanic (35)	146	0.52
Hispanic (15)	36	0.13
Blackfeet (0)	5	0.02
Central American Ind. (2)	5	0.02
Cherokee (5)	42	0.15
Chippewa (0)	1	<0.01
Choctaw (0)	6	0.02
Creek (0)	1	<0.01
Delaware (2)	2	0.01
Inupiat *(Alaska Native)* (0)	2	0.01
Iroquois (2)	8	0.03
Lumbee (0)	2	0.01
Navajo (4)	6	0.02
Seminole (1)	2	0.01
Sioux (1)	2	0.01
South American Ind. (0)	2	0.01
Spanish American Ind. (1)	1	<0.01
Yaqui (0)	1	<0.01
Asian (643)	832	2.99
Not Hispanic (632)	805	2.89
Hispanic (11)	27	0.10
Burmese (4)	4	0.01
Chinese, ex. Taiwanese (138)	166	0.60
Filipino (124)	159	0.57
Indian (143)	172	0.62
Indonesian (5)	5	0.02
Japanese (26)	59	0.21
Korean (47)	74	0.27
Laotian (5)	5	0.02
Malaysian (1)	3	0.01
Nepalese (6)	6	0.02
Pakistani (13)	13	0.05
Sri Lankan (4)	9	0.03
Taiwanese (9)	11	0.04
Thai (10)	19	0.07
Vietnamese (94)	110	0.39
Hawaii Native/Pacific Islander (5)	23	0.08
Not Hispanic (5)	23	0.08
Guamanian/Chamorro (1)	1	<0.01
Native Hawaiian (1)	10	0.04
Samoan (3)	3	0.01
White (24,214)	24,659	88.54
Not Hispanic (22,755)	23,104	82.95
Hispanic (1,459)	1,555	5.58

Winter Springs

Place Type: City
County: Seminole
Population: 33,282†

Ancestry‡	Population	%
African, Sub-Saharan (160)	160	0.48
African (160)	160	0.48
Alsatian (0)	39	0.12
American (1,590)	1,590	4.78
Arab (56)	81	0.24
Arab (8)	8	0.02
Lebanese (0)	25	0.08
Moroccan (48)	48	0.14
Armenian (10)	10	0.03
Austrian (18)	31	0.09
Belgian (25)	25	0.08
Brazilian (35)	48	0.14
British (159)	306	0.92
Canadian (120)	172	0.52
Croatian (0)	37	0.11
Czech (165)	346	1.04
Czechoslovakian (0)	35	0.11
Danish (57)	193	0.58
Dutch (160)	691	2.08
Eastern European (0)	39	0.12
English (1,192)	4,114	12.36
European (1,275)	1,526	4.58
Finnish (0)	35	0.11
French, ex. Basque (102)	1,076	3.23
French Canadian (73)	289	0.87
German (1,417)	5,253	15.78
Greek (32)	383	1.15
Guyanese (52)	52	0.16
Hungarian (37)	316	0.95
Iranian (161)	183	0.55
Irish (1,323)	4,817	14.47
Italian (1,344)	3,063	9.20
Latvian (0)	12	0.04
Lithuanian (24)	125	0.38
Macedonian (0)	58	0.17
Northern European (14)	14	0.04
Norwegian (170)	363	1.09
Polish (397)	1,392	4.18
Portuguese (21)	79	0.24
Romanian (25)	154	0.46
Russian (168)	549	1.65
Scandinavian (27)	61	0.18
Scotch-Irish (407)	1,148	3.45
Scottish (335)	921	2.77
Serbian (140)	156	0.47
Slavic (0)	19	0.06
Slovak (46)	148	0.44
Swedish (149)	521	1.57
Swiss (10)	55	0.17
Ukrainian (124)	196	0.59
Welsh (39)	301	0.90
West Indian, ex. Hispanic (429)	601	1.81
Bahamian (37)	37	0.11
Barbadian (7)	30	0.09
Belizean (0)	14	0.04
British West Indian (26)	50	0.15
Haitian (80)	112	0.34
Jamaican (183)	239	0.72
Trinidadian/Tobagonian (96)	119	0.36
Yugoslavian (15)	15	0.05

Hispanic Origin	Population	%
Hispanic or Latino (of any race)	4,978	14.96
Central American, ex. Mexican	238	0.72
Costa Rican	19	0.06
Guatemalan	28	0.08
Honduran	49	0.15
Nicaraguan	24	0.07
Panamanian	56	0.17
Salvadoran	52	0.16
Other Central American	10	0.03
Cuban	401	1.20
Dominican Republic	291	0.87
Mexican	358	1.08
Puerto Rican	2,492	7.49
South American	869	2.61
Argentinean	75	0.23
Bolivian	7	0.02
Chilean	15	0.05
Colombian	408	1.23
Ecuadorian	105	0.32
Peruvian	107	0.32
Uruguayan	17	0.05
Venezuelan	130	0.39
Other South American	5	0.02
Other Hispanic or Latino	329	0.99

Race*	Population	%
African-American/Black (1,831)	2,180	6.55
Not Hispanic (1,672)	1,938	5.82
Hispanic (159)	242	0.73
American Indian/Alaska Native (86)	238	0.72
Not Hispanic (63)	190	0.57
Hispanic (23)	48	0.14
Blackfeet (3)	12	0.04
Canadian/French Am. Ind. (0)	1	<0.01
Central American Ind. (0)	2	0.01
Cherokee (19)	81	0.24
Chickasaw (1)	1	<0.01
Chippewa (2)	5	0.02
Choctaw (3)	3	0.01
Comanche (0)	2	0.01
Creek (5)	6	0.02
Delaware (1)	1	<0.01
Houma (1)	1	<0.01
Iroquois (1)	5	0.02
Lumbee (2)	3	0.01
Menominee (0)	1	<0.01
Mexican American Ind. (4)	5	0.02
Ottawa (1)	2	0.01
Pueblo (2)	2	0.01
Seminole (3)	4	0.01
Sioux (1)	1	<0.01
South American Ind. (1)	1	<0.01
Asian (861)	1,057	3.18
Not Hispanic (838)	1,009	3.03
Hispanic (23)	48	0.14
Bangladeshi (5)	9	0.03
Cambodian (2)	2	0.01
Chinese, ex. Taiwanese (176)	215	0.65
Filipino (154)	209	0.63
Indian (243)	277	0.83
Indonesian (9)	11	0.03
Japanese (24)	50	0.15
Korean (61)	79	0.24
Laotian (9)	12	0.04
Malaysian (1)	1	<0.01
Nepalese (2)	2	0.01
Pakistani (16)	17	0.05
Sri Lankan (8)	8	0.02
Taiwanese (5)	6	0.02
Thai (18)	26	0.08
Vietnamese (90)	99	0.30
Hawaii Native/Pacific Islander (20)	53	0.16
Not Hispanic (15)	42	0.13
Hispanic (5)	11	0.03
Guamanian/Chamorro (8)	10	0.03
Native Hawaiian (6)	10	0.03
Samoan (2)	2	0.01
White (28,817)	29,518	88.69
Not Hispanic (25,099)	25,591	76.89
Hispanic (3,718)	3,927	11.80

World Golf Village

Place Type: CDP
County: St. Johns
Population: 12,310†

Ancestry‡	Population	%
American (1,420)	1,420	14.45
Austrian (10)	41	0.42
Belgian (0)	12	0.12
Brazilian (67)	67	0.68
British (14)	50	0.51
Canadian (60)	60	0.61
Croatian (0)	13	0.13
Czech (14)	14	0.14
Danish (28)	54	0.55
Dutch (17)	153	1.56
English (369)	1,030	10.48
Estonian (0)	30	0.31
European (49)	49	0.50
Finnish (9)	9	0.09
French, ex. Basque (95)	205	2.09
French Canadian (28)	109	1.11

*Notes: † The Census 2010 population figure is used to calculate the percentages in the Hispanic Origin and Race categories. Ancestry percentages are based on the 2006-2010 American Community Survey population (not shown); ‡ Numbers in parentheses indicate the number of people reporting a single ancestry; * Numbers in parentheses indicate the number of persons reporting this race alone, not in combination with any other race; Please refer to the Explanation of Data for more information.*

German (700)	1,656	16.85
Greek (30)	50	0.51
Hungarian (0)	54	0.55
Icelander (0)	8	0.08
Irish (334)	1,052	10.71
Israeli (0)	11	0.11
Italian (469)	931	9.48
Lithuanian (14)	14	0.14
Northern European (17)	17	0.17
Norwegian (38)	115	1.17
Pennsylvania German (12)	24	0.24
Polish (150)	303	3.08
Portuguese (0)	9	0.09
Russian (63)	151	1.54
Scotch-Irish (79)	154	1.57
Scottish (134)	293	2.98
Soviet Union (13)	13	0.13
Swedish (13)	28	0.28
Turkish (0)	11	0.11
Ukrainian (23)	76	0.77
Welsh (0)	24	0.24
Yugoslavian (12)	12	0.12

Hispanic Origin	Population	%
Hispanic or Latino (of any race)	936	7.60
Central American, ex. Mexican	121	0.98
Costa Rican	4	0.03
Guatemalan	27	0.22
Honduran	26	0.21
Nicaraguan	20	0.16
Panamanian	12	0.10
Salvadoran	32	0.26
Cuban	73	0.59
Dominican Republic	30	0.24
Mexican	175	1.42
Puerto Rican	222	1.80
South American	220	1.79
Argentinean	22	0.18
Bolivian	2	0.02
Chilean	14	0.11
Colombian	105	0.85
Ecuadorian	36	0.29
Peruvian	18	0.15
Uruguayan	1	0.01
Venezuelan	22	0.18
Other Hispanic or Latino	95	0.77

Race*	Population	%
African-American/Black (495)	570	4.63
Not Hispanic (479)	541	4.39
Hispanic (16)	29	0.24
American Indian/Alaska Native (29)	69	0.56
Not Hispanic (16)	44	0.36
Hispanic (13)	25	0.20
Blackfeet (0)	1	0.01
Central American Ind. (1)	1	0.01
Cherokee (2)	8	0.06
Chippewa (0)	1	0.01
Delaware (0)	3	0.02
Lumbee (4)	6	0.05
Mexican American Ind. (0)	3	0.02
Osage (1)	1	0.01
Seminole (0)	1	0.01
Sioux (0)	2	0.02
Tlingit-Haida *(Alaska Native)* (2)	2	0.02
Asian (417)	518	4.21
Not Hispanic (406)	500	4.06
Hispanic (11)	18	0.15
Bangladeshi (7)	7	0.06
Cambodian (17)	18	0.15
Chinese, ex. Taiwanese (58)	83	0.67
Filipino (115)	156	1.27
Indian (113)	119	0.97
Indonesian (3)	11	0.09
Japanese (8)	14	0.11
Korean (37)	49	0.40
Malaysian (1)	1	0.01
Nepalese (2)	2	0.02
Taiwanese (1)	1	0.01
Thai (10)	20	0.16
Vietnamese (20)	39	0.32
Hawaii Native/Pacific Islander (12)	31	0.25
Not Hispanic (10)	27	0.22
Hispanic (2)	4	0.03
Guamanian/Chamorro (4)	5	0.04
Native Hawaiian (6)	7	0.06
Samoan (1)	6	0.05
White (10,940)	11,146	90.54
Not Hispanic (10,261)	10,420	84.65
Hispanic (679)	726	5.90

Wright

Place Type: CDP
County: Okaloosa
Population: 23,127†

Ancestry‡	Population	%
African, Sub-Saharan (106)	154	0.65
African (78)	126	0.54
South African (28)	28	0.12
American (3,029)	3,029	12.86
Arab (57)	57	0.24
Arab (57)	57	0.24
Austrian (10)	47	0.20
Belgian (11)	11	0.05
Brazilian (15)	15	0.06
British (57)	96	0.41
Croatian (0)	16	0.07
Czech (0)	41	0.17
Danish (46)	81	0.34
Dutch (96)	405	1.72
English (994)	2,116	8.99
Estonian (27)	27	0.11
European (262)	293	1.24
Finnish (44)	104	0.44
French, ex. Basque (246)	1,015	4.31
French Canadian (121)	135	0.57
German (1,039)	3,446	14.63
Greek (122)	163	0.69
Guyanese (17)	17	0.07
Hungarian (40)	75	0.32
Iranian (8)	8	0.03
Irish (956)	2,473	10.50
Italian (268)	852	3.62
Norwegian (112)	332	1.41
Pennsylvania German (0)	11	0.05
Polish (102)	375	1.59
Portuguese (7)	20	0.08
Romanian (13)	13	0.06
Russian (12)	95	0.40
Scandinavian (11)	48	0.20
Scotch-Irish (114)	402	1.71
Scottish (155)	336	1.43
Slavic (12)	12	0.05
Slovak (15)	24	0.10
Swedish (68)	256	1.09
Ukrainian (48)	72	0.31
Welsh (60)	242	1.03
West Indian, ex. Hispanic (49)	171	0.73
Bahamian (0)	25	0.11
Haitian (27)	121	0.51
Jamaican (22)	25	0.11

Hispanic Origin	Population	%
Hispanic or Latino (of any race)	2,718	11.75
Central American, ex. Mexican	630	2.72
Costa Rican	8	0.03
Guatemalan	94	0.41
Honduran	343	1.48
Nicaraguan	20	0.09
Panamanian	82	0.35
Salvadoran	81	0.35
Other Central American	2	0.01
Cuban	95	0.41
Dominican Republic	44	0.19
Mexican	1,159	5.01
Puerto Rican	417	1.80
South American	112	0.48
Argentinean	1	<0.01
Bolivian	4	0.02
Chilean	10	0.04
Colombian	59	0.26
Ecuadorian	10	0.04
Peruvian	20	0.09
Uruguayan	4	0.02
Venezuelan	4	0.02
Other Hispanic or Latino	261	1.13

Race*	Population	%
African-American/Black (3,590)	4,094	17.70
Not Hispanic (3,492)	3,934	17.01
Hispanic (98)	160	0.69
American Indian/Alaska Native (123)	344	1.49
Not Hispanic (87)	280	1.21
Hispanic (36)	64	0.28
Apache (4)	6	0.03
Blackfeet (1)	11	0.05
Canadian/French Am. Ind. (1)	1	<0.01
Cherokee (28)	91	0.39
Chickasaw (0)	4	0.02
Chippewa (1)	3	0.01
Choctaw (3)	11	0.05
Comanche (1)	1	<0.01
Cree (0)	1	<0.01
Creek (7)	28	0.12
Houma (0)	3	0.01
Inupiat *(Alaska Native)* (1)	4	0.02
Iroquois (5)	7	0.03
Kiowa (0)	2	0.01
Lumbee (1)	3	0.01
Mexican American Ind. (20)	27	0.12
Navajo (1)	2	0.01
Osage (1)	1	<0.01
Seminole (3)	3	0.01
Shoshone (2)	2	0.01
Sioux (2)	9	0.04
South American Ind. (3)	4	0.02
Spanish American Ind. (1)	4	0.02
Yaqui (1)	2	0.01
Asian (984)	1,513	6.54
Not Hispanic (957)	1,411	6.10
Hispanic (27)	102	0.44
Bangladeshi (2)	2	0.01
Burmese (0)	1	<0.01
Cambodian (2)	2	0.01
Chinese, ex. Taiwanese (60)	100	0.43
Filipino (328)	554	2.40
Indian (33)	61	0.26
Indonesian (2)	3	0.01
Japanese (62)	148	0.64
Korean (157)	255	1.10
Laotian (8)	11	0.05
Pakistani (10)	14	0.06
Sri Lankan (1)	1	<0.01
Taiwanese (1)	1	<0.01
Thai (169)	239	1.03
Vietnamese (106)	137	0.59
Hawaii Native/Pacific Islander (53)	101	0.44
Not Hispanic (46)	76	0.33
Hispanic (7)	25	0.11
Fijian (1)	1	<0.01
Guamanian/Chamorro (22)	38	0.16
Native Hawaiian (10)	25	0.11
Samoan (5)	6	0.03
White (16,140)	17,193	74.34
Not Hispanic (14,815)	15,673	67.77
Hispanic (1,325)	1,520	6.57

Yulee

Place Type: CDP
County: Nassau
Population: 11,491†

Ancestry‡	Population	%
African, Sub-Saharan (194)	194	1.59
Cape Verdean (194)	194	1.59
American (3,607)	3,607	29.49
Brazilian (11)	11	0.09

*Notes: † The Census 2010 population figure is used to calculate the percentages in the Hispanic Origin and Race categories. Ancestry percentages are based on the 2006-2010 American Community Survey population (not shown); ‡ Numbers in parentheses indicate the number of people reporting a single ancestry; * Numbers in parentheses indicate the number of persons reporting this race alone, not in combination with any other race; Please refer to the Explanation of Data for more information.*

British (12)	12	0.10
Croatian (11)	11	0.09
Dutch (0)	45	0.37
English (274)	1,005	8.22
European (88)	88	0.72
French, ex. Basque (157)	439	3.59
French Canadian (46)	46	0.38
German (485)	1,703	13.92
Hungarian (0)	13	0.11
Irish (435)	1,699	13.89
Italian (147)	363	2.97
Lithuanian (31)	31	0.25
Norwegian (44)	44	0.36
Polish (0)	134	1.10
Portuguese (0)	26	0.21
Scandinavian (0)	31	0.25
Scotch-Irish (35)	109	0.89
Scottish (41)	238	1.95
Swedish (50)	66	0.54
Swiss (0)	139	1.14
Welsh (0)	87	0.71

Hispanic Origin	Population	%
Hispanic or Latino (of any race)	359	3.12
Central American, ex. Mexican	37	0.32
Costa Rican	4	0.03
Guatemalan	2	0.02
Honduran	7	0.06
Nicaraguan	3	0.03
Panamanian	8	0.07
Salvadoran	13	0.11
Cuban	25	0.22
Dominican Republic	5	0.04
Mexican	109	0.95
Puerto Rican	116	1.01
South American	22	0.19
Colombian	11	0.10
Peruvian	3	0.03
Uruguayan	1	0.01
Venezuelan	7	0.06
Other Hispanic or Latino	45	0.39

Race*	Population	%
African-American/Black (648)	706	6.14
Not Hispanic (627)	676	5.88
Hispanic (21)	30	0.26
American Indian/Alaska Native (49)	118	1.03
Not Hispanic (37)	100	0.87
Hispanic (12)	18	0.16
Apache (0)	1	0.01
Blackfeet (2)	5	0.04
Canadian/French Am. Ind. (1)	1	0.01
Cherokee (11)	36	0.31
Chickasaw (1)	1	0.01
Choctaw (4)	4	0.03
Comanche (0)	1	0.01
Creek (2)	7	0.06
Iroquois (2)	3	0.03
Lumbee (2)	2	0.02
Mexican American Ind. (5)	5	0.04
Osage (1)	2	0.02
Pueblo (2)	5	0.04
Seminole (1)	1	0.01
Sioux (0)	2	0.02
Asian (98)	145	1.26
Not Hispanic (87)	124	1.08
Hispanic (11)	21	0.18
Burmese (0)	1	0.01
Cambodian (6)	6	0.05
Chinese, ex. Taiwanese (13)	14	0.12
Filipino (51)	80	0.70
Indian (6)	7	0.06
Japanese (3)	13	0.11
Korean (1)	4	0.03
Thai (12)	13	0.11
Vietnamese (5)	6	0.05
Hawaii Native/Pacific Islander (7)	17	0.15
Not Hispanic (6)	16	0.14
Hispanic (1)	1	0.01
Guamanian/Chamorro (2)	2	0.02
Native Hawaiian (2)	2	0.02
Samoan (0)	4	0.03
White (10,399)	10,559	91.89
Not Hispanic (10,201)	10,336	89.95
Hispanic (198)	223	1.94

Zephyrhills

Place Type: City
County: Pasco
Population: 13,288†

Ancestry‡	Population	%
African, Sub-Saharan (0)	7	0.05
African (0)	7	0.05
American (1,017)	1,017	7.64
Arab (0)	23	0.17
Egyptian (0)	23	0.17
Brazilian (9)	9	0.07
Bulgarian (13)	13	0.10
Canadian (64)	64	0.48
Czech (0)	88	0.66
Czechoslovakian (27)	99	0.74
Danish (66)	149	1.12
Dutch (138)	427	3.21
English (873)	2,424	18.21
European (0)	16	0.12
Finnish (11)	59	0.44
French, ex. Basque (106)	801	6.02
French Canadian (250)	292	2.19
German (627)	2,296	17.24
Greek (81)	81	0.61
Hungarian (87)	114	0.86
Irish (503)	2,047	15.37
Italian (335)	663	4.98
Lithuanian (20)	126	0.95
Maltese (0)	21	0.16
Norwegian (15)	28	0.21
Pennsylvania German (29)	47	0.35
Polish (95)	348	2.61
Russian (29)	65	0.49
Scotch-Irish (184)	440	3.30
Scottish (110)	185	1.39
Serbian (0)	20	0.15
Slovak (11)	19	0.14
Swedish (12)	99	0.74
Swiss (0)	29	0.22
Ukrainian (0)	12	0.09
Welsh (26)	82	0.62
West Indian, ex. Hispanic (172)	214	1.61
Jamaican (55)	63	0.47
Trinidadian/Tobagonian (0)	17	0.13
West Indian (117)	134	1.01
Yugoslavian (0)	61	0.46

Hispanic Origin	Population	%
Hispanic or Latino (of any race)	1,386	10.43
Central American, ex. Mexican	76	0.57
Costa Rican	5	0.04
Guatemalan	10	0.08
Honduran	35	0.26
Nicaraguan	2	0.02
Panamanian	13	0.10
Salvadoran	11	0.08
Cuban	129	0.97
Dominican Republic	31	0.23
Mexican	337	2.54
Puerto Rican	656	4.94
South American	58	0.44
Argentinean	2	0.02
Chilean	1	0.01
Colombian	34	0.26
Ecuadorian	2	0.02
Peruvian	11	0.08
Venezuelan	8	0.06
Other Hispanic or Latino	99	0.75

Race*	Population	%
African-American/Black (648)	760	5.72
Not Hispanic (578)	673	5.06
Hispanic (70)	87	0.65
American Indian/Alaska Native (28)	109	0.82
Not Hispanic (22)	70	0.53
Hispanic (6)	39	0.29
Blackfeet (0)	2	0.02
Cherokee (3)	26	0.20
Chickasaw (1)	1	0.01
Chippewa (2)	2	0.02
Choctaw (1)	2	0.02
Creek (1)	2	0.02
Iroquois (0)	3	0.02
Menominee (0)	1	0.01
Ottawa (1)	1	0.01
Potawatomi (0)	1	0.01
Seminole (1)	1	0.01
Sioux (2)	5	0.04
South American Ind. (1)	1	0.01
Ute (1)	1	0.01
Yaqui (1)	1	0.01
Asian (187)	237	1.78
Not Hispanic (185)	222	1.67
Hispanic (2)	15	0.11
Cambodian (1)	1	0.01
Chinese, ex. Taiwanese (36)	46	0.35
Filipino (50)	67	0.50
Indian (53)	61	0.46
Indonesian (3)	3	0.02
Japanese (4)	8	0.06
Korean (4)	11	0.08
Laotian (1)	1	0.01
Pakistani (1)	1	0.01
Taiwanese (3)	3	0.02
Thai (3)	3	0.02
Vietnamese (22)	27	0.20
Hawaii Native/Pacific Islander (3)	14	0.11
Not Hispanic (3)	7	0.05
Hispanic (0)	7	0.05
Native Hawaiian (1)	7	0.05
White (11,789)	12,011	90.39
Not Hispanic (10,936)	11,090	83.46
Hispanic (853)	921	6.93

*Notes: † The Census 2010 population figure is used to calculate the percentages in the Hispanic Origin and Race categories. Ancestry percentages are based on the 2006-2010 American Community Survey population (not shown); ‡ Numbers in parentheses indicate the number of people reporting a single ancestry; * Numbers in parentheses indicate the number of persons reporting this race alone, not in combination with any other race; Please refer to the Explanation of Data for more information.*

GEORGIA

Place Type: State
Population: 9,687,653†

Ancestry‡	Population	%
Afghan (1,265)	1,364	0.01
African, Sub-Saharan (160,890)	183,695	1.94
African (111,988)	129,637	1.37
Cape Verdean (488)	802	0.01
Ethiopian (9,675)	10,060	0.11
Ghanaian (3,474)	3,644	0.04
Kenyan (1,929)	2,136	0.02
Liberian (2,319)	2,368	0.03
Nigerian (17,549)	19,679	0.21
Senegalese (273)	360	<0.01
Sierra Leonean (960)	1,003	0.01
Somalian (1,871)	2,093	0.02
South African (2,592)	3,424	0.04
Sudanese (489)	542	0.01
Ugandan (249)	249	<0.01
Zimbabwean (186)	208	<0.01
Other Sub-Saharan African (6,848)	7,490	0.08
Albanian (1,249)	1,477	0.02
Alsatian (36)	136	<0.01
American (1,012,372)	1,012,372	10.69
Arab (16,411)	24,675	0.26
Arab (2,472)	3,555	0.04
Egyptian (1,655)	2,085	0.02
Iraqi (815)	963	0.01
Jordanian (689)	736	0.01
Lebanese (5,016)	9,372	0.10
Moroccan (721)	992	0.01
Palestinian (813)	986	0.01
Syrian (1,001)	2,099	0.02
Other Arab (3,229)	3,887	0.04
Armenian (1,882)	2,964	0.03
Assyrian/Chaldean/Syriac (72)	342	<0.01
Australian (1,075)	1,937	0.02
Austrian (4,138)	12,371	0.13
Basque (62)	135	<0.01
Belgian (2,415)	5,063	0.05
Brazilian (10,157)	11,684	0.12
British (25,962)	43,905	0.46
Bulgarian (1,684)	1,866	0.02
Cajun (1,331)	2,024	0.02
Canadian (7,396)	12,702	0.13
Carpatho Rusyn (24)	129	<0.01
Celtic (776)	1,295	0.01
Croatian (1,602)	4,167	0.04
Cypriot (10)	30	<0.01
Czech (4,614)	15,034	0.16
Czechoslovakian (1,683)	4,341	0.05
Danish (4,014)	13,099	0.14
Dutch (19,672)	86,949	0.92
Eastern European (6,543)	7,570	0.08
English (430,183)	858,272	9.06
Estonian (128)	415	<0.01
European (82,001)	94,610	1.00
Finnish (2,116)	6,420	0.07
French, ex. Basque (36,883)	153,685	1.62
French Canadian (11,397)	24,648	0.26
German (246,365)	758,945	8.02
German Russian (286)	373	<0.01
Greek (9,331)	19,761	0.21
Guyanese (5,707)	7,485	0.08
Hungarian (6,120)	19,963	0.21
Icelander (326)	683	0.01
Iranian (7,778)	8,865	0.09
Irish (314,966)	862,101	9.10
Israeli (1,139)	1,795	0.02
Italian (82,745)	218,715	2.31
Latvian (551)	1,603	0.02
Lithuanian (3,033)	8,215	0.09
Luxemburger (160)	311	<0.01
Macedonian (123)	230	<0.01
Maltese (199)	329	<0.01
New Zealander (116)	208	<0.01
Northern European (4,249)	4,554	0.05
Norwegian (11,682)	35,864	0.38
Pennsylvania German (701)	1,325	0.01
Polish (33,022)	103,243	1.09
Portuguese (4,796)	12,995	0.14
Romanian (8,117)	11,109	0.12
Russian (19,993)	44,575	0.47
Scandinavian (2,919)	7,986	0.08
Scotch-Irish (95,224)	183,779	1.94
Scottish (75,763)	184,525	1.95
Serbian (840)	1,868	0.02
Slavic (492)	2,026	0.02
Slovak (2,320)	6,996	0.07
Slovene (359)	1,305	0.01
Soviet Union (9)	17	<0.01
Swedish (12,709)	44,257	0.47
Swiss (3,195)	12,015	0.13
Turkish (2,933)	4,126	0.04
Ukrainian (6,993)	12,538	0.13
Welsh (11,598)	41,220	0.44
West Indian, ex. Hispanic (78,747)	102,553	1.08
Bahamian (1,904)	2,871	0.03
Barbadian (1,245)	2,230	0.02
Belizean (620)	937	0.01
Bermudan (410)	452	<0.01
British West Indian (2,263)	3,105	0.03
Dutch West Indian (150)	850	0.01
Haitian (19,128)	22,360	0.24
Jamaican (38,744)	49,026	0.52
Trinidadian/Tobagonian (5,130)	6,991	0.07
U.S. Virgin Islander (1,331)	1,725	0.02
West Indian (7,745)	11,849	0.13
Other West Indian (77)	157	<0.01
Yugoslavian (7,647)	9,408	0.10

Hispanic Origin	Population	%
Hispanic or Latino (of any race)	853,689	8.81
Central American, ex. Mexican	106,987	1.10
Costa Rican	3,114	0.03
Guatemalan	36,874	0.38
Honduran	20,577	0.21
Nicaraguan	4,787	0.05
Panamanian	8,678	0.09
Salvadoran	32,107	0.33
Other Central American	850	0.01
Cuban	25,048	0.26
Dominican Republic	14,941	0.15
Mexican	519,502	5.36
Puerto Rican	71,987	0.74
South American	57,707	0.60
Argentinean	3,230	0.03
Bolivian	872	0.01
Chilean	2,249	0.02
Colombian	26,013	0.27
Ecuadorian	4,886	0.05
Paraguayan	360	<0.01
Peruvian	10,570	0.11
Uruguayan	2,708	0.03
Venezuelan	6,289	0.06
Other South American	530	0.01
Other Hispanic or Latino	57,517	0.59

Race*	Population	%
African-American/Black (2,950,435)	3,054,098	31.53
Not Hispanic (2,910,800)	2,997,627	30.94
Hispanic (39,635)	56,471	0.58
American Indian/Alaska Native (32,151)	84,024	0.87
Not Hispanic (21,279)	64,925	0.67
Hispanic (10,872)	19,099	0.20
Alaska Athabascan *(Ala. Nat.)* (52)	94	<0.01
Aleut *(Alaska Native)* (44)	84	<0.01
Apache (297)	897	0.01
Arapaho (9)	26	<0.01
Blackfeet (280)	1,952	0.02
Canadian/French Am. Ind. (63)	145	<0.01
Central American Ind. (331)	558	0.01
Cherokee (5,241)	21,525	0.22
Cheyenne (42)	108	<0.01
Chickasaw (128)	314	<0.01
Chippewa (416)	734	0.01
Choctaw (476)	1,419	0.01
Colville (6)	26	<0.01
Comanche (66)	170	<0.01
Cree (18)	87	<0.01
Creek (974)	2,370	0.02
Crow (18)	82	<0.01
Delaware (57)	196	<0.01
Hopi (32)	54	<0.01
Houma (78)	104	<0.01
Inupiat *(Alaska Native)* (63)	124	<0.01
Iroquois (310)	792	0.01
Kiowa (22)	55	<0.01
Lumbee (491)	765	0.01
Menominee (36)	51	<0.01
Mexican American Ind. (2,559)	3,796	0.04
Navajo (295)	653	0.01
Osage (61)	137	<0.01
Ottawa (37)	75	<0.01
Paiute (12)	33	<0.01
Pima (16)	50	<0.01
Potawatomi (121)	208	<0.01
Pueblo (77)	157	<0.01
Puget Sound Salish (16)	24	<0.01
Seminole (108)	664	0.01
Shoshone (11)	49	<0.01
Sioux (374)	1,027	0.01
South American Ind. (316)	872	0.01
Spanish American Ind. (210)	316	<0.01
Tlingit-Haida *(Alaska Native)* (32)	80	<0.01
Tohono O'Odham (34)	45	<0.01
Tsimshian *(Alaska Native)* (13)	18	<0.01
Ute (27)	41	<0.01
Yakama (13)	25	<0.01
Yaqui (24)	82	<0.01
Yuman (8)	14	<0.01
Yup'ik *(Alaska Native)* (13)	25	<0.01
Asian (314,467)	365,497	3.77
Not Hispanic (311,692)	357,791	3.69
Hispanic (2,775)	7,706	0.08
Bangladeshi (3,466)	3,966	0.04
Bhutanese (667)	1,703	0.02
Burmese (2,436)	2,646	0.03
Cambodian (4,528)	5,423	0.06
Chinese, ex. Taiwanese (42,420)	50,725	0.52
Filipino (17,923)	28,528	0.29
Hmong (3,460)	3,623	0.04
Indian (96,116)	105,444	1.09
Indonesian (1,652)	2,114	0.02
Japanese (7,658)	14,247	0.15
Korean (52,431)	60,836	0.63
Laotian (5,560)	6,638	0.07
Malaysian (405)	679	0.01
Nepalese (879)	1,959	0.02
Pakistani (9,868)	11,202	0.12
Sri Lankan (616)	743	0.01
Taiwanese (3,202)	3,819	0.04
Thai (3,377)	5,168	0.05
Vietnamese (45,263)	49,264	0.51
Hawaii Native/Pacific Islander (6,799)	15,577	0.16
Not Hispanic (5,152)	11,896	0.12
Hispanic (1,647)	3,681	0.04
Fijian (120)	189	<0.01
Guamanian/Chamorro (2,746)	3,856	0.04
Marshallese (113)	120	<0.01
Native Hawaiian (1,319)	3,976	0.04
Samoan (919)	1,828	0.02
Tongan (34)	93	<0.01
White (5,787,440)	5,951,521	61.43
Not Hispanic (5,413,920)	5,535,598	57.14
Hispanic (373,520)	415,923	4.29

*Notes: † The Census 2010 population figure is used to calculate the percentages in the Hispanic Origin and Race categories. Ancestry percentages are based on the 2006-2010 American Community Survey population (not shown); ‡ Numbers in parentheses indicate the number of people reporting a single ancestry; * Numbers in parentheses indicate the number of persons reporting this race alone, not in combination with any other race; Please refer to the Explanation of Data for more information.*

Acworth

Place Type: City
County: Cobb
Population: 20,425†

Ancestry‡	Population	%
African, Sub-Saharan (939)	1,204	6.23
African (665)	805	4.16
Ghanaian (19)	19	0.10
Kenyan (214)	214	1.11
Nigerian (41)	96	0.50
South African (0)	59	0.31
Other Sub-Saharan African (0)	11	0.06
American (2,289)	2,289	11.84
Arab (17)	72	0.37
Lebanese (17)	72	0.37
Armenian (0)	12	0.06
Belgian (0)	7	0.04
Brazilian (104)	134	0.69
British (19)	28	0.14
Bulgarian (13)	13	0.07
Cajun (7)	7	0.04
Czech (17)	33	0.17
Danish (10)	24	0.12
Dutch (22)	125	0.65
Eastern European (14)	14	0.07
English (752)	1,481	7.66
European (150)	150	0.78
Finnish (0)	63	0.33
French, ex. Basque (160)	377	1.95
French Canadian (33)	42	0.22
German (727)	1,492	7.72
Greek (10)	10	0.05
Guyanese (8)	22	0.11
Hungarian (30)	49	0.25
Icelander (0)	35	0.18
Irish (542)	1,372	7.10
Israeli (26)	79	0.41
Italian (138)	358	1.85
Lithuanian (11)	11	0.06
Norwegian (0)	54	0.28
Pennsylvania German (9)	9	0.05
Polish (11)	265	1.37
Portuguese (87)	101	0.52
Romanian (0)	9	0.05
Russian (37)	91	0.47
Scandinavian (0)	17	0.09
Scotch-Irish (163)	314	1.62
Scottish (101)	258	1.33
Slovak (8)	24	0.12
Swedish (8)	26	0.13
Swiss (0)	16	0.08
Turkish (49)	49	0.25
Welsh (27)	85	0.44
West Indian, ex. Hispanic (620)	663	3.43
British West Indian (33)	33	0.17
Haitian (442)	442	2.29
Jamaican (145)	177	0.92
Trinidadian/Tobagonian (0)	11	0.06
Yugoslavian (296)	326	1.69

Hispanic Origin	Population	%
Hispanic or Latino (of any race)	2,542	12.45
Central American, ex. Mexican	290	1.42
Costa Rican	4	0.02
Guatemalan	67	0.33
Honduran	95	0.47
Nicaraguan	13	0.06
Panamanian	29	0.14
Salvadoran	78	0.38
Other Central American	4	0.02
Cuban	66	0.32
Dominican Republic	73	0.36
Mexican	1,297	6.35
Puerto Rican	338	1.65
South American	305	1.49
Argentinean	4	0.02
Bolivian	16	0.08
Chilean	9	0.04
Colombian	152	0.74
Ecuadorian	48	0.24
Peruvian	33	0.16
Uruguayan	15	0.07
Venezuelan	27	0.13
Other South American	1	<0.01
Other Hispanic or Latino	173	0.85

Race*	Population	%
African-American/Black (5,232)	5,562	27.23
Not Hispanic (5,093)	5,356	26.22
Hispanic (139)	206	1.01
American Indian/Alaska Native (65)	190	0.93
Not Hispanic (43)	157	0.77
Hispanic (22)	33	0.16
Apache (1)	5	0.02
Arapaho (1)	1	<0.01
Blackfeet (1)	10	0.05
Cherokee (13)	63	0.31
Chippewa (0)	2	0.01
Choctaw (2)	2	0.01
Creek (2)	3	0.01
Crow (0)	1	<0.01
Iroquois (1)	1	<0.01
Lumbee (0)	5	0.02
Mexican American Ind. (1)	2	0.01
Ottawa (0)	2	0.01
Pueblo (1)	1	<0.01
Seminole (0)	1	<0.01
Sioux (1)	2	0.01
South American Ind. (2)	3	0.01
Asian (706)	844	4.13
Not Hispanic (694)	819	4.01
Hispanic (12)	25	0.12
Bangladeshi (2)	3	0.01
Cambodian (15)	21	0.10
Chinese, ex. Taiwanese (77)	94	0.46
Filipino (96)	125	0.61
Hmong (5)	6	0.03
Indian (183)	221	1.08
Indonesian (10)	13	0.06
Japanese (16)	34	0.17
Korean (52)	71	0.35
Laotian (25)	28	0.14
Malaysian (2)	2	0.01
Nepalese (4)	4	0.02
Pakistani (65)	65	0.32
Taiwanese (7)	7	0.03
Thai (9)	17	0.08
Vietnamese (101)	108	0.53
Hawaii Native/Pacific Islander (13)	32	0.16
Not Hispanic (9)	25	0.12
Hispanic (4)	7	0.03
Guamanian/Chamorro (6)	6	0.03
Native Hawaiian (2)	11	0.05
White (12,758)	13,242	64.83
Not Hispanic (11,503)	11,856	58.05
Hispanic (1,255)	1,386	6.79

Albany

Place Type: City
County: Dougherty
Population: 77,434†

Ancestry‡	Population	%
African, Sub-Saharan (749)	896	1.16
African (624)	771	1.00
Kenyan (29)	29	0.04
Liberian (15)	15	0.02
Nigerian (23)	23	0.03
Ugandan (58)	58	0.08
American (3,802)	3,802	4.92
Arab (0)	15	0.02
Lebanese (0)	15	0.02
Austrian (89)	101	0.13
British (87)	202	0.26
Celtic (7)	7	0.01
Croatian (0)	17	0.02
Czech (19)	19	0.02
Czechoslovakian (16)	16	0.02
Danish (0)	27	0.03
Dutch (148)	404	0.52
English (2,412)	4,117	5.33
European (413)	436	0.56
French, ex. Basque (129)	649	0.84
French Canadian (23)	50	0.06
German (829)	2,642	3.42
Greek (55)	69	0.09
Guyanese (87)	93	0.12
Hungarian (14)	27	0.03
Iranian (26)	26	0.03
Irish (1,128)	3,436	4.45
Italian (191)	577	0.75
Latvian (0)	7	0.01
Luxemburger (0)	10	0.01
Northern European (10)	10	0.01
Norwegian (0)	40	0.05
Polish (69)	200	0.26
Portuguese (0)	8	0.01
Romanian (0)	15	0.02
Russian (0)	41	0.05
Scandinavian (20)	20	0.03
Scotch-Irish (520)	841	1.09
Scottish (370)	522	0.68
Slavic (7)	7	0.01
Slovak (0)	16	0.02
Slovene (0)	12	0.02
Swedish (19)	19	0.02
Swiss (0)	145	0.19
Ukrainian (0)	38	0.05
Welsh (21)	97	0.13
West Indian, ex. Hispanic (208)	342	0.44
Bahamian (21)	21	0.03
Haitian (15)	48	0.06
Jamaican (113)	197	0.26
Trinidadian/Tobagonian (11)	11	0.01
West Indian (48)	65	0.08

Hispanic Origin	Population	%
Hispanic or Latino (of any race)	1,596	2.06
Central American, ex. Mexican	261	0.34
Costa Rican	9	0.01
Guatemalan	194	0.25
Honduran	18	0.02
Nicaraguan	5	0.01
Panamanian	15	0.02
Salvadoran	20	0.03
Cuban	68	0.09
Dominican Republic	36	0.05
Mexican	712	0.92
Puerto Rican	219	0.28
South American	85	0.11
Argentinean	4	0.01
Chilean	12	0.02
Colombian	43	0.06
Ecuadorian	14	0.02
Peruvian	7	0.01
Venezuelan	3	<0.01
Other South American	2	<0.01
Other Hispanic or Latino	215	0.28

Race*	Population	%
African-American/Black (55,456)	56,081	72.42
Not Hispanic (55,210)	55,753	72.00
Hispanic (246)	328	0.42
American Indian/Alaska Native (145)	434	0.56
Not Hispanic (131)	394	0.51
Hispanic (14)	40	0.05
Apache (0)	2	<0.01
Blackfeet (0)	9	0.01
Cherokee (25)	106	0.14
Cheyenne (1)	1	<0.01
Chickasaw (0)	1	<0.01
Chippewa (3)	5	0.01
Choctaw (0)	9	0.01
Comanche (2)	2	<0.01
Creek (3)	16	0.02
Iroquois (0)	2	<0.01
Mexican American Ind. (5)	8	0.01

*Notes: † The Census 2010 population figure is used to calculate the percentages in the Hispanic Origin and Race categories. Ancestry percentages are based on the 2006-2010 American Community Survey population (not shown); ‡ Numbers in parentheses indicate the number of people reporting a single ancestry; * Numbers in parentheses indicate the number of persons reporting this race alone, not in combination with any other race; Please refer to the Explanation of Data for more information.*

Navajo (2)	2	<0.01
Potawatomi (1)	1	<0.01
Seminole (1)	5	0.01
Sioux (2)	5	0.01
South American Ind. (1)	3	<0.01
Yaqui (1)	1	<0.01
Asian (636)	816	1.05
Not Hispanic (622)	785	1.01
Hispanic (14)	31	0.04
Burmese (2)	2	<0.01
Chinese, ex. Taiwanese (97)	116	0.15
Filipino (62)	123	0.16
Indian (254)	280	0.36
Indonesian (2)	2	<0.01
Japanese (26)	52	0.07
Korean (57)	72	0.09
Laotian (0)	1	<0.01
Nepalese (1)	2	<0.01
Pakistani (16)	16	0.02
Taiwanese (8)	9	0.01
Thai (8)	15	0.02
Vietnamese (84)	88	0.11
Hawaii Native/Pacific Islander (89)	138	0.18
Not Hispanic (42)	80	0.10
Hispanic (47)	58	0.07
Guamanian/Chamorro (71)	79	0.10
Native Hawaiian (10)	27	0.03
Samoan (3)	7	0.01
White (19,549)	20,115	25.98
Not Hispanic (19,020)	19,511	25.20
Hispanic (529)	604	0.78

Alpharetta

Place Type: City
County: Fulton
Population: 57,551†

Ancestry‡	Population	%
Afghan (33)	33	0.06
African, Sub-Saharan (458)	606	1.11
African (115)	198	0.36
Ghanaian (23)	23	0.04
Kenyan (24)	24	0.04
Liberian (37)	37	0.07
Nigerian (59)	73	0.13
South African (155)	175	0.32
Other Sub-Saharan African (45)	76	0.14
Albanian (0)	16	0.03
American (2,758)	2,758	5.04
Arab (275)	366	0.67
Arab (59)	59	0.11
Egyptian (49)	49	0.09
Lebanese (89)	172	0.31
Palestinian (7)	7	0.01
Syrian (0)	8	0.01
Other Arab (71)	71	0.13
Armenian (11)	31	0.06
Assyrian/Chaldean/Syriac (0)	44	0.08
Australian (9)	9	0.02
Austrian (29)	181	0.33
Brazilian (180)	180	0.33
British (404)	726	1.33
Cajun (0)	18	0.03
Canadian (78)	184	0.34
Croatian (0)	53	0.10
Czech (164)	354	0.65
Czechoslovakian (13)	102	0.19
Danish (30)	100	0.18
Dutch (372)	778	1.42
Eastern European (109)	109	0.20
English (2,822)	6,250	11.42
Estonian (12)	12	0.02
European (1,146)	1,262	2.31
Finnish (126)	165	0.30
French, ex. Basque (265)	965	1.76
French Canadian (67)	188	0.34
German (1,848)	6,067	11.09
Greek (20)	132	0.24
Guyanese (8)	8	0.01
Hungarian (92)	200	0.37
Iranian (317)	317	0.58
Irish (2,205)	6,176	11.29
Italian (1,216)	2,998	5.48
Latvian (0)	22	0.04
Lithuanian (242)	297	0.54
Macedonian (12)	12	0.02
Northern European (39)	39	0.07
Norwegian (101)	810	1.48
Pennsylvania German (13)	13	0.02
Polish (510)	1,549	2.83
Portuguese (23)	71	0.13
Romanian (13)	101	0.18
Russian (323)	761	1.39
Scandinavian (10)	42	0.08
Scotch-Irish (580)	1,232	2.25
Scottish (497)	1,439	2.63
Serbian (19)	46	0.08
Slavic (16)	16	0.03
Slovak (86)	213	0.39
Slovene (0)	26	0.05
Swedish (71)	513	0.94
Swiss (27)	92	0.17
Turkish (80)	89	0.16
Ukrainian (374)	548	1.00
Welsh (53)	256	0.47
West Indian, ex. Hispanic (490)	592	1.08
Bahamian (0)	3	0.01
Dutch West Indian (0)	14	0.03
Jamaican (320)	402	0.73
Trinidadian/Tobagonian (37)	37	0.07
U.S. Virgin Islander (133)	136	0.25

Hispanic Origin	Population	%
Hispanic or Latino (of any race)	4,892	8.50
Central American, ex. Mexican	387	0.67
Costa Rican	36	0.06
Guatemalan	98	0.17
Honduran	51	0.09
Nicaraguan	32	0.06
Panamanian	34	0.06
Salvadoran	135	0.23
Other Central American	1	<0.01
Cuban	268	0.47
Dominican Republic	114	0.20
Mexican	2,297	3.99
Puerto Rican	450	0.78
South American	977	1.70
Argentinean	59	0.10
Bolivian	8	0.01
Chilean	45	0.08
Colombian	403	0.70
Ecuadorian	45	0.08
Paraguayan	6	0.01
Peruvian	183	0.32
Uruguayan	35	0.06
Venezuelan	187	0.32
Other South American	6	0.01
Other Hispanic or Latino	399	0.69

Race*	Population	%
African-American/Black (6,245)	6,787	11.79
Not Hispanic (6,099)	6,536	11.36
Hispanic (146)	251	0.44
American Indian/Alaska Native (111)	364	0.63
Not Hispanic (70)	276	0.48
Hispanic (41)	88	0.15
Apache (1)	2	<0.01
Arapaho (0)	1	<0.01
Blackfeet (0)	7	0.01
Central American Ind. (2)	2	<0.01
Cherokee (16)	88	0.15
Chickasaw (0)	3	0.01
Chippewa (1)	1	<0.01
Choctaw (1)	7	0.01
Creek (2)	6	0.01
Crow (0)	2	<0.01
Delaware (0)	4	0.01
Hopi (0)	1	<0.01
Inupiat *(Alaska Native)* (1)	1	<0.01
Iroquois (0)	2	<0.01
Lumbee (2)	6	0.01
Mexican American Ind. (7)	19	0.03
Navajo (2)	6	0.01
Osage (1)	5	0.01
Potawatomi (1)	1	<0.01
Pueblo (1)	5	0.01
Seminole (0)	2	<0.01
Sioux (2)	4	0.01
South American Ind. (1)	5	0.01
Tlingit-Haida *(Alaska Native)* (0)	1	<0.01
Asian (7,690)	8,375	14.55
Not Hispanic (7,678)	8,321	14.46
Hispanic (12)	54	0.09
Bangladeshi (27)	28	0.05
Burmese (3)	3	0.01
Cambodian (11)	13	0.02
Chinese, ex. Taiwanese (1,149)	1,269	2.21
Filipino (167)	283	0.49
Hmong (5)	5	0.01
Indian (4,478)	4,630	8.05
Indonesian (34)	34	0.06
Japanese (97)	178	0.31
Korean (916)	986	1.71
Laotian (8)	16	0.03
Malaysian (8)	13	0.02
Nepalese (4)	4	0.01
Pakistani (242)	271	0.47
Sri Lankan (32)	33	0.06
Taiwanese (131)	137	0.24
Thai (43)	52	0.09
Vietnamese (208)	234	0.41
Hawaii Native/Pacific Islander (29)	101	0.18
Not Hispanic (28)	95	0.17
Hispanic (1)	6	0.01
Fijian (7)	8	0.01
Guamanian/Chamorro (0)	2	<0.01
Native Hawaiian (7)	29	0.05
Samoan (5)	11	0.02
White (40,310)	41,520	72.14
Not Hispanic (37,391)	38,284	66.52
Hispanic (2,919)	3,236	5.62

Americus

Place Type: City
County: Sumter
Population: 17,041†

Ancestry‡	Population	%
African, Sub-Saharan (800)	843	4.95
African (800)	843	4.95
American (831)	831	4.88
Austrian (0)	5	0.03
British (20)	20	0.12
Bulgarian (36)	36	0.21
Canadian (48)	92	0.54
Czech (0)	11	0.06
Danish (0)	7	0.04
Dutch (68)	237	1.39
English (572)	923	5.42
European (54)	100	0.59
French, ex. Basque (62)	200	1.17
French Canadian (70)	70	0.41
German (218)	488	2.87
Hungarian (70)	70	0.41
Irish (137)	591	3.47
Italian (37)	120	0.70
Norwegian (0)	6	0.04
Polish (0)	28	0.16
Russian (9)	9	0.05
Scotch-Irish (70)	121	0.71
Scottish (110)	226	1.33
Slovak (0)	11	0.06
Swedish (0)	7	0.04
Welsh (0)	10	0.06
West Indian, ex. Hispanic (81)	81	0.48
British West Indian (15)	15	0.09
Jamaican (66)	66	0.39

*Notes: † The Census 2010 population figure is used to calculate the percentages in the Hispanic Origin and Race categories. Ancestry percentages are based on the 2006-2010 American Community Survey population (not shown); ‡ Numbers in parentheses indicate the number of people reporting a single ancestry; * Numbers in parentheses indicate the number of persons reporting this race alone, not in combination with any other race; Please refer to the Explanation of Data for more information.*

Hispanic Origin	Population	%
Hispanic or Latino (of any race)	786	4.61
Central American, ex. Mexican	46	0.27
Costa Rican	1	0.01
Guatemalan	20	0.12
Honduran	19	0.11
Panamanian	2	0.01
Salvadoran	4	0.02
Cuban	22	0.13
Dominican Republic	1	0.01
Mexican	603	3.54
Puerto Rican	29	0.17
South American	19	0.11
Argentinean	6	0.04
Colombian	7	0.04
Paraguayan	3	0.02
Peruvian	2	0.01
Venezuelan	1	0.01
Other Hispanic or Latino	66	0.39

Race*	Population	%
African-American/Black (10,818)	10,937	64.18
Not Hispanic (10,752)	10,841	63.62
Hispanic (66)	96	0.56
American Indian/Alaska Native (53)	119	0.70
Not Hispanic (46)	94	0.55
Hispanic (7)	25	0.15
Blackfeet (0)	1	0.01
Central American Ind. (0)	1	0.01
Cherokee (7)	22	0.13
Creek (4)	9	0.05
Lumbee (2)	2	0.01
Mexican American Ind. (0)	6	0.04
Seminole (0)	4	0.02
Shoshone (0)	1	0.01
Sioux (0)	4	0.02
Asian (302)	338	1.98
Not Hispanic (302)	328	1.92
Hispanic (0)	10	0.06
Chinese, ex. Taiwanese (40)	43	0.25
Filipino (34)	47	0.28
Hmong (1)	1	0.01
Indian (121)	126	0.74
Japanese (0)	1	0.01
Korean (17)	20	0.12
Laotian (1)	1	0.01
Pakistani (7)	7	0.04
Sri Lankan (6)	6	0.04
Taiwanese (6)	7	0.04
Thai (2)	5	0.03
Vietnamese (13)	19	0.11
Hawaii Native/Pacific Islander (3)	11	0.06
Not Hispanic (3)	11	0.06
Guamanian/Chamorro (1)	2	0.01
Native Hawaiian (2)	7	0.04
White (5,219)	5,352	31.41
Not Hispanic (5,006)	5,111	29.99
Hispanic (213)	241	1.41

Athens-Clarke County

Place Type: Unified Government
County: Clarke
Population: 115,452†

Ancestry‡	Population	%
African, Sub-Saharan (1,581)	1,697	1.49
African (1,128)	1,213	1.07
Ethiopian (74)	74	0.07
Ghanaian (47)	68	0.06
Nigerian (160)	160	0.14
Senegalese (11)	11	0.01
South African (2)	2	<0.01
Sudanese (159)	159	0.14
Other Sub-Saharan African (0)	10	0.01
Albanian (78)	78	0.07
American (7,494)	7,494	6.60
Arab (320)	508	0.45
Arab (19)	54	0.05
Egyptian (63)	100	0.09
Iraqi (53)	53	0.05
Lebanese (133)	198	0.17
Palestinian (22)	44	0.04
Syrian (0)	8	0.01
Other Arab (30)	51	0.04
Armenian (37)	89	0.08
Australian (64)	77	0.07
Austrian (116)	255	0.22
Belgian (30)	72	0.06
Brazilian (0)	27	0.02
British (441)	1,015	0.89
Bulgarian (56)	56	0.05
Cajun (103)	103	0.09
Canadian (125)	228	0.20
Celtic (0)	7	0.01
Croatian (0)	78	0.07
Czech (108)	322	0.28
Czechoslovakian (37)	101	0.09
Danish (33)	186	0.16
Dutch (369)	1,152	1.01
Eastern European (102)	123	0.11
English (5,459)	12,419	10.93
European (1,297)	1,432	1.26
Finnish (47)	73	0.06
French, ex. Basque (478)	2,223	1.96
French Canadian (154)	314	0.28
German (3,417)	11,308	9.95
German Russian (25)	25	0.02
Greek (344)	494	0.43
Guyanese (60)	60	0.05
Hungarian (157)	492	0.43
Icelander (10)	66	0.06
Iranian (44)	65	0.06
Irish (3,432)	10,221	9.00
Israeli (0)	17	0.01
Italian (707)	2,620	2.31
Latvian (26)	52	0.05
Lithuanian (40)	156	0.14
Macedonian (26)	35	0.03
Northern European (93)	109	0.10
Norwegian (239)	825	0.73
Pennsylvania German (0)	6	0.01
Polish (798)	1,807	1.59
Portuguese (95)	142	0.12
Romanian (248)	293	0.26
Russian (469)	981	0.86
Scandinavian (38)	57	0.05
Scotch-Irish (1,682)	3,049	2.68
Scottish (1,698)	3,930	3.46
Serbian (61)	78	0.07
Slavic (9)	69	0.06
Slovak (52)	102	0.09
Slovene (17)	32	0.03
Swedish (300)	885	0.78
Swiss (34)	170	0.15
Turkish (47)	63	0.06
Ukrainian (39)	142	0.12
Welsh (366)	1,005	0.88
West Indian, ex. Hispanic (249)	485	0.43
Bahamian (8)	8	0.01
Barbadian (0)	53	0.05
British West Indian (18)	62	0.05
Haitian (55)	74	0.07
Jamaican (126)	214	0.19
Trinidadian/Tobagonian (20)	20	0.02
West Indian (22)	54	0.05
Yugoslavian (60)	77	0.07

Hispanic Origin	Population	%
Hispanic or Latino (of any race)	12,129	10.51
Central American, ex. Mexican	1,602	1.39
Costa Rican	48	0.04
Guatemalan	393	0.34
Honduran	117	0.10
Nicaraguan	37	0.03
Panamanian	49	0.04
Salvadoran	932	0.81
Other Central American	26	0.02
Cuban	315	0.27
Dominican Republic	64	0.06
Mexican	7,625	6.60
Puerto Rican	686	0.59
South American	1,058	0.92
Argentinean	91	0.08
Bolivian	28	0.02
Chilean	39	0.03
Colombian	204	0.18
Ecuadorian	64	0.06
Paraguayan	3	<0.01
Peruvian	529	0.46
Uruguayan	23	0.02
Venezuelan	72	0.06
Other South American	5	<0.01
Other Hispanic or Latino	779	0.67

Race*	Population	%
African-American/Black (30,733)	31,820	27.56
Not Hispanic (30,441)	31,374	27.17
Hispanic (292)	446	0.39
American Indian/Alaska Native (244)	706	0.61
Not Hispanic (138)	520	0.45
Hispanic (106)	186	0.16
Alaska Athabascan *(Ala. Nat.)* (2)	3	<0.01
Apache (2)	9	0.01
Blackfeet (0)	6	0.01
Canadian/French Am. Ind. (1)	2	<0.01
Central American Ind. (2)	3	<0.01
Cherokee (48)	201	0.17
Chickasaw (0)	4	<0.01
Chippewa (1)	3	<0.01
Choctaw (3)	11	0.01
Comanche (0)	3	<0.01
Creek (3)	12	0.01
Delaware (0)	1	<0.01
Inupiat *(Alaska Native)* (0)	6	0.01
Iroquois (3)	5	<0.01
Lumbee (3)	6	0.01
Mexican American Ind. (21)	24	0.02
Navajo (3)	5	<0.01
Puget Sound Salish (1)	1	<0.01
Seminole (0)	3	<0.01
Sioux (1)	6	0.01
South American Ind. (1)	3	<0.01
Tohono O'Odham (4)	4	<0.01
Yaqui (0)	1	<0.01
Yup'ik *(Alaska Native)* (0)	1	<0.01
Asian (4,865)	5,706	4.94
Not Hispanic (4,807)	5,591	4.84
Hispanic (58)	115	0.10
Bangladeshi (38)	46	0.04
Burmese (16)	22	0.02
Cambodian (18)	25	0.02
Chinese, ex. Taiwanese (1,126)	1,262	1.09
Filipino (318)	505	0.44
Hmong (22)	22	0.02
Indian (1,444)	1,570	1.36
Indonesian (9)	18	0.02
Japanese (132)	259	0.22
Korean (1,003)	1,128	0.98
Laotian (12)	27	0.02
Malaysian (10)	15	0.01
Nepalese (26)	27	0.02
Pakistani (124)	142	0.12
Sri Lankan (9)	11	0.01
Taiwanese (112)	127	0.11
Thai (38)	68	0.06
Vietnamese (268)	316	0.27
Hawaii Native/Pacific Islander (84)	187	0.16
Not Hispanic (48)	130	0.11
Hispanic (36)	57	0.05
Guamanian/Chamorro (41)	49	0.04
Marshallese (2)	3	<0.01
Native Hawaiian (18)	46	0.04
Samoan (9)	17	0.01
Tongan (1)	1	<0.01
White (71,294)	73,383	63.56
Not Hispanic (65,747)	67,304	58.30
Hispanic (5,547)	6,079	5.27

*Notes: † The Census 2010 population figure is used to calculate the percentages in the Hispanic Origin and Race categories. Ancestry percentages are based on the 2006-2010 American Community Survey population (not shown); ‡ Numbers in parentheses indicate the number of people reporting a single ancestry; * Numbers in parentheses indicate the number of persons reporting this race alone, not in combination with any other race; Please refer to the Explanation of Data for more information.*

Atlanta

Place Type: City
County: Fulton
Population: 420,003†

Ancestry‡	Population	%
Afghan (8)	8	<0.01
African, Sub-Saharan (13,124)	14,882	3.60
African (11,314)	12,994	3.14
Cape Verdean (53)	53	0.01
Ethiopian (487)	499	0.12
Ghanaian (91)	96	0.02
Kenyan (101)	101	0.02
Liberian (54)	54	0.01
Nigerian (356)	372	0.09
Senegalese (15)	15	<0.01
Somalian (78)	78	0.02
South African (192)	222	0.05
Other Sub-Saharan African (383)	398	0.10
Albanian (21)	45	0.01
Alsatian (8)	8	<0.01
American (21,935)	21,935	5.31
Arab (1,117)	1,578	0.38
Arab (67)	94	0.02
Egyptian (70)	166	0.04
Iraqi (38)	38	0.01
Lebanese (392)	636	0.15
Moroccan (37)	46	0.01
Palestinian (16)	70	0.02
Syrian (65)	78	0.02
Other Arab (432)	450	0.11
Armenian (146)	176	0.04
Assyrian/Chaldean/Syriac (13)	13	<0.01
Australian (26)	110	0.03
Austrian (291)	778	0.19
Belgian (109)	202	0.05
Brazilian (215)	246	0.06
British (1,782)	3,155	0.76
Bulgarian (180)	180	0.04
Cajun (16)	43	0.01
Canadian (271)	552	0.13
Carpatho Rusyn (0)	13	<0.01
Celtic (52)	52	0.01
Croatian (35)	168	0.04
Czech (228)	764	0.18
Czechoslovakian (74)	151	0.04
Danish (227)	678	0.16
Dutch (787)	2,528	0.61
Eastern European (1,086)	1,101	0.27
English (12,087)	30,071	7.27
European (5,235)	5,928	1.43
Finnish (121)	321	0.08
French, ex. Basque (1,662)	7,173	1.73
French Canadian (452)	1,012	0.24
German (7,828)	27,301	6.60
German Russian (21)	21	0.01
Greek (553)	956	0.23
Guyanese (173)	249	0.06
Hungarian (429)	1,147	0.28
Iranian (477)	516	0.12
Irish (7,134)	22,432	5.43
Israeli (81)	153	0.04
Italian (3,243)	8,287	2.00
Latvian (160)	261	0.06
Lithuanian (214)	556	0.13
Luxemburger (19)	19	<0.01
Macedonian (41)	41	0.01
Maltese (26)	26	0.01
Northern European (269)	269	0.07
Norwegian (488)	1,561	0.38
Pennsylvania German (10)	24	0.01
Polish (1,573)	5,220	1.26
Portuguese (138)	282	0.07
Romanian (184)	314	0.08
Russian (1,944)	3,892	0.94
Scandinavian (81)	255	0.06
Scotch-Irish (3,819)	7,472	1.81
Scottish (3,227)	8,305	2.01
Serbian (71)	101	0.02
Slavic (15)	45	0.01
Slovak (54)	286	0.07
Slovene (13)	73	0.02
Swedish (490)	2,176	0.53
Swiss (126)	396	0.10
Turkish (361)	411	0.10
Ukrainian (216)	560	0.14
Welsh (463)	1,888	0.46
West Indian, ex. Hispanic (2,491)	3,668	0.89
Bahamian (141)	154	0.04
Barbadian (126)	155	0.04
Belizean (23)	36	0.01
British West Indian (80)	139	0.03
Haitian (431)	722	0.17
Jamaican (1,105)	1,519	0.37
Trinidadian/Tobagonian (220)	250	0.06
U.S. Virgin Islander (0)	49	0.01
West Indian (365)	618	0.15
Other West Indian (0)	26	0.01
Yugoslavian (13)	121	0.03

Hispanic Origin	Population	%
Hispanic or Latino (of any race)	21,815	5.19
Central American, ex. Mexican	1,840	0.44
Costa Rican	126	0.03
Guatemalan	466	0.11
Honduran	518	0.12
Nicaraguan	113	0.03
Panamanian	376	0.09
Salvadoran	217	0.05
Other Central American	24	0.01
Cuban	1,333	0.32
Dominican Republic	473	0.11
Mexican	11,827	2.82
Puerto Rican	2,258	0.54
South American	2,335	0.56
Argentinean	256	0.06
Bolivian	43	0.01
Chilean	134	0.03
Colombian	989	0.24
Ecuadorian	137	0.03
Paraguayan	32	0.01
Peruvian	315	0.07
Uruguayan	58	0.01
Venezuelan	350	0.08
Other South American	21	0.01
Other Hispanic or Latino	1,749	0.42

Race*	Population	%
African-American/Black (226,894)	231,948	55.23
Not Hispanic (224,316)	228,575	54.42
Hispanic (2,578)	3,373	0.80
American Indian/Alaska Native (988)	3,363	0.80
Not Hispanic (754)	2,814	0.67
Hispanic (234)	549	0.13
Alaska Athabascan *(Ala. Nat.)* (2)	3	<0.01
Aleut *(Alaska Native)* (1)	1	<0.01
Apache (6)	20	<0.01
Blackfeet (11)	106	0.03
Canadian/French Am. Ind. (2)	7	<0.01
Central American Ind. (2)	7	<0.01
Cherokee (116)	836	0.20
Cheyenne (0)	1	<0.01
Chickasaw (7)	16	<0.01
Chippewa (11)	30	0.01
Choctaw (16)	68	0.02
Comanche (2)	6	<0.01
Cree (0)	5	<0.01
Creek (16)	71	0.02
Crow (0)	1	<0.01
Delaware (0)	6	<0.01
Hopi (1)	2	<0.01
Houma (1)	1	<0.01
Inupiat *(Alaska Native)* (4)	4	<0.01
Iroquois (8)	41	0.01
Kiowa (0)	2	<0.01
Lumbee (19)	29	0.01
Menominee (0)	1	<0.01
Mexican American Ind. (64)	87	0.02
Navajo (5)	17	<0.01
Osage (3)	6	<0.01
Ottawa (4)	11	<0.01
Paiute (1)	1	<0.01
Pima (3)	3	<0.01
Potawatomi (4)	9	<0.01
Pueblo (1)	3	<0.01
Seminole (5)	29	0.01
Shoshone (2)	3	<0.01
Sioux (12)	31	0.01
South American Ind. (8)	45	0.01
Spanish American Ind. (1)	6	<0.01
Tlingit-Haida *(Alaska Native)* (0)	5	<0.01
Tohono O'Odham (1)	2	<0.01
Tsimshian *(Alaska Native)* (1)	1	<0.01
Yaqui (0)	7	<0.01
Yuman (0)	1	<0.01
Asian (13,188)	15,954	3.80
Not Hispanic (13,098)	15,625	3.72
Hispanic (90)	329	0.08
Bangladeshi (132)	142	0.03
Bhutanese (3)	3	<0.01
Burmese (12)	19	<0.01
Cambodian (43)	59	0.01
Chinese, ex. Taiwanese (2,838)	3,417	0.81
Filipino (622)	1,083	0.26
Hmong (11)	13	<0.01
Indian (4,606)	5,141	1.22
Indonesian (83)	114	0.03
Japanese (520)	883	0.21
Korean (2,024)	2,493	0.59
Laotian (56)	76	0.02
Malaysian (26)	43	0.01
Nepalese (19)	22	0.01
Pakistani (372)	462	0.11
Sri Lankan (37)	49	0.01
Taiwanese (273)	321	0.08
Thai (198)	256	0.06
Vietnamese (731)	899	0.21
Hawaii Native/Pacific Islander (132)	458	0.11
Not Hispanic (115)	387	0.09
Hispanic (17)	71	0.02
Fijian (8)	13	<0.01
Guamanian/Chamorro (30)	69	0.02
Native Hawaiian (36)	113	0.03
Samoan (14)	56	0.01
Tongan (3)	6	<0.01
White (161,115)	166,869	39.73
Not Hispanic (152,377)	157,119	37.41
Hispanic (8,738)	9,750	2.32

Augusta-Richmond County

Place Type: Consolidated Government
County: Richmond
Population: 195,844†

Ancestry‡	Population	%
Afghan (13)	27	0.01
African, Sub-Saharan (2,616)	4,918	2.54
African (2,285)	4,490	2.32
Cape Verdean (10)	65	0.03
Ethiopian (157)	199	0.10
Kenyan (16)	16	0.01
Nigerian (91)	91	0.05
Somalian (12)	12	0.01
South African (33)	33	0.02
Other Sub-Saharan African (12)	12	0.01
American (14,917)	14,917	7.71
Arab (153)	354	0.18
Arab (0)	108	0.06
Egyptian (28)	28	0.01
Lebanese (41)	41	0.02
Moroccan (13)	13	0.01
Palestinian (55)	55	0.03
Syrian (16)	16	0.01
Other Arab (0)	93	0.05
Armenian (9)	27	0.01
Assyrian/Chaldean/Syriac (0)	130	0.07
Austrian (54)	209	0.11

*Notes: † The Census 2010 population figure is used to calculate the percentages in the Hispanic Origin and Race categories. Ancestry percentages are based on the 2006-2010 American Community Survey population (not shown); ‡ Numbers in parentheses indicate the number of people reporting a single ancestry; * Numbers in parentheses indicate the number of persons reporting this race alone, not in combination with any other race; Please refer to the Explanation of Data for more information.*

Ancestry (continued)	Population	%
Belgian (71)	106	0.05
British (386)	532	0.27
Cajun (54)	64	0.03
Canadian (61)	95	0.05
Croatian (19)	19	0.01
Czech (92)	274	0.14
Czechoslovakian (7)	31	0.02
Danish (5)	5	<0.01
Dutch (299)	1,058	0.55
Eastern European (22)	22	0.01
English (5,098)	10,310	5.33
Estonian (0)	8	<0.01
European (1,014)	1,259	0.65
Finnish (0)	27	0.01
French, ex. Basque (817)	2,767	1.43
French Canadian (248)	356	0.18
German (4,978)	12,893	6.66
Greek (144)	331	0.17
Guyanese (42)	56	0.03
Hungarian (78)	193	0.10
Iranian (12)	22	0.01
Irish (5,121)	13,190	6.82
Israeli (0)	10	0.01
Italian (1,022)	3,030	1.57
Latvian (0)	39	0.02
Lithuanian (0)	45	0.02
Northern European (128)	128	0.07
Norwegian (151)	494	0.26
Pennsylvania German (27)	55	0.03
Polish (544)	1,161	0.60
Portuguese (102)	469	0.24
Romanian (37)	37	0.02
Russian (152)	454	0.23
Scandinavian (93)	206	0.11
Scotch-Irish (1,719)	2,850	1.47
Scottish (956)	2,566	1.33
Serbian (11)	44	0.02
Slavic (0)	39	0.02
Slovak (8)	23	0.01
Slovene (11)	25	0.01
Swedish (196)	455	0.24
Swiss (14)	125	0.06
Turkish (20)	20	0.01
Ukrainian (74)	123	0.06
Welsh (146)	568	0.29
West Indian, ex. Hispanic (872)	1,766	0.91
Bahamian (0)	21	0.01
British West Indian (75)	120	0.06
Haitian (241)	420	0.22
Jamaican (304)	585	0.30
Trinidadian/Tobagonian (35)	100	0.05
U.S. Virgin Islander (0)	19	0.01
West Indian (217)	501	0.26

Hispanic Origin	Population	%
Hispanic or Latino (of any race)	8,053	4.11
Central American, ex. Mexican	746	0.38
Costa Rican	57	0.03
Guatemalan	55	0.03
Honduran	109	0.06
Nicaraguan	38	0.02
Panamanian	389	0.20
Salvadoran	93	0.05
Other Central American	5	<0.01
Cuban	278	0.14
Dominican Republic	217	0.11
Mexican	3,018	1.54
Puerto Rican	2,848	1.45
South American	278	0.14
Argentinean	20	0.01
Bolivian	3	<0.01
Chilean	13	0.01
Colombian	114	0.06
Ecuadorian	32	0.02
Paraguayan	9	<0.01
Peruvian	41	0.02
Uruguayan	6	<0.01
Venezuelan	35	0.02
Other South American	5	<0.01
Other Hispanic or Latino	668	0.34

Race*	Population	%
African-American/Black (107,182)	110,481	56.41
Not Hispanic (105,921)	108,666	55.49
Hispanic (1,261)	1,815	0.93
American Indian/Alaska Native (672)	1,878	0.96
Not Hispanic (557)	1,582	0.81
Hispanic (115)	296	0.15
Alaska Athabascan *(Ala. Nat.)* (0)	2	<0.01
Aleut *(Alaska Native)* (1)	1	<0.01
Apache (14)	36	0.02
Arapaho (1)	2	<0.01
Blackfeet (7)	42	0.02
Canadian/French Am. Ind. (1)	1	<0.01
Central American Ind. (1)	3	<0.01
Cherokee (140)	499	0.25
Cheyenne (1)	5	<0.01
Chickasaw (10)	20	0.01
Chippewa (11)	26	0.01
Choctaw (13)	42	0.02
Comanche (7)	7	<0.01
Cree (0)	3	<0.01
Creek (10)	34	0.02
Delaware (3)	7	<0.01
Hopi (2)	2	<0.01
Houma (1)	2	<0.01
Inupiat *(Alaska Native)* (1)	1	<0.01
Iroquois (6)	18	0.01
Kiowa (1)	6	<0.01
Lumbee (18)	23	0.01
Mexican American Ind. (21)	33	0.02
Navajo (17)	38	0.02
Osage (1)	2	<0.01
Pima (3)	3	<0.01
Potawatomi (0)	3	<0.01
Pueblo (5)	5	<0.01
Puget Sound Salish (2)	2	<0.01
Seminole (5)	14	0.01
Shoshone (0)	1	<0.01
Sioux (13)	26	0.01
South American Ind. (4)	19	0.01
Spanish American Ind. (1)	2	<0.01
Tsimshian *(Alaska Native)* (2)	2	<0.01
Yaqui (2)	5	<0.01
Yuman (0)	2	<0.01
Yup'ik *(Alaska Native)* (1)	1	<0.01
Asian (3,312)	4,638	2.37
Not Hispanic (3,259)	4,450	2.27
Hispanic (53)	188	0.10
Bangladeshi (6)	6	<0.01
Burmese (13)	16	0.01
Cambodian (15)	22	0.01
Chinese, ex. Taiwanese (612)	745	0.38
Filipino (497)	825	0.42
Hmong (2)	2	<0.01
Indian (585)	727	0.37
Indonesian (6)	12	0.01
Japanese (179)	375	0.19
Korean (708)	1,117	0.57
Laotian (27)	31	0.02
Malaysian (1)	1	<0.01
Nepalese (8)	8	<0.01
Pakistani (50)	71	0.04
Sri Lankan (2)	2	<0.01
Taiwanese (22)	25	0.01
Thai (88)	145	0.07
Vietnamese (314)	415	0.21
Hawaii Native/Pacific Islander (396)	662	0.34
Not Hispanic (370)	579	0.30
Hispanic (26)	83	0.04
Fijian (1)	4	<0.01
Guamanian/Chamorro (93)	135	0.07
Marshallese (1)	3	<0.01
Native Hawaiian (80)	168	0.09
Samoan (90)	133	0.07
White (76,573)	80,373	41.04
Not Hispanic (73,277)	76,488	39.06
Hispanic (3,296)	3,885	1.98

Bainbridge

Place Type: City
County: Decatur
Population: 12,697†

Ancestry‡	Population	%
African, Sub-Saharan (148)	148	1.18
African (128)	128	1.02
Ghanaian (20)	20	0.16
American (797)	797	6.34
Arab (25)	25	0.20
Palestinian (25)	25	0.20
British (14)	14	0.11
Dutch (24)	39	0.31
English (592)	781	6.21
European (22)	22	0.17
Finnish (0)	27	0.21
French, ex. Basque (23)	92	0.73
German (104)	325	2.58
Irish (258)	568	4.52
Italian (27)	54	0.43
Norwegian (0)	17	0.14
Polish (7)	7	0.06
Scotch-Irish (68)	75	0.60
Scottish (43)	55	0.44
Swedish (0)	6	0.05
Swiss (12)	12	0.10
West Indian, ex. Hispanic (26)	26	0.21
Jamaican (14)	14	0.11
Trinidadian/Tobagonian (12)	12	0.10

Hispanic Origin	Population	%
Hispanic or Latino (of any race)	521	4.10
Central American, ex. Mexican	41	0.32
Costa Rican	5	0.04
Guatemalan	26	0.20
Honduran	6	0.05
Nicaraguan	1	0.01
Panamanian	3	0.02
Cuban	12	0.09
Mexican	368	2.90
Puerto Rican	40	0.32
South American	2	0.02
Argentinean	2	0.02
Other Hispanic or Latino	58	0.46

Race*	Population	%
African-American/Black (6,945)	7,017	55.27
Not Hispanic (6,904)	6,972	54.91
Hispanic (41)	45	0.35
American Indian/Alaska Native (32)	93	0.73
Not Hispanic (14)	69	0.54
Hispanic (18)	24	0.19
Cherokee (1)	15	0.12
Cree (0)	1	0.01
Creek (2)	14	0.11
Hopi (0)	1	0.01
Iroquois (0)	1	0.01
Lumbee (2)	2	0.02
Mexican American Ind. (12)	12	0.09
Shoshone (0)	1	0.01
Asian (96)	123	0.97
Not Hispanic (91)	112	0.88
Hispanic (5)	11	0.09
Chinese, ex. Taiwanese (7)	7	0.06
Filipino (14)	19	0.15
Indian (44)	51	0.40
Japanese (3)	12	0.09
Korean (6)	14	0.11
Vietnamese (20)	20	0.16
Hawaii Native/Pacific Islander (0)	10	0.08
Not Hispanic (0)	9	0.07
Hispanic (0)	1	0.01
Guamanian/Chamorro (0)	1	0.01
Native Hawaiian (0)	6	0.05
White (5,215)	5,356	42.18
Not Hispanic (5,029)	5,133	40.43
Hispanic (186)	223	1.76

*Notes: † The Census 2010 population figure is used to calculate the percentages in the Hispanic Origin and Race categories. Ancestry percentages are based on the 2006-2010 American Community Survey population (not shown); ‡ Numbers in parentheses indicate the number of people reporting a single ancestry; * Numbers in parentheses indicate the number of persons reporting this race alone, not in combination with any other race; Please refer to the Explanation of Data for more information.*

Belvedere Park

Place Type: CDP
County: DeKalb
Population: 15,152†

Ancestry‡	Population	%
African, Sub-Saharan (145)	167	1.15
African (125)	147	1.01
Kenyan (20)	20	0.14
American (337)	337	2.32
Arab (36)	45	0.31
Iraqi (0)	9	0.06
Lebanese (18)	18	0.12
Syrian (10)	10	0.07
Other Arab (8)	8	0.06
Armenian (0)	9	0.06
Belgian (0)	10	0.07
Brazilian (0)	11	0.08
British (9)	29	0.20
Cajun (0)	9	0.06
Celtic (0)	16	0.11
Dutch (0)	106	0.73
English (92)	355	2.44
European (121)	121	0.83
French, ex. Basque (8)	38	0.26
French Canadian (8)	19	0.13
German (127)	408	2.81
Greek (51)	51	0.35
Guyanese (0)	26	0.18
Hungarian (0)	11	0.08
Irish (115)	360	2.48
Israeli (11)	11	0.08
Italian (8)	82	0.56
Lithuanian (0)	16	0.11
Northern European (7)	7	0.05
Norwegian (9)	9	0.06
Polish (19)	84	0.58
Romanian (0)	7	0.05
Russian (9)	62	0.43
Scotch-Irish (69)	182	1.25
Scottish (41)	129	0.89
Swedish (0)	10	0.07
Swiss (0)	11	0.08
Turkish (16)	16	0.11
Ukrainian (30)	30	0.21
Welsh (18)	109	0.75
West Indian, ex. Hispanic (138)	321	2.21
Barbadian (0)	13	0.09
Haitian (0)	41	0.28
Jamaican (121)	210	1.45
West Indian (17)	57	0.39

Hispanic Origin	Population	%
Hispanic or Latino (of any race)	523	3.45
Central American, ex. Mexican	46	0.30
Costa Rican	4	0.03
Guatemalan	9	0.06
Honduran	8	0.05
Nicaraguan	7	0.05
Panamanian	6	0.04
Salvadoran	12	0.08
Cuban	31	0.20
Dominican Republic	17	0.11
Mexican	254	1.68
Puerto Rican	89	0.59
South American	31	0.20
Argentinean	2	0.01
Chilean	4	0.03
Colombian	8	0.05
Peruvian	6	0.04
Uruguayan	1	0.01
Venezuelan	9	0.06
Other South American	1	0.01
Other Hispanic or Latino	55	0.36

Race*	Population	%
African-American/Black (11,557)	11,785	77.78
Not Hispanic (11,454)	11,643	76.84
Hispanic (103)	142	0.94
American Indian/Alaska Native (40)	138	0.91
Not Hispanic (36)	126	0.83
Hispanic (4)	12	0.08
Aleut *(Alaska Native)* (0)	4	0.03
Blackfeet (0)	13	0.09
Cherokee (8)	35	0.23
Choctaw (0)	7	0.05
Mexican American Ind. (2)	2	0.01
Navajo (1)	1	0.01
Seminole (0)	3	0.02
Sioux (1)	2	0.01
Asian (122)	187	1.23
Not Hispanic (120)	177	1.17
Hispanic (2)	10	0.07
Cambodian (3)	6	0.04
Chinese, ex. Taiwanese (15)	26	0.17
Filipino (7)	20	0.13
Hmong (6)	6	0.04
Indian (35)	44	0.29
Japanese (8)	18	0.12
Korean (13)	22	0.15
Laotian (4)	5	0.03
Pakistani (2)	2	0.01
Sri Lankan (1)	2	0.01
Taiwanese (1)	2	0.01
Vietnamese (18)	22	0.15
Hawaii Native/Pacific Islander (3)	19	0.13
Not Hispanic (3)	15	0.10
Hispanic (0)	4	0.03
Guamanian/Chamorro (0)	3	0.02
Marshallese (3)	3	0.02
Native Hawaiian (0)	3	0.02
White (2,912)	3,079	20.32
Not Hispanic (2,744)	2,880	19.01
Hispanic (168)	199	1.31

Braselton

Place Type: Town
County: Gwinnett
Population: 7,511†

Ancestry‡	Population	%
African, Sub-Saharan (8)	23	0.38
African (8)	23	0.38
American (631)	631	10.33
Arab (0)	101	1.65
Lebanese (0)	101	1.65
Austrian (0)	6	0.10
Belgian (47)	47	0.77
British (18)	21	0.34
Canadian (4)	4	0.07
Czech (0)	22	0.36
Czechoslovakian (0)	12	0.20
Danish (11)	34	0.56
Dutch (12)	38	0.62
English (411)	1,030	16.87
European (47)	47	0.77
Finnish (0)	21	0.34
French, ex. Basque (48)	105	1.72
French Canadian (21)	30	0.49
German (253)	715	11.71
Greek (14)	45	0.74
Hungarian (9)	9	0.15
Iranian (35)	78	1.28
Irish (273)	886	14.51
Israeli (0)	13	0.21
Italian (139)	454	7.43
Norwegian (0)	10	0.16
Polish (50)	74	1.21
Romanian (116)	116	1.90
Russian (2)	49	0.80
Scotch-Irish (76)	143	2.34
Scottish (97)	185	3.03
Slovak (0)	13	0.21
Swedish (0)	12	0.20
Swiss (8)	31	0.51
Welsh (26)	50	0.82
West Indian, ex. Hispanic (0)	16	0.26
Dutch West Indian (0)	16	0.26

Hispanic Origin	Population	%
Hispanic or Latino (of any race)	619	8.24
Central American, ex. Mexican	35	0.47
Costa Rican	4	0.05
Guatemalan	9	0.12
Honduran	6	0.08
Nicaraguan	2	0.03
Panamanian	1	0.01
Salvadoran	13	0.17
Cuban	37	0.49
Dominican Republic	21	0.28
Mexican	194	2.58
Puerto Rican	117	1.56
South American	178	2.37
Argentinean	7	0.09
Bolivian	1	0.01
Chilean	9	0.12
Colombian	120	1.60
Ecuadorian	10	0.13
Paraguayan	1	0.01
Peruvian	15	0.20
Uruguayan	1	0.01
Venezuelan	10	0.13
Other South American	4	0.05
Other Hispanic or Latino	37	0.49

Race*	Population	%
African-American/Black (662)	736	9.80
Not Hispanic (649)	714	9.51
Hispanic (13)	22	0.29
American Indian/Alaska Native (27)	64	0.85
Not Hispanic (13)	40	0.53
Hispanic (14)	24	0.32
Blackfeet (0)	3	0.04
Cherokee (0)	6	0.08
Chickasaw (0)	1	0.01
Chippewa (2)	2	0.03
Choctaw (0)	1	0.01
Creek (2)	6	0.08
Iroquois (0)	1	0.01
Lumbee (3)	3	0.04
Mexican American Ind. (3)	6	0.08
South American Ind. (9)	9	0.12
Ute (0)	1	0.01
Asian (291)	346	4.61
Not Hispanic (280)	329	4.38
Hispanic (11)	17	0.23
Bangladeshi (3)	3	0.04
Chinese, ex. Taiwanese (29)	36	0.48
Filipino (19)	28	0.37
Hmong (54)	54	0.72
Indian (47)	50	0.67
Indonesian (1)	1	0.01
Japanese (8)	18	0.24
Korean (63)	76	1.01
Laotian (2)	4	0.05
Pakistani (5)	5	0.07
Taiwanese (0)	1	0.01
Thai (2)	7	0.09
Vietnamese (47)	51	0.68
Hawaii Native/Pacific Islander (0)	6	0.08
Not Hispanic (0)	2	0.03
Hispanic (0)	4	0.05
Native Hawaiian (0)	3	0.04
White (6,228)	6,347	84.50
Not Hispanic (5,818)	5,914	78.74
Hispanic (410)	433	5.76

Brunswick

Place Type: City
County: Glynn
Population: 15,383†

Ancestry‡	Population	%
African, Sub-Saharan (254)	283	1.83
African (254)	283	1.83
American (741)	741	4.80
Arab (0)	10	0.06
Arab (0)	10	0.06

SECTION TWO

*Notes: † The Census 2010 population figure is used to calculate the percentages in the Hispanic Origin and Race categories. Ancestry percentages are based on the 2006-2010 American Community Survey population (not shown); ‡ Numbers in parentheses indicate the number of people reporting a single ancestry; * Numbers in parentheses indicate the number of persons reporting this race alone, not in combination with any other race; Please refer to the Explanation of Data for more information.*

Austrian (0)	10	0.06
Brazilian (22)	22	0.14
British (13)	43	0.28
Canadian (19)	19	0.12
Czechoslovakian (0)	59	0.38
Dutch (11)	81	0.52
English (160)	586	3.79
European (29)	29	0.19
French, ex. Basque (11)	90	0.58
French Canadian (10)	10	0.06
German (130)	477	3.09
Irish (286)	685	4.43
Italian (67)	225	1.46
Lithuanian (9)	9	0.06
Northern European (13)	13	0.08
Norwegian (8)	8	0.05
Pennsylvania German (17)	30	0.19
Polish (8)	60	0.39
Portuguese (40)	40	0.26
Russian (0)	59	0.38
Scotch-Irish (41)	51	0.33
Scottish (140)	313	2.03
Serbian (0)	10	0.06
Swedish (0)	33	0.21
Swiss (9)	9	0.06
Welsh (15)	27	0.17
West Indian, ex. Hispanic (20)	65	0.42
Belizean (9)	9	0.06
Haitian (0)	28	0.18
Jamaican (11)	28	0.18
Yugoslavian (0)	19	0.12

Hispanic Origin	Population	%
Hispanic or Latino (of any race)	1,733	11.27
Central American, ex. Mexican	117	0.76
Guatemalan	34	0.22
Honduran	41	0.27
Nicaraguan	7	0.05
Panamanian	3	0.02
Salvadoran	31	0.20
Other Central American	1	0.01
Cuban	20	0.13
Dominican Republic	8	0.05
Mexican	1,342	8.72
Puerto Rican	102	0.66
South American	41	0.27
Argentinean	3	0.02
Colombian	2	0.01
Ecuadorian	1	0.01
Peruvian	11	0.07
Uruguayan	23	0.15
Venezuelan	1	0.01
Other Hispanic or Latino	103	0.67

Race*	Population	%
African-American/Black (9,111)	9,301	60.46
Not Hispanic (9,053)	9,225	59.97
Hispanic (58)	76	0.49
American Indian/Alaska Native (53)	136	0.88
Not Hispanic (19)	98	0.64
Hispanic (34)	38	0.25
Apache (1)	1	0.01
Blackfeet (0)	3	0.02
Cherokee (13)	36	0.23
Chippewa (0)	1	0.01
Creek (0)	2	0.01
Inupiat *(Alaska Native)* (0)	1	0.01
Lumbee (0)	1	0.01
Mexican American Ind. (6)	6	0.04
Pueblo (5)	5	0.03
Seminole (0)	1	0.01
Sioux (0)	1	0.01
Spanish American Ind. (1)	1	0.01
Asian (87)	131	0.85
Not Hispanic (77)	115	0.75
Hispanic (10)	16	0.10
Cambodian (1)	1	0.01
Chinese, ex. Taiwanese (4)	18	0.12
Filipino (35)	45	0.29
Indian (20)	28	0.18
Japanese (4)	5	0.03
Korean (5)	11	0.07
Laotian (1)	3	0.02
Malaysian (1)	1	0.01
Pakistani (1)	2	0.01
Thai (1)	4	0.03
Vietnamese (10)	12	0.08
Hawaii Native/Pacific Islander (12)	26	0.17
Not Hispanic (10)	23	0.15
Hispanic (2)	3	0.02
Guamanian/Chamorro (5)	7	0.05
Native Hawaiian (0)	10	0.07
White (4,823)	5,055	32.86
Not Hispanic (4,233)	4,404	28.63
Hispanic (590)	651	4.23

Buford

Place Type: City
County: Gwinnett
Population: 12,225†

Ancestry‡	Population	%
American (1,384)	1,384	11.50
Arab (41)	41	0.34
Palestinian (41)	41	0.34
Armenian (43)	43	0.36
Canadian (13)	13	0.11
Czech (0)	18	0.15
Czechoslovakian (47)	73	0.61
Dutch (0)	80	0.66
English (379)	844	7.01
European (64)	64	0.53
Finnish (0)	17	0.14
French, ex. Basque (0)	141	1.17
French Canadian (11)	11	0.09
German (340)	900	7.48
Greek (0)	28	0.23
Hungarian (17)	17	0.14
Irish (348)	987	8.20
Italian (193)	349	2.90
Norwegian (0)	13	0.11
Polish (17)	65	0.54
Romanian (35)	35	0.29
Russian (115)	155	1.29
Scotch-Irish (22)	138	1.15
Scottish (49)	133	1.11
Swedish (0)	17	0.14
Ukrainian (18)	36	0.30
Welsh (33)	101	0.84
West Indian, ex. Hispanic (124)	132	1.10
Barbadian (8)	8	0.07
Dutch West Indian (0)	8	0.07
Jamaican (101)	101	0.84
West Indian (15)	15	0.12

Hispanic Origin	Population	%
Hispanic or Latino (of any race)	3,122	25.54
Central American, ex. Mexican	301	2.46
Costa Rican	15	0.12
Guatemalan	98	0.80
Honduran	66	0.54
Nicaraguan	4	0.03
Panamanian	3	0.02
Salvadoran	115	0.94
Cuban	41	0.34
Dominican Republic	17	0.14
Mexican	2,392	19.57
Puerto Rican	123	1.01
South American	127	1.04
Argentinean	5	0.04
Chilean	1	0.01
Colombian	60	0.49
Ecuadorian	7	0.06
Peruvian	41	0.34
Uruguayan	6	0.05
Venezuelan	7	0.06
Other Hispanic or Latino	121	0.99

Race*	Population	%
African-American/Black (1,684)	1,820	14.89
Not Hispanic (1,637)	1,743	14.26
Hispanic (47)	77	0.63
American Indian/Alaska Native (35)	83	0.68
Not Hispanic (15)	56	0.46
Hispanic (20)	27	0.22
Blackfeet (0)	4	0.03
Cherokee (3)	19	0.16
Choctaw (1)	2	0.02
Creek (0)	2	0.02
Houma (1)	1	0.01
Mexican American Ind. (6)	6	0.05
Navajo (1)	1	0.01
Sioux (6)	6	0.05
Asian (351)	410	3.35
Not Hispanic (347)	393	3.21
Hispanic (4)	17	0.14
Bangladeshi (2)	2	0.02
Cambodian (3)	3	0.02
Chinese, ex. Taiwanese (30)	36	0.29
Filipino (11)	19	0.16
Hmong (7)	9	0.07
Indian (68)	76	0.62
Indonesian (3)	4	0.03
Japanese (17)	19	0.16
Korean (102)	115	0.94
Laotian (10)	10	0.08
Malaysian (2)	2	0.02
Taiwanese (7)	7	0.06
Thai (6)	14	0.11
Vietnamese (78)	87	0.71
Hawaii Native/Pacific Islander (4)	8	0.07
Not Hispanic (2)	4	0.03
Hispanic (2)	4	0.03
Guamanian/Chamorro (2)	2	0.02
Native Hawaiian (1)	2	0.02
Samoan (1)	1	0.01
White (8,049)	8,316	68.02
Not Hispanic (6,904)	7,068	57.82
Hispanic (1,145)	1,248	10.21

Cairo

Place Type: City
County: Grady
Population: 9,607†

Ancestry‡	Population	%
African, Sub-Saharan (32)	32	0.34
Nigerian (32)	32	0.34
American (743)	743	7.78
Czechoslovakian (0)	13	0.14
Danish (0)	13	0.14
Dutch (0)	100	1.05
English (243)	476	4.99
French, ex. Basque (26)	56	0.59
French Canadian (9)	9	0.09
German (94)	278	2.91
Hungarian (0)	29	0.30
Irish (196)	537	5.62
Italian (13)	73	0.76
Polish (0)	24	0.25
Romanian (0)	29	0.30
Scandinavian (0)	29	0.30
Scotch-Irish (27)	36	0.38
Scottish (24)	45	0.47
Welsh (0)	6	0.06

Hispanic Origin	Population	%
Hispanic or Latino (of any race)	1,384	14.41
Central American, ex. Mexican	308	3.21
Guatemalan	292	3.04
Honduran	2	0.02
Panamanian	6	0.06
Salvadoran	4	0.04
Other Central American	4	0.04
Cuban	6	0.06
Dominican Republic	2	0.02
Mexican	991	10.32

*Notes: † The Census 2010 population figure is used to calculate the percentages in the Hispanic Origin and Race categories. Ancestry percentages are based on the 2006-2010 American Community Survey population (not shown); ‡ Numbers in parentheses indicate the number of people reporting a single ancestry; * Numbers in parentheses indicate the number of persons reporting this race alone, not in combination with any other race; Please refer to the Explanation of Data for more information.*

Puerto Rican	36	0.37
South American	3	0.03
Chilean	3	0.03
Other Hispanic or Latino	38	0.40

Race*	Population	%
African-American/Black (4,627)	4,713	49.06
Not Hispanic (4,601)	4,670	48.61
Hispanic (26)	43	0.45
American Indian/Alaska Native (56)	94	0.98
Not Hispanic (27)	58	0.60
Hispanic (29)	36	0.37
Apache (1)	1	0.01
Blackfeet (1)	4	0.04
Cherokee (2)	13	0.14
Choctaw (0)	1	0.01
Creek (16)	22	0.23
Crow (2)	4	0.04
Inupiat *(Alaska Native)* (0)	1	0.01
Iroquois (0)	1	0.01
Mexican American Ind. (10)	10	0.10
Sioux (0)	3	0.03
Spanish American Ind. (1)	1	0.01
Asian (64)	82	0.85
Not Hispanic (52)	68	0.71
Hispanic (12)	14	0.15
Chinese, ex. Taiwanese (10)	11	0.11
Filipino (6)	9	0.09
Indian (28)	30	0.31
Indonesian (0)	1	0.01
Japanese (0)	1	0.01
Korean (1)	1	0.01
Laotian (0)	1	0.01
Pakistani (5)	5	0.05
Vietnamese (9)	15	0.16
Hawaii Native/Pacific Islander (14)	20	0.21
Not Hispanic (10)	13	0.14
Hispanic (4)	7	0.07
Guamanian/Chamorro (12)	15	0.16
Native Hawaiian (2)	2	0.02
White (3,894)	4,049	42.15
Not Hispanic (3,416)	3,488	36.31
Hispanic (478)	561	5.84

Calhoun

Place Type: City
County: Gordon
Population: 15,650†

Ancestry‡	Population	%
American (1,531)	1,531	10.18
Arab (33)	33	0.22
Jordanian (28)	28	0.19
Lebanese (5)	5	0.03
British (0)	9	0.06
Czech (0)	8	0.05
Danish (39)	39	0.26
Dutch (24)	170	1.13
Eastern European (0)	52	0.35
English (764)	1,287	8.56
European (73)	73	0.49
French, ex. Basque (16)	179	1.19
French Canadian (41)	41	0.27
German (242)	690	4.59
Greek (0)	19	0.13
Hungarian (9)	9	0.06
Irish (555)	1,267	8.42
Italian (192)	225	1.50
Polish (0)	19	0.13
Scotch-Irish (53)	129	0.86
Scottish (161)	287	1.91
Welsh (16)	28	0.19
West Indian, ex. Hispanic (0)	10	0.07
Dutch West Indian (0)	10	0.07

Hispanic Origin	Population	%
Hispanic or Latino (of any race)	3,910	24.98
Central American, ex. Mexican	1,015	6.49
Costa Rican	22	0.14
Guatemalan	784	5.01
Honduran	94	0.60
Nicaraguan	13	0.08
Panamanian	4	0.03
Salvadoran	97	0.62
Other Central American	1	0.01
Cuban	20	0.13
Dominican Republic	3	0.02
Mexican	2,416	15.44
Puerto Rican	81	0.52
South American	49	0.31
Argentinean	2	0.01
Chilean	4	0.03
Colombian	22	0.14
Ecuadorian	6	0.04
Peruvian	12	0.08
Uruguayan	1	0.01
Venezuelan	2	0.01
Other Hispanic or Latino	326	2.08

Race*	Population	%
African-American/Black (1,063)	1,248	7.97
Not Hispanic (1,035)	1,185	7.57
Hispanic (28)	63	0.40
American Indian/Alaska Native (82)	128	0.82
Not Hispanic (45)	81	0.52
Hispanic (37)	47	0.30
Apache (8)	8	0.05
Central American Ind. (0)	3	0.02
Cherokee (12)	32	0.20
Chippewa (1)	1	0.01
Choctaw (2)	2	0.01
Creek (0)	4	0.03
Crow (0)	1	0.01
Lumbee (1)	1	0.01
Mexican American Ind. (9)	16	0.10
Navajo (7)	9	0.06
Sioux (0)	5	0.03
Tlingit-Haida *(Alaska Native)* (2)	2	0.01
Ute (4)	4	0.03
Asian (273)	311	1.99
Not Hispanic (261)	290	1.85
Hispanic (12)	21	0.13
Chinese, ex. Taiwanese (17)	28	0.18
Filipino (14)	14	0.09
Indian (136)	140	0.89
Indonesian (2)	2	0.01
Japanese (10)	10	0.06
Korean (11)	15	0.10
Laotian (0)	2	0.01
Nepalese (1)	1	0.01
Pakistani (16)	18	0.12
Taiwanese (6)	6	0.04
Thai (1)	3	0.02
Vietnamese (52)	71	0.45
Hawaii Native/Pacific Islander (39)	56	0.36
Not Hispanic (24)	33	0.21
Hispanic (15)	23	0.15
Guamanian/Chamorro (30)	34	0.22
Native Hawaiian (6)	12	0.08
Samoan (0)	1	0.01
White (11,472)	11,897	76.02
Not Hispanic (10,127)	10,345	66.10
Hispanic (1,345)	1,552	9.92

Candler-McAfee

Place Type: CDP
County: DeKalb
Population: 23,025†

Ancestry‡	Population	%
African, Sub-Saharan (351)	422	1.80
African (339)	410	1.75
Nigerian (12)	12	0.05
American (334)	334	1.43
Arab (9)	17	0.07
Lebanese (9)	17	0.07
Croatian (0)	11	0.05
Dutch (15)	48	0.21
Eastern European (8)	8	0.03
English (159)	275	1.18
European (37)	160	0.68
French, ex. Basque (12)	18	0.08
German (42)	165	0.71
Irish (6)	112	0.48
Italian (11)	68	0.29
Lithuanian (0)	5	0.02
Polish (7)	12	0.05
Portuguese (0)	14	0.06
Scotch-Irish (14)	67	0.29
Scottish (28)	74	0.32
Swedish (0)	6	0.03
Ukrainian (18)	18	0.08
Welsh (13)	13	0.06
West Indian, ex. Hispanic (195)	264	1.13
Belizean (13)	13	0.06
Haitian (44)	44	0.19
Jamaican (31)	69	0.30
Trinidadian/Tobagonian (50)	50	0.21
U.S. Virgin Islander (43)	43	0.18
West Indian (14)	45	0.19

Hispanic Origin	Population	%
Hispanic or Latino (of any race)	303	1.32
Central American, ex. Mexican	27	0.12
Guatemalan	6	0.03
Honduran	1	<0.01
Panamanian	13	0.06
Salvadoran	7	0.03
Cuban	19	0.08
Dominican Republic	11	0.05
Mexican	101	0.44
Puerto Rican	78	0.34
South American	15	0.07
Colombian	10	0.04
Paraguayan	1	<0.01
Peruvian	4	0.02
Other Hispanic or Latino	52	0.23

Race*	Population	%
African-American/Black (21,030)	21,301	92.51
Not Hispanic (20,926)	21,164	91.92
Hispanic (104)	137	0.60
American Indian/Alaska Native (63)	203	0.88
Not Hispanic (59)	190	0.83
Hispanic (4)	13	0.06
Apache (0)	1	<0.01
Blackfeet (0)	4	0.02
Cherokee (6)	48	0.21
Chickasaw (5)	6	0.03
Chippewa (4)	6	0.03
Choctaw (0)	3	0.01
Creek (2)	2	0.01
Iroquois (1)	1	<0.01
Lumbee (1)	1	<0.01
Ottawa (0)	4	0.02
Pueblo (1)	1	<0.01
Seminole (0)	2	0.01
Sioux (1)	1	<0.01
South American Ind. (1)	5	0.02
Asian (47)	80	0.35
Not Hispanic (47)	79	0.34
Hispanic (0)	1	<0.01
Bangladeshi (1)	1	<0.01
Cambodian (4)	4	0.02
Chinese, ex. Taiwanese (6)	14	0.06
Filipino (2)	3	0.01
Indian (5)	10	0.04
Japanese (1)	5	0.02
Korean (13)	19	0.08
Laotian (0)	2	0.01
Nepalese (2)	2	0.01
Taiwanese (2)	4	0.02
Vietnamese (6)	7	0.03
Hawaii Native/Pacific Islander (7)	10	0.04
Not Hispanic (6)	7	0.03
Hispanic (1)	3	0.01
Guamanian/Chamorro (7)	7	0.03
Native Hawaiian (0)	1	<0.01

SECTION TWO

*Notes: † The Census 2010 population figure is used to calculate the percentages in the Hispanic Origin and Race categories. Ancestry percentages are based on the 2006-2010 American Community Survey population (not shown); ‡ Numbers in parentheses indicate the number of people reporting a single ancestry; * Numbers in parentheses indicate the number of persons reporting this race alone, not in combination with any other race; Please refer to the Explanation of Data for more information.*

Samoan (0)	1	<0.01
White (1,463)	1,623	7.05
Not Hispanic (1,399)	1,545	6.71
Hispanic (64)	78	0.34

Canton

Place Type: City
County: Cherokee
Population: 22,958†

Ancestry‡	Population	%
African, Sub-Saharan (184)	221	1.06
African (114)	151	0.73
Cape Verdean (9)	9	0.04
Kenyan (34)	34	0.16
South African (27)	27	0.13
Albanian (12)	12	0.06
American (1,771)	1,771	8.52
Arab (0)	12	0.06
Egyptian (0)	12	0.06
Austrian (8)	47	0.23
Belgian (4)	4	0.02
Brazilian (11)	11	0.05
British (74)	74	0.36
Canadian (18)	26	0.13
Czech (50)	72	0.35
Czechoslovakian (12)	39	0.19
Dutch (18)	198	0.95
Eastern European (0)	7	0.03
English (903)	2,385	11.48
European (163)	187	0.90
French, ex. Basque (43)	286	1.38
French Canadian (54)	144	0.69
German (672)	2,595	12.49
Greek (9)	28	0.13
Guyanese (45)	45	0.22
Hungarian (0)	47	0.23
Irish (714)	2,464	11.86
Italian (333)	1,099	5.29
Latvian (10)	10	0.05
Lithuanian (0)	8	0.04
Norwegian (27)	165	0.79
Pennsylvania German (11)	11	0.05
Polish (124)	473	2.28
Portuguese (9)	9	0.04
Russian (0)	79	0.38
Scandinavian (11)	11	0.05
Scotch-Irish (293)	687	3.31
Scottish (302)	1,058	5.09
Slovak (0)	13	0.06
Swedish (32)	116	0.56
Swiss (0)	47	0.23
Ukrainian (39)	66	0.32
Welsh (6)	91	0.44
West Indian, ex. Hispanic (106)	106	0.51
Haitian (45)	45	0.22
Jamaican (5)	5	0.02
Trinidadian/Tobagonian (56)	56	0.27
Yugoslavian (44)	266	1.28

Hispanic Origin	Population	%
Hispanic or Latino (of any race)	5,156	22.46
Central American, ex. Mexican	1,638	7.13
Costa Rican	24	0.10
Guatemalan	1,385	6.03
Honduran	71	0.31
Nicaraguan	27	0.12
Panamanian	6	0.03
Salvadoran	115	0.50
Other Central American	10	0.04
Cuban	97	0.42
Dominican Republic	29	0.13
Mexican	2,542	11.07
Puerto Rican	256	1.12
South American	250	1.09
Argentinean	11	0.05
Bolivian	1	<0.01
Chilean	18	0.08
Colombian	102	0.44
Ecuadorian	13	0.06
Peruvian	37	0.16
Uruguayan	5	0.02
Venezuelan	61	0.27
Other South American	2	0.01
Other Hispanic or Latino	344	1.50

Race*	Population	%
African-American/Black (2,045)	2,369	10.32
Not Hispanic (1,991)	2,279	9.93
Hispanic (54)	90	0.39
American Indian/Alaska Native (182)	318	1.39
Not Hispanic (74)	143	0.62
Hispanic (108)	175	0.76
Blackfeet (0)	5	0.02
Central American Ind. (9)	26	0.11
Cherokee (25)	52	0.23
Cheyenne (1)	1	<0.01
Chickasaw (1)	1	<0.01
Chippewa (1)	7	0.03
Choctaw (2)	8	0.03
Creek (1)	2	0.01
Houma (3)	3	0.01
Inupiat *(Alaska Native)* (1)	1	<0.01
Iroquois (1)	1	<0.01
Lumbee (1)	2	0.01
Mexican American Ind. (59)	76	0.33
Navajo (1)	2	0.01
Ottawa (0)	3	0.01
Shoshone (0)	1	<0.01
Sioux (1)	1	<0.01
South American Ind. (0)	2	0.01
Yaqui (1)	1	<0.01
Asian (309)	440	1.92
Not Hispanic (298)	409	1.78
Hispanic (11)	31	0.14
Burmese (3)	3	0.01
Cambodian (1)	1	<0.01
Chinese, ex. Taiwanese (27)	51	0.22
Filipino (56)	81	0.35
Hmong (1)	2	0.01
Indian (84)	95	0.41
Indonesian (7)	8	0.03
Japanese (16)	39	0.17
Korean (28)	44	0.19
Laotian (12)	15	0.07
Pakistani (10)	12	0.05
Sri Lankan (1)	1	<0.01
Taiwanese (2)	2	0.01
Thai (11)	13	0.06
Vietnamese (34)	48	0.21
Hawaii Native/Pacific Islander (55)	83	0.36
Not Hispanic (21)	36	0.16
Hispanic (34)	47	0.20
Guamanian/Chamorro (46)	59	0.26
Native Hawaiian (6)	10	0.04
Samoan (2)	4	0.02
White (17,354)	17,915	78.03
Not Hispanic (14,913)	15,301	66.65
Hispanic (2,441)	2,614	11.39

Carrollton

Place Type: City
County: Carroll
Population: 24,388†

Ancestry‡	Population	%
African, Sub-Saharan (154)	202	0.83
African (62)	110	0.45
Kenyan (15)	15	0.06
Nigerian (61)	61	0.25
Sudanese (16)	16	0.07
American (3,873)	3,873	16.01
Arab (7)	23	0.10
Lebanese (0)	16	0.07
Other Arab (7)	7	0.03
Austrian (11)	11	0.05
Belgian (0)	7	0.03
British (45)	155	0.64
Bulgarian (0)	14	0.06
Carpatho Rusyn (0)	10	0.04
Croatian (0)	10	0.04
Czech (0)	78	0.32
Czechoslovakian (0)	13	0.05
Danish (0)	16	0.07
Dutch (8)	237	0.98
Eastern European (35)	35	0.14
English (799)	1,649	6.82
European (530)	547	2.26
French, ex. Basque (47)	307	1.27
French Canadian (10)	47	0.19
German (414)	1,469	6.07
Greek (21)	110	0.45
Hungarian (0)	84	0.35
Irish (778)	1,920	7.94
Italian (153)	424	1.75
Lithuanian (0)	11	0.05
Northern European (58)	58	0.24
Norwegian (20)	20	0.08
Polish (29)	136	0.56
Portuguese (16)	29	0.12
Scotch-Irish (281)	401	1.66
Scottish (202)	480	1.98
Swedish (7)	56	0.23
Swiss (0)	9	0.04
Turkish (34)	34	0.14
Welsh (83)	83	0.34
West Indian, ex. Hispanic (92)	112	0.46
British West Indian (28)	28	0.12
Jamaican (45)	65	0.27
Trinidadian/Tobagonian (19)	19	0.08

Hispanic Origin	Population	%
Hispanic or Latino (of any race)	2,633	10.80
Central American, ex. Mexican	1,102	4.52
Costa Rican	12	0.05
Guatemalan	197	0.81
Honduran	660	2.71
Nicaraguan	143	0.59
Panamanian	5	0.02
Salvadoran	81	0.33
Other Central American	4	0.02
Cuban	43	0.18
Dominican Republic	18	0.07
Mexican	1,069	4.38
Puerto Rican	125	0.51
South American	64	0.26
Argentinean	2	0.01
Bolivian	4	0.02
Chilean	9	0.04
Colombian	26	0.11
Ecuadorian	5	0.02
Peruvian	15	0.06
Uruguayan	1	<0.01
Venezuelan	2	0.01
Other Hispanic or Latino	212	0.87

Race*	Population	%
African-American/Black (7,773)	8,183	33.55
Not Hispanic (7,668)	8,000	32.80
Hispanic (105)	183	0.75
American Indian/Alaska Native (101)	240	0.98
Not Hispanic (57)	167	0.68
Hispanic (44)	73	0.30
Blackfeet (0)	4	0.02
Central American Ind. (12)	14	0.06
Cherokee (14)	51	0.21
Choctaw (1)	5	0.02
Comanche (0)	1	<0.01
Creek (0)	4	0.02
Kiowa (0)	1	<0.01
Lumbee (1)	1	<0.01
Mexican American Ind. (3)	3	0.01
Navajo (0)	1	<0.01
Osage (3)	3	0.01
Potawatomi (0)	4	0.02
Seminole (1)	2	0.01
Sioux (0)	2	0.01
South American Ind. (2)	2	0.01

*Notes: † The Census 2010 population figure is used to calculate the percentages in the Hispanic Origin and Race categories. Ancestry percentages are based on the 2006-2010 American Community Survey population (not shown); ‡ Numbers in parentheses indicate the number of people reporting a single ancestry; * Numbers in parentheses indicate the number of persons reporting this race alone, not in combination with any other race; Please refer to the Explanation of Data for more information.*

	Population	%
Spanish American Ind. (0)	2	0.01
Yup'ik *(Alaska Native)* (0)	2	0.01
Asian (346)	448	1.84
Not Hispanic (337)	438	1.80
Hispanic (9)	10	0.04
Bangladeshi (1)	1	<0.01
Cambodian (3)	6	0.02
Chinese, ex. Taiwanese (49)	60	0.25
Filipino (18)	44	0.18
Indian (152)	176	0.72
Indonesian (3)	4	0.02
Japanese (17)	24	0.10
Korean (26)	51	0.21
Laotian (6)	6	0.02
Pakistani (16)	19	0.08
Sri Lankan (4)	6	0.02
Taiwanese (12)	12	0.05
Thai (2)	3	0.01
Vietnamese (13)	18	0.07
Hawaii Native/Pacific Islander (9)	36	0.15
Not Hispanic (6)	25	0.10
Hispanic (3)	11	0.05
Fijian (1)	1	<0.01
Guamanian/Chamorro (0)	3	0.01
Marshallese (1)	1	<0.01
Native Hawaiian (2)	12	0.05
Tongan (0)	2	0.01
White (14,249)	14,812	60.73
Not Hispanic (13,143)	13,560	55.60
Hispanic (1,106)	1,252	5.13

Cartersville

Place Type: City
County: Bartow
Population: 19,731†

Ancestry‡	Population	%
African, Sub-Saharan (124)	124	0.64
African (64)	64	0.33
Nigerian (60)	60	0.31
American (2,498)	2,498	12.93
Austrian (28)	28	0.14
Belgian (306)	306	1.58
Brazilian (12)	12	0.06
British (37)	58	0.30
Canadian (0)	13	0.07
Danish (0)	23	0.12
Dutch (17)	232	1.20
Eastern European (11)	11	0.06
English (1,012)	1,955	10.12
European (195)	195	1.01
Finnish (0)	16	0.08
French, ex. Basque (106)	161	0.83
French Canadian (0)	17	0.09
German (546)	1,289	6.67
Greek (10)	27	0.14
Hungarian (12)	12	0.06
Irish (899)	1,738	8.99
Italian (149)	186	0.96
Lithuanian (0)	14	0.07
Norwegian (19)	90	0.47
Pennsylvania German (9)	9	0.05
Polish (11)	40	0.21
Russian (24)	105	0.54
Scandinavian (13)	13	0.07
Scotch-Irish (346)	478	2.47
Scottish (249)	354	1.83
Slovak (26)	38	0.20
Swedish (12)	12	0.06
Swiss (0)	25	0.13
Welsh (33)	118	0.61
West Indian, ex. Hispanic (0)	15	0.08
Jamaican (0)	15	0.08

Hispanic Origin	Population	%
Hispanic or Latino (of any race)	2,505	12.70
Central American, ex. Mexican	349	1.77
Costa Rican	4	0.02
Guatemalan	211	1.07
Honduran	54	0.27
Nicaraguan	8	0.04
Panamanian	1	0.01
Salvadoran	70	0.35
Other Central American	1	0.01
Cuban	26	0.13
Dominican Republic	6	0.03
Mexican	1,821	9.23
Puerto Rican	108	0.55
South American	45	0.23
Argentinean	1	0.01
Chilean	2	0.01
Colombian	13	0.07
Ecuadorian	20	0.10
Peruvian	1	0.01
Uruguayan	4	0.02
Venezuelan	4	0.02
Other Hispanic or Latino	150	0.76

Race*	Population	%
African-American/Black (3,648)	3,875	19.64
Not Hispanic (3,592)	3,800	19.26
Hispanic (56)	75	0.38
American Indian/Alaska Native (77)	260	1.32
Not Hispanic (45)	131	0.66
Hispanic (32)	129	0.65
Blackfeet (0)	1	0.01
Cherokee (16)	53	0.27
Choctaw (1)	2	0.01
Iroquois (1)	1	0.01
Lumbee (2)	2	0.01
Mexican American Ind. (12)	13	0.07
Pima (1)	1	0.01
Seminole (0)	3	0.02
Sioux (0)	1	0.01
Yaqui (0)	1	0.01
Yuman (0)	1	0.01
Asian (206)	263	1.33
Not Hispanic (196)	246	1.25
Hispanic (10)	17	0.09
Bangladeshi (2)	2	0.01
Chinese, ex. Taiwanese (34)	42	0.21
Filipino (20)	35	0.18
Indian (67)	86	0.44
Japanese (15)	18	0.09
Korean (16)	20	0.10
Laotian (3)	3	0.02
Pakistani (8)	13	0.07
Taiwanese (1)	1	0.01
Thai (2)	3	0.02
Vietnamese (25)	31	0.16
Hawaii Native/Pacific Islander (43)	55	0.28
Not Hispanic (42)	50	0.25
Hispanic (1)	5	0.03
Guamanian/Chamorro (9)	13	0.07
Native Hawaiian (8)	9	0.05
White (13,979)	14,466	73.32
Not Hispanic (13,003)	13,305	67.43
Hispanic (976)	1,161	5.88

Cedartown

Place Type: City
County: Polk
Population: 9,750†

Ancestry‡	Population	%
African, Sub-Saharan (20)	20	0.20
African (20)	20	0.20
American (781)	781	7.98
Austrian (0)	13	0.13
British (14)	14	0.14
Canadian (0)	53	0.54
Celtic (0)	11	0.11
Danish (0)	51	0.52
Dutch (0)	73	0.75
English (347)	672	6.86
European (64)	93	0.95
French, ex. Basque (11)	11	0.11
French Canadian (0)	13	0.13
German (117)	410	4.19
Irish (614)	1,186	12.11
Italian (36)	203	2.07
Scotch-Irish (94)	200	2.04
Scottish (86)	156	1.59
Welsh (16)	16	0.16
West Indian, ex. Hispanic (70)	70	0.71
Haitian (70)	70	0.71

Hispanic Origin	Population	%
Hispanic or Latino (of any race)	3,026	31.04
Central American, ex. Mexican	910	9.33
Guatemalan	895	9.18
Honduran	2	0.02
Nicaraguan	1	0.01
Panamanian	1	0.01
Salvadoran	10	0.10
Other Central American	1	0.01
Cuban	4	0.04
Dominican Republic	1	0.01
Mexican	1,823	18.70
Puerto Rican	17	0.17
South American	3	0.03
Colombian	2	0.02
Peruvian	1	0.01
Other Hispanic or Latino	268	2.75

Race*	Population	%
African-American/Black (1,829)	1,910	19.59
Not Hispanic (1,817)	1,885	19.33
Hispanic (12)	25	0.26
American Indian/Alaska Native (44)	107	1.10
Not Hispanic (25)	68	0.70
Hispanic (19)	39	0.40
Apache (3)	3	0.03
Central American Ind. (0)	5	0.05
Cherokee (11)	33	0.34
Comanche (0)	1	0.01
Creek (1)	1	0.01
Delaware (3)	5	0.05
Mexican American Ind. (6)	11	0.11
Navajo (0)	1	0.01
Spanish American Ind. (0)	1	0.01
Asian (98)	116	1.19
Not Hispanic (98)	116	1.19
Chinese, ex. Taiwanese (12)	14	0.14
Filipino (2)	4	0.04
Indian (65)	70	0.72
Japanese (1)	8	0.08
Korean (2)	5	0.05
Thai (0)	1	0.01
Vietnamese (14)	14	0.14
Hawaii Native/Pacific Islander (23)	31	0.32
Not Hispanic (10)	16	0.16
Hispanic (13)	15	0.15
Guamanian/Chamorro (23)	29	0.30
White (5,512)	5,696	58.42
Not Hispanic (4,629)	4,746	48.68
Hispanic (883)	950	9.74

Chamblee

Place Type: City
County: DeKalb
Population: 9,892†

Ancestry‡	Population	%
African, Sub-Saharan (156)	156	1.60
Ethiopian (51)	51	0.52
Other Sub-Saharan African (105)	105	1.08
American (100)	100	1.03
Arab (18)	18	0.18
Moroccan (18)	18	0.18
Belgian (0)	7	0.07
British (41)	199	2.04
Czech (0)	13	0.13
Dutch (15)	30	0.31
English (201)	776	7.96
European (152)	152	1.56
Finnish (34)	129	1.32

SECTION TWO

*Notes: † The Census 2010 population figure is used to calculate the percentages in the Hispanic Origin and Race categories. Ancestry percentages are based on the 2006-2010 American Community Survey population (not shown); ‡ Numbers in parentheses indicate the number of people reporting a single ancestry; * Numbers in parentheses indicate the number of persons reporting this race alone, not in combination with any other race; Please refer to the Explanation of Data for more information.*

Ancestry	Population	%
French, ex. Basque (24)	92	0.94
German (178)	663	6.80
Greek (13)	42	0.43
Hungarian (0)	16	0.16
Irish (138)	647	6.64
Italian (111)	187	1.92
Norwegian (0)	11	0.11
Polish (24)	43	0.44
Russian (62)	95	0.97
Scotch-Irish (53)	97	0.99
Scottish (10)	98	1.01
Serbian (0)	65	0.67
Ukrainian (9)	80	0.82
Welsh (0)	13	0.13
West Indian, ex. Hispanic (19)	19	0.19
Trinidadian/Tobagonian (19)	19	0.19

Hispanic Origin	Population	%
Hispanic or Latino (of any race)	5,782	58.45
Central American, ex. Mexican	3,521	35.59
Costa Rican	2	0.02
Guatemalan	3,056	30.89
Honduran	208	2.10
Nicaraguan	11	0.11
Panamanian	9	0.09
Salvadoran	166	1.68
Other Central American	69	0.70
Cuban	28	0.28
Dominican Republic	26	0.26
Mexican	1,740	17.59
Puerto Rican	47	0.48
South American	126	1.27
Argentinean	3	0.03
Bolivian	1	0.01
Chilean	1	0.01
Colombian	29	0.29
Ecuadorian	45	0.45
Peruvian	20	0.20
Uruguayan	5	0.05
Venezuelan	15	0.15
Other South American	7	0.07
Other Hispanic or Latino	294	2.97

Race*	Population	%
African-American/Black (697)	755	7.63
Not Hispanic (617)	652	6.59
Hispanic (80)	103	1.04
American Indian/Alaska Native (206)	296	2.99
Not Hispanic (15)	39	0.39
Hispanic (191)	257	2.60
Arapaho (1)	1	0.01
Blackfeet (0)	1	0.01
Central American Ind. (57)	57	0.58
Cherokee (1)	9	0.09
Chippewa (1)	1	0.01
Choctaw (2)	2	0.02
Kiowa (2)	2	0.02
Mexican American Ind. (86)	106	1.07
South American Ind. (0)	5	0.05
Spanish American Ind. (6)	6	0.06
Asian (795)	858	8.67
Not Hispanic (781)	831	8.40
Hispanic (14)	27	0.27
Bangladeshi (114)	127	1.28
Cambodian (11)	11	0.11
Chinese, ex. Taiwanese (131)	135	1.36
Filipino (28)	36	0.36
Indian (159)	171	1.73
Indonesian (17)	20	0.20
Japanese (11)	15	0.15
Korean (81)	92	0.93
Laotian (1)	1	0.01
Malaysian (1)	1	0.01
Pakistani (8)	8	0.08
Taiwanese (10)	10	0.10
Thai (4)	6	0.06
Vietnamese (179)	189	1.91
Hawaii Native/Pacific Islander (3)	14	0.14
Not Hispanic (3)	5	0.05
Hispanic (0)	9	0.09
Guamanian/Chamorro (0)	2	0.02
Native Hawaiian (0)	1	0.01
White (4,465)	4,780	48.32
Not Hispanic (2,587)	2,646	26.75
Hispanic (1,878)	2,134	21.57

Clarkston

Place Type: City
County: DeKalb
Population: 7,554†

Ancestry‡	Population	%
African, Sub-Saharan (2,273)	2,338	30.95
African (475)	475	6.29
Ethiopian (759)	824	10.91
Somalian (89)	89	1.18
South African (267)	267	3.53
Sudanese (144)	144	1.91
Other Sub-Saharan African (539)	539	7.13
American (86)	86	1.14
Arab (9)	9	0.12
Other Arab (9)	9	0.12
Czechoslovakian (18)	18	0.24
Dutch (0)	48	0.64
English (155)	232	3.07
European (15)	15	0.20
French, ex. Basque (0)	40	0.53
German (29)	76	1.01
Irish (25)	102	1.35
Italian (0)	28	0.37
Scotch-Irish (49)	77	1.02
Scottish (31)	37	0.49
Ukrainian (8)	8	0.11
West Indian, ex. Hispanic (336)	336	4.45
Jamaican (310)	310	4.10
Trinidadian/Tobagonian (8)	8	0.11
West Indian (18)	18	0.24

Hispanic Origin	Population	%
Hispanic or Latino (of any race)	211	2.79
Central American, ex. Mexican	53	0.70
Costa Rican	1	0.01
Guatemalan	25	0.33
Panamanian	8	0.11
Salvadoran	19	0.25
Cuban	33	0.44
Dominican Republic	3	0.04
Mexican	53	0.70
Puerto Rican	35	0.46
South American	17	0.23
Colombian	5	0.07
Peruvian	10	0.13
Venezuelan	2	0.03
Other Hispanic or Latino	17	0.23

Race*	Population	%
African-American/Black (4,413)	4,536	60.05
Not Hispanic (4,373)	4,487	59.40
Hispanic (40)	49	0.65
American Indian/Alaska Native (12)	57	0.75
Not Hispanic (11)	51	0.68
Hispanic (1)	6	0.08
Apache (0)	4	0.05
Blackfeet (0)	3	0.04
Central American Ind. (1)	1	0.01
Cherokee (1)	14	0.19
Choctaw (0)	1	0.01
Mexican American Ind. (0)	2	0.03
South American Ind. (0)	1	0.01
Asian (1,632)	1,827	24.19
Not Hispanic (1,617)	1,810	23.96
Hispanic (15)	17	0.23
Bhutanese (217)	530	7.02
Burmese (458)	501	6.63
Cambodian (11)	14	0.19
Chinese, ex. Taiwanese (19)	28	0.37
Filipino (7)	21	0.28
Indian (70)	104	1.38
Indonesian (1)	1	0.01
Japanese (0)	2	0.03
Korean (3)	10	0.13
Laotian (3)	3	0.04
Malaysian (6)	6	0.08
Nepalese (80)	381	5.04
Pakistani (6)	6	0.08
Sri Lankan (5)	5	0.07
Thai (14)	18	0.24
Vietnamese (361)	372	4.92
Hawaii Native/Pacific Islander (3)	12	0.16
Not Hispanic (3)	11	0.15
Hispanic (0)	1	0.01
Guamanian/Chamorro (0)	1	0.01
Samoan (3)	3	0.04
White (1,027)	1,237	16.38
Not Hispanic (990)	1,193	15.79
Hispanic (37)	44	0.58

College Park

Place Type: City
County: Fulton
Population: 13,942†

Ancestry‡	Population	%
African, Sub-Saharan (806)	810	5.80
African (626)	630	4.51
Ghanaian (180)	180	1.29
American (334)	334	2.39
Arab (49)	49	0.35
Arab (34)	34	0.24
Moroccan (15)	15	0.11
British (25)	75	0.54
Dutch (43)	43	0.31
English (109)	349	2.50
French, ex. Basque (0)	101	0.72
French Canadian (9)	9	0.06
German (62)	255	1.82
Hungarian (11)	11	0.08
Irish (115)	403	2.88
Italian (10)	61	0.44
Lithuanian (0)	45	0.32
Luxemburger (47)	47	0.34
Polish (24)	76	0.54
Romanian (0)	7	0.05
Russian (16)	78	0.56
Scotch-Irish (154)	214	1.53
Swedish (0)	17	0.12
West Indian, ex. Hispanic (336)	380	2.72
Jamaican (126)	170	1.22
Trinidadian/Tobagonian (35)	35	0.25
U.S. Virgin Islander (15)	15	0.11
West Indian (160)	160	1.14

Hispanic Origin	Population	%
Hispanic or Latino (of any race)	963	6.91
Central American, ex. Mexican	137	0.98
Costa Rican	4	0.03
Guatemalan	14	0.10
Honduran	66	0.47
Nicaraguan	1	0.01
Panamanian	11	0.08
Salvadoran	41	0.29
Cuban	20	0.14
Dominican Republic	23	0.16
Mexican	583	4.18
Puerto Rican	85	0.61
South American	20	0.14
Argentinean	4	0.03
Colombian	10	0.07
Ecuadorian	1	0.01
Paraguayan	1	0.01
Uruguayan	1	0.01
Venezuelan	1	0.01
Other South American	2	0.01
Other Hispanic or Latino	95	0.68

Race*	Population	%
African-American/Black (11,073)	11,312	81.14
Not Hispanic (10,950)	11,149	79.97

*Notes: † The Census 2010 population figure is used to calculate the percentages in the Hispanic Origin and Race categories. Ancestry percentages are based on the 2006-2010 American Community Survey population (not shown); ‡ Numbers in parentheses indicate the number of people reporting a single ancestry; * Numbers in parentheses indicate the number of persons reporting this race alone, not in combination with any other race; Please refer to the Explanation of Data for more information.*

Hispanic (123)	163	1.17
American Indian/Alaska Native (56)	168	1.20
Not Hispanic (36)	141	1.01
Hispanic (20)	27	0.19
Blackfeet (2)	5	0.04
Central American Ind. (0)	2	0.01
Cherokee (5)	31	0.22
Choctaw (0)	7	0.05
Creek (0)	1	0.01
Houma (3)	3	0.02
Iroquois (0)	3	0.02
Lumbee (1)	1	0.01
Mexican American Ind. (0)	2	0.01
Seminole (1)	3	0.02
Sioux (0)	1	0.01
South American Ind. (4)	5	0.04
Asian (126)	148	1.06
Not Hispanic (121)	143	1.03
Hispanic (5)	5	0.04
Bangladeshi (1)	1	0.01
Burmese (5)	5	0.04
Cambodian (10)	10	0.07
Chinese, ex. Taiwanese (16)	23	0.16
Filipino (19)	28	0.20
Indian (31)	34	0.24
Japanese (1)	3	0.02
Korean (3)	5	0.04
Laotian (4)	6	0.04
Nepalese (1)	1	0.01
Pakistani (6)	6	0.04
Taiwanese (1)	1	0.01
Thai (4)	5	0.04
Vietnamese (6)	13	0.09
Hawaii Native/Pacific Islander (5)	16	0.11
Not Hispanic (4)	14	0.10
Hispanic (1)	2	0.01
Guamanian/Chamorro (1)	1	0.01
Native Hawaiian (0)	3	0.02
Samoan (1)	1	0.01
White (1,814)	1,965	14.09
Not Hispanic (1,612)	1,735	12.44
Hispanic (202)	230	1.65

Columbus

Place Type: City
County: Muscogee
Population: 189,885†

Ancestry‡	Population	%
Afghan (25)	25	0.01
African, Sub-Saharan (1,203)	1,488	0.79
African (874)	1,152	0.61
Cape Verdean (18)	18	0.01
Ethiopian (58)	58	0.03
Liberian (0)	7	<0.01
Nigerian (207)	207	0.11
Other Sub-Saharan African (46)	46	0.02
Albanian (22)	22	0.01
American (11,893)	11,893	6.34
Arab (54)	121	0.06
Lebanese (51)	105	0.06
Syrian (3)	16	0.01
Armenian (0)	23	0.01
Assyrian/Chaldean/Syriac (8)	23	0.01
Australian (16)	82	0.04
Austrian (84)	174	0.09
Belgian (0)	22	0.01
Brazilian (34)	60	0.03
British (395)	735	0.39
Bulgarian (10)	42	0.02
Cajun (6)	20	0.01
Canadian (90)	291	0.16
Celtic (0)	55	0.03
Croatian (15)	27	0.01
Czech (33)	327	0.17
Czechoslovakian (0)	48	0.03
Danish (77)	169	0.09
Dutch (269)	1,425	0.76
Eastern European (57)	64	0.03
English (6,082)	12,631	6.73
Estonian (12)	12	0.01
European (1,164)	1,365	0.73
Finnish (22)	129	0.07
French, ex. Basque (708)	3,337	1.78
French Canadian (139)	301	0.16
German (5,034)	15,682	8.36
German Russian (13)	13	0.01
Greek (58)	222	0.12
Guyanese (29)	29	0.02
Hungarian (72)	262	0.14
Iranian (92)	92	0.05
Irish (5,929)	16,352	8.72
Italian (1,489)	4,044	2.16
Latvian (0)	11	0.01
Lithuanian (40)	108	0.06
Luxemburger (10)	10	0.01
Maltese (7)	7	<0.01
Northern European (52)	52	0.03
Norwegian (248)	536	0.29
Polish (796)	1,952	1.04
Portuguese (100)	402	0.21
Romanian (22)	62	0.03
Russian (252)	494	0.26
Scandinavian (45)	162	0.09
Scotch-Irish (1,516)	3,256	1.74
Scottish (1,200)	2,983	1.59
Serbian (11)	11	0.01
Slavic (0)	22	0.01
Slovak (18)	45	0.02
Slovene (9)	37	0.02
Swedish (314)	786	0.42
Swiss (21)	268	0.14
Turkish (34)	100	0.05
Ukrainian (49)	160	0.09
Welsh (181)	804	0.43
West Indian, ex. Hispanic (684)	1,397	0.74
Belizean (14)	14	0.01
Dutch West Indian (0)	30	0.02
Haitian (154)	318	0.17
Jamaican (277)	598	0.32
Trinidadian/Tobagonian (48)	99	0.05
U.S. Virgin Islander (31)	71	0.04
West Indian (160)	267	0.14
Yugoslavian (0)	65	0.03

Hispanic Origin	Population	%
Hispanic or Latino (of any race)	12,110	6.38
Central American, ex. Mexican	1,585	0.83
Costa Rican	33	0.02
Guatemalan	464	0.24
Honduran	186	0.10
Nicaraguan	80	0.04
Panamanian	696	0.37
Salvadoran	125	0.07
Other Central American	1	<0.01
Cuban	328	0.17
Dominican Republic	275	0.14
Mexican	4,792	2.52
Puerto Rican	3,301	1.74
South American	652	0.34
Argentinean	36	0.02
Bolivian	22	0.01
Chilean	28	0.01
Colombian	336	0.18
Ecuadorian	63	0.03
Paraguayan	15	0.01
Peruvian	107	0.06
Uruguayan	14	0.01
Venezuelan	21	0.01
Other South American	10	0.01
Other Hispanic or Latino	1,177	0.62

Race*	Population	%
African-American/Black (86,403)	89,897	47.34
Not Hispanic (85,119)	87,921	46.30
Hispanic (1,284)	1,976	1.04
American Indian/Alaska Native (731)	1,963	1.03
Not Hispanic (599)	1,612	0.85
Hispanic (132)	351	0.18
Alaska Athabascan *(Ala. Nat.)* (3)	6	<0.01
Aleut *(Alaska Native)* (1)	2	<0.01
Apache (6)	34	0.02
Blackfeet (7)	48	0.03
Central American Ind. (9)	16	0.01
Cherokee (136)	490	0.26
Cheyenne (0)	2	<0.01
Chickasaw (6)	9	<0.01
Chippewa (17)	25	0.01
Choctaw (14)	44	0.02
Comanche (0)	5	<0.01
Cree (1)	1	<0.01
Creek (31)	91	0.05
Crow (2)	2	<0.01
Delaware (0)	2	<0.01
Hopi (0)	1	<0.01
Houma (1)	2	<0.01
Inupiat *(Alaska Native)* (0)	7	<0.01
Iroquois (3)	17	0.01
Kiowa (0)	1	<0.01
Lumbee (11)	18	0.01
Menominee (5)	5	<0.01
Mexican American Ind. (32)	51	0.03
Navajo (24)	33	0.02
Paiute (3)	5	<0.01
Potawatomi (1)	3	<0.01
Pueblo (6)	7	<0.01
Puget Sound Salish (2)	3	<0.01
Seminole (2)	24	0.01
Sioux (14)	29	0.02
South American Ind. (6)	10	0.01
Spanish American Ind. (4)	4	<0.01
Yaqui (0)	4	<0.01
Yup'ik *(Alaska Native)* (1)	3	<0.01
Asian (4,128)	5,638	2.97
Not Hispanic (4,061)	5,378	2.83
Hispanic (67)	260	0.14
Bangladeshi (6)	7	<0.01
Burmese (8)	16	0.01
Cambodian (35)	46	0.02
Chinese, ex. Taiwanese (321)	482	0.25
Filipino (653)	1,058	0.56
Hmong (4)	4	<0.01
Indian (1,204)	1,341	0.71
Indonesian (29)	36	0.02
Japanese (219)	450	0.24
Korean (910)	1,398	0.74
Laotian (16)	20	0.01
Malaysian (3)	3	<0.01
Nepalese (8)	9	<0.01
Pakistani (94)	104	0.05
Sri Lankan (16)	19	0.01
Taiwanese (15)	21	0.01
Thai (69)	105	0.06
Vietnamese (373)	462	0.24
Hawaii Native/Pacific Islander (431)	778	0.41
Not Hispanic (378)	645	0.34
Hispanic (53)	133	0.07
Fijian (1)	3	<0.01
Guamanian/Chamorro (161)	247	0.13
Marshallese (11)	12	0.01
Native Hawaiian (82)	234	0.12
Samoan (118)	188	0.10
Tongan (1)	4	<0.01
White (87,870)	92,267	48.59
Not Hispanic (82,890)	86,267	45.43
Hispanic (4,980)	6,000	3.16

Conyers

Place Type: City
County: Rockdale
Population: 15,195†

Ancestry‡	Population	%
African, Sub-Saharan (80)	80	0.55
African (55)	55	0.38
Nigerian (25)	25	0.17
American (1,311)	1,311	9.00
Arab (18)	18	0.12

*Notes: † The Census 2010 population figure is used to calculate the percentages in the Hispanic Origin and Race categories. Ancestry percentages are based on the 2006-2010 American Community Survey population (not shown); ‡ Numbers in parentheses indicate the number of people reporting a single ancestry; * Numbers in parentheses indicate the number of persons reporting this race alone, not in combination with any other race; Please refer to the Explanation of Data for more information.*

Ancestry	Population	%
Arab (18)	18	0.12
Belgian (15)	15	0.10
British (25)	56	0.38
Canadian (27)	27	0.19
Czech (0)	37	0.25
Czechoslovakian (0)	21	0.14
Danish (15)	15	0.10
Dutch (0)	155	1.06
English (255)	639	4.38
French, ex. Basque (42)	159	1.09
German (429)	1,026	7.04
Guyanese (51)	51	0.35
Irish (236)	764	5.24
Italian (38)	128	0.88
Norwegian (0)	68	0.47
Polish (88)	110	0.75
Romanian (11)	11	0.08
Scotch-Irish (41)	71	0.49
Scottish (13)	121	0.83
Slovak (0)	15	0.10
Swiss (0)	28	0.19
Welsh (13)	75	0.51
West Indian, ex. Hispanic (388)	670	4.60
Haitian (48)	120	0.82
Jamaican (340)	503	3.45
U.S. Virgin Islander (0)	38	0.26
West Indian (0)	9	0.06

Hispanic Origin	Population	%
Hispanic or Latino (of any race)	2,475	16.29
Central American, ex. Mexican	126	0.83
Costa Rican	10	0.07
Guatemalan	24	0.16
Honduran	31	0.20
Nicaraguan	26	0.17
Panamanian	20	0.13
Salvadoran	15	0.10
Cuban	35	0.23
Dominican Republic	22	0.14
Mexican	1,975	13.00
Puerto Rican	124	0.82
South American	45	0.30
Argentinean	1	0.01
Chilean	3	0.02
Colombian	19	0.13
Ecuadorian	4	0.03
Peruvian	3	0.02
Uruguayan	7	0.05
Venezuelan	7	0.05
Other South American	1	0.01
Other Hispanic or Latino	148	0.97

Race*	Population	%
African-American/Black (8,598)	8,833	58.13
Not Hispanic (8,474)	8,662	57.01
Hispanic (124)	171	1.13
American Indian/Alaska Native (46)	113	0.74
Not Hispanic (32)	88	0.58
Hispanic (14)	25	0.16
Blackfeet (0)	6	0.04
Canadian/French Am. Ind. (0)	1	0.01
Cherokee (5)	30	0.20
Choctaw (1)	1	0.01
Creek (1)	2	0.01
Delaware (0)	2	0.01
Inupiat *(Alaska Native)* (0)	1	0.01
Mexican American Ind. (2)	2	0.01
Pueblo (1)	1	0.01
Shoshone (0)	1	0.01
Asian (213)	260	1.71
Not Hispanic (210)	251	1.65
Hispanic (3)	9	0.06
Bangladeshi (2)	2	0.01
Cambodian (21)	22	0.14
Chinese, ex. Taiwanese (23)	34	0.22
Filipino (25)	31	0.20
Hmong (2)	2	0.01
Indian (87)	97	0.64
Japanese (2)	9	0.06
Korean (21)	24	0.16
Laotian (1)	1	0.01
Thai (2)	2	0.01
Vietnamese (16)	18	0.12
Hawaii Native/Pacific Islander (17)	34	0.22
Not Hispanic (16)	31	0.20
Hispanic (1)	3	0.02
Guamanian/Chamorro (1)	1	0.01
Native Hawaiian (0)	3	0.02
Samoan (3)	8	0.05
White (4,539)	4,780	31.46
Not Hispanic (3,699)	3,870	25.47
Hispanic (840)	910	5.99

Cordele

Place Type: City
County: Crisp
Population: 11,147†

Ancestry‡	Population	%
African, Sub-Saharan (379)	379	3.38
African (379)	379	3.38
American (431)	431	3.84
Austrian (0)	11	0.10
British (13)	13	0.12
Canadian (0)	16	0.14
Czech (113)	113	1.01
Dutch (0)	33	0.29
English (227)	431	3.84
European (12)	12	0.11
French, ex. Basque (32)	50	0.45
German (68)	222	1.98
Hungarian (0)	11	0.10
Irish (115)	517	4.61
Italian (0)	53	0.47
Scotch-Irish (55)	64	0.57
Scottish (14)	32	0.29
West Indian, ex. Hispanic (0)	31	0.28
Dutch West Indian (0)	31	0.28

Hispanic Origin	Population	%
Hispanic or Latino (of any race)	369	3.31
Central American, ex. Mexican	24	0.22
Guatemalan	21	0.19
Salvadoran	3	0.03
Cuban	41	0.37
Dominican Republic	7	0.06
Mexican	249	2.23
Puerto Rican	12	0.11
South American	4	0.04
Colombian	4	0.04
Other Hispanic or Latino	32	0.29

Race*	Population	%
African-American/Black (7,419)	7,502	67.30
Not Hispanic (7,387)	7,469	67.00
Hispanic (32)	33	0.30
American Indian/Alaska Native (13)	38	0.34
Not Hispanic (11)	35	0.31
Hispanic (2)	3	0.03
Cherokee (2)	9	0.08
Creek (4)	4	0.04
Asian (140)	174	1.56
Not Hispanic (140)	173	1.55
Hispanic (0)	1	0.01
Chinese, ex. Taiwanese (9)	11	0.10
Filipino (2)	10	0.09
Indian (117)	125	1.12
Japanese (0)	5	0.04
Korean (3)	5	0.04
Laotian (1)	3	0.03
Pakistani (2)	2	0.02
Taiwanese (1)	1	0.01
Thai (0)	7	0.06
Vietnamese (5)	6	0.05
Hawaii Native/Pacific Islander (1)	5	0.04
Not Hispanic (1)	5	0.04
Guamanian/Chamorro (0)	1	0.01
Native Hawaiian (0)	1	0.01
Samoan (0)	1	0.01
White (3,228)	3,332	29.89
Not Hispanic (3,113)	3,212	28.81
Hispanic (115)	120	1.08

Country Club Estates

Place Type: CDP
County: Glynn
Population: 8,545†

Ancestry‡	Population	%
African, Sub-Saharan (40)	40	0.43
African (40)	40	0.43
American (271)	271	2.91
Austrian (21)	21	0.23
British (26)	38	0.41
Canadian (0)	10	0.11
Czech (0)	39	0.42
Dutch (9)	66	0.71
English (377)	761	8.18
European (0)	51	0.55
French, ex. Basque (50)	157	1.69
French Canadian (0)	28	0.30
German (138)	399	4.29
Irish (212)	824	8.86
Italian (25)	166	1.78
Norwegian (26)	49	0.53
Pennsylvania German (8)	8	0.09
Polish (40)	72	0.77
Russian (0)	21	0.23
Scotch-Irish (55)	115	1.24
Scottish (90)	100	1.08
Swedish (6)	27	0.29
Swiss (7)	7	0.08

Hispanic Origin	Population	%
Hispanic or Latino (of any race)	650	7.61
Central American, ex. Mexican	52	0.61
Costa Rican	1	0.01
Guatemalan	18	0.21
Honduran	14	0.16
Nicaraguan	5	0.06
Panamanian	10	0.12
Salvadoran	4	0.05
Cuban	11	0.13
Dominican Republic	8	0.09
Mexican	412	4.82
Puerto Rican	56	0.66
South American	34	0.40
Bolivian	1	0.01
Colombian	1	0.01
Peruvian	8	0.09
Uruguayan	20	0.23
Venezuelan	4	0.05
Other Hispanic or Latino	77	0.90

Race*	Population	%
African-American/Black (3,983)	4,094	47.91
Not Hispanic (3,934)	4,035	47.22
Hispanic (49)	59	0.69
American Indian/Alaska Native (23)	49	0.57
Not Hispanic (19)	41	0.48
Hispanic (4)	8	0.09
Cherokee (1)	9	0.11
Creek (2)	2	0.02
Iroquois (3)	3	0.04
Mexican American Ind. (3)	3	0.04
Potawatomi (3)	3	0.04
Asian (143)	173	2.02
Not Hispanic (143)	172	2.01
Hispanic (0)	1	0.01
Burmese (8)	8	0.09
Chinese, ex. Taiwanese (31)	32	0.37
Filipino (37)	58	0.68
Indian (24)	26	0.30
Japanese (2)	4	0.05
Korean (2)	3	0.04
Pakistani (6)	6	0.07
Thai (3)	3	0.04
Vietnamese (30)	33	0.39

*Notes: † The Census 2010 population figure is used to calculate the percentages in the Hispanic Origin and Race categories. Ancestry percentages are based on the 2006-2010 American Community Survey population (not shown); ‡ Numbers in parentheses indicate the number of people reporting a single ancestry; * Numbers in parentheses indicate the number of persons reporting this race alone, not in combination with any other race; Please refer to the Explanation of Data for more information.*

Hawaii Native/Pacific Islander (50)	68	0.80
Not Hispanic (45)	60	0.70
Hispanic (5)	8	0.09
Guamanian/Chamorro (2)	6	0.07
Native Hawaiian (6)	15	0.18
White (3,857)	4,000	46.81
Not Hispanic (3,590)	3,706	43.37
Hispanic (267)	294	3.44

Covington

Place Type: City
County: Newton
Population: 13,118†

Ancestry‡	Population	%
African, Sub-Saharan (310)	358	2.71
African (275)	307	2.33
Nigerian (0)	16	0.12
Other Sub-Saharan African (35)	35	0.27
American (1,192)	1,192	9.03
Austrian (0)	26	0.20
British (57)	172	1.30
Cajun (60)	60	0.45
Czech (36)	110	0.83
Dutch (8)	101	0.77
English (502)	1,206	9.14
European (30)	30	0.23
French, ex. Basque (7)	58	0.44
French Canadian (16)	41	0.31
German (257)	1,065	8.07
Greek (11)	35	0.27
Irish (441)	1,536	11.64
Italian (52)	147	1.11
Northern European (80)	80	0.61
Norwegian (0)	20	0.15
Polish (43)	59	0.45
Scotch-Irish (116)	150	1.14
Scottish (121)	197	1.49
Swedish (0)	66	0.50
Turkish (15)	55	0.42
Welsh (99)	113	0.86
West Indian, ex. Hispanic (38)	277	2.10
British West Indian (9)	184	1.39
Jamaican (18)	18	0.14
Trinidadian/Tobagonian (11)	11	0.08
West Indian (0)	64	0.48

Hispanic Origin	Population	%
Hispanic or Latino (of any race)	723	5.51
Central American, ex. Mexican	75	0.57
Guatemalan	14	0.11
Honduran	4	0.03
Nicaraguan	5	0.04
Panamanian	14	0.11
Salvadoran	38	0.29
Cuban	13	0.10
Dominican Republic	1	0.01
Mexican	482	3.67
Puerto Rican	74	0.56
South American	10	0.08
Chilean	1	0.01
Colombian	2	0.02
Peruvian	2	0.02
Uruguayan	3	0.02
Venezuelan	1	0.01
Other South American	1	0.01
Other Hispanic or Latino	68	0.52

Race*	Population	%
African-American/Black (6,222)	6,373	48.58
Not Hispanic (6,140)	6,272	47.81
Hispanic (82)	101	0.77
American Indian/Alaska Native (27)	71	0.54
Not Hispanic (26)	66	0.50
Hispanic (1)	5	0.04
Cherokee (1)	18	0.14
Choctaw (1)	1	0.01
Creek (0)	1	0.01
Inupiat *(Alaska Native)* (1)	1	0.01
Lumbee (4)	4	0.03
Mexican American Ind. (1)	1	0.01
Asian (87)	127	0.97
Not Hispanic (87)	121	0.92
Hispanic (0)	6	0.05
Chinese, ex. Taiwanese (14)	20	0.15
Filipino (3)	15	0.11
Hmong (1)	1	0.01
Indian (27)	41	0.31
Japanese (2)	6	0.05
Korean (10)	13	0.10
Pakistani (2)	3	0.02
Thai (6)	6	0.05
Vietnamese (18)	19	0.14
Hawaii Native/Pacific Islander (10)	19	0.14
Not Hispanic (10)	19	0.14
Samoan (10)	10	0.08
White (6,140)	6,324	48.21
Not Hispanic (5,919)	6,072	46.29
Hispanic (221)	252	1.92

Cusseta-Chattahoochee County

Place Type: Unified Government
County: Chattahoochee
Population: 11,267†

Ancestry‡	Population	%
African, Sub-Saharan (58)	58	0.50
African (16)	16	0.14
Senegalese (17)	17	0.15
South African (14)	14	0.12
Other Sub-Saharan African (11)	11	0.09
American (362)	362	3.09
Arab (11)	48	0.41
Jordanian (11)	11	0.09
Syrian (0)	37	0.32
Armenian (13)	13	0.11
Austrian (0)	43	0.37
Belgian (0)	2	0.02
Brazilian (0)	5	0.04
British (7)	33	0.28
Cajun (0)	4	0.03
Canadian (43)	43	0.37
Celtic (0)	37	0.32
Czech (2)	39	0.33
Danish (0)	18	0.15
Dutch (19)	70	0.60
English (248)	1,177	10.06
European (244)	265	2.26
Finnish (0)	37	0.32
French, ex. Basque (1)	270	2.31
French Canadian (45)	98	0.84
German (496)	2,047	17.49
Greek (0)	3	0.03
Hungarian (15)	63	0.54
Irish (485)	1,747	14.93
Italian (165)	796	6.80
Northern European (73)	83	0.71
Norwegian (40)	154	1.32
Polish (114)	369	3.15
Portuguese (25)	131	1.12
Romanian (0)	5	0.04
Russian (50)	83	0.71
Scandinavian (6)	35	0.30
Scotch-Irish (152)	362	3.09
Scottish (70)	367	3.14
Swedish (0)	96	0.82
Swiss (13)	32	0.27
Ukrainian (0)	34	0.29
Welsh (4)	101	0.86
West Indian, ex. Hispanic (9)	88	0.75
Jamaican (9)	88	0.75

Hispanic Origin	Population	%
Hispanic or Latino (of any race)	1,398	12.41
Central American, ex. Mexican	75	0.67
Costa Rican	2	0.02
Guatemalan	8	0.07
Honduran	10	0.09
Nicaraguan	2	0.02
Panamanian	35	0.31
Salvadoran	16	0.14
Other Central American	2	0.02
Cuban	54	0.48
Dominican Republic	39	0.35
Mexican	560	4.97
Puerto Rican	370	3.28
South American	191	1.70
Argentinean	1	0.01
Bolivian	2	0.02
Chilean	26	0.23
Colombian	90	0.80
Ecuadorian	24	0.21
Peruvian	38	0.34
Uruguayan	7	0.06
Venezuelan	3	0.03
Other Hispanic or Latino	109	0.97

Race*	Population	%
African-American/Black (2,123)	2,308	20.48
Not Hispanic (2,047)	2,209	19.61
Hispanic (76)	99	0.88
American Indian/Alaska Native (81)	194	1.72
Not Hispanic (67)	151	1.34
Hispanic (14)	43	0.38
Apache (7)	9	0.08
Blackfeet (1)	6	0.05
Central American Ind. (4)	4	0.04
Cherokee (10)	40	0.36
Chickasaw (0)	2	0.02
Chippewa (5)	8	0.07
Choctaw (0)	2	0.02
Comanche (2)	2	0.02
Creek (3)	4	0.04
Inupiat *(Alaska Native)* (0)	1	0.01
Lumbee (0)	2	0.02
Mexican American Ind. (2)	6	0.05
Osage (0)	3	0.03
Puget Sound Salish (1)	4	0.04
South American Ind. (0)	1	0.01
Tlingit-Haida *(Alaska Native)* (1)	1	0.01
Asian (246)	412	3.66
Not Hispanic (231)	365	3.24
Hispanic (15)	47	0.42
Bangladeshi (0)	1	0.01
Cambodian (6)	6	0.05
Chinese, ex. Taiwanese (32)	42	0.37
Filipino (66)	124	1.10
Hmong (9)	9	0.08
Indian (27)	36	0.32
Japanese (5)	30	0.27
Korean (61)	109	0.97
Laotian (2)	2	0.02
Nepalese (7)	7	0.06
Pakistani (0)	1	0.01
Taiwanese (2)	3	0.03
Thai (7)	12	0.11
Vietnamese (12)	25	0.22
Hawaii Native/Pacific Islander (72)	125	1.11
Not Hispanic (62)	105	0.93
Hispanic (10)	20	0.18
Guamanian/Chamorro (37)	42	0.37
Marshallese (5)	5	0.04
Native Hawaiian (9)	40	0.36
Samoan (12)	19	0.17
Tongan (0)	1	0.01
White (7,753)	8,176	72.57
Not Hispanic (7,089)	7,412	65.79
Hispanic (664)	764	6.78

Dallas

Place Type: City
County: Paulding
Population: 11,544†

*Notes: † The Census 2010 population figure is used to calculate the percentages in the Hispanic Origin and Race categories. Ancestry percentages are based on the 2006-2010 American Community Survey population (not shown); ‡ Numbers in parentheses indicate the number of people reporting a single ancestry; * Numbers in parentheses indicate the number of persons reporting this race alone, not in combination with any other race; Please refer to the Explanation of Data for more information.*

Ancestry‡	Population	%
African, Sub-Saharan (979)	1,044	9.71
African (979)	979	9.10
Cape Verdean (0)	65	0.60
American (873)	873	8.12
Arab (169)	169	1.57
Lebanese (169)	169	1.57
Austrian (0)	144	1.34
British (9)	9	0.08
Dutch (9)	51	0.47
English (84)	457	4.25
European (32)	32	0.30
Finnish (0)	66	0.61
French, ex. Basque (34)	261	2.43
French Canadian (15)	67	0.62
German (424)	916	8.52
Greek (21)	21	0.20
Irish (537)	1,081	10.05
Italian (132)	418	3.89
Northern European (77)	77	0.72
Norwegian (38)	106	0.99
Polish (68)	192	1.79
Portuguese (17)	24	0.22
Russian (0)	63	0.59
Scotch-Irish (12)	46	0.43
Scottish (31)	154	1.43
Swedish (0)	82	0.76
Welsh (0)	101	0.94
West Indian, ex. Hispanic (102)	102	0.95
Jamaican (87)	87	0.81
Trinidadian/Tobagonian (15)	15	0.14

Hispanic Origin	Population	%
Hispanic or Latino (of any race)	826	7.16
Central American, ex. Mexican	91	0.79
Costa Rican	10	0.09
Guatemalan	12	0.10
Honduran	18	0.16
Nicaraguan	10	0.09
Panamanian	11	0.10
Salvadoran	30	0.26
Cuban	32	0.28
Dominican Republic	62	0.54
Mexican	293	2.54
Puerto Rican	175	1.52
South American	91	0.79
Argentinean	5	0.04
Bolivian	5	0.04
Colombian	35	0.30
Ecuadorian	20	0.17
Peruvian	10	0.09
Uruguayan	7	0.06
Venezuelan	8	0.07
Other South American	1	0.01
Other Hispanic or Latino	82	0.71

Race*	Population	%
African-American/Black (3,598)	3,830	33.18
Not Hispanic (3,503)	3,700	32.05
Hispanic (95)	130	1.13
American Indian/Alaska Native (41)	122	1.06
Not Hispanic (31)	91	0.79
Hispanic (10)	31	0.27
Apache (0)	6	0.05
Blackfeet (1)	7	0.06
Cherokee (3)	39	0.34
Cheyenne (0)	1	0.01
Chippewa (0)	1	0.01
Creek (0)	4	0.03
Iroquois (0)	1	0.01
Lumbee (1)	1	0.01
Mexican American Ind. (1)	1	0.01
Navajo (0)	4	0.03
Sioux (1)	2	0.02
Spanish American Ind. (0)	1	0.01
Asian (152)	192	1.66
Not Hispanic (147)	179	1.55
Hispanic (5)	13	0.11
Bangladeshi (3)	3	0.03
Cambodian (2)	7	0.06
Chinese, ex. Taiwanese (9)	18	0.16
Filipino (6)	22	0.19
Indian (60)	65	0.56
Indonesian (1)	2	0.02
Japanese (6)	11	0.10
Korean (6)	13	0.11
Laotian (3)	7	0.06
Pakistani (10)	10	0.09
Thai (6)	6	0.05
Vietnamese (24)	26	0.23
Hawaii Native/Pacific Islander (5)	23	0.20
Not Hispanic (5)	23	0.20
Guamanian/Chamorro (0)	2	0.02
Native Hawaiian (3)	5	0.04
White (7,056)	7,324	63.44
Not Hispanic (6,726)	6,943	60.14
Hispanic (330)	381	3.30

Dalton

Place Type: City
County: Whitfield
Population: 33,128†

Ancestry‡	Population	%
African, Sub-Saharan (19)	19	0.06
African (19)	19	0.06
American (2,242)	2,242	6.93
Arab (274)	293	0.91
Arab (10)	10	0.03
Egyptian (95)	95	0.29
Iraqi (15)	15	0.05
Palestinian (154)	173	0.53
Australian (49)	49	0.15
Austrian (0)	10	0.03
British (118)	202	0.62
Dutch (42)	319	0.99
Eastern European (21)	21	0.06
English (948)	2,328	7.19
European (176)	206	0.64
French, ex. Basque (68)	344	1.06
French Canadian (0)	34	0.11
German (603)	1,559	4.82
Greek (0)	13	0.04
Guyanese (15)	15	0.05
Hungarian (14)	14	0.04
Irish (1,009)	2,614	8.07
Italian (94)	237	0.73
Norwegian (14)	14	0.04
Polish (7)	136	0.42
Russian (55)	191	0.59
Scandinavian (43)	85	0.26
Scotch-Irish (317)	589	1.82
Scottish (239)	678	2.09
Slovak (0)	13	0.04
Swedish (0)	29	0.09
Swiss (0)	10	0.03
Ukrainian (0)	12	0.04
Welsh (162)	264	0.82
West Indian, ex. Hispanic (133)	133	0.41
Jamaican (62)	62	0.19
West Indian (71)	71	0.22

Hispanic Origin	Population	%
Hispanic or Latino (of any race)	15,891	47.97
Central American, ex. Mexican	1,538	4.64
Costa Rican	9	0.03
Guatemalan	909	2.74
Honduran	101	0.30
Nicaraguan	51	0.15
Panamanian	18	0.05
Salvadoran	445	1.34
Other Central American	5	0.02
Cuban	139	0.42
Dominican Republic	84	0.25
Mexican	13,214	39.89
Puerto Rican	223	0.67
South American	103	0.31
Argentinean	6	0.02
Chilean	5	0.02
Colombian	30	0.09
Ecuadorian	3	0.01
Peruvian	32	0.10
Venezuelan	27	0.08
Other Hispanic or Latino	590	1.78

Race*	Population	%
African-American/Black (2,108)	2,408	7.27
Not Hispanic (1,974)	2,201	6.64
Hispanic (134)	207	0.62
American Indian/Alaska Native (212)	356	1.07
Not Hispanic (41)	114	0.34
Hispanic (171)	242	0.73
Apache (2)	7	0.02
Blackfeet (0)	1	<0.01
Central American Ind. (3)	5	0.02
Cherokee (11)	48	0.14
Chickasaw (0)	1	<0.01
Chippewa (4)	4	0.01
Creek (2)	2	0.01
Iroquois (1)	2	0.01
Lumbee (4)	4	0.01
Mexican American Ind. (43)	53	0.16
Navajo (2)	3	0.01
Sioux (3)	4	0.01
Ute (1)	1	<0.01
Asian (779)	896	2.70
Not Hispanic (749)	844	2.55
Hispanic (30)	52	0.16
Cambodian (9)	9	0.03
Chinese, ex. Taiwanese (121)	134	0.40
Filipino (34)	53	0.16
Indian (308)	346	1.04
Indonesian (3)	4	0.01
Japanese (37)	47	0.14
Korean (67)	72	0.22
Laotian (1)	1	<0.01
Pakistani (58)	65	0.20
Thai (3)	5	0.02
Vietnamese (107)	119	0.36
Hawaii Native/Pacific Islander (42)	70	0.21
Not Hispanic (12)	20	0.06
Hispanic (30)	50	0.15
Guamanian/Chamorro (28)	35	0.11
Marshallese (1)	1	<0.01
Native Hawaiian (2)	5	0.02
Samoan (1)	2	0.01
White (21,549)	22,479	67.85
Not Hispanic (14,055)	14,383	43.42
Hispanic (7,494)	8,096	24.44

Decatur

Place Type: City
County: DeKalb
Population: 19,335†

Ancestry‡	Population	%
African, Sub-Saharan (538)	538	2.82
African (70)	70	0.37
Ethiopian (232)	232	1.22
Somalian (236)	236	1.24
Alsatian (0)	13	0.07
American (633)	633	3.32
Arab (69)	189	0.99
Arab (14)	40	0.21
Lebanese (55)	135	0.71
Syrian (0)	14	0.07
Assyrian/Chaldean/Syriac (0)	9	0.05
Austrian (0)	100	0.52
Belgian (0)	6	0.03
Brazilian (0)	49	0.26
British (125)	196	1.03
Cajun (13)	13	0.07
Canadian (0)	7	0.04
Croatian (0)	30	0.16
Czech (0)	26	0.14
Czechoslovakian (29)	61	0.32
Danish (12)	89	0.47
Dutch (102)	293	1.54

*Notes: † The Census 2010 population figure is used to calculate the percentages in the Hispanic Origin and Race categories. Ancestry percentages are based on the 2006-2010 American Community Survey population (not shown); ‡ Numbers in parentheses indicate the number of people reporting a single ancestry; * Numbers in parentheses indicate the number of persons reporting this race alone, not in combination with any other race; Please refer to the Explanation of Data for more information.*

Eastern European (42)	97	0.51
English (978)	3,007	15.77
European (595)	630	3.31
Finnish (0)	30	0.16
French, ex. Basque (75)	575	3.02
French Canadian (50)	127	0.67
German (546)	2,296	12.04
Greek (10)	74	0.39
Hungarian (0)	39	0.20
Iranian (30)	30	0.16
Irish (869)	2,378	12.48
Italian (266)	682	3.58
Lithuanian (17)	17	0.09
Northern European (16)	23	0.12
Norwegian (50)	194	1.02
Polish (74)	360	1.89
Portuguese (0)	24	0.13
Romanian (9)	23	0.12
Russian (70)	206	1.08
Scandinavian (10)	39	0.20
Scotch-Irish (337)	1,114	5.84
Scottish (281)	764	4.01
Slavic (0)	11	0.06
Slovak (17)	27	0.14
Swedish (46)	304	1.59
Swiss (0)	115	0.60
Ukrainian (26)	37	0.19
Welsh (31)	184	0.97
West Indian, ex. Hispanic (29)	74	0.39
Belizean (0)	14	0.07
Haitian (15)	15	0.08
Jamaican (0)	31	0.16
West Indian (14)	14	0.07

Hispanic Origin	Population	%
Hispanic or Latino (of any race)	612	3.17
Central American, ex. Mexican	51	0.26
Costa Rican	10	0.05
Guatemalan	13	0.07
Honduran	5	0.03
Nicaraguan	3	0.02
Panamanian	13	0.07
Salvadoran	5	0.03
Other Central American	2	0.01
Cuban	72	0.37
Dominican Republic	16	0.08
Mexican	181	0.94
Puerto Rican	97	0.50
South American	115	0.59
Argentinean	18	0.09
Bolivian	7	0.04
Chilean	7	0.04
Colombian	29	0.15
Ecuadorian	6	0.03
Paraguayan	2	0.01
Peruvian	31	0.16
Uruguayan	3	0.02
Venezuelan	12	0.06
Other Hispanic or Latino	80	0.41

Race*	Population	%
African-American/Black (3,910)	4,095	21.18
Not Hispanic (3,858)	4,017	20.78
Hispanic (52)	78	0.40
American Indian/Alaska Native (45)	152	0.79
Not Hispanic (36)	132	0.68
Hispanic (9)	20	0.10
Apache (1)	3	0.02
Blackfeet (1)	5	0.03
Central American Ind. (0)	2	0.01
Cherokee (8)	24	0.12
Cheyenne (1)	1	0.01
Chippewa (2)	3	0.02
Choctaw (0)	7	0.04
Cree (0)	1	0.01
Creek (3)	8	0.04
Hopi (1)	1	0.01
Houma (0)	2	0.01
Iroquois (0)	6	0.03
Lumbee (2)	2	0.01
Mexican American Ind. (5)	5	0.03
Navajo (0)	2	0.01
Seminole (0)	1	0.01
Sioux (1)	1	0.01
South American Ind. (2)	3	0.02
Tlingit-Haida *(Alaska Native)* (0)	1	0.01
Tsimshian *(Alaska Native)* (0)	1	0.01
Asian (564)	773	4.00
Not Hispanic (554)	756	3.91
Hispanic (10)	17	0.09
Bangladeshi (1)	6	0.03
Cambodian (3)	3	0.02
Chinese, ex. Taiwanese (153)	205	1.06
Filipino (36)	62	0.32
Indian (146)	181	0.94
Indonesian (6)	6	0.03
Japanese (31)	62	0.32
Korean (77)	111	0.57
Laotian (3)	7	0.04
Malaysian (2)	2	0.01
Nepalese (1)	2	0.01
Pakistani (16)	22	0.11
Taiwanese (12)	15	0.08
Thai (7)	9	0.05
Vietnamese (30)	47	0.24
Hawaii Native/Pacific Islander (9)	26	0.13
Not Hispanic (9)	26	0.13
Guamanian/Chamorro (3)	4	0.02
Native Hawaiian (1)	7	0.04
Samoan (0)	3	0.02
White (14,215)	14,603	75.53
Not Hispanic (13,806)	14,151	73.19
Hispanic (409)	452	2.34

Dock Junction

Place Type: CDP
County: Glynn
Population: 7,721†

Ancestry‡	Population	%
African, Sub-Saharan (54)	66	0.88
African (54)	66	0.88
American (947)	947	12.56
Czech (19)	19	0.25
Danish (7)	7	0.09
Dutch (0)	95	1.26
English (206)	512	6.79
Finnish (0)	97	1.29
French, ex. Basque (10)	25	0.33
German (169)	460	6.10
Irish (387)	705	9.35
Italian (78)	214	2.84
Norwegian (0)	9	0.12
Polish (13)	42	0.56
Portuguese (29)	29	0.38
Russian (8)	8	0.11
Scotch-Irish (0)	62	0.82
Scottish (54)	246	3.26
Swedish (26)	205	2.72

Hispanic Origin	Population	%
Hispanic or Latino (of any race)	867	11.23
Central American, ex. Mexican	38	0.49
Guatemalan	6	0.08
Honduran	11	0.14
Nicaraguan	3	0.04
Panamanian	4	0.05
Salvadoran	14	0.18
Cuban	3	0.04
Dominican Republic	3	0.04
Mexican	726	9.40
Puerto Rican	60	0.78
South American	20	0.26
Chilean	2	0.03
Colombian	9	0.12
Peruvian	4	0.05
Uruguayan	3	0.04
Venezuelan	1	0.01
Other South American	1	0.01
Other Hispanic or Latino	17	0.22

Race*	Population	%
African-American/Black (2,158)	2,253	29.18
Not Hispanic (2,127)	2,216	28.70
Hispanic (31)	37	0.48
American Indian/Alaska Native (18)	47	0.61
Not Hispanic (14)	39	0.51
Hispanic (4)	8	0.10
Blackfeet (2)	2	0.03
Central American Ind. (0)	1	0.01
Cherokee (2)	16	0.21
Creek (0)	3	0.04
Lumbee (1)	1	0.01
Mexican American Ind. (2)	2	0.03
Asian (119)	146	1.89
Not Hispanic (115)	138	1.79
Hispanic (4)	8	0.10
Chinese, ex. Taiwanese (4)	9	0.12
Filipino (12)	21	0.27
Indian (63)	68	0.88
Indonesian (1)	1	0.01
Japanese (4)	5	0.06
Korean (14)	17	0.22
Thai (7)	8	0.10
Vietnamese (11)	12	0.16
Hawaii Native/Pacific Islander (0)	5	0.06
Not Hispanic (0)	5	0.06
Guamanian/Chamorro (0)	2	0.03
Native Hawaiian (0)	2	0.03
Samoan (0)	1	0.01
White (4,727)	4,862	62.97
Not Hispanic (4,461)	4,579	59.31
Hispanic (266)	283	3.67

Doraville

Place Type: City
County: DeKalb
Population: 8,330†

Ancestry‡	Population	%
African, Sub-Saharan (211)	211	2.54
African (16)	16	0.19
Ethiopian (195)	195	2.34
American (167)	167	2.01
Arab (0)	44	0.53
Lebanese (0)	44	0.53
Belgian (0)	9	0.11
British (26)	26	0.31
Czech (22)	36	0.43
Dutch (24)	56	0.67
English (92)	236	2.84
European (51)	51	0.61
Finnish (17)	22	0.26
French, ex. Basque (0)	230	2.76
French Canadian (0)	10	0.12
German (60)	409	4.92
Hungarian (0)	10	0.12
Irish (128)	287	3.45
Italian (25)	88	1.06
Latvian (0)	10	0.12
Polish (0)	19	0.23
Portuguese (0)	15	0.18
Russian (28)	164	1.97
Scotch-Irish (47)	133	1.60
Scottish (86)	165	1.98
Slovak (13)	13	0.16
Swedish (0)	9	0.11
Welsh (0)	17	0.20

Hispanic Origin	Population	%
Hispanic or Latino (of any race)	4,119	49.45
Central American, ex. Mexican	1,059	12.71
Costa Rican	2	0.02
Guatemalan	580	6.96
Honduran	256	3.07
Nicaraguan	19	0.23
Panamanian	1	0.01
Salvadoran	199	2.39

SECTION TWO

*Notes: † The Census 2010 population figure is used to calculate the percentages in the Hispanic Origin and Race categories. Ancestry percentages are based on the 2006-2010 American Community Survey population (not shown); ‡ Numbers in parentheses indicate the number of people reporting a single ancestry; * Numbers in parentheses indicate the number of persons reporting this race alone, not in combination with any other race; Please refer to the Explanation of Data for more information.*

Other Central American	2	0.02
Cuban	50	0.60
Dominican Republic	35	0.42
Mexican	2,350	28.21
Puerto Rican	65	0.78
South American	246	2.95
Argentinean	9	0.11
Bolivian	1	0.01
Chilean	18	0.22
Colombian	56	0.67
Ecuadorian	62	0.74
Peruvian	28	0.34
Uruguayan	61	0.73
Venezuelan	10	0.12
Other South American	1	0.01
Other Hispanic or Latino	314	3.77

Race*	Population	%
African-American/Black (797)	866	10.40
Not Hispanic (731)	773	9.28
Hispanic (66)	93	1.12
American Indian/Alaska Native (96)	155	1.86
Not Hispanic (16)	54	0.65
Hispanic (80)	101	1.21
Blackfeet (1)	1	0.01
Central American Ind. (0)	3	0.04
Cherokee (7)	19	0.23
Creek (1)	1	0.01
Mexican American Ind. (46)	61	0.73
Sioux (2)	11	0.13
South American Ind. (0)	1	0.01
Spanish American Ind. (2)	2	0.02
Asian (1,472)	1,537	18.45
Not Hispanic (1,464)	1,515	18.19
Hispanic (8)	22	0.26
Bangladeshi (168)	202	2.42
Cambodian (32)	42	0.50
Chinese, ex. Taiwanese (529)	548	6.58
Filipino (17)	21	0.25
Hmong (1)	1	0.01
Indian (195)	237	2.85
Japanese (7)	11	0.13
Korean (104)	112	1.34
Laotian (9)	13	0.16
Pakistani (28)	28	0.34
Taiwanese (8)	12	0.14
Thai (12)	14	0.17
Vietnamese (301)	317	3.81
Hawaii Native/Pacific Islander (14)	18	0.22
Not Hispanic (8)	10	0.12
Hispanic (6)	8	0.10
Guamanian/Chamorro (6)	7	0.08
White (3,664)	3,876	46.53
Not Hispanic (1,870)	1,933	23.21
Hispanic (1,794)	1,943	23.33

Douglas

Place Type: City
County: Coffee
Population: 11,589†

Ancestry‡	Population	%
African, Sub-Saharan (134)	145	1.26
African (134)	145	1.26
American (893)	893	7.78
Arab (0)	13	0.11
Jordanian (0)	13	0.11
British (2)	2	0.02
Dutch (9)	48	0.42
English (1,064)	1,203	10.48
European (9)	9	0.08
French, ex. Basque (21)	51	0.44
French Canadian (4)	4	0.03
German (77)	158	1.38
Irish (171)	417	3.63
Italian (77)	84	0.73
Polish (19)	19	0.17
Scotch-Irish (97)	128	1.12
Scottish (59)	117	1.02
Swedish (22)	22	0.19
Welsh (0)	31	0.27
West Indian, ex. Hispanic (28)	104	0.91
Haitian (14)	52	0.45
Jamaican (14)	52	0.45

Hispanic Origin	Population	%
Hispanic or Latino (of any race)	728	6.28
Central American, ex. Mexican	82	0.71
Guatemalan	56	0.48
Honduran	7	0.06
Nicaraguan	3	0.03
Panamanian	8	0.07
Salvadoran	8	0.07
Cuban	38	0.33
Dominican Republic	7	0.06
Mexican	485	4.19
Puerto Rican	40	0.35
South American	18	0.16
Colombian	14	0.12
Peruvian	3	0.03
Venezuelan	1	0.01
Other Hispanic or Latino	58	0.50

Race*	Population	%
African-American/Black (6,025)	6,130	52.89
Not Hispanic (6,001)	6,097	52.61
Hispanic (24)	33	0.28
American Indian/Alaska Native (19)	56	0.48
Not Hispanic (13)	48	0.41
Hispanic (6)	8	0.07
Cherokee (3)	16	0.14
Creek (2)	4	0.03
Lumbee (1)	2	0.02
Mexican American Ind. (1)	1	0.01
Seminole (0)	1	0.01
Asian (105)	117	1.01
Not Hispanic (105)	116	1.00
Hispanic (0)	1	0.01
Chinese, ex. Taiwanese (24)	24	0.21
Filipino (2)	4	0.03
Indian (56)	59	0.51
Japanese (1)	4	0.03
Korean (4)	5	0.04
Malaysian (2)	3	0.03
Pakistani (5)	5	0.04
Sri Lankan (2)	2	0.02
Thai (4)	4	0.03
Vietnamese (5)	6	0.05
Hawaii Native/Pacific Islander (13)	20	0.17
Not Hispanic (9)	15	0.13
Hispanic (4)	5	0.04
Guamanian/Chamorro (8)	10	0.09
Native Hawaiian (0)	2	0.02
White (4,819)	4,945	42.67
Not Hispanic (4,587)	4,693	40.50
Hispanic (232)	252	2.17

Douglasville

Place Type: City
County: Douglas
Population: 30,961†

Ancestry‡	Population	%
African, Sub-Saharan (4,883)	5,296	18.03
African (4,595)	5,008	17.05
Cape Verdean (14)	14	0.05
Ghanaian (11)	11	0.04
Nigerian (237)	237	0.81
Other Sub-Saharan African (26)	26	0.09
American (2,391)	2,391	8.14
Arab (14)	14	0.05
Other Arab (14)	14	0.05
Armenian (10)	10	0.03
Australian (21)	21	0.07
Austrian (53)	53	0.18
British (63)	63	0.21
Canadian (26)	26	0.09
Croatian (13)	48	0.16
Czech (0)	15	0.05
Danish (0)	88	0.30
Dutch (97)	356	1.21
Eastern European (32)	32	0.11
English (722)	1,750	5.96
European (132)	132	0.45
Finnish (10)	10	0.03
French, ex. Basque (59)	220	0.75
French Canadian (34)	131	0.45
German (566)	2,002	6.82
Guyanese (56)	56	0.19
Hungarian (0)	33	0.11
Irish (810)	2,223	7.57
Italian (150)	374	1.27
Lithuanian (0)	11	0.04
Norwegian (28)	87	0.30
Polish (74)	151	0.51
Romanian (0)	7	0.02
Russian (9)	31	0.11
Scotch-Irish (234)	298	1.01
Scottish (129)	559	1.90
Serbian (0)	35	0.12
Swedish (24)	52	0.18
Swiss (17)	40	0.14
West Indian, ex. Hispanic (500)	630	2.14
British West Indian (14)	14	0.05
Haitian (262)	262	0.89
Jamaican (177)	307	1.05
Trinidadian/Tobagonian (12)	12	0.04
West Indian (35)	35	0.12

Hispanic Origin	Population	%
Hispanic or Latino (of any race)	2,243	7.24
Central American, ex. Mexican	234	0.76
Costa Rican	4	0.01
Guatemalan	40	0.13
Honduran	56	0.18
Nicaraguan	8	0.03
Panamanian	58	0.19
Salvadoran	68	0.22
Cuban	69	0.22
Dominican Republic	74	0.24
Mexican	1,249	4.03
Puerto Rican	351	1.13
South American	118	0.38
Chilean	5	0.02
Colombian	36	0.12
Ecuadorian	21	0.07
Peruvian	29	0.09
Uruguayan	2	0.01
Venezuelan	25	0.08
Other Hispanic or Latino	148	0.48

Race*	Population	%
African-American/Black (17,297)	17,855	57.67
Not Hispanic (17,031)	17,503	56.53
Hispanic (266)	352	1.14
American Indian/Alaska Native (70)	287	0.93
Not Hispanic (65)	229	0.74
Hispanic (5)	58	0.19
Apache (2)	3	0.01
Blackfeet (1)	14	0.05
Central American Ind. (1)	7	0.02
Cherokee (15)	95	0.31
Cheyenne (0)	1	<0.01
Chickasaw (0)	1	<0.01
Chippewa (0)	1	<0.01
Choctaw (0)	4	0.01
Comanche (0)	1	<0.01
Creek (3)	4	0.01
Crow (0)	1	<0.01
Delaware (1)	2	0.01
Lumbee (1)	2	0.01
Mexican American Ind. (1)	6	0.02
Navajo (2)	2	0.01
Potawatomi (3)	3	0.01
Pueblo (2)	2	0.01
Sioux (0)	2	0.01
South American Ind. (0)	2	0.01
Asian (559)	673	2.17

*Notes: † The Census 2010 population figure is used to calculate the percentages in the Hispanic Origin and Race categories. Ancestry percentages are based on the 2006-2010 American Community Survey population (not shown); ‡ Numbers in parentheses indicate the number of people reporting a single ancestry; * Numbers in parentheses indicate the number of persons reporting this race alone, not in combination with any other race; Please refer to the Explanation of Data for more information.*

Race* (continued)	Population	%
Not Hispanic (554)	661	2.13
Hispanic (5)	12	0.04
Bangladeshi (12)	13	0.04
Burmese (4)	4	0.01
Cambodian (5)	7	0.02
Chinese, ex. Taiwanese (89)	110	0.36
Filipino (34)	60	0.19
Indian (209)	231	0.75
Indonesian (10)	10	0.03
Japanese (22)	42	0.14
Korean (49)	64	0.21
Laotian (4)	4	0.01
Malaysian (2)	2	0.01
Pakistani (37)	37	0.12
Sri Lankan (2)	2	0.01
Taiwanese (6)	6	0.02
Thai (8)	10	0.03
Vietnamese (43)	52	0.17
Hawaii Native/Pacific Islander (18)	61	0.20
Not Hispanic (15)	47	0.15
Hispanic (3)	14	0.05
Guamanian/Chamorro (4)	6	0.02
Native Hawaiian (9)	23	0.07
Samoan (1)	9	0.03
White (11,144)	11,807	38.14
Not Hispanic (10,331)	10,850	35.04
Hispanic (813)	957	3.09

Druid Hills

Place Type: CDP
County: DeKalb
Population: 14,568†

Ancestry‡	Population	%
African, Sub-Saharan (47)	128	0.88
African (24)	63	0.43
Ethiopian (11)	11	0.08
Nigerian (12)	54	0.37
Alsatian (0)	12	0.08
American (776)	776	5.31
Arab (17)	49	0.34
Arab (0)	10	0.07
Lebanese (17)	17	0.12
Syrian (0)	22	0.15
Australian (29)	29	0.20
Austrian (39)	89	0.61
British (288)	351	2.40
Cajun (99)	99	0.68
Canadian (48)	77	0.53
Celtic (12)	12	0.08
Croatian (30)	30	0.21
Czech (0)	27	0.18
Danish (11)	25	0.17
Dutch (31)	263	1.80
Eastern European (104)	104	0.71
English (943)	2,202	15.08
Estonian (0)	14	0.10
European (223)	241	1.65
French, ex. Basque (106)	598	4.10
French Canadian (10)	41	0.28
German (378)	1,607	11.00
Greek (56)	116	0.79
Guyanese (0)	18	0.12
Hungarian (13)	75	0.51
Iranian (41)	54	0.37
Irish (542)	1,649	11.29
Italian (244)	734	5.03
Lithuanian (21)	65	0.45
Northern European (16)	16	0.11
Norwegian (44)	116	0.79
Polish (263)	577	3.95
Portuguese (45)	100	0.68
Romanian (8)	18	0.12
Russian (138)	276	1.89
Scotch-Irish (325)	725	4.96
Scottish (250)	500	3.42
Slovene (13)	38	0.26
Swedish (48)	136	0.93
Swiss (0)	34	0.23
Ukrainian (42)	42	0.29
Welsh (20)	115	0.79
West Indian, ex. Hispanic (43)	63	0.43
Bahamian (0)	20	0.14
Haitian (7)	7	0.05
Jamaican (36)	36	0.25
Yugoslavian (16)	16	0.11

Hispanic Origin	Population	%
Hispanic or Latino (of any race)	419	2.88
Central American, ex. Mexican	47	0.32
Costa Rican	6	0.04
Guatemalan	13	0.09
Honduran	5	0.03
Nicaraguan	6	0.04
Panamanian	10	0.07
Salvadoran	7	0.05
Cuban	58	0.40
Dominican Republic	9	0.06
Mexican	92	0.63
Puerto Rican	54	0.37
South American	104	0.71
Argentinean	12	0.08
Bolivian	2	0.01
Chilean	9	0.06
Colombian	40	0.27
Ecuadorian	11	0.08
Paraguayan	2	0.01
Peruvian	14	0.10
Uruguayan	1	0.01
Venezuelan	13	0.09
Other Hispanic or Latino	55	0.38

Race*	Population	%
African-American/Black (1,118)	1,194	8.20
Not Hispanic (1,097)	1,167	8.01
Hispanic (21)	27	0.19
American Indian/Alaska Native (22)	80	0.55
Not Hispanic (19)	73	0.50
Hispanic (3)	7	0.05
Alaska Athabascan *(Ala. Nat.)* (2)	2	0.01
Apache (0)	3	0.02
Blackfeet (0)	3	0.02
Central American Ind. (0)	1	0.01
Cherokee (1)	25	0.17
Chickasaw (2)	2	0.01
Choctaw (1)	1	0.01
Creek (0)	4	0.03
Iroquois (1)	1	0.01
Mexican American Ind. (0)	1	0.01
Navajo (0)	1	0.01
Potawatomi (1)	2	0.01
Sioux (1)	1	0.01
South American Ind. (2)	4	0.03
Tlingit-Haida *(Alaska Native)* (0)	4	0.03
Asian (1,599)	1,803	12.38
Not Hispanic (1,594)	1,795	12.32
Hispanic (5)	8	0.05
Bangladeshi (2)	6	0.04
Burmese (4)	4	0.03
Cambodian (4)	5	0.03
Chinese, ex. Taiwanese (381)	465	3.19
Filipino (32)	62	0.43
Indian (500)	563	3.86
Indonesian (1)	1	0.01
Japanese (39)	65	0.45
Korean (336)	357	2.45
Laotian (2)	7	0.05
Nepalese (1)	1	0.01
Pakistani (61)	65	0.45
Sri Lankan (9)	9	0.06
Taiwanese (42)	53	0.36
Thai (13)	16	0.11
Vietnamese (113)	121	0.83
Hawaii Native/Pacific Islander (6)	16	0.11
Not Hispanic (6)	16	0.11
Native Hawaiian (6)	10	0.07
White (11,404)	11,685	80.21
Not Hispanic (11,103)	11,367	78.03
Hispanic (301)	318	2.18

Dublin

Place Type: City
County: Laurens
Population: 16,201†

Ancestry‡	Population	%
African, Sub-Saharan (132)	167	1.02
African (132)	159	0.97
Ghanaian (0)	8	0.05
American (1,481)	1,481	9.08
British (87)	111	0.68
Czech (0)	13	0.08
Danish (13)	13	0.08
Dutch (0)	5	0.03
English (760)	1,240	7.60
European (84)	149	0.91
French, ex. Basque (35)	98	0.60
French Canadian (22)	22	0.13
German (191)	456	2.80
Hungarian (0)	37	0.23
Irish (373)	870	5.33
Italian (50)	59	0.36
Norwegian (35)	48	0.29
Polish (32)	32	0.20
Portuguese (0)	18	0.11
Russian (17)	17	0.10
Scotch-Irish (121)	311	1.91
Scottish (116)	199	1.22
Swedish (17)	17	0.10
Swiss (0)	12	0.07
Welsh (0)	14	0.09
West Indian, ex. Hispanic (9)	9	0.06
Jamaican (9)	9	0.06

Hispanic Origin	Population	%
Hispanic or Latino (of any race)	324	2.00
Central American, ex. Mexican	17	0.10
Guatemalan	3	0.02
Honduran	2	0.01
Panamanian	9	0.06
Salvadoran	3	0.02
Cuban	21	0.13
Dominican Republic	13	0.08
Mexican	176	1.09
Puerto Rican	49	0.30
South American	12	0.07
Bolivian	1	0.01
Colombian	9	0.06
Peruvian	2	0.01
Other Hispanic or Latino	36	0.22

Race*	Population	%
African-American/Black (9,329)	9,461	58.40
Not Hispanic (9,302)	9,426	58.18
Hispanic (27)	35	0.22
American Indian/Alaska Native (26)	64	0.40
Not Hispanic (25)	61	0.38
Hispanic (1)	3	0.02
Apache (0)	2	0.01
Blackfeet (0)	4	0.02
Cherokee (6)	21	0.13
Sioux (0)	1	0.01
Asian (317)	362	2.23
Not Hispanic (317)	359	2.22
Hispanic (0)	3	0.02
Bangladeshi (3)	3	0.02
Chinese, ex. Taiwanese (36)	44	0.27
Filipino (18)	33	0.20
Indian (166)	171	1.06
Indonesian (4)	4	0.02
Japanese (39)	45	0.28
Korean (13)	15	0.09
Nepalese (6)	6	0.04
Pakistani (5)	5	0.03
Thai (0)	1	0.01
Vietnamese (15)	19	0.12
Hawaii Native/Pacific Islander (0)	10	0.06
Not Hispanic (0)	9	0.06
Hispanic (0)	1	0.01

*Notes: † The Census 2010 population figure is used to calculate the percentages in the Hispanic Origin and Race categories. Ancestry percentages are based on the 2006-2010 American Community Survey population (not shown); ‡ Numbers in parentheses indicate the number of people reporting a single ancestry; * Numbers in parentheses indicate the number of persons reporting this race alone, not in combination with any other race; Please refer to the Explanation of Data for more information.*

Native Hawaiian (0)	3	0.02
Samoan (0)	1	0.01
White (6,171)	6,295	38.86
Not Hispanic (6,057)	6,160	38.02
Hispanic (114)	135	0.83

Duluth

Place Type: City
County: Gwinnett
Population: 26,600†

Ancestry‡	Population	%
African, Sub-Saharan (331)	383	1.46
African (230)	282	1.07
Kenyan (13)	13	0.05
Nigerian (71)	71	0.27
South African (17)	17	0.06
Albanian (10)	10	0.04
Alsatian (0)	11	0.04
American (1,461)	1,461	5.55
Arab (47)	105	0.40
Egyptian (47)	47	0.18
Other Arab (0)	58	0.22
Armenian (23)	38	0.14
Austrian (29)	74	0.28
British (61)	106	0.40
Canadian (11)	45	0.17
Croatian (0)	8	0.03
Czech (12)	61	0.23
Czechoslovakian (0)	35	0.13
Danish (0)	7	0.03
Dutch (75)	279	1.06
Eastern European (0)	34	0.13
English (849)	2,094	7.96
European (353)	455	1.73
French, ex. Basque (127)	446	1.69
French Canadian (18)	71	0.27
German (392)	1,888	7.17
Greek (31)	31	0.12
Hungarian (10)	39	0.15
Iranian (119)	119	0.45
Irish (864)	2,497	9.49
Italian (176)	648	2.46
Latvian (0)	16	0.06
Lithuanian (30)	47	0.18
Northern European (21)	21	0.08
Norwegian (11)	70	0.27
Polish (124)	372	1.41
Portuguese (28)	28	0.11
Romanian (20)	40	0.15
Russian (130)	179	0.68
Scandinavian (29)	29	0.11
Scotch-Irish (214)	423	1.61
Scottish (143)	379	1.44
Serbian (19)	19	0.07
Slavic (12)	12	0.05
Slovak (13)	39	0.15
Swedish (61)	199	0.76
Swiss (0)	40	0.15
Turkish (0)	7	0.03
Ukrainian (56)	56	0.21
Welsh (11)	268	1.02
West Indian, ex. Hispanic (161)	174	0.66
Haitian (59)	59	0.22
Jamaican (90)	90	0.34
Trinidadian/Tobagonian (12)	12	0.05
West Indian (0)	13	0.05

Hispanic Origin	Population	%
Hispanic or Latino (of any race)	3,732	14.03
Central American, ex. Mexican	268	1.01
Costa Rican	26	0.10
Guatemalan	39	0.15
Honduran	48	0.18
Nicaraguan	24	0.09
Panamanian	36	0.14
Salvadoran	91	0.34
Other Central American	4	0.02
Cuban	126	0.47
Dominican Republic	106	0.40
Mexican	1,986	7.47
Puerto Rican	282	1.06
South American	769	2.89
Argentinean	23	0.09
Bolivian	1	<0.01
Chilean	18	0.07
Colombian	379	1.42
Ecuadorian	20	0.08
Paraguayan	6	0.02
Peruvian	187	0.70
Uruguayan	27	0.10
Venezuelan	105	0.39
Other South American	3	0.01
Other Hispanic or Latino	195	0.73

Race*	Population	%
African-American/Black (5,378)	5,756	21.64
Not Hispanic (5,196)	5,499	20.67
Hispanic (182)	257	0.97
American Indian/Alaska Native (111)	306	1.15
Not Hispanic (56)	178	0.67
Hispanic (55)	128	0.48
Apache (1)	2	0.01
Blackfeet (0)	2	0.01
Central American Ind. (3)	3	0.01
Cherokee (6)	39	0.15
Chippewa (6)	7	0.03
Choctaw (0)	3	0.01
Creek (4)	5	0.02
Inupiat *(Alaska Native)* (1)	1	<0.01
Iroquois (1)	3	0.01
Lumbee (1)	1	<0.01
Mexican American Ind. (10)	32	0.12
Navajo (0)	1	<0.01
Pima (1)	1	<0.01
Shoshone (1)	1	<0.01
Sioux (1)	4	0.02
South American Ind. (2)	6	0.02
Spanish American Ind. (0)	1	<0.01
Asian (5,920)	6,229	23.42
Not Hispanic (5,905)	6,196	23.29
Hispanic (15)	33	0.12
Bangladeshi (33)	41	0.15
Burmese (7)	7	0.03
Cambodian (9)	10	0.04
Chinese, ex. Taiwanese (894)	977	3.67
Filipino (101)	142	0.53
Hmong (2)	4	0.02
Indian (1,286)	1,359	5.11
Indonesian (43)	46	0.17
Japanese (150)	203	0.76
Korean (2,600)	2,683	10.09
Laotian (41)	55	0.21
Malaysian (15)	25	0.09
Nepalese (9)	9	0.03
Pakistani (129)	138	0.52
Sri Lankan (3)	3	0.01
Taiwanese (73)	82	0.31
Thai (14)	21	0.08
Vietnamese (387)	418	1.57
Hawaii Native/Pacific Islander (16)	38	0.14
Not Hispanic (15)	33	0.12
Hispanic (1)	5	0.02
Guamanian/Chamorro (4)	5	0.02
Native Hawaiian (4)	7	0.03
Samoan (0)	1	<0.01
White (12,949)	13,554	50.95
Not Hispanic (11,028)	11,458	43.08
Hispanic (1,921)	2,096	7.88

Dunwoody

Place Type: City
County: DeKalb
Population: 46,267†

Ancestry‡	Population	%
African, Sub-Saharan (496)	624	1.40
African (272)	388	0.87
Ethiopian (16)	16	0.04
Kenyan (90)	90	0.20
South African (71)	83	0.19
Other Sub-Saharan African (47)	47	0.11
Albanian (70)	70	0.16
American (3,304)	3,304	7.39
Arab (181)	387	0.87
Arab (46)	105	0.23
Egyptian (35)	35	0.08
Lebanese (64)	211	0.47
Other Arab (36)	36	0.08
Australian (14)	28	0.06
Austrian (13)	159	0.36
Belgian (23)	56	0.13
Brazilian (74)	137	0.31
British (517)	707	1.58
Bulgarian (22)	22	0.05
Canadian (47)	74	0.17
Celtic (27)	27	0.06
Croatian (0)	29	0.06
Czech (53)	140	0.31
Czechoslovakian (14)	62	0.14
Danish (17)	157	0.35
Dutch (105)	446	1.00
Eastern European (597)	609	1.36
English (2,742)	5,917	13.24
European (1,172)	1,333	2.98
French, ex. Basque (336)	981	2.20
French Canadian (82)	243	0.54
German (1,634)	5,095	11.40
Greek (184)	285	0.64
Guyanese (21)	21	0.05
Hungarian (51)	143	0.32
Iranian (34)	34	0.08
Irish (1,241)	4,543	10.17
Israeli (119)	165	0.37
Italian (828)	2,223	4.97
Latvian (0)	54	0.12
Lithuanian (15)	86	0.19
Luxemburger (0)	25	0.06
Northern European (46)	46	0.10
Norwegian (68)	366	0.82
Pennsylvania German (0)	16	0.04
Polish (295)	992	2.22
Portuguese (10)	103	0.23
Romanian (50)	117	0.26
Russian (693)	1,257	2.81
Scandinavian (86)	148	0.33
Scotch-Irish (688)	1,122	2.51
Scottish (518)	1,452	3.25
Slavic (17)	17	0.04
Slovak (33)	185	0.41
Slovene (14)	14	0.03
Swedish (213)	535	1.20
Swiss (63)	94	0.21
Turkish (60)	111	0.25
Ukrainian (48)	104	0.23
Welsh (62)	248	0.55
West Indian, ex. Hispanic (226)	307	0.69
Bahamian (10)	10	0.02
Haitian (27)	27	0.06
Jamaican (171)	232	0.52
Trinidadian/Tobagonian (18)	38	0.09
Yugoslavian (12)	12	0.03

Hispanic Origin	Population	%
Hispanic or Latino (of any race)	4,755	10.28
Central American, ex. Mexican	820	1.77
Costa Rican	18	0.04
Guatemalan	332	0.72
Honduran	197	0.43
Nicaraguan	35	0.08
Panamanian	42	0.09
Salvadoran	190	0.41
Other Central American	6	0.01
Cuban	181	0.39
Dominican Republic	66	0.14
Mexican	2,283	4.93
Puerto Rican	289	0.62
South American	729	1.58

*Notes: † The Census 2010 population figure is used to calculate the percentages in the Hispanic Origin and Race categories. Ancestry percentages are based on the 2006-2010 American Community Survey population (not shown); ‡ Numbers in parentheses indicate the number of people reporting a single ancestry; * Numbers in parentheses indicate the number of persons reporting this race alone, not in combination with any other race; Please refer to the Explanation of Data for more information.*

Argentinean	61	0.13
Bolivian	20	0.04
Chilean	57	0.12
Colombian	311	0.67
Ecuadorian	58	0.13
Paraguayan	2	<0.01
Peruvian	70	0.15
Uruguayan	28	0.06
Venezuelan	114	0.25
Other South American	8	0.02
Other Hispanic or Latino	387	0.84

Race*	Population	%
African-American/Black (5,851)	6,228	13.46
Not Hispanic (5,697)	6,010	12.99
Hispanic (154)	218	0.47
American Indian/Alaska Native (151)	361	0.78
Not Hispanic (99)	267	0.58
Hispanic (52)	94	0.20
Apache (3)	5	0.01
Blackfeet (1)	8	0.02
Central American Ind. (2)	2	<0.01
Cherokee (17)	66	0.14
Chickasaw (0)	2	<0.01
Choctaw (5)	13	0.03
Creek (2)	5	0.01
Iroquois (3)	4	0.01
Kiowa (0)	1	<0.01
Lumbee (1)	4	0.01
Mexican American Ind. (15)	19	0.04
Navajo (0)	3	0.01
Osage (0)	1	<0.01
Potawatomi (1)	1	<0.01
Seminole (0)	3	0.01
Sioux (0)	5	0.01
Asian (5,153)	5,609	12.12
Not Hispanic (5,139)	5,581	12.06
Hispanic (14)	28	0.06
Bangladeshi (40)	44	0.10
Bhutanese (47)	104	0.22
Cambodian (17)	24	0.05
Chinese, ex. Taiwanese (662)	768	1.66
Filipino (123)	170	0.37
Hmong (3)	3	0.01
Indian (2,595)	2,701	5.84
Indonesian (44)	51	0.11
Japanese (235)	301	0.65
Korean (801)	859	1.86
Laotian (15)	19	0.04
Malaysian (6)	14	0.03
Nepalese (23)	81	0.18
Pakistani (72)	79	0.17
Sri Lankan (9)	10	0.02
Taiwanese (85)	112	0.24
Thai (34)	45	0.10
Vietnamese (183)	204	0.44
Hawaii Native/Pacific Islander (57)	95	0.21
Not Hispanic (16)	49	0.11
Hispanic (41)	46	0.10
Guamanian/Chamorro (44)	48	0.10
Native Hawaiian (9)	13	0.03
Samoan (2)	7	0.02
White (32,287)	33,072	71.48
Not Hispanic (29,667)	30,222	65.32
Hispanic (2,620)	2,850	6.16

East Point

Place Type: City
County: Fulton
Population: 33,712†

Ancestry‡	Population	%
African, Sub-Saharan (1,091)	1,369	3.98
African (923)	974	2.83
Ghanaian (47)	123	0.36
Liberian (12)	12	0.03
Nigerian (79)	79	0.23
Somalian (0)	99	0.29
Sudanese (30)	30	0.09
Other Sub-Saharan African (0)	52	0.15
American (1,341)	1,341	3.90
Austrian (0)	8	0.02
Belgian (13)	13	0.04
British (8)	58	0.17
Canadian (0)	8	0.02
Dutch (10)	112	0.33
English (210)	599	1.74
European (82)	92	0.27
French, ex. Basque (28)	134	0.39
French Canadian (27)	42	0.12
German (69)	363	1.06
Greek (13)	32	0.09
Guyanese (0)	15	0.04
Irish (317)	743	2.16
Italian (66)	171	0.50
Lithuanian (21)	45	0.13
Norwegian (0)	5	0.01
Polish (34)	110	0.32
Portuguese (0)	44	0.13
Russian (15)	34	0.10
Scotch-Irish (165)	311	0.90
Scottish (151)	291	0.85
Swedish (40)	52	0.15
Welsh (0)	55	0.16
West Indian, ex. Hispanic (304)	360	1.05
Haitian (108)	108	0.31
Jamaican (82)	138	0.40
Trinidadian/Tobagonian (70)	70	0.20
West Indian (44)	44	0.13

Hispanic Origin	Population	%
Hispanic or Latino (of any race)	3,890	11.54
Central American, ex. Mexican	109	0.32
Costa Rican	7	0.02
Guatemalan	12	0.04
Honduran	42	0.12
Nicaraguan	3	0.01
Panamanian	29	0.09
Salvadoran	16	0.05
Cuban	77	0.23
Dominican Republic	32	0.09
Mexican	3,205	9.51
Puerto Rican	157	0.47
South American	42	0.12
Argentinean	1	<0.01
Bolivian	1	<0.01
Colombian	11	0.03
Ecuadorian	4	0.01
Peruvian	12	0.04
Uruguayan	3	0.01
Venezuelan	7	0.02
Other South American	3	0.01
Other Hispanic or Latino	268	0.79

Race*	Population	%
African-American/Black (25,165)	25,673	76.15
Not Hispanic (24,924)	25,350	75.20
Hispanic (241)	323	0.96
American Indian/Alaska Native (131)	318	0.94
Not Hispanic (94)	269	0.80
Hispanic (37)	49	0.15
Alaska Athabascan *(Ala. Nat.)* (1)	1	<0.01
Apache (0)	2	0.01
Blackfeet (0)	3	0.01
Central American Ind. (4)	4	0.01
Cherokee (9)	46	0.14
Chippewa (0)	2	0.01
Choctaw (0)	10	0.03
Comanche (0)	1	<0.01
Creek (0)	3	0.01
Iroquois (1)	1	<0.01
Kiowa (2)	2	0.01
Mexican American Ind. (11)	11	0.03
Potawatomi (0)	1	<0.01
Pueblo (1)	1	<0.01
Sioux (0)	2	0.01
South American Ind. (4)	4	0.01
Asian (268)	379	1.12
Not Hispanic (266)	368	1.09
Hispanic (2)	11	0.03
Bangladeshi (3)	3	0.01
Cambodian (8)	10	0.03
Chinese, ex. Taiwanese (27)	42	0.12
Filipino (55)	75	0.22
Indian (52)	76	0.23
Indonesian (0)	1	<0.01
Japanese (13)	26	0.08
Korean (11)	24	0.07
Laotian (2)	2	0.01
Malaysian (1)	1	<0.01
Pakistani (18)	19	0.06
Sri Lankan (1)	1	<0.01
Taiwanese (8)	10	0.03
Thai (5)	7	0.02
Vietnamese (40)	55	0.16
Hawaii Native/Pacific Islander (13)	45	0.13
Not Hispanic (11)	28	0.08
Hispanic (2)	17	0.05
Guamanian/Chamorro (7)	7	0.02
Native Hawaiian (4)	14	0.04
Samoan (0)	6	0.02
White (5,437)	5,849	17.35
Not Hispanic (3,978)	4,290	12.73
Hispanic (1,459)	1,559	4.62

Evans

Place Type: CDP
County: Columbia
Population: 29,011†

Ancestry‡	Population	%
African, Sub-Saharan (314)	314	1.13
African (29)	29	0.10
Nigerian (285)	285	1.03
American (4,420)	4,420	15.90
Arab (227)	299	1.08
Jordanian (86)	86	0.31
Lebanese (0)	48	0.17
Palestinian (98)	98	0.35
Other Arab (43)	67	0.24
Armenian (20)	79	0.28
Austrian (33)	150	0.54
Belgian (7)	7	0.03
British (61)	75	0.27
Cajun (14)	14	0.05
Canadian (0)	43	0.15
Croatian (9)	27	0.10
Czech (30)	69	0.25
Czechoslovakian (36)	76	0.27
Danish (23)	59	0.21
Dutch (105)	375	1.35
Eastern European (10)	10	0.04
English (1,800)	3,317	11.93
European (653)	700	2.52
Finnish (0)	21	0.08
French, ex. Basque (139)	650	2.34
French Canadian (109)	177	0.64
German (1,407)	3,727	13.41
Greek (27)	37	0.13
Hungarian (19)	227	0.82
Irish (1,197)	2,991	10.76
Italian (565)	1,297	4.67
Northern European (13)	13	0.05
Norwegian (143)	351	1.26
Polish (177)	398	1.43
Portuguese (0)	40	0.14
Romanian (41)	41	0.15
Russian (124)	166	0.60
Scotch-Irish (263)	559	2.01
Scottish (235)	692	2.49
Slovak (0)	38	0.14
Slovene (0)	30	0.11
Swedish (50)	140	0.50
Swiss (0)	80	0.29
Turkish (19)	57	0.21
Ukrainian (55)	77	0.28
Welsh (37)	217	0.78
West Indian, ex. Hispanic (12)	12	0.04

*Notes: † The Census 2010 population figure is used to calculate the percentages in the Hispanic Origin and Race categories. Ancestry percentages are based on the 2006-2010 American Community Survey population (not shown); ‡ Numbers in parentheses indicate the number of people reporting a single ancestry; * Numbers in parentheses indicate the number of persons reporting this race alone, not in combination with any other race; Please refer to the Explanation of Data for more information.*

Jamaican (12)	12	0.04

Hispanic Origin	Population	%
Hispanic or Latino (of any race)	1,104	3.81
Central American, ex. Mexican	110	0.38
Costa Rican	10	0.03
Guatemalan	7	0.02
Honduran	26	0.09
Nicaraguan	8	0.03
Panamanian	49	0.17
Salvadoran	9	0.03
Other Central American	1	<0.01
Cuban	61	0.21
Dominican Republic	24	0.08
Mexican	411	1.42
Puerto Rican	304	1.05
South American	105	0.36
Argentinean	1	<0.01
Bolivian	3	0.01
Chilean	8	0.03
Colombian	55	0.19
Ecuadorian	4	0.01
Paraguayan	1	<0.01
Peruvian	19	0.07
Uruguayan	1	<0.01
Venezuelan	10	0.03
Other South American	3	0.01
Other Hispanic or Latino	89	0.31

Race*	Population	%
African-American/Black (3,313)	3,547	12.23
Not Hispanic (3,276)	3,456	11.91
Hispanic (37)	91	0.31
American Indian/Alaska Native (69)	209	0.72
Not Hispanic (60)	176	0.61
Hispanic (9)	33	0.11
Apache (1)	2	0.01
Blackfeet (0)	1	<0.01
Cherokee (17)	64	0.22
Chippewa (7)	10	0.03
Choctaw (0)	3	0.01
Comanche (0)	1	<0.01
Cree (0)	1	<0.01
Creek (1)	6	0.02
Houma (3)	3	0.01
Inupiat *(Alaska Native)* (1)	1	<0.01
Iroquois (1)	5	0.02
Lumbee (1)	7	0.02
Mexican American Ind. (1)	2	0.01
Navajo (2)	7	0.02
Potawatomi (1)	1	<0.01
Shoshone (0)	3	0.01
Sioux (5)	5	0.02
South American Ind. (0)	4	0.01
Spanish American Ind. (1)	2	0.01
Asian (1,469)	1,785	6.15
Not Hispanic (1,458)	1,738	5.99
Hispanic (11)	47	0.16
Bangladeshi (11)	11	0.04
Cambodian (4)	4	0.01
Chinese, ex. Taiwanese (243)	266	0.92
Filipino (109)	171	0.59
Indian (557)	606	2.09
Indonesian (2)	4	0.01
Japanese (28)	79	0.27
Korean (296)	400	1.38
Laotian (0)	1	<0.01
Malaysian (3)	3	0.01
Nepalese (0)	1	<0.01
Pakistani (48)	54	0.19
Sri Lankan (3)	3	0.01
Taiwanese (9)	9	0.03
Thai (12)	32	0.11
Vietnamese (102)	113	0.39
Hawaii Native/Pacific Islander (23)	58	0.20
Not Hispanic (23)	54	0.19
Hispanic (0)	4	0.01
Guamanian/Chamorro (15)	18	0.06
Native Hawaiian (1)	15	0.05
Samoan (2)	7	0.02
White (23,180)	23,747	81.86
Not Hispanic (22,500)	22,974	79.19
Hispanic (680)	773	2.66

Fair Oaks

Place Type: CDP
County: Cobb
Population: 8,225†

Ancestry‡	Population	%
African, Sub-Saharan (179)	194	3.03
African (113)	113	1.77
Nigerian (0)	15	0.23
Other Sub-Saharan African (66)	66	1.03
American (421)	421	6.58
Brazilian (6)	12	0.19
British (16)	22	0.34
Dutch (0)	76	1.19
English (65)	194	3.03
European (0)	19	0.30
French, ex. Basque (15)	68	1.06
German (64)	203	3.17
Irish (68)	198	3.09
Italian (8)	53	0.83
Lithuanian (12)	20	0.31
Norwegian (16)	16	0.25
Polish (8)	8	0.12
Romanian (0)	15	0.23
Russian (19)	19	0.30
Scotch-Irish (19)	19	0.30
Scottish (14)	37	0.58
Ukrainian (10)	10	0.16
Welsh (0)	5	0.08
West Indian, ex. Hispanic (16)	16	0.25
Haitian (16)	16	0.25

Hispanic Origin	Population	%
Hispanic or Latino (of any race)	4,333	52.68
Central American, ex. Mexican	470	5.71
Costa Rican	6	0.07
Guatemalan	201	2.44
Honduran	83	1.01
Nicaraguan	25	0.30
Panamanian	2	0.02
Salvadoran	153	1.86
Cuban	14	0.17
Dominican Republic	9	0.11
Mexican	3,552	43.19
Puerto Rican	56	0.68
South American	50	0.61
Argentinean	4	0.05
Colombian	15	0.18
Ecuadorian	5	0.06
Peruvian	12	0.15
Uruguayan	10	0.12
Venezuelan	4	0.05
Other Hispanic or Latino	182	2.21

Race*	Population	%
African-American/Black (1,814)	1,991	24.21
Not Hispanic (1,736)	1,822	22.15
Hispanic (78)	169	2.05
American Indian/Alaska Native (75)	125	1.52
Not Hispanic (19)	51	0.62
Hispanic (56)	74	0.90
Apache (1)	1	0.01
Blackfeet (4)	5	0.06
Central American Ind. (0)	2	0.02
Cherokee (6)	23	0.28
Creek (1)	1	0.01
Iroquois (1)	4	0.05
Mexican American Ind. (25)	28	0.34
Navajo (1)	1	0.01
Asian (49)	62	0.75
Not Hispanic (48)	58	0.71
Hispanic (1)	4	0.05
Cambodian (1)	1	0.01
Chinese, ex. Taiwanese (0)	1	0.01
Filipino (6)	7	0.09
Indian (17)	20	0.24
Japanese (1)	4	0.05
Korean (3)	6	0.07
Laotian (2)	2	0.02
Pakistani (4)	4	0.05
Vietnamese (15)	15	0.18
Hawaii Native/Pacific Islander (6)	11	0.13
Hispanic (6)	11	0.13
Guamanian/Chamorro (6)	10	0.12
White (4,107)	4,423	53.78
Not Hispanic (1,954)	2,054	24.97
Hispanic (2,153)	2,369	28.80

Fairburn

Place Type: City
County: Fulton
Population: 12,950†

Ancestry‡	Population	%
African, Sub-Saharan (234)	234	2.03
African (58)	58	0.50
Ghanaian (32)	32	0.28
Nigerian (144)	144	1.25
American (608)	608	5.27
Austrian (10)	10	0.09
Belgian (8)	8	0.07
Dutch (0)	11	0.10
English (113)	136	1.18
French, ex. Basque (0)	64	0.55
French Canadian (9)	9	0.08
German (109)	291	2.52
Guyanese (51)	51	0.44
Hungarian (0)	8	0.07
Irish (159)	335	2.90
Italian (10)	59	0.51
Polish (9)	22	0.19
Russian (0)	16	0.14
Scotch-Irish (10)	10	0.09
Scottish (14)	76	0.66
Swedish (0)	7	0.06
Swiss (0)	49	0.42
Welsh (10)	20	0.17
West Indian, ex. Hispanic (178)	199	1.72
Haitian (0)	6	0.05
Jamaican (116)	116	1.01
U.S. Virgin Islander (6)	6	0.05
West Indian (56)	71	0.62

Hispanic Origin	Population	%
Hispanic or Latino (of any race)	1,545	11.93
Central American, ex. Mexican	109	0.84
Costa Rican	1	0.01
Guatemalan	20	0.15
Honduran	26	0.20
Nicaraguan	4	0.03
Panamanian	21	0.16
Salvadoran	35	0.27
Other Central American	2	0.02
Cuban	20	0.15
Dominican Republic	18	0.14
Mexican	1,157	8.93
Puerto Rican	106	0.82
South American	47	0.36
Argentinean	1	0.01
Chilean	4	0.03
Colombian	32	0.25
Peruvian	3	0.02
Venezuelan	3	0.02
Other South American	4	0.03
Other Hispanic or Latino	88	0.68

Race*	Population	%
African-American/Black (9,050)	9,236	71.32
Not Hispanic (8,966)	9,102	70.29
Hispanic (84)	134	1.03
American Indian/Alaska Native (57)	135	1.04
Not Hispanic (33)	99	0.76
Hispanic (24)	36	0.28
Blackfeet (0)	4	0.03

*Notes: † The Census 2010 population figure is used to calculate the percentages in the Hispanic Origin and Race categories. Ancestry percentages are based on the 2006-2010 American Community Survey population (not shown); ‡ Numbers in parentheses indicate the number of people reporting a single ancestry; * Numbers in parentheses indicate the number of persons reporting this race alone, not in combination with any other race; Please refer to the Explanation of Data for more information.*

Cherokee (8)	32	0.25
Chickasaw (1)	1	0.01
Choctaw (0)	7	0.05
Creek (0)	1	0.01
Iroquois (0)	4	0.03
Lumbee (3)	3	0.02
Mexican American Ind. (7)	7	0.05
Navajo (2)	2	0.02
Seminole (0)	5	0.04
South American Ind. (2)	2	0.02
Spanish American Ind. (5)	5	0.04
Yaqui (1)	1	0.01
Asian (222)	267	2.06
Not Hispanic (212)	248	1.92
Hispanic (10)	19	0.15
Bangladeshi (1)	4	0.03
Chinese, ex. Taiwanese (38)	43	0.33
Filipino (15)	21	0.16
Hmong (0)	1	0.01
Indian (58)	66	0.51
Indonesian (0)	2	0.02
Japanese (7)	9	0.07
Korean (9)	20	0.15
Laotian (5)	6	0.05
Pakistani (30)	33	0.25
Thai (2)	3	0.02
Vietnamese (37)	42	0.32
Hawaii Native/Pacific Islander (5)	10	0.08
Not Hispanic (4)	6	0.05
Hispanic (1)	4	0.03
Guamanian/Chamorro (4)	4	0.03
Samoan (1)	1	0.01
White (2,603)	2,741	21.17
Not Hispanic (1,986)	2,078	16.05
Hispanic (617)	663	5.12

Fayetteville

Place Type: City
County: Fayette
Population: 15,945†

Ancestry‡	Population	%
African, Sub-Saharan (616)	880	5.77
African (475)	739	4.84
Nigerian (81)	81	0.53
Sierra Leonean (60)	60	0.39
American (1,345)	1,345	8.81
Arab (48)	66	0.43
Lebanese (15)	29	0.19
Moroccan (33)	33	0.22
Syrian (0)	4	0.03
British (33)	155	1.02
Cajun (8)	19	0.12
Canadian (39)	109	0.71
Czech (0)	28	0.18
Czechoslovakian (10)	23	0.15
Danish (0)	37	0.24
Dutch (18)	106	0.69
English (1,089)	2,113	13.84
European (80)	80	0.52
Finnish (0)	27	0.18
French, ex. Basque (21)	236	1.55
French Canadian (7)	7	0.05
German (295)	1,178	7.72
Greek (45)	45	0.29
Hungarian (18)	73	0.48
Irish (478)	1,601	10.49
Italian (115)	415	2.72
Latvian (5)	24	0.16
Lithuanian (13)	19	0.12
Norwegian (93)	193	1.26
Pennsylvania German (0)	12	0.08
Polish (141)	258	1.69
Portuguese (9)	14	0.09
Russian (8)	41	0.27
Scandinavian (0)	20	0.13
Scotch-Irish (203)	467	3.06
Scottish (77)	409	2.68
Slovak (11)	11	0.07
Swedish (23)	54	0.35
Swiss (7)	17	0.11
Ukrainian (8)	8	0.05
Welsh (11)	61	0.40
West Indian, ex. Hispanic (180)	247	1.62
Haitian (123)	136	0.89
Jamaican (35)	89	0.58
Trinidadian/Tobagonian (14)	14	0.09
West Indian (8)	8	0.05

Hispanic Origin	Population	%
Hispanic or Latino (of any race)	766	4.80
Central American, ex. Mexican	78	0.49
Costa Rican	7	0.04
Guatemalan	17	0.11
Honduran	11	0.07
Nicaraguan	7	0.04
Panamanian	27	0.17
Salvadoran	3	0.02
Other Central American	6	0.04
Cuban	38	0.24
Dominican Republic	60	0.38
Mexican	233	1.46
Puerto Rican	182	1.14
South American	88	0.55
Argentinean	3	0.02
Chilean	3	0.02
Colombian	26	0.16
Ecuadorian	5	0.03
Peruvian	34	0.21
Uruguayan	4	0.03
Venezuelan	12	0.08
Other South American	1	0.01
Other Hispanic or Latino	87	0.55

Race*	Population	%
African-American/Black (5,402)	5,654	35.46
Not Hispanic (5,323)	5,536	34.72
Hispanic (79)	118	0.74
American Indian/Alaska Native (57)	147	0.92
Not Hispanic (43)	121	0.76
Hispanic (14)	26	0.16
Cherokee (18)	47	0.29
Choctaw (1)	4	0.03
Cree (0)	1	0.01
Creek (0)	2	0.01
Lumbee (1)	1	0.01
Mexican American Ind. (1)	2	0.01
Navajo (0)	1	0.01
Ottawa (1)	1	0.01
Seminole (1)	3	0.02
Shoshone (1)	3	0.02
Sioux (1)	1	0.01
South American Ind. (0)	1	0.01
Tohono O'Odham (3)	3	0.02
Yaqui (1)	3	0.02
Asian (1,055)	1,205	7.56
Not Hispanic (1,053)	1,197	7.51
Hispanic (2)	8	0.05
Bangladeshi (4)	5	0.03
Cambodian (15)	15	0.09
Chinese, ex. Taiwanese (120)	149	0.93
Filipino (57)	107	0.67
Indian (417)	446	2.80
Indonesian (4)	7	0.04
Japanese (28)	48	0.30
Korean (100)	132	0.83
Laotian (19)	27	0.17
Malaysian (1)	1	0.01
Nepalese (8)	8	0.05
Pakistani (170)	173	1.08
Taiwanese (4)	4	0.03
Thai (4)	6	0.04
Vietnamese (57)	59	0.37
Hawaii Native/Pacific Islander (13)	27	0.17
Not Hispanic (9)	23	0.14
Hispanic (4)	4	0.03
Guamanian/Chamorro (3)	3	0.02
Native Hawaiian (0)	17	0.11
Samoan (3)	8	0.05
White (8,762)	9,094	57.03
Not Hispanic (8,345)	8,618	54.05
Hispanic (417)	476	2.99

Fitzgerald

Place Type: City
County: Ben Hill
Population: 9,053†

Ancestry‡	Population	%
African, Sub-Saharan (69)	69	0.76
African (69)	69	0.76
American (499)	499	5.51
Arab (0)	10	0.11
Arab (0)	10	0.11
British (0)	68	0.75
Danish (0)	45	0.50
Dutch (16)	129	1.42
English (1,080)	1,471	16.24
European (14)	14	0.15
French, ex. Basque (19)	53	0.59
French Canadian (0)	3	0.03
German (33)	422	4.66
Irish (447)	843	9.31
Italian (47)	94	1.04
Lithuanian (20)	20	0.22
Norwegian (71)	71	0.78
Polish (0)	7	0.08
Scotch-Irish (37)	178	1.96
Scottish (87)	121	1.34
Welsh (0)	7	0.08
West Indian, ex. Hispanic (24)	24	0.26
Bermudan (24)	24	0.26

Hispanic Origin	Population	%
Hispanic or Latino (of any race)	388	4.29
Central American, ex. Mexican	10	0.11
Guatemalan	4	0.04
Honduran	3	0.03
Salvadoran	3	0.03
Cuban	5	0.06
Dominican Republic	1	0.01
Mexican	345	3.81
Puerto Rican	14	0.15
Other Hispanic or Latino	13	0.14

Race*	Population	%
African-American/Black (4,652)	4,724	52.18
Not Hispanic (4,638)	4,703	51.95
Hispanic (14)	21	0.23
American Indian/Alaska Native (33)	72	0.80
Not Hispanic (28)	60	0.66
Hispanic (5)	12	0.13
Aleut *(Alaska Native)* (0)	1	0.01
Apache (4)	5	0.06
Cherokee (1)	5	0.06
Mexican American Ind. (0)	2	0.02
South American Ind. (0)	2	0.02
Tsimshian *(Alaska Native)* (0)	1	0.01
Asian (79)	93	1.03
Not Hispanic (79)	93	1.03
Chinese, ex. Taiwanese (2)	3	0.03
Filipino (20)	24	0.27
Indian (51)	57	0.63
Japanese (4)	4	0.04
Thai (2)	4	0.04
Hawaii Native/Pacific Islander (2)	4	0.04
Not Hispanic (2)	4	0.04
Guamanian/Chamorro (2)	3	0.03
White (3,911)	4,025	44.46
Not Hispanic (3,807)	3,898	43.06
Hispanic (104)	127	1.40

Forest Park

Place Type: City
County: Clayton
Population: 18,468†

*Notes: † The Census 2010 population figure is used to calculate the percentages in the Hispanic Origin and Race categories. Ancestry percentages are based on the 2006-2010 American Community Survey population (not shown); ‡ Numbers in parentheses indicate the number of people reporting a single ancestry; * Numbers in parentheses indicate the number of persons reporting this race alone, not in combination with any other race; Please refer to the Explanation of Data for more information.*

Ancestry‡	Population	%
African, Sub-Saharan (273)	310	1.60
African (255)	292	1.51
Nigerian (18)	18	0.09
American (1,098)	1,098	5.68
Cajun (0)	15	0.08
Danish (10)	10	0.05
Dutch (16)	143	0.74
English (153)	384	1.99
European (57)	57	0.30
French, ex. Basque (21)	140	0.72
French Canadian (25)	56	0.29
German (223)	694	3.59
Greek (0)	10	0.05
Irish (151)	616	3.19
Italian (99)	182	0.94
Norwegian (0)	36	0.19
Polish (22)	49	0.25
Portuguese (11)	11	0.06
Russian (28)	90	0.47
Scandinavian (30)	62	0.32
Scotch-Irish (94)	120	0.62
Scottish (14)	98	0.51
Swedish (0)	8	0.04
Swiss (0)	7	0.04
Welsh (0)	27	0.14
West Indian, ex. Hispanic (451)	451	2.33
Bahamian (154)	154	0.80
Haitian (108)	108	0.56
Jamaican (148)	148	0.77
West Indian (41)	41	0.21

Hispanic Origin	Population	%
Hispanic or Latino (of any race)	6,343	34.35
Central American, ex. Mexican	434	2.35
Costa Rican	1	0.01
Guatemalan	116	0.63
Honduran	118	0.64
Nicaraguan	8	0.04
Panamanian	21	0.11
Salvadoran	169	0.92
Other Central American	1	0.01
Cuban	69	0.37
Dominican Republic	40	0.22
Mexican	5,378	29.12
Puerto Rican	133	0.72
South American	46	0.25
Argentinean	2	0.01
Chilean	3	0.02
Colombian	10	0.05
Ecuadorian	9	0.05
Peruvian	4	0.02
Uruguayan	16	0.09
Venezuelan	2	0.01
Other Hispanic or Latino	243	1.32

Race*	Population	%
African-American/Black (6,964)	7,204	39.01
Not Hispanic (6,808)	6,981	37.80
Hispanic (156)	223	1.21
American Indian/Alaska Native (85)	211	1.14
Not Hispanic (23)	117	0.63
Hispanic (62)	94	0.51
Apache (1)	1	0.01
Canadian/French Am. Ind. (1)	1	0.01
Central American Ind. (1)	2	0.01
Cherokee (10)	51	0.28
Chippewa (0)	1	0.01
Comanche (1)	1	0.01
Creek (0)	5	0.03
Iroquois (0)	6	0.03
Lumbee (0)	1	0.01
Mexican American Ind. (9)	13	0.07
Seminole (0)	1	0.01
Sioux (0)	3	0.02
Tlingit-Haida *(Alaska Native)* (1)	1	0.01
Asian (1,464)	1,514	8.20
Not Hispanic (1,448)	1,489	8.06
Hispanic (16)	25	0.14
Bangladeshi (5)	5	0.03
Cambodian (51)	62	0.34
Chinese, ex. Taiwanese (24)	41	0.22
Filipino (30)	38	0.21
Indian (59)	75	0.41
Japanese (0)	6	0.03
Korean (14)	15	0.08
Laotian (47)	59	0.32
Pakistani (3)	5	0.03
Thai (10)	24	0.13
Vietnamese (1,170)	1,224	6.63
Hawaii Native/Pacific Islander (11)	42	0.23
Not Hispanic (7)	20	0.11
Hispanic (4)	22	0.12
Guamanian/Chamorro (6)	7	0.04
Native Hawaiian (1)	10	0.05
Samoan (4)	6	0.03
White (5,855)	6,249	33.84
Not Hispanic (3,555)	3,753	20.32
Hispanic (2,300)	2,496	13.52

Fort Oglethorpe

Place Type: City
County: Catoosa
Population: 9,263†

Ancestry‡	Population	%
African, Sub-Saharan (8)	8	0.09
African (8)	8	0.09
American (1,461)	1,461	16.45
Canadian (0)	12	0.14
Croatian (0)	36	0.41
Danish (0)	15	0.17
Dutch (31)	103	1.16
English (439)	877	9.88
European (44)	53	0.60
French, ex. Basque (79)	193	2.17
French Canadian (33)	33	0.37
German (501)	970	10.92
Greek (9)	38	0.43
Iranian (15)	15	0.17
Irish (405)	1,551	17.47
Italian (37)	224	2.52
Luxemburger (11)	11	0.12
Norwegian (15)	15	0.17
Polish (28)	55	0.62
Russian (6)	31	0.35
Scotch-Irish (155)	208	2.34
Scottish (112)	272	3.06
Slovak (8)	8	0.09
Swiss (10)	10	0.11
Ukrainian (9)	9	0.10
Welsh (12)	30	0.34
West Indian, ex. Hispanic (6)	6	0.07
Jamaican (6)	6	0.07
Yugoslavian (53)	53	0.60

Hispanic Origin	Population	%
Hispanic or Latino (of any race)	246	2.66
Central American, ex. Mexican	13	0.14
Costa Rican	1	0.01
Guatemalan	3	0.03
Honduran	6	0.06
Nicaraguan	1	0.01
Panamanian	2	0.02
Cuban	8	0.09
Dominican Republic	5	0.05
Mexican	155	1.67
Puerto Rican	24	0.26
South American	10	0.11
Argentinean	4	0.04
Colombian	5	0.05
Other South American	1	0.01
Other Hispanic or Latino	31	0.33

Race*	Population	%
African-American/Black (438)	553	5.97
Not Hispanic (425)	536	5.79
Hispanic (13)	17	0.18
American Indian/Alaska Native (26)	93	1.00
Not Hispanic (26)	91	0.98
Hispanic (0)	2	0.02
Cherokee (13)	41	0.44
Chippewa (1)	1	0.01
Choctaw (2)	2	0.02
Creek (1)	2	0.02
Iroquois (1)	1	0.01
Lumbee (1)	1	0.01
Potawatomi (1)	2	0.02
Sioux (0)	1	0.01
Yaqui (0)	1	0.01
Asian (250)	287	3.10
Not Hispanic (243)	278	3.00
Hispanic (7)	9	0.10
Cambodian (1)	2	0.02
Chinese, ex. Taiwanese (16)	16	0.17
Filipino (7)	12	0.13
Indian (86)	97	1.05
Japanese (3)	4	0.04
Korean (46)	51	0.55
Laotian (55)	60	0.65
Nepalese (1)	1	0.01
Pakistani (4)	4	0.04
Thai (4)	8	0.09
Vietnamese (18)	27	0.29
Hawaii Native/Pacific Islander (8)	19	0.21
Not Hispanic (8)	15	0.16
Hispanic (0)	4	0.04
Guamanian/Chamorro (3)	3	0.03
Native Hawaiian (2)	5	0.05
Samoan (1)	1	0.01
White (8,206)	8,403	90.72
Not Hispanic (8,111)	8,285	89.44
Hispanic (95)	118	1.27

Fort Valley

Place Type: City
County: Peach
Population: 9,815†

Ancestry‡	Population	%
African, Sub-Saharan (203)	309	3.26
African (177)	283	2.99
Nigerian (26)	26	0.27
American (400)	400	4.22
British (0)	22	0.23
Dutch (0)	20	0.21
English (138)	222	2.34
European (35)	35	0.37
Finnish (0)	91	0.96
German (144)	322	3.40
Irish (94)	123	1.30
Italian (30)	45	0.47
Norwegian (22)	22	0.23
Polish (21)	21	0.22
Portuguese (29)	29	0.31
Scottish (0)	49	0.52
Ukrainian (10)	23	0.24
West Indian, ex. Hispanic (31)	42	0.44
Bahamian (19)	19	0.20
British West Indian (12)	12	0.13
Jamaican (0)	11	0.12

Hispanic Origin	Population	%
Hispanic or Latino (of any race)	570	5.81
Central American, ex. Mexican	27	0.28
Guatemalan	16	0.16
Honduran	1	0.01
Nicaraguan	1	0.01
Panamanian	1	0.01
Salvadoran	8	0.08
Cuban	5	0.05
Dominican Republic	14	0.14
Mexican	461	4.70
Puerto Rican	36	0.37
Other Hispanic or Latino	27	0.28

Race*	Population	%
African-American/Black (8,006)	8,124	82.77

*Notes: † The Census 2010 population figure is used to calculate the percentages in the Hispanic Origin and Race categories. Ancestry percentages are based on the 2006-2010 American Community Survey population (not shown); ‡ Numbers in parentheses indicate the number of people reporting a single ancestry; * Numbers in parentheses indicate the number of persons reporting this race alone, not in combination with any other race; Please refer to the Explanation of Data for more information.*

Not Hispanic (7,963)	8,062	82.14
Hispanic (43)	62	0.63
American Indian/Alaska Native (23)	72	0.73
Not Hispanic (22)	67	0.68
Hispanic (1)	5	0.05
Blackfeet (1)	5	0.05
Cherokee (7)	17	0.17
Creek (7)	10	0.10
Mexican American Ind. (1)	1	0.01
Pueblo (0)	1	0.01
Seminole (1)	2	0.02
Sioux (0)	1	0.01
Asian (25)	42	0.43
Not Hispanic (24)	39	0.40
Hispanic (1)	3	0.03
Chinese, ex. Taiwanese (10)	11	0.11
Filipino (1)	9	0.09
Indian (8)	10	0.10
Japanese (0)	4	0.04
Korean (3)	4	0.04
Vietnamese (1)	2	0.02
Hawaii Native/Pacific Islander (2)	9	0.09
Not Hispanic (2)	7	0.07
Hispanic (0)	2	0.02
Guamanian/Chamorro (1)	1	0.01
Native Hawaiian (1)	1	0.01
Samoan (0)	2	0.02
White (1,337)	1,451	14.78
Not Hispanic (1,116)	1,201	12.24
Hispanic (221)	250	2.55

Gainesville

Place Type: City
County: Hall
Population: 33,804†

Ancestry‡	Population	%
Afghan (56)	56	0.17
African, Sub-Saharan (57)	82	0.25
African (57)	82	0.25
American (3,903)	3,903	11.87
Arab (0)	32	0.10
Arab (0)	32	0.10
Austrian (12)	12	0.04
British (90)	144	0.44
Canadian (38)	38	0.12
Czech (0)	44	0.13
Danish (0)	13	0.04
Dutch (112)	337	1.02
Eastern European (24)	24	0.07
English (788)	1,624	4.94
European (182)	227	0.69
French, ex. Basque (63)	437	1.33
French Canadian (9)	21	0.06
German (591)	1,857	5.65
Greek (41)	41	0.12
Hungarian (26)	80	0.24
Irish (932)	2,224	6.76
Italian (186)	482	1.47
Luxemburger (13)	13	0.04
Norwegian (29)	139	0.42
Polish (39)	128	0.39
Portuguese (0)	13	0.04
Romanian (0)	21	0.06
Russian (0)	82	0.25
Scotch-Irish (329)	584	1.78
Scottish (158)	442	1.34
Slovak (25)	25	0.08
Swedish (0)	51	0.16
Swiss (17)	52	0.16
Ukrainian (9)	9	0.03
Welsh (13)	140	0.43
West Indian, ex. Hispanic (102)	114	0.35
Barbadian (19)	19	0.06
British West Indian (42)	42	0.13
Jamaican (23)	35	0.11
West Indian (18)	18	0.05

Hispanic Origin	Population	%
Hispanic or Latino (of any race)	14,058	41.59
Central American, ex. Mexican	1,844	5.45
Costa Rican	5	0.01
Guatemalan	321	0.95
Honduran	400	1.18
Nicaraguan	45	0.13
Panamanian	7	0.02
Salvadoran	1,037	3.07
Other Central American	29	0.09
Cuban	81	0.24
Dominican Republic	65	0.19
Mexican	10,940	32.36
Puerto Rican	350	1.04
South American	217	0.64
Argentinean	5	0.01
Bolivian	3	0.01
Chilean	12	0.04
Colombian	150	0.44
Ecuadorian	13	0.04
Peruvian	16	0.05
Uruguayan	7	0.02
Venezuelan	11	0.03
Other Hispanic or Latino	561	1.66

Race*	Population	%
African-American/Black (5,143)	5,488	16.23
Not Hispanic (4,940)	5,216	15.43
Hispanic (203)	272	0.80
American Indian/Alaska Native (219)	379	1.12
Not Hispanic (48)	154	0.46
Hispanic (171)	225	0.67
Blackfeet (0)	1	<0.01
Cherokee (7)	29	0.09
Chickasaw (0)	1	<0.01
Chippewa (2)	5	0.01
Choctaw (1)	2	0.01
Creek (3)	6	0.02
Iroquois (4)	5	0.01
Menominee (1)	1	<0.01
Mexican American Ind. (49)	67	0.20
Ottawa (1)	1	<0.01
Paiute (1)	1	<0.01
Pueblo (0)	2	0.01
Seminole (0)	2	0.01
Sioux (0)	1	<0.01
South American Ind. (0)	4	0.01
Spanish American Ind. (2)	2	0.01
Tlingit-Haida *(Alaska Native)* (2)	2	0.01
Yaqui (0)	1	<0.01
Asian (1,073)	1,209	3.58
Not Hispanic (1,070)	1,175	3.48
Hispanic (3)	34	0.10
Bangladeshi (3)	3	0.01
Cambodian (5)	9	0.03
Chinese, ex. Taiwanese (76)	95	0.28
Filipino (38)	69	0.20
Indian (87)	103	0.30
Japanese (24)	31	0.09
Korean (40)	60	0.18
Laotian (10)	11	0.03
Pakistani (19)	19	0.06
Taiwanese (14)	24	0.07
Thai (8)	17	0.05
Vietnamese (669)	700	2.07
Hawaii Native/Pacific Islander (72)	117	0.35
Not Hispanic (13)	46	0.14
Hispanic (59)	71	0.21
Guamanian/Chamorro (61)	64	0.19
Native Hawaiian (2)	27	0.08
Samoan (8)	8	0.02
White (18,333)	19,247	56.94
Not Hispanic (13,190)	13,568	40.14
Hispanic (5,143)	5,679	16.80

Garden City

Place Type: City
County: Chatham
Population: 8,778†

Ancestry‡	Population	%
African, Sub-Saharan (87)	87	0.97
African (79)	79	0.88
South African (8)	8	0.09
American (349)	349	3.89
Arab (22)	22	0.25
Other Arab (22)	22	0.25
Austrian (14)	47	0.52
Brazilian (24)	24	0.27
British (9)	9	0.10
Cajun (16)	16	0.18
Canadian (20)	20	0.22
Czech (0)	23	0.26
Czechoslovakian (7)	7	0.08
Danish (0)	19	0.21
Dutch (7)	31	0.35
English (340)	480	5.35
European (10)	10	0.11
French, ex. Basque (10)	43	0.48
French Canadian (0)	6	0.07
German (162)	319	3.56
Greek (0)	6	0.07
Hungarian (0)	10	0.11
Irish (282)	636	7.09
Italian (6)	86	0.96
Norwegian (7)	13	0.14
Polish (31)	46	0.51
Scotch-Irish (82)	128	1.43
Scottish (53)	101	1.13
Swiss (6)	6	0.07
Welsh (6)	6	0.07

Hispanic Origin	Population	%
Hispanic or Latino (of any race)	1,470	16.75
Central American, ex. Mexican	174	1.98
Costa Rican	3	0.03
Guatemalan	7	0.08
Honduran	138	1.57
Nicaraguan	4	0.05
Panamanian	3	0.03
Salvadoran	19	0.22
Cuban	19	0.22
Dominican Republic	14	0.16
Mexican	1,121	12.77
Puerto Rican	81	0.92
South American	3	0.03
Chilean	2	0.02
Venezuelan	1	0.01
Other Hispanic or Latino	58	0.66

Race*	Population	%
African-American/Black (3,285)	3,373	38.43
Not Hispanic (3,248)	3,319	37.81
Hispanic (37)	54	0.62
American Indian/Alaska Native (37)	75	0.85
Not Hispanic (25)	53	0.60
Hispanic (12)	22	0.25
Aleut *(Alaska Native)* (1)	1	0.01
Apache (0)	1	0.01
Blackfeet (2)	3	0.03
Central American Ind. (4)	4	0.05
Cherokee (10)	18	0.21
Creek (0)	1	0.01
Crow (0)	1	0.01
Lumbee (2)	3	0.03
Mexican American Ind. (5)	9	0.10
Navajo (0)	1	0.01
Pueblo (1)	2	0.02
Seminole (2)	2	0.02
Asian (120)	165	1.88
Not Hispanic (116)	157	1.79
Hispanic (4)	8	0.09
Chinese, ex. Taiwanese (23)	23	0.26
Filipino (13)	25	0.28

*Notes: † The Census 2010 population figure is used to calculate the percentages in the Hispanic Origin and Race categories. Ancestry percentages are based on the 2006-2010 American Community Survey population (not shown); ‡ Numbers in parentheses indicate the number of people reporting a single ancestry; * Numbers in parentheses indicate the number of persons reporting this race alone, not in combination with any other race; Please refer to the Explanation of Data for more information.*

Indian (56)	64	0.73
Indonesian (3)	3	0.03
Japanese (0)	6	0.07
Korean (3)	15	0.17
Laotian (2)	2	0.02
Vietnamese (16)	19	0.22
Hawaii Native/Pacific Islander (18)	28	0.32
Not Hispanic (11)	17	0.19
Hispanic (7)	11	0.13
Guamanian/Chamorro (0)	1	0.01
Native Hawaiian (0)	1	0.01
Samoan (1)	3	0.03
White (4,315)	4,501	51.28
Not Hispanic (3,769)	3,879	44.19
Hispanic (546)	622	7.09

Georgetown

Place Type: CDP
County: Chatham
Population: 11,823†

Ancestry‡	Population	%
African, Sub-Saharan (95)	111	0.91
African (39)	55	0.45
Cape Verdean (37)	37	0.30
Kenyan (19)	19	0.16
American (705)	705	5.77
Arab (37)	37	0.30
Egyptian (17)	17	0.14
Lebanese (20)	20	0.16
Armenian (12)	12	0.10
Belgian (8)	8	0.07
British (71)	71	0.58
Canadian (0)	16	0.13
Celtic (18)	18	0.15
Czech (5)	5	0.04
Czechoslovakian (10)	10	0.08
Dutch (0)	61	0.50
English (554)	896	7.34
European (152)	180	1.47
French, ex. Basque (79)	225	1.84
French Canadian (146)	239	1.96
German (325)	1,002	8.21
Irish (245)	1,001	8.20
Italian (168)	439	3.60
Norwegian (13)	13	0.11
Polish (111)	256	2.10
Portuguese (0)	74	0.61
Romanian (64)	64	0.52
Russian (0)	11	0.09
Scandinavian (47)	77	0.63
Scotch-Irish (42)	150	1.23
Scottish (108)	143	1.17
Slovak (29)	29	0.24
Swedish (0)	50	0.41
Swiss (0)	15	0.12
Welsh (95)	138	1.13
West Indian, ex. Hispanic (200)	224	1.83
Bahamian (45)	57	0.47
Haitian (92)	92	0.75
Jamaican (53)	53	0.43
West Indian (10)	10	0.08
Other West Indian (0)	12	0.10

Hispanic Origin	Population	%
Hispanic or Latino (of any race)	922	7.80
Central American, ex. Mexican	89	0.75
Costa Rican	8	0.07
Guatemalan	15	0.13
Honduran	9	0.08
Nicaraguan	9	0.08
Panamanian	34	0.29
Salvadoran	14	0.12
Cuban	34	0.29
Dominican Republic	20	0.17
Mexican	383	3.24
Puerto Rican	259	2.19
South American	59	0.50
Bolivian	4	0.03
Chilean	2	0.02
Colombian	28	0.24
Ecuadorian	8	0.07
Peruvian	13	0.11
Uruguayan	1	0.01
Venezuelan	3	0.03
Other Hispanic or Latino	78	0.66

Race*	Population	%
African-American/Black (3,267)	3,476	29.40
Not Hispanic (3,216)	3,387	28.65
Hispanic (51)	89	0.75
American Indian/Alaska Native (46)	123	1.04
Not Hispanic (35)	102	0.86
Hispanic (11)	21	0.18
Apache (1)	1	0.01
Blackfeet (1)	4	0.03
Cherokee (7)	22	0.19
Choctaw (2)	6	0.05
Creek (0)	1	0.01
Lumbee (7)	7	0.06
Mexican American Ind. (2)	2	0.02
Navajo (2)	2	0.02
Seminole (0)	3	0.03
Sioux (1)	4	0.03
South American Ind. (3)	3	0.03
Spanish American Ind. (1)	1	0.01
Tlingit-Haida *(Alaska Native)* (0)	2	0.02
Asian (416)	550	4.65
Not Hispanic (409)	529	4.47
Hispanic (7)	21	0.18
Chinese, ex. Taiwanese (45)	54	0.46
Filipino (89)	119	1.01
Indian (103)	116	0.98
Indonesian (1)	2	0.02
Japanese (27)	50	0.42
Korean (58)	97	0.82
Laotian (1)	4	0.03
Malaysian (6)	6	0.05
Taiwanese (3)	3	0.03
Thai (8)	11	0.09
Vietnamese (59)	65	0.55
Hawaii Native/Pacific Islander (20)	49	0.41
Not Hispanic (20)	41	0.35
Hispanic (0)	8	0.07
Guamanian/Chamorro (3)	5	0.04
Native Hawaiian (6)	19	0.16
Samoan (1)	4	0.03
White (7,341)	7,657	64.76
Not Hispanic (6,876)	7,133	60.33
Hispanic (465)	524	4.43

Griffin

Place Type: City
County: Spalding
Population: 23,643†

Ancestry‡	Population	%
African, Sub-Saharan (435)	435	1.84
African (341)	341	1.44
South African (94)	94	0.40
American (3,185)	3,185	13.50
Assyrian/Chaldean/Syriac (0)	8	0.03
British (20)	101	0.43
Croatian (15)	15	0.06
Czechoslovakian (14)	14	0.06
Dutch (58)	136	0.58
English (957)	1,565	6.63
European (153)	153	0.65
Finnish (16)	16	0.07
French, ex. Basque (48)	327	1.39
French Canadian (0)	11	0.05
German (271)	938	3.97
Greek (52)	59	0.25
Hungarian (14)	34	0.14
Iranian (17)	17	0.07
Irish (366)	1,406	5.96
Italian (34)	168	0.71
Macedonian (0)	10	0.04
Northern European (46)	46	0.19
Norwegian (0)	10	0.04
Polish (100)	189	0.80
Portuguese (20)	20	0.08
Romanian (9)	9	0.04
Russian (0)	25	0.11
Scandinavian (0)	53	0.22
Scotch-Irish (135)	433	1.83
Scottish (115)	380	1.61
Swedish (8)	8	0.03
Swiss (21)	21	0.09
Welsh (75)	110	0.47
West Indian, ex. Hispanic (30)	30	0.13
Trinidadian/Tobagonian (30)	30	0.13

Hispanic Origin	Population	%
Hispanic or Latino (of any race)	952	4.03
Central American, ex. Mexican	113	0.48
Costa Rican	1	<0.01
Guatemalan	21	0.09
Honduran	81	0.34
Nicaraguan	2	0.01
Panamanian	5	0.02
Salvadoran	3	0.01
Cuban	27	0.11
Dominican Republic	9	0.04
Mexican	629	2.66
Puerto Rican	70	0.30
South American	36	0.15
Argentinean	1	<0.01
Colombian	13	0.05
Ecuadorian	6	0.03
Peruvian	11	0.05
Venezuelan	5	0.02
Other Hispanic or Latino	68	0.29

Race*	Population	%
African-American/Black (12,331)	12,599	53.29
Not Hispanic (12,280)	12,528	52.99
Hispanic (51)	71	0.30
American Indian/Alaska Native (69)	202	0.85
Not Hispanic (49)	166	0.70
Hispanic (20)	36	0.15
Alaska Athabascan *(Ala. Nat.)* (0)	1	<0.01
Apache (0)	2	0.01
Blackfeet (0)	1	<0.01
Central American Ind. (5)	6	0.03
Cherokee (7)	43	0.18
Chippewa (0)	1	<0.01
Colville (0)	5	0.02
Cree (0)	1	<0.01
Creek (2)	3	0.01
Mexican American Ind. (10)	16	0.07
Seminole (1)	2	0.01
Sioux (6)	6	0.03
Spanish American Ind. (0)	2	0.01
Ute (1)	1	<0.01
Asian (259)	305	1.29
Not Hispanic (259)	297	1.26
Hispanic (0)	8	0.03
Chinese, ex. Taiwanese (49)	57	0.24
Filipino (31)	43	0.18
Hmong (5)	5	0.02
Indian (121)	135	0.57
Indonesian (3)	3	0.01
Japanese (3)	8	0.03
Korean (10)	19	0.08
Laotian (1)	3	0.01
Pakistani (5)	12	0.05
Thai (3)	3	0.01
Vietnamese (12)	17	0.07
Hawaii Native/Pacific Islander (12)	32	0.14
Not Hispanic (12)	27	0.11
Hispanic (0)	5	0.02
Guamanian/Chamorro (12)	17	0.07
Native Hawaiian (0)	3	0.01
White (10,121)	10,453	44.21
Not Hispanic (9,719)	9,993	42.27
Hispanic (402)	460	1.95

*Notes: † The Census 2010 population figure is used to calculate the percentages in the Hispanic Origin and Race categories. Ancestry percentages are based on the 2006-2010 American Community Survey population (not shown); ‡ Numbers in parentheses indicate the number of people reporting a single ancestry; * Numbers in parentheses indicate the number of persons reporting this race alone, not in combination with any other race; Please refer to the Explanation of Data for more information.*

Grovetown

Place Type: City
County: Columbia
Population: 11,216†

Ancestry‡	Population	%
African, Sub-Saharan (185)	211	2.05
African (185)	211	2.05
American (1,195)	1,195	11.61
British (17)	28	0.27
Canadian (20)	20	0.19
Czech (13)	20	0.19
Danish (11)	11	0.11
Dutch (12)	135	1.31
English (242)	583	5.67
European (28)	28	0.27
Finnish (20)	20	0.19
French, ex. Basque (20)	144	1.40
French Canadian (74)	74	0.72
German (335)	1,084	10.54
Greek (11)	11	0.11
Hungarian (50)	50	0.49
Iranian (0)	26	0.25
Irish (252)	700	6.80
Italian (40)	168	1.63
Lithuanian (10)	10	0.10
Norwegian (11)	35	0.34
Pennsylvania German (11)	22	0.21
Polish (29)	64	0.62
Portuguese (0)	15	0.15
Russian (0)	51	0.50
Scotch-Irish (23)	98	0.95
Scottish (129)	178	1.73
Swedish (0)	40	0.39
Welsh (27)	27	0.26
West Indian, ex. Hispanic (25)	25	0.24
Jamaican (25)	25	0.24

Hispanic Origin	Population	%
Hispanic or Latino (of any race)	1,552	13.84
Central American, ex. Mexican	105	0.94
Costa Rican	3	0.03
Guatemalan	15	0.13
Honduran	28	0.25
Nicaraguan	4	0.04
Panamanian	45	0.40
Salvadoran	10	0.09
Cuban	13	0.12
Dominican Republic	7	0.06
Mexican	915	8.16
Puerto Rican	380	3.39
South American	38	0.34
Argentinean	3	0.03
Colombian	23	0.21
Ecuadorian	7	0.06
Peruvian	3	0.03
Uruguayan	2	0.02
Other Hispanic or Latino	94	0.84

Race*	Population	%
African-American/Black (3,360)	3,658	32.61
Not Hispanic (3,251)	3,499	31.20
Hispanic (109)	159	1.42
American Indian/Alaska Native (65)	169	1.51
Not Hispanic (47)	123	1.10
Hispanic (18)	46	0.41
Aleut *(Alaska Native)* (0)	2	0.02
Apache (0)	2	0.02
Blackfeet (0)	2	0.02
Central American Ind. (1)	4	0.04
Cherokee (16)	40	0.36
Chippewa (1)	2	0.02
Choctaw (1)	1	0.01
Cree (0)	3	0.03
Creek (0)	1	0.01
Kiowa (0)	5	0.04
Lumbee (3)	3	0.03
Mexican American Ind. (8)	10	0.09
Navajo (1)	3	0.03
Ottawa (1)	1	0.01
Pueblo (0)	1	0.01
Sioux (2)	6	0.05
South American Ind. (1)	1	0.01
Asian (159)	323	2.88
Not Hispanic (156)	293	2.61
Hispanic (3)	30	0.27
Chinese, ex. Taiwanese (5)	23	0.21
Filipino (43)	108	0.96
Indian (18)	20	0.18
Indonesian (0)	1	0.01
Japanese (9)	45	0.40
Korean (58)	106	0.95
Laotian (6)	6	0.05
Pakistani (2)	6	0.05
Thai (0)	1	0.01
Vietnamese (11)	20	0.18
Hawaii Native/Pacific Islander (29)	59	0.53
Not Hispanic (27)	49	0.44
Hispanic (2)	10	0.09
Fijian (1)	1	0.01
Guamanian/Chamorro (12)	17	0.15
Native Hawaiian (4)	26	0.23
Samoan (8)	18	0.16
White (6,458)	6,918	61.68
Not Hispanic (5,767)	6,110	54.48
Hispanic (691)	808	7.20

Hinesville

Place Type: City
County: Liberty
Population: 33,437†

Ancestry‡	Population	%
African, Sub-Saharan (413)	535	1.63
African (256)	378	1.15
Nigerian (145)	145	0.44
South African (12)	12	0.04
American (1,686)	1,686	5.12
Arab (19)	29	0.09
Arab (14)	14	0.04
Lebanese (5)	15	0.05
Austrian (0)	21	0.06
Belgian (86)	98	0.30
British (105)	246	0.75
Canadian (13)	23	0.07
Czech (0)	72	0.22
Danish (0)	12	0.04
Dutch (71)	364	1.11
English (441)	1,224	3.72
European (14)	14	0.04
Finnish (20)	20	0.06
French, ex. Basque (95)	401	1.22
French Canadian (45)	117	0.36
German (1,018)	2,489	7.56
German Russian (27)	27	0.08
Guyanese (27)	27	0.08
Irish (418)	1,667	5.06
Italian (152)	686	2.08
Norwegian (46)	182	0.55
Polish (69)	551	1.67
Portuguese (19)	60	0.18
Russian (91)	103	0.31
Scandinavian (22)	22	0.07
Scotch-Irish (91)	313	0.95
Scottish (159)	599	1.82
Slavic (7)	7	0.02
Slovak (4)	4	0.01
Swedish (57)	177	0.54
Ukrainian (0)	11	0.03
Welsh (21)	87	0.26
West Indian, ex. Hispanic (293)	413	1.25
Barbadian (41)	62	0.19
Belizean (0)	66	0.20
Bermudan (11)	11	0.03
British West Indian (78)	78	0.24
Haitian (36)	48	0.15
Jamaican (95)	95	0.29
Trinidadian/Tobagonian (0)	21	0.06
West Indian (32)	32	0.10
Yugoslavian (0)	15	0.05

Hispanic Origin	Population	%
Hispanic or Latino (of any race)	3,843	11.49
Central American, ex. Mexican	341	1.02
Costa Rican	20	0.06
Guatemalan	10	0.03
Honduran	36	0.11
Nicaraguan	13	0.04
Panamanian	229	0.68
Salvadoran	32	0.10
Other Central American	1	<0.01
Cuban	94	0.28
Dominican Republic	100	0.30
Mexican	1,042	3.12
Puerto Rican	1,784	5.34
South American	180	0.54
Argentinean	8	0.02
Bolivian	1	<0.01
Chilean	3	0.01
Colombian	81	0.24
Ecuadorian	40	0.12
Peruvian	30	0.09
Uruguayan	1	<0.01
Venezuelan	15	0.04
Other South American	1	<0.01
Other Hispanic or Latino	302	0.90

Race*	Population	%
African-American/Black (15,859)	16,988	50.81
Not Hispanic (15,324)	16,184	48.40
Hispanic (535)	804	2.40
American Indian/Alaska Native (174)	468	1.40
Not Hispanic (134)	371	1.11
Hispanic (40)	97	0.29
Alaska Athabascan *(Ala. Nat.)* (2)	2	0.01
Apache (5)	18	0.05
Blackfeet (1)	7	0.02
Cherokee (31)	96	0.29
Chickasaw (2)	3	0.01
Chippewa (2)	4	0.01
Choctaw (1)	3	0.01
Creek (8)	17	0.05
Crow (0)	1	<0.01
Hopi (1)	1	<0.01
Inupiat *(Alaska Native)* (2)	2	0.01
Iroquois (5)	14	0.04
Kiowa (2)	2	0.01
Lumbee (11)	12	0.04
Menominee (3)	3	0.01
Mexican American Ind. (7)	10	0.03
Navajo (6)	12	0.04
Seminole (0)	12	0.04
Sioux (8)	12	0.04
South American Ind. (7)	12	0.04
Tsimshian *(Alaska Native)* (0)	1	<0.01
Asian (877)	1,331	3.98
Not Hispanic (824)	1,212	3.62
Hispanic (53)	119	0.36
Cambodian (11)	12	0.04
Chinese, ex. Taiwanese (98)	157	0.47
Filipino (217)	369	1.10
Hmong (7)	8	0.02
Indian (91)	110	0.33
Indonesian (2)	3	0.01
Japanese (37)	93	0.28
Korean (282)	444	1.33
Laotian (2)	6	0.02
Sri Lankan (2)	2	0.01
Taiwanese (1)	1	<0.01
Thai (26)	40	0.12
Vietnamese (58)	99	0.30
Hawaii Native/Pacific Islander (260)	435	1.30
Not Hispanic (233)	375	1.12
Hispanic (27)	60	0.18
Fijian (1)	1	<0.01
Guamanian/Chamorro (37)	66	0.20
Marshallese (13)	13	0.04
Native Hawaiian (46)	119	0.36

SECTION TWO

*Notes: † The Census 2010 population figure is used to calculate the percentages in the Hispanic Origin and Race categories. Ancestry percentages are based on the 2006-2010 American Community Survey population (not shown); ‡ Numbers in parentheses indicate the number of people reporting a single ancestry; * Numbers in parentheses indicate the number of persons reporting this race alone, not in combination with any other race; Please refer to the Explanation of Data for more information.*

Samoan (119)	171	0.51
Tongan (1)	3	0.01
White (13,371)	14,722	44.03
Not Hispanic (11,701)	12,748	38.13
Hispanic (1,670)	1,974	5.90

Holly Springs

Place Type: City
County: Cherokee
Population: 9,189†

Ancestry‡	Population	%
African, Sub-Saharan (51)	60	0.72
African (28)	37	0.44
South African (23)	23	0.28
American (864)	864	10.34
Armenian (0)	11	0.13
Austrian (0)	56	0.67
Basque (0)	15	0.18
British (28)	92	1.10
Canadian (18)	37	0.44
Czech (10)	10	0.12
Czechoslovakian (0)	28	0.34
Dutch (14)	133	1.59
English (364)	1,033	12.37
European (58)	58	0.69
French, ex. Basque (50)	211	2.53
French Canadian (9)	28	0.34
German (494)	1,480	17.72
Greek (22)	35	0.42
Hungarian (0)	22	0.26
Irish (356)	1,635	19.57
Italian (223)	549	6.57
Lithuanian (0)	16	0.19
Norwegian (12)	27	0.32
Polish (22)	53	0.63
Portuguese (0)	35	0.42
Romanian (8)	8	0.10
Russian (65)	163	1.95
Scotch-Irish (66)	247	2.96
Scottish (83)	113	1.35
Serbian (0)	10	0.12
Slovak (20)	20	0.24
Swedish (11)	22	0.26
Swiss (0)	10	0.12
Welsh (33)	40	0.48
West Indian, ex. Hispanic (148)	206	2.47
British West Indian (111)	111	1.33
Jamaican (26)	26	0.31
U.S. Virgin Islander (11)	11	0.13
West Indian (0)	58	0.69

Hispanic Origin	Population	%
Hispanic or Latino (of any race)	725	7.89
Central American, ex. Mexican	82	0.89
Guatemalan	20	0.22
Honduran	12	0.13
Nicaraguan	6	0.07
Panamanian	25	0.27
Salvadoran	19	0.21
Cuban	32	0.35
Dominican Republic	20	0.22
Mexican	396	4.31
Puerto Rican	87	0.95
South American	76	0.83
Argentinean	2	0.02
Chilean	4	0.04
Colombian	33	0.36
Ecuadorian	7	0.08
Peruvian	12	0.13
Uruguayan	3	0.03
Venezuelan	14	0.15
Other South American	1	0.01
Other Hispanic or Latino	32	0.35

Race*	Population	%
African-American/Black (659)	748	8.14
Not Hispanic (621)	694	7.55
Hispanic (38)	54	0.59
American Indian/Alaska Native (28)	61	0.66
Not Hispanic (19)	50	0.54
Hispanic (9)	11	0.12
Blackfeet (2)	3	0.03
Cherokee (0)	15	0.16
Chippewa (0)	2	0.02
Creek (6)	6	0.07
Iroquois (1)	1	0.01
Mexican American Ind. (9)	9	0.10
Seminole (0)	1	0.01
Asian (168)	230	2.50
Not Hispanic (166)	224	2.44
Hispanic (2)	6	0.07
Chinese, ex. Taiwanese (23)	31	0.34
Filipino (18)	28	0.30
Indian (41)	50	0.54
Indonesian (4)	4	0.04
Japanese (6)	17	0.19
Korean (27)	54	0.59
Laotian (2)	2	0.02
Malaysian (1)	1	0.01
Thai (5)	6	0.07
Vietnamese (33)	39	0.42
Hawaii Native/Pacific Islander (1)	6	0.07
Not Hispanic (1)	4	0.04
Hispanic (0)	2	0.02
Guamanian/Chamorro (1)	1	0.01
White (7,876)	8,056	87.67
Not Hispanic (7,474)	7,605	82.76
Hispanic (402)	451	4.91

Jefferson

Place Type: City
County: Jackson
Population: 9,432†

Ancestry‡	Population	%
American (1,436)	1,436	16.72
Austrian (0)	20	0.23
British (0)	88	1.02
Danish (0)	62	0.72
Dutch (42)	148	1.72
English (466)	697	8.12
European (98)	98	1.14
French, ex. Basque (45)	94	1.09
French Canadian (32)	63	0.73
German (368)	1,153	13.43
Irish (620)	1,022	11.90
Italian (21)	223	2.60
Lithuanian (72)	114	1.33
Norwegian (25)	25	0.29
Polish (29)	169	1.97
Portuguese (0)	44	0.51
Russian (108)	108	1.26
Scotch-Irish (198)	360	4.19
Scottish (138)	410	4.77
Swedish (0)	36	0.42
West Indian, ex. Hispanic (131)	131	1.53
Bahamian (19)	19	0.22
Haitian (112)	112	1.30

Hispanic Origin	Population	%
Hispanic or Latino (of any race)	707	7.50
Central American, ex. Mexican	43	0.46
Costa Rican	1	0.01
Guatemalan	12	0.13
Honduran	4	0.04
Nicaraguan	2	0.02
Panamanian	6	0.06
Salvadoran	18	0.19
Cuban	12	0.13
Dominican Republic	38	0.40
Mexican	349	3.70
Puerto Rican	103	1.09
South American	97	1.03
Chilean	8	0.08
Colombian	46	0.49
Ecuadorian	13	0.14
Paraguayan	1	0.01
Peruvian	26	0.28
Uruguayan	1	0.01
Venezuelan	2	0.02
Other Hispanic or Latino	65	0.69

Race*	Population	%
African-American/Black (940)	1,008	10.69
Not Hispanic (919)	978	10.37
Hispanic (21)	30	0.32
American Indian/Alaska Native (24)	80	0.85
Not Hispanic (18)	71	0.75
Hispanic (6)	9	0.10
Apache (0)	1	0.01
Canadian/French Am. Ind. (1)	1	0.01
Central American Ind. (2)	2	0.02
Cherokee (6)	36	0.38
Chippewa (0)	6	0.06
Creek (2)	4	0.04
Inupiat *(Alaska Native)* (1)	1	0.01
Lumbee (1)	1	0.01
Mexican American Ind. (1)	2	0.02
Asian (149)	173	1.83
Not Hispanic (147)	166	1.76
Hispanic (2)	7	0.07
Cambodian (2)	3	0.03
Chinese, ex. Taiwanese (11)	14	0.15
Filipino (23)	25	0.27
Hmong (20)	20	0.21
Indian (30)	32	0.34
Japanese (3)	8	0.08
Korean (12)	12	0.13
Laotian (7)	9	0.10
Sri Lankan (4)	5	0.05
Thai (0)	7	0.07
Vietnamese (31)	34	0.36
Hawaii Native/Pacific Islander (6)	10	0.11
Not Hispanic (6)	10	0.11
Guamanian/Chamorro (1)	1	0.01
Native Hawaiian (3)	3	0.03
Samoan (1)	1	0.01
White (7,837)	7,989	84.70
Not Hispanic (7,494)	7,604	80.62
Hispanic (343)	385	4.08

Jesup

Place Type: City
County: Wayne
Population: 10,214†

Ancestry‡	Population	%
African, Sub-Saharan (256)	323	3.17
African (247)	314	3.09
Other Sub-Saharan African (9)	9	0.09
American (935)	935	9.19
Arab (9)	9	0.09
Egyptian (9)	9	0.09
Brazilian (0)	33	0.32
British (0)	5	0.05
Czechoslovakian (13)	13	0.13
Danish (0)	6	0.06
Dutch (10)	29	0.28
English (343)	741	7.28
European (82)	82	0.81
French, ex. Basque (9)	121	1.19
German (122)	381	3.74
Hungarian (14)	14	0.14
Irish (312)	894	8.79
Italian (18)	57	0.56
Norwegian (7)	14	0.14
Polish (28)	28	0.28
Portuguese (50)	83	0.82
Russian (0)	12	0.12
Scotch-Irish (147)	234	2.30
Scottish (77)	129	1.27
Swedish (6)	12	0.12
Swiss (0)	6	0.06
Ukrainian (8)	8	0.08
Welsh (25)	48	0.47
West Indian, ex. Hispanic (70)	101	0.99

*Notes: † The Census 2010 population figure is used to calculate the percentages in the Hispanic Origin and Race categories. Ancestry percentages are based on the 2006-2010 American Community Survey population (not shown); ‡ Numbers in parentheses indicate the number of people reporting a single ancestry; * Numbers in parentheses indicate the number of persons reporting this race alone, not in combination with any other race; Please refer to the Explanation of Data for more information.*

British West Indian (8)	8	0.08
Haitian (19)	19	0.19
Jamaican (35)	45	0.44
West Indian (8)	29	0.28

Hispanic Origin	Population	%
Hispanic or Latino (of any race)	937	9.17
Central American, ex. Mexican	54	0.53
Guatemalan	10	0.10
Honduran	23	0.23
Nicaraguan	5	0.05
Panamanian	3	0.03
Salvadoran	13	0.13
Cuban	81	0.79
Dominican Republic	16	0.16
Mexican	473	4.63
Puerto Rican	201	1.97
South American	57	0.56
Argentinean	1	0.01
Chilean	1	0.01
Colombian	49	0.48
Ecuadorian	3	0.03
Peruvian	1	0.01
Uruguayan	2	0.02
Other Hispanic or Latino	55	0.54

Race*	Population	%
African-American/Black (4,094)	4,245	41.56
Not Hispanic (4,040)	4,165	40.78
Hispanic (54)	80	0.78
American Indian/Alaska Native (59)	143	1.40
Not Hispanic (35)	103	1.01
Hispanic (24)	40	0.39
Blackfeet (0)	5	0.05
Canadian/French Am. Ind. (1)	3	0.03
Central American Ind. (0)	2	0.02
Cherokee (3)	18	0.18
Cheyenne (1)	1	0.01
Chippewa (0)	1	0.01
Comanche (0)	1	0.01
Creek (1)	4	0.04
Delaware (0)	4	0.04
Mexican American Ind. (2)	3	0.03
Navajo (3)	3	0.03
Sioux (0)	1	0.01
South American Ind. (3)	5	0.05
Asian (91)	128	1.25
Not Hispanic (91)	118	1.16
Hispanic (0)	10	0.10
Chinese, ex. Taiwanese (0)	5	0.05
Filipino (6)	11	0.11
Indian (39)	43	0.42
Japanese (2)	3	0.03
Korean (1)	8	0.08
Laotian (0)	5	0.05
Pakistani (12)	12	0.12
Taiwanese (2)	2	0.02
Thai (2)	10	0.10
Vietnamese (27)	29	0.28
Hawaii Native/Pacific Islander (2)	10	0.10
Not Hispanic (2)	6	0.06
Hispanic (0)	4	0.04
Guamanian/Chamorro (0)	1	0.01
Native Hawaiian (2)	3	0.03
Samoan (0)	3	0.03
White (5,423)	5,640	55.22
Not Hispanic (4,926)	5,070	49.64
Hispanic (497)	570	5.58

Johns Creek

Place Type: City
County: Fulton
Population: 76,728†

Ancestry‡	Population	%
Afghan (23)	23	0.03
African, Sub-Saharan (728)	851	1.17
African (245)	327	0.45
Ethiopian (190)	190	0.26
Ghanaian (81)	81	0.11
Nigerian (87)	87	0.12
South African (37)	78	0.11
Other Sub-Saharan African (88)	88	0.12
American (4,213)	4,213	5.80
Arab (531)	619	0.85
Arab (0)	22	0.03
Egyptian (61)	119	0.16
Iraqi (37)	37	0.05
Jordanian (57)	57	0.08
Lebanese (23)	31	0.04
Moroccan (63)	63	0.09
Palestinian (13)	13	0.02
Other Arab (277)	277	0.38
Armenian (115)	124	0.17
Australian (83)	103	0.14
Austrian (53)	192	0.26
Belgian (57)	118	0.16
Brazilian (53)	73	0.10
British (480)	747	1.03
Bulgarian (72)	72	0.10
Canadian (119)	135	0.19
Croatian (26)	140	0.19
Czech (80)	255	0.35
Czechoslovakian (16)	94	0.13
Danish (60)	253	0.35
Dutch (147)	710	0.98
Eastern European (94)	106	0.15
English (2,563)	6,807	9.37
European (911)	1,293	1.78
Finnish (85)	180	0.25
French, ex. Basque (255)	1,485	2.04
French Canadian (56)	136	0.19
German (2,684)	7,658	10.54
Greek (219)	372	0.51
Hungarian (51)	218	0.30
Iranian (1,404)	1,508	2.07
Irish (1,941)	6,699	9.22
Israeli (201)	201	0.28
Italian (1,283)	3,509	4.83
Latvian (8)	8	0.01
Lithuanian (90)	133	0.18
Maltese (0)	11	0.02
Norwegian (121)	525	0.72
Pennsylvania German (13)	13	0.02
Polish (365)	1,778	2.45
Portuguese (36)	131	0.18
Romanian (20)	88	0.12
Russian (894)	1,591	2.19
Scandinavian (62)	106	0.15
Scotch-Irish (570)	1,461	2.01
Scottish (384)	1,323	1.82
Serbian (0)	41	0.06
Slovak (63)	223	0.31
Swedish (246)	789	1.09
Swiss (49)	143	0.20
Turkish (173)	241	0.33
Ukrainian (206)	269	0.37
Welsh (74)	311	0.43
West Indian, ex. Hispanic (613)	916	1.26
Bahamian (11)	11	0.02
Bermudan (18)	18	0.02
Haitian (59)	59	0.08
Jamaican (334)	518	0.71
Trinidadian/Tobagonian (74)	153	0.21
U.S. Virgin Islander (11)	51	0.07
West Indian (106)	106	0.15
Yugoslavian (36)	47	0.06

Hispanic Origin	Population	%
Hispanic or Latino (of any race)	4,000	5.21
Central American, ex. Mexican	245	0.32
Costa Rican	21	0.03
Guatemalan	64	0.08
Honduran	47	0.06
Nicaraguan	15	0.02
Panamanian	41	0.05
Salvadoran	55	0.07
Other Central American	2	<0.01
Cuban	298	0.39
Dominican Republic	126	0.16
Mexican	1,251	1.63
Puerto Rican	578	0.75
South American	1,120	1.46
Argentinean	68	0.09
Bolivian	17	0.02
Chilean	41	0.05
Colombian	559	0.73
Ecuadorian	50	0.07
Paraguayan	1	<0.01
Peruvian	189	0.25
Uruguayan	33	0.04
Venezuelan	158	0.21
Other South American	4	0.01
Other Hispanic or Latino	382	0.50

Race*	Population	%
African-American/Black (7,062)	7,704	10.04
Not Hispanic (6,925)	7,484	9.75
Hispanic (137)	220	0.29
American Indian/Alaska Native (94)	351	0.46
Not Hispanic (69)	291	0.38
Hispanic (25)	60	0.08
Apache (2)	2	<0.01
Arapaho (0)	1	<0.01
Blackfeet (1)	12	0.02
Cherokee (11)	64	0.08
Chickasaw (2)	6	0.01
Chippewa (0)	1	<0.01
Choctaw (1)	1	<0.01
Comanche (0)	3	<0.01
Creek (4)	5	0.01
Delaware (0)	3	<0.01
Kiowa (0)	1	<0.01
Lumbee (1)	2	<0.01
Mexican American Ind. (2)	10	0.01
Navajo (1)	2	<0.01
Paiute (0)	2	<0.01
Potawatomi (3)	3	<0.01
Puget Sound Salish (0)	1	<0.01
Seminole (1)	6	0.01
Sioux (4)	7	0.01
South American Ind. (4)	14	0.02
Spanish American Ind. (1)	1	<0.01
Yaqui (0)	1	<0.01
Yuman (1)	1	<0.01
Asian (17,925)	18,977	24.73
Not Hispanic (17,892)	18,899	24.63
Hispanic (33)	78	0.10
Bangladeshi (58)	71	0.09
Burmese (4)	4	0.01
Cambodian (48)	54	0.07
Chinese, ex. Taiwanese (3,998)	4,227	5.51
Filipino (282)	371	0.48
Hmong (5)	8	0.01
Indian (6,453)	6,685	8.71
Indonesian (95)	111	0.14
Japanese (360)	482	0.63
Korean (4,997)	5,138	6.70
Laotian (42)	51	0.07
Malaysian (18)	34	0.04
Nepalese (16)	19	0.02
Pakistani (367)	395	0.51
Sri Lankan (33)	46	0.06
Taiwanese (373)	412	0.54
Thai (58)	75	0.10
Vietnamese (417)	461	0.60
Hawaii Native/Pacific Islander (22)	76	0.10
Not Hispanic (22)	68	0.09
Hispanic (0)	8	0.01
Fijian (1)	1	<0.01
Guamanian/Chamorro (4)	10	0.01
Marshallese (1)	1	<0.01
Native Hawaiian (6)	21	0.03
Samoan (2)	3	<0.01
White (48,684)	50,194	65.42
Not Hispanic (45,978)	47,301	61.65
Hispanic (2,706)	2,893	3.77

*Notes: † The Census 2010 population figure is used to calculate the percentages in the Hispanic Origin and Race categories. Ancestry percentages are based on the 2006-2010 American Community Survey population (not shown); ‡ Numbers in parentheses indicate the number of people reporting a single ancestry; * Numbers in parentheses indicate the number of persons reporting this race alone, not in combination with any other race; Please refer to the Explanation of Data for more information.*

Kennesaw

Place Type: City
County: Cobb
Population: 29,783†

Ancestry‡	Population	%
African, Sub-Saharan (1,020)	1,035	3.66
African (691)	706	2.49
Ethiopian (47)	47	0.17
Ghanaian (119)	119	0.42
Kenyan (55)	55	0.19
Nigerian (17)	17	0.06
Other Sub-Saharan African (91)	91	0.32
American (3,244)	3,244	11.46
Arab (383)	411	1.45
Arab (344)	344	1.21
Lebanese (0)	28	0.10
Other Arab (39)	39	0.14
Austrian (12)	38	0.13
Brazilian (264)	264	0.93
British (26)	47	0.17
Canadian (49)	49	0.17
Croatian (0)	40	0.14
Czech (19)	87	0.31
Czechoslovakian (0)	22	0.08
Danish (35)	35	0.12
Dutch (50)	362	1.28
English (998)	2,460	8.69
European (212)	212	0.75
Finnish (82)	97	0.34
French, ex. Basque (113)	509	1.80
French Canadian (29)	68	0.24
German (633)	2,827	9.98
Guyanese (0)	43	0.15
Hungarian (36)	124	0.44
Iranian (38)	38	0.13
Irish (1,212)	3,237	11.43
Italian (574)	1,374	4.85
Latvian (13)	13	0.05
Lithuanian (13)	40	0.14
Luxemburger (0)	15	0.05
Northern European (30)	30	0.11
Norwegian (54)	222	0.78
Pennsylvania German (0)	14	0.05
Polish (93)	345	1.22
Romanian (29)	29	0.10
Russian (56)	201	0.71
Scandinavian (0)	12	0.04
Scotch-Irish (366)	531	1.88
Scottish (283)	623	2.20
Slavic (47)	47	0.17
Slovak (0)	29	0.10
Swedish (34)	201	0.71
Swiss (8)	24	0.08
Turkish (34)	34	0.12
Ukrainian (22)	22	0.08
Welsh (85)	163	0.58
West Indian, ex. Hispanic (894)	927	3.27
Bahamian (24)	72	0.25
British West Indian (11)	11	0.04
Haitian (511)	511	1.80
Jamaican (171)	186	0.66
Trinidadian/Tobagonian (82)	82	0.29
U.S. Virgin Islander (14)	14	0.05
West Indian (24)	32	0.11
Other West Indian (19)	19	0.07
Yugoslavian (17)	17	0.06

Hispanic Origin	Population	%
Hispanic or Latino (of any race)	3,230	10.85
Central American, ex. Mexican	309	1.04
Costa Rican	10	0.03
Guatemalan	97	0.33
Honduran	61	0.20
Nicaraguan	25	0.08
Panamanian	37	0.12
Salvadoran	77	0.26
Other Central American	2	0.01
Cuban	121	0.41
Dominican Republic	65	0.22
Mexican	1,617	5.43
Puerto Rican	326	1.09
South American	572	1.92
Argentinean	10	0.03
Bolivian	9	0.03
Chilean	13	0.04
Colombian	241	0.81
Ecuadorian	111	0.37
Peruvian	89	0.30
Uruguayan	8	0.03
Venezuelan	80	0.27
Other South American	11	0.04
Other Hispanic or Latino	220	0.74

Race*	Population	%
African-American/Black (6,647)	7,092	23.81
Not Hispanic (6,510)	6,885	23.12
Hispanic (137)	207	0.70
American Indian/Alaska Native (105)	276	0.93
Not Hispanic (73)	221	0.74
Hispanic (32)	55	0.18
Alaska Athabascan *(Ala. Nat.)* (0)	1	<0.01
Apache (2)	2	0.01
Blackfeet (1)	11	0.04
Cherokee (16)	79	0.27
Chickasaw (0)	6	0.02
Chippewa (2)	2	0.01
Choctaw (2)	5	0.02
Creek (0)	4	0.01
Crow (0)	3	0.01
Iroquois (0)	2	0.01
Lumbee (3)	4	0.01
Mexican American Ind. (5)	6	0.02
Paiute (0)	2	0.01
Potawatomi (0)	3	0.01
Sioux (2)	2	0.01
South American Ind. (1)	3	0.01
Spanish American Ind. (1)	3	0.01
Asian (1,568)	1,862	6.25
Not Hispanic (1,548)	1,812	6.08
Hispanic (20)	50	0.17
Bangladeshi (8)	9	0.03
Cambodian (15)	20	0.07
Chinese, ex. Taiwanese (147)	210	0.71
Filipino (166)	245	0.82
Hmong (8)	9	0.03
Indian (521)	560	1.88
Indonesian (18)	25	0.08
Japanese (89)	125	0.42
Korean (165)	203	0.68
Laotian (45)	48	0.16
Malaysian (0)	1	<0.01
Pakistani (102)	130	0.44
Sri Lankan (1)	1	<0.01
Taiwanese (11)	11	0.04
Thai (14)	25	0.08
Vietnamese (191)	231	0.78
Hawaii Native/Pacific Islander (14)	49	0.16
Not Hispanic (14)	42	0.14
Hispanic (0)	7	0.02
Guamanian/Chamorro (12)	15	0.05
Native Hawaiian (2)	21	0.07
Samoan (0)	1	<0.01
White (19,131)	19,854	66.66
Not Hispanic (17,546)	18,100	60.77
Hispanic (1,585)	1,754	5.89

Kingsland

Place Type: City
County: Camden
Population: 15,946†

Ancestry‡	Population	%
African, Sub-Saharan (110)	127	0.84
African (110)	127	0.84
American (1,084)	1,084	7.17
Austrian (0)	15	0.10
Brazilian (11)	11	0.07
British (25)	33	0.22
Cajun (12)	60	0.40
Czech (22)	22	0.15
Czechoslovakian (10)	33	0.22
Danish (14)	39	0.26
Dutch (0)	109	0.72
English (572)	1,105	7.31
European (53)	80	0.53
Finnish (0)	16	0.11
French, ex. Basque (40)	264	1.75
French Canadian (12)	34	0.23
German (615)	1,732	11.46
Greek (0)	23	0.15
Hungarian (0)	81	0.54
Iranian (8)	8	0.05
Irish (637)	1,856	12.28
Italian (221)	618	4.09
Lithuanian (0)	25	0.17
Norwegian (17)	95	0.63
Polish (257)	573	3.79
Romanian (29)	29	0.19
Russian (10)	20	0.13
Scotch-Irish (84)	183	1.21
Scottish (185)	522	3.45
Slovak (0)	19	0.13
Swedish (29)	107	0.71
Swiss (0)	9	0.06
Ukrainian (17)	24	0.16
Welsh (0)	132	0.87
West Indian, ex. Hispanic (25)	25	0.17
Barbadian (11)	11	0.07
British West Indian (14)	14	0.09

Hispanic Origin	Population	%
Hispanic or Latino (of any race)	883	5.54
Central American, ex. Mexican	35	0.22
Costa Rican	5	0.03
Guatemalan	5	0.03
Honduran	6	0.04
Nicaraguan	3	0.02
Panamanian	9	0.06
Salvadoran	7	0.04
Cuban	50	0.31
Dominican Republic	6	0.04
Mexican	310	1.94
Puerto Rican	324	2.03
South American	71	0.45
Argentinean	2	0.01
Chilean	5	0.03
Colombian	47	0.29
Ecuadorian	7	0.04
Peruvian	6	0.04
Venezuelan	4	0.03
Other Hispanic or Latino	87	0.55

Race*	Population	%
African-American/Black (3,685)	3,992	25.03
Not Hispanic (3,616)	3,880	24.33
Hispanic (69)	112	0.70
American Indian/Alaska Native (79)	230	1.44
Not Hispanic (70)	199	1.25
Hispanic (9)	31	0.19
Apache (0)	4	0.03
Blackfeet (2)	7	0.04
Central American Ind. (0)	1	0.01
Cherokee (12)	61	0.38
Chickasaw (1)	1	0.01
Chippewa (2)	5	0.03
Choctaw (5)	6	0.04
Creek (4)	7	0.04
Inupiat *(Alaska Native)* (0)	2	0.01
Lumbee (1)	1	0.01
Menominee (1)	1	0.01
Mexican American Ind. (2)	2	0.01
Navajo (0)	1	0.01
Osage (0)	4	0.03
Ottawa (0)	1	0.01
Pima (0)	1	0.01
Potawatomi (2)	4	0.03
Pueblo (2)	3	0.02

*Notes: † The Census 2010 population figure is used to calculate the percentages in the Hispanic Origin and Race categories. Ancestry percentages are based on the 2006-2010 American Community Survey population (not shown); ‡ Numbers in parentheses indicate the number of people reporting a single ancestry; * Numbers in parentheses indicate the number of persons reporting this race alone, not in combination with any other race; Please refer to the Explanation of Data for more information.*

Seminole (0)	4	0.03
Sioux (6)	7	0.04
South American Ind. (4)	11	0.07
Spanish American Ind. (2)	2	0.01
Tohono O'Odham (1)	1	0.01
Asian (361)	517	3.24
Not Hispanic (355)	495	3.10
Hispanic (6)	22	0.14
Bangladeshi (3)	3	0.02
Chinese, ex. Taiwanese (23)	46	0.29
Filipino (110)	198	1.24
Hmong (2)	2	0.01
Indian (121)	132	0.83
Indonesian (4)	5	0.03
Japanese (10)	37	0.23
Korean (12)	26	0.16
Laotian (2)	6	0.04
Pakistani (0)	1	0.01
Taiwanese (1)	3	0.02
Thai (2)	10	0.06
Vietnamese (47)	59	0.37
Hawaii Native/Pacific Islander (32)	64	0.40
Not Hispanic (31)	54	0.34
Hispanic (1)	10	0.06
Guamanian/Chamorro (13)	28	0.18
Marshallese (1)	3	0.02
Native Hawaiian (5)	28	0.18
Samoan (1)	2	0.01
White (11,052)	11,524	72.27
Not Hispanic (10,501)	10,907	68.40
Hispanic (551)	617	3.87

LaGrange

Place Type: City
County: Troup
Population: 29,588†

Ancestry‡	Population	%
African, Sub-Saharan (96)	96	0.33
African (96)	96	0.33
American (2,628)	2,628	9.04
Arab (39)	39	0.13
Lebanese (28)	28	0.10
Moroccan (11)	11	0.04
British (41)	74	0.25
Bulgarian (0)	17	0.06
Cajun (12)	12	0.04
Celtic (5)	5	0.02
Danish (0)	73	0.25
Dutch (20)	144	0.50
English (1,385)	2,969	10.21
European (206)	306	1.05
French, ex. Basque (88)	247	0.85
French Canadian (120)	141	0.49
German (539)	1,810	6.23
Greek (70)	70	0.24
Irish (958)	2,658	9.14
Italian (29)	105	0.36
Norwegian (0)	7	0.02
Polish (57)	97	0.33
Portuguese (0)	17	0.06
Romanian (45)	45	0.15
Russian (55)	100	0.34
Scandinavian (0)	15	0.05
Scotch-Irish (346)	531	1.83
Scottish (227)	632	2.17
Slovak (11)	11	0.04
Swedish (0)	46	0.16
Turkish (0)	17	0.06
Ukrainian (0)	36	0.12
Welsh (20)	76	0.26
West Indian, ex. Hispanic (41)	85	0.29
Jamaican (41)	66	0.23
West Indian (0)	19	0.07

Hispanic Origin	Population	%
Hispanic or Latino (of any race)	1,393	4.71
Central American, ex. Mexican	317	1.07
Costa Rican	7	0.02
Guatemalan	263	0.89
Honduran	23	0.08
Nicaraguan	8	0.03
Panamanian	4	0.01
Salvadoran	12	0.04
Cuban	14	0.05
Dominican Republic	22	0.07
Mexican	750	2.53
Puerto Rican	65	0.22
South American	36	0.12
Argentinean	5	0.02
Colombian	14	0.05
Ecuadorian	12	0.04
Peruvian	3	0.01
Venezuelan	2	0.01
Other Hispanic or Latino	189	0.64

Race*	Population	%
African-American/Black (14,207)	14,522	49.08
Not Hispanic (14,160)	14,444	48.82
Hispanic (47)	78	0.26
American Indian/Alaska Native (73)	181	0.61
Not Hispanic (49)	150	0.51
Hispanic (24)	31	0.10
Alaska Athabascan *(Ala. Nat.)* (2)	2	0.01
Apache (0)	2	0.01
Blackfeet (0)	3	0.01
Cherokee (12)	38	0.13
Chickasaw (0)	3	0.01
Chippewa (1)	1	<0.01
Choctaw (0)	5	0.02
Comanche (1)	1	<0.01
Creek (2)	2	0.01
Iroquois (0)	3	0.01
Menominee (0)	1	<0.01
Mexican American Ind. (3)	3	0.01
Navajo (0)	3	0.01
Seminole (0)	6	0.02
Sioux (0)	1	<0.01
South American Ind. (4)	4	0.01
Yup'ik *(Alaska Native)* (0)	3	0.01
Asian (728)	798	2.70
Not Hispanic (726)	796	2.69
Hispanic (2)	2	0.01
Bangladeshi (6)	6	0.02
Chinese, ex. Taiwanese (23)	36	0.12
Filipino (15)	27	0.09
Indian (118)	133	0.45
Japanese (20)	37	0.13
Korean (448)	471	1.59
Malaysian (1)	1	<0.01
Nepalese (2)	2	0.01
Pakistani (26)	26	0.09
Taiwanese (2)	2	0.01
Vietnamese (48)	51	0.17
Hawaii Native/Pacific Islander (43)	61	0.21
Not Hispanic (12)	22	0.07
Hispanic (31)	39	0.13
Guamanian/Chamorro (38)	45	0.15
Native Hawaiian (1)	9	0.03
White (13,172)	13,611	46.00
Not Hispanic (12,783)	13,150	44.44
Hispanic (389)	461	1.56

Lawrenceville

Place Type: City
County: Gwinnett
Population: 28,546†

Ancestry‡	Population	%
Afghan (31)	31	0.11
African, Sub-Saharan (1,247)	1,279	4.62
African (756)	756	2.73
Ethiopian (19)	19	0.07
Ghanaian (43)	43	0.16
Liberian (63)	63	0.23
Nigerian (352)	352	1.27
Somalian (14)	46	0.17
American (1,672)	1,672	6.04
Arab (20)	30	0.11
Egyptian (20)	20	0.07
Lebanese (0)	10	0.04
Austrian (19)	26	0.09
British (19)	57	0.21
Canadian (0)	28	0.10
Czech (11)	34	0.12
Czechoslovakian (0)	16	0.06
Danish (28)	34	0.12
Dutch (46)	213	0.77
English (678)	1,846	6.66
European (75)	129	0.47
Finnish (0)	46	0.17
French, ex. Basque (22)	276	1.00
French Canadian (10)	47	0.17
German (563)	1,670	6.03
Greek (0)	31	0.11
Guyanese (67)	67	0.24
Hungarian (29)	75	0.27
Iranian (9)	9	0.03
Irish (528)	2,129	7.68
Italian (285)	690	2.49
Lithuanian (27)	27	0.10
Northern European (30)	30	0.11
Norwegian (0)	89	0.32
Polish (91)	375	1.35
Portuguese (10)	103	0.37
Romanian (29)	38	0.14
Russian (0)	115	0.42
Scotch-Irish (234)	425	1.53
Scottish (147)	419	1.51
Serbian (17)	53	0.19
Slavic (0)	118	0.43
Swedish (22)	84	0.30
Swiss (0)	13	0.05
Ukrainian (9)	9	0.03
Welsh (36)	63	0.23
West Indian, ex. Hispanic (215)	317	1.14
Haitian (174)	174	0.63
Jamaican (29)	48	0.17
West Indian (12)	95	0.34
Yugoslavian (629)	629	2.27

Hispanic Origin	Population	%
Hispanic or Latino (of any race)	6,378	22.34
Central American, ex. Mexican	922	3.23
Costa Rican	9	0.03
Guatemalan	316	1.11
Honduran	156	0.55
Nicaraguan	25	0.09
Panamanian	28	0.10
Salvadoran	369	1.29
Other Central American	19	0.07
Cuban	178	0.62
Dominican Republic	177	0.62
Mexican	3,708	12.99
Puerto Rican	490	1.72
South American	473	1.66
Argentinean	5	0.02
Chilean	16	0.06
Colombian	223	0.78
Ecuadorian	34	0.12
Paraguayan	5	0.02
Peruvian	91	0.32
Uruguayan	49	0.17
Venezuelan	47	0.16
Other South American	3	0.01
Other Hispanic or Latino	430	1.51

Race*	Population	%
African-American/Black (9,134)	9,627	33.72
Not Hispanic (8,869)	9,256	32.42
Hispanic (265)	371	1.30
American Indian/Alaska Native (181)	336	1.18
Not Hispanic (62)	185	0.65
Hispanic (119)	151	0.53
Apache (0)	4	0.01
Blackfeet (1)	5	0.02
Canadian/French Am. Ind. (2)	2	0.01
Central American Ind. (0)	2	0.01

*Notes: † The Census 2010 population figure is used to calculate the percentages in the Hispanic Origin and Race categories. Ancestry percentages are based on the 2006-2010 American Community Survey population (not shown); ‡ Numbers in parentheses indicate the number of people reporting a single ancestry; * Numbers in parentheses indicate the number of persons reporting this race alone, not in combination with any other race; Please refer to the Explanation of Data for more information.*

SECTION TWO

Cherokee (15)	47	0.16
Chickasaw (0)	2	0.01
Chippewa (0)	2	0.01
Comanche (1)	1	<0.01
Creek (0)	2	0.01
Crow (0)	1	<0.01
Delaware (0)	3	0.01
Iroquois (1)	1	<0.01
Lumbee (5)	8	0.03
Mexican American Ind. (20)	31	0.11
Navajo (0)	1	<0.01
Seminole (0)	1	<0.01
Sioux (1)	2	0.01
South American Ind. (1)	1	<0.01
Asian (1,622)	1,835	6.43
Not Hispanic (1,608)	1,797	6.30
Hispanic (14)	38	0.13
Bangladeshi (23)	25	0.09
Cambodian (19)	33	0.12
Chinese, ex. Taiwanese (99)	128	0.45
Filipino (85)	119	0.42
Hmong (22)	22	0.08
Indian (312)	341	1.19
Japanese (4)	11	0.04
Korean (157)	190	0.67
Laotian (73)	97	0.34
Malaysian (3)	3	0.01
Pakistani (67)	77	0.27
Taiwanese (6)	6	0.02
Thai (18)	23	0.08
Vietnamese (662)	687	2.41
Hawaii Native/Pacific Islander (14)	51	0.18
Not Hispanic (13)	36	0.13
Hispanic (1)	15	0.05
Fijian (2)	3	0.01
Guamanian/Chamorro (7)	9	0.03
Native Hawaiian (1)	3	0.01
Samoan (1)	1	<0.01
White (13,692)	14,420	50.51
Not Hispanic (10,930)	11,358	39.79
Hispanic (2,762)	3,062	10.73

Lilburn

Place Type: City
County: Gwinnett
Population: 11,596†

Ancestry‡	Population	%
African, Sub-Saharan (328)	350	2.99
African (144)	166	1.42
Ethiopian (120)	120	1.02
Ghanaian (40)	40	0.34
Other Sub-Saharan African (24)	24	0.20
American (351)	351	2.99
Arab (82)	82	0.70
Arab (39)	39	0.33
Iraqi (27)	27	0.23
Other Arab (16)	16	0.14
Austrian (0)	12	0.10
British (10)	78	0.67
Canadian (0)	20	0.17
Czech (0)	23	0.20
Danish (0)	12	0.10
Dutch (15)	119	1.01
Eastern European (12)	12	0.10
English (350)	815	6.95
European (261)	290	2.47
Finnish (0)	11	0.09
French, ex. Basque (164)	323	2.75
German (115)	631	5.38
Greek (45)	77	0.66
Guyanese (51)	51	0.43
Hungarian (0)	42	0.36
Irish (223)	741	6.32
Italian (128)	276	2.35
Lithuanian (7)	7	0.06
Polish (5)	143	1.22
Romanian (28)	28	0.24
Russian (88)	95	0.81
Scotch-Irish (144)	245	2.09
Scottish (120)	196	1.67
Slovak (0)	21	0.18
Slovene (0)	10	0.09
Swedish (15)	53	0.45
Ukrainian (0)	15	0.13
Welsh (15)	61	0.52
West Indian, ex. Hispanic (25)	39	0.33
Jamaican (15)	15	0.13
Trinidadian/Tobagonian (0)	7	0.06
West Indian (10)	17	0.14
Yugoslavian (207)	207	1.77

Hispanic Origin	Population	%
Hispanic or Latino (of any race)	3,181	27.43
Central American, ex. Mexican	731	6.30
Costa Rican	11	0.09
Guatemalan	141	1.22
Honduran	130	1.12
Nicaraguan	22	0.19
Panamanian	2	0.02
Salvadoran	419	3.61
Other Central American	6	0.05
Cuban	59	0.51
Dominican Republic	75	0.65
Mexican	1,802	15.54
Puerto Rican	134	1.16
South American	191	1.65
Argentinean	25	0.22
Bolivian	4	0.03
Chilean	4	0.03
Colombian	91	0.78
Ecuadorian	9	0.08
Paraguayan	2	0.02
Peruvian	28	0.24
Uruguayan	15	0.13
Venezuelan	12	0.10
Other South American	1	0.01
Other Hispanic or Latino	189	1.63

Race*	Population	%
African-American/Black (1,900)	2,019	17.41
Not Hispanic (1,840)	1,937	16.70
Hispanic (60)	82	0.71
American Indian/Alaska Native (62)	135	1.16
Not Hispanic (21)	66	0.57
Hispanic (41)	69	0.60
Blackfeet (3)	4	0.03
Central American Ind. (0)	2	0.02
Cherokee (4)	18	0.16
Chickasaw (0)	2	0.02
Mexican American Ind. (25)	27	0.23
Pima (1)	1	0.01
Seminole (1)	5	0.04
Sioux (0)	2	0.02
South American Ind. (0)	2	0.02
Spanish American Ind. (4)	4	0.03
Asian (1,766)	1,860	16.04
Not Hispanic (1,763)	1,855	16.00
Hispanic (3)	5	0.04
Bangladeshi (76)	90	0.78
Cambodian (71)	78	0.67
Chinese, ex. Taiwanese (167)	176	1.52
Filipino (40)	50	0.43
Indian (551)	587	5.06
Indonesian (5)	5	0.04
Japanese (7)	17	0.15
Korean (95)	107	0.92
Laotian (25)	27	0.23
Pakistani (107)	115	0.99
Taiwanese (34)	35	0.30
Thai (25)	29	0.25
Vietnamese (500)	514	4.43
Hawaii Native/Pacific Islander (5)	12	0.10
Not Hispanic (3)	9	0.08
Hispanic (2)	3	0.03
Native Hawaiian (3)	6	0.05
Samoan (0)	1	0.01
White (6,113)	6,334	54.62
Not Hispanic (4,560)	4,689	40.44
Hispanic (1,553)	1,645	14.19

Lithia Springs

Place Type: CDP
County: Douglas
Population: 15,491†

Ancestry‡	Population	%
African, Sub-Saharan (2,675)	2,809	16.46
African (2,438)	2,572	15.07
Ghanaian (89)	89	0.52
Liberian (40)	40	0.23
Nigerian (20)	20	0.12
Senegalese (13)	13	0.08
Other Sub-Saharan African (75)	75	0.44
American (1,505)	1,505	8.82
Arab (17)	17	0.10
Other Arab (17)	17	0.10
Austrian (11)	11	0.06
Canadian (11)	11	0.06
Danish (31)	31	0.18
Dutch (10)	183	1.07
Eastern European (11)	11	0.06
English (548)	1,066	6.25
European (79)	79	0.46
French, ex. Basque (82)	313	1.83
French Canadian (14)	37	0.22
German (233)	579	3.39
Greek (13)	13	0.08
Guyanese (34)	34	0.20
Irish (267)	1,057	6.19
Italian (164)	326	1.91
Pennsylvania German (14)	14	0.08
Polish (8)	43	0.25
Russian (36)	36	0.21
Scotch-Irish (156)	210	1.23
Scottish (101)	226	1.32
Slavic (0)	12	0.07
Swedish (0)	19	0.11
Swiss (21)	21	0.12
West Indian, ex. Hispanic (78)	127	0.74
Haitian (22)	22	0.13
Jamaican (35)	84	0.49
Trinidadian/Tobagonian (21)	21	0.12

Hispanic Origin	Population	%
Hispanic or Latino (of any race)	2,724	17.58
Central American, ex. Mexican	319	2.06
Costa Rican	4	0.03
Guatemalan	62	0.40
Honduran	91	0.59
Nicaraguan	9	0.06
Panamanian	18	0.12
Salvadoran	130	0.84
Other Central American	5	0.03
Cuban	19	0.12
Dominican Republic	32	0.21
Mexican	2,041	13.18
Puerto Rican	120	0.77
South American	61	0.39
Argentinean	5	0.03
Chilean	2	0.01
Colombian	27	0.17
Ecuadorian	5	0.03
Paraguayan	3	0.02
Peruvian	6	0.04
Uruguayan	7	0.05
Venezuelan	5	0.03
Other South American	1	0.01
Other Hispanic or Latino	132	0.85

Race*	Population	%
African-American/Black (6,218)	6,472	41.78
Not Hispanic (6,122)	6,331	40.87
Hispanic (96)	141	0.91
American Indian/Alaska Native (57)	135	0.87
Not Hispanic (41)	101	0.65
Hispanic (16)	34	0.22
Apache (1)	1	0.01

*Notes: † The Census 2010 population figure is used to calculate the percentages in the Hispanic Origin and Race categories. Ancestry percentages are based on the 2006-2010 American Community Survey population (not shown); ‡ Numbers in parentheses indicate the number of people reporting a single ancestry; * Numbers in parentheses indicate the number of persons reporting this race alone, not in combination with any other race; Please refer to the Explanation of Data for more information.*

Blackfeet (1)	3	0.02
Canadian/French Am. Ind. (0)	1	0.01
Cherokee (15)	55	0.36
Chippewa (3)	3	0.02
Choctaw (0)	2	0.01
Houma (3)	3	0.02
Mexican American Ind. (0)	4	0.03
Seminole (0)	1	0.01
Sioux (1)	2	0.01
Asian (221)	253	1.63
Not Hispanic (217)	246	1.59
Hispanic (4)	7	0.05
Bangladeshi (8)	10	0.06
Cambodian (1)	1	0.01
Chinese, ex. Taiwanese (20)	20	0.13
Filipino (42)	53	0.34
Indian (71)	74	0.48
Indonesian (3)	3	0.02
Japanese (7)	17	0.11
Korean (16)	19	0.12
Laotian (1)	1	0.01
Pakistani (7)	9	0.06
Thai (2)	2	0.01
Vietnamese (34)	35	0.23
Hawaii Native/Pacific Islander (37)	62	0.40
Not Hispanic (37)	58	0.37
Hispanic (0)	4	0.03
Marshallese (24)	24	0.15
Native Hawaiian (10)	12	0.08
Samoan (3)	5	0.03
White (7,074)	7,399	47.76
Not Hispanic (6,063)	6,269	40.47
Hispanic (1,011)	1,130	7.29

Loganville

Place Type: City
County: Walton
Population: 10,458†

Ancestry‡	Population	%
African, Sub-Saharan (138)	138	1.43
African (116)	116	1.20
Nigerian (19)	19	0.20
Other Sub-Saharan African (3)	3	0.03
Albanian (121)	121	1.26
American (1,391)	1,391	14.43
Arab (19)	37	0.38
Egyptian (19)	19	0.20
Lebanese (0)	18	0.19
Belgian (11)	11	0.11
British (77)	134	1.39
Canadian (16)	16	0.17
Czech (0)	36	0.37
Dutch (0)	25	0.26
English (559)	1,037	10.76
European (52)	52	0.54
French, ex. Basque (20)	213	2.21
French Canadian (25)	25	0.26
German (474)	1,418	14.71
Greek (23)	23	0.24
Irish (479)	1,574	16.33
Italian (108)	242	2.51
Polish (11)	121	1.26
Russian (0)	8	0.08
Scandinavian (0)	27	0.28
Scotch-Irish (54)	374	3.88
Scottish (117)	202	2.10
Swedish (51)	51	0.53
Ukrainian (21)	21	0.22
Welsh (0)	34	0.35
West Indian, ex. Hispanic (417)	417	4.33
Jamaican (409)	409	4.24
West Indian (8)	8	0.08

Hispanic Origin	Population	%
Hispanic or Latino (of any race)	712	6.81
Central American, ex. Mexican	104	0.99
Costa Rican	5	0.05
Guatemalan	35	0.33
Honduran	13	0.12
Nicaraguan	6	0.06
Panamanian	5	0.05
Salvadoran	35	0.33
Other Central American	5	0.05
Cuban	44	0.42
Dominican Republic	24	0.23
Mexican	311	2.97
Puerto Rican	89	0.85
South American	100	0.96
Argentinean	2	0.02
Bolivian	1	0.01
Chilean	3	0.03
Colombian	62	0.59
Ecuadorian	20	0.19
Peruvian	3	0.03
Uruguayan	6	0.06
Other South American	3	0.03
Other Hispanic or Latino	40	0.38

Race*	Population	%
African-American/Black (2,316)	2,428	23.22
Not Hispanic (2,275)	2,367	22.63
Hispanic (41)	61	0.58
American Indian/Alaska Native (27)	74	0.71
Not Hispanic (23)	65	0.62
Hispanic (4)	9	0.09
Cherokee (3)	20	0.19
Cheyenne (0)	1	0.01
Creek (1)	4	0.04
Mexican American Ind. (1)	1	0.01
Seminole (0)	1	0.01
Sioux (0)	4	0.04
South American Ind. (0)	2	0.02
Yakama (1)	1	0.01
Asian (243)	313	2.99
Not Hispanic (240)	306	2.93
Hispanic (3)	7	0.07
Bangladeshi (12)	12	0.11
Cambodian (3)	5	0.05
Chinese, ex. Taiwanese (16)	29	0.28
Filipino (9)	26	0.25
Indian (103)	114	1.09
Indonesian (2)	2	0.02
Japanese (4)	9	0.09
Korean (21)	33	0.32
Laotian (6)	9	0.09
Pakistani (18)	21	0.20
Taiwanese (1)	1	0.01
Thai (1)	1	0.01
Vietnamese (34)	41	0.39
Hawaii Native/Pacific Islander (7)	22	0.21
Not Hispanic (7)	20	0.19
Hispanic (0)	2	0.02
Guamanian/Chamorro (0)	1	0.01
Native Hawaiian (0)	2	0.02
White (7,320)	7,491	71.63
Not Hispanic (6,969)	7,101	67.90
Hispanic (351)	390	3.73

Mableton

Place Type: CDP
County: Cobb
Population: 37,115†

Ancestry‡	Population	%
African, Sub-Saharan (1,212)	1,287	3.60
African (684)	718	2.01
Ethiopian (32)	32	0.09
Ghanaian (26)	26	0.07
Nigerian (470)	511	1.43
American (2,310)	2,310	6.47
Arab (39)	80	0.22
Arab (15)	15	0.04
Lebanese (0)	41	0.11
Syrian (24)	24	0.07
Armenian (11)	11	0.03
Belgian (18)	18	0.05
Brazilian (7)	7	0.02
British (24)	86	0.24
Canadian (8)	57	0.16
Czech (37)	44	0.12
Danish (18)	26	0.07
Dutch (29)	316	0.88
English (1,247)	2,580	7.22
European (596)	639	1.79
French, ex. Basque (83)	396	1.11
French Canadian (35)	61	0.17
German (492)	2,237	6.26
Greek (89)	192	0.54
Hungarian (0)	23	0.06
Icelander (20)	30	0.08
Iranian (0)	8	0.02
Irish (975)	2,633	7.37
Italian (238)	731	2.05
Northern European (16)	32	0.09
Norwegian (88)	169	0.47
Polish (39)	217	0.61
Portuguese (0)	18	0.05
Russian (83)	124	0.35
Scotch-Irish (221)	390	1.09
Scottish (173)	407	1.14
Slovak (11)	56	0.16
Swedish (34)	114	0.32
Swiss (22)	45	0.13
Ukrainian (86)	131	0.37
Welsh (27)	148	0.41
West Indian, ex. Hispanic (263)	422	1.18
Bahamian (10)	10	0.03
Belizean (9)	9	0.03
Haitian (38)	84	0.24
Jamaican (143)	212	0.59
Trinidadian/Tobagonian (63)	77	0.22
West Indian (0)	30	0.08

Hispanic Origin	Population	%
Hispanic or Latino (of any race)	6,864	18.49
Central American, ex. Mexican	1,127	3.04
Costa Rican	14	0.04
Guatemalan	89	0.24
Honduran	374	1.01
Nicaraguan	41	0.11
Panamanian	24	0.06
Salvadoran	583	1.57
Other Central American	2	0.01
Cuban	84	0.23
Dominican Republic	64	0.17
Mexican	4,493	12.11
Puerto Rican	357	0.96
South American	238	0.64
Argentinean	18	0.05
Bolivian	4	0.01
Chilean	5	0.01
Colombian	77	0.21
Ecuadorian	13	0.04
Peruvian	97	0.26
Uruguayan	1	<0.01
Venezuelan	23	0.06
Other Hispanic or Latino	501	1.35

Race*	Population	%
African-American/Black (14,660)	15,253	41.10
Not Hispanic (14,424)	14,911	40.18
Hispanic (236)	342	0.92
American Indian/Alaska Native (252)	515	1.39
Not Hispanic (101)	310	0.84
Hispanic (151)	205	0.55
Alaska Athabascan *(Ala. Nat.)* (1)	1	<0.01
Apache (1)	6	0.02
Blackfeet (1)	4	0.01
Central American Ind. (1)	1	<0.01
Cherokee (24)	106	0.29
Choctaw (1)	7	0.02
Creek (2)	6	0.02
Houma (1)	1	<0.01
Inupiat *(Alaska Native)* (7)	9	0.02
Iroquois (2)	5	0.01
Lumbee (2)	5	0.01
Mexican American Ind. (26)	34	0.09

*Notes: † The Census 2010 population figure is used to calculate the percentages in the Hispanic Origin and Race categories. Ancestry percentages are based on the 2006-2010 American Community Survey population (not shown); ‡ Numbers in parentheses indicate the number of people reporting a single ancestry; * Numbers in parentheses indicate the number of persons reporting this race alone, not in combination with any other race; Please refer to the Explanation of Data for more information.*

Navajo (0)	1	<0.01
Ottawa (2)	2	0.01
Paiute (1)	1	<0.01
Potawatomi (1)	1	<0.01
Sioux (1)	10	0.03
South American Ind. (0)	4	0.01
Spanish American Ind. (11)	11	0.03
Tlingit-Haida *(Alaska Native)* (0)	3	0.01
Yaqui (1)	1	<0.01
Asian (816)	1,035	2.79
Not Hispanic (810)	984	2.65
Hispanic (6)	51	0.14
Bangladeshi (9)	11	0.03
Cambodian (22)	25	0.07
Chinese, ex. Taiwanese (105)	152	0.41
Filipino (69)	108	0.29
Indian (345)	388	1.05
Indonesian (2)	4	0.01
Japanese (13)	35	0.09
Korean (66)	89	0.24
Laotian (7)	8	0.02
Malaysian (0)	8	0.02
Nepalese (2)	2	0.01
Pakistani (19)	23	0.06
Sri Lankan (9)	9	0.02
Taiwanese (5)	15	0.04
Thai (3)	8	0.02
Vietnamese (105)	117	0.32
Hawaii Native/Pacific Islander (22)	64	0.17
Not Hispanic (6)	32	0.09
Hispanic (16)	32	0.09
Fijian (1)	1	<0.01
Guamanian/Chamorro (11)	15	0.04
Native Hawaiian (1)	5	0.01
Samoan (9)	10	0.03
White (16,932)	17,785	47.92
Not Hispanic (14,090)	14,637	39.44
Hispanic (2,842)	3,148	8.48

Macon

Place Type: City
County: Bibb
Population: 91,351†

Ancestry‡	Population	%
African, Sub-Saharan (871)	948	1.03
African (633)	710	0.77
Ghanaian (33)	33	0.04
Nigerian (195)	195	0.21
Other Sub-Saharan African (10)	10	0.01
Alsatian (0)	7	0.01
American (4,084)	4,084	4.43
Arab (25)	79	0.09
Egyptian (0)	15	0.02
Lebanese (25)	64	0.07
Australian (0)	5	0.01
Austrian (13)	21	0.02
Brazilian (69)	69	0.07
British (191)	281	0.30
Cajun (14)	14	0.02
Canadian (21)	21	0.02
Czech (83)	125	0.14
Danish (7)	46	0.05
Dutch (72)	345	0.37
English (3,381)	6,058	6.56
European (215)	302	0.33
French, ex. Basque (221)	1,037	1.12
French Canadian (23)	89	0.10
German (1,065)	3,378	3.66
Greek (151)	182	0.20
Guyanese (10)	17	0.02
Hungarian (0)	60	0.07
Irish (2,245)	4,978	5.39
Italian (321)	680	0.74
Lithuanian (11)	21	0.02
Northern European (15)	15	0.02
Norwegian (36)	135	0.15
Polish (152)	316	0.34
Portuguese (14)	89	0.10
Romanian (9)	28	0.03
Russian (45)	150	0.16
Scandinavian (20)	54	0.06
Scotch-Irish (606)	1,149	1.25
Scottish (598)	1,259	1.36
Slovak (16)	35	0.04
Swedish (100)	189	0.20
Swiss (0)	8	0.01
Welsh (34)	119	0.13
West Indian, ex. Hispanic (265)	557	0.60
Barbadian (0)	7	0.01
Haitian (59)	115	0.12
Jamaican (152)	340	0.37
Trinidadian/Tobagonian (11)	52	0.06
West Indian (43)	43	0.05

Hispanic Origin	Population	%
Hispanic or Latino (of any race)	2,264	2.48
Central American, ex. Mexican	247	0.27
Costa Rican	14	0.02
Guatemalan	66	0.07
Honduran	79	0.09
Nicaraguan	32	0.04
Panamanian	4	<0.01
Salvadoran	40	0.04
Other Central American	12	0.01
Cuban	144	0.16
Dominican Republic	21	0.02
Mexican	1,143	1.25
Puerto Rican	276	0.30
South American	64	0.07
Argentinean	11	0.01
Bolivian	1	<0.01
Chilean	2	<0.01
Colombian	28	0.03
Ecuadorian	5	0.01
Peruvian	9	0.01
Venezuelan	7	0.01
Other South American	1	<0.01
Other Hispanic or Latino	369	0.40

Race*	Population	%
African-American/Black (62,060)	62,977	68.94
Not Hispanic (61,768)	62,572	68.50
Hispanic (292)	405	0.44
American Indian/Alaska Native (179)	521	0.57
Not Hispanic (146)	447	0.49
Hispanic (33)	74	0.08
Alaska Athabascan *(Ala. Nat.)* (0)	1	<0.01
Apache (1)	6	0.01
Blackfeet (1)	13	0.01
Canadian/French Am. Ind. (1)	1	<0.01
Central American Ind. (4)	4	<0.01
Cherokee (41)	152	0.17
Chickasaw (0)	1	<0.01
Chippewa (3)	4	<0.01
Choctaw (3)	9	0.01
Comanche (3)	3	<0.01
Creek (2)	12	0.01
Crow (0)	1	<0.01
Houma (2)	2	<0.01
Iroquois (2)	5	0.01
Lumbee (3)	3	<0.01
Mexican American Ind. (5)	6	0.01
Navajo (2)	6	0.01
Puget Sound Salish (1)	1	<0.01
Seminole (3)	7	0.01
Sioux (1)	1	<0.01
South American Ind. (3)	4	<0.01
Spanish American Ind. (1)	1	<0.01
Yakama (0)	1	<0.01
Yuman (1)	1	<0.01
Asian (701)	968	1.06
Not Hispanic (683)	926	1.01
Hispanic (18)	42	0.05
Bangladeshi (2)	2	<0.01
Burmese (2)	2	<0.01
Cambodian (3)	3	<0.01
Chinese, ex. Taiwanese (107)	135	0.15
Filipino (115)	184	0.20
Hmong (2)	2	<0.01
Indian (205)	272	0.30
Indonesian (7)	10	0.01
Japanese (19)	44	0.05
Korean (74)	120	0.13
Laotian (6)	6	0.01
Malaysian (4)	5	0.01
Nepalese (16)	16	0.02
Pakistani (25)	25	0.03
Sri Lankan (1)	2	<0.01
Taiwanese (3)	4	<0.01
Thai (11)	14	0.02
Vietnamese (47)	63	0.07
Hawaii Native/Pacific Islander (48)	136	0.15
Not Hispanic (28)	89	0.10
Hispanic (20)	47	0.05
Fijian (1)	2	<0.01
Guamanian/Chamorro (30)	37	0.04
Native Hawaiian (5)	31	0.03
Samoan (1)	11	0.01
White (26,087)	26,968	29.52
Not Hispanic (25,296)	26,056	28.52
Hispanic (791)	912	1.00

Marietta

Place Type: City
County: Cobb
Population: 56,579†

Ancestry‡	Population	%
African, Sub-Saharan (2,164)	2,340	4.09
African (1,797)	1,961	3.43
Liberian (12)	12	0.02
Nigerian (283)	283	0.49
Sierra Leonean (58)	58	0.10
South African (14)	26	0.05
Albanian (7)	7	0.01
American (3,345)	3,345	5.84
Arab (74)	94	0.16
Arab (0)	20	0.03
Moroccan (15)	15	0.03
Syrian (10)	10	0.02
Other Arab (49)	49	0.09
Armenian (0)	24	0.04
Austrian (25)	72	0.13
Belgian (10)	28	0.05
Brazilian (986)	986	1.72
British (280)	341	0.60
Bulgarian (130)	130	0.23
Cajun (0)	10	0.02
Canadian (31)	131	0.23
Croatian (0)	29	0.05
Czech (0)	48	0.08
Czechoslovakian (9)	54	0.09
Danish (0)	140	0.24
Dutch (93)	329	0.57
Eastern European (29)	29	0.05
English (2,012)	4,598	8.03
European (520)	520	0.91
Finnish (54)	54	0.09
French, ex. Basque (124)	728	1.27
French Canadian (74)	97	0.17
German (1,231)	3,786	6.61
Greek (257)	367	0.64
Guyanese (71)	71	0.12
Hungarian (36)	118	0.21
Iranian (81)	104	0.18
Irish (1,293)	3,921	6.85
Italian (514)	1,422	2.48
Lithuanian (37)	76	0.13
Luxemburger (14)	14	0.02
Northern European (30)	30	0.05
Norwegian (164)	237	0.41
Polish (306)	680	1.19
Portuguese (83)	83	0.14
Romanian (83)	98	0.17
Russian (44)	149	0.26
Scandinavian (18)	48	0.08
Scotch-Irish (719)	1,297	2.27

*Notes: † The Census 2010 population figure is used to calculate the percentages in the Hispanic Origin and Race categories. Ancestry percentages are based on the 2006-2010 American Community Survey population (not shown); ‡ Numbers in parentheses indicate the number of people reporting a single ancestry; * Numbers in parentheses indicate the number of persons reporting this race alone, not in combination with any other race; Please refer to the Explanation of Data for more information.*

Scottish (711)	1,349	2.36
Slavic (20)	48	0.08
Slovak (12)	34	0.06
Swedish (58)	211	0.37
Swiss (17)	51	0.09
Ukrainian (86)	128	0.22
Welsh (89)	246	0.43
West Indian, ex. Hispanic (957)	1,143	2.00
Barbadian (0)	18	0.03
Haitian (564)	564	0.99
Jamaican (216)	322	0.56
Trinidadian/Tobagonian (16)	36	0.06
West Indian (161)	203	0.35
Yugoslavian (0)	20	0.03

Hispanic Origin	Population	%
Hispanic or Latino (of any race)	11,633	20.56
Central American, ex. Mexican	2,088	3.69
Costa Rican	40	0.07
Guatemalan	1,152	2.04
Honduran	321	0.57
Nicaraguan	47	0.08
Panamanian	61	0.11
Salvadoran	460	0.81
Other Central American	7	0.01
Cuban	170	0.30
Dominican Republic	211	0.37
Mexican	7,330	12.96
Puerto Rican	609	1.08
South American	492	0.87
Argentinean	28	0.05
Bolivian	14	0.02
Chilean	23	0.04
Colombian	192	0.34
Ecuadorian	49	0.09
Peruvian	103	0.18
Uruguayan	18	0.03
Venezuelan	57	0.10
Other South American	8	0.01
Other Hispanic or Latino	733	1.30

Race*	Population	%
African-American/Black (17,804)	18,742	33.13
Not Hispanic (17,363)	18,125	32.03
Hispanic (441)	617	1.09
American Indian/Alaska Native (264)	602	1.06
Not Hispanic (109)	361	0.64
Hispanic (155)	241	0.43
Aleut *(Alaska Native)* (0)	2	<0.01
Apache (2)	2	<0.01
Blackfeet (1)	10	0.02
Central American Ind. (7)	11	0.02
Cherokee (17)	85	0.15
Cheyenne (0)	1	<0.01
Chickasaw (1)	2	<0.01
Chippewa (3)	6	0.01
Choctaw (7)	7	0.01
Colville (2)	2	<0.01
Creek (4)	12	0.02
Iroquois (0)	6	0.01
Lumbee (1)	1	<0.01
Mexican American Ind. (31)	50	0.09
Navajo (2)	4	0.01
Osage (2)	2	<0.01
Pueblo (0)	3	0.01
Puget Sound Salish (3)	3	0.01
Seminole (1)	4	0.01
Sioux (2)	2	<0.01
South American Ind. (1)	3	0.01
Spanish American Ind. (4)	4	0.01
Ute (0)	1	<0.01
Asian (1,671)	1,999	3.53
Not Hispanic (1,652)	1,929	3.41
Hispanic (19)	70	0.12
Bangladeshi (30)	30	0.05
Bhutanese (1)	1	<0.01
Cambodian (33)	39	0.07
Chinese, ex. Taiwanese (297)	347	0.61
Filipino (111)	177	0.31
Hmong (1)	1	<0.01
Indian (533)	580	1.03
Indonesian (12)	19	0.03
Japanese (52)	88	0.16
Korean (142)	190	0.34
Laotian (37)	43	0.08
Malaysian (2)	2	<0.01
Nepalese (36)	39	0.07
Pakistani (108)	114	0.20
Sri Lankan (7)	7	0.01
Taiwanese (6)	11	0.02
Thai (31)	35	0.06
Vietnamese (176)	194	0.34
Hawaii Native/Pacific Islander (48)	117	0.21
Not Hispanic (46)	101	0.18
Hispanic (2)	16	0.03
Fijian (1)	2	<0.01
Guamanian/Chamorro (13)	19	0.03
Marshallese (5)	5	0.01
Native Hawaiian (21)	35	0.06
Samoan (3)	5	0.01
White (29,806)	31,259	55.25
Not Hispanic (24,242)	25,105	44.37
Hispanic (5,564)	6,154	10.88

Martinez

Place Type: CDP
County: Columbia
Population: 35,795†

Ancestry‡	Population	%
African, Sub-Saharan (20)	20	0.06
Ugandan (20)	20	0.06
American (4,516)	4,516	12.94
Arab (101)	176	0.50
Arab (32)	43	0.12
Egyptian (28)	28	0.08
Lebanese (24)	66	0.19
Syrian (17)	39	0.11
Armenian (23)	114	0.33
Austrian (10)	84	0.24
Belgian (0)	27	0.08
Brazilian (13)	13	0.04
British (154)	197	0.56
Bulgarian (11)	11	0.03
Canadian (0)	27	0.08
Celtic (48)	53	0.15
Croatian (0)	76	0.22
Czech (45)	101	0.29
Danish (0)	113	0.32
Dutch (147)	780	2.24
English (1,804)	4,477	12.83
European (510)	584	1.67
French, ex. Basque (222)	1,121	3.21
French Canadian (46)	105	0.30
German (2,210)	5,030	14.41
Greek (96)	248	0.71
Hungarian (0)	30	0.09
Iranian (40)	52	0.15
Irish (1,398)	4,277	12.26
Italian (684)	1,082	3.10
Northern European (8)	17	0.05
Norwegian (48)	215	0.62
Pennsylvania German (0)	11	0.03
Polish (259)	806	2.31
Portuguese (19)	19	0.05
Romanian (12)	44	0.13
Russian (39)	104	0.30
Scotch-Irish (350)	753	2.16
Scottish (829)	1,301	3.73
Serbian (0)	13	0.04
Slovak (0)	16	0.05
Swedish (29)	198	0.57
Swiss (13)	71	0.20
Ukrainian (22)	34	0.10
Welsh (45)	292	0.84
West Indian, ex. Hispanic (14)	26	0.07
Trinidadian/Tobagonian (0)	12	0.03
West Indian (14)	14	0.04
Yugoslavian (0)	60	0.17

Hispanic Origin	Population	%
Hispanic or Latino (of any race)	1,530	4.27
Central American, ex. Mexican	147	0.41
Costa Rican	12	0.03
Guatemalan	15	0.04
Honduran	29	0.08
Nicaraguan	7	0.02
Panamanian	55	0.15
Salvadoran	25	0.07
Other Central American	4	0.01
Cuban	61	0.17
Dominican Republic	31	0.09
Mexican	582	1.63
Puerto Rican	435	1.22
South American	152	0.42
Argentinean	6	0.02
Bolivian	9	0.03
Chilean	13	0.04
Colombian	69	0.19
Ecuadorian	6	0.02
Paraguayan	3	0.01
Peruvian	16	0.04
Uruguayan	3	0.01
Venezuelan	25	0.07
Other South American	2	0.01
Other Hispanic or Latino	122	0.34

Race*	Population	%
African-American/Black (4,548)	4,949	13.83
Not Hispanic (4,464)	4,809	13.43
Hispanic (84)	140	0.39
American Indian/Alaska Native (107)	301	0.84
Not Hispanic (103)	270	0.75
Hispanic (4)	31	0.09
Apache (1)	1	<0.01
Blackfeet (4)	6	0.02
Canadian/French Am. Ind. (1)	1	<0.01
Central American Ind. (0)	4	0.01
Cherokee (28)	111	0.31
Cheyenne (0)	7	0.02
Chickasaw (2)	5	0.01
Chippewa (3)	5	0.01
Choctaw (5)	20	0.06
Comanche (2)	2	0.01
Cree (0)	1	<0.01
Creek (1)	10	0.03
Delaware (1)	1	<0.01
Houma (3)	3	0.01
Iroquois (5)	6	0.02
Kiowa (0)	1	<0.01
Lumbee (0)	1	<0.01
Mexican American Ind. (1)	1	<0.01
Navajo (0)	1	<0.01
Pueblo (1)	3	0.01
Seminole (0)	1	<0.01
Sioux (3)	9	0.03
Asian (1,970)	2,366	6.61
Not Hispanic (1,961)	2,321	6.48
Hispanic (9)	45	0.13
Bangladeshi (4)	4	0.01
Cambodian (8)	9	0.03
Chinese, ex. Taiwanese (327)	389	1.09
Filipino (97)	155	0.43
Hmong (2)	2	0.01
Indian (768)	818	2.29
Indonesian (1)	2	0.01
Japanese (38)	114	0.32
Korean (376)	470	1.31
Malaysian (5)	5	0.01
Nepalese (2)	2	0.01
Pakistani (96)	106	0.30
Sri Lankan (4)	4	0.01
Taiwanese (20)	20	0.06
Thai (33)	46	0.13
Vietnamese (146)	156	0.44
Hawaii Native/Pacific Islander (83)	135	0.38
Not Hispanic (80)	126	0.35
Hispanic (3)	9	0.03
Fijian (1)	1	<0.01
Guamanian/Chamorro (28)	40	0.11

*Notes: † The Census 2010 population figure is used to calculate the percentages in the Hispanic Origin and Race categories. Ancestry percentages are based on the 2006-2010 American Community Survey population (not shown); ‡ Numbers in parentheses indicate the number of people reporting a single ancestry; * Numbers in parentheses indicate the number of persons reporting this race alone, not in combination with any other race; Please refer to the Explanation of Data for more information.*

Native Hawaiian (10)	30	0.08
Samoan (5)	11	0.03
White (27,622)	28,524	79.69
Not Hispanic (26,740)	27,501	76.83
Hispanic (882)	1,023	2.86

McDonough

Place Type: City
County: Henry
Population: 22,084†

Ancestry‡	Population	%
African, Sub-Saharan (652)	980	4.86
African (396)	691	3.42
Nigerian (179)	212	1.05
Other Sub-Saharan African (77)	77	0.38
American (1,187)	1,187	5.88
British (56)	56	0.28
Danish (0)	23	0.11
Dutch (0)	90	0.45
English (213)	796	3.94
European (115)	158	0.78
Finnish (0)	11	0.05
French, ex. Basque (86)	364	1.80
French Canadian (7)	7	0.03
German (305)	1,653	8.19
Greek (0)	20	0.10
Guyanese (0)	10	0.05
Hungarian (0)	26	0.13
Irish (280)	1,669	8.27
Israeli (9)	9	0.04
Italian (100)	501	2.48
Lithuanian (0)	18	0.09
Norwegian (9)	18	0.09
Pennsylvania German (19)	19	0.09
Polish (25)	152	0.75
Portuguese (16)	143	0.71
Russian (0)	19	0.09
Scandinavian (0)	156	0.77
Scotch-Irish (197)	263	1.30
Scottish (62)	317	1.57
Slavic (0)	8	0.04
Slovak (0)	10	0.05
Swedish (0)	43	0.21
Welsh (33)	205	1.02
West Indian, ex. Hispanic (972)	1,321	6.55
Bahamian (29)	200	0.99
British West Indian (30)	30	0.15
Haitian (418)	440	2.18
Jamaican (321)	477	2.36
Trinidadian/Tobagonian (107)	107	0.53
U.S. Virgin Islander (38)	38	0.19
West Indian (29)	29	0.14
Yugoslavian (0)	7	0.03

Hispanic Origin	Population	%
Hispanic or Latino (of any race)	1,340	6.07
Central American, ex. Mexican	158	0.72
Costa Rican	13	0.06
Guatemalan	17	0.08
Honduran	11	0.05
Nicaraguan	18	0.08
Panamanian	57	0.26
Salvadoran	38	0.17
Other Central American	4	0.02
Cuban	74	0.34
Dominican Republic	86	0.39
Mexican	518	2.35
Puerto Rican	329	1.49
South American	105	0.48
Argentinean	2	0.01
Chilean	3	0.01
Colombian	47	0.21
Ecuadorian	16	0.07
Peruvian	29	0.13
Uruguayan	3	0.01
Venezuelan	4	0.02
Other South American	1	<0.01
Other Hispanic or Latino	70	0.32

Race*	Population	%
African-American/Black (12,857)	13,274	60.11
Not Hispanic (12,647)	12,987	58.81
Hispanic (210)	287	1.30
American Indian/Alaska Native (59)	194	0.88
Not Hispanic (51)	165	0.75
Hispanic (8)	29	0.13
Alaska Athabascan *(Ala. Nat.)* (2)	2	0.01
Apache (0)	2	0.01
Blackfeet (0)	4	0.02
Canadian/French Am. Ind. (1)	1	<0.01
Cherokee (6)	33	0.15
Chippewa (0)	1	<0.01
Choctaw (0)	3	0.01
Creek (1)	2	0.01
Delaware (1)	2	0.01
Iroquois (0)	1	<0.01
Lumbee (0)	6	0.03
Seminole (0)	1	<0.01
Sioux (0)	1	<0.01
South American Ind. (0)	9	0.04
Ute (0)	2	0.01
Asian (391)	506	2.29
Not Hispanic (387)	494	2.24
Hispanic (4)	12	0.05
Bangladeshi (6)	6	0.03
Cambodian (15)	22	0.10
Chinese, ex. Taiwanese (38)	46	0.21
Filipino (47)	75	0.34
Indian (112)	138	0.62
Indonesian (3)	4	0.02
Japanese (9)	20	0.09
Korean (34)	49	0.22
Laotian (26)	32	0.14
Pakistani (7)	7	0.03
Taiwanese (1)	1	<0.01
Thai (8)	24	0.11
Vietnamese (54)	56	0.25
Hawaii Native/Pacific Islander (18)	48	0.22
Not Hispanic (17)	46	0.21
Hispanic (1)	2	0.01
Guamanian/Chamorro (11)	12	0.05
Native Hawaiian (2)	8	0.04
Samoan (4)	8	0.04
White (7,695)	8,098	36.67
Not Hispanic (7,153)	7,458	33.77
Hispanic (542)	640	2.90

Milledgeville

Place Type: City
County: Baldwin
Population: 17,715†

Ancestry‡	Population	%
African, Sub-Saharan (44)	44	0.23
African (31)	31	0.16
Nigerian (13)	13	0.07
American (4,210)	4,210	21.89
Austrian (11)	19	0.10
Belgian (8)	8	0.04
British (51)	51	0.27
Celtic (19)	19	0.10
Danish (0)	9	0.05
Dutch (71)	209	1.09
English (565)	1,507	7.84
European (120)	120	0.62
Finnish (7)	7	0.04
French, ex. Basque (28)	391	2.03
French Canadian (28)	28	0.15
German (460)	1,336	6.95
Greek (0)	25	0.13
Hungarian (0)	36	0.19
Iranian (19)	19	0.10
Irish (848)	1,532	7.97
Italian (73)	270	1.40
Lithuanian (0)	35	0.18
Maltese (9)	9	0.05
Northern European (46)	46	0.24
Norwegian (0)	23	0.12
Polish (8)	83	0.43
Portuguese (19)	19	0.10
Romanian (131)	131	0.68
Russian (4)	13	0.07
Scotch-Irish (209)	359	1.87
Scottish (116)	425	2.21
Serbian (2)	2	0.01
Slovak (13)	65	0.34
Slovene (16)	16	0.08
Swedish (19)	141	0.73
Welsh (27)	145	0.75
West Indian, ex. Hispanic (27)	27	0.14
Haitian (16)	16	0.08
West Indian (11)	11	0.06
Yugoslavian (0)	36	0.19

Hispanic Origin	Population	%
Hispanic or Latino (of any race)	402	2.27
Central American, ex. Mexican	36	0.20
Costa Rican	2	0.01
Guatemalan	14	0.08
Honduran	5	0.03
Nicaraguan	3	0.02
Panamanian	5	0.03
Salvadoran	7	0.04
Cuban	38	0.21
Dominican Republic	4	0.02
Mexican	187	1.06
Puerto Rican	60	0.34
South American	40	0.23
Argentinean	1	0.01
Chilean	1	0.01
Colombian	15	0.08
Ecuadorian	10	0.06
Peruvian	5	0.03
Uruguayan	3	0.02
Venezuelan	5	0.03
Other Hispanic or Latino	37	0.21

Race*	Population	%
African-American/Black (7,483)	7,618	43.00
Not Hispanic (7,432)	7,558	42.66
Hispanic (51)	60	0.34
American Indian/Alaska Native (26)	105	0.59
Not Hispanic (23)	97	0.55
Hispanic (3)	8	0.05
Alaska Athabascan *(Ala. Nat.)* (1)	1	0.01
Apache (0)	1	0.01
Blackfeet (1)	7	0.04
Cherokee (8)	40	0.23
Choctaw (0)	1	0.01
Creek (0)	6	0.03
Mexican American Ind. (1)	1	0.01
Asian (308)	361	2.04
Not Hispanic (307)	359	2.03
Hispanic (1)	2	0.01
Bangladeshi (2)	2	0.01
Cambodian (0)	1	0.01
Chinese, ex. Taiwanese (27)	37	0.21
Filipino (43)	62	0.35
Hmong (1)	1	0.01
Indian (136)	144	0.81
Indonesian (1)	4	0.02
Japanese (8)	15	0.08
Korean (43)	49	0.28
Laotian (2)	3	0.02
Malaysian (0)	1	0.01
Pakistani (8)	9	0.05
Sri Lankan (2)	2	0.01
Thai (1)	2	0.01
Vietnamese (29)	29	0.16
Hawaii Native/Pacific Islander (11)	20	0.11
Not Hispanic (10)	19	0.11
Hispanic (1)	1	0.01
Fijian (0)	2	0.01
Guamanian/Chamorro (1)	1	0.01
Native Hawaiian (0)	3	0.02
Samoan (1)	2	0.01
Tongan (1)	1	0.01

*Notes: † The Census 2010 population figure is used to calculate the percentages in the Hispanic Origin and Race categories. Ancestry percentages are based on the 2006-2010 American Community Survey population (not shown); ‡ Numbers in parentheses indicate the number of people reporting a single ancestry; * Numbers in parentheses indicate the number of persons reporting this race alone, not in combination with any other race; Please refer to the Explanation of Data for more information.*

White (9,466)	9,679	54.64
Not Hispanic (9,287)	9,469	53.45
Hispanic (179)	210	1.19

Milton

Place Type: City
County: Fulton
Population: 32,661†

Ancestry‡	Population	%
African, Sub-Saharan (497)	553	1.90
African (70)	94	0.32
Ethiopian (9)	9	0.03
Nigerian (370)	370	1.27
South African (21)	53	0.18
Other Sub-Saharan African (27)	27	0.09
American (1,443)	1,443	4.95
Arab (255)	316	1.08
Arab (104)	104	0.36
Jordanian (0)	13	0.04
Lebanese (66)	101	0.35
Moroccan (44)	44	0.15
Syrian (41)	54	0.19
Armenian (34)	34	0.12
Austrian (24)	32	0.11
Belgian (23)	32	0.11
Brazilian (265)	275	0.94
British (194)	330	1.13
Canadian (199)	247	0.85
Croatian (0)	24	0.08
Czech (24)	129	0.44
Czechoslovakian (0)	8	0.03
Danish (27)	61	0.21
Dutch (76)	250	0.86
Eastern European (0)	11	0.04
English (1,214)	3,847	13.21
Estonian (0)	14	0.05
European (598)	650	2.23
French, ex. Basque (179)	941	3.23
French Canadian (34)	152	0.52
German (1,073)	4,442	15.25
Greek (42)	97	0.33
Hungarian (61)	174	0.60
Icelander (13)	51	0.18
Iranian (83)	83	0.28
Irish (1,256)	3,551	12.19
Israeli (0)	41	0.14
Italian (682)	1,819	6.24
Latvian (0)	13	0.04
Lithuanian (0)	83	0.28
Norwegian (108)	374	1.28
Polish (176)	866	2.97
Portuguese (22)	106	0.36
Romanian (24)	24	0.08
Russian (235)	605	2.08
Scandinavian (20)	20	0.07
Scotch-Irish (344)	659	2.26
Scottish (414)	1,231	4.23
Slovak (12)	94	0.32
Swedish (233)	495	1.70
Swiss (15)	56	0.19
Turkish (42)	42	0.14
Ukrainian (37)	155	0.53
Welsh (41)	210	0.72
West Indian, ex. Hispanic (260)	280	0.96
Jamaican (260)	280	0.96
Yugoslavian (0)	15	0.05

Hispanic Origin	Population	%
Hispanic or Latino (of any race)	1,959	6.00
Central American, ex. Mexican	107	0.33
Costa Rican	11	0.03
Guatemalan	14	0.04
Honduran	21	0.06
Nicaraguan	20	0.06
Panamanian	16	0.05
Salvadoran	21	0.06
Other Central American	4	0.01
Cuban	154	0.47
Dominican Republic	40	0.12
Mexican	670	2.05
Puerto Rican	254	0.78
South American	569	1.74
Argentinean	50	0.15
Bolivian	4	0.01
Chilean	8	0.02
Colombian	243	0.74
Ecuadorian	25	0.08
Peruvian	109	0.33
Uruguayan	17	0.05
Venezuelan	112	0.34
Other South American	1	<0.01
Other Hispanic or Latino	165	0.51

Race*	Population	%
African-American/Black (2,936)	3,237	9.91
Not Hispanic (2,865)	3,115	9.54
Hispanic (71)	122	0.37
American Indian/Alaska Native (62)	206	0.63
Not Hispanic (59)	172	0.53
Hispanic (3)	34	0.10
Apache (1)	2	0.01
Blackfeet (0)	2	0.01
Cherokee (14)	52	0.16
Chickasaw (2)	2	0.01
Chippewa (2)	3	0.01
Choctaw (4)	4	0.01
Creek (1)	1	<0.01
Crow (1)	1	<0.01
Houma (1)	3	0.01
Iroquois (2)	2	0.01
Lumbee (4)	4	0.01
Navajo (0)	2	0.01
Sioux (0)	1	<0.01
South American Ind. (0)	2	0.01
Spanish American Ind. (0)	3	0.01
Yakama (1)	1	<0.01
Yaqui (0)	3	0.01
Asian (3,399)	3,724	11.40
Not Hispanic (3,380)	3,682	11.27
Hispanic (19)	42	0.13
Bangladeshi (21)	23	0.07
Cambodian (3)	3	0.01
Chinese, ex. Taiwanese (382)	455	1.39
Filipino (138)	175	0.54
Hmong (1)	3	0.01
Indian (2,258)	2,332	7.14
Indonesian (30)	30	0.09
Japanese (30)	83	0.25
Korean (191)	247	0.76
Laotian (5)	7	0.02
Malaysian (2)	7	0.02
Nepalese (5)	7	0.02
Pakistani (130)	135	0.41
Sri Lankan (13)	14	0.04
Taiwanese (19)	31	0.09
Thai (14)	17	0.05
Vietnamese (74)	87	0.27
Hawaii Native/Pacific Islander (11)	37	0.11
Not Hispanic (9)	27	0.08
Hispanic (2)	10	0.03
Guamanian/Chamorro (1)	3	0.01
Native Hawaiian (7)	14	0.04
White (25,012)	25,589	78.35
Not Hispanic (23,653)	24,131	73.88
Hispanic (1,359)	1,458	4.46

Monroe

Place Type: City
County: Walton
Population: 13,234†

Ancestry‡	Population	%
African, Sub-Saharan (67)	67	0.51
African (50)	50	0.38
Nigerian (17)	17	0.13
American (2,280)	2,280	17.28
Arab (0)	20	0.15
Other Arab (0)	20	0.15
Austrian (7)	7	0.05
Canadian (0)	20	0.15
Czech (16)	33	0.25
Dutch (0)	78	0.59
English (372)	711	5.39
European (39)	39	0.30
French, ex. Basque (63)	123	0.93
French Canadian (0)	24	0.18
German (70)	373	2.83
Irish (309)	1,071	8.12
Italian (71)	128	0.97
Polish (0)	75	0.57
Russian (14)	41	0.31
Scandinavian (7)	7	0.05
Scotch-Irish (300)	467	3.54
Scottish (278)	504	3.82
Swedish (0)	61	0.46
West Indian, ex. Hispanic (26)	26	0.20
West Indian (26)	26	0.20

Hispanic Origin	Population	%
Hispanic or Latino (of any race)	447	3.38
Central American, ex. Mexican	36	0.27
Guatemalan	15	0.11
Honduran	8	0.06
Nicaraguan	11	0.08
Salvadoran	2	0.02
Cuban	20	0.15
Dominican Republic	48	0.36
Mexican	242	1.83
Puerto Rican	57	0.43
South American	8	0.06
Colombian	4	0.03
Peruvian	2	0.02
Venezuelan	2	0.02
Other Hispanic or Latino	36	0.27

Race*	Population	%
African-American/Black (5,610)	5,782	43.69
Not Hispanic (5,583)	5,745	43.41
Hispanic (27)	37	0.28
American Indian/Alaska Native (16)	78	0.59
Not Hispanic (12)	68	0.51
Hispanic (4)	10	0.08
Blackfeet (0)	2	0.02
Canadian/French Am. Ind. (0)	1	0.01
Cherokee (5)	18	0.14
Choctaw (0)	2	0.02
Comanche (0)	1	0.01
Osage (1)	1	0.01
Sioux (0)	5	0.04
South American Ind. (0)	3	0.02
Asian (100)	118	0.89
Not Hispanic (100)	115	0.87
Hispanic (0)	3	0.02
Chinese, ex. Taiwanese (11)	16	0.12
Filipino (24)	27	0.20
Hmong (4)	4	0.03
Indian (49)	53	0.40
Indonesian (1)	3	0.02
Korean (2)	2	0.02
Vietnamese (6)	6	0.05
Hawaii Native/Pacific Islander (6)	20	0.15
Not Hispanic (6)	19	0.14
Hispanic (0)	1	0.01
Guamanian/Chamorro (1)	1	0.01
Native Hawaiian (0)	1	0.01
Samoan (0)	2	0.02
Tongan (1)	1	0.01
White (7,055)	7,260	54.86
Not Hispanic (6,851)	7,034	53.15
Hispanic (204)	226	1.71

Moultrie

Place Type: City
County: Colquitt
Population: 14,268†

SECTION TWO

*Notes: † The Census 2010 population figure is used to calculate the percentages in the Hispanic Origin and Race categories. Ancestry percentages are based on the 2006-2010 American Community Survey population (not shown); ‡ Numbers in parentheses indicate the number of people reporting a single ancestry; * Numbers in parentheses indicate the number of persons reporting this race alone, not in combination with any other race; Please refer to the Explanation of Data for more information.*

Ancestry‡	Population	%
African, Sub-Saharan (202)	266	1.87
African (202)	266	1.87
American (1,646)	1,646	11.55
Arab (0)	6	0.04
Syrian (0)	6	0.04
British (42)	52	0.36
Croatian (73)	73	0.51
Dutch (0)	131	0.92
English (406)	674	4.73
European (44)	44	0.31
French, ex. Basque (54)	54	0.38
French Canadian (9)	47	0.33
German (150)	402	2.82
Greek (7)	42	0.29
Irish (205)	595	4.17
Italian (22)	124	0.87
Lithuanian (0)	46	0.32
Norwegian (37)	37	0.26
Polish (14)	97	0.68
Scotch-Irish (120)	162	1.14
Scottish (19)	128	0.90
West Indian, ex. Hispanic (146)	146	1.02
Jamaican (146)	146	1.02
Yugoslavian (0)	27	0.19

Hispanic Origin	Population	%
Hispanic or Latino (of any race)	1,453	10.18
Central American, ex. Mexican	69	0.48
Costa Rican	1	0.01
Guatemalan	53	0.37
Honduran	10	0.07
Panamanian	2	0.01
Salvadoran	3	0.02
Cuban	444	3.11
Dominican Republic	2	0.01
Mexican	841	5.89
Puerto Rican	31	0.22
South American	13	0.09
Argentinean	2	0.01
Bolivian	1	0.01
Chilean	3	0.02
Colombian	4	0.03
Ecuadorian	3	0.02
Other Hispanic or Latino	53	0.37

Race*	Population	%
African-American/Black (7,060)	7,201	50.47
Not Hispanic (7,016)	7,129	49.96
Hispanic (44)	72	0.50
American Indian/Alaska Native (41)	116	0.81
Not Hispanic (29)	93	0.65
Hispanic (12)	23	0.16
Apache (1)	1	0.01
Blackfeet (0)	1	0.01
Cherokee (9)	34	0.24
Creek (5)	5	0.04
Lumbee (5)	5	0.04
Mexican American Ind. (2)	2	0.01
Navajo (0)	1	0.01
Sioux (0)	1	0.01
Asian (98)	117	0.82
Not Hispanic (97)	114	0.80
Hispanic (1)	3	0.02
Chinese, ex. Taiwanese (8)	11	0.08
Filipino (2)	3	0.02
Indian (64)	69	0.48
Japanese (0)	1	0.01
Korean (2)	3	0.02
Laotian (1)	2	0.01
Malaysian (0)	2	0.01
Thai (1)	1	0.01
Vietnamese (10)	11	0.08
Hawaii Native/Pacific Islander (13)	25	0.18
Not Hispanic (9)	20	0.14
Hispanic (4)	5	0.04
Guamanian/Chamorro (7)	7	0.05
Native Hawaiian (4)	5	0.04
Samoan (0)	1	0.01
White (6,084)	6,251	43.81
Not Hispanic (5,487)	5,601	39.26
Hispanic (597)	650	4.56

Mountain Park

Place Type: CDP
County: Gwinnett
Population: 11,554†

Ancestry‡	Population	%
African, Sub-Saharan (283)	283	2.37
African (65)	65	0.54
Ethiopian (90)	90	0.75
Ghanaian (98)	98	0.82
Other Sub-Saharan African (30)	30	0.25
American (1,027)	1,027	8.60
Arab (111)	126	1.06
Egyptian (29)	29	0.24
Iraqi (82)	82	0.69
Lebanese (0)	15	0.13
Austrian (0)	70	0.59
British (50)	151	1.26
Bulgarian (25)	25	0.21
Canadian (27)	27	0.23
Croatian (13)	41	0.34
Czech (7)	43	0.36
Czechoslovakian (0)	47	0.39
Danish (7)	24	0.20
Dutch (11)	87	0.73
English (650)	1,300	10.89
European (166)	166	1.39
French, ex. Basque (79)	366	3.06
French Canadian (11)	59	0.49
German (360)	1,044	8.74
Guyanese (29)	29	0.24
Hungarian (10)	47	0.39
Irish (299)	910	7.62
Italian (141)	222	1.86
Lithuanian (0)	10	0.08
Northern European (35)	35	0.29
Norwegian (23)	51	0.43
Polish (100)	276	2.31
Portuguese (0)	65	0.54
Romanian (97)	97	0.81
Russian (15)	82	0.69
Scandinavian (8)	8	0.07
Scotch-Irish (213)	393	3.29
Scottish (299)	624	5.23
Slovak (0)	15	0.13
Swedish (66)	179	1.50
Swiss (0)	36	0.30
Welsh (0)	36	0.30
West Indian, ex. Hispanic (16)	27	0.23
Jamaican (16)	16	0.13
West Indian (0)	11	0.09
Yugoslavian (69)	69	0.58

Hispanic Origin	Population	%
Hispanic or Latino (of any race)	789	6.83
Central American, ex. Mexican	105	0.91
Costa Rican	2	0.02
Guatemalan	19	0.16
Honduran	18	0.16
Nicaraguan	9	0.08
Panamanian	5	0.04
Salvadoran	52	0.45
Cuban	45	0.39
Dominican Republic	19	0.16
Mexican	342	2.96
Puerto Rican	113	0.98
South American	98	0.85
Argentinean	3	0.03
Chilean	4	0.03
Colombian	34	0.29
Ecuadorian	19	0.16
Paraguayan	1	0.01
Peruvian	22	0.19
Uruguayan	11	0.10
Venezuelan	3	0.03
Other South American	1	0.01
Other Hispanic or Latino	67	0.58

Race*	Population	%
African-American/Black (1,699)	1,834	15.87
Not Hispanic (1,646)	1,757	15.21
Hispanic (53)	77	0.67
American Indian/Alaska Native (63)	110	0.95
Not Hispanic (40)	75	0.65
Hispanic (23)	35	0.30
Blackfeet (0)	1	0.01
Cherokee (11)	18	0.16
Chippewa (0)	1	0.01
Creek (5)	5	0.04
Mexican American Ind. (3)	3	0.03
South American Ind. (0)	5	0.04
Asian (1,364)	1,485	12.85
Not Hispanic (1,361)	1,479	12.80
Hispanic (3)	6	0.05
Bangladeshi (4)	6	0.05
Burmese (2)	2	0.02
Cambodian (31)	34	0.29
Chinese, ex. Taiwanese (205)	235	2.03
Filipino (16)	26	0.23
Hmong (5)	6	0.05
Indian (687)	728	6.30
Indonesian (0)	2	0.02
Japanese (16)	27	0.23
Korean (93)	98	0.85
Laotian (11)	12	0.10
Nepalese (4)	4	0.03
Pakistani (97)	109	0.94
Taiwanese (19)	27	0.23
Thai (6)	12	0.10
Vietnamese (123)	135	1.17
Hawaii Native/Pacific Islander (16)	21	0.18
Not Hispanic (10)	15	0.13
Hispanic (6)	6	0.05
Fijian (5)	5	0.04
Guamanian/Chamorro (6)	6	0.05
Samoan (5)	6	0.05
White (7,841)	8,071	69.85
Not Hispanic (7,448)	7,637	66.10
Hispanic (393)	434	3.76

Newnan

Place Type: City
County: Coweta
Population: 33,039†

Ancestry‡	Population	%
Afghan (72)	72	0.24
African, Sub-Saharan (128)	154	0.51
African (128)	154	0.51
American (5,250)	5,250	17.41
Arab (18)	18	0.06
Lebanese (11)	11	0.04
Palestinian (7)	7	0.02
Australian (0)	10	0.03
Belgian (8)	20	0.07
Brazilian (21)	44	0.15
British (106)	139	0.46
Cajun (38)	38	0.13
Canadian (17)	17	0.06
Croatian (0)	10	0.03
Czech (0)	39	0.13
Czechoslovakian (18)	18	0.06
Danish (17)	43	0.14
Dutch (46)	235	0.78
English (1,267)	2,338	7.75
European (454)	528	1.75
Finnish (13)	37	0.12
French, ex. Basque (137)	495	1.64
French Canadian (53)	159	0.53
German (770)	2,237	7.42
Greek (42)	86	0.29
Guyanese (0)	12	0.04
Hungarian (0)	51	0.17
Icelander (37)	37	0.12
Iranian (17)	17	0.06

*Notes: † The Census 2010 population figure is used to calculate the percentages in the Hispanic Origin and Race categories. Ancestry percentages are based on the 2006-2010 American Community Survey population (not shown); ‡ Numbers in parentheses indicate the number of people reporting a single ancestry; * Numbers in parentheses indicate the number of persons reporting this race alone, not in combination with any other race; Please refer to the Explanation of Data for more information.*

Ancestry	Population	%
Irish (890)	2,598	8.61
Italian (497)	1,049	3.48
Latvian (12)	36	0.12
Lithuanian (0)	17	0.06
Northern European (14)	14	0.05
Norwegian (40)	209	0.69
Polish (91)	221	0.73
Portuguese (0)	24	0.08
Russian (40)	71	0.24
Scandinavian (27)	45	0.15
Scotch-Irish (415)	599	1.99
Scottish (291)	691	2.29
Slovak (16)	16	0.05
Slovene (9)	9	0.03
Swedish (45)	122	0.40
Swiss (8)	18	0.06
Turkish (0)	17	0.06
Ukrainian (9)	9	0.03
Welsh (32)	116	0.38
West Indian, ex. Hispanic (64)	189	0.63
Belizean (0)	9	0.03
Jamaican (18)	32	0.11
Trinidadian/Tobagonian (46)	56	0.19
West Indian (0)	76	0.25
Other West Indian (0)	16	0.05
Yugoslavian (0)	35	0.12

Hispanic Origin	Population	%
Hispanic or Latino (of any race)	3,619	10.95
Central American, ex. Mexican	362	1.10
Costa Rican	53	0.16
Guatemalan	112	0.34
Honduran	54	0.16
Nicaraguan	33	0.10
Panamanian	35	0.11
Salvadoran	72	0.22
Other Central American	3	0.01
Cuban	92	0.28
Dominican Republic	91	0.28
Mexican	2,104	6.37
Puerto Rican	411	1.24
South American	388	1.17
Argentinean	11	0.03
Bolivian	3	0.01
Chilean	11	0.03
Colombian	144	0.44
Ecuadorian	48	0.15
Peruvian	149	0.45
Uruguayan	4	0.01
Venezuelan	15	0.05
Other South American	3	0.01
Other Hispanic or Latino	171	0.52

Race*	Population	%
African-American/Black (9,978)	10,429	31.57
Not Hispanic (9,825)	10,195	30.86
Hispanic (153)	234	0.71
American Indian/Alaska Native (89)	288	0.87
Not Hispanic (48)	220	0.67
Hispanic (41)	68	0.21
Apache (0)	3	0.01
Blackfeet (0)	8	0.02
Canadian/French Am. Ind. (0)	1	<0.01
Cherokee (17)	81	0.25
Chickasaw (1)	2	0.01
Chippewa (0)	2	0.01
Choctaw (4)	15	0.05
Cree (1)	1	<0.01
Creek (0)	4	0.01
Iroquois (1)	2	0.01
Lumbee (1)	3	0.01
Mexican American Ind. (14)	15	0.05
Navajo (0)	5	0.02
Seminole (0)	1	<0.01
Shoshone (0)	2	0.01
Sioux (2)	10	0.03
Spanish American Ind. (1)	1	<0.01
Asian (868)	1,119	3.39
Not Hispanic (850)	1,062	3.21
Hispanic (18)	57	0.17
Bangladeshi (16)	17	0.05
Cambodian (6)	8	0.02
Chinese, ex. Taiwanese (101)	126	0.38
Filipino (89)	152	0.46
Indian (228)	259	0.78
Indonesian (6)	6	0.02
Japanese (42)	81	0.25
Korean (270)	323	0.98
Laotian (8)	11	0.03
Pakistani (27)	40	0.12
Taiwanese (2)	2	0.01
Thai (14)	20	0.06
Vietnamese (40)	54	0.16
Hawaii Native/Pacific Islander (27)	81	0.25
Not Hispanic (19)	55	0.17
Hispanic (8)	26	0.08
Guamanian/Chamorro (18)	23	0.07
Native Hawaiian (3)	26	0.08
Samoan (1)	14	0.04
White (19,473)	20,210	61.17
Not Hispanic (17,943)	18,507	56.02
Hispanic (1,530)	1,703	5.15

Norcross

Place Type: City
County: Gwinnett
Population: 9,116†

Ancestry‡	Population	%
African, Sub-Saharan (123)	127	1.38
African (37)	41	0.45
Ethiopian (38)	38	0.41
Ghanaian (48)	48	0.52
American (358)	358	3.89
British (0)	65	0.71
Croatian (13)	13	0.14
Czech (15)	15	0.16
Dutch (39)	63	0.68
English (393)	620	6.73
European (187)	196	2.13
Finnish (7)	7	0.08
French, ex. Basque (0)	45	0.49
French Canadian (0)	44	0.48
German (98)	381	4.14
Greek (12)	12	0.13
Irish (61)	333	3.62
Italian (10)	42	0.46
Norwegian (0)	17	0.18
Polish (26)	75	0.81
Romanian (0)	26	0.28
Russian (0)	45	0.49
Scotch-Irish (29)	148	1.61
Scottish (33)	89	0.97
Swedish (0)	55	0.60
Ukrainian (0)	10	0.11
West Indian, ex. Hispanic (47)	50	0.54
Haitian (0)	3	0.03
Jamaican (47)	47	0.51
Yugoslavian (41)	41	0.45

Hispanic Origin	Population	%
Hispanic or Latino (of any race)	3,591	39.39
Central American, ex. Mexican	694	7.61
Costa Rican	12	0.13
Guatemalan	306	3.36
Honduran	116	1.27
Nicaraguan	20	0.22
Panamanian	12	0.13
Salvadoran	222	2.44
Other Central American	6	0.07
Cuban	36	0.39
Dominican Republic	36	0.39
Mexican	2,332	25.58
Puerto Rican	109	1.20
South American	156	1.71
Argentinean	1	0.01
Chilean	2	0.02
Colombian	80	0.88
Ecuadorian	15	0.16
Peruvian	30	0.33
Uruguayan	8	0.09
Venezuelan	20	0.22
Other Hispanic or Latino	228	2.50

Race*	Population	%
African-American/Black (1,801)	1,930	21.17
Not Hispanic (1,703)	1,798	19.72
Hispanic (98)	132	1.45
American Indian/Alaska Native (60)	124	1.36
Not Hispanic (19)	51	0.56
Hispanic (41)	73	0.80
Blackfeet (0)	4	0.04
Central American Ind. (1)	1	0.01
Cherokee (0)	16	0.18
Choctaw (0)	1	0.01
Crow (0)	1	0.01
Iroquois (0)	3	0.03
Lumbee (1)	1	0.01
Mexican American Ind. (5)	6	0.07
Potawatomi (4)	4	0.04
South American Ind. (0)	2	0.02
Spanish American Ind. (1)	1	0.01
Asian (1,167)	1,237	13.57
Not Hispanic (1,154)	1,220	13.38
Hispanic (13)	17	0.19
Bangladeshi (70)	74	0.81
Burmese (5)	5	0.05
Cambodian (17)	17	0.19
Chinese, ex. Taiwanese (265)	292	3.20
Filipino (23)	30	0.33
Hmong (8)	8	0.09
Indian (195)	207	2.27
Indonesian (11)	12	0.13
Japanese (13)	21	0.23
Korean (156)	172	1.89
Laotian (17)	19	0.21
Malaysian (1)	5	0.05
Pakistani (14)	16	0.18
Sri Lankan (1)	1	0.01
Taiwanese (25)	29	0.32
Thai (18)	22	0.24
Vietnamese (289)	308	3.38
Hawaii Native/Pacific Islander (11)	24	0.26
Not Hispanic (5)	14	0.15
Hispanic (6)	10	0.11
Guamanian/Chamorro (5)	6	0.07
Native Hawaiian (5)	8	0.09
Samoan (1)	8	0.09
White (3,722)	4,048	44.41
Not Hispanic (2,448)	2,569	28.18
Hispanic (1,274)	1,479	16.22

North Atlanta

Place Type: CDP
County: DeKalb
Population: 40,456†

Ancestry‡	Population	%
African, Sub-Saharan (837)	1,124	3.03
African (220)	465	1.25
Ethiopian (119)	119	0.32
Ghanaian (71)	71	0.19
Kenyan (0)	21	0.06
Liberian (23)	23	0.06
Nigerian (345)	345	0.93
Other Sub-Saharan African (59)	80	0.22
American (1,213)	1,213	3.27
Arab (45)	76	0.20
Arab (10)	10	0.03
Egyptian (28)	28	0.08
Lebanese (7)	7	0.02
Other Arab (0)	31	0.08
Armenian (22)	22	0.06
Australian (40)	59	0.16
Austrian (57)	191	0.52
Belgian (18)	43	0.12
Brazilian (72)	97	0.26
British (156)	255	0.69

*Notes: † The Census 2010 population figure is used to calculate the percentages in the Hispanic Origin and Race categories. Ancestry percentages are based on the 2006-2010 American Community Survey population (not shown); ‡ Numbers in parentheses indicate the number of people reporting a single ancestry; * Numbers in parentheses indicate the number of persons reporting this race alone, not in combination with any other race; Please refer to the Explanation of Data for more information.*

Canadian (247)	356	0.96
Croatian (0)	115	0.31
Czech (16)	64	0.17
Czechoslovakian (0)	13	0.04
Danish (33)	67	0.18
Dutch (73)	309	0.83
Eastern European (88)	88	0.24
English (1,847)	3,850	10.38
European (488)	515	1.39
French, ex. Basque (134)	802	2.16
French Canadian (24)	104	0.28
German (824)	3,467	9.35
Greek (88)	154	0.42
Guyanese (23)	23	0.06
Hungarian (45)	112	0.30
Icelander (6)	27	0.07
Iranian (34)	34	0.09
Irish (1,016)	3,201	8.63
Israeli (97)	97	0.26
Italian (431)	1,243	3.35
Latvian (8)	21	0.06
Lithuanian (10)	10	0.03
Maltese (11)	11	0.03
New Zealander (10)	30	0.08
Norwegian (70)	175	0.47
Polish (277)	751	2.03
Portuguese (0)	22	0.06
Romanian (7)	34	0.09
Russian (443)	678	1.83
Scandinavian (13)	60	0.16
Scotch-Irish (383)	652	1.76
Scottish (328)	692	1.87
Serbian (14)	14	0.04
Slovak (31)	43	0.12
Swedish (91)	249	0.67
Swiss (0)	58	0.16
Turkish (14)	37	0.10
Ukrainian (22)	53	0.14
Welsh (105)	264	0.71
West Indian, ex. Hispanic (68)	190	0.51
Bahamian (0)	27	0.07
Jamaican (44)	125	0.34
West Indian (24)	38	0.10
Yugoslavian (0)	3	0.01

Hispanic Origin	Population	%
Hispanic or Latino (of any race)	14,426	35.66
Central American, ex. Mexican	1,366	3.38
Costa Rican	21	0.05
Guatemalan	344	0.85
Honduran	471	1.16
Nicaraguan	183	0.45
Panamanian	24	0.06
Salvadoran	315	0.78
Other Central American	8	0.02
Cuban	145	0.36
Dominican Republic	65	0.16
Mexican	11,367	28.10
Puerto Rican	214	0.53
South American	551	1.36
Argentinean	34	0.08
Bolivian	13	0.03
Chilean	10	0.02
Colombian	173	0.43
Ecuadorian	37	0.09
Paraguayan	2	<0.01
Peruvian	200	0.49
Uruguayan	19	0.05
Venezuelan	62	0.15
Other South American	1	<0.01
Other Hispanic or Latino	718	1.77

Race*	Population	%
African-American/Black (4,402)	4,814	11.90
Not Hispanic (4,137)	4,379	10.82
Hispanic (265)	435	1.08
American Indian/Alaska Native (379)	981	2.42
Not Hispanic (74)	169	0.42
Hispanic (305)	812	2.01
Blackfeet (2)	8	0.02
Central American Ind. (9)	11	0.03
Cherokee (12)	45	0.11
Cheyenne (0)	3	0.01
Chickasaw (2)	6	0.01
Choctaw (2)	4	0.01
Creek (4)	7	0.02
Iroquois (0)	3	0.01
Lumbee (1)	1	<0.01
Mexican American Ind. (80)	508	1.26
Pima (0)	1	<0.01
Potawatomi (0)	2	<0.01
Pueblo (2)	2	<0.01
Sioux (2)	3	0.01
South American Ind. (1)	4	0.01
Spanish American Ind. (1)	3	0.01
Asian (1,919)	2,219	5.48
Not Hispanic (1,898)	2,172	5.37
Hispanic (21)	47	0.12
Bangladeshi (196)	214	0.53
Cambodian (5)	5	0.01
Chinese, ex. Taiwanese (394)	465	1.15
Filipino (67)	119	0.29
Indian (651)	736	1.82
Indonesian (34)	36	0.09
Japanese (62)	101	0.25
Korean (173)	210	0.52
Laotian (11)	13	0.03
Malaysian (2)	6	0.01
Nepalese (4)	4	0.01
Pakistani (72)	85	0.21
Sri Lankan (4)	4	0.01
Taiwanese (29)	40	0.10
Thai (14)	23	0.06
Vietnamese (104)	129	0.32
Hawaii Native/Pacific Islander (45)	76	0.19
Not Hispanic (19)	35	0.09
Hispanic (26)	41	0.10
Fijian (2)	2	<0.01
Guamanian/Chamorro (26)	26	0.06
Native Hawaiian (13)	20	0.05
Samoan (0)	1	<0.01
White (24,405)	25,980	64.22
Not Hispanic (19,287)	19,694	48.68
Hispanic (5,118)	6,286	15.54

North Decatur

Place Type: CDP
County: DeKalb
Population: 16,698†

Ancestry‡	Population	%
Afghan (52)	52	0.30
African, Sub-Saharan (60)	78	0.45
African (30)	48	0.27
Kenyan (14)	14	0.08
Other Sub-Saharan African (16)	16	0.09
American (938)	938	5.36
Arab (62)	62	0.35
Arab (13)	13	0.07
Egyptian (11)	11	0.06
Lebanese (14)	14	0.08
Palestinian (8)	8	0.05
Syrian (16)	16	0.09
Armenian (23)	23	0.13
Austrian (11)	26	0.15
Belgian (0)	8	0.05
Brazilian (19)	19	0.11
British (51)	82	0.47
Bulgarian (21)	21	0.12
Canadian (17)	24	0.14
Czech (16)	44	0.25
Czechoslovakian (0)	15	0.09
Danish (34)	122	0.70
Dutch (29)	232	1.32
Eastern European (35)	35	0.20
English (1,107)	2,642	15.09
European (387)	464	2.65
Finnish (0)	16	0.09
French, ex. Basque (121)	759	4.33
French Canadian (15)	41	0.23
German (489)	2,131	12.17
Greek (96)	100	0.57
Hungarian (23)	83	0.47
Iranian (36)	36	0.21
Irish (576)	2,061	11.77
Italian (299)	799	4.56
Lithuanian (0)	137	0.78
Northern European (93)	93	0.53
Norwegian (53)	124	0.71
Polish (69)	295	1.68
Romanian (0)	15	0.09
Russian (198)	435	2.48
Scandinavian (25)	51	0.29
Scotch-Irish (546)	1,021	5.83
Scottish (307)	708	4.04
Slovak (15)	28	0.16
Swedish (82)	187	1.07
Swiss (0)	10	0.06
Ukrainian (11)	44	0.25
Welsh (90)	303	1.73
West Indian, ex. Hispanic (40)	139	0.79
Bahamian (40)	124	0.71
Haitian (0)	15	0.09
Yugoslavian (0)	33	0.19

Hispanic Origin	Population	%
Hispanic or Latino (of any race)	663	3.97
Central American, ex. Mexican	62	0.37
Costa Rican	16	0.10
Guatemalan	12	0.07
Honduran	6	0.04
Nicaraguan	7	0.04
Panamanian	8	0.05
Salvadoran	13	0.08
Cuban	103	0.62
Dominican Republic	8	0.05
Mexican	185	1.11
Puerto Rican	90	0.54
South American	157	0.94
Argentinean	23	0.14
Bolivian	6	0.04
Chilean	6	0.04
Colombian	69	0.41
Ecuadorian	16	0.10
Peruvian	9	0.05
Uruguayan	2	0.01
Venezuelan	24	0.14
Other South American	2	0.01
Other Hispanic or Latino	58	0.35

Race*	Population	%
African-American/Black (2,036)	2,198	13.16
Not Hispanic (1,999)	2,123	12.71
Hispanic (37)	75	0.45
American Indian/Alaska Native (46)	131	0.78
Not Hispanic (34)	110	0.66
Hispanic (12)	21	0.13
Apache (0)	4	0.02
Blackfeet (0)	3	0.02
Central American Ind. (1)	2	0.01
Cherokee (10)	34	0.20
Chickasaw (0)	1	0.01
Choctaw (0)	4	0.02
Creek (0)	4	0.02
Iroquois (0)	1	0.01
Mexican American Ind. (1)	2	0.01
Navajo (3)	4	0.02
Ottawa (1)	1	0.01
Pima (1)	1	0.01
Shoshone (0)	1	0.01
Sioux (0)	1	0.01
South American Ind. (2)	4	0.02
Spanish American Ind. (1)	2	0.01
Asian (1,852)	2,065	12.37
Not Hispanic (1,845)	2,051	12.28
Hispanic (7)	14	0.08
Bangladeshi (17)	21	0.13
Bhutanese (35)	50	0.30
Burmese (1)	1	0.01

*Notes: † The Census 2010 population figure is used to calculate the percentages in the Hispanic Origin and Race categories. Ancestry percentages are based on the 2006-2010 American Community Survey population (not shown); ‡ Numbers in parentheses indicate the number of people reporting a single ancestry; * Numbers in parentheses indicate the number of persons reporting this race alone, not in combination with any other race; Please refer to the Explanation of Data for more information.*

Cambodian (3)	4	0.02
Chinese, ex. Taiwanese (387)	422	2.53
Filipino (24)	51	0.31
Indian (893)	962	5.76
Indonesian (14)	14	0.08
Japanese (36)	71	0.43
Korean (190)	210	1.26
Laotian (2)	2	0.01
Malaysian (1)	4	0.02
Nepalese (19)	35	0.21
Pakistani (85)	95	0.57
Sri Lankan (10)	10	0.06
Taiwanese (11)	12	0.07
Thai (18)	24	0.14
Vietnamese (47)	60	0.36
Hawaii Native/Pacific Islander (4)	19	0.11
Not Hispanic (4)	16	0.10
Hispanic (0)	3	0.02
Guamanian/Chamorro (0)	2	0.01
Marshallese (1)	1	0.01
Native Hawaiian (2)	5	0.03
Samoan (0)	3	0.02
Tongan (0)	5	0.03
White (12,133)	12,514	74.94
Not Hispanic (11,735)	12,042	72.12
Hispanic (398)	472	2.83

North Druid Hills

Place Type: CDP
County: DeKalb
Population: 18,947†

Ancestry‡	Population	%
African, Sub-Saharan (301)	301	1.64
African (142)	142	0.77
Ethiopian (41)	41	0.22
South African (32)	32	0.17
Other Sub-Saharan African (86)	86	0.47
American (1,305)	1,305	7.11
Arab (100)	111	0.60
Egyptian (35)	35	0.19
Lebanese (28)	39	0.21
Moroccan (37)	37	0.20
Armenian (0)	16	0.09
Austrian (0)	18	0.10
Belgian (9)	42	0.23
British (58)	112	0.61
Bulgarian (56)	58	0.32
Czech (5)	34	0.19
Danish (0)	52	0.28
Dutch (83)	151	0.82
Eastern European (308)	331	1.80
English (871)	2,223	12.11
European (325)	325	1.77
Finnish (0)	13	0.07
French, ex. Basque (109)	435	2.37
French Canadian (180)	219	1.19
German (670)	2,047	11.15
Greek (80)	96	0.52
Hungarian (33)	89	0.48
Iranian (38)	63	0.34
Irish (438)	1,486	8.09
Israeli (5)	16	0.09
Italian (144)	526	2.86
Latvian (19)	19	0.10
Lithuanian (12)	88	0.48
Maltese (0)	19	0.10
Northern European (0)	11	0.06
Norwegian (10)	90	0.49
Polish (104)	423	2.30
Portuguese (36)	78	0.42
Romanian (39)	39	0.21
Russian (233)	556	3.03
Scandinavian (0)	16	0.09
Scotch-Irish (501)	838	4.56
Scottish (198)	467	2.54
Slovene (15)	36	0.20
Swedish (9)	57	0.31
Swiss (0)	61	0.33
Ukrainian (21)	63	0.34
Welsh (50)	162	0.88
West Indian, ex. Hispanic (45)	54	0.29
Jamaican (45)	45	0.25
West Indian (0)	9	0.05

Hispanic Origin	Population	%
Hispanic or Latino (of any race)	1,844	9.73
Central American, ex. Mexican	113	0.60
Costa Rican	15	0.08
Guatemalan	14	0.07
Honduran	40	0.21
Nicaraguan	9	0.05
Panamanian	12	0.06
Salvadoran	21	0.11
Other Central American	2	0.01
Cuban	152	0.80
Dominican Republic	31	0.16
Mexican	995	5.25
Puerto Rican	133	0.70
South American	304	1.60
Argentinean	27	0.14
Bolivian	8	0.04
Chilean	34	0.18
Colombian	110	0.58
Ecuadorian	26	0.14
Peruvian	66	0.35
Uruguayan	6	0.03
Venezuelan	26	0.14
Other South American	1	0.01
Other Hispanic or Latino	116	0.61

Race*	Population	%
African-American/Black (2,435)	2,590	13.67
Not Hispanic (2,354)	2,476	13.07
Hispanic (81)	114	0.60
American Indian/Alaska Native (64)	158	0.83
Not Hispanic (38)	101	0.53
Hispanic (26)	57	0.30
Apache (1)	1	0.01
Blackfeet (1)	5	0.03
Canadian/French Am. Ind. (1)	1	0.01
Central American Ind. (2)	2	0.01
Cherokee (5)	30	0.16
Chickasaw (1)	2	0.01
Chippewa (1)	2	0.01
Choctaw (4)	7	0.04
Delaware (1)	1	0.01
Hopi (0)	2	0.01
Iroquois (0)	1	0.01
Lumbee (3)	3	0.02
Mexican American Ind. (2)	17	0.09
Pueblo (1)	1	0.01
Seminole (0)	1	0.01
Sioux (0)	1	0.01
South American Ind. (1)	5	0.03
Yaqui (0)	4	0.02
Asian (2,118)	2,301	12.14
Not Hispanic (2,110)	2,283	12.05
Hispanic (8)	18	0.10
Bangladeshi (46)	48	0.25
Burmese (3)	3	0.02
Cambodian (3)	8	0.04
Chinese, ex. Taiwanese (582)	627	3.31
Filipino (41)	72	0.38
Hmong (1)	1	0.01
Indian (742)	786	4.15
Indonesian (16)	20	0.11
Japanese (69)	85	0.45
Korean (268)	286	1.51
Laotian (8)	9	0.05
Malaysian (8)	8	0.04
Nepalese (40)	41	0.22
Pakistani (55)	61	0.32
Sri Lankan (10)	14	0.07
Taiwanese (50)	58	0.31
Thai (43)	54	0.29
Vietnamese (38)	43	0.23
Hawaii Native/Pacific Islander (4)	21	0.11
Not Hispanic (4)	14	0.07
Hispanic (0)	7	0.04
Fijian (0)	1	0.01
Native Hawaiian (2)	7	0.04
Samoan (0)	1	0.01
White (13,061)	13,436	70.91
Not Hispanic (12,228)	12,500	65.97
Hispanic (833)	936	4.94

Panthersville

Place Type: CDP
County: DeKalb
Population: 9,749†

Ancestry‡	Population	%
African, Sub-Saharan (172)	172	1.66
African (172)	172	1.66
American (123)	123	1.19
English (10)	10	0.10
European (10)	10	0.10
German (0)	42	0.41
Guyanese (30)	30	0.29
Irish (0)	29	0.28
Italian (9)	9	0.09
Norwegian (12)	12	0.12
West Indian, ex. Hispanic (208)	208	2.01
Haitian (153)	153	1.48
Jamaican (22)	22	0.21
Trinidadian/Tobagonian (33)	33	0.32

Hispanic Origin	Population	%
Hispanic or Latino (of any race)	106	1.09
Central American, ex. Mexican	11	0.11
Costa Rican	1	0.01
Honduran	2	0.02
Panamanian	5	0.05
Salvadoran	3	0.03
Cuban	4	0.04
Dominican Republic	10	0.10
Mexican	35	0.36
Puerto Rican	26	0.27
South American	3	0.03
Colombian	3	0.03
Other Hispanic or Latino	17	0.17

Race*	Population	%
African-American/Black (9,409)	9,503	97.48
Not Hispanic (9,357)	9,442	96.85
Hispanic (52)	61	0.63
American Indian/Alaska Native (14)	45	0.46
Not Hispanic (10)	41	0.42
Hispanic (4)	4	0.04
Apache (1)	1	0.01
Blackfeet (1)	3	0.03
Cherokee (1)	18	0.18
Iroquois (0)	1	0.01
Seminole (0)	3	0.03
Asian (25)	38	0.39
Not Hispanic (25)	38	0.39
Bangladeshi (11)	11	0.11
Chinese, ex. Taiwanese (2)	2	0.02
Filipino (2)	3	0.03
Indian (2)	3	0.03
Japanese (0)	3	0.03
Korean (1)	8	0.08
Thai (1)	2	0.02
Vietnamese (2)	2	0.02
Hawaii Native/Pacific Islander (2)	12	0.12
Not Hispanic (1)	9	0.09
Hispanic (1)	3	0.03
Guamanian/Chamorro (1)	7	0.07
Native Hawaiian (1)	2	0.02
Samoan (0)	1	0.01
White (166)	223	2.29
Not Hispanic (148)	202	2.07
Hispanic (18)	21	0.22

*Notes: † The Census 2010 population figure is used to calculate the percentages in the Hispanic Origin and Race categories. Ancestry percentages are based on the 2006-2010 American Community Survey population (not shown); ‡ Numbers in parentheses indicate the number of people reporting a single ancestry; * Numbers in parentheses indicate the number of persons reporting this race alone, not in combination with any other race; Please refer to the Explanation of Data for more information.*

Peachtree City

Place Type: City
County: Fayette
Population: 34,364†

Ancestry‡	Population	%
African, Sub-Saharan (108)	317	0.92
African (39)	103	0.30
Cape Verdean (15)	15	0.04
Nigerian (11)	11	0.03
Senegalese (43)	43	0.13
South African (0)	145	0.42
Albanian (0)	16	0.05
American (2,061)	2,061	6.00
Arab (191)	292	0.85
Arab (21)	35	0.10
Egyptian (81)	81	0.24
Lebanese (66)	132	0.38
Syrian (23)	44	0.13
Armenian (7)	15	0.04
Australian (0)	19	0.06
Austrian (11)	183	0.53
Belgian (43)	81	0.24
Brazilian (44)	44	0.13
British (58)	164	0.48
Canadian (106)	187	0.54
Celtic (0)	9	0.03
Croatian (18)	83	0.24
Czech (48)	260	0.76
Danish (21)	139	0.40
Dutch (216)	782	2.28
Eastern European (11)	11	0.03
English (1,894)	6,248	18.18
European (470)	482	1.40
Finnish (13)	48	0.14
French, ex. Basque (199)	1,715	4.99
French Canadian (43)	108	0.31
German (2,045)	6,948	20.21
Greek (20)	95	0.28
Hungarian (0)	184	0.54
Irish (1,260)	5,248	15.27
Italian (937)	2,644	7.69
Lithuanian (17)	78	0.23
Northern European (44)	44	0.13
Norwegian (191)	487	1.42
Polish (442)	1,389	4.04
Portuguese (65)	127	0.37
Romanian (33)	46	0.13
Russian (40)	223	0.65
Scandinavian (9)	19	0.06
Scotch-Irish (744)	1,384	4.03
Scottish (312)	1,020	2.97
Slovak (0)	44	0.13
Slovene (23)	23	0.07
Swedish (117)	723	2.10
Swiss (21)	106	0.31
Turkish (15)	15	0.04
Ukrainian (28)	176	0.51
Welsh (92)	464	1.35
West Indian, ex. Hispanic (397)	533	1.55
Bahamian (0)	89	0.26
British West Indian (0)	37	0.11
Haitian (34)	34	0.10
Jamaican (306)	306	0.89
U.S. Virgin Islander (40)	40	0.12
West Indian (17)	27	0.08
Yugoslavian (0)	148	0.43

Hispanic Origin	Population	%
Hispanic or Latino (of any race)	2,442	7.11
Central American, ex. Mexican	189	0.55
Costa Rican	15	0.04
Guatemalan	35	0.10
Honduran	37	0.11
Nicaraguan	20	0.06
Panamanian	43	0.13
Salvadoran	39	0.11
Cuban	135	0.39
Dominican Republic	28	0.08
Mexican	1,004	2.92
Puerto Rican	401	1.17
South American	435	1.27
Argentinean	29	0.08
Bolivian	6	0.02
Chilean	36	0.10
Colombian	153	0.45
Ecuadorian	16	0.05
Paraguayan	6	0.02
Peruvian	108	0.31
Uruguayan	47	0.14
Venezuelan	32	0.09
Other South American	2	0.01
Other Hispanic or Latino	250	0.73

Race*	Population	%
African-American/Black (2,557)	2,889	8.41
Not Hispanic (2,509)	2,799	8.15
Hispanic (48)	90	0.26
American Indian/Alaska Native (86)	263	0.77
Not Hispanic (64)	208	0.61
Hispanic (22)	55	0.16
Apache (0)	2	0.01
Blackfeet (1)	9	0.03
Cherokee (15)	64	0.19
Chickasaw (4)	6	0.02
Chippewa (1)	1	<0.01
Choctaw (4)	12	0.03
Creek (9)	14	0.04
Iroquois (1)	3	0.01
Lumbee (0)	3	0.01
Mexican American Ind. (7)	11	0.03
Navajo (1)	1	<0.01
Potawatomi (0)	1	<0.01
Seminole (0)	2	0.01
Sioux (1)	7	0.02
South American Ind. (1)	5	0.01
Tlingit-Haida *(Alaska Native)* (1)	1	<0.01
Asian (1,824)	2,179	6.34
Not Hispanic (1,811)	2,133	6.21
Hispanic (13)	46	0.13
Bangladeshi (12)	12	0.03
Burmese (12)	12	0.03
Cambodian (7)	10	0.03
Chinese, ex. Taiwanese (284)	339	0.99
Filipino (165)	256	0.74
Indian (508)	554	1.61
Indonesian (18)	23	0.07
Japanese (355)	425	1.24
Korean (232)	289	0.84
Laotian (4)	4	0.01
Malaysian (1)	2	0.01
Pakistani (53)	66	0.19
Sri Lankan (1)	1	<0.01
Taiwanese (22)	30	0.09
Thai (16)	21	0.06
Vietnamese (78)	99	0.29
Hawaii Native/Pacific Islander (23)	77	0.22
Not Hispanic (16)	60	0.17
Hispanic (7)	17	0.05
Guamanian/Chamorro (12)	20	0.06
Marshallese (2)	2	0.01
Native Hawaiian (2)	22	0.06
Samoan (1)	8	0.02
White (28,296)	28,992	84.37
Not Hispanic (26,790)	27,340	79.56
Hispanic (1,506)	1,652	4.81

Perry

Place Type: City
County: Houston
Population: 13,839†

Ancestry‡	Population	%
African, Sub-Saharan (31)	31	0.24
African (31)	31	0.24
American (1,812)	1,812	13.81
Austrian (18)	35	0.27
Brazilian (0)	7	0.05
British (47)	178	1.36
Cajun (32)	32	0.24
Canadian (19)	19	0.14
Czech (0)	37	0.28
Dutch (0)	92	0.70
English (466)	978	7.45
European (71)	71	0.54
Finnish (0)	8	0.06
French, ex. Basque (270)	385	2.93
French Canadian (21)	43	0.33
German (613)	1,373	10.47
Greek (0)	9	0.07
Irish (426)	1,108	8.45
Italian (65)	207	1.58
Northern European (18)	25	0.19
Norwegian (0)	19	0.14
Polish (61)	111	0.85
Portuguese (11)	20	0.15
Russian (33)	49	0.37
Scotch-Irish (78)	259	1.97
Scottish (96)	164	1.25
Slovak (0)	15	0.11
Swedish (19)	69	0.53
Ukrainian (15)	15	0.11
Welsh (14)	48	0.37

Hispanic Origin	Population	%
Hispanic or Latino (of any race)	411	2.97
Central American, ex. Mexican	33	0.24
Guatemalan	14	0.10
Honduran	7	0.05
Nicaraguan	3	0.02
Panamanian	6	0.04
Salvadoran	3	0.02
Cuban	19	0.14
Dominican Republic	12	0.09
Mexican	209	1.51
Puerto Rican	69	0.50
South American	20	0.14
Bolivian	1	0.01
Chilean	2	0.01
Colombian	14	0.10
Ecuadorian	2	0.01
Peruvian	1	0.01
Other Hispanic or Latino	49	0.35

Race*	Population	%
African-American/Black (4,965)	5,096	36.82
Not Hispanic (4,949)	5,065	36.60
Hispanic (16)	31	0.22
American Indian/Alaska Native (27)	86	0.62
Not Hispanic (20)	68	0.49
Hispanic (7)	18	0.13
Aleut *(Alaska Native)* (3)	3	0.02
Apache (0)	1	0.01
Arapaho (0)	1	0.01
Blackfeet (0)	1	0.01
Cherokee (2)	28	0.20
Chippewa (1)	1	0.01
Creek (2)	4	0.03
Iroquois (1)	1	0.01
Lumbee (0)	1	0.01
Mexican American Ind. (1)	4	0.03
Sioux (2)	2	0.01
Asian (279)	329	2.38
Not Hispanic (273)	321	2.32
Hispanic (6)	8	0.06
Bhutanese (4)	4	0.03
Burmese (3)	3	0.02
Chinese, ex. Taiwanese (10)	12	0.09
Filipino (31)	54	0.39
Hmong (4)	4	0.03
Indian (179)	182	1.32
Japanese (4)	10	0.07
Korean (6)	14	0.10
Pakistani (2)	2	0.01
Sri Lankan (1)	1	0.01
Thai (9)	9	0.07
Vietnamese (22)	24	0.17
Hawaii Native/Pacific Islander (4)	13	0.09

*Notes: † The Census 2010 population figure is used to calculate the percentages in the Hispanic Origin and Race categories. Ancestry percentages are based on the 2006-2010 American Community Survey population (not shown); ‡ Numbers in parentheses indicate the number of people reporting a single ancestry; * Numbers in parentheses indicate the number of persons reporting this race alone, not in combination with any other race; Please refer to the Explanation of Data for more information.*

Not Hispanic (2)	11	0.08
Hispanic (2)	2	0.01
Guamanian/Chamorro (3)	4	0.03
Native Hawaiian (1)	4	0.03
White (8,216)	8,402	60.71
Not Hispanic (7,982)	8,134	58.78
Hispanic (234)	268	1.94

Pooler

Place Type: City
County: Chatham
Population: 19,140†

Ancestry‡	Population	%
African, Sub-Saharan (43)	43	0.26
African (26)	26	0.16
Nigerian (17)	17	0.10
American (982)	982	5.89
Arab (28)	36	0.22
Syrian (0)	8	0.05
Other Arab (28)	28	0.17
Austrian (13)	13	0.08
Brazilian (12)	12	0.07
British (49)	49	0.29
Bulgarian (40)	40	0.24
Canadian (80)	105	0.63
Croatian (0)	11	0.07
Dutch (66)	108	0.65
English (519)	1,124	6.74
European (232)	232	1.39
Finnish (13)	29	0.17
French, ex. Basque (118)	280	1.68
French Canadian (20)	20	0.12
German (557)	1,651	9.90
Greek (7)	38	0.23
Guyanese (0)	13	0.08
Hungarian (16)	26	0.16
Irish (700)	1,730	10.37
Italian (150)	433	2.60
Norwegian (18)	29	0.17
Polish (54)	282	1.69
Portuguese (0)	73	0.44
Russian (31)	93	0.56
Scandinavian (32)	32	0.19
Scotch-Irish (194)	273	1.64
Scottish (163)	299	1.79
Serbian (0)	11	0.07
Slovak (0)	9	0.05
Swedish (33)	55	0.33
Swiss (16)	33	0.20
Turkish (96)	96	0.58
Ukrainian (23)	23	0.14
Welsh (0)	35	0.21
West Indian, ex. Hispanic (8)	16	0.10
Jamaican (8)	16	0.10

Hispanic Origin	Population	%
Hispanic or Latino (of any race)	1,255	6.56
Central American, ex. Mexican	138	0.72
Costa Rican	10	0.05
Guatemalan	11	0.06
Honduran	53	0.28
Nicaraguan	5	0.03
Panamanian	37	0.19
Salvadoran	21	0.11
Other Central American	1	0.01
Cuban	64	0.33
Dominican Republic	24	0.13
Mexican	382	2.00
Puerto Rican	395	2.06
South American	139	0.73
Argentinean	7	0.04
Bolivian	1	0.01
Chilean	2	0.01
Colombian	60	0.31
Ecuadorian	10	0.05
Peruvian	43	0.22
Venezuelan	12	0.06
Other South American	4	0.02
Other Hispanic or Latino	113	0.59

Race*	Population	%
African-American/Black (4,854)	5,093	26.61
Not Hispanic (4,781)	4,996	26.10
Hispanic (73)	97	0.51
American Indian/Alaska Native (33)	112	0.59
Not Hispanic (33)	104	0.54
Hispanic (0)	8	0.04
Apache (1)	1	0.01
Blackfeet (0)	2	0.01
Cherokee (8)	39	0.20
Delaware (0)	3	0.02
Iroquois (0)	2	0.01
Lumbee (0)	1	0.01
Navajo (1)	2	0.01
Ottawa (1)	1	0.01
Sioux (2)	9	0.05
South American Ind. (0)	1	0.01
Asian (730)	939	4.91
Not Hispanic (721)	892	4.66
Hispanic (9)	47	0.25
Bangladeshi (2)	2	0.01
Burmese (0)	4	0.02
Cambodian (6)	6	0.03
Chinese, ex. Taiwanese (140)	170	0.89
Filipino (55)	125	0.65
Indian (322)	335	1.75
Indonesian (2)	2	0.01
Japanese (29)	54	0.28
Korean (51)	88	0.46
Laotian (17)	20	0.10
Malaysian (1)	3	0.02
Pakistani (0)	3	0.02
Sri Lankan (4)	4	0.02
Taiwanese (1)	1	0.01
Thai (7)	20	0.10
Vietnamese (82)	92	0.48
Hawaii Native/Pacific Islander (25)	71	0.37
Not Hispanic (19)	42	0.22
Hispanic (6)	29	0.15
Fijian (2)	2	0.01
Guamanian/Chamorro (4)	13	0.07
Native Hawaiian (6)	23	0.12
Samoan (7)	8	0.04
Tongan (3)	3	0.02
White (12,525)	12,970	67.76
Not Hispanic (11,878)	12,220	63.85
Hispanic (647)	750	3.92

Powder Springs

Place Type: City
County: Cobb
Population: 13,940†

Ancestry‡	Population	%
African, Sub-Saharan (628)	691	5.02
African (509)	572	4.15
Nigerian (41)	41	0.30
Other Sub-Saharan African (78)	78	0.57
American (770)	770	5.59
Austrian (0)	33	0.24
Basque (19)	19	0.14
Brazilian (44)	44	0.32
British (51)	91	0.66
Cajun (15)	15	0.11
Czech (0)	76	0.55
Dutch (18)	77	0.56
Eastern European (12)	12	0.09
English (393)	880	6.39
European (41)	41	0.30
French, ex. Basque (70)	214	1.55
French Canadian (0)	15	0.11
German (166)	825	5.99
Greek (0)	28	0.20
Hungarian (14)	24	0.17
Irish (268)	979	7.11
Italian (73)	201	1.46
Latvian (0)	20	0.15
Lithuanian (0)	20	0.15
Norwegian (0)	74	0.54
Polish (29)	84	0.61
Portuguese (0)	20	0.15
Romanian (0)	13	0.09
Russian (0)	51	0.37
Scotch-Irish (182)	383	2.78
Scottish (194)	445	3.23
Serbian (17)	17	0.12
Slovak (0)	13	0.09
Swedish (0)	58	0.42
Swiss (0)	11	0.08
Ukrainian (0)	22	0.16
Welsh (0)	79	0.57
West Indian, ex. Hispanic (271)	284	2.06
Bahamian (23)	23	0.17
Haitian (139)	139	1.01
Jamaican (72)	85	0.62
Trinidadian/Tobagonian (37)	37	0.27
Yugoslavian (14)	31	0.23

Hispanic Origin	Population	%
Hispanic or Latino (of any race)	1,267	9.09
Central American, ex. Mexican	177	1.27
Costa Rican	6	0.04
Guatemalan	64	0.46
Honduran	28	0.20
Nicaraguan	2	0.01
Panamanian	15	0.11
Salvadoran	62	0.44
Cuban	29	0.21
Dominican Republic	66	0.47
Mexican	641	4.60
Puerto Rican	196	1.41
South American	90	0.65
Argentinean	1	0.01
Chilean	3	0.02
Colombian	48	0.34
Ecuadorian	13	0.09
Peruvian	16	0.11
Venezuelan	9	0.06
Other Hispanic or Latino	68	0.49

Race*	Population	%
African-American/Black (6,961)	7,235	51.90
Not Hispanic (6,850)	7,078	50.77
Hispanic (111)	157	1.13
American Indian/Alaska Native (25)	103	0.74
Not Hispanic (14)	86	0.62
Hispanic (11)	17	0.12
Alaska Athabascan *(Ala. Nat.)* (1)	1	0.01
Blackfeet (0)	2	0.01
Central American Ind. (1)	1	0.01
Cherokee (5)	44	0.32
Choctaw (0)	5	0.04
Creek (0)	2	0.01
Lumbee (0)	1	0.01
Mexican American Ind. (0)	1	0.01
Navajo (0)	4	0.03
Asian (147)	229	1.64
Not Hispanic (145)	219	1.57
Hispanic (2)	10	0.07
Cambodian (5)	5	0.04
Chinese, ex. Taiwanese (12)	19	0.14
Filipino (22)	48	0.34
Indian (32)	45	0.32
Indonesian (6)	9	0.06
Japanese (4)	9	0.06
Korean (9)	24	0.17
Laotian (2)	2	0.01
Malaysian (1)	1	0.01
Nepalese (1)	1	0.01
Pakistani (19)	23	0.16
Taiwanese (2)	2	0.01
Vietnamese (23)	27	0.19
Hawaii Native/Pacific Islander (4)	19	0.14
Not Hispanic (2)	9	0.06
Hispanic (2)	10	0.07
Guamanian/Chamorro (3)	3	0.02
Native Hawaiian (0)	7	0.05

SECTION TWO

*Notes: † The Census 2010 population figure is used to calculate the percentages in the Hispanic Origin and Race categories. Ancestry percentages are based on the 2006-2010 American Community Survey population (not shown); ‡ Numbers in parentheses indicate the number of people reporting a single ancestry; * Numbers in parentheses indicate the number of persons reporting this race alone, not in combination with any other race; Please refer to the Explanation of Data for more information.*

White (5,802)	6,095	43.72
Not Hispanic (5,304)	5,549	39.81
Hispanic (498)	546	3.92

Redan

Place Type: CDP
County: DeKalb
Population: 33,015†

Ancestry‡	Population	%
African, Sub-Saharan (1,478)	1,869	5.46
African (985)	1,279	3.74
Cape Verdean (18)	18	0.05
Nigerian (346)	397	1.16
Senegalese (10)	22	0.06
Somalian (48)	48	0.14
Sudanese (19)	19	0.06
Other Sub-Saharan African (52)	86	0.25
American (431)	431	1.26
Arab (0)	18	0.05
Other Arab (0)	18	0.05
British (11)	11	0.03
Dutch (0)	5	0.01
English (76)	294	0.86
European (0)	16	0.05
French, ex. Basque (27)	64	0.19
German (67)	157	0.46
Guyanese (452)	473	1.38
Irish (95)	476	1.39
Italian (35)	139	0.41
Polish (9)	49	0.14
Russian (0)	11	0.03
Scotch-Irish (103)	146	0.43
Scottish (14)	103	0.30
Swedish (22)	32	0.09
Welsh (0)	38	0.11
West Indian, ex. Hispanic (1,036)	1,221	3.57
Barbadian (9)	9	0.03
British West Indian (73)	73	0.21
Haitian (47)	59	0.17
Jamaican (742)	826	2.41
Trinidadian/Tobagonian (114)	156	0.46
West Indian (51)	98	0.29

Hispanic Origin	Population	%
Hispanic or Latino (of any race)	799	2.42
Central American, ex. Mexican	125	0.38
Costa Rican	13	0.04
Guatemalan	21	0.06
Honduran	19	0.06
Nicaraguan	5	0.02
Panamanian	60	0.18
Salvadoran	7	0.02
Cuban	64	0.19
Dominican Republic	38	0.12
Mexican	247	0.75
Puerto Rican	195	0.59
South American	33	0.10
Chilean	2	0.01
Colombian	15	0.05
Ecuadorian	1	<0.01
Peruvian	6	0.02
Venezuelan	9	0.03
Other Hispanic or Latino	97	0.29

Race*	Population	%
African-American/Black (30,992)	31,497	95.40
Not Hispanic (30,600)	31,031	93.99
Hispanic (392)	466	1.41
American Indian/Alaska Native (78)	248	0.75
Not Hispanic (70)	218	0.66
Hispanic (8)	30	0.09
Blackfeet (0)	7	0.02
Canadian/French Am. Ind. (0)	1	<0.01
Central American Ind. (3)	4	0.01
Cherokee (6)	37	0.11
Chickasaw (0)	1	<0.01
Choctaw (3)	10	0.03
Cree (0)	1	<0.01
Creek (1)	5	0.02
Delaware (1)	12	0.04
Iroquois (0)	1	<0.01
Mexican American Ind. (0)	1	<0.01
Navajo (1)	3	0.01
Osage (1)	1	<0.01
Pueblo (1)	1	<0.01
Seminole (1)	1	<0.01
Sioux (0)	4	0.01
South American Ind. (1)	1	<0.01
Tlingit-Haida *(Alaska Native)* (0)	1	<0.01
Asian (167)	239	0.72
Not Hispanic (166)	233	0.71
Hispanic (1)	6	0.02
Bangladeshi (11)	12	0.04
Cambodian (2)	9	0.03
Chinese, ex. Taiwanese (6)	29	0.09
Filipino (27)	37	0.11
Hmong (8)	8	0.02
Indian (40)	67	0.20
Japanese (9)	12	0.04
Korean (7)	16	0.05
Laotian (14)	16	0.05
Malaysian (1)	1	<0.01
Pakistani (1)	2	0.01
Thai (0)	2	0.01
Vietnamese (19)	25	0.08
Hawaii Native/Pacific Islander (8)	39	0.12
Not Hispanic (8)	37	0.11
Hispanic (0)	2	0.01
Fijian (1)	3	0.01
Guamanian/Chamorro (3)	4	0.01
Samoan (2)	7	0.02
White (990)	1,266	3.83
Not Hispanic (852)	1,087	3.29
Hispanic (138)	179	0.54

Richmond Hill

Place Type: City
County: Bryan
Population: 9,281†

Ancestry‡	Population	%
African, Sub-Saharan (17)	17	0.19
African (17)	17	0.19
American (458)	458	5.15
British (0)	19	0.21
Czech (0)	80	0.90
Danish (14)	67	0.75
Dutch (23)	348	3.91
English (187)	1,047	11.78
European (37)	37	0.42
French, ex. Basque (0)	201	2.26
French Canadian (48)	61	0.69
German (314)	1,429	16.07
Greek (0)	47	0.53
Hungarian (28)	28	0.31
Irish (329)	1,273	14.32
Italian (121)	328	3.69
Norwegian (18)	146	1.64
Polish (15)	172	1.93
Portuguese (0)	17	0.19
Russian (467)	497	5.59
Scotch-Irish (84)	237	2.67
Scottish (138)	433	4.87
Slovak (13)	13	0.15
Swedish (0)	93	1.05
Swiss (0)	20	0.22
Ukrainian (19)	101	1.14
Welsh (7)	92	1.03
West Indian, ex. Hispanic (194)	235	2.64
Barbadian (9)	9	0.10
British West Indian (58)	58	0.65
Jamaican (127)	127	1.43
West Indian (0)	41	0.46

Hispanic Origin	Population	%
Hispanic or Latino (of any race)	694	7.48
Central American, ex. Mexican	100	1.08
Costa Rican	9	0.10
Honduran	14	0.15
Nicaraguan	4	0.04
Panamanian	59	0.64
Salvadoran	8	0.09
Other Central American	6	0.06
Cuban	21	0.23
Dominican Republic	12	0.13
Mexican	201	2.17
Puerto Rican	262	2.82
South American	60	0.65
Chilean	1	0.01
Colombian	29	0.31
Ecuadorian	11	0.12
Peruvian	9	0.10
Uruguayan	3	0.03
Venezuelan	3	0.03
Other South American	4	0.04
Other Hispanic or Latino	38	0.41

Race*	Population	%
African-American/Black (1,568)	1,754	18.90
Not Hispanic (1,530)	1,675	18.05
Hispanic (38)	79	0.85
American Indian/Alaska Native (33)	88	0.95
Not Hispanic (23)	58	0.62
Hispanic (10)	30	0.32
Aleut *(Alaska Native)* (3)	3	0.03
Blackfeet (0)	1	0.01
Canadian/French Am. Ind. (1)	1	0.01
Cherokee (4)	17	0.18
Creek (1)	3	0.03
Menominee (1)	1	0.01
Mexican American Ind. (3)	4	0.04
Navajo (3)	4	0.04
Sioux (0)	1	0.01
South American Ind. (0)	7	0.08
Asian (269)	357	3.85
Not Hispanic (259)	340	3.66
Hispanic (10)	17	0.18
Bangladeshi (3)	4	0.04
Chinese, ex. Taiwanese (42)	57	0.61
Filipino (66)	89	0.96
Indian (54)	63	0.68
Japanese (13)	35	0.38
Korean (48)	68	0.73
Sri Lankan (3)	4	0.04
Taiwanese (2)	2	0.02
Thai (3)	3	0.03
Vietnamese (33)	37	0.40
Hawaii Native/Pacific Islander (14)	39	0.42
Not Hispanic (11)	31	0.33
Hispanic (3)	8	0.09
Guamanian/Chamorro (6)	10	0.11
Native Hawaiian (2)	14	0.15
Samoan (5)	9	0.10
White (6,888)	7,175	77.31
Not Hispanic (6,483)	6,705	72.24
Hispanic (405)	470	5.06

Rincon

Place Type: Town
County: Effingham
Population: 8,836†

Ancestry‡	Population	%
African, Sub-Saharan (10)	10	0.12
African (10)	10	0.12
American (641)	641	7.84
Austrian (17)	67	0.82
Belgian (22)	22	0.27
British (28)	28	0.34
Danish (0)	9	0.11
Dutch (66)	102	1.25
English (577)	975	11.93
European (64)	64	0.78
French, ex. Basque (0)	133	1.63
German (317)	1,064	13.02
Hungarian (158)	166	2.03

*Notes: † The Census 2010 population figure is used to calculate the percentages in the Hispanic Origin and Race categories. Ancestry percentages are based on the 2006-2010 American Community Survey population (not shown); ‡ Numbers in parentheses indicate the number of people reporting a single ancestry; * Numbers in parentheses indicate the number of persons reporting this race alone, not in combination with any other race; Please refer to the Explanation of Data for more information.*

Irish (531)	1,455	17.80
Italian (37)	250	3.06
Polish (15)	242	2.96
Russian (0)	58	0.71
Scotch-Irish (32)	57	0.70
Scottish (93)	153	1.87
Slovak (12)	30	0.37
Swedish (0)	17	0.21
Welsh (15)	15	0.18
Yugoslavian (16)	16	0.20

Hispanic Origin	Population	%
Hispanic or Latino (of any race)	421	4.76
Central American, ex. Mexican	25	0.28
Guatemalan	12	0.14
Honduran	3	0.03
Nicaraguan	1	0.01
Panamanian	7	0.08
Salvadoran	2	0.02
Cuban	11	0.12
Dominican Republic	17	0.19
Mexican	223	2.52
Puerto Rican	103	1.17
South American	17	0.19
Colombian	11	0.12
Ecuadorian	2	0.02
Peruvian	1	0.01
Venezuelan	3	0.03
Other Hispanic or Latino	25	0.28

Race*	Population	%
African-American/Black (1,866)	1,994	22.57
Not Hispanic (1,845)	1,959	22.17
Hispanic (21)	35	0.40
American Indian/Alaska Native (29)	120	1.36
Not Hispanic (26)	113	1.28
Hispanic (3)	7	0.08
Cherokee (7)	38	0.43
Creek (4)	5	0.06
Lumbee (0)	1	0.01
Mexican American Ind. (1)	1	0.01
Navajo (0)	4	0.05
Sioux (4)	4	0.05
Asian (170)	223	2.52
Not Hispanic (169)	219	2.48
Hispanic (1)	4	0.05
Chinese, ex. Taiwanese (25)	26	0.29
Filipino (12)	22	0.25
Indian (82)	85	0.96
Japanese (1)	9	0.10
Korean (7)	23	0.26
Laotian (0)	1	0.01
Malaysian (6)	7	0.08
Pakistani (0)	1	0.01
Taiwanese (0)	5	0.06
Thai (4)	5	0.06
Vietnamese (27)	32	0.36
Hawaii Native/Pacific Islander (2)	17	0.19
Not Hispanic (2)	12	0.14
Hispanic (0)	5	0.06
Native Hawaiian (0)	6	0.07
White (6,346)	6,576	74.42
Not Hispanic (6,129)	6,318	71.50
Hispanic (217)	258	2.92

Riverdale

Place Type: City
County: Clayton
Population: 15,134†

Ancestry‡	Population	%
African, Sub-Saharan (739)	750	4.99
African (117)	128	0.85
Ethiopian (49)	49	0.33
Ghanaian (14)	14	0.09
Nigerian (550)	550	3.66
Other Sub-Saharan African (9)	9	0.06
American (671)	671	4.46
Dutch (0)	16	0.11
English (124)	133	0.88
European (0)	11	0.07
French, ex. Basque (0)	16	0.11
French Canadian (9)	9	0.06
German (25)	72	0.48
Greek (0)	44	0.29
Irish (26)	286	1.90
Italian (229)	229	1.52
Polish (18)	18	0.12
Scotch-Irish (9)	18	0.12
Scottish (0)	22	0.15
Swedish (0)	61	0.41
West Indian, ex. Hispanic (391)	424	2.82
Haitian (217)	217	1.44
Jamaican (124)	135	0.90
Trinidadian/Tobagonian (11)	11	0.07
West Indian (39)	61	0.41

Hispanic Origin	Population	%
Hispanic or Latino (of any race)	905	5.98
Central American, ex. Mexican	109	0.72
Costa Rican	3	0.02
Guatemalan	17	0.11
Honduran	19	0.13
Nicaraguan	3	0.02
Panamanian	31	0.20
Salvadoran	20	0.13
Other Central American	16	0.11
Cuban	36	0.24
Dominican Republic	28	0.19
Mexican	502	3.32
Puerto Rican	121	0.80
South American	40	0.26
Chilean	3	0.02
Colombian	13	0.09
Peruvian	2	0.01
Uruguayan	14	0.09
Venezuelan	6	0.04
Other South American	2	0.01
Other Hispanic or Latino	69	0.46

Race*	Population	%
African-American/Black (12,112)	12,355	81.64
Not Hispanic (11,967)	12,163	80.37
Hispanic (145)	192	1.27
American Indian/Alaska Native (44)	126	0.83
Not Hispanic (37)	112	0.74
Hispanic (7)	14	0.09
Blackfeet (0)	1	0.01
Canadian/French Am. Ind. (1)	2	0.01
Cherokee (1)	10	0.07
Seminole (2)	4	0.03
Asian (1,027)	1,092	7.22
Not Hispanic (1,025)	1,082	7.15
Hispanic (2)	10	0.07
Cambodian (143)	165	1.09
Chinese, ex. Taiwanese (34)	46	0.30
Filipino (39)	49	0.32
Hmong (1)	5	0.03
Indian (116)	137	0.91
Indonesian (1)	1	0.01
Japanese (3)	8	0.05
Korean (14)	15	0.10
Laotian (62)	78	0.52
Pakistani (29)	29	0.19
Thai (2)	14	0.09
Vietnamese (520)	555	3.67
Hawaii Native/Pacific Islander (9)	32	0.21
Not Hispanic (9)	29	0.19
Hispanic (0)	3	0.02
Guamanian/Chamorro (1)	6	0.04
Native Hawaiian (2)	8	0.05
White (1,216)	1,409	9.31
Not Hispanic (918)	1,050	6.94
Hispanic (298)	359	2.37

Rome

Place Type: City
County: Floyd
Population: 36,303†

Ancestry‡	Population	%
African, Sub-Saharan (598)	666	1.84
African (558)	626	1.73
Nigerian (19)	19	0.05
Other Sub-Saharan African (21)	21	0.06
American (2,750)	2,750	7.58
Arab (50)	60	0.17
Arab (0)	10	0.03
Lebanese (13)	13	0.04
Palestinian (7)	7	0.02
Other Arab (30)	30	0.08
Austrian (7)	7	0.02
Brazilian (9)	9	0.02
British (35)	57	0.16
Bulgarian (41)	41	0.11
Canadian (0)	8	0.02
Croatian (11)	11	0.03
Czech (0)	1	<0.01
Dutch (18)	255	0.70
English (2,202)	3,946	10.88
European (178)	209	0.58
French, ex. Basque (85)	435	1.20
French Canadian (74)	89	0.25
German (665)	2,402	6.62
Greek (44)	304	0.84
Irish (1,051)	3,211	8.86
Italian (197)	704	1.94
Norwegian (22)	109	0.30
Polish (46)	232	0.64
Portuguese (12)	86	0.24
Russian (58)	120	0.33
Scandinavian (14)	32	0.09
Scotch-Irish (557)	851	2.35
Scottish (256)	596	1.64
Slavic (0)	62	0.17
Swedish (39)	85	0.23
Swiss (39)	59	0.16
Turkish (9)	9	0.02
Ukrainian (12)	56	0.15
Welsh (0)	120	0.33
West Indian, ex. Hispanic (60)	70	0.19
Bahamian (6)	6	0.02
Belizean (12)	12	0.03
Haitian (12)	12	0.03
Jamaican (30)	40	0.11

Hispanic Origin	Population	%
Hispanic or Latino (of any race)	5,892	16.23
Central American, ex. Mexican	2,444	6.73
Costa Rican	5	0.01
Guatemalan	2,234	6.15
Honduran	50	0.14
Nicaraguan	4	0.01
Panamanian	3	0.01
Salvadoran	147	0.40
Other Central American	1	<0.01
Cuban	24	0.07
Dominican Republic	12	0.03
Mexican	2,613	7.20
Puerto Rican	112	0.31
South American	105	0.29
Argentinean	3	0.01
Bolivian	3	0.01
Chilean	9	0.02
Colombian	61	0.17
Ecuadorian	12	0.03
Paraguayan	1	<0.01
Peruvian	13	0.04
Venezuelan	3	0.01
Other Hispanic or Latino	582	1.60

Race*	Population	%
African-American/Black (10,075)	10,501	28.93
Not Hispanic (9,991)	10,383	28.60

*Notes: † The Census 2010 population figure is used to calculate the percentages in the Hispanic Origin and Race categories. Ancestry percentages are based on the 2006-2010 American Community Survey population (not shown); ‡ Numbers in parentheses indicate the number of people reporting a single ancestry; * Numbers in parentheses indicate the number of persons reporting this race alone, not in combination with any other race; Please refer to the Explanation of Data for more information.*

Hispanic (84)	118	0.33
American Indian/Alaska Native (214)	382	1.05
Not Hispanic (88)	209	0.58
Hispanic (126)	173	0.48
Apache (0)	1	<0.01
Blackfeet (1)	5	0.01
Canadian/French Am. Ind. (1)	2	0.01
Central American Ind. (3)	5	0.01
Cherokee (13)	68	0.19
Choctaw (3)	5	0.01
Comanche (0)	1	<0.01
Creek (1)	5	0.01
Houma (1)	1	<0.01
Iroquois (1)	2	0.01
Kiowa (1)	1	<0.01
Lumbee (0)	1	<0.01
Mexican American Ind. (39)	49	0.13
Navajo (0)	1	<0.01
Ottawa (4)	4	0.01
Sioux (4)	6	0.02
South American Ind. (1)	1	<0.01
Asian (694)	831	2.29
Not Hispanic (690)	801	2.21
Hispanic (4)	30	0.08
Bangladeshi (5)	10	0.03
Burmese (1)	1	<0.01
Cambodian (1)	3	0.01
Chinese, ex. Taiwanese (64)	72	0.20
Filipino (31)	53	0.15
Indian (277)	325	0.90
Indonesian (2)	3	0.01
Japanese (20)	33	0.09
Korean (41)	45	0.12
Laotian (1)	1	<0.01
Pakistani (29)	34	0.09
Sri Lankan (12)	14	0.04
Taiwanese (1)	1	<0.01
Thai (3)	7	0.02
Vietnamese (177)	200	0.55
Hawaii Native/Pacific Islander (70)	106	0.29
Not Hispanic (17)	30	0.08
Hispanic (53)	76	0.21
Guamanian/Chamorro (65)	80	0.22
Marshallese (0)	1	<0.01
Native Hawaiian (4)	13	0.04
Samoan (0)	3	0.01
White (20,821)	21,613	59.54
Not Hispanic (18,974)	19,490	53.69
Hispanic (1,847)	2,123	5.85

Roswell

Place Type: City
County: Fulton
Population: 88,346†

Ancestry‡	Population	%
Afghan (8)	8	0.01
African, Sub-Saharan (764)	914	1.07
African (374)	459	0.54
Ethiopian (74)	74	0.09
Kenyan (32)	32	0.04
Nigerian (78)	78	0.09
Sierra Leonean (8)	8	0.01
South African (58)	80	0.09
Zimbabwean (8)	8	0.01
Other Sub-Saharan African (132)	175	0.20
Albanian (525)	525	0.61
American (5,285)	5,285	6.17
Arab (342)	549	0.64
Arab (32)	32	0.04
Egyptian (36)	36	0.04
Lebanese (149)	281	0.33
Syrian (55)	130	0.15
Other Arab (70)	70	0.08
Australian (97)	123	0.14
Austrian (71)	200	0.23
Belgian (13)	93	0.11
Brazilian (488)	567	0.66
British (714)	1,036	1.21
Bulgarian (35)	35	0.04
Cajun (0)	9	0.01
Canadian (198)	306	0.36
Croatian (26)	79	0.09
Czech (81)	334	0.39
Czechoslovakian (42)	98	0.11
Danish (202)	516	0.60
Dutch (131)	856	1.00
Eastern European (265)	307	0.36
English (4,739)	11,046	12.90
European (1,468)	1,655	1.93
Finnish (73)	136	0.16
French, ex. Basque (474)	1,831	2.14
French Canadian (152)	555	0.65
German (3,386)	10,656	12.44
German Russian (0)	15	0.02
Greek (148)	359	0.42
Guyanese (18)	18	0.02
Hungarian (161)	426	0.50
Iranian (274)	274	0.32
Irish (3,119)	9,602	11.21
Israeli (36)	78	0.09
Italian (1,827)	4,691	5.48
Latvian (0)	55	0.06
Lithuanian (77)	197	0.23
Northern European (30)	30	0.04
Norwegian (168)	633	0.74
Pennsylvania German (10)	10	0.01
Polish (705)	2,284	2.67
Portuguese (100)	249	0.29
Romanian (46)	97	0.11
Russian (754)	1,395	1.63
Scandinavian (45)	133	0.16
Scotch-Irish (1,024)	2,094	2.45
Scottish (836)	1,936	2.26
Serbian (29)	51	0.06
Slavic (10)	37	0.04
Slovak (29)	105	0.12
Slovene (0)	42	0.05
Swedish (88)	598	0.70
Swiss (170)	403	0.47
Turkish (306)	353	0.41
Ukrainian (246)	432	0.50
Welsh (136)	672	0.78
West Indian, ex. Hispanic (816)	869	1.01
Belizean (57)	77	0.09
Haitian (359)	359	0.42
Jamaican (366)	379	0.44
Trinidadian/Tobagonian (0)	20	0.02
West Indian (34)	34	0.04
Yugoslavian (226)	283	0.33

Hispanic Origin	Population	%
Hispanic or Latino (of any race)	14,699	16.64
Central American, ex. Mexican	1,021	1.16
Costa Rican	31	0.04
Guatemalan	251	0.28
Honduran	218	0.25
Nicaraguan	45	0.05
Panamanian	48	0.05
Salvadoran	419	0.47
Other Central American	9	0.01
Cuban	420	0.48
Dominican Republic	179	0.20
Mexican	10,144	11.48
Puerto Rican	699	0.79
South American	1,479	1.67
Argentinean	102	0.12
Bolivian	39	0.04
Chilean	55	0.06
Colombian	591	0.67
Ecuadorian	74	0.08
Paraguayan	3	<0.01
Peruvian	311	0.35
Uruguayan	107	0.12
Venezuelan	187	0.21
Other South American	10	0.01
Other Hispanic or Latino	757	0.86

Race*	Population	%
African-American/Black (10,373)	11,309	12.80
Not Hispanic (10,066)	10,803	12.23
Hispanic (307)	506	0.57
American Indian/Alaska Native (261)	626	0.71
Not Hispanic (130)	412	0.47
Hispanic (131)	214	0.24
Apache (5)	12	0.01
Blackfeet (7)	22	0.02
Canadian/French Am. Ind. (1)	1	<0.01
Central American Ind. (0)	5	0.01
Cherokee (34)	121	0.14
Chickasaw (0)	2	<0.01
Chippewa (2)	4	<0.01
Choctaw (4)	15	0.02
Colville (0)	1	<0.01
Comanche (0)	1	<0.01
Creek (5)	7	0.01
Crow (0)	1	<0.01
Delaware (0)	2	<0.01
Hopi (5)	5	0.01
Inupiat *(Alaska Native)* (0)	1	<0.01
Iroquois (4)	9	0.01
Lumbee (1)	7	0.01
Mexican American Ind. (49)	52	0.06
Navajo (1)	1	<0.01
Osage (6)	6	0.01
Pima (0)	1	<0.01
Potawatomi (1)	2	<0.01
Sioux (2)	4	<0.01
South American Ind. (10)	17	0.02
Spanish American Ind. (0)	4	<0.01
Tlingit-Haida *(Alaska Native)* (1)	1	<0.01
Ute (2)	2	<0.01
Asian (3,565)	4,304	4.87
Not Hispanic (3,545)	4,225	4.78
Hispanic (20)	79	0.09
Bangladeshi (38)	40	0.05
Burmese (11)	18	0.02
Cambodian (11)	18	0.02
Chinese, ex. Taiwanese (639)	784	0.89
Filipino (172)	284	0.32
Indian (1,356)	1,441	1.63
Indonesian (108)	132	0.15
Japanese (141)	253	0.29
Korean (499)	561	0.64
Laotian (16)	21	0.02
Malaysian (12)	18	0.02
Nepalese (1)	1	<0.01
Pakistani (136)	157	0.18
Sri Lankan (19)	23	0.03
Taiwanese (32)	39	0.04
Thai (45)	54	0.06
Vietnamese (219)	253	0.29
Hawaii Native/Pacific Islander (50)	145	0.16
Not Hispanic (38)	115	0.13
Hispanic (12)	30	0.03
Fijian (1)	3	<0.01
Guamanian/Chamorro (14)	29	0.03
Native Hawaiian (11)	34	0.04
Samoan (7)	15	0.02
Tongan (1)	1	<0.01
White (66,010)	67,870	76.82
Not Hispanic (58,008)	59,305	67.13
Hispanic (8,002)	8,565	9.69

Sandy Springs

Place Type: City
County: Fulton
Population: 93,853†

Ancestry‡	Population	%
African, Sub-Saharan (2,331)	2,544	2.80
African (1,390)	1,428	1.57
Ethiopian (34)	177	0.19
Ghanaian (12)	12	0.01
Kenyan (70)	70	0.08
Liberian (14)	14	0.02

*Notes: † The Census 2010 population figure is used to calculate the percentages in the Hispanic Origin and Race categories. Ancestry percentages are based on the 2006-2010 American Community Survey population (not shown); ‡ Numbers in parentheses indicate the number of people reporting a single ancestry; * Numbers in parentheses indicate the number of persons reporting this race alone, not in combination with any other race; Please refer to the Explanation of Data for more information.*

Ancestry	Population	%
Nigerian (287)	302	0.33
Sierra Leonean (30)	30	0.03
South African (265)	282	0.31
Other Sub-Saharan African (229)	229	0.25
Albanian (68)	68	0.07
American (7,320)	7,320	8.06
Arab (493)	791	0.87
Egyptian (0)	25	0.03
Lebanese (145)	351	0.39
Moroccan (143)	157	0.17
Palestinian (0)	13	0.01
Syrian (30)	41	0.05
Other Arab (175)	204	0.22
Armenian (81)	93	0.10
Australian (26)	94	0.10
Austrian (71)	316	0.35
Belgian (0)	71	0.08
Brazilian (1,776)	1,816	2.00
British (566)	904	1.00
Canadian (340)	370	0.41
Carpatho Rusyn (0)	11	0.01
Celtic (21)	39	0.04
Croatian (72)	94	0.10
Czech (39)	197	0.22
Czechoslovakian (29)	45	0.05
Danish (62)	207	0.23
Dutch (246)	875	0.96
Eastern European (652)	661	0.73
English (5,115)	10,718	11.80
European (1,474)	1,618	1.78
Finnish (50)	95	0.10
French, ex. Basque (502)	1,862	2.05
French Canadian (188)	378	0.42
German (2,671)	8,121	8.94
Greek (385)	527	0.58
Guyanese (60)	60	0.07
Hungarian (175)	521	0.57
Iranian (601)	615	0.68
Irish (2,933)	7,769	8.55
Israeli (65)	76	0.08
Italian (1,213)	2,823	3.11
Latvian (0)	13	0.01
Lithuanian (66)	252	0.28
Macedonian (0)	31	0.03
Northern European (60)	69	0.08
Norwegian (101)	429	0.47
Pennsylvania German (27)	40	0.04
Polish (806)	2,168	2.39
Portuguese (205)	419	0.46
Romanian (23)	128	0.14
Russian (1,564)	2,673	2.94
Scandinavian (74)	111	0.12
Scotch-Irish (1,011)	2,052	2.26
Scottish (919)	2,397	2.64
Serbian (57)	57	0.06
Slovak (7)	30	0.03
Slovene (0)	10	0.01
Swedish (202)	877	0.97
Swiss (12)	169	0.19
Turkish (186)	207	0.23
Ukrainian (141)	240	0.26
Welsh (156)	609	0.67
West Indian, ex. Hispanic (1,148)	1,260	1.39
Bahamian (41)	57	0.06
Haitian (341)	353	0.39
Jamaican (289)	373	0.41
Trinidadian/Tobagonian (92)	92	0.10
U.S. Virgin Islander (219)	219	0.24
West Indian (166)	166	0.18
Yugoslavian (523)	546	0.60

Hispanic Origin	Population	%
Hispanic or Latino (of any race)	13,368	14.24
Central American, ex. Mexican	859	0.92
Costa Rican	39	0.04
Guatemalan	163	0.17
Honduran	182	0.19
Nicaraguan	75	0.08
Panamanian	130	0.14
Salvadoran	256	0.27
Other Central American	14	0.01
Cuban	432	0.46
Dominican Republic	179	0.19
Mexican	9,010	9.60
Puerto Rican	773	0.82
South American	1,178	1.26
Argentinean	124	0.13
Bolivian	29	0.03
Chilean	60	0.06
Colombian	433	0.46
Ecuadorian	84	0.09
Paraguayan	15	0.02
Peruvian	162	0.17
Uruguayan	40	0.04
Venezuelan	209	0.22
Other South American	22	0.02
Other Hispanic or Latino	937	1.00

Race*	Population	%
African-American/Black (18,724)	19,980	21.29
Not Hispanic (18,092)	19,046	20.29
Hispanic (632)	934	1.00
American Indian/Alaska Native (275)	776	0.83
Not Hispanic (160)	583	0.62
Hispanic (115)	193	0.21
Apache (1)	2	<0.01
Blackfeet (3)	22	0.02
Central American Ind. (2)	2	<0.01
Cherokee (34)	180	0.19
Cheyenne (0)	1	<0.01
Chickasaw (0)	4	<0.01
Chippewa (6)	13	0.01
Choctaw (1)	9	0.01
Colville (1)	1	<0.01
Cree (0)	1	<0.01
Creek (5)	23	0.02
Delaware (2)	4	<0.01
Iroquois (1)	7	0.01
Kiowa (0)	2	<0.01
Lumbee (2)	5	0.01
Mexican American Ind. (17)	22	0.02
Navajo (0)	1	<0.01
Osage (0)	1	<0.01
Ottawa (0)	1	<0.01
Potawatomi (5)	5	0.01
Pueblo (1)	2	<0.01
Seminole (2)	11	0.01
Shoshone (0)	1	<0.01
Sioux (4)	8	0.01
South American Ind. (1)	5	0.01
Spanish American Ind. (1)	3	<0.01
Tohono O'Odham (0)	1	<0.01
Yaqui (1)	1	<0.01
Asian (4,702)	5,461	5.82
Not Hispanic (4,660)	5,378	5.73
Hispanic (42)	83	0.09
Bangladeshi (22)	22	0.02
Burmese (15)	16	0.02
Cambodian (12)	17	0.02
Chinese, ex. Taiwanese (597)	754	0.80
Filipino (209)	312	0.33
Hmong (6)	8	0.01
Indian (2,586)	2,721	2.90
Indonesian (47)	59	0.06
Japanese (191)	300	0.32
Korean (413)	487	0.52
Laotian (12)	22	0.02
Malaysian (8)	14	0.01
Nepalese (45)	50	0.05
Pakistani (106)	117	0.12
Sri Lankan (20)	21	0.02
Taiwanese (76)	82	0.09
Thai (60)	96	0.10
Vietnamese (121)	142	0.15
Hawaii Native/Pacific Islander (42)	149	0.16
Not Hispanic (33)	112	0.12
Hispanic (9)	37	0.04
Guamanian/Chamorro (3)	13	0.01
Native Hawaiian (21)	48	0.05
Samoan (4)	14	0.01
White (61,051)	62,983	67.11
Not Hispanic (55,066)	56,464	60.16
Hispanic (5,985)	6,519	6.95

Savannah

Place Type: City
County: Chatham
Population: 136,286†

Ancestry‡	Population	%
Afghan (11)	11	0.01
African, Sub-Saharan (1,390)	1,448	1.08
African (1,309)	1,362	1.01
Ethiopian (29)	29	0.02
Sierra Leonean (0)	5	<0.01
South African (52)	52	0.04
Albanian (12)	12	0.01
Alsatian (0)	6	<0.01
American (4,033)	4,033	3.00
Arab (179)	243	0.18
Arab (54)	63	0.05
Egyptian (11)	25	0.02
Jordanian (63)	63	0.05
Lebanese (30)	63	0.05
Moroccan (0)	8	0.01
Palestinian (9)	9	0.01
Syrian (12)	12	0.01
Armenian (14)	27	0.02
Assyrian/Chaldean/Syriac (9)	33	0.02
Australian (6)	6	<0.01
Austrian (132)	193	0.14
Belgian (8)	48	0.04
Brazilian (38)	38	0.03
British (317)	473	0.35
Bulgarian (13)	13	0.01
Canadian (117)	161	0.12
Croatian (0)	34	0.03
Czech (20)	165	0.12
Czechoslovakian (21)	40	0.03
Danish (9)	95	0.07
Dutch (118)	778	0.58
Eastern European (99)	109	0.08
English (4,290)	8,874	6.61
Estonian (7)	32	0.02
European (859)	917	0.68
Finnish (0)	71	0.05
French, ex. Basque (476)	1,623	1.21
French Canadian (170)	253	0.19
German (2,534)	7,064	5.26
Greek (210)	359	0.27
Guyanese (0)	10	0.01
Hungarian (22)	181	0.13
Iranian (53)	53	0.04
Irish (4,636)	9,918	7.38
Italian (1,034)	2,572	1.91
Latvian (14)	23	0.02
Lithuanian (26)	57	0.04
Maltese (0)	17	0.01
Northern European (19)	19	0.01
Norwegian (73)	255	0.19
Polish (430)	1,132	0.84
Portuguese (105)	148	0.11
Romanian (14)	81	0.06
Russian (200)	552	0.41
Scandinavian (9)	44	0.03
Scotch-Irish (861)	1,855	1.38
Scottish (601)	1,747	1.30
Serbian (0)	7	0.01
Slavic (10)	10	0.01
Slovak (45)	72	0.05
Slovene (0)	15	0.01
Swedish (259)	575	0.43
Swiss (54)	144	0.11
Turkish (52)	66	0.05
Ukrainian (77)	107	0.08
Welsh (161)	537	0.40
West Indian, ex. Hispanic (214)	442	0.33
Haitian (68)	102	0.08
Jamaican (99)	210	0.16

SECTION TWO

*Notes: † The Census 2010 population figure is used to calculate the percentages in the Hispanic Origin and Race categories. Ancestry percentages are based on the 2006-2010 American Community Survey population (not shown); ‡ Numbers in parentheses indicate the number of people reporting a single ancestry; * Numbers in parentheses indicate the number of persons reporting this race alone, not in combination with any other race; Please refer to the Explanation of Data for more information.*

Ancestry (cont.)	Population	%
Trinidadian/Tobagonian (18)	18	0.01
West Indian (29)	112	0.08
Yugoslavian (0)	30	0.02

Hispanic Origin	Population	%
Hispanic or Latino (of any race)	6,392	4.69
Central American, ex. Mexican	547	0.40
Costa Rican	41	0.03
Guatemalan	96	0.07
Honduran	126	0.09
Nicaraguan	49	0.04
Panamanian	166	0.12
Salvadoran	64	0.05
Other Central American	5	<0.01
Cuban	252	0.18
Dominican Republic	179	0.13
Mexican	2,876	2.11
Puerto Rican	1,401	1.03
South American	513	0.38
Argentinean	25	0.02
Bolivian	7	0.01
Chilean	26	0.02
Colombian	197	0.14
Ecuadorian	85	0.06
Paraguayan	2	<0.01
Peruvian	97	0.07
Uruguayan	7	0.01
Venezuelan	59	0.04
Other South American	8	0.01
Other Hispanic or Latino	624	0.46

Race*	Population	%
African-American/Black (75,507)	77,270	56.70
Not Hispanic (74,782)	76,271	55.96
Hispanic (725)	999	0.73
American Indian/Alaska Native (352)	1,074	0.79
Not Hispanic (315)	934	0.69
Hispanic (37)	140	0.10
Alaska Athabascan *(Ala. Nat.)* (1)	1	<0.01
Aleut *(Alaska Native)* (1)	4	<0.01
Apache (10)	20	0.01
Arapaho (0)	1	<0.01
Blackfeet (1)	20	0.01
Canadian/French Am. Ind. (0)	1	<0.01
Central American Ind. (0)	4	<0.01
Cherokee (51)	270	0.20
Cheyenne (0)	1	<0.01
Chickasaw (7)	12	0.01
Chippewa (3)	7	0.01
Choctaw (6)	13	0.01
Comanche (2)	5	<0.01
Cree (1)	2	<0.01
Creek (3)	19	0.01
Delaware (0)	4	<0.01
Hopi (0)	1	<0.01
Houma (1)	1	<0.01
Inupiat *(Alaska Native)* (2)	2	<0.01
Iroquois (1)	8	0.01
Lumbee (7)	12	0.01
Menominee (1)	1	<0.01
Mexican American Ind. (2)	7	0.01
Navajo (3)	9	0.01
Osage (0)	2	<0.01
Ottawa (0)	1	<0.01
Paiute (0)	2	<0.01
Pima (1)	3	<0.01
Pueblo (5)	9	0.01
Seminole (1)	8	0.01
Shoshone (0)	1	<0.01
Sioux (13)	32	0.02
South American Ind. (3)	18	0.01
Spanish American Ind. (0)	1	<0.01
Yakama (0)	2	<0.01
Yaqui (2)	2	<0.01
Yuman (1)	2	<0.01
Yup'ik *(Alaska Native)* (0)	1	<0.01
Asian (2,741)	3,524	2.59
Not Hispanic (2,697)	3,407	2.50
Hispanic (44)	117	0.09
Bangladeshi (1)	1	<0.01
Burmese (12)	12	0.01
Cambodian (16)	19	0.01
Chinese, ex. Taiwanese (446)	560	0.41
Filipino (399)	586	0.43
Hmong (2)	2	<0.01
Indian (527)	627	0.46
Indonesian (11)	15	0.01
Japanese (70)	176	0.13
Korean (371)	512	0.38
Laotian (34)	44	0.03
Malaysian (4)	8	0.01
Nepalese (23)	26	0.02
Pakistani (32)	41	0.03
Sri Lankan (1)	2	<0.01
Taiwanese (66)	76	0.06
Thai (55)	85	0.06
Vietnamese (530)	617	0.45
Hawaii Native/Pacific Islander (146)	312	0.23
Not Hispanic (130)	260	0.19
Hispanic (16)	52	0.04
Fijian (1)	4	<0.01
Guamanian/Chamorro (43)	69	0.05
Native Hawaiian (23)	98	0.07
Samoan (9)	28	0.02
White (52,190)	54,444	39.95
Not Hispanic (49,381)	51,251	37.61
Hispanic (2,809)	3,193	2.34

Scottdale

Place Type: CDP
County: DeKalb
Population: 10,631†

Ancestry‡	Population	%
African, Sub-Saharan (646)	699	7.15
African (95)	139	1.42
Ethiopian (201)	210	2.15
Somalian (303)	303	3.10
Other Sub-Saharan African (47)	47	0.48
American (287)	287	2.94
Arab (75)	75	0.77
Arab (29)	29	0.30
Lebanese (31)	31	0.32
Moroccan (15)	15	0.15
Austrian (0)	12	0.12
Belgian (0)	12	0.12
Brazilian (10)	10	0.10
British (20)	30	0.31
Celtic (0)	20	0.20
Dutch (22)	170	1.74
Eastern European (19)	30	0.31
English (310)	649	6.64
European (71)	93	0.95
French, ex. Basque (24)	228	2.33
French Canadian (56)	56	0.57
German (91)	550	5.63
Irish (60)	480	4.91
Italian (56)	193	1.98
Norwegian (17)	45	0.46
Polish (9)	107	1.10
Portuguese (0)	14	0.14
Romanian (13)	24	0.25
Russian (20)	53	0.54
Scotch-Irish (30)	197	2.02
Scottish (0)	122	1.25
Serbian (0)	34	0.35
Slavic (0)	12	0.12
Slovak (15)	15	0.15
Swedish (24)	64	0.66
Swiss (12)	18	0.18
Ukrainian (7)	22	0.23
Welsh (4)	79	0.81
West Indian, ex. Hispanic (124)	176	1.80
Bahamian (10)	10	0.10
Barbadian (27)	61	0.62
Belizean (0)	9	0.09
Jamaican (24)	24	0.25
U.S. Virgin Islander (0)	9	0.09
West Indian (63)	63	0.64

Hispanic Origin	Population	%
Hispanic or Latino (of any race)	564	5.31
Central American, ex. Mexican	64	0.60
Costa Rican	3	0.03
Guatemalan	10	0.09
Honduran	4	0.04
Nicaraguan	3	0.03
Panamanian	17	0.16
Salvadoran	25	0.24
Other Central American	2	0.02
Cuban	86	0.81
Dominican Republic	9	0.08
Mexican	265	2.49
Puerto Rican	34	0.32
South American	60	0.56
Colombian	38	0.36
Ecuadorian	3	0.03
Peruvian	10	0.09
Uruguayan	1	0.01
Venezuelan	8	0.08
Other Hispanic or Latino	46	0.43

Race*	Population	%
African-American/Black (4,072)	4,242	39.90
Not Hispanic (4,009)	4,162	39.15
Hispanic (63)	80	0.75
American Indian/Alaska Native (24)	132	1.24
Not Hispanic (21)	125	1.18
Hispanic (3)	7	0.07
Blackfeet (0)	10	0.09
Cherokee (4)	23	0.22
Creek (1)	4	0.04
Lumbee (0)	1	0.01
Mexican American Ind. (1)	1	0.01
Seminole (0)	5	0.05
Sioux (1)	1	0.01
South American Ind. (0)	3	0.03
Asian (2,455)	2,662	25.04
Not Hispanic (2,448)	2,652	24.95
Hispanic (7)	10	0.09
Bangladeshi (20)	25	0.24
Bhutanese (76)	354	3.33
Burmese (358)	412	3.88
Cambodian (5)	8	0.08
Chinese, ex. Taiwanese (40)	53	0.50
Filipino (15)	22	0.21
Indian (1,351)	1,481	13.93
Indonesian (0)	1	0.01
Japanese (9)	19	0.18
Korean (11)	20	0.19
Laotian (2)	3	0.03
Nepalese (12)	277	2.61
Pakistani (116)	128	1.20
Sri Lankan (11)	11	0.10
Taiwanese (3)	3	0.03
Thai (9)	14	0.13
Vietnamese (53)	55	0.52
Hawaii Native/Pacific Islander (2)	15	0.14
Not Hispanic (1)	14	0.13
Hispanic (1)	1	0.01
Guamanian/Chamorro (1)	1	0.01
Native Hawaiian (1)	3	0.03
White (3,432)	3,640	34.24
Not Hispanic (3,178)	3,349	31.50
Hispanic (254)	291	2.74

Skidaway Island

Place Type: CDP
County: Chatham
Population: 8,341†

Ancestry‡	Population	%
American (632)	632	7.83
Arab (86)	121	1.50
Arab (14)	28	0.35
Egyptian (72)	72	0.89
Lebanese (0)	21	0.26
Australian (0)	14	0.17
Austrian (15)	94	1.16

*Notes: † The Census 2010 population figure is used to calculate the percentages in the Hispanic Origin and Race categories. Ancestry percentages are based on the 2006-2010 American Community Survey population (not shown); ‡ Numbers in parentheses indicate the number of people reporting a single ancestry; * Numbers in parentheses indicate the number of persons reporting this race alone, not in combination with any other race; Please refer to the Explanation of Data for more information.*

British (15)	40	0.50
Canadian (0)	14	0.17
Czech (14)	71	0.88
Czechoslovakian (14)	14	0.17
Danish (25)	61	0.76
Dutch (173)	227	2.81
Eastern European (54)	54	0.67
English (708)	1,969	24.38
European (100)	100	1.24
French, ex. Basque (60)	304	3.76
German (524)	1,634	20.24
Greek (14)	14	0.17
Hungarian (0)	44	0.54
Irish (379)	1,345	16.66
Italian (107)	392	4.85
Lithuanian (0)	14	0.17
Norwegian (62)	139	1.72
Polish (79)	313	3.88
Romanian (47)	61	0.76
Russian (52)	163	2.02
Scandinavian (0)	16	0.20
Scotch-Irish (228)	360	4.46
Scottish (198)	622	7.70
Slovak (0)	23	0.28
Swedish (59)	200	2.48
Swiss (28)	86	1.07
Turkish (22)	22	0.27
Ukrainian (0)	15	0.19
Welsh (59)	152	1.88

Hispanic Origin	Population	%
Hispanic or Latino (of any race)	112	1.34
Central American, ex. Mexican	5	0.06
Guatemalan	5	0.06
Cuban	35	0.42
Dominican Republic	1	0.01
Mexican	22	0.26
Puerto Rican	19	0.23
South American	19	0.23
Argentinean	2	0.02
Colombian	4	0.05
Ecuadorian	3	0.04
Peruvian	6	0.07
Uruguayan	4	0.05
Other Hispanic or Latino	11	0.13

Race*	Population	%
African-American/Black (69)	80	0.96
Not Hispanic (65)	75	0.90
Hispanic (4)	5	0.06
American Indian/Alaska Native (7)	11	0.13
Not Hispanic (7)	11	0.13
Cherokee (3)	3	0.04
Iroquois (1)	1	0.01
Lumbee (1)	1	0.01
Asian (155)	173	2.07
Not Hispanic (154)	171	2.05
Hispanic (1)	2	0.02
Chinese, ex. Taiwanese (50)	56	0.67
Filipino (16)	25	0.30
Indian (40)	40	0.48
Japanese (5)	9	0.11
Korean (13)	14	0.17
Pakistani (17)	17	0.20
Thai (1)	3	0.04
Vietnamese (7)	9	0.11
Hawaii Native/Pacific Islander (3)	4	0.05
Not Hispanic (3)	4	0.05
Native Hawaiian (0)	1	0.01
White (8,046)	8,081	96.88
Not Hispanic (7,954)	7,987	95.76
Hispanic (92)	94	1.13

Smyrna

Place Type: City
County: Cobb
Population: 51,271†

Ancestry‡	Population	%
African, Sub-Saharan (1,306)	1,631	3.25
African (900)	1,181	2.35
Cape Verdean (0)	14	0.03
Ethiopian (86)	86	0.17
Kenyan (37)	37	0.07
Liberian (32)	32	0.06
Nigerian (110)	110	0.22
South African (47)	64	0.13
Zimbabwean (15)	15	0.03
Other Sub-Saharan African (79)	92	0.18
Albanian (0)	15	0.03
American (2,465)	2,465	4.91
Arab (150)	240	0.48
Arab (0)	62	0.12
Egyptian (11)	11	0.02
Jordanian (128)	128	0.25
Lebanese (11)	22	0.04
Other Arab (0)	17	0.03
Armenian (0)	29	0.06
Australian (0)	72	0.14
Austrian (0)	64	0.13
Belgian (0)	27	0.05
Brazilian (109)	164	0.33
British (120)	254	0.51
Bulgarian (19)	19	0.04
Canadian (29)	42	0.08
Carpatho Rusyn (15)	15	0.03
Croatian (33)	111	0.22
Czech (89)	266	0.53
Czechoslovakian (0)	24	0.05
Danish (9)	97	0.19
Dutch (255)	539	1.07
Eastern European (66)	74	0.15
English (1,572)	4,191	8.34
European (585)	690	1.37
Finnish (25)	41	0.08
French, ex. Basque (327)	1,197	2.38
French Canadian (70)	161	0.32
German (1,357)	4,893	9.74
Greek (78)	145	0.29
Guyanese (36)	36	0.07
Hungarian (43)	142	0.28
Iranian (54)	54	0.11
Irish (1,748)	4,628	9.21
Italian (570)	1,755	3.49
Latvian (16)	16	0.03
Lithuanian (10)	80	0.16
New Zealander (23)	23	0.05
Northern European (13)	13	0.03
Norwegian (54)	166	0.33
Polish (294)	1,033	2.06
Portuguese (42)	124	0.25
Romanian (9)	40	0.08
Russian (123)	409	0.81
Scandinavian (0)	21	0.04
Scotch-Irish (413)	648	1.29
Scottish (775)	1,440	2.87
Serbian (31)	73	0.15
Slavic (0)	18	0.04
Slovak (0)	11	0.02
Slovene (0)	33	0.07
Swedish (41)	199	0.40
Swiss (38)	175	0.35
Turkish (28)	28	0.06
Ukrainian (52)	77	0.15
Welsh (70)	226	0.45
West Indian, ex. Hispanic (986)	1,296	2.58
Barbadian (0)	30	0.06
British West Indian (16)	16	0.03
Haitian (522)	563	1.12
Jamaican (289)	414	0.82
Trinidadian/Tobagonian (0)	78	0.16
West Indian (159)	195	0.39
Yugoslavian (69)	78	0.16

Hispanic Origin	Population	%
Hispanic or Latino (of any race)	7,642	14.91
Central American, ex. Mexican	721	1.41
Costa Rican	44	0.09
Guatemalan	94	0.18
Honduran	123	0.24
Nicaraguan	25	0.05
Panamanian	77	0.15
Salvadoran	358	0.70
Cuban	177	0.35
Dominican Republic	103	0.20
Mexican	5,094	9.94
Puerto Rican	543	1.06
South American	486	0.95
Argentinean	53	0.10
Bolivian	6	0.01
Chilean	15	0.03
Colombian	195	0.38
Ecuadorian	34	0.07
Paraguayan	2	<0.01
Peruvian	88	0.17
Uruguayan	7	0.01
Venezuelan	77	0.15
Other South American	9	0.02
Other Hispanic or Latino	518	1.01

Race*	Population	%
African-American/Black (16,204)	17,071	33.30
Not Hispanic (15,801)	16,520	32.22
Hispanic (403)	551	1.07
American Indian/Alaska Native (182)	497	0.97
Not Hispanic (110)	386	0.75
Hispanic (72)	111	0.22
Apache (1)	4	0.01
Arapaho (1)	1	<0.01
Blackfeet (4)	11	0.02
Canadian/French Am. Ind. (0)	3	0.01
Cherokee (25)	129	0.25
Cheyenne (0)	1	<0.01
Chickasaw (3)	4	0.01
Chippewa (3)	4	0.01
Choctaw (1)	8	0.02
Comanche (1)	4	0.01
Cree (0)	3	0.01
Creek (1)	3	0.01
Crow (0)	1	<0.01
Iroquois (1)	7	0.01
Lumbee (5)	7	0.01
Mexican American Ind. (13)	14	0.03
Navajo (1)	4	0.01
Osage (0)	3	0.01
Ottawa (1)	1	<0.01
Pima (1)	2	<0.01
Potawatomi (2)	2	<0.01
Pueblo (0)	3	0.01
Seminole (0)	4	0.01
Sioux (2)	7	0.01
South American Ind. (8)	11	0.02
Spanish American Ind. (2)	4	0.01
Yakama (6)	6	0.01
Yaqui (1)	1	<0.01
Yuman (1)	2	<0.01
Asian (2,500)	2,900	5.66
Not Hispanic (2,476)	2,847	5.55
Hispanic (24)	53	0.10
Bangladeshi (28)	31	0.06
Cambodian (19)	20	0.04
Chinese, ex. Taiwanese (286)	361	0.70
Filipino (103)	182	0.35
Hmong (1)	1	<0.01
Indian (1,360)	1,433	2.79
Indonesian (20)	21	0.04
Japanese (53)	91	0.18
Korean (194)	249	0.49
Laotian (15)	15	0.03
Malaysian (3)	5	0.01
Nepalese (22)	23	0.04
Pakistani (67)	77	0.15
Sri Lankan (8)	9	0.02
Taiwanese (20)	30	0.06
Thai (28)	35	0.07
Vietnamese (207)	228	0.44
Hawaii Native/Pacific Islander (35)	79	0.15
Not Hispanic (24)	53	0.10

SECTION TWO

*Notes: † The Census 2010 population figure is used to calculate the percentages in the Hispanic Origin and Race categories. Ancestry percentages are based on the 2006-2010 American Community Survey population (not shown); ‡ Numbers in parentheses indicate the number of people reporting a single ancestry; * Numbers in parentheses indicate the number of persons reporting this race alone, not in combination with any other race; Please refer to the Explanation of Data for more information.*

Hispanic (11)	26	0.05
Fijian (8)	12	0.02
Guamanian/Chamorro (2)	4	0.01
Native Hawaiian (12)	22	0.04
Samoan (12)	23	0.04
White (27,593)	28,850	56.27
Not Hispanic (23,871)	24,744	48.26
Hispanic (3,722)	4,106	8.01

Snellville

Place Type: City
County: Gwinnett
Population: 18,242†

Ancestry‡	Population	%
African, Sub-Saharan (361)	481	2.63
African (241)	301	1.65
Ethiopian (69)	69	0.38
Nigerian (51)	111	0.61
American (1,093)	1,093	5.98
Arab (0)	16	0.09
Lebanese (0)	16	0.09
British (66)	129	0.71
Bulgarian (23)	23	0.13
Canadian (0)	21	0.11
Celtic (14)	14	0.08
Czech (51)	51	0.28
Danish (10)	47	0.26
Dutch (27)	172	0.94
English (1,149)	2,408	13.18
European (410)	424	2.32
Finnish (0)	79	0.43
French, ex. Basque (82)	274	1.50
French Canadian (0)	64	0.35
German (488)	2,016	11.03
German Russian (0)	12	0.07
Greek (0)	18	0.10
Guyanese (14)	14	0.08
Hungarian (0)	9	0.05
Irish (700)	1,993	10.91
Italian (245)	721	3.95
Northern European (20)	20	0.11
Norwegian (65)	134	0.73
Polish (126)	352	1.93
Romanian (113)	113	0.62
Russian (70)	196	1.07
Scandinavian (16)	83	0.45
Scotch-Irish (313)	516	2.82
Scottish (161)	546	2.99
Swedish (73)	249	1.36
Ukrainian (0)	15	0.08
Welsh (16)	33	0.18
West Indian, ex. Hispanic (484)	614	3.36
Barbadian (41)	41	0.22
British West Indian (22)	22	0.12
Haitian (127)	155	0.85
Jamaican (294)	365	2.00
West Indian (0)	31	0.17

Hispanic Origin	Population	%
Hispanic or Latino (of any race)	1,351	7.41
Central American, ex. Mexican	187	1.03
Costa Rican	7	0.04
Guatemalan	47	0.26
Honduran	19	0.10
Nicaraguan	9	0.05
Panamanian	18	0.10
Salvadoran	85	0.47
Other Central American	2	0.01
Cuban	96	0.53
Dominican Republic	66	0.36
Mexican	548	3.00
Puerto Rican	235	1.29
South American	113	0.62
Argentinean	15	0.08
Bolivian	3	0.02
Chilean	8	0.04
Colombian	33	0.18
Ecuadorian	11	0.06
Paraguayan	2	0.01
Peruvian	25	0.14
Uruguayan	7	0.04
Venezuelan	9	0.05
Other Hispanic or Latino	106	0.58

Race*	Population	%
African-American/Black (5,479)	5,755	31.55
Not Hispanic (5,345)	5,583	30.61
Hispanic (134)	172	0.94
American Indian/Alaska Native (52)	151	0.83
Not Hispanic (36)	119	0.65
Hispanic (16)	32	0.18
Apache (0)	1	0.01
Blackfeet (0)	5	0.03
Canadian/French Am. Ind. (1)	1	0.01
Central American Ind. (2)	3	0.02
Cherokee (7)	25	0.14
Chippewa (2)	2	0.01
Choctaw (4)	4	0.02
Creek (1)	1	0.01
Iroquois (2)	5	0.03
Lumbee (2)	4	0.02
Mexican American Ind. (1)	1	0.01
South American Ind. (2)	10	0.05
Asian (598)	739	4.05
Not Hispanic (592)	732	4.01
Hispanic (6)	7	0.04
Bangladeshi (17)	22	0.12
Cambodian (15)	15	0.08
Chinese, ex. Taiwanese (55)	72	0.39
Filipino (45)	78	0.43
Hmong (1)	3	0.02
Indian (282)	299	1.64
Japanese (8)	22	0.12
Korean (39)	50	0.27
Laotian (7)	8	0.04
Pakistani (32)	33	0.18
Taiwanese (6)	6	0.03
Thai (4)	7	0.04
Vietnamese (75)	87	0.48
Hawaii Native/Pacific Islander (16)	38	0.21
Not Hispanic (15)	37	0.20
Hispanic (1)	1	0.01
Fijian (8)	9	0.05
Guamanian/Chamorro (0)	1	0.01
Native Hawaiian (4)	11	0.06
Samoan (3)	7	0.04
White (11,122)	11,464	62.84
Not Hispanic (10,438)	10,719	58.76
Hispanic (684)	745	4.08

St. Marys

Place Type: City
County: Camden
Population: 17,121†

Ancestry‡	Population	%
African, Sub-Saharan (95)	111	0.66
African (95)	111	0.66
American (1,021)	1,021	6.07
Austrian (11)	53	0.31
Belgian (0)	64	0.38
British (11)	55	0.33
Cajun (8)	21	0.12
Canadian (31)	49	0.29
Czech (0)	73	0.43
Czechoslovakian (0)	10	0.06
Dutch (23)	95	0.56
English (715)	1,837	10.91
European (61)	61	0.36
Finnish (10)	31	0.18
French, ex. Basque (75)	342	2.03
French Canadian (20)	77	0.46
German (537)	2,233	13.27
Hungarian (26)	50	0.30
Irish (321)	1,729	10.27
Italian (255)	953	5.66
Lithuanian (0)	18	0.11
Norwegian (70)	193	1.15
Polish (48)	230	1.37
Portuguese (30)	57	0.34
Romanian (0)	21	0.12
Russian (20)	80	0.48
Scotch-Irish (107)	260	1.54
Scottish (257)	571	3.39
Serbian (0)	10	0.06
Slovene (9)	43	0.26
Swedish (47)	181	1.08
Swiss (0)	92	0.55
Turkish (43)	43	0.26
Welsh (0)	107	0.64
West Indian, ex. Hispanic (18)	35	0.21
Belizean (18)	18	0.11
Trinidadian/Tobagonian (0)	17	0.10

Hispanic Origin	Population	%
Hispanic or Latino (of any race)	1,029	6.01
Central American, ex. Mexican	54	0.32
Costa Rican	6	0.04
Guatemalan	9	0.05
Honduran	10	0.06
Nicaraguan	5	0.03
Panamanian	10	0.06
Salvadoran	14	0.08
Cuban	48	0.28
Dominican Republic	17	0.10
Mexican	327	1.91
Puerto Rican	447	2.61
South American	48	0.28
Argentinean	4	0.02
Chilean	4	0.02
Colombian	8	0.05
Ecuadorian	22	0.13
Peruvian	6	0.04
Other South American	4	0.02
Other Hispanic or Latino	88	0.51

Race*	Population	%
African-American/Black (3,198)	3,501	20.45
Not Hispanic (3,131)	3,390	19.80
Hispanic (67)	111	0.65
American Indian/Alaska Native (92)	265	1.55
Not Hispanic (79)	230	1.34
Hispanic (13)	35	0.20
Apache (4)	4	0.02
Blackfeet (6)	16	0.09
Cherokee (25)	76	0.44
Chickasaw (4)	4	0.02
Chippewa (2)	5	0.03
Choctaw (5)	12	0.07
Creek (6)	7	0.04
Iroquois (5)	6	0.04
Lumbee (7)	7	0.04
Mexican American Ind. (3)	3	0.02
Seminole (0)	4	0.02
South American Ind. (0)	5	0.03
Asian (234)	393	2.30
Not Hispanic (228)	359	2.10
Hispanic (6)	34	0.20
Burmese (1)	3	0.02
Chinese, ex. Taiwanese (12)	29	0.17
Filipino (143)	226	1.32
Indian (20)	33	0.19
Indonesian (0)	1	0.01
Japanese (21)	48	0.28
Korean (14)	26	0.15
Laotian (0)	2	0.01
Malaysian (0)	1	0.01
Thai (9)	12	0.07
Vietnamese (3)	3	0.02
Hawaii Native/Pacific Islander (15)	52	0.30
Not Hispanic (14)	35	0.20
Hispanic (1)	17	0.10
Guamanian/Chamorro (5)	10	0.06
Native Hawaiian (7)	22	0.13
Samoan (1)	9	0.05
White (12,705)	13,203	77.12
Not Hispanic (12,128)	12,531	73.19

*Notes: † The Census 2010 population figure is used to calculate the percentages in the Hispanic Origin and Race categories. Ancestry percentages are based on the 2006-2010 American Community Survey population (not shown); ‡ Numbers in parentheses indicate the number of people reporting a single ancestry; * Numbers in parentheses indicate the number of persons reporting this race alone, not in combination with any other race; Please refer to the Explanation of Data for more information.*

Hispanic (577)	672	3.93

St. Simons

Place Type: CDP
County: Glynn
Population: 12,743†

Ancestry‡	Population	%
American (1,408)	1,408	10.95
Arab (18)	36	0.28
Lebanese (0)	18	0.14
Syrian (18)	18	0.14
Armenian (13)	13	0.10
Austrian (13)	50	0.39
Belgian (18)	18	0.14
British (122)	224	1.74
Canadian (22)	43	0.33
Czech (0)	24	0.19
Danish (0)	14	0.11
Dutch (34)	159	1.24
Eastern European (23)	23	0.18
English (1,767)	3,116	24.24
European (56)	56	0.44
French, ex. Basque (224)	663	5.16
French Canadian (79)	132	1.03
German (812)	2,130	16.57
Greek (36)	68	0.53
Hungarian (14)	56	0.44
Irish (955)	1,964	15.28
Italian (155)	416	3.24
Lithuanian (0)	69	0.54
Northern European (54)	54	0.42
Norwegian (69)	116	0.90
Polish (76)	171	1.33
Portuguese (24)	27	0.21
Russian (0)	48	0.37
Scandinavian (17)	17	0.13
Scotch-Irish (346)	614	4.78
Scottish (173)	462	3.59
Slavic (0)	10	0.08
Slovak (42)	42	0.33
Swedish (45)	175	1.36
Swiss (13)	22	0.17
Ukrainian (21)	51	0.40
Welsh (41)	182	1.42

Hispanic Origin	Population	%
Hispanic or Latino (of any race)	284	2.23
Central American, ex. Mexican	16	0.13
Guatemalan	6	0.05
Honduran	4	0.03
Salvadoran	6	0.05
Cuban	15	0.12
Dominican Republic	7	0.05
Mexican	104	0.82
Puerto Rican	44	0.35
South American	27	0.21
Argentinean	4	0.03
Chilean	2	0.02
Colombian	12	0.09
Peruvian	5	0.04
Uruguayan	3	0.02
Venezuelan	1	0.01
Other Hispanic or Latino	71	0.56

Race*	Population	%
African-American/Black (352)	378	2.97
Not Hispanic (339)	362	2.84
Hispanic (13)	16	0.13
American Indian/Alaska Native (19)	55	0.43
Not Hispanic (17)	52	0.41
Hispanic (2)	3	0.02
Apache (0)	1	0.01
Blackfeet (2)	3	0.02
Cherokee (8)	17	0.13
Chickasaw (1)	1	0.01
Choctaw (0)	2	0.02
Comanche (0)	2	0.02
Delaware (1)	1	0.01
Iroquois (3)	3	0.02
Seminole (0)	1	0.01
Shoshone (0)	1	0.01
Asian (124)	159	1.25
Not Hispanic (117)	146	1.15
Hispanic (7)	13	0.10
Cambodian (6)	7	0.05
Chinese, ex. Taiwanese (28)	30	0.24
Filipino (26)	37	0.29
Indian (18)	20	0.16
Japanese (9)	18	0.14
Korean (1)	2	0.02
Malaysian (1)	1	0.01
Pakistani (0)	4	0.03
Sri Lankan (2)	2	0.02
Thai (9)	13	0.10
Vietnamese (18)	25	0.20
Hawaii Native/Pacific Islander (2)	3	0.02
Not Hispanic (2)	3	0.02
Native Hawaiian (2)	3	0.02
White (12,086)	12,170	95.50
Not Hispanic (11,889)	11,958	93.84
Hispanic (197)	212	1.66

Statesboro

Place Type: City
County: Bulloch
Population: 28,422†

Ancestry‡	Population	%
African, Sub-Saharan (422)	422	1.55
African (382)	382	1.40
Kenyan (21)	21	0.08
Nigerian (19)	19	0.07
American (720)	720	2.64
Arab (39)	136	0.50
Arab (23)	30	0.11
Iraqi (0)	21	0.08
Lebanese (16)	78	0.29
Other Arab (0)	7	0.03
Austrian (24)	24	0.09
Brazilian (17)	17	0.06
British (17)	46	0.17
Canadian (0)	19	0.07
Croatian (54)	62	0.23
Czech (0)	46	0.17
Czechoslovakian (33)	52	0.19
Danish (23)	51	0.19
Dutch (172)	309	1.13
Eastern European (43)	96	0.35
English (2,124)	3,686	13.52
European (59)	59	0.22
French, ex. Basque (60)	504	1.85
French Canadian (9)	21	0.08
German (983)	2,451	8.99
Greek (50)	249	0.91
Hungarian (34)	69	0.25
Iranian (16)	16	0.06
Irish (1,482)	3,629	13.31
Italian (390)	889	3.26
Latvian (0)	14	0.05
Norwegian (81)	158	0.58
Polish (104)	156	0.57
Portuguese (23)	40	0.15
Romanian (14)	14	0.05
Russian (75)	99	0.36
Scotch-Irish (432)	749	2.75
Scottish (273)	851	3.12
Slovene (0)	31	0.11
Swedish (18)	69	0.25
Swiss (13)	13	0.05
Turkish (23)	59	0.22
Welsh (43)	225	0.83
West Indian, ex. Hispanic (79)	165	0.61
Haitian (0)	51	0.19
Jamaican (22)	57	0.21
Trinidadian/Tobagonian (40)	40	0.15
West Indian (17)	17	0.06

Hispanic Origin	Population	%
Hispanic or Latino (of any race)	847	2.98
Central American, ex. Mexican	62	0.22
Costa Rican	9	0.03
Guatemalan	6	0.02
Honduran	22	0.08
Nicaraguan	5	0.02
Panamanian	17	0.06
Salvadoran	2	0.01
Other Central American	1	<0.01
Cuban	49	0.17
Dominican Republic	10	0.04
Mexican	393	1.38
Puerto Rican	156	0.55
South American	77	0.27
Argentinean	7	0.02
Bolivian	2	0.01
Chilean	6	0.02
Colombian	30	0.11
Ecuadorian	8	0.03
Peruvian	8	0.03
Uruguayan	1	<0.01
Venezuelan	10	0.04
Other South American	5	0.02
Other Hispanic or Latino	100	0.35

Race*	Population	%
African-American/Black (11,402)	11,710	41.20
Not Hispanic (11,303)	11,579	40.74
Hispanic (99)	131	0.46
American Indian/Alaska Native (51)	177	0.62
Not Hispanic (45)	156	0.55
Hispanic (6)	21	0.07
Apache (1)	1	<0.01
Blackfeet (0)	3	0.01
Central American Ind. (0)	1	<0.01
Cherokee (5)	39	0.14
Choctaw (1)	5	0.02
Comanche (0)	2	0.01
Creek (1)	3	0.01
Iroquois (0)	1	<0.01
Mexican American Ind. (3)	5	0.02
Navajo (1)	2	0.01
Seminole (0)	4	0.01
Sioux (1)	4	0.01
South American Ind. (0)	3	0.01
Tlingit-Haida *(Alaska Native)* (1)	1	<0.01
Asian (562)	691	2.43
Not Hispanic (556)	681	2.40
Hispanic (6)	10	0.04
Bangladeshi (8)	9	0.03
Cambodian (2)	2	0.01
Chinese, ex. Taiwanese (98)	120	0.42
Filipino (70)	109	0.38
Hmong (1)	1	<0.01
Indian (110)	125	0.44
Indonesian (1)	2	0.01
Japanese (7)	16	0.06
Korean (130)	158	0.56
Laotian (1)	1	<0.01
Malaysian (0)	1	<0.01
Nepalese (2)	2	0.01
Pakistani (5)	5	0.02
Taiwanese (8)	11	0.04
Thai (12)	16	0.06
Vietnamese (33)	35	0.12
Hawaii Native/Pacific Islander (46)	76	0.27
Not Hispanic (44)	67	0.24
Hispanic (2)	9	0.03
Guamanian/Chamorro (1)	2	0.01
Native Hawaiian (19)	28	0.10
Samoan (12)	24	0.08
White (15,457)	15,851	55.77
Not Hispanic (15,132)	15,478	54.46
Hispanic (325)	373	1.31

*Notes: † The Census 2010 population figure is used to calculate the percentages in the Hispanic Origin and Race categories. Ancestry percentages are based on the 2006-2010 American Community Survey population (not shown); ‡ Numbers in parentheses indicate the number of people reporting a single ancestry; * Numbers in parentheses indicate the number of persons reporting this race alone, not in combination with any other race; Please refer to the Explanation of Data for more information.*

Stockbridge

Place Type: City
County: Henry
Population: 25,636†

Ancestry‡	Population	%
Afghan (177)	177	0.75
African, Sub-Saharan (1,240)	1,327	5.60
African (665)	752	3.17
Ghanaian (23)	23	0.10
Liberian (110)	110	0.46
Nigerian (376)	376	1.59
Other Sub-Saharan African (66)	66	0.28
American (1,435)	1,435	6.06
Austrian (10)	20	0.08
Belgian (0)	16	0.07
British (70)	209	0.88
Bulgarian (25)	25	0.11
Canadian (29)	45	0.19
Czechoslovakian (0)	19	0.08
Danish (0)	14	0.06
Dutch (33)	54	0.23
English (540)	1,161	4.90
European (187)	187	0.79
French, ex. Basque (24)	167	0.70
French Canadian (63)	99	0.42
German (314)	968	4.09
Greek (68)	83	0.35
Guyanese (164)	164	0.69
Hungarian (8)	103	0.43
Irish (375)	1,357	5.73
Italian (125)	277	1.17
Lithuanian (13)	46	0.19
Pennsylvania German (17)	17	0.07
Polish (60)	264	1.11
Russian (43)	97	0.41
Scandinavian (0)	103	0.43
Scotch-Irish (82)	235	0.99
Scottish (221)	378	1.60
Slovak (14)	48	0.20
Swedish (8)	84	0.35
Turkish (0)	10	0.04
Ukrainian (18)	18	0.08
Welsh (107)	162	0.68
West Indian, ex. Hispanic (1,141)	1,334	5.63
Bahamian (39)	51	0.22
British West Indian (55)	88	0.37
Haitian (531)	531	2.24
Jamaican (311)	397	1.68
Trinidadian/Tobagonian (125)	125	0.53
West Indian (80)	142	0.60

Hispanic Origin	Population	%
Hispanic or Latino (of any race)	2,448	9.55
Central American, ex. Mexican	266	1.04
Costa Rican	10	0.04
Guatemalan	32	0.12
Honduran	43	0.17
Nicaraguan	13	0.05
Panamanian	84	0.33
Salvadoran	83	0.32
Other Central American	1	<0.01
Cuban	96	0.37
Dominican Republic	151	0.59
Mexican	1,053	4.11
Puerto Rican	525	2.05
South American	182	0.71
Argentinean	10	0.04
Chilean	9	0.04
Colombian	54	0.21
Ecuadorian	52	0.20
Peruvian	21	0.08
Uruguayan	22	0.09
Venezuelan	11	0.04
Other South American	3	0.01
Other Hispanic or Latino	175	0.68

Race*	Population	%
African-American/Black (14,281)	14,888	58.07
Not Hispanic (13,999)	14,480	56.48
Hispanic (282)	408	1.59
American Indian/Alaska Native (79)	269	1.05
Not Hispanic (66)	223	0.87
Hispanic (13)	46	0.18
Apache (0)	1	<0.01
Blackfeet (1)	16	0.06
Cherokee (7)	72	0.28
Chippewa (1)	2	0.01
Choctaw (0)	3	0.01
Creek (2)	8	0.03
Kiowa (0)	1	<0.01
Lumbee (0)	3	0.01
Mexican American Ind. (3)	4	0.02
Navajo (3)	3	0.01
Potawatomi (3)	3	0.01
Pueblo (2)	2	0.01
Seminole (0)	2	0.01
Sioux (0)	1	<0.01
South American Ind. (0)	4	0.02
Asian (1,951)	2,199	8.58
Not Hispanic (1,914)	2,136	8.33
Hispanic (37)	63	0.25
Bangladeshi (20)	24	0.09
Burmese (3)	3	0.01
Cambodian (42)	69	0.27
Chinese, ex. Taiwanese (95)	156	0.61
Filipino (118)	168	0.66
Indian (850)	916	3.57
Indonesian (1)	2	0.01
Japanese (33)	64	0.25
Korean (108)	146	0.57
Laotian (63)	80	0.31
Malaysian (0)	5	0.02
Pakistani (116)	127	0.50
Sri Lankan (3)	3	0.01
Taiwanese (13)	14	0.05
Thai (6)	16	0.06
Vietnamese (390)	409	1.60
Hawaii Native/Pacific Islander (21)	58	0.23
Not Hispanic (19)	46	0.18
Hispanic (2)	12	0.05
Guamanian/Chamorro (3)	3	0.01
Native Hawaiian (3)	19	0.07
Samoan (9)	21	0.08
White (7,382)	8,030	31.32
Not Hispanic (6,400)	6,891	26.88
Hispanic (982)	1,139	4.44

Sugar Hill

Place Type: City
County: Gwinnett
Population: 18,522†

Ancestry‡	Population	%
African, Sub-Saharan (37)	37	0.21
African (8)	8	0.05
Nigerian (20)	20	0.11
South African (9)	9	0.05
American (2,016)	2,016	11.47
Austrian (26)	48	0.27
British (93)	128	0.73
Canadian (24)	24	0.14
Celtic (25)	25	0.14
Czech (50)	79	0.45
Czechoslovakian (0)	26	0.15
Dutch (29)	341	1.94
English (470)	1,409	8.01
European (378)	487	2.77
French, ex. Basque (30)	192	1.09
French Canadian (25)	55	0.31
German (604)	1,971	11.21
German Russian (8)	8	0.05
Greek (0)	12	0.07
Hungarian (7)	66	0.38
Iranian (8)	8	0.05
Irish (435)	1,764	10.03
Italian (253)	646	3.67
Lithuanian (0)	29	0.16
Norwegian (27)	79	0.45
Polish (147)	413	2.35
Portuguese (10)	35	0.20
Romanian (125)	125	0.71
Russian (58)	69	0.39
Scandinavian (0)	42	0.24
Scotch-Irish (378)	631	3.59
Scottish (334)	578	3.29
Slovak (8)	8	0.05
Swedish (41)	189	1.08
Swiss (0)	11	0.06
Turkish (10)	10	0.06
Ukrainian (85)	85	0.48
Welsh (0)	56	0.32
West Indian, ex. Hispanic (162)	177	1.01
British West Indian (6)	6	0.03
Jamaican (144)	159	0.90
Trinidadian/Tobagonian (12)	12	0.07
Yugoslavian (184)	184	1.05

Hispanic Origin	Population	%
Hispanic or Latino (of any race)	3,636	19.63
Central American, ex. Mexican	421	2.27
Costa Rican	12	0.06
Guatemalan	92	0.50
Honduran	106	0.57
Nicaraguan	28	0.15
Panamanian	19	0.10
Salvadoran	164	0.89
Cuban	101	0.55
Dominican Republic	57	0.31
Mexican	2,194	11.85
Puerto Rican	234	1.26
South American	419	2.26
Argentinean	20	0.11
Bolivian	6	0.03
Chilean	14	0.08
Colombian	199	1.07
Ecuadorian	17	0.09
Paraguayan	3	0.02
Peruvian	97	0.52
Uruguayan	8	0.04
Venezuelan	53	0.29
Other South American	2	0.01
Other Hispanic or Latino	210	1.13

Race*	Population	%
African-American/Black (1,820)	1,994	10.77
Not Hispanic (1,747)	1,874	10.12
Hispanic (73)	120	0.65
American Indian/Alaska Native (59)	135	0.73
Not Hispanic (24)	87	0.47
Hispanic (35)	48	0.26
Blackfeet (0)	5	0.03
Cherokee (5)	29	0.16
Chippewa (0)	3	0.02
Choctaw (0)	1	0.01
Creek (1)	3	0.02
Hopi (2)	2	0.01
Houma (1)	3	0.02
Navajo (1)	2	0.01
Osage (0)	3	0.02
Paiute (0)	1	0.01
Seminole (2)	3	0.02
Sioux (1)	2	0.01
South American Ind. (3)	3	0.02
Asian (1,170)	1,306	7.05
Not Hispanic (1,148)	1,271	6.86
Hispanic (22)	35	0.19
Bangladeshi (13)	20	0.11
Cambodian (13)	15	0.08
Chinese, ex. Taiwanese (103)	114	0.62
Filipino (56)	78	0.42
Hmong (7)	7	0.04
Indian (247)	297	1.60
Indonesian (11)	11	0.06
Japanese (13)	32	0.17
Korean (507)	541	2.92
Laotian (21)	23	0.12
Malaysian (5)	6	0.03

*Notes: † The Census 2010 population figure is used to calculate the percentages in the Hispanic Origin and Race categories. Ancestry percentages are based on the 2006-2010 American Community Survey population (not shown); ‡ Numbers in parentheses indicate the number of people reporting a single ancestry; * Numbers in parentheses indicate the number of persons reporting this race alone, not in combination with any other race; Please refer to the Explanation of Data for more information.*

Pakistani (11)	14	0.08
Taiwanese (17)	17	0.09
Thai (1)	4	0.02
Vietnamese (100)	109	0.59
Hawaii Native/Pacific Islander (14)	23	0.12
Not Hispanic (8)	10	0.05
Hispanic (6)	13	0.07
Guamanian/Chamorro (0)	1	0.01
Native Hawaiian (5)	6	0.03
White (13,405)	13,790	74.45
Not Hispanic (11,630)	11,871	64.09
Hispanic (1,775)	1,919	10.36

Suwanee

Place Type: City
County: Gwinnett
Population: 15,355†

Ancestry‡	Population	%
African, Sub-Saharan (95)	109	0.75
African (52)	52	0.36
Cape Verdean (14)	28	0.19
Kenyan (14)	14	0.10
South African (15)	15	0.10
American (916)	916	6.30
Arab (101)	153	1.05
Egyptian (38)	38	0.26
Lebanese (6)	58	0.40
Other Arab (57)	57	0.39
Australian (0)	17	0.12
Belgian (9)	35	0.24
Brazilian (24)	24	0.17
British (38)	38	0.26
Canadian (16)	30	0.21
Croatian (0)	7	0.05
Czech (0)	10	0.07
Czechoslovakian (10)	10	0.07
Danish (12)	34	0.23
Dutch (0)	224	1.54
Eastern European (81)	81	0.56
English (584)	1,456	10.02
European (535)	535	3.68
Finnish (12)	57	0.39
French, ex. Basque (12)	246	1.69
French Canadian (40)	61	0.42
German (444)	1,533	10.55
Hungarian (12)	61	0.42
Iranian (75)	81	0.56
Irish (429)	1,554	10.69
Italian (292)	783	5.39
Norwegian (0)	54	0.37
Polish (191)	520	3.58
Portuguese (17)	89	0.61
Romanian (0)	36	0.25
Russian (0)	61	0.42
Scandinavian (0)	27	0.19
Scotch-Irish (195)	361	2.48
Scottish (111)	355	2.44
Slovak (0)	19	0.13
Soviet Union (0)	8	0.06
Swedish (54)	157	1.08
Swiss (10)	49	0.34
Ukrainian (11)	38	0.26
Welsh (51)	186	1.28
West Indian, ex. Hispanic (99)	121	0.83
Belizean (9)	9	0.06
Haitian (21)	21	0.14
Jamaican (69)	91	0.63
Yugoslavian (13)	13	0.09

Hispanic Origin	Population	%
Hispanic or Latino (of any race)	1,025	6.68
Central American, ex. Mexican	115	0.75
Costa Rican	27	0.18
Guatemalan	30	0.20
Honduran	8	0.05
Nicaraguan	4	0.03
Panamanian	5	0.03
Salvadoran	41	0.27
Cuban	98	0.64
Dominican Republic	45	0.29
Mexican	299	1.95
Puerto Rican	137	0.89
South American	245	1.60
Argentinean	17	0.11
Bolivian	5	0.03
Chilean	12	0.08
Colombian	130	0.85
Ecuadorian	14	0.09
Peruvian	41	0.27
Uruguayan	6	0.04
Venezuelan	20	0.13
Other Hispanic or Latino	86	0.56

Race*	Population	%
African-American/Black (1,655)	1,791	11.66
Not Hispanic (1,604)	1,725	11.23
Hispanic (51)	66	0.43
American Indian/Alaska Native (19)	82	0.53
Not Hispanic (14)	67	0.44
Hispanic (5)	15	0.10
Blackfeet (0)	2	0.01
Cherokee (4)	18	0.12
Chickasaw (1)	4	0.03
Choctaw (1)	2	0.01
Creek (1)	4	0.03
Lumbee (0)	2	0.01
Mexican American Ind. (5)	6	0.04
Navajo (1)	1	0.01
Sioux (0)	3	0.02
South American Ind. (0)	3	0.02
Asian (2,761)	2,939	19.14
Not Hispanic (2,752)	2,917	19.00
Hispanic (9)	22	0.14
Bangladeshi (17)	21	0.14
Burmese (11)	11	0.07
Cambodian (31)	41	0.27
Chinese, ex. Taiwanese (184)	243	1.58
Filipino (41)	64	0.42
Indian (602)	645	4.20
Indonesian (15)	21	0.14
Japanese (33)	63	0.41
Korean (1,467)	1,506	9.81
Laotian (31)	36	0.23
Malaysian (6)	7	0.05
Nepalese (4)	4	0.03
Pakistani (70)	76	0.49
Sri Lankan (8)	8	0.05
Taiwanese (17)	22	0.14
Thai (9)	11	0.07
Vietnamese (169)	181	1.18
Hawaii Native/Pacific Islander (8)	15	0.10
Not Hispanic (8)	13	0.08
Hispanic (0)	2	0.01
Fijian (0)	1	0.01
Guamanian/Chamorro (1)	1	0.01
Native Hawaiian (4)	6	0.04
Samoan (0)	1	0.01
White (10,356)	10,631	69.23
Not Hispanic (9,646)	9,864	64.24
Hispanic (710)	767	5.00

Thomaston

Place Type: City
County: Upson
Population: 9,170†

Ancestry‡	Population	%
African, Sub-Saharan (112)	112	1.21
African (59)	59	0.64
Nigerian (53)	53	0.57
American (1,245)	1,245	13.50
British (34)	34	0.37
Celtic (16)	16	0.17
Dutch (12)	48	0.52
English (587)	864	9.37
European (20)	20	0.22
Finnish (0)	29	0.31
French, ex. Basque (50)	186	2.02
French Canadian (0)	26	0.28
German (19)	284	3.08
Hungarian (0)	10	0.11
Irish (336)	731	7.92
Italian (72)	95	1.03
Norwegian (52)	52	0.56
Polish (0)	48	0.52
Scandinavian (4)	4	0.04
Scotch-Irish (105)	236	2.56
Scottish (102)	177	1.92
Swedish (8)	18	0.20
Welsh (8)	32	0.35
West Indian, ex. Hispanic (31)	31	0.34
Haitian (31)	31	0.34

Hispanic Origin	Population	%
Hispanic or Latino (of any race)	296	3.23
Central American, ex. Mexican	9	0.10
Guatemalan	1	0.01
Honduran	3	0.03
Salvadoran	5	0.05
Cuban	5	0.05
Dominican Republic	4	0.04
Mexican	238	2.60
Puerto Rican	7	0.08
South American	5	0.05
Argentinean	1	0.01
Ecuadorian	1	0.01
Peruvian	3	0.03
Other Hispanic or Latino	28	0.31

Race*	Population	%
African-American/Black (3,772)	3,848	41.96
Not Hispanic (3,748)	3,821	41.67
Hispanic (24)	27	0.29
American Indian/Alaska Native (20)	68	0.74
Not Hispanic (19)	65	0.71
Hispanic (1)	3	0.03
Blackfeet (1)	4	0.04
Cherokee (3)	25	0.27
Choctaw (0)	1	0.01
Creek (3)	3	0.03
Puget Sound Salish (0)	2	0.02
South American Ind. (0)	2	0.02
Asian (44)	59	0.64
Not Hispanic (43)	56	0.61
Hispanic (1)	3	0.03
Chinese, ex. Taiwanese (2)	2	0.02
Filipino (8)	12	0.13
Indian (24)	33	0.36
Korean (1)	4	0.04
Pakistani (1)	1	0.01
Thai (2)	2	0.02
Hawaii Native/Pacific Islander (3)	5	0.05
Not Hispanic (1)	2	0.02
Hispanic (2)	3	0.03
Guamanian/Chamorro (1)	1	0.01
Native Hawaiian (1)	2	0.02
White (5,025)	5,151	56.17
Not Hispanic (4,931)	5,042	54.98
Hispanic (94)	109	1.19

Thomasville

Place Type: City
County: Thomas
Population: 18,413†

Ancestry‡	Population	%
African, Sub-Saharan (137)	137	0.75
African (137)	137	0.75
American (1,351)	1,351	7.35
Armenian (0)	15	0.08
British (7)	48	0.26
Canadian (12)	12	0.07
Czech (0)	11	0.06
Czechoslovakian (18)	18	0.10
Danish (13)	25	0.14
Dutch (32)	78	0.42

*Notes: † The Census 2010 population figure is used to calculate the percentages in the Hispanic Origin and Race categories. Ancestry percentages are based on the 2006-2010 American Community Survey population (not shown); ‡ Numbers in parentheses indicate the number of people reporting a single ancestry; * Numbers in parentheses indicate the number of persons reporting this race alone, not in combination with any other race; Please refer to the Explanation of Data for more information.*

Eastern European (8)	41	0.22
English (556)	1,222	6.65
European (82)	82	0.45
French, ex. Basque (65)	236	1.28
French Canadian (40)	78	0.42
German (223)	886	4.82
Greek (14)	25	0.14
Hungarian (0)	21	0.11
Irish (251)	859	4.68
Italian (240)	424	2.31
New Zealander (9)	33	0.18
Northern European (30)	30	0.16
Norwegian (11)	81	0.44
Polish (29)	98	0.53
Portuguese (0)	28	0.15
Russian (0)	11	0.06
Scandinavian (21)	21	0.11
Scotch-Irish (192)	331	1.80
Scottish (179)	415	2.26
Slavic (0)	12	0.07
Slovak (0)	12	0.07
Swedish (14)	31	0.17
Swiss (0)	21	0.11
Welsh (53)	200	1.09

Hispanic Origin	Population	%
Hispanic or Latino (of any race)	418	2.27
Central American, ex. Mexican	38	0.21
Guatemalan	9	0.05
Honduran	6	0.03
Nicaraguan	2	0.01
Panamanian	8	0.04
Salvadoran	13	0.07
Cuban	40	0.22
Dominican Republic	8	0.04
Mexican	162	0.88
Puerto Rican	90	0.49
South American	21	0.11
Chilean	1	0.01
Colombian	14	0.08
Paraguayan	2	0.01
Peruvian	3	0.02
Venezuelan	1	0.01
Other Hispanic or Latino	59	0.32

Race*	Population	%
African-American/Black (9,904)	10,019	54.41
Not Hispanic (9,868)	9,961	54.10
Hispanic (36)	58	0.31
American Indian/Alaska Native (63)	134	0.73
Not Hispanic (61)	120	0.65
Hispanic (2)	14	0.08
Apache (1)	1	0.01
Central American Ind. (0)	2	0.01
Cherokee (8)	35	0.19
Cheyenne (0)	2	0.01
Choctaw (3)	3	0.02
Comanche (1)	5	0.03
Creek (11)	14	0.08
Lumbee (2)	2	0.01
Mexican American Ind. (0)	5	0.03
Navajo (0)	3	0.02
Osage (2)	2	0.01
Seminole (2)	3	0.02
Sioux (1)	4	0.02
Asian (154)	190	1.03
Not Hispanic (154)	189	1.03
Hispanic (0)	1	0.01
Chinese, ex. Taiwanese (4)	4	0.02
Filipino (23)	37	0.20
Indian (89)	91	0.49
Indonesian (3)	3	0.02
Japanese (0)	1	0.01
Korean (6)	8	0.04
Thai (1)	2	0.01
Vietnamese (27)	31	0.17
Hawaii Native/Pacific Islander (0)	11	0.06
Not Hispanic (0)	10	0.05
Hispanic (0)	1	0.01
Native Hawaiian (0)	6	0.03
White (7,919)	8,072	43.84
Not Hispanic (7,711)	7,836	42.56
Hispanic (208)	236	1.28

Tifton

Place Type: City
County: Tift
Population: 16,350†

Ancestry‡	Population	%
African, Sub-Saharan (84)	84	0.52
African (84)	84	0.52
American (2,979)	2,979	18.34
Arab (14)	14	0.09
Lebanese (14)	14	0.09
British (121)	121	0.75
Canadian (149)	189	1.16
Czech (0)	17	0.10
Dutch (0)	32	0.20
English (592)	839	5.17
European (131)	143	0.88
French, ex. Basque (21)	115	0.71
German (177)	649	4.00
Irish (528)	1,103	6.79
Italian (22)	22	0.14
Polish (28)	123	0.76
Portuguese (11)	11	0.07
Scotch-Irish (141)	277	1.71
Scottish (85)	192	1.18
Swedish (52)	52	0.32
Welsh (64)	83	0.51
West Indian, ex. Hispanic (27)	33	0.20
Dutch West Indian (0)	6	0.04
Haitian (27)	27	0.17

Hispanic Origin	Population	%
Hispanic or Latino (of any race)	1,861	11.38
Central American, ex. Mexican	58	0.35
Costa Rican	1	0.01
Guatemalan	10	0.06
Honduran	12	0.07
Panamanian	3	0.02
Salvadoran	32	0.20
Cuban	19	0.12
Dominican Republic	6	0.04
Mexican	1,606	9.82
Puerto Rican	54	0.33
South American	24	0.15
Argentinean	5	0.03
Bolivian	1	0.01
Colombian	7	0.04
Ecuadorian	6	0.04
Paraguayan	2	0.01
Venezuelan	3	0.02
Other Hispanic or Latino	94	0.57

Race*	Population	%
African-American/Black (5,934)	6,068	37.11
Not Hispanic (5,894)	6,019	36.81
Hispanic (40)	49	0.30
American Indian/Alaska Native (26)	63	0.39
Not Hispanic (19)	49	0.30
Hispanic (7)	14	0.09
Alaska Athabascan *(Ala. Nat.)* (1)	1	0.01
Cherokee (3)	17	0.10
Choctaw (0)	1	0.01
Lumbee (1)	3	0.02
Mexican American Ind. (2)	6	0.04
Navajo (0)	1	0.01
Asian (313)	350	2.14
Not Hispanic (311)	344	2.10
Hispanic (2)	6	0.04
Bangladeshi (5)	5	0.03
Cambodian (0)	1	0.01
Chinese, ex. Taiwanese (39)	48	0.29
Filipino (15)	22	0.13
Indian (162)	173	1.06
Japanese (4)	5	0.03
Korean (15)	16	0.10
Laotian (1)	1	0.01
Pakistani (13)	16	0.10
Thai (1)	2	0.01
Vietnamese (54)	57	0.35
Hawaii Native/Pacific Islander (8)	19	0.12
Not Hispanic (8)	16	0.10
Hispanic (0)	3	0.02
Fijian (2)	4	0.02
Guamanian/Chamorro (1)	1	0.01
Native Hawaiian (0)	2	0.01
Samoan (5)	9	0.06
White (8,552)	8,784	53.72
Not Hispanic (8,069)	8,213	50.23
Hispanic (483)	571	3.49

Toccoa

Place Type: City
County: Stephens
Population: 8,491†

Ancestry‡	Population	%
African, Sub-Saharan (141)	141	1.63
African (58)	58	0.67
Kenyan (9)	9	0.10
Liberian (74)	74	0.86
American (1,364)	1,364	15.78
Belgian (29)	29	0.34
British (39)	39	0.45
Czechoslovakian (0)	9	0.10
Dutch (10)	27	0.31
English (428)	742	8.58
European (120)	170	1.97
French, ex. Basque (111)	151	1.75
French Canadian (0)	17	0.20
German (268)	461	5.33
Greek (0)	53	0.61
Hungarian (19)	19	0.22
Irish (338)	632	7.31
Italian (18)	141	1.63
Macedonian (12)	12	0.14
Polish (0)	18	0.21
Scandinavian (9)	9	0.10
Scotch-Irish (99)	147	1.70
Scottish (83)	118	1.37
Swedish (0)	13	0.15

Hispanic Origin	Population	%
Hispanic or Latino (of any race)	208	2.45
Central American, ex. Mexican	14	0.16
Guatemalan	7	0.08
Nicaraguan	3	0.04
Panamanian	4	0.05
Cuban	7	0.08
Mexican	134	1.58
Puerto Rican	22	0.26
South American	10	0.12
Bolivian	3	0.04
Colombian	2	0.02
Ecuadorian	3	0.04
Peruvian	2	0.02
Other Hispanic or Latino	21	0.25

Race*	Population	%
African-American/Black (1,852)	2,015	23.73
Not Hispanic (1,843)	1,998	23.53
Hispanic (9)	17	0.20
American Indian/Alaska Native (33)	76	0.90
Not Hispanic (27)	67	0.79
Hispanic (6)	9	0.11
Apache (0)	1	0.01
Blackfeet (0)	1	0.01
Cherokee (11)	31	0.37
Choctaw (2)	2	0.02
Comanche (0)	2	0.02
Cree (0)	2	0.02
Iroquois (0)	1	0.01
Mexican American Ind. (2)	2	0.02
Seminole (0)	1	0.01
Sioux (1)	1	0.01

*Notes: † The Census 2010 population figure is used to calculate the percentages in the Hispanic Origin and Race categories. Ancestry percentages are based on the 2006-2010 American Community Survey population (not shown); ‡ Numbers in parentheses indicate the number of people reporting a single ancestry; * Numbers in parentheses indicate the number of persons reporting this race alone, not in combination with any other race; Please refer to the Explanation of Data for more information.*

South American Ind. (1)	1	0.01
Asian (96)	121	1.43
Not Hispanic (94)	118	1.39
Hispanic (2)	3	0.04
Bangladeshi (0)	2	0.02
Chinese, ex. Taiwanese (21)	26	0.31
Filipino (8)	15	0.18
Hmong (8)	8	0.09
Indian (37)	42	0.49
Japanese (0)	3	0.04
Korean (2)	2	0.02
Thai (2)	5	0.06
Vietnamese (12)	12	0.14
Hawaii Native/Pacific Islander (0)	1	0.01
Hispanic (0)	1	0.01
Guamanian/Chamorro (0)	1	0.01
White (6,209)	6,408	75.47
Not Hispanic (6,107)	6,288	74.05
Hispanic (102)	120	1.41

Tucker

Place Type: CDP
County: DeKalb
Population: 27,581†

Ancestry‡	Population	%
Afghan (100)	100	0.37
African, Sub-Saharan (366)	437	1.63
African (160)	184	0.69
Ethiopian (75)	75	0.28
Sierra Leonean (22)	22	0.08
Somalian (61)	108	0.40
Other Sub-Saharan African (48)	48	0.18
American (3,375)	3,375	12.59
Arab (32)	125	0.47
Egyptian (0)	11	0.04
Lebanese (32)	114	0.43
Armenian (205)	219	0.82
Austrian (9)	46	0.17
British (78)	179	0.67
Canadian (23)	49	0.18
Croatian (24)	76	0.28
Czech (0)	20	0.07
Czechoslovakian (38)	52	0.19
Danish (27)	94	0.35
Dutch (107)	337	1.26
Eastern European (105)	105	0.39
English (1,341)	2,507	9.35
European (463)	487	1.82
Finnish (0)	58	0.22
French, ex. Basque (93)	588	2.19
French Canadian (44)	78	0.29
German (879)	2,748	10.25
Greek (204)	230	0.86
Hungarian (9)	42	0.16
Icelander (0)	10	0.04
Iranian (16)	32	0.12
Irish (920)	2,530	9.44
Italian (236)	841	3.14
Latvian (0)	47	0.18
Lithuanian (9)	48	0.18
Norwegian (41)	233	0.87
Polish (215)	478	1.78
Portuguese (10)	34	0.13
Romanian (0)	34	0.13
Russian (144)	261	0.97
Scandinavian (0)	16	0.06
Scotch-Irish (329)	787	2.94
Scottish (348)	740	2.76
Serbian (36)	36	0.13
Slavic (0)	51	0.19
Slovak (12)	12	0.04
Swedish (82)	144	0.54
Swiss (0)	32	0.12
Turkish (0)	10	0.04
Ukrainian (86)	105	0.39
Welsh (39)	87	0.32
West Indian, ex. Hispanic (387)	450	1.68
Haitian (28)	41	0.15
Jamaican (266)	309	1.15
Trinidadian/Tobagonian (36)	43	0.16
West Indian (57)	57	0.21

Hispanic Origin	Population	%
Hispanic or Latino (of any race)	2,928	10.62
Central American, ex. Mexican	821	2.98
Costa Rican	14	0.05
Guatemalan	356	1.29
Honduran	92	0.33
Nicaraguan	27	0.10
Panamanian	13	0.05
Salvadoran	317	1.15
Other Central American	2	0.01
Cuban	189	0.69
Dominican Republic	99	0.36
Mexican	1,166	4.23
Puerto Rican	161	0.58
South American	318	1.15
Argentinean	19	0.07
Bolivian	6	0.02
Chilean	30	0.11
Colombian	100	0.36
Ecuadorian	24	0.09
Paraguayan	1	<0.01
Peruvian	98	0.36
Uruguayan	5	0.02
Venezuelan	35	0.13
Other Hispanic or Latino	174	0.63

Race*	Population	%
African-American/Black (6,146)	6,501	23.57
Not Hispanic (6,003)	6,285	22.79
Hispanic (143)	216	0.78
American Indian/Alaska Native (99)	241	0.87
Not Hispanic (57)	165	0.60
Hispanic (42)	76	0.28
Apache (0)	2	0.01
Blackfeet (0)	9	0.03
Canadian/French Am. Ind. (1)	1	<0.01
Cherokee (12)	49	0.18
Chippewa (1)	3	0.01
Choctaw (3)	8	0.03
Creek (3)	10	0.04
Iroquois (0)	7	0.03
Lumbee (1)	1	<0.01
Mexican American Ind. (2)	6	0.02
Navajo (1)	1	<0.01
Seminole (1)	3	0.01
Sioux (1)	1	<0.01
South American Ind. (1)	13	0.05
Spanish American Ind. (5)	5	0.02
Asian (2,036)	2,284	8.28
Not Hispanic (2,022)	2,243	8.13
Hispanic (14)	41	0.15
Bangladeshi (77)	83	0.30
Burmese (14)	14	0.05
Cambodian (68)	78	0.28
Chinese, ex. Taiwanese (334)	384	1.39
Filipino (60)	87	0.32
Hmong (1)	1	<0.01
Indian (531)	588	2.13
Indonesian (6)	10	0.04
Japanese (32)	49	0.18
Korean (208)	236	0.86
Laotian (51)	55	0.20
Malaysian (2)	3	0.01
Nepalese (8)	8	0.03
Pakistani (52)	66	0.24
Sri Lankan (13)	18	0.07
Taiwanese (58)	73	0.26
Thai (34)	47	0.17
Vietnamese (419)	440	1.60
Hawaii Native/Pacific Islander (21)	49	0.18
Not Hispanic (19)	39	0.14
Hispanic (2)	10	0.04
Guamanian/Chamorro (10)	11	0.04
Marshallese (1)	1	<0.01
Native Hawaiian (1)	7	0.03
Samoan (5)	9	0.03
Tongan (0)	1	<0.01
White (17,366)	17,953	65.09
Not Hispanic (15,951)	16,358	59.31
Hispanic (1,415)	1,595	5.78

Union City

Place Type: City
County: Fulton
Population: 19,456†

Ancestry‡	Population	%
African, Sub-Saharan (940)	951	5.32
African (927)	927	5.18
Cape Verdean (0)	11	0.06
Ethiopian (4)	4	0.02
Ghanaian (9)	9	0.05
American (876)	876	4.90
British (0)	15	0.08
Canadian (28)	28	0.16
Dutch (22)	51	0.29
English (91)	206	1.15
European (27)	27	0.15
French, ex. Basque (0)	31	0.17
German (86)	140	0.78
Greek (0)	15	0.08
Irish (62)	197	1.10
Italian (16)	60	0.34
Norwegian (7)	17	0.10
Polish (7)	17	0.10
Portuguese (0)	11	0.06
Scandinavian (0)	10	0.06
Scotch-Irish (31)	84	0.47
Scottish (22)	22	0.12
West Indian, ex. Hispanic (312)	367	2.05
Bahamian (58)	58	0.32
Barbadian (0)	30	0.17
Haitian (84)	84	0.47
Jamaican (74)	84	0.47
Trinidadian/Tobagonian (13)	13	0.07
West Indian (83)	98	0.55

Hispanic Origin	Population	%
Hispanic or Latino (of any race)	1,368	7.03
Central American, ex. Mexican	64	0.33
Costa Rican	2	0.01
Guatemalan	6	0.03
Honduran	5	0.03
Panamanian	21	0.11
Salvadoran	30	0.15
Cuban	25	0.13
Dominican Republic	38	0.20
Mexican	1,013	5.21
Puerto Rican	125	0.64
South American	30	0.15
Argentinean	2	0.01
Colombian	11	0.06
Ecuadorian	6	0.03
Peruvian	8	0.04
Uruguayan	2	0.01
Venezuelan	1	0.01
Other Hispanic or Latino	73	0.38

Race*	Population	%
African-American/Black (16,005)	16,350	84.04
Not Hispanic (15,852)	16,134	82.93
Hispanic (153)	216	1.11
American Indian/Alaska Native (45)	166	0.85
Not Hispanic (43)	149	0.77
Hispanic (2)	17	0.09
Apache (0)	1	0.01
Blackfeet (3)	4	0.02
Canadian/French Am. Ind. (0)	1	0.01
Central American Ind. (0)	1	0.01
Cherokee (5)	30	0.15
Chickasaw (0)	1	0.01
Choctaw (1)	4	0.02
Colville (0)	1	0.01
Creek (0)	1	0.01
Houma (3)	3	0.02

*Notes: † The Census 2010 population figure is used to calculate the percentages in the Hispanic Origin and Race categories. Ancestry percentages are based on the 2006-2010 American Community Survey population (not shown); ‡ Numbers in parentheses indicate the number of people reporting a single ancestry; * Numbers in parentheses indicate the number of persons reporting this race alone, not in combination with any other race; Please refer to the Explanation of Data for more information.*

Iroquois (0)	1	0.01
Lumbee (1)	1	0.01
Mexican American Ind. (2)	2	0.01
Potawatomi (1)	2	0.01
Sioux (0)	1	0.01
South American Ind. (0)	1	0.01
Asian (170)	240	1.23
Not Hispanic (148)	209	1.07
Hispanic (22)	31	0.16
Cambodian (8)	9	0.05
Chinese, ex. Taiwanese (30)	43	0.22
Filipino (26)	44	0.23
Indian (48)	61	0.31
Japanese (5)	18	0.09
Korean (12)	25	0.13
Laotian (12)	15	0.08
Nepalese (1)	1	0.01
Pakistani (5)	7	0.04
Taiwanese (2)	2	0.01
Thai (4)	6	0.03
Vietnamese (13)	13	0.07
Hawaii Native/Pacific Islander (1)	18	0.09
Not Hispanic (1)	12	0.06
Hispanic (0)	6	0.03
Guamanian/Chamorro (1)	2	0.01
Native Hawaiian (0)	2	0.01
Samoan (0)	2	0.01
White (2,166)	2,441	12.55
Not Hispanic (1,667)	1,872	9.62
Hispanic (499)	569	2.92

Valdosta

Place Type: City
County: Lowndes
Population: 54,518†

Ancestry‡	Population	%
African, Sub-Saharan (346)	412	0.79
African (270)	336	0.64
Ghanaian (55)	55	0.11
Liberian (21)	21	0.04
American (2,542)	2,542	4.86
Arab (170)	192	0.37
Lebanese (113)	135	0.26
Palestinian (57)	57	0.11
Austrian (35)	76	0.15
British (46)	120	0.23
Bulgarian (22)	22	0.04
Cajun (0)	11	0.02
Canadian (50)	50	0.10
Croatian (0)	20	0.04
Czech (10)	59	0.11
Czechoslovakian (0)	2	<0.01
Danish (8)	8	0.02
Dutch (91)	286	0.55
Eastern European (20)	28	0.05
English (1,739)	3,980	7.61
European (544)	583	1.11
Finnish (0)	9	0.02
French, ex. Basque (96)	740	1.41
French Canadian (79)	182	0.35
German (1,170)	3,741	7.15
German Russian (35)	35	0.07
Greek (90)	198	0.38
Hungarian (13)	90	0.17
Irish (2,018)	4,634	8.86
Italian (318)	881	1.68
Lithuanian (18)	43	0.08
Northern European (33)	33	0.06
Norwegian (51)	142	0.27
Pennsylvania German (10)	42	0.08
Polish (97)	303	0.58
Portuguese (8)	90	0.17
Russian (167)	276	0.53
Scandinavian (10)	10	0.02
Scotch-Irish (396)	795	1.52
Scottish (420)	1,037	1.98
Slovak (0)	43	0.08
Swedish (53)	214	0.41
Swiss (0)	6	0.01
Turkish (27)	49	0.09
Ukrainian (24)	34	0.06
Welsh (34)	122	0.23
West Indian, ex. Hispanic (296)	480	0.92
Belizean (37)	37	0.07
British West Indian (4)	4	0.01
Dutch West Indian (0)	45	0.09
Haitian (52)	132	0.25
Jamaican (80)	113	0.22
Trinidadian/Tobagonian (0)	13	0.02
West Indian (123)	136	0.26

Hispanic Origin	Population	%
Hispanic or Latino (of any race)	2,204	4.04
Central American, ex. Mexican	292	0.54
Costa Rican	3	0.01
Guatemalan	177	0.32
Honduran	37	0.07
Nicaraguan	7	0.01
Panamanian	41	0.08
Salvadoran	26	0.05
Other Central American	1	<0.01
Cuban	106	0.19
Dominican Republic	55	0.10
Mexican	978	1.79
Puerto Rican	332	0.61
South American	133	0.24
Argentinean	4	0.01
Bolivian	9	0.02
Chilean	7	0.01
Colombian	74	0.14
Ecuadorian	6	0.01
Paraguayan	6	0.01
Peruvian	19	0.03
Uruguayan	1	<0.01
Venezuelan	7	0.01
Other Hispanic or Latino	308	0.56

Race*	Population	%
African-American/Black (27,844)	28,452	52.19
Not Hispanic (27,620)	28,110	51.56
Hispanic (224)	342	0.63
American Indian/Alaska Native (187)	464	0.85
Not Hispanic (129)	350	0.64
Hispanic (58)	114	0.21
Aleut *(Alaska Native)* (3)	4	0.01
Apache (2)	3	0.01
Blackfeet (7)	15	0.03
Canadian/French Am. Ind. (0)	1	<0.01
Central American Ind. (0)	4	0.01
Cherokee (19)	98	0.18
Cheyenne (0)	4	0.01
Chippewa (8)	12	0.02
Choctaw (5)	6	0.01
Colville (0)	4	0.01
Cree (0)	1	<0.01
Creek (8)	14	0.03
Delaware (0)	1	<0.01
Houma (0)	1	<0.01
Iroquois (0)	4	0.01
Lumbee (1)	4	0.01
Mexican American Ind. (23)	26	0.05
Navajo (3)	6	0.01
Potawatomi (1)	6	0.01
Pueblo (0)	1	<0.01
Seminole (1)	3	0.01
Sioux (1)	4	0.01
South American Ind. (3)	6	0.01
Spanish American Ind. (12)	13	0.02
Tlingit-Haida *(Alaska Native)* (1)	1	<0.01
Ute (1)	1	<0.01
Yakama (0)	2	<0.01
Yuman (1)	1	<0.01
Asian (933)	1,221	2.24
Not Hispanic (919)	1,168	2.14
Hispanic (14)	53	0.10
Bangladeshi (3)	3	0.01
Burmese (10)	10	0.02
Cambodian (3)	5	0.01
Chinese, ex. Taiwanese (123)	141	0.26
Filipino (108)	197	0.36
Hmong (4)	5	0.01
Indian (412)	451	0.83
Indonesian (2)	4	0.01
Japanese (22)	58	0.11
Korean (79)	136	0.25
Laotian (4)	5	0.01
Malaysian (7)	8	0.01
Pakistani (12)	14	0.03
Taiwanese (4)	7	0.01
Thai (19)	42	0.08
Vietnamese (93)	100	0.18
Hawaii Native/Pacific Islander (51)	118	0.22
Not Hispanic (45)	91	0.17
Hispanic (6)	27	0.05
Guamanian/Chamorro (29)	45	0.08
Native Hawaiian (11)	25	0.05
Samoan (2)	5	0.01
White (23,596)	24,359	44.68
Not Hispanic (22,634)	23,259	42.66
Hispanic (962)	1,100	2.02

Vidalia

Place Type: City
County: Toombs
Population: 10,473†

Ancestry‡	Population	%
African, Sub-Saharan (0)	7	0.07
African (0)	7	0.07
American (1,419)	1,419	13.34
Arab (51)	51	0.48
Arab (35)	35	0.33
Egyptian (16)	16	0.15
Austrian (17)	17	0.16
British (29)	29	0.27
Czech (33)	33	0.31
Danish (19)	19	0.18
Dutch (22)	54	0.51
English (1,026)	1,568	14.74
European (37)	37	0.35
Finnish (0)	14	0.13
French, ex. Basque (42)	75	0.71
French Canadian (13)	13	0.12
German (170)	501	4.71
Greek (0)	50	0.47
Irish (184)	701	6.59
Italian (13)	84	0.79
Norwegian (19)	19	0.18
Polish (60)	124	1.17
Russian (53)	68	0.64
Scotch-Irish (79)	187	1.76
Scottish (21)	51	0.48
Swedish (9)	33	0.31
Welsh (35)	48	0.45

Hispanic Origin	Population	%
Hispanic or Latino (of any race)	479	4.57
Central American, ex. Mexican	25	0.24
Costa Rican	1	0.01
Guatemalan	13	0.12
Honduran	7	0.07
Nicaraguan	1	0.01
Panamanian	2	0.02
Salvadoran	1	0.01
Cuban	9	0.09
Dominican Republic	1	0.01
Mexican	363	3.47
Puerto Rican	28	0.27
South American	14	0.13
Colombian	8	0.08
Ecuadorian	5	0.05
Venezuelan	1	0.01
Other Hispanic or Latino	39	0.37

Race*	Population	%
African-American/Black (4,267)	4,331	41.35
Not Hispanic (4,245)	4,302	41.08

*Notes: † The Census 2010 population figure is used to calculate the percentages in the Hispanic Origin and Race categories. Ancestry percentages are based on the 2006-2010 American Community Survey population (not shown); ‡ Numbers in parentheses indicate the number of people reporting a single ancestry; * Numbers in parentheses indicate the number of persons reporting this race alone, not in combination with any other race; Please refer to the Explanation of Data for more information.*

Hispanic (22)	29	0.28
American Indian/Alaska Native (24)	52	0.50
Not Hispanic (21)	38	0.36
Hispanic (3)	14	0.13
Apache (0)	1	0.01
Blackfeet (0)	2	0.02
Cherokee (2)	7	0.07
Chippewa (0)	1	0.01
Choctaw (1)	1	0.01
Creek (1)	1	0.01
Ottawa (0)	1	0.01
South American Ind. (0)	1	0.01
Asian (145)	163	1.56
Not Hispanic (145)	157	1.50
Hispanic (0)	6	0.06
Cambodian (0)	6	0.06
Chinese, ex. Taiwanese (20)	20	0.19
Filipino (24)	26	0.25
Indian (75)	82	0.78
Japanese (0)	2	0.02
Korean (4)	10	0.10
Thai (2)	2	0.02
Vietnamese (18)	18	0.17
Hawaii Native/Pacific Islander (5)	5	0.05
Not Hispanic (5)	5	0.05
Fijian (5)	5	0.05
White (5,686)	5,789	55.28
Not Hispanic (5,474)	5,550	52.99
Hispanic (212)	239	2.28

Villa Rica

Place Type: City
County: Carroll
Population: 13,956†

Ancestry‡	Population	%
African, Sub-Saharan (585)	605	4.84
African (510)	530	4.24
Nigerian (75)	75	0.60
American (1,035)	1,035	8.28
Arab (7)	14	0.11
Arab (0)	7	0.06
Moroccan (7)	7	0.06
Australian (11)	11	0.09
Brazilian (9)	15	0.12
British (42)	42	0.34
Bulgarian (19)	19	0.15
Canadian (0)	7	0.06
Czech (0)	17	0.14
Czechoslovakian (44)	44	0.35
Dutch (76)	227	1.81
English (497)	1,018	8.14
European (70)	70	0.56
French, ex. Basque (171)	313	2.50
French Canadian (0)	11	0.09
German (261)	818	6.54
Greek (17)	17	0.14
Hungarian (6)	13	0.10
Irish (272)	1,125	8.99
Israeli (0)	7	0.06
Italian (260)	542	4.33
Polish (37)	61	0.49
Portuguese (15)	35	0.28
Scotch-Irish (78)	227	1.81
Scottish (138)	222	1.78
Slovak (21)	52	0.42
Swedish (11)	18	0.14
Ukrainian (3)	3	0.02
Welsh (9)	89	0.71
West Indian, ex. Hispanic (467)	467	3.73
British West Indian (14)	14	0.11
Haitian (337)	337	2.69
Jamaican (105)	105	0.84
Trinidadian/Tobagonian (11)	11	0.09

Hispanic Origin	Population	%
Hispanic or Latino (of any race)	1,064	7.62
Central American, ex. Mexican	98	0.70
Costa Rican	9	0.06
Guatemalan	23	0.16
Honduran	15	0.11
Nicaraguan	14	0.10
Panamanian	14	0.10
Salvadoran	20	0.14
Other Central American	3	0.02
Cuban	52	0.37
Dominican Republic	46	0.33
Mexican	380	2.72
Puerto Rican	260	1.86
South American	131	0.94
Argentinean	6	0.04
Chilean	8	0.06
Colombian	47	0.34
Ecuadorian	33	0.24
Peruvian	18	0.13
Venezuelan	13	0.09
Other South American	6	0.04
Other Hispanic or Latino	97	0.70

Race*	Population	%
African-American/Black (4,669)	4,919	35.25
Not Hispanic (4,598)	4,820	34.54
Hispanic (71)	99	0.71
American Indian/Alaska Native (45)	142	1.02
Not Hispanic (36)	119	0.85
Hispanic (9)	23	0.16
Apache (0)	1	0.01
Blackfeet (1)	1	0.01
Central American Ind. (1)	5	0.04
Cherokee (9)	47	0.34
Chippewa (1)	1	0.01
Creek (1)	5	0.04
Hopi (0)	1	0.01
Iroquois (0)	2	0.01
Lumbee (1)	1	0.01
Mexican American Ind. (0)	1	0.01
Navajo (1)	3	0.02
Seminole (1)	1	0.01
Asian (242)	317	2.27
Not Hispanic (239)	310	2.22
Hispanic (3)	7	0.05
Bangladeshi (3)	3	0.02
Chinese, ex. Taiwanese (27)	31	0.22
Filipino (14)	33	0.24
Hmong (1)	1	0.01
Indian (50)	74	0.53
Japanese (48)	57	0.41
Korean (22)	38	0.27
Laotian (9)	9	0.06
Pakistani (7)	8	0.06
Taiwanese (3)	3	0.02
Thai (6)	8	0.06
Vietnamese (29)	32	0.23
Hawaii Native/Pacific Islander (4)	18	0.13
Not Hispanic (3)	16	0.11
Hispanic (1)	2	0.01
Guamanian/Chamorro (1)	2	0.01
Native Hawaiian (0)	6	0.04
Samoan (2)	2	0.01
White (8,132)	8,451	60.55
Not Hispanic (7,641)	7,905	56.64
Hispanic (491)	546	3.91

Vinings

Place Type: CDP
County: Cobb
Population: 9,734†

Ancestry‡	Population	%
African, Sub-Saharan (144)	144	1.67
African (118)	118	1.37
Nigerian (16)	16	0.19
South African (10)	10	0.12
American (396)	396	4.61
Arab (31)	52	0.60
Egyptian (18)	18	0.21
Jordanian (0)	11	0.13
Lebanese (13)	23	0.27
Austrian (0)	37	0.43
British (49)	49	0.57
Bulgarian (34)	34	0.40
Canadian (0)	13	0.15
Croatian (12)	24	0.28
Danish (0)	7	0.08
Dutch (80)	217	2.52
Eastern European (41)	41	0.48
English (336)	770	8.96
European (335)	335	3.90
Finnish (0)	7	0.08
French, ex. Basque (61)	280	3.26
French Canadian (0)	45	0.52
German (255)	979	11.39
Hungarian (0)	16	0.19
Irish (351)	872	10.14
Italian (142)	314	3.65
Lithuanian (24)	41	0.48
Macedonian (0)	12	0.14
Northern European (23)	23	0.27
Norwegian (22)	84	0.98
Polish (45)	152	1.77
Portuguese (7)	69	0.80
Romanian (0)	11	0.13
Russian (23)	142	1.65
Scotch-Irish (173)	303	3.52
Scottish (114)	311	3.62
Swedish (37)	81	0.94
Swiss (0)	10	0.12
Turkish (26)	26	0.30
Ukrainian (0)	35	0.41
Welsh (11)	73	0.85
West Indian, ex. Hispanic (129)	175	2.04
British West Indian (0)	11	0.13
Dutch West Indian (15)	15	0.17
Jamaican (99)	99	1.15
Trinidadian/Tobagonian (15)	15	0.17
West Indian (0)	35	0.41

Hispanic Origin	Population	%
Hispanic or Latino (of any race)	502	5.16
Central American, ex. Mexican	23	0.24
Costa Rican	1	0.01
Guatemalan	2	0.02
Honduran	10	0.10
Nicaraguan	3	0.03
Panamanian	4	0.04
Salvadoran	3	0.03
Cuban	49	0.50
Dominican Republic	26	0.27
Mexican	197	2.02
Puerto Rican	88	0.90
South American	73	0.75
Argentinean	4	0.04
Chilean	1	0.01
Colombian	42	0.43
Ecuadorian	3	0.03
Paraguayan	1	0.01
Peruvian	13	0.13
Uruguayan	1	0.01
Venezuelan	7	0.07
Other South American	1	0.01
Other Hispanic or Latino	46	0.47

Race*	Population	%
African-American/Black (2,736)	2,879	29.58
Not Hispanic (2,679)	2,802	28.79
Hispanic (57)	77	0.79
American Indian/Alaska Native (18)	65	0.67
Not Hispanic (12)	51	0.52
Hispanic (6)	14	0.14
Blackfeet (0)	8	0.08
Canadian/French Am. Ind. (0)	1	0.01
Central American Ind. (0)	1	0.01
Cherokee (4)	20	0.21
Choctaw (0)	1	0.01
Delaware (0)	2	0.02
Iroquois (1)	2	0.02
Lumbee (1)	2	0.02
Mexican American Ind. (0)	1	0.01

SECTION TWO

*Notes: † The Census 2010 population figure is used to calculate the percentages in the Hispanic Origin and Race categories. Ancestry percentages are based on the 2006-2010 American Community Survey population (not shown); ‡ Numbers in parentheses indicate the number of people reporting a single ancestry; * Numbers in parentheses indicate the number of persons reporting this race alone, not in combination with any other race; Please refer to the Explanation of Data for more information.*

South American Ind. (0)	1	0.01
Asian (406)	492	5.05
Not Hispanic (402)	475	4.88
Hispanic (4)	17	0.17
Bangladeshi (4)	4	0.04
Cambodian (5)	5	0.05
Chinese, ex. Taiwanese (29)	41	0.42
Filipino (17)	41	0.42
Hmong (1)	1	0.01
Indian (252)	263	2.70
Indonesian (1)	3	0.03
Japanese (21)	29	0.30
Korean (36)	51	0.52
Laotian (1)	2	0.02
Malaysian (1)	1	0.01
Nepalese (2)	2	0.02
Pakistani (9)	10	0.10
Sri Lankan (5)	5	0.05
Taiwanese (1)	1	0.01
Thai (5)	6	0.06
Vietnamese (9)	17	0.17
Hawaii Native/Pacific Islander (6)	16	0.16
Not Hispanic (6)	14	0.14
Hispanic (0)	2	0.02
Native Hawaiian (0)	6	0.06
Samoan (2)	3	0.03
White (6,180)	6,346	65.19
Not Hispanic (5,913)	6,054	62.19
Hispanic (267)	292	3.00

Warner Robins

Place Type: City
County: Houston
Population: 66,588†

Ancestry‡	Population	%
African, Sub-Saharan (575)	671	1.06
African (500)	561	0.89
Nigerian (75)	75	0.12
Somalian (0)	35	0.06
American (7,682)	7,682	12.14
Arab (89)	89	0.14
Lebanese (13)	13	0.02
Other Arab (76)	76	0.12
Australian (192)	218	0.34
Austrian (17)	43	0.07
Belgian (0)	10	0.02
Brazilian (99)	99	0.16
British (174)	272	0.43
Cajun (19)	19	0.03
Canadian (30)	75	0.12
Czech (0)	176	0.28
Czechoslovakian (68)	68	0.11
Danish (50)	277	0.44
Dutch (54)	693	1.10
Eastern European (46)	84	0.13
English (1,900)	5,172	8.17
European (360)	553	0.87
Finnish (8)	40	0.06
French, ex. Basque (323)	1,630	2.58
French Canadian (62)	258	0.41
German (1,740)	5,800	9.17
Greek (72)	154	0.24
Hungarian (30)	125	0.20
Iranian (0)	75	0.12
Irish (1,674)	5,307	8.39
Italian (364)	1,069	1.69
Lithuanian (0)	15	0.02
Maltese (44)	44	0.07
Northern European (10)	26	0.04
Norwegian (31)	229	0.36
Polish (134)	512	0.81
Portuguese (53)	70	0.11
Romanian (59)	74	0.12
Russian (33)	201	0.32
Scandinavian (10)	26	0.04
Scotch-Irish (315)	1,178	1.86
Scottish (362)	1,267	2.00
Serbian (8)	8	0.01
Slavic (0)	34	0.05
Slovak (0)	31	0.05
Swedish (71)	362	0.57
Swiss (10)	10	0.02
Turkish (16)	45	0.07
Ukrainian (39)	79	0.12
Welsh (27)	136	0.21
West Indian, ex. Hispanic (374)	568	0.90
Barbadian (17)	31	0.05
Dutch West Indian (0)	9	0.01
Haitian (36)	96	0.15
Jamaican (299)	410	0.65
West Indian (22)	22	0.03
Yugoslavian (6)	6	0.01

Hispanic Origin	Population	%
Hispanic or Latino (of any race)	5,089	7.64
Central American, ex. Mexican	755	1.13
Costa Rican	18	0.03
Guatemalan	427	0.64
Honduran	107	0.16
Nicaraguan	6	0.01
Panamanian	127	0.19
Salvadoran	69	0.10
Other Central American	1	<0.01
Cuban	178	0.27
Dominican Republic	49	0.07
Mexican	2,690	4.04
Puerto Rican	748	1.12
South American	232	0.35
Argentinean	17	0.03
Bolivian	15	0.02
Chilean	7	0.01
Colombian	93	0.14
Ecuadorian	23	0.03
Paraguayan	2	<0.01
Peruvian	36	0.05
Uruguayan	14	0.02
Venezuelan	25	0.04
Other Hispanic or Latino	437	0.66

Race*	Population	%
African-American/Black (24,714)	25,822	38.78
Not Hispanic (24,379)	25,351	38.07
Hispanic (335)	471	0.71
American Indian/Alaska Native (234)	688	1.03
Not Hispanic (184)	576	0.87
Hispanic (50)	112	0.17
Alaska Athabascan *(Ala. Nat.)* (1)	4	0.01
Apache (6)	18	0.03
Blackfeet (2)	14	0.02
Canadian/French Am. Ind. (1)	1	<0.01
Cherokee (33)	188	0.28
Cheyenne (0)	1	<0.01
Chickasaw (0)	3	<0.01
Chippewa (2)	7	0.01
Choctaw (2)	8	0.01
Comanche (1)	3	<0.01
Creek (13)	27	0.04
Delaware (2)	2	<0.01
Iroquois (6)	8	0.01
Lumbee (10)	16	0.02
Mexican American Ind. (22)	36	0.05
Navajo (1)	2	<0.01
Pueblo (1)	1	<0.01
Seminole (0)	6	0.01
Sioux (7)	24	0.04
South American Ind. (3)	6	0.01
Tohono O'Odham (0)	4	0.01
Yaqui (0)	1	<0.01
Asian (1,752)	2,484	3.73
Not Hispanic (1,730)	2,406	3.61
Hispanic (22)	78	0.12
Bhutanese (0)	6	0.01
Burmese (42)	45	0.07
Cambodian (8)	9	0.01
Chinese, ex. Taiwanese (126)	174	0.26
Filipino (395)	688	1.03
Hmong (1)	3	<0.01
Indian (381)	448	0.67
Indonesian (2)	8	0.01
Japanese (80)	161	0.24
Korean (173)	308	0.46
Laotian (8)	16	0.02
Malaysian (0)	3	<0.01
Nepalese (5)	11	0.02
Pakistani (12)	15	0.02
Taiwanese (11)	13	0.02
Thai (71)	163	0.24
Vietnamese (362)	391	0.59
Hawaii Native/Pacific Islander (140)	235	0.35
Not Hispanic (59)	137	0.21
Hispanic (81)	98	0.15
Fijian (1)	1	<0.01
Guamanian/Chamorro (97)	118	0.18
Marshallese (1)	1	<0.01
Native Hawaiian (11)	51	0.08
Samoan (18)	31	0.05
Tongan (1)	5	0.01
White (35,407)	37,141	55.78
Not Hispanic (33,304)	34,732	52.16
Hispanic (2,103)	2,409	3.62

Waycross

Place Type: City
County: Ware
Population: 14,649†

Ancestry‡	Population	%
African, Sub-Saharan (63)	63	0.43
African (63)	63	0.43
American (1,542)	1,542	10.47
Austrian (0)	11	0.07
Croatian (0)	26	0.18
Dutch (19)	51	0.35
English (668)	1,453	9.87
European (41)	53	0.36
Finnish (18)	18	0.12
French, ex. Basque (10)	27	0.18
German (286)	746	5.07
Irish (324)	1,002	6.80
Italian (12)	30	0.20
Norwegian (2)	2	0.01
Pennsylvania German (16)	16	0.11
Russian (16)	27	0.18
Scotch-Irish (61)	197	1.34
Scottish (54)	169	1.15
Swedish (18)	34	0.23
Welsh (10)	21	0.14

Hispanic Origin	Population	%
Hispanic or Latino (of any race)	413	2.82
Central American, ex. Mexican	22	0.15
Costa Rican	2	0.01
Guatemalan	6	0.04
Honduran	12	0.08
Nicaraguan	1	0.01
Panamanian	1	0.01
Cuban	14	0.10
Dominican Republic	8	0.05
Mexican	239	1.63
Puerto Rican	82	0.56
South American	9	0.06
Argentinean	5	0.03
Colombian	2	0.01
Ecuadorian	1	0.01
Peruvian	1	0.01
Other Hispanic or Latino	39	0.27

Race*	Population	%
African-American/Black (8,072)	8,221	56.12
Not Hispanic (8,029)	8,163	55.72
Hispanic (43)	58	0.40
American Indian/Alaska Native (47)	133	0.91
Not Hispanic (38)	122	0.83
Hispanic (9)	11	0.08
Blackfeet (0)	1	0.01
Central American Ind. (1)	1	0.01
Cherokee (13)	54	0.37

*Notes: † The Census 2010 population figure is used to calculate the percentages in the Hispanic Origin and Race categories. Ancestry percentages are based on the 2006-2010 American Community Survey population (not shown); ‡ Numbers in parentheses indicate the number of people reporting a single ancestry; * Numbers in parentheses indicate the number of persons reporting this race alone, not in combination with any other race; Please refer to the Explanation of Data for more information.*

Choctaw (1)	1	0.01
Creek (0)	4	0.03
Navajo (2)	2	0.01
Seminole (0)	3	0.02
Sioux (1)	1	0.01
South American Ind. (1)	1	0.01
Asian (117)	145	0.99
Not Hispanic (116)	144	0.98
Hispanic (1)	1	0.01
Chinese, ex. Taiwanese (13)	16	0.11
Filipino (8)	14	0.10
Indian (56)	64	0.44
Indonesian (0)	2	0.01
Japanese (4)	8	0.05
Korean (3)	8	0.05
Pakistani (3)	5	0.03
Thai (2)	3	0.02
Vietnamese (24)	24	0.16
Hawaii Native/Pacific Islander (3)	11	0.08
Not Hispanic (3)	9	0.06
Hispanic (0)	2	0.01
Guamanian/Chamorro (0)	1	0.01
Native Hawaiian (1)	2	0.01
Samoan (2)	5	0.03
White (5,959)	6,185	42.22
Not Hispanic (5,801)	6,001	40.97
Hispanic (158)	184	1.26

Wilmington Island

Place Type: CDP
County: Chatham
Population: 15,138†

Ancestry‡	Population	%
American (1,459)	1,459	9.21
Austrian (18)	62	0.39
Belgian (0)	22	0.14
British (104)	135	0.85
Canadian (13)	43	0.27
Croatian (13)	13	0.08
Czech (24)	52	0.33
Dutch (0)	100	0.63
Eastern European (42)	42	0.27
English (1,198)	2,556	16.13
European (187)	187	1.18
Finnish (15)	29	0.18
French, ex. Basque (51)	315	1.99
French Canadian (0)	10	0.06
German (878)	2,665	16.81
Greek (73)	106	0.67
Hungarian (14)	72	0.45
Iranian (30)	30	0.19
Irish (1,458)	3,140	19.81
Italian (282)	841	5.31
Lithuanian (0)	13	0.08
Norwegian (73)	129	0.81
Polish (53)	168	1.06
Portuguese (0)	12	0.08
Romanian (36)	36	0.23
Russian (0)	47	0.30
Scandinavian (13)	118	0.74
Scotch-Irish (172)	463	2.92
Scottish (229)	664	4.19
Serbian (54)	54	0.34
Slovak (9)	87	0.55
Slovene (14)	14	0.09
Swedish (61)	106	0.67
Ukrainian (0)	44	0.28
Welsh (28)	182	1.15
West Indian, ex. Hispanic (19)	73	0.46
Barbadian (19)	73	0.46
Yugoslavian (0)	14	0.09

Hispanic Origin	Population	%
Hispanic or Latino (of any race)	464	3.07
Central American, ex. Mexican	18	0.12
Costa Rican	3	0.02
Guatemalan	5	0.03
Honduran	4	0.03
Nicaraguan	1	0.01
Panamanian	3	0.02
Salvadoran	1	0.01
Other Central American	1	0.01
Cuban	41	0.27
Dominican Republic	5	0.03
Mexican	174	1.15
Puerto Rican	98	0.65
South American	74	0.49
Argentinean	1	0.01
Bolivian	2	0.01
Chilean	1	0.01
Colombian	23	0.15
Ecuadorian	6	0.04
Peruvian	25	0.17
Venezuelan	16	0.11
Other Hispanic or Latino	54	0.36

Race*	Population	%
African-American/Black (568)	642	4.24
Not Hispanic (553)	620	4.10
Hispanic (15)	22	0.15
American Indian/Alaska Native (37)	98	0.65
Not Hispanic (32)	90	0.59
Hispanic (5)	8	0.05
Alaska Athabascan *(Ala. Nat.)* (3)	3	0.02
Apache (0)	1	0.01
Blackfeet (1)	2	0.01
Cherokee (9)	29	0.19
Chickasaw (1)	1	0.01
Chippewa (5)	6	0.04
Choctaw (0)	5	0.03
Cree (2)	2	0.01
Creek (4)	4	0.03
Iroquois (1)	1	0.01
Lumbee (0)	6	0.04
Seminole (0)	1	0.01
South American Ind. (1)	1	0.01
Asian (397)	481	3.18
Not Hispanic (393)	476	3.14
Hispanic (4)	5	0.03
Burmese (6)	6	0.04
Cambodian (1)	1	0.01
Chinese, ex. Taiwanese (100)	114	0.75
Filipino (18)	32	0.21
Indian (71)	84	0.55
Japanese (9)	22	0.15
Korean (16)	33	0.22
Laotian (1)	2	0.01
Pakistani (3)	6	0.04
Taiwanese (2)	2	0.01
Thai (5)	7	0.05
Vietnamese (153)	166	1.10
Hawaii Native/Pacific Islander (2)	11	0.07
Not Hispanic (2)	11	0.07
Native Hawaiian (0)	7	0.05
Samoan (1)	1	0.01
White (13,787)	13,986	92.39
Not Hispanic (13,477)	13,657	90.22
Hispanic (310)	329	2.17

Winder

Place Type: City
County: Barrow
Population: 14,099†

Ancestry‡	Population	%
African, Sub-Saharan (40)	40	0.29
African (40)	40	0.29
American (3,012)	3,012	22.00
Austrian (110)	110	0.80
Belgian (0)	14	0.10
British (19)	59	0.43
Croatian (0)	12	0.09
Dutch (31)	148	1.08
English (619)	882	6.44
European (129)	164	1.20
French, ex. Basque (134)	538	3.93
French Canadian (50)	124	0.91
German (337)	793	5.79
Greek (12)	12	0.09
Hungarian (34)	75	0.55
Irish (436)	1,536	11.22
Italian (110)	760	5.55
Norwegian (11)	87	0.64
Polish (0)	133	0.97
Russian (42)	42	0.31
Scotch-Irish (70)	260	1.90
Scottish (125)	176	1.29
Swedish (0)	16	0.12
Welsh (11)	30	0.22
West Indian, ex. Hispanic (168)	197	1.44
Bahamian (0)	29	0.21
Haitian (17)	17	0.12
Jamaican (133)	133	0.97
West Indian (18)	18	0.13

Hispanic Origin	Population	%
Hispanic or Latino (of any race)	1,381	9.80
Central American, ex. Mexican	187	1.33
Costa Rican	9	0.06
Guatemalan	63	0.45
Honduran	18	0.13
Nicaraguan	15	0.11
Panamanian	3	0.02
Salvadoran	78	0.55
Other Central American	1	0.01
Cuban	44	0.31
Dominican Republic	13	0.09
Mexican	896	6.36
Puerto Rican	95	0.67
South American	59	0.42
Argentinean	1	0.01
Chilean	1	0.01
Colombian	46	0.33
Ecuadorian	3	0.02
Peruvian	3	0.02
Venezuelan	5	0.04
Other Hispanic or Latino	87	0.62

Race*	Population	%
African-American/Black (2,568)	2,768	19.63
Not Hispanic (2,542)	2,724	19.32
Hispanic (26)	44	0.31
American Indian/Alaska Native (26)	115	0.82
Not Hispanic (20)	96	0.68
Hispanic (6)	19	0.13
Alaska Athabascan *(Ala. Nat.)* (0)	2	0.01
Apache (0)	6	0.04
Blackfeet (0)	8	0.06
Cherokee (7)	36	0.26
Choctaw (0)	3	0.02
Creek (1)	1	0.01
Lumbee (1)	1	0.01
Mexican American Ind. (0)	3	0.02
Navajo (2)	2	0.01
Sioux (1)	1	0.01
South American Ind. (1)	2	0.01
Asian (287)	343	2.43
Not Hispanic (285)	334	2.37
Hispanic (2)	9	0.06
Cambodian (22)	22	0.16
Chinese, ex. Taiwanese (12)	19	0.13
Filipino (2)	16	0.11
Hmong (157)	159	1.13
Indian (50)	56	0.40
Indonesian (1)	4	0.03
Japanese (2)	8	0.06
Korean (8)	18	0.13
Laotian (11)	12	0.09
Thai (1)	2	0.01
Vietnamese (7)	13	0.09
Hawaii Native/Pacific Islander (17)	25	0.18
Not Hispanic (13)	17	0.12
Hispanic (4)	8	0.06
Native Hawaiian (9)	11	0.08
Samoan (3)	3	0.02
White (10,117)	10,480	74.33
Not Hispanic (9,529)	9,806	69.55

*Notes: † The Census 2010 population figure is used to calculate the percentages in the Hispanic Origin and Race categories. Ancestry percentages are based on the 2006-2010 American Community Survey population (not shown); ‡ Numbers in parentheses indicate the number of people reporting a single ancestry; * Numbers in parentheses indicate the number of persons reporting this race alone, not in combination with any other race; Please refer to the Explanation of Data for more information.*

Hispanic (588)	674	4.78

Woodstock

Place Type: City
County: Cherokee
Population: 23,896†

Ancestry‡	Population	%
African, Sub-Saharan (91)	91	0.41
African (28)	28	0.13
South African (53)	53	0.24
Ugandan (10)	10	0.05
American (1,336)	1,336	6.07
Arab (147)	277	1.26
Egyptian (74)	131	0.59
Lebanese (30)	87	0.39
Moroccan (43)	51	0.23
Other Arab (0)	8	0.04
Armenian (16)	42	0.19
Assyrian/Chaldean/Syriac (28)	28	0.13
Austrian (16)	50	0.23
Brazilian (43)	43	0.20
British (85)	102	0.46
Cajun (16)	16	0.07
Canadian (91)	162	0.74
Croatian (7)	7	0.03
Czech (30)	94	0.43
Czechoslovakian (0)	5	0.02
Danish (0)	68	0.31
Dutch (78)	436	1.98
Eastern European (21)	21	0.10
English (885)	2,343	10.64
Estonian (0)	9	0.04
European (231)	254	1.15
Finnish (0)	14	0.06
French, ex. Basque (97)	662	3.01
French Canadian (9)	63	0.29
German (1,129)	4,273	19.40
Greek (59)	140	0.64
Guyanese (0)	10	0.05
Hungarian (59)	190	0.86
Icelander (44)	44	0.20
Iranian (187)	187	0.85
Irish (1,065)	3,496	15.87
Italian (525)	1,378	6.26
Lithuanian (14)	40	0.18
Norwegian (171)	265	1.20
Pennsylvania German (40)	40	0.18
Polish (113)	609	2.76
Portuguese (0)	106	0.48
Russian (135)	276	1.25
Scandinavian (10)	35	0.16
Scotch-Irish (333)	971	4.41
Scottish (141)	578	2.62
Slovak (10)	52	0.24
Swedish (46)	138	0.63
Swiss (40)	65	0.30
Turkish (10)	10	0.05
Ukrainian (97)	109	0.49
Welsh (61)	212	0.96
West Indian, ex. Hispanic (241)	294	1.33
Barbadian (17)	17	0.08
Haitian (89)	89	0.40
Jamaican (44)	80	0.36
Trinidadian/Tobagonian (91)	108	0.49

Hispanic Origin	Population	%
Hispanic or Latino (of any race)	2,325	9.73
Central American, ex. Mexican	282	1.18
Costa Rican	22	0.09
Guatemalan	62	0.26
Honduran	60	0.25
Nicaraguan	30	0.13
Panamanian	40	0.17
Salvadoran	68	0.28
Cuban	107	0.45
Dominican Republic	83	0.35
Mexican	803	3.36
Puerto Rican	218	0.91
South American	630	2.64
Argentinean	32	0.13
Bolivian	3	0.01
Chilean	25	0.10
Colombian	365	1.53
Ecuadorian	57	0.24
Paraguayan	6	0.03
Peruvian	56	0.23
Uruguayan	16	0.07
Venezuelan	69	0.29
Other South American	1	<0.01
Other Hispanic or Latino	202	0.85

Race*	Population	%
African-American/Black (2,440)	2,761	11.55
Not Hispanic (2,337)	2,605	10.90
Hispanic (103)	156	0.65
American Indian/Alaska Native (46)	193	0.81
Not Hispanic (42)	163	0.68
Hispanic (4)	30	0.13
Apache (0)	1	<0.01
Cherokee (11)	64	0.27
Choctaw (0)	3	0.01
Creek (2)	5	0.02
Delaware (1)	1	<0.01
Lumbee (2)	2	0.01
Mexican American Ind. (2)	6	0.03
Pueblo (0)	3	0.01
Sioux (2)	7	0.03
South American Ind. (0)	2	0.01
Spanish American Ind. (0)	1	<0.01
Tlingit-Haida *(Alaska Native)* (0)	1	<0.01
Asian (1,077)	1,338	5.60
Not Hispanic (1,069)	1,308	5.47
Hispanic (8)	30	0.13
Bangladeshi (6)	8	0.03
Burmese (4)	4	0.02
Cambodian (3)	6	0.03
Chinese, ex. Taiwanese (149)	195	0.82
Filipino (70)	116	0.49
Hmong (2)	3	0.01
Indian (445)	485	2.03
Indonesian (30)	31	0.13
Japanese (20)	44	0.18
Korean (131)	174	0.73
Laotian (18)	23	0.10
Malaysian (4)	6	0.03
Pakistani (28)	42	0.18
Taiwanese (15)	17	0.07
Thai (11)	16	0.07
Vietnamese (95)	106	0.44
Hawaii Native/Pacific Islander (4)	33	0.14
Not Hispanic (3)	31	0.13
Hispanic (1)	2	0.01
Guamanian/Chamorro (1)	4	0.02
Marshallese (2)	2	0.01
Native Hawaiian (0)	11	0.05
Samoan (0)	6	0.03
White (18,940)	19,541	81.78
Not Hispanic (17,472)	17,940	75.08
Hispanic (1,468)	1,601	6.70

*Notes: † The Census 2010 population figure is used to calculate the percentages in the Hispanic Origin and Race categories. Ancestry percentages are based on the 2006-2010 American Community Survey population (not shown); ‡ Numbers in parentheses indicate the number of people reporting a single ancestry; * Numbers in parentheses indicate the number of persons reporting this race alone, not in combination with any other race; Please refer to the Explanation of Data for more information.*

HAWAII

Place Type: State
Population: 1,360,301†

Ancestry‡	Population	%
Afghan (0)	13	<0.01
African, Sub-Saharan (1,071)	1,881	0.14
African (552)	1,082	0.08
Cape Verdean (23)	59	<0.01
Ethiopian (65)	65	<0.01
Ghanaian (13)	13	<0.01
Kenyan (158)	192	0.01
Liberian (95)	95	0.01
Nigerian (24)	24	<0.01
Somalian (38)	38	<0.01
South African (56)	184	0.01
Zimbabwean (26)	26	<0.01
Other Sub-Saharan African (21)	103	0.01
Albanian (0)	20	<0.01
Alsatian (0)	13	<0.01
American (10,350)	10,350	0.78
Arab (883)	1,853	0.14
Arab (220)	418	0.03
Egyptian (264)	335	0.03
Iraqi (16)	16	<0.01
Jordanian (0)	12	<0.01
Lebanese (110)	482	0.04
Moroccan (64)	118	0.01
Palestinian (23)	36	<0.01
Syrian (57)	216	0.02
Other Arab (129)	220	0.02
Armenian (211)	428	0.03
Assyrian/Chaldean/Syriac (0)	18	<0.01
Australian (252)	644	0.05
Austrian (398)	1,918	0.14
Basque (12)	310	0.02
Belgian (225)	664	0.05
Brazilian (523)	876	0.07
British (1,724)	3,458	0.26
Bulgarian (227)	294	0.02
Cajun (29)	110	0.01
Canadian (1,189)	2,006	0.15
Carpatho Rusyn (0)	57	<0.01
Celtic (119)	187	0.01
Croatian (248)	723	0.05
Cypriot (0)	12	<0.01
Czech (499)	2,175	0.16
Czechoslovakian (286)	551	0.04
Danish (1,040)	4,172	0.31
Dutch (1,742)	10,187	0.76
Eastern European (300)	340	0.03
English (13,564)	59,810	4.48
Estonian (35)	67	0.01
European (5,709)	7,362	0.55
Finnish (739)	1,477	0.11
French, ex. Basque (2,951)	22,963	1.72
French Canadian (1,220)	3,205	0.24
German (20,319)	89,726	6.73
German Russian (12)	23	<0.01
Greek (598)	1,957	0.15
Guyanese (25)	59	<0.01
Hungarian (853)	3,216	0.24
Icelander (68)	129	0.01
Iranian (247)	395	0.03
Irish (13,660)	66,244	4.97
Israeli (29)	148	0.01
Italian (8,381)	28,149	2.11
Latvian (112)	338	0.03
Lithuanian (259)	961	0.07
Luxemburger (0)	34	<0.01
Macedonian (34)	62	<0.01
Maltese (49)	176	0.01
New Zealander (75)	157	0.01
Northern European (648)	789	0.06
Norwegian (2,775)	10,203	0.77
Pennsylvania German (40)	193	0.01
Polish (3,730)	13,836	1.04
Portuguese (14,387)	58,791	4.41
Romanian (229)	816	0.06
Russian (1,761)	5,605	0.42
Scandinavian (1,082)	2,056	0.15
Scotch-Irish (3,266)	12,407	0.93
Scottish (3,239)	15,144	1.14
Serbian (251)	445	0.03
Slavic (39)	153	0.01
Slovak (211)	596	0.04
Slovene (81)	292	0.02
Swedish (2,598)	10,414	0.78
Swiss (551)	2,868	0.22
Turkish (155)	362	0.03
Ukrainian (425)	1,236	0.09
Welsh (646)	5,166	0.39
West Indian, ex. Hispanic (1,087)	2,051	0.15
Bahamian (89)	89	0.01
Barbadian (20)	123	0.01
Belizean (6)	28	<0.01
Bermudan (19)	22	<0.01
Dutch West Indian (0)	72	0.01
Haitian (372)	482	0.04
Jamaican (371)	771	0.06
Trinidadian/Tobagonian (16)	43	<0.01
U.S. Virgin Islander (12)	28	<0.01
West Indian (136)	343	0.03
Other West Indian (46)	50	<0.01
Yugoslavian (214)	589	0.04

Hispanic Origin	Population	%
Hispanic or Latino (of any race)	120,842	8.88
Central American, ex. Mexican	2,962	0.22
Costa Rican	289	0.02
Guatemalan	565	0.04
Honduran	390	0.03
Nicaraguan	336	0.02
Panamanian	527	0.04
Salvadoran	801	0.06
Other Central American	54	<0.01
Cuban	1,544	0.11
Dominican Republic	600	0.04
Mexican	35,415	2.60
Puerto Rican	44,116	3.24
South American	3,549	0.26
Argentinean	588	0.04
Bolivian	131	0.01
Chilean	408	0.03
Colombian	904	0.07
Ecuadorian	362	0.03
Paraguayan	24	<0.01
Peruvian	721	0.05
Uruguayan	63	<0.01
Venezuelan	287	0.02
Other South American	61	<0.01
Other Hispanic or Latino	32,656	2.40

Race*	Population	%
African-American/Black (21,424)	38,820	2.85
Not Hispanic (19,904)	33,564	2.47
Hispanic (1,520)	5,256	0.39
American Indian/Alaska Native (4,164)	33,470	2.46
Not Hispanic (2,823)	22,895	1.68
Hispanic (1,341)	10,575	0.78
Alaska Athabascan *(Ala. Nat.)* (29)	77	0.01
Aleut *(Alaska Native)* (43)	107	0.01
Apache (156)	1,068	0.08
Arapaho (9)	44	<0.01
Blackfeet (90)	1,309	0.10
Canadian/French Am. Ind. (31)	101	0.01
Central American Ind. (16)	65	<0.01
Cherokee (476)	8,024	0.59
Cheyenne (11)	120	0.01
Chickasaw (31)	161	0.01
Chippewa (77)	389	0.03
Choctaw (103)	842	0.06
Colville (3)	14	<0.01
Comanche (17)	124	0.01
Cree (15)	104	0.01
Creek (33)	204	0.01
Crow (3)	71	0.01
Delaware (15)	102	0.01
Hopi (3)	46	<0.01
Houma (0)	4	<0.01
Inupiat *(Alaska Native)* (22)	118	0.01
Iroquois (56)	493	0.04
Kiowa (10)	35	<0.01
Lumbee (29)	61	<0.01
Menominee (8)	35	<0.01
Mexican American Ind. (152)	424	0.03
Navajo (220)	656	0.05
Osage (17)	83	0.01
Ottawa (3)	27	<0.01
Paiute (15)	43	<0.01
Pima (13)	39	<0.01
Potawatomi (19)	71	0.01
Pueblo (81)	178	0.01
Puget Sound Salish (14)	58	<0.01
Seminole (18)	191	0.01
Shoshone (7)	118	0.01
Sioux (105)	777	0.06
South American Ind. (47)	240	0.02
Spanish American Ind. (20)	43	<0.01
Tlingit-Haida *(Alaska Native)* (42)	116	0.01
Tohono O'Odham (8)	28	<0.01
Tsimshian *(Alaska Native)* (0)	15	<0.01
Ute (3)	42	<0.01
Yakama (8)	41	<0.01
Yaqui (39)	146	0.01
Yuman (7)	57	<0.01
Yup'ik *(Alaska Native)* (37)	93	0.01
Asian (525,078)	780,968	57.41
Not Hispanic (513,294)	725,913	53.36
Hispanic (11,784)	55,055	4.05
Bangladeshi (60)	74	0.01
Bhutanese (7)	13	<0.01
Burmese (199)	281	0.02
Cambodian (464)	705	0.05
Chinese, ex. Taiwanese (53,963)	198,711	14.61
Filipino (197,497)	342,095	25.15
Hmong (70)	87	0.01
Indian (2,201)	4,737	0.35
Indonesian (399)	990	0.07
Japanese (185,502)	312,292	22.96
Korean (24,203)	48,699	3.58
Laotian (1,844)	2,620	0.19
Malaysian (86)	297	0.02
Nepalese (125)	146	0.01
Pakistani (174)	303	0.02
Sri Lankan (186)	231	0.02
Taiwanese (898)	1,161	0.09
Thai (2,006)	3,701	0.27
Vietnamese (9,779)	13,266	0.98
Hawaii Native/Pacific Isl. (135,422)	355,816	26.16
Not Hispanic (128,222)	311,205	22.88
Hispanic (7,200)	44,611	3.28
Fijian (282)	711	0.05
Guamanian/Chamorro (2,700)	6,647	0.49
Marshallese (6,316)	7,412	0.54
Native Hawaiian (80,337)	289,970	21.32
Samoan (18,287)	37,463	2.75
Tongan (4,830)	8,085	0.59
White (336,599)	564,323	41.49
Not Hispanic (309,343)	497,162	36.55
Hispanic (27,256)	67,161	4.94

*Notes: † The Census 2010 population figure is used to calculate the percentages in the Hispanic Origin and Race categories. Ancestry percentages are based on the 2006-2010 American Community Survey population (not shown); ‡ Numbers in parentheses indicate the number of people reporting a single ancestry; * Numbers in parentheses indicate the number of persons reporting this race alone, not in combination with any other race; Please refer to the Explanation of Data for more information.*

Ahuimanu

Place Type: CDP
County: Honolulu
Population: 8,810†

Ancestry‡	Population	%
American (106)	106	1.09
Arab (0)	21	0.22
Other Arab (0)	21	0.22
Austrian (0)	13	0.13
Basque (0)	13	0.13
British (24)	49	0.50
Danish (0)	9	0.09
Dutch (12)	60	0.61
English (48)	731	7.49
European (54)	67	0.69
French, ex. Basque (20)	305	3.13
French Canadian (0)	10	0.10
German (80)	973	9.97
Greek (0)	16	0.16
Irish (36)	513	5.26
Italian (25)	305	3.13
Lithuanian (0)	28	0.29
Northern European (11)	11	0.11
Norwegian (53)	79	0.81
Polish (28)	122	1.25
Portuguese (127)	427	4.38
Russian (10)	20	0.20
Scotch-Irish (0)	99	1.01
Scottish (13)	229	2.35
Swedish (0)	119	1.22
Swiss (0)	28	0.29
Welsh (0)	85	0.87
West Indian, ex. Hispanic (31)	45	0.46
Jamaican (31)	45	0.46

Hispanic Origin	Population	%
Hispanic or Latino (of any race)	832	9.44
Central American, ex. Mexican	20	0.23
Costa Rican	3	0.03
Guatemalan	3	0.03
Honduran	5	0.06
Nicaraguan	4	0.05
Panamanian	4	0.05
Salvadoran	1	0.01
Cuban	8	0.09
Dominican Republic	3	0.03
Mexican	180	2.04
Puerto Rican	346	3.93
South American	8	0.09
Chilean	3	0.03
Colombian	1	0.01
Ecuadorian	3	0.03
Peruvian	1	0.01
Other Hispanic or Latino	267	3.03

Race*	Population	%
African-American/Black (62)	169	1.92
Not Hispanic (58)	143	1.62
Hispanic (4)	26	0.30
American Indian/Alaska Native (6)	267	3.03
Not Hispanic (5)	185	2.10
Hispanic (1)	82	0.93
Aleut *(Alaska Native)* (0)	2	0.02
Apache (0)	8	0.09
Blackfeet (0)	16	0.18
Canadian/French Am. Ind. (1)	1	0.01
Cherokee (2)	69	0.78
Chippewa (1)	1	0.01
Choctaw (0)	4	0.05
Creek (0)	3	0.03
Iroquois (0)	3	0.03
Mexican American Ind. (0)	1	0.01
Navajo (0)	1	0.01
Osage (0)	3	0.03
Potawatomi (0)	1	0.01
Pueblo (0)	2	0.02
Seminole (0)	7	0.08
Sioux (0)	7	0.08
Asian (2,739)	5,381	61.08
Not Hispanic (2,678)	4,866	55.23
Hispanic (61)	515	5.85
Burmese (4)	4	0.05
Cambodian (2)	3	0.03
Chinese, ex. Taiwanese (303)	2,010	22.81
Filipino (348)	1,455	16.52
Indian (2)	14	0.16
Indonesian (3)	13	0.15
Japanese (1,549)	2,961	33.61
Korean (66)	334	3.79
Laotian (5)	16	0.18
Malaysian (2)	3	0.03
Nepalese (1)	1	0.01
Sri Lankan (1)	1	0.01
Taiwanese (1)	9	0.10
Thai (3)	21	0.24
Vietnamese (34)	57	0.65
Hawaii Native/Pacific Islander (842)	3,197	36.29
Not Hispanic (791)	2,731	31.00
Hispanic (51)	466	5.29
Fijian (0)	10	0.11
Guamanian/Chamorro (7)	36	0.41
Marshallese (16)	17	0.19
Native Hawaiian (680)	2,944	33.42
Samoan (48)	187	2.12
Tongan (23)	43	0.49
White (1,938)	4,423	50.20
Not Hispanic (1,789)	3,861	43.83
Hispanic (149)	562	6.38

Aiea

Place Type: CDP
County: Honolulu
Population: 9,338†

Ancestry‡	Population	%
American (38)	38	0.45
Czech (0)	9	0.11
Danish (7)	26	0.31
Dutch (21)	44	0.52
English (41)	242	2.88
European (171)	171	2.03
Finnish (0)	10	0.12
French, ex. Basque (12)	117	1.39
French Canadian (0)	9	0.11
German (151)	490	5.82
Irish (77)	267	3.17
Italian (38)	111	1.32
Lithuanian (0)	11	0.13
Norwegian (0)	52	0.62
Polish (8)	31	0.37
Portuguese (49)	325	3.86
Russian (0)	38	0.45
Scotch-Irish (0)	39	0.46
Scottish (0)	37	0.44
Swedish (22)	32	0.38
Welsh (0)	12	0.14
West Indian, ex. Hispanic (14)	14	0.17
West Indian (14)	14	0.17

Hispanic Origin	Population	%
Hispanic or Latino (of any race)	579	6.20
Central American, ex. Mexican	4	0.04
Panamanian	2	0.02
Salvadoran	2	0.02
Cuban	7	0.07
Mexican	126	1.35
Puerto Rican	200	2.14
South American	5	0.05
Colombian	5	0.05
Other Hispanic or Latino	237	2.54

Race*	Population	%
African-American/Black (61)	117	1.25
Not Hispanic (58)	98	1.05
Hispanic (3)	19	0.20
American Indian/Alaska Native (13)	125	1.34
Not Hispanic (6)	82	0.88
Hispanic (7)	43	0.46
Alaska Athabascan *(Ala. Nat.)* (0)	1	0.01
Aleut *(Alaska Native)* (0)	1	0.01
Apache (1)	2	0.02
Blackfeet (0)	2	0.02
Canadian/French Am. Ind. (0)	1	0.01
Cherokee (0)	38	0.41
Cheyenne (0)	1	0.01
Chippewa (0)	3	0.03
Choctaw (1)	2	0.02
Cree (0)	1	0.01
Inupiat *(Alaska Native)* (0)	1	0.01
Iroquois (0)	3	0.03
Navajo (1)	1	0.01
Pima (0)	1	0.01
Pueblo (0)	2	0.02
Sioux (0)	1	0.01
Yaqui (0)	1	0.01
Asian (5,387)	7,061	75.62
Not Hispanic (5,293)	6,679	71.52
Hispanic (94)	382	4.09
Burmese (0)	3	0.03
Cambodian (2)	2	0.02
Chinese, ex. Taiwanese (340)	1,432	15.34
Filipino (1,651)	2,578	27.61
Indian (13)	22	0.24
Indonesian (0)	5	0.05
Japanese (2,652)	3,714	39.77
Korean (147)	372	3.98
Laotian (9)	15	0.16
Taiwanese (12)	18	0.19
Thai (7)	16	0.17
Vietnamese (48)	66	0.71
Hawaii Native/Pacific Islander (531)	1,732	18.55
Not Hispanic (503)	1,498	16.04
Hispanic (28)	234	2.51
Fijian (5)	5	0.05
Guamanian/Chamorro (10)	25	0.27
Marshallese (5)	6	0.06
Native Hawaiian (338)	1,474	15.78
Samoan (91)	212	2.27
Tongan (15)	23	0.25
White (1,399)	2,763	29.59
Not Hispanic (1,322)	2,457	26.31
Hispanic (77)	306	3.28

East Honolulu

Place Type: CDP
County: Honolulu
Population: 49,914†

Ancestry‡	Population	%
African, Sub-Saharan (21)	65	0.13
African (0)	44	0.09
Ethiopian (21)	21	0.04
American (355)	355	0.72
Arab (69)	133	0.27
Egyptian (37)	52	0.11
Lebanese (0)	49	0.10
Other Arab (32)	32	0.07
Armenian (9)	41	0.08
Assyrian/Chaldean/Syriac (0)	15	0.03
Australian (30)	42	0.09
Austrian (55)	178	0.36
Belgian (6)	15	0.03
Brazilian (0)	17	0.03
British (48)	96	0.20
Canadian (54)	222	0.45
Croatian (15)	57	0.12
Czech (45)	89	0.18
Danish (64)	279	0.57
Dutch (151)	502	1.02
Eastern European (14)	14	0.03
English (517)	2,704	5.52
European (352)	451	0.92
Finnish (0)	27	0.06
French, ex. Basque (103)	929	1.90
French Canadian (102)	173	0.35
German (739)	3,571	7.29

*Notes: † The Census 2010 population figure is used to calculate the percentages in the Hispanic Origin and Race categories. Ancestry percentages are based on the 2006-2010 American Community Survey population (not shown); ‡ Numbers in parentheses indicate the number of people reporting a single ancestry; * Numbers in parentheses indicate the number of persons reporting this race alone, not in combination with any other race; Please refer to the Explanation of Data for more information.*

Ancestry	Population	%
Greek (86)	182	0.37
Hungarian (58)	113	0.23
Iranian (40)	40	0.08
Irish (815)	3,218	6.57
Israeli (0)	55	0.11
Italian (241)	920	1.88
Latvian (11)	22	0.04
Lithuanian (13)	35	0.07
Northern European (29)	29	0.06
Norwegian (69)	470	0.96
Polish (165)	444	0.91
Portuguese (371)	1,160	2.37
Russian (121)	327	0.67
Scandinavian (9)	9	0.02
Scotch-Irish (114)	510	1.04
Scottish (145)	640	1.31
Slovak (0)	7	0.01
Slovene (20)	20	0.04
Swedish (129)	502	1.02
Swiss (0)	41	0.08
Turkish (7)	7	0.01
Ukrainian (55)	128	0.26
Welsh (67)	258	0.53
West Indian, ex. Hispanic (0)	40	0.08
Haitian (0)	40	0.08
Yugoslavian (0)	87	0.18

Hispanic Origin	Population	%
Hispanic or Latino (of any race)	2,069	4.15
Central American, ex. Mexican	70	0.14
Costa Rican	15	0.03
Guatemalan	11	0.02
Honduran	2	<0.01
Nicaraguan	14	0.03
Panamanian	14	0.03
Salvadoran	14	0.03
Cuban	43	0.09
Dominican Republic	8	0.02
Mexican	616	1.23
Puerto Rican	452	0.91
South American	169	0.34
Argentinean	34	0.07
Bolivian	4	0.01
Chilean	34	0.07
Colombian	21	0.04
Ecuadorian	11	0.02
Paraguayan	1	<0.01
Peruvian	61	0.12
Uruguayan	1	<0.01
Venezuelan	2	<0.01
Other Hispanic or Latino	711	1.42

Race*	Population	%
African-American/Black (252)	575	1.15
Not Hispanic (246)	538	1.08
Hispanic (6)	37	0.07
American Indian/Alaska Native (67)	772	1.55
Not Hispanic (43)	605	1.21
Hispanic (24)	167	0.33
Alaska Athabascan *(Ala. Nat.)* (1)	2	<0.01
Apache (4)	20	0.04
Arapaho (1)	1	<0.01
Blackfeet (3)	31	0.06
Canadian/French Am. Ind. (0)	1	<0.01
Cherokee (7)	195	0.39
Cheyenne (0)	4	0.01
Chickasaw (1)	3	0.01
Chippewa (0)	12	0.02
Choctaw (3)	33	0.07
Comanche (0)	6	0.01
Creek (4)	7	0.01
Crow (0)	5	0.01
Hopi (0)	2	<0.01
Inupiat *(Alaska Native)* (0)	6	0.01
Iroquois (0)	12	0.02
Lumbee (3)	3	0.01
Mexican American Ind. (1)	12	0.02
Navajo (2)	10	0.02
Paiute (0)	1	<0.01
Potawatomi (0)	4	0.01
Pueblo (0)	5	0.01
Seminole (0)	9	0.02
Sioux (0)	18	0.04
South American Ind. (3)	4	0.01
Ute (0)	6	0.01
Yaqui (0)	5	0.01
Yup'ik *(Alaska Native)* (0)	1	<0.01
Asian (24,509)	32,752	65.62
Not Hispanic (24,327)	31,841	63.79
Hispanic (182)	911	1.83
Burmese (11)	17	0.03
Cambodian (19)	23	0.05
Chinese, ex. Taiwanese (4,867)	10,863	21.76
Filipino (1,245)	3,578	7.17
Indian (163)	253	0.51
Indonesian (25)	62	0.12
Japanese (13,324)	19,536	39.14
Korean (1,635)	3,116	6.24
Laotian (39)	75	0.15
Malaysian (2)	8	0.02
Pakistani (6)	9	0.02
Sri Lankan (8)	14	0.03
Taiwanese (130)	157	0.31
Thai (73)	146	0.29
Vietnamese (260)	455	0.91
Hawaii Native/Pacific Islander (1,415)	6,635	13.29
Not Hispanic (1,350)	6,083	12.19
Hispanic (65)	552	1.11
Fijian (2)	10	0.02
Guamanian/Chamorro (45)	139	0.28
Marshallese (10)	11	0.02
Native Hawaiian (1,134)	6,117	12.26
Samoan (101)	367	0.74
Tongan (46)	70	0.14
White (13,643)	21,655	43.38
Not Hispanic (13,018)	20,244	40.56
Hispanic (625)	1,411	2.83

Ewa Beach

Place Type: CDP
County: Honolulu
Population: 14,955†

Ancestry‡	Population	%
American (21)	21	0.14
Arab (0)	7	0.05
Lebanese (0)	7	0.05
Czechoslovakian (32)	32	0.21
Dutch (0)	74	0.48
English (0)	82	0.54
French, ex. Basque (31)	54	0.35
German (114)	518	3.39
Irish (29)	168	1.10
Italian (0)	20	0.13
Polish (0)	58	0.38
Portuguese (260)	959	6.27
Russian (0)	48	0.31
Scandinavian (0)	41	0.27
Scotch-Irish (0)	62	0.41
Swedish (10)	77	0.50
Swiss (0)	11	0.07
Welsh (24)	60	0.39

Hispanic Origin	Population	%
Hispanic or Latino (of any race)	1,658	11.09
Central American, ex. Mexican	23	0.15
Costa Rican	1	0.01
Guatemalan	12	0.08
Nicaraguan	1	0.01
Panamanian	5	0.03
Salvadoran	4	0.03
Cuban	10	0.07
Dominican Republic	2	0.01
Mexican	202	1.35
Puerto Rican	868	5.80
South American	15	0.10
Colombian	4	0.03
Peruvian	4	0.03
Venezuelan	3	0.02
Other South American	4	0.03
Other Hispanic or Latino	538	3.60

Race*	Population	%
African-American/Black (99)	348	2.33
Not Hispanic (90)	277	1.85
Hispanic (9)	71	0.47
American Indian/Alaska Native (19)	326	2.18
Not Hispanic (9)	201	1.34
Hispanic (10)	125	0.84
Apache (1)	19	0.13
Blackfeet (0)	22	0.15
Central American Ind. (1)	1	0.01
Cherokee (0)	57	0.38
Chickasaw (0)	1	0.01
Iroquois (1)	10	0.07
Kiowa (0)	1	0.01
Navajo (3)	18	0.12
Paiute (0)	1	0.01
Potawatomi (0)	1	0.01
Seminole (2)	3	0.02
Sioux (0)	10	0.07
Ute (0)	1	0.01
Yakama (0)	3	0.02
Yaqui (1)	2	0.01
Yuman (0)	1	0.01
Asian (7,573)	10,867	72.66
Not Hispanic (7,244)	9,790	65.46
Hispanic (329)	1,077	7.20
Cambodian (5)	5	0.03
Chinese, ex. Taiwanese (113)	1,812	12.12
Filipino (6,262)	8,650	57.84
Indian (8)	33	0.22
Japanese (661)	1,845	12.34
Korean (36)	263	1.76
Laotian (5)	11	0.07
Malaysian (0)	11	0.07
Thai (9)	19	0.13
Vietnamese (37)	43	0.29
Hawaii Native/Pacific Islander (1,925)	4,890	32.70
Not Hispanic (1,802)	4,075	27.25
Hispanic (123)	815	5.45
Fijian (17)	18	0.12
Guamanian/Chamorro (18)	91	0.61
Marshallese (34)	51	0.34
Native Hawaiian (907)	3,722	24.89
Samoan (689)	1,058	7.07
Tongan (84)	121	0.81
White (1,259)	3,884	25.97
Not Hispanic (1,070)	3,097	20.71
Hispanic (189)	787	5.26

Ewa Gentry

Place Type: CDP
County: Honolulu
Population: 22,690†

Ancestry‡	Population	%
American (229)	229	1.07
Arab (181)	181	0.84
Arab (181)	181	0.84
Australian (29)	97	0.45
Austrian (0)	12	0.06
British (0)	18	0.08
Canadian (20)	60	0.28
Croatian (0)	21	0.10
Czech (6)	6	0.03
Danish (0)	30	0.14
Dutch (15)	193	0.90
English (100)	467	2.17
European (74)	92	0.43
French, ex. Basque (25)	127	0.59
French Canadian (62)	73	0.34
German (316)	1,278	5.95
Guyanese (25)	25	0.12
Hungarian (8)	28	0.13
Irish (110)	702	3.27
Italian (143)	332	1.55
Luxemburger (0)	10	0.05

*Notes: † The Census 2010 population figure is used to calculate the percentages in the Hispanic Origin and Race categories. Ancestry percentages are based on the 2006-2010 American Community Survey population (not shown); ‡ Numbers in parentheses indicate the number of people reporting a single ancestry; * Numbers in parentheses indicate the number of persons reporting this race alone, not in combination with any other race; Please refer to the Explanation of Data for more information.*

Norwegian (18)	172	0.80
Polish (47)	88	0.41
Portuguese (75)	812	3.78
Russian (0)	21	0.10
Scandinavian (0)	12	0.06
Scotch-Irish (0)	86	0.40
Scottish (53)	225	1.05
Slavic (21)	21	0.10
Swedish (12)	60	0.28
Swiss (22)	56	0.26
Ukrainian (0)	9	0.04
Welsh (0)	17	0.08
West Indian, ex. Hispanic (41)	65	0.30
Haitian (23)	23	0.11
Jamaican (18)	31	0.14
Trinidadian/Tobagonian (0)	11	0.05
Yugoslavian (0)	9	0.04

Hispanic Origin	Population	%
Hispanic or Latino (of any race)	2,792	12.30
Central American, ex. Mexican	67	0.30
Costa Rican	2	0.01
Guatemalan	8	0.04
Honduran	5	0.02
Nicaraguan	14	0.06
Panamanian	15	0.07
Salvadoran	23	0.10
Cuban	46	0.20
Dominican Republic	26	0.11
Mexican	793	3.49
Puerto Rican	957	4.22
South American	70	0.31
Argentinean	5	0.02
Chilean	3	0.01
Colombian	17	0.07
Ecuadorian	21	0.09
Peruvian	20	0.09
Uruguayan	2	0.01
Venezuelan	2	0.01
Other Hispanic or Latino	833	3.67

Race*	Population	%
African-American/Black (817)	1,368	6.03
Not Hispanic (767)	1,174	5.17
Hispanic (50)	194	0.86
American Indian/Alaska Native (39)	568	2.50
Not Hispanic (24)	336	1.48
Hispanic (15)	232	1.02
Aleut *(Alaska Native)* (2)	4	0.02
Apache (3)	18	0.08
Blackfeet (2)	30	0.13
Central American Ind. (0)	3	0.01
Cherokee (3)	136	0.60
Cheyenne (0)	1	<0.01
Chickasaw (1)	2	0.01
Chippewa (1)	4	0.02
Choctaw (0)	5	0.02
Comanche (0)	3	0.01
Cree (2)	5	0.02
Creek (0)	4	0.02
Inupiat *(Alaska Native)* (0)	3	0.01
Iroquois (0)	8	0.04
Mexican American Ind. (3)	7	0.03
Navajo (4)	11	0.05
Osage (2)	2	0.01
Pima (0)	1	<0.01
Potawatomi (0)	1	<0.01
Pueblo (0)	2	0.01
Seminole (0)	4	0.02
Sioux (2)	11	0.05
South American Ind. (0)	5	0.02
Tlingit-Haida *(Alaska Native)* (2)	8	0.04
Asian (10,063)	15,205	67.01
Not Hispanic (9,663)	13,668	60.24
Hispanic (400)	1,537	6.77
Burmese (2)	4	0.02
Cambodian (12)	23	0.10
Chinese, ex. Taiwanese (337)	3,303	14.56
Filipino (6,499)	10,438	46.00
Indian (37)	75	0.33
Indonesian (9)	11	0.05
Japanese (1,631)	4,130	18.20
Korean (186)	715	3.15
Laotian (38)	72	0.32
Nepalese (4)	4	0.02
Pakistani (5)	8	0.04
Sri Lankan (0)	5	0.02
Taiwanese (5)	9	0.04
Thai (41)	100	0.44
Vietnamese (122)	195	0.86
Hawaii Native/Pacific Islander (1,584)	5,572	24.56
Not Hispanic (1,490)	4,583	20.20
Hispanic (94)	989	4.36
Fijian (5)	13	0.06
Guamanian/Chamorro (134)	272	1.20
Marshallese (79)	93	0.41
Native Hawaiian (616)	4,239	18.68
Samoan (516)	1,030	4.54
Tongan (37)	91	0.40
White (3,669)	7,941	35.00
Not Hispanic (3,194)	6,504	28.66
Hispanic (475)	1,437	6.33

Haiku-Pauwela

Place Type: CDP
County: Maui
Population: 8,118†

Ancestry‡	Population	%
American (149)	149	1.86
Arab (0)	26	0.32
Lebanese (0)	26	0.32
Austrian (0)	64	0.80
Brazilian (21)	58	0.72
British (61)	84	1.05
Cajun (0)	48	0.60
Canadian (0)	23	0.29
Czech (20)	91	1.13
Dutch (0)	97	1.21
English (214)	841	10.48
European (96)	96	1.20
Finnish (10)	10	0.12
French, ex. Basque (79)	570	7.11
French Canadian (0)	40	0.50
German (167)	1,114	13.89
Hungarian (65)	119	1.48
Irish (98)	558	6.96
Italian (105)	417	5.20
Lithuanian (28)	28	0.35
Northern European (14)	14	0.17
Norwegian (119)	167	2.08
Polish (0)	229	2.86
Portuguese (154)	566	7.06
Russian (0)	92	1.15
Scandinavian (160)	160	1.99
Scotch-Irish (135)	269	3.35
Scottish (24)	223	2.78
Slovak (27)	27	0.34
Swedish (71)	204	2.54
Swiss (0)	91	1.13
Welsh (0)	103	1.28
Yugoslavian (0)	5	0.06

Hispanic Origin	Population	%
Hispanic or Latino (of any race)	889	10.95
Central American, ex. Mexican	18	0.22
Costa Rican	3	0.04
Guatemalan	7	0.09
Honduran	2	0.02
Nicaraguan	1	0.01
Panamanian	1	0.01
Salvadoran	4	0.05
Cuban	22	0.27
Mexican	226	2.78
Puerto Rican	309	3.81
South American	93	1.15
Argentinean	58	0.71
Chilean	2	0.02
Colombian	10	0.12
Ecuadorian	1	0.01
Peruvian	9	0.11
Uruguayan	4	0.05
Venezuelan	9	0.11
Other Hispanic or Latino	221	2.72

Race*	Population	%
African-American/Black (27)	102	1.26
Not Hispanic (27)	87	1.07
Hispanic (0)	15	0.18
American Indian/Alaska Native (42)	277	3.41
Not Hispanic (26)	195	2.40
Hispanic (16)	82	1.01
Alaska Athabascan *(Ala. Nat.)* (0)	4	0.05
Aleut *(Alaska Native)* (0)	2	0.02
Apache (1)	6	0.07
Blackfeet (2)	14	0.17
Canadian/French Am. Ind. (1)	1	0.01
Central American Ind. (1)	1	0.01
Cherokee (4)	45	0.55
Cheyenne (0)	2	0.02
Chickasaw (1)	7	0.09
Chippewa (1)	3	0.04
Choctaw (0)	8	0.10
Comanche (0)	1	0.01
Cree (0)	3	0.04
Creek (0)	5	0.06
Iroquois (2)	6	0.07
Navajo (0)	1	0.01
Ottawa (1)	1	0.01
Paiute (1)	1	0.01
Potawatomi (0)	2	0.02
Pueblo (1)	1	0.01
Seminole (0)	2	0.02
Shoshone (0)	4	0.05
Sioux (0)	4	0.05
Tlingit-Haida *(Alaska Native)* (1)	2	0.02
Yup'ik *(Alaska Native)* (0)	1	0.01
Asian (659)	2,002	24.66
Not Hispanic (620)	1,687	20.78
Hispanic (39)	315	3.88
Burmese (1)	7	0.09
Cambodian (1)	1	0.01
Chinese, ex. Taiwanese (52)	636	7.83
Filipino (185)	884	10.89
Indian (6)	38	0.47
Indonesian (2)	16	0.20
Japanese (282)	789	9.72
Korean (23)	109	1.34
Laotian (0)	5	0.06
Malaysian (0)	2	0.02
Taiwanese (3)	8	0.10
Thai (14)	23	0.28
Vietnamese (2)	5	0.06
Hawaii Native/Pacific Islander (573)	1,853	22.83
Not Hispanic (538)	1,534	18.90
Hispanic (35)	319	3.93
Fijian (1)	3	0.04
Guamanian/Chamorro (3)	6	0.07
Marshallese (11)	15	0.18
Native Hawaiian (454)	1,698	20.92
Samoan (6)	34	0.42
Tongan (18)	26	0.32
White (4,825)	6,314	77.78
Not Hispanic (4,489)	5,679	69.96
Hispanic (336)	635	7.82

Halawa

Place Type: CDP
County: Honolulu
Population: 14,014†

Ancestry‡	Population	%
American (68)	68	0.49
Arab (27)	27	0.19
Lebanese (27)	27	0.19
Brazilian (15)	15	0.11
British (8)	8	0.06
Celtic (25)	25	0.18

*Notes: † The Census 2010 population figure is used to calculate the percentages in the Hispanic Origin and Race categories. Ancestry percentages are based on the 2006-2010 American Community Survey population (not shown); ‡ Numbers in parentheses indicate the number of people reporting a single ancestry; * Numbers in parentheses indicate the number of persons reporting this race alone, not in combination with any other race; Please refer to the Explanation of Data for more information.*

Czech (8)	8	0.06
Dutch (13)	82	0.59
English (22)	233	1.68
European (58)	58	0.42
Finnish (10)	10	0.07
French, ex. Basque (56)	245	1.76
French Canadian (30)	34	0.24
German (122)	641	4.62
Greek (16)	16	0.12
Hungarian (37)	75	0.54
Irish (104)	523	3.77
Italian (36)	185	1.33
Norwegian (0)	9	0.06
Polish (0)	59	0.42
Portuguese (80)	385	2.77
Scotch-Irish (11)	51	0.37
Scottish (0)	159	1.15
Slovak (0)	10	0.07
Swedish (16)	40	0.29
Swiss (8)	28	0.20
Welsh (0)	14	0.10
Yugoslavian (0)	8	0.06

Hispanic Origin	Population	%
Hispanic or Latino (of any race)	1,052	7.51
Central American, ex. Mexican	10	0.07
Guatemalan	2	0.01
Panamanian	4	0.03
Salvadoran	4	0.03
Cuban	7	0.05
Dominican Republic	4	0.03
Mexican	240	1.71
Puerto Rican	423	3.02
South American	17	0.12
Chilean	1	0.01
Colombian	12	0.09
Ecuadorian	2	0.01
Uruguayan	1	0.01
Other South American	1	0.01
Other Hispanic or Latino	351	2.50

Race*	Population	%
African-American/Black (209)	364	2.60
Not Hispanic (192)	319	2.28
Hispanic (17)	45	0.32
American Indian/Alaska Native (17)	230	1.64
Not Hispanic (9)	150	1.07
Hispanic (8)	80	0.57
Alaska Athabascan *(Ala. Nat.)* (0)	1	0.01
Apache (0)	7	0.05
Blackfeet (0)	10	0.07
Cherokee (4)	73	0.52
Chickasaw (0)	1	0.01
Chippewa (1)	3	0.02
Choctaw (0)	1	0.01
Creek (0)	4	0.03
Inupiat *(Alaska Native)* (0)	1	0.01
Mexican American Ind. (1)	10	0.07
Navajo (2)	3	0.02
Paiute (0)	2	0.01
Seminole (0)	3	0.02
Shoshone (0)	5	0.04
Sioux (1)	6	0.04
Spanish American Ind. (0)	1	0.01
Ute (1)	1	0.01
Yup'ik *(Alaska Native)* (1)	2	0.01
Asian (7,234)	9,772	69.73
Not Hispanic (7,090)	9,201	65.66
Hispanic (144)	571	4.07
Cambodian (4)	8	0.06
Chinese, ex. Taiwanese (574)	2,263	16.15
Filipino (2,865)	4,373	31.20
Indian (5)	31	0.22
Indonesian (0)	2	0.01
Japanese (2,572)	4,059	28.96
Korean (229)	515	3.67
Laotian (14)	17	0.12
Malaysian (1)	5	0.04
Pakistani (0)	1	0.01
Taiwanese (14)	16	0.11
Thai (28)	53	0.38
Vietnamese (252)	303	2.16
Hawaii Native/Pacific Islander (1,709)	3,782	26.99
Not Hispanic (1,633)	3,347	23.88
Hispanic (76)	435	3.10
Fijian (8)	15	0.11
Guamanian/Chamorro (34)	77	0.55
Marshallese (115)	128	0.91
Native Hawaiian (523)	2,453	17.50
Samoan (608)	952	6.79
Tongan (12)	44	0.31
White (1,730)	3,790	27.04
Not Hispanic (1,538)	3,270	23.33
Hispanic (192)	520	3.71

Hawaiian Paradise Park

Place Type: CDP
County: Hawaii
Population: 11,404†

Ancestry‡	Population	%
Dutch (0)	51	0.65
English (73)	551	7.03
European (0)	59	0.75
French, ex. Basque (22)	376	4.79
French Canadian (39)	89	1.13
German (317)	1,096	13.98
Irish (27)	451	5.75
Italian (194)	262	3.34
Norwegian (10)	78	0.99
Polish (85)	135	1.72
Portuguese (225)	854	10.89
Romanian (0)	11	0.14
Russian (72)	133	1.70
Scandinavian (24)	56	0.71
Scotch-Irish (14)	104	1.33
Scottish (26)	252	3.21
Swedish (0)	137	1.75
Swiss (24)	24	0.31
Welsh (0)	52	0.66
West Indian, ex. Hispanic (0)	25	0.32
Dutch West Indian (0)	25	0.32

Hispanic Origin	Population	%
Hispanic or Latino (of any race)	1,698	14.89
Central American, ex. Mexican	12	0.11
Guatemalan	1	0.01
Honduran	3	0.03
Nicaraguan	4	0.04
Panamanian	1	0.01
Salvadoran	3	0.03
Cuban	16	0.14
Dominican Republic	6	0.05
Mexican	338	2.96
Puerto Rican	898	7.87
South American	30	0.26
Argentinean	10	0.09
Chilean	3	0.03
Colombian	5	0.04
Ecuadorian	3	0.03
Peruvian	1	0.01
Other South American	8	0.07
Other Hispanic or Latino	398	3.49

Race*	Population	%
African-American/Black (89)	223	1.96
Not Hispanic (71)	175	1.53
Hispanic (18)	48	0.42
American Indian/Alaska Native (69)	554	4.86
Not Hispanic (42)	355	3.11
Hispanic (27)	199	1.75
Alaska Athabascan *(Ala. Nat.)* (1)	1	0.01
Aleut *(Alaska Native)* (0)	1	0.01
Apache (5)	19	0.17
Blackfeet (2)	30	0.26
Canadian/French Am. Ind. (0)	2	0.02
Cherokee (12)	127	1.11
Cheyenne (0)	8	0.07
Chickasaw (1)	1	0.01
Chippewa (2)	4	0.04
Choctaw (3)	30	0.26
Comanche (0)	4	0.04
Creek (0)	3	0.03
Delaware (0)	1	0.01
Hopi (1)	4	0.04
Inupiat *(Alaska Native)* (1)	1	0.01
Iroquois (0)	6	0.05
Mexican American Ind. (1)	6	0.05
Navajo (0)	4	0.04
Osage (1)	4	0.04
Paiute (0)	1	0.01
Potawatomi (0)	1	0.01
Puget Sound Salish (1)	2	0.02
Shoshone (0)	1	0.01
Sioux (2)	17	0.15
South American Ind. (1)	6	0.05
Tlingit-Haida *(Alaska Native)* (0)	2	0.02
Tohono O'Odham (0)	1	0.01
Ute (0)	1	0.01
Yakama (0)	1	0.01
Yaqui (0)	2	0.02
Yuman (1)	4	0.04
Asian (2,148)	4,965	43.54
Not Hispanic (2,037)	4,059	35.59
Hispanic (111)	906	7.94
Chinese, ex. Taiwanese (81)	1,494	13.10
Filipino (1,328)	3,135	27.49
Indian (19)	34	0.30
Indonesian (1)	8	0.07
Japanese (431)	1,533	13.44
Korean (36)	209	1.83
Malaysian (1)	3	0.03
Sri Lankan (0)	2	0.02
Taiwanese (1)	1	0.01
Thai (26)	32	0.28
Vietnamese (23)	38	0.33
Hawaii Native/Pacific Islander (1,341)	4,081	35.79
Not Hispanic (1,203)	3,213	28.17
Hispanic (138)	868	7.61
Fijian (1)	4	0.04
Guamanian/Chamorro (25)	70	0.61
Marshallese (4)	21	0.18
Native Hawaiian (980)	3,683	32.30
Samoan (60)	164	1.44
Tongan (32)	52	0.46
White (3,958)	6,660	58.40
Not Hispanic (3,618)	5,641	49.47
Hispanic (340)	1,019	8.94

Hilo

Place Type: CDP
County: Hawaii
Population: 43,263†

Ancestry‡	Population	%
African, Sub-Saharan (41)	120	0.25
African (15)	80	0.16
Cape Verdean (0)	14	0.03
Zimbabwean (26)	26	0.05
American (344)	344	0.70
Arab (28)	28	0.06
Palestinian (3)	3	0.01
Syrian (25)	25	0.05
Australian (14)	14	0.03
Austrian (0)	76	0.16
Basque (0)	18	0.04
British (8)	35	0.07
Canadian (3)	3	0.01
Czech (29)	50	0.10
Danish (0)	198	0.41
Dutch (26)	357	0.73
English (174)	1,319	2.70
European (172)	318	0.65
Finnish (8)	50	0.10
French, ex. Basque (122)	968	1.98
French Canadian (0)	115	0.24
German (488)	2,882	5.91
Greek (0)	11	0.02

*Notes: † The Census 2010 population figure is used to calculate the percentages in the Hispanic Origin and Race categories. Ancestry percentages are based on the 2006-2010 American Community Survey population (not shown); ‡ Numbers in parentheses indicate the number of people reporting a single ancestry; * Numbers in parentheses indicate the number of persons reporting this race alone, not in combination with any other race; Please refer to the Explanation of Data for more information.*

Guyanese (0)	24	0.05
Hungarian (0)	14	0.03
Irish (637)	2,059	4.22
Italian (161)	496	1.02
Latvian (0)	28	0.06
Lithuanian (0)	28	0.06
Norwegian (89)	171	0.35
Polish (126)	284	0.58
Portuguese (1,339)	4,207	8.62
Romanian (0)	9	0.02
Russian (127)	206	0.42
Scandinavian (0)	14	0.03
Scotch-Irish (112)	394	0.81
Scottish (152)	499	1.02
Slovak (0)	23	0.05
Slovene (15)	15	0.03
Swedish (83)	491	1.01
Swiss (0)	19	0.04
Ukrainian (34)	34	0.07
Welsh (42)	253	0.52

Hispanic Origin	Population	%
Hispanic or Latino (of any race)	4,501	10.40
Central American, ex. Mexican	42	0.10
Costa Rican	12	0.03
Guatemalan	3	0.01
Honduran	2	<0.01
Nicaraguan	3	0.01
Panamanian	4	0.01
Salvadoran	16	0.04
Other Central American	2	<0.01
Cuban	71	0.16
Dominican Republic	1	<0.01
Mexican	781	1.81
Puerto Rican	2,350	5.43
South American	78	0.18
Argentinean	8	0.02
Chilean	19	0.04
Colombian	13	0.03
Ecuadorian	15	0.03
Peruvian	14	0.03
Venezuelan	8	0.02
Other South American	1	<0.01
Other Hispanic or Latino	1,178	2.72

Race*	Population	%
African-American/Black (227)	653	1.51
Not Hispanic (198)	504	1.16
Hispanic (29)	149	0.34
American Indian/Alaska Native (132)	1,454	3.36
Not Hispanic (82)	889	2.05
Hispanic (50)	565	1.31
Aleut *(Alaska Native)* (3)	3	0.01
Apache (3)	42	0.10
Arapaho (0)	3	0.01
Blackfeet (2)	45	0.10
Canadian/French Am. Ind. (1)	3	0.01
Central American Ind. (0)	2	<0.01
Cherokee (21)	346	0.80
Cheyenne (0)	3	0.01
Chickasaw (1)	6	0.01
Chippewa (0)	22	0.05
Choctaw (1)	28	0.06
Comanche (1)	9	0.02
Cree (0)	7	0.02
Creek (0)	10	0.02
Crow (0)	3	0.01
Hopi (0)	1	<0.01
Inupiat *(Alaska Native)* (2)	8	0.02
Iroquois (4)	23	0.05
Menominee (0)	3	0.01
Mexican American Ind. (4)	11	0.03
Navajo (3)	24	0.06
Osage (0)	9	0.02
Ottawa (0)	2	<0.01
Paiute (4)	10	0.02
Pima (1)	1	<0.01
Potawatomi (1)	4	0.01
Pueblo (2)	9	0.02
Puget Sound Salish (0)	5	0.01
Seminole (0)	19	0.04
Shoshone (1)	8	0.02
Sioux (9)	34	0.08
South American Ind. (0)	5	0.01
Tlingit-Haida *(Alaska Native)* (3)	5	0.01
Tohono O'Odham (1)	4	0.01
Tsimshian *(Alaska Native)* (0)	1	<0.01
Yaqui (0)	4	0.01
Yup'ik *(Alaska Native)* (3)	3	0.01
Asian (14,833)	26,420	61.07
Not Hispanic (14,450)	23,823	55.07
Hispanic (383)	2,597	6.00
Bhutanese (2)	2	<0.01
Burmese (4)	8	0.02
Cambodian (4)	7	0.02
Chinese, ex. Taiwanese (618)	6,805	15.73
Filipino (2,637)	8,928	20.64
Hmong (3)	3	0.01
Indian (49)	139	0.32
Indonesian (16)	44	0.10
Japanese (9,550)	15,537	35.91
Korean (419)	1,342	3.10
Laotian (6)	8	0.02
Malaysian (0)	1	<0.01
Nepalese (1)	1	<0.01
Taiwanese (26)	31	0.07
Thai (46)	67	0.15
Vietnamese (105)	166	0.38
Hawaii Native/Pacific Islander (6,132)	16,587	38.34
Not Hispanic (5,771)	14,293	33.04
Hispanic (361)	2,294	5.30
Fijian (5)	24	0.06
Guamanian/Chamorro (43)	138	0.32
Marshallese (256)	289	0.67
Native Hawaiian (4,467)	14,694	33.96
Samoan (140)	486	1.12
Tongan (80)	172	0.40
White (7,617)	17,664	40.83
Not Hispanic (6,894)	14,931	34.51
Hispanic (723)	2,733	6.32

Holualoa

Place Type: CDP
County: Hawaii
Population: 8,538†

Ancestry‡	Population	%
American (250)	250	2.58
Arab (0)	8	0.08
Lebanese (0)	8	0.08
Austrian (9)	9	0.09
Belgian (14)	14	0.14
British (0)	23	0.24
Canadian (138)	195	2.01
Celtic (36)	36	0.37
Czech (25)	68	0.70
Danish (0)	26	0.27
Dutch (14)	249	2.57
English (121)	736	7.59
European (92)	101	1.04
French, ex. Basque (49)	115	1.19
French Canadian (8)	8	0.08
German (497)	1,382	14.24
German Russian (12)	12	0.12
Hungarian (12)	190	1.96
Iranian (32)	32	0.33
Irish (102)	1,079	11.12
Italian (115)	453	4.67
Norwegian (75)	123	1.27
Pennsylvania German (0)	15	0.15
Polish (45)	192	1.98
Portuguese (89)	371	3.82
Russian (0)	20	0.21
Scandinavian (74)	74	0.76
Scotch-Irish (80)	176	1.81
Scottish (81)	274	2.82
Slovak (14)	14	0.14
Swedish (164)	260	2.68
Swiss (42)	42	0.43
Turkish (0)	9	0.09
Ukrainian (14)	26	0.27
Welsh (0)	39	0.40
Yugoslavian (31)	31	0.32

Hispanic Origin	Population	%
Hispanic or Latino (of any race)	811	9.50
Central American, ex. Mexican	24	0.28
Costa Rican	3	0.04
Guatemalan	10	0.12
Honduran	5	0.06
Nicaraguan	2	0.02
Panamanian	1	0.01
Salvadoran	2	0.02
Other Central American	1	0.01
Cuban	10	0.12
Mexican	405	4.74
Puerto Rican	155	1.82
South American	50	0.59
Argentinean	6	0.07
Chilean	8	0.09
Colombian	8	0.09
Ecuadorian	9	0.11
Peruvian	16	0.19
Uruguayan	1	0.01
Other South American	2	0.02
Other Hispanic or Latino	167	1.96

Race*	Population	%
African-American/Black (58)	143	1.67
Not Hispanic (57)	129	1.51
Hispanic (1)	14	0.16
American Indian/Alaska Native (37)	296	3.47
Not Hispanic (27)	217	2.54
Hispanic (10)	79	0.93
Alaska Athabascan *(Ala. Nat.)* (1)	1	0.01
Aleut *(Alaska Native)* (1)	1	0.01
Apache (3)	25	0.29
Arapaho (0)	2	0.02
Blackfeet (1)	23	0.27
Canadian/French Am. Ind. (1)	1	0.01
Cherokee (2)	56	0.66
Cheyenne (0)	1	0.01
Chickasaw (0)	7	0.08
Chippewa (0)	5	0.06
Choctaw (1)	5	0.06
Comanche (1)	1	0.01
Creek (1)	2	0.02
Hopi (0)	1	0.01
Iroquois (1)	5	0.06
Mexican American Ind. (3)	9	0.11
Navajo (2)	12	0.14
Osage (1)	1	0.01
Paiute (1)	2	0.02
Pima (0)	2	0.02
Sioux (0)	13	0.15
Tlingit-Haida *(Alaska Native)* (1)	3	0.04
Asian (1,390)	2,583	30.25
Not Hispanic (1,348)	2,380	27.88
Hispanic (42)	203	2.38
Cambodian (8)	8	0.09
Chinese, ex. Taiwanese (80)	604	7.07
Filipino (614)	1,258	14.73
Indian (8)	25	0.29
Indonesian (0)	2	0.02
Japanese (497)	965	11.30
Korean (48)	101	1.18
Malaysian (1)	2	0.02
Pakistani (1)	1	0.01
Taiwanese (2)	2	0.02
Thai (31)	46	0.54
Vietnamese (27)	31	0.36
Hawaii Native/Pacific Islander (506)	1,592	18.65
Not Hispanic (475)	1,424	16.68
Hispanic (31)	168	1.97
Guamanian/Chamorro (8)	28	0.33
Marshallese (26)	34	0.40
Native Hawaiian (346)	1,379	16.15
Samoan (15)	58	0.68
Tongan (15)	36	0.42

*Notes: † The Census 2010 population figure is used to calculate the percentages in the Hispanic Origin and Race categories. Ancestry percentages are based on the 2006-2010 American Community Survey population (not shown); ‡ Numbers in parentheses indicate the number of people reporting a single ancestry; * Numbers in parentheses indicate the number of persons reporting this race alone, not in combination with any other race; Please refer to the Explanation of Data for more information.*

White (4,692)	5,912	69.24
Not Hispanic (4,403)	5,428	63.57
Hispanic (289)	484	5.67

Kahului

Place Type: CDP
County: Maui
Population: 26,337†

Ancestry‡	Population	%
American (14)	14	0.06
British (0)	38	0.15
Canadian (31)	55	0.22
Dutch (7)	87	0.35
English (83)	258	1.04
European (53)	66	0.27
French, ex. Basque (0)	59	0.24
French Canadian (0)	80	0.32
German (102)	453	1.83
Hungarian (6)	6	0.02
Irish (78)	171	0.69
Italian (128)	318	1.29
Lithuanian (0)	14	0.06
Norwegian (0)	68	0.28
Pennsylvania German (0)	6	0.02
Polish (16)	73	0.30
Portuguese (220)	1,938	7.84
Scotch-Irish (52)	88	0.36
Scottish (35)	83	0.34
Serbian (13)	13	0.05
Swedish (0)	60	0.24
Swiss (49)	161	0.65

Hispanic Origin	Population	%
Hispanic or Latino (of any race)	2,484	9.43
Central American, ex. Mexican	122	0.46
Costa Rican	14	0.05
Guatemalan	82	0.31
Honduran	7	0.03
Nicaraguan	5	0.02
Salvadoran	9	0.03
Other Central American	5	0.02
Cuban	16	0.06
Dominican Republic	3	0.01
Mexican	671	2.55
Puerto Rican	1,120	4.25
South American	18	0.07
Argentinean	1	<0.01
Colombian	9	0.03
Peruvian	7	0.03
Venezuelan	1	<0.01
Other Hispanic or Latino	534	2.03

Race*	Population	%
African-American/Black (111)	315	1.20
Not Hispanic (103)	268	1.02
Hispanic (8)	47	0.18
American Indian/Alaska Native (72)	489	1.86
Not Hispanic (41)	305	1.16
Hispanic (31)	184	0.70
Apache (2)	22	0.08
Arapaho (0)	1	<0.01
Blackfeet (3)	10	0.04
Canadian/French Am. Ind. (1)	3	0.01
Cherokee (7)	95	0.36
Chippewa (0)	3	0.01
Choctaw (1)	5	0.02
Cree (0)	1	<0.01
Crow (0)	1	<0.01
Delaware (1)	1	<0.01
Iroquois (0)	7	0.03
Mexican American Ind. (1)	5	0.02
Navajo (3)	6	0.02
Pima (1)	2	0.01
Pueblo (1)	4	0.02
Shoshone (0)	2	0.01
Sioux (2)	11	0.04
South American Ind. (0)	1	<0.01
Spanish American Ind. (0)	1	<0.01
Tlingit-Haida *(Alaska Native)* (0)	3	0.01
Tsimshian *(Alaska Native)* (0)	3	0.01
Ute (0)	3	0.01
Yakama (0)	4	0.02
Yaqui (0)	1	<0.01
Yuman (3)	3	0.01
Yup'ik *(Alaska Native)* (1)	4	0.02
Asian (13,992)	18,830	71.50
Not Hispanic (13,674)	17,524	66.54
Hispanic (318)	1,306	4.96
Burmese (4)	4	0.02
Cambodian (4)	7	0.03
Chinese, ex. Taiwanese (146)	2,456	9.33
Filipino (9,755)	13,099	49.74
Hmong (0)	1	<0.01
Indian (23)	66	0.25
Indonesian (5)	21	0.08
Japanese (3,115)	5,197	19.73
Korean (155)	475	1.80
Malaysian (1)	5	0.02
Pakistani (9)	9	0.03
Taiwanese (4)	5	0.02
Thai (9)	14	0.05
Vietnamese (89)	123	0.47
Hawaii Native/Pacific Islander (3,341)	7,672	29.13
Not Hispanic (3,191)	6,692	25.41
Hispanic (150)	980	3.72
Fijian (1)	6	0.02
Guamanian/Chamorro (17)	43	0.16
Marshallese (440)	521	1.98
Native Hawaiian (1,573)	5,634	21.39
Samoan (116)	306	1.16
Tongan (236)	316	1.20
White (2,620)	6,096	23.15
Not Hispanic (2,265)	5,035	19.12
Hispanic (355)	1,061	4.03

Kailua

Place Type: CDP
County: Hawaii
Population: 11,975†

Ancestry‡	Population	%
African, Sub-Saharan (19)	19	0.15
African (19)	19	0.15
American (88)	88	0.67
Armenian (0)	14	0.11
Belgian (0)	15	0.11
British (14)	39	0.30
Celtic (0)	13	0.10
Danish (12)	47	0.36
Dutch (15)	153	1.17
English (196)	798	6.11
European (144)	144	1.10
Finnish (0)	57	0.44
French, ex. Basque (70)	335	2.57
French Canadian (0)	15	0.11
German (256)	1,035	7.93
Hungarian (0)	27	0.21
Irish (108)	894	6.85
Italian (132)	367	2.81
Norwegian (47)	114	0.87
Polish (66)	127	0.97
Portuguese (198)	879	6.73
Romanian (0)	8	0.06
Russian (0)	34	0.26
Scandinavian (14)	14	0.11
Scotch-Irish (75)	336	2.57
Scottish (77)	182	1.39
Slovene (0)	17	0.13
Swedish (27)	320	2.45
Swiss (44)	93	0.71
Welsh (14)	87	0.67
West Indian, ex. Hispanic (0)	9	0.07
Jamaican (0)	9	0.07

Hispanic Origin	Population	%
Hispanic or Latino (of any race)	1,463	12.22
Central American, ex. Mexican	31	0.26
Guatemalan	6	0.05
Honduran	5	0.04
Panamanian	2	0.02
Salvadoran	8	0.07
Other Central American	10	0.08
Cuban	14	0.12
Dominican Republic	4	0.03
Mexican	675	5.64
Puerto Rican	424	3.54
South American	29	0.24
Argentinean	9	0.08
Bolivian	1	0.01
Chilean	6	0.05
Colombian	1	0.01
Peruvian	8	0.07
Venezuelan	4	0.03
Other Hispanic or Latino	286	2.39

Race*	Population	%
African-American/Black (53)	160	1.34
Not Hispanic (49)	134	1.12
Hispanic (4)	26	0.22
American Indian/Alaska Native (71)	372	3.11
Not Hispanic (38)	228	1.90
Hispanic (33)	144	1.20
Alaska Athabascan *(Ala. Nat.)* (1)	1	0.01
Aleut *(Alaska Native)* (2)	3	0.03
Apache (2)	7	0.06
Blackfeet (1)	21	0.18
Canadian/French Am. Ind. (1)	1	0.01
Cherokee (6)	93	0.78
Chickasaw (0)	6	0.05
Chippewa (0)	1	0.01
Choctaw (2)	15	0.13
Colville (0)	1	0.01
Cree (1)	1	0.01
Inupiat *(Alaska Native)* (1)	3	0.03
Iroquois (5)	11	0.09
Lumbee (2)	2	0.02
Mexican American Ind. (2)	5	0.04
Navajo (3)	7	0.06
Potawatomi (1)	3	0.03
Pueblo (5)	5	0.04
Seminole (0)	2	0.02
Shoshone (0)	1	0.01
Sioux (2)	11	0.09
South American Ind. (0)	1	0.01
Spanish American Ind. (0)	1	0.01
Tlingit-Haida *(Alaska Native)* (0)	1	0.01
Tohono O'Odham (0)	1	0.01
Ute (0)	1	0.01
Yaqui (0)	6	0.05
Asian (2,172)	4,364	36.44
Not Hispanic (2,093)	3,886	32.45
Hispanic (79)	478	3.99
Burmese (4)	6	0.05
Cambodian (5)	6	0.05
Chinese, ex. Taiwanese (100)	1,174	9.80
Filipino (1,117)	2,512	20.98
Indian (8)	30	0.25
Indonesian (2)	5	0.04
Japanese (538)	1,338	11.17
Korean (186)	274	2.29
Laotian (0)	1	0.01
Malaysian (0)	1	0.01
Pakistani (3)	3	0.03
Taiwanese (1)	4	0.03
Thai (31)	44	0.37
Vietnamese (22)	29	0.24
Hawaii Native/Pacific Islander (1,822)	4,099	34.23
Not Hispanic (1,740)	3,616	30.20
Hispanic (82)	483	4.03
Guamanian/Chamorro (19)	39	0.33
Marshallese (190)	212	1.77
Native Hawaiian (997)	3,181	26.56
Samoan (79)	230	1.92
Tongan (80)	122	1.02
White (4,400)	6,402	53.46
Not Hispanic (4,137)	5,743	47.96
Hispanic (263)	659	5.50

*Notes: † The Census 2010 population figure is used to calculate the percentages in the Hispanic Origin and Race categories. Ancestry percentages are based on the 2006-2010 American Community Survey population (not shown); ‡ Numbers in parentheses indicate the number of people reporting a single ancestry; * Numbers in parentheses indicate the number of persons reporting this race alone, not in combination with any other race; Please refer to the Explanation of Data for more information.*

Kailua

Place Type: CDP
County: Honolulu
Population: 38,635†

Ancestry‡	Population	%
African, Sub-Saharan (7)	19	0.05
African (7)	7	0.02
South African (0)	12	0.03
Alsatian (0)	13	0.03
American (779)	779	2.02
Arab (70)	84	0.22
Egyptian (14)	14	0.04
Lebanese (13)	27	0.07
Moroccan (43)	43	0.11
Australian (40)	72	0.19
Austrian (28)	69	0.18
Belgian (23)	63	0.16
Brazilian (0)	58	0.15
British (56)	181	0.47
Cajun (0)	19	0.05
Canadian (112)	120	0.31
Croatian (74)	74	0.19
Czech (59)	184	0.48
Czechoslovakian (12)	33	0.09
Danish (74)	226	0.59
Dutch (67)	474	1.23
Eastern European (33)	41	0.11
English (1,401)	4,251	11.03
European (388)	420	1.09
Finnish (33)	44	0.11
French, ex. Basque (32)	636	1.65
French Canadian (35)	143	0.37
German (946)	5,108	13.25
German Russian (0)	7	0.02
Greek (34)	205	0.53
Hungarian (32)	207	0.54
Icelander (0)	27	0.07
Iranian (26)	41	0.11
Irish (458)	3,354	8.70
Italian (314)	1,343	3.48
Lithuanian (11)	106	0.28
Maltese (0)	16	0.04
Northern European (90)	90	0.23
Norwegian (148)	700	1.82
Polish (134)	725	1.88
Portuguese (868)	2,619	6.80
Romanian (38)	64	0.17
Russian (130)	342	0.89
Scandinavian (18)	71	0.18
Scotch-Irish (104)	615	1.60
Scottish (158)	844	2.19
Slovak (22)	47	0.12
Slovene (10)	29	0.08
Swedish (56)	459	1.19
Swiss (12)	82	0.21
Ukrainian (29)	38	0.10
Welsh (7)	399	1.04
West Indian, ex. Hispanic (0)	4	0.01
Other West Indian (0)	4	0.01

Hispanic Origin	Population	%
Hispanic or Latino (of any race)	2,525	6.54
Central American, ex. Mexican	70	0.18
Costa Rican	6	0.02
Guatemalan	18	0.05
Honduran	6	0.02
Nicaraguan	8	0.02
Panamanian	14	0.04
Salvadoran	18	0.05
Cuban	46	0.12
Dominican Republic	13	0.03
Mexican	797	2.06
Puerto Rican	568	1.47
South American	132	0.34
Argentinean	23	0.06
Bolivian	12	0.03
Chilean	26	0.07
Colombian	21	0.05
Ecuadorian	3	0.01
Peruvian	34	0.09
Venezuelan	13	0.03
Other Hispanic or Latino	899	2.33

Race*	Population	%
African-American/Black (224)	640	1.66
Not Hispanic (209)	563	1.46
Hispanic (15)	77	0.20
American Indian/Alaska Native (91)	903	2.34
Not Hispanic (69)	732	1.89
Hispanic (22)	171	0.44
Alaska Athabascan *(Ala. Nat.)* (3)	6	0.02
Aleut *(Alaska Native)* (0)	3	0.01
Apache (6)	20	0.05
Arapaho (0)	1	<0.01
Blackfeet (0)	19	0.05
Cherokee (13)	257	0.67
Cheyenne (1)	2	0.01
Chickasaw (2)	5	0.01
Chippewa (3)	6	0.02
Choctaw (6)	33	0.09
Comanche (0)	1	<0.01
Creek (0)	8	0.02
Delaware (0)	12	0.03
Hopi (0)	5	0.01
Inupiat *(Alaska Native)* (1)	5	0.01
Iroquois (1)	21	0.05
Kiowa (0)	3	0.01
Lumbee (0)	3	0.01
Menominee (2)	2	0.01
Mexican American Ind. (2)	6	0.02
Navajo (1)	8	0.02
Potawatomi (0)	5	0.01
Pueblo (3)	4	0.01
Seminole (0)	12	0.03
Shoshone (1)	4	0.01
Sioux (3)	19	0.05
South American Ind. (3)	8	0.02
Spanish American Ind. (3)	4	0.01
Yakama (0)	2	0.01
Yaqui (1)	3	0.01
Yuman (1)	1	<0.01
Yup'ik *(Alaska Native)* (1)	1	<0.01
Asian (7,827)	15,851	41.03
Not Hispanic (7,700)	14,868	38.48
Hispanic (127)	983	2.54
Burmese (9)	14	0.04
Cambodian (18)	29	0.08
Chinese, ex. Taiwanese (999)	5,971	15.45
Filipino (1,170)	3,701	9.58
Hmong (2)	2	0.01
Indian (48)	91	0.24
Indonesian (6)	49	0.13
Japanese (4,179)	7,983	20.66
Korean (323)	1,120	2.90
Laotian (31)	41	0.11
Malaysian (1)	7	0.02
Nepalese (2)	2	0.01
Pakistani (2)	7	0.02
Sri Lankan (1)	3	0.01
Taiwanese (11)	14	0.04
Thai (35)	85	0.22
Vietnamese (125)	210	0.54
Hawaii Native/Pacific Islander (2,581)	9,732	25.19
Not Hispanic (2,447)	8,804	22.79
Hispanic (134)	928	2.40
Fijian (6)	17	0.04
Guamanian/Chamorro (41)	122	0.32
Marshallese (11)	30	0.08
Native Hawaiian (2,151)	9,028	23.37
Samoan (146)	569	1.47
Tongan (55)	133	0.34
White (17,015)	25,762	66.68
Not Hispanic (16,276)	24,003	62.13
Hispanic (739)	1,759	4.55

Kalaoa

Place Type: CDP
County: Hawaii
Population: 9,644†

Ancestry‡	Population	%
African, Sub-Saharan (6)	6	0.07
African (6)	6	0.07
American (84)	84	0.97
Armenian (0)	19	0.22
Basque (0)	53	0.61
Belgian (0)	15	0.17
Canadian (45)	45	0.52
Czech (0)	15	0.17
Danish (0)	30	0.35
Dutch (14)	51	0.59
English (345)	866	9.99
European (16)	16	0.18
Finnish (27)	36	0.42
French, ex. Basque (0)	121	1.40
German (447)	902	10.40
Irish (74)	701	8.09
Italian (33)	236	2.72
Lithuanian (0)	37	0.43
Norwegian (47)	108	1.25
Polish (102)	177	2.04
Portuguese (65)	500	5.77
Russian (0)	16	0.18
Scotch-Irish (14)	182	2.10
Scottish (74)	347	4.00
Slavic (0)	12	0.14
Slovene (0)	30	0.35
Swedish (31)	103	1.19
Swiss (10)	24	0.28
Turkish (18)	18	0.21
Ukrainian (0)	80	0.92
Welsh (0)	102	1.18
Yugoslavian (0)	23	0.27

Hispanic Origin	Population	%
Hispanic or Latino (of any race)	1,060	10.99
Central American, ex. Mexican	37	0.38
Costa Rican	5	0.05
Guatemalan	4	0.04
Honduran	4	0.04
Nicaraguan	1	0.01
Salvadoran	23	0.24
Cuban	9	0.09
Mexican	422	4.38
Puerto Rican	318	3.30
South American	31	0.32
Argentinean	3	0.03
Chilean	9	0.09
Colombian	8	0.08
Ecuadorian	8	0.08
Peruvian	2	0.02
Venezuelan	1	0.01
Other Hispanic or Latino	243	2.52

Race*	Population	%
African-American/Black (49)	125	1.30
Not Hispanic (46)	111	1.15
Hispanic (3)	14	0.15
American Indian/Alaska Native (29)	327	3.39
Not Hispanic (18)	246	2.55
Hispanic (11)	81	0.84
Alaska Athabascan *(Ala. Nat.)* (0)	5	0.05
Aleut *(Alaska Native)* (1)	1	0.01
Apache (0)	5	0.05
Blackfeet (4)	26	0.27
Cherokee (2)	82	0.85
Chickasaw (1)	5	0.05
Chippewa (0)	1	0.01
Choctaw (2)	10	0.10
Delaware (1)	5	0.05
Iroquois (0)	5	0.05
Mexican American Ind. (2)	11	0.11
Navajo (1)	8	0.08
Osage (0)	4	0.04

*Notes: † The Census 2010 population figure is used to calculate the percentages in the Hispanic Origin and Race categories. Ancestry percentages are based on the 2006-2010 American Community Survey population (not shown); ‡ Numbers in parentheses indicate the number of people reporting a single ancestry; * Numbers in parentheses indicate the number of persons reporting this race alone, not in combination with any other race; Please refer to the Explanation of Data for more information.*

Pueblo (0)	1	0.01
Puget Sound Salish (0)	1	0.01
Seminole (0)	1	0.01
Shoshone (0)	3	0.03
Sioux (0)	12	0.12
South American Ind. (1)	2	0.02
Spanish American Ind. (1)	1	0.01
Tlingit-Haida *(Alaska Native)* (1)	2	0.02
Tohono O'Odham (1)	1	0.01
Yup'ik *(Alaska Native)* (1)	1	0.01
Asian (1,267)	3,310	34.32
Not Hispanic (1,209)	2,921	30.29
Hispanic (58)	389	4.03
Burmese (1)	1	0.01
Cambodian (11)	11	0.11
Chinese, ex. Taiwanese (68)	1,105	11.46
Filipino (435)	1,592	16.51
Indian (8)	26	0.27
Indonesian (4)	9	0.09
Japanese (531)	1,329	13.78
Korean (40)	203	2.10
Laotian (1)	1	0.01
Taiwanese (2)	4	0.04
Thai (14)	26	0.27
Vietnamese (2)	8	0.08
Hawaii Native/Pacific Islander (1,071)	3,098	32.12
Not Hispanic (1,023)	2,710	28.10
Hispanic (48)	388	4.02
Fijian (0)	3	0.03
Guamanian/Chamorro (15)	30	0.31
Marshallese (49)	55	0.57
Native Hawaiian (722)	2,675	27.74
Samoan (44)	175	1.81
Tongan (69)	113	1.17
White (4,259)	6,295	65.27
Not Hispanic (4,013)	5,680	58.90
Hispanic (246)	615	6.38

Kaneohe

Place Type: CDP
County: Honolulu
Population: 34,597†

Ancestry‡	Population	%
African, Sub-Saharan (0)	28	0.08
African (0)	11	0.03
South African (0)	17	0.05
American (126)	126	0.37
Arab (29)	94	0.27
Arab (0)	39	0.11
Lebanese (18)	18	0.05
Syrian (11)	37	0.11
Armenian (0)	18	0.05
Austrian (0)	33	0.10
Belgian (15)	15	0.04
British (24)	29	0.08
Canadian (31)	64	0.19
Carpatho Rusyn (0)	40	0.12
Czech (5)	84	0.24
Czechoslovakian (0)	7	0.02
Danish (38)	87	0.25
Dutch (83)	150	0.44
Eastern European (5)	5	0.01
English (252)	1,355	3.94
European (164)	219	0.64
Finnish (14)	38	0.11
French, ex. Basque (40)	539	1.57
French Canadian (19)	19	0.06
German (305)	2,006	5.83
Hungarian (34)	94	0.27
Irish (282)	1,348	3.92
Italian (230)	823	2.39
Maltese (0)	29	0.08
Norwegian (25)	132	0.38
Pennsylvania German (0)	25	0.07
Polish (76)	224	0.65
Portuguese (394)	1,630	4.74
Romanian (0)	6	0.02
Russian (26)	68	0.20
Scandinavian (0)	10	0.03
Scotch-Irish (105)	510	1.48
Scottish (12)	300	0.87
Swedish (23)	77	0.22
Swiss (31)	82	0.24
Ukrainian (21)	46	0.13
Welsh (22)	136	0.40
West Indian, ex. Hispanic (63)	113	0.33
Jamaican (51)	101	0.29
Trinidadian/Tobagonian (12)	12	0.03
Yugoslavian (13)	13	0.04

Hispanic Origin	Population	%
Hispanic or Latino (of any race)	2,900	8.38
Central American, ex. Mexican	53	0.15
Costa Rican	14	0.04
Guatemalan	1	<0.01
Honduran	7	0.02
Nicaraguan	8	0.02
Panamanian	11	0.03
Salvadoran	11	0.03
Other Central American	1	<0.01
Cuban	27	0.08
Dominican Republic	11	0.03
Mexican	706	2.04
Puerto Rican	1,106	3.20
South American	50	0.14
Argentinean	4	0.01
Chilean	6	0.02
Colombian	6	0.02
Ecuadorian	11	0.03
Peruvian	15	0.04
Venezuelan	7	0.02
Other South American	1	<0.01
Other Hispanic or Latino	947	2.74

Race*	Population	%
African-American/Black (215)	543	1.57
Not Hispanic (194)	432	1.25
Hispanic (21)	111	0.32
American Indian/Alaska Native (88)	957	2.77
Not Hispanic (69)	674	1.95
Hispanic (19)	283	0.82
Aleut *(Alaska Native)* (0)	1	<0.01
Apache (2)	21	0.06
Arapaho (1)	3	0.01
Blackfeet (2)	23	0.07
Canadian/French Am. Ind. (0)	1	<0.01
Central American Ind. (0)	3	0.01
Cherokee (18)	291	0.84
Cheyenne (0)	1	<0.01
Chickasaw (0)	4	0.01
Chippewa (5)	10	0.03
Choctaw (2)	34	0.10
Comanche (0)	1	<0.01
Creek (0)	9	0.03
Delaware (0)	3	0.01
Hopi (0)	2	0.01
Inupiat *(Alaska Native)* (1)	1	<0.01
Iroquois (0)	11	0.03
Kiowa (0)	1	<0.01
Lumbee (1)	2	0.01
Mexican American Ind. (1)	9	0.03
Navajo (6)	17	0.05
Paiute (2)	2	0.01
Potawatomi (2)	2	0.01
Seminole (0)	9	0.03
Shoshone (0)	5	0.01
Sioux (6)	23	0.07
South American Ind. (0)	3	0.01
Tlingit-Haida *(Alaska Native)* (1)	2	0.01
Ute (0)	2	0.01
Yaqui (1)	4	0.01
Asian (12,754)	21,959	63.47
Not Hispanic (12,526)	20,385	58.92
Hispanic (228)	1,574	4.55
Bangladeshi (0)	1	<0.01
Bhutanese (1)	4	0.01
Burmese (5)	5	0.01
Cambodian (8)	9	0.03
Chinese, ex. Taiwanese (1,283)	7,527	21.76
Filipino (1,828)	5,590	16.16
Indian (38)	80	0.23
Indonesian (6)	16	0.05
Japanese (7,477)	12,759	36.88
Korean (304)	1,266	3.66
Laotian (11)	20	0.06
Malaysian (2)	16	0.05
Nepalese (2)	2	0.01
Pakistani (2)	14	0.04
Sri Lankan (4)	4	0.01
Taiwanese (5)	6	0.02
Thai (45)	78	0.23
Vietnamese (108)	195	0.56
Hawaii Native/Pacific Islander (3,177)	11,509	33.27
Not Hispanic (2,959)	10,022	28.97
Hispanic (218)	1,487	4.30
Fijian (7)	21	0.06
Guamanian/Chamorro (42)	155	0.45
Marshallese (21)	34	0.10
Native Hawaiian (2,601)	10,685	30.88
Samoan (251)	872	2.52
Tongan (66)	175	0.51
White (7,109)	15,434	44.61
Not Hispanic (6,549)	13,539	39.13
Hispanic (560)	1,895	5.48

Kaneohe Station

Place Type: CDP
County: Honolulu
Population: 9,517†

Ancestry‡	Population	%
African, Sub-Saharan (45)	45	0.44
African (45)	45	0.44
American (226)	226	2.22
Arab (9)	9	0.09
Syrian (9)	9	0.09
Austrian (33)	33	0.32
Belgian (11)	26	0.26
Brazilian (0)	39	0.38
British (29)	29	0.28
Czech (0)	11	0.11
Danish (0)	144	1.41
Dutch (45)	138	1.35
English (157)	667	6.54
European (0)	11	0.11
French, ex. Basque (60)	589	5.78
German (721)	2,219	21.77
Greek (0)	12	0.12
Hungarian (43)	75	0.74
Irish (615)	1,188	11.66
Italian (176)	781	7.66
Norwegian (33)	122	1.20
Polish (123)	333	3.27
Portuguese (9)	9	0.09
Russian (18)	83	0.81
Scandinavian (0)	12	0.12
Scotch-Irish (37)	107	1.05
Scottish (79)	405	3.97
Slovak (0)	23	0.23
Swedish (31)	132	1.30
Swiss (0)	29	0.28
Welsh (0)	25	0.25
West Indian, ex. Hispanic (24)	54	0.53
Belizean (0)	17	0.17
Jamaican (12)	12	0.12
Trinidadian/Tobagonian (0)	13	0.13
West Indian (12)	12	0.12

Hispanic Origin	Population	%
Hispanic or Latino (of any race)	1,890	19.86
Central American, ex. Mexican	106	1.11
Costa Rican	3	0.03
Guatemalan	23	0.24
Honduran	27	0.28
Nicaraguan	11	0.12
Panamanian	5	0.05
Salvadoran	34	0.36

*Notes: † The Census 2010 population figure is used to calculate the percentages in the Hispanic Origin and Race categories. Ancestry percentages are based on the 2006-2010 American Community Survey population (not shown); ‡ Numbers in parentheses indicate the number of people reporting a single ancestry; * Numbers in parentheses indicate the number of persons reporting this race alone, not in combination with any other race; Please refer to the Explanation of Data for more information.*

Other Central American	3	0.03
Cuban	36	0.38
Dominican Republic	30	0.32
Mexican	1,119	11.76
Puerto Rican	263	2.76
South American	110	1.16
Argentinean	5	0.05
Bolivian	5	0.05
Chilean	17	0.18
Colombian	58	0.61
Ecuadorian	11	0.12
Peruvian	11	0.12
Uruguayan	1	0.01
Venezuelan	2	0.02
Other Hispanic or Latino	226	2.37

Race*	Population	%
African-American/Black (699)	899	9.45
Not Hispanic (628)	779	8.19
Hispanic (71)	120	1.26
American Indian/Alaska Native (100)	216	2.27
Not Hispanic (80)	155	1.63
Hispanic (20)	61	0.64
Alaska Athabascan *(Ala. Nat.)* (3)	3	0.03
Aleut *(Alaska Native)* (1)	2	0.02
Apache (2)	4	0.04
Blackfeet (0)	6	0.06
Cherokee (3)	33	0.35
Chickasaw (1)	1	0.01
Chippewa (2)	2	0.02
Choctaw (5)	9	0.09
Creek (4)	10	0.11
Iroquois (2)	5	0.05
Kiowa (1)	1	0.01
Mexican American Ind. (3)	8	0.08
Navajo (14)	17	0.18
Potawatomi (2)	2	0.02
Pueblo (10)	10	0.11
Seminole (0)	1	0.01
Sioux (2)	6	0.06
South American Ind. (1)	1	0.01
Tlingit-Haida *(Alaska Native)* (0)	1	0.01
Tsimshian *(Alaska Native)* (0)	1	0.01
Yaqui (3)	4	0.04
Asian (370)	732	7.69
Not Hispanic (347)	634	6.66
Hispanic (23)	98	1.03
Cambodian (10)	15	0.16
Chinese, ex. Taiwanese (13)	89	0.94
Filipino (174)	339	3.56
Hmong (14)	14	0.15
Indian (8)	17	0.18
Indonesian (2)	9	0.09
Japanese (50)	169	1.78
Korean (27)	65	0.68
Laotian (7)	10	0.11
Nepalese (1)	1	0.01
Pakistani (0)	4	0.04
Taiwanese (1)	1	0.01
Thai (12)	16	0.17
Vietnamese (28)	53	0.56
Hawaii Native/Pacific Islander (68)	191	2.01
Not Hispanic (66)	150	1.58
Hispanic (2)	41	0.43
Guamanian/Chamorro (16)	30	0.32
Marshallese (1)	2	0.02
Native Hawaiian (20)	117	1.23
Samoan (14)	32	0.34
White (7,039)	7,651	80.39
Not Hispanic (6,008)	6,432	67.58
Hispanic (1,031)	1,219	12.81

Kapaa

Place Type: CDP
County: Kauai
Population: 10,699†

Ancestry‡	Population	%
American (50)	50	0.50
Austrian (0)	13	0.13
Czech (19)	19	0.19
Danish (0)	19	0.19
Dutch (0)	54	0.54
English (144)	491	4.88
European (41)	41	0.41
Finnish (10)	61	0.61
French, ex. Basque (0)	254	2.52
French Canadian (41)	52	0.52
German (300)	889	8.84
Irish (150)	456	4.53
Italian (113)	423	4.20
Maltese (30)	68	0.68
Northern European (72)	72	0.72
Norwegian (24)	63	0.63
Polish (16)	87	0.86
Portuguese (235)	581	5.78
Russian (12)	48	0.48
Scotch-Irish (42)	208	2.07
Scottish (109)	287	2.85
Slovak (20)	56	0.56
Swedish (0)	38	0.38
Swiss (0)	20	0.20
Ukrainian (0)	43	0.43
Welsh (26)	37	0.37
West Indian, ex. Hispanic (0)	39	0.39
Jamaican (0)	39	0.39

Hispanic Origin	Population	%
Hispanic or Latino (of any race)	1,215	11.36
Central American, ex. Mexican	18	0.17
Guatemalan	3	0.03
Honduran	4	0.04
Nicaraguan	1	0.01
Panamanian	4	0.04
Salvadoran	6	0.06
Cuban	10	0.09
Dominican Republic	1	0.01
Mexican	451	4.22
Puerto Rican	351	3.28
South American	27	0.25
Argentinean	1	0.01
Bolivian	1	0.01
Chilean	2	0.02
Colombian	10	0.09
Peruvian	8	0.07
Uruguayan	2	0.02
Venezuelan	3	0.03
Other Hispanic or Latino	357	3.34

Race*	Population	%
African-American/Black (46)	160	1.50
Not Hispanic (43)	129	1.21
Hispanic (3)	31	0.29
American Indian/Alaska Native (58)	457	4.27
Not Hispanic (31)	286	2.67
Hispanic (27)	171	1.60
Alaska Athabascan *(Ala. Nat.)* (0)	3	0.03
Aleut *(Alaska Native)* (0)	1	0.01
Apache (2)	26	0.24
Blackfeet (4)	18	0.17
Canadian/French Am. Ind. (0)	1	0.01
Central American Ind. (0)	1	0.01
Cherokee (8)	110	1.03
Chippewa (2)	2	0.02
Choctaw (1)	2	0.02
Comanche (1)	3	0.03
Cree (1)	1	0.01
Creek (0)	1	0.01
Crow (0)	2	0.02
Hopi (0)	3	0.03
Inupiat *(Alaska Native)* (1)	4	0.04
Iroquois (1)	5	0.05
Mexican American Ind. (5)	8	0.07
Navajo (0)	6	0.06
Paiute (0)	1	0.01
Pima (0)	1	0.01
Potawatomi (1)	2	0.02
Pueblo (0)	1	0.01
Puget Sound Salish (1)	4	0.04
Seminole (0)	3	0.03
Sioux (2)	12	0.11
South American Ind. (1)	4	0.04
Spanish American Ind. (0)	1	0.01
Yaqui (2)	7	0.07
Yuman (0)	17	0.16
Asian (2,906)	5,274	49.29
Not Hispanic (2,800)	4,755	44.44
Hispanic (106)	519	4.85
Cambodian (1)	1	0.01
Chinese, ex. Taiwanese (111)	1,101	10.29
Filipino (1,680)	3,276	30.62
Indian (20)	37	0.35
Indonesian (0)	9	0.08
Japanese (804)	1,862	17.40
Korean (25)	90	0.84
Laotian (5)	5	0.05
Sri Lankan (1)	1	0.01
Thai (16)	21	0.20
Vietnamese (4)	22	0.21
Hawaii Native/Pacific Islander (968)	3,112	29.09
Not Hispanic (894)	2,598	24.28
Hispanic (74)	514	4.80
Fijian (7)	7	0.07
Guamanian/Chamorro (9)	72	0.67
Marshallese (12)	22	0.21
Native Hawaiian (760)	2,817	26.33
Samoan (20)	84	0.79
Tongan (82)	110	1.03
White (3,509)	5,770	53.93
Not Hispanic (3,263)	5,061	47.30
Hispanic (246)	709	6.63

Kapolei

Place Type: CDP
County: Honolulu
Population: 15,186†

Ancestry‡	Population	%
American (94)	94	0.78
British (15)	15	0.12
Canadian (15)	15	0.12
Croatian (0)	33	0.27
Danish (0)	49	0.41
Dutch (0)	62	0.51
English (65)	477	3.96
European (115)	115	0.95
Finnish (0)	12	0.10
French, ex. Basque (47)	58	0.48
French Canadian (0)	12	0.10
German (33)	492	4.09
Hungarian (0)	13	0.11
Irish (130)	618	5.13
Italian (86)	172	1.43
Norwegian (86)	176	1.46
Polish (10)	75	0.62
Portuguese (39)	425	3.53
Russian (38)	53	0.44
Scotch-Irish (11)	65	0.54
Scottish (41)	78	0.65
Serbian (0)	32	0.27
Swedish (2)	6	0.05
Swiss (0)	9	0.07
Welsh (10)	10	0.08

Hispanic Origin	Population	%
Hispanic or Latino (of any race)	1,708	11.25
Central American, ex. Mexican	29	0.19
Costa Rican	1	0.01
Guatemalan	5	0.03
Honduran	7	0.05
Nicaraguan	2	0.01
Panamanian	6	0.04
Salvadoran	8	0.05
Cuban	15	0.10
Dominican Republic	13	0.09
Mexican	395	2.60
Puerto Rican	691	4.55
South American	29	0.19

*Notes: † The Census 2010 population figure is used to calculate the percentages in the Hispanic Origin and Race categories. Ancestry percentages are based on the 2006-2010 American Community Survey population (not shown); ‡ Numbers in parentheses indicate the number of people reporting a single ancestry; * Numbers in parentheses indicate the number of persons reporting this race alone, not in combination with any other race; Please refer to the Explanation of Data for more information.*

Argentinean	2	0.01
Bolivian	3	0.02
Colombian	7	0.05
Peruvian	6	0.04
Venezuelan	6	0.04
Other South American	5	0.03
Other Hispanic or Latino	536	3.53

Race*	Population	%
African-American/Black (275)	584	3.85
Not Hispanic (267)	491	3.23
Hispanic (8)	93	0.61
American Indian/Alaska Native (23)	425	2.80
Not Hispanic (8)	290	1.91
Hispanic (15)	135	0.89
Apache (0)	6	0.04
Arapaho (0)	4	0.03
Blackfeet (0)	15	0.10
Canadian/French Am. Ind. (0)	4	0.03
Cherokee (6)	125	0.82
Chippewa (0)	1	0.01
Choctaw (0)	2	0.01
Comanche (0)	2	0.01
Delaware (1)	1	0.01
Hopi (0)	1	0.01
Inupiat *(Alaska Native)* (1)	4	0.03
Iroquois (0)	9	0.06
Mexican American Ind. (0)	1	0.01
Navajo (0)	7	0.05
Osage (0)	1	0.01
Pueblo (1)	1	0.01
Puget Sound Salish (0)	1	0.01
Seminole (0)	2	0.01
Shoshone (0)	8	0.05
Sioux (0)	4	0.03
Yaqui (0)	2	0.01
Asian (5,222)	9,540	62.82
Not Hispanic (5,031)	8,567	56.41
Hispanic (191)	973	6.41
Burmese (0)	1	0.01
Cambodian (2)	3	0.02
Chinese, ex. Taiwanese (324)	2,833	18.66
Filipino (2,998)	5,663	37.29
Hmong (4)	4	0.03
Indian (7)	37	0.24
Indonesian (3)	8	0.05
Japanese (965)	2,706	17.82
Korean (156)	556	3.66
Laotian (82)	97	0.64
Malaysian (0)	3	0.02
Nepalese (2)	2	0.01
Sri Lankan (1)	1	0.01
Taiwanese (5)	6	0.04
Thai (19)	40	0.26
Vietnamese (71)	131	0.86
Hawaii Native/Pacific Islander (2,220)	6,396	42.12
Not Hispanic (2,081)	5,476	36.06
Hispanic (139)	920	6.06
Fijian (1)	13	0.09
Guamanian/Chamorro (79)	182	1.20
Marshallese (4)	8	0.05
Native Hawaiian (1,651)	5,673	37.36
Samoan (319)	755	4.97
Tongan (9)	34	0.22
White (1,969)	5,578	36.73
Not Hispanic (1,767)	4,729	31.14
Hispanic (202)	849	5.59

Kihei

Place Type: CDP
County: Maui
Population: 20,881†

Ancestry‡	Population	%
African, Sub-Saharan (21)	42	0.21
African (21)	42	0.21
Albanian (0)	15	0.08
American (230)	230	1.16
Arab (0)	21	0.11
Arab (0)	21	0.11
Australian (0)	11	0.06
Austrian (40)	52	0.26
Belgian (44)	44	0.22
Brazilian (0)	15	0.08
British (54)	115	0.58
Canadian (44)	44	0.22
Croatian (0)	17	0.09
Czech (9)	73	0.37
Danish (27)	91	0.46
Dutch (53)	463	2.33
Eastern European (12)	12	0.06
English (552)	1,746	8.79
Estonian (0)	32	0.16
European (40)	105	0.53
Finnish (69)	98	0.49
French, ex. Basque (176)	578	2.91
French Canadian (89)	291	1.47
German (741)	2,612	13.16
Greek (37)	93	0.47
Hungarian (44)	59	0.30
Iranian (16)	16	0.08
Irish (529)	1,915	9.64
Italian (505)	1,232	6.20
Northern European (11)	11	0.06
Norwegian (117)	211	1.06
Polish (77)	287	1.45
Portuguese (138)	626	3.15
Russian (48)	110	0.55
Scandinavian (79)	79	0.40
Scotch-Irish (112)	478	2.41
Scottish (110)	469	2.36
Slovak (16)	30	0.15
Slovene (21)	21	0.11
Swedish (88)	182	0.92
Swiss (0)	31	0.16
Welsh (32)	410	2.06
West Indian, ex. Hispanic (62)	62	0.31
Jamaican (62)	62	0.31
Yugoslavian (25)	37	0.19

Hispanic Origin	Population	%
Hispanic or Latino (of any race)	2,198	10.53
Central American, ex. Mexican	70	0.34
Costa Rican	19	0.09
Guatemalan	15	0.07
Honduran	10	0.05
Nicaraguan	8	0.04
Panamanian	1	<0.01
Salvadoran	15	0.07
Other Central American	2	0.01
Cuban	30	0.14
Dominican Republic	2	0.01
Mexican	1,168	5.59
Puerto Rican	420	2.01
South American	120	0.57
Argentinean	51	0.24
Bolivian	2	0.01
Chilean	9	0.04
Colombian	21	0.10
Ecuadorian	2	0.01
Paraguayan	1	<0.01
Peruvian	28	0.13
Uruguayan	1	<0.01
Venezuelan	5	0.02
Other Hispanic or Latino	388	1.86

Race*	Population	%
African-American/Black (244)	473	2.27
Not Hispanic (227)	421	2.02
Hispanic (17)	52	0.25
American Indian/Alaska Native (134)	609	2.92
Not Hispanic (96)	460	2.20
Hispanic (38)	149	0.71
Alaska Athabascan *(Ala. Nat.)* (1)	1	<0.01
Apache (0)	12	0.06
Blackfeet (3)	23	0.11
Cherokee (12)	110	0.53
Chickasaw (3)	4	0.02
Chippewa (4)	8	0.04
Choctaw (2)	21	0.10
Colville (1)	4	0.02
Comanche (1)	3	0.01
Cree (0)	3	0.01
Creek (0)	6	0.03
Crow (0)	1	<0.01
Delaware (2)	7	0.03
Hopi (0)	1	<0.01
Inupiat *(Alaska Native)* (4)	5	0.02
Iroquois (0)	9	0.04
Mexican American Ind. (12)	19	0.09
Navajo (4)	12	0.06
Paiute (1)	1	<0.01
Pueblo (1)	1	<0.01
Puget Sound Salish (0)	2	0.01
Shoshone (0)	7	0.03
Sioux (3)	14	0.07
South American Ind. (0)	3	0.01
Tsimshian *(Alaska Native)* (0)	3	0.01
Ute (0)	2	0.01
Yakama (1)	5	0.02
Yaqui (1)	3	0.01
Asian (4,533)	6,913	33.11
Not Hispanic (4,406)	6,404	30.67
Hispanic (127)	509	2.44
Burmese (8)	11	0.05
Cambodian (4)	6	0.03
Chinese, ex. Taiwanese (114)	1,116	5.34
Filipino (3,326)	4,927	23.60
Hmong (1)	1	<0.01
Indian (26)	63	0.30
Indonesian (5)	12	0.06
Japanese (585)	1,479	7.08
Korean (62)	239	1.14
Laotian (18)	25	0.12
Malaysian (0)	12	0.06
Nepalese (2)	2	0.01
Pakistani (0)	2	0.01
Sri Lankan (2)	2	0.01
Taiwanese (2)	3	0.01
Thai (30)	41	0.20
Vietnamese (61)	79	0.38
Hawaii Native/Pacific Islander (1,359)	3,343	16.01
Not Hispanic (1,275)	2,968	14.21
Hispanic (84)	375	1.80
Fijian (3)	6	0.03
Guamanian/Chamorro (60)	94	0.45
Marshallese (40)	45	0.22
Native Hawaiian (617)	2,485	11.90
Samoan (115)	222	1.06
Tongan (339)	437	2.09
White (10,582)	13,069	62.59
Not Hispanic (9,836)	11,906	57.02
Hispanic (746)	1,163	5.57

Lahaina

Place Type: CDP
County: Maui
Population: 11,704†

Ancestry‡	Population	%
African, Sub-Saharan (38)	38	0.36
Somalian (38)	38	0.36
American (40)	40	0.37
Belgian (22)	22	0.21
Croatian (14)	14	0.13
Czech (0)	43	0.40
Czechoslovakian (0)	8	0.07
Danish (28)	28	0.26
Dutch (42)	76	0.71
Eastern European (23)	23	0.22
English (31)	565	5.29
European (38)	38	0.36
French, ex. Basque (31)	430	4.03
French Canadian (0)	11	0.10
German (118)	681	6.38
Hungarian (0)	55	0.52
Irish (88)	445	4.17
Italian (121)	339	3.17

*Notes: † The Census 2010 population figure is used to calculate the percentages in the Hispanic Origin and Race categories. Ancestry percentages are based on the 2006-2010 American Community Survey population (not shown); ‡ Numbers in parentheses indicate the number of people reporting a single ancestry; * Numbers in parentheses indicate the number of persons reporting this race alone, not in combination with any other race; Please refer to the Explanation of Data for more information.*

New Zealander (11)	11	0.10
Norwegian (54)	93	0.87
Polish (12)	29	0.27
Portuguese (101)	380	3.56
Russian (0)	41	0.38
Scotch-Irish (24)	87	0.81
Scottish (0)	122	1.14
Serbian (10)	10	0.09
Swedish (0)	111	1.04
Welsh (19)	76	0.71
West Indian, ex. Hispanic (0)	18	0.17
West Indian (0)	18	0.17

Hispanic Origin	Population	%
Hispanic or Latino (of any race)	1,345	11.49
Central American, ex. Mexican	11	0.09
Costa Rican	5	0.04
Guatemalan	1	0.01
Honduran	1	0.01
Salvadoran	3	0.03
Other Central American	1	0.01
Cuban	7	0.06
Dominican Republic	8	0.07
Mexican	983	8.40
Puerto Rican	173	1.48
South American	23	0.20
Argentinean	7	0.06
Chilean	1	0.01
Colombian	7	0.06
Peruvian	2	0.02
Venezuelan	6	0.05
Other Hispanic or Latino	140	1.20

Race*	Population	%
African-American/Black (62)	134	1.14
Not Hispanic (60)	116	0.99
Hispanic (2)	18	0.15
American Indian/Alaska Native (37)	239	2.04
Not Hispanic (20)	176	1.50
Hispanic (17)	63	0.54
Aleut *(Alaska Native)* (0)	1	0.01
Apache (3)	8	0.07
Arapaho (0)	2	0.02
Blackfeet (0)	9	0.08
Canadian/French Am. Ind. (1)	2	0.02
Central American Ind. (0)	1	0.01
Cherokee (3)	47	0.40
Cheyenne (0)	2	0.02
Chickasaw (0)	3	0.03
Chippewa (0)	5	0.04
Choctaw (0)	5	0.04
Cree (1)	1	0.01
Creek (0)	6	0.05
Delaware (1)	1	0.01
Hopi (0)	2	0.02
Iroquois (0)	3	0.03
Menominee (0)	4	0.03
Mexican American Ind. (8)	13	0.11
Navajo (1)	4	0.03
Osage (0)	1	0.01
Ottawa (1)	1	0.01
Seminole (2)	3	0.03
Shoshone (1)	1	0.01
Sioux (0)	6	0.05
South American Ind. (0)	2	0.02
Spanish American Ind. (1)	1	0.01
Tlingit-Haida *(Alaska Native)* (0)	1	0.01
Ute (0)	2	0.02
Yaqui (0)	4	0.03
Yuman (0)	2	0.02
Asian (4,627)	6,342	54.19
Not Hispanic (4,578)	6,062	51.79
Hispanic (49)	280	2.39
Burmese (0)	1	0.01
Cambodian (0)	2	0.02
Chinese, ex. Taiwanese (36)	705	6.02
Filipino (3,571)	4,760	40.67
Indian (7)	28	0.24
Indonesian (4)	10	0.09
Japanese (634)	1,296	11.07
Korean (46)	146	1.25
Laotian (2)	7	0.06
Thai (10)	25	0.21
Vietnamese (133)	156	1.33
Hawaii Native/Pacific Islander (1,103)	2,611	22.31
Not Hispanic (1,081)	2,401	20.51
Hispanic (22)	210	1.79
Fijian (3)	4	0.03
Guamanian/Chamorro (2)	13	0.11
Marshallese (11)	15	0.13
Native Hawaiian (703)	2,146	18.34
Samoan (44)	130	1.11
Tongan (232)	328	2.80
White (3,182)	4,581	39.14
Not Hispanic (2,742)	3,917	33.47
Hispanic (440)	664	5.67

Maili

Place Type: CDP
County: Honolulu
Population: 9,488†

Ancestry‡	Population	%
American (123)	123	1.53
Australian (0)	24	0.30
Austrian (37)	84	1.04
Czech (0)	27	0.33
Danish (13)	13	0.16
Dutch (13)	68	0.84
English (0)	105	1.30
Finnish (11)	11	0.14
German (10)	320	3.97
Irish (14)	448	5.55
Italian (31)	78	0.97
Portuguese (75)	865	10.73
Russian (16)	57	0.71
Scotch-Irish (0)	16	0.20
Scottish (0)	41	0.51
Swedish (0)	19	0.24
West Indian, ex. Hispanic (56)	103	1.28
Jamaican (56)	103	1.28

Hispanic Origin	Population	%
Hispanic or Latino (of any race)	1,676	17.66
Central American, ex. Mexican	17	0.18
Costa Rican	1	0.01
Honduran	1	0.01
Panamanian	6	0.06
Salvadoran	9	0.09
Cuban	24	0.25
Dominican Republic	4	0.04
Mexican	316	3.33
Puerto Rican	850	8.96
South American	12	0.13
Argentinean	2	0.02
Colombian	1	0.01
Ecuadorian	2	0.02
Peruvian	1	0.01
Venezuelan	6	0.06
Other Hispanic or Latino	453	4.77

Race*	Population	%
African-American/Black (218)	527	5.55
Not Hispanic (202)	435	4.58
Hispanic (16)	92	0.97
American Indian/Alaska Native (23)	328	3.46
Not Hispanic (16)	191	2.01
Hispanic (7)	137	1.44
Alaska Athabascan *(Ala. Nat.)* (0)	2	0.02
Aleut *(Alaska Native)* (0)	3	0.03
Apache (1)	17	0.18
Blackfeet (0)	6	0.06
Canadian/French Am. Ind. (0)	2	0.02
Central American Ind. (0)	5	0.05
Cherokee (0)	65	0.69
Cheyenne (0)	1	0.01
Chickasaw (1)	1	0.01
Chippewa (1)	1	0.01
Choctaw (0)	4	0.04
Crow (0)	6	0.06
Iroquois (2)	9	0.09
Menominee (1)	9	0.09
Mexican American Ind. (3)	6	0.06
Navajo (0)	6	0.06
Sioux (0)	5	0.05
South American Ind. (0)	7	0.07
Yaqui (0)	2	0.02
Yup'ik *(Alaska Native)* (3)	5	0.05
Asian (1,685)	4,766	50.23
Not Hispanic (1,530)	3,824	40.30
Hispanic (155)	942	9.93
Chinese, ex. Taiwanese (72)	1,695	17.86
Filipino (1,180)	3,219	33.93
Indian (2)	15	0.16
Japanese (211)	1,046	11.02
Korean (29)	225	2.37
Laotian (14)	22	0.23
Malaysian (2)	3	0.03
Taiwanese (3)	3	0.03
Thai (8)	16	0.17
Vietnamese (7)	11	0.12
Hawaii Native/Pacific Islander (2,110)	5,441	57.35
Not Hispanic (1,914)	4,483	47.25
Hispanic (196)	958	10.10
Fijian (0)	8	0.08
Guamanian/Chamorro (30)	75	0.79
Marshallese (9)	15	0.16
Native Hawaiian (1,406)	4,616	48.65
Samoan (415)	917	9.66
Tongan (18)	56	0.59
White (1,377)	3,906	41.17
Not Hispanic (1,161)	3,009	31.71
Hispanic (216)	897	9.45

Makaha

Place Type: CDP
County: Honolulu
Population: 8,278†

Ancestry‡	Population	%
African, Sub-Saharan (0)	8	0.10
African (0)	8	0.10
American (9)	9	0.12
Armenian (10)	10	0.13
Austrian (0)	77	1.00
British (0)	10	0.13
Czech (0)	77	1.00
Danish (0)	20	0.26
Dutch (0)	39	0.51
English (28)	382	4.95
Finnish (9)	9	0.12
French, ex. Basque (9)	92	1.19
French Canadian (0)	8	0.10
German (80)	546	7.08
Hungarian (0)	22	0.29
Irish (22)	413	5.35
Italian (9)	47	0.61
Norwegian (0)	35	0.45
Polish (8)	19	0.25
Portuguese (65)	1,047	13.57
Romanian (11)	11	0.14
Russian (0)	11	0.14
Scotch-Irish (0)	45	0.58
Scottish (10)	10	0.13
Swedish (17)	94	1.22
Swiss (12)	12	0.16
Welsh (28)	28	0.36

Hispanic Origin	Population	%
Hispanic or Latino (of any race)	1,525	18.42
Central American, ex. Mexican	27	0.33
Costa Rican	2	0.02
Guatemalan	5	0.06
Honduran	8	0.10
Nicaraguan	4	0.05
Panamanian	6	0.07
Salvadoran	2	0.02
Cuban	8	0.10

*Notes: † The Census 2010 population figure is used to calculate the percentages in the Hispanic Origin and Race categories. Ancestry percentages are based on the 2006-2010 American Community Survey population (not shown); ‡ Numbers in parentheses indicate the number of people reporting a single ancestry; * Numbers in parentheses indicate the number of persons reporting this race alone, not in combination with any other race; Please refer to the Explanation of Data for more information.*

Dominican Republic	1	0.01
Mexican	210	2.54
Puerto Rican	905	10.93
South American	8	0.10
Colombian	1	0.01
Ecuadorian	1	0.01
Peruvian	6	0.07
Other Hispanic or Latino	366	4.42

Race*	Population	%
African-American/Black (112)	359	4.34
Not Hispanic (99)	291	3.52
Hispanic (13)	68	0.82
American Indian/Alaska Native (35)	385	4.65
Not Hispanic (24)	229	2.77
Hispanic (11)	156	1.88
Apache (1)	12	0.14
Blackfeet (2)	7	0.08
Central American Ind. (0)	1	0.01
Cherokee (4)	121	1.46
Chippewa (1)	6	0.07
Choctaw (0)	4	0.05
Creek (0)	3	0.04
Crow (0)	1	0.01
Delaware (1)	1	0.01
Inupiat *(Alaska Native)* (0)	3	0.04
Iroquois (0)	3	0.04
Mexican American Ind. (3)	9	0.11
Navajo (0)	3	0.04
Ottawa (0)	4	0.05
Pima (2)	6	0.07
Potawatomi (0)	1	0.01
Seminole (0)	2	0.02
Shoshone (0)	5	0.06
Sioux (1)	15	0.18
South American Ind. (0)	5	0.06
Spanish American Ind. (0)	3	0.04
Asian (1,033)	3,671	44.35
Not Hispanic (910)	2,884	34.84
Hispanic (123)	787	9.51
Cambodian (2)	2	0.02
Chinese, ex. Taiwanese (36)	1,467	17.72
Filipino (593)	2,285	27.60
Indian (3)	21	0.25
Indonesian (0)	4	0.05
Japanese (189)	940	11.36
Korean (27)	157	1.90
Laotian (0)	2	0.02
Nepalese (0)	2	0.02
Pakistani (1)	1	0.01
Taiwanese (2)	3	0.04
Thai (4)	20	0.24
Vietnamese (14)	22	0.27
Hawaii Native/Pacific Islander (1,986)	4,982	60.18
Not Hispanic (1,748)	3,993	48.24
Hispanic (238)	989	11.95
Guamanian/Chamorro (8)	54	0.65
Marshallese (51)	54	0.65
Native Hawaiian (1,462)	4,393	53.07
Samoan (293)	630	7.61
Tongan (42)	76	0.92
White (1,474)	3,873	46.79
Not Hispanic (1,308)	3,081	37.22
Hispanic (166)	792	9.57

Makakilo

Place Type: CDP
County: Honolulu
Population: 18,248†

Ancestry‡	Population	%
American (328)	328	1.92
Arab (92)	103	0.60
Egyptian (92)	92	0.54
Moroccan (0)	11	0.06
Armenian (25)	34	0.20
Australian (12)	12	0.07
Austrian (0)	13	0.08
Belgian (0)	26	0.15
British (29)	48	0.28
Bulgarian (11)	11	0.06
Canadian (38)	113	0.66
Croatian (13)	26	0.15
Czech (12)	12	0.07
Danish (0)	16	0.09
Dutch (24)	208	1.22
Eastern European (3)	3	0.02
English (113)	586	3.42
European (59)	59	0.34
Finnish (0)	2	0.01
French, ex. Basque (22)	265	1.55
French Canadian (0)	29	0.17
German (302)	1,125	6.57
Greek (28)	28	0.16
Irish (171)	893	5.22
Italian (152)	363	2.12
Lithuanian (0)	14	0.08
New Zealander (0)	17	0.10
Northern European (0)	26	0.15
Norwegian (8)	87	0.51
Pennsylvania German (9)	9	0.05
Polish (16)	284	1.66
Portuguese (178)	571	3.34
Russian (0)	25	0.15
Scandinavian (8)	8	0.05
Scotch-Irish (0)	80	0.47
Scottish (15)	149	0.87
Slovene (0)	13	0.08
Swedish (41)	203	1.19
Swiss (0)	63	0.37
Ukrainian (17)	34	0.20
Welsh (0)	12	0.07
West Indian, ex. Hispanic (315)	341	1.99
Dutch West Indian (0)	26	0.15
Haitian (282)	282	1.65
Other West Indian (33)	33	0.19
Yugoslavian (0)	18	0.11

Hispanic Origin	Population	%
Hispanic or Latino (of any race)	2,424	13.28
Central American, ex. Mexican	54	0.30
Costa Rican	2	0.01
Guatemalan	12	0.07
Honduran	12	0.07
Nicaraguan	3	0.02
Panamanian	15	0.08
Salvadoran	10	0.05
Cuban	29	0.16
Dominican Republic	17	0.09
Mexican	505	2.77
Puerto Rican	990	5.43
South American	84	0.46
Argentinean	2	0.01
Bolivian	6	0.03
Chilean	20	0.11
Colombian	17	0.09
Ecuadorian	12	0.07
Peruvian	13	0.07
Uruguayan	3	0.02
Venezuelan	11	0.06
Other Hispanic or Latino	745	4.08

Race*	Population	%
African-American/Black (535)	1,000	5.48
Not Hispanic (494)	866	4.75
Hispanic (41)	134	0.73
American Indian/Alaska Native (33)	518	2.84
Not Hispanic (21)	318	1.74
Hispanic (12)	200	1.10
Apache (0)	19	0.10
Arapaho (0)	4	0.02
Blackfeet (3)	40	0.22
Canadian/French Am. Ind. (2)	5	0.03
Cherokee (1)	131	0.72
Chickasaw (0)	2	0.01
Chippewa (0)	2	0.01
Choctaw (0)	11	0.06
Comanche (0)	1	0.01
Creek (0)	1	0.01
Iroquois (0)	2	0.01
Lumbee (1)	4	0.02
Mexican American Ind. (2)	3	0.02
Navajo (3)	7	0.04
Osage (0)	1	0.01
Ottawa (0)	1	0.01
Pima (2)	4	0.02
Potawatomi (0)	2	0.01
Pueblo (0)	10	0.05
Seminole (1)	2	0.01
Shoshone (0)	4	0.02
Sioux (6)	15	0.08
South American Ind. (0)	4	0.02
Spanish American Ind. (1)	1	0.01
Tlingit-Haida *(Alaska Native)* (1)	3	0.02
Ute (0)	7	0.04
Yaqui (1)	1	0.01
Asian (5,587)	10,511	57.60
Not Hispanic (5,278)	9,150	50.14
Hispanic (309)	1,361	7.46
Bangladeshi (1)	1	0.01
Burmese (2)	3	0.02
Cambodian (5)	8	0.04
Chinese, ex. Taiwanese (267)	2,960	16.22
Filipino (3,227)	6,454	35.37
Indian (14)	75	0.41
Indonesian (4)	12	0.07
Japanese (1,066)	3,110	17.04
Korean (212)	677	3.71
Laotian (16)	32	0.18
Malaysian (0)	3	0.02
Pakistani (0)	7	0.04
Sri Lankan (4)	4	0.02
Taiwanese (7)	8	0.04
Thai (38)	70	0.38
Vietnamese (50)	88	0.48
Hawaii Native/Pacific Islander (1,563)	5,581	30.58
Not Hispanic (1,403)	4,551	24.94
Hispanic (160)	1,030	5.64
Fijian (1)	16	0.09
Guamanian/Chamorro (75)	208	1.14
Marshallese (28)	32	0.18
Native Hawaiian (902)	4,616	25.30
Samoan (352)	976	5.35
Tongan (32)	87	0.48
White (4,352)	8,741	47.90
Not Hispanic (3,904)	7,406	40.59
Hispanic (448)	1,335	7.32

Mililani Mauka

Place Type: CDP
County: Honolulu
Population: 21,039†

Ancestry‡	Population	%
American (143)	143	0.69
Arab (0)	26	0.13
Lebanese (0)	13	0.06
Palestinian (0)	13	0.06
Australian (0)	62	0.30
Austrian (0)	19	0.09
British (0)	45	0.22
Canadian (10)	10	0.05
Celtic (0)	23	0.11
Czech (0)	8	0.04
Danish (76)	76	0.37
Dutch (0)	144	0.69
English (58)	610	2.93
European (46)	111	0.53
French, ex. Basque (26)	346	1.66
French Canadian (0)	22	0.11
German (189)	1,118	5.38
Greek (0)	8	0.04
Hungarian (12)	210	1.01
Irish (182)	651	3.13
Italian (102)	384	1.85
Northern European (30)	30	0.14
Norwegian (41)	149	0.72
Polish (81)	233	1.12

*Notes: † The Census 2010 population figure is used to calculate the percentages in the Hispanic Origin and Race categories. Ancestry percentages are based on the 2006-2010 American Community Survey population (not shown); ‡ Numbers in parentheses indicate the number of people reporting a single ancestry; * Numbers in parentheses indicate the number of persons reporting this race alone, not in combination with any other race; Please refer to the Explanation of Data for more information.*

Portuguese (73)	507	2.44
Russian (0)	49	0.24
Scandinavian (28)	140	0.67
Scotch-Irish (51)	209	1.00
Scottish (57)	103	0.50
Slavic (0)	7	0.03
Swedish (66)	246	1.18
Swiss (0)	33	0.16
West Indian, ex. Hispanic (0)	97	0.47
Jamaican (0)	97	0.47

Hispanic Origin	Population	%
Hispanic or Latino (of any race)	1,674	7.96
Central American, ex. Mexican	63	0.30
Costa Rican	1	<0.01
Guatemalan	3	0.01
Honduran	4	0.02
Nicaraguan	10	0.05
Panamanian	26	0.12
Salvadoran	19	0.09
Cuban	21	0.10
Dominican Republic	13	0.06
Mexican	493	2.34
Puerto Rican	556	2.64
South American	47	0.22
Argentinean	3	0.01
Chilean	1	<0.01
Colombian	24	0.11
Ecuadorian	5	0.02
Peruvian	11	0.05
Venezuelan	3	0.01
Other Hispanic or Latino	481	2.29

Race*	Population	%
African-American/Black (493)	715	3.40
Not Hispanic (471)	646	3.07
Hispanic (22)	69	0.33
American Indian/Alaska Native (46)	431	2.05
Not Hispanic (24)	285	1.35
Hispanic (22)	146	0.69
Apache (3)	22	0.10
Blackfeet (1)	21	0.10
Cherokee (3)	104	0.49
Chippewa (0)	3	0.01
Choctaw (0)	11	0.05
Colville (1)	1	<0.01
Comanche (0)	2	0.01
Creek (0)	2	0.01
Crow (1)	6	0.03
Inupiat *(Alaska Native)* (2)	2	0.01
Iroquois (0)	4	0.02
Kiowa (5)	5	0.02
Mexican American Ind. (0)	2	0.01
Navajo (10)	26	0.12
Potawatomi (1)	6	0.03
Pueblo (0)	4	0.02
Seminole (0)	3	0.01
Sioux (2)	6	0.03
South American Ind. (1)	13	0.06
Spanish American Ind. (1)	1	<0.01
Ute (1)	2	0.01
Yaqui (0)	3	0.01
Asian (10,587)	15,389	73.15
Not Hispanic (10,330)	14,506	68.95
Hispanic (257)	883	4.20
Burmese (4)	4	0.02
Cambodian (1)	4	0.02
Chinese, ex. Taiwanese (649)	3,677	17.48
Filipino (2,310)	5,230	24.86
Hmong (4)	4	0.02
Indian (32)	64	0.30
Indonesian (5)	19	0.09
Japanese (5,189)	9,047	43.00
Korean (442)	1,332	6.33
Laotian (17)	31	0.15
Malaysian (0)	3	0.01
Nepalese (0)	1	<0.01
Pakistani (6)	9	0.04
Sri Lankan (8)	8	0.04
Taiwanese (15)	24	0.11
Thai (37)	92	0.44
Vietnamese (64)	135	0.64
Hawaii Native/Pacific Islander (650)	3,587	17.05
Not Hispanic (616)	3,151	14.98
Hispanic (34)	436	2.07
Fijian (1)	5	0.02
Guamanian/Chamorro (54)	136	0.65
Marshallese (1)	4	0.02
Native Hawaiian (471)	3,256	15.48
Samoan (86)	223	1.06
Tongan (5)	13	0.06
White (3,659)	7,847	37.30
Not Hispanic (3,292)	6,891	32.75
Hispanic (367)	956	4.54

Mililani Town

Place Type: CDP
County: Honolulu
Population: 27,629†

Ancestry‡	Population	%
African, Sub-Saharan (25)	25	0.08
Ghanaian (13)	13	0.04
Other Sub-Saharan African (12)	12	0.04
American (67)	67	0.23
Austrian (0)	12	0.04
Basque (0)	63	0.21
Belgian (0)	13	0.04
British (43)	50	0.17
Canadian (22)	30	0.10
Czech (11)	35	0.12
Czechoslovakian (25)	25	0.08
Danish (13)	52	0.18
Dutch (40)	270	0.91
Eastern European (14)	29	0.10
English (228)	989	3.35
European (125)	151	0.51
Finnish (13)	24	0.08
French, ex. Basque (116)	653	2.21
French Canadian (57)	111	0.38
German (305)	1,612	5.46
Greek (9)	51	0.17
Hungarian (0)	58	0.20
Irish (192)	1,047	3.54
Italian (85)	497	1.68
Northern European (34)	34	0.12
Norwegian (58)	144	0.49
Polish (72)	269	0.91
Portuguese (134)	640	2.17
Russian (14)	51	0.17
Scandinavian (55)	55	0.19
Scotch-Irish (105)	284	0.96
Scottish (57)	293	0.99
Swedish (58)	169	0.57
Swiss (0)	17	0.06
Turkish (14)	62	0.21
Ukrainian (0)	18	0.06
Welsh (8)	38	0.13
Yugoslavian (0)	14	0.05

Hispanic Origin	Population	%
Hispanic or Latino (of any race)	2,559	9.26
Central American, ex. Mexican	46	0.17
Costa Rican	5	0.02
Guatemalan	3	0.01
Honduran	5	0.02
Nicaraguan	4	0.01
Panamanian	22	0.08
Salvadoran	7	0.03
Cuban	29	0.10
Dominican Republic	13	0.05
Mexican	621	2.25
Puerto Rican	926	3.35
South American	43	0.16
Argentinean	1	<0.01
Bolivian	4	0.01
Chilean	7	0.03
Colombian	9	0.03
Ecuadorian	5	0.02
Peruvian	10	0.04
Venezuelan	5	0.02
Other South American	2	0.01
Other Hispanic or Latino	881	3.19

Race*	Population	%
African-American/Black (566)	1,021	3.70
Not Hispanic (537)	883	3.20
Hispanic (29)	138	0.50
American Indian/Alaska Native (79)	701	2.54
Not Hispanic (54)	448	1.62
Hispanic (25)	253	0.92
Aleut *(Alaska Native)* (0)	5	0.02
Apache (5)	34	0.12
Blackfeet (3)	25	0.09
Cherokee (14)	196	0.71
Cheyenne (0)	3	0.01
Chickasaw (0)	1	<0.01
Chippewa (2)	9	0.03
Choctaw (2)	34	0.12
Comanche (0)	2	0.01
Creek (0)	1	<0.01
Crow (0)	2	0.01
Inupiat *(Alaska Native)* (0)	1	<0.01
Iroquois (2)	9	0.03
Kiowa (0)	1	<0.01
Mexican American Ind. (0)	3	0.01
Navajo (3)	6	0.02
Osage (0)	1	<0.01
Pueblo (1)	3	0.01
Puget Sound Salish (0)	1	<0.01
Seminole (4)	8	0.03
Sioux (1)	15	0.05
South American Ind. (3)	7	0.03
Spanish American Ind. (8)	9	0.03
Tlingit-Haida *(Alaska Native)* (0)	5	0.02
Tohono O'Odham (1)	1	<0.01
Yaqui (0)	1	<0.01
Yuman (0)	1	<0.01
Asian (12,761)	19,609	70.97
Not Hispanic (12,418)	18,075	65.42
Hispanic (343)	1,534	5.55
Bangladeshi (2)	2	0.01
Burmese (4)	5	0.02
Cambodian (3)	6	0.02
Chinese, ex. Taiwanese (769)	4,658	16.86
Filipino (3,139)	7,372	26.68
Indian (44)	85	0.31
Indonesian (4)	18	0.07
Japanese (6,415)	10,648	38.54
Korean (540)	1,457	5.27
Laotian (32)	51	0.18
Malaysian (1)	12	0.04
Pakistani (2)	11	0.04
Sri Lankan (4)	4	0.01
Taiwanese (19)	19	0.07
Thai (51)	118	0.43
Vietnamese (72)	132	0.48
Hawaii Native/Pacific Islander (1,414)	6,209	22.47
Not Hispanic (1,312)	5,239	18.96
Hispanic (102)	970	3.51
Fijian (1)	1	<0.01
Guamanian/Chamorro (96)	239	0.87
Marshallese (23)	45	0.16
Native Hawaiian (959)	5,400	19.54
Samoan (236)	609	2.20
Tongan (7)	27	0.10
White (4,717)	10,607	38.39
Not Hispanic (4,304)	9,149	33.11
Hispanic (413)	1,458	5.28

Nanakuli

Place Type: CDP
County: Honolulu
Population: 12,666†

Ancestry‡	Population	%
African, Sub-Saharan (23)	45	0.36
Cape Verdean (23)	45	0.36

*Notes: † The Census 2010 population figure is used to calculate the percentages in the Hispanic Origin and Race categories. Ancestry percentages are based on the 2006-2010 American Community Survey population (not shown); ‡ Numbers in parentheses indicate the number of people reporting a single ancestry; * Numbers in parentheses indicate the number of persons reporting this race alone, not in combination with any other race; Please refer to the Explanation of Data for more information.*

Australian (0)	12	0.09
Dutch (0)	38	0.30
English (15)	194	1.53
European (3)	6	0.05
Finnish (0)	13	0.10
French, ex. Basque (12)	229	1.81
French Canadian (20)	20	0.16
German (35)	590	4.66
Irish (10)	172	1.36
Italian (0)	125	0.99
Norwegian (29)	83	0.66
Polish (0)	20	0.16
Portuguese (76)	567	4.48
Russian (0)	25	0.20
Scotch-Irish (0)	11	0.09
Scottish (0)	9	0.07
Swedish (0)	8	0.06
Swiss (3)	8	0.06
West Indian, ex. Hispanic (0)	11	0.09
Jamaican (0)	11	0.09
Yugoslavian (0)	5	0.04

Hispanic Origin	Population	%
Hispanic or Latino (of any race)	1,493	11.79
Central American, ex. Mexican	5	0.04
Guatemalan	1	0.01
Nicaraguan	1	0.01
Panamanian	2	0.02
Salvadoran	1	0.01
Cuban	15	0.12
Dominican Republic	3	0.02
Mexican	199	1.57
Puerto Rican	782	6.17
South American	5	0.04
Argentinean	1	0.01
Colombian	2	0.02
Ecuadorian	1	0.01
Venezuelan	1	0.01
Other Hispanic or Latino	484	3.82

Race*	Population	%
African-American/Black (97)	381	3.01
Not Hispanic (89)	301	2.38
Hispanic (8)	80	0.63
American Indian/Alaska Native (29)	369	2.91
Not Hispanic (20)	224	1.77
Hispanic (9)	145	1.14
Aleut *(Alaska Native)* (1)	1	0.01
Apache (0)	7	0.06
Arapaho (0)	1	0.01
Blackfeet (0)	17	0.13
Cherokee (6)	102	0.81
Chickasaw (0)	3	0.02
Choctaw (4)	5	0.04
Iroquois (1)	2	0.02
Mexican American Ind. (8)	13	0.10
Pueblo (0)	1	0.01
Seminole (0)	4	0.03
Sioux (0)	4	0.03
South American Ind. (0)	2	0.02
Asian (1,159)	5,197	41.03
Not Hispanic (1,071)	4,408	34.80
Hispanic (88)	789	6.23
Burmese (1)	1	0.01
Chinese, ex. Taiwanese (49)	2,446	19.31
Filipino (820)	2,949	23.28
Indian (2)	22	0.17
Indonesian (0)	7	0.06
Japanese (136)	1,122	8.86
Korean (11)	154	1.22
Laotian (22)	31	0.24
Pakistani (2)	7	0.06
Thai (4)	14	0.11
Vietnamese (12)	19	0.15
Hawaii Native/Pacific Islander (5,265)	10,276	81.13
Not Hispanic (4,949)	9,142	72.18
Hispanic (316)	1,134	8.95
Fijian (2)	13	0.10
Guamanian/Chamorro (10)	75	0.59
Marshallese (12)	22	0.17
Native Hawaiian (3,970)	9,051	71.46
Samoan (791)	1,602	12.65
Tongan (43)	98	0.77
White (613)	3,829	30.23
Not Hispanic (537)	3,139	24.78
Hispanic (76)	690	5.45

Ocean Pointe

Place Type: CDP
County: Honolulu
Population: 8,361†

Ancestry‡	Population	%
African, Sub-Saharan (89)	89	1.46
African (89)	89	1.46
American (87)	87	1.43
Arab (0)	9	0.15
Moroccan (0)	9	0.15
Basque (0)	12	0.20
British (15)	80	1.32
Celtic (7)	7	0.12
Croatian (0)	34	0.56
Czech (0)	12	0.20
Danish (0)	18	0.30
Dutch (12)	46	0.76
English (23)	313	5.15
European (23)	31	0.51
Finnish (0)	11	0.18
French, ex. Basque (12)	95	1.56
French Canadian (26)	34	0.56
German (229)	712	11.71
Greek (0)	71	1.17
Hungarian (0)	13	0.21
Iranian (0)	26	0.43
Irish (44)	484	7.96
Italian (36)	317	5.22
Lithuanian (0)	24	0.39
Norwegian (0)	6	0.10
Polish (45)	167	2.75
Portuguese (0)	78	1.28
Russian (21)	75	1.23
Scotch-Irish (0)	7	0.12
Scottish (13)	63	1.04
Slovak (11)	21	0.35
Swedish (0)	17	0.28
Swiss (8)	17	0.28
Ukrainian (9)	19	0.31
Welsh (0)	13	0.21
West Indian, ex. Hispanic (15)	45	0.74
Jamaican (15)	45	0.74

Hispanic Origin	Population	%
Hispanic or Latino (of any race)	896	10.72
Central American, ex. Mexican	41	0.49
Guatemalan	4	0.05
Honduran	8	0.10
Nicaraguan	5	0.06
Panamanian	13	0.16
Salvadoran	11	0.13
Cuban	19	0.23
Dominican Republic	7	0.08
Mexican	341	4.08
Puerto Rican	237	2.83
South American	33	0.39
Argentinean	3	0.04
Bolivian	1	0.01
Colombian	13	0.16
Ecuadorian	3	0.04
Peruvian	8	0.10
Venezuelan	5	0.06
Other Hispanic or Latino	218	2.61

Race*	Population	%
African-American/Black (615)	836	10.00
Not Hispanic (577)	769	9.20
Hispanic (38)	67	0.80
American Indian/Alaska Native (49)	238	2.85
Not Hispanic (36)	186	2.22
Hispanic (13)	52	0.62
Aleut *(Alaska Native)* (1)	3	0.04
Blackfeet (1)	11	0.13
Cherokee (4)	66	0.79
Chickasaw (1)	3	0.04
Choctaw (1)	4	0.05
Cree (2)	4	0.05
Creek (8)	10	0.12
Delaware (0)	4	0.05
Hopi (0)	3	0.04
Iroquois (1)	3	0.04
Kiowa (0)	6	0.07
Mexican American Ind. (1)	1	0.01
Pima (1)	7	0.08
Potawatomi (2)	9	0.11
Pueblo (2)	2	0.02
Shoshone (1)	1	0.01
Sioux (1)	7	0.08
South American Ind. (2)	2	0.02
Tlingit-Haida *(Alaska Native)* (0)	1	0.01
Asian (2,547)	3,973	47.52
Not Hispanic (2,455)	3,609	43.16
Hispanic (92)	364	4.35
Cambodian (10)	11	0.13
Chinese, ex. Taiwanese (144)	806	9.64
Filipino (1,510)	2,514	30.07
Hmong (0)	1	0.01
Indian (13)	32	0.38
Indonesian (0)	1	0.01
Japanese (384)	1,076	12.87
Korean (77)	219	2.62
Laotian (20)	31	0.37
Pakistani (4)	8	0.10
Taiwanese (2)	2	0.02
Thai (23)	49	0.59
Vietnamese (64)	90	1.08
Hawaii Native/Pacific Islander (345)	1,251	14.96
Not Hispanic (321)	1,059	12.67
Hispanic (24)	192	2.30
Fijian (0)	1	0.01
Guamanian/Chamorro (54)	105	1.26
Marshallese (1)	3	0.04
Native Hawaiian (164)	969	11.59
Samoan (91)	169	2.02
Tongan (3)	17	0.20
White (2,889)	4,230	50.59
Not Hispanic (2,619)	3,700	44.25
Hispanic (270)	530	6.34

Pearl City

Place Type: CDP
County: Honolulu
Population: 47,698†

Ancestry‡	Population	%
African, Sub-Saharan (90)	90	0.20
Kenyan (74)	74	0.17
South African (16)	16	0.04
American (352)	352	0.79
Arab (0)	28	0.06
Lebanese (0)	28	0.06
Armenian (33)	63	0.14
Belgian (0)	14	0.03
Brazilian (33)	33	0.07
British (0)	12	0.03
Canadian (1)	1	<0.01
Celtic (0)	5	0.01
Czech (9)	100	0.22
Danish (15)	56	0.13
Dutch (95)	241	0.54
English (212)	948	2.13
European (24)	24	0.05
Finnish (0)	3	0.01
French, ex. Basque (51)	410	0.92
French Canadian (0)	16	0.04
German (383)	1,791	4.02
Greek (0)	28	0.06
Hungarian (7)	44	0.10
Irish (128)	1,293	2.91
Italian (124)	491	1.10

SECTION TWO

*Notes: † The Census 2010 population figure is used to calculate the percentages in the Hispanic Origin and Race categories. Ancestry percentages are based on the 2006-2010 American Community Survey population (not shown); ‡ Numbers in parentheses indicate the number of people reporting a single ancestry; * Numbers in parentheses indicate the number of persons reporting this race alone, not in combination with any other race; Please refer to the Explanation of Data for more information.*

Ancestry	Population	%
Lithuanian (0)	28	0.06
Northern European (11)	11	0.02
Norwegian (0)	134	0.30
Polish (51)	295	0.66
Portuguese (424)	1,620	3.64
Romanian (0)	18	0.04
Russian (0)	75	0.17
Scotch-Irish (87)	178	0.40
Scottish (18)	127	0.29
Slovak (23)	23	0.05
Swedish (65)	148	0.33
Swiss (0)	9	0.02
Turkish (11)	11	0.02
Welsh (21)	76	0.17
West Indian, ex. Hispanic (0)	2	<0.01
Haitian (0)	2	<0.01

Hispanic Origin	Population	%
Hispanic or Latino (of any race)	3,889	8.15
Central American, ex. Mexican	96	0.20
Costa Rican	2	<0.01
Guatemalan	5	0.01
Honduran	28	0.06
Nicaraguan	5	0.01
Panamanian	19	0.04
Salvadoran	36	0.08
Other Central American	1	<0.01
Cuban	34	0.07
Dominican Republic	38	0.08
Mexican	1,106	2.32
Puerto Rican	1,332	2.79
South American	96	0.20
Argentinean	6	0.01
Bolivian	4	0.01
Chilean	5	0.01
Colombian	32	0.07
Ecuadorian	17	0.04
Peruvian	14	0.03
Uruguayan	1	<0.01
Venezuelan	17	0.04
Other Hispanic or Latino	1,187	2.49

Race*	Population	%
African-American/Black (1,379)	1,957	4.10
Not Hispanic (1,294)	1,755	3.68
Hispanic (85)	202	0.42
American Indian/Alaska Native (131)	895	1.88
Not Hispanic (91)	585	1.23
Hispanic (40)	310	0.65
Aleut *(Alaska Native)* (4)	6	0.01
Apache (3)	21	0.04
Blackfeet (0)	36	0.08
Canadian/French Am. Ind. (0)	2	<0.01
Central American Ind. (0)	4	0.01
Cherokee (14)	220	0.46
Chickasaw (2)	2	<0.01
Chippewa (4)	10	0.02
Choctaw (2)	18	0.04
Colville (0)	2	<0.01
Comanche (2)	5	0.01
Creek (0)	3	0.01
Crow (0)	5	0.01
Delaware (0)	1	<0.01
Iroquois (2)	24	0.05
Mexican American Ind. (11)	16	0.03
Navajo (7)	21	0.04
Osage (4)	5	0.01
Pueblo (1)	3	0.01
Puget Sound Salish (0)	2	<0.01
Seminole (1)	2	<0.01
Shoshone (0)	3	0.01
Sioux (5)	11	0.02
South American Ind. (0)	3	0.01
Tlingit-Haida *(Alaska Native)* (1)	6	0.01
Tohono O'Odham (1)	2	<0.01
Yaqui (2)	2	<0.01
Yuman (0)	1	<0.01
Yup'ik *(Alaska Native)* (1)	1	<0.01
Asian (25,392)	34,051	71.39
Not Hispanic (24,905)	32,040	67.17
Hispanic (487)	2,011	4.22
Cambodian (18)	31	0.06
Chinese, ex. Taiwanese (1,617)	7,245	15.19
Filipino (6,218)	11,421	23.94
Hmong (5)	5	0.01
Indian (53)	130	0.27
Indonesian (17)	33	0.07
Japanese (13,596)	19,604	41.10
Korean (754)	1,974	4.14
Laotian (40)	81	0.17
Malaysian (0)	9	0.02
Nepalese (1)	1	<0.01
Pakistani (12)	16	0.03
Sri Lankan (1)	2	<0.01
Taiwanese (14)	26	0.05
Thai (73)	145	0.30
Vietnamese (218)	354	0.74
Hawaii Native/Pacific Islander (2,611)	9,078	19.03
Not Hispanic (2,457)	7,804	16.36
Hispanic (154)	1,274	2.67
Fijian (2)	19	0.04
Guamanian/Chamorro (76)	207	0.43
Marshallese (50)	70	0.15
Native Hawaiian (1,409)	7,464	15.65
Samoan (600)	1,187	2.49
Tongan (84)	119	0.25
White (7,619)	14,648	30.71
Not Hispanic (6,790)	12,657	26.54
Hispanic (829)	1,991	4.17

Pukalani

Place Type: CDP
County: Maui
Population: 7,574†

Ancestry‡	Population	%
American (134)	134	1.66
Arab (0)	12	0.15
Jordanian (0)	12	0.15
Danish (0)	54	0.67
Dutch (43)	193	2.39
English (12)	302	3.74
European (12)	12	0.15
Finnish (73)	73	0.90
French, ex. Basque (71)	94	1.16
French Canadian (0)	45	0.56
German (200)	599	7.42
Greek (0)	20	0.25
Irish (200)	529	6.55
Italian (105)	241	2.98
Norwegian (12)	29	0.36
Polish (0)	69	0.85
Portuguese (425)	1,065	13.19
Russian (10)	10	0.12
Scotch-Irish (0)	44	0.54
Scottish (35)	64	0.79
Swedish (13)	138	1.71
Swiss (0)	9	0.11
Welsh (0)	53	0.66

Hispanic Origin	Population	%
Hispanic or Latino (of any race)	907	11.98
Central American, ex. Mexican	27	0.36
Costa Rican	5	0.07
Guatemalan	16	0.21
Honduran	1	0.01
Nicaraguan	5	0.07
Cuban	5	0.07
Dominican Republic	4	0.05
Mexican	255	3.37
Puerto Rican	408	5.39
South American	25	0.33
Argentinean	6	0.08
Colombian	6	0.08
Ecuadorian	3	0.04
Peruvian	5	0.07
Uruguayan	5	0.07
Other Hispanic or Latino	183	2.42

Race*	Population	%
African-American/Black (28)	109	1.44
Not Hispanic (27)	92	1.21
Hispanic (1)	17	0.22
American Indian/Alaska Native (26)	216	2.85
Not Hispanic (15)	154	2.03
Hispanic (11)	62	0.82
Apache (3)	11	0.15
Blackfeet (1)	9	0.12
Cherokee (7)	50	0.66
Chippewa (0)	8	0.11
Choctaw (2)	7	0.09
Comanche (0)	3	0.04
Cree (1)	1	0.01
Iroquois (0)	1	0.01
Mexican American Ind. (5)	17	0.22
Navajo (0)	8	0.11
Osage (1)	1	0.01
Paiute (0)	2	0.03
Pima (0)	1	0.01
Pueblo (0)	1	0.01
Sioux (0)	3	0.04
Yaqui (0)	2	0.03
Yup'ik *(Alaska Native)* (0)	1	0.01
Asian (1,808)	3,618	47.77
Not Hispanic (1,725)	3,189	42.10
Hispanic (83)	429	5.66
Cambodian (1)	3	0.04
Chinese, ex. Taiwanese (55)	862	11.38
Filipino (556)	1,645	21.72
Hmong (0)	1	0.01
Indian (12)	21	0.28
Indonesian (2)	4	0.05
Japanese (969)	1,838	24.27
Korean (36)	180	2.38
Thai (5)	6	0.08
Vietnamese (2)	5	0.07
Hawaii Native/Pacific Islander (720)	2,392	31.58
Not Hispanic (667)	2,054	27.12
Hispanic (53)	338	4.46
Fijian (4)	13	0.17
Guamanian/Chamorro (4)	16	0.21
Marshallese (1)	4	0.05
Native Hawaiian (602)	2,209	29.17
Samoan (10)	70	0.92
Tongan (5)	25	0.33
White (2,513)	4,284	56.56
Not Hispanic (2,313)	3,756	49.59
Hispanic (200)	528	6.97

Royal Kunia

Place Type: CDP
County: Honolulu
Population: 14,525†

Ancestry‡	Population	%
African, Sub-Saharan (21)	21	0.13
African (21)	21	0.13
American (155)	155	0.99
Arab (22)	43	0.28
Arab (8)	29	0.19
Lebanese (14)	14	0.09
Austrian (0)	5	0.03
Dutch (0)	24	0.15
English (110)	409	2.62
European (0)	16	0.10
French, ex. Basque (43)	279	1.79
French Canadian (32)	89	0.57
German (61)	615	3.94
Greek (0)	12	0.08
Hungarian (0)	20	0.13
Irish (0)	160	1.03
Italian (89)	174	1.12
Northern European (0)	16	0.10
Norwegian (26)	130	0.83
Polish (14)	33	0.21
Portuguese (0)	391	2.51
Russian (0)	23	0.15

*Notes: † The Census 2010 population figure is used to calculate the percentages in the Hispanic Origin and Race categories. Ancestry percentages are based on the 2006-2010 American Community Survey population (not shown); ‡ Numbers in parentheses indicate the number of people reporting a single ancestry; * Numbers in parentheses indicate the number of persons reporting this race alone, not in combination with any other race; Please refer to the Explanation of Data for more information.*

Scotch-Irish (0)	66	0.42
Scottish (38)	198	1.27
Swedish (0)	22	0.14
Ukrainian (0)	5	0.03
Welsh (15)	67	0.43

Hispanic Origin	Population	%
Hispanic or Latino (of any race)	1,096	7.55
Central American, ex. Mexican	37	0.25
Costa Rican	1	0.01
Guatemalan	4	0.03
Honduran	5	0.03
Nicaraguan	9	0.06
Panamanian	7	0.05
Salvadoran	11	0.08
Cuban	10	0.07
Dominican Republic	11	0.08
Mexican	306	2.11
Puerto Rican	400	2.75
South American	29	0.20
Argentinean	5	0.03
Chilean	1	0.01
Colombian	9	0.06
Ecuadorian	9	0.06
Peruvian	5	0.03
Other Hispanic or Latino	303	2.09

Race*	Population	%
African-American/Black (264)	433	2.98
Not Hispanic (247)	376	2.59
Hispanic (17)	57	0.39
American Indian/Alaska Native (30)	216	1.49
Not Hispanic (21)	158	1.09
Hispanic (9)	58	0.40
Apache (0)	6	0.04
Blackfeet (0)	2	0.01
Canadian/French Am. Ind. (0)	4	0.03
Central American Ind. (1)	1	0.01
Cherokee (3)	48	0.33
Chickasaw (0)	3	0.02
Chippewa (2)	6	0.04
Choctaw (0)	3	0.02
Cree (1)	1	0.01
Creek (0)	4	0.03
Crow (0)	6	0.04
Iroquois (0)	2	0.01
Mexican American Ind. (2)	2	0.01
Navajo (1)	3	0.02
Pueblo (0)	1	0.01
Seminole (0)	2	0.01
Sioux (2)	3	0.02
South American Ind. (1)	2	0.01
Ute (1)	1	0.01
Yaqui (0)	2	0.01
Yup'ik *(Alaska Native)* (1)	1	0.01
Asian (8,476)	10,949	75.38
Not Hispanic (8,273)	10,356	71.30
Hispanic (203)	593	4.08
Burmese (1)	3	0.02
Cambodian (6)	8	0.06
Chinese, ex. Taiwanese (256)	1,686	11.61
Filipino (5,820)	7,703	53.03
Indian (10)	41	0.28
Indonesian (0)	1	0.01
Japanese (1,398)	2,709	18.65
Korean (168)	423	2.91
Laotian (21)	29	0.20
Malaysian (1)	4	0.03
Sri Lankan (2)	4	0.03
Taiwanese (1)	1	0.01
Thai (38)	59	0.41
Vietnamese (83)	132	0.91
Hawaii Native/Pacific Islander (1,056)	2,851	19.63
Not Hispanic (988)	2,494	17.17
Hispanic (68)	357	2.46
Fijian (4)	8	0.06
Guamanian/Chamorro (59)	122	0.84
Marshallese (52)	67	0.46
Native Hawaiian (401)	2,055	14.15
Samoan (399)	619	4.26
Tongan (34)	59	0.41
White (1,748)	3,618	24.91
Not Hispanic (1,525)	3,074	21.16
Hispanic (223)	544	3.75

Schofield Barracks

Place Type: CDP
County: Honolulu
Population: 16,370†

Ancestry‡	Population	%
African, Sub-Saharan (28)	28	0.23
African (15)	15	0.12
South African (13)	13	0.11
American (128)	128	1.06
Arab (0)	59	0.49
Arab (0)	59	0.49
Australian (0)	4	0.03
Belgian (0)	4	0.03
Czech (0)	9	0.07
Danish (70)	171	1.42
Dutch (38)	111	0.92
English (162)	710	5.90
European (77)	293	2.43
Finnish (31)	67	0.56
French, ex. Basque (51)	335	2.78
French Canadian (32)	60	0.50
German (922)	2,814	23.36
Greek (32)	54	0.45
Hungarian (30)	46	0.38
Irish (369)	1,800	14.95
Italian (159)	565	4.69
Norwegian (35)	156	1.30
Polish (23)	141	1.17
Portuguese (0)	10	0.08
Russian (0)	68	0.56
Scandinavian (0)	14	0.12
Scotch-Irish (59)	190	1.58
Scottish (14)	175	1.45
Slovene (0)	50	0.42
Swedish (0)	74	0.61
Turkish (14)	14	0.12
Welsh (18)	116	0.96
West Indian, ex. Hispanic (180)	180	1.49
Bahamian (87)	87	0.72
Haitian (40)	40	0.33
Jamaican (53)	53	0.44

Hispanic Origin	Population	%
Hispanic or Latino (of any race)	2,835	17.32
Central American, ex. Mexican	161	0.98
Costa Rican	18	0.11
Guatemalan	10	0.06
Honduran	35	0.21
Nicaraguan	11	0.07
Panamanian	36	0.22
Salvadoran	38	0.23
Other Central American	13	0.08
Cuban	54	0.33
Dominican Republic	68	0.42
Mexican	1,363	8.33
Puerto Rican	824	5.03
South American	88	0.54
Argentinean	11	0.07
Colombian	53	0.32
Ecuadorian	12	0.07
Paraguayan	1	0.01
Peruvian	9	0.05
Venezuelan	2	0.01
Other Hispanic or Latino	277	1.69

Race*	Population	%
African-American/Black (2,501)	3,071	18.76
Not Hispanic (2,358)	2,804	17.13
Hispanic (143)	267	1.63
American Indian/Alaska Native (250)	590	3.60
Not Hispanic (214)	470	2.87
Hispanic (36)	120	0.73
Alaska Athabascan *(Ala. Nat.)* (0)	2	0.01
Aleut *(Alaska Native)* (1)	1	0.01
Apache (11)	28	0.17
Arapaho (1)	1	0.01
Blackfeet (4)	16	0.10
Canadian/French Am. Ind. (2)	10	0.06
Cherokee (44)	104	0.64
Chickasaw (3)	3	0.02
Chippewa (6)	13	0.08
Choctaw (5)	13	0.08
Comanche (1)	1	0.01
Cree (0)	2	0.01
Creek (1)	1	0.01
Delaware (1)	1	0.01
Inupiat *(Alaska Native)* (0)	6	0.04
Iroquois (5)	10	0.06
Kiowa (1)	1	0.01
Lumbee (5)	7	0.04
Mexican American Ind. (0)	3	0.02
Navajo (31)	48	0.29
Ottawa (0)	1	0.01
Pima (0)	3	0.02
Pueblo (6)	6	0.04
Puget Sound Salish (1)	1	0.01
Sioux (3)	9	0.05
South American Ind. (1)	1	0.01
Tlingit-Haida *(Alaska Native)* (0)	6	0.04
Yakama (2)	4	0.02
Yup'ik *(Alaska Native)* (3)	3	0.02
Asian (517)	1,271	7.76
Not Hispanic (472)	1,107	6.76
Hispanic (45)	164	1.00
Cambodian (14)	18	0.11
Chinese, ex. Taiwanese (28)	154	0.94
Filipino (256)	604	3.69
Hmong (2)	2	0.01
Indian (9)	38	0.23
Indonesian (0)	2	0.01
Japanese (27)	190	1.16
Korean (82)	161	0.98
Laotian (17)	22	0.13
Nepalese (3)	4	0.02
Pakistani (3)	8	0.05
Sri Lankan (4)	4	0.02
Thai (11)	29	0.18
Vietnamese (26)	83	0.51
Hawaii Native/Pacific Islander (505)	872	5.33
Not Hispanic (488)	777	4.75
Hispanic (17)	95	0.58
Fijian (1)	2	0.01
Guamanian/Chamorro (142)	202	1.23
Marshallese (14)	14	0.09
Native Hawaiian (53)	364	2.22
Samoan (114)	162	0.99
Tongan (6)	8	0.05
White (9,853)	11,122	67.94
Not Hispanic (8,776)	9,703	59.27
Hispanic (1,077)	1,419	8.67

Urban Honolulu

Place Type: CDP
County: Honolulu
Population: 337,256†

Ancestry‡	Population	%
Afghan (0)	13	<0.01
African, Sub-Saharan (399)	490	0.15
African (264)	355	0.11
Ethiopian (19)	19	0.01
Liberian (95)	95	0.03
South African (21)	21	0.01
American (1,816)	1,816	0.55
Arab (223)	435	0.13
Arab (31)	31	0.01
Egyptian (56)	56	0.02
Iraqi (16)	16	<0.01
Lebanese (0)	79	0.02
Moroccan (0)	34	0.01
Palestinian (20)	20	0.01
Syrian (7)	80	0.02

*Notes: † The Census 2010 population figure is used to calculate the percentages in the Hispanic Origin and Race categories. Ancestry percentages are based on the 2006-2010 American Community Survey population (not shown); ‡ Numbers in parentheses indicate the number of people reporting a single ancestry; * Numbers in parentheses indicate the number of persons reporting this race alone, not in combination with any other race; Please refer to the Explanation of Data for more information.*

Other Arab (93)	119	0.04
Armenian (61)	83	0.03
Australian (70)	162	0.05
Austrian (74)	406	0.12
Basque (0)	22	0.01
Belgian (21)	52	0.02
Brazilian (224)	234	0.07
British (511)	871	0.26
Bulgarian (73)	73	0.02
Cajun (17)	17	0.01
Canadian (228)	302	0.09
Carpatho Rusyn (0)	13	<0.01
Celtic (29)	36	0.01
Croatian (31)	174	0.05
Czech (87)	346	0.10
Czechoslovakian (85)	148	0.04
Danish (209)	673	0.20
Dutch (308)	1,647	0.50
Eastern European (89)	101	0.03
English (2,467)	10,957	3.31
European (867)	994	0.30
Finnish (153)	330	0.10
French, ex. Basque (549)	3,804	1.15
French Canadian (172)	495	0.15
German (3,034)	13,979	4.23
German Russian (0)	4	<0.01
Greek (182)	644	0.19
Guyanese (0)	10	<0.01
Hungarian (170)	509	0.15
Icelander (58)	73	0.02
Iranian (63)	108	0.03
Irish (2,449)	11,343	3.43
Israeli (20)	27	0.01
Italian (1,465)	4,967	1.50
Latvian (79)	163	0.05
Lithuanian (28)	157	0.05
Luxemburger (0)	10	<0.01
Macedonian (0)	28	0.01
New Zealander (24)	31	0.01
Northern European (68)	75	0.02
Norwegian (629)	2,173	0.66
Pennsylvania German (12)	56	0.02
Polish (848)	2,800	0.85
Portuguese (1,821)	6,667	2.02
Romanian (107)	340	0.10
Russian (526)	1,146	0.35
Scandinavian (306)	425	0.13
Scotch-Irish (472)	1,926	0.58
Scottish (404)	2,664	0.81
Serbian (205)	268	0.08
Slavic (0)	29	0.01
Slovak (45)	164	0.05
Slovene (9)	21	0.01
Swedish (597)	1,800	0.54
Swiss (50)	592	0.18
Turkish (73)	122	0.04
Ukrainian (75)	178	0.05
Welsh (85)	1,002	0.30
West Indian, ex. Hispanic (61)	325	0.10
Barbadian (20)	123	0.04
Bermudan (19)	19	0.01
Dutch West Indian (0)	13	<0.01
Haitian (0)	26	0.01
Jamaican (10)	51	0.02
U.S. Virgin Islander (12)	28	0.01
West Indian (0)	65	0.02
Yugoslavian (74)	90	0.03

Hispanic Origin	Population	%
Hispanic or Latino (of any race)	18,301	5.43
Central American, ex. Mexican	619	0.18
Costa Rican	52	0.02
Guatemalan	100	0.03
Honduran	82	0.02
Nicaraguan	80	0.02
Panamanian	133	0.04
Salvadoran	163	0.05
Other Central American	9	<0.01
Cuban	307	0.09
Dominican Republic	133	0.04
Mexican	5,601	1.66
Puerto Rican	5,397	1.60
South American	818	0.24
Argentinean	129	0.04
Bolivian	29	0.01
Chilean	90	0.03
Colombian	208	0.06
Ecuadorian	80	0.02
Paraguayan	12	<0.01
Peruvian	183	0.05
Uruguayan	17	0.01
Venezuelan	61	0.02
Other South American	9	<0.01
Other Hispanic or Latino	5,426	1.61

Race*	Population	%
African-American/Black (4,974)	8,733	2.59
Not Hispanic (4,642)	7,710	2.29
Hispanic (332)	1,023	0.30
American Indian/Alaska Native (743)	5,691	1.69
Not Hispanic (517)	4,154	1.23
Hispanic (226)	1,537	0.46
Alaska Athabascan *(Ala. Nat.)* (11)	17	0.01
Aleut *(Alaska Native)* (8)	14	<0.01
Apache (28)	165	0.05
Arapaho (4)	11	<0.01
Blackfeet (14)	222	0.07
Canadian/French Am. Ind. (5)	16	<0.01
Central American Ind. (1)	9	<0.01
Cherokee (67)	1,321	0.39
Cheyenne (5)	27	0.01
Chickasaw (7)	36	0.01
Chippewa (16)	84	0.02
Choctaw (20)	136	0.04
Colville (1)	5	<0.01
Comanche (3)	29	0.01
Cree (1)	27	0.01
Creek (5)	31	0.01
Crow (0)	4	<0.01
Delaware (2)	21	0.01
Hopi (2)	9	<0.01
Houma (0)	1	<0.01
Inupiat *(Alaska Native)* (2)	23	0.01
Iroquois (4)	83	0.02
Kiowa (0)	8	<0.01
Lumbee (6)	7	<0.01
Menominee (2)	4	<0.01
Mexican American Ind. (19)	67	0.02
Navajo (48)	111	0.03
Osage (6)	16	<0.01
Ottawa (0)	3	<0.01
Paiute (2)	7	<0.01
Pima (2)	3	<0.01
Potawatomi (0)	6	<0.01
Pueblo (10)	33	0.01
Puget Sound Salish (6)	21	0.01
Seminole (2)	26	0.01
Shoshone (1)	11	<0.01
Sioux (18)	142	0.04
South American Ind. (14)	50	0.01
Spanish American Ind. (1)	5	<0.01
Tlingit-Haida *(Alaska Native)* (13)	26	0.01
Tohono O'Odham (2)	11	<0.01
Tsimshian *(Alaska Native)* (0)	3	<0.01
Ute (0)	4	<0.01
Yakama (2)	7	<0.01
Yaqui (7)	27	0.01
Yuman (2)	13	<0.01
Yup'ik *(Alaska Native)* (7)	38	0.01
Asian (184,950)	230,071	68.22
Not Hispanic (182,792)	222,126	65.86
Hispanic (2,158)	7,945	2.36
Bangladeshi (55)	66	0.02
Bhutanese (4)	6	<0.01
Burmese (81)	107	0.03
Cambodian (170)	277	0.08
Chinese, ex. Taiwanese (34,508)	63,881	18.94
Filipino (44,573)	64,964	19.26
Hmong (12)	20	0.01
Indian (986)	1,674	0.50
Indonesian (162)	279	0.08
Japanese (67,130)	95,201	28.23
Korean (14,566)	20,716	6.14
Laotian (870)	1,152	0.34
Malaysian (41)	98	0.03
Nepalese (90)	106	0.03
Pakistani (98)	139	0.04
Sri Lankan (114)	136	0.04
Taiwanese (523)	641	0.19
Thai (643)	1,073	0.32
Vietnamese (6,655)	8,307	2.46
Hawaii Native/Pacific Islander (28,260)	61,970	18.37
Not Hispanic (27,346)	56,359	16.71
Hispanic (914)	5,611	1.66
Fijian (63)	165	0.05
Guamanian/Chamorro (841)	1,596	0.47
Marshallese (1,629)	1,921	0.57
Native Hawaiian (10,847)	41,781	12.39
Samoan (5,067)	8,520	2.53
Tongan (1,154)	1,723	0.51
White (60,409)	99,213	29.42
Not Hispanic (55,762)	89,225	26.46
Hispanic (4,647)	9,988	2.96

Wahiawa

Place Type: CDP
County: Honolulu
Population: 17,821†

Ancestry‡	Population	%
African, Sub-Saharan (0)	16	0.09
Other Sub-Saharan African (0)	16	0.09
American (65)	65	0.38
Arab (17)	17	0.10
Egyptian (17)	17	0.10
Belgian (0)	13	0.08
British (7)	7	0.04
Danish (17)	17	0.10
Dutch (17)	17	0.10
English (74)	367	2.13
European (30)	30	0.17
Finnish (0)	12	0.07
French, ex. Basque (17)	120	0.70
French Canadian (0)	48	0.28
German (132)	712	4.14
Greek (16)	16	0.09
Hungarian (18)	33	0.19
Irish (90)	503	2.92
Italian (27)	207	1.20
Norwegian (9)	38	0.22
Pennsylvania German (13)	39	0.23
Polish (17)	17	0.10
Portuguese (212)	724	4.21
Russian (0)	41	0.24
Scotch-Irish (26)	118	0.69
Scottish (9)	35	0.20
Welsh (0)	8	0.05

Hispanic Origin	Population	%
Hispanic or Latino (of any race)	2,321	13.02
Central American, ex. Mexican	24	0.13
Costa Rican	1	0.01
Guatemalan	7	0.04
Honduran	1	0.01
Panamanian	5	0.03
Salvadoran	10	0.06
Cuban	36	0.20
Dominican Republic	3	0.02
Mexican	477	2.68
Puerto Rican	1,067	5.99
South American	26	0.15
Argentinean	11	0.06
Bolivian	2	0.01
Chilean	2	0.01
Ecuadorian	3	0.02
Peruvian	7	0.04
Uruguayan	1	0.01
Other Hispanic or Latino	688	3.86

*Notes: † The Census 2010 population figure is used to calculate the percentages in the Hispanic Origin and Race categories. Ancestry percentages are based on the 2006-2010 American Community Survey population (not shown); ‡ Numbers in parentheses indicate the number of people reporting a single ancestry; * Numbers in parentheses indicate the number of persons reporting this race alone, not in combination with any other race; Please refer to the Explanation of Data for more information.*

Race*	Population	%
African-American/Black (282)	690	3.87
Not Hispanic (229)	514	2.88
Hispanic (53)	176	0.99
American Indian/Alaska Native (46)	647	3.63
Not Hispanic (28)	373	2.09
Hispanic (18)	274	1.54
Apache (4)	33	0.19
Blackfeet (1)	41	0.23
Canadian/French Am. Ind. (0)	1	0.01
Cherokee (6)	166	0.93
Cheyenne (0)	6	0.03
Chickasaw (0)	1	0.01
Chippewa (0)	2	0.01
Choctaw (1)	9	0.05
Comanche (0)	1	0.01
Creek (0)	1	0.01
Crow (0)	1	0.01
Inupiat *(Alaska Native)* (0)	5	0.03
Iroquois (1)	4	0.02
Lumbee (0)	6	0.03
Mexican American Ind. (0)	6	0.03
Navajo (2)	13	0.07
Ottawa (0)	1	0.01
Pueblo (4)	4	0.02
Seminole (0)	1	0.01
Shoshone (0)	1	0.01
Sioux (2)	15	0.08
South American Ind. (0)	1	0.01
Yup'ik *(Alaska Native)* (0)	2	0.01
Asian (7,257)	12,085	67.81
Not Hispanic (7,009)	10,727	60.19
Hispanic (248)	1,358	7.62
Burmese (7)	8	0.04
Cambodian (19)	22	0.12
Chinese, ex. Taiwanese (163)	2,631	14.76
Filipino (3,412)	6,821	38.28
Indian (13)	47	0.26
Indonesian (2)	3	0.02
Japanese (2,652)	4,744	26.62
Korean (278)	822	4.61
Laotian (14)	22	0.12
Malaysian (0)	1	0.01
Pakistani (0)	4	0.02
Taiwanese (0)	6	0.03
Thai (14)	35	0.20
Vietnamese (15)	36	0.20
Hawaii Native/Pacific Islander (2,227)	6,296	35.33
Not Hispanic (2,098)	5,273	29.59
Hispanic (129)	1,023	5.74
Fijian (6)	14	0.08
Guamanian/Chamorro (29)	130	0.73
Marshallese (82)	109	0.61
Native Hawaiian (998)	4,771	26.77
Samoan (457)	935	5.25
Tongan (38)	109	0.61
White (2,028)	5,814	32.62
Not Hispanic (1,728)	4,632	25.99
Hispanic (300)	1,182	6.63

Waianae

Place Type: CDP
County: Honolulu
Population: 13,177†

Ancestry‡	Population	%
American (7)	7	0.06
British (0)	18	0.14
Canadian (0)	15	0.12
Danish (0)	21	0.17
Dutch (0)	86	0.68
English (87)	694	5.49
European (0)	27	0.21
French, ex. Basque (0)	32	0.25
German (13)	377	2.98
Hungarian (0)	144	1.14
Irish (21)	130	1.03
Italian (0)	48	0.38
Norwegian (0)	59	0.47
Portuguese (78)	958	7.58
Russian (0)	11	0.09
Scotch-Irish (0)	14	0.11
Scottish (0)	26	0.21
Swedish (0)	10	0.08
Ukrainian (0)	6	0.05

Hispanic Origin	Population	%
Hispanic or Latino (of any race)	2,099	15.93
Central American, ex. Mexican	5	0.04
Nicaraguan	5	0.04
Cuban	24	0.18
Dominican Republic	3	0.02
Mexican	243	1.84
Puerto Rican	1,188	9.02
South American	21	0.16
Colombian	12	0.09
Ecuadorian	1	0.01
Peruvian	2	0.02
Venezuelan	4	0.03
Other South American	2	0.02
Other Hispanic or Latino	615	4.67

Race*	Population	%
African-American/Black (111)	443	3.36
Not Hispanic (97)	344	2.61
Hispanic (14)	99	0.75
American Indian/Alaska Native (26)	585	4.44
Not Hispanic (16)	319	2.42
Hispanic (10)	266	2.02
Apache (0)	22	0.17
Blackfeet (2)	19	0.14
Cherokee (1)	138	1.05
Cheyenne (0)	7	0.05
Chickasaw (0)	7	0.05
Chippewa (1)	1	0.01
Choctaw (0)	7	0.05
Comanche (0)	3	0.02
Delaware (0)	6	0.05
Iroquois (0)	3	0.02
Mexican American Ind. (0)	10	0.08
Navajo (3)	13	0.10
Seminole (0)	3	0.02
Sioux (0)	21	0.16
South American Ind. (0)	8	0.06
Spanish American Ind. (0)	3	0.02
Yakama (0)	4	0.03
Asian (1,917)	6,497	49.31
Not Hispanic (1,783)	5,308	40.28
Hispanic (134)	1,189	9.02
Chinese, ex. Taiwanese (130)	2,682	20.35
Filipino (1,099)	3,933	29.85
Indian (4)	39	0.30
Indonesian (1)	5	0.04
Japanese (415)	1,696	12.87
Korean (12)	242	1.84
Laotian (29)	34	0.26
Thai (9)	10	0.08
Vietnamese (7)	24	0.18
Hawaii Native/Pacific Islander (4,035)	9,141	69.37
Not Hispanic (3,719)	7,743	58.76
Hispanic (316)	1,398	10.61
Fijian (0)	3	0.02
Guamanian/Chamorro (31)	107	0.81
Marshallese (96)	100	0.76
Native Hawaiian (2,908)	8,018	60.85
Samoan (396)	963	7.31
Tongan (37)	82	0.62
White (1,089)	4,820	36.58
Not Hispanic (912)	3,779	28.68
Hispanic (177)	1,041	7.90

Waihee-Waiehu

Place Type: CDP
County: Maui
Population: 8,841†

Ancestry‡	Population	%
American (51)	51	0.55
Canadian (0)	43	0.46
Dutch (0)	3	0.03
English (33)	225	2.43
European (11)	11	0.12
French, ex. Basque (0)	34	0.37
French Canadian (11)	11	0.12
German (12)	225	2.43
Irish (73)	232	2.50
Italian (235)	259	2.80
Norwegian (0)	44	0.47
Polish (41)	108	1.17
Portuguese (88)	623	6.72
Russian (0)	4	0.04
Scandinavian (48)	48	0.52
Scotch-Irish (10)	88	0.95
Scottish (0)	13	0.14
Slovene (0)	25	0.27
Swedish (0)	14	0.15

Hispanic Origin	Population	%
Hispanic or Latino (of any race)	867	9.81
Central American, ex. Mexican	7	0.08
Costa Rican	3	0.03
Guatemalan	1	0.01
Nicaraguan	1	0.01
Panamanian	1	0.01
Salvadoran	1	0.01
Cuban	2	0.02
Mexican	249	2.82
Puerto Rican	422	4.77
South American	8	0.09
Bolivian	3	0.03
Colombian	5	0.06
Other Hispanic or Latino	179	2.02

Race*	Population	%
African-American/Black (19)	89	1.01
Not Hispanic (12)	75	0.85
Hispanic (7)	14	0.16
American Indian/Alaska Native (19)	175	1.98
Not Hispanic (16)	105	1.19
Hispanic (3)	70	0.79
Apache (0)	3	0.03
Blackfeet (0)	2	0.02
Cherokee (3)	27	0.31
Chippewa (0)	2	0.02
Choctaw (1)	11	0.12
Creek (1)	1	0.01
Delaware (0)	2	0.02
Iroquois (0)	1	0.01
Mexican American Ind. (0)	1	0.01
Navajo (0)	4	0.05
Pueblo (1)	1	0.01
Sioux (0)	1	0.01
South American Ind. (0)	2	0.02
Spanish American Ind. (0)	1	0.01
Tlingit-Haida *(Alaska Native)* (0)	5	0.06
Tsimshian *(Alaska Native)* (0)	2	0.02
Asian (3,388)	5,555	62.83
Not Hispanic (3,295)	5,116	57.87
Hispanic (93)	439	4.97
Cambodian (7)	9	0.10
Chinese, ex. Taiwanese (63)	1,148	12.98
Filipino (2,425)	3,828	43.30
Indian (7)	18	0.20
Japanese (535)	1,358	15.36
Korean (81)	247	2.79
Laotian (4)	10	0.11
Malaysian (0)	6	0.07
Pakistani (1)	1	0.01
Sri Lankan (1)	1	0.01
Thai (4)	14	0.16
Vietnamese (13)	16	0.18
Hawaii Native/Pacific Islander (1,549)	3,737	42.27
Not Hispanic (1,464)	3,320	37.55
Hispanic (85)	417	4.72
Fijian (1)	6	0.07
Guamanian/Chamorro (4)	19	0.21

SECTION TWO

*Notes: † The Census 2010 population figure is used to calculate the percentages in the Hispanic Origin and Race categories. Ancestry percentages are based on the 2006-2010 American Community Survey population (not shown); ‡ Numbers in parentheses indicate the number of people reporting a single ancestry; * Numbers in parentheses indicate the number of persons reporting this race alone, not in combination with any other race; Please refer to the Explanation of Data for more information.*

	Population	%
Marshallese (40)	46	0.52
Native Hawaiian (1,357)	3,506	39.66
Samoan (33)	116	1.31
Tongan (48)	80	0.90
White (1,082)	2,684	30.36
Not Hispanic (950)	2,277	25.76
Hispanic (132)	407	4.60

Wailuku

Place Type: CDP
County: Maui
Population: 15,313†

Ancestry‡	Population	%
American (47)	47	0.30
Austrian (0)	21	0.14
British (24)	172	1.11
Czech (0)	37	0.24
Czechoslovakian (10)	21	0.14
Dutch (0)	7	0.05
English (121)	481	3.10
European (28)	28	0.18
Finnish (23)	67	0.43
French, ex. Basque (14)	228	1.47
French Canadian (17)	97	0.62
German (112)	862	5.55
Hungarian (0)	17	0.11
Irish (58)	713	4.59
Italian (172)	649	4.18
Luxemburger (0)	11	0.07
Norwegian (0)	11	0.07
Polish (69)	255	1.64
Portuguese (188)	1,017	6.55
Russian (50)	123	0.79
Scandinavian (0)	42	0.27
Scotch-Irish (27)	122	0.79
Scottish (0)	205	1.32
Slovak (8)	8	0.05
Swedish (0)	49	0.32
Swiss (8)	8	0.05
Ukrainian (12)	61	0.39
Welsh (0)	38	0.24
West Indian, ex. Hispanic (4)	8	0.05
West Indian (4)	8	0.05
Yugoslavian (4)	4	0.03

Hispanic Origin	Population	%
Hispanic or Latino (of any race)	1,572	10.27
Central American, ex. Mexican	27	0.18
Costa Rican	1	0.01
Guatemalan	13	0.08
Nicaraguan	10	0.07
Salvadoran	3	0.02
Cuban	17	0.11
Dominican Republic	1	0.01
Mexican	507	3.31
Puerto Rican	608	3.97
South American	42	0.27
Argentinean	10	0.07
Colombian	12	0.08
Ecuadorian	10	0.07
Peruvian	5	0.03
Venezuelan	5	0.03
Other Hispanic or Latino	370	2.42

Race*	Population	%
African-American/Black (91)	224	1.46
Not Hispanic (89)	178	1.16
Hispanic (2)	46	0.30
American Indian/Alaska Native (48)	404	2.64
Not Hispanic (23)	262	1.71
Hispanic (25)	142	0.93
Alaska Athabascan *(Ala. Nat.)* (1)	1	0.01
Aleut *(Alaska Native)* (0)	1	0.01
Apache (0)	14	0.09
Arapaho (0)	1	0.01
Blackfeet (0)	5	0.03
Cherokee (5)	73	0.48
Cheyenne (0)	5	0.03
Chickasaw (0)	1	0.01
Chippewa (0)	1	0.01
Choctaw (3)	10	0.07
Comanche (0)	4	0.03
Cree (0)	5	0.03
Creek (0)	4	0.03
Hopi (0)	1	0.01
Inupiat *(Alaska Native)* (1)	5	0.03
Iroquois (1)	4	0.03
Lumbee (0)	6	0.04
Mexican American Ind. (0)	2	0.01
Navajo (0)	7	0.05
Osage (0)	8	0.05
Ottawa (1)	4	0.03
Paiute (0)	1	0.01
Pueblo (1)	1	0.01
Seminole (1)	3	0.02
Shoshone (0)	2	0.01
Sioux (1)	9	0.06
South American Ind. (0)	7	0.05
Spanish American Ind. (1)	3	0.02
Tlingit-Haida *(Alaska Native)* (0)	1	0.01
Ute (0)	1	0.01
Yaqui (0)	1	0.01
Asian (5,693)	9,327	60.91
Not Hispanic (5,540)	8,571	55.97
Hispanic (153)	756	4.94
Burmese (0)	4	0.03
Cambodian (3)	3	0.02
Chinese, ex. Taiwanese (195)	1,962	12.81
Filipino (1,995)	4,154	27.13
Indian (28)	56	0.37
Indonesian (7)	17	0.11
Japanese (2,619)	4,445	29.03
Korean (273)	548	3.58
Laotian (17)	23	0.15
Malaysian (0)	1	0.01
Nepalese (1)	1	0.01
Taiwanese (2)	2	0.01
Thai (10)	18	0.12
Vietnamese (81)	117	0.76
Hawaii Native/Pacific Islander (1,655)	4,912	32.08
Not Hispanic (1,555)	4,291	28.02
Hispanic (100)	621	4.06
Fijian (3)	12	0.08
Guamanian/Chamorro (15)	39	0.25
Marshallese (91)	108	0.71
Native Hawaiian (1,299)	4,465	29.16
Samoan (44)	163	1.06
Tongan (59)	111	0.72
White (3,209)	6,168	40.28
Not Hispanic (2,861)	5,326	34.78
Hispanic (348)	842	5.50

Waimalu

Place Type: CDP
County: Honolulu
Population: 13,730†

Ancestry‡	Population	%
African, Sub-Saharan (93)	93	0.66
Kenyan (84)	84	0.59
Other Sub-Saharan African (9)	9	0.06
American (83)	83	0.59
Arab (0)	10	0.07
Other Arab (0)	10	0.07
British (29)	29	0.20
Canadian (0)	13	0.09
Czech (0)	62	0.44
Czechoslovakian (12)	12	0.08
Danish (0)	80	0.56
Dutch (0)	11	0.08
English (154)	481	3.40
European (0)	21	0.15
Finnish (37)	37	0.26
French, ex. Basque (35)	183	1.29
French Canadian (23)	64	0.45
German (176)	784	5.54
Irish (62)	401	2.83
Italian (96)	395	2.79
Norwegian (10)	48	0.34
Polish (23)	263	1.86
Portuguese (9)	408	2.88
Russian (0)	37	0.26
Scotch-Irish (16)	52	0.37
Scottish (0)	179	1.26
Swedish (36)	171	1.21
Swiss (0)	20	0.14
Ukrainian (60)	60	0.42
Welsh (0)	26	0.18
West Indian, ex. Hispanic (0)	9	0.06
West Indian (0)	9	0.06

Hispanic Origin	Population	%
Hispanic or Latino (of any race)	1,173	8.54
Central American, ex. Mexican	30	0.22
Costa Rican	1	0.01
Guatemalan	5	0.04
Honduran	1	0.01
Nicaraguan	5	0.04
Panamanian	7	0.05
Salvadoran	11	0.08
Cuban	16	0.12
Dominican Republic	5	0.04
Mexican	300	2.18
Puerto Rican	400	2.91
South American	39	0.28
Chilean	5	0.04
Colombian	10	0.07
Ecuadorian	11	0.08
Peruvian	5	0.04
Venezuelan	8	0.06
Other Hispanic or Latino	383	2.79

Race*	Population	%
African-American/Black (375)	604	4.40
Not Hispanic (359)	539	3.93
Hispanic (16)	65	0.47
American Indian/Alaska Native (37)	248	1.81
Not Hispanic (26)	168	1.22
Hispanic (11)	80	0.58
Apache (2)	13	0.09
Blackfeet (0)	8	0.06
Canadian/French Am. Ind. (1)	1	0.01
Cherokee (7)	62	0.45
Chickasaw (0)	2	0.01
Chippewa (1)	1	0.01
Choctaw (1)	2	0.01
Comanche (0)	3	0.02
Creek (1)	2	0.01
Crow (0)	4	0.03
Iroquois (0)	2	0.01
Mexican American Ind. (2)	3	0.02
Navajo (3)	5	0.04
Ottawa (0)	2	0.01
Shoshone (0)	2	0.01
Sioux (2)	4	0.03
Yakama (0)	2	0.01
Yup'ik *(Alaska Native)* (1)	1	0.01
Asian (6,756)	9,332	67.97
Not Hispanic (6,578)	8,689	63.28
Hispanic (178)	643	4.68
Burmese (1)	1	0.01
Cambodian (1)	4	0.03
Chinese, ex. Taiwanese (517)	2,020	14.71
Filipino (2,039)	3,538	25.77
Hmong (4)	4	0.03
Indian (24)	56	0.41
Indonesian (13)	15	0.11
Japanese (2,738)	4,342	31.62
Korean (557)	866	6.31
Laotian (28)	40	0.29
Malaysian (0)	3	0.02
Sri Lankan (3)	3	0.02
Taiwanese (7)	11	0.08
Thai (35)	76	0.55
Vietnamese (87)	128	0.93
Hawaii Native/Pacific Islander (1,052)	2,877	20.95
Not Hispanic (993)	2,490	18.14

*Notes: † The Census 2010 population figure is used to calculate the percentages in the Hispanic Origin and Race categories. Ancestry percentages are based on the 2006-2010 American Community Survey population (not shown); ‡ Numbers in parentheses indicate the number of people reporting a single ancestry; * Numbers in parentheses indicate the number of persons reporting this race alone, not in combination with any other race; Please refer to the Explanation of Data for more information.*

Hispanic (59)	387	2.82
Fijian (0)	2	0.01
Guamanian/Chamorro (31)	86	0.63
Marshallese (86)	100	0.73
Native Hawaiian (454)	2,118	15.43
Samoan (281)	504	3.67
Tongan (4)	23	0.17
White (2,379)	4,536	33.04
Not Hispanic (2,142)	3,929	28.62
Hispanic (237)	607	4.42

Waimea

Place Type: CDP
County: Hawaii
Population: 9,212†

Ancestry‡	Population	%
African, Sub-Saharan (0)	40	0.41
South African (0)	40	0.41
American (86)	86	0.88
Arab (0)	88	0.90
Egyptian (0)	28	0.29
Syrian (0)	60	0.61
Austrian (0)	16	0.16
Bulgarian (73)	140	1.43
Canadian (17)	17	0.17
Czechoslovakian (24)	24	0.25
Danish (0)	61	0.62
Dutch (0)	49	0.50
English (139)	882	9.02
European (52)	99	1.01
French, ex. Basque (0)	295	3.02
French Canadian (32)	32	0.33
German (270)	1,032	10.56
Hungarian (0)	123	1.26
Irish (62)	414	4.23
Italian (24)	257	2.63
Northern European (24)	24	0.25
Norwegian (11)	112	1.15
Polish (54)	207	2.12
Portuguese (97)	718	7.34
Russian (0)	364	3.72
Scotch-Irish (98)	133	1.36
Scottish (25)	222	2.27
Swedish (0)	106	1.08
Swiss (0)	25	0.26
Ukrainian (10)	10	0.10

Hispanic Origin	Population	%
Hispanic or Latino (of any race)	825	8.96
Central American, ex. Mexican	14	0.15
Guatemalan	6	0.07
Honduran	1	0.01
Nicaraguan	2	0.02
Panamanian	2	0.02
Salvadoran	3	0.03
Cuban	5	0.05
Mexican	222	2.41
Puerto Rican	401	4.35
South American	18	0.20
Argentinean	2	0.02
Bolivian	1	0.01
Chilean	5	0.05
Colombian	4	0.04
Ecuadorian	1	0.01
Peruvian	1	0.01
Uruguayan	3	0.03
Other South American	1	0.01
Other Hispanic or Latino	165	1.79

Race*	Population	%
African-American/Black (30)	80	0.87
Not Hispanic (27)	67	0.73
Hispanic (3)	13	0.14
American Indian/Alaska Native (22)	293	3.18
Not Hispanic (19)	205	2.23
Hispanic (3)	88	0.96
Aleut *(Alaska Native)* (1)	3	0.03
Apache (1)	8	0.09
Blackfeet (3)	22	0.24
Canadian/French Am. Ind. (0)	1	0.01
Cherokee (2)	68	0.74
Cheyenne (1)	5	0.05
Chickasaw (0)	1	0.01
Chippewa (0)	4	0.04
Choctaw (0)	6	0.07
Comanche (1)	1	0.01
Cree (0)	4	0.04
Creek (1)	2	0.02
Crow (0)	1	0.01
Delaware (0)	1	0.01
Inupiat *(Alaska Native)* (0)	5	0.05
Iroquois (0)	9	0.10
Menominee (0)	1	0.01
Mexican American Ind. (0)	3	0.03
Navajo (1)	3	0.03
Potawatomi (0)	1	0.01
Pueblo (0)	1	0.01
Seminole (0)	1	0.01
Shoshone (0)	2	0.02
Sioux (0)	4	0.04
Tlingit-Haida *(Alaska Native)* (0)	2	0.02
Yaqui (0)	2	0.02
Asian (1,597)	3,965	43.04
Not Hispanic (1,543)	3,582	38.88
Hispanic (54)	383	4.16
Burmese (1)	2	0.02
Cambodian (1)	1	0.01
Chinese, ex. Taiwanese (83)	1,320	14.33
Filipino (698)	1,955	21.22
Hmong (0)	3	0.03
Indian (3)	25	0.27
Indonesian (3)	4	0.04
Japanese (574)	1,488	16.15
Korean (56)	182	1.98
Malaysian (1)	6	0.07
Pakistani (4)	4	0.04
Taiwanese (7)	8	0.09
Thai (8)	12	0.13
Vietnamese (16)	19	0.21
Hawaii Native/Pacific Islander (1,456)	3,926	42.62
Not Hispanic (1,401)	3,542	38.45
Hispanic (55)	384	4.17
Fijian (2)	4	0.04
Guamanian/Chamorro (4)	20	0.22
Marshallese (154)	168	1.82
Native Hawaiian (1,140)	3,577	38.83
Samoan (29)	104	1.13
Tongan (4)	13	0.14
White (2,878)	5,212	56.58
Not Hispanic (2,708)	4,721	51.25
Hispanic (170)	491	5.33

Waipahu

Place Type: CDP
County: Honolulu
Population: 38,216†

Ancestry‡	Population	%
African, Sub-Saharan (14)	14	0.03
African (14)	14	0.03
American (78)	78	0.19
Arab (0)	12	0.03
Arab (0)	12	0.03
British (0)	15	0.04
Bulgarian (12)	12	0.03
Canadian (13)	37	0.09
Danish (38)	49	0.12
Dutch (0)	51	0.13
Eastern European (11)	11	0.03
English (119)	208	0.52
European (12)	12	0.03
French, ex. Basque (75)	124	0.31
German (196)	626	1.56
Iranian (11)	11	0.03
Irish (136)	591	1.47
Italian (46)	165	0.41
Norwegian (0)	11	0.03
Polish (40)	76	0.19
Portuguese (108)	623	1.55
Russian (0)	5	0.01
Scandinavian (12)	12	0.03
Scotch-Irish (11)	69	0.17
Scottish (0)	55	0.14
Swiss (0)	12	0.03
Welsh (15)	44	0.11

Hispanic Origin	Population	%
Hispanic or Latino (of any race)	2,229	5.83
Central American, ex. Mexican	37	0.10
Guatemalan	8	0.02
Honduran	8	0.02
Nicaraguan	1	<0.01
Panamanian	8	0.02
Salvadoran	12	0.03
Cuban	24	0.06
Dominican Republic	10	0.03
Mexican	359	0.94
Puerto Rican	937	2.45
South American	15	0.04
Argentinean	1	<0.01
Bolivian	3	0.01
Chilean	2	0.01
Colombian	3	0.01
Ecuadorian	5	0.01
Other South American	1	<0.01
Other Hispanic or Latino	847	2.22

Race*	Population	%
African-American/Black (319)	738	1.93
Not Hispanic (280)	559	1.46
Hispanic (39)	179	0.47
American Indian/Alaska Native (26)	441	1.15
Not Hispanic (19)	232	0.61
Hispanic (7)	209	0.55
Aleut *(Alaska Native)* (0)	2	0.01
Apache (1)	22	0.06
Blackfeet (2)	17	0.04
Cherokee (2)	119	0.31
Choctaw (0)	4	0.01
Comanche (0)	6	0.02
Creek (0)	4	0.01
Iroquois (0)	1	<0.01
Lumbee (1)	1	<0.01
Navajo (1)	6	0.02
Seminole (0)	5	0.01
Shoshone (0)	2	0.01
Sioux (2)	12	0.03
Yup'ik *(Alaska Native)* (0)	1	<0.01
Asian (25,628)	30,298	79.28
Not Hispanic (25,121)	28,838	75.46
Hispanic (507)	1,460	3.82
Bhutanese (0)	1	<0.01
Cambodian (2)	8	0.02
Chinese, ex. Taiwanese (257)	2,762	7.23
Filipino (21,122)	25,040	65.52
Hmong (2)	4	0.01
Indian (30)	89	0.23
Indonesian (0)	4	0.01
Japanese (2,748)	4,619	12.09
Korean (210)	553	1.45
Laotian (37)	66	0.17
Malaysian (0)	2	0.01
Pakistani (1)	1	<0.01
Sri Lankan (0)	1	<0.01
Taiwanese (0)	2	0.01
Thai (34)	58	0.15
Vietnamese (121)	165	0.43
Hawaii Native/Pacific Islander (5,173)	9,072	23.74
Not Hispanic (5,052)	8,211	21.49
Hispanic (121)	861	2.25
Fijian (0)	6	0.02
Guamanian/Chamorro (39)	136	0.36
Marshallese (829)	984	2.57
Native Hawaiian (857)	4,175	10.92
Samoan (2,051)	2,831	7.41
Tongan (211)	327	0.86
White (1,305)	4,540	11.88

*Notes: † The Census 2010 population figure is used to calculate the percentages in the Hispanic Origin and Race categories. Ancestry percentages are based on the 2006-2010 American Community Survey population (not shown); ‡ Numbers in parentheses indicate the number of people reporting a single ancestry; * Numbers in parentheses indicate the number of persons reporting this race alone, not in combination with any other race; Please refer to the Explanation of Data for more information.*

Not Hispanic (1,098)	3,634	9.51
Hispanic (207)	906	2.37

Waipio

Place Type: CDP
County: Honolulu
Population: 11,674†

Ancestry‡	Population	%
American (86)	86	0.68
Brazilian (9)	27	0.21
British (0)	23	0.18
Danish (0)	13	0.10
Dutch (24)	71	0.56
English (71)	228	1.81
European (23)	34	0.27
French, ex. Basque (0)	297	2.36
German (113)	528	4.20
Hungarian (0)	27	0.21
Irish (91)	628	4.99
Italian (0)	100	0.79
New Zealander (27)	27	0.21
Norwegian (55)	149	1.18
Polish (0)	64	0.51
Portuguese (30)	428	3.40
Romanian (19)	19	0.15
Scotch-Irish (33)	47	0.37
Scottish (20)	33	0.26
Swedish (0)	51	0.41
Turkish (0)	57	0.45
Welsh (0)	22	0.17
West Indian, ex. Hispanic (27)	27	0.21
West Indian (27)	27	0.21
Yugoslavian (9)	9	0.07

Hispanic Origin	Population	%
Hispanic or Latino (of any race)	1,012	8.67
Central American, ex. Mexican	19	0.16
Costa Rican	2	0.02
Guatemalan	1	0.01
Honduran	5	0.04
Nicaraguan	2	0.02
Panamanian	1	0.01
Salvadoran	8	0.07
Cuban	7	0.06
Dominican Republic	3	0.03
Mexican	278	2.38
Puerto Rican	322	2.76
South American	13	0.11
Argentinean	3	0.03
Ecuadorian	1	0.01
Peruvian	5	0.04
Venezuelan	4	0.03
Other Hispanic or Latino	370	3.17

Race*	Population	%
African-American/Black (179)	344	2.95
Not Hispanic (159)	297	2.54
Hispanic (20)	47	0.40
American Indian/Alaska Native (21)	229	1.96
Not Hispanic (17)	150	1.28
Hispanic (4)	79	0.68
Apache (0)	2	0.02
Arapaho (1)	1	0.01
Blackfeet (0)	5	0.04
Canadian/French Am. Ind. (1)	1	0.01
Cherokee (1)	40	0.34
Chippewa (0)	7	0.06
Choctaw (0)	5	0.04
Comanche (1)	1	0.01
Crow (0)	2	0.02
Delaware (0)	1	0.01
Mexican American Ind. (0)	2	0.02
Navajo (0)	1	0.01
Ottawa (0)	1	0.01
Paiute (0)	2	0.02
Pueblo (1)	2	0.02
Shoshone (0)	4	0.03
Sioux (0)	5	0.04
South American Ind. (0)	5	0.04
Yup'ik *(Alaska Native)* (0)	1	0.01
Asian (6,588)	9,058	77.59
Not Hispanic (6,372)	8,424	72.16
Hispanic (216)	634	5.43
Cambodian (2)	3	0.03
Chinese, ex. Taiwanese (334)	1,902	16.29
Filipino (2,644)	4,318	36.99
Indian (10)	26	0.22
Indonesian (0)	8	0.07
Japanese (2,474)	4,150	35.55
Korean (201)	535	4.58
Laotian (28)	42	0.36
Malaysian (1)	1	0.01
Sri Lankan (9)	9	0.08
Taiwanese (3)	5	0.04
Thai (15)	39	0.33
Vietnamese (40)	90	0.77
Hawaii Native/Pacific Islander (595)	2,335	20.00
Not Hispanic (554)	2,021	17.31
Hispanic (41)	314	2.69
Guamanian/Chamorro (14)	54	0.46
Marshallese (0)	7	0.06
Native Hawaiian (392)	2,005	17.17
Samoan (133)	287	2.46
Tongan (15)	32	0.27
White (1,351)	3,337	28.58
Not Hispanic (1,218)	2,879	24.66
Hispanic (133)	458	3.92

*Notes: † The Census 2010 population figure is used to calculate the percentages in the Hispanic Origin and Race categories. Ancestry percentages are based on the 2006-2010 American Community Survey population (not shown); ‡ Numbers in parentheses indicate the number of people reporting a single ancestry; * Numbers in parentheses indicate the number of persons reporting this race alone, not in combination with any other race; Please refer to the Explanation of Data for more information.*

IDAHO

Place Type: State
Population: 1,567,582[†]

Ancestry[‡]	Population	%
Afghan (193)	193	0.01
African, Sub-Saharan (1,904)	2,939	0.19
African (852)	1,433	0.09
Cape Verdean (40)	76	<0.01
Ethiopian (161)	201	0.01
Kenyan (12)	12	<0.01
Liberian (40)	40	<0.01
Nigerian (0)	14	<0.01
Senegalese (0)	19	<0.01
Somalian (300)	300	0.02
South African (99)	335	0.02
Sudanese (127)	127	0.01
Zimbabwean (15)	15	<0.01
Other Sub-Saharan African (258)	367	0.02
Albanian (124)	124	0.01
Alsatian (0)	18	<0.01
American (149,238)	149,238	9.77
Arab (829)	1,900	0.12
Arab (131)	335	0.02
Egyptian (101)	174	0.01
Iraqi (35)	39	<0.01
Jordanian (4)	71	<0.01
Lebanese (381)	770	0.05
Moroccan (1)	43	<0.01
Palestinian (36)	36	<0.01
Syrian (21)	178	0.01
Other Arab (119)	254	0.02
Armenian (366)	860	0.06
Assyrian/Chaldean/Syriac (10)	10	<0.01
Australian (207)	664	0.04
Austrian (907)	3,560	0.23
Basque (4,374)	7,264	0.48
Belgian (272)	1,520	0.10
Brazilian (219)	373	0.02
British (4,460)	9,256	0.61
Bulgarian (86)	220	0.01
Cajun (32)	150	0.01
Canadian (2,514)	5,158	0.34
Carpatho Rusyn (0)	20	<0.01
Celtic (218)	459	0.03
Croatian (419)	1,388	0.09
Cypriot (0)	26	<0.01
Czech (2,466)	8,079	0.53
Czechoslovakian (811)	1,760	0.12
Danish (9,863)	37,041	2.43
Dutch (9,713)	36,548	2.39
Eastern European (377)	483	0.03
English (101,673)	269,570	17.66
Estonian (43)	98	0.01
European (26,084)	29,128	1.91
Finnish (1,979)	5,134	0.34
French, ex. Basque (8,100)	47,063	3.08
French Canadian (3,057)	8,675	0.57
German (107,009)	309,212	20.25
German Russian (46)	91	0.01
Greek (2,027)	4,723	0.31
Guyanese (23)	23	<0.01
Hungarian (1,114)	4,009	0.26
Icelander (220)	694	0.05
Iranian (249)	393	0.03
Irish (42,708)	165,249	10.82
Israeli (9)	95	0.01
Italian (15,893)	46,471	3.04
Latvian (89)	376	0.02
Lithuanian (624)	1,509	0.10
Luxemburger (17)	161	0.01
Macedonian (17)	17	<0.01
Maltese (56)	94	0.01
New Zealander (124)	205	0.01
Northern European (1,954)	2,127	0.14
Norwegian (18,565)	53,092	3.48
Pennsylvania German (293)	632	0.04
Polish (6,499)	20,544	1.35
Portuguese (3,303)	7,916	0.52
Romanian (924)	1,431	0.09
Russian (3,317)	9,298	0.61
Scandinavian (4,826)	9,884	0.65
Scotch-Irish (10,945)	30,722	2.01
Scottish (14,436)	52,306	3.43
Serbian (96)	396	0.03
Slavic (237)	546	0.04
Slovak (312)	922	0.06
Slovene (101)	355	0.02
Swedish (14,785)	51,884	3.40
Swiss (2,995)	12,781	0.84
Turkish (328)	687	0.04
Ukrainian (1,875)	2,766	0.18
Welsh (5,024)	22,464	1.47
West Indian, ex. Hispanic (498)	875	0.06
Bahamian (7)	7	<0.01
Belizean (21)	21	<0.01
Dutch West Indian (71)	184	0.01
Haitian (245)	245	0.02
Jamaican (123)	315	0.02
Trinidadian/Tobagonian (1)	1	<0.01
West Indian (30)	102	0.01
Yugoslavian (2,317)	3,323	0.22

Hispanic Origin	Population	%
Hispanic or Latino (of any race)	175,901	11.22
Central American, ex. Mexican	3,494	0.22
Costa Rican	230	0.01
Guatemalan	1,168	0.07
Honduran	461	0.03
Nicaraguan	222	0.01
Panamanian	223	0.01
Salvadoran	1,159	0.07
Other Central American	31	<0.01
Cuban	825	0.05
Dominican Republic	185	0.01
Mexican	148,923	9.50
Puerto Rican	2,910	0.19
South American	3,707	0.24
Argentinean	366	0.02
Bolivian	122	0.01
Chilean	336	0.02
Colombian	734	0.05
Ecuadorian	274	0.02
Paraguayan	28	<0.01
Peruvian	1,560	0.10
Uruguayan	35	<0.01
Venezuelan	200	0.01
Other South American	52	<0.01
Other Hispanic or Latino	15,857	1.01

Race*	Population	%
African-American/Black (9,810)	15,940	1.02
Not Hispanic (8,875)	13,927	0.89
Hispanic (935)	2,013	0.13
American Indian/Alaska Native (21,441)	36,385	2.32
Not Hispanic (17,556)	29,445	1.88
Hispanic (3,885)	6,940	0.44
Alaska Athabascan *(Ala. Nat.)* (82)	144	0.01
Aleut *(Alaska Native)* (64)	121	0.01
Apache (231)	622	0.04
Arapaho (97)	135	0.01
Blackfeet (222)	671	0.04
Canadian/French Am. Ind. (65)	133	0.01
Central American Ind. (9)	17	<0.01
Cherokee (1,174)	4,089	0.26
Cheyenne (91)	182	0.01
Chickasaw (85)	185	0.01
Chippewa (444)	847	0.05
Choctaw (311)	841	0.05
Colville (204)	263	0.02
Comanche (36)	95	0.01
Cree (34)	119	0.01
Creek (74)	152	0.01
Crow (50)	99	0.01
Delaware (98)	185	0.01
Hopi (23)	46	<0.01
Houma (0)	1	<0.01
Inupiat *(Alaska Native)* (68)	112	0.01
Iroquois (88)	230	0.01
Kiowa (15)	26	<0.01
Lumbee (30)	60	<0.01
Menominee (12)	21	<0.01
Mexican American Ind. (586)	865	0.06
Navajo (780)	1,321	0.08
Osage (47)	129	0.01
Ottawa (34)	65	<0.01
Paiute (123)	188	0.01
Pima (31)	62	<0.01
Potawatomi (92)	182	0.01
Pueblo (52)	124	0.01
Puget Sound Salish (123)	185	0.01
Seminole (30)	80	0.01
Shoshone (568)	812	0.05
Sioux (506)	1,093	0.07
South American Ind. (55)	97	0.01
Spanish American Ind. (30)	52	<0.01
Tlingit-Haida *(Alaska Native)* (141)	256	0.02
Tohono O'Odham (38)	69	<0.01
Tsimshian *(Alaska Native)* (22)	43	<0.01
Ute (63)	125	0.01
Yakama (127)	160	0.01
Yaqui (38)	85	0.01
Yuman (16)	21	<0.01
Yup'ik *(Alaska Native)* (21)	43	<0.01
Asian (19,069)	29,698	1.89
Not Hispanic (18,529)	27,926	1.78
Hispanic (540)	1,772	0.11
Bangladeshi (36)	39	<0.01
Bhutanese (350)	423	0.03
Burmese (379)	399	0.03
Cambodian (134)	199	0.01
Chinese, ex. Taiwanese (3,821)	5,212	0.33
Filipino (3,022)	6,211	0.40
Hmong (26)	44	<0.01
Indian (2,152)	2,786	0.18
Indonesian (91)	216	0.01
Japanese (2,620)	5,698	0.36
Korean (1,670)	2,806	0.18
Laotian (717)	941	0.06
Malaysian (35)	55	<0.01
Nepalese (320)	376	0.02
Pakistani (121)	151	0.01
Sri Lankan (34)	46	<0.01
Taiwanese (214)	265	0.02
Thai (469)	799	0.05
Vietnamese (1,707)	2,154	0.14
Hawaii Native/Pacific Islander (2,317)	5,094	0.32
Not Hispanic (2,153)	4,414	0.28
Hispanic (164)	680	0.04
Fijian (36)	56	<0.01
Guamanian/Chamorro (543)	860	0.05
Marshallese (63)	75	<0.01
Native Hawaiian (637)	1,921	0.12
Samoan (387)	895	0.06
Tongan (176)	311	0.02
White (1,396,487)	1,432,824	91.40
Not Hispanic (1,316,243)	1,341,827	85.60
Hispanic (80,244)	90,997	5.80

*Notes: † The Census 2010 population figure is used to calculate the percentages in the Hispanic Origin and Race categories. Ancestry percentages are based on the 2006-2010 American Community Survey population (not shown); ‡ Numbers in parentheses indicate the number of people reporting a single ancestry; * Numbers in parentheses indicate the number of persons reporting this race alone, not in combination with any other race; Please refer to the Explanation of Data for more information.*

Ammon

Place Type: City
County: Bonneville
Population: 13,816†

Ancestry‡	Population	%
African, Sub-Saharan (0)	57	0.46
African (0)	57	0.46
American (1,852)	1,852	14.88
Arab (40)	40	0.32
Lebanese (40)	40	0.32
Austrian (0)	11	0.09
British (94)	170	1.37
Canadian (11)	11	0.09
Czech (8)	33	0.27
Czechoslovakian (0)	33	0.27
Danish (142)	449	3.61
Dutch (41)	132	1.06
English (1,540)	3,021	24.28
European (235)	235	1.89
French, ex. Basque (35)	412	3.31
French Canadian (54)	54	0.43
German (713)	1,963	15.78
Greek (31)	31	0.25
Hungarian (0)	11	0.09
Irish (257)	1,093	8.78
Italian (122)	223	1.79
Northern European (31)	31	0.25
Norwegian (85)	270	2.17
Polish (17)	123	0.99
Portuguese (92)	92	0.74
Scandinavian (129)	155	1.25
Scotch-Irish (4)	66	0.53
Scottish (186)	417	3.35
Slovene (8)	8	0.06
Swedish (115)	372	2.99
Swiss (44)	146	1.17
Welsh (53)	221	1.78

Hispanic Origin	Population	%
Hispanic or Latino (of any race)	884	6.40
Central American, ex. Mexican	29	0.21
Guatemalan	13	0.09
Honduran	7	0.05
Salvadoran	9	0.07
Cuban	3	0.02
Dominican Republic	1	0.01
Mexican	718	5.20
Puerto Rican	17	0.12
South American	23	0.17
Argentinean	1	0.01
Bolivian	3	0.02
Colombian	2	0.01
Ecuadorian	11	0.08
Peruvian	6	0.04
Other Hispanic or Latino	93	0.67

Race*	Population	%
African-American/Black (73)	131	0.95
Not Hispanic (66)	119	0.86
Hispanic (7)	12	0.09
American Indian/Alaska Native (67)	147	1.06
Not Hispanic (43)	106	0.77
Hispanic (24)	41	0.30
Alaska Athabascan *(Ala. Nat.)* (2)	2	0.01
Blackfeet (0)	8	0.06
Cherokee (6)	28	0.20
Chickasaw (0)	1	0.01
Chippewa (1)	2	0.01
Choctaw (0)	2	0.01
Crow (0)	1	0.01
Inupiat *(Alaska Native)* (0)	1	0.01
Iroquois (0)	1	0.01
Mexican American Ind. (6)	9	0.07
Navajo (12)	14	0.10
Osage (1)	1	0.01
Ottawa (0)	1	0.01
Paiute (0)	3	0.02
Puget Sound Salish (0)	1	0.01
Shoshone (0)	1	0.01
Sioux (1)	2	0.01
Tlingit-Haida *(Alaska Native)* (0)	1	0.01
Tsimshian *(Alaska Native)* (1)	1	0.01
Ute (0)	3	0.02
Asian (113)	170	1.23
Not Hispanic (113)	161	1.17
Hispanic (0)	9	0.07
Chinese, ex. Taiwanese (26)	33	0.24
Filipino (19)	23	0.17
Hmong (1)	4	0.03
Indian (10)	16	0.12
Japanese (27)	48	0.35
Korean (11)	18	0.13
Laotian (1)	2	0.01
Sri Lankan (1)	1	0.01
Taiwanese (0)	2	0.01
Thai (1)	5	0.04
Vietnamese (4)	6	0.04
Hawaii Native/Pacific Islander (9)	33	0.24
Not Hispanic (8)	27	0.20
Hispanic (1)	6	0.04
Guamanian/Chamorro (2)	7	0.05
Native Hawaiian (3)	13	0.09
Samoan (3)	12	0.09
Tongan (0)	1	0.01
White (13,002)	13,242	95.85
Not Hispanic (12,515)	12,684	91.81
Hispanic (487)	558	4.04

Blackfoot

Place Type: City
County: Bingham
Population: 11,899†

Ancestry‡	Population	%
African, Sub-Saharan (6)	6	0.05
African (6)	6	0.05
American (818)	818	7.10
Arab (12)	177	1.54
Arab (0)	136	1.18
Egyptian (12)	27	0.23
Lebanese (0)	14	0.12
Basque (7)	7	0.06
British (20)	30	0.26
Canadian (46)	46	0.40
Danish (98)	697	6.05
Dutch (0)	255	2.21
English (853)	2,079	18.04
European (138)	138	1.20
French, ex. Basque (6)	101	0.88
German (581)	1,542	13.38
Irish (161)	520	4.51
Italian (81)	210	1.82
Norwegian (35)	189	1.64
Polish (16)	35	0.30
Portuguese (13)	28	0.24
Romanian (15)	15	0.13
Russian (0)	13	0.11
Scandinavian (0)	22	0.19
Scotch-Irish (77)	244	2.12
Scottish (131)	667	5.79
Swedish (127)	508	4.41
Swiss (62)	260	2.26
Welsh (64)	193	1.67
Yugoslavian (14)	14	0.12

Hispanic Origin	Population	%
Hispanic or Latino (of any race)	2,192	18.42
Central American, ex. Mexican	11	0.09
Guatemalan	2	0.02
Panamanian	1	0.01
Salvadoran	8	0.07
Mexican	2,015	16.93
Puerto Rican	27	0.23
South American	15	0.13
Bolivian	2	0.02
Chilean	2	0.02
Colombian	3	0.03
Peruvian	6	0.05
Other South American	2	0.02
Other Hispanic or Latino	124	1.04

Race*	Population	%
African-American/Black (40)	84	0.71
Not Hispanic (24)	46	0.39
Hispanic (16)	38	0.32
American Indian/Alaska Native (418)	523	4.40
Not Hispanic (323)	381	3.20
Hispanic (95)	142	1.19
Apache (0)	5	0.04
Arapaho (3)	3	0.03
Blackfeet (13)	14	0.12
Canadian/French Am. Ind. (1)	2	0.02
Cherokee (7)	13	0.11
Cheyenne (5)	6	0.05
Chippewa (4)	8	0.07
Choctaw (1)	1	0.01
Cree (0)	4	0.03
Inupiat *(Alaska Native)* (0)	2	0.02
Iroquois (0)	2	0.02
Mexican American Ind. (5)	5	0.04
Navajo (44)	56	0.47
Paiute (0)	2	0.02
Shoshone (32)	39	0.33
Sioux (4)	7	0.06
Spanish American Ind. (2)	2	0.02
Ute (1)	1	0.01
Asian (125)	207	1.74
Not Hispanic (125)	192	1.61
Hispanic (0)	15	0.13
Chinese, ex. Taiwanese (34)	45	0.38
Filipino (13)	34	0.29
Indian (5)	6	0.05
Indonesian (1)	1	0.01
Japanese (46)	78	0.66
Korean (4)	14	0.12
Laotian (5)	10	0.08
Thai (1)	4	0.03
Vietnamese (11)	18	0.15
Hawaii Native/Pacific Islander (18)	38	0.32
Not Hispanic (14)	33	0.28
Hispanic (4)	5	0.04
Guamanian/Chamorro (4)	7	0.06
Marshallese (1)	1	0.01
Native Hawaiian (2)	12	0.10
Samoan (7)	13	0.11
Tongan (2)	6	0.05
White (9,893)	10,196	85.69
Not Hispanic (9,068)	9,215	77.44
Hispanic (825)	981	8.24

Boise City

Place Type: City
County: Ada
Population: 205,671†

Ancestry‡	Population	%
Afghan (40)	40	0.02
African, Sub-Saharan (904)	1,310	0.63
African (327)	540	0.26
Cape Verdean (15)	51	0.02
Ethiopian (59)	59	0.03
Liberian (40)	40	0.02
Somalian (274)	274	0.13
South African (0)	48	0.02
Zimbabwean (15)	15	0.01
Other Sub-Saharan African (174)	283	0.14
Albanian (39)	39	0.02
American (17,120)	17,120	8.29
Arab (217)	441	0.21
Arab (54)	71	0.03
Egyptian (31)	55	0.03
Iraqi (19)	19	0.01
Jordanian (0)	60	0.03
Lebanese (58)	73	0.04
Syrian (15)	82	0.04
Other Arab (40)	81	0.04

*Notes: † The Census 2010 population figure is used to calculate the percentages in the Hispanic Origin and Race categories. Ancestry percentages are based on the 2006-2010 American Community Survey population (not shown); ‡ Numbers in parentheses indicate the number of people reporting a single ancestry; * Numbers in parentheses indicate the number of persons reporting this race alone, not in combination with any other race; Please refer to the Explanation of Data for more information.*

Armenian (44)	141	0.07
Australian (0)	73	0.04
Austrian (144)	500	0.24
Basque (1,175)	1,763	0.85
Belgian (28)	209	0.10
Brazilian (41)	125	0.06
British (702)	1,576	0.76
Bulgarian (26)	52	0.03
Cajun (0)	63	0.03
Canadian (323)	678	0.33
Carpatho Rusyn (0)	20	0.01
Celtic (42)	102	0.05
Croatian (126)	264	0.13
Czech (577)	1,692	0.82
Czechoslovakian (100)	253	0.12
Danish (888)	3,555	1.72
Dutch (849)	3,976	1.93
Eastern European (111)	129	0.06
English (10,534)	32,660	15.82
European (3,472)	3,968	1.92
Finnish (155)	620	0.30
French, ex. Basque (1,236)	6,632	3.21
French Canadian (556)	1,313	0.64
German (11,788)	39,868	19.31
German Russian (0)	10	<0.01
Greek (330)	674	0.33
Hungarian (151)	637	0.31
Icelander (43)	158	0.08
Iranian (108)	132	0.06
Irish (6,976)	26,177	12.68
Israeli (0)	12	0.01
Italian (2,437)	7,447	3.61
Latvian (25)	85	0.04
Lithuanian (123)	365	0.18
Luxemburger (8)	39	0.02
New Zealander (12)	70	0.03
Northern European (418)	471	0.23
Norwegian (3,048)	8,127	3.94
Pennsylvania German (87)	110	0.05
Polish (1,295)	3,690	1.79
Portuguese (255)	1,025	0.50
Romanian (127)	241	0.12
Russian (720)	2,085	1.01
Scandinavian (534)	1,166	0.56
Scotch-Irish (1,747)	4,913	2.38
Scottish (2,240)	7,350	3.56
Serbian (0)	29	0.01
Slavic (135)	195	0.09
Slovak (39)	120	0.06
Slovene (30)	55	0.03
Swedish (1,843)	6,126	2.97
Swiss (392)	1,404	0.68
Turkish (59)	300	0.15
Ukrainian (248)	522	0.25
Welsh (561)	3,812	1.85
West Indian, ex. Hispanic (85)	151	0.07
Bahamian (7)	7	<0.01
Dutch West Indian (0)	10	<0.01
Haitian (35)	35	0.02
Jamaican (43)	99	0.05
Yugoslavian (1,446)	1,535	0.74

Hispanic Origin	**Population**	**%**
Hispanic or Latino (of any race)	14,606	7.10
Central American, ex. Mexican	483	0.23
Costa Rican	47	0.02
Guatemalan	147	0.07
Honduran	58	0.03
Nicaraguan	41	0.02
Panamanian	52	0.03
Salvadoran	131	0.06
Other Central American	7	<0.01
Cuban	197	0.10
Dominican Republic	21	0.01
Mexican	11,065	5.38
Puerto Rican	488	0.24
South American	529	0.26
Argentinean	62	0.03
Bolivian	11	0.01
Chilean	47	0.02
Colombian	204	0.10
Ecuadorian	57	0.03
Paraguayan	1	<0.01
Peruvian	97	0.05
Uruguayan	7	<0.01
Venezuelan	33	0.02
Other South American	10	<0.01
Other Hispanic or Latino	1,823	0.89

Race*	**Population**	**%**
African-American/Black (3,043)	4,226	2.05
Not Hispanic (2,901)	3,899	1.90
Hispanic (142)	327	0.16
American Indian/Alaska Native (1,404)	3,216	1.56
Not Hispanic (1,107)	2,502	1.22
Hispanic (297)	714	0.35
Alaska Athabascan *(Ala. Nat.)* (10)	15	0.01
Aleut *(Alaska Native)* (15)	26	0.01
Apache (37)	91	0.04
Arapaho (4)	8	<0.01
Blackfeet (13)	64	0.03
Canadian/French Am. Ind. (8)	12	0.01
Central American Ind. (0)	3	<0.01
Cherokee (111)	536	0.26
Cheyenne (17)	29	0.01
Chickasaw (14)	26	0.01
Chippewa (40)	82	0.04
Choctaw (39)	101	0.05
Colville (8)	10	<0.01
Comanche (9)	16	0.01
Cree (12)	24	0.01
Creek (15)	23	0.01
Crow (1)	12	0.01
Delaware (17)	30	0.01
Hopi (4)	5	<0.01
Inupiat *(Alaska Native)* (1)	3	<0.01
Iroquois (19)	39	0.02
Lumbee (9)	13	0.01
Menominee (0)	2	<0.01
Mexican American Ind. (39)	105	0.05
Navajo (51)	98	0.05
Osage (6)	12	0.01
Ottawa (5)	6	<0.01
Paiute (9)	14	0.01
Pima (8)	14	0.01
Potawatomi (13)	29	0.01
Pueblo (7)	14	0.01
Puget Sound Salish (11)	15	0.01
Seminole (7)	11	0.01
Shoshone (23)	53	0.03
Sioux (44)	143	0.07
South American Ind. (1)	9	<0.01
Spanish American Ind. (12)	16	0.01
Tlingit-Haida *(Alaska Native)* (25)	36	0.02
Tohono O'Odham (3)	5	<0.01
Tsimshian *(Alaska Native)* (1)	2	<0.01
Ute (5)	8	<0.01
Yakama (2)	2	<0.01
Yaqui (3)	10	<0.01
Yuman (3)	3	<0.01
Yup'ik *(Alaska Native)* (1)	8	<0.01
Asian (6,501)	8,892	4.32
Not Hispanic (6,398)	8,576	4.17
Hispanic (103)	316	0.15
Bangladeshi (12)	13	0.01
Bhutanese (118)	155	0.08
Burmese (283)	292	0.14
Cambodian (58)	67	0.03
Chinese, ex. Taiwanese (1,292)	1,626	0.79
Filipino (616)	1,154	0.56
Hmong (2)	3	<0.01
Indian (1,011)	1,175	0.57
Indonesian (23)	44	0.02
Japanese (560)	1,185	0.58
Korean (519)	740	0.36
Laotian (306)	366	0.18
Malaysian (13)	16	0.01
Nepalese (187)	211	0.10
Pakistani (34)	41	0.02
Sri Lankan (11)	16	0.01
Taiwanese (99)	116	0.06
Thai (161)	244	0.12
Vietnamese (806)	955	0.46
Hawaii Native/Pacific Islander (457)	882	0.43
Not Hispanic (432)	799	0.39
Hispanic (25)	83	0.04
Fijian (6)	8	<0.01
Guamanian/Chamorro (182)	260	0.13
Marshallese (17)	21	0.01
Native Hawaiian (89)	274	0.13
Samoan (59)	119	0.06
Tongan (6)	21	0.01
White (182,991)	188,702	91.75
Not Hispanic (175,310)	179,647	87.35
Hispanic (7,681)	9,055	4.40

Burley

Place Type: City
County: Cassia
Population: 10,345†

Ancestry‡	**Population**	**%**
American (658)	658	6.66
Armenian (0)	8	0.08
Basque (0)	8	0.08
British (16)	16	0.16
Canadian (51)	104	1.05
Celtic (8)	8	0.08
Croatian (0)	9	0.09
Czech (16)	95	0.96
Danish (70)	352	3.56
Dutch (31)	124	1.25
English (900)	1,789	18.10
European (110)	110	1.11
Finnish (0)	14	0.14
French, ex. Basque (27)	106	1.07
German (518)	1,204	12.18
Greek (16)	70	0.71
Hungarian (0)	53	0.54
Irish (96)	527	5.33
Italian (183)	246	2.49
Latvian (0)	74	0.75
Norwegian (62)	130	1.32
Polish (6)	42	0.43
Portuguese (18)	104	1.05
Russian (0)	14	0.14
Scandinavian (8)	8	0.08
Scotch-Irish (6)	154	1.56
Scottish (102)	314	3.18
Serbian (0)	9	0.09
Slovak (0)	9	0.09
Swedish (36)	170	1.72
Swiss (0)	54	0.55
Welsh (0)	41	0.41

Hispanic Origin	**Population**	**%**
Hispanic or Latino (of any race)	3,460	33.45
Central American, ex. Mexican	21	0.20
Costa Rican	1	0.01
Guatemalan	9	0.09
Honduran	5	0.05
Salvadoran	6	0.06
Cuban	3	0.03
Mexican	3,183	30.77
Puerto Rican	15	0.14
South American	11	0.11
Argentinean	1	0.01
Chilean	1	0.01
Colombian	2	0.02
Peruvian	3	0.03
Venezuelan	4	0.04
Other Hispanic or Latino	227	2.19

Race*	**Population**	**%**
African-American/Black (45)	81	0.78
Not Hispanic (24)	44	0.43
Hispanic (21)	37	0.36
American Indian/Alaska Native (103)	214	2.07
Not Hispanic (63)	132	1.28

*Notes: † The Census 2010 population figure is used to calculate the percentages in the Hispanic Origin and Race categories. Ancestry percentages are based on the 2006-2010 American Community Survey population (not shown); ‡ Numbers in parentheses indicate the number of people reporting a single ancestry; * Numbers in parentheses indicate the number of persons reporting this race alone, not in combination with any other race; Please refer to the Explanation of Data for more information.*

Hispanic (40)	82	0.79
Apache (0)	2	0.02
Arapaho (1)	3	0.03
Blackfeet (0)	1	0.01
Canadian/French Am. Ind. (0)	1	0.01
Cherokee (1)	31	0.30
Chippewa (1)	1	0.01
Choctaw (0)	1	0.01
Creek (1)	1	0.01
Iroquois (0)	3	0.03
Lumbee (1)	1	0.01
Mexican American Ind. (16)	25	0.24
Navajo (23)	43	0.42
Osage (2)	2	0.02
Ottawa (2)	2	0.02
Shoshone (2)	7	0.07
Sioux (3)	4	0.04
South American Ind. (0)	1	0.01
Yup'ik *(Alaska Native)* (0)	3	0.03
Asian (74)	128	1.24
Not Hispanic (72)	101	0.98
Hispanic (2)	27	0.26
Cambodian (1)	1	0.01
Chinese, ex. Taiwanese (9)	16	0.15
Filipino (28)	42	0.41
Indian (6)	11	0.11
Japanese (14)	29	0.28
Korean (5)	14	0.14
Vietnamese (6)	6	0.06
Hawaii Native/Pacific Islander (5)	18	0.17
Not Hispanic (5)	13	0.13
Hispanic (0)	5	0.05
Native Hawaiian (4)	9	0.09
Tongan (1)	4	0.04
White (7,984)	8,293	80.16
Not Hispanic (6,591)	6,708	64.84
Hispanic (1,393)	1,585	15.32

Caldwell

Place Type: City
County: Canyon
Population: 46,237†

Ancestry‡	Population	%
African, Sub-Saharan (62)	62	0.14
African (62)	62	0.14
American (9,247)	9,247	21.14
Armenian (23)	36	0.08
Australian (0)	19	0.04
Austrian (0)	65	0.15
Basque (67)	91	0.21
Belgian (0)	37	0.08
British (142)	248	0.57
Bulgarian (7)	7	0.02
Canadian (23)	57	0.13
Croatian (0)	14	0.03
Czech (46)	147	0.34
Danish (37)	604	1.38
Dutch (105)	865	1.98
English (1,687)	4,647	10.62
European (485)	556	1.27
Finnish (0)	12	0.03
French, ex. Basque (123)	1,173	2.68
French Canadian (34)	136	0.31
German (1,878)	6,296	14.39
Greek (34)	187	0.43
Hungarian (11)	220	0.50
Iranian (14)	14	0.03
Irish (701)	3,060	6.99
Italian (283)	855	1.95
Latvian (0)	6	0.01
Lithuanian (31)	31	0.07
Northern European (17)	17	0.04
Norwegian (221)	603	1.38
Pennsylvania German (16)	61	0.14
Polish (76)	455	1.04
Portuguese (106)	276	0.63
Romanian (26)	26	0.06
Russian (11)	70	0.16
Scandinavian (91)	191	0.44
Scotch-Irish (126)	668	1.53
Scottish (276)	1,027	2.35
Slovak (13)	26	0.06
Swedish (346)	685	1.57
Swiss (0)	58	0.13
Ukrainian (36)	36	0.08
Welsh (183)	322	0.74
West Indian, ex. Hispanic (0)	37	0.08
Jamaican (0)	37	0.08
Yugoslavian (0)	37	0.08

Hispanic Origin	Population	%
Hispanic or Latino (of any race)	16,347	35.35
Central American, ex. Mexican	235	0.51
Costa Rican	8	0.02
Guatemalan	92	0.20
Honduran	20	0.04
Nicaraguan	16	0.03
Panamanian	12	0.03
Salvadoran	87	0.19
Cuban	12	0.03
Dominican Republic	15	0.03
Mexican	14,580	31.53
Puerto Rican	125	0.27
South American	98	0.21
Argentinean	26	0.06
Bolivian	4	0.01
Chilean	5	0.01
Colombian	19	0.04
Ecuadorian	10	0.02
Peruvian	27	0.06
Venezuelan	2	<0.01
Other South American	5	0.01
Other Hispanic or Latino	1,282	2.77

Race*	Population	%
African-American/Black (300)	536	1.16
Not Hispanic (237)	391	0.85
Hispanic (63)	145	0.31
American Indian/Alaska Native (539)	1,015	2.20
Not Hispanic (291)	620	1.34
Hispanic (248)	395	0.85
Aleut *(Alaska Native)* (3)	3	0.01
Apache (9)	34	0.07
Arapaho (1)	1	<0.01
Blackfeet (5)	24	0.05
Cherokee (67)	186	0.40
Cheyenne (3)	3	0.01
Chickasaw (1)	2	<0.01
Chippewa (12)	18	0.04
Choctaw (23)	44	0.10
Colville (1)	1	<0.01
Cree (0)	1	<0.01
Creek (2)	7	0.02
Delaware (3)	9	0.02
Hopi (0)	2	<0.01
Inupiat *(Alaska Native)* (6)	14	0.03
Iroquois (2)	7	0.02
Kiowa (0)	2	<0.01
Mexican American Ind. (63)	74	0.16
Navajo (18)	30	0.06
Osage (1)	3	0.01
Paiute (15)	19	0.04
Pima (1)	1	<0.01
Potawatomi (2)	2	<0.01
Puget Sound Salish (2)	6	0.01
Seminole (0)	3	0.01
Shoshone (4)	4	0.01
Sioux (7)	21	0.05
South American Ind. (3)	6	0.01
Spanish American Ind. (0)	1	<0.01
Tlingit-Haida *(Alaska Native)* (4)	6	0.01
Tohono O'Odham (1)	5	0.01
Ute (0)	2	<0.01
Yakama (0)	3	0.01
Yaqui (12)	13	0.03
Yuman (0)	4	0.01
Yup'ik *(Alaska Native)* (1)	1	<0.01
Asian (406)	785	1.70
Not Hispanic (365)	677	1.46
Hispanic (41)	108	0.23
Bangladeshi (1)	1	<0.01
Burmese (2)	2	<0.01
Cambodian (5)	10	0.02
Chinese, ex. Taiwanese (94)	137	0.30
Filipino (92)	238	0.51
Indian (15)	40	0.09
Indonesian (3)	3	0.01
Japanese (76)	160	0.35
Korean (35)	79	0.17
Laotian (1)	4	0.01
Nepalese (3)	4	0.01
Pakistani (1)	1	<0.01
Sri Lankan (1)	3	0.01
Thai (14)	19	0.04
Vietnamese (35)	54	0.12
Hawaii Native/Pacific Islander (41)	160	0.35
Not Hispanic (32)	125	0.27
Hispanic (9)	35	0.08
Fijian (4)	4	0.01
Guamanian/Chamorro (3)	18	0.04
Marshallese (1)	2	<0.01
Native Hawaiian (15)	79	0.17
Samoan (4)	20	0.04
Tongan (4)	7	0.02
White (35,856)	37,353	80.79
Not Hispanic (28,099)	28,856	62.41
Hispanic (7,757)	8,497	18.38

Chubbuck

Place Type: City
County: Bannock
Population: 13,922†

Ancestry‡	Population	%
African, Sub-Saharan (20)	62	0.48
African (20)	62	0.48
American (1,002)	1,002	7.69
Arab (13)	58	0.44
Other Arab (13)	58	0.44
Austrian (11)	31	0.24
Basque (9)	9	0.07
British (46)	97	0.74
Canadian (49)	49	0.38
Czech (13)	61	0.47
Czechoslovakian (25)	25	0.19
Danish (54)	483	3.71
Dutch (185)	410	3.15
English (1,208)	2,757	21.15
European (215)	240	1.84
Finnish (29)	29	0.22
French, ex. Basque (9)	288	2.21
French Canadian (33)	67	0.51
German (1,011)	2,424	18.59
Greek (26)	26	0.20
Hungarian (0)	16	0.12
Iranian (0)	18	0.14
Irish (244)	1,203	9.23
Italian (76)	212	1.63
Northern European (22)	22	0.17
Norwegian (133)	541	4.15
Polish (84)	122	0.94
Portuguese (33)	106	0.81
Romanian (0)	6	0.05
Scandinavian (26)	67	0.51
Scotch-Irish (55)	146	1.12
Scottish (83)	535	4.10
Swedish (183)	646	4.96
Swiss (22)	125	0.96
Welsh (71)	286	2.19
Yugoslavian (12)	12	0.09

Hispanic Origin	Population	%
Hispanic or Latino (of any race)	1,050	7.54
Central American, ex. Mexican	10	0.07
Costa Rican	2	0.01
Guatemalan	5	0.04
Honduran	1	0.01

*Notes: † The Census 2010 population figure is used to calculate the percentages in the Hispanic Origin and Race categories. Ancestry percentages are based on the 2006-2010 American Community Survey population (not shown); ‡ Numbers in parentheses indicate the number of people reporting a single ancestry; * Numbers in parentheses indicate the number of persons reporting this race alone, not in combination with any other race; Please refer to the Explanation of Data for more information.*

Nicaraguan	1	0.01
Salvadoran	1	0.01
Cuban	4	0.03
Dominican Republic	1	0.01
Mexican	901	6.47
Puerto Rican	14	0.10
South American	15	0.11
Argentinean	1	0.01
Bolivian	3	0.02
Chilean	1	0.01
Colombian	3	0.02
Ecuadorian	1	0.01
Peruvian	4	0.03
Uruguayan	2	0.01
Other Hispanic or Latino	105	0.75

Race*	Population	%
African-American/Black (62)	145	1.04
Not Hispanic (61)	130	0.93
Hispanic (1)	15	0.11
American Indian/Alaska Native (339)	481	3.45
Not Hispanic (279)	373	2.68
Hispanic (60)	108	0.78
Apache (9)	10	0.07
Arapaho (6)	6	0.04
Blackfeet (0)	1	0.01
Cherokee (6)	21	0.15
Cheyenne (1)	1	0.01
Chippewa (3)	10	0.07
Choctaw (4)	8	0.06
Cree (1)	1	0.01
Crow (2)	2	0.01
Hopi (0)	2	0.01
Iroquois (1)	3	0.02
Lumbee (1)	1	0.01
Mexican American Ind. (0)	4	0.03
Navajo (22)	23	0.17
Ottawa (0)	1	0.01
Paiute (1)	1	0.01
Seminole (3)	3	0.02
Shoshone (36)	40	0.29
Sioux (27)	33	0.24
Tlingit-Haida *(Alaska Native)* (2)	2	0.01
Ute (4)	4	0.03
Yakama (1)	1	0.01
Asian (159)	243	1.75
Not Hispanic (155)	232	1.67
Hispanic (4)	11	0.08
Chinese, ex. Taiwanese (40)	51	0.37
Filipino (35)	59	0.42
Indian (8)	13	0.09
Japanese (22)	61	0.44
Korean (19)	26	0.19
Laotian (10)	12	0.09
Nepalese (4)	4	0.03
Taiwanese (1)	1	0.01
Thai (2)	5	0.04
Vietnamese (13)	13	0.09
Hawaii Native/Pacific Islander (36)	82	0.59
Not Hispanic (36)	77	0.55
Hispanic (0)	5	0.04
Fijian (3)	3	0.02
Guamanian/Chamorro (0)	5	0.04
Native Hawaiian (1)	23	0.17
Samoan (11)	24	0.17
Tongan (1)	5	0.04
White (12,596)	12,968	93.15
Not Hispanic (12,079)	12,322	88.51
Hispanic (517)	646	4.64

Coeur d'Alene

Place Type: City
County: Kootenai
Population: 44,137†

Ancestry‡	Population	%
American (4,421)	4,421	10.26
Arab (0)	20	0.05
Arab (0)	11	0.03
Lebanese (0)	9	0.02
Armenian (45)	65	0.15
Austrian (18)	108	0.25
Basque (13)	65	0.15
Belgian (21)	150	0.35
British (46)	164	0.38
Bulgarian (0)	59	0.14
Cajun (0)	10	0.02
Canadian (150)	252	0.58
Croatian (0)	44	0.10
Czech (82)	475	1.10
Czechoslovakian (42)	111	0.26
Danish (122)	699	1.62
Dutch (177)	1,035	2.40
Eastern European (29)	29	0.07
English (1,657)	5,785	13.42
Estonian (0)	11	0.03
European (776)	865	2.01
Finnish (28)	141	0.33
French, ex. Basque (385)	1,973	4.58
French Canadian (155)	471	1.09
German (4,307)	11,887	27.58
Greek (31)	187	0.43
Hungarian (46)	155	0.36
Icelander (9)	32	0.07
Irish (1,922)	7,439	17.26
Italian (788)	2,205	5.12
Latvian (17)	43	0.10
Lithuanian (20)	91	0.21
New Zealander (44)	44	0.10
Northern European (57)	57	0.13
Norwegian (984)	3,010	6.98
Pennsylvania German (0)	33	0.08
Polish (267)	1,033	2.40
Portuguese (284)	425	0.99
Russian (156)	321	0.74
Scandinavian (203)	361	0.84
Scotch-Irish (207)	1,058	2.45
Scottish (342)	1,271	2.95
Serbian (20)	77	0.18
Slavic (10)	10	0.02
Slovak (12)	83	0.19
Slovene (0)	5	0.01
Swedish (247)	1,808	4.20
Swiss (46)	353	0.82
Ukrainian (33)	44	0.10
Welsh (112)	462	1.07
West Indian, ex. Hispanic (0)	47	0.11
Dutch West Indian (0)	23	0.05
Jamaican (0)	24	0.06
Yugoslavian (36)	147	0.34

Hispanic Origin	Population	%
Hispanic or Latino (of any race)	1,911	4.33
Central American, ex. Mexican	87	0.20
Costa Rican	17	0.04
Guatemalan	21	0.05
Honduran	11	0.02
Nicaraguan	9	0.02
Panamanian	3	0.01
Salvadoran	26	0.06
Cuban	15	0.03
Dominican Republic	2	<0.01
Mexican	1,251	2.83
Puerto Rican	138	0.31
South American	53	0.12
Argentinean	8	0.02
Bolivian	1	<0.01
Chilean	3	0.01
Colombian	26	0.06
Ecuadorian	3	0.01
Peruvian	9	0.02
Uruguayan	1	<0.01
Venezuelan	2	<0.01
Other Hispanic or Latino	365	0.83

Race*	Population	%
African-American/Black (175)	411	0.93
Not Hispanic (165)	353	0.80
Hispanic (10)	58	0.13
American Indian/Alaska Native (520)	1,124	2.55
Not Hispanic (439)	961	2.18
Hispanic (81)	163	0.37
Alaska Athabascan *(Ala. Nat.)* (5)	10	0.02
Aleut *(Alaska Native)* (5)	13	0.03
Apache (11)	30	0.07
Arapaho (1)	1	<0.01
Blackfeet (14)	42	0.10
Canadian/French Am. Ind. (1)	5	0.01
Central American Ind. (1)	2	<0.01
Cherokee (30)	119	0.27
Cheyenne (1)	4	0.01
Chickasaw (6)	15	0.03
Chippewa (19)	48	0.11
Choctaw (11)	37	0.08
Colville (11)	20	0.05
Comanche (1)	1	<0.01
Cree (4)	5	0.01
Creek (3)	7	0.02
Crow (1)	3	0.01
Delaware (0)	1	<0.01
Hopi (1)	1	<0.01
Inupiat *(Alaska Native)* (1)	2	<0.01
Iroquois (9)	23	0.05
Lumbee (1)	1	<0.01
Mexican American Ind. (5)	11	0.02
Navajo (16)	31	0.07
Osage (2)	17	0.04
Ottawa (3)	4	0.01
Paiute (1)	1	<0.01
Pima (1)	1	<0.01
Pueblo (1)	3	0.01
Puget Sound Salish (3)	3	0.01
Seminole (0)	2	<0.01
Shoshone (0)	3	0.01
Sioux (12)	19	0.04
Spanish American Ind. (1)	1	<0.01
Tlingit-Haida *(Alaska Native)* (2)	10	0.02
Tohono O'Odham (0)	1	<0.01
Tsimshian *(Alaska Native)* (0)	1	<0.01
Yakama (2)	2	<0.01
Yaqui (0)	1	<0.01
Yup'ik *(Alaska Native)* (2)	2	<0.01
Asian (364)	640	1.45
Not Hispanic (352)	607	1.38
Hispanic (12)	33	0.07
Bangladeshi (3)	3	0.01
Burmese (7)	8	0.02
Cambodian (0)	1	<0.01
Chinese, ex. Taiwanese (57)	99	0.22
Filipino (74)	183	0.41
Hmong (1)	2	<0.01
Indian (57)	66	0.15
Indonesian (1)	9	0.02
Japanese (50)	129	0.29
Korean (52)	75	0.17
Laotian (2)	3	0.01
Pakistani (0)	1	<0.01
Thai (9)	13	0.03
Vietnamese (35)	41	0.09
Hawaii Native/Pacific Islander (63)	154	0.35
Not Hispanic (56)	139	0.31
Hispanic (7)	15	0.03
Fijian (2)	3	0.01
Guamanian/Chamorro (9)	22	0.05
Marshallese (1)	1	<0.01
Native Hawaiian (39)	82	0.19
Samoan (11)	25	0.06
Tongan (0)	1	<0.01
White (41,417)	42,574	96.46
Not Hispanic (40,211)	41,141	93.21
Hispanic (1,206)	1,433	3.25

Eagle

Place Type: City
County: Ada
Population: 19,908†

*Notes: † The Census 2010 population figure is used to calculate the percentages in the Hispanic Origin and Race categories. Ancestry percentages are based on the 2006-2010 American Community Survey population (not shown); ‡ Numbers in parentheses indicate the number of people reporting a single ancestry; * Numbers in parentheses indicate the number of persons reporting this race alone, not in combination with any other race; Please refer to the Explanation of Data for more information.*

Ancestry‡	Population	%
African, Sub-Saharan (32)	32	0.17
Ethiopian (32)	32	0.17
American (914)	914	4.87
Austrian (0)	44	0.23
Basque (38)	38	0.20
Belgian (0)	49	0.26
Brazilian (19)	19	0.10
British (98)	226	1.21
Bulgarian (15)	15	0.08
Canadian (38)	91	0.49
Croatian (0)	43	0.23
Czech (79)	204	1.09
Czechoslovakian (16)	32	0.17
Danish (111)	461	2.46
Dutch (190)	451	2.41
English (1,019)	3,661	19.52
European (644)	821	4.38
Finnish (20)	82	0.44
French, ex. Basque (108)	817	4.36
French Canadian (0)	122	0.65
German (1,214)	3,951	21.07
Greek (11)	49	0.26
Hungarian (14)	83	0.44
Icelander (0)	33	0.18
Iranian (40)	40	0.21
Irish (443)	2,351	12.54
Italian (146)	665	3.55
Lithuanian (7)	19	0.10
Norwegian (197)	660	3.52
Polish (60)	389	2.07
Portuguese (43)	98	0.52
Russian (34)	99	0.53
Scandinavian (68)	276	1.47
Scotch-Irish (175)	512	2.73
Scottish (190)	809	4.31
Slovak (15)	31	0.17
Slovene (0)	14	0.07
Swedish (270)	787	4.20
Swiss (92)	260	1.39
Welsh (118)	431	2.30

Hispanic Origin	Population	%
Hispanic or Latino (of any race)	927	4.66
Central American, ex. Mexican	31	0.16
Costa Rican	2	0.01
Guatemalan	7	0.04
Nicaraguan	2	0.01
Panamanian	3	0.02
Salvadoran	17	0.09
Cuban	15	0.08
Dominican Republic	2	0.01
Mexican	661	3.32
Puerto Rican	20	0.10
South American	55	0.28
Argentinean	11	0.06
Bolivian	4	0.02
Chilean	7	0.04
Colombian	10	0.05
Ecuadorian	3	0.02
Paraguayan	1	0.01
Peruvian	16	0.08
Venezuelan	3	0.02
Other Hispanic or Latino	143	0.72

Race*	Population	%
African-American/Black (60)	128	0.64
Not Hispanic (57)	118	0.59
Hispanic (3)	10	0.05
American Indian/Alaska Native (99)	236	1.19
Not Hispanic (92)	212	1.06
Hispanic (7)	24	0.12
Alaska Athabascan *(Ala. Nat.)* (7)	8	0.04
Aleut *(Alaska Native)* (1)	1	0.01
Apache (2)	8	0.04
Blackfeet (0)	2	0.01
Cherokee (10)	52	0.26
Cheyenne (1)	1	0.01
Chickasaw (3)	3	0.02
Chippewa (2)	6	0.03
Choctaw (3)	6	0.03
Colville (1)	1	0.01
Cree (0)	3	0.02
Creek (1)	2	0.01
Delaware (0)	4	0.02
Mexican American Ind. (0)	4	0.02
Navajo (4)	5	0.03
Osage (3)	3	0.02
Paiute (1)	1	0.01
Potawatomi (0)	1	0.01
Pueblo (1)	2	0.01
Puget Sound Salish (0)	1	0.01
Seminole (5)	5	0.03
Sioux (5)	5	0.03
South American Ind. (0)	1	0.01
Tlingit-Haida *(Alaska Native)* (1)	3	0.02
Asian (326)	493	2.48
Not Hispanic (319)	475	2.39
Hispanic (7)	18	0.09
Bangladeshi (4)	4	0.02
Burmese (2)	2	0.01
Cambodian (4)	4	0.02
Chinese, ex. Taiwanese (88)	112	0.56
Filipino (23)	78	0.39
Indian (48)	55	0.28
Indonesian (2)	2	0.01
Japanese (58)	107	0.54
Korean (39)	68	0.34
Laotian (1)	1	0.01
Nepalese (2)	3	0.02
Pakistani (6)	7	0.04
Taiwanese (15)	15	0.08
Thai (4)	5	0.03
Vietnamese (19)	26	0.13
Hawaii Native/Pacific Islander (23)	52	0.26
Not Hispanic (23)	52	0.26
Guamanian/Chamorro (6)	13	0.07
Native Hawaiian (6)	26	0.13
Samoan (7)	7	0.04
Tongan (1)	5	0.03
White (18,802)	19,185	96.37
Not Hispanic (18,150)	18,472	92.79
Hispanic (652)	713	3.58

Garden City

Place Type: City
County: Ada
Population: 10,972†

Ancestry‡	Population	%
American (1,179)	1,179	10.67
Arab (0)	8	0.07
Syrian (0)	8	0.07
Armenian (0)	26	0.24
Austrian (0)	20	0.18
Basque (56)	70	0.63
British (39)	74	0.67
Canadian (28)	89	0.81
Czech (0)	29	0.26
Danish (59)	139	1.26
Dutch (73)	279	2.52
English (505)	1,553	14.05
European (179)	187	1.69
Finnish (51)	71	0.64
French, ex. Basque (48)	309	2.80
French Canadian (19)	42	0.38
German (710)	1,994	18.04
Greek (41)	83	0.75
Hungarian (0)	17	0.15
Irish (300)	1,165	10.54
Italian (185)	343	3.10
Norwegian (81)	246	2.23
Polish (52)	113	1.02
Portuguese (10)	10	0.09
Russian (20)	63	0.57
Scandinavian (0)	10	0.09
Scotch-Irish (83)	269	2.43
Scottish (83)	358	3.24
Slovak (0)	15	0.14
Swedish (112)	218	1.97
Swiss (73)	106	0.96
Ukrainian (17)	17	0.15
Welsh (88)	274	2.48

Hispanic Origin	Population	%
Hispanic or Latino (of any race)	1,509	13.75
Central American, ex. Mexican	36	0.33
Costa Rican	3	0.03
Guatemalan	8	0.07
Honduran	1	0.01
Nicaraguan	8	0.07
Panamanian	5	0.05
Salvadoran	11	0.10
Cuban	8	0.07
Dominican Republic	9	0.08
Mexican	1,194	10.88
Puerto Rican	21	0.19
South American	33	0.30
Argentinean	4	0.04
Bolivian	1	0.01
Chilean	1	0.01
Colombian	8	0.07
Ecuadorian	5	0.05
Peruvian	12	0.11
Venezuelan	2	0.02
Other Hispanic or Latino	208	1.90

Race*	Population	%
African-American/Black (112)	154	1.40
Not Hispanic (100)	128	1.17
Hispanic (12)	26	0.24
American Indian/Alaska Native (119)	238	2.17
Not Hispanic (85)	168	1.53
Hispanic (34)	70	0.64
Apache (4)	10	0.09
Arapaho (2)	2	0.02
Blackfeet (4)	11	0.10
Canadian/French Am. Ind. (1)	2	0.02
Cherokee (16)	44	0.40
Cheyenne (1)	3	0.03
Chippewa (0)	7	0.06
Choctaw (0)	2	0.02
Comanche (0)	2	0.02
Creek (0)	1	0.01
Inupiat *(Alaska Native)* (1)	1	0.01
Iroquois (2)	3	0.03
Mexican American Ind. (1)	3	0.03
Navajo (9)	15	0.14
Ottawa (0)	3	0.03
Paiute (4)	4	0.04
Potawatomi (2)	6	0.05
Shoshone (4)	5	0.05
Sioux (3)	7	0.06
South American Ind. (0)	2	0.02
Tlingit-Haida *(Alaska Native)* (4)	4	0.04
Yakama (1)	1	0.01
Yaqui (1)	2	0.02
Asian (158)	251	2.29
Not Hispanic (150)	230	2.10
Hispanic (8)	21	0.19
Bhutanese (6)	9	0.08
Burmese (6)	6	0.05
Chinese, ex. Taiwanese (30)	41	0.37
Filipino (22)	46	0.42
Indian (13)	18	0.16
Japanese (22)	37	0.34
Korean (12)	27	0.25
Laotian (4)	4	0.04
Nepalese (0)	5	0.05
Sri Lankan (5)	5	0.05
Thai (5)	14	0.13
Vietnamese (19)	24	0.22
Hawaii Native/Pacific Islander (8)	21	0.19
Not Hispanic (7)	15	0.14
Hispanic (1)	6	0.05
Guamanian/Chamorro (1)	2	0.02
Native Hawaiian (4)	11	0.10
Samoan (1)	4	0.04
White (9,453)	9,781	89.15

*Notes: † The Census 2010 population figure is used to calculate the percentages in the Hispanic Origin and Race categories. Ancestry percentages are based on the 2006-2010 American Community Survey population (not shown); ‡ Numbers in parentheses indicate the number of people reporting a single ancestry; * Numbers in parentheses indicate the number of persons reporting this race alone, not in combination with any other race; Please refer to the Explanation of Data for more information.*

Not Hispanic (8,911)	9,106	82.99
Hispanic (542)	675	6.15

Hailey

Place Type: City
County: Blaine
Population: 7,960†

Ancestry‡	Population	%
American (626)	626	8.04
Austrian (0)	60	0.77
Basque (14)	14	0.18
Belgian (0)	18	0.23
British (13)	13	0.17
Bulgarian (21)	21	0.27
Croatian (15)	37	0.47
Czech (0)	53	0.68
Czechoslovakian (0)	15	0.19
Danish (16)	139	1.78
Dutch (18)	104	1.34
English (127)	757	9.72
European (270)	270	3.47
Finnish (0)	42	0.54
French, ex. Basque (0)	259	3.32
French Canadian (52)	52	0.67
German (768)	2,236	28.70
Greek (0)	32	0.41
Hungarian (18)	18	0.23
Irish (205)	939	12.05
Italian (25)	110	1.41
Norwegian (38)	92	1.18
Pennsylvania German (21)	21	0.27
Polish (0)	44	0.56
Portuguese (71)	71	0.91
Russian (0)	91	1.17
Scandinavian (33)	33	0.42
Scotch-Irish (11)	105	1.35
Scottish (61)	246	3.16
Slovak (14)	14	0.18
Swedish (40)	259	3.32
Swiss (0)	5	0.06
Ukrainian (63)	63	0.81
Welsh (42)	127	1.63
Yugoslavian (0)	34	0.44

Hispanic Origin	Population	%
Hispanic or Latino (of any race)	2,237	28.10
Central American, ex. Mexican	58	0.73
Costa Rican	5	0.06
Guatemalan	34	0.43
Honduran	6	0.08
Nicaraguan	1	0.01
Salvadoran	12	0.15
Cuban	1	0.01
Dominican Republic	1	0.01
Mexican	1,867	23.45
Puerto Rican	28	0.35
South American	193	2.42
Argentinean	4	0.05
Bolivian	3	0.04
Chilean	2	0.03
Colombian	4	0.05
Ecuadorian	1	0.01
Peruvian	179	2.25
Other Hispanic or Latino	89	1.12

Race*	Population	%
African-American/Black (14)	26	0.33
Not Hispanic (4)	11	0.14
Hispanic (10)	15	0.19
American Indian/Alaska Native (54)	90	1.13
Not Hispanic (15)	45	0.57
Hispanic (39)	45	0.57
Apache (3)	4	0.05
Cherokee (0)	4	0.05
Creek (3)	3	0.04
Inupiat *(Alaska Native)* (1)	1	0.01
Mexican American Ind. (5)	5	0.06
Navajo (3)	9	0.11
Shoshone (0)	1	0.01
South American Ind. (1)	2	0.03
Spanish American Ind. (1)	1	0.01
Asian (60)	86	1.08
Not Hispanic (56)	78	0.98
Hispanic (4)	8	0.10
Chinese, ex. Taiwanese (9)	12	0.15
Filipino (10)	20	0.25
Indian (6)	7	0.09
Japanese (9)	13	0.16
Korean (1)	1	0.01
Pakistani (1)	1	0.01
Thai (6)	7	0.09
Vietnamese (18)	21	0.26
Hawaii Native/Pacific Islander (10)	15	0.19
Not Hispanic (9)	11	0.14
Hispanic (1)	4	0.05
Native Hawaiian (5)	6	0.08
Samoan (1)	2	0.03
White (6,380)	6,521	81.92
Not Hispanic (5,568)	5,626	70.68
Hispanic (812)	895	11.24

Hayden

Place Type: City
County: Kootenai
Population: 13,294†

Ancestry‡	Population	%
American (2,101)	2,101	16.44
Arab (49)	95	0.74
Lebanese (49)	95	0.74
Austrian (0)	57	0.45
Basque (35)	173	1.35
British (13)	51	0.40
Canadian (12)	12	0.09
Celtic (0)	17	0.13
Czech (0)	51	0.40
Czechoslovakian (11)	11	0.09
Danish (110)	204	1.60
Dutch (127)	276	2.16
Eastern European (54)	61	0.48
English (520)	2,059	16.11
European (312)	326	2.55
Finnish (33)	84	0.66
French, ex. Basque (47)	712	5.57
French Canadian (45)	55	0.43
German (861)	3,136	24.53
Hungarian (18)	31	0.24
Irish (466)	1,625	12.71
Italian (333)	689	5.39
Latvian (13)	13	0.10
Lithuanian (15)	15	0.12
Norwegian (249)	651	5.09
Pennsylvania German (0)	14	0.11
Polish (163)	269	2.10
Portuguese (80)	94	0.74
Romanian (0)	15	0.12
Russian (0)	66	0.52
Scandinavian (50)	77	0.60
Scotch-Irish (135)	448	3.50
Scottish (56)	186	1.46
Serbian (0)	8	0.06
Slavic (10)	10	0.08
Swedish (210)	432	3.38
Swiss (15)	57	0.45
Ukrainian (27)	27	0.21
Welsh (22)	84	0.66

Hispanic Origin	Population	%
Hispanic or Latino (of any race)	562	4.23
Central American, ex. Mexican	30	0.23
Costa Rican	5	0.04
Guatemalan	13	0.10
Honduran	6	0.05
Panamanian	2	0.02
Salvadoran	4	0.03
Cuban	5	0.04
Dominican Republic	2	0.02
Mexican	357	2.69
Puerto Rican	30	0.23
South American	13	0.10
Argentinean	4	0.03
Colombian	4	0.03
Ecuadorian	3	0.02
Peruvian	1	0.01
Venezuelan	1	0.01
Other Hispanic or Latino	125	0.94

Race*	Population	%
African-American/Black (27)	58	0.44
Not Hispanic (19)	48	0.36
Hispanic (8)	10	0.08
American Indian/Alaska Native (123)	259	1.95
Not Hispanic (103)	228	1.72
Hispanic (20)	31	0.23
Alaska Athabascan *(Ala. Nat.)* (1)	1	0.01
Apache (2)	3	0.02
Blackfeet (8)	10	0.08
Canadian/French Am. Ind. (2)	3	0.02
Cherokee (17)	36	0.27
Chippewa (3)	12	0.09
Choctaw (6)	6	0.05
Colville (1)	4	0.03
Cree (0)	5	0.04
Crow (1)	1	0.01
Iroquois (0)	2	0.02
Kiowa (2)	2	0.02
Mexican American Ind. (3)	3	0.02
Navajo (2)	3	0.02
Paiute (0)	3	0.02
Potawatomi (1)	1	0.01
Shoshone (4)	4	0.03
Sioux (2)	18	0.14
Tlingit-Haida *(Alaska Native)* (4)	5	0.04
Tsimshian *(Alaska Native)* (1)	1	0.01
Ute (1)	2	0.02
Asian (114)	210	1.58
Not Hispanic (111)	190	1.43
Hispanic (3)	20	0.15
Chinese, ex. Taiwanese (22)	30	0.23
Filipino (37)	83	0.62
Indian (1)	1	0.01
Japanese (11)	29	0.22
Korean (14)	26	0.20
Thai (1)	5	0.04
Vietnamese (17)	31	0.23
Hawaii Native/Pacific Islander (12)	31	0.23
Not Hispanic (11)	27	0.20
Hispanic (1)	4	0.03
Fijian (2)	2	0.02
Guamanian/Chamorro (1)	4	0.03
Native Hawaiian (5)	17	0.13
Samoan (2)	3	0.02
White (12,642)	12,919	97.18
Not Hispanic (12,239)	12,470	93.80
Hispanic (403)	449	3.38

Idaho Falls

Place Type: City
County: Bonneville
Population: 56,813†

Ancestry‡	Population	%
African, Sub-Saharan (115)	139	0.25
Ethiopian (8)	8	0.01
Kenyan (12)	12	0.02
South African (39)	63	0.11
Other Sub-Saharan African (56)	56	0.10
American (4,549)	4,549	8.17
Arab (26)	117	0.21
Arab (26)	26	0.05
Lebanese (0)	78	0.14
Other Arab (0)	13	0.02
Armenian (0)	31	0.06
Austrian (0)	56	0.10
Basque (22)	61	0.11
Belgian (0)	12	0.02

SECTION TWO

*Notes: † The Census 2010 population figure is used to calculate the percentages in the Hispanic Origin and Race categories. Ancestry percentages are based on the 2006-2010 American Community Survey population (not shown); ‡ Numbers in parentheses indicate the number of people reporting a single ancestry; * Numbers in parentheses indicate the number of persons reporting this race alone, not in combination with any other race; Please refer to the Explanation of Data for more information.*

Ancestry	Population	%
British (256)	419	0.75
Cajun (0)	23	0.04
Canadian (131)	142	0.26
Celtic (24)	42	0.08
Czech (38)	131	0.24
Czechoslovakian (11)	18	0.03
Danish (623)	1,858	3.34
Dutch (198)	796	1.43
Eastern European (30)	30	0.05
English (5,611)	12,269	22.05
European (1,042)	1,152	2.07
Finnish (38)	189	0.34
French, ex. Basque (422)	1,713	3.08
French Canadian (69)	183	0.33
German (3,952)	9,787	17.59
Greek (121)	195	0.35
Hungarian (69)	95	0.17
Icelander (10)	51	0.09
Iranian (24)	61	0.11
Irish (1,356)	4,849	8.71
Israeli (0)	32	0.06
Italian (429)	1,595	2.87
Latvian (11)	11	0.02
Northern European (105)	105	0.19
Norwegian (521)	1,390	2.50
Pennsylvania German (12)	23	0.04
Polish (146)	675	1.21
Portuguese (113)	181	0.33
Romanian (50)	50	0.09
Russian (61)	166	0.30
Scandinavian (205)	304	0.55
Scotch-Irish (421)	989	1.78
Scottish (504)	2,116	3.80
Serbian (7)	7	0.01
Slovak (0)	25	0.04
Slovene (0)	18	0.03
Swedish (754)	2,001	3.60
Swiss (68)	522	0.94
Ukrainian (11)	67	0.12
Welsh (140)	1,059	1.90
West Indian, ex. Hispanic (17)	52	0.09
West Indian (17)	52	0.09
Yugoslavian (34)	40	0.07

Hispanic Origin	Population	%
Hispanic or Latino (of any race)	7,357	12.95
Central American, ex. Mexican	221	0.39
Costa Rican	14	0.02
Guatemalan	85	0.15
Honduran	31	0.05
Nicaraguan	8	0.01
Panamanian	2	<0.01
Salvadoran	78	0.14
Other Central American	3	0.01
Cuban	38	0.07
Dominican Republic	15	0.03
Mexican	6,296	11.08
Puerto Rican	91	0.16
South American	151	0.27
Argentinean	22	0.04
Bolivian	11	0.02
Chilean	28	0.05
Colombian	18	0.03
Ecuadorian	15	0.03
Paraguayan	1	<0.01
Peruvian	35	0.06
Uruguayan	3	0.01
Venezuelan	14	0.02
Other South American	4	0.01
Other Hispanic or Latino	545	0.96

Race*	Population	%
African-American/Black (396)	651	1.15
Not Hispanic (363)	592	1.04
Hispanic (33)	59	0.10
American Indian/Alaska Native (551)	1,081	1.90
Not Hispanic (379)	731	1.29
Hispanic (172)	350	0.62
Alaska Athabascan *(Ala. Nat.)* (3)	10	0.02
Aleut *(Alaska Native)* (0)	2	<0.01
Apache (1)	2	<0.01
Arapaho (24)	36	0.06
Blackfeet (7)	27	0.05
Canadian/French Am. Ind. (1)	1	<0.01
Central American Ind. (1)	3	0.01
Cherokee (32)	118	0.21
Chippewa (23)	36	0.06
Choctaw (1)	18	0.03
Colville (3)	3	0.01
Comanche (2)	3	0.01
Cree (1)	5	0.01
Creek (2)	4	0.01
Crow (1)	2	<0.01
Delaware (0)	1	<0.01
Hopi (0)	1	<0.01
Inupiat *(Alaska Native)* (2)	5	0.01
Iroquois (2)	2	<0.01
Lumbee (1)	1	<0.01
Mexican American Ind. (32)	52	0.09
Navajo (50)	68	0.12
Osage (0)	2	<0.01
Paiute (8)	8	0.01
Pima (0)	1	<0.01
Potawatomi (6)	9	0.02
Pueblo (3)	4	0.01
Puget Sound Salish (5)	5	0.01
Shoshone (20)	27	0.05
Sioux (12)	33	0.06
South American Ind. (3)	3	0.01
Spanish American Ind. (0)	2	<0.01
Tlingit-Haida *(Alaska Native)* (1)	2	<0.01
Tohono O'Odham (0)	3	0.01
Tsimshian *(Alaska Native)* (5)	5	0.01
Ute (2)	3	0.01
Yaqui (1)	6	0.01
Yup'ik *(Alaska Native)* (0)	2	<0.01
Asian (574)	879	1.55
Not Hispanic (565)	836	1.47
Hispanic (9)	43	0.08
Cambodian (1)	3	0.01
Chinese, ex. Taiwanese (140)	180	0.32
Filipino (49)	109	0.19
Indian (90)	107	0.19
Indonesian (1)	6	0.01
Japanese (167)	285	0.50
Korean (52)	99	0.17
Laotian (5)	9	0.02
Malaysian (4)	4	0.01
Pakistani (1)	3	0.01
Taiwanese (6)	6	0.01
Thai (9)	14	0.02
Vietnamese (32)	36	0.06
Hawaii Native/Pacific Islander (59)	120	0.21
Not Hispanic (56)	103	0.18
Hispanic (3)	17	0.03
Fijian (2)	2	<0.01
Guamanian/Chamorro (8)	11	0.02
Marshallese (3)	3	0.01
Native Hawaiian (24)	54	0.10
Samoan (7)	21	0.04
Tongan (0)	1	<0.01
White (50,711)	51,954	91.45
Not Hispanic (47,208)	48,029	84.54
Hispanic (3,503)	3,925	6.91

Jerome

Place Type: City
County: Jerome
Population: 10,890†

Ancestry‡	Population	%
Albanian (18)	18	0.18
American (924)	924	9.04
Armenian (8)	47	0.46
Austrian (0)	12	0.12
Basque (25)	35	0.34
Belgian (0)	12	0.12
British (24)	24	0.23
Canadian (0)	10	0.10
Celtic (14)	25	0.24
Danish (7)	108	1.06
Dutch (15)	272	2.66
English (298)	879	8.60
European (57)	57	0.56
Finnish (0)	29	0.28
French, ex. Basque (35)	212	2.07
French Canadian (9)	29	0.28
German (497)	1,296	12.68
Hungarian (0)	26	0.25
Irish (195)	692	6.77
Italian (40)	213	2.08
Norwegian (106)	213	2.08
Portuguese (22)	22	0.22
Scandinavian (6)	6	0.06
Scotch-Irish (109)	174	1.70
Scottish (37)	120	1.17
Swedish (51)	148	1.45
Swiss (59)	105	1.03
Welsh (86)	142	1.39

Hispanic Origin	Population	%
Hispanic or Latino (of any race)	3,739	34.33
Central American, ex. Mexican	83	0.76
Costa Rican	1	0.01
Guatemalan	29	0.27
Honduran	25	0.23
Nicaraguan	7	0.06
Salvadoran	21	0.19
Cuban	4	0.04
Dominican Republic	1	0.01
Mexican	3,342	30.69
Puerto Rican	35	0.32
South American	45	0.41
Argentinean	4	0.04
Chilean	4	0.04
Colombian	2	0.02
Ecuadorian	3	0.03
Peruvian	26	0.24
Venezuelan	1	0.01
Other South American	5	0.05
Other Hispanic or Latino	229	2.10

Race*	Population	%
African-American/Black (48)	86	0.79
Not Hispanic (31)	58	0.53
Hispanic (17)	28	0.26
American Indian/Alaska Native (197)	282	2.59
Not Hispanic (95)	157	1.44
Hispanic (102)	125	1.15
Apache (1)	1	0.01
Blackfeet (8)	9	0.08
Canadian/French Am. Ind. (1)	2	0.02
Central American Ind. (1)	1	0.01
Cherokee (12)	34	0.31
Chippewa (2)	4	0.04
Choctaw (4)	7	0.06
Colville (6)	6	0.06
Creek (0)	2	0.02
Iroquois (0)	1	0.01
Lumbee (0)	5	0.05
Mexican American Ind. (15)	18	0.17
Navajo (3)	5	0.05
Osage (1)	4	0.04
Paiute (3)	3	0.03
Pueblo (1)	1	0.01
Puget Sound Salish (1)	1	0.01
Shoshone (11)	18	0.17
Sioux (6)	11	0.10
South American Ind. (3)	3	0.03
Tohono O'Odham (0)	1	0.01
Asian (43)	76	0.70
Not Hispanic (34)	64	0.59
Hispanic (9)	12	0.11
Cambodian (1)	1	0.01
Chinese, ex. Taiwanese (17)	19	0.17
Filipino (10)	26	0.24
Indian (6)	7	0.06
Indonesian (1)	1	0.01
Japanese (3)	11	0.10

*Notes: † The Census 2010 population figure is used to calculate the percentages in the Hispanic Origin and Race categories. Ancestry percentages are based on the 2006-2010 American Community Survey population (not shown); ‡ Numbers in parentheses indicate the number of people reporting a single ancestry; * Numbers in parentheses indicate the number of persons reporting this race alone, not in combination with any other race; Please refer to the Explanation of Data for more information.*

Korean (1)	5	0.05
Laotian (0)	2	0.02
Thai (2)	3	0.03
Vietnamese (1)	1	0.01
Hawaii Native/Pacific Islander (14)	31	0.28
Not Hispanic (9)	19	0.17
Hispanic (5)	12	0.11
Guamanian/Chamorro (8)	8	0.07
Native Hawaiian (4)	6	0.06
Tongan (2)	8	0.07
White (8,526)	8,738	80.24
Not Hispanic (6,846)	6,967	63.98
Hispanic (1,680)	1,771	16.26

Kuna

Place Type: City
County: Ada
Population: 15,210†

Ancestry‡	Population	%
African, Sub-Saharan (83)	83	0.60
African (83)	83	0.60
Albanian (9)	9	0.07
American (1,326)	1,326	9.63
Arab (44)	75	0.54
Arab (0)	31	0.23
Other Arab (44)	44	0.32
Austrian (0)	16	0.12
Basque (71)	94	0.68
British (36)	103	0.75
Canadian (59)	82	0.60
Croatian (10)	152	1.10
Czech (12)	46	0.33
Danish (101)	221	1.61
Dutch (82)	240	1.74
Eastern European (0)	22	0.16
English (593)	1,593	11.57
European (271)	290	2.11
Finnish (24)	79	0.57
French, ex. Basque (64)	458	3.33
French Canadian (19)	67	0.49
German (797)	2,233	16.22
Greek (0)	7	0.05
Hungarian (0)	48	0.35
Irish (235)	1,460	10.61
Italian (70)	375	2.72
Lithuanian (9)	9	0.07
Northern European (47)	47	0.34
Norwegian (75)	241	1.75
Polish (38)	210	1.53
Portuguese (36)	82	0.60
Russian (62)	76	0.55
Scandinavian (22)	22	0.16
Scotch-Irish (11)	165	1.20
Scottish (79)	509	3.70
Serbian (0)	55	0.40
Slavic (0)	58	0.42
Slovak (0)	14	0.10
Slovene (0)	29	0.21
Swedish (81)	282	2.05
Swiss (11)	11	0.08
Ukrainian (42)	42	0.31
Welsh (10)	195	1.42

Hispanic Origin	Population	%
Hispanic or Latino (of any race)	1,305	8.58
Central American, ex. Mexican	32	0.21
Guatemalan	14	0.09
Panamanian	3	0.02
Salvadoran	15	0.10
Cuban	9	0.06
Dominican Republic	1	0.01
Mexican	1,057	6.95
Puerto Rican	34	0.22
South American	38	0.25
Argentinean	3	0.02
Chilean	10	0.07
Colombian	12	0.08
Peruvian	10	0.07
Venezuelan	3	0.02
Other Hispanic or Latino	134	0.88

Race*	Population	%
African-American/Black (94)	187	1.23
Not Hispanic (83)	163	1.07
Hispanic (11)	24	0.16
American Indian/Alaska Native (125)	280	1.84
Not Hispanic (100)	230	1.51
Hispanic (25)	50	0.33
Apache (12)	16	0.11
Blackfeet (8)	12	0.08
Cherokee (10)	41	0.27
Cheyenne (3)	4	0.03
Chickasaw (1)	3	0.02
Chippewa (1)	3	0.02
Choctaw (4)	11	0.07
Comanche (0)	2	0.01
Cree (0)	1	0.01
Creek (1)	1	0.01
Delaware (5)	8	0.05
Hopi (6)	6	0.04
Menominee (2)	4	0.03
Mexican American Ind. (1)	2	0.01
Navajo (7)	12	0.08
Osage (1)	3	0.02
Ottawa (0)	4	0.03
Paiute (1)	1	0.01
Pueblo (1)	5	0.03
Puget Sound Salish (1)	2	0.01
Shoshone (2)	3	0.02
Sioux (7)	12	0.08
Tlingit-Haida *(Alaska Native)* (1)	6	0.04
Asian (108)	255	1.68
Not Hispanic (105)	223	1.47
Hispanic (3)	32	0.21
Cambodian (2)	4	0.03
Chinese, ex. Taiwanese (17)	32	0.21
Filipino (40)	105	0.69
Indian (5)	6	0.04
Indonesian (0)	5	0.03
Japanese (13)	45	0.30
Korean (10)	25	0.16
Laotian (9)	20	0.13
Thai (5)	17	0.11
Vietnamese (0)	3	0.02
Hawaii Native/Pacific Islander (19)	58	0.38
Not Hispanic (18)	48	0.32
Hispanic (1)	10	0.07
Guamanian/Chamorro (1)	5	0.03
Native Hawaiian (11)	37	0.24
Samoan (5)	7	0.05
Tongan (1)	1	0.01
White (13,872)	14,290	93.95
Not Hispanic (13,258)	13,568	89.20
Hispanic (614)	722	4.75

Lewiston

Place Type: City
County: Nez Perce
Population: 31,894†

Ancestry‡	Population	%
African, Sub-Saharan (33)	33	0.10
Ethiopian (33)	33	0.10
Albanian (12)	12	0.04
American (2,576)	2,576	8.13
Arab (0)	42	0.13
Moroccan (0)	42	0.13
Austrian (34)	186	0.59
Basque (11)	73	0.23
Belgian (0)	10	0.03
British (39)	102	0.32
Cajun (16)	16	0.05
Canadian (9)	52	0.16
Croatian (0)	40	0.13
Czech (69)	159	0.50
Czechoslovakian (44)	55	0.17
Danish (103)	360	1.14
Dutch (134)	1,067	3.37
English (1,290)	4,314	13.62
European (270)	270	0.85
Finnish (31)	227	0.72
French, ex. Basque (145)	1,066	3.36
French Canadian (169)	337	1.06
German (3,438)	9,834	31.04
Greek (0)	34	0.11
Hungarian (0)	30	0.09
Icelander (0)	50	0.16
Irish (950)	4,736	14.95
Italian (409)	1,082	3.42
Northern European (7)	7	0.02
Norwegian (580)	1,582	4.99
Pennsylvania German (0)	21	0.07
Polish (87)	329	1.04
Romanian (6)	20	0.06
Russian (88)	264	0.83
Scandinavian (81)	144	0.45
Scotch-Irish (346)	841	2.65
Scottish (320)	935	2.95
Slovak (0)	10	0.03
Slovene (8)	19	0.06
Swedish (364)	1,348	4.25
Swiss (7)	137	0.43
Ukrainian (36)	44	0.14
Welsh (42)	492	1.55
Yugoslavian (50)	60	0.19

Hispanic Origin	Population	%
Hispanic or Latino (of any race)	904	2.83
Central American, ex. Mexican	36	0.11
Costa Rican	8	0.03
Guatemalan	6	0.02
Honduran	9	0.03
Nicaraguan	2	0.01
Panamanian	6	0.02
Salvadoran	5	0.02
Cuban	23	0.07
Dominican Republic	4	0.01
Mexican	585	1.83
Puerto Rican	50	0.16
South American	32	0.10
Argentinean	1	<0.01
Chilean	8	0.03
Colombian	3	0.01
Ecuadorian	3	0.01
Peruvian	16	0.05
Venezuelan	1	<0.01
Other Hispanic or Latino	174	0.55

Race*	Population	%
African-American/Black (106)	225	0.71
Not Hispanic (101)	207	0.65
Hispanic (5)	18	0.06
American Indian/Alaska Native (555)	996	3.12
Not Hispanic (503)	906	2.84
Hispanic (52)	90	0.28
Alaska Athabascan *(Ala. Nat.)* (9)	11	0.03
Aleut *(Alaska Native)* (2)	4	0.01
Apache (4)	9	0.03
Blackfeet (1)	9	0.03
Canadian/French Am. Ind. (0)	1	<0.01
Cherokee (16)	70	0.22
Cheyenne (3)	4	0.01
Chickasaw (2)	3	0.01
Chippewa (14)	29	0.09
Choctaw (9)	19	0.06
Colville (4)	6	0.02
Comanche (1)	2	0.01
Cree (0)	1	<0.01
Creek (1)	4	0.01
Crow (1)	4	0.01
Delaware (2)	4	0.01
Inupiat *(Alaska Native)* (5)	6	0.02
Iroquois (4)	7	0.02
Kiowa (3)	4	0.01
Menominee (4)	4	0.01
Mexican American Ind. (3)	3	0.01
Navajo (2)	6	0.02

*Notes: † The Census 2010 population figure is used to calculate the percentages in the Hispanic Origin and Race categories. Ancestry percentages are based on the 2006-2010 American Community Survey population (not shown); ‡ Numbers in parentheses indicate the number of people reporting a single ancestry; * Numbers in parentheses indicate the number of persons reporting this race alone, not in combination with any other race; Please refer to the Explanation of Data for more information.*

Paiute (3)	4	0.01
Pima (2)	2	0.01
Potawatomi (0)	1	<0.01
Puget Sound Salish (0)	6	0.02
Seminole (0)	1	<0.01
Shoshone (0)	1	<0.01
Sioux (12)	25	0.08
South American Ind. (1)	1	<0.01
Tlingit-Haida *(Alaska Native)* (4)	14	0.04
Tohono O'Odham (0)	1	<0.01
Tsimshian *(Alaska Native)* (1)	7	0.02
Ute (1)	5	0.02
Yakama (9)	13	0.04
Yuman (3)	3	0.01
Asian (255)	432	1.35
Not Hispanic (253)	410	1.29
Hispanic (2)	22	0.07
Bangladeshi (1)	1	<0.01
Cambodian (0)	1	<0.01
Chinese, ex. Taiwanese (67)	94	0.29
Filipino (49)	128	0.40
Hmong (0)	2	0.01
Indian (39)	49	0.15
Indonesian (4)	10	0.03
Japanese (36)	69	0.22
Korean (18)	39	0.12
Malaysian (5)	5	0.02
Nepalese (12)	12	0.04
Pakistani (1)	1	<0.01
Taiwanese (5)	5	0.02
Thai (3)	3	0.01
Vietnamese (12)	20	0.06
Hawaii Native/Pacific Islander (30)	90	0.28
Not Hispanic (28)	79	0.25
Hispanic (2)	11	0.03
Guamanian/Chamorro (3)	6	0.02
Native Hawaiian (12)	42	0.13
Samoan (14)	33	0.10
White (29,942)	30,664	96.14
Not Hispanic (29,452)	30,058	94.24
Hispanic (490)	606	1.90

Meridian

Place Type: City
County: Ada
Population: 75,092†

Ancestry‡	Population	%
Afghan (44)	44	0.06
African, Sub-Saharan (27)	39	0.06
African (14)	26	0.04
South African (13)	13	0.02
Albanian (40)	40	0.06
Alsatian (0)	18	0.03
American (5,375)	5,375	7.80
Arab (38)	38	0.06
Egyptian (11)	11	0.02
Lebanese (17)	17	0.02
Palestinian (10)	10	0.01
Armenian (0)	50	0.07
Assyrian/Chaldean/Syriac (10)	10	0.01
Australian (38)	243	0.35
Austrian (0)	29	0.04
Basque (351)	683	0.99
Belgian (15)	98	0.14
Brazilian (67)	89	0.13
British (161)	451	0.65
Cajun (0)	11	0.02
Canadian (136)	294	0.43
Celtic (16)	26	0.04
Croatian (22)	66	0.10
Czech (76)	277	0.40
Czechoslovakian (115)	141	0.20
Danish (180)	983	1.43
Dutch (300)	1,424	2.07
Eastern European (36)	74	0.11
English (3,229)	10,677	15.48
European (1,243)	1,339	1.94
Finnish (17)	182	0.26
French, ex. Basque (371)	1,873	2.72
French Canadian (58)	309	0.45
German (4,851)	13,850	20.09
Greek (163)	257	0.37
Guyanese (23)	23	0.03
Hungarian (94)	251	0.36
Icelander (9)	18	0.03
Irish (1,709)	6,921	10.04
Italian (1,100)	2,811	4.08
Lithuanian (77)	127	0.18
Luxemburger (0)	16	0.02
Maltese (31)	45	0.07
Northern European (41)	41	0.06
Norwegian (669)	2,157	3.13
Polish (340)	1,091	1.58
Portuguese (187)	424	0.61
Romanian (128)	157	0.23
Russian (270)	478	0.69
Scandinavian (371)	753	1.09
Scotch-Irish (484)	1,354	1.96
Scottish (692)	2,386	3.46
Slavic (0)	9	0.01
Slovak (30)	37	0.05
Slovene (25)	35	0.05
Swedish (641)	2,554	3.70
Swiss (56)	485	0.70
Turkish (27)	35	0.05
Ukrainian (649)	649	0.94
Welsh (193)	789	1.14
Yugoslavian (75)	143	0.21

Hispanic Origin	Population	%
Hispanic or Latino (of any race)	5,111	6.81
Central American, ex. Mexican	186	0.25
Costa Rican	6	0.01
Guatemalan	68	0.09
Honduran	33	0.04
Nicaraguan	4	0.01
Panamanian	17	0.02
Salvadoran	57	0.08
Other Central American	1	<0.01
Cuban	84	0.11
Dominican Republic	19	0.03
Mexican	3,770	5.02
Puerto Rican	186	0.25
South American	243	0.32
Argentinean	31	0.04
Bolivian	8	0.01
Chilean	26	0.03
Colombian	80	0.11
Ecuadorian	15	0.02
Paraguayan	7	0.01
Peruvian	45	0.06
Uruguayan	11	0.01
Venezuelan	16	0.02
Other South American	4	0.01
Other Hispanic or Latino	623	0.83

Race*	Population	%
African-American/Black (573)	1,001	1.33
Not Hispanic (518)	881	1.17
Hispanic (55)	120	0.16
American Indian/Alaska Native (375)	898	1.20
Not Hispanic (271)	689	0.92
Hispanic (104)	209	0.28
Alaska Athabascan *(Ala. Nat.)* (5)	9	0.01
Apache (5)	11	0.01
Arapaho (0)	1	<0.01
Blackfeet (6)	20	0.03
Canadian/French Am. Ind. (1)	2	<0.01
Cherokee (36)	141	0.19
Cheyenne (0)	7	0.01
Chickasaw (0)	2	<0.01
Chippewa (15)	29	0.04
Choctaw (19)	51	0.07
Colville (2)	2	<0.01
Comanche (5)	14	0.02
Cree (0)	5	0.01
Creek (5)	15	0.02
Crow (1)	1	<0.01
Delaware (5)	8	0.01
Inupiat *(Alaska Native)* (2)	6	0.01
Iroquois (2)	7	0.01
Mexican American Ind. (18)	23	0.03
Navajo (8)	23	0.03
Osage (2)	10	0.01
Ottawa (1)	6	0.01
Paiute (2)	3	<0.01
Pima (2)	2	<0.01
Potawatomi (2)	17	0.02
Pueblo (2)	3	<0.01
Puget Sound Salish (1)	3	<0.01
Seminole (0)	2	<0.01
Shoshone (7)	13	0.02
Sioux (16)	35	0.05
South American Ind. (3)	3	<0.01
Tlingit-Haida *(Alaska Native)* (4)	5	0.01
Tohono O'Odham (4)	6	0.01
Ute (2)	7	0.01
Yakama (1)	4	0.01
Yaqui (0)	5	0.01
Yuman (1)	1	<0.01
Yup'ik *(Alaska Native)* (2)	3	<0.01
Asian (1,345)	2,165	2.88
Not Hispanic (1,312)	2,059	2.74
Hispanic (33)	106	0.14
Bangladeshi (3)	3	<0.01
Cambodian (2)	7	0.01
Chinese, ex. Taiwanese (217)	380	0.51
Filipino (224)	436	0.58
Hmong (7)	11	0.01
Indian (151)	205	0.27
Indonesian (9)	16	0.02
Japanese (167)	410	0.55
Korean (130)	247	0.33
Laotian (80)	125	0.17
Malaysian (0)	4	0.01
Nepalese (7)	8	0.01
Pakistani (23)	28	0.04
Sri Lankan (5)	6	0.01
Taiwanese (10)	18	0.02
Thai (29)	54	0.07
Vietnamese (191)	244	0.32
Hawaii Native/Pacific Islander (106)	282	0.38
Not Hispanic (102)	246	0.33
Hispanic (4)	36	0.05
Fijian (1)	6	0.01
Guamanian/Chamorro (18)	37	0.05
Marshallese (12)	15	0.02
Native Hawaiian (33)	112	0.15
Samoan (17)	62	0.08
Tongan (17)	36	0.05
White (69,071)	71,148	94.75
Not Hispanic (66,123)	67,640	90.08
Hispanic (2,948)	3,508	4.67

Moscow

Place Type: City
County: Latah
Population: 23,800†

Ancestry‡	Population	%
Afghan (8)	8	0.03
African, Sub-Saharan (20)	39	0.17
African (20)	20	0.09
Senegalese (0)	19	0.08
American (650)	650	2.79
Arab (21)	21	0.09
Egyptian (10)	10	0.04
Lebanese (11)	11	0.05
Armenian (0)	51	0.22
Australian (20)	20	0.09
Austrian (0)	53	0.23
Basque (60)	60	0.26
Belgian (10)	42	0.18
Brazilian (9)	9	0.04
British (42)	204	0.88
Cajun (16)	16	0.07
Canadian (19)	73	0.31

*Notes: † The Census 2010 population figure is used to calculate the percentages in the Hispanic Origin and Race categories. Ancestry percentages are based on the 2006-2010 American Community Survey population (not shown); ‡ Numbers in parentheses indicate the number of people reporting a single ancestry; * Numbers in parentheses indicate the number of persons reporting this race alone, not in combination with any other race; Please refer to the Explanation of Data for more information.*

Celtic (12)	38	0.16
Croatian (7)	20	0.09
Czech (106)	211	0.91
Czechoslovakian (10)	30	0.13
Danish (98)	474	2.04
Dutch (193)	513	2.21
Eastern European (25)	25	0.11
English (1,202)	4,147	17.83
European (520)	652	2.80
Finnish (11)	96	0.41
French, ex. Basque (132)	1,034	4.44
French Canadian (36)	136	0.58
German (1,760)	6,369	27.38
Greek (14)	60	0.26
Hungarian (41)	41	0.18
Iranian (26)	26	0.11
Irish (713)	3,406	14.64
Italian (158)	1,203	5.17
Lithuanian (45)	83	0.36
Luxemburger (0)	10	0.04
Northern European (97)	97	0.42
Norwegian (365)	1,561	6.71
Polish (184)	577	2.48
Portuguese (26)	129	0.55
Romanian (42)	42	0.18
Russian (87)	226	0.97
Scandinavian (77)	140	0.60
Scotch-Irish (282)	686	2.95
Scottish (331)	1,110	4.77
Slavic (0)	17	0.07
Slovak (35)	51	0.22
Slovene (0)	22	0.09
Swedish (240)	1,209	5.20
Swiss (15)	214	0.92
Ukrainian (33)	74	0.32
Welsh (76)	708	3.04
West Indian, ex. Hispanic (39)	39	0.17
Jamaican (39)	39	0.17
Yugoslavian (0)	16	0.07

Hispanic Origin	Population	%
Hispanic or Latino (of any race)	1,091	4.58
Central American, ex. Mexican	49	0.21
Costa Rican	8	0.03
Guatemalan	10	0.04
Nicaraguan	7	0.03
Panamanian	10	0.04
Salvadoran	14	0.06
Cuban	18	0.08
Mexican	731	3.07
Puerto Rican	60	0.25
South American	77	0.32
Argentinean	6	0.03
Bolivian	2	0.01
Chilean	7	0.03
Colombian	13	0.05
Ecuadorian	20	0.08
Peruvian	25	0.11
Venezuelan	3	0.01
Other South American	1	<0.01
Other Hispanic or Latino	156	0.66

Race*	Population	%
African-American/Black (271)	410	1.72
Not Hispanic (266)	391	1.64
Hispanic (5)	19	0.08
American Indian/Alaska Native (152)	340	1.43
Not Hispanic (135)	295	1.24
Hispanic (17)	45	0.19
Alaska Athabascan *(Ala. Nat.)* (1)	2	0.01
Aleut *(Alaska Native)* (0)	1	<0.01
Apache (1)	7	0.03
Arapaho (1)	1	<0.01
Blackfeet (1)	5	0.02
Canadian/French Am. Ind. (1)	2	0.01
Cherokee (12)	45	0.19
Chickasaw (0)	3	0.01
Chippewa (6)	14	0.06
Choctaw (1)	12	0.05
Colville (5)	6	0.03
Cree (1)	2	0.01
Creek (2)	2	0.01
Crow (0)	1	<0.01
Delaware (0)	1	<0.01
Hopi (1)	1	<0.01
Inupiat *(Alaska Native)* (3)	4	0.02
Iroquois (2)	5	0.02
Lumbee (1)	1	<0.01
Mexican American Ind. (3)	8	0.03
Navajo (6)	14	0.06
Osage (0)	4	0.02
Ottawa (1)	1	<0.01
Potawatomi (0)	1	<0.01
Puget Sound Salish (3)	6	0.03
Shoshone (1)	2	0.01
Sioux (4)	12	0.05
Tlingit-Haida *(Alaska Native)* (7)	15	0.06
Tohono O'Odham (1)	1	<0.01
Tsimshian *(Alaska Native)* (1)	1	<0.01
Ute (3)	7	0.03
Yakama (1)	3	0.01
Yaqui (0)	1	<0.01
Yup'ik *(Alaska Native)* (1)	1	<0.01
Asian (729)	989	4.16
Not Hispanic (721)	967	4.06
Hispanic (8)	22	0.09
Bangladeshi (8)	10	0.04
Burmese (10)	10	0.04
Cambodian (2)	6	0.03
Chinese, ex. Taiwanese (245)	283	1.19
Filipino (62)	124	0.52
Indian (114)	139	0.58
Indonesian (2)	9	0.04
Japanese (54)	139	0.58
Korean (73)	105	0.44
Laotian (1)	2	0.01
Malaysian (1)	3	0.01
Nepalese (47)	47	0.20
Pakistani (4)	4	0.02
Sri Lankan (5)	5	0.02
Taiwanese (29)	32	0.13
Thai (12)	22	0.09
Vietnamese (27)	36	0.15
Hawaii Native/Pacific Islander (40)	87	0.37
Not Hispanic (36)	75	0.32
Hispanic (4)	12	0.05
Guamanian/Chamorro (4)	7	0.03
Native Hawaiian (17)	32	0.13
Samoan (7)	17	0.07
Tongan (2)	4	0.02
White (21,624)	22,243	93.46
Not Hispanic (20,982)	21,508	90.37
Hispanic (642)	735	3.09

Mountain Home

Place Type: City
County: Elmore
Population: 14,206†

Ancestry‡	Population	%
American (1,344)	1,344	9.92
Arab (29)	29	0.21
Lebanese (29)	29	0.21
Basque (77)	192	1.42
British (100)	145	1.07
Canadian (0)	42	0.31
Croatian (0)	9	0.07
Czech (0)	40	0.30
Czechoslovakian (23)	23	0.17
Danish (46)	124	0.92
Dutch (51)	129	0.95
English (604)	1,677	12.38
European (131)	152	1.12
Finnish (21)	33	0.24
French, ex. Basque (48)	343	2.53
French Canadian (31)	60	0.44
German (1,018)	3,122	23.04
Greek (0)	32	0.24
Hungarian (9)	45	0.33
Irish (430)	1,993	14.71
Italian (165)	784	5.79
Lithuanian (9)	9	0.07
Northern European (10)	10	0.07
Norwegian (159)	503	3.71
Polish (139)	385	2.84
Portuguese (39)	39	0.29
Russian (13)	76	0.56
Scandinavian (11)	11	0.08
Scotch-Irish (32)	156	1.15
Scottish (142)	214	1.58
Slovak (0)	64	0.47
Slovene (0)	11	0.08
Swedish (67)	286	2.11
Swiss (13)	20	0.15
Turkish (33)	33	0.24
Ukrainian (0)	35	0.26
Welsh (43)	150	1.11
West Indian, ex. Hispanic (0)	9	0.07
Jamaican (0)	9	0.07
Yugoslavian (11)	11	0.08

Hispanic Origin	Population	%
Hispanic or Latino (of any race)	1,692	11.91
Central American, ex. Mexican	27	0.19
Costa Rican	1	0.01
Guatemalan	5	0.04
Honduran	4	0.03
Nicaraguan	3	0.02
Panamanian	9	0.06
Salvadoran	5	0.04
Cuban	13	0.09
Dominican Republic	4	0.03
Mexican	1,344	9.46
Puerto Rican	81	0.57
South American	34	0.24
Chilean	3	0.02
Colombian	12	0.08
Ecuadorian	6	0.04
Paraguayan	1	0.01
Peruvian	5	0.04
Venezuelan	6	0.04
Other South American	1	0.01
Other Hispanic or Latino	189	1.33

Race*	Population	%
African-American/Black (470)	637	4.48
Not Hispanic (455)	589	4.15
Hispanic (15)	48	0.34
American Indian/Alaska Native (136)	353	2.48
Not Hispanic (116)	280	1.97
Hispanic (20)	73	0.51
Apache (3)	14	0.10
Blackfeet (2)	19	0.13
Canadian/French Am. Ind. (6)	6	0.04
Cherokee (11)	45	0.32
Cheyenne (0)	2	0.01
Chickasaw (5)	8	0.06
Chippewa (5)	10	0.07
Choctaw (3)	7	0.05
Colville (1)	1	0.01
Creek (0)	3	0.02
Delaware (2)	2	0.01
Hopi (0)	1	0.01
Iroquois (4)	4	0.03
Lumbee (1)	4	0.03
Menominee (1)	1	0.01
Mexican American Ind. (10)	14	0.10
Navajo (9)	28	0.20
Osage (0)	2	0.01
Ottawa (2)	3	0.02
Paiute (3)	5	0.04
Potawatomi (0)	4	0.03
Pueblo (0)	1	0.01
Puget Sound Salish (4)	5	0.04
Seminole (2)	2	0.01
Shoshone (3)	6	0.04
Sioux (6)	23	0.16
South American Ind. (0)	2	0.01
Tsimshian *(Alaska Native)* (0)	1	0.01

*Notes: † The Census 2010 population figure is used to calculate the percentages in the Hispanic Origin and Race categories. Ancestry percentages are based on the 2006-2010 American Community Survey population (not shown); ‡ Numbers in parentheses indicate the number of people reporting a single ancestry; * Numbers in parentheses indicate the number of persons reporting this race alone, not in combination with any other race; Please refer to the Explanation of Data for more information.*

Yakama (0)	3	0.02
Yaqui (0)	1	0.01
Yup'ik *(Alaska Native)* (1)	1	0.01
Asian (409)	642	4.52
Not Hispanic (398)	600	4.22
Hispanic (11)	42	0.30
Burmese (1)	1	0.01
Chinese, ex. Taiwanese (126)	147	1.03
Filipino (136)	245	1.72
Indian (12)	17	0.12
Indonesian (2)	8	0.06
Japanese (29)	63	0.44
Korean (39)	74	0.52
Laotian (2)	7	0.05
Thai (26)	44	0.31
Vietnamese (10)	18	0.13
Hawaii Native/Pacific Islander (79)	126	0.89
Not Hispanic (76)	108	0.76
Hispanic (3)	18	0.13
Guamanian/Chamorro (44)	58	0.41
Native Hawaiian (16)	35	0.25
Samoan (0)	4	0.03
Tongan (3)	4	0.03
White (11,817)	12,379	87.14
Not Hispanic (10,967)	11,398	80.23
Hispanic (850)	981	6.91

Nampa

Place Type: City
County: Canyon
Population: 81,557†

Ancestry‡	Population	%
African, Sub-Saharan (144)	144	0.18
Somalian (26)	26	0.03
Sudanese (118)	118	0.15
American (15,510)	15,510	19.80
Arab (8)	13	0.02
Egyptian (8)	8	0.01
Lebanese (0)	5	0.01
Armenian (38)	52	0.07
Australian (0)	8	0.01
Austrian (40)	175	0.22
Basque (166)	407	0.52
Belgian (0)	29	0.04
Brazilian (10)	10	0.01
British (96)	281	0.36
Canadian (139)	387	0.49
Celtic (13)	13	0.02
Croatian (38)	64	0.08
Czech (57)	250	0.32
Czechoslovakian (35)	147	0.19
Danish (221)	886	1.13
Dutch (511)	1,708	2.18
Eastern European (0)	15	0.02
English (3,188)	8,568	10.94
European (1,321)	1,527	1.95
Finnish (100)	268	0.34
French, ex. Basque (347)	1,971	2.52
French Canadian (193)	502	0.64
German (4,916)	13,160	16.80
German Russian (24)	24	0.03
Greek (0)	115	0.15
Hungarian (44)	204	0.26
Icelander (0)	40	0.05
Irish (1,924)	7,124	9.10
Italian (646)	1,653	2.11
Lithuanian (0)	52	0.07
Luxemburger (0)	14	0.02
New Zealander (26)	26	0.03
Northern European (25)	25	0.03
Norwegian (756)	1,752	2.24
Pennsylvania German (42)	77	0.10
Polish (368)	975	1.24
Portuguese (110)	371	0.47
Romanian (215)	236	0.30
Russian (374)	570	0.73
Scandinavian (143)	395	0.50
Scotch-Irish (524)	1,344	1.72
Scottish (602)	2,077	2.65
Slavic (45)	45	0.06
Slovak (12)	27	0.03
Slovene (0)	38	0.05
Swedish (454)	1,576	2.01
Swiss (119)	423	0.54
Ukrainian (125)	125	0.16
Welsh (133)	822	1.05
West Indian, ex. Hispanic (215)	242	0.31
Dutch West Indian (10)	37	0.05
Haitian (192)	192	0.25
Jamaican (13)	13	0.02
Yugoslavian (84)	146	0.19

Hispanic Origin	Population	%
Hispanic or Latino (of any race)	18,653	22.87
Central American, ex. Mexican	534	0.65
Costa Rican	12	0.01
Guatemalan	142	0.17
Honduran	94	0.12
Nicaraguan	21	0.03
Panamanian	15	0.02
Salvadoran	241	0.30
Other Central American	9	0.01
Cuban	27	0.03
Dominican Republic	17	0.02
Mexican	16,237	19.91
Puerto Rican	244	0.30
South American	204	0.25
Argentinean	49	0.06
Bolivian	13	0.02
Chilean	18	0.02
Colombian	51	0.06
Ecuadorian	12	0.01
Peruvian	47	0.06
Venezuelan	13	0.02
Other South American	1	<0.01
Other Hispanic or Latino	1,390	1.70

Race*	Population	%
African-American/Black (593)	997	1.22
Not Hispanic (500)	818	1.00
Hispanic (93)	179	0.22
American Indian/Alaska Native (954)	1,819	2.23
Not Hispanic (552)	1,206	1.48
Hispanic (402)	613	0.75
Alaska Athabascan *(Ala. Nat.)* (7)	11	0.01
Aleut *(Alaska Native)* (1)	2	<0.01
Apache (19)	43	0.05
Arapaho (0)	1	<0.01
Blackfeet (5)	25	0.03
Canadian/French Am. Ind. (8)	26	0.03
Cherokee (106)	285	0.35
Cheyenne (6)	15	0.02
Chickasaw (9)	19	0.02
Chippewa (13)	24	0.03
Choctaw (16)	51	0.06
Colville (0)	1	<0.01
Comanche (2)	7	0.01
Cree (0)	1	<0.01
Creek (4)	8	0.01
Crow (3)	4	<0.01
Delaware (16)	22	0.03
Hopi (2)	2	<0.01
Inupiat *(Alaska Native)* (1)	2	<0.01
Iroquois (2)	11	0.01
Menominee (2)	3	<0.01
Mexican American Ind. (67)	85	0.10
Navajo (45)	82	0.10
Osage (0)	1	<0.01
Ottawa (9)	11	0.01
Paiute (4)	5	0.01
Pima (0)	5	0.01
Potawatomi (6)	10	0.01
Pueblo (3)	4	<0.01
Puget Sound Salish (12)	21	0.03
Seminole (0)	2	<0.01
Shoshone (18)	26	0.03
Sioux (27)	55	0.07
South American Ind. (1)	5	0.01
Spanish American Ind. (9)	11	0.01
Tlingit-Haida *(Alaska Native)* (12)	12	0.01
Tsimshian *(Alaska Native)* (0)	2	<0.01
Ute (4)	11	0.01
Yakama (1)	1	<0.01
Yaqui (3)	5	0.01
Yup'ik *(Alaska Native)* (1)	4	<0.01
Asian (722)	1,326	1.63
Not Hispanic (671)	1,143	1.40
Hispanic (51)	183	0.22
Cambodian (7)	11	0.01
Chinese, ex. Taiwanese (110)	162	0.20
Filipino (152)	410	0.50
Hmong (0)	2	<0.01
Indian (49)	71	0.09
Indonesian (4)	12	0.01
Japanese (120)	276	0.34
Korean (53)	127	0.16
Laotian (58)	81	0.10
Malaysian (4)	4	<0.01
Nepalese (1)	1	<0.01
Pakistani (0)	1	<0.01
Taiwanese (5)	12	0.01
Thai (18)	27	0.03
Vietnamese (79)	100	0.12
Hawaii Native/Pacific Islander (292)	476	0.58
Not Hispanic (270)	400	0.49
Hispanic (22)	76	0.09
Fijian (3)	10	0.01
Guamanian/Chamorro (20)	27	0.03
Marshallese (7)	9	0.01
Native Hawaiian (61)	142	0.17
Samoan (65)	94	0.12
Tongan (65)	87	0.11
White (67,618)	70,070	85.92
Not Hispanic (59,291)	60,737	74.47
Hispanic (8,327)	9,333	11.44

Pocatello

Place Type: City
County: Bannock
Population: 54,255†

Ancestry‡	Population	%
African, Sub-Saharan (72)	142	0.27
African (72)	72	0.14
South African (0)	70	0.13
American (3,643)	3,643	6.84
Arab (51)	60	0.11
Arab (39)	39	0.07
Lebanese (12)	21	0.04
Australian (0)	12	0.02
Austrian (24)	163	0.31
Basque (53)	90	0.17
Belgian (0)	27	0.05
British (195)	383	0.72
Cajun (0)	11	0.02
Canadian (197)	384	0.72
Croatian (0)	8	0.02
Cypriot (0)	26	0.05
Czech (86)	356	0.67
Czechoslovakian (10)	26	0.05
Danish (855)	2,334	4.38
Dutch (202)	923	1.73
English (4,907)	12,111	22.74
European (1,488)	1,584	2.97
Finnish (38)	106	0.20
French, ex. Basque (233)	1,420	2.67
French Canadian (16)	162	0.30
German (3,125)	8,954	16.81
German Russian (9)	21	0.04
Greek (162)	314	0.59
Hungarian (18)	93	0.17
Icelander (12)	12	0.02
Iranian (12)	41	0.08
Irish (1,847)	5,031	9.45
Italian (775)	2,252	4.23
Lithuanian (11)	33	0.06
Maltese (7)	7	0.01

*Notes: † The Census 2010 population figure is used to calculate the percentages in the Hispanic Origin and Race categories. Ancestry percentages are based on the 2006-2010 American Community Survey population (not shown); ‡ Numbers in parentheses indicate the number of people reporting a single ancestry; * Numbers in parentheses indicate the number of persons reporting this race alone, not in combination with any other race; Please refer to the Explanation of Data for more information.*

Northern European (80)	91	0.17
Norwegian (589)	1,368	2.57
Pennsylvania German (15)	25	0.05
Polish (187)	651	1.22
Portuguese (44)	84	0.16
Romanian (37)	37	0.07
Russian (46)	170	0.32
Scandinavian (249)	553	1.04
Scotch-Irish (236)	1,193	2.24
Scottish (392)	1,967	3.69
Slovene (13)	13	0.02
Swedish (549)	1,861	3.49
Swiss (101)	737	1.38
Turkish (0)	15	0.03
Ukrainian (42)	51	0.10
Welsh (438)	1,418	2.66
West Indian, ex. Hispanic (44)	44	0.08
Dutch West Indian (30)	30	0.06
Jamaican (14)	14	0.03
Yugoslavian (0)	58	0.11

Hispanic Origin	Population	%
Hispanic or Latino (of any race)	3,909	7.20
Central American, ex. Mexican	48	0.09
Costa Rican	4	0.01
Guatemalan	9	0.02
Honduran	11	0.02
Nicaraguan	7	0.01
Panamanian	6	0.01
Salvadoran	11	0.02
Cuban	19	0.04
Dominican Republic	1	<0.01
Mexican	3,052	5.63
Puerto Rican	139	0.26
South American	113	0.21
Argentinean	3	0.01
Bolivian	12	0.02
Chilean	10	0.02
Colombian	43	0.08
Ecuadorian	11	0.02
Peruvian	25	0.05
Uruguayan	2	<0.01
Venezuelan	6	0.01
Other South American	1	<0.01
Other Hispanic or Latino	537	0.99

Race*	Population	%
African-American/Black (527)	829	1.53
Not Hispanic (501)	758	1.40
Hispanic (26)	71	0.13
American Indian/Alaska Native (914)	1,437	2.65
Not Hispanic (750)	1,135	2.09
Hispanic (164)	302	0.56
Alaska Athabascan *(Ala. Nat.)* (2)	4	0.01
Aleut *(Alaska Native)* (4)	7	0.01
Apache (9)	20	0.04
Arapaho (13)	21	0.04
Blackfeet (4)	14	0.03
Canadian/French Am. Ind. (4)	6	0.01
Central American Ind. (2)	2	<0.01
Cherokee (31)	95	0.18
Cheyenne (5)	7	0.01
Chippewa (24)	34	0.06
Choctaw (12)	18	0.03
Colville (1)	1	<0.01
Cree (1)	9	0.02
Creek (7)	9	0.02
Crow (6)	7	0.01
Delaware (0)	3	0.01
Hopi (2)	3	0.01
Inupiat *(Alaska Native)* (7)	7	0.01
Iroquois (7)	8	0.01
Kiowa (0)	1	<0.01
Lumbee (0)	2	<0.01
Mexican American Ind. (15)	24	0.04
Navajo (51)	73	0.13
Osage (1)	1	<0.01
Ottawa (0)	4	0.01
Paiute (7)	7	0.01
Potawatomi (4)	6	0.01
Pueblo (5)	8	0.01
Puget Sound Salish (1)	6	0.01
Shoshone (57)	89	0.16
Sioux (31)	51	0.09
South American Ind. (0)	1	<0.01
Tlingit-Haida *(Alaska Native)* (9)	21	0.04
Tohono O'Odham (5)	7	0.01
Ute (2)	4	0.01
Yakama (3)	3	0.01
Yaqui (0)	6	0.01
Yup'ik *(Alaska Native)* (1)	2	<0.01
Asian (850)	1,244	2.29
Not Hispanic (835)	1,199	2.21
Hispanic (15)	45	0.08
Bangladeshi (3)	3	0.01
Burmese (5)	5	0.01
Cambodian (5)	11	0.02
Chinese, ex. Taiwanese (209)	291	0.54
Filipino (130)	225	0.41
Hmong (1)	2	<0.01
Indian (111)	137	0.25
Indonesian (2)	7	0.01
Japanese (110)	249	0.46
Korean (66)	99	0.18
Laotian (32)	41	0.08
Malaysian (1)	6	0.01
Nepalese (42)	43	0.08
Pakistani (28)	32	0.06
Taiwanese (7)	9	0.02
Thai (17)	26	0.05
Vietnamese (26)	37	0.07
Hawaii Native/Pacific Islander (129)	254	0.47
Not Hispanic (112)	226	0.42
Hispanic (17)	28	0.05
Fijian (1)	1	<0.01
Guamanian/Chamorro (17)	25	0.05
Marshallese (2)	2	<0.01
Native Hawaiian (36)	87	0.16
Samoan (37)	84	0.15
Tongan (7)	9	0.02
White (49,087)	50,472	93.03
Not Hispanic (47,088)	48,045	88.55
Hispanic (1,999)	2,427	4.47

Post Falls

Place Type: City
County: Kootenai
Population: 27,574†

Ancestry‡	Population	%
African, Sub-Saharan (8)	24	0.09
African (8)	24	0.09
American (2,957)	2,957	11.30
Arab (54)	78	0.30
Iraqi (16)	16	0.06
Lebanese (27)	27	0.10
Other Arab (11)	35	0.13
Armenian (8)	8	0.03
Australian (0)	3	0.01
Austrian (12)	80	0.31
Basque (24)	65	0.25
Belgian (0)	43	0.16
British (26)	99	0.38
Canadian (81)	90	0.34
Celtic (12)	12	0.05
Czech (52)	143	0.55
Czechoslovakian (23)	59	0.23
Danish (45)	553	2.11
Dutch (69)	521	1.99
English (804)	3,145	12.01
European (629)	641	2.45
Finnish (133)	252	0.96
French, ex. Basque (130)	1,017	3.88
French Canadian (139)	351	1.34
German (2,602)	7,282	27.82
Greek (0)	63	0.24
Hungarian (45)	127	0.49
Icelander (49)	66	0.25
Irish (958)	4,234	16.17
Italian (340)	707	2.70
Lithuanian (22)	22	0.08
New Zealander (16)	16	0.06
Northern European (24)	24	0.09
Norwegian (392)	1,820	6.95
Polish (100)	565	2.16
Portuguese (236)	268	1.02
Romanian (6)	6	0.02
Russian (134)	273	1.04
Scandinavian (33)	167	0.64
Scotch-Irish (284)	738	2.82
Scottish (107)	694	2.65
Serbian (0)	41	0.16
Slovene (0)	12	0.05
Swedish (386)	1,465	5.60
Swiss (28)	150	0.57
Ukrainian (18)	28	0.11
Welsh (43)	272	1.04
West Indian, ex. Hispanic (13)	76	0.29
Dutch West Indian (13)	41	0.16
Jamaican (0)	35	0.13

Hispanic Origin	Population	%
Hispanic or Latino (of any race)	1,280	4.64
Central American, ex. Mexican	31	0.11
Costa Rican	2	0.01
Guatemalan	10	0.04
Honduran	2	0.01
Nicaraguan	6	0.02
Panamanian	2	0.01
Salvadoran	9	0.03
Cuban	8	0.03
Dominican Republic	4	0.01
Mexican	888	3.22
Puerto Rican	75	0.27
South American	37	0.13
Argentinean	3	0.01
Chilean	2	0.01
Colombian	15	0.05
Ecuadorian	2	0.01
Paraguayan	1	<0.01
Peruvian	13	0.05
Venezuelan	1	<0.01
Other Hispanic or Latino	237	0.86

Race*	Population	%
African-American/Black (117)	236	0.86
Not Hispanic (102)	201	0.73
Hispanic (15)	35	0.13
American Indian/Alaska Native (260)	614	2.23
Not Hispanic (230)	512	1.86
Hispanic (30)	102	0.37
Alaska Athabascan *(Ala. Nat.)* (2)	5	0.02
Aleut *(Alaska Native)* (1)	4	0.01
Apache (5)	13	0.05
Blackfeet (12)	29	0.11
Canadian/French Am. Ind. (5)	10	0.04
Cherokee (14)	74	0.27
Cheyenne (0)	4	0.01
Chickasaw (4)	5	0.02
Chippewa (22)	34	0.12
Choctaw (4)	14	0.05
Colville (9)	16	0.06
Creek (0)	2	0.01
Crow (1)	1	<0.01
Inupiat *(Alaska Native)* (4)	8	0.03
Iroquois (1)	2	0.01
Lumbee (1)	1	<0.01
Mexican American Ind. (1)	6	0.02
Navajo (12)	21	0.08
Osage (0)	2	0.01
Paiute (2)	3	0.01
Pima (1)	7	0.03
Pueblo (0)	3	0.01
Puget Sound Salish (5)	6	0.02
Seminole (0)	2	0.01
Shoshone (4)	7	0.03
Sioux (4)	18	0.07
South American Ind. (3)	3	0.01
Tlingit-Haida *(Alaska Native)* (2)	6	0.02

*Notes: † The Census 2010 population figure is used to calculate the percentages in the Hispanic Origin and Race categories. Ancestry percentages are based on the 2006-2010 American Community Survey population (not shown); ‡ Numbers in parentheses indicate the number of people reporting a single ancestry; * Numbers in parentheses indicate the number of persons reporting this race alone, not in combination with any other race; Please refer to the Explanation of Data for more information.*

Race* (continued)	Population	%
Ute (0)	1	<0.01
Yakama (2)	2	0.01
Yaqui (1)	1	<0.01
Yup'ik *(Alaska Native)* (1)	2	0.01
Asian (202)	410	1.49
Not Hispanic (192)	375	1.36
Hispanic (10)	35	0.13
Cambodian (2)	2	0.01
Chinese, ex. Taiwanese (20)	40	0.15
Filipino (65)	162	0.59
Hmong (4)	4	0.01
Indian (38)	48	0.17
Indonesian (3)	5	0.02
Japanese (30)	88	0.32
Korean (11)	32	0.12
Laotian (1)	3	0.01
Taiwanese (2)	2	0.01
Thai (6)	9	0.03
Vietnamese (8)	10	0.04
Hawaii Native/Pacific Islander (18)	69	0.25
Not Hispanic (16)	65	0.24
Hispanic (2)	4	0.01
Guamanian/Chamorro (1)	2	0.01
Native Hawaiian (8)	42	0.15
Samoan (5)	6	0.02
Tongan (0)	2	0.01
White (25,926)	26,652	96.66
Not Hispanic (25,144)	25,702	93.21
Hispanic (782)	950	3.45

Rexburg

Place Type: City
County: Madison
Population: 25,484†

Ancestry‡	Population	%
African, Sub-Saharan (68)	68	0.28
African (59)	59	0.24
South African (9)	9	0.04
American (1,083)	1,083	4.42
Armenian (0)	16	0.07
Australian (0)	25	0.10
Austrian (0)	18	0.07
Basque (12)	12	0.05
Belgian (31)	31	0.13
British (252)	526	2.15
Canadian (28)	39	0.16
Celtic (0)	21	0.09
Croatian (0)	45	0.18
Czech (0)	51	0.21
Czechoslovakian (0)	23	0.09
Danish (590)	1,597	6.51
Dutch (221)	843	3.44
English (3,766)	8,722	35.58
Estonian (0)	10	0.04
European (892)	962	3.92
Finnish (0)	17	0.07
French, ex. Basque (244)	967	3.94
French Canadian (87)	250	1.02
German (1,019)	3,702	15.10
Greek (12)	62	0.25
Hungarian (20)	99	0.40
Irish (409)	1,636	6.67
Italian (151)	474	1.93
Latvian (0)	22	0.09
New Zealander (7)	16	0.07
Northern European (116)	116	0.47
Norwegian (183)	871	3.55
Pennsylvania German (0)	14	0.06
Polish (76)	197	0.80
Portuguese (16)	174	0.71
Romanian (11)	11	0.04
Russian (37)	56	0.23
Scandinavian (152)	479	1.95
Scotch-Irish (131)	462	1.88
Scottish (171)	1,054	4.30
Swedish (331)	1,140	4.65
Swiss (155)	495	2.02
Welsh (198)	971	3.96
Yugoslavian (0)	89	0.36

Hispanic Origin	Population	%
Hispanic or Latino (of any race)	1,435	5.63
Central American, ex. Mexican	91	0.36
Costa Rican	10	0.04
Guatemalan	32	0.13
Honduran	6	0.02
Nicaraguan	5	0.02
Panamanian	7	0.03
Salvadoran	30	0.12
Other Central American	1	<0.01
Cuban	29	0.11
Dominican Republic	12	0.05
Mexican	982	3.85
Puerto Rican	62	0.24
South American	156	0.61
Argentinean	16	0.06
Bolivian	11	0.04
Chilean	26	0.10
Colombian	25	0.10
Ecuadorian	17	0.07
Paraguayan	4	0.02
Peruvian	32	0.13
Uruguayan	3	0.01
Venezuelan	22	0.09
Other Hispanic or Latino	103	0.40

Race*	Population	%
African-American/Black (161)	201	0.79
Not Hispanic (156)	193	0.76
Hispanic (5)	8	0.03
American Indian/Alaska Native (60)	172	0.67
Not Hispanic (44)	133	0.52
Hispanic (16)	39	0.15
Alaska Athabascan *(Ala. Nat.)* (1)	3	0.01
Aleut *(Alaska Native)* (2)	2	0.01
Apache (3)	5	0.02
Arapaho (0)	1	<0.01
Blackfeet (0)	1	<0.01
Central American Ind. (1)	1	<0.01
Cherokee (2)	19	0.07
Chickasaw (1)	3	0.01
Chippewa (1)	2	0.01
Choctaw (0)	5	0.02
Comanche (0)	2	0.01
Creek (1)	2	0.01
Inupiat *(Alaska Native)* (1)	3	0.01
Iroquois (0)	2	0.01
Mexican American Ind. (0)	2	0.01
Navajo (9)	15	0.06
Potawatomi (0)	1	<0.01
Pueblo (1)	1	<0.01
Puget Sound Salish (1)	1	<0.01
Sioux (9)	12	0.05
South American Ind. (5)	5	0.02
Tohono O'Odham (0)	1	<0.01
Asian (305)	492	1.93
Not Hispanic (301)	475	1.86
Hispanic (4)	17	0.07
Bangladeshi (1)	1	<0.01
Cambodian (2)	2	0.01
Chinese, ex. Taiwanese (53)	86	0.34
Filipino (40)	90	0.35
Hmong (8)	12	0.05
Indian (7)	16	0.06
Indonesian (1)	5	0.02
Japanese (39)	116	0.46
Korean (105)	118	0.46
Laotian (2)	3	0.01
Nepalese (5)	5	0.02
Pakistani (0)	1	<0.01
Sri Lankan (2)	4	0.02
Taiwanese (12)	14	0.05
Thai (10)	11	0.04
Vietnamese (4)	8	0.03
Hawaii Native/Pacific Islander (48)	128	0.50
Not Hispanic (44)	109	0.43
Hispanic (4)	19	0.07
Fijian (1)	1	<0.01
Native Hawaiian (13)	64	0.25
Samoan (12)	27	0.11
Tongan (8)	15	0.06
White (23,901)	24,306	95.38
Not Hispanic (23,151)	23,456	92.04
Hispanic (750)	850	3.34

Twin Falls

Place Type: City
County: Twin Falls
Population: 44,125†

Ancestry‡	Population	%
African, Sub-Saharan (168)	248	0.58
African (143)	183	0.43
Cape Verdean (25)	25	0.06
Ethiopian (0)	40	0.09
American (2,598)	2,598	6.12
Armenian (36)	47	0.11
Australian (48)	48	0.11
Austrian (38)	52	0.12
Basque (230)	259	0.61
Belgian (56)	56	0.13
Brazilian (0)	12	0.03
British (117)	206	0.49
Bulgarian (14)	14	0.03
Canadian (91)	138	0.33
Croatian (0)	72	0.17
Czech (159)	317	0.75
Czechoslovakian (36)	67	0.16
Danish (333)	1,041	2.45
Dutch (540)	1,300	3.06
English (2,052)	5,634	13.27
Estonian (43)	43	0.10
European (608)	608	1.43
Finnish (8)	22	0.05
French, ex. Basque (402)	1,473	3.47
French Canadian (69)	165	0.39
German (3,940)	8,187	19.28
Greek (67)	122	0.29
Hungarian (0)	39	0.09
Irish (1,652)	4,827	11.37
Italian (336)	1,124	2.65
Norwegian (767)	1,563	3.68
Pennsylvania German (15)	39	0.09
Polish (115)	397	0.94
Portuguese (191)	367	0.86
Romanian (12)	12	0.03
Russian (70)	171	0.40
Scandinavian (50)	114	0.27
Scotch-Irish (205)	489	1.15
Scottish (521)	1,368	3.22
Serbian (31)	89	0.21
Slovak (16)	16	0.04
Slovene (8)	8	0.02
Swedish (389)	1,181	2.78
Swiss (46)	145	0.34
Turkish (159)	159	0.37
Ukrainian (12)	24	0.06
Welsh (49)	332	0.78
Yugoslavian (190)	190	0.45

Hispanic Origin	Population	%
Hispanic or Latino (of any race)	5,765	13.07
Central American, ex. Mexican	76	0.17
Costa Rican	6	0.01
Guatemalan	21	0.05
Honduran	3	0.01
Nicaraguan	10	0.02
Panamanian	2	<0.01
Salvadoran	34	0.08
Cuban	14	0.03
Dominican Republic	3	0.01
Mexican	4,983	11.29
Puerto Rican	58	0.13
South American	119	0.27
Argentinean	24	0.05
Bolivian	1	<0.01
Chilean	11	0.02

*Notes: † The Census 2010 population figure is used to calculate the percentages in the Hispanic Origin and Race categories. Ancestry percentages are based on the 2006-2010 American Community Survey population (not shown); ‡ Numbers in parentheses indicate the number of people reporting a single ancestry; * Numbers in parentheses indicate the number of persons reporting this race alone, not in combination with any other race; Please refer to the Explanation of Data for more information.*

Colombian	13	0.03
Ecuadorian	3	0.01
Peruvian	52	0.12
Venezuelan	15	0.03
Other Hispanic or Latino	512	1.16

Race*	Population	%
African-American/Black (288)	436	0.99
Not Hispanic (257)	373	0.85
Hispanic (31)	63	0.14
American Indian/Alaska Native (371)	751	1.70
Not Hispanic (263)	540	1.22
Hispanic (108)	211	0.48
Alaska Athabascan *(Ala. Nat.)* (3)	6	0.01
Apache (4)	17	0.04
Arapaho (1)	1	<0.01
Blackfeet (6)	22	0.05
Canadian/French Am. Ind. (1)	1	<0.01
Cherokee (47)	134	0.30
Cheyenne (1)	3	0.01
Chickasaw (3)	3	0.01
Chippewa (16)	23	0.05
Choctaw (6)	20	0.05
Creek (2)	4	0.01
Crow (2)	4	0.01
Delaware (0)	1	<0.01
Inupiat *(Alaska Native)* (1)	1	<0.01
Iroquois (0)	2	<0.01
Lumbee (0)	3	0.01
Mexican American Ind. (13)	16	0.04
Navajo (24)	47	0.11
Osage (0)	2	<0.01
Ottawa (1)	1	<0.01
Paiute (4)	5	0.01
Pima (1)	5	0.01
Potawatomi (3)	4	0.01
Pueblo (1)	1	<0.01
Puget Sound Salish (3)	6	0.01
Seminole (1)	5	0.01
Shoshone (14)	29	0.07
Sioux (19)	44	0.10
Tlingit-Haida *(Alaska Native)* (1)	1	<0.01
Tohono O'Odham (8)	10	0.02
Tsimshian *(Alaska Native)* (2)	2	<0.01
Ute (2)	7	0.02
Yup'ik *(Alaska Native)* (1)	1	<0.01
Asian (788)	1,088	2.47
Not Hispanic (770)	1,037	2.35
Hispanic (18)	51	0.12
Bhutanese (223)	256	0.58
Burmese (53)	61	0.14
Cambodian (13)	22	0.05
Chinese, ex. Taiwanese (116)	139	0.32
Filipino (70)	143	0.32
Indian (30)	64	0.15
Indonesian (0)	1	<0.01
Japanese (69)	108	0.24
Korean (27)	56	0.13
Laotian (30)	39	0.09
Malaysian (1)	1	<0.01
Nepalese (5)	22	0.05
Taiwanese (2)	2	<0.01
Thai (15)	26	0.06
Vietnamese (74)	89	0.20
Hawaii Native/Pacific Islander (59)	123	0.28
Not Hispanic (56)	103	0.23
Hispanic (3)	20	0.05
Fijian (3)	3	0.01
Guamanian/Chamorro (7)	14	0.03
Native Hawaiian (18)	45	0.10
Samoan (12)	19	0.04
Tongan (1)	1	<0.01
White (39,068)	40,078	90.83
Not Hispanic (36,248)	36,917	83.66
Hispanic (2,820)	3,161	7.16

SECTION TWO

*Notes: † The Census 2010 population figure is used to calculate the percentages in the Hispanic Origin and Race categories. Ancestry percentages are based on the 2006-2010 American Community Survey population (not shown); ‡ Numbers in parentheses indicate the number of people reporting a single ancestry; * Numbers in parentheses indicate the number of persons reporting this race alone, not in combination with any other race; Please refer to the Explanation of Data for more information.*

ILLINOIS

Place Type: State
Population: 12,830,632†

Ancestry‡	Population	%
Afghan (988)	1,058	0.01
African, Sub-Saharan (67,978)	80,211	0.63
African (42,006)	50,756	0.40
Cape Verdean (80)	197	<0.01
Ethiopian (3,090)	3,306	0.03
Ghanaian (3,842)	3,934	0.03
Kenyan (760)	863	0.01
Liberian (365)	439	<0.01
Nigerian (11,674)	13,217	0.10
Senegalese (62)	62	<0.01
Sierra Leonean (485)	497	<0.01
Somalian (708)	839	0.01
South African (1,058)	1,623	0.01
Sudanese (541)	585	<0.01
Ugandan (79)	117	<0.01
Zimbabwean (132)	146	<0.01
Other Sub-Saharan African (3,096)	3,630	0.03
Albanian (7,385)	8,794	0.07
Alsatian (172)	669	0.01
American (587,066)	587,066	4.61
Arab (55,460)	71,622	0.56
Arab (16,645)	19,609	0.15
Egyptian (4,415)	5,053	0.04
Iraqi (3,513)	4,332	0.03
Jordanian (4,208)	4,755	0.04
Lebanese (5,524)	11,409	0.09
Moroccan (2,566)	3,159	0.02
Palestinian (8,695)	9,810	0.08
Syrian (2,905)	4,734	0.04
Other Arab (6,989)	8,761	0.07
Armenian (4,519)	8,357	0.07
Assyrian/Chaldean/Syriac (13,746)	17,225	0.14
Australian (1,125)	2,719	0.02
Austrian (9,169)	41,675	0.33
Basque (186)	569	<0.01
Belgian (10,999)	33,847	0.27
Brazilian (3,373)	5,648	0.04
British (16,707)	36,600	0.29
Bulgarian (12,183)	14,058	0.11
Cajun (224)	612	<0.01
Canadian (6,813)	15,620	0.12
Carpatho Rusyn (26)	91	<0.01
Celtic (403)	980	0.01
Croatian (15,769)	44,065	0.35
Cypriot (159)	171	<0.01
Czech (34,757)	128,879	1.01
Czechoslovakian (7,590)	17,974	0.14
Danish (11,332)	53,218	0.42
Dutch (50,239)	201,329	1.58
Eastern European (16,848)	18,969	0.15
English (233,152)	836,287	6.56
Estonian (538)	947	0.01
European (96,902)	107,785	0.85
Finnish (4,814)	18,771	0.15
French, ex. Basque (38,474)	272,074	2.13
French Canadian (11,475)	37,197	0.29
German (885,614)	2,634,885	20.67
German Russian (160)	523	<0.01
Greek (56,674)	105,569	0.83
Guyanese (577)	897	0.01
Hungarian (14,609)	55,195	0.43
Icelander (433)	1,165	0.01
Iranian (7,390)	9,708	0.08
Irish (416,169)	1,648,856	12.94
Israeli (2,829)	4,197	0.03
Italian (288,615)	810,398	6.36
Latvian (3,359)	6,982	0.05
Lithuanian (38,465)	92,913	0.73
Luxemburger (1,664)	6,688	0.05
Macedonian (3,137)	4,372	0.03
Maltese (127)	356	<0.01
New Zealander (351)	542	<0.01
Northern European (5,809)	6,547	0.05
Norwegian (45,991)	173,334	1.36
Pennsylvania German (3,049)	5,327	0.04
Polish (436,077)	979,781	7.69
Portuguese (2,738)	9,579	0.08
Romanian (22,091)	34,691	0.27
Russian (60,501)	136,208	1.07
Scandinavian (7,294)	16,473	0.13
Scotch-Irish (48,149)	142,246	1.12
Scottish (40,521)	160,166	1.26
Serbian (13,999)	21,258	0.17
Slavic (2,087)	5,900	0.05
Slovak (13,847)	41,893	0.33
Slovene (4,953)	14,745	0.12
Soviet Union (88)	102	<0.01
Swedish (73,449)	302,369	2.37
Swiss (7,416)	41,435	0.33
Turkish (4,062)	5,949	0.05
Ukrainian (28,637)	50,346	0.40
Welsh (9,118)	52,576	0.41
West Indian, ex. Hispanic (21,918)	29,090	0.23
Bahamian (186)	333	<0.01
Barbadian (354)	506	<0.01
Belizean (3,784)	4,851	0.04
Bermudan (0)	59	<0.01
British West Indian (194)	345	<0.01
Dutch West Indian (123)	259	<0.01
Haitian (6,376)	7,639	0.06
Jamaican (8,824)	11,721	0.09
Trinidadian/Tobagonian (683)	1,069	0.01
U.S. Virgin Islander (151)	157	<0.01
West Indian (1,234)	2,142	0.02
Other West Indian (9)	9	<0.01
Yugoslavian (14,105)	20,954	0.16

Hispanic Origin	Population	%
Hispanic or Latino (of any race)	2,027,578	15.80
Central American, ex. Mexican	70,000	0.55
Costa Rican	1,874	0.01
Guatemalan	35,321	0.28
Honduran	12,023	0.09
Nicaraguan	3,078	0.02
Panamanian	2,843	0.02
Salvadoran	14,217	0.11
Other Central American	644	0.01
Cuban	22,541	0.18
Dominican Republic	5,691	0.04
Mexican	1,602,403	12.49
Puerto Rican	182,989	1.43
South American	67,862	0.53
Argentinean	5,294	0.04
Bolivian	2,304	0.02
Chilean	2,753	0.02
Colombian	19,345	0.15
Ecuadorian	22,816	0.18
Paraguayan	423	<0.01
Peruvian	10,213	0.08
Uruguayan	737	0.01
Venezuelan	3,283	0.03
Other South American	694	0.01
Other Hispanic or Latino	76,092	0.59

Race*	Population	%
African-American/Black (1,866,414)	1,974,113	15.39
Not Hispanic (1,832,924)	1,919,384	14.96
Hispanic (33,490)	54,729	0.43
American Indian/Alaska Native (43,963)	101,451	0.79
Not Hispanic (18,849)	60,948	0.48
Hispanic (25,114)	40,503	0.32
Alaska Athabascan *(Ala. Nat.)* (44)	86	<0.01
Aleut *(Alaska Native)* (53)	97	<0.01
Apache (536)	1,521	0.01
Arapaho (30)	93	<0.01
Blackfeet (361)	2,752	0.02
Canadian/French Am. Ind. (103)	279	<0.01
Central American Ind. (211)	424	<0.01
Cherokee (3,462)	17,033	0.13
Cheyenne (59)	224	<0.01
Chickasaw (88)	351	<0.01
Chippewa (1,352)	2,740	0.02
Choctaw (530)	1,934	0.02
Colville (7)	16	<0.01
Comanche (88)	251	<0.01
Cree (59)	197	<0.01
Creek (189)	599	<0.01
Crow (34)	147	<0.01
Delaware (70)	186	<0.01
Hopi (41)	99	<0.01
Houma (19)	28	<0.01
Inupiat *(Alaska Native)* (89)	173	<0.01
Iroquois (569)	1,336	0.01
Kiowa (57)	95	<0.01
Lumbee (106)	205	<0.01
Menominee (205)	390	<0.01
Mexican American Ind. (5,153)	7,421	0.06
Navajo (506)	1,063	0.01
Osage (69)	238	<0.01
Ottawa (124)	222	<0.01
Paiute (30)	55	<0.01
Pima (46)	85	<0.01
Potawatomi (294)	625	<0.01
Pueblo (124)	230	<0.01
Puget Sound Salish (32)	56	<0.01
Seminole (58)	316	<0.01
Shoshone (26)	107	<0.01
Sioux (829)	2,270	0.02
South American Ind. (559)	1,402	0.01
Spanish American Ind. (357)	535	<0.01
Tlingit-Haida *(Alaska Native)* (49)	86	<0.01
Tohono O'Odham (36)	47	<0.01
Tsimshian *(Alaska Native)* (4)	7	<0.01
Ute (18)	72	<0.01
Yakama (8)	17	<0.01
Yaqui (100)	193	<0.01
Yuman (20)	33	<0.01
Yup'ik *(Alaska Native)* (26)	49	<0.01
Asian (586,934)	668,694	5.21
Not Hispanic (580,586)	652,951	5.09
Hispanic (6,348)	15,743	0.12
Bangladeshi (1,895)	2,088	0.02
Bhutanese (467)	559	<0.01
Burmese (2,675)	2,950	0.02
Cambodian (3,526)	4,366	0.03
Chinese, ex. Taiwanese (98,269)	112,951	0.88
Filipino (114,724)	139,090	1.08
Hmong (572)	651	0.01
Indian (188,328)	203,669	1.59
Indonesian (1,144)	1,665	0.01
Japanese (17,542)	28,623	0.22
Korean (61,469)	70,263	0.55
Laotian (5,822)	7,102	0.06
Malaysian (635)	939	0.01
Nepalese (1,277)	1,459	0.01
Pakistani (29,646)	33,000	0.26
Sri Lankan (1,148)	1,320	0.01
Taiwanese (5,600)	6,705	0.05
Thai (7,430)	9,800	0.08
Vietnamese (25,036)	29,101	0.23
Hawaii Native/Pacific Islander (4,050)	13,546	0.11
Not Hispanic (2,977)	9,816	0.08
Hispanic (1,073)	3,730	0.03
Fijian (80)	133	<0.01
Guamanian/Chamorro (1,100)	1,928	0.02
Marshallese (32)	41	<0.01
Native Hawaiian (1,122)	3,636	0.03
Samoan (492)	1,191	0.01
Tongan (44)	82	<0.01
White (9,177,877)	9,423,048	73.44
Not Hispanic (8,167,753)	8,324,628	64.88
Hispanic (1,010,124)	1,098,420	8.56

*Notes: † The Census 2010 population figure is used to calculate the percentages in the Hispanic Origin and Race categories. Ancestry percentages are based on the 2006-2010 American Community Survey population (not shown); ‡ Numbers in parentheses indicate the number of people reporting a single ancestry; * Numbers in parentheses indicate the number of persons reporting this race alone, not in combination with any other race; Please refer to the Explanation of Data for more information.*

Addison

Place Type: Village
County: DuPage
Population: 36,942†

Ancestry‡	Population	%
African, Sub-Saharan (25)	37	0.10
African (25)	37	0.10
Albanian (420)	526	1.43
American (452)	452	1.23
Arab (492)	492	1.34
Arab (191)	191	0.52
Egyptian (167)	167	0.46
Palestinian (26)	26	0.07
Syrian (108)	108	0.29
Armenian (10)	10	0.03
Austrian (13)	48	0.13
Belgian (15)	67	0.18
Brazilian (57)	57	0.16
British (17)	55	0.15
Bulgarian (40)	40	0.11
Canadian (0)	74	0.20
Carpatho Rusyn (0)	5	0.01
Croatian (53)	72	0.20
Czech (210)	749	2.04
Czechoslovakian (35)	35	0.10
Danish (36)	190	0.52
Dutch (33)	191	0.52
Eastern European (31)	31	0.08
English (74)	712	1.94
European (69)	79	0.22
Finnish (0)	99	0.27
French, ex. Basque (57)	476	1.30
French Canadian (0)	12	0.03
German (1,041)	3,769	10.28
Greek (703)	921	2.51
Hungarian (16)	27	0.07
Irish (479)	2,564	6.99
Italian (3,063)	5,441	14.84
Latvian (12)	12	0.03
Lithuanian (135)	170	0.46
Macedonian (22)	22	0.06
Norwegian (38)	463	1.26
Polish (2,743)	4,554	12.42
Romanian (98)	110	0.30
Russian (51)	108	0.29
Scandinavian (15)	15	0.04
Scotch-Irish (180)	258	0.70
Scottish (12)	197	0.54
Serbian (67)	67	0.18
Slovak (0)	22	0.06
Swedish (107)	412	1.12
Swiss (0)	27	0.07
Ukrainian (50)	94	0.26
Welsh (19)	87	0.24
West Indian, ex. Hispanic (0)	8	0.02
Haitian (0)	8	0.02
Yugoslavian (0)	21	0.06

Hispanic Origin	Population	%
Hispanic or Latino (of any race)	14,813	40.10
Central American, ex. Mexican	561	1.52
Costa Rican	3	0.01
Guatemalan	418	1.13
Honduran	42	0.11
Nicaraguan	16	0.04
Salvadoran	70	0.19
Other Central American	12	0.03
Cuban	150	0.41
Dominican Republic	2	0.01
Mexican	12,863	34.82
Puerto Rican	493	1.33
South American	265	0.72
Argentinean	15	0.04
Bolivian	4	0.01
Chilean	8	0.02
Colombian	86	0.23
Ecuadorian	85	0.23
Paraguayan	2	0.01
Peruvian	30	0.08
Uruguayan	3	0.01
Venezuelan	22	0.06
Other South American	10	0.03
Other Hispanic or Latino	479	1.30

Race*	Population	%
African-American/Black (1,441)	1,604	4.34
Not Hispanic (1,355)	1,464	3.96
Hispanic (86)	140	0.38
American Indian/Alaska Native (198)	339	0.92
Not Hispanic (55)	124	0.34
Hispanic (143)	215	0.58
Apache (6)	10	0.03
Central American Ind. (0)	5	0.01
Cherokee (10)	38	0.10
Chickasaw (0)	3	0.01
Chippewa (0)	3	0.01
Choctaw (0)	2	0.01
Mexican American Ind. (40)	47	0.13
Navajo (2)	3	0.01
Potawatomi (0)	1	<0.01
Sioux (4)	4	0.01
Spanish American Ind. (0)	2	0.01
Yup'ik *(Alaska Native)* (0)	1	<0.01
Asian (2,730)	2,993	8.10
Not Hispanic (2,706)	2,939	7.96
Hispanic (24)	54	0.15
Bangladeshi (5)	6	0.02
Burmese (15)	15	0.04
Cambodian (28)	32	0.09
Chinese, ex. Taiwanese (117)	156	0.42
Filipino (547)	638	1.73
Indian (1,482)	1,556	4.21
Indonesian (4)	4	0.01
Japanese (26)	45	0.12
Korean (73)	89	0.24
Laotian (15)	23	0.06
Pakistani (162)	183	0.50
Sri Lankan (1)	4	0.01
Taiwanese (14)	15	0.04
Thai (19)	20	0.05
Vietnamese (136)	143	0.39
Hawaii Native/Pacific Islander (3)	46	0.12
Not Hispanic (3)	35	0.09
Hispanic (0)	11	0.03
Native Hawaiian (1)	16	0.04
Samoan (2)	2	0.01
White (24,962)	25,760	69.73
Not Hispanic (17,562)	17,833	48.27
Hispanic (7,400)	7,927	21.46

Algonquin

Place Type: Village
County: McHenry
Population: 30,046†

Ancestry‡	Population	%
African, Sub-Saharan (62)	62	0.21
African (62)	62	0.21
American (797)	797	2.71
Arab (0)	30	0.10
Lebanese (0)	30	0.10
Austrian (13)	131	0.45
Belgian (0)	23	0.08
British (62)	87	0.30
Canadian (71)	85	0.29
Croatian (0)	89	0.30
Czech (107)	393	1.34
Czechoslovakian (78)	169	0.57
Danish (8)	224	0.76
Dutch (136)	757	2.57
English (416)	1,985	6.75
European (189)	228	0.78
Finnish (0)	115	0.39
French, ex. Basque (67)	1,052	3.58
French Canadian (37)	222	0.75
German (2,481)	8,890	30.23
Greek (164)	321	1.09
Hungarian (64)	298	1.01
Irish (996)	4,717	16.04
Italian (1,093)	3,742	12.72
Latvian (4)	4	0.01
Lithuanian (29)	157	0.53
Luxemburger (0)	10	0.03
Northern European (22)	22	0.07
Norwegian (159)	859	2.92
Polish (1,624)	4,971	16.90
Portuguese (7)	21	0.07
Romanian (65)	119	0.40
Russian (100)	364	1.24
Scandinavian (33)	87	0.30
Scotch-Irish (148)	276	0.94
Scottish (119)	521	1.77
Serbian (28)	85	0.29
Slavic (0)	6	0.02
Slovak (32)	76	0.26
Slovene (21)	21	0.07
Swedish (181)	1,248	4.24
Swiss (51)	79	0.27
Ukrainian (39)	84	0.29
Welsh (8)	31	0.11
Yugoslavian (13)	13	0.04

Hispanic Origin	Population	%
Hispanic or Latino (of any race)	2,045	6.81
Central American, ex. Mexican	83	0.28
Costa Rican	9	0.03
Guatemalan	36	0.12
Honduran	12	0.04
Nicaraguan	3	0.01
Panamanian	5	0.02
Salvadoran	18	0.06
Cuban	65	0.22
Dominican Republic	2	0.01
Mexican	1,312	4.37
Puerto Rican	254	0.85
South American	210	0.70
Argentinean	26	0.09
Bolivian	6	0.02
Chilean	5	0.02
Colombian	75	0.25
Ecuadorian	49	0.16
Paraguayan	2	0.01
Peruvian	26	0.09
Uruguayan	1	<0.01
Venezuelan	12	0.04
Other South American	8	0.03
Other Hispanic or Latino	119	0.40

Race*	Population	%
African-American/Black (525)	632	2.10
Not Hispanic (507)	595	1.98
Hispanic (18)	37	0.12
American Indian/Alaska Native (58)	146	0.49
Not Hispanic (43)	113	0.38
Hispanic (15)	33	0.11
Apache (2)	2	0.01
Arapaho (0)	2	0.01
Blackfeet (0)	1	<0.01
Canadian/French Am. Ind. (1)	1	<0.01
Central American Ind. (1)	1	<0.01
Cherokee (4)	23	0.08
Chippewa (6)	15	0.05
Choctaw (1)	4	0.01
Comanche (0)	1	<0.01
Iroquois (0)	3	0.01
Mexican American Ind. (1)	8	0.03
Osage (1)	1	<0.01
Ottawa (2)	2	0.01
Potawatomi (2)	2	0.01
Pueblo (0)	1	<0.01
Seminole (0)	3	0.01
Sioux (5)	5	0.02
South American Ind. (1)	1	<0.01
Tlingit-Haida *(Alaska Native)* (0)	1	<0.01
Asian (2,179)	2,453	8.16
Not Hispanic (2,174)	2,424	8.07
Hispanic (5)	29	0.10

*Notes: † The Census 2010 population figure is used to calculate the percentages in the Hispanic Origin and Race categories. Ancestry percentages are based on the 2006-2010 American Community Survey population (not shown); ‡ Numbers in parentheses indicate the number of people reporting a single ancestry; * Numbers in parentheses indicate the number of persons reporting this race alone, not in combination with any other race; Please refer to the Explanation of Data for more information.*

Bangladeshi (12)	12	0.04
Burmese (4)	4	0.01
Cambodian (5)	7	0.02
Chinese, ex. Taiwanese (197)	246	0.82
Filipino (506)	612	2.04
Hmong (1)	3	0.01
Indian (873)	927	3.09
Indonesian (1)	1	<0.01
Japanese (39)	74	0.25
Korean (168)	212	0.71
Laotian (29)	38	0.13
Malaysian (7)	8	0.03
Pakistani (147)	168	0.56
Sri Lankan (5)	7	0.02
Taiwanese (12)	16	0.05
Thai (14)	33	0.11
Vietnamese (65)	74	0.25
Hawaii Native/Pacific Islander (11)	27	0.09
Not Hispanic (11)	23	0.08
Hispanic (0)	4	0.01
Fijian (1)	1	<0.01
Guamanian/Chamorro (2)	9	0.03
Native Hawaiian (6)	8	0.03
Samoan (2)	4	0.01
White (26,214)	26,670	88.76
Not Hispanic (24,847)	25,189	83.83
Hispanic (1,367)	1,481	4.93

Alsip

Place Type: Village
County: Cook
Population: 19,277†

Ancestry‡	Population	%
African, Sub-Saharan (117)	117	0.61
African (95)	95	0.50
Ethiopian (22)	22	0.11
American (468)	468	2.45
Arab (295)	350	1.83
Arab (67)	90	0.47
Lebanese (88)	88	0.46
Palestinian (118)	132	0.69
Other Arab (22)	40	0.21
Assyrian/Chaldean/Syriac (3)	3	0.02
Austrian (8)	8	0.04
Belgian (0)	13	0.07
British (0)	13	0.07
Bulgarian (0)	11	0.06
Canadian (12)	12	0.06
Croatian (108)	167	0.87
Czech (0)	179	0.94
Czechoslovakian (14)	14	0.07
Danish (18)	81	0.42
Dutch (226)	543	2.84
Eastern European (0)	13	0.07
English (108)	658	3.44
European (52)	52	0.27
Finnish (0)	9	0.05
French, ex. Basque (23)	183	0.96
French Canadian (29)	64	0.33
German (766)	3,756	19.63
Greek (160)	417	2.18
Hungarian (0)	69	0.36
Irish (839)	3,601	18.82
Italian (382)	1,363	7.12
Lithuanian (192)	455	2.38
Norwegian (9)	114	0.60
Polish (1,213)	3,334	17.42
Romanian (43)	43	0.22
Russian (0)	77	0.40
Scandinavian (22)	36	0.19
Scotch-Irish (44)	306	1.60
Scottish (26)	178	0.93
Slavic (17)	17	0.09
Slovak (0)	45	0.24
Slovene (0)	13	0.07
Swedish (42)	338	1.77
Swiss (11)	11	0.06
Ukrainian (73)	93	0.49
Yugoslavian (16)	62	0.32

Hispanic Origin	Population	%
Hispanic or Latino (of any race)	3,842	19.93
Central American, ex. Mexican	71	0.37
Guatemalan	39	0.20
Honduran	8	0.04
Nicaraguan	11	0.06
Salvadoran	13	0.07
Cuban	29	0.15
Dominican Republic	2	0.01
Mexican	3,362	17.44
Puerto Rican	224	1.16
South American	69	0.36
Argentinean	3	0.02
Bolivian	3	0.02
Chilean	7	0.04
Colombian	9	0.05
Ecuadorian	21	0.11
Peruvian	23	0.12
Uruguayan	2	0.01
Other South American	1	0.01
Other Hispanic or Latino	85	0.44

Race*	Population	%
African-American/Black (3,495)	3,628	18.82
Not Hispanic (3,451)	3,548	18.41
Hispanic (44)	80	0.42
American Indian/Alaska Native (71)	154	0.80
Not Hispanic (18)	79	0.41
Hispanic (53)	75	0.39
Apache (4)	10	0.05
Blackfeet (1)	2	0.01
Cherokee (9)	26	0.13
Chippewa (0)	1	0.01
Choctaw (0)	1	0.01
Creek (1)	2	0.01
Kiowa (0)	2	0.01
Mexican American Ind. (5)	8	0.04
Osage (3)	3	0.02
Asian (440)	548	2.84
Not Hispanic (434)	524	2.72
Hispanic (6)	24	0.12
Chinese, ex. Taiwanese (10)	14	0.07
Filipino (243)	283	1.47
Indian (89)	107	0.56
Japanese (6)	10	0.05
Korean (19)	33	0.17
Laotian (1)	8	0.04
Pakistani (25)	25	0.13
Thai (8)	8	0.04
Vietnamese (21)	21	0.11
Hawaii Native/Pacific Islander (21)	31	0.16
Not Hispanic (5)	14	0.07
Hispanic (16)	17	0.09
Fijian (1)	1	0.01
Guamanian/Chamorro (7)	7	0.04
Native Hawaiian (9)	10	0.05
White (13,105)	13,539	70.23
Not Hispanic (11,272)	11,468	59.49
Hispanic (1,833)	2,071	10.74

Alton

Place Type: City
County: Madison
Population: 27,865†

Ancestry‡	Population	%
African, Sub-Saharan (151)	174	0.61
African (151)	174	0.61
American (1,593)	1,593	5.61
Arab (99)	107	0.38
Arab (13)	21	0.07
Lebanese (9)	9	0.03
Palestinian (77)	77	0.27
Austrian (7)	13	0.05
Belgian (8)	8	0.03
Brazilian (58)	58	0.20
British (19)	26	0.09
Croatian (62)	130	0.46
Czech (69)	82	0.29
Czechoslovakian (15)	31	0.11
Danish (0)	37	0.13
Dutch (118)	429	1.51
English (1,079)	3,063	10.79
European (142)	197	0.69
Finnish (0)	38	0.13
French, ex. Basque (62)	702	2.47
French Canadian (18)	57	0.20
German (2,624)	6,765	23.84
German Russian (16)	16	0.06
Greek (200)	240	0.85
Hungarian (43)	51	0.18
Irish (944)	3,604	12.70
Italian (543)	1,203	4.24
Lithuanian (0)	16	0.06
Macedonian (0)	8	0.03
Northern European (14)	53	0.19
Norwegian (40)	166	0.58
Polish (82)	544	1.92
Portuguese (0)	17	0.06
Romanian (0)	14	0.05
Russian (9)	32	0.11
Scandinavian (8)	8	0.03
Scotch-Irish (119)	443	1.56
Scottish (110)	384	1.35
Slovak (16)	25	0.09
Swedish (58)	223	0.79
Swiss (32)	116	0.41
Ukrainian (50)	50	0.18
Welsh (0)	138	0.49
Yugoslavian (16)	30	0.11

Hispanic Origin	Population	%
Hispanic or Latino (of any race)	536	1.92
Central American, ex. Mexican	18	0.06
Guatemalan	1	<0.01
Honduran	7	0.03
Panamanian	4	0.01
Salvadoran	6	0.02
Cuban	18	0.06
Dominican Republic	9	0.03
Mexican	360	1.29
Puerto Rican	42	0.15
South American	29	0.10
Argentinean	2	0.01
Bolivian	1	<0.01
Chilean	5	0.02
Colombian	7	0.03
Ecuadorian	1	<0.01
Peruvian	7	0.03
Venezuelan	6	0.02
Other Hispanic or Latino	60	0.22

Race*	Population	%
African-American/Black (7,421)	8,187	29.38
Not Hispanic (7,375)	8,120	29.14
Hispanic (46)	67	0.24
American Indian/Alaska Native (63)	297	1.07
Not Hispanic (53)	268	0.96
Hispanic (10)	29	0.10
Apache (0)	7	0.03
Arapaho (1)	1	<0.01
Blackfeet (3)	15	0.05
Cherokee (8)	97	0.35
Cheyenne (0)	2	0.01
Chippewa (7)	16	0.06
Choctaw (0)	4	0.01
Creek (3)	3	0.01
Inupiat *(Alaska Native)* (0)	1	<0.01
Iroquois (0)	2	0.01
Lumbee (1)	3	0.01
Menominee (4)	4	0.01
Mexican American Ind. (1)	1	<0.01
Navajo (0)	4	0.01
Potawatomi (0)	1	<0.01
Seminole (0)	2	0.01
Sioux (2)	8	0.03
Asian (140)	236	0.85

*Notes: † The Census 2010 population figure is used to calculate the percentages in the Hispanic Origin and Race categories. Ancestry percentages are based on the 2006-2010 American Community Survey population (not shown); ‡ Numbers in parentheses indicate the number of people reporting a single ancestry; * Numbers in parentheses indicate the number of persons reporting this race alone, not in combination with any other race; Please refer to the Explanation of Data for more information.*

Not Hispanic (138)	226	0.81
Hispanic (2)	10	0.04
Chinese, ex. Taiwanese (23)	35	0.13
Filipino (24)	69	0.25
Indian (30)	35	0.13
Indonesian (1)	2	0.01
Japanese (10)	24	0.09
Korean (21)	37	0.13
Nepalese (0)	1	<0.01
Pakistani (1)	2	0.01
Taiwanese (2)	2	0.01
Thai (4)	4	0.01
Vietnamese (20)	21	0.08
Hawaii Native/Pacific Islander (5)	26	0.09
Not Hispanic (3)	22	0.08
Hispanic (2)	4	0.01
Guamanian/Chamorro (1)	3	0.01
Native Hawaiian (3)	14	0.05
Samoan (0)	2	0.01
White (19,082)	20,012	71.82
Not Hispanic (18,785)	19,657	70.54
Hispanic (297)	355	1.27

Antioch

Place Type: Village
County: Lake
Population: 14,430†

Ancestry‡	Population	%
African, Sub-Saharan (38)	69	0.51
African (38)	69	0.51
American (347)	347	2.57
Arab (0)	11	0.08
Lebanese (0)	11	0.08
Austrian (34)	91	0.67
Belgian (0)	15	0.11
Brazilian (34)	34	0.25
Canadian (12)	12	0.09
Celtic (7)	29	0.21
Croatian (41)	124	0.92
Czech (10)	145	1.07
Czechoslovakian (27)	48	0.36
Danish (11)	108	0.80
Dutch (10)	211	1.56
English (226)	1,433	10.60
European (112)	112	0.83
Finnish (24)	91	0.67
French, ex. Basque (48)	314	2.32
French Canadian (26)	70	0.52
German (1,137)	4,877	36.08
Greek (103)	321	2.37
Hungarian (22)	114	0.84
Irish (525)	2,978	22.03
Italian (256)	1,022	7.56
Latvian (16)	32	0.24
Lithuanian (17)	38	0.28
Norwegian (120)	549	4.06
Polish (505)	1,540	11.39
Portuguese (14)	50	0.37
Romanian (80)	80	0.59
Russian (94)	225	1.66
Scotch-Irish (10)	120	0.89
Scottish (37)	327	2.42
Slovak (36)	231	1.71
Slovene (20)	20	0.15
Swedish (133)	802	5.93
Swiss (24)	80	0.59
Turkish (0)	15	0.11
Ukrainian (12)	61	0.45
Welsh (0)	91	0.67
West Indian, ex. Hispanic (69)	120	0.89
Haitian (0)	27	0.20
Jamaican (12)	36	0.27
West Indian (57)	57	0.42
Yugoslavian (16)	31	0.23

Hispanic Origin	Population	%
Hispanic or Latino (of any race)	1,231	8.53
Central American, ex. Mexican	75	0.52
Costa Rican	2	0.01
Guatemalan	23	0.16
Honduran	10	0.07
Panamanian	12	0.08
Salvadoran	24	0.17
Other Central American	4	0.03
Cuban	22	0.15
Dominican Republic	4	0.03
Mexican	827	5.73
Puerto Rican	197	1.37
South American	57	0.40
Argentinean	5	0.03
Colombian	22	0.15
Ecuadorian	9	0.06
Peruvian	21	0.15
Other Hispanic or Latino	49	0.34

Race*	Population	%
African-American/Black (444)	529	3.67
Not Hispanic (418)	498	3.45
Hispanic (26)	31	0.21
American Indian/Alaska Native (24)	81	0.56
Not Hispanic (20)	74	0.51
Hispanic (4)	7	0.05
Apache (0)	2	0.01
Blackfeet (1)	1	0.01
Canadian/French Am. Ind. (0)	2	0.01
Cherokee (3)	21	0.15
Cheyenne (0)	1	0.01
Chippewa (1)	9	0.06
Choctaw (0)	1	0.01
Iroquois (1)	3	0.02
Menominee (1)	1	0.01
Mexican American Ind. (1)	1	0.01
Navajo (0)	1	0.01
Potawatomi (0)	1	0.01
Asian (538)	654	4.53
Not Hispanic (525)	614	4.26
Hispanic (13)	40	0.28
Cambodian (3)	3	0.02
Chinese, ex. Taiwanese (61)	76	0.53
Filipino (263)	327	2.27
Indian (110)	126	0.87
Indonesian (0)	2	0.01
Japanese (8)	19	0.13
Korean (27)	38	0.26
Malaysian (4)	4	0.03
Pakistani (9)	9	0.06
Taiwanese (4)	5	0.03
Thai (7)	14	0.10
Vietnamese (27)	35	0.24
Hawaii Native/Pacific Islander (14)	28	0.19
Not Hispanic (13)	24	0.17
Hispanic (1)	4	0.03
Guamanian/Chamorro (13)	17	0.12
Native Hawaiian (0)	1	0.01
Samoan (0)	1	0.01
Tongan (1)	4	0.03
White (12,813)	13,092	90.73
Not Hispanic (11,972)	12,177	84.39
Hispanic (841)	915	6.34

Arlington Heights

Place Type: Village
County: Cook
Population: 75,101†

Ancestry‡	Population	%
African, Sub-Saharan (91)	113	0.15
African (44)	44	0.06
Nigerian (35)	57	0.08
Other Sub-Saharan African (12)	12	0.02
Albanian (142)	176	0.23
Alsatian (0)	12	0.02
American (2,097)	2,097	2.80
Arab (58)	157	0.21
Arab (22)	82	0.11
Egyptian (7)	22	0.03
Lebanese (0)	9	0.01
Palestinian (18)	18	0.02
Syrian (11)	11	0.01
Other Arab (0)	15	0.02
Armenian (112)	156	0.21
Assyrian/Chaldean/Syriac (19)	58	0.08
Austrian (150)	732	0.98
Belgian (16)	173	0.23
Brazilian (0)	57	0.08
British (205)	459	0.61
Bulgarian (675)	754	1.01
Canadian (38)	46	0.06
Croatian (126)	323	0.43
Czech (218)	1,161	1.55
Czechoslovakian (95)	117	0.16
Danish (121)	645	0.86
Dutch (277)	929	1.24
Eastern European (145)	161	0.21
English (965)	5,336	7.12
Estonian (34)	34	0.05
European (908)	982	1.31
Finnish (22)	153	0.20
French, ex. Basque (120)	1,500	2.00
French Canadian (39)	173	0.23
German (5,600)	20,088	26.80
Greek (986)	1,599	2.13
Hungarian (130)	475	0.63
Icelander (0)	15	0.02
Iranian (10)	106	0.14
Irish (3,424)	14,141	18.86
Israeli (60)	74	0.10
Italian (3,379)	8,782	11.71
Latvian (0)	27	0.04
Lithuanian (201)	510	0.68
Luxemburger (20)	122	0.16
Macedonian (0)	10	0.01
Northern European (48)	48	0.06
Norwegian (383)	1,657	2.21
Pennsylvania German (0)	37	0.05
Polish (6,196)	12,420	16.57
Portuguese (34)	81	0.11
Romanian (417)	548	0.73
Russian (943)	1,800	2.40
Scandinavian (89)	117	0.16
Scotch-Irish (266)	952	1.27
Scottish (381)	1,440	1.92
Serbian (225)	307	0.41
Slovak (81)	388	0.52
Slovene (99)	150	0.20
Swedish (895)	3,191	4.26
Swiss (0)	191	0.25
Turkish (0)	27	0.04
Ukrainian (320)	626	0.84
Welsh (71)	369	0.49
West Indian, ex. Hispanic (61)	71	0.09
Belizean (9)	9	0.01
Haitian (52)	52	0.07
West Indian (0)	10	0.01
Yugoslavian (65)	81	0.11

Hispanic Origin	Population	%
Hispanic or Latino (of any race)	4,306	5.73
Central American, ex. Mexican	202	0.27
Costa Rican	7	0.01
Guatemalan	90	0.12
Honduran	32	0.04
Nicaraguan	17	0.02
Panamanian	15	0.02
Salvadoran	40	0.05
Other Central American	1	<0.01
Cuban	162	0.22
Dominican Republic	36	0.05
Mexican	2,850	3.79
Puerto Rican	375	0.50
South American	443	0.59
Argentinean	53	0.07
Bolivian	7	0.01
Chilean	13	0.02
Colombian	138	0.18
Ecuadorian	115	0.15
Paraguayan	4	0.01

*Notes: † The Census 2010 population figure is used to calculate the percentages in the Hispanic Origin and Race categories. Ancestry percentages are based on the 2006-2010 American Community Survey population (not shown); ‡ Numbers in parentheses indicate the number of people reporting a single ancestry; * Numbers in parentheses indicate the number of persons reporting this race alone, not in combination with any other race; Please refer to the Explanation of Data for more information.*

	Population	%
Peruvian	69	0.09
Uruguayan	9	0.01
Venezuelan	32	0.04
Other South American	3	<0.01
Other Hispanic or Latino	238	0.32

Race*	Population	%
African-American/Black (984)	1,176	1.57
Not Hispanic (936)	1,083	1.44
Hispanic (48)	93	0.12
American Indian/Alaska Native (95)	237	0.32
Not Hispanic (48)	158	0.21
Hispanic (47)	79	0.11
Apache (0)	1	<0.01
Blackfeet (0)	6	0.01
Canadian/French Am. Ind. (0)	2	<0.01
Central American Ind. (1)	2	<0.01
Cherokee (13)	42	0.06
Chippewa (6)	19	0.03
Choctaw (1)	4	0.01
Iroquois (1)	3	<0.01
Kiowa (1)	1	<0.01
Mexican American Ind. (6)	17	0.02
Navajo (2)	3	<0.01
Ottawa (2)	2	<0.01
Sioux (1)	9	0.01
South American Ind. (4)	8	0.01
Asian (5,349)	5,992	7.98
Not Hispanic (5,320)	5,930	7.90
Hispanic (29)	62	0.08
Bangladeshi (6)	6	0.01
Cambodian (7)	10	0.01
Chinese, ex. Taiwanese (673)	813	1.08
Filipino (748)	955	1.27
Indian (1,586)	1,677	2.23
Indonesian (14)	20	0.03
Japanese (670)	819	1.09
Korean (1,104)	1,193	1.59
Laotian (7)	14	0.02
Malaysian (8)	16	0.02
Pakistani (109)	118	0.16
Taiwanese (70)	82	0.11
Thai (45)	59	0.08
Vietnamese (160)	191	0.25
Hawaii Native/Pacific Islander (8)	44	0.06
Not Hispanic (7)	40	0.05
Hispanic (1)	4	0.01
Guamanian/Chamorro (4)	5	0.01
Native Hawaiian (2)	17	0.02
Samoan (1)	2	<0.01
White (66,266)	67,261	89.56
Not Hispanic (63,532)	64,320	85.64
Hispanic (2,734)	2,941	3.92

Aurora

Place Type: City
County: Kane
Population: 197,899†

Ancestry‡	Population	%
Afghan (261)	261	0.14
African, Sub-Saharan (800)	977	0.51
African (236)	395	0.21
Nigerian (354)	372	0.20
Sierra Leonean (8)	8	<0.01
Other Sub-Saharan African (202)	202	0.11
Albanian (369)	467	0.25
Alsatian (0)	15	0.01
American (2,674)	2,674	1.40
Arab (326)	570	0.30
Arab (118)	118	0.06
Egyptian (45)	77	0.04
Jordanian (13)	26	0.01
Lebanese (35)	126	0.07
Palestinian (115)	115	0.06
Syrian (0)	12	0.01
Other Arab (0)	96	0.05
Armenian (0)	23	0.01
Assyrian/Chaldean/Syriac (26)	37	0.02
Australian (0)	12	0.01
Austrian (151)	389	0.20
Belgian (102)	290	0.15
Brazilian (12)	186	0.10
British (259)	619	0.33
Bulgarian (39)	54	0.03
Canadian (141)	357	0.19
Croatian (31)	246	0.13
Czech (456)	1,429	0.75
Czechoslovakian (113)	244	0.13
Danish (119)	707	0.37
Dutch (344)	1,799	0.94
Eastern European (248)	297	0.16
English (2,025)	9,343	4.91
Estonian (0)	10	0.01
European (1,287)	1,374	0.72
Finnish (0)	193	0.10
French, ex. Basque (445)	2,674	1.40
French Canadian (161)	565	0.30
German (8,935)	31,118	16.34
German Russian (0)	6	<0.01
Greek (410)	1,065	0.56
Guyanese (0)	20	0.01
Hungarian (209)	924	0.49
Icelander (0)	11	0.01
Iranian (188)	188	0.10
Irish (3,076)	18,380	9.65
Italian (2,974)	9,132	4.80
Latvian (17)	116	0.06
Lithuanian (280)	979	0.51
Luxemburger (168)	608	0.32
Macedonian (14)	14	0.01
Northern European (68)	68	0.04
Norwegian (483)	2,157	1.13
Pennsylvania German (7)	25	0.01
Polish (2,715)	9,369	4.92
Portuguese (89)	276	0.14
Romanian (437)	1,266	0.66
Russian (509)	1,340	0.70
Scandinavian (37)	202	0.11
Scotch-Irish (317)	1,361	0.71
Scottish (364)	2,105	1.11
Serbian (39)	138	0.07
Slavic (24)	36	0.02
Slovak (102)	421	0.22
Slovene (16)	77	0.04
Swedish (601)	3,178	1.67
Swiss (65)	397	0.21
Turkish (23)	109	0.06
Ukrainian (292)	509	0.27
Welsh (233)	954	0.50
West Indian, ex. Hispanic (55)	133	0.07
Haitian (32)	32	0.02
Jamaican (16)	94	0.05
West Indian (7)	7	<0.01
Yugoslavian (63)	212	0.11

Hispanic Origin	Population	%
Hispanic or Latino (of any race)	81,809	41.34
Central American, ex. Mexican	1,086	0.55
Costa Rican	13	0.01
Guatemalan	386	0.20
Honduran	211	0.11
Nicaraguan	98	0.05
Panamanian	60	0.03
Salvadoran	289	0.15
Other Central American	29	0.01
Cuban	318	0.16
Dominican Republic	110	0.06
Mexican	72,924	36.85
Puerto Rican	3,867	1.95
South American	1,010	0.51
Argentinean	133	0.07
Bolivian	96	0.05
Chilean	42	0.02
Colombian	311	0.16
Ecuadorian	135	0.07
Paraguayan	3	<0.01
Peruvian	187	0.09
Uruguayan	5	<0.01
Venezuelan	94	0.05
Other South American	4	<0.01
Other Hispanic or Latino	2,494	1.26

Race*	Population	%
African-American/Black (21,202)	23,545	11.90
Not Hispanic (20,348)	21,960	11.10
Hispanic (854)	1,585	0.80
American Indian/Alaska Native (1,004)	1,868	0.94
Not Hispanic (246)	738	0.37
Hispanic (758)	1,130	0.57
Aleut *(Alaska Native)* (1)	1	<0.01
Apache (7)	25	0.01
Blackfeet (5)	31	0.02
Canadian/French Am. Ind. (2)	3	<0.01
Central American Ind. (1)	6	<0.01
Cherokee (42)	187	0.09
Cheyenne (0)	3	<0.01
Chickasaw (2)	4	<0.01
Chippewa (10)	23	0.01
Choctaw (5)	16	0.01
Comanche (1)	4	<0.01
Cree (0)	2	<0.01
Creek (1)	6	<0.01
Crow (2)	3	<0.01
Hopi (8)	14	0.01
Inupiat *(Alaska Native)* (4)	10	0.01
Iroquois (9)	15	0.01
Lumbee (4)	4	<0.01
Menominee (0)	1	<0.01
Mexican American Ind. (164)	222	0.11
Navajo (20)	26	0.01
Ottawa (0)	2	<0.01
Pima (3)	5	<0.01
Potawatomi (7)	11	0.01
Pueblo (0)	5	<0.01
Sioux (11)	29	0.01
South American Ind. (8)	17	0.01
Spanish American Ind. (19)	28	0.01
Tlingit-Haida *(Alaska Native)* (1)	1	<0.01
Ute (0)	2	<0.01
Yaqui (7)	12	0.01
Asian (13,248)	14,809	7.48
Not Hispanic (13,105)	14,444	7.30
Hispanic (143)	365	0.18
Bangladeshi (93)	95	0.05
Bhutanese (61)	81	0.04
Burmese (198)	206	0.10
Cambodian (51)	76	0.04
Chinese, ex. Taiwanese (1,388)	1,636	0.83
Filipino (2,058)	2,529	1.28
Hmong (92)	97	0.05
Indian (6,464)	6,828	3.45
Indonesian (39)	55	0.03
Japanese (110)	264	0.13
Korean (648)	801	0.40
Laotian (128)	151	0.08
Malaysian (23)	25	0.01
Nepalese (23)	31	0.02
Pakistani (755)	829	0.42
Sri Lankan (70)	72	0.04
Taiwanese (67)	80	0.04
Thai (86)	143	0.07
Vietnamese (533)	601	0.30
Hawaii Native/Pacific Islander (65)	202	0.10
Not Hispanic (53)	152	0.08
Hispanic (12)	50	0.03
Fijian (1)	4	<0.01
Guamanian/Chamorro (19)	38	0.02
Native Hawaiian (10)	44	0.02
Samoan (2)	9	<0.01
Tongan (2)	2	<0.01
White (118,172)	123,599	62.46
Not Hispanic (78,924)	81,537	41.20
Hispanic (39,248)	42,062	21.25

SECTION TWO

*Notes: † The Census 2010 population figure is used to calculate the percentages in the Hispanic Origin and Race categories. Ancestry percentages are based on the 2006-2010 American Community Survey population (not shown); ‡ Numbers in parentheses indicate the number of people reporting a single ancestry; * Numbers in parentheses indicate the number of persons reporting this race alone, not in combination with any other race; Please refer to the Explanation of Data for more information.*

Barrington

Place Type: Village
County: Cook
Population: 10,327†

Ancestry‡	Population	%
African, Sub-Saharan (0)	16	0.15
South African (0)	16	0.15
American (691)	691	6.48
Arab (0)	28	0.26
Lebanese (0)	28	0.26
Australian (0)	11	0.10
Austrian (32)	55	0.52
Belgian (0)	35	0.33
British (0)	36	0.34
Canadian (0)	35	0.33
Croatian (12)	35	0.33
Czech (52)	84	0.79
Czechoslovakian (0)	17	0.16
Danish (33)	165	1.55
Dutch (63)	173	1.62
English (347)	1,456	13.66
European (70)	80	0.75
Finnish (9)	84	0.79
French, ex. Basque (42)	260	2.44
French Canadian (0)	60	0.56
German (701)	2,680	25.14
Greek (179)	322	3.02
Hungarian (14)	90	0.84
Irish (690)	2,460	23.07
Italian (442)	1,463	13.72
Lithuanian (0)	10	0.09
Luxemburger (0)	44	0.41
Norwegian (91)	329	3.09
Polish (207)	929	8.71
Romanian (7)	7	0.07
Russian (12)	94	0.88
Scandinavian (22)	44	0.41
Scotch-Irish (182)	443	4.15
Scottish (55)	326	3.06
Serbian (61)	61	0.57
Slovak (36)	71	0.67
Swedish (86)	598	5.61
Swiss (0)	97	0.91
Ukrainian (28)	73	0.68
Welsh (9)	9	0.08

Hispanic Origin	Population	%
Hispanic or Latino (of any race)	468	4.53
Central American, ex. Mexican	17	0.16
Costa Rican	2	0.02
Guatemalan	10	0.10
Honduran	3	0.03
Nicaraguan	1	0.01
Salvadoran	1	0.01
Cuban	18	0.17
Dominican Republic	3	0.03
Mexican	339	3.28
Puerto Rican	21	0.20
South American	40	0.39
Chilean	6	0.06
Colombian	14	0.14
Ecuadorian	5	0.05
Peruvian	5	0.05
Uruguayan	1	0.01
Venezuelan	9	0.09
Other Hispanic or Latino	30	0.29

Race*	Population	%
African-American/Black (100)	142	1.38
Not Hispanic (96)	128	1.24
Hispanic (4)	14	0.14
American Indian/Alaska Native (21)	44	0.43
Not Hispanic (14)	35	0.34
Hispanic (7)	9	0.09
Aleut *(Alaska Native)* (1)	1	0.01
Cherokee (1)	7	0.07
Chippewa (2)	2	0.02
Creek (0)	2	0.02
Iroquois (0)	1	0.01
Mexican American Ind. (1)	1	0.01
Navajo (1)	3	0.03
Puget Sound Salish (0)	2	0.02
Sioux (1)	1	0.01
Asian (379)	476	4.61
Not Hispanic (378)	466	4.51
Hispanic (1)	10	0.10
Chinese, ex. Taiwanese (126)	144	1.39
Filipino (42)	68	0.66
Indian (84)	111	1.07
Japanese (16)	24	0.23
Korean (74)	82	0.79
Malaysian (0)	4	0.04
Pakistani (7)	7	0.07
Taiwanese (4)	12	0.12
Thai (4)	4	0.04
Vietnamese (7)	14	0.14
Hawaii Native/Pacific Islander (0)	5	0.05
Not Hispanic (0)	5	0.05
Native Hawaiian (0)	2	0.02
White (9,509)	9,653	93.47
Not Hispanic (9,232)	9,343	90.47
Hispanic (277)	310	3.00

Bartlett

Place Type: Village
County: DuPage
Population: 41,208†

Ancestry‡	Population	%
African, Sub-Saharan (129)	129	0.32
African (58)	58	0.14
Nigerian (47)	47	0.12
South African (24)	24	0.06
American (1,214)	1,214	3.03
Arab (13)	27	0.07
Lebanese (0)	14	0.03
Other Arab (13)	13	0.03
Armenian (0)	43	0.11
Assyrian/Chaldean/Syriac (124)	185	0.46
Australian (0)	14	0.03
Austrian (46)	158	0.39
Belgian (43)	124	0.31
British (51)	95	0.24
Canadian (9)	18	0.04
Croatian (45)	121	0.30
Czech (271)	1,006	2.51
Danish (18)	189	0.47
Dutch (98)	350	0.87
Eastern European (0)	12	0.03
English (332)	2,128	5.30
European (466)	466	1.16
Finnish (23)	146	0.36
French, ex. Basque (54)	985	2.46
French Canadian (73)	119	0.30
German (2,509)	11,276	28.10
Greek (320)	561	1.40
Hungarian (80)	269	0.67
Irish (1,241)	6,453	16.08
Israeli (11)	11	0.03
Italian (2,205)	6,929	17.27
Latvian (21)	21	0.05
Lithuanian (290)	515	1.28
Luxemburger (0)	45	0.11
Macedonian (80)	80	0.20
Norwegian (191)	713	1.78
Polish (2,302)	5,953	14.84
Portuguese (5)	5	0.01
Romanian (20)	43	0.11
Russian (38)	260	0.65
Scandinavian (13)	90	0.22
Scotch-Irish (182)	482	1.20
Scottish (102)	604	1.51
Serbian (15)	55	0.14
Slovak (22)	166	0.41
Slovene (0)	25	0.06
Swedish (266)	1,437	3.58
Swiss (22)	188	0.47
Turkish (0)	63	0.16
Ukrainian (85)	199	0.50
Welsh (31)	209	0.52
Yugoslavian (38)	38	0.09

Hispanic Origin	Population	%
Hispanic or Latino (of any race)	3,557	8.63
Central American, ex. Mexican	180	0.44
Costa Rican	4	0.01
Guatemalan	107	0.26
Honduran	16	0.04
Nicaraguan	7	0.02
Panamanian	3	0.01
Salvadoran	43	0.10
Cuban	103	0.25
Dominican Republic	12	0.03
Mexican	2,502	6.07
Puerto Rican	364	0.88
South American	247	0.60
Argentinean	25	0.06
Bolivian	5	0.01
Chilean	15	0.04
Colombian	98	0.24
Ecuadorian	35	0.08
Paraguayan	2	<0.01
Peruvian	37	0.09
Uruguayan	10	0.02
Venezuelan	15	0.04
Other South American	5	0.01
Other Hispanic or Latino	149	0.36

Race*	Population	%
African-American/Black (966)	1,141	2.77
Not Hispanic (917)	1,059	2.57
Hispanic (49)	82	0.20
American Indian/Alaska Native (100)	253	0.61
Not Hispanic (36)	148	0.36
Hispanic (64)	105	0.25
Alaska Athabascan *(Ala. Nat.)* (0)	3	0.01
Apache (1)	1	<0.01
Arapaho (0)	2	<0.01
Blackfeet (0)	7	0.02
Canadian/French Am. Ind. (1)	1	<0.01
Central American Ind. (0)	2	<0.01
Cherokee (17)	50	0.12
Cheyenne (1)	1	<0.01
Chippewa (0)	3	0.01
Choctaw (2)	4	0.01
Crow (0)	3	0.01
Mexican American Ind. (7)	10	0.02
Potawatomi (0)	3	0.01
Pueblo (0)	4	0.01
Sioux (1)	8	0.02
South American Ind. (0)	2	<0.01
Tohono O'Odham (1)	1	<0.01
Asian (5,918)	6,327	15.35
Not Hispanic (5,895)	6,267	15.21
Hispanic (23)	60	0.15
Bangladeshi (22)	22	0.05
Burmese (10)	12	0.03
Cambodian (17)	27	0.07
Chinese, ex. Taiwanese (324)	386	0.94
Filipino (1,315)	1,454	3.53
Indian (3,010)	3,120	7.57
Indonesian (1)	1	<0.01
Japanese (70)	127	0.31
Korean (316)	342	0.83
Laotian (87)	90	0.22
Malaysian (19)	19	0.05
Pakistani (444)	482	1.17
Taiwanese (25)	30	0.07
Thai (17)	24	0.06
Vietnamese (134)	157	0.38
Hawaii Native/Pacific Islander (12)	39	0.09
Not Hispanic (7)	28	0.07
Hispanic (5)	11	0.03
Guamanian/Chamorro (1)	4	0.01
Native Hawaiian (9)	20	0.05
Samoan (1)	6	0.01
White (32,397)	33,038	80.17

*Notes: † The Census 2010 population figure is used to calculate the percentages in the Hispanic Origin and Race categories. Ancestry percentages are based on the 2006-2010 American Community Survey population (not shown); ‡ Numbers in parentheses indicate the number of people reporting a single ancestry; * Numbers in parentheses indicate the number of persons reporting this race alone, not in combination with any other race; Please refer to the Explanation of Data for more information.*

Not Hispanic (30,169)	30,625	74.32
Hispanic (2,228)	2,413	5.86

Batavia

Place Type: City
County: Kane
Population: 26,045†

Ancestry‡	Population	%
African, Sub-Saharan (38)	38	0.15
African (18)	18	0.07
Nigerian (6)	6	0.02
South African (14)	14	0.05
American (948)	948	3.66
Austrian (22)	103	0.40
Belgian (35)	149	0.57
Brazilian (30)	30	0.12
British (42)	87	0.34
Canadian (0)	29	0.11
Carpatho Rusyn (14)	14	0.05
Croatian (16)	65	0.25
Czech (151)	712	2.75
Czechoslovakian (0)	29	0.11
Danish (51)	444	1.71
Dutch (208)	810	3.12
Eastern European (11)	11	0.04
English (634)	2,988	11.53
European (366)	380	1.47
Finnish (0)	31	0.12
French, ex. Basque (96)	1,014	3.91
French Canadian (14)	232	0.89
German (2,814)	9,480	36.57
Greek (69)	164	0.63
Hungarian (66)	171	0.66
Irish (1,022)	4,732	18.25
Italian (802)	2,638	10.18
Latvian (0)	87	0.34
Lithuanian (77)	256	0.99
Luxemburger (10)	19	0.07
Norwegian (206)	1,078	4.16
Polish (846)	2,733	10.54
Portuguese (0)	48	0.19
Romanian (14)	110	0.42
Russian (118)	245	0.95
Scandinavian (29)	29	0.11
Scotch-Irish (73)	409	1.58
Scottish (16)	410	1.58
Serbian (14)	76	0.29
Slavic (0)	14	0.05
Slovak (81)	258	1.00
Slovene (0)	28	0.11
Swedish (667)	1,906	7.35
Swiss (14)	118	0.46
Ukrainian (32)	126	0.49
Welsh (32)	141	0.54
Yugoslavian (10)	10	0.04

Hispanic Origin	Population	%
Hispanic or Latino (of any race)	1,775	6.82
Central American, ex. Mexican	42	0.16
Guatemalan	21	0.08
Honduran	8	0.03
Nicaraguan	4	0.02
Salvadoran	9	0.03
Cuban	50	0.19
Dominican Republic	3	0.01
Mexican	1,385	5.32
Puerto Rican	159	0.61
South American	59	0.23
Argentinean	13	0.05
Chilean	1	<0.01
Colombian	20	0.08
Ecuadorian	12	0.05
Paraguayan	1	<0.01
Peruvian	5	0.02
Uruguayan	2	0.01
Venezuelan	5	0.02
Other Hispanic or Latino	77	0.30

Race*	Population	%
African-American/Black (636)	779	2.99
Not Hispanic (611)	731	2.81
Hispanic (25)	48	0.18
American Indian/Alaska Native (60)	115	0.44
Not Hispanic (38)	78	0.30
Hispanic (22)	37	0.14
Aleut *(Alaska Native)* (0)	1	<0.01
Apache (1)	3	0.01
Blackfeet (0)	1	<0.01
Cherokee (9)	26	0.10
Chippewa (1)	2	0.01
Choctaw (1)	1	<0.01
Cree (1)	1	<0.01
Creek (0)	1	<0.01
Inupiat *(Alaska Native)* (1)	1	<0.01
Iroquois (1)	5	0.02
Lumbee (3)	3	0.01
Mexican American Ind. (1)	5	0.02
Navajo (1)	1	<0.01
Ottawa (1)	1	<0.01
Seminole (0)	1	<0.01
Asian (473)	628	2.41
Not Hispanic (469)	602	2.31
Hispanic (4)	26	0.10
Bangladeshi (4)	4	0.02
Cambodian (6)	9	0.03
Chinese, ex. Taiwanese (105)	133	0.51
Filipino (63)	108	0.41
Hmong (6)	6	0.02
Indian (98)	112	0.43
Indonesian (0)	2	0.01
Japanese (20)	44	0.17
Korean (55)	69	0.26
Laotian (12)	23	0.09
Pakistani (37)	37	0.14
Sri Lankan (7)	9	0.03
Taiwanese (5)	6	0.02
Thai (6)	9	0.03
Vietnamese (35)	48	0.18
Hawaii Native/Pacific Islander (4)	15	0.06
Not Hispanic (3)	11	0.04
Hispanic (1)	4	0.02
Guamanian/Chamorro (0)	2	0.01
Native Hawaiian (4)	9	0.03
White (23,934)	24,304	93.32
Not Hispanic (22,840)	23,112	88.74
Hispanic (1,094)	1,192	4.58

Beach Park

Place Type: Village
County: Lake
Population: 13,638†

Ancestry‡	Population	%
African, Sub-Saharan (11)	11	0.08
Ghanaian (11)	11	0.08
American (283)	283	2.13
Arab (12)	12	0.09
Lebanese (12)	12	0.09
Austrian (0)	23	0.17
Belgian (36)	52	0.39
British (19)	68	0.51
Canadian (27)	41	0.31
Croatian (60)	148	1.11
Czech (0)	88	0.66
Czechoslovakian (0)	14	0.11
Danish (24)	107	0.80
Dutch (48)	223	1.67
English (255)	1,118	8.40
European (83)	83	0.62
Finnish (200)	421	3.16
French, ex. Basque (45)	220	1.65
French Canadian (33)	98	0.74
German (346)	2,548	19.14
Greek (26)	153	1.15
Hungarian (0)	25	0.19
Irish (230)	1,600	12.02
Italian (130)	689	5.17
Latvian (0)	14	0.11
Lithuanian (45)	235	1.76
Luxemburger (14)	14	0.11
Northern European (29)	29	0.22
Norwegian (11)	174	1.31
Polish (360)	1,040	7.81
Romanian (31)	64	0.48
Russian (0)	68	0.51
Scandinavian (0)	8	0.06
Scotch-Irish (27)	121	0.91
Scottish (11)	119	0.89
Slavic (0)	26	0.20
Slovak (11)	85	0.64
Slovene (36)	96	0.72
Swedish (105)	285	2.14
Swiss (0)	38	0.29
Ukrainian (34)	34	0.26
Welsh (8)	48	0.36
West Indian, ex. Hispanic (68)	68	0.51
Belizean (25)	25	0.19
Jamaican (43)	43	0.32
Yugoslavian (14)	14	0.11

Hispanic Origin	Population	%
Hispanic or Latino (of any race)	3,420	25.08
Central American, ex. Mexican	182	1.33
Costa Rican	2	0.01
Guatemalan	36	0.26
Honduran	73	0.54
Nicaraguan	6	0.04
Salvadoran	65	0.48
Cuban	20	0.15
Dominican Republic	4	0.03
Mexican	2,640	19.36
Puerto Rican	388	2.84
South American	76	0.56
Argentinean	1	0.01
Chilean	1	0.01
Colombian	53	0.39
Ecuadorian	7	0.05
Peruvian	11	0.08
Venezuelan	3	0.02
Other Hispanic or Latino	110	0.81

Race*	Population	%
African-American/Black (1,455)	1,633	11.97
Not Hispanic (1,420)	1,555	11.40
Hispanic (35)	78	0.57
American Indian/Alaska Native (85)	173	1.27
Not Hispanic (35)	93	0.68
Hispanic (50)	80	0.59
Aleut *(Alaska Native)* (0)	4	0.03
Apache (2)	6	0.04
Blackfeet (1)	1	0.01
Cherokee (0)	23	0.17
Chippewa (5)	8	0.06
Choctaw (2)	5	0.04
Creek (0)	1	0.01
Menominee (1)	1	0.01
Mexican American Ind. (12)	22	0.16
Navajo (2)	2	0.01
Shoshone (0)	1	0.01
Sioux (1)	2	0.01
South American Ind. (3)	4	0.03
Yaqui (4)	4	0.03
Asian (773)	903	6.62
Not Hispanic (760)	857	6.28
Hispanic (13)	46	0.34
Cambodian (27)	37	0.27
Chinese, ex. Taiwanese (18)	28	0.21
Filipino (531)	602	4.41
Indian (100)	116	0.85
Japanese (14)	39	0.29
Korean (18)	26	0.19
Malaysian (1)	1	0.01
Pakistani (14)	16	0.12
Sri Lankan (0)	2	0.01
Thai (8)	19	0.14
Vietnamese (19)	22	0.16

*Notes: † The Census 2010 population figure is used to calculate the percentages in the Hispanic Origin and Race categories. Ancestry percentages are based on the 2006-2010 American Community Survey population (not shown); ‡ Numbers in parentheses indicate the number of people reporting a single ancestry; * Numbers in parentheses indicate the number of persons reporting this race alone, not in combination with any other race; Please refer to the Explanation of Data for more information.*

Hawaii Native/Pacific Islander (6)	17	0.12
Not Hispanic (1)	11	0.08
Hispanic (5)	6	0.04
Samoan (1)	3	0.02
White (9,398)	9,797	71.84
Not Hispanic (7,706)	7,938	58.21
Hispanic (1,692)	1,859	13.63

Belleville

Place Type: City
County: St. Clair
Population: 44,478†

Ancestry‡	Population	%
African, Sub-Saharan (133)	164	0.37
African (133)	164	0.37
American (1,790)	1,790	4.07
Arab (9)	38	0.09
Lebanese (0)	29	0.07
Moroccan (9)	9	0.02
Armenian (0)	11	0.03
Austrian (0)	50	0.11
Basque (13)	13	0.03
Belgian (14)	35	0.08
British (116)	157	0.36
Bulgarian (0)	32	0.07
Cajun (0)	7	0.02
Canadian (38)	48	0.11
Croatian (46)	172	0.39
Czech (59)	270	0.61
Czechoslovakian (45)	56	0.13
Danish (0)	13	0.03
Dutch (82)	806	1.83
Eastern European (16)	16	0.04
English (996)	3,598	8.19
European (2,132)	2,261	5.15
Finnish (0)	10	0.02
French, ex. Basque (121)	1,893	4.31
French Canadian (60)	235	0.53
German (5,924)	14,197	32.31
Greek (36)	168	0.38
Hungarian (0)	96	0.22
Icelander (54)	54	0.12
Irish (1,334)	5,527	12.58
Italian (327)	1,234	2.81
Lithuanian (46)	116	0.26
Norwegian (164)	367	0.84
Polish (329)	1,266	2.88
Romanian (14)	94	0.21
Russian (51)	189	0.43
Scandinavian (0)	30	0.07
Scotch-Irish (135)	449	1.02
Scottish (109)	565	1.29
Slavic (12)	48	0.11
Slovak (46)	109	0.25
Swedish (122)	489	1.11
Swiss (0)	70	0.16
Turkish (12)	38	0.09
Ukrainian (13)	62	0.14
Welsh (35)	314	0.71
West Indian, ex. Hispanic (57)	57	0.13
Jamaican (57)	57	0.13

Hispanic Origin	Population	%
Hispanic or Latino (of any race)	1,163	2.61
Central American, ex. Mexican	39	0.09
Costa Rican	3	0.01
Guatemalan	13	0.03
Honduran	3	0.01
Nicaraguan	3	0.01
Panamanian	12	0.03
Salvadoran	5	0.01
Cuban	17	0.04
Dominican Republic	8	0.02
Mexican	675	1.52
Puerto Rican	193	0.43
South American	42	0.09
Argentinean	1	<0.01
Bolivian	1	<0.01
Chilean	2	<0.01
Colombian	18	0.04
Ecuadorian	5	0.01
Peruvian	10	0.02
Venezuelan	5	0.01
Other Hispanic or Latino	189	0.42

Race*	Population	%
African-American/Black (11,314)	12,061	27.12
Not Hispanic (11,231)	11,926	26.81
Hispanic (83)	135	0.30
American Indian/Alaska Native (142)	397	0.89
Not Hispanic (113)	344	0.77
Hispanic (29)	53	0.12
Alaska Athabascan *(Ala. Nat.)* (2)	4	0.01
Aleut *(Alaska Native)* (2)	2	<0.01
Apache (2)	5	0.01
Blackfeet (0)	7	0.02
Cherokee (23)	101	0.23
Chickasaw (1)	1	<0.01
Chippewa (2)	5	0.01
Choctaw (3)	8	0.02
Comanche (2)	2	<0.01
Creek (2)	2	<0.01
Inupiat *(Alaska Native)* (1)	1	<0.01
Iroquois (6)	6	0.01
Lumbee (0)	3	0.01
Mexican American Ind. (8)	11	0.02
Navajo (4)	7	0.02
Osage (1)	2	<0.01
Potawatomi (3)	6	0.01
Seminole (5)	5	0.01
Sioux (3)	6	0.01
South American Ind. (1)	1	<0.01
Spanish American Ind. (0)	1	<0.01
Tlingit-Haida *(Alaska Native)* (1)	5	0.01
Yaqui (1)	1	<0.01
Asian (436)	755	1.70
Not Hispanic (424)	724	1.63
Hispanic (12)	31	0.07
Burmese (0)	1	<0.01
Cambodian (4)	6	0.01
Chinese, ex. Taiwanese (54)	75	0.17
Filipino (129)	269	0.60
Indian (61)	71	0.16
Indonesian (0)	2	<0.01
Japanese (32)	83	0.19
Korean (57)	100	0.22
Laotian (0)	5	0.01
Nepalese (3)	5	0.01
Pakistani (16)	18	0.04
Taiwanese (2)	3	0.01
Thai (22)	54	0.12
Vietnamese (39)	55	0.12
Hawaii Native/Pacific Islander (30)	81	0.18
Not Hispanic (25)	73	0.16
Hispanic (5)	8	0.02
Guamanian/Chamorro (10)	24	0.05
Marshallese (1)	1	<0.01
Native Hawaiian (12)	30	0.07
Samoan (1)	6	0.01
White (31,029)	32,143	72.27
Not Hispanic (30,345)	31,349	70.48
Hispanic (684)	794	1.79

Bellwood

Place Type: Village
County: Cook
Population: 19,071†

Ancestry‡	Population	%
African, Sub-Saharan (274)	313	1.64
African (247)	286	1.50
Other Sub-Saharan African (27)	27	0.14
American (62)	62	0.32
Brazilian (16)	16	0.08
British (7)	7	0.04
Czech (11)	11	0.06
Czechoslovakian (0)	6	0.03
Dutch (0)	50	0.26
English (5)	107	0.56
French, ex. Basque (0)	56	0.29
French Canadian (0)	19	0.10
German (105)	347	1.82
Hungarian (0)	6	0.03
Irish (132)	201	1.05
Italian (128)	270	1.41
Lithuanian (13)	21	0.11
Norwegian (0)	33	0.17
Polish (79)	107	0.56
Portuguese (4)	4	0.02
Romanian (15)	15	0.08
Scotch-Irish (0)	11	0.06
Serbian (0)	3	0.02
Slovak (0)	24	0.13
Swedish (0)	43	0.22
Welsh (0)	8	0.04
West Indian, ex. Hispanic (69)	85	0.44
Jamaican (23)	39	0.20
West Indian (46)	46	0.24

Hispanic Origin	Population	%
Hispanic or Latino (of any race)	3,596	18.86
Central American, ex. Mexican	82	0.43
Guatemalan	49	0.26
Honduran	11	0.06
Nicaraguan	11	0.06
Panamanian	5	0.03
Salvadoran	6	0.03
Cuban	24	0.13
Dominican Republic	3	0.02
Mexican	3,060	16.05
Puerto Rican	312	1.64
South American	34	0.18
Argentinean	4	0.02
Chilean	3	0.02
Colombian	11	0.06
Ecuadorian	6	0.03
Peruvian	6	0.03
Venezuelan	4	0.02
Other Hispanic or Latino	81	0.42

Race*	Population	%
African-American/Black (14,407)	14,593	76.52
Not Hispanic (14,240)	14,391	75.46
Hispanic (167)	202	1.06
American Indian/Alaska Native (43)	135	0.71
Not Hispanic (16)	73	0.38
Hispanic (27)	62	0.33
Blackfeet (0)	1	0.01
Cherokee (1)	7	0.04
Cheyenne (1)	1	0.01
Chickasaw (0)	1	0.01
Chippewa (3)	11	0.06
Choctaw (3)	3	0.02
Creek (0)	1	0.01
Lumbee (0)	1	0.01
Mexican American Ind. (1)	9	0.05
Potawatomi (0)	3	0.02
Sioux (0)	7	0.04
South American Ind. (0)	1	0.01
Asian (123)	174	0.91
Not Hispanic (116)	144	0.76
Hispanic (7)	30	0.16
Chinese, ex. Taiwanese (5)	6	0.03
Filipino (22)	40	0.21
Indian (64)	77	0.40
Japanese (4)	7	0.04
Korean (1)	6	0.03
Laotian (1)	1	0.01
Pakistani (9)	9	0.05
Thai (3)	6	0.03
Vietnamese (9)	10	0.05
Hawaii Native/Pacific Islander (1)	14	0.07
Not Hispanic (1)	12	0.06
Hispanic (0)	2	0.01
Guamanian/Chamorro (1)	1	0.01
Samoan (0)	4	0.02
White (2,648)	2,876	15.08

*Notes: † The Census 2010 population figure is used to calculate the percentages in the Hispanic Origin and Race categories. Ancestry percentages are based on the 2006-2010 American Community Survey population (not shown); ‡ Numbers in parentheses indicate the number of people reporting a single ancestry; * Numbers in parentheses indicate the number of persons reporting this race alone, not in combination with any other race; Please refer to the Explanation of Data for more information.*

Not Hispanic (907)	1,017	5.33
Hispanic (1,741)	1,859	9.75

Belvidere

Place Type: City
County: Boone
Population: 25,585†

Ancestry‡	Population	%
African, Sub-Saharan (59)	59	0.23
Nigerian (59)	59	0.23
Albanian (21)	21	0.08
American (2,240)	2,240	8.85
Arab (61)	117	0.46
Arab (0)	39	0.15
Egyptian (0)	17	0.07
Syrian (16)	16	0.06
Other Arab (45)	45	0.18
Austrian (0)	91	0.36
British (14)	30	0.12
Canadian (0)	52	0.21
Croatian (43)	43	0.17
Czech (10)	129	0.51
Czechoslovakian (21)	36	0.14
Danish (35)	234	0.92
Dutch (67)	501	1.98
Eastern European (13)	13	0.05
English (545)	2,047	8.09
European (101)	113	0.45
Finnish (0)	10	0.04
French, ex. Basque (28)	399	1.58
French Canadian (21)	62	0.25
German (1,533)	4,706	18.60
Greek (16)	176	0.70
Hungarian (8)	141	0.56
Irish (763)	3,023	11.95
Italian (407)	1,328	5.25
Luxemburger (0)	25	0.10
Northern European (14)	14	0.06
Norwegian (415)	1,127	4.45
Pennsylvania German (16)	16	0.06
Polish (332)	933	3.69
Russian (6)	101	0.40
Scandinavian (24)	35	0.14
Scotch-Irish (87)	208	0.82
Scottish (36)	234	0.92
Slovak (0)	16	0.06
Swedish (401)	1,247	4.93
Swiss (50)	126	0.50
Ukrainian (0)	14	0.06
Welsh (24)	75	0.30
Yugoslavian (0)	16	0.06

Hispanic Origin	Population	%
Hispanic or Latino (of any race)	7,838	30.64
Central American, ex. Mexican	89	0.35
Costa Rican	1	<0.01
Guatemalan	30	0.12
Honduran	3	0.01
Nicaraguan	13	0.05
Panamanian	6	0.02
Salvadoran	36	0.14
Cuban	24	0.09
Dominican Republic	34	0.13
Mexican	7,169	28.02
Puerto Rican	291	1.14
South American	56	0.22
Argentinean	1	<0.01
Colombian	25	0.10
Ecuadorian	12	0.05
Peruvian	12	0.05
Other South American	6	0.02
Other Hispanic or Latino	175	0.68

Race*	Population	%
African-American/Black (671)	872	3.41
Not Hispanic (599)	758	2.96
Hispanic (72)	114	0.45
American Indian/Alaska Native (137)	440	1.72
Not Hispanic (35)	130	0.51
Hispanic (102)	310	1.21
Apache (8)	8	0.03
Cherokee (6)	54	0.21
Chippewa (3)	9	0.04
Choctaw (1)	2	0.01
Cree (0)	2	0.01
Inupiat *(Alaska Native)* (1)	1	<0.01
Mexican American Ind. (33)	53	0.21
Navajo (1)	5	0.02
Ottawa (1)	1	<0.01
Potawatomi (0)	3	0.01
Puget Sound Salish (2)	2	0.01
Seminole (0)	2	0.01
Shoshone (0)	1	<0.01
Sioux (0)	4	0.02
South American Ind. (0)	5	0.02
Tlingit-Haida *(Alaska Native)* (1)	1	<0.01
Yaqui (0)	1	<0.01
Asian (256)	360	1.41
Not Hispanic (243)	331	1.29
Hispanic (13)	29	0.11
Chinese, ex. Taiwanese (28)	50	0.20
Filipino (82)	118	0.46
Indian (42)	56	0.22
Japanese (8)	24	0.09
Korean (17)	27	0.11
Laotian (20)	25	0.10
Malaysian (2)	2	0.01
Pakistani (10)	10	0.04
Sri Lankan (2)	2	0.01
Thai (9)	14	0.05
Vietnamese (22)	26	0.10
Hawaii Native/Pacific Islander (1)	23	0.09
Not Hispanic (0)	14	0.05
Hispanic (1)	9	0.04
Guamanian/Chamorro (0)	7	0.03
Native Hawaiian (1)	7	0.03
Samoan (0)	1	<0.01
White (19,934)	20,746	81.09
Not Hispanic (16,527)	16,833	65.79
Hispanic (3,407)	3,913	15.29

Bensenville

Place Type: Village
County: DuPage
Population: 18,352†

Ancestry‡	Population	%
African, Sub-Saharan (45)	45	0.24
African (45)	45	0.24
American (179)	179	0.96
Arab (330)	337	1.81
Arab (23)	23	0.12
Jordanian (307)	307	1.65
Lebanese (0)	7	0.04
Austrian (40)	147	0.79
Brazilian (227)	227	1.22
Bulgarian (60)	60	0.32
Croatian (36)	36	0.19
Czech (51)	79	0.42
Czechoslovakian (10)	33	0.18
Danish (0)	10	0.05
Dutch (12)	89	0.48
English (122)	501	2.68
European (46)	46	0.25
Finnish (0)	13	0.07
French, ex. Basque (6)	179	0.96
French Canadian (15)	24	0.13
German (566)	2,195	11.76
Greek (245)	294	1.58
Hungarian (46)	94	0.50
Irish (350)	1,494	8.01
Italian (653)	1,110	5.95
Lithuanian (12)	41	0.22
Norwegian (0)	162	0.87
Polish (1,044)	1,690	9.06
Portuguese (0)	13	0.07
Romanian (18)	32	0.17
Russian (9)	101	0.54
Scandinavian (0)	50	0.27
Scotch-Irish (10)	68	0.36
Scottish (10)	63	0.34
Slovak (0)	11	0.06
Slovene (0)	43	0.23
Swedish (25)	276	1.48
Turkish (39)	39	0.21
Ukrainian (25)	25	0.13
Welsh (0)	29	0.16
West Indian, ex. Hispanic (61)	61	0.33
British West Indian (5)	5	0.03
Haitian (35)	35	0.19
West Indian (21)	21	0.11
Yugoslavian (57)	78	0.42

Hispanic Origin	Population	%
Hispanic or Latino (of any race)	8,781	47.85
Central American, ex. Mexican	1,072	5.84
Costa Rican	9	0.05
Guatemalan	969	5.28
Honduran	25	0.14
Nicaraguan	6	0.03
Panamanian	13	0.07
Salvadoran	49	0.27
Other Central American	1	0.01
Cuban	46	0.25
Dominican Republic	3	0.02
Mexican	6,867	37.42
Puerto Rican	383	2.09
South American	169	0.92
Argentinean	24	0.13
Bolivian	1	0.01
Chilean	3	0.02
Colombian	46	0.25
Ecuadorian	32	0.17
Peruvian	47	0.26
Venezuelan	15	0.08
Other South American	1	0.01
Other Hispanic or Latino	241	1.31

Race*	Population	%
African-American/Black (646)	734	4.00
Not Hispanic (590)	645	3.51
Hispanic (56)	89	0.48
American Indian/Alaska Native (179)	309	1.68
Not Hispanic (31)	74	0.40
Hispanic (148)	235	1.28
Aleut *(Alaska Native)* (0)	1	0.01
Blackfeet (0)	5	0.03
Cherokee (8)	28	0.15
Chippewa (3)	8	0.04
Houma (1)	1	0.01
Inupiat *(Alaska Native)* (0)	1	0.01
Iroquois (7)	7	0.04
Lumbee (2)	3	0.02
Mexican American Ind. (35)	45	0.25
Navajo (1)	2	0.01
Osage (0)	2	0.01
Potawatomi (2)	2	0.01
Sioux (0)	2	0.01
South American Ind. (2)	4	0.02
Spanish American Ind. (5)	5	0.03
Yaqui (5)	5	0.03
Asian (888)	995	5.42
Not Hispanic (872)	960	5.23
Hispanic (16)	35	0.19
Bangladeshi (2)	2	0.01
Cambodian (1)	1	0.01
Chinese, ex. Taiwanese (39)	54	0.29
Filipino (291)	326	1.78
Indian (365)	410	2.23
Japanese (19)	31	0.17
Korean (34)	36	0.20
Laotian (2)	4	0.02
Malaysian (3)	3	0.02
Pakistani (54)	54	0.29
Taiwanese (2)	2	0.01
Thai (0)	3	0.02
Vietnamese (46)	51	0.28

*Notes: † The Census 2010 population figure is used to calculate the percentages in the Hispanic Origin and Race categories. Ancestry percentages are based on the 2006-2010 American Community Survey population (not shown); ‡ Numbers in parentheses indicate the number of people reporting a single ancestry; * Numbers in parentheses indicate the number of persons reporting this race alone, not in combination with any other race; Please refer to the Explanation of Data for more information.*

Hawaii Native/Pacific Islander (3)	22	0.12
Not Hispanic (2)	13	0.07
Hispanic (1)	9	0.05
Native Hawaiian (2)	5	0.03
Samoan (0)	2	0.01
White (12,345)	12,796	69.73
Not Hispanic (7,857)	7,982	43.49
Hispanic (4,488)	4,814	26.23

Berwyn

Place Type: City
County: Cook
Population: 56,657†

Ancestry‡	Population	%
African, Sub-Saharan (131)	155	0.28
African (115)	139	0.25
South African (16)	16	0.03
Albanian (0)	9	0.02
American (481)	481	0.87
Arab (191)	204	0.37
Arab (64)	64	0.12
Egyptian (14)	14	0.03
Jordanian (31)	31	0.06
Lebanese (0)	13	0.02
Moroccan (82)	82	0.15
Armenian (9)	9	0.02
Austrian (34)	151	0.27
Belgian (13)	49	0.09
Brazilian (10)	22	0.04
Canadian (13)	26	0.05
Croatian (134)	231	0.42
Czech (746)	1,864	3.35
Czechoslovakian (163)	346	0.62
Danish (20)	72	0.13
Dutch (63)	243	0.44
Eastern European (13)	13	0.02
English (173)	1,153	2.07
Estonian (12)	12	0.02
European (25)	25	0.04
Finnish (10)	33	0.06
French, ex. Basque (55)	637	1.15
French Canadian (31)	109	0.20
German (927)	4,978	8.96
Greek (147)	321	0.58
Hungarian (28)	61	0.11
Iranian (0)	8	0.01
Irish (1,033)	4,905	8.82
Italian (1,722)	4,694	8.44
Lithuanian (196)	441	0.79
Norwegian (41)	388	0.70
Pennsylvania German (24)	50	0.09
Polish (1,586)	4,633	8.34
Portuguese (9)	9	0.02
Romanian (13)	32	0.06
Russian (39)	217	0.39
Scandinavian (0)	6	0.01
Scotch-Irish (50)	258	0.46
Scottish (70)	467	0.84
Serbian (34)	54	0.10
Slavic (0)	11	0.02
Slovak (52)	93	0.17
Slovene (17)	57	0.10
Swedish (18)	333	0.60
Swiss (0)	47	0.08
Turkish (8)	8	0.01
Ukrainian (137)	194	0.35
Welsh (10)	64	0.12
West Indian, ex. Hispanic (81)	159	0.29
Haitian (32)	32	0.06
Jamaican (23)	101	0.18
Trinidadian/Tobagonian (26)	26	0.05
Yugoslavian (89)	166	0.30

Hispanic Origin	Population	%
Hispanic or Latino (of any race)	33,676	59.44
Central American, ex. Mexican	825	1.46
Costa Rican	15	0.03
Guatemalan	476	0.84
Honduran	95	0.17
Nicaraguan	41	0.07
Panamanian	16	0.03
Salvadoran	182	0.32
Cuban	167	0.29
Dominican Republic	47	0.08
Mexican	28,185	49.75
Puerto Rican	2,918	5.15
South American	856	1.51
Argentinean	79	0.14
Bolivian	34	0.06
Chilean	36	0.06
Colombian	276	0.49
Ecuadorian	257	0.45
Paraguayan	7	0.01
Peruvian	128	0.23
Uruguayan	16	0.03
Venezuelan	18	0.03
Other South American	5	0.01
Other Hispanic or Latino	678	1.20

Race*	Population	%
African-American/Black (3,627)	4,007	7.07
Not Hispanic (3,373)	3,564	6.29
Hispanic (254)	443	0.78
American Indian/Alaska Native (335)	605	1.07
Not Hispanic (66)	205	0.36
Hispanic (269)	400	0.71
Alaska Athabascan *(Ala. Nat.)* (0)	1	<0.01
Apache (13)	18	0.03
Blackfeet (1)	11	0.02
Canadian/French Am. Ind. (0)	1	<0.01
Central American Ind. (5)	7	0.01
Cherokee (9)	51	0.09
Chippewa (9)	22	0.04
Choctaw (4)	14	0.02
Comanche (0)	1	<0.01
Creek (0)	1	<0.01
Inupiat *(Alaska Native)* (1)	1	<0.01
Iroquois (4)	6	0.01
Kiowa (3)	3	0.01
Lumbee (0)	3	0.01
Menominee (3)	6	0.01
Mexican American Ind. (74)	102	0.18
Navajo (6)	7	0.01
Ottawa (2)	2	<0.01
Pima (1)	1	<0.01
Sioux (3)	16	0.03
South American Ind. (12)	26	0.05
Spanish American Ind. (0)	5	0.01
Yaqui (0)	3	0.01
Yup'ik *(Alaska Native)* (1)	1	<0.01
Asian (1,425)	1,766	3.12
Not Hispanic (1,362)	1,586	2.80
Hispanic (63)	180	0.32
Burmese (3)	3	0.01
Cambodian (10)	20	0.04
Chinese, ex. Taiwanese (133)	192	0.34
Filipino (802)	923	1.63
Hmong (1)	1	<0.01
Indian (130)	182	0.32
Indonesian (6)	6	0.01
Japanese (19)	53	0.09
Korean (32)	44	0.08
Laotian (7)	8	0.01
Malaysian (2)	2	<0.01
Pakistani (49)	65	0.11
Sri Lankan (1)	1	<0.01
Taiwanese (1)	1	<0.01
Thai (49)	55	0.10
Vietnamese (138)	159	0.28
Hawaii Native/Pacific Islander (17)	80	0.14
Not Hispanic (2)	33	0.06
Hispanic (15)	47	0.08
Fijian (1)	4	0.01
Guamanian/Chamorro (4)	4	0.01
Native Hawaiian (0)	8	0.01
Samoan (1)	8	0.01
White (34,270)	35,893	63.35
Not Hispanic (17,592)	18,019	31.80
Hispanic (16,678)	17,874	31.55

Bethalto

Place Type: Village
County: Madison
Population: 9,521†

Ancestry‡	Population	%
American (986)	986	10.35
Austrian (0)	28	0.29
Belgian (8)	8	0.08
British (24)	24	0.25
Croatian (39)	58	0.61
Czech (0)	10	0.10
Czechoslovakian (11)	11	0.12
Danish (0)	8	0.08
Dutch (15)	319	3.35
English (444)	1,131	11.87
European (114)	114	1.20
French, ex. Basque (61)	258	2.71
French Canadian (11)	11	0.12
German (1,412)	3,118	32.71
Greek (39)	93	0.98
Hungarian (23)	42	0.44
Irish (305)	1,390	14.58
Italian (372)	801	8.40
Lithuanian (0)	29	0.30
Northern European (31)	31	0.33
Polish (66)	172	1.80
Russian (266)	279	2.93
Scotch-Irish (122)	203	2.13
Scottish (15)	92	0.97
Swedish (23)	103	1.08
Swiss (0)	21	0.22
Welsh (0)	39	0.41
Yugoslavian (9)	9	0.09

Hispanic Origin	Population	%
Hispanic or Latino (of any race)	181	1.90
Central American, ex. Mexican	7	0.07
Guatemalan	5	0.05
Panamanian	2	0.02
Cuban	3	0.03
Mexican	133	1.40
Puerto Rican	9	0.09
South American	1	0.01
Colombian	1	0.01
Other Hispanic or Latino	28	0.29

Race*	Population	%
African-American/Black (80)	124	1.30
Not Hispanic (80)	123	1.29
Hispanic (0)	1	0.01
American Indian/Alaska Native (14)	51	0.54
Not Hispanic (14)	51	0.54
Blackfeet (1)	3	0.03
Cherokee (4)	12	0.13
Menominee (4)	4	0.04
Potawatomi (1)	1	0.01
Sioux (0)	5	0.05
Asian (51)	64	0.67
Not Hispanic (49)	61	0.64
Hispanic (2)	3	0.03
Chinese, ex. Taiwanese (13)	14	0.15
Filipino (12)	16	0.17
Indian (5)	7	0.07
Japanese (7)	10	0.11
Korean (3)	5	0.05
Thai (2)	2	0.02
Vietnamese (4)	4	0.04
Hawaii Native/Pacific Islander (4)	7	0.07
Not Hispanic (4)	7	0.07
Native Hawaiian (4)	6	0.06
White (9,213)	9,304	97.72
Not Hispanic (9,102)	9,184	96.46
Hispanic (111)	120	1.26

*Notes: † The Census 2010 population figure is used to calculate the percentages in the Hispanic Origin and Race categories. Ancestry percentages are based on the 2006-2010 American Community Survey population (not shown); ‡ Numbers in parentheses indicate the number of people reporting a single ancestry; * Numbers in parentheses indicate the number of persons reporting this race alone, not in combination with any other race; Please refer to the Explanation of Data for more information.*

Bloomingdale

Place Type: Village
County: DuPage
Population: 22,018†

Ancestry‡	Population	%
African, Sub-Saharan (31)	31	0.14
African (31)	31	0.14
Albanian (9)	9	0.04
American (416)	416	1.90
Arab (52)	52	0.24
Lebanese (42)	42	0.19
Other Arab (10)	10	0.05
Armenian (0)	16	0.07
Assyrian/Chaldean/Syriac (14)	14	0.06
Australian (0)	24	0.11
Austrian (88)	202	0.92
Belgian (21)	42	0.19
British (31)	52	0.24
Bulgarian (72)	72	0.33
Canadian (20)	82	0.37
Croatian (14)	96	0.44
Czech (199)	580	2.65
Czechoslovakian (35)	88	0.40
Danish (24)	81	0.37
Dutch (36)	168	0.77
English (168)	1,016	4.64
Estonian (18)	36	0.16
European (45)	45	0.21
Finnish (0)	44	0.20
French, ex. Basque (24)	470	2.15
French Canadian (21)	56	0.26
German (1,319)	5,163	23.60
Greek (409)	744	3.40
Hungarian (28)	87	0.40
Irish (496)	3,372	15.41
Israeli (0)	22	0.10
Italian (2,354)	5,683	25.98
Latvian (12)	12	0.05
Lithuanian (35)	95	0.43
Luxemburger (0)	14	0.06
Macedonian (16)	16	0.07
Northern European (8)	8	0.04
Norwegian (76)	366	1.67
Polish (1,473)	3,384	15.47
Portuguese (0)	37	0.17
Romanian (0)	7	0.03
Russian (0)	119	0.54
Scandinavian (11)	32	0.15
Scotch-Irish (74)	198	0.91
Scottish (7)	76	0.35
Serbian (16)	48	0.22
Slavic (4)	19	0.09
Slovak (14)	25	0.11
Slovene (0)	10	0.05
Swedish (127)	813	3.72
Turkish (15)	15	0.07
Ukrainian (164)	318	1.45
Welsh (32)	132	0.60
Yugoslavian (32)	42	0.19

Hispanic Origin	Population	%
Hispanic or Latino (of any race)	1,916	8.70
Central American, ex. Mexican	92	0.42
Costa Rican	1	<0.01
Guatemalan	53	0.24
Honduran	18	0.08
Nicaraguan	3	0.01
Panamanian	8	0.04
Salvadoran	8	0.04
Other Central American	1	<0.01
Cuban	63	0.29
Dominican Republic	13	0.06
Mexican	1,263	5.74
Puerto Rican	228	1.04
South American	173	0.79
Argentinean	14	0.06
Bolivian	9	0.04
Chilean	1	<0.01
Colombian	62	0.28
Ecuadorian	60	0.27
Paraguayan	3	0.01
Peruvian	17	0.08
Venezuelan	7	0.03
Other Hispanic or Latino	84	0.38

Race*	Population	%
African-American/Black (818)	918	4.17
Not Hispanic (783)	863	3.92
Hispanic (35)	55	0.25
American Indian/Alaska Native (45)	113	0.51
Not Hispanic (29)	87	0.40
Hispanic (16)	26	0.12
Blackfeet (0)	2	0.01
Cherokee (5)	9	0.04
Chippewa (2)	5	0.02
Choctaw (6)	7	0.03
Creek (0)	1	<0.01
Iroquois (2)	3	0.01
Menominee (0)	3	0.01
Mexican American Ind. (10)	13	0.06
Navajo (1)	1	<0.01
Potawatomi (3)	5	0.02
Sioux (0)	3	0.01
South American Ind. (1)	1	<0.01
Tlingit-Haida *(Alaska Native)* (0)	1	<0.01
Yaqui (0)	2	0.01
Asian (2,791)	2,981	13.54
Not Hispanic (2,770)	2,948	13.39
Hispanic (21)	33	0.15
Bangladeshi (5)	5	0.02
Cambodian (8)	11	0.05
Chinese, ex. Taiwanese (191)	234	1.06
Filipino (683)	752	3.42
Hmong (1)	3	0.01
Indian (1,328)	1,383	6.28
Indonesian (5)	5	0.02
Japanese (86)	107	0.49
Korean (123)	132	0.60
Laotian (3)	5	0.02
Malaysian (0)	1	<0.01
Nepalese (1)	1	<0.01
Pakistani (191)	213	0.97
Taiwanese (23)	27	0.12
Thai (8)	9	0.04
Vietnamese (62)	77	0.35
Hawaii Native/Pacific Islander (5)	22	0.10
Not Hispanic (5)	16	0.07
Hispanic (0)	6	0.03
Guamanian/Chamorro (1)	1	<0.01
Native Hawaiian (0)	5	0.02
Samoan (2)	2	0.01
White (17,472)	17,795	80.82
Not Hispanic (16,216)	16,445	74.69
Hispanic (1,256)	1,350	6.13

Bloomington

Place Type: City
County: McLean
Population: 76,610†

Ancestry‡	Population	%
African, Sub-Saharan (331)	365	0.49
African (264)	264	0.35
Ethiopian (18)	41	0.05
Ghanaian (17)	17	0.02
Kenyan (10)	10	0.01
Nigerian (10)	10	0.01
Other Sub-Saharan African (12)	23	0.03
Alsatian (0)	8	0.01
American (8,005)	8,005	10.69
Arab (24)	203	0.27
Arab (0)	11	0.01
Lebanese (24)	69	0.09
Palestinian (0)	8	0.01
Syrian (0)	83	0.11
Other Arab (0)	32	0.04
Armenian (8)	8	0.01
Australian (12)	12	0.02
Austrian (7)	126	0.17
Belgian (52)	185	0.25
British (155)	380	0.51
Bulgarian (14)	14	0.02
Canadian (0)	89	0.12
Celtic (15)	15	0.02
Croatian (17)	194	0.26
Czech (89)	437	0.58
Czechoslovakian (50)	90	0.12
Danish (61)	273	0.36
Dutch (322)	1,285	1.72
Eastern European (62)	69	0.09
English (2,777)	8,376	11.19
Estonian (12)	12	0.02
European (769)	905	1.21
Finnish (0)	102	0.14
French, ex. Basque (226)	1,815	2.42
French Canadian (58)	171	0.23
German (7,694)	20,952	27.99
German Russian (0)	11	0.01
Greek (113)	154	0.21
Hungarian (129)	190	0.25
Irish (2,941)	11,242	15.02
Israeli (0)	10	0.01
Italian (801)	2,707	3.62
Latvian (16)	28	0.04
Lithuanian (44)	202	0.27
Luxemburger (0)	11	0.01
Macedonian (0)	9	0.01
Northern European (31)	31	0.04
Norwegian (363)	1,211	1.62
Pennsylvania German (0)	44	0.06
Polish (561)	2,344	3.13
Portuguese (20)	132	0.18
Romanian (31)	31	0.04
Russian (64)	192	0.26
Scandinavian (29)	68	0.09
Scotch-Irish (506)	1,404	1.88
Scottish (356)	1,576	2.11
Slavic (0)	19	0.03
Slovak (88)	300	0.40
Slovene (15)	63	0.08
Swedish (447)	1,505	2.01
Swiss (40)	421	0.56
Turkish (65)	96	0.13
Ukrainian (173)	192	0.26
Welsh (229)	581	0.78
West Indian, ex. Hispanic (45)	75	0.10
Belizean (0)	14	0.02
British West Indian (11)	11	0.01
Dutch West Indian (11)	11	0.01
Haitian (10)	17	0.02
Jamaican (0)	9	0.01
U.S. Virgin Islander (13)	13	0.02
Yugoslavian (0)	8	0.01

Hispanic Origin	Population	%
Hispanic or Latino (of any race)	4,308	5.62
Central American, ex. Mexican	413	0.54
Costa Rican	2	<0.01
Guatemalan	301	0.39
Honduran	26	0.03
Nicaraguan	2	<0.01
Panamanian	17	0.02
Salvadoran	64	0.08
Other Central American	1	<0.01
Cuban	81	0.11
Dominican Republic	12	0.02
Mexican	3,077	4.02
Puerto Rican	259	0.34
South American	160	0.21
Argentinean	9	0.01
Bolivian	11	0.01
Chilean	18	0.02
Colombian	53	0.07
Ecuadorian	15	0.02
Paraguayan	7	0.01
Peruvian	30	0.04
Venezuelan	17	0.02

*Notes: † The Census 2010 population figure is used to calculate the percentages in the Hispanic Origin and Race categories. Ancestry percentages are based on the 2006-2010 American Community Survey population (not shown); ‡ Numbers in parentheses indicate the number of people reporting a single ancestry; * Numbers in parentheses indicate the number of persons reporting this race alone, not in combination with any other race; Please refer to the Explanation of Data for more information.*

Other Hispanic or Latino	306	0.40

Race*	Population	%
African-American/Black (7,770)	9,050	11.81
Not Hispanic (7,663)	8,833	11.53
Hispanic (107)	217	0.28
American Indian/Alaska Native (231)	608	0.79
Not Hispanic (170)	493	0.64
Hispanic (61)	115	0.15
Aleut *(Alaska Native)* (3)	3	<0.01
Apache (3)	6	0.01
Blackfeet (1)	17	0.02
Central American Ind. (0)	2	<0.01
Cherokee (26)	131	0.17
Cheyenne (0)	2	<0.01
Chickasaw (2)	6	0.01
Chippewa (6)	13	0.02
Choctaw (5)	15	0.02
Colville (1)	1	<0.01
Comanche (1)	1	<0.01
Cree (1)	2	<0.01
Creek (1)	5	0.01
Iroquois (2)	4	0.01
Mexican American Ind. (21)	32	0.04
Navajo (1)	3	<0.01
Osage (0)	1	<0.01
Potawatomi (8)	14	0.02
Puget Sound Salish (1)	1	<0.01
Shoshone (0)	1	<0.01
Sioux (13)	30	0.04
South American Ind. (3)	3	<0.01
Yakama (1)	1	<0.01
Yup'ik *(Alaska Native)* (1)	1	<0.01
Asian (5,343)	5,890	7.69
Not Hispanic (5,315)	5,815	7.59
Hispanic (28)	75	0.10
Bangladeshi (14)	15	0.02
Burmese (5)	5	0.01
Cambodian (5)	8	0.01
Chinese, ex. Taiwanese (428)	526	0.69
Filipino (234)	362	0.47
Indian (3,968)	4,090	5.34
Indonesian (8)	18	0.02
Japanese (96)	167	0.22
Korean (176)	250	0.33
Laotian (1)	4	0.01
Malaysian (0)	8	0.01
Nepalese (5)	5	0.01
Pakistani (82)	98	0.13
Sri Lankan (0)	1	<0.01
Taiwanese (27)	34	0.04
Thai (30)	47	0.06
Vietnamese (172)	207	0.27
Hawaii Native/Pacific Islander (28)	74	0.10
Not Hispanic (23)	52	0.07
Hispanic (5)	22	0.03
Fijian (2)	2	<0.01
Guamanian/Chamorro (8)	10	0.01
Native Hawaiian (10)	20	0.03
Samoan (2)	5	0.01
Tongan (2)	2	<0.01
White (59,353)	61,325	80.05
Not Hispanic (57,141)	58,841	76.81
Hispanic (2,212)	2,484	3.24

Blue Island

Place Type: City
County: Cook
Population: 23,706†

Ancestry‡	Population	%
African, Sub-Saharan (125)	125	0.54
African (101)	101	0.44
Ghanaian (12)	12	0.05
Nigerian (12)	12	0.05
American (172)	172	0.75
Austrian (7)	16	0.07
Belgian (10)	10	0.04
British (0)	15	0.07
Czech (6)	64	0.28
Czechoslovakian (0)	19	0.08
Danish (0)	10	0.04
Dutch (88)	236	1.03
English (187)	372	1.62
Finnish (0)	10	0.04
French, ex. Basque (25)	139	0.60
French Canadian (21)	45	0.20
German (527)	2,097	9.12
Greek (31)	63	0.27
Hungarian (11)	133	0.58
Icelander (0)	15	0.07
Irish (390)	1,246	5.42
Italian (497)	913	3.97
Lithuanian (91)	230	1.00
Luxemburger (0)	20	0.09
Northern European (23)	23	0.10
Norwegian (26)	52	0.23
Pennsylvania German (0)	10	0.04
Polish (344)	1,279	5.56
Russian (0)	21	0.09
Scotch-Irish (11)	94	0.41
Scottish (0)	148	0.64
Serbian (0)	6	0.03
Slovak (60)	130	0.57
Swedish (98)	232	1.01
Swiss (0)	9	0.04
Turkish (35)	35	0.15
Ukrainian (9)	39	0.17
Welsh (0)	7	0.03
West Indian, ex. Hispanic (15)	15	0.07
Jamaican (15)	15	0.07
Yugoslavian (0)	14	0.06

Hispanic Origin	Population	%
Hispanic or Latino (of any race)	11,133	46.96
Central American, ex. Mexican	169	0.71
Costa Rican	5	0.02
Guatemalan	102	0.43
Honduran	18	0.08
Nicaraguan	9	0.04
Panamanian	2	0.01
Salvadoran	33	0.14
Cuban	25	0.11
Dominican Republic	6	0.03
Mexican	10,330	43.58
Puerto Rican	227	0.96
South American	106	0.45
Argentinean	46	0.19
Chilean	1	<0.01
Colombian	17	0.07
Ecuadorian	13	0.05
Peruvian	21	0.09
Uruguayan	2	0.01
Venezuelan	6	0.03
Other Hispanic or Latino	270	1.14

Race*	Population	%
African-American/Black (7,304)	7,578	31.97
Not Hispanic (7,173)	7,346	30.99
Hispanic (131)	232	0.98
American Indian/Alaska Native (195)	341	1.44
Not Hispanic (42)	124	0.52
Hispanic (153)	217	0.92
Apache (2)	12	0.05
Blackfeet (0)	2	0.01
Central American Ind. (0)	1	<0.01
Cherokee (5)	28	0.12
Chickasaw (0)	1	<0.01
Chippewa (10)	13	0.05
Choctaw (1)	4	0.02
Crow (0)	1	<0.01
Iroquois (0)	1	<0.01
Menominee (0)	1	<0.01
Mexican American Ind. (18)	24	0.10
Navajo (9)	9	0.04
Potawatomi (0)	1	<0.01
Sioux (2)	8	0.03
South American Ind. (4)	6	0.03
Spanish American Ind. (0)	2	0.01
Asian (87)	149	0.63
Not Hispanic (79)	119	0.50
Hispanic (8)	30	0.13
Chinese, ex. Taiwanese (12)	20	0.08
Filipino (30)	40	0.17
Indian (15)	24	0.10
Indonesian (2)	2	0.01
Japanese (5)	13	0.05
Korean (5)	10	0.04
Laotian (0)	2	0.01
Pakistani (12)	12	0.05
Thai (0)	2	0.01
Vietnamese (2)	4	0.02
Hawaii Native/Pacific Islander (21)	39	0.16
Not Hispanic (6)	15	0.06
Hispanic (15)	24	0.10
Guamanian/Chamorro (19)	24	0.10
Native Hawaiian (1)	5	0.02
Samoan (1)	1	<0.01
White (9,780)	10,355	43.68
Not Hispanic (4,990)	5,183	21.86
Hispanic (4,790)	5,172	21.82

Bolingbrook

Place Type: Village
County: Will
Population: 73,366†

Ancestry‡	Population	%
African, Sub-Saharan (1,195)	1,497	2.06
African (664)	870	1.20
Ghanaian (287)	314	0.43
Kenyan (0)	12	0.02
Nigerian (160)	171	0.24
Sierra Leonean (43)	43	0.06
South African (0)	17	0.02
Other Sub-Saharan African (41)	70	0.10
Albanian (48)	54	0.07
American (1,296)	1,296	1.78
Arab (75)	172	0.24
Arab (7)	20	0.03
Lebanese (13)	84	0.12
Moroccan (55)	55	0.08
Other Arab (0)	13	0.02
Armenian (22)	35	0.05
Assyrian/Chaldean/Syriac (69)	172	0.24
Austrian (40)	159	0.22
Belgian (28)	131	0.18
Brazilian (44)	44	0.06
British (107)	262	0.36
Bulgarian (90)	90	0.12
Canadian (63)	193	0.27
Croatian (39)	158	0.22
Czech (417)	1,080	1.49
Czechoslovakian (28)	63	0.09
Danish (0)	191	0.26
Dutch (139)	817	1.12
Eastern European (11)	37	0.05
English (531)	3,042	4.19
European (234)	282	0.39
Finnish (101)	196	0.27
French, ex. Basque (98)	1,041	1.43
French Canadian (26)	169	0.23
German (2,178)	10,413	14.33
Greek (178)	498	0.69
Hungarian (62)	443	0.61
Iranian (98)	122	0.17
Irish (1,622)	8,387	11.54
Italian (1,156)	4,612	6.35
Latvian (0)	26	0.04
Lithuanian (304)	640	0.88
Luxemburger (0)	12	0.02
New Zealander (18)	68	0.09
Norwegian (196)	798	1.10
Polish (2,137)	7,074	9.74
Portuguese (0)	18	0.02
Romanian (133)	142	0.20
Russian (31)	166	0.23
Scandinavian (21)	27	0.04

*Notes: † The Census 2010 population figure is used to calculate the percentages in the Hispanic Origin and Race categories. Ancestry percentages are based on the 2006-2010 American Community Survey population (not shown); ‡ Numbers in parentheses indicate the number of people reporting a single ancestry; * Numbers in parentheses indicate the number of persons reporting this race alone, not in combination with any other race; Please refer to the Explanation of Data for more information.*

Scotch-Irish (218)	605	0.83
Scottish (209)	807	1.11
Serbian (129)	224	0.31
Slavic (0)	47	0.06
Slovak (64)	234	0.32
Slovene (26)	114	0.16
Swedish (198)	1,093	1.50
Swiss (9)	78	0.11
Turkish (26)	39	0.05
Ukrainian (22)	102	0.14
Welsh (73)	307	0.42
West Indian, ex. Hispanic (106)	197	0.27
Barbadian (18)	18	0.02
Belizean (0)	64	0.09
British West Indian (9)	9	0.01
Jamaican (79)	96	0.13
West Indian (0)	10	0.01
Yugoslavian (8)	86	0.12

Hispanic Origin	Population	%
Hispanic or Latino (of any race)	17,957	24.48
Central American, ex. Mexican	460	0.63
Costa Rican	14	0.02
Guatemalan	262	0.36
Honduran	46	0.06
Nicaraguan	25	0.03
Panamanian	41	0.06
Salvadoran	71	0.10
Other Central American	1	<0.01
Cuban	117	0.16
Dominican Republic	29	0.04
Mexican	15,256	20.79
Puerto Rican	1,254	1.71
South American	405	0.55
Argentinean	23	0.03
Bolivian	29	0.04
Chilean	4	0.01
Colombian	140	0.19
Ecuadorian	75	0.10
Paraguayan	3	<0.01
Peruvian	99	0.13
Uruguayan	3	<0.01
Venezuelan	28	0.04
Other South American	1	<0.01
Other Hispanic or Latino	436	0.59

Race*	Population	%
African-American/Black (14,999)	15,996	21.80
Not Hispanic (14,735)	15,519	21.15
Hispanic (264)	477	0.65
American Indian/Alaska Native (230)	581	0.79
Not Hispanic (94)	353	0.48
Hispanic (136)	228	0.31
Apache (6)	14	0.02
Arapaho (0)	6	0.01
Blackfeet (0)	8	0.01
Canadian/French Am. Ind. (1)	1	<0.01
Central American Ind. (1)	5	0.01
Cherokee (21)	107	0.15
Chickasaw (0)	3	<0.01
Chippewa (7)	12	0.02
Choctaw (0)	4	0.01
Comanche (1)	1	<0.01
Creek (2)	4	0.01
Crow (0)	1	<0.01
Iroquois (4)	12	0.02
Lumbee (3)	3	<0.01
Mexican American Ind. (25)	36	0.05
Navajo (3)	3	<0.01
Ottawa (0)	2	<0.01
Potawatomi (5)	8	0.01
Shoshone (0)	2	<0.01
Sioux (2)	12	0.02
South American Ind. (1)	4	0.01
Yaqui (1)	1	<0.01
Yuman (0)	1	<0.01
Asian (8,357)	9,178	12.51
Not Hispanic (8,264)	8,979	12.24
Hispanic (93)	199	0.27
Bangladeshi (36)	37	0.05
Cambodian (100)	125	0.17
Chinese, ex. Taiwanese (754)	887	1.21
Filipino (2,878)	3,222	4.39
Hmong (6)	7	0.01
Indian (2,791)	2,996	4.08
Indonesian (9)	13	0.02
Japanese (55)	115	0.16
Korean (278)	327	0.45
Laotian (35)	49	0.07
Malaysian (3)	5	0.01
Nepalese (14)	20	0.03
Pakistani (792)	835	1.14
Sri Lankan (14)	16	0.02
Taiwanese (37)	40	0.05
Thai (67)	111	0.15
Vietnamese (227)	277	0.38
Hawaii Native/Pacific Islander (15)	78	0.11
Not Hispanic (9)	55	0.07
Hispanic (6)	23	0.03
Fijian (1)	1	<0.01
Guamanian/Chamorro (3)	6	0.01
Marshallese (1)	1	<0.01
Native Hawaiian (3)	23	0.03
Samoan (1)	6	0.01
White (39,819)	41,835	57.02
Not Hispanic (30,587)	31,853	43.42
Hispanic (9,232)	9,982	13.61

Boulder Hill

Place Type: CDP
County: Kendall
Population: 8,108†

Ancestry‡	Population	%
African, Sub-Saharan (11)	11	0.13
African (11)	11	0.13
Albanian (0)	9	0.10
American (244)	244	2.82
Armenian (26)	26	0.30
Austrian (13)	13	0.15
British (8)	25	0.29
Czech (38)	92	1.06
Danish (10)	57	0.66
Dutch (0)	118	1.37
English (163)	778	9.00
European (84)	93	1.08
Finnish (0)	50	0.58
French, ex. Basque (117)	281	3.25
French Canadian (12)	76	0.88
German (553)	2,528	29.26
German Russian (0)	40	0.46
Greek (8)	61	0.71
Hungarian (26)	62	0.72
Irish (144)	1,431	16.56
Italian (144)	632	7.31
Lithuanian (37)	108	1.25
Luxemburger (15)	15	0.17
Norwegian (35)	174	2.01
Pennsylvania German (0)	19	0.22
Polish (93)	595	6.89
Romanian (108)	122	1.41
Russian (42)	42	0.49
Scotch-Irish (19)	70	0.81
Scottish (49)	122	1.41
Slovak (10)	20	0.23
Swedish (17)	146	1.69
Swiss (0)	9	0.10
Welsh (0)	63	0.73
West Indian, ex. Hispanic (0)	20	0.23
British West Indian (0)	10	0.12
Dutch West Indian (0)	10	0.12
Yugoslavian (0)	26	0.30

Hispanic Origin	Population	%
Hispanic or Latino (of any race)	1,805	22.26
Central American, ex. Mexican	13	0.16
Guatemalan	5	0.06
Nicaraguan	2	0.02
Salvadoran	6	0.07
Cuban	9	0.11
Mexican	1,591	19.62
Puerto Rican	135	1.67
South American	11	0.14
Argentinean	3	0.04
Colombian	7	0.09
Ecuadorian	1	0.01
Other Hispanic or Latino	46	0.57

Race*	Population	%
African-American/Black (359)	429	5.29
Not Hispanic (351)	405	5.00
Hispanic (8)	24	0.30
American Indian/Alaska Native (39)	82	1.01
Not Hispanic (10)	36	0.44
Hispanic (29)	46	0.57
Apache (0)	1	0.01
Cherokee (5)	12	0.15
Chickasaw (0)	1	0.01
Chippewa (4)	4	0.05
Cree (0)	1	0.01
Iroquois (0)	2	0.02
Mexican American Ind. (7)	7	0.09
Tohono O'Odham (1)	1	0.01
Yuman (0)	1	0.01
Yup'ik *(Alaska Native)* (0)	4	0.05
Asian (60)	123	1.52
Not Hispanic (52)	108	1.33
Hispanic (8)	15	0.19
Chinese, ex. Taiwanese (10)	14	0.17
Filipino (9)	17	0.21
Indian (9)	15	0.19
Indonesian (0)	1	0.01
Japanese (4)	24	0.30
Korean (9)	15	0.19
Laotian (8)	11	0.14
Pakistani (1)	3	0.04
Thai (2)	4	0.05
Vietnamese (5)	6	0.07
Hawaii Native/Pacific Islander (3)	9	0.11
Not Hispanic (2)	7	0.09
Hispanic (1)	2	0.02
Guamanian/Chamorro (3)	3	0.04
Native Hawaiian (0)	2	0.02
White (6,847)	7,044	86.88
Not Hispanic (5,755)	5,882	72.55
Hispanic (1,092)	1,162	14.33

Bourbonnais

Place Type: Village
County: Kankakee
Population: 18,631†

Ancestry‡	Population	%
African, Sub-Saharan (56)	91	0.50
African (41)	56	0.31
Ethiopian (15)	35	0.19
American (596)	596	3.29
Arab (0)	11	0.06
Egyptian (0)	11	0.06
Austrian (0)	21	0.12
Belgian (0)	109	0.60
British (32)	52	0.29
Bulgarian (0)	13	0.07
Canadian (0)	10	0.06
Croatian (0)	18	0.10
Czech (13)	135	0.75
Danish (34)	134	0.74
Dutch (372)	797	4.40
English (532)	1,692	9.35
European (50)	62	0.34
Finnish (15)	15	0.08
French, ex. Basque (423)	1,631	9.01
French Canadian (101)	228	1.26
German (1,722)	5,748	31.76
Greek (42)	276	1.52
Hungarian (45)	111	0.61
Irish (393)	2,695	14.89
Italian (452)	1,200	6.63

*Notes: † The Census 2010 population figure is used to calculate the percentages in the Hispanic Origin and Race categories. Ancestry percentages are based on the 2006-2010 American Community Survey population (not shown); ‡ Numbers in parentheses indicate the number of people reporting a single ancestry; * Numbers in parentheses indicate the number of persons reporting this race alone, not in combination with any other race; Please refer to the Explanation of Data for more information.*

Latvian (16)	16	0.09
Lithuanian (42)	108	0.60
Luxemburger (0)	14	0.08
Macedonian (0)	13	0.07
Norwegian (104)	434	2.40
Polish (499)	1,341	7.41
Russian (0)	62	0.34
Scotch-Irish (120)	236	1.30
Scottish (53)	213	1.18
Slovene (0)	11	0.06
Swedish (127)	430	2.38
Ukrainian (0)	14	0.08
Welsh (10)	62	0.34
West Indian, ex. Hispanic (37)	72	0.40
Bahamian (17)	17	0.09
Jamaican (11)	46	0.25
Trinidadian/Tobagonian (9)	9	0.05

Hispanic Origin	Population	%
Hispanic or Latino (of any race)	898	4.82
Central American, ex. Mexican	20	0.11
Guatemalan	10	0.05
Nicaraguan	2	0.01
Panamanian	1	0.01
Salvadoran	7	0.04
Cuban	18	0.10
Dominican Republic	1	0.01
Mexican	686	3.68
Puerto Rican	77	0.41
South American	36	0.19
Argentinean	6	0.03
Bolivian	2	0.01
Chilean	2	0.01
Colombian	7	0.04
Ecuadorian	13	0.07
Peruvian	3	0.02
Venezuelan	3	0.02
Other Hispanic or Latino	60	0.32

Race*	Population	%
African-American/Black (1,392)	1,594	8.56
Not Hispanic (1,385)	1,564	8.39
Hispanic (7)	30	0.16
American Indian/Alaska Native (35)	149	0.80
Not Hispanic (20)	123	0.66
Hispanic (15)	26	0.14
Alaska Athabascan *(Ala. Nat.)* (3)	3	0.02
Apache (1)	2	0.01
Arapaho (0)	1	0.01
Blackfeet (1)	2	0.01
Cherokee (0)	30	0.16
Chippewa (1)	5	0.03
Choctaw (4)	11	0.06
Iroquois (0)	6	0.03
Lumbee (0)	1	0.01
Mexican American Ind. (10)	11	0.06
Navajo (0)	1	0.01
Potawatomi (0)	3	0.02
Shoshone (1)	3	0.02
Sioux (1)	5	0.03
Yaqui (2)	2	0.01
Asian (353)	443	2.38
Not Hispanic (351)	439	2.36
Hispanic (2)	4	0.02
Chinese, ex. Taiwanese (44)	58	0.31
Filipino (80)	112	0.60
Indian (134)	151	0.81
Japanese (5)	13	0.07
Korean (39)	48	0.26
Laotian (1)	3	0.02
Pakistani (8)	13	0.07
Taiwanese (1)	1	0.01
Thai (2)	6	0.03
Vietnamese (26)	29	0.16
Hawaii Native/Pacific Islander (9)	14	0.08
Not Hispanic (9)	13	0.07
Hispanic (0)	1	0.01
Native Hawaiian (1)	3	0.02
Samoan (8)	8	0.04
White (16,144)	16,512	88.63
Not Hispanic (15,614)	15,911	85.40
Hispanic (530)	601	3.23

Bradley

Place Type: Village
County: Kankakee
Population: 15,895†

Ancestry‡	Population	%
American (586)	586	3.81
Arab (18)	27	0.18
Egyptian (18)	18	0.12
Other Arab (0)	9	0.06
Austrian (10)	23	0.15
British (11)	55	0.36
Canadian (18)	30	0.19
Croatian (0)	6	0.04
Czech (21)	88	0.57
Czechoslovakian (0)	6	0.04
Danish (55)	118	0.77
Dutch (80)	358	2.33
English (247)	1,326	8.61
European (25)	25	0.16
Finnish (17)	17	0.11
French, ex. Basque (522)	2,150	13.97
French Canadian (182)	343	2.23
German (1,114)	4,263	27.69
Greek (0)	34	0.22
Irish (461)	2,422	15.73
Italian (849)	1,835	11.92
Lithuanian (0)	18	0.12
Northern European (22)	22	0.14
Norwegian (49)	164	1.07
Pennsylvania German (11)	11	0.07
Polish (279)	806	5.24
Portuguese (0)	33	0.21
Scandinavian (0)	45	0.29
Scotch-Irish (64)	216	1.40
Scottish (20)	175	1.14
Serbian (0)	12	0.08
Slavic (0)	6	0.04
Slovak (46)	162	1.05
Slovene (0)	9	0.06
Swedish (85)	462	3.00
Swiss (0)	8	0.05
Turkish (0)	9	0.06
Welsh (18)	58	0.38

Hispanic Origin	Population	%
Hispanic or Latino (of any race)	1,190	7.49
Central American, ex. Mexican	30	0.19
Guatemalan	23	0.14
Honduran	5	0.03
Nicaraguan	1	0.01
Salvadoran	1	0.01
Cuban	3	0.02
Dominican Republic	1	0.01
Mexican	982	6.18
Puerto Rican	78	0.49
South American	23	0.14
Bolivian	2	0.01
Chilean	2	0.01
Colombian	12	0.08
Ecuadorian	2	0.01
Peruvian	5	0.03
Other Hispanic or Latino	73	0.46

Race*	Population	%
African-American/Black (998)	1,181	7.43
Not Hispanic (976)	1,130	7.11
Hispanic (22)	51	0.32
American Indian/Alaska Native (38)	107	0.67
Not Hispanic (31)	88	0.55
Hispanic (7)	19	0.12
Apache (6)	7	0.04
Blackfeet (1)	8	0.05
Cherokee (7)	29	0.18
Chippewa (3)	3	0.02
Choctaw (1)	1	0.01
Houma (1)	2	0.01
Mexican American Ind. (1)	1	0.01
Ottawa (1)	1	0.01
Sioux (0)	1	0.01
Yaqui (3)	4	0.03
Yup'ik *(Alaska Native)* (1)	1	0.01
Asian (185)	219	1.38
Not Hispanic (184)	216	1.36
Hispanic (1)	3	0.02
Chinese, ex. Taiwanese (26)	32	0.20
Filipino (53)	69	0.43
Hmong (6)	6	0.04
Indian (55)	60	0.38
Japanese (4)	9	0.06
Korean (21)	27	0.17
Laotian (1)	2	0.01
Pakistani (1)	2	0.01
Vietnamese (12)	14	0.09
Hawaii Native/Pacific Islander (6)	9	0.06
Not Hispanic (5)	8	0.05
Hispanic (1)	1	0.01
Native Hawaiian (6)	8	0.05
Samoan (0)	1	0.01
White (13,872)	14,172	89.16
Not Hispanic (13,263)	13,474	84.77
Hispanic (609)	698	4.39

Bridgeview

Place Type: Village
County: Cook
Population: 16,446†

Ancestry‡	Population	%
African, Sub-Saharan (16)	43	0.27
African (16)	43	0.27
Albanian (11)	11	0.07
American (434)	434	2.69
Arab (1,691)	2,010	12.45
Arab (587)	786	4.87
Egyptian (224)	224	1.39
Jordanian (225)	225	1.39
Moroccan (65)	65	0.40
Palestinian (284)	284	1.76
Other Arab (306)	426	2.64
Austrian (0)	18	0.11
Brazilian (19)	19	0.12
Canadian (7)	51	0.32
Croatian (55)	136	0.84
Czech (54)	349	2.16
Czechoslovakian (0)	17	0.11
Danish (0)	33	0.20
Dutch (58)	232	1.44
Eastern European (30)	30	0.19
English (85)	487	3.02
European (39)	39	0.24
French, ex. Basque (36)	216	1.34
French Canadian (34)	97	0.60
German (500)	2,247	13.92
Greek (0)	288	1.78
Hungarian (12)	12	0.07
Irish (532)	2,927	18.13
Italian (413)	1,217	7.54
Lithuanian (80)	235	1.46
Macedonian (0)	56	0.35
Northern European (0)	38	0.24
Norwegian (59)	87	0.54
Polish (2,616)	4,156	25.74
Portuguese (13)	13	0.08
Romanian (0)	9	0.06
Russian (0)	66	0.41
Scandinavian (0)	8	0.05
Scotch-Irish (19)	32	0.20
Scottish (0)	93	0.58
Serbian (13)	13	0.08
Slavic (6)	6	0.04
Slovak (95)	150	0.93
Slovene (36)	36	0.22
Swedish (11)	257	1.59
Turkish (10)	10	0.06

*Notes: † The Census 2010 population figure is used to calculate the percentages in the Hispanic Origin and Race categories. Ancestry percentages are based on the 2006-2010 American Community Survey population (not shown); ‡ Numbers in parentheses indicate the number of people reporting a single ancestry; * Numbers in parentheses indicate the number of persons reporting this race alone, not in combination with any other race; Please refer to the Explanation of Data for more information.*

Ukrainian (13)	47	0.29
Welsh (0)	25	0.15

Hispanic Origin	Population	%
Hispanic or Latino (of any race)	2,578	15.68
Central American, ex. Mexican	46	0.28
Guatemalan	25	0.15
Honduran	3	0.02
Nicaraguan	9	0.05
Salvadoran	9	0.05
Cuban	11	0.07
Dominican Republic	4	0.02
Mexican	2,148	13.06
Puerto Rican	192	1.17
South American	52	0.32
Chilean	1	0.01
Colombian	19	0.12
Ecuadorian	18	0.11
Peruvian	8	0.05
Venezuelan	5	0.03
Other South American	1	0.01
Other Hispanic or Latino	125	0.76

Race*	Population	%
African-American/Black (481)	534	3.25
Not Hispanic (450)	490	2.98
Hispanic (31)	44	0.27
American Indian/Alaska Native (26)	85	0.52
Not Hispanic (11)	58	0.35
Hispanic (15)	27	0.16
Arapaho (1)	2	0.01
Cherokee (1)	10	0.06
Chippewa (0)	2	0.01
Mexican American Ind. (0)	2	0.01
Navajo (0)	1	0.01
Potawatomi (0)	1	0.01
Sioux (1)	4	0.02
Asian (503)	722	4.39
Not Hispanic (489)	700	4.26
Hispanic (14)	22	0.13
Bangladeshi (20)	23	0.14
Chinese, ex. Taiwanese (18)	22	0.13
Filipino (136)	162	0.99
Indian (152)	168	1.02
Japanese (1)	10	0.06
Korean (10)	10	0.06
Laotian (0)	1	0.01
Malaysian (0)	4	0.02
Pakistani (121)	126	0.77
Thai (9)	11	0.07
Vietnamese (4)	4	0.02
Hawaii Native/Pacific Islander (2)	17	0.10
Not Hispanic (2)	13	0.08
Hispanic (0)	4	0.02
Native Hawaiian (2)	3	0.02
White (13,890)	14,326	87.11
Not Hispanic (12,574)	12,880	78.32
Hispanic (1,316)	1,446	8.79

Broadview

Place Type: Village
County: Cook
Population: 7,932†

Ancestry‡	Population	%
African, Sub-Saharan (92)	106	1.34
African (92)	106	1.34
American (46)	46	0.58
Arab (15)	15	0.19
Jordanian (15)	15	0.19
Belgian (0)	15	0.19
Croatian (0)	14	0.18
Czech (73)	73	0.92
Czechoslovakian (8)	8	0.10
Dutch (33)	47	0.59
English (0)	55	0.69
French, ex. Basque (0)	5	0.06
French Canadian (4)	4	0.05
German (60)	237	2.99
Hungarian (0)	31	0.39
Irish (0)	159	2.01
Italian (110)	162	2.04
Latvian (0)	15	0.19
Lithuanian (0)	5	0.06
Polish (73)	202	2.55
Russian (0)	30	0.38
Scottish (0)	12	0.15
Slovak (14)	14	0.18
Ukrainian (0)	42	0.53
West Indian, ex. Hispanic (73)	73	0.92
Jamaican (70)	70	0.88
Trinidadian/Tobagonian (3)	3	0.04

Hispanic Origin	Population	%
Hispanic or Latino (of any race)	682	8.60
Central American, ex. Mexican	17	0.21
Guatemalan	13	0.16
Panamanian	3	0.04
Other Central American	1	0.01
Cuban	11	0.14
Dominican Republic	3	0.04
Mexican	530	6.68
Puerto Rican	86	1.08
South American	8	0.10
Argentinean	1	0.01
Ecuadorian	2	0.03
Venezuelan	5	0.06
Other Hispanic or Latino	27	0.34

Race*	Population	%
African-American/Black (6,047)	6,169	77.77
Not Hispanic (6,001)	6,091	76.79
Hispanic (46)	78	0.98
American Indian/Alaska Native (8)	46	0.58
Not Hispanic (4)	38	0.48
Hispanic (4)	8	0.10
Blackfeet (0)	1	0.01
Cherokee (0)	4	0.05
Chippewa (1)	1	0.01
Choctaw (1)	1	0.01
South American Ind. (1)	1	0.01
Asian (108)	119	1.50
Not Hispanic (99)	108	1.36
Hispanic (9)	11	0.14
Bangladeshi (1)	1	0.01
Chinese, ex. Taiwanese (12)	13	0.16
Filipino (49)	54	0.68
Indian (16)	20	0.25
Indonesian (8)	8	0.10
Japanese (4)	8	0.10
Korean (2)	2	0.03
Pakistani (5)	5	0.06
Thai (3)	3	0.04
Vietnamese (6)	7	0.09
Hawaii Native/Pacific Islander (3)	3	0.04
Not Hispanic (3)	3	0.04
White (1,352)	1,436	18.10
Not Hispanic (1,035)	1,087	13.70
Hispanic (317)	349	4.40

Brookfield

Place Type: Village
County: Cook
Population: 18,978†

Ancestry‡	Population	%
African, Sub-Saharan (49)	56	0.30
African (0)	7	0.04
Nigerian (49)	49	0.26
Albanian (16)	23	0.12
American (237)	237	1.26
Arab (154)	203	1.08
Arab (32)	32	0.17
Lebanese (0)	49	0.26
Palestinian (112)	112	0.60
Other Arab (10)	10	0.05
Austrian (6)	105	0.56
Belgian (9)	21	0.11
British (9)	37	0.20
Canadian (17)	17	0.09
Croatian (72)	191	1.02
Czech (595)	1,651	8.78
Czechoslovakian (83)	93	0.49
Danish (25)	79	0.42
Dutch (111)	297	1.58
English (180)	943	5.01
European (91)	134	0.71
Finnish (0)	6	0.03
French, ex. Basque (58)	403	2.14
French Canadian (12)	46	0.24
German (771)	5,086	27.04
Greek (147)	334	1.78
Hungarian (0)	152	0.81
Irish (971)	4,186	22.26
Italian (698)	1,985	10.55
Lithuanian (186)	354	1.88
Luxemburger (0)	60	0.32
Northern European (25)	50	0.27
Norwegian (46)	232	1.23
Polish (1,207)	3,143	16.71
Portuguese (0)	32	0.17
Romanian (9)	51	0.27
Russian (22)	63	0.33
Scandinavian (0)	25	0.13
Scotch-Irish (125)	310	1.65
Scottish (87)	351	1.87
Serbian (26)	54	0.29
Slovak (61)	199	1.06
Slovene (8)	29	0.15
Swedish (52)	383	2.04
Swiss (35)	75	0.40
Turkish (12)	46	0.24
Ukrainian (39)	155	0.82
Welsh (11)	74	0.39
West Indian, ex. Hispanic (0)	14	0.07
Haitian (0)	14	0.07
Yugoslavian (279)	279	1.48

Hispanic Origin	Population	%
Hispanic or Latino (of any race)	3,069	16.17
Central American, ex. Mexican	81	0.43
Costa Rican	6	0.03
Guatemalan	51	0.27
Honduran	6	0.03
Nicaraguan	1	0.01
Panamanian	5	0.03
Salvadoran	12	0.06
Cuban	33	0.17
Dominican Republic	7	0.04
Mexican	2,439	12.85
Puerto Rican	277	1.46
South American	119	0.63
Argentinean	28	0.15
Bolivian	7	0.04
Chilean	3	0.02
Colombian	26	0.14
Ecuadorian	13	0.07
Paraguayan	13	0.07
Peruvian	18	0.09
Venezuelan	6	0.03
Other South American	5	0.03
Other Hispanic or Latino	113	0.60

Race*	Population	%
African-American/Black (476)	570	3.00
Not Hispanic (456)	528	2.78
Hispanic (20)	42	0.22
American Indian/Alaska Native (42)	148	0.78
Not Hispanic (11)	84	0.44
Hispanic (31)	64	0.34
Apache (1)	1	0.01
Blackfeet (0)	1	0.01
Cherokee (2)	34	0.18
Chippewa (3)	8	0.04
Choctaw (0)	15	0.08
Delaware (0)	1	0.01
Iroquois (1)	6	0.03
Menominee (1)	1	0.01

SECTION TWO

*Notes: † The Census 2010 population figure is used to calculate the percentages in the Hispanic Origin and Race categories. Ancestry percentages are based on the 2006-2010 American Community Survey population (not shown); ‡ Numbers in parentheses indicate the number of people reporting a single ancestry; * Numbers in parentheses indicate the number of persons reporting this race alone, not in combination with any other race; Please refer to the Explanation of Data for more information.*

Mexican American Ind. (6)	6	0.03
Navajo (1)	1	0.01
Ottawa (0)	4	0.02
Potawatomi (0)	2	0.01
Sioux (0)	2	0.01
South American Ind. (0)	2	0.01
Ute (0)	1	0.01
Asian (285)	419	2.21
Not Hispanic (285)	404	2.13
Hispanic (0)	15	0.08
Bangladeshi (1)	1	0.01
Cambodian (1)	2	0.01
Chinese, ex. Taiwanese (50)	70	0.37
Filipino (86)	142	0.75
Hmong (0)	1	0.01
Indian (67)	90	0.47
Indonesian (0)	1	0.01
Japanese (11)	36	0.19
Korean (16)	20	0.11
Nepalese (3)	3	0.02
Pakistani (1)	1	0.01
Thai (15)	18	0.09
Vietnamese (28)	33	0.17
Hawaii Native/Pacific Islander (5)	25	0.13
Not Hispanic (0)	12	0.06
Hispanic (5)	13	0.07
Guamanian/Chamorro (0)	3	0.02
Native Hawaiian (0)	8	0.04
White (16,830)	17,238	90.83
Not Hispanic (14,888)	15,127	79.71
Hispanic (1,942)	2,111	11.12

Buffalo Grove

Place Type: Village
County: Lake
Population: 41,496†

Ancestry‡	Population	%
African, Sub-Saharan (0)	14	0.03
Zimbabwean (0)	14	0.03
American (2,282)	2,282	5.45
Arab (11)	24	0.06
Iraqi (11)	11	0.03
Lebanese (0)	13	0.03
Armenian (21)	71	0.17
Assyrian/Chaldean/Syriac (42)	55	0.13
Australian (0)	15	0.04
Austrian (43)	196	0.47
Belgian (0)	40	0.10
Brazilian (21)	43	0.10
British (36)	191	0.46
Bulgarian (78)	78	0.19
Canadian (18)	50	0.12
Croatian (22)	22	0.05
Czech (0)	222	0.53
Czechoslovakian (98)	134	0.32
Danish (18)	150	0.36
Dutch (108)	295	0.70
Eastern European (564)	577	1.38
English (376)	2,433	5.81
European (529)	566	1.35
Finnish (38)	278	0.66
French, ex. Basque (43)	442	1.06
French Canadian (29)	108	0.26
German (1,364)	5,957	14.23
Greek (208)	421	1.01
Hungarian (97)	499	1.19
Icelander (11)	11	0.03
Iranian (106)	116	0.28
Irish (595)	3,426	8.18
Israeli (44)	44	0.11
Italian (1,046)	2,351	5.62
Latvian (123)	170	0.41
Lithuanian (293)	439	1.05
Luxemburger (9)	45	0.11
Norwegian (82)	404	0.97
Polish (1,653)	4,402	10.52
Portuguese (0)	36	0.09
Romanian (140)	466	1.11
Russian (3,894)	6,299	15.05
Scandinavian (22)	52	0.12
Scotch-Irish (65)	251	0.60
Scottish (140)	559	1.34
Serbian (90)	105	0.25
Slavic (42)	42	0.10
Slovak (31)	81	0.19
Slovene (65)	201	0.48
Soviet Union (18)	18	0.04
Swedish (262)	947	2.26
Swiss (0)	83	0.20
Turkish (52)	100	0.24
Ukrainian (1,053)	1,311	3.13
Welsh (14)	76	0.18
Yugoslavian (0)	70	0.17

Hispanic Origin	Population	%
Hispanic or Latino (of any race)	2,040	4.92
Central American, ex. Mexican	128	0.31
Costa Rican	6	0.01
Guatemalan	75	0.18
Honduran	11	0.03
Nicaraguan	5	0.01
Panamanian	1	<0.01
Salvadoran	30	0.07
Cuban	75	0.18
Dominican Republic	9	0.02
Mexican	1,356	3.27
Puerto Rican	141	0.34
South American	229	0.55
Argentinean	32	0.08
Bolivian	7	0.02
Chilean	10	0.02
Colombian	74	0.18
Ecuadorian	38	0.09
Paraguayan	3	0.01
Peruvian	42	0.10
Venezuelan	23	0.06
Other Hispanic or Latino	102	0.25

Race*	Population	%
African-American/Black (416)	534	1.29
Not Hispanic (405)	501	1.21
Hispanic (11)	33	0.08
American Indian/Alaska Native (67)	145	0.35
Not Hispanic (32)	89	0.21
Hispanic (35)	56	0.13
Apache (1)	1	<0.01
Blackfeet (0)	5	0.01
Canadian/French Am. Ind. (1)	1	<0.01
Central American Ind. (1)	1	<0.01
Cherokee (3)	12	0.03
Chickasaw (1)	1	<0.01
Chippewa (3)	6	0.01
Choctaw (0)	2	<0.01
Creek (0)	2	<0.01
Mexican American Ind. (4)	6	0.01
Navajo (3)	3	0.01
Potawatomi (0)	3	0.01
Sioux (3)	4	0.01
South American Ind. (0)	5	0.01
Yuman (1)	3	0.01
Asian (6,639)	7,053	17.00
Not Hispanic (6,625)	7,007	16.89
Hispanic (14)	46	0.11
Bangladeshi (13)	15	0.04
Burmese (1)	1	<0.01
Cambodian (4)	4	0.01
Chinese, ex. Taiwanese (1,433)	1,552	3.74
Filipino (499)	595	1.43
Indian (2,171)	2,250	5.42
Indonesian (7)	11	0.03
Japanese (436)	498	1.20
Korean (1,709)	1,780	4.29
Laotian (2)	2	<0.01
Malaysian (6)	10	0.02
Nepalese (5)	5	0.01
Pakistani (98)	110	0.27
Sri Lankan (8)	9	0.02
Taiwanese (65)	83	0.20
Thai (30)	36	0.09
Vietnamese (46)	59	0.14
Hawaii Native/Pacific Islander (18)	53	0.13
Not Hispanic (17)	52	0.13
Hispanic (1)	1	<0.01
Guamanian/Chamorro (1)	5	0.01
Native Hawaiian (13)	21	0.05
White (33,122)	33,635	81.06
Not Hispanic (31,813)	32,193	77.58
Hispanic (1,309)	1,442	3.48

Burbank

Place Type: City
County: Cook
Population: 28,925†

Ancestry‡	Population	%
Albanian (15)	15	0.05
American (629)	629	2.21
Arab (1,542)	1,558	5.48
Arab (524)	532	1.87
Egyptian (27)	27	0.09
Jordanian (40)	40	0.14
Palestinian (612)	620	2.18
Other Arab (339)	339	1.19
Assyrian/Chaldean/Syriac (24)	38	0.13
Austrian (70)	196	0.69
Belgian (0)	22	0.08
Brazilian (12)	12	0.04
British (15)	33	0.12
Croatian (97)	202	0.71
Czech (254)	604	2.12
Danish (14)	86	0.30
Dutch (19)	201	0.71
English (235)	766	2.69
French, ex. Basque (20)	149	0.52
French Canadian (13)	53	0.19
German (705)	3,328	11.71
Greek (245)	514	1.81
Hungarian (14)	69	0.24
Irish (796)	3,563	12.53
Israeli (26)	26	0.09
Italian (723)	2,008	7.06
Lithuanian (424)	845	2.97
Luxemburger (0)	7	0.02
Northern European (41)	41	0.14
Norwegian (25)	178	0.63
Polish (7,023)	9,415	33.12
Russian (18)	106	0.37
Scandinavian (7)	20	0.07
Scotch-Irish (15)	48	0.17
Scottish (0)	58	0.20
Serbian (0)	35	0.12
Slavic (8)	14	0.05
Slovak (62)	133	0.47
Slovene (31)	109	0.38
Swedish (48)	299	1.05
Swiss (0)	42	0.15
Ukrainian (9)	17	0.06
Welsh (0)	123	0.43
West Indian, ex. Hispanic (27)	27	0.09
Haitian (27)	27	0.09
Yugoslavian (0)	12	0.04

Hispanic Origin	Population	%
Hispanic or Latino (of any race)	7,680	26.55
Central American, ex. Mexican	142	0.49
Costa Rican	2	0.01
Guatemalan	83	0.29
Honduran	24	0.08
Nicaraguan	6	0.02
Panamanian	5	0.02
Salvadoran	21	0.07
Other Central American	1	<0.01
Cuban	33	0.11
Dominican Republic	4	0.01
Mexican	6,678	23.09
Puerto Rican	421	1.46
South American	151	0.52

*Notes: † The Census 2010 population figure is used to calculate the percentages in the Hispanic Origin and Race categories. Ancestry percentages are based on the 2006-2010 American Community Survey population (not shown); ‡ Numbers in parentheses indicate the number of people reporting a single ancestry; * Numbers in parentheses indicate the number of persons reporting this race alone, not in combination with any other race; Please refer to the Explanation of Data for more information.*

Argentinean	9	0.03
Bolivian	5	0.02
Chilean	1	<0.01
Colombian	56	0.19
Ecuadorian	52	0.18
Paraguayan	3	0.01
Peruvian	20	0.07
Uruguayan	2	0.01
Venezuelan	3	0.01
Other Hispanic or Latino	251	0.87

Race*	Population	%
African-American/Black (544)	609	2.11
Not Hispanic (494)	534	1.85
Hispanic (50)	75	0.26
American Indian/Alaska Native (114)	228	0.79
Not Hispanic (35)	98	0.34
Hispanic (79)	130	0.45
Apache (6)	10	0.03
Blackfeet (0)	2	0.01
Canadian/French Am. Ind. (2)	2	0.01
Cherokee (0)	24	0.08
Chippewa (5)	8	0.03
Inupiat *(Alaska Native)* (1)	1	<0.01
Iroquois (0)	1	<0.01
Menominee (1)	3	0.01
Mexican American Ind. (17)	26	0.09
Navajo (0)	4	0.01
Ottawa (1)	1	<0.01
Sioux (0)	3	0.01
South American Ind. (2)	8	0.03
Spanish American Ind. (3)	7	0.02
Asian (726)	948	3.28
Not Hispanic (701)	888	3.07
Hispanic (25)	60	0.21
Bangladeshi (1)	1	<0.01
Cambodian (3)	3	0.01
Chinese, ex. Taiwanese (48)	63	0.22
Filipino (246)	269	0.93
Indian (174)	186	0.64
Japanese (11)	30	0.10
Korean (9)	20	0.07
Pakistani (36)	45	0.16
Taiwanese (1)	1	<0.01
Thai (29)	29	0.10
Vietnamese (151)	155	0.54
Hawaii Native/Pacific Islander (12)	40	0.14
Not Hispanic (4)	23	0.08
Hispanic (8)	17	0.06
Guamanian/Chamorro (6)	6	0.02
Native Hawaiian (1)	1	<0.01
Samoan (0)	1	<0.01
White (23,634)	24,217	83.72
Not Hispanic (19,656)	19,951	68.97
Hispanic (3,978)	4,266	14.75

Burr Ridge

Place Type: Village
County: DuPage
Population: 10,559†

Ancestry‡	Population	%
African, Sub-Saharan (122)	122	1.16
Ghanaian (122)	122	1.16
American (91)	91	0.87
Arab (411)	433	4.12
Arab (189)	200	1.90
Egyptian (100)	100	0.95
Lebanese (32)	32	0.30
Palestinian (28)	28	0.27
Syrian (62)	73	0.69
Austrian (0)	94	0.89
British (19)	19	0.18
Canadian (0)	35	0.33
Croatian (45)	150	1.43
Czech (128)	250	2.38
Czechoslovakian (16)	36	0.34
Danish (0)	76	0.72
Dutch (70)	175	1.67
English (149)	732	6.97
European (63)	63	0.60
Finnish (10)	23	0.22
French, ex. Basque (25)	154	1.47
French Canadian (24)	24	0.23
German (366)	1,873	17.83
Greek (101)	325	3.09
Hungarian (24)	62	0.59
Icelander (0)	15	0.14
Iranian (37)	37	0.35
Irish (498)	2,112	20.10
Italian (291)	1,039	9.89
Lithuanian (169)	328	3.12
Norwegian (42)	140	1.33
Polish (562)	1,388	13.21
Portuguese (53)	72	0.69
Russian (70)	144	1.37
Scandinavian (38)	85	0.81
Scotch-Irish (39)	58	0.55
Scottish (0)	242	2.30
Serbian (13)	36	0.34
Slovak (12)	62	0.59
Slovene (15)	44	0.42
Swedish (46)	222	2.11
Swiss (0)	39	0.37
Ukrainian (13)	29	0.28
Welsh (0)	11	0.10

Hispanic Origin	Population	%
Hispanic or Latino (of any race)	430	4.07
Central American, ex. Mexican	21	0.20
Costa Rican	2	0.02
Guatemalan	6	0.06
Honduran	5	0.05
Nicaraguan	1	0.01
Panamanian	7	0.07
Cuban	32	0.30
Dominican Republic	1	0.01
Mexican	260	2.46
Puerto Rican	24	0.23
South American	55	0.52
Argentinean	4	0.04
Bolivian	2	0.02
Chilean	1	0.01
Colombian	20	0.19
Ecuadorian	3	0.03
Paraguayan	4	0.04
Peruvian	10	0.09
Venezuelan	11	0.10
Other Hispanic or Latino	37	0.35

Race*	Population	%
African-American/Black (209)	230	2.18
Not Hispanic (207)	227	2.15
Hispanic (2)	3	0.03
American Indian/Alaska Native (5)	26	0.25
Not Hispanic (4)	23	0.22
Hispanic (1)	3	0.03
Blackfeet (0)	2	0.02
Central American Ind. (1)	1	0.01
Cherokee (0)	1	0.01
Chippewa (2)	2	0.02
Choctaw (0)	3	0.03
Navajo (1)	1	0.01
Spanish American Ind. (0)	1	0.01
Asian (1,568)	1,724	16.33
Not Hispanic (1,563)	1,708	16.18
Hispanic (5)	16	0.15
Bangladeshi (7)	7	0.07
Burmese (5)	5	0.05
Chinese, ex. Taiwanese (188)	204	1.93
Filipino (137)	159	1.51
Indian (935)	968	9.17
Japanese (5)	10	0.09
Korean (59)	83	0.79
Malaysian (1)	2	0.02
Pakistani (157)	174	1.65
Sri Lankan (1)	3	0.03
Taiwanese (33)	39	0.37
Thai (9)	14	0.13
Vietnamese (5)	10	0.09
Hawaii Native/Pacific Islander (0)	9	0.09
Not Hispanic (0)	7	0.07
Hispanic (0)	2	0.02
White (8,487)	8,644	81.86
Not Hispanic (8,167)	8,303	78.63
Hispanic (320)	341	3.23

Cahokia

Place Type: Village
County: St. Clair
Population: 15,241†

Ancestry‡	Population	%
African, Sub-Saharan (13)	13	0.08
African (13)	13	0.08
American (400)	400	2.60
Arab (8)	8	0.05
Egyptian (8)	8	0.05
Austrian (0)	13	0.08
British (0)	11	0.07
Canadian (0)	6	0.04
Czech (17)	35	0.23
Danish (0)	32	0.21
Dutch (16)	154	1.00
English (222)	662	4.30
European (1,138)	1,138	7.39
French, ex. Basque (55)	311	2.02
French Canadian (6)	6	0.04
German (484)	1,260	8.18
Hungarian (0)	32	0.21
Irish (191)	958	6.22
Italian (114)	177	1.15
Norwegian (10)	29	0.19
Polish (99)	109	0.71
Romanian (11)	11	0.07
Scotch-Irish (25)	191	1.24
Scottish (15)	43	0.28
Slavic (23)	23	0.15
Swedish (12)	37	0.24
Swiss (0)	13	0.08
Welsh (18)	18	0.12

Hispanic Origin	Population	%
Hispanic or Latino (of any race)	298	1.96
Central American, ex. Mexican	9	0.06
Guatemalan	3	0.02
Honduran	1	0.01
Panamanian	4	0.03
Salvadoran	1	0.01
Cuban	4	0.03
Mexican	237	1.56
Puerto Rican	16	0.10
South American	1	0.01
Peruvian	1	0.01
Other Hispanic or Latino	31	0.20

Race*	Population	%
African-American/Black (9,484)	9,732	63.85
Not Hispanic (9,455)	9,685	63.55
Hispanic (29)	47	0.31
American Indian/Alaska Native (30)	75	0.49
Not Hispanic (30)	75	0.49
Aleut *(Alaska Native)* (1)	1	0.01
Blackfeet (2)	2	0.01
Cherokee (9)	24	0.16
Cheyenne (1)	1	0.01
Choctaw (0)	1	0.01
Cree (0)	2	0.01
Shoshone (3)	3	0.02
Sioux (0)	2	0.01
Asian (30)	58	0.38
Not Hispanic (29)	57	0.37
Hispanic (1)	1	0.01
Chinese, ex. Taiwanese (3)	12	0.08
Filipino (2)	3	0.02
Indian (6)	15	0.10
Japanese (3)	7	0.05
Korean (7)	7	0.05

SECTION TWO

*Notes: † The Census 2010 population figure is used to calculate the percentages in the Hispanic Origin and Race categories. Ancestry percentages are based on the 2006-2010 American Community Survey population (not shown); ‡ Numbers in parentheses indicate the number of people reporting a single ancestry; * Numbers in parentheses indicate the number of persons reporting this race alone, not in combination with any other race; Please refer to the Explanation of Data for more information.*

Thai (3)	4	0.03
Vietnamese (1)	1	0.01
Hawaii Native/Pacific Islander (2)	7	0.05
Not Hispanic (2)	7	0.05
Guamanian/Chamorro (2)	5	0.03
Native Hawaiian (0)	1	0.01
White (5,232)	5,494	36.05
Not Hispanic (5,126)	5,363	35.19
Hispanic (106)	131	0.86

Calumet City

Place Type: City
County: Cook
Population: 37,042†

Ancestry‡	Population	%
African, Sub-Saharan (534)	588	1.59
African (178)	232	0.63
Ghanaian (4)	4	0.01
Nigerian (352)	352	0.95
American (491)	491	1.33
Arab (35)	56	0.15
Arab (35)	56	0.15
Austrian (0)	12	0.03
Belgian (14)	14	0.04
Canadian (0)	12	0.03
Croatian (42)	88	0.24
Czech (14)	72	0.19
Danish (0)	39	0.11
Dutch (64)	150	0.41
English (128)	373	1.01
European (12)	26	0.07
French, ex. Basque (14)	92	0.25
French Canadian (0)	9	0.02
German (296)	1,220	3.30
Greek (95)	113	0.31
Hungarian (29)	72	0.19
Irish (310)	936	2.53
Israeli (23)	23	0.06
Italian (452)	749	2.03
Lithuanian (38)	61	0.16
Macedonian (8)	8	0.02
Norwegian (36)	86	0.23
Polish (1,247)	2,122	5.74
Romanian (0)	7	0.02
Russian (0)	24	0.06
Scotch-Irish (13)	110	0.30
Scottish (21)	60	0.16
Serbian (23)	118	0.32
Slavic (11)	11	0.03
Slovak (34)	199	0.54
Slovene (0)	7	0.02
Swedish (30)	86	0.23
Swiss (0)	30	0.08
Welsh (8)	73	0.20
West Indian, ex. Hispanic (773)	809	2.19
Belizean (0)	12	0.03
Haitian (223)	223	0.60
Jamaican (456)	468	1.27
Trinidadian/Tobagonian (0)	12	0.03
West Indian (94)	94	0.25
Yugoslavian (27)	27	0.07

Hispanic Origin	Population	%
Hispanic or Latino (of any race)	5,574	15.05
Central American, ex. Mexican	97	0.26
Costa Rican	3	0.01
Guatemalan	59	0.16
Honduran	4	0.01
Nicaraguan	6	0.02
Panamanian	6	0.02
Salvadoran	19	0.05
Cuban	15	0.04
Dominican Republic	10	0.03
Mexican	4,965	13.40
Puerto Rican	275	0.74
South American	13	0.04
Colombian	6	0.02
Ecuadorian	1	<0.01
Peruvian	6	0.02
Other Hispanic or Latino	199	0.54

Race*	Population	%
African-American/Black (26,136)	26,633	71.90
Not Hispanic (25,888)	26,282	70.95
Hispanic (248)	351	0.95
American Indian/Alaska Native (233)	449	1.21
Not Hispanic (58)	231	0.62
Hispanic (175)	218	0.59
Apache (1)	1	<0.01
Blackfeet (1)	9	0.02
Cherokee (5)	33	0.09
Chickasaw (0)	1	<0.01
Chippewa (1)	9	0.02
Choctaw (0)	9	0.02
Crow (0)	1	<0.01
Iroquois (0)	2	0.01
Menominee (2)	2	0.01
Mexican American Ind. (12)	13	0.04
Potawatomi (0)	2	0.01
Sioux (0)	9	0.02
Asian (116)	188	0.51
Not Hispanic (108)	173	0.47
Hispanic (8)	15	0.04
Chinese, ex. Taiwanese (24)	33	0.09
Filipino (29)	42	0.11
Indian (12)	17	0.05
Indonesian (0)	2	0.01
Japanese (11)	24	0.06
Korean (18)	27	0.07
Pakistani (1)	1	<0.01
Thai (1)	6	0.02
Vietnamese (18)	21	0.06
Hawaii Native/Pacific Islander (7)	27	0.07
Not Hispanic (7)	21	0.06
Hispanic (0)	6	0.02
Fijian (4)	4	0.01
Native Hawaiian (0)	4	0.01
Samoan (0)	4	0.01
White (7,101)	7,540	20.36
Not Hispanic (4,928)	5,194	14.02
Hispanic (2,173)	2,346	6.33

Calumet Park

Place Type: Village
County: Cook
Population: 7,835†

Ancestry‡	Population	%
African, Sub-Saharan (66)	97	1.22
African (66)	66	0.83
Nigerian (0)	31	0.39
American (222)	222	2.80
Brazilian (0)	16	0.20
Dutch (0)	38	0.48
English (8)	42	0.53
French, ex. Basque (0)	15	0.19
French Canadian (0)	43	0.54
German (0)	148	1.87
Irish (8)	172	2.17
Italian (0)	115	1.45
Lithuanian (19)	27	0.34
Luxemburger (0)	13	0.16
Norwegian (0)	16	0.20
Polish (31)	89	1.12
Portuguese (0)	8	0.10
Romanian (0)	48	0.61
Russian (87)	87	1.10
Scotch-Irish (21)	48	0.61
Swedish (0)	9	0.11
West Indian, ex. Hispanic (47)	58	0.73
Haitian (24)	24	0.30
Jamaican (23)	34	0.43

Hispanic Origin	Population	%
Hispanic or Latino (of any race)	536	6.84
Central American, ex. Mexican	23	0.29
Guatemalan	18	0.23
Nicaraguan	4	0.05
Panamanian	1	0.01
Cuban	1	0.01
Mexican	454	5.79
Puerto Rican	26	0.33
South American	8	0.10
Argentinean	6	0.08
Peruvian	1	0.01
Other South American	1	0.01
Other Hispanic or Latino	24	0.31

Race*	Population	%
African-American/Black (6,920)	6,968	88.93
Not Hispanic (6,893)	6,931	88.46
Hispanic (27)	37	0.47
American Indian/Alaska Native (12)	38	0.49
Not Hispanic (6)	24	0.31
Hispanic (6)	14	0.18
Blackfeet (0)	3	0.04
Cherokee (0)	2	0.03
Chickasaw (0)	2	0.03
Choctaw (0)	1	0.01
Mexican American Ind. (2)	2	0.03
Sioux (0)	1	0.01
Yaqui (0)	2	0.03
Asian (37)	42	0.54
Not Hispanic (24)	28	0.36
Hispanic (13)	14	0.18
Chinese, ex. Taiwanese (1)	1	0.01
Filipino (5)	8	0.10
Indian (27)	28	0.36
Korean (1)	1	0.01
Thai (1)	1	0.01
Vietnamese (2)	3	0.04
Hawaii Native/Pacific Islander (2)	6	0.08
Not Hispanic (2)	6	0.08
White (519)	570	7.28
Not Hispanic (322)	349	4.45
Hispanic (197)	221	2.82

Campton Hills

Place Type: Village
County: Kane
Population: 11,131†

Ancestry‡	Population	%
Albanian (11)	34	0.32
American (474)	474	4.40
Austrian (6)	93	0.86
Belgian (32)	47	0.44
British (40)	40	0.37
Canadian (0)	114	1.06
Croatian (0)	40	0.37
Czech (60)	249	2.31
Czechoslovakian (30)	49	0.45
Danish (15)	56	0.52
Dutch (26)	166	1.54
English (143)	962	8.92
European (142)	167	1.55
French, ex. Basque (35)	423	3.92
French Canadian (15)	115	1.07
German (1,034)	3,796	35.21
Greek (68)	152	1.41
Hungarian (44)	96	0.89
Irish (505)	2,216	20.56
Italian (334)	1,532	14.21
Latvian (21)	21	0.19
Lithuanian (27)	147	1.36
Luxemburger (29)	29	0.27
Norwegian (107)	371	3.44
Polish (401)	1,479	13.72
Russian (0)	73	0.68
Scotch-Irish (112)	298	2.76
Scottish (69)	377	3.50
Slavic (0)	8	0.07
Slovak (17)	107	0.99
Slovene (17)	17	0.16
Swedish (247)	697	6.47
Swiss (0)	72	0.67

*Notes: † The Census 2010 population figure is used to calculate the percentages in the Hispanic Origin and Race categories. Ancestry percentages are based on the 2006-2010 American Community Survey population (not shown); ‡ Numbers in parentheses indicate the number of people reporting a single ancestry; * Numbers in parentheses indicate the number of persons reporting this race alone, not in combination with any other race; Please refer to the Explanation of Data for more information.*

Ukrainian (0)	35	0.32
Welsh (0)	79	0.73

Hispanic Origin	Population	%
Hispanic or Latino (of any race)	406	3.65
Central American, ex. Mexican	18	0.16
Costa Rican	2	0.02
Guatemalan	11	0.10
Honduran	5	0.04
Cuban	39	0.35
Mexican	231	2.08
Puerto Rican	49	0.44
South American	33	0.30
Argentinean	7	0.06
Bolivian	5	0.04
Chilean	1	0.01
Colombian	5	0.04
Ecuadorian	12	0.11
Peruvian	3	0.03
Other Hispanic or Latino	36	0.32

Race*	Population	%
African-American/Black (61)	86	0.77
Not Hispanic (57)	77	0.69
Hispanic (4)	9	0.08
American Indian/Alaska Native (20)	41	0.37
Not Hispanic (12)	31	0.28
Hispanic (8)	10	0.09
Blackfeet (0)	2	0.02
Cherokee (1)	1	0.01
Chickasaw (4)	7	0.06
Chippewa (1)	1	0.01
Choctaw (1)	1	0.01
Creek (0)	1	0.01
Mexican American Ind. (2)	2	0.02
Pueblo (4)	4	0.04
Asian (198)	271	2.43
Not Hispanic (197)	262	2.35
Hispanic (1)	9	0.08
Cambodian (0)	4	0.04
Chinese, ex. Taiwanese (26)	50	0.45
Filipino (29)	55	0.49
Indian (80)	90	0.81
Japanese (8)	28	0.25
Korean (17)	21	0.19
Laotian (1)	1	0.01
Nepalese (1)	1	0.01
Pakistani (10)	10	0.09
Sri Lankan (1)	3	0.03
Thai (1)	8	0.07
Vietnamese (7)	11	0.10
Hawaii Native/Pacific Islander (7)	7	0.06
Not Hispanic (6)	6	0.05
Hispanic (1)	1	0.01
Native Hawaiian (7)	7	0.06
White (10,616)	10,743	96.51
Not Hispanic (10,341)	10,437	93.77
Hispanic (275)	306	2.75

Canton

Place Type: City
County: Fulton
Population: 14,704†

Ancestry‡	Population	%
African, Sub-Saharan (59)	59	0.40
African (59)	59	0.40
American (2,583)	2,583	17.50
Arab (9)	9	0.06
Syrian (9)	9	0.06
Austrian (13)	13	0.09
Belgian (0)	20	0.14
British (32)	32	0.22
Celtic (10)	10	0.07
Croatian (112)	180	1.22
Czech (68)	77	0.52
Czechoslovakian (0)	10	0.07
Danish (25)	32	0.22
Dutch (56)	371	2.51
English (837)	1,943	13.16
European (226)	248	1.68
Finnish (0)	9	0.06
French, ex. Basque (78)	529	3.58
German (949)	2,840	19.24
Greek (37)	67	0.45
Hungarian (0)	30	0.20
Iranian (0)	14	0.09
Irish (572)	1,798	12.18
Italian (138)	568	3.85
Lithuanian (33)	42	0.28
Norwegian (30)	107	0.72
Polish (197)	328	2.22
Scotch-Irish (59)	167	1.13
Scottish (127)	415	2.81
Serbian (0)	10	0.07
Slavic (17)	17	0.12
Slovak (0)	8	0.05
Swedish (141)	210	1.42
Swiss (0)	22	0.15
Ukrainian (9)	31	0.21
Welsh (56)	200	1.35
West Indian, ex. Hispanic (17)	17	0.12
Dutch West Indian (8)	8	0.05
Jamaican (9)	9	0.06
Yugoslavian (7)	52	0.35

Hispanic Origin	Population	%
Hispanic or Latino (of any race)	662	4.50
Central American, ex. Mexican	15	0.10
Guatemalan	5	0.03
Honduran	7	0.05
Salvadoran	2	0.01
Other Central American	1	0.01
Cuban	10	0.07
Mexican	453	3.08
Puerto Rican	37	0.25
South American	12	0.08
Argentinean	3	0.02
Bolivian	1	0.01
Colombian	4	0.03
Ecuadorian	3	0.02
Peruvian	1	0.01
Other Hispanic or Latino	135	0.92

Race*	Population	%
African-American/Black (1,204)	1,266	8.61
Not Hispanic (1,203)	1,262	8.58
Hispanic (1)	4	0.03
American Indian/Alaska Native (76)	135	0.92
Not Hispanic (37)	94	0.64
Hispanic (39)	41	0.28
Blackfeet (2)	10	0.07
Cherokee (5)	26	0.18
Chippewa (4)	4	0.03
Choctaw (0)	1	0.01
Cree (0)	1	0.01
Iroquois (9)	10	0.07
Mexican American Ind. (2)	2	0.01
Sioux (1)	4	0.03
Asian (67)	88	0.60
Not Hispanic (66)	87	0.59
Hispanic (1)	1	0.01
Chinese, ex. Taiwanese (13)	13	0.09
Filipino (8)	13	0.09
Indian (9)	10	0.07
Indonesian (1)	2	0.01
Japanese (5)	6	0.04
Korean (3)	7	0.05
Pakistani (6)	8	0.05
Sri Lankan (1)	1	0.01
Thai (4)	4	0.03
Vietnamese (12)	17	0.12
Hawaii Native/Pacific Islander (1)	3	0.02
Not Hispanic (1)	2	0.01
Hispanic (0)	1	0.01
Native Hawaiian (0)	1	0.01
Samoan (1)	1	0.01
White (12,666)	12,805	87.09
Not Hispanic (12,595)	12,724	86.53
Hispanic (71)	81	0.55

Carbondale

Place Type: City
County: Jackson
Population: 25,902†

Ancestry‡	Population	%
African, Sub-Saharan (154)	173	0.67
African (99)	99	0.38
Ethiopian (0)	19	0.07
Nigerian (55)	55	0.21
American (634)	634	2.46
Arab (203)	256	0.99
Arab (41)	41	0.16
Egyptian (35)	35	0.14
Lebanese (34)	87	0.34
Moroccan (19)	19	0.07
Syrian (42)	42	0.16
Other Arab (32)	32	0.12
Australian (13)	13	0.05
Austrian (52)	96	0.37
Belgian (17)	28	0.11
British (13)	51	0.20
Bulgarian (0)	18	0.07
Canadian (46)	81	0.31
Croatian (10)	22	0.09
Cypriot (15)	15	0.06
Czech (0)	105	0.41
Czechoslovakian (0)	11	0.04
Danish (0)	145	0.56
Dutch (88)	366	1.42
Eastern European (57)	82	0.32
English (642)	1,987	7.72
European (154)	167	0.65
French, ex. Basque (122)	559	2.17
French Canadian (72)	116	0.45
German (2,263)	5,801	22.54
Greek (130)	163	0.63
Hungarian (32)	32	0.12
Iranian (132)	154	0.60
Irish (879)	2,974	11.56
Italian (275)	948	3.68
Latvian (0)	53	0.21
Lithuanian (73)	159	0.62
Northern European (8)	8	0.03
Norwegian (210)	287	1.12
Polish (284)	838	3.26
Portuguese (5)	5	0.02
Romanian (14)	59	0.23
Russian (71)	216	0.84
Scotch-Irish (148)	451	1.75
Scottish (210)	513	1.99
Serbian (16)	29	0.11
Slovak (0)	26	0.10
Slovene (0)	19	0.07
Swedish (78)	449	1.74
Swiss (0)	79	0.31
Turkish (35)	35	0.14
Ukrainian (0)	12	0.05
Welsh (15)	87	0.34
West Indian, ex. Hispanic (33)	46	0.18
Haitian (33)	33	0.13
West Indian (0)	13	0.05

Hispanic Origin	Population	%
Hispanic or Latino (of any race)	1,410	5.44
Central American, ex. Mexican	157	0.61
Costa Rican	2	0.01
Guatemalan	72	0.28
Honduran	33	0.13
Nicaraguan	8	0.03
Panamanian	19	0.07
Salvadoran	23	0.09
Cuban	47	0.18
Dominican Republic	13	0.05
Mexican	817	3.15
Puerto Rican	134	0.52
South American	129	0.50

*Notes: † The Census 2010 population figure is used to calculate the percentages in the Hispanic Origin and Race categories. Ancestry percentages are based on the 2006-2010 American Community Survey population (not shown); ‡ Numbers in parentheses indicate the number of people reporting a single ancestry; * Numbers in parentheses indicate the number of persons reporting this race alone, not in combination with any other race; Please refer to the Explanation of Data for more information.*

Argentinean	8	0.03
Chilean	12	0.05
Colombian	59	0.23
Ecuadorian	9	0.03
Paraguayan	1	<0.01
Peruvian	28	0.11
Uruguayan	1	<0.01
Venezuelan	11	0.04
Other Hispanic or Latino	113	0.44

Race*	Population	%
African-American/Black (6,636)	7,058	27.25
Not Hispanic (6,560)	6,938	26.79
Hispanic (76)	120	0.46
American Indian/Alaska Native (96)	337	1.30
Not Hispanic (69)	283	1.09
Hispanic (27)	54	0.21
Aleut *(Alaska Native)* (0)	1	<0.01
Apache (1)	1	<0.01
Blackfeet (3)	20	0.08
Canadian/French Am. Ind. (1)	2	0.01
Cherokee (14)	72	0.28
Chickasaw (0)	7	0.03
Chippewa (1)	4	0.02
Choctaw (4)	9	0.03
Comanche (0)	1	<0.01
Creek (0)	1	<0.01
Iroquois (1)	6	0.02
Menominee (0)	2	0.01
Mexican American Ind. (2)	2	0.01
Navajo (1)	6	0.02
Osage (1)	1	<0.01
Pueblo (1)	1	<0.01
Seminole (0)	2	0.01
Sioux (1)	5	0.02
South American Ind. (0)	6	0.02
Spanish American Ind. (0)	1	<0.01
Tohono O'Odham (2)	2	0.01
Asian (1,466)	1,761	6.80
Not Hispanic (1,448)	1,729	6.68
Hispanic (18)	32	0.12
Bangladeshi (20)	21	0.08
Burmese (2)	2	0.01
Cambodian (4)	4	0.02
Chinese, ex. Taiwanese (334)	366	1.41
Filipino (74)	115	0.44
Indian (435)	474	1.83
Indonesian (13)	13	0.05
Japanese (68)	108	0.42
Korean (223)	243	0.94
Laotian (1)	1	<0.01
Malaysian (47)	52	0.20
Nepalese (30)	31	0.12
Pakistani (59)	75	0.29
Sri Lankan (25)	25	0.10
Taiwanese (48)	48	0.19
Thai (9)	21	0.08
Vietnamese (48)	57	0.22
Hawaii Native/Pacific Islander (21)	56	0.22
Not Hispanic (17)	39	0.15
Hispanic (4)	17	0.07
Fijian (0)	1	<0.01
Guamanian/Chamorro (14)	17	0.07
Native Hawaiian (5)	16	0.06
Samoan (0)	3	0.01
Tongan (1)	1	<0.01
White (16,169)	16,884	65.18
Not Hispanic (15,571)	16,200	62.54
Hispanic (598)	684	2.64

Carol Stream

Place Type: Village
County: DuPage
Population: 39,711†

Ancestry‡	Population	%
African, Sub-Saharan (332)	332	0.84
African (228)	228	0.57
Ethiopian (70)	70	0.18
Other Sub-Saharan African (34)	34	0.09
Albanian (80)	87	0.22
American (1,099)	1,099	2.77
Arab (211)	219	0.55
Egyptian (12)	12	0.03
Lebanese (26)	34	0.09
Moroccan (37)	37	0.09
Syrian (136)	136	0.34
Armenian (30)	39	0.10
Australian (17)	17	0.04
Austrian (29)	143	0.36
Belgian (24)	71	0.18
Brazilian (124)	161	0.41
British (55)	97	0.24
Bulgarian (85)	85	0.21
Canadian (10)	19	0.05
Croatian (43)	148	0.37
Czech (129)	566	1.42
Czechoslovakian (39)	39	0.10
Danish (76)	185	0.47
Dutch (111)	443	1.11
Eastern European (22)	22	0.06
English (417)	2,257	5.68
European (168)	168	0.42
Finnish (0)	80	0.20
French, ex. Basque (62)	849	2.14
French Canadian (57)	224	0.56
German (2,017)	8,899	22.39
Greek (73)	221	0.56
Hungarian (43)	177	0.45
Iranian (38)	38	0.10
Irish (1,284)	5,905	14.86
Italian (1,763)	5,059	12.73
Lithuanian (63)	186	0.47
Macedonian (11)	35	0.09
Norwegian (133)	622	1.57
Pennsylvania German (10)	10	0.03
Polish (1,722)	4,482	11.28
Portuguese (12)	50	0.13
Russian (166)	489	1.23
Scandinavian (16)	27	0.07
Scotch-Irish (31)	317	0.80
Scottish (103)	644	1.62
Slavic (4)	4	0.01
Slovak (19)	87	0.22
Slovene (8)	8	0.02
Swedish (239)	1,093	2.75
Swiss (8)	113	0.28
Ukrainian (178)	450	1.13
Welsh (0)	61	0.15
West Indian, ex. Hispanic (17)	17	0.04
West Indian (17)	17	0.04
Yugoslavian (0)	18	0.05

Hispanic Origin	Population	%
Hispanic or Latino (of any race)	5,633	14.18
Central American, ex. Mexican	246	0.62
Guatemalan	132	0.33
Honduran	19	0.05
Nicaraguan	11	0.03
Panamanian	12	0.03
Salvadoran	72	0.18
Cuban	115	0.29
Dominican Republic	12	0.03
Mexican	4,389	11.05
Puerto Rican	505	1.27
South American	192	0.48
Argentinean	8	0.02
Bolivian	4	0.01
Chilean	9	0.02
Colombian	76	0.19
Ecuadorian	31	0.08
Paraguayan	1	<0.01
Peruvian	54	0.14
Venezuelan	8	0.02
Other South American	1	<0.01
Other Hispanic or Latino	174	0.44

Race*	Population	%
African-American/Black (2,438)	2,675	6.74
Not Hispanic (2,333)	2,521	6.35
Hispanic (105)	154	0.39
American Indian/Alaska Native (116)	255	0.64
Not Hispanic (44)	132	0.33
Hispanic (72)	123	0.31
Apache (1)	3	0.01
Blackfeet (0)	6	0.02
Canadian/French Am. Ind. (1)	2	0.01
Cherokee (3)	35	0.09
Chickasaw (0)	1	<0.01
Chippewa (2)	4	0.01
Choctaw (0)	2	0.01
Creek (0)	3	0.01
Iroquois (1)	4	0.01
Mexican American Ind. (9)	16	0.04
Navajo (1)	2	0.01
Osage (0)	1	<0.01
Sioux (1)	1	<0.01
Spanish American Ind. (8)	14	0.04
Asian (5,810)	6,359	16.01
Not Hispanic (5,778)	6,264	15.77
Hispanic (32)	95	0.24
Bangladeshi (16)	22	0.06
Burmese (30)	30	0.08
Cambodian (69)	81	0.20
Chinese, ex. Taiwanese (177)	228	0.57
Filipino (1,202)	1,334	3.36
Indian (2,753)	2,929	7.38
Indonesian (1)	3	0.01
Japanese (57)	93	0.23
Korean (177)	201	0.51
Laotian (23)	37	0.09
Malaysian (1)	4	0.01
Nepalese (4)	4	0.01
Pakistani (335)	376	0.95
Taiwanese (20)	22	0.06
Thai (38)	42	0.11
Vietnamese (790)	804	2.02
Hawaii Native/Pacific Islander (7)	45	0.11
Not Hispanic (4)	26	0.07
Hispanic (3)	19	0.05
Guamanian/Chamorro (2)	11	0.03
Native Hawaiian (4)	11	0.03
White (28,061)	28,872	72.71
Not Hispanic (25,106)	25,616	64.51
Hispanic (2,955)	3,256	8.20

Carpentersville

Place Type: Village
County: Kane
Population: 37,691†

Ancestry‡	Population	%
African, Sub-Saharan (33)	97	0.26
African (33)	97	0.26
American (638)	638	1.72
Arab (0)	120	0.32
Arab (0)	60	0.16
Palestinian (0)	60	0.16
Assyrian/Chaldean/Syriac (0)	10	0.03
Austrian (12)	65	0.18
Belgian (9)	58	0.16
Brazilian (23)	48	0.13
British (20)	31	0.08
Bulgarian (0)	107	0.29
Canadian (0)	16	0.04
Croatian (0)	64	0.17
Czech (18)	194	0.52
Czechoslovakian (41)	82	0.22
Danish (28)	170	0.46
Dutch (27)	255	0.69
Eastern European (24)	24	0.06
English (286)	1,430	3.86
European (115)	164	0.44
Finnish (0)	30	0.08
French, ex. Basque (54)	452	1.22
French Canadian (20)	81	0.22
German (1,683)	6,030	16.26
Greek (108)	137	0.37

*Notes: † The Census 2010 population figure is used to calculate the percentages in the Hispanic Origin and Race categories. Ancestry percentages are based on the 2006-2010 American Community Survey population (not shown); ‡ Numbers in parentheses indicate the number of people reporting a single ancestry; * Numbers in parentheses indicate the number of persons reporting this race alone, not in combination with any other race; Please refer to the Explanation of Data for more information.*

Ancestry	Population	%
Hungarian (0)	117	0.32
Irish (441)	2,886	7.78
Italian (597)	1,927	5.19
Latvian (0)	10	0.03
Lithuanian (13)	117	0.32
Northern European (20)	20	0.05
Norwegian (184)	558	1.50
Polish (1,426)	2,898	7.81
Portuguese (117)	117	0.32
Romanian (10)	42	0.11
Russian (48)	343	0.92
Scandinavian (0)	11	0.03
Scotch-Irish (71)	281	0.76
Scottish (38)	250	0.67
Serbian (63)	63	0.17
Slavic (0)	10	0.03
Slovak (19)	35	0.09
Swedish (131)	590	1.59
Swiss (15)	77	0.21
Ukrainian (65)	93	0.25
Welsh (0)	85	0.23
Yugoslavian (0)	18	0.05

Hispanic Origin	Population	%
Hispanic or Latino (of any race)	18,877	50.08
Central American, ex. Mexican	748	1.98
Costa Rican	18	0.05
Guatemalan	173	0.46
Honduran	43	0.11
Nicaraguan	23	0.06
Panamanian	12	0.03
Salvadoran	478	1.27
Other Central American	1	<0.01
Cuban	33	0.09
Dominican Republic	18	0.05
Mexican	16,794	44.56
Puerto Rican	601	1.59
South American	205	0.54
Argentinean	14	0.04
Bolivian	3	0.01
Chilean	9	0.02
Colombian	99	0.26
Ecuadorian	29	0.08
Peruvian	42	0.11
Venezuelan	7	0.02
Other South American	2	0.01
Other Hispanic or Latino	478	1.27

Race*	Population	%
African-American/Black (2,566)	2,881	7.64
Not Hispanic (2,399)	2,612	6.93
Hispanic (167)	269	0.71
American Indian/Alaska Native (206)	360	0.96
Not Hispanic (42)	144	0.38
Hispanic (164)	216	0.57
Alaska Athabascan *(Ala. Nat.)* (0)	1	<0.01
Aleut *(Alaska Native)* (0)	1	<0.01
Apache (0)	3	0.01
Blackfeet (0)	5	0.01
Central American Ind. (1)	2	0.01
Cherokee (9)	45	0.12
Chippewa (4)	4	0.01
Choctaw (5)	5	0.01
Comanche (0)	6	0.02
Creek (0)	4	0.01
Delaware (5)	5	0.01
Iroquois (3)	12	0.03
Menominee (0)	7	0.02
Mexican American Ind. (41)	49	0.13
Ottawa (0)	1	<0.01
Potawatomi (1)	2	0.01
Sioux (3)	7	0.02
South American Ind. (0)	4	0.01
Yakama (1)	1	<0.01
Asian (2,081)	2,338	6.20
Not Hispanic (2,022)	2,228	5.91
Hispanic (59)	110	0.29
Burmese (5)	5	0.01
Cambodian (4)	11	0.03
Chinese, ex. Taiwanese (124)	168	0.45
Filipino (629)	750	1.99
Hmong (3)	3	0.01
Indian (695)	767	2.03
Indonesian (6)	6	0.02
Japanese (45)	61	0.16
Korean (138)	151	0.40
Laotian (68)	82	0.22
Malaysian (0)	1	<0.01
Nepalese (4)	4	0.01
Pakistani (127)	141	0.37
Sri Lankan (0)	1	<0.01
Taiwanese (16)	16	0.04
Thai (20)	23	0.06
Vietnamese (79)	94	0.25
Hawaii Native/Pacific Islander (15)	32	0.08
Not Hispanic (0)	5	0.01
Hispanic (15)	27	0.07
Guamanian/Chamorro (0)	1	<0.01
Native Hawaiian (3)	10	0.03
Samoan (0)	2	0.01
White (23,719)	24,787	65.76
Not Hispanic (13,810)	14,221	37.73
Hispanic (9,909)	10,566	28.03

Cary

Place Type: Village
County: McHenry
Population: 18,271†

Ancestry‡	Population	%
American (452)	452	2.49
Arab (15)	24	0.13
Lebanese (0)	9	0.05
Palestinian (15)	15	0.08
Armenian (20)	33	0.18
Assyrian/Chaldean/Syriac (11)	36	0.20
Austrian (74)	231	1.27
Basque (0)	25	0.14
Belgian (20)	74	0.41
British (56)	92	0.51
Bulgarian (0)	27	0.15
Croatian (37)	121	0.67
Czech (27)	299	1.65
Czechoslovakian (8)	8	0.04
Danish (26)	98	0.54
Dutch (52)	389	2.14
Eastern European (85)	121	0.67
English (277)	1,456	8.01
European (199)	199	1.10
French, ex. Basque (46)	677	3.73
French Canadian (11)	78	0.43
German (1,872)	6,753	37.17
Greek (138)	383	2.11
Hungarian (24)	285	1.57
Irish (527)	3,455	19.02
Israeli (10)	10	0.06
Italian (587)	2,371	13.05
Lithuanian (50)	77	0.42
Norwegian (138)	521	2.87
Pennsylvania German (17)	17	0.09
Polish (933)	2,903	15.98
Portuguese (0)	20	0.11
Romanian (14)	38	0.21
Russian (17)	248	1.37
Scandinavian (89)	148	0.81
Scotch-Irish (74)	163	0.90
Scottish (35)	268	1.48
Serbian (0)	60	0.33
Slavic (11)	11	0.06
Slovak (27)	107	0.59
Slovene (10)	54	0.30
Swedish (179)	678	3.73
Swiss (0)	89	0.49
Ukrainian (13)	40	0.22
Welsh (9)	108	0.59
West Indian, ex. Hispanic (0)	7	0.04
Jamaican (0)	7	0.04
Yugoslavian (0)	67	0.37

Hispanic Origin	Population	%
Hispanic or Latino (of any race)	1,626	8.90
Central American, ex. Mexican	49	0.27
Costa Rican	17	0.09
Guatemalan	17	0.09
Honduran	5	0.03
Nicaraguan	1	0.01
Panamanian	6	0.03
Salvadoran	3	0.02
Cuban	15	0.08
Dominican Republic	2	0.01
Mexican	1,372	7.51
Puerto Rican	67	0.37
South American	60	0.33
Argentinean	2	0.01
Chilean	8	0.04
Colombian	9	0.05
Ecuadorian	8	0.04
Peruvian	22	0.12
Uruguayan	1	0.01
Venezuelan	10	0.05
Other Hispanic or Latino	61	0.33

Race*	Population	%
African-American/Black (120)	191	1.05
Not Hispanic (113)	183	1.00
Hispanic (7)	8	0.04
American Indian/Alaska Native (30)	88	0.48
Not Hispanic (10)	57	0.31
Hispanic (20)	31	0.17
Blackfeet (0)	6	0.03
Cherokee (3)	26	0.14
Chippewa (0)	1	0.01
Cree (0)	1	0.01
Creek (0)	1	0.01
Iroquois (5)	5	0.03
Mexican American Ind. (4)	4	0.02
Navajo (0)	2	0.01
Ottawa (2)	2	0.01
Pueblo (0)	2	0.01
Seminole (0)	1	0.01
Sioux (0)	6	0.03
Yaqui (0)	1	0.01
Asian (445)	597	3.27
Not Hispanic (440)	587	3.21
Hispanic (5)	10	0.05
Cambodian (4)	4	0.02
Chinese, ex. Taiwanese (68)	100	0.55
Filipino (98)	134	0.73
Indian (160)	175	0.96
Japanese (16)	49	0.27
Korean (54)	72	0.39
Malaysian (5)	5	0.03
Pakistani (1)	2	0.01
Taiwanese (7)	8	0.04
Thai (6)	14	0.08
Vietnamese (8)	15	0.08
Hawaii Native/Pacific Islander (2)	6	0.03
Not Hispanic (2)	6	0.03
Native Hawaiian (0)	1	0.01
Samoan (1)	1	0.01
White (16,786)	17,075	93.45
Not Hispanic (15,801)	16,035	87.76
Hispanic (985)	1,040	5.69

Centralia

Place Type: City
County: Marion
Population: 13,032†

Ancestry‡	Population	%
African, Sub-Saharan (29)	44	0.33
African (29)	32	0.24
Ghanaian (0)	6	0.05
Nigerian (0)	6	0.05
American (916)	916	6.91
Austrian (0)	13	0.10
Belgian (21)	57	0.43
Brazilian (3)	7	0.05

SECTION TWO

*Notes: † The Census 2010 population figure is used to calculate the percentages in the Hispanic Origin and Race categories. Ancestry percentages are based on the 2006-2010 American Community Survey population (not shown); ‡ Numbers in parentheses indicate the number of people reporting a single ancestry; * Numbers in parentheses indicate the number of persons reporting this race alone, not in combination with any other race; Please refer to the Explanation of Data for more information.*

British (12)	12	0.09
Bulgarian (0)	14	0.11
Canadian (3)	3	0.02
Czech (0)	10	0.08
Danish (0)	11	0.08
Dutch (84)	305	2.30
English (786)	1,657	12.51
European (23)	23	0.17
Finnish (0)	7	0.05
French, ex. Basque (145)	408	3.08
French Canadian (0)	19	0.14
German (1,385)	3,414	25.77
Greek (10)	10	0.08
Hungarian (12)	401	3.03
Irish (360)	1,997	15.07
Italian (192)	392	2.96
Lithuanian (0)	3	0.02
Norwegian (0)	17	0.13
Polish (106)	349	2.63
Portuguese (0)	10	0.08
Romanian (9)	9	0.07
Russian (8)	20	0.15
Scandinavian (0)	17	0.13
Scotch-Irish (151)	320	2.42
Scottish (42)	165	1.25
Slavic (0)	10	0.08
Slovak (0)	9	0.07
Swedish (19)	90	0.68
Swiss (0)	38	0.29
Welsh (11)	143	1.08
West Indian, ex. Hispanic (0)	7	0.05
Trinidadian/Tobagonian (0)	7	0.05

Hispanic Origin	Population	%
Hispanic or Latino (of any race)	281	2.16
Central American, ex. Mexican	22	0.17
Guatemalan	5	0.04
Honduran	5	0.04
Nicaraguan	4	0.03
Panamanian	5	0.04
Salvadoran	1	0.01
Other Central American	2	0.02
Cuban	4	0.03
Dominican Republic	4	0.03
Mexican	195	1.50
Puerto Rican	17	0.13
South American	7	0.05
Colombian	1	0.01
Peruvian	5	0.04
Uruguayan	1	0.01
Other Hispanic or Latino	32	0.25

Race*	Population	%
African-American/Black (1,334)	1,571	12.05
Not Hispanic (1,317)	1,539	11.81
Hispanic (17)	32	0.25
American Indian/Alaska Native (51)	115	0.88
Not Hispanic (42)	101	0.78
Hispanic (9)	14	0.11
Apache (0)	1	0.01
Blackfeet (0)	6	0.05
Canadian/French Am. Ind. (1)	4	0.03
Cherokee (12)	32	0.25
Cheyenne (1)	1	0.01
Chippewa (1)	1	0.01
Choctaw (1)	1	0.01
Comanche (0)	3	0.02
Crow (0)	1	0.01
Inupiat *(Alaska Native)* (0)	1	0.01
Mexican American Ind. (2)	4	0.03
Navajo (0)	3	0.02
Osage (1)	1	0.01
Seminole (0)	1	0.01
Sioux (1)	1	0.01
Yakama (1)	1	0.01
Asian (93)	124	0.95
Not Hispanic (93)	122	0.94
Hispanic (0)	2	0.02
Chinese, ex. Taiwanese (17)	17	0.13
Filipino (17)	22	0.17
Indian (37)	42	0.32
Indonesian (0)	5	0.04
Japanese (3)	9	0.07
Korean (2)	6	0.05
Laotian (1)	1	0.01
Nepalese (2)	2	0.02
Pakistani (3)	5	0.04
Thai (4)	8	0.06
Vietnamese (5)	5	0.04
Hawaii Native/Pacific Islander (1)	9	0.07
Not Hispanic (1)	8	0.06
Hispanic (0)	1	0.01
Native Hawaiian (0)	4	0.03
White (11,124)	11,442	87.80
Not Hispanic (10,999)	11,274	86.51
Hispanic (125)	168	1.29

Champaign

Place Type: City
County: Champaign
Population: 81,055†

Ancestry‡	Population	%
African, Sub-Saharan (3,180)	3,208	4.04
African (3,030)	3,045	3.83
Nigerian (63)	76	0.10
Other Sub-Saharan African (87)	87	0.11
American (8,172)	8,172	10.29
Arab (188)	247	0.31
Arab (33)	33	0.04
Egyptian (65)	65	0.08
Iraqi (22)	30	0.04
Jordanian (0)	24	0.03
Lebanese (20)	39	0.05
Syrian (0)	8	0.01
Other Arab (48)	48	0.06
Assyrian/Chaldean/Syriac (0)	16	0.02
Australian (15)	15	0.02
Austrian (70)	313	0.39
Belgian (47)	121	0.15
Brazilian (167)	239	0.30
British (256)	501	0.63
Canadian (51)	137	0.17
Celtic (6)	6	0.01
Croatian (28)	86	0.11
Czech (141)	491	0.62
Czechoslovakian (81)	126	0.16
Danish (15)	144	0.18
Dutch (180)	1,045	1.32
Eastern European (124)	162	0.20
English (1,790)	6,475	8.15
Estonian (0)	17	0.02
European (2,322)	2,373	2.99
Finnish (22)	65	0.08
French, ex. Basque (141)	1,291	1.63
French Canadian (68)	199	0.25
German (5,713)	16,461	20.72
Greek (292)	489	0.62
Hungarian (90)	319	0.40
Icelander (0)	9	0.01
Iranian (123)	149	0.19
Irish (2,520)	9,671	12.18
Israeli (51)	51	0.06
Italian (764)	3,146	3.96
Latvian (0)	23	0.03
Lithuanian (136)	342	0.43
Luxemburger (0)	50	0.06
Maltese (24)	24	0.03
Northern European (6)	6	0.01
Norwegian (286)	986	1.24
Pennsylvania German (33)	81	0.10
Polish (1,269)	3,632	4.57
Portuguese (42)	90	0.11
Romanian (100)	156	0.20
Russian (386)	1,127	1.42
Scandinavian (71)	136	0.17
Scotch-Irish (195)	1,009	1.27
Scottish (392)	1,389	1.75
Serbian (8)	8	0.01
Slavic (15)	22	0.03
Slovak (35)	169	0.21
Slovene (14)	35	0.04
Swedish (390)	1,659	2.09
Swiss (39)	332	0.42
Turkish (177)	263	0.33
Ukrainian (233)	373	0.47
Welsh (116)	433	0.55
West Indian, ex. Hispanic (174)	198	0.25
Jamaican (74)	98	0.12
Trinidadian/Tobagonian (19)	19	0.02
U.S. Virgin Islander (81)	81	0.10
Yugoslavian (18)	31	0.04

Hispanic Origin	Population	%
Hispanic or Latino (of any race)	5,111	6.31
Central American, ex. Mexican	344	0.42
Costa Rican	29	0.04
Guatemalan	217	0.27
Honduran	23	0.03
Nicaraguan	17	0.02
Panamanian	18	0.02
Salvadoran	39	0.05
Other Central American	1	<0.01
Cuban	125	0.15
Dominican Republic	34	0.04
Mexican	3,310	4.08
Puerto Rican	415	0.51
South American	481	0.59
Argentinean	73	0.09
Bolivian	25	0.03
Chilean	41	0.05
Colombian	132	0.16
Ecuadorian	59	0.07
Paraguayan	8	0.01
Peruvian	91	0.11
Uruguayan	8	0.01
Venezuelan	41	0.05
Other South American	3	<0.01
Other Hispanic or Latino	402	0.50

Race*	Population	%
African-American/Black (12,680)	13,834	17.07
Not Hispanic (12,474)	13,520	16.68
Hispanic (206)	314	0.39
American Indian/Alaska Native (205)	593	0.73
Not Hispanic (143)	453	0.56
Hispanic (62)	140	0.17
Aleut *(Alaska Native)* (1)	1	<0.01
Apache (7)	10	0.01
Blackfeet (0)	19	0.02
Central American Ind. (2)	2	<0.01
Cherokee (30)	139	0.17
Cheyenne (0)	3	<0.01
Chickasaw (7)	8	0.01
Chippewa (4)	11	0.01
Choctaw (4)	13	0.02
Cree (0)	4	<0.01
Creek (1)	6	0.01
Delaware (2)	4	<0.01
Hopi (1)	4	<0.01
Inupiat *(Alaska Native)* (1)	2	<0.01
Iroquois (1)	7	0.01
Kiowa (1)	1	<0.01
Menominee (1)	1	<0.01
Mexican American Ind. (11)	25	0.03
Navajo (8)	12	0.01
Osage (3)	3	<0.01
Ottawa (1)	3	<0.01
Pima (1)	3	<0.01
Potawatomi (2)	7	0.01
Pueblo (5)	5	0.01
Sioux (3)	10	0.01
South American Ind. (8)	13	0.02
Spanish American Ind. (0)	1	<0.01
Yaqui (0)	2	<0.01
Asian (8,566)	9,544	11.77
Not Hispanic (8,510)	9,442	11.65
Hispanic (56)	102	0.13
Bangladeshi (47)	56	0.07

*Notes: † The Census 2010 population figure is used to calculate the percentages in the Hispanic Origin and Race categories. Ancestry percentages are based on the 2006-2010 American Community Survey population (not shown); ‡ Numbers in parentheses indicate the number of people reporting a single ancestry; * Numbers in parentheses indicate the number of persons reporting this race alone, not in combination with any other race; Please refer to the Explanation of Data for more information.*

Race* (continued)	Population	%
Burmese (16)	18	0.02
Cambodian (15)	26	0.03
Chinese, ex. Taiwanese (2,068)	2,302	2.84
Filipino (572)	755	0.93
Hmong (8)	9	0.01
Indian (2,162)	2,308	2.85
Indonesian (9)	15	0.02
Japanese (214)	379	0.47
Korean (1,930)	2,060	2.54
Laotian (74)	89	0.11
Malaysian (44)	46	0.06
Nepalese (34)	39	0.05
Pakistani (154)	174	0.21
Sri Lankan (27)	31	0.04
Taiwanese (234)	272	0.34
Thai (99)	126	0.16
Vietnamese (618)	687	0.85
Hawaii Native/Pacific Islander (58)	173	0.21
Not Hispanic (56)	151	0.19
Hispanic (2)	22	0.03
Fijian (0)	2	<0.01
Guamanian/Chamorro (1)	7	0.01
Native Hawaiian (19)	37	0.05
Samoan (10)	23	0.03
Tongan (1)	2	<0.01
White (54,918)	56,978	70.30
Not Hispanic (52,533)	54,308	67.00
Hispanic (2,385)	2,670	3.29

Channahon

Place Type: Village
County: Will
Population: 12,560†

Ancestry‡	Population	%
American (476)	476	3.90
Arab (87)	87	0.71
Palestinian (87)	87	0.71
Austrian (0)	57	0.47
Belgian (15)	15	0.12
Canadian (15)	15	0.12
Croatian (192)	446	3.65
Czech (29)	90	0.74
Czechoslovakian (0)	40	0.33
Danish (10)	37	0.30
Dutch (86)	365	2.99
English (127)	922	7.55
European (125)	125	1.02
Finnish (15)	15	0.12
French, ex. Basque (13)	472	3.86
French Canadian (16)	93	0.76
German (496)	3,512	28.75
Greek (0)	45	0.37
Hungarian (0)	132	1.08
Irish (795)	3,564	29.18
Italian (447)	1,957	16.02
Lithuanian (13)	165	1.35
Norwegian (42)	283	2.32
Polish (590)	2,068	16.93
Romanian (49)	64	0.52
Russian (44)	85	0.70
Scotch-Irish (58)	257	2.10
Scottish (0)	93	0.76
Serbian (0)	7	0.06
Slavic (0)	12	0.10
Slovak (61)	238	1.95
Slovene (43)	268	2.19
Swedish (60)	396	3.24
Ukrainian (0)	35	0.29
Welsh (14)	29	0.24
Yugoslavian (19)	101	0.83

Hispanic Origin	Population	%
Hispanic or Latino (of any race)	1,020	8.12
Central American, ex. Mexican	16	0.13
Guatemalan	13	0.10
Honduran	1	0.01
Nicaraguan	1	0.01
Salvadoran	1	0.01
Cuban	9	0.07
Dominican Republic	4	0.03
Mexican	868	6.91
Puerto Rican	70	0.56
South American	13	0.10
Argentinean	2	0.02
Colombian	5	0.04
Ecuadorian	3	0.02
Peruvian	2	0.02
Other South American	1	0.01
Other Hispanic or Latino	40	0.32

Race*	Population	%
African-American/Black (159)	190	1.51
Not Hispanic (156)	181	1.44
Hispanic (3)	9	0.07
American Indian/Alaska Native (19)	56	0.45
Not Hispanic (6)	32	0.25
Hispanic (13)	24	0.19
Apache (0)	3	0.02
Cherokee (6)	20	0.16
Chippewa (1)	2	0.02
Comanche (0)	1	0.01
Iroquois (0)	2	0.02
Ottawa (0)	1	0.01
Potawatomi (0)	4	0.03
Asian (93)	156	1.24
Not Hispanic (87)	144	1.15
Hispanic (6)	12	0.10
Chinese, ex. Taiwanese (19)	28	0.22
Filipino (28)	56	0.45
Indian (10)	16	0.13
Japanese (3)	6	0.05
Korean (4)	9	0.07
Laotian (1)	6	0.05
Thai (2)	4	0.03
Vietnamese (13)	17	0.14
Hawaii Native/Pacific Islander (1)	5	0.04
Not Hispanic (1)	5	0.04
Native Hawaiian (1)	5	0.04
White (11,873)	12,028	95.76
Not Hispanic (11,168)	11,271	89.74
Hispanic (705)	757	6.03

Charleston

Place Type: City
County: Coles
Population: 21,838†

Ancestry‡	Population	%
African, Sub-Saharan (49)	73	0.34
African (19)	34	0.16
Nigerian (30)	30	0.14
South African (0)	9	0.04
Albanian (44)	44	0.20
American (2,225)	2,225	10.23
Arab (0)	16	0.07
Syrian (0)	16	0.07
Austrian (12)	12	0.06
Belgian (0)	33	0.15
British (42)	117	0.54
Canadian (6)	24	0.11
Czech (40)	108	0.50
Czechoslovakian (0)	14	0.06
Danish (0)	7	0.03
Dutch (133)	407	1.87
English (734)	1,721	7.91
European (621)	652	3.00
French, ex. Basque (52)	328	1.51
French Canadian (12)	78	0.36
German (1,882)	5,245	24.12
Greek (0)	37	0.17
Hungarian (0)	58	0.27
Iranian (12)	12	0.06
Irish (941)	3,489	16.04
Italian (352)	1,062	4.88
Latvian (0)	9	0.04
Lithuanian (18)	29	0.13
Norwegian (48)	201	0.92
Polish (473)	1,221	5.61
Romanian (0)	22	0.10
Russian (0)	72	0.33
Scotch-Irish (275)	513	2.36
Scottish (117)	334	1.54
Serbian (0)	11	0.05
Slovak (10)	10	0.05
Slovene (0)	31	0.14
Swedish (292)	433	1.99
Swiss (11)	163	0.75
Turkish (0)	16	0.07
Ukrainian (10)	20	0.09
Welsh (15)	105	0.48

Hispanic Origin	Population	%
Hispanic or Latino (of any race)	651	2.98
Central American, ex. Mexican	38	0.17
Costa Rican	1	<0.01
Guatemalan	18	0.08
Honduran	3	0.01
Nicaraguan	1	<0.01
Panamanian	3	0.01
Salvadoran	12	0.05
Cuban	20	0.09
Dominican Republic	3	0.01
Mexican	404	1.85
Puerto Rican	64	0.29
South American	37	0.17
Argentinean	1	<0.01
Bolivian	2	0.01
Chilean	10	0.05
Colombian	7	0.03
Ecuadorian	8	0.04
Paraguayan	2	0.01
Peruvian	3	0.01
Venezuelan	3	0.01
Other South American	1	<0.01
Other Hispanic or Latino	85	0.39

Race*	Population	%
African-American/Black (1,537)	1,713	7.84
Not Hispanic (1,512)	1,675	7.67
Hispanic (25)	38	0.17
American Indian/Alaska Native (38)	123	0.56
Not Hispanic (25)	100	0.46
Hispanic (13)	23	0.11
Aleut *(Alaska Native)* (0)	1	<0.01
Apache (0)	3	0.01
Blackfeet (1)	4	0.02
Cherokee (8)	29	0.13
Chickasaw (0)	3	0.01
Chippewa (2)	6	0.03
Creek (0)	3	0.01
Inupiat *(Alaska Native)* (0)	1	<0.01
Iroquois (1)	2	0.01
Kiowa (1)	1	<0.01
Mexican American Ind. (6)	6	0.03
Navajo (0)	1	<0.01
Osage (0)	3	0.01
Pima (3)	3	0.01
Potawatomi (2)	2	0.01
Sioux (1)	3	0.01
South American Ind. (1)	1	<0.01
Spanish American Ind. (1)	3	0.01
Asian (355)	458	2.10
Not Hispanic (348)	443	2.03
Hispanic (7)	15	0.07
Bangladeshi (3)	3	0.01
Cambodian (1)	2	0.01
Chinese, ex. Taiwanese (63)	79	0.36
Filipino (60)	94	0.43
Indian (93)	111	0.51
Japanese (17)	33	0.15
Korean (49)	68	0.31
Malaysian (0)	1	<0.01
Nepalese (6)	7	0.03
Pakistani (9)	10	0.05
Sri Lankan (5)	5	0.02
Taiwanese (9)	12	0.05
Thai (3)	5	0.02

SECTION TWO

*Notes: † The Census 2010 population figure is used to calculate the percentages in the Hispanic Origin and Race categories. Ancestry percentages are based on the 2006-2010 American Community Survey population (not shown); ‡ Numbers in parentheses indicate the number of people reporting a single ancestry; * Numbers in parentheses indicate the number of persons reporting this race alone, not in combination with any other race; Please refer to the Explanation of Data for more information.*

Vietnamese (23)	30	0.14
Hawaii Native/Pacific Islander (9)	31	0.14
Not Hispanic (7)	25	0.11
Hispanic (2)	6	0.03
Guamanian/Chamorro (2)	3	0.01
Native Hawaiian (0)	9	0.04
Samoan (3)	4	0.02
Tongan (1)	1	<0.01
White (19,365)	19,699	90.21
Not Hispanic (18,960)	19,253	88.16
Hispanic (405)	446	2.04

Chatham

Place Type: Village
County: Sangamon
Population: 11,500†

Ancestry‡	Population	%
American (1,016)	1,016	9.14
Austrian (0)	25	0.22
British (39)	50	0.45
Celtic (0)	42	0.38
Croatian (0)	26	0.23
Czech (0)	25	0.22
Danish (14)	55	0.49
Dutch (15)	199	1.79
English (590)	1,501	13.50
European (163)	188	1.69
French, ex. Basque (53)	418	3.76
French Canadian (0)	34	0.31
German (1,781)	4,004	36.01
Greek (10)	97	0.87
Hungarian (0)	11	0.10
Irish (573)	2,066	18.58
Italian (224)	702	6.31
Lithuanian (62)	92	0.83
Northern European (14)	14	0.13
Norwegian (38)	61	0.55
Polish (63)	446	4.01
Portuguese (9)	72	0.65
Russian (0)	20	0.18
Scotch-Irish (71)	205	1.84
Scottish (66)	188	1.69
Serbian (0)	15	0.13
Slovak (0)	8	0.07
Slovene (10)	10	0.09
Swedish (42)	217	1.95
Swiss (0)	42	0.38
Welsh (27)	79	0.71
West Indian, ex. Hispanic (17)	17	0.15
Haitian (17)	17	0.15

Hispanic Origin	Population	%
Hispanic or Latino (of any race)	227	1.97
Central American, ex. Mexican	12	0.10
Guatemalan	2	0.02
Honduran	4	0.03
Salvadoran	5	0.04
Other Central American	1	0.01
Cuban	6	0.05
Dominican Republic	4	0.03
Mexican	122	1.06
Puerto Rican	32	0.28
South American	24	0.21
Argentinean	4	0.03
Colombian	5	0.04
Ecuadorian	3	0.03
Peruvian	6	0.05
Uruguayan	2	0.02
Venezuelan	4	0.03
Other Hispanic or Latino	27	0.23

Race*	Population	%
African-American/Black (284)	369	3.21
Not Hispanic (276)	358	3.11
Hispanic (8)	11	0.10
American Indian/Alaska Native (10)	38	0.33
Not Hispanic (9)	37	0.32
Hispanic (1)	1	0.01
Blackfeet (0)	1	0.01
Central American Ind. (1)	1	0.01
Cherokee (2)	7	0.06
Choctaw (1)	3	0.03
Pueblo (2)	2	0.02
Asian (213)	275	2.39
Not Hispanic (211)	273	2.37
Hispanic (2)	2	0.02
Chinese, ex. Taiwanese (56)	64	0.56
Filipino (32)	42	0.37
Indian (57)	61	0.53
Japanese (7)	13	0.11
Korean (13)	30	0.26
Laotian (6)	13	0.11
Malaysian (1)	2	0.02
Pakistani (11)	11	0.10
Taiwanese (16)	20	0.17
Vietnamese (7)	7	0.06
Hawaii Native/Pacific Islander (8)	18	0.16
Not Hispanic (8)	18	0.16
Guamanian/Chamorro (3)	6	0.05
Native Hawaiian (0)	7	0.06
Samoan (5)	5	0.04
White (10,760)	10,928	95.03
Not Hispanic (10,594)	10,752	93.50
Hispanic (166)	176	1.53

Chester

Place Type: City
County: Randolph
Population: 8,586†

Ancestry‡	Population	%
African, Sub-Saharan (0)	21	0.25
African (0)	11	0.13
Nigerian (0)	10	0.12
American (285)	285	3.35
Arab (0)	18	0.21
Lebanese (0)	18	0.21
Belgian (0)	9	0.11
British (27)	42	0.49
Canadian (11)	11	0.13
Czech (0)	12	0.14
Dutch (44)	112	1.32
English (232)	484	5.69
French, ex. Basque (26)	283	3.33
French Canadian (0)	28	0.33
German (873)	1,676	19.69
Irish (202)	527	6.19
Italian (99)	143	1.68
Lithuanian (23)	23	0.27
Norwegian (10)	17	0.20
Polish (44)	98	1.15
Scotch-Irish (8)	32	0.38
Scottish (32)	63	0.74
Swedish (10)	42	0.49
Turkish (26)	35	0.41
Welsh (0)	23	0.27
West Indian, ex. Hispanic (20)	20	0.24
Belizean (11)	11	0.13
Jamaican (9)	9	0.11
Yugoslavian (9)	9	0.11

Hispanic Origin	Population	%
Hispanic or Latino (of any race)	521	6.07
Central American, ex. Mexican	10	0.12
Costa Rican	1	0.01
Guatemalan	4	0.05
Honduran	2	0.02
Salvadoran	3	0.03
Cuban	6	0.07
Mexican	248	2.89
Puerto Rican	39	0.45
South American	1	0.01
Colombian	1	0.01
Other Hispanic or Latino	217	2.53

Race*	Population	%
African-American/Black (2,397)	2,430	28.30
Not Hispanic (2,388)	2,421	28.20
Hispanic (9)	9	0.10
American Indian/Alaska Native (12)	48	0.56
Not Hispanic (7)	37	0.43
Hispanic (5)	11	0.13
Blackfeet (0)	2	0.02
Cherokee (1)	12	0.14
Choctaw (0)	3	0.03
Iroquois (0)	2	0.02
Mexican American Ind. (1)	1	0.01
Asian (26)	30	0.35
Not Hispanic (26)	29	0.34
Hispanic (0)	1	0.01
Chinese, ex. Taiwanese (5)	5	0.06
Filipino (3)	4	0.05
Indian (6)	6	0.07
Korean (2)	2	0.02
Thai (1)	1	0.01
Vietnamese (6)	6	0.07
Hawaii Native/Pacific Islander (1)	2	0.02
Hispanic (1)	2	0.02
Native Hawaiian (0)	1	0.01
Samoan (1)	1	0.01
White (5,798)	5,870	68.37
Not Hispanic (5,584)	5,636	65.64
Hispanic (214)	234	2.73

Chicago Heights

Place Type: City
County: Cook
Population: 30,276†

Ancestry‡	Population	%
African, Sub-Saharan (206)	219	0.72
African (152)	165	0.54
Nigerian (54)	54	0.18
American (435)	435	1.43
Austrian (11)	11	0.04
Belgian (12)	57	0.19
Brazilian (0)	10	0.03
Bulgarian (8)	8	0.03
Croatian (11)	50	0.16
Czech (6)	59	0.19
Czechoslovakian (9)	9	0.03
Danish (0)	28	0.09
Dutch (22)	203	0.67
English (94)	558	1.83
European (13)	13	0.04
Finnish (7)	29	0.10
French, ex. Basque (11)	204	0.67
French Canadian (12)	46	0.15
German (595)	2,204	7.25
Greek (59)	102	0.34
Hungarian (41)	79	0.26
Iranian (31)	31	0.10
Irish (436)	1,483	4.88
Italian (1,246)	2,516	8.27
Lithuanian (49)	210	0.69
Norwegian (0)	55	0.18
Polish (524)	1,296	4.26
Portuguese (0)	10	0.03
Russian (0)	11	0.04
Scotch-Irish (30)	67	0.22
Scottish (11)	114	0.37
Slovak (81)	149	0.49
Slovene (6)	15	0.05
Swedish (64)	238	0.78
Swiss (9)	19	0.06
Ukrainian (0)	58	0.19
Welsh (0)	17	0.06
West Indian, ex. Hispanic (0)	12	0.04
West Indian (0)	12	0.04
Yugoslavian (5)	5	0.02

Hispanic Origin	Population	%
Hispanic or Latino (of any race)	10,254	33.87
Central American, ex. Mexican	68	0.22
Costa Rican	5	0.02
Guatemalan	26	0.09

*Notes: † The Census 2010 population figure is used to calculate the percentages in the Hispanic Origin and Race categories. Ancestry percentages are based on the 2006-2010 American Community Survey population (not shown); ‡ Numbers in parentheses indicate the number of people reporting a single ancestry; * Numbers in parentheses indicate the number of persons reporting this race alone, not in combination with any other race; Please refer to the Explanation of Data for more information.*

Honduran	32	0.11
Panamanian	4	0.01
Salvadoran	1	<0.01
Cuban	21	0.07
Dominican Republic	8	0.03
Mexican	9,438	31.17
Puerto Rican	281	0.93
South American	64	0.21
Argentinean	11	0.04
Colombian	21	0.07
Ecuadorian	2	0.01
Peruvian	18	0.06
Uruguayan	12	0.04
Other Hispanic or Latino	374	1.24

Race*	Population	%
African-American/Black (12,573)	13,074	43.18
Not Hispanic (12,370)	12,707	41.97
Hispanic (203)	367	1.21
American Indian/Alaska Native (181)	321	1.06
Not Hispanic (44)	156	0.52
Hispanic (137)	165	0.54
Apache (1)	1	<0.01
Blackfeet (0)	6	0.02
Canadian/French Am. Ind. (0)	1	<0.01
Cherokee (7)	34	0.11
Chippewa (1)	10	0.03
Choctaw (0)	8	0.03
Cree (0)	1	<0.01
Mexican American Ind. (20)	26	0.09
Navajo (0)	1	<0.01
Shoshone (0)	1	<0.01
Sioux (3)	10	0.03
Spanish American Ind. (0)	5	0.02
Yuman (1)	1	<0.01
Asian (107)	184	0.61
Not Hispanic (87)	151	0.50
Hispanic (20)	33	0.11
Bangladeshi (4)	4	0.01
Chinese, ex. Taiwanese (10)	21	0.07
Filipino (32)	51	0.17
Indian (24)	34	0.11
Japanese (11)	14	0.05
Korean (5)	16	0.05
Laotian (0)	1	<0.01
Pakistani (1)	2	0.01
Thai (0)	2	0.01
Vietnamese (11)	13	0.04
Hawaii Native/Pacific Islander (10)	37	0.12
Not Hispanic (8)	23	0.08
Hispanic (2)	14	0.05
Guamanian/Chamorro (1)	2	0.01
Native Hawaiian (6)	18	0.06
Samoan (0)	2	0.01
White (11,506)	12,159	40.16
Not Hispanic (7,062)	7,362	24.32
Hispanic (4,444)	4,797	15.84

Chicago Ridge

Place Type: Village
County: Cook
Population: 14,305†

Ancestry‡	Population	%
Afghan (13)	13	0.09
African, Sub-Saharan (140)	140	0.99
African (86)	86	0.61
Sudanese (54)	54	0.38
American (255)	255	1.80
Arab (1,427)	1,605	11.35
Arab (733)	766	5.42
Jordanian (33)	130	0.92
Palestinian (586)	598	4.23
Other Arab (75)	111	0.78
Austrian (0)	26	0.18
Croatian (54)	198	1.40
Czech (55)	189	1.34
Danish (19)	29	0.21
Dutch (147)	223	1.58
English (82)	418	2.96
European (50)	50	0.35
French, ex. Basque (0)	235	1.66
French Canadian (24)	78	0.55
German (475)	2,410	17.04
Greek (142)	295	2.09
Hungarian (0)	11	0.08
Irish (1,056)	3,536	25.00
Italian (372)	1,436	10.15
Latvian (0)	30	0.21
Lithuanian (70)	295	2.09
Norwegian (30)	191	1.35
Polish (1,257)	2,464	17.42
Romanian (22)	22	0.16
Russian (54)	130	0.92
Scotch-Irish (36)	140	0.99
Scottish (33)	56	0.40
Serbian (53)	53	0.37
Slovak (54)	121	0.86
Slovene (0)	24	0.17
Swedish (32)	139	0.98
Turkish (0)	97	0.69
Ukrainian (0)	27	0.19
Welsh (0)	25	0.18
West Indian, ex. Hispanic (13)	13	0.09
Belizean (13)	13	0.09
Yugoslavian (92)	92	0.65

Hispanic Origin	Population	%
Hispanic or Latino (of any race)	1,776	12.42
Central American, ex. Mexican	24	0.17
Costa Rican	1	0.01
Guatemalan	9	0.06
Honduran	5	0.03
Nicaraguan	3	0.02
Salvadoran	6	0.04
Cuban	10	0.07
Mexican	1,427	9.98
Puerto Rican	151	1.06
South American	43	0.30
Argentinean	10	0.07
Bolivian	4	0.03
Chilean	1	0.01
Colombian	14	0.10
Ecuadorian	5	0.03
Peruvian	7	0.05
Uruguayan	1	0.01
Venezuelan	1	0.01
Other Hispanic or Latino	121	0.85

Race*	Population	%
African-American/Black (1,006)	1,121	7.84
Not Hispanic (977)	1,064	7.44
Hispanic (29)	57	0.40
American Indian/Alaska Native (40)	99	0.69
Not Hispanic (19)	66	0.46
Hispanic (21)	33	0.23
Apache (0)	1	0.01
Blackfeet (0)	2	0.01
Cherokee (4)	23	0.16
Chippewa (0)	7	0.05
Choctaw (1)	7	0.05
Creek (0)	2	0.01
Mexican American Ind. (0)	2	0.01
Navajo (0)	2	0.01
Sioux (0)	2	0.01
Asian (257)	444	3.10
Not Hispanic (254)	416	2.91
Hispanic (3)	28	0.20
Cambodian (2)	2	0.01
Chinese, ex. Taiwanese (10)	25	0.17
Filipino (113)	133	0.93
Indian (23)	41	0.29
Indonesian (1)	1	0.01
Japanese (4)	4	0.03
Korean (3)	9	0.06
Laotian (1)	1	0.01
Malaysian (5)	5	0.03
Pakistani (21)	24	0.17
Thai (4)	6	0.04
Vietnamese (34)	42	0.29
Hawaii Native/Pacific Islander (5)	14	0.10
Not Hispanic (5)	13	0.09
Hispanic (0)	1	0.01
Fijian (3)	3	0.02
Samoan (2)	2	0.01
White (11,883)	12,265	85.74
Not Hispanic (10,952)	11,235	78.54
Hispanic (931)	1,030	7.20

Chicago

Place Type: City
County: Cook
Population: 2,695,598†

Ancestry‡	Population	%
Afghan (223)	234	0.01
African, Sub-Saharan (31,194)	36,226	1.34
African (18,104)	21,971	0.81
Cape Verdean (22)	22	<0.01
Ethiopian (2,136)	2,224	0.08
Ghanaian (1,826)	1,873	0.07
Kenyan (456)	456	0.02
Liberian (58)	102	<0.01
Nigerian (5,645)	6,193	0.23
Sierra Leonean (209)	221	0.01
Somalian (510)	637	0.02
South African (211)	375	0.01
Sudanese (195)	225	0.01
Ugandan (39)	39	<0.01
Zimbabwean (107)	107	<0.01
Other Sub-Saharan African (1,676)	1,781	0.07
Albanian (1,499)	1,699	0.06
Alsatian (39)	96	<0.01
American (34,496)	34,496	1.28
Arab (13,702)	16,946	0.63
Arab (3,850)	4,311	0.16
Egyptian (827)	1,010	0.04
Iraqi (1,318)	1,592	0.06
Jordanian (899)	948	0.04
Lebanese (990)	1,936	0.07
Moroccan (836)	1,014	0.04
Palestinian (1,874)	2,219	0.08
Syrian (784)	1,029	0.04
Other Arab (2,324)	2,887	0.11
Armenian (706)	1,256	0.05
Assyrian/Chaldean/Syriac (3,653)	4,646	0.17
Australian (212)	561	0.02
Austrian (1,166)	7,125	0.26
Basque (72)	259	0.01
Belgian (705)	2,597	0.10
Brazilian (984)	1,439	0.05
British (2,697)	5,392	0.20
Bulgarian (2,922)	3,223	0.12
Cajun (42)	99	<0.01
Canadian (1,176)	2,179	0.08
Carpatho Rusyn (0)	25	<0.01
Celtic (42)	155	0.01
Croatian (3,116)	7,104	0.26
Cypriot (122)	122	<0.01
Czech (3,306)	12,642	0.47
Czechoslovakian (884)	2,450	0.09
Danish (1,099)	5,565	0.21
Dutch (3,430)	14,116	0.52
Eastern European (5,362)	5,967	0.22
English (12,819)	64,585	2.39
Estonian (131)	202	0.01
European (15,353)	17,169	0.64
Finnish (853)	2,609	0.10
French, ex. Basque (3,518)	25,053	0.93
French Canadian (1,564)	4,592	0.17
German (51,511)	205,863	7.61
German Russian (46)	106	<0.01
Greek (11,174)	17,672	0.65
Guyanese (94)	272	0.01
Hungarian (2,700)	8,760	0.32
Icelander (71)	207	0.01
Iranian (1,735)	2,222	0.08
Irish (63,543)	201,693	7.46

SECTION TWO

*Notes: † The Census 2010 population figure is used to calculate the percentages in the Hispanic Origin and Race categories. Ancestry percentages are based on the 2006-2010 American Community Survey population (not shown); ‡ Numbers in parentheses indicate the number of people reporting a single ancestry; * Numbers in parentheses indicate the number of persons reporting this race alone, not in combination with any other race; Please refer to the Explanation of Data for more information.*

Israeli (822)	1,411	0.05
Italian (39,947)	102,842	3.80
Latvian (842)	1,505	0.06
Lithuanian (5,099)	12,503	0.46
Luxemburger (234)	657	0.02
Macedonian (304)	495	0.02
Maltese (22)	70	<0.01
New Zealander (181)	205	0.01
Northern European (1,402)	1,551	0.06
Norwegian (3,187)	14,090	0.52
Pennsylvania German (131)	200	0.01
Polish (100,880)	176,295	6.52
Portuguese (354)	1,187	0.04
Romanian (7,237)	9,121	0.34
Russian (12,700)	28,264	1.05
Scandinavian (805)	1,792	0.07
Scotch-Irish (4,221)	13,218	0.49
Scottish (3,852)	16,230	0.60
Serbian (3,708)	5,286	0.20
Slavic (535)	1,157	0.04
Slovak (1,859)	4,761	0.18
Slovene (540)	1,432	0.05
Soviet Union (19)	19	<0.01
Swedish (5,864)	26,075	0.96
Swiss (715)	3,481	0.13
Turkish (1,281)	1,598	0.06
Ukrainian (8,223)	12,513	0.46
Welsh (651)	5,904	0.22
West Indian, ex. Hispanic (8,397)	11,174	0.41
Bahamian (22)	22	<0.01
Barbadian (75)	154	0.01
Belizean (1,847)	2,273	0.08
Bermudan (0)	24	<0.01
British West Indian (57)	103	<0.01
Haitian (2,288)	2,734	0.10
Jamaican (3,412)	4,601	0.17
Trinidadian/Tobagonian (341)	533	0.02
U.S. Virgin Islander (32)	32	<0.01
West Indian (323)	698	0.03
Yugoslavian (5,621)	6,612	0.24

Hispanic Origin	Population	%
Hispanic or Latino (of any race)	778,862	28.89
Central American, ex. Mexican	31,263	1.16
Costa Rican	681	0.03
Guatemalan	17,973	0.67
Honduran	5,021	0.19
Nicaraguan	1,239	0.05
Panamanian	883	0.03
Salvadoran	5,204	0.19
Other Central American	262	0.01
Cuban	8,331	0.31
Dominican Republic	2,737	0.10
Mexican	578,100	21.45
Puerto Rican	102,703	3.81
South American	32,129	1.19
Argentinean	1,743	0.06
Bolivian	626	0.02
Chilean	876	0.03
Colombian	7,547	0.28
Ecuadorian	15,466	0.57
Paraguayan	101	<0.01
Peruvian	4,075	0.15
Uruguayan	267	0.01
Venezuelan	1,121	0.04
Other South American	307	0.01
Other Hispanic or Latino	23,599	0.88

Race*	Population	%
African-American/Black (887,608)	913,009	33.87
Not Hispanic (872,286)	889,783	33.01
Hispanic (15,322)	23,226	0.86
American Indian/Alaska Native (13,337)	26,933	1.00
Not Hispanic (4,097)	12,449	0.46
Hispanic (9,240)	14,484	0.54
Alaska Athabascan *(Ala. Nat.)* (4)	11	<0.01
Aleut *(Alaska Native)* (4)	8	<0.01
Apache (135)	350	0.01
Arapaho (9)	20	<0.01
Blackfeet (65)	590	0.02
Canadian/French Am. Ind. (22)	55	<0.01
Central American Ind. (92)	203	0.01
Cherokee (458)	2,639	0.10
Cheyenne (11)	27	<0.01
Chickasaw (10)	56	<0.01
Chippewa (382)	659	0.02
Choctaw (120)	513	0.02
Colville (2)	5	<0.01
Comanche (21)	47	<0.01
Cree (16)	54	<0.01
Creek (22)	139	0.01
Crow (4)	17	<0.01
Delaware (3)	25	<0.01
Hopi (6)	26	<0.01
Houma (1)	3	<0.01
Inupiat *(Alaska Native)* (18)	30	<0.01
Iroquois (170)	359	0.01
Kiowa (13)	23	<0.01
Lumbee (13)	25	<0.01
Menominee (66)	117	<0.01
Mexican American Ind. (1,924)	2,810	0.10
Navajo (122)	261	0.01
Osage (9)	31	<0.01
Ottawa (21)	41	<0.01
Paiute (6)	9	<0.01
Pima (6)	16	<0.01
Potawatomi (56)	115	<0.01
Pueblo (36)	71	<0.01
Puget Sound Salish (5)	8	<0.01
Seminole (10)	80	<0.01
Shoshone (6)	17	<0.01
Sioux (163)	385	0.01
South American Ind. (290)	743	0.03
Spanish American Ind. (156)	225	0.01
Tlingit-Haida *(Alaska Native)* (13)	15	<0.01
Tohono O'Odham (1)	4	<0.01
Tsimshian *(Alaska Native)* (1)	1	<0.01
Ute (5)	8	<0.01
Yakama (0)	3	<0.01
Yaqui (34)	58	<0.01
Yuman (11)	15	<0.01
Yup'ik *(Alaska Native)* (7)	10	<0.01
Asian (147,164)	166,770	6.19
Not Hispanic (144,903)	161,439	5.99
Hispanic (2,261)	5,331	0.20
Bangladeshi (624)	679	0.03
Bhutanese (276)	339	0.01
Burmese (648)	711	0.03
Cambodian (1,204)	1,404	0.05
Chinese, ex. Taiwanese (42,060)	46,446	1.72
Filipino (29,664)	35,188	1.31
Hmong (85)	97	<0.01
Indian (29,948)	33,528	1.24
Indonesian (294)	430	0.02
Japanese (4,347)	7,044	0.26
Korean (11,422)	13,418	0.50
Laotian (414)	529	0.02
Malaysian (110)	165	0.01
Nepalese (534)	627	0.02
Pakistani (7,008)	7,926	0.29
Sri Lankan (335)	376	0.01
Taiwanese (1,111)	1,319	0.05
Thai (2,658)	3,168	0.12
Vietnamese (8,930)	10,118	0.38
Hawaii Native/Pacific Islander (1,013)	3,770	0.14
Not Hispanic (557)	2,186	0.08
Hispanic (456)	1,584	0.06
Fijian (12)	18	<0.01
Guamanian/Chamorro (361)	592	0.02
Marshallese (2)	5	<0.01
Native Hawaiian (242)	731	0.03
Samoan (94)	281	0.01
Tongan (5)	10	<0.01
White (1,212,835)	1,270,097	47.12
Not Hispanic (854,717)	881,920	32.72
Hispanic (358,118)	388,177	14.40

Cicero

Place Type: Town
County: Cook
Population: 83,891†

Ancestry‡	Population	%
American (233)	233	0.28
Arab (195)	220	0.26
Arab (110)	135	0.16
Moroccan (14)	14	0.02
Palestinian (55)	55	0.07
Other Arab (16)	16	0.02
Austrian (5)	47	0.06
British (0)	49	0.06
Bulgarian (46)	46	0.06
Canadian (23)	23	0.03
Celtic (0)	14	0.02
Croatian (11)	68	0.08
Czech (400)	863	1.04
Czechoslovakian (50)	75	0.09
Danish (39)	55	0.07
Dutch (0)	127	0.15
Eastern European (32)	32	0.04
English (58)	451	0.54
Estonian (27)	27	0.03
European (66)	66	0.08
French, ex. Basque (17)	429	0.51
French Canadian (31)	55	0.07
German (400)	1,951	2.34
Greek (26)	36	0.04
Hungarian (0)	51	0.06
Irish (360)	2,168	2.60
Italian (609)	1,690	2.03
Latvian (9)	9	0.01
Lithuanian (106)	130	0.16
Macedonian (23)	23	0.03
Norwegian (0)	31	0.04
Polish (1,032)	2,065	2.48
Portuguese (99)	231	0.28
Romanian (46)	75	0.09
Russian (0)	73	0.09
Scotch-Irish (33)	69	0.08
Scottish (24)	183	0.22
Serbian (36)	45	0.05
Slovak (80)	89	0.11
Swedish (7)	138	0.17
Swiss (0)	16	0.02
Ukrainian (31)	107	0.13
Welsh (0)	52	0.06
West Indian, ex. Hispanic (32)	100	0.12
Belizean (0)	68	0.08
Jamaican (32)	32	0.04
Yugoslavian (54)	91	0.11

Hispanic Origin	Population	%
Hispanic or Latino (of any race)	72,609	86.55
Central American, ex. Mexican	1,293	1.54
Costa Rican	21	0.03
Guatemalan	650	0.77
Honduran	205	0.24
Nicaraguan	105	0.13
Panamanian	22	0.03
Salvadoran	278	0.33
Other Central American	12	0.01
Cuban	137	0.16
Dominican Republic	150	0.18
Mexican	65,694	78.31
Puerto Rican	2,782	3.32
South American	719	0.86
Argentinean	48	0.06
Bolivian	13	0.02
Chilean	12	0.01
Colombian	145	0.17
Ecuadorian	365	0.44
Paraguayan	3	<0.01
Peruvian	85	0.10
Uruguayan	6	0.01
Venezuelan	35	0.04
Other South American	7	0.01

*Notes: † The Census 2010 population figure is used to calculate the percentages in the Hispanic Origin and Race categories. Ancestry percentages are based on the 2006-2010 American Community Survey population (not shown); ‡ Numbers in parentheses indicate the number of people reporting a single ancestry; * Numbers in parentheses indicate the number of persons reporting this race alone, not in combination with any other race; Please refer to the Explanation of Data for more information.*

Other Hispanic or Latino	1,834	2.19

Race*	Population	%
African-American/Black (3,154)	3,508	4.18
Not Hispanic (2,690)	2,781	3.32
Hispanic (464)	727	0.87
American Indian/Alaska Native (693)	1,024	1.22
Not Hispanic (56)	102	0.12
Hispanic (637)	922	1.10
Alaska Athabascan *(Ala. Nat.)* (0)	4	<0.01
Apache (6)	9	0.01
Arapaho (1)	1	<0.01
Blackfeet (1)	1	<0.01
Canadian/French Am. Ind. (0)	2	<0.01
Central American Ind. (6)	6	0.01
Cherokee (11)	22	0.03
Cheyenne (0)	5	0.01
Chippewa (5)	8	0.01
Choctaw (4)	4	<0.01
Comanche (0)	1	<0.01
Creek (0)	2	<0.01
Delaware (1)	2	<0.01
Iroquois (2)	4	<0.01
Menominee (6)	6	0.01
Mexican American Ind. (169)	256	0.31
Navajo (9)	17	0.02
Paiute (1)	1	<0.01
Potawatomi (1)	1	<0.01
Pueblo (2)	2	<0.01
Sioux (5)	5	0.01
South American Ind. (4)	16	0.02
Spanish American Ind. (6)	6	0.01
Yup'ik *(Alaska Native)* (0)	1	<0.01
Asian (510)	718	0.86
Not Hispanic (467)	574	0.68
Hispanic (43)	144	0.17
Bangladeshi (3)	3	<0.01
Cambodian (13)	16	0.02
Chinese, ex. Taiwanese (60)	73	0.09
Filipino (247)	320	0.38
Indian (38)	65	0.08
Indonesian (5)	5	0.01
Japanese (6)	18	0.02
Korean (13)	23	0.03
Malaysian (0)	2	<0.01
Pakistani (10)	23	0.03
Sri Lankan (2)	5	0.01
Thai (24)	25	0.03
Vietnamese (50)	64	0.08
Hawaii Native/Pacific Islander (53)	118	0.14
Not Hispanic (26)	31	0.04
Hispanic (27)	87	0.10
Guamanian/Chamorro (22)	29	0.03
Native Hawaiian (10)	18	0.02
Samoan (12)	13	0.02
White (43,579)	46,142	55.00
Not Hispanic (7,696)	7,917	9.44
Hispanic (35,883)	38,225	45.57

Clarendon Hills

Place Type: Village
County: DuPage
Population: 8,427†

Ancestry‡	Population	%
American (243)	243	2.94
Arab (17)	17	0.21
Iraqi (17)	17	0.21
Assyrian/Chaldean/Syriac (0)	17	0.21
Austrian (0)	94	1.14
Belgian (40)	155	1.87
British (77)	373	4.51
Canadian (28)	46	0.56
Croatian (35)	87	1.05
Czech (88)	218	2.63
Danish (10)	78	0.94
Dutch (32)	88	1.06
Eastern European (14)	14	0.17
English (114)	409	4.94
European (41)	80	0.97
Finnish (0)	34	0.41
French, ex. Basque (0)	214	2.59
French Canadian (0)	12	0.15
German (426)	1,732	20.93
Greek (51)	271	3.27
Hungarian (0)	23	0.28
Irish (740)	2,277	27.52
Italian (293)	1,121	13.55
Lithuanian (38)	154	1.86
Luxemburger (12)	24	0.29
Macedonian (11)	33	0.40
Norwegian (15)	189	2.28
Polish (157)	865	10.45
Portuguese (0)	39	0.47
Russian (47)	90	1.09
Scotch-Irish (60)	205	2.48
Scottish (0)	330	3.99
Slovak (19)	49	0.59
Slovene (13)	54	0.65
Swedish (29)	452	5.46
Swiss (94)	151	1.82
Welsh (12)	37	0.45

Hispanic Origin	Population	%
Hispanic or Latino (of any race)	426	5.06
Central American, ex. Mexican	19	0.23
Costa Rican	3	0.04
Guatemalan	8	0.09
Honduran	1	0.01
Panamanian	2	0.02
Salvadoran	5	0.06
Cuban	29	0.34
Dominican Republic	6	0.07
Mexican	261	3.10
Puerto Rican	22	0.26
South American	38	0.45
Argentinean	9	0.11
Bolivian	1	0.01
Chilean	9	0.11
Colombian	6	0.07
Ecuadorian	7	0.08
Paraguayan	2	0.02
Peruvian	2	0.02
Venezuelan	2	0.02
Other Hispanic or Latino	51	0.61

Race*	Population	%
African-American/Black (149)	178	2.11
Not Hispanic (145)	170	2.02
Hispanic (4)	8	0.09
American Indian/Alaska Native (3)	33	0.39
Not Hispanic (3)	27	0.32
Hispanic (0)	6	0.07
Blackfeet (1)	5	0.06
Cherokee (1)	7	0.08
Choctaw (0)	1	0.01
Creek (0)	1	0.01
Mexican American Ind. (0)	3	0.04
Asian (433)	518	6.15
Not Hispanic (432)	510	6.05
Hispanic (1)	8	0.09
Burmese (11)	11	0.13
Chinese, ex. Taiwanese (162)	182	2.16
Filipino (52)	82	0.97
Indian (105)	120	1.42
Indonesian (1)	1	0.01
Japanese (13)	21	0.25
Korean (35)	45	0.53
Pakistani (14)	16	0.19
Taiwanese (4)	4	0.05
Thai (2)	7	0.08
Vietnamese (10)	12	0.14
Hawaii Native/Pacific Islander (2)	3	0.04
Not Hispanic (1)	2	0.02
Hispanic (1)	1	0.01
Samoan (1)	1	0.01
White (7,601)	7,743	91.88
Not Hispanic (7,286)	7,397	87.78
Hispanic (315)	346	4.11

Collinsville

Place Type: City
County: Madison
Population: 25,579†

Ancestry‡	Population	%
African, Sub-Saharan (28)	36	0.14
African (0)	8	0.03
Kenyan (28)	28	0.11
American (1,464)	1,464	5.76
Arab (15)	21	0.08
Jordanian (15)	15	0.06
Lebanese (0)	6	0.02
Armenian (23)	23	0.09
Austrian (48)	123	0.48
Belgian (0)	54	0.21
British (22)	111	0.44
Bulgarian (0)	12	0.05
Croatian (65)	183	0.72
Czech (56)	235	0.92
Czechoslovakian (43)	55	0.22
Danish (9)	42	0.17
Dutch (122)	558	2.20
Eastern European (0)	15	0.06
English (1,032)	2,455	9.66
European (450)	614	2.42
Finnish (0)	98	0.39
French, ex. Basque (211)	959	3.77
French Canadian (19)	33	0.13
German (2,996)	7,456	29.33
Greek (53)	53	0.21
Hungarian (22)	109	0.43
Irish (1,151)	3,930	15.46
Italian (894)	1,941	7.64
Lithuanian (67)	406	1.60
Northern European (51)	51	0.20
Norwegian (32)	69	0.27
Polish (229)	923	3.63
Portuguese (0)	47	0.18
Romanian (13)	45	0.18
Russian (9)	38	0.15
Scotch-Irish (168)	452	1.78
Scottish (134)	332	1.31
Serbian (10)	37	0.15
Slavic (0)	27	0.11
Slovak (10)	46	0.18
Swedish (57)	228	0.90
Swiss (28)	60	0.24
Ukrainian (10)	44	0.17
Welsh (90)	241	0.95
West Indian, ex. Hispanic (0)	6	0.02
Trinidadian/Tobagonian (0)	6	0.02
Yugoslavian (0)	11	0.04

Hispanic Origin	Population	%
Hispanic or Latino (of any race)	1,112	4.35
Central American, ex. Mexican	43	0.17
Costa Rican	3	0.01
Guatemalan	13	0.05
Honduran	8	0.03
Nicaraguan	1	<0.01
Panamanian	14	0.05
Salvadoran	3	0.01
Other Central American	1	<0.01
Cuban	5	0.02
Dominican Republic	4	0.02
Mexican	845	3.30
Puerto Rican	61	0.24
South American	30	0.12
Argentinean	1	<0.01
Bolivian	5	0.02
Chilean	6	0.02
Colombian	6	0.02
Ecuadorian	3	0.01
Peruvian	6	0.02
Venezuelan	3	0.01
Other Hispanic or Latino	124	0.48

SECTION TWO

*Notes: † The Census 2010 population figure is used to calculate the percentages in the Hispanic Origin and Race categories. Ancestry percentages are based on the 2006-2010 American Community Survey population (not shown); ‡ Numbers in parentheses indicate the number of people reporting a single ancestry; * Numbers in parentheses indicate the number of persons reporting this race alone, not in combination with any other race; Please refer to the Explanation of Data for more information.*

Race*	Population	%
African-American/Black (2,567)	2,862	11.19
Not Hispanic (2,544)	2,826	11.05
Hispanic (23)	36	0.14
American Indian/Alaska Native (58)	198	0.77
Not Hispanic (44)	169	0.66
Hispanic (14)	29	0.11
Apache (1)	4	0.02
Arapaho (0)	4	0.02
Blackfeet (4)	7	0.03
Central American Ind. (0)	2	0.01
Cherokee (18)	62	0.24
Chickasaw (0)	2	0.01
Chippewa (1)	4	0.02
Choctaw (2)	11	0.04
Creek (0)	1	<0.01
Iroquois (0)	2	0.01
Mexican American Ind. (11)	12	0.05
Navajo (0)	1	<0.01
Pueblo (0)	1	<0.01
Puget Sound Salish (0)	1	<0.01
Seminole (0)	1	<0.01
Sioux (2)	3	0.01
Spanish American Ind. (2)	4	0.02
Asian (196)	291	1.14
Not Hispanic (196)	288	1.13
Hispanic (0)	3	0.01
Cambodian (1)	1	<0.01
Chinese, ex. Taiwanese (33)	38	0.15
Filipino (38)	65	0.25
Indian (24)	28	0.11
Indonesian (1)	1	<0.01
Japanese (16)	40	0.16
Korean (44)	55	0.22
Laotian (1)	4	0.02
Pakistani (2)	2	0.01
Taiwanese (2)	2	0.01
Thai (9)	22	0.09
Vietnamese (8)	12	0.05
Hawaii Native/Pacific Islander (12)	27	0.11
Not Hispanic (12)	27	0.11
Fijian (1)	4	0.02
Guamanian/Chamorro (1)	2	0.01
Native Hawaiian (3)	6	0.02
Samoan (2)	3	0.01
White (21,830)	22,361	87.42
Not Hispanic (21,186)	21,624	84.54
Hispanic (644)	737	2.88

Columbia

Place Type: City
County: Monroe
Population: 9,707†

Ancestry‡	Population	%
American (358)	358	3.78
Austrian (0)	7	0.07
British (0)	15	0.16
Croatian (9)	9	0.10
Czech (16)	87	0.92
Danish (12)	42	0.44
Dutch (25)	226	2.39
English (208)	995	10.51
European (102)	102	1.08
French, ex. Basque (59)	670	7.08
German (2,540)	5,142	54.30
Hungarian (40)	120	1.27
Irish (228)	1,666	17.59
Italian (172)	381	4.02
Lithuanian (0)	29	0.31
Norwegian (11)	49	0.52
Polish (83)	384	4.06
Romanian (0)	10	0.11
Russian (102)	128	1.35
Scandinavian (0)	14	0.15
Scotch-Irish (77)	106	1.12
Scottish (84)	142	1.50
Slovak (9)	34	0.36
Swedish (0)	23	0.24
Swiss (48)	98	1.03
Ukrainian (0)	10	0.11
Welsh (0)	48	0.51

Hispanic Origin	Population	%
Hispanic or Latino (of any race)	190	1.96
Central American, ex. Mexican	14	0.14
Guatemalan	12	0.12
Panamanian	2	0.02
Cuban	1	0.01
Dominican Republic	3	0.03
Mexican	118	1.22
Puerto Rican	12	0.12
South American	12	0.12
Bolivian	2	0.02
Chilean	1	0.01
Colombian	2	0.02
Peruvian	2	0.02
Venezuelan	2	0.02
Other South American	3	0.03
Other Hispanic or Latino	30	0.31

Race*	Population	%
African-American/Black (36)	55	0.57
Not Hispanic (33)	49	0.50
Hispanic (3)	6	0.06
American Indian/Alaska Native (12)	36	0.37
Not Hispanic (11)	34	0.35
Hispanic (1)	2	0.02
Arapaho (1)	1	0.01
Cherokee (5)	12	0.12
Delaware (0)	1	0.01
Mexican American Ind. (0)	1	0.01
Osage (0)	1	0.01
Potawatomi (0)	5	0.05
Pueblo (0)	1	0.01
Seminole (1)	1	0.01
Sioux (1)	3	0.03
Asian (65)	92	0.95
Not Hispanic (63)	88	0.91
Hispanic (2)	4	0.04
Cambodian (3)	4	0.04
Chinese, ex. Taiwanese (8)	8	0.08
Filipino (6)	12	0.12
Indian (20)	24	0.25
Indonesian (0)	2	0.02
Japanese (2)	3	0.03
Korean (16)	25	0.26
Malaysian (1)	1	0.01
Pakistani (1)	1	0.01
Thai (6)	11	0.11
Hawaii Native/Pacific Islander (0)	1	0.01
Hispanic (0)	1	0.01
Native Hawaiian (0)	1	0.01
White (9,454)	9,537	98.25
Not Hispanic (9,340)	9,406	96.90
Hispanic (114)	131	1.35

Country Club Hills

Place Type: City
County: Cook
Population: 16,541†

Ancestry‡	Population	%
African, Sub-Saharan (299)	299	1.84
African (105)	105	0.64
Nigerian (194)	194	1.19
American (102)	102	0.63
Austrian (0)	30	0.18
Belgian (0)	7	0.04
Croatian (21)	36	0.22
Czech (0)	8	0.05
Czechoslovakian (0)	113	0.69
Danish (5)	34	0.21
Dutch (0)	18	0.11
English (90)	234	1.44
European (42)	52	0.32
Finnish (0)	30	0.18
French, ex. Basque (12)	112	0.69
French Canadian (0)	24	0.15
German (56)	324	1.99
Greek (0)	56	0.34
Irish (34)	156	0.96
Italian (34)	73	0.45
Lithuanian (16)	42	0.26
Northern European (19)	19	0.12
Norwegian (14)	79	0.49
Polish (40)	181	1.11
Russian (0)	12	0.07
Scandinavian (10)	10	0.06
Scotch-Irish (0)	50	0.31
Scottish (13)	51	0.31
Serbian (0)	20	0.12
Slovak (0)	126	0.77
Swedish (39)	139	0.85
Swiss (0)	29	0.18
Ukrainian (9)	30	0.18
Welsh (0)	7	0.04
West Indian, ex. Hispanic (55)	84	0.52
Jamaican (55)	84	0.52

Hispanic Origin	Population	%
Hispanic or Latino (of any race)	461	2.79
Central American, ex. Mexican	10	0.06
Guatemalan	6	0.04
Honduran	2	0.01
Salvadoran	1	0.01
Other Central American	1	0.01
Cuban	7	0.04
Dominican Republic	1	0.01
Mexican	299	1.81
Puerto Rican	116	0.70
South American	10	0.06
Colombian	2	0.01
Ecuadorian	6	0.04
Uruguayan	2	0.01
Other Hispanic or Latino	18	0.11

Race*	Population	%
African-American/Black (14,413)	14,648	88.56
Not Hispanic (14,299)	14,491	87.61
Hispanic (114)	157	0.95
American Indian/Alaska Native (40)	133	0.80
Not Hispanic (34)	118	0.71
Hispanic (6)	15	0.09
Apache (0)	2	0.01
Blackfeet (1)	5	0.03
Cherokee (3)	25	0.15
Choctaw (0)	6	0.04
Cree (0)	1	0.01
Creek (2)	2	0.01
Iroquois (1)	2	0.01
Mexican American Ind. (0)	5	0.03
Ottawa (0)	2	0.01
Seminole (0)	6	0.04
Asian (163)	211	1.28
Not Hispanic (162)	208	1.26
Hispanic (1)	3	0.02
Burmese (1)	1	0.01
Chinese, ex. Taiwanese (10)	14	0.08
Filipino (79)	99	0.60
Indian (10)	17	0.10
Indonesian (0)	1	0.01
Japanese (3)	9	0.05
Korean (4)	5	0.03
Laotian (8)	8	0.05
Malaysian (1)	2	0.01
Nepalese (3)	3	0.02
Taiwanese (0)	1	0.01
Thai (3)	5	0.03
Vietnamese (36)	36	0.22
Hawaii Native/Pacific Islander (6)	17	0.10
Not Hispanic (2)	12	0.07
Hispanic (4)	5	0.03
Native Hawaiian (5)	6	0.04
White (1,442)	1,619	9.79
Not Hispanic (1,343)	1,484	8.97
Hispanic (99)	135	0.82

*Notes: † The Census 2010 population figure is used to calculate the percentages in the Hispanic Origin and Race categories. Ancestry percentages are based on the 2006-2010 American Community Survey population (not shown); ‡ Numbers in parentheses indicate the number of people reporting a single ancestry; * Numbers in parentheses indicate the number of persons reporting this race alone, not in combination with any other race; Please refer to the Explanation of Data for more information.*

Crest Hill

Place Type: City
County: Will
Population: 20,837†

Ancestry‡	Population	%
African, Sub-Saharan (175)	275	1.35
African (164)	264	1.30
Nigerian (11)	11	0.05
American (500)	500	2.46
Arab (112)	112	0.55
Arab (23)	23	0.11
Lebanese (74)	74	0.36
Moroccan (15)	15	0.07
Austrian (11)	22	0.11
Belgian (0)	20	0.10
British (7)	29	0.14
Canadian (46)	46	0.23
Celtic (10)	10	0.05
Croatian (103)	344	1.69
Czech (42)	549	2.70
Czechoslovakian (33)	63	0.31
Danish (0)	129	0.64
Dutch (87)	383	1.89
Eastern European (16)	16	0.08
English (233)	1,114	5.48
European (24)	24	0.12
Finnish (0)	15	0.07
French, ex. Basque (67)	598	2.94
French Canadian (60)	144	0.71
German (720)	4,419	21.75
Greek (29)	185	0.91
Guyanese (21)	21	0.10
Hungarian (6)	63	0.31
Iranian (0)	28	0.14
Irish (519)	3,034	14.94
Israeli (0)	6	0.03
Italian (699)	2,140	10.54
Lithuanian (166)	411	2.02
Norwegian (73)	247	1.22
Polish (761)	2,634	12.97
Russian (100)	183	0.90
Scandinavian (8)	27	0.13
Scotch-Irish (150)	212	1.04
Scottish (35)	173	0.85
Slavic (0)	76	0.37
Slovak (74)	222	1.09
Slovene (45)	346	1.70
Swedish (125)	601	2.96
Swiss (0)	66	0.32
Turkish (49)	78	0.38
Ukrainian (81)	168	0.83
Welsh (0)	74	0.36
West Indian, ex. Hispanic (27)	60	0.30
Barbadian (27)	27	0.13
Belizean (0)	19	0.09
Jamaican (0)	14	0.07
Yugoslavian (35)	35	0.17

Hispanic Origin	Population	%
Hispanic or Latino (of any race)	3,732	17.91
Central American, ex. Mexican	89	0.43
Costa Rican	4	0.02
Guatemalan	42	0.20
Honduran	18	0.09
Nicaraguan	4	0.02
Panamanian	6	0.03
Salvadoran	15	0.07
Cuban	23	0.11
Dominican Republic	4	0.02
Mexican	3,133	15.04
Puerto Rican	265	1.27
South American	65	0.31
Argentinean	1	<0.01
Bolivian	1	<0.01
Chilean	2	0.01
Colombian	22	0.11
Ecuadorian	20	0.10
Peruvian	15	0.07
Venezuelan	2	0.01
Other South American	2	0.01
Other Hispanic or Latino	153	0.73

Race*	Population	%
African-American/Black (4,537)	4,768	22.88
Not Hispanic (4,494)	4,683	22.47
Hispanic (43)	85	0.41
American Indian/Alaska Native (56)	122	0.59
Not Hispanic (30)	76	0.36
Hispanic (26)	46	0.22
Apache (1)	2	0.01
Blackfeet (0)	2	0.01
Cherokee (5)	26	0.12
Chippewa (0)	1	<0.01
Choctaw (0)	2	0.01
Creek (0)	1	<0.01
Hopi (1)	1	<0.01
Iroquois (4)	6	0.03
Lumbee (2)	2	0.01
Mexican American Ind. (7)	11	0.05
Sioux (0)	2	0.01
Tlingit-Haida *(Alaska Native)* (0)	2	0.01
Ute (1)	1	<0.01
Asian (516)	583	2.80
Not Hispanic (496)	551	2.64
Hispanic (20)	32	0.15
Bangladeshi (6)	6	0.03
Cambodian (9)	9	0.04
Chinese, ex. Taiwanese (49)	54	0.26
Filipino (235)	266	1.28
Hmong (1)	4	0.02
Indian (85)	91	0.44
Japanese (13)	26	0.12
Korean (29)	34	0.16
Laotian (22)	28	0.13
Nepalese (2)	2	0.01
Pakistani (24)	25	0.12
Sri Lankan (4)	4	0.02
Thai (5)	13	0.06
Vietnamese (17)	17	0.08
Hawaii Native/Pacific Islander (4)	8	0.04
Not Hispanic (4)	5	0.02
Hispanic (0)	3	0.01
Guamanian/Chamorro (1)	1	<0.01
Native Hawaiian (1)	2	0.01
White (14,070)	14,474	69.46
Not Hispanic (11,800)	12,035	57.76
Hispanic (2,270)	2,439	11.71

Crestwood

Place Type: Village
County: Cook
Population: 10,950†

Ancestry‡	Population	%
American (48)	48	0.44
Arab (143)	143	1.31
Jordanian (143)	143	1.31
Austrian (9)	59	0.54
Belgian (0)	56	0.51
Brazilian (128)	128	1.17
Bulgarian (3)	3	0.03
Canadian (0)	30	0.27
Croatian (14)	95	0.87
Czech (75)	253	2.32
Czechoslovakian (18)	91	0.83
Danish (0)	66	0.60
Dutch (164)	368	3.37
English (24)	253	2.32
Finnish (0)	16	0.15
French, ex. Basque (0)	407	3.73
French Canadian (13)	46	0.42
German (411)	2,241	20.52
Greek (120)	192	1.76
Hungarian (22)	137	1.25
Irish (832)	2,606	23.86
Italian (719)	1,722	15.77
Lithuanian (128)	270	2.47
Luxemburger (0)	16	0.15
Norwegian (98)	170	1.56
Polish (891)	1,977	18.10
Russian (24)	61	0.56
Scotch-Irish (23)	125	1.14
Scottish (0)	77	0.70
Serbian (0)	8	0.07
Slovak (17)	61	0.56
Swedish (139)	333	3.05
Ukrainian (22)	70	0.64
Welsh (0)	36	0.33
Yugoslavian (0)	7	0.06

Hispanic Origin	Population	%
Hispanic or Latino (of any race)	892	8.15
Central American, ex. Mexican	8	0.07
Costa Rican	1	0.01
Guatemalan	4	0.04
Nicaraguan	1	0.01
Salvadoran	2	0.02
Cuban	8	0.07
Dominican Republic	3	0.03
Mexican	721	6.58
Puerto Rican	85	0.78
South American	14	0.13
Argentinean	3	0.03
Colombian	1	0.01
Ecuadorian	6	0.05
Paraguayan	2	0.02
Peruvian	1	0.01
Venezuelan	1	0.01
Other Hispanic or Latino	53	0.48

Race*	Population	%
African-American/Black (750)	799	7.30
Not Hispanic (740)	780	7.12
Hispanic (10)	19	0.17
American Indian/Alaska Native (18)	63	0.58
Not Hispanic (13)	44	0.40
Hispanic (5)	19	0.17
Cherokee (2)	15	0.14
Chickasaw (0)	1	0.01
Chippewa (1)	7	0.06
Comanche (0)	1	0.01
Hopi (0)	1	0.01
Iroquois (1)	1	0.01
Mexican American Ind. (3)	3	0.03
Navajo (0)	3	0.03
Ottawa (1)	1	0.01
Sioux (0)	1	0.01
Spanish American Ind. (1)	1	0.01
Asian (106)	166	1.52
Not Hispanic (105)	154	1.41
Hispanic (1)	12	0.11
Chinese, ex. Taiwanese (10)	13	0.12
Filipino (50)	65	0.59
Indian (16)	31	0.28
Japanese (3)	12	0.11
Korean (5)	11	0.10
Nepalese (1)	1	0.01
Pakistani (2)	2	0.02
Thai (5)	10	0.09
Vietnamese (11)	11	0.10
Hawaii Native/Pacific Islander (3)	4	0.04
Not Hispanic (1)	2	0.02
Hispanic (2)	2	0.02
Guamanian/Chamorro (3)	3	0.03
White (9,536)	9,711	88.68
Not Hispanic (9,073)	9,181	83.84
Hispanic (463)	530	4.84

Crete

Place Type: Village
County: Will
Population: 8,259†

Ancestry‡	Population	%
African, Sub-Saharan (57)	57	0.68
African (57)	57	0.68

SECTION TWO

*Notes: † The Census 2010 population figure is used to calculate the percentages in the Hispanic Origin and Race categories. Ancestry percentages are based on the 2006-2010 American Community Survey population (not shown); ‡ Numbers in parentheses indicate the number of people reporting a single ancestry; * Numbers in parentheses indicate the number of persons reporting this race alone, not in combination with any other race; Please refer to the Explanation of Data for more information.*

American (197)	197	2.33
Armenian (0)	104	1.23
British (0)	11	0.13
Croatian (0)	34	0.40
Czech (21)	96	1.14
Danish (79)	92	1.09
Dutch (305)	610	7.23
English (118)	732	8.67
European (25)	25	0.30
French, ex. Basque (17)	176	2.08
German (835)	2,148	25.44
Greek (22)	39	0.46
Hungarian (23)	36	0.43
Irish (295)	1,100	13.03
Italian (296)	830	9.83
Lithuanian (40)	52	0.62
Norwegian (16)	42	0.50
Polish (425)	912	10.80
Romanian (0)	23	0.27
Russian (0)	13	0.15
Scotch-Irish (40)	147	1.74
Scottish (60)	84	1.00
Serbian (27)	27	0.32
Slovak (45)	135	1.60
Swedish (96)	235	2.78
Swiss (0)	51	0.60
Turkish (0)	33	0.39
Ukrainian (11)	23	0.27
Welsh (0)	12	0.14
Yugoslavian (5)	33	0.39

Hispanic Origin	Population	%
Hispanic or Latino (of any race)	523	6.33
Central American, ex. Mexican	28	0.34
Guatemalan	22	0.27
Honduran	2	0.02
Panamanian	2	0.02
Salvadoran	2	0.02
Cuban	7	0.08
Mexican	379	4.59
Puerto Rican	64	0.77
South American	15	0.18
Argentinean	5	0.06
Colombian	3	0.04
Peruvian	1	0.01
Venezuelan	3	0.04
Other South American	3	0.04
Other Hispanic or Latino	30	0.36

Race*	Population	%
African-American/Black (2,322)	2,418	29.28
Not Hispanic (2,293)	2,367	28.66
Hispanic (29)	51	0.62
American Indian/Alaska Native (21)	74	0.90
Not Hispanic (18)	63	0.76
Hispanic (3)	11	0.13
Blackfeet (0)	1	0.01
Canadian/French Am. Ind. (0)	2	0.02
Cherokee (4)	12	0.15
Chickasaw (1)	9	0.11
Chippewa (1)	1	0.01
Choctaw (1)	7	0.08
Comanche (0)	2	0.02
Creek (0)	2	0.02
Houma (1)	1	0.01
Ottawa (3)	5	0.06
Potawatomi (1)	1	0.01
Pueblo (0)	1	0.01
Seminole (0)	1	0.01
Asian (87)	135	1.63
Not Hispanic (87)	134	1.62
Hispanic (0)	1	0.01
Cambodian (1)	2	0.02
Chinese, ex. Taiwanese (11)	26	0.31
Filipino (23)	38	0.46
Indian (31)	38	0.46
Japanese (1)	9	0.11
Korean (8)	14	0.17
Pakistani (3)	3	0.04
Thai (2)	7	0.08
Hawaii Native/Pacific Islander (5)	12	0.15
Not Hispanic (5)	12	0.15
Fijian (4)	4	0.05
Native Hawaiian (0)	6	0.07
Samoan (1)	1	0.01
White (5,436)	5,589	67.67
Not Hispanic (5,177)	5,291	64.06
Hispanic (259)	298	3.61

Crystal Lake

Place Type: City
County: McHenry
Population: 40,743†

Ancestry‡	Population	%
African, Sub-Saharan (193)	310	0.76
African (141)	243	0.59
Nigerian (52)	52	0.13
Other Sub-Saharan African (0)	15	0.04
American (1,515)	1,515	3.69
Arab (20)	69	0.17
Lebanese (20)	69	0.17
Assyrian/Chaldean/Syriac (47)	47	0.11
Australian (8)	8	0.02
Austrian (29)	188	0.46
Belgian (15)	72	0.18
British (110)	205	0.50
Canadian (61)	177	0.43
Croatian (18)	83	0.20
Czech (160)	640	1.56
Czechoslovakian (42)	75	0.18
Danish (37)	257	0.63
Dutch (143)	651	1.59
Eastern European (45)	45	0.11
English (751)	3,322	8.09
Estonian (14)	14	0.03
European (376)	445	1.08
Finnish (0)	120	0.29
French, ex. Basque (36)	1,177	2.87
French Canadian (74)	304	0.74
German (3,689)	13,620	33.18
Greek (59)	250	0.61
Hungarian (68)	325	0.79
Icelander (8)	8	0.02
Iranian (25)	25	0.06
Irish (1,404)	8,543	20.81
Italian (1,083)	5,313	12.94
Latvian (25)	37	0.09
Lithuanian (71)	356	0.87
Luxemburger (15)	15	0.04
Northern European (12)	12	0.03
Norwegian (175)	1,503	3.66
Polish (1,675)	5,928	14.44
Portuguese (0)	54	0.13
Romanian (87)	150	0.37
Russian (174)	694	1.69
Scandinavian (55)	79	0.19
Scotch-Irish (149)	554	1.35
Scottish (48)	604	1.47
Serbian (0)	34	0.08
Slovak (70)	102	0.25
Slovene (37)	65	0.16
Swedish (287)	1,498	3.65
Swiss (9)	182	0.44
Ukrainian (67)	209	0.51
Welsh (65)	326	0.79
West Indian, ex. Hispanic (24)	41	0.10
Barbadian (15)	15	0.04
West Indian (9)	26	0.06
Yugoslavian (54)	102	0.25

Hispanic Origin	Population	%
Hispanic or Latino (of any race)	4,770	11.71
Central American, ex. Mexican	170	0.42
Costa Rican	11	0.03
Guatemalan	77	0.19
Honduran	34	0.08
Nicaraguan	4	0.01
Panamanian	11	0.03
Salvadoran	33	0.08
Cuban	60	0.15
Dominican Republic	24	0.06
Mexican	3,801	9.33
Puerto Rican	321	0.79
South American	161	0.40
Argentinean	14	0.03
Bolivian	15	0.04
Chilean	4	0.01
Colombian	58	0.14
Ecuadorian	23	0.06
Peruvian	28	0.07
Venezuelan	18	0.04
Other South American	1	<0.01
Other Hispanic or Latino	233	0.57

Race*	Population	%
African-American/Black (398)	634	1.56
Not Hispanic (377)	569	1.40
Hispanic (21)	65	0.16
American Indian/Alaska Native (172)	333	0.82
Not Hispanic (54)	188	0.46
Hispanic (118)	145	0.36
Apache (2)	3	0.01
Blackfeet (1)	7	0.02
Central American Ind. (1)	1	<0.01
Cherokee (9)	39	0.10
Chippewa (11)	24	0.06
Choctaw (0)	1	<0.01
Comanche (1)	5	0.01
Cree (1)	2	<0.01
Creek (0)	1	<0.01
Inupiat *(Alaska Native)* (0)	4	0.01
Iroquois (7)	12	0.03
Menominee (4)	10	0.02
Mexican American Ind. (11)	13	0.03
Navajo (5)	6	0.01
Potawatomi (0)	5	0.01
Pueblo (0)	1	<0.01
Sioux (0)	2	<0.01
South American Ind. (0)	2	<0.01
Asian (1,023)	1,315	3.23
Not Hispanic (1,012)	1,280	3.14
Hispanic (11)	35	0.09
Bangladeshi (10)	13	0.03
Burmese (2)	3	0.01
Cambodian (1)	5	0.01
Chinese, ex. Taiwanese (152)	202	0.50
Filipino (207)	308	0.76
Indian (344)	389	0.95
Indonesian (2)	8	0.02
Japanese (34)	76	0.19
Korean (90)	145	0.36
Laotian (24)	30	0.07
Pakistani (48)	63	0.15
Sri Lankan (1)	1	<0.01
Thai (12)	16	0.04
Vietnamese (60)	64	0.16
Hawaii Native/Pacific Islander (10)	34	0.08
Not Hispanic (7)	19	0.05
Hispanic (3)	15	0.04
Guamanian/Chamorro (1)	3	0.01
Native Hawaiian (4)	11	0.03
Samoan (0)	2	<0.01
White (36,748)	37,410	91.82
Not Hispanic (33,951)	34,454	84.56
Hispanic (2,797)	2,956	7.26

Danville

Place Type: City
County: Vermilion
Population: 33,027†

Ancestry‡	Population	%
African, Sub-Saharan (513)	539	1.62
African (513)	539	1.62
American (5,369)	5,369	16.15
Arab (52)	179	0.54
Egyptian (11)	35	0.11

*Notes: † The Census 2010 population figure is used to calculate the percentages in the Hispanic Origin and Race categories. Ancestry percentages are based on the 2006-2010 American Community Survey population (not shown); ‡ Numbers in parentheses indicate the number of people reporting a single ancestry; * Numbers in parentheses indicate the number of persons reporting this race alone, not in combination with any other race; Please refer to the Explanation of Data for more information.*

Ancestry	Population	%
Iraqi (0)	66	0.20
Jordanian (26)	26	0.08
Moroccan (0)	11	0.03
Palestinian (0)	15	0.05
Other Arab (15)	26	0.08
Armenian (0)	12	0.04
Assyrian/Chaldean/Syriac (0)	66	0.20
Australian (9)	9	0.03
Austrian (0)	46	0.14
Belgian (19)	91	0.27
British (7)	43	0.13
Cajun (32)	32	0.10
Canadian (0)	10	0.03
Croatian (0)	15	0.05
Czech (10)	93	0.28
Czechoslovakian (35)	35	0.11
Danish (17)	46	0.14
Dutch (137)	609	1.83
English (928)	2,461	7.40
European (151)	185	0.56
Finnish (11)	11	0.03
French, ex. Basque (172)	759	2.28
French Canadian (18)	102	0.31
German (1,724)	4,839	14.56
Greek (16)	41	0.12
Hungarian (32)	82	0.25
Iranian (0)	27	0.08
Irish (714)	2,590	7.79
Italian (282)	457	1.37
Latvian (14)	14	0.04
Lithuanian (51)	165	0.50
Northern European (12)	12	0.04
Norwegian (59)	214	0.64
Polish (258)	642	1.93
Portuguese (36)	71	0.21
Romanian (0)	7	0.02
Russian (12)	12	0.04
Scotch-Irish (169)	502	1.51
Scottish (108)	391	1.18
Slavic (7)	7	0.02
Slovak (40)	106	0.32
Swedish (105)	350	1.05
Swiss (9)	54	0.16
Ukrainian (0)	21	0.06
Welsh (116)	264	0.79
West Indian, ex. Hispanic (44)	89	0.27
Jamaican (44)	89	0.27
Yugoslavian (6)	25	0.08

Hispanic Origin	Population	%
Hispanic or Latino (of any race)	2,154	6.52
Central American, ex. Mexican	30	0.09
Costa Rican	1	<0.01
Guatemalan	12	0.04
Honduran	1	<0.01
Nicaraguan	5	0.02
Panamanian	7	0.02
Salvadoran	4	0.01
Cuban	15	0.05
Dominican Republic	3	0.01
Mexican	1,555	4.71
Puerto Rican	127	0.38
South American	19	0.06
Colombian	7	0.02
Ecuadorian	6	0.02
Paraguayan	1	<0.01
Peruvian	4	0.01
Venezuelan	1	<0.01
Other Hispanic or Latino	405	1.23

Race*	Population	%
African-American/Black (9,963)	10,763	32.59
Not Hispanic (9,808)	10,527	31.87
Hispanic (155)	236	0.71
American Indian/Alaska Native (93)	318	0.96
Not Hispanic (71)	268	0.81
Hispanic (22)	50	0.15
Apache (0)	4	0.01
Blackfeet (2)	13	0.04
Cherokee (15)	77	0.23
Cheyenne (1)	2	0.01
Chickasaw (0)	1	<0.01
Chippewa (0)	2	0.01
Choctaw (0)	1	<0.01
Comanche (0)	2	0.01
Cree (4)	7	0.02
Creek (1)	1	<0.01
Crow (1)	2	0.01
Delaware (0)	1	<0.01
Iroquois (0)	1	<0.01
Kiowa (0)	1	<0.01
Menominee (1)	1	<0.01
Mexican American Ind. (2)	2	0.01
Potawatomi (2)	2	0.01
Pueblo (0)	1	<0.01
Sioux (1)	5	0.02
South American Ind. (0)	1	<0.01
Tohono O'Odham (3)	3	0.01
Ute (0)	4	0.01
Asian (399)	502	1.52
Not Hispanic (394)	486	1.47
Hispanic (5)	16	0.05
Bangladeshi (1)	1	<0.01
Burmese (1)	1	<0.01
Chinese, ex. Taiwanese (41)	51	0.15
Filipino (92)	111	0.34
Hmong (19)	19	0.06
Indian (158)	180	0.55
Japanese (8)	26	0.08
Korean (19)	29	0.09
Laotian (1)	2	0.01
Nepalese (2)	2	0.01
Pakistani (3)	3	0.01
Sri Lankan (4)	4	0.01
Taiwanese (1)	1	<0.01
Thai (9)	12	0.04
Vietnamese (30)	33	0.10
Hawaii Native/Pacific Islander (7)	26	0.08
Not Hispanic (5)	20	0.06
Hispanic (2)	6	0.02
Guamanian/Chamorro (2)	3	0.01
Native Hawaiian (0)	8	0.02
Samoan (2)	5	0.02
White (20,654)	21,673	65.62
Not Hispanic (19,626)	20,474	61.99
Hispanic (1,028)	1,199	3.63

Darien

Place Type: City
County: DuPage
Population: 22,086†

Ancestry‡	Population	%
African, Sub-Saharan (68)	68	0.31
African (36)	36	0.16
Nigerian (32)	32	0.14
Albanian (0)	12	0.05
American (302)	302	1.36
Arab (42)	127	0.57
Moroccan (18)	18	0.08
Palestinian (24)	109	0.49
Austrian (0)	93	0.42
Belgian (16)	112	0.51
British (72)	168	0.76
Bulgarian (63)	63	0.28
Canadian (52)	107	0.48
Croatian (43)	179	0.81
Czech (539)	1,274	5.75
Czechoslovakian (55)	198	0.89
Danish (10)	69	0.31
Dutch (123)	263	1.19
English (155)	1,099	4.96
European (136)	136	0.61
Finnish (17)	42	0.19
French, ex. Basque (23)	477	2.15
French Canadian (0)	39	0.18
German (1,279)	5,296	23.90
Greek (139)	190	0.86
Hungarian (49)	236	1.06
Iranian (34)	34	0.15
Irish (957)	3,711	16.74
Italian (1,065)	3,170	14.30
Latvian (0)	24	0.11
Lithuanian (686)	853	3.85
Luxemburger (0)	10	0.05
Macedonian (169)	169	0.76
Northern European (17)	17	0.08
Norwegian (51)	527	2.38
Polish (2,012)	3,640	16.42
Portuguese (11)	33	0.15
Romanian (131)	131	0.59
Russian (56)	150	0.68
Scandinavian (0)	9	0.04
Scotch-Irish (14)	83	0.37
Scottish (113)	368	1.66
Serbian (195)	217	0.98
Slovak (257)	362	1.63
Slovene (16)	69	0.31
Swedish (65)	720	3.25
Swiss (16)	75	0.34
Ukrainian (16)	28	0.13
Welsh (0)	93	0.42
West Indian, ex. Hispanic (19)	19	0.09
Barbadian (9)	9	0.04
Jamaican (10)	10	0.05
Yugoslavian (0)	28	0.13

Hispanic Origin	Population	%
Hispanic or Latino (of any race)	1,386	6.28
Central American, ex. Mexican	36	0.16
Costa Rican	2	0.01
Guatemalan	20	0.09
Honduran	4	0.02
Panamanian	3	0.01
Salvadoran	7	0.03
Cuban	45	0.20
Dominican Republic	7	0.03
Mexican	1,025	4.64
Puerto Rican	91	0.41
South American	110	0.50
Argentinean	12	0.05
Bolivian	6	0.03
Chilean	8	0.04
Colombian	21	0.10
Ecuadorian	26	0.12
Peruvian	19	0.09
Uruguayan	2	0.01
Venezuelan	16	0.07
Other Hispanic or Latino	72	0.33

Race*	Population	%
African-American/Black (706)	793	3.59
Not Hispanic (695)	766	3.47
Hispanic (11)	27	0.12
American Indian/Alaska Native (28)	74	0.34
Not Hispanic (15)	58	0.26
Hispanic (13)	16	0.07
Blackfeet (0)	2	0.01
Cherokee (1)	14	0.06
Choctaw (3)	5	0.02
Creek (0)	1	<0.01
Iroquois (1)	6	0.03
Lumbee (2)	2	0.01
Mexican American Ind. (4)	4	0.02
Sioux (0)	1	<0.01
Asian (2,619)	2,856	12.93
Not Hispanic (2,603)	2,818	12.76
Hispanic (16)	38	0.17
Bangladeshi (3)	4	0.02
Burmese (1)	3	0.01
Chinese, ex. Taiwanese (461)	511	2.31
Filipino (672)	763	3.45
Indian (1,012)	1,066	4.83
Japanese (28)	48	0.22
Korean (113)	132	0.60
Laotian (2)	5	0.02
Malaysian (1)	6	0.03
Pakistani (111)	114	0.52
Sri Lankan (2)	2	0.01

*Notes: † The Census 2010 population figure is used to calculate the percentages in the Hispanic Origin and Race categories. Ancestry percentages are based on the 2006-2010 American Community Survey population (not shown); ‡ Numbers in parentheses indicate the number of people reporting a single ancestry; * Numbers in parentheses indicate the number of persons reporting this race alone, not in combination with any other race; Please refer to the Explanation of Data for more information.*

Taiwanese (53)	57	0.26
Thai (37)	44	0.20
Vietnamese (45)	52	0.24
Hawaii Native/Pacific Islander (4)	15	0.07
Not Hispanic (4)	13	0.06
Hispanic (0)	2	0.01
Guamanian/Chamorro (2)	4	0.02
Native Hawaiian (1)	1	<0.01
Samoan (1)	5	0.02
White (17,985)	18,268	82.71
Not Hispanic (17,063)	17,273	78.21
Hispanic (922)	995	4.51

DeKalb

Place Type: City
County: DeKalb
Population: 43,862†

Ancestry‡	Population	%
African, Sub-Saharan (137)	277	0.63
African (117)	183	0.42
Nigerian (4)	78	0.18
Sudanese (16)	16	0.04
Albanian (17)	30	0.07
American (1,002)	1,002	2.28
Arab (46)	68	0.15
Lebanese (35)	44	0.10
Palestinian (11)	11	0.03
Syrian (0)	13	0.03
Armenian (26)	40	0.09
Australian (14)	14	0.03
Austrian (15)	188	0.43
Belgian (0)	195	0.44
British (86)	215	0.49
Bulgarian (68)	68	0.15
Canadian (44)	118	0.27
Croatian (10)	86	0.20
Czech (77)	367	0.83
Czechoslovakian (0)	26	0.06
Danish (155)	456	1.04
Dutch (103)	724	1.65
Eastern European (44)	44	0.10
English (642)	3,261	7.41
European (441)	476	1.08
Finnish (62)	197	0.45
French, ex. Basque (113)	885	2.01
French Canadian (85)	180	0.41
German (3,090)	10,975	24.95
Greek (134)	277	0.63
Hungarian (46)	132	0.30
Iranian (13)	173	0.39
Irish (1,467)	6,984	15.87
Italian (824)	2,846	6.47
Latvian (16)	16	0.04
Lithuanian (167)	440	1.00
Luxemburger (20)	20	0.05
Northern European (60)	60	0.14
Norwegian (442)	1,513	3.44
Pennsylvania German (0)	14	0.03
Polish (974)	3,454	7.85
Portuguese (0)	28	0.06
Romanian (0)	58	0.13
Russian (102)	476	1.08
Scandinavian (62)	121	0.28
Scotch-Irish (206)	732	1.66
Scottish (55)	642	1.46
Serbian (80)	142	0.32
Slovak (36)	134	0.30
Slovene (24)	24	0.05
Swedish (394)	2,365	5.38
Swiss (31)	189	0.43
Turkish (0)	13	0.03
Ukrainian (90)	191	0.43
Welsh (15)	207	0.47
West Indian, ex. Hispanic (23)	60	0.14
Belizean (0)	15	0.03
Haitian (23)	31	0.07
Jamaican (0)	14	0.03
Yugoslavian (25)	68	0.15

Hispanic Origin	Population	%
Hispanic or Latino (of any race)	5,504	12.55
Central American, ex. Mexican	122	0.28
Costa Rican	9	0.02
Guatemalan	54	0.12
Honduran	24	0.05
Nicaraguan	12	0.03
Panamanian	12	0.03
Salvadoran	9	0.02
Other Central American	2	<0.01
Cuban	72	0.16
Dominican Republic	17	0.04
Mexican	4,550	10.37
Puerto Rican	319	0.73
South American	148	0.34
Argentinean	16	0.04
Bolivian	3	0.01
Chilean	11	0.03
Colombian	43	0.10
Ecuadorian	20	0.05
Paraguayan	2	<0.01
Peruvian	44	0.10
Venezuelan	9	0.02
Other Hispanic or Latino	276	0.63

Race*	Population	%
African-American/Black (5,596)	6,046	13.78
Not Hispanic (5,494)	5,870	13.38
Hispanic (102)	176	0.40
American Indian/Alaska Native (115)	332	0.76
Not Hispanic (48)	198	0.45
Hispanic (67)	134	0.31
Apache (1)	2	<0.01
Blackfeet (6)	15	0.03
Cherokee (7)	69	0.16
Cheyenne (0)	1	<0.01
Chippewa (3)	9	0.02
Choctaw (0)	5	0.01
Creek (0)	1	<0.01
Delaware (2)	2	<0.01
Inupiat *(Alaska Native)* (0)	1	<0.01
Iroquois (6)	7	0.02
Mexican American Ind. (27)	41	0.09
Navajo (2)	5	0.01
Potawatomi (3)	6	0.01
Pueblo (0)	1	<0.01
Seminole (0)	1	<0.01
Shoshone (0)	3	0.01
Sioux (2)	9	0.02
South American Ind. (1)	6	0.01
Yaqui (0)	1	<0.01
Asian (1,796)	2,089	4.76
Not Hispanic (1,769)	2,040	4.65
Hispanic (27)	49	0.11
Bangladeshi (1)	1	<0.01
Burmese (6)	6	0.01
Cambodian (32)	39	0.09
Chinese, ex. Taiwanese (342)	403	0.92
Filipino (217)	281	0.64
Indian (587)	626	1.43
Indonesian (7)	10	0.02
Japanese (49)	97	0.22
Korean (208)	258	0.59
Laotian (20)	21	0.05
Malaysian (13)	16	0.04
Nepalese (8)	8	0.02
Pakistani (76)	81	0.18
Sri Lankan (10)	10	0.02
Taiwanese (21)	22	0.05
Thai (30)	37	0.08
Vietnamese (111)	129	0.29
Hawaii Native/Pacific Islander (11)	43	0.10
Not Hispanic (8)	33	0.08
Hispanic (3)	10	0.02
Guamanian/Chamorro (2)	4	0.01
Native Hawaiian (3)	18	0.04
Samoan (1)	2	<0.01
Tongan (1)	2	<0.01
White (32,856)	33,762	76.97
Not Hispanic (30,238)	30,876	70.39
Hispanic (2,618)	2,886	6.58

Decatur

Place Type: City
County: Macon
Population: 76,122†

Ancestry‡	Population	%
African, Sub-Saharan (145)	169	0.22
African (145)	169	0.22
American (11,484)	11,484	15.03
Arab (172)	172	0.23
Arab (152)	152	0.20
Egyptian (11)	11	0.01
Moroccan (9)	9	0.01
Australian (0)	45	0.06
Austrian (41)	149	0.19
Belgian (59)	105	0.14
British (126)	231	0.30
Canadian (44)	125	0.16
Croatian (17)	94	0.12
Czech (67)	194	0.25
Danish (36)	118	0.15
Dutch (225)	1,233	1.61
Eastern European (10)	10	0.01
English (2,879)	7,427	9.72
European (483)	548	0.72
Finnish (0)	11	0.01
French, ex. Basque (317)	1,477	1.93
French Canadian (58)	209	0.27
German (5,963)	15,437	20.20
Greek (128)	341	0.45
Hungarian (66)	231	0.30
Iranian (29)	29	0.04
Irish (2,614)	9,737	12.74
Italian (511)	1,740	2.28
Lithuanian (0)	36	0.05
Luxemburger (0)	21	0.03
Maltese (0)	11	0.01
Northern European (9)	9	0.01
Norwegian (187)	555	0.73
Pennsylvania German (51)	51	0.07
Polish (467)	1,558	2.04
Portuguese (75)	90	0.12
Russian (23)	60	0.08
Scandinavian (0)	28	0.04
Scotch-Irish (606)	1,194	1.56
Scottish (485)	1,176	1.54
Serbian (6)	6	0.01
Slavic (21)	28	0.04
Slovak (9)	77	0.10
Swedish (219)	706	0.92
Swiss (53)	176	0.23
Ukrainian (23)	83	0.11
Welsh (102)	368	0.48
West Indian, ex. Hispanic (75)	100	0.13
Haitian (65)	65	0.09
Jamaican (10)	24	0.03
Trinidadian/Tobagonian (0)	11	0.01
Yugoslavian (0)	10	0.01

Hispanic Origin	Population	%
Hispanic or Latino (of any race)	1,650	2.17
Central American, ex. Mexican	80	0.11
Costa Rican	10	0.01
Guatemalan	17	0.02
Honduran	10	0.01
Nicaraguan	21	0.03
Panamanian	14	0.02
Salvadoran	7	0.01
Other Central American	1	<0.01
Cuban	50	0.07
Dominican Republic	16	0.02
Mexican	1,055	1.39
Puerto Rican	163	0.21
South American	55	0.07
Argentinean	4	0.01
Bolivian	2	<0.01
Chilean	4	0.01

*Notes: † The Census 2010 population figure is used to calculate the percentages in the Hispanic Origin and Race categories. Ancestry percentages are based on the 2006-2010 American Community Survey population (not shown); ‡ Numbers in parentheses indicate the number of people reporting a single ancestry; * Numbers in parentheses indicate the number of persons reporting this race alone, not in combination with any other race; Please refer to the Explanation of Data for more information.*

Colombian	18	0.02
Ecuadorian	3	<0.01
Peruvian	15	0.02
Venezuelan	9	0.01
Other Hispanic or Latino	231	0.30

Race*	Population	%
African-American/Black (17,704)	19,491	25.60
Not Hispanic (17,600)	19,291	25.34
Hispanic (104)	200	0.26
American Indian/Alaska Native (173)	621	0.82
Not Hispanic (155)	561	0.74
Hispanic (18)	60	0.08
Alaska Athabascan *(Ala. Nat.)* (1)	1	<0.01
Aleut *(Alaska Native)* (0)	3	<0.01
Apache (8)	16	0.02
Blackfeet (3)	31	0.04
Cherokee (24)	161	0.21
Cheyenne (0)	2	<0.01
Chickasaw (0)	3	<0.01
Chippewa (9)	13	0.02
Choctaw (5)	9	0.01
Cree (0)	1	<0.01
Creek (0)	7	0.01
Delaware (0)	2	<0.01
Iroquois (1)	3	<0.01
Mexican American Ind. (1)	7	0.01
Navajo (8)	17	0.02
Osage (0)	1	<0.01
Paiute (3)	5	0.01
Potawatomi (4)	4	0.01
Seminole (0)	1	<0.01
Sioux (6)	22	0.03
South American Ind. (0)	2	<0.01
Spanish American Ind. (0)	1	<0.01
Asian (704)	904	1.19
Not Hispanic (695)	873	1.15
Hispanic (9)	31	0.04
Burmese (1)	1	<0.01
Cambodian (2)	3	<0.01
Chinese, ex. Taiwanese (78)	94	0.12
Filipino (131)	183	0.24
Indian (302)	318	0.42
Indonesian (4)	12	0.02
Japanese (14)	30	0.04
Korean (55)	61	0.08
Laotian (2)	4	0.01
Malaysian (1)	1	<0.01
Pakistani (32)	34	0.04
Sri Lankan (1)	1	<0.01
Taiwanese (2)	2	<0.01
Thai (9)	11	0.01
Vietnamese (49)	68	0.09
Hawaii Native/Pacific Islander (23)	91	0.12
Not Hispanic (18)	76	0.10
Hispanic (5)	15	0.02
Guamanian/Chamorro (1)	9	0.01
Native Hawaiian (4)	11	0.01
Samoan (4)	9	0.01
White (54,509)	56,669	74.44
Not Hispanic (53,749)	55,734	73.22
Hispanic (760)	935	1.23

Deerfield

Place Type: Village
County: Lake
Population: 18,225†

Ancestry‡	Population	%
African, Sub-Saharan (20)	20	0.11
South African (20)	20	0.11
American (2,239)	2,239	12.17
Arab (29)	66	0.36
Egyptian (19)	19	0.10
Lebanese (0)	11	0.06
Palestinian (0)	12	0.07
Syrian (10)	24	0.13
Armenian (38)	38	0.21
Assyrian/Chaldean/Syriac (0)	14	0.08
Austrian (0)	173	0.94
Belgian (9)	47	0.26
British (81)	107	0.58
Bulgarian (116)	125	0.68
Canadian (20)	41	0.22
Croatian (21)	30	0.16
Czech (20)	72	0.39
Czechoslovakian (8)	18	0.10
Danish (0)	39	0.21
Dutch (73)	172	0.93
Eastern European (618)	618	3.36
English (331)	1,391	7.56
European (466)	466	2.53
Finnish (22)	37	0.20
French, ex. Basque (19)	358	1.95
French Canadian (7)	59	0.32
German (667)	2,791	15.16
Greek (128)	187	1.02
Hungarian (44)	232	1.26
Iranian (29)	29	0.16
Irish (390)	1,552	8.43
Israeli (30)	65	0.35
Italian (414)	1,017	5.53
Latvian (17)	105	0.57
Lithuanian (49)	180	0.98
Luxemburger (0)	10	0.05
Northern European (36)	62	0.34
Norwegian (103)	212	1.15
Polish (760)	2,080	11.30
Romanian (79)	197	1.07
Russian (1,720)	3,318	18.03
Scandinavian (24)	52	0.28
Scotch-Irish (44)	182	0.99
Scottish (54)	371	2.02
Slavic (0)	31	0.17
Slovak (28)	82	0.45
Slovene (7)	16	0.09
Swedish (104)	472	2.56
Swiss (0)	53	0.29
Ukrainian (76)	95	0.52
Welsh (0)	86	0.47
Yugoslavian (0)	9	0.05

Hispanic Origin	Population	%
Hispanic or Latino (of any race)	510	2.80
Central American, ex. Mexican	26	0.14
Costa Rican	3	0.02
Guatemalan	17	0.09
Honduran	4	0.02
Salvadoran	2	0.01
Cuban	32	0.18
Dominican Republic	6	0.03
Mexican	265	1.45
Puerto Rican	56	0.31
South American	78	0.43
Argentinean	12	0.07
Bolivian	4	0.02
Chilean	1	0.01
Colombian	36	0.20
Ecuadorian	13	0.07
Paraguayan	1	0.01
Peruvian	10	0.05
Venezuelan	1	0.01
Other Hispanic or Latino	47	0.26

Race*	Population	%
African-American/Black (94)	119	0.65
Not Hispanic (93)	113	0.62
Hispanic (1)	6	0.03
American Indian/Alaska Native (17)	43	0.24
Not Hispanic (4)	27	0.15
Hispanic (13)	16	0.09
Blackfeet (0)	1	0.01
Cherokee (3)	11	0.06
Comanche (1)	1	0.01
Iroquois (0)	2	0.01
Mexican American Ind. (5)	8	0.04
Seminole (0)	2	0.01
Shoshone (0)	3	0.02
Asian (665)	792	4.35
Not Hispanic (660)	783	4.30
Hispanic (5)	9	0.05
Bangladeshi (1)	2	0.01
Chinese, ex. Taiwanese (202)	237	1.30
Filipino (71)	101	0.55
Indian (108)	117	0.64
Indonesian (1)	1	0.01
Japanese (62)	89	0.49
Korean (159)	189	1.04
Laotian (1)	1	0.01
Pakistani (13)	16	0.09
Taiwanese (10)	17	0.09
Thai (6)	9	0.05
Vietnamese (6)	10	0.05
Hawaii Native/Pacific Islander (3)	7	0.04
Not Hispanic (2)	6	0.03
Hispanic (1)	1	0.01
Guamanian/Chamorro (1)	1	0.01
Native Hawaiian (1)	4	0.02
Samoan (1)	1	0.01
White (17,124)	17,296	94.90
Not Hispanic (16,767)	16,921	92.84
Hispanic (357)	375	2.06

Des Plaines

Place Type: City
County: Cook
Population: 58,364†

Ancestry‡	Population	%
African, Sub-Saharan (49)	49	0.09
African (37)	37	0.06
Nigerian (12)	12	0.02
Albanian (147)	234	0.41
American (1,236)	1,236	2.15
Arab (213)	354	0.62
Arab (31)	114	0.20
Egyptian (44)	66	0.12
Iraqi (25)	61	0.11
Moroccan (100)	100	0.17
Palestinian (6)	6	0.01
Other Arab (7)	7	0.01
Armenian (33)	44	0.08
Assyrian/Chaldean/Syriac (461)	614	1.07
Australian (9)	57	0.10
Austrian (104)	295	0.51
Belgian (24)	69	0.12
British (19)	44	0.08
Bulgarian (383)	389	0.68
Cajun (0)	11	0.02
Canadian (27)	121	0.21
Celtic (5)	5	0.01
Croatian (235)	351	0.61
Czech (289)	742	1.29
Czechoslovakian (10)	92	0.16
Danish (61)	279	0.49
Dutch (83)	425	0.74
Eastern European (32)	32	0.06
English (347)	2,086	3.64
Estonian (10)	10	0.02
European (244)	267	0.47
Finnish (9)	110	0.19
French, ex. Basque (108)	1,019	1.78
French Canadian (0)	150	0.26
German (3,866)	11,836	20.64
Greek (1,221)	1,559	2.72
Hungarian (111)	251	0.44
Icelander (14)	14	0.02
Iranian (11)	61	0.11
Irish (2,008)	7,675	13.38
Italian (2,610)	5,675	9.89
Latvian (54)	54	0.09
Lithuanian (118)	400	0.70
Luxemburger (59)	144	0.25
Macedonian (8)	23	0.04
Northern European (12)	12	0.02
Norwegian (294)	1,002	1.75
Pennsylvania German (0)	19	0.03
Polish (6,110)	9,648	16.82

SECTION TWO

*Notes: † The Census 2010 population figure is used to calculate the percentages in the Hispanic Origin and Race categories. Ancestry percentages are based on the 2006-2010 American Community Survey population (not shown); ‡ Numbers in parentheses indicate the number of people reporting a single ancestry; * Numbers in parentheses indicate the number of persons reporting this race alone, not in combination with any other race; Please refer to the Explanation of Data for more information.*

Portuguese (0)	7	0.01
Romanian (676)	867	1.51
Russian (310)	545	0.95
Scandinavian (22)	22	0.04
Scotch-Irish (38)	322	0.56
Scottish (126)	443	0.77
Serbian (172)	282	0.49
Slavic (22)	22	0.04
Slovak (84)	198	0.35
Slovene (45)	56	0.10
Swedish (459)	1,901	3.31
Swiss (0)	101	0.18
Turkish (82)	155	0.27
Ukrainian (238)	401	0.70
Welsh (0)	177	0.31
Yugoslavian (320)	381	0.66

Hispanic Origin	Population	%
Hispanic or Latino (of any race)	10,053	17.22
Central American, ex. Mexican	445	0.76
Costa Rican	28	0.05
Guatemalan	184	0.32
Honduran	29	0.05
Nicaraguan	24	0.04
Panamanian	10	0.02
Salvadoran	165	0.28
Other Central American	5	0.01
Cuban	149	0.26
Dominican Republic	19	0.03
Mexican	8,001	13.71
Puerto Rican	615	1.05
South American	492	0.84
Argentinean	27	0.05
Bolivian	27	0.05
Chilean	28	0.05
Colombian	139	0.24
Ecuadorian	165	0.28
Paraguayan	1	<0.01
Peruvian	70	0.12
Uruguayan	3	0.01
Venezuelan	23	0.04
Other South American	9	0.02
Other Hispanic or Latino	332	0.57

Race*	Population	%
African-American/Black (1,039)	1,285	2.20
Not Hispanic (963)	1,160	1.99
Hispanic (76)	125	0.21
American Indian/Alaska Native (369)	588	1.01
Not Hispanic (63)	199	0.34
Hispanic (306)	389	0.67
Aleut *(Alaska Native)* (1)	5	0.01
Apache (1)	6	0.01
Blackfeet (0)	4	0.01
Canadian/French Am. Ind. (1)	2	<0.01
Central American Ind. (1)	1	<0.01
Cherokee (6)	39	0.07
Chickasaw (0)	1	<0.01
Chippewa (5)	11	0.02
Choctaw (1)	3	0.01
Creek (1)	1	<0.01
Delaware (0)	1	<0.01
Inupiat *(Alaska Native)* (0)	2	<0.01
Iroquois (4)	10	0.02
Menominee (1)	5	0.01
Mexican American Ind. (59)	75	0.13
Navajo (0)	2	<0.01
Potawatomi (2)	3	0.01
Pueblo (0)	2	<0.01
Seminole (0)	2	<0.01
Sioux (2)	12	0.02
South American Ind. (2)	3	0.01
Spanish American Ind. (12)	13	0.02
Tohono O'Odham (3)	3	0.01
Asian (6,674)	7,292	12.49
Not Hispanic (6,613)	7,146	12.24
Hispanic (61)	146	0.25
Bangladeshi (5)	6	0.01
Burmese (4)	5	0.01
Cambodian (103)	105	0.18
Chinese, ex. Taiwanese (370)	432	0.74
Filipino (1,689)	1,851	3.17
Indian (2,995)	3,214	5.51
Indonesian (2)	4	0.01
Japanese (151)	212	0.36
Korean (621)	664	1.14
Laotian (11)	13	0.02
Malaysian (1)	1	<0.01
Nepalese (8)	8	0.01
Pakistani (314)	375	0.64
Sri Lankan (8)	10	0.02
Taiwanese (26)	27	0.05
Thai (38)	53	0.09
Vietnamese (159)	171	0.29
Hawaii Native/Pacific Islander (9)	78	0.13
Not Hispanic (9)	63	0.11
Hispanic (0)	15	0.03
Marshallese (1)	1	<0.01
Native Hawaiian (4)	16	0.03
Samoan (2)	9	0.02
White (45,133)	46,247	79.24
Not Hispanic (39,689)	40,347	69.13
Hispanic (5,444)	5,900	10.11

Dixon

Place Type: City
County: Lee
Population: 15,733†

Ancestry‡	Population	%
African, Sub-Saharan (18)	18	0.12
Nigerian (18)	18	0.12
American (1,314)	1,314	8.51
Arab (0)	8	0.05
Syrian (0)	8	0.05
Austrian (10)	10	0.06
Belgian (23)	23	0.15
British (0)	29	0.19
Canadian (0)	6	0.04
Celtic (8)	8	0.05
Croatian (0)	11	0.07
Czech (17)	97	0.63
Czechoslovakian (26)	26	0.17
Danish (0)	36	0.23
Dutch (96)	768	4.97
Eastern European (38)	38	0.25
English (215)	1,070	6.93
European (124)	124	0.80
French, ex. Basque (23)	535	3.47
French Canadian (15)	15	0.10
German (2,041)	4,949	32.05
Greek (11)	104	0.67
Hungarian (0)	21	0.14
Irish (970)	2,723	17.64
Italian (265)	591	3.83
Lithuanian (20)	34	0.22
Northern European (32)	32	0.21
Norwegian (78)	322	2.09
Pennsylvania German (21)	21	0.14
Polish (79)	383	2.48
Portuguese (0)	72	0.47
Romanian (12)	26	0.17
Russian (163)	201	1.30
Scotch-Irish (18)	208	1.35
Scottish (55)	107	0.69
Swedish (221)	443	2.87
Swiss (21)	100	0.65
Ukrainian (12)	12	0.08
Welsh (13)	99	0.64
West Indian, ex. Hispanic (4)	4	0.03
Jamaican (4)	4	0.03
Yugoslavian (12)	12	0.08

Hispanic Origin	Population	%
Hispanic or Latino (of any race)	1,051	6.68
Central American, ex. Mexican	15	0.10
Costa Rican	1	0.01
Guatemalan	6	0.04
Honduran	2	0.01
Nicaraguan	2	0.01
Salvadoran	4	0.03
Cuban	12	0.08
Mexican	730	4.64
Puerto Rican	77	0.49
South American	24	0.15
Chilean	2	0.01
Colombian	14	0.09
Ecuadorian	1	0.01
Peruvian	4	0.03
Venezuelan	3	0.02
Other Hispanic or Latino	193	1.23

Race*	Population	%
African-American/Black (1,598)	1,746	11.10
Not Hispanic (1,583)	1,712	10.88
Hispanic (15)	34	0.22
American Indian/Alaska Native (37)	99	0.63
Not Hispanic (25)	62	0.39
Hispanic (12)	37	0.24
Apache (0)	1	0.01
Blackfeet (1)	5	0.03
Cherokee (2)	18	0.11
Chippewa (1)	2	0.01
Choctaw (1)	1	0.01
Comanche (3)	3	0.02
Inupiat *(Alaska Native)* (1)	1	0.01
Iroquois (0)	1	0.01
Mexican American Ind. (8)	14	0.09
Pueblo (0)	1	0.01
Sioux (2)	3	0.02
South American Ind. (0)	1	0.01
Asian (152)	197	1.25
Not Hispanic (152)	197	1.25
Chinese, ex. Taiwanese (23)	27	0.17
Filipino (44)	55	0.35
Indian (24)	27	0.17
Japanese (7)	18	0.11
Korean (13)	18	0.11
Laotian (10)	10	0.06
Pakistani (4)	6	0.04
Thai (8)	12	0.08
Vietnamese (13)	13	0.08
Hawaii Native/Pacific Islander (6)	10	0.06
Not Hispanic (2)	5	0.03
Hispanic (4)	5	0.03
Guamanian/Chamorro (4)	7	0.04
Native Hawaiian (1)	2	0.01
White (13,193)	13,470	85.62
Not Hispanic (12,698)	12,900	81.99
Hispanic (495)	570	3.62

Dolton

Place Type: Village
County: Cook
Population: 23,153†

Ancestry‡	Population	%
African, Sub-Saharan (359)	359	1.54
African (225)	225	0.96
Nigerian (134)	134	0.57
American (578)	578	2.48
Austrian (9)	16	0.07
British (0)	8	0.03
Canadian (10)	10	0.04
Croatian (0)	10	0.04
Czech (0)	13	0.06
Czechoslovakian (0)	9	0.04
Danish (0)	14	0.06
Dutch (123)	165	0.71
English (106)	206	0.88
French, ex. Basque (0)	14	0.06
German (202)	383	1.64
Greek (7)	7	0.03
Hungarian (12)	18	0.08
Irish (45)	234	1.00
Italian (143)	206	0.88
Lithuanian (0)	29	0.12
Northern European (30)	30	0.13

*Notes: † The Census 2010 population figure is used to calculate the percentages in the Hispanic Origin and Race categories. Ancestry percentages are based on the 2006-2010 American Community Survey population (not shown); ‡ Numbers in parentheses indicate the number of people reporting a single ancestry; * Numbers in parentheses indicate the number of persons reporting this race alone, not in combination with any other race; Please refer to the Explanation of Data for more information.*

Norwegian (0)	9	0.04
Polish (143)	222	0.95
Scotch-Irish (0)	13	0.06
Scottish (0)	27	0.12
Serbian (12)	12	0.05
Slovak (0)	42	0.18
Slovene (0)	10	0.04
Swedish (8)	47	0.20
West Indian, ex. Hispanic (131)	162	0.69
Belizean (36)	36	0.15
Haitian (65)	65	0.28
Jamaican (30)	61	0.26

Hispanic Origin	Population	%
Hispanic or Latino (of any race)	622	2.69
Central American, ex. Mexican	15	0.06
Guatemalan	3	0.01
Honduran	2	0.01
Panamanian	5	0.02
Salvadoran	5	0.02
Cuban	11	0.05
Dominican Republic	7	0.03
Mexican	437	1.89
Puerto Rican	93	0.40
South American	5	0.02
Colombian	1	<0.01
Other South American	4	0.02
Other Hispanic or Latino	54	0.23

Race*	Population	%
African-American/Black (21,046)	21,318	92.07
Not Hispanic (20,932)	21,164	91.41
Hispanic (114)	154	0.67
American Indian/Alaska Native (28)	138	0.60
Not Hispanic (14)	121	0.52
Hispanic (14)	17	0.07
Apache (1)	1	<0.01
Blackfeet (0)	6	0.03
Cherokee (1)	37	0.16
Chippewa (0)	1	<0.01
Choctaw (0)	1	<0.01
Mexican American Ind. (2)	2	0.01
Asian (68)	117	0.51
Not Hispanic (68)	111	0.48
Hispanic (0)	6	0.03
Chinese, ex. Taiwanese (0)	4	0.02
Filipino (44)	64	0.28
Indian (9)	17	0.07
Japanese (5)	16	0.07
Korean (5)	10	0.04
Pakistani (0)	1	<0.01
Thai (1)	2	0.01
Hawaii Native/Pacific Islander (3)	14	0.06
Not Hispanic (3)	14	0.06
Samoan (0)	1	<0.01
White (1,438)	1,604	6.93
Not Hispanic (1,226)	1,376	5.94
Hispanic (212)	228	0.98

Downers Grove

Place Type: Village
County: DuPage
Population: 47,833†

Ancestry‡	Population	%
Afghan (16)	33	0.07
African, Sub-Saharan (28)	36	0.08
African (19)	27	0.06
Other Sub-Saharan African (9)	9	0.02
Albanian (13)	13	0.03
Alsatian (0)	16	0.03
American (1,140)	1,140	2.38
Arab (216)	327	0.68
Arab (136)	153	0.32
Iraqi (0)	12	0.03
Jordanian (35)	35	0.07
Lebanese (23)	93	0.19
Moroccan (12)	12	0.03
Palestinian (10)	10	0.02
Other Arab (0)	12	0.03
Armenian (13)	44	0.09
Austrian (71)	288	0.60
Belgian (32)	130	0.27
British (163)	414	0.86
Bulgarian (34)	34	0.07
Canadian (80)	142	0.30
Celtic (16)	16	0.03
Croatian (133)	446	0.93
Czech (688)	2,278	4.75
Czechoslovakian (134)	291	0.61
Danish (63)	482	1.01
Dutch (602)	1,495	3.12
Eastern European (37)	37	0.08
English (789)	4,164	8.69
European (375)	375	0.78
Finnish (0)	174	0.36
French, ex. Basque (85)	1,052	2.19
French Canadian (25)	226	0.47
German (2,946)	12,493	26.06
Greek (161)	613	1.28
Guyanese (82)	82	0.17
Hungarian (59)	311	0.65
Icelander (0)	12	0.03
Iranian (33)	33	0.07
Irish (2,632)	10,475	21.85
Israeli (0)	55	0.11
Italian (1,957)	6,577	13.72
Latvian (19)	19	0.04
Lithuanian (500)	865	1.80
Macedonian (125)	125	0.26
Northern European (0)	31	0.06
Norwegian (175)	821	1.71
Polish (2,613)	7,492	15.63
Portuguese (44)	44	0.09
Romanian (29)	76	0.16
Russian (129)	443	0.92
Scandinavian (79)	162	0.34
Scotch-Irish (173)	679	1.42
Scottish (181)	729	1.52
Serbian (94)	140	0.29
Slavic (12)	52	0.11
Slovak (199)	526	1.10
Slovene (73)	82	0.17
Swedish (461)	1,671	3.49
Swiss (17)	187	0.39
Ukrainian (210)	353	0.74
Welsh (42)	228	0.48
West Indian, ex. Hispanic (14)	14	0.03
Trinidadian/Tobagonian (14)	14	0.03
Yugoslavian (14)	38	0.08

Hispanic Origin	Population	%
Hispanic or Latino (of any race)	2,468	5.16
Central American, ex. Mexican	70	0.15
Costa Rican	8	0.02
Guatemalan	45	0.09
Honduran	1	<0.01
Nicaraguan	5	0.01
Panamanian	4	0.01
Salvadoran	4	0.01
Other Central American	3	0.01
Cuban	77	0.16
Dominican Republic	8	0.02
Mexican	1,771	3.70
Puerto Rican	243	0.51
South American	180	0.38
Argentinean	27	0.06
Bolivian	13	0.03
Chilean	27	0.06
Colombian	43	0.09
Ecuadorian	17	0.04
Paraguayan	2	<0.01
Peruvian	36	0.08
Uruguayan	1	<0.01
Venezuelan	13	0.03
Other South American	1	<0.01
Other Hispanic or Latino	119	0.25

Race*	Population	%
African-American/Black (1,424)	1,637	3.42
Not Hispanic (1,388)	1,568	3.28
Hispanic (36)	69	0.14
American Indian/Alaska Native (77)	204	0.43
Not Hispanic (37)	137	0.29
Hispanic (40)	67	0.14
Aleut *(Alaska Native)* (1)	1	<0.01
Apache (1)	3	0.01
Blackfeet (0)	5	0.01
Cherokee (8)	42	0.09
Cheyenne (0)	1	<0.01
Chickasaw (0)	1	<0.01
Chippewa (5)	12	0.03
Choctaw (5)	6	0.01
Creek (0)	3	0.01
Iroquois (4)	6	0.01
Mexican American Ind. (3)	8	0.02
Ottawa (0)	1	<0.01
Sioux (0)	6	0.01
South American Ind. (3)	5	0.01
Spanish American Ind. (0)	1	<0.01
Ute (1)	2	<0.01
Asian (2,635)	3,040	6.36
Not Hispanic (2,623)	3,006	6.28
Hispanic (12)	34	0.07
Bangladeshi (4)	4	0.01
Burmese (0)	5	0.01
Cambodian (5)	8	0.02
Chinese, ex. Taiwanese (503)	596	1.25
Filipino (537)	671	1.40
Hmong (2)	3	0.01
Indian (1,010)	1,075	2.25
Indonesian (1)	4	0.01
Japanese (49)	105	0.22
Korean (159)	186	0.39
Laotian (1)	2	<0.01
Malaysian (2)	3	0.01
Nepalese (1)	1	<0.01
Pakistani (124)	135	0.28
Sri Lankan (2)	3	0.01
Taiwanese (56)	59	0.12
Thai (24)	40	0.08
Vietnamese (86)	107	0.22
Hawaii Native/Pacific Islander (4)	34	0.07
Not Hispanic (4)	33	0.07
Hispanic (0)	1	<0.01
Guamanian/Chamorro (0)	2	<0.01
Native Hawaiian (3)	15	0.03
Samoan (0)	1	<0.01
White (42,356)	43,042	89.98
Not Hispanic (40,631)	41,185	86.10
Hispanic (1,725)	1,857	3.88

East Moline

Place Type: City
County: Rock Island
Population: 21,302†

Ancestry‡	Population	%
African, Sub-Saharan (482)	493	2.31
African (431)	442	2.07
Somalian (12)	12	0.06
Other Sub-Saharan African (39)	39	0.18
American (791)	791	3.70
Arab (204)	204	0.95
Arab (19)	19	0.09
Egyptian (13)	13	0.06
Moroccan (172)	172	0.80
Armenian (0)	82	0.38
Austrian (19)	98	0.46
Belgian (425)	816	3.82
British (0)	9	0.04
Canadian (14)	14	0.07
Croatian (28)	70	0.33
Czech (75)	134	0.63
Czechoslovakian (0)	9	0.04
Danish (34)	75	0.35

*Notes: † The Census 2010 population figure is used to calculate the percentages in the Hispanic Origin and Race categories. Ancestry percentages are based on the 2006-2010 American Community Survey population (not shown); ‡ Numbers in parentheses indicate the number of people reporting a single ancestry; * Numbers in parentheses indicate the number of persons reporting this race alone, not in combination with any other race; Please refer to the Explanation of Data for more information.*

Dutch (105)	326	1.53
Eastern European (47)	47	0.22
English (468)	1,466	6.86
European (73)	96	0.45
Finnish (0)	10	0.05
French, ex. Basque (194)	606	2.84
French Canadian (48)	88	0.41
German (1,756)	4,521	21.16
Greek (39)	77	0.36
Hungarian (0)	13	0.06
Irish (763)	2,384	11.16
Italian (259)	708	3.31
Lithuanian (0)	6	0.03
Luxemburger (11)	23	0.11
Northern European (9)	9	0.04
Norwegian (46)	175	0.82
Pennsylvania German (34)	34	0.16
Polish (48)	280	1.31
Russian (9)	25	0.12
Scandinavian (14)	84	0.39
Scotch-Irish (112)	253	1.18
Scottish (70)	250	1.17
Serbian (15)	30	0.14
Slovak (23)	35	0.16
Swedish (394)	1,274	5.96
Swiss (0)	19	0.09
Welsh (0)	113	0.53
Yugoslavian (0)	13	0.06

Hispanic Origin	Population	%
Hispanic or Latino (of any race)	4,050	19.01
Central American, ex. Mexican	41	0.19
Guatemalan	13	0.06
Honduran	19	0.09
Salvadoran	9	0.04
Cuban	19	0.09
Dominican Republic	2	0.01
Mexican	3,650	17.13
Puerto Rican	50	0.23
South American	18	0.08
Argentinean	2	0.01
Bolivian	3	0.01
Chilean	1	<0.01
Colombian	7	0.03
Ecuadorian	1	<0.01
Peruvian	1	<0.01
Venezuelan	3	0.01
Other Hispanic or Latino	270	1.27

Race*	Population	%
African-American/Black (2,730)	3,119	14.64
Not Hispanic (2,619)	2,925	13.73
Hispanic (111)	194	0.91
American Indian/Alaska Native (67)	205	0.96
Not Hispanic (37)	132	0.62
Hispanic (30)	73	0.34
Apache (3)	5	0.02
Blackfeet (0)	5	0.02
Cherokee (2)	51	0.24
Cheyenne (0)	2	0.01
Chippewa (2)	6	0.03
Choctaw (0)	3	0.01
Comanche (0)	1	<0.01
Creek (1)	1	<0.01
Lumbee (0)	1	<0.01
Mexican American Ind. (7)	15	0.07
Osage (0)	1	<0.01
Seminole (0)	1	<0.01
Sioux (4)	9	0.04
South American Ind. (0)	1	<0.01
Spanish American Ind. (1)	2	0.01
Tlingit-Haida *(Alaska Native)* (1)	1	<0.01
Yaqui (1)	2	0.01
Asian (433)	525	2.46
Not Hispanic (422)	496	2.33
Hispanic (11)	29	0.14
Burmese (34)	34	0.16
Cambodian (0)	3	0.01
Chinese, ex. Taiwanese (28)	45	0.21
Filipino (23)	41	0.19
Indian (197)	211	0.99
Japanese (5)	9	0.04
Korean (9)	19	0.09
Laotian (38)	49	0.23
Nepalese (8)	10	0.05
Pakistani (8)	8	0.04
Taiwanese (1)	1	<0.01
Thai (6)	11	0.05
Vietnamese (57)	72	0.34
Hawaii Native/Pacific Islander (14)	19	0.09
Not Hispanic (14)	19	0.09
Native Hawaiian (0)	3	0.01
Samoan (14)	14	0.07
White (15,534)	16,161	75.87
Not Hispanic (13,686)	14,108	66.23
Hispanic (1,848)	2,053	9.64

East Peoria

Place Type: City
County: Tazewell
Population: 23,402†

Ancestry‡	Population	%
American (4,226)	4,226	18.20
Arab (112)	224	0.96
Lebanese (112)	224	0.96
Austrian (2)	2	0.01
Belgian (34)	34	0.15
British (71)	99	0.43
Canadian (3)	76	0.33
Croatian (18)	51	0.22
Czech (32)	42	0.18
Danish (17)	110	0.47
Dutch (130)	445	1.92
English (995)	2,696	11.61
European (154)	210	0.90
Finnish (36)	68	0.29
French, ex. Basque (99)	767	3.30
French Canadian (0)	36	0.16
German (3,134)	7,043	30.33
Greek (4)	31	0.13
Hungarian (12)	60	0.26
Irish (834)	3,176	13.68
Italian (414)	782	3.37
Lithuanian (35)	38	0.16
Luxemburger (0)	13	0.06
Norwegian (121)	237	1.02
Pennsylvania German (0)	9	0.04
Polish (199)	364	1.57
Portuguese (29)	29	0.12
Romanian (12)	12	0.05
Russian (43)	65	0.28
Scotch-Irish (271)	628	2.70
Scottish (158)	584	2.51
Slovak (53)	53	0.23
Swedish (135)	445	1.92
Swiss (15)	123	0.53
Ukrainian (29)	58	0.25
Welsh (0)	72	0.31
Yugoslavian (14)	27	0.12

Hispanic Origin	Population	%
Hispanic or Latino (of any race)	517	2.21
Central American, ex. Mexican	26	0.11
Costa Rican	3	0.01
Guatemalan	4	0.02
Honduran	2	0.01
Nicaraguan	3	0.01
Panamanian	9	0.04
Salvadoran	5	0.02
Cuban	6	0.03
Mexican	372	1.59
Puerto Rican	50	0.21
South American	18	0.08
Argentinean	2	0.01
Bolivian	2	0.01
Chilean	1	<0.01
Colombian	3	0.01
Ecuadorian	5	0.02
Peruvian	5	0.02
Other Hispanic or Latino	45	0.19

Race*	Population	%
African-American/Black (236)	387	1.65
Not Hispanic (228)	377	1.61
Hispanic (8)	10	0.04
American Indian/Alaska Native (71)	212	0.91
Not Hispanic (53)	183	0.78
Hispanic (18)	29	0.12
Apache (0)	1	<0.01
Blackfeet (0)	4	0.02
Central American Ind. (1)	1	<0.01
Cherokee (14)	57	0.24
Chickasaw (0)	2	0.01
Chippewa (0)	6	0.03
Choctaw (1)	3	0.01
Comanche (1)	3	0.01
Inupiat *(Alaska Native)* (1)	1	<0.01
Iroquois (0)	6	0.03
Mexican American Ind. (4)	9	0.04
Potawatomi (8)	8	0.03
Seminole (2)	9	0.04
Sioux (2)	3	0.01
Tlingit-Haida *(Alaska Native)* (1)	1	<0.01
Tsimshian *(Alaska Native)* (0)	1	<0.01
Yup'ik *(Alaska Native)* (3)	3	0.01
Asian (239)	301	1.29
Not Hispanic (238)	295	1.26
Hispanic (1)	6	0.03
Cambodian (2)	3	0.01
Chinese, ex. Taiwanese (43)	48	0.21
Filipino (57)	81	0.35
Indian (60)	63	0.27
Japanese (5)	9	0.04
Korean (18)	33	0.14
Laotian (4)	7	0.03
Taiwanese (3)	3	0.01
Thai (1)	1	<0.01
Vietnamese (42)	44	0.19
Hawaii Native/Pacific Islander (8)	19	0.08
Not Hispanic (8)	15	0.06
Hispanic (0)	4	0.02
Native Hawaiian (7)	13	0.06
Samoan (1)	4	0.02
White (22,335)	22,724	97.10
Not Hispanic (21,985)	22,321	95.38
Hispanic (350)	403	1.72

East St. Louis

Place Type: City
County: St. Clair
Population: 27,006†

Ancestry‡	Population	%
African, Sub-Saharan (354)	484	1.74
African (354)	484	1.74
American (174)	174	0.63
English (22)	86	0.31
French, ex. Basque (0)	54	0.19
German (42)	79	0.28
Hungarian (0)	9	0.03
Irish (17)	105	0.38
Italian (0)	48	0.17
Lithuanian (6)	6	0.02
Norwegian (7)	7	0.03
Polish (67)	67	0.24
Scotch-Irish (18)	18	0.06
Scottish (0)	17	0.06
Swedish (0)	6	0.02
West Indian, ex. Hispanic (9)	9	0.03
West Indian (9)	9	0.03

Hispanic Origin	Population	%
Hispanic or Latino (of any race)	133	0.49
Central American, ex. Mexican	3	0.01
Guatemalan	1	<0.01
Nicaraguan	1	<0.01
Salvadoran	1	<0.01

*Notes: † The Census 2010 population figure is used to calculate the percentages in the Hispanic Origin and Race categories. Ancestry percentages are based on the 2006-2010 American Community Survey population (not shown); ‡ Numbers in parentheses indicate the number of people reporting a single ancestry; * Numbers in parentheses indicate the number of persons reporting this race alone, not in combination with any other race; Please refer to the Explanation of Data for more information.*

Cuban	8	0.03
Dominican Republic	5	0.02
Mexican	53	0.20
Puerto Rican	15	0.06
Other Hispanic or Latino	49	0.18

Race*	Population	%
African-American/Black (26,454)	26,665	98.74
Not Hispanic (26,378)	26,574	98.40
Hispanic (76)	91	0.34
American Indian/Alaska Native (28)	138	0.51
Not Hispanic (22)	126	0.47
Hispanic (6)	12	0.04
Arapaho (0)	1	<0.01
Blackfeet (0)	23	0.09
Cherokee (2)	30	0.11
Chickasaw (0)	2	0.01
Choctaw (1)	1	<0.01
Creek (0)	1	<0.01
Navajo (1)	1	<0.01
Seminole (0)	1	<0.01
Shoshone (0)	1	<0.01
Sioux (0)	4	0.01
Asian (26)	59	0.22
Not Hispanic (24)	57	0.21
Hispanic (2)	2	0.01
Chinese, ex. Taiwanese (8)	15	0.06
Filipino (4)	12	0.04
Indian (1)	18	0.07
Japanese (4)	7	0.03
Korean (1)	3	0.01
Laotian (0)	3	0.01
Vietnamese (2)	7	0.03
Hawaii Native/Pacific Islander (4)	18	0.07
Not Hispanic (3)	17	0.06
Hispanic (1)	1	<0.01
Guamanian/Chamorro (0)	5	0.02
Native Hawaiian (2)	10	0.04
Samoan (1)	2	0.01
White (241)	342	1.27
Not Hispanic (219)	319	1.18
Hispanic (22)	23	0.09

Edwardsville

Place Type: City
County: Madison
Population: 24,293†

Ancestry‡	Population	%
African, Sub-Saharan (176)	188	0.80
African (120)	120	0.51
Ghanaian (8)	8	0.03
Nigerian (24)	36	0.15
Other Sub-Saharan African (24)	24	0.10
American (1,067)	1,067	4.55
Arab (37)	37	0.16
Egyptian (15)	15	0.06
Jordanian (8)	8	0.03
Other Arab (14)	14	0.06
Austrian (40)	81	0.35
Belgian (9)	34	0.14
British (99)	146	0.62
Bulgarian (116)	129	0.55
Canadian (8)	31	0.13
Croatian (0)	32	0.14
Czech (134)	298	1.27
Czechoslovakian (46)	97	0.41
Danish (0)	78	0.33
Dutch (217)	597	2.55
English (779)	2,411	10.28
European (257)	277	1.18
French, ex. Basque (195)	680	2.90
French Canadian (61)	123	0.52
German (4,001)	8,531	36.38
Greek (56)	145	0.62
Hungarian (31)	96	0.41
Irish (1,110)	3,246	13.84
Italian (730)	1,391	5.93
Lithuanian (0)	65	0.28
Northern European (19)	19	0.08
Norwegian (96)	230	0.98
Polish (234)	773	3.30
Portuguese (0)	29	0.12
Romanian (29)	29	0.12
Russian (8)	75	0.32
Scandinavian (59)	59	0.25
Scotch-Irish (122)	390	1.66
Scottish (106)	337	1.44
Serbian (0)	8	0.03
Slovak (9)	31	0.13
Swedish (84)	566	2.41
Swiss (37)	151	0.64
Turkish (63)	76	0.32
Ukrainian (10)	25	0.11
Welsh (67)	197	0.84
Yugoslavian (47)	53	0.23

Hispanic Origin	Population	%
Hispanic or Latino (of any race)	473	1.95
Central American, ex. Mexican	38	0.16
Costa Rican	7	0.03
Guatemalan	15	0.06
Honduran	3	0.01
Nicaraguan	9	0.04
Panamanian	3	0.01
Salvadoran	1	<0.01
Cuban	22	0.09
Dominican Republic	5	0.02
Mexican	259	1.07
Puerto Rican	55	0.23
South American	38	0.16
Argentinean	6	0.02
Bolivian	2	0.01
Colombian	17	0.07
Ecuadorian	9	0.04
Peruvian	3	0.01
Other South American	1	<0.01
Other Hispanic or Latino	56	0.23

Race*	Population	%
African-American/Black (2,008)	2,247	9.25
Not Hispanic (1,983)	2,213	9.11
Hispanic (25)	34	0.14
American Indian/Alaska Native (43)	136	0.56
Not Hispanic (38)	122	0.50
Hispanic (5)	14	0.06
Apache (0)	6	0.02
Arapaho (0)	1	<0.01
Blackfeet (0)	6	0.02
Cherokee (11)	41	0.17
Chickasaw (1)	2	0.01
Chippewa (2)	5	0.02
Choctaw (6)	8	0.03
Comanche (0)	1	<0.01
Creek (0)	5	0.02
Iroquois (0)	1	<0.01
Kiowa (1)	1	<0.01
Mexican American Ind. (3)	3	0.01
Potawatomi (1)	1	<0.01
Shoshone (1)	2	0.01
Sioux (0)	3	0.01
South American Ind. (1)	2	0.01
Asian (586)	719	2.96
Not Hispanic (579)	709	2.92
Hispanic (7)	10	0.04
Bangladeshi (1)	1	<0.01
Burmese (4)	7	0.03
Chinese, ex. Taiwanese (123)	148	0.61
Filipino (46)	79	0.33
Indian (220)	230	0.95
Indonesian (1)	2	0.01
Japanese (15)	45	0.19
Korean (62)	82	0.34
Laotian (1)	1	<0.01
Malaysian (1)	2	0.01
Nepalese (3)	3	0.01
Pakistani (44)	46	0.19
Sri Lankan (3)	3	0.01
Taiwanese (7)	8	0.03
Thai (13)	19	0.08
Vietnamese (14)	20	0.08
Hawaii Native/Pacific Islander (19)	36	0.15
Not Hispanic (14)	31	0.13
Hispanic (5)	5	0.02
Guamanian/Chamorro (11)	15	0.06
Native Hawaiian (5)	12	0.05
Samoan (1)	3	0.01
White (21,055)	21,490	88.46
Not Hispanic (20,737)	21,144	87.04
Hispanic (318)	346	1.42

Effingham

Place Type: City
County: Effingham
Population: 12,328†

Ancestry‡	Population	%
Alsatian (0)	9	0.07
American (893)	893	7.39
Arab (34)	34	0.28
Egyptian (34)	34	0.28
Austrian (0)	26	0.22
British (37)	78	0.65
Canadian (91)	91	0.75
Dutch (0)	143	1.18
English (707)	1,228	10.17
European (96)	96	0.79
Finnish (0)	20	0.17
French, ex. Basque (102)	297	2.46
German (3,182)	4,645	38.46
Greek (7)	68	0.56
Hungarian (0)	19	0.16
Iranian (60)	74	0.61
Irish (323)	1,330	11.01
Italian (63)	159	1.32
Lithuanian (7)	7	0.06
Norwegian (17)	80	0.66
Polish (0)	124	1.03
Portuguese (0)	7	0.06
Scandinavian (0)	8	0.07
Scotch-Irish (159)	295	2.44
Scottish (75)	225	1.86
Swedish (72)	178	1.47
Swiss (0)	50	0.41

Hispanic Origin	Population	%
Hispanic or Latino (of any race)	398	3.23
Central American, ex. Mexican	19	0.15
Guatemalan	5	0.04
Honduran	4	0.03
Nicaraguan	5	0.04
Panamanian	4	0.03
Salvadoran	1	0.01
Cuban	4	0.03
Dominican Republic	2	0.02
Mexican	296	2.40
Puerto Rican	19	0.15
South American	15	0.12
Colombian	9	0.07
Ecuadorian	2	0.02
Peruvian	3	0.02
Venezuelan	1	0.01
Other Hispanic or Latino	43	0.35

Race*	Population	%
African-American/Black (47)	96	0.78
Not Hispanic (44)	89	0.72
Hispanic (3)	7	0.06
American Indian/Alaska Native (26)	59	0.48
Not Hispanic (13)	46	0.37
Hispanic (13)	13	0.11
Blackfeet (0)	1	0.01
Cherokee (5)	13	0.11
Chippewa (0)	1	0.01
Choctaw (1)	1	0.01
Delaware (0)	1	0.01
Kiowa (3)	3	0.02
Tsimshian *(Alaska Native)* (1)	1	0.01

*Notes: † The Census 2010 population figure is used to calculate the percentages in the Hispanic Origin and Race categories. Ancestry percentages are based on the 2006-2010 American Community Survey population (not shown); ‡ Numbers in parentheses indicate the number of people reporting a single ancestry; * Numbers in parentheses indicate the number of persons reporting this race alone, not in combination with any other race; Please refer to the Explanation of Data for more information.*

Asian (89)	117	0.95
Not Hispanic (89)	116	0.94
Hispanic (0)	1	0.01
Chinese, ex. Taiwanese (2)	6	0.05
Filipino (11)	16	0.13
Indian (42)	50	0.41
Japanese (3)	5	0.04
Korean (6)	12	0.10
Pakistani (9)	11	0.09
Sri Lankan (2)	2	0.02
Taiwanese (0)	3	0.02
Vietnamese (9)	15	0.12
Hawaii Native/Pacific Islander (6)	15	0.12
Not Hispanic (6)	13	0.11
Hispanic (0)	2	0.02
Guamanian/Chamorro (1)	5	0.04
Native Hawaiian (5)	6	0.05
White (11,838)	11,950	96.93
Not Hispanic (11,668)	11,761	95.40
Hispanic (170)	189	1.53

Elgin

Place Type: City
County: Kane
Population: 108,188†

Ancestry‡	Population	%
African, Sub-Saharan (278)	351	0.33
African (118)	191	0.18
Ethiopian (130)	130	0.12
Nigerian (28)	28	0.03
Other Sub-Saharan African (2)	2	<0.01
American (1,704)	1,704	1.59
Arab (173)	301	0.28
Arab (0)	16	0.01
Egyptian (22)	45	0.04
Lebanese (50)	139	0.13
Syrian (91)	91	0.09
Other Arab (10)	10	0.01
Armenian (89)	89	0.08
Assyrian/Chaldean/Syriac (220)	263	0.25
Australian (0)	12	0.01
Austrian (175)	316	0.30
Basque (45)	58	0.05
Belgian (22)	201	0.19
Brazilian (15)	23	0.02
British (76)	269	0.25
Bulgarian (30)	30	0.03
Canadian (75)	130	0.12
Croatian (57)	189	0.18
Czech (268)	969	0.91
Czechoslovakian (74)	83	0.08
Danish (21)	477	0.45
Dutch (117)	950	0.89
Eastern European (24)	57	0.05
English (888)	5,690	5.33
European (531)	573	0.54
Finnish (21)	131	0.12
French, ex. Basque (129)	2,594	2.43
French Canadian (111)	254	0.24
German (5,227)	20,264	18.97
Greek (219)	551	0.52
Hungarian (151)	544	0.51
Icelander (0)	18	0.02
Irish (1,667)	9,498	8.89
Israeli (35)	35	0.03
Italian (2,051)	6,096	5.71
Latvian (0)	42	0.04
Lithuanian (81)	209	0.20
Luxemburger (25)	106	0.10
Macedonian (0)	24	0.02
Northern European (19)	19	0.02
Norwegian (328)	1,798	1.68
Pennsylvania German (24)	39	0.04
Polish (2,146)	6,145	5.75
Portuguese (0)	17	0.02
Romanian (0)	62	0.06
Russian (190)	606	0.57
Scandinavian (77)	294	0.28
Scotch-Irish (259)	1,228	1.15
Scottish (365)	1,285	1.20
Serbian (65)	87	0.08
Slovak (36)	113	0.11
Slovene (11)	22	0.02
Swedish (278)	2,441	2.28
Swiss (61)	450	0.42
Turkish (0)	9	0.01
Ukrainian (108)	230	0.22
Welsh (68)	340	0.32
West Indian, ex. Hispanic (31)	31	0.03
Jamaican (17)	17	0.02
West Indian (14)	14	0.01
Yugoslavian (31)	31	0.03

Hispanic Origin	Population	%
Hispanic or Latino (of any race)	47,121	43.55
Central American, ex. Mexican	888	0.82
Costa Rican	15	0.01
Guatemalan	356	0.33
Honduran	87	0.08
Nicaraguan	20	0.02
Panamanian	21	0.02
Salvadoran	387	0.36
Other Central American	2	<0.01
Cuban	204	0.19
Dominican Republic	66	0.06
Mexican	41,265	38.14
Puerto Rican	2,973	2.75
South American	637	0.59
Argentinean	30	0.03
Bolivian	11	0.01
Chilean	27	0.02
Colombian	253	0.23
Ecuadorian	152	0.14
Peruvian	117	0.11
Uruguayan	3	<0.01
Venezuelan	41	0.04
Other South American	3	<0.01
Other Hispanic or Latino	1,088	1.01

Race*	Population	%
African-American/Black (7,982)	9,269	8.57
Not Hispanic (7,467)	8,299	7.67
Hispanic (515)	970	0.90
American Indian/Alaska Native (1,468)	2,220	2.05
Not Hispanic (144)	405	0.37
Hispanic (1,324)	1,815	1.68
Apache (12)	14	0.01
Blackfeet (1)	16	0.01
Canadian/French Am. Ind. (1)	5	<0.01
Central American Ind. (4)	4	<0.01
Cherokee (23)	101	0.09
Chippewa (14)	30	0.03
Choctaw (8)	11	0.01
Cree (3)	3	<0.01
Creek (1)	8	0.01
Crow (0)	2	<0.01
Inupiat *(Alaska Native)* (0)	1	<0.01
Iroquois (3)	10	0.01
Kiowa (1)	3	<0.01
Lumbee (2)	3	<0.01
Menominee (2)	5	<0.01
Mexican American Ind. (245)	292	0.27
Navajo (4)	6	0.01
Osage (0)	7	0.01
Ottawa (3)	5	<0.01
Paiute (3)	3	<0.01
Pima (0)	1	<0.01
Potawatomi (2)	14	0.01
Seminole (3)	9	0.01
Sioux (11)	32	0.03
South American Ind. (11)	35	0.03
Spanish American Ind. (16)	18	0.02
Tohono O'Odham (1)	2	<0.01
Asian (5,809)	6,551	6.06
Not Hispanic (5,675)	6,250	5.78
Hispanic (134)	301	0.28
Burmese (10)	13	0.01
Cambodian (57)	72	0.07
Chinese, ex. Taiwanese (338)	492	0.45
Filipino (1,453)	1,699	1.57
Hmong (19)	20	0.02
Indian (1,425)	1,559	1.44
Indonesian (7)	15	0.01
Japanese (97)	164	0.15
Korean (181)	260	0.24
Laotian (1,304)	1,445	1.34
Malaysian (4)	14	0.01
Nepalese (7)	7	0.01
Pakistani (267)	301	0.28
Sri Lankan (1)	1	<0.01
Taiwanese (13)	16	0.01
Thai (85)	109	0.10
Vietnamese (275)	320	0.30
Hawaii Native/Pacific Islander (37)	139	0.13
Not Hispanic (19)	71	0.07
Hispanic (18)	68	0.06
Fijian (1)	1	<0.01
Guamanian/Chamorro (1)	13	0.01
Marshallese (1)	1	<0.01
Native Hawaiian (9)	31	0.03
Samoan (13)	22	0.02
White (71,347)	74,584	68.94
Not Hispanic (46,089)	47,429	43.84
Hispanic (25,258)	27,155	25.10

Elk Grove Village

Place Type: Village
County: Cook
Population: 33,127†

Ancestry‡	Population	%
Alsatian (0)	54	0.16
American (595)	595	1.80
Arab (70)	142	0.43
Arab (0)	18	0.05
Iraqi (38)	38	0.11
Syrian (32)	86	0.26
Assyrian/Chaldean/Syriac (108)	125	0.38
Austrian (32)	182	0.55
Belgian (34)	120	0.36
British (62)	62	0.19
Bulgarian (90)	141	0.43
Canadian (58)	90	0.27
Croatian (49)	117	0.35
Czech (69)	571	1.73
Czechoslovakian (40)	65	0.20
Danish (40)	215	0.65
Dutch (100)	275	0.83
Eastern European (9)	9	0.03
English (326)	1,747	5.28
European (109)	109	0.33
Finnish (0)	11	0.03
French, ex. Basque (54)	627	1.90
French Canadian (26)	69	0.21
German (1,541)	7,531	22.77
Greek (191)	523	1.58
Hungarian (9)	117	0.35
Icelander (13)	13	0.04
Iranian (64)	64	0.19
Irish (1,074)	5,895	17.82
Italian (1,702)	4,666	14.11
Latvian (79)	162	0.49
Lithuanian (109)	268	0.81
Luxemburger (10)	80	0.24
Northern European (17)	17	0.05
Norwegian (119)	732	2.21
Pennsylvania German (24)	24	0.07
Polish (3,751)	6,843	20.69
Portuguese (11)	11	0.03
Romanian (233)	248	0.75
Russian (141)	416	1.26
Scandinavian (7)	17	0.05
Scotch-Irish (146)	286	0.86
Scottish (32)	265	0.80
Serbian (67)	76	0.23
Slovak (72)	72	0.22
Swedish (259)	1,200	3.63

*Notes: † The Census 2010 population figure is used to calculate the percentages in the Hispanic Origin and Race categories. Ancestry percentages are based on the 2006-2010 American Community Survey population (not shown); ‡ Numbers in parentheses indicate the number of people reporting a single ancestry; * Numbers in parentheses indicate the number of persons reporting this race alone, not in combination with any other race; Please refer to the Explanation of Data for more information.*

Swiss (11)	60	0.18
Turkish (0)	20	0.06
Ukrainian (61)	115	0.35
Welsh (70)	175	0.53
West Indian, ex. Hispanic (66)	66	0.20
Belizean (24)	24	0.07
Trinidadian/Tobagonian (42)	42	0.13
Yugoslavian (0)	7	0.02

Hispanic Origin	Population	%
Hispanic or Latino (of any race)	3,149	9.51
Central American, ex. Mexican	126	0.38
Costa Rican	1	<0.01
Guatemalan	55	0.17
Honduran	20	0.06
Nicaraguan	6	0.02
Panamanian	11	0.03
Salvadoran	26	0.08
Other Central American	7	0.02
Cuban	54	0.16
Dominican Republic	16	0.05
Mexican	2,252	6.80
Puerto Rican	312	0.94
South American	238	0.72
Argentinean	26	0.08
Bolivian	4	0.01
Chilean	15	0.05
Colombian	67	0.20
Ecuadorian	82	0.25
Paraguayan	1	<0.01
Peruvian	37	0.11
Uruguayan	3	0.01
Venezuelan	2	0.01
Other South American	1	<0.01
Other Hispanic or Latino	151	0.46

Race*	Population	%
African-American/Black (472)	594	1.79
Not Hispanic (449)	552	1.67
Hispanic (23)	42	0.13
American Indian/Alaska Native (100)	188	0.57
Not Hispanic (44)	112	0.34
Hispanic (56)	76	0.23
Apache (3)	5	0.02
Blackfeet (2)	7	0.02
Canadian/French Am. Ind. (0)	1	<0.01
Cherokee (10)	30	0.09
Cheyenne (0)	1	<0.01
Chippewa (10)	12	0.04
Creek (0)	6	0.02
Hopi (3)	3	0.01
Iroquois (2)	4	0.01
Menominee (1)	1	<0.01
Mexican American Ind. (14)	21	0.06
Navajo (1)	3	0.01
Ottawa (1)	1	<0.01
Seminole (1)	1	<0.01
Sioux (0)	1	<0.01
Spanish American Ind. (0)	1	<0.01
Yaqui (0)	2	0.01
Asian (3,348)	3,704	11.18
Not Hispanic (3,327)	3,652	11.02
Hispanic (21)	52	0.16
Burmese (1)	2	0.01
Cambodian (5)	5	0.02
Chinese, ex. Taiwanese (308)	376	1.14
Filipino (508)	610	1.84
Hmong (1)	1	<0.01
Indian (1,422)	1,494	4.51
Indonesian (4)	4	0.01
Japanese (512)	589	1.78
Korean (332)	371	1.12
Nepalese (7)	7	0.02
Pakistani (67)	78	0.24
Sri Lankan (2)	2	0.01
Taiwanese (50)	52	0.16
Thai (21)	35	0.11
Vietnamese (25)	36	0.11
Hawaii Native/Pacific Islander (4)	26	0.08
Not Hispanic (4)	24	0.07
Hispanic (0)	2	0.01
Guamanian/Chamorro (0)	3	0.01
Native Hawaiian (3)	11	0.03
Samoan (0)	1	<0.01
Tongan (1)	1	<0.01
White (27,464)	27,963	84.41
Not Hispanic (25,671)	26,018	78.54
Hispanic (1,793)	1,945	5.87

Elmhurst

Place Type: City
County: DuPage
Population: 44,121†

Ancestry‡	Population	%
African, Sub-Saharan (40)	59	0.13
South African (0)	19	0.04
Other Sub-Saharan African (40)	40	0.09
Albanian (129)	129	0.29
American (1,025)	1,025	2.34
Arab (234)	311	0.71
Arab (0)	9	0.02
Egyptian (31)	31	0.07
Jordanian (48)	48	0.11
Lebanese (24)	33	0.08
Syrian (0)	59	0.13
Other Arab (131)	131	0.30
Armenian (0)	12	0.03
Assyrian/Chaldean/Syriac (0)	48	0.11
Australian (0)	12	0.03
Austrian (33)	204	0.47
Belgian (24)	89	0.20
Brazilian (13)	21	0.05
British (306)	637	1.46
Bulgarian (40)	60	0.14
Canadian (11)	18	0.04
Croatian (100)	265	0.61
Czech (391)	971	2.22
Czechoslovakian (17)	83	0.19
Danish (55)	364	0.83
Dutch (329)	941	2.15
Eastern European (74)	94	0.21
English (495)	2,576	5.89
Estonian (0)	21	0.05
European (196)	219	0.50
Finnish (11)	58	0.13
French, ex. Basque (89)	952	2.18
French Canadian (43)	134	0.31
German (3,449)	13,126	30.00
Greek (378)	791	1.81
Guyanese (79)	79	0.18
Hungarian (61)	269	0.61
Irish (3,491)	10,849	24.80
Italian (2,275)	6,915	15.80
Latvian (80)	137	0.31
Lithuanian (162)	437	1.00
Luxemburger (0)	129	0.29
Northern European (35)	35	0.08
Norwegian (340)	1,153	2.64
Polish (1,792)	5,039	11.52
Portuguese (33)	111	0.25
Romanian (185)	200	0.46
Russian (246)	610	1.39
Scandinavian (74)	87	0.20
Scotch-Irish (131)	657	1.50
Scottish (165)	667	1.52
Serbian (105)	143	0.33
Slavic (0)	7	0.02
Slovak (66)	263	0.60
Slovene (15)	135	0.31
Swedish (312)	1,699	3.88
Swiss (27)	142	0.32
Ukrainian (131)	356	0.81
Welsh (10)	79	0.18
West Indian, ex. Hispanic (15)	15	0.03
Haitian (15)	15	0.03
Yugoslavian (57)	76	0.17

Hispanic Origin	Population	%
Hispanic or Latino (of any race)	2,898	6.57
Central American, ex. Mexican	190	0.43
Costa Rican	10	0.02
Guatemalan	156	0.35
Honduran	7	0.02
Nicaraguan	1	<0.01
Panamanian	9	0.02
Salvadoran	5	0.01
Other Central American	2	<0.01
Cuban	174	0.39
Dominican Republic	8	0.02
Mexican	1,829	4.15
Puerto Rican	344	0.78
South American	217	0.49
Argentinean	13	0.03
Bolivian	28	0.06
Chilean	5	0.01
Colombian	55	0.12
Ecuadorian	39	0.09
Paraguayan	7	0.02
Peruvian	53	0.12
Uruguayan	2	<0.01
Venezuelan	15	0.03
Other Hispanic or Latino	136	0.31

Race*	Population	%
African-American/Black (841)	1,002	2.27
Not Hispanic (815)	950	2.15
Hispanic (26)	52	0.12
American Indian/Alaska Native (53)	160	0.36
Not Hispanic (27)	104	0.24
Hispanic (26)	56	0.13
Aleut *(Alaska Native)* (2)	2	<0.01
Apache (0)	2	<0.01
Cherokee (1)	21	0.05
Chickasaw (0)	1	<0.01
Chippewa (2)	9	0.02
Choctaw (1)	3	0.01
Comanche (1)	1	<0.01
Creek (0)	1	<0.01
Delaware (1)	2	<0.01
Hopi (0)	1	<0.01
Houma (1)	1	<0.01
Iroquois (0)	1	<0.01
Menominee (4)	8	0.02
Mexican American Ind. (7)	11	0.02
Seminole (0)	1	<0.01
Sioux (1)	2	<0.01
South American Ind. (5)	15	0.03
Ute (0)	1	<0.01
Yaqui (0)	2	<0.01
Asian (2,272)	2,642	5.99
Not Hispanic (2,244)	2,583	5.85
Hispanic (28)	59	0.13
Bangladeshi (1)	1	<0.01
Burmese (2)	5	0.01
Chinese, ex. Taiwanese (252)	337	0.76
Filipino (322)	431	0.98
Indian (1,244)	1,351	3.06
Indonesian (1)	1	<0.01
Japanese (53)	93	0.21
Korean (127)	156	0.35
Laotian (1)	4	0.01
Malaysian (2)	12	0.03
Nepalese (8)	8	0.02
Pakistani (75)	94	0.21
Sri Lankan (4)	5	0.01
Taiwanese (37)	49	0.11
Thai (14)	24	0.05
Vietnamese (44)	57	0.13
Hawaii Native/Pacific Islander (5)	24	0.05
Not Hispanic (4)	21	0.05
Hispanic (1)	3	0.01
Guamanian/Chamorro (3)	4	0.01
Native Hawaiian (2)	10	0.02
White (39,478)	40,094	90.87
Not Hispanic (37,549)	38,026	86.19
Hispanic (1,929)	2,068	4.69

*Notes: † The Census 2010 population figure is used to calculate the percentages in the Hispanic Origin and Race categories. Ancestry percentages are based on the 2006-2010 American Community Survey population (not shown); ‡ Numbers in parentheses indicate the number of people reporting a single ancestry; * Numbers in parentheses indicate the number of persons reporting this race alone, not in combination with any other race; Please refer to the Explanation of Data for more information.*

Elmwood Park

Place Type: Village
County: Cook
Population: 24,883†

Ancestry‡	Population	%
African, Sub-Saharan (0)	9	0.04
African (0)	9	0.04
Albanian (89)	89	0.36
American (594)	594	2.40
Arab (282)	290	1.17
Jordanian (33)	33	0.13
Palestinian (145)	145	0.59
Syrian (0)	8	0.03
Other Arab (104)	104	0.42
Assyrian/Chaldean/Syriac (40)	58	0.23
Austrian (24)	162	0.66
Belgian (22)	38	0.15
Brazilian (10)	20	0.08
Bulgarian (35)	35	0.14
Croatian (131)	168	0.68
Czech (164)	348	1.41
Czechoslovakian (0)	10	0.04
Danish (11)	87	0.35
Dutch (31)	110	0.45
English (53)	785	3.18
European (44)	57	0.23
Finnish (12)	49	0.20
French, ex. Basque (100)	318	1.29
French Canadian (0)	82	0.33
German (686)	3,126	12.65
Greek (571)	740	2.99
Hungarian (81)	132	0.53
Irish (860)	3,118	12.62
Italian (3,908)	5,806	23.50
Lithuanian (0)	111	0.45
Norwegian (88)	266	1.08
Polish (4,543)	5,916	23.94
Romanian (50)	61	0.25
Russian (78)	179	0.72
Scotch-Irish (29)	119	0.48
Scottish (53)	237	0.96
Serbian (0)	11	0.04
Slavic (24)	36	0.15
Slovak (46)	82	0.33
Swedish (55)	371	1.50
Swiss (0)	38	0.15
Ukrainian (347)	503	2.04
Welsh (10)	62	0.25
West Indian, ex. Hispanic (0)	9	0.04
Barbadian (0)	9	0.04
Yugoslavian (0)	10	0.04

Hispanic Origin	Population	%
Hispanic or Latino (of any race)	5,729	23.02
Central American, ex. Mexican	359	1.44
Costa Rican	11	0.04
Guatemalan	219	0.88
Honduran	39	0.16
Nicaraguan	17	0.07
Panamanian	14	0.06
Salvadoran	53	0.21
Other Central American	6	0.02
Cuban	82	0.33
Dominican Republic	38	0.15
Mexican	2,840	11.41
Puerto Rican	1,735	6.97
South American	489	1.97
Argentinean	81	0.33
Bolivian	8	0.03
Chilean	10	0.04
Colombian	142	0.57
Ecuadorian	137	0.55
Peruvian	77	0.31
Uruguayan	6	0.02
Venezuelan	26	0.10
Other South American	2	0.01
Other Hispanic or Latino	186	0.75

Race*	Population	%
African-American/Black (481)	600	2.41
Not Hispanic (398)	460	1.85
Hispanic (83)	140	0.56
American Indian/Alaska Native (70)	137	0.55
Not Hispanic (24)	53	0.21
Hispanic (46)	84	0.34
Apache (2)	2	0.01
Blackfeet (0)	2	0.01
Central American Ind. (0)	2	0.01
Cherokee (1)	8	0.03
Chickasaw (3)	3	0.01
Chippewa (4)	6	0.02
Comanche (0)	1	<0.01
Iroquois (3)	7	0.03
Lumbee (1)	1	<0.01
Mexican American Ind. (12)	12	0.05
Navajo (1)	6	0.02
Potawatomi (0)	2	0.01
South American Ind. (1)	5	0.02
Spanish American Ind. (1)	2	0.01
Asian (579)	714	2.87
Not Hispanic (570)	666	2.68
Hispanic (9)	48	0.19
Burmese (0)	1	<0.01
Cambodian (0)	4	0.02
Chinese, ex. Taiwanese (38)	49	0.20
Filipino (358)	424	1.70
Indian (81)	102	0.41
Indonesian (4)	4	0.02
Japanese (19)	22	0.09
Korean (28)	35	0.14
Laotian (2)	2	0.01
Pakistani (4)	4	0.02
Sri Lankan (1)	1	<0.01
Taiwanese (5)	5	0.02
Thai (13)	19	0.08
Vietnamese (13)	17	0.07
Hawaii Native/Pacific Islander (5)	36	0.14
Not Hispanic (1)	24	0.10
Hispanic (4)	12	0.05
Guamanian/Chamorro (3)	5	0.02
Native Hawaiian (1)	6	0.02
White (21,102)	21,580	86.73
Not Hispanic (17,929)	18,119	72.82
Hispanic (3,173)	3,461	13.91

Evanston

Place Type: City
County: Cook
Population: 74,486†

Ancestry‡	Population	%
African, Sub-Saharan (579)	686	0.93
African (347)	430	0.58
Ethiopian (11)	11	0.01
Nigerian (120)	130	0.18
South African (27)	27	0.04
Ugandan (27)	41	0.06
Other Sub-Saharan African (47)	47	0.06
American (2,009)	2,009	2.72
Arab (153)	375	0.51
Arab (20)	37	0.05
Egyptian (44)	44	0.06
Iraqi (0)	14	0.02
Lebanese (59)	178	0.24
Moroccan (17)	17	0.02
Palestinian (0)	17	0.02
Syrian (13)	42	0.06
Other Arab (0)	26	0.04
Armenian (89)	174	0.24
Assyrian/Chaldean/Syriac (29)	54	0.07
Australian (22)	35	0.05
Austrian (75)	528	0.71
Basque (14)	14	0.02
Belgian (51)	369	0.50
Brazilian (47)	118	0.16
British (205)	732	0.99
Bulgarian (55)	84	0.11
Canadian (98)	169	0.23
Croatian (68)	135	0.18
Czech (139)	631	0.85
Czechoslovakian (25)	79	0.11
Danish (35)	343	0.46
Dutch (304)	1,150	1.56
Eastern European (787)	854	1.16
English (1,009)	6,226	8.43
Estonian (60)	73	0.10
European (1,341)	1,549	2.10
Finnish (0)	97	0.13
French, ex. Basque (179)	1,878	2.54
French Canadian (109)	286	0.39
German (2,850)	12,775	17.29
German Russian (0)	62	0.08
Greek (310)	886	1.20
Hungarian (198)	576	0.78
Icelander (0)	11	0.01
Iranian (58)	86	0.12
Irish (2,111)	9,193	12.44
Israeli (99)	129	0.17
Italian (896)	3,687	4.99
Latvian (11)	86	0.12
Lithuanian (99)	524	0.71
Luxemburger (82)	132	0.18
Macedonian (0)	23	0.03
New Zealander (0)	15	0.02
Northern European (97)	181	0.24
Norwegian (357)	1,725	2.33
Polish (1,266)	4,765	6.45
Portuguese (34)	112	0.15
Romanian (362)	499	0.68
Russian (1,325)	3,244	4.39
Scandinavian (83)	122	0.17
Scotch-Irish (541)	1,417	1.92
Scottish (394)	1,848	2.50
Serbian (92)	101	0.14
Slavic (28)	53	0.07
Slovak (64)	247	0.33
Slovene (14)	137	0.19
Soviet Union (0)	14	0.02
Swedish (491)	2,448	3.31
Swiss (72)	388	0.53
Turkish (141)	152	0.21
Ukrainian (147)	547	0.74
Welsh (77)	501	0.68
West Indian, ex. Hispanic (1,938)	2,476	3.35
Bahamian (8)	44	0.06
Belizean (318)	358	0.48
British West Indian (0)	25	0.03
Haitian (551)	781	1.06
Jamaican (1,029)	1,181	1.60
West Indian (32)	87	0.12
Yugoslavian (15)	52	0.07

Hispanic Origin	Population	%
Hispanic or Latino (of any race)	6,739	9.05
Central American, ex. Mexican	438	0.59
Costa Rican	24	0.03
Guatemalan	181	0.24
Honduran	33	0.04
Nicaraguan	30	0.04
Panamanian	52	0.07
Salvadoran	108	0.14
Other Central American	10	0.01
Cuban	278	0.37
Dominican Republic	59	0.08
Mexican	4,310	5.79
Puerto Rican	483	0.65
South American	708	0.95
Argentinean	134	0.18
Bolivian	22	0.03
Chilean	81	0.11
Colombian	179	0.24
Ecuadorian	94	0.13
Paraguayan	8	0.01
Peruvian	103	0.14
Uruguayan	12	0.02
Venezuelan	63	0.08

*Notes: † The Census 2010 population figure is used to calculate the percentages in the Hispanic Origin and Race categories. Ancestry percentages are based on the 2006-2010 American Community Survey population (not shown); ‡ Numbers in parentheses indicate the number of people reporting a single ancestry; * Numbers in parentheses indicate the number of persons reporting this race alone, not in combination with any other race; Please refer to the Explanation of Data for more information.*

Other South American	12	0.02
Other Hispanic or Latino	463	0.62

Race*	Population	%
African-American/Black (13,474)	14,878	19.97
Not Hispanic (13,139)	14,338	19.25
Hispanic (335)	540	0.72
American Indian/Alaska Native (175)	671	0.90
Not Hispanic (96)	486	0.65
Hispanic (79)	185	0.25
Apache (3)	12	0.02
Arapaho (1)	1	<0.01
Blackfeet (0)	25	0.03
Canadian/French Am. Ind. (0)	3	<0.01
Central American Ind. (1)	6	0.01
Cherokee (13)	131	0.18
Chickasaw (1)	6	0.01
Chippewa (3)	16	0.02
Choctaw (1)	25	0.03
Cree (4)	4	0.01
Creek (0)	1	<0.01
Delaware (1)	2	<0.01
Hopi (0)	2	<0.01
Iroquois (0)	12	0.02
Lumbee (0)	2	<0.01
Menominee (1)	1	<0.01
Mexican American Ind. (29)	54	0.07
Navajo (1)	3	<0.01
Ottawa (0)	3	<0.01
Potawatomi (1)	1	<0.01
Pueblo (1)	4	0.01
Seminole (0)	11	0.01
Shoshone (0)	1	<0.01
Sioux (5)	13	0.02
South American Ind. (3)	13	0.02
Spanish American Ind. (0)	2	<0.01
Tlingit-Haida *(Alaska Native)* (1)	4	0.01
Tohono O'Odham (1)	1	<0.01
Ute (1)	2	<0.01
Yaqui (2)	3	<0.01
Asian (6,416)	7,576	10.17
Not Hispanic (6,355)	7,436	9.98
Hispanic (61)	140	0.19
Bangladeshi (19)	20	0.03
Bhutanese (5)	5	0.01
Burmese (2)	2	<0.01
Cambodian (9)	17	0.02
Chinese, ex. Taiwanese (1,981)	2,322	3.12
Filipino (496)	748	1.00
Hmong (2)	2	<0.01
Indian (1,467)	1,678	2.25
Indonesian (17)	26	0.03
Japanese (341)	560	0.75
Korean (1,100)	1,239	1.66
Laotian (4)	6	0.01
Malaysian (7)	20	0.03
Nepalese (10)	10	0.01
Pakistani (197)	245	0.33
Sri Lankan (6)	6	0.01
Taiwanese (252)	290	0.39
Thai (102)	138	0.19
Vietnamese (124)	159	0.21
Hawaii Native/Pacific Islander (16)	106	0.14
Not Hispanic (13)	95	0.13
Hispanic (3)	11	0.01
Fijian (1)	2	<0.01
Guamanian/Chamorro (5)	8	0.01
Native Hawaiian (5)	32	0.04
Samoan (1)	3	<0.01
White (48,872)	51,233	68.78
Not Hispanic (45,551)	47,492	63.76
Hispanic (3,321)	3,741	5.02

Evergreen Park

Place Type: Village
County: Cook
Population: 19,852†

Ancestry‡	Population	%
African, Sub-Saharan (186)	228	1.15
African (117)	159	0.80
Nigerian (69)	69	0.35
American (209)	209	1.05
Arab (55)	154	0.78
Arab (20)	71	0.36
Jordanian (6)	6	0.03
Other Arab (29)	77	0.39
Austrian (51)	119	0.60
Belgian (0)	18	0.09
British (32)	56	0.28
Canadian (0)	20	0.10
Croatian (106)	223	1.13
Czech (31)	239	1.21
Czechoslovakian (29)	37	0.19
Danish (0)	11	0.06
Dutch (238)	604	3.05
English (151)	988	4.99
European (51)	51	0.26
Finnish (21)	21	0.11
French, ex. Basque (0)	372	1.88
French Canadian (13)	95	0.48
German (879)	3,932	19.84
Greek (78)	234	1.18
Hungarian (0)	62	0.31
Irish (2,181)	5,839	29.47
Italian (393)	2,029	10.24
Lithuanian (192)	476	2.40
Luxemburger (0)	6	0.03
Norwegian (11)	126	0.64
Polish (624)	1,816	9.16
Romanian (78)	78	0.39
Russian (9)	73	0.37
Scandinavian (10)	32	0.16
Scotch-Irish (87)	193	0.97
Scottish (18)	136	0.69
Serbian (9)	9	0.05
Slovak (65)	142	0.72
Swedish (47)	464	2.34
Swiss (8)	52	0.26
Ukrainian (49)	71	0.36
Welsh (12)	135	0.68
West Indian, ex. Hispanic (44)	130	0.66
Jamaican (44)	130	0.66
Yugoslavian (12)	21	0.11

Hispanic Origin	Population	%
Hispanic or Latino (of any race)	2,035	10.25
Central American, ex. Mexican	33	0.17
Guatemalan	13	0.07
Honduran	2	0.01
Nicaraguan	5	0.03
Panamanian	2	0.01
Salvadoran	11	0.06
Cuban	22	0.11
Dominican Republic	12	0.06
Mexican	1,631	8.22
Puerto Rican	226	1.14
South American	31	0.16
Argentinean	10	0.05
Bolivian	1	0.01
Colombian	7	0.04
Ecuadorian	5	0.03
Paraguayan	3	0.02
Peruvian	4	0.02
Uruguayan	1	0.01
Other Hispanic or Latino	80	0.40

Race*	Population	%
African-American/Black (3,704)	3,868	19.48
Not Hispanic (3,651)	3,786	19.07
Hispanic (53)	82	0.41
American Indian/Alaska Native (48)	140	0.71
Not Hispanic (33)	112	0.56
Hispanic (15)	28	0.14
Apache (0)	1	0.01
Arapaho (0)	1	0.01
Cherokee (0)	26	0.13
Chippewa (4)	7	0.04
Choctaw (0)	8	0.04
Iroquois (0)	1	0.01
Mexican American Ind. (10)	13	0.07
Navajo (0)	1	0.01
Potawatomi (0)	1	0.01
Sioux (0)	1	0.01
Spanish American Ind. (1)	1	0.01
Asian (233)	316	1.59
Not Hispanic (227)	303	1.53
Hispanic (6)	13	0.07
Chinese, ex. Taiwanese (24)	31	0.16
Filipino (107)	157	0.79
Indian (53)	59	0.30
Indonesian (1)	1	0.01
Japanese (3)	17	0.09
Korean (9)	13	0.07
Laotian (3)	4	0.02
Malaysian (0)	3	0.02
Pakistani (9)	9	0.05
Thai (2)	4	0.02
Vietnamese (11)	13	0.07
Hawaii Native/Pacific Islander (3)	16	0.08
Not Hispanic (1)	10	0.05
Hispanic (2)	6	0.03
Guamanian/Chamorro (2)	5	0.03
Native Hawaiian (0)	1	0.01
Samoan (1)	3	0.02
White (14,715)	15,055	75.84
Not Hispanic (13,630)	13,847	69.75
Hispanic (1,085)	1,208	6.09

Fairview Heights

Place Type: City
County: St. Clair
Population: 17,078†

Ancestry‡	Population	%
Afghan (0)	4	0.02
African, Sub-Saharan (54)	54	0.33
African (37)	37	0.22
Senegalese (17)	17	0.10
American (1,136)	1,136	6.88
Arab (0)	60	0.36
Syrian (0)	36	0.22
Other Arab (0)	24	0.15
Armenian (9)	18	0.11
Austrian (20)	100	0.61
Belgian (11)	27	0.16
British (64)	64	0.39
Croatian (13)	57	0.35
Czech (27)	82	0.50
Czechoslovakian (0)	10	0.06
Danish (0)	100	0.61
Dutch (37)	177	1.07
English (355)	1,336	8.10
European (301)	332	2.01
French, ex. Basque (35)	467	2.83
French Canadian (27)	40	0.24
German (1,625)	4,164	25.23
Greek (12)	70	0.42
Hungarian (11)	68	0.41
Irish (598)	2,123	12.86
Italian (244)	855	5.18
Lithuanian (26)	46	0.28
Macedonian (0)	29	0.18
Norwegian (49)	101	0.61
Polish (100)	327	1.98
Romanian (0)	12	0.07
Russian (0)	20	0.12
Scandinavian (0)	76	0.46
Scotch-Irish (111)	267	1.62
Scottish (83)	281	1.70
Serbian (11)	18	0.11
Slavic (0)	13	0.08
Slovak (0)	26	0.16
Slovene (0)	6	0.04
Swedish (99)	204	1.24
Swiss (0)	13	0.08
Ukrainian (31)	31	0.19

SECTION TWO

*Notes: † The Census 2010 population figure is used to calculate the percentages in the Hispanic Origin and Race categories. Ancestry percentages are based on the 2006-2010 American Community Survey population (not shown); ‡ Numbers in parentheses indicate the number of people reporting a single ancestry; * Numbers in parentheses indicate the number of persons reporting this race alone, not in combination with any other race; Please refer to the Explanation of Data for more information.*

Welsh (8)	179	1.08
West Indian, ex. Hispanic (0)	58	0.35
Jamaican (0)	58	0.35
Yugoslavian (0)	13	0.08

Hispanic Origin	Population	%
Hispanic or Latino (of any race)	519	3.04
Central American, ex. Mexican	17	0.10
Costa Rican	1	0.01
Guatemalan	3	0.02
Nicaraguan	4	0.02
Panamanian	4	0.02
Salvadoran	5	0.03
Cuban	13	0.08
Dominican Republic	5	0.03
Mexican	325	1.90
Puerto Rican	63	0.37
South American	22	0.13
Argentinean	1	0.01
Bolivian	3	0.02
Chilean	2	0.01
Colombian	8	0.05
Ecuadorian	3	0.02
Peruvian	5	0.03
Other Hispanic or Latino	74	0.43

Race*	Population	%
African-American/Black (4,536)	4,753	27.83
Not Hispanic (4,518)	4,712	27.59
Hispanic (18)	41	0.24
American Indian/Alaska Native (55)	154	0.90
Not Hispanic (47)	131	0.77
Hispanic (8)	23	0.13
Alaska Athabascan *(Ala. Nat.)* (2)	2	0.01
Apache (0)	1	0.01
Arapaho (0)	2	0.01
Blackfeet (2)	3	0.02
Canadian/French Am. Ind. (1)	2	0.01
Cherokee (14)	54	0.32
Cheyenne (1)	1	0.01
Chickasaw (0)	1	0.01
Chippewa (1)	1	0.01
Choctaw (0)	4	0.02
Kiowa (0)	2	0.01
Lumbee (0)	1	0.01
Menominee (3)	3	0.02
Mexican American Ind. (1)	3	0.02
Navajo (6)	6	0.04
Potawatomi (0)	1	0.01
Pueblo (1)	1	0.01
Seminole (0)	1	0.01
Sioux (2)	7	0.04
Asian (468)	612	3.58
Not Hispanic (464)	599	3.51
Hispanic (4)	13	0.08
Chinese, ex. Taiwanese (61)	83	0.49
Filipino (107)	174	1.02
Indian (105)	118	0.69
Japanese (20)	28	0.16
Korean (60)	87	0.51
Laotian (4)	4	0.02
Nepalese (3)	3	0.02
Pakistani (11)	12	0.07
Sri Lankan (3)	3	0.02
Taiwanese (5)	9	0.05
Thai (40)	42	0.25
Vietnamese (35)	39	0.23
Hawaii Native/Pacific Islander (8)	33	0.19
Not Hispanic (8)	32	0.19
Hispanic (0)	1	0.01
Guamanian/Chamorro (0)	5	0.03
Native Hawaiian (7)	14	0.08
Samoan (1)	5	0.03
White (11,399)	11,776	68.95
Not Hispanic (11,123)	11,447	67.03
Hispanic (276)	329	1.93

Flossmoor

Place Type: Village
County: Cook
Population: 9,464†

Ancestry‡	Population	%
Afghan (47)	47	0.51
African, Sub-Saharan (261)	334	3.62
African (102)	113	1.23
Nigerian (159)	221	2.40
American (148)	148	1.61
Austrian (23)	74	0.80
Belgian (0)	27	0.29
Carpatho Rusyn (0)	10	0.11
Croatian (13)	50	0.54
Czech (7)	29	0.31
Danish (19)	62	0.67
Dutch (58)	322	3.49
Eastern European (87)	87	0.94
English (130)	586	6.36
European (99)	99	1.07
French, ex. Basque (53)	161	1.75
French Canadian (0)	17	0.18
German (368)	1,081	11.73
German Russian (10)	30	0.33
Greek (27)	77	0.84
Hungarian (0)	10	0.11
Iranian (8)	8	0.09
Irish (248)	1,169	12.68
Italian (197)	530	5.75
Lithuanian (24)	146	1.58
Norwegian (25)	87	0.94
Polish (354)	789	8.56
Russian (177)	419	4.55
Scandinavian (0)	7	0.08
Scotch-Irish (62)	144	1.56
Scottish (12)	141	1.53
Slovak (32)	42	0.46
Slovene (0)	15	0.16
Swedish (30)	222	2.41
Swiss (0)	54	0.59
Ukrainian (17)	17	0.18
Welsh (8)	19	0.21
West Indian, ex. Hispanic (12)	12	0.13
Haitian (12)	12	0.13

Hispanic Origin	Population	%
Hispanic or Latino (of any race)	303	3.20
Central American, ex. Mexican	23	0.24
Costa Rican	3	0.03
Guatemalan	1	0.01
Honduran	6	0.06
Nicaraguan	1	0.01
Panamanian	11	0.12
Salvadoran	1	0.01
Cuban	1	0.01
Dominican Republic	1	0.01
Mexican	176	1.86
Puerto Rican	51	0.54
South American	40	0.42
Argentinean	3	0.03
Chilean	1	0.01
Colombian	17	0.18
Ecuadorian	4	0.04
Peruvian	9	0.10
Uruguayan	5	0.05
Venezuelan	1	0.01
Other Hispanic or Latino	11	0.12

Race*	Population	%
African-American/Black (4,521)	4,651	49.14
Not Hispanic (4,462)	4,581	48.40
Hispanic (59)	70	0.74
American Indian/Alaska Native (7)	65	0.69
Not Hispanic (6)	61	0.64
Hispanic (1)	4	0.04
Cherokee (2)	9	0.10
Chickasaw (0)	7	0.07
Choctaw (0)	5	0.05
Creek (0)	5	0.05
Iroquois (0)	1	0.01
Shoshone (0)	1	0.01
Ute (0)	1	0.01
Asian (240)	303	3.20
Not Hispanic (240)	298	3.15
Hispanic (0)	5	0.05
Chinese, ex. Taiwanese (47)	64	0.68
Filipino (26)	34	0.36
Indian (105)	113	1.19
Japanese (4)	9	0.10
Korean (26)	37	0.39
Pakistani (3)	5	0.05
Taiwanese (1)	2	0.02
Thai (7)	7	0.07
Vietnamese (13)	13	0.14
Hawaii Native/Pacific Islander (2)	3	0.03
Not Hispanic (2)	3	0.03
Native Hawaiian (1)	1	0.01
White (4,393)	4,564	48.22
Not Hispanic (4,235)	4,377	46.25
Hispanic (158)	187	1.98

Forest Park

Place Type: Village
County: Cook
Population: 14,167†

Ancestry‡	Population	%
African, Sub-Saharan (220)	220	1.54
African (211)	211	1.48
Nigerian (9)	9	0.06
American (163)	163	1.14
Arab (54)	54	0.38
Lebanese (11)	11	0.08
Other Arab (43)	43	0.30
Austrian (0)	54	0.38
Belgian (12)	12	0.08
Brazilian (11)	11	0.08
British (8)	8	0.06
Bulgarian (15)	15	0.11
Canadian (13)	13	0.09
Croatian (0)	12	0.08
Czech (36)	185	1.30
Czechoslovakian (26)	59	0.41
Danish (12)	57	0.40
Dutch (71)	218	1.53
English (104)	467	3.27
European (73)	73	0.51
Finnish (0)	16	0.11
French, ex. Basque (9)	207	1.45
French Canadian (17)	72	0.50
German (627)	1,845	12.92
Greek (114)	173	1.21
Irish (804)	1,975	13.83
Italian (439)	1,235	8.65
Lithuanian (40)	63	0.44
Norwegian (58)	190	1.33
Polish (230)	630	4.41
Portuguese (0)	27	0.19
Romanian (30)	30	0.21
Russian (103)	138	0.97
Scotch-Irish (62)	91	0.64
Scottish (42)	116	0.81
Slovene (53)	53	0.37
Swedish (51)	136	0.95
Swiss (0)	12	0.08
Welsh (0)	56	0.39
West Indian, ex. Hispanic (18)	31	0.22
Belizean (18)	18	0.13
West Indian (0)	13	0.09
Yugoslavian (0)	11	0.08

Hispanic Origin	Population	%
Hispanic or Latino (of any race)	1,398	9.87
Central American, ex. Mexican	69	0.49
Guatemalan	25	0.18
Honduran	8	0.06
Nicaraguan	14	0.10

*Notes: † The Census 2010 population figure is used to calculate the percentages in the Hispanic Origin and Race categories. Ancestry percentages are based on the 2006-2010 American Community Survey population (not shown); ‡ Numbers in parentheses indicate the number of people reporting a single ancestry; * Numbers in parentheses indicate the number of persons reporting this race alone, not in combination with any other race; Please refer to the Explanation of Data for more information.*

Panamanian	6	0.04
Salvadoran	15	0.11
Other Central American	1	0.01
Cuban	44	0.31
Dominican Republic	4	0.03
Mexican	885	6.25
Puerto Rican	224	1.58
South American	96	0.68
Argentinean	11	0.08
Chilean	12	0.08
Colombian	23	0.16
Ecuadorian	13	0.09
Peruvian	24	0.17
Uruguayan	1	0.01
Venezuelan	9	0.06
Other South American	3	0.02
Other Hispanic or Latino	76	0.54

Race*	Population	%
African-American/Black (4,583)	4,791	33.82
Not Hispanic (4,504)	4,675	33.00
Hispanic (79)	116	0.82
American Indian/Alaska Native (38)	115	0.81
Not Hispanic (27)	94	0.66
Hispanic (11)	21	0.15
Apache (0)	1	0.01
Cherokee (3)	25	0.18
Cheyenne (0)	2	0.01
Chickasaw (0)	1	0.01
Chippewa (5)	6	0.04
Choctaw (1)	2	0.01
Cree (1)	1	0.01
Creek (1)	4	0.03
Iroquois (0)	1	0.01
Mexican American Ind. (2)	4	0.03
Navajo (1)	1	0.01
Potawatomi (0)	1	0.01
Seminole (0)	3	0.02
Sioux (1)	2	0.01
South American Ind. (0)	1	0.01
Spanish American Ind. (0)	1	0.01
Asian (847)	1,002	7.07
Not Hispanic (841)	986	6.96
Hispanic (6)	16	0.11
Bangladeshi (1)	2	0.01
Cambodian (2)	2	0.01
Chinese, ex. Taiwanese (100)	128	0.90
Filipino (241)	292	2.06
Indian (288)	313	2.21
Indonesian (3)	5	0.04
Japanese (25)	51	0.36
Korean (47)	61	0.43
Laotian (2)	2	0.01
Nepalese (2)	3	0.02
Pakistani (30)	33	0.23
Sri Lankan (7)	7	0.05
Taiwanese (8)	9	0.06
Thai (31)	33	0.23
Vietnamese (20)	25	0.18
Hawaii Native/Pacific Islander (3)	9	0.06
Not Hispanic (2)	6	0.04
Hispanic (1)	3	0.02
Fijian (1)	1	0.01
Guamanian/Chamorro (1)	3	0.02
Native Hawaiian (0)	1	0.01
Samoan (1)	1	0.01
White (7,814)	8,126	57.36
Not Hispanic (7,048)	7,292	51.47
Hispanic (766)	834	5.89

Fox Lake

Place Type: Village
County: Lake
Population: 10,579†

Ancestry‡	Population	%
American (327)	327	3.11
Austrian (0)	17	0.16
Belgian (50)	184	1.75
Canadian (48)	60	0.57
Croatian (42)	143	1.36
Czech (26)	204	1.94
Czechoslovakian (21)	21	0.20
Danish (24)	105	1.00
Dutch (27)	169	1.61
Eastern European (9)	9	0.09
English (138)	539	5.13
European (63)	63	0.60
French, ex. Basque (0)	270	2.57
French Canadian (9)	38	0.36
German (1,117)	3,428	32.60
Greek (54)	102	0.97
Hungarian (12)	95	0.90
Icelander (0)	13	0.12
Irish (485)	2,489	23.67
Italian (342)	1,474	14.02
Lithuanian (26)	101	0.96
Luxemburger (18)	18	0.17
Northern European (16)	16	0.15
Norwegian (104)	404	3.84
Polish (947)	2,292	21.80
Russian (26)	44	0.42
Scandinavian (14)	34	0.32
Scotch-Irish (80)	193	1.84
Scottish (44)	189	1.80
Slovak (12)	25	0.24
Swedish (59)	463	4.40
Swiss (7)	18	0.17
Ukrainian (0)	11	0.10
Welsh (10)	21	0.20

Hispanic Origin	Population	%
Hispanic or Latino (of any race)	940	8.89
Central American, ex. Mexican	33	0.31
Costa Rican	3	0.03
Guatemalan	10	0.09
Honduran	3	0.03
Nicaraguan	2	0.02
Panamanian	6	0.06
Salvadoran	9	0.09
Cuban	12	0.11
Dominican Republic	5	0.05
Mexican	728	6.88
Puerto Rican	94	0.89
South American	18	0.17
Argentinean	2	0.02
Colombian	9	0.09
Peruvian	6	0.06
Other South American	1	0.01
Other Hispanic or Latino	50	0.47

Race*	Population	%
African-American/Black (103)	155	1.47
Not Hispanic (96)	130	1.23
Hispanic (7)	25	0.24
American Indian/Alaska Native (33)	96	0.91
Not Hispanic (26)	73	0.69
Hispanic (7)	23	0.22
Apache (0)	5	0.05
Arapaho (0)	1	0.01
Blackfeet (0)	3	0.03
Cherokee (7)	16	0.15
Chippewa (5)	9	0.09
Choctaw (1)	2	0.02
Comanche (0)	3	0.03
Mexican American Ind. (2)	3	0.03
Navajo (0)	1	0.01
Sioux (6)	19	0.18
Asian (101)	159	1.50
Not Hispanic (97)	145	1.37
Hispanic (4)	14	0.13
Cambodian (1)	1	0.01
Chinese, ex. Taiwanese (19)	20	0.19
Filipino (35)	60	0.57
Indian (24)	30	0.28
Indonesian (1)	6	0.06
Japanese (2)	14	0.13
Korean (7)	11	0.10
Pakistani (1)	3	0.03
Sri Lankan (2)	2	0.02
Taiwanese (2)	3	0.03
Thai (2)	4	0.04
Vietnamese (3)	4	0.04
Hawaii Native/Pacific Islander (2)	9	0.09
Not Hispanic (1)	6	0.06
Hispanic (1)	3	0.03
Guamanian/Chamorro (0)	3	0.03
Native Hawaiian (0)	3	0.03
Samoan (2)	3	0.03
White (9,819)	10,029	94.80
Not Hispanic (9,289)	9,413	88.98
Hispanic (530)	616	5.82

Frankfort Square

Place Type: CDP
County: Will
Population: 9,276†

Ancestry‡	Population	%
Albanian (32)	32	0.34
American (290)	290	3.04
Arab (22)	22	0.23
Lebanese (22)	22	0.23
Belgian (0)	87	0.91
British (13)	13	0.14
Croatian (15)	120	1.26
Czech (61)	401	4.21
Danish (0)	41	0.43
Dutch (118)	323	3.39
English (79)	593	6.23
European (33)	33	0.35
French, ex. Basque (44)	211	2.22
French Canadian (0)	35	0.37
German (643)	3,028	31.79
Greek (63)	174	1.83
Hungarian (26)	60	0.63
Irish (629)	2,869	30.12
Italian (250)	1,591	16.70
Lithuanian (36)	310	3.25
Norwegian (13)	63	0.66
Polish (490)	2,334	24.50
Russian (0)	52	0.55
Scotch-Irish (55)	109	1.14
Scottish (9)	66	0.69
Slovak (0)	22	0.23
Slovene (0)	11	0.12
Swedish (30)	206	2.16
Swiss (0)	134	1.41
Welsh (0)	16	0.17
West Indian, ex. Hispanic (0)	12	0.13
Jamaican (0)	12	0.13

Hispanic Origin	Population	%
Hispanic or Latino (of any race)	643	6.93
Central American, ex. Mexican	8	0.09
Guatemalan	5	0.05
Honduran	1	0.01
Panamanian	2	0.02
Cuban	10	0.11
Dominican Republic	3	0.03
Mexican	507	5.47
Puerto Rican	69	0.74
South American	14	0.15
Argentinean	2	0.02
Bolivian	4	0.04
Colombian	3	0.03
Ecuadorian	4	0.04
Other South American	1	0.01
Other Hispanic or Latino	32	0.34

Race*	Population	%
African-American/Black (115)	135	1.46
Not Hispanic (113)	131	1.41
Hispanic (2)	4	0.04
American Indian/Alaska Native (14)	33	0.36
Not Hispanic (10)	25	0.27
Hispanic (4)	8	0.09
Apache (1)	3	0.03

SECTION TWO

*Notes: † The Census 2010 population figure is used to calculate the percentages in the Hispanic Origin and Race categories. Ancestry percentages are based on the 2006-2010 American Community Survey population (not shown); ‡ Numbers in parentheses indicate the number of people reporting a single ancestry; * Numbers in parentheses indicate the number of persons reporting this race alone, not in combination with any other race; Please refer to the Explanation of Data for more information.*

Blackfeet (0)	1	0.01
Cherokee (0)	5	0.05
Chippewa (2)	2	0.02
Hopi (1)	3	0.03
Mexican American Ind. (1)	3	0.03
Potawatomi (0)	2	0.02
Asian (144)	206	2.22
Not Hispanic (141)	194	2.09
Hispanic (3)	12	0.13
Burmese (1)	4	0.04
Chinese, ex. Taiwanese (19)	28	0.30
Filipino (54)	78	0.84
Indian (32)	33	0.36
Indonesian (0)	4	0.04
Japanese (7)	15	0.16
Korean (15)	25	0.27
Pakistani (4)	4	0.04
Taiwanese (1)	2	0.02
Thai (5)	6	0.06
Vietnamese (2)	2	0.02
Hawaii Native/Pacific Islander (1)	8	0.09
Not Hispanic (1)	4	0.04
Hispanic (0)	4	0.04
Native Hawaiian (1)	4	0.04
White (8,701)	8,824	95.13
Not Hispanic (8,275)	8,354	90.06
Hispanic (426)	470	5.07

Frankfort

Place Type: Village
County: Will
Population: 17,782†

Ancestry‡	Population	%
African, Sub-Saharan (240)	292	1.71
African (16)	16	0.09
Nigerian (224)	276	1.62
American (164)	164	0.96
Arab (32)	113	0.66
Lebanese (0)	46	0.27
Palestinian (19)	54	0.32
Syrian (13)	13	0.08
Austrian (29)	188	1.10
Belgian (0)	134	0.79
Brazilian (0)	9	0.05
British (57)	75	0.44
Croatian (53)	185	1.08
Czech (20)	399	2.34
Czechoslovakian (18)	18	0.11
Danish (12)	221	1.30
Dutch (125)	428	2.51
English (194)	1,292	7.58
European (288)	288	1.69
Finnish (0)	9	0.05
French, ex. Basque (55)	680	3.99
French Canadian (36)	133	0.78
German (981)	4,812	28.21
Greek (58)	462	2.71
Hungarian (54)	253	1.48
Iranian (0)	12	0.07
Irish (871)	4,771	27.97
Italian (460)	2,185	12.81
Latvian (0)	14	0.08
Lithuanian (115)	345	2.02
Norwegian (31)	313	1.84
Polish (953)	3,261	19.12
Romanian (14)	14	0.08
Russian (38)	159	0.93
Scandinavian (0)	20	0.12
Scotch-Irish (70)	308	1.81
Scottish (35)	176	1.03
Serbian (14)	28	0.16
Slavic (0)	21	0.12
Slovak (0)	158	0.93
Slovene (27)	93	0.55
Swedish (52)	586	3.44
Swiss (0)	12	0.07
Turkish (0)	12	0.07
Ukrainian (22)	46	0.27
Welsh (14)	160	0.94
West Indian, ex. Hispanic (0)	12	0.07
Trinidadian/Tobagonian (0)	12	0.07

Hispanic Origin	Population	%
Hispanic or Latino (of any race)	815	4.58
Central American, ex. Mexican	27	0.15
Costa Rican	5	0.03
Guatemalan	11	0.06
Honduran	3	0.02
Nicaraguan	4	0.02
Panamanian	4	0.02
Cuban	16	0.09
Mexican	622	3.50
Puerto Rican	73	0.41
South American	34	0.19
Argentinean	7	0.04
Chilean	1	0.01
Colombian	16	0.09
Ecuadorian	3	0.02
Peruvian	3	0.02
Venezuelan	4	0.02
Other Hispanic or Latino	43	0.24

Race*	Population	%
African-American/Black (1,090)	1,144	6.43
Not Hispanic (1,085)	1,133	6.37
Hispanic (5)	11	0.06
American Indian/Alaska Native (25)	66	0.37
Not Hispanic (16)	54	0.30
Hispanic (9)	12	0.07
Arapaho (0)	2	0.01
Cherokee (5)	19	0.11
Chippewa (2)	2	0.01
Choctaw (0)	3	0.02
Crow (0)	1	0.01
Mexican American Ind. (4)	7	0.04
Potawatomi (1)	1	0.01
Shoshone (0)	4	0.02
Asian (465)	555	3.12
Not Hispanic (462)	539	3.03
Hispanic (3)	16	0.09
Burmese (4)	4	0.02
Chinese, ex. Taiwanese (58)	84	0.47
Filipino (93)	121	0.68
Indian (155)	169	0.95
Indonesian (1)	1	0.01
Japanese (6)	26	0.15
Korean (52)	64	0.36
Pakistani (39)	39	0.22
Taiwanese (2)	5	0.03
Thai (10)	10	0.06
Vietnamese (21)	22	0.12
Hawaii Native/Pacific Islander (2)	8	0.04
Not Hispanic (2)	3	0.02
Hispanic (0)	5	0.03
Native Hawaiian (0)	1	0.01
White (15,822)	16,001	89.98
Not Hispanic (15,234)	15,372	86.45
Hispanic (588)	629	3.54

Franklin Park

Place Type: Village
County: Cook
Population: 18,333†

Ancestry‡	Population	%
African, Sub-Saharan (0)	22	0.12
African (0)	22	0.12
Albanian (56)	56	0.31
American (248)	248	1.35
Arab (40)	40	0.22
Arab (40)	40	0.22
Armenian (0)	22	0.12
Austrian (7)	28	0.15
British (0)	28	0.15
Bulgarian (88)	88	0.48
Celtic (10)	10	0.05
Croatian (0)	10	0.05
Czech (54)	143	0.78
Danish (0)	66	0.36
Dutch (36)	159	0.87
English (30)	330	1.80
Finnish (0)	6	0.03
French, ex. Basque (66)	173	0.94
French Canadian (8)	33	0.18
German (478)	2,007	10.94
Greek (11)	161	0.88
Hungarian (24)	108	0.59
Iranian (102)	102	0.56
Irish (330)	1,594	8.69
Italian (1,249)	2,234	12.18
Lithuanian (0)	27	0.15
Norwegian (73)	228	1.24
Polish (2,553)	3,424	18.66
Portuguese (8)	8	0.04
Romanian (140)	186	1.01
Russian (12)	48	0.26
Scotch-Irish (11)	119	0.65
Scottish (0)	27	0.15
Slovak (11)	49	0.27
Swedish (55)	272	1.48
Swiss (0)	13	0.07
Ukrainian (115)	151	0.82
Yugoslavian (111)	111	0.61

Hispanic Origin	Population	%
Hispanic or Latino (of any race)	7,902	43.10
Central American, ex. Mexican	387	2.11
Costa Rican	1	0.01
Guatemalan	273	1.49
Honduran	39	0.21
Nicaraguan	17	0.09
Panamanian	9	0.05
Salvadoran	48	0.26
Cuban	88	0.48
Dominican Republic	20	0.11
Mexican	6,212	33.88
Puerto Rican	829	4.52
South American	204	1.11
Argentinean	10	0.05
Bolivian	5	0.03
Chilean	2	0.01
Colombian	73	0.40
Ecuadorian	63	0.34
Peruvian	42	0.23
Uruguayan	3	0.02
Venezuelan	6	0.03
Other Hispanic or Latino	162	0.88

Race*	Population	%
African-American/Black (233)	324	1.77
Not Hispanic (167)	198	1.08
Hispanic (66)	126	0.69
American Indian/Alaska Native (68)	137	0.75
Not Hispanic (24)	50	0.27
Hispanic (44)	87	0.47
Apache (0)	1	0.01
Blackfeet (1)	1	0.01
Central American Ind. (1)	1	0.01
Cherokee (1)	12	0.07
Chippewa (3)	7	0.04
Choctaw (5)	5	0.03
Cree (0)	2	0.01
Creek (0)	3	0.02
Iroquois (1)	1	0.01
Mexican American Ind. (10)	22	0.12
Seminole (4)	7	0.04
Sioux (1)	4	0.02
South American Ind. (0)	8	0.04
Asian (565)	635	3.46
Not Hispanic (543)	595	3.25
Hispanic (22)	40	0.22
Cambodian (4)	4	0.02
Chinese, ex. Taiwanese (33)	42	0.23
Filipino (356)	386	2.11
Indian (38)	41	0.22
Japanese (10)	20	0.11
Korean (18)	18	0.10

*Notes: † The Census 2010 population figure is used to calculate the percentages in the Hispanic Origin and Race categories. Ancestry percentages are based on the 2006-2010 American Community Survey population (not shown); ‡ Numbers in parentheses indicate the number of people reporting a single ancestry; * Numbers in parentheses indicate the number of persons reporting this race alone, not in combination with any other race; Please refer to the Explanation of Data for more information.*

Laotian (10)	10	0.05
Pakistani (14)	14	0.08
Taiwanese (5)	5	0.03
Thai (13)	15	0.08
Vietnamese (50)	54	0.29
Hawaii Native/Pacific Islander (4)	9	0.05
Not Hispanic (1)	2	0.01
Hispanic (3)	7	0.04
Guamanian/Chamorro (3)	3	0.02
White (13,703)	14,129	77.07
Not Hispanic (9,573)	9,678	52.79
Hispanic (4,130)	4,451	24.28

Freeport

Place Type: City
County: Stephenson
Population: 25,638†

Ancestry‡	Population	%
African, Sub-Saharan (13)	24	0.09
Ethiopian (13)	13	0.05
South African (0)	11	0.04
Albanian (0)	38	0.15
American (2,052)	2,052	7.99
Austrian (0)	59	0.23
Belgian (0)	12	0.05
British (40)	49	0.19
Canadian (0)	10	0.04
Croatian (10)	37	0.14
Czech (27)	159	0.62
Danish (72)	188	0.73
Dutch (96)	1,135	4.42
English (571)	2,536	9.87
European (186)	197	0.77
Finnish (27)	43	0.17
French, ex. Basque (77)	948	3.69
French Canadian (4)	73	0.28
German (4,384)	10,329	40.21
Greek (50)	61	0.24
Hungarian (49)	130	0.51
Irish (401)	2,818	10.97
Italian (201)	577	2.25
Lithuanian (0)	17	0.07
Luxemburger (0)	26	0.10
Norwegian (143)	616	2.40
Pennsylvania German (42)	50	0.19
Polish (235)	526	2.05
Portuguese (0)	30	0.12
Romanian (10)	51	0.20
Russian (13)	100	0.39
Scandinavian (29)	69	0.27
Scotch-Irish (78)	245	0.95
Scottish (13)	155	0.60
Slovak (0)	26	0.10
Slovene (0)	8	0.03
Swedish (204)	1,040	4.05
Swiss (134)	406	1.58
Turkish (18)	18	0.07
Ukrainian (18)	18	0.07
Welsh (9)	111	0.43
West Indian, ex. Hispanic (45)	45	0.18
Jamaican (45)	45	0.18
Yugoslavian (43)	140	0.55

Hispanic Origin	Population	%
Hispanic or Latino (of any race)	1,056	4.12
Central American, ex. Mexican	45	0.18
Guatemalan	7	0.03
Honduran	20	0.08
Nicaraguan	1	<0.01
Panamanian	13	0.05
Salvadoran	4	0.02
Cuban	25	0.10
Dominican Republic	4	0.02
Mexican	786	3.07
Puerto Rican	121	0.47
South American	15	0.06
Argentinean	3	0.01
Colombian	3	0.01
Paraguayan	1	<0.01
Peruvian	8	0.03
Other Hispanic or Latino	60	0.23

Race*	Population	%
African-American/Black (4,155)	4,865	18.98
Not Hispanic (4,108)	4,776	18.63
Hispanic (47)	89	0.35
American Indian/Alaska Native (55)	210	0.82
Not Hispanic (45)	187	0.73
Hispanic (10)	23	0.09
Apache (1)	4	0.02
Blackfeet (4)	15	0.06
Cherokee (12)	63	0.25
Chippewa (1)	2	0.01
Choctaw (1)	2	0.01
Creek (1)	1	<0.01
Iroquois (1)	2	0.01
Mexican American Ind. (1)	4	0.02
Osage (0)	1	<0.01
Sioux (1)	8	0.03
Asian (218)	296	1.15
Not Hispanic (216)	291	1.14
Hispanic (2)	5	0.02
Cambodian (1)	1	<0.01
Chinese, ex. Taiwanese (20)	46	0.18
Filipino (52)	76	0.30
Indian (73)	89	0.35
Indonesian (1)	2	0.01
Japanese (7)	24	0.09
Korean (25)	28	0.11
Laotian (6)	7	0.03
Pakistani (2)	3	0.01
Taiwanese (2)	2	0.01
Thai (3)	3	0.01
Vietnamese (17)	19	0.07
Hawaii Native/Pacific Islander (8)	32	0.12
Not Hispanic (8)	30	0.12
Hispanic (0)	2	0.01
Fijian (0)	1	<0.01
Guamanian/Chamorro (0)	2	0.01
Marshallese (1)	1	<0.01
Native Hawaiian (7)	19	0.07
Samoan (0)	4	0.02
White (19,775)	20,689	80.70
Not Hispanic (19,313)	20,136	78.54
Hispanic (462)	553	2.16

Gages Lake

Place Type: CDP
County: Lake
Population: 10,198†

Ancestry‡	Population	%
African, Sub-Saharan (44)	44	0.43
African (44)	44	0.43
Alsatian (0)	11	0.11
American (182)	182	1.79
Arab (0)	28	0.28
Lebanese (0)	7	0.07
Syrian (0)	21	0.21
Assyrian/Chaldean/Syriac (8)	8	0.08
Australian (19)	19	0.19
Austrian (0)	64	0.63
Belgian (12)	47	0.46
British (57)	77	0.76
Canadian (0)	12	0.12
Croatian (9)	71	0.70
Czech (39)	121	1.19
Danish (11)	124	1.22
Dutch (50)	177	1.74
English (146)	1,108	10.90
European (100)	100	0.98
Finnish (8)	33	0.32
French, ex. Basque (38)	342	3.36
French Canadian (8)	27	0.27
German (647)	2,703	26.59
German Russian (10)	10	0.10
Greek (54)	82	0.81
Hungarian (9)	52	0.51
Irish (255)	1,561	15.36
Israeli (12)	23	0.23
Italian (152)	737	7.25
Latvian (11)	11	0.11
Lithuanian (31)	81	0.80
Luxemburger (0)	10	0.10
Northern European (5)	5	0.05
Norwegian (65)	233	2.29
Polish (311)	928	9.13
Romanian (11)	22	0.22
Russian (255)	502	4.94
Scandinavian (26)	26	0.26
Scotch-Irish (38)	190	1.87
Scottish (67)	310	3.05
Serbian (0)	45	0.44
Slavic (0)	12	0.12
Slovak (19)	44	0.43
Slovene (0)	21	0.21
Swedish (45)	378	3.72
Swiss (10)	30	0.30
Turkish (167)	167	1.64
Ukrainian (22)	33	0.32
Welsh (10)	84	0.83
West Indian, ex. Hispanic (7)	7	0.07
Trinidadian/Tobagonian (7)	7	0.07
Yugoslavian (0)	95	0.93

Hispanic Origin	Population	%
Hispanic or Latino (of any race)	872	8.55
Central American, ex. Mexican	73	0.72
Costa Rican	3	0.03
Guatemalan	22	0.22
Honduran	22	0.22
Nicaraguan	1	0.01
Panamanian	14	0.14
Salvadoran	11	0.11
Cuban	22	0.22
Dominican Republic	15	0.15
Mexican	591	5.80
Puerto Rican	105	1.03
South American	32	0.31
Argentinean	7	0.07
Colombian	9	0.09
Ecuadorian	3	0.03
Paraguayan	2	0.02
Peruvian	11	0.11
Other Hispanic or Latino	34	0.33

Race*	Population	%
African-American/Black (390)	490	4.80
Not Hispanic (367)	455	4.46
Hispanic (23)	35	0.34
American Indian/Alaska Native (34)	68	0.67
Not Hispanic (17)	40	0.39
Hispanic (17)	28	0.27
Cherokee (2)	11	0.11
Chippewa (2)	3	0.03
Choctaw (1)	4	0.04
Comanche (0)	3	0.03
Iroquois (2)	2	0.02
Mexican American Ind. (4)	7	0.07
Ottawa (0)	1	0.01
Seminole (0)	1	0.01
Asian (614)	703	6.89
Not Hispanic (608)	697	6.83
Hispanic (6)	6	0.06
Bangladeshi (5)	5	0.05
Burmese (1)	1	0.01
Cambodian (9)	11	0.11
Chinese, ex. Taiwanese (89)	103	1.01
Filipino (140)	177	1.74
Indian (180)	186	1.82
Japanese (21)	40	0.39
Korean (101)	118	1.16
Malaysian (4)	7	0.07
Pakistani (18)	22	0.22
Sri Lankan (1)	1	0.01
Taiwanese (1)	1	0.01
Thai (16)	20	0.20

*Notes: † The Census 2010 population figure is used to calculate the percentages in the Hispanic Origin and Race categories. Ancestry percentages are based on the 2006-2010 American Community Survey population (not shown); ‡ Numbers in parentheses indicate the number of people reporting a single ancestry; * Numbers in parentheses indicate the number of persons reporting this race alone, not in combination with any other race; Please refer to the Explanation of Data for more information.*

Vietnamese (14)	19	0.19
Hawaii Native/Pacific Islander (5)	13	0.13
Not Hispanic (5)	13	0.13
Native Hawaiian (4)	7	0.07
Samoan (0)	1	0.01
White (8,599)	8,842	86.70
Not Hispanic (8,121)	8,295	81.34
Hispanic (478)	547	5.36

Galesburg

Place Type: City
County: Knox
Population: 32,195†

Ancestry‡	Population	%
African, Sub-Saharan (499)	627	1.95
African (472)	600	1.86
Nigerian (27)	27	0.08
American (2,144)	2,144	6.66
Arab (22)	62	0.19
Iraqi (22)	22	0.07
Lebanese (0)	20	0.06
Other Arab (0)	20	0.06
Armenian (15)	15	0.05
Australian (0)	9	0.03
Austrian (0)	44	0.14
Belgian (10)	39	0.12
British (62)	122	0.38
Bulgarian (9)	9	0.03
Croatian (24)	39	0.12
Czech (52)	148	0.46
Danish (67)	182	0.57
Dutch (177)	996	3.10
Eastern European (0)	20	0.06
English (1,295)	3,206	9.96
European (276)	276	0.86
Finnish (28)	43	0.13
French, ex. Basque (87)	623	1.94
French Canadian (13)	40	0.12
German (1,926)	6,595	20.50
Greek (36)	89	0.28
Hungarian (18)	61	0.19
Irish (1,458)	4,564	14.18
Israeli (14)	14	0.04
Italian (495)	1,126	3.50
Lithuanian (16)	39	0.12
Maltese (0)	15	0.05
Northern European (21)	21	0.07
Norwegian (72)	247	0.77
Pennsylvania German (34)	34	0.11
Polish (140)	463	1.44
Portuguese (0)	82	0.25
Romanian (0)	36	0.11
Russian (47)	138	0.43
Scotch-Irish (295)	670	2.08
Scottish (175)	430	1.34
Slovak (17)	17	0.05
Swedish (1,424)	3,141	9.76
Swiss (9)	49	0.15
Ukrainian (22)	78	0.24
Welsh (130)	224	0.70
West Indian, ex. Hispanic (34)	128	0.40
Bahamian (21)	97	0.30
Belizean (0)	9	0.03
Jamaican (13)	22	0.07
Yugoslavian (9)	18	0.06

Hispanic Origin	Population	%
Hispanic or Latino (of any race)	2,237	6.95
Central American, ex. Mexican	48	0.15
Guatemalan	15	0.05
Honduran	4	0.01
Nicaraguan	14	0.04
Panamanian	2	0.01
Salvadoran	13	0.04
Cuban	26	0.08
Dominican Republic	8	0.02
Mexican	1,734	5.39
Puerto Rican	110	0.34
South American	17	0.05
Argentinean	2	0.01
Bolivian	1	<0.01
Chilean	4	0.01
Colombian	4	0.01
Ecuadorian	2	0.01
Peruvian	1	<0.01
Venezuelan	2	0.01
Other South American	1	<0.01
Other Hispanic or Latino	294	0.91

Race*	Population	%
African-American/Black (3,698)	4,405	13.68
Not Hispanic (3,630)	4,256	13.22
Hispanic (68)	149	0.46
American Indian/Alaska Native (80)	265	0.82
Not Hispanic (56)	221	0.69
Hispanic (24)	44	0.14
Aleut *(Alaska Native)* (1)	2	0.01
Apache (0)	2	0.01
Blackfeet (1)	13	0.04
Central American Ind. (4)	4	0.01
Cherokee (13)	65	0.20
Cheyenne (0)	1	<0.01
Chippewa (1)	3	0.01
Choctaw (4)	5	0.02
Cree (0)	1	<0.01
Creek (1)	2	0.01
Crow (1)	1	<0.01
Delaware (0)	2	0.01
Iroquois (0)	4	0.01
Mexican American Ind. (1)	9	0.03
Navajo (0)	5	0.02
Osage (0)	1	<0.01
Potawatomi (0)	1	<0.01
Pueblo (1)	1	<0.01
Seminole (1)	1	<0.01
Sioux (0)	3	0.01
Spanish American Ind. (0)	2	0.01
Asian (290)	392	1.22
Not Hispanic (284)	369	1.15
Hispanic (6)	23	0.07
Chinese, ex. Taiwanese (54)	82	0.25
Filipino (61)	86	0.27
Hmong (1)	3	0.01
Indian (81)	95	0.30
Indonesian (0)	1	<0.01
Japanese (16)	48	0.15
Korean (30)	34	0.11
Laotian (0)	5	0.02
Pakistani (6)	6	0.02
Sri Lankan (1)	1	<0.01
Thai (0)	3	0.01
Vietnamese (19)	23	0.07
Hawaii Native/Pacific Islander (9)	26	0.08
Not Hispanic (7)	21	0.07
Hispanic (2)	5	0.02
Guamanian/Chamorro (1)	6	0.02
Native Hawaiian (5)	13	0.04
Samoan (1)	1	<0.01
White (26,121)	27,107	84.20
Not Hispanic (25,114)	25,908	80.47
Hispanic (1,007)	1,199	3.72

Geneva

Place Type: City
County: Kane
Population: 21,495†

Ancestry‡	Population	%
African, Sub-Saharan (34)	34	0.16
African (34)	34	0.16
Albanian (0)	22	0.10
American (552)	552	2.57
Arab (0)	65	0.30
Lebanese (0)	53	0.25
Other Arab (0)	12	0.06
Armenian (0)	12	0.06
Austrian (16)	108	0.50
Belgian (12)	94	0.44
British (79)	156	0.73
Canadian (34)	71	0.33
Celtic (0)	26	0.12
Croatian (78)	294	1.37
Czech (102)	552	2.57
Czechoslovakian (80)	190	0.89
Danish (61)	255	1.19
Dutch (145)	405	1.89
Eastern European (51)	51	0.24
English (527)	2,576	12.01
European (305)	330	1.54
Finnish (0)	47	0.22
French, ex. Basque (97)	781	3.64
French Canadian (117)	195	0.91
German (1,991)	6,699	31.23
Greek (127)	352	1.64
Hungarian (0)	140	0.65
Iranian (40)	76	0.35
Irish (955)	4,609	21.49
Italian (819)	2,820	13.15
Lithuanian (30)	274	1.28
Luxemburger (0)	50	0.23
Northern European (27)	27	0.13
Norwegian (150)	768	3.58
Pennsylvania German (11)	11	0.05
Polish (592)	2,259	10.53
Portuguese (11)	67	0.31
Romanian (0)	15	0.07
Russian (191)	232	1.08
Scandinavian (24)	119	0.55
Scotch-Irish (97)	366	1.71
Scottish (13)	400	1.86
Serbian (0)	16	0.07
Slovak (13)	135	0.63
Slovene (17)	17	0.08
Swedish (460)	1,469	6.85
Swiss (12)	84	0.39
Ukrainian (228)	356	1.66
Welsh (60)	183	0.85
West Indian, ex. Hispanic (0)	28	0.13
West Indian (0)	28	0.13
Yugoslavian (0)	11	0.05

Hispanic Origin	Population	%
Hispanic or Latino (of any race)	1,043	4.85
Central American, ex. Mexican	45	0.21
Costa Rican	5	0.02
Guatemalan	23	0.11
Honduran	4	0.02
Nicaraguan	5	0.02
Panamanian	8	0.04
Cuban	38	0.18
Dominican Republic	1	<0.01
Mexican	775	3.61
Puerto Rican	74	0.34
South American	46	0.21
Argentinean	10	0.05
Bolivian	10	0.05
Chilean	6	0.03
Colombian	4	0.02
Ecuadorian	5	0.02
Paraguayan	1	<0.01
Peruvian	8	0.04
Venezuelan	2	0.01
Other Hispanic or Latino	64	0.30

Race*	Population	%
African-American/Black (109)	168	0.78
Not Hispanic (103)	158	0.74
Hispanic (6)	10	0.05
American Indian/Alaska Native (14)	61	0.28
Not Hispanic (3)	34	0.16
Hispanic (11)	27	0.13
Blackfeet (0)	1	<0.01
Cherokee (0)	16	0.07
Cree (0)	1	<0.01
Delaware (0)	1	<0.01
Mexican American Ind. (5)	11	0.05
Ottawa (1)	1	<0.01

*Notes: † The Census 2010 population figure is used to calculate the percentages in the Hispanic Origin and Race categories. Ancestry percentages are based on the 2006-2010 American Community Survey population (not shown); ‡ Numbers in parentheses indicate the number of people reporting a single ancestry; * Numbers in parentheses indicate the number of persons reporting this race alone, not in combination with any other race; Please refer to the Explanation of Data for more information.*

Potawatomi (0)	1	<0.01
Sioux (0)	1	<0.01
Asian (472)	602	2.80
Not Hispanic (461)	585	2.72
Hispanic (11)	17	0.08
Cambodian (10)	10	0.05
Chinese, ex. Taiwanese (92)	114	0.53
Filipino (109)	154	0.72
Indian (115)	129	0.60
Indonesian (1)	1	<0.01
Japanese (21)	39	0.18
Korean (71)	97	0.45
Laotian (12)	15	0.07
Pakistani (10)	15	0.07
Taiwanese (3)	4	0.02
Thai (3)	3	0.01
Vietnamese (14)	14	0.07
Hawaii Native/Pacific Islander (4)	7	0.03
Not Hispanic (3)	3	0.01
Hispanic (1)	4	0.02
Native Hawaiian (4)	4	0.02
White (20,371)	20,628	95.97
Not Hispanic (19,651)	19,861	92.40
Hispanic (720)	767	3.57

Glen Carbon

Place Type: Village
County: Madison
Population: 12,934†

Ancestry‡	Population	%
African, Sub-Saharan (80)	80	0.65
Ethiopian (12)	12	0.10
Ghanaian (17)	17	0.14
Nigerian (51)	51	0.41
Albanian (0)	11	0.09
American (679)	679	5.52
Arab (88)	88	0.72
Egyptian (88)	88	0.72
Armenian (0)	14	0.11
Austrian (0)	14	0.11
Belgian (0)	29	0.24
British (0)	31	0.25
Bulgarian (0)	40	0.33
Canadian (0)	13	0.11
Croatian (48)	74	0.60
Czech (23)	85	0.69
Czechoslovakian (41)	69	0.56
Danish (0)	13	0.11
Dutch (18)	151	1.23
English (243)	1,022	8.31
European (42)	57	0.46
Finnish (0)	47	0.38
French, ex. Basque (163)	702	5.71
French Canadian (19)	30	0.24
German (2,006)	4,167	33.87
Greek (46)	89	0.72
Hungarian (41)	79	0.64
Iranian (10)	10	0.08
Irish (614)	1,768	14.37
Italian (126)	634	5.15
Lithuanian (28)	99	0.80
Macedonian (0)	9	0.07
Northern European (7)	7	0.06
Norwegian (91)	248	2.02
Pennsylvania German (0)	9	0.07
Polish (118)	545	4.43
Romanian (27)	61	0.50
Russian (68)	208	1.69
Scandinavian (0)	26	0.21
Scotch-Irish (62)	152	1.24
Scottish (93)	212	1.72
Slavic (0)	13	0.11
Slovak (10)	31	0.25
Swedish (43)	144	1.17
Swiss (26)	121	0.98
Turkish (0)	12	0.10
Welsh (10)	60	0.49
West Indian, ex. Hispanic (10)	10	0.08
Belizean (10)	10	0.08
Yugoslavian (0)	8	0.07

Hispanic Origin	Population	%
Hispanic or Latino (of any race)	283	2.19
Central American, ex. Mexican	6	0.05
Costa Rican	2	0.02
Guatemalan	1	0.01
Honduran	1	0.01
Panamanian	2	0.02
Cuban	2	0.02
Dominican Republic	8	0.06
Mexican	175	1.35
Puerto Rican	26	0.20
South American	19	0.15
Argentinean	1	0.01
Chilean	1	0.01
Colombian	6	0.05
Ecuadorian	2	0.02
Peruvian	8	0.06
Venezuelan	1	0.01
Other Hispanic or Latino	47	0.36

Race*	Population	%
African-American/Black (961)	1,062	8.21
Not Hispanic (953)	1,052	8.13
Hispanic (8)	10	0.08
American Indian/Alaska Native (45)	95	0.73
Not Hispanic (40)	88	0.68
Hispanic (5)	7	0.05
Apache (1)	1	0.01
Blackfeet (1)	8	0.06
Cherokee (4)	35	0.27
Chippewa (1)	2	0.02
Choctaw (3)	3	0.02
Comanche (2)	3	0.02
Mexican American Ind. (1)	1	0.01
Potawatomi (1)	1	0.01
Puget Sound Salish (5)	5	0.04
Sioux (8)	11	0.09
South American Ind. (1)	1	0.01
Asian (260)	342	2.64
Not Hispanic (254)	336	2.60
Hispanic (6)	6	0.05
Bangladeshi (8)	10	0.08
Chinese, ex. Taiwanese (65)	79	0.61
Filipino (30)	43	0.33
Indian (64)	84	0.65
Indonesian (0)	2	0.02
Japanese (10)	19	0.15
Korean (29)	38	0.29
Malaysian (0)	1	0.01
Nepalese (5)	5	0.04
Pakistani (10)	16	0.12
Taiwanese (10)	11	0.09
Thai (15)	17	0.13
Vietnamese (3)	3	0.02
Hawaii Native/Pacific Islander (4)	18	0.14
Not Hispanic (4)	18	0.14
Guamanian/Chamorro (2)	4	0.03
Native Hawaiian (0)	2	0.02
Samoan (2)	7	0.05
White (11,348)	11,555	89.34
Not Hispanic (11,162)	11,352	87.77
Hispanic (186)	203	1.57

Glen Ellyn

Place Type: Village
County: DuPage
Population: 27,450†

Ancestry‡	Population	%
Afghan (305)	305	1.11
African, Sub-Saharan (293)	293	1.07
Ethiopian (14)	14	0.05
Sudanese (157)	157	0.57
Other Sub-Saharan African (122)	122	0.45
Albanian (77)	77	0.28
American (606)	606	2.21
Arab (11)	197	0.72
Lebanese (11)	166	0.61
Syrian (0)	31	0.11
Armenian (0)	13	0.05
Austrian (78)	123	0.45
Basque (10)	10	0.04
Belgian (12)	36	0.13
British (139)	236	0.86
Canadian (18)	34	0.12
Croatian (12)	76	0.28
Czech (192)	993	3.62
Czechoslovakian (32)	91	0.33
Danish (65)	214	0.78
Dutch (312)	807	2.95
Eastern European (10)	10	0.04
English (662)	3,160	11.53
European (481)	561	2.05
Finnish (60)	123	0.45
French, ex. Basque (88)	916	3.34
French Canadian (19)	144	0.53
German (1,998)	8,556	31.23
Greek (148)	434	1.58
Hungarian (43)	144	0.53
Iranian (21)	21	0.08
Irish (1,634)	6,753	24.65
Italian (501)	2,742	10.01
Latvian (0)	16	0.06
Lithuanian (50)	276	1.01
Luxemburger (6)	62	0.23
Northern European (40)	52	0.19
Norwegian (137)	646	2.36
Polish (659)	2,639	9.63
Romanian (73)	118	0.43
Russian (120)	299	1.09
Scandinavian (27)	127	0.46
Scotch-Irish (98)	421	1.54
Scottish (120)	684	2.50
Serbian (10)	62	0.23
Slavic (0)	42	0.15
Slovak (38)	122	0.45
Slovene (22)	48	0.18
Swedish (347)	1,568	5.72
Swiss (17)	183	0.67
Ukrainian (60)	139	0.51
Welsh (94)	265	0.97
Yugoslavian (0)	18	0.07

Hispanic Origin	Population	%
Hispanic or Latino (of any race)	1,801	6.56
Central American, ex. Mexican	87	0.32
Costa Rican	4	0.01
Guatemalan	43	0.16
Honduran	7	0.03
Nicaraguan	3	0.01
Panamanian	9	0.03
Salvadoran	21	0.08
Cuban	75	0.27
Dominican Republic	4	0.01
Mexican	1,276	4.65
Puerto Rican	105	0.38
South American	153	0.56
Argentinean	14	0.05
Bolivian	12	0.04
Chilean	4	0.01
Colombian	45	0.16
Ecuadorian	28	0.10
Paraguayan	2	0.01
Peruvian	36	0.13
Uruguayan	1	<0.01
Venezuelan	11	0.04
Other Hispanic or Latino	101	0.37

Race*	Population	%
African-American/Black (810)	910	3.32
Not Hispanic (786)	864	3.15
Hispanic (24)	46	0.17
American Indian/Alaska Native (36)	109	0.40
Not Hispanic (20)	77	0.28
Hispanic (16)	32	0.12
Blackfeet (0)	3	0.01

SECTION TWO

*Notes: † The Census 2010 population figure is used to calculate the percentages in the Hispanic Origin and Race categories. Ancestry percentages are based on the 2006-2010 American Community Survey population (not shown); ‡ Numbers in parentheses indicate the number of people reporting a single ancestry; * Numbers in parentheses indicate the number of persons reporting this race alone, not in combination with any other race; Please refer to the Explanation of Data for more information.*

Cherokee (1)	13	0.05
Cheyenne (0)	1	<0.01
Chippewa (5)	6	0.02
Choctaw (1)	1	<0.01
Comanche (0)	1	<0.01
Creek (0)	2	0.01
Delaware (0)	1	<0.01
Iroquois (2)	7	0.03
Lumbee (0)	3	0.01
Menominee (0)	1	<0.01
Mexican American Ind. (2)	2	0.01
Navajo (0)	3	0.01
Sioux (3)	3	0.01
South American Ind. (2)	3	0.01
Asian (1,780)	2,021	7.36
Not Hispanic (1,774)	2,001	7.29
Hispanic (6)	20	0.07
Bangladeshi (3)	6	0.02
Bhutanese (4)	4	0.01
Burmese (220)	226	0.82
Cambodian (3)	3	0.01
Chinese, ex. Taiwanese (147)	191	0.70
Filipino (96)	166	0.60
Indian (679)	762	2.78
Indonesian (3)	9	0.03
Japanese (49)	84	0.31
Korean (108)	129	0.47
Pakistani (283)	334	1.22
Sri Lankan (5)	5	0.02
Taiwanese (23)	27	0.10
Thai (18)	21	0.08
Vietnamese (42)	54	0.20
Hawaii Native/Pacific Islander (3)	17	0.06
Not Hispanic (3)	14	0.05
Hispanic (0)	3	0.01
Native Hawaiian (0)	6	0.02
Samoan (2)	2	0.01
White (23,810)	24,213	88.21
Not Hispanic (22,667)	22,998	83.78
Hispanic (1,143)	1,215	4.43

Glencoe

Place Type: Village
County: Cook
Population: 8,723†

Ancestry‡	Population	%
American (425)	425	4.93
Arab (0)	12	0.14
Palestinian (0)	12	0.14
Austrian (33)	167	1.94
Belgian (0)	6	0.07
Brazilian (11)	11	0.13
British (49)	88	1.02
Canadian (0)	17	0.20
Czech (0)	77	0.89
Czechoslovakian (0)	11	0.13
Danish (20)	96	1.11
Eastern European (201)	201	2.33
English (130)	850	9.85
European (347)	358	4.15
Finnish (0)	14	0.16
French, ex. Basque (18)	267	3.09
German (380)	1,653	19.16
Greek (23)	51	0.59
Hungarian (53)	145	1.68
Irish (415)	1,212	14.05
Israeli (42)	53	0.61
Italian (212)	599	6.94
Latvian (9)	9	0.10
Lithuanian (180)	289	3.35
Norwegian (0)	44	0.51
Polish (179)	703	8.15
Portuguese (0)	29	0.34
Romanian (63)	119	1.38
Russian (546)	1,479	17.14
Scandinavian (34)	34	0.39
Scotch-Irish (16)	68	0.79
Scottish (16)	240	2.78
Slavic (0)	28	0.32
Slovak (0)	28	0.32
Swedish (19)	145	1.68
Swiss (12)	12	0.14
Ukrainian (8)	56	0.65
Welsh (0)	48	0.56
Yugoslavian (21)	84	0.97

Hispanic Origin	Population	%
Hispanic or Latino (of any race)	232	2.66
Central American, ex. Mexican	32	0.37
Costa Rican	5	0.06
Guatemalan	5	0.06
Honduran	3	0.03
Nicaraguan	4	0.05
Panamanian	12	0.14
Salvadoran	3	0.03
Cuban	11	0.13
Dominican Republic	4	0.05
Mexican	93	1.07
Puerto Rican	24	0.28
South American	51	0.58
Argentinean	16	0.18
Bolivian	4	0.05
Chilean	3	0.03
Colombian	11	0.13
Ecuadorian	4	0.05
Peruvian	9	0.10
Uruguayan	4	0.05
Other Hispanic or Latino	17	0.19

Race*	Population	%
African-American/Black (107)	141	1.62
Not Hispanic (105)	137	1.57
Hispanic (2)	4	0.05
American Indian/Alaska Native (8)	24	0.28
Not Hispanic (5)	19	0.22
Hispanic (3)	5	0.06
Apache (0)	3	0.03
Canadian/French Am. Ind. (0)	1	0.01
Cherokee (0)	7	0.08
Chippewa (0)	3	0.03
Mexican American Ind. (3)	3	0.03
Asian (235)	323	3.70
Not Hispanic (234)	312	3.58
Hispanic (1)	11	0.13
Bangladeshi (1)	1	0.01
Burmese (1)	4	0.05
Chinese, ex. Taiwanese (83)	112	1.28
Filipino (8)	20	0.23
Hmong (4)	4	0.05
Indian (54)	67	0.77
Japanese (9)	26	0.30
Korean (43)	48	0.55
Pakistani (11)	11	0.13
Sri Lankan (1)	1	0.01
Taiwanese (2)	6	0.07
Thai (5)	7	0.08
Vietnamese (5)	13	0.15
Hawaii Native/Pacific Islander (1)	1	0.01
Not Hispanic (1)	1	0.01
White (8,201)	8,316	95.33
Not Hispanic (8,024)	8,125	93.14
Hispanic (177)	191	2.19

Glendale Heights

Place Type: Village
County: DuPage
Population: 34,208†

Ancestry‡	Population	%
African, Sub-Saharan (161)	161	0.48
African (126)	126	0.37
Ethiopian (35)	35	0.10
Albanian (163)	163	0.48
American (455)	455	1.35
Arab (0)	32	0.10
Arab (0)	16	0.05
Lebanese (0)	16	0.05
Assyrian/Chaldean/Syriac (21)	21	0.06
Austrian (36)	62	0.18
Belgian (41)	60	0.18
Bulgarian (212)	212	0.63
Canadian (0)	122	0.36
Croatian (10)	25	0.07
Czech (60)	380	1.13
Czechoslovakian (0)	57	0.17
Danish (49)	95	0.28
Dutch (63)	191	0.57
Eastern European (4)	4	0.01
English (353)	957	2.84
European (82)	131	0.39
Finnish (0)	58	0.17
French, ex. Basque (24)	451	1.34
French Canadian (44)	59	0.18
German (1,233)	4,438	13.18
Greek (12)	135	0.40
Hungarian (19)	128	0.38
Irish (567)	2,500	7.43
Italian (1,112)	2,492	7.40
Latvian (8)	20	0.06
Lithuanian (102)	161	0.48
Norwegian (110)	373	1.11
Polish (1,284)	2,681	7.96
Romanian (9)	18	0.05
Russian (45)	122	0.36
Scandinavian (8)	8	0.02
Scotch-Irish (62)	204	0.61
Scottish (118)	265	0.79
Serbian (60)	60	0.18
Slavic (0)	9	0.03
Slovak (0)	62	0.18
Slovene (0)	51	0.15
Swedish (99)	344	1.02
Ukrainian (160)	236	0.70
Welsh (0)	21	0.06
West Indian, ex. Hispanic (26)	26	0.08
Barbadian (26)	26	0.08
Yugoslavian (50)	121	0.36

Hispanic Origin	Population	%
Hispanic or Latino (of any race)	10,512	30.73
Central American, ex. Mexican	550	1.61
Costa Rican	13	0.04
Guatemalan	357	1.04
Honduran	63	0.18
Nicaraguan	14	0.04
Panamanian	6	0.02
Salvadoran	93	0.27
Other Central American	4	0.01
Cuban	79	0.23
Dominican Republic	3	0.01
Mexican	8,685	25.39
Puerto Rican	465	1.36
South American	323	0.94
Argentinean	35	0.10
Bolivian	12	0.04
Chilean	12	0.04
Colombian	99	0.29
Ecuadorian	76	0.22
Paraguayan	4	0.01
Peruvian	61	0.18
Uruguayan	3	0.01
Venezuelan	17	0.05
Other South American	4	0.01
Other Hispanic or Latino	407	1.19

Race*	Population	%
African-American/Black (2,005)	2,266	6.62
Not Hispanic (1,939)	2,135	6.24
Hispanic (66)	131	0.38
American Indian/Alaska Native (206)	392	1.15
Not Hispanic (61)	182	0.53
Hispanic (145)	210	0.61
Apache (1)	1	<0.01
Arapaho (0)	1	<0.01
Blackfeet (0)	2	0.01
Cherokee (7)	32	0.09
Chippewa (4)	9	0.03

*Notes: † The Census 2010 population figure is used to calculate the percentages in the Hispanic Origin and Race categories. Ancestry percentages are based on the 2006-2010 American Community Survey population (not shown); ‡ Numbers in parentheses indicate the number of people reporting a single ancestry; * Numbers in parentheses indicate the number of persons reporting this race alone, not in combination with any other race; Please refer to the Explanation of Data for more information.*

Cree (0)	4	0.01
Creek (1)	1	<0.01
Crow (0)	1	<0.01
Iroquois (2)	5	0.01
Lumbee (4)	4	0.01
Mexican American Ind. (30)	50	0.15
Navajo (2)	4	0.01
Osage (1)	5	0.01
Ottawa (1)	1	<0.01
Potawatomi (0)	1	<0.01
Puget Sound Salish (1)	1	<0.01
Sioux (1)	2	0.01
South American Ind. (1)	2	0.01
Tohono O'Odham (0)	1	<0.01
Asian (7,575)	8,024	23.46
Not Hispanic (7,528)	7,940	23.21
Hispanic (47)	84	0.25
Bangladeshi (22)	23	0.07
Bhutanese (14)	14	0.04
Burmese (26)	27	0.08
Cambodian (106)	128	0.37
Chinese, ex. Taiwanese (183)	239	0.70
Filipino (1,864)	2,027	5.93
Hmong (4)	5	0.01
Indian (2,998)	3,215	9.40
Indonesian (0)	2	0.01
Japanese (42)	76	0.22
Korean (154)	171	0.50
Laotian (13)	22	0.06
Malaysian (4)	6	0.02
Nepalese (8)	9	0.03
Pakistani (792)	877	2.56
Sri Lankan (5)	6	0.02
Taiwanese (10)	11	0.03
Thai (34)	42	0.12
Vietnamese (1,042)	1,077	3.15
Hawaii Native/Pacific Islander (24)	68	0.20
Not Hispanic (19)	43	0.13
Hispanic (5)	25	0.07
Fijian (8)	9	0.03
Guamanian/Chamorro (5)	5	0.01
Native Hawaiian (3)	14	0.04
Samoan (1)	6	0.02
White (17,953)	18,819	55.01
Not Hispanic (13,438)	13,842	40.46
Hispanic (4,515)	4,977	14.55

Glenview

Place Type: Village
County: Cook
Population: 44,692†

Ancestry‡	Population	%
African, Sub-Saharan (11)	22	0.05
Ethiopian (11)	22	0.05
American (1,705)	1,705	3.91
Arab (216)	295	0.68
Arab (37)	55	0.13
Egyptian (10)	10	0.02
Iraqi (64)	82	0.19
Lebanese (78)	108	0.25
Palestinian (27)	27	0.06
Other Arab (0)	13	0.03
Armenian (72)	153	0.35
Assyrian/Chaldean/Syriac (275)	303	0.69
Australian (0)	27	0.06
Austrian (144)	406	0.93
Belgian (31)	175	0.40
Brazilian (35)	68	0.16
British (53)	119	0.27
Bulgarian (0)	74	0.17
Canadian (0)	17	0.04
Croatian (169)	194	0.44
Czech (91)	459	1.05
Czechoslovakian (42)	72	0.16
Danish (67)	202	0.46
Dutch (87)	455	1.04
Eastern European (483)	596	1.37
English (627)	3,051	6.99
European (432)	475	1.09
Finnish (21)	208	0.48
French, ex. Basque (113)	866	1.98
French Canadian (0)	100	0.23
German (2,119)	8,293	19.00
Greek (803)	1,332	3.05
Hungarian (160)	514	1.18
Iranian (185)	261	0.60
Irish (1,981)	6,812	15.61
Israeli (0)	11	0.03
Italian (1,057)	3,307	7.58
Latvian (77)	102	0.23
Lithuanian (226)	452	1.04
Luxemburger (0)	50	0.11
Macedonian (9)	9	0.02
Northern European (67)	67	0.15
Norwegian (105)	758	1.74
Polish (2,724)	5,133	11.76
Portuguese (12)	45	0.10
Romanian (316)	355	0.81
Russian (1,469)	2,477	5.67
Scandinavian (70)	238	0.55
Scotch-Irish (116)	389	0.89
Scottish (151)	826	1.89
Serbian (84)	94	0.22
Slovak (47)	47	0.11
Slovene (27)	52	0.12
Swedish (351)	1,578	3.62
Swiss (34)	343	0.79
Turkish (14)	14	0.03
Ukrainian (618)	741	1.70
Welsh (22)	205	0.47
West Indian, ex. Hispanic (17)	28	0.06
Belizean (11)	11	0.03
Bermudan (0)	11	0.03
Haitian (6)	6	0.01
Yugoslavian (30)	30	0.07

Hispanic Origin	Population	%
Hispanic or Latino (of any race)	2,584	5.78
Central American, ex. Mexican	105	0.23
Costa Rican	2	<0.01
Guatemalan	71	0.16
Honduran	8	0.02
Nicaraguan	7	0.02
Salvadoran	17	0.04
Cuban	133	0.30
Dominican Republic	11	0.02
Mexican	1,607	3.60
Puerto Rican	223	0.50
South American	370	0.83
Argentinean	39	0.09
Bolivian	23	0.05
Chilean	20	0.04
Colombian	150	0.34
Ecuadorian	65	0.15
Paraguayan	5	0.01
Peruvian	43	0.10
Uruguayan	5	0.01
Venezuelan	12	0.03
Other South American	8	0.02
Other Hispanic or Latino	135	0.30

Race*	Population	%
African-American/Black (451)	559	1.25
Not Hispanic (431)	518	1.16
Hispanic (20)	41	0.09
American Indian/Alaska Native (54)	126	0.28
Not Hispanic (25)	85	0.19
Hispanic (29)	41	0.09
Apache (0)	1	<0.01
Blackfeet (0)	2	<0.01
Central American Ind. (3)	3	0.01
Cherokee (2)	24	0.05
Chippewa (5)	6	0.01
Choctaw (2)	2	<0.01
Creek (1)	2	<0.01
Inupiat *(Alaska Native)* (5)	5	0.01
Iroquois (1)	2	<0.01
Menominee (0)	1	<0.01
Mexican American Ind. (10)	15	0.03
Sioux (0)	3	0.01
South American Ind. (0)	3	0.01
Asian (5,569)	6,052	13.54
Not Hispanic (5,535)	5,996	13.42
Hispanic (34)	56	0.13
Bangladeshi (9)	12	0.03
Burmese (4)	4	0.01
Cambodian (19)	23	0.05
Chinese, ex. Taiwanese (706)	858	1.92
Filipino (565)	701	1.57
Hmong (2)	4	0.01
Indian (1,288)	1,375	3.08
Indonesian (3)	4	0.01
Japanese (217)	331	0.74
Korean (2,240)	2,321	5.19
Laotian (1)	3	0.01
Malaysian (5)	5	0.01
Pakistani (175)	194	0.43
Sri Lankan (5)	5	0.01
Taiwanese (72)	82	0.18
Thai (65)	75	0.17
Vietnamese (39)	58	0.13
Hawaii Native/Pacific Islander (27)	54	0.12
Not Hispanic (21)	46	0.10
Hispanic (6)	8	0.02
Fijian (1)	1	<0.01
Guamanian/Chamorro (2)	3	0.01
Native Hawaiian (9)	15	0.03
Samoan (1)	1	<0.01
Tongan (2)	2	<0.01
White (37,201)	37,825	84.63
Not Hispanic (35,434)	35,972	80.49
Hispanic (1,767)	1,853	4.15

Glenwood

Place Type: Village
County: Cook
Population: 8,969†

Ancestry‡	Population	%
African, Sub-Saharan (110)	136	1.56
African (105)	131	1.50
Cape Verdean (5)	5	0.06
American (33)	33	0.38
Croatian (0)	23	0.26
Czech (14)	129	1.48
Czechoslovakian (0)	12	0.14
Danish (0)	60	0.69
Dutch (36)	113	1.29
Eastern European (11)	11	0.13
English (77)	164	1.88
European (45)	54	0.62
Finnish (14)	14	0.16
French, ex. Basque (8)	174	1.99
French Canadian (0)	10	0.11
German (261)	918	10.51
Hungarian (0)	20	0.23
Irish (95)	412	4.72
Italian (143)	336	3.85
Lithuanian (27)	74	0.85
Norwegian (32)	89	1.02
Polish (162)	403	4.62
Scandinavian (13)	13	0.15
Scotch-Irish (0)	79	0.90
Scottish (0)	34	0.39
Slovak (13)	25	0.29
Swedish (8)	53	0.61
Swiss (0)	7	0.08
West Indian, ex. Hispanic (13)	28	0.32
Belizean (13)	13	0.15
Jamaican (0)	15	0.17

Hispanic Origin	Population	%
Hispanic or Latino (of any race)	665	7.41
Central American, ex. Mexican	10	0.11
Costa Rican	1	0.01
Guatemalan	3	0.03
Panamanian	6	0.07

*Notes: † The Census 2010 population figure is used to calculate the percentages in the Hispanic Origin and Race categories. Ancestry percentages are based on the 2006-2010 American Community Survey population (not shown); ‡ Numbers in parentheses indicate the number of people reporting a single ancestry; * Numbers in parentheses indicate the number of persons reporting this race alone, not in combination with any other race; Please refer to the Explanation of Data for more information.*

Cuban	10	0.11
Dominican Republic	3	0.03
Mexican	522	5.82
Puerto Rican	73	0.81
South American	5	0.06
Argentinean	2	0.02
Chilean	1	0.01
Colombian	2	0.02
Other Hispanic or Latino	42	0.47

Race*	Population	%
African-American/Black (5,979)	6,128	68.32
Not Hispanic (5,909)	6,031	67.24
Hispanic (70)	97	1.08
American Indian/Alaska Native (12)	59	0.66
Not Hispanic (10)	51	0.57
Hispanic (2)	8	0.09
Apache (0)	1	0.01
Blackfeet (0)	2	0.02
Cherokee (0)	19	0.21
Choctaw (0)	2	0.02
Creek (0)	1	0.01
Mexican American Ind. (1)	1	0.01
Potawatomi (1)	3	0.03
Asian (27)	47	0.52
Not Hispanic (27)	47	0.52
Chinese, ex. Taiwanese (8)	9	0.10
Filipino (2)	10	0.11
Indian (0)	3	0.03
Indonesian (2)	2	0.02
Japanese (5)	8	0.09
Korean (1)	4	0.04
Sri Lankan (1)	1	0.01
Vietnamese (8)	8	0.09
Hawaii Native/Pacific Islander (9)	20	0.22
Not Hispanic (8)	18	0.20
Hispanic (1)	2	0.02
Guamanian/Chamorro (0)	1	0.01
Native Hawaiian (1)	2	0.02
Samoan (7)	9	0.10
White (2,447)	2,592	28.90
Not Hispanic (2,186)	2,298	25.62
Hispanic (261)	294	3.28

Godfrey

Place Type: Village
County: Madison
Population: 17,982†

Ancestry‡	Population	%
African, Sub-Saharan (14)	26	0.15
Ghanaian (14)	26	0.15
American (1,219)	1,219	6.84
Belgian (24)	24	0.13
British (9)	9	0.05
Croatian (7)	67	0.38
Czech (9)	63	0.35
Czechoslovakian (0)	15	0.08
Danish (0)	8	0.04
Dutch (83)	379	2.13
English (909)	2,478	13.91
European (167)	167	0.94
Finnish (0)	8	0.04
French, ex. Basque (190)	718	4.03
French Canadian (16)	16	0.09
German (3,815)	7,284	40.88
Greek (0)	21	0.12
Hungarian (20)	20	0.11
Irish (878)	2,838	15.93
Italian (258)	785	4.41
Lithuanian (31)	31	0.17
Norwegian (88)	98	0.55
Pennsylvania German (23)	23	0.13
Polish (302)	429	2.41
Russian (0)	15	0.08
Scandinavian (24)	24	0.13
Scotch-Irish (144)	434	2.44
Scottish (60)	296	1.66
Slovak (10)	10	0.06
Swedish (36)	69	0.39
Swiss (26)	63	0.35
Turkish (42)	42	0.24
Ukrainian (34)	34	0.19
Welsh (17)	203	1.14
Yugoslavian (10)	10	0.06

Hispanic Origin	Population	%
Hispanic or Latino (of any race)	270	1.50
Central American, ex. Mexican	28	0.16
Costa Rican	1	0.01
Guatemalan	12	0.07
Honduran	7	0.04
Nicaraguan	1	0.01
Panamanian	6	0.03
Salvadoran	1	0.01
Cuban	15	0.08
Mexican	163	0.91
Puerto Rican	26	0.14
South American	15	0.08
Bolivian	1	0.01
Chilean	5	0.03
Colombian	4	0.02
Peruvian	5	0.03
Other Hispanic or Latino	23	0.13

Race*	Population	%
African-American/Black (841)	967	5.38
Not Hispanic (830)	953	5.30
Hispanic (11)	14	0.08
American Indian/Alaska Native (45)	100	0.56
Not Hispanic (42)	97	0.54
Hispanic (3)	3	0.02
Cherokee (12)	31	0.17
Cheyenne (1)	1	0.01
Choctaw (0)	1	0.01
Crow (0)	1	0.01
Delaware (1)	1	0.01
Mexican American Ind. (2)	2	0.01
Navajo (2)	4	0.02
Potawatomi (0)	2	0.01
Shoshone (0)	3	0.02
Sioux (10)	17	0.09
Yaqui (0)	4	0.02
Asian (134)	186	1.03
Not Hispanic (133)	184	1.02
Hispanic (1)	2	0.01
Cambodian (1)	1	0.01
Chinese, ex. Taiwanese (32)	35	0.19
Filipino (12)	27	0.15
Indian (12)	14	0.08
Japanese (13)	33	0.18
Korean (21)	28	0.16
Laotian (4)	4	0.02
Pakistani (1)	1	0.01
Taiwanese (6)	6	0.03
Thai (9)	13	0.07
Vietnamese (11)	14	0.08
Hawaii Native/Pacific Islander (3)	9	0.05
Not Hispanic (3)	9	0.05
Guamanian/Chamorro (2)	2	0.01
Native Hawaiian (1)	5	0.03
Samoan (0)	2	0.01
White (16,652)	16,883	93.89
Not Hispanic (16,467)	16,683	92.78
Hispanic (185)	200	1.11

Granite City

Place Type: City
County: Madison
Population: 29,849†

Ancestry‡	Population	%
African, Sub-Saharan (102)	136	0.45
African (102)	136	0.45
American (3,235)	3,235	10.61
Arab (41)	61	0.20
Arab (41)	41	0.13
Lebanese (0)	20	0.07
Armenian (51)	96	0.31
Belgian (28)	41	0.13
Brazilian (36)	36	0.12
British (10)	51	0.17
Bulgarian (105)	202	0.66
Canadian (12)	12	0.04
Croatian (94)	363	1.19
Czech (35)	94	0.31
Czechoslovakian (20)	20	0.07
Danish (12)	52	0.17
Dutch (78)	694	2.28
Eastern European (11)	34	0.11
English (937)	2,921	9.58
European (943)	957	3.14
French, ex. Basque (194)	1,514	4.97
French Canadian (28)	46	0.15
German (2,629)	7,144	23.44
German Russian (0)	11	0.04
Greek (108)	292	0.96
Hungarian (116)	481	1.58
Icelander (0)	14	0.05
Irish (1,299)	5,487	18.00
Italian (742)	2,037	6.68
Lithuanian (29)	64	0.21
Macedonian (43)	148	0.49
Norwegian (9)	51	0.17
Polish (267)	946	3.10
Portuguese (0)	6	0.02
Romanian (9)	47	0.15
Russian (58)	79	0.26
Scandinavian (0)	10	0.03
Scotch-Irish (310)	494	1.62
Scottish (90)	451	1.48
Serbian (0)	10	0.03
Slavic (0)	110	0.36
Slovak (42)	198	0.65
Swedish (8)	106	0.35
Swiss (0)	53	0.17
Ukrainian (0)	61	0.20
Welsh (44)	283	0.93
Yugoslavian (31)	41	0.13

Hispanic Origin	Population	%
Hispanic or Latino (of any race)	1,489	4.99
Central American, ex. Mexican	43	0.14
Guatemalan	3	0.01
Honduran	8	0.03
Nicaraguan	6	0.02
Panamanian	12	0.04
Salvadoran	13	0.04
Other Central American	1	<0.01
Cuban	17	0.06
Dominican Republic	4	0.01
Mexican	1,262	4.23
Puerto Rican	61	0.20
South American	7	0.02
Argentinean	3	0.01
Colombian	2	0.01
Ecuadorian	1	<0.01
Peruvian	1	<0.01
Other Hispanic or Latino	95	0.32

Race*	Population	%
African-American/Black (1,632)	1,931	6.47
Not Hispanic (1,618)	1,891	6.34
Hispanic (14)	40	0.13
American Indian/Alaska Native (114)	295	0.99
Not Hispanic (87)	250	0.84
Hispanic (27)	45	0.15
Alaska Athabascan *(Ala. Nat.)* (0)	1	<0.01
Aleut *(Alaska Native)* (1)	3	0.01
Apache (2)	3	0.01
Blackfeet (3)	19	0.06
Canadian/French Am. Ind. (3)	8	0.03
Cherokee (36)	114	0.38
Cheyenne (1)	1	<0.01
Chickasaw (1)	4	0.01
Chippewa (8)	8	0.03
Choctaw (2)	4	0.01
Creek (1)	2	0.01

*Notes: † The Census 2010 population figure is used to calculate the percentages in the Hispanic Origin and Race categories. Ancestry percentages are based on the 2006-2010 American Community Survey population (not shown); ‡ Numbers in parentheses indicate the number of people reporting a single ancestry; * Numbers in parentheses indicate the number of persons reporting this race alone, not in combination with any other race; Please refer to the Explanation of Data for more information.*

Delaware (0)	1	<0.01
Hopi (1)	3	0.01
Iroquois (1)	1	<0.01
Lumbee (1)	5	0.02
Mexican American Ind. (4)	5	0.02
Navajo (0)	2	0.01
Osage (1)	1	<0.01
Paiute (3)	3	0.01
Potawatomi (0)	1	<0.01
Seminole (0)	3	0.01
Sioux (1)	9	0.03
Yaqui (0)	1	<0.01
Asian (156)	253	0.85
Not Hispanic (144)	225	0.75
Hispanic (12)	28	0.09
Burmese (4)	4	0.01
Cambodian (0)	2	0.01
Chinese, ex. Taiwanese (18)	24	0.08
Filipino (45)	70	0.23
Indian (21)	44	0.15
Japanese (13)	25	0.08
Korean (32)	47	0.16
Laotian (11)	22	0.07
Pakistani (2)	2	0.01
Thai (5)	8	0.03
Vietnamese (2)	3	0.01
Hawaii Native/Pacific Islander (11)	44	0.15
Not Hispanic (10)	30	0.10
Hispanic (1)	14	0.05
Guamanian/Chamorro (1)	2	0.01
Native Hawaiian (4)	18	0.06
Samoan (1)	2	0.01
White (26,722)	27,309	91.49
Not Hispanic (25,994)	26,460	88.65
Hispanic (728)	849	2.84

Grayslake

Place Type: Village
County: Lake
Population: 20,957†

Ancestry‡	Population	%
African, Sub-Saharan (68)	68	0.33
African (68)	68	0.33
American (836)	836	4.04
Armenian (0)	14	0.07
Assyrian/Chaldean/Syriac (0)	12	0.06
Australian (0)	18	0.09
Austrian (10)	49	0.24
Belgian (0)	11	0.05
British (13)	72	0.35
Bulgarian (58)	71	0.34
Canadian (18)	18	0.09
Croatian (15)	78	0.38
Czech (75)	294	1.42
Czechoslovakian (24)	46	0.22
Danish (12)	128	0.62
Dutch (21)	341	1.65
Eastern European (123)	135	0.65
English (333)	1,397	6.76
European (223)	235	1.14
Finnish (59)	59	0.29
French, ex. Basque (28)	421	2.04
French Canadian (60)	151	0.73
German (1,892)	6,290	30.43
Greek (49)	227	1.10
Hungarian (72)	193	0.93
Iranian (12)	12	0.06
Irish (828)	3,943	19.08
Italian (425)	2,056	9.95
Latvian (14)	14	0.07
Lithuanian (72)	178	0.86
Luxemburger (10)	27	0.13
Norwegian (255)	620	3.00
Polish (963)	2,784	13.47
Romanian (0)	49	0.24
Russian (289)	532	2.57
Scandinavian (49)	60	0.29
Scotch-Irish (57)	186	0.90
Scottish (154)	270	1.31
Serbian (14)	26	0.13
Slavic (0)	15	0.07
Slovak (20)	66	0.32
Slovene (12)	19	0.09
Swedish (184)	931	4.50
Swiss (0)	20	0.10
Turkish (30)	60	0.29
Ukrainian (28)	70	0.34
Welsh (19)	36	0.17
Yugoslavian (11)	30	0.15

Hispanic Origin	Population	%
Hispanic or Latino (of any race)	1,853	8.84
Central American, ex. Mexican	112	0.53
Costa Rican	1	<0.01
Guatemalan	34	0.16
Honduran	21	0.10
Nicaraguan	2	0.01
Panamanian	9	0.04
Salvadoran	44	0.21
Other Central American	1	<0.01
Cuban	72	0.34
Dominican Republic	9	0.04
Mexican	1,178	5.62
Puerto Rican	222	1.06
South American	148	0.71
Argentinean	14	0.07
Bolivian	10	0.05
Chilean	8	0.04
Colombian	51	0.24
Ecuadorian	31	0.15
Paraguayan	1	<0.01
Peruvian	24	0.11
Venezuelan	9	0.04
Other Hispanic or Latino	112	0.53

Race*	Population	%
African-American/Black (691)	835	3.98
Not Hispanic (667)	786	3.75
Hispanic (24)	49	0.23
American Indian/Alaska Native (53)	144	0.69
Not Hispanic (35)	102	0.49
Hispanic (18)	42	0.20
Blackfeet (0)	10	0.05
Central American Ind. (1)	2	0.01
Cherokee (4)	38	0.18
Chippewa (1)	5	0.02
Choctaw (0)	1	<0.01
Cree (1)	2	0.01
Iroquois (2)	5	0.02
Menominee (1)	1	<0.01
Mexican American Ind. (4)	6	0.03
Navajo (1)	1	<0.01
Potawatomi (3)	3	0.01
South American Ind. (1)	3	0.01
Ute (0)	4	0.02
Asian (1,415)	1,644	7.84
Not Hispanic (1,406)	1,618	7.72
Hispanic (9)	26	0.12
Bangladeshi (10)	10	0.05
Cambodian (9)	11	0.05
Chinese, ex. Taiwanese (191)	265	1.26
Filipino (273)	348	1.66
Hmong (0)	1	<0.01
Indian (537)	566	2.70
Indonesian (0)	5	0.02
Japanese (51)	95	0.45
Korean (198)	228	1.09
Laotian (6)	8	0.04
Malaysian (4)	4	0.02
Nepalese (8)	8	0.04
Pakistani (44)	53	0.25
Sri Lankan (5)	6	0.03
Taiwanese (5)	8	0.04
Thai (15)	24	0.11
Vietnamese (22)	33	0.16
Hawaii Native/Pacific Islander (5)	21	0.10
Not Hispanic (3)	12	0.06
Hispanic (2)	9	0.04
Guamanian/Chamorro (0)	5	0.02
Native Hawaiian (3)	8	0.04
Samoan (2)	4	0.02
White (17,548)	18,034	86.05
Not Hispanic (16,578)	16,929	80.78
Hispanic (970)	1,105	5.27

Gurnee

Place Type: Village
County: Lake
Population: 31,295†

Ancestry‡	Population	%
African, Sub-Saharan (42)	53	0.17
African (36)	47	0.15
Ethiopian (6)	6	0.02
American (1,010)	1,010	3.25
Arab (124)	133	0.43
Arab (22)	22	0.07
Egyptian (69)	69	0.22
Lebanese (9)	13	0.04
Syrian (24)	24	0.08
Other Arab (0)	5	0.02
Armenian (26)	59	0.19
Assyrian/Chaldean/Syriac (40)	78	0.25
Austrian (0)	130	0.42
Belgian (36)	84	0.27
Brazilian (20)	20	0.06
British (42)	105	0.34
Canadian (9)	111	0.36
Celtic (13)	13	0.04
Croatian (92)	319	1.03
Czech (69)	471	1.52
Danish (68)	285	0.92
Dutch (24)	407	1.31
Eastern European (128)	128	0.41
English (449)	2,441	7.86
European (247)	265	0.85
Finnish (18)	125	0.40
French, ex. Basque (136)	561	1.81
French Canadian (25)	153	0.49
German (1,913)	7,139	22.98
German Russian (10)	22	0.07
Greek (314)	686	2.21
Hungarian (36)	174	0.56
Iranian (35)	35	0.11
Irish (852)	4,661	15.00
Italian (714)	2,621	8.44
Latvian (0)	12	0.04
Lithuanian (78)	468	1.51
Luxemburger (10)	25	0.08
Macedonian (0)	6	0.02
Northern European (18)	18	0.06
Norwegian (106)	600	1.93
Pennsylvania German (12)	12	0.04
Polish (1,148)	3,313	10.66
Portuguese (0)	120	0.39
Romanian (48)	251	0.81
Russian (126)	397	1.28
Scotch-Irish (196)	384	1.24
Scottish (155)	629	2.02
Serbian (168)	168	0.54
Slavic (10)	75	0.24
Slovak (18)	73	0.23
Slovene (55)	167	0.54
Swedish (208)	1,250	4.02
Swiss (44)	152	0.49
Turkish (6)	6	0.02
Ukrainian (12)	49	0.16
Welsh (13)	125	0.40
West Indian, ex. Hispanic (187)	209	0.67
Belizean (122)	122	0.39
British West Indian (4)	4	0.01
Haitian (24)	35	0.11
Jamaican (37)	37	0.12
West Indian (0)	11	0.04
Yugoslavian (37)	146	0.47

*Notes: † The Census 2010 population figure is used to calculate the percentages in the Hispanic Origin and Race categories. Ancestry percentages are based on the 2006-2010 American Community Survey population (not shown); ‡ Numbers in parentheses indicate the number of people reporting a single ancestry; * Numbers in parentheses indicate the number of persons reporting this race alone, not in combination with any other race; Please refer to the Explanation of Data for more information.*

Hispanic Origin	Population	%
Hispanic or Latino (of any race)	3,665	11.71
Central American, ex. Mexican	275	0.88
Costa Rican	3	0.01
Guatemalan	66	0.21
Honduran	94	0.30
Nicaraguan	11	0.04
Panamanian	18	0.06
Salvadoran	78	0.25
Other Central American	5	0.02
Cuban	76	0.24
Dominican Republic	13	0.04
Mexican	2,298	7.34
Puerto Rican	511	1.63
South American	306	0.98
Argentinean	31	0.10
Bolivian	13	0.04
Chilean	7	0.02
Colombian	145	0.46
Ecuadorian	41	0.13
Peruvian	46	0.15
Uruguayan	5	0.02
Venezuelan	12	0.04
Other South American	6	0.02
Other Hispanic or Latino	186	0.59

Race*	Population	%
African-American/Black (2,443)	2,740	8.76
Not Hispanic (2,362)	2,582	8.25
Hispanic (81)	158	0.50
American Indian/Alaska Native (93)	266	0.85
Not Hispanic (57)	175	0.56
Hispanic (36)	91	0.29
Apache (0)	4	0.01
Arapaho (1)	2	0.01
Blackfeet (2)	10	0.03
Canadian/French Am. Ind. (1)	1	<0.01
Cherokee (12)	56	0.18
Chippewa (5)	16	0.05
Choctaw (1)	6	0.02
Cree (0)	1	<0.01
Iroquois (0)	3	0.01
Kiowa (5)	6	0.02
Lumbee (6)	6	0.02
Mexican American Ind. (7)	11	0.04
Navajo (1)	1	<0.01
Osage (1)	1	<0.01
Pima (0)	3	0.01
Seminole (0)	1	<0.01
Sioux (0)	5	0.02
South American Ind. (4)	9	0.03
Asian (3,625)	4,037	12.90
Not Hispanic (3,601)	3,959	12.65
Hispanic (24)	78	0.25
Bangladeshi (22)	23	0.07
Burmese (4)	4	0.01
Cambodian (17)	26	0.08
Chinese, ex. Taiwanese (466)	562	1.80
Filipino (1,095)	1,287	4.11
Indian (1,274)	1,345	4.30
Indonesian (5)	8	0.03
Japanese (59)	112	0.36
Korean (294)	333	1.06
Laotian (4)	7	0.02
Malaysian (13)	17	0.05
Nepalese (1)	2	0.01
Pakistani (141)	160	0.51
Sri Lankan (16)	17	0.05
Taiwanese (16)	18	0.06
Thai (16)	21	0.07
Vietnamese (67)	80	0.26
Hawaii Native/Pacific Islander (14)	61	0.19
Not Hispanic (14)	56	0.18
Hispanic (0)	5	0.02
Fijian (1)	2	0.01
Guamanian/Chamorro (6)	14	0.04
Native Hawaiian (2)	15	0.05
Samoan (2)	5	0.02
White (22,924)	23,760	75.92
Not Hispanic (20,872)	21,452	68.55
Hispanic (2,052)	2,308	7.37

Hanover Park

Place Type: Village
County: Cook
Population: 37,973†

Ancestry‡	Population	%
African, Sub-Saharan (333)	367	0.97
African (31)	65	0.17
Ghanaian (233)	233	0.62
Other Sub-Saharan African (69)	69	0.18
Albanian (149)	149	0.39
American (454)	454	1.20
Arab (57)	57	0.15
Syrian (57)	57	0.15
Armenian (0)	12	0.03
Assyrian/Chaldean/Syriac (119)	119	0.32
Austrian (43)	55	0.15
Belgian (45)	66	0.17
Brazilian (51)	51	0.14
British (19)	53	0.14
Bulgarian (47)	55	0.15
Canadian (0)	189	0.50
Croatian (49)	73	0.19
Czech (94)	434	1.15
Czechoslovakian (11)	55	0.15
Danish (0)	98	0.26
Dutch (71)	319	0.85
Eastern European (21)	21	0.06
English (296)	1,142	3.03
European (54)	54	0.14
Finnish (22)	50	0.13
French, ex. Basque (9)	491	1.30
French Canadian (32)	32	0.08
German (1,119)	5,361	14.20
Greek (35)	126	0.33
Hungarian (13)	151	0.40
Iranian (170)	170	0.45
Irish (818)	3,316	8.79
Italian (718)	2,151	5.70
Latvian (8)	8	0.02
Lithuanian (57)	82	0.22
Luxemburger (6)	6	0.02
Northern European (13)	13	0.03
Norwegian (198)	622	1.65
Polish (1,538)	3,860	10.23
Romanian (50)	189	0.50
Russian (90)	160	0.42
Scandinavian (0)	14	0.04
Scotch-Irish (10)	94	0.25
Scottish (68)	364	0.96
Serbian (48)	96	0.25
Slavic (0)	12	0.03
Slovak (0)	23	0.06
Swedish (45)	355	0.94
Swiss (0)	29	0.08
Ukrainian (37)	118	0.31
Welsh (0)	132	0.35
West Indian, ex. Hispanic (91)	99	0.26
Belizean (28)	28	0.07
Haitian (23)	23	0.06
Jamaican (40)	48	0.13
Yugoslavian (229)	265	0.70

Hispanic Origin	Population	%
Hispanic or Latino (of any race)	14,532	38.27
Central American, ex. Mexican	437	1.15
Costa Rican	7	0.02
Guatemalan	223	0.59
Honduran	35	0.09
Nicaraguan	15	0.04
Panamanian	4	0.01
Salvadoran	149	0.39
Other Central American	4	0.01
Cuban	86	0.23
Dominican Republic	40	0.11
Mexican	12,691	33.42
Puerto Rican	572	1.51
South American	316	0.83
Argentinean	22	0.06
Bolivian	5	0.01
Chilean	12	0.03
Colombian	139	0.37
Ecuadorian	77	0.20
Peruvian	43	0.11
Uruguayan	1	<0.01
Venezuelan	13	0.03
Other South American	4	0.01
Other Hispanic or Latino	390	1.03

Race*	Population	%
African-American/Black (2,674)	3,035	7.99
Not Hispanic (2,509)	2,765	7.28
Hispanic (165)	270	0.71
American Indian/Alaska Native (397)	614	1.62
Not Hispanic (62)	197	0.52
Hispanic (335)	417	1.10
Apache (7)	8	0.02
Arapaho (0)	2	0.01
Canadian/French Am. Ind. (0)	1	<0.01
Cherokee (6)	50	0.13
Chickasaw (0)	2	0.01
Chippewa (4)	14	0.04
Choctaw (1)	6	0.02
Creek (0)	2	0.01
Mexican American Ind. (28)	39	0.10
Navajo (1)	1	<0.01
Ottawa (1)	6	0.02
Potawatomi (2)	4	0.01
Sioux (2)	4	0.01
South American Ind. (6)	14	0.04
Spanish American Ind. (5)	5	0.01
Asian (5,764)	6,199	16.32
Not Hispanic (5,711)	6,074	16.00
Hispanic (53)	125	0.33
Bangladeshi (2)	2	0.01
Burmese (7)	7	0.02
Cambodian (112)	125	0.33
Chinese, ex. Taiwanese (168)	201	0.53
Filipino (1,308)	1,458	3.84
Hmong (37)	37	0.10
Indian (2,960)	3,151	8.30
Indonesian (1)	3	0.01
Japanese (67)	121	0.32
Korean (162)	199	0.52
Laotian (59)	69	0.18
Pakistani (599)	631	1.66
Taiwanese (8)	10	0.03
Thai (18)	19	0.05
Vietnamese (90)	106	0.28
Hawaii Native/Pacific Islander (9)	45	0.12
Not Hispanic (5)	29	0.08
Hispanic (4)	16	0.04
Guamanian/Chamorro (5)	6	0.02
Native Hawaiian (3)	12	0.03
Samoan (0)	1	<0.01
White (22,207)	23,223	61.16
Not Hispanic (14,423)	14,891	39.21
Hispanic (7,784)	8,332	21.94

Harrisburg

Place Type: City
County: Saline
Population: 9,017†

Ancestry‡	Population	%
African, Sub-Saharan (46)	46	0.51
African (46)	46	0.51
American (1,207)	1,207	13.51
Arab (19)	19	0.21
Egyptian (19)	19	0.21
British (8)	8	0.09
Canadian (10)	10	0.11
Czech (0)	17	0.19
Dutch (77)	250	2.80
English (646)	973	10.89
European (27)	40	0.45

*Notes: † The Census 2010 population figure is used to calculate the percentages in the Hispanic Origin and Race categories. Ancestry percentages are based on the 2006-2010 American Community Survey population (not shown); ‡ Numbers in parentheses indicate the number of people reporting a single ancestry; * Numbers in parentheses indicate the number of persons reporting this race alone, not in combination with any other race; Please refer to the Explanation of Data for more information.*

Finnish (0)	12	0.13
French, ex. Basque (56)	194	2.17
German (441)	1,370	15.34
Hungarian (57)	249	2.79
Irish (419)	1,351	15.12
Italian (87)	117	1.31
Lithuanian (32)	173	1.94
Norwegian (0)	18	0.20
Polish (72)	112	1.25
Russian (0)	28	0.31
Scotch-Irish (141)	305	3.41
Scottish (63)	141	1.58
Slovene (18)	18	0.20
Swedish (0)	47	0.53
Swiss (0)	15	0.17
Ukrainian (0)	11	0.12
Welsh (10)	75	0.84
West Indian, ex. Hispanic (0)	8	0.09
Dutch West Indian (0)	8	0.09
Yugoslavian (0)	15	0.17

Hispanic Origin	Population	%
Hispanic or Latino (of any race)	209	2.32
Central American, ex. Mexican	8	0.09
Costa Rican	1	0.01
Guatemalan	1	0.01
Panamanian	6	0.07
Cuban	3	0.03
Dominican Republic	1	0.01
Mexican	131	1.45
Puerto Rican	27	0.30
South American	2	0.02
Peruvian	2	0.02
Other Hispanic or Latino	37	0.41

Race*	Population	%
African-American/Black (589)	751	8.33
Not Hispanic (578)	724	8.03
Hispanic (11)	27	0.30
American Indian/Alaska Native (45)	124	1.38
Not Hispanic (42)	110	1.22
Hispanic (3)	14	0.16
Apache (2)	2	0.02
Blackfeet (1)	5	0.06
Cherokee (9)	34	0.38
Chippewa (0)	1	0.01
Kiowa (0)	1	0.01
Lumbee (1)	1	0.01
Mexican American Ind. (1)	2	0.02
Navajo (2)	6	0.07
Osage (1)	2	0.02
Seminole (0)	1	0.01
Shoshone (0)	1	0.01
Sioux (1)	2	0.02
Tlingit-Haida *(Alaska Native)* (0)	1	0.01
Asian (74)	92	1.02
Not Hispanic (73)	89	0.99
Hispanic (1)	3	0.03
Cambodian (1)	1	0.01
Chinese, ex. Taiwanese (23)	29	0.32
Filipino (12)	17	0.19
Indian (13)	16	0.18
Japanese (5)	14	0.16
Korean (0)	1	0.01
Vietnamese (13)	17	0.19
Hawaii Native/Pacific Islander (8)	14	0.16
Not Hispanic (0)	4	0.04
Hispanic (8)	10	0.11
Guamanian/Chamorro (8)	9	0.10
Native Hawaiian (0)	4	0.04
White (7,983)	8,218	91.14
Not Hispanic (7,887)	8,100	89.83
Hispanic (96)	118	1.31

Harvard

Place Type: City
County: McHenry
Population: 9,447†

Ancestry‡	Population	%
American (364)	364	4.22
Arab (28)	28	0.32
Arab (28)	28	0.32
Austrian (0)	84	0.97
Belgian (0)	21	0.24
Cajun (14)	14	0.16
Croatian (0)	96	1.11
Czech (0)	32	0.37
Danish (14)	53	0.61
Dutch (18)	134	1.55
English (138)	468	5.43
Estonian (0)	22	0.26
European (59)	59	0.68
Finnish (0)	13	0.15
French, ex. Basque (30)	207	2.40
German (669)	1,846	21.41
Irish (494)	1,376	15.96
Italian (101)	515	5.97
Lithuanian (0)	37	0.43
Norwegian (56)	287	3.33
Pennsylvania German (0)	14	0.16
Polish (275)	731	8.48
Portuguese (0)	12	0.14
Russian (0)	14	0.16
Scandinavian (45)	45	0.52
Scotch-Irish (20)	65	0.75
Scottish (25)	106	1.23
Swedish (96)	246	2.85
Ukrainian (0)	55	0.64
Welsh (0)	11	0.13

Hispanic Origin	Population	%
Hispanic or Latino (of any race)	4,270	45.20
Central American, ex. Mexican	35	0.37
Costa Rican	1	0.01
Guatemalan	11	0.12
Honduran	4	0.04
Salvadoran	19	0.20
Cuban	19	0.20
Mexican	3,968	42.00
Puerto Rican	52	0.55
South American	17	0.18
Chilean	1	0.01
Colombian	4	0.04
Ecuadorian	8	0.08
Venezuelan	4	0.04
Other Hispanic or Latino	179	1.89

Race*	Population	%
African-American/Black (85)	138	1.46
Not Hispanic (64)	107	1.13
Hispanic (21)	31	0.33
American Indian/Alaska Native (76)	149	1.58
Not Hispanic (16)	73	0.77
Hispanic (60)	76	0.80
Apache (4)	4	0.04
Blackfeet (0)	3	0.03
Canadian/French Am. Ind. (0)	1	0.01
Cherokee (5)	27	0.29
Cheyenne (0)	1	0.01
Chippewa (2)	7	0.07
Choctaw (1)	1	0.01
Lumbee (1)	1	0.01
Menominee (1)	3	0.03
Mexican American Ind. (10)	15	0.16
Potawatomi (0)	9	0.10
Pueblo (3)	3	0.03
Sioux (2)	6	0.06
South American Ind. (2)	2	0.02
Asian (70)	103	1.09
Not Hispanic (63)	90	0.95
Hispanic (7)	13	0.14
Chinese, ex. Taiwanese (6)	11	0.12
Filipino (18)	31	0.33
Indian (24)	28	0.30
Indonesian (1)	1	0.01
Japanese (2)	6	0.06
Korean (5)	6	0.06
Malaysian (1)	3	0.03
Pakistani (5)	5	0.05
Thai (2)	2	0.02
Vietnamese (3)	4	0.04
Hawaii Native/Pacific Islander (6)	12	0.13
Not Hispanic (0)	3	0.03
Hispanic (6)	9	0.10
Guamanian/Chamorro (6)	6	0.06
Native Hawaiian (0)	1	0.01
Samoan (0)	2	0.02
White (6,759)	7,030	74.42
Not Hispanic (4,901)	5,020	53.14
Hispanic (1,858)	2,010	21.28

Harvey

Place Type: City
County: Cook
Population: 25,282†

Ancestry‡	Population	%
African, Sub-Saharan (509)	541	2.12
African (341)	373	1.46
Ghanaian (110)	110	0.43
Nigerian (58)	58	0.23
Albanian (17)	35	0.14
American (165)	165	0.65
Arab (0)	61	0.24
Moroccan (0)	61	0.24
Armenian (10)	10	0.04
British (25)	25	0.10
Dutch (0)	21	0.08
English (10)	90	0.35
French, ex. Basque (0)	8	0.03
German (60)	194	0.76
Greek (15)	15	0.06
Hungarian (1)	10	0.04
Irish (30)	169	0.66
Italian (25)	33	0.13
Lithuanian (0)	32	0.13
Norwegian (0)	61	0.24
Polish (100)	106	0.42
Russian (0)	3	0.01
Scotch-Irish (10)	60	0.24
Scottish (0)	12	0.05
Slovak (0)	7	0.03
Swedish (0)	8	0.03
West Indian, ex. Hispanic (11)	40	0.16
Jamaican (11)	40	0.16

Hispanic Origin	Population	%
Hispanic or Latino (of any race)	4,799	18.98
Central American, ex. Mexican	95	0.38
Guatemalan	49	0.19
Honduran	12	0.05
Nicaraguan	10	0.04
Panamanian	7	0.03
Salvadoran	17	0.07
Cuban	8	0.03
Dominican Republic	3	0.01
Mexican	4,332	17.13
Puerto Rican	105	0.42
South American	15	0.06
Argentinean	6	0.02
Colombian	4	0.02
Ecuadorian	2	0.01
Peruvian	1	<0.01
Venezuelan	2	0.01
Other Hispanic or Latino	241	0.95

Race*	Population	%
African-American/Black (19,170)	19,506	77.15
Not Hispanic (19,046)	19,293	76.31
Hispanic (124)	213	0.84
American Indian/Alaska Native (72)	198	0.78
Not Hispanic (33)	127	0.50
Hispanic (39)	71	0.28
Apache (0)	10	0.04
Blackfeet (0)	4	0.02
Canadian/French Am. Ind. (0)	1	<0.01
Cherokee (1)	29	0.11

*Notes: † The Census 2010 population figure is used to calculate the percentages in the Hispanic Origin and Race categories. Ancestry percentages are based on the 2006-2010 American Community Survey population (not shown); ‡ Numbers in parentheses indicate the number of people reporting a single ancestry; * Numbers in parentheses indicate the number of persons reporting this race alone, not in combination with any other race; Please refer to the Explanation of Data for more information.*

Cheyenne (0)	1	<0.01
Chippewa (0)	1	<0.01
Choctaw (0)	5	0.02
Creek (1)	1	<0.01
Iroquois (1)	5	0.02
Menominee (0)	2	0.01
Mexican American Ind. (5)	5	0.02
Navajo (3)	4	0.02
Potawatomi (0)	1	<0.01
Sioux (3)	4	0.02
Asian (216)	267	1.06
Not Hispanic (199)	235	0.93
Hispanic (17)	32	0.13
Cambodian (0)	4	0.02
Chinese, ex. Taiwanese (0)	7	0.03
Filipino (17)	30	0.12
Indian (185)	206	0.81
Japanese (2)	3	0.01
Korean (0)	4	0.02
Laotian (1)	1	<0.01
Pakistani (3)	3	0.01
Hawaii Native/Pacific Islander (10)	30	0.12
Not Hispanic (10)	23	0.09
Hispanic (0)	7	0.03
Fijian (1)	2	0.01
Guamanian/Chamorro (0)	5	0.02
Native Hawaiian (0)	13	0.05
Samoan (8)	9	0.04
White (2,516)	2,797	11.06
Not Hispanic (913)	1,097	4.34
Hispanic (1,603)	1,700	6.72

Harwood Heights

Place Type: Village
County: Cook
Population: 8,612†

Ancestry‡	Population	%
American (171)	171	2.02
Arab (70)	96	1.13
Egyptian (26)	52	0.61
Palestinian (44)	44	0.52
Assyrian/Chaldean/Syriac (10)	30	0.35
Austrian (0)	5	0.06
Brazilian (0)	169	2.00
Bulgarian (121)	121	1.43
Croatian (54)	54	0.64
Czech (11)	70	0.83
Dutch (0)	59	0.70
English (128)	243	2.87
European (25)	25	0.30
Finnish (21)	21	0.25
French, ex. Basque (5)	105	1.24
French Canadian (5)	5	0.06
German (309)	902	10.66
Greek (141)	174	2.06
Hungarian (3)	53	0.63
Irish (146)	720	8.51
Italian (1,041)	1,635	19.32
Lithuanian (0)	34	0.40
Luxemburger (10)	15	0.18
Norwegian (23)	63	0.74
Pennsylvania German (0)	10	0.12
Polish (1,761)	2,319	27.40
Romanian (19)	19	0.22
Russian (0)	49	0.58
Scotch-Irish (13)	23	0.27
Serbian (319)	319	3.77
Slavic (11)	11	0.13
Slovak (85)	85	1.00
Slovene (10)	10	0.12
Swedish (40)	91	1.08
Ukrainian (180)	224	2.65
West Indian, ex. Hispanic (70)	75	0.89
Belizean (70)	75	0.89
Yugoslavian (51)	51	0.60

Hispanic Origin	Population	%
Hispanic or Latino (of any race)	1,069	12.41
Central American, ex. Mexican	67	0.78
Guatemalan	51	0.59
Honduran	4	0.05
Panamanian	1	0.01
Salvadoran	10	0.12
Other Central American	1	0.01
Cuban	28	0.33
Dominican Republic	2	0.02
Mexican	493	5.72
Puerto Rican	304	3.53
South American	126	1.46
Argentinean	14	0.16
Colombian	31	0.36
Ecuadorian	48	0.56
Peruvian	21	0.24
Uruguayan	1	0.01
Venezuelan	7	0.08
Other South American	4	0.05
Other Hispanic or Latino	49	0.57

Race*	Population	%
African-American/Black (56)	91	1.06
Not Hispanic (53)	79	0.92
Hispanic (3)	12	0.14
American Indian/Alaska Native (24)	64	0.74
Not Hispanic (14)	47	0.55
Hispanic (10)	17	0.20
Arapaho (5)	5	0.06
Cherokee (2)	15	0.17
Chippewa (0)	1	0.01
Choctaw (4)	6	0.07
Mexican American Ind. (1)	3	0.03
Navajo (0)	1	0.01
Sioux (1)	3	0.03
South American Ind. (0)	1	0.01
Asian (620)	693	8.05
Not Hispanic (610)	663	7.70
Hispanic (10)	30	0.35
Cambodian (11)	15	0.17
Chinese, ex. Taiwanese (53)	59	0.69
Filipino (344)	389	4.52
Indian (109)	114	1.32
Indonesian (3)	3	0.03
Japanese (4)	8	0.09
Korean (35)	37	0.43
Laotian (2)	3	0.03
Pakistani (1)	2	0.02
Taiwanese (2)	3	0.03
Thai (10)	12	0.14
Vietnamese (22)	23	0.27
Hawaii Native/Pacific Islander (4)	13	0.15
Not Hispanic (1)	8	0.09
Hispanic (3)	5	0.06
Guamanian/Chamorro (2)	2	0.02
Native Hawaiian (0)	1	0.01
White (7,330)	7,503	87.12
Not Hispanic (6,747)	6,847	79.51
Hispanic (583)	656	7.62

Hawthorn Woods

Place Type: Village
County: Lake
Population: 7,663†

Ancestry‡	Population	%
American (174)	174	2.35
Arab (60)	60	0.81
Other Arab (60)	60	0.81
Armenian (41)	91	1.23
Austrian (0)	47	0.63
Belgian (20)	71	0.96
British (24)	101	1.36
Canadian (8)	43	0.58
Czech (20)	31	0.42
Danish (7)	57	0.77
Dutch (0)	64	0.86
Eastern European (90)	90	1.22
English (121)	479	6.47
European (73)	73	0.99
Finnish (0)	55	0.74
French, ex. Basque (28)	155	2.09
French Canadian (47)	124	1.67
German (645)	2,154	29.09
Greek (17)	70	0.95
Hungarian (34)	47	0.63
Irish (329)	1,118	15.10
Italian (255)	942	12.72
Latvian (13)	13	0.18
Lithuanian (18)	39	0.53
Luxemburger (0)	31	0.42
Norwegian (59)	140	1.89
Polish (311)	624	8.43
Portuguese (21)	85	1.15
Romanian (37)	37	0.50
Russian (184)	236	3.19
Scotch-Irish (29)	54	0.73
Scottish (31)	170	2.30
Serbian (60)	69	0.93
Slavic (13)	13	0.18
Swedish (145)	510	6.89
Swiss (0)	86	1.16
Ukrainian (159)	176	2.38
Welsh (0)	64	0.86
Yugoslavian (53)	53	0.72

Hispanic Origin	Population	%
Hispanic or Latino (of any race)	288	3.76
Central American, ex. Mexican	20	0.26
Costa Rican	2	0.03
Guatemalan	6	0.08
Honduran	5	0.07
Nicaraguan	7	0.09
Cuban	14	0.18
Dominican Republic	4	0.05
Mexican	134	1.75
Puerto Rican	32	0.42
South American	62	0.81
Argentinean	19	0.25
Bolivian	3	0.04
Chilean	4	0.05
Colombian	8	0.10
Ecuadorian	2	0.03
Paraguayan	1	0.01
Peruvian	14	0.18
Venezuelan	11	0.14
Other Hispanic or Latino	22	0.29

Race*	Population	%
African-American/Black (107)	130	1.70
Not Hispanic (104)	127	1.66
Hispanic (3)	3	0.04
American Indian/Alaska Native (10)	16	0.21
Not Hispanic (10)	11	0.14
Hispanic (0)	5	0.07
Chippewa (1)	2	0.03
Creek (2)	2	0.03
Mexican American Ind. (0)	2	0.03
Asian (510)	610	7.96
Not Hispanic (509)	606	7.91
Hispanic (1)	4	0.05
Bangladeshi (1)	1	0.01
Cambodian (3)	3	0.04
Chinese, ex. Taiwanese (109)	125	1.63
Filipino (43)	74	0.97
Indian (177)	194	2.53
Indonesian (4)	4	0.05
Japanese (9)	32	0.42
Korean (117)	139	1.81
Pakistani (22)	23	0.30
Taiwanese (4)	7	0.09
Thai (1)	1	0.01
Vietnamese (10)	12	0.16
Hawaii Native/Pacific Islander (1)	4	0.05
Not Hispanic (1)	4	0.05
Native Hawaiian (1)	1	0.01
White (6,850)	6,974	91.01
Not Hispanic (6,630)	6,737	87.92
Hispanic (220)	237	3.09

*Notes: † The Census 2010 population figure is used to calculate the percentages in the Hispanic Origin and Race categories. Ancestry percentages are based on the 2006-2010 American Community Survey population (not shown); ‡ Numbers in parentheses indicate the number of people reporting a single ancestry; * Numbers in parentheses indicate the number of persons reporting this race alone, not in combination with any other race; Please refer to the Explanation of Data for more information.*

Hazel Crest

Place Type: Village
County: Cook
Population: 14,100†

Ancestry‡	Population	%
African, Sub-Saharan (411)	429	3.01
African (187)	195	1.37
Nigerian (224)	234	1.64
American (99)	99	0.69
Austrian (22)	33	0.23
Belgian (8)	15	0.11
Croatian (9)	19	0.13
Czech (22)	34	0.24
Dutch (70)	86	0.60
English (44)	133	0.93
French, ex. Basque (0)	22	0.15
French Canadian (19)	67	0.47
German (248)	570	3.99
Guyanese (17)	17	0.12
Hungarian (0)	11	0.08
Irish (68)	258	1.81
Italian (90)	122	0.85
Norwegian (22)	22	0.15
Polish (134)	167	1.17
Russian (28)	38	0.27
Scandinavian (0)	10	0.07
Scotch-Irish (8)	30	0.21
Scottish (0)	21	0.15
Swedish (10)	40	0.28
Ukrainian (11)	11	0.08
Welsh (0)	38	0.27
West Indian, ex. Hispanic (76)	76	0.53
Belizean (10)	10	0.07
Jamaican (47)	47	0.33
West Indian (19)	19	0.13

Hispanic Origin	Population	%
Hispanic or Latino (of any race)	527	3.74
Central American, ex. Mexican	14	0.10
Guatemalan	7	0.05
Honduran	1	0.01
Panamanian	6	0.04
Cuban	18	0.13
Dominican Republic	6	0.04
Mexican	407	2.89
Puerto Rican	60	0.43
South American	3	0.02
Peruvian	2	0.01
Venezuelan	1	0.01
Other Hispanic or Latino	19	0.13

Race*	Population	%
African-American/Black (12,009)	12,238	86.79
Not Hispanic (11,935)	12,131	86.04
Hispanic (74)	107	0.76
American Indian/Alaska Native (33)	118	0.84
Not Hispanic (26)	107	0.76
Hispanic (7)	11	0.08
Apache (1)	1	0.01
Blackfeet (0)	2	0.01
Cherokee (5)	21	0.15
Comanche (0)	1	0.01
Creek (1)	1	0.01
Mexican American Ind. (5)	6	0.04
Potawatomi (0)	1	0.01
Ute (0)	1	0.01
Asian (92)	140	0.99
Not Hispanic (91)	132	0.94
Hispanic (1)	8	0.06
Burmese (0)	5	0.04
Chinese, ex. Taiwanese (8)	12	0.09
Filipino (31)	38	0.27
Indian (15)	29	0.21
Japanese (2)	9	0.06
Korean (11)	19	0.13
Pakistani (5)	6	0.04
Taiwanese (1)	1	0.01
Thai (3)	3	0.02
Vietnamese (11)	12	0.09
Hawaii Native/Pacific Islander (0)	3	0.02
Not Hispanic (0)	3	0.02
Samoan (0)	2	0.01
White (1,443)	1,623	11.51
Not Hispanic (1,269)	1,422	10.09
Hispanic (174)	201	1.43

Herrin

Place Type: City
County: Williamson
Population: 12,501†

Ancestry‡	Population	%
American (1,183)	1,183	9.61
Belgian (36)	51	0.41
British (74)	102	0.83
Bulgarian (42)	55	0.45
Croatian (0)	12	0.10
Czech (22)	61	0.50
Danish (14)	79	0.64
Dutch (261)	412	3.35
English (877)	1,911	15.52
European (112)	121	0.98
Finnish (8)	8	0.06
French, ex. Basque (70)	304	2.47
French Canadian (12)	12	0.10
German (1,067)	3,106	25.23
Hungarian (47)	88	0.71
Irish (574)	1,931	15.68
Italian (570)	1,307	10.62
Lithuanian (9)	25	0.20
Norwegian (12)	43	0.35
Polish (126)	339	2.75
Portuguese (39)	57	0.46
Scandinavian (0)	32	0.26
Scotch-Irish (80)	130	1.06
Scottish (101)	168	1.36
Swedish (9)	52	0.42
Swiss (0)	12	0.10
Welsh (69)	100	0.81

Hispanic Origin	Population	%
Hispanic or Latino (of any race)	264	2.11
Central American, ex. Mexican	17	0.14
Costa Rican	3	0.02
Guatemalan	2	0.02
Honduran	1	0.01
Salvadoran	11	0.09
Cuban	2	0.02
Mexican	173	1.38
Puerto Rican	34	0.27
South American	4	0.03
Colombian	1	0.01
Peruvian	1	0.01
Venezuelan	2	0.02
Other Hispanic or Latino	34	0.27

Race*	Population	%
African-American/Black (313)	430	3.44
Not Hispanic (311)	426	3.41
Hispanic (2)	4	0.03
American Indian/Alaska Native (24)	114	0.91
Not Hispanic (20)	107	0.86
Hispanic (4)	7	0.06
Alaska Athabascan *(Ala. Nat.)* (1)	3	0.02
Apache (0)	3	0.02
Blackfeet (0)	3	0.02
Cherokee (7)	38	0.30
Cheyenne (0)	1	0.01
Chippewa (0)	1	0.01
Choctaw (0)	2	0.02
Cree (0)	2	0.02
Iroquois (0)	1	0.01
Kiowa (3)	3	0.02
Lumbee (1)	1	0.01
Mexican American Ind. (2)	3	0.02
Navajo (0)	1	0.01
Sioux (0)	4	0.03
Tlingit-Haida *(Alaska Native)* (2)	2	0.02
Asian (126)	154	1.23
Not Hispanic (126)	153	1.22
Hispanic (0)	1	0.01
Cambodian (0)	1	0.01
Chinese, ex. Taiwanese (41)	43	0.34
Filipino (29)	39	0.31
Indian (17)	25	0.20
Japanese (10)	12	0.10
Korean (3)	7	0.06
Pakistani (4)	4	0.03
Taiwanese (2)	2	0.02
Thai (7)	9	0.07
Vietnamese (10)	10	0.08
Hawaii Native/Pacific Islander (2)	9	0.07
Not Hispanic (2)	8	0.06
Hispanic (0)	1	0.01
Native Hawaiian (1)	4	0.03
Samoan (1)	4	0.03
White (11,728)	11,970	95.75
Not Hispanic (11,541)	11,764	94.10
Hispanic (187)	206	1.65

Hickory Hills

Place Type: City
County: Cook
Population: 14,049†

Ancestry‡	Population	%
Afghan (15)	44	0.31
African, Sub-Saharan (88)	88	0.63
African (88)	88	0.63
Albanian (84)	84	0.60
American (332)	332	2.37
Arab (1,465)	1,595	11.39
Arab (662)	727	5.19
Egyptian (155)	209	1.49
Jordanian (180)	180	1.29
Moroccan (69)	69	0.49
Palestinian (274)	274	1.96
Other Arab (125)	136	0.97
Austrian (10)	97	0.69
Belgian (14)	35	0.25
British (12)	12	0.09
Bulgarian (0)	7	0.05
Celtic (0)	13	0.09
Croatian (0)	9	0.06
Czech (183)	543	3.88
Czechoslovakian (12)	22	0.16
Danish (0)	14	0.10
Dutch (61)	236	1.69
English (91)	383	2.73
European (34)	34	0.24
French, ex. Basque (0)	141	1.01
French Canadian (0)	28	0.20
German (372)	1,803	12.87
Greek (161)	188	1.34
Hungarian (0)	65	0.46
Irish (576)	2,292	16.37
Italian (517)	1,164	8.31
Lithuanian (226)	490	3.50
Macedonian (0)	8	0.06
New Zealander (9)	9	0.06
Norwegian (0)	77	0.55
Polish (3,082)	4,052	28.93
Romanian (0)	57	0.41
Russian (9)	59	0.42
Scotch-Irish (167)	210	1.50
Scottish (10)	60	0.43
Slavic (0)	8	0.06
Slovak (65)	100	0.71
Slovene (20)	63	0.45
Swedish (75)	165	1.18
Turkish (34)	34	0.24

Hispanic Origin	Population	%
Hispanic or Latino (of any race)	1,777	12.65
Central American, ex. Mexican	31	0.22
Costa Rican	3	0.02

*Notes: † The Census 2010 population figure is used to calculate the percentages in the Hispanic Origin and Race categories. Ancestry percentages are based on the 2006-2010 American Community Survey population (not shown); ‡ Numbers in parentheses indicate the number of people reporting a single ancestry; * Numbers in parentheses indicate the number of persons reporting this race alone, not in combination with any other race; Please refer to the Explanation of Data for more information.*

Guatemalan	23	0.16
Honduran	1	0.01
Nicaraguan	3	0.02
Salvadoran	1	0.01
Cuban	13	0.09
Mexican	1,516	10.79
Puerto Rican	109	0.78
South American	38	0.27
Argentinean	8	0.06
Bolivian	4	0.03
Chilean	1	0.01
Colombian	15	0.11
Ecuadorian	4	0.03
Peruvian	2	0.01
Venezuelan	4	0.03
Other Hispanic or Latino	70	0.50

Race*	Population	%
African-American/Black (472)	527	3.75
Not Hispanic (449)	500	3.56
Hispanic (23)	27	0.19
American Indian/Alaska Native (16)	53	0.38
Not Hispanic (10)	40	0.28
Hispanic (6)	13	0.09
Apache (2)	2	0.01
Cherokee (0)	9	0.06
Chippewa (2)	4	0.03
Iroquois (4)	8	0.06
Menominee (1)	1	0.01
Navajo (1)	1	0.01
Asian (365)	476	3.39
Not Hispanic (359)	459	3.27
Hispanic (6)	17	0.12
Bangladeshi (6)	6	0.04
Chinese, ex. Taiwanese (23)	25	0.18
Filipino (101)	109	0.78
Indian (126)	148	1.05
Indonesian (2)	2	0.01
Japanese (6)	16	0.11
Korean (23)	25	0.18
Malaysian (1)	1	0.01
Pakistani (41)	47	0.33
Sri Lankan (2)	2	0.01
Thai (11)	11	0.08
Vietnamese (17)	19	0.14
Hawaii Native/Pacific Islander (0)	6	0.04
Not Hispanic (0)	5	0.04
Hispanic (0)	1	0.01
Native Hawaiian (0)	1	0.01
White (12,364)	12,625	89.86
Not Hispanic (11,241)	11,422	81.30
Hispanic (1,123)	1,203	8.56

Highland Park

Place Type: City
County: Lake
Population: 29,763†

Ancestry‡	Population	%
African, Sub-Saharan (57)	57	0.19
African (9)	9	0.03
South African (48)	48	0.16
American (2,200)	2,200	7.31
Arab (186)	216	0.72
Arab (23)	23	0.08
Egyptian (21)	21	0.07
Iraqi (132)	132	0.44
Moroccan (0)	30	0.10
Syrian (10)	10	0.03
Armenian (23)	36	0.12
Austrian (46)	369	1.23
Belgian (0)	72	0.24
British (64)	169	0.56
Bulgarian (13)	13	0.04
Canadian (85)	166	0.55
Croatian (154)	225	0.75
Cypriot (8)	8	0.03
Czech (63)	235	0.78
Czechoslovakian (0)	11	0.04
Danish (11)	141	0.47
Dutch (22)	290	0.96
Eastern European (837)	980	3.26
English (490)	1,794	5.96
European (888)	908	3.02
Finnish (0)	10	0.03
French, ex. Basque (68)	455	1.51
French Canadian (31)	83	0.28
German (1,629)	5,129	17.05
Greek (95)	162	0.54
Hungarian (99)	394	1.31
Iranian (0)	14	0.05
Irish (551)	2,709	9.01
Israeli (128)	143	0.48
Italian (1,263)	2,155	7.16
Latvian (17)	59	0.20
Lithuanian (70)	433	1.44
Luxemburger (0)	37	0.12
Maltese (0)	25	0.08
Northern European (26)	26	0.09
Norwegian (103)	411	1.37
Pennsylvania German (0)	16	0.05
Polish (992)	2,999	9.97
Romanian (304)	530	1.76
Russian (3,248)	6,049	20.11
Scandinavian (0)	13	0.04
Scotch-Irish (87)	234	0.78
Scottish (98)	369	1.23
Slavic (0)	30	0.10
Slovak (0)	38	0.13
Slovene (13)	54	0.18
Swedish (95)	450	1.50
Swiss (0)	43	0.14
Turkish (27)	98	0.33
Ukrainian (248)	374	1.24
Welsh (0)	25	0.08
West Indian, ex. Hispanic (44)	44	0.15
Haitian (44)	44	0.15
Yugoslavian (19)	34	0.11

Hispanic Origin	Population	%
Hispanic or Latino (of any race)	2,167	7.28
Central American, ex. Mexican	137	0.46
Costa Rican	10	0.03
Guatemalan	70	0.24
Honduran	29	0.10
Nicaraguan	1	<0.01
Panamanian	6	0.02
Salvadoran	21	0.07
Cuban	54	0.18
Dominican Republic	20	0.07
Mexican	1,564	5.25
Puerto Rican	94	0.32
South American	177	0.59
Argentinean	30	0.10
Bolivian	12	0.04
Chilean	13	0.04
Colombian	83	0.28
Ecuadorian	9	0.03
Paraguayan	3	0.01
Peruvian	13	0.04
Uruguayan	7	0.02
Venezuelan	7	0.02
Other Hispanic or Latino	121	0.41

Race*	Population	%
African-American/Black (548)	638	2.14
Not Hispanic (516)	596	2.00
Hispanic (32)	42	0.14
American Indian/Alaska Native (54)	125	0.42
Not Hispanic (22)	72	0.24
Hispanic (32)	53	0.18
Apache (0)	3	0.01
Blackfeet (0)	1	<0.01
Canadian/French Am. Ind. (3)	3	0.01
Cherokee (6)	21	0.07
Chickasaw (0)	6	0.02
Chippewa (1)	2	0.01
Choctaw (0)	2	0.01
Creek (4)	6	0.02
Crow (0)	1	<0.01
Lumbee (1)	1	<0.01
Mexican American Ind. (6)	14	0.05
Potawatomi (1)	1	<0.01
Sioux (0)	1	<0.01
Asian (864)	1,077	3.62
Not Hispanic (848)	1,048	3.52
Hispanic (16)	29	0.10
Burmese (3)	3	0.01
Cambodian (2)	6	0.02
Chinese, ex. Taiwanese (193)	255	0.86
Filipino (160)	231	0.78
Indian (185)	226	0.76
Indonesian (1)	4	0.01
Japanese (62)	105	0.35
Korean (143)	171	0.57
Laotian (1)	1	<0.01
Malaysian (1)	1	<0.01
Pakistani (17)	17	0.06
Sri Lankan (2)	5	0.02
Taiwanese (7)	10	0.03
Thai (19)	31	0.10
Vietnamese (10)	21	0.07
Hawaii Native/Pacific Islander (9)	28	0.09
Not Hispanic (9)	25	0.08
Hispanic (0)	3	0.01
Guamanian/Chamorro (4)	8	0.03
Native Hawaiian (1)	16	0.05
Samoan (0)	3	0.01
White (27,099)	27,517	92.45
Not Hispanic (25,845)	26,156	87.88
Hispanic (1,254)	1,361	4.57

Highland

Place Type: City
County: Madison
Population: 9,919†

Ancestry‡	Population	%
American (671)	671	7.13
Belgian (0)	10	0.11
British (0)	62	0.66
Czech (0)	10	0.11
Dutch (16)	219	2.33
English (197)	757	8.04
European (69)	69	0.73
French, ex. Basque (78)	495	5.26
French Canadian (6)	6	0.06
German (2,560)	4,785	50.82
Hungarian (21)	29	0.31
Irish (459)	1,346	14.29
Italian (105)	321	3.41
Lithuanian (0)	9	0.10
Polish (26)	232	2.46
Russian (0)	17	0.18
Scotch-Irish (102)	208	2.21
Scottish (17)	97	1.03
Slovak (11)	45	0.48
Swedish (19)	85	0.90
Swiss (78)	576	6.12
Welsh (0)	45	0.48

Hispanic Origin	Population	%
Hispanic or Latino (of any race)	138	1.39
Central American, ex. Mexican	24	0.24
Costa Rican	1	0.01
Guatemalan	5	0.05
Honduran	8	0.08
Panamanian	8	0.08
Salvadoran	2	0.02
Mexican	72	0.73
Puerto Rican	10	0.10
South American	5	0.05
Chilean	1	0.01
Colombian	1	0.01
Venezuelan	3	0.03
Other Hispanic or Latino	27	0.27

*Notes: † The Census 2010 population figure is used to calculate the percentages in the Hispanic Origin and Race categories. Ancestry percentages are based on the 2006-2010 American Community Survey population (not shown); ‡ Numbers in parentheses indicate the number of people reporting a single ancestry; * Numbers in parentheses indicate the number of persons reporting this race alone, not in combination with any other race; Please refer to the Explanation of Data for more information.*

Race*	Population	%
African-American/Black (21)	47	0.47
Not Hispanic (21)	47	0.47
American Indian/Alaska Native (17)	57	0.57
Not Hispanic (17)	54	0.54
Hispanic (0)	3	0.03
Blackfeet (0)	2	0.02
Cherokee (3)	14	0.14
Chickasaw (0)	1	0.01
Chippewa (2)	2	0.02
Choctaw (0)	1	0.01
Comanche (1)	1	0.01
Lumbee (0)	1	0.01
Navajo (0)	1	0.01
Potawatomi (0)	1	0.01
Shoshone (0)	1	0.01
Sioux (0)	4	0.04
Asian (89)	136	1.37
Not Hispanic (89)	133	1.34
Hispanic (0)	3	0.03
Burmese (2)	2	0.02
Chinese, ex. Taiwanese (32)	40	0.40
Filipino (9)	25	0.25
Indian (8)	10	0.10
Indonesian (0)	1	0.01
Japanese (4)	10	0.10
Korean (12)	21	0.21
Pakistani (4)	4	0.04
Taiwanese (2)	2	0.02
Thai (4)	6	0.06
Vietnamese (11)	11	0.11
Hawaii Native/Pacific Islander (6)	9	0.09
Not Hispanic (3)	5	0.05
Hispanic (3)	4	0.04
Guamanian/Chamorro (3)	3	0.03
Samoan (1)	3	0.03
White (9,621)	9,742	98.22
Not Hispanic (9,542)	9,645	97.24
Hispanic (79)	97	0.98

Hillside

Place Type: Village
County: Cook
Population: 8,157†

Ancestry‡	Population	%
African, Sub-Saharan (46)	58	0.72
African (39)	39	0.48
Nigerian (7)	19	0.23
Arab (11)	61	0.75
Syrian (11)	61	0.75
Czech (50)	173	2.14
Dutch (6)	71	0.88
English (6)	143	1.77
European (16)	16	0.20
French, ex. Basque (0)	30	0.37
German (356)	720	8.90
Greek (83)	83	1.03
Hungarian (0)	14	0.17
Irish (148)	589	7.28
Italian (194)	277	3.42
Lithuanian (0)	18	0.22
Luxemburger (0)	10	0.12
Norwegian (0)	15	0.19
Polish (93)	241	2.98
Portuguese (30)	30	0.37
Romanian (44)	44	0.54
Russian (0)	18	0.22
Scotch-Irish (9)	9	0.11
Scottish (6)	6	0.07
Slovak (0)	6	0.07
Swedish (0)	22	0.27
Swiss (33)	36	0.45
Ukrainian (0)	23	0.28
Welsh (0)	22	0.27
Yugoslavian (11)	11	0.14

Hispanic Origin	Population	%
Hispanic or Latino (of any race)	2,252	27.61
Central American, ex. Mexican	42	0.51
Costa Rican	2	0.02
Guatemalan	30	0.37
Nicaraguan	2	0.02
Panamanian	1	0.01
Salvadoran	7	0.09
Cuban	13	0.16
Dominican Republic	6	0.07
Mexican	1,926	23.61
Puerto Rican	196	2.40
South American	48	0.59
Argentinean	2	0.02
Chilean	4	0.05
Colombian	12	0.15
Ecuadorian	17	0.21
Peruvian	9	0.11
Uruguayan	2	0.02
Venezuelan	2	0.02
Other Hispanic or Latino	21	0.26

Race*	Population	%
African-American/Black (3,525)	3,632	44.53
Not Hispanic (3,485)	3,546	43.47
Hispanic (40)	86	1.05
American Indian/Alaska Native (23)	65	0.80
Not Hispanic (6)	29	0.36
Hispanic (17)	36	0.44
Apache (2)	2	0.02
Cherokee (4)	6	0.07
Cheyenne (0)	1	0.01
Mexican American Ind. (5)	7	0.09
South American Ind. (0)	2	0.02
Yaqui (0)	2	0.02
Asian (273)	318	3.90
Not Hispanic (269)	309	3.79
Hispanic (4)	9	0.11
Chinese, ex. Taiwanese (11)	20	0.25
Filipino (99)	110	1.35
Indian (123)	138	1.69
Japanese (3)	7	0.09
Korean (4)	11	0.13
Pakistani (11)	12	0.15
Thai (9)	10	0.12
Vietnamese (7)	7	0.09
Hawaii Native/Pacific Islander (3)	9	0.11
Not Hispanic (3)	7	0.09
Hispanic (0)	2	0.02
Guamanian/Chamorro (0)	2	0.02
Native Hawaiian (3)	3	0.04
Samoan (0)	2	0.02
White (3,079)	3,269	40.08
Not Hispanic (2,022)	2,098	25.72
Hispanic (1,057)	1,171	14.36

Hinsdale

Place Type: Village
County: DuPage
Population: 16,816†

Ancestry‡	Population	%
African, Sub-Saharan (29)	29	0.17
African (29)	29	0.17
American (618)	618	3.72
Arab (21)	72	0.43
Lebanese (0)	10	0.06
Moroccan (0)	41	0.25
Palestinian (21)	21	0.13
Armenian (15)	58	0.35
Assyrian/Chaldean/Syriac (0)	13	0.08
Austrian (10)	77	0.46
Belgian (9)	41	0.25
British (105)	190	1.14
Canadian (11)	96	0.58
Croatian (47)	230	1.38
Czech (128)	399	2.40
Czechoslovakian (68)	68	0.41
Danish (0)	60	0.36
Dutch (146)	456	2.74
Eastern European (29)	29	0.17
English (514)	2,108	12.67
European (118)	125	0.75
Finnish (10)	49	0.29
French, ex. Basque (12)	477	2.87
French Canadian (39)	105	0.63
German (1,032)	4,396	26.43
Greek (158)	311	1.87
Hungarian (48)	100	0.60
Iranian (19)	27	0.16
Irish (920)	3,674	22.09
Italian (501)	1,786	10.74
Lithuanian (132)	313	1.88
Luxemburger (0)	14	0.08
Northern European (62)	62	0.37
Norwegian (167)	616	3.70
Polish (574)	2,216	13.32
Portuguese (10)	10	0.06
Russian (36)	138	0.83
Scandinavian (30)	38	0.23
Scotch-Irish (117)	300	1.80
Scottish (142)	536	3.22
Serbian (11)	31	0.19
Slavic (0)	9	0.05
Slovak (13)	43	0.26
Slovene (6)	32	0.19
Swedish (145)	576	3.46
Swiss (0)	18	0.11
Ukrainian (9)	33	0.20
Welsh (0)	93	0.56

Hispanic Origin	Population	%
Hispanic or Latino (of any race)	592	3.52
Central American, ex. Mexican	14	0.08
Costa Rican	5	0.03
Guatemalan	2	0.01
Honduran	1	0.01
Nicaraguan	1	0.01
Panamanian	5	0.03
Cuban	52	0.31
Dominican Republic	1	0.01
Mexican	289	1.72
Puerto Rican	94	0.56
South American	75	0.45
Argentinean	14	0.08
Bolivian	11	0.07
Chilean	2	0.01
Colombian	19	0.11
Ecuadorian	8	0.05
Paraguayan	2	0.01
Peruvian	11	0.07
Uruguayan	4	0.02
Venezuelan	3	0.02
Other South American	1	0.01
Other Hispanic or Latino	67	0.40

Race*	Population	%
African-American/Black (216)	252	1.50
Not Hispanic (212)	242	1.44
Hispanic (4)	10	0.06
American Indian/Alaska Native (6)	39	0.23
Not Hispanic (6)	37	0.22
Hispanic (0)	2	0.01
Alaska Athabascan *(Ala. Nat.)* (1)	1	0.01
Cherokee (0)	11	0.07
Chippewa (2)	2	0.01
Choctaw (0)	3	0.02
Comanche (0)	3	0.02
Iroquois (0)	1	0.01
Mexican American Ind. (1)	1	0.01
Asian (1,077)	1,285	7.64
Not Hispanic (1,075)	1,274	7.58
Hispanic (2)	11	0.07
Burmese (1)	1	0.01
Cambodian (3)	8	0.05
Chinese, ex. Taiwanese (372)	437	2.60
Filipino (177)	209	1.24
Indian (250)	288	1.71
Indonesian (3)	4	0.02
Japanese (25)	48	0.29
Korean (124)	157	0.93

*Notes: † The Census 2010 population figure is used to calculate the percentages in the Hispanic Origin and Race categories. Ancestry percentages are based on the 2006-2010 American Community Survey population (not shown); ‡ Numbers in parentheses indicate the number of people reporting a single ancestry; * Numbers in parentheses indicate the number of persons reporting this race alone, not in combination with any other race; Please refer to the Explanation of Data for more information.*

Pakistani (46)	55	0.33
Sri Lankan (3)	4	0.02
Taiwanese (16)	26	0.15
Thai (11)	12	0.07
Vietnamese (8)	19	0.11
Hawaii Native/Pacific Islander (9)	12	0.07
Not Hispanic (5)	8	0.05
Hispanic (4)	4	0.02
Native Hawaiian (7)	7	0.04
White (15,135)	15,385	91.49
Not Hispanic (14,663)	14,881	88.49
Hispanic (472)	504	3.00

Hoffman Estates

Place Type: Village
County: Cook
Population: 51,895†

Ancestry‡	Population	%
African, Sub-Saharan (175)	175	0.34
African (175)	175	0.34
Albanian (65)	65	0.13
American (715)	715	1.40
Arab (219)	239	0.47
Arab (11)	11	0.02
Egyptian (164)	164	0.32
Lebanese (37)	57	0.11
Other Arab (7)	7	0.01
Armenian (77)	89	0.17
Assyrian/Chaldean/Syriac (114)	114	0.22
Austrian (11)	189	0.37
Belgian (0)	110	0.21
British (0)	65	0.13
Bulgarian (36)	49	0.10
Canadian (11)	83	0.16
Croatian (14)	77	0.15
Czech (216)	623	1.22
Czechoslovakian (21)	29	0.06
Danish (43)	344	0.67
Dutch (100)	335	0.65
Eastern European (74)	74	0.14
English (468)	2,170	4.24
European (291)	299	0.58
Finnish (19)	65	0.13
French, ex. Basque (104)	978	1.91
French Canadian (76)	328	0.64
German (2,168)	8,675	16.94
Greek (631)	863	1.69
Hungarian (49)	124	0.24
Iranian (234)	293	0.57
Irish (1,476)	5,754	11.24
Italian (1,561)	4,281	8.36
Latvian (0)	50	0.10
Lithuanian (184)	461	0.90
Luxemburger (21)	86	0.17
Macedonian (12)	12	0.02
Northern European (74)	74	0.14
Norwegian (221)	986	1.93
Pennsylvania German (7)	7	0.01
Polish (3,474)	7,198	14.06
Portuguese (15)	24	0.05
Romanian (240)	333	0.65
Russian (301)	694	1.36
Scandinavian (71)	102	0.20
Scotch-Irish (246)	462	0.90
Scottish (97)	417	0.81
Serbian (69)	69	0.13
Slavic (0)	13	0.03
Slovak (28)	296	0.58
Slovene (21)	21	0.04
Swedish (243)	1,473	2.88
Swiss (41)	101	0.20
Turkish (92)	92	0.18
Ukrainian (257)	343	0.67
Welsh (14)	197	0.38
West Indian, ex. Hispanic (18)	18	0.04
Jamaican (18)	18	0.04
Yugoslavian (85)	85	0.17

Hispanic Origin	Population	%
Hispanic or Latino (of any race)	7,297	14.06
Central American, ex. Mexican	326	0.63
Costa Rican	7	0.01
Guatemalan	133	0.26
Honduran	31	0.06
Nicaraguan	17	0.03
Panamanian	13	0.03
Salvadoran	125	0.24
Cuban	114	0.22
Dominican Republic	30	0.06
Mexican	5,522	10.64
Puerto Rican	584	1.13
South American	439	0.85
Argentinean	23	0.04
Bolivian	17	0.03
Chilean	15	0.03
Colombian	115	0.22
Ecuadorian	130	0.25
Peruvian	111	0.21
Uruguayan	11	0.02
Venezuelan	16	0.03
Other South American	1	<0.01
Other Hispanic or Latino	282	0.54

Race*	Population	%
African-American/Black (2,478)	2,765	5.33
Not Hispanic (2,393)	2,624	5.06
Hispanic (85)	141	0.27
American Indian/Alaska Native (120)	288	0.55
Not Hispanic (60)	185	0.36
Hispanic (60)	103	0.20
Apache (0)	1	<0.01
Arapaho (1)	2	<0.01
Blackfeet (1)	10	0.02
Canadian/French Am. Ind. (1)	1	<0.01
Cherokee (4)	29	0.06
Chickasaw (0)	5	0.01
Chippewa (2)	4	0.01
Choctaw (5)	10	0.02
Iroquois (1)	1	<0.01
Mexican American Ind. (11)	21	0.04
Navajo (1)	4	0.01
Pima (2)	2	<0.01
Potawatomi (3)	3	0.01
Pueblo (3)	3	0.01
Seminole (0)	1	<0.01
Sioux (1)	6	0.01
South American Ind. (0)	3	0.01
Yaqui (1)	1	<0.01
Yuman (0)	2	<0.01
Asian (11,760)	12,555	24.19
Not Hispanic (11,701)	12,439	23.97
Hispanic (59)	116	0.22
Bangladeshi (19)	20	0.04
Burmese (3)	3	0.01
Cambodian (18)	26	0.05
Chinese, ex. Taiwanese (1,039)	1,160	2.24
Filipino (1,369)	1,541	2.97
Hmong (8)	8	0.02
Indian (5,738)	5,985	11.53
Indonesian (10)	15	0.03
Japanese (786)	885	1.71
Korean (1,514)	1,602	3.09
Laotian (44)	51	0.10
Malaysian (2)	15	0.03
Nepalese (4)	4	0.01
Pakistani (651)	712	1.37
Sri Lankan (3)	5	0.01
Taiwanese (104)	137	0.26
Thai (78)	101	0.19
Vietnamese (113)	125	0.24
Hawaii Native/Pacific Islander (8)	83	0.16
Not Hispanic (4)	66	0.13
Hispanic (4)	17	0.03
Guamanian/Chamorro (2)	2	<0.01
Native Hawaiian (2)	25	0.05
Samoan (0)	1	<0.01
White (33,270)	34,214	65.93
Not Hispanic (29,357)	30,014	57.84
Hispanic (3,913)	4,200	8.09

Homer Glen

Place Type: Village
County: Will
Population: 24,220†

Ancestry‡	Population	%
Albanian (54)	54	0.22
American (374)	374	1.51
Arab (474)	514	2.08
Arab (317)	317	1.28
Iraqi (13)	13	0.05
Lebanese (30)	46	0.19
Palestinian (114)	114	0.46
Other Arab (0)	24	0.10
Armenian (0)	8	0.03
Austrian (55)	207	0.84
Belgian (0)	21	0.08
Brazilian (41)	41	0.17
British (0)	79	0.32
Bulgarian (15)	15	0.06
Canadian (0)	12	0.05
Croatian (98)	278	1.12
Czech (101)	768	3.11
Czechoslovakian (0)	30	0.12
Danish (0)	55	0.22
Dutch (132)	406	1.64
Eastern European (72)	72	0.29
English (194)	1,065	4.31
European (131)	172	0.70
French, ex. Basque (41)	471	1.91
French Canadian (0)	81	0.33
German (738)	4,604	18.62
Greek (246)	435	1.76
Hungarian (42)	182	0.74
Iranian (13)	13	0.05
Irish (1,264)	6,168	24.95
Israeli (241)	241	0.97
Italian (1,310)	3,446	13.94
Latvian (13)	41	0.17
Lithuanian (817)	1,167	4.72
Luxemburger (0)	9	0.04
Macedonian (31)	57	0.23
Northern European (11)	11	0.04
Norwegian (0)	127	0.51
Polish (3,323)	6,952	28.12
Portuguese (0)	6	0.02
Romanian (0)	18	0.07
Russian (141)	331	1.34
Scandinavian (0)	9	0.04
Scotch-Irish (56)	182	0.74
Scottish (29)	182	0.74
Slavic (0)	15	0.06
Slovak (58)	230	0.93
Slovene (9)	24	0.10
Swedish (297)	895	3.62
Swiss (0)	39	0.16
Turkish (7)	21	0.08
Ukrainian (28)	52	0.21
Welsh (10)	14	0.06
Yugoslavian (28)	61	0.25

Hispanic Origin	Population	%
Hispanic or Latino (of any race)	1,189	4.91
Central American, ex. Mexican	18	0.07
Costa Rican	1	<0.01
Guatemalan	6	0.02
Nicaraguan	1	<0.01
Panamanian	3	0.01
Salvadoran	4	0.02
Other Central American	3	0.01
Cuban	17	0.07
Mexican	958	3.96
Puerto Rican	99	0.41
South American	45	0.19
Argentinean	6	0.02
Chilean	2	0.01
Colombian	8	0.03

*Notes: † The Census 2010 population figure is used to calculate the percentages in the Hispanic Origin and Race categories. Ancestry percentages are based on the 2006-2010 American Community Survey population (not shown); ‡ Numbers in parentheses indicate the number of people reporting a single ancestry; * Numbers in parentheses indicate the number of persons reporting this race alone, not in combination with any other race; Please refer to the Explanation of Data for more information.*

Ecuadorian	18	0.07
Peruvian	3	0.01
Uruguayan	2	0.01
Venezuelan	6	0.02
Other Hispanic or Latino	52	0.21

Race*	Population	%
African-American/Black (139)	165	0.68
Not Hispanic (134)	157	0.65
Hispanic (5)	8	0.03
American Indian/Alaska Native (19)	47	0.19
Not Hispanic (14)	37	0.15
Hispanic (5)	10	0.04
Blackfeet (0)	1	<0.01
Canadian/French Am. Ind. (0)	1	<0.01
Cherokee (4)	11	0.05
Chippewa (7)	7	0.03
Inupiat *(Alaska Native)* (2)	2	0.01
Iroquois (0)	1	<0.01
Mexican American Ind. (3)	3	0.01
Ottawa (0)	3	0.01
Asian (423)	589	2.43
Not Hispanic (422)	581	2.40
Hispanic (1)	8	0.03
Chinese, ex. Taiwanese (39)	48	0.20
Filipino (150)	183	0.76
Indian (113)	124	0.51
Japanese (5)	19	0.08
Korean (52)	66	0.27
Laotian (1)	1	<0.01
Malaysian (1)	1	<0.01
Pakistani (14)	14	0.06
Taiwanese (2)	2	0.01
Thai (13)	17	0.07
Vietnamese (17)	19	0.08
Hawaii Native/Pacific Islander (5)	10	0.04
Not Hispanic (4)	9	0.04
Hispanic (1)	1	<0.01
Guamanian/Chamorro (2)	2	0.01
Samoan (2)	2	0.01
White (23,134)	23,371	96.49
Not Hispanic (22,215)	22,410	92.53
Hispanic (919)	961	3.97

Homewood

Place Type: Village
County: Cook
Population: 19,323†

Ancestry‡	Population	%
African, Sub-Saharan (286)	334	1.73
African (79)	100	0.52
Nigerian (180)	180	0.93
Other Sub-Saharan African (27)	54	0.28
American (298)	298	1.54
Armenian (0)	99	0.51
Austrian (27)	74	0.38
Belgian (0)	45	0.23
British (41)	41	0.21
Celtic (9)	9	0.05
Croatian (0)	30	0.16
Czech (20)	86	0.44
Czechoslovakian (0)	48	0.25
Danish (14)	79	0.41
Dutch (182)	608	3.15
Eastern European (19)	19	0.10
English (316)	1,380	7.14
European (143)	156	0.81
Finnish (14)	61	0.32
French, ex. Basque (62)	568	2.94
French Canadian (6)	171	0.88
German (840)	3,896	20.16
Greek (8)	77	0.40
Hungarian (26)	196	1.01
Iranian (0)	12	0.06
Irish (810)	3,594	18.59
Italian (599)	1,405	7.27
Latvian (0)	24	0.12
Lithuanian (12)	179	0.93
Luxemburger (0)	34	0.18
Macedonian (0)	26	0.13
Northern European (12)	12	0.06
Norwegian (25)	270	1.40
Pennsylvania German (15)	15	0.08
Polish (371)	1,364	7.06
Portuguese (0)	36	0.19
Romanian (12)	12	0.06
Russian (137)	318	1.65
Scotch-Irish (117)	328	1.70
Scottish (159)	372	1.92
Serbian (0)	20	0.10
Slovak (30)	82	0.42
Slovene (9)	33	0.17
Swedish (164)	685	3.54
Swiss (28)	166	0.86
Ukrainian (0)	9	0.05
Welsh (12)	129	0.67
West Indian, ex. Hispanic (20)	27	0.14
Belizean (7)	14	0.07
Jamaican (13)	13	0.07

Hispanic Origin	Population	%
Hispanic or Latino (of any race)	1,133	5.86
Central American, ex. Mexican	29	0.15
Costa Rican	7	0.04
Guatemalan	14	0.07
Honduran	2	0.01
Nicaraguan	3	0.02
Panamanian	1	0.01
Salvadoran	2	0.01
Cuban	22	0.11
Dominican Republic	6	0.03
Mexican	840	4.35
Puerto Rican	141	0.73
South American	33	0.17
Argentinean	13	0.07
Colombian	7	0.04
Ecuadorian	4	0.02
Peruvian	9	0.05
Other Hispanic or Latino	62	0.32

Race*	Population	%
African-American/Black (6,594)	6,935	35.89
Not Hispanic (6,520)	6,827	35.33
Hispanic (74)	108	0.56
American Indian/Alaska Native (22)	146	0.76
Not Hispanic (17)	113	0.58
Hispanic (5)	33	0.17
Blackfeet (0)	11	0.06
Canadian/French Am. Ind. (1)	1	0.01
Central American Ind. (0)	4	0.02
Cherokee (1)	14	0.07
Chickasaw (0)	1	0.01
Chippewa (0)	4	0.02
Choctaw (0)	6	0.03
Creek (0)	1	0.01
Iroquois (0)	3	0.02
Mexican American Ind. (0)	1	0.01
Navajo (0)	3	0.02
Pueblo (0)	1	0.01
Seminole (0)	1	0.01
Sioux (0)	4	0.02
Tohono O'Odham (0)	1	0.01
Asian (274)	380	1.97
Not Hispanic (270)	360	1.86
Hispanic (4)	20	0.10
Chinese, ex. Taiwanese (52)	67	0.35
Filipino (75)	111	0.57
Indian (48)	57	0.29
Indonesian (0)	1	0.01
Japanese (20)	35	0.18
Korean (23)	36	0.19
Malaysian (1)	1	0.01
Pakistani (14)	18	0.09
Taiwanese (4)	4	0.02
Thai (13)	16	0.08
Vietnamese (15)	15	0.08
Hawaii Native/Pacific Islander (1)	7	0.04
Not Hispanic (1)	7	0.04
Fijian (1)	1	0.01
Native Hawaiian (0)	4	0.02
White (11,498)	11,927	61.72
Not Hispanic (10,922)	11,250	58.22
Hispanic (576)	677	3.50

Huntley

Place Type: Village
County: McHenry
Population: 24,291†

Ancestry‡	Population	%
African, Sub-Saharan (340)	368	1.73
African (0)	28	0.13
Nigerian (340)	340	1.60
American (533)	533	2.51
Arab (19)	19	0.09
Lebanese (19)	19	0.09
Armenian (10)	20	0.09
Australian (0)	12	0.06
Austrian (47)	215	1.01
Belgian (28)	90	0.42
Brazilian (39)	39	0.18
British (0)	10	0.05
Bulgarian (0)	10	0.05
Canadian (134)	157	0.74
Croatian (53)	173	0.81
Czech (111)	429	2.02
Czechoslovakian (8)	23	0.11
Danish (0)	134	0.63
Dutch (100)	340	1.60
Eastern European (18)	25	0.12
English (334)	1,794	8.44
European (194)	238	1.12
Finnish (15)	43	0.20
French, ex. Basque (35)	506	2.38
French Canadian (36)	88	0.41
German (2,276)	7,151	33.63
Greek (128)	257	1.21
Hungarian (42)	121	0.57
Icelander (0)	11	0.05
Irish (896)	3,680	17.31
Italian (1,191)	2,917	13.72
Lithuanian (62)	140	0.66
Luxemburger (9)	40	0.19
Norwegian (95)	547	2.57
Pennsylvania German (0)	10	0.05
Polish (1,011)	3,654	17.19
Portuguese (0)	39	0.18
Romanian (0)	21	0.10
Russian (61)	209	0.98
Scotch-Irish (49)	261	1.23
Scottish (143)	431	2.03
Serbian (12)	24	0.11
Slavic (0)	11	0.05
Slovak (25)	62	0.29
Swedish (248)	933	4.39
Swiss (0)	35	0.16
Ukrainian (41)	121	0.57
Welsh (0)	92	0.43

Hispanic Origin	Population	%
Hispanic or Latino (of any race)	1,862	7.67
Central American, ex. Mexican	74	0.30
Guatemalan	43	0.18
Honduran	8	0.03
Nicaraguan	1	<0.01
Salvadoran	22	0.09
Cuban	39	0.16
Dominican Republic	4	0.02
Mexican	1,203	4.95
Puerto Rican	274	1.13
South American	185	0.76
Argentinean	12	0.05
Bolivian	4	0.02
Chilean	6	0.02
Colombian	49	0.20
Ecuadorian	60	0.25
Paraguayan	1	<0.01

SECTION TWO

*Notes: † The Census 2010 population figure is used to calculate the percentages in the Hispanic Origin and Race categories. Ancestry percentages are based on the 2006-2010 American Community Survey population (not shown); ‡ Numbers in parentheses indicate the number of people reporting a single ancestry; * Numbers in parentheses indicate the number of persons reporting this race alone, not in combination with any other race; Please refer to the Explanation of Data for more information.*

Peruvian	44	0.18
Venezuelan	9	0.04
Other Hispanic or Latino	83	0.34

Race*	Population	%
African-American/Black (301)	399	1.64
Not Hispanic (293)	380	1.56
Hispanic (8)	19	0.08
American Indian/Alaska Native (74)	121	0.50
Not Hispanic (40)	78	0.32
Hispanic (34)	43	0.18
Alaska Athabascan *(Ala. Nat.)* (1)	1	<0.01
Aleut *(Alaska Native)* (3)	3	0.01
Blackfeet (3)	5	0.02
Cherokee (0)	18	0.07
Chippewa (1)	3	0.01
Inupiat *(Alaska Native)* (1)	1	<0.01
Lumbee (2)	2	0.01
Mexican American Ind. (5)	5	0.02
Navajo (0)	2	0.01
Ottawa (2)	2	0.01
Pueblo (0)	1	<0.01
Shoshone (0)	1	<0.01
Sioux (5)	5	0.02
South American Ind. (1)	1	<0.01
Asian (1,266)	1,447	5.96
Not Hispanic (1,254)	1,418	5.84
Hispanic (12)	29	0.12
Bangladeshi (0)	4	0.02
Burmese (3)	3	0.01
Cambodian (0)	1	<0.01
Chinese, ex. Taiwanese (72)	97	0.40
Filipino (560)	659	2.71
Indian (293)	322	1.33
Indonesian (11)	15	0.06
Japanese (23)	50	0.21
Korean (91)	106	0.44
Laotian (52)	59	0.24
Pakistani (47)	56	0.23
Sri Lankan (9)	9	0.04
Taiwanese (5)	5	0.02
Thai (10)	10	0.04
Vietnamese (51)	53	0.22
Hawaii Native/Pacific Islander (1)	24	0.10
Not Hispanic (1)	21	0.09
Hispanic (0)	3	0.01
Guamanian/Chamorro (0)	1	<0.01
Native Hawaiian (1)	12	0.05
White (21,741)	22,113	91.03
Not Hispanic (20,524)	20,794	85.60
Hispanic (1,217)	1,319	5.43

Island Lake

Place Type: Village
County: McHenry
Population: 8,080†

Ancestry‡	Population	%
African, Sub-Saharan (0)	12	0.15
African (0)	12	0.15
American (485)	485	5.90
Arab (11)	48	0.58
Arab (11)	48	0.58
Austrian (52)	52	0.63
Belgian (11)	23	0.28
British (36)	87	1.06
Croatian (0)	71	0.86
Czech (39)	374	4.55
Czechoslovakian (19)	30	0.36
Danish (11)	80	0.97
Dutch (48)	144	1.75
English (70)	512	6.23
European (65)	65	0.79
French, ex. Basque (13)	164	1.99
French Canadian (36)	79	0.96
German (752)	2,413	29.34
Greek (90)	309	3.76
Hungarian (9)	74	0.90
Irish (260)	1,459	17.74
Italian (265)	798	9.70
Lithuanian (18)	70	0.85
Norwegian (29)	213	2.59
Pennsylvania German (0)	12	0.15
Polish (319)	1,126	13.69
Russian (29)	102	1.24
Scandinavian (3)	3	0.04
Scotch-Irish (9)	67	0.81
Scottish (33)	86	1.05
Serbian (0)	24	0.29
Slavic (0)	13	0.16
Slovak (9)	49	0.60
Swedish (62)	403	4.90
Swiss (0)	9	0.11
Ukrainian (18)	69	0.84
Welsh (46)	138	1.68
Yugoslavian (0)	12	0.15

Hispanic Origin	Population	%
Hispanic or Latino (of any race)	1,130	13.99
Central American, ex. Mexican	26	0.32
Costa Rican	2	0.02
Guatemalan	17	0.21
Honduran	1	0.01
Nicaraguan	1	0.01
Salvadoran	1	0.01
Other Central American	4	0.05
Cuban	9	0.11
Dominican Republic	6	0.07
Mexican	963	11.92
Puerto Rican	39	0.48
South American	33	0.41
Argentinean	2	0.02
Bolivian	4	0.05
Colombian	10	0.12
Ecuadorian	5	0.06
Peruvian	12	0.15
Other Hispanic or Latino	54	0.67

Race*	Population	%
African-American/Black (88)	122	1.51
Not Hispanic (78)	105	1.30
Hispanic (10)	17	0.21
American Indian/Alaska Native (12)	32	0.40
Not Hispanic (6)	20	0.25
Hispanic (6)	12	0.15
Blackfeet (0)	1	0.01
Cherokee (1)	10	0.12
Chippewa (0)	2	0.02
Creek (1)	1	0.01
Ottawa (2)	2	0.02
Asian (153)	198	2.45
Not Hispanic (151)	192	2.38
Hispanic (2)	6	0.07
Cambodian (1)	1	0.01
Chinese, ex. Taiwanese (25)	36	0.45
Filipino (44)	66	0.82
Indian (45)	48	0.59
Japanese (7)	14	0.17
Korean (12)	14	0.17
Laotian (1)	1	0.01
Pakistani (4)	6	0.07
Thai (3)	3	0.04
Vietnamese (5)	13	0.16
Hawaii Native/Pacific Islander (2)	5	0.06
Not Hispanic (1)	3	0.04
Hispanic (1)	2	0.02
Guamanian/Chamorro (1)	2	0.02
Samoan (1)	1	0.01
White (7,305)	7,435	92.02
Not Hispanic (6,623)	6,701	82.93
Hispanic (682)	734	9.08

Itasca

Place Type: Village
County: DuPage
Population: 8,649†

Ancestry‡	Population	%
American (223)	223	2.66
Austrian (0)	41	0.49
British (0)	50	0.60
Bulgarian (73)	73	0.87
Canadian (0)	14	0.17
Croatian (0)	16	0.19
Czech (15)	61	0.73
Czechoslovakian (18)	48	0.57
Danish (30)	77	0.92
Dutch (26)	122	1.45
Eastern European (26)	26	0.31
English (19)	307	3.66
European (20)	20	0.24
Finnish (0)	12	0.14
French, ex. Basque (22)	266	3.17
German (577)	2,063	24.59
Greek (142)	263	3.13
Hungarian (0)	93	1.11
Icelander (7)	7	0.08
Irish (394)	1,077	12.84
Italian (823)	1,612	19.21
Latvian (29)	29	0.35
Lithuanian (39)	64	0.76
Northern European (40)	40	0.48
Norwegian (15)	160	1.91
Polish (837)	1,508	17.97
Portuguese (21)	21	0.25
Romanian (37)	80	0.95
Russian (0)	38	0.45
Scandinavian (0)	26	0.31
Scotch-Irish (20)	60	0.72
Scottish (0)	81	0.97
Slavic (0)	6	0.07
Slovene (0)	11	0.13
Swedish (35)	296	3.53
Swiss (0)	8	0.10
Ukrainian (15)	46	0.55
Welsh (0)	27	0.32
Yugoslavian (0)	12	0.14

Hispanic Origin	Population	%
Hispanic or Latino (of any race)	919	10.63
Central American, ex. Mexican	33	0.38
Guatemalan	23	0.27
Honduran	1	0.01
Nicaraguan	1	0.01
Panamanian	3	0.03
Salvadoran	5	0.06
Cuban	30	0.35
Dominican Republic	3	0.03
Mexican	660	7.63
Puerto Rican	122	1.41
South American	40	0.46
Argentinean	1	0.01
Bolivian	1	0.01
Chilean	2	0.02
Colombian	21	0.24
Ecuadorian	14	0.16
Other South American	1	0.01
Other Hispanic or Latino	31	0.36

Race*	Population	%
African-American/Black (184)	215	2.49
Not Hispanic (176)	202	2.34
Hispanic (8)	13	0.15
American Indian/Alaska Native (17)	56	0.65
Not Hispanic (10)	32	0.37
Hispanic (7)	24	0.28
Canadian/French Am. Ind. (1)	1	0.01
Cherokee (1)	13	0.15
Inupiat *(Alaska Native)* (0)	2	0.02
Mexican American Ind. (0)	1	0.01
Osage (0)	5	0.06
Sioux (1)	6	0.07
Tohono O'Odham (2)	2	0.02
Yaqui (1)	1	0.01
Asian (731)	789	9.12
Not Hispanic (727)	778	9.00
Hispanic (4)	11	0.13

*Notes: † The Census 2010 population figure is used to calculate the percentages in the Hispanic Origin and Race categories. Ancestry percentages are based on the 2006-2010 American Community Survey population (not shown); ‡ Numbers in parentheses indicate the number of people reporting a single ancestry; * Numbers in parentheses indicate the number of persons reporting this race alone, not in combination with any other race; Please refer to the Explanation of Data for more information.*

	Population	%
Bangladeshi (13)	13	0.15
Burmese (2)	2	0.02
Chinese, ex. Taiwanese (76)	83	0.96
Filipino (98)	117	1.35
Indian (336)	354	4.09
Indonesian (0)	1	0.01
Japanese (49)	56	0.65
Korean (85)	90	1.04
Laotian (6)	6	0.07
Nepalese (2)	2	0.02
Pakistani (24)	30	0.35
Taiwanese (4)	7	0.08
Thai (16)	18	0.21
Vietnamese (6)	6	0.07
Hawaii Native/Pacific Islander (1)	13	0.15
Not Hispanic (1)	13	0.15
Native Hawaiian (1)	1	0.01
White (7,271)	7,397	85.52
Not Hispanic (6,707)	6,786	78.46
Hispanic (564)	611	7.06

Jacksonville

Place Type: City
County: Morgan
Population: 19,446†

Ancestry‡	Population	%
African, Sub-Saharan (189)	198	1.02
African (150)	150	0.77
Ethiopian (6)	6	0.03
Ghanaian (8)	8	0.04
Nigerian (0)	9	0.05
South African (25)	25	0.13
Alsatian (0)	40	0.21
American (4,436)	4,436	22.86
Arab (0)	24	0.12
Jordanian (0)	9	0.05
Lebanese (0)	15	0.08
Austrian (15)	28	0.14
Belgian (14)	14	0.07
British (35)	68	0.35
Cajun (0)	14	0.07
Canadian (29)	29	0.15
Celtic (10)	20	0.10
Croatian (32)	44	0.23
Czech (44)	141	0.73
Czechoslovakian (0)	44	0.23
Danish (13)	63	0.32
Dutch (72)	447	2.30
English (728)	2,404	12.39
Estonian (0)	13	0.07
European (38)	54	0.28
Finnish (0)	39	0.20
French, ex. Basque (88)	405	2.09
French Canadian (16)	16	0.08
German (2,038)	4,692	24.18
Greek (30)	79	0.41
Hungarian (0)	9	0.05
Iranian (0)	12	0.06
Irish (543)	2,721	14.02
Italian (88)	288	1.48
Lithuanian (0)	20	0.10
Northern European (24)	24	0.12
Norwegian (48)	240	1.24
Polish (118)	374	1.93
Portuguese (97)	274	1.41
Romanian (0)	10	0.05
Scandinavian (18)	49	0.25
Scotch-Irish (154)	400	2.06
Scottish (79)	254	1.31
Serbian (0)	12	0.06
Slovak (0)	8	0.04
Swedish (93)	229	1.18
Swiss (0)	35	0.18
Welsh (11)	82	0.42
Yugoslavian (0)	23	0.12

Hispanic Origin	Population	%
Hispanic or Latino (of any race)	585	3.01
Central American, ex. Mexican	15	0.08
Costa Rican	1	0.01
Guatemalan	9	0.05
Honduran	1	0.01
Nicaraguan	2	0.01
Panamanian	2	0.01
Cuban	18	0.09
Dominican Republic	4	0.02
Mexican	305	1.57
Puerto Rican	72	0.37
South American	18	0.09
Argentinean	4	0.02
Bolivian	2	0.01
Colombian	9	0.05
Ecuadorian	2	0.01
Other South American	1	0.01
Other Hispanic or Latino	153	0.79

Race*	Population	%
African-American/Black (1,992)	2,332	11.99
Not Hispanic (1,978)	2,290	11.78
Hispanic (14)	42	0.22
American Indian/Alaska Native (54)	126	0.65
Not Hispanic (45)	111	0.57
Hispanic (9)	15	0.08
Apache (6)	7	0.04
Blackfeet (3)	8	0.04
Cherokee (11)	36	0.19
Chickasaw (1)	1	0.01
Chippewa (5)	5	0.03
Choctaw (0)	1	0.01
Inupiat *(Alaska Native)* (0)	1	0.01
Iroquois (3)	3	0.02
Mexican American Ind. (1)	1	0.01
Navajo (3)	3	0.02
Osage (1)	1	0.01
Ottawa (1)	1	0.01
Seminole (2)	2	0.01
Sioux (2)	7	0.04
South American Ind. (1)	1	0.01
Asian (129)	174	0.89
Not Hispanic (125)	165	0.85
Hispanic (4)	9	0.05
Cambodian (3)	3	0.02
Chinese, ex. Taiwanese (15)	24	0.12
Filipino (35)	49	0.25
Indian (41)	47	0.24
Japanese (7)	22	0.11
Korean (4)	7	0.04
Laotian (0)	6	0.03
Nepalese (1)	1	0.01
Pakistani (8)	8	0.04
Thai (3)	9	0.05
Vietnamese (2)	3	0.02
Hawaii Native/Pacific Islander (0)	13	0.07
Not Hispanic (0)	12	0.06
Hispanic (0)	1	0.01
Guamanian/Chamorro (0)	1	0.01
Native Hawaiian (0)	10	0.05
Samoan (0)	1	0.01
White (16,592)	17,035	87.60
Not Hispanic (16,270)	16,667	85.71
Hispanic (322)	368	1.89

Jerseyville

Place Type: City
County: Jersey
Population: 8,465†

Ancestry‡	Population	%
American (739)	739	8.70
Austrian (0)	38	0.45
Croatian (26)	26	0.31
Danish (0)	30	0.35
Dutch (41)	267	3.14
Eastern European (12)	12	0.14
English (288)	726	8.55
French, ex. Basque (138)	307	3.61
German (1,691)	3,210	37.79
Greek (22)	22	0.26
Irish (268)	1,111	13.08
Italian (248)	292	3.44
Norwegian (0)	23	0.27
Polish (62)	183	2.15
Portuguese (17)	17	0.20
Scotch-Irish (25)	40	0.47
Scottish (55)	266	3.13
Slovak (0)	40	0.47
Swedish (69)	190	2.24
Ukrainian (10)	10	0.12
Welsh (32)	49	0.58

Hispanic Origin	Population	%
Hispanic or Latino (of any race)	89	1.05
Central American, ex. Mexican	2	0.02
Guatemalan	2	0.02
Cuban	1	0.01
Mexican	71	0.84
Puerto Rican	1	0.01
South American	6	0.07
Argentinean	2	0.02
Bolivian	1	0.01
Ecuadorian	1	0.01
Peruvian	1	0.01
Venezuelan	1	0.01
Other Hispanic or Latino	8	0.09

Race*	Population	%
African-American/Black (20)	68	0.80
Not Hispanic (20)	66	0.78
Hispanic (0)	2	0.02
American Indian/Alaska Native (18)	70	0.83
Not Hispanic (16)	66	0.78
Hispanic (2)	4	0.05
Apache (0)	3	0.04
Blackfeet (1)	8	0.09
Cherokee (2)	30	0.35
Cheyenne (0)	1	0.01
Chippewa (0)	1	0.01
Comanche (2)	2	0.02
Navajo (0)	3	0.04
Seminole (1)	1	0.01
Sioux (1)	5	0.06
South American Ind. (1)	1	0.01
Yaqui (0)	1	0.01
Asian (41)	58	0.69
Not Hispanic (41)	58	0.69
Chinese, ex. Taiwanese (8)	10	0.12
Filipino (9)	12	0.14
Indian (3)	4	0.05
Japanese (2)	6	0.07
Korean (4)	10	0.12
Pakistani (1)	1	0.01
Thai (7)	7	0.08
Vietnamese (6)	6	0.07
Hawaii Native/Pacific Islander (2)	6	0.07
Not Hispanic (2)	6	0.07
Native Hawaiian (2)	6	0.07
White (8,244)	8,368	98.85
Not Hispanic (8,183)	8,294	97.98
Hispanic (61)	74	0.87

Joliet

Place Type: City
County: Will
Population: 147,433†

Ancestry‡	Population	%
African, Sub-Saharan (678)	955	0.66
African (581)	837	0.58
Ghanaian (26)	26	0.02
Nigerian (42)	63	0.04
South African (29)	29	0.02
Albanian (48)	48	0.03
Alsatian (0)	15	0.01
American (2,512)	2,512	1.73
Arab (608)	694	0.48
Arab (320)	331	0.23

*Notes: † The Census 2010 population figure is used to calculate the percentages in the Hispanic Origin and Race categories. Ancestry percentages are based on the 2006-2010 American Community Survey population (not shown); ‡ Numbers in parentheses indicate the number of people reporting a single ancestry; * Numbers in parentheses indicate the number of persons reporting this race alone, not in combination with any other race; Please refer to the Explanation of Data for more information.*

SECTION TWO

Egyptian (119)	133	0.09
Jordanian (0)	14	0.01
Lebanese (105)	105	0.07
Moroccan (9)	9	0.01
Palestinian (33)	80	0.06
Syrian (9)	9	0.01
Other Arab (13)	13	0.01
Armenian (7)	32	0.02
Assyrian/Chaldean/Syriac (0)	28	0.02
Austrian (65)	306	0.21
Belgian (39)	88	0.06
Brazilian (0)	53	0.04
British (106)	289	0.20
Bulgarian (10)	10	0.01
Canadian (32)	80	0.06
Celtic (0)	27	0.02
Croatian (259)	1,196	0.82
Czech (254)	1,474	1.02
Czechoslovakian (48)	84	0.06
Danish (59)	464	0.32
Dutch (225)	1,311	0.90
Eastern European (33)	55	0.04
English (1,024)	6,635	4.58
European (625)	694	0.48
Finnish (30)	81	0.06
French, ex. Basque (200)	2,385	1.64
French Canadian (107)	304	0.21
German (4,859)	23,053	15.90
German Russian (0)	29	0.02
Greek (445)	1,225	0.84
Guyanese (19)	19	0.01
Hungarian (159)	782	0.54
Icelander (0)	34	0.02
Irish (4,615)	21,088	14.54
Italian (3,491)	13,198	9.10
Lithuanian (594)	1,678	1.16
Luxemburger (14)	33	0.02
Macedonian (34)	34	0.02
Norwegian (387)	1,862	1.28
Pennsylvania German (0)	34	0.02
Polish (4,763)	14,334	9.89
Portuguese (33)	201	0.14
Romanian (118)	294	0.20
Russian (189)	621	0.43
Scandinavian (52)	220	0.15
Scotch-Irish (280)	1,214	0.84
Scottish (318)	1,556	1.07
Serbian (87)	305	0.21
Slavic (58)	153	0.11
Slovak (506)	1,601	1.10
Slovene (487)	1,830	1.26
Swedish (342)	2,493	1.72
Swiss (38)	180	0.12
Ukrainian (48)	145	0.10
Welsh (86)	459	0.32
West Indian, ex. Hispanic (69)	94	0.06
Dutch West Indian (0)	13	0.01
Haitian (55)	55	0.04
Jamaican (0)	12	0.01
Trinidadian/Tobagonian (14)	14	0.01
Yugoslavian (11)	26	0.02

Hispanic Origin	Population	%
Hispanic or Latino (of any race)	41,042	27.84
Central American, ex. Mexican	588	0.40
Costa Rican	17	0.01
Guatemalan	323	0.22
Honduran	69	0.05
Nicaraguan	26	0.02
Panamanian	42	0.03
Salvadoran	109	0.07
Other Central American	2	<0.01
Cuban	151	0.10
Dominican Republic	88	0.06
Mexican	36,570	24.80
Puerto Rican	2,084	1.41
South American	485	0.33
Argentinean	25	0.02
Bolivian	23	0.02
Chilean	15	0.01
Colombian	167	0.11
Ecuadorian	95	0.06
Paraguayan	9	0.01
Peruvian	102	0.07
Uruguayan	10	0.01
Venezuelan	39	0.03
Other Hispanic or Latino	1,076	0.73

Race*	Population	%
African-American/Black (23,562)	25,255	17.13
Not Hispanic (23,025)	24,271	16.46
Hispanic (537)	984	0.67
American Indian/Alaska Native (475)	1,176	0.80
Not Hispanic (192)	636	0.43
Hispanic (283)	540	0.37
Alaska Athabascan *(Ala. Nat.)* (1)	1	<0.01
Aleut *(Alaska Native)* (0)	2	<0.01
Apache (7)	28	0.02
Blackfeet (5)	31	0.02
Canadian/French Am. Ind. (3)	3	<0.01
Cherokee (34)	194	0.13
Cheyenne (2)	4	<0.01
Chickasaw (3)	4	<0.01
Chippewa (16)	29	0.02
Choctaw (1)	23	0.02
Comanche (1)	1	<0.01
Cree (0)	1	<0.01
Creek (12)	17	0.01
Crow (1)	1	<0.01
Hopi (1)	2	<0.01
Inupiat *(Alaska Native)* (1)	3	<0.01
Iroquois (9)	18	0.01
Mexican American Ind. (67)	110	0.07
Navajo (9)	24	0.02
Ottawa (0)	2	<0.01
Potawatomi (6)	11	0.01
Pueblo (0)	1	<0.01
Seminole (0)	1	<0.01
Sioux (6)	25	0.02
South American Ind. (4)	13	0.01
Spanish American Ind. (10)	14	0.01
Ute (4)	4	<0.01
Asian (2,841)	3,584	2.43
Not Hispanic (2,747)	3,347	2.27
Hispanic (94)	237	0.16
Bangladeshi (5)	9	0.01
Burmese (11)	12	0.01
Cambodian (100)	110	0.07
Chinese, ex. Taiwanese (154)	247	0.17
Filipino (990)	1,269	0.86
Hmong (22)	24	0.02
Indian (617)	706	0.48
Indonesian (8)	12	0.01
Japanese (50)	146	0.10
Korean (134)	212	0.14
Laotian (201)	221	0.15
Malaysian (5)	9	0.01
Pakistani (190)	214	0.15
Sri Lankan (0)	5	<0.01
Taiwanese (17)	18	0.01
Thai (38)	58	0.04
Vietnamese (211)	246	0.17
Hawaii Native/Pacific Islander (30)	116	0.08
Not Hispanic (18)	59	0.04
Hispanic (12)	57	0.04
Fijian (0)	2	<0.01
Guamanian/Chamorro (7)	12	0.01
Marshallese (1)	1	<0.01
Native Hawaiian (5)	22	0.01
Samoan (9)	13	0.01
Tongan (2)	2	<0.01
White (99,494)	103,279	70.05
Not Hispanic (78,159)	80,019	54.27
Hispanic (21,335)	23,260	15.78

Justice

Place Type: Village
County: Cook
Population: 12,926†

Ancestry‡	Population	%
African, Sub-Saharan (198)	198	1.57
African (93)	93	0.74
Nigerian (105)	105	0.83
American (506)	506	4.01
Arab (660)	671	5.31
Arab (270)	281	2.22
Egyptian (262)	262	2.07
Lebanese (21)	21	0.17
Palestinian (107)	107	0.85
Austrian (7)	34	0.27
Brazilian (18)	18	0.14
Croatian (0)	73	0.58
Czech (168)	489	3.87
Danish (24)	37	0.29
Dutch (80)	149	1.18
English (120)	423	3.35
European (29)	29	0.23
French, ex. Basque (0)	130	1.03
French Canadian (0)	21	0.17
German (132)	1,267	10.03
Greek (0)	61	0.48
Hungarian (0)	93	0.74
Irish (508)	1,490	11.79
Italian (222)	792	6.27
Lithuanian (86)	217	1.72
Norwegian (15)	57	0.45
Polish (2,526)	3,666	29.02
Romanian (40)	94	0.74
Russian (0)	69	0.55
Scotch-Irish (42)	54	0.43
Scottish (0)	11	0.09
Slovak (13)	26	0.21
Slovene (0)	19	0.15
Swedish (13)	50	0.40
Ukrainian (25)	62	0.49
West Indian, ex. Hispanic (0)	66	0.52
Haitian (0)	66	0.52
Yugoslavian (8)	8	0.06

Hispanic Origin	Population	%
Hispanic or Latino (of any race)	1,595	12.34
Central American, ex. Mexican	19	0.15
Costa Rican	4	0.03
Guatemalan	2	0.02
Honduran	1	0.01
Nicaraguan	2	0.02
Panamanian	1	0.01
Other Central American	9	0.07
Cuban	25	0.19
Dominican Republic	5	0.04
Mexican	1,345	10.41
Puerto Rican	133	1.03
South American	18	0.14
Argentinean	5	0.04
Colombian	5	0.04
Ecuadorian	4	0.03
Peruvian	1	0.01
Venezuelan	3	0.02
Other Hispanic or Latino	50	0.39

Race*	Population	%
African-American/Black (2,926)	3,028	23.43
Not Hispanic (2,863)	2,938	22.73
Hispanic (63)	90	0.70
American Indian/Alaska Native (40)	102	0.79
Not Hispanic (15)	51	0.39
Hispanic (25)	51	0.39
Apache (0)	4	0.03
Cherokee (2)	17	0.13
Chippewa (1)	1	0.01
Iroquois (2)	2	0.02
Mexican American Ind. (4)	16	0.12
Navajo (5)	5	0.04
Sioux (1)	3	0.02
Asian (230)	316	2.44
Not Hispanic (222)	306	2.37
Hispanic (8)	10	0.08
Chinese, ex. Taiwanese (7)	15	0.12
Filipino (72)	80	0.62

*Notes: † The Census 2010 population figure is used to calculate the percentages in the Hispanic Origin and Race categories. Ancestry percentages are based on the 2006-2010 American Community Survey population (not shown); ‡ Numbers in parentheses indicate the number of people reporting a single ancestry; * Numbers in parentheses indicate the number of persons reporting this race alone, not in combination with any other race; Please refer to the Explanation of Data for more information.*

Indian (90)	101	0.78
Japanese (1)	5	0.04
Korean (13)	16	0.12
Pakistani (26)	33	0.26
Thai (4)	4	0.03
Vietnamese (5)	5	0.04
Hawaii Native/Pacific Islander (6)	19	0.15
Not Hispanic (1)	13	0.10
Hispanic (5)	6	0.05
Native Hawaiian (1)	3	0.02
White (8,977)	9,212	71.27
Not Hispanic (8,038)	8,196	63.41
Hispanic (939)	1,016	7.86

Kankakee

Place Type: City
County: Kankakee
Population: 27,537†

Ancestry‡	Population	%
African, Sub-Saharan (62)	62	0.22
African (37)	37	0.13
Other Sub-Saharan African (25)	25	0.09
American (904)	904	3.28
Austrian (0)	13	0.05
Belgian (8)	46	0.17
British (0)	35	0.13
Canadian (10)	10	0.04
Croatian (0)	12	0.04
Czech (32)	84	0.30
Danish (38)	91	0.33
Dutch (81)	402	1.46
Eastern European (14)	32	0.12
English (257)	1,130	4.09
European (162)	177	0.64
Finnish (12)	12	0.04
French, ex. Basque (374)	1,823	6.61
French Canadian (112)	254	0.92
German (945)	3,907	14.16
German Russian (0)	21	0.08
Greek (53)	96	0.35
Hungarian (9)	15	0.05
Irish (484)	2,161	7.83
Italian (208)	651	2.36
Latvian (9)	16	0.06
Lithuanian (14)	40	0.14
Norwegian (25)	84	0.30
Polish (205)	438	1.59
Portuguese (8)	8	0.03
Romanian (0)	9	0.03
Scotch-Irish (18)	150	0.54
Scottish (45)	225	0.82
Serbian (15)	64	0.23
Slovak (8)	39	0.14
Slovene (0)	10	0.04
Swedish (39)	277	1.00
Swiss (0)	41	0.15
Welsh (14)	153	0.55
Yugoslavian (0)	6	0.02

Hispanic Origin	Population	%
Hispanic or Latino (of any race)	5,107	18.55
Central American, ex. Mexican	35	0.13
Guatemalan	8	0.03
Honduran	3	0.01
Panamanian	17	0.06
Salvadoran	7	0.03
Cuban	18	0.07
Dominican Republic	3	0.01
Mexican	4,583	16.64
Puerto Rican	168	0.61
South American	40	0.15
Bolivian	2	0.01
Chilean	1	<0.01
Colombian	5	0.02
Ecuadorian	26	0.09
Paraguayan	2	0.01
Peruvian	4	0.01
Other Hispanic or Latino	260	0.94

Race*	Population	%
African-American/Black (11,244)	11,825	42.94
Not Hispanic (11,128)	11,630	42.23
Hispanic (116)	195	0.71
American Indian/Alaska Native (87)	246	0.89
Not Hispanic (54)	167	0.61
Hispanic (33)	79	0.29
Apache (2)	3	0.01
Blackfeet (1)	10	0.04
Canadian/French Am. Ind. (2)	3	0.01
Cherokee (11)	58	0.21
Cheyenne (0)	2	0.01
Chippewa (0)	5	0.02
Choctaw (0)	4	0.01
Cree (0)	2	0.01
Creek (0)	3	0.01
Inupiat *(Alaska Native)* (0)	1	<0.01
Iroquois (0)	2	0.01
Menominee (2)	2	0.01
Mexican American Ind. (7)	7	0.03
Navajo (0)	1	<0.01
Potawatomi (0)	2	0.01
Seminole (0)	1	<0.01
Sioux (1)	6	0.02
South American Ind. (0)	1	<0.01
Spanish American Ind. (2)	2	0.01
Asian (181)	261	0.95
Not Hispanic (175)	230	0.84
Hispanic (6)	31	0.11
Burmese (2)	2	0.01
Chinese, ex. Taiwanese (59)	67	0.24
Filipino (56)	76	0.28
Indian (25)	51	0.19
Japanese (1)	6	0.02
Korean (13)	20	0.07
Laotian (0)	2	0.01
Pakistani (9)	10	0.04
Sri Lankan (1)	1	<0.01
Thai (0)	1	<0.01
Vietnamese (11)	16	0.06
Hawaii Native/Pacific Islander (3)	16	0.06
Not Hispanic (3)	9	0.03
Hispanic (0)	7	0.03
Guamanian/Chamorro (1)	1	<0.01
Native Hawaiian (2)	10	0.04
White (12,563)	13,355	48.50
Not Hispanic (10,432)	10,974	39.85
Hispanic (2,131)	2,381	8.65

Kewanee

Place Type: City
County: Henry
Population: 12,916†

Ancestry‡	Population	%
African, Sub-Saharan (55)	80	0.61
African (47)	72	0.55
Sudanese (8)	8	0.06
American (778)	778	5.98
Arab (0)	25	0.19
Lebanese (0)	25	0.19
Australian (0)	6	0.05
Austrian (34)	53	0.41
Belgian (260)	560	4.30
British (20)	22	0.17
Bulgarian (13)	13	0.10
Cajun (15)	15	0.12
Canadian (0)	9	0.07
Czech (0)	24	0.18
Danish (0)	7	0.05
Dutch (169)	451	3.47
English (501)	1,337	10.27
European (48)	53	0.41
Finnish (0)	13	0.10
French, ex. Basque (68)	307	2.36
French Canadian (0)	22	0.17
German (1,434)	3,757	28.87
Greek (8)	33	0.25
Hungarian (0)	9	0.07
Irish (454)	1,811	13.92
Italian (122)	381	2.93
Lithuanian (68)	87	0.67
Luxemburger (9)	18	0.14
Norwegian (47)	122	0.94
Polish (203)	466	3.58
Russian (12)	32	0.25
Scotch-Irish (45)	125	0.96
Scottish (55)	188	1.44
Serbian (0)	12	0.09
Swedish (202)	956	7.35
Turkish (0)	6	0.05
Welsh (17)	95	0.73
West Indian, ex. Hispanic (50)	50	0.38
Belizean (50)	50	0.38

Hispanic Origin	Population	%
Hispanic or Latino (of any race)	1,350	10.45
Central American, ex. Mexican	25	0.19
Guatemalan	2	0.02
Nicaraguan	16	0.12
Salvadoran	7	0.05
Cuban	5	0.04
Mexican	1,201	9.30
Puerto Rican	57	0.44
South American	7	0.05
Colombian	5	0.04
Ecuadorian	2	0.02
Other Hispanic or Latino	55	0.43

Race*	Population	%
African-American/Black (633)	841	6.51
Not Hispanic (614)	800	6.19
Hispanic (19)	41	0.32
American Indian/Alaska Native (38)	93	0.72
Not Hispanic (26)	78	0.60
Hispanic (12)	15	0.12
Blackfeet (0)	3	0.02
Cherokee (3)	22	0.17
Cheyenne (0)	3	0.02
Chippewa (1)	1	0.01
Iroquois (0)	1	0.01
Kiowa (1)	1	0.01
Navajo (6)	7	0.05
Paiute (1)	1	0.01
Shoshone (0)	1	0.01
Sioux (0)	4	0.03
South American Ind. (0)	1	0.01
Asian (51)	73	0.57
Not Hispanic (51)	73	0.57
Chinese, ex. Taiwanese (13)	16	0.12
Filipino (21)	28	0.22
Indian (7)	13	0.10
Japanese (1)	4	0.03
Korean (7)	10	0.08
Taiwanese (1)	1	0.01
Hawaii Native/Pacific Islander (4)	8	0.06
Not Hispanic (4)	7	0.05
Hispanic (0)	1	0.01
Guamanian/Chamorro (3)	4	0.03
Native Hawaiian (0)	2	0.02
White (11,241)	11,557	89.48
Not Hispanic (10,626)	10,866	84.13
Hispanic (615)	691	5.35

La Grange Park

Place Type: Village
County: Cook
Population: 13,579†

Ancestry‡	Population	%
American (230)	230	1.72
Arab (107)	198	1.48
Arab (0)	26	0.19
Egyptian (12)	12	0.09
Lebanese (0)	65	0.49
Other Arab (95)	95	0.71
Armenian (9)	33	0.25

*Notes: † The Census 2010 population figure is used to calculate the percentages in the Hispanic Origin and Race categories. Ancestry percentages are based on the 2006-2010 American Community Survey population (not shown); ‡ Numbers in parentheses indicate the number of people reporting a single ancestry; * Numbers in parentheses indicate the number of persons reporting this race alone, not in combination with any other race; Please refer to the Explanation of Data for more information.*

Assyrian/Chaldean/Syriac (12)	23	0.17
Austrian (0)	47	0.35
Belgian (0)	10	0.07
British (10)	20	0.15
Croatian (59)	178	1.33
Czech (235)	966	7.22
Czechoslovakian (59)	127	0.95
Dutch (37)	258	1.93
English (118)	1,047	7.82
European (74)	84	0.63
Finnish (0)	62	0.46
French, ex. Basque (26)	406	3.03
French Canadian (0)	22	0.16
German (576)	2,705	20.21
Greek (30)	99	0.74
Hungarian (18)	48	0.36
Irish (889)	3,411	25.48
Italian (626)	1,804	13.48
Latvian (24)	24	0.18
Lithuanian (127)	258	1.93
Luxemburger (0)	72	0.54
Macedonian (6)	6	0.04
Norwegian (58)	440	3.29
Polish (733)	2,208	16.49
Portuguese (9)	9	0.07
Romanian (116)	116	0.87
Russian (40)	97	0.72
Scandinavian (0)	13	0.10
Scotch-Irish (58)	132	0.99
Scottish (31)	193	1.44
Serbian (115)	115	0.86
Slovak (57)	114	0.85
Slovene (32)	128	0.96
Swedish (32)	243	1.82
Swiss (10)	63	0.47
Ukrainian (32)	113	0.84
Welsh (0)	47	0.35
Yugoslavian (88)	88	0.66

Hispanic Origin	Population	%
Hispanic or Latino (of any race)	929	6.84
Central American, ex. Mexican	23	0.17
Guatemalan	13	0.10
Honduran	3	0.02
Nicaraguan	1	0.01
Panamanian	3	0.02
Salvadoran	3	0.02
Cuban	25	0.18
Dominican Republic	2	0.01
Mexican	691	5.09
Puerto Rican	89	0.66
South American	46	0.34
Argentinean	3	0.02
Bolivian	5	0.04
Chilean	2	0.01
Colombian	10	0.07
Ecuadorian	10	0.07
Paraguayan	1	0.01
Peruvian	9	0.07
Venezuelan	1	0.01
Other South American	5	0.04
Other Hispanic or Latino	53	0.39

Race*	Population	%
African-American/Black (530)	598	4.40
Not Hispanic (525)	574	4.23
Hispanic (5)	24	0.18
American Indian/Alaska Native (19)	69	0.51
Not Hispanic (12)	50	0.37
Hispanic (7)	19	0.14
Blackfeet (1)	3	0.02
Cherokee (0)	8	0.06
Chippewa (0)	3	0.02
Crow (0)	1	0.01
Iroquois (1)	2	0.01
Mexican American Ind. (3)	7	0.05
Navajo (0)	1	0.01
Osage (2)	2	0.01
Ottawa (1)	1	0.01
Puget Sound Salish (1)	1	0.01
Sioux (2)	5	0.04
South American Ind. (0)	3	0.02
Asian (263)	362	2.67
Not Hispanic (258)	345	2.54
Hispanic (5)	17	0.13
Cambodian (1)	2	0.01
Chinese, ex. Taiwanese (42)	62	0.46
Filipino (57)	91	0.67
Indian (79)	93	0.68
Japanese (9)	22	0.16
Korean (23)	31	0.23
Laotian (2)	2	0.01
Malaysian (1)	1	0.01
Pakistani (5)	7	0.05
Taiwanese (1)	3	0.02
Thai (12)	12	0.09
Vietnamese (14)	16	0.12
Hawaii Native/Pacific Islander (1)	4	0.03
Not Hispanic (1)	3	0.02
Hispanic (0)	1	0.01
Guamanian/Chamorro (0)	1	0.01
Native Hawaiian (0)	1	0.01
White (12,279)	12,502	92.07
Not Hispanic (11,671)	11,830	87.12
Hispanic (608)	672	4.95

La Grange

Place Type: Village
County: Cook
Population: 15,550†

Ancestry‡	Population	%
American (354)	354	2.29
Arab (84)	84	0.54
Arab (75)	75	0.49
Egyptian (9)	9	0.06
Australian (0)	18	0.12
Austrian (34)	94	0.61
Belgian (10)	46	0.30
Brazilian (0)	9	0.06
British (35)	53	0.34
Canadian (15)	25	0.16
Croatian (91)	244	1.58
Czech (171)	731	4.74
Czechoslovakian (100)	159	1.03
Danish (18)	111	0.72
Dutch (50)	325	2.11
Eastern European (9)	9	0.06
English (250)	1,869	12.11
Estonian (26)	50	0.32
European (141)	169	1.10
Finnish (11)	24	0.16
French, ex. Basque (10)	504	3.27
French Canadian (0)	43	0.28
German (751)	3,841	24.89
Greek (55)	251	1.63
Hungarian (0)	37	0.24
Irish (1,542)	4,713	30.54
Italian (461)	1,946	12.61
Lithuanian (217)	389	2.52
Luxemburger (0)	27	0.17
Macedonian (118)	128	0.83
Northern European (29)	36	0.23
Norwegian (19)	243	1.57
Pennsylvania German (0)	9	0.06
Polish (607)	2,019	13.08
Portuguese (0)	9	0.06
Romanian (36)	92	0.60
Russian (9)	91	0.59
Scandinavian (21)	21	0.14
Scotch-Irish (99)	244	1.58
Scottish (68)	381	2.47
Serbian (68)	87	0.56
Slavic (28)	28	0.18
Slovak (27)	127	0.82
Slovene (8)	57	0.37
Swedish (68)	378	2.45
Swiss (0)	39	0.25
Turkish (26)	26	0.17
Ukrainian (16)	48	0.31
Welsh (10)	107	0.69
Yugoslavian (75)	94	0.61

Hispanic Origin	Population	%
Hispanic or Latino (of any race)	998	6.42
Central American, ex. Mexican	40	0.26
Costa Rican	4	0.03
Guatemalan	29	0.19
Honduran	4	0.03
Nicaraguan	1	0.01
Panamanian	1	0.01
Salvadoran	1	0.01
Cuban	24	0.15
Dominican Republic	8	0.05
Mexican	765	4.92
Puerto Rican	73	0.47
South American	48	0.31
Argentinean	6	0.04
Colombian	20	0.13
Ecuadorian	8	0.05
Peruvian	4	0.03
Uruguayan	2	0.01
Venezuelan	2	0.01
Other South American	6	0.04
Other Hispanic or Latino	40	0.26

Race*	Population	%
African-American/Black (759)	824	5.30
Not Hispanic (751)	804	5.17
Hispanic (8)	20	0.13
American Indian/Alaska Native (21)	67	0.43
Not Hispanic (10)	44	0.28
Hispanic (11)	23	0.15
Cherokee (2)	17	0.11
Chippewa (1)	1	0.01
Choctaw (0)	1	0.01
Iroquois (1)	1	0.01
Mexican American Ind. (2)	7	0.05
Seminole (1)	1	0.01
Tlingit-Haida *(Alaska Native)* (1)	1	0.01
Asian (214)	361	2.32
Not Hispanic (213)	327	2.10
Hispanic (1)	34	0.22
Cambodian (1)	1	0.01
Chinese, ex. Taiwanese (56)	92	0.59
Filipino (51)	95	0.61
Indian (45)	62	0.40
Indonesian (0)	1	0.01
Japanese (10)	36	0.23
Korean (28)	45	0.29
Pakistani (1)	5	0.03
Taiwanese (5)	5	0.03
Thai (6)	16	0.10
Vietnamese (1)	2	0.01
Hawaii Native/Pacific Islander (0)	7	0.05
Not Hispanic (0)	2	0.01
Hispanic (0)	5	0.03
Guamanian/Chamorro (0)	1	0.01
Native Hawaiian (0)	6	0.04
Samoan (0)	5	0.03
White (13,983)	14,246	91.61
Not Hispanic (13,361)	13,550	87.14
Hispanic (622)	696	4.48

LaSalle

Place Type: City
County: LaSalle
Population: 9,609†

Ancestry‡	Population	%
American (400)	400	4.12
Arab (41)	41	0.42
Lebanese (41)	41	0.42
Austrian (37)	83	0.86
Belgian (2)	41	0.42
British (0)	39	0.40
Czech (16)	50	0.52
Czechoslovakian (2)	2	0.02

*Notes: † The Census 2010 population figure is used to calculate the percentages in the Hispanic Origin and Race categories. Ancestry percentages are based on the 2006-2010 American Community Survey population (not shown); ‡ Numbers in parentheses indicate the number of people reporting a single ancestry; * Numbers in parentheses indicate the number of persons reporting this race alone, not in combination with any other race; Please refer to the Explanation of Data for more information.*

Danish (0)	31	0.32
Dutch (9)	231	2.38
English (177)	539	5.56
European (52)	52	0.54
Finnish (17)	17	0.18
French, ex. Basque (59)	390	4.02
French Canadian (11)	11	0.11
German (884)	3,502	36.11
Hungarian (0)	11	0.11
Irish (343)	1,556	16.05
Italian (405)	1,282	13.22
Latvian (0)	7	0.07
Lithuanian (45)	104	1.07
Northern European (9)	9	0.09
Norwegian (57)	119	1.23
Polish (518)	1,602	16.52
Portuguese (0)	37	0.38
Romanian (108)	108	1.11
Russian (0)	62	0.64
Scotch-Irish (21)	179	1.85
Scottish (39)	173	1.78
Slavic (8)	21	0.22
Slovak (52)	101	1.04
Slovene (79)	209	2.16
Swedish (44)	400	4.12
Swiss (0)	20	0.21
Ukrainian (0)	35	0.36
Welsh (0)	10	0.10
West Indian, ex. Hispanic (0)	10	0.10
Bahamian (0)	10	0.10

Hispanic Origin	Population	%
Hispanic or Latino (of any race)	1,369	14.25
Central American, ex. Mexican	20	0.21
Guatemalan	13	0.14
Honduran	1	0.01
Nicaraguan	1	0.01
Salvadoran	5	0.05
Cuban	4	0.04
Mexican	1,181	12.29
Puerto Rican	93	0.97
South American	8	0.08
Colombian	8	0.08
Other Hispanic or Latino	63	0.66

Race*	Population	%
African-American/Black (160)	263	2.74
Not Hispanic (152)	242	2.52
Hispanic (8)	21	0.22
American Indian/Alaska Native (26)	68	0.71
Not Hispanic (23)	58	0.60
Hispanic (3)	10	0.10
Apache (1)	1	0.01
Blackfeet (0)	3	0.03
Cherokee (3)	20	0.21
Choctaw (1)	5	0.05
Creek (1)	1	0.01
Delaware (3)	3	0.03
Mexican American Ind. (1)	2	0.02
Navajo (1)	2	0.02
Sioux (0)	2	0.02
Tlingit-Haida *(Alaska Native)* (2)	2	0.02
Asian (85)	125	1.30
Not Hispanic (82)	111	1.16
Hispanic (3)	14	0.15
Cambodian (6)	8	0.08
Chinese, ex. Taiwanese (11)	23	0.24
Filipino (19)	38	0.40
Indian (16)	18	0.19
Japanese (6)	8	0.08
Korean (5)	8	0.08
Laotian (11)	11	0.11
Vietnamese (2)	5	0.05
Hawaii Native/Pacific Islander (0)	9	0.09
Not Hispanic (0)	8	0.08
Hispanic (0)	1	0.01
Native Hawaiian (0)	8	0.08
White (8,574)	8,778	91.35
Not Hispanic (7,836)	7,978	83.03
Hispanic (738)	800	8.33

Lake Forest

Place Type: City
County: Lake
Population: 19,375†

Ancestry‡	Population	%
African, Sub-Saharan (13)	13	0.07
Somalian (13)	13	0.07
American (1,064)	1,064	5.49
Arab (40)	57	0.29
Arab (15)	15	0.08
Lebanese (14)	14	0.07
Syrian (11)	20	0.10
Other Arab (0)	8	0.04
Armenian (107)	131	0.68
Assyrian/Chaldean/Syriac (0)	18	0.09
Australian (65)	65	0.34
Austrian (88)	216	1.11
Belgian (16)	74	0.38
Brazilian (8)	8	0.04
British (31)	203	1.05
Canadian (26)	48	0.25
Croatian (47)	71	0.37
Czech (66)	207	1.07
Czechoslovakian (0)	22	0.11
Danish (7)	194	1.00
Dutch (99)	527	2.72
Eastern European (27)	27	0.14
English (918)	2,795	14.41
European (182)	227	1.17
Finnish (26)	58	0.30
French, ex. Basque (55)	610	3.14
French Canadian (115)	215	1.11
German (1,286)	5,249	27.06
Greek (227)	301	1.55
Hungarian (15)	97	0.50
Iranian (0)	12	0.06
Irish (1,154)	3,666	18.90
Italian (913)	1,845	9.51
Latvian (9)	9	0.05
Lithuanian (26)	115	0.59
Luxemburger (12)	31	0.16
Northern European (63)	74	0.38
Norwegian (121)	392	2.02
Polish (538)	1,280	6.60
Portuguese (8)	8	0.04
Romanian (71)	112	0.58
Russian (110)	264	1.36
Scandinavian (49)	95	0.49
Scotch-Irish (141)	704	3.63
Scottish (224)	859	4.43
Serbian (10)	10	0.05
Slovak (17)	26	0.13
Slovene (10)	22	0.11
Swedish (141)	750	3.87
Swiss (15)	236	1.22
Turkish (6)	6	0.03
Ukrainian (90)	143	0.74
Welsh (17)	176	0.91
West Indian, ex. Hispanic (14)	14	0.07
Haitian (7)	7	0.04
Jamaican (7)	7	0.04
Yugoslavian (0)	10	0.05

Hispanic Origin	Population	%
Hispanic or Latino (of any race)	542	2.80
Central American, ex. Mexican	41	0.21
Costa Rican	6	0.03
Guatemalan	17	0.09
Honduran	4	0.02
Nicaraguan	10	0.05
Panamanian	3	0.02
Salvadoran	1	0.01
Cuban	52	0.27
Dominican Republic	9	0.05
Mexican	212	1.09
Puerto Rican	40	0.21
South American	119	0.61
Argentinean	7	0.04
Bolivian	2	0.01
Chilean	8	0.04
Colombian	61	0.31
Ecuadorian	10	0.05
Paraguayan	3	0.02
Peruvian	17	0.09
Venezuelan	11	0.06
Other Hispanic or Latino	69	0.36

Race*	Population	%
African-American/Black (213)	246	1.27
Not Hispanic (196)	226	1.17
Hispanic (17)	20	0.10
American Indian/Alaska Native (28)	75	0.39
Not Hispanic (19)	64	0.33
Hispanic (9)	11	0.06
Apache (2)	2	0.01
Blackfeet (0)	2	0.01
Cherokee (2)	11	0.06
Chippewa (1)	3	0.02
Choctaw (0)	12	0.06
Crow (1)	3	0.02
Hopi (1)	1	0.01
Iroquois (3)	4	0.02
Mexican American Ind. (2)	2	0.01
Navajo (0)	1	0.01
Sioux (2)	5	0.03
Asian (904)	1,066	5.50
Not Hispanic (899)	1,052	5.43
Hispanic (5)	14	0.07
Bangladeshi (5)	8	0.04
Burmese (1)	1	0.01
Cambodian (2)	2	0.01
Chinese, ex. Taiwanese (195)	262	1.35
Filipino (77)	123	0.63
Indian (252)	309	1.59
Indonesian (4)	8	0.04
Japanese (39)	75	0.39
Korean (202)	220	1.14
Laotian (2)	2	0.01
Nepalese (7)	7	0.04
Pakistani (19)	26	0.13
Sri Lankan (7)	7	0.04
Taiwanese (21)	25	0.13
Thai (6)	16	0.08
Vietnamese (16)	20	0.10
Hawaii Native/Pacific Islander (1)	12	0.06
Not Hispanic (1)	11	0.06
Hispanic (0)	1	0.01
Guamanian/Chamorro (0)	2	0.01
Native Hawaiian (1)	6	0.03
White (17,846)	18,077	93.30
Not Hispanic (17,474)	17,683	91.27
Hispanic (372)	394	2.03

Lake Villa

Place Type: Village
County: Lake
Population: 8,741†

Ancestry‡	Population	%
American (305)	305	3.61
Arab (0)	14	0.17
Lebanese (0)	14	0.17
Armenian (37)	78	0.92
Assyrian/Chaldean/Syriac (0)	60	0.71
Austrian (37)	118	1.39
Brazilian (7)	7	0.08
British (19)	19	0.22
Bulgarian (10)	10	0.12
Canadian (9)	9	0.11
Croatian (0)	38	0.45
Czech (40)	163	1.93
Danish (0)	59	0.70
Dutch (7)	125	1.48
Eastern European (7)	7	0.08
English (135)	674	7.97
European (152)	182	2.15
Finnish (12)	70	0.83

SECTION TWO

*Notes: † The Census 2010 population figure is used to calculate the percentages in the Hispanic Origin and Race categories. Ancestry percentages are based on the 2006-2010 American Community Survey population (not shown); ‡ Numbers in parentheses indicate the number of people reporting a single ancestry; * Numbers in parentheses indicate the number of persons reporting this race alone, not in combination with any other race; Please refer to the Explanation of Data for more information.*

French, ex. Basque (46)	287	3.39
French Canadian (0)	18	0.21
German (522)	2,437	28.81
Greek (50)	129	1.52
Hungarian (47)	89	1.05
Iranian (14)	14	0.17
Irish (250)	1,816	21.47
Israeli (7)	7	0.08
Italian (54)	524	6.19
Latvian (0)	22	0.26
Lithuanian (19)	56	0.66
Norwegian (73)	199	2.35
Pennsylvania German (0)	12	0.14
Polish (421)	1,344	15.89
Russian (78)	149	1.76
Scandinavian (33)	57	0.67
Scotch-Irish (56)	132	1.56
Scottish (10)	124	1.47
Serbian (15)	15	0.18
Slavic (7)	11	0.13
Slovak (0)	28	0.33
Swedish (79)	380	4.49
Swiss (7)	7	0.08
Ukrainian (7)	28	0.33
Welsh (0)	59	0.70
Yugoslavian (0)	14	0.17

Hispanic Origin	Population	%
Hispanic or Latino (of any race)	714	8.17
Central American, ex. Mexican	31	0.35
Guatemalan	5	0.06
Honduran	7	0.08
Nicaraguan	1	0.01
Panamanian	8	0.09
Salvadoran	10	0.11
Cuban	20	0.23
Dominican Republic	7	0.08
Mexican	453	5.18
Puerto Rican	127	1.45
South American	43	0.49
Argentinean	1	0.01
Bolivian	1	0.01
Chilean	2	0.02
Colombian	23	0.26
Ecuadorian	13	0.15
Peruvian	1	0.01
Venezuelan	1	0.01
Other South American	1	0.01
Other Hispanic or Latino	33	0.38

Race*	Population	%
African-American/Black (344)	396	4.53
Not Hispanic (335)	376	4.30
Hispanic (9)	20	0.23
American Indian/Alaska Native (18)	41	0.47
Not Hispanic (8)	25	0.29
Hispanic (10)	16	0.18
Apache (4)	5	0.06
Central American Ind. (1)	1	0.01
Cherokee (0)	5	0.06
Chippewa (5)	7	0.08
Creek (0)	1	0.01
Hopi (1)	1	0.01
Iroquois (0)	1	0.01
Lumbee (0)	2	0.02
Menominee (1)	1	0.01
Mexican American Ind. (2)	2	0.02
Seminole (0)	1	0.01
Asian (438)	524	5.99
Not Hispanic (437)	515	5.89
Hispanic (1)	9	0.10
Cambodian (12)	12	0.14
Chinese, ex. Taiwanese (47)	59	0.67
Filipino (204)	233	2.67
Indian (114)	117	1.34
Japanese (8)	20	0.23
Korean (31)	41	0.47
Laotian (2)	2	0.02
Pakistani (1)	3	0.03
Sri Lankan (3)	4	0.05
Taiwanese (0)	4	0.05
Thai (3)	3	0.03
Vietnamese (11)	12	0.14
Hawaii Native/Pacific Islander (0)	9	0.10
Not Hispanic (0)	8	0.09
Hispanic (0)	1	0.01
Native Hawaiian (0)	4	0.05
Samoan (0)	2	0.02
White (7,537)	7,690	87.98
Not Hispanic (7,109)	7,227	82.68
Hispanic (428)	463	5.30

Lake Zurich

Place Type: Village
County: Lake
Population: 19,631†

Ancestry‡	Population	%
African, Sub-Saharan (9)	9	0.05
South African (9)	9	0.05
American (704)	704	3.60
Arab (51)	114	0.58
Arab (51)	69	0.35
Lebanese (0)	18	0.09
Palestinian (0)	17	0.09
Syrian (0)	10	0.05
Armenian (9)	49	0.25
Assyrian/Chaldean/Syriac (0)	48	0.25
Australian (0)	7	0.04
Austrian (38)	98	0.50
Belgian (27)	141	0.72
Brazilian (35)	35	0.18
British (22)	90	0.46
Bulgarian (77)	77	0.39
Croatian (8)	92	0.47
Czech (37)	358	1.83
Czechoslovakian (11)	47	0.24
Danish (32)	172	0.88
Dutch (68)	317	1.62
Eastern European (10)	10	0.05
English (268)	1,620	8.28
European (205)	205	1.05
Finnish (0)	10	0.05
French, ex. Basque (26)	452	2.31
French Canadian (5)	73	0.37
German (1,136)	5,627	28.78
Greek (186)	291	1.49
Hungarian (36)	136	0.70
Icelander (0)	34	0.17
Iranian (14)	14	0.07
Irish (642)	3,460	17.69
Italian (516)	2,090	10.69
Lithuanian (100)	254	1.30
Luxemburger (11)	57	0.29
Northern European (10)	19	0.10
Norwegian (70)	535	2.74
Pennsylvania German (11)	11	0.06
Polish (1,097)	3,385	17.31
Portuguese (0)	5	0.03
Romanian (120)	136	0.70
Russian (198)	450	2.30
Scandinavian (0)	69	0.35
Scotch-Irish (119)	328	1.68
Scottish (74)	346	1.77
Serbian (75)	86	0.44
Slovak (39)	244	1.25
Slovene (0)	12	0.06
Swedish (79)	948	4.85
Swiss (9)	107	0.55
Ukrainian (180)	236	1.21
Welsh (25)	65	0.33
Yugoslavian (17)	17	0.09

Hispanic Origin	Population	%
Hispanic or Latino (of any race)	1,521	7.75
Central American, ex. Mexican	60	0.31
Costa Rican	2	0.01
Guatemalan	22	0.11
Honduran	2	0.01
Nicaraguan	4	0.02
Panamanian	5	0.03
Salvadoran	25	0.13
Cuban	33	0.17
Dominican Republic	5	0.03
Mexican	1,095	5.58
Puerto Rican	114	0.58
South American	93	0.47
Argentinean	9	0.05
Bolivian	2	0.01
Chilean	3	0.02
Colombian	29	0.15
Ecuadorian	23	0.12
Peruvian	18	0.09
Venezuelan	9	0.05
Other Hispanic or Latino	121	0.62

Race*	Population	%
African-American/Black (189)	256	1.30
Not Hispanic (165)	218	1.11
Hispanic (24)	38	0.19
American Indian/Alaska Native (23)	53	0.27
Not Hispanic (10)	35	0.18
Hispanic (13)	18	0.09
Apache (2)	2	0.01
Canadian/French Am. Ind. (0)	1	0.01
Cherokee (5)	15	0.08
Chippewa (0)	2	0.01
Choctaw (1)	1	0.01
Inupiat *(Alaska Native)* (1)	1	0.01
Lumbee (0)	3	0.02
Menominee (0)	3	0.02
Mexican American Ind. (4)	5	0.03
Potawatomi (1)	1	0.01
Pueblo (0)	1	0.01
Asian (1,444)	1,630	8.30
Not Hispanic (1,440)	1,609	8.20
Hispanic (4)	21	0.11
Chinese, ex. Taiwanese (464)	502	2.56
Filipino (66)	117	0.60
Indian (572)	609	3.10
Indonesian (0)	1	0.01
Japanese (35)	77	0.39
Korean (201)	232	1.18
Laotian (0)	3	0.02
Malaysian (3)	4	0.02
Nepalese (9)	11	0.06
Pakistani (16)	19	0.10
Taiwanese (1)	4	0.02
Thai (15)	16	0.08
Vietnamese (27)	32	0.16
Hawaii Native/Pacific Islander (12)	16	0.08
Not Hispanic (11)	15	0.08
Hispanic (1)	1	0.01
Guamanian/Chamorro (3)	3	0.02
Native Hawaiian (1)	2	0.01
Samoan (2)	2	0.01
White (17,015)	17,320	88.23
Not Hispanic (16,223)	16,451	83.80
Hispanic (792)	869	4.43

Lake in the Hills

Place Type: Village
County: McHenry
Population: 28,965†

Ancestry‡	Population	%
African, Sub-Saharan (16)	16	0.06
African (16)	16	0.06
American (666)	666	2.33
Arab (155)	173	0.60
Arab (28)	28	0.10
Egyptian (9)	9	0.03
Lebanese (15)	15	0.05
Palestinian (7)	14	0.05
Syrian (0)	11	0.04
Other Arab (96)	96	0.34
Assyrian/Chaldean/Syriac (63)	63	0.22
Austrian (9)	129	0.45

*Notes: † The Census 2010 population figure is used to calculate the percentages in the Hispanic Origin and Race categories. Ancestry percentages are based on the 2006-2010 American Community Survey population (not shown); ‡ Numbers in parentheses indicate the number of people reporting a single ancestry; * Numbers in parentheses indicate the number of persons reporting this race alone, not in combination with any other race; Please refer to the Explanation of Data for more information.*

Belgian (14)	14	0.05
British (14)	59	0.21
Bulgarian (0)	32	0.11
Croatian (0)	29	0.10
Czech (88)	517	1.81
Czechoslovakian (13)	20	0.07
Danish (52)	273	0.95
Dutch (40)	508	1.78
Eastern European (14)	41	0.14
English (398)	1,713	5.99
European (260)	335	1.17
Finnish (8)	16	0.06
French, ex. Basque (54)	740	2.59
French Canadian (0)	84	0.29
German (1,989)	7,958	27.83
Greek (44)	154	0.54
Hungarian (64)	318	1.11
Iranian (17)	17	0.06
Irish (855)	5,027	17.58
Israeli (0)	11	0.04
Italian (1,833)	4,330	15.14
Lithuanian (0)	161	0.56
Luxemburger (0)	14	0.05
Norwegian (173)	712	2.49
Polish (2,354)	5,160	18.04
Portuguese (14)	82	0.29
Romanian (381)	443	1.55
Russian (56)	259	0.91
Scandinavian (67)	81	0.28
Scotch-Irish (129)	195	0.68
Scottish (57)	416	1.45
Serbian (11)	43	0.15
Slovak (20)	54	0.19
Swedish (65)	890	3.11
Swiss (0)	31	0.11
Turkish (23)	23	0.08
Ukrainian (80)	143	0.50
Welsh (0)	89	0.31
West Indian, ex. Hispanic (15)	26	0.09
Haitian (0)	11	0.04
Jamaican (15)	15	0.05
Yugoslavian (123)	154	0.54

Hispanic Origin	Population	%
Hispanic or Latino (of any race)	3,358	11.59
Central American, ex. Mexican	156	0.54
Costa Rican	3	0.01
Guatemalan	65	0.22
Honduran	23	0.08
Nicaraguan	9	0.03
Panamanian	5	0.02
Salvadoran	51	0.18
Cuban	89	0.31
Dominican Republic	11	0.04
Mexican	2,259	7.80
Puerto Rican	445	1.54
South American	246	0.85
Argentinean	13	0.04
Bolivian	8	0.03
Chilean	12	0.04
Colombian	81	0.28
Ecuadorian	33	0.11
Peruvian	76	0.26
Venezuelan	21	0.07
Other South American	2	0.01
Other Hispanic or Latino	152	0.52

Race*	Population	%
African-American/Black (578)	743	2.57
Not Hispanic (546)	671	2.32
Hispanic (32)	72	0.25
American Indian/Alaska Native (75)	184	0.64
Not Hispanic (33)	106	0.37
Hispanic (42)	78	0.27
Blackfeet (0)	2	0.01
Cherokee (3)	18	0.06
Chippewa (0)	5	0.02
Choctaw (2)	2	0.01
Creek (0)	1	<0.01
Crow (0)	1	<0.01
Delaware (0)	4	0.01
Iroquois (1)	5	0.02
Mexican American Ind. (15)	21	0.07
Navajo (2)	6	0.02
Osage (0)	1	<0.01
Ottawa (2)	4	0.01
Potawatomi (0)	3	0.01
Shoshone (1)	1	<0.01
Sioux (11)	15	0.05
South American Ind. (7)	12	0.04
Asian (1,519)	1,764	6.09
Not Hispanic (1,512)	1,740	6.01
Hispanic (7)	24	0.08
Bangladeshi (4)	8	0.03
Burmese (5)	5	0.02
Chinese, ex. Taiwanese (99)	134	0.46
Filipino (447)	526	1.82
Indian (563)	592	2.04
Indonesian (2)	8	0.03
Japanese (32)	85	0.29
Korean (104)	125	0.43
Laotian (11)	16	0.06
Pakistani (109)	112	0.39
Taiwanese (5)	5	0.02
Thai (15)	21	0.07
Vietnamese (90)	111	0.38
Hawaii Native/Pacific Islander (12)	38	0.13
Not Hispanic (12)	37	0.13
Hispanic (0)	1	<0.01
Guamanian/Chamorro (8)	12	0.04
Native Hawaiian (4)	21	0.07
White (25,117)	25,683	88.67
Not Hispanic (23,078)	23,461	81.00
Hispanic (2,039)	2,222	7.67

Lansing

Place Type: Village
County: Cook
Population: 28,331[†]

Ancestry[‡]	Population	%
African, Sub-Saharan (58)	111	0.40
African (9)	62	0.22
Nigerian (49)	49	0.17
Albanian (20)	39	0.14
American (523)	523	1.87
Arab (134)	155	0.55
Moroccan (123)	123	0.44
Palestinian (11)	32	0.11
Austrian (44)	124	0.44
Belgian (0)	20	0.07
Brazilian (11)	32	0.11
British (13)	37	0.13
Bulgarian (16)	16	0.06
Canadian (18)	32	0.11
Croatian (216)	471	1.68
Czech (97)	211	0.75
Czechoslovakian (0)	12	0.04
Danish (13)	62	0.22
Dutch (1,852)	2,662	9.51
Eastern European (32)	32	0.11
English (97)	897	3.20
European (16)	35	0.12
Finnish (7)	14	0.05
French, ex. Basque (0)	442	1.58
French Canadian (14)	81	0.29
German (1,625)	4,907	17.52
Greek (73)	254	0.91
Hungarian (35)	123	0.44
Irish (854)	3,415	12.19
Italian (827)	1,941	6.93
Latvian (0)	12	0.04
Lithuanian (69)	327	1.17
Macedonian (0)	8	0.03
Northern European (18)	18	0.06
Norwegian (43)	210	0.75
Polish (1,480)	4,005	14.30
Portuguese (0)	17	0.06
Romanian (0)	48	0.17
Russian (9)	35	0.12
Scandinavian (17)	44	0.16
Scotch-Irish (27)	192	0.69
Scottish (0)	169	0.60
Serbian (272)	441	1.57
Slavic (10)	20	0.07
Slovak (75)	183	0.65
Slovene (0)	23	0.08
Swedish (189)	492	1.76
Swiss (0)	71	0.25
Ukrainian (136)	147	0.52
Welsh (0)	30	0.11
West Indian, ex. Hispanic (151)	164	0.59
Bahamian (35)	35	0.12
Haitian (0)	13	0.05
Jamaican (31)	31	0.11
Trinidadian/Tobagonian (85)	85	0.30
Yugoslavian (13)	13	0.05

Hispanic Origin	Population	%
Hispanic or Latino (of any race)	4,103	14.48
Central American, ex. Mexican	68	0.24
Costa Rican	4	0.01
Guatemalan	32	0.11
Honduran	11	0.04
Nicaraguan	8	0.03
Panamanian	2	0.01
Salvadoran	11	0.04
Cuban	23	0.08
Dominican Republic	7	0.02
Mexican	3,548	12.52
Puerto Rican	246	0.87
South American	49	0.17
Argentinean	1	<0.01
Bolivian	1	<0.01
Colombian	7	0.02
Ecuadorian	16	0.06
Peruvian	14	0.05
Uruguayan	3	0.01
Venezuelan	7	0.02
Other Hispanic or Latino	162	0.57

Race*	Population	%
African-American/Black (8,949)	9,242	32.62
Not Hispanic (8,847)	9,085	32.07
Hispanic (102)	157	0.55
American Indian/Alaska Native (65)	189	0.67
Not Hispanic (38)	134	0.47
Hispanic (27)	55	0.19
Alaska Athabascan *(Ala. Nat.)* (0)	1	<0.01
Aleut *(Alaska Native)* (0)	1	<0.01
Apache (0)	4	0.01
Blackfeet (1)	2	0.01
Central American Ind. (0)	1	<0.01
Cherokee (3)	27	0.10
Chickasaw (0)	1	<0.01
Chippewa (2)	4	0.01
Choctaw (1)	4	0.01
Colville (0)	2	0.01
Creek (0)	2	0.01
Iroquois (0)	1	<0.01
Mexican American Ind. (11)	17	0.06
Navajo (2)	2	0.01
Pima (5)	5	0.02
Potawatomi (1)	5	0.02
Pueblo (2)	2	0.01
Seminole (1)	2	0.01
Sioux (0)	1	<0.01
South American Ind. (5)	5	0.02
Spanish American Ind. (0)	1	<0.01
Ute (0)	3	0.01
Yuman (4)	4	0.01
Asian (267)	349	1.23
Not Hispanic (255)	321	1.13
Hispanic (12)	28	0.10
Burmese (0)	4	0.01
Chinese, ex. Taiwanese (17)	22	0.08
Filipino (68)	84	0.30
Indian (82)	93	0.33
Indonesian (1)	1	<0.01

SECTION TWO

*Notes: † The Census 2010 population figure is used to calculate the percentages in the Hispanic Origin and Race categories. Ancestry percentages are based on the 2006-2010 American Community Survey population (not shown); ‡ Numbers in parentheses indicate the number of people reporting a single ancestry; * Numbers in parentheses indicate the number of persons reporting this race alone, not in combination with any other race; Please refer to the Explanation of Data for more information.*

Japanese (14)	31	0.11
Korean (23)	31	0.11
Laotian (4)	6	0.02
Pakistani (16)	16	0.06
Sri Lankan (1)	2	0.01
Thai (11)	21	0.07
Vietnamese (21)	26	0.09
Hawaii Native/Pacific Islander (5)	18	0.06
Not Hispanic (5)	9	0.03
Hispanic (0)	9	0.03
Guamanian/Chamorro (1)	1	<0.01
Native Hawaiian (0)	3	0.01
Samoan (0)	1	<0.01
White (16,696)	17,216	60.77
Not Hispanic (14,681)	14,992	52.92
Hispanic (2,015)	2,224	7.85

Lemont

Place Type: Village
County: Cook
Population: 16,000†

Ancestry‡	Population	%
African, Sub-Saharan (0)	12	0.08
Cape Verdean (0)	12	0.08
Albanian (0)	45	0.29
American (171)	171	1.12
Arab (45)	45	0.29
Lebanese (45)	45	0.29
Armenian (27)	27	0.18
Assyrian/Chaldean/Syriac (29)	29	0.19
Austrian (57)	218	1.42
Brazilian (22)	22	0.14
British (36)	36	0.23
Bulgarian (10)	10	0.07
Croatian (35)	322	2.10
Czech (104)	726	4.74
Czechoslovakian (26)	26	0.17
Danish (0)	35	0.23
Dutch (64)	329	2.15
English (317)	770	5.03
European (41)	54	0.35
French, ex. Basque (33)	407	2.66
French Canadian (16)	97	0.63
German (432)	2,937	19.17
Greek (25)	118	0.77
Hungarian (13)	90	0.59
Irish (979)	3,116	20.34
Italian (793)	2,597	16.95
Latvian (0)	28	0.18
Lithuanian (784)	1,131	7.38
Luxemburger (0)	12	0.08
Macedonian (8)	8	0.05
Norwegian (32)	79	0.52
Polish (2,346)	4,685	30.58
Romanian (38)	53	0.35
Russian (37)	57	0.37
Scotch-Irish (87)	204	1.33
Scottish (15)	130	0.85
Slavic (54)	117	0.76
Slovak (17)	76	0.50
Slovene (63)	303	1.98
Swedish (41)	499	3.26
Swiss (12)	27	0.18
Ukrainian (20)	67	0.44
Welsh (0)	60	0.39
Yugoslavian (17)	50	0.33

Hispanic Origin	Population	%
Hispanic or Latino (of any race)	822	5.14
Central American, ex. Mexican	18	0.11
Costa Rican	2	0.01
Guatemalan	10	0.06
Honduran	1	0.01
Panamanian	1	0.01
Salvadoran	4	0.03
Cuban	24	0.15
Mexican	661	4.13
Puerto Rican	52	0.33
South American	32	0.20
Argentinean	3	0.02
Bolivian	3	0.02
Colombian	13	0.08
Ecuadorian	5	0.03
Peruvian	6	0.04
Venezuelan	2	0.01
Other Hispanic or Latino	35	0.22

Race*	Population	%
African-American/Black (58)	90	0.56
Not Hispanic (58)	89	0.56
Hispanic (0)	1	0.01
American Indian/Alaska Native (14)	59	0.37
Not Hispanic (9)	51	0.32
Hispanic (5)	8	0.05
Aleut *(Alaska Native)* (1)	1	0.01
Blackfeet (0)	4	0.03
Canadian/French Am. Ind. (0)	3	0.02
Cherokee (3)	13	0.08
Chippewa (1)	4	0.03
Choctaw (0)	1	0.01
Colville (0)	1	0.01
Hopi (3)	3	0.02
Lumbee (1)	1	0.01
Mexican American Ind. (0)	1	0.01
Navajo (1)	1	0.01
Ottawa (0)	5	0.03
Seminole (0)	1	0.01
Sioux (0)	1	0.01
Asian (260)	314	1.96
Not Hispanic (258)	307	1.92
Hispanic (2)	7	0.04
Chinese, ex. Taiwanese (48)	61	0.38
Filipino (70)	94	0.59
Indian (98)	106	0.66
Japanese (0)	6	0.04
Korean (21)	29	0.18
Pakistani (4)	5	0.03
Thai (6)	8	0.05
Vietnamese (4)	4	0.03
Hawaii Native/Pacific Islander (2)	3	0.02
Not Hispanic (2)	3	0.02
White (15,340)	15,511	96.94
Not Hispanic (14,719)	14,844	92.78
Hispanic (621)	667	4.17

Libertyville

Place Type: Village
County: Lake
Population: 20,315†

Ancestry‡	Population	%
African, Sub-Saharan (0)	13	0.06
African (0)	13	0.06
American (1,043)	1,043	5.08
Arab (28)	44	0.21
Egyptian (28)	28	0.14
Lebanese (0)	9	0.04
Other Arab (0)	7	0.03
Armenian (143)	193	0.94
Assyrian/Chaldean/Syriac (6)	6	0.03
Austrian (37)	136	0.66
Basque (0)	41	0.20
Belgian (6)	24	0.12
British (115)	161	0.78
Canadian (27)	46	0.22
Croatian (22)	70	0.34
Czech (85)	281	1.37
Czechoslovakian (45)	45	0.22
Danish (34)	293	1.43
Dutch (139)	546	2.66
Eastern European (20)	20	0.10
English (435)	2,076	10.11
Estonian (0)	9	0.04
European (562)	588	2.86
Finnish (71)	179	0.87
French, ex. Basque (46)	505	2.46
French Canadian (26)	89	0.43
German (1,529)	6,161	30.01
Greek (233)	412	2.01
Hungarian (42)	145	0.71
Iranian (0)	11	0.05
Irish (657)	3,453	16.82
Italian (643)	2,161	10.53
Lithuanian (65)	188	0.92
Luxemburger (0)	10	0.05
New Zealander (14)	14	0.07
Northern European (12)	19	0.09
Norwegian (112)	577	2.81
Polish (618)	1,959	9.54
Portuguese (7)	30	0.15
Romanian (5)	74	0.36
Russian (150)	590	2.87
Scandinavian (28)	69	0.34
Scotch-Irish (161)	517	2.52
Scottish (55)	497	2.42
Serbian (219)	219	1.07
Slavic (0)	13	0.06
Slovak (10)	69	0.34
Slovene (13)	39	0.19
Swedish (230)	814	3.96
Swiss (72)	265	1.29
Turkish (17)	17	0.08
Ukrainian (80)	146	0.71
Welsh (19)	239	1.16
West Indian, ex. Hispanic (8)	8	0.04
Haitian (8)	8	0.04
Yugoslavian (38)	38	0.19

Hispanic Origin	Population	%
Hispanic or Latino (of any race)	836	4.12
Central American, ex. Mexican	76	0.37
Costa Rican	1	<0.01
Guatemalan	19	0.09
Honduran	14	0.07
Nicaraguan	8	0.04
Panamanian	6	0.03
Salvadoran	28	0.14
Cuban	51	0.25
Dominican Republic	9	0.04
Mexican	470	2.31
Puerto Rican	101	0.50
South American	86	0.42
Argentinean	14	0.07
Bolivian	3	0.01
Chilean	2	0.01
Colombian	43	0.21
Ecuadorian	1	<0.01
Peruvian	9	0.04
Uruguayan	4	0.02
Venezuelan	9	0.04
Other South American	1	<0.01
Other Hispanic or Latino	43	0.21

Race*	Population	%
African-American/Black (249)	316	1.56
Not Hispanic (232)	293	1.44
Hispanic (17)	23	0.11
American Indian/Alaska Native (32)	105	0.52
Not Hispanic (14)	74	0.36
Hispanic (18)	31	0.15
Apache (0)	1	<0.01
Canadian/French Am. Ind. (0)	1	<0.01
Cherokee (3)	21	0.10
Chickasaw (0)	1	<0.01
Chippewa (4)	8	0.04
Choctaw (0)	1	<0.01
Creek (1)	1	<0.01
Inupiat *(Alaska Native)* (1)	1	<0.01
Iroquois (1)	2	0.01
Mexican American Ind. (16)	19	0.09
Osage (2)	2	0.01
Sioux (0)	3	0.01
Asian (1,164)	1,357	6.68
Not Hispanic (1,154)	1,334	6.57
Hispanic (10)	23	0.11
Burmese (1)	1	<0.01
Cambodian (3)	3	0.01

*Notes: † The Census 2010 population figure is used to calculate the percentages in the Hispanic Origin and Race categories. Ancestry percentages are based on the 2006-2010 American Community Survey population (not shown); ‡ Numbers in parentheses indicate the number of people reporting a single ancestry; * Numbers in parentheses indicate the number of persons reporting this race alone, not in combination with any other race; Please refer to the Explanation of Data for more information.*

	Population	%
Chinese, ex. Taiwanese (432)	482	2.37
Filipino (99)	156	0.77
Indian (332)	369	1.82
Indonesian (6)	7	0.03
Japanese (45)	66	0.32
Korean (136)	158	0.78
Nepalese (1)	1	<0.01
Pakistani (9)	11	0.05
Taiwanese (32)	38	0.19
Thai (16)	18	0.09
Vietnamese (25)	29	0.14
Hawaii Native/Pacific Islander (8)	17	0.08
Not Hispanic (4)	13	0.06
Hispanic (4)	4	0.02
Fijian (3)	3	0.01
Marshallese (1)	4	0.02
Native Hawaiian (2)	5	0.02
Samoan (0)	3	0.01
White (18,303)	18,616	91.64
Not Hispanic (17,777)	18,029	88.75
Hispanic (526)	587	2.89

Lincoln

Place Type: City
County: Logan
Population: 14,504†

Ancestry‡	Population	%
African, Sub-Saharan (30)	36	0.25
African (30)	36	0.25
American (2,708)	2,708	18.75
Arab (12)	28	0.19
Lebanese (12)	12	0.08
Syrian (0)	16	0.11
Austrian (8)	14	0.10
Belgian (23)	40	0.28
British (34)	77	0.53
Canadian (6)	129	0.89
Celtic (15)	15	0.10
Croatian (0)	14	0.10
Czech (22)	88	0.61
Danish (0)	42	0.29
Dutch (46)	353	2.44
English (464)	1,622	11.23
European (64)	96	0.66
French, ex. Basque (87)	421	2.92
French Canadian (11)	11	0.08
German (1,855)	4,473	30.97
Greek (0)	9	0.06
Hungarian (47)	72	0.50
Irish (544)	2,026	14.03
Italian (202)	470	3.25
Lithuanian (0)	45	0.31
Norwegian (90)	128	0.89
Pennsylvania German (16)	23	0.16
Polish (55)	236	1.63
Russian (0)	19	0.13
Scandinavian (4)	52	0.36
Scotch-Irish (66)	155	1.07
Scottish (102)	253	1.75
Slovene (0)	9	0.06
Swedish (87)	282	1.95
Swiss (6)	86	0.60
Welsh (10)	115	0.80
West Indian, ex. Hispanic (0)	14	0.10
Jamaican (0)	14	0.10

Hispanic Origin	Population	%
Hispanic or Latino (of any race)	336	2.32
Central American, ex. Mexican	18	0.12
Costa Rican	1	0.01
Guatemalan	4	0.03
Panamanian	3	0.02
Salvadoran	8	0.06
Other Central American	2	0.01
Cuban	6	0.04
Dominican Republic	3	0.02
Mexican	216	1.49
Puerto Rican	29	0.20
South American	24	0.17
Argentinean	1	0.01
Bolivian	1	0.01
Chilean	4	0.03
Colombian	11	0.08
Ecuadorian	1	0.01
Paraguayan	4	0.03
Peruvian	2	0.01
Other Hispanic or Latino	40	0.28

Race*	Population	%
African-American/Black (551)	696	4.80
Not Hispanic (528)	659	4.54
Hispanic (23)	37	0.26
American Indian/Alaska Native (30)	95	0.65
Not Hispanic (27)	84	0.58
Hispanic (3)	11	0.08
Apache (2)	3	0.02
Blackfeet (0)	6	0.04
Cherokee (3)	15	0.10
Cheyenne (0)	1	0.01
Cree (0)	1	0.01
Creek (0)	1	0.01
Inupiat *(Alaska Native)* (1)	4	0.03
Iroquois (3)	4	0.03
Potawatomi (0)	1	0.01
Seminole (0)	1	0.01
Sioux (0)	1	0.01
Asian (118)	166	1.14
Not Hispanic (118)	161	1.11
Hispanic (0)	5	0.03
Chinese, ex. Taiwanese (18)	21	0.14
Filipino (33)	48	0.33
Indian (17)	27	0.19
Japanese (3)	14	0.10
Korean (7)	8	0.06
Laotian (0)	2	0.01
Malaysian (0)	1	0.01
Taiwanese (6)	7	0.05
Thai (2)	4	0.03
Vietnamese (25)	26	0.18
Hawaii Native/Pacific Islander (0)	7	0.05
Not Hispanic (0)	5	0.03
Hispanic (0)	2	0.01
Native Hawaiian (0)	1	0.01
White (13,472)	13,721	94.60
Not Hispanic (13,262)	13,478	92.93
Hispanic (210)	243	1.68

Lincolnwood

Place Type: Village
County: Cook
Population: 12,590†

Ancestry‡	Population	%
African, Sub-Saharan (51)	51	0.41
African (51)	51	0.41
Albanian (78)	78	0.63
American (376)	376	3.03
Arab (268)	277	2.23
Arab (99)	99	0.80
Iraqi (13)	22	0.18
Lebanese (24)	24	0.19
Palestinian (34)	34	0.27
Syrian (13)	13	0.10
Other Arab (85)	85	0.68
Armenian (44)	54	0.43
Assyrian/Chaldean/Syriac (884)	905	7.29
Austrian (50)	131	1.05
Bulgarian (20)	20	0.16
Canadian (0)	7	0.06
Croatian (236)	249	2.00
Czechoslovakian (0)	21	0.17
Danish (8)	21	0.17
Dutch (0)	12	0.10
Eastern European (43)	43	0.35
English (58)	234	1.88
European (27)	48	0.39
French, ex. Basque (12)	56	0.45
French Canadian (0)	16	0.13
German (282)	837	6.74
Greek (889)	964	7.76
Hungarian (71)	166	1.34
Iranian (30)	30	0.24
Irish (87)	565	4.55
Israeli (53)	75	0.60
Italian (178)	339	2.73
Latvian (47)	101	0.81
Lithuanian (54)	171	1.38
Norwegian (14)	89	0.72
Polish (463)	767	6.17
Romanian (482)	605	4.87
Russian (480)	750	6.04
Scandinavian (12)	12	0.10
Scotch-Irish (20)	61	0.49
Scottish (17)	73	0.59
Serbian (173)	206	1.66
Swedish (24)	99	0.80
Ukrainian (17)	44	0.35
Welsh (0)	19	0.15
West Indian, ex. Hispanic (119)	119	0.96
Jamaican (119)	119	0.96
Yugoslavian (94)	134	1.08

Hispanic Origin	Population	%
Hispanic or Latino (of any race)	859	6.82
Central American, ex. Mexican	68	0.54
Costa Rican	9	0.07
Guatemalan	37	0.29
Honduran	3	0.02
Nicaraguan	6	0.05
Panamanian	3	0.02
Salvadoran	10	0.08
Cuban	93	0.74
Dominican Republic	2	0.02
Mexican	346	2.75
Puerto Rican	78	0.62
South American	197	1.56
Argentinean	18	0.14
Bolivian	14	0.11
Chilean	8	0.06
Colombian	58	0.46
Ecuadorian	54	0.43
Peruvian	29	0.23
Uruguayan	3	0.02
Venezuelan	9	0.07
Other South American	4	0.03
Other Hispanic or Latino	75	0.60

Race*	Population	%
African-American/Black (134)	165	1.31
Not Hispanic (129)	152	1.21
Hispanic (5)	13	0.10
American Indian/Alaska Native (9)	43	0.34
Not Hispanic (6)	23	0.18
Hispanic (3)	20	0.16
Cherokee (0)	7	0.06
Creek (1)	1	0.01
Sioux (0)	1	0.01
Asian (3,358)	3,639	28.90
Not Hispanic (3,338)	3,596	28.56
Hispanic (20)	43	0.34
Bangladeshi (21)	34	0.27
Chinese, ex. Taiwanese (222)	294	2.34
Filipino (526)	572	4.54
Indian (1,054)	1,151	9.14
Indonesian (4)	4	0.03
Japanese (99)	116	0.92
Korean (437)	456	3.62
Nepalese (3)	3	0.02
Pakistani (531)	580	4.61
Sri Lankan (3)	3	0.02
Taiwanese (6)	9	0.07
Thai (64)	77	0.61
Vietnamese (225)	278	2.21
Hawaii Native/Pacific Islander (3)	21	0.17
Not Hispanic (0)	14	0.11
Hispanic (3)	7	0.06
Guamanian/Chamorro (3)	7	0.06

*Notes: † The Census 2010 population figure is used to calculate the percentages in the Hispanic Origin and Race categories. Ancestry percentages are based on the 2006-2010 American Community Survey population (not shown); ‡ Numbers in parentheses indicate the number of people reporting a single ancestry; * Numbers in parentheses indicate the number of persons reporting this race alone, not in combination with any other race; Please refer to the Explanation of Data for more information.*

White (8,425)	8,706	69.15
Not Hispanic (7,938)	8,152	64.75
Hispanic (487)	554	4.40

Lindenhurst

Place Type: Village
County: Lake
Population: 14,462†

Ancestry‡	Population	%
American (453)	453	3.18
Arab (33)	60	0.42
Moroccan (23)	23	0.16
Syrian (10)	37	0.26
Armenian (0)	25	0.18
Australian (20)	20	0.14
Austrian (26)	174	1.22
Belgian (11)	65	0.46
British (78)	126	0.89
Croatian (7)	31	0.22
Czech (106)	352	2.47
Danish (22)	260	1.83
Dutch (101)	533	3.75
Eastern European (117)	140	0.98
English (344)	1,408	9.90
European (85)	153	1.08
Finnish (36)	122	0.86
French, ex. Basque (35)	372	2.61
French Canadian (52)	102	0.72
German (1,210)	4,323	30.39
Greek (153)	304	2.14
Hungarian (27)	200	1.41
Iranian (41)	41	0.29
Irish (486)	2,697	18.96
Italian (407)	1,607	11.30
Lithuanian (19)	124	0.87
Norwegian (40)	670	4.71
Polish (705)	1,792	12.60
Romanian (22)	71	0.50
Russian (49)	128	0.90
Scandinavian (20)	43	0.30
Scotch-Irish (78)	230	1.62
Scottish (62)	223	1.57
Serbian (59)	80	0.56
Slavic (12)	43	0.30
Slovak (0)	54	0.38
Slovene (20)	55	0.39
Swedish (62)	499	3.51
Swiss (0)	48	0.34
Ukrainian (11)	22	0.15
Welsh (13)	105	0.74

Hispanic Origin	Population	%
Hispanic or Latino (of any race)	984	6.80
Central American, ex. Mexican	44	0.30
Costa Rican	1	0.01
Guatemalan	18	0.12
Honduran	7	0.05
Nicaraguan	3	0.02
Panamanian	6	0.04
Salvadoran	9	0.06
Cuban	28	0.19
Dominican Republic	15	0.10
Mexican	602	4.16
Puerto Rican	166	1.15
South American	78	0.54
Argentinean	5	0.03
Chilean	9	0.06
Colombian	43	0.30
Ecuadorian	17	0.12
Peruvian	3	0.02
Venezuelan	1	0.01
Other Hispanic or Latino	51	0.35

Race*	Population	%
African-American/Black (341)	423	2.92
Not Hispanic (332)	409	2.83
Hispanic (9)	14	0.10
American Indian/Alaska Native (35)	98	0.68
Not Hispanic (29)	84	0.58
Hispanic (6)	14	0.10
Apache (1)	4	0.03
Blackfeet (0)	4	0.03
Cherokee (2)	22	0.15
Chippewa (6)	10	0.07
Choctaw (4)	5	0.03
Hopi (0)	2	0.01
Menominee (4)	4	0.03
Mexican American Ind. (0)	1	0.01
Navajo (0)	1	0.01
Ottawa (0)	3	0.02
Potawatomi (5)	6	0.04
Sioux (2)	10	0.07
South American Ind. (1)	1	0.01
Asian (656)	794	5.49
Not Hispanic (655)	782	5.41
Hispanic (1)	12	0.08
Bangladeshi (6)	6	0.04
Cambodian (3)	3	0.02
Chinese, ex. Taiwanese (51)	78	0.54
Filipino (187)	244	1.69
Hmong (6)	6	0.04
Indian (228)	255	1.76
Japanese (18)	45	0.31
Korean (74)	80	0.55
Malaysian (0)	1	0.01
Pakistani (48)	50	0.35
Taiwanese (3)	3	0.02
Thai (5)	5	0.03
Vietnamese (13)	14	0.10
Hawaii Native/Pacific Islander (4)	17	0.12
Not Hispanic (4)	16	0.11
Hispanic (0)	1	0.01
Guamanian/Chamorro (2)	8	0.06
Native Hawaiian (1)	7	0.05
White (12,846)	13,125	90.76
Not Hispanic (12,182)	12,418	85.87
Hispanic (664)	707	4.89

Lisle

Place Type: Village
County: DuPage
Population: 22,390†

Ancestry‡	Population	%
African, Sub-Saharan (41)	60	0.27
African (0)	19	0.09
Ghanaian (41)	41	0.18
Albanian (34)	34	0.15
American (388)	388	1.74
Arab (37)	60	0.27
Egyptian (13)	13	0.06
Lebanese (16)	29	0.13
Syrian (0)	10	0.04
Other Arab (8)	8	0.04
Austrian (17)	51	0.23
Belgian (0)	56	0.25
British (0)	221	0.99
Canadian (9)	81	0.36
Croatian (111)	253	1.14
Czech (254)	753	3.38
Czechoslovakian (24)	90	0.40
Danish (15)	122	0.55
Dutch (33)	123	0.55
Eastern European (12)	12	0.05
English (389)	1,407	6.31
European (234)	382	1.71
Finnish (0)	45	0.20
French, ex. Basque (52)	598	2.68
French Canadian (10)	102	0.46
German (1,377)	4,978	22.33
Greek (24)	178	0.80
Hungarian (35)	165	0.74
Iranian (15)	15	0.07
Irish (1,242)	4,077	18.29
Italian (683)	2,369	10.63
Lithuanian (199)	337	1.51
Northern European (26)	26	0.12
Norwegian (48)	298	1.34
Pennsylvania German (19)	19	0.09
Polish (950)	2,758	12.37
Portuguese (15)	43	0.19
Romanian (27)	103	0.46
Russian (160)	292	1.31
Scandinavian (0)	22	0.10
Scotch-Irish (30)	118	0.53
Scottish (60)	284	1.27
Serbian (172)	172	0.77
Slavic (25)	37	0.17
Slovak (229)	336	1.51
Swedish (55)	481	2.16
Swiss (17)	161	0.72
Turkish (41)	41	0.18
Ukrainian (188)	290	1.30
Welsh (0)	104	0.47
Yugoslavian (7)	22	0.10

Hispanic Origin	Population	%
Hispanic or Latino (of any race)	1,690	7.55
Central American, ex. Mexican	50	0.22
Costa Rican	3	0.01
Guatemalan	27	0.12
Honduran	3	0.01
Nicaraguan	1	<0.01
Panamanian	5	0.02
Salvadoran	11	0.05
Cuban	45	0.20
Dominican Republic	6	0.03
Mexican	1,256	5.61
Puerto Rican	126	0.56
South American	132	0.59
Argentinean	5	0.02
Bolivian	13	0.06
Chilean	7	0.03
Colombian	42	0.19
Ecuadorian	26	0.12
Peruvian	23	0.10
Uruguayan	2	0.01
Venezuelan	12	0.05
Other South American	2	0.01
Other Hispanic or Latino	75	0.33

Race*	Population	%
African-American/Black (1,261)	1,437	6.42
Not Hispanic (1,214)	1,366	6.10
Hispanic (47)	71	0.32
American Indian/Alaska Native (20)	107	0.48
Not Hispanic (13)	81	0.36
Hispanic (7)	26	0.12
Apache (0)	3	0.01
Blackfeet (0)	2	0.01
Cherokee (1)	38	0.17
Chickasaw (0)	2	0.01
Chippewa (3)	4	0.02
Creek (0)	2	0.01
Delaware (0)	4	0.02
Iroquois (0)	1	<0.01
Mexican American Ind. (2)	9	0.04
Pueblo (1)	1	<0.01
Sioux (1)	3	0.01
South American Ind. (0)	1	<0.01
Yaqui (0)	1	<0.01
Asian (2,674)	2,892	12.92
Not Hispanic (2,665)	2,857	12.76
Hispanic (9)	35	0.16
Bangladeshi (4)	4	0.02
Burmese (3)	3	0.01
Cambodian (3)	7	0.03
Chinese, ex. Taiwanese (879)	943	4.21
Filipino (270)	342	1.53
Hmong (2)	2	0.01
Indian (986)	1,039	4.64
Indonesian (5)	5	0.02
Japanese (41)	67	0.30
Korean (205)	221	0.99
Laotian (1)	1	<0.01
Malaysian (7)	12	0.05
Nepalese (3)	3	0.01

*Notes: † The Census 2010 population figure is used to calculate the percentages in the Hispanic Origin and Race categories. Ancestry percentages are based on the 2006-2010 American Community Survey population (not shown); ‡ Numbers in parentheses indicate the number of people reporting a single ancestry; * Numbers in parentheses indicate the number of persons reporting this race alone, not in combination with any other race; Please refer to the Explanation of Data for more information.*

Pakistani (61)	72	0.32
Sri Lankan (16)	20	0.09
Taiwanese (97)	117	0.52
Thai (2)	11	0.05
Vietnamese (31)	38	0.17
Hawaii Native/Pacific Islander (8)	33	0.15
Not Hispanic (5)	25	0.11
Hispanic (3)	8	0.04
Fijian (0)	1	<0.01
Guamanian/Chamorro (3)	7	0.03
Native Hawaiian (0)	8	0.04
Samoan (2)	4	0.02
White (17,392)	17,800	79.50
Not Hispanic (16,398)	16,714	74.65
Hispanic (994)	1,086	4.85

Lockport

Place Type: City
County: Will
Population: 24,839†

Ancestry‡	Population	%
African, Sub-Saharan (0)	11	0.05
African (0)	11	0.05
Albanian (0)	72	0.30
American (509)	509	2.13
Arab (412)	508	2.13
Arab (324)	407	1.71
Lebanese (0)	13	0.05
Palestinian (88)	88	0.37
Armenian (0)	11	0.05
Austrian (31)	208	0.87
Belgian (0)	11	0.05
Brazilian (10)	10	0.04
British (95)	212	0.89
Bulgarian (0)	15	0.06
Canadian (27)	65	0.27
Croatian (43)	393	1.65
Czech (117)	483	2.03
Czechoslovakian (0)	30	0.13
Danish (6)	40	0.17
Dutch (191)	739	3.10
English (388)	1,417	5.94
European (97)	108	0.45
Finnish (0)	53	0.22
French, ex. Basque (64)	435	1.82
French Canadian (6)	76	0.32
German (1,092)	6,249	26.21
Greek (164)	412	1.73
Hungarian (31)	91	0.38
Irish (1,392)	5,830	24.45
Italian (949)	3,988	16.73
Latvian (0)	11	0.05
Lithuanian (271)	645	2.71
Macedonian (25)	25	0.10
Norwegian (12)	53	0.22
Polish (2,209)	5,937	24.90
Romanian (14)	14	0.06
Russian (28)	200	0.84
Scandinavian (0)	12	0.05
Scotch-Irish (38)	197	0.83
Scottish (31)	216	0.91
Serbian (48)	48	0.20
Slavic (0)	20	0.08
Slovak (85)	210	0.88
Slovene (54)	194	0.81
Swedish (160)	668	2.80
Swiss (0)	17	0.07
Ukrainian (0)	29	0.12
Welsh (6)	62	0.26
West Indian, ex. Hispanic (35)	35	0.15
West Indian (35)	35	0.15
Yugoslavian (13)	24	0.10

Hispanic Origin	Population	%
Hispanic or Latino (of any race)	2,025	8.15
Central American, ex. Mexican	31	0.12
Costa Rican	1	<0.01
Guatemalan	10	0.04
Honduran	4	0.02
Nicaraguan	11	0.04
Salvadoran	5	0.02
Cuban	24	0.10
Dominican Republic	3	0.01
Mexican	1,670	6.72
Puerto Rican	148	0.60
South American	49	0.20
Argentinean	5	0.02
Chilean	3	0.01
Colombian	16	0.06
Ecuadorian	18	0.07
Peruvian	2	0.01
Venezuelan	4	0.02
Other South American	1	<0.01
Other Hispanic or Latino	100	0.40

Race*	Population	%
African-American/Black (350)	438	1.76
Not Hispanic (329)	409	1.65
Hispanic (21)	29	0.12
American Indian/Alaska Native (37)	124	0.50
Not Hispanic (31)	106	0.43
Hispanic (6)	18	0.07
Apache (1)	1	<0.01
Blackfeet (1)	3	0.01
Cherokee (4)	16	0.06
Cheyenne (0)	3	0.01
Chippewa (2)	6	0.02
Choctaw (0)	3	0.01
Iroquois (3)	3	0.01
Lumbee (1)	1	<0.01
Menominee (0)	2	0.01
Mexican American Ind. (1)	2	0.01
Potawatomi (1)	1	<0.01
Pueblo (3)	3	0.01
Sioux (2)	9	0.04
Asian (334)	444	1.79
Not Hispanic (329)	430	1.73
Hispanic (5)	14	0.06
Chinese, ex. Taiwanese (37)	45	0.18
Filipino (150)	213	0.86
Indian (64)	74	0.30
Indonesian (2)	2	0.01
Japanese (9)	17	0.07
Korean (29)	40	0.16
Pakistani (11)	11	0.04
Taiwanese (1)	3	0.01
Thai (2)	3	0.01
Vietnamese (21)	26	0.10
Hawaii Native/Pacific Islander (7)	10	0.04
Not Hispanic (6)	9	0.04
Hispanic (1)	1	<0.01
Guamanian/Chamorro (0)	1	<0.01
Native Hawaiian (2)	3	0.01
White (23,237)	23,564	94.87
Not Hispanic (21,854)	22,092	88.94
Hispanic (1,383)	1,472	5.93

Lombard

Place Type: Village
County: DuPage
Population: 43,165†

Ancestry‡	Population	%
African, Sub-Saharan (47)	47	0.11
African (47)	47	0.11
Albanian (173)	173	0.40
American (1,051)	1,051	2.46
Arab (202)	248	0.58
Arab (53)	53	0.12
Iraqi (30)	30	0.07
Jordanian (15)	15	0.04
Lebanese (54)	86	0.20
Moroccan (15)	29	0.07
Palestinian (21)	21	0.05
Other Arab (14)	14	0.03
Armenian (13)	13	0.03
Austrian (27)	199	0.47
Belgian (86)	138	0.32
British (9)	100	0.23
Bulgarian (44)	97	0.23
Canadian (13)	91	0.21
Croatian (66)	374	0.88
Czech (425)	1,128	2.64
Czechoslovakian (72)	159	0.37
Danish (42)	367	0.86
Dutch (554)	1,239	2.90
Eastern European (82)	105	0.25
English (396)	3,230	7.56
European (217)	247	0.58
Finnish (7)	36	0.08
French, ex. Basque (39)	577	1.35
French Canadian (56)	143	0.33
German (2,935)	11,830	27.69
Greek (352)	603	1.41
Hungarian (45)	84	0.20
Icelander (0)	6	0.01
Iranian (25)	25	0.06
Irish (1,690)	9,147	21.41
Italian (2,213)	6,405	14.99
Lithuanian (126)	383	0.90
Luxemburger (13)	36	0.08
Northern European (9)	9	0.02
Norwegian (121)	830	1.94
Pennsylvania German (22)	22	0.05
Polish (1,899)	5,899	13.81
Romanian (26)	26	0.06
Russian (4)	460	1.08
Scandinavian (44)	89	0.21
Scotch-Irish (100)	796	1.86
Scottish (76)	397	0.93
Serbian (49)	76	0.18
Slovak (65)	470	1.10
Swedish (205)	1,244	2.91
Swiss (36)	106	0.25
Ukrainian (106)	247	0.58
Welsh (56)	220	0.51
Yugoslavian (105)	105	0.25

Hispanic Origin	Population	%
Hispanic or Latino (of any race)	3,487	8.08
Central American, ex. Mexican	160	0.37
Costa Rican	11	0.03
Guatemalan	62	0.14
Honduran	59	0.14
Nicaraguan	9	0.02
Panamanian	4	0.01
Salvadoran	15	0.03
Cuban	95	0.22
Dominican Republic	13	0.03
Mexican	2,561	5.93
Puerto Rican	270	0.63
South American	197	0.46
Argentinean	19	0.04
Bolivian	9	0.02
Chilean	12	0.03
Colombian	55	0.13
Ecuadorian	45	0.10
Peruvian	36	0.08
Uruguayan	3	0.01
Venezuelan	15	0.03
Other South American	3	0.01
Other Hispanic or Latino	191	0.44

Race*	Population	%
African-American/Black (1,967)	2,232	5.17
Not Hispanic (1,925)	2,162	5.01
Hispanic (42)	70	0.16
American Indian/Alaska Native (55)	167	0.39
Not Hispanic (24)	115	0.27
Hispanic (31)	52	0.12
Apache (0)	5	0.01
Blackfeet (0)	1	<0.01
Cherokee (2)	22	0.05
Chickasaw (1)	1	<0.01
Chippewa (3)	4	0.01
Choctaw (0)	2	<0.01
Cree (0)	2	<0.01

*Notes: † The Census 2010 population figure is used to calculate the percentages in the Hispanic Origin and Race categories. Ancestry percentages are based on the 2006-2010 American Community Survey population (not shown); ‡ Numbers in parentheses indicate the number of people reporting a single ancestry; * Numbers in parentheses indicate the number of persons reporting this race alone, not in combination with any other race; Please refer to the Explanation of Data for more information.*

Creek (0)	1	<0.01
Iroquois (1)	6	0.01
Lumbee (1)	2	<0.01
Menominee (2)	2	<0.01
Mexican American Ind. (8)	13	0.03
Osage (0)	3	0.01
Ottawa (3)	3	0.01
Pima (0)	3	0.01
Seminole (0)	1	<0.01
Sioux (1)	1	<0.01
South American Ind. (0)	2	<0.01
Spanish American Ind. (1)	1	<0.01
Yup'ik *(Alaska Native)* (0)	1	<0.01
Asian (4,217)	4,634	10.74
Not Hispanic (4,207)	4,596	10.65
Hispanic (10)	38	0.09
Bangladeshi (15)	15	0.03
Burmese (2)	2	<0.01
Cambodian (9)	9	0.02
Chinese, ex. Taiwanese (222)	282	0.65
Filipino (729)	836	1.94
Indian (2,161)	2,312	5.36
Indonesian (7)	9	0.02
Japanese (67)	109	0.25
Korean (120)	156	0.36
Laotian (4)	6	0.01
Malaysian (4)	4	0.01
Pakistani (653)	710	1.64
Sri Lankan (1)	1	<0.01
Taiwanese (26)	32	0.07
Thai (20)	27	0.06
Vietnamese (53)	62	0.14
Hawaii Native/Pacific Islander (5)	33	0.08
Not Hispanic (4)	30	0.07
Hispanic (1)	3	0.01
Fijian (1)	2	<0.01
Guamanian/Chamorro (2)	9	0.02
Native Hawaiian (1)	8	0.02
Samoan (1)	2	<0.01
Tongan (0)	1	<0.01
White (34,851)	35,526	82.30
Not Hispanic (32,790)	33,329	77.21
Hispanic (2,061)	2,197	5.09

Long Grove

Place Type: Village
County: Lake
Population: 8,043†

Ancestry‡	Population	%
African, Sub-Saharan (5)	5	0.06
South African (5)	5	0.06
American (499)	499	6.34
Arab (12)	65	0.83
Arab (6)	6	0.08
Lebanese (0)	35	0.44
Palestinian (6)	6	0.08
Syrian (0)	18	0.23
Assyrian/Chaldean/Syriac (0)	10	0.13
Austrian (0)	46	0.58
British (31)	64	0.81
Bulgarian (14)	14	0.18
Croatian (13)	78	0.99
Czech (10)	79	1.00
Czechoslovakian (4)	4	0.05
Danish (17)	56	0.71
Dutch (10)	96	1.22
Eastern European (128)	128	1.63
English (133)	657	8.35
European (214)	214	2.72
French, ex. Basque (9)	160	2.03
French Canadian (0)	51	0.65
German (354)	1,462	18.59
Greek (16)	75	0.95
Hungarian (8)	60	0.76
Iranian (18)	18	0.23
Irish (109)	949	12.06
Italian (362)	878	11.16
Latvian (11)	21	0.27
Lithuanian (58)	108	1.37
New Zealander (16)	16	0.20
Northern European (11)	32	0.41
Norwegian (24)	94	1.20
Polish (380)	933	11.86
Portuguese (8)	8	0.10
Romanian (0)	27	0.34
Russian (341)	704	8.95
Scotch-Irish (43)	62	0.79
Scottish (37)	155	1.97
Slavic (6)	20	0.25
Slovak (24)	112	1.42
Slovene (0)	15	0.19
Swedish (40)	181	2.30
Swiss (16)	80	1.02
Ukrainian (37)	68	0.86
Welsh (9)	34	0.43
Yugoslavian (4)	4	0.05

Hispanic Origin	Population	%
Hispanic or Latino (of any race)	258	3.21
Central American, ex. Mexican	7	0.09
Guatemalan	7	0.09
Cuban	21	0.26
Mexican	168	2.09
Puerto Rican	9	0.11
South American	39	0.48
Argentinean	2	0.02
Bolivian	1	0.01
Chilean	1	0.01
Colombian	16	0.20
Ecuadorian	8	0.10
Paraguayan	1	0.01
Peruvian	2	0.02
Venezuelan	8	0.10
Other Hispanic or Latino	14	0.17

Race*	Population	%
African-American/Black (99)	119	1.48
Not Hispanic (97)	116	1.44
Hispanic (2)	3	0.04
American Indian/Alaska Native (1)	24	0.30
Not Hispanic (1)	20	0.25
Hispanic (0)	4	0.05
Cherokee (0)	12	0.15
Chippewa (1)	1	0.01
Mexican American Ind. (0)	4	0.05
Asian (961)	1,047	13.02
Not Hispanic (959)	1,045	12.99
Hispanic (2)	2	0.02
Chinese, ex. Taiwanese (298)	318	3.95
Filipino (51)	74	0.92
Indian (246)	268	3.33
Japanese (25)	38	0.47
Korean (269)	294	3.66
Laotian (2)	2	0.02
Pakistani (18)	20	0.25
Sri Lankan (6)	6	0.07
Taiwanese (10)	14	0.17
Thai (1)	5	0.06
Vietnamese (10)	13	0.16
Hawaii Native/Pacific Islander (0)	7	0.09
Not Hispanic (0)	7	0.09
Native Hawaiian (0)	4	0.05
White (6,750)	6,882	85.57
Not Hispanic (6,597)	6,708	83.40
Hispanic (153)	174	2.16

Loves Park

Place Type: City
County: Winnebago
Population: 23,996†

Ancestry‡	Population	%
African, Sub-Saharan (9)	9	0.04
Other Sub-Saharan African (9)	9	0.04
Albanian (0)	10	0.04
American (2,971)	2,971	12.52
Arab (0)	15	0.06
Other Arab (0)	15	0.06
Armenian (16)	51	0.21
Austrian (9)	61	0.26
Belgian (0)	17	0.07
British (35)	102	0.43
Canadian (0)	21	0.09
Croatian (0)	37	0.16
Czech (35)	172	0.73
Czechoslovakian (9)	25	0.11
Danish (12)	146	0.62
Dutch (136)	417	1.76
English (517)	2,133	8.99
European (233)	292	1.23
Finnish (11)	37	0.16
French, ex. Basque (100)	768	3.24
French Canadian (39)	93	0.39
German (1,511)	6,060	25.54
Hungarian (0)	18	0.08
Irish (691)	3,561	15.01
Italian (850)	2,186	9.21
Lithuanian (7)	61	0.26
Norwegian (294)	1,130	4.76
Pennsylvania German (7)	7	0.03
Polish (318)	1,151	4.85
Portuguese (0)	6	0.03
Romanian (0)	80	0.34
Russian (222)	240	1.01
Scandinavian (17)	17	0.07
Scotch-Irish (77)	245	1.03
Scottish (78)	368	1.55
Serbian (18)	18	0.08
Slovak (0)	25	0.11
Slovene (12)	12	0.05
Swedish (674)	2,154	9.08
Swiss (23)	61	0.26
Ukrainian (0)	48	0.20
Welsh (13)	120	0.51
Yugoslavian (79)	79	0.33

Hispanic Origin	Population	%
Hispanic or Latino (of any race)	1,606	6.69
Central American, ex. Mexican	23	0.10
Costa Rican	3	0.01
Guatemalan	11	0.05
Honduran	1	<0.01
Panamanian	4	0.02
Salvadoran	4	0.02
Cuban	26	0.11
Dominican Republic	9	0.04
Mexican	1,259	5.25
Puerto Rican	138	0.58
South American	85	0.35
Argentinean	6	0.03
Bolivian	4	0.02
Chilean	11	0.05
Colombian	31	0.13
Ecuadorian	9	0.04
Paraguayan	2	0.01
Peruvian	13	0.05
Uruguayan	6	0.03
Venezuelan	3	0.01
Other Hispanic or Latino	66	0.28

Race*	Population	%
African-American/Black (944)	1,166	4.86
Not Hispanic (930)	1,129	4.70
Hispanic (14)	37	0.15
American Indian/Alaska Native (64)	169	0.70
Not Hispanic (48)	134	0.56
Hispanic (16)	35	0.15
Blackfeet (0)	1	<0.01
Cherokee (8)	32	0.13
Cheyenne (0)	1	<0.01
Chippewa (6)	12	0.05
Choctaw (0)	9	0.04
Creek (0)	3	0.01
Crow (0)	1	<0.01
Houma (2)	2	0.01
Inupiat *(Alaska Native)* (1)	4	0.02
Iroquois (2)	4	0.02

*Notes: † The Census 2010 population figure is used to calculate the percentages in the Hispanic Origin and Race categories. Ancestry percentages are based on the 2006-2010 American Community Survey population (not shown); ‡ Numbers in parentheses indicate the number of people reporting a single ancestry; * Numbers in parentheses indicate the number of persons reporting this race alone, not in combination with any other race; Please refer to the Explanation of Data for more information.*

	Population	%
Mexican American Ind. (0)	1	<0.01
Navajo (1)	2	0.01
Seminole (0)	2	0.01
Shoshone (5)	5	0.02
Sioux (6)	13	0.05
South American Ind. (0)	5	0.02
Spanish American Ind. (1)	1	<0.01
Ute (0)	1	<0.01
Yaqui (1)	2	0.01
Asian (628)	785	3.27
Not Hispanic (625)	772	3.22
Hispanic (3)	13	0.05
Burmese (5)	5	0.02
Cambodian (1)	3	0.01
Chinese, ex. Taiwanese (54)	80	0.33
Filipino (187)	223	0.93
Indian (128)	153	0.64
Indonesian (5)	8	0.03
Japanese (25)	50	0.21
Korean (62)	92	0.38
Laotian (47)	65	0.27
Pakistani (13)	15	0.06
Taiwanese (0)	1	<0.01
Thai (14)	27	0.11
Vietnamese (49)	60	0.25
Hawaii Native/Pacific Islander (3)	19	0.08
Not Hispanic (3)	15	0.06
Hispanic (0)	4	0.02
Native Hawaiian (1)	7	0.03
Samoan (1)	5	0.02
White (21,311)	21,812	90.90
Not Hispanic (20,346)	20,727	86.38
Hispanic (965)	1,085	4.52

Lynwood

Place Type: Village
County: Cook
Population: 9,007†

Ancestry‡	Population	%
African, Sub-Saharan (35)	152	1.74
African (18)	30	0.34
Liberian (0)	26	0.30
Nigerian (17)	96	1.10
American (135)	135	1.55
Belgian (28)	28	0.32
British (0)	30	0.34
Croatian (0)	50	0.57
Czechoslovakian (16)	52	0.60
Dutch (150)	197	2.26
English (131)	304	3.48
European (56)	56	0.64
French, ex. Basque (13)	110	1.26
German (142)	649	7.44
Greek (35)	45	0.52
Irish (117)	465	5.33
Italian (55)	357	4.09
Lithuanian (16)	91	1.04
Norwegian (0)	13	0.15
Polish (118)	487	5.58
Russian (0)	32	0.37
Scotch-Irish (19)	98	1.12
Scottish (21)	21	0.24
Slovak (11)	66	0.76
Slovene (10)	10	0.11
Swedish (0)	16	0.18
Ukrainian (0)	12	0.14
Welsh (0)	65	0.74
West Indian, ex. Hispanic (112)	112	1.28
Haitian (112)	112	1.28

Hispanic Origin	Population	%
Hispanic or Latino (of any race)	657	7.29
Central American, ex. Mexican	5	0.06
Guatemalan	1	0.01
Panamanian	4	0.04
Cuban	4	0.04
Dominican Republic	4	0.04
Mexican	554	6.15
Puerto Rican	63	0.70
South American	8	0.09
Argentinean	1	0.01
Bolivian	3	0.03
Colombian	2	0.02
Paraguayan	1	0.01
Peruvian	1	0.01
Other Hispanic or Latino	19	0.21

Race*	Population	%
African-American/Black (5,940)	6,086	67.57
Not Hispanic (5,886)	6,006	66.68
Hispanic (54)	80	0.89
American Indian/Alaska Native (26)	73	0.81
Not Hispanic (9)	49	0.54
Hispanic (17)	24	0.27
Apache (0)	1	0.01
Blackfeet (0)	4	0.04
Cherokee (1)	9	0.10
Choctaw (0)	1	0.01
Creek (1)	3	0.03
Navajo (0)	3	0.03
Sioux (0)	1	0.01
South American Ind. (0)	2	0.02
Asian (47)	69	0.77
Not Hispanic (47)	63	0.70
Hispanic (0)	6	0.07
Cambodian (1)	1	0.01
Chinese, ex. Taiwanese (1)	5	0.06
Filipino (14)	16	0.18
Indian (9)	15	0.17
Japanese (0)	6	0.07
Korean (2)	4	0.04
Laotian (4)	4	0.04
Pakistani (6)	8	0.09
Vietnamese (5)	6	0.07
White (2,590)	2,724	30.24
Not Hispanic (2,265)	2,359	26.19
Hispanic (325)	365	4.05

Lyons

Place Type: Village
County: Cook
Population: 10,729†

Ancestry‡	Population	%
American (87)	87	0.83
Arab (93)	93	0.88
Lebanese (36)	36	0.34
Palestinian (57)	57	0.54
Austrian (0)	22	0.21
Brazilian (15)	82	0.78
Celtic (0)	8	0.08
Croatian (64)	198	1.88
Czech (281)	604	5.74
Czechoslovakian (20)	20	0.19
Dutch (18)	80	0.76
English (22)	312	2.96
European (8)	8	0.08
French, ex. Basque (12)	66	0.63
German (354)	1,451	13.78
Greek (16)	37	0.35
Hungarian (0)	59	0.56
Irish (291)	1,360	12.92
Italian (193)	518	4.92
Lithuanian (135)	284	2.70
Macedonian (14)	14	0.13
Norwegian (0)	47	0.45
Polish (698)	1,945	18.47
Romanian (0)	31	0.29
Russian (15)	130	1.23
Scotch-Irish (0)	72	0.68
Scottish (15)	37	0.35
Serbian (106)	118	1.12
Slovak (14)	185	1.76
Swedish (0)	276	2.62
Welsh (0)	8	0.08
Yugoslavian (0)	41	0.39

Hispanic Origin	Population	%
Hispanic or Latino (of any race)	4,113	38.34
Central American, ex. Mexican	85	0.79
Costa Rican	1	0.01
Guatemalan	49	0.46
Honduran	11	0.10
Nicaraguan	13	0.12
Panamanian	1	0.01
Salvadoran	8	0.07
Other Central American	2	0.02
Cuban	32	0.30
Mexican	3,495	32.58
Puerto Rican	305	2.84
South American	93	0.87
Argentinean	2	0.02
Bolivian	3	0.03
Chilean	9	0.08
Colombian	25	0.23
Ecuadorian	27	0.25
Peruvian	23	0.21
Other South American	4	0.04
Other Hispanic or Latino	103	0.96

Race*	Population	%
African-American/Black (452)	507	4.73
Not Hispanic (419)	463	4.32
Hispanic (33)	44	0.41
American Indian/Alaska Native (82)	103	0.96
Not Hispanic (16)	28	0.26
Hispanic (66)	75	0.70
Blackfeet (0)	2	0.02
Cherokee (1)	7	0.07
Chippewa (1)	1	0.01
Crow (1)	3	0.03
Iroquois (1)	1	0.01
Menominee (3)	3	0.03
Mexican American Ind. (9)	9	0.08
Yaqui (1)	1	0.01
Asian (149)	206	1.92
Not Hispanic (143)	196	1.83
Hispanic (6)	10	0.09
Bangladeshi (2)	2	0.02
Burmese (0)	1	0.01
Cambodian (3)	3	0.03
Chinese, ex. Taiwanese (20)	27	0.25
Filipino (49)	60	0.56
Indian (32)	37	0.34
Japanese (3)	8	0.07
Korean (8)	8	0.07
Pakistani (1)	3	0.03
Thai (3)	5	0.05
Vietnamese (21)	23	0.21
Hawaii Native/Pacific Islander (1)	11	0.10
Not Hispanic (1)	11	0.10
Native Hawaiian (0)	3	0.03
Samoan (1)	1	0.01
White (8,037)	8,290	77.27
Not Hispanic (5,889)	6,001	55.93
Hispanic (2,148)	2,289	21.33

Machesney Park

Place Type: Village
County: Winnebago
Population: 23,499†

Ancestry‡	Population	%
African, Sub-Saharan (12)	12	0.05
Other Sub-Saharan African (12)	12	0.05
Albanian (66)	66	0.29
American (2,788)	2,788	12.08
Arab (0)	19	0.08
Syrian (0)	19	0.08
Austrian (12)	39	0.17
Belgian (35)	106	0.46
Cajun (12)	35	0.15
Canadian (9)	9	0.04
Celtic (0)	21	0.09
Croatian (33)	62	0.27
Czech (43)	132	0.57

*Notes: † The Census 2010 population figure is used to calculate the percentages in the Hispanic Origin and Race categories. Ancestry percentages are based on the 2006-2010 American Community Survey population (not shown); ‡ Numbers in parentheses indicate the number of people reporting a single ancestry; * Numbers in parentheses indicate the number of persons reporting this race alone, not in combination with any other race; Please refer to the Explanation of Data for more information.*

Danish (11)	77	0.33
Dutch (67)	357	1.55
English (500)	2,185	9.47
European (84)	106	0.46
Finnish (0)	64	0.28
French, ex. Basque (59)	863	3.74
French Canadian (32)	68	0.29
German (2,489)	7,610	32.99
Greek (41)	118	0.51
Hungarian (18)	18	0.08
Irish (978)	4,080	17.69
Italian (921)	2,160	9.36
Lithuanian (54)	181	0.78
Northern European (28)	28	0.12
Norwegian (305)	1,020	4.42
Polish (167)	962	4.17
Romanian (11)	21	0.09
Russian (29)	135	0.59
Scandinavian (17)	29	0.13
Scotch-Irish (30)	131	0.57
Scottish (68)	274	1.19
Serbian (178)	200	0.87
Slovak (0)	9	0.04
Swedish (382)	1,904	8.25
Swiss (17)	138	0.60
Ukrainian (26)	64	0.28
Welsh (0)	94	0.41
Yugoslavian (24)	46	0.20

Hispanic Origin	Population	%
Hispanic or Latino (of any race)	1,172	4.99
Central American, ex. Mexican	26	0.11
Costa Rican	3	0.01
Guatemalan	9	0.04
Nicaraguan	4	0.02
Panamanian	1	<0.01
Salvadoran	9	0.04
Cuban	22	0.09
Dominican Republic	3	0.01
Mexican	919	3.91
Puerto Rican	93	0.40
South American	45	0.19
Argentinean	4	0.02
Chilean	11	0.05
Colombian	16	0.07
Ecuadorian	5	0.02
Peruvian	5	0.02
Uruguayan	2	0.01
Venezuelan	1	<0.01
Other South American	1	<0.01
Other Hispanic or Latino	64	0.27

Race*	Population	%
African-American/Black (666)	901	3.83
Not Hispanic (652)	863	3.67
Hispanic (14)	38	0.16
American Indian/Alaska Native (57)	166	0.71
Not Hispanic (51)	136	0.58
Hispanic (6)	30	0.13
Apache (0)	3	0.01
Blackfeet (1)	5	0.02
Cherokee (8)	30	0.13
Chickasaw (0)	1	<0.01
Chippewa (8)	11	0.05
Comanche (1)	2	0.01
Creek (0)	1	<0.01
Crow (0)	2	0.01
Iroquois (2)	2	0.01
Menominee (1)	1	<0.01
Mexican American Ind. (0)	1	<0.01
Navajo (0)	1	<0.01
Ottawa (1)	1	<0.01
Puget Sound Salish (0)	3	0.01
Seminole (0)	1	<0.01
Sioux (9)	9	0.04
Asian (365)	481	2.05
Not Hispanic (359)	473	2.01
Hispanic (6)	8	0.03
Chinese, ex. Taiwanese (42)	46	0.20
Filipino (94)	132	0.56
Hmong (1)	1	<0.01
Indian (70)	82	0.35
Japanese (11)	25	0.11
Korean (30)	40	0.17
Laotian (32)	41	0.17
Pakistani (11)	11	0.05
Thai (7)	19	0.08
Vietnamese (57)	71	0.30
Hawaii Native/Pacific Islander (7)	22	0.09
Not Hispanic (6)	19	0.08
Hispanic (1)	3	0.01
Guamanian/Chamorro (2)	2	0.01
Native Hawaiian (2)	15	0.06
Samoan (2)	2	0.01
White (21,494)	21,988	93.57
Not Hispanic (20,837)	21,222	90.31
Hispanic (657)	766	3.26

Macomb

Place Type: City
County: McDonough
Population: 19,288†

Ancestry‡	Population	%
African, Sub-Saharan (22)	22	0.11
African (10)	10	0.05
Liberian (12)	12	0.06
American (2,545)	2,545	13.20
Armenian (0)	23	0.12
Austrian (0)	153	0.79
Belgian (10)	49	0.25
British (46)	85	0.44
Canadian (0)	17	0.09
Croatian (9)	25	0.13
Czech (28)	138	0.72
Czechoslovakian (0)	13	0.07
Danish (1)	38	0.20
Dutch (146)	450	2.33
English (760)	2,209	11.46
European (114)	122	0.63
Finnish (14)	25	0.13
French, ex. Basque (36)	372	1.93
French Canadian (97)	108	0.56
German (1,804)	4,903	25.43
Greek (14)	41	0.21
Hungarian (0)	43	0.22
Irish (582)	2,802	14.53
Israeli (0)	15	0.08
Italian (400)	1,432	7.43
Lithuanian (17)	58	0.30
Luxemburger (0)	15	0.08
Norwegian (123)	273	1.42
Pennsylvania German (16)	21	0.11
Polish (389)	1,069	5.54
Portuguese (11)	11	0.06
Romanian (9)	23	0.12
Russian (32)	112	0.58
Scandinavian (14)	26	0.13
Scotch-Irish (161)	460	2.39
Scottish (172)	463	2.40
Serbian (0)	26	0.13
Slavic (0)	10	0.05
Slovak (12)	36	0.19
Swedish (127)	556	2.88
Swiss (0)	46	0.24
Ukrainian (0)	28	0.15
Welsh (0)	115	0.60
West Indian, ex. Hispanic (0)	28	0.15
Bahamian (0)	14	0.07
Jamaican (0)	14	0.07
Yugoslavian (11)	11	0.06

Hispanic Origin	Population	%
Hispanic or Latino (of any race)	700	3.63
Central American, ex. Mexican	31	0.16
Costa Rican	12	0.06
Guatemalan	6	0.03
Honduran	2	0.01
Nicaraguan	1	0.01
Panamanian	5	0.03
Salvadoran	5	0.03
Cuban	25	0.13
Dominican Republic	7	0.04
Mexican	476	2.47
Puerto Rican	91	0.47
South American	27	0.14
Argentinean	3	0.02
Bolivian	3	0.02
Chilean	2	0.01
Colombian	11	0.06
Ecuadorian	3	0.02
Peruvian	5	0.03
Other Hispanic or Latino	43	0.22

Race*	Population	%
African-American/Black (1,573)	1,787	9.26
Not Hispanic (1,527)	1,725	8.94
Hispanic (46)	62	0.32
American Indian/Alaska Native (45)	159	0.82
Not Hispanic (28)	132	0.68
Hispanic (17)	27	0.14
Apache (2)	5	0.03
Blackfeet (0)	6	0.03
Cherokee (8)	50	0.26
Chippewa (0)	1	0.01
Choctaw (0)	2	0.01
Comanche (0)	1	0.01
Crow (0)	1	0.01
Iroquois (3)	5	0.03
Mexican American Ind. (4)	6	0.03
Osage (0)	1	0.01
Asian (470)	605	3.14
Not Hispanic (462)	587	3.04
Hispanic (8)	18	0.09
Burmese (8)	10	0.05
Cambodian (2)	3	0.02
Chinese, ex. Taiwanese (93)	102	0.53
Filipino (44)	63	0.33
Indian (136)	149	0.77
Indonesian (3)	3	0.02
Japanese (39)	54	0.28
Korean (79)	98	0.51
Laotian (0)	3	0.02
Malaysian (1)	2	0.01
Nepalese (11)	13	0.07
Pakistani (10)	12	0.06
Sri Lankan (0)	1	0.01
Taiwanese (11)	11	0.06
Thai (2)	3	0.02
Vietnamese (9)	13	0.07
Hawaii Native/Pacific Islander (1)	16	0.08
Not Hispanic (1)	13	0.07
Hispanic (0)	3	0.02
Guamanian/Chamorro (0)	1	0.01
Samoan (0)	1	0.01
White (16,543)	16,974	88.00
Not Hispanic (16,145)	16,533	85.72
Hispanic (398)	441	2.29

Manteno

Place Type: Village
County: Kankakee
Population: 9,204†

Ancestry‡	Population	%
American (231)	231	2.70
Armenian (0)	35	0.41
Belgian (0)	36	0.42
Brazilian (25)	25	0.29
Canadian (0)	35	0.41
Czech (0)	97	1.13
Czechoslovakian (0)	26	0.30
Danish (0)	27	0.32
Dutch (130)	366	4.28
Eastern European (14)	14	0.16
English (253)	735	8.60
European (10)	10	0.12
French, ex. Basque (110)	599	7.01

*Notes: † The Census 2010 population figure is used to calculate the percentages in the Hispanic Origin and Race categories. Ancestry percentages are based on the 2006-2010 American Community Survey population (not shown); ‡ Numbers in parentheses indicate the number of people reporting a single ancestry; * Numbers in parentheses indicate the number of persons reporting this race alone, not in combination with any other race; Please refer to the Explanation of Data for more information.*

Ancestry (continued)	Population	%
French Canadian (89)	130	1.52
German (739)	2,911	34.04
Greek (11)	11	0.13
Hungarian (14)	25	0.29
Irish (360)	2,097	24.52
Italian (300)	1,002	11.72
Lithuanian (44)	142	1.66
Macedonian (0)	13	0.15
Norwegian (13)	124	1.45
Polish (247)	961	11.24
Romanian (11)	62	0.73
Scotch-Irish (29)	113	1.32
Scottish (25)	45	0.53
Serbian (0)	14	0.16
Swedish (45)	221	2.58
Ukrainian (14)	25	0.29
Welsh (102)	102	1.19

Hispanic Origin	Population	%
Hispanic or Latino (of any race)	521	5.66
Central American, ex. Mexican	11	0.12
Costa Rican	4	0.04
Guatemalan	1	0.01
Honduran	1	0.01
Nicaraguan	1	0.01
Salvadoran	4	0.04
Cuban	4	0.04
Mexican	439	4.77
Puerto Rican	31	0.34
South American	8	0.09
Bolivian	1	0.01
Colombian	5	0.05
Ecuadorian	2	0.02
Other Hispanic or Latino	28	0.30

Race*	Population	%
African-American/Black (108)	156	1.69
Not Hispanic (104)	147	1.60
Hispanic (4)	9	0.10
American Indian/Alaska Native (24)	54	0.59
Not Hispanic (20)	39	0.42
Hispanic (4)	15	0.16
Apache (1)	1	0.01
Cherokee (5)	13	0.14
Chippewa (0)	1	0.01
Choctaw (0)	1	0.01
Delaware (0)	4	0.04
Iroquois (1)	1	0.01
Mexican American Ind. (1)	3	0.03
Potawatomi (0)	3	0.03
Sioux (3)	6	0.07
Asian (55)	78	0.85
Not Hispanic (48)	68	0.74
Hispanic (7)	10	0.11
Chinese, ex. Taiwanese (11)	11	0.12
Filipino (21)	30	0.33
Indian (1)	2	0.02
Japanese (4)	6	0.07
Korean (8)	16	0.17
Sri Lankan (4)	4	0.04
Thai (6)	6	0.07
Vietnamese (0)	1	0.01
Hawaii Native/Pacific Islander (2)	3	0.03
Not Hispanic (2)	3	0.03
Native Hawaiian (2)	3	0.03
White (8,796)	8,912	96.83
Not Hispanic (8,426)	8,506	92.42
Hispanic (370)	406	4.41

Marengo

Place Type: City
County: McHenry
Population: 7,648†

Ancestry‡	Population	%
American (269)	269	3.41
Austrian (14)	58	0.74
Belgian (0)	56	0.71
British (18)	31	0.39
Bulgarian (6)	6	0.08
Canadian (34)	45	0.57
Croatian (31)	31	0.39
Czech (12)	91	1.15
Danish (0)	13	0.16
Dutch (69)	158	2.00
English (134)	493	6.26
Finnish (0)	30	0.38
French, ex. Basque (9)	173	2.20
French Canadian (12)	39	0.49
German (1,208)	3,082	39.11
Greek (0)	29	0.37
Hungarian (30)	47	0.60
Irish (188)	1,338	16.98
Italian (210)	668	8.48
Lithuanian (0)	60	0.76
Norwegian (42)	178	2.26
Polish (122)	632	8.02
Romanian (13)	13	0.16
Russian (17)	94	1.19
Scandinavian (0)	36	0.46
Scotch-Irish (28)	71	0.90
Scottish (22)	64	0.81
Slovak (0)	7	0.09
Slovene (10)	10	0.13
Swedish (74)	364	4.62
Swiss (5)	20	0.25
Ukrainian (14)	71	0.90
Welsh (0)	19	0.24
Yugoslavian (0)	34	0.43

Hispanic Origin	Population	%
Hispanic or Latino (of any race)	1,172	15.32
Central American, ex. Mexican	25	0.33
Guatemalan	12	0.16
Honduran	4	0.05
Nicaraguan	1	0.01
Salvadoran	8	0.10
Cuban	8	0.10
Dominican Republic	2	0.03
Mexican	1,034	13.52
Puerto Rican	48	0.63
South American	13	0.17
Colombian	4	0.05
Peruvian	9	0.12
Other Hispanic or Latino	42	0.55

Race*	Population	%
African-American/Black (50)	96	1.26
Not Hispanic (41)	75	0.98
Hispanic (9)	21	0.27
American Indian/Alaska Native (41)	71	0.93
Not Hispanic (16)	35	0.46
Hispanic (25)	36	0.47
Apache (0)	1	0.01
Blackfeet (0)	2	0.03
Cherokee (3)	11	0.14
Chickasaw (1)	1	0.01
Chippewa (6)	6	0.08
Menominee (0)	2	0.03
Mexican American Ind. (5)	7	0.09
Navajo (0)	2	0.03
Asian (39)	60	0.78
Not Hispanic (37)	56	0.73
Hispanic (2)	4	0.05
Chinese, ex. Taiwanese (5)	14	0.18
Filipino (11)	21	0.27
Indian (5)	5	0.07
Japanese (4)	5	0.07
Korean (2)	5	0.07
Laotian (1)	1	0.01
Thai (5)	9	0.12
Vietnamese (0)	1	0.01
Hawaii Native/Pacific Islander (1)	1	0.01
Not Hispanic (1)	1	0.01
Native Hawaiian (1)	1	0.01
White (6,782)	6,915	90.42
Not Hispanic (6,305)	6,370	83.29
Hispanic (477)	545	7.13

Marion

Place Type: City
County: Williamson
Population: 17,193†

Ancestry‡	Population	%
African, Sub-Saharan (87)	104	0.61
African (71)	71	0.42
Nigerian (16)	33	0.19
American (1,577)	1,577	9.27
Arab (15)	27	0.16
Egyptian (15)	15	0.09
Lebanese (0)	12	0.07
Austrian (0)	17	0.10
Belgian (17)	17	0.10
British (15)	116	0.68
Canadian (46)	46	0.27
Croatian (0)	32	0.19
Czech (13)	150	0.88
Czechoslovakian (35)	35	0.21
Danish (0)	70	0.41
Dutch (0)	388	2.28
English (1,387)	2,704	15.90
European (177)	206	1.21
Finnish (0)	8	0.05
French, ex. Basque (115)	541	3.18
French Canadian (36)	62	0.36
German (1,479)	3,789	22.28
Greek (17)	17	0.10
Guyanese (0)	12	0.07
Hungarian (17)	28	0.16
Irish (849)	2,690	15.82
Israeli (10)	10	0.06
Italian (545)	811	4.77
Lithuanian (0)	14	0.08
Norwegian (33)	208	1.22
Pennsylvania German (16)	16	0.09
Polish (47)	292	1.72
Russian (48)	64	0.38
Scandinavian (12)	12	0.07
Scotch-Irish (86)	294	1.73
Scottish (143)	348	2.05
Serbian (0)	36	0.21
Slavic (15)	15	0.09
Slovak (18)	29	0.17
Swedish (41)	193	1.14
Swiss (0)	10	0.06
Ukrainian (93)	93	0.55
Welsh (12)	66	0.39
Yugoslavian (9)	9	0.05

Hispanic Origin	Population	%
Hispanic or Latino (of any race)	445	2.59
Central American, ex. Mexican	25	0.15
Costa Rican	1	0.01
Guatemalan	8	0.05
Honduran	3	0.02
Nicaraguan	2	0.01
Panamanian	4	0.02
Salvadoran	7	0.04
Cuban	2	0.01
Dominican Republic	1	0.01
Mexican	283	1.65
Puerto Rican	40	0.23
South American	20	0.12
Argentinean	3	0.02
Bolivian	4	0.02
Colombian	11	0.06
Ecuadorian	1	0.01
Peruvian	1	0.01
Other Hispanic or Latino	74	0.43

Race*	Population	%
African-American/Black (1,278)	1,487	8.65
Not Hispanic (1,261)	1,455	8.46
Hispanic (17)	32	0.19
American Indian/Alaska Native (69)	145	0.84
Not Hispanic (60)	134	0.78
Hispanic (9)	11	0.06

*Notes: † The Census 2010 population figure is used to calculate the percentages in the Hispanic Origin and Race categories. Ancestry percentages are based on the 2006-2010 American Community Survey population (not shown); ‡ Numbers in parentheses indicate the number of people reporting a single ancestry; * Numbers in parentheses indicate the number of persons reporting this race alone, not in combination with any other race; Please refer to the Explanation of Data for more information.*

Apache (1)	6	0.03
Blackfeet (2)	10	0.06
Central American Ind. (1)	1	0.01
Cherokee (16)	46	0.27
Cheyenne (0)	3	0.02
Chippewa (0)	3	0.02
Choctaw (0)	1	0.01
Creek (2)	2	0.01
Delaware (0)	1	0.01
Iroquois (0)	1	0.01
Navajo (0)	2	0.01
Ottawa (2)	2	0.01
Pima (1)	1	0.01
Puget Sound Salish (1)	1	0.01
Seminole (0)	1	0.01
Shoshone (0)	1	0.01
Sioux (7)	8	0.05
South American Ind. (0)	1	0.01
Asian (262)	316	1.84
Not Hispanic (261)	311	1.81
Hispanic (1)	5	0.03
Cambodian (12)	12	0.07
Chinese, ex. Taiwanese (26)	27	0.16
Filipino (46)	63	0.37
Indian (84)	93	0.54
Japanese (40)	45	0.26
Korean (2)	9	0.05
Laotian (0)	1	0.01
Malaysian (0)	5	0.03
Pakistani (3)	3	0.02
Sri Lankan (5)	5	0.03
Thai (18)	18	0.10
Vietnamese (21)	27	0.16
Hawaii Native/Pacific Islander (4)	13	0.08
Not Hispanic (4)	13	0.08
Guamanian/Chamorro (0)	1	0.01
Native Hawaiian (3)	5	0.03
Samoan (1)	3	0.02
White (15,093)	15,400	89.57
Not Hispanic (14,832)	15,117	87.93
Hispanic (261)	283	1.65

Markham

Place Type: City
County: Cook
Population: 12,508†

Ancestry‡	Population	%
African, Sub-Saharan (124)	136	1.10
African (82)	94	0.76
Ghanaian (15)	15	0.12
Nigerian (27)	27	0.22
American (72)	72	0.58
Austrian (0)	9	0.07
Croatian (0)	24	0.19
Czech (0)	13	0.10
Czechoslovakian (0)	13	0.10
Dutch (9)	91	0.73
English (47)	166	1.34
Finnish (0)	14	0.11
French, ex. Basque (0)	94	0.76
German (76)	364	2.93
Hungarian (9)	28	0.23
Irish (64)	318	2.56
Italian (31)	161	1.30
Lithuanian (0)	12	0.10
Polish (103)	231	1.86
Scotch-Irish (35)	105	0.85
Scottish (0)	50	0.40
Swedish (0)	49	0.39
Ukrainian (10)	36	0.29
Welsh (0)	9	0.07
West Indian, ex. Hispanic (31)	92	0.74
Bahamian (11)	11	0.09
Belizean (0)	22	0.18
Haitian (0)	10	0.08
Jamaican (20)	49	0.39

Hispanic Origin	Population	%
Hispanic or Latino (of any race)	837	6.69
Central American, ex. Mexican	16	0.13
Guatemalan	2	0.02
Honduran	9	0.07
Panamanian	1	0.01
Salvadoran	4	0.03
Cuban	3	0.02
Mexican	705	5.64
Puerto Rican	63	0.50
South American	9	0.07
Ecuadorian	4	0.03
Peruvian	2	0.02
Uruguayan	1	0.01
Other South American	2	0.02
Other Hispanic or Latino	41	0.33

Race*	Population	%
African-American/Black (10,129)	10,329	82.58
Not Hispanic (10,076)	10,253	81.97
Hispanic (53)	76	0.61
American Indian/Alaska Native (26)	105	0.84
Not Hispanic (15)	86	0.69
Hispanic (11)	19	0.15
Blackfeet (0)	3	0.02
Central American Ind. (2)	2	0.02
Cherokee (4)	23	0.18
Choctaw (1)	7	0.06
Creek (0)	1	0.01
Iroquois (0)	1	0.01
Lumbee (0)	5	0.04
Mexican American Ind. (9)	10	0.08
Navajo (1)	1	0.01
Asian (85)	108	0.86
Not Hispanic (84)	102	0.82
Hispanic (1)	6	0.05
Burmese (6)	6	0.05
Cambodian (1)	3	0.02
Chinese, ex. Taiwanese (5)	7	0.06
Filipino (26)	37	0.30
Indian (16)	20	0.16
Indonesian (2)	2	0.02
Japanese (2)	4	0.03
Korean (4)	12	0.10
Laotian (10)	11	0.09
Pakistani (2)	6	0.05
Vietnamese (4)	4	0.03
Hawaii Native/Pacific Islander (8)	16	0.13
Not Hispanic (8)	11	0.09
Hispanic (0)	5	0.04
Guamanian/Chamorro (0)	1	0.01
Native Hawaiian (3)	5	0.04
Samoan (5)	6	0.05
White (1,594)	1,773	14.17
Not Hispanic (1,275)	1,396	11.16
Hispanic (319)	377	3.01

Matteson

Place Type: Village
County: Cook
Population: 19,009†

Ancestry‡	Population	%
African, Sub-Saharan (204)	217	1.22
African (112)	125	0.70
Ghanaian (36)	36	0.20
Nigerian (56)	56	0.32
American (202)	202	1.14
Austrian (12)	32	0.18
Croatian (9)	21	0.12
Czech (9)	9	0.05
Danish (0)	26	0.15
Dutch (53)	115	0.65
English (156)	390	2.20
French, ex. Basque (9)	118	0.66
German (313)	1,195	6.73
German Russian (33)	33	0.19
Greek (0)	36	0.20
Hungarian (0)	11	0.06
Irish (264)	968	5.45
Italian (194)	431	2.43
Lithuanian (26)	62	0.35
Luxemburger (0)	3	0.02
Norwegian (0)	67	0.38
Polish (322)	502	2.83
Russian (13)	22	0.12
Scandinavian (0)	7	0.04
Scotch-Irish (12)	35	0.20
Scottish (14)	103	0.58
Slovak (0)	48	0.27
Slovene (10)	10	0.06
Swedish (47)	171	0.96
Welsh (0)	17	0.10
West Indian, ex. Hispanic (108)	116	0.65
Belizean (12)	12	0.07
Haitian (46)	46	0.26
Jamaican (50)	50	0.28
West Indian (0)	8	0.05
Yugoslavian (13)	13	0.07

Hispanic Origin	Population	%
Hispanic or Latino (of any race)	813	4.28
Central American, ex. Mexican	17	0.09
Costa Rican	1	0.01
Guatemalan	5	0.03
Honduran	3	0.02
Panamanian	5	0.03
Salvadoran	3	0.02
Cuban	7	0.04
Dominican Republic	5	0.03
Mexican	577	3.04
Puerto Rican	141	0.74
South American	6	0.03
Colombian	2	0.01
Ecuadorian	1	0.01
Peruvian	3	0.02
Other Hispanic or Latino	60	0.32

Race*	Population	%
African-American/Black (14,952)	15,291	80.44
Not Hispanic (14,833)	15,119	79.54
Hispanic (119)	172	0.90
American Indian/Alaska Native (39)	144	0.76
Not Hispanic (13)	97	0.51
Hispanic (26)	47	0.25
Apache (0)	6	0.03
Blackfeet (1)	5	0.03
Central American Ind. (0)	1	0.01
Cherokee (0)	21	0.11
Cheyenne (0)	2	0.01
Chickasaw (0)	4	0.02
Chippewa (1)	2	0.01
Choctaw (0)	3	0.02
Mexican American Ind. (3)	3	0.02
Sioux (2)	12	0.06
Asian (193)	241	1.27
Not Hispanic (187)	232	1.22
Hispanic (6)	9	0.05
Chinese, ex. Taiwanese (16)	22	0.12
Filipino (74)	93	0.49
Hmong (0)	1	0.01
Indian (56)	62	0.33
Japanese (6)	13	0.07
Korean (9)	17	0.09
Laotian (5)	5	0.03
Pakistani (0)	2	0.01
Taiwanese (1)	1	0.01
Thai (1)	1	0.01
Vietnamese (21)	21	0.11
Hawaii Native/Pacific Islander (9)	27	0.14
Not Hispanic (8)	25	0.13
Hispanic (1)	2	0.01
Fijian (1)	1	0.01
Guamanian/Chamorro (2)	2	0.01
Native Hawaiian (1)	12	0.06
Samoan (5)	9	0.05
White (3,089)	3,384	17.80
Not Hispanic (2,784)	3,022	15.90
Hispanic (305)	362	1.90

*Notes: † The Census 2010 population figure is used to calculate the percentages in the Hispanic Origin and Race categories. Ancestry percentages are based on the 2006-2010 American Community Survey population (not shown); ‡ Numbers in parentheses indicate the number of people reporting a single ancestry; * Numbers in parentheses indicate the number of persons reporting this race alone, not in combination with any other race; Please refer to the Explanation of Data for more information.*

Mattoon

Place Type: City
County: Coles
Population: 18,555†

Ancestry‡	Population	%
African, Sub-Saharan (6)	6	0.03
African (6)	6	0.03
American (1,752)	1,752	9.89
British (22)	77	0.43
Croatian (0)	14	0.08
Czech (9)	37	0.21
Danish (19)	69	0.39
Dutch (52)	335	1.89
English (819)	1,973	11.13
European (61)	61	0.34
French, ex. Basque (95)	651	3.67
French Canadian (74)	147	0.83
German (1,865)	4,637	26.17
Greek (10)	10	0.06
Irish (974)	3,007	16.97
Italian (121)	286	1.61
Lithuanian (7)	7	0.04
Norwegian (40)	112	0.63
Polish (25)	252	1.42
Portuguese (14)	42	0.24
Romanian (0)	21	0.12
Russian (9)	9	0.05
Scandinavian (11)	11	0.06
Scotch-Irish (114)	218	1.23
Scottish (102)	254	1.43
Slovak (0)	14	0.08
Swedish (50)	180	1.02
Swiss (9)	44	0.25
Welsh (10)	46	0.26

Hispanic Origin	Population	%
Hispanic or Latino (of any race)	331	1.78
Central American, ex. Mexican	14	0.08
Costa Rican	1	0.01
Guatemalan	6	0.03
Nicaraguan	1	0.01
Salvadoran	5	0.03
Other Central American	1	0.01
Cuban	1	0.01
Dominican Republic	4	0.02
Mexican	217	1.17
Puerto Rican	36	0.19
South American	21	0.11
Chilean	5	0.03
Colombian	8	0.04
Ecuadorian	4	0.02
Peruvian	1	0.01
Other South American	3	0.02
Other Hispanic or Latino	38	0.20

Race*	Population	%
African-American/Black (449)	635	3.42
Not Hispanic (433)	608	3.28
Hispanic (16)	27	0.15
American Indian/Alaska Native (39)	138	0.74
Not Hispanic (32)	116	0.63
Hispanic (7)	22	0.12
Alaska Athabascan *(Ala. Nat.)* (1)	1	0.01
Apache (1)	5	0.03
Blackfeet (0)	2	0.01
Cherokee (8)	36	0.19
Cheyenne (0)	3	0.02
Chippewa (3)	3	0.02
Choctaw (0)	1	0.01
Comanche (1)	2	0.01
Creek (1)	1	0.01
Crow (0)	3	0.02
Mexican American Ind. (1)	4	0.02
Pueblo (1)	1	0.01
Shoshone (0)	1	0.01
Sioux (2)	3	0.02
South American Ind. (0)	1	0.01
Asian (125)	157	0.85
Not Hispanic (124)	156	0.84
Hispanic (1)	1	0.01
Bangladeshi (4)	4	0.02
Chinese, ex. Taiwanese (29)	29	0.16
Filipino (19)	32	0.17
Hmong (15)	15	0.08
Indian (26)	30	0.16
Indonesian (1)	1	0.01
Japanese (4)	11	0.06
Korean (11)	16	0.09
Malaysian (0)	2	0.01
Pakistani (2)	2	0.01
Thai (1)	1	0.01
Vietnamese (12)	12	0.06
Hawaii Native/Pacific Islander (2)	12	0.06
Not Hispanic (1)	8	0.04
Hispanic (1)	4	0.02
Guamanian/Chamorro (2)	6	0.03
Native Hawaiian (0)	1	0.01
White (17,528)	17,825	96.07
Not Hispanic (17,342)	17,610	94.91
Hispanic (186)	215	1.16

Maywood

Place Type: Village
County: Cook
Population: 24,090†

Ancestry‡	Population	%
African, Sub-Saharan (350)	433	1.78
African (305)	378	1.55
Liberian (45)	45	0.18
Other Sub-Saharan African (0)	10	0.04
Alsatian (0)	20	0.08
American (149)	149	0.61
Belgian (0)	52	0.21
British (20)	20	0.08
Czech (0)	19	0.08
Czechoslovakian (3)	3	0.01
Dutch (30)	30	0.12
English (19)	64	0.26
French, ex. Basque (0)	122	0.50
French Canadian (26)	47	0.19
German (162)	307	1.26
Irish (64)	252	1.04
Italian (21)	108	0.44
Latvian (13)	13	0.05
Lithuanian (7)	13	0.05
Norwegian (12)	54	0.22
Polish (60)	79	0.32
Portuguese (0)	19	0.08
Russian (19)	19	0.08
Swedish (0)	14	0.06
Welsh (0)	9	0.04
West Indian, ex. Hispanic (260)	278	1.14
Barbadian (129)	129	0.53
Belizean (6)	6	0.02
Haitian (47)	47	0.19
Jamaican (54)	72	0.30
Trinidadian/Tobagonian (24)	24	0.10
Yugoslavian (8)	8	0.03

Hispanic Origin	Population	%
Hispanic or Latino (of any race)	4,999	20.75
Central American, ex. Mexican	134	0.56
Guatemalan	70	0.29
Honduran	18	0.07
Nicaraguan	2	0.01
Panamanian	7	0.03
Salvadoran	27	0.11
Other Central American	10	0.04
Cuban	29	0.12
Dominican Republic	17	0.07
Mexican	4,252	17.65
Puerto Rican	380	1.58
South American	55	0.23
Argentinean	3	0.01
Chilean	2	0.01
Colombian	10	0.04
Ecuadorian	26	0.11
Peruvian	7	0.03
Venezuelan	7	0.03
Other Hispanic or Latino	132	0.55

Race*	Population	%
African-American/Black (17,924)	18,221	75.64
Not Hispanic (17,781)	18,018	74.79
Hispanic (143)	203	0.84
American Indian/Alaska Native (84)	203	0.84
Not Hispanic (25)	128	0.53
Hispanic (59)	75	0.31
Blackfeet (0)	1	<0.01
Cherokee (5)	18	0.07
Chippewa (2)	5	0.02
Choctaw (0)	5	0.02
Mexican American Ind. (4)	7	0.03
Sioux (0)	1	<0.01
South American Ind. (0)	2	0.01
Asian (122)	151	0.63
Not Hispanic (118)	142	0.59
Hispanic (4)	9	0.04
Chinese, ex. Taiwanese (4)	7	0.03
Filipino (39)	59	0.24
Indian (54)	58	0.24
Indonesian (4)	4	0.02
Japanese (0)	1	<0.01
Korean (6)	6	0.02
Laotian (2)	2	0.01
Pakistani (4)	4	0.02
Vietnamese (1)	2	0.01
Hawaii Native/Pacific Islander (0)	8	0.03
Not Hispanic (0)	4	0.02
Hispanic (0)	4	0.02
Native Hawaiian (0)	4	0.02
Samoan (0)	1	<0.01
White (3,024)	3,336	13.85
Not Hispanic (891)	1,054	4.38
Hispanic (2,133)	2,282	9.47

McHenry

Place Type: City
County: McHenry
Population: 26,992†

Ancestry‡	Population	%
American (1,226)	1,226	4.62
Assyrian/Chaldean/Syriac (0)	14	0.05
Austrian (26)	111	0.42
Belgian (20)	70	0.26
British (16)	52	0.20
Cajun (0)	10	0.04
Croatian (40)	131	0.49
Czech (104)	658	2.48
Czechoslovakian (12)	52	0.20
Danish (39)	123	0.46
Dutch (190)	402	1.52
Eastern European (51)	51	0.19
English (522)	2,028	7.65
European (174)	266	1.00
Finnish (8)	60	0.23
French, ex. Basque (67)	502	1.89
French Canadian (32)	138	0.52
German (2,789)	9,852	37.15
Greek (30)	136	0.51
Hungarian (12)	125	0.47
Iranian (12)	12	0.05
Irish (947)	4,908	18.51
Italian (497)	2,201	8.30
Lithuanian (13)	173	0.65
Luxemburger (0)	22	0.08
Northern European (60)	60	0.23
Norwegian (131)	899	3.39
Polish (918)	4,363	16.45
Portuguese (9)	82	0.31
Romanian (54)	72	0.27
Russian (75)	360	1.36
Scandinavian (32)	87	0.33
Scotch-Irish (125)	399	1.50

*Notes: † The Census 2010 population figure is used to calculate the percentages in the Hispanic Origin and Race categories. Ancestry percentages are based on the 2006-2010 American Community Survey population (not shown); ‡ Numbers in parentheses indicate the number of people reporting a single ancestry; * Numbers in parentheses indicate the number of persons reporting this race alone, not in combination with any other race; Please refer to the Explanation of Data for more information.*

Scottish (130)	256	0.97
Serbian (12)	89	0.34
Slovak (20)	78	0.29
Slovene (6)	23	0.09
Swedish (292)	1,372	5.17
Swiss (16)	82	0.31
Ukrainian (31)	83	0.31
Welsh (18)	262	0.99
Yugoslavian (54)	54	0.20

Hispanic Origin	Population	%
Hispanic or Latino (of any race)	3,450	12.78
Central American, ex. Mexican	80	0.30
Costa Rican	5	0.02
Guatemalan	28	0.10
Honduran	13	0.05
Nicaraguan	4	0.01
Panamanian	11	0.04
Salvadoran	17	0.06
Other Central American	2	0.01
Cuban	35	0.13
Dominican Republic	3	0.01
Mexican	2,976	11.03
Puerto Rican	196	0.73
South American	52	0.19
Argentinean	1	<0.01
Bolivian	1	<0.01
Chilean	5	0.02
Colombian	25	0.09
Ecuadorian	2	0.01
Paraguayan	3	0.01
Peruvian	13	0.05
Venezuelan	1	<0.01
Other South American	1	<0.01
Other Hispanic or Latino	108	0.40

Race*	Population	%
African-American/Black (200)	299	1.11
Not Hispanic (173)	253	0.94
Hispanic (27)	46	0.17
American Indian/Alaska Native (94)	204	0.76
Not Hispanic (45)	121	0.45
Hispanic (49)	83	0.31
Apache (6)	8	0.03
Blackfeet (0)	3	0.01
Canadian/French Am. Ind. (1)	1	<0.01
Central American Ind. (1)	1	<0.01
Cherokee (8)	34	0.13
Chickasaw (1)	1	<0.01
Chippewa (9)	13	0.05
Iroquois (0)	4	0.01
Menominee (0)	3	0.01
Mexican American Ind. (4)	5	0.02
Potawatomi (4)	4	0.01
Sioux (2)	8	0.03
South American Ind. (0)	3	0.01
Asian (420)	508	1.88
Not Hispanic (411)	490	1.82
Hispanic (9)	18	0.07
Cambodian (5)	5	0.02
Chinese, ex. Taiwanese (73)	87	0.32
Filipino (158)	203	0.75
Hmong (4)	4	0.01
Indian (95)	100	0.37
Japanese (7)	17	0.06
Korean (15)	27	0.10
Laotian (1)	1	<0.01
Pakistani (9)	9	0.03
Thai (9)	18	0.07
Vietnamese (32)	32	0.12
Hawaii Native/Pacific Islander (5)	26	0.10
Not Hispanic (5)	21	0.08
Hispanic (0)	5	0.02
Guamanian/Chamorro (0)	3	0.01
Native Hawaiian (2)	6	0.02
Samoan (1)	6	0.02
White (24,372)	24,767	91.76
Not Hispanic (22,661)	22,890	84.80
Hispanic (1,711)	1,877	6.95

Melrose Park

Place Type: Village
County: Cook
Population: 25,411†

Ancestry‡	Population	%
African, Sub-Saharan (70)	98	0.40
African (2)	30	0.12
Sudanese (29)	29	0.12
Other Sub-Saharan African (39)	39	0.16
American (200)	200	0.81
Arab (75)	75	0.30
Arab (28)	28	0.11
Lebanese (9)	9	0.04
Moroccan (1)	1	<0.01
Syrian (37)	37	0.15
Assyrian/Chaldean/Syriac (8)	8	0.03
Brazilian (17)	34	0.14
Croatian (26)	26	0.11
Czech (24)	119	0.48
Danish (0)	10	0.04
Dutch (0)	50	0.20
English (72)	176	0.71
European (139)	139	0.56
Finnish (0)	34	0.14
French, ex. Basque (0)	65	0.26
French Canadian (0)	43	0.17
German (327)	864	3.49
Greek (21)	29	0.12
Hungarian (37)	47	0.19
Irish (204)	606	2.45
Italian (1,977)	2,717	10.99
Lithuanian (72)	111	0.45
Norwegian (0)	35	0.14
Polish (764)	1,160	4.69
Romanian (23)	23	0.09
Russian (17)	17	0.07
Scandinavian (7)	19	0.08
Scotch-Irish (27)	27	0.11
Scottish (0)	8	0.03
Slovak (32)	60	0.24
Swedish (29)	111	0.45
Welsh (0)	17	0.07

Hispanic Origin	Population	%
Hispanic or Latino (of any race)	17,675	69.56
Central American, ex. Mexican	441	1.74
Costa Rican	8	0.03
Guatemalan	297	1.17
Honduran	27	0.11
Nicaraguan	21	0.08
Panamanian	2	0.01
Salvadoran	84	0.33
Other Central American	2	0.01
Cuban	237	0.93
Dominican Republic	54	0.21
Mexican	15,141	59.58
Puerto Rican	1,095	4.31
South American	320	1.26
Argentinean	11	0.04
Bolivian	11	0.04
Chilean	4	0.02
Colombian	111	0.44
Ecuadorian	75	0.30
Peruvian	90	0.35
Uruguayan	6	0.02
Venezuelan	12	0.05
Other Hispanic or Latino	387	1.52

Race*	Population	%
African-American/Black (1,489)	1,631	6.42
Not Hispanic (1,334)	1,398	5.50
Hispanic (155)	233	0.92
American Indian/Alaska Native (118)	214	0.84
Not Hispanic (22)	63	0.25
Hispanic (96)	151	0.59
Blackfeet (0)	2	0.01
Central American Ind. (0)	1	<0.01
Cherokee (5)	17	0.07
Chippewa (3)	4	0.02
Choctaw (0)	1	<0.01
Iroquois (2)	5	0.02
Menominee (0)	2	0.01
Mexican American Ind. (20)	33	0.13
Navajo (1)	1	<0.01
Osage (0)	2	0.01
Pima (0)	1	<0.01
Seminole (1)	1	<0.01
Sioux (5)	11	0.04
South American Ind. (1)	3	0.01
Asian (456)	522	2.05
Not Hispanic (430)	478	1.88
Hispanic (26)	44	0.17
Burmese (3)	3	0.01
Cambodian (14)	14	0.06
Chinese, ex. Taiwanese (38)	47	0.18
Filipino (188)	214	0.84
Indian (75)	101	0.40
Indonesian (1)	2	0.01
Japanese (7)	15	0.06
Korean (8)	9	0.04
Laotian (5)	5	0.02
Pakistani (20)	20	0.08
Sri Lankan (2)	2	0.01
Thai (22)	27	0.11
Vietnamese (60)	64	0.25
Hawaii Native/Pacific Islander (5)	22	0.09
Not Hispanic (5)	9	0.04
Hispanic (0)	13	0.05
Guamanian/Chamorro (5)	9	0.04
Samoan (0)	1	<0.01
White (14,472)	15,160	59.66
Not Hispanic (5,768)	5,869	23.10
Hispanic (8,704)	9,291	36.56

Midlothian

Place Type: Village
County: Cook
Population: 14,819†

Ancestry‡	Population	%
African, Sub-Saharan (0)	16	0.11
African (0)	16	0.11
American (225)	225	1.54
Arab (74)	87	0.60
Arab (12)	25	0.17
Egyptian (34)	34	0.23
Jordanian (28)	28	0.19
Armenian (0)	36	0.25
Australian (0)	9	0.06
Austrian (0)	22	0.15
Bulgarian (13)	13	0.09
Canadian (0)	18	0.12
Croatian (59)	160	1.10
Czech (84)	329	2.26
Czechoslovakian (0)	20	0.14
Danish (0)	18	0.12
Dutch (187)	398	2.73
English (72)	627	4.30
European (132)	132	0.91
Finnish (0)	7	0.05
French, ex. Basque (24)	298	2.04
French Canadian (0)	141	0.97
German (503)	3,336	22.88
Greek (63)	143	0.98
Hungarian (0)	17	0.12
Irish (617)	3,435	23.56
Israeli (28)	28	0.19
Italian (259)	1,407	9.65
Lithuanian (91)	327	2.24
Norwegian (0)	35	0.24
Pennsylvania German (0)	57	0.39
Polish (682)	2,107	14.45
Romanian (25)	57	0.39
Russian (0)	15	0.10
Scandinavian (10)	10	0.07
Scotch-Irish (41)	112	0.77
Scottish (9)	116	0.80

*Notes: † The Census 2010 population figure is used to calculate the percentages in the Hispanic Origin and Race categories. Ancestry percentages are based on the 2006-2010 American Community Survey population (not shown); ‡ Numbers in parentheses indicate the number of people reporting a single ancestry; * Numbers in parentheses indicate the number of persons reporting this race alone, not in combination with any other race; Please refer to the Explanation of Data for more information.*

Ancestry	Population	%
Serbian (16)	16	0.11
Slovak (0)	47	0.32
Swedish (73)	357	2.45
Welsh (0)	55	0.38

Hispanic Origin	Population	%
Hispanic or Latino (of any race)	3,043	20.53
Central American, ex. Mexican	50	0.34
Costa Rican	6	0.04
Guatemalan	27	0.18
Honduran	8	0.05
Nicaraguan	6	0.04
Panamanian	2	0.01
Salvadoran	1	0.01
Cuban	7	0.05
Dominican Republic	2	0.01
Mexican	2,705	18.25
Puerto Rican	161	1.09
South American	49	0.33
Argentinean	17	0.11
Bolivian	1	0.01
Chilean	1	0.01
Colombian	5	0.03
Ecuadorian	8	0.05
Peruvian	12	0.08
Uruguayan	2	0.01
Venezuelan	1	0.01
Other South American	2	0.01
Other Hispanic or Latino	69	0.47

Race*	Population	%
African-American/Black (1,662)	1,815	12.25
Not Hispanic (1,635)	1,749	11.80
Hispanic (27)	66	0.45
American Indian/Alaska Native (48)	117	0.79
Not Hispanic (15)	59	0.40
Hispanic (33)	58	0.39
Apache (0)	2	0.01
Blackfeet (0)	7	0.05
Canadian/French Am. Ind. (0)	1	0.01
Central American Ind. (1)	1	0.01
Cherokee (8)	24	0.16
Chippewa (1)	1	0.01
Choctaw (1)	1	0.01
Inupiat *(Alaska Native)* (0)	1	0.01
Iroquois (4)	5	0.03
Menominee (0)	3	0.02
Mexican American Ind. (9)	14	0.09
Paiute (0)	1	0.01
Asian (215)	290	1.96
Not Hispanic (206)	273	1.84
Hispanic (9)	17	0.11
Chinese, ex. Taiwanese (14)	21	0.14
Filipino (111)	148	1.00
Indian (48)	55	0.37
Japanese (0)	3	0.02
Korean (5)	8	0.05
Laotian (4)	4	0.03
Pakistani (1)	2	0.01
Thai (5)	8	0.05
Vietnamese (16)	17	0.11
Hawaii Native/Pacific Islander (4)	14	0.09
Not Hispanic (4)	11	0.07
Hispanic (0)	3	0.02
Native Hawaiian (0)	5	0.03
Samoan (3)	3	0.02
White (10,982)	11,367	76.71
Not Hispanic (9,682)	9,877	66.65
Hispanic (1,300)	1,490	10.05

Minooka

Place Type: Village
County: Grundy
Population: 10,924†

Ancestry‡	Population	%
Albanian (0)	22	0.23
American (136)	136	1.43
Austrian (19)	61	0.64
Belgian (0)	15	0.16
British (19)	48	0.50
Croatian (10)	55	0.58
Czech (33)	128	1.34
Czechoslovakian (0)	52	0.55
Danish (13)	68	0.71
Dutch (19)	75	0.79
Eastern European (75)	75	0.79
English (120)	662	6.95
European (67)	90	0.95
French, ex. Basque (17)	377	3.96
French Canadian (0)	24	0.25
German (990)	3,184	33.44
Greek (13)	128	1.34
Hungarian (0)	44	0.46
Irish (374)	2,141	22.48
Italian (352)	1,324	13.90
Lithuanian (25)	113	1.19
Luxemburger (0)	9	0.09
Norwegian (67)	181	1.90
Polish (460)	1,360	14.28
Romanian (0)	22	0.23
Russian (15)	51	0.54
Scandinavian (19)	49	0.51
Scotch-Irish (0)	91	0.96
Scottish (136)	201	2.11
Serbian (0)	11	0.12
Slavic (9)	56	0.59
Slovak (0)	58	0.61
Slovene (58)	82	0.86
Swedish (13)	226	2.37
Swiss (12)	31	0.33
Ukrainian (6)	6	0.06
Welsh (0)	31	0.33

Hispanic Origin	Population	%
Hispanic or Latino (of any race)	1,391	12.73
Central American, ex. Mexican	31	0.28
Costa Rican	4	0.04
Guatemalan	19	0.17
Honduran	3	0.03
Nicaraguan	1	0.01
Salvadoran	4	0.04
Cuban	18	0.16
Mexican	1,091	9.99
Puerto Rican	158	1.45
South American	30	0.27
Argentinean	16	0.15
Bolivian	4	0.04
Colombian	3	0.03
Ecuadorian	1	0.01
Peruvian	5	0.05
Venezuelan	1	0.01
Other Hispanic or Latino	63	0.58

Race*	Population	%
African-American/Black (355)	422	3.86
Not Hispanic (338)	388	3.55
Hispanic (17)	34	0.31
American Indian/Alaska Native (22)	50	0.46
Not Hispanic (14)	37	0.34
Hispanic (8)	13	0.12
Apache (0)	1	0.01
Blackfeet (1)	1	0.01
Canadian/French Am. Ind. (1)	1	0.01
Cherokee (3)	21	0.19
Chippewa (3)	4	0.04
Cree (0)	5	0.05
Creek (0)	1	0.01
Kiowa (1)	2	0.02
Lumbee (2)	2	0.02
Mexican American Ind. (0)	1	0.01
Seminole (0)	1	0.01
Asian (133)	219	2.00
Not Hispanic (125)	197	1.80
Hispanic (8)	22	0.20
Bangladeshi (5)	5	0.05
Burmese (1)	1	0.01
Cambodian (1)	2	0.02
Chinese, ex. Taiwanese (11)	21	0.19
Filipino (37)	61	0.56
Indian (17)	27	0.25
Indonesian (1)	2	0.02
Japanese (0)	7	0.06
Korean (19)	37	0.34
Laotian (2)	4	0.04
Pakistani (22)	24	0.22
Taiwanese (1)	1	0.01
Thai (2)	5	0.05
Vietnamese (11)	16	0.15
Hawaii Native/Pacific Islander (2)	7	0.06
Not Hispanic (0)	5	0.05
Hispanic (2)	2	0.02
Guamanian/Chamorro (1)	1	0.01
Native Hawaiian (0)	3	0.03
Samoan (1)	1	0.01
White (9,730)	9,946	91.05
Not Hispanic (8,916)	9,038	82.74
Hispanic (814)	908	8.31

Mokena

Place Type: Village
County: Will
Population: 18,740†

Ancestry‡	Population	%
American (312)	312	1.72
Arab (68)	128	0.70
Arab (0)	29	0.16
Palestinian (41)	41	0.23
Syrian (27)	58	0.32
Australian (0)	23	0.13
Austrian (36)	125	0.69
British (9)	19	0.10
Croatian (83)	212	1.17
Czech (70)	390	2.15
Czechoslovakian (0)	96	0.53
Danish (8)	53	0.29
Dutch (208)	666	3.67
Eastern European (11)	24	0.13
English (129)	1,038	5.71
European (117)	117	0.64
French, ex. Basque (59)	788	4.34
French Canadian (0)	90	0.50
German (1,138)	5,532	30.46
Greek (288)	455	2.50
Hungarian (39)	93	0.51
Irish (1,658)	5,356	29.49
Italian (568)	2,840	15.64
Latvian (0)	10	0.06
Lithuanian (149)	463	2.55
Norwegian (76)	262	1.44
Polish (1,109)	3,684	20.28
Romanian (0)	22	0.12
Russian (33)	246	1.35
Scandinavian (0)	14	0.08
Scotch-Irish (20)	154	0.85
Scottish (45)	170	0.94
Serbian (34)	64	0.35
Slovak (26)	148	0.81
Slovene (26)	44	0.24
Swedish (160)	727	4.00
Swiss (13)	55	0.30
Ukrainian (13)	105	0.58
Welsh (6)	102	0.56

Hispanic Origin	Population	%
Hispanic or Latino (of any race)	903	4.82
Central American, ex. Mexican	17	0.09
Guatemalan	14	0.07
Honduran	1	0.01
Salvadoran	1	0.01
Other Central American	1	0.01
Cuban	21	0.11
Mexican	750	4.00
Puerto Rican	63	0.34
South American	12	0.06
Colombian	7	0.04
Ecuadorian	2	0.01

SECTION TWO

*Notes: † The Census 2010 population figure is used to calculate the percentages in the Hispanic Origin and Race categories. Ancestry percentages are based on the 2006-2010 American Community Survey population (not shown); ‡ Numbers in parentheses indicate the number of people reporting a single ancestry; * Numbers in parentheses indicate the number of persons reporting this race alone, not in combination with any other race; Please refer to the Explanation of Data for more information.*

Peruvian	3	0.02
Other Hispanic or Latino	40	0.21

Race*	Population	%
African-American/Black (242)	296	1.58
Not Hispanic (238)	283	1.51
Hispanic (4)	13	0.07
American Indian/Alaska Native (24)	81	0.43
Not Hispanic (21)	65	0.35
Hispanic (3)	16	0.09
Blackfeet (0)	4	0.02
Cherokee (0)	10	0.05
Chippewa (2)	6	0.03
Choctaw (0)	6	0.03
Creek (1)	1	0.01
Iroquois (1)	1	0.01
Lumbee (0)	1	0.01
Mexican American Ind. (0)	3	0.02
Navajo (3)	4	0.02
Osage (0)	1	0.01
Potawatomi (4)	7	0.04
Sioux (2)	2	0.01
Spanish American Ind. (0)	1	0.01
Asian (382)	447	2.39
Not Hispanic (381)	444	2.37
Hispanic (1)	3	0.02
Cambodian (1)	1	0.01
Chinese, ex. Taiwanese (55)	69	0.37
Filipino (74)	99	0.53
Indian (107)	126	0.67
Japanese (12)	21	0.11
Korean (85)	94	0.50
Malaysian (1)	1	0.01
Pakistani (3)	7	0.04
Thai (0)	1	0.01
Vietnamese (25)	31	0.17
Hawaii Native/Pacific Islander (5)	11	0.06
Not Hispanic (5)	11	0.06
Guamanian/Chamorro (0)	1	0.01
Native Hawaiian (4)	7	0.04
Samoan (0)	2	0.01
White (17,715)	17,904	95.54
Not Hispanic (17,046)	17,180	91.68
Hispanic (669)	724	3.86

Moline

Place Type: City
County: Rock Island
Population: 43,483†

Ancestry‡	Population	%
African, Sub-Saharan (110)	246	0.57
African (95)	123	0.28
Senegalese (6)	6	0.01
Other Sub-Saharan African (9)	117	0.27
American (2,256)	2,256	5.21
Arab (95)	95	0.22
Lebanese (7)	7	0.02
Moroccan (88)	88	0.20
Austrian (11)	21	0.05
Belgian (1,096)	2,722	6.28
British (84)	157	0.36
Canadian (9)	19	0.04
Celtic (11)	11	0.03
Croatian (121)	174	0.40
Czech (76)	262	0.60
Czechoslovakian (8)	78	0.18
Danish (55)	321	0.74
Dutch (99)	881	2.03
English (832)	4,056	9.36
European (230)	242	0.56
Finnish (27)	41	0.09
French, ex. Basque (80)	997	2.30
French Canadian (33)	127	0.29
German (3,613)	11,227	25.91
Greek (82)	317	0.73
Hungarian (0)	79	0.18
Irish (1,927)	6,229	14.38
Italian (440)	1,386	3.20
Lithuanian (36)	134	0.31
Northern European (20)	20	0.05
Norwegian (276)	862	1.99
Pennsylvania German (0)	36	0.08
Polish (382)	1,008	2.33
Romanian (48)	99	0.23
Russian (202)	294	0.68
Scandinavian (0)	35	0.08
Scotch-Irish (282)	976	2.25
Scottish (182)	856	1.98
Serbian (18)	47	0.11
Slavic (0)	34	0.08
Slovak (10)	53	0.12
Slovene (0)	11	0.03
Swedish (934)	3,277	7.56
Swiss (14)	131	0.30
Welsh (28)	168	0.39
Yugoslavian (57)	79	0.18

Hispanic Origin	Population	%
Hispanic or Latino (of any race)	6,764	15.56
Central American, ex. Mexican	86	0.20
Costa Rican	7	0.02
Guatemalan	18	0.04
Honduran	26	0.06
Nicaraguan	5	0.01
Panamanian	1	<0.01
Salvadoran	27	0.06
Other Central American	2	<0.01
Cuban	22	0.05
Dominican Republic	2	<0.01
Mexican	6,227	14.32
Puerto Rican	89	0.20
South American	40	0.09
Argentinean	2	<0.01
Bolivian	1	<0.01
Chilean	10	0.02
Colombian	15	0.03
Ecuadorian	5	0.01
Paraguayan	1	<0.01
Venezuelan	6	0.01
Other Hispanic or Latino	298	0.69

Race*	Population	%
African-American/Black (2,251)	2,835	6.52
Not Hispanic (2,168)	2,641	6.07
Hispanic (83)	194	0.45
American Indian/Alaska Native (113)	562	1.29
Not Hispanic (72)	223	0.51
Hispanic (41)	339	0.78
Apache (2)	3	0.01
Blackfeet (0)	9	0.02
Canadian/French Am. Ind. (0)	1	<0.01
Central American Ind. (2)	2	<0.01
Cherokee (19)	67	0.15
Chickasaw (0)	2	<0.01
Chippewa (4)	8	0.02
Choctaw (0)	6	0.01
Cree (0)	3	0.01
Crow (0)	3	0.01
Delaware (2)	2	<0.01
Iroquois (1)	2	<0.01
Mexican American Ind. (7)	9	0.02
Navajo (5)	5	0.01
Osage (0)	2	<0.01
Potawatomi (1)	1	<0.01
Shoshone (0)	1	<0.01
Sioux (9)	24	0.06
Ute (0)	1	<0.01
Asian (1,034)	1,204	2.77
Not Hispanic (1,023)	1,173	2.70
Hispanic (11)	31	0.07
Bangladeshi (5)	5	0.01
Bhutanese (6)	10	0.02
Burmese (91)	94	0.22
Cambodian (8)	14	0.03
Chinese, ex. Taiwanese (62)	79	0.18
Filipino (52)	80	0.18
Indian (599)	624	1.44
Indonesian (3)	4	0.01
Japanese (18)	32	0.07
Korean (47)	78	0.18
Laotian (1)	6	0.01
Malaysian (3)	4	0.01
Nepalese (14)	18	0.04
Pakistani (12)	17	0.04
Thai (17)	20	0.05
Vietnamese (55)	64	0.15
Hawaii Native/Pacific Islander (9)	37	0.09
Not Hispanic (7)	33	0.08
Hispanic (2)	4	0.01
Guamanian/Chamorro (4)	9	0.02
Native Hawaiian (2)	8	0.02
Samoan (1)	1	<0.01
White (36,103)	37,162	85.46
Not Hispanic (32,674)	33,372	76.75
Hispanic (3,429)	3,790	8.72

Monmouth

Place Type: City
County: Warren
Population: 9,444†

Ancestry‡	Population	%
African, Sub-Saharan (31)	31	0.33
African (31)	31	0.33
American (415)	415	4.42
British (7)	39	0.42
Czech (0)	23	0.24
Czechoslovakian (17)	17	0.18
Danish (13)	56	0.60
Dutch (28)	247	2.63
Eastern European (0)	15	0.16
English (275)	813	8.66
European (45)	45	0.48
French, ex. Basque (25)	148	1.58
French Canadian (19)	31	0.33
German (648)	1,893	20.16
Greek (49)	174	1.85
Hungarian (0)	14	0.15
Irish (413)	1,296	13.80
Italian (118)	279	2.97
Lithuanian (0)	10	0.11
Norwegian (51)	95	1.01
Pennsylvania German (10)	21	0.22
Polish (108)	318	3.39
Russian (0)	25	0.27
Scandinavian (9)	9	0.10
Scotch-Irish (35)	190	2.02
Scottish (56)	289	3.08
Slovak (0)	10	0.11
Swedish (293)	619	6.59
Swiss (10)	35	0.37
Welsh (53)	80	0.85

Hispanic Origin	Population	%
Hispanic or Latino (of any race)	1,358	14.38
Central American, ex. Mexican	67	0.71
Guatemalan	47	0.50
Honduran	8	0.08
Salvadoran	12	0.13
Cuban	10	0.11
Mexican	1,200	12.71
Puerto Rican	9	0.10
South American	1	0.01
Ecuadorian	1	0.01
Other Hispanic or Latino	71	0.75

Race*	Population	%
African-American/Black (272)	387	4.10
Not Hispanic (258)	365	3.86
Hispanic (14)	22	0.23
American Indian/Alaska Native (32)	73	0.77
Not Hispanic (22)	58	0.61
Hispanic (10)	15	0.16
Blackfeet (3)	4	0.04
Cherokee (0)	7	0.07
Comanche (1)	4	0.04
Delaware (1)	1	0.01

*Notes: † The Census 2010 population figure is used to calculate the percentages in the Hispanic Origin and Race categories. Ancestry percentages are based on the 2006-2010 American Community Survey population (not shown); ‡ Numbers in parentheses indicate the number of people reporting a single ancestry; * Numbers in parentheses indicate the number of persons reporting this race alone, not in combination with any other race; Please refer to the Explanation of Data for more information.*

Race*	Population	%
Menominee (1)	7	0.07
Ottawa (1)	1	0.01
Paiute (4)	4	0.04
Sioux (0)	2	0.02
Asian (66)	76	0.80
Not Hispanic (65)	75	0.79
Hispanic (1)	1	0.01
Burmese (8)	8	0.08
Chinese, ex. Taiwanese (17)	18	0.19
Filipino (4)	4	0.04
Indian (10)	11	0.12
Indonesian (2)	2	0.02
Japanese (4)	7	0.07
Korean (9)	10	0.11
Laotian (1)	1	0.01
Pakistani (3)	3	0.03
Thai (0)	1	0.01
Vietnamese (4)	7	0.07
Hawaii Native/Pacific Islander (8)	13	0.14
Not Hispanic (4)	8	0.08
Hispanic (4)	5	0.05
Guamanian/Chamorro (8)	9	0.10
Samoan (0)	3	0.03
White (8,094)	8,296	87.84
Not Hispanic (7,576)	7,720	81.75
Hispanic (518)	576	6.10

Montgomery

Place Type: Village
County: Kendall
Population: 18,438†

Ancestry‡	Population	%
African, Sub-Saharan (286)	553	3.47
African (30)	115	0.72
Cape Verdean (44)	134	0.84
Ghanaian (36)	36	0.23
South African (71)	163	1.02
Other Sub-Saharan African (105)	105	0.66
American (546)	546	3.42
Assyrian/Chaldean/Syriac (0)	12	0.08
Austrian (0)	37	0.23
Belgian (21)	35	0.22
British (27)	43	0.27
Croatian (0)	9	0.06
Czech (39)	149	0.93
Czechoslovakian (13)	37	0.23
Danish (28)	94	0.59
Dutch (39)	205	1.28
Eastern European (19)	19	0.12
English (376)	1,158	7.26
European (26)	111	0.70
Finnish (0)	6	0.04
French, ex. Basque (36)	330	2.07
French Canadian (28)	60	0.38
German (1,058)	3,792	23.76
Greek (68)	118	0.74
Hungarian (50)	147	0.92
Irish (275)	2,069	12.97
Italian (268)	1,180	7.39
Lithuanian (10)	63	0.39
Luxemburger (32)	32	0.20
Macedonian (14)	38	0.24
Norwegian (42)	312	1.96
Polish (572)	1,393	8.73
Portuguese (0)	19	0.12
Romanian (0)	45	0.28
Russian (13)	147	0.92
Scotch-Irish (12)	137	0.86
Scottish (40)	100	0.63
Serbian (0)	13	0.08
Slavic (0)	15	0.09
Slovak (0)	24	0.15
Swedish (75)	324	2.03
Swiss (33)	58	0.36
Welsh (0)	17	0.11

Hispanic Origin	Population	%
Hispanic or Latino (of any race)	4,923	26.70
Central American, ex. Mexican	91	0.49
Costa Rican	4	0.02
Guatemalan	42	0.23
Honduran	15	0.08
Nicaraguan	11	0.06
Panamanian	3	0.02
Salvadoran	16	0.09
Cuban	57	0.31
Mexican	4,083	22.14
Puerto Rican	424	2.30
South American	100	0.54
Argentinean	8	0.04
Bolivian	8	0.04
Chilean	11	0.06
Colombian	34	0.18
Ecuadorian	20	0.11
Peruvian	14	0.08
Venezuelan	5	0.03
Other Hispanic or Latino	168	0.91

Race*	Population	%
African-American/Black (1,539)	1,770	9.60
Not Hispanic (1,464)	1,642	8.91
Hispanic (75)	128	0.69
American Indian/Alaska Native (69)	147	0.80
Not Hispanic (10)	50	0.27
Hispanic (59)	97	0.53
Aleut *(Alaska Native)* (1)	1	0.01
Apache (0)	1	0.01
Blackfeet (2)	5	0.03
Cherokee (4)	18	0.10
Chippewa (0)	4	0.02
Crow (0)	1	0.01
Houma (1)	1	0.01
Inupiat *(Alaska Native)* (0)	2	0.01
Menominee (0)	1	0.01
Mexican American Ind. (10)	15	0.08
Pueblo (0)	1	0.01
Sioux (0)	1	0.01
South American Ind. (0)	1	0.01
Spanish American Ind. (1)	2	0.01
Asian (588)	726	3.94
Not Hispanic (585)	705	3.82
Hispanic (3)	21	0.11
Burmese (0)	2	0.01
Cambodian (2)	2	0.01
Chinese, ex. Taiwanese (35)	47	0.25
Filipino (249)	294	1.59
Hmong (8)	8	0.04
Indian (169)	184	1.00
Japanese (8)	39	0.21
Korean (18)	30	0.16
Laotian (18)	21	0.11
Pakistani (38)	41	0.22
Sri Lankan (4)	4	0.02
Thai (4)	8	0.04
Vietnamese (27)	35	0.19
Hawaii Native/Pacific Islander (6)	18	0.10
Not Hispanic (4)	13	0.07
Hispanic (2)	5	0.03
Guamanian/Chamorro (0)	5	0.03
Native Hawaiian (0)	2	0.01
Samoan (2)	2	0.01
White (13,888)	14,428	78.25
Not Hispanic (11,119)	11,402	61.84
Hispanic (2,769)	3,026	16.41

Morris

Place Type: City
County: Grundy
Population: 13,636†

Ancestry‡	Population	%
African, Sub-Saharan (42)	42	0.31
Nigerian (42)	42	0.31
American (376)	376	2.78
Arab (8)	8	0.06
Lebanese (8)	8	0.06
Assyrian/Chaldean/Syriac (8)	8	0.06
Australian (0)	14	0.10
Austrian (0)	10	0.07
Belgian (0)	54	0.40
British (0)	8	0.06
Canadian (24)	61	0.45
Croatian (16)	34	0.25
Czech (39)	125	0.92
Czechoslovakian (0)	17	0.13
Danish (106)	164	1.21
Dutch (7)	172	1.27
English (193)	1,201	8.87
European (80)	112	0.83
Finnish (0)	23	0.17
French, ex. Basque (0)	278	2.05
French Canadian (22)	42	0.31
German (994)	3,854	28.48
Greek (19)	83	0.61
Hungarian (0)	18	0.13
Irish (702)	2,782	20.56
Italian (256)	1,325	9.79
Lithuanian (16)	41	0.30
Luxemburger (6)	6	0.04
Macedonian (0)	28	0.21
Northern European (31)	31	0.23
Norwegian (530)	1,399	10.34
Pennsylvania German (0)	37	0.27
Polish (185)	1,048	7.74
Portuguese (21)	21	0.16
Russian (0)	12	0.09
Scandinavian (68)	68	0.50
Scotch-Irish (149)	500	3.69
Scottish (44)	443	3.27
Slavic (0)	43	0.32
Slovak (16)	150	1.11
Slovene (12)	44	0.33
Swedish (63)	453	3.35
Swiss (0)	15	0.11
Turkish (40)	40	0.30
Welsh (0)	61	0.45
Yugoslavian (0)	28	0.21

Hispanic Origin	Population	%
Hispanic or Latino (of any race)	1,306	9.58
Central American, ex. Mexican	12	0.09
Costa Rican	3	0.02
Guatemalan	4	0.03
Honduran	3	0.02
Salvadoran	2	0.01
Cuban	9	0.07
Mexican	1,156	8.48
Puerto Rican	49	0.36
South American	12	0.09
Argentinean	2	0.01
Colombian	1	0.01
Paraguayan	6	0.04
Peruvian	1	0.01
Venezuelan	2	0.01
Other Hispanic or Latino	68	0.50

Race*	Population	%
African-American/Black (140)	219	1.61
Not Hispanic (124)	193	1.42
Hispanic (16)	26	0.19
American Indian/Alaska Native (33)	66	0.48
Not Hispanic (21)	47	0.34
Hispanic (12)	19	0.14
Apache (0)	1	0.01
Blackfeet (1)	4	0.03
Cherokee (9)	15	0.11
Inupiat *(Alaska Native)* (0)	1	0.01
Mexican American Ind. (1)	3	0.02
Ottawa (1)	1	0.01
Sioux (1)	3	0.02
Yaqui (1)	1	0.01
Yuman (1)	2	0.01
Asian (98)	129	0.95
Not Hispanic (96)	120	0.88
Hispanic (2)	9	0.07
Burmese (3)	3	0.02
Cambodian (1)	3	0.02

*Notes: † The Census 2010 population figure is used to calculate the percentages in the Hispanic Origin and Race categories. Ancestry percentages are based on the 2006-2010 American Community Survey population (not shown); ‡ Numbers in parentheses indicate the number of people reporting a single ancestry; * Numbers in parentheses indicate the number of persons reporting this race alone, not in combination with any other race; Please refer to the Explanation of Data for more information.*

Chinese, ex. Taiwanese (15)	15	0.11
Filipino (25)	33	0.24
Indian (26)	27	0.20
Japanese (1)	7	0.05
Korean (9)	14	0.10
Laotian (3)	3	0.02
Nepalese (1)	1	0.01
Pakistani (1)	1	0.01
Taiwanese (8)	8	0.06
Thai (0)	1	0.01
Vietnamese (1)	9	0.07
Hawaii Native/Pacific Islander (4)	7	0.05
Not Hispanic (3)	6	0.04
Hispanic (1)	1	0.01
Guamanian/Chamorro (2)	4	0.03
Native Hawaiian (0)	1	0.01
White (12,702)	12,873	94.40
Not Hispanic (11,962)	12,071	88.52
Hispanic (740)	802	5.88

Morton Grove

Place Type: Village
County: Cook
Population: 23,270†

Ancestry‡	Population	%
African, Sub-Saharan (0)	146	0.64
Other Sub-Saharan African (0)	146	0.64
Albanian (45)	45	0.20
American (501)	501	2.19
Arab (305)	345	1.51
Arab (68)	85	0.37
Iraqi (49)	72	0.31
Jordanian (10)	10	0.04
Lebanese (146)	146	0.64
Palestinian (12)	12	0.05
Other Arab (20)	20	0.09
Armenian (119)	141	0.62
Assyrian/Chaldean/Syriac (469)	533	2.33
Austrian (57)	109	0.48
Belgian (20)	50	0.22
Brazilian (9)	9	0.04
British (0)	35	0.15
Bulgarian (50)	50	0.22
Croatian (41)	41	0.18
Czech (29)	170	0.74
Czechoslovakian (11)	11	0.05
Danish (0)	54	0.24
Dutch (0)	82	0.36
Eastern European (70)	70	0.31
English (143)	763	3.34
European (24)	24	0.10
Finnish (5)	16	0.07
French, ex. Basque (50)	367	1.60
French Canadian (6)	51	0.22
German (1,260)	3,452	15.10
Greek (834)	1,109	4.85
Hungarian (97)	215	0.94
Iranian (51)	58	0.25
Irish (675)	2,238	9.79
Israeli (0)	10	0.04
Italian (434)	1,209	5.29
Latvian (0)	12	0.05
Lithuanian (61)	161	0.70
Luxemburger (12)	80	0.35
New Zealander (0)	12	0.05
Northern European (9)	9	0.04
Norwegian (62)	307	1.34
Polish (1,801)	2,798	12.24
Romanian (569)	624	2.73
Russian (498)	964	4.22
Scandinavian (15)	15	0.07
Scotch-Irish (35)	155	0.68
Scottish (37)	179	0.78
Serbian (142)	183	0.80
Slavic (11)	34	0.15
Slovak (30)	30	0.13
Slovene (21)	31	0.14
Soviet Union (21)	21	0.09
Swedish (167)	434	1.90
Swiss (0)	11	0.05
Turkish (0)	8	0.03
Ukrainian (270)	329	1.44
Welsh (0)	19	0.08
Yugoslavian (214)	227	0.99

Hispanic Origin	Population	%
Hispanic or Latino (of any race)	1,504	6.46
Central American, ex. Mexican	90	0.39
Costa Rican	1	<0.01
Guatemalan	58	0.25
Honduran	8	0.03
Nicaraguan	4	0.02
Panamanian	2	0.01
Salvadoran	17	0.07
Cuban	89	0.38
Dominican Republic	2	0.01
Mexican	805	3.46
Puerto Rican	221	0.95
South American	223	0.96
Argentinean	8	0.03
Bolivian	9	0.04
Chilean	5	0.02
Colombian	52	0.22
Ecuadorian	81	0.35
Peruvian	50	0.21
Uruguayan	12	0.05
Venezuelan	6	0.03
Other Hispanic or Latino	74	0.32

Race*	Population	%
African-American/Black (280)	385	1.65
Not Hispanic (279)	361	1.55
Hispanic (1)	24	0.10
American Indian/Alaska Native (42)	106	0.46
Not Hispanic (32)	81	0.35
Hispanic (10)	25	0.11
Apache (1)	1	<0.01
Blackfeet (2)	3	0.01
Cherokee (3)	15	0.06
Chippewa (1)	1	<0.01
Choctaw (0)	1	<0.01
Creek (0)	1	<0.01
Iroquois (1)	1	<0.01
Menominee (0)	1	<0.01
Mexican American Ind. (3)	3	0.01
Navajo (2)	2	0.01
Potawatomi (1)	1	<0.01
Sioux (1)	5	0.02
Asian (6,527)	6,933	29.79
Not Hispanic (6,498)	6,884	29.58
Hispanic (29)	49	0.21
Bangladeshi (18)	23	0.10
Burmese (8)	14	0.06
Cambodian (24)	31	0.13
Chinese, ex. Taiwanese (500)	576	2.48
Filipino (1,713)	1,835	7.89
Indian (2,182)	2,309	9.92
Indonesian (9)	9	0.04
Japanese (101)	138	0.59
Korean (1,029)	1,069	4.59
Laotian (2)	2	0.01
Malaysian (0)	1	<0.01
Nepalese (5)	5	0.02
Pakistani (412)	466	2.00
Sri Lankan (2)	5	0.02
Taiwanese (41)	50	0.21
Thai (78)	89	0.38
Vietnamese (205)	237	1.02
Hawaii Native/Pacific Islander (10)	33	0.14
Not Hispanic (9)	30	0.13
Hispanic (1)	3	0.01
Guamanian/Chamorro (0)	1	<0.01
Native Hawaiian (0)	2	0.01
Samoan (1)	1	<0.01
Tongan (0)	5	0.02
White (15,402)	15,867	68.19
Not Hispanic (14,426)	14,795	63.58
Hispanic (976)	1,072	4.61

Morton

Place Type: Village
County: Tazewell
Population: 16,267†

Ancestry‡	Population	%
Afghan (12)	12	0.08
American (1,834)	1,834	11.47
Arab (45)	54	0.34
Lebanese (45)	54	0.34
Belgian (80)	117	0.73
British (35)	50	0.31
Bulgarian (25)	39	0.24
Canadian (0)	14	0.09
Croatian (11)	60	0.38
Czech (0)	98	0.61
Czechoslovakian (0)	64	0.40
Danish (0)	53	0.33
Dutch (42)	336	2.10
English (844)	2,418	15.13
European (214)	240	1.50
French, ex. Basque (36)	677	4.23
French Canadian (0)	12	0.08
German (3,459)	6,824	42.69
Greek (10)	58	0.36
Hungarian (64)	139	0.87
Irish (487)	2,042	12.77
Italian (243)	643	4.02
Lithuanian (15)	22	0.14
Northern European (11)	11	0.07
Norwegian (112)	174	1.09
Pennsylvania German (7)	31	0.19
Polish (126)	527	3.30
Romanian (0)	11	0.07
Russian (10)	10	0.06
Scandinavian (12)	23	0.14
Scotch-Irish (52)	163	1.02
Scottish (52)	301	1.88
Serbian (11)	11	0.07
Slovak (0)	24	0.15
Slovene (0)	27	0.17
Swedish (141)	393	2.46
Swiss (21)	297	1.86
Welsh (12)	112	0.70
Yugoslavian (9)	22	0.14

Hispanic Origin	Population	%
Hispanic or Latino (of any race)	271	1.67
Central American, ex. Mexican	8	0.05
Guatemalan	6	0.04
Nicaraguan	1	0.01
Salvadoran	1	0.01
Cuban	9	0.06
Dominican Republic	2	0.01
Mexican	183	1.12
Puerto Rican	22	0.14
South American	15	0.09
Chilean	4	0.02
Colombian	3	0.02
Ecuadorian	5	0.03
Peruvian	2	0.01
Venezuelan	1	0.01
Other Hispanic or Latino	32	0.20

Race*	Population	%
African-American/Black (112)	166	1.02
Not Hispanic (110)	160	0.98
Hispanic (2)	6	0.04
American Indian/Alaska Native (30)	66	0.41
Not Hispanic (29)	64	0.39
Hispanic (1)	2	0.01
Apache (2)	4	0.02
Blackfeet (0)	1	0.01
Cherokee (2)	17	0.10
Chickasaw (2)	3	0.02
Chippewa (0)	1	0.01
Choctaw (1)	3	0.02
Comanche (0)	1	0.01
Creek (0)	3	0.02

*Notes: † The Census 2010 population figure is used to calculate the percentages in the Hispanic Origin and Race categories. Ancestry percentages are based on the 2006-2010 American Community Survey population (not shown); ‡ Numbers in parentheses indicate the number of people reporting a single ancestry; * Numbers in parentheses indicate the number of persons reporting this race alone, not in combination with any other race; Please refer to the Explanation of Data for more information.*

Iroquois (1)	1	0.01
Potawatomi (1)	2	0.01
Sioux (1)	5	0.03
Asian (210)	264	1.62
Not Hispanic (208)	257	1.58
Hispanic (2)	7	0.04
Burmese (1)	2	0.01
Chinese, ex. Taiwanese (46)	56	0.34
Filipino (28)	41	0.25
Indian (83)	90	0.55
Indonesian (1)	1	0.01
Japanese (4)	11	0.07
Korean (23)	32	0.20
Malaysian (1)	1	0.01
Pakistani (2)	2	0.01
Taiwanese (1)	1	0.01
Thai (2)	2	0.01
Vietnamese (12)	21	0.13
Hawaii Native/Pacific Islander (3)	10	0.06
Not Hispanic (3)	10	0.06
Guamanian/Chamorro (0)	4	0.02
Native Hawaiian (3)	6	0.04
White (15,661)	15,814	97.22
Not Hispanic (15,488)	15,622	96.03
Hispanic (173)	192	1.18

Mount Prospect

Place Type: Village
County: Cook
Population: 54,167†

Ancestry‡	Population	%
African, Sub-Saharan (91)	120	0.22
African (81)	110	0.20
Other Sub-Saharan African (10)	10	0.02
Albanian (84)	95	0.18
Alsatian (14)	29	0.05
American (1,106)	1,106	2.05
Arab (139)	191	0.35
Arab (53)	80	0.15
Egyptian (18)	18	0.03
Lebanese (45)	54	0.10
Palestinian (0)	16	0.03
Other Arab (23)	23	0.04
Armenian (111)	223	0.41
Assyrian/Chaldean/Syriac (307)	355	0.66
Austrian (71)	361	0.67
Belgian (11)	39	0.07
Brazilian (14)	30	0.06
British (42)	131	0.24
Bulgarian (902)	926	1.72
Canadian (11)	85	0.16
Croatian (129)	301	0.56
Czech (176)	831	1.54
Czechoslovakian (67)	81	0.15
Danish (27)	314	0.58
Dutch (125)	667	1.24
Eastern European (67)	73	0.14
English (401)	1,958	3.64
European (357)	357	0.66
Finnish (9)	9	0.02
French, ex. Basque (65)	891	1.65
French Canadian (37)	114	0.21
German (3,286)	11,827	21.97
Greek (846)	1,303	2.42
Hungarian (142)	353	0.66
Icelander (0)	9	0.02
Iranian (65)	82	0.15
Irish (1,474)	6,885	12.79
Italian (2,263)	5,061	9.40
Latvian (26)	34	0.06
Lithuanian (207)	369	0.69
Luxemburger (0)	23	0.04
Macedonian (8)	8	0.01
Northern European (61)	61	0.11
Norwegian (173)	983	1.83
Pennsylvania German (0)	13	0.02
Polish (5,687)	9,709	18.03
Portuguese (13)	13	0.02
Romanian (319)	474	0.88
Russian (119)	712	1.32
Scandinavian (33)	46	0.09
Scotch-Irish (149)	456	0.85
Scottish (106)	510	0.95
Serbian (103)	111	0.21
Slavic (0)	22	0.04
Slovak (80)	161	0.30
Slovene (0)	33	0.06
Swedish (438)	1,525	2.83
Swiss (10)	83	0.15
Turkish (160)	160	0.30
Ukrainian (199)	335	0.62
Welsh (29)	386	0.72
West Indian, ex. Hispanic (318)	331	0.61
Haitian (295)	308	0.57
Jamaican (23)	23	0.04
Yugoslavian (207)	244	0.45

Hispanic Origin	Population	%
Hispanic or Latino (of any race)	8,408	15.52
Central American, ex. Mexican	310	0.57
Costa Rican	4	0.01
Guatemalan	137	0.25
Honduran	18	0.03
Nicaraguan	17	0.03
Panamanian	13	0.02
Salvadoran	115	0.21
Other Central American	6	0.01
Cuban	170	0.31
Dominican Republic	14	0.03
Mexican	6,932	12.80
Puerto Rican	452	0.83
South American	319	0.59
Argentinean	22	0.04
Bolivian	10	0.02
Chilean	15	0.03
Colombian	93	0.17
Ecuadorian	89	0.16
Paraguayan	2	<0.01
Peruvian	65	0.12
Uruguayan	2	<0.01
Venezuelan	16	0.03
Other South American	5	0.01
Other Hispanic or Latino	211	0.39

Race*	Population	%
African-American/Black (1,282)	1,506	2.78
Not Hispanic (1,230)	1,409	2.60
Hispanic (52)	97	0.18
American Indian/Alaska Native (196)	359	0.66
Not Hispanic (47)	169	0.31
Hispanic (149)	190	0.35
Apache (1)	1	<0.01
Blackfeet (0)	5	0.01
Central American Ind. (0)	1	<0.01
Cherokee (1)	28	0.05
Chippewa (2)	9	0.02
Choctaw (0)	2	<0.01
Comanche (1)	1	<0.01
Creek (0)	1	<0.01
Crow (0)	1	<0.01
Iroquois (3)	6	0.01
Menominee (1)	1	<0.01
Mexican American Ind. (12)	20	0.04
Navajo (0)	1	<0.01
Ottawa (1)	1	<0.01
Potawatomi (2)	3	0.01
Seminole (0)	1	<0.01
Sioux (1)	3	0.01
South American Ind. (3)	4	0.01
Spanish American Ind. (0)	1	<0.01
Yaqui (0)	3	0.01
Asian (6,339)	6,844	12.63
Not Hispanic (6,312)	6,782	12.52
Hispanic (27)	62	0.11
Bangladeshi (9)	10	0.02
Burmese (4)	4	0.01
Cambodian (18)	21	0.04
Chinese, ex. Taiwanese (384)	474	0.88
Filipino (857)	1,007	1.86
Hmong (1)	1	<0.01
Indian (3,183)	3,314	6.12
Indonesian (9)	10	0.02
Japanese (229)	306	0.56
Korean (1,047)	1,101	2.03
Laotian (11)	12	0.02
Malaysian (6)	6	0.01
Nepalese (8)	8	0.01
Pakistani (147)	173	0.32
Taiwanese (20)	22	0.04
Thai (28)	37	0.07
Vietnamese (141)	157	0.29
Hawaii Native/Pacific Islander (16)	67	0.12
Not Hispanic (11)	49	0.09
Hispanic (5)	18	0.03
Guamanian/Chamorro (6)	18	0.03
Native Hawaiian (6)	19	0.04
Samoan (1)	2	<0.01
White (41,715)	42,591	78.63
Not Hispanic (37,355)	37,930	70.02
Hispanic (4,360)	4,661	8.60

Mount Vernon

Place Type: City
County: Jefferson
Population: 15,277†

Ancestry‡	Population	%
African, Sub-Saharan (12)	12	0.08
African (12)	12	0.08
American (1,393)	1,393	9.28
Australian (0)	15	0.10
Belgian (9)	9	0.06
British (9)	20	0.13
Bulgarian (0)	38	0.25
Canadian (0)	42	0.28
Croatian (4)	10	0.07
Czech (8)	43	0.29
Czechoslovakian (45)	45	0.30
Danish (0)	34	0.23
Dutch (22)	265	1.77
English (924)	1,929	12.86
European (70)	70	0.47
French, ex. Basque (39)	415	2.77
French Canadian (4)	62	0.41
German (1,252)	3,636	24.24
Greek (10)	36	0.24
Hungarian (0)	10	0.07
Irish (547)	2,287	15.24
Italian (99)	425	2.83
Northern European (0)	8	0.05
Norwegian (27)	65	0.43
Pennsylvania German (0)	7	0.05
Polish (68)	128	0.85
Romanian (18)	18	0.12
Russian (10)	10	0.07
Scandinavian (0)	3	0.02
Scotch-Irish (133)	243	1.62
Scottish (145)	364	2.43
Slavic (0)	25	0.17
Swedish (16)	124	0.83
Swiss (10)	39	0.26
Welsh (10)	80	0.53
West Indian, ex. Hispanic (7)	7	0.05
Jamaican (7)	7	0.05
Yugoslavian (16)	16	0.11

Hispanic Origin	Population	%
Hispanic or Latino (of any race)	369	2.42
Central American, ex. Mexican	14	0.09
Guatemalan	1	0.01
Honduran	2	0.01
Panamanian	5	0.03
Salvadoran	6	0.04
Cuban	4	0.03
Dominican Republic	1	0.01
Mexican	189	1.24
Puerto Rican	100	0.65

SECTION TWO

*Notes: † The Census 2010 population figure is used to calculate the percentages in the Hispanic Origin and Race categories. Ancestry percentages are based on the 2006-2010 American Community Survey population (not shown); ‡ Numbers in parentheses indicate the number of people reporting a single ancestry; * Numbers in parentheses indicate the number of persons reporting this race alone, not in combination with any other race; Please refer to the Explanation of Data for more information.*

South American	9	0.06
Colombian	2	0.01
Ecuadorian	5	0.03
Peruvian	2	0.01
Other Hispanic or Latino	52	0.34

Race*	Population	%
African-American/Black (2,250)	2,516	16.47
Not Hispanic (2,203)	2,443	15.99
Hispanic (47)	73	0.48
American Indian/Alaska Native (42)	126	0.82
Not Hispanic (34)	109	0.71
Hispanic (8)	17	0.11
Apache (2)	5	0.03
Blackfeet (0)	5	0.03
Cherokee (9)	43	0.28
Chippewa (1)	1	0.01
Choctaw (1)	1	0.01
Cree (0)	1	0.01
Creek (1)	2	0.01
Iroquois (1)	2	0.01
Mexican American Ind. (0)	1	0.01
Pima (0)	1	0.01
Ute (0)	2	0.01
Asian (160)	199	1.30
Not Hispanic (160)	198	1.30
Hispanic (0)	1	0.01
Chinese, ex. Taiwanese (19)	24	0.16
Filipino (29)	46	0.30
Hmong (7)	7	0.05
Indian (58)	68	0.45
Japanese (2)	10	0.07
Korean (13)	17	0.11
Laotian (2)	4	0.03
Pakistani (5)	5	0.03
Taiwanese (6)	6	0.04
Thai (1)	1	0.01
Vietnamese (12)	12	0.08
Hawaii Native/Pacific Islander (4)	17	0.11
Not Hispanic (4)	16	0.10
Hispanic (0)	1	0.01
Native Hawaiian (4)	14	0.09
Samoan (0)	2	0.01
White (12,315)	12,688	83.05
Not Hispanic (12,138)	12,467	81.61
Hispanic (177)	221	1.45

Mundelein

Place Type: Village
County: Lake
Population: 31,064†

Ancestry‡	Population	%
African, Sub-Saharan (58)	73	0.23
African (21)	36	0.12
Nigerian (8)	8	0.03
Other Sub-Saharan African (29)	29	0.09
American (1,909)	1,909	6.13
Arab (37)	56	0.18
Lebanese (0)	19	0.06
Syrian (37)	37	0.12
Assyrian/Chaldean/Syriac (18)	27	0.09
Austrian (9)	98	0.31
Basque (17)	31	0.10
Belgian (19)	37	0.12
British (12)	63	0.20
Bulgarian (155)	155	0.50
Canadian (19)	55	0.18
Croatian (60)	70	0.22
Czech (42)	386	1.24
Czechoslovakian (19)	31	0.10
Danish (22)	312	1.00
Dutch (92)	305	0.98
English (244)	1,553	4.99
Estonian (11)	11	0.04
European (161)	192	0.62
Finnish (48)	98	0.31
French, ex. Basque (52)	831	2.67
French Canadian (19)	92	0.30
German (1,449)	5,957	19.13
Greek (194)	448	1.44
Hungarian (0)	50	0.16
Iranian (48)	99	0.32
Irish (660)	3,377	10.84
Italian (696)	1,991	6.39
Latvian (132)	229	0.74
Lithuanian (43)	104	0.33
Luxemburger (0)	30	0.10
Macedonian (0)	11	0.04
Maltese (14)	14	0.04
Norwegian (155)	517	1.66
Polish (1,106)	2,885	9.26
Portuguese (0)	10	0.03
Romanian (280)	326	1.05
Russian (732)	1,029	3.30
Scandinavian (44)	90	0.29
Scotch-Irish (58)	190	0.61
Scottish (139)	318	1.02
Serbian (11)	64	0.21
Slovak (32)	66	0.21
Slovene (38)	90	0.29
Swedish (129)	781	2.51
Swiss (17)	130	0.42
Ukrainian (87)	188	0.60
Welsh (28)	150	0.48
Yugoslavian (7)	7	0.02

Hispanic Origin	Population	%
Hispanic or Latino (of any race)	9,344	30.08
Central American, ex. Mexican	254	0.82
Costa Rican	2	0.01
Guatemalan	95	0.31
Honduran	35	0.11
Nicaraguan	4	0.01
Panamanian	2	0.01
Salvadoran	115	0.37
Other Central American	1	<0.01
Cuban	56	0.18
Dominican Republic	10	0.03
Mexican	8,353	26.89
Puerto Rican	256	0.82
South American	223	0.72
Argentinean	16	0.05
Bolivian	7	0.02
Chilean	12	0.04
Colombian	103	0.33
Ecuadorian	25	0.08
Paraguayan	1	<0.01
Peruvian	42	0.14
Uruguayan	2	0.01
Venezuelan	13	0.04
Other South American	2	0.01
Other Hispanic or Latino	192	0.62

Race*	Population	%
African-American/Black (471)	597	1.92
Not Hispanic (416)	504	1.62
Hispanic (55)	93	0.30
American Indian/Alaska Native (203)	330	1.06
Not Hispanic (28)	97	0.31
Hispanic (175)	233	0.75
Apache (2)	3	0.01
Blackfeet (1)	2	0.01
Cherokee (4)	21	0.07
Chippewa (3)	8	0.03
Choctaw (1)	3	0.01
Creek (0)	2	0.01
Crow (0)	2	0.01
Iroquois (0)	5	0.02
Mexican American Ind. (56)	62	0.20
Navajo (2)	4	0.01
Ottawa (1)	1	<0.01
Sioux (2)	11	0.04
South American Ind. (2)	5	0.02
Spanish American Ind. (1)	1	<0.01
Asian (2,724)	3,014	9.70
Not Hispanic (2,719)	2,964	9.54
Hispanic (5)	50	0.16
Bangladeshi (5)	6	0.02
Cambodian (44)	49	0.16
Chinese, ex. Taiwanese (372)	438	1.41
Filipino (646)	761	2.45
Indian (885)	925	2.98
Indonesian (4)	7	0.02
Japanese (59)	102	0.33
Korean (472)	509	1.64
Laotian (3)	3	0.01
Malaysian (1)	3	0.01
Nepalese (4)	4	0.01
Pakistani (47)	48	0.15
Sri Lankan (7)	7	0.02
Taiwanese (25)	32	0.10
Thai (15)	21	0.07
Vietnamese (74)	92	0.30
Hawaii Native/Pacific Islander (10)	33	0.11
Not Hispanic (6)	26	0.08
Hispanic (4)	7	0.02
Guamanian/Chamorro (1)	1	<0.01
Native Hawaiian (5)	14	0.05
Samoan (3)	5	0.02
White (22,457)	23,134	74.47
Not Hispanic (18,123)	18,462	59.43
Hispanic (4,334)	4,672	15.04

Murphysboro

Place Type: City
County: Jackson
Population: 7,970†

Ancestry‡	Population	%
African, Sub-Saharan (112)	112	1.34
African (112)	112	1.34
American (698)	698	8.33
Czech (11)	24	0.29
Dutch (115)	209	2.50
English (208)	639	7.63
European (12)	12	0.14
French, ex. Basque (61)	248	2.96
French Canadian (22)	60	0.72
German (937)	2,161	25.80
Greek (0)	29	0.35
Hungarian (0)	11	0.13
Irish (268)	1,220	14.57
Italian (197)	359	4.29
Lithuanian (0)	42	0.50
Norwegian (16)	16	0.19
Polish (28)	36	0.43
Portuguese (0)	10	0.12
Russian (22)	33	0.39
Scandinavian (0)	10	0.12
Scotch-Irish (28)	94	1.12
Scottish (9)	60	0.72
Swedish (22)	50	0.60
Ukrainian (0)	27	0.32
Welsh (20)	68	0.81
West Indian, ex. Hispanic (0)	90	1.07
West Indian (0)	90	1.07

Hispanic Origin	Population	%
Hispanic or Latino (of any race)	236	2.96
Central American, ex. Mexican	16	0.20
Costa Rican	1	0.01
Guatemalan	8	0.10
Honduran	1	0.01
Nicaraguan	1	0.01
Panamanian	3	0.04
Salvadoran	1	0.01
Other Central American	1	0.01
Cuban	2	0.03
Mexican	166	2.08
Puerto Rican	24	0.30
South American	7	0.09
Colombian	2	0.03
Ecuadorian	5	0.06
Other Hispanic or Latino	21	0.26

Race*	Population	%
African-American/Black (1,216)	1,363	17.10

*Notes: † The Census 2010 population figure is used to calculate the percentages in the Hispanic Origin and Race categories. Ancestry percentages are based on the 2006-2010 American Community Survey population (not shown); ‡ Numbers in parentheses indicate the number of people reporting a single ancestry; * Numbers in parentheses indicate the number of persons reporting this race alone, not in combination with any other race; Please refer to the Explanation of Data for more information.*

Not Hispanic (1,206)	1,346	16.89
Hispanic (10)	17	0.21
American Indian/Alaska Native (32)	103	1.29
Not Hispanic (23)	92	1.15
Hispanic (9)	11	0.14
Aleut *(Alaska Native)* (1)	1	0.01
Apache (0)	4	0.05
Arapaho (0)	1	0.01
Blackfeet (0)	1	0.01
Canadian/French Am. Ind. (0)	1	0.01
Central American Ind. (0)	1	0.01
Cherokee (10)	50	0.63
Cheyenne (0)	4	0.05
Chickasaw (0)	1	0.01
Chippewa (1)	3	0.04
Choctaw (0)	1	0.01
Iroquois (0)	1	0.01
Mexican American Ind. (1)	2	0.03
Navajo (1)	1	0.01
Asian (43)	64	0.80
Not Hispanic (42)	62	0.78
Hispanic (1)	2	0.03
Chinese, ex. Taiwanese (1)	3	0.04
Filipino (3)	10	0.13
Indian (13)	16	0.20
Japanese (6)	9	0.11
Korean (5)	6	0.08
Malaysian (2)	2	0.03
Pakistani (2)	2	0.03
Sri Lankan (0)	1	0.01
Taiwanese (2)	2	0.03
Thai (2)	4	0.05
Vietnamese (1)	1	0.01
Hawaii Native/Pacific Islander (1)	8	0.10
Not Hispanic (1)	8	0.10
Guamanian/Chamorro (0)	1	0.01
Native Hawaiian (0)	2	0.03
Samoan (0)	2	0.03
White (6,360)	6,570	82.43
Not Hispanic (6,247)	6,441	80.82
Hispanic (113)	129	1.62

Naperville

Place Type: City
County: DuPage
Population: 141,853†

Ancestry‡	Population	%
African, Sub-Saharan (460)	634	0.45
African (108)	135	0.10
Ghanaian (110)	110	0.08
Kenyan (18)	55	0.04
Nigerian (91)	133	0.09
South African (125)	179	0.13
Other Sub-Saharan African (8)	22	0.02
Albanian (60)	60	0.04
Alsatian (32)	59	0.04
American (3,568)	3,568	2.53
Arab (1,209)	1,759	1.25
Arab (157)	266	0.19
Egyptian (143)	157	0.11
Jordanian (0)	42	0.03
Lebanese (209)	367	0.26
Moroccan (182)	235	0.17
Palestinian (294)	336	0.24
Syrian (15)	89	0.06
Other Arab (209)	267	0.19
Armenian (23)	108	0.08
Assyrian/Chaldean/Syriac (56)	74	0.05
Australian (65)	114	0.08
Austrian (44)	666	0.47
Belgian (66)	443	0.31
Brazilian (119)	313	0.22
British (389)	1,104	0.78
Bulgarian (55)	62	0.04
Cajun (0)	14	0.01
Canadian (480)	734	0.52
Celtic (0)	9	0.01
Croatian (290)	1,020	0.72
Czech (809)	3,566	2.53
Czechoslovakian (116)	266	0.19
Danish (107)	1,049	0.74
Dutch (508)	2,210	1.57
Eastern European (210)	278	0.20
English (2,285)	12,476	8.86
European (2,330)	2,659	1.89
Finnish (78)	379	0.27
French, ex. Basque (481)	3,333	2.37
French Canadian (129)	768	0.55
German (7,562)	32,930	23.38
Greek (931)	1,872	1.33
Guyanese (116)	116	0.08
Hungarian (256)	798	0.57
Icelander (9)	31	0.02
Iranian (461)	510	0.36
Irish (5,996)	25,848	18.35
Italian (3,586)	14,744	10.47
Latvian (46)	283	0.20
Lithuanian (879)	2,734	1.94
Luxemburger (24)	92	0.07
Macedonian (282)	295	0.21
Maltese (13)	64	0.05
New Zealander (13)	13	0.01
Northern European (71)	71	0.05
Norwegian (470)	2,831	2.01
Pennsylvania German (10)	18	0.01
Polish (4,945)	15,623	11.09
Portuguese (25)	169	0.12
Romanian (91)	331	0.24
Russian (730)	1,979	1.41
Scandinavian (182)	324	0.23
Scotch-Irish (767)	2,240	1.59
Scottish (504)	2,657	1.89
Serbian (92)	301	0.21
Slavic (0)	20	0.01
Slovak (340)	1,015	0.72
Slovene (0)	178	0.13
Swedish (861)	4,354	3.09
Swiss (62)	647	0.46
Turkish (102)	112	0.08
Ukrainian (459)	915	0.65
Welsh (129)	847	0.60
West Indian, ex. Hispanic (63)	121	0.09
Bahamian (21)	21	0.01
Jamaican (30)	46	0.03
Trinidadian/Tobagonian (12)	54	0.04
Yugoslavian (21)	77	0.05

Hispanic Origin	Population	%
Hispanic or Latino (of any race)	7,574	5.34
Central American, ex. Mexican	320	0.23
Costa Rican	26	0.02
Guatemalan	135	0.10
Honduran	42	0.03
Nicaraguan	31	0.02
Panamanian	35	0.02
Salvadoran	49	0.03
Other Central American	2	<0.01
Cuban	286	0.20
Dominican Republic	66	0.05
Mexican	4,767	3.36
Puerto Rican	853	0.60
South American	798	0.56
Argentinean	111	0.08
Bolivian	27	0.02
Chilean	65	0.05
Colombian	262	0.18
Ecuadorian	96	0.07
Paraguayan	9	0.01
Peruvian	109	0.08
Uruguayan	9	0.01
Venezuelan	108	0.08
Other South American	2	<0.01
Other Hispanic or Latino	484	0.34

Race*	Population	%
African-American/Black (6,612)	7,463	5.26
Not Hispanic (6,504)	7,225	5.09
Hispanic (108)	238	0.17
American Indian/Alaska Native (212)	688	0.49
Not Hispanic (122)	497	0.35
Hispanic (90)	191	0.13
Alaska Athabascan *(Ala. Nat.)* (1)	1	<0.01
Apache (3)	15	0.01
Arapaho (0)	1	<0.01
Blackfeet (0)	10	0.01
Canadian/French Am. Ind. (0)	2	<0.01
Central American Ind. (6)	8	0.01
Cherokee (31)	161	0.11
Chickasaw (0)	4	<0.01
Chippewa (2)	21	0.01
Choctaw (5)	12	0.01
Creek (0)	3	<0.01
Inupiat *(Alaska Native)* (2)	2	<0.01
Iroquois (4)	12	0.01
Lumbee (0)	3	<0.01
Mexican American Ind. (11)	27	0.02
Navajo (4)	17	0.01
Osage (3)	7	<0.01
Potawatomi (4)	4	<0.01
Pueblo (3)	3	<0.01
Puget Sound Salish (0)	1	<0.01
Seminole (1)	6	<0.01
Sioux (7)	20	0.01
South American Ind. (2)	7	<0.01
Spanish American Ind. (1)	1	<0.01
Ute (0)	5	<0.01
Yup'ik *(Alaska Native)* (0)	1	<0.01
Asian (21,170)	23,042	16.24
Not Hispanic (21,094)	22,868	16.12
Hispanic (76)	174	0.12
Bangladeshi (71)	77	0.05
Bhutanese (1)	1	<0.01
Burmese (17)	25	0.02
Cambodian (13)	24	0.02
Chinese, ex. Taiwanese (4,966)	5,487	3.87
Filipino (1,287)	1,716	1.21
Hmong (2)	2	<0.01
Indian (10,469)	10,917	7.70
Indonesian (31)	49	0.03
Japanese (252)	480	0.34
Korean (1,661)	1,864	1.31
Laotian (14)	28	0.02
Malaysian (13)	16	0.01
Nepalese (15)	15	0.01
Pakistani (968)	1,060	0.75
Sri Lankan (53)	62	0.04
Taiwanese (503)	597	0.42
Thai (73)	116	0.08
Vietnamese (277)	332	0.23
Hawaii Native/Pacific Islander (32)	146	0.10
Not Hispanic (32)	136	0.10
Hispanic (0)	10	0.01
Fijian (4)	7	<0.01
Guamanian/Chamorro (5)	14	0.01
Native Hawaiian (6)	43	0.03
Samoan (1)	10	0.01
Tongan (1)	3	<0.01
White (108,447)	111,144	78.35
Not Hispanic (103,603)	105,833	74.61
Hispanic (4,844)	5,311	3.74

New Lenox

Place Type: Village
County: Will
Population: 24,394†

Ancestry‡	Population	%
American (337)	337	1.41
Armenian (0)	16	0.07
Australian (0)	14	0.06
Austrian (57)	104	0.43
Belgian (0)	133	0.56
British (100)	115	0.48
Canadian (14)	14	0.06
Croatian (109)	407	1.70
Czech (129)	711	2.97
Czechoslovakian (26)	68	0.28

*Notes: † The Census 2010 population figure is used to calculate the percentages in the Hispanic Origin and Race categories. Ancestry percentages are based on the 2006-2010 American Community Survey population (not shown); ‡ Numbers in parentheses indicate the number of people reporting a single ancestry; * Numbers in parentheses indicate the number of persons reporting this race alone, not in combination with any other race; Please refer to the Explanation of Data for more information.*

Ancestry (continued)	Population	%
Danish (8)	91	0.38
Dutch (331)	911	3.80
Eastern European (40)	40	0.17
English (436)	1,770	7.39
European (186)	186	0.78
Finnish (0)	66	0.28
French, ex. Basque (15)	747	3.12
French Canadian (36)	136	0.57
German (2,120)	7,959	33.24
Greek (173)	361	1.51
Hungarian (33)	162	0.68
Icelander (0)	55	0.23
Irish (1,207)	6,186	25.83
Italian (1,114)	4,377	18.28
Lithuanian (181)	735	3.07
Luxemburger (0)	24	0.10
Norwegian (71)	261	1.09
Pennsylvania German (0)	14	0.06
Polish (1,131)	4,463	18.64
Russian (35)	279	1.17
Scandinavian (32)	84	0.35
Scotch-Irish (79)	268	1.12
Scottish (56)	304	1.27
Serbian (11)	33	0.14
Slavic (0)	27	0.11
Slovak (145)	266	1.11
Slovene (11)	19	0.08
Swedish (225)	1,248	5.21
Swiss (21)	118	0.49
Ukrainian (0)	59	0.25
Welsh (11)	79	0.33
Yugoslavian (11)	28	0.12

Hispanic Origin	Population	%
Hispanic or Latino (of any race)	1,396	5.72
Central American, ex. Mexican	20	0.08
Guatemalan	15	0.06
Honduran	4	0.02
Nicaraguan	1	<0.01
Cuban	32	0.13
Dominican Republic	4	0.02
Mexican	1,129	4.63
Puerto Rican	107	0.44
South American	34	0.14
Bolivian	4	0.02
Colombian	16	0.07
Paraguayan	3	0.01
Peruvian	10	0.04
Other South American	1	<0.01
Other Hispanic or Latino	70	0.29

Race*	Population	%
African-American/Black (165)	237	0.97
Not Hispanic (158)	224	0.92
Hispanic (7)	13	0.05
American Indian/Alaska Native (45)	124	0.51
Not Hispanic (23)	90	0.37
Hispanic (22)	34	0.14
Apache (2)	2	0.01
Blackfeet (0)	3	0.01
Cherokee (2)	29	0.12
Chippewa (0)	11	0.05
Choctaw (0)	2	0.01
Hopi (0)	2	0.01
Iroquois (6)	10	0.04
Kiowa (1)	2	0.01
Mexican American Ind. (6)	6	0.02
Sioux (2)	6	0.02
South American Ind. (3)	10	0.04
Asian (186)	271	1.11
Not Hispanic (180)	257	1.05
Hispanic (6)	14	0.06
Bangladeshi (1)	2	0.01
Burmese (2)	3	0.01
Chinese, ex. Taiwanese (52)	76	0.31
Filipino (36)	70	0.29
Indian (19)	25	0.10
Japanese (9)	26	0.11
Korean (27)	43	0.18
Malaysian (1)	1	<0.01
Taiwanese (1)	3	0.01
Thai (5)	6	0.02
Vietnamese (23)	24	0.10
Hawaii Native/Pacific Islander (1)	11	0.05
Not Hispanic (1)	11	0.05
Guamanian/Chamorro (0)	1	<0.01
Native Hawaiian (1)	6	0.02
White (23,473)	23,738	97.31
Not Hispanic (22,432)	22,627	92.76
Hispanic (1,041)	1,111	4.55

Niles

Place Type: Village
County: Cook
Population: 29,803†

Ancestry‡	Population	%
African, Sub-Saharan (180)	180	0.61
African (21)	21	0.07
Nigerian (159)	159	0.54
Albanian (0)	21	0.07
American (376)	376	1.28
Arab (525)	765	2.60
Arab (28)	55	0.19
Iraqi (249)	391	1.33
Jordanian (90)	90	0.31
Lebanese (71)	133	0.45
Moroccan (0)	9	0.03
Palestinian (23)	23	0.08
Syrian (64)	64	0.22
Armenian (121)	121	0.41
Assyrian/Chaldean/Syriac (1,236)	1,483	5.03
Austrian (61)	168	0.57
Belgian (10)	10	0.03
British (0)	7	0.02
Canadian (0)	18	0.06
Croatian (29)	48	0.16
Czech (58)	220	0.75
Czechoslovakian (0)	27	0.09
Danish (47)	69	0.23
Dutch (27)	103	0.35
English (96)	600	2.04
European (15)	29	0.10
Finnish (33)	45	0.15
French, ex. Basque (39)	452	1.53
French Canadian (0)	18	0.06
German (1,362)	3,430	11.64
Greek (967)	1,107	3.76
Hungarian (43)	122	0.41
Icelander (26)	78	0.26
Iranian (20)	41	0.14
Irish (837)	2,263	7.68
Israeli (19)	19	0.06
Italian (1,245)	1,938	6.58
Latvian (9)	9	0.03
Lithuanian (0)	41	0.14
Luxemburger (13)	58	0.20
Northern European (7)	7	0.02
Norwegian (38)	205	0.70
Polish (5,076)	6,747	22.90
Portuguese (0)	32	0.11
Romanian (327)	358	1.22
Russian (733)	915	3.11
Scotch-Irish (25)	65	0.22
Scottish (33)	83	0.28
Serbian (498)	498	1.69
Slavic (106)	120	0.41
Slovak (7)	53	0.18
Slovene (8)	37	0.13
Swedish (84)	389	1.32
Swiss (0)	10	0.03
Turkish (0)	20	0.07
Ukrainian (217)	235	0.80
Welsh (0)	12	0.04
West Indian, ex. Hispanic (0)	18	0.06
Belizean (0)	18	0.06
Yugoslavian (303)	327	1.11

Hispanic Origin	Population	%
Hispanic or Latino (of any race)	2,582	8.66
Central American, ex. Mexican	127	0.43
Costa Rican	2	0.01
Guatemalan	85	0.29
Honduran	15	0.05
Nicaraguan	1	<0.01
Panamanian	4	0.01
Salvadoran	19	0.06
Other Central American	1	<0.01
Cuban	87	0.29
Dominican Republic	14	0.05
Mexican	1,439	4.83
Puerto Rican	372	1.25
South American	402	1.35
Argentinean	12	0.04
Bolivian	24	0.08
Chilean	7	0.02
Colombian	94	0.32
Ecuadorian	203	0.68
Paraguayan	3	0.01
Peruvian	47	0.16
Uruguayan	2	0.01
Venezuelan	10	0.03
Other Hispanic or Latino	141	0.47

Race*	Population	%
African-American/Black (411)	494	1.66
Not Hispanic (388)	463	1.55
Hispanic (23)	31	0.10
American Indian/Alaska Native (33)	104	0.35
Not Hispanic (20)	74	0.25
Hispanic (13)	30	0.10
Blackfeet (1)	2	0.01
Cherokee (4)	14	0.05
Chippewa (0)	1	<0.01
Choctaw (2)	7	0.02
Iroquois (1)	1	<0.01
Mexican American Ind. (1)	4	0.01
Navajo (0)	2	0.01
Seminole (0)	3	0.01
Asian (4,977)	5,393	18.10
Not Hispanic (4,950)	5,332	17.89
Hispanic (27)	61	0.20
Bangladeshi (8)	13	0.04
Burmese (16)	18	0.06
Cambodian (6)	12	0.04
Chinese, ex. Taiwanese (254)	309	1.04
Filipino (1,351)	1,461	4.90
Indian (1,589)	1,711	5.74
Japanese (62)	82	0.28
Korean (909)	929	3.12
Laotian (5)	6	0.02
Nepalese (19)	20	0.07
Pakistani (376)	413	1.39
Taiwanese (13)	15	0.05
Thai (70)	81	0.27
Vietnamese (107)	123	0.41
Hawaii Native/Pacific Islander (8)	30	0.10
Not Hispanic (1)	21	0.07
Hispanic (7)	9	0.03
Guamanian/Chamorro (4)	5	0.02
Native Hawaiian (0)	1	<0.01
Samoan (0)	2	0.01
White (22,728)	23,180	77.78
Not Hispanic (21,332)	21,666	72.70
Hispanic (1,396)	1,514	5.08

Normal

Place Type: Town
County: McLean
Population: 52,497†

Ancestry‡	Population	%
African, Sub-Saharan (330)	388	0.75
African (159)	208	0.40
Ethiopian (23)	23	0.04
Ghanaian (1)	1	<0.01
Nigerian (68)	68	0.13

*Notes: † The Census 2010 population figure is used to calculate the percentages in the Hispanic Origin and Race categories. Ancestry percentages are based on the 2006-2010 American Community Survey population (not shown); ‡ Numbers in parentheses indicate the number of people reporting a single ancestry; * Numbers in parentheses indicate the number of persons reporting this race alone, not in combination with any other race; Please refer to the Explanation of Data for more information.*

South African (0)	9	0.02
Other Sub-Saharan African (79)	79	0.15
Albanian (38)	38	0.07
Alsatian (0)	13	0.03
American (4,384)	4,384	8.49
Arab (17)	95	0.18
Lebanese (17)	95	0.18
Armenian (19)	46	0.09
Austrian (26)	145	0.28
Belgian (27)	162	0.31
British (39)	185	0.36
Canadian (29)	58	0.11
Croatian (29)	143	0.28
Czech (69)	455	0.88
Czechoslovakian (21)	63	0.12
Danish (47)	289	0.56
Dutch (242)	932	1.81
Eastern European (25)	25	0.05
English (1,446)	4,945	9.58
European (449)	494	0.96
Finnish (14)	47	0.09
French, ex. Basque (180)	1,299	2.52
French Canadian (52)	141	0.27
German (6,093)	16,582	32.13
Greek (116)	314	0.61
Hungarian (19)	210	0.41
Iranian (48)	48	0.09
Irish (2,206)	8,434	16.34
Israeli (0)	25	0.05
Italian (574)	3,057	5.92
Latvian (0)	17	0.03
Lithuanian (24)	110	0.21
Northern European (14)	14	0.03
Norwegian (351)	988	1.91
Pennsylvania German (0)	34	0.07
Polish (589)	2,606	5.05
Romanian (17)	81	0.16
Russian (105)	285	0.55
Scandinavian (16)	52	0.10
Scotch-Irish (312)	905	1.75
Scottish (388)	1,129	2.19
Slavic (0)	12	0.02
Slovak (22)	201	0.39
Slovene (0)	101	0.20
Swedish (341)	1,314	2.55
Swiss (61)	392	0.76
Turkish (18)	44	0.09
Ukrainian (16)	75	0.15
Welsh (86)	342	0.66
West Indian, ex. Hispanic (36)	36	0.07
Barbadian (13)	13	0.03
Jamaican (8)	8	0.02
West Indian (15)	15	0.03

Hispanic Origin	Population	%
Hispanic or Latino (of any race)	2,133	4.06
Central American, ex. Mexican	110	0.21
Costa Rican	9	0.02
Guatemalan	54	0.10
Honduran	14	0.03
Panamanian	10	0.02
Salvadoran	23	0.04
Cuban	62	0.12
Dominican Republic	22	0.04
Mexican	1,418	2.70
Puerto Rican	230	0.44
South American	140	0.27
Argentinean	15	0.03
Bolivian	6	0.01
Chilean	21	0.04
Colombian	51	0.10
Ecuadorian	13	0.02
Paraguayan	3	0.01
Peruvian	23	0.04
Uruguayan	1	<0.01
Venezuelan	7	0.01
Other Hispanic or Latino	151	0.29

Race*	Population	%
African-American/Black (4,257)	4,918	9.37
Not Hispanic (4,201)	4,796	9.14
Hispanic (56)	122	0.23
American Indian/Alaska Native (79)	273	0.52
Not Hispanic (59)	220	0.42
Hispanic (20)	53	0.10
Apache (4)	8	0.02
Blackfeet (2)	7	0.01
Canadian/French Am. Ind. (4)	4	0.01
Central American Ind. (1)	4	0.01
Cherokee (22)	82	0.16
Chippewa (3)	5	0.01
Choctaw (1)	11	0.02
Cree (1)	1	<0.01
Creek (1)	6	0.01
Iroquois (1)	2	<0.01
Mexican American Ind. (2)	7	0.01
Navajo (1)	3	0.01
Potawatomi (2)	4	0.01
Pueblo (0)	1	<0.01
Seminole (0)	3	0.01
Shoshone (0)	2	<0.01
Sioux (0)	1	<0.01
South American Ind. (0)	4	0.01
Tohono O'Odham (1)	1	<0.01
Yaqui (1)	1	<0.01
Yuman (0)	1	<0.01
Asian (1,687)	2,043	3.89
Not Hispanic (1,673)	2,002	3.81
Hispanic (14)	41	0.08
Bangladeshi (7)	7	0.01
Burmese (7)	9	0.02
Cambodian (2)	6	0.01
Chinese, ex. Taiwanese (317)	378	0.72
Filipino (128)	226	0.43
Indian (763)	806	1.54
Indonesian (1)	7	0.01
Japanese (66)	131	0.25
Korean (167)	216	0.41
Laotian (5)	7	0.01
Malaysian (1)	2	<0.01
Nepalese (22)	22	0.04
Pakistani (38)	42	0.08
Sri Lankan (16)	21	0.04
Taiwanese (11)	12	0.02
Thai (24)	35	0.07
Vietnamese (81)	101	0.19
Hawaii Native/Pacific Islander (23)	51	0.10
Not Hispanic (21)	42	0.08
Hispanic (2)	9	0.02
Fijian (2)	2	<0.01
Guamanian/Chamorro (3)	6	0.01
Native Hawaiian (9)	16	0.03
Samoan (6)	11	0.02
White (44,660)	45,768	87.18
Not Hispanic (43,313)	44,263	84.32
Hispanic (1,347)	1,505	2.87

Norridge

Place Type: Village
County: Cook
Population: 14,572†

Ancestry‡	Population	%
Albanian (55)	55	0.38
American (109)	109	0.76
Arab (26)	26	0.18
Palestinian (26)	26	0.18
Armenian (186)	186	1.29
Austrian (41)	87	0.60
Celtic (15)	15	0.10
Czech (21)	66	0.46
Czechoslovakian (0)	25	0.17
Dutch (18)	18	0.12
English (64)	264	1.83
European (65)	65	0.45
Finnish (0)	10	0.07
French, ex. Basque (22)	79	0.55
French Canadian (0)	5	0.03
German (639)	2,049	14.22
Greek (532)	719	4.99
Hungarian (0)	26	0.18
Irish (388)	1,417	9.83
Italian (2,289)	3,448	23.92
Lithuanian (41)	50	0.35
Macedonian (74)	74	0.51
Norwegian (8)	32	0.22
Polish (3,960)	5,070	35.17
Romanian (63)	170	1.18
Russian (42)	86	0.60
Scotch-Irish (10)	82	0.57
Scottish (0)	30	0.21
Serbian (22)	71	0.49
Slavic (15)	15	0.10
Slovak (21)	33	0.23
Slovene (0)	13	0.09
Swedish (128)	417	2.89
Swiss (10)	10	0.07
Ukrainian (106)	106	0.74
Welsh (0)	29	0.20
Yugoslavian (114)	137	0.95

Hispanic Origin	Population	%
Hispanic or Latino (of any race)	1,073	7.36
Central American, ex. Mexican	50	0.34
Costa Rican	1	0.01
Guatemalan	34	0.23
Honduran	2	0.01
Panamanian	1	0.01
Salvadoran	12	0.08
Cuban	33	0.23
Dominican Republic	13	0.09
Mexican	500	3.43
Puerto Rican	277	1.90
South American	129	0.89
Argentinean	25	0.17
Bolivian	4	0.03
Chilean	2	0.01
Colombian	34	0.23
Ecuadorian	49	0.34
Peruvian	13	0.09
Venezuelan	2	0.01
Other Hispanic or Latino	71	0.49

Race*	Population	%
African-American/Black (73)	86	0.59
Not Hispanic (63)	74	0.51
Hispanic (10)	12	0.08
American Indian/Alaska Native (18)	37	0.25
Not Hispanic (8)	22	0.15
Hispanic (10)	15	0.10
Blackfeet (0)	1	0.01
Cherokee (1)	6	0.04
Chippewa (0)	1	0.01
Menominee (1)	2	0.01
Mexican American Ind. (1)	6	0.04
Navajo (2)	2	0.01
Potawatomi (0)	1	0.01
South American Ind. (5)	5	0.03
Asian (586)	644	4.42
Not Hispanic (574)	625	4.29
Hispanic (12)	19	0.13
Chinese, ex. Taiwanese (31)	36	0.25
Filipino (344)	358	2.46
Indian (103)	116	0.80
Japanese (4)	12	0.08
Korean (30)	32	0.22
Pakistani (22)	22	0.15
Thai (15)	17	0.12
Vietnamese (35)	35	0.24
Hawaii Native/Pacific Islander (1)	7	0.05
Not Hispanic (1)	6	0.04
Hispanic (0)	1	0.01
Native Hawaiian (0)	4	0.03
Samoan (1)	2	0.01
White (13,406)	13,547	92.97
Not Hispanic (12,745)	12,830	88.05
Hispanic (661)	717	4.92

*Notes: † The Census 2010 population figure is used to calculate the percentages in the Hispanic Origin and Race categories. Ancestry percentages are based on the 2006-2010 American Community Survey population (not shown); ‡ Numbers in parentheses indicate the number of people reporting a single ancestry; * Numbers in parentheses indicate the number of persons reporting this race alone, not in combination with any other race; Please refer to the Explanation of Data for more information.*

North Aurora

Place Type: Village
County: Kane
Population: 16,760†

Ancestry‡	Population	%
African, Sub-Saharan (98)	118	0.75
African (76)	76	0.48
South African (22)	42	0.27
Albanian (17)	17	0.11
American (440)	440	2.81
Arab (41)	41	0.26
Palestinian (10)	10	0.06
Other Arab (31)	31	0.20
Assyrian/Chaldean/Syriac (0)	15	0.10
Austrian (0)	32	0.20
Belgian (13)	24	0.15
Brazilian (24)	32	0.20
British (10)	29	0.18
Cajun (8)	32	0.20
Canadian (0)	20	0.13
Czech (80)	313	2.00
Czechoslovakian (0)	8	0.05
Danish (28)	98	0.63
Dutch (37)	296	1.89
Eastern European (11)	20	0.13
English (192)	1,075	6.86
European (346)	374	2.39
Finnish (16)	34	0.22
French, ex. Basque (0)	346	2.21
French Canadian (6)	44	0.28
German (1,282)	4,118	26.26
Greek (101)	269	1.72
Hungarian (65)	111	0.71
Irish (393)	2,075	13.23
Italian (417)	1,212	7.73
Latvian (0)	5	0.03
Lithuanian (8)	64	0.41
Luxemburger (19)	56	0.36
Northern European (32)	32	0.20
Norwegian (177)	587	3.74
Pennsylvania German (9)	20	0.13
Polish (297)	1,307	8.34
Portuguese (0)	8	0.05
Romanian (15)	54	0.34
Russian (39)	172	1.10
Scandinavian (24)	24	0.15
Scotch-Irish (24)	237	1.51
Scottish (80)	198	1.26
Slavic (0)	18	0.11
Slovak (16)	35	0.22
Slovene (0)	51	0.33
Swedish (170)	753	4.80
Swiss (0)	18	0.11
Ukrainian (13)	42	0.27
Welsh (0)	37	0.24
West Indian, ex. Hispanic (20)	26	0.17
Jamaican (17)	23	0.15
Trinidadian/Tobagonian (3)	3	0.02
Yugoslavian (7)	35	0.22

Hispanic Origin	Population	%
Hispanic or Latino (of any race)	2,514	15.00
Central American, ex. Mexican	70	0.42
Costa Rican	4	0.02
Guatemalan	40	0.24
Honduran	13	0.08
Nicaraguan	1	0.01
Panamanian	6	0.04
Salvadoran	6	0.04
Cuban	30	0.18
Dominican Republic	12	0.07
Mexican	2,054	12.26
Puerto Rican	204	1.22
South American	80	0.48
Argentinean	3	0.02
Bolivian	4	0.02
Chilean	8	0.05
Colombian	33	0.20
Ecuadorian	16	0.10
Paraguayan	2	0.01
Peruvian	5	0.03
Venezuelan	9	0.05
Other Hispanic or Latino	64	0.38

Race*	Population	%
African-American/Black (872)	998	5.95
Not Hispanic (836)	930	5.55
Hispanic (36)	68	0.41
American Indian/Alaska Native (36)	114	0.68
Not Hispanic (16)	59	0.35
Hispanic (20)	55	0.33
Apache (1)	2	0.01
Blackfeet (0)	9	0.05
Cherokee (6)	24	0.14
Cheyenne (0)	1	0.01
Chippewa (1)	7	0.04
Creek (1)	3	0.02
Iroquois (0)	1	0.01
Lumbee (0)	1	0.01
Mexican American Ind. (1)	1	0.01
Sioux (0)	3	0.02
Asian (822)	1,013	6.04
Not Hispanic (804)	971	5.79
Hispanic (18)	42	0.25
Burmese (4)	5	0.03
Cambodian (4)	4	0.02
Chinese, ex. Taiwanese (85)	112	0.67
Filipino (204)	255	1.52
Hmong (14)	14	0.08
Indian (219)	251	1.50
Indonesian (5)	5	0.03
Japanese (12)	44	0.26
Korean (62)	86	0.51
Laotian (71)	90	0.54
Pakistani (35)	47	0.28
Sri Lankan (1)	3	0.02
Taiwanese (5)	10	0.06
Thai (7)	19	0.11
Vietnamese (45)	56	0.33
Hawaii Native/Pacific Islander (6)	14	0.08
Not Hispanic (4)	6	0.04
Hispanic (2)	8	0.05
Guamanian/Chamorro (1)	1	0.01
Native Hawaiian (4)	5	0.03
Samoan (0)	1	0.01
White (13,621)	14,063	83.91
Not Hispanic (12,285)	12,551	74.89
Hispanic (1,336)	1,512	9.02

North Chicago

Place Type: City
County: Lake
Population: 32,574†

Ancestry‡	Population	%
African, Sub-Saharan (302)	416	1.26
African (285)	399	1.21
Nigerian (17)	17	0.05
American (514)	514	1.56
Arab (184)	184	0.56
Egyptian (87)	87	0.26
Iraqi (9)	9	0.03
Lebanese (40)	40	0.12
Other Arab (48)	48	0.15
Austrian (25)	25	0.08
Belgian (0)	60	0.18
Brazilian (27)	77	0.23
British (0)	121	0.37
Canadian (0)	61	0.18
Croatian (165)	165	0.50
Czech (0)	50	0.15
Czechoslovakian (20)	20	0.06
Danish (79)	140	0.42
Dutch (63)	242	0.73
Eastern European (9)	24	0.07
English (104)	607	1.84
European (55)	113	0.34
Finnish (39)	39	0.12
French, ex. Basque (107)	342	1.04
French Canadian (34)	137	0.42
German (1,327)	3,703	11.22
Greek (79)	168	0.51
Guyanese (0)	50	0.15
Hungarian (0)	10	0.03
Irish (1,150)	3,113	9.43
Israeli (0)	49	0.15
Italian (304)	1,331	4.03
Latvian (24)	24	0.07
Lithuanian (12)	12	0.04
Luxemburger (0)	23	0.07
Norwegian (56)	249	0.75
Polish (338)	756	2.29
Portuguese (19)	294	0.89
Romanian (10)	10	0.03
Russian (14)	120	0.36
Scotch-Irish (112)	455	1.38
Scottish (114)	351	1.06
Serbian (44)	92	0.28
Slovak (13)	13	0.04
Slovene (10)	10	0.03
Swedish (33)	161	0.49
Swiss (12)	22	0.07
Ukrainian (12)	12	0.04
Welsh (62)	170	0.51
West Indian, ex. Hispanic (551)	706	2.14
Belizean (68)	217	0.66
British West Indian (43)	43	0.13
Haitian (66)	66	0.20
Jamaican (374)	374	1.13
West Indian (0)	6	0.02

Hispanic Origin	Population	%
Hispanic or Latino (of any race)	8,857	27.19
Central American, ex. Mexican	383	1.18
Costa Rican	7	0.02
Guatemalan	65	0.20
Honduran	157	0.48
Nicaraguan	22	0.07
Panamanian	20	0.06
Salvadoran	104	0.32
Other Central American	8	0.02
Cuban	74	0.23
Dominican Republic	63	0.19
Mexican	6,915	21.23
Puerto Rican	731	2.24
South American	165	0.51
Argentinean	10	0.03
Bolivian	6	0.02
Chilean	5	0.02
Colombian	83	0.25
Ecuadorian	22	0.07
Peruvian	33	0.10
Venezuelan	4	0.01
Other South American	2	0.01
Other Hispanic or Latino	526	1.61

Race*	Population	%
African-American/Black (9,746)	10,366	31.82
Not Hispanic (9,469)	9,939	30.51
Hispanic (277)	427	1.31
American Indian/Alaska Native (231)	511	1.57
Not Hispanic (120)	335	1.03
Hispanic (111)	176	0.54
Alaska Athabascan *(Ala. Nat.)* (2)	2	0.01
Apache (2)	10	0.03
Blackfeet (2)	11	0.03
Cherokee (20)	68	0.21
Cheyenne (0)	3	0.01
Chickasaw (4)	5	0.02
Chippewa (6)	8	0.02
Choctaw (9)	16	0.05
Comanche (0)	1	<0.01
Creek (3)	6	0.02
Crow (2)	2	0.01
Delaware (2)	3	0.01
Hopi (1)	2	0.01
Iroquois (1)	3	0.01

*Notes: † The Census 2010 population figure is used to calculate the percentages in the Hispanic Origin and Race categories. Ancestry percentages are based on the 2006-2010 American Community Survey population (not shown); ‡ Numbers in parentheses indicate the number of people reporting a single ancestry; * Numbers in parentheses indicate the number of persons reporting this race alone, not in combination with any other race; Please refer to the Explanation of Data for more information.*

Kiowa (1)	1	<0.01
Lumbee (0)	1	<0.01
Menominee (2)	2	0.01
Mexican American Ind. (21)	26	0.08
Navajo (14)	16	0.05
Osage (1)	3	0.01
Ottawa (1)	1	<0.01
Paiute (0)	2	0.01
Potawatomi (2)	2	0.01
Pueblo (2)	4	0.01
Puget Sound Salish (1)	3	0.01
Sioux (2)	11	0.03
Spanish American Ind. (1)	1	<0.01
Tlingit-Haida *(Alaska Native)* (1)	1	<0.01
Tohono O'Odham (0)	1	<0.01
Ute (0)	2	0.01
Yaqui (0)	1	<0.01
Yup'ik *(Alaska Native)* (1)	3	0.01
Asian (1,224)	1,690	5.19
Not Hispanic (1,190)	1,590	4.88
Hispanic (34)	100	0.31
Bangladeshi (2)	2	0.01
Cambodian (17)	19	0.06
Chinese, ex. Taiwanese (166)	224	0.69
Filipino (537)	716	2.20
Hmong (18)	18	0.06
Indian (132)	151	0.46
Indonesian (5)	5	0.02
Japanese (46)	131	0.40
Korean (82)	137	0.42
Laotian (5)	7	0.02
Malaysian (0)	1	<0.01
Nepalese (2)	3	0.01
Pakistani (19)	20	0.06
Sri Lankan (3)	6	0.02
Taiwanese (5)	6	0.02
Thai (8)	22	0.07
Vietnamese (50)	70	0.21
Hawaii Native/Pacific Islander (43)	223	0.68
Not Hispanic (39)	183	0.56
Hispanic (4)	40	0.12
Fijian (2)	5	0.02
Guamanian/Chamorro (10)	19	0.06
Native Hawaiian (13)	56	0.17
Samoan (13)	27	0.08
White (15,601)	16,591	50.93
Not Hispanic (11,838)	12,534	38.48
Hispanic (3,763)	4,057	12.45

Northbrook

Place Type: Village
County: Cook
Population: 33,170†

Ancestry‡	Population	%
African, Sub-Saharan (17)	61	0.19
African (0)	28	0.09
South African (17)	33	0.10
Albanian (0)	8	0.02
Alsatian (0)	15	0.05
American (1,751)	1,751	5.32
Arab (187)	238	0.72
Egyptian (69)	69	0.21
Iraqi (9)	9	0.03
Lebanese (28)	50	0.15
Moroccan (0)	21	0.06
Syrian (81)	81	0.25
Other Arab (0)	8	0.02
Armenian (32)	67	0.20
Assyrian/Chaldean/Syriac (86)	86	0.26
Australian (0)	23	0.07
Austrian (37)	319	0.97
Belgian (0)	49	0.15
British (77)	258	0.78
Canadian (53)	100	0.30
Celtic (0)	14	0.04
Czech (55)	151	0.46
Czechoslovakian (14)	14	0.04
Danish (48)	164	0.50
Dutch (165)	504	1.53
Eastern European (507)	578	1.76
English (523)	2,416	7.34
Estonian (0)	34	0.10
European (692)	743	2.26
Finnish (0)	24	0.07
French, ex. Basque (26)	435	1.32
French Canadian (12)	48	0.15
German (1,537)	5,277	16.03
Greek (842)	1,011	3.07
Hungarian (108)	340	1.03
Iranian (186)	207	0.63
Irish (1,286)	3,611	10.97
Israeli (72)	118	0.36
Italian (611)	1,479	4.49
Latvian (86)	183	0.56
Lithuanian (102)	399	1.21
Luxemburger (13)	33	0.10
Macedonian (0)	8	0.02
Northern European (22)	22	0.07
Norwegian (249)	678	2.06
Polish (1,407)	3,397	10.32
Portuguese (15)	36	0.11
Romanian (197)	445	1.35
Russian (2,386)	4,261	12.94
Scandinavian (8)	28	0.09
Scotch-Irish (114)	325	0.99
Scottish (75)	486	1.48
Serbian (233)	300	0.91
Slovak (27)	54	0.16
Swedish (179)	706	2.14
Swiss (46)	119	0.36
Turkish (77)	77	0.23
Ukrainian (472)	655	1.99
Welsh (55)	198	0.60
West Indian, ex. Hispanic (0)	59	0.18
Jamaican (0)	59	0.18
Yugoslavian (9)	30	0.09

Hispanic Origin	Population	%
Hispanic or Latino (of any race)	828	2.50
Central American, ex. Mexican	48	0.14
Costa Rican	2	0.01
Guatemalan	18	0.05
Honduran	6	0.02
Nicaraguan	4	0.01
Panamanian	3	0.01
Salvadoran	15	0.05
Cuban	90	0.27
Dominican Republic	4	0.01
Mexican	346	1.04
Puerto Rican	84	0.25
South American	168	0.51
Argentinean	35	0.11
Bolivian	8	0.02
Chilean	2	0.01
Colombian	54	0.16
Ecuadorian	27	0.08
Paraguayan	2	0.01
Peruvian	26	0.08
Uruguayan	2	0.01
Venezuelan	12	0.04
Other Hispanic or Latino	88	0.27

Race*	Population	%
African-American/Black (210)	270	0.81
Not Hispanic (201)	249	0.75
Hispanic (9)	21	0.06
American Indian/Alaska Native (12)	52	0.16
Not Hispanic (8)	42	0.13
Hispanic (4)	10	0.03
Cherokee (2)	7	0.02
Chippewa (0)	3	0.01
Osage (0)	1	<0.01
Asian (3,875)	4,171	12.57
Not Hispanic (3,869)	4,143	12.49
Hispanic (6)	28	0.08
Bangladeshi (16)	16	0.05
Burmese (15)	15	0.05
Cambodian (1)	1	<0.01
Chinese, ex. Taiwanese (622)	712	2.15
Filipino (284)	366	1.10
Indian (577)	607	1.83
Indonesian (4)	5	0.02
Japanese (120)	158	0.48
Korean (1,931)	2,005	6.04
Laotian (2)	2	0.01
Nepalese (4)	4	0.01
Pakistani (97)	101	0.30
Taiwanese (80)	91	0.27
Thai (40)	46	0.14
Vietnamese (12)	21	0.06
Hawaii Native/Pacific Islander (4)	13	0.04
Not Hispanic (4)	13	0.04
Fijian (0)	1	<0.01
Guamanian/Chamorro (3)	3	0.01
Native Hawaiian (0)	6	0.02
Samoan (0)	1	<0.01
White (28,549)	28,915	87.17
Not Hispanic (27,892)	28,210	85.05
Hispanic (657)	705	2.13

Northlake

Place Type: City
County: Cook
Population: 12,323†

Ancestry‡	Population	%
African, Sub-Saharan (0)	13	0.11
Other Sub-Saharan African (0)	13	0.11
American (195)	195	1.60
Austrian (0)	24	0.20
Belgian (0)	9	0.07
British (0)	11	0.09
Bulgarian (7)	7	0.06
Croatian (0)	8	0.07
Czech (82)	92	0.76
Danish (0)	134	1.10
Dutch (17)	49	0.40
English (122)	396	3.26
European (13)	26	0.21
Finnish (6)	35	0.29
French, ex. Basque (0)	66	0.54
French Canadian (9)	35	0.29
German (243)	1,012	8.33
Greek (44)	44	0.36
Hungarian (11)	22	0.18
Irish (392)	1,048	8.62
Italian (577)	1,024	8.42
Lithuanian (10)	10	0.08
Norwegian (28)	111	0.91
Polish (822)	1,216	10.00
Romanian (0)	34	0.28
Russian (8)	40	0.33
Scandinavian (17)	51	0.42
Scotch-Irish (29)	29	0.24
Scottish (0)	23	0.19
Serbian (24)	24	0.20
Swedish (33)	132	1.09
Ukrainian (9)	9	0.07
Welsh (9)	22	0.18
West Indian, ex. Hispanic (11)	11	0.09
West Indian (11)	11	0.09

Hispanic Origin	Population	%
Hispanic or Latino (of any race)	6,520	52.91
Central American, ex. Mexican	361	2.93
Costa Rican	3	0.02
Guatemalan	285	2.31
Honduran	16	0.13
Nicaraguan	8	0.06
Panamanian	1	0.01
Salvadoran	42	0.34
Other Central American	6	0.05
Cuban	122	0.99
Dominican Republic	9	0.07
Mexican	5,257	42.66
Puerto Rican	522	4.24
South American	104	0.84

SECTION TWO

*Notes: † The Census 2010 population figure is used to calculate the percentages in the Hispanic Origin and Race categories. Ancestry percentages are based on the 2006-2010 American Community Survey population (not shown); ‡ Numbers in parentheses indicate the number of people reporting a single ancestry; * Numbers in parentheses indicate the number of persons reporting this race alone, not in combination with any other race; Please refer to the Explanation of Data for more information.*

Argentinean	2	0.02
Bolivian	5	0.04
Chilean	6	0.05
Colombian	42	0.34
Ecuadorian	15	0.12
Peruvian	32	0.26
Venezuelan	2	0.02
Other Hispanic or Latino	145	1.18

Race*	Population	%
African-American/Black (397)	459	3.72
Not Hispanic (365)	392	3.18
Hispanic (32)	67	0.54
American Indian/Alaska Native (57)	93	0.75
Not Hispanic (6)	27	0.22
Hispanic (51)	66	0.54
Blackfeet (0)	8	0.06
Central American Ind. (6)	7	0.06
Cherokee (1)	6	0.05
Chippewa (0)	1	0.01
Inupiat *(Alaska Native)* (0)	2	0.02
Lumbee (3)	3	0.02
Menominee (1)	1	0.01
Mexican American Ind. (16)	17	0.14
Navajo (0)	1	0.01
Pueblo (0)	2	0.02
Sioux (1)	2	0.02
Spanish American Ind. (1)	1	0.01
Asian (344)	371	3.01
Not Hispanic (328)	350	2.84
Hispanic (16)	21	0.17
Cambodian (1)	1	0.01
Chinese, ex. Taiwanese (17)	20	0.16
Filipino (158)	174	1.41
Indian (78)	81	0.66
Japanese (8)	10	0.08
Korean (10)	11	0.09
Laotian (3)	3	0.02
Malaysian (0)	1	0.01
Pakistani (8)	8	0.06
Thai (7)	7	0.06
Vietnamese (52)	52	0.42
Hawaii Native/Pacific Islander (4)	16	0.13
Not Hispanic (4)	12	0.10
Hispanic (0)	4	0.03
Native Hawaiian (1)	2	0.02
Samoan (1)	1	0.01
White (8,250)	8,571	69.55
Not Hispanic (5,008)	5,070	41.14
Hispanic (3,242)	3,501	28.41

O'Fallon

Place Type: City
County: St. Clair
Population: 28,281†

Ancestry‡	Population	%
African, Sub-Saharan (56)	126	0.47
African (17)	51	0.19
Cape Verdean (9)	9	0.03
Kenyan (12)	32	0.12
Nigerian (18)	34	0.13
American (1,441)	1,441	5.33
Armenian (72)	72	0.27
Australian (4)	4	0.01
Austrian (0)	86	0.32
Belgian (11)	11	0.04
British (54)	168	0.62
Bulgarian (39)	39	0.14
Cajun (0)	8	0.03
Canadian (17)	100	0.37
Croatian (39)	78	0.29
Czech (16)	177	0.65
Czechoslovakian (7)	14	0.05
Danish (15)	222	0.82
Dutch (179)	527	1.95
Eastern European (16)	16	0.06
English (783)	3,262	12.06
European (507)	530	1.96
Finnish (39)	81	0.30
French, ex. Basque (111)	1,171	4.33
French Canadian (45)	172	0.64
German (3,102)	8,481	31.36
Greek (55)	135	0.50
Hungarian (21)	222	0.82
Irish (668)	3,469	12.83
Italian (431)	1,360	5.03
Lithuanian (20)	123	0.45
Macedonian (13)	13	0.05
Northern European (11)	11	0.04
Norwegian (123)	413	1.53
Pennsylvania German (8)	24	0.09
Polish (163)	925	3.42
Portuguese (24)	43	0.16
Romanian (0)	44	0.16
Russian (99)	211	0.78
Scandinavian (12)	53	0.20
Scotch-Irish (140)	363	1.34
Scottish (115)	470	1.74
Slavic (0)	25	0.09
Slovak (84)	168	0.62
Swedish (67)	201	0.74
Swiss (33)	338	1.25
Ukrainian (16)	36	0.13
Welsh (27)	115	0.43
West Indian, ex. Hispanic (45)	88	0.33
Haitian (0)	27	0.10
Trinidadian/Tobagonian (37)	37	0.14
West Indian (8)	24	0.09

Hispanic Origin	Population	%
Hispanic or Latino (of any race)	982	3.47
Central American, ex. Mexican	81	0.29
Costa Rican	6	0.02
Guatemalan	21	0.07
Honduran	4	0.01
Nicaraguan	8	0.03
Panamanian	32	0.11
Salvadoran	10	0.04
Cuban	31	0.11
Dominican Republic	17	0.06
Mexican	546	1.93
Puerto Rican	144	0.51
South American	59	0.21
Argentinean	10	0.04
Bolivian	5	0.02
Chilean	1	<0.01
Colombian	23	0.08
Ecuadorian	3	0.01
Peruvian	9	0.03
Venezuelan	8	0.03
Other Hispanic or Latino	104	0.37

Race*	Population	%
African-American/Black (4,404)	4,829	17.08
Not Hispanic (4,372)	4,762	16.84
Hispanic (32)	67	0.24
American Indian/Alaska Native (69)	246	0.87
Not Hispanic (60)	222	0.78
Hispanic (9)	24	0.08
Alaska Athabascan *(Ala. Nat.)* (2)	3	0.01
Aleut *(Alaska Native)* (2)	2	0.01
Blackfeet (2)	4	0.01
Canadian/French Am. Ind. (3)	3	0.01
Central American Ind. (2)	3	0.01
Cherokee (14)	54	0.19
Chickasaw (0)	3	0.01
Chippewa (0)	7	0.02
Choctaw (4)	9	0.03
Comanche (2)	2	0.01
Creek (0)	1	<0.01
Hopi (0)	1	<0.01
Iroquois (0)	1	<0.01
Kiowa (0)	3	0.01
Menominee (1)	1	<0.01
Mexican American Ind. (3)	5	0.02
Navajo (2)	7	0.02
Osage (3)	3	0.01
Ottawa (0)	1	<0.01
Seminole (0)	1	<0.01
Sioux (0)	5	0.02
Tlingit-Haida *(Alaska Native)* (2)	7	0.02
Asian (785)	1,127	3.99
Not Hispanic (772)	1,091	3.86
Hispanic (13)	36	0.13
Bangladeshi (4)	8	0.03
Chinese, ex. Taiwanese (76)	110	0.39
Filipino (224)	361	1.28
Indian (128)	150	0.53
Japanese (55)	99	0.35
Korean (162)	244	0.86
Laotian (8)	13	0.05
Malaysian (0)	8	0.03
Pakistani (6)	6	0.02
Taiwanese (6)	7	0.02
Thai (31)	54	0.19
Vietnamese (33)	51	0.18
Hawaii Native/Pacific Islander (28)	64	0.23
Not Hispanic (26)	55	0.19
Hispanic (2)	9	0.03
Guamanian/Chamorro (14)	22	0.08
Marshallese (1)	1	<0.01
Native Hawaiian (4)	21	0.07
Samoan (8)	10	0.04
White (21,872)	22,615	79.97
Not Hispanic (21,279)	21,950	77.61
Hispanic (593)	665	2.35

Oak Brook

Place Type: Village
County: DuPage
Population: 7,883†

Ancestry‡	Population	%
African, Sub-Saharan (79)	79	1.00
African (79)	79	1.00
Albanian (27)	27	0.34
American (103)	103	1.30
Arab (92)	136	1.72
Arab (16)	16	0.20
Lebanese (35)	35	0.44
Moroccan (12)	36	0.46
Syrian (20)	30	0.38
Other Arab (9)	19	0.24
Austrian (0)	54	0.68
Belgian (23)	51	0.65
British (0)	31	0.39
Canadian (0)	9	0.11
Croatian (29)	105	1.33
Czech (87)	213	2.69
Czechoslovakian (27)	27	0.34
Danish (23)	113	1.43
Dutch (164)	232	2.93
English (61)	462	5.84
European (12)	12	0.15
French, ex. Basque (64)	187	2.37
French Canadian (1)	80	1.01
German (263)	1,267	16.03
Greek (194)	321	4.06
Hungarian (32)	32	0.40
Iranian (209)	244	3.09
Irish (150)	836	10.58
Italian (738)	1,237	15.65
Lithuanian (33)	49	0.62
Northern European (85)	85	1.08
Norwegian (13)	97	1.23
Polish (234)	533	6.74
Romanian (15)	15	0.19
Russian (38)	72	0.91
Scandinavian (8)	8	0.10
Scotch-Irish (19)	58	0.73
Scottish (45)	130	1.64
Slovak (0)	10	0.13
Slovene (0)	12	0.15
Swedish (16)	142	1.80
Swiss (0)	55	0.70
Ukrainian (34)	80	1.01
Welsh (0)	45	0.57

*Notes: † The Census 2010 population figure is used to calculate the percentages in the Hispanic Origin and Race categories. Ancestry percentages are based on the 2006-2010 American Community Survey population (not shown); ‡ Numbers in parentheses indicate the number of people reporting a single ancestry; * Numbers in parentheses indicate the number of persons reporting this race alone, not in combination with any other race; Please refer to the Explanation of Data for more information.*

Yugoslavian (37)	37	0.47

Hispanic Origin	Population	%
Hispanic or Latino (of any race)	339	4.30
Central American, ex. Mexican	19	0.24
Guatemalan	9	0.11
Salvadoran	10	0.13
Cuban	31	0.39
Dominican Republic	3	0.04
Mexican	151	1.92
Puerto Rican	20	0.25
South American	99	1.26
Argentinean	11	0.14
Bolivian	16	0.20
Chilean	15	0.19
Colombian	18	0.23
Ecuadorian	21	0.27
Paraguayan	2	0.03
Peruvian	8	0.10
Venezuelan	4	0.05
Other South American	4	0.05
Other Hispanic or Latino	16	0.20

Race*	Population	%
African-American/Black (155)	170	2.16
Not Hispanic (154)	169	2.14
Hispanic (1)	1	0.01
American Indian/Alaska Native (5)	21	0.27
Not Hispanic (2)	18	0.23
Hispanic (3)	3	0.04
Cherokee (1)	10	0.13
Chippewa (0)	1	0.01
Iroquois (0)	2	0.03
Lumbee (0)	1	0.01
Mexican American Ind. (2)	2	0.03
Asian (1,832)	1,974	25.04
Not Hispanic (1,830)	1,966	24.94
Hispanic (2)	8	0.10
Bangladeshi (7)	7	0.09
Burmese (5)	5	0.06
Chinese, ex. Taiwanese (221)	239	3.03
Filipino (102)	142	1.80
Indian (1,066)	1,116	14.16
Indonesian (3)	4	0.05
Japanese (12)	23	0.29
Korean (71)	76	0.96
Pakistani (195)	215	2.73
Sri Lankan (12)	15	0.19
Taiwanese (75)	79	1.00
Thai (14)	15	0.19
Vietnamese (10)	11	0.14
Hawaii Native/Pacific Islander (0)	7	0.09
Not Hispanic (0)	6	0.08
Hispanic (0)	1	0.01
White (5,661)	5,798	73.55
Not Hispanic (5,395)	5,526	70.10
Hispanic (266)	272	3.45

Oak Forest

Place Type: City
County: Cook
Population: 27,962†

Ancestry‡	Population	%
American (641)	641	2.32
Arab (197)	395	1.43
Arab (42)	136	0.49
Jordanian (151)	201	0.73
Palestinian (4)	58	0.21
Armenian (9)	47	0.17
Austrian (0)	217	0.78
Belgian (0)	28	0.10
British (25)	25	0.09
Bulgarian (50)	50	0.18
Croatian (79)	335	1.21
Czech (67)	532	1.92
Czechoslovakian (0)	117	0.42
Danish (8)	88	0.32
Dutch (315)	1,025	3.70
English (73)	1,224	4.42
European (120)	143	0.52
Finnish (0)	11	0.04
French, ex. Basque (45)	610	2.20
French Canadian (10)	67	0.24
German (1,385)	5,939	21.45
Greek (120)	292	1.05
Guyanese (10)	10	0.04
Hungarian (36)	321	1.16
Irish (2,660)	7,717	27.87
Italian (1,180)	4,243	15.33
Lithuanian (534)	1,001	3.62
Luxemburger (0)	50	0.18
Norwegian (121)	492	1.78
Polish (1,546)	4,867	17.58
Russian (10)	169	0.61
Scandinavian (10)	10	0.04
Scotch-Irish (80)	321	1.16
Scottish (24)	219	0.79
Serbian (0)	73	0.26
Slavic (0)	8	0.03
Slovak (41)	47	0.17
Swedish (195)	1,337	4.83
Swiss (0)	32	0.12
Ukrainian (21)	104	0.38
Welsh (0)	52	0.19
West Indian, ex. Hispanic (5)	5	0.02
Haitian (5)	5	0.02
Yugoslavian (0)	20	0.07

Hispanic Origin	Population	%
Hispanic or Latino (of any race)	3,753	13.42
Central American, ex. Mexican	43	0.15
Costa Rican	1	<0.01
Guatemalan	19	0.07
Honduran	12	0.04
Nicaraguan	3	0.01
Panamanian	4	0.01
Salvadoran	3	0.01
Other Central American	1	<0.01
Cuban	24	0.09
Dominican Republic	8	0.03
Mexican	3,172	11.34
Puerto Rican	269	0.96
South American	116	0.41
Argentinean	17	0.06
Chilean	3	0.01
Colombian	41	0.15
Ecuadorian	11	0.04
Peruvian	28	0.10
Uruguayan	8	0.03
Venezuelan	6	0.02
Other South American	2	0.01
Other Hispanic or Latino	121	0.43

Race*	Population	%
African-American/Black (1,268)	1,437	5.14
Not Hispanic (1,248)	1,379	4.93
Hispanic (20)	58	0.21
American Indian/Alaska Native (56)	171	0.61
Not Hispanic (29)	120	0.43
Hispanic (27)	51	0.18
Apache (1)	2	0.01
Blackfeet (0)	9	0.03
Cherokee (6)	28	0.10
Cheyenne (0)	1	<0.01
Chippewa (6)	10	0.04
Choctaw (1)	1	<0.01
Creek (2)	2	0.01
Menominee (1)	2	0.01
Mexican American Ind. (6)	9	0.03
Navajo (1)	1	<0.01
Osage (0)	1	<0.01
Ottawa (0)	1	<0.01
Potawatomi (1)	1	<0.01
Shoshone (0)	3	0.01
Sioux (1)	3	0.01
Yaqui (0)	4	0.01
Asian (1,079)	1,285	4.60
Not Hispanic (1,076)	1,270	4.54
Hispanic (3)	15	0.05
Chinese, ex. Taiwanese (31)	61	0.22
Filipino (474)	535	1.91
Indian (409)	446	1.60
Japanese (18)	34	0.12
Korean (18)	32	0.11
Laotian (5)	10	0.04
Malaysian (5)	5	0.02
Pakistani (43)	46	0.16
Thai (14)	20	0.07
Vietnamese (33)	35	0.13
Hawaii Native/Pacific Islander (4)	28	0.10
Not Hispanic (1)	25	0.09
Hispanic (3)	3	0.01
Guamanian/Chamorro (4)	5	0.02
Native Hawaiian (0)	2	0.01
Samoan (0)	1	<0.01
White (23,330)	23,891	85.44
Not Hispanic (21,445)	21,762	77.83
Hispanic (1,885)	2,129	7.61

Oak Lawn

Place Type: Village
County: Cook
Population: 56,690†

Ancestry‡	Population	%
African, Sub-Saharan (111)	178	0.32
African (24)	91	0.16
Ethiopian (77)	77	0.14
Sudanese (10)	10	0.02
Albanian (52)	52	0.09
American (860)	860	1.54
Arab (2,517)	2,764	4.95
Arab (1,246)	1,415	2.53
Egyptian (88)	88	0.16
Jordanian (220)	254	0.45
Lebanese (28)	28	0.05
Moroccan (118)	137	0.25
Palestinian (725)	739	1.32
Syrian (10)	21	0.04
Other Arab (82)	82	0.15
Austrian (193)	411	0.74
Belgian (0)	49	0.09
Brazilian (0)	9	0.02
British (30)	45	0.08
Bulgarian (15)	27	0.05
Canadian (27)	43	0.08
Celtic (11)	11	0.02
Croatian (265)	577	1.03
Czech (155)	1,005	1.80
Czechoslovakian (78)	145	0.26
Danish (44)	284	0.51
Dutch (349)	1,045	1.87
Eastern European (4)	4	0.01
English (296)	1,738	3.11
Estonian (0)	15	0.03
European (160)	172	0.31
Finnish (0)	44	0.08
French, ex. Basque (82)	806	1.44
French Canadian (83)	252	0.45
German (1,731)	10,189	18.25
Greek (870)	1,162	2.08
Guyanese (11)	11	0.02
Hungarian (36)	438	0.78
Iranian (0)	8	0.01
Irish (5,081)	14,106	25.27
Israeli (103)	122	0.22
Italian (2,067)	6,249	11.19
Lithuanian (1,098)	2,267	4.06
Luxemburger (14)	48	0.09
Macedonian (24)	24	0.04
Northern European (13)	13	0.02
Norwegian (172)	620	1.11
Polish (5,809)	11,843	21.21
Romanian (258)	315	0.56
Russian (66)	204	0.37
Scandinavian (0)	11	0.02
Scotch-Irish (95)	296	0.53

*Notes: † The Census 2010 population figure is used to calculate the percentages in the Hispanic Origin and Race categories. Ancestry percentages are based on the 2006-2010 American Community Survey population (not shown); ‡ Numbers in parentheses indicate the number of people reporting a single ancestry; * Numbers in parentheses indicate the number of persons reporting this race alone, not in combination with any other race; Please refer to the Explanation of Data for more information.*

Scottish (67)	547	0.98
Serbian (79)	79	0.14
Slavic (0)	76	0.14
Slovak (159)	616	1.10
Slovene (26)	46	0.08
Swedish (245)	897	1.61
Swiss (50)	79	0.14
Ukrainian (98)	326	0.58
Welsh (0)	226	0.40
West Indian, ex. Hispanic (11)	23	0.04
British West Indian (0)	12	0.02
Haitian (11)	11	0.02
Yugoslavian (9)	9	0.02

Hispanic Origin	Population	%
Hispanic or Latino (of any race)	8,108	14.30
Central American, ex. Mexican	169	0.30
Costa Rican	8	0.01
Guatemalan	86	0.15
Honduran	24	0.04
Nicaraguan	9	0.02
Panamanian	6	0.01
Salvadoran	36	0.06
Cuban	58	0.10
Dominican Republic	13	0.02
Mexican	6,856	12.09
Puerto Rican	580	1.02
South American	213	0.38
Argentinean	16	0.03
Bolivian	23	0.04
Chilean	10	0.02
Colombian	73	0.13
Ecuadorian	55	0.10
Peruvian	21	0.04
Uruguayan	3	0.01
Venezuelan	10	0.02
Other South American	2	<0.01
Other Hispanic or Latino	219	0.39

Race*	Population	%
African-American/Black (2,946)	3,152	5.56
Not Hispanic (2,893)	3,055	5.39
Hispanic (53)	97	0.17
American Indian/Alaska Native (139)	308	0.54
Not Hispanic (54)	168	0.30
Hispanic (85)	140	0.25
Apache (4)	13	0.02
Blackfeet (0)	4	0.01
Cherokee (7)	51	0.09
Chickasaw (1)	1	<0.01
Choctaw (0)	2	<0.01
Inupiat *(Alaska Native)* (2)	2	<0.01
Iroquois (1)	9	0.02
Mexican American Ind. (27)	36	0.06
Navajo (2)	6	0.01
Pima (0)	1	<0.01
Shoshone (1)	2	<0.01
Sioux (0)	8	0.01
South American Ind. (1)	3	0.01
Asian (1,234)	1,624	2.86
Not Hispanic (1,207)	1,558	2.75
Hispanic (27)	66	0.12
Bangladeshi (4)	4	0.01
Burmese (7)	11	0.02
Chinese, ex. Taiwanese (73)	96	0.17
Filipino (553)	646	1.14
Indian (228)	265	0.47
Indonesian (2)	5	0.01
Japanese (23)	56	0.10
Korean (44)	67	0.12
Laotian (4)	6	0.01
Pakistani (80)	85	0.15
Thai (39)	41	0.07
Vietnamese (107)	119	0.21
Hawaii Native/Pacific Islander (19)	55	0.10
Not Hispanic (14)	45	0.08
Hispanic (5)	10	0.02
Guamanian/Chamorro (5)	6	0.01
Native Hawaiian (4)	10	0.02
Samoan (1)	4	0.01
White (48,279)	49,247	86.87
Not Hispanic (43,680)	44,283	78.11
Hispanic (4,599)	4,964	8.76

Oak Park

Place Type: Village
County: Cook
Population: 51,878†

Ancestry‡	Population	%
Afghan (0)	9	0.02
African, Sub-Saharan (291)	448	0.87
African (224)	376	0.73
Ethiopian (0)	5	0.01
Ghanaian (17)	17	0.03
Nigerian (50)	50	0.10
Albanian (0)	17	0.03
Alsatian (0)	40	0.08
American (1,122)	1,122	2.18
Arab (150)	265	0.52
Arab (58)	83	0.16
Egyptian (24)	41	0.08
Iraqi (0)	10	0.02
Lebanese (13)	43	0.08
Syrian (0)	10	0.02
Other Arab (55)	78	0.15
Armenian (22)	45	0.09
Assyrian/Chaldean/Syriac (7)	16	0.03
Australian (5)	5	0.01
Austrian (41)	203	0.39
Belgian (32)	48	0.09
Brazilian (0)	15	0.03
British (193)	385	0.75
Bulgarian (18)	50	0.10
Canadian (93)	153	0.30
Croatian (32)	111	0.22
Cypriot (0)	12	0.02
Czech (210)	895	1.74
Czechoslovakian (0)	21	0.04
Danish (23)	224	0.44
Dutch (234)	842	1.64
Eastern European (310)	328	0.64
English (982)	5,023	9.77
European (680)	789	1.53
Finnish (39)	174	0.34
French, ex. Basque (217)	1,472	2.86
French Canadian (60)	365	0.71
German (2,325)	10,013	19.47
Greek (242)	581	1.13
Guyanese (0)	11	0.02
Hungarian (34)	210	0.41
Iranian (19)	74	0.14
Irish (2,638)	9,760	18.98
Israeli (12)	12	0.02
Italian (1,359)	4,437	8.63
Latvian (133)	190	0.37
Lithuanian (112)	375	0.73
Luxemburger (0)	5	0.01
Maltese (12)	12	0.02
Northern European (118)	134	0.26
Norwegian (138)	779	1.51
Polish (1,299)	3,986	7.75
Portuguese (0)	39	0.08
Romanian (98)	248	0.48
Russian (451)	1,231	2.39
Scandinavian (7)	83	0.16
Scotch-Irish (301)	882	1.72
Scottish (226)	1,042	2.03
Serbian (141)	236	0.46
Slavic (14)	34	0.07
Slovak (66)	268	0.52
Slovene (62)	208	0.40
Swedish (213)	1,349	2.62
Swiss (17)	207	0.40
Turkish (21)	39	0.08
Ukrainian (73)	232	0.45
Welsh (18)	432	0.84
West Indian, ex. Hispanic (236)	304	0.59
Bahamian (7)	7	0.01
Haitian (42)	64	0.12
Jamaican (80)	113	0.22
West Indian (107)	120	0.23
Yugoslavian (57)	65	0.13

Hispanic Origin	Population	%
Hispanic or Latino (of any race)	3,521	6.79
Central American, ex. Mexican	198	0.38
Costa Rican	6	0.01
Guatemalan	87	0.17
Honduran	23	0.04
Nicaraguan	22	0.04
Panamanian	34	0.07
Salvadoran	22	0.04
Other Central American	4	0.01
Cuban	134	0.26
Dominican Republic	47	0.09
Mexican	1,858	3.58
Puerto Rican	555	1.07
South American	477	0.92
Argentinean	77	0.15
Bolivian	20	0.04
Chilean	49	0.09
Colombian	116	0.22
Ecuadorian	58	0.11
Paraguayan	10	0.02
Peruvian	91	0.18
Uruguayan	15	0.03
Venezuelan	31	0.06
Other South American	10	0.02
Other Hispanic or Latino	252	0.49

Race*	Population	%
African-American/Black (11,233)	12,235	23.58
Not Hispanic (11,023)	11,872	22.88
Hispanic (210)	363	0.70
American Indian/Alaska Native (93)	416	0.80
Not Hispanic (65)	303	0.58
Hispanic (28)	113	0.22
Apache (3)	4	0.01
Blackfeet (0)	10	0.02
Canadian/French Am. Ind. (0)	1	<0.01
Central American Ind. (1)	1	<0.01
Cherokee (3)	84	0.16
Chippewa (2)	12	0.02
Choctaw (1)	10	0.02
Comanche (1)	5	0.01
Cree (0)	1	<0.01
Creek (0)	2	<0.01
Crow (0)	1	<0.01
Delaware (0)	1	<0.01
Iroquois (1)	4	0.01
Lumbee (1)	2	<0.01
Menominee (0)	3	0.01
Mexican American Ind. (7)	18	0.03
Navajo (2)	3	0.01
Osage (1)	2	<0.01
Ottawa (2)	3	0.01
Seminole (1)	1	<0.01
Sioux (1)	5	0.01
South American Ind. (4)	19	0.04
Spanish American Ind. (0)	1	<0.01
Tlingit-Haida *(Alaska Native)* (1)	1	<0.01
Asian (2,511)	3,219	6.20
Not Hispanic (2,474)	3,142	6.06
Hispanic (37)	77	0.15
Bangladeshi (7)	8	0.02
Burmese (6)	6	0.01
Cambodian (5)	9	0.02
Chinese, ex. Taiwanese (614)	793	1.53
Filipino (430)	601	1.16
Indian (669)	845	1.63
Indonesian (9)	12	0.02
Japanese (186)	314	0.61
Korean (205)	275	0.53
Laotian (12)	19	0.04
Malaysian (9)	11	0.02
Nepalese (13)	14	0.03
Pakistani (38)	55	0.11
Sri Lankan (18)	21	0.04

*Notes: † The Census 2010 population figure is used to calculate the percentages in the Hispanic Origin and Race categories. Ancestry percentages are based on the 2006-2010 American Community Survey population (not shown); ‡ Numbers in parentheses indicate the number of people reporting a single ancestry; * Numbers in parentheses indicate the number of persons reporting this race alone, not in combination with any other race; Please refer to the Explanation of Data for more information.*

	Population	%
Taiwanese (31)	45	0.09
Thai (66)	93	0.18
Vietnamese (75)	102	0.20
Hawaii Native/Pacific Islander (16)	52	0.10
Not Hispanic (15)	44	0.08
Hispanic (1)	8	0.02
Guamanian/Chamorro (3)	5	0.01
Native Hawaiian (7)	22	0.04
Samoan (3)	5	0.01
White (35,121)	36,676	70.70
Not Hispanic (33,076)	34,374	66.26
Hispanic (2,045)	2,302	4.44

Olney

Place Type: City
County: Richland
Population: 9,115†

Ancestry‡	Population	%
American (998)	998	11.40
Arab (15)	25	0.29
Arab (0)	10	0.11
Palestinian (15)	15	0.17
British (20)	20	0.23
Czech (0)	12	0.14
Dutch (49)	210	2.40
English (559)	1,186	13.54
European (148)	169	1.93
Finnish (0)	24	0.27
French, ex. Basque (50)	170	1.94
French Canadian (0)	14	0.16
German (1,056)	2,156	24.62
Hungarian (0)	19	0.22
Icelander (0)	40	0.46
Irish (251)	812	9.27
Italian (13)	70	0.80
Polish (57)	165	1.88
Russian (11)	19	0.22
Scandinavian (0)	8	0.09
Scotch-Irish (71)	178	2.03
Scottish (70)	132	1.51
Serbian (12)	12	0.14
Slovak (11)	25	0.29
Swedish (0)	29	0.33
Swiss (12)	54	0.62
Ukrainian (9)	9	0.10
Welsh (0)	23	0.26

Hispanic Origin	Population	%
Hispanic or Latino (of any race)	141	1.55
Central American, ex. Mexican	11	0.12
Guatemalan	5	0.05
Panamanian	6	0.07
Cuban	4	0.04
Mexican	78	0.86
Puerto Rican	16	0.18
South American	7	0.08
Chilean	1	0.01
Colombian	2	0.02
Peruvian	4	0.04
Other Hispanic or Latino	25	0.27

Race*	Population	%
African-American/Black (60)	100	1.10
Not Hispanic (60)	99	1.09
Hispanic (0)	1	0.01
American Indian/Alaska Native (15)	38	0.42
Not Hispanic (15)	36	0.39
Hispanic (0)	2	0.02
Blackfeet (0)	2	0.02
Cherokee (5)	15	0.16
Chippewa (0)	1	0.01
Navajo (0)	1	0.01
Sioux (0)	1	0.01
Asian (98)	125	1.37
Not Hispanic (98)	125	1.37
Chinese, ex. Taiwanese (21)	23	0.25
Filipino (27)	38	0.42
Indian (21)	22	0.24
Indonesian (11)	11	0.12
Japanese (3)	9	0.10
Korean (8)	15	0.16
Thai (1)	2	0.02
Vietnamese (4)	4	0.04
Hawaii Native/Pacific Islander (1)	9	0.10
Not Hispanic (1)	9	0.10
Guamanian/Chamorro (1)	1	0.01
Native Hawaiian (0)	3	0.03
Samoan (0)	1	0.01
White (8,790)	8,889	97.52
Not Hispanic (8,706)	8,792	96.46
Hispanic (84)	97	1.06

Orland Park

Place Type: Village
County: Cook
Population: 56,767†

Ancestry‡	Population	%
African, Sub-Saharan (45)	56	0.10
African (45)	56	0.10
Albanian (170)	170	0.31
American (1,155)	1,155	2.10
Arab (2,258)	2,393	4.34
Arab (1,023)	1,104	2.00
Egyptian (22)	22	0.04
Iraqi (18)	18	0.03
Jordanian (316)	316	0.57
Lebanese (66)	86	0.16
Palestinian (563)	563	1.02
Syrian (38)	55	0.10
Other Arab (212)	229	0.42
Armenian (12)	12	0.02
Australian (0)	15	0.03
Austrian (126)	387	0.70
Belgian (11)	88	0.16
Brazilian (25)	25	0.05
British (15)	30	0.05
Bulgarian (13)	13	0.02
Canadian (46)	78	0.14
Croatian (239)	840	1.52
Czech (231)	1,159	2.10
Czechoslovakian (79)	149	0.27
Danish (66)	373	0.68
Dutch (815)	1,504	2.73
Eastern European (24)	24	0.04
English (487)	2,409	4.37
European (195)	265	0.48
Finnish (31)	69	0.13
French, ex. Basque (16)	768	1.39
French Canadian (50)	163	0.30
German (2,043)	10,706	19.43
Greek (1,345)	1,744	3.17
Hungarian (109)	364	0.66
Icelander (10)	10	0.02
Iranian (28)	28	0.05
Irish (4,845)	14,774	26.81
Italian (2,867)	7,670	13.92
Latvian (23)	23	0.04
Lithuanian (866)	1,425	2.59
Luxemburger (0)	23	0.04
Macedonian (75)	75	0.14
Northern European (19)	19	0.03
Norwegian (161)	570	1.03
Polish (4,567)	10,058	18.25
Romanian (12)	54	0.10
Russian (276)	607	1.10
Scandinavian (0)	65	0.12
Scotch-Irish (113)	392	0.71
Scottish (135)	542	0.98
Serbian (156)	457	0.83
Slavic (15)	35	0.06
Slovak (35)	198	0.36
Slovene (12)	98	0.18
Swedish (215)	1,277	2.32
Swiss (10)	118	0.21
Turkish (37)	37	0.07
Ukrainian (105)	294	0.53
Welsh (0)	112	0.20
West Indian, ex. Hispanic (18)	37	0.07
Belizean (18)	37	0.07
Yugoslavian (13)	33	0.06

Hispanic Origin	Population	%
Hispanic or Latino (of any race)	3,528	6.21
Central American, ex. Mexican	83	0.15
Guatemalan	56	0.10
Honduran	18	0.03
Nicaraguan	2	<0.01
Salvadoran	6	0.01
Other Central American	1	<0.01
Cuban	51	0.09
Dominican Republic	3	0.01
Mexican	2,883	5.08
Puerto Rican	181	0.32
South American	140	0.25
Argentinean	10	0.02
Bolivian	15	0.03
Chilean	11	0.02
Colombian	49	0.09
Ecuadorian	24	0.04
Paraguayan	3	0.01
Peruvian	14	0.02
Uruguayan	2	<0.01
Venezuelan	9	0.02
Other South American	3	0.01
Other Hispanic or Latino	187	0.33

Race*	Population	%
African-American/Black (945)	1,050	1.85
Not Hispanic (936)	1,034	1.82
Hispanic (9)	16	0.03
American Indian/Alaska Native (51)	163	0.29
Not Hispanic (20)	110	0.19
Hispanic (31)	53	0.09
Apache (0)	1	<0.01
Arapaho (0)	1	<0.01
Central American Ind. (2)	2	<0.01
Cherokee (2)	33	0.06
Chippewa (1)	6	0.01
Choctaw (0)	4	0.01
Creek (1)	1	<0.01
Iroquois (4)	4	0.01
Menominee (0)	2	<0.01
Mexican American Ind. (5)	9	0.02
Navajo (0)	2	<0.01
Osage (0)	3	0.01
Ottawa (3)	6	0.01
Potawatomi (0)	4	0.01
Sioux (0)	2	<0.01
Asian (2,788)	3,238	5.70
Not Hispanic (2,777)	3,199	5.64
Hispanic (11)	39	0.07
Bangladeshi (3)	7	0.01
Burmese (1)	1	<0.01
Cambodian (1)	3	0.01
Chinese, ex. Taiwanese (238)	267	0.47
Filipino (843)	939	1.65
Indian (906)	988	1.74
Indonesian (3)	7	0.01
Japanese (21)	39	0.07
Korean (339)	395	0.70
Laotian (2)	2	<0.01
Malaysian (3)	5	0.01
Pakistani (197)	219	0.39
Taiwanese (21)	24	0.04
Thai (39)	49	0.09
Vietnamese (87)	98	0.17
Hawaii Native/Pacific Islander (5)	38	0.07
Not Hispanic (3)	35	0.06
Hispanic (2)	3	0.01
Guamanian/Chamorro (3)	5	0.01
Native Hawaiian (2)	9	0.02
Samoan (0)	1	<0.01
White (51,234)	51,944	91.50
Not Hispanic (48,851)	49,389	87.00
Hispanic (2,383)	2,555	4.50

SECTION TWO

*Notes: † The Census 2010 population figure is used to calculate the percentages in the Hispanic Origin and Race categories. Ancestry percentages are based on the 2006-2010 American Community Survey population (not shown); ‡ Numbers in parentheses indicate the number of people reporting a single ancestry; * Numbers in parentheses indicate the number of persons reporting this race alone, not in combination with any other race; Please refer to the Explanation of Data for more information.*

Oswego

Place Type: Village
County: Kendall
Population: 30,355†

Ancestry‡	Population	%
African, Sub-Saharan (0)	49	0.18
African (0)	49	0.18
Albanian (14)	14	0.05
American (859)	859	3.10
Arab (100)	166	0.60
Arab (16)	16	0.06
Egyptian (12)	12	0.04
Lebanese (0)	66	0.24
Palestinian (72)	72	0.26
Austrian (0)	38	0.14
Basque (14)	28	0.10
Belgian (37)	115	0.41
British (18)	48	0.17
Cajun (0)	14	0.05
Canadian (13)	24	0.09
Croatian (18)	85	0.31
Czech (202)	449	1.62
Czechoslovakian (22)	61	0.22
Danish (25)	103	0.37
Dutch (67)	395	1.43
Eastern European (41)	50	0.18
English (364)	2,207	7.96
European (351)	374	1.35
Finnish (0)	39	0.14
French, ex. Basque (56)	1,021	3.68
French Canadian (0)	13	0.05
German (2,067)	7,983	28.80
Greek (167)	307	1.11
Guyanese (0)	15	0.05
Hungarian (21)	222	0.80
Irish (830)	4,699	16.95
Israeli (15)	15	0.05
Italian (812)	2,776	10.01
Lithuanian (55)	157	0.57
Luxemburger (0)	7	0.03
Norwegian (74)	479	1.73
Polish (720)	2,734	9.86
Portuguese (0)	9	0.03
Romanian (14)	103	0.37
Russian (131)	291	1.05
Scandinavian (14)	79	0.29
Scotch-Irish (155)	479	1.73
Scottish (286)	825	2.98
Serbian (0)	33	0.12
Slavic (0)	16	0.06
Slovak (68)	221	0.80
Slovene (14)	14	0.05
Swedish (59)	575	2.07
Swiss (0)	132	0.48
Ukrainian (111)	165	0.60
Welsh (0)	71	0.26
Yugoslavian (45)	263	0.95

Hispanic Origin	Population	%
Hispanic or Latino (of any race)	3,556	11.71
Central American, ex. Mexican	84	0.28
Costa Rican	1	<0.01
Guatemalan	47	0.15
Honduran	5	0.02
Nicaraguan	7	0.02
Panamanian	7	0.02
Salvadoran	14	0.05
Other Central American	3	0.01
Cuban	49	0.16
Dominican Republic	5	0.02
Mexican	2,668	8.79
Puerto Rican	459	1.51
South American	155	0.51
Argentinean	13	0.04
Bolivian	14	0.05
Chilean	3	0.01
Colombian	53	0.17
Ecuadorian	37	0.12
Paraguayan	3	0.01
Peruvian	26	0.09
Venezuelan	2	0.01
Other South American	4	0.01
Other Hispanic or Latino	136	0.45

Race*	Population	%
African-American/Black (1,565)	1,772	5.84
Not Hispanic (1,518)	1,682	5.54
Hispanic (47)	90	0.30
American Indian/Alaska Native (74)	170	0.56
Not Hispanic (26)	103	0.34
Hispanic (48)	67	0.22
Aleut *(Alaska Native)* (0)	2	0.01
Blackfeet (0)	7	0.02
Cherokee (10)	27	0.09
Cheyenne (1)	1	<0.01
Chickasaw (0)	3	0.01
Chippewa (2)	6	0.02
Choctaw (1)	8	0.03
Comanche (0)	1	<0.01
Creek (0)	2	0.01
Delaware (0)	2	0.01
Inupiat *(Alaska Native)* (0)	2	0.01
Iroquois (1)	3	0.01
Mexican American Ind. (3)	13	0.04
Navajo (0)	1	<0.01
Sioux (0)	2	0.01
Yup'ik *(Alaska Native)* (3)	8	0.03
Asian (1,042)	1,331	4.38
Not Hispanic (1,022)	1,283	4.23
Hispanic (20)	48	0.16
Cambodian (3)	7	0.02
Chinese, ex. Taiwanese (160)	202	0.67
Filipino (253)	354	1.17
Indian (338)	360	1.19
Indonesian (5)	6	0.02
Japanese (13)	51	0.17
Korean (59)	103	0.34
Laotian (11)	12	0.04
Nepalese (2)	2	0.01
Pakistani (77)	85	0.28
Sri Lankan (2)	7	0.02
Taiwanese (6)	11	0.04
Thai (9)	11	0.04
Vietnamese (72)	94	0.31
Hawaii Native/Pacific Islander (10)	18	0.06
Not Hispanic (9)	17	0.06
Hispanic (1)	1	<0.01
Guamanian/Chamorro (1)	1	<0.01
Native Hawaiian (2)	7	0.02
White (25,998)	26,634	87.74
Not Hispanic (23,700)	24,150	79.56
Hispanic (2,298)	2,484	8.18

Ottawa

Place Type: City
County: LaSalle
Population: 18,768†

Ancestry‡	Population	%
African, Sub-Saharan (104)	119	0.62
African (104)	119	0.62
American (897)	897	4.66
Armenian (10)	31	0.16
Australian (0)	9	0.05
Austrian (0)	48	0.25
Belgian (0)	52	0.27
British (9)	32	0.17
Canadian (0)	14	0.07
Croatian (0)	39	0.20
Czech (0)	93	0.48
Czechoslovakian (0)	17	0.09
Danish (64)	159	0.83
Dutch (49)	458	2.38
Eastern European (0)	11	0.06
English (459)	2,084	10.82
European (232)	232	1.20
French, ex. Basque (64)	735	3.82
French Canadian (4)	27	0.14
German (1,661)	5,889	30.57
Greek (18)	81	0.42
Hungarian (0)	78	0.40
Irish (870)	4,354	22.60
Italian (745)	1,751	9.09
Lithuanian (26)	104	0.54
Norwegian (486)	1,607	8.34
Pennsylvania German (8)	31	0.16
Polish (147)	736	3.82
Portuguese (0)	32	0.17
Romanian (9)	88	0.46
Russian (34)	88	0.46
Scandinavian (16)	35	0.18
Scotch-Irish (105)	244	1.27
Scottish (90)	298	1.55
Serbian (6)	6	0.03
Slavic (0)	60	0.31
Slovak (19)	183	0.95
Slovene (21)	21	0.11
Swedish (64)	434	2.25
Swiss (0)	17	0.09
Ukrainian (0)	18	0.09
Welsh (0)	41	0.21
Yugoslavian (0)	72	0.37

Hispanic Origin	Population	%
Hispanic or Latino (of any race)	1,406	7.49
Central American, ex. Mexican	13	0.07
Costa Rican	2	0.01
Guatemalan	8	0.04
Honduran	1	0.01
Salvadoran	2	0.01
Cuban	1	0.01
Dominican Republic	2	0.01
Mexican	1,204	6.42
Puerto Rican	87	0.46
South American	28	0.15
Argentinean	6	0.03
Bolivian	1	0.01
Colombian	16	0.09
Venezuelan	5	0.03
Other Hispanic or Latino	71	0.38

Race*	Population	%
African-American/Black (382)	485	2.58
Not Hispanic (357)	456	2.43
Hispanic (25)	29	0.15
American Indian/Alaska Native (58)	146	0.78
Not Hispanic (43)	112	0.60
Hispanic (15)	34	0.18
Aleut *(Alaska Native)* (1)	1	0.01
Apache (1)	1	0.01
Blackfeet (1)	9	0.05
Cherokee (14)	37	0.20
Cheyenne (1)	1	0.01
Chickasaw (2)	2	0.01
Chippewa (1)	2	0.01
Choctaw (1)	2	0.01
Creek (0)	1	0.01
Mexican American Ind. (2)	7	0.04
Potawatomi (1)	5	0.03
Seminole (0)	1	0.01
Sioux (5)	5	0.03
Yup'ik *(Alaska Native)* (1)	3	0.02
Asian (173)	217	1.16
Not Hispanic (172)	213	1.13
Hispanic (1)	4	0.02
Cambodian (4)	4	0.02
Chinese, ex. Taiwanese (32)	35	0.19
Filipino (41)	61	0.33
Indian (24)	27	0.14
Indonesian (0)	1	0.01
Japanese (12)	21	0.11
Korean (12)	14	0.07
Laotian (3)	5	0.03
Pakistani (8)	8	0.04
Taiwanese (2)	3	0.02
Thai (7)	10	0.05
Vietnamese (23)	27	0.14

*Notes: † The Census 2010 population figure is used to calculate the percentages in the Hispanic Origin and Race categories. Ancestry percentages are based on the 2006-2010 American Community Survey population (not shown); ‡ Numbers in parentheses indicate the number of people reporting a single ancestry; * Numbers in parentheses indicate the number of persons reporting this race alone, not in combination with any other race; Please refer to the Explanation of Data for more information.*

Hawaii Native/Pacific Islander (2)	12	0.06
Not Hispanic (2)	12	0.06
Guamanian/Chamorro (1)	2	0.01
Native Hawaiian (1)	8	0.04
White (17,528)	17,807	94.88
Not Hispanic (16,566)	16,774	89.38
Hispanic (962)	1,033	5.50

Palatine

Place Type: Village
County: Cook
Population: 68,557†

Ancestry‡	Population	%
African, Sub-Saharan (298)	322	0.48
African (100)	111	0.16
Ghanaian (28)	28	0.04
Kenyan (19)	32	0.05
Nigerian (151)	151	0.22
Albanian (67)	67	0.10
Alsatian (9)	9	0.01
American (1,365)	1,365	2.02
Arab (124)	149	0.22
Arab (17)	31	0.05
Egyptian (20)	31	0.05
Iraqi (42)	42	0.06
Lebanese (31)	31	0.05
Palestinian (14)	14	0.02
Armenian (66)	82	0.12
Assyrian/Chaldean/Syriac (22)	36	0.05
Australian (18)	38	0.06
Austrian (57)	362	0.54
Belgian (0)	135	0.20
Brazilian (37)	91	0.13
British (79)	242	0.36
Bulgarian (267)	267	0.40
Canadian (81)	131	0.19
Croatian (33)	159	0.24
Czech (111)	650	0.96
Czechoslovakian (13)	59	0.09
Danish (65)	722	1.07
Dutch (231)	966	1.43
Eastern European (194)	194	0.29
English (807)	3,707	5.50
European (278)	314	0.47
Finnish (14)	144	0.21
French, ex. Basque (99)	1,409	2.09
French Canadian (14)	126	0.19
German (3,805)	14,535	21.56
Greek (418)	709	1.05
Hungarian (106)	400	0.59
Iranian (11)	59	0.09
Irish (2,523)	10,714	15.89
Israeli (45)	45	0.07
Italian (2,440)	7,027	10.42
Latvian (35)	65	0.10
Lithuanian (155)	378	0.56
Luxemburger (19)	73	0.11
Macedonian (24)	40	0.06
Norwegian (197)	1,230	1.82
Polish (4,475)	9,622	14.27
Portuguese (13)	54	0.08
Romanian (139)	170	0.25
Russian (731)	1,452	2.15
Scandinavian (32)	154	0.23
Scotch-Irish (197)	723	1.07
Scottish (143)	906	1.34
Serbian (86)	109	0.16
Slavic (39)	51	0.08
Slovak (98)	341	0.51
Slovene (15)	115	0.17
Swedish (536)	2,447	3.63
Swiss (63)	212	0.31
Turkish (29)	29	0.04
Ukrainian (435)	620	0.92
Welsh (57)	300	0.45
West Indian, ex. Hispanic (118)	126	0.19
British West Indian (0)	8	0.01
Haitian (45)	45	0.07
Jamaican (62)	62	0.09
West Indian (11)	11	0.02
Yugoslavian (26)	33	0.05

Hispanic Origin	Population	%
Hispanic or Latino (of any race)	12,347	18.01
Central American, ex. Mexican	484	0.71
Costa Rican	22	0.03
Guatemalan	165	0.24
Honduran	101	0.15
Nicaraguan	18	0.03
Panamanian	16	0.02
Salvadoran	153	0.22
Other Central American	9	0.01
Cuban	109	0.16
Dominican Republic	14	0.02
Mexican	10,256	14.96
Puerto Rican	484	0.71
South American	532	0.78
Argentinean	37	0.05
Bolivian	7	0.01
Chilean	23	0.03
Colombian	162	0.24
Ecuadorian	74	0.11
Paraguayan	10	0.01
Peruvian	189	0.28
Uruguayan	1	<0.01
Venezuelan	24	0.04
Other South American	5	0.01
Other Hispanic or Latino	468	0.68

Race*	Population	%
African-American/Black (1,869)	2,208	3.22
Not Hispanic (1,798)	2,055	3.00
Hispanic (71)	153	0.22
American Indian/Alaska Native (190)	455	0.66
Not Hispanic (61)	216	0.32
Hispanic (129)	239	0.35
Apache (3)	5	0.01
Blackfeet (2)	9	0.01
Cherokee (8)	59	0.09
Chickasaw (1)	1	<0.01
Chippewa (11)	21	0.03
Choctaw (3)	8	0.01
Creek (1)	7	0.01
Crow (0)	1	<0.01
Hopi (0)	1	<0.01
Inupiat *(Alaska Native)* (1)	1	<0.01
Iroquois (2)	6	0.01
Kiowa (4)	4	0.01
Menominee (0)	1	<0.01
Mexican American Ind. (27)	47	0.07
Navajo (1)	1	<0.01
Ottawa (4)	6	0.01
Potawatomi (6)	7	0.01
Puget Sound Salish (1)	1	<0.01
Seminole (0)	1	<0.01
Sioux (1)	9	0.01
South American Ind. (8)	22	0.03
Spanish American Ind. (0)	6	0.01
Asian (7,077)	7,704	11.24
Not Hispanic (7,043)	7,623	11.12
Hispanic (34)	81	0.12
Bangladeshi (16)	16	0.02
Burmese (9)	11	0.02
Cambodian (12)	19	0.03
Chinese, ex. Taiwanese (1,112)	1,249	1.82
Filipino (702)	874	1.27
Hmong (1)	3	<0.01
Indian (2,695)	2,836	4.14
Indonesian (17)	18	0.03
Japanese (567)	683	1.00
Korean (1,094)	1,175	1.71
Laotian (11)	14	0.02
Malaysian (8)	15	0.02
Nepalese (6)	6	0.01
Pakistani (379)	422	0.62
Sri Lankan (11)	12	0.02
Taiwanese (77)	88	0.13
Thai (27)	37	0.05
Vietnamese (142)	167	0.24
Hawaii Native/Pacific Islander (23)	68	0.10
Not Hispanic (19)	57	0.08
Hispanic (4)	11	0.02
Guamanian/Chamorro (5)	11	0.02
Native Hawaiian (2)	14	0.02
Samoan (2)	13	0.02
Tongan (1)	3	<0.01
White (52,736)	54,068	78.87
Not Hispanic (46,246)	47,024	68.59
Hispanic (6,490)	7,044	10.27

Palos Heights

Place Type: City
County: Cook
Population: 12,515†

Ancestry‡	Population	%
American (410)	410	3.36
Arab (59)	139	1.14
Arab (42)	42	0.34
Jordanian (0)	23	0.19
Lebanese (12)	46	0.38
Palestinian (5)	23	0.19
Syrian (0)	5	0.04
Armenian (11)	11	0.09
Austrian (33)	98	0.80
Belgian (38)	47	0.39
British (32)	53	0.43
Canadian (11)	11	0.09
Croatian (25)	122	1.00
Czech (123)	190	1.56
Czechoslovakian (9)	30	0.25
Danish (0)	25	0.21
Dutch (694)	924	7.58
English (146)	699	5.74
European (76)	88	0.72
French, ex. Basque (24)	250	2.05
French Canadian (10)	23	0.19
German (601)	2,848	23.37
Greek (244)	433	3.55
Hungarian (0)	89	0.73
Irish (1,453)	3,523	28.91
Italian (361)	1,183	9.71
Lithuanian (272)	547	4.49
Luxemburger (0)	11	0.09
Norwegian (46)	165	1.35
Polish (1,019)	2,085	17.11
Portuguese (11)	25	0.21
Russian (43)	115	0.94
Scotch-Irish (45)	120	0.98
Scottish (119)	231	1.90
Slovak (104)	166	1.36
Slovene (10)	10	0.08
Swedish (70)	383	3.14
Swiss (15)	96	0.79
Ukrainian (9)	35	0.29
Welsh (22)	54	0.44
Yugoslavian (0)	13	0.11

Hispanic Origin	Population	%
Hispanic or Latino (of any race)	474	3.79
Central American, ex. Mexican	17	0.14
Guatemalan	1	0.01
Honduran	4	0.03
Panamanian	8	0.06
Salvadoran	4	0.03
Cuban	13	0.10
Mexican	353	2.82
Puerto Rican	26	0.21
South American	36	0.29
Argentinean	9	0.07
Colombian	11	0.09
Ecuadorian	7	0.06
Peruvian	1	0.01
Uruguayan	5	0.04
Venezuelan	3	0.02
Other Hispanic or Latino	29	0.23

*Notes: † The Census 2010 population figure is used to calculate the percentages in the Hispanic Origin and Race categories. Ancestry percentages are based on the 2006-2010 American Community Survey population (not shown); ‡ Numbers in parentheses indicate the number of people reporting a single ancestry; * Numbers in parentheses indicate the number of persons reporting this race alone, not in combination with any other race; Please refer to the Explanation of Data for more information.*

Race*	Population	%
African-American/Black (210)	231	1.85
Not Hispanic (208)	228	1.82
Hispanic (2)	3	0.02
American Indian/Alaska Native (7)	31	0.25
Not Hispanic (6)	29	0.23
Hispanic (1)	2	0.02
Apache (0)	2	0.02
Cherokee (0)	8	0.06
Chickasaw (0)	2	0.02
Creek (0)	1	0.01
Inupiat *(Alaska Native)* (1)	1	0.01
Mexican American Ind. (0)	1	0.01
Asian (254)	323	2.58
Not Hispanic (249)	315	2.52
Hispanic (5)	8	0.06
Chinese, ex. Taiwanese (29)	39	0.31
Filipino (101)	116	0.93
Indian (45)	57	0.46
Indonesian (0)	1	0.01
Japanese (12)	19	0.15
Korean (22)	25	0.20
Laotian (2)	4	0.03
Pakistani (10)	15	0.12
Taiwanese (16)	16	0.13
Thai (6)	6	0.05
Vietnamese (5)	5	0.04
Hawaii Native/Pacific Islander (1)	10	0.08
Not Hispanic (1)	10	0.08
White (11,791)	11,925	95.29
Not Hispanic (11,456)	11,556	92.34
Hispanic (335)	369	2.95

Palos Hills

Place Type: City
County: Cook
Population: 17,484†

Ancestry‡	Population	%
African, Sub-Saharan (18)	18	0.10
Nigerian (18)	18	0.10
American (388)	388	2.23
Arab (1,448)	1,536	8.84
Arab (607)	637	3.67
Jordanian (114)	114	0.66
Palestinian (272)	330	1.90
Other Arab (455)	455	2.62
Armenian (0)	19	0.11
Austrian (14)	91	0.52
Belgian (15)	15	0.09
Bulgarian (47)	47	0.27
Canadian (9)	9	0.05
Croatian (72)	204	1.17
Czech (93)	460	2.65
Czechoslovakian (11)	28	0.16
Danish (30)	30	0.17
Dutch (98)	165	0.95
Eastern European (18)	18	0.10
English (38)	409	2.36
European (27)	27	0.16
Finnish (0)	11	0.06
French, ex. Basque (54)	205	1.18
French Canadian (0)	30	0.17
German (458)	2,621	15.09
Greek (912)	1,289	7.42
Hungarian (24)	147	0.85
Irish (511)	2,437	14.03
Italian (772)	1,490	8.58
Lithuanian (747)	1,012	5.83
Northern European (15)	15	0.09
Norwegian (7)	98	0.56
Polish (2,734)	4,193	24.14
Portuguese (0)	15	0.09
Romanian (48)	118	0.68
Russian (38)	313	1.80
Scandinavian (70)	116	0.67
Scotch-Irish (31)	126	0.73
Scottish (11)	97	0.56
Serbian (0)	13	0.07
Slavic (31)	31	0.18
Slovak (28)	154	0.89
Slovene (0)	14	0.08
Swedish (88)	274	1.58
Ukrainian (57)	241	1.39
West Indian, ex. Hispanic (15)	15	0.09
Jamaican (15)	15	0.09
Yugoslavian (0)	8	0.05

Hispanic Origin	Population	%
Hispanic or Latino (of any race)	1,292	7.39
Central American, ex. Mexican	21	0.12
Guatemalan	15	0.09
Honduran	1	0.01
Nicaraguan	2	0.01
Salvadoran	3	0.02
Cuban	12	0.07
Dominican Republic	9	0.05
Mexican	1,061	6.07
Puerto Rican	72	0.41
South American	36	0.21
Argentinean	10	0.06
Colombian	10	0.06
Ecuadorian	2	0.01
Peruvian	2	0.01
Uruguayan	4	0.02
Venezuelan	8	0.05
Other Hispanic or Latino	81	0.46

Race*	Population	%
African-American/Black (949)	1,011	5.78
Not Hispanic (926)	977	5.59
Hispanic (23)	34	0.19
American Indian/Alaska Native (36)	66	0.38
Not Hispanic (14)	38	0.22
Hispanic (22)	28	0.16
Blackfeet (0)	3	0.02
Cherokee (9)	18	0.10
Chippewa (0)	3	0.02
Choctaw (0)	1	0.01
Cree (0)	1	0.01
Iroquois (2)	3	0.02
Lumbee (1)	1	0.01
Navajo (0)	1	0.01
Potawatomi (1)	1	0.01
Pueblo (0)	1	0.01
Asian (453)	579	3.31
Not Hispanic (450)	562	3.21
Hispanic (3)	17	0.10
Burmese (1)	1	0.01
Chinese, ex. Taiwanese (22)	32	0.18
Filipino (107)	123	0.70
Indian (128)	133	0.76
Japanese (7)	14	0.08
Korean (68)	79	0.45
Laotian (2)	3	0.02
Pakistani (36)	36	0.21
Taiwanese (6)	6	0.03
Thai (22)	24	0.14
Vietnamese (7)	9	0.05
Hawaii Native/Pacific Islander (4)	12	0.07
Not Hispanic (4)	11	0.06
Hispanic (0)	1	0.01
Marshallese (1)	1	0.01
Native Hawaiian (0)	1	0.01
Samoan (1)	2	0.01
White (15,397)	15,650	89.51
Not Hispanic (14,591)	14,774	84.50
Hispanic (806)	876	5.01

Paris

Place Type: City
County: Edgar
Population: 8,837†

Ancestry‡	Population	%
American (1,237)	1,237	13.70
British (28)	82	0.91
Bulgarian (0)	16	0.18
Cajun (15)	15	0.17
Canadian (6)	6	0.07
Czech (29)	55	0.61
Danish (7)	27	0.30
Dutch (27)	211	2.34
English (470)	1,098	12.16
European (12)	53	0.59
French, ex. Basque (57)	200	2.22
German (844)	2,153	23.85
Irish (297)	1,289	14.28
Italian (21)	142	1.57
Northern European (9)	9	0.10
Norwegian (61)	61	0.68
Polish (24)	78	0.86
Scotch-Irish (78)	149	1.65
Scottish (160)	226	2.50
Serbian (13)	13	0.14
Slovak (0)	10	0.11
Swedish (29)	50	0.55
Swiss (15)	29	0.32
Welsh (28)	28	0.31

Hispanic Origin	Population	%
Hispanic or Latino (of any race)	112	1.27
Central American, ex. Mexican	2	0.02
Salvadoran	2	0.02
Cuban	7	0.08
Mexican	73	0.83
Puerto Rican	9	0.10
South American	8	0.09
Colombian	6	0.07
Ecuadorian	1	0.01
Uruguayan	1	0.01
Other Hispanic or Latino	13	0.15

Race*	Population	%
African-American/Black (40)	70	0.79
Not Hispanic (39)	69	0.78
Hispanic (1)	1	0.01
American Indian/Alaska Native (12)	43	0.49
Not Hispanic (10)	41	0.46
Hispanic (2)	2	0.02
Blackfeet (0)	1	0.01
Cherokee (1)	13	0.15
Crow (0)	3	0.03
Iroquois (0)	1	0.01
Kiowa (1)	1	0.01
Asian (20)	34	0.38
Not Hispanic (20)	33	0.37
Hispanic (0)	1	0.01
Chinese, ex. Taiwanese (2)	2	0.02
Filipino (4)	6	0.07
Indian (4)	7	0.08
Japanese (3)	6	0.07
Korean (0)	2	0.02
Pakistani (7)	7	0.08
Vietnamese (0)	1	0.01
Hawaii Native/Pacific Islander (2)	2	0.02
Not Hispanic (2)	2	0.02
Guamanian/Chamorro (1)	1	0.01
Samoan (1)	1	0.01
White (8,649)	8,719	98.66
Not Hispanic (8,580)	8,644	97.82
Hispanic (69)	75	0.85

Park City

Place Type: City
County: Lake
Population: 7,570†

Ancestry‡	Population	%
African, Sub-Saharan (13)	222	2.92
African (0)	164	2.16
Nigerian (13)	58	0.76
American (170)	170	2.24
Armenian (11)	11	0.14
Austrian (0)	10	0.13
Belgian (11)	11	0.14

*Notes: † The Census 2010 population figure is used to calculate the percentages in the Hispanic Origin and Race categories. Ancestry percentages are based on the 2006-2010 American Community Survey population (not shown); ‡ Numbers in parentheses indicate the number of people reporting a single ancestry; * Numbers in parentheses indicate the number of persons reporting this race alone, not in combination with any other race; Please refer to the Explanation of Data for more information.*

Croatian (13)	13	0.17
Czechoslovakian (0)	10	0.13
Danish (0)	10	0.13
Dutch (0)	11	0.14
English (80)	100	1.32
European (22)	22	0.29
Finnish (54)	54	0.71
French, ex. Basque (0)	33	0.43
French Canadian (0)	11	0.14
German (220)	449	5.91
Greek (0)	10	0.13
Hungarian (9)	39	0.51
Iranian (0)	19	0.25
Irish (123)	308	4.05
Israeli (0)	19	0.25
Italian (61)	161	2.12
Lithuanian (0)	19	0.25
Norwegian (0)	62	0.82
Polish (111)	238	3.13
Russian (11)	11	0.14
Scotch-Irish (63)	73	0.96
Scottish (0)	15	0.20
Slovak (0)	11	0.14
Slovene (10)	10	0.13
Swedish (0)	39	0.51
Ukrainian (39)	82	1.08
West Indian, ex. Hispanic (40)	40	0.53
Belizean (40)	40	0.53

Hispanic Origin	Population	%
Hispanic or Latino (of any race)	4,933	65.17
Central American, ex. Mexican	217	2.87
Guatemalan	48	0.63
Honduran	95	1.25
Nicaraguan	12	0.16
Panamanian	3	0.04
Salvadoran	46	0.61
Other Central American	13	0.17
Cuban	8	0.11
Dominican Republic	4	0.05
Mexican	4,279	56.53
Puerto Rican	214	2.83
South American	49	0.65
Argentinean	8	0.11
Bolivian	2	0.03
Chilean	3	0.04
Colombian	25	0.33
Ecuadorian	1	0.01
Peruvian	5	0.07
Venezuelan	4	0.05
Other South American	1	0.01
Other Hispanic or Latino	162	2.14

Race*	Population	%
African-American/Black (559)	633	8.36
Not Hispanic (529)	581	7.68
Hispanic (30)	52	0.69
American Indian/Alaska Native (73)	113	1.49
Not Hispanic (7)	39	0.52
Hispanic (66)	74	0.98
Aleut *(Alaska Native)* (1)	1	0.01
Apache (1)	3	0.04
Blackfeet (0)	3	0.04
Central American Ind. (1)	1	0.01
Cherokee (1)	27	0.36
Chickasaw (0)	4	0.05
Chippewa (0)	2	0.03
Delaware (0)	1	0.01
Mexican American Ind. (8)	8	0.11
Sioux (0)	7	0.09
Spanish American Ind. (1)	1	0.01
Asian (405)	464	6.13
Not Hispanic (386)	431	5.69
Hispanic (19)	33	0.44
Cambodian (45)	54	0.71
Chinese, ex. Taiwanese (13)	23	0.30
Filipino (204)	235	3.10
Indian (79)	104	1.37
Japanese (1)	8	0.11
Korean (12)	16	0.21
Laotian (2)	3	0.04
Malaysian (1)	2	0.03
Pakistani (10)	20	0.26
Thai (1)	2	0.03
Vietnamese (7)	12	0.16
Hawaii Native/Pacific Islander (10)	15	0.20
Not Hispanic (9)	13	0.17
Hispanic (1)	2	0.03
Native Hawaiian (0)	3	0.04
White (3,446)	3,698	48.85
Not Hispanic (1,564)	1,650	21.80
Hispanic (1,882)	2,048	27.05

Park Forest

Place Type: Village
County: Cook
Population: 21,975†

Ancestry‡	Population	%
African, Sub-Saharan (255)	280	1.25
African (112)	137	0.61
Nigerian (143)	143	0.64
American (247)	247	1.11
Arab (6)	6	0.03
Palestinian (6)	6	0.03
Austrian (0)	39	0.17
British (52)	52	0.23
Canadian (6)	6	0.03
Croatian (18)	37	0.17
Czech (9)	90	0.40
Czechoslovakian (19)	53	0.24
Danish (0)	18	0.08
Dutch (9)	308	1.38
Eastern European (63)	63	0.28
English (276)	1,190	5.33
European (199)	199	0.89
Finnish (16)	16	0.07
French, ex. Basque (13)	186	0.83
French Canadian (16)	98	0.44
German (757)	2,869	12.85
Greek (0)	31	0.14
Hungarian (57)	150	0.67
Icelander (0)	24	0.11
Irish (526)	2,016	9.03
Italian (340)	888	3.98
Latvian (0)	16	0.07
Lithuanian (56)	217	0.97
Norwegian (7)	97	0.43
Pennsylvania German (0)	5	0.02
Polish (232)	810	3.63
Romanian (0)	14	0.06
Russian (31)	46	0.21
Scotch-Irish (46)	245	1.10
Scottish (87)	212	0.95
Slovak (6)	69	0.31
Swedish (69)	359	1.61
Swiss (0)	10	0.04
Ukrainian (27)	34	0.15
Welsh (0)	35	0.16
West Indian, ex. Hispanic (42)	115	0.52
Jamaican (42)	115	0.52
Yugoslavian (0)	12	0.05

Hispanic Origin	Population	%
Hispanic or Latino (of any race)	1,407	6.40
Central American, ex. Mexican	25	0.11
Costa Rican	6	0.03
Guatemalan	5	0.02
Honduran	1	<0.01
Nicaraguan	1	<0.01
Panamanian	4	0.02
Salvadoran	7	0.03
Other Central American	1	<0.01
Cuban	38	0.17
Dominican Republic	5	0.02
Mexican	1,033	4.70
Puerto Rican	194	0.88
South American	29	0.13
Argentinean	4	0.02
Chilean	3	0.01
Colombian	10	0.05
Ecuadorian	2	0.01
Peruvian	8	0.04
Uruguayan	1	<0.01
Other South American	1	<0.01
Other Hispanic or Latino	83	0.38

Race*	Population	%
African-American/Black (13,144)	13,765	62.64
Not Hispanic (12,977)	13,486	61.37
Hispanic (167)	279	1.27
American Indian/Alaska Native (69)	247	1.12
Not Hispanic (37)	179	0.81
Hispanic (32)	68	0.31
Arapaho (0)	4	0.02
Blackfeet (1)	11	0.05
Cherokee (8)	54	0.25
Chippewa (5)	7	0.03
Choctaw (0)	20	0.09
Creek (1)	5	0.02
Iroquois (0)	2	0.01
Menominee (0)	1	<0.01
Mexican American Ind. (3)	3	0.01
Navajo (0)	1	<0.01
Ottawa (0)	1	<0.01
Potawatomi (1)	3	0.01
Seminole (0)	2	0.01
Sioux (0)	6	0.03
Asian (166)	254	1.16
Not Hispanic (157)	229	1.04
Hispanic (9)	25	0.11
Chinese, ex. Taiwanese (27)	36	0.16
Filipino (43)	69	0.31
Hmong (1)	2	0.01
Indian (54)	61	0.28
Indonesian (2)	2	0.01
Japanese (6)	22	0.10
Korean (14)	25	0.11
Laotian (6)	10	0.05
Pakistani (2)	2	0.01
Thai (7)	10	0.05
Vietnamese (1)	4	0.02
Hawaii Native/Pacific Islander (10)	28	0.13
Not Hispanic (10)	28	0.13
Guamanian/Chamorro (0)	3	0.01
Native Hawaiian (2)	10	0.05
Samoan (8)	12	0.05
White (7,338)	7,938	36.12
Not Hispanic (6,759)	7,228	32.89
Hispanic (579)	710	3.23

Park Ridge

Place Type: City
County: Cook
Population: 37,480†

Ancestry‡	Population	%
Albanian (8)	17	0.05
Alsatian (0)	11	0.03
American (881)	881	2.37
Arab (286)	298	0.80
Egyptian (11)	23	0.06
Jordanian (168)	168	0.45
Lebanese (26)	26	0.07
Syrian (81)	81	0.22
Armenian (29)	60	0.16
Assyrian/Chaldean/Syriac (167)	255	0.69
Australian (48)	48	0.13
Austrian (16)	212	0.57
Basque (0)	10	0.03
Belgian (25)	125	0.34
British (21)	58	0.16
Bulgarian (85)	85	0.23
Cajun (11)	11	0.03
Canadian (56)	96	0.26
Celtic (6)	20	0.05
Croatian (0)	13	0.04
Czech (65)	415	1.12

*Notes: † The Census 2010 population figure is used to calculate the percentages in the Hispanic Origin and Race categories. Ancestry percentages are based on the 2006-2010 American Community Survey population (not shown); ‡ Numbers in parentheses indicate the number of people reporting a single ancestry; * Numbers in parentheses indicate the number of persons reporting this race alone, not in combination with any other race; Please refer to the Explanation of Data for more information.*

Czechoslovakian (30)	66	0.18
Danish (55)	239	0.64
Dutch (94)	435	1.17
Eastern European (80)	80	0.22
English (364)	2,382	6.42
European (344)	392	1.06
Finnish (14)	80	0.22
French, ex. Basque (112)	685	1.85
French Canadian (35)	182	0.49
German (2,258)	8,817	23.76
Greek (762)	1,134	3.06
Hungarian (66)	245	0.66
Icelander (8)	8	0.02
Iranian (46)	46	0.12
Irish (3,213)	7,848	21.15
Italian (2,871)	5,657	15.24
Latvian (105)	105	0.28
Lithuanian (105)	194	0.52
Luxemburger (0)	10	0.03
Norwegian (272)	1,069	2.88
Polish (4,327)	7,624	20.54
Portuguese (0)	22	0.06
Romanian (108)	145	0.39
Russian (128)	567	1.53
Scandinavian (0)	29	0.08
Scotch-Irish (181)	643	1.73
Scottish (68)	529	1.43
Serbian (78)	98	0.26
Slavic (10)	20	0.05
Slovak (113)	171	0.46
Slovene (18)	24	0.06
Swedish (298)	1,404	3.78
Swiss (24)	197	0.53
Turkish (56)	56	0.15
Ukrainian (335)	606	1.63
Welsh (40)	230	0.62
West Indian, ex. Hispanic (11)	11	0.03
U.S. Virgin Islander (11)	11	0.03
Yugoslavian (152)	200	0.54

Hispanic Origin	Population	%
Hispanic or Latino (of any race)	1,774	4.73
Central American, ex. Mexican	90	0.24
Costa Rican	4	0.01
Guatemalan	62	0.17
Honduran	3	0.01
Nicaraguan	3	0.01
Panamanian	11	0.03
Salvadoran	7	0.02
Cuban	155	0.41
Dominican Republic	14	0.04
Mexican	882	2.35
Puerto Rican	277	0.74
South American	227	0.61
Argentinean	34	0.09
Bolivian	16	0.04
Chilean	7	0.02
Colombian	66	0.18
Ecuadorian	52	0.14
Paraguayan	1	<0.01
Peruvian	33	0.09
Uruguayan	4	0.01
Venezuelan	12	0.03
Other South American	2	0.01
Other Hispanic or Latino	129	0.34

Race*	Population	%
African-American/Black (178)	244	0.65
Not Hispanic (168)	227	0.61
Hispanic (10)	17	0.05
American Indian/Alaska Native (29)	100	0.27
Not Hispanic (19)	79	0.21
Hispanic (10)	21	0.06
Blackfeet (0)	5	0.01
Cherokee (4)	21	0.06
Chippewa (2)	8	0.02
Choctaw (0)	1	<0.01
Comanche (1)	1	<0.01
Creek (0)	2	0.01
Iroquois (1)	1	<0.01
Lumbee (2)	2	0.01
Menominee (2)	2	0.01
Mexican American Ind. (5)	5	0.01
Navajo (1)	2	0.01
Potawatomi (0)	1	<0.01
Seminole (0)	6	0.02
Sioux (1)	3	0.01
South American Ind. (0)	1	<0.01
Tohono O'Odham (1)	1	<0.01
Asian (1,402)	1,688	4.50
Not Hispanic (1,373)	1,616	4.31
Hispanic (29)	72	0.19
Bangladeshi (18)	18	0.05
Cambodian (3)	5	0.01
Chinese, ex. Taiwanese (233)	305	0.81
Filipino (414)	538	1.44
Indian (302)	337	0.90
Indonesian (1)	1	<0.01
Japanese (98)	147	0.39
Korean (141)	189	0.50
Laotian (1)	3	0.01
Malaysian (0)	1	<0.01
Pakistani (33)	37	0.10
Sri Lankan (1)	1	<0.01
Taiwanese (16)	17	0.05
Thai (28)	30	0.08
Vietnamese (17)	24	0.06
Hawaii Native/Pacific Islander (5)	17	0.05
Not Hispanic (4)	11	0.03
Hispanic (1)	6	0.02
Guamanian/Chamorro (1)	1	<0.01
Native Hawaiian (4)	15	0.04
White (35,014)	35,480	94.66
Not Hispanic (33,744)	34,091	90.96
Hispanic (1,270)	1,389	3.71

Pekin

Place Type: City
County: Tazewell
Population: 34,094†

Ancestry‡	Population	%
African, Sub-Saharan (70)	107	0.32
African (70)	107	0.32
American (5,931)	5,931	17.58
Arab (92)	100	0.30
Arab (28)	28	0.08
Lebanese (13)	21	0.06
Moroccan (40)	40	0.12
Palestinian (11)	11	0.03
Australian (24)	24	0.07
Austrian (5)	22	0.07
Belgian (21)	30	0.09
British (8)	37	0.11
Canadian (20)	30	0.09
Croatian (35)	57	0.17
Czech (43)	164	0.49
Danish (68)	200	0.59
Dutch (199)	845	2.50
English (1,369)	3,493	10.35
European (212)	212	0.63
Finnish (12)	24	0.07
French, ex. Basque (297)	1,186	3.52
French Canadian (23)	23	0.07
German (4,697)	10,551	31.28
Greek (16)	58	0.17
Hungarian (0)	15	0.04
Irish (1,708)	5,024	14.89
Italian (921)	1,825	5.41
Norwegian (92)	206	0.61
Polish (131)	676	2.00
Portuguese (12)	25	0.07
Romanian (34)	47	0.14
Russian (26)	62	0.18
Scandinavian (21)	21	0.06
Scotch-Irish (196)	435	1.29
Scottish (265)	745	2.21
Slavic (0)	24	0.07
Slovak (19)	60	0.18
Swedish (150)	590	1.75
Swiss (38)	230	0.68
Ukrainian (18)	18	0.05
Welsh (23)	107	0.32
West Indian, ex. Hispanic (19)	19	0.06
Jamaican (19)	19	0.06
Yugoslavian (0)	19	0.06

Hispanic Origin	Population	%
Hispanic or Latino (of any race)	818	2.40
Central American, ex. Mexican	10	0.03
Guatemalan	2	0.01
Honduran	1	<0.01
Nicaraguan	1	<0.01
Panamanian	1	<0.01
Salvadoran	5	0.01
Cuban	12	0.04
Dominican Republic	5	0.01
Mexican	568	1.67
Puerto Rican	77	0.23
South American	31	0.09
Argentinean	1	<0.01
Chilean	5	0.01
Colombian	14	0.04
Ecuadorian	1	<0.01
Peruvian	8	0.02
Uruguayan	1	<0.01
Venezuelan	1	<0.01
Other Hispanic or Latino	115	0.34

Race*	Population	%
African-American/Black (710)	876	2.57
Not Hispanic (700)	854	2.50
Hispanic (10)	22	0.06
American Indian/Alaska Native (153)	321	0.94
Not Hispanic (130)	275	0.81
Hispanic (23)	46	0.13
Aleut *(Alaska Native)* (1)	2	0.01
Apache (2)	5	0.01
Arapaho (1)	1	<0.01
Blackfeet (2)	12	0.04
Canadian/French Am. Ind. (1)	2	0.01
Central American Ind. (2)	2	0.01
Cherokee (10)	48	0.14
Cheyenne (0)	1	<0.01
Chippewa (26)	28	0.08
Choctaw (3)	14	0.04
Comanche (3)	7	0.02
Cree (1)	1	<0.01
Creek (1)	1	<0.01
Inupiat *(Alaska Native)* (1)	1	<0.01
Iroquois (2)	8	0.02
Menominee (7)	7	0.02
Mexican American Ind. (4)	6	0.02
Navajo (2)	2	0.01
Pueblo (1)	2	0.01
Seminole (0)	1	<0.01
Sioux (13)	15	0.04
Tlingit-Haida *(Alaska Native)* (0)	1	<0.01
Asian (214)	312	0.92
Not Hispanic (213)	307	0.90
Hispanic (1)	5	0.01
Burmese (1)	1	<0.01
Chinese, ex. Taiwanese (36)	44	0.13
Filipino (35)	63	0.18
Hmong (13)	13	0.04
Indian (16)	25	0.07
Indonesian (0)	1	<0.01
Japanese (16)	31	0.09
Korean (16)	32	0.09
Laotian (6)	6	0.02
Pakistani (18)	18	0.05
Sri Lankan (1)	1	<0.01
Taiwanese (1)	1	<0.01
Thai (11)	21	0.06
Vietnamese (35)	45	0.13
Hawaii Native/Pacific Islander (7)	33	0.10
Not Hispanic (7)	27	0.08
Hispanic (0)	6	0.02
Guamanian/Chamorro (2)	2	0.01

*Notes: † The Census 2010 population figure is used to calculate the percentages in the Hispanic Origin and Race categories. Ancestry percentages are based on the 2006-2010 American Community Survey population (not shown); ‡ Numbers in parentheses indicate the number of people reporting a single ancestry; * Numbers in parentheses indicate the number of persons reporting this race alone, not in combination with any other race; Please refer to the Explanation of Data for more information.*

Native Hawaiian (2)	16	0.05
Samoan (0)	3	0.01
White (32,285)	32,734	96.01
Not Hispanic (31,817)	32,191	94.42
Hispanic (468)	543	1.59

Peoria

Place Type: City
County: Peoria
Population: 115,007†

Ancestry‡	Population	%
Afghan (71)	71	0.06
African, Sub-Saharan (413)	489	0.43
African (136)	212	0.19
Ghanaian (236)	236	0.21
Nigerian (18)	18	0.02
South African (13)	13	0.01
Sudanese (10)	10	0.01
Albanian (0)	15	0.01
Alsatian (0)	13	0.01
American (4,712)	4,712	4.14
Arab (692)	1,002	0.88
Arab (110)	110	0.10
Jordanian (18)	18	0.02
Lebanese (564)	874	0.77
Austrian (17)	217	0.19
Belgian (152)	465	0.41
Brazilian (71)	144	0.13
British (140)	341	0.30
Canadian (27)	77	0.07
Celtic (0)	12	0.01
Croatian (54)	162	0.14
Czech (135)	749	0.66
Czechoslovakian (10)	72	0.06
Danish (77)	386	0.34
Dutch (134)	1,746	1.53
Eastern European (77)	101	0.09
English (2,566)	10,009	8.79
European (926)	1,028	0.90
Finnish (14)	64	0.06
French, ex. Basque (664)	3,579	3.14
French Canadian (301)	515	0.45
German (8,867)	26,263	23.07
Greek (230)	352	0.31
Guyanese (11)	22	0.02
Hungarian (131)	436	0.38
Iranian (56)	86	0.08
Irish (3,834)	15,136	13.29
Italian (1,641)	4,211	3.70
Latvian (12)	12	0.01
Lithuanian (160)	319	0.28
Luxemburger (0)	62	0.05
Macedonian (18)	18	0.02
Northern European (0)	13	0.01
Norwegian (408)	1,408	1.24
Pennsylvania German (11)	28	0.02
Polish (649)	2,654	2.33
Portuguese (14)	103	0.09
Romanian (53)	95	0.08
Russian (122)	391	0.34
Scandinavian (105)	227	0.20
Scotch-Irish (585)	1,755	1.54
Scottish (558)	1,670	1.47
Serbian (72)	222	0.19
Slavic (31)	57	0.05
Slovak (64)	276	0.24
Slovene (65)	105	0.09
Swedish (566)	2,798	2.46
Swiss (158)	729	0.64
Ukrainian (51)	120	0.11
Welsh (127)	669	0.59
West Indian, ex. Hispanic (326)	346	0.30
Dutch West Indian (0)	9	0.01
Haitian (313)	313	0.27
Jamaican (13)	24	0.02
Yugoslavian (22)	115	0.10

Hispanic Origin	Population	%
Hispanic or Latino (of any race)	5,628	4.89
Central American, ex. Mexican	185	0.16
Costa Rican	6	0.01
Guatemalan	79	0.07
Honduran	31	0.03
Nicaraguan	9	0.01
Panamanian	21	0.02
Salvadoran	37	0.03
Other Central American	2	<0.01
Cuban	122	0.11
Dominican Republic	24	0.02
Mexican	4,422	3.84
Puerto Rican	299	0.26
South American	197	0.17
Argentinean	18	0.02
Bolivian	16	0.01
Chilean	20	0.02
Colombian	76	0.07
Ecuadorian	16	0.01
Paraguayan	2	<0.01
Peruvian	16	0.01
Uruguayan	5	<0.01
Venezuelan	27	0.02
Other South American	1	<0.01
Other Hispanic or Latino	379	0.33

Race*	Population	%
African-American/Black (30,991)	33,877	29.46
Not Hispanic (30,705)	33,328	28.98
Hispanic (286)	549	0.48
American Indian/Alaska Native (360)	1,021	0.89
Not Hispanic (233)	815	0.71
Hispanic (127)	206	0.18
Alaska Athabascan *(Ala. Nat.)* (2)	3	<0.01
Apache (4)	10	0.01
Arapaho (1)	2	<0.01
Blackfeet (3)	30	0.03
Central American Ind. (1)	3	<0.01
Cherokee (51)	215	0.19
Chickasaw (0)	11	0.01
Chippewa (4)	24	0.02
Choctaw (8)	21	0.02
Cree (1)	5	<0.01
Creek (2)	4	<0.01
Crow (0)	4	<0.01
Delaware (3)	4	<0.01
Houma (2)	2	<0.01
Inupiat *(Alaska Native)* (1)	1	<0.01
Iroquois (2)	5	<0.01
Lumbee (2)	6	0.01
Menominee (1)	3	<0.01
Mexican American Ind. (13)	17	0.01
Navajo (3)	16	0.01
Osage (1)	2	<0.01
Ottawa (4)	7	0.01
Pima (2)	2	<0.01
Potawatomi (1)	1	<0.01
Puget Sound Salish (4)	4	<0.01
Seminole (0)	4	<0.01
Shoshone (0)	1	<0.01
Sioux (11)	26	0.02
Spanish American Ind. (0)	1	<0.01
Yaqui (2)	2	<0.01
Yup'ik *(Alaska Native)* (1)	1	<0.01
Asian (5,240)	5,927	5.15
Not Hispanic (5,214)	5,864	5.10
Hispanic (26)	63	0.05
Bangladeshi (50)	51	0.04
Burmese (20)	21	0.02
Cambodian (1)	1	<0.01
Chinese, ex. Taiwanese (959)	1,081	0.94
Filipino (371)	521	0.45
Hmong (1)	1	<0.01
Indian (2,528)	2,673	2.32
Indonesian (28)	31	0.03
Japanese (106)	201	0.17
Korean (288)	361	0.31
Laotian (57)	76	0.07
Malaysian (14)	17	0.01
Nepalese (19)	19	0.02
Pakistani (226)	246	0.21
Sri Lankan (26)	27	0.02
Taiwanese (35)	43	0.04
Thai (28)	54	0.05
Vietnamese (366)	439	0.38
Hawaii Native/Pacific Islander (29)	125	0.11
Not Hispanic (27)	112	0.10
Hispanic (2)	13	0.01
Guamanian/Chamorro (4)	24	0.02
Native Hawaiian (15)	46	0.04
Samoan (3)	9	0.01
White (71,740)	75,399	65.56
Not Hispanic (69,454)	72,633	63.16
Hispanic (2,286)	2,766	2.41

Peru

Place Type: City
County: LaSalle
Population: 10,295†

Ancestry‡	Population	%
African, Sub-Saharan (99)	113	1.10
African (99)	99	0.97
Ethiopian (0)	14	0.14
American (582)	582	5.68
Austrian (9)	45	0.44
Belgian (11)	31	0.30
British (0)	26	0.25
Croatian (17)	43	0.42
Czech (11)	86	0.84
Danish (0)	10	0.10
Dutch (21)	101	0.99
English (239)	946	9.24
Estonian (24)	24	0.23
European (83)	114	1.11
Finnish (0)	41	0.40
French, ex. Basque (29)	241	2.35
German (942)	3,466	33.85
Greek (16)	36	0.35
Irish (451)	1,865	18.21
Italian (597)	1,574	15.37
Lithuanian (0)	61	0.60
Norwegian (18)	113	1.10
Polish (545)	1,807	17.65
Romanian (10)	20	0.20
Russian (0)	9	0.09
Scotch-Irish (38)	197	1.92
Scottish (41)	218	2.13
Slavic (10)	19	0.19
Slovak (31)	61	0.60
Slovene (31)	105	1.03
Swedish (40)	192	1.88
Swiss (0)	19	0.19
Turkish (18)	18	0.18
Welsh (7)	35	0.34
Yugoslavian (0)	10	0.10

Hispanic Origin	Population	%
Hispanic or Latino (of any race)	633	6.15
Central American, ex. Mexican	10	0.10
Costa Rican	4	0.04
Honduran	2	0.02
Salvadoran	3	0.03
Other Central American	1	0.01
Cuban	2	0.02
Mexican	526	5.11
Puerto Rican	41	0.40
South American	10	0.10
Bolivian	1	0.01
Chilean	1	0.01
Colombian	8	0.08
Other Hispanic or Latino	44	0.43

Race*	Population	%
African-American/Black (72)	129	1.25
Not Hispanic (71)	122	1.19
Hispanic (1)	7	0.07
American Indian/Alaska Native (27)	60	0.58

*Notes: † The Census 2010 population figure is used to calculate the percentages in the Hispanic Origin and Race categories. Ancestry percentages are based on the 2006-2010 American Community Survey population (not shown); ‡ Numbers in parentheses indicate the number of people reporting a single ancestry; * Numbers in parentheses indicate the number of persons reporting this race alone, not in combination with any other race; Please refer to the Explanation of Data for more information.*

Not Hispanic (15)	44	0.43
Hispanic (12)	16	0.16
Apache (0)	4	0.04
Blackfeet (0)	1	0.01
Canadian/French Am. Ind. (0)	1	0.01
Cherokee (3)	15	0.15
Chippewa (1)	1	0.01
Choctaw (1)	3	0.03
Creek (0)	1	0.01
Iroquois (0)	3	0.03
Mexican American Ind. (2)	3	0.03
Navajo (1)	1	0.01
Sioux (2)	2	0.02
Asian (167)	195	1.89
Not Hispanic (167)	190	1.85
Hispanic (0)	5	0.05
Chinese, ex. Taiwanese (44)	45	0.44
Filipino (25)	34	0.33
Indian (41)	44	0.43
Japanese (25)	31	0.30
Korean (5)	11	0.11
Thai (1)	1	0.01
Vietnamese (15)	15	0.15
Hawaii Native/Pacific Islander (0)	3	0.03
Not Hispanic (0)	2	0.02
Hispanic (0)	1	0.01
Guamanian/Chamorro (0)	1	0.01
Native Hawaiian (0)	2	0.02
White (9,665)	9,803	95.22
Not Hispanic (9,303)	9,406	91.36
Hispanic (362)	397	3.86

Plainfield

Place Type: Village
County: Will
Population: 39,581†

Ancestry‡	Population	%
African, Sub-Saharan (78)	104	0.29
African (11)	11	0.03
South African (26)	52	0.15
Other Sub-Saharan African (41)	41	0.11
Albanian (0)	85	0.24
American (864)	864	2.42
Arab (229)	325	0.91
Arab (128)	186	0.52
Iraqi (18)	18	0.05
Lebanese (12)	43	0.12
Syrian (0)	7	0.02
Other Arab (71)	71	0.20
Austrian (9)	128	0.36
Belgian (8)	30	0.08
British (84)	105	0.29
Bulgarian (140)	140	0.39
Canadian (68)	114	0.32
Croatian (28)	262	0.73
Czech (303)	1,111	3.11
Czechoslovakian (42)	119	0.33
Danish (16)	199	0.56
Dutch (171)	772	2.16
Eastern European (79)	91	0.25
English (497)	2,521	7.06
European (121)	130	0.36
Finnish (21)	85	0.24
French, ex. Basque (97)	789	2.21
French Canadian (40)	234	0.66
German (1,508)	7,815	21.89
Greek (236)	496	1.39
Hungarian (120)	274	0.77
Iranian (25)	65	0.18
Irish (1,172)	7,614	21.32
Italian (1,209)	5,712	16.00
Lithuanian (47)	364	1.02
Luxemburger (0)	12	0.03
Macedonian (83)	83	0.23
Northern European (13)	13	0.04
Norwegian (226)	735	2.06
Polish (1,315)	4,608	12.90
Portuguese (0)	23	0.06
Romanian (41)	41	0.11
Russian (41)	114	0.32
Scandinavian (31)	31	0.09
Scotch-Irish (112)	320	0.90
Scottish (63)	485	1.36
Serbian (14)	79	0.22
Slavic (30)	46	0.13
Slovak (51)	180	0.50
Slovene (74)	123	0.34
Swedish (245)	1,045	2.93
Swiss (12)	50	0.14
Ukrainian (72)	104	0.29
Welsh (0)	162	0.45
West Indian, ex. Hispanic (16)	16	0.04
Haitian (16)	16	0.04

Hispanic Origin	Population	%
Hispanic or Latino (of any race)	4,247	10.73
Central American, ex. Mexican	116	0.29
Costa Rican	1	<0.01
Guatemalan	75	0.19
Honduran	11	0.03
Nicaraguan	1	<0.01
Panamanian	7	0.02
Salvadoran	20	0.05
Other Central American	1	<0.01
Cuban	88	0.22
Dominican Republic	17	0.04
Mexican	3,124	7.89
Puerto Rican	516	1.30
South American	221	0.56
Argentinean	29	0.07
Bolivian	8	0.02
Chilean	2	0.01
Colombian	83	0.21
Ecuadorian	33	0.08
Paraguayan	1	<0.01
Peruvian	26	0.07
Uruguayan	3	0.01
Venezuelan	32	0.08
Other South American	4	0.01
Other Hispanic or Latino	165	0.42

Race*	Population	%
African-American/Black (2,202)	2,453	6.20
Not Hispanic (2,155)	2,372	5.99
Hispanic (47)	81	0.20
American Indian/Alaska Native (89)	199	0.50
Not Hispanic (46)	134	0.34
Hispanic (43)	65	0.16
Apache (0)	2	0.01
Arapaho (1)	1	<0.01
Blackfeet (1)	10	0.03
Canadian/French Am. Ind. (0)	3	0.01
Cherokee (12)	49	0.12
Chickasaw (0)	1	<0.01
Chippewa (4)	5	0.01
Choctaw (1)	2	0.01
Comanche (0)	4	0.01
Cree (1)	1	<0.01
Creek (1)	2	0.01
Delaware (0)	2	0.01
Iroquois (0)	2	0.01
Lumbee (0)	3	0.01
Mexican American Ind. (10)	11	0.03
Potawatomi (5)	5	0.01
Sioux (0)	2	0.01
South American Ind. (4)	4	0.01
Asian (3,016)	3,449	8.71
Not Hispanic (2,993)	3,360	8.49
Hispanic (23)	89	0.22
Bangladeshi (11)	12	0.03
Burmese (3)	6	0.02
Cambodian (16)	17	0.04
Chinese, ex. Taiwanese (274)	348	0.88
Filipino (731)	936	2.36
Hmong (8)	9	0.02
Indian (1,183)	1,284	3.24
Indonesian (3)	3	0.01
Japanese (25)	60	0.15
Korean (166)	198	0.50
Laotian (33)	43	0.11
Nepalese (1)	2	0.01
Pakistani (273)	323	0.82
Sri Lankan (4)	4	0.01
Taiwanese (17)	21	0.05
Thai (20)	45	0.11
Vietnamese (131)	161	0.41
Hawaii Native/Pacific Islander (16)	61	0.15
Not Hispanic (12)	47	0.12
Hispanic (4)	14	0.04
Fijian (0)	1	<0.01
Guamanian/Chamorro (4)	12	0.03
Native Hawaiian (8)	29	0.07
Samoan (0)	7	0.02
Tongan (0)	4	0.01
White (32,347)	33,115	83.66
Not Hispanic (29,415)	29,982	75.75
Hispanic (2,932)	3,133	7.92

Plano

Place Type: City
County: Kendall
Population: 10,856†

Ancestry‡	Population	%
American (440)	440	4.65
Arab (19)	19	0.20
Palestinian (19)	19	0.20
Austrian (0)	14	0.15
British (15)	29	0.31
Croatian (0)	19	0.20
Czech (27)	148	1.56
Danish (0)	44	0.46
Dutch (26)	81	0.86
English (154)	511	5.39
European (63)	63	0.67
French, ex. Basque (0)	380	4.01
French Canadian (0)	66	0.70
German (620)	1,707	18.02
Greek (5)	20	0.21
Hungarian (51)	236	2.49
Irish (113)	1,092	11.53
Italian (164)	729	7.70
Lithuanian (38)	38	0.40
Norwegian (57)	202	2.13
Polish (377)	873	9.22
Russian (8)	39	0.41
Scotch-Irish (0)	113	1.19
Scottish (0)	44	0.46
Slovak (0)	27	0.29
Slovene (11)	40	0.42
Swedish (70)	201	2.12
Swiss (0)	39	0.41
Ukrainian (33)	33	0.35
Welsh (15)	15	0.16
West Indian, ex. Hispanic (0)	22	0.23
Haitian (0)	22	0.23

Hispanic Origin	Population	%
Hispanic or Latino (of any race)	3,382	31.15
Central American, ex. Mexican	43	0.40
Costa Rican	4	0.04
Guatemalan	16	0.15
Honduran	1	0.01
Nicaraguan	12	0.11
Panamanian	2	0.02
Salvadoran	8	0.07
Cuban	13	0.12
Dominican Republic	1	0.01
Mexican	2,984	27.49
Puerto Rican	185	1.70
South American	73	0.67
Argentinean	2	0.02
Bolivian	6	0.06
Chilean	7	0.06
Colombian	29	0.27
Ecuadorian	16	0.15
Peruvian	2	0.02

*Notes: † The Census 2010 population figure is used to calculate the percentages in the Hispanic Origin and Race categories. Ancestry percentages are based on the 2006-2010 American Community Survey population (not shown); ‡ Numbers in parentheses indicate the number of people reporting a single ancestry; * Numbers in parentheses indicate the number of persons reporting this race alone, not in combination with any other race; Please refer to the Explanation of Data for more information.*

Uruguayan	1	0.01
Venezuelan	4	0.04
Other South American	6	0.06
Other Hispanic or Latino	83	0.76

Race*	Population	%
African-American/Black (796)	921	8.48
Not Hispanic (754)	841	7.75
Hispanic (42)	80	0.74
American Indian/Alaska Native (28)	83	0.76
Not Hispanic (12)	40	0.37
Hispanic (16)	43	0.40
Blackfeet (0)	1	0.01
Cherokee (2)	27	0.25
Choctaw (0)	3	0.03
Creek (1)	1	0.01
Iroquois (1)	4	0.04
Mexican American Ind. (4)	10	0.09
Navajo (0)	2	0.02
Pima (1)	1	0.01
Sioux (1)	1	0.01
Spanish American Ind. (0)	1	0.01
Yaqui (1)	1	0.01
Asian (192)	232	2.14
Not Hispanic (182)	209	1.93
Hispanic (10)	23	0.21
Cambodian (1)	3	0.03
Chinese, ex. Taiwanese (7)	10	0.09
Filipino (109)	126	1.16
Hmong (1)	1	0.01
Indian (22)	25	0.23
Japanese (9)	15	0.14
Korean (8)	10	0.09
Laotian (1)	1	0.01
Taiwanese (6)	6	0.06
Thai (4)	4	0.04
Vietnamese (19)	22	0.20
Hawaii Native/Pacific Islander (9)	13	0.12
Not Hispanic (9)	12	0.11
Hispanic (0)	1	0.01
Native Hawaiian (1)	3	0.03
White (8,097)	8,400	77.38
Not Hispanic (6,379)	6,496	59.84
Hispanic (1,718)	1,904	17.54

Pontiac

Place Type: City
County: Livingston
Population: 11,931†

Ancestry‡	Population	%
African, Sub-Saharan (266)	287	2.35
African (244)	265	2.17
Nigerian (7)	7	0.06
Sudanese (15)	15	0.12
Albanian (34)	34	0.28
American (1,313)	1,313	10.75
Arab (11)	11	0.09
Iraqi (11)	11	0.09
Austrian (0)	12	0.10
Belgian (0)	7	0.06
British (8)	27	0.22
Canadian (0)	23	0.19
Croatian (10)	49	0.40
Czech (10)	72	0.59
Czechoslovakian (17)	29	0.24
Danish (9)	97	0.79
Dutch (21)	272	2.23
English (382)	1,024	8.38
European (126)	126	1.03
French, ex. Basque (78)	430	3.52
French Canadian (53)	75	0.61
German (1,003)	3,531	28.91
Greek (14)	41	0.34
Irish (379)	2,160	17.68
Italian (248)	574	4.70
Lithuanian (29)	40	0.33
Luxemburger (0)	14	0.11
Norwegian (80)	247	2.02
Polish (99)	356	2.91
Portuguese (0)	8	0.07
Russian (0)	7	0.06
Scandinavian (0)	10	0.08
Scotch-Irish (30)	157	1.29
Scottish (26)	177	1.45
Slavic (0)	56	0.46
Slovak (17)	68	0.56
Slovene (0)	27	0.22
Swedish (85)	424	3.47
Swiss (8)	38	0.31
Turkish (6)	6	0.05
Welsh (7)	35	0.29
Yugoslavian (0)	17	0.14

Hispanic Origin	Population	%
Hispanic or Latino (of any race)	749	6.28
Central American, ex. Mexican	12	0.10
Guatemalan	6	0.05
Honduran	3	0.03
Nicaraguan	2	0.02
Salvadoran	1	0.01
Cuban	2	0.02
Mexican	479	4.01
Puerto Rican	45	0.38
South American	15	0.13
Argentinean	1	0.01
Colombian	1	0.01
Ecuadorian	1	0.01
Peruvian	1	0.01
Venezuelan	11	0.09
Other Hispanic or Latino	196	1.64

Race*	Population	%
African-American/Black (1,191)	1,300	10.90
Not Hispanic (1,173)	1,265	10.60
Hispanic (18)	35	0.29
American Indian/Alaska Native (35)	84	0.70
Not Hispanic (29)	72	0.60
Hispanic (6)	12	0.10
Apache (2)	4	0.03
Blackfeet (0)	15	0.13
Cherokee (13)	27	0.23
Chippewa (0)	4	0.03
Iroquois (1)	1	0.01
Mexican American Ind. (0)	3	0.03
Pima (0)	1	0.01
Asian (78)	90	0.75
Not Hispanic (76)	88	0.74
Hispanic (2)	2	0.02
Chinese, ex. Taiwanese (8)	9	0.08
Filipino (18)	22	0.18
Indian (19)	20	0.17
Japanese (1)	1	0.01
Korean (5)	7	0.06
Laotian (1)	2	0.02
Thai (0)	2	0.02
Vietnamese (8)	8	0.07
Hawaii Native/Pacific Islander (0)	7	0.06
Not Hispanic (0)	7	0.06
Samoan (0)	1	0.01
White (10,197)	10,396	87.13
Not Hispanic (9,750)	9,881	82.82
Hispanic (447)	515	4.32

Princeton

Place Type: City
County: Bureau
Population: 7,660†

Ancestry‡	Population	%
American (771)	771	9.78
Austrian (11)	22	0.28
Belgian (33)	55	0.70
British (9)	29	0.37
Czech (10)	63	0.80
Czechoslovakian (18)	18	0.23
Danish (7)	88	1.12
Dutch (35)	232	2.94
English (298)	887	11.25
Finnish (0)	40	0.51
French, ex. Basque (49)	217	2.75
French Canadian (0)	10	0.13
German (1,046)	2,803	35.55
German Russian (12)	12	0.15
Hungarian (0)	29	0.37
Irish (351)	1,109	14.07
Italian (165)	380	4.82
Lithuanian (8)	8	0.10
Norwegian (28)	103	1.31
Pennsylvania German (9)	17	0.22
Polish (125)	396	5.02
Russian (0)	7	0.09
Scandinavian (0)	29	0.37
Scotch-Irish (32)	130	1.65
Scottish (45)	219	2.78
Slovak (49)	67	0.85
Slovene (7)	7	0.09
Swedish (362)	1,179	14.95
Swiss (0)	16	0.20
Ukrainian (13)	13	0.16
Welsh (0)	22	0.28
Yugoslavian (0)	10	0.13

Hispanic Origin	Population	%
Hispanic or Latino (of any race)	203	2.65
Central American, ex. Mexican	7	0.09
Honduran	3	0.04
Salvadoran	4	0.05
Cuban	4	0.05
Mexican	153	2.00
Puerto Rican	26	0.34
South American	5	0.07
Bolivian	3	0.04
Colombian	1	0.01
Peruvian	1	0.01
Other Hispanic or Latino	8	0.10

Race*	Population	%
African-American/Black (43)	75	0.98
Not Hispanic (42)	73	0.95
Hispanic (1)	2	0.03
American Indian/Alaska Native (13)	47	0.61
Not Hispanic (13)	47	0.61
Blackfeet (2)	8	0.10
Cherokee (0)	11	0.14
Cheyenne (1)	1	0.01
Choctaw (0)	1	0.01
Menominee (0)	1	0.01
Pueblo (1)	1	0.01
Sioux (1)	2	0.03
Asian (71)	82	1.07
Not Hispanic (69)	80	1.04
Hispanic (2)	2	0.03
Chinese, ex. Taiwanese (10)	11	0.14
Filipino (36)	39	0.51
Indian (5)	8	0.10
Japanese (4)	4	0.05
Korean (5)	10	0.13
Thai (5)	6	0.08
Vietnamese (4)	4	0.05
Hawaii Native/Pacific Islander (4)	10	0.13
Not Hispanic (4)	6	0.08
Hispanic (0)	4	0.05
Guamanian/Chamorro (2)	4	0.05
Native Hawaiian (2)	2	0.03
White (7,398)	7,476	97.60
Not Hispanic (7,256)	7,325	95.63
Hispanic (142)	151	1.97

Prospect Heights

Place Type: City
County: Cook
Population: 16,256†

Ancestry‡	Population	%
African, Sub-Saharan (96)	96	0.59
Kenyan (47)	47	0.29

SECTION TWO

*Notes: † The Census 2010 population figure is used to calculate the percentages in the Hispanic Origin and Race categories. Ancestry percentages are based on the 2006-2010 American Community Survey population (not shown); ‡ Numbers in parentheses indicate the number of people reporting a single ancestry; * Numbers in parentheses indicate the number of persons reporting this race alone, not in combination with any other race; Please refer to the Explanation of Data for more information.*

South African (49)	49	0.30
American (240)	240	1.48
Arab (112)	172	1.06
Arab (20)	20	0.12
Moroccan (36)	85	0.52
Palestinian (17)	17	0.10
Syrian (0)	11	0.07
Other Arab (39)	39	0.24
Armenian (0)	19	0.12
Assyrian/Chaldean/Syriac (38)	81	0.50
Australian (0)	24	0.15
Austrian (47)	61	0.38
Belgian (17)	17	0.10
British (49)	49	0.30
Bulgarian (99)	99	0.61
Canadian (12)	12	0.07
Croatian (16)	16	0.10
Czech (66)	91	0.56
Danish (10)	93	0.57
Dutch (17)	273	1.68
English (96)	833	5.13
Finnish (0)	16	0.10
French, ex. Basque (28)	149	0.92
French Canadian (17)	60	0.37
German (711)	2,313	14.23
Greek (381)	413	2.54
Hungarian (14)	64	0.39
Iranian (58)	70	0.43
Irish (515)	1,496	9.21
Israeli (14)	14	0.09
Italian (647)	1,075	6.61
Latvian (11)	11	0.07
Lithuanian (10)	10	0.06
Luxemburger (0)	22	0.14
Norwegian (95)	194	1.19
Polish (2,339)	3,028	18.63
Romanian (58)	58	0.36
Russian (72)	186	1.14
Scandinavian (14)	14	0.09
Scotch-Irish (75)	132	0.81
Scottish (57)	83	0.51
Serbian (100)	100	0.62
Slavic (34)	34	0.21
Swedish (48)	343	2.11
Swiss (17)	62	0.38
Ukrainian (286)	373	2.30
Welsh (0)	13	0.08

Hispanic Origin	Population	%
Hispanic or Latino (of any race)	4,846	29.81
Central American, ex. Mexican	116	0.71
Costa Rican	3	0.02
Guatemalan	24	0.15
Honduran	15	0.09
Nicaraguan	2	0.01
Panamanian	5	0.03
Salvadoran	67	0.41
Cuban	24	0.15
Dominican Republic	11	0.07
Mexican	4,454	27.40
Puerto Rican	56	0.34
South American	68	0.42
Argentinean	8	0.05
Chilean	3	0.02
Colombian	20	0.12
Ecuadorian	29	0.18
Peruvian	6	0.04
Venezuelan	1	0.01
Other South American	1	0.01
Other Hispanic or Latino	117	0.72

Race*	Population	%
African-American/Black (246)	295	1.81
Not Hispanic (181)	209	1.29
Hispanic (65)	86	0.53
American Indian/Alaska Native (109)	165	1.02
Not Hispanic (9)	29	0.18
Hispanic (100)	136	0.84
Cherokee (2)	8	0.05
Chippewa (0)	2	0.01
Choctaw (1)	1	0.01
Iroquois (0)	1	0.01
Menominee (1)	1	0.01
Mexican American Ind. (23)	25	0.15
Navajo (2)	5	0.03
Potawatomi (1)	3	0.02
Pueblo (0)	1	0.01
Sioux (4)	4	0.02
South American Ind. (4)	4	0.02
Spanish American Ind. (0)	2	0.01
Asian (1,281)	1,352	8.32
Not Hispanic (1,273)	1,337	8.22
Hispanic (8)	15	0.09
Burmese (0)	2	0.01
Chinese, ex. Taiwanese (75)	84	0.52
Filipino (173)	203	1.25
Indian (762)	775	4.77
Indonesian (1)	1	0.01
Japanese (32)	40	0.25
Korean (157)	166	1.02
Pakistani (27)	29	0.18
Taiwanese (5)	5	0.03
Thai (5)	7	0.04
Vietnamese (11)	11	0.07
Hawaii Native/Pacific Islander (2)	12	0.07
Not Hispanic (2)	8	0.05
Hispanic (0)	4	0.02
Native Hawaiian (1)	3	0.02
Samoan (0)	1	0.01
White (12,237)	12,516	76.99
Not Hispanic (9,822)	9,916	61.00
Hispanic (2,415)	2,600	15.99

Quincy

Place Type: City
County: Adams
Population: 40,633†

Ancestry‡	Population	%
African, Sub-Saharan (15)	24	0.06
African (15)	24	0.06
American (4,580)	4,580	11.31
Arab (0)	22	0.05
Lebanese (0)	11	0.03
Other Arab (0)	11	0.03
Armenian (0)	12	0.03
Belgian (0)	11	0.03
Brazilian (5)	5	0.01
British (95)	122	0.30
Canadian (8)	22	0.05
Celtic (1)	1	<0.01
Croatian (0)	31	0.08
Czech (15)	127	0.31
Czechoslovakian (36)	47	0.12
Danish (117)	155	0.38
Dutch (102)	447	1.10
English (1,265)	3,735	9.22
European (184)	184	0.45
Finnish (0)	49	0.12
French, ex. Basque (290)	970	2.40
French Canadian (74)	131	0.32
German (8,769)	16,339	40.35
Greek (53)	78	0.19
Hungarian (0)	30	0.07
Irish (1,023)	5,487	13.55
Italian (256)	699	1.73
Lithuanian (10)	25	0.06
Norwegian (70)	259	0.64
Polish (158)	758	1.87
Portuguese (14)	40	0.10
Romanian (6)	6	0.01
Russian (38)	90	0.22
Scandinavian (13)	13	0.03
Scotch-Irish (280)	729	1.80
Scottish (205)	640	1.58
Slovak (13)	96	0.24
Swedish (130)	481	1.19
Swiss (55)	216	0.53
Welsh (56)	185	0.46
West Indian, ex. Hispanic (5)	5	0.01
Haitian (5)	5	0.01

Hispanic Origin	Population	%
Hispanic or Latino (of any race)	584	1.44
Central American, ex. Mexican	43	0.11
Costa Rican	2	<0.01
Guatemalan	11	0.03
Honduran	6	0.01
Nicaraguan	1	<0.01
Panamanian	13	0.03
Salvadoran	10	0.02
Cuban	22	0.05
Dominican Republic	5	0.01
Mexican	361	0.89
Puerto Rican	69	0.17
South American	24	0.06
Argentinean	1	<0.01
Bolivian	1	<0.01
Chilean	2	<0.01
Colombian	16	0.04
Ecuadorian	1	<0.01
Peruvian	2	<0.01
Venezuelan	1	<0.01
Other Hispanic or Latino	60	0.15

Race*	Population	%
African-American/Black (2,197)	2,839	6.99
Not Hispanic (2,160)	2,774	6.83
Hispanic (37)	65	0.16
American Indian/Alaska Native (75)	255	0.63
Not Hispanic (71)	237	0.58
Hispanic (4)	18	0.04
Alaska Athabascan *(Ala. Nat.)* (2)	2	<0.01
Apache (1)	3	0.01
Blackfeet (4)	12	0.03
Cherokee (21)	57	0.14
Chickasaw (0)	2	<0.01
Chippewa (4)	12	0.03
Choctaw (1)	1	<0.01
Cree (1)	1	<0.01
Creek (0)	2	<0.01
Crow (0)	1	<0.01
Iroquois (4)	11	0.03
Lumbee (1)	1	<0.01
Mexican American Ind. (1)	1	<0.01
Navajo (1)	1	<0.01
Osage (1)	1	<0.01
Potawatomi (1)	1	<0.01
Shoshone (1)	1	<0.01
Sioux (1)	11	0.03
Asian (368)	459	1.13
Not Hispanic (359)	448	1.10
Hispanic (9)	11	0.03
Cambodian (1)	3	0.01
Chinese, ex. Taiwanese (82)	90	0.22
Filipino (81)	107	0.26
Indian (69)	91	0.22
Indonesian (4)	4	0.01
Japanese (14)	29	0.07
Korean (8)	13	0.03
Laotian (29)	35	0.09
Nepalese (4)	4	0.01
Pakistani (8)	9	0.02
Sri Lankan (1)	1	<0.01
Taiwanese (11)	12	0.03
Thai (4)	10	0.02
Vietnamese (34)	37	0.09
Hawaii Native/Pacific Islander (9)	25	0.06
Not Hispanic (9)	25	0.06
Guamanian/Chamorro (0)	1	<0.01
Native Hawaiian (7)	20	0.05
Samoan (1)	1	<0.01
White (36,904)	37,765	92.94
Not Hispanic (36,564)	37,348	91.92
Hispanic (340)	417	1.03

*Notes: † The Census 2010 population figure is used to calculate the percentages in the Hispanic Origin and Race categories. Ancestry percentages are based on the 2006-2010 American Community Survey population (not shown); ‡ Numbers in parentheses indicate the number of people reporting a single ancestry; * Numbers in parentheses indicate the number of persons reporting this race alone, not in combination with any other race; Please refer to the Explanation of Data for more information.*

Rantoul

Place Type: Village
County: Champaign
Population: 12,941†

Ancestry‡	Population	%
African, Sub-Saharan (231)	231	1.84
African (231)	231	1.84
Albanian (122)	122	0.97
American (1,097)	1,097	8.74
Arab (17)	25	0.20
Arab (0)	8	0.06
Jordanian (9)	9	0.07
Palestinian (8)	8	0.06
British (26)	53	0.42
Celtic (8)	8	0.06
Croatian (13)	13	0.10
Czech (0)	13	0.10
Czechoslovakian (10)	10	0.08
Danish (15)	49	0.39
Dutch (9)	217	1.73
English (442)	1,100	8.76
European (93)	100	0.80
Finnish (0)	28	0.22
French, ex. Basque (20)	260	2.07
French Canadian (8)	26	0.21
German (1,438)	2,998	23.89
Irish (478)	1,406	11.20
Italian (103)	389	3.10
Lithuanian (0)	23	0.18
Norwegian (75)	322	2.57
Pennsylvania German (0)	16	0.13
Polish (34)	268	2.14
Portuguese (17)	17	0.14
Scandinavian (9)	40	0.32
Scotch-Irish (13)	73	0.58
Scottish (102)	185	1.47
Swedish (51)	145	1.16
Swiss (0)	45	0.36
Ukrainian (0)	15	0.12
Welsh (13)	36	0.29
West Indian, ex. Hispanic (33)	79	0.63
Haitian (33)	79	0.63
Yugoslavian (42)	42	0.33

Hispanic Origin	Population	%
Hispanic or Latino (of any race)	1,252	9.67
Central American, ex. Mexican	82	0.63
Guatemalan	37	0.29
Honduran	20	0.15
Nicaraguan	15	0.12
Panamanian	10	0.08
Cuban	5	0.04
Mexican	931	7.19
Puerto Rican	153	1.18
South American	9	0.07
Bolivian	3	0.02
Chilean	2	0.02
Peruvian	2	0.02
Other South American	2	0.02
Other Hispanic or Latino	72	0.56

Race*	Population	%
African-American/Black (2,940)	3,361	25.97
Not Hispanic (2,877)	3,241	25.04
Hispanic (63)	120	0.93
American Indian/Alaska Native (75)	166	1.28
Not Hispanic (35)	115	0.89
Hispanic (40)	51	0.39
Aleut *(Alaska Native)* (4)	4	0.03
Blackfeet (0)	6	0.05
Central American Ind. (0)	1	0.01
Cherokee (4)	30	0.23
Chippewa (8)	10	0.08
Choctaw (0)	5	0.04
Delaware (0)	1	0.01
Iroquois (0)	3	0.02
Mexican American Ind. (8)	8	0.06
Navajo (3)	3	0.02
Potawatomi (2)	5	0.04
Seminole (0)	1	0.01
Sioux (0)	1	0.01
Asian (215)	324	2.50
Not Hispanic (212)	316	2.44
Hispanic (3)	8	0.06
Burmese (1)	1	0.01
Cambodian (6)	6	0.05
Chinese, ex. Taiwanese (13)	15	0.12
Filipino (69)	114	0.88
Indian (46)	64	0.49
Japanese (14)	48	0.37
Korean (15)	22	0.17
Laotian (7)	10	0.08
Pakistani (3)	9	0.07
Thai (7)	18	0.14
Vietnamese (6)	9	0.07
Hawaii Native/Pacific Islander (9)	31	0.24
Not Hispanic (7)	28	0.22
Hispanic (2)	3	0.02
Guamanian/Chamorro (1)	3	0.02
Native Hawaiian (6)	16	0.12
Samoan (0)	2	0.02
White (8,597)	9,119	70.47
Not Hispanic (8,045)	8,492	65.62
Hispanic (552)	627	4.85

Richton Park

Place Type: Village
County: Cook
Population: 13,646†

Ancestry‡	Population	%
African, Sub-Saharan (206)	251	1.88
African (172)	191	1.43
Ethiopian (22)	22	0.17
Nigerian (12)	38	0.29
American (71)	71	0.53
Canadian (0)	32	0.24
Croatian (7)	23	0.17
Czech (0)	49	0.37
Dutch (7)	22	0.17
English (76)	207	1.55
French, ex. Basque (17)	71	0.53
German (147)	594	4.46
Guyanese (14)	14	0.11
Hungarian (14)	14	0.11
Irish (118)	573	4.30
Italian (180)	259	1.94
Lithuanian (8)	8	0.06
Norwegian (13)	13	0.10
Polish (190)	358	2.69
Scotch-Irish (0)	52	0.39
Scottish (0)	33	0.25
Swedish (37)	95	0.71
Ukrainian (9)	9	0.07
West Indian, ex. Hispanic (97)	97	0.73
Haitian (26)	26	0.20
Jamaican (71)	71	0.53

Hispanic Origin	Population	%
Hispanic or Latino (of any race)	477	3.50
Central American, ex. Mexican	25	0.18
Guatemalan	13	0.10
Panamanian	1	0.01
Salvadoran	11	0.08
Cuban	6	0.04
Dominican Republic	4	0.03
Mexican	329	2.41
Puerto Rican	72	0.53
South American	21	0.15
Argentinean	7	0.05
Colombian	5	0.04
Ecuadorian	8	0.06
Other South American	1	0.01
Other Hispanic or Latino	20	0.15

Race*	Population	%
African-American/Black (11,244)	11,548	84.63
Not Hispanic (11,156)	11,429	83.75
Hispanic (88)	119	0.87
American Indian/Alaska Native (15)	98	0.72
Not Hispanic (12)	92	0.67
Hispanic (3)	6	0.04
Blackfeet (0)	10	0.07
Cherokee (0)	9	0.07
Chippewa (1)	4	0.03
Choctaw (2)	9	0.07
Crow (0)	1	0.01
Mexican American Ind. (1)	2	0.01
Navajo (0)	2	0.01
Potawatomi (1)	1	0.01
Pueblo (0)	1	0.01
Asian (136)	185	1.36
Not Hispanic (136)	183	1.34
Hispanic (0)	2	0.01
Cambodian (3)	3	0.02
Chinese, ex. Taiwanese (17)	33	0.24
Filipino (88)	109	0.80
Indian (12)	17	0.12
Japanese (3)	5	0.04
Korean (1)	5	0.04
Laotian (4)	4	0.03
Pakistani (3)	3	0.02
Vietnamese (4)	5	0.04
Hawaii Native/Pacific Islander (8)	13	0.10
Not Hispanic (8)	13	0.10
Native Hawaiian (8)	10	0.07
White (1,733)	1,985	14.55
Not Hispanic (1,543)	1,765	12.93
Hispanic (190)	220	1.61

River Forest

Place Type: Village
County: Cook
Population: 11,172†

Ancestry‡	Population	%
American (280)	280	2.51
Arab (18)	38	0.34
Arab (18)	18	0.16
Moroccan (0)	10	0.09
Syrian (0)	10	0.09
Austrian (0)	27	0.24
Brazilian (15)	30	0.27
British (61)	89	0.80
Canadian (0)	20	0.18
Celtic (0)	10	0.09
Croatian (11)	84	0.75
Czech (0)	211	1.89
Danish (0)	42	0.38
Dutch (11)	81	0.73
Eastern European (46)	71	0.64
English (205)	1,216	10.89
European (279)	331	2.96
Finnish (0)	32	0.29
French, ex. Basque (39)	152	1.36
French Canadian (16)	27	0.24
German (622)	2,879	25.78
Greek (94)	94	0.84
Hungarian (49)	286	2.56
Icelander (0)	11	0.10
Iranian (91)	102	0.91
Irish (798)	2,717	24.33
Israeli (6)	6	0.05
Italian (665)	1,636	14.65
Lithuanian (12)	131	1.17
Macedonian (0)	9	0.08
Northern European (14)	28	0.25
Norwegian (31)	178	1.59
Pennsylvania German (9)	9	0.08
Polish (315)	933	8.36
Russian (149)	336	3.01
Scandinavian (66)	104	0.93
Scotch-Irish (38)	125	1.12
Scottish (75)	162	1.45
Serbian (0)	25	0.22
Slovak (0)	19	0.17

*Notes: † The Census 2010 population figure is used to calculate the percentages in the Hispanic Origin and Race categories. Ancestry percentages are based on the 2006-2010 American Community Survey population (not shown); ‡ Numbers in parentheses indicate the number of people reporting a single ancestry; * Numbers in parentheses indicate the number of persons reporting this race alone, not in combination with any other race; Please refer to the Explanation of Data for more information.*

Swedish (103)	452	4.05
Swiss (10)	103	0.92
Turkish (8)	8	0.07
Ukrainian (12)	112	1.00
West Indian, ex. Hispanic (32)	32	0.29
Jamaican (32)	32	0.29

Hispanic Origin	Population	%
Hispanic or Latino (of any race)	670	6.00
Central American, ex. Mexican	50	0.45
Costa Rican	2	0.02
Guatemalan	22	0.20
Honduran	4	0.04
Nicaraguan	15	0.13
Panamanian	1	0.01
Salvadoran	6	0.05
Cuban	36	0.32
Mexican	286	2.56
Puerto Rican	85	0.76
South American	124	1.11
Argentinean	15	0.13
Bolivian	25	0.22
Chilean	10	0.09
Colombian	18	0.16
Ecuadorian	25	0.22
Paraguayan	2	0.02
Peruvian	20	0.18
Uruguayan	1	0.01
Venezuelan	4	0.04
Other South American	4	0.04
Other Hispanic or Latino	89	0.80

Race*	Population	%
African-American/Black (751)	832	7.45
Not Hispanic (733)	800	7.16
Hispanic (18)	32	0.29
American Indian/Alaska Native (10)	60	0.54
Not Hispanic (4)	40	0.36
Hispanic (6)	20	0.18
Aleut *(Alaska Native)* (0)	1	0.01
Apache (1)	1	0.01
Central American Ind. (0)	1	0.01
Cherokee (0)	19	0.17
Chippewa (1)	3	0.03
Choctaw (0)	5	0.04
Creek (0)	1	0.01
Mexican American Ind. (2)	3	0.03
Sioux (0)	1	0.01
South American Ind. (1)	5	0.04
Asian (505)	608	5.44
Not Hispanic (505)	600	5.37
Hispanic (0)	8	0.07
Burmese (1)	3	0.03
Cambodian (1)	4	0.04
Chinese, ex. Taiwanese (141)	178	1.59
Filipino (88)	109	0.98
Indian (121)	136	1.22
Japanese (22)	41	0.37
Korean (58)	69	0.62
Laotian (0)	1	0.01
Malaysian (1)	1	0.01
Nepalese (7)	7	0.06
Pakistani (0)	3	0.03
Sri Lankan (11)	11	0.10
Taiwanese (10)	12	0.11
Thai (17)	18	0.16
Vietnamese (7)	14	0.13
Hawaii Native/Pacific Islander (5)	9	0.08
Not Hispanic (2)	6	0.05
Hispanic (3)	3	0.03
Fijian (0)	1	0.01
Guamanian/Chamorro (4)	5	0.04
Native Hawaiian (1)	1	0.01
White (9,475)	9,678	86.63
Not Hispanic (9,050)	9,200	82.35
Hispanic (425)	478	4.28

River Grove

Place Type: Village
County: Cook
Population: 10,227†

Ancestry‡	Population	%
Albanian (58)	58	0.57
American (311)	311	3.05
Arab (38)	38	0.37
Moroccan (29)	29	0.28
Palestinian (9)	9	0.09
Armenian (0)	9	0.09
Assyrian/Chaldean/Syriac (8)	8	0.08
Austrian (0)	34	0.33
British (0)	8	0.08
Bulgarian (54)	54	0.53
Canadian (28)	28	0.27
Croatian (31)	31	0.30
Czech (59)	125	1.23
Danish (0)	18	0.18
Dutch (35)	71	0.70
English (30)	142	1.39
French, ex. Basque (0)	143	1.40
French Canadian (10)	92	0.90
German (271)	978	9.59
Greek (141)	164	1.61
Hungarian (0)	32	0.31
Iranian (37)	37	0.36
Irish (381)	962	9.43
Italian (654)	1,309	12.83
Lithuanian (9)	44	0.43
Luxemburger (0)	9	0.09
Norwegian (63)	125	1.23
Polish (3,000)	3,374	33.08
Romanian (35)	35	0.34
Russian (12)	53	0.52
Scandinavian (0)	10	0.10
Scotch-Irish (11)	37	0.36
Scottish (24)	79	0.77
Slovak (13)	13	0.13
Slovene (8)	16	0.16
Swedish (26)	219	2.15
Ukrainian (238)	238	2.33

Hispanic Origin	Population	%
Hispanic or Latino (of any race)	1,901	18.59
Central American, ex. Mexican	87	0.85
Costa Rican	6	0.06
Guatemalan	43	0.42
Honduran	9	0.09
Nicaraguan	4	0.04
Panamanian	2	0.02
Salvadoran	23	0.22
Cuban	45	0.44
Dominican Republic	2	0.02
Mexican	1,016	9.93
Puerto Rican	562	5.50
South American	129	1.26
Argentinean	16	0.16
Bolivian	6	0.06
Colombian	36	0.35
Ecuadorian	45	0.44
Peruvian	23	0.22
Uruguayan	1	0.01
Other South American	2	0.02
Other Hispanic or Latino	60	0.59

Race*	Population	%
African-American/Black (158)	194	1.90
Not Hispanic (131)	144	1.41
Hispanic (27)	50	0.49
American Indian/Alaska Native (46)	98	0.96
Not Hispanic (18)	49	0.48
Hispanic (28)	49	0.48
Cherokee (5)	24	0.23
Cree (0)	2	0.02
Menominee (1)	4	0.04
Mexican American Ind. (1)	5	0.05
Navajo (2)	2	0.02
Pueblo (2)	2	0.02
Sioux (4)	6	0.06
South American Ind. (3)	7	0.07
Asian (225)	278	2.72
Not Hispanic (219)	263	2.57
Hispanic (6)	15	0.15
Chinese, ex. Taiwanese (19)	23	0.22
Filipino (136)	160	1.56
Indian (16)	19	0.19
Japanese (5)	5	0.05
Korean (9)	9	0.09
Laotian (3)	3	0.03
Pakistani (8)	9	0.09
Thai (2)	2	0.02
Vietnamese (15)	17	0.17
Hawaii Native/Pacific Islander (4)	13	0.13
Not Hispanic (4)	10	0.10
Hispanic (0)	3	0.03
Guamanian/Chamorro (0)	2	0.02
Native Hawaiian (0)	1	0.01
White (8,944)	9,114	89.12
Not Hispanic (7,847)	7,936	77.60
Hispanic (1,097)	1,178	11.52

Riverdale

Place Type: Village
County: Cook
Population: 13,549†

Ancestry‡	Population	%
African, Sub-Saharan (355)	412	3.02
African (275)	332	2.44
Nigerian (80)	80	0.59
American (92)	92	0.68
Czech (7)	9	0.07
Dutch (3)	19	0.14
English (90)	115	0.84
French, ex. Basque (0)	57	0.42
German (42)	103	0.76
Hungarian (0)	10	0.07
Irish (59)	174	1.28
Italian (35)	92	0.68
Lithuanian (15)	15	0.11
Norwegian (0)	16	0.12
Polish (23)	132	0.97
Scotch-Irish (0)	9	0.07
Scottish (12)	21	0.15
Slovak (5)	5	0.04
Swedish (0)	37	0.27
West Indian, ex. Hispanic (52)	55	0.40
Haitian (13)	13	0.10
Jamaican (32)	32	0.23
Trinidadian/Tobagonian (7)	10	0.07

Hispanic Origin	Population	%
Hispanic or Latino (of any race)	237	1.75
Central American, ex. Mexican	7	0.05
Guatemalan	2	0.01
Honduran	3	0.02
Salvadoran	2	0.01
Cuban	13	0.10
Dominican Republic	2	0.01
Mexican	122	0.90
Puerto Rican	70	0.52
South American	1	0.01
Argentinean	1	0.01
Other Hispanic or Latino	22	0.16

Race*	Population	%
African-American/Black (12,694)	12,852	94.86
Not Hispanic (12,610)	12,749	94.10
Hispanic (84)	103	0.76
American Indian/Alaska Native (24)	74	0.55
Not Hispanic (24)	74	0.55
Blackfeet (0)	1	0.01
Cherokee (0)	15	0.11
Chickasaw (0)	1	0.01
Chippewa (0)	1	0.01
Creek (0)	1	0.01

*Notes: † The Census 2010 population figure is used to calculate the percentages in the Hispanic Origin and Race categories. Ancestry percentages are based on the 2006-2010 American Community Survey population (not shown); ‡ Numbers in parentheses indicate the number of people reporting a single ancestry; * Numbers in parentheses indicate the number of persons reporting this race alone, not in combination with any other race; Please refer to the Explanation of Data for more information.*

	Population	%
Houma (0)	1	0.01
Asian (13)	35	0.26
Not Hispanic (13)	32	0.24
Hispanic (0)	3	0.02
Chinese, ex. Taiwanese (1)	6	0.04
Filipino (2)	3	0.02
Indian (9)	17	0.13
Japanese (0)	1	0.01
Korean (0)	4	0.03
Vietnamese (1)	1	0.01
Hawaii Native/Pacific Islander (0)	9	0.07
Not Hispanic (0)	8	0.06
Hispanic (0)	1	0.01
Guamanian/Chamorro (0)	1	0.01
Native Hawaiian (0)	1	0.01
White (581)	669	4.94
Not Hispanic (511)	591	4.36
Hispanic (70)	78	0.58

Riverside

Place Type: Village
County: Cook
Population: 8,875†

Ancestry‡	Population	%
Albanian (16)	16	0.18
American (120)	120	1.37
Arab (0)	10	0.11
Lebanese (0)	10	0.11
Austrian (34)	222	2.54
Belgian (22)	39	0.45
British (0)	21	0.24
Bulgarian (0)	32	0.37
Celtic (9)	9	0.10
Croatian (60)	81	0.93
Czech (272)	725	8.30
Czechoslovakian (37)	134	1.53
Danish (0)	20	0.23
Dutch (16)	71	0.81
English (36)	455	5.21
European (66)	66	0.76
Finnish (0)	13	0.15
French, ex. Basque (0)	185	2.12
German (362)	2,130	24.38
Greek (118)	206	2.36
Hungarian (31)	115	1.32
Irish (452)	1,722	19.71
Italian (399)	1,062	12.16
Latvian (0)	13	0.15
Lithuanian (254)	365	4.18
Luxemburger (0)	27	0.31
Norwegian (8)	118	1.35
Polish (511)	1,613	18.46
Russian (18)	62	0.71
Scotch-Irish (81)	188	2.15
Scottish (19)	253	2.90
Serbian (0)	47	0.54
Slavic (0)	11	0.13
Slovak (11)	11	0.13
Slovene (11)	67	0.77
Swedish (28)	107	1.22
Swiss (10)	48	0.55
Ukrainian (9)	60	0.69
Welsh (10)	45	0.52
Yugoslavian (11)	11	0.13

Hispanic Origin	Population	%
Hispanic or Latino (of any race)	935	10.54
Central American, ex. Mexican	29	0.33
Costa Rican	2	0.02
Guatemalan	15	0.17
Honduran	4	0.05
Nicaraguan	4	0.05
Panamanian	3	0.03
Salvadoran	1	0.01
Cuban	17	0.19
Dominican Republic	1	0.01
Mexican	699	7.88
Puerto Rican	95	1.07
South American	60	0.68
Argentinean	12	0.14
Bolivian	13	0.15
Chilean	2	0.02
Colombian	5	0.06
Ecuadorian	8	0.09
Paraguayan	3	0.03
Peruvian	11	0.12
Venezuelan	6	0.07
Other Hispanic or Latino	34	0.38

Race*	Population	%
African-American/Black (111)	139	1.57
Not Hispanic (110)	127	1.43
Hispanic (1)	12	0.14
American Indian/Alaska Native (17)	45	0.51
Not Hispanic (7)	22	0.25
Hispanic (10)	23	0.26
Canadian/French Am. Ind. (0)	1	0.01
Cherokee (0)	1	0.01
Cheyenne (4)	5	0.06
Chippewa (0)	5	0.06
Choctaw (0)	1	0.01
Iroquois (2)	2	0.02
Mexican American Ind. (0)	2	0.02
Sioux (3)	3	0.03
South American Ind. (0)	1	0.01
Asian (188)	249	2.81
Not Hispanic (184)	234	2.64
Hispanic (4)	15	0.17
Chinese, ex. Taiwanese (74)	88	0.99
Filipino (48)	61	0.69
Indian (17)	24	0.27
Indonesian (2)	2	0.02
Japanese (8)	27	0.30
Korean (15)	21	0.24
Laotian (1)	1	0.01
Pakistani (1)	1	0.01
Thai (4)	4	0.05
Vietnamese (11)	11	0.12
Hawaii Native/Pacific Islander (3)	6	0.07
Not Hispanic (1)	4	0.05
Hispanic (2)	2	0.02
Native Hawaiian (0)	2	0.02
Samoan (3)	3	0.03
White (8,107)	8,247	92.92
Not Hispanic (7,535)	7,611	85.76
Hispanic (572)	636	7.17

Robinson

Place Type: City
County: Crawford
Population: 7,713†

Ancestry‡	Population	%
African, Sub-Saharan (30)	67	0.86
African (30)	67	0.86
American (969)	969	12.41
Arab (1)	1	0.01
Moroccan (1)	1	0.01
Belgian (0)	15	0.19
British (9)	19	0.24
Czechoslovakian (0)	8	0.10
Dutch (94)	448	5.74
English (275)	729	9.34
European (9)	22	0.28
French, ex. Basque (73)	202	2.59
French Canadian (0)	17	0.22
German (906)	2,290	29.33
Hungarian (28)	51	0.65
Irish (238)	1,060	13.58
Italian (70)	296	3.79
Lithuanian (1)	1	0.01
Norwegian (13)	21	0.27
Polish (70)	293	3.75
Russian (8)	8	0.10
Scotch-Irish (49)	97	1.24
Scottish (25)	78	1.00
Swedish (0)	57	0.73
Swiss (0)	29	0.37
Welsh (0)	46	0.59

Hispanic Origin	Population	%
Hispanic or Latino (of any race)	274	3.55
Cuban	2	0.03
Mexican	134	1.74
Puerto Rican	10	0.13
South American	4	0.05
Colombian	2	0.03
Peruvian	1	0.01
Uruguayan	1	0.01
Other Hispanic or Latino	124	1.61

Race*	Population	%
African-American/Black (877)	926	12.01
Not Hispanic (867)	912	11.82
Hispanic (10)	14	0.18
American Indian/Alaska Native (11)	36	0.47
Not Hispanic (10)	35	0.45
Hispanic (1)	1	0.01
Apache (0)	1	0.01
Blackfeet (0)	2	0.03
Cherokee (5)	22	0.29
Chippewa (1)	1	0.01
Iroquois (0)	2	0.03
Asian (58)	78	1.01
Not Hispanic (56)	75	0.97
Hispanic (2)	3	0.04
Chinese, ex. Taiwanese (9)	15	0.19
Filipino (15)	27	0.35
Indian (6)	6	0.08
Japanese (3)	10	0.13
Korean (9)	9	0.12
Thai (4)	4	0.05
Vietnamese (5)	6	0.08
Hawaii Native/Pacific Islander (1)	3	0.04
Not Hispanic (1)	3	0.04
Native Hawaiian (1)	1	0.01
White (6,533)	6,634	86.01
Not Hispanic (6,414)	6,500	84.27
Hispanic (119)	134	1.74

Rochelle

Place Type: City
County: Ogle
Population: 9,574†

Ancestry‡	Population	%
American (587)	587	6.12
Austrian (0)	11	0.11
British (0)	11	0.11
Czech (0)	30	0.31
Danish (13)	71	0.74
Dutch (24)	61	0.64
English (294)	694	7.23
European (13)	13	0.14
Finnish (0)	11	0.11
French, ex. Basque (45)	247	2.57
French Canadian (58)	191	1.99
German (1,033)	2,792	29.09
Greek (43)	43	0.45
Irish (350)	1,264	13.17
Italian (155)	584	6.09
Norwegian (102)	349	3.64
Polish (80)	280	2.92
Scotch-Irish (42)	56	0.58
Scottish (81)	119	1.24
Slovak (0)	87	0.91
Swedish (35)	311	3.24
Welsh (0)	41	0.43

Hispanic Origin	Population	%
Hispanic or Latino (of any race)	2,254	23.54
Central American, ex. Mexican	75	0.78
Costa Rican	1	0.01
Guatemalan	38	0.40
Honduran	5	0.05
Nicaraguan	4	0.04

*Notes: † The Census 2010 population figure is used to calculate the percentages in the Hispanic Origin and Race categories. Ancestry percentages are based on the 2006-2010 American Community Survey population (not shown); ‡ Numbers in parentheses indicate the number of people reporting a single ancestry; * Numbers in parentheses indicate the number of persons reporting this race alone, not in combination with any other race; Please refer to the Explanation of Data for more information.*

Panamanian	2	0.02
Salvadoran	25	0.26
Cuban	42	0.44
Mexican	1,965	20.52
Puerto Rican	23	0.24
South American	19	0.20
Chilean	2	0.02
Colombian	6	0.06
Ecuadorian	2	0.02
Peruvian	6	0.06
Other South American	3	0.03
Other Hispanic or Latino	130	1.36

Race*	Population	%
African-American/Black (217)	295	3.08
Not Hispanic (208)	270	2.82
Hispanic (9)	25	0.26
American Indian/Alaska Native (30)	60	0.63
Not Hispanic (21)	48	0.50
Hispanic (9)	12	0.13
Apache (1)	1	0.01
Cherokee (6)	9	0.09
Choctaw (0)	5	0.05
Creek (1)	1	0.01
Iroquois (0)	1	0.01
Mexican American Ind. (4)	4	0.04
Navajo (1)	6	0.06
Sioux (2)	7	0.07
South American Ind. (1)	2	0.02
Asian (72)	93	0.97
Not Hispanic (65)	84	0.88
Hispanic (7)	9	0.09
Chinese, ex. Taiwanese (9)	12	0.13
Filipino (10)	17	0.18
Indian (31)	33	0.34
Japanese (2)	6	0.06
Korean (8)	8	0.08
Laotian (2)	3	0.03
Taiwanese (0)	3	0.03
Vietnamese (5)	5	0.05
Hawaii Native/Pacific Islander (5)	9	0.09
Not Hispanic (1)	2	0.02
Hispanic (4)	7	0.07
Guamanian/Chamorro (4)	4	0.04
Native Hawaiian (0)	1	0.01
White (8,134)	8,329	87.00
Not Hispanic (6,918)	7,024	73.37
Hispanic (1,216)	1,305	13.63

Rock Falls

Place Type: City
County: Whiteside
Population: 9,266†

Ancestry‡	Population	%
Albanian (50)	50	0.54
Alsatian (7)	7	0.08
American (608)	608	6.58
Austrian (3)	12	0.13
Belgian (38)	59	0.64
British (24)	24	0.26
Cajun (0)	7	0.08
Czech (3)	117	1.27
Czechoslovakian (8)	8	0.09
Danish (22)	39	0.42
Dutch (186)	355	3.84
English (163)	668	7.23
European (14)	14	0.15
Finnish (21)	77	0.83
French, ex. Basque (24)	194	2.10
French Canadian (8)	8	0.09
German (1,044)	2,430	26.31
Greek (9)	21	0.23
Hungarian (0)	40	0.43
Irish (431)	1,183	12.81
Italian (118)	341	3.69
Maltese (0)	3	0.03
Norwegian (54)	228	2.47
Pennsylvania German (10)	13	0.14
Polish (43)	205	2.22
Russian (0)	14	0.15
Scandinavian (8)	8	0.09
Scotch-Irish (27)	90	0.97
Scottish (40)	138	1.49
Slovak (26)	26	0.28
Swedish (178)	476	5.15
Swiss (11)	23	0.25
Turkish (5)	5	0.05
Welsh (15)	15	0.16

Hispanic Origin	Population	%
Hispanic or Latino (of any race)	1,395	15.06
Central American, ex. Mexican	8	0.09
Guatemalan	6	0.06
Honduran	1	0.01
Salvadoran	1	0.01
Cuban	8	0.09
Mexican	1,216	13.12
Puerto Rican	91	0.98
South American	1	0.01
Bolivian	1	0.01
Other Hispanic or Latino	71	0.77

Race*	Population	%
African-American/Black (138)	293	3.16
Not Hispanic (122)	222	2.40
Hispanic (16)	71	0.77
American Indian/Alaska Native (39)	98	1.06
Not Hispanic (19)	57	0.62
Hispanic (20)	41	0.44
Apache (1)	3	0.03
Canadian/French Am. Ind. (0)	1	0.01
Cherokee (4)	12	0.13
Chippewa (1)	5	0.05
Choctaw (0)	1	0.01
Creek (0)	3	0.03
Inupiat *(Alaska Native)* (0)	1	0.01
Mexican American Ind. (3)	11	0.12
Navajo (1)	4	0.04
Osage (1)	3	0.03
Sioux (1)	8	0.09
Yaqui (0)	1	0.01
Asian (28)	46	0.50
Not Hispanic (26)	40	0.43
Hispanic (2)	6	0.06
Chinese, ex. Taiwanese (8)	9	0.10
Filipino (3)	6	0.06
Indian (5)	8	0.09
Japanese (2)	2	0.02
Korean (6)	8	0.09
Laotian (3)	3	0.03
Pakistani (1)	1	0.01
Vietnamese (0)	3	0.03
Hawaii Native/Pacific Islander (5)	10	0.11
Not Hispanic (0)	5	0.05
Hispanic (5)	5	0.05
Guamanian/Chamorro (3)	3	0.03
Native Hawaiian (2)	3	0.03
Samoan (0)	1	0.01
White (8,475)	8,739	94.31
Not Hispanic (7,541)	7,699	83.09
Hispanic (934)	1,040	11.22

Rock Island

Place Type: City
County: Rock Island
Population: 39,018†

Ancestry‡	Population	%
African, Sub-Saharan (410)	459	1.18
African (339)	388	1.00
Liberian (11)	11	0.03
Nigerian (60)	60	0.15
American (1,616)	1,616	4.16
Arab (0)	12	0.03
Arab (0)	12	0.03
Austrian (40)	134	0.35
Belgian (634)	1,408	3.63
Brazilian (0)	36	0.09
British (33)	65	0.17
Bulgarian (13)	13	0.03
Canadian (0)	24	0.06
Celtic (0)	10	0.03
Croatian (73)	181	0.47
Czech (155)	392	1.01
Danish (19)	250	0.64
Dutch (25)	579	1.49
Eastern European (50)	50	0.13
English (669)	2,852	7.35
European (272)	312	0.80
Finnish (11)	75	0.19
French, ex. Basque (61)	709	1.83
French Canadian (9)	82	0.21
German (3,317)	9,208	23.72
Greek (203)	260	0.67
Hungarian (17)	63	0.16
Icelander (0)	13	0.03
Irish (1,021)	4,658	12.00
Italian (488)	1,472	3.79
Lithuanian (52)	145	0.37
Luxemburger (0)	1	<0.01
New Zealander (14)	14	0.04
Northern European (9)	9	0.02
Norwegian (143)	481	1.24
Pennsylvania German (27)	27	0.07
Polish (466)	1,007	2.59
Portuguese (32)	41	0.11
Romanian (57)	70	0.18
Russian (10)	99	0.26
Scandinavian (9)	44	0.11
Scotch-Irish (301)	693	1.79
Scottish (97)	542	1.40
Slovak (0)	46	0.12
Slovene (10)	22	0.06
Swedish (630)	2,117	5.45
Swiss (18)	215	0.55
Ukrainian (10)	18	0.05
Welsh (10)	145	0.37
West Indian, ex. Hispanic (32)	40	0.10
Belizean (19)	19	0.05
Haitian (6)	14	0.04
Jamaican (7)	7	0.02
Yugoslavian (55)	55	0.14

Hispanic Origin	Population	%
Hispanic or Latino (of any race)	3,664	9.39
Central American, ex. Mexican	37	0.09
Guatemalan	12	0.03
Honduran	6	0.02
Nicaraguan	1	<0.01
Panamanian	12	0.03
Salvadoran	5	0.01
Other Central American	1	<0.01
Cuban	34	0.09
Dominican Republic	3	0.01
Mexican	3,303	8.47
Puerto Rican	100	0.26
South American	27	0.07
Argentinean	3	0.01
Chilean	2	0.01
Colombian	10	0.03
Ecuadorian	7	0.02
Peruvian	4	0.01
Venezuelan	1	<0.01
Other Hispanic or Latino	160	0.41

Race*	Population	%
African-American/Black (7,122)	8,039	20.60
Not Hispanic (6,987)	7,755	19.88
Hispanic (135)	284	0.73
American Indian/Alaska Native (104)	434	1.11
Not Hispanic (84)	331	0.85
Hispanic (20)	103	0.26
Aleut *(Alaska Native)* (0)	1	<0.01
Apache (5)	13	0.03
Blackfeet (5)	50	0.13
Cherokee (10)	108	0.28
Cheyenne (0)	2	0.01

*Notes: † The Census 2010 population figure is used to calculate the percentages in the Hispanic Origin and Race categories. Ancestry percentages are based on the 2006-2010 American Community Survey population (not shown); ‡ Numbers in parentheses indicate the number of people reporting a single ancestry; * Numbers in parentheses indicate the number of persons reporting this race alone, not in combination with any other race; Please refer to the Explanation of Data for more information.*

Chickasaw (0)	1	<0.01
Chippewa (11)	13	0.03
Choctaw (0)	15	0.04
Comanche (0)	1	<0.01
Creek (2)	3	0.01
Delaware (0)	2	0.01
Iroquois (1)	5	0.01
Kiowa (0)	2	0.01
Menominee (2)	2	0.01
Mexican American Ind. (0)	12	0.03
Navajo (2)	5	0.01
Osage (0)	3	0.01
Pima (1)	1	<0.01
Potawatomi (3)	3	0.01
Seminole (1)	2	0.01
Sioux (8)	15	0.04
Ute (0)	2	0.01
Asian (687)	881	2.26
Not Hispanic (680)	855	2.19
Hispanic (7)	26	0.07
Bhutanese (24)	29	0.07
Burmese (252)	282	0.72
Cambodian (1)	1	<0.01
Chinese, ex. Taiwanese (41)	64	0.16
Filipino (48)	87	0.22
Indian (106)	139	0.36
Indonesian (1)	1	<0.01
Japanese (17)	40	0.10
Korean (34)	64	0.16
Laotian (6)	13	0.03
Nepalese (36)	47	0.12
Pakistani (3)	4	0.01
Sri Lankan (3)	3	0.01
Taiwanese (0)	1	<0.01
Thai (15)	34	0.09
Vietnamese (49)	62	0.16
Hawaii Native/Pacific Islander (8)	30	0.08
Not Hispanic (8)	30	0.08
Guamanian/Chamorro (2)	7	0.02
Native Hawaiian (0)	6	0.02
Samoan (2)	5	0.01
White (28,224)	29,505	75.62
Not Hispanic (26,464)	27,421	70.28
Hispanic (1,760)	2,084	5.34

Rockford

Place Type: City
County: Winnebago
Population: 152,871†

Ancestry‡	Population	%
African, Sub-Saharan (388)	474	0.31
African (331)	372	0.24
Ethiopian (9)	45	0.03
Ghanaian (10)	10	0.01
Nigerian (0)	9	0.01
Sierra Leonean (13)	13	0.01
South African (14)	14	0.01
Sudanese (11)	11	0.01
Albanian (0)	40	0.03
American (12,203)	12,203	7.90
Arab (554)	697	0.45
Arab (397)	397	0.26
Iraqi (125)	125	0.08
Jordanian (9)	27	0.02
Lebanese (10)	71	0.05
Palestinian (13)	17	0.01
Syrian (0)	60	0.04
Austrian (100)	235	0.15
Basque (1)	1	<0.01
Belgian (79)	269	0.17
Brazilian (0)	9	0.01
British (180)	369	0.24
Canadian (42)	95	0.06
Croatian (70)	116	0.08
Czech (119)	629	0.41
Czechoslovakian (58)	133	0.09
Danish (327)	1,067	0.69
Dutch (395)	2,584	1.67
Eastern European (16)	16	0.01
English (2,200)	10,118	6.55
Estonian (7)	25	0.02
European (517)	588	0.38
Finnish (55)	336	0.22
French, ex. Basque (327)	3,268	2.11
French Canadian (200)	485	0.31
German (8,977)	29,971	19.40
German Russian (0)	68	0.04
Greek (91)	315	0.20
Hungarian (71)	412	0.27
Iranian (16)	26	0.02
Irish (2,946)	16,387	10.61
Italian (4,622)	10,137	6.56
Latvian (24)	58	0.04
Lithuanian (275)	827	0.54
Luxemburger (8)	18	0.01
Macedonian (116)	116	0.08
Northern European (66)	85	0.06
Norwegian (1,140)	4,532	2.93
Pennsylvania German (87)	113	0.07
Polish (1,775)	4,787	3.10
Portuguese (0)	51	0.03
Romanian (13)	78	0.05
Russian (183)	433	0.28
Scandinavian (324)	588	0.38
Scotch-Irish (422)	1,348	0.87
Scottish (340)	1,513	0.98
Serbian (66)	155	0.10
Slavic (16)	64	0.04
Slovak (76)	131	0.08
Swedish (4,608)	12,535	8.11
Swiss (141)	625	0.40
Turkish (49)	66	0.04
Ukrainian (157)	317	0.21
Welsh (98)	569	0.37
West Indian, ex. Hispanic (64)	157	0.10
Bahamian (21)	21	0.01
Jamaican (10)	62	0.04
West Indian (33)	74	0.05
Yugoslavian (277)	375	0.24

Hispanic Origin	Population	%
Hispanic or Latino (of any race)	24,085	15.76
Central American, ex. Mexican	510	0.33
Costa Rican	29	0.02
Guatemalan	240	0.16
Honduran	92	0.06
Nicaraguan	23	0.02
Panamanian	23	0.02
Salvadoran	100	0.07
Other Central American	3	<0.01
Cuban	418	0.27
Dominican Republic	42	0.03
Mexican	20,019	13.10
Puerto Rican	1,323	0.87
South American	494	0.32
Argentinean	38	0.02
Bolivian	26	0.02
Chilean	29	0.02
Colombian	211	0.14
Ecuadorian	53	0.03
Paraguayan	1	<0.01
Peruvian	81	0.05
Uruguayan	32	0.02
Venezuelan	21	0.01
Other South American	2	<0.01
Other Hispanic or Latino	1,279	0.84

Race*	Population	%
African-American/Black (31,359)	34,438	22.53
Not Hispanic (30,695)	33,293	21.78
Hispanic (664)	1,145	0.75
American Indian/Alaska Native (614)	1,703	1.11
Not Hispanic (308)	1,100	0.72
Hispanic (306)	603	0.39
Alaska Athabascan *(Ala. Nat.)* (1)	1	<0.01
Aleut *(Alaska Native)* (0)	1	<0.01
Apache (6)	22	0.01
Arapaho (1)	2	<0.01
Blackfeet (4)	58	0.04
Canadian/French Am. Ind. (0)	5	<0.01
Central American Ind. (1)	6	<0.01
Cherokee (52)	259	0.17
Cheyenne (1)	3	<0.01
Chippewa (17)	42	0.03
Choctaw (2)	25	0.02
Comanche (3)	13	0.01
Cree (2)	3	<0.01
Creek (3)	11	0.01
Crow (7)	10	0.01
Delaware (0)	5	<0.01
Inupiat *(Alaska Native)* (1)	4	<0.01
Iroquois (13)	23	0.02
Kiowa (0)	1	<0.01
Lumbee (1)	1	<0.01
Menominee (1)	1	<0.01
Mexican American Ind. (65)	88	0.06
Navajo (7)	21	0.01
Ottawa (2)	2	<0.01
Paiute (0)	4	<0.01
Pima (4)	4	<0.01
Potawatomi (2)	8	0.01
Puget Sound Salish (0)	4	<0.01
Seminole (0)	3	<0.01
Sioux (20)	46	0.03
South American Ind. (2)	12	0.01
Spanish American Ind. (4)	4	<0.01
Tsimshian *(Alaska Native)* (1)	1	<0.01
Yaqui (1)	1	<0.01
Asian (4,443)	5,272	3.45
Not Hispanic (4,390)	5,115	3.35
Hispanic (53)	157	0.10
Bangladeshi (20)	22	0.01
Bhutanese (1)	1	<0.01
Burmese (389)	403	0.26
Cambodian (6)	18	0.01
Chinese, ex. Taiwanese (333)	453	0.30
Filipino (581)	768	0.50
Hmong (26)	30	0.02
Indian (825)	948	0.62
Indonesian (12)	14	0.01
Japanese (100)	208	0.14
Korean (240)	303	0.20
Laotian (903)	1,027	0.67
Malaysian (4)	9	0.01
Nepalese (0)	3	<0.01
Pakistani (133)	153	0.10
Sri Lankan (10)	10	0.01
Taiwanese (11)	13	0.01
Thai (85)	122	0.08
Vietnamese (490)	586	0.38
Hawaii Native/Pacific Islander (41)	163	0.11
Not Hispanic (36)	117	0.08
Hispanic (5)	46	0.03
Guamanian/Chamorro (8)	17	0.01
Native Hawaiian (19)	56	0.04
Samoan (2)	16	0.01
White (99,517)	104,370	68.27
Not Hispanic (89,349)	92,788	60.70
Hispanic (10,168)	11,582	7.58

Rockton

Place Type: Village
County: Winnebago
Population: 7,685†

Ancestry‡	Population	%
American (708)	708	9.72
Austrian (0)	25	0.34
Belgian (0)	19	0.26
Brazilian (25)	25	0.34
British (0)	13	0.18
Canadian (45)	56	0.77
Croatian (0)	12	0.16
Czech (12)	66	0.91
Danish (24)	91	1.25
Dutch (26)	124	1.70
English (173)	945	12.97

*Notes: † The Census 2010 population figure is used to calculate the percentages in the Hispanic Origin and Race categories. Ancestry percentages are based on the 2006-2010 American Community Survey population (not shown); ‡ Numbers in parentheses indicate the number of people reporting a single ancestry; * Numbers in parentheses indicate the number of persons reporting this race alone, not in combination with any other race; Please refer to the Explanation of Data for more information.*

Ancestry	Population	%
European (158)	158	2.17
Finnish (0)	108	1.48
French, ex. Basque (16)	179	2.46
French Canadian (0)	12	0.16
German (832)	2,577	35.36
Greek (0)	12	0.16
Hungarian (0)	40	0.55
Irish (290)	1,340	18.39
Italian (169)	630	8.65
Norwegian (156)	634	8.70
Polish (83)	314	4.31
Scandinavian (22)	33	0.45
Scotch-Irish (33)	199	2.73
Scottish (16)	70	0.96
Slovene (12)	28	0.38
Swedish (197)	521	7.15
Swiss (0)	69	0.95
Welsh (11)	40	0.55
Yugoslavian (15)	15	0.21

Hispanic Origin	Population	%
Hispanic or Latino (of any race)	278	3.62
Central American, ex. Mexican	8	0.10
Guatemalan	3	0.04
Panamanian	1	0.01
Salvadoran	4	0.05
Cuban	12	0.16
Mexican	208	2.71
Puerto Rican	16	0.21
South American	16	0.21
Chilean	2	0.03
Colombian	8	0.10
Ecuadorian	1	0.01
Peruvian	1	0.01
Venezuelan	4	0.05
Other Hispanic or Latino	18	0.23

Race*	Population	%
African-American/Black (105)	153	1.99
Not Hispanic (101)	137	1.78
Hispanic (4)	16	0.21
American Indian/Alaska Native (10)	45	0.59
Not Hispanic (9)	43	0.56
Hispanic (1)	2	0.03
Apache (1)	1	0.01
Blackfeet (0)	5	0.07
Cherokee (0)	7	0.09
Chippewa (1)	6	0.08
Iroquois (0)	1	0.01
Osage (2)	2	0.03
Yakama (0)	1	0.01
Asian (85)	124	1.61
Not Hispanic (84)	122	1.59
Hispanic (1)	2	0.03
Cambodian (6)	6	0.08
Chinese, ex. Taiwanese (13)	20	0.26
Filipino (12)	19	0.25
Indian (7)	9	0.12
Japanese (2)	11	0.14
Korean (11)	20	0.26
Laotian (3)	4	0.05
Taiwanese (4)	5	0.07
Thai (0)	1	0.01
Vietnamese (21)	30	0.39
Hawaii Native/Pacific Islander (1)	2	0.03
Not Hispanic (1)	2	0.03
Native Hawaiian (1)	1	0.01
White (7,307)	7,442	96.84
Not Hispanic (7,101)	7,204	93.74
Hispanic (206)	238	3.10

Rolling Meadows

Place Type: City
County: Cook
Population: 24,099†

Ancestry‡	Population	%
African, Sub-Saharan (42)	42	0.18
African (42)	42	0.18
Albanian (76)	100	0.42
American (420)	420	1.78
Arab (12)	32	0.14
Egyptian (12)	12	0.05
Syrian (0)	20	0.08
Armenian (65)	104	0.44
Assyrian/Chaldean/Syriac (54)	72	0.31
Australian (0)	8	0.03
Austrian (22)	65	0.28
Belgian (0)	51	0.22
British (0)	105	0.44
Bulgarian (246)	246	1.04
Cajun (0)	27	0.11
Canadian (14)	31	0.13
Croatian (10)	29	0.12
Czech (47)	170	0.72
Czechoslovakian (8)	45	0.19
Danish (23)	124	0.53
Dutch (31)	158	0.67
Eastern European (22)	22	0.09
English (363)	1,218	5.16
European (258)	301	1.28
Finnish (0)	45	0.19
French, ex. Basque (61)	435	1.84
French Canadian (8)	57	0.24
German (1,699)	5,037	21.34
Greek (181)	412	1.75
Hungarian (15)	55	0.23
Iranian (0)	16	0.07
Irish (605)	2,679	11.35
Italian (692)	2,407	10.20
Latvian (0)	13	0.06
Lithuanian (76)	203	0.86
Luxemburger (31)	62	0.26
Macedonian (20)	70	0.30
Northern European (43)	43	0.18
Norwegian (136)	624	2.64
Pennsylvania German (0)	13	0.06
Polish (1,649)	3,252	13.78
Portuguese (0)	107	0.45
Romanian (54)	54	0.23
Russian (102)	241	1.02
Scotch-Irish (104)	179	0.76
Scottish (89)	351	1.49
Serbian (53)	53	0.22
Slovak (0)	10	0.04
Slovene (0)	39	0.17
Swedish (213)	893	3.78
Swiss (0)	14	0.06
Ukrainian (0)	11	0.05
Welsh (0)	72	0.31
West Indian, ex. Hispanic (28)	56	0.24
Jamaican (28)	56	0.24
Yugoslavian (54)	62	0.26

Hispanic Origin	Population	%
Hispanic or Latino (of any race)	6,334	26.28
Central American, ex. Mexican	234	0.97
Costa Rican	2	0.01
Guatemalan	55	0.23
Honduran	18	0.07
Panamanian	6	0.02
Salvadoran	153	0.63
Cuban	31	0.13
Dominican Republic	5	0.02
Mexican	5,444	22.59
Puerto Rican	190	0.79
South American	162	0.67
Argentinean	7	0.03
Bolivian	8	0.03
Chilean	9	0.04
Colombian	41	0.17
Ecuadorian	59	0.24
Peruvian	32	0.13
Venezuelan	6	0.02
Other Hispanic or Latino	268	1.11

Race*	Population	%
African-American/Black (569)	671	2.78
Not Hispanic (514)	602	2.50
Hispanic (55)	69	0.29
American Indian/Alaska Native (81)	342	1.42
Not Hispanic (8)	58	0.24
Hispanic (73)	284	1.18
Apache (0)	5	0.02
Blackfeet (0)	2	0.01
Central American Ind. (1)	1	<0.01
Cherokee (0)	17	0.07
Chippewa (0)	4	0.02
Choctaw (1)	1	<0.01
Mexican American Ind. (27)	30	0.12
Sioux (0)	3	0.01
South American Ind. (0)	5	0.02
Spanish American Ind. (0)	1	<0.01
Asian (1,977)	2,164	8.98
Not Hispanic (1,961)	2,130	8.84
Hispanic (16)	34	0.14
Bangladeshi (2)	2	0.01
Burmese (1)	5	0.02
Cambodian (1)	1	<0.01
Chinese, ex. Taiwanese (276)	319	1.32
Filipino (305)	377	1.56
Indian (509)	544	2.26
Indonesian (4)	4	0.02
Japanese (189)	226	0.94
Korean (443)	461	1.91
Laotian (4)	4	0.02
Malaysian (1)	2	0.01
Nepalese (13)	13	0.05
Pakistani (73)	91	0.38
Sri Lankan (4)	5	0.02
Taiwanese (33)	42	0.17
Thai (13)	20	0.08
Vietnamese (28)	41	0.17
Hawaii Native/Pacific Islander (6)	32	0.13
Not Hispanic (6)	17	0.07
Hispanic (0)	15	0.06
Guamanian/Chamorro (0)	3	0.01
Native Hawaiian (5)	10	0.04
Samoan (1)	1	<0.01
White (18,725)	19,418	80.58
Not Hispanic (14,948)	15,201	63.08
Hispanic (3,777)	4,217	17.50

Romeoville

Place Type: Village
County: Will
Population: 39,680†

Ancestry‡	Population	%
African, Sub-Saharan (591)	608	1.62
African (129)	146	0.39
Ethiopian (192)	192	0.51
Ghanaian (78)	78	0.21
Nigerian (87)	87	0.23
Sierra Leonean (105)	105	0.28
American (493)	493	1.32
Arab (218)	218	0.58
Arab (154)	154	0.41
Egyptian (32)	32	0.09
Palestinian (32)	32	0.09
Austrian (59)	76	0.20
Belgian (74)	74	0.20
Brazilian (0)	3	0.01
British (17)	39	0.10
Cajun (0)	1	<0.01
Canadian (44)	44	0.12
Carpatho Rusyn (0)	13	0.03
Croatian (9)	153	0.41
Czech (97)	501	1.34
Czechoslovakian (42)	56	0.15
Danish (0)	104	0.28
Dutch (88)	434	1.16
English (266)	1,255	3.35
European (70)	70	0.19
Finnish (30)	30	0.08
French, ex. Basque (0)	819	2.18
French Canadian (0)	28	0.07
German (940)	5,803	15.48

*Notes: † The Census 2010 population figure is used to calculate the percentages in the Hispanic Origin and Race categories. Ancestry percentages are based on the 2006-2010 American Community Survey population (not shown); ‡ Numbers in parentheses indicate the number of people reporting a single ancestry; * Numbers in parentheses indicate the number of persons reporting this race alone, not in combination with any other race; Please refer to the Explanation of Data for more information.*

Greek (35)	378	1.01
Hungarian (12)	67	0.18
Irish (1,165)	5,743	15.32
Italian (993)	3,820	10.19
Lithuanian (256)	486	1.30
Luxemburger (0)	19	0.05
Macedonian (8)	24	0.06
Norwegian (45)	274	0.73
Pennsylvania German (17)	17	0.05
Polish (2,377)	4,536	12.10
Portuguese (0)	3	0.01
Romanian (17)	34	0.09
Russian (0)	174	0.46
Scandinavian (26)	26	0.07
Scotch-Irish (59)	347	0.93
Scottish (73)	154	0.41
Serbian (54)	85	0.23
Slovak (51)	85	0.23
Slovene (13)	101	0.27
Swedish (59)	611	1.63
Swiss (0)	52	0.14
Ukrainian (14)	94	0.25
Welsh (12)	102	0.27
West Indian, ex. Hispanic (114)	165	0.44
Dutch West Indian (0)	10	0.03
Haitian (96)	137	0.37
West Indian (18)	18	0.05

Hispanic Origin	Population	%
Hispanic or Latino (of any race)	11,883	29.95
Central American, ex. Mexican	275	0.69
Costa Rican	13	0.03
Guatemalan	148	0.37
Honduran	47	0.12
Nicaraguan	11	0.03
Panamanian	7	0.02
Salvadoran	48	0.12
Other Central American	1	<0.01
Cuban	58	0.15
Dominican Republic	20	0.05
Mexican	9,992	25.18
Puerto Rican	931	2.35
South American	301	0.76
Argentinean	12	0.03
Bolivian	21	0.05
Chilean	15	0.04
Colombian	80	0.20
Ecuadorian	88	0.22
Paraguayan	1	<0.01
Peruvian	70	0.18
Uruguayan	3	0.01
Venezuelan	10	0.03
Other South American	1	<0.01
Other Hispanic or Latino	306	0.77

Race*	Population	%
African-American/Black (4,675)	5,052	12.73
Not Hispanic (4,545)	4,835	12.18
Hispanic (130)	217	0.55
American Indian/Alaska Native (209)	455	1.15
Not Hispanic (61)	224	0.56
Hispanic (148)	231	0.58
Apache (0)	6	0.02
Blackfeet (1)	19	0.05
Canadian/French Am. Ind. (3)	7	0.02
Central American Ind. (1)	1	<0.01
Cherokee (14)	66	0.17
Cheyenne (0)	1	<0.01
Chickasaw (1)	1	<0.01
Chippewa (6)	11	0.03
Choctaw (5)	8	0.02
Comanche (1)	1	<0.01
Cree (1)	6	0.02
Lumbee (0)	2	0.01
Mexican American Ind. (30)	39	0.10
Navajo (5)	5	0.01
Potawatomi (1)	6	0.02
Pueblo (0)	1	<0.01
Sioux (1)	7	0.02
South American Ind. (10)	10	0.03
Spanish American Ind. (2)	2	0.01
Yaqui (2)	2	0.01
Asian (2,525)	2,854	7.19
Not Hispanic (2,486)	2,771	6.98
Hispanic (39)	83	0.21
Bangladeshi (1)	2	0.01
Burmese (1)	4	0.01
Cambodian (21)	38	0.10
Chinese, ex. Taiwanese (112)	153	0.39
Filipino (1,326)	1,490	3.76
Indian (354)	402	1.01
Indonesian (7)	8	0.02
Japanese (17)	45	0.11
Korean (60)	75	0.19
Laotian (36)	41	0.10
Malaysian (10)	11	0.03
Nepalese (3)	3	0.01
Pakistani (299)	341	0.86
Sri Lankan (7)	11	0.03
Taiwanese (10)	10	0.03
Thai (37)	51	0.13
Vietnamese (131)	143	0.36
Hawaii Native/Pacific Islander (5)	56	0.14
Not Hispanic (3)	35	0.09
Hispanic (2)	21	0.05
Guamanian/Chamorro (1)	2	0.01
Native Hawaiian (1)	14	0.04
Samoan (0)	1	<0.01
Tongan (1)	1	<0.01
White (26,178)	27,145	68.41
Not Hispanic (19,992)	20,530	51.74
Hispanic (6,186)	6,615	16.67

Roscoe

Place Type: Village
County: Winnebago
Population: 10,785†

Ancestry‡	Population	%
African, Sub-Saharan (43)	54	0.53
African (30)	30	0.30
Ugandan (13)	24	0.24
American (1,805)	1,805	17.76
Austrian (0)	9	0.09
Belgian (0)	33	0.32
British (18)	33	0.32
Canadian (0)	10	0.10
Czech (31)	112	1.10
Czechoslovakian (11)	111	1.09
Danish (25)	130	1.28
Dutch (9)	151	1.49
English (242)	1,049	10.32
European (101)	101	0.99
Finnish (0)	18	0.18
French, ex. Basque (7)	236	2.32
French Canadian (34)	64	0.63
German (880)	3,045	29.96
Greek (9)	9	0.09
Irish (335)	1,500	14.76
Italian (329)	774	7.62
Lithuanian (14)	73	0.72
Norwegian (56)	428	4.21
Pennsylvania German (0)	11	0.11
Polish (50)	357	3.51
Portuguese (0)	24	0.24
Russian (0)	90	0.89
Scandinavian (0)	17	0.17
Scotch-Irish (44)	116	1.14
Scottish (52)	213	2.10
Slovene (12)	12	0.12
Swedish (160)	678	6.67
Swiss (0)	48	0.47
Ukrainian (9)	9	0.09
Welsh (37)	104	1.02

Hispanic Origin	Population	%
Hispanic or Latino (of any race)	491	4.55
Central American, ex. Mexican	19	0.18
Guatemalan	14	0.13
Nicaraguan	3	0.03
Salvadoran	2	0.02
Cuban	6	0.06
Dominican Republic	4	0.04
Mexican	361	3.35
Puerto Rican	55	0.51
South American	21	0.19
Argentinean	1	0.01
Bolivian	1	0.01
Colombian	10	0.09
Ecuadorian	9	0.08
Other Hispanic or Latino	25	0.23

Race*	Population	%
African-American/Black (330)	418	3.88
Not Hispanic (325)	400	3.71
Hispanic (5)	18	0.17
American Indian/Alaska Native (16)	65	0.60
Not Hispanic (12)	58	0.54
Hispanic (4)	7	0.06
Canadian/French Am. Ind. (0)	4	0.04
Cherokee (1)	15	0.14
Cheyenne (0)	1	0.01
Chippewa (3)	3	0.03
Mexican American Ind. (0)	1	0.01
Navajo (0)	1	0.01
Osage (0)	1	0.01
Puget Sound Salish (0)	3	0.03
Sioux (0)	3	0.03
Asian (231)	299	2.77
Not Hispanic (230)	294	2.73
Hispanic (1)	5	0.05
Chinese, ex. Taiwanese (40)	51	0.47
Filipino (37)	60	0.56
Indian (42)	50	0.46
Indonesian (0)	1	0.01
Japanese (16)	31	0.29
Korean (41)	51	0.47
Laotian (1)	3	0.03
Malaysian (1)	1	0.01
Pakistani (5)	6	0.06
Sri Lankan (5)	5	0.05
Thai (7)	10	0.09
Vietnamese (27)	33	0.31
Hawaii Native/Pacific Islander (0)	5	0.05
Not Hispanic (0)	4	0.04
Hispanic (0)	1	0.01
Native Hawaiian (0)	1	0.01
White (9,832)	10,028	92.98
Not Hispanic (9,544)	9,699	89.93
Hispanic (288)	329	3.05

Roselle

Place Type: Village
County: DuPage
Population: 22,763†

Ancestry‡	Population	%
African, Sub-Saharan (0)	15	0.07
Cape Verdean (0)	15	0.07
American (703)	703	3.09
Arab (198)	213	0.94
Arab (40)	40	0.18
Egyptian (76)	76	0.33
Lebanese (61)	61	0.27
Palestinian (21)	21	0.09
Syrian (0)	15	0.07
Armenian (9)	49	0.22
Assyrian/Chaldean/Syriac (72)	109	0.48
Austrian (0)	206	0.91
Belgian (0)	56	0.25
British (5)	83	0.37
Bulgarian (161)	161	0.71
Canadian (0)	11	0.05
Croatian (49)	79	0.35
Czech (51)	437	1.92
Czechoslovakian (8)	55	0.24
Danish (0)	109	0.48
Dutch (61)	294	1.29

SECTION TWO

*Notes: † The Census 2010 population figure is used to calculate the percentages in the Hispanic Origin and Race categories. Ancestry percentages are based on the 2006-2010 American Community Survey population (not shown); ‡ Numbers in parentheses indicate the number of people reporting a single ancestry; * Numbers in parentheses indicate the number of persons reporting this race alone, not in combination with any other race; Please refer to the Explanation of Data for more information.*

English (204)	1,453	6.39
European (94)	109	0.48
Finnish (15)	80	0.35
French, ex. Basque (56)	564	2.48
French Canadian (10)	44	0.19
German (1,285)	6,337	27.88
Greek (56)	349	1.54
Hungarian (21)	96	0.42
Iranian (27)	27	0.12
Irish (539)	3,893	17.12
Israeli (0)	17	0.07
Italian (1,478)	3,809	16.76
Latvian (14)	37	0.16
Lithuanian (151)	280	1.23
Luxemburger (0)	104	0.46
Northern European (30)	30	0.13
Norwegian (81)	413	1.82
Polish (2,297)	4,344	19.11
Portuguese (0)	10	0.04
Romanian (99)	205	0.90
Russian (100)	256	1.13
Scandinavian (35)	53	0.23
Scotch-Irish (31)	132	0.58
Scottish (109)	444	1.95
Serbian (9)	24	0.11
Slavic (0)	13	0.06
Slovak (47)	84	0.37
Slovene (21)	28	0.12
Swedish (47)	452	1.99
Swiss (0)	76	0.33
Ukrainian (52)	101	0.44
Welsh (7)	81	0.36
Yugoslavian (36)	96	0.42

Hispanic Origin	Population	%
Hispanic or Latino (of any race)	1,867	8.20
Central American, ex. Mexican	86	0.38
Guatemalan	51	0.22
Honduran	12	0.05
Nicaraguan	5	0.02
Panamanian	3	0.01
Salvadoran	15	0.07
Cuban	76	0.33
Dominican Republic	2	0.01
Mexican	1,245	5.47
Puerto Rican	212	0.93
South American	179	0.79
Argentinean	20	0.09
Bolivian	2	0.01
Chilean	22	0.10
Colombian	55	0.24
Ecuadorian	57	0.25
Peruvian	21	0.09
Venezuelan	1	<0.01
Other South American	1	<0.01
Other Hispanic or Latino	67	0.29

Race*	Population	%
African-American/Black (584)	683	3.00
Not Hispanic (577)	665	2.92
Hispanic (7)	18	0.08
American Indian/Alaska Native (34)	119	0.52
Not Hispanic (21)	90	0.40
Hispanic (13)	29	0.13
Alaska Athabascan *(Ala. Nat.)* (0)	3	0.01
Blackfeet (1)	4	0.02
Cherokee (6)	17	0.07
Chippewa (2)	4	0.02
Choctaw (1)	3	0.01
Iroquois (0)	3	0.01
Menominee (1)	3	0.01
Mexican American Ind. (2)	3	0.01
Sioux (0)	3	0.01
Asian (2,075)	2,284	10.03
Not Hispanic (2,058)	2,249	9.88
Hispanic (17)	35	0.15
Bangladeshi (8)	8	0.04
Burmese (1)	1	<0.01
Cambodian (4)	4	0.02
Chinese, ex. Taiwanese (166)	198	0.87
Filipino (344)	405	1.78
Hmong (2)	2	0.01
Indian (1,000)	1,063	4.67
Indonesian (9)	13	0.06
Japanese (111)	137	0.60
Korean (151)	168	0.74
Laotian (4)	10	0.04
Pakistani (145)	155	0.68
Sri Lankan (5)	5	0.02
Taiwanese (17)	20	0.09
Thai (25)	29	0.13
Vietnamese (42)	47	0.21
Hawaii Native/Pacific Islander (7)	33	0.14
Not Hispanic (7)	22	0.10
Hispanic (0)	11	0.05
Fijian (3)	5	0.02
Guamanian/Chamorro (3)	3	0.01
Native Hawaiian (1)	6	0.03
Samoan (0)	4	0.02
White (19,161)	19,537	85.83
Not Hispanic (17,885)	18,149	79.73
Hispanic (1,276)	1,388	6.10

Round Lake Beach

Place Type: Village
County: Lake
Population: 28,175†

Ancestry‡	Population	%
African, Sub-Saharan (0)	16	0.06
African (0)	16	0.06
American (481)	481	1.72
Arab (14)	14	0.05
Syrian (14)	14	0.05
Austrian (0)	60	0.21
Belgian (35)	35	0.12
British (16)	50	0.18
Czech (65)	175	0.62
Danish (28)	108	0.39
Dutch (12)	247	0.88
English (103)	1,014	3.62
European (127)	127	0.45
Finnish (52)	115	0.41
French, ex. Basque (15)	535	1.91
French Canadian (8)	22	0.08
German (1,131)	4,263	15.22
Greek (10)	17	0.06
Hungarian (55)	86	0.31
Irish (520)	2,834	10.12
Italian (293)	906	3.24
Latvian (16)	16	0.06
Lithuanian (17)	63	0.22
Luxemburger (0)	32	0.11
Maltese (8)	8	0.03
Northern European (45)	45	0.16
Norwegian (66)	299	1.07
Pennsylvania German (10)	21	0.07
Polish (913)	2,605	9.30
Portuguese (0)	16	0.06
Romanian (0)	28	0.10
Russian (112)	318	1.14
Scandinavian (23)	71	0.25
Scotch-Irish (65)	203	0.72
Scottish (94)	438	1.56
Slavic (0)	12	0.04
Slovak (20)	20	0.07
Slovene (9)	9	0.03
Swedish (84)	441	1.57
Swiss (0)	6	0.02
Turkish (0)	32	0.11
Ukrainian (10)	51	0.18
Welsh (8)	21	0.07
West Indian, ex. Hispanic (38)	103	0.37
British West Indian (38)	38	0.14
Jamaican (0)	49	0.17
West Indian (0)	16	0.06

Hispanic Origin	Population	%
Hispanic or Latino (of any race)	13,530	48.02
Central American, ex. Mexican	357	1.27
Guatemalan	130	0.46
Honduran	54	0.19
Nicaraguan	8	0.03
Panamanian	13	0.05
Salvadoran	151	0.54
Other Central American	1	<0.01
Cuban	45	0.16
Dominican Republic	11	0.04
Mexican	12,194	43.28
Puerto Rican	415	1.47
South American	225	0.80
Argentinean	29	0.10
Bolivian	18	0.06
Chilean	15	0.05
Colombian	87	0.31
Ecuadorian	34	0.12
Peruvian	24	0.09
Uruguayan	7	0.02
Venezuelan	11	0.04
Other Hispanic or Latino	283	1.00

Race*	Population	%
African-American/Black (1,198)	1,463	5.19
Not Hispanic (1,076)	1,263	4.48
Hispanic (122)	200	0.71
American Indian/Alaska Native (374)	525	1.86
Not Hispanic (58)	141	0.50
Hispanic (316)	384	1.36
Apache (2)	7	0.02
Blackfeet (4)	6	0.02
Canadian/French Am. Ind. (1)	4	0.01
Central American Ind. (3)	3	0.01
Cherokee (15)	59	0.21
Cheyenne (0)	2	0.01
Chippewa (10)	20	0.07
Choctaw (0)	5	0.02
Creek (2)	3	0.01
Delaware (0)	3	0.01
Hopi (1)	1	<0.01
Iroquois (7)	12	0.04
Menominee (0)	1	<0.01
Mexican American Ind. (48)	64	0.23
Navajo (0)	2	0.01
Ottawa (1)	1	<0.01
Pueblo (1)	1	<0.01
Sioux (2)	6	0.02
South American Ind. (3)	3	0.01
Spanish American Ind. (17)	17	0.06
Yaqui (1)	1	<0.01
Asian (844)	1,045	3.71
Not Hispanic (838)	1,000	3.55
Hispanic (6)	45	0.16
Bangladeshi (4)	4	0.01
Cambodian (30)	33	0.12
Chinese, ex. Taiwanese (59)	97	0.34
Filipino (324)	407	1.44
Hmong (15)	19	0.07
Indian (221)	250	0.89
Japanese (23)	44	0.16
Korean (41)	58	0.21
Laotian (2)	6	0.02
Malaysian (3)	3	0.01
Pakistani (40)	44	0.16
Sri Lankan (1)	1	<0.01
Taiwanese (0)	1	<0.01
Thai (14)	24	0.09
Vietnamese (43)	47	0.17
Hawaii Native/Pacific Islander (7)	50	0.18
Not Hispanic (7)	39	0.14
Hispanic (0)	11	0.04
Guamanian/Chamorro (1)	10	0.04
Native Hawaiian (0)	1	<0.01
Samoan (3)	12	0.04
White (19,359)	20,205	71.71
Not Hispanic (12,212)	12,588	44.68
Hispanic (7,147)	7,617	27.03

*Notes: † The Census 2010 population figure is used to calculate the percentages in the Hispanic Origin and Race categories. Ancestry percentages are based on the 2006-2010 American Community Survey population (not shown); ‡ Numbers in parentheses indicate the number of people reporting a single ancestry; * Numbers in parentheses indicate the number of persons reporting this race alone, not in combination with any other race; Please refer to the Explanation of Data for more information.*

Round Lake Park

Place Type: Village
County: Lake
Population: 7,505†

Ancestry‡	Population	%
American (188)	188	2.60
Austrian (0)	41	0.57
Belgian (0)	47	0.65
Czech (0)	31	0.43
Danish (0)	28	0.39
Dutch (38)	89	1.23
Eastern European (12)	12	0.17
English (104)	318	4.40
European (21)	21	0.29
Finnish (39)	39	0.54
French, ex. Basque (21)	178	2.46
French Canadian (0)	55	0.76
German (502)	1,827	25.26
Greek (41)	52	0.72
Irish (192)	1,313	18.16
Italian (226)	610	8.43
Lithuanian (8)	30	0.41
Norwegian (84)	498	6.89
Pennsylvania German (12)	12	0.17
Polish (189)	712	9.85
Romanian (0)	13	0.18
Russian (8)	54	0.75
Scotch-Irish (0)	41	0.57
Scottish (0)	75	1.04
Serbian (11)	11	0.15
Slovak (23)	23	0.32
Slovene (8)	8	0.11
Swedish (57)	170	2.35
Swiss (0)	24	0.33
Ukrainian (0)	8	0.11
Welsh (0)	10	0.14

Hispanic Origin	Population	%
Hispanic or Latino (of any race)	2,899	38.63
Central American, ex. Mexican	77	1.03
Costa Rican	2	0.03
Guatemalan	23	0.31
Honduran	13	0.17
Nicaraguan	6	0.08
Panamanian	4	0.05
Salvadoran	28	0.37
Other Central American	1	0.01
Cuban	3	0.04
Mexican	2,654	35.36
Puerto Rican	75	1.00
South American	26	0.35
Chilean	1	0.01
Colombian	9	0.12
Ecuadorian	6	0.08
Peruvian	10	0.13
Other Hispanic or Latino	64	0.85

Race*	Population	%
African-American/Black (256)	311	4.14
Not Hispanic (226)	258	3.44
Hispanic (30)	53	0.71
American Indian/Alaska Native (126)	168	2.24
Not Hispanic (20)	42	0.56
Hispanic (106)	126	1.68
Blackfeet (0)	7	0.09
Cherokee (6)	10	0.13
Chickasaw (0)	1	0.01
Chippewa (1)	4	0.05
Choctaw (0)	4	0.05
Iroquois (0)	1	0.01
Menominee (2)	2	0.03
Mexican American Ind. (23)	23	0.31
Ottawa (0)	1	0.01
South American Ind. (0)	1	0.01
Asian (83)	108	1.44
Not Hispanic (82)	95	1.27
Hispanic (1)	13	0.17
Cambodian (7)	7	0.09
Chinese, ex. Taiwanese (2)	7	0.09
Filipino (39)	49	0.65
Indian (9)	9	0.12
Japanese (6)	9	0.12
Korean (8)	11	0.15
Laotian (5)	5	0.07
Taiwanese (2)	2	0.03
Thai (4)	4	0.05
Vietnamese (1)	4	0.05
Hawaii Native/Pacific Islander (1)	8	0.11
Not Hispanic (1)	8	0.11
Guamanian/Chamorro (1)	5	0.07
Samoan (0)	2	0.03
White (5,371)	5,548	73.92
Not Hispanic (4,189)	4,255	56.70
Hispanic (1,182)	1,293	17.23

Round Lake

Place Type: Village
County: Lake
Population: 18,289†

Ancestry‡	Population	%
African, Sub-Saharan (47)	47	0.29
African (6)	6	0.04
Kenyan (5)	5	0.03
Nigerian (36)	36	0.22
American (430)	430	2.66
Arab (102)	114	0.71
Lebanese (10)	10	0.06
Moroccan (23)	23	0.14
Palestinian (69)	69	0.43
Syrian (0)	12	0.07
Assyrian/Chaldean/Syriac (48)	48	0.30
Austrian (0)	22	0.14
Belgian (10)	21	0.13
British (0)	31	0.19
Bulgarian (31)	31	0.19
Canadian (12)	23	0.14
Croatian (0)	18	0.11
Czech (0)	57	0.35
Danish (30)	147	0.91
Dutch (35)	206	1.27
English (129)	572	3.54
European (162)	229	1.42
French, ex. Basque (23)	252	1.56
French Canadian (31)	65	0.40
German (733)	2,716	16.80
Greek (12)	55	0.34
Hungarian (30)	162	1.00
Iranian (80)	80	0.49
Irish (309)	1,672	10.34
Italian (323)	910	5.63
Latvian (56)	56	0.35
Lithuanian (0)	17	0.11
Maltese (18)	18	0.11
Norwegian (95)	275	1.70
Polish (549)	1,484	9.18
Romanian (102)	126	0.78
Russian (203)	314	1.94
Scotch-Irish (11)	98	0.61
Scottish (57)	169	1.05
Serbian (15)	56	0.35
Swedish (28)	358	2.21
Swiss (16)	37	0.23
Ukrainian (75)	106	0.66
Welsh (20)	45	0.28
West Indian, ex. Hispanic (346)	361	2.23
Belizean (12)	27	0.17
Jamaican (334)	334	2.07

Hispanic Origin	Population	%
Hispanic or Latino (of any race)	4,631	25.32
Central American, ex. Mexican	211	1.15
Costa Rican	2	0.01
Guatemalan	96	0.52
Honduran	21	0.11
Nicaraguan	2	0.01
Panamanian	7	0.04
Salvadoran	79	0.43
Other Central American	4	0.02
Cuban	41	0.22
Dominican Republic	11	0.06
Mexican	3,761	20.56
Puerto Rican	329	1.80
South American	157	0.86
Argentinean	14	0.08
Bolivian	7	0.04
Chilean	3	0.02
Colombian	63	0.34
Ecuadorian	49	0.27
Peruvian	18	0.10
Venezuelan	3	0.02
Other Hispanic or Latino	121	0.66

Race*	Population	%
African-American/Black (873)	1,046	5.72
Not Hispanic (828)	972	5.31
Hispanic (45)	74	0.40
American Indian/Alaska Native (92)	165	0.90
Not Hispanic (27)	66	0.36
Hispanic (65)	99	0.54
Apache (0)	1	0.01
Blackfeet (1)	2	0.01
Cherokee (1)	15	0.08
Chippewa (4)	8	0.04
Choctaw (1)	2	0.01
Creek (0)	5	0.03
Mexican American Ind. (3)	6	0.03
Navajo (2)	4	0.02
Ottawa (0)	1	0.01
Sioux (1)	2	0.01
South American Ind. (0)	5	0.03
Tlingit-Haida *(Alaska Native)* (1)	1	0.01
Asian (2,340)	2,574	14.07
Not Hispanic (2,310)	2,525	13.81
Hispanic (30)	49	0.27
Bangladeshi (3)	5	0.03
Burmese (1)	4	0.02
Cambodian (17)	20	0.11
Chinese, ex. Taiwanese (137)	188	1.03
Filipino (901)	1,021	5.58
Hmong (6)	6	0.03
Indian (647)	677	3.70
Indonesian (8)	8	0.04
Japanese (14)	45	0.25
Korean (350)	375	2.05
Malaysian (1)	2	0.01
Nepalese (1)	1	0.01
Pakistani (63)	71	0.39
Sri Lankan (16)	16	0.09
Taiwanese (9)	11	0.06
Thai (4)	11	0.06
Vietnamese (111)	133	0.73
Hawaii Native/Pacific Islander (14)	47	0.26
Not Hispanic (12)	35	0.19
Hispanic (2)	12	0.07
Guamanian/Chamorro (2)	2	0.01
Native Hawaiian (1)	10	0.05
Samoan (5)	11	0.06
White (12,603)	13,101	71.63
Not Hispanic (10,066)	10,392	56.82
Hispanic (2,537)	2,709	14.81

Sauk Village

Place Type: Village
County: Cook
Population: 10,506†

Ancestry‡	Population	%
African, Sub-Saharan (53)	129	1.25
African (43)	119	1.15
Nigerian (10)	10	0.10
American (116)	116	1.12
Assyrian/Chaldean/Syriac (7)	16	0.15
Canadian (0)	12	0.12
Croatian (35)	79	0.76
Czech (7)	7	0.07

*Notes: † The Census 2010 population figure is used to calculate the percentages in the Hispanic Origin and Race categories. Ancestry percentages are based on the 2006-2010 American Community Survey population (not shown); ‡ Numbers in parentheses indicate the number of people reporting a single ancestry; * Numbers in parentheses indicate the number of persons reporting this race alone, not in combination with any other race; Please refer to the Explanation of Data for more information.*

Ancestry	Population	%
Czechoslovakian (0)	10	0.10
Danish (6)	6	0.06
Dutch (55)	105	1.01
English (50)	246	2.37
French, ex. Basque (63)	110	1.06
French Canadian (4)	21	0.20
German (164)	628	6.06
Greek (44)	103	0.99
Hungarian (28)	73	0.70
Irish (179)	1,006	9.71
Italian (95)	254	2.45
Lithuanian (58)	91	0.88
Norwegian (16)	16	0.15
Polish (185)	451	4.35
Romanian (8)	24	0.23
Russian (0)	6	0.06
Scandinavian (9)	9	0.09
Scottish (11)	11	0.11
Slovak (8)	27	0.26
Swedish (8)	31	0.30
West Indian, ex. Hispanic (16)	25	0.24
Dutch West Indian (16)	16	0.15
Haitian (0)	9	0.09

Hispanic Origin	Population	%
Hispanic or Latino (of any race)	1,171	11.15
Central American, ex. Mexican	30	0.29
Guatemalan	5	0.05
Honduran	12	0.11
Nicaraguan	1	0.01
Panamanian	7	0.07
Salvadoran	5	0.05
Cuban	4	0.04
Dominican Republic	4	0.04
Mexican	935	8.90
Puerto Rican	113	1.08
South American	3	0.03
Argentinean	1	0.01
Bolivian	1	0.01
Uruguayan	1	0.01
Other Hispanic or Latino	82	0.78

Race*	Population	%
African-American/Black (6,584)	6,884	65.52
Not Hispanic (6,511)	6,748	64.23
Hispanic (73)	136	1.29
American Indian/Alaska Native (22)	101	0.96
Not Hispanic (13)	71	0.68
Hispanic (9)	30	0.29
Apache (1)	8	0.08
Blackfeet (1)	2	0.02
Central American Ind. (1)	1	0.01
Cherokee (1)	17	0.16
Chippewa (1)	1	0.01
Choctaw (0)	4	0.04
Cree (0)	1	0.01
Creek (0)	2	0.02
Iroquois (0)	1	0.01
Mexican American Ind. (1)	2	0.02
Osage (0)	5	0.05
Sioux (0)	2	0.02
Yaqui (1)	1	0.01
Asian (36)	54	0.51
Not Hispanic (30)	47	0.45
Hispanic (6)	7	0.07
Bhutanese (1)	1	0.01
Burmese (2)	2	0.02
Chinese, ex. Taiwanese (2)	10	0.10
Filipino (15)	27	0.26
Indian (5)	6	0.06
Japanese (1)	4	0.04
Korean (0)	2	0.02
Thai (1)	1	0.01
Vietnamese (2)	5	0.05
Hawaii Native/Pacific Islander (3)	5	0.05
Not Hispanic (2)	2	0.02
Hispanic (1)	3	0.03
Native Hawaiian (2)	4	0.04
Samoan (1)	1	0.01
White (2,946)	3,277	31.19
Not Hispanic (2,496)	2,721	25.90
Hispanic (450)	556	5.29

Schaumburg

Place Type: Village
County: Cook
Population: 74,227†

Ancestry‡	Population	%
African, Sub-Saharan (324)	334	0.46
African (39)	49	0.07
Kenyan (88)	88	0.12
Nigerian (105)	105	0.14
Senegalese (39)	39	0.05
Sierra Leonean (53)	53	0.07
Albanian (27)	27	0.04
American (1,210)	1,210	1.65
Arab (528)	684	0.93
Arab (0)	80	0.11
Egyptian (14)	14	0.02
Iraqi (217)	217	0.30
Jordanian (10)	10	0.01
Lebanese (110)	177	0.24
Moroccan (48)	48	0.07
Syrian (83)	92	0.13
Other Arab (46)	46	0.06
Armenian (101)	130	0.18
Assyrian/Chaldean/Syriac (35)	59	0.08
Australian (28)	42	0.06
Austrian (25)	265	0.36
Belgian (34)	241	0.33
Brazilian (0)	11	0.02
British (162)	332	0.45
Bulgarian (207)	207	0.28
Cajun (0)	24	0.03
Canadian (52)	125	0.17
Croatian (87)	273	0.37
Czech (322)	1,159	1.58
Czechoslovakian (42)	86	0.12
Danish (38)	259	0.35
Dutch (132)	963	1.31
Eastern European (33)	46	0.06
English (603)	3,875	5.28
Estonian (0)	17	0.02
European (595)	639	0.87
Finnish (45)	144	0.20
French, ex. Basque (167)	1,472	2.01
French Canadian (69)	232	0.32
German (4,694)	16,982	23.16
Greek (721)	1,317	1.80
Guyanese (41)	41	0.06
Hungarian (215)	631	0.86
Iranian (170)	224	0.31
Irish (1,649)	10,048	13.70
Israeli (33)	41	0.06
Italian (3,155)	8,459	11.54
Latvian (8)	43	0.06
Lithuanian (65)	357	0.49
Luxemburger (15)	69	0.09
Northern European (77)	90	0.12
Norwegian (376)	1,676	2.29
Polish (5,853)	11,923	16.26
Portuguese (15)	15	0.02
Romanian (182)	262	0.36
Russian (388)	1,071	1.46
Scandinavian (45)	113	0.15
Scotch-Irish (357)	889	1.21
Scottish (260)	810	1.10
Serbian (69)	151	0.21
Slavic (0)	18	0.02
Slovak (73)	161	0.22
Slovene (79)	154	0.21
Swedish (342)	2,209	3.01
Swiss (18)	189	0.26
Turkish (25)	51	0.07
Ukrainian (211)	435	0.59
Welsh (23)	258	0.35
West Indian, ex. Hispanic (0)	10	0.01
Jamaican (0)	10	0.01
Yugoslavian (133)	180	0.25

Hispanic Origin	Population	%
Hispanic or Latino (of any race)	6,554	8.83
Central American, ex. Mexican	356	0.48
Costa Rican	10	0.01
Guatemalan	150	0.20
Honduran	46	0.06
Nicaraguan	26	0.04
Panamanian	20	0.03
Salvadoran	92	0.12
Other Central American	12	0.02
Cuban	148	0.20
Dominican Republic	38	0.05
Mexican	4,375	5.89
Puerto Rican	715	0.96
South American	590	0.79
Argentinean	60	0.08
Bolivian	9	0.01
Chilean	31	0.04
Colombian	211	0.28
Ecuadorian	132	0.18
Paraguayan	2	<0.01
Peruvian	106	0.14
Uruguayan	3	<0.01
Venezuelan	24	0.03
Other South American	12	0.02
Other Hispanic or Latino	332	0.45

Race*	Population	%
African-American/Black (3,123)	3,563	4.80
Not Hispanic (2,987)	3,359	4.53
Hispanic (136)	204	0.27
American Indian/Alaska Native (162)	423	0.57
Not Hispanic (112)	306	0.41
Hispanic (50)	117	0.16
Apache (2)	2	<0.01
Blackfeet (1)	10	0.01
Central American Ind. (2)	2	<0.01
Cherokee (8)	57	0.08
Chickasaw (0)	1	<0.01
Chippewa (3)	9	0.01
Choctaw (6)	13	0.02
Creek (4)	10	0.01
Delaware (3)	3	<0.01
Iroquois (2)	5	0.01
Lumbee (1)	1	<0.01
Menominee (0)	1	<0.01
Mexican American Ind. (11)	14	0.02
Navajo (0)	3	<0.01
Osage (0)	1	<0.01
Ottawa (1)	1	<0.01
Paiute (0)	3	<0.01
Potawatomi (1)	2	<0.01
Sioux (3)	12	0.02
South American Ind. (3)	6	0.01
Ute (1)	1	<0.01
Asian (14,731)	15,744	21.21
Not Hispanic (14,675)	15,608	21.03
Hispanic (56)	136	0.18
Bangladeshi (34)	36	0.05
Burmese (12)	13	0.02
Cambodian (32)	33	0.04
Chinese, ex. Taiwanese (1,168)	1,306	1.76
Filipino (1,339)	1,597	2.15
Hmong (3)	3	<0.01
Indian (7,988)	8,303	11.19
Indonesian (30)	36	0.05
Japanese (1,044)	1,216	1.64
Korean (1,892)	1,994	2.69
Laotian (12)	18	0.02
Malaysian (14)	21	0.03
Nepalese (16)	16	0.02
Pakistani (515)	550	0.74
Sri Lankan (18)	20	0.03
Taiwanese (97)	104	0.14
Thai (104)	131	0.18
Vietnamese (109)	125	0.17
Hawaii Native/Pacific Islander (23)	93	0.13
Not Hispanic (18)	74	0.10

*Notes: † The Census 2010 population figure is used to calculate the percentages in the Hispanic Origin and Race categories. Ancestry percentages are based on the 2006-2010 American Community Survey population (not shown); ‡ Numbers in parentheses indicate the number of people reporting a single ancestry; * Numbers in parentheses indicate the number of persons reporting this race alone, not in combination with any other race; Please refer to the Explanation of Data for more information.*

Hispanic (5)	19	0.03
Fijian (1)	3	<0.01
Guamanian/Chamorro (5)	6	0.01
Native Hawaiian (6)	30	0.04
Samoan (6)	11	0.01
Tongan (0)	3	<0.01
White (52,281)	53,580	72.18
Not Hispanic (48,385)	49,375	66.52
Hispanic (3,896)	4,205	5.67

Schiller Park

Place Type: Village
County: Cook
Population: 11,793†

Ancestry‡	Population	%
Albanian (97)	97	0.83
American (243)	243	2.08
Arab (108)	108	0.93
Syrian (108)	108	0.93
Armenian (0)	13	0.11
Assyrian/Chaldean/Syriac (100)	100	0.86
Austrian (31)	104	0.89
Bulgarian (318)	318	2.73
Croatian (29)	29	0.25
Czech (156)	216	1.85
Danish (0)	37	0.32
Dutch (0)	58	0.50
English (0)	137	1.17
European (37)	46	0.39
French, ex. Basque (0)	123	1.05
German (50)	811	6.95
Greek (365)	453	3.88
Hungarian (19)	31	0.27
Irish (239)	1,011	8.66
Italian (821)	1,470	12.60
Lithuanian (29)	57	0.49
Macedonian (64)	64	0.55
Norwegian (24)	54	0.46
Pennsylvania German (0)	15	0.13
Polish (2,616)	3,034	26.00
Romanian (56)	69	0.59
Russian (12)	25	0.21
Scotch-Irish (80)	106	0.91
Scottish (11)	37	0.32
Slovak (50)	73	0.63
Swedish (74)	123	1.05
Ukrainian (196)	221	1.89
Welsh (0)	15	0.13
Yugoslavian (64)	64	0.55

Hispanic Origin	Population	%
Hispanic or Latino (of any race)	2,843	24.11
Central American, ex. Mexican	130	1.10
Costa Rican	12	0.10
Guatemalan	81	0.69
Honduran	11	0.09
Nicaraguan	3	0.03
Panamanian	2	0.02
Salvadoran	21	0.18
Cuban	52	0.44
Dominican Republic	3	0.03
Mexican	2,031	17.22
Puerto Rican	416	3.53
South American	152	1.29
Argentinean	23	0.20
Bolivian	2	0.02
Chilean	6	0.05
Colombian	62	0.53
Ecuadorian	44	0.37
Peruvian	13	0.11
Venezuelan	2	0.02
Other Hispanic or Latino	59	0.50

Race*	Population	%
African-American/Black (220)	258	2.19
Not Hispanic (189)	205	1.74
Hispanic (31)	53	0.45
American Indian/Alaska Native (61)	84	0.71
Not Hispanic (21)	37	0.31
Hispanic (40)	47	0.40
Blackfeet (1)	1	0.01
Cherokee (5)	9	0.08
Chippewa (0)	1	0.01
Iroquois (0)	2	0.02
Menominee (2)	3	0.03
Mexican American Ind. (19)	19	0.16
Sioux (2)	5	0.04
South American Ind. (6)	6	0.05
Spanish American Ind. (3)	3	0.03
Asian (698)	791	6.71
Not Hispanic (691)	750	6.36
Hispanic (7)	41	0.35
Burmese (0)	4	0.03
Chinese, ex. Taiwanese (15)	20	0.17
Filipino (300)	322	2.73
Indian (225)	246	2.09
Indonesian (6)	6	0.05
Japanese (13)	23	0.20
Korean (6)	7	0.06
Laotian (25)	25	0.21
Pakistani (48)	48	0.41
Taiwanese (6)	6	0.05
Thai (5)	5	0.04
Vietnamese (31)	31	0.26
Hawaii Native/Pacific Islander (1)	8	0.07
Not Hispanic (0)	5	0.04
Hispanic (1)	3	0.03
Guamanian/Chamorro (0)	1	0.01
Native Hawaiian (0)	1	0.01
Samoan (1)	1	0.01
White (9,514)	9,685	82.12
Not Hispanic (7,935)	7,996	67.80
Hispanic (1,579)	1,689	14.32

Shiloh

Place Type: Village
County: St. Clair
Population: 12,651†

Ancestry‡	Population	%
African, Sub-Saharan (111)	111	0.92
African (65)	65	0.54
Other Sub-Saharan African (46)	46	0.38
American (533)	533	4.44
Australian (43)	250	2.08
Austrian (12)	45	0.37
Canadian (0)	17	0.14
Croatian (0)	15	0.12
Czech (35)	136	1.13
Danish (59)	83	0.69
Dutch (72)	145	1.21
English (342)	1,055	8.78
European (230)	230	1.91
French, ex. Basque (157)	562	4.68
French Canadian (23)	23	0.19
German (1,549)	3,506	29.18
Greek (0)	304	2.53
Hungarian (15)	27	0.22
Irish (264)	1,394	11.60
Italian (195)	526	4.38
Northern European (14)	14	0.12
Norwegian (76)	103	0.86
Polish (34)	217	1.81
Portuguese (16)	16	0.13
Russian (0)	14	0.12
Scotch-Irish (14)	150	1.25
Scottish (107)	306	2.55
Swedish (55)	314	2.61
Swiss (0)	95	0.79
Turkish (42)	42	0.35
Ukrainian (39)	66	0.55
Welsh (0)	145	1.21
West Indian, ex. Hispanic (52)	126	1.05
West Indian (52)	126	1.05

Hispanic Origin	Population	%
Hispanic or Latino (of any race)	403	3.19
Central American, ex. Mexican	17	0.13
Costa Rican	1	0.01
Guatemalan	6	0.05
Honduran	2	0.02
Panamanian	8	0.06
Cuban	15	0.12
Dominican Republic	6	0.05
Mexican	224	1.77
Puerto Rican	79	0.62
South American	11	0.09
Bolivian	1	0.01
Chilean	2	0.02
Colombian	2	0.02
Ecuadorian	2	0.02
Venezuelan	4	0.03
Other Hispanic or Latino	51	0.40

Race*	Population	%
African-American/Black (2,753)	2,979	23.55
Not Hispanic (2,732)	2,939	23.23
Hispanic (21)	40	0.32
American Indian/Alaska Native (20)	89	0.70
Not Hispanic (15)	78	0.62
Hispanic (5)	11	0.09
Apache (1)	1	0.01
Cherokee (7)	31	0.25
Chippewa (2)	2	0.02
Choctaw (1)	1	0.01
Creek (0)	4	0.03
Lumbee (1)	2	0.02
Navajo (1)	1	0.01
Sioux (0)	1	0.01
Yaqui (1)	1	0.01
Yuman (1)	1	0.01
Asian (380)	543	4.29
Not Hispanic (377)	531	4.20
Hispanic (3)	12	0.09
Bangladeshi (2)	2	0.02
Cambodian (4)	5	0.04
Chinese, ex. Taiwanese (44)	67	0.53
Filipino (93)	164	1.30
Indian (58)	62	0.49
Indonesian (4)	4	0.03
Japanese (9)	32	0.25
Korean (94)	126	1.00
Laotian (1)	3	0.02
Pakistani (15)	15	0.12
Taiwanese (2)	2	0.02
Thai (26)	39	0.31
Vietnamese (10)	19	0.15
Hawaii Native/Pacific Islander (25)	62	0.49
Not Hispanic (23)	56	0.44
Hispanic (2)	6	0.05
Guamanian/Chamorro (7)	14	0.11
Native Hawaiian (6)	29	0.23
Samoan (2)	8	0.06
White (8,973)	9,311	73.60
Not Hispanic (8,702)	9,013	71.24
Hispanic (271)	298	2.36

Shorewood

Place Type: Village
County: Will
Population: 15,615†

Ancestry‡	Population	%
African, Sub-Saharan (136)	152	1.03
African (136)	152	1.03
American (137)	137	0.93
Australian (0)	13	0.09
Austrian (38)	157	1.07
British (18)	29	0.20
Croatian (99)	385	2.62
Czech (14)	78	0.53
Czechoslovakian (19)	19	0.13
Danish (12)	63	0.43
Dutch (29)	185	1.26
English (222)	1,049	7.13
European (107)	107	0.73

*Notes: † The Census 2010 population figure is used to calculate the percentages in the Hispanic Origin and Race categories. Ancestry percentages are based on the 2006-2010 American Community Survey population (not shown); ‡ Numbers in parentheses indicate the number of people reporting a single ancestry; * Numbers in parentheses indicate the number of persons reporting this race alone, not in combination with any other race; Please refer to the Explanation of Data for more information.*

Finnish (26)	49	0.33
French, ex. Basque (14)	493	3.35
French Canadian (29)	66	0.45
German (977)	4,020	27.31
Greek (72)	238	1.62
Hungarian (16)	71	0.48
Iranian (0)	12	0.08
Irish (766)	3,104	21.09
Italian (559)	2,260	15.36
Lithuanian (98)	145	0.99
Norwegian (85)	292	1.98
Pennsylvania German (0)	16	0.11
Polish (523)	1,830	12.43
Romanian (0)	22	0.15
Russian (35)	137	0.93
Scotch-Irish (13)	87	0.59
Scottish (22)	204	1.39
Serbian (12)	24	0.16
Slovak (67)	172	1.17
Slovene (172)	352	2.39
Swedish (62)	378	2.57
Swiss (0)	14	0.10
Welsh (12)	101	0.69
Yugoslavian (9)	9	0.06

Hispanic Origin	Population	%
Hispanic or Latino (of any race)	1,681	10.77
Central American, ex. Mexican	18	0.12
Costa Rican	2	0.01
Guatemalan	11	0.07
Honduran	3	0.02
Salvadoran	2	0.01
Cuban	31	0.20
Dominican Republic	5	0.03
Mexican	1,348	8.63
Puerto Rican	175	1.12
South American	37	0.24
Argentinean	4	0.03
Bolivian	3	0.02
Chilean	3	0.02
Colombian	5	0.03
Ecuadorian	3	0.02
Peruvian	12	0.08
Venezuelan	7	0.04
Other Hispanic or Latino	67	0.43

Race*	Population	%
African-American/Black (825)	952	6.10
Not Hispanic (813)	913	5.85
Hispanic (12)	39	0.25
American Indian/Alaska Native (31)	79	0.51
Not Hispanic (17)	55	0.35
Hispanic (14)	24	0.15
Alaska Athabascan *(Ala. Nat.)* (3)	3	0.02
Apache (1)	2	0.01
Blackfeet (2)	6	0.04
Cherokee (5)	13	0.08
Chippewa (0)	1	0.01
Iroquois (1)	4	0.03
Navajo (1)	1	0.01
Spanish American Ind. (0)	1	0.01
Asian (272)	356	2.28
Not Hispanic (267)	347	2.22
Hispanic (5)	9	0.06
Bangladeshi (2)	2	0.01
Cambodian (8)	11	0.07
Chinese, ex. Taiwanese (18)	20	0.13
Filipino (55)	99	0.63
Indian (63)	73	0.47
Indonesian (1)	1	0.01
Japanese (7)	17	0.11
Korean (39)	45	0.29
Laotian (2)	8	0.05
Pakistani (10)	10	0.06
Thai (2)	8	0.05
Vietnamese (58)	63	0.40
Hawaii Native/Pacific Islander (7)	18	0.12
Not Hispanic (7)	18	0.12
Guamanian/Chamorro (3)	3	0.02
Native Hawaiian (0)	3	0.02
White (13,695)	13,929	89.20
Not Hispanic (12,614)	12,784	81.87
Hispanic (1,081)	1,145	7.33

Skokie

Place Type: Village
County: Cook
Population: 64,784†

Ancestry‡	Population	%
African, Sub-Saharan (371)	433	0.68
African (176)	208	0.33
Ethiopian (23)	23	0.04
Liberian (35)	35	0.05
Nigerian (74)	74	0.12
South African (63)	79	0.12
Sudanese (0)	14	0.02
Albanian (135)	135	0.21
American (2,241)	2,241	3.51
Arab (1,282)	1,643	2.57
Arab (101)	128	0.20
Egyptian (0)	20	0.03
Iraqi (709)	898	1.41
Jordanian (16)	16	0.03
Lebanese (132)	221	0.35
Palestinian (63)	63	0.10
Syrian (131)	158	0.25
Other Arab (130)	139	0.22
Armenian (341)	372	0.58
Assyrian/Chaldean/Syriac (3,620)	3,833	6.01
Austrian (95)	212	0.33
Belgian (8)	64	0.10
Brazilian (13)	13	0.02
British (93)	139	0.22
Bulgarian (205)	205	0.32
Canadian (35)	51	0.08
Croatian (227)	337	0.53
Czech (57)	312	0.49
Czechoslovakian (7)	19	0.03
Danish (24)	165	0.26
Dutch (98)	333	0.52
Eastern European (584)	592	0.93
English (441)	1,670	2.62
European (504)	570	0.89
Finnish (11)	21	0.03
French, ex. Basque (125)	515	0.81
French Canadian (0)	58	0.09
German (1,867)	6,040	9.46
Greek (1,378)	1,666	2.61
Guyanese (43)	43	0.07
Hungarian (304)	668	1.05
Iranian (248)	294	0.46
Irish (1,084)	3,563	5.58
Israeli (321)	497	0.78
Italian (435)	1,594	2.50
Latvian (64)	140	0.22
Lithuanian (176)	550	0.86
Luxemburger (0)	33	0.05
Macedonian (188)	229	0.36
Northern European (30)	30	0.05
Norwegian (34)	255	0.40
Polish (1,797)	4,292	6.72
Portuguese (0)	11	0.02
Romanian (1,248)	1,582	2.48
Russian (2,347)	4,794	7.51
Scandinavian (28)	73	0.11
Scotch-Irish (58)	288	0.45
Scottish (39)	325	0.51
Serbian (242)	325	0.51
Slavic (11)	11	0.02
Slovak (52)	61	0.10
Slovene (16)	38	0.06
Soviet Union (20)	20	0.03
Swedish (189)	746	1.17
Swiss (11)	149	0.23
Ukrainian (943)	1,223	1.92
Welsh (14)	123	0.19
West Indian, ex. Hispanic (1,059)	1,073	1.68
Belizean (22)	36	0.06
Haitian (891)	891	1.40
Jamaican (146)	146	0.23
Yugoslavian (223)	281	0.44

Hispanic Origin	Population	%
Hispanic or Latino (of any race)	5,728	8.84
Central American, ex. Mexican	497	0.77
Costa Rican	15	0.02
Guatemalan	284	0.44
Honduran	51	0.08
Nicaraguan	26	0.04
Panamanian	25	0.04
Salvadoran	87	0.13
Other Central American	9	0.01
Cuban	476	0.73
Dominican Republic	33	0.05
Mexican	2,854	4.41
Puerto Rican	754	1.16
South American	822	1.27
Argentinean	74	0.11
Bolivian	59	0.09
Chilean	29	0.04
Colombian	220	0.34
Ecuadorian	195	0.30
Paraguayan	2	<0.01
Peruvian	161	0.25
Uruguayan	12	0.02
Venezuelan	40	0.06
Other South American	30	0.05
Other Hispanic or Latino	292	0.45

Race*	Population	%
African-American/Black (4,701)	5,294	8.17
Not Hispanic (4,566)	5,028	7.76
Hispanic (135)	266	0.41
American Indian/Alaska Native (120)	349	0.54
Not Hispanic (70)	246	0.38
Hispanic (50)	103	0.16
Alaska Athabascan *(Ala. Nat.)* (1)	2	<0.01
Apache (3)	4	0.01
Blackfeet (1)	6	0.01
Central American Ind. (3)	6	0.01
Cherokee (4)	54	0.08
Cheyenne (0)	1	<0.01
Chippewa (5)	10	0.02
Choctaw (1)	6	0.01
Creek (0)	6	0.01
Crow (0)	5	0.01
Iroquois (1)	2	<0.01
Mexican American Ind. (11)	17	0.03
Navajo (5)	8	0.01
Potawatomi (1)	2	<0.01
Pueblo (0)	1	<0.01
Seminole (0)	1	<0.01
Sioux (6)	8	0.01
South American Ind. (0)	12	0.02
Spanish American Ind. (1)	1	<0.01
Tlingit-Haida *(Alaska Native)* (1)	1	<0.01
Asian (16,549)	17,996	27.78
Not Hispanic (16,437)	17,752	27.40
Hispanic (112)	244	0.38
Bangladeshi (91)	98	0.15
Burmese (12)	14	0.02
Cambodian (136)	162	0.25
Chinese, ex. Taiwanese (1,503)	1,726	2.66
Filipino (4,505)	4,896	7.56
Hmong (8)	10	0.02
Indian (4,283)	4,624	7.14
Indonesian (36)	41	0.06
Japanese (304)	431	0.67
Korean (1,771)	1,880	2.90
Laotian (23)	37	0.06
Malaysian (22)	37	0.06
Nepalese (43)	48	0.07
Pakistani (1,990)	2,121	3.27
Sri Lankan (46)	52	0.08
Taiwanese (69)	78	0.12
Thai (208)	234	0.36
Vietnamese (717)	794	1.23
Hawaii Native/Pacific Islander (13)	139	0.21

*Notes: † The Census 2010 population figure is used to calculate the percentages in the Hispanic Origin and Race categories. Ancestry percentages are based on the 2006-2010 American Community Survey population (not shown); ‡ Numbers in parentheses indicate the number of people reporting a single ancestry; * Numbers in parentheses indicate the number of persons reporting this race alone, not in combination with any other race; Please refer to the Explanation of Data for more information.*

Not Hispanic (13)	122	0.19
Hispanic (0)	17	0.03
Fijian (2)	3	<0.01
Guamanian/Chamorro (0)	4	0.01
Marshallese (4)	4	0.01
Native Hawaiian (2)	11	0.02
White (39,045)	40,807	62.99
Not Hispanic (35,955)	37,310	57.59
Hispanic (3,090)	3,497	5.40

South Beloit

Place Type: City
County: Winnebago
Population: 7,892†

Ancestry‡	Population	%
American (909)	909	12.03
Austrian (0)	13	0.17
British (0)	10	0.13
Canadian (10)	10	0.13
Croatian (9)	9	0.12
Czech (26)	33	0.44
Danish (5)	18	0.24
Dutch (11)	74	0.98
English (105)	607	8.03
European (6)	21	0.28
French, ex. Basque (13)	71	0.94
German (963)	2,426	32.09
Irish (252)	1,056	13.97
Italian (222)	778	10.29
Lithuanian (11)	11	0.15
Northern European (22)	22	0.29
Norwegian (150)	506	6.69
Polish (30)	243	3.21
Russian (0)	11	0.15
Scotch-Irish (24)	88	1.16
Scottish (84)	148	1.96
Swedish (103)	489	6.47
Swiss (19)	110	1.46
Welsh (0)	38	0.50

Hispanic Origin	Population	%
Hispanic or Latino (of any race)	608	7.70
Central American, ex. Mexican	10	0.13
Guatemalan	2	0.03
Honduran	3	0.04
Salvadoran	5	0.06
Cuban	12	0.15
Dominican Republic	1	0.01
Mexican	477	6.04
Puerto Rican	38	0.48
South American	14	0.18
Colombian	3	0.04
Ecuadorian	5	0.06
Peruvian	1	0.01
Venezuelan	5	0.06
Other Hispanic or Latino	56	0.71

Race*	Population	%
African-American/Black (317)	428	5.42
Not Hispanic (311)	414	5.25
Hispanic (6)	14	0.18
American Indian/Alaska Native (30)	80	1.01
Not Hispanic (16)	54	0.68
Hispanic (14)	26	0.33
Apache (1)	5	0.06
Cherokee (0)	16	0.20
Chippewa (2)	4	0.05
Iroquois (1)	1	0.01
Mexican American Ind. (0)	7	0.09
Sioux (1)	1	0.01
Asian (128)	180	2.28
Not Hispanic (128)	173	2.19
Hispanic (0)	7	0.09
Burmese (7)	7	0.09
Cambodian (2)	4	0.05
Chinese, ex. Taiwanese (9)	13	0.16
Filipino (11)	42	0.53
Indian (24)	27	0.34
Indonesian (3)	6	0.08
Japanese (1)	5	0.06
Korean (9)	14	0.18
Laotian (2)	4	0.05
Malaysian (1)	1	0.01
Pakistani (4)	5	0.06
Taiwanese (1)	1	0.01
Thai (3)	5	0.06
Vietnamese (41)	41	0.52
Hawaii Native/Pacific Islander (3)	16	0.20
Not Hispanic (3)	12	0.15
Hispanic (0)	4	0.05
Guamanian/Chamorro (1)	1	0.01
Native Hawaiian (2)	12	0.15
Samoan (0)	2	0.03
White (6,898)	7,117	90.18
Not Hispanic (6,642)	6,814	86.34
Hispanic (256)	303	3.84

South Elgin

Place Type: Village
County: Kane
Population: 21,985†

Ancestry‡	Population	%
African, Sub-Saharan (11)	11	0.05
Ghanaian (11)	11	0.05
Albanian (16)	16	0.08
American (763)	763	3.59
Arab (265)	292	1.38
Lebanese (0)	27	0.13
Syrian (151)	151	0.71
Other Arab (114)	114	0.54
Assyrian/Chaldean/Syriac (71)	101	0.48
Austrian (26)	64	0.30
Belgian (13)	128	0.60
Brazilian (0)	14	0.07
British (0)	9	0.04
Croatian (12)	37	0.17
Czech (13)	330	1.55
Czechoslovakian (0)	64	0.30
Danish (14)	273	1.29
Dutch (23)	179	0.84
Eastern European (12)	12	0.06
English (187)	1,564	7.37
Estonian (8)	8	0.04
European (142)	181	0.85
Finnish (13)	92	0.43
French, ex. Basque (93)	475	2.24
French Canadian (25)	184	0.87
German (2,049)	6,585	31.01
Greek (102)	247	1.16
Hungarian (0)	84	0.40
Irish (446)	3,461	16.30
Italian (944)	2,566	12.08
Latvian (9)	9	0.04
Lithuanian (95)	207	0.97
Norwegian (104)	583	2.75
Polish (722)	2,915	13.73
Romanian (0)	9	0.04
Russian (79)	127	0.60
Scandinavian (0)	24	0.11
Scotch-Irish (130)	254	1.20
Scottish (39)	319	1.50
Slovene (0)	10	0.05
Swedish (194)	741	3.49
Swiss (10)	10	0.05
Ukrainian (0)	40	0.19
Welsh (15)	64	0.30

Hispanic Origin	Population	%
Hispanic or Latino (of any race)	3,402	15.47
Central American, ex. Mexican	100	0.45
Costa Rican	3	0.01
Guatemalan	56	0.25
Honduran	10	0.05
Nicaraguan	5	0.02
Panamanian	7	0.03
Salvadoran	17	0.08
Other Central American	2	0.01
Cuban	34	0.15
Dominican Republic	11	0.05
Mexican	2,651	12.06
Puerto Rican	411	1.87
South American	90	0.41
Argentinean	4	0.02
Bolivian	4	0.02
Chilean	5	0.02
Colombian	41	0.19
Ecuadorian	23	0.10
Peruvian	12	0.05
Uruguayan	1	<0.01
Other Hispanic or Latino	105	0.48

Race*	Population	%
African-American/Black (740)	910	4.14
Not Hispanic (679)	804	3.66
Hispanic (61)	106	0.48
American Indian/Alaska Native (94)	216	0.98
Not Hispanic (17)	96	0.44
Hispanic (77)	120	0.55
Apache (0)	1	<0.01
Blackfeet (0)	5	0.02
Central American Ind. (2)	2	0.01
Cherokee (6)	25	0.11
Chippewa (1)	5	0.02
Choctaw (0)	4	0.02
Cree (0)	1	<0.01
Iroquois (0)	5	0.02
Kiowa (1)	1	<0.01
Mexican American Ind. (16)	17	0.08
Potawatomi (1)	11	0.05
Sioux (0)	8	0.04
South American Ind. (2)	2	0.01
Spanish American Ind. (0)	2	0.01
Asian (1,545)	1,797	8.17
Not Hispanic (1,515)	1,735	7.89
Hispanic (30)	62	0.28
Burmese (2)	2	0.01
Cambodian (7)	10	0.05
Chinese, ex. Taiwanese (112)	148	0.67
Filipino (441)	557	2.53
Indian (284)	312	1.42
Indonesian (2)	5	0.02
Japanese (9)	30	0.14
Korean (69)	91	0.41
Laotian (366)	402	1.83
Malaysian (0)	2	0.01
Nepalese (5)	5	0.02
Pakistani (89)	94	0.43
Taiwanese (5)	10	0.05
Thai (16)	24	0.11
Vietnamese (67)	86	0.39
Hawaii Native/Pacific Islander (7)	26	0.12
Not Hispanic (7)	22	0.10
Hispanic (0)	4	0.02
Guamanian/Chamorro (4)	4	0.02
Native Hawaiian (1)	14	0.06
Samoan (1)	2	0.01
White (17,875)	18,447	83.91
Not Hispanic (15,936)	16,307	74.17
Hispanic (1,939)	2,140	9.73

South Holland

Place Type: Village
County: Cook
Population: 22,030†

Ancestry‡	Population	%
African, Sub-Saharan (517)	542	2.48
African (368)	383	1.75
Nigerian (95)	105	0.48
Sierra Leonean (54)	54	0.25
American (142)	142	0.65
Arab (0)	46	0.21
Lebanese (0)	19	0.09
Moroccan (0)	27	0.12
Austrian (12)	34	0.16

SECTION TWO

*Notes: † The Census 2010 population figure is used to calculate the percentages in the Hispanic Origin and Race categories. Ancestry percentages are based on the 2006-2010 American Community Survey population (not shown); ‡ Numbers in parentheses indicate the number of people reporting a single ancestry; * Numbers in parentheses indicate the number of persons reporting this race alone, not in combination with any other race; Please refer to the Explanation of Data for more information.*

British (14)	29	0.13
Canadian (0)	9	0.04
Croatian (43)	73	0.33
Czech (0)	31	0.14
Czechoslovakian (9)	9	0.04
Danish (12)	12	0.05
Dutch (1,022)	1,222	5.59
Eastern European (8)	8	0.04
English (165)	341	1.56
European (0)	20	0.09
French, ex. Basque (33)	110	0.50
French Canadian (9)	51	0.23
German (273)	808	3.69
Hungarian (31)	66	0.30
Irish (193)	521	2.38
Italian (189)	514	2.35
Lithuanian (20)	102	0.47
Norwegian (30)	68	0.31
Pennsylvania German (0)	12	0.05
Polish (462)	698	3.19
Russian (6)	78	0.36
Scotch-Irish (24)	31	0.14
Scottish (35)	121	0.55
Serbian (26)	52	0.24
Slovak (6)	6	0.03
Swedish (44)	146	0.67
Ukrainian (23)	67	0.31
Welsh (0)	25	0.11
West Indian, ex. Hispanic (153)	213	0.97
Belizean (12)	24	0.11
Dutch West Indian (0)	8	0.04
Haitian (100)	120	0.55
Jamaican (41)	61	0.28
Yugoslavian (18)	38	0.17

Hispanic Origin	Population	%
Hispanic or Latino (of any race)	1,274	5.78
Central American, ex. Mexican	37	0.17
Guatemalan	10	0.05
Honduran	11	0.05
Panamanian	1	<0.01
Salvadoran	11	0.05
Other Central American	4	0.02
Cuban	25	0.11
Dominican Republic	2	0.01
Mexican	1,088	4.94
Puerto Rican	78	0.35
South American	12	0.05
Argentinean	2	0.01
Colombian	5	0.02
Peruvian	1	<0.01
Other South American	4	0.02
Other Hispanic or Latino	32	0.15

Race*	Population	%
African-American/Black (16,350)	16,625	75.47
Not Hispanic (16,263)	16,497	74.88
Hispanic (87)	128	0.58
American Indian/Alaska Native (45)	144	0.65
Not Hispanic (34)	113	0.51
Hispanic (11)	31	0.14
Apache (1)	1	<0.01
Blackfeet (0)	4	0.02
Central American Ind. (0)	2	0.01
Cherokee (5)	29	0.13
Chickasaw (0)	1	<0.01
Choctaw (0)	8	0.04
Cree (0)	2	0.01
Creek (0)	1	<0.01
Crow (0)	2	0.01
Mexican American Ind. (1)	5	0.02
Ottawa (8)	8	0.04
South American Ind. (2)	2	0.01
Ute (0)	1	<0.01
Asian (135)	183	0.83
Not Hispanic (135)	181	0.82
Hispanic (0)	2	0.01
Chinese, ex. Taiwanese (26)	27	0.12
Filipino (45)	57	0.26
Indian (24)	35	0.16
Indonesian (1)	2	0.01
Japanese (12)	21	0.10
Korean (8)	18	0.08
Laotian (1)	1	<0.01
Pakistani (0)	1	<0.01
Thai (7)	7	0.03
Hawaii Native/Pacific Islander (1)	11	0.05
Not Hispanic (1)	10	0.05
Hispanic (0)	1	<0.01
Native Hawaiian (0)	5	0.02
White (4,508)	4,718	21.42
Not Hispanic (4,023)	4,198	19.06
Hispanic (485)	520	2.36

Springfield

Place Type: City
County: Sangamon
Population: 116,250†

Ancestry‡	Population	%
African, Sub-Saharan (591)	749	0.65
African (409)	537	0.47
Ghanaian (58)	58	0.05
Nigerian (124)	154	0.13
American (9,384)	9,384	8.15
Arab (389)	567	0.49
Arab (104)	108	0.09
Egyptian (15)	29	0.03
Jordanian (22)	22	0.02
Lebanese (42)	42	0.04
Moroccan (7)	7	0.01
Syrian (155)	235	0.20
Other Arab (44)	124	0.11
Assyrian/Chaldean/Syriac (15)	15	0.01
Austrian (76)	239	0.21
Belgian (110)	289	0.25
Brazilian (0)	19	0.02
British (192)	384	0.33
Bulgarian (4)	19	0.02
Canadian (29)	66	0.06
Croatian (39)	258	0.22
Czech (130)	445	0.39
Czechoslovakian (47)	183	0.16
Danish (34)	255	0.22
Dutch (188)	1,655	1.44
Eastern European (31)	37	0.03
English (4,232)	13,247	11.51
Estonian (10)	10	0.01
European (617)	691	0.60
Finnish (25)	25	0.02
French, ex. Basque (571)	3,255	2.83
French Canadian (23)	144	0.13
German (10,961)	30,854	26.80
German Russian (0)	11	0.01
Greek (157)	255	0.22
Hungarian (106)	393	0.34
Iranian (19)	19	0.02
Irish (4,182)	16,364	14.21
Italian (3,061)	7,362	6.40
Latvian (0)	44	0.04
Lithuanian (548)	973	0.85
Luxemburger (0)	19	0.02
Northern European (45)	115	0.10
Norwegian (349)	963	0.84
Pennsylvania German (47)	59	0.05
Polish (892)	2,578	2.24
Portuguese (125)	282	0.24
Romanian (13)	36	0.03
Russian (158)	464	0.40
Scandinavian (107)	152	0.13
Scotch-Irish (763)	2,407	2.09
Scottish (594)	2,251	1.96
Serbian (14)	14	0.01
Slavic (38)	129	0.11
Slovak (80)	430	0.37
Slovene (56)	96	0.08
Swedish (332)	1,351	1.17
Swiss (71)	366	0.32
Turkish (19)	19	0.02
Ukrainian (75)	180	0.16
Welsh (141)	877	0.76
West Indian, ex. Hispanic (60)	154	0.13
Dutch West Indian (0)	14	0.01
Haitian (0)	7	0.01
Jamaican (46)	115	0.10
West Indian (14)	18	0.02
Yugoslavian (0)	70	0.06

Hispanic Origin	Population	%
Hispanic or Latino (of any race)	2,325	2.00
Central American, ex. Mexican	153	0.13
Costa Rican	14	0.01
Guatemalan	41	0.04
Honduran	28	0.02
Nicaraguan	25	0.02
Panamanian	28	0.02
Salvadoran	17	0.01
Cuban	47	0.04
Dominican Republic	21	0.02
Mexican	1,287	1.11
Puerto Rican	374	0.32
South American	179	0.15
Argentinean	5	<0.01
Bolivian	20	0.02
Chilean	27	0.02
Colombian	37	0.03
Ecuadorian	30	0.03
Peruvian	45	0.04
Venezuelan	12	0.01
Other South American	3	<0.01
Other Hispanic or Latino	264	0.23

Race*	Population	%
African-American/Black (21,510)	23,683	20.37
Not Hispanic (21,344)	23,404	20.13
Hispanic (166)	279	0.24
American Indian/Alaska Native (239)	889	0.76
Not Hispanic (205)	797	0.69
Hispanic (34)	92	0.08
Alaska Athabascan *(Ala. Nat.)* (1)	1	<0.01
Apache (3)	11	0.01
Blackfeet (6)	55	0.05
Canadian/French Am. Ind. (3)	4	<0.01
Central American Ind. (1)	1	<0.01
Cherokee (36)	248	0.21
Cheyenne (0)	2	<0.01
Chickasaw (2)	6	0.01
Chippewa (3)	11	0.01
Choctaw (1)	27	0.02
Comanche (0)	1	<0.01
Cree (0)	1	<0.01
Creek (4)	7	0.01
Crow (1)	5	<0.01
Delaware (1)	1	<0.01
Iroquois (7)	9	0.01
Lumbee (1)	7	0.01
Menominee (11)	12	0.01
Mexican American Ind. (7)	17	0.01
Navajo (3)	4	<0.01
Osage (0)	1	<0.01
Ottawa (1)	1	<0.01
Pima (0)	1	<0.01
Potawatomi (4)	5	<0.01
Pueblo (2)	2	<0.01
Seminole (1)	5	<0.01
Sioux (12)	26	0.02
South American Ind. (2)	2	<0.01
Ute (1)	1	<0.01
Yaqui (0)	1	<0.01
Asian (2,555)	3,047	2.62
Not Hispanic (2,538)	3,002	2.58
Hispanic (17)	45	0.04
Bangladeshi (11)	11	0.01
Burmese (12)	16	0.01
Cambodian (9)	13	0.01
Chinese, ex. Taiwanese (485)	549	0.47
Filipino (244)	363	0.31
Hmong (2)	3	<0.01
Indian (1,005)	1,091	0.94

*Notes: † The Census 2010 population figure is used to calculate the percentages in the Hispanic Origin and Race categories. Ancestry percentages are based on the 2006-2010 American Community Survey population (not shown); ‡ Numbers in parentheses indicate the number of people reporting a single ancestry; * Numbers in parentheses indicate the number of persons reporting this race alone, not in combination with any other race; Please refer to the Explanation of Data for more information.*

	Population	%
Indonesian (8)	8	0.01
Japanese (53)	118	0.10
Korean (174)	251	0.22
Laotian (32)	43	0.04
Malaysian (5)	6	0.01
Nepalese (14)	14	0.01
Pakistani (110)	122	0.10
Sri Lankan (6)	6	0.01
Taiwanese (54)	62	0.05
Thai (36)	61	0.05
Vietnamese (218)	240	0.21
Hawaii Native/Pacific Islander (25)	85	0.07
Not Hispanic (23)	78	0.07
Hispanic (2)	7	0.01
Fijian (3)	4	<0.01
Guamanian/Chamorro (3)	7	0.01
Native Hawaiian (4)	21	0.02
Samoan (6)	14	0.01
White (88,092)	90,846	78.15
Not Hispanic (86,781)	89,342	76.85
Hispanic (1,311)	1,504	1.29

St. Charles

Place Type: City
County: Kane
Population: 32,974†

Ancestry‡	Population	%
Afghan (25)	25	0.08
African, Sub-Saharan (6)	6	0.02
African (6)	6	0.02
American (825)	825	2.55
Arab (0)	12	0.04
Other Arab (0)	12	0.04
Armenian (0)	9	0.03
Australian (0)	6	0.02
Austrian (115)	426	1.32
Belgian (94)	292	0.90
Brazilian (44)	44	0.14
British (63)	88	0.27
Canadian (55)	116	0.36
Celtic (14)	14	0.04
Croatian (26)	53	0.16
Czech (111)	456	1.41
Czechoslovakian (0)	63	0.19
Danish (47)	392	1.21
Dutch (118)	578	1.78
Eastern European (14)	14	0.04
English (823)	3,743	11.56
European (266)	370	1.14
Finnish (12)	171	0.53
French, ex. Basque (111)	1,059	3.27
French Canadian (34)	60	0.19
German (2,574)	10,543	32.55
Greek (77)	179	0.55
Hungarian (15)	210	0.65
Irish (1,043)	6,434	19.86
Italian (1,702)	4,328	13.36
Latvian (14)	14	0.04
Lithuanian (146)	275	0.85
Luxemburger (30)	72	0.22
Macedonian (33)	33	0.10
Maltese (0)	23	0.07
Norwegian (266)	1,139	3.52
Polish (1,073)	3,805	11.75
Romanian (68)	122	0.38
Russian (42)	337	1.04
Scandinavian (55)	91	0.28
Scotch-Irish (157)	701	2.16
Scottish (91)	812	2.51
Serbian (0)	10	0.03
Slavic (12)	12	0.04
Slovak (41)	194	0.60
Slovene (67)	109	0.34
Swedish (280)	1,625	5.02
Swiss (25)	264	0.82
Ukrainian (191)	378	1.17
Welsh (66)	369	1.14
Yugoslavian (10)	34	0.10

Hispanic Origin	Population	%
Hispanic or Latino (of any race)	3,349	10.16
Central American, ex. Mexican	73	0.22
Costa Rican	3	0.01
Guatemalan	41	0.12
Honduran	9	0.03
Nicaraguan	2	0.01
Panamanian	5	0.02
Salvadoran	13	0.04
Cuban	67	0.20
Dominican Republic	4	0.01
Mexican	2,716	8.24
Puerto Rican	207	0.63
South American	103	0.31
Argentinean	5	0.02
Bolivian	4	0.01
Chilean	7	0.02
Colombian	33	0.10
Ecuadorian	26	0.08
Peruvian	13	0.04
Venezuelan	13	0.04
Other South American	2	0.01
Other Hispanic or Latino	179	0.54

Race*	Population	%
African-American/Black (824)	965	2.93
Not Hispanic (785)	903	2.74
Hispanic (39)	62	0.19
American Indian/Alaska Native (62)	172	0.52
Not Hispanic (34)	109	0.33
Hispanic (28)	63	0.19
Apache (0)	3	0.01
Arapaho (0)	2	0.01
Blackfeet (1)	4	0.01
Cherokee (7)	31	0.09
Chippewa (4)	8	0.02
Choctaw (2)	6	0.02
Comanche (3)	3	0.01
Creek (0)	1	<0.01
Iroquois (2)	3	0.01
Mexican American Ind. (7)	11	0.03
Navajo (1)	1	<0.01
Osage (0)	3	0.01
Ottawa (0)	1	<0.01
Pueblo (0)	1	<0.01
Sioux (0)	1	<0.01
Tlingit-Haida *(Alaska Native)* (1)	1	<0.01
Asian (1,045)	1,219	3.70
Not Hispanic (1,034)	1,194	3.62
Hispanic (11)	25	0.08
Burmese (25)	25	0.08
Cambodian (4)	4	0.01
Chinese, ex. Taiwanese (136)	174	0.53
Filipino (253)	324	0.98
Hmong (4)	7	0.02
Indian (356)	387	1.17
Indonesian (2)	5	0.02
Japanese (30)	43	0.13
Korean (70)	97	0.29
Laotian (30)	37	0.11
Nepalese (2)	4	0.01
Pakistani (31)	35	0.11
Taiwanese (4)	4	0.01
Thai (11)	16	0.05
Vietnamese (40)	55	0.17
Hawaii Native/Pacific Islander (17)	26	0.08
Not Hispanic (15)	22	0.07
Hispanic (2)	4	0.01
Guamanian/Chamorro (1)	1	<0.01
Native Hawaiian (0)	4	0.01
Tongan (5)	5	0.02
White (29,293)	29,774	90.30
Not Hispanic (27,378)	27,697	84.00
Hispanic (1,915)	2,077	6.30

Steger

Place Type: Village
County: Will
Population: 9,570†

Ancestry‡	Population	%
African, Sub-Saharan (46)	46	0.47
African (17)	17	0.17
Nigerian (29)	29	0.30
American (258)	258	2.65
Arab (0)	23	0.24
Lebanese (0)	23	0.24
Assyrian/Chaldean/Syriac (13)	13	0.13
Austrian (0)	59	0.61
Belgian (0)	30	0.31
British (0)	14	0.14
Croatian (13)	24	0.25
Czech (39)	118	1.21
Danish (0)	16	0.16
Dutch (54)	257	2.64
English (56)	537	5.52
European (59)	100	1.03
French, ex. Basque (29)	232	2.38
French Canadian (24)	90	0.92
German (479)	2,096	21.53
Greek (0)	133	1.37
Hungarian (10)	30	0.31
Irish (165)	1,386	14.24
Italian (379)	1,355	13.92
Latvian (0)	10	0.10
Lithuanian (0)	55	0.57
New Zealander (12)	12	0.12
Norwegian (24)	77	0.79
Polish (448)	978	10.05
Portuguese (33)	44	0.45
Russian (0)	56	0.58
Scotch-Irish (19)	119	1.22
Scottish (47)	208	2.14
Serbian (0)	26	0.27
Slavic (7)	7	0.07
Slovak (17)	29	0.30
Swedish (51)	303	3.11
Ukrainian (0)	9	0.09
Welsh (9)	24	0.25

Hispanic Origin	Population	%
Hispanic or Latino (of any race)	1,357	14.18
Central American, ex. Mexican	16	0.17
Costa Rican	2	0.02
Guatemalan	9	0.09
Honduran	2	0.02
Panamanian	1	0.01
Salvadoran	2	0.02
Cuban	9	0.09
Dominican Republic	6	0.06
Mexican	1,180	12.33
Puerto Rican	72	0.75
South American	14	0.15
Argentinean	2	0.02
Bolivian	1	0.01
Colombian	4	0.04
Ecuadorian	4	0.04
Peruvian	3	0.03
Other Hispanic or Latino	60	0.63

Race*	Population	%
African-American/Black (1,869)	2,001	20.91
Not Hispanic (1,818)	1,930	20.17
Hispanic (51)	71	0.74
American Indian/Alaska Native (29)	114	1.19
Not Hispanic (8)	77	0.80
Hispanic (21)	37	0.39
Apache (0)	8	0.08
Blackfeet (0)	6	0.06
Cherokee (4)	36	0.38
Choctaw (0)	3	0.03
Comanche (0)	3	0.03
Creek (1)	1	0.01
Lumbee (0)	1	0.01

SECTION TWO

*Notes: † The Census 2010 population figure is used to calculate the percentages in the Hispanic Origin and Race categories. Ancestry percentages are based on the 2006-2010 American Community Survey population (not shown); ‡ Numbers in parentheses indicate the number of people reporting a single ancestry; * Numbers in parentheses indicate the number of persons reporting this race alone, not in combination with any other race; Please refer to the Explanation of Data for more information.*

Mexican American Ind. (3)	3	0.03
Navajo (0)	2	0.02
Potawatomi (0)	1	0.01
Sioux (0)	4	0.04
Asian (96)	119	1.24
Not Hispanic (96)	118	1.23
Hispanic (0)	1	0.01
Cambodian (2)	2	0.02
Chinese, ex. Taiwanese (1)	1	0.01
Filipino (43)	48	0.50
Indian (13)	16	0.17
Japanese (3)	12	0.13
Korean (5)	10	0.10
Thai (8)	9	0.09
Vietnamese (15)	15	0.16
Hawaii Native/Pacific Islander (0)	3	0.03
Not Hispanic (0)	3	0.03
White (6,854)	7,123	74.43
Not Hispanic (6,103)	6,267	65.49
Hispanic (751)	856	8.94

Sterling

Place Type: City
County: Whiteside
Population: 15,370†

Ancestry‡	Population	%
African, Sub-Saharan (172)	172	1.11
African (172)	172	1.11
Albanian (34)	34	0.22
American (698)	698	4.52
Arab (10)	10	0.06
Other Arab (10)	10	0.06
Belgian (0)	61	0.39
British (15)	15	0.10
Canadian (15)	45	0.29
Czech (10)	116	0.75
Danish (27)	120	0.78
Dutch (63)	478	3.09
English (374)	878	5.68
European (130)	154	1.00
Finnish (0)	18	0.12
French, ex. Basque (62)	399	2.58
French Canadian (19)	59	0.38
German (1,608)	4,195	27.15
Greek (11)	37	0.24
Hungarian (12)	43	0.28
Irish (827)	2,194	14.20
Italian (207)	475	3.07
Lithuanian (0)	28	0.18
Macedonian (0)	14	0.09
Norwegian (47)	242	1.57
Polish (173)	559	3.62
Portuguese (0)	71	0.46
Russian (15)	39	0.25
Scandinavian (36)	36	0.23
Scotch-Irish (21)	113	0.73
Scottish (59)	131	0.85
Swedish (79)	368	2.38
Swiss (11)	18	0.12
Ukrainian (0)	2	0.01
Welsh (0)	21	0.14

Hispanic Origin	Population	%
Hispanic or Latino (of any race)	3,715	24.17
Central American, ex. Mexican	19	0.12
Guatemalan	10	0.07
Nicaraguan	1	0.01
Panamanian	3	0.02
Salvadoran	5	0.03
Cuban	17	0.11
Dominican Republic	4	0.03
Mexican	3,326	21.64
Puerto Rican	189	1.23
South American	30	0.20
Argentinean	8	0.05
Bolivian	3	0.02
Colombian	7	0.05
Ecuadorian	4	0.03
Peruvian	8	0.05
Other Hispanic or Latino	130	0.85

Race*	Population	%
African-American/Black (464)	694	4.52
Not Hispanic (411)	556	3.62
Hispanic (53)	138	0.90
American Indian/Alaska Native (68)	183	1.19
Not Hispanic (15)	97	0.63
Hispanic (53)	86	0.56
Apache (1)	9	0.06
Blackfeet (1)	6	0.04
Cherokee (6)	35	0.23
Chippewa (1)	2	0.01
Choctaw (0)	1	0.01
Crow (3)	3	0.02
Delaware (0)	1	0.01
Iroquois (0)	1	0.01
Mexican American Ind. (10)	15	0.10
Navajo (2)	7	0.05
Seminole (0)	1	0.01
Sioux (1)	8	0.05
South American Ind. (1)	4	0.03
Spanish American Ind. (0)	4	0.03
Tlingit-Haida *(Alaska Native)* (0)	1	0.01
Asian (107)	154	1.00
Not Hispanic (102)	140	0.91
Hispanic (5)	14	0.09
Burmese (3)	3	0.02
Chinese, ex. Taiwanese (13)	13	0.08
Filipino (23)	32	0.21
Indian (18)	23	0.15
Indonesian (1)	1	0.01
Japanese (1)	6	0.04
Korean (13)	18	0.12
Laotian (2)	4	0.03
Nepalese (1)	2	0.01
Pakistani (5)	9	0.06
Thai (1)	4	0.03
Vietnamese (24)	29	0.19
Hawaii Native/Pacific Islander (1)	14	0.09
Not Hispanic (0)	9	0.06
Hispanic (1)	5	0.03
Native Hawaiian (0)	3	0.02
White (12,678)	13,240	86.14
Not Hispanic (10,855)	11,088	72.14
Hispanic (1,823)	2,152	14.00

Streamwood

Place Type: Village
County: Cook
Population: 39,858†

Ancestry‡	Population	%
African, Sub-Saharan (46)	46	0.12
African (17)	17	0.04
Nigerian (11)	11	0.03
South African (18)	18	0.05
American (623)	623	1.59
Arab (108)	212	0.54
Arab (41)	114	0.29
Iraqi (10)	19	0.05
Jordanian (52)	52	0.13
Lebanese (0)	22	0.06
Syrian (5)	5	0.01
Armenian (32)	32	0.08
Assyrian/Chaldean/Syriac (42)	65	0.17
Austrian (81)	134	0.34
Belgian (0)	20	0.05
Brazilian (14)	42	0.11
British (10)	50	0.13
Bulgarian (171)	171	0.44
Canadian (24)	59	0.15
Croatian (13)	42	0.11
Czech (60)	352	0.90
Czechoslovakian (10)	51	0.13
Danish (11)	99	0.25
Dutch (30)	330	0.84
Eastern European (24)	24	0.06
English (172)	1,301	3.31
European (192)	239	0.61
Finnish (40)	317	0.81
French, ex. Basque (45)	511	1.30
French Canadian (0)	80	0.20
German (1,931)	6,746	17.18
Greek (134)	385	0.98
Hungarian (62)	258	0.66
Icelander (9)	9	0.02
Iranian (24)	24	0.06
Irish (713)	3,506	8.93
Italian (1,318)	3,794	9.66
Lithuanian (32)	135	0.34
Macedonian (204)	204	0.52
Northern European (25)	25	0.06
Norwegian (65)	370	0.94
Polish (2,512)	4,580	11.66
Portuguese (0)	14	0.04
Romanian (30)	30	0.08
Russian (90)	238	0.61
Scandinavian (51)	148	0.38
Scotch-Irish (63)	218	0.56
Scottish (14)	250	0.64
Serbian (67)	67	0.17
Slavic (0)	25	0.06
Slovak (36)	91	0.23
Slovene (10)	29	0.07
Swedish (180)	767	1.95
Swiss (0)	61	0.16
Turkish (0)	11	0.03
Ukrainian (149)	201	0.51
Welsh (15)	66	0.17
West Indian, ex. Hispanic (36)	61	0.16
Jamaican (36)	36	0.09
West Indian (0)	25	0.06
Yugoslavian (214)	243	0.62

Hispanic Origin	Population	%
Hispanic or Latino (of any race)	11,238	28.20
Central American, ex. Mexican	434	1.09
Costa Rican	4	0.01
Guatemalan	134	0.34
Honduran	29	0.07
Nicaraguan	23	0.06
Panamanian	10	0.03
Salvadoran	234	0.59
Cuban	57	0.14
Dominican Republic	29	0.07
Mexican	9,416	23.62
Puerto Rican	555	1.39
South American	410	1.03
Argentinean	15	0.04
Bolivian	20	0.05
Chilean	28	0.07
Colombian	131	0.33
Ecuadorian	126	0.32
Paraguayan	5	0.01
Peruvian	63	0.16
Uruguayan	1	<0.01
Venezuelan	15	0.04
Other South American	6	0.02
Other Hispanic or Latino	337	0.85

Race*	Population	%
African-American/Black (1,798)	2,063	5.18
Not Hispanic (1,655)	1,852	4.65
Hispanic (143)	211	0.53
American Indian/Alaska Native (348)	570	1.43
Not Hispanic (34)	140	0.35
Hispanic (314)	430	1.08
Apache (1)	4	0.01
Blackfeet (1)	1	<0.01
Cherokee (6)	30	0.08
Chickasaw (0)	3	0.01
Chippewa (3)	8	0.02
Choctaw (2)	4	0.01
Creek (1)	1	<0.01
Delaware (0)	2	0.01
Iroquois (0)	2	0.01
Kiowa (1)	1	<0.01

*Notes: † The Census 2010 population figure is used to calculate the percentages in the Hispanic Origin and Race categories. Ancestry percentages are based on the 2006-2010 American Community Survey population (not shown); ‡ Numbers in parentheses indicate the number of people reporting a single ancestry; * Numbers in parentheses indicate the number of persons reporting this race alone, not in combination with any other race; Please refer to the Explanation of Data for more information.*

	Population	%
Menominee (0)	1	<0.01
Mexican American Ind. (63)	68	0.17
Osage (1)	4	0.01
Ottawa (0)	4	0.01
Pima (1)	2	0.01
Potawatomi (0)	1	<0.01
Sioux (0)	9	0.02
South American Ind. (1)	4	0.01
Asian (5,978)	6,458	16.20
Not Hispanic (5,935)	6,361	15.96
Hispanic (43)	97	0.24
Bangladeshi (2)	2	0.01
Burmese (12)	13	0.03
Cambodian (42)	66	0.17
Chinese, ex. Taiwanese (281)	345	0.87
Filipino (1,637)	1,786	4.48
Hmong (2)	2	0.01
Indian (2,817)	2,962	7.43
Indonesian (8)	11	0.03
Japanese (123)	206	0.52
Korean (330)	361	0.91
Laotian (58)	74	0.19
Malaysian (5)	6	0.02
Nepalese (15)	15	0.04
Pakistani (345)	373	0.94
Taiwanese (9)	13	0.03
Thai (47)	61	0.15
Vietnamese (116)	133	0.33
Hawaii Native/Pacific Islander (14)	51	0.13
Not Hispanic (9)	28	0.07
Hispanic (5)	23	0.06
Guamanian/Chamorro (4)	4	0.01
Native Hawaiian (2)	5	0.01
Samoan (4)	7	0.02
White (26,305)	27,237	68.34
Not Hispanic (20,262)	20,751	52.06
Hispanic (6,043)	6,486	16.27

Streator

Place Type: City
County: LaSalle
Population: 13,710†

Ancestry‡	Population	%
American (882)	882	6.68
Arab (7)	7	0.05
Arab (7)	7	0.05
Austrian (0)	15	0.11
British (0)	7	0.05
Canadian (9)	9	0.07
Czech (51)	84	0.64
Czechoslovakian (51)	161	1.22
Danish (9)	50	0.38
Dutch (0)	175	1.33
Eastern European (97)	97	0.74
English (226)	816	6.18
European (41)	41	0.31
French, ex. Basque (96)	256	1.94
French Canadian (7)	66	0.50
German (1,247)	4,074	30.88
Greek (0)	99	0.75
Irish (703)	2,404	18.22
Italian (492)	874	6.62
Lithuanian (0)	13	0.10
Norwegian (143)	420	3.18
Pennsylvania German (0)	15	0.11
Polish (176)	657	4.98
Russian (10)	49	0.37
Scandinavian (57)	121	0.92
Scotch-Irish (34)	128	0.97
Scottish (0)	100	0.76
Slavic (0)	8	0.06
Slovak (460)	1,596	12.10
Swedish (33)	249	1.89
Swiss (0)	43	0.33
Turkish (7)	7	0.05
Welsh (27)	77	0.58

Hispanic Origin	Population	%
Hispanic or Latino (of any race)	1,422	10.37
Central American, ex. Mexican	15	0.11
Guatemalan	8	0.06
Honduran	4	0.03
Salvadoran	3	0.02
Cuban	3	0.02
Mexican	1,250	9.12
Puerto Rican	89	0.65
South American	6	0.04
Chilean	1	0.01
Colombian	5	0.04
Other Hispanic or Latino	59	0.43

Race*	Population	%
African-American/Black (340)	484	3.53
Not Hispanic (326)	448	3.27
Hispanic (14)	36	0.26
American Indian/Alaska Native (42)	81	0.59
Not Hispanic (24)	57	0.42
Hispanic (18)	24	0.18
Apache (0)	4	0.03
Cherokee (7)	20	0.15
Chickasaw (1)	1	0.01
Mexican American Ind. (3)	3	0.02
Sioux (12)	12	0.09
Spanish American Ind. (4)	4	0.03
Asian (60)	89	0.65
Not Hispanic (57)	86	0.63
Hispanic (3)	3	0.02
Cambodian (1)	2	0.01
Chinese, ex. Taiwanese (13)	13	0.09
Filipino (19)	34	0.25
Indian (6)	11	0.08
Indonesian (0)	4	0.03
Japanese (2)	5	0.04
Korean (4)	5	0.04
Vietnamese (15)	15	0.11
Hawaii Native/Pacific Islander (3)	8	0.06
Not Hispanic (0)	4	0.03
Hispanic (3)	4	0.03
Guamanian/Chamorro (2)	2	0.01
Native Hawaiian (0)	1	0.01
White (12,505)	12,790	93.29
Not Hispanic (11,680)	11,873	86.60
Hispanic (825)	917	6.69

Sugar Grove

Place Type: Village
County: Kane
Population: 8,997†

Ancestry‡	Population	%
American (248)	248	3.02
Arab (0)	22	0.27
Arab (0)	11	0.13
Syrian (0)	11	0.13
Austrian (0)	100	1.22
Belgian (0)	32	0.39
British (15)	15	0.18
Bulgarian (12)	12	0.15
Canadian (0)	21	0.26
Croatian (0)	32	0.39
Czech (62)	198	2.41
Czechoslovakian (9)	19	0.23
Danish (0)	19	0.23
Dutch (34)	114	1.39
English (175)	897	10.94
European (44)	55	0.67
Finnish (0)	10	0.12
French, ex. Basque (30)	312	3.80
French Canadian (8)	52	0.63
German (832)	2,921	35.61
Greek (113)	287	3.50
Hungarian (19)	64	0.78
Icelander (0)	11	0.13
Irish (323)	1,337	16.30
Italian (342)	691	8.42
Lithuanian (0)	27	0.33
Luxemburger (0)	17	0.21
Norwegian (175)	560	6.83
Polish (198)	722	8.80
Romanian (29)	58	0.71
Russian (0)	10	0.12
Scandinavian (0)	11	0.13
Scotch-Irish (11)	65	0.79
Scottish (0)	236	2.88
Slavic (21)	21	0.26
Slovak (0)	75	0.91
Swedish (30)	208	2.54
Swiss (0)	19	0.23
Ukrainian (15)	15	0.18
Welsh (0)	26	0.32
Yugoslavian (0)	10	0.12

Hispanic Origin	Population	%
Hispanic or Latino (of any race)	698	7.76
Central American, ex. Mexican	12	0.13
Guatemalan	8	0.09
Panamanian	1	0.01
Salvadoran	3	0.03
Cuban	20	0.22
Dominican Republic	4	0.04
Mexican	520	5.78
Puerto Rican	78	0.87
South American	28	0.31
Argentinean	10	0.11
Chilean	1	0.01
Colombian	7	0.08
Ecuadorian	7	0.08
Paraguayan	1	0.01
Peruvian	1	0.01
Uruguayan	1	0.01
Other Hispanic or Latino	36	0.40

Race*	Population	%
African-American/Black (143)	184	2.05
Not Hispanic (137)	174	1.93
Hispanic (6)	10	0.11
American Indian/Alaska Native (16)	40	0.44
Not Hispanic (12)	34	0.38
Hispanic (4)	6	0.07
Aleut *(Alaska Native)* (0)	1	0.01
Blackfeet (1)	1	0.01
Cherokee (1)	4	0.04
Chippewa (0)	4	0.04
Crow (0)	1	0.01
Mexican American Ind. (1)	1	0.01
Yup'ik *(Alaska Native)* (1)	1	0.01
Asian (155)	218	2.42
Not Hispanic (153)	208	2.31
Hispanic (2)	10	0.11
Cambodian (1)	1	0.01
Chinese, ex. Taiwanese (25)	39	0.43
Filipino (36)	59	0.66
Indian (31)	47	0.52
Japanese (8)	17	0.19
Korean (16)	23	0.26
Pakistani (6)	6	0.07
Taiwanese (1)	1	0.01
Thai (3)	5	0.06
Vietnamese (18)	20	0.22
White (8,387)	8,507	94.55
Not Hispanic (7,881)	7,979	88.69
Hispanic (506)	528	5.87

Summit

Place Type: Village
County: Cook
Population: 11,054†

Ancestry‡	Population	%
Albanian (90)	90	0.83
American (259)	259	2.38
Austrian (0)	15	0.14
Croatian (33)	46	0.42
Czech (10)	81	0.75
Dutch (9)	28	0.26

*Notes: † The Census 2010 population figure is used to calculate the percentages in the Hispanic Origin and Race categories. Ancestry percentages are based on the 2006-2010 American Community Survey population (not shown); ‡ Numbers in parentheses indicate the number of people reporting a single ancestry; * Numbers in parentheses indicate the number of persons reporting this race alone, not in combination with any other race; Please refer to the Explanation of Data for more information.*

Ancestry	Population	%
English (37)	187	1.72
Estonian (21)	21	0.19
Finnish (0)	21	0.19
French, ex. Basque (8)	94	0.87
German (61)	695	6.40
Greek (18)	18	0.17
Irish (76)	568	5.23
Italian (52)	276	2.54
Lithuanian (28)	100	0.92
Macedonian (0)	10	0.09
Norwegian (0)	20	0.18
Polish (301)	714	6.57
Russian (10)	25	0.23
Scotch-Irish (0)	8	0.07
Scottish (11)	11	0.10
Serbian (30)	30	0.28
Slovak (11)	34	0.31
Swedish (0)	18	0.17
Ukrainian (0)	8	0.07
Yugoslavian (0)	19	0.17

Hispanic Origin	Population	%
Hispanic or Latino (of any race)	7,042	63.71
Central American, ex. Mexican	149	1.35
Costa Rican	1	0.01
Guatemalan	57	0.52
Honduran	3	0.03
Nicaraguan	1	0.01
Salvadoran	87	0.79
Cuban	9	0.08
Dominican Republic	3	0.03
Mexican	6,500	58.80
Puerto Rican	164	1.48
South American	41	0.37
Argentinean	1	0.01
Colombian	13	0.12
Ecuadorian	10	0.09
Paraguayan	3	0.03
Peruvian	7	0.06
Uruguayan	7	0.06
Other Hispanic or Latino	176	1.59

Race*	Population	%
African-American/Black (1,038)	1,091	9.87
Not Hispanic (1,011)	1,036	9.37
Hispanic (27)	55	0.50
American Indian/Alaska Native (89)	181	1.64
Not Hispanic (28)	79	0.71
Hispanic (61)	102	0.92
Apache (0)	1	0.01
Blackfeet (0)	8	0.07
Central American Ind. (0)	1	0.01
Cherokee (3)	15	0.14
Chippewa (7)	10	0.09
Choctaw (0)	7	0.06
Iroquois (3)	3	0.03
Mexican American Ind. (22)	26	0.24
Navajo (4)	4	0.04
Ottawa (1)	1	0.01
Tohono O'Odham (4)	4	0.04
Asian (215)	281	2.54
Not Hispanic (199)	257	2.32
Hispanic (16)	24	0.22
Chinese, ex. Taiwanese (11)	12	0.11
Filipino (16)	22	0.20
Indian (107)	143	1.29
Japanese (1)	2	0.02
Korean (2)	3	0.03
Pakistani (54)	61	0.55
Thai (2)	3	0.03
Vietnamese (16)	19	0.17
Hawaii Native/Pacific Islander (7)	11	0.10
Not Hispanic (0)	1	0.01
Hispanic (7)	10	0.09
Guamanian/Chamorro (6)	6	0.05
White (6,386)	6,716	60.76
Not Hispanic (2,662)	2,727	24.67
Hispanic (3,724)	3,989	36.09

Swansea

Place Type: Village
County: St. Clair
Population: 13,430†

Ancestry‡	Population	%
African, Sub-Saharan (49)	49	0.38
African (28)	28	0.22
Ethiopian (21)	21	0.16
American (441)	441	3.41
Armenian (11)	29	0.22
Australian (9)	9	0.07
Austrian (12)	37	0.29
Belgian (0)	13	0.10
British (27)	85	0.66
Canadian (14)	14	0.11
Croatian (0)	21	0.16
Czech (9)	89	0.69
Czechoslovakian (0)	15	0.12
Dutch (12)	212	1.64
Eastern European (15)	15	0.12
English (374)	1,390	10.74
European (612)	612	4.73
French, ex. Basque (57)	530	4.10
French Canadian (0)	55	0.43
German (2,246)	4,603	35.57
Hungarian (8)	40	0.31
Irish (317)	1,789	13.82
Italian (111)	512	3.96
Lithuanian (83)	83	0.64
Norwegian (55)	175	1.35
Pennsylvania German (11)	26	0.20
Polish (145)	456	3.52
Portuguese (0)	20	0.15
Russian (10)	10	0.08
Scandinavian (0)	54	0.42
Scotch-Irish (103)	194	1.50
Scottish (37)	116	0.90
Slavic (15)	15	0.12
Slovak (19)	48	0.37
Slovene (12)	22	0.17
Swedish (22)	132	1.02
Swiss (0)	95	0.73
Ukrainian (0)	25	0.19
Welsh (0)	65	0.50

Hispanic Origin	Population	%
Hispanic or Latino (of any race)	309	2.30
Central American, ex. Mexican	25	0.19
Costa Rican	8	0.06
Guatemalan	3	0.02
Nicaraguan	2	0.01
Panamanian	6	0.04
Salvadoran	6	0.04
Cuban	10	0.07
Mexican	161	1.20
Puerto Rican	59	0.44
South American	12	0.09
Chilean	1	0.01
Colombian	7	0.05
Ecuadorian	4	0.03
Other Hispanic or Latino	42	0.31

Race*	Population	%
African-American/Black (2,225)	2,377	17.70
Not Hispanic (2,209)	2,355	17.54
Hispanic (16)	22	0.16
American Indian/Alaska Native (23)	65	0.48
Not Hispanic (21)	63	0.47
Hispanic (2)	2	0.01
Cherokee (4)	12	0.09
Choctaw (1)	5	0.04
Crow (0)	1	0.01
Hopi (1)	1	0.01
Inupiat *(Alaska Native)* (1)	1	0.01
Iroquois (0)	1	0.01
Osage (1)	1	0.01
Spanish American Ind. (1)	1	0.01
Asian (244)	361	2.69
Not Hispanic (235)	341	2.54
Hispanic (9)	20	0.15
Chinese, ex. Taiwanese (38)	56	0.42
Filipino (60)	99	0.74
Indian (39)	46	0.34
Japanese (10)	23	0.17
Korean (34)	57	0.42
Laotian (0)	1	0.01
Malaysian (0)	1	0.01
Pakistani (18)	22	0.16
Sri Lankan (0)	2	0.01
Taiwanese (2)	3	0.02
Thai (6)	11	0.08
Vietnamese (25)	27	0.20
Hawaii Native/Pacific Islander (25)	39	0.29
Not Hispanic (24)	35	0.26
Hispanic (1)	4	0.03
Guamanian/Chamorro (17)	18	0.13
Marshallese (1)	1	0.01
Native Hawaiian (3)	12	0.09
Samoan (2)	4	0.03
White (10,540)	10,812	80.51
Not Hispanic (10,349)	10,590	78.85
Hispanic (191)	222	1.65

Sycamore

Place Type: City
County: DeKalb
Population: 17,519†

Ancestry‡	Population	%
African, Sub-Saharan (25)	46	0.27
Kenyan (25)	46	0.27
American (703)	703	4.18
Arab (64)	182	1.08
Jordanian (48)	48	0.29
Other Arab (16)	134	0.80
Armenian (15)	66	0.39
Austrian (66)	103	0.61
Belgian (0)	20	0.12
British (20)	58	0.35
Canadian (0)	28	0.17
Croatian (0)	11	0.07
Czech (97)	316	1.88
Danish (19)	132	0.79
Dutch (31)	187	1.11
English (325)	1,551	9.23
European (144)	157	0.93
Finnish (8)	36	0.21
French, ex. Basque (23)	375	2.23
French Canadian (0)	79	0.47
German (1,750)	6,038	35.94
Greek (192)	219	1.30
Hungarian (0)	54	0.32
Iranian (9)	18	0.11
Irish (1,014)	3,514	20.92
Israeli (18)	18	0.11
Italian (318)	1,042	6.20
Lithuanian (62)	124	0.74
Luxemburger (0)	23	0.14
Norwegian (247)	664	3.95
Pennsylvania German (22)	54	0.32
Polish (413)	1,160	6.90
Portuguese (0)	11	0.07
Russian (34)	86	0.51
Scandinavian (74)	139	0.83
Scotch-Irish (65)	172	1.02
Scottish (44)	196	1.17
Serbian (36)	36	0.21
Slovak (0)	11	0.07
Slovene (0)	11	0.07
Swedish (359)	1,341	7.98
Swiss (0)	13	0.08
Ukrainian (15)	15	0.09
Welsh (0)	61	0.36
Yugoslavian (10)	10	0.06

Hispanic Origin	Population	%
Hispanic or Latino (of any race)	1,229	7.02

*Notes: † The Census 2010 population figure is used to calculate the percentages in the Hispanic Origin and Race categories. Ancestry percentages are based on the 2006-2010 American Community Survey population (not shown); ‡ Numbers in parentheses indicate the number of people reporting a single ancestry; * Numbers in parentheses indicate the number of persons reporting this race alone, not in combination with any other race; Please refer to the Explanation of Data for more information.*

Central American, ex. Mexican	14	0.08
Costa Rican	3	0.02
Guatemalan	7	0.04
Honduran	2	0.01
Nicaraguan	1	0.01
Panamanian	1	0.01
Cuban	32	0.18
Dominican Republic	1	0.01
Mexican	991	5.66
Puerto Rican	93	0.53
South American	30	0.17
Argentinean	5	0.03
Chilean	1	0.01
Colombian	6	0.03
Ecuadorian	8	0.05
Peruvian	2	0.01
Venezuelan	8	0.05
Other Hispanic or Latino	68	0.39

Race*	Population	%
African-American/Black (509)	627	3.58
Not Hispanic (493)	595	3.40
Hispanic (16)	32	0.18
American Indian/Alaska Native (34)	104	0.59
Not Hispanic (14)	68	0.39
Hispanic (20)	36	0.21
Apache (0)	5	0.03
Blackfeet (0)	8	0.05
Cherokee (1)	15	0.09
Chippewa (1)	11	0.06
Choctaw (1)	4	0.02
Iroquois (2)	5	0.03
Mexican American Ind. (5)	9	0.05
Navajo (4)	9	0.05
Osage (1)	1	0.01
Potawatomi (0)	1	0.01
Seminole (0)	3	0.02
Sioux (0)	3	0.02
Yaqui (0)	1	0.01
Asian (260)	364	2.08
Not Hispanic (254)	351	2.00
Hispanic (6)	13	0.07
Bangladeshi (9)	9	0.05
Burmese (2)	2	0.01
Chinese, ex. Taiwanese (56)	72	0.41
Filipino (32)	58	0.33
Indian (39)	44	0.25
Japanese (12)	29	0.17
Korean (28)	41	0.23
Laotian (17)	24	0.14
Malaysian (1)	3	0.02
Pakistani (35)	35	0.20
Taiwanese (0)	5	0.03
Thai (2)	5	0.03
Vietnamese (19)	23	0.13
Hawaii Native/Pacific Islander (2)	11	0.06
Not Hispanic (2)	10	0.06
Hispanic (0)	1	0.01
Native Hawaiian (2)	5	0.03
Samoan (0)	1	0.01
White (16,009)	16,308	93.09
Not Hispanic (15,267)	15,491	88.42
Hispanic (742)	817	4.66

Taylorville

Place Type: City
County: Christian
Population: 11,246†

Ancestry‡	Population	%
African, Sub-Saharan (38)	38	0.30
African (28)	28	0.22
Nigerian (10)	10	0.08
Albanian (12)	12	0.09
American (1,418)	1,418	11.19
Australian (0)	14	0.11
Austrian (0)	54	0.43
Belgian (0)	62	0.49
British (10)	10	0.08
Canadian (10)	10	0.08
Croatian (16)	16	0.13
Czech (14)	120	0.95
Czechoslovakian (22)	34	0.27
Danish (24)	36	0.28
Dutch (53)	324	2.56
Eastern European (67)	67	0.53
English (504)	1,267	10.00
European (18)	29	0.23
Finnish (0)	20	0.16
French, ex. Basque (123)	428	3.38
French Canadian (14)	36	0.28
German (837)	2,765	21.83
Greek (9)	19	0.15
Hungarian (0)	11	0.09
Irish (890)	2,159	17.04
Israeli (9)	9	0.07
Italian (163)	481	3.80
Lithuanian (0)	37	0.29
New Zealander (0)	13	0.10
Norwegian (32)	57	0.45
Polish (90)	300	2.37
Scotch-Irish (109)	253	2.00
Scottish (35)	101	0.80
Slovak (12)	49	0.39
Swedish (29)	154	1.22
Swiss (22)	33	0.26
Welsh (10)	19	0.15

Hispanic Origin	Population	%
Hispanic or Latino (of any race)	186	1.65
Central American, ex. Mexican	14	0.12
Guatemalan	1	0.01
Salvadoran	12	0.11
Other Central American	1	0.01
Cuban	1	0.01
Mexican	122	1.08
Puerto Rican	12	0.11
South American	9	0.08
Chilean	5	0.04
Colombian	1	0.01
Peruvian	3	0.03
Other Hispanic or Latino	28	0.25

Race*	Population	%
African-American/Black (92)	158	1.40
Not Hispanic (92)	153	1.36
Hispanic (0)	5	0.04
American Indian/Alaska Native (20)	66	0.59
Not Hispanic (12)	56	0.50
Hispanic (8)	10	0.09
Apache (1)	8	0.07
Blackfeet (0)	7	0.06
Cherokee (3)	19	0.17
Chippewa (1)	2	0.02
Choctaw (3)	6	0.05
Mexican American Ind. (4)	4	0.04
Navajo (1)	1	0.01
Sioux (1)	4	0.04
South American Ind. (1)	1	0.01
Asian (65)	82	0.73
Not Hispanic (63)	73	0.65
Hispanic (2)	9	0.08
Chinese, ex. Taiwanese (12)	13	0.12
Filipino (21)	33	0.29
Indian (18)	18	0.16
Indonesian (1)	1	0.01
Japanese (4)	4	0.04
Korean (3)	5	0.04
Thai (0)	1	0.01
Vietnamese (3)	3	0.03
Hawaii Native/Pacific Islander (7)	13	0.12
Not Hispanic (6)	9	0.08
Hispanic (1)	4	0.04
Guamanian/Chamorro (0)	1	0.01
Native Hawaiian (1)	3	0.03
Samoan (0)	1	0.01
White (10,880)	11,014	97.94
Not Hispanic (10,763)	10,877	96.72
Hispanic (117)	137	1.22

Tinley Park

Place Type: Village
County: Cook
Population: 56,703†

Ancestry‡	Population	%
African, Sub-Saharan (193)	193	0.35
African (193)	193	0.35
Albanian (10)	10	0.02
American (1,190)	1,190	2.17
Arab (1,274)	1,358	2.47
Arab (884)	902	1.64
Jordanian (101)	101	0.18
Lebanese (29)	29	0.05
Palestinian (62)	95	0.17
Other Arab (198)	231	0.42
Armenian (28)	67	0.12
Austrian (185)	566	1.03
Belgian (15)	42	0.08
British (0)	50	0.09
Bulgarian (28)	28	0.05
Canadian (12)	37	0.07
Celtic (22)	42	0.08
Croatian (166)	394	0.72
Czech (334)	1,409	2.56
Czechoslovakian (12)	104	0.19
Danish (36)	207	0.38
Dutch (746)	1,517	2.76
Eastern European (49)	49	0.09
English (508)	3,135	5.71
European (201)	315	0.57
Finnish (0)	78	0.14
French, ex. Basque (71)	1,228	2.24
French Canadian (38)	193	0.35
German (2,606)	12,421	22.61
Greek (448)	1,065	1.94
Hungarian (49)	233	0.42
Irish (3,462)	13,718	24.97
Israeli (37)	37	0.07
Italian (2,134)	7,333	13.35
Latvian (35)	35	0.06
Lithuanian (489)	1,503	2.74
Norwegian (99)	451	0.82
Pennsylvania German (11)	11	0.02
Polish (3,838)	10,148	18.47
Russian (65)	485	0.88
Scandinavian (42)	56	0.10
Scotch-Irish (246)	686	1.25
Scottish (83)	452	0.82
Serbian (61)	74	0.13
Slovak (78)	487	0.89
Slovene (5)	24	0.04
Swedish (228)	1,818	3.31
Swiss (49)	175	0.32
Turkish (15)	15	0.03
Ukrainian (190)	619	1.13
Welsh (17)	96	0.17
West Indian, ex. Hispanic (146)	169	0.31
Belizean (7)	7	0.01
Haitian (12)	35	0.06
West Indian (127)	127	0.23
Yugoslavian (45)	45	0.08

Hispanic Origin	Population	%
Hispanic or Latino (of any race)	3,898	6.87
Central American, ex. Mexican	70	0.12
Costa Rican	9	0.02
Guatemalan	43	0.08
Honduran	7	0.01
Nicaraguan	7	0.01
Salvadoran	3	0.01
Other Central American	1	<0.01
Cuban	37	0.07
Dominican Republic	15	0.03
Mexican	3,220	5.68
Puerto Rican	255	0.45
South American	107	0.19
Argentinean	17	0.03
Bolivian	5	0.01

*Notes: † The Census 2010 population figure is used to calculate the percentages in the Hispanic Origin and Race categories. Ancestry percentages are based on the 2006-2010 American Community Survey population (not shown); ‡ Numbers in parentheses indicate the number of people reporting a single ancestry; * Numbers in parentheses indicate the number of persons reporting this race alone, not in combination with any other race; Please refer to the Explanation of Data for more information.*

Colombian	30	0.05
Ecuadorian	27	0.05
Paraguayan	2	<0.01
Peruvian	16	0.03
Uruguayan	1	<0.01
Venezuelan	9	0.02
Other Hispanic or Latino	194	0.34

Race*	Population	%
African-American/Black (2,085)	2,223	3.92
Not Hispanic (2,062)	2,176	3.84
Hispanic (23)	47	0.08
American Indian/Alaska Native (80)	212	0.37
Not Hispanic (52)	158	0.28
Hispanic (28)	54	0.10
Apache (0)	5	0.01
Blackfeet (1)	8	0.01
Cherokee (7)	33	0.06
Chippewa (3)	5	0.01
Choctaw (1)	3	0.01
Creek (0)	1	<0.01
Iroquois (0)	1	<0.01
Menominee (1)	1	<0.01
Mexican American Ind. (7)	9	0.02
Navajo (6)	8	0.01
Potawatomi (1)	1	<0.01
Shoshone (0)	3	0.01
Sioux (2)	3	0.01
Tlingit-Haida *(Alaska Native)* (1)	1	<0.01
Ute (0)	1	<0.01
Asian (2,208)	2,602	4.59
Not Hispanic (2,199)	2,571	4.53
Hispanic (9)	31	0.05
Bangladeshi (5)	6	0.01
Burmese (10)	15	0.03
Cambodian (2)	2	<0.01
Chinese, ex. Taiwanese (223)	266	0.47
Filipino (783)	887	1.56
Indian (711)	785	1.38
Indonesian (2)	2	<0.01
Japanese (21)	48	0.08
Korean (101)	127	0.22
Laotian (20)	27	0.05
Malaysian (3)	3	0.01
Nepalese (0)	3	0.01
Pakistani (108)	128	0.23
Sri Lankan (9)	9	0.02
Taiwanese (4)	7	0.01
Thai (50)	60	0.11
Vietnamese (101)	109	0.19
Hawaii Native/Pacific Islander (10)	45	0.08
Not Hispanic (6)	37	0.07
Hispanic (4)	8	0.01
Guamanian/Chamorro (5)	7	0.01
Native Hawaiian (0)	12	0.02
Samoan (4)	5	0.01
White (50,332)	51,088	90.10
Not Hispanic (47,858)	48,383	85.33
Hispanic (2,474)	2,705	4.77

Troy

Place Type: City
County: Madison
Population: 9,888†

Ancestry‡	Population	%
African, Sub-Saharan (30)	30	0.31
African (30)	30	0.31
American (552)	552	5.66
Arab (21)	21	0.22
Arab (11)	11	0.11
Moroccan (10)	10	0.10
Australian (0)	54	0.55
British (31)	67	0.69
Bulgarian (0)	12	0.12
Croatian (0)	46	0.47
Czech (32)	83	0.85
Danish (0)	57	0.58
Dutch (94)	226	2.32
English (181)	745	7.64
European (25)	46	0.47
Finnish (0)	5	0.05
French, ex. Basque (16)	347	3.56
French Canadian (10)	10	0.10
German (1,592)	3,608	37.02
Greek (26)	101	1.04
Hungarian (0)	85	0.87
Irish (401)	1,315	13.49
Italian (214)	654	6.71
Macedonian (16)	16	0.16
Northern European (12)	12	0.12
Norwegian (33)	195	2.00
Polish (120)	263	2.70
Russian (29)	51	0.52
Scotch-Irish (52)	125	1.28
Scottish (14)	107	1.10
Serbian (0)	11	0.11
Slavic (0)	14	0.14
Slovak (0)	10	0.10
Swedish (9)	59	0.61
Swiss (0)	11	0.11
Welsh (0)	20	0.21
Yugoslavian (0)	12	0.12

Hispanic Origin	Population	%
Hispanic or Latino (of any race)	259	2.62
Central American, ex. Mexican	13	0.13
Guatemalan	5	0.05
Honduran	1	0.01
Panamanian	7	0.07
Cuban	2	0.02
Dominican Republic	1	0.01
Mexican	167	1.69
Puerto Rican	18	0.18
South American	10	0.10
Chilean	1	0.01
Colombian	5	0.05
Ecuadorian	1	0.01
Peruvian	1	0.01
Venezuelan	2	0.02
Other Hispanic or Latino	48	0.49

Race*	Population	%
African-American/Black (199)	273	2.76
Not Hispanic (196)	262	2.65
Hispanic (3)	11	0.11
American Indian/Alaska Native (32)	94	0.95
Not Hispanic (28)	88	0.89
Hispanic (4)	6	0.06
Blackfeet (0)	9	0.09
Cherokee (13)	38	0.38
Chickasaw (1)	2	0.02
Choctaw (0)	6	0.06
Seminole (2)	2	0.02
Asian (103)	164	1.66
Not Hispanic (98)	152	1.54
Hispanic (5)	12	0.12
Burmese (1)	3	0.03
Chinese, ex. Taiwanese (14)	16	0.16
Filipino (19)	52	0.53
Indian (14)	16	0.16
Japanese (8)	20	0.20
Korean (18)	23	0.23
Laotian (1)	1	0.01
Malaysian (0)	1	0.01
Nepalese (8)	8	0.08
Pakistani (1)	1	0.01
Thai (0)	3	0.03
Vietnamese (14)	14	0.14
Hawaii Native/Pacific Islander (10)	13	0.13
Not Hispanic (9)	11	0.11
Hispanic (1)	2	0.02
Guamanian/Chamorro (1)	3	0.03
Native Hawaiian (5)	6	0.06
Samoan (0)	1	0.01
White (9,283)	9,459	95.66
Not Hispanic (9,126)	9,281	93.86
Hispanic (157)	178	1.80

Urbana

Place Type: City
County: Champaign
Population: 41,250†

Ancestry‡	Population	%
African, Sub-Saharan (1,574)	1,594	3.91
African (1,356)	1,356	3.32
Ghanaian (83)	83	0.20
Kenyan (22)	22	0.05
Nigerian (51)	71	0.17
South African (21)	21	0.05
Zimbabwean (25)	25	0.06
Other Sub-Saharan African (16)	16	0.04
American (3,767)	3,767	9.23
Arab (340)	392	0.96
Egyptian (48)	48	0.12
Iraqi (57)	57	0.14
Jordanian (49)	49	0.12
Lebanese (6)	26	0.06
Moroccan (34)	34	0.08
Palestinian (27)	27	0.07
Other Arab (119)	151	0.37
Armenian (18)	18	0.04
Australian (22)	22	0.05
Austrian (103)	158	0.39
Basque (0)	20	0.05
Belgian (66)	143	0.35
Brazilian (50)	64	0.16
British (141)	333	0.82
Bulgarian (31)	52	0.13
Canadian (50)	71	0.17
Celtic (8)	8	0.02
Croatian (0)	45	0.11
Czech (14)	176	0.43
Czechoslovakian (13)	60	0.15
Danish (38)	122	0.30
Dutch (79)	367	0.90
Eastern European (42)	42	0.10
English (746)	3,282	8.04
European (873)	919	2.25
Finnish (9)	33	0.08
French, ex. Basque (85)	709	1.74
French Canadian (71)	152	0.37
German (2,467)	7,725	18.93
Greek (41)	203	0.50
Hungarian (0)	35	0.09
Icelander (105)	105	0.26
Iranian (63)	63	0.15
Irish (772)	4,330	10.61
Israeli (73)	73	0.18
Italian (354)	1,511	3.70
Lithuanian (8)	154	0.38
Luxemburger (0)	15	0.04
Northern European (26)	26	0.06
Norwegian (89)	359	0.88
Polish (423)	1,534	3.76
Portuguese (0)	14	0.03
Romanian (57)	71	0.17
Russian (343)	617	1.51
Scandinavian (38)	50	0.12
Scotch-Irish (225)	571	1.40
Scottish (148)	683	1.67
Serbian (26)	57	0.14
Slovak (39)	67	0.16
Swedish (153)	800	1.96
Swiss (71)	239	0.59
Turkish (145)	155	0.38
Ukrainian (12)	42	0.10
Welsh (14)	180	0.44
West Indian, ex. Hispanic (44)	80	0.20
Haitian (31)	31	0.08
Jamaican (0)	36	0.09
West Indian (13)	13	0.03
Yugoslavian (42)	66	0.16

Hispanic Origin	Population	%
Hispanic or Latino (of any race)	2,165	5.25
Central American, ex. Mexican	235	0.57

*Notes: † The Census 2010 population figure is used to calculate the percentages in the Hispanic Origin and Race categories. Ancestry percentages are based on the 2006-2010 American Community Survey population (not shown); ‡ Numbers in parentheses indicate the number of people reporting a single ancestry; * Numbers in parentheses indicate the number of persons reporting this race alone, not in combination with any other race; Please refer to the Explanation of Data for more information.*

Costa Rican	15	0.04
Guatemalan	129	0.31
Honduran	39	0.09
Nicaraguan	6	0.01
Panamanian	16	0.04
Salvadoran	27	0.07
Other Central American	3	0.01
Cuban	72	0.17
Dominican Republic	20	0.05
Mexican	1,074	2.60
Puerto Rican	210	0.51
South American	315	0.76
Argentinean	51	0.12
Bolivian	19	0.05
Chilean	16	0.04
Colombian	109	0.26
Ecuadorian	41	0.10
Paraguayan	8	0.02
Peruvian	39	0.09
Uruguayan	2	<0.01
Venezuelan	24	0.06
Other South American	6	0.01
Other Hispanic or Latino	239	0.58

Race*	Population	%
African-American/Black (6,726)	7,238	17.55
Not Hispanic (6,651)	7,104	17.22
Hispanic (75)	134	0.32
American Indian/Alaska Native (111)	318	0.77
Not Hispanic (59)	211	0.51
Hispanic (52)	107	0.26
Apache (1)	3	0.01
Arapaho (1)	1	<0.01
Blackfeet (0)	7	0.02
Canadian/French Am. Ind. (0)	1	<0.01
Central American Ind. (2)	4	0.01
Cherokee (11)	56	0.14
Chippewa (2)	8	0.02
Choctaw (4)	13	0.03
Comanche (0)	1	<0.01
Creek (2)	4	0.01
Delaware (2)	2	<0.01
Iroquois (4)	8	0.02
Lumbee (1)	1	<0.01
Mexican American Ind. (26)	33	0.08
Navajo (2)	3	0.01
Osage (0)	1	<0.01
Potawatomi (2)	2	<0.01
Pueblo (1)	1	<0.01
Puget Sound Salish (1)	2	<0.01
Seminole (1)	2	<0.01
Sioux (1)	6	0.01
South American Ind. (3)	7	0.02
Yaqui (0)	1	<0.01
Asian (7,328)	7,895	19.14
Not Hispanic (7,305)	7,843	19.01
Hispanic (23)	52	0.13
Bangladeshi (24)	24	0.06
Burmese (5)	6	0.01
Cambodian (24)	30	0.07
Chinese, ex. Taiwanese (2,902)	3,067	7.44
Filipino (225)	306	0.74
Hmong (1)	1	<0.01
Indian (1,229)	1,289	3.12
Indonesian (66)	80	0.19
Japanese (158)	235	0.57
Korean (1,542)	1,598	3.87
Laotian (80)	93	0.23
Malaysian (32)	35	0.08
Nepalese (17)	17	0.04
Pakistani (159)	165	0.40
Sri Lankan (22)	23	0.06
Taiwanese (387)	422	1.02
Thai (90)	101	0.24
Vietnamese (179)	203	0.49
Hawaii Native/Pacific Islander (58)	107	0.26
Not Hispanic (57)	100	0.24
Hispanic (1)	7	0.02
Guamanian/Chamorro (3)	8	0.02
Native Hawaiian (1)	12	0.03
Samoan (2)	4	0.01
White (24,902)	25,998	63.03
Not Hispanic (23,809)	24,740	59.98
Hispanic (1,093)	1,258	3.05

Vernon Hills

Place Type: Village
County: Lake
Population: 25,113†

Ancestry‡	Population	%
American (1,303)	1,303	5.34
Arab (189)	189	0.77
Arab (13)	13	0.05
Egyptian (42)	42	0.17
Jordanian (61)	61	0.25
Lebanese (13)	13	0.05
Syrian (15)	15	0.06
Other Arab (45)	45	0.18
Armenian (0)	11	0.05
Austrian (60)	189	0.77
Belgian (65)	103	0.42
British (36)	88	0.36
Bulgarian (40)	52	0.21
Canadian (12)	12	0.05
Croatian (0)	47	0.19
Czech (72)	281	1.15
Czechoslovakian (22)	31	0.13
Danish (30)	54	0.22
Dutch (7)	131	0.54
Eastern European (201)	201	0.82
English (188)	1,227	5.03
Estonian (0)	31	0.13
European (118)	140	0.57
Finnish (13)	75	0.31
French, ex. Basque (21)	390	1.60
French Canadian (31)	59	0.24
German (1,178)	3,782	15.51
Greek (104)	170	0.70
Hungarian (45)	219	0.90
Irish (938)	2,663	10.92
Israeli (57)	57	0.23
Italian (768)	1,650	6.77
Latvian (8)	15	0.06
Lithuanian (247)	369	1.51
Norwegian (88)	383	1.57
Polish (780)	2,061	8.45
Portuguese (14)	14	0.06
Romanian (51)	115	0.47
Russian (1,187)	2,089	8.57
Scandinavian (10)	32	0.13
Scotch-Irish (36)	131	0.54
Scottish (78)	382	1.57
Serbian (12)	12	0.05
Slovak (15)	44	0.18
Soviet Union (10)	10	0.04
Swedish (80)	555	2.28
Swiss (18)	29	0.12
Turkish (15)	52	0.21
Ukrainian (495)	565	2.32
Welsh (9)	99	0.41
Yugoslavian (56)	56	0.23

Hispanic Origin	Population	%
Hispanic or Latino (of any race)	2,860	11.39
Central American, ex. Mexican	128	0.51
Costa Rican	6	0.02
Guatemalan	56	0.22
Honduran	7	0.03
Nicaraguan	6	0.02
Panamanian	6	0.02
Salvadoran	47	0.19
Cuban	46	0.18
Dominican Republic	2	0.01
Mexican	2,195	8.74
Puerto Rican	147	0.59
South American	223	0.89
Argentinean	17	0.07
Bolivian	12	0.05
Chilean	8	0.03
Colombian	98	0.39
Ecuadorian	29	0.12
Paraguayan	3	0.01
Peruvian	32	0.13
Uruguayan	2	0.01
Venezuelan	20	0.08
Other South American	2	0.01
Other Hispanic or Latino	119	0.47

Race*	Population	%
African-American/Black (549)	630	2.51
Not Hispanic (527)	593	2.36
Hispanic (22)	37	0.15
American Indian/Alaska Native (44)	114	0.45
Not Hispanic (19)	58	0.23
Hispanic (25)	56	0.22
Apache (3)	3	0.01
Blackfeet (1)	1	<0.01
Cherokee (3)	9	0.04
Chippewa (1)	4	0.02
Choctaw (0)	2	0.01
Iroquois (1)	1	<0.01
Mexican American Ind. (1)	7	0.03
Sioux (1)	1	<0.01
South American Ind. (0)	2	0.01
Spanish American Ind. (1)	1	<0.01
Asian (4,858)	5,162	20.56
Not Hispanic (4,848)	5,130	20.43
Hispanic (10)	32	0.13
Bangladeshi (18)	20	0.08
Burmese (9)	11	0.04
Cambodian (10)	11	0.04
Chinese, ex. Taiwanese (1,186)	1,265	5.04
Filipino (422)	509	2.03
Indian (1,348)	1,414	5.63
Indonesian (2)	2	0.01
Japanese (159)	196	0.78
Korean (1,381)	1,429	5.69
Malaysian (2)	2	0.01
Pakistani (135)	139	0.55
Sri Lankan (1)	1	<0.01
Taiwanese (45)	52	0.21
Thai (21)	29	0.12
Vietnamese (48)	61	0.24
Hawaii Native/Pacific Islander (11)	32	0.13
Not Hispanic (10)	31	0.12
Hispanic (1)	1	<0.01
Native Hawaiian (2)	15	0.06
Samoan (9)	11	0.04
White (17,927)	18,379	73.19
Not Hispanic (16,434)	16,775	66.80
Hispanic (1,493)	1,604	6.39

Villa Park

Place Type: Village
County: DuPage
Population: 21,904†

Ancestry‡	Population	%
African, Sub-Saharan (52)	52	0.23
African (9)	9	0.04
Nigerian (31)	31	0.14
Other Sub-Saharan African (12)	12	0.05
Albanian (168)	168	0.76
American (543)	543	2.44
Arab (27)	66	0.30
Arab (27)	27	0.12
Lebanese (0)	25	0.11
Syrian (0)	14	0.06
Assyrian/Chaldean/Syriac (20)	20	0.09
Austrian (0)	145	0.65
Belgian (13)	30	0.13
British (22)	141	0.63
Canadian (33)	59	0.27
Croatian (115)	161	0.72
Czech (91)	603	2.71
Czechoslovakian (44)	70	0.31
Danish (7)	77	0.35

*Notes: † The Census 2010 population figure is used to calculate the percentages in the Hispanic Origin and Race categories. Ancestry percentages are based on the 2006-2010 American Community Survey population (not shown); ‡ Numbers in parentheses indicate the number of people reporting a single ancestry; * Numbers in parentheses indicate the number of persons reporting this race alone, not in combination with any other race; Please refer to the Explanation of Data for more information.*

Dutch (228)	706	3.17
Eastern European (31)	31	0.14
English (214)	1,372	6.17
European (165)	195	0.88
Finnish (38)	102	0.46
French, ex. Basque (14)	477	2.14
French Canadian (22)	63	0.28
German (1,348)	5,481	24.63
Greek (28)	166	0.75
Hungarian (10)	73	0.33
Iranian (41)	41	0.18
Irish (1,050)	4,849	21.79
Italian (722)	2,679	12.04
Latvian (21)	63	0.28
Lithuanian (20)	131	0.59
Luxemburger (0)	9	0.04
Norwegian (118)	378	1.70
Pennsylvania German (0)	16	0.07
Polish (762)	2,383	10.71
Romanian (48)	98	0.44
Russian (0)	91	0.41
Scandinavian (14)	34	0.15
Scotch-Irish (174)	353	1.59
Scottish (77)	439	1.97
Serbian (85)	97	0.44
Slavic (11)	28	0.13
Slovak (24)	121	0.54
Slovene (0)	20	0.09
Swedish (218)	734	3.30
Swiss (0)	57	0.26
Ukrainian (48)	109	0.49
Welsh (13)	188	0.84
Yugoslavian (217)	251	1.13

Hispanic Origin	Population	%
Hispanic or Latino (of any race)	3,894	17.78
Central American, ex. Mexican	124	0.57
Costa Rican	1	<0.01
Guatemalan	77	0.35
Honduran	22	0.10
Nicaraguan	5	0.02
Panamanian	8	0.04
Salvadoran	11	0.05
Cuban	78	0.36
Dominican Republic	7	0.03
Mexican	3,215	14.68
Puerto Rican	235	1.07
South American	79	0.36
Argentinean	11	0.05
Bolivian	4	0.02
Chilean	7	0.03
Colombian	14	0.06
Ecuadorian	13	0.06
Peruvian	29	0.13
Venezuelan	1	<0.01
Other Hispanic or Latino	156	0.71

Race*	Population	%
African-American/Black (933)	1,059	4.83
Not Hispanic (908)	999	4.56
Hispanic (25)	60	0.27
American Indian/Alaska Native (67)	179	0.82
Not Hispanic (26)	110	0.50
Hispanic (41)	69	0.32
Apache (2)	6	0.03
Blackfeet (0)	6	0.03
Cherokee (0)	28	0.13
Chippewa (6)	8	0.04
Choctaw (0)	2	0.01
Comanche (1)	3	0.01
Iroquois (2)	2	0.01
Mexican American Ind. (6)	9	0.04
Seminole (0)	1	<0.01
South American Ind. (0)	1	<0.01
Spanish American Ind. (5)	5	0.02
Ute (0)	5	0.02
Asian (1,141)	1,300	5.93
Not Hispanic (1,129)	1,261	5.76
Hispanic (12)	39	0.18
Bangladeshi (3)	4	0.02
Cambodian (1)	1	<0.01
Chinese, ex. Taiwanese (65)	91	0.42
Filipino (182)	237	1.08
Indian (553)	610	2.78
Indonesian (7)	10	0.05
Japanese (10)	30	0.14
Korean (26)	39	0.18
Laotian (6)	8	0.04
Malaysian (1)	1	<0.01
Pakistani (198)	220	1.00
Taiwanese (3)	4	0.02
Thai (5)	6	0.03
Vietnamese (19)	24	0.11
Hawaii Native/Pacific Islander (1)	22	0.10
Not Hispanic (1)	21	0.10
Hispanic (0)	1	<0.01
Guamanian/Chamorro (1)	1	<0.01
Native Hawaiian (0)	15	0.07
Samoan (0)	1	<0.01
White (17,741)	18,131	82.77
Not Hispanic (15,639)	15,877	72.48
Hispanic (2,102)	2,254	10.29

Warrenville

Place Type: City
County: DuPage
Population: 13,140†

Ancestry‡	Population	%
African, Sub-Saharan (0)	45	0.34
Nigerian (0)	45	0.34
Albanian (0)	8	0.06
American (304)	304	2.30
Arab (61)	129	0.98
Egyptian (61)	61	0.46
Lebanese (0)	68	0.51
Austrian (15)	78	0.59
Belgian (18)	29	0.22
British (81)	103	0.78
Bulgarian (0)	31	0.23
Canadian (61)	73	0.55
Croatian (17)	112	0.85
Czech (40)	127	0.96
Danish (0)	68	0.51
Dutch (42)	147	1.11
English (323)	1,215	9.19
European (145)	195	1.48
Finnish (9)	9	0.07
French, ex. Basque (23)	315	2.38
French Canadian (9)	38	0.29
German (742)	3,521	26.65
Greek (216)	224	1.70
Hungarian (33)	166	1.26
Irish (623)	2,140	16.19
Italian (439)	1,264	9.57
Latvian (0)	33	0.25
Lithuanian (17)	149	1.13
Macedonian (0)	31	0.23
Norwegian (48)	149	1.13
Pennsylvania German (0)	30	0.23
Polish (457)	1,094	8.28
Romanian (8)	8	0.06
Russian (0)	60	0.45
Scandinavian (12)	76	0.58
Scotch-Irish (46)	159	1.20
Scottish (0)	204	1.54
Serbian (0)	35	0.26
Slovak (30)	47	0.36
Slovene (20)	39	0.30
Swedish (58)	568	4.30
Swiss (13)	23	0.17
Ukrainian (10)	37	0.28
Welsh (0)	14	0.11

Hispanic Origin	Population	%
Hispanic or Latino (of any race)	2,752	20.94
Central American, ex. Mexican	22	0.17
Guatemalan	10	0.08
Honduran	2	0.02
Nicaraguan	3	0.02
Panamanian	1	0.01
Salvadoran	6	0.05
Cuban	11	0.08
Mexican	2,479	18.87
Puerto Rican	80	0.61
South American	46	0.35
Argentinean	3	0.02
Bolivian	4	0.03
Colombian	20	0.15
Ecuadorian	7	0.05
Peruvian	7	0.05
Venezuelan	5	0.04
Other Hispanic or Latino	114	0.87

Race*	Population	%
African-American/Black (514)	606	4.61
Not Hispanic (501)	585	4.45
Hispanic (13)	21	0.16
American Indian/Alaska Native (80)	150	1.14
Not Hispanic (22)	67	0.51
Hispanic (58)	83	0.63
Blackfeet (1)	3	0.02
Cherokee (5)	18	0.14
Chippewa (2)	3	0.02
Creek (1)	1	0.01
Iroquois (4)	7	0.05
Menominee (0)	3	0.02
Mexican American Ind. (18)	25	0.19
Navajo (2)	2	0.02
Ottawa (0)	1	0.01
Potawatomi (0)	1	0.01
Sioux (0)	1	0.01
Spanish American Ind. (1)	2	0.02
Asian (486)	569	4.33
Not Hispanic (482)	557	4.24
Hispanic (4)	12	0.09
Cambodian (29)	33	0.25
Chinese, ex. Taiwanese (54)	61	0.46
Filipino (61)	85	0.65
Hmong (4)	4	0.03
Indian (141)	160	1.22
Japanese (12)	36	0.27
Korean (83)	89	0.68
Laotian (5)	10	0.08
Malaysian (1)	1	0.01
Nepalese (7)	9	0.07
Pakistani (15)	16	0.12
Taiwanese (6)	12	0.09
Thai (19)	26	0.20
Vietnamese (26)	36	0.27
Hawaii Native/Pacific Islander (3)	18	0.14
Not Hispanic (3)	13	0.10
Hispanic (0)	5	0.04
Guamanian/Chamorro (0)	4	0.03
Native Hawaiian (1)	5	0.04
Tongan (2)	2	0.02
White (10,800)	11,051	84.10
Not Hispanic (9,176)	9,332	71.02
Hispanic (1,624)	1,719	13.08

Washington

Place Type: City
County: Tazewell
Population: 15,134†

Ancestry‡	Population	%
American (1,656)	1,656	11.46
Arab (130)	274	1.90
Lebanese (130)	274	1.90
Australian (33)	33	0.23
Austrian (11)	42	0.29
Belgian (29)	69	0.48
British (23)	50	0.35
Croatian (0)	9	0.06
Czech (11)	21	0.15
Czechoslovakian (12)	12	0.08
Danish (0)	40	0.28
Dutch (34)	270	1.87

*Notes: † The Census 2010 population figure is used to calculate the percentages in the Hispanic Origin and Race categories. Ancestry percentages are based on the 2006-2010 American Community Survey population (not shown); ‡ Numbers in parentheses indicate the number of people reporting a single ancestry; * Numbers in parentheses indicate the number of persons reporting this race alone, not in combination with any other race; Please refer to the Explanation of Data for more information.*

Ancestry	Population	%
English (569)	1,953	13.51
European (146)	171	1.18
Finnish (12)	23	0.16
French, ex. Basque (103)	482	3.33
French Canadian (21)	75	0.52
German (2,196)	5,192	35.92
Greek (17)	38	0.26
Hungarian (0)	13	0.09
Irish (900)	2,575	17.81
Italian (409)	763	5.28
Lithuanian (133)	198	1.37
Norwegian (117)	218	1.51
Pennsylvania German (26)	26	0.18
Polish (133)	387	2.68
Romanian (0)	10	0.07
Russian (52)	63	0.44
Scandinavian (32)	62	0.43
Scotch-Irish (67)	245	1.69
Scottish (78)	292	2.02
Slavic (0)	10	0.07
Slovak (0)	8	0.06
Slovene (0)	7	0.05
Swedish (82)	306	2.12
Swiss (15)	90	0.62
Ukrainian (12)	12	0.08
Welsh (48)	131	0.91
Yugoslavian (32)	46	0.32

Hispanic Origin	Population	%
Hispanic or Latino (of any race)	248	1.64
Central American, ex. Mexican	13	0.09
Guatemalan	4	0.03
Honduran	1	0.01
Nicaraguan	1	0.01
Panamanian	6	0.04
Salvadoran	1	0.01
Cuban	9	0.06
Mexican	174	1.15
Puerto Rican	10	0.07
South American	12	0.08
Chilean	1	0.01
Colombian	5	0.03
Ecuadorian	1	0.01
Peruvian	1	0.01
Uruguayan	1	0.01
Other South American	3	0.02
Other Hispanic or Latino	30	0.20

Race*	Population	%
African-American/Black (78)	163	1.08
Not Hispanic (76)	156	1.03
Hispanic (2)	7	0.05
American Indian/Alaska Native (19)	57	0.38
Not Hispanic (19)	56	0.37
Hispanic (0)	1	0.01
Alaska Athabascan *(Ala. Nat.)* (1)	1	0.01
Blackfeet (0)	2	0.01
Central American Ind. (0)	1	0.01
Cherokee (11)	19	0.13
Choctaw (0)	1	0.01
Comanche (1)	1	0.01
Iroquois (0)	1	0.01
Sioux (1)	5	0.03
Asian (153)	216	1.43
Not Hispanic (152)	213	1.41
Hispanic (1)	3	0.02
Cambodian (1)	3	0.02
Chinese, ex. Taiwanese (37)	46	0.30
Filipino (14)	31	0.20
Indian (22)	35	0.23
Japanese (9)	25	0.17
Korean (39)	45	0.30
Laotian (1)	1	0.01
Thai (0)	2	0.01
Vietnamese (15)	23	0.15
Hawaii Native/Pacific Islander (7)	14	0.09
Not Hispanic (6)	13	0.09
Hispanic (1)	1	0.01
Guamanian/Chamorro (1)	1	0.01
Native Hawaiian (0)	7	0.05
Samoan (3)	3	0.02
Tongan (1)	1	0.01
White (14,627)	14,806	97.83
Not Hispanic (14,436)	14,607	96.52
Hispanic (191)	199	1.31

Waterloo

Place Type: City
County: Monroe
Population: 9,811†

Ancestry‡	Population	%
African, Sub-Saharan (0)	14	0.15
African (0)	14	0.15
American (823)	823	8.54
Austrian (0)	11	0.11
Croatian (0)	12	0.12
Czech (0)	65	0.67
Czechoslovakian (0)	43	0.45
Danish (8)	8	0.08
Dutch (18)	226	2.34
Eastern European (9)	9	0.09
English (414)	1,085	11.26
European (157)	157	1.63
French, ex. Basque (61)	893	9.26
French Canadian (12)	22	0.23
German (2,696)	4,732	49.09
Irish (266)	1,377	14.28
Italian (163)	352	3.65
Lithuanian (12)	51	0.53
Norwegian (0)	11	0.11
Polish (80)	289	3.00
Portuguese (0)	3	0.03
Romanian (0)	19	0.20
Russian (23)	23	0.24
Scotch-Irish (41)	93	0.96
Scottish (8)	125	1.30
Serbian (0)	42	0.44
Swedish (15)	15	0.16
Swiss (14)	14	0.15
Ukrainian (8)	52	0.54
Welsh (0)	28	0.29

Hispanic Origin	Population	%
Hispanic or Latino (of any race)	149	1.52
Central American, ex. Mexican	1	0.01
Guatemalan	1	0.01
Cuban	2	0.02
Mexican	97	0.99
Puerto Rican	5	0.05
South American	7	0.07
Colombian	2	0.02
Venezuelan	5	0.05
Other Hispanic or Latino	37	0.38

Race*	Population	%
African-American/Black (13)	34	0.35
Not Hispanic (13)	33	0.34
Hispanic (0)	1	0.01
American Indian/Alaska Native (35)	73	0.74
Not Hispanic (29)	66	0.67
Hispanic (6)	7	0.07
Blackfeet (3)	9	0.09
Cherokee (13)	36	0.37
Choctaw (1)	2	0.02
Cree (0)	2	0.02
Lumbee (1)	1	0.01
Mexican American Ind. (3)	3	0.03
Asian (33)	56	0.57
Not Hispanic (33)	56	0.57
Chinese, ex. Taiwanese (11)	15	0.15
Filipino (5)	12	0.12
Indian (5)	7	0.07
Indonesian (1)	2	0.02
Japanese (1)	8	0.08
Korean (4)	7	0.07
Thai (1)	3	0.03
Vietnamese (2)	2	0.02
Hawaii Native/Pacific Islander (6)	11	0.11
Not Hispanic (6)	11	0.11
Native Hawaiian (0)	4	0.04
White (9,609)	9,695	98.82
Not Hispanic (9,498)	9,579	97.64
Hispanic (111)	116	1.18

Wauconda

Place Type: Village
County: Lake
Population: 13,603†

Ancestry‡	Population	%
American (637)	637	4.90
Arab (62)	112	0.86
Egyptian (6)	20	0.15
Lebanese (0)	36	0.28
Moroccan (18)	18	0.14
Palestinian (38)	38	0.29
Armenian (8)	32	0.25
Assyrian/Chaldean/Syriac (0)	17	0.13
Austrian (13)	102	0.78
Belgian (0)	124	0.95
British (0)	16	0.12
Canadian (12)	12	0.09
Croatian (0)	47	0.36
Czech (178)	240	1.84
Czechoslovakian (14)	29	0.22
Danish (6)	65	0.50
Dutch (19)	184	1.41
Eastern European (18)	18	0.14
English (142)	772	5.93
European (205)	212	1.63
Finnish (0)	23	0.18
French, ex. Basque (0)	229	1.76
French Canadian (17)	110	0.85
German (884)	3,319	25.51
Greek (35)	57	0.44
Hungarian (23)	167	1.28
Irish (458)	2,077	15.97
Israeli (34)	34	0.26
Italian (516)	1,344	10.33
Lithuanian (12)	124	0.95
Norwegian (50)	450	3.46
Polish (462)	1,474	11.33
Portuguese (7)	16	0.12
Romanian (20)	44	0.34
Russian (69)	128	0.98
Scandinavian (51)	68	0.52
Scotch-Irish (96)	151	1.16
Scottish (59)	218	1.68
Serbian (0)	40	0.31
Slovak (0)	68	0.52
Slovene (33)	104	0.80
Swedish (115)	551	4.24
Swiss (0)	69	0.53
Ukrainian (97)	103	0.79
Welsh (0)	49	0.38
Yugoslavian (18)	18	0.14

Hispanic Origin	Population	%
Hispanic or Latino (of any race)	2,424	17.82
Central American, ex. Mexican	64	0.47
Costa Rican	3	0.02
Guatemalan	29	0.21
Honduran	2	0.01
Nicaraguan	8	0.06
Salvadoran	19	0.14
Other Central American	3	0.02
Cuban	12	0.09
Dominican Republic	2	0.01
Mexican	2,113	15.53
Puerto Rican	91	0.67
South American	51	0.37
Argentinean	3	0.02
Bolivian	2	0.01
Colombian	18	0.13
Ecuadorian	11	0.08
Peruvian	15	0.11
Venezuelan	1	0.01

*Notes: † The Census 2010 population figure is used to calculate the percentages in the Hispanic Origin and Race categories. Ancestry percentages are based on the 2006-2010 American Community Survey population (not shown); ‡ Numbers in parentheses indicate the number of people reporting a single ancestry; * Numbers in parentheses indicate the number of persons reporting this race alone, not in combination with any other race; Please refer to the Explanation of Data for more information.*

Other South American	1	0.01
Other Hispanic or Latino	91	0.67

Race*	Population	%
African-American/Black (121)	164	1.21
Not Hispanic (107)	137	1.01
Hispanic (14)	27	0.20
American Indian/Alaska Native (19)	50	0.37
Not Hispanic (9)	25	0.18
Hispanic (10)	25	0.18
Blackfeet (1)	1	0.01
Cherokee (1)	5	0.04
Cheyenne (0)	1	0.01
Chickasaw (0)	1	0.01
Chippewa (2)	4	0.03
Mexican American Ind. (5)	5	0.04
Navajo (2)	2	0.01
South American Ind. (0)	3	0.02
Spanish American Ind. (0)	1	0.01
Tohono O'Odham (1)	1	0.01
Asian (574)	699	5.14
Not Hispanic (564)	678	4.98
Hispanic (10)	21	0.15
Burmese (2)	2	0.01
Cambodian (1)	1	0.01
Chinese, ex. Taiwanese (65)	86	0.63
Filipino (186)	238	1.75
Indian (181)	205	1.51
Indonesian (4)	5	0.04
Japanese (15)	28	0.21
Korean (56)	67	0.49
Laotian (0)	1	0.01
Pakistani (14)	18	0.13
Taiwanese (1)	1	0.01
Thai (5)	9	0.07
Vietnamese (29)	33	0.24
Hawaii Native/Pacific Islander (8)	14	0.10
Not Hispanic (2)	7	0.05
Hispanic (6)	7	0.05
Guamanian/Chamorro (6)	7	0.05
Native Hawaiian (2)	2	0.01
Samoan (0)	1	0.01
White (11,559)	11,782	86.61
Not Hispanic (10,317)	10,452	76.84
Hispanic (1,242)	1,330	9.78

Waukegan

Place Type: City
County: Lake
Population: 89,078†

Ancestry‡	Population	%
African, Sub-Saharan (507)	574	0.64
African (481)	548	0.61
Ghanaian (16)	16	0.02
South African (10)	10	0.01
American (920)	920	1.03
Arab (58)	58	0.06
Arab (31)	31	0.03
Moroccan (27)	27	0.03
Armenian (105)	172	0.19
Austrian (0)	103	0.12
Belgian (39)	219	0.25
British (27)	97	0.11
Bulgarian (20)	27	0.03
Canadian (0)	13	0.01
Celtic (0)	17	0.02
Croatian (66)	253	0.28
Czech (28)	204	0.23
Czechoslovakian (18)	29	0.03
Danish (78)	264	0.30
Dutch (84)	511	0.57
Eastern European (46)	77	0.09
English (538)	2,197	2.46
European (290)	395	0.44
Finnish (272)	886	0.99
French, ex. Basque (76)	813	0.91
French Canadian (5)	108	0.12
German (1,543)	6,744	7.55
Greek (157)	340	0.38
Hungarian (30)	62	0.07
Icelander (14)	23	0.03
Iranian (0)	33	0.04
Irish (873)	4,124	4.61
Italian (851)	2,273	2.54
Lithuanian (135)	436	0.49
Luxemburger (0)	31	0.03
Macedonian (40)	49	0.05
Norwegian (168)	855	0.96
Pennsylvania German (0)	10	0.01
Polish (841)	2,391	2.68
Romanian (143)	150	0.17
Russian (42)	125	0.14
Scandinavian (13)	49	0.05
Scotch-Irish (234)	507	0.57
Scottish (102)	631	0.71
Serbian (225)	225	0.25
Slavic (30)	73	0.08
Slovak (67)	117	0.13
Slovene (61)	304	0.34
Swedish (315)	1,267	1.42
Swiss (9)	103	0.12
Turkish (58)	58	0.06
Ukrainian (77)	206	0.23
Welsh (0)	144	0.16
West Indian, ex. Hispanic (887)	1,126	1.26
Belizean (475)	536	0.60
Haitian (43)	43	0.05
Jamaican (351)	529	0.59
West Indian (18)	18	0.02
Yugoslavian (21)	98	0.11

Hispanic Origin	Population	%
Hispanic or Latino (of any race)	47,612	53.45
Central American, ex. Mexican	3,653	4.10
Costa Rican	3	<0.01
Guatemalan	340	0.38
Honduran	2,311	2.59
Nicaraguan	39	0.04
Panamanian	29	0.03
Salvadoran	887	1.00
Other Central American	44	0.05
Cuban	136	0.15
Dominican Republic	103	0.12
Mexican	38,636	43.37
Puerto Rican	2,918	3.28
South American	546	0.61
Argentinean	8	0.01
Bolivian	12	0.01
Chilean	21	0.02
Colombian	358	0.40
Ecuadorian	76	0.09
Paraguayan	5	0.01
Peruvian	44	0.05
Uruguayan	5	0.01
Venezuelan	16	0.02
Other South American	1	<0.01
Other Hispanic or Latino	1,620	1.82

Race*	Population	%
African-American/Black (17,081)	18,333	20.58
Not Hispanic (16,240)	17,078	19.17
Hispanic (841)	1,255	1.41
American Indian/Alaska Native (1,042)	1,628	1.83
Not Hispanic (173)	470	0.53
Hispanic (869)	1,158	1.30
Apache (12)	21	0.02
Arapaho (0)	1	<0.01
Blackfeet (8)	32	0.04
Canadian/French Am. Ind. (0)	1	<0.01
Central American Ind. (10)	23	0.03
Cherokee (19)	130	0.15
Cheyenne (0)	1	<0.01
Chippewa (21)	37	0.04
Choctaw (5)	20	0.02
Comanche (0)	4	<0.01
Creek (0)	4	<0.01
Hopi (1)	1	<0.01
Iroquois (1)	5	0.01
Kiowa (0)	1	<0.01
Lumbee (1)	1	<0.01
Menominee (0)	1	<0.01
Mexican American Ind. (154)	192	0.22
Navajo (7)	16	0.02
Potawatomi (0)	3	<0.01
Pueblo (3)	3	<0.01
Seminole (0)	2	<0.01
Sioux (1)	3	<0.01
South American Ind. (17)	32	0.04
Spanish American Ind. (29)	36	0.04
Tlingit-Haida *(Alaska Native)* (0)	1	<0.01
Tohono O'Odham (2)	2	<0.01
Ute (2)	2	<0.01
Yakama (1)	1	<0.01
Yaqui (5)	7	0.01
Asian (3,825)	4,401	4.94
Not Hispanic (3,722)	4,123	4.63
Hispanic (103)	278	0.31
Bangladeshi (3)	3	<0.01
Burmese (1)	1	<0.01
Cambodian (36)	50	0.06
Chinese, ex. Taiwanese (247)	310	0.35
Filipino (1,958)	2,230	2.50
Hmong (10)	11	0.01
Indian (1,084)	1,184	1.33
Indonesian (7)	11	0.01
Japanese (38)	84	0.09
Korean (157)	220	0.25
Laotian (10)	11	0.01
Malaysian (1)	5	0.01
Nepalese (9)	9	0.01
Pakistani (78)	93	0.10
Sri Lankan (3)	6	0.01
Taiwanese (21)	21	0.02
Thai (24)	41	0.05
Vietnamese (54)	72	0.08
Hawaii Native/Pacific Islander (52)	156	0.18
Not Hispanic (26)	82	0.09
Hispanic (26)	74	0.08
Guamanian/Chamorro (28)	35	0.04
Native Hawaiian (4)	35	0.04
Samoan (2)	3	<0.01
Tongan (1)	2	<0.01
White (41,552)	44,475	49.93
Not Hispanic (19,370)	20,407	22.91
Hispanic (22,182)	24,068	27.02

West Chicago

Place Type: City
County: DuPage
Population: 27,086†

Ancestry‡	Population	%
American (440)	440	1.67
Arab (369)	465	1.76
Arab (0)	29	0.11
Iraqi (91)	91	0.35
Lebanese (191)	258	0.98
Palestinian (28)	28	0.11
Other Arab (59)	59	0.22
Armenian (9)	9	0.03
Austrian (12)	56	0.21
Belgian (13)	41	0.16
British (19)	73	0.28
Canadian (4)	4	0.02
Croatian (0)	20	0.08
Czech (205)	587	2.23
Czechoslovakian (11)	36	0.14
Danish (0)	85	0.32
Dutch (62)	309	1.17
English (181)	1,086	4.12
European (140)	175	0.66
Finnish (0)	10	0.04
French, ex. Basque (0)	294	1.12
French Canadian (0)	14	0.05
German (807)	3,532	13.41
Greek (82)	236	0.90
Hungarian (0)	142	0.54

*Notes: † The Census 2010 population figure is used to calculate the percentages in the Hispanic Origin and Race categories. Ancestry percentages are based on the 2006-2010 American Community Survey population (not shown); ‡ Numbers in parentheses indicate the number of people reporting a single ancestry; * Numbers in parentheses indicate the number of persons reporting this race alone, not in combination with any other race; Please refer to the Explanation of Data for more information.*

Icelander (11)	11	0.04
Irish (314)	1,868	7.09
Italian (480)	1,568	5.95
Latvian (17)	17	0.06
Lithuanian (55)	152	0.58
Luxemburger (4)	4	0.02
Northern European (26)	26	0.10
Norwegian (76)	387	1.47
Polish (600)	1,755	6.66
Romanian (19)	28	0.11
Russian (163)	176	0.67
Scandinavian (11)	139	0.53
Scotch-Irish (53)	262	0.99
Scottish (118)	382	1.45
Slovene (12)	12	0.05
Swedish (64)	458	1.74
Swiss (0)	106	0.40
Ukrainian (21)	29	0.11
Welsh (0)	107	0.41
Yugoslavian (0)	14	0.05

Hispanic Origin	Population	%
Hispanic or Latino (of any race)	13,837	51.09
Central American, ex. Mexican	103	0.38
Costa Rican	2	0.01
Guatemalan	47	0.17
Honduran	14	0.05
Nicaraguan	4	0.01
Panamanian	10	0.04
Salvadoran	22	0.08
Other Central American	4	0.01
Cuban	182	0.67
Dominican Republic	8	0.03
Mexican	12,797	47.25
Puerto Rican	186	0.69
South American	98	0.36
Argentinean	9	0.03
Bolivian	15	0.06
Chilean	1	<0.01
Colombian	13	0.05
Ecuadorian	30	0.11
Peruvian	14	0.05
Uruguayan	2	0.01
Venezuelan	10	0.04
Other South American	4	0.01
Other Hispanic or Latino	463	1.71

Race*	Population	%
African-American/Black (684)	827	3.05
Not Hispanic (580)	651	2.40
Hispanic (104)	176	0.65
American Indian/Alaska Native (157)	252	0.93
Not Hispanic (31)	90	0.33
Hispanic (126)	162	0.60
Apache (1)	7	0.03
Blackfeet (3)	4	0.01
Cherokee (2)	32	0.12
Chickasaw (1)	1	<0.01
Chippewa (2)	2	0.01
Choctaw (8)	8	0.03
Comanche (0)	1	<0.01
Cree (0)	1	<0.01
Creek (2)	2	0.01
Iroquois (1)	1	<0.01
Menominee (0)	3	0.01
Mexican American Ind. (20)	22	0.08
Osage (0)	3	0.01
Sioux (3)	5	0.02
South American Ind. (0)	2	0.01
Spanish American Ind. (4)	6	0.02
Asian (1,597)	1,763	6.51
Not Hispanic (1,584)	1,726	6.37
Hispanic (13)	37	0.14
Burmese (3)	4	0.01
Cambodian (36)	37	0.14
Chinese, ex. Taiwanese (46)	62	0.23
Filipino (449)	503	1.86
Indian (696)	764	2.82
Indonesian (0)	1	<0.01
Japanese (7)	18	0.07
Korean (66)	85	0.31
Laotian (7)	9	0.03
Malaysian (0)	2	0.01
Nepalese (3)	4	0.01
Pakistani (80)	88	0.32
Thai (1)	4	0.01
Vietnamese (145)	155	0.57
Hawaii Native/Pacific Islander (14)	23	0.08
Not Hispanic (11)	17	0.06
Hispanic (3)	6	0.02
Guamanian/Chamorro (3)	4	0.01
Marshallese (2)	2	0.01
Native Hawaiian (0)	3	0.01
White (18,307)	18,937	69.91
Not Hispanic (10,770)	10,987	40.56
Hispanic (7,537)	7,950	29.35

West Frankfort

Place Type: City
County: Franklin
Population: 8,182†

Ancestry‡	Population	%
American (940)	940	10.80
Austrian (0)	35	0.40
British (12)	31	0.36
Bulgarian (10)	10	0.11
Croatian (0)	32	0.37
Czech (0)	9	0.10
Czechoslovakian (14)	14	0.16
Dutch (56)	297	3.41
English (870)	1,510	17.36
European (78)	78	0.90
French, ex. Basque (10)	153	1.76
French Canadian (62)	62	0.71
German (440)	1,585	18.22
Greek (0)	132	1.52
Irish (548)	1,575	18.10
Italian (246)	320	3.68
Lithuanian (65)	102	1.17
Norwegian (34)	34	0.39
Polish (161)	411	4.72
Russian (0)	9	0.10
Scotch-Irish (332)	467	5.37
Scottish (88)	232	2.67
Slovak (10)	44	0.51
Slovene (13)	39	0.45
Swedish (0)	38	0.44
Swiss (0)	10	0.11
Ukrainian (10)	10	0.11
Welsh (0)	56	0.64
Yugoslavian (0)	11	0.13

Hispanic Origin	Population	%
Hispanic or Latino (of any race)	137	1.67
Central American, ex. Mexican	7	0.09
Costa Rican	2	0.02
Guatemalan	2	0.02
Honduran	1	0.01
Panamanian	1	0.01
Salvadoran	1	0.01
Cuban	4	0.05
Dominican Republic	5	0.06
Mexican	93	1.14
Puerto Rican	9	0.11
South American	2	0.02
Colombian	2	0.02
Other Hispanic or Latino	17	0.21

Race*	Population	%
African-American/Black (33)	56	0.68
Not Hispanic (33)	54	0.66
Hispanic (0)	2	0.02
American Indian/Alaska Native (24)	71	0.87
Not Hispanic (24)	65	0.79
Hispanic (0)	6	0.07
Apache (2)	4	0.05
Blackfeet (0)	3	0.04
Cherokee (6)	26	0.32
Chippewa (0)	1	0.01
Choctaw (1)	1	0.01
Iroquois (1)	1	0.01
Menominee (3)	3	0.04
Navajo (0)	1	0.01
Potawatomi (1)	3	0.04
Sioux (4)	5	0.06
Asian (53)	65	0.79
Not Hispanic (53)	65	0.79
Bangladeshi (1)	1	0.01
Chinese, ex. Taiwanese (17)	20	0.24
Filipino (15)	23	0.28
Indian (13)	15	0.18
Japanese (1)	2	0.02
Korean (3)	5	0.06
Thai (2)	2	0.02
Hawaii Native/Pacific Islander (2)	4	0.05
Not Hispanic (2)	4	0.05
Guamanian/Chamorro (0)	1	0.01
Native Hawaiian (2)	3	0.04
White (7,950)	8,035	98.20
Not Hispanic (7,853)	7,926	96.87
Hispanic (97)	109	1.33

Westchester

Place Type: Village
County: Cook
Population: 16,718†

Ancestry‡	Population	%
African, Sub-Saharan (97)	117	0.71
African (66)	66	0.40
Nigerian (31)	51	0.31
American (247)	247	1.49
Arab (59)	59	0.36
Other Arab (59)	59	0.36
Armenian (0)	27	0.16
Austrian (10)	89	0.54
British (16)	26	0.16
Canadian (6)	18	0.11
Croatian (46)	128	0.77
Czech (342)	836	5.05
Czechoslovakian (122)	213	1.29
Danish (24)	166	1.00
Dutch (38)	245	1.48
English (121)	709	4.29
European (51)	85	0.51
Finnish (0)	37	0.22
French, ex. Basque (11)	254	1.54
French Canadian (0)	51	0.31
German (529)	2,270	13.72
Greek (239)	365	2.21
Hungarian (28)	52	0.31
Irish (833)	2,292	13.86
Italian (1,327)	2,457	14.85
Lithuanian (61)	148	0.89
Norwegian (48)	169	1.02
Polish (946)	2,202	13.31
Romanian (13)	13	0.08
Russian (23)	54	0.33
Scandinavian (20)	31	0.19
Scotch-Irish (19)	175	1.06
Scottish (42)	166	1.00
Serbian (35)	58	0.35
Slovak (45)	114	0.69
Slovene (17)	17	0.10
Swedish (62)	353	2.13
Swiss (0)	12	0.07
Ukrainian (40)	161	0.97
West Indian, ex. Hispanic (22)	22	0.13
Jamaican (22)	22	0.13
Yugoslavian (14)	39	0.24

Hispanic Origin	Population	%
Hispanic or Latino (of any race)	2,485	14.86
Central American, ex. Mexican	91	0.54
Guatemalan	62	0.37
Honduran	14	0.08
Nicaraguan	2	0.01

*Notes: † The Census 2010 population figure is used to calculate the percentages in the Hispanic Origin and Race categories. Ancestry percentages are based on the 2006-2010 American Community Survey population (not shown); ‡ Numbers in parentheses indicate the number of people reporting a single ancestry; * Numbers in parentheses indicate the number of persons reporting this race alone, not in combination with any other race; Please refer to the Explanation of Data for more information.*

Panamanian	1	0.01
Salvadoran	12	0.07
Cuban	41	0.25
Dominican Republic	6	0.04
Mexican	1,879	11.24
Puerto Rican	273	1.63
South American	136	0.81
Argentinean	11	0.07
Bolivian	1	0.01
Chilean	7	0.04
Colombian	60	0.36
Ecuadorian	36	0.22
Peruvian	13	0.08
Uruguayan	1	0.01
Venezuelan	3	0.02
Other South American	4	0.02
Other Hispanic or Latino	59	0.35

Race*	Population	%
African-American/Black (2,389)	2,484	14.86
Not Hispanic (2,349)	2,429	14.53
Hispanic (40)	55	0.33
American Indian/Alaska Native (44)	107	0.64
Not Hispanic (21)	61	0.36
Hispanic (23)	46	0.28
Apache (0)	1	0.01
Blackfeet (0)	1	0.01
Cherokee (1)	5	0.03
Chickasaw (0)	4	0.02
Chippewa (0)	5	0.03
Iroquois (0)	2	0.01
Menominee (0)	2	0.01
Mexican American Ind. (1)	4	0.02
Navajo (3)	5	0.03
Pueblo (3)	7	0.04
Sioux (0)	4	0.02
Asian (664)	744	4.45
Not Hispanic (659)	726	4.34
Hispanic (5)	18	0.11
Bangladeshi (0)	1	0.01
Cambodian (1)	1	0.01
Chinese, ex. Taiwanese (74)	88	0.53
Filipino (339)	382	2.28
Indian (94)	112	0.67
Indonesian (5)	6	0.04
Japanese (13)	25	0.15
Korean (28)	33	0.20
Laotian (1)	3	0.02
Pakistani (23)	26	0.16
Sri Lankan (2)	2	0.01
Taiwanese (4)	4	0.02
Thai (22)	22	0.13
Vietnamese (30)	33	0.20
Hawaii Native/Pacific Islander (6)	15	0.09
Not Hispanic (1)	4	0.02
Hispanic (5)	11	0.07
Guamanian/Chamorro (2)	2	0.01
Native Hawaiian (4)	6	0.04
White (12,434)	12,691	75.91
Not Hispanic (11,018)	11,174	66.84
Hispanic (1,416)	1,517	9.07

Western Springs

Place Type: Village
County: Cook
Population: 12,975†

Ancestry‡	Population	%
American (250)	250	1.98
Arab (30)	369	2.92
Arab (9)	54	0.43
Egyptian (0)	39	0.31
Jordanian (21)	21	0.17
Lebanese (0)	251	1.98
Other Arab (0)	4	0.03
Armenian (0)	21	0.17
Australian (0)	8	0.06
Austrian (30)	136	1.07
Belgian (0)	20	0.16
British (16)	47	0.37
Canadian (75)	75	0.59
Croatian (11)	75	0.59
Czech (161)	450	3.56
Czechoslovakian (34)	83	0.66
Danish (29)	71	0.56
Dutch (79)	254	2.01
Eastern European (21)	21	0.17
English (291)	1,636	12.93
European (263)	281	2.22
French, ex. Basque (20)	286	2.26
French Canadian (38)	73	0.58
German (887)	3,702	29.25
Greek (24)	260	2.05
Hungarian (19)	67	0.53
Iranian (14)	57	0.45
Irish (1,097)	3,953	31.23
Italian (489)	1,823	14.40
Latvian (52)	74	0.58
Lithuanian (32)	113	0.89
Luxemburger (0)	19	0.15
Norwegian (76)	262	2.07
Polish (516)	1,318	10.41
Romanian (0)	20	0.16
Russian (36)	139	1.10
Scandinavian (0)	12	0.09
Scotch-Irish (101)	274	2.16
Scottish (66)	329	2.60
Slavic (21)	41	0.32
Slovak (60)	143	1.13
Swedish (150)	617	4.87
Swiss (0)	39	0.31
Ukrainian (36)	89	0.70
Welsh (0)	39	0.31

Hispanic Origin	Population	%
Hispanic or Latino (of any race)	361	2.78
Central American, ex. Mexican	24	0.18
Costa Rican	3	0.02
Guatemalan	17	0.13
Honduran	3	0.02
Panamanian	1	0.01
Cuban	34	0.26
Dominican Republic	6	0.05
Mexican	191	1.47
Puerto Rican	36	0.28
South American	38	0.29
Argentinean	3	0.02
Chilean	3	0.02
Colombian	17	0.13
Ecuadorian	8	0.06
Paraguayan	1	0.01
Peruvian	5	0.04
Venezuelan	1	0.01
Other Hispanic or Latino	32	0.25

Race*	Population	%
African-American/Black (46)	71	0.55
Not Hispanic (43)	63	0.49
Hispanic (3)	8	0.06
American Indian/Alaska Native (11)	28	0.22
Not Hispanic (5)	17	0.13
Hispanic (6)	11	0.08
Blackfeet (0)	3	0.02
Chippewa (0)	1	0.01
Mexican American Ind. (2)	3	0.02
Navajo (1)	2	0.02
Sioux (0)	1	0.01
Asian (180)	246	1.90
Not Hispanic (179)	231	1.78
Hispanic (1)	15	0.12
Bangladeshi (3)	3	0.02
Cambodian (3)	4	0.03
Chinese, ex. Taiwanese (54)	67	0.52
Filipino (34)	58	0.45
Indian (29)	41	0.32
Japanese (7)	21	0.16
Korean (22)	31	0.24
Laotian (0)	1	0.01
Pakistani (6)	6	0.05
Taiwanese (5)	5	0.04
Thai (4)	6	0.05
Vietnamese (5)	11	0.08
Hawaii Native/Pacific Islander (1)	9	0.07
Not Hispanic (1)	7	0.05
Hispanic (0)	2	0.02
Native Hawaiian (0)	5	0.04
White (12,554)	12,658	97.56
Not Hispanic (12,294)	12,376	95.38
Hispanic (260)	282	2.17

Westmont

Place Type: Village
County: DuPage
Population: 24,685†

Ancestry‡	Population	%
African, Sub-Saharan (73)	110	0.45
African (73)	73	0.30
Nigerian (0)	37	0.15
Albanian (0)	8	0.03
American (433)	433	1.77
Arab (464)	532	2.17
Arab (231)	246	1.00
Egyptian (160)	160	0.65
Lebanese (52)	87	0.36
Palestinian (0)	3	0.01
Other Arab (21)	36	0.15
Armenian (47)	47	0.19
Austrian (38)	137	0.56
Belgian (12)	12	0.05
British (15)	54	0.22
Bulgarian (30)	57	0.23
Canadian (0)	21	0.09
Croatian (143)	284	1.16
Czech (440)	1,135	4.63
Czechoslovakian (113)	159	0.65
Danish (28)	168	0.69
Dutch (159)	485	1.98
Eastern European (17)	31	0.13
English (192)	1,105	4.51
Estonian (0)	15	0.06
European (196)	196	0.80
French, ex. Basque (60)	335	1.37
French Canadian (0)	41	0.17
German (1,299)	4,555	18.60
Greek (220)	403	1.65
Hungarian (0)	345	1.41
Iranian (56)	56	0.23
Irish (646)	3,228	13.18
Italian (836)	1,988	8.12
Latvian (11)	11	0.04
Lithuanian (282)	463	1.89
Luxemburger (0)	23	0.09
Norwegian (92)	327	1.34
Pennsylvania German (0)	16	0.07
Polish (1,513)	3,312	13.52
Romanian (37)	234	0.96
Russian (83)	312	1.27
Scandinavian (0)	12	0.05
Scotch-Irish (23)	129	0.53
Scottish (57)	286	1.17
Serbian (43)	70	0.29
Slovak (60)	240	0.98
Slovene (0)	19	0.08
Swedish (97)	578	2.36
Swiss (0)	17	0.07
Ukrainian (11)	49	0.20
Welsh (0)	40	0.16
West Indian, ex. Hispanic (87)	87	0.36
Belizean (72)	72	0.29
West Indian (15)	15	0.06
Yugoslavian (107)	151	0.62

Hispanic Origin	Population	%
Hispanic or Latino (of any race)	2,757	11.17
Central American, ex. Mexican	75	0.30
Costa Rican	2	0.01
Guatemalan	41	0.17

*Notes: † The Census 2010 population figure is used to calculate the percentages in the Hispanic Origin and Race categories. Ancestry percentages are based on the 2006-2010 American Community Survey population (not shown); ‡ Numbers in parentheses indicate the number of people reporting a single ancestry; * Numbers in parentheses indicate the number of persons reporting this race alone, not in combination with any other race; Please refer to the Explanation of Data for more information.*

Honduran	1	<0.01
Nicaraguan	14	0.06
Panamanian	2	0.01
Salvadoran	15	0.06
Cuban	37	0.15
Dominican Republic	9	0.04
Mexican	2,246	9.10
Puerto Rican	146	0.59
South American	91	0.37
Argentinean	14	0.06
Bolivian	17	0.07
Chilean	3	0.01
Colombian	26	0.11
Ecuadorian	19	0.08
Peruvian	10	0.04
Uruguayan	1	<0.01
Venezuelan	1	<0.01
Other Hispanic or Latino	153	0.62

Race*	Population	%
African-American/Black (2,140)	2,311	9.36
Not Hispanic (2,107)	2,243	9.09
Hispanic (33)	68	0.28
American Indian/Alaska Native (83)	197	0.80
Not Hispanic (37)	124	0.50
Hispanic (46)	73	0.30
Apache (2)	2	0.01
Blackfeet (1)	5	0.02
Canadian/French Am. Ind. (0)	1	<0.01
Central American Ind. (0)	3	0.01
Cherokee (5)	20	0.08
Chippewa (1)	10	0.04
Choctaw (4)	6	0.02
Comanche (0)	1	<0.01
Creek (0)	1	<0.01
Iroquois (0)	1	<0.01
Mexican American Ind. (16)	25	0.10
Navajo (0)	3	0.01
Osage (1)	2	0.01
Potawatomi (1)	2	0.01
Sioux (1)	3	0.01
Asian (3,089)	3,343	13.54
Not Hispanic (3,068)	3,301	13.37
Hispanic (21)	42	0.17
Burmese (10)	13	0.05
Cambodian (2)	2	0.01
Chinese, ex. Taiwanese (682)	737	2.99
Filipino (586)	667	2.70
Indian (1,312)	1,360	5.51
Indonesian (5)	5	0.02
Japanese (26)	40	0.16
Korean (110)	127	0.51
Laotian (6)	10	0.04
Malaysian (2)	4	0.02
Nepalese (8)	8	0.03
Pakistani (112)	126	0.51
Sri Lankan (10)	10	0.04
Taiwanese (89)	108	0.44
Thai (25)	35	0.14
Vietnamese (35)	37	0.15
Hawaii Native/Pacific Islander (6)	29	0.12
Not Hispanic (6)	23	0.09
Hispanic (0)	6	0.02
Guamanian/Chamorro (0)	1	<0.01
Native Hawaiian (0)	4	0.02
White (17,937)	18,393	74.51
Not Hispanic (16,274)	16,583	67.18
Hispanic (1,663)	1,810	7.33

Wheaton

Place Type: City
County: DuPage
Population: 52,894†

Ancestry‡	Population	%
African, Sub-Saharan (230)	239	0.45
African (21)	30	0.06
Kenyan (9)	9	0.02
Nigerian (30)	30	0.06
Somalian (134)	134	0.25
Sudanese (36)	36	0.07
Albanian (199)	212	0.40
American (1,206)	1,206	2.27
Arab (76)	199	0.37
Egyptian (14)	14	0.03
Lebanese (40)	155	0.29
Palestinian (9)	9	0.02
Syrian (0)	8	0.02
Other Arab (13)	13	0.02
Armenian (162)	224	0.42
Assyrian/Chaldean/Syriac (9)	50	0.09
Australian (0)	34	0.06
Austrian (107)	313	0.59
Belgian (102)	213	0.40
Brazilian (0)	11	0.02
British (319)	601	1.13
Canadian (35)	85	0.16
Croatian (49)	146	0.27
Czech (251)	791	1.49
Czechoslovakian (78)	172	0.32
Danish (82)	538	1.01
Dutch (327)	1,202	2.26
Eastern European (30)	30	0.06
English (1,317)	6,664	12.54
European (925)	1,145	2.15
Finnish (58)	145	0.27
French, ex. Basque (288)	1,566	2.95
French Canadian (37)	302	0.57
German (3,674)	14,873	27.99
Greek (272)	657	1.24
Guyanese (7)	7	0.01
Hungarian (50)	342	0.64
Icelander (0)	16	0.03
Irish (2,089)	9,656	18.17
Israeli (53)	53	0.10
Italian (1,902)	5,622	10.58
Latvian (0)	103	0.19
Lithuanian (344)	835	1.57
Luxemburger (0)	62	0.12
Macedonian (0)	12	0.02
Northern European (126)	135	0.25
Norwegian (331)	1,598	3.01
Polish (1,653)	5,226	9.83
Portuguese (0)	14	0.03
Romanian (94)	159	0.30
Russian (595)	986	1.86
Scandinavian (154)	330	0.62
Scotch-Irish (411)	1,284	2.42
Scottish (222)	1,270	2.39
Serbian (84)	163	0.31
Slavic (0)	43	0.08
Slovak (106)	306	0.58
Slovene (27)	47	0.09
Swedish (620)	2,653	4.99
Swiss (0)	322	0.61
Turkish (147)	147	0.28
Ukrainian (136)	338	0.64
Welsh (26)	378	0.71
West Indian, ex. Hispanic (36)	91	0.17
Belizean (0)	10	0.02
Haitian (14)	23	0.04
Jamaican (22)	58	0.11
Yugoslavian (219)	285	0.54

Hispanic Origin	Population	%
Hispanic or Latino (of any race)	2,617	4.95
Central American, ex. Mexican	150	0.28
Costa Rican	13	0.02
Guatemalan	71	0.13
Honduran	18	0.03
Nicaraguan	15	0.03
Panamanian	11	0.02
Salvadoran	21	0.04
Other Central American	1	<0.01
Cuban	149	0.28
Dominican Republic	11	0.02
Mexican	1,503	2.84
Puerto Rican	290	0.55
South American	358	0.68
Argentinean	42	0.08
Bolivian	40	0.08
Chilean	29	0.05
Colombian	129	0.24
Ecuadorian	47	0.09
Peruvian	39	0.07
Uruguayan	4	0.01
Venezuelan	28	0.05
Other Hispanic or Latino	156	0.29

Race*	Population	%
African-American/Black (2,357)	2,644	5.00
Not Hispanic (2,324)	2,565	4.85
Hispanic (33)	79	0.15
American Indian/Alaska Native (97)	268	0.51
Not Hispanic (55)	186	0.35
Hispanic (42)	82	0.16
Apache (0)	4	0.01
Blackfeet (1)	11	0.02
Canadian/French Am. Ind. (0)	7	0.01
Central American Ind. (1)	1	<0.01
Cherokee (4)	49	0.09
Chippewa (2)	17	0.03
Choctaw (1)	4	0.01
Comanche (0)	1	<0.01
Cree (1)	1	<0.01
Crow (1)	1	<0.01
Delaware (1)	1	<0.01
Hopi (0)	1	<0.01
Iroquois (4)	6	0.01
Mexican American Ind. (14)	21	0.04
Navajo (0)	2	<0.01
Pueblo (0)	1	<0.01
Shoshone (0)	2	<0.01
Sioux (2)	11	0.02
South American Ind. (2)	3	0.01
Spanish American Ind. (2)	2	<0.01
Yup'ik *(Alaska Native)* (1)	1	<0.01
Asian (2,721)	3,313	6.26
Not Hispanic (2,708)	3,267	6.18
Hispanic (13)	46	0.09
Bangladeshi (0)	3	0.01
Bhutanese (68)	68	0.13
Burmese (230)	245	0.46
Cambodian (33)	43	0.08
Chinese, ex. Taiwanese (398)	574	1.09
Filipino (302)	446	0.84
Hmong (8)	10	0.02
Indian (616)	715	1.35
Indonesian (6)	11	0.02
Japanese (73)	150	0.28
Korean (332)	393	0.74
Laotian (3)	3	0.01
Malaysian (3)	5	0.01
Nepalese (26)	27	0.05
Pakistani (154)	176	0.33
Sri Lankan (0)	1	<0.01
Taiwanese (48)	75	0.14
Thai (21)	33	0.06
Vietnamese (288)	327	0.62
Hawaii Native/Pacific Islander (13)	57	0.11
Not Hispanic (12)	51	0.10
Hispanic (1)	6	0.01
Guamanian/Chamorro (2)	2	<0.01
Native Hawaiian (3)	18	0.03
Samoan (2)	3	0.01
White (46,165)	47,131	89.10
Not Hispanic (44,232)	45,045	85.16
Hispanic (1,933)	2,086	3.94

Wheeling

Place Type: Village
County: Cook
Population: 37,648†

Ancestry‡	Population	%
African, Sub-Saharan (17)	17	0.05
African (17)	17	0.05
American (511)	511	1.38

*Notes: † The Census 2010 population figure is used to calculate the percentages in the Hispanic Origin and Race categories. Ancestry percentages are based on the 2006-2010 American Community Survey population (not shown); ‡ Numbers in parentheses indicate the number of people reporting a single ancestry; * Numbers in parentheses indicate the number of persons reporting this race alone, not in combination with any other race; Please refer to the Explanation of Data for more information.*

Arab (127)	163	0.44
Arab (69)	69	0.19
Syrian (17)	53	0.14
Other Arab (41)	41	0.11
Armenian (16)	36	0.10
Assyrian/Chaldean/Syriac (17)	17	0.05
Austrian (9)	65	0.18
Belgian (23)	103	0.28
British (18)	74	0.20
Bulgarian (351)	351	0.95
Canadian (12)	97	0.26
Croatian (17)	17	0.05
Czech (47)	255	0.69
Czechoslovakian (34)	46	0.12
Danish (0)	43	0.12
Dutch (70)	166	0.45
Eastern European (93)	93	0.25
English (183)	889	2.40
European (272)	272	0.73
Finnish (0)	28	0.08
French, ex. Basque (16)	217	0.59
French Canadian (0)	110	0.30
German (1,620)	5,437	14.68
Greek (165)	286	0.77
Hungarian (99)	257	0.69
Irish (517)	2,947	7.96
Israeli (13)	13	0.04
Italian (612)	1,493	4.03
Latvian (11)	21	0.06
Lithuanian (218)	435	1.17
Luxemburger (0)	18	0.05
Macedonian (14)	31	0.08
Norwegian (70)	150	0.41
Polish (2,472)	3,899	10.53
Portuguese (26)	39	0.11
Romanian (201)	235	0.63
Russian (2,107)	2,904	7.84
Scotch-Irish (48)	179	0.48
Scottish (45)	281	0.76
Serbian (108)	108	0.29
Slovak (43)	136	0.37
Swedish (132)	963	2.60
Swiss (20)	70	0.19
Ukrainian (534)	610	1.65
Welsh (0)	45	0.12
West Indian, ex. Hispanic (58)	58	0.16
Haitian (58)	58	0.16
Yugoslavian (49)	49	0.13

Hispanic Origin	Population	%
Hispanic or Latino (of any race)	11,758	31.23
Central American, ex. Mexican	329	0.87
Costa Rican	3	0.01
Guatemalan	121	0.32
Honduran	33	0.09
Nicaraguan	2	0.01
Panamanian	3	0.01
Salvadoran	167	0.44
Cuban	55	0.15
Dominican Republic	17	0.05
Mexican	10,517	27.94
Puerto Rican	254	0.67
South American	283	0.75
Argentinean	49	0.13
Bolivian	2	0.01
Chilean	9	0.02
Colombian	66	0.18
Ecuadorian	77	0.20
Paraguayan	2	0.01
Peruvian	52	0.14
Venezuelan	26	0.07
Other Hispanic or Latino	303	0.80

Race*	Population	%
African-American/Black (898)	1,039	2.76
Not Hispanic (806)	913	2.43
Hispanic (92)	126	0.33
American Indian/Alaska Native (291)	456	1.21
Not Hispanic (39)	141	0.37
Hispanic (252)	315	0.84
Apache (0)	1	<0.01
Blackfeet (0)	1	<0.01
Cherokee (6)	35	0.09
Chippewa (4)	6	0.02
Choctaw (1)	1	<0.01
Iroquois (1)	6	0.02
Lumbee (1)	1	<0.01
Mexican American Ind. (44)	49	0.13
Navajo (1)	2	0.01
Seminole (1)	1	<0.01
Sioux (3)	9	0.02
South American Ind. (4)	4	0.01
Asian (4,861)	5,181	13.76
Not Hispanic (4,826)	5,098	13.54
Hispanic (35)	83	0.22
Bangladeshi (23)	27	0.07
Burmese (22)	28	0.07
Cambodian (52)	71	0.19
Chinese, ex. Taiwanese (291)	360	0.96
Filipino (754)	850	2.26
Indian (2,287)	2,371	6.30
Indonesian (5)	6	0.02
Japanese (72)	99	0.26
Korean (945)	985	2.62
Laotian (7)	10	0.03
Malaysian (2)	2	0.01
Nepalese (3)	5	0.01
Pakistani (112)	125	0.33
Sri Lankan (5)	6	0.02
Taiwanese (16)	20	0.05
Thai (39)	52	0.14
Vietnamese (108)	117	0.31
Hawaii Native/Pacific Islander (5)	29	0.08
Not Hispanic (2)	18	0.05
Hispanic (3)	11	0.03
Guamanian/Chamorro (1)	3	0.01
Native Hawaiian (1)	8	0.02
Samoan (2)	5	0.01
Tongan (1)	2	0.01
White (25,220)	26,000	69.06
Not Hispanic (19,701)	20,063	53.29
Hispanic (5,519)	5,937	15.77

Willowbrook

Place Type: Village
County: DuPage
Population: 8,540†

Ancestry‡	Population	%
American (121)	121	1.42
Arab (155)	173	2.02
Arab (122)	122	1.43
Lebanese (0)	18	0.21
Other Arab (33)	33	0.39
Assyrian/Chaldean/Syriac (13)	13	0.15
Austrian (9)	42	0.49
Belgian (0)	14	0.16
Bulgarian (162)	162	1.90
Croatian (114)	218	2.55
Czech (175)	397	4.65
Czechoslovakian (14)	36	0.42
Danish (24)	46	0.54
Dutch (112)	165	1.93
English (86)	518	6.06
European (34)	34	0.40
Finnish (11)	25	0.29
French, ex. Basque (14)	221	2.59
French Canadian (0)	26	0.30
German (378)	1,471	17.21
Greek (97)	129	1.51
Hungarian (13)	88	1.03
Iranian (49)	49	0.57
Irish (579)	1,240	14.51
Italian (403)	880	10.30
Lithuanian (209)	327	3.83
Macedonian (144)	214	2.50
Norwegian (41)	177	2.07
Polish (453)	1,015	11.88
Portuguese (0)	15	0.18
Russian (45)	169	1.98
Scotch-Irish (13)	151	1.77
Scottish (28)	207	2.42
Serbian (0)	14	0.16
Slovak (12)	25	0.29
Swedish (67)	278	3.25
Ukrainian (0)	177	2.07
Welsh (0)	66	0.77
Yugoslavian (38)	48	0.56

Hispanic Origin	Population	%
Hispanic or Latino (of any race)	487	5.70
Central American, ex. Mexican	11	0.13
Guatemalan	8	0.09
Nicaraguan	1	0.01
Panamanian	1	0.01
Salvadoran	1	0.01
Cuban	18	0.21
Dominican Republic	1	0.01
Mexican	356	4.17
Puerto Rican	36	0.42
South American	48	0.56
Argentinean	4	0.05
Bolivian	1	0.01
Chilean	1	0.01
Colombian	9	0.11
Ecuadorian	11	0.13
Peruvian	15	0.18
Venezuelan	7	0.08
Other Hispanic or Latino	17	0.20

Race*	Population	%
African-American/Black (405)	440	5.15
Not Hispanic (400)	430	5.04
Hispanic (5)	10	0.12
American Indian/Alaska Native (5)	26	0.30
Not Hispanic (4)	19	0.22
Hispanic (1)	7	0.08
Cherokee (2)	10	0.12
Chickasaw (0)	1	0.01
Mexican American Ind. (0)	2	0.02
Pueblo (0)	2	0.02
Sioux (0)	2	0.02
South American Ind. (0)	1	0.01
Yaqui (0)	1	0.01
Asian (1,154)	1,235	14.46
Not Hispanic (1,151)	1,224	14.33
Hispanic (3)	11	0.13
Cambodian (1)	1	0.01
Chinese, ex. Taiwanese (196)	216	2.53
Filipino (237)	266	3.11
Hmong (3)	3	0.04
Indian (458)	475	5.56
Indonesian (1)	1	0.01
Japanese (12)	24	0.28
Korean (75)	86	1.01
Malaysian (0)	1	0.01
Pakistani (42)	44	0.52
Sri Lankan (3)	3	0.04
Taiwanese (45)	59	0.69
Thai (20)	26	0.30
Vietnamese (9)	11	0.13
Hawaii Native/Pacific Islander (2)	14	0.16
Not Hispanic (2)	12	0.14
Hispanic (0)	2	0.02
Guamanian/Chamorro (0)	1	0.01
Native Hawaiian (2)	4	0.05
Samoan (0)	1	0.01
White (6,721)	6,846	80.16
Not Hispanic (6,378)	6,471	75.77
Hispanic (343)	375	4.39

Wilmette

Place Type: Village
County: Cook
Population: 27,087†

Ancestry‡	Population	%
African, Sub-Saharan (13)	26	0.10

*Notes: † The Census 2010 population figure is used to calculate the percentages in the Hispanic Origin and Race categories. Ancestry percentages are based on the 2006-2010 American Community Survey population (not shown); ‡ Numbers in parentheses indicate the number of people reporting a single ancestry; * Numbers in parentheses indicate the number of persons reporting this race alone, not in combination with any other race; Please refer to the Explanation of Data for more information.*

South African (13)	26	0.10
Alsatian (10)	10	0.04
American (1,273)	1,273	4.73
Arab (80)	106	0.39
Arab (14)	14	0.05
Egyptian (10)	10	0.04
Lebanese (36)	62	0.23
Syrian (20)	20	0.07
Armenian (9)	9	0.03
Assyrian/Chaldean/Syriac (59)	59	0.22
Australian (19)	19	0.07
Austrian (52)	257	0.95
Belgian (65)	174	0.65
British (117)	165	0.61
Bulgarian (106)	106	0.39
Canadian (26)	44	0.16
Celtic (7)	26	0.10
Croatian (68)	112	0.42
Czech (76)	231	0.86
Czechoslovakian (9)	50	0.19
Danish (62)	186	0.69
Dutch (77)	386	1.43
Eastern European (301)	349	1.30
English (601)	3,337	12.39
European (587)	610	2.27
Finnish (12)	27	0.10
French, ex. Basque (32)	801	2.97
French Canadian (15)	87	0.32
German (1,420)	6,041	22.43
Greek (331)	616	2.29
Hungarian (45)	261	0.97
Icelander (0)	8	0.03
Iranian (109)	132	0.49
Irish (1,465)	5,497	20.41
Israeli (16)	39	0.14
Italian (462)	1,693	6.29
Latvian (8)	31	0.12
Lithuanian (122)	383	1.42
Luxemburger (0)	27	0.10
Northern European (40)	61	0.23
Norwegian (153)	618	2.30
Polish (783)	1,905	7.07
Romanian (200)	313	1.16
Russian (783)	1,650	6.13
Scandinavian (9)	74	0.27
Scotch-Irish (133)	476	1.77
Scottish (214)	1,019	3.78
Serbian (46)	122	0.45
Slovak (10)	53	0.20
Slovene (9)	9	0.03
Swedish (274)	1,234	4.58
Swiss (25)	131	0.49
Turkish (10)	20	0.07
Ukrainian (94)	271	1.01
Welsh (49)	273	1.01
West Indian, ex. Hispanic (0)	18	0.07
Belizean (0)	18	0.07
Yugoslavian (36)	36	0.13

Hispanic Origin	Population	%
Hispanic or Latino (of any race)	902	3.33
Central American, ex. Mexican	66	0.24
Costa Rican	1	<0.01
Guatemalan	37	0.14
Honduran	12	0.04
Nicaraguan	5	0.02
Panamanian	1	<0.01
Salvadoran	10	0.04
Cuban	97	0.36
Dominican Republic	5	0.02
Mexican	302	1.11
Puerto Rican	77	0.28
South American	249	0.92
Argentinean	41	0.15
Bolivian	31	0.11
Chilean	18	0.07
Colombian	92	0.34
Ecuadorian	16	0.06
Paraguayan	3	0.01
Peruvian	38	0.14
Uruguayan	1	<0.01
Venezuelan	4	0.01
Other South American	5	0.02
Other Hispanic or Latino	106	0.39

Race*	Population	%
African-American/Black (215)	275	1.02
Not Hispanic (208)	261	0.96
Hispanic (7)	14	0.05
American Indian/Alaska Native (16)	69	0.25
Not Hispanic (10)	51	0.19
Hispanic (6)	18	0.07
Cherokee (1)	17	0.06
Chippewa (1)	5	0.02
Choctaw (0)	2	0.01
Creek (0)	2	0.01
Lumbee (3)	3	0.01
Menominee (1)	1	<0.01
Mexican American Ind. (3)	4	0.01
Navajo (1)	1	<0.01
Osage (0)	2	0.01
Sioux (0)	1	<0.01
Spanish American Ind. (1)	1	<0.01
Asian (2,917)	3,370	12.44
Not Hispanic (2,909)	3,342	12.34
Hispanic (8)	28	0.10
Bangladeshi (7)	7	0.03
Burmese (3)	3	0.01
Cambodian (8)	12	0.04
Chinese, ex. Taiwanese (862)	997	3.68
Filipino (213)	281	1.04
Hmong (1)	1	<0.01
Indian (351)	426	1.57
Indonesian (3)	6	0.02
Japanese (188)	294	1.09
Korean (857)	935	3.45
Malaysian (8)	9	0.03
Nepalese (1)	1	<0.01
Pakistani (121)	126	0.47
Sri Lankan (3)	3	0.01
Taiwanese (95)	107	0.40
Thai (96)	111	0.41
Vietnamese (26)	37	0.14
Hawaii Native/Pacific Islander (8)	24	0.09
Not Hispanic (7)	19	0.07
Hispanic (1)	5	0.02
Guamanian/Chamorro (2)	2	0.01
Native Hawaiian (0)	6	0.02
White (23,148)	23,669	87.38
Not Hispanic (22,471)	22,951	84.73
Hispanic (677)	718	2.65

Winfield

Place Type: Village
County: DuPage
Population: 9,080†

Ancestry‡	Population	%
American (232)	232	2.57
Arab (80)	80	0.88
Syrian (80)	80	0.88
Assyrian/Chaldean/Syriac (0)	33	0.37
Austrian (0)	46	0.51
Belgian (26)	39	0.43
British (0)	28	0.31
Canadian (40)	65	0.72
Croatian (60)	78	0.86
Czech (103)	213	2.36
Czechoslovakian (23)	68	0.75
Danish (82)	161	1.78
Dutch (81)	245	2.71
English (194)	1,019	11.27
European (86)	86	0.95
French, ex. Basque (17)	302	3.34
French Canadian (33)	59	0.65
German (729)	2,640	29.20
Greek (35)	35	0.39
Hungarian (0)	35	0.39
Iranian (38)	80	0.88
Irish (354)	1,835	20.30
Italian (355)	1,128	12.48
Lithuanian (46)	127	1.40
Norwegian (23)	111	1.23
Polish (380)	1,210	13.38
Portuguese (35)	35	0.39
Russian (132)	340	3.76
Scandinavian (33)	131	1.45
Scotch-Irish (146)	355	3.93
Scottish (94)	203	2.25
Slovak (33)	67	0.74
Slovene (40)	65	0.72
Swedish (103)	314	3.47
Swiss (0)	46	0.51
Ukrainian (0)	47	0.52
Welsh (0)	129	1.43
Yugoslavian (0)	18	0.20

Hispanic Origin	Population	%
Hispanic or Latino (of any race)	492	5.42
Central American, ex. Mexican	24	0.26
Costa Rican	1	0.01
Guatemalan	8	0.09
Honduran	6	0.07
Nicaraguan	1	0.01
Panamanian	4	0.04
Salvadoran	4	0.04
Cuban	38	0.42
Dominican Republic	4	0.04
Mexican	333	3.67
Puerto Rican	22	0.24
South American	45	0.50
Bolivian	1	0.01
Colombian	9	0.10
Ecuadorian	8	0.09
Paraguayan	2	0.02
Peruvian	24	0.26
Venezuelan	1	0.01
Other Hispanic or Latino	26	0.29

Race*	Population	%
African-American/Black (140)	166	1.83
Not Hispanic (139)	164	1.81
Hispanic (1)	2	0.02
American Indian/Alaska Native (13)	55	0.61
Not Hispanic (8)	49	0.54
Hispanic (5)	6	0.07
Apache (2)	2	0.02
Blackfeet (0)	1	0.01
Cherokee (1)	17	0.19
Chippewa (1)	1	0.01
Choctaw (0)	2	0.02
Inupiat *(Alaska Native)* (1)	2	0.02
Iroquois (1)	1	0.01
Menominee (1)	3	0.03
Sioux (0)	2	0.02
Asian (308)	395	4.35
Not Hispanic (302)	383	4.22
Hispanic (6)	12	0.13
Cambodian (6)	12	0.13
Chinese, ex. Taiwanese (39)	64	0.70
Filipino (50)	85	0.94
Indian (94)	104	1.15
Indonesian (1)	1	0.01
Japanese (15)	26	0.29
Korean (45)	52	0.57
Pakistani (25)	27	0.30
Taiwanese (3)	5	0.06
Thai (2)	3	0.03
Vietnamese (17)	19	0.21
Hawaii Native/Pacific Islander (3)	8	0.09
Not Hispanic (3)	8	0.09
Marshallese (1)	1	0.01
Native Hawaiian (1)	2	0.02
Samoan (1)	1	0.01
White (8,321)	8,484	93.44
Not Hispanic (7,983)	8,118	89.41
Hispanic (338)	366	4.03

*Notes: † The Census 2010 population figure is used to calculate the percentages in the Hispanic Origin and Race categories. Ancestry percentages are based on the 2006-2010 American Community Survey population (not shown); ‡ Numbers in parentheses indicate the number of people reporting a single ancestry; * Numbers in parentheses indicate the number of persons reporting this race alone, not in combination with any other race; Please refer to the Explanation of Data for more information.*

Winnetka

Place Type: Village
County: Cook
Population: 12,187†

Ancestry‡	Population	%
African, Sub-Saharan (14)	14	0.12
Other Sub-Saharan African (14)	14	0.12
Albanian (38)	38	0.31
American (616)	616	5.09
Arab (20)	74	0.61
Lebanese (0)	54	0.45
Syrian (20)	20	0.17
Armenian (23)	55	0.45
Austrian (7)	101	0.83
British (73)	133	1.10
Bulgarian (27)	27	0.22
Canadian (41)	86	0.71
Croatian (12)	87	0.72
Czech (0)	166	1.37
Czechoslovakian (0)	14	0.12
Danish (20)	85	0.70
Dutch (52)	272	2.25
Eastern European (59)	110	0.91
English (551)	2,395	19.77
European (172)	232	1.92
Finnish (6)	6	0.05
French, ex. Basque (20)	561	4.63
French Canadian (0)	28	0.23
German (700)	3,117	25.73
Greek (82)	245	2.02
Hungarian (48)	179	1.48
Irish (552)	2,510	20.72
Italian (115)	816	6.74
Latvian (21)	21	0.17
Lithuanian (12)	52	0.43
Luxemburger (18)	79	0.65
Northern European (52)	52	0.43
Norwegian (28)	380	3.14
Polish (121)	459	3.79
Romanian (17)	26	0.21
Russian (223)	510	4.21
Scandinavian (24)	24	0.20
Scotch-Irish (70)	248	2.05
Scottish (155)	598	4.94
Slavic (0)	10	0.08
Slovak (12)	33	0.27
Swedish (125)	340	2.81
Swiss (117)	186	1.54
Ukrainian (27)	36	0.30
Welsh (113)	202	1.67

Hispanic Origin	Population	%
Hispanic or Latino (of any race)	271	2.22
Central American, ex. Mexican	16	0.13
Guatemalan	14	0.11
Panamanian	2	0.02
Cuban	25	0.21
Dominican Republic	5	0.04
Mexican	110	0.90
Puerto Rican	30	0.25
South American	54	0.44
Argentinean	15	0.12
Bolivian	5	0.04
Chilean	7	0.06
Colombian	14	0.11
Ecuadorian	6	0.05
Peruvian	4	0.03
Venezuelan	2	0.02
Other South American	1	0.01
Other Hispanic or Latino	31	0.25

Race*	Population	%
African-American/Black (33)	53	0.43
Not Hispanic (31)	51	0.42
Hispanic (2)	2	0.02
American Indian/Alaska Native (11)	20	0.16
Not Hispanic (9)	18	0.15
Hispanic (2)	2	0.02
Cherokee (0)	1	0.01
Iroquois (0)	4	0.03
Lumbee (0)	1	0.01
Menominee (0)	1	0.01
Sioux (1)	1	0.01
Asian (403)	501	4.11
Not Hispanic (400)	495	4.06
Hispanic (3)	6	0.05
Bangladeshi (4)	4	0.03
Burmese (1)	2	0.02
Chinese, ex. Taiwanese (106)	134	1.10
Filipino (25)	44	0.36
Indian (83)	100	0.82
Japanese (37)	53	0.43
Korean (92)	119	0.98
Laotian (1)	1	0.01
Nepalese (2)	2	0.02
Pakistani (10)	13	0.11
Taiwanese (6)	6	0.05
Thai (4)	7	0.06
Vietnamese (4)	9	0.07
Hawaii Native/Pacific Islander (3)	4	0.03
Not Hispanic (3)	4	0.03
White (11,554)	11,690	95.92
Not Hispanic (11,334)	11,453	93.98
Hispanic (220)	237	1.94

Wood Dale

Place Type: City
County: DuPage
Population: 13,770†

Ancestry‡	Population	%
African, Sub-Saharan (17)	27	0.20
African (17)	27	0.20
American (257)	257	1.88
Arab (54)	54	0.39
Jordanian (54)	54	0.39
Assyrian/Chaldean/Syriac (12)	36	0.26
Australian (30)	30	0.22
Austrian (14)	81	0.59
Belgian (11)	11	0.08
Brazilian (0)	29	0.21
British (10)	70	0.51
Canadian (0)	49	0.36
Croatian (0)	12	0.09
Czech (99)	307	2.24
Czechoslovakian (14)	14	0.10
Danish (13)	65	0.48
Dutch (0)	88	0.64
English (211)	652	4.77
European (80)	80	0.58
French, ex. Basque (11)	306	2.24
German (555)	2,553	18.67
Greek (158)	226	1.65
Hungarian (18)	57	0.42
Irish (283)	1,369	10.01
Italian (933)	1,725	12.61
Latvian (33)	46	0.34
Lithuanian (11)	35	0.26
Luxemburger (26)	26	0.19
Norwegian (56)	230	1.68
Polish (2,657)	4,061	29.69
Romanian (158)	173	1.26
Russian (18)	139	1.02
Scandinavian (0)	14	0.10
Scotch-Irish (48)	189	1.38
Scottish (25)	103	0.75
Slovak (12)	24	0.18
Slovene (0)	11	0.08
Swedish (34)	220	1.61
Swiss (0)	12	0.09
Ukrainian (35)	185	1.35
Welsh (0)	10	0.07
West Indian, ex. Hispanic (0)	12	0.09
Trinidadian/Tobagonian (0)	12	0.09
Yugoslavian (34)	34	0.25

Hispanic Origin	Population	%
Hispanic or Latino (of any race)	2,796	20.31
Central American, ex. Mexican	121	0.88
Costa Rican	4	0.03
Guatemalan	89	0.65
Honduran	18	0.13
Nicaraguan	2	0.01
Panamanian	3	0.02
Salvadoran	3	0.02
Other Central American	2	0.01
Cuban	43	0.31
Dominican Republic	4	0.03
Mexican	2,260	16.41
Puerto Rican	182	1.32
South American	96	0.70
Argentinean	6	0.04
Chilean	11	0.08
Colombian	26	0.19
Ecuadorian	30	0.22
Peruvian	9	0.07
Venezuelan	14	0.10
Other Hispanic or Latino	90	0.65

Race*	Population	%
African-American/Black (168)	229	1.66
Not Hispanic (158)	195	1.42
Hispanic (10)	34	0.25
American Indian/Alaska Native (30)	84	0.61
Not Hispanic (9)	46	0.33
Hispanic (21)	38	0.28
Apache (0)	1	0.01
Blackfeet (0)	2	0.01
Cherokee (2)	19	0.14
Chippewa (1)	7	0.05
Choctaw (6)	6	0.04
Creek (0)	1	0.01
Crow (0)	1	0.01
Iroquois (0)	1	0.01
Mexican American Ind. (9)	16	0.12
Ottawa (0)	1	0.01
Seminole (0)	4	0.03
Sioux (0)	1	0.01
South American Ind. (3)	7	0.05
Asian (721)	817	5.93
Not Hispanic (721)	809	5.88
Hispanic (0)	8	0.06
Cambodian (1)	1	0.01
Chinese, ex. Taiwanese (43)	63	0.46
Filipino (135)	167	1.21
Indian (324)	335	2.43
Japanese (40)	55	0.40
Korean (41)	41	0.30
Laotian (0)	2	0.01
Nepalese (2)	2	0.01
Pakistani (88)	95	0.69
Sri Lankan (3)	3	0.02
Taiwanese (4)	6	0.04
Thai (3)	5	0.04
Vietnamese (15)	18	0.13
Hawaii Native/Pacific Islander (2)	10	0.07
Not Hispanic (0)	4	0.03
Hispanic (2)	6	0.04
Guamanian/Chamorro (0)	1	0.01
White (11,489)	11,744	85.29
Not Hispanic (9,918)	10,049	72.98
Hispanic (1,571)	1,695	12.31

Wood River

Place Type: City
County: Madison
Population: 10,657†

Ancestry‡	Population	%
American (948)	948	8.76
Arab (5)	5	0.05
Egyptian (5)	5	0.05
Austrian (0)	38	0.35
Belgian (0)	14	0.13
British (18)	69	0.64

*Notes: † The Census 2010 population figure is used to calculate the percentages in the Hispanic Origin and Race categories. Ancestry percentages are based on the 2006-2010 American Community Survey population (not shown); ‡ Numbers in parentheses indicate the number of people reporting a single ancestry; * Numbers in parentheses indicate the number of persons reporting this race alone, not in combination with any other race; Please refer to the Explanation of Data for more information.*

Ancestry (continued)	Population	%
Croatian (82)	143	1.32
Czech (0)	11	0.10
Czechoslovakian (0)	13	0.12
Danish (20)	33	0.31
Dutch (38)	237	2.19
Eastern European (21)	21	0.19
English (576)	1,116	10.32
European (88)	88	0.81
French, ex. Basque (11)	425	3.93
French Canadian (9)	33	0.31
German (1,179)	3,010	27.83
Greek (69)	69	0.64
Hungarian (0)	42	0.39
Irish (456)	1,501	13.88
Italian (282)	564	5.21
Lithuanian (79)	79	0.73
Norwegian (9)	14	0.13
Polish (125)	545	5.04
Portuguese (12)	12	0.11
Russian (19)	84	0.78
Scotch-Irish (82)	167	1.54
Scottish (55)	116	1.07
Swedish (30)	91	0.84
Swiss (0)	18	0.17
Welsh (0)	18	0.17

Hispanic Origin	Population	%
Hispanic or Latino (of any race)	203	1.90
Central American, ex. Mexican	6	0.06
Costa Rican	1	0.01
Guatemalan	1	0.01
Honduran	3	0.03
Panamanian	1	0.01
Cuban	4	0.04
Mexican	143	1.34
Puerto Rican	11	0.10
South American	4	0.04
Chilean	2	0.02
Ecuadorian	1	0.01
Venezuelan	1	0.01
Other Hispanic or Latino	35	0.33

Race*	Population	%
African-American/Black (155)	224	2.10
Not Hispanic (152)	216	2.03
Hispanic (3)	8	0.08
American Indian/Alaska Native (24)	58	0.54
Not Hispanic (23)	54	0.51
Hispanic (1)	4	0.04
Apache (1)	2	0.02
Blackfeet (0)	9	0.08
Cherokee (13)	23	0.22
Chickasaw (2)	2	0.02
Chippewa (0)	2	0.02
Iroquois (1)	1	0.01
Sioux (0)	1	0.01
Spanish American Ind. (0)	1	0.01
Asian (56)	78	0.73
Not Hispanic (55)	74	0.69
Hispanic (1)	4	0.04
Chinese, ex. Taiwanese (2)	9	0.08
Filipino (20)	24	0.23
Indian (13)	22	0.21
Japanese (2)	9	0.08
Korean (2)	3	0.03
Laotian (3)	4	0.04
Thai (4)	6	0.06
Vietnamese (0)	1	0.01
Hawaii Native/Pacific Islander (1)	1	0.01
Not Hispanic (1)	1	0.01
White (10,262)	10,373	97.34
Not Hispanic (10,110)	10,212	95.82
Hispanic (152)	161	1.51

Woodridge

Place Type: Village
County: DuPage
Population: 32,971†

Ancestry‡	Population	%
African, Sub-Saharan (386)	386	1.19
African (13)	13	0.04
Ethiopian (97)	97	0.30
Ghanaian (276)	276	0.85
Albanian (25)	25	0.08
American (642)	642	1.98
Arab (265)	434	1.34
Arab (77)	77	0.24
Egyptian (120)	120	0.37
Jordanian (29)	29	0.09
Lebanese (0)	148	0.46
Syrian (29)	50	0.15
Other Arab (10)	10	0.03
Austrian (0)	68	0.21
Belgian (13)	27	0.08
Brazilian (58)	75	0.23
British (106)	334	1.03
Bulgarian (73)	73	0.22
Canadian (0)	12	0.04
Croatian (91)	239	0.74
Czech (318)	1,067	3.29
Czechoslovakian (91)	176	0.54
Danish (33)	324	1.00
Dutch (166)	746	2.30
Eastern European (48)	48	0.15
English (251)	1,851	5.70
Estonian (15)	15	0.05
European (93)	93	0.29
Finnish (0)	9	0.03
French, ex. Basque (38)	477	1.47
French Canadian (39)	98	0.30
German (1,586)	6,715	20.68
Greek (95)	644	1.98
Hungarian (29)	185	0.57
Irish (1,089)	4,377	13.48
Italian (892)	3,367	10.37
Latvian (0)	11	0.03
Lithuanian (915)	1,229	3.78
Luxemburger (0)	10	0.03
Macedonian (139)	139	0.43
Norwegian (135)	367	1.13
Pennsylvania German (14)	14	0.04
Polish (1,458)	3,992	12.29
Portuguese (0)	24	0.07
Romanian (171)	181	0.56
Russian (90)	165	0.51
Scandinavian (48)	72	0.22
Scotch-Irish (105)	318	0.98
Scottish (13)	164	0.51
Serbian (73)	85	0.26
Slavic (47)	65	0.20
Slovak (34)	195	0.60
Slovene (10)	20	0.06
Swedish (54)	557	1.72
Swiss (18)	77	0.24
Turkish (34)	72	0.22
Ukrainian (0)	64	0.20
Welsh (31)	194	0.60
West Indian, ex. Hispanic (271)	271	0.83
Jamaican (271)	271	0.83
Yugoslavian (0)	15	0.05

Hispanic Origin	Population	%
Hispanic or Latino (of any race)	4,425	13.42
Central American, ex. Mexican	109	0.33
Costa Rican	6	0.02
Guatemalan	52	0.16
Honduran	19	0.06
Panamanian	7	0.02
Salvadoran	25	0.08
Cuban	42	0.13
Dominican Republic	11	0.03
Mexican	3,622	10.99
Puerto Rican	323	0.98
South American	157	0.48
Argentinean	26	0.08
Bolivian	4	0.01
Chilean	7	0.02
Colombian	44	0.13
Ecuadorian	33	0.10
Paraguayan	2	0.01
Peruvian	23	0.07
Uruguayan	1	<0.01
Venezuelan	16	0.05
Other South American	1	<0.01
Other Hispanic or Latino	161	0.49

Race*	Population	%
African-American/Black (2,938)	3,234	9.81
Not Hispanic (2,858)	3,099	9.40
Hispanic (80)	135	0.41
American Indian/Alaska Native (96)	227	0.69
Not Hispanic (37)	146	0.44
Hispanic (59)	81	0.25
Alaska Athabascan *(Ala. Nat.)* (1)	1	<0.01
Aleut *(Alaska Native)* (1)	4	0.01
Blackfeet (5)	8	0.02
Cherokee (2)	37	0.11
Chippewa (1)	3	0.01
Choctaw (0)	3	0.01
Comanche (1)	1	<0.01
Creek (0)	5	0.02
Crow (0)	2	0.01
Delaware (0)	1	<0.01
Iroquois (4)	9	0.03
Mexican American Ind. (14)	15	0.05
Navajo (1)	1	<0.01
Potawatomi (0)	1	<0.01
Pueblo (0)	2	0.01
Seminole (0)	3	0.01
South American Ind. (1)	1	<0.01
Spanish American Ind. (1)	1	<0.01
Tohono O'Odham (0)	1	<0.01
Yaqui (3)	3	0.01
Asian (4,127)	4,435	13.45
Not Hispanic (4,092)	4,377	13.28
Hispanic (35)	58	0.18
Bangladeshi (7)	7	0.02
Burmese (5)	5	0.02
Cambodian (7)	10	0.03
Chinese, ex. Taiwanese (484)	539	1.63
Filipino (1,076)	1,211	3.67
Hmong (2)	3	0.01
Indian (1,858)	1,943	5.89
Indonesian (14)	17	0.05
Japanese (39)	59	0.18
Korean (179)	197	0.60
Laotian (7)	14	0.04
Nepalese (1)	1	<0.01
Pakistani (196)	209	0.63
Sri Lankan (9)	10	0.03
Taiwanese (53)	67	0.20
Thai (26)	38	0.12
Vietnamese (69)	85	0.26
Hawaii Native/Pacific Islander (11)	44	0.13
Not Hispanic (3)	30	0.09
Hispanic (8)	14	0.04
Fijian (0)	1	<0.01
Guamanian/Chamorro (0)	4	0.01
Native Hawaiian (0)	4	0.01
Samoan (8)	9	0.03
White (23,426)	24,053	72.95
Not Hispanic (20,942)	21,373	64.82
Hispanic (2,484)	2,680	8.13

Woodstock

Place Type: City
County: McHenry
Population: 24,770†

Ancestry‡	Population	%
African, Sub-Saharan (46)	88	0.36
African (46)	60	0.25
South African (0)	28	0.11
Albanian (33)	33	0.14
American (1,053)	1,053	4.31
Armenian (0)	21	0.09
Austrian (43)	72	0.29

*Notes: † The Census 2010 population figure is used to calculate the percentages in the Hispanic Origin and Race categories. Ancestry percentages are based on the 2006-2010 American Community Survey population (not shown); ‡ Numbers in parentheses indicate the number of people reporting a single ancestry; * Numbers in parentheses indicate the number of persons reporting this race alone, not in combination with any other race; Please refer to the Explanation of Data for more information.*

Ancestry (cont.)	Population	%
Belgian (13)	66	0.27
Brazilian (104)	178	0.73
British (50)	111	0.45
Bulgarian (0)	13	0.05
Canadian (26)	36	0.15
Croatian (0)	12	0.05
Czech (88)	239	0.98
Czechoslovakian (15)	50	0.20
Danish (41)	237	0.97
Dutch (61)	280	1.15
Eastern European (0)	17	0.07
English (322)	1,778	7.28
European (151)	199	0.82
Finnish (13)	31	0.13
French, ex. Basque (63)	707	2.90
French Canadian (12)	63	0.26
German (2,087)	7,378	30.22
Greek (64)	82	0.34
Hungarian (9)	81	0.33
Irish (1,013)	4,214	17.26
Italian (482)	1,588	6.50
Lithuanian (43)	142	0.58
Luxemburger (9)	54	0.22
Northern European (14)	14	0.06
Norwegian (188)	896	3.67
Polish (546)	1,988	8.14
Portuguese (0)	12	0.05
Romanian (0)	47	0.19
Russian (14)	112	0.46
Scandinavian (25)	73	0.30
Scotch-Irish (98)	325	1.33
Scottish (109)	434	1.78
Serbian (39)	39	0.16
Slovak (0)	10	0.04
Slovene (0)	28	0.11
Swedish (148)	833	3.41
Swiss (35)	79	0.32
Ukrainian (35)	63	0.26
Welsh (0)	170	0.70
West Indian, ex. Hispanic (33)	54	0.22
Belizean (18)	25	0.10
British West Indian (0)	14	0.06
Haitian (15)	15	0.06
Yugoslavian (88)	114	0.47

Hispanic Origin	Population	%
Hispanic or Latino (of any race)	5,852	23.63
Central American, ex. Mexican	111	0.45
Guatemalan	37	0.15
Honduran	19	0.08
Nicaraguan	8	0.03
Panamanian	2	0.01
Salvadoran	45	0.18
Cuban	29	0.12
Dominican Republic	2	0.01
Mexican	5,129	20.71
Puerto Rican	201	0.81
South American	70	0.28
Argentinean	3	0.01
Chilean	8	0.03
Colombian	25	0.10
Ecuadorian	11	0.04
Peruvian	11	0.04
Venezuelan	12	0.05
Other Hispanic or Latino	310	1.25

Race*	Population	%
African-American/Black (562)	717	2.89
Not Hispanic (513)	632	2.55
Hispanic (49)	85	0.34
American Indian/Alaska Native (97)	225	0.91
Not Hispanic (40)	132	0.53
Hispanic (57)	93	0.38
Apache (1)	6	0.02
Blackfeet (0)	5	0.02
Canadian/French Am. Ind. (1)	1	<0.01
Cherokee (11)	39	0.16
Chippewa (6)	12	0.05
Delaware (0)	3	0.01
Iroquois (2)	5	0.02
Lumbee (0)	1	<0.01
Mexican American Ind. (3)	10	0.04
Navajo (1)	5	0.02
Potawatomi (1)	6	0.02
Seminole (1)	2	0.01
Sioux (2)	8	0.03
South American Ind. (2)	2	0.01
Yaqui (0)	2	0.01
Asian (578)	686	2.77
Not Hispanic (562)	663	2.68
Hispanic (16)	23	0.09
Bangladeshi (2)	2	0.01
Chinese, ex. Taiwanese (47)	67	0.27
Filipino (212)	249	1.01
Indian (195)	205	0.83
Indonesian (1)	1	<0.01
Japanese (11)	32	0.13
Korean (37)	40	0.16
Laotian (9)	10	0.04
Pakistani (21)	32	0.13
Sri Lankan (4)	4	0.02
Taiwanese (1)	2	0.01
Thai (7)	12	0.05
Vietnamese (2)	7	0.03
Hawaii Native/Pacific Islander (17)	31	0.13
Not Hispanic (15)	24	0.10
Hispanic (2)	7	0.03
Guamanian/Chamorro (1)	3	0.01
Native Hawaiian (9)	12	0.05
White (20,675)	21,161	85.43
Not Hispanic (17,478)	17,749	71.66
Hispanic (3,197)	3,412	13.77

Worth

Place Type: Village
County: Cook
Population: 10,789†

Ancestry‡	Population	%
American (403)	403	3.77
Arab (292)	344	3.22
Arab (61)	61	0.57
Jordanian (17)	34	0.32
Palestinian (214)	249	2.33
Austrian (9)	35	0.33
Belgian (0)	8	0.07
British (0)	16	0.15
Canadian (21)	21	0.20
Croatian (0)	24	0.22
Czech (40)	343	3.21
Czechoslovakian (25)	25	0.23
Danish (0)	65	0.61
Dutch (98)	378	3.54
English (32)	449	4.21
European (73)	73	0.68
Finnish (0)	32	0.30
French, ex. Basque (11)	212	1.99
French Canadian (15)	15	0.14
German (480)	1,894	17.74
Greek (111)	226	2.12
Hungarian (9)	57	0.53
Iranian (0)	7	0.07
Irish (536)	2,114	19.80
Italian (513)	1,058	9.91
Latvian (26)	26	0.24
Lithuanian (203)	540	5.06
Northern European (9)	9	0.08
Norwegian (10)	94	0.88
Pennsylvania German (0)	9	0.08
Polish (1,497)	2,539	23.78
Portuguese (12)	12	0.11
Russian (6)	133	1.25
Scotch-Irish (13)	80	0.75
Scottish (99)	239	2.24
Slavic (8)	8	0.07
Slovak (22)	78	0.73
Slovene (15)	15	0.14
Swedish (22)	250	2.34
Ukrainian (9)	40	0.37
Welsh (0)	8	0.07
Yugoslavian (0)	39	0.37

Hispanic Origin	Population	%
Hispanic or Latino (of any race)	1,230	11.40
Central American, ex. Mexican	41	0.38
Costa Rican	4	0.04
Guatemalan	13	0.12
Honduran	9	0.08
Nicaraguan	3	0.03
Panamanian	1	0.01
Salvadoran	11	0.10
Cuban	3	0.03
Dominican Republic	3	0.03
Mexican	1,010	9.36
Puerto Rican	85	0.79
South American	30	0.28
Argentinean	2	0.02
Bolivian	2	0.02
Colombian	11	0.10
Ecuadorian	7	0.06
Paraguayan	3	0.03
Peruvian	2	0.02
Venezuelan	3	0.03
Other Hispanic or Latino	58	0.54

Race*	Population	%
African-American/Black (279)	319	2.96
Not Hispanic (266)	294	2.72
Hispanic (13)	25	0.23
American Indian/Alaska Native (17)	47	0.44
Not Hispanic (13)	35	0.32
Hispanic (4)	12	0.11
Arapaho (0)	1	0.01
Cherokee (2)	16	0.15
Chippewa (0)	2	0.02
Osage (0)	1	0.01
Sioux (1)	7	0.06
Asian (205)	268	2.48
Not Hispanic (198)	256	2.37
Hispanic (7)	12	0.11
Chinese, ex. Taiwanese (17)	21	0.19
Filipino (83)	98	0.91
Hmong (1)	1	0.01
Indian (31)	36	0.33
Japanese (1)	8	0.07
Korean (9)	17	0.16
Laotian (6)	6	0.06
Pakistani (7)	8	0.07
Taiwanese (1)	1	0.01
Thai (5)	8	0.07
Vietnamese (31)	31	0.29
Hawaii Native/Pacific Islander (1)	14	0.13
Not Hispanic (1)	13	0.12
Hispanic (0)	1	0.01
Guamanian/Chamorro (0)	1	0.01
Native Hawaiian (1)	6	0.06
White (9,710)	9,902	91.78
Not Hispanic (8,942)	9,054	83.92
Hispanic (768)	848	7.86

Yorkville

Place Type: City
County: Kendall
Population: 16,921†

Ancestry‡	Population	%
African, Sub-Saharan (28)	28	0.19
Ethiopian (28)	28	0.19
American (615)	615	4.08
Armenian (0)	11	0.07
Austrian (15)	25	0.17
Belgian (0)	27	0.18
Canadian (0)	33	0.22
Croatian (10)	48	0.32
Czech (101)	344	2.28
Czechoslovakian (0)	53	0.35
Danish (0)	23	0.15
Dutch (75)	257	1.71

*Notes: † The Census 2010 population figure is used to calculate the percentages in the Hispanic Origin and Race categories. Ancestry percentages are based on the 2006-2010 American Community Survey population (not shown); ‡ Numbers in parentheses indicate the number of people reporting a single ancestry; * Numbers in parentheses indicate the number of persons reporting this race alone, not in combination with any other race; Please refer to the Explanation of Data for more information.*

English (541)	1,570	10.42
European (73)	73	0.48
Finnish (56)	62	0.41
French, ex. Basque (8)	412	2.73
French Canadian (19)	49	0.33
German (1,666)	4,333	28.76
Greek (7)	127	0.84
Hungarian (41)	115	0.76
Irish (396)	2,345	15.57
Italian (556)	1,759	11.68
Latvian (0)	77	0.51
Lithuanian (60)	225	1.49
Luxemburger (15)	33	0.22
Norwegian (339)	786	5.22
Polish (196)	1,073	7.12
Portuguese (0)	22	0.15
Romanian (0)	104	0.69
Russian (59)	59	0.39
Scandinavian (31)	31	0.21
Scotch-Irish (36)	288	1.91
Scottish (24)	275	1.83
Serbian (0)	21	0.14
Slovak (16)	44	0.29
Slovene (14)	48	0.32
Swedish (234)	702	4.66
Swiss (42)	154	1.02
Turkish (0)	27	0.18
Ukrainian (40)	163	1.08
Welsh (8)	106	0.70

Hispanic Origin	Population	%
Hispanic or Latino (of any race)	1,791	10.58
Central American, ex. Mexican	46	0.27
Costa Rican	3	0.02
Guatemalan	29	0.17
Nicaraguan	2	0.01
Panamanian	2	0.01
Salvadoran	10	0.06
Cuban	26	0.15
Dominican Republic	3	0.02
Mexican	1,411	8.34
Puerto Rican	202	1.19
South American	58	0.34
Argentinean	15	0.09
Colombian	23	0.14
Ecuadorian	14	0.08
Peruvian	6	0.04
Other Hispanic or Latino	45	0.27

Race*	Population	%
African-American/Black (562)	684	4.04
Not Hispanic (541)	638	3.77
Hispanic (21)	46	0.27
American Indian/Alaska Native (36)	80	0.47
Not Hispanic (18)	55	0.33
Hispanic (18)	25	0.15
Apache (0)	5	0.03
Blackfeet (0)	2	0.01
Central American Ind. (2)	2	0.01
Cherokee (8)	23	0.14
Cheyenne (1)	2	0.01
Chippewa (1)	6	0.04
Choctaw (0)	2	0.01
Creek (1)	1	0.01
Mexican American Ind. (7)	7	0.04
Sioux (1)	2	0.01
Spanish American Ind. (1)	1	0.01
Tohono O'Odham (2)	2	0.01
Ute (0)	1	0.01
Asian (261)	358	2.12
Not Hispanic (256)	334	1.97
Hispanic (5)	24	0.14
Cambodian (4)	4	0.02
Chinese, ex. Taiwanese (45)	58	0.34
Filipino (58)	94	0.56
Indian (93)	105	0.62
Indonesian (0)	6	0.04
Japanese (4)	25	0.15
Korean (18)	28	0.17
Laotian (4)	4	0.02
Pakistani (5)	11	0.07
Taiwanese (1)	1	0.01
Thai (5)	8	0.05
Vietnamese (14)	22	0.13
Hawaii Native/Pacific Islander (2)	8	0.05
Not Hispanic (2)	5	0.03
Hispanic (0)	3	0.02
Guamanian/Chamorro (0)	1	0.01
Samoan (2)	2	0.01
White (15,362)	15,628	92.36
Not Hispanic (14,109)	14,293	84.47
Hispanic (1,253)	1,335	7.89

Zion

Place Type: City
County: Lake
Population: 24,413[†]

Ancestry[‡]	Population	%
African, Sub-Saharan (51)	157	0.64
African (51)	157	0.64
American (674)	674	2.77
Armenian (0)	10	0.04
Austrian (37)	46	0.19
Belgian (31)	49	0.20
British (33)	33	0.14
Bulgarian (6)	6	0.02
Canadian (0)	11	0.05
Croatian (11)	67	0.27
Czech (26)	100	0.41
Czechoslovakian (12)	53	0.22
Danish (62)	207	0.85
Dutch (70)	366	1.50
Eastern European (33)	33	0.14
English (264)	1,184	4.86
European (252)	366	1.50
Finnish (73)	293	1.20
French, ex. Basque (92)	454	1.86
French Canadian (30)	46	0.19
German (542)	2,937	12.05
German Russian (23)	23	0.09
Greek (12)	61	0.25
Hungarian (0)	47	0.19
Irish (1,056)	2,921	11.98
Italian (198)	613	2.51
Lithuanian (36)	94	0.39
Norwegian (125)	266	1.09
Polish (172)	946	3.88
Romanian (21)	21	0.09
Russian (18)	140	0.57
Scotch-Irish (11)	143	0.59
Scottish (110)	325	1.33
Serbian (20)	37	0.15
Slavic (12)	23	0.09
Slovene (25)	44	0.18
Swedish (100)	643	2.64
Swiss (9)	58	0.24
Ukrainian (0)	7	0.03
Welsh (0)	173	0.71
West Indian, ex. Hispanic (175)	191	0.78
Belizean (86)	102	0.42
Jamaican (89)	89	0.37

Hispanic Origin	Population	%
Hispanic or Latino (of any race)	6,758	27.68
Central American, ex. Mexican	373	1.53
Costa Rican	4	0.02
Guatemalan	89	0.36
Honduran	184	0.75
Nicaraguan	12	0.05
Panamanian	18	0.07
Salvadoran	57	0.23
Other Central American	9	0.04
Cuban	38	0.16
Dominican Republic	24	0.10
Mexican	5,120	20.97
Puerto Rican	870	3.56
South American	70	0.29
Argentinean	3	0.01
Chilean	4	0.02
Colombian	37	0.15
Ecuadorian	2	0.01
Peruvian	14	0.06
Uruguayan	1	<0.01
Venezuelan	5	0.02
Other South American	4	0.02
Other Hispanic or Latino	263	1.08

Race*	Population	%
African-American/Black (7,566)	8,250	33.79
Not Hispanic (7,391)	7,917	32.43
Hispanic (175)	333	1.36
American Indian/Alaska Native (107)	306	1.25
Not Hispanic (53)	193	0.79
Hispanic (54)	113	0.46
Aleut *(Alaska Native)* (0)	1	<0.01
Apache (0)	4	0.02
Blackfeet (0)	4	0.02
Canadian/French Am. Ind. (1)	1	<0.01
Central American Ind. (1)	1	<0.01
Cherokee (5)	50	0.20
Cheyenne (0)	1	<0.01
Chippewa (7)	18	0.07
Choctaw (0)	1	<0.01
Comanche (0)	1	<0.01
Creek (1)	1	<0.01
Crow (0)	1	<0.01
Iroquois (1)	5	0.02
Lumbee (1)	1	<0.01
Menominee (4)	4	0.02
Mexican American Ind. (14)	17	0.07
Navajo (5)	5	0.02
Sioux (2)	7	0.03
South American Ind. (0)	1	<0.01
Spanish American Ind. (0)	1	<0.01
Tlingit-Haida *(Alaska Native)* (1)	1	<0.01
Asian (563)	801	3.28
Not Hispanic (546)	739	3.03
Hispanic (17)	62	0.25
Cambodian (20)	23	0.09
Chinese, ex. Taiwanese (29)	49	0.20
Filipino (380)	514	2.11
Indian (47)	71	0.29
Japanese (22)	65	0.27
Korean (14)	20	0.08
Nepalese (5)	5	0.02
Pakistani (11)	12	0.05
Taiwanese (1)	5	0.02
Thai (4)	11	0.05
Vietnamese (15)	26	0.11
Hawaii Native/Pacific Islander (14)	56	0.23
Not Hispanic (10)	46	0.19
Hispanic (4)	10	0.04
Guamanian/Chamorro (6)	8	0.03
Native Hawaiian (1)	8	0.03
Samoan (2)	5	0.02
White (11,938)	12,950	53.05
Not Hispanic (8,787)	9,412	38.55
Hispanic (3,151)	3,538	14.49

*Notes: † The Census 2010 population figure is used to calculate the percentages in the Hispanic Origin and Race categories. Ancestry percentages are based on the 2006-2010 American Community Survey population (not shown); ‡ Numbers in parentheses indicate the number of people reporting a single ancestry; * Numbers in parentheses indicate the number of persons reporting this race alone, not in combination with any other race; Please refer to the Explanation of Data for more information.*

INDIANA

Place Type: State
Population: 6,483,802[†]

Ancestry[‡]	Population	%
Afghan (242)	261	<0.01
African, Sub-Saharan (65,151)	79,021	1.23
African (56,028)	68,814	1.07
Cape Verdean (9)	28	<0.01
Ethiopian (1,265)	1,431	0.02
Ghanaian (303)	322	0.01
Kenyan (647)	663	0.01
Liberian (732)	771	0.01
Nigerian (3,000)	3,311	0.05
Senegalese (179)	193	<0.01
Sierra Leonean (0)	41	<0.01
Somalian (586)	626	0.01
South African (376)	600	0.01
Sudanese (422)	433	0.01
Ugandan (69)	109	<0.01
Zimbabwean (149)	162	<0.01
Other Sub-Saharan African (1,386)	1,517	0.02
Albanian (458)	703	0.01
Alsatian (82)	300	<0.01
American (644,285)	644,285	10.04
Arab (10,118)	15,838	0.25
Arab (2,653)	3,625	0.06
Egyptian (1,080)	1,376	0.02
Iraqi (304)	594	0.01
Jordanian (521)	596	0.01
Lebanese (2,109)	4,417	0.07
Moroccan (406)	571	0.01
Palestinian (774)	885	0.01
Syrian (839)	2,104	0.03
Other Arab (1,432)	1,670	0.03
Armenian (479)	1,080	0.02
Assyrian/Chaldean/Syriac (199)	453	0.01
Australian (687)	1,313	0.02
Austrian (2,431)	9,059	0.14
Basque (3)	81	<0.01
Belgian (4,026)	13,481	0.21
Brazilian (1,192)	1,706	0.03
British (10,920)	23,647	0.37
Bulgarian (676)	1,359	0.02
Cajun (301)	666	0.01
Canadian (4,537)	9,085	0.14
Carpatho Rusyn (24)	62	<0.01
Celtic (252)	636	0.01
Croatian (4,180)	13,306	0.21
Cypriot (88)	88	<0.01
Czech (4,832)	18,523	0.29
Czechoslovakian (2,305)	5,115	0.08
Danish (3,532)	13,281	0.21
Dutch (37,596)	144,391	2.25
Eastern European (2,179)	2,605	0.04
English (248,297)	623,154	9.71
Estonian (51)	365	0.01
European (51,753)	58,511	0.91
Finnish (1,411)	5,241	0.08
French, ex. Basque (34,177)	167,332	2.61
French Canadian (6,999)	17,621	0.27
German (740,501)	1,692,418	26.37
German Russian (34)	194	<0.01
Greek (11,608)	23,572	0.37
Guyanese (81)	158	<0.01
Hungarian (12,566)	38,908	0.61
Icelander (146)	292	<0.01
Iranian (1,687)	2,332	0.04
Irish (234,713)	827,853	12.90
Israeli (343)	483	0.01
Italian (64,626)	185,128	2.88
Latvian (814)	1,490	0.02
Lithuanian (4,371)	11,699	0.18
Luxemburger (94)	591	0.01
Macedonian (3,873)	5,064	0.08
Maltese (43)	197	<0.01
New Zealander (221)	318	<0.01
Northern European (3,042)	3,363	0.05
Norwegian (10,599)	36,566	0.57
Pennsylvania German (10,066)	13,018	0.20
Polish (76,354)	210,729	3.28
Portuguese (1,567)	4,720	0.07
Romanian (4,190)	8,644	0.13
Russian (9,274)	25,824	0.40
Scandinavian (2,637)	6,406	0.10
Scotch-Irish (38,900)	95,439	1.49
Scottish (42,470)	123,773	1.93
Serbian (6,179)	11,326	0.18
Slavic (922)	2,352	0.04
Slovak (7,358)	21,051	0.33
Slovene (996)	2,873	0.04
Swedish (16,589)	65,409	1.02
Swiss (14,649)	44,777	0.70
Turkish (1,124)	1,592	0.02
Ukrainian (4,411)	9,005	0.14
Welsh (9,294)	38,925	0.61
West Indian, ex. Hispanic (3,921)	6,151	0.10
Bahamian (68)	109	<0.01
Barbadian (41)	97	<0.01
Belizean (79)	147	<0.01
Bermudan (42)	42	<0.01
British West Indian (212)	347	0.01
Dutch West Indian (51)	294	<0.01
Haitian (1,290)	1,721	0.03
Jamaican (1,605)	2,228	0.03
Trinidadian/Tobagonian (156)	233	<0.01
U.S. Virgin Islander (8)	8	<0.01
West Indian (290)	804	0.01
Other West Indian (79)	121	<0.01
Yugoslavian (4,274)	6,328	0.10

Hispanic Origin	Population	%
Hispanic or Latino (of any race)	389,707	6.01
Central American, ex. Mexican	22,093	0.34
Costa Rican	592	0.01
Guatemalan	5,933	0.09
Honduran	5,345	0.08
Nicaraguan	1,431	0.02
Panamanian	1,218	0.02
Salvadoran	7,401	0.11
Other Central American	173	<0.01
Cuban	4,042	0.06
Dominican Republic	2,340	0.04
Mexican	295,373	4.56
Puerto Rican	30,304	0.47
South American	10,032	0.15
Argentinean	1,027	0.02
Bolivian	425	0.01
Chilean	647	0.01
Colombian	2,854	0.04
Ecuadorian	1,092	0.02
Paraguayan	88	<0.01
Peruvian	2,225	0.03
Uruguayan	150	<0.01
Venezuelan	1,440	0.02
Other South American	84	<0.01
Other Hispanic or Latino	25,523	0.39

Race*	Population	%
African-American/Black (591,397)	654,415	10.09
Not Hispanic (582,140)	638,353	9.85
Hispanic (9,257)	16,062	0.25
American Indian/Alaska Native (18,462)	49,738	0.77
Not Hispanic (14,165)	41,469	0.64
Hispanic (4,297)	8,269	0.13
Alaska Athabascan *(Ala. Nat.)* (23)	36	<0.01
Aleut *(Alaska Native)* (40)	55	<0.01
Apache (277)	824	0.01
Arapaho (20)	43	<0.01
Blackfeet (375)	2,065	0.03
Canadian/French Am. Ind. (101)	248	<0.01
Central American Ind. (87)	152	<0.01
Cherokee (3,036)	12,583	0.19
Cheyenne (43)	157	<0.01
Chickasaw (83)	195	<0.01
Chippewa (618)	1,208	0.02
Choctaw (323)	852	0.01
Colville (11)	14	<0.01
Comanche (64)	142	<0.01
Cree (38)	115	<0.01
Creek (186)	375	0.01
Crow (36)	122	<0.01
Delaware (77)	196	<0.01
Hopi (20)	60	<0.01
Houma (29)	43	<0.01
Inupiat *(Alaska Native)* (42)	95	<0.01
Iroquois (255)	640	0.01
Kiowa (24)	35	<0.01
Lumbee (101)	189	<0.01
Menominee (40)	71	<0.01
Mexican American Ind. (938)	1,441	0.02
Navajo (230)	547	0.01
Osage (39)	114	<0.01
Ottawa (82)	164	<0.01
Paiute (18)	36	<0.01
Pima (12)	24	<0.01
Potawatomi (368)	724	0.01
Pueblo (62)	132	<0.01
Puget Sound Salish (13)	19	<0.01
Seminole (27)	149	<0.01
Shoshone (26)	75	<0.01
Sioux (508)	1,340	0.02
South American Ind. (99)	257	<0.01
Spanish American Ind. (91)	137	<0.01
Tlingit-Haida *(Alaska Native)* (43)	65	<0.01
Tohono O'Odham (11)	26	<0.01
Tsimshian *(Alaska Native)* (3)	5	<0.01
Ute (33)	56	<0.01
Yakama (5)	7	<0.01
Yaqui (22)	50	<0.01
Yuman (8)	13	<0.01
Yup'ik *(Alaska Native)* (21)	29	<0.01
Asian (102,474)	126,750	1.95
Not Hispanic (101,444)	123,750	1.91
Hispanic (1,030)	3,000	0.05
Bangladeshi (480)	539	0.01
Bhutanese (1)	3	<0.01
Burmese (7,523)	7,868	0.12
Cambodian (816)	1,019	0.02
Chinese, ex. Taiwanese (21,100)	24,468	0.38
Filipino (10,652)	16,988	0.26
Hmong (175)	218	<0.01
Indian (27,598)	30,947	0.48
Indonesian (547)	823	0.01
Japanese (4,896)	8,437	0.13
Korean (10,322)	13,685	0.21
Laotian (1,129)	1,466	0.02
Malaysian (332)	471	0.01
Nepalese (253)	278	<0.01
Pakistani (2,685)	3,098	0.05
Sri Lankan (331)	372	0.01
Taiwanese (1,387)	1,646	0.03
Thai (1,432)	2,176	0.03
Vietnamese (6,845)	8,175	0.13
Hawaii Native/Pacific Islander (2,348)	6,385	0.10
Not Hispanic (1,853)	5,116	0.08
Hispanic (495)	1,269	0.02
Fijian (15)	35	<0.01
Guamanian/Chamorro (636)	1,113	0.02
Marshallese (71)	82	<0.01
Native Hawaiian (728)	2,223	0.03
Samoan (326)	830	0.01
Tongan (60)	114	<0.01
White (5,467,906)	5,583,367	86.11
Not Hispanic (5,286,453)	5,377,916	82.94
Hispanic (181,453)	205,451	3.17

*Notes: † The Census 2010 population figure is used to calculate the percentages in the Hispanic Origin and Race categories. Ancestry percentages are based on the 2006-2010 American Community Survey population (not shown); ‡ Numbers in parentheses indicate the number of people reporting a single ancestry; * Numbers in parentheses indicate the number of persons reporting this race alone, not in combination with any other race; Please refer to the Explanation of Data for more information.*

Anderson

Place Type: City
County: Madison
Population: 56,129†

Ancestry‡	Population	%
African, Sub-Saharan (628)	648	1.14
African (523)	543	0.96
Ethiopian (18)	18	0.03
Kenyan (43)	43	0.08
Sudanese (18)	18	0.03
Other Sub-Saharan African (26)	26	0.05
American (5,914)	5,914	10.42
Arab (12)	24	0.04
Moroccan (12)	24	0.04
Australian (12)	12	0.02
Austrian (44)	103	0.18
Belgian (0)	23	0.04
British (73)	153	0.27
Canadian (21)	50	0.09
Celtic (0)	12	0.02
Croatian (9)	59	0.10
Czech (25)	45	0.08
Czechoslovakian (12)	12	0.02
Danish (0)	33	0.06
Dutch (429)	1,593	2.81
English (2,333)	4,934	8.69
European (290)	313	0.55
Finnish (13)	35	0.06
French, ex. Basque (493)	1,268	2.23
French Canadian (18)	66	0.12
German (4,469)	10,377	18.28
Greek (82)	126	0.22
Hungarian (41)	83	0.15
Irish (1,989)	6,464	11.39
Italian (364)	869	1.53
Luxemburger (0)	6	0.01
Norwegian (62)	167	0.29
Pennsylvania German (0)	12	0.02
Polish (295)	917	1.62
Portuguese (21)	26	0.05
Romanian (17)	17	0.03
Russian (21)	61	0.11
Scandinavian (0)	75	0.13
Scotch-Irish (302)	792	1.40
Scottish (453)	861	1.52
Serbian (0)	12	0.02
Slavic (0)	13	0.02
Slovak (23)	23	0.04
Slovene (0)	9	0.02
Swedish (160)	302	0.53
Swiss (30)	113	0.20
Turkish (10)	33	0.06
Ukrainian (0)	22	0.04
Welsh (94)	399	0.70
West Indian, ex. Hispanic (42)	56	0.10
Jamaican (29)	29	0.05
Other West Indian (13)	27	0.05
Yugoslavian (0)	12	0.02

Hispanic Origin	Population	%
Hispanic or Latino (of any race)	2,719	4.84
Central American, ex. Mexican	115	0.20
Costa Rican	1	<0.01
Guatemalan	59	0.11
Honduran	16	0.03
Nicaraguan	19	0.03
Panamanian	1	<0.01
Salvadoran	19	0.03
Cuban	26	0.05
Dominican Republic	15	0.03
Mexican	2,199	3.92
Puerto Rican	118	0.21
South American	23	0.04
Argentinean	3	0.01
Bolivian	3	0.01
Chilean	3	0.01
Colombian	6	0.01
Ecuadorian	2	<0.01
Peruvian	3	0.01
Venezuelan	3	0.01
Other Hispanic or Latino	223	0.40

Race*	Population	%
African-American/Black (8,532)	9,500	16.93
Not Hispanic (8,470)	9,376	16.70
Hispanic (62)	124	0.22
American Indian/Alaska Native (185)	528	0.94
Not Hispanic (134)	432	0.77
Hispanic (51)	96	0.17
Apache (7)	9	0.02
Blackfeet (1)	32	0.06
Canadian/French Am. Ind. (0)	1	<0.01
Central American Ind. (0)	7	0.01
Cherokee (44)	127	0.23
Cheyenne (1)	4	0.01
Chickasaw (0)	1	<0.01
Chippewa (3)	6	0.01
Choctaw (5)	10	0.02
Creek (2)	3	0.01
Delaware (0)	6	0.01
Hopi (0)	1	<0.01
Inupiat *(Alaska Native)* (0)	1	<0.01
Iroquois (0)	7	0.01
Kiowa (1)	1	<0.01
Mexican American Ind. (16)	30	0.05
Navajo (2)	11	0.02
Osage (2)	2	<0.01
Potawatomi (3)	7	0.01
Seminole (0)	2	<0.01
Shoshone (0)	1	<0.01
Sioux (3)	11	0.02
Spanish American Ind. (1)	2	<0.01
Ute (4)	4	0.01
Asian (265)	401	0.71
Not Hispanic (264)	383	0.68
Hispanic (1)	18	0.03
Chinese, ex. Taiwanese (46)	58	0.10
Filipino (50)	76	0.14
Indian (39)	53	0.09
Japanese (19)	57	0.10
Korean (32)	58	0.10
Laotian (0)	2	<0.01
Malaysian (1)	1	<0.01
Pakistani (1)	1	<0.01
Taiwanese (0)	2	<0.01
Thai (7)	11	0.02
Vietnamese (37)	46	0.08
Hawaii Native/Pacific Islander (25)	54	0.10
Not Hispanic (22)	43	0.08
Hispanic (3)	11	0.02
Guamanian/Chamorro (5)	8	0.01
Native Hawaiian (5)	22	0.04
Samoan (8)	11	0.02
White (44,204)	45,548	81.15
Not Hispanic (43,181)	44,327	78.97
Hispanic (1,023)	1,221	2.18

Angola

Place Type: City
County: Steuben
Population: 8,612†

Ancestry‡	Population	%
African, Sub-Saharan (11)	11	0.13
African (11)	11	0.13
American (639)	639	7.59
Arab (0)	4	0.05
Syrian (0)	4	0.05
Austrian (35)	71	0.84
Croatian (0)	9	0.11
Czech (0)	133	1.58
Czechoslovakian (0)	37	0.44
Danish (0)	18	0.21
Dutch (58)	274	3.25
English (285)	951	11.29
European (41)	41	0.49
French, ex. Basque (0)	173	2.05
French Canadian (14)	37	0.44
German (1,499)	2,802	33.26
Greek (77)	104	1.23
Hungarian (0)	41	0.49
Irish (182)	868	10.30
Italian (180)	345	4.10
Lithuanian (10)	10	0.12
Norwegian (30)	59	0.70
Polish (168)	335	3.98
Portuguese (11)	11	0.13
Romanian (22)	22	0.26
Russian (17)	17	0.20
Scotch-Irish (0)	137	1.63
Scottish (88)	195	2.31
Slovak (0)	9	0.11
Slovene (0)	10	0.12
Swedish (10)	53	0.63
Swiss (11)	21	0.25
Welsh (11)	88	1.04

Hispanic Origin	Population	%
Hispanic or Latino (of any race)	542	6.29
Central American, ex. Mexican	18	0.21
Honduran	1	0.01
Salvadoran	17	0.20
Cuban	3	0.03
Mexican	426	4.95
Puerto Rican	41	0.48
South American	11	0.13
Argentinean	3	0.03
Bolivian	1	0.01
Chilean	1	0.01
Colombian	3	0.03
Ecuadorian	1	0.01
Peruvian	1	0.01
Venezuelan	1	0.01
Other Hispanic or Latino	43	0.50

Race*	Population	%
African-American/Black (120)	164	1.90
Not Hispanic (101)	141	1.64
Hispanic (19)	23	0.27
American Indian/Alaska Native (24)	71	0.82
Not Hispanic (19)	65	0.75
Hispanic (5)	6	0.07
Blackfeet (0)	1	0.01
Cherokee (2)	9	0.10
Chickasaw (0)	1	0.01
Chippewa (1)	4	0.05
Choctaw (0)	1	0.01
Iroquois (2)	4	0.05
Navajo (3)	6	0.07
Ottawa (1)	1	0.01
Sioux (0)	3	0.03
Asian (73)	107	1.24
Not Hispanic (71)	103	1.20
Hispanic (2)	4	0.05
Bangladeshi (1)	1	0.01
Chinese, ex. Taiwanese (16)	18	0.21
Filipino (8)	18	0.21
Indian (9)	11	0.13
Japanese (2)	4	0.05
Korean (13)	17	0.20
Malaysian (2)	3	0.03
Nepalese (4)	4	0.05
Pakistani (12)	13	0.15
Taiwanese (0)	1	0.01
Thai (3)	5	0.06
Vietnamese (1)	2	0.02
Hawaii Native/Pacific Islander (7)	11	0.13
Not Hispanic (2)	5	0.06
Hispanic (5)	6	0.07
Guamanian/Chamorro (6)	7	0.08
Native Hawaiian (1)	2	0.02
White (8,064)	8,203	95.25
Not Hispanic (7,754)	7,866	91.34
Hispanic (310)	337	3.91

*Notes: † The Census 2010 population figure is used to calculate the percentages in the Hispanic Origin and Race categories. Ancestry percentages are based on the 2006-2010 American Community Survey population (not shown); ‡ Numbers in parentheses indicate the number of people reporting a single ancestry; * Numbers in parentheses indicate the number of persons reporting this race alone, not in combination with any other race; Please refer to the Explanation of Data for more information.*

Auburn

Place Type: City
County: DeKalb
Population: 12,731†

Ancestry‡	Population	%
Alsatian (0)	12	0.10
American (1,248)	1,248	10.00
Belgian (16)	46	0.37
British (9)	46	0.37
Canadian (16)	20	0.16
Croatian (0)	14	0.11
Czech (0)	11	0.09
Czechoslovakian (15)	15	0.12
Dutch (54)	335	2.68
English (373)	1,107	8.87
European (44)	44	0.35
French, ex. Basque (107)	491	3.93
French Canadian (0)	16	0.13
German (2,358)	4,535	36.33
Greek (25)	25	0.20
Hungarian (0)	7	0.06
Irish (286)	1,143	9.16
Italian (121)	444	3.56
Norwegian (0)	62	0.50
Pennsylvania German (25)	85	0.68
Polish (58)	388	3.11
Scandinavian (12)	12	0.10
Scotch-Irish (82)	192	1.54
Scottish (50)	293	2.35
Slovak (32)	66	0.53
Swedish (0)	99	0.79
Swiss (29)	126	1.01
Ukrainian (0)	88	0.71
Welsh (27)	123	0.99

Hispanic Origin	Population	%
Hispanic or Latino (of any race)	332	2.61
Central American, ex. Mexican	11	0.09
Costa Rican	2	0.02
Guatemalan	6	0.05
Honduran	2	0.02
Salvadoran	1	0.01
Cuban	3	0.02
Mexican	271	2.13
Puerto Rican	15	0.12
South American	5	0.04
Chilean	2	0.02
Colombian	1	0.01
Peruvian	1	0.01
Venezuelan	1	0.01
Other Hispanic or Latino	27	0.21

Race*	Population	%
African-American/Black (57)	100	0.79
Not Hispanic (53)	92	0.72
Hispanic (4)	8	0.06
American Indian/Alaska Native (24)	59	0.46
Not Hispanic (22)	53	0.42
Hispanic (2)	6	0.05
Aleut *(Alaska Native)* (1)	1	0.01
Blackfeet (2)	3	0.02
Cherokee (12)	15	0.12
Chippewa (1)	1	0.01
Choctaw (1)	1	0.01
Iroquois (0)	1	0.01
Mexican American Ind. (2)	4	0.03
Sioux (0)	3	0.02
Asian (93)	104	0.82
Not Hispanic (91)	102	0.80
Hispanic (2)	2	0.02
Cambodian (4)	4	0.03
Chinese, ex. Taiwanese (18)	19	0.15
Filipino (20)	24	0.19
Indian (18)	18	0.14
Indonesian (1)	1	0.01
Japanese (2)	2	0.02
Korean (6)	7	0.05
Laotian (1)	1	0.01
Pakistani (3)	4	0.03
Thai (3)	3	0.02
Vietnamese (10)	13	0.10
Hawaii Native/Pacific Islander (0)	2	0.02
Not Hispanic (0)	2	0.02
Guamanian/Chamorro (0)	1	0.01
White (12,341)	12,458	97.86
Not Hispanic (12,134)	12,221	95.99
Hispanic (207)	237	1.86

Avon

Place Type: Town
County: Hendricks
Population: 12,446†

Ancestry‡	Population	%
African, Sub-Saharan (100)	124	1.06
African (72)	96	0.82
Nigerian (28)	28	0.24
American (979)	979	8.40
Arab (92)	136	1.17
Arab (92)	92	0.79
Lebanese (0)	12	0.10
Syrian (0)	32	0.27
Armenian (0)	11	0.09
Australian (17)	17	0.15
Belgian (0)	31	0.27
British (16)	16	0.14
Bulgarian (10)	21	0.18
Czech (27)	43	0.37
Dutch (44)	225	1.93
English (740)	1,548	13.28
European (139)	139	1.19
Finnish (14)	14	0.12
French, ex. Basque (68)	236	2.03
French Canadian (0)	35	0.30
German (1,179)	3,032	26.02
Greek (62)	95	0.82
Hungarian (0)	55	0.47
Irish (670)	1,835	15.75
Italian (198)	473	4.06
Latvian (14)	14	0.12
Lithuanian (24)	40	0.34
Norwegian (0)	32	0.27
Pennsylvania German (33)	41	0.35
Polish (142)	496	4.26
Portuguese (0)	28	0.24
Russian (14)	14	0.12
Scotch-Irish (12)	74	0.64
Scottish (59)	277	2.38
Serbian (0)	15	0.13
Slovak (0)	67	0.57
Swedish (0)	42	0.36
Swiss (86)	129	1.11
Welsh (0)	51	0.44
West Indian, ex. Hispanic (59)	77	0.66
British West Indian (59)	77	0.66

Hispanic Origin	Population	%
Hispanic or Latino (of any race)	531	4.27
Central American, ex. Mexican	41	0.33
Costa Rican	7	0.06
Guatemalan	8	0.06
Honduran	3	0.02
Nicaraguan	6	0.05
Panamanian	1	0.01
Salvadoran	13	0.10
Other Central American	3	0.02
Cuban	5	0.04
Dominican Republic	23	0.18
Mexican	304	2.44
Puerto Rican	80	0.64
South American	43	0.35
Argentinean	1	0.01
Bolivian	3	0.02
Chilean	3	0.02
Colombian	12	0.10
Ecuadorian	2	0.02
Peruvian	19	0.15
Uruguayan	3	0.02
Other Hispanic or Latino	35	0.28

Race*	Population	%
African-American/Black (731)	849	6.82
Not Hispanic (724)	830	6.67
Hispanic (7)	19	0.15
American Indian/Alaska Native (43)	90	0.72
Not Hispanic (26)	72	0.58
Hispanic (17)	18	0.14
Blackfeet (0)	6	0.05
Central American Ind. (2)	2	0.02
Cherokee (1)	13	0.10
Cheyenne (1)	1	0.01
Chippewa (0)	1	0.01
Choctaw (0)	1	0.01
Cree (0)	1	0.01
Creek (0)	1	0.01
Mexican American Ind. (2)	2	0.02
Potawatomi (2)	3	0.02
Pueblo (0)	1	0.01
Sioux (5)	7	0.06
Yakama (1)	1	0.01
Asian (414)	503	4.04
Not Hispanic (410)	495	3.98
Hispanic (4)	8	0.06
Bangladeshi (4)	4	0.03
Cambodian (1)	1	0.01
Chinese, ex. Taiwanese (40)	43	0.35
Filipino (94)	129	1.04
Indian (126)	148	1.19
Indonesian (2)	2	0.02
Japanese (17)	24	0.19
Korean (27)	37	0.30
Laotian (1)	1	0.01
Pakistani (44)	53	0.43
Taiwanese (10)	11	0.09
Thai (2)	5	0.04
Vietnamese (36)	42	0.34
Hawaii Native/Pacific Islander (11)	22	0.18
Not Hispanic (11)	22	0.18
Guamanian/Chamorro (5)	5	0.04
Native Hawaiian (5)	12	0.10
Samoan (1)	2	0.02
White (10,789)	11,049	88.78
Not Hispanic (10,486)	10,705	86.01
Hispanic (303)	344	2.76

Bedford

Place Type: City
County: Lawrence
Population: 13,413†

Ancestry‡	Population	%
American (1,968)	1,968	14.56
Arab (1)	1	0.01
Arab (1)	1	0.01
Austrian (0)	11	0.08
Belgian (11)	11	0.08
British (9)	25	0.18
Czech (0)	8	0.06
Dutch (11)	193	1.43
English (534)	1,202	8.89
European (17)	91	0.67
Finnish (0)	44	0.33
French, ex. Basque (92)	289	2.14
French Canadian (29)	50	0.37
German (1,189)	2,625	19.42
Greek (16)	16	0.12
Hungarian (0)	16	0.12
Irish (820)	1,862	13.78
Italian (103)	382	2.83
Lithuanian (0)	9	0.07
Norwegian (39)	72	0.53
Pennsylvania German (26)	26	0.19
Polish (51)	201	1.49
Russian (0)	8	0.06
Scotch-Irish (206)	410	3.03
Scottish (111)	319	2.36

*Notes: † The Census 2010 population figure is used to calculate the percentages in the Hispanic Origin and Race categories. Ancestry percentages are based on the 2006-2010 American Community Survey population (not shown); ‡ Numbers in parentheses indicate the number of people reporting a single ancestry; * Numbers in parentheses indicate the number of persons reporting this race alone, not in combination with any other race; Please refer to the Explanation of Data for more information.*

Ancestry	Population	%
Swedish (7)	42	0.31
Welsh (9)	107	0.79
West Indian, ex. Hispanic (11)	11	0.08
Dutch West Indian (11)	11	0.08
Yugoslavian (9)	9	0.07

Hispanic Origin	Population	%
Hispanic or Latino (of any race)	243	1.81
Central American, ex. Mexican	7	0.05
Costa Rican	1	0.01
Guatemalan	3	0.02
Nicaraguan	1	0.01
Salvadoran	2	0.01
Cuban	4	0.03
Mexican	196	1.46
Puerto Rican	10	0.07
South American	7	0.05
Colombian	4	0.03
Peruvian	1	0.01
Venezuelan	1	0.01
Other South American	1	0.01
Other Hispanic or Latino	19	0.14

Race*	Population	%
African-American/Black (106)	153	1.14
Not Hispanic (103)	148	1.10
Hispanic (3)	5	0.04
American Indian/Alaska Native (37)	123	0.92
Not Hispanic (35)	112	0.84
Hispanic (2)	11	0.08
Apache (0)	1	0.01
Blackfeet (1)	4	0.03
Canadian/French Am. Ind. (1)	3	0.02
Cherokee (7)	40	0.30
Chippewa (2)	4	0.03
Delaware (1)	1	0.01
Iroquois (3)	3	0.02
Lumbee (5)	10	0.07
Navajo (0)	1	0.01
Sioux (1)	8	0.06
Spanish American Ind. (1)	1	0.01
Ute (1)	1	0.01
Asian (120)	152	1.13
Not Hispanic (120)	143	1.07
Hispanic (0)	9	0.07
Chinese, ex. Taiwanese (33)	43	0.32
Filipino (24)	40	0.30
Indian (40)	43	0.32
Japanese (4)	8	0.06
Korean (3)	4	0.03
Vietnamese (12)	14	0.10
Hawaii Native/Pacific Islander (3)	10	0.07
Not Hispanic (3)	10	0.07
Guamanian/Chamorro (0)	1	0.01
Native Hawaiian (2)	3	0.02
Samoan (0)	1	0.01
White (12,902)	13,081	97.52
Not Hispanic (12,751)	12,900	96.18
Hispanic (151)	181	1.35

Beech Grove

Place Type: City
County: Marion
Population: 14,192†

Ancestry‡	Population	%
African, Sub-Saharan (0)	157	1.12
African (0)	157	1.12
American (1,303)	1,303	9.29
Austrian (13)	49	0.35
Brazilian (15)	15	0.11
British (0)	69	0.49
Canadian (17)	29	0.21
Czech (0)	19	0.14
Danish (0)	37	0.26
Dutch (70)	245	1.75
English (548)	1,497	10.67
European (228)	253	1.80
French, ex. Basque (38)	494	3.52
French Canadian (53)	53	0.38
German (1,633)	4,147	29.56
Greek (16)	55	0.39
Irish (885)	2,626	18.72
Italian (262)	681	4.85
Norwegian (12)	26	0.19
Polish (16)	94	0.67
Portuguese (9)	9	0.06
Scotch-Irish (98)	417	2.97
Scottish (88)	211	1.50
Slovak (9)	9	0.06
Swedish (0)	74	0.53
Swiss (23)	49	0.35
Welsh (49)	112	0.80

Hispanic Origin	Population	%
Hispanic or Latino (of any race)	589	4.15
Central American, ex. Mexican	28	0.20
Guatemalan	4	0.03
Honduran	13	0.09
Nicaraguan	1	0.01
Panamanian	5	0.04
Salvadoran	5	0.04
Cuban	7	0.05
Dominican Republic	4	0.03
Mexican	428	3.02
Puerto Rican	45	0.32
South American	18	0.13
Bolivian	2	0.01
Chilean	1	0.01
Colombian	3	0.02
Ecuadorian	3	0.02
Peruvian	7	0.05
Venezuelan	1	0.01
Other South American	1	0.01
Other Hispanic or Latino	59	0.42

Race*	Population	%
African-American/Black (461)	587	4.14
Not Hispanic (442)	563	3.97
Hispanic (19)	24	0.17
American Indian/Alaska Native (46)	123	0.87
Not Hispanic (37)	107	0.75
Hispanic (9)	16	0.11
Apache (1)	2	0.01
Blackfeet (1)	8	0.06
Cherokee (6)	17	0.12
Chippewa (1)	1	0.01
Choctaw (0)	5	0.04
Delaware (3)	3	0.02
Iroquois (1)	1	0.01
Mexican American Ind. (1)	1	0.01
Navajo (1)	2	0.01
Potawatomi (3)	4	0.03
Shoshone (0)	1	0.01
Sioux (4)	7	0.05
Asian (100)	153	1.08
Not Hispanic (96)	137	0.97
Hispanic (4)	16	0.11
Bangladeshi (4)	4	0.03
Chinese, ex. Taiwanese (11)	17	0.12
Filipino (36)	52	0.37
Indian (19)	25	0.18
Japanese (9)	15	0.11
Korean (10)	25	0.18
Pakistani (7)	7	0.05
Thai (0)	1	0.01
Vietnamese (2)	4	0.03
Hawaii Native/Pacific Islander (5)	16	0.11
Not Hispanic (3)	9	0.06
Hispanic (2)	7	0.05
Fijian (0)	2	0.01
Guamanian/Chamorro (2)	2	0.01
Native Hawaiian (2)	4	0.03
Samoan (1)	1	0.01
White (12,984)	13,258	93.42
Not Hispanic (12,766)	12,981	91.47
Hispanic (218)	277	1.95

Bloomington

Place Type: City
County: Monroe
Population: 80,405†

Ancestry‡	Population	%
Afghan (59)	59	0.08
African, Sub-Saharan (498)	593	0.76
African (417)	508	0.65
Ethiopian (4)	5	0.01
Nigerian (14)	14	0.02
South African (63)	63	0.08
Other Sub-Saharan African (0)	3	<0.01
Albanian (20)	20	0.03
Alsatian (0)	19	0.02
American (3,411)	3,411	4.35
Arab (363)	548	0.70
Arab (187)	187	0.24
Egyptian (8)	21	0.03
Iraqi (30)	30	0.04
Jordanian (0)	10	0.01
Lebanese (67)	167	0.21
Moroccan (27)	27	0.03
Syrian (13)	75	0.10
Other Arab (31)	31	0.04
Armenian (14)	37	0.05
Australian (18)	46	0.06
Austrian (70)	439	0.56
Belgian (23)	155	0.20
Brazilian (40)	69	0.09
British (181)	729	0.93
Bulgarian (29)	29	0.04
Canadian (71)	138	0.18
Croatian (48)	171	0.22
Czech (129)	478	0.61
Czechoslovakian (19)	85	0.11
Danish (127)	353	0.45
Dutch (483)	1,696	2.16
Eastern European (296)	354	0.45
English (2,870)	8,739	11.13
Estonian (0)	15	0.02
European (1,245)	1,404	1.79
Finnish (12)	42	0.05
French, ex. Basque (581)	2,654	3.38
French Canadian (73)	305	0.39
German (5,754)	19,499	24.84
Greek (227)	551	0.70
Hungarian (165)	767	0.98
Icelander (21)	41	0.05
Iranian (187)	201	0.26
Irish (3,083)	10,941	13.94
Israeli (91)	168	0.21
Italian (1,043)	3,669	4.67
Latvian (10)	10	0.01
Lithuanian (82)	362	0.46
Macedonian (48)	62	0.08
Northern European (62)	98	0.12
Norwegian (240)	1,150	1.47
Pennsylvania German (21)	58	0.07
Polish (952)	3,792	4.83
Portuguese (9)	52	0.07
Romanian (110)	270	0.34
Russian (341)	1,268	1.62
Scandinavian (25)	161	0.21
Scotch-Irish (826)	2,163	2.76
Scottish (576)	2,274	2.90
Serbian (49)	155	0.20
Slavic (0)	23	0.03
Slovak (37)	194	0.25
Slovene (10)	65	0.08
Swedish (305)	1,462	1.86
Swiss (98)	457	0.58
Turkish (111)	111	0.14
Ukrainian (122)	232	0.30
Welsh (171)	840	1.07
West Indian, ex. Hispanic (57)	96	0.12
Dutch West Indian (0)	23	0.03
Jamaican (57)	57	0.07

*Notes: † The Census 2010 population figure is used to calculate the percentages in the Hispanic Origin and Race categories. Ancestry percentages are based on the 2006-2010 American Community Survey population (not shown); ‡ Numbers in parentheses indicate the number of people reporting a single ancestry; * Numbers in parentheses indicate the number of persons reporting this race alone, not in combination with any other race; Please refer to the Explanation of Data for more information.*

Ancestry	Population	%
West Indian (0)	16	0.02
Yugoslavian (17)	50	0.06

Hispanic Origin	Population	%
Hispanic or Latino (of any race)	2,823	3.51
Central American, ex. Mexican	165	0.21
Costa Rican	21	0.03
Guatemalan	38	0.05
Honduran	21	0.03
Nicaraguan	28	0.03
Panamanian	22	0.03
Salvadoran	31	0.04
Other Central American	4	<0.01
Cuban	126	0.16
Dominican Republic	43	0.05
Mexican	1,506	1.87
Puerto Rican	348	0.43
South American	349	0.43
Argentinean	57	0.07
Bolivian	11	0.01
Chilean	36	0.04
Colombian	85	0.11
Ecuadorian	30	0.04
Paraguayan	5	0.01
Peruvian	67	0.08
Uruguayan	5	0.01
Venezuelan	53	0.07
Other Hispanic or Latino	286	0.36

Race*	Population	%
African-American/Black (3,671)	4,618	5.74
Not Hispanic (3,562)	4,423	5.50
Hispanic (109)	195	0.24
American Indian/Alaska Native (214)	699	0.87
Not Hispanic (176)	591	0.74
Hispanic (38)	108	0.13
Alaska Athabascan *(Ala. Nat.)* (1)	1	<0.01
Aleut *(Alaska Native)* (0)	2	<0.01
Apache (4)	11	0.01
Blackfeet (0)	26	0.03
Canadian/French Am. Ind. (0)	1	<0.01
Central American Ind. (1)	2	<0.01
Cherokee (37)	161	0.20
Chickasaw (2)	2	<0.01
Chippewa (10)	21	0.03
Choctaw (8)	19	0.02
Cree (0)	1	<0.01
Creek (4)	5	0.01
Delaware (5)	8	0.01
Hopi (1)	2	<0.01
Inupiat *(Alaska Native)* (0)	3	<0.01
Iroquois (5)	9	0.01
Lumbee (4)	4	<0.01
Menominee (1)	2	<0.01
Mexican American Ind. (6)	14	0.02
Navajo (3)	9	0.01
Osage (0)	2	<0.01
Ottawa (1)	1	<0.01
Potawatomi (3)	10	0.01
Pueblo (0)	3	<0.01
Puget Sound Salish (5)	5	0.01
Seminole (0)	3	<0.01
Shoshone (0)	1	<0.01
Sioux (9)	24	0.03
South American Ind. (2)	4	<0.01
Spanish American Ind. (3)	21	0.03
Tlingit-Haida *(Alaska Native)* (0)	1	<0.01
Tohono O'Odham (3)	8	0.01
Yakama (3)	3	<0.01
Yup'ik *(Alaska Native)* (0)	1	<0.01
Asian (6,399)	7,368	9.16
Not Hispanic (6,378)	7,298	9.08
Hispanic (21)	70	0.09
Bangladeshi (21)	27	0.03
Burmese (17)	18	0.02
Cambodian (5)	9	0.01
Chinese, ex. Taiwanese (2,004)	2,230	2.77
Filipino (161)	312	0.39
Hmong (4)	5	0.01
Indian (1,263)	1,390	1.73
Indonesian (71)	78	0.10
Japanese (242)	395	0.49
Korean (1,696)	1,807	2.25
Laotian (6)	8	0.01
Malaysian (49)	59	0.07
Nepalese (19)	19	0.02
Pakistani (76)	87	0.11
Sri Lankan (38)	40	0.05
Taiwanese (235)	260	0.32
Thai (83)	103	0.13
Vietnamese (168)	203	0.25
Hawaii Native/Pacific Islander (42)	120	0.15
Not Hispanic (37)	95	0.12
Hispanic (5)	25	0.03
Fijian (1)	1	<0.01
Guamanian/Chamorro (11)	24	0.03
Native Hawaiian (11)	37	0.05
Samoan (6)	16	0.02
White (66,751)	68,936	85.74
Not Hispanic (65,189)	67,128	83.49
Hispanic (1,562)	1,808	2.25

Bluffton

Place Type: City
County: Wells
Population: 9,897†

Ancestry‡	Population	%
American (843)	843	8.84
Belgian (0)	17	0.18
British (35)	71	0.74
Canadian (6)	6	0.06
Czech (9)	9	0.09
Danish (30)	58	0.61
Dutch (63)	337	3.54
English (762)	1,354	14.21
European (49)	49	0.51
Finnish (0)	47	0.49
French, ex. Basque (68)	192	2.01
French Canadian (31)	73	0.77
German (1,690)	3,407	35.75
Hungarian (16)	16	0.17
Irish (334)	1,147	12.03
Italian (113)	368	3.86
Pennsylvania German (32)	32	0.34
Polish (43)	239	2.51
Russian (0)	10	0.10
Scandinavian (14)	30	0.31
Scotch-Irish (30)	41	0.43
Scottish (66)	157	1.65
Serbian (13)	13	0.14
Slovak (9)	9	0.09
Swedish (0)	26	0.27
Swiss (195)	526	5.52
Welsh (8)	64	0.67

Hispanic Origin	Population	%
Hispanic or Latino (of any race)	328	3.31
Central American, ex. Mexican	15	0.15
Guatemalan	1	0.01
Panamanian	5	0.05
Salvadoran	9	0.09
Cuban	2	0.02
Mexican	236	2.38
Puerto Rican	26	0.26
South American	14	0.14
Colombian	12	0.12
Ecuadorian	2	0.02
Other Hispanic or Latino	35	0.35

Race*	Population	%
African-American/Black (69)	115	1.16
Not Hispanic (65)	103	1.04
Hispanic (4)	12	0.12
American Indian/Alaska Native (41)	74	0.75
Not Hispanic (38)	64	0.65
Hispanic (3)	10	0.10
Blackfeet (2)	3	0.03
Cherokee (11)	29	0.29
Cheyenne (1)	2	0.02
Chippewa (1)	1	0.01
Creek (1)	3	0.03
Iroquois (1)	1	0.01
Mexican American Ind. (1)	1	0.01
Sioux (6)	6	0.06
South American Ind. (0)	1	0.01
Asian (50)	72	0.73
Not Hispanic (49)	71	0.72
Hispanic (1)	1	0.01
Cambodian (4)	6	0.06
Chinese, ex. Taiwanese (15)	15	0.15
Filipino (15)	20	0.20
Hmong (0)	1	0.01
Indian (0)	4	0.04
Korean (8)	11	0.11
Taiwanese (1)	1	0.01
Vietnamese (4)	4	0.04
Hawaii Native/Pacific Islander (3)	4	0.04
Not Hispanic (3)	4	0.04
Guamanian/Chamorro (1)	2	0.02
Native Hawaiian (1)	1	0.01
White (9,499)	9,603	97.03
Not Hispanic (9,326)	9,406	95.04
Hispanic (173)	197	1.99

Brazil

Place Type: City
County: Clay
Population: 7,912†

Ancestry‡	Population	%
American (1,759)	1,759	23.35
British (0)	150	1.99
Canadian (53)	53	0.70
Dutch (0)	63	0.84
English (330)	725	9.63
European (57)	57	0.76
French, ex. Basque (48)	459	6.09
German (407)	1,321	17.54
Hungarian (0)	14	0.19
Irish (202)	901	11.96
Italian (58)	195	2.59
Norwegian (0)	15	0.20
Polish (43)	83	1.10
Russian (9)	9	0.12
Scotch-Irish (131)	226	3.00
Scottish (23)	115	1.53
Swiss (0)	23	0.31
Welsh (28)	86	1.14
Yugoslavian (0)	23	0.31

Hispanic Origin	Population	%
Hispanic or Latino (of any race)	123	1.55
Central American, ex. Mexican	2	0.03
Honduran	1	0.01
Panamanian	1	0.01
Cuban	4	0.05
Mexican	90	1.14
Puerto Rican	6	0.08
South American	2	0.03
Colombian	2	0.03
Other Hispanic or Latino	19	0.24

Race*	Population	%
African-American/Black (51)	90	1.14
Not Hispanic (50)	88	1.11
Hispanic (1)	2	0.03
American Indian/Alaska Native (11)	35	0.44
Not Hispanic (11)	32	0.40
Hispanic (0)	3	0.04
Cherokee (4)	14	0.18
Cree (1)	1	0.01
Sioux (0)	1	0.01
Asian (37)	47	0.59
Not Hispanic (37)	47	0.59
Chinese, ex. Taiwanese (10)	11	0.14
Filipino (2)	2	0.03
Indian (18)	21	0.27

*Notes: † The Census 2010 population figure is used to calculate the percentages in the Hispanic Origin and Race categories. Ancestry percentages are based on the 2006-2010 American Community Survey population (not shown); ‡ Numbers in parentheses indicate the number of people reporting a single ancestry; * Numbers in parentheses indicate the number of persons reporting this race alone, not in combination with any other race; Please refer to the Explanation of Data for more information.*

Japanese (1)	2	0.03
Korean (2)	2	0.03
Vietnamese (4)	4	0.05
Hawaii Native/Pacific Islander (2)	5	0.06
Not Hispanic (2)	5	0.06
Native Hawaiian (2)	4	0.05
Samoan (0)	1	0.01
White (7,682)	7,764	98.13
Not Hispanic (7,614)	7,687	97.16
Hispanic (68)	77	0.97

Brownsburg

Place Type: Town
County: Hendricks
Population: 21,285†

Ancestry‡	Population	%
American (1,845)	1,845	8.97
Arab (11)	76	0.37
Jordanian (11)	34	0.17
Lebanese (0)	42	0.20
Armenian (0)	14	0.07
Austrian (25)	25	0.12
British (13)	62	0.30
Canadian (7)	18	0.09
Celtic (15)	15	0.07
Croatian (27)	27	0.13
Czech (0)	37	0.18
Czechoslovakian (0)	37	0.18
Danish (33)	99	0.48
Dutch (111)	276	1.34
English (1,969)	3,595	17.47
European (284)	303	1.47
Finnish (0)	36	0.17
French, ex. Basque (80)	543	2.64
French Canadian (51)	151	0.73
German (2,285)	5,895	28.65
Greek (11)	42	0.20
Hungarian (89)	89	0.43
Iranian (38)	38	0.18
Irish (1,200)	3,161	15.36
Italian (99)	627	3.05
Lithuanian (13)	53	0.26
Macedonian (25)	32	0.16
Northern European (14)	14	0.07
Norwegian (152)	344	1.67
Pennsylvania German (11)	11	0.05
Polish (220)	511	2.48
Portuguese (14)	30	0.15
Romanian (33)	33	0.16
Russian (61)	120	0.58
Scandinavian (0)	35	0.17
Scotch-Irish (243)	429	2.09
Scottish (180)	826	4.01
Serbian (11)	11	0.05
Slovak (37)	89	0.43
Slovene (0)	12	0.06
Swedish (37)	172	0.84
Swiss (13)	30	0.15
Ukrainian (16)	16	0.08
Welsh (34)	213	1.04
Yugoslavian (103)	119	0.58

Hispanic Origin	Population	%
Hispanic or Latino (of any race)	635	2.98
Central American, ex. Mexican	46	0.22
Costa Rican	1	<0.01
Guatemalan	12	0.06
Honduran	12	0.06
Nicaraguan	4	0.02
Panamanian	2	0.01
Salvadoran	15	0.07
Cuban	10	0.05
Dominican Republic	23	0.11
Mexican	401	1.88
Puerto Rican	58	0.27
South American	58	0.27
Argentinean	5	0.02
Bolivian	4	0.02
Chilean	12	0.06
Colombian	7	0.03
Ecuadorian	7	0.03
Peruvian	17	0.08
Venezuelan	6	0.03
Other Hispanic or Latino	39	0.18

Race*	Population	%
African-American/Black (462)	600	2.82
Not Hispanic (442)	572	2.69
Hispanic (20)	28	0.13
American Indian/Alaska Native (31)	85	0.40
Not Hispanic (28)	80	0.38
Hispanic (3)	5	0.02
Alaska Athabascan *(Ala. Nat.)* (0)	2	0.01
Blackfeet (0)	2	0.01
Cherokee (4)	22	0.10
Chickasaw (2)	2	0.01
Chippewa (1)	1	<0.01
Delaware (2)	3	0.01
Iroquois (0)	4	0.02
Mexican American Ind. (2)	3	0.01
Navajo (1)	2	0.01
Sioux (2)	7	0.03
Asian (337)	428	2.01
Not Hispanic (333)	419	1.97
Hispanic (4)	9	0.04
Bangladeshi (5)	5	0.02
Burmese (4)	4	0.02
Chinese, ex. Taiwanese (38)	42	0.20
Filipino (39)	73	0.34
Indian (135)	142	0.67
Indonesian (0)	2	0.01
Japanese (16)	28	0.13
Korean (18)	35	0.16
Laotian (0)	3	0.01
Malaysian (1)	1	<0.01
Pakistani (12)	17	0.08
Thai (7)	7	0.03
Vietnamese (52)	53	0.25
Hawaii Native/Pacific Islander (12)	21	0.10
Not Hispanic (8)	17	0.08
Hispanic (4)	4	0.02
Guamanian/Chamorro (5)	6	0.03
Native Hawaiian (1)	7	0.03
Samoan (4)	4	0.02
White (19,874)	20,163	94.73
Not Hispanic (19,546)	19,796	93.00
Hispanic (328)	367	1.72

Carmel

Place Type: City
County: Hamilton
Population: 79,191†

Ancestry‡	Population	%
Afghan (18)	37	0.05
African, Sub-Saharan (83)	255	0.33
African (58)	95	0.12
Ethiopian (12)	12	0.02
South African (13)	137	0.18
Sudanese (0)	11	0.01
American (4,712)	4,712	6.14
Arab (378)	563	0.73
Arab (86)	101	0.13
Egyptian (164)	164	0.21
Jordanian (8)	8	0.01
Lebanese (40)	160	0.21
Moroccan (13)	36	0.05
Palestinian (24)	24	0.03
Other Arab (43)	70	0.09
Armenian (0)	21	0.03
Australian (31)	42	0.05
Austrian (32)	161	0.21
Belgian (26)	352	0.46
Brazilian (0)	11	0.01
British (449)	626	0.82
Bulgarian (0)	16	0.02
Canadian (77)	166	0.22
Carpatho Rusyn (0)	16	0.02
Celtic (14)	14	0.02
Croatian (23)	175	0.23
Czech (33)	336	0.44
Czechoslovakian (60)	115	0.15
Danish (161)	597	0.78
Dutch (320)	1,777	2.31
Eastern European (149)	164	0.21
English (3,161)	11,352	14.79
Estonian (0)	13	0.02
European (1,056)	1,241	1.62
Finnish (14)	70	0.09
French, ex. Basque (305)	2,214	2.88
French Canadian (128)	225	0.29
German (7,760)	21,955	28.60
Greek (192)	485	0.63
Hungarian (86)	504	0.66
Icelander (0)	12	0.02
Iranian (203)	253	0.33
Irish (3,191)	12,211	15.91
Italian (1,290)	3,728	4.86
Latvian (129)	129	0.17
Lithuanian (57)	120	0.16
Luxemburger (0)	22	0.03
Macedonian (55)	104	0.14
Northern European (105)	105	0.14
Norwegian (335)	995	1.30
Pennsylvania German (15)	42	0.05
Polish (680)	3,117	4.06
Portuguese (22)	112	0.15
Romanian (112)	200	0.26
Russian (676)	1,522	1.98
Scandinavian (74)	90	0.12
Scotch-Irish (468)	1,430	1.86
Scottish (684)	2,632	3.43
Serbian (21)	40	0.05
Slovak (103)	356	0.46
Slovene (17)	109	0.14
Swedish (222)	1,414	1.84
Swiss (49)	431	0.56
Turkish (69)	69	0.09
Ukrainian (161)	271	0.35
Welsh (83)	628	0.82
West Indian, ex. Hispanic (39)	55	0.07
Haitian (0)	16	0.02
Jamaican (39)	39	0.05
Yugoslavian (51)	67	0.09

Hispanic Origin	Population	%
Hispanic or Latino (of any race)	2,009	2.54
Central American, ex. Mexican	181	0.23
Costa Rican	8	0.01
Guatemalan	87	0.11
Honduran	9	0.01
Nicaraguan	20	0.03
Panamanian	28	0.04
Salvadoran	28	0.04
Other Central American	1	<0.01
Cuban	101	0.13
Dominican Republic	40	0.05
Mexican	944	1.19
Puerto Rican	226	0.29
South American	310	0.39
Argentinean	38	0.05
Bolivian	12	0.02
Chilean	22	0.03
Colombian	125	0.16
Ecuadorian	17	0.02
Paraguayan	3	<0.01
Peruvian	49	0.06
Uruguayan	3	<0.01
Venezuelan	40	0.05
Other South American	1	<0.01
Other Hispanic or Latino	207	0.26

Race*	Population	%
African-American/Black (2,354)	2,767	3.49
Not Hispanic (2,299)	2,674	3.38
Hispanic (55)	93	0.12
American Indian/Alaska Native (130)	354	0.45

*Notes: † The Census 2010 population figure is used to calculate the percentages in the Hispanic Origin and Race categories. Ancestry percentages are based on the 2006-2010 American Community Survey population (not shown); ‡ Numbers in parentheses indicate the number of people reporting a single ancestry; * Numbers in parentheses indicate the number of persons reporting this race alone, not in combination with any other race; Please refer to the Explanation of Data for more information.*

	Population	%
Not Hispanic (104)	304	0.38
Hispanic (26)	50	0.06
Apache (6)	6	0.01
Blackfeet (4)	16	0.02
Central American Ind. (1)	2	<0.01
Cherokee (17)	57	0.07
Chippewa (4)	6	0.01
Choctaw (5)	11	0.01
Comanche (0)	3	<0.01
Cree (3)	3	<0.01
Creek (0)	1	<0.01
Crow (1)	1	<0.01
Hopi (2)	4	0.01
Inupiat *(Alaska Native)* (1)	1	<0.01
Iroquois (1)	8	0.01
Lumbee (2)	2	<0.01
Mexican American Ind. (16)	21	0.03
Navajo (1)	4	0.01
Osage (3)	3	<0.01
Ottawa (1)	5	0.01
Potawatomi (3)	11	0.01
Seminole (0)	1	<0.01
Sioux (3)	5	0.01
South American Ind. (1)	1	<0.01
Spanish American Ind. (2)	2	<0.01
Ute (0)	1	<0.01
Yaqui (2)	2	<0.01
Yup'ik *(Alaska Native)* (0)	1	<0.01
Asian (7,009)	7,838	9.90
Not Hispanic (6,988)	7,790	9.84
Hispanic (21)	48	0.06
Bangladeshi (34)	35	0.04
Burmese (1)	8	0.01
Cambodian (17)	22	0.03
Chinese, ex. Taiwanese (2,557)	2,754	3.48
Filipino (265)	411	0.52
Hmong (27)	27	0.03
Indian (2,384)	2,526	3.19
Indonesian (32)	41	0.05
Japanese (320)	415	0.52
Korean (583)	684	0.86
Laotian (9)	9	0.01
Malaysian (7)	17	0.02
Nepalese (12)	12	0.02
Pakistani (186)	211	0.27
Sri Lankan (30)	35	0.04
Taiwanese (145)	177	0.22
Thai (24)	42	0.05
Vietnamese (236)	279	0.35
Hawaii Native/Pacific Islander (20)	87	0.11
Not Hispanic (17)	77	0.10
Hispanic (3)	10	0.01
Guamanian/Chamorro (5)	11	0.01
Native Hawaiian (8)	33	0.04
Samoan (5)	16	0.02
White (67,654)	68,938	87.05
Not Hispanic (66,295)	67,446	85.17
Hispanic (1,359)	1,492	1.88

Cedar Lake

Place Type: Town
County: Lake
Population: 11,560†

Ancestry‡	Population	%
Albanian (0)	14	0.13
American (782)	782	7.02
Arab (0)	19	0.17
Lebanese (0)	19	0.17
Belgian (21)	82	0.74
Brazilian (11)	11	0.10
British (14)	14	0.13
Croatian (11)	155	1.39
Czech (0)	26	0.23
Danish (0)	27	0.24
Dutch (238)	576	5.17
Eastern European (0)	33	0.30
English (302)	971	8.72
European (90)	90	0.81
French, ex. Basque (39)	315	2.83
French Canadian (16)	56	0.50
German (770)	3,355	30.13
Greek (10)	10	0.09
Hungarian (7)	71	0.64
Irish (551)	1,862	16.72
Italian (130)	1,154	10.36
Lithuanian (50)	124	1.11
Northern European (65)	65	0.58
Norwegian (24)	49	0.44
Polish (913)	1,667	14.97
Russian (10)	72	0.65
Scotch-Irish (47)	145	1.30
Scottish (6)	81	0.73
Serbian (62)	204	1.83
Slovak (43)	307	2.76
Slovene (0)	10	0.09
Swedish (101)	336	3.02
Swiss (0)	13	0.12
Ukrainian (25)	25	0.22
Welsh (55)	67	0.60
Yugoslavian (13)	63	0.57

Hispanic Origin	Population	%
Hispanic or Latino (of any race)	754	6.52
Central American, ex. Mexican	1	0.01
Guatemalan	1	0.01
Cuban	7	0.06
Dominican Republic	3	0.03
Mexican	598	5.17
Puerto Rican	94	0.81
South American	18	0.16
Argentinean	1	0.01
Chilean	7	0.06
Colombian	3	0.03
Ecuadorian	6	0.05
Venezuelan	1	0.01
Other Hispanic or Latino	33	0.29

Race*	Population	%
African-American/Black (53)	85	0.74
Not Hispanic (50)	79	0.68
Hispanic (3)	6	0.05
American Indian/Alaska Native (29)	94	0.81
Not Hispanic (22)	77	0.67
Hispanic (7)	17	0.15
Alaska Athabascan *(Ala. Nat.)* (0)	5	0.04
Apache (1)	1	0.01
Blackfeet (1)	2	0.02
Cherokee (6)	32	0.28
Cheyenne (0)	2	0.02
Chippewa (4)	7	0.06
Choctaw (0)	2	0.02
Creek (0)	1	0.01
Mexican American Ind. (4)	4	0.03
Navajo (1)	2	0.02
Pima (1)	3	0.03
Sioux (0)	2	0.02
Tlingit-Haida *(Alaska Native)* (0)	1	0.01
Asian (45)	88	0.76
Not Hispanic (42)	74	0.64
Hispanic (3)	14	0.12
Chinese, ex. Taiwanese (9)	9	0.08
Filipino (19)	32	0.28
Hmong (1)	1	0.01
Indian (2)	5	0.04
Indonesian (0)	5	0.04
Japanese (2)	11	0.10
Korean (4)	9	0.08
Thai (3)	5	0.04
Vietnamese (1)	7	0.06
Hawaii Native/Pacific Islander (3)	9	0.08
Not Hispanic (3)	6	0.05
Hispanic (0)	3	0.03
Native Hawaiian (2)	3	0.03
Samoan (0)	1	0.01
White (10,965)	11,150	96.45
Not Hispanic (10,563)	10,679	92.38
Hispanic (402)	471	4.07

Charlestown

Place Type: City
County: Clark
Population: 7,585†

Ancestry‡	Population	%
American (1,038)	1,038	13.89
British (33)	33	0.44
Canadian (0)	10	0.13
Danish (14)	44	0.59
Dutch (8)	177	2.37
English (418)	822	11.00
European (0)	21	0.28
French, ex. Basque (0)	107	1.43
French Canadian (0)	9	0.12
German (925)	1,870	25.03
Hungarian (0)	11	0.15
Icelander (17)	25	0.33
Irish (152)	909	12.17
Italian (58)	99	1.32
Lithuanian (19)	19	0.25
Scandinavian (0)	25	0.33
Scotch-Irish (21)	74	0.99
Scottish (95)	146	1.95
Serbian (15)	15	0.20
Slovene (0)	11	0.15
Swedish (42)	51	0.68
Welsh (15)	67	0.90

Hispanic Origin	Population	%
Hispanic or Latino (of any race)	628	8.28
Central American, ex. Mexican	79	1.04
Costa Rican	3	0.04
Guatemalan	3	0.04
Honduran	22	0.29
Nicaraguan	2	0.03
Panamanian	4	0.05
Salvadoran	45	0.59
Cuban	5	0.07
Mexican	462	6.09
Puerto Rican	22	0.29
South American	15	0.20
Argentinean	8	0.11
Bolivian	5	0.07
Colombian	1	0.01
Ecuadorian	1	0.01
Other Hispanic or Latino	45	0.59

Race*	Population	%
African-American/Black (163)	243	3.20
Not Hispanic (153)	227	2.99
Hispanic (10)	16	0.21
American Indian/Alaska Native (21)	50	0.66
Not Hispanic (18)	44	0.58
Hispanic (3)	6	0.08
Apache (0)	1	0.01
Blackfeet (1)	2	0.03
Cherokee (6)	18	0.24
Chippewa (0)	1	0.01
Choctaw (1)	2	0.03
Comanche (1)	1	0.01
Houma (4)	4	0.05
Menominee (0)	1	0.01
Asian (20)	36	0.47
Not Hispanic (18)	34	0.45
Hispanic (2)	2	0.03
Chinese, ex. Taiwanese (3)	3	0.04
Filipino (10)	13	0.17
Indian (2)	4	0.05
Korean (4)	8	0.11
Taiwanese (0)	2	0.03
Thai (1)	1	0.01
Vietnamese (0)	2	0.03
Hawaii Native/Pacific Islander (1)	7	0.09
Not Hispanic (1)	7	0.09
Guamanian/Chamorro (1)	2	0.03
Native Hawaiian (0)	4	0.05
White (6,822)	6,976	91.97
Not Hispanic (6,632)	6,749	88.98

*Notes: † The Census 2010 population figure is used to calculate the percentages in the Hispanic Origin and Race categories. Ancestry percentages are based on the 2006-2010 American Community Survey population (not shown); ‡ Numbers in parentheses indicate the number of people reporting a single ancestry; * Numbers in parentheses indicate the number of persons reporting this race alone, not in combination with any other race; Please refer to the Explanation of Data for more information.*

Hispanic (190)	227	2.99

Chesterton

Place Type: Town
County: Porter
Population: 13,068†

Ancestry‡	Population	%
African, Sub-Saharan (19)	19	0.14
Sudanese (19)	19	0.14
American (814)	814	6.19
Arab (12)	34	0.26
Lebanese (12)	34	0.26
Armenian (49)	207	1.57
Austrian (0)	36	0.27
Brazilian (38)	38	0.29
British (12)	28	0.21
Canadian (43)	83	0.63
Croatian (0)	112	0.85
Czech (42)	120	0.91
Czechoslovakian (28)	83	0.63
Danish (15)	32	0.24
Dutch (65)	201	1.53
English (151)	1,295	9.84
European (191)	207	1.57
French, ex. Basque (12)	152	1.16
French Canadian (48)	95	0.72
German (1,280)	3,960	30.10
Greek (43)	176	1.34
Hungarian (98)	305	2.32
Irish (589)	2,444	18.58
Italian (268)	1,014	7.71
Lithuanian (39)	50	0.38
Norwegian (94)	148	1.13
Pennsylvania German (0)	37	0.28
Polish (438)	1,520	11.56
Romanian (0)	43	0.33
Russian (0)	123	0.94
Scotch-Irish (19)	234	1.78
Scottish (149)	373	2.84
Serbian (0)	17	0.13
Slavic (42)	42	0.32
Slovak (161)	360	2.74
Slovene (0)	40	0.30
Swedish (158)	419	3.19
Swiss (0)	18	0.14
Ukrainian (0)	70	0.53
Welsh (20)	80	0.61
Yugoslavian (40)	55	0.42

Hispanic Origin	Population	%
Hispanic or Latino (of any race)	899	6.88
Central American, ex. Mexican	11	0.08
Costa Rican	1	0.01
Guatemalan	6	0.05
Honduran	2	0.02
Nicaraguan	1	0.01
Salvadoran	1	0.01
Cuban	6	0.05
Dominican Republic	4	0.03
Mexican	659	5.04
Puerto Rican	131	1.00
South American	37	0.28
Argentinean	8	0.06
Bolivian	1	0.01
Chilean	3	0.02
Colombian	2	0.02
Ecuadorian	3	0.02
Peruvian	15	0.11
Venezuelan	5	0.04
Other Hispanic or Latino	51	0.39

Race*	Population	%
African-American/Black (179)	249	1.91
Not Hispanic (172)	230	1.76
Hispanic (7)	19	0.15
American Indian/Alaska Native (33)	98	0.75
Not Hispanic (23)	77	0.59
Hispanic (10)	21	0.16
Alaska Athabascan *(Ala. Nat.)* (1)	1	0.01
Blackfeet (2)	4	0.03
Cherokee (7)	28	0.21
Chickasaw (1)	1	0.01
Chippewa (2)	3	0.02
Creek (3)	7	0.05
Iroquois (2)	6	0.05
Mexican American Ind. (1)	1	0.01
Navajo (0)	2	0.02
Osage (0)	2	0.02
Sioux (2)	2	0.02
South American Ind. (4)	4	0.03
Ute (1)	1	0.01
Asian (280)	322	2.46
Not Hispanic (272)	308	2.36
Hispanic (8)	14	0.11
Burmese (1)	1	0.01
Chinese, ex. Taiwanese (30)	33	0.25
Filipino (17)	24	0.18
Indian (142)	150	1.15
Indonesian (0)	1	0.01
Japanese (12)	26	0.20
Korean (24)	31	0.24
Pakistani (18)	21	0.16
Taiwanese (1)	4	0.03
Thai (12)	14	0.11
Vietnamese (3)	5	0.04
Hawaii Native/Pacific Islander (2)	9	0.07
Not Hispanic (2)	7	0.05
Hispanic (0)	2	0.02
Native Hawaiian (1)	4	0.03
White (12,118)	12,330	94.35
Not Hispanic (11,536)	11,683	89.40
Hispanic (582)	647	4.95

Clarksville

Place Type: Town
County: Clark
Population: 21,724†

Ancestry‡	Population	%
American (1,935)	1,935	8.43
Belgian (0)	45	0.20
Brazilian (95)	95	0.41
British (80)	91	0.40
Cajun (0)	55	0.24
Croatian (0)	28	0.12
Czechoslovakian (30)	30	0.13
Dutch (45)	316	1.38
English (1,027)	2,226	9.70
European (91)	91	0.40
French, ex. Basque (91)	556	2.42
French Canadian (14)	14	0.06
German (2,125)	5,061	22.06
Greek (9)	9	0.04
Hungarian (9)	9	0.04
Irish (1,003)	3,225	14.05
Italian (212)	479	2.09
Norwegian (0)	105	0.46
Polish (149)	301	1.31
Portuguese (0)	9	0.04
Russian (0)	27	0.12
Scandinavian (39)	39	0.17
Scotch-Irish (146)	452	1.97
Scottish (85)	279	1.22
Serbian (25)	25	0.11
Swedish (10)	65	0.28
Swiss (21)	48	0.21
Welsh (0)	57	0.25

Hispanic Origin	Population	%
Hispanic or Latino (of any race)	2,056	9.46
Central American, ex. Mexican	108	0.50
Costa Rican	1	<0.01
Guatemalan	17	0.08
Honduran	43	0.20
Nicaraguan	2	0.01
Panamanian	7	0.03
Salvadoran	38	0.17
Cuban	33	0.15
Dominican Republic	11	0.05
Mexican	1,642	7.56
Puerto Rican	76	0.35
South American	8	0.04
Colombian	1	<0.01
Ecuadorian	4	0.02
Peruvian	3	0.01
Other Hispanic or Latino	178	0.82

Race*	Population	%
African-American/Black (1,221)	1,562	7.19
Not Hispanic (1,178)	1,498	6.90
Hispanic (43)	64	0.29
American Indian/Alaska Native (75)	178	0.82
Not Hispanic (54)	139	0.64
Hispanic (21)	39	0.18
Apache (2)	3	0.01
Blackfeet (4)	7	0.03
Cherokee (15)	56	0.26
Choctaw (1)	5	0.02
Creek (2)	2	0.01
Delaware (0)	3	0.01
Iroquois (1)	2	0.01
Lumbee (1)	1	<0.01
Mexican American Ind. (10)	12	0.06
Navajo (6)	6	0.03
Osage (0)	1	<0.01
Pima (3)	3	0.01
Potawatomi (0)	1	<0.01
Seminole (2)	2	0.01
Shoshone (0)	1	<0.01
Sioux (0)	4	0.02
South American Ind. (0)	1	<0.01
Asian (155)	221	1.02
Not Hispanic (150)	209	0.96
Hispanic (5)	12	0.06
Bangladeshi (0)	1	<0.01
Burmese (5)	5	0.02
Cambodian (5)	6	0.03
Chinese, ex. Taiwanese (17)	21	0.10
Filipino (29)	46	0.21
Indian (42)	50	0.23
Indonesian (0)	1	<0.01
Japanese (14)	21	0.10
Korean (12)	19	0.09
Laotian (1)	3	0.01
Pakistani (1)	1	<0.01
Sri Lankan (4)	4	0.02
Taiwanese (4)	4	0.02
Thai (3)	7	0.03
Vietnamese (13)	16	0.07
Hawaii Native/Pacific Islander (8)	22	0.10
Not Hispanic (5)	19	0.09
Hispanic (3)	3	0.01
Guamanian/Chamorro (2)	5	0.02
Native Hawaiian (2)	9	0.04
Samoan (3)	4	0.02
White (18,477)	18,982	87.38
Not Hispanic (17,783)	18,212	83.83
Hispanic (694)	770	3.54

Columbia City

Place Type: City
County: Whitley
Population: 8,750†

Ancestry‡	Population	%
American (1,217)	1,217	14.83
Arab (27)	67	0.82
Arab (0)	40	0.49
Palestinian (27)	27	0.33
Australian (0)	6	0.07
Austrian (0)	18	0.22
Belgian (0)	8	0.10
Brazilian (14)	14	0.17
British (23)	23	0.28
Canadian (12)	12	0.15
Danish (17)	74	0.90

*Notes: † The Census 2010 population figure is used to calculate the percentages in the Hispanic Origin and Race categories. Ancestry percentages are based on the 2006-2010 American Community Survey population (not shown); ‡ Numbers in parentheses indicate the number of people reporting a single ancestry; * Numbers in parentheses indicate the number of persons reporting this race alone, not in combination with any other race; Please refer to the Explanation of Data for more information.*

Ancestry	Population	%
Dutch (20)	139	1.69
English (231)	607	7.40
European (18)	18	0.22
French, ex. Basque (84)	263	3.20
French Canadian (0)	11	0.13
German (1,473)	2,795	34.06
Irish (243)	1,081	13.17
Italian (91)	190	2.32
Lithuanian (0)	11	0.13
Norwegian (9)	9	0.11
Polish (11)	22	0.27
Portuguese (0)	10	0.12
Russian (0)	7	0.09
Scotch-Irish (54)	122	1.49
Scottish (41)	111	1.35
Slavic (16)	16	0.19
Slovene (0)	46	0.56
Swedish (60)	72	0.88
Swiss (17)	124	1.51
Welsh (28)	74	0.90
Yugoslavian (0)	13	0.16

Hispanic Origin	Population	%
Hispanic or Latino (of any race)	189	2.16
Central American, ex. Mexican	6	0.07
Guatemalan	3	0.03
Honduran	1	0.01
Salvadoran	2	0.02
Mexican	150	1.71
Puerto Rican	19	0.22
South American	2	0.02
Colombian	2	0.02
Other Hispanic or Latino	12	0.14

Race*	Population	%
African-American/Black (43)	81	0.93
Not Hispanic (42)	80	0.91
Hispanic (1)	1	0.01
American Indian/Alaska Native (22)	66	0.75
Not Hispanic (17)	60	0.69
Hispanic (5)	6	0.07
Blackfeet (0)	1	0.01
Cherokee (1)	23	0.26
Chippewa (0)	1	0.01
Comanche (1)	1	0.01
Navajo (2)	3	0.03
Osage (1)	1	0.01
Pueblo (0)	1	0.01
Sioux (0)	2	0.02
Spanish American Ind. (1)	1	0.01
Asian (43)	65	0.74
Not Hispanic (43)	65	0.74
Chinese, ex. Taiwanese (18)	19	0.22
Filipino (11)	15	0.17
Indian (9)	9	0.10
Indonesian (0)	2	0.02
Japanese (2)	9	0.10
Korean (2)	5	0.06
Pakistani (1)	5	0.06
Vietnamese (0)	1	0.01
Hawaii Native/Pacific Islander (0)	2	0.02
Not Hispanic (0)	2	0.02
White (8,462)	8,585	98.11
Not Hispanic (8,344)	8,446	96.53
Hispanic (118)	139	1.59

Columbus

Place Type: City
County: Bartholomew
Population: 44,061†

Ancestry‡	Population	%
African, Sub-Saharan (15)	44	0.10
African (5)	34	0.08
Ghanaian (10)	10	0.02
American (3,866)	3,866	8.93
Arab (59)	77	0.18
Arab (0)	11	0.03
Egyptian (20)	20	0.05
Lebanese (0)	7	0.02
Moroccan (39)	39	0.09
Armenian (20)	28	0.06
Austrian (0)	12	0.03
Belgian (9)	20	0.05
Brazilian (23)	23	0.05
British (249)	320	0.74
Cajun (36)	36	0.08
Canadian (28)	101	0.23
Croatian (18)	44	0.10
Czech (0)	93	0.21
Czechoslovakian (0)	21	0.05
Danish (46)	222	0.51
Dutch (332)	764	1.76
English (2,312)	5,704	13.17
European (365)	435	1.00
Finnish (30)	58	0.13
French, ex. Basque (360)	1,081	2.50
French Canadian (37)	106	0.24
German (5,588)	12,338	28.49
Greek (32)	70	0.16
Hungarian (91)	149	0.34
Irish (1,495)	5,207	12.02
Italian (477)	1,017	2.35
Lithuanian (0)	30	0.07
Macedonian (0)	8	0.02
Northern European (17)	17	0.04
Norwegian (43)	363	0.84
Pennsylvania German (42)	54	0.12
Polish (233)	1,220	2.82
Romanian (176)	176	0.41
Russian (19)	181	0.42
Scandinavian (106)	229	0.53
Scotch-Irish (378)	1,110	2.56
Scottish (453)	1,401	3.23
Serbian (0)	11	0.03
Slovak (11)	52	0.12
Slovene (8)	8	0.02
Swedish (78)	395	0.91
Swiss (35)	244	0.56
Ukrainian (13)	44	0.10
Welsh (45)	307	0.71
West Indian, ex. Hispanic (29)	40	0.09
Haitian (11)	11	0.03
Jamaican (0)	11	0.03
West Indian (10)	10	0.02
Other West Indian (8)	8	0.02
Yugoslavian (21)	21	0.05

Hispanic Origin	Population	%
Hispanic or Latino (of any race)	2,575	5.84
Central American, ex. Mexican	127	0.29
Costa Rican	4	0.01
Guatemalan	82	0.19
Honduran	18	0.04
Nicaraguan	1	<0.01
Panamanian	2	<0.01
Salvadoran	14	0.03
Other Central American	6	0.01
Cuban	20	0.05
Dominican Republic	8	0.02
Mexican	2,042	4.63
Puerto Rican	153	0.35
South American	84	0.19
Argentinean	16	0.04
Bolivian	2	<0.01
Chilean	7	0.02
Colombian	19	0.04
Ecuadorian	10	0.02
Peruvian	12	0.03
Uruguayan	3	0.01
Venezuelan	15	0.03
Other Hispanic or Latino	141	0.32

Race*	Population	%
African-American/Black (1,178)	1,588	3.60
Not Hispanic (1,144)	1,523	3.46
Hispanic (34)	65	0.15
American Indian/Alaska Native (104)	293	0.66
Not Hispanic (80)	239	0.54
Hispanic (24)	54	0.12
Apache (1)	3	0.01
Arapaho (1)	1	<0.01
Blackfeet (1)	16	0.04
Canadian/French Am. Ind. (0)	1	<0.01
Central American Ind. (5)	8	0.02
Cherokee (9)	89	0.20
Chippewa (4)	4	0.01
Choctaw (3)	3	0.01
Crow (0)	1	<0.01
Delaware (0)	1	<0.01
Iroquois (1)	2	<0.01
Menominee (0)	1	<0.01
Mexican American Ind. (10)	18	0.04
Navajo (1)	4	0.01
Ottawa (2)	2	<0.01
Potawatomi (1)	1	<0.01
Pueblo (1)	1	<0.01
Seminole (1)	1	<0.01
Sioux (4)	6	0.01
South American Ind. (0)	1	<0.01
Asian (2,467)	2,625	5.96
Not Hispanic (2,464)	2,607	5.92
Hispanic (3)	18	0.04
Bangladeshi (16)	17	0.04
Chinese, ex. Taiwanese (388)	422	0.96
Filipino (58)	85	0.19
Hmong (4)	4	0.01
Indian (1,344)	1,381	3.13
Indonesian (9)	12	0.03
Japanese (369)	402	0.91
Korean (59)	83	0.19
Laotian (4)	5	0.01
Malaysian (6)	6	0.01
Nepalese (3)	3	0.01
Pakistani (14)	15	0.03
Sri Lankan (4)	4	0.01
Taiwanese (26)	30	0.07
Thai (13)	21	0.05
Vietnamese (110)	118	0.27
Hawaii Native/Pacific Islander (31)	86	0.20
Not Hispanic (22)	70	0.16
Hispanic (9)	16	0.04
Guamanian/Chamorro (10)	15	0.03
Native Hawaiian (17)	50	0.11
Samoan (0)	1	<0.01
Tongan (1)	2	<0.01
White (38,305)	39,132	88.81
Not Hispanic (37,018)	37,672	85.50
Hispanic (1,287)	1,460	3.31

Connersville

Place Type: City
County: Fayette
Population: 13,481†

Ancestry‡	Population	%
African, Sub-Saharan (25)	25	0.18
African (25)	25	0.18
American (1,821)	1,821	13.37
British (25)	40	0.29
Canadian (16)	16	0.12
Dutch (27)	144	1.06
English (690)	1,141	8.38
European (28)	55	0.40
French, ex. Basque (95)	188	1.38
German (1,226)	2,431	17.85
Greek (32)	32	0.24
Hungarian (20)	20	0.15
Irish (658)	1,665	12.23
Italian (27)	133	0.98
Norwegian (11)	50	0.37
Pennsylvania German (0)	8	0.06
Polish (47)	114	0.84
Scotch-Irish (69)	195	1.43
Scottish (228)	257	1.89
Slovak (0)	9	0.07
Swedish (7)	21	0.15
Welsh (21)	56	0.41

*Notes: † The Census 2010 population figure is used to calculate the percentages in the Hispanic Origin and Race categories. Ancestry percentages are based on the 2006-2010 American Community Survey population (not shown); ‡ Numbers in parentheses indicate the number of people reporting a single ancestry; * Numbers in parentheses indicate the number of persons reporting this race alone, not in combination with any other race; Please refer to the Explanation of Data for more information.*

SECTION TWO

West Indian, ex. Hispanic (0)	11	0.08
Dutch West Indian (0)	11	0.08

Hispanic Origin	Population	%
Hispanic or Latino (of any race)	138	1.02
Central American, ex. Mexican	10	0.07
Guatemalan	6	0.04
Panamanian	3	0.02
Salvadoran	1	0.01
Cuban	4	0.03
Mexican	74	0.55
Puerto Rican	15	0.11
South American	11	0.08
Peruvian	4	0.03
Venezuelan	7	0.05
Other Hispanic or Latino	24	0.18

Race*	Population	%
African-American/Black (286)	376	2.79
Not Hispanic (283)	373	2.77
Hispanic (3)	3	0.02
American Indian/Alaska Native (23)	84	0.62
Not Hispanic (21)	82	0.61
Hispanic (2)	2	0.01
Apache (0)	1	0.01
Cherokee (4)	25	0.19
Iroquois (0)	3	0.02
Mexican American Ind. (2)	2	0.01
Navajo (1)	1	0.01
Shoshone (1)	1	0.01
Sioux (0)	2	0.01
Asian (43)	57	0.42
Not Hispanic (42)	55	0.41
Hispanic (1)	2	0.01
Cambodian (1)	1	0.01
Chinese, ex. Taiwanese (13)	14	0.10
Filipino (6)	9	0.07
Indian (10)	12	0.09
Indonesian (4)	4	0.03
Japanese (1)	2	0.01
Korean (4)	4	0.03
Pakistani (1)	1	0.01
Vietnamese (1)	3	0.02
Hawaii Native/Pacific Islander (0)	5	0.04
Not Hispanic (0)	5	0.04
Native Hawaiian (0)	3	0.02
White (12,906)	13,079	97.02
Not Hispanic (12,820)	12,981	96.29
Hispanic (86)	98	0.73

Crawfordsville

Place Type: City
County: Montgomery
Population: 15,915†

Ancestry‡	Population	%
Albanian (34)	34	0.21
American (2,909)	2,909	18.30
British (15)	38	0.24
Cajun (11)	11	0.07
Canadian (13)	22	0.14
Croatian (0)	38	0.24
Czechoslovakian (37)	74	0.47
Danish (0)	6	0.04
Dutch (56)	442	2.78
English (652)	1,430	9.00
European (121)	121	0.76
Finnish (0)	19	0.12
French, ex. Basque (22)	194	1.22
French Canadian (0)	29	0.18
German (1,052)	3,268	20.56
Irish (577)	2,518	15.84
Italian (306)	497	3.13
Latvian (0)	13	0.08
Norwegian (10)	117	0.74
Polish (54)	188	1.18
Romanian (45)	91	0.57
Scandinavian (26)	26	0.16
Scotch-Irish (105)	324	2.04
Scottish (77)	317	1.99
Slavic (0)	6	0.04
Slovak (12)	23	0.14
Slovene (0)	11	0.07
Swedish (0)	70	0.44
Swiss (0)	10	0.06
Ukrainian (39)	39	0.25
Welsh (60)	138	0.87

Hispanic Origin	Population	%
Hispanic or Latino (of any race)	1,310	8.23
Central American, ex. Mexican	48	0.30
Guatemalan	38	0.24
Honduran	6	0.04
Salvadoran	4	0.03
Cuban	8	0.05
Mexican	1,160	7.29
Puerto Rican	22	0.14
South American	27	0.17
Argentinean	6	0.04
Bolivian	1	0.01
Chilean	4	0.03
Colombian	12	0.08
Ecuadorian	1	0.01
Peruvian	2	0.01
Venezuelan	1	0.01
Other Hispanic or Latino	45	0.28

Race*	Population	%
African-American/Black (271)	384	2.41
Not Hispanic (253)	363	2.28
Hispanic (18)	21	0.13
American Indian/Alaska Native (59)	122	0.77
Not Hispanic (45)	96	0.60
Hispanic (14)	26	0.16
Apache (0)	6	0.04
Blackfeet (1)	3	0.02
Cherokee (13)	34	0.21
Cheyenne (1)	1	0.01
Choctaw (1)	1	0.01
Crow (1)	1	0.01
Iroquois (3)	6	0.04
Kiowa (1)	2	0.01
Mexican American Ind. (4)	7	0.04
Navajo (0)	1	0.01
Pueblo (3)	3	0.02
Seminole (1)	1	0.01
Sioux (1)	1	0.01
Asian (143)	174	1.09
Not Hispanic (139)	168	1.06
Hispanic (4)	6	0.04
Bangladeshi (5)	5	0.03
Chinese, ex. Taiwanese (52)	54	0.34
Filipino (12)	24	0.15
Indian (35)	36	0.23
Japanese (10)	18	0.11
Korean (12)	19	0.12
Malaysian (0)	1	0.01
Nepalese (1)	1	0.01
Pakistani (1)	1	0.01
Thai (1)	1	0.01
Vietnamese (13)	14	0.09
Hawaii Native/Pacific Islander (5)	17	0.11
Not Hispanic (5)	14	0.09
Hispanic (0)	3	0.02
Guamanian/Chamorro (0)	1	0.01
Native Hawaiian (3)	7	0.04
Samoan (1)	2	0.01
White (14,664)	14,908	93.67
Not Hispanic (13,961)	14,151	88.92
Hispanic (703)	757	4.76

Crown Point

Place Type: City
County: Lake
Population: 27,317†

Ancestry‡	Population	%
African, Sub-Saharan (323)	375	1.44
African (236)	267	1.02
Ethiopian (13)	13	0.05
Nigerian (74)	95	0.36
Albanian (8)	8	0.03
American (1,396)	1,396	5.35
Arab (128)	156	0.60
Arab (0)	14	0.05
Lebanese (28)	28	0.11
Moroccan (9)	9	0.03
Palestinian (71)	71	0.27
Syrian (20)	27	0.10
Other Arab (0)	7	0.03
Armenian (24)	24	0.09
Australian (18)	18	0.07
Austrian (0)	61	0.23
Belgian (26)	58	0.22
British (0)	27	0.10
Bulgarian (8)	8	0.03
Canadian (17)	44	0.17
Croatian (169)	585	2.24
Czech (92)	361	1.38
Czechoslovakian (26)	65	0.25
Danish (13)	103	0.39
Dutch (328)	989	3.79
Eastern European (26)	26	0.10
English (430)	1,825	7.00
European (159)	159	0.61
Finnish (9)	28	0.11
French, ex. Basque (46)	475	1.82
French Canadian (0)	32	0.12
German (2,327)	6,802	26.08
Greek (427)	661	2.53
Hungarian (101)	396	1.52
Irish (997)	3,824	14.66
Italian (501)	1,647	6.32
Lithuanian (46)	125	0.48
Macedonian (862)	901	3.46
Maltese (0)	48	0.18
Norwegian (23)	155	0.59
Pennsylvania German (0)	30	0.12
Polish (1,066)	3,046	11.68
Portuguese (16)	16	0.06
Romanian (63)	118	0.45
Russian (72)	296	1.14
Scandinavian (0)	42	0.16
Scotch-Irish (51)	286	1.10
Scottish (77)	437	1.68
Serbian (246)	337	1.29
Slavic (30)	30	0.12
Slovak (230)	489	1.88
Slovene (15)	15	0.06
Swedish (173)	611	2.34
Swiss (10)	52	0.20
Turkish (0)	10	0.04
Ukrainian (0)	16	0.06
Welsh (0)	36	0.14
West Indian, ex. Hispanic (14)	59	0.23
Bahamian (0)	14	0.05
Jamaican (14)	45	0.17
Yugoslavian (41)	79	0.30

Hispanic Origin	Population	%
Hispanic or Latino (of any race)	2,213	8.10
Central American, ex. Mexican	35	0.13
Costa Rican	2	0.01
Guatemalan	12	0.04
Honduran	7	0.03
Nicaraguan	5	0.02
Panamanian	7	0.03
Salvadoran	2	0.01
Cuban	21	0.08
Dominican Republic	8	0.03
Mexican	1,735	6.35
Puerto Rican	230	0.84
South American	40	0.15
Argentinean	6	0.02
Chilean	1	<0.01
Colombian	21	0.08
Ecuadorian	8	0.03
Venezuelan	4	0.01

*Notes: † The Census 2010 population figure is used to calculate the percentages in the Hispanic Origin and Race categories. Ancestry percentages are based on the 2006-2010 American Community Survey population (not shown); ‡ Numbers in parentheses indicate the number of people reporting a single ancestry; * Numbers in parentheses indicate the number of persons reporting this race alone, not in combination with any other race; Please refer to the Explanation of Data for more information.*

Other Hispanic or Latino	144	0.53

Race*	Population	%
African-American/Black (1,711)	1,867	6.83
Not Hispanic (1,687)	1,801	6.59
Hispanic (24)	66	0.24
American Indian/Alaska Native (52)	136	0.50
Not Hispanic (29)	94	0.34
Hispanic (23)	42	0.15
Apache (4)	4	0.01
Blackfeet (1)	1	<0.01
Canadian/French Am. Ind. (1)	1	<0.01
Cherokee (1)	19	0.07
Chippewa (5)	8	0.03
Choctaw (2)	3	0.01
Comanche (0)	1	<0.01
Cree (0)	1	<0.01
Creek (1)	1	<0.01
Crow (1)	1	<0.01
Delaware (1)	3	0.01
Mexican American Ind. (7)	7	0.03
Navajo (0)	5	0.02
Potawatomi (0)	1	<0.01
Sioux (2)	2	0.01
South American Ind. (0)	4	0.01
Asian (484)	582	2.13
Not Hispanic (475)	563	2.06
Hispanic (9)	19	0.07
Bangladeshi (6)	6	0.02
Chinese, ex. Taiwanese (87)	108	0.40
Filipino (140)	179	0.66
Hmong (1)	2	0.01
Indian (83)	91	0.33
Indonesian (1)	3	0.01
Japanese (8)	20	0.07
Korean (24)	39	0.14
Laotian (1)	1	<0.01
Pakistani (58)	63	0.23
Thai (26)	37	0.14
Vietnamese (24)	26	0.10
Hawaii Native/Pacific Islander (3)	13	0.05
Not Hispanic (2)	7	0.03
Hispanic (1)	6	0.02
Guamanian/Chamorro (1)	3	0.01
Native Hawaiian (1)	1	<0.01
White (24,107)	24,503	89.70
Not Hispanic (22,606)	22,852	83.65
Hispanic (1,501)	1,651	6.04

Danville

Place Type: Town
County: Hendricks
Population: 9,001†

Ancestry‡	Population	%
American (722)	722	8.31
Belgian (0)	15	0.17
British (35)	49	0.56
Czech (0)	15	0.17
Danish (0)	15	0.17
Dutch (49)	182	2.09
English (1,247)	2,044	23.52
European (103)	113	1.30
French, ex. Basque (0)	189	2.17
German (961)	2,648	30.46
Greek (0)	51	0.59
Hungarian (8)	8	0.09
Irish (388)	1,759	20.24
Italian (41)	172	1.98
Norwegian (16)	16	0.18
Polish (41)	41	0.47
Portuguese (0)	15	0.17
Romanian (0)	60	0.69
Russian (15)	28	0.32
Scandinavian (17)	30	0.35
Scotch-Irish (172)	215	2.47
Scottish (170)	372	4.28
Serbian (11)	11	0.13
Slavic (10)	10	0.12
Swedish (0)	68	0.78
Welsh (0)	55	0.63
Yugoslavian (10)	10	0.12

Hispanic Origin	Population	%
Hispanic or Latino (of any race)	165	1.83
Central American, ex. Mexican	15	0.17
Costa Rican	1	0.01
Guatemalan	7	0.08
Nicaraguan	5	0.06
Panamanian	1	0.01
Salvadoran	1	0.01
Cuban	1	0.01
Dominican Republic	3	0.03
Mexican	107	1.19
Puerto Rican	21	0.23
South American	8	0.09
Argentinean	2	0.02
Chilean	1	0.01
Ecuadorian	1	0.01
Peruvian	2	0.02
Venezuelan	2	0.02
Other Hispanic or Latino	10	0.11

Race*	Population	%
African-American/Black (73)	133	1.48
Not Hispanic (73)	132	1.47
Hispanic (0)	1	0.01
American Indian/Alaska Native (19)	57	0.63
Not Hispanic (19)	56	0.62
Hispanic (0)	1	0.01
Blackfeet (1)	2	0.02
Canadian/French Am. Ind. (4)	4	0.04
Cherokee (1)	14	0.16
Chippewa (0)	1	0.01
Creek (0)	1	0.01
Iroquois (0)	1	0.01
Pueblo (1)	2	0.02
Asian (38)	58	0.64
Not Hispanic (37)	57	0.63
Hispanic (1)	1	0.01
Chinese, ex. Taiwanese (12)	12	0.13
Filipino (7)	15	0.17
Indian (5)	7	0.08
Indonesian (1)	1	0.01
Japanese (5)	12	0.13
Korean (5)	8	0.09
Malaysian (1)	1	0.01
Thai (1)	1	0.01
Vietnamese (1)	1	0.01
Hawaii Native/Pacific Islander (1)	2	0.02
Not Hispanic (1)	2	0.02
White (8,714)	8,824	98.03
Not Hispanic (8,601)	8,694	96.59
Hispanic (113)	130	1.44

Decatur

Place Type: City
County: Adams
Population: 9,405†

Ancestry‡	Population	%
American (798)	798	8.06
Czech (22)	64	0.65
Dutch (47)	160	1.62
English (328)	756	7.64
European (19)	19	0.19
French, ex. Basque (60)	292	2.95
German (2,272)	4,078	41.19
Irish (362)	1,140	11.51
Italian (60)	70	0.71
Lithuanian (0)	21	0.21
Norwegian (13)	76	0.77
Pennsylvania German (16)	16	0.16
Polish (106)	181	1.83
Romanian (0)	13	0.13
Scotch-Irish (13)	31	0.31
Scottish (43)	84	0.85
Swedish (45)	97	0.98
Swiss (61)	332	3.35

Hispanic Origin	Population	%
Hispanic or Latino (of any race)	790	8.40
Central American, ex. Mexican	6	0.06
Guatemalan	3	0.03
Salvadoran	3	0.03
Cuban	1	0.01
Dominican Republic	1	0.01
Mexican	697	7.41
Puerto Rican	17	0.18
South American	3	0.03
Colombian	2	0.02
Ecuadorian	1	0.01
Other Hispanic or Latino	65	0.69

Race*	Population	%
African-American/Black (51)	89	0.95
Not Hispanic (47)	75	0.80
Hispanic (4)	14	0.15
American Indian/Alaska Native (35)	55	0.58
Not Hispanic (26)	43	0.46
Hispanic (9)	12	0.13
Apache (1)	1	0.01
Blackfeet (1)	3	0.03
Cherokee (2)	8	0.09
Lumbee (1)	1	0.01
Mexican American Ind. (2)	2	0.02
Ottawa (1)	1	0.01
Tlingit-Haida *(Alaska Native)* (1)	1	0.01
Asian (34)	53	0.56
Not Hispanic (34)	52	0.55
Hispanic (0)	1	0.01
Cambodian (2)	2	0.02
Chinese, ex. Taiwanese (17)	17	0.18
Filipino (4)	7	0.07
Indian (6)	6	0.06
Japanese (3)	6	0.06
Korean (2)	14	0.15
Hawaii Native/Pacific Islander (2)	7	0.07
Not Hispanic (2)	5	0.05
Hispanic (0)	2	0.02
Guamanian/Chamorro (2)	5	0.05
Native Hawaiian (0)	1	0.01
White (8,908)	9,039	96.11
Not Hispanic (8,437)	8,504	90.42
Hispanic (471)	535	5.69

Dyer

Place Type: Town
County: Lake
Population: 16,390†

Ancestry‡	Population	%
African, Sub-Saharan (9)	28	0.18
Cape Verdean (9)	28	0.18
American (903)	903	5.66
Arab (155)	229	1.44
Egyptian (52)	52	0.33
Jordanian (25)	25	0.16
Lebanese (18)	42	0.26
Moroccan (0)	30	0.19
Palestinian (14)	24	0.15
Syrian (21)	21	0.13
Other Arab (25)	35	0.22
Austrian (11)	23	0.14
Belgian (0)	44	0.28
British (0)	7	0.04
Canadian (22)	93	0.58
Croatian (73)	227	1.42
Czech (67)	148	0.93
Czechoslovakian (12)	39	0.24
Danish (15)	85	0.53
Dutch (601)	1,096	6.87
English (641)	1,623	10.17
European (106)	140	0.88
French, ex. Basque (17)	285	1.79
French Canadian (0)	44	0.28
German (1,053)	3,616	22.66

SECTION TWO

*Notes: † The Census 2010 population figure is used to calculate the percentages in the Hispanic Origin and Race categories. Ancestry percentages are based on the 2006-2010 American Community Survey population (not shown); ‡ Numbers in parentheses indicate the number of people reporting a single ancestry; * Numbers in parentheses indicate the number of persons reporting this race alone, not in combination with any other race; Please refer to the Explanation of Data for more information.*

Greek (94)	216	1.35
Hungarian (38)	281	1.76
Irish (524)	2,553	16.00
Italian (572)	1,567	9.82
Lithuanian (53)	200	1.25
Northern European (8)	26	0.16
Norwegian (14)	66	0.41
Polish (867)	2,496	15.64
Portuguese (25)	77	0.48
Romanian (41)	63	0.39
Russian (143)	282	1.77
Scandinavian (0)	85	0.53
Scotch-Irish (34)	174	1.09
Scottish (33)	203	1.27
Serbian (125)	152	0.95
Slavic (0)	12	0.08
Slovak (164)	341	2.14
Slovene (22)	64	0.40
Swedish (0)	194	1.22
Swiss (0)	31	0.19
Ukrainian (28)	110	0.69
Welsh (37)	57	0.36
Yugoslavian (54)	127	0.80

Hispanic Origin	Population	%
Hispanic or Latino (of any race)	1,520	9.27
Central American, ex. Mexican	20	0.12
Costa Rican	1	0.01
Guatemalan	11	0.07
Honduran	6	0.04
Salvadoran	1	0.01
Other Central American	1	0.01
Cuban	12	0.07
Mexican	1,247	7.61
Puerto Rican	138	0.84
South American	36	0.22
Argentinean	8	0.05
Bolivian	1	0.01
Chilean	2	0.01
Colombian	2	0.01
Ecuadorian	18	0.11
Peruvian	4	0.02
Venezuelan	1	0.01
Other Hispanic or Latino	67	0.41

Race*	Population	%
African-American/Black (410)	491	3.00
Not Hispanic (403)	468	2.86
Hispanic (7)	23	0.14
American Indian/Alaska Native (39)	90	0.55
Not Hispanic (28)	64	0.39
Hispanic (11)	26	0.16
Apache (1)	4	0.02
Arapaho (0)	1	0.01
Blackfeet (0)	2	0.01
Cherokee (10)	18	0.11
Crow (0)	1	0.01
Delaware (1)	2	0.01
Iroquois (3)	7	0.04
Lumbee (0)	1	0.01
Navajo (3)	3	0.02
Potawatomi (1)	2	0.01
Sioux (4)	7	0.04
South American Ind. (2)	2	0.01
Asian (481)	573	3.50
Not Hispanic (481)	558	3.40
Hispanic (0)	15	0.09
Bangladeshi (7)	9	0.05
Chinese, ex. Taiwanese (29)	34	0.21
Filipino (144)	175	1.07
Indian (194)	215	1.31
Japanese (10)	16	0.10
Korean (40)	44	0.27
Laotian (1)	1	0.01
Malaysian (1)	5	0.03
Pakistani (14)	16	0.10
Taiwanese (7)	10	0.06
Thai (11)	15	0.09
Vietnamese (16)	22	0.13
Hawaii Native/Pacific Islander (3)	13	0.08
Not Hispanic (3)	13	0.08
Native Hawaiian (0)	2	0.01
Samoan (2)	4	0.02
White (14,768)	15,019	91.64
Not Hispanic (13,766)	13,922	84.94
Hispanic (1,002)	1,097	6.69

East Chicago

Place Type: City
County: Lake
Population: 29,698†

Ancestry‡	Population	%
African, Sub-Saharan (595)	595	1.97
African (595)	595	1.97
American (171)	171	0.57
Arab (27)	27	0.09
Jordanian (9)	9	0.03
Palestinian (18)	18	0.06
Armenian (0)	20	0.07
Assyrian/Chaldean/Syriac (0)	10	0.03
Canadian (0)	1	<0.01
Croatian (10)	138	0.46
Czech (8)	20	0.07
Czechoslovakian (15)	36	0.12
Danish (0)	10	0.03
Dutch (0)	22	0.07
English (28)	86	0.28
French, ex. Basque (12)	40	0.13
French Canadian (7)	7	0.02
German (113)	357	1.18
Hungarian (47)	290	0.96
Irish (80)	497	1.64
Italian (16)	164	0.54
Lithuanian (10)	52	0.17
Luxemburger (0)	9	0.03
Polish (503)	623	2.06
Romanian (0)	21	0.07
Russian (31)	73	0.24
Scottish (68)	68	0.23
Serbian (11)	18	0.06
Slovak (9)	120	0.40
Swedish (0)	10	0.03
Ukrainian (10)	10	0.03
West Indian, ex. Hispanic (18)	146	0.48
British West Indian (0)	64	0.21
Trinidadian/Tobagonian (18)	18	0.06
West Indian (0)	64	0.21

Hispanic Origin	Population	%
Hispanic or Latino (of any race)	15,105	50.86
Central American, ex. Mexican	160	0.54
Costa Rican	2	0.01
Guatemalan	40	0.13
Honduran	43	0.14
Nicaraguan	1	<0.01
Panamanian	1	<0.01
Salvadoran	69	0.23
Other Central American	4	0.01
Cuban	41	0.14
Dominican Republic	30	0.10
Mexican	11,819	39.80
Puerto Rican	2,528	8.51
South American	44	0.15
Argentinean	7	0.02
Colombian	11	0.04
Ecuadorian	11	0.04
Peruvian	8	0.03
Uruguayan	7	0.02
Other Hispanic or Latino	483	1.63

Race*	Population	%
African-American/Black (12,736)	13,135	44.23
Not Hispanic (12,125)	12,330	41.52
Hispanic (611)	805	2.71
American Indian/Alaska Native (187)	330	1.11
Not Hispanic (46)	121	0.41
Hispanic (141)	209	0.70
Apache (2)	3	0.01
Arapaho (0)	3	0.01
Blackfeet (2)	15	0.05
Canadian/French Am. Ind. (5)	6	0.02
Cherokee (3)	39	0.13
Chippewa (1)	1	<0.01
Choctaw (0)	1	<0.01
Houma (1)	2	0.01
Inupiat *(Alaska Native)* (0)	1	<0.01
Iroquois (0)	1	<0.01
Mexican American Ind. (37)	48	0.16
Sioux (1)	2	0.01
South American Ind. (4)	18	0.06
Asian (34)	75	0.25
Not Hispanic (28)	35	0.12
Hispanic (6)	40	0.13
Chinese, ex. Taiwanese (1)	8	0.03
Filipino (10)	14	0.05
Indian (14)	24	0.08
Japanese (1)	4	0.01
Korean (1)	1	<0.01
Laotian (0)	1	<0.01
Pakistani (5)	7	0.02
Thai (2)	2	0.01
Hawaii Native/Pacific Islander (12)	34	0.11
Not Hispanic (4)	18	0.06
Hispanic (8)	16	0.05
Fijian (0)	3	0.01
Guamanian/Chamorro (2)	3	0.01
Native Hawaiian (5)	9	0.03
Samoan (3)	12	0.04
White (10,530)	11,151	37.55
Not Hispanic (2,140)	2,299	7.74
Hispanic (8,390)	8,852	29.81

Elkhart

Place Type: City
County: Elkhart
Population: 50,949†

Ancestry‡	Population	%
African, Sub-Saharan (296)	409	0.79
African (235)	305	0.59
Kenyan (61)	61	0.12
Zimbabwean (0)	13	0.03
Other Sub-Saharan African (0)	30	0.06
American (2,012)	2,012	3.88
Arab (109)	109	0.21
Arab (23)	23	0.04
Lebanese (9)	9	0.02
Moroccan (16)	16	0.03
Other Arab (61)	61	0.12
Austrian (0)	38	0.07
Belgian (18)	123	0.24
Brazilian (30)	92	0.18
British (41)	111	0.21
Canadian (15)	79	0.15
Croatian (0)	17	0.03
Czech (106)	195	0.38
Czechoslovakian (14)	14	0.03
Danish (21)	53	0.10
Dutch (374)	1,346	2.60
Eastern European (9)	9	0.02
English (1,054)	3,278	6.32
European (207)	207	0.40
Finnish (34)	48	0.09
French, ex. Basque (155)	1,022	1.97
French Canadian (35)	203	0.39
German (3,461)	9,960	19.21
Greek (51)	82	0.16
Hungarian (111)	258	0.50
Irish (1,183)	5,091	9.82
Italian (711)	1,611	3.11
Latvian (11)	11	0.02
Lithuanian (21)	21	0.04
Northern European (26)	26	0.05
Norwegian (55)	299	0.58
Pennsylvania German (226)	347	0.67
Polish (487)	1,234	2.38
Portuguese (42)	42	0.08

*Notes: † The Census 2010 population figure is used to calculate the percentages in the Hispanic Origin and Race categories. Ancestry percentages are based on the 2006-2010 American Community Survey population (not shown); ‡ Numbers in parentheses indicate the number of people reporting a single ancestry; * Numbers in parentheses indicate the number of persons reporting this race alone, not in combination with any other race; Please refer to the Explanation of Data for more information.*

Romanian (11)	40	0.08
Russian (27)	162	0.31
Scandinavian (60)	60	0.12
Scotch-Irish (331)	647	1.25
Scottish (137)	679	1.31
Slovak (0)	11	0.02
Slovene (18)	18	0.03
Swedish (105)	422	0.81
Swiss (64)	504	0.97
Ukrainian (29)	39	0.08
Welsh (44)	213	0.41
West Indian, ex. Hispanic (121)	121	0.23
Jamaican (121)	121	0.23

Hispanic Origin	Population	%
Hispanic or Latino (of any race)	11,451	22.48
Central American, ex. Mexican	912	1.79
Costa Rican	1	<0.01
Guatemalan	93	0.18
Honduran	390	0.77
Nicaraguan	14	0.03
Panamanian	2	<0.01
Salvadoran	400	0.79
Other Central American	12	0.02
Cuban	26	0.05
Dominican Republic	19	0.04
Mexican	9,313	18.28
Puerto Rican	392	0.77
South American	121	0.24
Argentinean	10	0.02
Bolivian	29	0.06
Chilean	6	0.01
Colombian	24	0.05
Ecuadorian	7	0.01
Paraguayan	2	<0.01
Peruvian	20	0.04
Uruguayan	1	<0.01
Venezuelan	22	0.04
Other Hispanic or Latino	668	1.31

Race*	Population	%
African-American/Black (7,862)	9,108	17.88
Not Hispanic (7,705)	8,843	17.36
Hispanic (157)	265	0.52
American Indian/Alaska Native (290)	706	1.39
Not Hispanic (154)	482	0.95
Hispanic (136)	224	0.44
Apache (0)	5	0.01
Blackfeet (5)	31	0.06
Canadian/French Am. Ind. (0)	5	0.01
Central American Ind. (1)	4	0.01
Cherokee (28)	120	0.24
Cheyenne (0)	3	0.01
Chickasaw (2)	2	<0.01
Chippewa (4)	14	0.03
Choctaw (4)	12	0.02
Comanche (2)	2	<0.01
Cree (1)	4	0.01
Creek (0)	4	0.01
Crow (0)	4	0.01
Iroquois (3)	5	0.01
Lumbee (7)	8	0.02
Mexican American Ind. (32)	55	0.11
Navajo (3)	7	0.01
Ottawa (4)	6	0.01
Paiute (0)	3	0.01
Potawatomi (14)	28	0.05
Sioux (7)	21	0.04
South American Ind. (3)	4	0.01
Spanish American Ind. (2)	3	0.01
Asian (452)	660	1.30
Not Hispanic (430)	625	1.23
Hispanic (22)	35	0.07
Bangladeshi (3)	3	0.01
Cambodian (49)	66	0.13
Chinese, ex. Taiwanese (43)	77	0.15
Filipino (46)	76	0.15
Indian (93)	115	0.23
Indonesian (1)	8	0.02
Japanese (10)	32	0.06
Korean (37)	60	0.12
Laotian (87)	115	0.23
Malaysian (0)	1	<0.01
Pakistani (9)	15	0.03
Sri Lankan (4)	4	0.01
Taiwanese (1)	1	<0.01
Thai (11)	22	0.04
Vietnamese (12)	24	0.05
Hawaii Native/Pacific Islander (33)	71	0.14
Not Hispanic (20)	44	0.09
Hispanic (13)	27	0.05
Guamanian/Chamorro (11)	17	0.03
Marshallese (1)	1	<0.01
Native Hawaiian (6)	19	0.04
Samoan (5)	8	0.02
Tongan (6)	6	0.01
White (33,672)	35,539	69.75
Not Hispanic (29,565)	30,987	60.82
Hispanic (4,107)	4,552	8.93

Elwood

Place Type: City
County: Madison
Population: 8,614†

Ancestry‡	Population	%
American (1,103)	1,103	12.41
Austrian (26)	53	0.60
Czech (0)	32	0.36
Dutch (24)	95	1.07
English (313)	702	7.90
European (12)	12	0.14
Finnish (0)	28	0.32
French, ex. Basque (61)	372	4.19
French Canadian (92)	92	1.04
German (996)	2,060	23.19
Greek (38)	38	0.43
Hungarian (0)	10	0.11
Irish (564)	1,338	15.06
Italian (44)	57	0.64
Pennsylvania German (12)	12	0.14
Polish (0)	29	0.33
Portuguese (0)	8	0.09
Russian (0)	55	0.62
Scotch-Irish (52)	145	1.63
Scottish (52)	111	1.25
Serbian (78)	78	0.88
Swedish (20)	42	0.47
Turkish (25)	73	0.82
Welsh (71)	92	1.04

Hispanic Origin	Population	%
Hispanic or Latino (of any race)	286	3.32
Central American, ex. Mexican	7	0.08
Guatemalan	4	0.05
Honduran	2	0.02
Salvadoran	1	0.01
Dominican Republic	4	0.05
Mexican	243	2.82
Puerto Rican	1	0.01
Other Hispanic or Latino	31	0.36

Race*	Population	%
African-American/Black (18)	70	0.81
Not Hispanic (18)	69	0.80
Hispanic (0)	1	0.01
American Indian/Alaska Native (16)	50	0.58
Not Hispanic (14)	46	0.53
Hispanic (2)	4	0.05
Apache (0)	2	0.02
Blackfeet (0)	2	0.02
Canadian/French Am. Ind. (1)	1	0.01
Cherokee (5)	13	0.15
Cheyenne (1)	5	0.06
Delaware (0)	3	0.03
Menominee (0)	2	0.02
Sioux (1)	1	0.01
Asian (30)	42	0.49
Not Hispanic (30)	40	0.46
Hispanic (0)	2	0.02
Chinese, ex. Taiwanese (9)	9	0.10
Filipino (7)	13	0.15
Japanese (10)	14	0.16
Korean (3)	3	0.03
Laotian (0)	2	0.02
Vietnamese (0)	2	0.02
Hawaii Native/Pacific Islander (4)	13	0.15
Not Hispanic (4)	9	0.10
Hispanic (0)	4	0.05
Guamanian/Chamorro (1)	2	0.02
Native Hawaiian (0)	3	0.03
Samoan (1)	2	0.02
Tongan (2)	5	0.06
White (8,333)	8,456	98.17
Not Hispanic (8,162)	8,257	95.86
Hispanic (171)	199	2.31

Evansville

Place Type: City
County: Vanderburgh
Population: 117,429†

Ancestry‡	Population	%
African, Sub-Saharan (120)	233	0.20
African (90)	160	0.14
Ethiopian (0)	34	0.03
Nigerian (8)	17	0.01
Ugandan (14)	14	0.01
Other Sub-Saharan African (8)	8	0.01
American (23,162)	23,162	19.60
Arab (79)	117	0.10
Arab (7)	7	0.01
Iraqi (16)	16	0.01
Jordanian (15)	15	0.01
Lebanese (0)	27	0.02
Palestinian (30)	30	0.03
Syrian (0)	11	0.01
Other Arab (11)	11	0.01
Armenian (70)	78	0.07
Australian (39)	39	0.03
Austrian (9)	109	0.09
Belgian (0)	75	0.06
Brazilian (62)	62	0.05
British (257)	446	0.38
Cajun (0)	12	0.01
Canadian (61)	71	0.06
Celtic (0)	23	0.02
Croatian (0)	47	0.04
Czech (39)	152	0.13
Czechoslovakian (44)	73	0.06
Danish (8)	133	0.11
Dutch (466)	1,856	1.57
Eastern European (0)	14	0.01
English (4,204)	9,922	8.40
European (672)	768	0.65
Finnish (18)	80	0.07
French, ex. Basque (892)	2,952	2.50
French Canadian (99)	110	0.09
German (18,318)	33,828	28.62
Greek (52)	135	0.11
Guyanese (0)	49	0.04
Hungarian (56)	136	0.12
Iranian (20)	20	0.02
Irish (3,732)	14,073	11.91
Italian (622)	2,111	1.79
Latvian (12)	12	0.01
Lithuanian (0)	83	0.07
Northern European (17)	34	0.03
Norwegian (132)	375	0.32
Pennsylvania German (21)	33	0.03
Polish (462)	1,485	1.26
Portuguese (63)	95	0.08
Romanian (0)	10	0.01
Russian (177)	381	0.32
Scandinavian (17)	25	0.02
Scotch-Irish (666)	1,964	1.66
Scottish (823)	2,023	1.71
Serbian (13)	13	0.01

SECTION TWO

*Notes: † The Census 2010 population figure is used to calculate the percentages in the Hispanic Origin and Race categories. Ancestry percentages are based on the 2006-2010 American Community Survey population (not shown); ‡ Numbers in parentheses indicate the number of people reporting a single ancestry; * Numbers in parentheses indicate the number of persons reporting this race alone, not in combination with any other race; Please refer to the Explanation of Data for more information.*

Slavic (0)	11	0.01
Slovak (55)	157	0.13
Swedish (203)	477	0.40
Swiss (11)	216	0.18
Turkish (11)	25	0.02
Ukrainian (129)	129	0.11
Welsh (82)	380	0.32
West Indian, ex. Hispanic (23)	55	0.05
Haitian (0)	11	0.01
Jamaican (23)	44	0.04

Hispanic Origin	Population	%
Hispanic or Latino (of any race)	3,014	2.57
Central American, ex. Mexican	178	0.15
Costa Rican	7	0.01
Guatemalan	31	0.03
Honduran	31	0.03
Nicaraguan	35	0.03
Panamanian	24	0.02
Salvadoran	45	0.04
Other Central American	5	<0.01
Cuban	64	0.05
Dominican Republic	24	0.02
Mexican	2,073	1.77
Puerto Rican	245	0.21
South American	118	0.10
Argentinean	9	0.01
Bolivian	4	<0.01
Chilean	4	<0.01
Colombian	32	0.03
Ecuadorian	9	0.01
Paraguayan	2	<0.01
Peruvian	33	0.03
Venezuelan	24	0.02
Other South American	1	<0.01
Other Hispanic or Latino	312	0.27

Race*	Population	%
African-American/Black (14,766)	17,089	14.55
Not Hispanic (14,672)	16,871	14.37
Hispanic (94)	218	0.19
American Indian/Alaska Native (312)	916	0.78
Not Hispanic (269)	831	0.71
Hispanic (43)	85	0.07
Alaska Athabascan *(Ala. Nat.)* (0)	1	<0.01
Apache (6)	23	0.02
Arapaho (1)	1	<0.01
Blackfeet (5)	39	0.03
Canadian/French Am. Ind. (1)	2	<0.01
Central American Ind. (1)	1	<0.01
Cherokee (71)	283	0.24
Cheyenne (4)	11	0.01
Chickasaw (1)	3	<0.01
Chippewa (12)	18	0.02
Choctaw (5)	16	0.01
Colville (1)	1	<0.01
Comanche (0)	2	<0.01
Cree (0)	2	<0.01
Crow (0)	1	<0.01
Delaware (4)	6	0.01
Hopi (0)	1	<0.01
Houma (2)	4	<0.01
Inupiat *(Alaska Native)* (0)	1	<0.01
Iroquois (3)	14	0.01
Kiowa (0)	1	<0.01
Lumbee (1)	11	0.01
Mexican American Ind. (5)	7	0.01
Navajo (3)	10	0.01
Osage (2)	2	<0.01
Potawatomi (0)	1	<0.01
Pueblo (1)	3	<0.01
Seminole (1)	3	<0.01
Sioux (25)	52	0.04
South American Ind. (2)	4	<0.01
Spanish American Ind. (1)	1	<0.01
Yaqui (0)	1	<0.01
Asian (1,160)	1,578	1.34
Not Hispanic (1,149)	1,544	1.31
Hispanic (11)	34	0.03
Bangladeshi (6)	6	0.01
Burmese (1)	1	<0.01
Cambodian (2)	3	<0.01
Chinese, ex. Taiwanese (254)	319	0.27
Filipino (161)	248	0.21
Indian (307)	369	0.31
Indonesian (6)	12	0.01
Japanese (69)	135	0.11
Korean (102)	162	0.14
Laotian (2)	2	<0.01
Malaysian (13)	17	0.01
Nepalese (14)	23	0.02
Pakistani (5)	10	0.01
Taiwanese (6)	10	0.01
Thai (23)	40	0.03
Vietnamese (155)	194	0.17
Hawaii Native/Pacific Islander (84)	176	0.15
Not Hispanic (72)	150	0.13
Hispanic (12)	26	0.02
Guamanian/Chamorro (18)	30	0.03
Marshallese (44)	49	0.04
Native Hawaiian (12)	49	0.04
Samoan (5)	20	0.02
White (96,266)	99,372	84.62
Not Hispanic (94,961)	97,793	83.28
Hispanic (1,305)	1,579	1.34

Fishers

Place Type: Town
County: Hamilton
Population: 76,794†

Ancestry‡	Population	%
Afghan (15)	15	0.02
African, Sub-Saharan (240)	258	0.36
African (102)	111	0.15
Nigerian (79)	79	0.11
Senegalese (13)	13	0.02
Other Sub-Saharan African (46)	55	0.08
Albanian (0)	10	0.01
American (3,929)	3,929	5.48
Arab (450)	580	0.81
Arab (207)	235	0.33
Egyptian (113)	125	0.17
Jordanian (25)	37	0.05
Lebanese (73)	135	0.19
Syrian (32)	32	0.04
Other Arab (0)	16	0.02
Armenian (10)	10	0.01
Australian (0)	36	0.05
Austrian (46)	233	0.32
Belgian (74)	165	0.23
Brazilian (10)	24	0.03
British (228)	451	0.63
Cajun (0)	22	0.03
Canadian (95)	195	0.27
Celtic (14)	14	0.02
Croatian (19)	84	0.12
Czech (105)	513	0.72
Czechoslovakian (27)	41	0.06
Danish (129)	282	0.39
Dutch (353)	1,512	2.11
Eastern European (75)	75	0.10
English (3,213)	9,173	12.79
European (1,290)	1,428	1.99
Finnish (13)	83	0.12
French, ex. Basque (468)	2,611	3.64
French Canadian (108)	382	0.53
German (8,414)	20,883	29.11
Greek (206)	637	0.89
Hungarian (127)	463	0.65
Iranian (161)	181	0.25
Irish (3,090)	10,537	14.69
Israeli (21)	21	0.03
Italian (1,156)	3,343	4.66
Latvian (13)	13	0.02
Lithuanian (24)	166	0.23
Macedonian (0)	10	0.01
New Zealander (14)	14	0.02
Northern European (24)	24	0.03
Norwegian (335)	843	1.17
Pennsylvania German (12)	27	0.04
Polish (774)	2,912	4.06
Portuguese (59)	185	0.26
Romanian (85)	109	0.15
Russian (142)	350	0.49
Scandinavian (97)	183	0.26
Scotch-Irish (518)	1,293	1.80
Scottish (656)	2,188	3.05
Serbian (29)	47	0.07
Slavic (12)	50	0.07
Slovak (36)	63	0.09
Slovene (48)	54	0.08
Swedish (283)	1,288	1.80
Swiss (143)	576	0.80
Ukrainian (39)	97	0.14
Welsh (393)	930	1.30
West Indian, ex. Hispanic (13)	58	0.08
British West Indian (13)	13	0.02
Jamaican (0)	45	0.06
Yugoslavian (90)	133	0.19

Hispanic Origin	Population	%
Hispanic or Latino (of any race)	2,638	3.44
Central American, ex. Mexican	162	0.21
Costa Rican	9	0.01
Guatemalan	54	0.07
Honduran	16	0.02
Nicaraguan	13	0.02
Panamanian	39	0.05
Salvadoran	28	0.04
Other Central American	3	<0.01
Cuban	90	0.12
Dominican Republic	46	0.06
Mexican	1,389	1.81
Puerto Rican	349	0.45
South American	359	0.47
Argentinean	29	0.04
Bolivian	5	0.01
Chilean	15	0.02
Colombian	127	0.17
Ecuadorian	9	0.01
Paraguayan	3	<0.01
Peruvian	62	0.08
Uruguayan	7	0.01
Venezuelan	93	0.12
Other South American	9	0.01
Other Hispanic or Latino	243	0.32

Race*	Population	%
African-American/Black (4,299)	4,958	6.46
Not Hispanic (4,228)	4,837	6.30
Hispanic (71)	121	0.16
American Indian/Alaska Native (126)	302	0.39
Not Hispanic (109)	267	0.35
Hispanic (17)	35	0.05
Apache (4)	9	0.01
Blackfeet (2)	4	0.01
Central American Ind. (0)	1	<0.01
Cherokee (20)	61	0.08
Chickasaw (0)	1	<0.01
Chippewa (5)	9	0.01
Choctaw (0)	6	0.01
Cree (0)	1	<0.01
Creek (1)	1	<0.01
Delaware (0)	2	<0.01
Iroquois (3)	6	0.01
Kiowa (1)	1	<0.01
Lumbee (5)	6	0.01
Menominee (1)	2	<0.01
Mexican American Ind. (3)	3	<0.01
Navajo (0)	2	<0.01
Ottawa (1)	1	<0.01
Paiute (2)	3	<0.01
Potawatomi (6)	7	0.01
Pueblo (0)	1	<0.01
Sioux (7)	9	0.01
South American Ind. (0)	10	0.01
Tlingit-Haida *(Alaska Native)* (1)	1	<0.01
Asian (4,188)	4,930	6.42

*Notes: † The Census 2010 population figure is used to calculate the percentages in the Hispanic Origin and Race categories. Ancestry percentages are based on the 2006-2010 American Community Survey population (not shown); ‡ Numbers in parentheses indicate the number of people reporting a single ancestry; * Numbers in parentheses indicate the number of persons reporting this race alone, not in combination with any other race; Please refer to the Explanation of Data for more information.*

Not Hispanic (4,174)	4,883	6.36
Hispanic (14)	47	0.06
Bangladeshi (31)	35	0.05
Bhutanese (1)	3	<0.01
Burmese (2)	6	0.01
Cambodian (9)	14	0.02
Chinese, ex. Taiwanese (703)	818	1.07
Filipino (241)	391	0.51
Hmong (11)	11	0.01
Indian (1,639)	1,785	2.32
Indonesian (46)	53	0.07
Japanese (220)	316	0.41
Korean (457)	575	0.75
Laotian (19)	25	0.03
Malaysian (8)	10	0.01
Nepalese (18)	18	0.02
Pakistani (177)	189	0.25
Sri Lankan (10)	11	0.01
Taiwanese (40)	45	0.06
Thai (24)	47	0.06
Vietnamese (383)	439	0.57
Hawaii Native/Pacific Islander (19)	58	0.08
Not Hispanic (14)	46	0.06
Hispanic (5)	12	0.02
Guamanian/Chamorro (3)	6	0.01
Native Hawaiian (5)	16	0.02
Samoan (4)	11	0.01
Tongan (3)	6	0.01
White (65,754)	67,165	87.46
Not Hispanic (64,058)	65,289	85.02
Hispanic (1,696)	1,876	2.44

Fort Wayne

Place Type: City
County: Allen
Population: 253,691†

Ancestry‡	Population	%
Afghan (20)	20	0.01
African, Sub-Saharan (13,049)	13,249	5.22
African (12,562)	12,753	5.03
Ethiopian (47)	47	0.02
Kenyan (27)	27	0.01
Nigerian (138)	138	0.05
Somalian (68)	68	0.03
South African (43)	52	0.02
Other Sub-Saharan African (164)	164	0.06
Albanian (33)	33	0.01
Alsatian (8)	8	<0.01
American (25,688)	25,688	10.12
Arab (475)	664	0.26
Arab (207)	222	0.09
Egyptian (8)	8	<0.01
Iraqi (44)	54	0.02
Jordanian (10)	10	<0.01
Lebanese (121)	235	0.09
Moroccan (10)	10	<0.01
Syrian (54)	104	0.04
Other Arab (21)	21	0.01
Armenian (81)	81	0.03
Assyrian/Chaldean/Syriac (10)	10	<0.01
Australian (27)	54	0.02
Austrian (105)	250	0.10
Belgian (27)	220	0.09
Brazilian (0)	21	0.01
British (375)	767	0.30
Bulgarian (126)	156	0.06
Canadian (295)	681	0.27
Celtic (8)	30	0.01
Croatian (150)	244	0.10
Czech (224)	837	0.33
Czechoslovakian (53)	130	0.05
Danish (182)	601	0.24
Dutch (872)	3,612	1.42
Eastern European (101)	110	0.04
English (6,224)	19,734	7.78
Estonian (0)	12	<0.01
European (1,501)	1,608	0.63
Finnish (18)	185	0.07
French, ex. Basque (1,952)	9,917	3.91
French Canadian (321)	813	0.32
German (36,666)	76,622	30.20
Greek (380)	732	0.29
Hungarian (350)	1,122	0.44
Icelander (0)	9	<0.01
Iranian (8)	8	<0.01
Irish (8,309)	28,352	11.17
Israeli (34)	34	0.01
Italian (2,543)	6,703	2.64
Latvian (70)	70	0.03
Lithuanian (39)	278	0.11
Luxemburger (0)	36	0.01
Macedonian (328)	580	0.23
New Zealander (0)	11	<0.01
Northern European (96)	96	0.04
Norwegian (393)	1,488	0.59
Pennsylvania German (190)	255	0.10
Polish (1,714)	5,438	2.14
Portuguese (175)	324	0.13
Romanian (184)	387	0.15
Russian (344)	913	0.36
Scandinavian (153)	269	0.11
Scotch-Irish (998)	3,125	1.23
Scottish (1,270)	4,615	1.82
Serbian (0)	75	0.03
Slavic (47)	92	0.04
Slovak (196)	468	0.18
Slovene (0)	37	0.01
Swedish (460)	1,940	0.76
Swiss (615)	2,499	0.98
Turkish (46)	46	0.02
Ukrainian (155)	293	0.12
Welsh (248)	1,388	0.55
West Indian, ex. Hispanic (567)	665	0.26
British West Indian (74)	74	0.03
Haitian (346)	377	0.15
Jamaican (147)	196	0.08
West Indian (0)	18	0.01
Yugoslavian (1,385)	1,443	0.57

Hispanic Origin	Population	%
Hispanic or Latino (of any race)	20,200	7.96
Central American, ex. Mexican	1,346	0.53
Costa Rican	38	0.01
Guatemalan	729	0.29
Honduran	129	0.05
Nicaraguan	37	0.01
Panamanian	38	0.01
Salvadoran	369	0.15
Other Central American	6	<0.01
Cuban	174	0.07
Dominican Republic	72	0.03
Mexican	15,545	6.13
Puerto Rican	939	0.37
South American	651	0.26
Argentinean	36	0.01
Bolivian	15	0.01
Chilean	18	0.01
Colombian	235	0.09
Ecuadorian	159	0.06
Paraguayan	4	<0.01
Peruvian	128	0.05
Uruguayan	10	<0.01
Venezuelan	45	0.02
Other South American	1	<0.01
Other Hispanic or Latino	1,473	0.58

Race*	Population	%
African-American/Black (39,085)	44,499	17.54
Not Hispanic (38,514)	43,301	17.07
Hispanic (571)	1,198	0.47
American Indian/Alaska Native (939)	2,669	1.05
Not Hispanic (730)	2,172	0.86
Hispanic (209)	497	0.20
Alaska Athabascan *(Ala. Nat.)* (4)	4	<0.01
Aleut *(Alaska Native)* (1)	1	<0.01
Apache (15)	43	0.02
Arapaho (2)	3	<0.01
Blackfeet (18)	110	0.04
Canadian/French Am. Ind. (2)	4	<0.01
Central American Ind. (5)	11	<0.01
Cherokee (126)	481	0.19
Cheyenne (2)	6	<0.01
Chickasaw (5)	13	0.01
Chippewa (28)	63	0.02
Choctaw (19)	55	0.02
Comanche (3)	4	<0.01
Cree (1)	9	<0.01
Creek (6)	18	0.01
Crow (1)	12	<0.01
Delaware (1)	12	<0.01
Hopi (2)	7	<0.01
Houma (0)	3	<0.01
Inupiat *(Alaska Native)* (3)	3	<0.01
Iroquois (20)	41	0.02
Kiowa (3)	3	<0.01
Lumbee (1)	2	<0.01
Menominee (0)	1	<0.01
Mexican American Ind. (42)	67	0.03
Navajo (8)	26	0.01
Osage (1)	1	<0.01
Ottawa (9)	15	0.01
Paiute (0)	1	<0.01
Pima (4)	7	<0.01
Potawatomi (7)	26	0.01
Pueblo (2)	7	<0.01
Seminole (0)	11	<0.01
Sioux (21)	68	0.03
South American Ind. (4)	9	<0.01
Spanish American Ind. (2)	3	<0.01
Tlingit-Haida *(Alaska Native)* (2)	4	<0.01
Ute (1)	2	<0.01
Yaqui (3)	5	<0.01
Yup'ik *(Alaska Native)* (1)	2	<0.01
Asian (8,379)	9,768	3.85
Not Hispanic (8,279)	9,548	3.76
Hispanic (100)	220	0.09
Bangladeshi (37)	40	0.02
Burmese (3,653)	3,819	1.51
Cambodian (38)	46	0.02
Chinese, ex. Taiwanese (493)	643	0.25
Filipino (520)	823	0.32
Indian (1,183)	1,426	0.56
Indonesian (18)	26	0.01
Japanese (128)	252	0.10
Korean (313)	474	0.19
Laotian (290)	369	0.15
Malaysian (19)	41	0.02
Nepalese (10)	11	<0.01
Pakistani (114)	161	0.06
Sri Lankan (17)	19	0.01
Taiwanese (33)	47	0.02
Thai (132)	202	0.08
Vietnamese (818)	939	0.37
Hawaii Native/Pacific Islander (154)	354	0.14
Not Hispanic (91)	249	0.10
Hispanic (63)	105	0.04
Fijian (2)	2	<0.01
Guamanian/Chamorro (67)	102	0.04
Marshallese (1)	1	<0.01
Native Hawaiian (41)	119	0.05
Samoan (13)	38	0.01
Tongan (0)	1	<0.01
White (186,763)	194,759	76.77
Not Hispanic (178,436)	184,757	72.83
Hispanic (8,327)	10,002	3.94

Frankfort

Place Type: City
County: Clinton
Population: 16,422†

Ancestry‡	Population	%
American (1,571)	1,571	9.54
Belgian (27)	104	0.63
British (12)	26	0.16
Canadian (16)	16	0.10
Croatian (11)	11	0.07

*Notes: † The Census 2010 population figure is used to calculate the percentages in the Hispanic Origin and Race categories. Ancestry percentages are based on the 2006-2010 American Community Survey population (not shown); ‡ Numbers in parentheses indicate the number of people reporting a single ancestry; * Numbers in parentheses indicate the number of persons reporting this race alone, not in combination with any other race; Please refer to the Explanation of Data for more information.*

Danish (17)	29	0.18
Dutch (33)	195	1.18
English (775)	1,496	9.09
European (43)	49	0.30
Finnish (0)	12	0.07
French, ex. Basque (128)	158	0.96
German (1,348)	3,131	19.02
Hungarian (11)	38	0.23
Irish (578)	1,531	9.30
Italian (96)	221	1.34
Norwegian (0)	8	0.05
Pennsylvania German (16)	16	0.10
Polish (115)	232	1.41
Romanian (10)	10	0.06
Scandinavian (22)	22	0.13
Scotch-Irish (93)	194	1.18
Scottish (280)	383	2.33
Swedish (61)	186	1.13
Swiss (0)	21	0.13
Welsh (21)	81	0.49

Hispanic Origin	Population	%
Hispanic or Latino (of any race)	4,098	24.95
Central American, ex. Mexican	110	0.67
Costa Rican	1	0.01
Guatemalan	53	0.32
Honduran	9	0.05
Nicaraguan	2	0.01
Panamanian	1	0.01
Salvadoran	44	0.27
Cuban	4	0.02
Mexican	3,693	22.49
Puerto Rican	44	0.27
South American	12	0.07
Argentinean	3	0.02
Colombian	9	0.05
Other Hispanic or Latino	235	1.43

Race*	Population	%
African-American/Black (105)	159	0.97
Not Hispanic (101)	138	0.84
Hispanic (4)	21	0.13
American Indian/Alaska Native (57)	131	0.80
Not Hispanic (22)	67	0.41
Hispanic (35)	64	0.39
Apache (2)	2	0.01
Blackfeet (0)	1	0.01
Cherokee (4)	30	0.18
Cheyenne (0)	1	0.01
Chickasaw (1)	1	0.01
Chippewa (2)	3	0.02
Choctaw (3)	3	0.02
Inupiat *(Alaska Native)* (3)	4	0.02
Mexican American Ind. (5)	7	0.04
Ottawa (1)	1	0.01
Potawatomi (0)	1	0.01
Sioux (1)	1	0.01
South American Ind. (0)	1	0.01
Asian (29)	68	0.41
Not Hispanic (24)	42	0.26
Hispanic (5)	26	0.16
Chinese, ex. Taiwanese (2)	3	0.02
Filipino (8)	27	0.16
Indian (7)	9	0.05
Japanese (2)	3	0.02
Korean (6)	7	0.04
Laotian (0)	1	0.01
Thai (1)	5	0.03
Vietnamese (0)	1	0.01
Hawaii Native/Pacific Islander (1)	18	0.11
Not Hispanic (1)	6	0.04
Hispanic (0)	12	0.07
Native Hawaiian (1)	3	0.02
Samoan (0)	2	0.01
White (13,775)	14,048	85.54
Not Hispanic (12,055)	12,160	74.05
Hispanic (1,720)	1,888	11.50

Franklin

Place Type: City
County: Johnson
Population: 23,712†

Ancestry‡	Population	%
African, Sub-Saharan (46)	46	0.20
Ghanaian (46)	46	0.20
American (2,751)	2,751	12.22
Arab (24)	24	0.11
Moroccan (24)	24	0.11
Austrian (0)	25	0.11
British (47)	172	0.76
Celtic (0)	17	0.08
Croatian (0)	6	0.03
Czech (13)	53	0.24
Danish (9)	19	0.08
Dutch (64)	357	1.59
English (1,211)	2,836	12.60
Estonian (0)	17	0.08
European (106)	179	0.80
French, ex. Basque (195)	496	2.20
French Canadian (43)	64	0.28
German (2,822)	6,240	27.72
Greek (0)	71	0.32
Hungarian (38)	98	0.44
Iranian (0)	9	0.04
Irish (945)	3,800	16.88
Italian (153)	558	2.48
Latvian (10)	10	0.04
Lithuanian (0)	23	0.10
Northern European (13)	13	0.06
Norwegian (59)	225	1.00
Pennsylvania German (14)	14	0.06
Polish (15)	183	0.81
Portuguese (0)	13	0.06
Russian (50)	59	0.26
Scandinavian (36)	36	0.16
Scotch-Irish (184)	622	2.76
Scottish (265)	446	1.98
Serbian (15)	15	0.07
Slovak (11)	38	0.17
Swedish (47)	218	0.97
Swiss (8)	18	0.08
Turkish (36)	36	0.16
Welsh (0)	121	0.54
West Indian, ex. Hispanic (0)	9	0.04
Jamaican (0)	9	0.04
Yugoslavian (32)	32	0.14

Hispanic Origin	Population	%
Hispanic or Latino (of any race)	586	2.47
Central American, ex. Mexican	35	0.15
Costa Rican	2	0.01
Guatemalan	3	0.01
Honduran	18	0.08
Nicaraguan	4	0.02
Panamanian	3	0.01
Salvadoran	5	0.02
Cuban	11	0.05
Dominican Republic	5	0.02
Mexican	426	1.80
Puerto Rican	53	0.22
South American	20	0.08
Argentinean	1	<0.01
Colombian	2	0.01
Ecuadorian	4	0.02
Peruvian	12	0.05
Venezuelan	1	<0.01
Other Hispanic or Latino	36	0.15

Race*	Population	%
African-American/Black (325)	520	2.19
Not Hispanic (311)	490	2.07
Hispanic (14)	30	0.13
American Indian/Alaska Native (62)	143	0.60
Not Hispanic (54)	122	0.51
Hispanic (8)	21	0.09
Alaska Athabascan *(Ala. Nat.)* (0)	1	<0.01
Apache (3)	6	0.03
Blackfeet (2)	5	0.02
Central American Ind. (0)	1	<0.01
Cherokee (11)	32	0.13
Chickasaw (1)	1	<0.01
Chippewa (0)	8	0.03
Choctaw (0)	1	<0.01
Crow (1)	6	0.03
Ottawa (0)	1	<0.01
Pueblo (1)	1	<0.01
Sioux (1)	5	0.02
Tohono O'Odham (0)	1	<0.01
Asian (184)	266	1.12
Not Hispanic (182)	255	1.08
Hispanic (2)	11	0.05
Burmese (1)	1	<0.01
Cambodian (2)	6	0.03
Chinese, ex. Taiwanese (43)	49	0.21
Filipino (25)	59	0.25
Indian (60)	68	0.29
Indonesian (2)	5	0.02
Japanese (13)	24	0.10
Korean (13)	22	0.09
Thai (2)	5	0.02
Vietnamese (14)	16	0.07
Hawaii Native/Pacific Islander (2)	24	0.10
Not Hispanic (2)	18	0.08
Hispanic (0)	6	0.03
Guamanian/Chamorro (0)	5	0.02
Native Hawaiian (1)	11	0.05
Samoan (0)	2	0.01
White (22,514)	22,883	96.50
Not Hispanic (22,233)	22,541	95.06
Hispanic (281)	342	1.44

Gary

Place Type: City
County: Lake
Population: 80,294†

Ancestry‡	Population	%
African, Sub-Saharan (1,504)	1,824	2.16
African (1,278)	1,527	1.81
Ethiopian (121)	121	0.14
Ghanaian (10)	10	0.01
Liberian (0)	11	0.01
Nigerian (95)	155	0.18
American (1,013)	1,013	1.20
Arab (18)	18	0.02
Moroccan (18)	18	0.02
Austrian (0)	30	0.04
Belgian (12)	43	0.05
Brazilian (21)	30	0.04
British (26)	68	0.08
Canadian (0)	19	0.02
Croatian (100)	187	0.22
Czech (24)	24	0.03
Danish (0)	29	0.03
Dutch (71)	315	0.37
Eastern European (37)	37	0.04
English (724)	1,454	1.72
European (42)	42	0.05
Finnish (7)	7	0.01
French, ex. Basque (15)	207	0.25
French Canadian (10)	19	0.02
German (600)	2,519	2.98
Greek (89)	164	0.19
Hungarian (65)	167	0.20
Irish (730)	2,537	3.01
Italian (152)	530	0.63
Lithuanian (46)	162	0.19
Maltese (10)	10	0.01
Norwegian (16)	194	0.23
Polish (375)	1,164	1.38
Romanian (0)	9	0.01
Russian (0)	46	0.05
Scotch-Irish (34)	169	0.20
Scottish (67)	204	0.24
Serbian (9)	9	0.01

*Notes: † The Census 2010 population figure is used to calculate the percentages in the Hispanic Origin and Race categories. Ancestry percentages are based on the 2006-2010 American Community Survey population (not shown); ‡ Numbers in parentheses indicate the number of people reporting a single ancestry; * Numbers in parentheses indicate the number of persons reporting this race alone, not in combination with any other race; Please refer to the Explanation of Data for more information.*

Slavic (0)	12	0.01
Slovak (43)	209	0.25
Swedish (27)	98	0.12
Swiss (0)	24	0.03
Turkish (12)	12	0.01
Ukrainian (20)	31	0.04
Welsh (0)	90	0.11
West Indian, ex. Hispanic (198)	265	0.31
Haitian (0)	14	0.02
Jamaican (173)	192	0.23
West Indian (0)	34	0.04
Other West Indian (25)	25	0.03
Yugoslavian (17)	24	0.03

Hispanic Origin	Population	%
Hispanic or Latino (of any race)	4,128	5.14
Central American, ex. Mexican	47	0.06
Guatemalan	19	0.02
Honduran	12	0.01
Nicaraguan	2	<0.01
Panamanian	9	0.01
Salvadoran	5	0.01
Cuban	61	0.08
Dominican Republic	24	0.03
Mexican	2,553	3.18
Puerto Rican	1,223	1.52
South American	14	0.02
Argentinean	1	<0.01
Bolivian	1	<0.01
Chilean	1	<0.01
Colombian	8	0.01
Peruvian	2	<0.01
Venezuelan	1	<0.01
Other Hispanic or Latino	206	0.26

Race*	Population	%
African-American/Black (68,107)	69,508	86.57
Not Hispanic (67,363)	68,449	85.25
Hispanic (744)	1,059	1.32
American Indian/Alaska Native (241)	760	0.95
Not Hispanic (197)	659	0.82
Hispanic (44)	101	0.13
Apache (9)	16	0.02
Blackfeet (5)	43	0.05
Canadian/French Am. Ind. (0)	1	<0.01
Central American Ind. (2)	3	<0.01
Cherokee (12)	153	0.19
Chickasaw (0)	4	<0.01
Chippewa (5)	11	0.01
Choctaw (3)	27	0.03
Comanche (1)	2	<0.01
Cree (4)	7	0.01
Creek (2)	20	0.02
Delaware (0)	2	<0.01
Houma (4)	4	<0.01
Iroquois (2)	5	0.01
Lumbee (3)	3	<0.01
Menominee (1)	6	0.01
Mexican American Ind. (6)	15	0.02
Navajo (1)	6	0.01
Paiute (0)	1	<0.01
Potawatomi (1)	1	<0.01
Seminole (0)	12	0.01
Sioux (4)	17	0.02
South American Ind. (1)	3	<0.01
Asian (164)	345	0.43
Not Hispanic (156)	309	0.38
Hispanic (8)	36	0.04
Bangladeshi (0)	1	<0.01
Cambodian (7)	7	0.01
Chinese, ex. Taiwanese (23)	86	0.11
Filipino (42)	75	0.09
Indian (23)	52	0.06
Japanese (11)	34	0.04
Korean (24)	42	0.05
Laotian (6)	6	0.01
Pakistani (6)	9	0.01
Thai (2)	4	<0.01
Vietnamese (7)	19	0.02
Hawaii Native/Pacific Islander (8)	46	0.06
Not Hispanic (5)	32	0.04
Hispanic (3)	14	0.02
Guamanian/Chamorro (1)	6	0.01
Native Hawaiian (1)	4	<0.01
Samoan (3)	15	0.02
White (8,619)	9,685	12.06
Not Hispanic (7,151)	7,969	9.92
Hispanic (1,468)	1,716	2.14

Goshen

Place Type: City
County: Elkhart
Population: 31,719†

Ancestry‡	Population	%
African, Sub-Saharan (62)	71	0.23
African (20)	20	0.06
Ethiopian (7)	7	0.02
Kenyan (35)	35	0.11
Sierra Leonean (0)	9	0.03
Alsatian (0)	24	0.08
American (1,846)	1,846	5.91
Austrian (0)	12	0.04
Belgian (0)	33	0.11
Brazilian (59)	59	0.19
British (27)	81	0.26
Canadian (62)	62	0.20
Czech (43)	72	0.23
Danish (23)	90	0.29
Dutch (270)	742	2.37
Eastern European (14)	14	0.04
English (553)	1,872	5.99
European (466)	492	1.57
Finnish (0)	11	0.04
French, ex. Basque (168)	760	2.43
French Canadian (27)	51	0.16
German (3,934)	8,850	28.31
Greek (14)	21	0.07
Guyanese (10)	10	0.03
Hungarian (33)	33	0.11
Irish (700)	2,311	7.39
Italian (100)	339	1.08
Lithuanian (15)	15	0.05
Norwegian (17)	110	0.35
Pennsylvania German (203)	215	0.69
Polish (145)	742	2.37
Portuguese (33)	33	0.11
Russian (173)	235	0.75
Scandinavian (15)	15	0.05
Scotch-Irish (137)	278	0.89
Scottish (138)	431	1.38
Serbian (9)	9	0.03
Slavic (16)	16	0.05
Slovak (15)	35	0.11
Swedish (181)	350	1.12
Swiss (212)	1,482	4.74
Ukrainian (73)	85	0.27
Welsh (12)	101	0.32
West Indian, ex. Hispanic (56)	56	0.18
Haitian (14)	14	0.04
Jamaican (42)	42	0.13
Yugoslavian (0)	16	0.05

Hispanic Origin	Population	%
Hispanic or Latino (of any race)	8,903	28.07
Central American, ex. Mexican	310	0.98
Costa Rican	14	0.04
Guatemalan	71	0.22
Honduran	124	0.39
Nicaraguan	6	0.02
Panamanian	4	0.01
Salvadoran	91	0.29
Cuban	28	0.09
Dominican Republic	9	0.03
Mexican	7,781	24.53
Puerto Rican	347	1.09
South American	88	0.28
Argentinean	4	0.01
Bolivian	29	0.09
Chilean	5	0.02
Colombian	17	0.05
Ecuadorian	14	0.04
Paraguayan	3	0.01
Peruvian	6	0.02
Uruguayan	1	<0.01
Venezuelan	9	0.03
Other Hispanic or Latino	340	1.07

Race*	Population	%
African-American/Black (815)	1,140	3.59
Not Hispanic (740)	998	3.15
Hispanic (75)	142	0.45
American Indian/Alaska Native (163)	318	1.00
Not Hispanic (72)	181	0.57
Hispanic (91)	137	0.43
Aleut *(Alaska Native)* (1)	1	<0.01
Blackfeet (2)	8	0.03
Canadian/French Am. Ind. (1)	4	0.01
Cherokee (10)	59	0.19
Chickasaw (1)	1	<0.01
Chippewa (4)	13	0.04
Choctaw (6)	7	0.02
Delaware (0)	4	0.01
Iroquois (2)	4	0.01
Mexican American Ind. (23)	35	0.11
Navajo (2)	4	0.01
Paiute (0)	1	<0.01
Potawatomi (1)	2	0.01
Pueblo (1)	6	0.02
Sioux (5)	6	0.02
South American Ind. (0)	6	0.02
Spanish American Ind. (5)	5	0.02
Yup'ik *(Alaska Native)* (3)	3	0.01
Asian (381)	486	1.53
Not Hispanic (376)	467	1.47
Hispanic (5)	19	0.06
Bangladeshi (11)	11	0.03
Cambodian (62)	71	0.22
Chinese, ex. Taiwanese (62)	67	0.21
Filipino (40)	59	0.19
Indian (43)	54	0.17
Indonesian (7)	17	0.05
Japanese (9)	24	0.08
Korean (32)	48	0.15
Laotian (13)	23	0.07
Malaysian (0)	1	<0.01
Nepalese (9)	10	0.03
Pakistani (12)	15	0.05
Sri Lankan (10)	10	0.03
Thai (3)	7	0.02
Vietnamese (51)	69	0.22
Hawaii Native/Pacific Islander (11)	35	0.11
Not Hispanic (9)	21	0.07
Hispanic (2)	14	0.04
Guamanian/Chamorro (3)	6	0.02
Marshallese (4)	4	0.01
Native Hawaiian (1)	2	0.01
Samoan (1)	1	<0.01
White (24,812)	25,596	80.70
Not Hispanic (21,140)	21,567	67.99
Hispanic (3,672)	4,029	12.70

Granger

Place Type: CDP
County: St. Joseph
Population: 30,465†

Ancestry‡	Population	%
African, Sub-Saharan (164)	164	0.58
African (126)	126	0.44
Other Sub-Saharan African (38)	38	0.13
American (1,308)	1,308	4.61
Arab (155)	316	1.11
Lebanese (66)	227	0.80
Syrian (16)	16	0.06
Other Arab (73)	73	0.26
Armenian (0)	12	0.04
Australian (0)	7	0.02

*Notes: † The Census 2010 population figure is used to calculate the percentages in the Hispanic Origin and Race categories. Ancestry percentages are based on the 2006-2010 American Community Survey population (not shown); ‡ Numbers in parentheses indicate the number of people reporting a single ancestry; * Numbers in parentheses indicate the number of persons reporting this race alone, not in combination with any other race; Please refer to the Explanation of Data for more information.*

Austrian (38)	219	0.77
Belgian (115)	347	1.22
Brazilian (11)	11	0.04
British (0)	33	0.12
Canadian (86)	201	0.71
Celtic (0)	10	0.04
Croatian (11)	36	0.13
Czech (43)	172	0.61
Czechoslovakian (16)	47	0.17
Danish (23)	165	0.58
Dutch (283)	795	2.80
Eastern European (8)	8	0.03
English (1,084)	3,439	12.12
European (714)	756	2.67
Finnish (22)	122	0.43
French, ex. Basque (96)	558	1.97
French Canadian (87)	191	0.67
German (2,878)	8,608	30.35
Greek (139)	278	0.98
Hungarian (249)	655	2.31
Iranian (84)	124	0.44
Irish (1,068)	4,792	16.89
Italian (482)	1,819	6.41
Lithuanian (37)	107	0.38
Luxemburger (0)	26	0.09
Northern European (73)	85	0.30
Norwegian (157)	587	2.07
Pennsylvania German (22)	22	0.08
Polish (1,268)	3,502	12.35
Portuguese (0)	128	0.45
Romanian (40)	40	0.14
Russian (122)	291	1.03
Scandinavian (13)	54	0.19
Scotch-Irish (160)	501	1.77
Scottish (68)	672	2.37
Serbian (34)	55	0.19
Slavic (0)	20	0.07
Slovak (9)	16	0.06
Slovene (14)	59	0.21
Swedish (186)	670	2.36
Swiss (7)	158	0.56
Turkish (0)	23	0.08
Ukrainian (0)	27	0.10
Welsh (34)	181	0.64
West Indian, ex. Hispanic (49)	79	0.28
Jamaican (49)	79	0.28
Yugoslavian (17)	17	0.06

Hispanic Origin	Population	%
Hispanic or Latino (of any race)	733	2.41
Central American, ex. Mexican	40	0.13
Costa Rican	1	<0.01
Guatemalan	17	0.06
Honduran	8	0.03
Nicaraguan	5	0.02
Panamanian	3	0.01
Salvadoran	6	0.02
Cuban	20	0.07
Dominican Republic	7	0.02
Mexican	410	1.35
Puerto Rican	79	0.26
South American	87	0.29
Argentinean	7	0.02
Chilean	11	0.04
Colombian	28	0.09
Ecuadorian	8	0.03
Paraguayan	4	0.01
Peruvian	19	0.06
Venezuelan	10	0.03
Other Hispanic or Latino	90	0.30

Race*	Population	%
African-American/Black (773)	938	3.08
Not Hispanic (766)	913	3.00
Hispanic (7)	25	0.08
American Indian/Alaska Native (41)	157	0.52
Not Hispanic (33)	129	0.42
Hispanic (8)	28	0.09
Apache (0)	1	<0.01
Blackfeet (1)	5	0.02
Canadian/French Am. Ind. (0)	12	0.04
Cherokee (5)	31	0.10
Chippewa (1)	6	0.02
Choctaw (4)	8	0.03
Creek (3)	3	0.01
Delaware (0)	3	0.01
Inupiat *(Alaska Native)* (0)	1	<0.01
Mexican American Ind. (5)	5	0.02
Navajo (0)	1	<0.01
Potawatomi (5)	16	0.05
Sioux (0)	4	0.01
South American Ind. (0)	2	0.01
Asian (1,403)	1,608	5.28
Not Hispanic (1,400)	1,594	5.23
Hispanic (3)	14	0.05
Cambodian (4)	4	0.01
Chinese, ex. Taiwanese (387)	420	1.38
Filipino (91)	135	0.44
Indian (466)	502	1.65
Indonesian (10)	12	0.04
Japanese (39)	72	0.24
Korean (179)	223	0.73
Laotian (18)	18	0.06
Malaysian (1)	1	<0.01
Pakistani (86)	91	0.30
Sri Lankan (9)	9	0.03
Taiwanese (16)	16	0.05
Thai (10)	18	0.06
Vietnamese (62)	70	0.23
Hawaii Native/Pacific Islander (29)	55	0.18
Not Hispanic (29)	49	0.16
Hispanic (0)	6	0.02
Guamanian/Chamorro (3)	12	0.04
Marshallese (2)	2	0.01
Native Hawaiian (1)	10	0.03
Samoan (7)	16	0.05
Tongan (1)	1	<0.01
White (27,512)	27,968	91.80
Not Hispanic (27,036)	27,419	90.00
Hispanic (476)	549	1.80

Greencastle

Place Type: City
County: Putnam
Population: 10,326†

Ancestry‡	Population	%
African, Sub-Saharan (55)	103	0.99
African (13)	47	0.45
Ghanaian (14)	14	0.14
Nigerian (14)	14	0.14
Senegalese (0)	14	0.14
South African (14)	14	0.14
American (1,877)	1,877	18.12
Arab (67)	101	0.98
Arab (57)	91	0.88
Lebanese (10)	10	0.10
British (23)	23	0.22
Canadian (14)	28	0.27
Celtic (15)	15	0.14
Croatian (0)	13	0.13
Czech (28)	98	0.95
Czechoslovakian (0)	13	0.13
Dutch (35)	383	3.70
English (706)	1,462	14.12
European (167)	167	1.61
French, ex. Basque (41)	341	3.29
German (1,135)	2,666	25.74
Greek (13)	27	0.26
Hungarian (0)	9	0.09
Irish (266)	1,156	11.16
Italian (227)	355	3.43
Norwegian (22)	58	0.56
Polish (0)	98	0.95
Scandinavian (31)	45	0.43
Scotch-Irish (94)	408	3.94
Scottish (80)	226	2.18
Serbian (0)	13	0.13
Slovak (14)	14	0.14
Swedish (31)	156	1.51
Swiss (66)	148	1.43
Welsh (14)	59	0.57
Yugoslavian (0)	20	0.19

Hispanic Origin	Population	%
Hispanic or Latino (of any race)	257	2.49
Central American, ex. Mexican	18	0.17
Guatemalan	4	0.04
Honduran	1	0.01
Nicaraguan	5	0.05
Panamanian	5	0.05
Salvadoran	3	0.03
Cuban	4	0.04
Dominican Republic	1	0.01
Mexican	164	1.59
Puerto Rican	46	0.45
South American	7	0.07
Chilean	1	0.01
Colombian	4	0.04
Paraguayan	1	0.01
Peruvian	1	0.01
Other Hispanic or Latino	17	0.16

Race*	Population	%
African-American/Black (281)	354	3.43
Not Hispanic (271)	343	3.32
Hispanic (10)	11	0.11
American Indian/Alaska Native (27)	66	0.64
Not Hispanic (24)	54	0.52
Hispanic (3)	12	0.12
Apache (0)	5	0.05
Blackfeet (2)	4	0.04
Cherokee (3)	11	0.11
Choctaw (1)	1	0.01
Creek (3)	3	0.03
Delaware (0)	1	0.01
Iroquois (1)	1	0.01
Navajo (0)	4	0.04
Sioux (1)	1	0.01
South American Ind. (1)	1	0.01
Asian (198)	245	2.37
Not Hispanic (194)	234	2.27
Hispanic (4)	11	0.11
Chinese, ex. Taiwanese (61)	74	0.72
Filipino (10)	14	0.14
Indian (20)	25	0.24
Indonesian (0)	1	0.01
Japanese (65)	77	0.75
Korean (13)	27	0.26
Laotian (2)	5	0.05
Malaysian (0)	1	0.01
Pakistani (4)	4	0.04
Thai (2)	4	0.04
Vietnamese (11)	19	0.18
Hawaii Native/Pacific Islander (5)	17	0.16
Not Hispanic (3)	11	0.11
Hispanic (2)	6	0.06
Native Hawaiian (3)	13	0.13
White (9,546)	9,716	94.09
Not Hispanic (9,418)	9,557	92.55
Hispanic (128)	159	1.54

Greenfield

Place Type: City
County: Hancock
Population: 20,602†

Ancestry‡	Population	%
African, Sub-Saharan (0)	6	0.03
African (0)	6	0.03
American (2,207)	2,207	11.18
Arab (17)	17	0.09
Egyptian (17)	17	0.09
Austrian (0)	48	0.24
British (87)	157	0.80
Bulgarian (12)	12	0.06
Canadian (0)	7	0.04
Celtic (0)	12	0.06

*Notes: † The Census 2010 population figure is used to calculate the percentages in the Hispanic Origin and Race categories. Ancestry percentages are based on the 2006-2010 American Community Survey population (not shown); ‡ Numbers in parentheses indicate the number of people reporting a single ancestry; * Numbers in parentheses indicate the number of persons reporting this race alone, not in combination with any other race; Please refer to the Explanation of Data for more information.*

Croatian (10)	10	0.05
Czechoslovakian (0)	30	0.15
Danish (0)	6	0.03
Dutch (144)	312	1.58
English (950)	1,867	9.46
European (163)	163	0.83
French, ex. Basque (67)	526	2.67
French Canadian (48)	48	0.24
German (1,977)	5,238	26.55
Greek (17)	17	0.09
Hungarian (0)	12	0.06
Irish (786)	2,739	13.88
Italian (101)	308	1.56
Lithuanian (14)	14	0.07
Northern European (40)	40	0.20
Norwegian (23)	174	0.88
Pennsylvania German (13)	13	0.07
Polish (10)	262	1.33
Russian (10)	25	0.13
Scotch-Irish (94)	211	1.07
Scottish (148)	306	1.55
Slovene (0)	12	0.06
Swedish (0)	142	0.72
Swiss (0)	83	0.42
Ukrainian (6)	41	0.21
Welsh (26)	126	0.64
Yugoslavian (14)	14	0.07

Hispanic Origin	Population	%
Hispanic or Latino (of any race)	368	1.79
Central American, ex. Mexican	8	0.04
Costa Rican	1	<0.01
Guatemalan	3	0.01
Honduran	2	0.01
Nicaraguan	1	<0.01
Panamanian	1	<0.01
Cuban	8	0.04
Dominican Republic	1	<0.01
Mexican	275	1.33
Puerto Rican	19	0.09
South American	27	0.13
Argentinean	3	0.01
Bolivian	1	<0.01
Chilean	2	0.01
Ecuadorian	2	0.01
Peruvian	8	0.04
Venezuelan	11	0.05
Other Hispanic or Latino	30	0.15

Race*	Population	%
African-American/Black (121)	209	1.01
Not Hispanic (118)	203	0.99
Hispanic (3)	6	0.03
American Indian/Alaska Native (54)	154	0.75
Not Hispanic (42)	134	0.65
Hispanic (12)	20	0.10
Apache (0)	1	<0.01
Arapaho (1)	1	<0.01
Blackfeet (2)	6	0.03
Cherokee (8)	42	0.20
Choctaw (4)	6	0.03
Comanche (0)	1	<0.01
Crow (4)	4	0.02
Delaware (0)	1	<0.01
Hopi (0)	1	<0.01
Iroquois (1)	6	0.03
Lumbee (2)	2	0.01
Mexican American Ind. (3)	3	0.01
Pima (0)	1	<0.01
Potawatomi (0)	1	<0.01
Sioux (1)	4	0.02
Asian (174)	221	1.07
Not Hispanic (174)	221	1.07
Chinese, ex. Taiwanese (29)	41	0.20
Filipino (45)	55	0.27
Indian (36)	38	0.18
Japanese (20)	33	0.16
Korean (10)	21	0.10
Laotian (4)	4	0.02
Pakistani (1)	2	0.01
Taiwanese (5)	5	0.02
Thai (2)	2	0.01
Vietnamese (15)	17	0.08
Hawaii Native/Pacific Islander (5)	13	0.06
Not Hispanic (3)	11	0.05
Hispanic (2)	2	0.01
Guamanian/Chamorro (2)	2	0.01
Native Hawaiian (2)	8	0.04
White (19,909)	20,161	97.86
Not Hispanic (19,670)	19,879	96.49
Hispanic (239)	282	1.37

Greensburg

Place Type: City
County: Decatur
Population: 11,492†

Ancestry‡	Population	%
American (1,768)	1,768	15.80
Arab (0)	35	0.31
Lebanese (0)	35	0.31
British (40)	40	0.36
Canadian (8)	8	0.07
Dutch (62)	290	2.59
English (480)	974	8.70
European (29)	29	0.26
Finnish (0)	30	0.27
French, ex. Basque (32)	145	1.30
French Canadian (3)	3	0.03
German (1,801)	2,969	26.53
Greek (20)	20	0.18
Irish (545)	1,202	10.74
Italian (57)	118	1.05
Norwegian (0)	31	0.28
Polish (38)	57	0.51
Russian (0)	14	0.13
Scotch-Irish (49)	129	1.15
Scottish (25)	99	0.88
Swedish (0)	33	0.29
Welsh (22)	22	0.20

Hispanic Origin	Population	%
Hispanic or Latino (of any race)	273	2.38
Central American, ex. Mexican	8	0.07
Guatemalan	6	0.05
Honduran	2	0.02
Cuban	5	0.04
Dominican Republic	6	0.05
Mexican	210	1.83
Puerto Rican	11	0.10
South American	5	0.04
Colombian	2	0.02
Peruvian	1	0.01
Venezuelan	2	0.02
Other Hispanic or Latino	28	0.24

Race*	Population	%
African-American/Black (50)	72	0.63
Not Hispanic (46)	63	0.55
Hispanic (4)	9	0.08
American Indian/Alaska Native (26)	82	0.71
Not Hispanic (23)	72	0.63
Hispanic (3)	10	0.09
Apache (2)	5	0.04
Blackfeet (5)	10	0.09
Cherokee (6)	28	0.24
Iroquois (1)	6	0.05
Kiowa (1)	1	0.01
Mexican American Ind. (0)	2	0.02
Potawatomi (2)	2	0.02
Sioux (1)	1	0.01
Yaqui (1)	1	0.01
Asian (154)	172	1.50
Not Hispanic (147)	162	1.41
Hispanic (7)	10	0.09
Chinese, ex. Taiwanese (18)	32	0.28
Filipino (31)	41	0.36
Indian (35)	36	0.31
Japanese (45)	48	0.42
Korean (8)	16	0.14
Vietnamese (8)	8	0.07
Hawaii Native/Pacific Islander (3)	3	0.03
Not Hispanic (3)	3	0.03
Native Hawaiian (3)	3	0.03
White (11,048)	11,151	97.03
Not Hispanic (10,891)	10,979	95.54
Hispanic (157)	172	1.50

Greenwood

Place Type: City
County: Johnson
Population: 49,791†

Ancestry‡	Population	%
African, Sub-Saharan (57)	57	0.12
African (31)	31	0.07
Kenyan (26)	26	0.05
Albanian (14)	37	0.08
American (4,055)	4,055	8.53
Arab (154)	190	0.40
Arab (0)	18	0.04
Jordanian (101)	101	0.21
Lebanese (11)	11	0.02
Other Arab (42)	60	0.13
Austrian (11)	54	0.11
Belgian (10)	31	0.07
British (135)	323	0.68
Bulgarian (6)	6	0.01
Cajun (0)	72	0.15
Canadian (62)	181	0.38
Croatian (34)	80	0.17
Czech (24)	50	0.11
Czechoslovakian (0)	12	0.03
Danish (47)	112	0.24
Dutch (330)	1,034	2.17
English (1,785)	5,214	10.96
European (416)	473	0.99
Finnish (0)	80	0.17
French, ex. Basque (227)	1,012	2.13
French Canadian (205)	302	0.63
German (5,239)	13,472	28.32
Greek (46)	152	0.32
Hungarian (100)	414	0.87
Iranian (0)	22	0.05
Irish (2,388)	7,639	16.06
Italian (534)	2,125	4.47
Lithuanian (0)	17	0.04
Northern European (44)	44	0.09
Norwegian (141)	392	0.82
Pennsylvania German (22)	32	0.07
Polish (474)	1,355	2.85
Portuguese (17)	83	0.17
Romanian (35)	68	0.14
Russian (89)	174	0.37
Scandinavian (0)	27	0.06
Scotch-Irish (344)	857	1.80
Scottish (522)	1,197	2.52
Serbian (0)	17	0.04
Slavic (9)	16	0.03
Slovak (35)	48	0.10
Slovene (49)	75	0.16
Swedish (151)	606	1.27
Swiss (174)	287	0.60
Ukrainian (0)	14	0.03
Welsh (38)	412	0.87
West Indian, ex. Hispanic (27)	27	0.06
Jamaican (27)	27	0.06

Hispanic Origin	Population	%
Hispanic or Latino (of any race)	2,476	4.97
Central American, ex. Mexican	96	0.19
Costa Rican	1	<0.01
Guatemalan	24	0.05
Honduran	29	0.06
Nicaraguan	6	0.01
Panamanian	9	0.02
Salvadoran	24	0.05
Other Central American	3	0.01

SECTION TWO

*Notes: † The Census 2010 population figure is used to calculate the percentages in the Hispanic Origin and Race categories. Ancestry percentages are based on the 2006-2010 American Community Survey population (not shown); ‡ Numbers in parentheses indicate the number of people reporting a single ancestry; * Numbers in parentheses indicate the number of persons reporting this race alone, not in combination with any other race; Please refer to the Explanation of Data for more information.*

Hispanic Origin (cont.)	Population	%
Cuban	16	0.03
Dominican Republic	21	0.04
Mexican	1,928	3.87
Puerto Rican	195	0.39
South American	109	0.22
Argentinean	5	0.01
Bolivian	7	0.01
Chilean	4	0.01
Colombian	22	0.04
Ecuadorian	2	<0.01
Paraguayan	1	<0.01
Peruvian	34	0.07
Venezuelan	34	0.07
Other Hispanic or Latino	111	0.22

Race*	Population	%
African-American/Black (845)	1,224	2.46
Not Hispanic (827)	1,174	2.36
Hispanic (18)	50	0.10
American Indian/Alaska Native (128)	377	0.76
Not Hispanic (100)	320	0.64
Hispanic (28)	57	0.11
Aleut *(Alaska Native)* (0)	2	<0.01
Apache (1)	3	0.01
Blackfeet (3)	15	0.03
Cherokee (21)	110	0.22
Cheyenne (1)	3	0.01
Chippewa (1)	7	0.01
Choctaw (1)	4	0.01
Comanche (0)	3	0.01
Creek (2)	4	0.01
Crow (1)	2	<0.01
Iroquois (4)	8	0.02
Mexican American Ind. (4)	8	0.02
Navajo (4)	6	0.01
Ottawa (0)	1	<0.01
Potawatomi (2)	2	<0.01
Sioux (5)	8	0.02
Tohono O'Odham (0)	2	<0.01
Yaqui (1)	1	<0.01
Asian (1,866)	2,170	4.36
Not Hispanic (1,861)	2,153	4.32
Hispanic (5)	17	0.03
Bangladeshi (1)	2	<0.01
Burmese (3)	3	0.01
Chinese, ex. Taiwanese (162)	194	0.39
Filipino (124)	213	0.43
Indian (1,302)	1,381	2.77
Indonesian (8)	8	0.02
Japanese (54)	95	0.19
Korean (62)	85	0.17
Laotian (1)	2	<0.01
Malaysian (1)	1	<0.01
Nepalese (4)	4	0.01
Pakistani (17)	21	0.04
Taiwanese (10)	12	0.02
Thai (10)	15	0.03
Vietnamese (75)	90	0.18
Hawaii Native/Pacific Islander (25)	70	0.14
Not Hispanic (25)	57	0.11
Hispanic (0)	13	0.03
Guamanian/Chamorro (3)	10	0.02
Native Hawaiian (5)	15	0.03
Samoan (6)	10	0.02
White (44,841)	45,742	91.87
Not Hispanic (43,603)	44,332	89.04
Hispanic (1,238)	1,410	2.83

Griffith

Place Type: Town
County: Lake
Population: 16,893†

Ancestry‡	Population	%
African, Sub-Saharan (108)	130	0.77
African (108)	130	0.77
American (943)	943	5.56
Arab (99)	112	0.66
Arab (29)	29	0.17
Lebanese (48)	48	0.28
Syrian (0)	13	0.08
Other Arab (22)	22	0.13
Australian (0)	17	0.10
Austrian (36)	52	0.31
British (15)	24	0.14
Croatian (93)	157	0.93
Czech (10)	105	0.62
Czechoslovakian (0)	42	0.25
Danish (42)	55	0.32
Dutch (118)	450	2.65
English (452)	1,693	9.98
European (179)	179	1.06
Finnish (0)	14	0.08
French, ex. Basque (111)	546	3.22
French Canadian (12)	84	0.50
German (1,041)	4,066	23.98
Greek (15)	82	0.48
Hungarian (79)	308	1.82
Irish (495)	2,442	14.40
Italian (278)	866	5.11
Latvian (0)	38	0.22
Lithuanian (29)	148	0.87
Macedonian (10)	26	0.15
Norwegian (20)	69	0.41
Polish (859)	2,235	13.18
Portuguese (0)	14	0.08
Romanian (24)	49	0.29
Russian (80)	198	1.17
Scotch-Irish (57)	233	1.37
Scottish (25)	213	1.26
Serbian (53)	93	0.55
Slovak (151)	319	1.88
Swedish (30)	324	1.91
Swiss (0)	22	0.13
Ukrainian (34)	106	0.63
Welsh (12)	122	0.72
Yugoslavian (41)	67	0.40

Hispanic Origin	Population	%
Hispanic or Latino (of any race)	2,248	13.31
Central American, ex. Mexican	22	0.13
Guatemalan	14	0.08
Nicaraguan	3	0.02
Panamanian	1	0.01
Salvadoran	4	0.02
Cuban	7	0.04
Mexican	1,791	10.60
Puerto Rican	284	1.68
South American	30	0.18
Argentinean	3	0.02
Chilean	1	0.01
Colombian	11	0.07
Ecuadorian	2	0.01
Peruvian	13	0.08
Other Hispanic or Latino	114	0.67

Race*	Population	%
African-American/Black (2,848)	3,009	17.81
Not Hispanic (2,775)	2,909	17.22
Hispanic (73)	100	0.59
American Indian/Alaska Native (45)	148	0.88
Not Hispanic (38)	120	0.71
Hispanic (7)	28	0.17
Apache (0)	3	0.02
Arapaho (0)	1	0.01
Blackfeet (0)	2	0.01
Canadian/French Am. Ind. (0)	2	0.01
Cherokee (5)	40	0.24
Chippewa (0)	3	0.02
Choctaw (1)	4	0.02
Hopi (0)	1	0.01
Iroquois (0)	1	0.01
Navajo (1)	1	0.01
Potawatomi (4)	4	0.02
Shoshone (0)	1	0.01
Sioux (2)	12	0.07
South American Ind. (3)	3	0.02
Spanish American Ind. (1)	1	0.01
Asian (133)	177	1.05
Not Hispanic (121)	160	0.95
Hispanic (12)	17	0.10
Burmese (1)	1	0.01
Cambodian (1)	1	0.01
Chinese, ex. Taiwanese (38)	39	0.23
Filipino (36)	63	0.37
Indian (20)	22	0.13
Japanese (3)	5	0.03
Korean (14)	21	0.12
Pakistani (0)	1	0.01
Thai (1)	1	0.01
Vietnamese (18)	22	0.13
Hawaii Native/Pacific Islander (5)	17	0.10
Not Hispanic (4)	15	0.09
Hispanic (1)	2	0.01
Guamanian/Chamorro (3)	7	0.04
Native Hawaiian (1)	2	0.01
Samoan (0)	7	0.04
White (12,797)	13,141	77.79
Not Hispanic (11,459)	11,642	68.92
Hispanic (1,338)	1,499	8.87

Hammond

Place Type: City
County: Lake
Population: 80,830†

Ancestry‡	Population	%
African, Sub-Saharan (354)	421	0.52
African (354)	398	0.49
Nigerian (0)	10	0.01
Other Sub-Saharan African (0)	13	0.02
Albanian (0)	61	0.08
Alsatian (0)	18	0.02
American (2,149)	2,149	2.64
Arab (180)	272	0.33
Arab (52)	144	0.18
Egyptian (83)	83	0.10
Jordanian (30)	30	0.04
Other Arab (15)	15	0.02
Armenian (18)	27	0.03
Assyrian/Chaldean/Syriac (7)	7	0.01
Australian (21)	21	0.03
Austrian (8)	59	0.07
Belgian (12)	27	0.03
Brazilian (0)	13	0.02
British (30)	79	0.10
Canadian (10)	55	0.07
Celtic (0)	7	0.01
Croatian (230)	908	1.12
Czech (94)	369	0.45
Czechoslovakian (61)	101	0.12
Danish (12)	85	0.10
Dutch (205)	1,088	1.34
Eastern European (180)	180	0.22
English (879)	3,228	3.97
Estonian (0)	18	0.02
European (122)	150	0.18
Finnish (25)	153	0.19
French, ex. Basque (215)	1,407	1.73
French Canadian (103)	345	0.42
German (2,610)	9,601	11.81
Greek (438)	881	1.08
Guyanese (14)	14	0.02
Hungarian (298)	827	1.02
Irish (1,741)	8,337	10.25
Italian (835)	2,841	3.49
Lithuanian (107)	242	0.30
Macedonian (0)	9	0.01
Northern European (49)	49	0.06
Norwegian (77)	322	0.40
Pennsylvania German (18)	76	0.09
Polish (3,706)	7,497	9.22
Portuguese (0)	64	0.08
Romanian (16)	77	0.09
Russian (89)	275	0.34
Scandinavian (17)	65	0.08
Scotch-Irish (223)	574	0.71
Scottish (30)	627	0.77

*Notes: † The Census 2010 population figure is used to calculate the percentages in the Hispanic Origin and Race categories. Ancestry percentages are based on the 2006-2010 American Community Survey population (not shown); ‡ Numbers in parentheses indicate the number of people reporting a single ancestry; * Numbers in parentheses indicate the number of persons reporting this race alone, not in combination with any other race; Please refer to the Explanation of Data for more information.*

Ancestry	Population	%
Serbian (228)	572	0.70
Slavic (0)	22	0.03
Slovak (705)	1,791	2.20
Swedish (222)	1,016	1.25
Swiss (12)	81	0.10
Turkish (0)	8	0.01
Ukrainian (129)	244	0.30
Welsh (59)	241	0.30
West Indian, ex. Hispanic (42)	135	0.17
Haitian (42)	86	0.11
Jamaican (0)	49	0.06

Hispanic Origin	Population	%
Hispanic or Latino (of any race)	27,563	34.10
Central American, ex. Mexican	526	0.65
Costa Rican	18	0.02
Guatemalan	172	0.21
Honduran	117	0.14
Nicaraguan	19	0.02
Panamanian	21	0.03
Salvadoran	174	0.22
Other Central American	5	0.01
Cuban	140	0.17
Dominican Republic	10	0.01
Mexican	22,684	28.06
Puerto Rican	3,081	3.81
South American	141	0.17
Argentinean	29	0.04
Chilean	5	0.01
Colombian	36	0.04
Ecuadorian	12	0.01
Paraguayan	1	<0.01
Peruvian	40	0.05
Uruguayan	6	0.01
Venezuelan	12	0.01
Other Hispanic or Latino	981	1.21

Race*	Population	%
African-American/Black (18,224)	19,336	23.92
Not Hispanic (17,568)	18,369	22.73
Hispanic (656)	967	1.20
American Indian/Alaska Native (411)	930	1.15
Not Hispanic (145)	489	0.60
Hispanic (266)	441	0.55
Apache (5)	19	0.02
Arapaho (1)	1	<0.01
Blackfeet (7)	24	0.03
Canadian/French Am. Ind. (1)	1	<0.01
Cherokee (40)	182	0.23
Chickasaw (0)	2	<0.01
Chippewa (6)	21	0.03
Choctaw (4)	18	0.02
Comanche (1)	3	<0.01
Creek (8)	10	0.01
Crow (1)	4	<0.01
Iroquois (1)	6	0.01
Menominee (0)	1	<0.01
Mexican American Ind. (44)	69	0.09
Navajo (1)	4	<0.01
Ottawa (2)	3	<0.01
Potawatomi (1)	6	0.01
Puget Sound Salish (0)	2	<0.01
Seminole (0)	3	<0.01
Shoshone (6)	6	0.01
Sioux (7)	12	0.01
South American Ind. (2)	9	0.01
Spanish American Ind. (3)	3	<0.01
Ute (6)	7	0.01
Yaqui (3)	3	<0.01
Asian (804)	1,059	1.31
Not Hispanic (753)	931	1.15
Hispanic (51)	128	0.16
Bangladeshi (1)	2	<0.01
Cambodian (5)	5	0.01
Chinese, ex. Taiwanese (385)	422	0.52
Filipino (126)	203	0.25
Indian (118)	135	0.17
Indonesian (2)	4	<0.01
Japanese (11)	54	0.07
Korean (34)	55	0.07
Nepalese (1)	1	<0.01
Pakistani (40)	44	0.05
Sri Lankan (1)	1	<0.01
Taiwanese (3)	3	<0.01
Thai (12)	19	0.02
Vietnamese (35)	48	0.06
Hawaii Native/Pacific Islander (24)	97	0.12
Not Hispanic (9)	47	0.06
Hispanic (15)	50	0.06
Fijian (0)	1	<0.01
Guamanian/Chamorro (4)	9	0.01
Native Hawaiian (8)	30	0.04
Samoan (8)	21	0.03
White (47,984)	50,206	62.11
Not Hispanic (33,534)	34,532	42.72
Hispanic (14,450)	15,674	19.39

Highland

Place Type: Town
County: Lake
Population: 23,727†

Ancestry‡	Population	%
African, Sub-Saharan (15)	15	0.06
African (15)	15	0.06
American (1,292)	1,292	5.45
Arab (337)	337	1.42
Arab (326)	326	1.37
Lebanese (11)	11	0.05
Austrian (0)	81	0.34
Belgian (11)	49	0.21
British (16)	26	0.11
Bulgarian (57)	57	0.24
Canadian (23)	57	0.24
Croatian (189)	663	2.80
Czech (36)	60	0.25
Czechoslovakian (28)	50	0.21
Danish (0)	15	0.06
Dutch (700)	1,729	7.29
English (293)	1,639	6.91
European (157)	198	0.84
French, ex. Basque (63)	527	2.22
French Canadian (0)	12	0.05
German (1,400)	4,887	20.61
Greek (254)	473	1.99
Hungarian (321)	707	2.98
Irish (689)	3,538	14.92
Italian (373)	1,310	5.53
Latvian (0)	10	0.04
Lithuanian (204)	258	1.09
Luxemburger (0)	10	0.04
Norwegian (32)	162	0.68
Pennsylvania German (11)	11	0.05
Polish (1,598)	3,947	16.65
Portuguese (0)	8	0.03
Romanian (103)	211	0.89
Russian (12)	155	0.65
Scandinavian (0)	14	0.06
Scotch-Irish (125)	284	1.20
Scottish (33)	426	1.80
Serbian (194)	259	1.09
Slavic (19)	40	0.17
Slovak (374)	896	3.78
Slovene (0)	17	0.07
Swedish (158)	660	2.78
Swiss (0)	9	0.04
Ukrainian (125)	155	0.65
Welsh (20)	108	0.46
Yugoslavian (16)	58	0.24

Hispanic Origin	Population	%
Hispanic or Latino (of any race)	3,047	12.84
Central American, ex. Mexican	42	0.18
Costa Rican	2	0.01
Guatemalan	17	0.07
Honduran	3	0.01
Nicaraguan	4	0.02
Panamanian	8	0.03
Salvadoran	8	0.03
Cuban	14	0.06
Dominican Republic	1	<0.01
Mexican	2,394	10.09
Puerto Rican	428	1.80
South American	29	0.12
Argentinean	4	0.02
Bolivian	3	0.01
Chilean	1	<0.01
Colombian	7	0.03
Paraguayan	1	<0.01
Peruvian	13	0.05
Other Hispanic or Latino	139	0.59

Race*	Population	%
African-American/Black (997)	1,125	4.74
Not Hispanic (965)	1,065	4.49
Hispanic (32)	60	0.25
American Indian/Alaska Native (49)	155	0.65
Not Hispanic (24)	102	0.43
Hispanic (25)	53	0.22
Apache (1)	6	0.03
Arapaho (0)	2	0.01
Blackfeet (0)	3	0.01
Central American Ind. (1)	1	<0.01
Cherokee (6)	39	0.16
Cheyenne (0)	1	<0.01
Chickasaw (2)	2	0.01
Chippewa (4)	7	0.03
Choctaw (1)	1	<0.01
Creek (1)	3	0.01
Iroquois (3)	4	0.02
Mexican American Ind. (4)	6	0.03
Navajo (0)	1	<0.01
Ottawa (0)	3	0.01
Potawatomi (0)	4	0.02
Seminole (0)	2	0.01
Sioux (1)	1	<0.01
South American Ind. (1)	3	0.01
Tlingit-Haida *(Alaska Native)* (5)	5	0.02
Asian (380)	508	2.14
Not Hispanic (371)	473	1.99
Hispanic (9)	35	0.15
Bangladeshi (1)	1	<0.01
Chinese, ex. Taiwanese (47)	53	0.22
Filipino (89)	131	0.55
Hmong (2)	2	0.01
Indian (138)	153	0.64
Indonesian (9)	10	0.04
Japanese (10)	30	0.13
Korean (39)	59	0.25
Laotian (5)	5	0.02
Pakistani (8)	8	0.03
Taiwanese (1)	1	<0.01
Thai (2)	4	0.02
Vietnamese (22)	24	0.10
Hawaii Native/Pacific Islander (1)	14	0.06
Not Hispanic (1)	12	0.05
Hispanic (0)	2	0.01
Guamanian/Chamorro (0)	2	0.01
Native Hawaiian (1)	6	0.03
White (21,027)	21,446	90.39
Not Hispanic (19,039)	19,282	81.27
Hispanic (1,988)	2,164	9.12

Hobart

Place Type: City
County: Lake
Population: 29,059†

Ancestry‡	Population	%
African, Sub-Saharan (225)	241	0.85
African (195)	211	0.74
Ethiopian (30)	30	0.11
Albanian (6)	13	0.05
American (1,392)	1,392	4.90
Assyrian/Chaldean/Syriac (42)	42	0.15
Austrian (13)	26	0.09
Brazilian (26)	26	0.09
British (0)	32	0.11

SECTION TWO

*Notes: † The Census 2010 population figure is used to calculate the percentages in the Hispanic Origin and Race categories. Ancestry percentages are based on the 2006-2010 American Community Survey population (not shown); ‡ Numbers in parentheses indicate the number of people reporting a single ancestry; * Numbers in parentheses indicate the number of persons reporting this race alone, not in combination with any other race; Please refer to the Explanation of Data for more information.*

Bulgarian (10)	10	0.04
Canadian (0)	36	0.13
Croatian (142)	483	1.70
Czech (90)	236	0.83
Czechoslovakian (66)	178	0.63
Danish (18)	169	0.60
Dutch (86)	570	2.01
Eastern European (78)	78	0.27
English (541)	2,282	8.04
European (450)	450	1.59
Finnish (0)	23	0.08
French, ex. Basque (92)	726	2.56
French Canadian (11)	70	0.25
German (1,870)	6,628	23.35
Greek (196)	451	1.59
Hungarian (287)	632	2.23
Irish (813)	3,925	13.83
Italian (531)	1,571	5.53
Lithuanian (15)	210	0.74
Macedonian (180)	221	0.78
Northern European (15)	15	0.05
Norwegian (51)	352	1.24
Pennsylvania German (18)	18	0.06
Polish (662)	2,926	10.31
Romanian (91)	145	0.51
Russian (65)	189	0.67
Scandinavian (10)	21	0.07
Scotch-Irish (127)	301	1.06
Scottish (196)	606	2.13
Serbian (239)	614	2.16
Slavic (28)	28	0.10
Slovak (261)	689	2.43
Slovene (10)	10	0.04
Swedish (121)	634	2.23
Swiss (0)	27	0.10
Ukrainian (59)	157	0.55
Welsh (45)	312	1.10

Hispanic Origin	Population	%
Hispanic or Latino (of any race)	4,026	13.85
Central American, ex. Mexican	47	0.16
Costa Rican	1	<0.01
Guatemalan	5	0.02
Honduran	14	0.05
Nicaraguan	13	0.04
Panamanian	7	0.02
Salvadoran	7	0.02
Cuban	36	0.12
Dominican Republic	11	0.04
Mexican	2,876	9.90
Puerto Rican	850	2.93
South American	40	0.14
Argentinean	7	0.02
Bolivian	2	0.01
Chilean	1	<0.01
Colombian	17	0.06
Ecuadorian	8	0.03
Peruvian	4	0.01
Venezuelan	1	<0.01
Other Hispanic or Latino	166	0.57

Race*	Population	%
African-American/Black (2,025)	2,268	7.80
Not Hispanic (1,947)	2,124	7.31
Hispanic (78)	144	0.50
American Indian/Alaska Native (107)	266	0.92
Not Hispanic (81)	198	0.68
Hispanic (26)	68	0.23
Apache (0)	5	0.02
Blackfeet (0)	12	0.04
Central American Ind. (0)	1	<0.01
Cherokee (20)	57	0.20
Chippewa (2)	8	0.03
Choctaw (0)	1	<0.01
Comanche (1)	2	0.01
Creek (0)	3	0.01
Iroquois (2)	2	0.01
Kiowa (2)	2	0.01
Lumbee (1)	1	<0.01
Menominee (0)	2	0.01
Mexican American Ind. (2)	4	0.01
Navajo (0)	1	<0.01
Ottawa (0)	1	<0.01
Potawatomi (1)	1	<0.01
Pueblo (1)	1	<0.01
Seminole (0)	1	<0.01
Sioux (5)	7	0.02
Tlingit-Haida *(Alaska Native)* (0)	1	<0.01
Asian (298)	413	1.42
Not Hispanic (280)	372	1.28
Hispanic (18)	41	0.14
Bangladeshi (3)	3	0.01
Chinese, ex. Taiwanese (48)	60	0.21
Filipino (102)	152	0.52
Indian (64)	71	0.24
Indonesian (1)	4	0.01
Japanese (6)	20	0.07
Korean (23)	34	0.12
Pakistani (17)	21	0.07
Taiwanese (0)	4	0.01
Thai (7)	18	0.06
Vietnamese (12)	19	0.07
Hawaii Native/Pacific Islander (4)	17	0.06
Not Hispanic (3)	14	0.05
Hispanic (1)	3	0.01
Guamanian/Chamorro (1)	3	0.01
Native Hawaiian (2)	10	0.03
Samoan (0)	1	<0.01
White (24,786)	25,395	87.39
Not Hispanic (22,338)	22,663	77.99
Hispanic (2,448)	2,732	9.40

Huntington

Place Type: City
County: Huntington
Population: 17,391†

Ancestry‡	Population	%
American (2,145)	2,145	12.27
Arab (11)	11	0.06
Egyptian (11)	11	0.06
Belgian (0)	24	0.14
British (24)	73	0.42
Canadian (31)	31	0.18
Croatian (15)	25	0.14
Danish (11)	42	0.24
Dutch (164)	572	3.27
English (1,009)	2,293	13.12
European (103)	103	0.59
French, ex. Basque (105)	570	3.26
French Canadian (45)	92	0.53
German (2,873)	6,550	37.47
Greek (11)	11	0.06
Hungarian (0)	9	0.05
Irish (664)	2,966	16.97
Italian (140)	383	2.19
Lithuanian (11)	93	0.53
Norwegian (8)	90	0.51
Pennsylvania German (0)	10	0.06
Polish (96)	293	1.68
Romanian (0)	13	0.07
Russian (0)	37	0.21
Scandinavian (26)	30	0.17
Scotch-Irish (47)	185	1.06
Scottish (83)	310	1.77
Slovak (0)	16	0.09
Swedish (36)	221	1.26
Swiss (21)	120	0.69
Ukrainian (21)	43	0.25
Welsh (18)	75	0.43

Hispanic Origin	Population	%
Hispanic or Latino (of any race)	420	2.42
Central American, ex. Mexican	27	0.16
Guatemalan	18	0.10
Honduran	5	0.03
Salvadoran	4	0.02
Cuban	5	0.03
Mexican	283	1.63
Puerto Rican	34	0.20
South American	9	0.05
Argentinean	1	0.01
Chilean	1	0.01
Colombian	2	0.01
Ecuadorian	2	0.01
Peruvian	2	0.01
Venezuelan	1	0.01
Other Hispanic or Latino	62	0.36

Race*	Population	%
African-American/Black (99)	178	1.02
Not Hispanic (95)	170	0.98
Hispanic (4)	8	0.05
American Indian/Alaska Native (77)	161	0.93
Not Hispanic (66)	133	0.76
Hispanic (11)	28	0.16
Apache (3)	5	0.03
Blackfeet (1)	3	0.02
Central American Ind. (1)	1	0.01
Cherokee (15)	29	0.17
Crow (0)	1	0.01
Delaware (3)	3	0.02
Iroquois (0)	1	0.01
Mexican American Ind. (3)	3	0.02
Navajo (0)	1	0.01
Osage (0)	3	0.02
Sioux (2)	4	0.02
Asian (90)	141	0.81
Not Hispanic (90)	133	0.76
Hispanic (0)	8	0.05
Burmese (1)	1	0.01
Cambodian (3)	3	0.02
Chinese, ex. Taiwanese (24)	29	0.17
Filipino (9)	21	0.12
Indian (31)	37	0.21
Japanese (4)	14	0.08
Korean (9)	23	0.13
Malaysian (1)	1	0.01
Pakistani (0)	1	0.01
Taiwanese (1)	3	0.02
Thai (1)	5	0.03
Vietnamese (1)	1	0.01
Hawaii Native/Pacific Islander (6)	11	0.06
Not Hispanic (4)	9	0.05
Hispanic (2)	2	0.01
Guamanian/Chamorro (4)	6	0.03
Native Hawaiian (1)	3	0.02
Samoan (1)	2	0.01
White (16,768)	17,001	97.76
Not Hispanic (16,525)	16,701	96.03
Hispanic (243)	300	1.73

Indianapolis

Place Type: City
County: Marion
Population: 820,445†

Ancestry‡	Population	%
Afghan (29)	29	<0.01
African, Sub-Saharan (34,151)	43,672	5.39
African (29,012)	38,288	4.73
Ethiopian (443)	443	0.05
Ghanaian (154)	154	0.02
Kenyan (63)	63	0.01
Liberian (687)	687	0.08
Nigerian (1,907)	2,048	0.25
Senegalese (150)	150	0.02
Somalian (432)	432	0.05
South African (20)	43	0.01
Sudanese (376)	376	0.05
Ugandan (14)	54	0.01
Zimbabwean (149)	149	0.02
Other Sub-Saharan African (744)	785	0.10
Albanian (51)	105	0.01
Alsatian (0)	12	<0.01
American (52,433)	52,433	6.47
Arab (1,818)	2,776	0.34
Arab (433)	542	0.07

*Notes: † The Census 2010 population figure is used to calculate the percentages in the Hispanic Origin and Race categories. Ancestry percentages are based on the 2006-2010 American Community Survey population (not shown); ‡ Numbers in parentheses indicate the number of people reporting a single ancestry; * Numbers in parentheses indicate the number of persons reporting this race alone, not in combination with any other race; Please refer to the Explanation of Data for more information.*

Egyptian (147)	158	0.02
Iraqi (132)	192	0.02
Jordanian (152)	182	0.02
Lebanese (410)	826	0.10
Moroccan (96)	141	0.02
Palestinian (12)	45	0.01
Syrian (77)	239	0.03
Other Arab (359)	451	0.06
Armenian (34)	158	0.02
Assyrian/Chaldean/Syriac (44)	44	0.01
Australian (189)	258	0.03
Austrian (325)	1,084	0.13
Belgian (276)	866	0.11
Brazilian (121)	259	0.03
British (1,698)	3,547	0.44
Bulgarian (18)	80	0.01
Cajun (29)	52	0.01
Canadian (702)	1,392	0.17
Celtic (0)	8	<0.01
Croatian (94)	412	0.05
Czech (366)	1,484	0.18
Czechoslovakian (226)	393	0.05
Danish (513)	1,483	0.18
Dutch (2,739)	11,553	1.43
Eastern European (299)	332	0.04
English (24,751)	67,644	8.35
Estonian (15)	99	0.01
European (7,714)	9,215	1.14
Finnish (177)	436	0.05
French, ex. Basque (3,373)	15,735	1.94
French Canadian (515)	1,565	0.19
German (58,139)	149,656	18.48
German Russian (11)	11	<0.01
Greek (1,089)	2,372	0.29
Hungarian (951)	2,960	0.37
Iranian (325)	455	0.06
Irish (29,177)	93,959	11.60
Israeli (55)	107	0.01
Italian (7,266)	20,396	2.52
Latvian (142)	275	0.03
Lithuanian (298)	1,175	0.15
Luxemburger (34)	97	0.01
Macedonian (127)	265	0.03
Maltese (22)	56	0.01
New Zealander (35)	35	<0.01
Northern European (560)	584	0.07
Norwegian (967)	3,636	0.45
Pennsylvania German (256)	355	0.04
Polish (3,961)	12,731	1.57
Portuguese (86)	414	0.05
Romanian (629)	1,001	0.12
Russian (1,361)	3,280	0.41
Scandinavian (590)	1,199	0.15
Scotch-Irish (5,103)	10,956	1.35
Scottish (4,801)	14,050	1.73
Serbian (258)	777	0.10
Slavic (134)	455	0.06
Slovak (344)	1,058	0.13
Slovene (203)	497	0.06
Swedish (1,395)	5,593	0.69
Swiss (481)	2,276	0.28
Turkish (160)	243	0.03
Ukrainian (395)	792	0.10
Welsh (1,266)	4,603	0.57
West Indian, ex. Hispanic (1,133)	1,846	0.23
Bahamian (8)	8	<0.01
Barbadian (13)	55	0.01
Belizean (28)	51	0.01
British West Indian (0)	13	<0.01
Dutch West Indian (0)	38	<0.01
Haitian (394)	635	0.08
Jamaican (510)	589	0.07
Trinidadian/Tobagonian (72)	110	0.01
West Indian (96)	335	0.04
Other West Indian (12)	12	<0.01
Yugoslavian (327)	531	0.07

Hispanic Origin	Population	%
Hispanic or Latino (of any race)	77,352	9.43
Central American, ex. Mexican	7,746	0.94
Costa Rican	125	0.02
Guatemalan	1,616	0.20
Honduran	2,302	0.28
Nicaraguan	668	0.08
Panamanian	274	0.03
Salvadoran	2,695	0.33
Other Central American	66	0.01
Cuban	739	0.09
Dominican Republic	1,124	0.14
Mexican	56,771	6.92
Puerto Rican	3,431	0.42
South American	2,068	0.25
Argentinean	207	0.03
Bolivian	47	0.01
Chilean	83	0.01
Colombian	587	0.07
Ecuadorian	160	0.02
Paraguayan	11	<0.01
Peruvian	611	0.07
Uruguayan	29	<0.01
Venezuelan	314	0.04
Other South American	19	<0.01
Other Hispanic or Latino	5,473	0.67

Race*	Population	%
African-American/Black (225,355)	239,354	29.17
Not Hispanic (223,053)	235,521	28.71
Hispanic (2,302)	3,833	0.47
American Indian/Alaska Native (2,611)	7,323	0.89
Not Hispanic (1,760)	5,844	0.71
Hispanic (851)	1,479	0.18
Alaska Athabascan *(Ala. Nat.)* (2)	3	<0.01
Aleut *(Alaska Native)* (12)	14	<0.01
Apache (43)	98	0.01
Arapaho (4)	4	<0.01
Blackfeet (63)	354	0.04
Canadian/French Am. Ind. (10)	22	<0.01
Central American Ind. (6)	11	<0.01
Cherokee (378)	1,682	0.21
Cheyenne (1)	18	<0.01
Chickasaw (6)	12	<0.01
Chippewa (64)	134	0.02
Choctaw (26)	99	0.01
Comanche (11)	28	<0.01
Cree (0)	13	<0.01
Creek (14)	31	<0.01
Crow (1)	11	<0.01
Delaware (8)	27	<0.01
Hopi (4)	13	<0.01
Houma (3)	3	<0.01
Inupiat *(Alaska Native)* (9)	20	<0.01
Iroquois (33)	96	0.01
Kiowa (2)	5	<0.01
Lumbee (8)	17	<0.01
Menominee (4)	5	<0.01
Mexican American Ind. (187)	263	0.03
Navajo (40)	100	0.01
Osage (4)	15	<0.01
Ottawa (3)	15	<0.01
Paiute (0)	5	<0.01
Pima (0)	1	<0.01
Potawatomi (54)	88	0.01
Pueblo (10)	26	<0.01
Seminole (2)	17	<0.01
Shoshone (2)	7	<0.01
Sioux (55)	201	0.02
South American Ind. (14)	39	<0.01
Spanish American Ind. (19)	23	<0.01
Tlingit-Haida *(Alaska Native)* (4)	6	<0.01
Tohono O'Odham (1)	2	<0.01
Tsimshian *(Alaska Native)* (1)	1	<0.01
Ute (2)	4	<0.01
Yakama (0)	1	<0.01
Yaqui (3)	5	<0.01
Yuman (2)	4	<0.01
Yup'ik *(Alaska Native)* (0)	2	<0.01
Asian (17,236)	21,294	2.60
Not Hispanic (17,053)	20,777	2.53
Hispanic (183)	517	0.06
Bangladeshi (115)	128	0.02
Burmese (3,476)	3,622	0.44
Cambodian (85)	118	0.01
Chinese, ex. Taiwanese (2,666)	3,197	0.39
Filipino (1,628)	2,608	0.32
Hmong (15)	24	<0.01
Indian (4,739)	5,358	0.65
Indonesian (76)	142	0.02
Japanese (517)	1,094	0.13
Korean (1,043)	1,558	0.19
Laotian (115)	142	0.02
Malaysian (29)	44	0.01
Nepalese (45)	46	0.01
Pakistani (544)	625	0.08
Sri Lankan (34)	42	0.01
Taiwanese (144)	160	0.02
Thai (226)	352	0.04
Vietnamese (1,138)	1,347	0.16
Hawaii Native/Pacific Islander (384)	1,129	0.14
Not Hispanic (274)	820	0.10
Hispanic (110)	309	0.04
Fijian (3)	5	<0.01
Guamanian/Chamorro (128)	216	0.03
Native Hawaiian (114)	361	0.04
Samoan (71)	145	0.02
Tongan (5)	10	<0.01
White (507,005)	526,672	64.19
Not Hispanic (480,960)	496,520	60.52
Hispanic (26,045)	30,152	3.68

Jasper

Place Type: City
County: Dubois
Population: 15,038†

Ancestry‡	Population	%
African, Sub-Saharan (15)	48	0.33
African (15)	48	0.33
American (1,382)	1,382	9.48
Arab (43)	43	0.30
Other Arab (43)	43	0.30
British (10)	39	0.27
Canadian (28)	28	0.19
Croatian (42)	42	0.29
Czechoslovakian (0)	12	0.08
Danish (0)	21	0.14
Dutch (59)	424	2.91
English (473)	1,008	6.92
European (131)	153	1.05
French, ex. Basque (56)	181	1.24
German (5,856)	7,627	52.34
Greek (17)	23	0.16
Irish (425)	1,410	9.68
Italian (44)	228	1.56
Maltese (0)	9	0.06
Norwegian (11)	112	0.77
Polish (0)	88	0.60
Portuguese (0)	19	0.13
Russian (16)	38	0.26
Scotch-Irish (103)	204	1.40
Scottish (25)	112	0.77
Swedish (0)	103	0.71
Swiss (77)	205	1.41
Welsh (13)	25	0.17
West Indian, ex. Hispanic (36)	47	0.32
Jamaican (36)	47	0.32

Hispanic Origin	Population	%
Hispanic or Latino (of any race)	1,153	7.67
Central American, ex. Mexican	342	2.27
Guatemalan	32	0.21
Honduran	19	0.13
Panamanian	1	0.01
Salvadoran	290	1.93
Cuban	9	0.06
Dominican Republic	1	0.01
Mexican	596	3.96
Puerto Rican	29	0.19
South American	8	0.05
Argentinean	1	0.01

*Notes: † The Census 2010 population figure is used to calculate the percentages in the Hispanic Origin and Race categories. Ancestry percentages are based on the 2006-2010 American Community Survey population (not shown); ‡ Numbers in parentheses indicate the number of people reporting a single ancestry; * Numbers in parentheses indicate the number of persons reporting this race alone, not in combination with any other race; Please refer to the Explanation of Data for more information.*

SECTION TWO

Bolivian	1	0.01
Chilean	2	0.01
Colombian	4	0.03
Other Hispanic or Latino	168	1.12

Race*	Population	%
African-American/Black (57)	91	0.61
Not Hispanic (52)	82	0.55
Hispanic (5)	9	0.06
American Indian/Alaska Native (27)	59	0.39
Not Hispanic (21)	51	0.34
Hispanic (6)	8	0.05
Arapaho (3)	3	0.02
Blackfeet (0)	2	0.01
Cherokee (1)	12	0.08
Comanche (0)	1	0.01
Inupiat *(Alaska Native)* (1)	1	0.01
Mexican American Ind. (1)	1	0.01
Sioux (1)	3	0.02
Asian (131)	155	1.03
Not Hispanic (131)	155	1.03
Chinese, ex. Taiwanese (23)	24	0.16
Filipino (10)	22	0.15
Indian (59)	65	0.43
Indonesian (1)	1	0.01
Japanese (1)	4	0.03
Korean (7)	7	0.05
Taiwanese (0)	1	0.01
Thai (1)	1	0.01
Vietnamese (23)	23	0.15
Hawaii Native/Pacific Islander (5)	5	0.03
Not Hispanic (4)	4	0.03
Hispanic (1)	1	0.01
Native Hawaiian (5)	5	0.03
White (14,075)	14,209	94.49
Not Hispanic (13,582)	13,665	90.87
Hispanic (493)	544	3.62

Jeffersonville

Place Type: City
County: Clark
Population: 44,953†

Ancestry‡	Population	%
African, Sub-Saharan (65)	98	0.23
African (65)	98	0.23
American (5,374)	5,374	12.75
Arab (31)	54	0.13
Lebanese (19)	42	0.10
Moroccan (12)	12	0.03
Australian (14)	14	0.03
Austrian (0)	20	0.05
British (25)	84	0.20
Cajun (20)	29	0.07
Canadian (17)	63	0.15
Celtic (8)	25	0.06
Croatian (236)	236	0.56
Czech (14)	70	0.17
Danish (0)	33	0.08
Dutch (173)	665	1.58
English (1,826)	3,973	9.43
European (350)	361	0.86
French, ex. Basque (239)	1,246	2.96
French Canadian (66)	108	0.26
German (4,155)	9,921	23.54
Greek (0)	17	0.04
Hungarian (97)	185	0.44
Irish (2,087)	6,311	14.97
Italian (323)	1,104	2.62
Norwegian (34)	77	0.18
Pennsylvania German (0)	14	0.03
Polish (212)	589	1.40
Portuguese (0)	68	0.16
Romanian (85)	96	0.23
Russian (17)	207	0.49
Scotch-Irish (400)	729	1.73
Scottish (468)	1,085	2.57
Slovak (48)	99	0.23
Swedish (16)	64	0.15
Swiss (17)	225	0.53
Ukrainian (0)	12	0.03
Welsh (13)	102	0.24
West Indian, ex. Hispanic (13)	32	0.08
Haitian (13)	32	0.08
Yugoslavian (17)	29	0.07

Hispanic Origin	Population	%
Hispanic or Latino (of any race)	1,828	4.07
Central American, ex. Mexican	126	0.28
Costa Rican	6	0.01
Guatemalan	26	0.06
Honduran	39	0.09
Nicaraguan	7	0.02
Panamanian	9	0.02
Salvadoran	39	0.09
Cuban	72	0.16
Dominican Republic	3	0.01
Mexican	1,198	2.67
Puerto Rican	217	0.48
South American	74	0.16
Argentinean	6	0.01
Bolivian	4	0.01
Chilean	2	<0.01
Colombian	18	0.04
Ecuadorian	11	0.02
Peruvian	17	0.04
Venezuelan	16	0.04
Other Hispanic or Latino	138	0.31

Race*	Population	%
African-American/Black (5,953)	6,862	15.26
Not Hispanic (5,889)	6,742	15.00
Hispanic (64)	120	0.27
American Indian/Alaska Native (129)	413	0.92
Not Hispanic (111)	372	0.83
Hispanic (18)	41	0.09
Apache (3)	4	0.01
Blackfeet (5)	12	0.03
Canadian/French Am. Ind. (4)	5	0.01
Cherokee (28)	149	0.33
Cheyenne (0)	1	<0.01
Chickasaw (1)	8	0.02
Chippewa (3)	8	0.02
Choctaw (7)	16	0.04
Comanche (0)	1	<0.01
Creek (5)	9	0.02
Delaware (1)	1	<0.01
Inupiat *(Alaska Native)* (4)	4	0.01
Iroquois (1)	2	<0.01
Mexican American Ind. (11)	11	0.02
Navajo (0)	2	<0.01
Ottawa (0)	4	0.01
Potawatomi (2)	3	0.01
Seminole (1)	1	<0.01
Sioux (4)	9	0.02
Asian (513)	705	1.57
Not Hispanic (506)	682	1.52
Hispanic (7)	23	0.05
Burmese (1)	1	<0.01
Cambodian (5)	5	0.01
Chinese, ex. Taiwanese (66)	85	0.19
Filipino (99)	168	0.37
Indian (93)	127	0.28
Indonesian (1)	2	<0.01
Japanese (26)	46	0.10
Korean (53)	87	0.19
Laotian (1)	3	0.01
Malaysian (1)	1	<0.01
Pakistani (23)	26	0.06
Sri Lankan (1)	1	<0.01
Taiwanese (18)	19	0.04
Thai (13)	19	0.04
Vietnamese (33)	39	0.09
Hawaii Native/Pacific Islander (22)	83	0.18
Not Hispanic (17)	75	0.17
Hispanic (5)	8	0.02
Guamanian/Chamorro (8)	18	0.04
Native Hawaiian (8)	31	0.07
Samoan (2)	6	0.01
White (36,144)	37,370	83.13
Not Hispanic (35,292)	36,395	80.96
Hispanic (852)	975	2.17

Kendallville

Place Type: City
County: Noble
Population: 9,862†

Ancestry‡	Population	%
American (981)	981	10.15
Austrian (0)	15	0.16
Belgian (6)	27	0.28
British (19)	19	0.20
Canadian (12)	12	0.12
Czech (13)	39	0.40
Danish (0)	66	0.68
Dutch (61)	174	1.80
English (402)	908	9.39
European (0)	7	0.07
French, ex. Basque (46)	379	3.92
French Canadian (55)	80	0.83
German (1,175)	3,013	31.17
Irish (276)	1,086	11.24
Italian (12)	221	2.29
Lithuanian (0)	11	0.11
Norwegian (7)	48	0.50
Pennsylvania German (14)	25	0.26
Polish (89)	190	1.97
Russian (21)	21	0.22
Scotch-Irish (57)	193	2.00
Scottish (37)	227	2.35
Swedish (28)	126	1.30
Swiss (45)	76	0.79
Welsh (0)	41	0.42

Hispanic Origin	Population	%
Hispanic or Latino (of any race)	507	5.14
Central American, ex. Mexican	6	0.06
Guatemalan	1	0.01
Salvadoran	5	0.05
Cuban	1	0.01
Mexican	440	4.46
Puerto Rican	9	0.09
South American	2	0.02
Colombian	2	0.02
Other Hispanic or Latino	49	0.50

Race*	Population	%
African-American/Black (51)	97	0.98
Not Hispanic (48)	87	0.88
Hispanic (3)	10	0.10
American Indian/Alaska Native (18)	68	0.69
Not Hispanic (17)	65	0.66
Hispanic (1)	3	0.03
Blackfeet (1)	2	0.02
Canadian/French Am. Ind. (0)	2	0.02
Cherokee (3)	29	0.29
Chippewa (0)	1	0.01
Iroquois (1)	1	0.01
Potawatomi (0)	1	0.01
Sioux (7)	9	0.09
Asian (54)	94	0.95
Not Hispanic (54)	94	0.95
Cambodian (4)	4	0.04
Chinese, ex. Taiwanese (12)	12	0.12
Filipino (7)	21	0.21
Indian (5)	7	0.07
Japanese (2)	2	0.02
Korean (3)	3	0.03
Laotian (1)	1	0.01
Pakistani (1)	1	0.01
Thai (2)	2	0.02
Vietnamese (17)	29	0.29
Hawaii Native/Pacific Islander (0)	5	0.05
Not Hispanic (0)	5	0.05
Native Hawaiian (0)	1	0.01
White (9,278)	9,449	95.81
Not Hispanic (9,090)	9,225	93.54

*Notes: † The Census 2010 population figure is used to calculate the percentages in the Hispanic Origin and Race categories. Ancestry percentages are based on the 2006-2010 American Community Survey population (not shown); ‡ Numbers in parentheses indicate the number of people reporting a single ancestry; * Numbers in parentheses indicate the number of persons reporting this race alone, not in combination with any other race; Please refer to the Explanation of Data for more information.*

Hispanic (188)	224	2.27

Kokomo

Place Type: City
County: Howard
Population: 45,468†

Ancestry‡	Population	%
African, Sub-Saharan (66)	302	0.66
African (66)	302	0.66
Albanian (0)	11	0.02
American (6,617)	6,617	14.42
Arab (23)	57	0.12
Arab (0)	25	0.05
Lebanese (11)	11	0.02
Palestinian (12)	12	0.03
Syrian (0)	9	0.02
Australian (0)	7	0.02
Austrian (7)	7	0.02
Belgian (0)	49	0.11
Brazilian (9)	9	0.02
British (153)	224	0.49
Cajun (0)	18	0.04
Canadian (17)	59	0.13
Czech (34)	80	0.17
Czechoslovakian (13)	31	0.07
Danish (13)	25	0.05
Dutch (109)	1,066	2.32
English (2,063)	4,428	9.65
European (166)	274	0.60
Finnish (0)	54	0.12
French, ex. Basque (234)	814	1.77
French Canadian (55)	324	0.71
German (3,549)	8,897	19.39
Greek (201)	262	0.57
Hungarian (87)	237	0.52
Irish (1,066)	4,113	8.96
Italian (251)	767	1.67
Lithuanian (37)	57	0.12
Norwegian (104)	261	0.57
Pennsylvania German (16)	43	0.09
Polish (255)	620	1.35
Portuguese (0)	21	0.05
Romanian (87)	129	0.28
Russian (10)	30	0.07
Scotch-Irish (241)	559	1.22
Scottish (155)	645	1.41
Serbian (0)	21	0.05
Slovak (13)	58	0.13
Swedish (130)	546	1.19
Swiss (43)	184	0.40
Ukrainian (22)	45	0.10
Welsh (51)	247	0.54
West Indian, ex. Hispanic (10)	10	0.02
British West Indian (10)	10	0.02

Hispanic Origin	Population	%
Hispanic or Latino (of any race)	1,501	3.30
Central American, ex. Mexican	46	0.10
Costa Rican	4	0.01
Guatemalan	6	0.01
Honduran	16	0.04
Nicaraguan	1	<0.01
Panamanian	8	0.02
Salvadoran	11	0.02
Cuban	21	0.05
Dominican Republic	2	<0.01
Mexican	1,058	2.33
Puerto Rican	154	0.34
South American	31	0.07
Bolivian	1	<0.01
Chilean	9	0.02
Colombian	12	0.03
Ecuadorian	1	<0.01
Peruvian	1	<0.01
Venezuelan	6	0.01
Other South American	1	<0.01
Other Hispanic or Latino	189	0.42

Race*	Population	%
African-American/Black (4,852)	5,852	12.87
Not Hispanic (4,776)	5,696	12.53
Hispanic (76)	156	0.34
American Indian/Alaska Native (175)	502	1.10
Not Hispanic (146)	439	0.97
Hispanic (29)	63	0.14
Apache (2)	7	0.02
Arapaho (1)	1	<0.01
Blackfeet (10)	18	0.04
Canadian/French Am. Ind. (0)	1	<0.01
Cherokee (30)	150	0.33
Chippewa (13)	19	0.04
Choctaw (2)	9	0.02
Colville (2)	2	<0.01
Comanche (0)	1	<0.01
Cree (0)	2	<0.01
Creek (0)	2	<0.01
Crow (1)	1	<0.01
Hopi (1)	2	<0.01
Iroquois (2)	3	0.01
Lumbee (0)	1	<0.01
Mexican American Ind. (0)	8	0.02
Navajo (1)	5	0.01
Potawatomi (0)	2	<0.01
Pueblo (0)	2	<0.01
Seminole (0)	3	0.01
Shoshone (1)	1	<0.01
Sioux (9)	18	0.04
South American Ind. (1)	1	<0.01
Spanish American Ind. (2)	2	<0.01
Ute (0)	1	<0.01
Asian (451)	607	1.34
Not Hispanic (449)	586	1.29
Hispanic (2)	21	0.05
Bangladeshi (4)	4	0.01
Chinese, ex. Taiwanese (119)	149	0.33
Filipino (112)	142	0.31
Indian (80)	101	0.22
Japanese (8)	45	0.10
Korean (23)	54	0.12
Nepalese (1)	1	<0.01
Pakistani (13)	14	0.03
Sri Lankan (4)	4	0.01
Taiwanese (2)	3	0.01
Thai (5)	12	0.03
Vietnamese (63)	68	0.15
Hawaii Native/Pacific Islander (11)	51	0.11
Not Hispanic (10)	47	0.10
Hispanic (1)	4	0.01
Guamanian/Chamorro (2)	4	0.01
Native Hawaiian (4)	27	0.06
Samoan (5)	12	0.03
White (37,981)	39,362	86.57
Not Hispanic (37,207)	38,431	84.52
Hispanic (774)	931	2.05

La Porte

Place Type: City
County: LaPorte
Population: 22,053†

Ancestry‡	Population	%
African, Sub-Saharan (50)	55	0.25
African (50)	55	0.25
American (1,305)	1,305	5.88
Arab (13)	40	0.18
Lebanese (13)	40	0.18
Armenian (21)	36	0.16
Austrian (0)	23	0.10
Belgian (26)	111	0.50
British (25)	169	0.76
Croatian (8)	30	0.14
Czech (62)	150	0.68
Czechoslovakian (0)	24	0.11
Danish (0)	51	0.23
Dutch (209)	613	2.76
English (544)	1,894	8.53
European (275)	291	1.31
Finnish (0)	65	0.29
French, ex. Basque (68)	354	1.60
French Canadian (49)	49	0.22
German (2,486)	6,794	30.61
Greek (0)	38	0.17
Hungarian (11)	90	0.41
Iranian (16)	16	0.07
Irish (863)	3,448	15.54
Italian (129)	601	2.71
Lithuanian (31)	102	0.46
Norwegian (34)	79	0.36
Pennsylvania German (0)	14	0.06
Polish (964)	2,309	10.40
Romanian (9)	9	0.04
Russian (35)	91	0.41
Scandinavian (11)	11	0.05
Scotch-Irish (64)	411	1.85
Scottish (69)	385	1.73
Serbian (14)	59	0.27
Slavic (24)	24	0.11
Slovak (52)	99	0.45
Slovene (0)	14	0.06
Swedish (144)	480	2.16
Swiss (10)	30	0.14
Ukrainian (39)	48	0.22
Welsh (13)	102	0.46
West Indian, ex. Hispanic (15)	15	0.07
Haitian (15)	15	0.07

Hispanic Origin	Population	%
Hispanic or Latino (of any race)	2,460	11.15
Central American, ex. Mexican	22	0.10
Guatemalan	4	0.02
Honduran	1	<0.01
Nicaraguan	1	<0.01
Panamanian	5	0.02
Salvadoran	11	0.05
Cuban	5	0.02
Dominican Republic	1	<0.01
Mexican	2,222	10.08
Puerto Rican	75	0.34
South American	20	0.09
Argentinean	1	<0.01
Colombian	9	0.04
Ecuadorian	3	0.01
Peruvian	2	0.01
Venezuelan	2	0.01
Other South American	3	0.01
Other Hispanic or Latino	115	0.52

Race*	Population	%
African-American/Black (672)	923	4.19
Not Hispanic (646)	880	3.99
Hispanic (26)	43	0.19
American Indian/Alaska Native (58)	155	0.70
Not Hispanic (41)	128	0.58
Hispanic (17)	27	0.12
Apache (1)	4	0.02
Blackfeet (1)	18	0.08
Cherokee (9)	45	0.20
Chickasaw (1)	1	<0.01
Chippewa (6)	8	0.04
Crow (0)	2	0.01
Iroquois (0)	2	0.01
Mexican American Ind. (9)	11	0.05
Navajo (1)	1	<0.01
Potawatomi (2)	2	0.01
Sioux (1)	4	0.02
Tohono O'Odham (1)	1	<0.01
Asian (100)	173	0.78
Not Hispanic (94)	152	0.69
Hispanic (6)	21	0.10
Chinese, ex. Taiwanese (21)	21	0.10
Filipino (22)	37	0.17
Indian (32)	49	0.22
Indonesian (1)	1	<0.01
Japanese (8)	20	0.09
Korean (7)	16	0.07
Taiwanese (1)	1	<0.01

*Notes: † The Census 2010 population figure is used to calculate the percentages in the Hispanic Origin and Race categories. Ancestry percentages are based on the 2006-2010 American Community Survey population (not shown); ‡ Numbers in parentheses indicate the number of people reporting a single ancestry; * Numbers in parentheses indicate the number of persons reporting this race alone, not in combination with any other race; Please refer to the Explanation of Data for more information.*

Thai (1)	3	0.01
Vietnamese (5)	5	0.02
Hawaii Native/Pacific Islander (2)	10	0.05
Not Hispanic (0)	6	0.03
Hispanic (2)	4	0.02
Guamanian/Chamorro (2)	3	0.01
White (19,549)	20,110	91.19
Not Hispanic (18,414)	18,780	85.16
Hispanic (1,135)	1,330	6.03

Lafayette

Place Type: City
County: Tippecanoe
Population: 67,140†

Ancestry‡	Population	%
African, Sub-Saharan (177)	247	0.37
African (66)	105	0.16
Kenyan (33)	33	0.05
Liberian (32)	32	0.05
Nigerian (23)	23	0.03
Other Sub-Saharan African (23)	54	0.08
American (4,832)	4,832	7.30
Arab (14)	25	0.04
Lebanese (14)	14	0.02
Other Arab (0)	11	0.02
Assyrian/Chaldean/Syriac (8)	30	0.05
Austrian (6)	79	0.12
Belgian (20)	100	0.15
Brazilian (8)	31	0.05
British (163)	331	0.50
Cajun (11)	22	0.03
Canadian (34)	34	0.05
Croatian (0)	33	0.05
Czech (40)	84	0.13
Czechoslovakian (0)	36	0.05
Danish (9)	74	0.11
Dutch (663)	2,127	3.22
Eastern European (29)	40	0.06
English (2,659)	6,889	10.41
European (543)	672	1.02
Finnish (40)	63	0.10
French, ex. Basque (322)	1,964	2.97
French Canadian (110)	177	0.27
German (6,095)	16,791	25.38
Greek (94)	147	0.22
Hungarian (132)	247	0.37
Irish (2,843)	10,032	15.17
Italian (789)	1,624	2.46
Lithuanian (11)	45	0.07
Luxemburger (0)	45	0.07
New Zealander (68)	68	0.10
Northern European (77)	77	0.12
Norwegian (35)	249	0.38
Pennsylvania German (0)	61	0.09
Polish (693)	1,900	2.87
Portuguese (27)	27	0.04
Romanian (28)	61	0.09
Russian (84)	391	0.59
Scandinavian (26)	36	0.05
Scotch-Irish (519)	1,115	1.69
Scottish (610)	1,572	2.38
Slavic (0)	27	0.04
Slovak (23)	44	0.07
Swedish (80)	556	0.84
Swiss (78)	302	0.46
Turkish (49)	49	0.07
Ukrainian (45)	94	0.14
Welsh (88)	360	0.54
West Indian, ex. Hispanic (8)	26	0.04
Dutch West Indian (0)	8	0.01
Haitian (0)	10	0.02
U.S. Virgin Islander (8)	8	0.01

Hispanic Origin	Population	%
Hispanic or Latino (of any race)	8,107	12.07
Central American, ex. Mexican	283	0.42
Costa Rican	12	0.02
Guatemalan	81	0.12
Honduran	10	0.01
Nicaraguan	16	0.02
Panamanian	26	0.04
Salvadoran	138	0.21
Cuban	78	0.12
Dominican Republic	33	0.05
Mexican	6,965	10.37
Puerto Rican	253	0.38
South American	130	0.19
Argentinean	16	0.02
Bolivian	12	0.02
Chilean	13	0.02
Colombian	39	0.06
Ecuadorian	23	0.03
Peruvian	18	0.03
Venezuelan	9	0.01
Other Hispanic or Latino	365	0.54

Race*	Population	%
African-American/Black (4,164)	4,987	7.43
Not Hispanic (4,050)	4,752	7.08
Hispanic (114)	235	0.35
American Indian/Alaska Native (245)	672	1.00
Not Hispanic (171)	544	0.81
Hispanic (74)	128	0.19
Alaska Athabascan *(Ala. Nat.)* (4)	4	0.01
Aleut *(Alaska Native)* (1)	2	<0.01
Apache (2)	12	0.02
Blackfeet (6)	27	0.04
Canadian/French Am. Ind. (2)	3	<0.01
Cherokee (39)	195	0.29
Cheyenne (1)	4	0.01
Chickasaw (0)	3	<0.01
Chippewa (8)	12	0.02
Choctaw (7)	9	0.01
Comanche (1)	3	<0.01
Cree (1)	1	<0.01
Creek (0)	4	0.01
Crow (2)	2	<0.01
Delaware (1)	3	<0.01
Houma (6)	6	0.01
Inupiat *(Alaska Native)* (1)	1	<0.01
Iroquois (8)	14	0.02
Lumbee (5)	5	0.01
Mexican American Ind. (23)	24	0.04
Navajo (0)	2	<0.01
Ottawa (4)	5	0.01
Potawatomi (1)	6	0.01
Seminole (0)	5	0.01
Sioux (12)	23	0.03
South American Ind. (0)	7	0.01
Tlingit-Haida *(Alaska Native)* (0)	5	0.01
Ute (0)	1	<0.01
Yaqui (1)	1	<0.01
Yuman (0)	1	<0.01
Asian (925)	1,224	1.82
Not Hispanic (908)	1,160	1.73
Hispanic (17)	64	0.10
Bangladeshi (5)	5	0.01
Burmese (6)	8	0.01
Cambodian (1)	1	<0.01
Chinese, ex. Taiwanese (188)	226	0.34
Filipino (111)	200	0.30
Indian (196)	225	0.34
Indonesian (9)	9	0.01
Japanese (71)	107	0.16
Korean (190)	239	0.36
Laotian (6)	11	0.02
Malaysian (3)	4	0.01
Nepalese (3)	3	<0.01
Pakistani (10)	13	0.02
Taiwanese (19)	20	0.03
Thai (12)	25	0.04
Vietnamese (63)	79	0.12
Hawaii Native/Pacific Islander (20)	73	0.11
Not Hispanic (14)	55	0.08
Hispanic (6)	18	0.03
Guamanian/Chamorro (17)	20	0.03
Native Hawaiian (3)	18	0.03
Samoan (0)	13	0.02
Tongan (0)	1	<0.01
White (56,108)	57,759	86.03
Not Hispanic (52,557)	53,754	80.06
Hispanic (3,551)	4,005	5.97

Lake Station

Place Type: City
County: Lake
Population: 12,572†

Ancestry‡	Population	%
American (861)	861	6.71
Arab (18)	18	0.14
Jordanian (18)	18	0.14
Austrian (0)	44	0.34
British (33)	33	0.26
Bulgarian (0)	15	0.12
Croatian (0)	57	0.44
Czech (13)	42	0.33
Czechoslovakian (0)	25	0.19
Danish (0)	11	0.09
Dutch (38)	257	2.00
English (234)	686	5.35
European (27)	27	0.21
French, ex. Basque (145)	367	2.86
German (532)	2,029	15.81
Greek (44)	89	0.69
Hungarian (21)	83	0.65
Irish (345)	2,194	17.10
Italian (293)	441	3.44
Lithuanian (0)	16	0.12
Northern European (4)	4	0.03
Norwegian (44)	93	0.72
Polish (278)	672	5.24
Romanian (0)	44	0.34
Russian (34)	34	0.26
Scotch-Irish (21)	174	1.36
Scottish (30)	154	1.20
Serbian (29)	108	0.84
Slovak (25)	40	0.31
Swedish (59)	159	1.24
Welsh (24)	127	0.99
West Indian, ex. Hispanic (26)	26	0.20
Jamaican (26)	26	0.20

Hispanic Origin	Population	%
Hispanic or Latino (of any race)	3,517	27.97
Central American, ex. Mexican	27	0.21
Guatemalan	12	0.10
Honduran	5	0.04
Nicaraguan	4	0.03
Panamanian	3	0.02
Salvadoran	3	0.02
Cuban	19	0.15
Dominican Republic	2	0.02
Mexican	2,522	20.06
Puerto Rican	843	6.71
South American	4	0.03
Ecuadorian	2	0.02
Peruvian	2	0.02
Other Hispanic or Latino	100	0.80

Race*	Population	%
African-American/Black (455)	628	5.00
Not Hispanic (373)	489	3.89
Hispanic (82)	139	1.11
American Indian/Alaska Native (66)	182	1.45
Not Hispanic (40)	133	1.06
Hispanic (26)	49	0.39
Blackfeet (2)	7	0.06
Cherokee (3)	40	0.32
Cheyenne (1)	1	0.01
Chippewa (1)	2	0.02
Cree (0)	1	0.01
Creek (6)	7	0.06
Delaware (0)	1	0.01
Iroquois (2)	7	0.06
Lumbee (1)	2	0.02
Mexican American Ind. (1)	3	0.02

*Notes: † The Census 2010 population figure is used to calculate the percentages in the Hispanic Origin and Race categories. Ancestry percentages are based on the 2006-2010 American Community Survey population (not shown); ‡ Numbers in parentheses indicate the number of people reporting a single ancestry; * Numbers in parentheses indicate the number of persons reporting this race alone, not in combination with any other race; Please refer to the Explanation of Data for more information.*

Navajo (0)	1	0.01
Osage (0)	1	0.01
Ottawa (0)	1	0.01
Pueblo (1)	2	0.02
Sioux (2)	12	0.10
South American Ind. (2)	5	0.04
Spanish American Ind. (1)	1	0.01
Yaqui (1)	1	0.01
Asian (40)	66	0.52
Not Hispanic (35)	55	0.44
Hispanic (5)	11	0.09
Chinese, ex. Taiwanese (1)	1	0.01
Filipino (10)	16	0.13
Indian (6)	19	0.15
Japanese (3)	5	0.04
Korean (1)	4	0.03
Pakistani (9)	9	0.07
Thai (5)	7	0.06
Vietnamese (1)	1	0.01
Hawaii Native/Pacific Islander (3)	11	0.09
Not Hispanic (0)	3	0.02
Hispanic (3)	8	0.06
Guamanian/Chamorro (1)	3	0.02
Native Hawaiian (2)	3	0.02
Samoan (0)	3	0.02
White (10,023)	10,499	83.51
Not Hispanic (8,385)	8,585	68.29
Hispanic (1,638)	1,914	15.22

Lawrence

Place Type: City
County: Marion
Population: 46,001†

Ancestry‡	Population	%
African, Sub-Saharan (1,587)	1,653	3.72
African (1,561)	1,595	3.59
Nigerian (26)	26	0.06
Somalian (0)	32	0.07
American (3,051)	3,051	6.87
Arab (26)	109	0.25
Arab (12)	68	0.15
Lebanese (14)	24	0.05
Other Arab (0)	17	0.04
Assyrian/Chaldean/Syriac (0)	10	0.02
Austrian (19)	55	0.12
Belgian (8)	8	0.02
Brazilian (21)	21	0.05
British (120)	203	0.46
Canadian (11)	37	0.08
Celtic (15)	15	0.03
Croatian (36)	53	0.12
Czech (19)	55	0.12
Czechoslovakian (0)	38	0.09
Danish (11)	126	0.28
Dutch (216)	714	1.61
English (1,174)	3,634	8.18
European (443)	537	1.21
Finnish (36)	57	0.13
French, ex. Basque (213)	866	1.95
French Canadian (52)	81	0.18
German (2,997)	8,644	19.46
German Russian (11)	11	0.02
Greek (172)	232	0.52
Hungarian (0)	106	0.24
Iranian (11)	11	0.02
Irish (1,080)	5,187	11.68
Italian (456)	1,494	3.36
Latvian (10)	10	0.02
Lithuanian (17)	42	0.09
Luxemburger (0)	12	0.03
Macedonian (62)	103	0.23
Northern European (80)	80	0.18
Norwegian (72)	295	0.66
Pennsylvania German (77)	77	0.17
Polish (147)	621	1.40
Portuguese (50)	108	0.24
Russian (55)	106	0.24
Scandinavian (16)	16	0.04
Scotch-Irish (210)	429	0.97
Scottish (297)	967	2.18
Slavic (0)	26	0.06
Slovak (28)	38	0.09
Swedish (83)	419	0.94
Swiss (54)	155	0.35
Turkish (0)	17	0.04
Ukrainian (24)	33	0.07
Welsh (47)	454	1.02
West Indian, ex. Hispanic (35)	60	0.14
Belizean (0)	25	0.06
Jamaican (35)	35	0.08
Yugoslavian (17)	17	0.04

Hispanic Origin	Population	%
Hispanic or Latino (of any race)	5,155	11.21
Central American, ex. Mexican	481	1.05
Costa Rican	6	0.01
Guatemalan	140	0.30
Honduran	161	0.35
Nicaraguan	67	0.15
Panamanian	25	0.05
Salvadoran	80	0.17
Other Central American	2	<0.01
Cuban	48	0.10
Dominican Republic	28	0.06
Mexican	3,827	8.32
Puerto Rican	329	0.72
South American	164	0.36
Argentinean	8	0.02
Bolivian	1	<0.01
Chilean	4	0.01
Colombian	41	0.09
Ecuadorian	18	0.04
Paraguayan	2	<0.01
Peruvian	46	0.10
Uruguayan	2	<0.01
Venezuelan	40	0.09
Other South American	2	<0.01
Other Hispanic or Latino	278	0.60

Race*	Population	%
African-American/Black (11,865)	12,900	28.04
Not Hispanic (11,703)	12,650	27.50
Hispanic (162)	250	0.54
American Indian/Alaska Native (163)	482	1.05
Not Hispanic (102)	364	0.79
Hispanic (61)	118	0.26
Apache (2)	12	0.03
Arapaho (1)	1	<0.01
Blackfeet (2)	16	0.03
Canadian/French Am. Ind. (0)	1	<0.01
Central American Ind. (1)	1	<0.01
Cherokee (23)	105	0.23
Cheyenne (0)	2	<0.01
Chippewa (11)	13	0.03
Choctaw (2)	5	0.01
Comanche (0)	3	0.01
Creek (5)	5	0.01
Iroquois (6)	10	0.02
Lumbee (1)	2	<0.01
Mexican American Ind. (6)	15	0.03
Potawatomi (1)	3	0.01
Pueblo (1)	5	0.01
Shoshone (0)	1	<0.01
Sioux (5)	15	0.03
South American Ind. (1)	1	<0.01
Spanish American Ind. (6)	9	0.02
Asian (655)	997	2.17
Not Hispanic (649)	965	2.10
Hispanic (6)	32	0.07
Bangladeshi (5)	5	0.01
Cambodian (12)	14	0.03
Chinese, ex. Taiwanese (96)	148	0.32
Filipino (131)	204	0.44
Indian (62)	92	0.20
Indonesian (3)	6	0.01
Japanese (35)	91	0.20
Korean (178)	283	0.62
Malaysian (0)	2	<0.01
Nepalese (9)	10	0.02
Pakistani (16)	16	0.03
Taiwanese (6)	12	0.03
Thai (15)	24	0.05
Vietnamese (67)	84	0.18
Hawaii Native/Pacific Islander (59)	94	0.20
Not Hispanic (48)	80	0.17
Hispanic (11)	14	0.03
Guamanian/Chamorro (22)	28	0.06
Marshallese (1)	1	<0.01
Native Hawaiian (17)	30	0.07
Samoan (12)	18	0.04
White (29,056)	30,446	66.19
Not Hispanic (26,887)	28,079	61.04
Hispanic (2,169)	2,367	5.15

Lebanon

Place Type: City
County: Boone
Population: 15,792†

Ancestry‡	Population	%
African, Sub-Saharan (0)	19	0.12
African (0)	19	0.12
Albanian (13)	13	0.08
American (1,151)	1,151	7.30
Arab (38)	60	0.38
Egyptian (27)	38	0.24
Lebanese (0)	11	0.07
Other Arab (11)	11	0.07
Basque (0)	10	0.06
Belgian (20)	32	0.20
Bulgarian (0)	54	0.34
Canadian (51)	51	0.32
Czech (0)	49	0.31
Czechoslovakian (41)	41	0.26
Danish (14)	59	0.37
Dutch (62)	413	2.62
English (1,716)	2,881	18.27
European (51)	60	0.38
Finnish (0)	32	0.20
French, ex. Basque (157)	630	4.00
French Canadian (30)	30	0.19
German (1,904)	4,099	25.99
Greek (0)	15	0.10
Hungarian (0)	22	0.14
Irish (780)	2,182	13.84
Italian (95)	330	2.09
Macedonian (0)	8	0.05
Norwegian (39)	94	0.60
Pennsylvania German (10)	31	0.20
Polish (196)	289	1.83
Romanian (0)	15	0.10
Russian (0)	27	0.17
Scotch-Irish (205)	340	2.16
Scottish (412)	725	4.60
Swedish (49)	84	0.53
Swiss (0)	12	0.08
Ukrainian (35)	62	0.39
West Indian, ex. Hispanic (0)	14	0.09
Dutch West Indian (0)	14	0.09
Yugoslavian (50)	50	0.32

Hispanic Origin	Population	%
Hispanic or Latino (of any race)	489	3.10
Central American, ex. Mexican	11	0.07
Guatemalan	3	0.02
Honduran	2	0.01
Nicaraguan	3	0.02
Salvadoran	3	0.02
Cuban	3	0.02
Dominican Republic	6	0.04
Mexican	384	2.43
Puerto Rican	25	0.16
South American	20	0.13
Argentinean	6	0.04
Colombian	11	0.07
Ecuadorian	1	0.01
Peruvian	2	0.01

*Notes: † The Census 2010 population figure is used to calculate the percentages in the Hispanic Origin and Race categories. Ancestry percentages are based on the 2006-2010 American Community Survey population (not shown); ‡ Numbers in parentheses indicate the number of people reporting a single ancestry; * Numbers in parentheses indicate the number of persons reporting this race alone, not in combination with any other race; Please refer to the Explanation of Data for more information.*

Other Hispanic or Latino	40	0.25

Race*	Population	%
African-American/Black (85)	167	1.06
Not Hispanic (83)	157	0.99
Hispanic (2)	10	0.06
American Indian/Alaska Native (29)	111	0.70
Not Hispanic (23)	104	0.66
Hispanic (6)	7	0.04
Apache (0)	1	0.01
Blackfeet (1)	6	0.04
Canadian/French Am. Ind. (0)	1	0.01
Cherokee (4)	31	0.20
Cheyenne (0)	1	0.01
Chippewa (0)	2	0.01
Choctaw (1)	1	0.01
Comanche (0)	1	0.01
Delaware (2)	2	0.01
Inupiat *(Alaska Native)* (0)	2	0.01
Mexican American Ind. (0)	1	0.01
Osage (0)	1	0.01
Paiute (2)	4	0.03
Potawatomi (0)	1	0.01
Sioux (3)	6	0.04
Asian (100)	137	0.87
Not Hispanic (99)	132	0.84
Hispanic (1)	5	0.03
Chinese, ex. Taiwanese (23)	26	0.16
Filipino (16)	33	0.21
Hmong (1)	4	0.03
Indian (19)	23	0.15
Indonesian (1)	2	0.01
Japanese (2)	4	0.03
Korean (5)	10	0.06
Pakistani (5)	5	0.03
Thai (1)	1	0.01
Vietnamese (16)	21	0.13
Hawaii Native/Pacific Islander (4)	9	0.06
Not Hispanic (3)	8	0.05
Hispanic (1)	1	0.01
Native Hawaiian (1)	3	0.02
Samoan (1)	2	0.01
White (15,171)	15,398	97.51
Not Hispanic (14,901)	15,088	95.54
Hispanic (270)	310	1.96

Logansport

Place Type: City
County: Cass
Population: 18,396†

Ancestry‡	Population	%
African, Sub-Saharan (66)	66	0.36
African (66)	66	0.36
American (2,616)	2,616	14.45
Australian (0)	12	0.07
Belgian (0)	19	0.10
British (0)	23	0.13
Canadian (11)	31	0.17
Czech (7)	7	0.04
Danish (13)	65	0.36
Dutch (53)	268	1.48
English (513)	1,302	7.19
European (45)	45	0.25
French, ex. Basque (77)	362	2.00
French Canadian (0)	39	0.22
German (1,176)	3,281	18.13
Greek (0)	8	0.04
Hungarian (14)	37	0.20
Irish (527)	1,747	9.65
Italian (323)	633	3.50
Lithuanian (14)	14	0.08
Norwegian (0)	8	0.04
Pennsylvania German (0)	8	0.04
Polish (215)	392	2.17
Russian (15)	29	0.16
Scotch-Irish (42)	83	0.46
Scottish (11)	104	0.57
Serbian (7)	7	0.04
Swedish (0)	89	0.49
Swiss (6)	29	0.16
Ukrainian (4)	10	0.06
Welsh (16)	59	0.33

Hispanic Origin	Population	%
Hispanic or Latino (of any race)	3,973	21.60
Central American, ex. Mexican	641	3.48
Guatemalan	412	2.24
Honduran	54	0.29
Nicaraguan	7	0.04
Panamanian	2	0.01
Salvadoran	166	0.90
Cuban	57	0.31
Dominican Republic	42	0.23
Mexican	2,847	15.48
Puerto Rican	59	0.32
South American	62	0.34
Argentinean	3	0.02
Colombian	7	0.04
Ecuadorian	7	0.04
Peruvian	45	0.24
Other Hispanic or Latino	265	1.44

Race*	Population	%
African-American/Black (420)	583	3.17
Not Hispanic (377)	516	2.80
Hispanic (43)	67	0.36
American Indian/Alaska Native (140)	206	1.12
Not Hispanic (49)	95	0.52
Hispanic (91)	111	0.60
Aleut *(Alaska Native)* (1)	1	0.01
Arapaho (0)	1	0.01
Canadian/French Am. Ind. (1)	2	0.01
Central American Ind. (27)	27	0.15
Cherokee (6)	17	0.09
Cheyenne (0)	4	0.02
Chippewa (5)	6	0.03
Choctaw (0)	1	0.01
Cree (2)	2	0.01
Creek (0)	1	0.01
Crow (0)	2	0.01
Iroquois (1)	1	0.01
Mexican American Ind. (20)	32	0.17
Navajo (1)	1	0.01
Potawatomi (0)	2	0.01
Sioux (2)	4	0.02
Tlingit-Haida *(Alaska Native)* (1)	1	0.01
Asian (311)	359	1.95
Not Hispanic (302)	330	1.79
Hispanic (9)	29	0.16
Burmese (142)	144	0.78
Chinese, ex. Taiwanese (25)	32	0.17
Filipino (26)	36	0.20
Indian (13)	19	0.10
Indonesian (1)	1	0.01
Japanese (2)	8	0.04
Korean (2)	6	0.03
Laotian (36)	43	0.23
Pakistani (0)	3	0.02
Thai (11)	11	0.06
Vietnamese (35)	36	0.20
Hawaii Native/Pacific Islander (21)	34	0.18
Not Hispanic (2)	9	0.05
Hispanic (19)	25	0.14
Guamanian/Chamorro (15)	16	0.09
Native Hawaiian (6)	10	0.05
Tongan (0)	5	0.03
White (14,838)	15,203	82.64
Not Hispanic (13,450)	13,649	74.20
Hispanic (1,388)	1,554	8.45

Lowell

Place Type: Town
County: Lake
Population: 9,276†

Ancestry‡	Population	%
American (749)	749	8.36
Austrian (0)	52	0.58
Belgian (0)	15	0.17
British (24)	24	0.27
Croatian (44)	118	1.32
Czech (0)	48	0.54
Danish (17)	64	0.71
Dutch (86)	405	4.52
Eastern European (19)	19	0.21
English (187)	750	8.37
European (46)	46	0.51
French, ex. Basque (50)	330	3.68
French Canadian (0)	15	0.17
German (962)	3,055	34.08
Greek (25)	39	0.44
Hungarian (31)	172	1.92
Iranian (0)	9	0.10
Irish (497)	1,722	19.21
Italian (172)	576	6.43
Lithuanian (0)	129	1.44
Macedonian (17)	17	0.19
Northern European (12)	12	0.13
Norwegian (46)	134	1.49
Pennsylvania German (0)	23	0.26
Polish (366)	1,046	11.67
Romanian (0)	28	0.31
Russian (16)	136	1.52
Scotch-Irish (13)	226	2.52
Scottish (100)	389	4.34
Serbian (61)	141	1.57
Slavic (13)	13	0.15
Slovak (43)	170	1.90
Slovene (9)	19	0.21
Swedish (27)	208	2.32
Ukrainian (0)	50	0.56
Welsh (0)	25	0.28

Hispanic Origin	Population	%
Hispanic or Latino (of any race)	640	6.90
Central American, ex. Mexican	6	0.06
Guatemalan	2	0.02
Honduran	4	0.04
Cuban	3	0.03
Mexican	555	5.98
Puerto Rican	48	0.52
South American	7	0.08
Chilean	1	0.01
Colombian	2	0.02
Peruvian	4	0.04
Other Hispanic or Latino	21	0.23

Race*	Population	%
African-American/Black (49)	74	0.80
Not Hispanic (48)	68	0.73
Hispanic (1)	6	0.06
American Indian/Alaska Native (33)	81	0.87
Not Hispanic (28)	75	0.81
Hispanic (5)	6	0.06
Apache (1)	2	0.02
Blackfeet (0)	4	0.04
Canadian/French Am. Ind. (0)	1	0.01
Cherokee (3)	20	0.22
Chippewa (3)	5	0.05
Delaware (0)	3	0.03
Inupiat *(Alaska Native)* (2)	2	0.02
Iroquois (6)	6	0.06
Navajo (0)	1	0.01
Potawatomi (3)	4	0.04
Sioux (1)	2	0.02
Asian (24)	33	0.36
Not Hispanic (24)	33	0.36
Chinese, ex. Taiwanese (1)	1	0.01
Filipino (6)	9	0.10
Indian (2)	3	0.03
Japanese (3)	3	0.03
Korean (7)	9	0.10
Taiwanese (1)	1	0.01
Thai (4)	7	0.08
Hawaii Native/Pacific Islander (5)	6	0.06
Not Hispanic (2)	3	0.03
Hispanic (3)	3	0.03

*Notes: † The Census 2010 population figure is used to calculate the percentages in the Hispanic Origin and Race categories. Ancestry percentages are based on the 2006-2010 American Community Survey population (not shown); ‡ Numbers in parentheses indicate the number of people reporting a single ancestry; * Numbers in parentheses indicate the number of persons reporting this race alone, not in combination with any other race; Please refer to the Explanation of Data for more information.*

Native Hawaiian (3)	3	0.03
White (8,894)	9,006	97.09
Not Hispanic (8,456)	8,529	91.95
Hispanic (438)	477	5.14

Madison

Place Type: City
County: Jefferson
Population: 11,967†

Ancestry‡	Population	%
American (1,848)	1,848	15.42
Arab (10)	10	0.08
Arab (10)	10	0.08
Armenian (15)	15	0.13
Austrian (0)	16	0.13
British (0)	29	0.24
Canadian (8)	8	0.07
Celtic (14)	14	0.12
Croatian (7)	43	0.36
Dutch (11)	139	1.16
English (584)	1,342	11.20
European (0)	15	0.13
French, ex. Basque (64)	318	2.65
French Canadian (44)	96	0.80
German (1,246)	2,882	24.04
Greek (24)	53	0.44
Hungarian (17)	125	1.04
Irish (465)	1,607	13.41
Italian (87)	179	1.49
Lithuanian (18)	18	0.15
Norwegian (0)	3	0.03
Polish (38)	66	0.55
Russian (0)	12	0.10
Scandinavian (12)	22	0.18
Scotch-Irish (209)	365	3.05
Scottish (146)	267	2.23
Slovak (0)	95	0.79
Swedish (39)	56	0.47
Swiss (13)	99	0.83
Ukrainian (17)	34	0.28
Welsh (41)	116	0.97

Hispanic Origin	Population	%
Hispanic or Latino (of any race)	203	1.70
Central American, ex. Mexican	6	0.05
Guatemalan	2	0.02
Honduran	3	0.03
Salvadoran	1	0.01
Cuban	3	0.03
Mexican	148	1.24
Puerto Rican	34	0.28
South American	5	0.04
Argentinean	2	0.02
Bolivian	1	0.01
Colombian	2	0.02
Other Hispanic or Latino	7	0.06

Race*	Population	%
African-American/Black (338)	449	3.75
Not Hispanic (334)	439	3.67
Hispanic (4)	10	0.08
American Indian/Alaska Native (22)	70	0.58
Not Hispanic (22)	69	0.58
Hispanic (0)	1	0.01
Blackfeet (1)	3	0.03
Canadian/French Am. Ind. (0)	1	0.01
Cherokee (6)	12	0.10
Chickasaw (1)	1	0.01
Chippewa (3)	3	0.03
Delaware (0)	1	0.01
Inupiat *(Alaska Native)* (1)	3	0.03
Iroquois (0)	3	0.03
Paiute (0)	1	0.01
Potawatomi (1)	1	0.01
Sioux (1)	6	0.05
Asian (145)	177	1.48
Not Hispanic (145)	175	1.46
Hispanic (0)	2	0.02
Chinese, ex. Taiwanese (45)	46	0.38
Filipino (22)	32	0.27
Indian (24)	32	0.27
Indonesian (3)	3	0.03
Japanese (35)	41	0.34
Korean (5)	6	0.05
Pakistani (2)	2	0.02
Thai (0)	1	0.01
Vietnamese (5)	8	0.07
Hawaii Native/Pacific Islander (1)	2	0.02
Not Hispanic (1)	2	0.02
Native Hawaiian (1)	1	0.01
White (11,188)	11,374	95.04
Not Hispanic (11,071)	11,239	93.92
Hispanic (117)	135	1.13

Marion

Place Type: City
County: Grant
Population: 29,948†

Ancestry‡	Population	%
African, Sub-Saharan (100)	129	0.42
African (100)	129	0.42
American (3,196)	3,196	10.41
Arab (9)	29	0.09
Lebanese (0)	12	0.04
Syrian (9)	17	0.06
Austrian (29)	29	0.09
Belgian (0)	30	0.10
British (116)	148	0.48
Canadian (33)	60	0.20
Czech (21)	38	0.12
Danish (0)	9	0.03
Dutch (94)	556	1.81
English (1,256)	2,678	8.72
European (92)	92	0.30
Finnish (0)	10	0.03
French, ex. Basque (102)	748	2.44
French Canadian (30)	34	0.11
German (2,433)	5,749	18.72
Greek (0)	38	0.12
Hungarian (9)	77	0.25
Iranian (41)	41	0.13
Irish (865)	2,904	9.46
Italian (263)	554	1.80
Lithuanian (9)	9	0.03
Norwegian (59)	83	0.27
Pennsylvania German (8)	39	0.13
Polish (57)	464	1.51
Portuguese (41)	41	0.13
Russian (11)	11	0.04
Scandinavian (9)	24	0.08
Scotch-Irish (208)	340	1.11
Scottish (129)	304	0.99
Slovak (58)	103	0.34
Swedish (95)	242	0.79
Swiss (0)	96	0.31
Ukrainian (12)	12	0.04
Welsh (74)	172	0.56
West Indian, ex. Hispanic (21)	40	0.13
Dutch West Indian (0)	19	0.06
Other West Indian (21)	21	0.07

Hispanic Origin	Population	%
Hispanic or Latino (of any race)	1,656	5.53
Central American, ex. Mexican	30	0.10
Costa Rican	2	0.01
Guatemalan	6	0.02
Honduran	6	0.02
Nicaraguan	7	0.02
Panamanian	1	<0.01
Salvadoran	8	0.03
Cuban	32	0.11
Dominican Republic	1	<0.01
Mexican	1,308	4.37
Puerto Rican	91	0.30
South American	22	0.07
Argentinean	1	<0.01
Bolivian	2	0.01
Colombian	4	0.01
Ecuadorian	4	0.01
Peruvian	4	0.01
Uruguayan	1	<0.01
Venezuelan	4	0.01
Other South American	2	0.01
Other Hispanic or Latino	172	0.57

Race*	Population	%
African-American/Black (4,406)	5,159	17.23
Not Hispanic (4,337)	5,015	16.75
Hispanic (69)	144	0.48
American Indian/Alaska Native (109)	267	0.89
Not Hispanic (105)	242	0.81
Hispanic (4)	25	0.08
Apache (0)	4	0.01
Blackfeet (1)	14	0.05
Canadian/French Am. Ind. (2)	2	0.01
Cherokee (23)	74	0.25
Cheyenne (1)	2	0.01
Chickasaw (0)	1	<0.01
Chippewa (1)	5	0.02
Choctaw (3)	6	0.02
Crow (1)	3	0.01
Hopi (1)	1	<0.01
Lumbee (1)	6	0.02
Mexican American Ind. (2)	2	0.01
Navajo (3)	4	0.01
Potawatomi (2)	2	0.01
Sioux (1)	8	0.03
Asian (221)	332	1.11
Not Hispanic (221)	318	1.06
Hispanic (0)	14	0.05
Cambodian (7)	7	0.02
Chinese, ex. Taiwanese (18)	37	0.12
Filipino (65)	89	0.30
Indian (69)	76	0.25
Japanese (6)	29	0.10
Korean (20)	45	0.15
Pakistani (4)	5	0.02
Taiwanese (0)	1	<0.01
Thai (5)	8	0.03
Vietnamese (19)	25	0.08
Hawaii Native/Pacific Islander (6)	35	0.12
Not Hispanic (4)	24	0.08
Hispanic (2)	11	0.04
Fijian (0)	6	0.02
Guamanian/Chamorro (1)	4	0.01
Native Hawaiian (1)	12	0.04
Samoan (3)	6	0.02
White (23,400)	24,387	81.43
Not Hispanic (22,704)	23,529	78.57
Hispanic (696)	858	2.86

Martinsville

Place Type: City
County: Morgan
Population: 11,828†

Ancestry‡	Population	%
American (1,828)	1,828	15.32
British (35)	35	0.29
Canadian (12)	23	0.19
Czechoslovakian (25)	44	0.37
Dutch (56)	354	2.97
English (504)	1,009	8.45
European (22)	134	1.12
Finnish (15)	41	0.34
French, ex. Basque (51)	301	2.52
German (870)	3,045	25.51
Greek (43)	160	1.34
Hungarian (1)	26	0.22
Irish (401)	1,925	16.13
Italian (78)	213	1.78
Norwegian (0)	14	0.12
Polish (0)	66	0.55
Romanian (10)	10	0.08
Russian (0)	5	0.04

*Notes: † The Census 2010 population figure is used to calculate the percentages in the Hispanic Origin and Race categories. Ancestry percentages are based on the 2006-2010 American Community Survey population (not shown); ‡ Numbers in parentheses indicate the number of people reporting a single ancestry; * Numbers in parentheses indicate the number of persons reporting this race alone, not in combination with any other race; Please refer to the Explanation of Data for more information.*

Scotch-Irish (79)	248	2.08
Scottish (43)	160	1.34
Slovak (17)	17	0.14
Swedish (12)	51	0.43
Swiss (0)	12	0.10
Welsh (0)	55	0.46

Hispanic Origin	Population	%
Hispanic or Latino (of any race)	154	1.30
Central American, ex. Mexican	18	0.15
Guatemalan	14	0.12
Honduran	1	0.01
Panamanian	3	0.03
Cuban	1	0.01
Dominican Republic	1	0.01
Mexican	107	0.90
Puerto Rican	19	0.16
Other Hispanic or Latino	8	0.07

Race*	Population	%
African-American/Black (24)	55	0.46
Not Hispanic (24)	54	0.46
Hispanic (0)	1	0.01
American Indian/Alaska Native (38)	87	0.74
Not Hispanic (32)	79	0.67
Hispanic (6)	8	0.07
Arapaho (1)	1	0.01
Cherokee (6)	23	0.19
Chickasaw (1)	1	0.01
Choctaw (0)	3	0.03
Comanche (1)	1	0.01
Houma (0)	3	0.03
Mexican American Ind. (3)	3	0.03
Navajo (1)	2	0.02
Sioux (1)	6	0.05
Asian (43)	61	0.52
Not Hispanic (43)	61	0.52
Chinese, ex. Taiwanese (8)	12	0.10
Filipino (19)	26	0.22
Indian (7)	9	0.08
Japanese (1)	1	0.01
Korean (5)	7	0.06
Pakistani (0)	1	0.01
Taiwanese (0)	2	0.02
Thai (0)	3	0.03
Vietnamese (0)	1	0.01
Hawaii Native/Pacific Islander (15)	25	0.21
Not Hispanic (15)	25	0.21
Guamanian/Chamorro (0)	2	0.02
Native Hawaiian (0)	3	0.03
Samoan (0)	6	0.05
White (11,529)	11,642	98.43
Not Hispanic (11,448)	11,554	97.68
Hispanic (81)	88	0.74

Merrillville

Place Type: Town
County: Lake
Population: 35,246†

Ancestry‡	Population	%
African, Sub-Saharan (902)	902	2.62
African (867)	867	2.52
Ethiopian (7)	7	0.02
Ghanaian (18)	18	0.05
Nigerian (10)	10	0.03
American (1,090)	1,090	3.17
Arab (99)	99	0.29
Arab (24)	24	0.07
Jordanian (9)	9	0.03
Syrian (66)	66	0.19
Assyrian/Chaldean/Syriac (21)	21	0.06
Austrian (21)	21	0.06
British (16)	42	0.12
Bulgarian (50)	50	0.15
Croatian (158)	359	1.04
Czech (51)	177	0.51
Czechoslovakian (0)	4	0.01
Danish (0)	68	0.20
Dutch (67)	621	1.80
Eastern European (14)	14	0.04
English (498)	1,727	5.02
European (125)	137	0.40
Finnish (29)	51	0.15
French, ex. Basque (50)	324	0.94
French Canadian (12)	55	0.16
German (1,230)	3,818	11.09
Greek (212)	263	0.76
Hungarian (275)	490	1.42
Irish (448)	2,952	8.57
Italian (681)	1,387	4.03
Lithuanian (9)	135	0.39
Macedonian (138)	158	0.46
Northern European (37)	37	0.11
Norwegian (52)	111	0.32
Pennsylvania German (0)	12	0.03
Polish (847)	1,919	5.57
Romanian (17)	33	0.10
Russian (56)	143	0.42
Scandinavian (0)	11	0.03
Scotch-Irish (40)	323	0.94
Scottish (67)	209	0.61
Serbian (126)	247	0.72
Slavic (14)	26	0.08
Slovak (383)	576	1.67
Slovene (31)	31	0.09
Swedish (52)	249	0.72
Swiss (0)	50	0.15
Ukrainian (23)	49	0.14
Welsh (27)	95	0.28
West Indian, ex. Hispanic (31)	31	0.09
Jamaican (31)	31	0.09
Yugoslavian (43)	43	0.12

Hispanic Origin	Population	%
Hispanic or Latino (of any race)	4,533	12.86
Central American, ex. Mexican	53	0.15
Costa Rican	2	0.01
Guatemalan	9	0.03
Honduran	9	0.03
Nicaraguan	17	0.05
Panamanian	8	0.02
Salvadoran	8	0.02
Cuban	18	0.05
Dominican Republic	16	0.05
Mexican	3,355	9.52
Puerto Rican	817	2.32
South American	57	0.16
Argentinean	7	0.02
Bolivian	1	<0.01
Chilean	7	0.02
Colombian	5	0.01
Ecuadorian	18	0.05
Peruvian	14	0.04
Venezuelan	3	0.01
Other South American	2	0.01
Other Hispanic or Latino	217	0.62

Race*	Population	%
African-American/Black (15,673)	16,337	46.35
Not Hispanic (15,410)	15,889	45.08
Hispanic (263)	448	1.27
American Indian/Alaska Native (70)	275	0.78
Not Hispanic (47)	187	0.53
Hispanic (23)	88	0.25
Aleut *(Alaska Native)* (1)	1	<0.01
Apache (1)	2	0.01
Blackfeet (5)	18	0.05
Central American Ind. (1)	4	0.01
Cherokee (5)	41	0.12
Chickasaw (0)	3	0.01
Chippewa (3)	11	0.03
Choctaw (0)	9	0.03
Creek (0)	1	<0.01
Crow (0)	2	0.01
Inupiat *(Alaska Native)* (0)	8	0.02
Iroquois (0)	2	0.01
Mexican American Ind. (1)	8	0.02
Navajo (1)	1	<0.01
Potawatomi (0)	4	0.01
Pueblo (1)	1	<0.01
Seminole (0)	1	<0.01
Sioux (2)	4	0.01
South American Ind. (0)	3	0.01
Yaqui (0)	1	<0.01
Asian (421)	617	1.75
Not Hispanic (412)	580	1.65
Hispanic (9)	37	0.10
Bangladeshi (3)	4	0.01
Cambodian (0)	1	<0.01
Chinese, ex. Taiwanese (44)	57	0.16
Filipino (165)	254	0.72
Indian (72)	92	0.26
Indonesian (9)	9	0.03
Japanese (13)	24	0.07
Korean (17)	33	0.09
Laotian (2)	2	0.01
Malaysian (1)	3	0.01
Pakistani (24)	32	0.09
Sri Lankan (2)	2	0.01
Taiwanese (2)	2	0.01
Thai (9)	16	0.05
Vietnamese (36)	46	0.13
Hawaii Native/Pacific Islander (6)	32	0.09
Not Hispanic (4)	19	0.05
Hispanic (2)	13	0.04
Guamanian/Chamorro (0)	7	0.02
Native Hawaiian (2)	3	0.01
Samoan (2)	3	0.01
White (16,338)	17,219	48.85
Not Hispanic (14,095)	14,669	41.62
Hispanic (2,243)	2,550	7.23

Michigan City

Place Type: City
County: LaPorte
Population: 31,479†

Ancestry‡	Population	%
African, Sub-Saharan (569)	645	2.04
African (553)	629	1.99
Ethiopian (8)	8	0.03
Nigerian (8)	8	0.03
Albanian (26)	26	0.08
American (1,243)	1,243	3.93
Arab (202)	330	1.04
Arab (8)	18	0.06
Lebanese (180)	288	0.91
Moroccan (7)	7	0.02
Palestinian (7)	7	0.02
Syrian (0)	10	0.03
Assyrian/Chaldean/Syriac (0)	18	0.06
Austrian (13)	41	0.13
Belgian (8)	8	0.03
British (48)	48	0.15
Canadian (24)	61	0.19
Celtic (9)	9	0.03
Croatian (0)	23	0.07
Czech (23)	134	0.42
Czechoslovakian (7)	16	0.05
Danish (28)	133	0.42
Dutch (148)	689	2.18
English (556)	2,038	6.45
European (316)	327	1.03
Finnish (15)	15	0.05
French, ex. Basque (116)	707	2.24
French Canadian (37)	133	0.42
German (2,524)	6,819	21.57
Greek (99)	139	0.44
Hungarian (63)	205	0.65
Iranian (44)	44	0.14
Irish (863)	3,769	11.92
Italian (246)	1,044	3.30
Lithuanian (44)	94	0.30
Northern European (24)	24	0.08
Norwegian (59)	200	0.63
Pennsylvania German (24)	24	0.08
Polish (1,171)	3,027	9.58

*Notes: † The Census 2010 population figure is used to calculate the percentages in the Hispanic Origin and Race categories. Ancestry percentages are based on the 2006-2010 American Community Survey population (not shown); ‡ Numbers in parentheses indicate the number of people reporting a single ancestry; * Numbers in parentheses indicate the number of persons reporting this race alone, not in combination with any other race; Please refer to the Explanation of Data for more information.*

Portuguese (0)	37	0.12
Romanian (9)	54	0.17
Russian (40)	90	0.28
Scandinavian (16)	52	0.16
Scotch-Irish (80)	192	0.61
Scottish (134)	394	1.25
Slovak (7)	30	0.09
Slovene (0)	10	0.03
Swedish (98)	480	1.52
Swiss (0)	73	0.23
Ukrainian (28)	60	0.19
Welsh (10)	131	0.41
West Indian, ex. Hispanic (36)	44	0.14
Bermudan (9)	9	0.03
Haitian (13)	13	0.04
Jamaican (14)	22	0.07
Yugoslavian (0)	35	0.11

Hispanic Origin	Population	%
Hispanic or Latino (of any race)	1,843	5.85
Central American, ex. Mexican	46	0.15
Costa Rican	2	0.01
Guatemalan	15	0.05
Honduran	5	0.02
Nicaraguan	10	0.03
Panamanian	11	0.03
Salvadoran	3	0.01
Cuban	18	0.06
Dominican Republic	2	0.01
Mexican	1,400	4.45
Puerto Rican	233	0.74
South American	15	0.05
Argentinean	1	<0.01
Peruvian	12	0.04
Uruguayan	2	0.01
Other Hispanic or Latino	129	0.41

Race*	Population	%
African-American/Black (8,856)	9,686	30.77
Not Hispanic (8,741)	9,477	30.11
Hispanic (115)	209	0.66
American Indian/Alaska Native (120)	354	1.12
Not Hispanic (97)	289	0.92
Hispanic (23)	65	0.21
Aleut *(Alaska Native)* (1)	1	<0.01
Apache (2)	17	0.05
Blackfeet (1)	28	0.09
Canadian/French Am. Ind. (1)	1	<0.01
Cherokee (18)	81	0.26
Cheyenne (0)	1	<0.01
Chickasaw (1)	1	<0.01
Chippewa (3)	12	0.04
Choctaw (3)	6	0.02
Comanche (1)	1	<0.01
Iroquois (0)	4	0.01
Mexican American Ind. (4)	5	0.02
Navajo (0)	4	0.01
Potawatomi (1)	6	0.02
Shoshone (0)	2	0.01
Sioux (2)	13	0.04
South American Ind. (0)	1	<0.01
Spanish American Ind. (1)	1	<0.01
Asian (229)	320	1.02
Not Hispanic (226)	308	0.98
Hispanic (3)	12	0.04
Cambodian (2)	2	0.01
Chinese, ex. Taiwanese (51)	56	0.18
Filipino (36)	64	0.20
Indian (65)	77	0.24
Indonesian (1)	4	0.01
Japanese (7)	30	0.10
Korean (15)	21	0.07
Pakistani (15)	18	0.06
Thai (3)	3	0.01
Vietnamese (23)	25	0.08
Hawaii Native/Pacific Islander (8)	30	0.10
Not Hispanic (3)	21	0.07
Hispanic (5)	9	0.03
Native Hawaiian (1)	12	0.04
Samoan (4)	6	0.02
White (20,435)	21,485	68.25
Not Hispanic (19,595)	20,451	64.97
Hispanic (840)	1,034	3.28

Mishawaka

Place Type: City
County: St. Joseph
Population: 48,252†

Ancestry‡	Population	%
African, Sub-Saharan (416)	437	0.91
African (357)	357	0.75
Ghanaian (51)	51	0.11
Sierra Leonean (0)	21	0.04
Ugandan (8)	8	0.02
Albanian (9)	9	0.02
Alsatian (0)	12	0.03
American (2,478)	2,478	5.17
Arab (321)	475	0.99
Arab (53)	116	0.24
Egyptian (15)	15	0.03
Iraqi (0)	45	0.09
Lebanese (134)	166	0.35
Palestinian (119)	119	0.25
Syrian (0)	14	0.03
Assyrian/Chaldean/Syriac (0)	52	0.11
Austrian (27)	183	0.38
Belgian (485)	1,831	3.82
Brazilian (0)	33	0.07
British (98)	224	0.47
Cajun (0)	21	0.04
Canadian (0)	20	0.04
Celtic (16)	16	0.03
Croatian (23)	30	0.06
Czech (33)	121	0.25
Czechoslovakian (20)	56	0.12
Danish (52)	245	0.51
Dutch (233)	1,499	3.13
Eastern European (34)	34	0.07
English (1,046)	4,681	9.77
Estonian (0)	37	0.08
European (268)	307	0.64
Finnish (27)	52	0.11
French, ex. Basque (289)	1,835	3.83
French Canadian (55)	278	0.58
German (4,284)	13,286	27.74
German Russian (0)	10	0.02
Greek (35)	104	0.22
Hungarian (548)	1,337	2.79
Iranian (0)	9	0.02
Irish (1,850)	7,382	15.41
Italian (944)	2,342	4.89
Lithuanian (21)	77	0.16
Macedonian (0)	96	0.20
Northern European (45)	73	0.15
Norwegian (109)	428	0.89
Pennsylvania German (76)	129	0.27
Polish (1,771)	4,612	9.63
Portuguese (0)	62	0.13
Romanian (16)	30	0.06
Russian (41)	311	0.65
Scandinavian (41)	66	0.14
Scotch-Irish (247)	847	1.77
Scottish (259)	764	1.60
Serbian (32)	48	0.10
Slavic (13)	29	0.06
Slovak (0)	103	0.22
Slovene (23)	34	0.07
Swedish (249)	1,045	2.18
Swiss (31)	299	0.62
Ukrainian (23)	93	0.19
Welsh (44)	186	0.39
West Indian, ex. Hispanic (55)	80	0.17
Jamaican (20)	45	0.09
West Indian (35)	35	0.07
Yugoslavian (435)	446	0.93

Hispanic Origin	Population	%
Hispanic or Latino (of any race)	2,175	4.51
Central American, ex. Mexican	103	0.21
Costa Rican	4	0.01
Guatemalan	26	0.05
Honduran	28	0.06
Nicaraguan	2	<0.01
Panamanian	13	0.03
Salvadoran	30	0.06
Cuban	35	0.07
Dominican Republic	13	0.03
Mexican	1,607	3.33
Puerto Rican	180	0.37
South American	100	0.21
Argentinean	9	0.02
Chilean	4	0.01
Colombian	26	0.05
Ecuadorian	9	0.02
Peruvian	7	0.01
Uruguayan	6	0.01
Venezuelan	36	0.07
Other South American	3	0.01
Other Hispanic or Latino	137	0.28

Race*	Population	%
African-American/Black (3,326)	4,103	8.50
Not Hispanic (3,250)	3,965	8.22
Hispanic (76)	138	0.29
American Indian/Alaska Native (200)	550	1.14
Not Hispanic (173)	489	1.01
Hispanic (27)	61	0.13
Aleut *(Alaska Native)* (0)	1	<0.01
Apache (2)	6	0.01
Arapaho (1)	1	<0.01
Blackfeet (1)	11	0.02
Canadian/French Am. Ind. (2)	4	0.01
Cherokee (24)	115	0.24
Cheyenne (1)	1	<0.01
Chickasaw (3)	7	0.01
Chippewa (6)	13	0.03
Choctaw (0)	9	0.02
Cree (0)	2	<0.01
Creek (5)	7	0.01
Crow (0)	2	<0.01
Delaware (0)	6	0.01
Hopi (1)	1	<0.01
Iroquois (1)	3	0.01
Menominee (2)	2	<0.01
Mexican American Ind. (11)	14	0.03
Navajo (1)	1	<0.01
Ottawa (3)	6	0.01
Potawatomi (26)	58	0.12
Pueblo (1)	1	<0.01
Puget Sound Salish (1)	2	<0.01
Seminole (0)	2	<0.01
Sioux (1)	13	0.03
South American Ind. (0)	2	<0.01
Yup'ik *(Alaska Native)* (1)	1	<0.01
Asian (937)	1,138	2.36
Not Hispanic (933)	1,116	2.31
Hispanic (4)	22	0.05
Bangladeshi (1)	1	<0.01
Cambodian (21)	32	0.07
Chinese, ex. Taiwanese (252)	283	0.59
Filipino (45)	90	0.19
Indian (232)	263	0.55
Indonesian (1)	1	<0.01
Japanese (41)	57	0.12
Korean (131)	167	0.35
Laotian (13)	19	0.04
Malaysian (1)	1	<0.01
Pakistani (35)	39	0.08
Sri Lankan (3)	3	0.01
Taiwanese (14)	15	0.03
Thai (11)	11	0.02
Vietnamese (103)	120	0.25
Hawaii Native/Pacific Islander (45)	85	0.18
Not Hispanic (42)	79	0.16
Hispanic (3)	6	0.01
Guamanian/Chamorro (5)	8	0.02
Native Hawaiian (17)	30	0.06
Samoan (5)	9	0.02

*Notes: † The Census 2010 population figure is used to calculate the percentages in the Hispanic Origin and Race categories. Ancestry percentages are based on the 2006-2010 American Community Survey population (not shown); ‡ Numbers in parentheses indicate the number of people reporting a single ancestry; * Numbers in parentheses indicate the number of persons reporting this race alone, not in combination with any other race; Please refer to the Explanation of Data for more information.*

SECTION TWO

Tongan (6)	8	0.02
White (41,538)	42,848	88.80
Not Hispanic (40,430)	41,534	86.08
Hispanic (1,108)	1,314	2.72

Mooresville

Place Type: Town
County: Morgan
Population: 9,326†

Ancestry‡	Population	%
American (1,083)	1,083	11.59
Belgian (0)	26	0.28
Dutch (136)	311	3.33
English (668)	1,233	13.19
European (67)	67	0.72
French, ex. Basque (17)	201	2.15
French Canadian (43)	54	0.58
German (713)	2,373	25.39
Greek (0)	34	0.36
Irish (418)	1,417	15.16
Italian (109)	162	1.73
Northern European (0)	12	0.13
Norwegian (11)	68	0.73
Pennsylvania German (0)	11	0.12
Polish (116)	265	2.83
Romanian (19)	67	0.72
Scandinavian (0)	66	0.71
Scotch-Irish (25)	247	2.64
Scottish (100)	295	3.16
Swedish (0)	84	0.90
Swiss (0)	37	0.40
Ukrainian (0)	24	0.26
Welsh (13)	27	0.29

Hispanic Origin	Population	%
Hispanic or Latino (of any race)	100	1.07
Central American, ex. Mexican	11	0.12
Costa Rican	1	0.01
Honduran	3	0.03
Panamanian	7	0.08
Mexican	53	0.57
Puerto Rican	9	0.10
South American	11	0.12
Argentinean	1	0.01
Colombian	3	0.03
Ecuadorian	2	0.02
Peruvian	4	0.04
Venezuelan	1	0.01
Other Hispanic or Latino	16	0.17

Race*	Population	%
African-American/Black (26)	76	0.81
Not Hispanic (26)	76	0.81
American Indian/Alaska Native (19)	60	0.64
Not Hispanic (19)	59	0.63
Hispanic (0)	1	0.01
Apache (0)	1	0.01
Blackfeet (2)	2	0.02
Cherokee (5)	25	0.27
Choctaw (2)	5	0.05
Comanche (4)	4	0.04
Inupiat *(Alaska Native)* (2)	2	0.02
Shoshone (0)	1	0.01
Sioux (1)	7	0.08
Asian (44)	64	0.69
Not Hispanic (42)	62	0.66
Hispanic (2)	2	0.02
Cambodian (2)	2	0.02
Chinese, ex. Taiwanese (19)	21	0.23
Filipino (7)	16	0.17
Japanese (5)	10	0.11
Korean (3)	8	0.09
Vietnamese (6)	6	0.06
Hawaii Native/Pacific Islander (2)	7	0.08
Not Hispanic (2)	7	0.08
Guamanian/Chamorro (1)	6	0.06
Native Hawaiian (1)	1	0.01
White (9,096)	9,207	98.72
Not Hispanic (9,032)	9,136	97.96
Hispanic (64)	71	0.76

Muncie

Place Type: City
County: Delaware
Population: 70,085†

Ancestry‡	Population	%
African, Sub-Saharan (668)	875	1.25
African (546)	737	1.05
Kenyan (14)	14	0.02
South African (0)	16	0.02
Other Sub-Saharan African (108)	108	0.15
Albanian (57)	57	0.08
Alsatian (0)	22	0.03
American (6,079)	6,079	8.68
Arab (7)	204	0.29
Arab (0)	84	0.12
Egyptian (0)	14	0.02
Iraqi (0)	14	0.02
Moroccan (0)	13	0.02
Palestinian (7)	7	0.01
Syrian (0)	66	0.09
Other Arab (0)	6	0.01
Australian (14)	27	0.04
Austrian (9)	45	0.06
Belgian (0)	110	0.16
British (225)	372	0.53
Bulgarian (9)	9	0.01
Canadian (125)	194	0.28
Celtic (10)	10	0.01
Croatian (0)	103	0.15
Czech (63)	87	0.12
Danish (36)	119	0.17
Dutch (245)	1,417	2.02
English (2,398)	6,521	9.31
European (449)	525	0.75
Finnish (26)	42	0.06
French, ex. Basque (286)	1,865	2.66
French Canadian (26)	64	0.09
German (5,967)	14,993	21.41
Greek (143)	214	0.31
Hungarian (78)	175	0.25
Iranian (72)	78	0.11
Irish (2,747)	9,462	13.51
Israeli (13)	24	0.03
Italian (867)	1,965	2.81
Latvian (0)	9	0.01
Lithuanian (64)	77	0.11
Luxemburger (0)	32	0.05
Macedonian (12)	23	0.03
New Zealander (0)	18	0.03
Northern European (17)	17	0.02
Norwegian (47)	422	0.60
Pennsylvania German (0)	14	0.02
Polish (413)	1,148	1.64
Portuguese (0)	12	0.02
Romanian (40)	59	0.08
Russian (59)	162	0.23
Scandinavian (0)	14	0.02
Scotch-Irish (395)	930	1.33
Scottish (318)	1,264	1.81
Serbian (0)	15	0.02
Slavic (22)	22	0.03
Slovak (30)	118	0.17
Swedish (144)	494	0.71
Swiss (84)	326	0.47
Turkish (34)	34	0.05
Ukrainian (0)	30	0.04
Welsh (78)	511	0.73
West Indian, ex. Hispanic (41)	41	0.06
Barbadian (28)	28	0.04
Jamaican (13)	13	0.02
Yugoslavian (12)	27	0.04

Hispanic Origin	Population	%
Hispanic or Latino (of any race)	1,579	2.25
Central American, ex. Mexican	62	0.09
Costa Rican	5	0.01
Guatemalan	9	0.01
Honduran	12	0.02
Nicaraguan	3	<0.01
Panamanian	21	0.03
Salvadoran	11	0.02
Other Central American	1	<0.01
Cuban	38	0.05
Dominican Republic	21	0.03
Mexican	1,061	1.51
Puerto Rican	133	0.19
South American	63	0.09
Argentinean	7	0.01
Bolivian	5	0.01
Chilean	11	0.02
Colombian	6	0.01
Ecuadorian	2	<0.01
Paraguayan	1	<0.01
Peruvian	12	0.02
Uruguayan	2	<0.01
Venezuelan	13	0.02
Other South American	4	0.01
Other Hispanic or Latino	201	0.29

Race*	Population	%
African-American/Black (7,655)	8,829	12.60
Not Hispanic (7,569)	8,664	12.36
Hispanic (86)	165	0.24
American Indian/Alaska Native (203)	650	0.93
Not Hispanic (174)	577	0.82
Hispanic (29)	73	0.10
Apache (0)	12	0.02
Arapaho (0)	1	<0.01
Blackfeet (5)	42	0.06
Cherokee (51)	182	0.26
Chippewa (2)	5	0.01
Choctaw (1)	3	<0.01
Cree (1)	5	0.01
Creek (0)	2	<0.01
Crow (2)	2	<0.01
Delaware (0)	2	<0.01
Iroquois (5)	7	0.01
Lumbee (3)	3	<0.01
Menominee (1)	1	<0.01
Mexican American Ind. (9)	11	0.02
Navajo (4)	7	0.01
Osage (0)	1	<0.01
Potawatomi (5)	5	0.01
Pueblo (0)	1	<0.01
Puget Sound Salish (1)	1	<0.01
Seminole (1)	2	<0.01
Shoshone (0)	6	0.01
Sioux (8)	20	0.03
South American Ind. (2)	4	0.01
Spanish American Ind. (2)	2	<0.01
Asian (849)	1,173	1.67
Not Hispanic (839)	1,143	1.63
Hispanic (10)	30	0.04
Bangladeshi (21)	23	0.03
Burmese (2)	2	<0.01
Chinese, ex. Taiwanese (250)	282	0.40
Filipino (74)	143	0.20
Hmong (2)	2	<0.01
Indian (196)	248	0.35
Indonesian (2)	2	<0.01
Japanese (48)	86	0.12
Korean (111)	142	0.20
Laotian (2)	3	<0.01
Malaysian (1)	3	<0.01
Nepalese (10)	13	0.02
Pakistani (12)	14	0.02
Sri Lankan (4)	4	0.01
Taiwanese (22)	25	0.04
Thai (9)	16	0.02
Vietnamese (51)	62	0.09
Hawaii Native/Pacific Islander (42)	138	0.20
Not Hispanic (39)	126	0.18
Hispanic (3)	12	0.02
Fijian (0)	1	<0.01
Guamanian/Chamorro (3)	12	0.02

*Notes: † The Census 2010 population figure is used to calculate the percentages in the Hispanic Origin and Race categories. Ancestry percentages are based on the 2006-2010 American Community Survey population (not shown); ‡ Numbers in parentheses indicate the number of people reporting a single ancestry; * Numbers in parentheses indicate the number of persons reporting this race alone, not in combination with any other race; Please refer to the Explanation of Data for more information.*

	Population	%
Native Hawaiian (15)	44	0.06
Samoan (9)	19	0.03
Tongan (1)	3	<0.01
White (58,853)	60,636	86.52
Not Hispanic (58,018)	59,588	85.02
Hispanic (835)	1,048	1.50

Munster

Place Type: Town
County: Lake
Population: 23,603†

Ancestry‡	Population	%
Afghan (3)	3	0.01
Albanian (10)	10	0.04
American (658)	658	2.83
Arab (144)	144	0.62
Jordanian (13)	13	0.06
Palestinian (96)	96	0.41
Syrian (35)	35	0.15
Austrian (12)	77	0.33
Belgian (9)	18	0.08
British (10)	29	0.12
Bulgarian (0)	55	0.24
Carpatho Rusyn (11)	11	0.05
Croatian (167)	516	2.22
Czech (19)	32	0.14
Czechoslovakian (0)	71	0.31
Danish (20)	105	0.45
Dutch (618)	1,068	4.59
English (497)	1,611	6.93
Estonian (0)	33	0.14
European (183)	183	0.79
Finnish (0)	78	0.34
French, ex. Basque (93)	759	3.26
French Canadian (0)	97	0.42
German (1,194)	4,650	20.00
Greek (495)	784	3.37
Hungarian (146)	248	1.07
Irish (799)	3,765	16.19
Italian (680)	1,829	7.87
Latvian (0)	23	0.10
Lithuanian (51)	274	1.18
Macedonian (118)	145	0.62
Norwegian (30)	136	0.58
Pennsylvania German (0)	11	0.05
Polish (1,628)	3,822	16.44
Portuguese (0)	12	0.05
Romanian (37)	153	0.66
Russian (131)	335	1.44
Scandinavian (10)	10	0.04
Scotch-Irish (28)	112	0.48
Scottish (41)	230	0.99
Serbian (844)	984	4.23
Slavic (18)	35	0.15
Slovak (380)	814	3.50
Slovene (23)	51	0.22
Swedish (200)	698	3.00
Swiss (11)	28	0.12
Turkish (33)	33	0.14
Ukrainian (35)	70	0.30
Welsh (49)	198	0.85
West Indian, ex. Hispanic (31)	31	0.13
Belizean (31)	31	0.13
Yugoslavian (71)	81	0.35

Hispanic Origin	Population	%
Hispanic or Latino (of any race)	2,410	10.21
Central American, ex. Mexican	34	0.14
Costa Rican	2	0.01
Guatemalan	12	0.05
Honduran	10	0.04
Nicaraguan	5	0.02
Salvadoran	5	0.02
Cuban	18	0.08
Dominican Republic	9	0.04
Mexican	1,965	8.33
Puerto Rican	216	0.92
South American	83	0.35
Argentinean	6	0.03
Bolivian	1	<0.01
Chilean	4	0.02
Colombian	21	0.09
Ecuadorian	24	0.10
Peruvian	22	0.09
Uruguayan	2	0.01
Venezuelan	3	0.01
Other Hispanic or Latino	85	0.36

Race*	Population	%
African-American/Black (821)	916	3.88
Not Hispanic (806)	878	3.72
Hispanic (15)	38	0.16
American Indian/Alaska Native (47)	122	0.52
Not Hispanic (29)	87	0.37
Hispanic (18)	35	0.15
Alaska Athabascan *(Ala. Nat.)* (1)	1	<0.01
Apache (1)	5	0.02
Blackfeet (2)	4	0.02
Canadian/French Am. Ind. (0)	2	0.01
Cherokee (8)	45	0.19
Chippewa (0)	1	<0.01
Choctaw (0)	2	0.01
Lumbee (0)	3	0.01
Menominee (0)	2	0.01
Mexican American Ind. (2)	2	0.01
Navajo (3)	3	0.01
Ottawa (0)	1	<0.01
Sioux (3)	6	0.03
Tlingit-Haida *(Alaska Native)* (1)	1	<0.01
Tohono O'Odham (1)	1	<0.01
Asian (1,377)	1,536	6.51
Not Hispanic (1,369)	1,514	6.41
Hispanic (8)	22	0.09
Bangladeshi (13)	13	0.06
Chinese, ex. Taiwanese (173)	178	0.75
Filipino (227)	268	1.14
Indian (690)	718	3.04
Indonesian (0)	1	<0.01
Japanese (16)	31	0.13
Korean (114)	128	0.54
Laotian (1)	1	<0.01
Malaysian (3)	5	0.02
Nepalese (13)	14	0.06
Pakistani (51)	55	0.23
Taiwanese (20)	20	0.08
Thai (16)	27	0.11
Vietnamese (18)	19	0.08
Hawaii Native/Pacific Islander (3)	14	0.06
Not Hispanic (2)	13	0.06
Hispanic (1)	1	<0.01
Fijian (1)	1	<0.01
Guamanian/Chamorro (0)	1	<0.01
Native Hawaiian (1)	2	0.01
Samoan (0)	2	0.01
White (20,208)	20,589	87.23
Not Hispanic (18,689)	18,935	80.22
Hispanic (1,519)	1,654	7.01

New Albany

Place Type: City
County: Floyd
Population: 36,372†

Ancestry‡	Population	%
African, Sub-Saharan (9)	30	0.08
African (9)	30	0.08
American (3,223)	3,223	8.85
Arab (24)	56	0.15
Lebanese (11)	43	0.12
Palestinian (13)	13	0.04
Armenian (0)	8	0.02
Basque (0)	17	0.05
Belgian (16)	16	0.04
British (81)	127	0.35
Bulgarian (0)	7	0.02
Canadian (0)	18	0.05
Celtic (0)	14	0.04
Croatian (33)	66	0.18
Czech (0)	19	0.05
Czechoslovakian (0)	8	0.02
Danish (0)	40	0.11
Dutch (156)	665	1.83
English (1,458)	3,635	9.98
European (373)	411	1.13
French, ex. Basque (183)	1,396	3.83
French Canadian (52)	52	0.14
German (3,502)	8,711	23.91
Greek (16)	34	0.09
Hungarian (0)	63	0.17
Irish (1,789)	5,146	14.12
Italian (191)	625	1.72
Lithuanian (11)	45	0.12
Norwegian (83)	160	0.44
Polish (79)	293	0.80
Portuguese (0)	43	0.12
Romanian (0)	60	0.16
Russian (15)	35	0.10
Scandinavian (19)	19	0.05
Scotch-Irish (263)	806	2.21
Scottish (274)	826	2.27
Slavic (0)	11	0.03
Swedish (14)	68	0.19
Swiss (45)	176	0.48
Ukrainian (0)	20	0.05
Welsh (86)	216	0.59

Hispanic Origin	Population	%
Hispanic or Latino (of any race)	1,338	3.68
Central American, ex. Mexican	79	0.22
Costa Rican	2	0.01
Guatemalan	20	0.05
Honduran	25	0.07
Panamanian	11	0.03
Salvadoran	20	0.05
Other Central American	1	<0.01
Cuban	21	0.06
Dominican Republic	3	0.01
Mexican	1,004	2.76
Puerto Rican	109	0.30
South American	29	0.08
Argentinean	1	<0.01
Bolivian	1	<0.01
Chilean	2	0.01
Colombian	6	0.02
Ecuadorian	8	0.02
Peruvian	6	0.02
Venezuelan	5	0.01
Other Hispanic or Latino	93	0.26

Race*	Population	%
African-American/Black (3,159)	3,857	10.60
Not Hispanic (3,114)	3,776	10.38
Hispanic (45)	81	0.22
American Indian/Alaska Native (82)	307	0.84
Not Hispanic (75)	284	0.78
Hispanic (7)	23	0.06
Apache (3)	6	0.02
Blackfeet (2)	15	0.04
Central American Ind. (1)	2	0.01
Cherokee (29)	118	0.32
Chickasaw (2)	4	0.01
Chippewa (3)	6	0.02
Choctaw (5)	11	0.03
Creek (0)	2	0.01
Iroquois (0)	1	<0.01
Lumbee (2)	2	0.01
Mexican American Ind. (3)	4	0.01
Navajo (0)	2	0.01
Potawatomi (1)	2	0.01
Seminole (0)	3	0.01
Sioux (3)	7	0.02
Tlingit-Haida *(Alaska Native)* (0)	1	<0.01
Asian (248)	375	1.03
Not Hispanic (243)	362	1.00
Hispanic (5)	13	0.04
Cambodian (1)	5	0.01
Chinese, ex. Taiwanese (40)	56	0.15

SECTION TWO

*Notes: † The Census 2010 population figure is used to calculate the percentages in the Hispanic Origin and Race categories. Ancestry percentages are based on the 2006-2010 American Community Survey population (not shown); ‡ Numbers in parentheses indicate the number of people reporting a single ancestry; * Numbers in parentheses indicate the number of persons reporting this race alone, not in combination with any other race; Please refer to the Explanation of Data for more information.*

Filipino (44)	75	0.21
Hmong (1)	4	0.01
Indian (48)	60	0.16
Indonesian (0)	2	0.01
Japanese (10)	27	0.07
Korean (19)	49	0.13
Laotian (3)	4	0.01
Pakistani (32)	32	0.09
Taiwanese (5)	6	0.02
Thai (2)	8	0.02
Vietnamese (19)	25	0.07
Hawaii Native/Pacific Islander (8)	38	0.10
Not Hispanic (8)	31	0.09
Hispanic (0)	7	0.02
Guamanian/Chamorro (1)	5	0.01
Native Hawaiian (7)	18	0.05
Samoan (0)	6	0.02
White (31,194)	32,179	88.47
Not Hispanic (30,615)	31,462	86.50
Hispanic (579)	717	1.97

New Castle

Place Type: City
County: Henry
Population: 18,114†

Ancestry‡	Population	%
American (2,243)	2,243	12.32
Austrian (0)	11	0.06
British (29)	39	0.21
Croatian (0)	12	0.07
Czech (0)	48	0.26
Czechoslovakian (29)	29	0.16
Danish (0)	45	0.25
Dutch (143)	377	2.07
English (903)	1,367	7.51
European (130)	143	0.79
Finnish (0)	10	0.05
French, ex. Basque (81)	293	1.61
German (1,659)	3,052	16.76
Greek (0)	12	0.07
Hungarian (46)	70	0.38
Irish (690)	2,094	11.50
Italian (113)	282	1.55
Northern European (36)	36	0.20
Norwegian (19)	79	0.43
Polish (54)	104	0.57
Portuguese (35)	35	0.19
Russian (8)	8	0.04
Scandinavian (15)	43	0.24
Scotch-Irish (185)	223	1.22
Scottish (215)	444	2.44
Slovak (0)	9	0.05
Swedish (20)	42	0.23
Swiss (0)	7	0.04
Welsh (0)	21	0.12
West Indian, ex. Hispanic (0)	11	0.06
Dutch West Indian (0)	11	0.06

Hispanic Origin	Population	%
Hispanic or Latino (of any race)	309	1.71
Central American, ex. Mexican	6	0.03
Guatemalan	2	0.01
Panamanian	1	0.01
Salvadoran	3	0.02
Cuban	21	0.12
Dominican Republic	2	0.01
Mexican	203	1.12
Puerto Rican	21	0.12
South American	7	0.04
Colombian	1	0.01
Peruvian	4	0.02
Venezuelan	2	0.01
Other Hispanic or Latino	49	0.27

Race*	Population	%
African-American/Black (347)	515	2.84
Not Hispanic (346)	504	2.78
Hispanic (1)	11	0.06
American Indian/Alaska Native (37)	164	0.91
Not Hispanic (31)	148	0.82
Hispanic (6)	16	0.09
Apache (0)	1	0.01
Blackfeet (1)	8	0.04
Cherokee (6)	41	0.23
Chippewa (1)	2	0.01
Choctaw (1)	2	0.01
Mexican American Ind. (2)	2	0.01
Ottawa (0)	1	0.01
Seminole (0)	2	0.01
Sioux (1)	5	0.03
South American Ind. (1)	1	0.01
Ute (1)	1	0.01
Asian (73)	110	0.61
Not Hispanic (72)	105	0.58
Hispanic (1)	5	0.03
Chinese, ex. Taiwanese (11)	24	0.13
Filipino (3)	10	0.06
Indian (33)	37	0.20
Japanese (3)	4	0.02
Korean (6)	12	0.07
Malaysian (1)	1	0.01
Pakistani (3)	3	0.02
Thai (1)	1	0.01
Vietnamese (11)	12	0.07
Hawaii Native/Pacific Islander (2)	11	0.06
Not Hispanic (2)	10	0.06
Hispanic (0)	1	0.01
Guamanian/Chamorro (1)	1	0.01
Native Hawaiian (1)	6	0.03
White (17,227)	17,539	96.83
Not Hispanic (17,051)	17,323	95.63
Hispanic (176)	216	1.19

New Haven

Place Type: City
County: Allen
Population: 14,794†

Ancestry‡	Population	%
African, Sub-Saharan (222)	222	1.60
African (222)	222	1.60
American (2,066)	2,066	14.91
Arab (54)	108	0.78
Egyptian (17)	71	0.51
Lebanese (37)	37	0.27
Austrian (14)	14	0.10
British (24)	61	0.44
Celtic (0)	9	0.06
Czech (0)	18	0.13
Czechoslovakian (5)	13	0.09
Dutch (48)	215	1.55
English (326)	1,106	7.98
European (80)	80	0.58
Finnish (0)	11	0.08
French, ex. Basque (272)	912	6.58
French Canadian (16)	26	0.19
German (2,403)	5,192	37.47
Greek (11)	11	0.08
Hungarian (30)	62	0.45
Icelander (0)	7	0.05
Irish (352)	1,976	14.26
Italian (289)	597	4.31
Macedonian (17)	17	0.12
Norwegian (38)	161	1.16
Pennsylvania German (12)	12	0.09
Polish (130)	359	2.59
Romanian (0)	27	0.19
Russian (0)	7	0.05
Scandinavian (0)	32	0.23
Scotch-Irish (35)	77	0.56
Scottish (149)	451	3.25
Slovak (0)	17	0.12
Swedish (0)	50	0.36
Swiss (48)	207	1.49
Ukrainian (0)	108	0.78
Welsh (19)	46	0.33

Hispanic Origin	Population	%
Hispanic or Latino (of any race)	464	3.14
Central American, ex. Mexican	24	0.16
Guatemalan	18	0.12
Nicaraguan	1	0.01
Panamanian	1	0.01
Salvadoran	4	0.03
Cuban	3	0.02
Dominican Republic	1	0.01
Mexican	337	2.28
Puerto Rican	31	0.21
South American	8	0.05
Argentinean	1	0.01
Colombian	5	0.03
Paraguayan	1	0.01
Peruvian	1	0.01
Other Hispanic or Latino	60	0.41

Race*	Population	%
African-American/Black (489)	621	4.20
Not Hispanic (475)	592	4.00
Hispanic (14)	29	0.20
American Indian/Alaska Native (54)	130	0.88
Not Hispanic (40)	90	0.61
Hispanic (14)	40	0.27
Apache (1)	2	0.01
Blackfeet (6)	10	0.07
Cherokee (6)	30	0.20
Cheyenne (0)	1	0.01
Chippewa (5)	6	0.04
Choctaw (0)	2	0.01
Creek (2)	2	0.01
Mexican American Ind. (1)	4	0.03
Osage (2)	5	0.03
Potawatomi (1)	1	0.01
Asian (63)	94	0.64
Not Hispanic (63)	87	0.59
Hispanic (0)	7	0.05
Burmese (3)	5	0.03
Chinese, ex. Taiwanese (14)	19	0.13
Filipino (19)	31	0.21
Indian (10)	13	0.09
Japanese (1)	1	0.01
Korean (7)	8	0.05
Laotian (2)	4	0.03
Thai (1)	2	0.01
Vietnamese (2)	6	0.04
Hawaii Native/Pacific Islander (8)	13	0.09
Not Hispanic (8)	12	0.08
Hispanic (0)	1	0.01
Native Hawaiian (7)	7	0.05
Samoan (1)	1	0.01
White (13,792)	14,035	94.87
Not Hispanic (13,532)	13,715	92.71
Hispanic (260)	320	2.16

Noblesville

Place Type: City
County: Hamilton
Population: 51,969†

Ancestry‡	Population	%
African, Sub-Saharan (155)	278	0.57
African (98)	221	0.45
Kenyan (57)	57	0.12
Albanian (40)	40	0.08
American (4,429)	4,429	9.09
Arab (55)	183	0.38
Arab (0)	113	0.23
Egyptian (30)	30	0.06
Lebanese (13)	18	0.04
Moroccan (12)	12	0.02
Syrian (0)	10	0.02
Australian (14)	14	0.03
Austrian (25)	25	0.05
Belgian (32)	247	0.51
Brazilian (28)	28	0.06
British (102)	213	0.44
Bulgarian (29)	41	0.08

*Notes: † The Census 2010 population figure is used to calculate the percentages in the Hispanic Origin and Race categories. Ancestry percentages are based on the 2006-2010 American Community Survey population (not shown); ‡ Numbers in parentheses indicate the number of people reporting a single ancestry; * Numbers in parentheses indicate the number of persons reporting this race alone, not in combination with any other race; Please refer to the Explanation of Data for more information.*

Canadian (32)	57	0.12
Celtic (0)	15	0.03
Croatian (17)	56	0.11
Czech (68)	109	0.22
Czechoslovakian (84)	108	0.22
Danish (24)	71	0.15
Dutch (352)	1,089	2.24
Eastern European (126)	126	0.26
English (1,576)	5,811	11.93
European (875)	1,091	2.24
Finnish (53)	67	0.14
French, ex. Basque (320)	1,734	3.56
French Canadian (90)	186	0.38
German (5,244)	13,766	28.26
Greek (100)	174	0.36
Hungarian (60)	207	0.42
Iranian (56)	131	0.27
Irish (1,929)	7,262	14.91
Italian (726)	2,728	5.60
Latvian (41)	167	0.34
Lithuanian (9)	46	0.09
Macedonian (12)	25	0.05
Northern European (24)	24	0.05
Norwegian (100)	621	1.27
Pennsylvania German (69)	83	0.17
Polish (653)	1,516	3.11
Portuguese (27)	27	0.06
Romanian (33)	62	0.13
Russian (142)	216	0.44
Scandinavian (14)	83	0.17
Scotch-Irish (220)	817	1.68
Scottish (383)	1,261	2.59
Serbian (24)	70	0.14
Slovak (45)	139	0.29
Slovene (12)	12	0.02
Swedish (132)	695	1.43
Swiss (41)	212	0.44
Turkish (26)	52	0.11
Ukrainian (191)	436	0.90
Welsh (132)	497	1.02
West Indian, ex. Hispanic (75)	75	0.15
Bermudan (19)	19	0.04
Haitian (12)	12	0.02
Jamaican (31)	31	0.06
Trinidadian/Tobagonian (13)	13	0.03
Yugoslavian (121)	121	0.25

Hispanic Origin	Population	%
Hispanic or Latino (of any race)	2,209	4.25
Central American, ex. Mexican	244	0.47
Costa Rican	19	0.04
Guatemalan	59	0.11
Honduran	31	0.06
Nicaraguan	14	0.03
Panamanian	10	0.02
Salvadoran	111	0.21
Cuban	43	0.08
Dominican Republic	40	0.08
Mexican	1,245	2.40
Puerto Rican	210	0.40
South American	253	0.49
Argentinean	19	0.04
Bolivian	11	0.02
Chilean	11	0.02
Colombian	68	0.13
Ecuadorian	4	0.01
Peruvian	41	0.08
Uruguayan	2	<0.01
Venezuelan	97	0.19
Other Hispanic or Latino	174	0.33

Race*	Population	%
African-American/Black (1,896)	2,300	4.43
Not Hispanic (1,840)	2,196	4.23
Hispanic (56)	104	0.20
American Indian/Alaska Native (109)	281	0.54
Not Hispanic (87)	243	0.47
Hispanic (22)	38	0.07
Apache (0)	5	0.01
Blackfeet (6)	16	0.03
Cherokee (13)	58	0.11
Chippewa (10)	18	0.03
Choctaw (1)	5	0.01
Creek (4)	8	0.02
Crow (1)	1	<0.01
Inupiat *(Alaska Native)* (0)	1	<0.01
Mexican American Ind. (9)	10	0.02
Navajo (5)	5	0.01
Osage (1)	1	<0.01
Potawatomi (1)	1	<0.01
Seminole (0)	1	<0.01
Shoshone (0)	1	<0.01
Sioux (6)	11	0.02
South American Ind. (1)	2	<0.01
Ute (2)	2	<0.01
Yaqui (0)	1	<0.01
Asian (874)	1,149	2.21
Not Hispanic (864)	1,128	2.17
Hispanic (10)	21	0.04
Bangladeshi (12)	12	0.02
Cambodian (21)	26	0.05
Chinese, ex. Taiwanese (125)	157	0.30
Filipino (114)	198	0.38
Hmong (12)	14	0.03
Indian (241)	262	0.50
Indonesian (12)	15	0.03
Japanese (43)	86	0.17
Korean (94)	143	0.28
Laotian (4)	13	0.03
Malaysian (5)	5	0.01
Pakistani (11)	12	0.02
Sri Lankan (7)	7	0.01
Taiwanese (2)	2	<0.01
Thai (12)	24	0.05
Vietnamese (123)	139	0.27
Hawaii Native/Pacific Islander (35)	80	0.15
Not Hispanic (24)	61	0.12
Hispanic (11)	19	0.04
Guamanian/Chamorro (2)	7	0.01
Marshallese (1)	1	<0.01
Native Hawaiian (27)	51	0.10
Samoan (3)	11	0.02
Tongan (1)	1	<0.01
White (47,333)	48,170	92.69
Not Hispanic (46,089)	46,797	90.05
Hispanic (1,244)	1,373	2.64

Peru

Place Type: City
County: Miami
Population: 11,417†

Ancestry‡	Population	%
African, Sub-Saharan (59)	59	0.51
African (51)	51	0.44
South African (8)	8	0.07
American (1,459)	1,459	12.62
Armenian (11)	11	0.10
British (5)	11	0.10
Canadian (20)	42	0.36
Croatian (0)	11	0.10
Czech (8)	59	0.51
Danish (0)	53	0.46
Dutch (68)	251	2.17
English (312)	879	7.60
European (96)	133	1.15
French, ex. Basque (46)	207	1.79
French Canadian (64)	149	1.29
German (1,427)	3,110	26.90
Greek (0)	54	0.47
Hungarian (36)	114	0.99
Irish (318)	1,766	15.27
Italian (438)	550	4.76
Lithuanian (18)	63	0.54
Northern European (8)	8	0.07
Norwegian (11)	37	0.32
Pennsylvania German (34)	34	0.29
Polish (32)	105	0.91
Romanian (0)	18	0.16
Russian (0)	8	0.07
Scandinavian (0)	7	0.06
Scotch-Irish (15)	139	1.20
Scottish (21)	154	1.33
Swedish (41)	77	0.67
Swiss (0)	23	0.20
Welsh (17)	65	0.56

Hispanic Origin	Population	%
Hispanic or Latino (of any race)	274	2.40
Central American, ex. Mexican	12	0.11
Honduran	8	0.07
Salvadoran	4	0.04
Cuban	10	0.09
Mexican	195	1.71
Puerto Rican	46	0.40
South American	2	0.02
Peruvian	2	0.02
Other Hispanic or Latino	9	0.08

Race*	Population	%
African-American/Black (280)	402	3.52
Not Hispanic (265)	376	3.29
Hispanic (15)	26	0.23
American Indian/Alaska Native (146)	244	2.14
Not Hispanic (131)	227	1.99
Hispanic (15)	17	0.15
Apache (0)	1	0.01
Blackfeet (2)	9	0.08
Cherokee (16)	34	0.30
Chippewa (4)	7	0.06
Choctaw (6)	6	0.05
Cree (1)	1	0.01
Iroquois (0)	1	0.01
Mexican American Ind. (1)	1	0.01
Potawatomi (2)	3	0.03
Sioux (0)	4	0.04
South American Ind. (2)	2	0.02
Ute (1)	1	0.01
Asian (47)	87	0.76
Not Hispanic (47)	87	0.76
Chinese, ex. Taiwanese (15)	16	0.14
Filipino (11)	21	0.18
Indian (4)	7	0.06
Indonesian (2)	3	0.03
Japanese (4)	10	0.09
Korean (5)	18	0.16
Taiwanese (1)	2	0.02
Thai (3)	5	0.04
Vietnamese (1)	2	0.02
Hawaii Native/Pacific Islander (2)	9	0.08
Not Hispanic (2)	9	0.08
Guamanian/Chamorro (0)	2	0.02
Marshallese (1)	1	0.01
Native Hawaiian (0)	5	0.04
Samoan (1)	1	0.01
White (10,626)	10,885	95.34
Not Hispanic (10,451)	10,688	93.61
Hispanic (175)	197	1.73

Plainfield

Place Type: Town
County: Hendricks
Population: 27,631†

Ancestry‡	Population	%
African, Sub-Saharan (307)	327	1.23
African (112)	132	0.50
Ethiopian (82)	82	0.31
Kenyan (9)	9	0.03
Nigerian (84)	84	0.32
Other Sub-Saharan African (20)	20	0.08
American (2,303)	2,303	8.64
Arab (63)	81	0.30
Lebanese (0)	18	0.07
Moroccan (9)	9	0.03
Syrian (54)	54	0.20
Australian (20)	20	0.08
Austrian (27)	36	0.14

SECTION TWO

*Notes: † The Census 2010 population figure is used to calculate the percentages in the Hispanic Origin and Race categories. Ancestry percentages are based on the 2006-2010 American Community Survey population (not shown); ‡ Numbers in parentheses indicate the number of people reporting a single ancestry; * Numbers in parentheses indicate the number of persons reporting this race alone, not in combination with any other race; Please refer to the Explanation of Data for more information.*

Belgian (22)	124	0.47
Brazilian (149)	149	0.56
British (56)	106	0.40
Cajun (13)	23	0.09
Canadian (34)	34	0.13
Celtic (0)	21	0.08
Croatian (24)	37	0.14
Czech (10)	66	0.25
Danish (6)	55	0.21
Dutch (171)	544	2.04
English (2,139)	3,754	14.09
European (127)	137	0.51
Finnish (0)	15	0.06
French, ex. Basque (131)	591	2.22
French Canadian (30)	150	0.56
German (2,879)	6,770	25.41
Greek (19)	99	0.37
Hungarian (25)	54	0.20
Icelander (10)	31	0.12
Irish (1,562)	4,108	15.42
Italian (298)	776	2.91
Lithuanian (39)	124	0.47
Norwegian (36)	124	0.47
Pennsylvania German (9)	9	0.03
Polish (123)	435	1.63
Portuguese (9)	50	0.19
Romanian (17)	63	0.24
Russian (22)	120	0.45
Scotch-Irish (411)	682	2.56
Scottish (341)	852	3.20
Slavic (34)	34	0.13
Slovak (0)	30	0.11
Swedish (0)	173	0.65
Swiss (0)	20	0.08
Turkish (0)	11	0.04
Ukrainian (25)	25	0.09
Welsh (10)	103	0.39
West Indian, ex. Hispanic (9)	9	0.03
Haitian (9)	9	0.03

Hispanic Origin	Population	%
Hispanic or Latino (of any race)	1,115	4.04
Central American, ex. Mexican	156	0.56
Costa Rican	11	0.04
Guatemalan	28	0.10
Honduran	52	0.19
Nicaraguan	6	0.02
Panamanian	9	0.03
Salvadoran	50	0.18
Cuban	14	0.05
Dominican Republic	29	0.10
Mexican	636	2.30
Puerto Rican	71	0.26
South American	101	0.37
Argentinean	3	0.01
Colombian	21	0.08
Ecuadorian	8	0.03
Peruvian	63	0.23
Venezuelan	6	0.02
Other Hispanic or Latino	108	0.39

Race*	Population	%
African-American/Black (2,193)	2,404	8.70
Not Hispanic (2,173)	2,369	8.57
Hispanic (20)	35	0.13
American Indian/Alaska Native (49)	167	0.60
Not Hispanic (41)	142	0.51
Hispanic (8)	25	0.09
Apache (0)	5	0.02
Blackfeet (1)	7	0.03
Cherokee (8)	40	0.14
Chippewa (1)	3	0.01
Choctaw (1)	7	0.03
Cree (2)	3	0.01
Delaware (0)	3	0.01
Iroquois (3)	3	0.01
Mexican American Ind. (6)	9	0.03
Potawatomi (1)	2	0.01
South American Ind. (0)	1	<0.01
Ute (1)	3	0.01
Yaqui (1)	1	<0.01
Asian (919)	1,075	3.89
Not Hispanic (910)	1,050	3.80
Hispanic (9)	25	0.09
Chinese, ex. Taiwanese (55)	70	0.25
Filipino (75)	122	0.44
Indian (547)	595	2.15
Indonesian (12)	14	0.05
Japanese (13)	28	0.10
Korean (28)	50	0.18
Laotian (8)	8	0.03
Nepalese (3)	3	0.01
Pakistani (98)	103	0.37
Sri Lankan (2)	2	0.01
Taiwanese (7)	11	0.04
Thai (3)	6	0.02
Vietnamese (40)	49	0.18
Hawaii Native/Pacific Islander (0)	24	0.09
Not Hispanic (0)	19	0.07
Hispanic (0)	5	0.02
Guamanian/Chamorro (0)	1	<0.01
Native Hawaiian (0)	12	0.04
Samoan (0)	5	0.02
White (23,555)	23,983	86.80
Not Hispanic (22,961)	23,327	84.42
Hispanic (594)	656	2.37

Plymouth

Place Type: City
County: Marshall
Population: 10,033†

Ancestry‡	Population	%
American (457)	457	4.55
Arab (0)	12	0.12
Egyptian (0)	12	0.12
Belgian (10)	16	0.16
British (18)	18	0.18
Croatian (0)	7	0.07
Czech (66)	150	1.49
Dutch (8)	157	1.56
English (169)	673	6.70
European (12)	12	0.12
French, ex. Basque (41)	157	1.56
French Canadian (7)	7	0.07
German (1,109)	2,651	26.39
Greek (9)	17	0.17
Iranian (0)	11	0.11
Irish (430)	1,243	12.38
Italian (10)	201	2.00
Lithuanian (13)	38	0.38
Norwegian (12)	12	0.12
Pennsylvania German (16)	27	0.27
Polish (162)	587	5.84
Portuguese (23)	85	0.85
Romanian (47)	59	0.59
Russian (0)	8	0.08
Scandinavian (0)	14	0.14
Scotch-Irish (26)	202	2.01
Scottish (43)	115	1.14
Swedish (41)	108	1.08
Swiss (13)	48	0.48
Ukrainian (5)	5	0.05
Welsh (0)	46	0.46

Hispanic Origin	Population	%
Hispanic or Latino (of any race)	2,004	19.97
Central American, ex. Mexican	206	2.05
Guatemalan	3	0.03
Honduran	199	1.98
Nicaraguan	1	0.01
Salvadoran	3	0.03
Cuban	9	0.09
Dominican Republic	8	0.08
Mexican	1,501	14.96
Puerto Rican	47	0.47
South American	12	0.12
Ecuadorian	1	0.01
Peruvian	11	0.11
Other Hispanic or Latino	221	2.20

Race*	Population	%
African-American/Black (94)	172	1.71
Not Hispanic (74)	132	1.32
Hispanic (20)	40	0.40
American Indian/Alaska Native (59)	123	1.23
Not Hispanic (30)	86	0.86
Hispanic (29)	37	0.37
Apache (0)	1	0.01
Blackfeet (1)	9	0.09
Canadian/French Am. Ind. (0)	1	0.01
Cherokee (9)	40	0.40
Cree (0)	3	0.03
Iroquois (2)	2	0.02
Mexican American Ind. (0)	5	0.05
Navajo (1)	4	0.04
Potawatomi (0)	3	0.03
Asian (46)	71	0.71
Not Hispanic (46)	70	0.70
Hispanic (0)	1	0.01
Chinese, ex. Taiwanese (14)	14	0.14
Filipino (7)	14	0.14
Indian (5)	15	0.15
Indonesian (2)	2	0.02
Japanese (2)	9	0.09
Korean (1)	6	0.06
Laotian (1)	3	0.03
Pakistani (1)	1	0.01
Taiwanese (2)	2	0.02
Vietnamese (8)	8	0.08
Hawaii Native/Pacific Islander (1)	4	0.04
Not Hispanic (0)	3	0.03
Hispanic (1)	1	0.01
Guamanian/Chamorro (1)	1	0.01
Native Hawaiian (0)	2	0.02
White (8,744)	8,981	89.51
Not Hispanic (7,740)	7,877	78.51
Hispanic (1,004)	1,104	11.00

Portage

Place Type: City
County: Porter
Population: 36,828†

Ancestry‡	Population	%
Afghan (13)	13	0.04
African, Sub-Saharan (277)	356	0.98
African (277)	356	0.98
Albanian (0)	18	0.05
Alsatian (0)	11	0.03
American (2,027)	2,027	5.59
Arab (46)	46	0.13
Arab (18)	18	0.05
Jordanian (28)	28	0.08
Austrian (0)	23	0.06
Belgian (14)	49	0.14
British (18)	65	0.18
Bulgarian (0)	14	0.04
Cajun (15)	25	0.07
Canadian (57)	57	0.16
Celtic (0)	14	0.04
Croatian (165)	297	0.82
Czech (48)	108	0.30
Czechoslovakian (27)	104	0.29
Danish (9)	37	0.10
Dutch (164)	833	2.30
Eastern European (19)	19	0.05
English (752)	2,398	6.61
European (240)	262	0.72
Finnish (10)	104	0.29
French, ex. Basque (294)	1,128	3.11
French Canadian (73)	226	0.62
German (1,706)	7,106	19.58
Greek (395)	528	1.45
Hungarian (155)	668	1.84
Iranian (0)	99	0.27
Irish (1,574)	6,088	16.78
Israeli (5)	5	0.01

*Notes: † The Census 2010 population figure is used to calculate the percentages in the Hispanic Origin and Race categories. Ancestry percentages are based on the 2006-2010 American Community Survey population (not shown); ‡ Numbers in parentheses indicate the number of people reporting a single ancestry; * Numbers in parentheses indicate the number of persons reporting this race alone, not in combination with any other race; Please refer to the Explanation of Data for more information.*

Italian (667)	1,587	4.37
Lithuanian (24)	43	0.12
Macedonian (165)	181	0.50
Norwegian (125)	351	0.97
Pennsylvania German (0)	16	0.04
Polish (1,645)	3,667	10.10
Romanian (76)	233	0.64
Russian (70)	364	1.00
Scandinavian (23)	23	0.06
Scotch-Irish (286)	593	1.63
Scottish (223)	632	1.74
Serbian (113)	268	0.74
Slavic (26)	42	0.12
Slovak (200)	766	2.11
Slovene (74)	218	0.60
Swedish (177)	786	2.17
Swiss (0)	40	0.11
Ukrainian (23)	145	0.40
Welsh (9)	120	0.33
West Indian, ex. Hispanic (0)	13	0.04
Trinidadian/Tobagonian (0)	13	0.04
Yugoslavian (14)	54	0.15

Hispanic Origin	Population	%
Hispanic or Latino (of any race)	6,044	16.41
Central American, ex. Mexican	66	0.18
Guatemalan	33	0.09
Nicaraguan	4	0.01
Panamanian	15	0.04
Salvadoran	13	0.04
Other Central American	1	<0.01
Cuban	29	0.08
Dominican Republic	11	0.03
Mexican	4,011	10.89
Puerto Rican	1,608	4.37
South American	50	0.14
Argentinean	1	<0.01
Bolivian	17	0.05
Chilean	4	0.01
Colombian	7	0.02
Ecuadorian	6	0.02
Peruvian	7	0.02
Venezuelan	8	0.02
Other Hispanic or Latino	269	0.73

Race*	Population	%
African-American/Black (2,681)	3,039	8.25
Not Hispanic (2,553)	2,809	7.63
Hispanic (128)	230	0.62
American Indian/Alaska Native (162)	387	1.05
Not Hispanic (110)	281	0.76
Hispanic (52)	106	0.29
Apache (0)	6	0.02
Blackfeet (5)	35	0.10
Canadian/French Am. Ind. (3)	4	0.01
Central American Ind. (0)	2	0.01
Cherokee (21)	90	0.24
Cheyenne (0)	1	<0.01
Chippewa (17)	26	0.07
Choctaw (3)	9	0.02
Cree (1)	1	<0.01
Creek (3)	8	0.02
Delaware (0)	1	<0.01
Hopi (0)	2	0.01
Houma (2)	2	0.01
Iroquois (1)	1	<0.01
Menominee (1)	1	<0.01
Mexican American Ind. (6)	15	0.04
Navajo (0)	3	0.01
Osage (0)	5	0.01
Potawatomi (2)	4	0.01
Pueblo (2)	3	0.01
Seminole (1)	1	<0.01
Sioux (4)	8	0.02
South American Ind. (4)	7	0.02
Spanish American Ind. (0)	1	<0.01
Tohono O'Odham (1)	1	<0.01
Yaqui (1)	1	<0.01
Asian (337)	477	1.30
Not Hispanic (321)	436	1.18
Hispanic (16)	41	0.11
Cambodian (5)	5	0.01
Chinese, ex. Taiwanese (65)	91	0.25
Filipino (84)	115	0.31
Indian (64)	76	0.21
Japanese (18)	42	0.11
Korean (18)	39	0.11
Pakistani (21)	23	0.06
Taiwanese (2)	3	0.01
Thai (16)	26	0.07
Vietnamese (34)	45	0.12
Hawaii Native/Pacific Islander (9)	32	0.09
Not Hispanic (7)	28	0.08
Hispanic (2)	4	0.01
Guamanian/Chamorro (2)	4	0.01
Native Hawaiian (1)	9	0.02
Samoan (4)	4	0.01
White (30,788)	31,648	85.93
Not Hispanic (27,236)	27,720	75.27
Hispanic (3,552)	3,928	10.67

Princeton

Place Type: City
County: Gibson
Population: 8,644†

Ancestry‡	Population	%
American (2,023)	2,023	23.44
Australian (0)	124	1.44
Belgian (0)	27	0.31
British (40)	76	0.88
Dutch (0)	143	1.66
English (341)	746	8.64
European (28)	28	0.32
French, ex. Basque (240)	462	5.35
French Canadian (41)	41	0.48
German (862)	1,830	21.20
Greek (0)	101	1.17
Irish (522)	1,192	13.81
Italian (63)	277	3.21
New Zealander (0)	35	0.41
Norwegian (13)	26	0.30
Polish (57)	162	1.88
Portuguese (0)	100	1.16
Scotch-Irish (78)	264	3.06
Scottish (14)	32	0.37
Swedish (0)	39	0.45
Swiss (0)	12	0.14
Ukrainian (0)	100	1.16
Welsh (0)	4	0.05
West Indian, ex. Hispanic (6)	6	0.07
Jamaican (6)	6	0.07

Hispanic Origin	Population	%
Hispanic or Latino (of any race)	213	2.46
Central American, ex. Mexican	5	0.06
Salvadoran	5	0.06
Cuban	3	0.03
Dominican Republic	5	0.06
Mexican	150	1.74
Puerto Rican	21	0.24
South American	7	0.08
Argentinean	1	0.01
Colombian	4	0.05
Peruvian	2	0.02
Other Hispanic or Latino	22	0.25

Race*	Population	%
African-American/Black (400)	586	6.78
Not Hispanic (394)	572	6.62
Hispanic (6)	14	0.16
American Indian/Alaska Native (21)	97	1.12
Not Hispanic (18)	89	1.03
Hispanic (3)	8	0.09
Apache (0)	2	0.02
Blackfeet (1)	12	0.14
Canadian/French Am. Ind. (0)	4	0.05
Cherokee (3)	40	0.46
Chippewa (1)	1	0.01
Choctaw (0)	1	0.01
Comanche (1)	1	0.01
Creek (0)	1	0.01
Crow (0)	1	0.01
Mexican American Ind. (1)	3	0.03
Navajo (0)	1	0.01
Asian (59)	68	0.79
Not Hispanic (59)	67	0.78
Hispanic (0)	1	0.01
Chinese, ex. Taiwanese (4)	4	0.05
Filipino (8)	13	0.15
Indian (28)	28	0.32
Japanese (9)	10	0.12
Korean (2)	3	0.03
Thai (2)	2	0.02
Vietnamese (6)	6	0.07
Hawaii Native/Pacific Islander (3)	4	0.05
Not Hispanic (2)	2	0.02
Hispanic (1)	2	0.02
Fijian (1)	2	0.02
Guamanian/Chamorro (1)	1	0.01
Native Hawaiian (1)	1	0.01
White (7,813)	8,061	93.26
Not Hispanic (7,706)	7,929	91.73
Hispanic (107)	132	1.53

Purdue University

Place Type: CDP
County: Tippecanoe
Population: 12,183†

Ancestry‡	Population	%
African, Sub-Saharan (116)	116	0.89
African (47)	47	0.36
Ethiopian (46)	46	0.35
Nigerian (23)	23	0.18
American (95)	95	0.73
Arab (63)	101	0.78
Arab (13)	13	0.10
Egyptian (24)	24	0.19
Jordanian (13)	13	0.10
Lebanese (13)	39	0.30
Syrian (0)	12	0.09
Assyrian/Chaldean/Syriac (0)	14	0.11
Australian (73)	89	0.69
Austrian (0)	14	0.11
Belgian (10)	24	0.19
British (59)	139	1.07
Bulgarian (1)	1	0.01
Canadian (0)	26	0.20
Celtic (0)	13	0.10
Croatian (0)	25	0.19
Czech (0)	42	0.32
Danish (13)	38	0.29
Dutch (67)	233	1.80
English (207)	901	6.95
European (132)	138	1.06
Finnish (29)	29	0.22
French, ex. Basque (61)	412	3.18
French Canadian (0)	40	0.31
German (1,199)	3,728	28.76
Greek (60)	68	0.52
Hungarian (14)	147	1.13
Icelander (0)	18	0.14
Iranian (10)	10	0.08
Irish (363)	1,699	13.11
Italian (296)	940	7.25
Latvian (1)	1	0.01
Lithuanian (0)	2	0.02
Luxemburger (0)	13	0.10
Norwegian (42)	154	1.19
Pennsylvania German (12)	12	0.09
Polish (218)	908	7.01
Portuguese (0)	11	0.08
Romanian (27)	28	0.22
Russian (13)	88	0.68
Scotch-Irish (94)	309	2.38
Scottish (73)	251	1.94
Serbian (13)	26	0.20

*Notes: † The Census 2010 population figure is used to calculate the percentages in the Hispanic Origin and Race categories. Ancestry percentages are based on the 2006-2010 American Community Survey population (not shown); ‡ Numbers in parentheses indicate the number of people reporting a single ancestry; * Numbers in parentheses indicate the number of persons reporting this race alone, not in combination with any other race; Please refer to the Explanation of Data for more information.*

Ancestry	Population	%
Swedish (27)	250	1.93
Swiss (53)	168	1.30
Turkish (16)	16	0.12
Ukrainian (0)	7	0.05
Welsh (33)	87	0.67
West Indian, ex. Hispanic (33)	69	0.53
Bahamian (13)	13	0.10
British West Indian (0)	8	0.06
Haitian (7)	7	0.05
Jamaican (13)	27	0.21
Other West Indian (0)	14	0.11
Yugoslavian (0)	14	0.11

Hispanic Origin	Population	%
Hispanic or Latino (of any race)	436	3.58
Central American, ex. Mexican	64	0.53
Costa Rican	12	0.10
Guatemalan	5	0.04
Honduran	7	0.06
Nicaraguan	7	0.06
Panamanian	17	0.14
Salvadoran	16	0.13
Cuban	14	0.11
Dominican Republic	2	0.02
Mexican	177	1.45
Puerto Rican	54	0.44
South American	87	0.71
Argentinean	12	0.10
Bolivian	4	0.03
Chilean	8	0.07
Colombian	29	0.24
Ecuadorian	9	0.07
Paraguayan	2	0.02
Peruvian	11	0.09
Venezuelan	12	0.10
Other Hispanic or Latino	38	0.31

Race*	Population	%
African-American/Black (446)	511	4.19
Not Hispanic (428)	484	3.97
Hispanic (18)	27	0.22
American Indian/Alaska Native (17)	62	0.51
Not Hispanic (12)	49	0.40
Hispanic (5)	13	0.11
Apache (1)	1	0.01
Blackfeet (0)	1	0.01
Cherokee (4)	15	0.12
Chippewa (1)	1	0.01
Creek (0)	1	0.01
Iroquois (0)	1	0.01
Potawatomi (0)	1	0.01
Asian (2,798)	2,973	24.40
Not Hispanic (2,786)	2,951	24.22
Hispanic (12)	22	0.18
Bangladeshi (30)	31	0.25
Burmese (2)	3	0.02
Cambodian (2)	2	0.02
Chinese, ex. Taiwanese (1,215)	1,285	10.55
Filipino (32)	58	0.48
Indian (579)	616	5.06
Indonesian (17)	23	0.19
Japanese (26)	43	0.35
Korean (510)	542	4.45
Laotian (1)	1	0.01
Malaysian (18)	19	0.16
Nepalese (11)	11	0.09
Pakistani (87)	93	0.76
Sri Lankan (18)	18	0.15
Taiwanese (108)	118	0.97
Thai (28)	32	0.26
Vietnamese (41)	50	0.41
Hawaii Native/Pacific Islander (5)	21	0.17
Not Hispanic (4)	16	0.13
Hispanic (1)	5	0.04
Guamanian/Chamorro (1)	4	0.03
Native Hawaiian (2)	8	0.07
Samoan (1)	3	0.02
Tongan (1)	1	0.01
White (8,520)	8,730	71.66
Not Hispanic (8,256)	8,442	69.29
Hispanic (264)	288	2.36

Richmond

Place Type: City
County: Wayne
Population: 36,812†

Ancestry‡	Population	%
African, Sub-Saharan (147)	167	0.45
African (147)	167	0.45
American (3,589)	3,589	9.67
Arab (33)	33	0.09
Lebanese (17)	17	0.05
Palestinian (9)	9	0.02
Other Arab (7)	7	0.02
Armenian (14)	14	0.04
Austrian (0)	11	0.03
Belgian (0)	40	0.11
British (62)	198	0.53
Canadian (98)	105	0.28
Croatian (15)	15	0.04
Czech (15)	64	0.17
Danish (0)	43	0.12
Dutch (126)	883	2.38
Eastern European (10)	10	0.03
English (1,747)	4,355	11.73
European (289)	323	0.87
French, ex. Basque (53)	334	0.90
French Canadian (8)	41	0.11
German (3,828)	8,618	23.21
Greek (75)	101	0.27
Guyanese (7)	30	0.08
Hungarian (75)	175	0.47
Iranian (11)	11	0.03
Irish (1,384)	4,314	11.62
Italian (566)	1,173	3.16
Lithuanian (11)	19	0.05
Macedonian (93)	93	0.25
Maltese (11)	22	0.06
Northern European (33)	33	0.09
Norwegian (10)	98	0.26
Pennsylvania German (0)	13	0.04
Polish (97)	319	0.86
Portuguese (0)	15	0.04
Russian (49)	49	0.13
Scandinavian (13)	13	0.04
Scotch-Irish (254)	689	1.86
Scottish (302)	616	1.66
Slavic (16)	16	0.04
Slovak (14)	14	0.04
Slovene (0)	7	0.02
Swedish (21)	96	0.26
Swiss (52)	128	0.34
Turkish (0)	13	0.04
Ukrainian (13)	13	0.04
Welsh (61)	134	0.36
West Indian, ex. Hispanic (12)	15	0.04
Dutch West Indian (0)	3	0.01
Haitian (6)	6	0.02
Jamaican (6)	6	0.02
Yugoslavian (0)	14	0.04

Hispanic Origin	Population	%
Hispanic or Latino (of any race)	1,496	4.06
Central American, ex. Mexican	53	0.14
Costa Rican	2	0.01
Guatemalan	16	0.04
Honduran	12	0.03
Panamanian	11	0.03
Salvadoran	8	0.02
Other Central American	4	0.01
Cuban	27	0.07
Dominican Republic	4	0.01
Mexican	1,083	2.94
Puerto Rican	132	0.36
South American	81	0.22
Argentinean	2	0.01
Bolivian	1	<0.01
Chilean	7	0.02
Colombian	27	0.07
Ecuadorian	13	0.04
Peruvian	29	0.08
Uruguayan	1	<0.01
Venezuelan	1	<0.01
Other Hispanic or Latino	116	0.32

Race*	Population	%
African-American/Black (3,184)	4,177	11.35
Not Hispanic (3,121)	4,078	11.08
Hispanic (63)	99	0.27
American Indian/Alaska Native (102)	446	1.21
Not Hispanic (83)	398	1.08
Hispanic (19)	48	0.13
Apache (1)	7	0.02
Blackfeet (2)	25	0.07
Canadian/French Am. Ind. (0)	3	0.01
Central American Ind. (0)	2	0.01
Cherokee (24)	128	0.35
Chippewa (3)	8	0.02
Choctaw (1)	3	0.01
Comanche (1)	1	<0.01
Creek (0)	2	0.01
Crow (0)	1	<0.01
Hopi (1)	3	0.01
Houma (1)	1	<0.01
Iroquois (6)	8	0.02
Lumbee (0)	1	<0.01
Mexican American Ind. (7)	13	0.04
Navajo (2)	7	0.02
Pima (0)	2	0.01
Potawatomi (1)	1	<0.01
Seminole (0)	1	<0.01
Sioux (1)	7	0.02
Spanish American Ind. (5)	8	0.02
Asian (404)	559	1.52
Not Hispanic (399)	547	1.49
Hispanic (5)	12	0.03
Cambodian (2)	6	0.02
Chinese, ex. Taiwanese (58)	67	0.18
Filipino (92)	137	0.37
Indian (111)	124	0.34
Indonesian (2)	2	0.01
Japanese (47)	63	0.17
Korean (14)	20	0.05
Laotian (11)	16	0.04
Nepalese (1)	2	0.01
Pakistani (12)	12	0.03
Sri Lankan (1)	2	0.01
Taiwanese (2)	3	0.01
Thai (2)	3	0.01
Vietnamese (24)	30	0.08
Hawaii Native/Pacific Islander (37)	118	0.32
Not Hispanic (32)	110	0.30
Hispanic (5)	8	0.02
Guamanian/Chamorro (4)	4	0.01
Native Hawaiian (6)	22	0.06
Samoan (2)	3	0.01
White (30,897)	32,221	87.53
Not Hispanic (30,282)	31,456	85.45
Hispanic (615)	765	2.08

Schererville

Place Type: Town
County: Lake
Population: 29,243†

Ancestry‡	Population	%
African, Sub-Saharan (87)	111	0.39
African (44)	56	0.20
Ghanaian (0)	12	0.04
South African (43)	43	0.15
American (1,270)	1,270	4.46
Arab (604)	668	2.35
Arab (212)	216	0.76
Egyptian (159)	159	0.56
Palestinian (233)	293	1.03
Armenian (25)	25	0.09
Assyrian/Chaldean/Syriac (19)	19	0.07

*Notes: † The Census 2010 population figure is used to calculate the percentages in the Hispanic Origin and Race categories. Ancestry percentages are based on the 2006-2010 American Community Survey population (not shown); ‡ Numbers in parentheses indicate the number of people reporting a single ancestry; * Numbers in parentheses indicate the number of persons reporting this race alone, not in combination with any other race; Please refer to the Explanation of Data for more information.*

Ancestry	Population	%
Austrian (25)	90	0.32
Belgian (22)	37	0.13
British (20)	37	0.13
Carpatho Rusyn (13)	13	0.05
Croatian (255)	664	2.33
Czech (32)	197	0.69
Czechoslovakian (22)	28	0.10
Danish (0)	27	0.09
Dutch (572)	1,131	3.97
English (373)	1,970	6.92
European (74)	116	0.41
Finnish (0)	25	0.09
French, ex. Basque (20)	447	1.57
French Canadian (8)	114	0.40
German (1,980)	6,618	23.24
Greek (496)	571	2.01
Hungarian (164)	523	1.84
Irish (846)	3,605	12.66
Italian (846)	2,160	7.58
Lithuanian (123)	263	0.92
Macedonian (385)	401	1.41
Norwegian (104)	231	0.81
Pennsylvania German (16)	75	0.26
Polish (1,996)	4,977	17.48
Romanian (250)	368	1.29
Russian (181)	269	0.94
Scandinavian (0)	24	0.08
Scotch-Irish (173)	414	1.45
Scottish (65)	361	1.27
Serbian (686)	859	3.02
Slavic (22)	67	0.24
Slovak (252)	1,051	3.69
Swedish (53)	630	2.21
Swiss (0)	96	0.34
Turkish (9)	18	0.06
Ukrainian (25)	82	0.29
Welsh (24)	145	0.51
Yugoslavian (36)	110	0.39

Hispanic Origin	Population	%
Hispanic or Latino (of any race)	3,098	10.59
Central American, ex. Mexican	51	0.17
Costa Rican	1	<0.01
Guatemalan	22	0.08
Honduran	2	0.01
Nicaraguan	9	0.03
Panamanian	3	0.01
Salvadoran	14	0.05
Cuban	19	0.06
Dominican Republic	4	0.01
Mexican	2,444	8.36
Puerto Rican	333	1.14
South American	68	0.23
Argentinean	8	0.03
Bolivian	13	0.04
Chilean	3	0.01
Colombian	10	0.03
Ecuadorian	16	0.05
Peruvian	15	0.05
Uruguayan	2	0.01
Venezuelan	1	<0.01
Other Hispanic or Latino	179	0.61

Race*	Population	%
African-American/Black (1,590)	1,748	5.98
Not Hispanic (1,552)	1,676	5.73
Hispanic (38)	72	0.25
American Indian/Alaska Native (55)	147	0.50
Not Hispanic (43)	99	0.34
Hispanic (12)	48	0.16
Apache (0)	4	0.01
Blackfeet (1)	6	0.02
Canadian/French Am. Ind. (2)	5	0.02
Cherokee (6)	28	0.10
Chippewa (5)	8	0.03
Choctaw (2)	2	0.01
Cree (0)	2	0.01
Creek (5)	5	0.02
Hopi (1)	1	<0.01
Iroquois (0)	1	<0.01
Kiowa (0)	1	<0.01
Lumbee (3)	3	0.01
Mexican American Ind. (7)	12	0.04
Paiute (3)	3	0.01
Sioux (0)	5	0.02
South American Ind. (0)	1	<0.01
Spanish American Ind. (0)	4	0.01
Tlingit-Haida *(Alaska Native)* (0)	1	<0.01
Tsimshian *(Alaska Native)* (1)	1	<0.01
Yup'ik *(Alaska Native)* (0)	1	<0.01
Asian (823)	968	3.31
Not Hispanic (813)	941	3.22
Hispanic (10)	27	0.09
Burmese (4)	4	0.01
Cambodian (7)	9	0.03
Chinese, ex. Taiwanese (82)	104	0.36
Filipino (151)	209	0.71
Indian (327)	338	1.16
Indonesian (1)	4	0.01
Japanese (11)	27	0.09
Korean (96)	109	0.37
Pakistani (54)	64	0.22
Taiwanese (2)	2	0.01
Thai (10)	10	0.03
Vietnamese (54)	59	0.20
Hawaii Native/Pacific Islander (3)	19	0.06
Not Hispanic (2)	16	0.05
Hispanic (1)	3	0.01
Native Hawaiian (2)	4	0.01
White (25,397)	25,856	88.42
Not Hispanic (23,411)	23,672	80.95
Hispanic (1,986)	2,184	7.47

Seymour

Place Type: City
County: Jackson
Population: 17,503†

Ancestry‡	Population	%
American (2,212)	2,212	12.34
Arab (0)	42	0.23
Egyptian (0)	42	0.23
Australian (0)	9	0.05
British (0)	9	0.05
Czechoslovakian (39)	39	0.22
Dutch (73)	321	1.79
English (824)	1,585	8.84
European (49)	49	0.27
Finnish (0)	19	0.11
French, ex. Basque (34)	272	1.52
French Canadian (12)	64	0.36
German (2,893)	5,384	30.04
Greek (36)	36	0.20
Irish (448)	2,627	14.66
Italian (169)	284	1.58
Norwegian (18)	93	0.52
Polish (6)	84	0.47
Scandinavian (0)	8	0.04
Scotch-Irish (86)	160	0.89
Scottish (92)	303	1.69
Serbian (0)	9	0.05
Swedish (0)	10	0.06
Turkish (0)	5	0.03
Welsh (0)	169	0.94
Yugoslavian (0)	6	0.03

Hispanic Origin	Population	%
Hispanic or Latino (of any race)	2,014	11.51
Central American, ex. Mexican	93	0.53
Guatemalan	32	0.18
Honduran	48	0.27
Nicaraguan	6	0.03
Panamanian	2	0.01
Salvadoran	5	0.03
Cuban	6	0.03
Mexican	1,640	9.37
Puerto Rican	55	0.31
South American	8	0.05
Colombian	1	0.01
Ecuadorian	5	0.03
Peruvian	1	0.01
Venezuelan	1	0.01
Other Hispanic or Latino	212	1.21

Race*	Population	%
African-American/Black (223)	330	1.89
Not Hispanic (210)	307	1.75
Hispanic (13)	23	0.13
American Indian/Alaska Native (43)	132	0.75
Not Hispanic (38)	111	0.63
Hispanic (5)	21	0.12
Blackfeet (1)	5	0.03
Central American Ind. (1)	4	0.02
Cherokee (12)	42	0.24
Chippewa (1)	1	0.01
Choctaw (2)	3	0.02
Iroquois (0)	1	0.01
Kiowa (0)	1	0.01
Mexican American Ind. (0)	1	0.01
Potawatomi (1)	1	0.01
Sioux (2)	4	0.02
Asian (210)	240	1.37
Not Hispanic (208)	238	1.36
Hispanic (2)	2	0.01
Chinese, ex. Taiwanese (19)	21	0.12
Filipino (33)	46	0.26
Indian (22)	27	0.15
Indonesian (2)	6	0.03
Japanese (83)	88	0.50
Korean (10)	10	0.06
Malaysian (1)	1	0.01
Pakistani (10)	11	0.06
Thai (4)	4	0.02
Vietnamese (23)	27	0.15
Hawaii Native/Pacific Islander (18)	27	0.15
Not Hispanic (9)	15	0.09
Hispanic (9)	12	0.07
Guamanian/Chamorro (16)	17	0.10
Native Hawaiian (2)	6	0.03
White (15,809)	16,093	91.94
Not Hispanic (14,805)	14,999	85.69
Hispanic (1,004)	1,094	6.25

Shelbyville

Place Type: City
County: Shelby
Population: 19,191†

Ancestry‡	Population	%
American (2,240)	2,240	11.87
Arab (14)	47	0.25
Lebanese (0)	12	0.06
Syrian (14)	35	0.19
Armenian (11)	11	0.06
Belgian (0)	39	0.21
British (20)	30	0.16
Canadian (0)	15	0.08
Czech (34)	34	0.18
Danish (0)	14	0.07
Dutch (49)	370	1.96
English (844)	1,549	8.21
European (105)	105	0.56
Finnish (0)	23	0.12
French, ex. Basque (183)	425	2.25
French Canadian (0)	18	0.10
German (2,246)	4,398	23.30
Irish (840)	1,931	10.23
Italian (107)	226	1.20
Latvian (0)	11	0.06
Norwegian (12)	12	0.06
Pennsylvania German (0)	18	0.10
Polish (33)	165	0.87
Romanian (0)	27	0.14
Russian (24)	80	0.42
Scandinavian (31)	31	0.16
Scotch-Irish (130)	277	1.47
Scottish (107)	508	2.69
Slovene (0)	10	0.05

SECTION TWO

*Notes: † The Census 2010 population figure is used to calculate the percentages in the Hispanic Origin and Race categories. Ancestry percentages are based on the 2006-2010 American Community Survey population (not shown); ‡ Numbers in parentheses indicate the number of people reporting a single ancestry; * Numbers in parentheses indicate the number of persons reporting this race alone, not in combination with any other race; Please refer to the Explanation of Data for more information.*

Swedish (39)	211	1.12
Swiss (0)	9	0.05
Ukrainian (14)	20	0.11
Welsh (46)	155	0.82

Hispanic Origin	Population	%
Hispanic or Latino (of any race)	1,360	7.09
Central American, ex. Mexican	29	0.15
Costa Rican	1	0.01
Guatemalan	10	0.05
Honduran	12	0.06
Salvadoran	5	0.03
Other Central American	1	0.01
Cuban	3	0.02
Dominican Republic	10	0.05
Mexican	1,206	6.28
Puerto Rican	30	0.16
South American	32	0.17
Argentinean	1	0.01
Chilean	2	0.01
Colombian	4	0.02
Ecuadorian	1	0.01
Peruvian	24	0.13
Other Hispanic or Latino	50	0.26

Race*	Population	%
African-American/Black (372)	507	2.64
Not Hispanic (348)	472	2.46
Hispanic (24)	35	0.18
American Indian/Alaska Native (38)	118	0.61
Not Hispanic (33)	97	0.51
Hispanic (5)	21	0.11
Apache (1)	1	0.01
Blackfeet (1)	4	0.02
Canadian/French Am. Ind. (1)	1	0.01
Cherokee (12)	45	0.23
Chippewa (3)	3	0.02
Choctaw (0)	1	0.01
Delaware (1)	1	0.01
Lumbee (1)	1	0.01
Sioux (7)	11	0.06
Asian (186)	238	1.24
Not Hispanic (185)	224	1.17
Hispanic (1)	14	0.07
Cambodian (4)	4	0.02
Chinese, ex. Taiwanese (33)	39	0.20
Filipino (18)	42	0.22
Indian (17)	21	0.11
Japanese (92)	99	0.52
Korean (10)	14	0.07
Malaysian (0)	2	0.01
Pakistani (1)	1	0.01
Thai (4)	4	0.02
Vietnamese (1)	5	0.03
Hawaii Native/Pacific Islander (7)	15	0.08
Not Hispanic (3)	7	0.04
Hispanic (4)	8	0.04
Fijian (0)	1	0.01
Guamanian/Chamorro (6)	6	0.03
Native Hawaiian (0)	4	0.02
Tongan (1)	1	0.01
White (17,646)	17,956	93.56
Not Hispanic (17,025)	17,247	89.87
Hispanic (621)	709	3.69

South Bend

Place Type: City
County: St. Joseph
Population: 101,168†

Ancestry‡	Population	%
African, Sub-Saharan (979)	1,287	1.26
African (699)	952	0.93
Kenyan (202)	218	0.21
Liberian (0)	28	0.03
Sierra Leonean (0)	11	0.01
Other Sub-Saharan African (78)	78	0.08
American (3,845)	3,845	3.77
Arab (72)	131	0.13
Arab (27)	27	0.03
Iraqi (23)	33	0.03
Lebanese (9)	33	0.03
Moroccan (0)	6	0.01
Syrian (0)	19	0.02
Other Arab (13)	13	0.01
Armenian (8)	44	0.04
Austrian (89)	275	0.27
Belgian (397)	871	0.85
Brazilian (10)	50	0.05
British (158)	336	0.33
Bulgarian (22)	47	0.05
Canadian (66)	126	0.12
Celtic (10)	10	0.01
Croatian (23)	295	0.29
Czech (35)	264	0.26
Czechoslovakian (42)	84	0.08
Danish (20)	88	0.09
Dutch (249)	2,222	2.18
Eastern European (13)	66	0.06
English (1,797)	6,318	6.19
Estonian (0)	8	0.01
European (680)	796	0.78
Finnish (33)	93	0.09
French, ex. Basque (209)	2,323	2.28
French Canadian (84)	422	0.41
German (5,733)	19,199	18.81
Greek (89)	308	0.30
Hungarian (1,068)	2,904	2.85
Iranian (13)	13	0.01
Irish (2,788)	12,089	11.84
Italian (1,079)	3,341	3.27
Latvian (10)	10	0.01
Lithuanian (55)	176	0.17
Luxemburger (13)	13	0.01
Northern European (62)	62	0.06
Norwegian (116)	459	0.45
Pennsylvania German (48)	140	0.14
Polish (4,876)	10,370	10.16
Portuguese (23)	54	0.05
Romanian (68)	88	0.09
Russian (238)	730	0.72
Scandinavian (35)	150	0.15
Scotch-Irish (314)	1,065	1.04
Scottish (213)	1,319	1.29
Serbian (71)	165	0.16
Slavic (10)	10	0.01
Slovak (42)	131	0.13
Slovene (0)	9	0.01
Swedish (291)	1,638	1.60
Swiss (141)	343	0.34
Turkish (50)	104	0.10
Ukrainian (58)	214	0.21
Welsh (92)	372	0.36
West Indian, ex. Hispanic (98)	117	0.11
Bahamian (0)	9	0.01
British West Indian (15)	15	0.01
Dutch West Indian (11)	11	0.01
Jamaican (12)	12	0.01
Trinidadian/Tobagonian (39)	39	0.04
West Indian (21)	31	0.03
Yugoslavian (364)	514	0.50

Hispanic Origin	Population	%
Hispanic or Latino (of any race)	13,116	12.96
Central American, ex. Mexican	292	0.29
Costa Rican	7	0.01
Guatemalan	66	0.07
Honduran	49	0.05
Nicaraguan	46	0.05
Panamanian	21	0.02
Salvadoran	98	0.10
Other Central American	5	<0.01
Cuban	111	0.11
Dominican Republic	42	0.04
Mexican	11,025	10.90
Puerto Rican	525	0.52
South American	275	0.27
Argentinean	33	0.03
Bolivian	10	0.01
Chilean	27	0.03
Colombian	53	0.05
Ecuadorian	47	0.05
Paraguayan	10	0.01
Peruvian	17	0.02
Uruguayan	5	<0.01
Venezuelan	73	0.07
Other Hispanic or Latino	846	0.84

Race*	Population	%
African-American/Black (26,906)	29,667	29.32
Not Hispanic (26,496)	28,893	28.56
Hispanic (410)	774	0.77
American Indian/Alaska Native (478)	1,334	1.32
Not Hispanic (310)	1,029	1.02
Hispanic (168)	305	0.30
Apache (6)	29	0.03
Arapaho (0)	1	<0.01
Blackfeet (14)	74	0.07
Canadian/French Am. Ind. (1)	5	<0.01
Central American Ind. (3)	8	0.01
Cherokee (54)	281	0.28
Cheyenne (0)	1	<0.01
Chickasaw (3)	6	0.01
Chippewa (12)	29	0.03
Choctaw (5)	23	0.02
Colville (1)	1	<0.01
Comanche (0)	1	<0.01
Cree (0)	1	<0.01
Creek (0)	4	<0.01
Delaware (1)	1	<0.01
Inupiat *(Alaska Native)* (0)	1	<0.01
Iroquois (0)	4	<0.01
Lumbee (4)	10	0.01
Menominee (1)	1	<0.01
Mexican American Ind. (31)	54	0.05
Navajo (1)	8	0.01
Ottawa (0)	3	<0.01
Paiute (3)	3	<0.01
Potawatomi (38)	74	0.07
Pueblo (0)	4	<0.01
Seminole (0)	5	<0.01
Shoshone (0)	1	<0.01
Sioux (4)	9	0.01
South American Ind. (2)	3	<0.01
Spanish American Ind. (8)	11	0.01
Tlingit-Haida *(Alaska Native)* (3)	4	<0.01
Asian (1,318)	1,824	1.80
Not Hispanic (1,295)	1,742	1.72
Hispanic (23)	82	0.08
Bangladeshi (1)	2	<0.01
Cambodian (76)	80	0.08
Chinese, ex. Taiwanese (258)	360	0.36
Filipino (205)	345	0.34
Hmong (2)	2	<0.01
Indian (211)	266	0.26
Indonesian (11)	14	0.01
Japanese (44)	102	0.10
Korean (107)	164	0.16
Laotian (34)	53	0.05
Malaysian (2)	3	<0.01
Nepalese (3)	4	<0.01
Pakistani (12)	16	0.02
Sri Lankan (8)	9	0.01
Taiwanese (17)	19	0.02
Thai (24)	37	0.04
Vietnamese (242)	267	0.26
Hawaii Native/Pacific Islander (64)	185	0.18
Not Hispanic (55)	156	0.15
Hispanic (9)	29	0.03
Guamanian/Chamorro (12)	20	0.02
Native Hawaiian (17)	55	0.05
Samoan (17)	55	0.05
Tongan (11)	20	0.02
White (61,199)	64,797	64.05
Not Hispanic (56,474)	59,298	58.61
Hispanic (4,725)	5,499	5.44

*Notes: † The Census 2010 population figure is used to calculate the percentages in the Hispanic Origin and Race categories. Ancestry percentages are based on the 2006-2010 American Community Survey population (not shown); ‡ Numbers in parentheses indicate the number of people reporting a single ancestry; * Numbers in parentheses indicate the number of persons reporting this race alone, not in combination with any other race; Please refer to the Explanation of Data for more information.*

Speedway

Place Type: Town
County: Marion
Population: 11,812†

Ancestry‡	Population	%
African, Sub-Saharan (476)	709	5.94
African (368)	581	4.87
Ethiopian (26)	46	0.39
Kenyan (22)	22	0.18
Nigerian (40)	40	0.34
Other Sub-Saharan African (20)	20	0.17
American (1,175)	1,175	9.85
Arab (6)	31	0.26
Lebanese (6)	13	0.11
Syrian (0)	18	0.15
British (37)	37	0.31
Canadian (12)	12	0.10
Croatian (0)	12	0.10
Czech (33)	33	0.28
Czechoslovakian (0)	45	0.38
Danish (0)	28	0.23
Dutch (59)	325	2.72
English (517)	1,215	10.18
European (94)	102	0.85
Finnish (0)	8	0.07
French, ex. Basque (28)	418	3.50
French Canadian (16)	16	0.13
German (1,326)	2,959	24.80
Greek (10)	22	0.18
Iranian (0)	34	0.28
Irish (653)	1,663	13.94
Italian (95)	194	1.63
Macedonian (10)	10	0.08
New Zealander (19)	19	0.16
Norwegian (0)	59	0.49
Polish (0)	108	0.91
Romanian (15)	15	0.13
Scotch-Irish (115)	182	1.53
Scottish (84)	159	1.33
Slovak (13)	25	0.21
Slovene (18)	18	0.15
Swedish (50)	78	0.65
Swiss (19)	85	0.71
Ukrainian (56)	69	0.58
Welsh (15)	64	0.54
Yugoslavian (12)	12	0.10

Hispanic Origin	Population	%
Hispanic or Latino (of any race)	893	7.56
Central American, ex. Mexican	93	0.79
Guatemalan	11	0.09
Honduran	33	0.28
Nicaraguan	3	0.03
Panamanian	19	0.16
Salvadoran	26	0.22
Other Central American	1	0.01
Cuban	28	0.24
Dominican Republic	32	0.27
Mexican	620	5.25
Puerto Rican	41	0.35
South American	31	0.26
Argentinean	2	0.02
Colombian	4	0.03
Ecuadorian	6	0.05
Peruvian	14	0.12
Uruguayan	1	0.01
Venezuelan	4	0.03
Other Hispanic or Latino	48	0.41

Race*	Population	%
African-American/Black (1,978)	2,136	18.08
Not Hispanic (1,956)	2,093	17.72
Hispanic (22)	43	0.36
American Indian/Alaska Native (37)	107	0.91
Not Hispanic (33)	99	0.84
Hispanic (4)	8	0.07
Apache (0)	3	0.03
Blackfeet (1)	5	0.04
Canadian/French Am. Ind. (0)	4	0.03
Cherokee (12)	27	0.23
Chippewa (1)	1	0.01
Choctaw (0)	3	0.03
Colville (4)	4	0.03
Lumbee (1)	2	0.02
Navajo (1)	1	0.01
Sioux (0)	1	0.01
Ute (0)	1	0.01
Asian (242)	295	2.50
Not Hispanic (242)	295	2.50
Bangladeshi (1)	1	0.01
Burmese (42)	42	0.36
Cambodian (4)	5	0.04
Chinese, ex. Taiwanese (58)	63	0.53
Filipino (18)	39	0.33
Indian (67)	74	0.63
Japanese (4)	18	0.15
Korean (12)	13	0.11
Pakistani (4)	4	0.03
Sri Lankan (3)	3	0.03
Taiwanese (4)	4	0.03
Thai (17)	17	0.14
Vietnamese (3)	3	0.03
Hawaii Native/Pacific Islander (3)	5	0.04
Not Hispanic (2)	4	0.03
Hispanic (1)	1	0.01
Guamanian/Chamorro (1)	3	0.03
Native Hawaiian (2)	2	0.02
White (8,762)	8,997	76.17
Not Hispanic (8,432)	8,634	73.10
Hispanic (330)	363	3.07

St. John

Place Type: Town
County: Lake
Population: 14,850†

Ancestry‡	Population	%
American (575)	575	4.19
Arab (43)	43	0.31
Palestinian (43)	43	0.31
Austrian (0)	10	0.07
Belgian (0)	33	0.24
Canadian (34)	34	0.25
Carpatho Rusyn (0)	9	0.07
Croatian (120)	328	2.39
Czech (36)	178	1.30
Czechoslovakian (34)	67	0.49
Danish (0)	22	0.16
Dutch (605)	1,255	9.14
English (136)	889	6.47
European (22)	30	0.22
Finnish (11)	24	0.17
French, ex. Basque (39)	384	2.80
French Canadian (0)	69	0.50
German (1,032)	3,814	27.77
Greek (123)	333	2.42
Hungarian (40)	182	1.33
Irish (359)	2,229	16.23
Italian (545)	1,555	11.32
Lithuanian (125)	242	1.76
Macedonian (97)	109	0.79
Northern European (24)	24	0.17
Norwegian (17)	125	0.91
Polish (917)	2,401	17.48
Romanian (12)	44	0.32
Russian (9)	71	0.52
Scandinavian (0)	8	0.06
Scotch-Irish (61)	159	1.16
Scottish (59)	129	0.94
Serbian (245)	439	3.20
Slavic (0)	7	0.05
Slovak (137)	425	3.09
Slovene (13)	29	0.21
Swedish (82)	437	3.18
Swiss (0)	67	0.49
Ukrainian (48)	107	0.78
Welsh (0)	17	0.12
West Indian, ex. Hispanic (10)	10	0.07
Jamaican (10)	10	0.07
Yugoslavian (11)	11	0.08

Hispanic Origin	Population	%
Hispanic or Latino (of any race)	1,222	8.23
Central American, ex. Mexican	13	0.09
Guatemalan	4	0.03
Honduran	9	0.06
Cuban	6	0.04
Mexican	1,021	6.88
Puerto Rican	106	0.71
South American	30	0.20
Argentinean	2	0.01
Bolivian	2	0.01
Colombian	9	0.06
Ecuadorian	1	0.01
Paraguayan	2	0.01
Peruvian	9	0.06
Venezuelan	5	0.03
Other Hispanic or Latino	46	0.31

Race*	Population	%
African-American/Black (199)	241	1.62
Not Hispanic (183)	222	1.49
Hispanic (16)	19	0.13
American Indian/Alaska Native (19)	50	0.34
Not Hispanic (16)	44	0.30
Hispanic (3)	6	0.04
Cherokee (5)	15	0.10
Chickasaw (2)	2	0.01
Chippewa (1)	5	0.03
Delaware (0)	1	0.01
Iroquois (0)	6	0.04
Mexican American Ind. (1)	2	0.01
Navajo (0)	1	0.01
Osage (3)	3	0.02
Sioux (0)	1	0.01
Yup'ik *(Alaska Native)* (0)	1	0.01
Asian (187)	232	1.56
Not Hispanic (183)	227	1.53
Hispanic (4)	5	0.03
Chinese, ex. Taiwanese (23)	31	0.21
Filipino (61)	69	0.46
Indian (44)	51	0.34
Indonesian (0)	1	0.01
Japanese (1)	7	0.05
Korean (19)	25	0.17
Pakistani (17)	17	0.11
Thai (6)	7	0.05
Vietnamese (13)	19	0.13
Hawaii Native/Pacific Islander (10)	12	0.08
Not Hispanic (6)	7	0.05
Hispanic (4)	5	0.03
Native Hawaiian (10)	11	0.07
White (13,892)	14,071	94.75
Not Hispanic (13,113)	13,229	89.08
Hispanic (779)	842	5.67

Terre Haute

Place Type: City
County: Vigo
Population: 60,785†

Ancestry‡	Population	%
African, Sub-Saharan (691)	806	1.33
African (685)	800	1.32
Somalian (6)	6	0.01
American (11,657)	11,657	19.29
Arab (453)	525	0.87
Arab (108)	117	0.19
Jordanian (6)	6	0.01
Lebanese (24)	24	0.04
Syrian (74)	137	0.23
Other Arab (241)	241	0.40
Austrian (25)	85	0.14
Belgian (35)	75	0.12
British (90)	153	0.25
Canadian (33)	62	0.10

SECTION TWO

*Notes: † The Census 2010 population figure is used to calculate the percentages in the Hispanic Origin and Race categories. Ancestry percentages are based on the 2006-2010 American Community Survey population (not shown); ‡ Numbers in parentheses indicate the number of people reporting a single ancestry; * Numbers in parentheses indicate the number of persons reporting this race alone, not in combination with any other race; Please refer to the Explanation of Data for more information.*

Croatian (51)	85	0.14
Czech (69)	232	0.38
Czechoslovakian (43)	53	0.09
Danish (38)	75	0.12
Dutch (335)	1,355	2.24
Eastern European (26)	26	0.04
English (2,093)	5,550	9.18
Estonian (0)	53	0.09
European (396)	484	0.80
Finnish (32)	32	0.05
French, ex. Basque (487)	1,765	2.92
French Canadian (31)	85	0.14
German (5,115)	13,440	22.24
Greek (15)	52	0.09
Hungarian (135)	438	0.72
Icelander (0)	13	0.02
Irish (2,031)	7,200	11.91
Israeli (13)	13	0.02
Italian (848)	1,814	3.00
Latvian (69)	118	0.20
Lithuanian (33)	110	0.18
Northern European (0)	3	<0.01
Norwegian (51)	196	0.32
Pennsylvania German (2)	15	0.02
Polish (251)	1,184	1.96
Romanian (178)	263	0.44
Russian (7)	256	0.42
Scandinavian (41)	50	0.08
Scotch-Irish (308)	884	1.46
Scottish (348)	1,286	2.13
Serbian (24)	66	0.11
Slavic (0)	32	0.05
Slovak (22)	60	0.10
Slovene (16)	16	0.03
Swedish (86)	475	0.79
Swiss (42)	165	0.27
Turkish (8)	23	0.04
Ukrainian (20)	20	0.03
Welsh (122)	591	0.98
West Indian, ex. Hispanic (27)	27	0.04
Haitian (27)	27	0.04
Yugoslavian (27)	55	0.09

Hispanic Origin	Population	%
Hispanic or Latino (of any race)	1,893	3.11
Central American, ex. Mexican	63	0.10
Costa Rican	3	<0.01
Guatemalan	16	0.03
Honduran	22	0.04
Nicaraguan	2	<0.01
Panamanian	8	0.01
Salvadoran	12	0.02
Cuban	46	0.08
Dominican Republic	10	0.02
Mexican	1,469	2.42
Puerto Rican	140	0.23
South American	70	0.12
Argentinean	12	0.02
Bolivian	6	0.01
Chilean	6	0.01
Colombian	28	0.05
Ecuadorian	4	0.01
Peruvian	5	0.01
Venezuelan	9	0.01
Other Hispanic or Latino	95	0.16

Race*	Population	%
African-American/Black (6,644)	7,819	12.86
Not Hispanic (6,587)	7,705	12.68
Hispanic (57)	114	0.19
American Indian/Alaska Native (259)	685	1.13
Not Hispanic (231)	632	1.04
Hispanic (28)	53	0.09
Apache (1)	8	0.01
Blackfeet (2)	24	0.04
Canadian/French Am. Ind. (1)	1	<0.01
Cherokee (34)	159	0.26
Cheyenne (0)	6	0.01
Chickasaw (0)	4	0.01
Chippewa (2)	3	<0.01
Choctaw (3)	9	0.01
Comanche (0)	2	<0.01
Cree (8)	9	0.01
Creek (7)	8	0.01
Delaware (0)	1	<0.01
Houma (2)	2	<0.01
Iroquois (0)	4	0.01
Kiowa (2)	2	<0.01
Lumbee (0)	2	<0.01
Menominee (1)	1	<0.01
Mexican American Ind. (13)	20	0.03
Navajo (1)	6	0.01
Osage (1)	1	<0.01
Potawatomi (5)	6	0.01
Seminole (0)	1	<0.01
Sioux (15)	34	0.06
Tlingit-Haida *(Alaska Native)* (0)	1	<0.01
Ute (1)	1	<0.01
Yaqui (0)	3	<0.01
Asian (879)	1,092	1.80
Not Hispanic (876)	1,081	1.78
Hispanic (3)	11	0.02
Bangladeshi (2)	2	<0.01
Cambodian (1)	1	<0.01
Chinese, ex. Taiwanese (222)	254	0.42
Filipino (104)	159	0.26
Hmong (5)	7	0.01
Indian (213)	242	0.40
Indonesian (2)	5	0.01
Japanese (65)	112	0.18
Korean (118)	141	0.23
Malaysian (1)	9	0.01
Nepalese (5)	5	0.01
Pakistani (2)	6	0.01
Sri Lankan (0)	1	<0.01
Taiwanese (52)	55	0.09
Thai (7)	9	0.01
Vietnamese (28)	41	0.07
Hawaii Native/Pacific Islander (26)	79	0.13
Not Hispanic (22)	73	0.12
Hispanic (4)	6	0.01
Guamanian/Chamorro (8)	11	0.02
Native Hawaiian (10)	44	0.07
Samoan (2)	13	0.02
Tongan (0)	2	<0.01
White (50,750)	52,377	86.17
Not Hispanic (49,456)	50,949	83.82
Hispanic (1,294)	1,428	2.35

Valparaiso

Place Type: City
County: Porter
Population: 31,730†

Ancestry‡	Population	%
African, Sub-Saharan (96)	103	0.33
African (96)	96	0.31
Ghanaian (0)	7	0.02
American (1,281)	1,281	4.13
Arab (48)	80	0.26
Egyptian (0)	8	0.03
Lebanese (36)	57	0.18
Syrian (0)	3	0.01
Other Arab (12)	12	0.04
Assyrian/Chaldean/Syriac (20)	20	0.06
Australian (13)	24	0.08
Austrian (29)	192	0.62
Belgian (0)	18	0.06
British (39)	76	0.25
Bulgarian (12)	12	0.04
Canadian (19)	77	0.25
Croatian (141)	263	0.85
Czech (144)	288	0.93
Czechoslovakian (15)	65	0.21
Danish (77)	278	0.90
Dutch (212)	690	2.23
Eastern European (9)	21	0.07
English (682)	3,595	11.60
European (423)	451	1.46
Finnish (18)	18	0.06
French, ex. Basque (96)	1,006	3.25
French Canadian (49)	120	0.39
German (3,828)	10,693	34.50
Greek (220)	265	0.86
Hungarian (395)	744	2.40
Icelander (18)	18	0.06
Irish (1,223)	5,671	18.30
Italian (613)	1,785	5.76
Lithuanian (171)	271	0.87
Macedonian (19)	95	0.31
Norwegian (81)	302	0.97
Polish (839)	2,511	8.10
Romanian (55)	109	0.35
Russian (32)	318	1.03
Scandinavian (14)	55	0.18
Scotch-Irish (176)	485	1.57
Scottish (216)	755	2.44
Serbian (212)	421	1.36
Slavic (0)	82	0.26
Slovak (195)	530	1.71
Slovene (0)	17	0.05
Swedish (148)	906	2.92
Swiss (14)	90	0.29
Ukrainian (41)	76	0.25
Welsh (73)	377	1.22
West Indian, ex. Hispanic (19)	33	0.11
Jamaican (10)	10	0.03
West Indian (9)	23	0.07
Yugoslavian (8)	45	0.15

Hispanic Origin	Population	%
Hispanic or Latino (of any race)	2,263	7.13
Central American, ex. Mexican	54	0.17
Costa Rican	3	0.01
Guatemalan	31	0.10
Honduran	10	0.03
Nicaraguan	3	0.01
Panamanian	2	0.01
Salvadoran	4	0.01
Other Central American	1	<0.01
Cuban	16	0.05
Dominican Republic	8	0.03
Mexican	1,655	5.22
Puerto Rican	259	0.82
South American	93	0.29
Argentinean	4	0.01
Bolivian	8	0.03
Chilean	30	0.09
Colombian	13	0.04
Ecuadorian	12	0.04
Paraguayan	1	<0.01
Peruvian	20	0.06
Uruguayan	1	<0.01
Venezuelan	2	0.01
Other South American	2	0.01
Other Hispanic or Latino	178	0.56

Race*	Population	%
African-American/Black (1,036)	1,277	4.02
Not Hispanic (1,003)	1,214	3.83
Hispanic (33)	63	0.20
American Indian/Alaska Native (107)	281	0.89
Not Hispanic (72)	203	0.64
Hispanic (35)	78	0.25
Apache (2)	5	0.02
Blackfeet (1)	7	0.02
Canadian/French Am. Ind. (0)	1	<0.01
Central American Ind. (1)	2	0.01
Cherokee (9)	65	0.20
Chippewa (8)	13	0.04
Choctaw (1)	5	0.02
Comanche (0)	1	<0.01
Cree (1)	1	<0.01
Creek (0)	8	0.03
Delaware (1)	2	0.01
Iroquois (2)	5	0.02
Mexican American Ind. (12)	18	0.06
Navajo (3)	12	0.04
Ottawa (2)	2	0.01

*Notes: † The Census 2010 population figure is used to calculate the percentages in the Hispanic Origin and Race categories. Ancestry percentages are based on the 2006-2010 American Community Survey population (not shown); ‡ Numbers in parentheses indicate the number of people reporting a single ancestry; * Numbers in parentheses indicate the number of persons reporting this race alone, not in combination with any other race; Please refer to the Explanation of Data for more information.*

Potawatomi (6)	10	0.03
Seminole (0)	3	0.01
Shoshone (0)	1	<0.01
Sioux (4)	13	0.04
South American Ind. (1)	4	0.01
Tlingit-Haida *(Alaska Native)* (1)	1	<0.01
Tohono O'Odham (3)	3	0.01
Yaqui (0)	5	0.02
Asian (667)	880	2.77
Not Hispanic (667)	863	2.72
Hispanic (0)	17	0.05
Bangladeshi (3)	3	0.01
Cambodian (1)	1	<0.01
Chinese, ex. Taiwanese (256)	284	0.90
Filipino (90)	155	0.49
Indian (111)	141	0.44
Japanese (18)	56	0.18
Korean (44)	65	0.20
Laotian (5)	6	0.02
Pakistani (26)	26	0.08
Sri Lankan (3)	6	0.02
Taiwanese (7)	7	0.02
Thai (7)	16	0.05
Vietnamese (79)	82	0.26
Hawaii Native/Pacific Islander (19)	32	0.10
Not Hispanic (17)	25	0.08
Hispanic (2)	7	0.02
Guamanian/Chamorro (13)	13	0.04
Marshallese (1)	1	<0.01
Native Hawaiian (1)	4	0.01
Samoan (0)	1	<0.01
White (28,512)	29,134	91.82
Not Hispanic (27,155)	27,623	87.06
Hispanic (1,357)	1,511	4.76

Vincennes

Place Type: City
County: Knox
Population: 18,423†

Ancestry‡	Population	%
American (3,021)	3,021	16.45
Arab (12)	12	0.07
Syrian (12)	12	0.07
Austrian (0)	54	0.29
Belgian (46)	71	0.39
British (8)	53	0.29
Canadian (13)	29	0.16
Croatian (0)	14	0.08
Czech (0)	35	0.19
Czechoslovakian (0)	49	0.27
Dutch (46)	235	1.28
English (714)	1,608	8.75
European (58)	85	0.46
French, ex. Basque (290)	1,161	6.32
French Canadian (10)	10	0.05
German (1,819)	4,554	24.79
Greek (52)	62	0.34
Hungarian (25)	64	0.35
Irish (711)	2,694	14.67
Italian (165)	454	2.47
Lithuanian (0)	26	0.14
Pennsylvania German (0)	9	0.05
Polish (29)	43	0.23
Russian (14)	14	0.08
Scandinavian (12)	12	0.07
Scotch-Irish (145)	220	1.20
Scottish (90)	226	1.23
Serbian (34)	34	0.19
Swedish (0)	43	0.23
Swiss (39)	39	0.21
Ukrainian (0)	14	0.08
Welsh (22)	134	0.73
West Indian, ex. Hispanic (34)	34	0.19
Bahamian (34)	34	0.19

Hispanic Origin	Population	%
Hispanic or Latino (of any race)	353	1.92
Central American, ex. Mexican	7	0.04
Costa Rican	1	0.01
Guatemalan	4	0.02
Honduran	1	0.01
Salvadoran	1	0.01
Cuban	8	0.04
Mexican	255	1.38
Puerto Rican	33	0.18
South American	13	0.07
Argentinean	1	0.01
Colombian	6	0.03
Peruvian	1	0.01
Uruguayan	1	0.01
Venezuelan	3	0.02
Other South American	1	0.01
Other Hispanic or Latino	37	0.20

Race*	Population	%
African-American/Black (866)	1,036	5.62
Not Hispanic (859)	1,017	5.52
Hispanic (7)	19	0.10
American Indian/Alaska Native (47)	135	0.73
Not Hispanic (41)	124	0.67
Hispanic (6)	11	0.06
Blackfeet (2)	9	0.05
Canadian/French Am. Ind. (0)	5	0.03
Cherokee (11)	39	0.21
Cheyenne (4)	5	0.03
Chickasaw (0)	1	0.01
Chippewa (3)	6	0.03
Choctaw (2)	2	0.01
Creek (1)	1	0.01
Iroquois (0)	1	0.01
Mexican American Ind. (3)	4	0.02
Navajo (0)	4	0.02
Osage (0)	1	0.01
Sioux (0)	4	0.02
Tohono O'Odham (0)	1	0.01
Asian (136)	168	0.91
Not Hispanic (135)	165	0.90
Hispanic (1)	3	0.02
Burmese (6)	6	0.03
Chinese, ex. Taiwanese (21)	29	0.16
Filipino (25)	36	0.20
Indian (20)	20	0.11
Japanese (13)	19	0.10
Korean (32)	34	0.18
Malaysian (2)	2	0.01
Pakistani (1)	1	0.01
Thai (4)	6	0.03
Vietnamese (9)	9	0.05
Hawaii Native/Pacific Islander (5)	10	0.05
Not Hispanic (5)	10	0.05
Native Hawaiian (5)	6	0.03
Samoan (0)	2	0.01
White (16,939)	17,224	93.49
Not Hispanic (16,754)	17,003	92.29
Hispanic (185)	221	1.20

Wabash

Place Type: City
County: Wabash
Population: 10,666†

Ancestry‡	Population	%
African, Sub-Saharan (21)	21	0.19
African (21)	21	0.19
American (2,352)	2,352	21.68
Belgian (0)	10	0.09
Czechoslovakian (40)	40	0.37
Dutch (101)	303	2.79
English (349)	897	8.27
European (63)	68	0.63
French, ex. Basque (76)	374	3.45
German (1,323)	2,689	24.79
Greek (9)	9	0.08
Hungarian (27)	27	0.25
Irish (524)	1,301	11.99
Italian (90)	179	1.65
Northern European (11)	11	0.10
Norwegian (23)	40	0.37
Pennsylvania German (10)	10	0.09
Polish (43)	93	0.86
Scotch-Irish (82)	159	1.47
Scottish (20)	120	1.11
Slovak (9)	36	0.33
Swedish (14)	43	0.40
Swiss (11)	21	0.19
Welsh (24)	82	0.76

Hispanic Origin	Population	%
Hispanic or Latino (of any race)	208	1.95
Central American, ex. Mexican	9	0.08
Guatemalan	8	0.08
Honduran	1	0.01
Cuban	1	0.01
Mexican	170	1.59
Puerto Rican	9	0.08
South American	1	0.01
Bolivian	1	0.01
Other Hispanic or Latino	18	0.17

Race*	Population	%
African-American/Black (45)	72	0.68
Not Hispanic (44)	71	0.67
Hispanic (1)	1	0.01
American Indian/Alaska Native (104)	186	1.74
Not Hispanic (103)	185	1.73
Hispanic (1)	1	0.01
Apache (1)	1	0.01
Blackfeet (0)	3	0.03
Cherokee (8)	38	0.36
Chippewa (1)	1	0.01
Choctaw (2)	3	0.03
Kiowa (0)	2	0.02
Menominee (1)	1	0.01
Navajo (1)	3	0.03
Osage (1)	2	0.02
Potawatomi (0)	1	0.01
Pueblo (2)	2	0.02
Sioux (2)	2	0.02
Yuman (0)	2	0.02
Asian (52)	58	0.54
Not Hispanic (52)	58	0.54
Cambodian (2)	2	0.02
Chinese, ex. Taiwanese (11)	12	0.11
Filipino (5)	6	0.06
Indian (18)	18	0.17
Japanese (6)	7	0.07
Korean (3)	4	0.04
Laotian (5)	5	0.05
Sri Lankan (1)	1	0.01
Vietnamese (1)	3	0.03
Hawaii Native/Pacific Islander (0)	1	0.01
Not Hispanic (0)	1	0.01
White (10,271)	10,397	97.48
Not Hispanic (10,142)	10,254	96.14
Hispanic (129)	143	1.34

Warsaw

Place Type: City
County: Kosciusko
Population: 13,559†

Ancestry‡	Population	%
African, Sub-Saharan (31)	78	0.58
African (15)	62	0.46
South African (16)	16	0.12
American (825)	825	6.17
Arab (0)	11	0.08
Other Arab (0)	11	0.08
Austrian (0)	19	0.14
Belgian (0)	78	0.58
British (10)	10	0.07
Canadian (6)	26	0.19
Czech (12)	12	0.09
Danish (0)	21	0.16
Dutch (110)	469	3.50
English (641)	1,535	11.47

*Notes: † The Census 2010 population figure is used to calculate the percentages in the Hispanic Origin and Race categories. Ancestry percentages are based on the 2006-2010 American Community Survey population (not shown); ‡ Numbers in parentheses indicate the number of people reporting a single ancestry; * Numbers in parentheses indicate the number of persons reporting this race alone, not in combination with any other race; Please refer to the Explanation of Data for more information.*

Ancestry	Population	%
European (40)	40	0.30
Finnish (12)	12	0.09
French, ex. Basque (62)	458	3.42
French Canadian (25)	67	0.50
German (1,542)	3,710	27.73
Greek (44)	175	1.31
Hungarian (0)	13	0.10
Irish (696)	1,854	13.86
Italian (176)	579	4.33
Latvian (0)	8	0.06
Northern European (12)	12	0.09
Norwegian (7)	31	0.23
Pennsylvania German (0)	10	0.07
Polish (113)	378	2.82
Russian (0)	43	0.32
Scotch-Irish (55)	177	1.32
Scottish (101)	278	2.08
Swedish (47)	177	1.32
Swiss (7)	102	0.76
Welsh (28)	105	0.78

Hispanic Origin	Population	%
Hispanic or Latino (of any race)	1,407	10.38
Central American, ex. Mexican	29	0.21
Guatemalan	20	0.15
Honduran	5	0.04
Panamanian	3	0.02
Salvadoran	1	0.01
Dominican Republic	4	0.03
Mexican	1,223	9.02
Puerto Rican	38	0.28
South American	50	0.37
Argentinean	10	0.07
Chilean	1	0.01
Colombian	13	0.10
Ecuadorian	7	0.05
Peruvian	16	0.12
Venezuelan	3	0.02
Other Hispanic or Latino	63	0.46

Race*	Population	%
African-American/Black (213)	293	2.16
Not Hispanic (206)	281	2.07
Hispanic (7)	12	0.09
American Indian/Alaska Native (63)	126	0.93
Not Hispanic (40)	92	0.68
Hispanic (23)	34	0.25
Apache (1)	3	0.02
Blackfeet (2)	7	0.05
Cherokee (5)	24	0.18
Chippewa (3)	4	0.03
Choctaw (1)	1	0.01
Iroquois (0)	3	0.02
Mexican American Ind. (6)	6	0.04
Navajo (4)	4	0.03
Potawatomi (1)	4	0.03
Seminole (0)	1	0.01
Spanish American Ind. (2)	2	0.01
Yakama (0)	1	0.01
Asian (294)	340	2.51
Not Hispanic (293)	336	2.48
Hispanic (1)	4	0.03
Cambodian (4)	8	0.06
Chinese, ex. Taiwanese (50)	55	0.41
Filipino (21)	30	0.22
Indian (185)	193	1.42
Japanese (9)	16	0.12
Korean (7)	11	0.08
Nepalese (4)	4	0.03
Pakistani (0)	1	0.01
Thai (7)	7	0.05
Vietnamese (6)	12	0.09
Hawaii Native/Pacific Islander (4)	19	0.14
Not Hispanic (4)	14	0.10
Hispanic (0)	5	0.04
Native Hawaiian (2)	11	0.08
White (12,131)	12,381	91.31
Not Hispanic (11,416)	11,579	85.40
Hispanic (715)	802	5.91

Washington

Place Type: City
County: Daviess
Population: 11,509†

Ancestry‡	Population	%
American (1,715)	1,715	15.03
British (19)	44	0.39
Canadian (28)	28	0.25
Czech (9)	22	0.19
Danish (0)	107	0.94
Dutch (61)	216	1.89
English (598)	1,230	10.78
European (46)	46	0.40
French, ex. Basque (22)	244	2.14
German (1,495)	3,049	26.72
Greek (9)	9	0.08
Irish (533)	1,694	14.85
Italian (55)	162	1.42
Polish (41)	82	0.72
Romanian (0)	6	0.05
Scotch-Irish (170)	319	2.80
Scottish (29)	85	0.74
Serbian (0)	11	0.10
Swedish (0)	56	0.49
Swiss (11)	23	0.20
Welsh (10)	10	0.09
West Indian, ex. Hispanic (0)	63	0.55
Jamaican (0)	63	0.55

Hispanic Origin	Population	%
Hispanic or Latino (of any race)	1,107	9.62
Central American, ex. Mexican	237	2.06
Costa Rican	1	0.01
Guatemalan	66	0.57
Honduran	10	0.09
Nicaraguan	4	0.03
Panamanian	1	0.01
Salvadoran	154	1.34
Other Central American	1	0.01
Cuban	8	0.07
Dominican Republic	5	0.04
Mexican	760	6.60
Puerto Rican	36	0.31
South American	12	0.10
Colombian	3	0.03
Ecuadorian	1	0.01
Peruvian	8	0.07
Other Hispanic or Latino	49	0.43

Race*	Population	%
African-American/Black (123)	209	1.82
Not Hispanic (116)	191	1.66
Hispanic (7)	18	0.16
American Indian/Alaska Native (34)	74	0.64
Not Hispanic (29)	61	0.53
Hispanic (5)	13	0.11
Cherokee (8)	22	0.19
Chippewa (0)	1	0.01
Choctaw (3)	7	0.06
Comanche (0)	1	0.01
Lumbee (1)	2	0.02
Mexican American Ind. (2)	3	0.03
Sioux (4)	4	0.03
South American Ind. (1)	1	0.01
Yup'ik *(Alaska Native)* (3)	3	0.03
Asian (122)	141	1.23
Not Hispanic (122)	141	1.23
Burmese (79)	80	0.70
Chinese, ex. Taiwanese (8)	8	0.07
Filipino (10)	22	0.19
Indian (8)	8	0.07
Japanese (2)	6	0.05
Korean (5)	6	0.05
Pakistani (5)	5	0.04
Thai (2)	2	0.02
Vietnamese (1)	1	0.01
Hawaii Native/Pacific Islander (8)	17	0.15
Not Hispanic (6)	14	0.12
Hispanic (2)	3	0.03
Guamanian/Chamorro (1)	1	0.01
Native Hawaiian (5)	12	0.10
White (10,267)	10,471	90.98
Not Hispanic (9,980)	10,114	87.88
Hispanic (287)	357	3.10

West Lafayette

Place Type: City
County: Tippecanoe
Population: 29,596†

Ancestry‡	Population	%
African, Sub-Saharan (285)	310	1.06
African (107)	132	0.45
Ethiopian (26)	26	0.09
Kenyan (29)	29	0.10
Nigerian (49)	49	0.17
Sudanese (9)	9	0.03
Other Sub-Saharan African (65)	65	0.22
Albanian (80)	80	0.27
American (584)	584	1.99
Arab (60)	80	0.27
Arab (5)	5	0.02
Egyptian (18)	29	0.10
Jordanian (11)	11	0.04
Lebanese (13)	13	0.04
Syrian (0)	9	0.03
Other Arab (13)	13	0.04
Armenian (15)	15	0.05
Assyrian/Chaldean/Syriac (0)	15	0.05
Australian (7)	7	0.02
Austrian (65)	146	0.50
Belgian (42)	127	0.43
Brazilian (104)	104	0.35
British (165)	250	0.85
Bulgarian (13)	38	0.13
Canadian (30)	117	0.40
Croatian (0)	167	0.57
Cypriot (61)	61	0.21
Czech (172)	342	1.17
Czechoslovakian (17)	17	0.06
Danish (27)	122	0.42
Dutch (143)	433	1.48
Eastern European (10)	10	0.03
English (974)	3,145	10.72
Estonian (8)	8	0.03
European (417)	484	1.65
Finnish (24)	58	0.20
French, ex. Basque (82)	733	2.50
French Canadian (7)	60	0.20
German (2,766)	8,087	27.56
Greek (117)	181	0.62
Hungarian (40)	195	0.66
Iranian (27)	32	0.11
Irish (1,021)	4,067	13.86
Italian (584)	1,422	4.85
Latvian (0)	18	0.06
Lithuanian (0)	54	0.18
Macedonian (9)	9	0.03
New Zealander (26)	26	0.09
Northern European (14)	14	0.05
Norwegian (78)	349	1.19
Pennsylvania German (9)	9	0.03
Polish (365)	1,213	4.13
Portuguese (0)	28	0.10
Romanian (33)	96	0.33
Russian (312)	545	1.86
Scandinavian (0)	13	0.04
Scotch-Irish (72)	418	1.42
Scottish (194)	655	2.23
Serbian (28)	41	0.14
Slovak (32)	97	0.33
Slovene (23)	36	0.12
Swedish (119)	444	1.51
Swiss (65)	295	1.01
Turkish (99)	99	0.34
Ukrainian (0)	56	0.19
Welsh (32)	341	1.16

*Notes: † The Census 2010 population figure is used to calculate the percentages in the Hispanic Origin and Race categories. Ancestry percentages are based on the 2006-2010 American Community Survey population (not shown); ‡ Numbers in parentheses indicate the number of people reporting a single ancestry; * Numbers in parentheses indicate the number of persons reporting this race alone, not in combination with any other race; Please refer to the Explanation of Data for more information.*

West Indian, ex. Hispanic (9)	22	0.07
Jamaican (9)	9	0.03
Trinidadian/Tobagonian (0)	13	0.04
Yugoslavian (11)	28	0.10

Hispanic Origin	Population	%
Hispanic or Latino (of any race)	1,051	3.55
Central American, ex. Mexican	100	0.34
Costa Rican	10	0.03
Guatemalan	26	0.09
Honduran	17	0.06
Nicaraguan	2	0.01
Panamanian	28	0.09
Salvadoran	17	0.06
Cuban	24	0.08
Dominican Republic	12	0.04
Mexican	445	1.50
Puerto Rican	116	0.39
South American	241	0.81
Argentinean	53	0.18
Bolivian	17	0.06
Chilean	15	0.05
Colombian	94	0.32
Ecuadorian	17	0.06
Peruvian	26	0.09
Uruguayan	4	0.01
Venezuelan	15	0.05
Other Hispanic or Latino	113	0.38

Race*	Population	%
African-American/Black (813)	971	3.28
Not Hispanic (797)	933	3.15
Hispanic (16)	38	0.13
American Indian/Alaska Native (40)	118	0.40
Not Hispanic (37)	104	0.35
Hispanic (3)	14	0.05
Apache (0)	1	<0.01
Canadian/French Am. Ind. (0)	1	<0.01
Central American Ind. (1)	1	<0.01
Cherokee (8)	28	0.09
Cheyenne (0)	1	<0.01
Chippewa (1)	3	0.01
Choctaw (0)	1	<0.01
Cree (1)	1	<0.01
Creek (0)	2	0.01
Delaware (0)	1	<0.01
Hopi (1)	1	<0.01
Inupiat *(Alaska Native)* (1)	1	<0.01
Iroquois (0)	2	0.01
Lumbee (0)	2	0.01
Mexican American Ind. (1)	3	0.01
Navajo (0)	2	0.01
Ottawa (0)	1	<0.01
Pueblo (1)	3	0.01
Sioux (0)	2	0.01
South American Ind. (1)	3	0.01
Yup'ik *(Alaska Native)* (1)	1	<0.01
Asian (5,128)	5,498	18.58
Not Hispanic (5,116)	5,477	18.51
Hispanic (12)	21	0.07
Bangladeshi (16)	21	0.07
Burmese (3)	3	0.01
Cambodian (1)	1	<0.01
Chinese, ex. Taiwanese (1,747)	1,852	6.26
Filipino (89)	145	0.49
Hmong (1)	1	<0.01
Indian (1,572)	1,624	5.49
Indonesian (44)	49	0.17
Japanese (163)	206	0.70
Korean (853)	894	3.02
Laotian (1)	2	0.01
Malaysian (121)	135	0.46
Nepalese (7)	8	0.03
Pakistani (63)	74	0.25
Sri Lankan (40)	40	0.14
Taiwanese (182)	211	0.71
Thai (59)	65	0.22
Vietnamese (70)	94	0.32
Hawaii Native/Pacific Islander (5)	47	0.16
Not Hispanic (3)	45	0.15
Hispanic (2)	2	0.01
Guamanian/Chamorro (2)	3	0.01
Native Hawaiian (0)	10	0.03
Samoan (0)	1	<0.01
Tongan (1)	1	<0.01
White (22,736)	23,259	78.59
Not Hispanic (22,003)	22,468	75.92
Hispanic (733)	791	2.67

Westfield

Place Type: Town
County: Hamilton
Population: 30,068†

Ancestry‡	Population	%
African, Sub-Saharan (18)	28	0.10
African (18)	18	0.06
South African (0)	10	0.04
American (2,432)	2,432	8.77
Arab (0)	85	0.31
Iraqi (0)	14	0.05
Lebanese (0)	38	0.14
Syrian (0)	33	0.12
Austrian (29)	44	0.16
Belgian (30)	58	0.21
Brazilian (50)	50	0.18
British (78)	203	0.73
Canadian (38)	82	0.30
Croatian (0)	92	0.33
Czech (28)	117	0.42
Danish (37)	113	0.41
Dutch (121)	954	3.44
Eastern European (12)	58	0.21
English (1,433)	3,324	11.98
European (470)	518	1.87
Finnish (28)	55	0.20
French, ex. Basque (108)	681	2.45
French Canadian (70)	118	0.43
German (3,085)	8,736	31.49
Greek (25)	144	0.52
Hungarian (25)	571	2.06
Irish (916)	3,959	14.27
Italian (546)	1,459	5.26
Latvian (39)	39	0.14
Lithuanian (17)	67	0.24
Norwegian (42)	340	1.23
Polish (196)	983	3.54
Portuguese (0)	28	0.10
Romanian (65)	93	0.34
Russian (228)	311	1.12
Scandinavian (31)	82	0.30
Scotch-Irish (135)	395	1.42
Scottish (317)	832	3.00
Serbian (0)	65	0.23
Slovak (23)	89	0.32
Slovene (12)	84	0.30
Swedish (77)	601	2.17
Swiss (59)	175	0.63
Ukrainian (27)	43	0.15
Welsh (60)	299	1.08
West Indian, ex. Hispanic (23)	43	0.15
Belizean (11)	31	0.11
West Indian (12)	12	0.04

Hispanic Origin	Population	%
Hispanic or Latino (of any race)	1,746	5.81
Central American, ex. Mexican	122	0.41
Costa Rican	1	<0.01
Guatemalan	31	0.10
Honduran	28	0.09
Nicaraguan	5	0.02
Panamanian	11	0.04
Salvadoran	35	0.12
Other Central American	11	0.04
Cuban	32	0.11
Dominican Republic	19	0.06
Mexican	1,291	4.29
Puerto Rican	64	0.21
South American	103	0.34
Argentinean	7	0.02
Bolivian	5	0.02
Chilean	8	0.03
Colombian	29	0.10
Ecuadorian	3	0.01
Paraguayan	1	<0.01
Peruvian	15	0.05
Venezuelan	35	0.12
Other Hispanic or Latino	115	0.38

Race*	Population	%
African-American/Black (657)	818	2.72
Not Hispanic (643)	795	2.64
Hispanic (14)	23	0.08
American Indian/Alaska Native (69)	158	0.53
Not Hispanic (53)	121	0.40
Hispanic (16)	37	0.12
Apache (2)	2	0.01
Blackfeet (2)	7	0.02
Canadian/French Am. Ind. (1)	1	<0.01
Central American Ind. (0)	1	<0.01
Cherokee (12)	37	0.12
Chippewa (4)	9	0.03
Choctaw (1)	1	<0.01
Inupiat *(Alaska Native)* (1)	1	<0.01
Iroquois (1)	1	<0.01
Kiowa (1)	1	<0.01
Mexican American Ind. (6)	7	0.02
Navajo (6)	6	0.02
Osage (0)	3	0.01
Spanish American Ind. (0)	3	0.01
Asian (737)	915	3.04
Not Hispanic (732)	896	2.98
Hispanic (5)	19	0.06
Burmese (1)	2	0.01
Cambodian (56)	58	0.19
Chinese, ex. Taiwanese (119)	136	0.45
Filipino (70)	107	0.36
Hmong (43)	52	0.17
Indian (192)	218	0.73
Indonesian (9)	11	0.04
Japanese (29)	61	0.20
Korean (74)	100	0.33
Laotian (2)	2	0.01
Malaysian (1)	1	<0.01
Nepalese (5)	5	0.02
Pakistani (26)	32	0.11
Taiwanese (7)	7	0.02
Thai (9)	10	0.03
Vietnamese (64)	80	0.27
Hawaii Native/Pacific Islander (8)	13	0.04
Not Hispanic (4)	7	0.02
Hispanic (4)	6	0.02
Guamanian/Chamorro (3)	3	0.01
Native Hawaiian (5)	6	0.02
Samoan (0)	1	<0.01
White (27,321)	27,777	92.38
Not Hispanic (26,435)	26,804	89.14
Hispanic (886)	973	3.24

York

Place Type: Town
County: Delaware
Population: 9,405†

Ancestry‡	Population	%
Afghan (57)	57	0.62
American (957)	957	10.37
Australian (0)	15	0.16
Austrian (10)	23	0.25
British (31)	40	0.43
Canadian (12)	12	0.13
Danish (9)	9	0.10
Dutch (22)	240	2.60
English (439)	1,021	11.07
European (90)	90	0.98
Finnish (0)	17	0.18
French, ex. Basque (0)	140	1.52
German (1,362)	2,977	32.26

*Notes: † The Census 2010 population figure is used to calculate the percentages in the Hispanic Origin and Race categories. Ancestry percentages are based on the 2006-2010 American Community Survey population (not shown); ‡ Numbers in parentheses indicate the number of people reporting a single ancestry; * Numbers in parentheses indicate the number of persons reporting this race alone, not in combination with any other race; Please refer to the Explanation of Data for more information.*

Greek (17)	45	0.49
Irish (290)	1,350	14.63
Israeli (11)	11	0.12
Italian (79)	149	1.61
Lithuanian (13)	13	0.14
Norwegian (10)	30	0.33
Pennsylvania German (22)	37	0.40
Polish (60)	225	2.44
Russian (17)	30	0.33
Scotch-Irish (93)	117	1.27
Scottish (109)	223	2.42
Swedish (0)	35	0.38
Swiss (0)	84	0.91
Ukrainian (12)	12	0.13
Welsh (7)	62	0.67

Hispanic Origin	Population	%
Hispanic or Latino (of any race)	123	1.31
Central American, ex. Mexican	7	0.07
Guatemalan	3	0.03
Nicaraguan	3	0.03
Other Central American	1	0.01
Cuban	1	0.01
Dominican Republic	1	0.01
Mexican	76	0.81
Puerto Rican	6	0.06
South American	11	0.12
Bolivian	4	0.04
Chilean	3	0.03
Peruvian	4	0.04
Other Hispanic or Latino	21	0.22

Race*	Population	%
African-American/Black (148)	199	2.12
Not Hispanic (142)	193	2.05
Hispanic (6)	6	0.06
American Indian/Alaska Native (21)	29	0.31
Not Hispanic (13)	21	0.22
Hispanic (8)	8	0.09
Central American Ind. (1)	1	0.01
Cherokee (10)	13	0.14
Chickasaw (1)	1	0.01
Crow (1)	1	0.01
Iroquois (1)	1	0.01
Mexican American Ind. (2)	2	0.02
Asian (143)	176	1.87
Not Hispanic (140)	173	1.84
Hispanic (3)	3	0.03
Bangladeshi (2)	2	0.02
Chinese, ex. Taiwanese (28)	28	0.30
Filipino (36)	39	0.41
Indian (52)	55	0.58
Japanese (6)	18	0.19
Korean (10)	17	0.18
Taiwanese (1)	1	0.01
Thai (1)	1	0.01
Vietnamese (6)	6	0.06
Hawaii Native/Pacific Islander (2)	5	0.05
Not Hispanic (2)	5	0.05
Guamanian/Chamorro (1)	1	0.01
Native Hawaiian (1)	2	0.02
White (8,960)	9,055	96.28
Not Hispanic (8,889)	8,976	95.44
Hispanic (71)	79	0.84

Zionsville

Place Type: Town
County: Boone
Population: 14,160†

Ancestry‡	Population	%
American (635)	635	4.72
Arab (15)	78	0.58
Lebanese (0)	31	0.23
Syrian (0)	32	0.24
Other Arab (15)	15	0.11
Austrian (0)	52	0.39
Belgian (25)	47	0.35
British (103)	120	0.89
Canadian (38)	85	0.63
Croatian (0)	33	0.25
Czech (41)	141	1.05
Czechoslovakian (58)	58	0.43
Danish (15)	24	0.18
Dutch (78)	329	2.45
Eastern European (33)	63	0.47
English (1,255)	2,693	20.03
European (413)	461	3.43
Finnish (41)	46	0.34
French, ex. Basque (53)	597	4.44
French Canadian (49)	95	0.71
German (1,659)	4,150	30.87
Greek (27)	27	0.20
Hungarian (39)	159	1.18
Iranian (15)	27	0.20
Irish (656)	2,288	17.02
Italian (263)	901	6.70
Lithuanian (12)	63	0.47
New Zealander (13)	13	0.10
Northern European (56)	56	0.42
Norwegian (27)	109	0.81
Polish (63)	269	2.00
Romanian (0)	48	0.36
Russian (31)	140	1.04
Scandinavian (0)	10	0.07
Scotch-Irish (139)	221	1.64
Scottish (176)	390	2.90
Serbian (0)	15	0.11
Slavic (105)	119	0.89
Slovak (141)	247	1.84
Slovene (8)	39	0.29
Swedish (65)	193	1.44
Swiss (12)	61	0.45
Ukrainian (38)	99	0.74
Welsh (32)	102	0.76

Hispanic Origin	Population	%
Hispanic or Latino (of any race)	304	2.15
Central American, ex. Mexican	39	0.28
Costa Rican	2	0.01
Guatemalan	18	0.13
Honduran	7	0.05
Nicaraguan	1	0.01
Salvadoran	10	0.07
Other Central American	1	0.01
Cuban	19	0.13
Dominican Republic	1	0.01
Mexican	114	0.81
Puerto Rican	45	0.32
South American	52	0.37
Argentinean	10	0.07
Chilean	4	0.03
Colombian	21	0.15
Ecuadorian	4	0.03
Paraguayan	1	0.01
Peruvian	3	0.02
Uruguayan	1	0.01
Venezuelan	8	0.06
Other Hispanic or Latino	34	0.24

Race*	Population	%
African-American/Black (176)	228	1.61
Not Hispanic (173)	218	1.54
Hispanic (3)	10	0.07
American Indian/Alaska Native (21)	56	0.40
Not Hispanic (18)	53	0.37
Hispanic (3)	3	0.02
Blackfeet (0)	1	0.01
Cherokee (3)	19	0.13
Cheyenne (1)	1	0.01
Chippewa (0)	2	0.01
Choctaw (2)	3	0.02
Creek (0)	1	0.01
Crow (0)	1	0.01
Lumbee (0)	2	0.01
Potawatomi (0)	2	0.01
Seminole (0)	1	0.01
Asian (384)	485	3.43
Not Hispanic (384)	483	3.41
Hispanic (0)	2	0.01
Bangladeshi (1)	1	0.01
Cambodian (1)	1	0.01
Chinese, ex. Taiwanese (156)	170	1.20
Filipino (18)	36	0.25
Indian (88)	100	0.71
Indonesian (0)	3	0.02
Japanese (17)	38	0.27
Korean (37)	61	0.43
Malaysian (1)	1	0.01
Pakistani (17)	17	0.12
Taiwanese (13)	16	0.11
Thai (3)	4	0.03
Vietnamese (17)	17	0.12
Hawaii Native/Pacific Islander (2)	8	0.06
Not Hispanic (2)	8	0.06
Native Hawaiian (0)	1	0.01
White (13,314)	13,495	95.30
Not Hispanic (13,093)	13,261	93.65
Hispanic (221)	234	1.65

*Notes: † The Census 2010 population figure is used to calculate the percentages in the Hispanic Origin and Race categories. Ancestry percentages are based on the 2006-2010 American Community Survey population (not shown); ‡ Numbers in parentheses indicate the number of people reporting a single ancestry; * Numbers in parentheses indicate the number of persons reporting this race alone, not in combination with any other race; Please refer to the Explanation of Data for more information.*

IOWA

Place Type: State
Population: 3,046,355[†]

Ancestry[‡]	Population	%
Afghan (202)	202	0.01
African, Sub-Saharan (12,392)	15,454	0.51
African (7,979)	10,567	0.35
Ethiopian (787)	798	0.03
Ghanaian (97)	110	<0.01
Kenyan (475)	580	0.02
Liberian (262)	322	0.01
Nigerian (452)	604	0.02
Senegalese (26)	26	<0.01
Sierra Leonean (23)	23	<0.01
Somalian (239)	239	0.01
South African (200)	229	0.01
Sudanese (1,162)	1,178	0.04
Ugandan (150)	150	<0.01
Zimbabwean (27)	27	<0.01
Other Sub-Saharan African (513)	601	0.02
Albanian (477)	606	0.02
Alsatian (33)	102	<0.01
American (169,175)	169,175	5.61
Arab (3,273)	5,304	0.18
Arab (422)	696	0.02
Egyptian (718)	791	0.03
Iraqi (353)	353	0.01
Jordanian (162)	162	0.01
Lebanese (845)	1,976	0.07
Moroccan (52)	90	<0.01
Palestinian (206)	206	0.01
Syrian (167)	582	0.02
Other Arab (348)	448	0.01
Armenian (183)	415	0.01
Assyrian/Chaldean/Syriac (10)	17	<0.01
Australian (304)	829	0.03
Austrian (897)	4,718	0.16
Basque (34)	48	<0.01
Belgian (3,028)	8,265	0.27
Brazilian (439)	629	0.02
British (3,368)	7,841	0.26
Bulgarian (312)	584	0.02
Cajun (76)	348	0.01
Canadian (1,663)	3,406	0.11
Carpatho Rusyn (8)	20	<0.01
Celtic (129)	299	0.01
Croatian (1,682)	3,961	0.13
Cypriot (8)	16	<0.01
Czech (20,468)	62,486	2.07
Czechoslovakian (2,785)	5,659	0.19
Danish (20,531)	66,290	2.20
Dutch (58,496)	147,978	4.91
Eastern European (649)	852	0.03
English (89,724)	297,232	9.85
Estonian (54)	117	<0.01
European (26,560)	29,301	0.97
Finnish (891)	3,043	0.10
French, ex. Basque (12,454)	81,806	2.71
French Canadian (3,568)	10,232	0.34
German (536,712)	1,195,559	39.64
German Russian (0)	101	<0.01
Greek (2,723)	7,202	0.24
Guyanese (25)	72	<0.01
Hungarian (1,284)	4,143	0.14
Icelander (159)	249	0.01
Iranian (600)	891	0.03
Irish (107,270)	464,920	15.41
Israeli (312)	331	0.01
Italian (22,155)	66,844	2.22
Latvian (421)	942	0.03
Lithuanian (1,073)	2,882	0.10
Luxemburger (1,675)	5,983	0.20
Macedonian (33)	46	<0.01
Maltese (19)	43	<0.01
New Zealander (59)	85	<0.01
Northern European (2,981)	3,242	0.11
Norwegian (63,526)	169,885	5.63
Pennsylvania German (2,716)	4,659	0.15
Polish (10,974)	40,744	1.35
Portuguese (732)	2,120	0.07
Romanian (777)	1,394	0.05
Russian (3,391)	10,765	0.36
Scandinavian (4,906)	9,463	0.31
Scotch-Irish (15,408)	46,067	1.53
Scottish (12,718)	50,647	1.68
Serbian (506)	1,043	0.03
Slavic (194)	576	0.02
Slovak (499)	1,878	0.06
Slovene (190)	512	0.02
Swedish (26,521)	98,447	3.26
Swiss (3,326)	15,924	0.53
Turkish (442)	820	0.03
Ukrainian (1,551)	2,825	0.09
Welsh (4,587)	22,794	0.76
West Indian, ex. Hispanic (1,132)	1,944	0.06
Bahamian (10)	129	<0.01
Barbadian (30)	30	<0.01
Belizean (41)	52	<0.01
Bermudan (0)	7	<0.01
British West Indian (148)	158	0.01
Dutch West Indian (62)	185	0.01
Haitian (226)	276	0.01
Jamaican (318)	760	0.03
Trinidadian/Tobagonian (143)	156	0.01
U.S. Virgin Islander (26)	26	<0.01
West Indian (124)	161	0.01
Other West Indian (4)	4	<0.01
Yugoslavian (7,604)	8,581	0.28

Hispanic Origin	Population	%
Hispanic or Latino (of any race)	151,544	4.97
Central American, ex. Mexican	13,289	0.44
Costa Rican	255	0.01
Guatemalan	4,917	0.16
Honduran	1,539	0.05
Nicaraguan	472	0.02
Panamanian	413	0.01
Salvadoran	5,601	0.18
Other Central American	92	<0.01
Cuban	1,226	0.04
Dominican Republic	429	0.01
Mexican	117,090	3.84
Puerto Rican	4,885	0.16
South American	3,754	0.12
Argentinean	344	0.01
Bolivian	171	0.01
Chilean	329	0.01
Colombian	1,026	0.03
Ecuadorian	795	0.03
Paraguayan	69	<0.01
Peruvian	607	0.02
Uruguayan	61	<0.01
Venezuelan	310	0.01
Other South American	42	<0.01
Other Hispanic or Latino	10,871	0.36

Race*	Population	%
African-American/Black (89,148)	113,225	3.72
Not Hispanic (86,906)	108,852	3.57
Hispanic (2,242)	4,373	0.14
American Indian/Alaska Native (11,084)	24,511	0.80
Not Hispanic (8,581)	19,863	0.65
Hispanic (2,503)	4,648	0.15
Alaska Athabascan (*Ala. Nat.*) (18)	34	<0.01
Aleut (*Alaska Native*) (21)	33	<0.01
Apache (105)	346	0.01
Arapaho (17)	30	<0.01
Blackfeet (109)	583	0.02
Canadian/French Am. Ind. (24)	61	<0.01
Central American Ind. (39)	67	<0.01
Cherokee (768)	3,338	0.11
Cheyenne (41)	116	<0.01
Chickasaw (47)	107	<0.01
Chippewa (367)	710	0.02
Choctaw (120)	349	0.01
Colville (2)	6	<0.01
Comanche (40)	84	<0.01
Cree (17)	42	<0.01
Creek (59)	137	<0.01
Crow (20)	56	<0.01
Delaware (10)	30	<0.01
Hopi (13)	33	<0.01
Houma (3)	8	<0.01
Inupiat (*Alaska Native*) (26)	64	<0.01
Iroquois (79)	200	0.01
Kiowa (37)	80	<0.01
Lumbee (27)	57	<0.01
Menominee (24)	42	<0.01
Mexican American Ind. (486)	751	0.02
Navajo (112)	272	0.01
Osage (19)	52	<0.01
Ottawa (13)	29	<0.01
Paiute (14)	25	<0.01
Pima (19)	23	<0.01
Potawatomi (75)	135	<0.01
Pueblo (15)	28	<0.01
Puget Sound Salish (11)	17	<0.01
Seminole (22)	91	<0.01
Shoshone (8)	16	<0.01
Sioux (1,417)	2,725	0.09
South American Ind. (44)	100	<0.01
Spanish American Ind. (38)	55	<0.01
Tlingit-Haida (*Alaska Native*) (22)	34	<0.01
Tohono O'Odham (7)	20	<0.01
Tsimshian (*Alaska Native*) (4)	9	<0.01
Ute (5)	25	<0.01
Yakama (4)	9	<0.01
Yaqui (17)	43	<0.01
Yuman (0)	5	<0.01
Yup'ik (*Alaska Native*) (8)	12	<0.01
Asian (53,094)	64,512	2.12
Not Hispanic (52,597)	63,185	2.07
Hispanic (497)	1,327	0.04
Bangladeshi (137)	163	0.01
Bhutanese (62)	80	<0.01
Burmese (1,165)	1,260	0.04
Cambodian (747)	1,057	0.03
Chinese, ex. Taiwanese (9,309)	10,912	0.36
Filipino (3,558)	6,026	0.20
Hmong (491)	534	0.02
Indian (11,081)	12,525	0.41
Indonesian (177)	287	0.01
Japanese (1,332)	2,854	0.09
Korean (5,537)	7,375	0.24
Laotian (4,687)	5,744	0.19
Malaysian (230)	304	0.01
Nepalese (539)	598	0.02
Pakistani (815)	967	0.03
Sri Lankan (138)	180	0.01
Taiwanese (507)	601	0.02
Thai (1,432)	2,212	0.07
Vietnamese (8,347)	9,543	0.31
Hawaii Native/Pacific Islander (2,003)	3,847	0.13
Not Hispanic (1,797)	3,290	0.11
Hispanic (206)	557	0.02
Fijian (5)	21	<0.01
Guamanian/Chamorro (313)	572	0.02
Marshallese (391)	406	0.01
Native Hawaiian (381)	1,109	0.04
Samoan (128)	300	0.01
Tongan (23)	50	<0.01
White (2,781,561)	2,830,454	92.91
Not Hispanic (2,701,123)	2,739,834	89.94
Hispanic (80,438)	90,620	2.97

*Notes: † The Census 2010 population figure is used to calculate the percentages in the Hispanic Origin and Race categories. Ancestry percentages are based on the 2006-2010 American Community Survey population (not shown); ‡ Numbers in parentheses indicate the number of people reporting a single ancestry; * Numbers in parentheses indicate the number of persons reporting this race alone, not in combination with any other race; Please refer to the Explanation of Data for more information.*

Altoona

Place Type: City
County: Polk
Population: 14,541†

Ancestry‡	Population	%
African, Sub-Saharan (0)	26	0.19
Liberian (0)	26	0.19
American (864)	864	6.28
Arab (80)	80	0.58
Arab (40)	40	0.29
Iraqi (20)	20	0.15
Lebanese (20)	20	0.15
Austrian (0)	18	0.13
Belgian (53)	53	0.39
British (20)	69	0.50
Canadian (0)	11	0.08
Croatian (8)	41	0.30
Czech (45)	102	0.74
Czechoslovakian (0)	24	0.17
Danish (59)	225	1.64
Dutch (396)	1,147	8.34
English (389)	1,239	9.01
European (80)	90	0.65
Finnish (10)	40	0.29
French, ex. Basque (155)	543	3.95
French Canadian (8)	41	0.30
German (1,972)	4,659	33.87
Greek (39)	125	0.91
Hungarian (0)	17	0.12
Irish (411)	1,751	12.73
Italian (147)	493	3.58
Lithuanian (0)	7	0.05
Northern European (32)	32	0.23
Norwegian (273)	575	4.18
Polish (77)	201	1.46
Russian (11)	55	0.40
Scandinavian (16)	43	0.31
Scotch-Irish (20)	136	0.99
Scottish (72)	245	1.78
Swedish (347)	594	4.32
Swiss (0)	38	0.28
Welsh (33)	77	0.56

Hispanic Origin	Population	%
Hispanic or Latino (of any race)	420	2.89
Central American, ex. Mexican	21	0.14
Costa Rican	4	0.03
Guatemalan	7	0.05
Panamanian	3	0.02
Salvadoran	7	0.05
Cuban	8	0.06
Dominican Republic	2	0.01
Mexican	305	2.10
Puerto Rican	36	0.25
South American	19	0.13
Colombian	3	0.02
Ecuadorian	8	0.06
Peruvian	7	0.05
Venezuelan	1	0.01
Other Hispanic or Latino	29	0.20

Race*	Population	%
African-American/Black (162)	253	1.74
Not Hispanic (159)	241	1.66
Hispanic (3)	12	0.08
American Indian/Alaska Native (21)	57	0.39
Not Hispanic (15)	45	0.31
Hispanic (6)	12	0.08
Apache (2)	2	0.01
Cherokee (1)	2	0.01
Choctaw (0)	1	0.01
Comanche (2)	2	0.01
Menominee (1)	1	0.01
Mexican American Ind. (1)	1	0.01
Navajo (0)	3	0.02
Seminole (1)	5	0.03
Sioux (3)	9	0.06
Asian (167)	240	1.65
Not Hispanic (166)	237	1.63
Hispanic (1)	3	0.02
Cambodian (3)	6	0.04
Chinese, ex. Taiwanese (8)	18	0.12
Filipino (16)	35	0.24
Hmong (10)	10	0.07
Indian (12)	15	0.10
Indonesian (0)	2	0.01
Japanese (3)	4	0.03
Korean (23)	37	0.25
Laotian (33)	42	0.29
Pakistani (0)	3	0.02
Thai (10)	17	0.12
Vietnamese (34)	36	0.25
Hawaii Native/Pacific Islander (24)	47	0.32
Not Hispanic (24)	47	0.32
Guamanian/Chamorro (0)	5	0.03
Native Hawaiian (0)	2	0.01
Tongan (0)	1	0.01
White (13,828)	14,021	96.42
Not Hispanic (13,573)	13,732	94.44
Hispanic (255)	289	1.99

Ames

Place Type: City
County: Story
Population: 58,965†

Ancestry‡	Population	%
Afghan (47)	47	0.08
African, Sub-Saharan (619)	882	1.54
African (393)	604	1.05
Ethiopian (20)	20	0.03
Ghanaian (13)	13	0.02
Kenyan (0)	45	0.08
Nigerian (139)	139	0.24
Senegalese (9)	9	0.02
Zimbabwean (16)	16	0.03
Other Sub-Saharan African (29)	36	0.06
Albanian (0)	13	0.02
Alsatian (0)	29	0.05
American (1,444)	1,444	2.52
Arab (232)	336	0.59
Arab (40)	40	0.07
Egyptian (100)	148	0.26
Jordanian (62)	62	0.11
Lebanese (0)	56	0.10
Palestinian (22)	22	0.04
Other Arab (8)	8	0.01
Armenian (0)	9	0.02
Australian (8)	8	0.01
Austrian (27)	128	0.22
Belgian (110)	195	0.34
Brazilian (0)	16	0.03
British (96)	331	0.58
Cajun (0)	19	0.03
Canadian (98)	145	0.25
Celtic (11)	11	0.02
Croatian (11)	25	0.04
Czech (315)	1,167	2.04
Czechoslovakian (135)	355	0.62
Danish (515)	1,819	3.17
Dutch (613)	1,798	3.14
Eastern European (43)	43	0.07
English (1,541)	5,837	10.18
European (922)	1,016	1.77
Finnish (10)	47	0.08
French, ex. Basque (240)	1,678	2.93
French Canadian (35)	79	0.14
German (8,382)	20,682	36.07
Greek (121)	155	0.27
Guyanese (0)	38	0.07
Hungarian (92)	209	0.36
Iranian (13)	21	0.04
Irish (1,790)	7,487	13.06
Italian (377)	1,367	2.38
Latvian (0)	14	0.02
Lithuanian (38)	45	0.08
Luxemburger (12)	93	0.16
New Zealander (15)	15	0.03
Northern European (205)	208	0.36
Norwegian (1,665)	4,339	7.57
Polish (356)	1,267	2.21
Portuguese (75)	138	0.24
Romanian (23)	23	0.04
Russian (142)	449	0.78
Scandinavian (210)	380	0.66
Scotch-Irish (355)	880	1.53
Scottish (355)	1,600	2.79
Serbian (0)	13	0.02
Slavic (8)	29	0.05
Slovak (0)	24	0.04
Slovene (0)	47	0.08
Swedish (442)	2,603	4.54
Swiss (44)	446	0.78
Turkish (118)	129	0.22
Ukrainian (135)	219	0.38
Welsh (54)	446	0.78
West Indian, ex. Hispanic (88)	88	0.15
British West Indian (88)	88	0.15
Yugoslavian (109)	176	0.31

Hispanic Origin	Population	%
Hispanic or Latino (of any race)	2,027	3.44
Central American, ex. Mexican	167	0.28
Costa Rican	16	0.03
Guatemalan	67	0.11
Honduran	24	0.04
Nicaraguan	5	0.01
Panamanian	26	0.04
Salvadoran	27	0.05
Other Central American	2	<0.01
Cuban	45	0.08
Dominican Republic	15	0.03
Mexican	1,108	1.88
Puerto Rican	250	0.42
South American	271	0.46
Argentinean	32	0.05
Bolivian	8	0.01
Chilean	21	0.04
Colombian	68	0.12
Ecuadorian	38	0.06
Paraguayan	5	0.01
Peruvian	49	0.08
Uruguayan	23	0.04
Venezuelan	23	0.04
Other South American	4	0.01
Other Hispanic or Latino	171	0.29

Race*	Population	%
African-American/Black (1,993)	2,455	4.16
Not Hispanic (1,941)	2,345	3.98
Hispanic (52)	110	0.19
American Indian/Alaska Native (103)	338	0.57
Not Hispanic (77)	267	0.45
Hispanic (26)	71	0.12
Alaska Athabascan *(Ala. Nat.)* (1)	1	<0.01
Apache (3)	10	0.02
Arapaho (0)	1	<0.01
Blackfeet (1)	3	0.01
Cherokee (6)	55	0.09
Chickasaw (3)	3	0.01
Chippewa (4)	11	0.02
Choctaw (0)	3	0.01
Comanche (1)	1	<0.01
Creek (0)	4	0.01
Crow (0)	1	<0.01
Delaware (3)	7	0.01
Iroquois (0)	2	<0.01
Kiowa (1)	1	<0.01
Mexican American Ind. (3)	10	0.02
Osage (0)	1	<0.01
Potawatomi (0)	1	<0.01
Pueblo (0)	1	<0.01
Seminole (0)	1	<0.01
Sioux (13)	23	0.04
South American Ind. (7)	13	0.02
Yaqui (2)	2	<0.01
Asian (5,175)	5,689	9.65

*Notes: † The Census 2010 population figure is used to calculate the percentages in the Hispanic Origin and Race categories. Ancestry percentages are based on the 2006-2010 American Community Survey population (not shown); ‡ Numbers in parentheses indicate the number of people reporting a single ancestry; * Numbers in parentheses indicate the number of persons reporting this race alone, not in combination with any other race; Please refer to the Explanation of Data for more information.*

	Population	%
Not Hispanic (5,162)	5,650	9.58
Hispanic (13)	39	0.07
Bangladeshi (21)	23	0.04
Burmese (1)	1	<0.01
Cambodian (11)	23	0.04
Chinese, ex. Taiwanese (2,473)	2,581	4.38
Filipino (114)	177	0.30
Hmong (10)	11	0.02
Indian (904)	973	1.65
Indonesian (54)	63	0.11
Japanese (82)	150	0.25
Korean (690)	753	1.28
Laotian (61)	84	0.14
Malaysian (94)	114	0.19
Nepalese (34)	36	0.06
Pakistani (81)	91	0.15
Sri Lankan (41)	53	0.09
Taiwanese (117)	127	0.22
Thai (72)	104	0.18
Vietnamese (186)	226	0.38
Hawaii Native/Pacific Islander (17)	57	0.10
Not Hispanic (14)	45	0.08
Hispanic (3)	12	0.02
Guamanian/Chamorro (6)	12	0.02
Marshallese (1)	1	<0.01
Native Hawaiian (8)	21	0.04
Samoan (0)	3	0.01
Tongan (1)	1	<0.01
White (49,838)	50,904	86.33
Not Hispanic (48,639)	49,539	84.01
Hispanic (1,199)	1,365	2.31

Ankeny

Place Type: City
County: Polk
Population: 45,582†

Ancestry‡	Population	%
African, Sub-Saharan (77)	77	0.18
African (45)	45	0.11
Kenyan (10)	10	0.02
Sudanese (22)	22	0.05
American (1,935)	1,935	4.58
Arab (88)	261	0.62
Arab (11)	11	0.03
Lebanese (0)	142	0.34
Palestinian (67)	67	0.16
Syrian (0)	31	0.07
Other Arab (10)	10	0.02
Austrian (0)	61	0.14
Basque (13)	13	0.03
Belgian (59)	86	0.20
British (27)	140	0.33
Bulgarian (14)	29	0.07
Canadian (0)	12	0.03
Croatian (0)	81	0.19
Czech (172)	704	1.67
Czechoslovakian (27)	51	0.12
Danish (304)	944	2.24
Dutch (765)	2,019	4.78
English (1,536)	4,783	11.33
European (638)	638	1.51
Finnish (15)	29	0.07
French, ex. Basque (286)	1,412	3.35
French Canadian (22)	48	0.11
German (7,083)	16,795	39.79
Greek (28)	98	0.23
Hungarian (43)	81	0.19
Iranian (0)	21	0.05
Irish (1,208)	5,975	14.16
Italian (798)	1,997	4.73
Latvian (0)	12	0.03
Lithuanian (21)	64	0.15
Luxemburger (0)	6	0.01
Northern European (22)	22	0.05
Norwegian (1,245)	3,796	8.99
Pennsylvania German (29)	93	0.22
Polish (192)	754	1.79
Portuguese (14)	60	0.14
Romanian (0)	23	0.05
Russian (115)	165	0.39
Scandinavian (154)	276	0.65
Scotch-Irish (158)	493	1.17
Scottish (193)	747	1.77
Serbian (0)	14	0.03
Slavic (9)	9	0.02
Slovak (13)	38	0.09
Slovene (12)	12	0.03
Swedish (452)	1,523	3.61
Swiss (10)	137	0.32
Turkish (8)	25	0.06
Ukrainian (0)	29	0.07
Welsh (59)	318	0.75
Yugoslavian (274)	281	0.67

Hispanic Origin	Population	%
Hispanic or Latino (of any race)	1,033	2.27
Central American, ex. Mexican	87	0.19
Costa Rican	7	0.02
Guatemalan	37	0.08
Honduran	5	0.01
Nicaraguan	3	0.01
Panamanian	7	0.02
Salvadoran	28	0.06
Cuban	20	0.04
Dominican Republic	4	0.01
Mexican	659	1.45
Puerto Rican	87	0.19
South American	78	0.17
Argentinean	9	0.02
Bolivian	11	0.02
Chilean	9	0.02
Colombian	25	0.05
Ecuadorian	7	0.02
Paraguayan	1	<0.01
Peruvian	5	0.01
Venezuelan	11	0.02
Other Hispanic or Latino	98	0.21

Race*	Population	%
African-American/Black (548)	759	1.67
Not Hispanic (540)	739	1.62
Hispanic (8)	20	0.04
American Indian/Alaska Native (63)	194	0.43
Not Hispanic (56)	172	0.38
Hispanic (7)	22	0.05
Apache (1)	1	<0.01
Arapaho (3)	3	0.01
Blackfeet (1)	4	0.01
Canadian/French Am. Ind. (0)	1	<0.01
Cherokee (8)	33	0.07
Cheyenne (0)	1	<0.01
Chippewa (2)	3	0.01
Choctaw (0)	4	0.01
Creek (2)	2	<0.01
Crow (0)	1	<0.01
Iroquois (7)	8	0.02
Lumbee (0)	1	<0.01
Mexican American Ind. (2)	5	0.01
Navajo (1)	7	0.02
Osage (3)	3	0.01
Ottawa (1)	1	<0.01
Seminole (2)	3	0.01
Sioux (4)	13	0.03
South American Ind. (0)	1	<0.01
Yaqui (0)	5	0.01
Yup'ik *(Alaska Native)* (0)	1	<0.01
Asian (914)	1,133	2.49
Not Hispanic (908)	1,116	2.45
Hispanic (6)	17	0.04
Bangladeshi (1)	3	0.01
Burmese (8)	12	0.03
Cambodian (6)	8	0.02
Chinese, ex. Taiwanese (182)	215	0.47
Filipino (73)	119	0.26
Hmong (9)	10	0.02
Indian (137)	161	0.35
Indonesian (1)	4	0.01
Japanese (16)	48	0.11
Korean (108)	154	0.34
Laotian (82)	109	0.24
Malaysian (1)	6	0.01
Pakistani (28)	28	0.06
Taiwanese (4)	8	0.02
Thai (31)	50	0.11
Vietnamese (163)	187	0.41
Hawaii Native/Pacific Islander (23)	37	0.08
Not Hispanic (22)	33	0.07
Hispanic (1)	4	0.01
Guamanian/Chamorro (2)	3	0.01
Marshallese (0)	1	<0.01
Native Hawaiian (19)	22	0.05
Samoan (0)	3	0.01
White (43,188)	43,754	95.99
Not Hispanic (42,497)	42,983	94.30
Hispanic (691)	771	1.69

Bettendorf

Place Type: City
County: Scott
Population: 33,217†

Ancestry‡	Population	%
African, Sub-Saharan (0)	136	0.42
African (0)	136	0.42
American (1,419)	1,419	4.37
Arab (0)	20	0.06
Lebanese (0)	20	0.06
Armenian (82)	97	0.30
Australian (0)	24	0.07
Austrian (14)	80	0.25
Belgian (117)	473	1.46
British (34)	174	0.54
Cajun (2)	2	0.01
Canadian (61)	61	0.19
Croatian (19)	125	0.38
Czech (74)	362	1.11
Czechoslovakian (20)	37	0.11
Danish (100)	467	1.44
Dutch (260)	1,127	3.47
Eastern European (13)	48	0.15
English (773)	3,920	12.07
European (952)	1,022	3.15
Finnish (17)	54	0.17
French, ex. Basque (97)	889	2.74
French Canadian (9)	34	0.10
German (4,778)	11,859	36.50
Greek (51)	162	0.50
Hungarian (38)	110	0.34
Irish (1,642)	6,431	19.79
Italian (288)	1,119	3.44
Latvian (8)	8	0.02
Lithuanian (22)	31	0.10
Luxemburger (13)	28	0.09
Northern European (112)	130	0.40
Norwegian (286)	909	2.80
Pennsylvania German (8)	8	0.02
Polish (176)	743	2.29
Romanian (24)	35	0.11
Russian (53)	271	0.83
Scandinavian (34)	65	0.20
Scotch-Irish (170)	632	1.95
Scottish (198)	692	2.13
Serbian (12)	20	0.06
Slavic (9)	9	0.03
Slovak (20)	33	0.10
Slovene (0)	9	0.03
Swedish (358)	1,224	3.77
Swiss (85)	242	0.74
Turkish (35)	148	0.46
Ukrainian (41)	101	0.31
Welsh (15)	250	0.77
West Indian, ex. Hispanic (10)	22	0.07
Belizean (10)	10	0.03
Jamaican (0)	12	0.04

Hispanic Origin	Population	%
Hispanic or Latino (of any race)	1,205	3.63

*Notes: † The Census 2010 population figure is used to calculate the percentages in the Hispanic Origin and Race categories. Ancestry percentages are based on the 2006-2010 American Community Survey population (not shown); ‡ Numbers in parentheses indicate the number of people reporting a single ancestry; * Numbers in parentheses indicate the number of persons reporting this race alone, not in combination with any other race; Please refer to the Explanation of Data for more information.*

Central American, ex. Mexican	37	0.11
Costa Rican	5	0.02
Guatemalan	5	0.02
Honduran	3	0.01
Nicaraguan	6	0.02
Panamanian	14	0.04
Salvadoran	4	0.01
Cuban	14	0.04
Dominican Republic	4	0.01
Mexican	949	2.86
Puerto Rican	56	0.17
South American	76	0.23
Argentinean	7	0.02
Bolivian	3	0.01
Chilean	2	0.01
Colombian	30	0.09
Ecuadorian	10	0.03
Paraguayan	1	<0.01
Peruvian	17	0.05
Venezuelan	5	0.02
Other South American	1	<0.01
Other Hispanic or Latino	69	0.21

Race*	Population	%
African-American/Black (747)	1,003	3.02
Not Hispanic (731)	955	2.88
Hispanic (16)	48	0.14
American Indian/Alaska Native (65)	213	0.64
Not Hispanic (54)	172	0.52
Hispanic (11)	41	0.12
Alaska Athabascan *(Ala. Nat.)* (1)	1	<0.01
Apache (0)	1	<0.01
Blackfeet (2)	12	0.04
Canadian/French Am. Ind. (0)	1	<0.01
Cherokee (6)	52	0.16
Cheyenne (1)	1	<0.01
Chickasaw (0)	2	0.01
Chippewa (5)	12	0.04
Choctaw (3)	6	0.02
Hopi (1)	1	<0.01
Iroquois (1)	3	0.01
Kiowa (0)	3	0.01
Mexican American Ind. (7)	10	0.03
Navajo (2)	2	0.01
Osage (0)	1	<0.01
Shoshone (0)	1	<0.01
Sioux (3)	14	0.04
South American Ind. (1)	1	<0.01
Tlingit-Haida *(Alaska Native)* (0)	1	<0.01
Asian (1,025)	1,200	3.61
Not Hispanic (1,021)	1,186	3.57
Hispanic (4)	14	0.04
Bangladeshi (4)	7	0.02
Burmese (4)	4	0.01
Chinese, ex. Taiwanese (135)	158	0.48
Filipino (43)	69	0.21
Indian (531)	569	1.71
Indonesian (1)	1	<0.01
Japanese (34)	65	0.20
Korean (124)	163	0.49
Laotian (7)	7	0.02
Malaysian (3)	3	0.01
Nepalese (17)	17	0.05
Pakistani (42)	50	0.15
Sri Lankan (3)	3	0.01
Taiwanese (3)	3	0.01
Thai (9)	16	0.05
Vietnamese (40)	48	0.14
Hawaii Native/Pacific Islander (17)	33	0.10
Not Hispanic (15)	29	0.09
Hispanic (2)	4	0.01
Guamanian/Chamorro (0)	2	0.01
Native Hawaiian (7)	18	0.05
Samoan (2)	4	0.01
White (30,540)	31,063	93.52
Not Hispanic (29,688)	30,108	90.64
Hispanic (852)	955	2.88

Boone

Place Type: City
County: Boone
Population: 12,661†

Ancestry‡	Population	%
African, Sub-Saharan (70)	91	0.71
African (70)	91	0.71
American (663)	663	5.19
Arab (9)	23	0.18
Lebanese (9)	23	0.18
Austrian (21)	21	0.16
Belgian (35)	45	0.35
British (0)	33	0.26
Celtic (0)	14	0.11
Croatian (10)	10	0.08
Czech (67)	203	1.59
Czechoslovakian (21)	21	0.16
Danish (55)	194	1.52
Dutch (6)	194	1.52
English (391)	1,263	9.90
European (150)	189	1.48
French, ex. Basque (64)	412	3.23
French Canadian (16)	90	0.71
German (1,721)	4,702	36.84
Greek (14)	49	0.38
Irish (348)	1,638	12.83
Italian (147)	404	3.17
Northern European (47)	47	0.37
Norwegian (328)	1,104	8.65
Pennsylvania German (0)	7	0.05
Polish (23)	174	1.36
Portuguese (0)	45	0.35
Russian (0)	39	0.31
Scandinavian (6)	6	0.05
Scotch-Irish (18)	90	0.71
Scottish (109)	279	2.19
Serbian (26)	26	0.20
Swedish (391)	1,398	10.95
Swiss (27)	93	0.73
Welsh (0)	411	3.22
West Indian, ex. Hispanic (0)	48	0.38
Jamaican (0)	48	0.38

Hispanic Origin	Population	%
Hispanic or Latino (of any race)	252	1.99
Central American, ex. Mexican	10	0.08
Guatemalan	2	0.02
Nicaraguan	1	0.01
Panamanian	4	0.03
Salvadoran	3	0.02
Cuban	8	0.06
Dominican Republic	1	0.01
Mexican	179	1.41
Puerto Rican	16	0.13
South American	6	0.05
Bolivian	1	0.01
Chilean	2	0.02
Colombian	1	0.01
Peruvian	2	0.02
Other Hispanic or Latino	32	0.25

Race*	Population	%
African-American/Black (100)	171	1.35
Not Hispanic (97)	164	1.30
Hispanic (3)	7	0.06
American Indian/Alaska Native (37)	82	0.65
Not Hispanic (35)	75	0.59
Hispanic (2)	7	0.06
Apache (0)	2	0.02
Blackfeet (0)	4	0.03
Cherokee (2)	13	0.10
Chickasaw (0)	2	0.02
Chippewa (1)	2	0.02
Choctaw (6)	6	0.05
Lumbee (5)	6	0.05
Menominee (0)	1	0.01
Navajo (1)	2	0.02
Sioux (3)	7	0.06
Spanish American Ind. (1)	1	0.01
Asian (56)	91	0.72
Not Hispanic (56)	85	0.67
Hispanic (0)	6	0.05
Cambodian (2)	2	0.02
Chinese, ex. Taiwanese (9)	11	0.09
Filipino (6)	16	0.13
Indian (16)	21	0.17
Japanese (1)	7	0.06
Korean (10)	14	0.11
Pakistani (1)	1	0.01
Thai (1)	8	0.06
Vietnamese (9)	11	0.09
Hawaii Native/Pacific Islander (1)	6	0.05
Not Hispanic (1)	6	0.05
Guamanian/Chamorro (1)	2	0.02
Native Hawaiian (0)	3	0.02
White (12,238)	12,393	97.88
Not Hispanic (12,085)	12,214	96.47
Hispanic (153)	179	1.41

Burlington

Place Type: City
County: Des Moines
Population: 25,663†

Ancestry‡	Population	%
African, Sub-Saharan (470)	781	3.05
African (470)	781	3.05
American (2,372)	2,372	9.26
Arab (22)	22	0.09
Syrian (22)	22	0.09
Austrian (11)	11	0.04
Belgian (26)	47	0.18
British (47)	69	0.27
Bulgarian (0)	9	0.04
Czech (13)	83	0.32
Czechoslovakian (9)	17	0.07
Danish (107)	313	1.22
Dutch (191)	650	2.54
Eastern European (10)	10	0.04
English (791)	2,523	9.85
European (259)	290	1.13
Finnish (0)	11	0.04
French, ex. Basque (163)	1,054	4.12
French Canadian (15)	15	0.06
German (4,144)	9,132	35.67
Greek (11)	48	0.19
Hungarian (11)	31	0.12
Iranian (30)	30	0.12
Irish (673)	4,152	16.22
Italian (96)	475	1.86
Lithuanian (11)	33	0.13
Luxemburger (0)	26	0.10
Norwegian (128)	466	1.82
Pennsylvania German (0)	20	0.08
Polish (68)	249	0.97
Russian (7)	15	0.06
Scandinavian (0)	22	0.09
Scotch-Irish (160)	551	2.15
Scottish (110)	373	1.46
Slovak (0)	31	0.12
Swedish (330)	1,071	4.18
Swiss (0)	70	0.27
Ukrainian (13)	48	0.19
Welsh (0)	181	0.71
West Indian, ex. Hispanic (0)	13	0.05
Dutch West Indian (0)	13	0.05
Yugoslavian (11)	19	0.07

Hispanic Origin	Population	%
Hispanic or Latino (of any race)	789	3.07
Central American, ex. Mexican	13	0.05
Costa Rican	1	<0.01
Guatemalan	2	0.01
Honduran	2	0.01
Nicaraguan	2	0.01
Salvadoran	6	0.02
Cuban	2	0.01

*Notes: † The Census 2010 population figure is used to calculate the percentages in the Hispanic Origin and Race categories. Ancestry percentages are based on the 2006-2010 American Community Survey population (not shown); ‡ Numbers in parentheses indicate the number of people reporting a single ancestry; * Numbers in parentheses indicate the number of persons reporting this race alone, not in combination with any other race; Please refer to the Explanation of Data for more information.*

Dominican Republic	15	0.06
Mexican	620	2.42
Puerto Rican	38	0.15
South American	16	0.06
Argentinean	2	0.01
Chilean	1	<0.01
Colombian	5	0.02
Ecuadorian	3	0.01
Peruvian	2	0.01
Venezuelan	3	0.01
Other Hispanic or Latino	85	0.33

Race*	Population	%
African-American/Black (1,838)	2,337	9.11
Not Hispanic (1,797)	2,255	8.79
Hispanic (41)	82	0.32
American Indian/Alaska Native (70)	225	0.88
Not Hispanic (66)	197	0.77
Hispanic (4)	28	0.11
Blackfeet (6)	12	0.05
Cherokee (11)	44	0.17
Cheyenne (3)	4	0.02
Chickasaw (1)	1	<0.01
Chippewa (1)	1	<0.01
Choctaw (0)	1	<0.01
Comanche (1)	1	<0.01
Creek (1)	1	<0.01
Delaware (0)	1	<0.01
Iroquois (2)	7	0.03
Kiowa (2)	3	0.01
Mexican American Ind. (0)	1	<0.01
Navajo (1)	1	<0.01
Potawatomi (1)	1	<0.01
Seminole (0)	1	<0.01
Sioux (9)	19	0.07
Asian (196)	279	1.09
Not Hispanic (195)	272	1.06
Hispanic (1)	7	0.03
Chinese, ex. Taiwanese (39)	57	0.22
Filipino (28)	62	0.24
Indian (42)	44	0.17
Japanese (12)	21	0.08
Korean (29)	46	0.18
Laotian (12)	14	0.05
Nepalese (6)	7	0.03
Pakistani (1)	1	<0.01
Sri Lankan (1)	1	<0.01
Taiwanese (2)	2	0.01
Thai (5)	8	0.03
Vietnamese (6)	13	0.05
Hawaii Native/Pacific Islander (16)	29	0.11
Not Hispanic (13)	26	0.10
Hispanic (3)	3	0.01
Guamanian/Chamorro (8)	10	0.04
Native Hawaiian (7)	12	0.05
Samoan (1)	5	0.02
White (22,628)	23,340	90.95
Not Hispanic (22,142)	22,757	88.68
Hispanic (486)	583	2.27

Carroll

Place Type: City
County: Carroll
Population: 10,103†

Ancestry‡	Population	%
American (528)	528	5.26
Australian (0)	14	0.14
Austrian (0)	13	0.13
Bulgarian (0)	8	0.08
Czech (9)	39	0.39
Czechoslovakian (0)	13	0.13
Danish (33)	298	2.97
Dutch (28)	170	1.69
English (205)	672	6.69
European (0)	10	0.10
French, ex. Basque (180)	282	2.81
German (3,656)	5,986	59.58
Irish (161)	1,480	14.73
Italian (68)	121	1.20
Luxemburger (7)	7	0.07
Norwegian (48)	284	2.83
Pennsylvania German (10)	10	0.10
Polish (12)	26	0.26
Russian (0)	26	0.26
Scandinavian (33)	38	0.38
Scotch-Irish (50)	98	0.98
Scottish (26)	67	0.67
Swedish (21)	182	1.81
Swiss (15)	47	0.47
Welsh (0)	51	0.51

Hispanic Origin	Population	%
Hispanic or Latino (of any race)	239	2.37
Central American, ex. Mexican	28	0.28
Guatemalan	12	0.12
Honduran	3	0.03
Nicaraguan	2	0.02
Salvadoran	11	0.11
Mexican	190	1.88
Puerto Rican	4	0.04
Other Hispanic or Latino	17	0.17

Race*	Population	%
African-American/Black (55)	122	1.21
Not Hispanic (55)	121	1.20
Hispanic (0)	1	0.01
American Indian/Alaska Native (8)	55	0.54
Not Hispanic (8)	55	0.54
Blackfeet (0)	1	0.01
Cherokee (1)	9	0.09
Chippewa (0)	2	0.02
Creek (0)	1	0.01
Iroquois (0)	1	0.01
Navajo (0)	1	0.01
Sioux (0)	4	0.04
Asian (68)	86	0.85
Not Hispanic (68)	85	0.84
Hispanic (0)	1	0.01
Chinese, ex. Taiwanese (22)	23	0.23
Filipino (8)	10	0.10
Indian (11)	15	0.15
Japanese (0)	7	0.07
Korean (12)	15	0.15
Laotian (2)	2	0.02
Pakistani (4)	4	0.04
Vietnamese (9)	9	0.09
Hawaii Native/Pacific Islander (1)	4	0.04
Hispanic (1)	4	0.04
Guamanian/Chamorro (1)	1	0.01
Native Hawaiian (0)	3	0.03
Samoan (0)	1	0.01
White (9,694)	9,816	97.16
Not Hispanic (9,618)	9,727	96.28
Hispanic (76)	89	0.88

Cedar Falls

Place Type: City
County: Black Hawk
Population: 39,260†

Ancestry‡	Population	%
African, Sub-Saharan (113)	200	0.52
African (37)	118	0.31
Kenyan (34)	34	0.09
Nigerian (0)	6	0.02
Other Sub-Saharan African (42)	42	0.11
American (3,762)	3,762	9.85
Arab (8)	8	0.02
Lebanese (8)	8	0.02
Armenian (0)	14	0.04
Austrian (0)	10	0.03
Basque (0)	5	0.01
Belgian (0)	25	0.07
British (37)	52	0.14
Bulgarian (10)	10	0.03
Canadian (0)	12	0.03
Croatian (0)	12	0.03
Czech (177)	601	1.57
Czechoslovakian (29)	29	0.08
Danish (386)	1,134	2.97
Dutch (364)	1,324	3.47
English (841)	3,804	9.96
European (399)	436	1.14
Finnish (27)	99	0.26
French, ex. Basque (75)	1,019	2.67
French Canadian (26)	44	0.12
German (8,026)	16,838	44.10
Greek (0)	41	0.11
Icelander (11)	11	0.03
Irish (1,206)	4,998	13.09
Italian (291)	830	2.17
Lithuanian (78)	89	0.23
Luxemburger (29)	124	0.32
Northern European (171)	171	0.45
Norwegian (939)	2,909	7.62
Pennsylvania German (52)	133	0.35
Polish (147)	464	1.22
Russian (63)	130	0.34
Scandinavian (167)	235	0.62
Scotch-Irish (178)	686	1.80
Scottish (126)	912	2.39
Slovak (0)	125	0.33
Swedish (415)	1,106	2.90
Swiss (31)	182	0.48
Ukrainian (0)	9	0.02
Welsh (88)	277	0.73
West Indian, ex. Hispanic (0)	43	0.11
Jamaican (0)	43	0.11
Yugoslavian (62)	89	0.23

Hispanic Origin	Population	%
Hispanic or Latino (of any race)	771	1.96
Central American, ex. Mexican	48	0.12
Costa Rican	2	0.01
Guatemalan	14	0.04
Honduran	6	0.02
Nicaraguan	2	0.01
Panamanian	6	0.02
Salvadoran	15	0.04
Other Central American	3	0.01
Cuban	14	0.04
Dominican Republic	4	0.01
Mexican	486	1.24
Puerto Rican	67	0.17
South American	84	0.21
Argentinean	13	0.03
Bolivian	4	0.01
Chilean	12	0.03
Colombian	25	0.06
Ecuadorian	2	0.01
Paraguayan	2	0.01
Peruvian	19	0.05
Venezuelan	6	0.02
Other South American	1	<0.01
Other Hispanic or Latino	68	0.17

Race*	Population	%
African-American/Black (814)	1,075	2.74
Not Hispanic (794)	1,044	2.66
Hispanic (20)	31	0.08
American Indian/Alaska Native (60)	193	0.49
Not Hispanic (43)	167	0.43
Hispanic (17)	26	0.07
Blackfeet (4)	8	0.02
Cherokee (12)	35	0.09
Chippewa (3)	11	0.03
Choctaw (4)	6	0.02
Delaware (1)	1	<0.01
Mexican American Ind. (4)	5	0.01
Navajo (0)	1	<0.01
Osage (0)	4	0.01
Potawatomi (1)	4	0.01
Sioux (4)	10	0.03
Asian (888)	1,108	2.82
Not Hispanic (879)	1,092	2.78
Hispanic (9)	16	0.04
Bangladeshi (12)	13	0.03

*Notes: † The Census 2010 population figure is used to calculate the percentages in the Hispanic Origin and Race categories. Ancestry percentages are based on the 2006-2010 American Community Survey population (not shown); ‡ Numbers in parentheses indicate the number of people reporting a single ancestry; * Numbers in parentheses indicate the number of persons reporting this race alone, not in combination with any other race; Please refer to the Explanation of Data for more information.*

Cambodian (0)	1	<0.01
Chinese, ex. Taiwanese (249)	279	0.71
Filipino (29)	72	0.18
Indian (246)	278	0.71
Indonesian (5)	5	0.01
Japanese (35)	68	0.17
Korean (123)	164	0.42
Laotian (13)	22	0.06
Malaysian (0)	1	<0.01
Nepalese (3)	3	0.01
Pakistani (53)	69	0.18
Sri Lankan (3)	7	0.02
Taiwanese (14)	16	0.04
Thai (8)	13	0.03
Vietnamese (35)	50	0.13
Hawaii Native/Pacific Islander (1)	28	0.07
Not Hispanic (1)	26	0.07
Hispanic (0)	2	0.01
Guamanian/Chamorro (0)	2	0.01
Native Hawaiian (0)	14	0.04
White (36,651)	37,274	94.94
Not Hispanic (36,193)	36,730	93.56
Hispanic (458)	544	1.39

Cedar Rapids

Place Type: City
County: Linn
Population: 126,326†

Ancestry‡	Population	%
Afghan (36)	36	0.03
African, Sub-Saharan (666)	750	0.60
African (409)	479	0.38
Ghanaian (56)	56	0.04
Nigerian (8)	8	0.01
Sudanese (128)	128	0.10
Other Sub-Saharan African (65)	79	0.06
Albanian (13)	39	0.03
American (5,178)	5,178	4.13
Arab (486)	663	0.53
Arab (34)	52	0.04
Egyptian (84)	84	0.07
Iraqi (27)	27	0.02
Jordanian (51)	51	0.04
Lebanese (237)	330	0.26
Moroccan (6)	6	<0.01
Syrian (36)	92	0.07
Other Arab (11)	21	0.02
Austrian (36)	439	0.35
Belgian (86)	454	0.36
British (133)	477	0.38
Bulgarian (20)	20	0.02
Cajun (0)	58	0.05
Canadian (101)	163	0.13
Croatian (10)	67	0.05
Czech (3,014)	8,665	6.91
Czechoslovakian (344)	551	0.44
Danish (387)	1,715	1.37
Dutch (736)	4,245	3.38
English (3,471)	12,087	9.63
European (1,098)	1,224	0.98
Finnish (77)	194	0.15
French, ex. Basque (456)	3,861	3.08
French Canadian (141)	445	0.35
German (19,248)	49,660	39.59
Greek (205)	395	0.31
Hungarian (20)	234	0.19
Iranian (61)	69	0.06
Irish (5,062)	23,304	18.58
Israeli (0)	10	0.01
Italian (1,158)	2,842	2.27
Latvian (0)	108	0.09
Lithuanian (161)	305	0.24
Luxemburger (33)	233	0.19
Maltese (0)	14	0.01
New Zealander (0)	15	0.01
Northern European (41)	41	0.03
Norwegian (2,315)	6,543	5.22
Pennsylvania German (120)	184	0.15
Polish (442)	1,716	1.37
Portuguese (0)	76	0.06
Romanian (30)	64	0.05
Russian (118)	844	0.67
Scandinavian (106)	391	0.31
Scotch-Irish (614)	1,925	1.53
Scottish (485)	2,224	1.77
Serbian (8)	8	0.01
Slavic (48)	64	0.05
Slovak (25)	65	0.05
Slovene (22)	59	0.05
Swedish (547)	2,828	2.25
Swiss (210)	786	0.63
Turkish (0)	17	0.01
Ukrainian (21)	99	0.08
Welsh (130)	1,056	0.84
West Indian, ex. Hispanic (314)	370	0.29
Bahamian (0)	56	0.04
Barbadian (25)	25	0.02
Haitian (195)	195	0.16
Jamaican (14)	14	0.01
West Indian (80)	80	0.06
Yugoslavian (99)	132	0.11

Hispanic Origin	Population	%
Hispanic or Latino (of any race)	4,176	3.31
Central American, ex. Mexican	318	0.25
Costa Rican	35	0.03
Guatemalan	108	0.09
Honduran	42	0.03
Nicaraguan	41	0.03
Panamanian	28	0.02
Salvadoran	59	0.05
Other Central American	5	<0.01
Cuban	61	0.05
Dominican Republic	24	0.02
Mexican	2,928	2.32
Puerto Rican	280	0.22
South American	185	0.15
Argentinean	20	0.02
Bolivian	10	0.01
Chilean	25	0.02
Colombian	49	0.04
Ecuadorian	27	0.02
Paraguayan	3	<0.01
Peruvian	29	0.02
Uruguayan	2	<0.01
Venezuelan	19	0.02
Other South American	1	<0.01
Other Hispanic or Latino	380	0.30

Race*	Population	%
African-American/Black (7,046)	9,310	7.37
Not Hispanic (6,880)	8,996	7.12
Hispanic (166)	314	0.25
American Indian/Alaska Native (392)	1,114	0.88
Not Hispanic (338)	970	0.77
Hispanic (54)	144	0.11
Alaska Athabascan *(Ala. Nat.)* (1)	1	<0.01
Aleut *(Alaska Native)* (1)	1	<0.01
Apache (3)	15	0.01
Arapaho (2)	2	<0.01
Blackfeet (0)	22	0.02
Canadian/French Am. Ind. (1)	1	<0.01
Central American Ind. (1)	1	<0.01
Cherokee (34)	173	0.14
Cheyenne (0)	4	<0.01
Chickasaw (13)	16	0.01
Chippewa (25)	34	0.03
Choctaw (3)	10	0.01
Colville (1)	1	<0.01
Comanche (1)	4	<0.01
Cree (0)	1	<0.01
Creek (4)	9	0.01
Crow (0)	2	<0.01
Delaware (0)	1	<0.01
Hopi (0)	1	<0.01
Inupiat *(Alaska Native)* (0)	3	<0.01
Iroquois (4)	21	0.02
Kiowa (1)	1	<0.01
Lumbee (5)	5	<0.01
Menominee (5)	8	0.01
Mexican American Ind. (7)	18	0.01
Navajo (14)	27	0.02
Osage (0)	2	<0.01
Ottawa (2)	2	<0.01
Pima (0)	1	<0.01
Potawatomi (7)	7	0.01
Pueblo (3)	3	<0.01
Seminole (3)	4	<0.01
Shoshone (2)	4	<0.01
Sioux (36)	96	0.08
South American Ind. (5)	10	0.01
Tlingit-Haida *(Alaska Native)* (3)	6	<0.01
Tohono O'Odham (4)	6	<0.01
Ute (0)	2	<0.01
Yaqui (1)	3	<0.01
Yuman (0)	1	<0.01
Asian (2,796)	3,513	2.78
Not Hispanic (2,779)	3,454	2.73
Hispanic (17)	59	0.05
Bangladeshi (14)	16	0.01
Burmese (8)	8	0.01
Cambodian (9)	24	0.02
Chinese, ex. Taiwanese (355)	465	0.37
Filipino (200)	364	0.29
Hmong (2)	2	<0.01
Indian (1,080)	1,140	0.90
Indonesian (15)	22	0.02
Japanese (76)	146	0.12
Korean (266)	385	0.30
Laotian (109)	151	0.12
Malaysian (4)	9	0.01
Nepalese (33)	33	0.03
Pakistani (60)	71	0.06
Sri Lankan (9)	15	0.01
Taiwanese (12)	22	0.02
Thai (39)	84	0.07
Vietnamese (381)	451	0.36
Hawaii Native/Pacific Islander (147)	250	0.20
Not Hispanic (132)	224	0.18
Hispanic (15)	26	0.02
Fijian (1)	6	<0.01
Guamanian/Chamorro (10)	27	0.02
Marshallese (22)	25	0.02
Native Hawaiian (26)	53	0.04
Samoan (12)	19	0.02
Tongan (1)	5	<0.01
White (111,144)	114,533	90.66
Not Hispanic (108,696)	111,714	88.43
Hispanic (2,448)	2,819	2.23

Charles City

Place Type: City
County: Floyd
Population: 7,652†

Ancestry‡	Population	%
American (427)	427	5.57
Belgian (0)	8	0.10
British (0)	11	0.14
Cajun (0)	10	0.13
Canadian (4)	4	0.05
Czech (26)	122	1.59
Czechoslovakian (11)	11	0.14
Danish (81)	131	1.71
Dutch (16)	233	3.04
English (165)	605	7.89
European (66)	66	0.86
French, ex. Basque (59)	217	2.83
French Canadian (12)	33	0.43
German (2,189)	3,841	50.10
Irish (199)	811	10.58
Italian (0)	78	1.02
Norwegian (344)	601	7.84
Polish (14)	14	0.18
Portuguese (0)	19	0.25
Scotch-Irish (17)	102	1.33
Scottish (2)	30	0.39

*Notes: † The Census 2010 population figure is used to calculate the percentages in the Hispanic Origin and Race categories. Ancestry percentages are based on the 2006-2010 American Community Survey population (not shown); ‡ Numbers in parentheses indicate the number of people reporting a single ancestry; * Numbers in parentheses indicate the number of persons reporting this race alone, not in combination with any other race; Please refer to the Explanation of Data for more information.*

Swedish (99)	172	2.24
Swiss (15)	47	0.61
Welsh (20)	44	0.57

Hispanic Origin	Population	%
Hispanic or Latino (of any race)	201	2.63
Central American, ex. Mexican	6	0.08
Costa Rican	4	0.05
Guatemalan	1	0.01
Honduran	1	0.01
Cuban	3	0.04
Dominican Republic	8	0.10
Mexican	164	2.14
Puerto Rican	3	0.04
South American	6	0.08
Ecuadorian	5	0.07
Venezuelan	1	0.01
Other Hispanic or Latino	11	0.14

Race*	Population	%
African-American/Black (191)	226	2.95
Not Hispanic (188)	222	2.90
Hispanic (3)	4	0.05
American Indian/Alaska Native (12)	24	0.31
Not Hispanic (8)	18	0.24
Hispanic (4)	6	0.08
Cherokee (3)	7	0.09
Chippewa (4)	4	0.05
Comanche (2)	2	0.03
Crow (0)	1	0.01
Shoshone (0)	1	0.01
Sioux (0)	1	0.01
Asian (195)	217	2.84
Not Hispanic (192)	206	2.69
Hispanic (3)	11	0.14
Chinese, ex. Taiwanese (9)	9	0.12
Filipino (170)	184	2.40
Indian (3)	4	0.05
Indonesian (2)	5	0.07
Japanese (1)	3	0.04
Korean (3)	6	0.08
Vietnamese (1)	2	0.03
Hawaii Native/Pacific Islander (4)	9	0.12
Not Hispanic (4)	8	0.10
Hispanic (0)	1	0.01
Guamanian/Chamorro (1)	1	0.01
Native Hawaiian (1)	2	0.03
Samoan (1)	1	0.01
White (7,091)	7,168	93.67
Not Hispanic (6,994)	7,054	92.19
Hispanic (97)	114	1.49

Clear Lake

Place Type: City
County: Cerro Gordo
Population: 7,777†

Ancestry‡	Population	%
American (393)	393	5.04
Arab (44)	44	0.56
Egyptian (34)	34	0.44
Syrian (10)	10	0.13
Belgian (0)	15	0.19
British (17)	17	0.22
Croatian (0)	20	0.26
Czech (55)	262	3.36
Czechoslovakian (11)	45	0.58
Danish (47)	179	2.30
Dutch (56)	202	2.59
English (384)	978	12.54
European (37)	37	0.47
Finnish (9)	58	0.74
French, ex. Basque (84)	314	4.03
French Canadian (17)	34	0.44
German (1,382)	3,299	42.30
Greek (12)	20	0.26
Hungarian (13)	13	0.17
Iranian (10)	16	0.21
Irish (235)	883	11.32
Italian (24)	95	1.22
Norwegian (449)	1,078	13.82
Polish (26)	185	2.37
Russian (0)	13	0.17
Scandinavian (25)	37	0.47
Scotch-Irish (0)	123	1.58
Scottish (15)	134	1.72
Swedish (61)	341	4.37
Swiss (12)	99	1.27
Ukrainian (0)	62	0.79
Welsh (0)	51	0.65
West Indian, ex. Hispanic (0)	18	0.23
Jamaican (0)	18	0.23

Hispanic Origin	Population	%
Hispanic or Latino (of any race)	174	2.24
Central American, ex. Mexican	14	0.18
Costa Rican	1	0.01
Guatemalan	8	0.10
Honduran	1	0.01
Nicaraguan	2	0.03
Salvadoran	2	0.03
Cuban	1	0.01
Mexican	131	1.68
Puerto Rican	7	0.09
South American	3	0.04
Argentinean	2	0.03
Peruvian	1	0.01
Other Hispanic or Latino	18	0.23

Race*	Population	%
African-American/Black (35)	79	1.02
Not Hispanic (34)	78	1.00
Hispanic (1)	1	0.01
American Indian/Alaska Native (9)	42	0.54
Not Hispanic (7)	40	0.51
Hispanic (2)	2	0.03
Apache (1)	2	0.03
Cherokee (3)	8	0.10
Chippewa (0)	1	0.01
Choctaw (0)	1	0.01
Creek (0)	2	0.03
Lumbee (0)	1	0.01
Pima (1)	1	0.01
Sioux (0)	2	0.03
Tsimshian *(Alaska Native)* (0)	1	0.01
Asian (95)	132	1.70
Not Hispanic (91)	127	1.63
Hispanic (4)	5	0.06
Bangladeshi (0)	4	0.05
Cambodian (1)	1	0.01
Chinese, ex. Taiwanese (27)	28	0.36
Filipino (12)	32	0.41
Indian (11)	11	0.14
Indonesian (1)	1	0.01
Japanese (3)	6	0.08
Korean (11)	17	0.22
Laotian (24)	27	0.35
Vietnamese (0)	1	0.01
Hawaii Native/Pacific Islander (1)	7	0.09
Not Hispanic (1)	7	0.09
Guamanian/Chamorro (1)	1	0.01
Native Hawaiian (0)	1	0.01
White (7,488)	7,597	97.69
Not Hispanic (7,361)	7,465	95.99
Hispanic (127)	132	1.70

Clinton

Place Type: City
County: Clinton
Population: 26,885†

Ancestry‡	Population	%
African, Sub-Saharan (196)	242	0.90
African (196)	242	0.90
Alsatian (0)	9	0.03
American (1,746)	1,746	6.46
Arab (25)	25	0.09
Other Arab (25)	25	0.09
Armenian (0)	8	0.03
Austrian (0)	62	0.23
Belgian (31)	56	0.21
Brazilian (0)	13	0.05
British (0)	9	0.03
Bulgarian (0)	10	0.04
Canadian (55)	77	0.29
Croatian (0)	11	0.04
Czech (63)	232	0.86
Czechoslovakian (0)	9	0.03
Danish (259)	824	3.05
Dutch (306)	1,679	6.21
English (720)	2,274	8.42
European (166)	186	0.69
Finnish (0)	35	0.13
French, ex. Basque (84)	852	3.15
French Canadian (29)	178	0.66
German (4,648)	10,800	39.98
Greek (57)	188	0.70
Irish (1,304)	4,615	17.08
Italian (151)	807	2.99
Lithuanian (41)	54	0.20
Luxemburger (0)	30	0.11
Norwegian (150)	808	2.99
Pennsylvania German (12)	73	0.27
Polish (125)	627	2.32
Portuguese (11)	11	0.04
Romanian (0)	10	0.04
Russian (12)	98	0.36
Scandinavian (0)	33	0.12
Scotch-Irish (65)	251	0.93
Scottish (109)	395	1.46
Swedish (298)	918	3.40
Swiss (13)	59	0.22
Ukrainian (0)	23	0.09
Welsh (15)	162	0.60
Yugoslavian (21)	49	0.18

Hispanic Origin	Population	%
Hispanic or Latino (of any race)	883	3.28
Central American, ex. Mexican	7	0.03
Costa Rican	1	<0.01
Guatemalan	4	0.01
Panamanian	1	<0.01
Salvadoran	1	<0.01
Cuban	25	0.09
Mexican	711	2.64
Puerto Rican	36	0.13
South American	28	0.10
Argentinean	5	0.02
Bolivian	3	0.01
Chilean	4	0.01
Colombian	4	0.01
Ecuadorian	7	0.03
Peruvian	2	0.01
Venezuelan	3	0.01
Other Hispanic or Latino	76	0.28

Race*	Population	%
African-American/Black (1,166)	1,547	5.75
Not Hispanic (1,136)	1,500	5.58
Hispanic (30)	47	0.17
American Indian/Alaska Native (95)	253	0.94
Not Hispanic (88)	229	0.85
Hispanic (7)	24	0.09
Alaska Athabascan *(Ala. Nat.)* (0)	1	<0.01
Aleut *(Alaska Native)* (1)	1	<0.01
Apache (1)	5	0.02
Blackfeet (0)	2	0.01
Canadian/French Am. Ind. (0)	1	<0.01
Cherokee (10)	50	0.19
Cheyenne (1)	1	<0.01
Chickasaw (1)	1	<0.01
Chippewa (14)	19	0.07
Choctaw (5)	9	0.03
Cree (1)	1	<0.01
Crow (0)	1	<0.01
Delaware (2)	3	0.01
Iroquois (0)	1	<0.01
Menominee (4)	4	0.01

SECTION TWO

*Notes: † The Census 2010 population figure is used to calculate the percentages in the Hispanic Origin and Race categories. Ancestry percentages are based on the 2006-2010 American Community Survey population (not shown); ‡ Numbers in parentheses indicate the number of people reporting a single ancestry; * Numbers in parentheses indicate the number of persons reporting this race alone, not in combination with any other race; Please refer to the Explanation of Data for more information.*

Mexican American Ind. (0)	2	0.01
Navajo (2)	2	0.01
Sioux (7)	11	0.04
Tlingit-Haida *(Alaska Native)* (1)	1	<0.01
Yup'ik *(Alaska Native)* (2)	2	0.01
Asian (200)	268	1.00
Not Hispanic (197)	261	0.97
Hispanic (3)	7	0.03
Chinese, ex. Taiwanese (35)	41	0.15
Filipino (24)	48	0.18
Hmong (2)	2	0.01
Indian (57)	67	0.25
Indonesian (0)	3	0.01
Japanese (6)	13	0.05
Korean (43)	58	0.22
Laotian (7)	8	0.03
Nepalese (1)	1	<0.01
Pakistani (1)	5	0.02
Thai (2)	5	0.02
Vietnamese (10)	15	0.06
Hawaii Native/Pacific Islander (8)	16	0.06
Not Hispanic (5)	9	0.03
Hispanic (3)	7	0.03
Guamanian/Chamorro (1)	2	0.01
Native Hawaiian (3)	5	0.02
White (24,467)	25,104	93.38
Not Hispanic (24,007)	24,537	91.27
Hispanic (460)	567	2.11

Clive

Place Type: City
County: Polk
Population: 15,447†

Ancestry‡	Population	%
African, Sub-Saharan (165)	165	1.10
African (62)	62	0.41
Sudanese (103)	103	0.69
American (597)	597	3.99
Arab (0)	11	0.07
Lebanese (0)	11	0.07
Armenian (0)	67	0.45
Austrian (12)	83	0.56
Belgian (7)	24	0.16
British (24)	100	0.67
Canadian (47)	47	0.31
Czech (84)	191	1.28
Danish (54)	260	1.74
Dutch (178)	663	4.43
Eastern European (48)	48	0.32
English (416)	1,552	10.38
European (260)	268	1.79
French, ex. Basque (24)	330	2.21
French Canadian (16)	52	0.35
German (2,254)	5,562	37.20
Greek (0)	38	0.25
Hungarian (21)	56	0.37
Irish (457)	2,759	18.45
Italian (291)	709	4.74
Lithuanian (0)	28	0.19
Luxemburger (0)	14	0.09
Northern European (52)	52	0.35
Norwegian (295)	907	6.07
Polish (102)	383	2.56
Portuguese (0)	14	0.09
Russian (101)	112	0.75
Scandinavian (53)	159	1.06
Scotch-Irish (0)	47	0.31
Scottish (83)	334	2.23
Serbian (0)	28	0.19
Slovak (20)	35	0.23
Swedish (34)	570	3.81
Swiss (0)	84	0.56
Ukrainian (21)	54	0.36
Welsh (40)	113	0.76
Yugoslavian (366)	366	2.45

Hispanic Origin	Population	%
Hispanic or Latino (of any race)	1,166	7.55
Central American, ex. Mexican	111	0.72
Costa Rican	7	0.05
Guatemalan	27	0.17
Honduran	5	0.03
Nicaraguan	4	0.03
Panamanian	9	0.06
Salvadoran	59	0.38
Cuban	10	0.06
Dominican Republic	2	0.01
Mexican	820	5.31
Puerto Rican	28	0.18
South American	129	0.84
Argentinean	5	0.03
Bolivian	3	0.02
Chilean	11	0.07
Colombian	8	0.05
Ecuadorian	84	0.54
Paraguayan	3	0.02
Peruvian	9	0.06
Venezuelan	3	0.02
Other South American	3	0.02
Other Hispanic or Latino	66	0.43

Race*	Population	%
African-American/Black (337)	424	2.74
Not Hispanic (329)	410	2.65
Hispanic (8)	14	0.09
American Indian/Alaska Native (26)	83	0.54
Not Hispanic (21)	69	0.45
Hispanic (5)	14	0.09
Apache (0)	2	0.01
Blackfeet (0)	2	0.01
Central American Ind. (1)	1	0.01
Cherokee (1)	13	0.08
Chippewa (0)	1	0.01
Choctaw (6)	7	0.05
Comanche (0)	1	0.01
Iroquois (1)	1	0.01
Kiowa (2)	4	0.03
Mexican American Ind. (4)	6	0.04
Sioux (3)	4	0.03
South American Ind. (0)	3	0.02
Asian (616)	700	4.53
Not Hispanic (614)	687	4.45
Hispanic (2)	13	0.08
Burmese (28)	28	0.18
Cambodian (0)	1	0.01
Chinese, ex. Taiwanese (88)	106	0.69
Filipino (16)	22	0.14
Indian (248)	257	1.66
Japanese (5)	17	0.11
Korean (43)	57	0.37
Laotian (9)	15	0.10
Malaysian (1)	3	0.02
Pakistani (10)	10	0.06
Sri Lankan (6)	6	0.04
Taiwanese (12)	12	0.08
Thai (28)	33	0.21
Vietnamese (90)	105	0.68
Hawaii Native/Pacific Islander (3)	7	0.05
Not Hispanic (2)	6	0.04
Hispanic (1)	1	0.01
Native Hawaiian (2)	3	0.02
White (13,613)	13,910	90.05
Not Hispanic (13,109)	13,288	86.02
Hispanic (504)	622	4.03

Coralville

Place Type: City
County: Johnson
Population: 18,907†

Ancestry‡	Population	%
African, Sub-Saharan (535)	570	3.13
African (417)	452	2.49
Ethiopian (55)	55	0.30
Kenyan (8)	8	0.04
Nigerian (5)	5	0.03
Sudanese (50)	50	0.27
American (509)	509	2.80
Arab (392)	392	2.16
Arab (18)	18	0.10
Egyptian (248)	248	1.36
Iraqi (19)	19	0.10
Jordanian (38)	38	0.21
Lebanese (19)	19	0.10
Other Arab (50)	50	0.27
Austrian (12)	30	0.16
Belgian (25)	25	0.14
British (51)	73	0.40
Cajun (0)	49	0.27
Canadian (16)	23	0.13
Czech (124)	452	2.49
Czechoslovakian (12)	12	0.07
Danish (131)	328	1.80
Dutch (122)	726	3.99
Eastern European (24)	32	0.18
English (383)	1,970	10.83
European (302)	369	2.03
Finnish (0)	16	0.09
French, ex. Basque (127)	711	3.91
French Canadian (86)	129	0.71
German (2,210)	6,253	34.38
Greek (32)	67	0.37
Hungarian (10)	40	0.22
Irish (446)	2,700	14.85
Italian (124)	606	3.33
Lithuanian (10)	37	0.20
Luxemburger (0)	30	0.16
Norwegian (175)	674	3.71
Polish (115)	464	2.55
Portuguese (0)	10	0.05
Russian (28)	153	0.84
Scandinavian (28)	37	0.20
Scotch-Irish (75)	265	1.46
Scottish (68)	488	2.68
Slavic (34)	34	0.19
Slovak (0)	9	0.05
Slovene (0)	16	0.09
Swedish (152)	611	3.36
Swiss (0)	21	0.12
Turkish (19)	19	0.10
Welsh (0)	128	0.70
West Indian, ex. Hispanic (40)	92	0.51
Belizean (21)	21	0.12
Jamaican (19)	71	0.39
Yugoslavian (11)	55	0.30

Hispanic Origin	Population	%
Hispanic or Latino (of any race)	957	5.06
Central American, ex. Mexican	137	0.72
Costa Rican	3	0.02
Guatemalan	27	0.14
Honduran	45	0.24
Nicaraguan	8	0.04
Panamanian	8	0.04
Salvadoran	46	0.24
Cuban	11	0.06
Dominican Republic	5	0.03
Mexican	585	3.09
Puerto Rican	48	0.25
South American	82	0.43
Argentinean	13	0.07
Chilean	7	0.04
Colombian	21	0.11
Ecuadorian	18	0.10
Peruvian	15	0.08
Venezuelan	8	0.04
Other Hispanic or Latino	89	0.47

Race*	Population	%
African-American/Black (1,492)	1,741	9.21
Not Hispanic (1,476)	1,715	9.07
Hispanic (16)	26	0.14
American Indian/Alaska Native (59)	151	0.80
Not Hispanic (48)	128	0.68
Hispanic (11)	23	0.12
Apache (1)	1	0.01
Blackfeet (1)	5	0.03

*Notes: † The Census 2010 population figure is used to calculate the percentages in the Hispanic Origin and Race categories. Ancestry percentages are based on the 2006-2010 American Community Survey population (not shown); ‡ Numbers in parentheses indicate the number of people reporting a single ancestry; * Numbers in parentheses indicate the number of persons reporting this race alone, not in combination with any other race; Please refer to the Explanation of Data for more information.*

Central American Ind. (0)	1	0.01
Cherokee (1)	23	0.12
Chickasaw (0)	2	0.01
Chippewa (1)	2	0.01
Choctaw (1)	1	0.01
Comanche (0)	1	0.01
Cree (0)	1	0.01
Crow (0)	1	0.01
Inupiat *(Alaska Native)* (0)	3	0.02
Iroquois (1)	3	0.02
Kiowa (1)	4	0.02
Mexican American Ind. (5)	5	0.03
Navajo (0)	1	0.01
Sioux (4)	7	0.04
Tlingit-Haida *(Alaska Native)* (1)	1	0.01
Tohono O'Odham (1)	1	0.01
Yakama (1)	1	0.01
Yup'ik *(Alaska Native)* (1)	1	0.01
Asian (1,467)	1,627	8.61
Not Hispanic (1,457)	1,610	8.52
Hispanic (10)	17	0.09
Bangladeshi (5)	6	0.03
Burmese (3)	3	0.02
Cambodian (2)	2	0.01
Chinese, ex. Taiwanese (391)	417	2.21
Filipino (48)	73	0.39
Hmong (3)	3	0.02
Indian (467)	501	2.65
Indonesian (3)	4	0.02
Japanese (44)	77	0.41
Korean (266)	280	1.48
Laotian (5)	8	0.04
Malaysian (9)	11	0.06
Nepalese (11)	11	0.06
Pakistani (49)	51	0.27
Taiwanese (23)	28	0.15
Thai (19)	20	0.11
Vietnamese (79)	91	0.48
Hawaii Native/Pacific Islander (12)	21	0.11
Not Hispanic (12)	17	0.09
Hispanic (0)	4	0.02
Guamanian/Chamorro (3)	3	0.02
Native Hawaiian (2)	4	0.02
Samoan (2)	3	0.02
White (15,014)	15,452	81.73
Not Hispanic (14,468)	14,865	78.62
Hispanic (546)	587	3.10

Council Bluffs

Place Type: City
County: Pottawattamie
Population: 62,230†

Ancestry‡	Population	%
African, Sub-Saharan (43)	141	0.23
African (0)	98	0.16
Sudanese (28)	28	0.05
Other Sub-Saharan African (15)	15	0.02
Alsatian (0)	9	0.01
American (3,059)	3,059	4.99
Arab (9)	44	0.07
Lebanese (9)	23	0.04
Syrian (0)	21	0.03
Austrian (9)	28	0.05
Belgian (0)	32	0.05
British (95)	139	0.23
Canadian (0)	32	0.05
Croatian (44)	98	0.16
Czech (317)	990	1.61
Czechoslovakian (91)	135	0.22
Danish (1,185)	3,910	6.37
Dutch (286)	1,531	2.50
English (1,894)	6,097	9.94
European (478)	544	0.89
Finnish (19)	29	0.05
French, ex. Basque (234)	1,934	3.15
French Canadian (75)	239	0.39
German (7,324)	22,408	36.53
Greek (43)	108	0.18
Hungarian (22)	61	0.10
Iranian (10)	10	0.02
Irish (2,362)	11,291	18.41
Israeli (10)	10	0.02
Italian (541)	1,899	3.10
Lithuanian (14)	23	0.04
Luxemburger (0)	33	0.05
Macedonian (18)	18	0.03
New Zealander (0)	6	0.01
Norwegian (540)	1,789	2.92
Pennsylvania German (45)	131	0.21
Polish (325)	1,105	1.80
Portuguese (0)	91	0.15
Romanian (11)	11	0.02
Russian (0)	83	0.14
Scandinavian (43)	109	0.18
Scotch-Irish (292)	1,308	2.13
Scottish (212)	739	1.20
Serbian (14)	23	0.04
Slovak (9)	9	0.01
Swedish (480)	1,968	3.21
Swiss (21)	235	0.38
Turkish (31)	31	0.05
Ukrainian (23)	23	0.04
Welsh (246)	791	1.29
West Indian, ex. Hispanic (51)	62	0.10
British West Indian (41)	41	0.07
Haitian (10)	21	0.03
Yugoslavian (52)	77	0.13

Hispanic Origin	Population	%
Hispanic or Latino (of any race)	5,277	8.48
Central American, ex. Mexican	433	0.70
Costa Rican	5	0.01
Guatemalan	56	0.09
Honduran	42	0.07
Nicaraguan	12	0.02
Panamanian	11	0.02
Salvadoran	306	0.49
Other Central American	1	<0.01
Cuban	38	0.06
Dominican Republic	3	<0.01
Mexican	4,220	6.78
Puerto Rican	76	0.12
South American	36	0.06
Argentinean	5	0.01
Chilean	9	0.01
Colombian	5	0.01
Ecuadorian	2	<0.01
Peruvian	13	0.02
Venezuelan	2	<0.01
Other Hispanic or Latino	471	0.76

Race*	Population	%
African-American/Black (1,159)	1,705	2.74
Not Hispanic (1,110)	1,610	2.59
Hispanic (49)	95	0.15
American Indian/Alaska Native (357)	811	1.30
Not Hispanic (257)	645	1.04
Hispanic (100)	166	0.27
Alaska Athabascan *(Ala. Nat.)* (2)	2	<0.01
Aleut *(Alaska Native)* (2)	2	<0.01
Apache (11)	21	0.03
Blackfeet (4)	16	0.03
Canadian/French Am. Ind. (0)	1	<0.01
Central American Ind. (1)	6	0.01
Cherokee (29)	128	0.21
Cheyenne (0)	4	0.01
Chickasaw (1)	3	<0.01
Chippewa (9)	15	0.02
Choctaw (0)	5	0.01
Creek (3)	6	0.01
Delaware (0)	2	<0.01
Hopi (0)	1	<0.01
Iroquois (8)	15	0.02
Lumbee (1)	3	<0.01
Mexican American Ind. (22)	25	0.04
Navajo (0)	9	0.01
Potawatomi (5)	5	0.01
Puget Sound Salish (1)	1	<0.01
Seminole (0)	5	0.01
Sioux (37)	93	0.15
South American Ind. (4)	4	0.01
Spanish American Ind. (6)	6	0.01
Ute (0)	2	<0.01
Yup'ik *(Alaska Native)* (0)	1	<0.01
Asian (462)	679	1.09
Not Hispanic (441)	627	1.01
Hispanic (21)	52	0.08
Burmese (2)	2	<0.01
Cambodian (1)	1	<0.01
Chinese, ex. Taiwanese (47)	62	0.10
Filipino (129)	214	0.34
Indian (37)	60	0.10
Indonesian (1)	1	<0.01
Japanese (35)	81	0.13
Korean (51)	82	0.13
Laotian (8)	11	0.02
Nepalese (1)	1	<0.01
Sri Lankan (4)	4	0.01
Taiwanese (2)	2	<0.01
Thai (14)	24	0.04
Vietnamese (112)	132	0.21
Hawaii Native/Pacific Islander (24)	65	0.10
Not Hispanic (22)	58	0.09
Hispanic (2)	7	0.01
Guamanian/Chamorro (9)	17	0.03
Native Hawaiian (8)	18	0.03
Samoan (1)	6	0.01
White (56,539)	57,901	93.04
Not Hispanic (54,065)	55,026	88.42
Hispanic (2,474)	2,875	4.62

Creston

Place Type: City
County: Union
Population: 7,834†

Ancestry‡	Population	%
African, Sub-Saharan (10)	10	0.13
Sudanese (10)	10	0.13
American (883)	883	11.41
Austrian (0)	15	0.19
British (0)	28	0.36
Czech (94)	158	2.04
Danish (61)	83	1.07
Dutch (120)	379	4.90
English (382)	1,093	14.13
European (50)	57	0.74
French, ex. Basque (8)	149	1.93
French Canadian (33)	45	0.58
German (835)	2,146	27.73
Greek (0)	29	0.37
Irish (418)	1,231	15.91
Italian (66)	93	1.20
Northern European (9)	9	0.12
Norwegian (44)	90	1.16
Pennsylvania German (14)	14	0.18
Polish (14)	53	0.68
Scotch-Irish (115)	215	2.78
Scottish (29)	120	1.55
Swedish (128)	310	4.01
Swiss (0)	26	0.34
Ukrainian (18)	29	0.37
Welsh (52)	166	2.15

Hispanic Origin	Population	%
Hispanic or Latino (of any race)	183	2.34
Central American, ex. Mexican	6	0.08
Honduran	5	0.06
Salvadoran	1	0.01
Cuban	1	0.01
Dominican Republic	1	0.01
Mexican	130	1.66
Puerto Rican	9	0.11
South American	12	0.15
Bolivian	1	0.01
Colombian	4	0.05
Ecuadorian	6	0.08

*Notes: † The Census 2010 population figure is used to calculate the percentages in the Hispanic Origin and Race categories. Ancestry percentages are based on the 2006-2010 American Community Survey population (not shown); ‡ Numbers in parentheses indicate the number of people reporting a single ancestry; * Numbers in parentheses indicate the number of persons reporting this race alone, not in combination with any other race; Please refer to the Explanation of Data for more information.*

Peruvian	1	0.01
Other Hispanic or Latino	24	0.31

Race*	Population	%
African-American/Black (81)	113	1.44
Not Hispanic (81)	107	1.37
Hispanic (0)	6	0.08
American Indian/Alaska Native (24)	62	0.79
Not Hispanic (15)	40	0.51
Hispanic (9)	22	0.28
Apache (0)	1	0.01
Cherokee (1)	5	0.06
Cheyenne (0)	1	0.01
Chippewa (0)	3	0.04
Iroquois (0)	1	0.01
Navajo (0)	7	0.09
Sioux (3)	9	0.11
Yakama (0)	1	0.01
Asian (49)	73	0.93
Not Hispanic (48)	68	0.87
Hispanic (1)	5	0.06
Chinese, ex. Taiwanese (14)	18	0.23
Filipino (11)	18	0.23
Hmong (4)	4	0.05
Indian (9)	11	0.14
Japanese (1)	4	0.05
Korean (7)	19	0.24
Pakistani (1)	4	0.05
Taiwanese (1)	1	0.01
Thai (1)	1	0.01
Vietnamese (0)	3	0.04
Hawaii Native/Pacific Islander (2)	9	0.11
Not Hispanic (2)	4	0.05
Hispanic (0)	5	0.06
Guamanian/Chamorro (1)	6	0.08
Native Hawaiian (0)	2	0.03
White (7,523)	7,613	97.18
Not Hispanic (7,429)	7,502	95.76
Hispanic (94)	111	1.42

Davenport

Place Type: City
County: Scott
Population: 99,685†

Ancestry‡	Population	%
African, Sub-Saharan (622)	702	0.71
African (518)	598	0.61
Ethiopian (23)	23	0.02
Kenyan (23)	23	0.02
Liberian (26)	26	0.03
Nigerian (32)	32	0.03
Albanian (42)	42	0.04
American (5,869)	5,869	5.97
Arab (159)	180	0.18
Egyptian (9)	17	0.02
Lebanese (122)	135	0.14
Moroccan (28)	28	0.03
Armenian (46)	67	0.07
Assyrian/Chaldean/Syriac (10)	10	0.01
Australian (23)	23	0.02
Austrian (32)	164	0.17
Belgian (396)	1,023	1.04
Brazilian (106)	113	0.11
British (41)	205	0.21
Cajun (12)	12	0.01
Canadian (54)	189	0.19
Celtic (10)	10	0.01
Croatian (131)	243	0.25
Czech (289)	1,082	1.10
Czechoslovakian (101)	224	0.23
Danish (142)	866	0.88
Dutch (587)	2,009	2.04
Eastern European (13)	36	0.04
English (2,115)	7,289	7.41
Estonian (8)	8	0.01
European (821)	886	0.90
Finnish (17)	35	0.04
French, ex. Basque (439)	2,659	2.70
French Canadian (167)	408	0.41
German (14,069)	34,092	34.67
German Russian (0)	3	<0.01
Greek (194)	537	0.55
Hungarian (77)	164	0.17
Iranian (110)	137	0.14
Irish (3,090)	15,293	15.55
Italian (676)	2,249	2.29
Latvian (0)	23	0.02
Lithuanian (47)	91	0.09
Luxemburger (0)	45	0.05
Maltese (12)	12	0.01
Northern European (49)	49	0.05
Norwegian (611)	2,106	2.14
Pennsylvania German (52)	75	0.08
Polish (519)	1,846	1.88
Portuguese (36)	36	0.04
Romanian (29)	29	0.03
Russian (127)	356	0.36
Scandinavian (77)	123	0.13
Scotch-Irish (424)	1,258	1.28
Scottish (332)	1,215	1.24
Serbian (43)	43	0.04
Slavic (0)	50	0.05
Slovak (11)	65	0.07
Slovene (0)	41	0.04
Swedish (769)	2,848	2.90
Swiss (114)	502	0.51
Turkish (17)	17	0.02
Ukrainian (74)	136	0.14
Welsh (87)	461	0.47
West Indian, ex. Hispanic (7)	16	0.02
Haitian (0)	9	0.01
Trinidadian/Tobagonian (7)	7	0.01
Yugoslavian (10)	32	0.03

Hispanic Origin	Population	%
Hispanic or Latino (of any race)	7,255	7.28
Central American, ex. Mexican	102	0.10
Costa Rican	6	0.01
Guatemalan	29	0.03
Honduran	17	0.02
Nicaraguan	12	0.01
Panamanian	16	0.02
Salvadoran	19	0.02
Other Central American	3	<0.01
Cuban	64	0.06
Dominican Republic	14	0.01
Mexican	6,244	6.26
Puerto Rican	307	0.31
South American	101	0.10
Argentinean	8	0.01
Bolivian	12	0.01
Chilean	13	0.01
Colombian	29	0.03
Ecuadorian	11	0.01
Paraguayan	1	<0.01
Peruvian	16	0.02
Uruguayan	1	<0.01
Venezuelan	9	0.01
Other South American	1	<0.01
Other Hispanic or Latino	423	0.42

Race*	Population	%
African-American/Black (10,759)	13,259	13.30
Not Hispanic (10,465)	12,633	12.67
Hispanic (294)	626	0.63
American Indian/Alaska Native (380)	1,198	1.20
Not Hispanic (270)	959	0.96
Hispanic (110)	239	0.24
Apache (7)	39	0.04
Arapaho (0)	1	<0.01
Blackfeet (6)	49	0.05
Canadian/French Am. Ind. (3)	6	0.01
Central American Ind. (1)	1	<0.01
Cherokee (48)	212	0.21
Cheyenne (1)	7	0.01
Chickasaw (2)	8	0.01
Chippewa (19)	33	0.03
Choctaw (3)	12	0.01
Comanche (3)	6	0.01
Creek (0)	6	0.01
Crow (0)	3	<0.01
Delaware (0)	1	<0.01
Hopi (0)	4	<0.01
Inupiat *(Alaska Native)* (7)	8	0.01
Iroquois (2)	12	0.01
Kiowa (14)	31	0.03
Lumbee (0)	1	<0.01
Menominee (1)	8	0.01
Mexican American Ind. (14)	33	0.03
Navajo (8)	20	0.02
Ottawa (0)	2	<0.01
Pima (2)	2	<0.01
Potawatomi (2)	2	<0.01
Pueblo (1)	1	<0.01
Puget Sound Salish (0)	4	<0.01
Seminole (0)	6	0.01
Sioux (25)	62	0.06
South American Ind. (3)	3	<0.01
Spanish American Ind. (2)	2	<0.01
Tohono O'Odham (1)	1	<0.01
Tsimshian *(Alaska Native)* (0)	4	<0.01
Yaqui (1)	4	<0.01
Asian (2,170)	2,650	2.66
Not Hispanic (2,140)	2,585	2.59
Hispanic (30)	65	0.07
Bangladeshi (3)	3	<0.01
Burmese (9)	10	0.01
Cambodian (14)	16	0.02
Chinese, ex. Taiwanese (194)	264	0.26
Filipino (132)	240	0.24
Indian (257)	312	0.31
Indonesian (4)	5	0.01
Japanese (54)	129	0.13
Korean (185)	265	0.27
Laotian (9)	27	0.03
Nepalese (36)	38	0.04
Pakistani (28)	36	0.04
Sri Lankan (2)	2	<0.01
Taiwanese (8)	16	0.02
Thai (36)	61	0.06
Vietnamese (1,095)	1,190	1.19
Hawaii Native/Pacific Islander (46)	126	0.13
Not Hispanic (36)	108	0.11
Hispanic (10)	18	0.02
Fijian (1)	1	<0.01
Guamanian/Chamorro (5)	16	0.02
Native Hawaiian (14)	50	0.05
Samoan (6)	24	0.02
White (80,401)	83,908	84.17
Not Hispanic (76,404)	79,156	79.41
Hispanic (3,997)	4,752	4.77

Decorah

Place Type: City
County: Winneshiek
Population: 8,127†

Ancestry‡	Population	%
African, Sub-Saharan (79)	90	1.11
African (40)	51	0.63
Ghanaian (11)	11	0.14
Liberian (11)	11	0.14
Nigerian (17)	17	0.21
American (187)	187	2.30
Arab (0)	16	0.20
Lebanese (0)	16	0.20
Austrian (22)	43	0.53
Belgian (0)	7	0.09
British (32)	42	0.52
Canadian (0)	6	0.07
Czech (69)	246	3.03
Czechoslovakian (24)	34	0.42
Danish (31)	134	1.65
Dutch (12)	95	1.17
English (162)	874	10.77
European (42)	52	0.64
Finnish (25)	74	0.91

*Notes: † The Census 2010 population figure is used to calculate the percentages in the Hispanic Origin and Race categories. Ancestry percentages are based on the 2006-2010 American Community Survey population (not shown); ‡ Numbers in parentheses indicate the number of people reporting a single ancestry; * Numbers in parentheses indicate the number of persons reporting this race alone, not in combination with any other race; Please refer to the Explanation of Data for more information.*

Ancestry	Population	%
French, ex. Basque (7)	206	2.54
French Canadian (21)	54	0.67
German (1,112)	3,573	44.03
Greek (0)	8	0.10
Irish (181)	1,220	15.03
Italian (24)	57	0.70
Lithuanian (27)	27	0.33
Luxemburger (0)	13	0.16
Norwegian (1,050)	2,395	29.51
Polish (29)	115	1.42
Russian (6)	17	0.21
Scandinavian (53)	73	0.90
Scotch-Irish (9)	65	0.80
Scottish (17)	148	1.82
Swedish (106)	487	6.00
Swiss (9)	28	0.35
Welsh (0)	29	0.36

Hispanic Origin	Population	%
Hispanic or Latino (of any race)	165	2.03
Central American, ex. Mexican	27	0.33
Guatemalan	19	0.23
Honduran	1	0.01
Panamanian	4	0.05
Salvadoran	3	0.04
Cuban	5	0.06
Dominican Republic	6	0.07
Mexican	80	0.98
Puerto Rican	9	0.11
South American	21	0.26
Bolivian	2	0.02
Colombian	7	0.09
Ecuadorian	3	0.04
Peruvian	9	0.11
Other Hispanic or Latino	17	0.21

Race*	Population	%
African-American/Black (123)	157	1.93
Not Hispanic (120)	149	1.83
Hispanic (3)	8	0.10
American Indian/Alaska Native (4)	14	0.17
Not Hispanic (4)	11	0.14
Hispanic (0)	3	0.04
Cherokee (1)	1	0.01
Chippewa (0)	2	0.02
Comanche (0)	1	0.01
Sioux (0)	1	0.01
Tlingit-Haida *(Alaska Native)* (0)	1	0.01
Tohono O'Odham (0)	1	0.01
Tsimshian *(Alaska Native)* (1)	1	0.01
Asian (180)	218	2.68
Not Hispanic (178)	213	2.62
Hispanic (2)	5	0.06
Cambodian (0)	2	0.02
Chinese, ex. Taiwanese (40)	49	0.60
Filipino (5)	10	0.12
Indian (36)	43	0.53
Indonesian (4)	5	0.06
Japanese (4)	7	0.09
Korean (50)	55	0.68
Laotian (11)	15	0.18
Nepalese (6)	6	0.07
Pakistani (0)	1	0.01
Taiwanese (0)	1	0.01
Thai (0)	1	0.01
Vietnamese (15)	20	0.25
Hawaii Native/Pacific Islander (3)	7	0.09
Not Hispanic (2)	6	0.07
Hispanic (1)	1	0.01
Guamanian/Chamorro (1)	1	0.01
Native Hawaiian (1)	2	0.02
Samoan (0)	2	0.02
White (7,686)	7,755	95.42
Not Hispanic (7,589)	7,648	94.11
Hispanic (97)	107	1.32

Denison

Place Type: City
County: Crawford
Population: 8,298†

Ancestry‡	Population	%
African, Sub-Saharan (39)	39	0.48
Somalian (14)	14	0.17
Sudanese (12)	12	0.15
Other Sub-Saharan African (13)	13	0.16
American (132)	132	1.63
British (0)	26	0.32
Canadian (9)	9	0.11
Croatian (0)	27	0.33
Czech (159)	185	2.29
Danish (100)	226	2.80
Dutch (20)	87	1.08
English (66)	357	4.42
European (23)	23	0.28
Finnish (0)	27	0.33
French, ex. Basque (0)	46	0.57
French Canadian (0)	32	0.40
German (1,717)	3,150	39.00
Greek (15)	15	0.19
Hungarian (0)	66	0.82
Irish (114)	615	7.61
Italian (0)	67	0.83
Norwegian (52)	379	4.69
Polish (7)	66	0.82
Scotch-Irish (0)	33	0.41
Scottish (0)	65	0.80
Swedish (25)	169	2.09
Welsh (0)	33	0.41

Hispanic Origin	Population	%
Hispanic or Latino (of any race)	3,490	42.06
Central American, ex. Mexican	788	9.50
Guatemalan	205	2.47
Honduran	36	0.43
Nicaraguan	14	0.17
Panamanian	1	0.01
Salvadoran	531	6.40
Other Central American	1	0.01
Cuban	3	0.04
Mexican	2,480	29.89
Puerto Rican	2	0.02
South American	2	0.02
Colombian	2	0.02
Other Hispanic or Latino	215	2.59

Race*	Population	%
African-American/Black (190)	226	2.72
Not Hispanic (178)	205	2.47
Hispanic (12)	21	0.25
American Indian/Alaska Native (46)	87	1.05
Not Hispanic (16)	27	0.33
Hispanic (30)	60	0.72
Apache (2)	3	0.04
Canadian/French Am. Ind. (1)	1	0.01
Central American Ind. (0)	5	0.06
Cherokee (0)	2	0.02
Iroquois (0)	1	0.01
Menominee (1)	1	0.01
Mexican American Ind. (3)	11	0.13
Potawatomi (1)	4	0.05
Sioux (4)	8	0.10
Asian (84)	96	1.16
Not Hispanic (83)	92	1.11
Hispanic (1)	4	0.05
Cambodian (3)	3	0.04
Chinese, ex. Taiwanese (5)	9	0.11
Filipino (2)	7	0.08
Hmong (8)	8	0.10
Indian (3)	3	0.04
Korean (6)	8	0.10
Laotian (27)	31	0.37
Thai (10)	17	0.20
Vietnamese (8)	12	0.14
Hawaii Native/Pacific Islander (15)	18	0.22
Not Hispanic (7)	9	0.11
Hispanic (8)	9	0.11
Guamanian/Chamorro (14)	16	0.19
Native Hawaiian (0)	1	0.01
Samoan (1)	1	0.01
White (5,861)	6,022	72.57
Not Hispanic (4,471)	4,510	54.35
Hispanic (1,390)	1,512	18.22

Des Moines

Place Type: City
County: Polk
Population: 203,433†

Ancestry‡	Population	%
Afghan (102)	102	0.05
African, Sub-Saharan (2,038)	2,294	1.14
African (874)	999	0.49
Ethiopian (103)	114	0.06
Ghanaian (17)	17	0.01
Kenyan (75)	126	0.06
Liberian (152)	152	0.08
Nigerian (67)	136	0.07
Sierra Leonean (23)	23	0.01
Somalian (195)	195	0.10
South African (12)	12	0.01
Sudanese (396)	396	0.20
Other Sub-Saharan African (124)	124	0.06
Albanian (0)	28	0.01
Alsatian (0)	10	<0.01
American (8,780)	8,780	4.34
Arab (349)	507	0.25
Arab (61)	94	0.05
Egyptian (13)	13	0.01
Iraqi (217)	217	0.11
Lebanese (32)	128	0.06
Syrian (9)	26	0.01
Other Arab (17)	29	0.01
Armenian (0)	17	0.01
Assyrian/Chaldean/Syriac (0)	7	<0.01
Austrian (66)	226	0.11
Basque (11)	11	0.01
Belgian (87)	430	0.21
Brazilian (8)	16	0.01
British (344)	607	0.30
Bulgarian (84)	84	0.04
Canadian (68)	117	0.06
Celtic (0)	18	0.01
Croatian (218)	385	0.19
Cypriot (8)	16	0.01
Czech (492)	2,013	1.00
Czechoslovakian (30)	156	0.08
Danish (693)	2,393	1.18
Dutch (2,139)	8,169	4.04
Eastern European (56)	84	0.04
English (5,847)	19,201	9.50
Estonian (25)	43	0.02
European (1,995)	2,097	1.04
Finnish (105)	260	0.13
French, ex. Basque (601)	4,219	2.09
French Canadian (110)	344	0.17
German (16,776)	49,043	24.27
German Russian (0)	37	0.02
Greek (97)	362	0.18
Guyanese (10)	10	<0.01
Hungarian (107)	242	0.12
Iranian (16)	16	0.01
Irish (7,392)	29,511	14.60
Italian (3,742)	9,152	4.53
Latvian (95)	224	0.11
Lithuanian (67)	311	0.15
Luxemburger (76)	222	0.11
Northern European (119)	153	0.08
Norwegian (2,777)	7,129	3.53
Pennsylvania German (63)	101	0.05
Polish (645)	2,144	1.06
Portuguese (79)	174	0.09
Romanian (67)	107	0.05
Russian (274)	718	0.36

*Notes: † The Census 2010 population figure is used to calculate the percentages in the Hispanic Origin and Race categories. Ancestry percentages are based on the 2006-2010 American Community Survey population (not shown); ‡ Numbers in parentheses indicate the number of people reporting a single ancestry; * Numbers in parentheses indicate the number of persons reporting this race alone, not in combination with any other race; Please refer to the Explanation of Data for more information.*

Scandinavian (332)	867	0.43
Scotch-Irish (1,268)	3,594	1.78
Scottish (1,010)	3,712	1.84
Serbian (85)	140	0.07
Slavic (4)	23	0.01
Slovak (34)	101	0.05
Slovene (0)	15	0.01
Swedish (1,330)	5,226	2.59
Swiss (148)	632	0.31
Turkish (0)	12	0.01
Ukrainian (28)	37	0.02
Welsh (311)	1,677	0.83
West Indian, ex. Hispanic (57)	290	0.14
Bahamian (10)	64	0.03
Dutch West Indian (0)	27	0.01
Jamaican (47)	199	0.10
Yugoslavian (1,259)	1,347	0.67

Hispanic Origin	Population	%
Hispanic or Latino (of any race)	24,334	11.96
Central American, ex. Mexican	2,480	1.22
Costa Rican	34	0.02
Guatemalan	544	0.27
Honduran	266	0.13
Nicaraguan	71	0.03
Panamanian	23	0.01
Salvadoran	1,515	0.74
Other Central American	27	0.01
Cuban	137	0.07
Dominican Republic	59	0.03
Mexican	19,167	9.42
Puerto Rican	531	0.26
South American	394	0.19
Argentinean	18	0.01
Bolivian	15	0.01
Chilean	21	0.01
Colombian	91	0.04
Ecuadorian	152	0.07
Paraguayan	2	<0.01
Peruvian	71	0.03
Venezuelan	13	0.01
Other South American	11	0.01
Other Hispanic or Latino	1,566	0.77

Race*	Population	%
African-American/Black (20,842)	24,555	12.07
Not Hispanic (20,430)	23,743	11.67
Hispanic (412)	812	0.40
American Indian/Alaska Native (1,008)	2,389	1.17
Not Hispanic (601)	1,684	0.83
Hispanic (407)	705	0.35
Alaska Athabascan *(Ala. Nat.)* (1)	2	<0.01
Aleut *(Alaska Native)* (4)	4	<0.01
Apache (5)	27	0.01
Arapaho (0)	4	<0.01
Blackfeet (18)	80	0.04
Canadian/French Am. Ind. (1)	6	<0.01
Central American Ind. (7)	8	<0.01
Cherokee (75)	353	0.17
Cheyenne (4)	8	<0.01
Chickasaw (4)	6	<0.01
Chippewa (38)	73	0.04
Choctaw (12)	40	0.02
Colville (1)	3	<0.01
Comanche (7)	10	<0.01
Cree (3)	4	<0.01
Creek (5)	17	0.01
Crow (2)	4	<0.01
Delaware (1)	1	<0.01
Hopi (0)	2	<0.01
Inupiat *(Alaska Native)* (6)	8	<0.01
Iroquois (4)	11	0.01
Kiowa (5)	5	<0.01
Lumbee (0)	1	<0.01
Menominee (0)	1	<0.01
Mexican American Ind. (79)	130	0.06
Navajo (15)	20	0.01
Osage (1)	6	<0.01
Ottawa (3)	4	<0.01
Potawatomi (11)	13	0.01
Pueblo (2)	3	<0.01
Puget Sound Salish (2)	2	<0.01
Seminole (1)	6	<0.01
Shoshone (1)	2	<0.01
Sioux (81)	195	0.10
South American Ind. (1)	4	<0.01
Spanish American Ind. (9)	15	0.01
Tlingit-Haida *(Alaska Native)* (1)	3	<0.01
Tohono O'Odham (0)	2	<0.01
Ute (1)	5	<0.01
Yakama (0)	1	<0.01
Yaqui (3)	4	<0.01
Asian (8,990)	10,392	5.11
Not Hispanic (8,923)	10,205	5.02
Hispanic (67)	187	0.09
Bangladeshi (5)	8	<0.01
Bhutanese (61)	79	0.04
Burmese (766)	810	0.40
Cambodian (374)	488	0.24
Chinese, ex. Taiwanese (424)	609	0.30
Filipino (294)	527	0.26
Hmong (170)	181	0.09
Indian (531)	731	0.36
Indonesian (9)	25	0.01
Japanese (86)	203	0.10
Korean (285)	463	0.23
Laotian (1,899)	2,269	1.12
Malaysian (39)	48	0.02
Nepalese (170)	213	0.10
Pakistani (35)	41	0.02
Sri Lankan (5)	9	<0.01
Taiwanese (6)	12	0.01
Thai (597)	806	0.40
Vietnamese (2,383)	2,626	1.29
Hawaii Native/Pacific Islander (149)	327	0.16
Not Hispanic (127)	261	0.13
Hispanic (22)	66	0.03
Fijian (1)	1	<0.01
Guamanian/Chamorro (45)	64	0.03
Native Hawaiian (44)	108	0.05
Samoan (14)	36	0.02
White (155,469)	161,365	79.32
Not Hispanic (143,413)	147,960	72.73
Hispanic (12,056)	13,405	6.59

Dubuque

Place Type: City
County: Dubuque
Population: 57,637[†]

Ancestry[‡]	Population	%
African, Sub-Saharan (128)	233	0.41
African (128)	233	0.41
Alsatian (9)	9	0.02
American (3,409)	3,409	5.93
Arab (0)	77	0.13
Arab (0)	47	0.08
Lebanese (0)	30	0.05
Austrian (9)	320	0.56
Belgian (34)	147	0.26
British (47)	63	0.11
Bulgarian (9)	9	0.02
Canadian (37)	63	0.11
Carpatho Rusyn (8)	8	0.01
Croatian (9)	46	0.08
Czech (112)	503	0.87
Czechoslovakian (0)	9	0.02
Danish (60)	224	0.39
Dutch (245)	1,354	2.35
English (1,120)	4,473	7.78
European (446)	446	0.78
Finnish (9)	9	0.02
French, ex. Basque (138)	1,870	3.25
French Canadian (281)	401	0.70
German (14,027)	29,864	51.93
German Russian (0)	12	0.02
Greek (163)	488	0.85
Hungarian (29)	132	0.23
Irish (2,687)	13,364	23.24
Italian (290)	1,426	2.48
Lithuanian (0)	53	0.09
Luxemburger (169)	563	0.98
Northern European (0)	4	0.01
Norwegian (334)	1,400	2.43
Pennsylvania German (0)	23	0.04
Polish (211)	801	1.39
Portuguese (0)	19	0.03
Romanian (137)	137	0.24
Russian (50)	131	0.23
Scandinavian (133)	183	0.32
Scotch-Irish (199)	418	0.73
Scottish (93)	618	1.07
Serbian (0)	27	0.05
Slavic (17)	27	0.05
Slovak (0)	10	0.02
Slovene (22)	32	0.06
Swedish (223)	1,008	1.75
Swiss (82)	460	0.80
Turkish (0)	9	0.02
Ukrainian (3)	9	0.02
Welsh (63)	301	0.52
West Indian, ex. Hispanic (9)	9	0.02
Jamaican (9)	9	0.02
Yugoslavian (25)	51	0.09

Hispanic Origin	Population	%
Hispanic or Latino (of any race)	1,383	2.40
Central American, ex. Mexican	70	0.12
Guatemalan	36	0.06
Honduran	8	0.01
Nicaraguan	1	<0.01
Panamanian	7	0.01
Salvadoran	18	0.03
Cuban	31	0.05
Dominican Republic	11	0.02
Mexican	881	1.53
Puerto Rican	143	0.25
South American	108	0.19
Argentinean	6	0.01
Bolivian	6	0.01
Chilean	3	0.01
Colombian	46	0.08
Ecuadorian	17	0.03
Peruvian	26	0.05
Venezuelan	3	0.01
Other South American	1	<0.01
Other Hispanic or Latino	139	0.24

Race*	Population	%
African-American/Black (2,302)	2,854	4.95
Not Hispanic (2,256)	2,785	4.83
Hispanic (46)	69	0.12
American Indian/Alaska Native (155)	412	0.71
Not Hispanic (123)	360	0.62
Hispanic (32)	52	0.09
Alaska Athabascan *(Ala. Nat.)* (1)	1	<0.01
Aleut *(Alaska Native)* (1)	3	0.01
Apache (3)	12	0.02
Blackfeet (1)	12	0.02
Canadian/French Am. Ind. (3)	5	0.01
Cherokee (12)	36	0.06
Cheyenne (1)	1	<0.01
Chippewa (12)	22	0.04
Choctaw (2)	12	0.02
Comanche (3)	9	0.02
Creek (0)	2	<0.01
Iroquois (4)	12	0.02
Mexican American Ind. (11)	11	0.02
Navajo (0)	1	<0.01
Paiute (0)	1	<0.01
Potawatomi (0)	3	0.01
Seminole (0)	1	<0.01
Sioux (11)	31	0.05
South American Ind. (0)	1	<0.01
Spanish American Ind. (1)	1	<0.01
Asian (659)	874	1.52
Not Hispanic (652)	860	1.49
Hispanic (7)	14	0.02
Bangladeshi (4)	4	0.01

*Notes: † The Census 2010 population figure is used to calculate the percentages in the Hispanic Origin and Race categories. Ancestry percentages are based on the 2006-2010 American Community Survey population (not shown); ‡ Numbers in parentheses indicate the number of people reporting a single ancestry; * Numbers in parentheses indicate the number of persons reporting this race alone, not in combination with any other race; Please refer to the Explanation of Data for more information.*

Cambodian (1)	3	0.01
Chinese, ex. Taiwanese (81)	108	0.19
Filipino (107)	151	0.26
Indian (238)	275	0.48
Indonesian (0)	4	0.01
Japanese (27)	70	0.12
Korean (72)	109	0.19
Nepalese (29)	30	0.05
Pakistani (11)	17	0.03
Sri Lankan (5)	5	0.01
Taiwanese (23)	24	0.04
Thai (6)	14	0.02
Vietnamese (34)	61	0.11
Hawaii Native/Pacific Islander (268)	306	0.53
Not Hispanic (266)	296	0.51
Hispanic (2)	10	0.02
Guamanian/Chamorro (2)	5	0.01
Marshallese (224)	231	0.40
Native Hawaiian (14)	35	0.06
Samoan (0)	2	<0.01
White (52,869)	53,807	93.35
Not Hispanic (52,007)	52,849	91.69
Hispanic (862)	958	1.66

Fairfield

Place Type: City
County: Jefferson
Population: 9,464†

Ancestry‡	Population	%
African, Sub-Saharan (108)	108	1.14
Ethiopian (108)	108	1.14
American (559)	559	5.91
Arab (72)	72	0.76
Egyptian (33)	33	0.35
Jordanian (11)	11	0.12
Other Arab (28)	28	0.30
Australian (52)	52	0.55
Austrian (17)	17	0.18
Belgian (0)	13	0.14
British (37)	54	0.57
Canadian (35)	103	1.09
Croatian (0)	16	0.17
Czech (50)	160	1.69
Czechoslovakian (11)	11	0.12
Danish (46)	103	1.09
Dutch (135)	500	5.29
Eastern European (13)	27	0.29
English (327)	1,111	11.76
European (82)	82	0.87
Finnish (0)	28	0.30
French, ex. Basque (31)	346	3.66
French Canadian (53)	64	0.68
German (607)	2,120	22.43
Greek (0)	36	0.38
Iranian (96)	96	1.02
Irish (438)	1,380	14.60
Israeli (40)	40	0.42
Italian (45)	296	3.13
Latvian (0)	20	0.21
Lithuanian (0)	10	0.11
Northern European (33)	33	0.35
Norwegian (67)	111	1.17
Pennsylvania German (15)	15	0.16
Polish (25)	92	0.97
Portuguese (0)	28	0.30
Romanian (0)	25	0.26
Russian (25)	121	1.28
Scandinavian (0)	22	0.23
Scotch-Irish (168)	386	4.08
Scottish (43)	235	2.49
Swedish (21)	167	1.77
Swiss (0)	54	0.57
Ukrainian (0)	19	0.20
Welsh (0)	59	0.62

Hispanic Origin	Population	%
Hispanic or Latino (of any race)	344	3.63
Central American, ex. Mexican	16	0.17
Guatemalan	11	0.12
Panamanian	2	0.02
Salvadoran	3	0.03
Cuban	2	0.02
Dominican Republic	4	0.04
Mexican	205	2.17
Puerto Rican	30	0.32
South American	43	0.45
Argentinean	8	0.08
Bolivian	3	0.03
Chilean	2	0.02
Colombian	8	0.08
Ecuadorian	7	0.07
Peruvian	4	0.04
Uruguayan	1	0.01
Venezuelan	10	0.11
Other Hispanic or Latino	44	0.46

Race*	Population	%
African-American/Black (191)	249	2.63
Not Hispanic (176)	227	2.40
Hispanic (15)	22	0.23
American Indian/Alaska Native (18)	96	1.01
Not Hispanic (16)	85	0.90
Hispanic (2)	11	0.12
Apache (0)	2	0.02
Blackfeet (0)	8	0.08
Canadian/French Am. Ind. (1)	2	0.02
Cherokee (4)	33	0.35
Chippewa (0)	3	0.03
Choctaw (3)	4	0.04
Creek (1)	1	0.01
Hopi (0)	1	0.01
Iroquois (1)	2	0.02
Mexican American Ind. (0)	3	0.03
Sioux (1)	4	0.04
South American Ind. (0)	1	0.01
Asian (372)	444	4.69
Not Hispanic (368)	435	4.60
Hispanic (4)	9	0.10
Burmese (1)	1	0.01
Cambodian (3)	4	0.04
Chinese, ex. Taiwanese (83)	104	1.10
Filipino (30)	44	0.46
Indian (140)	167	1.76
Japanese (8)	15	0.16
Korean (12)	13	0.14
Laotian (14)	14	0.15
Malaysian (2)	3	0.03
Nepalese (37)	39	0.41
Pakistani (8)	11	0.12
Sri Lankan (2)	2	0.02
Taiwanese (8)	9	0.10
Thai (3)	3	0.03
Vietnamese (2)	2	0.02
Hawaii Native/Pacific Islander (1)	5	0.05
Not Hispanic (1)	3	0.03
Hispanic (0)	2	0.02
Native Hawaiian (0)	1	0.01
Samoan (0)	1	0.01
White (8,545)	8,726	92.20
Not Hispanic (8,370)	8,521	90.04
Hispanic (175)	205	2.17

Fort Dodge

Place Type: City
County: Webster
Population: 25,206†

Ancestry‡	Population	%
African, Sub-Saharan (691)	773	3.05
African (658)	740	2.92
Sudanese (33)	33	0.13
Albanian (0)	8	0.03
American (724)	724	2.86
Austrian (24)	35	0.14
Belgian (0)	12	0.05
British (16)	16	0.06
Canadian (0)	19	0.08
Croatian (33)	33	0.13
Czech (310)	748	2.95
Czechoslovakian (11)	157	0.62
Danish (127)	357	1.41
Dutch (172)	599	2.37
English (635)	1,845	7.29
European (184)	184	0.73
Finnish (0)	35	0.14
French, ex. Basque (66)	691	2.73
French Canadian (0)	71	0.28
German (3,614)	9,106	35.96
Greek (0)	21	0.08
Irish (1,031)	4,270	16.86
Italian (356)	633	2.50
Lithuanian (0)	57	0.23
Luxemburger (16)	32	0.13
Northern European (19)	19	0.08
Norwegian (1,093)	2,206	8.71
Polish (9)	163	0.64
Russian (33)	70	0.28
Scandinavian (29)	73	0.29
Scotch-Irish (162)	411	1.62
Scottish (162)	466	1.84
Swedish (370)	1,533	6.05
Swiss (13)	76	0.30
Ukrainian (10)	17	0.07
Welsh (14)	133	0.53
West Indian, ex. Hispanic (6)	6	0.02
Jamaican (6)	6	0.02
Yugoslavian (6)	13	0.05

Hispanic Origin	Population	%
Hispanic or Latino (of any race)	1,270	5.04
Central American, ex. Mexican	38	0.15
Guatemalan	16	0.06
Honduran	10	0.04
Salvadoran	12	0.05
Cuban	5	0.02
Dominican Republic	8	0.03
Mexican	1,015	4.03
Puerto Rican	60	0.24
South American	28	0.11
Chilean	4	0.02
Colombian	9	0.04
Ecuadorian	9	0.04
Peruvian	3	0.01
Uruguayan	3	0.01
Other Hispanic or Latino	116	0.46

Race*	Population	%
African-American/Black (1,376)	1,722	6.83
Not Hispanic (1,353)	1,670	6.63
Hispanic (23)	52	0.21
American Indian/Alaska Native (89)	181	0.72
Not Hispanic (71)	150	0.60
Hispanic (18)	31	0.12
Alaska Athabascan *(Ala. Nat.)* (1)	1	<0.01
Apache (1)	5	0.02
Blackfeet (0)	4	0.02
Cherokee (2)	25	0.10
Cheyenne (0)	3	0.01
Chippewa (1)	6	0.02
Choctaw (0)	1	<0.01
Comanche (0)	3	0.01
Creek (0)	1	<0.01
Hopi (1)	3	0.01
Inupiat *(Alaska Native)* (0)	1	<0.01
Iroquois (2)	2	0.01
Mexican American Ind. (7)	7	0.03
Navajo (0)	7	0.03
Potawatomi (1)	3	0.01
Sioux (4)	12	0.05
Tlingit-Haida *(Alaska Native)* (1)	1	<0.01
Tsimshian *(Alaska Native)* (3)	3	0.01
Ute (0)	2	0.01
Asian (212)	276	1.09
Not Hispanic (207)	271	1.08
Hispanic (5)	5	0.02
Bangladeshi (1)	1	<0.01
Chinese, ex. Taiwanese (55)	61	0.24

*Notes: † The Census 2010 population figure is used to calculate the percentages in the Hispanic Origin and Race categories. Ancestry percentages are based on the 2006-2010 American Community Survey population (not shown); ‡ Numbers in parentheses indicate the number of people reporting a single ancestry; * Numbers in parentheses indicate the number of persons reporting this race alone, not in combination with any other race; Please refer to the Explanation of Data for more information.*

Filipino (41)	59	0.23
Hmong (3)	3	0.01
Indian (18)	22	0.09
Indonesian (1)	2	0.01
Japanese (8)	15	0.06
Korean (26)	37	0.15
Laotian (4)	6	0.02
Taiwanese (5)	5	0.02
Thai (2)	6	0.02
Vietnamese (32)	35	0.14
Hawaii Native/Pacific Islander (5)	30	0.12
Not Hispanic (3)	28	0.11
Hispanic (2)	2	0.01
Guamanian/Chamorro (0)	1	<0.01
Native Hawaiian (2)	19	0.08
Samoan (2)	8	0.03
Tongan (1)	2	0.01
White (22,622)	23,151	91.85
Not Hispanic (21,835)	22,265	88.33
Hispanic (787)	886	3.52

Fort Madison

Place Type: City
County: Lee
Population: 11,051†

Ancestry‡	Population	%
African, Sub-Saharan (183)	212	1.91
African (183)	212	1.91
American (1,047)	1,047	9.44
Arab (8)	8	0.07
Moroccan (8)	8	0.07
Austrian (15)	15	0.14
Belgian (18)	68	0.61
British (0)	12	0.11
Czech (19)	54	0.49
Czechoslovakian (8)	8	0.07
Danish (13)	13	0.12
Dutch (19)	200	1.80
English (218)	771	6.95
European (158)	158	1.42
French, ex. Basque (39)	226	2.04
French Canadian (0)	10	0.09
German (1,936)	3,667	33.05
Greek (0)	8	0.07
Irish (433)	1,681	15.15
Italian (90)	239	2.15
Norwegian (41)	271	2.44
Pennsylvania German (9)	9	0.08
Polish (26)	39	0.35
Scandinavian (10)	10	0.09
Scotch-Irish (97)	246	2.22
Scottish (85)	181	1.63
Slavic (0)	11	0.10
Swedish (87)	271	2.44
Swiss (0)	9	0.08
Welsh (0)	26	0.23
Yugoslavian (27)	31	0.28

Hispanic Origin	Population	%
Hispanic or Latino (of any race)	735	6.65
Central American, ex. Mexican	4	0.04
Honduran	1	0.01
Panamanian	3	0.03
Cuban	7	0.06
Dominican Republic	5	0.05
Mexican	670	6.06
Puerto Rican	17	0.15
South American	3	0.03
Colombian	2	0.02
Peruvian	1	0.01
Other Hispanic or Latino	29	0.26

Race*	Population	%
African-American/Black (612)	758	6.86
Not Hispanic (598)	718	6.50
Hispanic (14)	40	0.36
American Indian/Alaska Native (42)	115	1.04
Not Hispanic (40)	105	0.95
Hispanic (2)	10	0.09
Blackfeet (1)	6	0.05
Cherokee (3)	21	0.19
Chippewa (1)	2	0.02
Choctaw (1)	2	0.02
Crow (2)	2	0.02
Iroquois (1)	1	0.01
Mexican American Ind. (0)	2	0.02
Navajo (1)	2	0.02
Osage (0)	1	0.01
Ottawa (0)	6	0.05
Pueblo (0)	1	0.01
Sioux (3)	5	0.05
Tlingit-Haida *(Alaska Native)* (3)	3	0.03
Asian (61)	97	0.88
Not Hispanic (60)	91	0.82
Hispanic (1)	6	0.05
Chinese, ex. Taiwanese (10)	15	0.14
Filipino (21)	29	0.26
Indian (11)	17	0.15
Indonesian (0)	2	0.02
Japanese (4)	12	0.11
Korean (3)	8	0.07
Laotian (1)	1	0.01
Sri Lankan (1)	1	0.01
Vietnamese (6)	9	0.08
Hawaii Native/Pacific Islander (7)	17	0.15
Not Hispanic (3)	10	0.09
Hispanic (4)	7	0.06
Guamanian/Chamorro (0)	1	0.01
Native Hawaiian (1)	6	0.05
Samoan (6)	6	0.05
White (9,872)	10,127	91.64
Not Hispanic (9,403)	9,598	86.85
Hispanic (469)	529	4.79

Grimes

Place Type: City
County: Polk
Population: 8,246†

Ancestry‡	Population	%
American (281)	281	3.67
Austrian (0)	14	0.18
Belgian (10)	49	0.64
British (7)	7	0.09
Bulgarian (0)	10	0.13
Czech (16)	78	1.02
Danish (0)	166	2.17
Dutch (44)	241	3.15
English (105)	553	7.23
European (70)	85	1.11
French, ex. Basque (66)	164	2.14
French Canadian (17)	28	0.37
German (1,103)	2,942	38.44
Greek (10)	74	0.97
Irish (302)	1,730	22.61
Italian (76)	171	2.23
Latvian (10)	10	0.13
Lithuanian (28)	28	0.37
Norwegian (178)	562	7.34
Polish (85)	128	1.67
Russian (0)	21	0.27
Scotch-Irish (63)	173	2.26
Scottish (20)	50	0.65
Serbian (0)	7	0.09
Slovak (0)	45	0.59
Swedish (123)	504	6.59
Swiss (10)	10	0.13
Ukrainian (12)	12	0.16
Welsh (16)	33	0.43
Yugoslavian (104)	104	1.36

Hispanic Origin	Population	%
Hispanic or Latino (of any race)	205	2.49
Central American, ex. Mexican	6	0.07
Guatemalan	2	0.02
Panamanian	3	0.04
Salvadoran	1	0.01
Cuban	1	0.01
Mexican	167	2.03
Puerto Rican	5	0.06
South American	7	0.08
Colombian	4	0.05
Ecuadorian	2	0.02
Venezuelan	1	0.01
Other Hispanic or Latino	19	0.23

Race*	Population	%
African-American/Black (87)	121	1.47
Not Hispanic (83)	116	1.41
Hispanic (4)	5	0.06
American Indian/Alaska Native (16)	32	0.39
Not Hispanic (16)	31	0.38
Hispanic (0)	1	0.01
Blackfeet (0)	3	0.04
Canadian/French Am. Ind. (0)	1	0.01
Cherokee (1)	1	0.01
Chippewa (1)	1	0.01
Choctaw (2)	2	0.02
Comanche (0)	2	0.02
Cree (0)	1	0.01
Creek (4)	6	0.07
Delaware (0)	1	0.01
Potawatomi (1)	1	0.01
Seminole (0)	1	0.01
Sioux (2)	3	0.04
Asian (139)	176	2.13
Not Hispanic (139)	175	2.12
Hispanic (0)	1	0.01
Cambodian (2)	2	0.02
Chinese, ex. Taiwanese (22)	26	0.32
Filipino (8)	20	0.24
Hmong (1)	1	0.01
Indian (37)	44	0.53
Indonesian (1)	1	0.01
Japanese (4)	6	0.07
Korean (17)	19	0.23
Laotian (16)	23	0.28
Taiwanese (1)	3	0.04
Thai (3)	10	0.12
Vietnamese (17)	24	0.29
Hawaii Native/Pacific Islander (2)	3	0.04
Not Hispanic (2)	3	0.04
Native Hawaiian (2)	2	0.02
White (7,835)	7,935	96.23
Not Hispanic (7,723)	7,797	94.55
Hispanic (112)	138	1.67

Grinnell

Place Type: City
County: Poweshiek
Population: 9,218†

Ancestry‡	Population	%
African, Sub-Saharan (42)	53	0.57
African (32)	43	0.46
Sudanese (10)	10	0.11
American (407)	407	4.39
Armenian (0)	10	0.11
Australian (0)	10	0.11
Austrian (0)	10	0.11
Belgian (19)	19	0.21
Brazilian (0)	19	0.21
British (21)	63	0.68
Czech (11)	101	1.09
Czechoslovakian (15)	15	0.16
Danish (40)	195	2.10
Dutch (71)	412	4.45
Eastern European (11)	22	0.24
English (313)	1,258	13.58
European (108)	129	1.39
Finnish (9)	9	0.10
French, ex. Basque (41)	351	3.79
French Canadian (0)	10	0.11
German (1,288)	3,642	39.31
Greek (18)	41	0.44
Hungarian (0)	21	0.23

*Notes: † The Census 2010 population figure is used to calculate the percentages in the Hispanic Origin and Race categories. Ancestry percentages are based on the 2006-2010 American Community Survey population (not shown); ‡ Numbers in parentheses indicate the number of people reporting a single ancestry; * Numbers in parentheses indicate the number of persons reporting this race alone, not in combination with any other race; Please refer to the Explanation of Data for more information.*

Irish (354)	1,312	14.16
Italian (36)	160	1.73
Lithuanian (0)	33	0.36
Luxemburger (0)	8	0.09
Northern European (8)	8	0.09
Norwegian (141)	332	3.58
Pennsylvania German (10)	48	0.52
Polish (29)	166	1.79
Portuguese (0)	10	0.11
Romanian (10)	32	0.35
Russian (0)	34	0.37
Scandinavian (36)	47	0.51
Scotch-Irish (135)	313	3.38
Scottish (62)	308	3.32
Serbian (0)	11	0.12
Swedish (80)	612	6.61
Swiss (8)	47	0.51
Ukrainian (24)	32	0.35
Welsh (26)	49	0.53

Hispanic Origin	Population	%
Hispanic or Latino (of any race)	292	3.17
Central American, ex. Mexican	28	0.30
Costa Rican	3	0.03
Guatemalan	5	0.05
Honduran	4	0.04
Nicaraguan	1	0.01
Salvadoran	12	0.13
Other Central American	3	0.03
Cuban	5	0.05
Dominican Republic	4	0.04
Mexican	182	1.97
Puerto Rican	11	0.12
South American	27	0.29
Argentinean	4	0.04
Bolivian	2	0.02
Chilean	3	0.03
Colombian	5	0.05
Ecuadorian	7	0.08
Peruvian	3	0.03
Venezuelan	2	0.02
Other South American	1	0.01
Other Hispanic or Latino	35	0.38

Race*	Population	%
African-American/Black (182)	255	2.77
Not Hispanic (175)	245	2.66
Hispanic (7)	10	0.11
American Indian/Alaska Native (30)	79	0.86
Not Hispanic (24)	63	0.68
Hispanic (6)	16	0.17
Arapaho (0)	1	0.01
Central American Ind. (0)	1	0.01
Cherokee (3)	14	0.15
Chippewa (1)	2	0.02
Choctaw (0)	2	0.02
Creek (1)	1	0.01
Mexican American Ind. (2)	3	0.03
Navajo (2)	4	0.04
Sioux (1)	3	0.03
Asian (246)	340	3.69
Not Hispanic (242)	326	3.54
Hispanic (4)	14	0.15
Bangladeshi (5)	5	0.05
Burmese (0)	1	0.01
Cambodian (13)	14	0.15
Chinese, ex. Taiwanese (94)	112	1.22
Filipino (10)	23	0.25
Indian (40)	59	0.64
Indonesian (0)	1	0.01
Japanese (9)	34	0.37
Korean (31)	44	0.48
Laotian (7)	7	0.08
Nepalese (3)	3	0.03
Pakistani (0)	2	0.02
Taiwanese (6)	6	0.07
Vietnamese (16)	21	0.23
Hawaii Native/Pacific Islander (21)	26	0.28
Not Hispanic (21)	26	0.28
Native Hawaiian (0)	3	0.03
Samoan (0)	1	0.01
White (8,468)	8,648	93.82
Not Hispanic (8,291)	8,446	91.63
Hispanic (177)	202	2.19

Indianola

Place Type: City
County: Warren
Population: 14,782†

Ancestry‡	Population	%
African, Sub-Saharan (11)	11	0.08
African (11)	11	0.08
American (932)	932	6.41
Arab (8)	37	0.25
Other Arab (8)	37	0.25
Australian (8)	18	0.12
Austrian (0)	25	0.17
Belgian (0)	25	0.17
British (0)	30	0.21
Canadian (24)	31	0.21
Croatian (38)	80	0.55
Czech (40)	102	0.70
Czechoslovakian (11)	20	0.14
Danish (290)	375	2.58
Dutch (186)	695	4.78
English (862)	2,065	14.20
European (163)	192	1.32
Finnish (0)	19	0.13
French, ex. Basque (46)	499	3.43
French Canadian (6)	40	0.27
German (2,097)	4,897	33.67
Hungarian (14)	80	0.55
Irish (533)	1,979	13.61
Italian (128)	496	3.41
Latvian (10)	22	0.15
Northern European (46)	46	0.32
Norwegian (248)	726	4.99
Polish (71)	259	1.78
Portuguese (0)	14	0.10
Russian (93)	111	0.76
Scandinavian (41)	53	0.36
Scotch-Irish (73)	281	1.93
Scottish (180)	344	2.36
Slovak (0)	17	0.12
Swedish (257)	618	4.25
Swiss (8)	59	0.41
Ukrainian (52)	64	0.44
Welsh (16)	120	0.82
Yugoslavian (12)	12	0.08

Hispanic Origin	Population	%
Hispanic or Latino (of any race)	218	1.47
Central American, ex. Mexican	8	0.05
Costa Rican	1	0.01
Guatemalan	3	0.02
Panamanian	1	0.01
Salvadoran	3	0.02
Cuban	6	0.04
Mexican	153	1.04
Puerto Rican	14	0.09
South American	18	0.12
Argentinean	5	0.03
Chilean	5	0.03
Colombian	3	0.02
Ecuadorian	3	0.02
Paraguayan	1	0.01
Venezuelan	1	0.01
Other Hispanic or Latino	19	0.13

Race*	Population	%
African-American/Black (77)	150	1.01
Not Hispanic (77)	148	1.00
Hispanic (0)	2	0.01
American Indian/Alaska Native (36)	94	0.64
Not Hispanic (35)	84	0.57
Hispanic (1)	10	0.07
Alaska Athabascan *(Ala. Nat.)* (0)	2	0.01
Blackfeet (0)	1	0.01
Cherokee (15)	32	0.22
Chippewa (2)	2	0.01
Comanche (0)	1	0.01
Delaware (0)	1	0.01
Mexican American Ind. (0)	2	0.01
Sioux (6)	10	0.07
South American Ind. (0)	2	0.01
Asian (107)	157	1.06
Not Hispanic (107)	154	1.04
Hispanic (0)	3	0.02
Cambodian (2)	2	0.01
Chinese, ex. Taiwanese (18)	21	0.14
Filipino (26)	36	0.24
Hmong (7)	7	0.05
Indian (5)	13	0.09
Japanese (1)	8	0.05
Korean (23)	32	0.22
Laotian (1)	2	0.01
Nepalese (2)	2	0.01
Sri Lankan (2)	3	0.02
Thai (9)	20	0.14
Vietnamese (7)	9	0.06
Hawaii Native/Pacific Islander (7)	19	0.13
Not Hispanic (6)	18	0.12
Hispanic (1)	1	0.01
Guamanian/Chamorro (1)	1	0.01
Native Hawaiian (3)	9	0.06
Samoan (1)	6	0.04
White (14,320)	14,503	98.11
Not Hispanic (14,160)	14,317	96.85
Hispanic (160)	186	1.26

Iowa City

Place Type: City
County: Johnson
Population: 67,862†

Ancestry‡	Population	%
African, Sub-Saharan (696)	760	1.14
African (493)	544	0.81
Ethiopian (64)	64	0.10
Ghanaian (0)	13	0.02
Kenyan (60)	60	0.09
South African (22)	22	0.03
Sudanese (57)	57	0.09
American (1,612)	1,612	2.41
Arab (285)	429	0.64
Arab (45)	45	0.07
Egyptian (108)	108	0.16
Lebanese (9)	105	0.16
Palestinian (46)	46	0.07
Syrian (14)	62	0.09
Other Arab (63)	63	0.09
Armenian (11)	34	0.05
Australian (0)	13	0.02
Austrian (47)	186	0.28
Basque (8)	8	0.01
Belgian (68)	286	0.43
Brazilian (49)	49	0.07
British (179)	397	0.59
Bulgarian (22)	45	0.07
Canadian (77)	150	0.22
Celtic (13)	13	0.02
Croatian (28)	87	0.13
Czech (659)	2,243	3.36
Czechoslovakian (22)	99	0.15
Danish (150)	915	1.37
Dutch (411)	1,623	2.43
Eastern European (106)	116	0.17
English (1,367)	6,660	9.98
European (999)	1,119	1.68
Finnish (0)	151	0.23
French, ex. Basque (206)	1,604	2.40
French Canadian (43)	213	0.32
German (8,388)	23,784	35.63
Greek (108)	293	0.44
Guyanese (15)	24	0.04
Hungarian (11)	174	0.26
Iranian (97)	243	0.36

SECTION TWO

*Notes: † The Census 2010 population figure is used to calculate the percentages in the Hispanic Origin and Race categories. Ancestry percentages are based on the 2006-2010 American Community Survey population (not shown); ‡ Numbers in parentheses indicate the number of people reporting a single ancestry; * Numbers in parentheses indicate the number of persons reporting this race alone, not in combination with any other race; Please refer to the Explanation of Data for more information.*

	Population	%
Irish (2,712)	12,326	18.46
Israeli (63)	63	0.09
Italian (773)	2,673	4.00
Latvian (55)	80	0.12
Lithuanian (9)	122	0.18
Luxemburger (18)	52	0.08
New Zealander (12)	12	0.02
Northern European (218)	235	0.35
Norwegian (786)	2,632	3.94
Pennsylvania German (30)	54	0.08
Polish (677)	2,335	3.50
Portuguese (10)	106	0.16
Romanian (150)	196	0.29
Russian (308)	641	0.96
Scandinavian (131)	332	0.50
Scotch-Irish (446)	1,107	1.66
Scottish (373)	1,597	2.39
Serbian (10)	37	0.06
Slavic (0)	5	0.01
Slovak (35)	139	0.21
Slovene (25)	25	0.04
Swedish (552)	2,594	3.89
Swiss (29)	499	0.75
Turkish (172)	226	0.34
Ukrainian (12)	61	0.09
Welsh (60)	555	0.83
West Indian, ex. Hispanic (0)	43	0.06
Belizean (0)	11	0.02
British West Indian (0)	10	0.01
Jamaican (0)	22	0.03
Yugoslavian (24)	24	0.04

Hispanic Origin	Population	%
Hispanic or Latino (of any race)	3,627	5.34
Central American, ex. Mexican	433	0.64
Costa Rican	16	0.02
Guatemalan	120	0.18
Honduran	136	0.20
Nicaraguan	14	0.02
Panamanian	15	0.02
Salvadoran	130	0.19
Other Central American	2	<0.01
Cuban	86	0.13
Dominican Republic	32	0.05
Mexican	2,218	3.27
Puerto Rican	265	0.39
South American	323	0.48
Argentinean	42	0.06
Bolivian	14	0.02
Chilean	44	0.06
Colombian	88	0.13
Ecuadorian	42	0.06
Paraguayan	1	<0.01
Peruvian	44	0.06
Uruguayan	6	0.01
Venezuelan	41	0.06
Other South American	1	<0.01
Other Hispanic or Latino	270	0.40

Race*	Population	%
African-American/Black (3,912)	4,568	6.73
Not Hispanic (3,805)	4,400	6.48
Hispanic (107)	168	0.25
American Indian/Alaska Native (144)	497	0.73
Not Hispanic (107)	397	0.59
Hispanic (37)	100	0.15
Aleut *(Alaska Native)* (1)	1	<0.01
Apache (2)	4	0.01
Blackfeet (1)	9	0.01
Canadian/French Am. Ind. (0)	2	<0.01
Central American Ind. (0)	1	<0.01
Cherokee (13)	78	0.11
Cheyenne (0)	2	<0.01
Chickasaw (3)	6	0.01
Chippewa (5)	23	0.03
Choctaw (4)	14	0.02
Comanche (3)	4	0.01
Creek (3)	5	0.01
Crow (0)	3	<0.01
Delaware (0)	1	<0.01
Inupiat *(Alaska Native)* (1)	1	<0.01
Iroquois (5)	6	0.01
Lumbee (1)	2	<0.01
Mexican American Ind. (13)	17	0.03
Navajo (6)	8	0.01
Osage (0)	1	<0.01
Potawatomi (0)	8	0.01
Pueblo (0)	2	<0.01
Seminole (0)	1	<0.01
Sioux (9)	32	0.05
South American Ind. (1)	7	0.01
Spanish American Ind. (2)	4	0.01
Tlingit-Haida *(Alaska Native)* (1)	1	<0.01
Yaqui (1)	1	<0.01
Asian (4,680)	5,330	7.85
Not Hispanic (4,655)	5,253	7.74
Hispanic (25)	77	0.11
Bangladeshi (20)	24	0.04
Burmese (7)	7	0.01
Cambodian (27)	34	0.05
Chinese, ex. Taiwanese (1,718)	1,898	2.80
Filipino (133)	237	0.35
Hmong (3)	3	<0.01
Indian (817)	900	1.33
Indonesian (17)	22	0.03
Japanese (181)	305	0.45
Korean (803)	900	1.33
Laotian (126)	145	0.21
Malaysian (37)	48	0.07
Nepalese (33)	34	0.05
Pakistani (69)	79	0.12
Sri Lankan (25)	27	0.04
Taiwanese (144)	154	0.23
Thai (77)	98	0.14
Vietnamese (318)	366	0.54
Hawaii Native/Pacific Islander (28)	90	0.13
Not Hispanic (26)	78	0.11
Hispanic (2)	12	0.02
Fijian (0)	1	<0.01
Guamanian/Chamorro (5)	13	0.02
Native Hawaiian (6)	28	0.04
Samoan (8)	21	0.03
Tongan (1)	2	<0.01
White (56,004)	57,523	84.76
Not Hispanic (54,103)	55,378	81.60
Hispanic (1,901)	2,145	3.16

Johnston

Place Type: City
County: Polk
Population: 17,278†

Ancestry‡	Population	%
American (655)	655	4.17
Arab (11)	104	0.66
Lebanese (0)	56	0.36
Palestinian (11)	11	0.07
Syrian (0)	37	0.24
Armenian (0)	10	0.06
Australian (19)	19	0.12
Belgian (41)	107	0.68
British (0)	9	0.06
Canadian (29)	29	0.18
Croatian (11)	49	0.31
Czech (81)	314	2.00
Czechoslovakian (0)	23	0.15
Danish (137)	448	2.85
Dutch (364)	759	4.83
Eastern European (15)	15	0.10
English (478)	1,967	12.51
Estonian (11)	11	0.07
European (134)	186	1.18
French, ex. Basque (108)	587	3.73
French Canadian (32)	32	0.20
German (2,538)	6,112	38.87
Greek (29)	75	0.48
Irish (797)	2,927	18.62
Italian (270)	762	4.85
Latvian (9)	9	0.06
Lithuanian (91)	91	0.58
Luxemburger (0)	9	0.06
Northern European (48)	48	0.31
Norwegian (289)	681	4.33
Polish (30)	334	2.12
Russian (9)	14	0.09
Scandinavian (9)	61	0.39
Scotch-Irish (120)	179	1.14
Scottish (48)	486	3.09
Slavic (0)	10	0.06
Slovak (0)	22	0.14
Swedish (153)	698	4.44
Swiss (0)	9	0.06
Welsh (0)	282	1.79
Yugoslavian (245)	245	1.56

Hispanic Origin	Population	%
Hispanic or Latino (of any race)	350	2.03
Central American, ex. Mexican	26	0.15
Costa Rican	2	0.01
Guatemalan	9	0.05
Honduran	7	0.04
Panamanian	7	0.04
Salvadoran	1	0.01
Cuban	6	0.03
Dominican Republic	3	0.02
Mexican	218	1.26
Puerto Rican	30	0.17
South American	44	0.25
Argentinean	10	0.06
Chilean	4	0.02
Colombian	16	0.09
Ecuadorian	5	0.03
Peruvian	5	0.03
Uruguayan	1	0.01
Venezuelan	3	0.02
Other Hispanic or Latino	23	0.13

Race*	Population	%
African-American/Black (376)	472	2.73
Not Hispanic (370)	464	2.69
Hispanic (6)	8	0.05
American Indian/Alaska Native (13)	52	0.30
Not Hispanic (7)	41	0.24
Hispanic (6)	11	0.06
Apache (0)	1	0.01
Cherokee (1)	9	0.05
Chippewa (2)	4	0.02
Cree (0)	3	0.02
Creek (0)	2	0.01
Kiowa (0)	2	0.01
Mexican American Ind. (0)	1	0.01
Sioux (2)	2	0.01
Yuman (0)	2	0.01
Asian (800)	910	5.27
Not Hispanic (800)	902	5.22
Hispanic (0)	8	0.05
Bangladeshi (11)	11	0.06
Cambodian (0)	4	0.02
Chinese, ex. Taiwanese (256)	272	1.57
Filipino (21)	42	0.24
Indian (281)	312	1.81
Japanese (9)	12	0.07
Korean (56)	73	0.42
Laotian (15)	21	0.12
Malaysian (1)	1	0.01
Nepalese (0)	1	0.01
Pakistani (4)	4	0.02
Taiwanese (4)	4	0.02
Thai (15)	28	0.16
Vietnamese (100)	113	0.65
Hawaii Native/Pacific Islander (3)	15	0.09
Not Hispanic (1)	13	0.08
Hispanic (2)	2	0.01
Guamanian/Chamorro (0)	3	0.02
Native Hawaiian (2)	4	0.02
Samoan (0)	1	0.01
White (15,727)	15,954	92.34
Not Hispanic (15,487)	15,688	90.80
Hispanic (240)	266	1.54

*Notes: † The Census 2010 population figure is used to calculate the percentages in the Hispanic Origin and Race categories. Ancestry percentages are based on the 2006-2010 American Community Survey population (not shown); ‡ Numbers in parentheses indicate the number of people reporting a single ancestry; * Numbers in parentheses indicate the number of persons reporting this race alone, not in combination with any other race; Please refer to the Explanation of Data for more information.*

Keokuk

Place Type: City
County: Lee
Population: 10,780†

Ancestry‡	Population	%
American (1,311)	1,311	12.14
Australian (10)	10	0.09
British (16)	55	0.51
Cajun (0)	28	0.26
Canadian (0)	40	0.37
Croatian (0)	9	0.08
Czech (4)	17	0.16
Czechoslovakian (9)	9	0.08
Danish (0)	19	0.18
Dutch (31)	261	2.42
English (521)	1,181	10.93
European (30)	30	0.28
French, ex. Basque (47)	256	2.37
French Canadian (0)	70	0.65
German (1,295)	3,588	33.22
Greek (8)	23	0.21
Hungarian (0)	15	0.14
Irish (644)	2,172	20.11
Italian (16)	78	0.72
Norwegian (25)	95	0.88
Pennsylvania German (0)	8	0.07
Polish (81)	109	1.01
Scotch-Irish (24)	102	0.94
Scottish (50)	139	1.29
Swedish (88)	226	2.09
Swiss (0)	18	0.17
Welsh (0)	33	0.31

Hispanic Origin	Population	%
Hispanic or Latino (of any race)	193	1.79
Central American, ex. Mexican	8	0.07
Costa Rican	1	0.01
Guatemalan	2	0.02
Honduran	1	0.01
Nicaraguan	2	0.02
Panamanian	2	0.02
Cuban	5	0.05
Mexican	128	1.19
Puerto Rican	24	0.22
South American	7	0.06
Colombian	2	0.02
Peruvian	3	0.03
Other South American	2	0.02
Other Hispanic or Latino	21	0.19

Race*	Population	%
African-American/Black (427)	605	5.61
Not Hispanic (420)	592	5.49
Hispanic (7)	13	0.12
American Indian/Alaska Native (19)	102	0.95
Not Hispanic (15)	87	0.81
Hispanic (4)	15	0.14
Blackfeet (0)	4	0.04
Cherokee (2)	27	0.25
Cheyenne (0)	1	0.01
Chickasaw (0)	1	0.01
Choctaw (0)	3	0.03
Lumbee (1)	1	0.01
Menominee (0)	1	0.01
Mexican American Ind. (2)	7	0.06
Navajo (0)	2	0.02
Sioux (3)	9	0.08
Tlingit-Haida *(Alaska Native)* (0)	1	0.01
Yaqui (0)	4	0.04
Asian (86)	122	1.13
Not Hispanic (85)	117	1.09
Hispanic (1)	5	0.05
Chinese, ex. Taiwanese (16)	18	0.17
Filipino (9)	27	0.25
Indian (18)	20	0.19
Japanese (2)	3	0.03
Korean (18)	23	0.21
Laotian (5)	5	0.05
Pakistani (1)	1	0.01
Thai (4)	4	0.04
Vietnamese (8)	11	0.10
Hawaii Native/Pacific Islander (2)	21	0.19
Not Hispanic (2)	18	0.17
Hispanic (0)	3	0.03
Native Hawaiian (1)	16	0.15
Samoan (1)	3	0.03
White (9,908)	10,206	94.68
Not Hispanic (9,786)	10,058	93.30
Hispanic (122)	148	1.37

Le Mars

Place Type: City
County: Plymouth
Population: 9,826†

Ancestry‡	Population	%
American (707)	707	7.27
British (0)	18	0.19
Czech (6)	80	0.82
Czechoslovakian (11)	31	0.32
Danish (40)	177	1.82
Dutch (427)	880	9.05
English (229)	653	6.72
European (21)	21	0.22
French, ex. Basque (0)	220	2.26
French Canadian (23)	34	0.35
German (3,072)	5,246	53.98
Irish (156)	1,223	12.58
Italian (8)	41	0.42
Lithuanian (0)	16	0.16
Luxemburger (67)	419	4.31
Norwegian (56)	286	2.94
Polish (27)	107	1.10
Russian (0)	14	0.14
Scandinavian (17)	17	0.17
Scotch-Irish (17)	57	0.59
Scottish (103)	129	1.33
Swedish (22)	193	1.99
Swiss (0)	7	0.07
Welsh (38)	51	0.52
West Indian, ex. Hispanic (136)	136	1.40
Trinidadian/Tobagonian (136)	136	1.40

Hispanic Origin	Population	%
Hispanic or Latino (of any race)	530	5.39
Central American, ex. Mexican	40	0.41
Costa Rican	2	0.02
Guatemalan	24	0.24
Honduran	7	0.07
Panamanian	1	0.01
Salvadoran	6	0.06
Cuban	2	0.02
Mexican	391	3.98
Puerto Rican	24	0.24
South American	9	0.09
Chilean	1	0.01
Colombian	3	0.03
Ecuadorian	2	0.02
Peruvian	3	0.03
Other Hispanic or Latino	64	0.65

Race*	Population	%
African-American/Black (53)	94	0.96
Not Hispanic (50)	85	0.87
Hispanic (3)	9	0.09
American Indian/Alaska Native (29)	63	0.64
Not Hispanic (24)	51	0.52
Hispanic (5)	12	0.12
Blackfeet (0)	3	0.03
Cherokee (2)	5	0.05
Cheyenne (0)	1	0.01
Chippewa (1)	1	0.01
Choctaw (0)	2	0.02
Mexican American Ind. (3)	3	0.03
Sioux (4)	19	0.19
Asian (73)	103	1.05
Not Hispanic (73)	102	1.04
Hispanic (0)	1	0.01
Chinese, ex. Taiwanese (8)	10	0.10
Filipino (9)	17	0.17
Hmong (0)	1	0.01
Indian (9)	18	0.18
Japanese (2)	4	0.04
Korean (16)	20	0.20
Laotian (1)	6	0.06
Malaysian (2)	4	0.04
Pakistani (3)	3	0.03
Thai (1)	5	0.05
Vietnamese (17)	20	0.20
Hawaii Native/Pacific Islander (2)	7	0.07
Not Hispanic (2)	7	0.07
Native Hawaiian (1)	2	0.02
Samoan (1)	1	0.01
White (9,255)	9,380	95.46
Not Hispanic (9,052)	9,141	93.03
Hispanic (203)	239	2.43

Marion

Place Type: City
County: Linn
Population: 34,768†

Ancestry‡	Population	%
African, Sub-Saharan (167)	167	0.50
African (120)	120	0.36
Ethiopian (47)	47	0.14
American (1,652)	1,652	4.96
Arab (44)	94	0.28
Lebanese (44)	79	0.24
Syrian (0)	15	0.05
Armenian (11)	11	0.03
Australian (0)	14	0.04
Austrian (20)	50	0.15
Belgian (89)	143	0.43
British (75)	101	0.30
Canadian (0)	15	0.05
Croatian (22)	29	0.09
Czech (541)	1,778	5.34
Czechoslovakian (41)	141	0.42
Danish (135)	513	1.54
Dutch (505)	1,537	4.62
English (1,082)	3,508	10.54
European (375)	424	1.27
Finnish (0)	16	0.05
French, ex. Basque (149)	1,181	3.55
French Canadian (30)	82	0.25
German (5,562)	14,239	42.77
Greek (37)	75	0.23
Hungarian (16)	147	0.44
Iranian (9)	37	0.11
Irish (1,134)	5,852	17.58
Italian (199)	783	2.35
Latvian (0)	9	0.03
Lithuanian (16)	16	0.05
Luxemburger (0)	15	0.05
Northern European (8)	8	0.02
Norwegian (442)	1,717	5.16
Pennsylvania German (0)	9	0.03
Polish (164)	611	1.84
Romanian (29)	29	0.09
Russian (91)	129	0.39
Scandinavian (34)	181	0.54
Scotch-Irish (162)	754	2.26
Scottish (135)	786	2.36
Slovak (0)	17	0.05
Swedish (226)	908	2.73
Swiss (21)	153	0.46
Welsh (37)	354	1.06

Hispanic Origin	Population	%
Hispanic or Latino (of any race)	687	1.98
Central American, ex. Mexican	46	0.13
Guatemalan	21	0.06
Honduran	16	0.05
Nicaraguan	2	0.01
Panamanian	5	0.01

SECTION TWO

*Notes: † The Census 2010 population figure is used to calculate the percentages in the Hispanic Origin and Race categories. Ancestry percentages are based on the 2006-2010 American Community Survey population (not shown); ‡ Numbers in parentheses indicate the number of people reporting a single ancestry; * Numbers in parentheses indicate the number of persons reporting this race alone, not in combination with any other race; Please refer to the Explanation of Data for more information.*

Salvadoran	2	0.01
Cuban	15	0.04
Dominican Republic	6	0.02
Mexican	443	1.27
Puerto Rican	40	0.12
South American	51	0.15
Argentinean	2	0.01
Bolivian	1	<0.01
Chilean	2	0.01
Colombian	17	0.05
Ecuadorian	6	0.02
Paraguayan	5	0.01
Peruvian	7	0.02
Uruguayan	1	<0.01
Venezuelan	6	0.02
Other South American	4	0.01
Other Hispanic or Latino	86	0.25

Race*	Population	%
African-American/Black (704)	1,038	2.99
Not Hispanic (692)	998	2.87
Hispanic (12)	40	0.12
American Indian/Alaska Native (87)	260	0.75
Not Hispanic (75)	225	0.65
Hispanic (12)	35	0.10
Apache (1)	9	0.03
Blackfeet (1)	7	0.02
Canadian/French Am. Ind. (1)	1	<0.01
Cherokee (13)	55	0.16
Cheyenne (0)	1	<0.01
Chippewa (5)	6	0.02
Choctaw (4)	9	0.03
Cree (5)	5	0.01
Creek (0)	2	0.01
Houma (2)	2	0.01
Inupiat *(Alaska Native)* (0)	1	<0.01
Iroquois (0)	2	0.01
Menominee (0)	2	0.01
Mexican American Ind. (4)	7	0.02
Navajo (2)	4	0.01
Paiute (0)	1	<0.01
Potawatomi (0)	1	<0.01
Seminole (0)	2	0.01
Sioux (7)	23	0.07
Ute (4)	5	0.01
Asian (539)	685	1.97
Not Hispanic (536)	668	1.92
Hispanic (3)	17	0.05
Bangladeshi (8)	9	0.03
Cambodian (2)	2	0.01
Chinese, ex. Taiwanese (70)	95	0.27
Filipino (56)	103	0.30
Indian (197)	224	0.64
Japanese (19)	28	0.08
Korean (67)	93	0.27
Laotian (20)	30	0.09
Malaysian (0)	1	<0.01
Nepalese (2)	2	0.01
Pakistani (13)	13	0.04
Taiwanese (3)	6	0.02
Thai (4)	9	0.03
Vietnamese (62)	76	0.22
Hawaii Native/Pacific Islander (17)	32	0.09
Not Hispanic (14)	27	0.08
Hispanic (3)	5	0.01
Guamanian/Chamorro (4)	4	0.01
Native Hawaiian (5)	7	0.02
Samoan (2)	6	0.02
Tongan (2)	2	0.01
White (32,588)	33,216	95.54
Not Hispanic (32,180)	32,722	94.12
Hispanic (408)	494	1.42

Marshalltown

Place Type: City
County: Marshall
Population: 27,552†

Ancestry‡	Population	%
African, Sub-Saharan (165)	181	0.67
African (43)	43	0.16
Sudanese (73)	89	0.33
Other Sub-Saharan African (49)	49	0.18
American (1,228)	1,228	4.53
Arab (18)	35	0.13
Arab (18)	35	0.13
Austrian (0)	31	0.11
Belgian (25)	25	0.09
Brazilian (17)	48	0.18
British (15)	41	0.15
Canadian (14)	14	0.05
Croatian (33)	103	0.38
Czech (175)	560	2.07
Czechoslovakian (45)	55	0.20
Danish (80)	411	1.52
Dutch (197)	1,020	3.76
English (637)	2,690	9.93
European (384)	405	1.49
Finnish (0)	19	0.07
French, ex. Basque (154)	759	2.80
French Canadian (0)	46	0.17
German (3,279)	8,092	29.86
Hungarian (0)	28	0.10
Irish (935)	3,270	12.07
Israeli (47)	47	0.17
Italian (84)	398	1.47
Northern European (8)	8	0.03
Norwegian (500)	1,323	4.88
Pennsylvania German (24)	59	0.22
Polish (95)	268	0.99
Portuguese (5)	5	0.02
Scandinavian (9)	18	0.07
Scotch-Irish (164)	607	2.24
Scottish (86)	513	1.89
Slovak (0)	12	0.04
Swedish (57)	353	1.30
Swiss (30)	75	0.28
Turkish (33)	33	0.12
Ukrainian (15)	15	0.06
Welsh (17)	168	0.62
West Indian, ex. Hispanic (7)	7	0.03
British West Indian (7)	7	0.03

Hispanic Origin	Population	%
Hispanic or Latino (of any race)	6,632	24.07
Central American, ex. Mexican	283	1.03
Costa Rican	1	<0.01
Guatemalan	111	0.40
Honduran	32	0.12
Nicaraguan	2	0.01
Panamanian	2	0.01
Salvadoran	135	0.49
Cuban	14	0.05
Dominican Republic	3	0.01
Mexican	6,003	21.79
Puerto Rican	70	0.25
South American	20	0.07
Argentinean	1	<0.01
Chilean	2	0.01
Colombian	8	0.03
Peruvian	5	0.02
Uruguayan	1	<0.01
Venezuelan	3	0.01
Other Hispanic or Latino	239	0.87

Race*	Population	%
African-American/Black (608)	857	3.11
Not Hispanic (568)	777	2.82
Hispanic (40)	80	0.29
American Indian/Alaska Native (160)	272	0.99
Not Hispanic (79)	160	0.58
Hispanic (81)	112	0.41
Apache (1)	2	0.01
Blackfeet (0)	4	0.01
Canadian/French Am. Ind. (1)	2	0.01
Central American Ind. (2)	2	0.01
Cherokee (2)	14	0.05
Chippewa (1)	4	0.01
Choctaw (0)	5	0.02
Creek (2)	2	0.01
Houma (0)	1	<0.01
Lumbee (0)	1	<0.01
Menominee (5)	5	0.02
Mexican American Ind. (13)	14	0.05
Paiute (0)	3	0.01
Potawatomi (1)	3	0.01
Pueblo (0)	1	<0.01
Puget Sound Salish (1)	2	0.01
Sioux (11)	18	0.07
South American Ind. (0)	2	0.01
Asian (467)	592	2.15
Not Hispanic (457)	575	2.09
Hispanic (10)	17	0.06
Burmese (134)	151	0.55
Cambodian (7)	8	0.03
Chinese, ex. Taiwanese (47)	53	0.19
Filipino (39)	64	0.23
Indian (85)	101	0.37
Indonesian (7)	9	0.03
Japanese (3)	18	0.07
Korean (28)	34	0.12
Laotian (48)	67	0.24
Malaysian (0)	1	<0.01
Pakistani (5)	5	0.02
Sri Lankan (4)	7	0.03
Thai (9)	17	0.06
Vietnamese (32)	37	0.13
Hawaii Native/Pacific Islander (45)	56	0.20
Not Hispanic (34)	44	0.16
Hispanic (11)	12	0.04
Guamanian/Chamorro (8)	9	0.03
Marshallese (5)	5	0.02
Native Hawaiian (6)	15	0.05
Samoan (7)	7	0.03
White (23,371)	23,994	87.09
Not Hispanic (19,360)	19,705	71.52
Hispanic (4,011)	4,289	15.57

Mason City

Place Type: City
County: Cerro Gordo
Population: 28,079†

Ancestry‡	Population	%
African, Sub-Saharan (24)	124	0.44
African (24)	124	0.44
American (1,065)	1,065	3.79
Arab (46)	46	0.16
Egyptian (46)	46	0.16
Australian (0)	46	0.16
Austrian (0)	36	0.13
Belgian (16)	52	0.18
British (16)	16	0.06
Bulgarian (6)	6	0.02
Croatian (0)	39	0.14
Czech (165)	708	2.52
Czechoslovakian (23)	65	0.23
Danish (133)	736	2.62
Dutch (206)	837	2.98
English (908)	3,012	10.71
European (262)	359	1.28
Finnish (14)	21	0.07
French, ex. Basque (76)	762	2.71
French Canadian (0)	18	0.06
German (4,557)	11,633	41.36
Greek (165)	287	1.02
Hungarian (0)	32	0.11
Iranian (20)	20	0.07
Irish (964)	3,895	13.85
Italian (224)	580	2.06
Luxemburger (9)	9	0.03
Northern European (14)	14	0.05
Norwegian (1,689)	4,218	15.00
Pennsylvania German (29)	29	0.10
Polish (234)	433	1.54
Portuguese (30)	66	0.23
Romanian (30)	93	0.33

*Notes: † The Census 2010 population figure is used to calculate the percentages in the Hispanic Origin and Race categories. Ancestry percentages are based on the 2006-2010 American Community Survey population (not shown); ‡ Numbers in parentheses indicate the number of people reporting a single ancestry; * Numbers in parentheses indicate the number of persons reporting this race alone, not in combination with any other race; Please refer to the Explanation of Data for more information.*

Ancestry	Population	%
Russian (21)	154	0.55
Scandinavian (50)	122	0.43
Scotch-Irish (151)	383	1.36
Scottish (239)	563	2.00
Serbian (12)	176	0.63
Slovak (14)	36	0.13
Slovene (0)	44	0.16
Swedish (183)	869	3.09
Swiss (29)	116	0.41
Welsh (49)	182	0.65
Yugoslavian (323)	334	1.19

Hispanic Origin	Population	%
Hispanic or Latino (of any race)	1,419	5.05
Central American, ex. Mexican	51	0.18
Costa Rican	1	<0.01
Guatemalan	23	0.08
Honduran	7	0.02
Nicaraguan	3	0.01
Panamanian	8	0.03
Salvadoran	9	0.03
Cuban	2	0.01
Dominican Republic	1	<0.01
Mexican	1,181	4.21
Puerto Rican	38	0.14
South American	19	0.07
Argentinean	2	0.01
Chilean	4	0.01
Colombian	2	0.01
Ecuadorian	7	0.02
Paraguayan	2	0.01
Peruvian	2	0.01
Other Hispanic or Latino	127	0.45

Race*	Population	%
African-American/Black (509)	777	2.77
Not Hispanic (487)	735	2.62
Hispanic (22)	42	0.15
American Indian/Alaska Native (75)	193	0.69
Not Hispanic (55)	156	0.56
Hispanic (20)	37	0.13
Apache (1)	1	<0.01
Blackfeet (1)	13	0.05
Cherokee (16)	53	0.19
Chickasaw (1)	1	<0.01
Chippewa (3)	9	0.03
Choctaw (0)	4	0.01
Creek (2)	2	0.01
Iroquois (1)	2	0.01
Lumbee (0)	4	0.01
Mexican American Ind. (6)	10	0.04
Navajo (0)	2	0.01
Sioux (2)	5	0.02
South American Ind. (4)	4	0.01
Asian (247)	326	1.16
Not Hispanic (242)	313	1.11
Hispanic (5)	13	0.05
Cambodian (3)	4	0.01
Chinese, ex. Taiwanese (58)	65	0.23
Filipino (18)	38	0.14
Indian (57)	64	0.23
Indonesian (1)	1	<0.01
Japanese (7)	22	0.08
Korean (29)	40	0.14
Laotian (17)	20	0.07
Pakistani (8)	8	0.03
Sri Lankan (3)	3	0.01
Taiwanese (1)	2	0.01
Thai (8)	10	0.04
Vietnamese (34)	41	0.15
Hawaii Native/Pacific Islander (7)	27	0.10
Not Hispanic (6)	22	0.08
Hispanic (1)	5	0.02
Fijian (0)	3	0.01
Guamanian/Chamorro (3)	3	0.01
Native Hawaiian (0)	6	0.02
Samoan (3)	6	0.02
White (26,345)	26,865	95.68
Not Hispanic (25,450)	25,848	92.05
Hispanic (895)	1,017	3.62

Mount Pleasant

Place Type: City
County: Henry
Population: 8,668†

Ancestry‡	Population	%
African, Sub-Saharan (22)	23	0.26
African (20)	21	0.24
Nigerian (2)	2	0.02
American (725)	725	8.29
Austrian (0)	8	0.09
British (0)	44	0.50
Czech (46)	95	1.09
Czechoslovakian (5)	5	0.06
Danish (1)	16	0.18
Dutch (30)	231	2.64
English (243)	757	8.66
European (77)	77	0.88
French, ex. Basque (70)	299	3.42
French Canadian (98)	237	2.71
German (1,222)	2,896	33.12
Hungarian (0)	8	0.09
Irish (395)	1,321	15.11
Italian (123)	230	2.63
Luxemburger (10)	10	0.11
Norwegian (62)	287	3.28
Pennsylvania German (40)	40	0.46
Polish (14)	69	0.79
Russian (0)	35	0.40
Scotch-Irish (98)	189	2.16
Scottish (47)	137	1.57
Swedish (146)	542	6.20
Swiss (32)	65	0.74
Turkish (9)	29	0.33
Ukrainian (0)	2	0.02
Welsh (0)	48	0.55

Hispanic Origin	Population	%
Hispanic or Latino (of any race)	578	6.67
Central American, ex. Mexican	83	0.96
Guatemalan	49	0.57
Honduran	14	0.16
Salvadoran	20	0.23
Cuban	1	0.01
Dominican Republic	2	0.02
Mexican	391	4.51
Puerto Rican	30	0.35
South American	19	0.22
Argentinean	10	0.12
Bolivian	1	0.01
Chilean	2	0.02
Colombian	1	0.01
Ecuadorian	3	0.03
Venezuelan	2	0.02
Other Hispanic or Latino	52	0.60

Race*	Population	%
African-American/Black (373)	461	5.32
Not Hispanic (361)	442	5.10
Hispanic (12)	19	0.22
American Indian/Alaska Native (37)	93	1.07
Not Hispanic (27)	79	0.91
Hispanic (10)	14	0.16
Apache (0)	1	0.01
Blackfeet (0)	2	0.02
Cherokee (2)	16	0.18
Cheyenne (0)	1	0.01
Chickasaw (0)	3	0.03
Chippewa (3)	3	0.03
Creek (0)	1	0.01
Crow (1)	1	0.01
Mexican American Ind. (1)	1	0.01
Navajo (1)	1	0.01
Sioux (8)	13	0.15
Asian (382)	432	4.98
Not Hispanic (371)	419	4.83
Hispanic (11)	13	0.15
Cambodian (2)	3	0.03
Chinese, ex. Taiwanese (60)	66	0.76
Filipino (11)	17	0.20
Hmong (5)	5	0.06
Indian (12)	19	0.22
Japanese (3)	5	0.06
Korean (1)	9	0.10
Laotian (122)	138	1.59
Pakistani (4)	4	0.05
Thai (12)	18	0.21
Vietnamese (122)	135	1.56
Hawaii Native/Pacific Islander (22)	30	0.35
Not Hispanic (20)	25	0.29
Hispanic (2)	5	0.06
Guamanian/Chamorro (8)	9	0.10
Native Hawaiian (0)	3	0.03
Samoan (8)	9	0.10
White (7,431)	7,638	88.12
Not Hispanic (7,125)	7,298	84.19
Hispanic (306)	340	3.92

Muscatine

Place Type: City
County: Muscatine
Population: 22,886†

Ancestry‡	Population	%
African, Sub-Saharan (52)	85	0.37
African (35)	68	0.30
Senegalese (17)	17	0.07
American (1,418)	1,418	6.21
Austrian (10)	22	0.10
Belgian (6)	43	0.19
Brazilian (70)	70	0.31
British (13)	19	0.08
Bulgarian (0)	37	0.16
Czech (65)	166	0.73
Czechoslovakian (13)	45	0.20
Danish (76)	252	1.10
Dutch (199)	785	3.44
English (961)	2,457	10.77
European (169)	214	0.94
Finnish (8)	32	0.14
French, ex. Basque (122)	632	2.77
French Canadian (13)	43	0.19
German (3,832)	8,164	35.78
Greek (25)	45	0.20
Hungarian (58)	82	0.36
Irish (791)	2,950	12.93
Italian (50)	365	1.60
Northern European (15)	15	0.07
Norwegian (148)	333	1.46
Pennsylvania German (26)	51	0.22
Polish (84)	201	0.88
Portuguese (9)	28	0.12
Romanian (17)	17	0.07
Russian (33)	184	0.81
Scandinavian (24)	24	0.11
Scotch-Irish (125)	337	1.48
Scottish (73)	452	1.98
Swedish (184)	553	2.42
Swiss (12)	12	0.05
Welsh (38)	60	0.26
West Indian, ex. Hispanic (26)	26	0.11
U.S. Virgin Islander (26)	26	0.11

Hispanic Origin	Population	%
Hispanic or Latino (of any race)	3,794	16.58
Central American, ex. Mexican	236	1.03
Guatemalan	40	0.17
Honduran	51	0.22
Nicaraguan	9	0.04
Panamanian	7	0.03
Salvadoran	129	0.56
Cuban	9	0.04
Mexican	3,190	13.94
Puerto Rican	105	0.46
South American	30	0.13
Argentinean	5	0.02
Bolivian	1	<0.01
Chilean	9	0.04

*Notes: † The Census 2010 population figure is used to calculate the percentages in the Hispanic Origin and Race categories. Ancestry percentages are based on the 2006-2010 American Community Survey population (not shown); ‡ Numbers in parentheses indicate the number of people reporting a single ancestry; * Numbers in parentheses indicate the number of persons reporting this race alone, not in combination with any other race; Please refer to the Explanation of Data for more information.*

Colombian	9	0.04
Peruvian	3	0.01
Uruguayan	2	0.01
Other South American	1	<0.01
Other Hispanic or Latino	224	0.98

Race*	Population	%
African-American/Black (535)	687	3.00
Not Hispanic (485)	621	2.71
Hispanic (50)	66	0.29
American Indian/Alaska Native (108)	228	1.00
Not Hispanic (58)	148	0.65
Hispanic (50)	80	0.35
Apache (2)	9	0.04
Blackfeet (3)	6	0.03
Central American Ind. (1)	1	<0.01
Cherokee (10)	28	0.12
Cheyenne (0)	3	0.01
Chickasaw (0)	1	<0.01
Chippewa (2)	8	0.03
Choctaw (8)	13	0.06
Comanche (0)	1	<0.01
Inupiat *(Alaska Native)* (0)	1	<0.01
Menominee (1)	1	<0.01
Mexican American Ind. (7)	14	0.06
Navajo (1)	4	0.02
Potawatomi (1)	3	0.01
Seminole (2)	3	0.01
Sioux (8)	15	0.07
Spanish American Ind. (0)	2	0.01
Asian (187)	255	1.11
Not Hispanic (186)	243	1.06
Hispanic (1)	12	0.05
Bangladeshi (1)	1	<0.01
Burmese (0)	1	<0.01
Cambodian (1)	3	0.01
Chinese, ex. Taiwanese (35)	46	0.20
Filipino (29)	48	0.21
Hmong (0)	2	0.01
Indian (57)	65	0.28
Indonesian (1)	1	<0.01
Japanese (2)	13	0.06
Korean (16)	26	0.11
Laotian (5)	8	0.03
Malaysian (1)	1	<0.01
Nepalese (1)	1	<0.01
Pakistani (4)	8	0.03
Sri Lankan (1)	1	<0.01
Taiwanese (2)	2	0.01
Thai (5)	8	0.03
Vietnamese (17)	22	0.10
Hawaii Native/Pacific Islander (4)	18	0.08
Not Hispanic (4)	13	0.06
Hispanic (0)	5	0.02
Fijian (0)	4	0.02
Guamanian/Chamorro (1)	5	0.02
Native Hawaiian (0)	1	<0.01
Samoan (2)	4	0.02
Tongan (0)	3	0.01
White (20,087)	20,568	89.87
Not Hispanic (18,076)	18,326	80.08
Hispanic (2,011)	2,242	9.80

Newton

Place Type: City
County: Jasper
Population: 15,254†

Ancestry‡	Population	%
American (846)	846	5.50
Austrian (0)	19	0.12
British (10)	39	0.25
Croatian (10)	10	0.07
Czech (30)	80	0.52
Czechoslovakian (0)	54	0.35
Danish (101)	336	2.19
Dutch (491)	1,077	7.01
English (544)	1,986	12.92
European (133)	133	0.87
French, ex. Basque (64)	469	3.05
French Canadian (0)	37	0.24
German (1,853)	4,586	29.84
Greek (34)	34	0.22
Hungarian (14)	25	0.16
Irish (767)	2,297	14.94
Italian (10)	202	1.31
Lithuanian (0)	12	0.08
Luxemburger (0)	12	0.08
Northern European (22)	22	0.14
Norwegian (290)	851	5.54
Pennsylvania German (10)	10	0.07
Polish (27)	217	1.41
Portuguese (20)	20	0.13
Romanian (0)	15	0.10
Russian (15)	80	0.52
Scandinavian (0)	14	0.09
Scotch-Irish (119)	453	2.95
Scottish (34)	155	1.01
Slavic (0)	13	0.08
Swedish (77)	269	1.75
Swiss (0)	18	0.12
Ukrainian (26)	26	0.17
Welsh (75)	278	1.81
Yugoslavian (25)	25	0.16

Hispanic Origin	Population	%
Hispanic or Latino (of any race)	262	1.72
Central American, ex. Mexican	11	0.07
Guatemalan	1	0.01
Honduran	1	0.01
Nicaraguan	1	0.01
Panamanian	5	0.03
Salvadoran	3	0.02
Cuban	1	0.01
Mexican	184	1.21
Puerto Rican	24	0.16
South American	11	0.07
Argentinean	1	0.01
Colombian	8	0.05
Peruvian	1	0.01
Venezuelan	1	0.01
Other Hispanic or Latino	31	0.20

Race*	Population	%
African-American/Black (113)	177	1.16
Not Hispanic (111)	168	1.10
Hispanic (2)	9	0.06
American Indian/Alaska Native (52)	111	0.73
Not Hispanic (52)	107	0.70
Hispanic (0)	4	0.03
Apache (0)	2	0.01
Blackfeet (1)	1	0.01
Cherokee (13)	31	0.20
Chickasaw (3)	4	0.03
Chippewa (4)	6	0.04
Choctaw (0)	2	0.01
Creek (0)	3	0.02
Osage (0)	2	0.01
Potawatomi (1)	1	0.01
Seminole (2)	3	0.02
Sioux (4)	12	0.08
Asian (95)	137	0.90
Not Hispanic (95)	136	0.89
Hispanic (0)	1	0.01
Cambodian (5)	6	0.04
Chinese, ex. Taiwanese (15)	17	0.11
Filipino (13)	20	0.13
Indian (26)	30	0.20
Japanese (0)	12	0.08
Korean (11)	17	0.11
Laotian (11)	11	0.07
Malaysian (1)	3	0.02
Pakistani (1)	1	0.01
Thai (6)	13	0.09
Vietnamese (1)	3	0.02
Hawaii Native/Pacific Islander (3)	8	0.05
Not Hispanic (3)	7	0.05
Hispanic (0)	1	0.01
Fijian (1)	1	0.01
Native Hawaiian (2)	5	0.03
White (14,749)	14,926	97.85
Not Hispanic (14,581)	14,724	96.53
Hispanic (168)	202	1.32

North Liberty

Place Type: City
County: Johnson
Population: 13,374†

Ancestry‡	Population	%
African, Sub-Saharan (0)	14	0.12
African (0)	14	0.12
American (444)	444	3.73
Arab (27)	40	0.34
Lebanese (27)	40	0.34
Austrian (12)	29	0.24
Belgian (11)	29	0.24
British (0)	27	0.23
Czech (98)	456	3.84
Czechoslovakian (30)	40	0.34
Danish (19)	256	2.15
Dutch (57)	353	2.97
English (425)	1,378	11.59
European (154)	222	1.87
French, ex. Basque (30)	474	3.99
French Canadian (15)	25	0.21
German (1,541)	5,247	44.13
Greek (0)	70	0.59
Iranian (15)	15	0.13
Irish (416)	2,416	20.32
Italian (34)	281	2.36
Lithuanian (0)	14	0.12
Northern European (31)	31	0.26
Norwegian (214)	797	6.70
Polish (60)	287	2.41
Romanian (0)	14	0.12
Russian (0)	45	0.38
Scandinavian (19)	35	0.29
Scotch-Irish (14)	187	1.57
Scottish (51)	159	1.34
Slovak (10)	10	0.08
Swedish (30)	156	1.31
Swiss (0)	136	1.14
Ukrainian (0)	18	0.15
Welsh (15)	108	0.91
West Indian, ex. Hispanic (0)	48	0.40
Jamaican (0)	18	0.15
West Indian (0)	30	0.25

Hispanic Origin	Population	%
Hispanic or Latino (of any race)	462	3.45
Central American, ex. Mexican	29	0.22
Costa Rican	4	0.03
Guatemalan	9	0.07
Honduran	6	0.04
Nicaraguan	2	0.01
Salvadoran	8	0.06
Cuban	11	0.08
Dominican Republic	1	0.01
Mexican	320	2.39
Puerto Rican	42	0.31
South American	29	0.22
Argentinean	2	0.01
Chilean	5	0.04
Colombian	9	0.07
Ecuadorian	3	0.02
Peruvian	3	0.02
Uruguayan	1	0.01
Venezuelan	6	0.04
Other Hispanic or Latino	30	0.22

Race*	Population	%
African-American/Black (608)	757	5.66
Not Hispanic (597)	732	5.47
Hispanic (11)	25	0.19
American Indian/Alaska Native (25)	79	0.59
Not Hispanic (20)	65	0.49
Hispanic (5)	14	0.10

*Notes: † The Census 2010 population figure is used to calculate the percentages in the Hispanic Origin and Race categories. Ancestry percentages are based on the 2006-2010 American Community Survey population (not shown); ‡ Numbers in parentheses indicate the number of people reporting a single ancestry; * Numbers in parentheses indicate the number of persons reporting this race alone, not in combination with any other race; Please refer to the Explanation of Data for more information.*

Blackfeet (1)	1	0.01
Cherokee (2)	15	0.11
Chippewa (3)	3	0.02
Choctaw (0)	3	0.02
Iroquois (2)	3	0.02
Menominee (1)	1	0.01
Mexican American Ind. (0)	4	0.03
Potawatomi (1)	2	0.01
Puget Sound Salish (1)	1	0.01
Shoshone (1)	1	0.01
Sioux (4)	6	0.04
South American Ind. (0)	1	0.01
Asian (246)	345	2.58
Not Hispanic (246)	341	2.55
Hispanic (0)	4	0.03
Cambodian (1)	2	0.01
Chinese, ex. Taiwanese (33)	45	0.34
Filipino (16)	29	0.22
Hmong (1)	1	0.01
Indian (89)	100	0.75
Japanese (4)	19	0.14
Korean (37)	51	0.38
Laotian (15)	23	0.17
Nepalese (2)	2	0.01
Pakistani (5)	5	0.04
Sri Lankan (1)	1	0.01
Taiwanese (6)	10	0.07
Thai (12)	18	0.13
Vietnamese (9)	17	0.13
Hawaii Native/Pacific Islander (3)	10	0.07
Not Hispanic (2)	8	0.06
Hispanic (1)	2	0.01
Guamanian/Chamorro (2)	4	0.03
Native Hawaiian (0)	4	0.03
Samoan (0)	1	0.01
White (12,067)	12,357	92.40
Not Hispanic (11,773)	12,020	89.88
Hispanic (294)	337	2.52

Norwalk

Place Type: City
County: Warren
Population: 8,945†

Ancestry‡	Population	%
Afghan (9)	9	0.10
American (415)	415	4.81
Arab (0)	16	0.19
Lebanese (0)	16	0.19
Belgian (9)	31	0.36
British (70)	70	0.81
Czech (74)	166	1.93
Danish (37)	329	3.82
Dutch (114)	569	6.60
English (379)	1,032	11.97
European (183)	205	2.38
Finnish (0)	12	0.14
French, ex. Basque (96)	390	4.52
German (1,294)	3,529	40.93
Irish (377)	1,670	19.37
Italian (105)	332	3.85
Northern European (12)	12	0.14
Norwegian (122)	319	3.70
Polish (0)	58	0.67
Russian (9)	9	0.10
Scotch-Irish (10)	119	1.38
Scottish (5)	145	1.68
Swedish (148)	447	5.18
Swiss (12)	31	0.36
Ukrainian (0)	8	0.09
Welsh (31)	151	1.75
Yugoslavian (13)	13	0.15

Hispanic Origin	Population	%
Hispanic or Latino (of any race)	228	2.55
Central American, ex. Mexican	16	0.18
Guatemalan	2	0.02
Honduran	10	0.11
Nicaraguan	1	0.01
Panamanian	3	0.03
Cuban	5	0.06
Dominican Republic	3	0.03
Mexican	159	1.78
Puerto Rican	8	0.09
South American	7	0.08
Colombian	3	0.03
Ecuadorian	1	0.01
Peruvian	3	0.03
Other Hispanic or Latino	30	0.34

Race*	Population	%
African-American/Black (47)	80	0.89
Not Hispanic (47)	78	0.87
Hispanic (0)	2	0.02
American Indian/Alaska Native (15)	47	0.53
Not Hispanic (11)	36	0.40
Hispanic (4)	11	0.12
Apache (0)	4	0.04
Blackfeet (0)	1	0.01
Cherokee (2)	13	0.15
Chippewa (3)	3	0.03
Hopi (0)	4	0.04
Mexican American Ind. (0)	3	0.03
Seminole (0)	2	0.02
Sioux (0)	1	0.01
Yup'ik *(Alaska Native)* (1)	1	0.01
Asian (57)	97	1.08
Not Hispanic (56)	93	1.04
Hispanic (1)	4	0.04
Cambodian (1)	1	0.01
Chinese, ex. Taiwanese (9)	20	0.22
Filipino (13)	22	0.25
Hmong (2)	2	0.02
Indian (7)	10	0.11
Japanese (2)	5	0.06
Korean (4)	16	0.18
Laotian (1)	1	0.01
Pakistani (8)	9	0.10
Thai (1)	1	0.01
Vietnamese (8)	10	0.11
Hawaii Native/Pacific Islander (2)	9	0.10
Not Hispanic (2)	8	0.09
Hispanic (0)	1	0.01
Guamanian/Chamorro (2)	2	0.02
Native Hawaiian (0)	7	0.08
White (8,671)	8,782	98.18
Not Hispanic (8,499)	8,593	96.06
Hispanic (172)	189	2.11

Oskaloosa

Place Type: City
County: Mahaska
Population: 11,463†

Ancestry‡	Population	%
African, Sub-Saharan (99)	99	0.87
African (99)	99	0.87
American (869)	869	7.63
Austrian (0)	20	0.18
British (27)	35	0.31
Czech (11)	22	0.19
Danish (22)	48	0.42
Dutch (1,010)	1,882	16.52
English (484)	1,448	12.71
European (39)	52	0.46
French, ex. Basque (88)	421	3.70
French Canadian (19)	50	0.44
German (1,087)	2,899	25.45
Greek (13)	13	0.11
Hungarian (27)	36	0.32
Irish (591)	1,941	17.04
Italian (60)	395	3.47
Northern European (20)	20	0.18
Norwegian (114)	402	3.53
Pennsylvania German (8)	31	0.27
Polish (46)	109	0.96
Portuguese (2)	2	0.02
Russian (0)	11	0.10
Scandinavian (9)	26	0.23
Scotch-Irish (138)	287	2.52
Scottish (73)	218	1.91
Swedish (23)	231	2.03
Swiss (10)	16	0.14
Welsh (0)	57	0.50
Yugoslavian (10)	10	0.09

Hispanic Origin	Population	%
Hispanic or Latino (of any race)	270	2.36
Central American, ex. Mexican	11	0.10
Guatemalan	2	0.02
Nicaraguan	6	0.05
Panamanian	1	0.01
Salvadoran	2	0.02
Cuban	6	0.05
Dominican Republic	1	0.01
Mexican	186	1.62
Puerto Rican	20	0.17
South American	12	0.10
Argentinean	1	0.01
Colombian	1	0.01
Peruvian	7	0.06
Venezuelan	3	0.03
Other Hispanic or Latino	34	0.30

Race*	Population	%
African-American/Black (229)	315	2.75
Not Hispanic (226)	310	2.70
Hispanic (3)	5	0.04
American Indian/Alaska Native (31)	82	0.72
Not Hispanic (24)	71	0.62
Hispanic (7)	11	0.10
Apache (1)	1	0.01
Blackfeet (1)	1	0.01
Canadian/French Am. Ind. (0)	1	0.01
Cherokee (6)	22	0.19
Chippewa (2)	3	0.03
Choctaw (0)	1	0.01
Creek (0)	1	0.01
Iroquois (0)	2	0.02
Lumbee (3)	3	0.03
Mexican American Ind. (6)	6	0.05
Navajo (1)	1	0.01
Potawatomi (1)	3	0.03
Sioux (0)	3	0.03
Yaqui (0)	3	0.03
Asian (196)	249	2.17
Not Hispanic (191)	242	2.11
Hispanic (5)	7	0.06
Burmese (1)	1	0.01
Cambodian (5)	17	0.15
Chinese, ex. Taiwanese (12)	13	0.11
Filipino (53)	63	0.55
Hmong (18)	22	0.19
Indian (20)	26	0.23
Japanese (21)	25	0.22
Korean (10)	22	0.19
Laotian (33)	35	0.31
Pakistani (0)	1	0.01
Thai (5)	11	0.10
Vietnamese (5)	9	0.08
Hawaii Native/Pacific Islander (2)	11	0.10
Not Hispanic (2)	10	0.09
Hispanic (0)	1	0.01
Guamanian/Chamorro (0)	1	0.01
Native Hawaiian (2)	9	0.08
Tongan (0)	1	0.01
White (10,696)	10,890	95.00
Not Hispanic (10,562)	10,735	93.65
Hispanic (134)	155	1.35

Ottumwa

Place Type: City
County: Wapello
Population: 25,023†

Ancestry‡	Population	%
African, Sub-Saharan (151)	151	0.61

*Notes: † The Census 2010 population figure is used to calculate the percentages in the Hispanic Origin and Race categories. Ancestry percentages are based on the 2006-2010 American Community Survey population (not shown); ‡ Numbers in parentheses indicate the number of people reporting a single ancestry; * Numbers in parentheses indicate the number of persons reporting this race alone, not in combination with any other race; Please refer to the Explanation of Data for more information.*

SECTION TWO

	Population	%
African (72)	72	0.29
Other Sub-Saharan African (79)	79	0.32
American (2,366)	2,366	9.51
Arab (24)	94	0.38
Arab (24)	94	0.38
Australian (0)	11	0.04
Austrian (12)	21	0.08
Belgian (0)	36	0.14
Brazilian (15)	15	0.06
British (11)	23	0.09
Cajun (0)	29	0.12
Canadian (10)	76	0.31
Croatian (13)	21	0.08
Czech (70)	144	0.58
Czechoslovakian (16)	34	0.14
Danish (58)	142	0.57
Dutch (186)	1,353	5.44
English (1,212)	3,217	12.93
European (56)	56	0.22
French, ex. Basque (95)	492	1.98
French Canadian (28)	28	0.11
German (2,199)	5,566	22.36
Greek (56)	220	0.88
Hungarian (0)	62	0.25
Irish (1,516)	4,400	17.68
Italian (177)	467	1.88
Lithuanian (0)	9	0.04
Luxemburger (8)	8	0.03
Norwegian (150)	457	1.84
Pennsylvania German (23)	37	0.15
Polish (46)	91	0.37
Portuguese (0)	50	0.20
Russian (0)	58	0.23
Scandinavian (41)	82	0.33
Scotch-Irish (86)	357	1.43
Scottish (213)	588	2.36
Swedish (167)	632	2.54
Swiss (0)	18	0.07
Ukrainian (0)	33	0.13
Welsh (99)	439	1.76
Yugoslavian (151)	170	0.68

Hispanic Origin	Population	%
Hispanic or Latino (of any race)	2,840	11.35
Central American, ex. Mexican	445	1.78
Costa Rican	3	0.01
Guatemalan	188	0.75
Honduran	55	0.22
Nicaraguan	13	0.05
Panamanian	1	<0.01
Salvadoran	180	0.72
Other Central American	5	0.02
Cuban	12	0.05
Dominican Republic	5	0.02
Mexican	2,122	8.48
Puerto Rican	61	0.24
South American	17	0.07
Chilean	2	0.01
Colombian	3	0.01
Ecuadorian	4	0.02
Paraguayan	5	0.02
Peruvian	3	0.01
Other Hispanic or Latino	178	0.71

Race*	Population	%
African-American/Black (469)	646	2.58
Not Hispanic (435)	595	2.38
Hispanic (34)	51	0.20
American Indian/Alaska Native (144)	268	1.07
Not Hispanic (65)	166	0.66
Hispanic (79)	102	0.41
Apache (4)	17	0.07
Blackfeet (2)	12	0.05
Cherokee (6)	35	0.14
Cheyenne (1)	1	<0.01
Chippewa (3)	3	0.01
Choctaw (0)	2	0.01
Creek (0)	1	<0.01
Iroquois (0)	1	<0.01
Kiowa (0)	1	<0.01
Mexican American Ind. (24)	26	0.10
Navajo (2)	7	0.03
Osage (0)	1	<0.01
Potawatomi (0)	1	<0.01
Puget Sound Salish (0)	1	<0.01
Sioux (5)	10	0.04
Spanish American Ind. (6)	6	0.02
Asian (213)	291	1.16
Not Hispanic (209)	281	1.12
Hispanic (4)	10	0.04
Bangladeshi (2)	2	0.01
Cambodian (1)	4	0.02
Chinese, ex. Taiwanese (25)	32	0.13
Filipino (44)	57	0.23
Indian (30)	43	0.17
Indonesian (0)	1	<0.01
Japanese (21)	32	0.13
Korean (25)	40	0.16
Laotian (38)	41	0.16
Pakistani (4)	4	0.02
Taiwanese (9)	9	0.04
Thai (1)	8	0.03
Vietnamese (8)	13	0.05
Hawaii Native/Pacific Islander (47)	69	0.28
Not Hispanic (42)	54	0.22
Hispanic (5)	15	0.06
Guamanian/Chamorro (13)	24	0.10
Marshallese (17)	17	0.07
Native Hawaiian (2)	8	0.03
Samoan (6)	14	0.06
White (22,559)	22,975	91.82
Not Hispanic (21,102)	21,406	85.55
Hispanic (1,457)	1,569	6.27

Pella

Place Type: City
County: Marion
Population: 10,352†

Ancestry‡	Population	%
African, Sub-Saharan (49)	49	0.47
African (49)	49	0.47
American (571)	571	5.51
Austrian (0)	23	0.22
Belgian (0)	69	0.67
British (43)	43	0.42
Canadian (11)	11	0.11
Czech (54)	175	1.69
Danish (59)	175	1.69
Dutch (3,554)	4,538	43.81
English (135)	706	6.82
European (77)	77	0.74
French, ex. Basque (55)	234	2.26
German (769)	2,701	26.07
Greek (10)	10	0.10
Irish (251)	1,109	10.71
Italian (36)	164	1.58
Norwegian (113)	316	3.05
Polish (0)	93	0.90
Romanian (0)	10	0.10
Russian (0)	25	0.24
Scotch-Irish (42)	169	1.63
Scottish (0)	62	0.60
Slovak (0)	13	0.13
Swedish (34)	216	2.09
Turkish (0)	25	0.24
Welsh (19)	85	0.82
West Indian, ex. Hispanic (12)	32	0.31
Haitian (12)	32	0.31

Hispanic Origin	Population	%
Hispanic or Latino (of any race)	175	1.69
Central American, ex. Mexican	13	0.13
Guatemalan	7	0.07
Panamanian	3	0.03
Salvadoran	3	0.03
Cuban	4	0.04
Mexican	98	0.95
Puerto Rican	26	0.25
South American	16	0.15
Argentinean	3	0.03
Bolivian	1	0.01
Chilean	1	0.01
Colombian	3	0.03
Ecuadorian	6	0.06
Peruvian	1	0.01
Venezuelan	1	0.01
Other Hispanic or Latino	18	0.17

Race*	Population	%
African-American/Black (74)	127	1.23
Not Hispanic (68)	116	1.12
Hispanic (6)	11	0.11
American Indian/Alaska Native (24)	60	0.58
Not Hispanic (15)	45	0.43
Hispanic (9)	15	0.14
Blackfeet (0)	5	0.05
Cherokee (1)	6	0.06
Chickasaw (0)	2	0.02
Chippewa (6)	7	0.07
Choctaw (1)	4	0.04
Hopi (5)	5	0.05
Mexican American Ind. (1)	4	0.04
Navajo (1)	1	0.01
Sioux (0)	4	0.04
Asian (238)	295	2.85
Not Hispanic (238)	294	2.84
Hispanic (0)	1	0.01
Cambodian (20)	24	0.23
Chinese, ex. Taiwanese (30)	32	0.31
Filipino (44)	55	0.53
Hmong (20)	25	0.24
Indian (49)	54	0.52
Indonesian (1)	1	0.01
Japanese (3)	8	0.08
Korean (18)	21	0.20
Laotian (28)	33	0.32
Malaysian (2)	2	0.02
Pakistani (0)	1	0.01
Taiwanese (2)	2	0.02
Thai (3)	12	0.12
Vietnamese (9)	14	0.14
Hawaii Native/Pacific Islander (2)	4	0.04
Not Hispanic (2)	4	0.04
Fijian (0)	1	0.01
Native Hawaiian (1)	2	0.02
Samoan (1)	2	0.02
White (9,838)	9,963	96.24
Not Hispanic (9,728)	9,835	95.01
Hispanic (110)	128	1.24

Perry

Place Type: City
County: Dallas
Population: 7,702†

Ancestry‡	Population	%
American (456)	456	5.92
Belgian (0)	10	0.13
British (16)	16	0.21
Canadian (12)	12	0.16
Croatian (12)	12	0.16
Czech (0)	26	0.34
Danish (0)	145	1.88
Dutch (37)	238	3.09
Eastern European (9)	9	0.12
English (147)	668	8.67
European (14)	14	0.18
French, ex. Basque (39)	137	1.78
German (772)	1,982	25.72
Icelander (24)	42	0.55
Irish (287)	910	11.81
Italian (10)	45	0.58
Norwegian (77)	193	2.50
Polish (10)	20	0.26
Scandinavian (10)	10	0.13
Scotch-Irish (23)	103	1.34
Scottish (0)	73	0.95

*Notes: † The Census 2010 population figure is used to calculate the percentages in the Hispanic Origin and Race categories. Ancestry percentages are based on the 2006-2010 American Community Survey population (not shown); ‡ Numbers in parentheses indicate the number of people reporting a single ancestry; * Numbers in parentheses indicate the number of persons reporting this race alone, not in combination with any other race; Please refer to the Explanation of Data for more information.*

Ancestry	Population	%
Swedish (11)	88	1.14
Welsh (0)	124	1.61
West Indian, ex. Hispanic (0)	10	0.13
Dutch West Indian (0)	10	0.13
Yugoslavian (0)	10	0.13

Hispanic Origin	Population	%
Hispanic or Latino (of any race)	2,692	34.95
Central American, ex. Mexican	722	9.37
Costa Rican	1	0.01
Guatemalan	257	3.34
Honduran	9	0.12
Nicaraguan	31	0.40
Panamanian	2	0.03
Salvadoran	422	5.48
Cuban	9	0.12
Dominican Republic	21	0.27
Mexican	1,631	21.18
Puerto Rican	38	0.49
South American	16	0.21
Argentinean	4	0.05
Bolivian	4	0.05
Colombian	5	0.06
Ecuadorian	1	0.01
Peruvian	1	0.01
Venezuelan	1	0.01
Other Hispanic or Latino	255	3.31

Race*	Population	%
African-American/Black (141)	183	2.38
Not Hispanic (120)	154	2.00
Hispanic (21)	29	0.38
American Indian/Alaska Native (35)	102	1.32
Not Hispanic (18)	51	0.66
Hispanic (17)	51	0.66
Apache (0)	3	0.04
Blackfeet (0)	1	0.01
Cherokee (3)	12	0.16
Chickasaw (1)	1	0.01
Chippewa (1)	4	0.05
Mexican American Ind. (4)	6	0.08
Osage (1)	1	0.01
Sioux (9)	9	0.12
Spanish American Ind. (0)	3	0.04
Asian (64)	94	1.22
Not Hispanic (60)	79	1.03
Hispanic (4)	15	0.19
Burmese (2)	5	0.06
Cambodian (2)	2	0.03
Chinese, ex. Taiwanese (8)	14	0.18
Filipino (2)	9	0.12
Indian (8)	11	0.14
Japanese (0)	3	0.04
Korean (3)	6	0.08
Laotian (1)	1	0.01
Thai (1)	1	0.01
Vietnamese (33)	36	0.47
Hawaii Native/Pacific Islander (11)	22	0.29
Not Hispanic (10)	12	0.16
Hispanic (1)	10	0.13
Guamanian/Chamorro (1)	1	0.01
Native Hawaiian (0)	1	0.01
White (6,095)	6,341	82.33
Not Hispanic (4,709)	4,782	62.09
Hispanic (1,386)	1,559	20.24

Pleasant Hill

Place Type: City
County: Polk
Population: 8,785†

Ancestry‡	Population	%
African, Sub-Saharan (42)	42	0.52
African (21)	21	0.26
Sudanese (21)	21	0.26
American (706)	706	8.72
Arab (13)	20	0.25
Arab (0)	7	0.09
Lebanese (13)	13	0.16
British (0)	42	0.52
Czech (0)	8	0.10
Danish (12)	71	0.88
Dutch (206)	731	9.02
English (174)	902	11.14
European (91)	102	1.26
Finnish (18)	18	0.22
French, ex. Basque (38)	233	2.88
German (975)	2,488	30.72
Greek (0)	32	0.40
Irish (301)	1,450	17.90
Italian (201)	305	3.77
Northern European (38)	38	0.47
Norwegian (114)	518	6.40
Pennsylvania German (0)	14	0.17
Polish (18)	88	1.09
Russian (0)	17	0.21
Scotch-Irish (7)	139	1.72
Scottish (52)	180	2.22
Slovak (12)	12	0.15
Swedish (197)	513	6.33
Swiss (0)	31	0.38
Turkish (0)	14	0.17
Ukrainian (0)	17	0.21
Welsh (63)	72	0.89

Hispanic Origin	Population	%
Hispanic or Latino (of any race)	397	4.52
Central American, ex. Mexican	31	0.35
Guatemalan	3	0.03
Honduran	1	0.01
Nicaraguan	4	0.05
Salvadoran	23	0.26
Cuban	5	0.06
Mexican	296	3.37
Puerto Rican	14	0.16
South American	25	0.28
Argentinean	3	0.03
Chilean	1	0.01
Colombian	5	0.06
Ecuadorian	4	0.05
Peruvian	10	0.11
Venezuelan	2	0.02
Other Hispanic or Latino	26	0.30

Race*	Population	%
African-American/Black (235)	323	3.68
Not Hispanic (235)	319	3.63
Hispanic (0)	4	0.05
American Indian/Alaska Native (28)	81	0.92
Not Hispanic (25)	70	0.80
Hispanic (3)	11	0.13
Apache (0)	1	0.01
Blackfeet (1)	1	0.01
Cherokee (6)	11	0.13
Chickasaw (0)	1	0.01
Chippewa (1)	2	0.02
Choctaw (0)	1	0.01
Comanche (0)	1	0.01
Mexican American Ind. (0)	2	0.02
Potawatomi (1)	1	0.01
Pueblo (0)	1	0.01
Sioux (1)	2	0.02
Asian (220)	281	3.20
Not Hispanic (214)	261	2.97
Hispanic (6)	20	0.23
Burmese (5)	5	0.06
Cambodian (5)	9	0.10
Chinese, ex. Taiwanese (22)	35	0.40
Filipino (20)	38	0.43
Hmong (7)	7	0.08
Indian (20)	23	0.26
Japanese (5)	11	0.13
Korean (13)	21	0.24
Laotian (48)	63	0.72
Thai (28)	31	0.35
Vietnamese (34)	38	0.43
Hawaii Native/Pacific Islander (0)	5	0.06
Not Hispanic (0)	2	0.02
Hispanic (0)	3	0.03
White (7,991)	8,206	93.41
Not Hispanic (7,741)	7,896	89.88
Hispanic (250)	310	3.53

Sioux City

Place Type: City
County: Woodbury
Population: 82,684†

Ancestry‡	Population	%
African, Sub-Saharan (692)	890	1.08
African (440)	625	0.76
Ethiopian (199)	199	0.24
Nigerian (19)	19	0.02
Other Sub-Saharan African (34)	47	0.06
American (2,847)	2,847	3.47
Arab (69)	176	0.21
Lebanese (60)	72	0.09
Syrian (9)	104	0.13
Australian (14)	14	0.02
Austrian (22)	131	0.16
Belgian (39)	107	0.13
Brazilian (47)	67	0.08
British (31)	121	0.15
Canadian (31)	55	0.07
Celtic (17)	17	0.02
Czech (336)	878	1.07
Czechoslovakian (45)	85	0.10
Danish (596)	1,835	2.23
Dutch (1,114)	3,449	4.20
Eastern European (18)	18	0.02
English (1,551)	6,344	7.73
European (396)	483	0.59
Finnish (46)	86	0.10
French, ex. Basque (576)	3,090	3.76
French Canadian (274)	770	0.94
German (10,742)	26,728	32.55
German Russian (0)	25	0.03
Greek (104)	152	0.19
Hungarian (32)	32	0.04
Irish (2,596)	12,425	15.13
Italian (324)	1,188	1.45
Latvian (26)	26	0.03
Lithuanian (77)	176	0.21
Luxemburger (138)	412	0.50
Macedonian (0)	8	0.01
Northern European (85)	85	0.10
Norwegian (1,482)	4,767	5.81
Pennsylvania German (29)	64	0.08
Polish (609)	2,240	2.73
Portuguese (50)	50	0.06
Romanian (0)	29	0.04
Russian (197)	864	1.05
Scandinavian (300)	503	0.61
Scotch-Irish (381)	967	1.18
Scottish (343)	1,192	1.45
Slavic (0)	12	0.01
Slovak (25)	44	0.05
Slovene (0)	15	0.02
Swedish (592)	2,805	3.42
Swiss (0)	219	0.27
Ukrainian (12)	118	0.14
Welsh (35)	274	0.33
West Indian, ex. Hispanic (0)	14	0.02
Jamaican (0)	9	0.01
West Indian (0)	5	0.01
Yugoslavian (12)	12	0.01

Hispanic Origin	Population	%
Hispanic or Latino (of any race)	13,598	16.45
Central American, ex. Mexican	1,889	2.28
Costa Rican	2	<0.01
Guatemalan	1,244	1.50
Honduran	76	0.09
Nicaraguan	75	0.09
Panamanian	17	0.02
Salvadoran	467	0.56
Other Central American	8	0.01
Cuban	42	0.05

*Notes: † The Census 2010 population figure is used to calculate the percentages in the Hispanic Origin and Race categories. Ancestry percentages are based on the 2006-2010 American Community Survey population (not shown); ‡ Numbers in parentheses indicate the number of people reporting a single ancestry; * Numbers in parentheses indicate the number of persons reporting this race alone, not in combination with any other race; Please refer to the Explanation of Data for more information.*

Dominican Republic	11	0.01
Mexican	10,561	12.77
Puerto Rican	198	0.24
South American	92	0.11
Argentinean	3	<0.01
Bolivian	8	0.01
Chilean	15	0.02
Colombian	30	0.04
Ecuadorian	13	0.02
Peruvian	19	0.02
Venezuelan	4	<0.01
Other Hispanic or Latino	805	0.97

Race*	Population	%
African-American/Black (2,371)	3,578	4.33
Not Hispanic (2,302)	3,391	4.10
Hispanic (69)	187	0.23
American Indian/Alaska Native (2,134)	3,071	3.71
Not Hispanic (1,685)	2,380	2.88
Hispanic (449)	691	0.84
Alaska Athabascan *(Ala. Nat.)* (2)	2	<0.01
Aleut *(Alaska Native)* (0)	1	<0.01
Apache (5)	9	0.01
Arapaho (1)	4	<0.01
Blackfeet (2)	9	0.01
Canadian/French Am. Ind. (1)	1	<0.01
Central American Ind. (12)	13	0.02
Cherokee (16)	61	0.07
Cheyenne (3)	8	0.01
Chickasaw (0)	1	<0.01
Chippewa (24)	42	0.05
Choctaw (0)	4	<0.01
Comanche (0)	2	<0.01
Creek (1)	1	<0.01
Crow (1)	2	<0.01
Hopi (5)	7	0.01
Inupiat *(Alaska Native)* (2)	5	0.01
Iroquois (4)	4	<0.01
Mexican American Ind. (84)	112	0.14
Navajo (11)	24	0.03
Ottawa (1)	1	<0.01
Paiute (1)	2	<0.01
Pima (7)	7	0.01
Potawatomi (4)	5	0.01
Pueblo (0)	2	<0.01
Puget Sound Salish (1)	1	<0.01
Seminole (0)	2	<0.01
Shoshone (2)	2	<0.01
Sioux (580)	887	1.07
South American Ind. (1)	2	<0.01
Tlingit-Haida *(Alaska Native)* (2)	2	<0.01
Yaqui (1)	1	<0.01
Asian (2,258)	2,704	3.27
Not Hispanic (2,231)	2,629	3.18
Hispanic (27)	75	0.09
Cambodian (126)	170	0.21
Chinese, ex. Taiwanese (101)	157	0.19
Filipino (108)	195	0.24
Hmong (18)	21	0.03
Indian (71)	121	0.15
Indonesian (2)	6	0.01
Japanese (33)	67	0.08
Korean (92)	150	0.18
Laotian (207)	266	0.32
Malaysian (0)	5	0.01
Nepalese (1)	3	<0.01
Pakistani (48)	58	0.07
Sri Lankan (1)	4	<0.01
Taiwanese (3)	3	<0.01
Thai (11)	46	0.06
Vietnamese (1,284)	1,416	1.71
Hawaii Native/Pacific Islander (102)	192	0.23
Not Hispanic (98)	153	0.19
Hispanic (4)	39	0.05
Guamanian/Chamorro (13)	40	0.05
Native Hawaiian (19)	48	0.06
Samoan (1)	5	0.01
Tongan (3)	3	<0.01
White (66,641)	69,346	83.87
Not Hispanic (60,748)	62,503	75.59
Hispanic (5,893)	6,843	8.28

Spencer

Place Type: City
County: Clay
Population: 11,233†

Ancestry‡	Population	%
American (552)	552	4.93
Canadian (0)	16	0.14
Croatian (0)	11	0.10
Czech (0)	27	0.24
Czechoslovakian (0)	10	0.09
Danish (128)	423	3.78
Dutch (240)	676	6.04
Eastern European (12)	12	0.11
English (351)	951	8.50
European (44)	59	0.53
Finnish (0)	15	0.13
French, ex. Basque (29)	275	2.46
French Canadian (21)	43	0.38
German (2,461)	5,049	45.11
Irish (293)	1,511	13.50
Italian (30)	124	1.11
Luxemburger (0)	12	0.11
Norwegian (439)	953	8.51
Pennsylvania German (19)	26	0.23
Polish (0)	116	1.04
Portuguese (0)	12	0.11
Scotch-Irish (15)	108	0.96
Scottish (0)	82	0.73
Swedish (164)	499	4.46
Swiss (0)	26	0.23
Ukrainian (0)	37	0.33
Welsh (52)	126	1.13
West Indian, ex. Hispanic (23)	23	0.21
West Indian (23)	23	0.21

Hispanic Origin	Population	%
Hispanic or Latino (of any race)	390	3.47
Central American, ex. Mexican	39	0.35
Guatemalan	5	0.04
Honduran	13	0.12
Nicaraguan	1	0.01
Panamanian	2	0.02
Salvadoran	18	0.16
Cuban	2	0.02
Mexican	269	2.39
Puerto Rican	17	0.15
South American	4	0.04
Argentinean	1	0.01
Chilean	2	0.02
Peruvian	1	0.01
Other Hispanic or Latino	59	0.53

Race*	Population	%
African-American/Black (60)	118	1.05
Not Hispanic (59)	113	1.01
Hispanic (1)	5	0.04
American Indian/Alaska Native (32)	61	0.54
Not Hispanic (31)	60	0.53
Hispanic (1)	1	0.01
Blackfeet (0)	3	0.03
Cherokee (1)	3	0.03
Chippewa (7)	11	0.10
Sioux (7)	9	0.08
South American Ind. (1)	1	0.01
Asian (78)	100	0.89
Not Hispanic (77)	99	0.88
Hispanic (1)	1	0.01
Cambodian (0)	2	0.02
Chinese, ex. Taiwanese (5)	9	0.08
Filipino (11)	17	0.15
Indian (4)	4	0.04
Japanese (1)	2	0.02
Korean (13)	20	0.18
Laotian (28)	36	0.32
Thai (1)	4	0.04
Vietnamese (7)	8	0.07
Hawaii Native/Pacific Islander (1)	4	0.04
Not Hispanic (0)	3	0.03
Hispanic (1)	1	0.01
Native Hawaiian (0)	3	0.03
White (10,779)	10,906	97.09
Not Hispanic (10,573)	10,671	95.00
Hispanic (206)	235	2.09

Storm Lake

Place Type: City
County: Buena Vista
Population: 10,600†

Ancestry‡	Population	%
African, Sub-Saharan (218)	218	2.10
African (148)	148	1.43
Sudanese (70)	70	0.68
American (241)	241	2.33
Austrian (0)	24	0.23
Belgian (0)	12	0.12
British (10)	13	0.13
Canadian (0)	9	0.09
Czech (22)	75	0.72
Czechoslovakian (126)	136	1.31
Danish (110)	262	2.53
Dutch (19)	184	1.78
English (137)	710	6.86
European (39)	61	0.59
Finnish (0)	37	0.36
French, ex. Basque (9)	171	1.65
French Canadian (8)	21	0.20
German (1,151)	2,752	26.57
Greek (0)	13	0.13
Hungarian (11)	11	0.11
Irish (125)	819	7.91
Italian (138)	266	2.57
Luxemburger (0)	20	0.19
New Zealander (16)	16	0.15
Northern European (8)	8	0.08
Norwegian (116)	329	3.18
Polish (0)	37	0.36
Portuguese (13)	13	0.13
Russian (0)	10	0.10
Scandinavian (10)	10	0.10
Scotch-Irish (43)	101	0.98
Scottish (0)	32	0.31
Swedish (180)	422	4.07
Swiss (0)	27	0.26
Ukrainian (28)	28	0.27
Welsh (0)	47	0.45

Hispanic Origin	Population	%
Hispanic or Latino (of any race)	3,822	36.06
Central American, ex. Mexican	461	4.35
Guatemalan	120	1.13
Honduran	56	0.53
Nicaraguan	6	0.06
Salvadoran	272	2.57
Other Central American	7	0.07
Cuban	17	0.16
Dominican Republic	1	0.01
Mexican	3,115	29.39
Puerto Rican	32	0.30
South American	28	0.26
Argentinean	9	0.08
Bolivian	1	0.01
Colombian	5	0.05
Ecuadorian	1	0.01
Peruvian	11	0.10
Venezuelan	1	0.01
Other Hispanic or Latino	168	1.58

Race*	Population	%
African-American/Black (468)	508	4.79
Not Hispanic (439)	470	4.43
Hispanic (29)	38	0.36
American Indian/Alaska Native (43)	77	0.73
Not Hispanic (12)	28	0.26
Hispanic (31)	49	0.46

*Notes: † The Census 2010 population figure is used to calculate the percentages in the Hispanic Origin and Race categories. Ancestry percentages are based on the 2006-2010 American Community Survey population (not shown); ‡ Numbers in parentheses indicate the number of people reporting a single ancestry; * Numbers in parentheses indicate the number of persons reporting this race alone, not in combination with any other race; Please refer to the Explanation of Data for more information.*

Aleut *(Alaska Native)* (1)	1	0.01
Central American Ind. (2)	2	0.02
Cherokee (0)	4	0.04
Iroquois (3)	3	0.03
Mexican American Ind. (6)	16	0.15
Sioux (3)	11	0.10
Spanish American Ind. (0)	1	0.01
Asian (1,043)	1,097	10.35
Not Hispanic (1,027)	1,074	10.13
Hispanic (16)	23	0.22
Bangladeshi (1)	1	0.01
Burmese (75)	82	0.77
Cambodian (1)	5	0.05
Chinese, ex. Taiwanese (24)	30	0.28
Filipino (11)	17	0.16
Hmong (84)	88	0.83
Indian (64)	83	0.78
Japanese (3)	6	0.06
Korean (12)	12	0.11
Laotian (513)	562	5.30
Taiwanese (2)	2	0.02
Thai (28)	47	0.44
Vietnamese (84)	90	0.85
Hawaii Native/Pacific Islander (93)	105	0.99
Not Hispanic (90)	98	0.92
Hispanic (3)	7	0.07
Guamanian/Chamorro (7)	7	0.07
Native Hawaiian (11)	21	0.20
White (7,255)	7,463	70.41
Not Hispanic (5,111)	5,177	48.84
Hispanic (2,144)	2,286	21.57

Urbandale

Place Type: City
County: Polk
Population: 39,463†

Ancestry‡	Population	%
African, Sub-Saharan (591)	733	1.95
African (256)	312	0.83
Kenyan (77)	77	0.21
Liberian (73)	88	0.23
Nigerian (0)	56	0.15
South African (48)	48	0.13
Sudanese (94)	94	0.25
Ugandan (29)	29	0.08
Other Sub-Saharan African (14)	29	0.08
Albanian (10)	33	0.09
American (1,395)	1,395	3.72
Arab (9)	63	0.17
Lebanese (9)	38	0.10
Syrian (0)	25	0.07
Australian (49)	147	0.39
Austrian (16)	93	0.25
Belgian (72)	129	0.34
British (86)	137	0.37
Bulgarian (13)	13	0.03
Canadian (16)	158	0.42
Celtic (0)	23	0.06
Croatian (0)	50	0.13
Czech (164)	636	1.70
Czechoslovakian (0)	79	0.21
Danish (191)	866	2.31
Dutch (333)	1,606	4.28
Eastern European (7)	7	0.02
English (1,504)	4,920	13.12
European (595)	672	1.79
Finnish (15)	54	0.14
French, ex. Basque (173)	1,168	3.11
French Canadian (52)	309	0.82
German (4,949)	13,790	36.77
Greek (130)	199	0.53
Hungarian (13)	13	0.03
Iranian (11)	11	0.03
Irish (1,468)	6,526	17.40
Italian (573)	1,754	4.68
Lithuanian (13)	41	0.11
Luxemburger (31)	63	0.17
Macedonian (10)	10	0.03
Northern European (77)	95	0.25
Norwegian (1,032)	2,835	7.56
Pennsylvania German (63)	108	0.29
Polish (170)	470	1.25
Portuguese (13)	113	0.30
Romanian (9)	36	0.10
Russian (69)	175	0.47
Scandinavian (118)	175	0.47
Scotch-Irish (112)	597	1.59
Scottish (154)	674	1.80
Serbian (105)	116	0.31
Slovak (14)	49	0.13
Swedish (393)	1,910	5.09
Swiss (0)	25	0.07
Ukrainian (0)	39	0.10
Welsh (119)	405	1.08
Yugoslavian (904)	919	2.45

Hispanic Origin	Population	%
Hispanic or Latino (of any race)	1,221	3.09
Central American, ex. Mexican	83	0.21
Costa Rican	6	0.02
Guatemalan	30	0.08
Honduran	12	0.03
Nicaraguan	3	0.01
Panamanian	7	0.02
Salvadoran	24	0.06
Other Central American	1	<0.01
Cuban	22	0.06
Dominican Republic	1	<0.01
Mexican	884	2.24
Puerto Rican	35	0.09
South American	112	0.28
Argentinean	22	0.06
Bolivian	4	0.01
Chilean	7	0.02
Colombian	19	0.05
Ecuadorian	40	0.10
Peruvian	7	0.02
Venezuelan	11	0.03
Other South American	2	0.01
Other Hispanic or Latino	84	0.21

Race*	Population	%
African-American/Black (1,092)	1,383	3.50
Not Hispanic (1,081)	1,348	3.42
Hispanic (11)	35	0.09
American Indian/Alaska Native (45)	158	0.40
Not Hispanic (34)	128	0.32
Hispanic (11)	30	0.08
Blackfeet (3)	4	0.01
Cherokee (3)	18	0.05
Chickasaw (1)	1	<0.01
Chippewa (0)	1	<0.01
Choctaw (4)	8	0.02
Cree (0)	1	<0.01
Delaware (0)	1	<0.01
Inupiat *(Alaska Native)* (1)	1	<0.01
Mexican American Ind. (4)	8	0.02
Osage (3)	7	0.02
Ottawa (2)	5	0.01
Paiute (1)	1	<0.01
Potawatomi (0)	4	0.01
Sioux (1)	5	0.01
South American Ind. (2)	5	0.01
Asian (1,383)	1,613	4.09
Not Hispanic (1,382)	1,599	4.05
Hispanic (1)	14	0.04
Bangladeshi (9)	9	0.02
Cambodian (8)	13	0.03
Chinese, ex. Taiwanese (180)	224	0.57
Filipino (58)	118	0.30
Hmong (4)	4	0.01
Indian (423)	444	1.13
Indonesian (1)	1	<0.01
Japanese (36)	61	0.15
Korean (120)	152	0.39
Laotian (49)	58	0.15
Malaysian (0)	2	0.01
Nepalese (22)	23	0.06
Pakistani (11)	17	0.04
Sri Lankan (2)	2	0.01
Taiwanese (11)	11	0.03
Thai (41)	60	0.15
Vietnamese (361)	398	1.01
Hawaii Native/Pacific Islander (11)	40	0.10
Not Hispanic (11)	39	0.10
Hispanic (0)	1	<0.01
Guamanian/Chamorro (1)	1	<0.01
Native Hawaiian (4)	15	0.04
Samoan (1)	2	0.01
White (35,950)	36,543	92.60
Not Hispanic (35,133)	35,647	90.33
Hispanic (817)	896	2.27

Waterloo

Place Type: City
County: Black Hawk
Population: 68,406†

Ancestry‡	Population	%
African, Sub-Saharan (621)	807	1.19
African (517)	703	1.04
Nigerian (74)	74	0.11
Somalian (30)	30	0.04
Albanian (39)	39	0.06
American (3,855)	3,855	5.68
Arab (18)	27	0.04
Egyptian (0)	9	0.01
Iraqi (9)	9	0.01
Other Arab (9)	9	0.01
Austrian (10)	64	0.09
Belgian (32)	110	0.16
Brazilian (24)	24	0.04
British (68)	151	0.22
Bulgarian (34)	44	0.06
Canadian (19)	33	0.05
Celtic (28)	28	0.04
Croatian (143)	170	0.25
Czech (414)	1,174	1.73
Czechoslovakian (9)	30	0.04
Danish (440)	1,353	1.99
Dutch (368)	1,554	2.29
Eastern European (16)	16	0.02
English (1,282)	4,883	7.19
European (304)	411	0.61
Finnish (22)	51	0.08
French, ex. Basque (226)	1,701	2.51
French Canadian (83)	302	0.44
German (10,217)	24,591	36.22
Greek (59)	125	0.18
Hungarian (0)	89	0.13
Icelander (41)	41	0.06
Iranian (13)	35	0.05
Irish (1,991)	9,521	14.02
Italian (453)	1,091	1.61
Lithuanian (0)	10	0.01
Luxemburger (8)	44	0.06
Northern European (60)	60	0.09
Norwegian (1,198)	3,337	4.92
Pennsylvania German (20)	73	0.11
Polish (176)	767	1.13
Portuguese (0)	29	0.04
Romanian (39)	47	0.07
Russian (46)	181	0.27
Scandinavian (43)	80	0.12
Scotch-Irish (232)	926	1.36
Scottish (127)	941	1.39
Serbian (50)	57	0.08
Slovak (0)	31	0.05
Slovene (0)	6	0.01
Swedish (235)	1,153	1.70
Swiss (0)	245	0.36
Turkish (0)	16	0.02
Ukrainian (31)	85	0.13
Welsh (74)	313	0.46
West Indian, ex. Hispanic (68)	87	0.13
Dutch West Indian (43)	43	0.06
Jamaican (25)	44	0.06

*Notes: † The Census 2010 population figure is used to calculate the percentages in the Hispanic Origin and Race categories. Ancestry percentages are based on the 2006-2010 American Community Survey population (not shown); ‡ Numbers in parentheses indicate the number of people reporting a single ancestry; * Numbers in parentheses indicate the number of persons reporting this race alone, not in combination with any other race; Please refer to the Explanation of Data for more information.*

Yugoslavian (2,282)	2,330	3.43

Hispanic Origin	Population	%
Hispanic or Latino (of any race)	3,827	5.59
Central American, ex. Mexican	397	0.58
Guatemalan	193	0.28
Honduran	61	0.09
Nicaraguan	3	<0.01
Panamanian	7	0.01
Salvadoran	131	0.19
Other Central American	2	<0.01
Cuban	23	0.03
Dominican Republic	18	0.03
Mexican	2,864	4.19
Puerto Rican	133	0.19
South American	72	0.11
Argentinean	7	0.01
Bolivian	8	0.01
Chilean	7	0.01
Colombian	22	0.03
Ecuadorian	3	<0.01
Paraguayan	1	<0.01
Peruvian	11	0.02
Venezuelan	13	0.02
Other Hispanic or Latino	320	0.47

Race*	Population	%
African-American/Black (10,606)	11,947	17.46
Not Hispanic (10,488)	11,741	17.16
Hispanic (118)	206	0.30
American Indian/Alaska Native (200)	571	0.83
Not Hispanic (145)	465	0.68
Hispanic (55)	106	0.15
Alaska Athabascan *(Ala. Nat.)* (0)	1	<0.01
Apache (2)	3	<0.01
Blackfeet (1)	5	0.01
Canadian/French Am. Ind. (1)	1	<0.01
Central American Ind. (1)	8	0.01
Cherokee (10)	89	0.13
Cheyenne (3)	4	0.01
Chickasaw (0)	4	0.01
Chippewa (12)	32	0.05
Choctaw (2)	7	0.01
Cree (0)	3	<0.01
Creek (1)	1	<0.01
Crow (0)	3	<0.01
Inupiat *(Alaska Native)* (0)	3	<0.01
Iroquois (2)	2	<0.01
Mexican American Ind. (21)	26	0.04
Navajo (1)	14	0.02
Osage (0)	1	<0.01
Pima (1)	2	<0.01
Potawatomi (0)	1	<0.01
Seminole (0)	1	<0.01
Sioux (6)	15	0.02
South American Ind. (0)	2	<0.01
Spanish American Ind. (1)	2	<0.01
Tlingit-Haida *(Alaska Native)* (1)	1	<0.01
Yaqui (2)	3	<0.01
Asian (722)	1,025	1.50
Not Hispanic (710)	981	1.43
Hispanic (12)	44	0.06
Cambodian (2)	13	0.02
Chinese, ex. Taiwanese (92)	134	0.20
Filipino (56)	137	0.20
Hmong (1)	2	<0.01
Indian (177)	209	0.31
Indonesian (1)	2	<0.01
Japanese (20)	48	0.07
Korean (86)	132	0.19
Laotian (13)	30	0.04
Malaysian (4)	4	0.01
Nepalese (0)	2	<0.01
Pakistani (36)	50	0.07
Taiwanese (8)	11	0.02
Thai (11)	21	0.03
Vietnamese (166)	189	0.28
Hawaii Native/Pacific Islander (197)	260	0.38
Not Hispanic (171)	230	0.34
Hispanic (26)	30	0.04
Guamanian/Chamorro (35)	39	0.06
Marshallese (102)	106	0.15
Native Hawaiian (24)	44	0.06
Samoan (2)	3	<0.01
Tongan (1)	4	0.01
White (52,864)	54,722	80.00
Not Hispanic (51,254)	52,849	77.26
Hispanic (1,610)	1,873	2.74

Waukee

Place Type: City
County: Dallas
Population: 13,790†

Ancestry‡	Population	%
African, Sub-Saharan (10)	63	0.51
African (10)	63	0.51
American (564)	564	4.58
Belgian (66)	132	1.07
British (9)	48	0.39
Czech (6)	87	0.71
Czechoslovakian (10)	85	0.69
Danish (45)	214	1.74
Dutch (228)	771	6.27
English (428)	1,512	12.29
European (215)	215	1.75
Finnish (0)	50	0.41
French, ex. Basque (24)	234	1.90
French Canadian (13)	54	0.44
German (2,253)	5,546	45.07
Greek (13)	13	0.11
Irish (458)	1,996	16.22
Italian (56)	263	2.14
Latvian (12)	12	0.10
Lithuanian (46)	112	0.91
Luxemburger (0)	12	0.10
Northern European (33)	33	0.27
Norwegian (310)	855	6.95
Pennsylvania German (9)	27	0.22
Polish (65)	351	2.85
Romanian (13)	13	0.11
Russian (10)	66	0.54
Scandinavian (96)	112	0.91
Scotch-Irish (87)	130	1.06
Scottish (45)	181	1.47
Slavic (13)	57	0.46
Swedish (86)	756	6.14
Swiss (68)	221	1.80
Ukrainian (15)	15	0.12
Welsh (51)	174	1.41
Yugoslavian (27)	27	0.22

Hispanic Origin	Population	%
Hispanic or Latino (of any race)	412	2.99
Central American, ex. Mexican	18	0.13
Guatemalan	6	0.04
Honduran	1	0.01
Nicaraguan	6	0.04
Panamanian	5	0.04
Cuban	11	0.08
Mexican	267	1.94
Puerto Rican	19	0.14
South American	40	0.29
Bolivian	1	0.01
Colombian	7	0.05
Ecuadorian	16	0.12
Paraguayan	5	0.04
Peruvian	5	0.04
Venezuelan	6	0.04
Other Hispanic or Latino	57	0.41

Race*	Population	%
African-American/Black (174)	246	1.78
Not Hispanic (173)	244	1.77
Hispanic (1)	2	0.01
American Indian/Alaska Native (21)	44	0.32
Not Hispanic (10)	29	0.21
Hispanic (11)	15	0.11
Blackfeet (4)	5	0.04
Cherokee (2)	5	0.04
Comanche (5)	5	0.04
Navajo (0)	2	0.01
Paiute (2)	2	0.01
Potawatomi (0)	1	0.01
Sioux (0)	1	0.01
Asian (364)	416	3.02
Not Hispanic (361)	411	2.98
Hispanic (3)	5	0.04
Cambodian (4)	6	0.04
Chinese, ex. Taiwanese (39)	46	0.33
Filipino (21)	29	0.21
Indian (161)	174	1.26
Indonesian (6)	8	0.06
Japanese (6)	11	0.08
Korean (34)	42	0.30
Laotian (43)	52	0.38
Nepalese (4)	4	0.03
Pakistani (3)	4	0.03
Thai (11)	21	0.15
Vietnamese (22)	25	0.18
Hawaii Native/Pacific Islander (8)	14	0.10
Not Hispanic (8)	14	0.10
Native Hawaiian (4)	7	0.05
Samoan (4)	5	0.04
White (12,943)	13,084	94.88
Not Hispanic (12,681)	12,804	92.85
Hispanic (262)	280	2.03

Waverly

Place Type: City
County: Bremer
Population: 9,874†

Ancestry‡	Population	%
American (559)	559	5.73
Australian (9)	9	0.09
British (0)	26	0.27
Bulgarian (10)	10	0.10
Czech (52)	114	1.17
Danish (86)	272	2.79
Dutch (193)	403	4.13
English (266)	1,134	11.63
European (38)	48	0.49
French, ex. Basque (0)	102	1.05
French Canadian (9)	65	0.67
German (3,115)	5,480	56.18
Hungarian (13)	49	0.50
Irish (295)	1,223	12.54
Italian (31)	183	1.88
Lithuanian (8)	8	0.08
Norwegian (345)	760	7.79
Pennsylvania German (9)	29	0.30
Polish (0)	10	0.10
Portuguese (0)	18	0.18
Russian (0)	10	0.10
Scandinavian (59)	75	0.77
Scotch-Irish (64)	92	0.94
Scottish (46)	196	2.01
Swedish (45)	232	2.38
Swiss (9)	47	0.48
Welsh (0)	63	0.65

Hispanic Origin	Population	%
Hispanic or Latino (of any race)	132	1.34
Central American, ex. Mexican	12	0.12
Costa Rican	1	0.01
Guatemalan	6	0.06
Honduran	2	0.02
Nicaraguan	2	0.02
Salvadoran	1	0.01
Cuban	3	0.03
Dominican Republic	1	0.01
Mexican	91	0.92
Puerto Rican	8	0.08
South American	4	0.04
Colombian	2	0.02
Venezuelan	2	0.02
Other Hispanic or Latino	13	0.13

*Notes: † The Census 2010 population figure is used to calculate the percentages in the Hispanic Origin and Race categories. Ancestry percentages are based on the 2006-2010 American Community Survey population (not shown); ‡ Numbers in parentheses indicate the number of people reporting a single ancestry; * Numbers in parentheses indicate the number of persons reporting this race alone, not in combination with any other race; Please refer to the Explanation of Data for more information.*

Race*	Population	%
African-American/Black (165)	225	2.28
Not Hispanic (160)	215	2.18
Hispanic (5)	10	0.10
American Indian/Alaska Native (9)	43	0.44
Not Hispanic (4)	28	0.28
Hispanic (5)	15	0.15
Cherokee (0)	2	0.02
Choctaw (0)	1	0.01
Mexican American Ind. (2)	2	0.02
Navajo (0)	1	0.01
Sioux (0)	2	0.02
Asian (122)	164	1.66
Not Hispanic (121)	160	1.62
Hispanic (1)	4	0.04
Burmese (2)	2	0.02
Cambodian (2)	4	0.04
Chinese, ex. Taiwanese (23)	27	0.27
Filipino (13)	32	0.32
Hmong (1)	1	0.01
Indian (27)	31	0.31
Japanese (19)	24	0.24
Korean (17)	21	0.21
Laotian (5)	6	0.06
Nepalese (2)	2	0.02
Thai (3)	4	0.04
Vietnamese (0)	2	0.02
Hawaii Native/Pacific Islander (0)	7	0.07
Not Hispanic (0)	6	0.06
Hispanic (0)	1	0.01
Guamanian/Chamorro (0)	1	0.01
Native Hawaiian (0)	3	0.03
White (9,409)	9,535	96.57
Not Hispanic (9,335)	9,447	95.68
Hispanic (74)	88	0.89

Webster City

Place Type: City
County: Hamilton
Population: 8,070†

Ancestry‡	Population	%
American (326)	326	4.01
British (18)	43	0.53
Canadian (0)	11	0.14
Czech (11)	144	1.77
Danish (38)	242	2.98
Dutch (39)	394	4.85
English (236)	870	10.71
European (18)	18	0.22
French, ex. Basque (117)	390	4.80
German (1,191)	2,795	34.40
Irish (359)	1,188	14.62
Italian (50)	286	3.52
Norwegian (517)	1,133	13.94
Pennsylvania German (11)	11	0.14
Polish (10)	88	1.08
Scandinavian (32)	77	0.95
Scotch-Irish (56)	161	1.98
Scottish (27)	126	1.55
Swedish (109)	383	4.71
Swiss (14)	44	0.54
Welsh (10)	10	0.12

Hispanic Origin	Population	%
Hispanic or Latino (of any race)	601	7.45
Central American, ex. Mexican	37	0.46
Guatemalan	18	0.22
Honduran	8	0.10
Panamanian	1	0.01
Salvadoran	10	0.12
Mexican	516	6.39
Puerto Rican	18	0.22
South American	1	0.01
Chilean	1	0.01
Other Hispanic or Latino	29	0.36

Race*	Population	%
African-American/Black (32)	78	0.97
Not Hispanic (28)	73	0.90
Hispanic (4)	5	0.06
American Indian/Alaska Native (15)	58	0.72
Not Hispanic (9)	43	0.53
Hispanic (6)	15	0.19
Aleut *(Alaska Native)* (0)	3	0.04
Blackfeet (0)	1	0.01
Canadian/French Am. Ind. (0)	1	0.01
Cherokee (2)	6	0.07
Choctaw (0)	1	0.01
Mexican American Ind. (2)	3	0.04
Navajo (0)	1	0.01
Sioux (0)	3	0.04
Yaqui (0)	2	0.02
Asian (273)	308	3.82
Not Hispanic (273)	308	3.82
Cambodian (3)	5	0.06
Chinese, ex. Taiwanese (17)	17	0.21
Filipino (7)	19	0.24
Indian (21)	23	0.29
Japanese (2)	2	0.02
Korean (3)	15	0.19
Laotian (208)	217	2.69
Malaysian (1)	1	0.01
Thai (0)	3	0.04
Hawaii Native/Pacific Islander (0)	2	0.02
Not Hispanic (0)	2	0.02
Fijian (0)	1	0.01
Native Hawaiian (0)	1	0.01
Tongan (0)	1	0.01
White (7,327)	7,463	92.48
Not Hispanic (7,050)	7,152	88.62
Hispanic (277)	311	3.85

West Des Moines

Place Type: City
County: Polk
Population: 56,609†

Ancestry‡	Population	%
Afghan (8)	8	0.01
African, Sub-Saharan (258)	306	0.56
African (71)	71	0.13
Ethiopian (26)	26	0.05
Kenyan (161)	161	0.29
Liberian (0)	19	0.03
South African (0)	29	0.05
Albanian (342)	342	0.62
American (2,323)	2,323	4.24
Arab (156)	211	0.39
Arab (51)	51	0.09
Iraqi (13)	13	0.02
Lebanese (52)	78	0.14
Moroccan (0)	29	0.05
Other Arab (40)	40	0.07
Austrian (63)	231	0.42
Belgian (36)	87	0.16
British (139)	235	0.43
Cajun (0)	29	0.05
Canadian (14)	111	0.20
Croatian (165)	204	0.37
Czech (166)	625	1.14
Czechoslovakian (53)	84	0.15
Danish (248)	1,015	1.85
Dutch (795)	2,293	4.19
Eastern European (55)	55	0.10
English (2,067)	6,460	11.80
European (909)	1,007	1.84
Finnish (45)	135	0.25
French, ex. Basque (211)	1,250	2.28
French Canadian (54)	135	0.25
German (7,355)	18,782	34.32
Greek (117)	307	0.56
Hungarian (90)	99	0.18
Icelander (17)	33	0.06
Iranian (23)	23	0.04
Irish (2,092)	8,954	16.36
Israeli (0)	9	0.02
Italian (1,085)	2,160	3.95
Latvian (77)	77	0.14
Lithuanian (0)	141	0.26
Northern European (146)	159	0.29
Norwegian (988)	2,878	5.26
Pennsylvania German (17)	125	0.23
Polish (245)	966	1.76
Romanian (13)	32	0.06
Russian (287)	561	1.03
Scandinavian (105)	311	0.57
Scotch-Irish (419)	976	1.78
Scottish (232)	909	1.66
Serbian (10)	19	0.03
Slavic (0)	9	0.02
Slovak (15)	150	0.27
Slovene (0)	10	0.02
Swedish (576)	1,924	3.52
Swiss (27)	228	0.42
Ukrainian (83)	95	0.17
Welsh (194)	601	1.10
West Indian, ex. Hispanic (138)	157	0.29
Jamaican (138)	157	0.29
Yugoslavian (615)	716	1.31

Hispanic Origin	Population	%
Hispanic or Latino (of any race)	2,930	5.18
Central American, ex. Mexican	218	0.39
Costa Rican	3	0.01
Guatemalan	82	0.14
Honduran	44	0.08
Nicaraguan	14	0.02
Panamanian	13	0.02
Salvadoran	60	0.11
Other Central American	2	<0.01
Cuban	32	0.06
Dominican Republic	22	0.04
Mexican	2,053	3.63
Puerto Rican	112	0.20
South American	290	0.51
Argentinean	7	0.01
Bolivian	6	0.01
Chilean	2	<0.01
Colombian	66	0.12
Ecuadorian	152	0.27
Paraguayan	3	0.01
Peruvian	29	0.05
Uruguayan	1	<0.01
Venezuelan	23	0.04
Other South American	1	<0.01
Other Hispanic or Latino	203	0.36

Race*	Population	%
African-American/Black (1,872)	2,324	4.11
Not Hispanic (1,839)	2,264	4.00
Hispanic (33)	60	0.11
American Indian/Alaska Native (88)	275	0.49
Not Hispanic (61)	219	0.39
Hispanic (27)	56	0.10
Alaska Athabascan *(Ala. Nat.)* (0)	1	<0.01
Apache (1)	2	<0.01
Blackfeet (2)	15	0.03
Canadian/French Am. Ind. (1)	2	<0.01
Central American Ind. (2)	3	0.01
Cherokee (14)	70	0.12
Cheyenne (2)	5	0.01
Chickasaw (0)	6	0.01
Chippewa (6)	7	0.01
Choctaw (1)	4	0.01
Comanche (2)	2	<0.01
Cree (0)	1	<0.01
Creek (0)	1	<0.01
Iroquois (2)	3	0.01
Mexican American Ind. (5)	7	0.01
Navajo (1)	2	<0.01
Pima (1)	1	<0.01
Seminole (1)	3	0.01
Sioux (6)	16	0.03
South American Ind. (0)	2	<0.01
Tlingit-Haida *(Alaska Native)* (0)	3	0.01
Tohono O'Odham (1)	1	<0.01
Yaqui (1)	1	<0.01

*Notes: † The Census 2010 population figure is used to calculate the percentages in the Hispanic Origin and Race categories. Ancestry percentages are based on the 2006-2010 American Community Survey population (not shown); ‡ Numbers in parentheses indicate the number of people reporting a single ancestry; * Numbers in parentheses indicate the number of persons reporting this race alone, not in combination with any other race; Please refer to the Explanation of Data for more information.*

Asian (2,709)	3,078	5.44
Not Hispanic (2,695)	3,054	5.39
Hispanic (14)	24	0.04
Bangladeshi (5)	5	0.01
Burmese (2)	5	0.01
Cambodian (10)	21	0.04
Chinese, ex. Taiwanese (328)	401	0.71
Filipino (122)	188	0.33
Hmong (8)	10	0.02
Indian (1,300)	1,347	2.38
Indonesian (5)	14	0.02
Japanese (43)	96	0.17
Korean (235)	313	0.55
Laotian (72)	97	0.17
Malaysian (4)	6	0.01
Nepalese (51)	51	0.09
Pakistani (89)	92	0.16
Sri Lankan (7)	10	0.02
Taiwanese (13)	24	0.04
Thai (52)	79	0.14
Vietnamese (257)	299	0.53
Hawaii Native/Pacific Islander (22)	84	0.15
Not Hispanic (22)	58	0.10
Hispanic (0)	26	0.05
Guamanian/Chamorro (4)	11	0.02
Native Hawaiian (9)	25	0.04
Samoan (2)	2	<0.01
Tongan (1)	1	<0.01
White (50,020)	50,958	90.02
Not Hispanic (48,098)	48,914	86.41
Hispanic (1,922)	2,044	3.61

*Notes: † The Census 2010 population figure is used to calculate the percentages in the Hispanic Origin and Race categories. Ancestry percentages are based on the 2006-2010 American Community Survey population (not shown); ‡ Numbers in parentheses indicate the number of people reporting a single ancestry; * Numbers in parentheses indicate the number of persons reporting this race alone, not in combination with any other race; Please refer to the Explanation of Data for more information.*

KANSAS

Place Type: State
Population: 2,853,118[†]

Ancestry[‡]	Population	%
Afghan (71)	95	<0.01
African, Sub-Saharan (12,772)	15,821	0.56
African (7,787)	10,346	0.37
Cape Verdean (0)	13	<0.01
Ethiopian (1,102)	1,122	0.04
Ghanaian (33)	33	<0.01
Kenyan (1,126)	1,270	0.05
Liberian (33)	33	<0.01
Nigerian (379)	517	0.02
Senegalese (131)	131	<0.01
Sierra Leonean (10)	10	<0.01
Somalian (478)	478	0.02
South African (232)	318	0.01
Sudanese (350)	362	0.01
Ugandan (62)	76	<0.01
Zimbabwean (74)	74	<0.01
Other Sub-Saharan African (975)	1,038	0.04
Albanian (28)	107	<0.01
Alsatian (25)	39	<0.01
American (190,250)	190,250	6.77
Arab (5,310)	7,880	0.28
Arab (1,173)	1,382	0.05
Egyptian (593)	777	0.03
Iraqi (258)	262	0.01
Jordanian (267)	438	0.02
Lebanese (1,842)	3,196	0.11
Moroccan (269)	310	0.01
Palestinian (237)	245	0.01
Syrian (276)	632	0.02
Other Arab (395)	638	0.02
Armenian (260)	669	0.02
Assyrian/Chaldean/Syriac (13)	30	<0.01
Australian (176)	608	0.02
Austrian (1,430)	6,158	0.22
Basque (26)	99	<0.01
Belgian (1,625)	5,165	0.18
Brazilian (601)	851	0.03
British (5,145)	10,664	0.38
Bulgarian (226)	383	0.01
Cajun (277)	577	0.02
Canadian (1,697)	3,517	0.13
Celtic (178)	286	0.01
Croatian (2,865)	6,494	0.23
Cypriot (16)	16	<0.01
Czech (8,438)	26,489	0.94
Czechoslovakian (2,012)	3,873	0.14
Danish (4,120)	16,188	0.58
Dutch (12,507)	66,230	2.36
Eastern European (1,173)	1,471	0.05
English (104,592)	312,695	11.13
Estonian (28)	57	<0.01
European (30,354)	35,572	1.27
Finnish (710)	2,010	0.07
French, ex. Basque (16,823)	93,887	3.34
French Canadian (4,597)	10,270	0.37
German (371,132)	863,661	30.74
German Russian (1,252)	1,650	0.06
Greek (1,542)	4,147	0.15
Guyanese (80)	145	0.01
Hungarian (1,006)	4,340	0.15
Icelander (235)	437	0.02
Iranian (1,336)	1,633	0.06
Irish (94,550)	387,825	13.80
Israeli (77)	155	0.01
Italian (20,693)	65,265	2.32
Latvian (193)	327	0.01
Lithuanian (799)	2,177	0.08
Luxemburger (144)	511	0.02
Macedonian (125)	193	0.01
Maltese (9)	50	<0.01
New Zealander (107)	126	<0.01
Northern European (2,044)	2,156	0.08
Norwegian (10,284)	31,788	1.13
Pennsylvania German (2,232)	3,826	0.14
Polish (10,226)	40,253	1.43
Portuguese (868)	2,693	0.10
Romanian (647)	1,230	0.04
Russian (6,264)	23,465	0.84
Scandinavian (1,799)	3,774	0.13
Scotch-Irish (20,837)	57,792	2.06
Scottish (17,524)	61,226	2.18
Serbian (421)	856	0.03
Slavic (371)	1,024	0.04
Slovak (521)	1,606	0.06
Slovene (426)	1,358	0.05
Swedish (20,920)	69,209	2.46
Swiss (3,396)	15,153	0.54
Turkish (336)	739	0.03
Ukrainian (1,696)	2,823	0.10
Welsh (4,760)	22,702	0.81
West Indian, ex. Hispanic (1,775)	3,056	0.11
Bahamian (0)	12	<0.01
Barbadian (137)	283	0.01
Belizean (0)	12	<0.01
Bermudan (11)	25	<0.01
British West Indian (91)	91	<0.01
Dutch West Indian (147)	622	0.02
Haitian (583)	664	0.02
Jamaican (423)	812	0.03
Trinidadian/Tobagonian (189)	239	0.01
U.S. Virgin Islander (9)	9	<0.01
West Indian (185)	287	0.01
Yugoslavian (453)	1,035	0.04

Hispanic Origin	Population	%
Hispanic or Latino (of any race)	300,042	10.52
Central American, ex. Mexican	15,293	0.54
Costa Rican	385	0.01
Guatemalan	5,538	0.19
Honduran	2,689	0.09
Nicaraguan	537	0.02
Panamanian	888	0.03
Salvadoran	5,108	0.18
Other Central American	148	0.01
Cuban	2,723	0.10
Dominican Republic	764	0.03
Mexican	247,297	8.67
Puerto Rican	9,247	0.32
South American	5,845	0.20
Argentinean	531	0.02
Bolivian	332	0.01
Chilean	346	0.01
Colombian	1,769	0.06
Ecuadorian	701	0.02
Paraguayan	212	0.01
Peruvian	1,151	0.04
Uruguayan	83	<0.01
Venezuelan	639	0.02
Other South American	81	<0.01
Other Hispanic or Latino	18,873	0.66

Race*	Population	%
African-American/Black (167,864)	202,149	7.09
Not Hispanic (162,700)	192,089	6.73
Hispanic (5,164)	10,060	0.35
American Indian/Alaska Native (28,150)	59,130	2.07
Not Hispanic (23,073)	49,659	1.74
Hispanic (5,077)	9,471	0.33
Alaska Athabascan *(Ala. Nat.)* (26)	50	<0.01
Aleut *(Alaska Native)* (57)	88	<0.01
Apache (466)	1,048	0.04
Arapaho (105)	173	0.01
Blackfeet (193)	1,123	0.04
Canadian/French Am. Ind. (35)	95	<0.01
Central American Ind. (32)	65	<0.01
Cherokee (5,642)	15,772	0.55
Cheyenne (157)	324	0.01
Chickasaw (312)	643	0.02
Chippewa (360)	726	0.03
Choctaw (1,156)	2,604	0.09
Colville (8)	17	<0.01
Comanche (212)	445	0.02
Cree (18)	72	<0.01
Creek (766)	1,777	0.06
Crow (77)	165	0.01
Delaware (336)	657	0.02
Hopi (33)	64	<0.01
Houma (6)	15	<0.01
Inupiat *(Alaska Native)* (43)	63	<0.01
Iroquois (413)	788	0.03
Kiowa (233)	365	0.01
Lumbee (69)	118	<0.01
Menominee (41)	72	<0.01
Mexican American Ind. (774)	1,274	0.04
Navajo (731)	1,192	0.04
Osage (407)	898	0.03
Ottawa (63)	119	<0.01
Paiute (39)	80	<0.01
Pima (39)	55	<0.01
Potawatomi (2,511)	3,852	0.14
Pueblo (109)	189	0.01
Puget Sound Salish (20)	28	<0.01
Seminole (172)	468	0.02
Shoshone (32)	77	<0.01
Sioux (898)	1,703	0.06
South American Ind. (65)	136	<0.01
Spanish American Ind. (45)	56	<0.01
Tlingit-Haida *(Alaska Native)* (41)	74	<0.01
Tohono O'Odham (27)	37	<0.01
Tsimshian *(Alaska Native)* (5)	11	<0.01
Ute (39)	71	<0.01
Yakama (26)	32	<0.01
Yaqui (43)	81	<0.01
Yuman (21)	29	<0.01
Yup'ik *(Alaska Native)* (11)	32	<0.01
Asian (67,762)	83,930	2.94
Not Hispanic (66,967)	81,491	2.86
Hispanic (795)	2,439	0.09
Bangladeshi (497)	531	0.02
Bhutanese (161)	163	0.01
Burmese (1,119)	1,204	0.04
Cambodian (1,045)	1,409	0.05
Chinese, ex. Taiwanese (10,517)	12,677	0.44
Filipino (5,545)	9,399	0.33
Hmong (1,645)	1,732	0.06
Indian (13,848)	15,644	0.55
Indonesian (253)	380	0.01
Japanese (1,671)	4,178	0.15
Korean (5,234)	7,756	0.27
Laotian (4,539)	5,406	0.19
Malaysian (221)	321	0.01
Nepalese (504)	545	0.02
Pakistani (1,633)	1,925	0.07
Sri Lankan (285)	307	0.01
Taiwanese (640)	807	0.03
Thai (969)	1,576	0.06
Vietnamese (14,015)	16,074	0.56
Hawaii Native/Pacific Islander (2,238)	4,938	0.17
Not Hispanic (1,978)	4,104	0.14
Hispanic (260)	834	0.03
Fijian (30)	44	<0.01
Guamanian/Chamorro (571)	1,002	0.04
Marshallese (61)	80	<0.01
Native Hawaiian (505)	1,554	0.05
Samoan (325)	657	0.02
Tongan (29)	58	<0.01
White (2,391,044)	2,468,364	86.51
Not Hispanic (2,230,539)	2,289,938	80.26
Hispanic (160,505)	178,426	6.25

*Notes: † The Census 2010 population figure is used to calculate the percentages in the Hispanic Origin and Race categories. Ancestry percentages are based on the 2006-2010 American Community Survey population (not shown); ‡ Numbers in parentheses indicate the number of people reporting a single ancestry; * Numbers in parentheses indicate the number of persons reporting this race alone, not in combination with any other race; Please refer to the Explanation of Data for more information.*

Andover

Place Type: City
County: Butler
Population: 11,791†

Ancestry‡	Population	%
American (1,225)	1,225	11.14
Arab (30)	44	0.40
Lebanese (5)	5	0.05
Moroccan (8)	8	0.07
Syrian (17)	31	0.28
Austrian (0)	12	0.11
British (10)	19	0.17
Cajun (52)	52	0.47
Canadian (11)	11	0.10
Czech (30)	61	0.55
Czechoslovakian (0)	9	0.08
Danish (12)	105	0.96
Dutch (13)	145	1.32
English (562)	1,415	12.87
European (167)	185	1.68
French, ex. Basque (33)	352	3.20
French Canadian (0)	36	0.33
German (1,430)	4,150	37.75
Greek (67)	81	0.74
Hungarian (8)	43	0.39
Iranian (13)	32	0.29
Irish (278)	1,732	15.76
Italian (89)	250	2.27
Norwegian (72)	176	1.60
Polish (111)	205	1.86
Portuguese (10)	49	0.45
Russian (7)	71	0.65
Scandinavian (13)	119	1.08
Scotch-Irish (27)	100	0.91
Scottish (23)	315	2.87
Swedish (16)	242	2.20
Swiss (0)	74	0.67
Welsh (40)	59	0.54

Hispanic Origin	Population	%
Hispanic or Latino (of any race)	564	4.78
Central American, ex. Mexican	26	0.22
Guatemalan	16	0.14
Nicaraguan	2	0.02
Panamanian	4	0.03
Salvadoran	4	0.03
Cuban	13	0.11
Dominican Republic	1	0.01
Mexican	410	3.48
Puerto Rican	34	0.29
South American	27	0.23
Colombian	9	0.08
Ecuadorian	1	0.01
Paraguayan	1	0.01
Peruvian	12	0.10
Venezuelan	4	0.03
Other Hispanic or Latino	53	0.45

Race*	Population	%
African-American/Black (122)	196	1.66
Not Hispanic (117)	185	1.57
Hispanic (5)	11	0.09
American Indian/Alaska Native (69)	199	1.69
Not Hispanic (63)	176	1.49
Hispanic (6)	23	0.20
Apache (5)	7	0.06
Blackfeet (0)	8	0.07
Cherokee (26)	74	0.63
Cheyenne (0)	1	0.01
Chickasaw (6)	6	0.05
Chippewa (1)	2	0.02
Choctaw (2)	17	0.14
Creek (2)	3	0.03
Iroquois (1)	1	0.01
Mexican American Ind. (2)	2	0.02
Osage (2)	11	0.09
Potawatomi (0)	2	0.02
Pueblo (0)	1	0.01
Sioux (1)	4	0.03
Tohono O'Odham (1)	2	0.02
Asian (217)	296	2.51
Not Hispanic (215)	284	2.41
Hispanic (2)	12	0.10
Cambodian (3)	3	0.03
Chinese, ex. Taiwanese (64)	69	0.59
Filipino (14)	42	0.36
Hmong (5)	5	0.04
Indian (37)	46	0.39
Indonesian (1)	1	0.01
Japanese (5)	17	0.14
Korean (11)	16	0.14
Laotian (7)	10	0.08
Malaysian (2)	2	0.02
Nepalese (13)	13	0.11
Sri Lankan (2)	2	0.02
Taiwanese (1)	2	0.02
Thai (2)	10	0.08
Vietnamese (39)	52	0.44
Hawaii Native/Pacific Islander (9)	15	0.13
Not Hispanic (7)	8	0.07
Hispanic (2)	7	0.06
Guamanian/Chamorro (1)	5	0.04
Native Hawaiian (2)	3	0.03
Samoan (2)	2	0.02
White (10,971)	11,242	95.34
Not Hispanic (10,578)	10,796	91.56
Hispanic (393)	446	3.78

Arkansas City

Place Type: City
County: Cowley
Population: 12,415†

Ancestry‡	Population	%
American (1,035)	1,035	8.42
Austrian (0)	10	0.08
Canadian (0)	7	0.06
Czech (0)	53	0.43
Danish (0)	18	0.15
Dutch (68)	556	4.52
English (368)	1,378	11.21
European (44)	121	0.98
French, ex. Basque (162)	465	3.78
French Canadian (0)	18	0.15
German (841)	2,590	21.06
Greek (9)	9	0.07
Irish (150)	1,305	10.61
Italian (45)	170	1.38
Norwegian (18)	57	0.46
Polish (66)	159	1.29
Portuguese (0)	28	0.23
Romanian (0)	7	0.06
Russian (0)	26	0.21
Scotch-Irish (75)	239	1.94
Scottish (212)	505	4.11
Slavic (0)	7	0.06
Swedish (19)	158	1.28
Welsh (19)	53	0.43
West Indian, ex. Hispanic (17)	17	0.14
Jamaican (17)	17	0.14

Hispanic Origin	Population	%
Hispanic or Latino (of any race)	2,149	17.31
Central American, ex. Mexican	351	2.83
Guatemalan	237	1.91
Honduran	3	0.02
Panamanian	2	0.02
Salvadoran	109	0.88
Cuban	1	0.01
Mexican	1,660	13.37
Puerto Rican	23	0.19
South American	8	0.06
Colombian	5	0.04
Ecuadorian	1	0.01
Venezuelan	2	0.02
Other Hispanic or Latino	106	0.85

Race*	Population	%
African-American/Black (487)	674	5.43
Not Hispanic (469)	624	5.03
Hispanic (18)	50	0.40
American Indian/Alaska Native (334)	630	5.07
Not Hispanic (285)	557	4.49
Hispanic (49)	73	0.59
Apache (6)	15	0.12
Blackfeet (0)	9	0.07
Central American Ind. (0)	4	0.03
Cherokee (66)	163	1.31
Cheyenne (4)	6	0.05
Chickasaw (8)	16	0.13
Chippewa (1)	9	0.07
Choctaw (5)	13	0.10
Comanche (0)	1	0.01
Creek (6)	23	0.19
Delaware (3)	4	0.03
Iroquois (5)	11	0.09
Kiowa (2)	4	0.03
Mexican American Ind. (18)	19	0.15
Navajo (7)	20	0.16
Osage (10)	27	0.22
Ottawa (1)	1	0.01
Potawatomi (7)	13	0.10
Seminole (9)	14	0.11
Sioux (4)	8	0.06
South American Ind. (1)	1	0.01
Asian (79)	117	0.94
Not Hispanic (73)	109	0.88
Hispanic (6)	8	0.06
Cambodian (3)	3	0.02
Chinese, ex. Taiwanese (17)	18	0.14
Filipino (16)	22	0.18
Indian (1)	4	0.03
Japanese (4)	14	0.11
Korean (3)	5	0.04
Laotian (21)	21	0.17
Thai (1)	5	0.04
Vietnamese (11)	14	0.11
Hawaii Native/Pacific Islander (15)	24	0.19
Not Hispanic (12)	16	0.13
Hispanic (3)	8	0.06
Guamanian/Chamorro (4)	8	0.06
Marshallese (7)	7	0.06
Native Hawaiian (2)	3	0.02
White (9,852)	10,395	83.73
Not Hispanic (8,990)	9,402	75.73
Hispanic (862)	993	8.00

Atchison

Place Type: City
County: Atchison
Population: 11,021†

Ancestry‡	Population	%
African, Sub-Saharan (0)	15	0.14
Nigerian (0)	15	0.14
American (677)	677	6.18
Austrian (0)	20	0.18
British (18)	39	0.36
Croatian (25)	25	0.23
Czech (37)	159	1.45
Czechoslovakian (18)	30	0.27
Danish (0)	31	0.28
Dutch (51)	162	1.48
English (332)	1,095	10.00
Estonian (0)	10	0.09
European (151)	359	3.28
French, ex. Basque (123)	425	3.88
French Canadian (0)	12	0.11
German (1,378)	3,569	32.60
German Russian (9)	9	0.08
Irish (850)	2,192	20.02
Italian (73)	238	2.17
Norwegian (47)	85	0.78
Pennsylvania German (14)	14	0.13
Polish (46)	118	1.08

*Notes: † The Census 2010 population figure is used to calculate the percentages in the Hispanic Origin and Race categories. Ancestry percentages are based on the 2006-2010 American Community Survey population (not shown); ‡ Numbers in parentheses indicate the number of people reporting a single ancestry; * Numbers in parentheses indicate the number of persons reporting this race alone, not in combination with any other race; Please refer to the Explanation of Data for more information.*

Ancestry	Population	%
Russian (0)	18	0.16
Scandinavian (20)	20	0.18
Scotch-Irish (95)	215	1.96
Scottish (111)	243	2.22
Swedish (51)	139	1.27
Swiss (0)	32	0.29
Welsh (0)	9	0.08
Yugoslavian (0)	26	0.24

Hispanic Origin	Population	%
Hispanic or Latino (of any race)	302	2.74
Central American, ex. Mexican	8	0.07
Guatemalan	2	0.02
Honduran	1	0.01
Nicaraguan	2	0.02
Panamanian	1	0.01
Salvadoran	2	0.02
Dominican Republic	1	0.01
Mexican	214	1.94
Puerto Rican	27	0.24
South American	8	0.07
Chilean	2	0.02
Venezuelan	5	0.05
Other South American	1	0.01
Other Hispanic or Latino	44	0.40

Race*	Population	%
African-American/Black (789)	991	8.99
Not Hispanic (780)	974	8.84
Hispanic (9)	17	0.15
American Indian/Alaska Native (65)	179	1.62
Not Hispanic (61)	169	1.53
Hispanic (4)	10	0.09
Apache (2)	3	0.03
Blackfeet (1)	6	0.05
Cherokee (9)	40	0.36
Cheyenne (3)	3	0.03
Chippewa (2)	2	0.02
Choctaw (3)	4	0.04
Comanche (4)	4	0.04
Creek (4)	5	0.05
Crow (1)	3	0.03
Delaware (0)	6	0.05
Kiowa (0)	1	0.01
Mexican American Ind. (1)	6	0.05
Osage (0)	2	0.02
Potawatomi (3)	8	0.07
Sioux (6)	7	0.06
Yakama (1)	1	0.01
Asian (54)	77	0.70
Not Hispanic (54)	77	0.70
Chinese, ex. Taiwanese (18)	18	0.16
Filipino (9)	16	0.15
Indian (4)	9	0.08
Japanese (3)	9	0.08
Korean (7)	8	0.07
Pakistani (2)	2	0.02
Thai (5)	5	0.05
Vietnamese (6)	8	0.07
Hawaii Native/Pacific Islander (8)	20	0.18
Not Hispanic (8)	19	0.17
Hispanic (0)	1	0.01
Guamanian/Chamorro (1)	2	0.02
Native Hawaiian (6)	14	0.13
Samoan (1)	2	0.02
White (9,686)	10,013	90.85
Not Hispanic (9,503)	9,793	88.86
Hispanic (183)	220	2.00

Augusta

Place Type: City
County: Butler
Population: 9,274†

Ancestry‡	Population	%
American (873)	873	9.54
Austrian (0)	5	0.05
British (0)	86	0.94
Czechoslovakian (0)	31	0.34
Danish (0)	43	0.47
Dutch (48)	107	1.17
English (391)	1,163	12.71
European (178)	178	1.95
French, ex. Basque (68)	245	2.68
French Canadian (0)	23	0.25
German (1,146)	2,738	29.93
Irish (239)	1,252	13.68
Italian (24)	123	1.34
Norwegian (20)	49	0.54
Polish (27)	61	0.67
Russian (10)	24	0.26
Scotch-Irish (61)	110	1.20
Scottish (59)	222	2.43
Slavic (0)	8	0.09
Swedish (28)	115	1.26
Swiss (19)	58	0.63
Welsh (0)	147	1.61
West Indian, ex. Hispanic (0)	9	0.10
Dutch West Indian (0)	9	0.10

Hispanic Origin	Population	%
Hispanic or Latino (of any race)	368	3.97
Central American, ex. Mexican	8	0.09
Guatemalan	3	0.03
Honduran	3	0.03
Panamanian	2	0.02
Cuban	2	0.02
Mexican	312	3.36
Puerto Rican	9	0.10
South American	3	0.03
Colombian	2	0.02
Venezuelan	1	0.01
Other Hispanic or Latino	34	0.37

Race*	Population	%
African-American/Black (35)	85	0.92
Not Hispanic (31)	79	0.85
Hispanic (4)	6	0.06
American Indian/Alaska Native (116)	220	2.37
Not Hispanic (107)	202	2.18
Hispanic (9)	18	0.19
Apache (1)	1	0.01
Blackfeet (0)	1	0.01
Cherokee (38)	81	0.87
Cheyenne (1)	2	0.02
Chickasaw (2)	2	0.02
Chippewa (3)	5	0.05
Choctaw (7)	20	0.22
Colville (0)	1	0.01
Comanche (2)	3	0.03
Creek (7)	13	0.14
Delaware (4)	9	0.10
Iroquois (6)	6	0.06
Kiowa (4)	6	0.06
Osage (3)	3	0.03
Potawatomi (1)	7	0.08
Pueblo (1)	2	0.02
Seminole (3)	5	0.05
Sioux (2)	2	0.02
Ute (1)	2	0.02
Asian (58)	90	0.97
Not Hispanic (56)	81	0.87
Hispanic (2)	9	0.10
Bangladeshi (11)	12	0.13
Cambodian (0)	1	0.01
Chinese, ex. Taiwanese (8)	10	0.11
Filipino (8)	26	0.28
Indian (7)	8	0.09
Japanese (4)	7	0.08
Korean (1)	5	0.05
Laotian (6)	6	0.06
Thai (2)	2	0.02
Vietnamese (11)	13	0.14
Hawaii Native/Pacific Islander (9)	19	0.20
Not Hispanic (9)	15	0.16
Hispanic (0)	4	0.04
Guamanian/Chamorro (7)	7	0.08
Native Hawaiian (1)	7	0.08
Samoan (0)	5	0.05
Tongan (0)	1	0.01
White (8,739)	8,952	96.53
Not Hispanic (8,536)	8,699	93.80
Hispanic (203)	253	2.73

Chanute

Place Type: City
County: Neosho
Population: 9,119†

Ancestry‡	Population	%
African, Sub-Saharan (224)	224	2.45
African (224)	224	2.45
American (608)	608	6.65
Arab (18)	18	0.20
Syrian (18)	18	0.20
Austrian (12)	12	0.13
Belgian (14)	58	0.63
British (10)	10	0.11
Czech (9)	28	0.31
Czechoslovakian (11)	19	0.21
Danish (0)	47	0.51
Dutch (24)	446	4.88
English (269)	830	9.08
French, ex. Basque (42)	463	5.07
French Canadian (17)	25	0.27
German (1,359)	3,150	34.46
Greek (27)	34	0.37
Irish (313)	1,572	17.20
Italian (23)	103	1.13
Norwegian (0)	8	0.09
Pennsylvania German (8)	8	0.09
Polish (6)	154	1.68
Scotch-Irish (61)	222	2.43
Scottish (9)	169	1.85
Slavic (0)	11	0.12
Swedish (145)	346	3.79
Ukrainian (8)	8	0.09
Welsh (7)	78	0.85

Hispanic Origin	Population	%
Hispanic or Latino (of any race)	496	5.44
Central American, ex. Mexican	19	0.21
Guatemalan	17	0.19
Honduran	1	0.01
Nicaraguan	1	0.01
Cuban	4	0.04
Mexican	426	4.67
Puerto Rican	8	0.09
South American	2	0.02
Colombian	1	0.01
Ecuadorian	1	0.01
Other Hispanic or Latino	37	0.41

Race*	Population	%
African-American/Black (177)	251	2.75
Not Hispanic (172)	236	2.59
Hispanic (5)	15	0.16
American Indian/Alaska Native (108)	189	2.07
Not Hispanic (88)	168	1.84
Hispanic (20)	21	0.23
Apache (3)	5	0.05
Blackfeet (0)	1	0.01
Cherokee (45)	87	0.95
Chippewa (1)	1	0.01
Choctaw (2)	4	0.04
Creek (1)	1	0.01
Crow (0)	1	0.01
Delaware (0)	1	0.01
Iroquois (2)	2	0.02
Lumbee (0)	1	0.01
Navajo (0)	1	0.01
Osage (5)	6	0.07
Potawatomi (9)	9	0.10
Sioux (2)	5	0.05
Asian (69)	96	1.05
Not Hispanic (69)	94	1.03
Hispanic (0)	2	0.02
Cambodian (2)	2	0.02

*Notes: † The Census 2010 population figure is used to calculate the percentages in the Hispanic Origin and Race categories. Ancestry percentages are based on the 2006-2010 American Community Survey population (not shown); ‡ Numbers in parentheses indicate the number of people reporting a single ancestry; * Numbers in parentheses indicate the number of persons reporting this race alone, not in combination with any other race; Please refer to the Explanation of Data for more information.*

Chinese, ex. Taiwanese (11)	18	0.20
Filipino (34)	36	0.39
Indian (5)	6	0.07
Japanese (5)	7	0.08
Korean (8)	19	0.21
Pakistani (3)	3	0.03
Taiwanese (1)	1	0.01
Hawaii Native/Pacific Islander (6)	16	0.18
Not Hispanic (2)	12	0.13
Hispanic (4)	4	0.04
Guamanian/Chamorro (5)	10	0.11
Native Hawaiian (1)	2	0.02
Samoan (0)	2	0.02
Tongan (0)	1	0.01
White (8,426)	8,610	94.42
Not Hispanic (8,126)	8,275	90.74
Hispanic (300)	335	3.67

Coffeyville

Place Type: City
County: Montgomery
Population: 10,295†

Ancestry‡	Population	%
African, Sub-Saharan (83)	83	0.80
African (83)	83	0.80
American (876)	876	8.44
Austrian (0)	7	0.07
British (14)	26	0.25
Croatian (9)	9	0.09
Czech (0)	8	0.08
Danish (32)	86	0.83
Dutch (6)	277	2.67
English (501)	872	8.40
European (66)	66	0.64
French, ex. Basque (16)	246	2.37
French Canadian (34)	58	0.56
German (746)	2,171	20.92
Greek (0)	24	0.23
Irish (348)	1,596	15.38
Italian (25)	291	2.80
Latvian (1)	4	0.04
Norwegian (37)	69	0.66
Polish (13)	178	1.71
Scotch-Irish (14)	140	1.35
Scottish (27)	97	0.93
Swedish (11)	113	1.09
Swiss (0)	9	0.09
Ukrainian (22)	22	0.21
Welsh (15)	24	0.23
West Indian, ex. Hispanic (0)	22	0.21
Dutch West Indian (0)	22	0.21

Hispanic Origin	Population	%
Hispanic or Latino (of any race)	765	7.43
Central American, ex. Mexican	66	0.64
Guatemalan	54	0.52
Honduran	2	0.02
Nicaraguan	3	0.03
Panamanian	4	0.04
Salvadoran	3	0.03
Cuban	4	0.04
Dominican Republic	1	0.01
Mexican	556	5.40
Puerto Rican	19	0.18
South American	11	0.11
Argentinean	3	0.03
Bolivian	1	0.01
Chilean	1	0.01
Peruvian	1	0.01
Venezuelan	1	0.01
Other South American	4	0.04
Other Hispanic or Latino	108	1.05

Race*	Population	%
African-American/Black (1,200)	1,434	13.93
Not Hispanic (1,181)	1,386	13.46
Hispanic (19)	48	0.47
American Indian/Alaska Native (515)	975	9.47
Not Hispanic (485)	922	8.96
Hispanic (30)	53	0.51
Apache (2)	7	0.07
Blackfeet (0)	6	0.06
Cherokee (246)	544	5.28
Chickasaw (0)	4	0.04
Chippewa (1)	1	0.01
Choctaw (14)	29	0.28
Comanche (1)	1	0.01
Creek (19)	26	0.25
Delaware (14)	23	0.22
Hopi (3)	3	0.03
Iroquois (10)	11	0.11
Kiowa (1)	1	0.01
Menominee (0)	3	0.03
Mexican American Ind. (9)	13	0.13
Navajo (8)	8	0.08
Osage (6)	28	0.27
Ottawa (3)	3	0.03
Potawatomi (21)	25	0.24
Pueblo (0)	2	0.02
Sioux (2)	3	0.03
South American Ind. (2)	2	0.02
Asian (75)	106	1.03
Not Hispanic (75)	104	1.01
Hispanic (0)	2	0.02
Chinese, ex. Taiwanese (11)	13	0.13
Filipino (12)	22	0.21
Indian (21)	24	0.23
Japanese (4)	12	0.12
Korean (4)	7	0.07
Pakistani (1)	1	0.01
Taiwanese (5)	5	0.05
Thai (1)	5	0.05
Vietnamese (1)	1	0.01
Hawaii Native/Pacific Islander (21)	33	0.32
Not Hispanic (16)	28	0.27
Hispanic (5)	5	0.05
Guamanian/Chamorro (14)	14	0.14
Native Hawaiian (3)	6	0.06
Samoan (4)	10	0.10
Tongan (0)	1	0.01
White (7,441)	8,087	78.55
Not Hispanic (7,148)	7,722	75.01
Hispanic (293)	365	3.55

Derby

Place Type: City
County: Sedgwick
Population: 22,158†

Ancestry‡	Population	%
American (1,549)	1,549	7.41
Arab (78)	113	0.54
Arab (56)	56	0.27
Egyptian (9)	9	0.04
Lebanese (13)	48	0.23
Austrian (21)	71	0.34
Belgian (12)	91	0.44
Brazilian (21)	27	0.13
British (69)	118	0.56
Canadian (0)	15	0.07
Croatian (10)	10	0.05
Czech (152)	303	1.45
Danish (88)	164	0.78
Dutch (104)	521	2.49
English (1,016)	3,487	16.68
European (294)	304	1.45
French, ex. Basque (144)	879	4.20
French Canadian (0)	43	0.21
German (2,663)	6,915	33.07
Greek (16)	61	0.29
Hungarian (31)	41	0.20
Irish (720)	2,960	14.16
Italian (100)	410	1.96
Northern European (30)	42	0.20
Norwegian (80)	395	1.89
Pennsylvania German (109)	117	0.56
Polish (62)	497	2.38
Portuguese (24)	68	0.33
Russian (0)	47	0.22
Scandinavian (49)	49	0.23
Scotch-Irish (68)	300	1.43
Scottish (109)	632	3.02
Swedish (57)	311	1.49
Swiss (13)	45	0.22
Turkish (8)	8	0.04
Ukrainian (8)	53	0.25
Welsh (24)	151	0.72
West Indian, ex. Hispanic (0)	132	0.63
Jamaican (0)	132	0.63

Hispanic Origin	Population	%
Hispanic or Latino (of any race)	1,163	5.25
Central American, ex. Mexican	41	0.19
Costa Rican	7	0.03
Guatemalan	10	0.05
Honduran	3	0.01
Panamanian	14	0.06
Salvadoran	7	0.03
Cuban	14	0.06
Dominican Republic	7	0.03
Mexican	840	3.79
Puerto Rican	115	0.52
South American	22	0.10
Argentinean	1	<0.01
Bolivian	2	0.01
Colombian	4	0.02
Ecuadorian	9	0.04
Paraguayan	2	0.01
Venezuelan	2	0.01
Other South American	2	0.01
Other Hispanic or Latino	124	0.56

Race*	Population	%
African-American/Black (410)	604	2.73
Not Hispanic (389)	563	2.54
Hispanic (21)	41	0.19
American Indian/Alaska Native (214)	424	1.91
Not Hispanic (187)	373	1.68
Hispanic (27)	51	0.23
Apache (8)	13	0.06
Blackfeet (2)	3	0.01
Cherokee (42)	104	0.47
Cheyenne (1)	2	0.01
Chickasaw (6)	9	0.04
Chippewa (2)	5	0.02
Choctaw (17)	26	0.12
Comanche (1)	2	0.01
Creek (18)	27	0.12
Delaware (2)	4	0.02
Inupiat *(Alaska Native)* (1)	1	<0.01
Iroquois (1)	4	0.02
Kiowa (6)	6	0.03
Lumbee (4)	4	0.02
Mexican American Ind. (2)	4	0.02
Navajo (10)	20	0.09
Osage (5)	7	0.03
Potawatomi (16)	17	0.08
Seminole (1)	6	0.03
Sioux (4)	11	0.05
South American Ind. (1)	1	<0.01
Tohono O'Odham (1)	1	<0.01
Ute (0)	4	0.02
Asian (345)	579	2.61
Not Hispanic (337)	551	2.49
Hispanic (8)	28	0.13
Bangladeshi (4)	4	0.02
Cambodian (5)	8	0.04
Chinese, ex. Taiwanese (40)	65	0.29
Filipino (89)	154	0.70
Indian (9)	32	0.14
Japanese (34)	74	0.33
Korean (22)	83	0.37
Laotian (42)	50	0.23
Pakistani (1)	6	0.03
Taiwanese (0)	12	0.05
Thai (19)	26	0.12
Vietnamese (51)	91	0.41

*Notes: † The Census 2010 population figure is used to calculate the percentages in the Hispanic Origin and Race categories. Ancestry percentages are based on the 2006-2010 American Community Survey population (not shown); ‡ Numbers in parentheses indicate the number of people reporting a single ancestry; * Numbers in parentheses indicate the number of persons reporting this race alone, not in combination with any other race; Please refer to the Explanation of Data for more information.*

Hawaii Native/Pacific Islander (30)	47	0.21
Not Hispanic (24)	41	0.19
Hispanic (6)	6	0.03
Guamanian/Chamorro (2)	2	0.01
Native Hawaiian (16)	23	0.10
Samoan (10)	11	0.05
White (20,301)	20,939	94.50
Not Hispanic (19,494)	20,003	90.27
Hispanic (807)	936	4.22

Dodge City

Place Type: City
County: Ford
Population: 27,340†

Ancestry‡	Population	%
African, Sub-Saharan (171)	171	0.65
Somalian (171)	171	0.65
American (939)	939	3.57
Arab (41)	52	0.20
Arab (41)	41	0.16
Egyptian (0)	11	0.04
Austrian (16)	36	0.14
British (41)	41	0.16
Czech (12)	34	0.13
Czechoslovakian (12)	12	0.05
Danish (27)	52	0.20
Dutch (110)	561	2.13
English (433)	1,563	5.94
European (29)	49	0.19
French, ex. Basque (41)	294	1.12
French Canadian (5)	13	0.05
German (2,368)	4,962	18.87
German Russian (10)	10	0.04
Irish (344)	1,714	6.52
Italian (17)	343	1.30
Norwegian (0)	70	0.27
Pennsylvania German (13)	13	0.05
Polish (0)	119	0.45
Russian (30)	93	0.35
Scotch-Irish (33)	97	0.37
Scottish (84)	266	1.01
Swedish (58)	159	0.60
Swiss (0)	46	0.17
Ukrainian (0)	13	0.05
Welsh (0)	55	0.21

Hispanic Origin	Population	%
Hispanic or Latino (of any race)	15,730	57.53
Central American, ex. Mexican	1,446	5.29
Costa Rican	3	0.01
Guatemalan	1,043	3.81
Honduran	62	0.23
Nicaraguan	14	0.05
Panamanian	1	<0.01
Salvadoran	316	1.16
Other Central American	7	0.03
Cuban	227	0.83
Dominican Republic	5	0.02
Mexican	13,105	47.93
Puerto Rican	140	0.51
South American	50	0.18
Argentinean	2	0.01
Bolivian	2	0.01
Chilean	1	<0.01
Colombian	24	0.09
Ecuadorian	7	0.03
Peruvian	10	0.04
Uruguayan	1	<0.01
Venezuelan	3	0.01
Other Hispanic or Latino	757	2.77

Race*	Population	%
African-American/Black (672)	855	3.13
Not Hispanic (566)	701	2.56
Hispanic (106)	154	0.56
American Indian/Alaska Native (290)	487	1.78
Not Hispanic (92)	204	0.75
Hispanic (198)	283	1.04
Aleut *(Alaska Native)* (2)	2	0.01
Apache (4)	4	0.01
Arapaho (2)	5	0.02
Blackfeet (3)	7	0.03
Central American Ind. (7)	7	0.03
Cherokee (22)	55	0.20
Chickasaw (0)	8	0.03
Chippewa (2)	3	0.01
Choctaw (0)	9	0.03
Comanche (0)	1	<0.01
Cree (0)	2	0.01
Creek (6)	15	0.05
Iroquois (0)	3	0.01
Mexican American Ind. (24)	31	0.11
Navajo (17)	23	0.08
Osage (1)	2	0.01
Potawatomi (5)	6	0.02
Pueblo (3)	6	0.02
Seminole (0)	1	<0.01
Sioux (3)	10	0.04
South American Ind. (0)	4	0.01
Tlingit-Haida *(Alaska Native)* (2)	2	0.01
Asian (435)	556	2.03
Not Hispanic (416)	487	1.78
Hispanic (19)	69	0.25
Burmese (1)	3	0.01
Cambodian (1)	9	0.03
Chinese, ex. Taiwanese (22)	33	0.12
Filipino (17)	45	0.16
Indian (45)	59	0.22
Indonesian (0)	1	<0.01
Japanese (3)	13	0.05
Korean (5)	10	0.04
Laotian (75)	93	0.34
Nepalese (2)	3	0.01
Pakistani (17)	24	0.09
Taiwanese (2)	4	0.01
Thai (7)	8	0.03
Vietnamese (224)	250	0.91
Hawaii Native/Pacific Islander (53)	89	0.33
Not Hispanic (35)	63	0.23
Hispanic (18)	26	0.10
Guamanian/Chamorro (33)	45	0.16
Native Hawaiian (3)	11	0.04
Samoan (15)	28	0.10
White (19,817)	20,516	75.04
Not Hispanic (10,173)	10,432	38.16
Hispanic (9,644)	10,084	36.88

El Dorado

Place Type: City
County: Butler
Population: 13,021†

Ancestry‡	Population	%
African, Sub-Saharan (46)	46	0.35
Kenyan (46)	46	0.35
Albanian (0)	12	0.09
American (927)	927	7.13
Arab (7)	7	0.05
Other Arab (7)	7	0.05
Austrian (14)	33	0.25
British (9)	21	0.16
Czech (82)	105	0.81
Czechoslovakian (11)	11	0.08
Danish (0)	34	0.26
Dutch (12)	229	1.76
English (799)	1,973	15.17
European (74)	74	0.57
French, ex. Basque (70)	353	2.71
German (1,751)	3,830	29.45
Greek (8)	8	0.06
Hungarian (0)	17	0.13
Irish (397)	1,725	13.27
Italian (45)	213	1.64
Northern European (8)	8	0.06
Norwegian (12)	41	0.32
Polish (21)	131	1.01
Portuguese (0)	48	0.37
Romanian (0)	20	0.15
Russian (0)	225	1.73
Scotch-Irish (150)	421	3.24
Scottish (103)	424	3.26
Swedish (38)	202	1.55
Swiss (0)	39	0.30
Welsh (8)	111	0.85

Hispanic Origin	Population	%
Hispanic or Latino (of any race)	607	4.66
Central American, ex. Mexican	19	0.15
Guatemalan	8	0.06
Panamanian	7	0.05
Salvadoran	4	0.03
Cuban	13	0.10
Dominican Republic	1	0.01
Mexican	476	3.66
Puerto Rican	23	0.18
South American	2	0.02
Colombian	1	0.01
Venezuelan	1	0.01
Other Hispanic or Latino	73	0.56

Race*	Population	%
African-American/Black (301)	419	3.22
Not Hispanic (297)	408	3.13
Hispanic (4)	11	0.08
American Indian/Alaska Native (147)	328	2.52
Not Hispanic (135)	294	2.26
Hispanic (12)	34	0.26
Apache (2)	5	0.04
Blackfeet (1)	5	0.04
Cherokee (38)	110	0.84
Cheyenne (0)	1	0.01
Chickasaw (1)	5	0.04
Chippewa (1)	4	0.03
Choctaw (6)	23	0.18
Colville (0)	2	0.02
Comanche (2)	2	0.02
Cree (0)	3	0.02
Creek (5)	7	0.05
Delaware (5)	11	0.08
Inupiat *(Alaska Native)* (3)	3	0.02
Iroquois (3)	4	0.03
Navajo (2)	11	0.08
Osage (3)	11	0.08
Ottawa (1)	1	0.01
Potawatomi (1)	3	0.02
Seminole (1)	1	0.01
Sioux (2)	9	0.07
Spanish American Ind. (0)	1	0.01
Asian (46)	76	0.58
Not Hispanic (43)	72	0.55
Hispanic (3)	4	0.03
Bangladeshi (1)	1	0.01
Burmese (1)	5	0.04
Chinese, ex. Taiwanese (13)	16	0.12
Filipino (5)	10	0.08
Indian (7)	8	0.06
Indonesian (0)	1	0.01
Japanese (1)	7	0.05
Korean (4)	9	0.07
Laotian (1)	3	0.02
Vietnamese (9)	10	0.08
Hawaii Native/Pacific Islander (11)	27	0.21
Not Hispanic (11)	27	0.21
Guamanian/Chamorro (8)	13	0.10
Native Hawaiian (1)	8	0.06
Tongan (1)	3	0.02
White (11,950)	12,312	94.55
Not Hispanic (11,629)	11,916	91.51
Hispanic (321)	396	3.04

Emporia

Place Type: City
County: Lyon
Population: 24,916†

*Notes: † The Census 2010 population figure is used to calculate the percentages in the Hispanic Origin and Race categories. Ancestry percentages are based on the 2006-2010 American Community Survey population (not shown); ‡ Numbers in parentheses indicate the number of people reporting a single ancestry; * Numbers in parentheses indicate the number of persons reporting this race alone, not in combination with any other race; Please refer to the Explanation of Data for more information.*

Ancestry‡	Population	%
African, Sub-Saharan (36)	54	0.21
Nigerian (0)	18	0.07
Somalian (36)	36	0.14
American (1,324)	1,324	5.10
Arab (41)	41	0.16
Arab (8)	8	0.03
Lebanese (9)	9	0.03
Other Arab (24)	24	0.09
Belgian (23)	70	0.27
British (13)	13	0.05
Canadian (37)	37	0.14
Croatian (13)	13	0.05
Czech (55)	139	0.54
Czechoslovakian (0)	37	0.14
Danish (31)	153	0.59
Dutch (209)	675	2.60
English (812)	2,184	8.42
European (569)	687	2.65
Finnish (46)	55	0.21
French, ex. Basque (70)	510	1.97
French Canadian (11)	26	0.10
German (3,110)	6,894	26.57
Iranian (25)	25	0.10
Irish (534)	2,639	10.17
Italian (51)	186	0.72
Latvian (0)	10	0.04
Norwegian (96)	223	0.86
Pennsylvania German (17)	57	0.22
Polish (57)	283	1.09
Portuguese (34)	52	0.20
Russian (0)	105	0.40
Scotch-Irish (94)	331	1.28
Scottish (87)	452	1.74
Swedish (70)	383	1.48
Swiss (20)	82	0.32
Welsh (149)	421	1.62

Hispanic Origin	Population	%
Hispanic or Latino (of any race)	6,331	25.41
Central American, ex. Mexican	770	3.09
Costa Rican	2	0.01
Guatemalan	57	0.23
Honduran	15	0.06
Nicaraguan	10	0.04
Panamanian	3	0.01
Salvadoran	680	2.73
Other Central American	3	0.01
Cuban	40	0.16
Dominican Republic	14	0.06
Mexican	4,872	19.55
Puerto Rican	51	0.20
South American	108	0.43
Argentinean	1	<0.01
Bolivian	2	0.01
Colombian	12	0.05
Ecuadorian	70	0.28
Paraguayan	3	0.01
Peruvian	12	0.05
Venezuelan	8	0.03
Other Hispanic or Latino	476	1.91

Race*	Population	%
African-American/Black (791)	1,080	4.33
Not Hispanic (711)	927	3.72
Hispanic (80)	153	0.61
American Indian/Alaska Native (198)	390	1.57
Not Hispanic (109)	247	0.99
Hispanic (89)	143	0.57
Apache (3)	6	0.02
Blackfeet (0)	2	0.01
Canadian/French Am. Ind. (4)	11	0.04
Cherokee (36)	92	0.37
Chickasaw (5)	7	0.03
Chippewa (4)	7	0.03
Choctaw (7)	16	0.06
Colville (1)	1	<0.01
Creek (3)	6	0.02
Delaware (1)	4	0.02
Hopi (1)	1	<0.01
Iroquois (2)	2	0.01
Mexican American Ind. (16)	19	0.08
Navajo (3)	3	0.01
Osage (0)	1	<0.01
Potawatomi (5)	13	0.05
Seminole (0)	1	<0.01
Sioux (4)	10	0.04
South American Ind. (1)	1	<0.01
Asian (771)	908	3.64
Not Hispanic (749)	860	3.45
Hispanic (22)	48	0.19
Bangladeshi (5)	5	0.02
Cambodian (24)	35	0.14
Chinese, ex. Taiwanese (264)	273	1.10
Filipino (21)	46	0.18
Hmong (1)	1	<0.01
Indian (51)	78	0.31
Japanese (41)	62	0.25
Korean (92)	116	0.47
Laotian (65)	88	0.35
Malaysian (2)	5	0.02
Nepalese (1)	1	<0.01
Pakistani (21)	24	0.10
Sri Lankan (6)	8	0.03
Taiwanese (0)	1	<0.01
Thai (2)	8	0.03
Vietnamese (120)	135	0.54
Hawaii Native/Pacific Islander (15)	37	0.15
Not Hispanic (9)	20	0.08
Hispanic (6)	17	0.07
Fijian (2)	2	0.01
Guamanian/Chamorro (1)	6	0.02
Native Hawaiian (2)	8	0.03
Samoan (6)	7	0.03
White (19,738)	20,449	82.07
Not Hispanic (16,537)	16,962	68.08
Hispanic (3,201)	3,487	14.00

Fort Riley

Place Type: CDP
County: Riley
Population: 7,761†

Ancestry‡	Population	%
African, Sub-Saharan (25)	69	0.82
African (25)	69	0.82
American (170)	170	2.02
Arab (7)	20	0.24
Other Arab (7)	20	0.24
Austrian (3)	3	0.04
Czech (3)	5	0.06
Danish (0)	29	0.34
Dutch (26)	121	1.44
English (460)	575	6.83
European (120)	132	1.57
French, ex. Basque (78)	212	2.52
French Canadian (89)	136	1.61
German (970)	1,786	21.20
Hungarian (0)	10	0.12
Irish (448)	980	11.63
Italian (126)	504	5.98
Norwegian (0)	51	0.61
Pennsylvania German (12)	12	0.14
Polish (60)	189	2.24
Portuguese (0)	25	0.30
Russian (27)	27	0.32
Scandinavian (14)	14	0.17
Scotch-Irish (71)	136	1.61
Scottish (194)	290	3.44
Swedish (0)	42	0.50
Turkish (13)	13	0.15
Welsh (0)	17	0.20
West Indian, ex. Hispanic (13)	49	0.58
Jamaican (13)	49	0.58

Hispanic Origin	Population	%
Hispanic or Latino (of any race)	951	12.25
Central American, ex. Mexican	37	0.48
Costa Rican	1	0.01
Guatemalan	3	0.04
Honduran	6	0.08
Nicaraguan	11	0.14
Panamanian	4	0.05
Salvadoran	11	0.14
Other Central American	1	0.01
Cuban	27	0.35
Dominican Republic	16	0.21
Mexican	490	6.31
Puerto Rican	241	3.11
South American	32	0.41
Bolivian	4	0.05
Chilean	1	0.01
Colombian	9	0.12
Ecuadorian	8	0.10
Peruvian	7	0.09
Venezuelan	2	0.03
Other South American	1	0.01
Other Hispanic or Latino	108	1.39

Race*	Population	%
African-American/Black (1,235)	1,396	17.99
Not Hispanic (1,184)	1,312	16.91
Hispanic (51)	84	1.08
American Indian/Alaska Native (86)	143	1.84
Not Hispanic (80)	115	1.48
Hispanic (6)	28	0.36
Apache (0)	2	0.03
Blackfeet (1)	2	0.03
Cherokee (17)	22	0.28
Cheyenne (0)	2	0.03
Chickasaw (2)	2	0.03
Chippewa (0)	3	0.04
Choctaw (3)	3	0.04
Colville (3)	3	0.04
Comanche (4)	4	0.05
Creek (0)	1	0.01
Navajo (9)	16	0.21
Sioux (5)	12	0.15
South American Ind. (1)	2	0.03
Tlingit-Haida *(Alaska Native)* (1)	1	0.01
Yup'ik *(Alaska Native)* (0)	1	0.01
Asian (185)	284	3.66
Not Hispanic (181)	261	3.36
Hispanic (4)	23	0.30
Chinese, ex. Taiwanese (1)	20	0.26
Filipino (45)	79	1.02
Hmong (1)	1	0.01
Indian (67)	72	0.93
Japanese (8)	23	0.30
Korean (20)	56	0.72
Thai (1)	3	0.04
Vietnamese (5)	5	0.06
Hawaii Native/Pacific Islander (50)	84	1.08
Not Hispanic (36)	65	0.84
Hispanic (14)	19	0.24
Guamanian/Chamorro (15)	20	0.26
Marshallese (0)	1	0.01
Native Hawaiian (6)	17	0.22
Samoan (11)	16	0.21
Tongan (1)	4	0.05
White (5,631)	5,936	76.48
Not Hispanic (5,079)	5,276	67.98
Hispanic (552)	660	8.50

Fort Scott

Place Type: City
County: Bourbon
Population: 8,087†

Ancestry‡	Population	%
American (1,737)	1,737	21.38
Belgian (0)	9	0.11
British (0)	10	0.12
Dutch (9)	205	2.52
English (310)	762	9.38
European (48)	179	2.20
Finnish (12)	27	0.33
French, ex. Basque (28)	124	1.53

*Notes: † The Census 2010 population figure is used to calculate the percentages in the Hispanic Origin and Race categories. Ancestry percentages are based on the 2006-2010 American Community Survey population (not shown); ‡ Numbers in parentheses indicate the number of people reporting a single ancestry; * Numbers in parentheses indicate the number of persons reporting this race alone, not in combination with any other race; Please refer to the Explanation of Data for more information.*

German (703)	1,731	21.30
Irish (217)	898	11.05
Italian (65)	172	2.12
Norwegian (11)	72	0.89
Polish (12)	68	0.84
Russian (0)	13	0.16
Scotch-Irish (60)	136	1.67
Scottish (24)	169	2.08
Swedish (32)	108	1.33
Swiss (0)	60	0.74
Welsh (7)	147	1.81

Hispanic Origin	Population	%
Hispanic or Latino (of any race)	206	2.55
Central American, ex. Mexican	4	0.05
Guatemalan	2	0.02
Honduran	1	0.01
Salvadoran	1	0.01
Cuban	6	0.07
Mexican	140	1.73
Puerto Rican	15	0.19
South American	3	0.04
Colombian	1	0.01
Peruvian	2	0.02
Other Hispanic or Latino	38	0.47

Race*	Population	%
African-American/Black (377)	477	5.90
Not Hispanic (364)	458	5.66
Hispanic (13)	19	0.23
American Indian/Alaska Native (63)	162	2.00
Not Hispanic (53)	144	1.78
Hispanic (10)	18	0.22
Apache (1)	4	0.05
Blackfeet (1)	3	0.04
Central American Ind. (0)	1	0.01
Cherokee (16)	58	0.72
Cheyenne (0)	2	0.02
Chickasaw (2)	2	0.02
Chippewa (1)	2	0.02
Choctaw (3)	5	0.06
Comanche (0)	2	0.02
Cree (0)	1	0.01
Iroquois (0)	1	0.01
Navajo (4)	4	0.05
Osage (2)	3	0.04
Potawatomi (3)	5	0.06
Sioux (0)	1	0.01
Asian (50)	78	0.96
Not Hispanic (50)	77	0.95
Hispanic (0)	1	0.01
Chinese, ex. Taiwanese (10)	11	0.14
Filipino (22)	25	0.31
Indian (8)	10	0.12
Japanese (3)	10	0.12
Korean (3)	4	0.05
Laotian (2)	5	0.06
Thai (0)	4	0.05
Vietnamese (2)	7	0.09
Hawaii Native/Pacific Islander (5)	17	0.21
Not Hispanic (5)	16	0.20
Hispanic (0)	1	0.01
Guamanian/Chamorro (0)	7	0.09
Native Hawaiian (5)	10	0.12
White (7,306)	7,521	93.00
Not Hispanic (7,197)	7,389	91.37
Hispanic (109)	132	1.63

Garden City

Place Type: City
County: Finney
Population: 26,658†

Ancestry‡	Population	%
African, Sub-Saharan (268)	436	1.67
African (148)	316	1.21
Somalian (120)	120	0.46
American (946)	946	3.63
Arab (0)	8	0.03
Lebanese (0)	8	0.03
Austrian (0)	22	0.08
British (56)	103	0.40
Czech (22)	98	0.38
Danish (29)	95	0.36
Dutch (77)	319	1.22
English (384)	1,324	5.08
European (96)	96	0.37
French, ex. Basque (73)	504	1.93
French Canadian (5)	43	0.17
German (2,590)	5,237	20.10
Greek (0)	29	0.11
Irish (484)	1,834	7.04
Italian (37)	176	0.68
Norwegian (42)	109	0.42
Polish (53)	287	1.10
Russian (0)	83	0.32
Scotch-Irish (111)	461	1.77
Scottish (32)	269	1.03
Swedish (85)	137	0.53
Swiss (0)	14	0.05
Ukrainian (0)	26	0.10
Welsh (17)	109	0.42

Hispanic Origin	Population	%
Hispanic or Latino (of any race)	12,946	48.56
Central American, ex. Mexican	868	3.26
Costa Rican	4	0.02
Guatemalan	144	0.54
Honduran	51	0.19
Nicaraguan	18	0.07
Panamanian	1	<0.01
Salvadoran	648	2.43
Other Central American	2	0.01
Cuban	19	0.07
Dominican Republic	3	0.01
Mexican	11,245	42.18
Puerto Rican	58	0.22
South American	45	0.17
Argentinean	6	0.02
Bolivian	3	0.01
Chilean	1	<0.01
Colombian	14	0.05
Ecuadorian	6	0.02
Peruvian	12	0.05
Venezuelan	3	0.01
Other Hispanic or Latino	708	2.66

Race*	Population	%
African-American/Black (759)	981	3.68
Not Hispanic (641)	786	2.95
Hispanic (118)	195	0.73
American Indian/Alaska Native (245)	386	1.45
Not Hispanic (105)	194	0.73
Hispanic (140)	192	0.72
Apache (11)	25	0.09
Blackfeet (1)	3	0.01
Canadian/French Am. Ind. (0)	1	<0.01
Central American Ind. (1)	1	<0.01
Cherokee (32)	64	0.24
Chippewa (1)	3	0.01
Choctaw (3)	8	0.03
Creek (5)	6	0.02
Crow (0)	1	<0.01
Mexican American Ind. (29)	39	0.15
Navajo (13)	22	0.08
Ottawa (0)	1	<0.01
Potawatomi (8)	17	0.06
Pueblo (2)	4	0.02
Shoshone (0)	1	<0.01
Sioux (1)	12	0.05
South American Ind. (4)	4	0.02
Spanish American Ind. (6)	6	0.02
Ute (1)	1	<0.01
Yaqui (4)	4	0.02
Asian (1,175)	1,264	4.74
Not Hispanic (1,146)	1,207	4.53
Hispanic (29)	57	0.21
Bangladeshi (1)	1	<0.01
Burmese (441)	465	1.74
Cambodian (5)	5	0.02
Chinese, ex. Taiwanese (31)	45	0.17
Filipino (42)	64	0.24
Hmong (1)	1	<0.01
Indian (48)	77	0.29
Indonesian (1)	1	<0.01
Japanese (8)	20	0.08
Korean (32)	46	0.17
Laotian (103)	119	0.45
Nepalese (3)	3	0.01
Pakistani (1)	1	<0.01
Thai (2)	5	0.02
Vietnamese (380)	408	1.53
Hawaii Native/Pacific Islander (13)	46	0.17
Not Hispanic (11)	30	0.11
Hispanic (2)	16	0.06
Guamanian/Chamorro (1)	9	0.03
Native Hawaiian (0)	8	0.03
Samoan (4)	9	0.03
White (19,910)	20,596	77.26
Not Hispanic (11,463)	11,735	44.02
Hispanic (8,447)	8,861	33.24

Gardner

Place Type: City
County: Johnson
Population: 19,123†

Ancestry‡	Population	%
African, Sub-Saharan (31)	31	0.18
Ethiopian (31)	31	0.18
American (1,420)	1,420	8.10
Armenian (31)	31	0.18
Austrian (0)	60	0.34
Belgian (22)	75	0.43
British (11)	119	0.68
Croatian (11)	44	0.25
Czech (28)	72	0.41
Danish (15)	57	0.32
Dutch (86)	380	2.17
English (399)	1,899	10.83
European (210)	269	1.53
Finnish (0)	16	0.09
French, ex. Basque (86)	767	4.37
French Canadian (5)	11	0.06
German (1,911)	5,806	33.10
Greek (29)	29	0.17
Iranian (17)	17	0.10
Irish (497)	2,776	15.83
Italian (159)	605	3.45
Latvian (7)	21	0.12
Luxemburger (0)	7	0.04
Norwegian (37)	116	0.66
Polish (41)	349	1.99
Russian (21)	158	0.90
Scandinavian (0)	71	0.40
Scotch-Irish (82)	489	2.79
Scottish (81)	563	3.21
Swedish (91)	467	2.66
Swiss (26)	37	0.21
Welsh (42)	168	0.96
West Indian, ex. Hispanic (15)	29	0.17
West Indian (15)	29	0.17

Hispanic Origin	Population	%
Hispanic or Latino (of any race)	1,184	6.19
Central American, ex. Mexican	79	0.41
Costa Rican	3	0.02
Guatemalan	34	0.18
Honduran	9	0.05
Nicaraguan	3	0.02
Panamanian	8	0.04
Salvadoran	22	0.12
Cuban	23	0.12
Dominican Republic	1	0.01
Mexican	899	4.70
Puerto Rican	55	0.29
South American	43	0.22
Argentinean	2	0.01

*Notes: † The Census 2010 population figure is used to calculate the percentages in the Hispanic Origin and Race categories. Ancestry percentages are based on the 2006-2010 American Community Survey population (not shown); ‡ Numbers in parentheses indicate the number of people reporting a single ancestry; * Numbers in parentheses indicate the number of persons reporting this race alone, not in combination with any other race; Please refer to the Explanation of Data for more information.*

Bolivian	5	0.03
Chilean	1	0.01
Colombian	9	0.05
Ecuadorian	14	0.07
Paraguayan	1	0.01
Peruvian	4	0.02
Venezuelan	5	0.03
Other South American	2	0.01
Other Hispanic or Latino	84	0.44

Race*	Population	%
African-American/Black (568)	782	4.09
Not Hispanic (553)	751	3.93
Hispanic (15)	31	0.16
American Indian/Alaska Native (97)	252	1.32
Not Hispanic (81)	226	1.18
Hispanic (16)	26	0.14
Apache (1)	1	0.01
Blackfeet (5)	13	0.07
Cherokee (30)	110	0.58
Chickasaw (3)	8	0.04
Chippewa (1)	1	0.01
Choctaw (7)	8	0.04
Creek (3)	7	0.04
Delaware (0)	1	0.01
Hopi (0)	2	0.01
Iroquois (3)	3	0.02
Kiowa (0)	1	0.01
Mexican American Ind. (7)	8	0.04
Navajo (1)	2	0.01
Potawatomi (1)	2	0.01
Sioux (2)	9	0.05
South American Ind. (1)	1	0.01
Ute (1)	1	0.01
Asian (368)	506	2.65
Not Hispanic (366)	494	2.58
Hispanic (2)	12	0.06
Cambodian (2)	4	0.02
Chinese, ex. Taiwanese (27)	45	0.24
Filipino (24)	66	0.35
Hmong (19)	19	0.10
Indian (36)	51	0.27
Japanese (3)	28	0.15
Korean (17)	42	0.22
Laotian (168)	189	0.99
Pakistani (2)	4	0.02
Taiwanese (3)	3	0.02
Thai (5)	14	0.07
Vietnamese (18)	31	0.16
Hawaii Native/Pacific Islander (8)	20	0.10
Not Hispanic (8)	16	0.08
Hispanic (0)	4	0.02
Guamanian/Chamorro (3)	8	0.04
Native Hawaiian (3)	3	0.02
Samoan (1)	5	0.03
Tongan (0)	1	0.01
White (17,161)	17,703	92.57
Not Hispanic (16,444)	16,901	88.38
Hispanic (717)	802	4.19

Great Bend

Place Type: City
County: Barton
Population: 15,995†

Ancestry‡	Population	%
African, Sub-Saharan (46)	46	0.29
African (46)	46	0.29
American (980)	980	6.23
Arab (0)	51	0.32
Arab (0)	41	0.26
Syrian (0)	10	0.06
Austrian (11)	70	0.45
British (16)	16	0.10
Canadian (0)	11	0.07
Czech (59)	292	1.86
Czechoslovakian (13)	121	0.77
Danish (0)	105	0.67
Dutch (43)	190	1.21
English (707)	1,684	10.71
European (111)	111	0.71
French, ex. Basque (58)	400	2.54
French Canadian (29)	94	0.60
German (3,048)	5,791	36.82
Irish (494)	1,710	10.87
Italian (92)	199	1.27
Norwegian (6)	36	0.23
Pennsylvania German (34)	45	0.29
Polish (34)	112	0.71
Russian (25)	217	1.38
Scandinavian (4)	4	0.03
Scotch-Irish (111)	220	1.40
Scottish (78)	222	1.41
Slavic (14)	24	0.15
Swedish (77)	240	1.53
Swiss (25)	116	0.74
Welsh (0)	27	0.17

Hispanic Origin	Population	%
Hispanic or Latino (of any race)	3,164	19.78
Central American, ex. Mexican	49	0.31
Guatemalan	11	0.07
Honduran	10	0.06
Nicaraguan	3	0.02
Panamanian	5	0.03
Salvadoran	17	0.11
Other Central American	3	0.02
Cuban	9	0.06
Mexican	2,889	18.06
Puerto Rican	18	0.11
South American	15	0.09
Argentinean	1	0.01
Colombian	4	0.03
Ecuadorian	5	0.03
Peruvian	3	0.02
Other South American	2	0.01
Other Hispanic or Latino	184	1.15

Race*	Population	%
African-American/Black (276)	401	2.51
Not Hispanic (245)	340	2.13
Hispanic (31)	61	0.38
American Indian/Alaska Native (99)	212	1.33
Not Hispanic (65)	153	0.96
Hispanic (34)	59	0.37
Apache (2)	3	0.02
Arapaho (3)	3	0.02
Blackfeet (0)	6	0.04
Canadian/French Am. Ind. (2)	2	0.01
Cherokee (12)	36	0.23
Cheyenne (2)	3	0.02
Chickasaw (4)	10	0.06
Chippewa (8)	11	0.07
Choctaw (2)	10	0.06
Comanche (0)	2	0.01
Creek (1)	7	0.04
Crow (0)	1	0.01
Delaware (0)	1	0.01
Iroquois (0)	1	0.01
Mexican American Ind. (0)	4	0.03
Navajo (1)	2	0.01
Ottawa (0)	1	0.01
Pima (0)	1	0.01
Potawatomi (2)	3	0.02
Seminole (3)	3	0.02
Sioux (2)	6	0.04
Tlingit-Haida *(Alaska Native)* (2)	3	0.02
Asian (39)	76	0.48
Not Hispanic (39)	71	0.44
Hispanic (0)	5	0.03
Chinese, ex. Taiwanese (6)	8	0.05
Filipino (9)	11	0.07
Indian (4)	11	0.07
Indonesian (0)	2	0.01
Japanese (0)	4	0.03
Korean (3)	5	0.03
Thai (2)	5	0.03
Vietnamese (15)	19	0.12
Hawaii Native/Pacific Islander (14)	21	0.13
Not Hispanic (8)	14	0.09
Hispanic (6)	7	0.04
Guamanian/Chamorro (2)	2	0.01
Native Hawaiian (10)	12	0.08
White (13,442)	13,767	86.07
Not Hispanic (12,250)	12,441	77.78
Hispanic (1,192)	1,326	8.29

Hays

Place Type: City
County: Ellis
Population: 20,510†

Ancestry‡	Population	%
African, Sub-Saharan (22)	22	0.11
Nigerian (22)	22	0.11
American (707)	707	3.49
Arab (0)	13	0.06
Syrian (0)	13	0.06
Austrian (0)	46	0.23
Belgian (0)	12	0.06
British (16)	34	0.17
Canadian (14)	66	0.33
Czech (52)	294	1.45
Czechoslovakian (0)	13	0.06
Danish (68)	158	0.78
Dutch (27)	286	1.41
English (633)	1,947	9.61
European (101)	116	0.57
Finnish (10)	10	0.05
French, ex. Basque (130)	855	4.22
French Canadian (112)	152	0.75
German (6,478)	11,456	56.55
German Russian (282)	308	1.52
Greek (0)	21	0.10
Hungarian (0)	5	0.02
Irish (520)	2,678	13.22
Italian (40)	250	1.23
Lithuanian (16)	16	0.08
Luxemburger (19)	19	0.09
Northern European (74)	74	0.37
Norwegian (52)	268	1.32
Pennsylvania German (0)	15	0.07
Polish (77)	344	1.70
Russian (45)	531	2.62
Scotch-Irish (160)	404	1.99
Scottish (111)	395	1.95
Serbian (15)	22	0.11
Swedish (147)	496	2.45
Swiss (16)	50	0.25
Welsh (11)	33	0.16
West Indian, ex. Hispanic (0)	10	0.05
Bahamian (0)	10	0.05

Hispanic Origin	Population	%
Hispanic or Latino (of any race)	963	4.70
Central American, ex. Mexican	17	0.08
Costa Rican	1	<0.01
Honduran	5	0.02
Nicaraguan	5	0.02
Panamanian	3	0.01
Salvadoran	3	0.01
Cuban	6	0.03
Dominican Republic	1	<0.01
Mexican	808	3.94
Puerto Rican	17	0.08
South American	35	0.17
Argentinean	1	<0.01
Bolivian	9	0.04
Chilean	5	0.02
Colombian	14	0.07
Peruvian	4	0.02
Uruguayan	1	<0.01
Venezuelan	1	<0.01
Other Hispanic or Latino	79	0.39

Race*	Population	%
African-American/Black (227)	371	1.81
Not Hispanic (217)	351	1.71

*Notes: † The Census 2010 population figure is used to calculate the percentages in the Hispanic Origin and Race categories. Ancestry percentages are based on the 2006-2010 American Community Survey population (not shown); ‡ Numbers in parentheses indicate the number of people reporting a single ancestry; * Numbers in parentheses indicate the number of persons reporting this race alone, not in combination with any other race; Please refer to the Explanation of Data for more information.*

Hispanic (10)	20	0.10
American Indian/Alaska Native (57)	189	0.92
Not Hispanic (50)	159	0.78
Hispanic (7)	30	0.15
Apache (2)	5	0.02
Blackfeet (4)	18	0.09
Cherokee (7)	45	0.22
Cheyenne (1)	1	<0.01
Chippewa (2)	2	0.01
Choctaw (6)	18	0.09
Comanche (1)	1	<0.01
Creek (0)	1	<0.01
Delaware (1)	2	0.01
Mexican American Ind. (1)	2	0.01
Navajo (1)	2	0.01
Osage (3)	3	0.01
Paiute (0)	2	0.01
Potawatomi (5)	7	0.03
Seminole (2)	2	0.01
Shoshone (0)	1	<0.01
Sioux (1)	6	0.03
Asian (377)	432	2.11
Not Hispanic (376)	428	2.09
Hispanic (1)	4	0.02
Chinese, ex. Taiwanese (217)	220	1.07
Filipino (13)	26	0.13
Indian (32)	37	0.18
Indonesian (1)	3	0.01
Japanese (20)	28	0.14
Korean (13)	27	0.13
Laotian (2)	7	0.03
Pakistani (26)	27	0.13
Taiwanese (11)	11	0.05
Thai (6)	10	0.05
Vietnamese (24)	26	0.13
Hawaii Native/Pacific Islander (5)	17	0.08
Not Hispanic (4)	13	0.06
Hispanic (1)	4	0.02
Guamanian/Chamorro (2)	3	0.01
Native Hawaiian (2)	9	0.04
White (19,036)	19,391	94.54
Not Hispanic (18,596)	18,863	91.97
Hispanic (440)	528	2.57

Haysville

Place Type: City
County: Sedgwick
Population: 10,826†

Ancestry‡	Population	%
American (611)	611	5.91
Arab (8)	8	0.08
Syrian (8)	8	0.08
Austrian (0)	10	0.10
Brazilian (12)	24	0.23
British (15)	36	0.35
Czech (12)	109	1.05
Czechoslovakian (9)	9	0.09
Danish (0)	9	0.09
Dutch (65)	372	3.60
English (397)	996	9.63
European (184)	249	2.41
French, ex. Basque (22)	429	4.15
French Canadian (23)	23	0.22
German (1,864)	3,708	35.84
Iranian (10)	10	0.10
Irish (447)	1,684	16.28
Italian (102)	233	2.25
Norwegian (16)	25	0.24
Polish (25)	151	1.46
Portuguese (11)	11	0.11
Russian (10)	10	0.10
Scotch-Irish (0)	55	0.53
Scottish (43)	101	0.98
Swedish (76)	137	1.32
Swiss (13)	49	0.47
Welsh (18)	60	0.58

Hispanic Origin	Population	%
Hispanic or Latino (of any race)	500	4.62
Central American, ex. Mexican	18	0.17
Guatemalan	5	0.05
Honduran	8	0.07
Panamanian	1	0.01
Salvadoran	4	0.04
Cuban	4	0.04
Mexican	409	3.78
Puerto Rican	25	0.23
South American	9	0.08
Argentinean	2	0.02
Chilean	1	0.01
Colombian	1	0.01
Ecuadorian	2	0.02
Peruvian	3	0.03
Other Hispanic or Latino	35	0.32

Race*	Population	%
African-American/Black (66)	146	1.35
Not Hispanic (64)	141	1.30
Hispanic (2)	5	0.05
American Indian/Alaska Native (128)	301	2.78
Not Hispanic (114)	264	2.44
Hispanic (14)	37	0.34
Apache (2)	10	0.09
Blackfeet (0)	2	0.02
Cherokee (25)	87	0.80
Cheyenne (0)	2	0.02
Chickasaw (0)	1	0.01
Chippewa (2)	5	0.05
Choctaw (2)	14	0.13
Comanche (10)	18	0.17
Creek (10)	14	0.13
Delaware (2)	2	0.02
Iroquois (1)	4	0.04
Kiowa (1)	2	0.02
Mexican American Ind. (1)	1	0.01
Navajo (3)	5	0.05
Osage (4)	13	0.12
Ottawa (0)	1	0.01
Potawatomi (2)	7	0.06
Seminole (0)	2	0.02
Sioux (0)	5	0.05
Yaqui (1)	1	0.01
Asian (95)	178	1.64
Not Hispanic (93)	166	1.53
Hispanic (2)	12	0.11
Cambodian (2)	5	0.05
Chinese, ex. Taiwanese (6)	16	0.15
Filipino (25)	49	0.45
Indian (4)	9	0.08
Japanese (4)	19	0.18
Korean (10)	19	0.18
Laotian (14)	17	0.16
Pakistani (0)	3	0.03
Taiwanese (1)	1	0.01
Thai (3)	10	0.09
Vietnamese (18)	32	0.30
Hawaii Native/Pacific Islander (1)	13	0.12
Not Hispanic (1)	9	0.08
Hispanic (0)	4	0.04
Guamanian/Chamorro (0)	1	0.01
Native Hawaiian (1)	4	0.04
White (10,031)	10,389	95.96
Not Hispanic (9,745)	10,034	92.68
Hispanic (286)	355	3.28

Hutchinson

Place Type: City
County: Reno
Population: 42,080†

Ancestry‡	Population	%
African, Sub-Saharan (33)	64	0.15
African (33)	52	0.12
Nigerian (0)	12	0.03
American (3,128)	3,128	7.50
Arab (251)	288	0.69
Lebanese (244)	244	0.58
Moroccan (7)	16	0.04
Syrian (0)	28	0.07
Australian (0)	12	0.03
Austrian (12)	48	0.12
Belgian (30)	30	0.07
British (98)	135	0.32
Cajun (0)	78	0.19
Canadian (0)	13	0.03
Czech (127)	315	0.75
Czechoslovakian (9)	50	0.12
Danish (10)	183	0.44
Dutch (342)	1,549	3.71
Eastern European (27)	27	0.06
English (1,925)	4,448	10.66
European (248)	293	0.70
Finnish (0)	8	0.02
French, ex. Basque (310)	1,291	3.09
French Canadian (84)	172	0.41
German (6,102)	13,474	32.29
Greek (0)	22	0.05
Hungarian (0)	30	0.07
Irish (1,113)	5,256	12.60
Italian (138)	419	1.00
Lithuanian (0)	21	0.05
Northern European (13)	13	0.03
Norwegian (192)	332	0.80
Pennsylvania German (132)	263	0.63
Polish (71)	309	0.74
Portuguese (26)	42	0.10
Romanian (0)	15	0.04
Russian (69)	224	0.54
Scandinavian (44)	94	0.23
Scotch-Irish (256)	788	1.89
Scottish (248)	769	1.84
Swedish (517)	1,349	3.23
Swiss (0)	151	0.36
Turkish (7)	7	0.02
Ukrainian (0)	27	0.06
Welsh (61)	227	0.54
West Indian, ex. Hispanic (107)	121	0.29
Jamaican (107)	121	0.29

Hispanic Origin	Population	%
Hispanic or Latino (of any race)	4,446	10.57
Central American, ex. Mexican	98	0.23
Costa Rican	6	0.01
Guatemalan	17	0.04
Honduran	41	0.10
Panamanian	8	0.02
Salvadoran	24	0.06
Other Central American	2	<0.01
Cuban	10	0.02
Dominican Republic	2	<0.01
Mexican	3,958	9.41
Puerto Rican	83	0.20
South American	17	0.04
Argentinean	1	<0.01
Chilean	1	<0.01
Colombian	6	0.01
Peruvian	6	0.01
Venezuelan	3	0.01
Other Hispanic or Latino	278	0.66

Race*	Population	%
African-American/Black (1,821)	2,432	5.78
Not Hispanic (1,744)	2,263	5.38
Hispanic (77)	169	0.40
American Indian/Alaska Native (276)	656	1.56
Not Hispanic (230)	547	1.30
Hispanic (46)	109	0.26
Alaska Athabascan *(Ala. Nat.)* (2)	2	<0.01
Aleut *(Alaska Native)* (2)	2	<0.01
Apache (7)	14	0.03
Arapaho (0)	1	<0.01
Blackfeet (2)	19	0.05
Cherokee (68)	211	0.50
Cheyenne (3)	5	0.01
Chickasaw (1)	7	0.02
Chippewa (0)	10	0.02

*Notes: † The Census 2010 population figure is used to calculate the percentages in the Hispanic Origin and Race categories. Ancestry percentages are based on the 2006-2010 American Community Survey population (not shown); ‡ Numbers in parentheses indicate the number of people reporting a single ancestry; * Numbers in parentheses indicate the number of persons reporting this race alone, not in combination with any other race; Please refer to the Explanation of Data for more information.*

Choctaw (6)	12	0.03
Comanche (3)	3	0.01
Cree (0)	1	<0.01
Creek (6)	13	0.03
Crow (0)	3	0.01
Delaware (5)	10	0.02
Hopi (1)	1	<0.01
Iroquois (3)	3	0.01
Kiowa (1)	3	0.01
Lumbee (0)	1	<0.01
Mexican American Ind. (2)	4	0.01
Navajo (13)	17	0.04
Osage (3)	6	0.01
Paiute (5)	5	0.01
Pima (0)	2	<0.01
Potawatomi (9)	17	0.04
Pueblo (0)	2	<0.01
Seminole (0)	2	<0.01
Sioux (8)	14	0.03
South American Ind. (0)	1	<0.01
Tlingit-Haida *(Alaska Native)* (5)	5	0.01
Tohono O'Odham (3)	3	0.01
Yaqui (0)	1	<0.01
Asian (237)	365	0.87
Not Hispanic (228)	337	0.80
Hispanic (9)	28	0.07
Cambodian (2)	2	<0.01
Chinese, ex. Taiwanese (37)	44	0.10
Filipino (54)	98	0.23
Hmong (2)	5	0.01
Indian (48)	62	0.15
Japanese (15)	31	0.07
Korean (15)	40	0.10
Laotian (4)	4	0.01
Nepalese (1)	1	<0.01
Pakistani (15)	16	0.04
Sri Lankan (1)	1	<0.01
Taiwanese (3)	4	0.01
Thai (4)	12	0.03
Vietnamese (16)	27	0.06
Hawaii Native/Pacific Islander (8)	27	0.06
Not Hispanic (7)	18	0.04
Hispanic (1)	9	0.02
Fijian (2)	4	0.01
Guamanian/Chamorro (1)	2	<0.01
Native Hawaiian (4)	10	0.02
Samoan (1)	1	<0.01
Tongan (0)	1	<0.01
White (36,968)	38,238	90.87
Not Hispanic (34,484)	35,366	84.04
Hispanic (2,484)	2,872	6.83

Independence

Place Type: City
County: Montgomery
Population: 9,483†

Ancestry‡	Population	%
African, Sub-Saharan (27)	27	0.28
African (27)	27	0.28
American (685)	685	7.21
Arab (9)	9	0.09
Other Arab (9)	9	0.09
Austrian (0)	48	0.50
Basque (0)	8	0.08
British (72)	93	0.98
Canadian (22)	39	0.41
Czech (0)	19	0.20
Danish (0)	14	0.15
Dutch (0)	303	3.19
English (591)	1,265	13.31
European (59)	100	1.05
French, ex. Basque (54)	620	6.52
German (834)	2,517	26.48
German Russian (0)	9	0.09
Greek (10)	32	0.34
Irish (769)	1,548	16.29
Italian (73)	260	2.74
Norwegian (46)	214	2.25
Polish (13)	159	1.67
Russian (0)	48	0.50
Scotch-Irish (58)	254	2.67
Scottish (11)	78	0.82
Swedish (27)	214	2.25
Swiss (13)	23	0.24
Welsh (26)	89	0.94
West Indian, ex. Hispanic (0)	17	0.18
Dutch West Indian (0)	17	0.18

Hispanic Origin	Population	%
Hispanic or Latino (of any race)	615	6.49
Central American, ex. Mexican	14	0.15
Guatemalan	10	0.11
Honduran	1	0.01
Panamanian	1	0.01
Salvadoran	2	0.02
Cuban	2	0.02
Dominican Republic	2	0.02
Mexican	505	5.33
Puerto Rican	40	0.42
South American	21	0.22
Argentinean	3	0.03
Colombian	11	0.12
Peruvian	1	0.01
Venezuelan	6	0.06
Other Hispanic or Latino	31	0.33

Race*	Population	%
African-American/Black (614)	793	8.36
Not Hispanic (603)	757	7.98
Hispanic (11)	36	0.38
American Indian/Alaska Native (156)	356	3.75
Not Hispanic (132)	318	3.35
Hispanic (24)	38	0.40
Apache (2)	3	0.03
Arapaho (1)	4	0.04
Blackfeet (0)	2	0.02
Cherokee (71)	175	1.85
Choctaw (10)	16	0.17
Creek (5)	11	0.12
Delaware (1)	6	0.06
Iroquois (0)	3	0.03
Kiowa (1)	1	0.01
Mexican American Ind. (0)	5	0.05
Navajo (4)	5	0.05
Osage (4)	17	0.18
Potawatomi (7)	11	0.12
Puget Sound Salish (0)	1	0.01
Seminole (1)	2	0.02
Sioux (0)	1	0.01
Tlingit-Haida *(Alaska Native)* (2)	4	0.04
Tsimshian *(Alaska Native)* (1)	2	0.02
Yaqui (4)	4	0.04
Asian (85)	117	1.23
Not Hispanic (82)	105	1.11
Hispanic (3)	12	0.13
Burmese (9)	9	0.09
Chinese, ex. Taiwanese (19)	27	0.28
Filipino (16)	30	0.32
Indian (19)	20	0.21
Japanese (4)	5	0.05
Korean (1)	1	0.01
Malaysian (3)	3	0.03
Pakistani (4)	4	0.04
Thai (1)	1	0.01
Vietnamese (9)	13	0.14
Hawaii Native/Pacific Islander (3)	14	0.15
Not Hispanic (3)	12	0.13
Hispanic (0)	2	0.02
Guamanian/Chamorro (1)	3	0.03
Native Hawaiian (1)	6	0.06
Samoan (0)	1	0.01
White (7,981)	8,368	88.24
Not Hispanic (7,705)	8,005	84.41
Hispanic (276)	363	3.83

Junction City

Place Type: City
County: Geary
Population: 23,353†

Ancestry‡	Population	%
African, Sub-Saharan (105)	172	0.83
African (105)	172	0.83
American (759)	759	3.66
Arab (159)	159	0.77
Arab (14)	14	0.07
Iraqi (145)	145	0.70
Australian (0)	25	0.12
Austrian (9)	9	0.04
British (30)	58	0.28
Cajun (0)	20	0.10
Czech (19)	96	0.46
Czechoslovakian (17)	28	0.13
Danish (13)	36	0.17
Dutch (110)	375	1.81
English (628)	1,465	7.06
European (217)	305	1.47
Finnish (0)	8	0.04
French, ex. Basque (115)	525	2.53
French Canadian (10)	16	0.08
German (2,261)	4,539	21.88
Greek (49)	49	0.24
Hungarian (0)	56	0.27
Irish (656)	1,975	9.52
Italian (138)	402	1.94
Luxemburger (0)	11	0.05
Norwegian (52)	124	0.60
Polish (28)	154	0.74
Portuguese (8)	8	0.04
Russian (70)	100	0.48
Scotch-Irish (85)	143	0.69
Scottish (19)	108	0.52
Slovak (0)	25	0.12
Swedish (73)	310	1.49
Swiss (27)	72	0.35
Turkish (28)	28	0.13
Ukrainian (0)	14	0.07
Welsh (0)	46	0.22
West Indian, ex. Hispanic (26)	56	0.27
Haitian (19)	38	0.18
Jamaican (0)	11	0.05
Trinidadian/Tobagonian (7)	7	0.03
Yugoslavian (0)	29	0.14

Hispanic Origin	Population	%
Hispanic or Latino (of any race)	3,025	12.95
Central American, ex. Mexican	254	1.09
Costa Rican	13	0.06
Guatemalan	13	0.06
Honduran	45	0.19
Nicaraguan	22	0.09
Panamanian	112	0.48
Salvadoran	47	0.20
Other Central American	2	0.01
Cuban	29	0.12
Dominican Republic	106	0.45
Mexican	1,346	5.76
Puerto Rican	948	4.06
South American	99	0.42
Bolivian	4	0.02
Chilean	11	0.05
Colombian	39	0.17
Ecuadorian	24	0.10
Peruvian	19	0.08
Venezuelan	2	0.01
Other Hispanic or Latino	243	1.04

Race*	Population	%
African-American/Black (5,199)	6,157	26.36
Not Hispanic (4,951)	5,736	24.56
Hispanic (248)	421	1.80
American Indian/Alaska Native (213)	528	2.26
Not Hispanic (177)	453	1.94
Hispanic (36)	75	0.32

*Notes: † The Census 2010 population figure is used to calculate the percentages in the Hispanic Origin and Race categories. Ancestry percentages are based on the 2006-2010 American Community Survey population (not shown); ‡ Numbers in parentheses indicate the number of people reporting a single ancestry; * Numbers in parentheses indicate the number of persons reporting this race alone, not in combination with any other race; Please refer to the Explanation of Data for more information.*

Aleut *(Alaska Native)* (1)	1	<0.01
Apache (3)	10	0.04
Arapaho (1)	1	<0.01
Blackfeet (7)	33	0.14
Central American Ind. (0)	2	0.01
Cherokee (34)	117	0.50
Cheyenne (0)	3	0.01
Chickasaw (1)	5	0.02
Chippewa (7)	14	0.06
Choctaw (7)	8	0.03
Comanche (10)	12	0.05
Creek (4)	13	0.06
Crow (4)	7	0.03
Hopi (4)	4	0.02
Inupiat *(Alaska Native)* (4)	5	0.02
Iroquois (1)	4	0.02
Kiowa (1)	1	<0.01
Lumbee (7)	9	0.04
Menominee (1)	1	<0.01
Mexican American Ind. (4)	10	0.04
Navajo (7)	18	0.08
Potawatomi (3)	9	0.04
Pueblo (3)	4	0.02
Puget Sound Salish (2)	2	0.01
Seminole (1)	2	0.01
Sioux (7)	14	0.06
South American Ind. (5)	10	0.04
Tlingit-Haida *(Alaska Native)* (1)	1	<0.01
Yakama (1)	1	<0.01
Yaqui (1)	2	0.01
Yup'ik *(Alaska Native)* (0)	1	<0.01
Asian (910)	1,449	6.20
Not Hispanic (886)	1,346	5.76
Hispanic (24)	103	0.44
Burmese (5)	5	0.02
Cambodian (28)	31	0.13
Chinese, ex. Taiwanese (46)	81	0.35
Filipino (256)	423	1.81
Indian (42)	71	0.30
Indonesian (1)	5	0.02
Japanese (51)	142	0.61
Korean (324)	517	2.21
Laotian (5)	7	0.03
Nepalese (12)	12	0.05
Pakistani (5)	6	0.03
Sri Lankan (2)	3	0.01
Taiwanese (9)	9	0.04
Thai (18)	37	0.16
Vietnamese (56)	76	0.33
Hawaii Native/Pacific Islander (215)	362	1.55
Not Hispanic (208)	312	1.34
Hispanic (7)	50	0.21
Fijian (1)	4	0.02
Guamanian/Chamorro (54)	70	0.30
Native Hawaiian (30)	118	0.51
Samoan (39)	55	0.24
Tongan (1)	2	0.01
White (14,172)	15,594	66.78
Not Hispanic (12,736)	13,854	59.32
Hispanic (1,436)	1,740	7.45

Kansas City

Place Type: City
County: Wyandotte
Population: 145,786†

Ancestry‡	Population	%
African, Sub-Saharan (2,051)	2,368	1.64
African (1,206)	1,523	1.06
Ethiopian (132)	132	0.09
Kenyan (28)	28	0.02
Liberian (33)	33	0.02
Nigerian (16)	16	0.01
Senegalese (97)	97	0.07
Sudanese (193)	193	0.13
Other Sub-Saharan African (346)	346	0.24
American (5,373)	5,373	3.73
Arab (76)	87	0.06
Arab (67)	67	0.05
Moroccan (9)	20	0.01
Australian (0)	77	0.05
Austrian (40)	201	0.14
Basque (0)	17	0.01
Belgian (32)	114	0.08
Brazilian (11)	11	0.01
British (132)	200	0.14
Bulgarian (35)	35	0.02
Cajun (0)	4	<0.01
Canadian (21)	122	0.08
Croatian (989)	1,767	1.23
Czech (96)	337	0.23
Czechoslovakian (39)	78	0.05
Danish (54)	379	0.26
Dutch (197)	2,010	1.40
Eastern European (17)	17	0.01
English (2,524)	7,884	5.47
Estonian (0)	5	<0.01
European (628)	797	0.55
French, ex. Basque (285)	2,051	1.42
French Canadian (103)	193	0.13
German (6,512)	19,509	13.55
Greek (66)	140	0.10
Hungarian (26)	87	0.06
Iranian (11)	11	0.01
Irish (2,963)	12,179	8.46
Italian (688)	2,107	1.46
Latvian (9)	9	0.01
Lithuanian (98)	288	0.20
Luxemburger (0)	26	0.02
Northern European (13)	13	0.01
Norwegian (216)	538	0.37
Pennsylvania German (30)	41	0.03
Polish (672)	1,735	1.20
Portuguese (0)	124	0.09
Romanian (0)	9	0.01
Russian (93)	491	0.34
Scandinavian (41)	97	0.07
Scotch-Irish (567)	1,732	1.20
Scottish (323)	1,724	1.20
Serbian (67)	67	0.05
Slavic (67)	88	0.06
Slovak (43)	111	0.08
Slovene (115)	283	0.20
Swedish (385)	1,470	1.02
Swiss (34)	197	0.14
Turkish (30)	92	0.06
Ukrainian (32)	77	0.05
Welsh (169)	476	0.33
West Indian, ex. Hispanic (343)	377	0.26
Barbadian (107)	107	0.07
Dutch West Indian (10)	19	0.01
Haitian (45)	45	0.03
Jamaican (131)	131	0.09
U.S. Virgin Islander (9)	9	0.01
West Indian (41)	66	0.05
Yugoslavian (204)	290	0.20

Hispanic Origin	Population	%
Hispanic or Latino (of any race)	40,522	27.80
Central American, ex. Mexican	2,636	1.81
Costa Rican	22	0.02
Guatemalan	917	0.63
Honduran	778	0.53
Nicaraguan	62	0.04
Panamanian	32	0.02
Salvadoran	800	0.55
Other Central American	25	0.02
Cuban	247	0.17
Dominican Republic	76	0.05
Mexican	34,764	23.85
Puerto Rican	397	0.27
South American	347	0.24
Argentinean	21	0.01
Bolivian	14	0.01
Chilean	25	0.02
Colombian	110	0.08
Ecuadorian	77	0.05
Paraguayan	1	<0.01
Peruvian	49	0.03
Uruguayan	4	<0.01
Venezuelan	40	0.03
Other South American	6	<0.01
Other Hispanic or Latino	2,055	1.41

Race*	Population	%
African-American/Black (39,080)	41,889	28.73
Not Hispanic (38,403)	40,711	27.93
Hispanic (677)	1,178	0.81
American Indian/Alaska Native (1,196)	2,790	1.91
Not Hispanic (702)	1,970	1.35
Hispanic (494)	820	0.56
Aleut *(Alaska Native)* (1)	2	<0.01
Apache (30)	53	0.04
Blackfeet (9)	104	0.07
Canadian/French Am. Ind. (1)	7	<0.01
Central American Ind. (5)	10	0.01
Cherokee (157)	573	0.39
Cheyenne (4)	12	0.01
Chickasaw (7)	13	0.01
Chippewa (7)	26	0.02
Choctaw (77)	148	0.10
Comanche (0)	3	<0.01
Cree (0)	3	<0.01
Creek (15)	72	0.05
Crow (4)	5	<0.01
Delaware (13)	26	0.02
Hopi (0)	3	<0.01
Inupiat *(Alaska Native)* (3)	3	<0.01
Iroquois (18)	57	0.04
Kiowa (2)	3	<0.01
Lumbee (4)	5	<0.01
Mexican American Ind. (82)	121	0.08
Navajo (9)	25	0.02
Osage (13)	21	0.01
Ottawa (0)	1	<0.01
Paiute (0)	5	<0.01
Pima (2)	2	<0.01
Potawatomi (46)	67	0.05
Pueblo (4)	5	<0.01
Seminole (10)	17	0.01
Shoshone (0)	1	<0.01
Sioux (23)	63	0.04
South American Ind. (5)	8	0.01
Spanish American Ind. (0)	1	<0.01
Tlingit-Haida *(Alaska Native)* (3)	5	<0.01
Tohono O'Odham (2)	2	<0.01
Ute (0)	2	<0.01
Yakama (1)	2	<0.01
Yaqui (2)	8	0.01
Yup'ik *(Alaska Native)* (1)	1	<0.01
Asian (3,887)	4,439	3.04
Not Hispanic (3,815)	4,251	2.92
Hispanic (72)	188	0.13
Bangladeshi (16)	16	0.01
Bhutanese (142)	144	0.10
Burmese (540)	578	0.40
Cambodian (18)	25	0.02
Chinese, ex. Taiwanese (239)	285	0.20
Filipino (145)	260	0.18
Hmong (1,316)	1,355	0.93
Indian (291)	385	0.26
Indonesian (6)	11	0.01
Japanese (30)	84	0.06
Korean (122)	188	0.13
Laotian (424)	468	0.32
Malaysian (10)	10	0.01
Nepalese (33)	36	0.02
Pakistani (18)	24	0.02
Sri Lankan (2)	2	<0.01
Taiwanese (14)	17	0.01
Thai (49)	66	0.05
Vietnamese (192)	253	0.17
Hawaii Native/Pacific Islander (157)	332	0.23
Not Hispanic (136)	240	0.16
Hispanic (21)	92	0.06
Fijian (1)	1	<0.01
Guamanian/Chamorro (31)	61	0.04
Marshallese (0)	2	<0.01
Native Hawaiian (27)	81	0.06

*Notes: † The Census 2010 population figure is used to calculate the percentages in the Hispanic Origin and Race categories. Ancestry percentages are based on the 2006-2010 American Community Survey population (not shown); ‡ Numbers in parentheses indicate the number of people reporting a single ancestry; * Numbers in parentheses indicate the number of persons reporting this race alone, not in combination with any other race; Please refer to the Explanation of Data for more information.*

Samoan (9)	19	0.01
Tongan (0)	2	<0.01
White (76,034)	80,518	55.23
Not Hispanic (58,655)	61,386	42.11
Hispanic (17,379)	19,132	13.12

Lansing

Place Type: City
County: Leavenworth
Population: 11,265†

Ancestry‡	Population	%
African, Sub-Saharan (277)	362	3.30
African (242)	327	2.98
Ghanaian (5)	5	0.05
Other Sub-Saharan African (30)	30	0.27
American (608)	608	5.55
Arab (13)	13	0.12
Egyptian (3)	3	0.03
Moroccan (10)	10	0.09
Armenian (8)	8	0.07
Belgian (0)	37	0.34
British (57)	83	0.76
Canadian (29)	29	0.26
Croatian (0)	116	1.06
Czech (0)	26	0.24
Czechoslovakian (58)	66	0.60
Danish (0)	10	0.09
Dutch (29)	386	3.52
Eastern European (0)	17	0.16
English (443)	814	7.43
European (29)	118	1.08
French, ex. Basque (46)	526	4.80
French Canadian (43)	162	1.48
German (852)	2,879	26.27
Greek (0)	4	0.04
Hungarian (0)	20	0.18
Irish (623)	2,238	20.42
Italian (101)	507	4.63
Lithuanian (0)	69	0.63
Norwegian (6)	118	1.08
Polish (140)	345	3.15
Scandinavian (0)	9	0.08
Scotch-Irish (99)	283	2.58
Scottish (26)	99	0.90
Swedish (0)	151	1.38
Swiss (9)	106	0.97
Welsh (42)	66	0.60
West Indian, ex. Hispanic (0)	9	0.08
Jamaican (0)	9	0.08

Hispanic Origin	Population	%
Hispanic or Latino (of any race)	578	5.13
Central American, ex. Mexican	27	0.24
Guatemalan	3	0.03
Honduran	4	0.04
Nicaraguan	5	0.04
Panamanian	13	0.12
Salvadoran	2	0.02
Cuban	25	0.22
Dominican Republic	4	0.04
Mexican	328	2.91
Puerto Rican	76	0.67
South American	14	0.12
Chilean	2	0.02
Colombian	6	0.05
Ecuadorian	4	0.04
Peruvian	2	0.02
Other Hispanic or Latino	104	0.92

Race*	Population	%
African-American/Black (1,492)	1,623	14.41
Not Hispanic (1,465)	1,573	13.96
Hispanic (27)	50	0.44
American Indian/Alaska Native (91)	179	1.59
Not Hispanic (81)	154	1.37
Hispanic (10)	25	0.22
Apache (2)	6	0.05
Blackfeet (3)	7	0.06
Cherokee (14)	40	0.36
Cheyenne (0)	1	0.01
Chippewa (4)	5	0.04
Choctaw (5)	11	0.10
Creek (1)	2	0.02
Delaware (0)	2	0.02
Houma (1)	1	0.01
Iroquois (2)	4	0.04
Mexican American Ind. (2)	5	0.04
Navajo (1)	4	0.04
Potawatomi (1)	3	0.03
Seminole (0)	1	0.01
Sioux (2)	3	0.03
South American Ind. (1)	1	0.01
Ute (0)	3	0.03
Asian (223)	339	3.01
Not Hispanic (223)	328	2.91
Hispanic (0)	11	0.10
Cambodian (1)	1	0.01
Chinese, ex. Taiwanese (24)	42	0.37
Filipino (24)	54	0.48
Indian (51)	55	0.49
Japanese (29)	40	0.36
Korean (63)	111	0.99
Pakistani (1)	2	0.02
Thai (0)	3	0.03
Vietnamese (9)	13	0.12
Hawaii Native/Pacific Islander (13)	48	0.43
Not Hispanic (12)	39	0.35
Hispanic (1)	9	0.08
Guamanian/Chamorro (5)	21	0.19
Native Hawaiian (7)	16	0.14
Samoan (1)	5	0.04
White (9,040)	9,326	82.79
Not Hispanic (8,631)	8,870	78.74
Hispanic (409)	456	4.05

Lawrence

Place Type: City
County: Douglas
Population: 87,643†

Ancestry‡	Population	%
African, Sub-Saharan (415)	621	0.72
African (317)	494	0.57
Kenyan (64)	64	0.07
Senegalese (34)	34	0.04
Other Sub-Saharan African (0)	29	0.03
American (2,779)	2,779	3.22
Arab (374)	498	0.58
Arab (179)	179	0.21
Egyptian (23)	40	0.05
Lebanese (99)	128	0.15
Syrian (11)	23	0.03
Other Arab (62)	128	0.15
Armenian (14)	61	0.07
Australian (25)	54	0.06
Austrian (106)	234	0.27
Belgian (30)	139	0.16
Brazilian (14)	35	0.04
British (294)	638	0.74
Bulgarian (0)	8	0.01
Cajun (34)	42	0.05
Canadian (23)	78	0.09
Celtic (44)	57	0.07
Croatian (51)	153	0.18
Czech (101)	931	1.08
Czechoslovakian (60)	87	0.10
Danish (167)	677	0.78
Dutch (434)	1,699	1.97
Eastern European (80)	141	0.16
English (2,554)	10,711	12.39
European (2,118)	2,565	2.97
Finnish (73)	135	0.16
French, ex. Basque (459)	3,227	3.73
French Canadian (119)	202	0.23
German (9,083)	26,767	30.97
German Russian (8)	16	0.02
Greek (85)	282	0.33
Hungarian (88)	398	0.46
Icelander (0)	25	0.03
Iranian (157)	195	0.23
Irish (3,098)	13,680	15.83
Israeli (23)	35	0.04
Italian (934)	2,674	3.09
Lithuanian (21)	100	0.12
Luxemburger (13)	76	0.09
Northern European (199)	224	0.26
Norwegian (306)	1,239	1.43
Pennsylvania German (13)	33	0.04
Polish (335)	1,821	2.11
Portuguese (37)	125	0.14
Romanian (28)	50	0.06
Russian (328)	1,183	1.37
Scandinavian (43)	182	0.21
Scotch-Irish (820)	2,040	2.36
Scottish (487)	2,700	3.12
Serbian (10)	28	0.03
Slavic (28)	118	0.14
Slovak (27)	174	0.20
Slovene (0)	6	0.01
Swedish (690)	2,703	3.13
Swiss (151)	597	0.69
Turkish (39)	75	0.09
Ukrainian (38)	90	0.10
Welsh (200)	960	1.11
West Indian, ex. Hispanic (19)	28	0.03
Barbadian (0)	8	0.01
Jamaican (19)	19	0.02
West Indian (0)	1	<0.01
Yugoslavian (14)	59	0.07

Hispanic Origin	Population	%
Hispanic or Latino (of any race)	5,006	5.71
Central American, ex. Mexican	234	0.27
Costa Rican	46	0.05
Guatemalan	32	0.04
Honduran	37	0.04
Nicaraguan	16	0.02
Panamanian	52	0.06
Salvadoran	50	0.06
Other Central American	1	<0.01
Cuban	125	0.14
Dominican Republic	30	0.03
Mexican	3,545	4.04
Puerto Rican	249	0.28
South American	387	0.44
Argentinean	30	0.03
Bolivian	36	0.04
Chilean	27	0.03
Colombian	70	0.08
Ecuadorian	35	0.04
Paraguayan	29	0.03
Peruvian	77	0.09
Uruguayan	20	0.02
Venezuelan	59	0.07
Other South American	4	<0.01
Other Hispanic or Latino	436	0.50

Race*	Population	%
African-American/Black (4,095)	5,573	6.36
Not Hispanic (3,948)	5,274	6.02
Hispanic (147)	299	0.34
American Indian/Alaska Native (2,700)	4,036	4.61
Not Hispanic (2,425)	3,562	4.06
Hispanic (275)	474	0.54
Alaska Athabascan *(Ala. Nat.)* (4)	8	0.01
Aleut *(Alaska Native)* (7)	11	0.01
Apache (56)	73	0.08
Arapaho (41)	44	0.05
Blackfeet (3)	34	0.04
Canadian/French Am. Ind. (1)	2	<0.01
Central American Ind. (0)	4	<0.01
Cherokee (201)	474	0.54
Cheyenne (29)	37	0.04
Chickasaw (14)	36	0.04
Chippewa (46)	87	0.10
Choctaw (116)	217	0.25
Colville (1)	1	<0.01

*Notes: † The Census 2010 population figure is used to calculate the percentages in the Hispanic Origin and Race categories. Ancestry percentages are based on the 2006-2010 American Community Survey population (not shown); ‡ Numbers in parentheses indicate the number of people reporting a single ancestry; * Numbers in parentheses indicate the number of persons reporting this race alone, not in combination with any other race; Please refer to the Explanation of Data for more information.*

	Population	%
Comanche (27)	39	0.04
Cree (4)	5	0.01
Creek (102)	197	0.22
Crow (34)	38	0.04
Delaware (24)	35	0.04
Hopi (11)	14	0.02
Inupiat *(Alaska Native)* (7)	14	0.02
Iroquois (30)	52	0.06
Kiowa (43)	56	0.06
Lumbee (0)	1	<0.01
Menominee (23)	28	0.03
Mexican American Ind. (24)	44	0.05
Navajo (266)	336	0.38
Osage (29)	43	0.05
Ottawa (2)	8	0.01
Paiute (13)	25	0.03
Pima (18)	19	0.02
Potawatomi (122)	179	0.20
Pueblo (30)	36	0.04
Puget Sound Salish (5)	11	0.01
Seminole (43)	81	0.09
Shoshone (11)	17	0.02
Sioux (216)	284	0.32
South American Ind. (6)	15	0.02
Spanish American Ind. (1)	5	0.01
Tlingit-Haida *(Alaska Native)* (9)	13	0.01
Tohono O'Odham (5)	6	0.01
Tsimshian *(Alaska Native)* (0)	1	<0.01
Ute (19)	21	0.02
Yakama (13)	14	0.02
Yaqui (2)	3	<0.01
Yuman (18)	18	0.02
Yup'ik *(Alaska Native)* (1)	6	0.01
Asian (3,971)	4,932	5.63
Not Hispanic (3,941)	4,849	5.53
Hispanic (30)	83	0.09
Bangladeshi (20)	22	0.03
Bhutanese (4)	4	<0.01
Burmese (35)	45	0.05
Cambodian (9)	16	0.02
Chinese, ex. Taiwanese (1,338)	1,515	1.73
Filipino (173)	349	0.40
Hmong (9)	10	0.01
Indian (700)	797	0.91
Indonesian (22)	46	0.05
Japanese (187)	369	0.42
Korean (511)	643	0.73
Laotian (220)	269	0.31
Malaysian (24)	30	0.03
Nepalese (27)	30	0.03
Pakistani (55)	70	0.08
Sri Lankan (40)	40	0.05
Taiwanese (87)	114	0.13
Thai (45)	76	0.09
Vietnamese (301)	367	0.42
Hawaii Native/Pacific Islander (57)	169	0.19
Not Hispanic (51)	149	0.17
Hispanic (6)	20	0.02
Guamanian/Chamorro (9)	19	0.02
Native Hawaiian (21)	62	0.07
Samoan (15)	18	0.02
Tongan (3)	4	<0.01
White (71,872)	75,105	85.69
Not Hispanic (69,114)	71,857	81.99
Hispanic (2,758)	3,248	3.71

Leavenworth

Place Type: City
County: Leavenworth
Population: 35,251†

Ancestry‡	Population	%
African, Sub-Saharan (786)	1,080	3.07
African (777)	1,071	3.04
Kenyan (9)	9	0.03
American (2,478)	2,478	7.04
Arab (116)	116	0.33
Moroccan (20)	20	0.06
Palestinian (96)	96	0.27
Austrian (19)	96	0.27
Belgian (25)	43	0.12
Brazilian (4)	4	0.01
British (119)	127	0.36
Cajun (14)	34	0.10
Canadian (12)	30	0.09
Croatian (9)	68	0.19
Czech (78)	211	0.60
Czechoslovakian (0)	24	0.07
Danish (27)	179	0.51
Dutch (92)	579	1.65
English (782)	3,053	8.68
Estonian (28)	28	0.08
European (636)	781	2.22
Finnish (58)	105	0.30
French, ex. Basque (145)	1,158	3.29
French Canadian (138)	377	1.07
German (2,413)	8,430	23.97
German Russian (14)	14	0.04
Greek (34)	52	0.15
Hungarian (21)	105	0.30
Irish (1,079)	5,482	15.59
Italian (211)	1,417	4.03
Lithuanian (17)	25	0.07
Luxemburger (5)	5	0.01
Northern European (36)	36	0.10
Norwegian (60)	400	1.14
Polish (115)	962	2.73
Portuguese (27)	36	0.10
Russian (39)	163	0.46
Scandinavian (38)	45	0.13
Scotch-Irish (194)	750	2.13
Scottish (94)	875	2.49
Slavic (0)	30	0.09
Slovak (13)	13	0.04
Swedish (119)	569	1.62
Swiss (18)	369	1.05
Ukrainian (8)	35	0.10
Welsh (72)	291	0.83
West Indian, ex. Hispanic (20)	71	0.20
Dutch West Indian (0)	15	0.04
Haitian (9)	9	0.03
Jamaican (11)	47	0.13

Hispanic Origin	Population	%
Hispanic or Latino (of any race)	2,867	8.13
Central American, ex. Mexican	125	0.35
Costa Rican	8	0.02
Guatemalan	13	0.04
Honduran	33	0.09
Nicaraguan	7	0.02
Panamanian	44	0.12
Salvadoran	20	0.06
Cuban	46	0.13
Dominican Republic	35	0.10
Mexican	1,891	5.36
Puerto Rican	403	1.14
South American	105	0.30
Argentinean	10	0.03
Bolivian	5	0.01
Chilean	18	0.05
Colombian	39	0.11
Ecuadorian	18	0.05
Paraguayan	6	0.02
Peruvian	9	0.03
Other Hispanic or Latino	262	0.74

Race*	Population	%
African-American/Black (5,338)	6,177	17.52
Not Hispanic (5,215)	5,931	16.83
Hispanic (123)	246	0.70
American Indian/Alaska Native (304)	698	1.98
Not Hispanic (267)	615	1.74
Hispanic (37)	83	0.24
Aleut *(Alaska Native)* (0)	1	<0.01
Apache (6)	23	0.07
Arapaho (1)	1	<0.01
Blackfeet (0)	16	0.05
Central American Ind. (0)	1	<0.01
Cherokee (53)	202	0.57
Cheyenne (2)	3	0.01
Chickasaw (1)	1	<0.01
Chippewa (10)	10	0.03
Choctaw (7)	21	0.06
Colville (1)	1	<0.01
Comanche (0)	7	0.02
Cree (3)	6	0.02
Creek (1)	5	0.01
Crow (3)	3	0.01
Delaware (1)	5	0.01
Hopi (1)	1	<0.01
Inupiat *(Alaska Native)* (3)	8	0.02
Iroquois (1)	7	0.02
Kiowa (1)	1	<0.01
Lumbee (7)	8	0.02
Menominee (1)	1	<0.01
Mexican American Ind. (4)	6	0.02
Navajo (13)	16	0.05
Osage (6)	13	0.04
Pima (3)	3	0.01
Potawatomi (8)	11	0.03
Pueblo (1)	1	<0.01
Seminole (1)	6	0.02
Sioux (33)	42	0.12
South American Ind. (0)	8	0.02
Yaqui (2)	6	0.02
Asian (622)	1,048	2.97
Not Hispanic (612)	999	2.83
Hispanic (10)	49	0.14
Burmese (1)	1	<0.01
Cambodian (4)	4	0.01
Chinese, ex. Taiwanese (57)	101	0.29
Filipino (120)	244	0.69
Hmong (1)	4	0.01
Indian (55)	80	0.23
Indonesian (5)	12	0.03
Japanese (35)	107	0.30
Korean (241)	365	1.04
Laotian (4)	4	0.01
Nepalese (7)	9	0.03
Pakistani (10)	10	0.03
Sri Lankan (3)	3	0.01
Taiwanese (3)	5	0.01
Thai (23)	31	0.09
Vietnamese (26)	40	0.11
Hawaii Native/Pacific Islander (76)	175	0.50
Not Hispanic (73)	161	0.46
Hispanic (3)	14	0.04
Guamanian/Chamorro (15)	28	0.08
Marshallese (3)	3	0.01
Native Hawaiian (33)	76	0.22
Samoan (21)	43	0.12
White (26,574)	27,953	79.30
Not Hispanic (24,872)	26,007	73.78
Hispanic (1,702)	1,946	5.52

Leawood

Place Type: City
County: Johnson
Population: 31,867†

Ancestry‡	Population	%
African, Sub-Saharan (95)	95	0.30
South African (95)	95	0.30
American (1,319)	1,319	4.21
Arab (30)	123	0.39
Egyptian (11)	32	0.10
Lebanese (9)	70	0.22
Syrian (0)	11	0.04
Other Arab (10)	10	0.03
Armenian (0)	23	0.07
Assyrian/Chaldean/Syriac (13)	13	0.04
Austrian (61)	225	0.72
Belgian (21)	42	0.13
British (223)	396	1.26
Cajun (13)	13	0.04
Canadian (29)	47	0.15
Celtic (12)	12	0.04
Croatian (43)	155	0.49

*Notes: † The Census 2010 population figure is used to calculate the percentages in the Hispanic Origin and Race categories. Ancestry percentages are based on the 2006-2010 American Community Survey population (not shown); ‡ Numbers in parentheses indicate the number of people reporting a single ancestry; * Numbers in parentheses indicate the number of persons reporting this race alone, not in combination with any other race; Please refer to the Explanation of Data for more information.*

SECTION TWO

Ancestry	Population	%
Czech (69)	266	0.85
Czechoslovakian (11)	11	0.04
Danish (140)	373	1.19
Dutch (87)	404	1.29
Eastern European (255)	291	0.93
English (1,549)	5,214	16.65
European (462)	470	1.50
Finnish (19)	57	0.18
French, ex. Basque (148)	1,228	3.92
French Canadian (104)	183	0.58
German (2,618)	9,860	31.48
Greek (62)	178	0.57
Hungarian (37)	124	0.40
Iranian (178)	187	0.60
Irish (1,502)	6,014	19.20
Italian (973)	1,923	6.14
Latvian (24)	24	0.08
Lithuanian (34)	105	0.34
Luxemburger (0)	13	0.04
Northern European (88)	88	0.28
Norwegian (255)	784	2.50
Polish (349)	1,103	3.52
Romanian (42)	42	0.13
Russian (566)	974	3.11
Scandinavian (22)	53	0.17
Scotch-Irish (321)	799	2.55
Scottish (377)	1,212	3.87
Serbian (27)	68	0.22
Slavic (59)	121	0.39
Slovak (22)	27	0.09
Slovene (0)	34	0.11
Swedish (239)	1,064	3.40
Swiss (34)	180	0.57
Turkish (21)	21	0.07
Ukrainian (96)	121	0.39
Welsh (36)	306	0.98

Hispanic Origin	Population	%
Hispanic or Latino (of any race)	687	2.16
Central American, ex. Mexican	59	0.19
Costa Rican	8	0.03
Guatemalan	19	0.06
Honduran	11	0.03
Nicaraguan	1	<0.01
Panamanian	9	0.03
Salvadoran	10	0.03
Other Central American	1	<0.01
Cuban	37	0.12
Dominican Republic	10	0.03
Mexican	381	1.20
Puerto Rican	43	0.13
South American	98	0.31
Argentinean	7	0.02
Bolivian	1	<0.01
Chilean	4	0.01
Colombian	29	0.09
Ecuadorian	7	0.02
Peruvian	32	0.10
Venezuelan	18	0.06
Other Hispanic or Latino	59	0.19

Race*	Population	%
African-American/Black (613)	715	2.24
Not Hispanic (603)	697	2.19
Hispanic (10)	18	0.06
American Indian/Alaska Native (40)	153	0.48
Not Hispanic (37)	141	0.44
Hispanic (3)	12	0.04
Central American Ind. (1)	1	<0.01
Cherokee (11)	51	0.16
Chickasaw (1)	1	<0.01
Chippewa (0)	1	<0.01
Choctaw (1)	4	0.01
Creek (3)	6	0.02
Delaware (3)	7	0.02
Houma (0)	3	0.01
Iroquois (4)	5	0.02
Menominee (0)	1	<0.01
Mexican American Ind. (1)	2	0.01
Navajo (0)	5	0.02
Osage (2)	3	0.01
Potawatomi (0)	1	<0.01
Sioux (1)	2	0.01
South American Ind. (0)	1	<0.01
Asian (1,209)	1,439	4.52
Not Hispanic (1,203)	1,427	4.48
Hispanic (6)	12	0.04
Burmese (4)	4	0.01
Cambodian (4)	4	0.01
Chinese, ex. Taiwanese (285)	322	1.01
Filipino (73)	103	0.32
Indian (493)	547	1.72
Indonesian (3)	3	0.01
Japanese (26)	58	0.18
Korean (110)	142	0.45
Malaysian (4)	5	0.02
Nepalese (1)	2	0.01
Pakistani (68)	81	0.25
Sri Lankan (5)	6	0.02
Taiwanese (15)	15	0.05
Thai (18)	26	0.08
Vietnamese (54)	66	0.21
Hawaii Native/Pacific Islander (12)	26	0.08
Not Hispanic (11)	23	0.07
Hispanic (1)	3	0.01
Guamanian/Chamorro (4)	6	0.02
Native Hawaiian (3)	7	0.02
Samoan (1)	2	0.01
White (29,409)	29,843	93.65
Not Hispanic (28,861)	29,259	91.82
Hispanic (548)	584	1.83

Lenexa

Place Type: City
County: Johnson
Population: 48,190†

Ancestry‡	Population	%
African, Sub-Saharan (465)	485	1.03
African (299)	299	0.63
Ethiopian (105)	105	0.22
Kenyan (40)	40	0.08
Nigerian (10)	10	0.02
South African (0)	20	0.04
Other Sub-Saharan African (11)	11	0.02
American (2,310)	2,310	4.91
Arab (50)	151	0.32
Arab (0)	14	0.03
Lebanese (50)	82	0.17
Syrian (0)	55	0.12
Armenian (28)	81	0.17
Austrian (14)	88	0.19
Belgian (69)	303	0.64
British (101)	433	0.92
Cajun (34)	47	0.10
Canadian (48)	274	0.58
Croatian (187)	343	0.73
Czech (91)	554	1.18
Czechoslovakian (36)	88	0.19
Danish (92)	366	0.78
Dutch (227)	847	1.80
Eastern European (95)	112	0.24
English (1,819)	6,713	14.26
European (673)	819	1.74
Finnish (30)	95	0.20
French, ex. Basque (281)	2,041	4.33
French Canadian (63)	237	0.50
German (4,339)	14,295	30.36
German Russian (0)	23	0.05
Greek (110)	183	0.39
Hungarian (32)	124	0.26
Iranian (0)	56	0.12
Irish (1,968)	7,218	15.33
Italian (550)	1,882	4.00
Latvian (0)	11	0.02
Lithuanian (9)	9	0.02
Luxemburger (0)	9	0.02
Macedonian (0)	42	0.09
New Zealander (0)	10	0.02
Northern European (45)	45	0.10
Norwegian (263)	780	1.66
Pennsylvania German (0)	63	0.13
Polish (289)	940	2.00
Portuguese (9)	86	0.18
Romanian (52)	73	0.16
Russian (390)	761	1.62
Scandinavian (14)	31	0.07
Scotch-Irish (617)	1,244	2.64
Scottish (326)	1,107	2.35
Serbian (0)	23	0.05
Slavic (0)	17	0.04
Slovak (49)	113	0.24
Slovene (8)	148	0.31
Swedish (479)	1,414	3.00
Swiss (60)	262	0.56
Turkish (21)	41	0.09
Ukrainian (49)	73	0.16
Welsh (82)	528	1.12
West Indian, ex. Hispanic (9)	9	0.02
Haitian (9)	9	0.02
Yugoslavian (0)	12	0.03

Hispanic Origin	Population	%
Hispanic or Latino (of any race)	3,510	7.28
Central American, ex. Mexican	305	0.63
Costa Rican	13	0.03
Guatemalan	129	0.27
Honduran	79	0.16
Nicaraguan	5	0.01
Panamanian	20	0.04
Salvadoran	58	0.12
Other Central American	1	<0.01
Cuban	57	0.12
Dominican Republic	11	0.02
Mexican	2,575	5.34
Puerto Rican	122	0.25
South American	211	0.44
Argentinean	25	0.05
Bolivian	9	0.02
Chilean	9	0.02
Colombian	74	0.15
Ecuadorian	17	0.04
Paraguayan	1	<0.01
Peruvian	57	0.12
Venezuelan	19	0.04
Other Hispanic or Latino	229	0.48

Race*	Population	%
African-American/Black (2,809)	3,291	6.83
Not Hispanic (2,748)	3,178	6.59
Hispanic (61)	113	0.23
American Indian/Alaska Native (177)	490	1.02
Not Hispanic (146)	417	0.87
Hispanic (31)	73	0.15
Apache (8)	18	0.04
Blackfeet (2)	13	0.03
Canadian/French Am. Ind. (0)	1	<0.01
Central American Ind. (1)	1	<0.01
Cherokee (39)	155	0.32
Chickasaw (1)	2	<0.01
Chippewa (6)	7	0.01
Choctaw (10)	26	0.05
Comanche (1)	2	<0.01
Creek (4)	7	0.01
Delaware (0)	1	<0.01
Inupiat *(Alaska Native)* (2)	5	0.01
Iroquois (1)	8	0.02
Mexican American Ind. (11)	13	0.03
Navajo (3)	4	0.01
Osage (4)	6	0.01
Ottawa (1)	1	<0.01
Potawatomi (8)	16	0.03
Pueblo (3)	3	0.01
Seminole (1)	3	0.01
Sioux (5)	19	0.04
Tlingit-Haida *(Alaska Native)* (0)	4	0.01
Tohono O'Odham (1)	1	<0.01
Tsimshian *(Alaska Native)* (3)	7	0.01
Yakama (1)	1	<0.01

*Notes: † The Census 2010 population figure is used to calculate the percentages in the Hispanic Origin and Race categories. Ancestry percentages are based on the 2006-2010 American Community Survey population (not shown); ‡ Numbers in parentheses indicate the number of people reporting a single ancestry; * Numbers in parentheses indicate the number of persons reporting this race alone, not in combination with any other race; Please refer to the Explanation of Data for more information.*

Yup'ik *(Alaska Native)* (0)	3	0.01
Asian (1,810)	2,184	4.53
Not Hispanic (1,805)	2,159	4.48
Hispanic (5)	25	0.05
Bangladeshi (7)	7	0.01
Burmese (3)	3	0.01
Cambodian (11)	16	0.03
Chinese, ex. Taiwanese (280)	335	0.70
Filipino (157)	245	0.51
Hmong (10)	10	0.02
Indian (643)	691	1.43
Indonesian (8)	8	0.02
Japanese (41)	111	0.23
Korean (183)	223	0.46
Laotian (48)	64	0.13
Malaysian (9)	11	0.02
Nepalese (39)	41	0.09
Pakistani (53)	75	0.16
Sri Lankan (3)	3	0.01
Taiwanese (22)	27	0.06
Thai (14)	27	0.06
Vietnamese (196)	234	0.49
Hawaii Native/Pacific Islander (42)	102	0.21
Not Hispanic (37)	77	0.16
Hispanic (5)	25	0.05
Fijian (1)	2	<0.01
Guamanian/Chamorro (18)	26	0.05
Native Hawaiian (8)	25	0.05
Samoan (3)	9	0.02
White (40,692)	41,775	86.69
Not Hispanic (38,837)	39,694	82.37
Hispanic (1,855)	2,081	4.32

Liberal

Place Type: City
County: Seward
Population: 20,525[†]

Ancestry[‡]	Population	%
American (706)	706	3.48
Arab (0)	22	0.11
Lebanese (0)	10	0.05
Other Arab (0)	12	0.06
Austrian (0)	31	0.15
Brazilian (45)	45	0.22
British (0)	39	0.19
Canadian (44)	44	0.22
Czech (0)	62	0.31
Czechoslovakian (0)	7	0.03
Danish (0)	28	0.14
Dutch (24)	196	0.97
English (352)	1,036	5.10
European (11)	18	0.09
French, ex. Basque (7)	291	1.43
French Canadian (0)	9	0.04
German (1,126)	2,315	11.40
Irish (264)	1,069	5.26
Italian (28)	107	0.53
Norwegian (24)	50	0.25
Pennsylvania German (5)	15	0.07
Polish (6)	17	0.08
Portuguese (80)	80	0.39
Russian (35)	50	0.25
Scotch-Irish (14)	232	1.14
Scottish (33)	139	0.68
Slovak (0)	8	0.04
Swedish (47)	155	0.76
Swiss (18)	18	0.09
Turkish (0)	17	0.08
Welsh (0)	11	0.05

Hispanic Origin	Population	%
Hispanic or Latino (of any race)	12,044	58.68
Central American, ex. Mexican	1,019	4.96
Costa Rican	2	0.01
Guatemalan	781	3.81
Honduran	68	0.33
Nicaraguan	50	0.24
Panamanian	1	<0.01
Salvadoran	108	0.53
Other Central American	9	0.04
Cuban	55	0.27
Dominican Republic	11	0.05
Mexican	10,454	50.93
Puerto Rican	47	0.23
South American	15	0.07
Argentinean	4	0.02
Colombian	5	0.02
Ecuadorian	1	<0.01
Paraguayan	2	0.01
Peruvian	1	<0.01
Venezuelan	2	0.01
Other Hispanic or Latino	443	2.16

Race*	Population	%
African-American/Black (759)	918	4.47
Not Hispanic (675)	790	3.85
Hispanic (84)	128	0.62
American Indian/Alaska Native (162)	349	1.70
Not Hispanic (64)	195	0.95
Hispanic (98)	154	0.75
Aleut *(Alaska Native)* (0)	1	<0.01
Apache (0)	5	0.02
Blackfeet (0)	2	0.01
Central American Ind. (2)	8	0.04
Cherokee (14)	63	0.31
Cheyenne (0)	3	0.01
Chickasaw (0)	3	0.01
Choctaw (8)	17	0.08
Comanche (0)	3	0.01
Cree (1)	2	0.01
Delaware (1)	2	0.01
Hopi (1)	1	<0.01
Iroquois (0)	2	0.01
Menominee (0)	2	0.01
Mexican American Ind. (34)	39	0.19
Navajo (4)	5	0.02
Osage (0)	2	0.01
Ottawa (1)	6	0.03
Paiute (2)	2	0.01
Potawatomi (5)	10	0.05
Pueblo (0)	8	0.04
South American Ind. (1)	2	0.01
Asian (595)	672	3.27
Not Hispanic (578)	637	3.10
Hispanic (17)	35	0.17
Cambodian (20)	21	0.10
Chinese, ex. Taiwanese (33)	35	0.17
Filipino (30)	35	0.17
Indian (42)	61	0.30
Japanese (5)	11	0.05
Korean (5)	8	0.04
Laotian (83)	95	0.46
Malaysian (0)	1	<0.01
Pakistani (2)	3	0.01
Thai (0)	1	<0.01
Vietnamese (341)	376	1.83
Hawaii Native/Pacific Islander (43)	50	0.24
Not Hispanic (31)	34	0.17
Hispanic (12)	16	0.08
Guamanian/Chamorro (27)	32	0.16
Native Hawaiian (3)	4	0.02
Samoan (12)	12	0.06
White (14,086)	14,656	71.41
Not Hispanic (6,834)	7,087	34.53
Hispanic (7,252)	7,569	36.88

Manhattan

Place Type: City
County: Riley
Population: 52,281[†]

Ancestry[‡]	Population	%
African, Sub-Saharan (544)	567	1.12
African (324)	347	0.69
Ethiopian (75)	75	0.15
Ghanaian (14)	14	0.03
Nigerian (22)	22	0.04
Sudanese (10)	10	0.02
Ugandan (39)	39	0.08
Other Sub-Saharan African (60)	60	0.12
American (1,688)	1,688	3.34
Arab (152)	168	0.33
Egyptian (79)	79	0.16
Lebanese (0)	16	0.03
Other Arab (73)	73	0.14
Australian (14)	14	0.03
Austrian (0)	82	0.16
Belgian (26)	45	0.09
Brazilian (17)	56	0.11
British (77)	255	0.50
Cajun (12)	12	0.02
Canadian (22)	35	0.07
Croatian (19)	42	0.08
Czech (144)	493	0.97
Czechoslovakian (7)	35	0.07
Danish (172)	472	0.93
Dutch (100)	884	1.75
Eastern European (45)	45	0.09
English (2,298)	5,423	10.72
European (564)	602	1.19
Finnish (14)	64	0.13
French, ex. Basque (448)	1,716	3.39
French Canadian (54)	134	0.26
German (12,438)	20,725	40.95
Greek (46)	126	0.25
Hungarian (70)	79	0.16
Iranian (0)	11	0.02
Irish (2,606)	6,959	13.75
Italian (465)	1,174	2.32
Lithuanian (34)	61	0.12
Maltese (0)	6	0.01
Norwegian (364)	735	1.45
Pennsylvania German (0)	32	0.06
Polish (399)	893	1.76
Portuguese (29)	124	0.25
Romanian (28)	94	0.19
Russian (141)	418	0.83
Scandinavian (15)	51	0.10
Scotch-Irish (389)	880	1.74
Scottish (714)	1,422	2.81
Serbian (23)	23	0.05
Slavic (0)	25	0.05
Slovak (13)	45	0.09
Slovene (11)	11	0.02
Swedish (511)	1,621	3.20
Swiss (78)	222	0.44
Ukrainian (39)	39	0.08
Welsh (52)	416	0.82
West Indian, ex. Hispanic (74)	130	0.26
Belizean (0)	12	0.02
Haitian (43)	43	0.08
Trinidadian/Tobagonian (31)	67	0.13
West Indian (0)	8	0.02
Yugoslavian (12)	12	0.02

Hispanic Origin	Population	%
Hispanic or Latino (of any race)	3,053	5.84
Central American, ex. Mexican	186	0.36
Costa Rican	17	0.03
Guatemalan	32	0.06
Honduran	25	0.05
Nicaraguan	16	0.03
Panamanian	59	0.11
Salvadoran	37	0.07
Cuban	46	0.09
Dominican Republic	29	0.06
Mexican	1,954	3.74
Puerto Rican	350	0.67
South American	206	0.39
Argentinean	19	0.04
Bolivian	9	0.02
Chilean	8	0.02
Colombian	81	0.15
Ecuadorian	14	0.03
Paraguayan	21	0.04
Peruvian	37	0.07
Venezuelan	15	0.03

*Notes: † The Census 2010 population figure is used to calculate the percentages in the Hispanic Origin and Race categories. Ancestry percentages are based on the 2006-2010 American Community Survey population (not shown); ‡ Numbers in parentheses indicate the number of people reporting a single ancestry; * Numbers in parentheses indicate the number of persons reporting this race alone, not in combination with any other race; Please refer to the Explanation of Data for more information.*

Other South American	2	<0.01
Other Hispanic or Latino	282	0.54

Race*	Population	%
African-American/Black (2,886)	3,672	7.02
Not Hispanic (2,770)	3,469	6.64
Hispanic (116)	203	0.39
American Indian/Alaska Native (261)	677	1.29
Not Hispanic (212)	571	1.09
Hispanic (49)	106	0.20
Aleut *(Alaska Native)* (0)	1	<0.01
Apache (2)	7	0.01
Arapaho (1)	1	<0.01
Blackfeet (1)	9	0.02
Cherokee (40)	153	0.29
Cheyenne (0)	1	<0.01
Chickasaw (4)	8	0.02
Chippewa (3)	3	0.01
Choctaw (9)	34	0.07
Comanche (3)	5	0.01
Cree (0)	1	<0.01
Creek (9)	26	0.05
Crow (1)	6	0.01
Delaware (1)	2	<0.01
Inupiat *(Alaska Native)* (0)	1	<0.01
Iroquois (0)	4	0.01
Kiowa (1)	2	<0.01
Lumbee (6)	7	0.01
Mexican American Ind. (8)	14	0.03
Navajo (11)	22	0.04
Osage (8)	14	0.03
Ottawa (3)	3	0.01
Paiute (0)	1	<0.01
Potawatomi (32)	60	0.11
Pueblo (2)	3	0.01
Puget Sound Salish (1)	1	<0.01
Seminole (1)	5	0.01
Sioux (7)	20	0.04
South American Ind. (6)	6	0.01
Tohono O'Odham (0)	3	0.01
Yaqui (1)	1	<0.01
Yuman (3)	3	0.01
Asian (2,689)	3,304	6.32
Not Hispanic (2,669)	3,249	6.21
Hispanic (20)	55	0.11
Bangladeshi (21)	23	0.04
Burmese (2)	2	<0.01
Cambodian (12)	17	0.03
Chinese, ex. Taiwanese (1,146)	1,213	2.32
Filipino (176)	286	0.55
Hmong (8)	8	0.02
Indian (473)	520	0.99
Indonesian (6)	13	0.02
Japanese (103)	191	0.37
Korean (348)	492	0.94
Laotian (9)	12	0.02
Malaysian (9)	11	0.02
Nepalese (70)	77	0.15
Pakistani (30)	37	0.07
Sri Lankan (39)	39	0.07
Taiwanese (50)	59	0.11
Thai (38)	58	0.11
Vietnamese (83)	126	0.24
Hawaii Native/Pacific Islander (83)	162	0.31
Not Hispanic (81)	152	0.29
Hispanic (2)	10	0.02
Fijian (0)	1	<0.01
Guamanian/Chamorro (35)	42	0.08
Marshallese (2)	2	<0.01
Native Hawaiian (13)	42	0.08
Samoan (25)	47	0.09
Tongan (1)	4	0.01
White (43,645)	45,280	86.61
Not Hispanic (41,914)	43,299	82.82
Hispanic (1,731)	1,981	3.79

McPherson

Place Type: City
County: McPherson
Population: 13,155†

Ancestry‡	Population	%
American (974)	974	7.34
Arab (11)	11	0.08
Lebanese (11)	11	0.08
Austrian (30)	43	0.32
Belgian (15)	46	0.35
British (3)	25	0.19
Cajun (8)	8	0.06
Canadian (0)	15	0.11
Croatian (0)	40	0.30
Czech (44)	169	1.27
Czechoslovakian (11)	24	0.18
Danish (0)	70	0.53
Dutch (37)	344	2.59
English (535)	1,772	13.36
European (143)	299	2.25
Finnish (0)	10	0.08
French, ex. Basque (55)	255	1.92
French Canadian (39)	52	0.39
German (2,630)	5,303	39.98
German Russian (0)	60	0.45
Greek (17)	17	0.13
Irish (157)	1,324	9.98
Italian (59)	185	1.39
Norwegian (81)	195	1.47
Pennsylvania German (27)	27	0.20
Polish (30)	165	1.24
Russian (38)	205	1.55
Scotch-Irish (63)	247	1.86
Scottish (93)	398	3.00
Swedish (359)	854	6.44
Swiss (29)	220	1.66
Ukrainian (30)	30	0.23
Welsh (37)	133	1.00

Hispanic Origin	Population	%
Hispanic or Latino (of any race)	634	4.82
Central American, ex. Mexican	34	0.26
Guatemalan	25	0.19
Salvadoran	9	0.07
Cuban	5	0.04
Dominican Republic	1	0.01
Mexican	448	3.41
Puerto Rican	27	0.21
South American	12	0.09
Argentinean	2	0.02
Bolivian	1	0.01
Chilean	3	0.02
Colombian	2	0.02
Paraguayan	1	0.01
Peruvian	1	0.01
Other South American	2	0.02
Other Hispanic or Latino	107	0.81

Race*	Population	%
African-American/Black (201)	320	2.43
Not Hispanic (195)	310	2.36
Hispanic (6)	10	0.08
American Indian/Alaska Native (55)	153	1.16
Not Hispanic (44)	135	1.03
Hispanic (11)	18	0.14
Apache (0)	1	0.01
Blackfeet (0)	5	0.04
Canadian/French Am. Ind. (0)	1	0.01
Cherokee (13)	37	0.28
Cheyenne (1)	6	0.05
Chickasaw (2)	3	0.02
Chippewa (1)	5	0.04
Choctaw (4)	7	0.05
Comanche (1)	1	0.01
Creek (1)	2	0.02
Delaware (1)	3	0.02
Iroquois (0)	1	0.01
Mexican American Ind. (3)	3	0.02
Navajo (3)	4	0.03
Potawatomi (2)	9	0.07
Sioux (7)	13	0.10
South American Ind. (0)	1	0.01
Asian (105)	145	1.10
Not Hispanic (103)	137	1.04
Hispanic (2)	8	0.06
Chinese, ex. Taiwanese (6)	9	0.07
Filipino (23)	44	0.33
Indian (30)	30	0.23
Japanese (3)	6	0.05
Korean (12)	19	0.14
Laotian (0)	2	0.02
Pakistani (2)	2	0.02
Sri Lankan (5)	5	0.04
Vietnamese (21)	23	0.17
Hawaii Native/Pacific Islander (14)	25	0.19
Not Hispanic (13)	20	0.15
Hispanic (1)	5	0.04
Guamanian/Chamorro (5)	10	0.08
Native Hawaiian (4)	9	0.07
Samoan (4)	4	0.03
White (12,265)	12,540	95.32
Not Hispanic (11,919)	12,150	92.36
Hispanic (346)	390	2.96

Merriam

Place Type: City
County: Johnson
Population: 11,003†

Ancestry‡	Population	%
African, Sub-Saharan (84)	115	1.04
African (84)	115	1.04
American (407)	407	3.66
Arab (55)	55	0.50
Arab (55)	55	0.50
Armenian (0)	7	0.06
Austrian (0)	12	0.11
Basque (11)	11	0.10
Belgian (36)	62	0.56
British (63)	114	1.03
Canadian (0)	11	0.10
Croatian (15)	69	0.62
Czech (28)	51	0.46
Czechoslovakian (0)	9	0.08
Danish (14)	32	0.29
Dutch (0)	163	1.47
Eastern European (10)	10	0.09
English (386)	1,387	12.49
European (151)	151	1.36
Finnish (0)	52	0.47
French, ex. Basque (44)	357	3.21
French Canadian (41)	132	1.19
German (968)	2,974	26.78
Hungarian (11)	41	0.37
Irish (560)	1,904	17.14
Italian (26)	267	2.40
Norwegian (12)	247	2.22
Polish (81)	361	3.25
Russian (11)	65	0.59
Scandinavian (0)	10	0.09
Scotch-Irish (175)	279	2.51
Scottish (86)	258	2.32
Slavic (9)	22	0.20
Slovene (11)	11	0.10
Swedish (149)	337	3.03
Swiss (18)	58	0.52
Welsh (25)	118	1.06
Yugoslavian (0)	28	0.25

Hispanic Origin	Population	%
Hispanic or Latino (of any race)	1,176	10.69
Central American, ex. Mexican	82	0.75
Costa Rican	2	0.02
Guatemalan	37	0.34
Honduran	16	0.15
Nicaraguan	2	0.02
Panamanian	6	0.05

*Notes: † The Census 2010 population figure is used to calculate the percentages in the Hispanic Origin and Race categories. Ancestry percentages are based on the 2006-2010 American Community Survey population (not shown); ‡ Numbers in parentheses indicate the number of people reporting a single ancestry; * Numbers in parentheses indicate the number of persons reporting this race alone, not in combination with any other race; Please refer to the Explanation of Data for more information.*

Salvadoran	19	0.17
Cuban	7	0.06
Dominican Republic	2	0.02
Mexican	904	8.22
Puerto Rican	29	0.26
South American	42	0.38
Argentinean	3	0.03
Bolivian	3	0.03
Chilean	1	0.01
Colombian	14	0.13
Ecuadorian	8	0.07
Peruvian	6	0.05
Uruguayan	4	0.04
Venezuelan	3	0.03
Other Hispanic or Latino	110	1.00

Race*	Population	%
African-American/Black (666)	780	7.09
Not Hispanic (655)	747	6.79
Hispanic (11)	33	0.30
American Indian/Alaska Native (51)	184	1.67
Not Hispanic (30)	131	1.19
Hispanic (21)	53	0.48
Apache (0)	1	0.01
Arapaho (0)	2	0.02
Blackfeet (0)	3	0.03
Central American Ind. (0)	3	0.03
Cherokee (12)	56	0.51
Cheyenne (5)	5	0.05
Chippewa (0)	1	0.01
Choctaw (1)	8	0.07
Creek (0)	2	0.02
Delaware (0)	1	0.01
Iroquois (0)	5	0.05
Kiowa (0)	1	0.01
Mexican American Ind. (3)	19	0.17
Navajo (1)	5	0.05
Osage (0)	1	0.01
Potawatomi (4)	6	0.05
Seminole (0)	2	0.02
Sioux (1)	3	0.03
South American Ind. (0)	2	0.02
Asian (282)	369	3.35
Not Hispanic (280)	363	3.30
Hispanic (2)	6	0.05
Chinese, ex. Taiwanese (51)	68	0.62
Filipino (16)	42	0.38
Hmong (18)	26	0.24
Indian (50)	52	0.47
Japanese (14)	30	0.27
Korean (30)	44	0.40
Laotian (40)	46	0.42
Pakistani (3)	3	0.03
Sri Lankan (4)	5	0.05
Taiwanese (3)	5	0.05
Thai (6)	6	0.05
Vietnamese (39)	46	0.42
Hawaii Native/Pacific Islander (6)	22	0.20
Not Hispanic (4)	19	0.17
Hispanic (2)	3	0.03
Guamanian/Chamorro (3)	5	0.05
Native Hawaiian (1)	7	0.06
Tongan (1)	2	0.02
White (9,172)	9,531	86.62
Not Hispanic (8,590)	8,822	80.18
Hispanic (582)	709	6.44

Mission

Place Type: City
County: Johnson
Population: 9,323†

Ancestry‡	Population	%
African, Sub-Saharan (0)	97	1.02
African (0)	82	0.86
South African (0)	15	0.16
American (386)	386	4.07
Arab (12)	12	0.13
Arab (12)	12	0.13
Austrian (27)	112	1.18
Belgian (0)	14	0.15
Brazilian (51)	51	0.54
Canadian (15)	30	0.32
Croatian (28)	68	0.72
Czech (0)	41	0.43
Danish (7)	65	0.69
Dutch (12)	89	0.94
English (297)	1,503	15.85
European (261)	276	2.91
French, ex. Basque (47)	268	2.83
French Canadian (0)	13	0.14
German (982)	2,823	29.77
Greek (12)	12	0.13
Guyanese (22)	22	0.23
Hungarian (0)	55	0.58
Irish (375)	1,760	18.56
Israeli (0)	43	0.45
Italian (53)	377	3.98
Latvian (11)	23	0.24
Lithuanian (0)	14	0.15
Northern European (12)	12	0.13
Norwegian (112)	163	1.72
Polish (129)	283	2.98
Portuguese (0)	16	0.17
Russian (0)	50	0.53
Scandinavian (0)	13	0.14
Scotch-Irish (220)	488	5.15
Scottish (45)	139	1.47
Swedish (45)	279	2.94
Swiss (14)	92	0.97
Welsh (0)	87	0.92

Hispanic Origin	Population	%
Hispanic or Latino (of any race)	767	8.23
Central American, ex. Mexican	43	0.46
Costa Rican	1	0.01
Guatemalan	20	0.21
Honduran	7	0.08
Nicaraguan	5	0.05
Panamanian	7	0.08
Salvadoran	3	0.03
Cuban	10	0.11
Mexican	602	6.46
Puerto Rican	24	0.26
South American	42	0.45
Argentinean	2	0.02
Chilean	1	0.01
Colombian	8	0.09
Ecuadorian	8	0.09
Paraguayan	2	0.02
Peruvian	16	0.17
Venezuelan	3	0.03
Other South American	2	0.02
Other Hispanic or Latino	46	0.49

Race*	Population	%
African-American/Black (512)	603	6.47
Not Hispanic (490)	579	6.21
Hispanic (22)	24	0.26
American Indian/Alaska Native (35)	126	1.35
Not Hispanic (33)	113	1.21
Hispanic (2)	13	0.14
Apache (0)	7	0.08
Blackfeet (1)	3	0.03
Canadian/French Am. Ind. (0)	1	0.01
Cherokee (7)	30	0.32
Chickasaw (0)	1	0.01
Choctaw (2)	13	0.14
Cree (0)	1	0.01
Creek (2)	2	0.02
Delaware (1)	5	0.05
Iroquois (0)	1	0.01
Mexican American Ind. (0)	1	0.01
Navajo (4)	7	0.08
Potawatomi (4)	7	0.08
Pueblo (0)	2	0.02
Seminole (1)	1	0.01
Sioux (1)	2	0.02
Asian (367)	452	4.85
Not Hispanic (363)	440	4.72
Hispanic (4)	12	0.13
Bangladeshi (7)	7	0.08
Burmese (0)	1	0.01
Cambodian (1)	1	0.01
Chinese, ex. Taiwanese (21)	32	0.34
Filipino (19)	32	0.34
Hmong (4)	5	0.05
Indian (184)	192	2.06
Japanese (13)	27	0.29
Korean (45)	60	0.64
Laotian (3)	8	0.09
Pakistani (34)	34	0.36
Taiwanese (2)	2	0.02
Thai (10)	12	0.13
Vietnamese (21)	28	0.30
Hawaii Native/Pacific Islander (2)	6	0.06
Not Hispanic (2)	6	0.06
Native Hawaiian (2)	4	0.04
White (7,883)	8,138	87.29
Not Hispanic (7,440)	7,635	81.89
Hispanic (443)	503	5.40

Newton

Place Type: City
County: Harvey
Population: 19,132†

Ancestry‡	Population	%
Afghan (0)	24	0.13
African, Sub-Saharan (37)	56	0.30
African (13)	21	0.11
Ethiopian (13)	24	0.13
Other Sub-Saharan African (11)	11	0.06
American (1,233)	1,233	6.57
Austrian (0)	11	0.06
Belgian (20)	20	0.11
Brazilian (0)	11	0.06
British (0)	18	0.10
Canadian (26)	73	0.39
Croatian (0)	12	0.06
Czech (11)	31	0.17
Czechoslovakian (8)	19	0.10
Danish (22)	62	0.33
Dutch (121)	688	3.67
English (696)	1,918	10.22
European (326)	339	1.81
Finnish (42)	50	0.27
French, ex. Basque (113)	632	3.37
French Canadian (11)	34	0.18
German (3,124)	6,082	32.40
German Russian (0)	9	0.05
Hungarian (0)	16	0.09
Irish (555)	2,287	12.18
Italian (66)	97	0.52
Latvian (13)	13	0.07
Norwegian (26)	67	0.36
Pennsylvania German (28)	53	0.28
Polish (57)	166	0.88
Russian (33)	270	1.44
Scandinavian (53)	100	0.53
Scotch-Irish (64)	374	1.99
Scottish (124)	304	1.62
Swedish (86)	452	2.41
Swiss (101)	222	1.18
Ukrainian (12)	22	0.12
Welsh (0)	140	0.75
West Indian, ex. Hispanic (40)	40	0.21
Haitian (40)	40	0.21
Yugoslavian (31)	31	0.17

Hispanic Origin	Population	%
Hispanic or Latino (of any race)	3,116	16.29
Central American, ex. Mexican	107	0.56
Costa Rican	3	0.02
Guatemalan	9	0.05
Honduran	63	0.33
Nicaraguan	3	0.02
Panamanian	1	0.01

SECTION TWO

*Notes: † The Census 2010 population figure is used to calculate the percentages in the Hispanic Origin and Race categories. Ancestry percentages are based on the 2006-2010 American Community Survey population (not shown); ‡ Numbers in parentheses indicate the number of people reporting a single ancestry; * Numbers in parentheses indicate the number of persons reporting this race alone, not in combination with any other race; Please refer to the Explanation of Data for more information.*

Salvadoran	26	0.14
Other Central American	2	0.01
Cuban	31	0.16
Dominican Republic	1	0.01
Mexican	2,785	14.56
Puerto Rican	31	0.16
South American	17	0.09
Argentinean	3	0.02
Bolivian	1	0.01
Colombian	6	0.03
Ecuadorian	4	0.02
Peruvian	3	0.02
Other Hispanic or Latino	144	0.75

Race*	Population	%
African-American/Black (427)	660	3.45
Not Hispanic (399)	588	3.07
Hispanic (28)	72	0.38
American Indian/Alaska Native (168)	382	2.00
Not Hispanic (119)	296	1.55
Hispanic (49)	86	0.45
Aleut *(Alaska Native)* (1)	3	0.02
Apache (5)	18	0.09
Blackfeet (2)	5	0.03
Cherokee (29)	92	0.48
Cheyenne (3)	3	0.02
Chickasaw (1)	4	0.02
Chippewa (7)	14	0.07
Choctaw (6)	21	0.11
Comanche (0)	4	0.02
Creek (1)	3	0.02
Delaware (5)	10	0.05
Iroquois (2)	4	0.02
Mexican American Ind. (13)	20	0.10
Navajo (2)	6	0.03
Osage (1)	1	0.01
Potawatomi (7)	9	0.05
Pueblo (3)	3	0.02
Seminole (1)	1	0.01
Shoshone (0)	1	0.01
Sioux (2)	3	0.02
Asian (146)	204	1.07
Not Hispanic (144)	198	1.03
Hispanic (2)	6	0.03
Cambodian (1)	1	0.01
Chinese, ex. Taiwanese (34)	49	0.26
Filipino (19)	34	0.18
Indian (17)	28	0.15
Indonesian (3)	3	0.02
Japanese (3)	13	0.07
Korean (11)	16	0.08
Laotian (2)	4	0.02
Pakistani (1)	1	0.01
Sri Lankan (0)	1	0.01
Thai (2)	2	0.01
Vietnamese (48)	62	0.32
Hawaii Native/Pacific Islander (8)	20	0.10
Not Hispanic (8)	14	0.07
Hispanic (0)	6	0.03
Guamanian/Chamorro (2)	3	0.02
Marshallese (1)	2	0.01
Native Hawaiian (1)	5	0.03
Samoan (3)	5	0.03
White (16,912)	17,443	91.17
Not Hispanic (14,938)	15,315	80.05
Hispanic (1,974)	2,128	11.12

Olathe

Place Type: City
County: Johnson
Population: 125,872†

Ancestry‡	Population	%
Afghan (13)	13	0.01
African, Sub-Saharan (1,632)	1,749	1.45
African (532)	559	0.46
Ethiopian (325)	325	0.27
Kenyan (335)	388	0.32
Nigerian (77)	88	0.07
Sierra Leonean (10)	10	0.01
Somalian (123)	123	0.10
Sudanese (133)	133	0.11
Zimbabwean (74)	74	0.06
Other Sub-Saharan African (23)	49	0.04
American (6,701)	6,701	5.55
Arab (94)	342	0.28
Egyptian (25)	64	0.05
Jordanian (10)	15	0.01
Lebanese (0)	166	0.14
Syrian (49)	77	0.06
Other Arab (10)	20	0.02
Armenian (0)	24	0.02
Australian (10)	62	0.05
Austrian (40)	371	0.31
Belgian (209)	659	0.55
Brazilian (53)	114	0.09
British (342)	566	0.47
Cajun (0)	10	0.01
Canadian (151)	238	0.20
Croatian (115)	268	0.22
Czech (335)	1,119	0.93
Czechoslovakian (105)	127	0.11
Danish (186)	645	0.53
Dutch (450)	3,129	2.59
Eastern European (40)	40	0.03
English (4,150)	14,439	11.96
European (2,047)	2,267	1.88
Finnish (34)	87	0.07
French, ex. Basque (700)	3,571	2.96
French Canadian (238)	642	0.53
German (12,905)	37,323	30.90
German Russian (70)	127	0.11
Greek (152)	411	0.34
Guyanese (0)	10	0.01
Hungarian (18)	197	0.16
Icelander (20)	67	0.06
Iranian (29)	47	0.04
Irish (4,010)	18,267	15.12
Italian (1,263)	4,795	3.97
Latvian (32)	32	0.03
Lithuanian (109)	220	0.18
Luxemburger (0)	9	0.01
Northern European (155)	155	0.13
Norwegian (696)	2,377	1.97
Pennsylvania German (46)	86	0.07
Polish (561)	2,507	2.08
Portuguese (66)	151	0.13
Romanian (50)	79	0.07
Russian (227)	695	0.58
Scandinavian (109)	287	0.24
Scotch-Irish (1,158)	2,838	2.35
Scottish (993)	3,104	2.57
Serbian (20)	36	0.03
Slavic (20)	84	0.07
Slovak (32)	118	0.10
Slovene (9)	136	0.11
Swedish (799)	3,130	2.59
Swiss (157)	674	0.56
Ukrainian (251)	305	0.25
Welsh (290)	1,225	1.01
West Indian, ex. Hispanic (154)	171	0.14
British West Indian (36)	36	0.03
Dutch West Indian (0)	17	0.01
Haitian (109)	109	0.09
Trinidadian/Tobagonian (9)	9	0.01
Yugoslavian (0)	59	0.05

Hispanic Origin	Population	%
Hispanic or Latino (of any race)	12,794	10.16
Central American, ex. Mexican	689	0.55
Costa Rican	44	0.03
Guatemalan	161	0.13
Honduran	255	0.20
Nicaraguan	19	0.02
Panamanian	42	0.03
Salvadoran	162	0.13
Other Central American	6	<0.01
Cuban	143	0.11
Dominican Republic	76	0.06
Mexican	9,995	7.94
Puerto Rican	441	0.35
South American	536	0.43
Argentinean	53	0.04
Bolivian	28	0.02
Chilean	21	0.02
Colombian	166	0.13
Ecuadorian	56	0.04
Paraguayan	9	0.01
Peruvian	115	0.09
Uruguayan	9	0.01
Venezuelan	75	0.06
Other South American	4	<0.01
Other Hispanic or Latino	914	0.73

Race*	Population	%
African-American/Black (6,703)	8,323	6.61
Not Hispanic (6,474)	7,888	6.27
Hispanic (229)	435	0.35
American Indian/Alaska Native (545)	1,352	1.07
Not Hispanic (436)	1,126	0.89
Hispanic (109)	226	0.18
Aleut *(Alaska Native)* (2)	2	<0.01
Apache (6)	19	0.02
Arapaho (5)	8	0.01
Blackfeet (4)	26	0.02
Canadian/French Am. Ind. (0)	1	<0.01
Cherokee (139)	397	0.32
Cheyenne (1)	3	<0.01
Chickasaw (6)	22	0.02
Chippewa (8)	19	0.02
Choctaw (22)	53	0.04
Comanche (4)	6	<0.01
Cree (0)	2	<0.01
Creek (11)	27	0.02
Crow (1)	4	<0.01
Delaware (7)	19	0.02
Hopi (0)	1	<0.01
Inupiat *(Alaska Native)* (1)	1	<0.01
Iroquois (7)	24	0.02
Kiowa (0)	1	<0.01
Lumbee (0)	5	<0.01
Mexican American Ind. (18)	28	0.02
Navajo (8)	21	0.02
Osage (11)	22	0.02
Ottawa (3)	5	<0.01
Potawatomi (14)	31	0.02
Pueblo (5)	10	0.01
Seminole (1)	15	0.01
Shoshone (2)	2	<0.01
Sioux (13)	34	0.03
South American Ind. (1)	10	0.01
Spanish American Ind. (1)	1	<0.01
Tlingit-Haida *(Alaska Native)* (1)	1	<0.01
Tohono O'Odham (1)	1	<0.01
Ute (0)	1	<0.01
Yup'ik *(Alaska Native)* (1)	1	<0.01
Asian (5,137)	6,197	4.92
Not Hispanic (5,100)	6,082	4.83
Hispanic (37)	115	0.09
Bangladeshi (16)	19	0.02
Burmese (4)	4	<0.01
Cambodian (21)	34	0.03
Chinese, ex. Taiwanese (865)	1,017	0.81
Filipino (393)	626	0.50
Hmong (31)	36	0.03
Indian (1,622)	1,737	1.38
Indonesian (33)	37	0.03
Japanese (88)	255	0.20
Korean (324)	495	0.39
Laotian (569)	633	0.50
Malaysian (26)	30	0.02
Nepalese (50)	51	0.04
Pakistani (190)	206	0.16
Sri Lankan (7)	8	0.01
Taiwanese (21)	33	0.03
Thai (75)	108	0.09
Vietnamese (542)	641	0.51
Hawaii Native/Pacific Islander (83)	207	0.16
Not Hispanic (77)	182	0.14

*Notes: † The Census 2010 population figure is used to calculate the percentages in the Hispanic Origin and Race categories. Ancestry percentages are based on the 2006-2010 American Community Survey population (not shown); ‡ Numbers in parentheses indicate the number of people reporting a single ancestry; * Numbers in parentheses indicate the number of persons reporting this race alone, not in combination with any other race; Please refer to the Explanation of Data for more information.*

Hispanic (6)	25	0.02
Fijian (1)	2	<0.01
Guamanian/Chamorro (14)	42	0.03
Marshallese (1)	2	<0.01
Native Hawaiian (14)	62	0.05
Samoan (12)	18	0.01
Tongan (1)	1	<0.01
White (104,559)	107,898	85.72
Not Hispanic (97,840)	100,468	79.82
Hispanic (6,719)	7,430	5.90

Ottawa

Place Type: City
County: Franklin
Population: 12,649†

Ancestry‡	Population	%
American (762)	762	6.07
Austrian (0)	58	0.46
British (73)	73	0.58
Canadian (0)	26	0.21
Czech (27)	63	0.50
Danish (32)	46	0.37
Dutch (59)	481	3.83
English (425)	1,314	10.47
European (167)	167	1.33
Finnish (17)	62	0.49
French, ex. Basque (80)	480	3.82
German (1,310)	4,219	33.61
German Russian (10)	21	0.17
Hungarian (0)	11	0.09
Irish (494)	2,147	17.10
Italian (72)	93	0.74
Lithuanian (13)	38	0.30
Northern European (8)	8	0.06
Norwegian (9)	133	1.06
Pennsylvania German (20)	20	0.16
Polish (16)	167	1.33
Russian (8)	203	1.62
Scotch-Irish (78)	206	1.64
Scottish (124)	451	3.59
Swedish (71)	428	3.41
Swiss (13)	20	0.16
Turkish (0)	7	0.06
Welsh (9)	153	1.22

Hispanic Origin	Population	%
Hispanic or Latino (of any race)	634	5.01
Central American, ex. Mexican	20	0.16
Guatemalan	2	0.02
Honduran	6	0.05
Nicaraguan	1	0.01
Panamanian	6	0.05
Salvadoran	5	0.04
Cuban	17	0.13
Dominican Republic	1	0.01
Mexican	538	4.25
Puerto Rican	20	0.16
South American	10	0.08
Argentinean	2	0.02
Colombian	4	0.03
Paraguayan	4	0.03
Other Hispanic or Latino	28	0.22

Race*	Population	%
African-American/Black (274)	447	3.53
Not Hispanic (272)	429	3.39
Hispanic (2)	18	0.14
American Indian/Alaska Native (120)	344	2.72
Not Hispanic (107)	281	2.22
Hispanic (13)	63	0.50
Apache (1)	10	0.08
Blackfeet (1)	6	0.05
Cherokee (29)	91	0.72
Cheyenne (1)	1	0.01
Chickasaw (1)	6	0.05
Chippewa (4)	9	0.07
Choctaw (3)	8	0.06
Creek (3)	18	0.14
Delaware (1)	4	0.03
Iroquois (3)	6	0.05
Kiowa (3)	3	0.02
Menominee (3)	3	0.02
Navajo (1)	5	0.04
Osage (0)	3	0.02
Ottawa (9)	9	0.07
Potawatomi (9)	14	0.11
Seminole (0)	2	0.02
Sioux (5)	9	0.07
Asian (49)	102	0.81
Not Hispanic (49)	87	0.69
Hispanic (0)	15	0.12
Chinese, ex. Taiwanese (15)	17	0.13
Filipino (14)	28	0.22
Indian (9)	16	0.13
Japanese (1)	16	0.13
Korean (4)	10	0.08
Laotian (3)	3	0.02
Vietnamese (2)	11	0.09
Hawaii Native/Pacific Islander (1)	10	0.08
Not Hispanic (1)	4	0.03
Hispanic (0)	6	0.05
Guamanian/Chamorro (0)	1	0.01
Native Hawaiian (1)	9	0.07
White (11,510)	11,972	94.65
Not Hispanic (11,217)	11,560	91.39
Hispanic (293)	412	3.26

Overland Park

Place Type: City
County: Johnson
Population: 173,372†

Ancestry‡	Population	%
Afghan (25)	25	0.01
African, Sub-Saharan (979)	1,268	0.74
African (623)	827	0.49
Ethiopian (37)	37	0.02
Kenyan (72)	112	0.07
Nigerian (13)	27	0.02
Somalian (15)	15	0.01
South African (10)	41	0.02
Other Sub-Saharan African (209)	209	0.12
Albanian (16)	16	0.01
Alsatian (15)	25	0.01
American (9,285)	9,285	5.45
Arab (1,001)	1,320	0.77
Arab (394)	394	0.23
Egyptian (210)	210	0.12
Jordanian (136)	284	0.17
Lebanese (86)	210	0.12
Palestinian (96)	96	0.06
Syrian (59)	59	0.03
Other Arab (20)	67	0.04
Armenian (28)	113	0.07
Assyrian/Chaldean/Syriac (0)	17	0.01
Australian (10)	26	0.02
Austrian (222)	622	0.36
Belgian (204)	575	0.34
Brazilian (96)	109	0.06
British (526)	1,191	0.70
Bulgarian (79)	147	0.09
Cajun (0)	84	0.05
Canadian (139)	292	0.17
Celtic (44)	59	0.03
Croatian (277)	1,131	0.66
Cypriot (11)	11	0.01
Czech (372)	1,736	1.02
Czechoslovakian (202)	318	0.19
Danish (243)	1,595	0.94
Dutch (774)	3,555	2.08
Eastern European (328)	343	0.20
English (6,159)	23,474	13.77
Estonian (0)	14	0.01
European (2,660)	2,886	1.69
Finnish (30)	177	0.10
French, ex. Basque (979)	6,763	3.97
French Canadian (255)	464	0.27
German (17,510)	51,466	30.18
German Russian (27)	27	0.02
Greek (249)	714	0.42
Guyanese (12)	12	0.01
Hungarian (130)	625	0.37
Icelander (11)	11	0.01
Iranian (495)	538	0.32
Irish (7,958)	28,990	17.00
Israeli (54)	62	0.04
Italian (2,431)	7,328	4.30
Latvian (13)	76	0.04
Lithuanian (78)	230	0.13
Luxemburger (37)	114	0.07
Macedonian (14)	14	0.01
New Zealander (13)	13	0.01
Northern European (341)	354	0.21
Norwegian (899)	3,202	1.88
Pennsylvania German (75)	129	0.08
Polish (1,280)	4,236	2.48
Portuguese (70)	261	0.15
Romanian (162)	269	0.16
Russian (1,299)	3,050	1.79
Scandinavian (213)	484	0.28
Scotch-Irish (1,278)	4,101	2.41
Scottish (1,361)	4,880	2.86
Serbian (55)	108	0.06
Slavic (54)	108	0.06
Slovak (73)	194	0.11
Slovene (72)	174	0.10
Swedish (1,177)	5,063	2.97
Swiss (181)	1,151	0.68
Turkish (73)	120	0.07
Ukrainian (714)	918	0.54
Welsh (393)	2,249	1.32
West Indian, ex. Hispanic (66)	141	0.08
Haitian (24)	24	0.01
Jamaican (42)	117	0.07
Yugoslavian (59)	70	0.04

Hispanic Origin	Population	%
Hispanic or Latino (of any race)	10,911	6.29
Central American, ex. Mexican	749	0.43
Costa Rican	33	0.02
Guatemalan	326	0.19
Honduran	156	0.09
Nicaraguan	11	0.01
Panamanian	50	0.03
Salvadoran	165	0.10
Other Central American	8	<0.01
Cuban	244	0.14
Dominican Republic	53	0.03
Mexican	7,682	4.43
Puerto Rican	390	0.22
South American	960	0.55
Argentinean	120	0.07
Bolivian	44	0.03
Chilean	49	0.03
Colombian	310	0.18
Ecuadorian	83	0.05
Paraguayan	27	0.02
Peruvian	197	0.11
Uruguayan	10	0.01
Venezuelan	99	0.06
Other South American	21	0.01
Other Hispanic or Latino	833	0.48

Race*	Population	%
African-American/Black (7,518)	9,131	5.27
Not Hispanic (7,357)	8,731	5.04
Hispanic (161)	400	0.23
American Indian/Alaska Native (570)	1,652	0.95
Not Hispanic (465)	1,377	0.79
Hispanic (105)	275	0.16
Aleut *(Alaska Native)* (2)	3	<0.01
Apache (8)	27	0.02
Arapaho (0)	1	<0.01
Blackfeet (3)	55	0.03
Canadian/French Am. Ind. (2)	5	<0.01
Central American Ind. (0)	3	<0.01
Cherokee (124)	455	0.26

*Notes: † The Census 2010 population figure is used to calculate the percentages in the Hispanic Origin and Race categories. Ancestry percentages are based on the 2006-2010 American Community Survey population (not shown); ‡ Numbers in parentheses indicate the number of people reporting a single ancestry; * Numbers in parentheses indicate the number of persons reporting this race alone, not in combination with any other race; Please refer to the Explanation of Data for more information.*

Cheyenne (1)	7	<0.01
Chickasaw (11)	22	0.01
Chippewa (16)	29	0.02
Choctaw (34)	102	0.06
Comanche (4)	13	0.01
Creek (19)	48	0.03
Crow (3)	10	0.01
Delaware (14)	33	0.02
Hopi (4)	5	<0.01
Houma (1)	5	<0.01
Inupiat *(Alaska Native)* (1)	1	<0.01
Iroquois (5)	13	0.01
Kiowa (3)	4	<0.01
Lumbee (3)	5	<0.01
Mexican American Ind. (28)	46	0.03
Navajo (4)	18	0.01
Osage (13)	37	0.02
Ottawa (3)	3	<0.01
Paiute (1)	1	<0.01
Potawatomi (34)	46	0.03
Pueblo (3)	5	<0.01
Puget Sound Salish (0)	1	<0.01
Seminole (6)	14	0.01
Shoshone (1)	6	<0.01
Sioux (23)	63	0.04
South American Ind. (6)	9	0.01
Yaqui (1)	4	<0.01
Asian (10,909)	12,359	7.13
Not Hispanic (10,846)	12,204	7.04
Hispanic (63)	155	0.09
Bangladeshi (73)	83	0.05
Bhutanese (13)	13	0.01
Burmese (18)	24	0.01
Cambodian (17)	26	0.01
Chinese, ex. Taiwanese (2,118)	2,350	1.36
Filipino (530)	836	0.48
Hmong (60)	61	0.04
Indian (4,781)	4,998	2.88
Indonesian (45)	64	0.04
Japanese (221)	397	0.23
Korean (1,061)	1,228	0.71
Laotian (103)	127	0.07
Malaysian (35)	50	0.03
Nepalese (72)	77	0.04
Pakistani (492)	535	0.31
Sri Lankan (40)	44	0.03
Taiwanese (203)	234	0.13
Thai (69)	115	0.07
Vietnamese (725)	843	0.49
Hawaii Native/Pacific Islander (83)	265	0.15
Not Hispanic (64)	214	0.12
Hispanic (19)	51	0.03
Fijian (1)	2	<0.01
Guamanian/Chamorro (25)	33	0.02
Native Hawaiian (17)	84	0.05
Samoan (10)	35	0.02
Tongan (1)	1	<0.01
White (146,304)	150,038	86.54
Not Hispanic (140,087)	143,091	82.53
Hispanic (6,217)	6,947	4.01

Parsons

Place Type: City
County: Labette
Population: 10,500†

Ancestry‡	Population	%
African, Sub-Saharan (0)	25	0.23
African (0)	25	0.23
American (993)	993	9.31
Austrian (0)	12	0.11
Belgian (9)	20	0.19
British (10)	10	0.09
Croatian (31)	31	0.29
Czech (19)	41	0.38
Danish (13)	13	0.12
Dutch (31)	237	2.22
English (354)	979	9.18
European (30)	30	0.28
French, ex. Basque (105)	351	3.29
German (1,011)	2,557	23.98
Hungarian (7)	81	0.76
Irish (415)	1,879	17.62
Italian (72)	318	2.98
Lithuanian (0)	13	0.12
Norwegian (24)	24	0.23
Polish (33)	185	1.74
Russian (9)	31	0.29
Scandinavian (0)	13	0.12
Scotch-Irish (75)	139	1.30
Scottish (45)	205	1.92
Swedish (74)	93	0.87
Swiss (0)	10	0.09
Welsh (7)	30	0.28
West Indian, ex. Hispanic (34)	34	0.32
Jamaican (34)	34	0.32

Hispanic Origin	Population	%
Hispanic or Latino (of any race)	597	5.69
Central American, ex. Mexican	13	0.12
Guatemalan	4	0.04
Honduran	2	0.02
Panamanian	5	0.05
Salvadoran	2	0.02
Cuban	7	0.07
Mexican	528	5.03
Puerto Rican	10	0.10
South American	2	0.02
Venezuelan	2	0.02
Other Hispanic or Latino	37	0.35

Race*	Population	%
African-American/Black (907)	1,179	11.23
Not Hispanic (895)	1,151	10.96
Hispanic (12)	28	0.27
American Indian/Alaska Native (142)	335	3.19
Not Hispanic (112)	280	2.67
Hispanic (30)	55	0.52
Apache (1)	7	0.07
Arapaho (7)	10	0.10
Blackfeet (2)	5	0.05
Canadian/French Am. Ind. (1)	1	0.01
Central American Ind. (1)	1	0.01
Cherokee (61)	144	1.37
Chickasaw (1)	1	0.01
Chippewa (2)	2	0.02
Choctaw (2)	24	0.23
Cree (1)	2	0.02
Creek (1)	3	0.03
Crow (0)	1	0.01
Delaware (10)	14	0.13
Inupiat *(Alaska Native)* (1)	1	0.01
Iroquois (1)	3	0.03
Lumbee (1)	1	0.01
Mexican American Ind. (10)	15	0.14
Pima (0)	3	0.03
Potawatomi (3)	4	0.04
Sioux (1)	3	0.03
Yakama (0)	2	0.02
Yuman (0)	3	0.03
Asian (65)	87	0.83
Not Hispanic (65)	82	0.78
Hispanic (0)	5	0.05
Chinese, ex. Taiwanese (10)	16	0.15
Filipino (11)	18	0.17
Indian (27)	33	0.31
Japanese (1)	3	0.03
Korean (1)	3	0.03
Sri Lankan (0)	2	0.02
Thai (3)	3	0.03
Vietnamese (7)	8	0.08
Hawaii Native/Pacific Islander (2)	6	0.06
Not Hispanic (2)	3	0.03
Hispanic (0)	3	0.03
Native Hawaiian (1)	1	0.01
Samoan (0)	3	0.03
Tongan (1)	1	0.01
White (8,848)	9,269	88.28
Not Hispanic (8,425)	8,797	83.78
Hispanic (423)	472	4.50

Pittsburg

Place Type: City
County: Crawford
Population: 20,233†

Ancestry‡	Population	%
African, Sub-Saharan (123)	123	0.61
African (123)	123	0.61
American (5,054)	5,054	25.19
Arab (66)	104	0.52
Lebanese (35)	62	0.31
Other Arab (31)	42	0.21
Armenian (42)	42	0.21
Australian (17)	17	0.08
Austrian (0)	50	0.25
Belgian (0)	83	0.41
Brazilian (12)	12	0.06
British (24)	41	0.20
Cajun (0)	12	0.06
Canadian (90)	90	0.45
Croatian (8)	24	0.12
Czech (11)	44	0.22
Czechoslovakian (9)	9	0.04
Danish (0)	28	0.14
Dutch (50)	446	2.22
English (604)	2,068	10.31
European (351)	362	1.80
Finnish (0)	7	0.03
French, ex. Basque (120)	590	2.94
French Canadian (39)	62	0.31
German (1,734)	3,926	19.57
Greek (8)	46	0.23
Hungarian (21)	21	0.10
Iranian (10)	10	0.05
Irish (421)	1,915	9.55
Italian (624)	1,152	5.74
Northern European (0)	18	0.09
Norwegian (17)	63	0.31
Polish (115)	207	1.03
Russian (11)	92	0.46
Scotch-Irish (325)	710	3.54
Scottish (153)	366	1.82
Slovak (0)	14	0.07
Swedish (18)	204	1.02
Swiss (0)	59	0.29
Welsh (74)	195	0.97
West Indian, ex. Hispanic (0)	15	0.07
Dutch West Indian (0)	15	0.07
Yugoslavian (57)	73	0.36

Hispanic Origin	Population	%
Hispanic or Latino (of any race)	1,350	6.67
Central American, ex. Mexican	192	0.95
Guatemalan	118	0.58
Honduran	5	0.02
Nicaraguan	4	0.02
Panamanian	1	<0.01
Salvadoran	64	0.32
Cuban	5	0.02
Dominican Republic	2	0.01
Mexican	937	4.63
Puerto Rican	41	0.20
South American	60	0.30
Argentinean	1	<0.01
Bolivian	3	0.01
Chilean	6	0.03
Colombian	10	0.05
Ecuadorian	3	0.01
Paraguayan	27	0.13
Peruvian	3	0.01
Venezuelan	6	0.03
Other South American	1	<0.01
Other Hispanic or Latino	113	0.56

Race*	Population	%
African-American/Black (662)	948	4.69
Not Hispanic (636)	910	4.50

*Notes: † The Census 2010 population figure is used to calculate the percentages in the Hispanic Origin and Race categories. Ancestry percentages are based on the 2006-2010 American Community Survey population (not shown); ‡ Numbers in parentheses indicate the number of people reporting a single ancestry; * Numbers in parentheses indicate the number of persons reporting this race alone, not in combination with any other race; Please refer to the Explanation of Data for more information.*

Hispanic (26)	38	0.19
American Indian/Alaska Native (173)	426	2.11
Not Hispanic (164)	397	1.96
Hispanic (9)	29	0.14
Apache (3)	11	0.05
Blackfeet (0)	10	0.05
Cherokee (52)	157	0.78
Chickasaw (2)	3	0.01
Chippewa (4)	4	0.02
Choctaw (11)	29	0.14
Comanche (0)	2	0.01
Creek (5)	8	0.04
Delaware (1)	2	0.01
Iroquois (6)	13	0.06
Lumbee (0)	1	<0.01
Menominee (1)	1	<0.01
Mexican American Ind. (3)	9	0.04
Navajo (1)	3	0.01
Osage (2)	3	0.01
Potawatomi (9)	17	0.08
Pueblo (1)	3	0.01
Seminole (0)	1	<0.01
Shoshone (1)	1	<0.01
Sioux (7)	10	0.05
Spanish American Ind. (0)	1	<0.01
Tlingit-Haida *(Alaska Native)* (1)	1	<0.01
Yup'ik *(Alaska Native)* (0)	5	0.02
Asian (412)	526	2.60
Not Hispanic (405)	505	2.50
Hispanic (7)	21	0.10
Chinese, ex. Taiwanese (174)	181	0.89
Filipino (23)	41	0.20
Hmong (2)	2	0.01
Indian (80)	89	0.44
Japanese (8)	21	0.10
Korean (48)	57	0.28
Laotian (1)	2	0.01
Malaysian (5)	7	0.03
Nepalese (1)	2	0.01
Pakistani (1)	1	<0.01
Sri Lankan (8)	8	0.04
Taiwanese (27)	28	0.14
Thai (21)	31	0.15
Vietnamese (5)	8	0.04
Hawaii Native/Pacific Islander (69)	107	0.53
Not Hispanic (61)	89	0.44
Hispanic (8)	18	0.09
Guamanian/Chamorro (11)	14	0.07
Marshallese (28)	34	0.17
Native Hawaiian (4)	11	0.05
Samoan (3)	9	0.04
White (17,621)	18,263	90.26
Not Hispanic (17,006)	17,571	86.84
Hispanic (615)	692	3.42

Prairie Village

Place Type: City
County: Johnson
Population: 21,447†

Ancestry‡	Population	%
Afghan (14)	14	0.06
African, Sub-Saharan (91)	91	0.42
African (30)	30	0.14
South African (61)	61	0.28
American (1,154)	1,154	5.31
Arab (9)	41	0.19
Lebanese (9)	30	0.14
Syrian (0)	11	0.05
Armenian (10)	78	0.36
Austrian (60)	114	0.52
Belgian (20)	74	0.34
British (70)	269	1.24
Canadian (12)	24	0.11
Celtic (0)	11	0.05
Croatian (51)	137	0.63
Czech (34)	241	1.11
Czechoslovakian (11)	43	0.20
Danish (127)	332	1.53
Dutch (81)	506	2.33
Eastern European (42)	54	0.25
English (1,207)	4,035	18.57
European (368)	420	1.93
Finnish (0)	10	0.05
French, ex. Basque (307)	743	3.42
French Canadian (40)	90	0.41
German (2,238)	6,442	29.65
Greek (0)	10	0.05
Hungarian (21)	92	0.42
Irish (1,182)	4,012	18.47
Italian (418)	1,120	5.15
Lithuanian (13)	41	0.19
Northern European (83)	83	0.38
Norwegian (96)	438	2.02
Polish (163)	593	2.73
Portuguese (0)	32	0.15
Romanian (0)	18	0.08
Russian (158)	394	1.81
Scandinavian (22)	38	0.17
Scotch-Irish (252)	757	3.48
Scottish (209)	844	3.88
Serbian (23)	23	0.11
Slovak (28)	40	0.18
Slovene (23)	51	0.23
Swedish (106)	613	2.82
Swiss (175)	537	2.47
Ukrainian (11)	11	0.05
Welsh (99)	521	2.40

Hispanic Origin	Population	%
Hispanic or Latino (of any race)	730	3.40
Central American, ex. Mexican	51	0.24
Costa Rican	6	0.03
Guatemalan	21	0.10
Honduran	6	0.03
Nicaraguan	2	0.01
Panamanian	3	0.01
Salvadoran	11	0.05
Other Central American	2	0.01
Cuban	31	0.14
Dominican Republic	1	<0.01
Mexican	477	2.22
Puerto Rican	38	0.18
South American	78	0.36
Argentinean	9	0.04
Bolivian	5	0.02
Chilean	10	0.05
Colombian	16	0.07
Ecuadorian	13	0.06
Peruvian	21	0.10
Venezuelan	4	0.02
Other Hispanic or Latino	54	0.25

Race*	Population	%
African-American/Black (214)	295	1.38
Not Hispanic (210)	279	1.30
Hispanic (4)	16	0.07
American Indian/Alaska Native (40)	140	0.65
Not Hispanic (38)	129	0.60
Hispanic (2)	11	0.05
Arapaho (1)	1	<0.01
Blackfeet (0)	4	0.02
Canadian/French Am. Ind. (1)	1	<0.01
Cherokee (11)	45	0.21
Cheyenne (0)	1	<0.01
Chickasaw (2)	3	0.01
Chippewa (1)	2	0.01
Choctaw (3)	11	0.05
Creek (2)	4	0.02
Delaware (0)	3	0.01
Iroquois (0)	1	<0.01
Kiowa (1)	1	<0.01
Menominee (0)	1	<0.01
Mexican American Ind. (1)	2	0.01
Osage (1)	1	<0.01
Paiute (0)	4	0.02
Potawatomi (4)	4	0.02
Sioux (0)	9	0.04
South American Ind. (0)	3	0.01
Asian (305)	453	2.11
Not Hispanic (303)	435	2.03
Hispanic (2)	18	0.08
Bangladeshi (4)	4	0.02
Chinese, ex. Taiwanese (114)	138	0.64
Filipino (35)	67	0.31
Hmong (1)	1	<0.01
Indian (49)	66	0.31
Indonesian (1)	3	0.01
Japanese (19)	50	0.23
Korean (34)	54	0.25
Laotian (1)	3	0.01
Malaysian (1)	1	<0.01
Pakistani (8)	11	0.05
Sri Lankan (1)	1	<0.01
Taiwanese (11)	11	0.05
Thai (4)	9	0.04
Vietnamese (14)	20	0.09
Hawaii Native/Pacific Islander (2)	16	0.07
Not Hispanic (2)	15	0.07
Hispanic (0)	1	<0.01
Guamanian/Chamorro (0)	1	<0.01
Native Hawaiian (1)	7	0.03
Samoan (1)	1	<0.01
White (20,435)	20,738	96.69
Not Hispanic (19,877)	20,139	93.90
Hispanic (558)	599	2.79

Salina

Place Type: City
County: Saline
Population: 47,707†

Ancestry‡	Population	%
African, Sub-Saharan (42)	103	0.22
African (0)	61	0.13
Kenyan (27)	27	0.06
Nigerian (15)	15	0.03
American (2,650)	2,650	5.62
Arab (0)	37	0.08
Lebanese (0)	21	0.04
Moroccan (0)	16	0.03
Austrian (25)	72	0.15
Basque (9)	9	0.02
Belgian (13)	29	0.06
British (22)	115	0.24
Canadian (42)	42	0.09
Croatian (64)	64	0.14
Czech (269)	670	1.42
Czechoslovakian (40)	57	0.12
Danish (204)	675	1.43
Dutch (280)	1,473	3.13
English (1,331)	4,066	8.63
European (435)	480	1.02
Finnish (33)	60	0.13
French, ex. Basque (404)	2,126	4.51
French Canadian (243)	360	0.76
German (7,774)	16,241	34.46
German Russian (27)	27	0.06
Greek (28)	72	0.15
Hungarian (0)	42	0.09
Irish (1,183)	5,319	11.29
Italian (206)	618	1.31
New Zealander (8)	8	0.02
Northern European (10)	10	0.02
Norwegian (215)	477	1.01
Pennsylvania German (30)	41	0.09
Polish (152)	850	1.80
Portuguese (0)	20	0.04
Russian (48)	456	0.97
Scandinavian (96)	110	0.23
Scotch-Irish (243)	849	1.80
Scottish (332)	999	2.12
Slovak (0)	25	0.05
Swedish (941)	2,326	4.94
Swiss (32)	71	0.15
Turkish (14)	14	0.03
Welsh (68)	263	0.56
West Indian, ex. Hispanic (0)	29	0.06

*Notes: † The Census 2010 population figure is used to calculate the percentages in the Hispanic Origin and Race categories. Ancestry percentages are based on the 2006-2010 American Community Survey population (not shown); ‡ Numbers in parentheses indicate the number of people reporting a single ancestry; * Numbers in parentheses indicate the number of persons reporting this race alone, not in combination with any other race; Please refer to the Explanation of Data for more information.*

Ancestry	Population	%
Haitian (0)	29	0.06
Yugoslavian (0)	17	0.04

Hispanic Origin	Population	%
Hispanic or Latino (of any race)	5,112	10.72
Central American, ex. Mexican	117	0.25
Costa Rican	1	<0.01
Guatemalan	14	0.03
Honduran	51	0.11
Nicaraguan	1	<0.01
Panamanian	18	0.04
Salvadoran	32	0.07
Cuban	43	0.09
Dominican Republic	7	0.01
Mexican	4,514	9.46
Puerto Rican	144	0.30
South American	49	0.10
Argentinean	10	0.02
Bolivian	1	<0.01
Chilean	2	<0.01
Colombian	14	0.03
Ecuadorian	3	0.01
Peruvian	7	0.01
Venezuelan	12	0.03
Other Hispanic or Latino	238	0.50

Race*	Population	%
African-American/Black (1,782)	2,611	5.47
Not Hispanic (1,714)	2,451	5.14
Hispanic (68)	160	0.34
American Indian/Alaska Native (261)	643	1.35
Not Hispanic (209)	522	1.09
Hispanic (52)	121	0.25
Alaska Athabascan *(Ala. Nat.)* (0)	2	<0.01
Apache (10)	20	0.04
Arapaho (1)	1	<0.01
Blackfeet (3)	15	0.03
Canadian/French Am. Ind. (0)	1	<0.01
Cherokee (49)	144	0.30
Cheyenne (2)	5	0.01
Chickasaw (2)	2	<0.01
Chippewa (2)	17	0.04
Choctaw (10)	25	0.05
Comanche (1)	8	0.02
Creek (1)	12	0.03
Crow (3)	5	0.01
Delaware (2)	2	<0.01
Iroquois (5)	10	0.02
Kiowa (1)	1	<0.01
Mexican American Ind. (7)	11	0.02
Navajo (7)	12	0.03
Osage (0)	1	<0.01
Ottawa (0)	3	0.01
Potawatomi (10)	20	0.04
Pueblo (1)	6	0.01
Seminole (0)	6	0.01
Sioux (12)	25	0.05
South American Ind. (0)	1	<0.01
Yakama (1)	1	<0.01
Yup'ik *(Alaska Native)* (1)	1	<0.01
Asian (1,095)	1,460	3.06
Not Hispanic (1,077)	1,402	2.94
Hispanic (18)	58	0.12
Cambodian (29)	40	0.08
Chinese, ex. Taiwanese (62)	100	0.21
Filipino (91)	169	0.35
Hmong (1)	1	<0.01
Indian (81)	105	0.22
Indonesian (3)	5	0.01
Japanese (36)	73	0.15
Korean (87)	160	0.34
Laotian (197)	239	0.50
Malaysian (0)	1	<0.01
Nepalese (1)	1	<0.01
Pakistani (7)	10	0.02
Taiwanese (7)	8	0.02
Thai (47)	88	0.18
Vietnamese (368)	432	0.91
Hawaii Native/Pacific Islander (24)	75	0.16
Not Hispanic (19)	63	0.13
Hispanic (5)	12	0.03
Guamanian/Chamorro (0)	4	0.01
Native Hawaiian (11)	29	0.06
Samoan (3)	9	0.02
Tongan (0)	3	0.01
White (41,116)	42,595	89.28
Not Hispanic (38,274)	39,470	82.73
Hispanic (2,842)	3,125	6.55

Shawnee

Place Type: City
County: Johnson
Population: 62,209†

Ancestry‡	Population	%
African, Sub-Saharan (575)	575	0.96
African (273)	273	0.45
Ethiopian (302)	302	0.50
American (4,585)	4,585	7.63
Arab (82)	115	0.19
Egyptian (41)	41	0.07
Iraqi (29)	29	0.05
Lebanese (12)	30	0.05
Syrian (0)	15	0.02
Australian (0)	12	0.02
Austrian (22)	176	0.29
Basque (0)	18	0.03
Belgian (202)	365	0.61
British (165)	347	0.58
Bulgarian (7)	7	0.01
Canadian (44)	105	0.17
Croatian (189)	404	0.67
Czech (174)	498	0.83
Czechoslovakian (94)	104	0.17
Danish (66)	573	0.95
Dutch (414)	1,227	2.04
Eastern European (0)	11	0.02
English (2,350)	7,322	12.19
European (870)	941	1.57
Finnish (10)	129	0.21
French, ex. Basque (358)	2,241	3.73
French Canadian (129)	281	0.47
German (6,430)	17,610	29.32
German Russian (13)	13	0.02
Greek (50)	147	0.24
Hungarian (71)	208	0.35
Icelander (107)	136	0.23
Irish (2,265)	9,344	15.56
Israeli (0)	12	0.02
Italian (755)	1,999	3.33
Lithuanian (0)	56	0.09
Northern European (73)	73	0.12
Norwegian (396)	816	1.36
Pennsylvania German (11)	11	0.02
Polish (294)	1,191	1.98
Portuguese (18)	82	0.14
Romanian (40)	40	0.07
Russian (107)	233	0.39
Scandinavian (59)	59	0.10
Scotch-Irish (401)	1,079	1.80
Scottish (367)	1,375	2.29
Serbian (34)	114	0.19
Slovak (32)	196	0.33
Slovene (14)	48	0.08
Swedish (398)	1,385	2.31
Swiss (27)	365	0.61
Ukrainian (26)	67	0.11
Welsh (95)	650	1.08
West Indian, ex. Hispanic (125)	222	0.37
Barbadian (30)	95	0.16
British West Indian (17)	17	0.03
Haitian (69)	69	0.11
Jamaican (9)	25	0.04
West Indian (0)	16	0.03
Yugoslavian (0)	11	0.02

Hispanic Origin	Population	%
Hispanic or Latino (of any race)	4,652	7.48
Central American, ex. Mexican	371	0.60
Costa Rican	9	0.01
Guatemalan	174	0.28
Honduran	70	0.11
Nicaraguan	3	<0.01
Panamanian	25	0.04
Salvadoran	82	0.13
Other Central American	8	0.01
Cuban	73	0.12
Dominican Republic	6	0.01
Mexican	3,505	5.63
Puerto Rican	145	0.23
South American	216	0.35
Argentinean	26	0.04
Bolivian	17	0.03
Chilean	4	0.01
Colombian	78	0.13
Ecuadorian	16	0.03
Paraguayan	3	<0.01
Peruvian	39	0.06
Venezuelan	32	0.05
Other South American	1	<0.01
Other Hispanic or Latino	336	0.54

Race*	Population	%
African-American/Black (3,294)	3,890	6.25
Not Hispanic (3,227)	3,766	6.05
Hispanic (67)	124	0.20
American Indian/Alaska Native (243)	717	1.15
Not Hispanic (186)	587	0.94
Hispanic (57)	130	0.21
Apache (3)	11	0.02
Blackfeet (5)	13	0.02
Canadian/French Am. Ind. (0)	1	<0.01
Cherokee (50)	198	0.32
Cheyenne (2)	2	<0.01
Chickasaw (8)	13	0.02
Chippewa (1)	5	0.01
Choctaw (11)	37	0.06
Colville (1)	1	<0.01
Comanche (0)	4	0.01
Creek (5)	12	0.02
Crow (2)	3	<0.01
Delaware (5)	14	0.02
Hopi (1)	1	<0.01
Iroquois (5)	16	0.03
Kiowa (3)	3	<0.01
Lumbee (1)	4	0.01
Mexican American Ind. (12)	49	0.08
Navajo (1)	5	0.01
Osage (5)	10	0.02
Ottawa (1)	1	<0.01
Potawatomi (5)	14	0.02
Pueblo (1)	1	<0.01
Seminole (1)	7	0.01
Sioux (8)	27	0.04
Spanish American Ind. (1)	1	<0.01
Tlingit-Haida *(Alaska Native)* (1)	5	0.01
Yaqui (0)	2	<0.01
Yup'ik *(Alaska Native)* (1)	3	<0.01
Asian (1,895)	2,411	3.88
Not Hispanic (1,876)	2,367	3.80
Hispanic (19)	44	0.07
Bangladeshi (6)	7	0.01
Burmese (1)	1	<0.01
Cambodian (9)	14	0.02
Chinese, ex. Taiwanese (245)	325	0.52
Filipino (161)	298	0.48
Hmong (25)	25	0.04
Indian (676)	755	1.21
Indonesian (6)	16	0.03
Japanese (36)	110	0.18
Korean (192)	265	0.43
Laotian (132)	165	0.27
Malaysian (9)	10	0.02
Nepalese (1)	1	<0.01
Pakistani (32)	35	0.06
Sri Lankan (1)	1	<0.01
Taiwanese (20)	22	0.04
Thai (23)	33	0.05
Vietnamese (228)	310	0.50

*Notes: † The Census 2010 population figure is used to calculate the percentages in the Hispanic Origin and Race categories. Ancestry percentages are based on the 2006-2010 American Community Survey population (not shown); ‡ Numbers in parentheses indicate the number of people reporting a single ancestry; * Numbers in parentheses indicate the number of persons reporting this race alone, not in combination with any other race; Please refer to the Explanation of Data for more information.*

Hawaii Native/Pacific Islander (51)	102	0.16
Not Hispanic (46)	96	0.15
Hispanic (5)	6	0.01
Fijian (2)	3	<0.01
Guamanian/Chamorro (7)	10	0.02
Marshallese (4)	5	0.01
Native Hawaiian (14)	34	0.05
Samoan (6)	17	0.03
Tongan (1)	1	<0.01
White (53,712)	55,139	88.64
Not Hispanic (50,862)	52,009	83.60
Hispanic (2,850)	3,130	5.03

Topeka

Place Type: City
County: Shawnee
Population: 127,473†

Ancestry‡	Population	%
African, Sub-Saharan (574)	775	0.61
African (529)	666	0.53
Ethiopian (26)	26	0.02
Nigerian (12)	62	0.05
Ugandan (0)	14	0.01
Other Sub-Saharan African (7)	7	0.01
American (7,382)	7,382	5.85
Arab (132)	199	0.16
Arab (10)	10	0.01
Egyptian (110)	143	0.11
Lebanese (12)	46	0.04
Armenian (0)	12	0.01
Australian (4)	14	0.01
Austrian (41)	148	0.12
Belgian (162)	265	0.21
Brazilian (44)	44	0.03
British (256)	493	0.39
Canadian (12)	91	0.07
Croatian (88)	97	0.08
Czech (246)	738	0.59
Czechoslovakian (57)	217	0.17
Danish (219)	755	0.60
Dutch (361)	2,729	2.16
Eastern European (12)	12	0.01
English (4,108)	12,778	10.13
European (876)	1,116	0.88
Finnish (11)	17	0.01
French, ex. Basque (540)	4,143	3.28
French Canadian (225)	542	0.43
German (13,969)	35,431	28.09
German Russian (211)	220	0.17
Greek (9)	47	0.04
Hungarian (64)	121	0.10
Icelander (0)	32	0.03
Irish (3,907)	17,288	13.71
Italian (763)	2,586	2.05
Lithuanian (59)	106	0.08
Luxemburger (15)	15	0.01
Macedonian (89)	89	0.07
Northern European (77)	93	0.07
Norwegian (459)	1,399	1.11
Pennsylvania German (62)	111	0.09
Polish (385)	1,320	1.05
Portuguese (8)	8	0.01
Romanian (61)	119	0.09
Russian (246)	1,356	1.08
Scandinavian (105)	231	0.18
Scotch-Irish (1,219)	2,853	2.26
Scottish (635)	2,524	2.00
Slavic (0)	19	0.02
Slovak (11)	22	0.02
Slovene (17)	47	0.04
Swedish (855)	2,854	2.26
Swiss (55)	414	0.33
Turkish (18)	65	0.05
Ukrainian (0)	59	0.05
Welsh (243)	1,070	0.85
West Indian, ex. Hispanic (28)	28	0.02
Bermudan (8)	8	0.01
Haitian (20)	20	0.02
Yugoslavian (0)	11	0.01

Hispanic Origin	Population	%
Hispanic or Latino (of any race)	17,026	13.36
Central American, ex. Mexican	286	0.22
Costa Rican	20	0.02
Guatemalan	106	0.08
Honduran	21	0.02
Nicaraguan	17	0.01
Panamanian	41	0.03
Salvadoran	74	0.06
Other Central American	7	0.01
Cuban	82	0.06
Dominican Republic	54	0.04
Mexican	14,803	11.61
Puerto Rican	790	0.62
South American	213	0.17
Argentinean	13	0.01
Bolivian	18	0.01
Chilean	18	0.01
Colombian	79	0.06
Ecuadorian	13	0.01
Paraguayan	15	0.01
Peruvian	14	0.01
Uruguayan	3	<0.01
Venezuelan	31	0.02
Other South American	9	0.01
Other Hispanic or Latino	798	0.63

Race*	Population	%
African-American/Black (14,423)	17,918	14.06
Not Hispanic (13,775)	16,629	13.05
Hispanic (648)	1,289	1.01
American Indian/Alaska Native (1,758)	3,938	3.09
Not Hispanic (1,374)	3,082	2.42
Hispanic (384)	856	0.67
Alaska Athabascan *(Ala. Nat.)* (5)	9	0.01
Aleut *(Alaska Native)* (3)	8	0.01
Apache (25)	60	0.05
Arapaho (5)	12	0.01
Blackfeet (12)	64	0.05
Canadian/French Am. Ind. (2)	3	<0.01
Central American Ind. (1)	1	<0.01
Cherokee (205)	672	0.53
Cheyenne (5)	10	0.01
Chickasaw (7)	28	0.02
Chippewa (11)	27	0.02
Choctaw (38)	85	0.07
Comanche (10)	18	0.01
Cree (0)	2	<0.01
Creek (25)	53	0.04
Crow (1)	10	0.01
Delaware (5)	6	<0.01
Hopi (1)	2	<0.01
Inupiat *(Alaska Native)* (0)	1	<0.01
Iroquois (16)	24	0.02
Kiowa (6)	6	<0.01
Lumbee (6)	9	0.01
Menominee (1)	5	<0.01
Mexican American Ind. (54)	108	0.08
Navajo (45)	79	0.06
Osage (14)	32	0.03
Ottawa (2)	3	<0.01
Paiute (1)	2	<0.01
Potawatomi (500)	873	0.68
Pueblo (2)	4	<0.01
Seminole (3)	14	0.01
Shoshone (1)	2	<0.01
Sioux (58)	112	0.09
South American Ind. (3)	7	0.01
Spanish American Ind. (2)	2	<0.01
Tlingit-Haida *(Alaska Native)* (0)	1	<0.01
Ute (3)	5	<0.01
Yaqui (2)	5	<0.01
Asian (1,717)	2,461	1.93
Not Hispanic (1,687)	2,314	1.82
Hispanic (30)	147	0.12
Bangladeshi (23)	27	0.02
Burmese (1)	1	<0.01
Cambodian (10)	13	0.01
Chinese, ex. Taiwanese (374)	473	0.37
Filipino (320)	526	0.41
Hmong (2)	3	<0.01
Indian (522)	584	0.46
Indonesian (10)	10	0.01
Japanese (71)	241	0.19
Korean (129)	273	0.21
Laotian (7)	19	0.01
Malaysian (1)	2	<0.01
Pakistani (64)	80	0.06
Sri Lankan (1)	1	<0.01
Taiwanese (24)	24	0.02
Thai (31)	50	0.04
Vietnamese (64)	97	0.08
Hawaii Native/Pacific Islander (93)	230	0.18
Not Hispanic (86)	189	0.15
Hispanic (7)	41	0.03
Fijian (4)	5	<0.01
Guamanian/Chamorro (11)	29	0.02
Native Hawaiian (37)	103	0.08
Samoan (22)	59	0.05
White (97,172)	102,698	80.56
Not Hispanic (88,839)	92,945	72.91
Hispanic (8,333)	9,753	7.65

Wellington

Place Type: City
County: Sumner
Population: 8,172†

Ancestry‡	Population	%
American (590)	590	7.21
Austrian (0)	10	0.12
Belgian (0)	20	0.24
Czech (61)	227	2.77
Czechoslovakian (0)	26	0.32
Danish (8)	8	0.10
Dutch (118)	380	4.64
English (355)	952	11.63
European (149)	155	1.89
French, ex. Basque (76)	252	3.08
French Canadian (0)	23	0.28
German (766)	2,329	28.45
Greek (0)	20	0.24
Irish (209)	1,189	14.52
Italian (0)	27	0.33
Lithuanian (8)	8	0.10
Norwegian (155)	180	2.20
Polish (0)	17	0.21
Russian (0)	21	0.26
Scotch-Irish (94)	315	3.85
Scottish (48)	216	2.64
Swedish (116)	226	2.76
Swiss (12)	28	0.34
Welsh (24)	65	0.79

Hispanic Origin	Population	%
Hispanic or Latino (of any race)	676	8.27
Cuban	1	0.01
Mexican	639	7.82
Puerto Rican	13	0.16
Other Hispanic or Latino	23	0.28

Race*	Population	%
African-American/Black (139)	213	2.61
Not Hispanic (131)	195	2.39
Hispanic (8)	18	0.22
American Indian/Alaska Native (122)	275	3.37
Not Hispanic (105)	241	2.95
Hispanic (17)	34	0.42
Apache (3)	4	0.05
Arapaho (0)	1	0.01
Blackfeet (0)	3	0.04
Cherokee (43)	94	1.15
Cheyenne (1)	2	0.02
Chippewa (1)	5	0.06
Choctaw (6)	16	0.20
Comanche (0)	1	0.01
Cree (0)	3	0.04

SECTION TWO

*Notes: † The Census 2010 population figure is used to calculate the percentages in the Hispanic Origin and Race categories. Ancestry percentages are based on the 2006-2010 American Community Survey population (not shown); ‡ Numbers in parentheses indicate the number of people reporting a single ancestry; * Numbers in parentheses indicate the number of persons reporting this race alone, not in combination with any other race; Please refer to the Explanation of Data for more information.*

Creek (0)	3	0.04
Iroquois (2)	3	0.04
Kiowa (4)	4	0.05
Mexican American Ind. (1)	1	0.01
Navajo (3)	3	0.04
Osage (8)	13	0.16
Potawatomi (2)	12	0.15
Seminole (2)	2	0.02
Sioux (1)	9	0.11
Asian (25)	43	0.53
Not Hispanic (25)	42	0.51
Hispanic (0)	1	0.01
Chinese, ex. Taiwanese (7)	8	0.10
Filipino (5)	7	0.09
Indian (0)	1	0.01
Japanese (1)	5	0.06
Korean (1)	5	0.06
Laotian (3)	4	0.05
Thai (5)	9	0.11
Vietnamese (1)	1	0.01
Hawaii Native/Pacific Islander (1)	6	0.07
Not Hispanic (1)	6	0.07
Native Hawaiian (1)	5	0.06
White (7,439)	7,714	94.40
Not Hispanic (7,019)	7,228	88.45
Hispanic (420)	486	5.95

Wichita

Place Type: City
County: Sedgwick
Population: 382,368†

Ancestry‡	Population	%
Afghan (19)	19	0.01
African, Sub-Saharan (2,274)	2,816	0.75
African (1,356)	1,808	0.48
Cape Verdean (0)	13	<0.01
Ethiopian (45)	54	0.01
Kenyan (383)	429	0.11
Nigerian (155)	168	0.04
Somalian (13)	13	<0.01
South African (27)	27	0.01
Sudanese (14)	23	0.01
Ugandan (23)	23	0.01
Other Sub-Saharan African (258)	258	0.07
Albanian (12)	70	0.02
Alsatian (10)	10	<0.01
American (21,334)	21,334	5.71
Arab (1,578)	2,327	0.62
Arab (100)	203	0.05
Egyptian (58)	73	0.02
Iraqi (10)	10	<0.01
Jordanian (119)	133	0.04
Lebanese (866)	1,388	0.37
Moroccan (192)	192	0.05
Palestinian (45)	45	0.01
Syrian (71)	120	0.03
Other Arab (117)	163	0.04
Armenian (7)	80	0.02
Australian (12)	119	0.03
Austrian (110)	576	0.15
Belgian (34)	189	0.05
Brazilian (119)	137	0.04
British (511)	1,174	0.31
Bulgarian (39)	68	0.02
Cajun (23)	45	0.01
Canadian (285)	481	0.13
Celtic (0)	23	0.01
Croatian (75)	187	0.05
Czech (613)	2,469	0.66
Czechoslovakian (349)	651	0.17
Danish (406)	1,639	0.44
Dutch (1,633)	8,318	2.23
Eastern European (54)	127	0.03
English (14,441)	39,129	10.47
European (4,069)	4,651	1.24
Finnish (65)	252	0.07
French, ex. Basque (2,146)	11,359	3.04
French Canadian (532)	1,112	0.30
German (35,135)	89,797	24.03
German Russian (105)	174	0.05
Greek (150)	399	0.11
Guyanese (0)	26	0.01
Hungarian (182)	609	0.16
Icelander (77)	102	0.03
Iranian (264)	283	0.08
Irish (10,806)	45,232	12.10
Italian (2,668)	7,346	1.97
Latvian (40)	40	0.01
Lithuanian (111)	174	0.05
Luxemburger (0)	76	0.02
Macedonian (14)	14	<0.01
Maltese (9)	44	0.01
New Zealander (53)	62	0.02
Northern European (116)	129	0.03
Norwegian (883)	3,662	0.98
Pennsylvania German (276)	557	0.15
Polish (688)	3,756	1.01
Portuguese (85)	425	0.11
Romanian (10)	50	0.01
Russian (475)	2,361	0.63
Scandinavian (320)	568	0.15
Scotch-Irish (2,980)	7,956	2.13
Scottish (2,219)	7,087	1.90
Serbian (24)	71	0.02
Slavic (17)	112	0.03
Slovak (21)	71	0.02
Slovene (43)	109	0.03
Swedish (1,631)	5,808	1.55
Swiss (357)	1,300	0.35
Turkish (46)	94	0.03
Ukrainian (72)	169	0.05
Welsh (570)	2,768	0.74
West Indian, ex. Hispanic (290)	574	0.15
Barbadian (0)	73	0.02
British West Indian (8)	8	<0.01
Dutch West Indian (0)	137	0.04
Haitian (119)	128	0.03
Jamaican (20)	44	0.01
Trinidadian/Tobagonian (121)	133	0.04
West Indian (22)	51	0.01
Yugoslavian (19)	99	0.03

Hispanic Origin	Population	%
Hispanic or Latino (of any race)	58,348	15.26
Central American, ex. Mexican	2,277	0.60
Costa Rican	43	0.01
Guatemalan	435	0.11
Honduran	467	0.12
Nicaraguan	146	0.04
Panamanian	128	0.03
Salvadoran	1,021	0.27
Other Central American	37	0.01
Cuban	422	0.11
Dominican Republic	84	0.02
Mexican	49,700	13.00
Puerto Rican	1,553	0.41
South American	944	0.25
Argentinean	77	0.02
Bolivian	72	0.02
Chilean	72	0.02
Colombian	252	0.07
Ecuadorian	88	0.02
Paraguayan	38	0.01
Peruvian	219	0.06
Uruguayan	11	<0.01
Venezuelan	112	0.03
Other South American	3	<0.01
Other Hispanic or Latino	3,368	0.88

Race*	Population	%
African-American/Black (43,807)	51,470	13.46
Not Hispanic (42,676)	49,113	12.84
Hispanic (1,131)	2,357	0.62
American Indian/Alaska Native (4,560)	10,084	2.64
Not Hispanic (3,424)	7,993	2.09
Hispanic (1,136)	2,091	0.55
Alaska Athabascan *(Ala. Nat.)* (7)	12	<0.01
Aleut *(Alaska Native)* (16)	24	0.01
Apache (105)	206	0.05
Arapaho (24)	50	0.01
Blackfeet (42)	182	0.05
Canadian/French Am. Ind. (10)	19	<0.01
Central American Ind. (8)	11	<0.01
Cherokee (964)	2,696	0.71
Cheyenne (40)	68	0.02
Chickasaw (86)	149	0.04
Chippewa (53)	100	0.03
Choctaw (193)	488	0.13
Colville (0)	5	<0.01
Comanche (58)	138	0.04
Cree (1)	14	<0.01
Creek (194)	557	0.15
Crow (2)	12	<0.01
Delaware (53)	90	0.02
Hopi (2)	14	<0.01
Houma (0)	1	<0.01
Inupiat *(Alaska Native)* (7)	8	<0.01
Iroquois (45)	89	0.02
Kiowa (102)	174	0.05
Lumbee (5)	16	<0.01
Menominee (4)	8	<0.01
Mexican American Ind. (202)	323	0.08
Navajo (81)	166	0.04
Osage (91)	189	0.05
Ottawa (7)	11	<0.01
Paiute (3)	4	<0.01
Pima (9)	15	<0.01
Potawatomi (116)	184	0.05
Pueblo (16)	29	0.01
Puget Sound Salish (8)	8	<0.01
Seminole (43)	147	0.04
Shoshone (5)	18	<0.01
Sioux (152)	312	0.08
South American Ind. (9)	17	<0.01
Spanish American Ind. (20)	21	0.01
Tlingit-Haida *(Alaska Native)* (4)	4	<0.01
Tohono O'Odham (7)	10	<0.01
Tsimshian *(Alaska Native)* (1)	1	<0.01
Ute (4)	12	<0.01
Yakama (1)	3	<0.01
Yaqui (14)	23	0.01
Yuman (0)	3	<0.01
Yup'ik *(Alaska Native)* (2)	2	<0.01
Asian (18,466)	21,541	5.63
Not Hispanic (18,272)	20,978	5.49
Hispanic (194)	563	0.15
Bangladeshi (230)	236	0.06
Bhutanese (2)	2	<0.01
Burmese (23)	23	0.01
Cambodian (705)	936	0.24
Chinese, ex. Taiwanese (1,375)	1,887	0.49
Filipino (1,074)	1,783	0.47
Hmong (36)	52	0.01
Indian (1,795)	2,164	0.57
Indonesian (41)	56	0.01
Japanese (213)	593	0.16
Korean (542)	848	0.22
Laotian (1,305)	1,594	0.42
Malaysian (61)	102	0.03
Nepalese (160)	174	0.05
Pakistani (396)	473	0.12
Sri Lankan (106)	115	0.03
Taiwanese (57)	97	0.03
Thai (210)	325	0.08
Vietnamese (9,014)	9,902	2.59
Hawaii Native/Pacific Islander (336)	711	0.19
Not Hispanic (311)	592	0.15
Hispanic (25)	119	0.03
Fijian (14)	17	<0.01
Guamanian/Chamorro (62)	133	0.03
Marshallese (6)	9	<0.01
Native Hawaiian (72)	196	0.05
Samoan (34)	78	0.02
Tongan (5)	6	<0.01
White (275,080)	289,470	75.70
Not Hispanic (246,744)	257,465	67.33
Hispanic (28,336)	32,005	8.37

*Notes: † The Census 2010 population figure is used to calculate the percentages in the Hispanic Origin and Race categories. Ancestry percentages are based on the 2006-2010 American Community Survey population (not shown); ‡ Numbers in parentheses indicate the number of people reporting a single ancestry; * Numbers in parentheses indicate the number of persons reporting this race alone, not in combination with any other race; Please refer to the Explanation of Data for more information.*

Winfield

Place Type: City
County: Cowley
Population: 12,301†

Ancestry‡	Population	%
African, Sub-Saharan (56)	56	0.46
African (56)	56	0.46
American (1,165)	1,165	9.49
Arab (15)	15	0.12
Lebanese (15)	15	0.12
Belgian (54)	54	0.44
British (26)	56	0.46
Cajun (0)	10	0.08
Czech (6)	53	0.43
Dutch (32)	204	1.66
English (383)	1,311	10.68
European (0)	9	0.07
Finnish (11)	11	0.09
French, ex. Basque (83)	637	5.19
French Canadian (37)	46	0.37
German (1,245)	2,872	23.41
Irish (296)	1,537	12.53
Italian (64)	243	1.98
Northern European (28)	28	0.23
Norwegian (51)	226	1.84
Pennsylvania German (39)	49	0.40
Polish (36)	137	1.12
Russian (16)	70	0.57
Scotch-Irish (75)	170	1.39
Scottish (108)	314	2.56
Swedish (18)	133	1.08
Swiss (0)	64	0.52
Turkish (0)	38	0.31
Welsh (12)	35	0.29
West Indian, ex. Hispanic (21)	21	0.17
Trinidadian/Tobagonian (21)	21	0.17

Hispanic Origin	Population	%
Hispanic or Latino (of any race)	750	6.10
Central American, ex. Mexican	19	0.15
Costa Rican	2	0.02
Guatemalan	8	0.07
Honduran	1	0.01
Nicaraguan	5	0.04
Salvadoran	3	0.02
Cuban	10	0.08
Dominican Republic	2	0.02
Mexican	627	5.10
Puerto Rican	19	0.15
South American	9	0.07
Argentinean	1	0.01
Bolivian	1	0.01
Colombian	2	0.02
Peruvian	3	0.02
Venezuelan	2	0.02
Other Hispanic or Latino	64	0.52

Race*	Population	%
African-American/Black (481)	649	5.28
Not Hispanic (469)	614	4.99
Hispanic (12)	35	0.28
American Indian/Alaska Native (154)	311	2.53
Not Hispanic (144)	289	2.35
Hispanic (10)	22	0.18
Aleut *(Alaska Native)* (2)	2	0.02
Apache (3)	4	0.03
Blackfeet (0)	5	0.04
Canadian/French Am. Ind. (0)	1	0.01
Cherokee (40)	103	0.84
Cheyenne (1)	1	0.01
Chickasaw (0)	3	0.02
Chippewa (3)	3	0.02
Choctaw (5)	14	0.11
Comanche (1)	1	0.01
Creek (8)	19	0.15
Delaware (2)	4	0.03
Iroquois (1)	4	0.03
Mexican American Ind. (1)	1	0.01
Navajo (4)	5	0.04
Osage (4)	11	0.09
Pima (0)	1	0.01
Potawatomi (3)	7	0.06
Pueblo (1)	1	0.01
Seminole (2)	6	0.05
Sioux (7)	9	0.07
Spanish American Ind. (0)	2	0.02
Tlingit-Haida *(Alaska Native)* (2)	2	0.02
Asian (479)	535	4.35
Not Hispanic (477)	530	4.31
Hispanic (2)	5	0.04
Burmese (1)	1	0.01
Cambodian (0)	2	0.02
Chinese, ex. Taiwanese (24)	44	0.36
Filipino (21)	31	0.25
Indian (23)	53	0.43
Japanese (4)	11	0.09
Korean (4)	7	0.06
Laotian (292)	356	2.89
Malaysian (0)	1	0.01
Pakistani (0)	4	0.03
Thai (1)	2	0.02
Vietnamese (38)	52	0.42
Hawaii Native/Pacific Islander (1)	9	0.07
Not Hispanic (0)	3	0.02
Hispanic (1)	6	0.05
Guamanian/Chamorro (0)	4	0.03
White (10,547)	10,933	88.88
Not Hispanic (10,126)	10,435	84.83
Hispanic (421)	498	4.05

*Notes: † The Census 2010 population figure is used to calculate the percentages in the Hispanic Origin and Race categories. Ancestry percentages are based on the 2006-2010 American Community Survey population (not shown); ‡ Numbers in parentheses indicate the number of people reporting a single ancestry; * Numbers in parentheses indicate the number of persons reporting this race alone, not in combination with any other race; Please refer to the Explanation of Data for more information.*

KENTUCKY

Place Type: State
Population: 4,339,367†

Ancestry‡	Population	%
Afghan (104)	157	<0.01
African, Sub-Saharan (19,709)	23,400	0.55
African (15,914)	19,102	0.45
Cape Verdean (29)	33	<0.01
Ethiopian (459)	651	0.02
Ghanaian (94)	94	<0.01
Kenyan (204)	204	<0.01
Liberian (348)	431	0.01
Nigerian (340)	358	0.01
Senegalese (72)	93	<0.01
Sierra Leonean (10)	10	<0.01
Somalian (914)	914	0.02
South African (151)	224	0.01
Sudanese (274)	316	0.01
Ugandan (40)	40	<0.01
Zimbabwean (25)	25	<0.01
Other Sub-Saharan African (835)	905	0.02
Albanian (544)	581	0.01
Alsatian (82)	138	<0.01
American (846,598)	846,598	19.75
Arab (6,566)	9,623	0.22
Arab (1,633)	1,858	0.04
Egyptian (367)	462	0.01
Iraqi (290)	315	0.01
Jordanian (612)	684	0.02
Lebanese (1,701)	3,823	0.09
Moroccan (271)	321	0.01
Palestinian (497)	576	0.01
Syrian (477)	692	0.02
Other Arab (718)	892	0.02
Armenian (546)	931	0.02
Assyrian/Chaldean/Syriac (20)	42	<0.01
Australian (419)	1,012	0.02
Austrian (1,175)	3,504	0.08
Basque (37)	113	<0.01
Belgian (549)	1,445	0.03
Brazilian (645)	788	0.02
British (9,547)	17,099	0.40
Bulgarian (257)	432	0.01
Cajun (167)	459	0.01
Canadian (1,966)	3,661	0.09
Carpatho Rusyn (15)	15	<0.01
Celtic (270)	553	0.01
Croatian (566)	1,291	0.03
Cypriot (19)	19	<0.01
Czech (1,775)	5,009	0.12
Czechoslovakian (510)	1,076	0.03
Danish (1,404)	4,682	0.11
Dutch (12,027)	58,584	1.37
Eastern European (1,247)	1,576	0.04
English (256,185)	494,312	11.53
Estonian (55)	142	<0.01
European (28,237)	32,836	0.77
Finnish (781)	2,243	0.05
French, ex. Basque (19,262)	79,830	1.86
French Canadian (3,701)	8,390	0.20
German (266,368)	682,836	15.93
German Russian (74)	206	<0.01
Greek (3,048)	6,669	0.16
Guyanese (120)	131	<0.01
Hungarian (2,295)	6,878	0.16
Icelander (17)	51	<0.01
Iranian (1,376)	1,627	0.04
Irish (204,133)	586,154	13.68
Israeli (60)	113	<0.01
Italian (31,926)	88,876	2.07
Latvian (173)	530	0.01
Lithuanian (676)	1,924	0.04
Luxemburger (61)	176	<0.01
Macedonian (28)	54	<0.01
Maltese (52)	100	<0.01
New Zealander (23)	103	<0.01
Northern European (978)	1,049	0.02
Norwegian (5,359)	13,878	0.32
Pennsylvania German (1,174)	1,724	0.04
Polish (13,330)	40,567	0.95
Portuguese (765)	2,944	0.07
Romanian (964)	1,836	0.04
Russian (4,197)	10,491	0.24
Scandinavian (998)	2,634	0.06
Scotch-Irish (47,655)	90,125	2.10
Scottish (34,959)	85,608	2.00
Serbian (206)	401	0.01
Slavic (259)	661	0.02
Slovak (1,039)	2,743	0.06
Slovene (221)	515	0.01
Swedish (5,049)	18,107	0.42
Swiss (3,087)	10,855	0.25
Turkish (874)	1,030	0.02
Ukrainian (2,463)	3,837	0.09
Welsh (5,908)	22,649	0.53
West Indian, ex. Hispanic (2,907)	4,830	0.11
Bahamian (0)	67	<0.01
Barbadian (216)	256	0.01
Belizean (57)	69	<0.01
Bermudan (0)	13	<0.01
British West Indian (21)	34	<0.01
Dutch West Indian (185)	509	0.01
Haitian (826)	1,121	0.03
Jamaican (1,064)	1,708	0.04
Trinidadian/Tobagonian (182)	283	0.01
U.S. Virgin Islander (9)	9	<0.01
West Indian (347)	750	0.02
Other West Indian (0)	11	<0.01
Yugoslavian (4,817)	5,427	0.13

Hispanic Origin	Population	%
Hispanic or Latino (of any race)	132,836	3.06
Central American, ex. Mexican	11,479	0.26
Costa Rican	253	0.01
Guatemalan	5,231	0.12
Honduran	2,012	0.05
Nicaraguan	526	0.01
Panamanian	1,019	0.02
Salvadoran	2,351	0.05
Other Central American	87	<0.01
Cuban	9,323	0.21
Dominican Republic	1,065	0.02
Mexican	82,110	1.89
Puerto Rican	11,454	0.26
South American	5,405	0.12
Argentinean	481	0.01
Bolivian	227	0.01
Chilean	332	0.01
Colombian	1,729	0.04
Ecuadorian	615	0.01
Paraguayan	52	<0.01
Peruvian	1,174	0.03
Uruguayan	93	<0.01
Venezuelan	637	0.01
Other South American	65	<0.01
Other Hispanic or Latino	12,000	0.28

Race*	Population	%
African-American/Black (337,520)	376,213	8.67
Not Hispanic (333,075)	369,025	8.50
Hispanic (4,445)	7,188	0.17
American Indian/Alaska Native (10,120)	31,355	0.72
Not Hispanic (8,642)	28,170	0.65
Hispanic (1,478)	3,185	0.07
Alaska Athabascan *(Ala. Nat.)* (26)	41	<0.01
Aleut *(Alaska Native)* (21)	39	<0.01
Apache (154)	417	0.01
Arapaho (5)	14	<0.01
Blackfeet (155)	986	0.02
Canadian/French Am. Ind. (42)	78	<0.01
Central American Ind. (36)	70	<0.01
Cherokee (2,783)	10,731	0.25
Cheyenne (29)	105	<0.01
Chickasaw (52)	149	<0.01
Chippewa (224)	406	0.01
Choctaw (181)	487	0.01
Colville (3)	7	<0.01
Comanche (30)	74	<0.01
Cree (20)	54	<0.01
Creek (90)	247	0.01
Crow (16)	66	<0.01
Delaware (25)	97	<0.01
Hopi (12)	45	<0.01
Houma (5)	10	<0.01
Inupiat *(Alaska Native)* (31)	44	<0.01
Iroquois (153)	369	0.01
Kiowa (17)	32	<0.01
Lumbee (94)	147	<0.01
Menominee (4)	13	<0.01
Mexican American Ind. (462)	681	0.02
Navajo (133)	307	0.01
Osage (28)	76	<0.01
Ottawa (39)	65	<0.01
Paiute (12)	20	<0.01
Pima (13)	21	<0.01
Potawatomi (59)	87	<0.01
Pueblo (43)	68	<0.01
Puget Sound Salish (9)	13	<0.01
Seminole (44)	160	<0.01
Shoshone (11)	29	<0.01
Sioux (257)	625	0.01
South American Ind. (45)	115	<0.01
Spanish American Ind. (26)	39	<0.01
Tlingit-Haida *(Alaska Native)* (16)	28	<0.01
Tohono O'Odham (8)	23	<0.01
Tsimshian *(Alaska Native)* (10)	13	<0.01
Ute (12)	25	<0.01
Yakama (2)	3	<0.01
Yaqui (16)	22	<0.01
Yuman (4)	7	<0.01
Yup'ik *(Alaska Native)* (7)	17	<0.01
Asian (48,930)	62,029	1.43
Not Hispanic (48,338)	60,537	1.40
Hispanic (592)	1,492	0.03
Bangladeshi (172)	196	<0.01
Bhutanese (215)	336	0.01
Burmese (1,420)	1,524	0.04
Cambodian (755)	910	0.02
Chinese, ex. Taiwanese (8,618)	10,024	0.23
Filipino (5,188)	8,402	0.19
Hmong (49)	71	<0.01
Indian (12,501)	14,253	0.33
Indonesian (244)	341	0.01
Japanese (4,124)	6,197	0.14
Korean (4,917)	7,264	0.17
Laotian (436)	567	0.01
Malaysian (68)	118	<0.01
Nepalese (555)	695	0.02
Pakistani (1,253)	1,402	0.03
Sri Lankan (173)	206	<0.01
Taiwanese (420)	504	0.01
Thai (820)	1,235	0.03
Vietnamese (5,046)	5,813	0.13
Hawaii Native/Pacific Islander (2,501)	5,111	0.12
Not Hispanic (2,074)	4,235	0.10
Hispanic (427)	876	0.02
Fijian (26)	35	<0.01
Guamanian/Chamorro (866)	1,287	0.03
Marshallese (28)	37	<0.01
Native Hawaiian (541)	1,505	0.03
Samoan (368)	704	0.02
Tongan (20)	42	<0.01
White (3,809,537)	3,878,336	89.38
Not Hispanic (3,745,655)	3,805,193	87.69
Hispanic (63,882)	73,143	1.69

*Notes: † The Census 2010 population figure is used to calculate the percentages in the Hispanic Origin and Race categories. Ancestry percentages are based on the 2006-2010 American Community Survey population (not shown); ‡ Numbers in parentheses indicate the number of people reporting a single ancestry; * Numbers in parentheses indicate the number of persons reporting this race alone, not in combination with any other race; Please refer to the Explanation of Data for more information.*

Alexandria

Place Type: City
County: Campbell
Population: 8,477†

Ancestry‡	Population	%
American (1,239)	1,239	14.79
Armenian (9)	19	0.23
Belgian (0)	11	0.13
Czech (0)	11	0.13
Danish (13)	69	0.82
Dutch (27)	191	2.28
English (331)	916	10.94
European (33)	33	0.39
French, ex. Basque (18)	232	2.77
German (1,564)	3,192	38.11
Greek (0)	73	0.87
Hungarian (0)	31	0.37
Irish (272)	1,551	18.52
Italian (122)	333	3.98
Norwegian (0)	49	0.59
Polish (0)	111	1.33
Russian (9)	30	0.36
Scotch-Irish (22)	75	0.90
Scottish (33)	126	1.50
Welsh (0)	34	0.41

Hispanic Origin	Population	%
Hispanic or Latino (of any race)	89	1.05
Central American, ex. Mexican	7	0.08
Guatemalan	3	0.04
Honduran	2	0.02
Nicaraguan	1	0.01
Panamanian	1	0.01
Cuban	2	0.02
Dominican Republic	1	0.01
Mexican	33	0.39
Puerto Rican	17	0.20
South American	14	0.17
Argentinean	4	0.05
Bolivian	4	0.05
Colombian	3	0.04
Ecuadorian	1	0.01
Peruvian	1	0.01
Venezuelan	1	0.01
Other Hispanic or Latino	15	0.18

Race*	Population	%
African-American/Black (48)	75	0.88
Not Hispanic (42)	68	0.80
Hispanic (6)	7	0.08
American Indian/Alaska Native (12)	37	0.44
Not Hispanic (10)	35	0.41
Hispanic (2)	2	0.02
Cherokee (5)	17	0.20
Choctaw (1)	1	0.01
Asian (61)	90	1.06
Not Hispanic (60)	85	1.00
Hispanic (1)	5	0.06
Chinese, ex. Taiwanese (11)	17	0.20
Filipino (9)	16	0.19
Indian (14)	24	0.28
Japanese (1)	2	0.02
Korean (8)	12	0.14
Sri Lankan (2)	4	0.05
Taiwanese (1)	1	0.01
Thai (1)	1	0.01
Vietnamese (13)	14	0.17
Hawaii Native/Pacific Islander (0)	5	0.06
Not Hispanic (0)	4	0.05
Hispanic (0)	1	0.01
Native Hawaiian (0)	5	0.06
White (8,248)	8,341	98.40
Not Hispanic (8,195)	8,273	97.59
Hispanic (53)	68	0.80

Ashland

Place Type: City
County: Boyd
Population: 21,684†

Ancestry‡	Population	%
African, Sub-Saharan (87)	87	0.40
African (87)	87	0.40
Albanian (37)	37	0.17
American (3,492)	3,492	16.16
Arab (0)	21	0.10
Lebanese (0)	21	0.10
Austrian (11)	22	0.10
Belgian (0)	7	0.03
British (90)	176	0.81
Bulgarian (9)	19	0.09
Canadian (14)	22	0.10
Czechoslovakian (9)	9	0.04
Danish (0)	11	0.05
Dutch (126)	395	1.83
English (1,400)	3,120	14.44
European (99)	99	0.46
French, ex. Basque (60)	389	1.80
French Canadian (11)	23	0.11
German (1,037)	3,292	15.23
Greek (25)	68	0.31
Hungarian (9)	14	0.06
Irish (1,633)	4,100	18.97
Italian (89)	232	1.07
Lithuanian (14)	14	0.06
Norwegian (11)	59	0.27
Polish (20)	113	0.52
Portuguese (65)	65	0.30
Romanian (0)	71	0.33
Russian (14)	35	0.16
Scandinavian (23)	34	0.16
Scotch-Irish (232)	699	3.23
Scottish (140)	454	2.10
Slavic (0)	24	0.11
Swedish (0)	37	0.17
Swiss (10)	20	0.09
Welsh (52)	129	0.60
West Indian, ex. Hispanic (203)	229	1.06
Haitian (0)	26	0.12
Jamaican (203)	203	0.94

Hispanic Origin	Population	%
Hispanic or Latino (of any race)	317	1.46
Central American, ex. Mexican	20	0.09
Costa Rican	1	<0.01
Guatemalan	17	0.08
Honduran	1	<0.01
Nicaraguan	1	<0.01
Cuban	8	0.04
Mexican	219	1.01
Puerto Rican	19	0.09
South American	18	0.08
Argentinean	1	<0.01
Chilean	10	0.05
Colombian	6	0.03
Peruvian	1	<0.01
Other Hispanic or Latino	33	0.15

Race*	Population	%
African-American/Black (601)	817	3.77
Not Hispanic (595)	807	3.72
Hispanic (6)	10	0.05
American Indian/Alaska Native (60)	173	0.80
Not Hispanic (57)	167	0.77
Hispanic (3)	6	0.03
Apache (1)	1	<0.01
Blackfeet (1)	4	0.02
Canadian/French Am. Ind. (0)	1	<0.01
Cherokee (20)	59	0.27
Crow (3)	3	0.01
Iroquois (0)	1	<0.01
Mexican American Ind. (2)	2	0.01
Navajo (1)	4	0.02
Sioux (2)	2	0.01
Tlingit-Haida *(Alaska Native)* (0)	1	<0.01
Asian (134)	200	0.92
Not Hispanic (133)	190	0.88
Hispanic (1)	10	0.05
Burmese (3)	3	0.01
Chinese, ex. Taiwanese (24)	37	0.17
Filipino (33)	46	0.21
Indian (33)	36	0.17
Indonesian (1)	3	0.01
Japanese (5)	9	0.04
Korean (8)	25	0.12
Laotian (1)	4	0.02
Malaysian (3)	3	0.01
Pakistani (5)	6	0.03
Thai (1)	6	0.03
Vietnamese (11)	11	0.05
Hawaii Native/Pacific Islander (1)	18	0.08
Not Hispanic (0)	16	0.07
Hispanic (1)	2	0.01
Guamanian/Chamorro (1)	1	<0.01
Native Hawaiian (0)	4	0.02
White (20,353)	20,751	95.70
Not Hispanic (20,168)	20,525	94.66
Hispanic (185)	226	1.04

Bardstown

Place Type: City
County: Nelson
Population: 11,700†

Ancestry‡	Population	%
African, Sub-Saharan (67)	67	0.58
African (67)	67	0.58
American (2,681)	2,681	23.21
Armenian (37)	37	0.32
Dutch (17)	41	0.35
English (875)	1,677	14.52
European (108)	113	0.98
French, ex. Basque (14)	368	3.19
French Canadian (40)	40	0.35
German (397)	1,369	11.85
Icelander (14)	14	0.12
Irish (386)	1,563	13.53
Italian (84)	259	2.24
Polish (37)	218	1.89
Portuguese (0)	14	0.12
Scotch-Irish (30)	147	1.27
Scottish (50)	152	1.32
Slovak (14)	14	0.12
Swedish (8)	24	0.21
Ukrainian (34)	52	0.45
Welsh (0)	73	0.63

Hispanic Origin	Population	%
Hispanic or Latino (of any race)	434	3.71
Central American, ex. Mexican	21	0.18
Guatemalan	6	0.05
Honduran	5	0.04
Nicaraguan	8	0.07
Panamanian	2	0.02
Cuban	10	0.09
Dominican Republic	5	0.04
Mexican	314	2.68
Puerto Rican	49	0.42
South American	3	0.03
Colombian	3	0.03
Other Hispanic or Latino	32	0.27

Race*	Population	%
African-American/Black (1,450)	1,647	14.08
Not Hispanic (1,443)	1,635	13.97
Hispanic (7)	12	0.10
American Indian/Alaska Native (24)	67	0.57
Not Hispanic (21)	61	0.52
Hispanic (3)	6	0.05
Apache (0)	3	0.03
Blackfeet (2)	2	0.02
Cherokee (11)	39	0.33
Chippewa (0)	4	0.03

*Notes: † The Census 2010 population figure is used to calculate the percentages in the Hispanic Origin and Race categories. Ancestry percentages are based on the 2006-2010 American Community Survey population (not shown); ‡ Numbers in parentheses indicate the number of people reporting a single ancestry; * Numbers in parentheses indicate the number of persons reporting this race alone, not in combination with any other race; Please refer to the Explanation of Data for more information.*

Mexican American Ind. (1)	1	0.01
Asian (88)	107	0.91
Not Hispanic (86)	105	0.90
Hispanic (2)	2	0.02
Chinese, ex. Taiwanese (24)	26	0.22
Filipino (14)	20	0.17
Indian (4)	4	0.03
Indonesian (0)	1	0.01
Japanese (33)	37	0.32
Korean (6)	7	0.06
Pakistani (0)	1	0.01
Thai (0)	2	0.02
Vietnamese (4)	5	0.04
Hawaii Native/Pacific Islander (1)	14	0.12
Not Hispanic (0)	5	0.04
Hispanic (1)	9	0.08
Native Hawaiian (1)	4	0.03
Samoan (0)	1	0.01
White (9,630)	9,940	84.96
Not Hispanic (9,453)	9,697	82.88
Hispanic (177)	243	2.08

Berea

Place Type: City
County: Madison
Population: 13,561†

Ancestry‡	Population	%
African, Sub-Saharan (64)	64	0.48
African (64)	64	0.48
Albanian (26)	26	0.20
American (2,529)	2,529	19.08
Arab (15)	28	0.21
Syrian (0)	13	0.10
Other Arab (15)	15	0.11
British (82)	149	1.12
Bulgarian (13)	13	0.10
Canadian (8)	8	0.06
Croatian (34)	34	0.26
Danish (16)	128	0.97
Dutch (28)	151	1.14
English (591)	1,896	14.30
European (270)	270	2.04
Finnish (0)	17	0.13
French, ex. Basque (87)	578	4.36
French Canadian (0)	77	0.58
German (613)	2,034	15.35
Greek (0)	10	0.08
Hungarian (50)	50	0.38
Irish (679)	1,909	14.40
Italian (54)	320	2.41
Lithuanian (0)	13	0.10
Norwegian (0)	23	0.17
Polish (0)	156	1.18
Russian (18)	44	0.33
Scotch-Irish (317)	501	3.78
Scottish (159)	405	3.06
Slovak (8)	8	0.06
Swedish (14)	26	0.20
Ukrainian (28)	28	0.21
Welsh (9)	76	0.57
West Indian, ex. Hispanic (27)	34	0.26
Dutch West Indian (0)	7	0.05
West Indian (27)	27	0.20

Hispanic Origin	Population	%
Hispanic or Latino (of any race)	360	2.65
Central American, ex. Mexican	43	0.32
Guatemalan	6	0.04
Honduran	8	0.06
Nicaraguan	12	0.09
Panamanian	13	0.10
Salvadoran	4	0.03
Cuban	4	0.03
Dominican Republic	3	0.02
Mexican	227	1.67
Puerto Rican	33	0.24
South American	18	0.13
Argentinean	3	0.02
Bolivian	1	0.01
Colombian	5	0.04
Ecuadorian	3	0.02
Paraguayan	1	0.01
Peruvian	4	0.03
Uruguayan	1	0.01
Other Hispanic or Latino	32	0.24

Race*	Population	%
African-American/Black (547)	715	5.27
Not Hispanic (535)	689	5.08
Hispanic (12)	26	0.19
American Indian/Alaska Native (69)	176	1.30
Not Hispanic (55)	147	1.08
Hispanic (14)	29	0.21
Alaska Athabascan *(Ala. Nat.)* (1)	1	0.01
Apache (2)	4	0.03
Blackfeet (5)	10	0.07
Central American Ind. (0)	2	0.01
Cherokee (27)	68	0.50
Chippewa (3)	3	0.02
Choctaw (1)	1	0.01
Creek (1)	2	0.01
Crow (0)	1	0.01
Iroquois (2)	2	0.01
Lumbee (1)	1	0.01
Mexican American Ind. (6)	12	0.09
Pima (0)	2	0.01
Sioux (0)	2	0.01
South American Ind. (1)	1	0.01
Asian (167)	231	1.70
Not Hispanic (167)	229	1.69
Hispanic (0)	2	0.01
Bangladeshi (3)	3	0.02
Burmese (0)	1	0.01
Chinese, ex. Taiwanese (41)	42	0.31
Filipino (16)	28	0.21
Indian (25)	33	0.24
Indonesian (5)	5	0.04
Japanese (38)	52	0.38
Korean (8)	18	0.13
Malaysian (1)	1	0.01
Nepalese (4)	5	0.04
Sri Lankan (1)	1	0.01
Taiwanese (5)	7	0.05
Thai (1)	3	0.02
Vietnamese (9)	9	0.07
Hawaii Native/Pacific Islander (8)	8	0.06
Not Hispanic (8)	8	0.06
Native Hawaiian (6)	6	0.04
White (12,304)	12,630	93.13
Not Hispanic (12,135)	12,404	91.47
Hispanic (169)	226	1.67

Bowling Green

Place Type: City
County: Warren
Population: 58,067†

Ancestry‡	Population	%
African, Sub-Saharan (170)	290	0.51
African (142)	262	0.46
Cape Verdean (21)	21	0.04
Zimbabwean (7)	7	0.01
American (4,356)	4,356	7.72
Arab (161)	190	0.34
Arab (58)	58	0.10
Egyptian (0)	16	0.03
Lebanese (24)	37	0.07
Syrian (9)	9	0.02
Other Arab (70)	70	0.12
Austrian (0)	39	0.07
Basque (8)	8	0.01
British (135)	234	0.41
Canadian (59)	116	0.21
Croatian (70)	94	0.17
Czech (31)	123	0.22
Danish (33)	113	0.20
Dutch (164)	809	1.43
English (2,281)	5,139	9.11
European (318)	420	0.74
Finnish (20)	20	0.04
French, ex. Basque (254)	1,107	1.96
French Canadian (47)	81	0.14
German (2,505)	6,967	12.35
Greek (1)	93	0.16
Hungarian (60)	98	0.17
Irish (2,833)	7,099	12.59
Italian (355)	1,180	2.09
Latvian (0)	25	0.04
Northern European (11)	11	0.02
Norwegian (25)	185	0.33
Polish (136)	642	1.14
Portuguese (9)	70	0.12
Russian (71)	196	0.35
Scandinavian (28)	44	0.08
Scotch-Irish (707)	1,283	2.27
Scottish (603)	1,252	2.22
Slovak (11)	25	0.04
Swedish (44)	232	0.41
Swiss (26)	66	0.12
Turkish (16)	16	0.03
Ukrainian (70)	107	0.19
Welsh (23)	264	0.47
West Indian, ex. Hispanic (18)	56	0.10
Bahamian (0)	11	0.02
Jamaican (18)	31	0.05
West Indian (0)	14	0.02
Yugoslavian (1,321)	1,345	2.38

Hispanic Origin	Population	%
Hispanic or Latino (of any race)	3,749	6.46
Central American, ex. Mexican	998	1.72
Costa Rican	5	0.01
Guatemalan	155	0.27
Honduran	167	0.29
Nicaraguan	18	0.03
Panamanian	19	0.03
Salvadoran	633	1.09
Other Central American	1	<0.01
Cuban	100	0.17
Dominican Republic	27	0.05
Mexican	1,981	3.41
Puerto Rican	146	0.25
South American	123	0.21
Argentinean	7	0.01
Bolivian	2	<0.01
Chilean	4	0.01
Colombian	60	0.10
Ecuadorian	7	0.01
Peruvian	29	0.05
Uruguayan	1	<0.01
Venezuelan	13	0.02
Other Hispanic or Latino	374	0.64

Race*	Population	%
African-American/Black (8,071)	8,896	15.32
Not Hispanic (7,989)	8,747	15.06
Hispanic (82)	149	0.26
American Indian/Alaska Native (158)	410	0.71
Not Hispanic (136)	349	0.60
Hispanic (22)	61	0.11
Alaska Athabascan *(Ala. Nat.)* (2)	2	<0.01
Apache (1)	6	0.01
Blackfeet (3)	15	0.03
Central American Ind. (0)	1	<0.01
Cherokee (37)	122	0.21
Cheyenne (3)	3	0.01
Chickasaw (1)	1	<0.01
Chippewa (6)	6	0.01
Choctaw (1)	4	0.01
Comanche (3)	4	0.01
Creek (0)	2	<0.01
Mexican American Ind. (4)	9	0.02
Navajo (1)	3	0.01
Osage (4)	4	0.01
Ottawa (1)	2	<0.01
Sioux (0)	4	0.01
Yakama (1)	1	<0.01

*Notes: † The Census 2010 population figure is used to calculate the percentages in the Hispanic Origin and Race categories. Ancestry percentages are based on the 2006-2010 American Community Survey population (not shown); ‡ Numbers in parentheses indicate the number of people reporting a single ancestry; * Numbers in parentheses indicate the number of persons reporting this race alone, not in combination with any other race; Please refer to the Explanation of Data for more information.*

Yaqui (1)	1	<0.01
Asian (2,416)	2,722	4.69
Not Hispanic (2,386)	2,664	4.59
Hispanic (30)	58	0.10
Bangladeshi (3)	3	0.01
Bhutanese (19)	19	0.03
Burmese (653)	694	1.20
Cambodian (108)	135	0.23
Chinese, ex. Taiwanese (258)	285	0.49
Filipino (76)	125	0.22
Indian (315)	347	0.60
Indonesian (3)	3	0.01
Japanese (145)	180	0.31
Korean (141)	167	0.29
Laotian (50)	53	0.09
Malaysian (1)	1	<0.01
Nepalese (13)	21	0.04
Pakistani (20)	20	0.03
Sri Lankan (4)	4	0.01
Taiwanese (30)	32	0.06
Thai (126)	148	0.25
Vietnamese (348)	363	0.63
Hawaii Native/Pacific Islander (106)	159	0.27
Not Hispanic (93)	144	0.25
Hispanic (13)	15	0.03
Guamanian/Chamorro (21)	26	0.04
Marshallese (2)	2	<0.01
Native Hawaiian (14)	26	0.04
Samoan (2)	7	0.01
White (44,013)	45,382	78.15
Not Hispanic (42,404)	43,466	74.85
Hispanic (1,609)	1,916	3.30

Burlington

Place Type: CDP
County: Boone
Population: 15,926†

Ancestry‡	Population	%
American (1,373)	1,373	8.74
Austrian (13)	44	0.28
British (76)	92	0.59
Canadian (0)	15	0.10
Croatian (0)	17	0.11
Cypriot (19)	19	0.12
Dutch (45)	375	2.39
Eastern European (0)	19	0.12
English (928)	2,493	15.88
European (69)	69	0.44
French, ex. Basque (125)	282	1.80
French Canadian (19)	48	0.31
German (1,913)	4,721	30.07
Greek (50)	60	0.38
Hungarian (15)	48	0.31
Irish (766)	3,029	19.29
Italian (181)	525	3.34
Norwegian (54)	54	0.34
Polish (50)	322	2.05
Russian (10)	29	0.18
Scandinavian (0)	44	0.28
Scotch-Irish (214)	269	1.71
Scottish (268)	497	3.17
Slovene (9)	9	0.06
Swedish (43)	140	0.89
Ukrainian (12)	59	0.38
Welsh (10)	61	0.39

Hispanic Origin	Population	%
Hispanic or Latino (of any race)	485	3.05
Central American, ex. Mexican	28	0.18
Guatemalan	17	0.11
Honduran	4	0.03
Panamanian	4	0.03
Salvadoran	3	0.02
Cuban	15	0.09
Mexican	239	1.50
Puerto Rican	65	0.41
South American	31	0.19
Argentinean	1	0.01
Bolivian	2	0.01
Colombian	4	0.03
Peruvian	10	0.06
Venezuelan	11	0.07
Other South American	3	0.02
Other Hispanic or Latino	107	0.67

Race*	Population	%
African-American/Black (438)	558	3.50
Not Hispanic (426)	540	3.39
Hispanic (12)	18	0.11
American Indian/Alaska Native (47)	137	0.86
Not Hispanic (39)	116	0.73
Hispanic (8)	21	0.13
Blackfeet (0)	5	0.03
Cherokee (10)	58	0.36
Cheyenne (1)	1	0.01
Chippewa (1)	1	0.01
Choctaw (4)	6	0.04
Lumbee (0)	1	0.01
Mexican American Ind. (1)	1	0.01
Osage (1)	1	0.01
Seminole (0)	1	0.01
Sioux (1)	1	0.01
Spanish American Ind. (4)	4	0.03
Asian (182)	240	1.51
Not Hispanic (179)	236	1.48
Hispanic (3)	4	0.03
Burmese (0)	2	0.01
Chinese, ex. Taiwanese (25)	25	0.16
Filipino (32)	48	0.30
Indian (16)	23	0.14
Indonesian (1)	2	0.01
Japanese (64)	82	0.51
Korean (13)	23	0.14
Pakistani (9)	10	0.06
Thai (4)	6	0.04
Vietnamese (14)	16	0.10
Hawaii Native/Pacific Islander (21)	27	0.17
Not Hispanic (20)	26	0.16
Hispanic (1)	1	0.01
Guamanian/Chamorro (2)	6	0.04
Marshallese (1)	1	0.01
Native Hawaiian (11)	17	0.11
Samoan (2)	2	0.01
White (14,816)	15,098	94.80
Not Hispanic (14,517)	14,755	92.65
Hispanic (299)	343	2.15

Campbellsville

Place Type: City
County: Taylor
Population: 9,108†

Ancestry‡	Population	%
African, Sub-Saharan (102)	113	1.21
African (86)	97	1.03
Sudanese (16)	16	0.17
American (1,610)	1,610	17.17
Brazilian (64)	64	0.68
British (12)	12	0.13
Danish (12)	12	0.13
Dutch (19)	45	0.48
English (400)	794	8.47
European (52)	77	0.82
French, ex. Basque (49)	140	1.49
German (473)	1,374	14.65
Irish (371)	1,271	13.56
Italian (32)	123	1.31
Polish (12)	118	1.26
Russian (0)	12	0.13
Scotch-Irish (46)	110	1.17
Scottish (88)	196	2.09
Swedish (0)	39	0.42
Welsh (0)	28	0.30

Hispanic Origin	Population	%
Hispanic or Latino (of any race)	190	2.09
Central American, ex. Mexican	8	0.09
Guatemalan	2	0.02
Honduran	1	0.01
Nicaraguan	1	0.01
Panamanian	1	0.01
Salvadoran	3	0.03
Cuban	3	0.03
Dominican Republic	1	0.01
Mexican	125	1.37
Puerto Rican	16	0.18
South American	16	0.18
Argentinean	2	0.02
Chilean	6	0.07
Colombian	1	0.01
Venezuelan	7	0.08
Other Hispanic or Latino	21	0.23

Race*	Population	%
African-American/Black (867)	1,023	11.23
Not Hispanic (862)	1,016	11.16
Hispanic (5)	7	0.08
American Indian/Alaska Native (10)	55	0.60
Not Hispanic (10)	55	0.60
Apache (2)	2	0.02
Blackfeet (0)	6	0.07
Cherokee (3)	11	0.12
Chippewa (1)	1	0.01
Choctaw (0)	1	0.01
Navajo (0)	1	0.01
Asian (52)	59	0.65
Not Hispanic (51)	57	0.63
Hispanic (1)	2	0.02
Chinese, ex. Taiwanese (11)	11	0.12
Filipino (2)	4	0.04
Indian (10)	10	0.11
Japanese (9)	9	0.10
Korean (12)	17	0.19
Sri Lankan (1)	1	0.01
Vietnamese (1)	1	0.01
Hawaii Native/Pacific Islander (7)	10	0.11
Not Hispanic (7)	10	0.11
Guamanian/Chamorro (6)	6	0.07
Native Hawaiian (1)	1	0.01
White (7,868)	8,077	88.68
Not Hispanic (7,771)	7,973	87.54
Hispanic (97)	104	1.14

Covington

Place Type: City
County: Kenton
Population: 40,640†

Ancestry‡	Population	%
African, Sub-Saharan (28)	28	0.07
African (28)	28	0.07
Albanian (16)	33	0.08
American (5,303)	5,303	12.92
Arab (81)	113	0.28
Jordanian (50)	50	0.12
Lebanese (22)	44	0.11
Moroccan (9)	9	0.02
Other Arab (0)	10	0.02
Armenian (0)	9	0.02
Australian (0)	9	0.02
Austrian (9)	59	0.14
Belgian (17)	17	0.04
British (321)	422	1.03
Canadian (53)	89	0.22
Celtic (0)	14	0.03
Czech (33)	84	0.20
Danish (0)	10	0.02
Dutch (91)	540	1.32
English (1,705)	3,813	9.29
European (97)	128	0.31
French, ex. Basque (95)	726	1.77
French Canadian (9)	47	0.11
German (4,412)	10,642	25.92
Greek (37)	76	0.19
Hungarian (10)	67	0.16
Irish (1,539)	5,992	14.60

*Notes: † The Census 2010 population figure is used to calculate the percentages in the Hispanic Origin and Race categories. Ancestry percentages are based on the 2006-2010 American Community Survey population (not shown); ‡ Numbers in parentheses indicate the number of people reporting a single ancestry; * Numbers in parentheses indicate the number of persons reporting this race alone, not in combination with any other race; Please refer to the Explanation of Data for more information.*

Italian (508)	1,324	3.22
Lithuanian (0)	63	0.15
Maltese (0)	9	0.02
Norwegian (17)	90	0.22
Polish (122)	521	1.27
Romanian (17)	17	0.04
Russian (0)	104	0.25
Scandinavian (0)	104	0.25
Scotch-Irish (270)	845	2.06
Scottish (171)	852	2.08
Serbian (0)	11	0.03
Slavic (0)	9	0.02
Slovak (8)	75	0.18
Slovene (0)	23	0.06
Swedish (20)	100	0.24
Swiss (25)	49	0.12
Turkish (12)	45	0.11
Welsh (150)	465	1.13
West Indian, ex. Hispanic (62)	80	0.19
Dutch West Indian (14)	14	0.03
Jamaican (24)	42	0.10
West Indian (24)	24	0.06

Hispanic Origin	Population	%
Hispanic or Latino (of any race)	1,450	3.57
Central American, ex. Mexican	349	0.86
Costa Rican	2	<0.01
Guatemalan	306	0.75
Honduran	21	0.05
Panamanian	10	0.02
Salvadoran	10	0.02
Cuban	31	0.08
Dominican Republic	14	0.03
Mexican	613	1.51
Puerto Rican	117	0.29
South American	53	0.13
Argentinean	3	0.01
Bolivian	1	<0.01
Chilean	5	0.01
Colombian	18	0.04
Ecuadorian	7	0.02
Peruvian	6	0.01
Venezuelan	13	0.03
Other Hispanic or Latino	273	0.67

Race*	Population	%
African-American/Black (4,844)	5,723	14.08
Not Hispanic (4,778)	5,592	13.76
Hispanic (66)	131	0.32
American Indian/Alaska Native (104)	418	1.03
Not Hispanic (82)	369	0.91
Hispanic (22)	49	0.12
Aleut *(Alaska Native)* (0)	1	<0.01
Apache (0)	6	0.01
Blackfeet (7)	35	0.09
Central American Ind. (8)	15	0.04
Cherokee (20)	128	0.31
Cheyenne (1)	3	0.01
Chippewa (2)	2	<0.01
Choctaw (0)	11	0.03
Creek (1)	1	<0.01
Iroquois (9)	9	0.02
Lumbee (1)	2	<0.01
Mexican American Ind. (5)	6	0.01
Navajo (1)	1	<0.01
Ottawa (1)	1	<0.01
Sioux (0)	5	0.01
South American Ind. (1)	1	<0.01
Tohono O'Odham (0)	1	<0.01
Yup'ik *(Alaska Native)* (0)	1	<0.01
Asian (218)	327	0.80
Not Hispanic (180)	285	0.70
Hispanic (38)	42	0.10
Chinese, ex. Taiwanese (19)	37	0.09
Filipino (67)	92	0.23
Indian (36)	46	0.11
Indonesian (1)	4	0.01
Japanese (18)	40	0.10
Korean (20)	34	0.08
Laotian (8)	8	0.02
Nepalese (0)	1	<0.01
Pakistani (1)	2	<0.01
Taiwanese (0)	1	<0.01
Thai (9)	9	0.02
Vietnamese (26)	33	0.08
Hawaii Native/Pacific Islander (60)	96	0.24
Not Hispanic (45)	72	0.18
Hispanic (15)	24	0.06
Guamanian/Chamorro (24)	31	0.08
Native Hawaiian (11)	17	0.04
Samoan (2)	5	0.01
White (33,323)	34,539	84.99
Not Hispanic (32,831)	33,910	83.44
Hispanic (492)	629	1.55

Danville

Place Type: City
County: Boyle
Population: 16,218†

Ancestry‡	Population	%
African, Sub-Saharan (51)	51	0.32
African (51)	51	0.32
American (3,416)	3,416	21.28
Arab (12)	36	0.22
Lebanese (12)	36	0.22
Armenian (0)	7	0.04
Austrian (0)	13	0.08
Belgian (23)	52	0.32
British (104)	167	1.04
Canadian (15)	15	0.09
Danish (0)	14	0.09
Dutch (35)	335	2.09
Eastern European (0)	93	0.58
English (904)	2,226	13.87
European (53)	66	0.41
Finnish (8)	8	0.05
French, ex. Basque (61)	216	1.35
French Canadian (39)	72	0.45
German (540)	2,477	15.43
Greek (0)	18	0.11
Hungarian (13)	28	0.17
Iranian (11)	11	0.07
Irish (657)	2,138	13.32
Italian (71)	438	2.73
Lithuanian (0)	18	0.11
Northern European (8)	8	0.05
Norwegian (21)	44	0.27
Polish (24)	144	0.90
Portuguese (0)	9	0.06
Romanian (12)	12	0.07
Russian (11)	11	0.07
Scandinavian (12)	12	0.07
Scotch-Irish (445)	736	4.58
Scottish (113)	358	2.23
Slovak (11)	19	0.12
Slovene (17)	24	0.15
Swedish (80)	89	0.55
Swiss (0)	43	0.27
Welsh (79)	242	1.51

Hispanic Origin	Population	%
Hispanic or Latino (of any race)	635	3.92
Central American, ex. Mexican	52	0.32
Costa Rican	3	0.02
Guatemalan	13	0.08
Honduran	13	0.08
Nicaraguan	5	0.03
Panamanian	9	0.06
Salvadoran	9	0.06
Cuban	13	0.08
Dominican Republic	7	0.04
Mexican	440	2.71
Puerto Rican	53	0.33
South American	15	0.09
Argentinean	1	0.01
Bolivian	1	0.01
Colombian	11	0.07
Paraguayan	1	0.01
Peruvian	1	0.01
Other Hispanic or Latino	55	0.34

Race*	Population	%
African-American/Black (1,771)	2,071	12.77
Not Hispanic (1,756)	2,022	12.47
Hispanic (15)	49	0.30
American Indian/Alaska Native (40)	132	0.81
Not Hispanic (33)	109	0.67
Hispanic (7)	23	0.14
Blackfeet (0)	7	0.04
Cherokee (8)	44	0.27
Chippewa (0)	1	0.01
Choctaw (0)	2	0.01
Comanche (0)	1	0.01
Delaware (0)	1	0.01
Iroquois (0)	1	0.01
Lumbee (1)	2	0.01
Mexican American Ind. (4)	4	0.02
Sioux (5)	9	0.06
Asian (163)	227	1.40
Not Hispanic (158)	214	1.32
Hispanic (5)	13	0.08
Bangladeshi (3)	3	0.02
Cambodian (16)	17	0.10
Chinese, ex. Taiwanese (56)	67	0.41
Filipino (5)	25	0.15
Indian (25)	33	0.20
Japanese (7)	12	0.07
Korean (23)	29	0.18
Laotian (1)	2	0.01
Nepalese (2)	2	0.01
Pakistani (10)	10	0.06
Taiwanese (7)	7	0.04
Thai (1)	3	0.02
Vietnamese (1)	2	0.01
Hawaii Native/Pacific Islander (3)	14	0.09
Not Hispanic (3)	13	0.08
Hispanic (0)	1	0.01
Native Hawaiian (1)	6	0.04
Samoan (2)	3	0.02
White (13,487)	13,900	85.71
Not Hispanic (13,208)	13,568	83.66
Hispanic (279)	332	2.05

Edgewood

Place Type: City
County: Kenton
Population: 8,575†

Ancestry‡	Population	%
American (689)	689	7.92
Arab (0)	9	0.10
Lebanese (0)	9	0.10
Austrian (11)	49	0.56
British (26)	26	0.30
Canadian (10)	10	0.11
Croatian (10)	10	0.11
Czech (9)	9	0.10
Czechoslovakian (10)	10	0.11
Danish (38)	38	0.44
Dutch (59)	212	2.44
English (408)	1,204	13.84
European (38)	77	0.89
French, ex. Basque (42)	466	5.36
French Canadian (22)	22	0.25
German (1,914)	4,031	46.34
Greek (41)	60	0.69
Hungarian (6)	80	0.92
Irish (436)	1,981	22.78
Italian (154)	574	6.60
Norwegian (44)	66	0.76
Polish (36)	89	1.02
Russian (0)	18	0.21
Scotch-Irish (137)	241	2.77
Scottish (103)	234	2.69
Slavic (8)	8	0.09
Swedish (18)	49	0.56
Swiss (11)	21	0.24

*Notes: † The Census 2010 population figure is used to calculate the percentages in the Hispanic Origin and Race categories. Ancestry percentages are based on the 2006-2010 American Community Survey population (not shown); ‡ Numbers in parentheses indicate the number of people reporting a single ancestry; * Numbers in parentheses indicate the number of persons reporting this race alone, not in combination with any other race; Please refer to the Explanation of Data for more information.*

Welsh (33)	56	0.64

Hispanic Origin	Population	%
Hispanic or Latino (of any race)	89	1.04
Central American, ex. Mexican	4	0.05
Guatemalan	3	0.03
Panamanian	1	0.01
Cuban	3	0.03
Dominican Republic	1	0.01
Mexican	29	0.34
Puerto Rican	26	0.30
South American	17	0.20
Argentinean	5	0.06
Colombian	2	0.02
Ecuadorian	6	0.07
Paraguayan	1	0.01
Peruvian	2	0.02
Uruguayan	1	0.01
Other Hispanic or Latino	9	0.10

Race*	Population	%
African-American/Black (45)	72	0.84
Not Hispanic (44)	69	0.80
Hispanic (1)	3	0.03
American Indian/Alaska Native (4)	18	0.21
Not Hispanic (4)	18	0.21
Cherokee (1)	4	0.05
Iroquois (1)	1	0.01
South American Ind. (1)	3	0.03
Asian (103)	123	1.43
Not Hispanic (102)	119	1.39
Hispanic (1)	4	0.05
Chinese, ex. Taiwanese (11)	15	0.17
Filipino (26)	34	0.40
Indian (16)	17	0.20
Japanese (4)	9	0.10
Korean (10)	18	0.21
Pakistani (11)	11	0.13
Taiwanese (2)	2	0.02
Thai (1)	1	0.01
Vietnamese (17)	18	0.21
Hawaii Native/Pacific Islander (10)	15	0.17
Not Hispanic (10)	14	0.16
Hispanic (0)	1	0.01
Guamanian/Chamorro (6)	7	0.08
Samoan (1)	1	0.01
Tongan (2)	2	0.02
White (8,323)	8,384	97.77
Not Hispanic (8,264)	8,315	96.97
Hispanic (59)	69	0.80

Elizabethtown

Place Type: City
County: Hardin
Population: 28,531†

Ancestry‡	Population	%
African, Sub-Saharan (51)	73	0.27
African (51)	73	0.27
American (3,492)	3,492	13.02
Austrian (0)	15	0.06
Belgian (0)	20	0.07
British (51)	96	0.36
Canadian (30)	41	0.15
Celtic (33)	33	0.12
Croatian (0)	14	0.05
Czech (23)	41	0.15
Dutch (91)	304	1.13
Eastern European (24)	24	0.09
English (1,762)	3,594	13.40
European (179)	226	0.84
Finnish (8)	8	0.03
French, ex. Basque (76)	512	1.91
French Canadian (87)	99	0.37
German (1,430)	3,827	14.27
Greek (13)	13	0.05
Guyanese (46)	57	0.21
Hungarian (0)	13	0.05
Irish (988)	3,515	13.10
Italian (307)	1,063	3.96
Northern European (11)	11	0.04
Norwegian (33)	89	0.33
Pennsylvania German (0)	17	0.06
Polish (106)	458	1.71
Portuguese (11)	11	0.04
Russian (0)	26	0.10
Scotch-Irish (357)	538	2.01
Scottish (376)	773	2.88
Swedish (33)	83	0.31
Swiss (0)	9	0.03
Ukrainian (16)	65	0.24
Welsh (64)	128	0.48
West Indian, ex. Hispanic (27)	62	0.23
Barbadian (0)	11	0.04
Jamaican (27)	51	0.19

Hispanic Origin	Population	%
Hispanic or Latino (of any race)	1,215	4.26
Central American, ex. Mexican	85	0.30
Costa Rican	2	0.01
Guatemalan	14	0.05
Honduran	8	0.03
Nicaraguan	14	0.05
Panamanian	35	0.12
Salvadoran	12	0.04
Cuban	42	0.15
Dominican Republic	17	0.06
Mexican	675	2.37
Puerto Rican	273	0.96
South American	29	0.10
Argentinean	2	0.01
Bolivian	3	0.01
Chilean	1	<0.01
Colombian	5	0.02
Ecuadorian	8	0.03
Peruvian	9	0.03
Uruguayan	1	<0.01
Other Hispanic or Latino	94	0.33

Race*	Population	%
African-American/Black (3,321)	3,866	13.55
Not Hispanic (3,255)	3,754	13.16
Hispanic (66)	112	0.39
American Indian/Alaska Native (98)	266	0.93
Not Hispanic (88)	245	0.86
Hispanic (10)	21	0.07
Alaska Athabascan *(Ala. Nat.)* (1)	1	<0.01
Apache (4)	5	0.02
Blackfeet (1)	5	0.02
Cherokee (21)	90	0.32
Cheyenne (1)	1	<0.01
Chickasaw (0)	1	<0.01
Chippewa (2)	4	0.01
Choctaw (3)	4	0.01
Comanche (1)	4	0.01
Creek (0)	1	<0.01
Iroquois (6)	13	0.05
Kiowa (1)	1	<0.01
Lumbee (3)	5	0.02
Mexican American Ind. (2)	4	0.01
Navajo (4)	5	0.02
Osage (0)	2	0.01
Ottawa (0)	1	<0.01
Pima (1)	1	<0.01
Potawatomi (0)	3	0.01
Sioux (7)	11	0.04
South American Ind. (1)	1	<0.01
Tohono O'Odham (0)	2	0.01
Asian (748)	1,018	3.57
Not Hispanic (741)	995	3.49
Hispanic (7)	23	0.08
Bangladeshi (1)	1	<0.01
Cambodian (10)	14	0.05
Chinese, ex. Taiwanese (37)	52	0.18
Filipino (130)	215	0.75
Indian (136)	157	0.55
Indonesian (2)	8	0.03
Japanese (103)	149	0.52
Korean (126)	212	0.74
Laotian (23)	30	0.11
Pakistani (90)	98	0.34
Taiwanese (3)	3	0.01
Thai (5)	11	0.04
Vietnamese (46)	56	0.20
Hawaii Native/Pacific Islander (52)	131	0.46
Not Hispanic (47)	119	0.42
Hispanic (5)	12	0.04
Fijian (1)	1	<0.01
Guamanian/Chamorro (27)	49	0.17
Marshallese (5)	5	0.02
Native Hawaiian (3)	24	0.08
Samoan (8)	23	0.08
Tongan (1)	6	0.02
White (22,952)	23,814	83.47
Not Hispanic (22,294)	23,048	80.78
Hispanic (658)	766	2.68

Elsmere

Place Type: City
County: Kenton
Population: 8,451†

Ancestry‡	Population	%
African, Sub-Saharan (88)	88	1.05
Ethiopian (88)	88	1.05
American (1,088)	1,088	12.93
Austrian (0)	13	0.15
Czech (25)	25	0.30
Danish (0)	16	0.19
Dutch (19)	99	1.18
English (173)	499	5.93
French, ex. Basque (45)	136	1.62
French Canadian (0)	11	0.13
German (818)	1,912	22.73
Greek (8)	8	0.10
Irish (394)	1,646	19.57
Italian (264)	464	5.52
Lithuanian (17)	17	0.20
Polish (9)	9	0.11
Romanian (0)	4	0.05
Scandinavian (0)	17	0.20
Scotch-Irish (32)	117	1.39
Scottish (59)	194	2.31
Swedish (0)	15	0.18
Swiss (0)	15	0.18
Welsh (0)	19	0.23
West Indian, ex. Hispanic (13)	41	0.49
West Indian (13)	41	0.49
Yugoslavian (11)	11	0.13

Hispanic Origin	Population	%
Hispanic or Latino (of any race)	691	8.18
Central American, ex. Mexican	47	0.56
Guatemalan	28	0.33
Honduran	10	0.12
Nicaraguan	4	0.05
Salvadoran	5	0.06
Cuban	6	0.07
Dominican Republic	6	0.07
Mexican	516	6.11
Puerto Rican	49	0.58
South American	25	0.30
Colombian	8	0.09
Ecuadorian	12	0.14
Peruvian	4	0.05
Other South American	1	0.01
Other Hispanic or Latino	42	0.50

Race*	Population	%
African-American/Black (602)	774	9.16
Not Hispanic (594)	750	8.87
Hispanic (8)	24	0.28
American Indian/Alaska Native (35)	71	0.84
Not Hispanic (20)	43	0.51
Hispanic (15)	28	0.33
Apache (0)	2	0.02
Central American Ind. (0)	1	0.01
Cherokee (4)	10	0.12

*Notes: † The Census 2010 population figure is used to calculate the percentages in the Hispanic Origin and Race categories. Ancestry percentages are based on the 2006-2010 American Community Survey population (not shown); ‡ Numbers in parentheses indicate the number of people reporting a single ancestry; * Numbers in parentheses indicate the number of persons reporting this race alone, not in combination with any other race; Please refer to the Explanation of Data for more information.*

Chippewa (2)	2	0.02
Lumbee (1)	1	0.01
Sioux (6)	7	0.08
Asian (38)	64	0.76
Not Hispanic (38)	64	0.76
Chinese, ex. Taiwanese (9)	13	0.15
Filipino (2)	10	0.12
Indian (5)	12	0.14
Japanese (5)	11	0.13
Korean (5)	6	0.07
Laotian (2)	6	0.07
Thai (0)	4	0.05
Vietnamese (3)	7	0.08
Hawaii Native/Pacific Islander (13)	20	0.24
Not Hispanic (13)	17	0.20
Hispanic (0)	3	0.04
Fijian (1)	1	0.01
Guamanian/Chamorro (1)	2	0.02
Native Hawaiian (2)	6	0.07
Samoan (5)	6	0.07
White (7,120)	7,391	87.46
Not Hispanic (6,875)	7,076	83.73
Hispanic (245)	315	3.73

Erlanger

Place Type: City
County: Kenton
Population: 18,082†

Ancestry‡	Population	%
African, Sub-Saharan (107)	113	0.63
African (0)	6	0.03
Somalian (107)	107	0.60
American (1,906)	1,906	10.71
Arab (0)	47	0.26
Lebanese (0)	31	0.17
Moroccan (0)	8	0.04
Other Arab (0)	8	0.04
Austrian (0)	11	0.06
Belgian (0)	10	0.06
British (53)	65	0.37
Canadian (28)	28	0.16
Croatian (0)	25	0.14
Czechoslovakian (0)	11	0.06
Danish (0)	8	0.04
Dutch (74)	390	2.19
Eastern European (17)	17	0.10
English (807)	1,920	10.79
European (146)	161	0.90
French, ex. Basque (115)	629	3.53
French Canadian (0)	7	0.04
German (2,832)	6,459	36.29
Greek (0)	16	0.09
Hungarian (74)	127	0.71
Irish (1,219)	4,074	22.89
Italian (151)	521	2.93
Latvian (0)	16	0.09
Norwegian (13)	56	0.31
Polish (42)	195	1.10
Romanian (0)	8	0.04
Scotch-Irish (102)	353	1.98
Scottish (54)	219	1.23
Swedish (29)	107	0.60
Swiss (40)	97	0.55
Welsh (37)	101	0.57
West Indian, ex. Hispanic (37)	37	0.21
West Indian (37)	37	0.21

Hispanic Origin	Population	%
Hispanic or Latino (of any race)	562	3.11
Central American, ex. Mexican	91	0.50
Guatemalan	59	0.33
Honduran	14	0.08
Panamanian	9	0.05
Salvadoran	9	0.05
Cuban	12	0.07
Dominican Republic	5	0.03
Mexican	302	1.67
Puerto Rican	43	0.24
South American	33	0.18
Argentinean	1	0.01
Chilean	1	0.01
Colombian	9	0.05
Ecuadorian	3	0.02
Peruvian	14	0.08
Uruguayan	3	0.02
Venezuelan	2	0.01
Other Hispanic or Latino	76	0.42

Race*	Population	%
African-American/Black (550)	770	4.26
Not Hispanic (544)	753	4.16
Hispanic (6)	17	0.09
American Indian/Alaska Native (22)	100	0.55
Not Hispanic (19)	89	0.49
Hispanic (3)	11	0.06
Apache (0)	1	0.01
Blackfeet (0)	1	0.01
Cherokee (5)	24	0.13
Choctaw (1)	1	0.01
Creek (1)	1	0.01
Delaware (0)	4	0.02
Inupiat *(Alaska Native)* (1)	1	0.01
Lumbee (1)	1	0.01
Sioux (0)	1	0.01
Spanish American Ind. (1)	1	0.01
Asian (150)	210	1.16
Not Hispanic (150)	208	1.15
Hispanic (0)	2	0.01
Bangladeshi (2)	2	0.01
Cambodian (2)	2	0.01
Chinese, ex. Taiwanese (30)	35	0.19
Filipino (13)	32	0.18
Indian (30)	39	0.22
Japanese (23)	38	0.21
Korean (10)	20	0.11
Nepalese (4)	4	0.02
Pakistani (10)	10	0.06
Thai (4)	5	0.03
Vietnamese (16)	19	0.11
Hawaii Native/Pacific Islander (25)	51	0.28
Not Hispanic (25)	44	0.24
Hispanic (0)	7	0.04
Guamanian/Chamorro (3)	12	0.07
Native Hawaiian (7)	10	0.06
Samoan (1)	6	0.03
White (16,686)	17,042	94.25
Not Hispanic (16,429)	16,748	92.62
Hispanic (257)	294	1.63

Florence

Place Type: City
County: Boone
Population: 29,951†

Ancestry‡	Population	%
African, Sub-Saharan (412)	445	1.52
African (217)	250	0.85
Nigerian (68)	68	0.23
Somalian (127)	127	0.43
American (2,521)	2,521	8.62
Arab (80)	80	0.27
Arab (45)	45	0.15
Lebanese (35)	35	0.12
Armenian (0)	15	0.05
Australian (0)	106	0.36
Austrian (10)	10	0.03
Belgian (0)	10	0.03
British (76)	200	0.68
Bulgarian (17)	21	0.07
Canadian (16)	16	0.05
Carpatho Rusyn (15)	15	0.05
Croatian (13)	28	0.10
Czech (0)	12	0.04
Danish (14)	14	0.05
Dutch (288)	749	2.56
English (1,284)	3,056	10.45
European (115)	115	0.39
Finnish (62)	114	0.39
French, ex. Basque (190)	986	3.37
French Canadian (42)	55	0.19
German (4,322)	9,412	32.19
Greek (38)	92	0.31
Hungarian (75)	110	0.38
Irish (1,320)	5,161	17.65
Italian (356)	1,099	3.76
Northern European (9)	9	0.03
Norwegian (42)	153	0.52
Polish (149)	524	1.79
Portuguese (12)	43	0.15
Romanian (0)	33	0.11
Russian (37)	170	0.58
Scotch-Irish (334)	764	2.61
Scottish (352)	810	2.77
Slovak (15)	15	0.05
Swedish (56)	109	0.37
Swiss (0)	15	0.05
Ukrainian (9)	24	0.08
Welsh (63)	343	1.17
West Indian, ex. Hispanic (57)	163	0.56
Barbadian (7)	7	0.02
West Indian (50)	156	0.53
Yugoslavian (115)	130	0.44

Hispanic Origin	Population	%
Hispanic or Latino (of any race)	1,634	5.46
Central American, ex. Mexican	156	0.52
Guatemalan	90	0.30
Honduran	22	0.07
Nicaraguan	10	0.03
Panamanian	3	0.01
Salvadoran	29	0.10
Other Central American	2	0.01
Cuban	29	0.10
Dominican Republic	33	0.11
Mexican	979	3.27
Puerto Rican	140	0.47
South American	168	0.56
Argentinean	20	0.07
Chilean	6	0.02
Colombian	48	0.16
Ecuadorian	42	0.14
Paraguayan	1	<0.01
Peruvian	39	0.13
Uruguayan	1	<0.01
Venezuelan	10	0.03
Other South American	1	<0.01
Other Hispanic or Latino	129	0.43

Race*	Population	%
African-American/Black (1,356)	1,707	5.70
Not Hispanic (1,338)	1,659	5.54
Hispanic (18)	48	0.16
American Indian/Alaska Native (65)	194	0.65
Not Hispanic (56)	168	0.56
Hispanic (9)	26	0.09
Apache (1)	2	0.01
Blackfeet (0)	10	0.03
Canadian/French Am. Ind. (2)	2	0.01
Central American Ind. (2)	3	0.01
Cherokee (11)	46	0.15
Cheyenne (0)	2	0.01
Chickasaw (0)	1	<0.01
Chippewa (1)	1	<0.01
Choctaw (0)	2	0.01
Cree (0)	1	<0.01
Creek (2)	4	0.01
Mexican American Ind. (1)	1	<0.01
Navajo (3)	7	0.02
Potawatomi (1)	1	<0.01
Pueblo (2)	2	0.01
Seminole (0)	1	<0.01
Sioux (7)	14	0.05
South American Ind. (0)	1	<0.01
Yup'ik *(Alaska Native)* (0)	4	0.01
Asian (897)	1,070	3.57
Not Hispanic (887)	1,054	3.52
Hispanic (10)	16	0.05

*Notes: † The Census 2010 population figure is used to calculate the percentages in the Hispanic Origin and Race categories. Ancestry percentages are based on the 2006-2010 American Community Survey population (not shown); ‡ Numbers in parentheses indicate the number of people reporting a single ancestry; * Numbers in parentheses indicate the number of persons reporting this race alone, not in combination with any other race; Please refer to the Explanation of Data for more information.*

Bangladeshi (5)	5	0.02
Burmese (19)	20	0.07
Cambodian (1)	2	0.01
Chinese, ex. Taiwanese (93)	105	0.35
Filipino (50)	81	0.27
Hmong (1)	1	<0.01
Indian (303)	327	1.09
Indonesian (9)	9	0.03
Japanese (239)	292	0.97
Korean (63)	88	0.29
Laotian (2)	2	0.01
Pakistani (1)	6	0.02
Sri Lankan (2)	2	0.01
Thai (15)	20	0.07
Vietnamese (80)	87	0.29
Hawaii Native/Pacific Islander (49)	86	0.29
Not Hispanic (41)	74	0.25
Hispanic (8)	12	0.04
Guamanian/Chamorro (11)	20	0.07
Marshallese (3)	3	0.01
Native Hawaiian (10)	21	0.07
Samoan (13)	13	0.04
White (26,100)	26,700	89.15
Not Hispanic (25,365)	25,875	86.39
Hispanic (735)	825	2.75

Fort Campbell North

Place Type: CDP
County: Christian
Population: 13,685†

Ancestry‡	Population	%
African, Sub-Saharan (145)	145	1.10
African (145)	145	1.10
American (1,688)	1,688	12.82
Brazilian (13)	46	0.35
British (124)	128	0.97
Czech (137)	165	1.25
Czechoslovakian (21)	37	0.28
Danish (0)	50	0.38
Dutch (50)	136	1.03
Eastern European (0)	18	0.14
English (333)	701	5.32
European (32)	32	0.24
Finnish (0)	46	0.35
French, ex. Basque (17)	173	1.31
French Canadian (3)	19	0.14
German (646)	1,807	13.72
Greek (7)	32	0.24
Hungarian (0)	40	0.30
Irish (597)	1,442	10.95
Italian (245)	694	5.27
Lithuanian (0)	32	0.24
Norwegian (14)	77	0.58
Polish (235)	513	3.90
Portuguese (0)	82	0.62
Russian (15)	35	0.27
Scandinavian (0)	18	0.14
Scotch-Irish (157)	318	2.41
Scottish (150)	352	2.67
Slovene (3)	3	0.02
Swedish (19)	181	1.37
Ukrainian (0)	12	0.09
West Indian, ex. Hispanic (70)	191	1.45
Haitian (0)	47	0.36
Jamaican (30)	78	0.59
West Indian (40)	66	0.50

Hispanic Origin	Population	%
Hispanic or Latino (of any race)	2,057	15.03
Central American, ex. Mexican	103	0.75
Costa Rican	1	0.01
Guatemalan	5	0.04
Honduran	10	0.07
Nicaraguan	12	0.09
Panamanian	27	0.20
Salvadoran	48	0.35
Cuban	53	0.39
Dominican Republic	39	0.28
Mexican	1,011	7.39
Puerto Rican	570	4.17
South American	67	0.49
Argentinean	7	0.05
Bolivian	1	0.01
Colombian	23	0.17
Ecuadorian	9	0.07
Peruvian	23	0.17
Venezuelan	4	0.03
Other Hispanic or Latino	214	1.56

Race*	Population	%
African-American/Black (2,255)	2,663	19.46
Not Hispanic (2,121)	2,436	17.80
Hispanic (134)	227	1.66
American Indian/Alaska Native (165)	328	2.40
Not Hispanic (127)	250	1.83
Hispanic (38)	78	0.57
Aleut *(Alaska Native)* (0)	3	0.02
Apache (5)	10	0.07
Blackfeet (1)	8	0.06
Canadian/French Am. Ind. (3)	4	0.03
Cherokee (11)	40	0.29
Cheyenne (0)	3	0.02
Chickasaw (4)	5	0.04
Chippewa (7)	8	0.06
Choctaw (0)	2	0.01
Creek (7)	8	0.06
Iroquois (1)	16	0.12
Lumbee (2)	4	0.03
Mexican American Ind. (8)	19	0.14
Navajo (10)	16	0.12
Potawatomi (1)	1	0.01
Puget Sound Salish (1)	1	0.01
Seminole (0)	3	0.02
Sioux (3)	9	0.07
South American Ind. (1)	3	0.02
Tlingit-Haida *(Alaska Native)* (2)	3	0.02
Yup'ik *(Alaska Native)* (5)	5	0.04
Asian (188)	379	2.77
Not Hispanic (179)	335	2.45
Hispanic (9)	44	0.32
Cambodian (3)	5	0.04
Chinese, ex. Taiwanese (15)	25	0.18
Filipino (81)	171	1.25
Hmong (5)	5	0.04
Indian (11)	21	0.15
Japanese (11)	48	0.35
Korean (36)	88	0.64
Laotian (3)	3	0.02
Nepalese (2)	2	0.01
Taiwanese (0)	3	0.02
Thai (9)	10	0.07
Vietnamese (7)	8	0.06
Hawaii Native/Pacific Islander (194)	275	2.01
Not Hispanic (177)	242	1.77
Hispanic (17)	33	0.24
Fijian (0)	4	0.03
Guamanian/Chamorro (65)	84	0.61
Marshallese (7)	7	0.05
Native Hawaiian (20)	54	0.39
Samoan (32)	43	0.31
Tongan (1)	4	0.03
White (9,527)	10,195	74.50
Not Hispanic (8,472)	8,950	65.40
Hispanic (1,055)	1,245	9.10

Fort Knox

Place Type: CDP
County: Hardin
Population: 10,124†

Ancestry‡	Population	%
African, Sub-Saharan (149)	172	1.44
African (135)	158	1.32
Other Sub-Saharan African (14)	14	0.12
Albanian (11)	16	0.13
American (545)	545	4.57
Arab (68)	80	0.67
Arab (68)	68	0.57
Lebanese (0)	12	0.10
Armenian (7)	7	0.06
Belgian (0)	76	0.64
British (21)	48	0.40
Cajun (0)	15	0.13
Celtic (6)	6	0.05
Czech (31)	76	0.64
Czechoslovakian (13)	13	0.11
Danish (0)	14	0.12
Dutch (25)	89	0.75
English (425)	1,434	12.02
European (91)	104	0.87
French, ex. Basque (23)	397	3.33
French Canadian (19)	54	0.45
German (770)	3,272	27.42
Greek (0)	11	0.09
Irish (476)	1,884	15.79
Italian (72)	337	2.82
Norwegian (11)	67	0.56
Polish (71)	433	3.63
Russian (16)	163	1.37
Scandinavian (0)	12	0.10
Scotch-Irish (60)	166	1.39
Scottish (56)	266	2.23
Swedish (47)	93	0.78
Swiss (0)	36	0.30
Welsh (59)	133	1.11
West Indian, ex. Hispanic (39)	75	0.63
Bahamian (0)	36	0.30
Haitian (39)	39	0.33

Hispanic Origin	Population	%
Hispanic or Latino (of any race)	1,424	14.07
Central American, ex. Mexican	84	0.83
Costa Rican	5	0.05
Guatemalan	7	0.07
Honduran	7	0.07
Nicaraguan	9	0.09
Panamanian	41	0.40
Salvadoran	15	0.15
Cuban	24	0.24
Dominican Republic	22	0.22
Mexican	782	7.72
Puerto Rican	372	3.67
South American	37	0.37
Argentinean	3	0.03
Chilean	1	0.01
Colombian	21	0.21
Ecuadorian	8	0.08
Peruvian	2	0.02
Other South American	2	0.02
Other Hispanic or Latino	103	1.02

Race*	Population	%
African-American/Black (1,677)	1,955	19.31
Not Hispanic (1,568)	1,777	17.55
Hispanic (109)	178	1.76
American Indian/Alaska Native (111)	234	2.31
Not Hispanic (82)	180	1.78
Hispanic (29)	54	0.53
Apache (2)	2	0.02
Blackfeet (1)	2	0.02
Cherokee (18)	52	0.51
Chickasaw (1)	1	0.01
Chippewa (7)	9	0.09
Choctaw (6)	7	0.07
Comanche (2)	2	0.02
Iroquois (3)	5	0.05
Lumbee (3)	6	0.06
Mexican American Ind. (1)	3	0.03
Navajo (5)	6	0.06
Osage (0)	1	0.01
Pueblo (9)	11	0.11
Seminole (0)	1	0.01
Sioux (0)	7	0.07
South American Ind. (0)	4	0.04
Yaqui (1)	1	0.01
Asian (168)	322	3.18
Not Hispanic (165)	302	2.98

*Notes: † The Census 2010 population figure is used to calculate the percentages in the Hispanic Origin and Race categories. Ancestry percentages are based on the 2006-2010 American Community Survey population (not shown); ‡ Numbers in parentheses indicate the number of people reporting a single ancestry; * Numbers in parentheses indicate the number of persons reporting this race alone, not in combination with any other race; Please refer to the Explanation of Data for more information.*

Hispanic (3)	20	0.20
Cambodian (1)	3	0.03
Chinese, ex. Taiwanese (17)	31	0.31
Filipino (80)	145	1.43
Hmong (2)	3	0.03
Indian (6)	16	0.16
Japanese (9)	49	0.48
Korean (29)	63	0.62
Laotian (4)	5	0.05
Nepalese (2)	2	0.02
Thai (3)	8	0.08
Vietnamese (7)	9	0.09
Hawaii Native/Pacific Islander (59)	93	0.92
Not Hispanic (53)	75	0.74
Hispanic (6)	18	0.18
Fijian (8)	9	0.09
Guamanian/Chamorro (14)	16	0.16
Native Hawaiian (11)	37	0.37
Samoan (13)	15	0.15
Tongan (1)	1	0.01
White (7,247)	7,697	76.03
Not Hispanic (6,430)	6,775	66.92
Hispanic (817)	922	9.11

Fort Mitchell

Place Type: City
County: Kenton
Population: 8,207†

Ancestry‡	Population	%
African, Sub-Saharan (182)	182	2.23
African (182)	182	2.23
American (1,144)	1,144	13.99
Austrian (12)	24	0.29
British (21)	21	0.26
Canadian (0)	49	0.60
Czech (0)	56	0.68
Dutch (28)	100	1.22
English (138)	800	9.78
European (90)	90	1.10
French, ex. Basque (43)	302	3.69
German (1,463)	2,934	35.88
Greek (106)	134	1.64
Hungarian (0)	11	0.13
Irish (432)	1,562	19.10
Italian (157)	462	5.65
Maltese (0)	12	0.15
Norwegian (19)	32	0.39
Polish (17)	192	2.35
Russian (8)	20	0.24
Scotch-Irish (127)	321	3.93
Scottish (42)	192	2.35
Slovak (0)	12	0.15
Swedish (14)	28	0.34
Swiss (0)	32	0.39
Welsh (27)	56	0.68

Hispanic Origin	Population	%
Hispanic or Latino (of any race)	233	2.84
Central American, ex. Mexican	19	0.23
Costa Rican	1	0.01
Guatemalan	16	0.19
Panamanian	1	0.01
Salvadoran	1	0.01
Cuban	6	0.07
Dominican Republic	3	0.04
Mexican	131	1.60
Puerto Rican	27	0.33
South American	18	0.22
Colombian	1	0.01
Ecuadorian	2	0.02
Peruvian	8	0.10
Uruguayan	2	0.02
Venezuelan	5	0.06
Other Hispanic or Latino	29	0.35

Race*	Population	%
African-American/Black (200)	244	2.97
Not Hispanic (199)	243	2.96
Hispanic (1)	1	0.01
American Indian/Alaska Native (11)	30	0.37
Not Hispanic (11)	29	0.35
Hispanic (0)	1	0.01
Blackfeet (0)	1	0.01
Cherokee (0)	11	0.13
Chippewa (4)	4	0.05
Cree (1)	1	0.01
Navajo (1)	2	0.02
Seminole (0)	1	0.01
Asian (209)	244	2.97
Not Hispanic (208)	241	2.94
Hispanic (1)	3	0.04
Cambodian (2)	2	0.02
Chinese, ex. Taiwanese (27)	27	0.33
Filipino (23)	32	0.39
Indian (116)	130	1.58
Japanese (11)	14	0.17
Korean (7)	10	0.12
Malaysian (1)	1	0.01
Sri Lankan (1)	2	0.02
Taiwanese (4)	9	0.11
Thai (1)	2	0.02
Vietnamese (10)	10	0.12
Hawaii Native/Pacific Islander (4)	5	0.06
Not Hispanic (4)	5	0.06
Guamanian/Chamorro (0)	1	0.01
White (7,587)	7,678	93.55
Not Hispanic (7,444)	7,528	91.73
Hispanic (143)	150	1.83

Fort Thomas

Place Type: City
County: Campbell
Population: 16,325†

Ancestry‡	Population	%
African, Sub-Saharan (0)	19	0.12
African (0)	19	0.12
American (1,325)	1,325	8.19
Arab (59)	59	0.36
Lebanese (49)	49	0.30
Moroccan (10)	10	0.06
Brazilian (54)	78	0.48
British (34)	71	0.44
Cajun (7)	7	0.04
Canadian (0)	6	0.04
Croatian (0)	33	0.20
Czech (8)	16	0.10
Danish (3)	3	0.02
Dutch (20)	383	2.37
English (794)	2,319	14.33
European (175)	199	1.23
French, ex. Basque (55)	463	2.86
German (2,972)	7,511	46.42
Greek (43)	60	0.37
Hungarian (7)	45	0.28
Irish (846)	3,408	21.06
Italian (209)	677	4.18
Latvian (0)	30	0.19
Lithuanian (27)	27	0.17
Norwegian (18)	69	0.43
Polish (32)	174	1.08
Portuguese (0)	24	0.15
Romanian (0)	13	0.08
Scandinavian (0)	15	0.09
Scotch-Irish (186)	579	3.58
Scottish (136)	414	2.56
Slavic (11)	11	0.07
Slovak (0)	19	0.12
Swedish (0)	157	0.97
Swiss (41)	105	0.65
Ukrainian (27)	45	0.28
Welsh (7)	101	0.62

Hispanic Origin	Population	%
Hispanic or Latino (of any race)	234	1.43
Central American, ex. Mexican	30	0.18
Guatemalan	22	0.13
Honduran	2	0.01
Panamanian	3	0.02
Salvadoran	3	0.02
Cuban	8	0.05
Dominican Republic	5	0.03
Mexican	99	0.61
Puerto Rican	24	0.15
South American	28	0.17
Argentinean	1	0.01
Bolivian	1	0.01
Chilean	4	0.02
Colombian	4	0.02
Ecuadorian	4	0.02
Peruvian	9	0.06
Venezuelan	3	0.02
Other South American	2	0.01
Other Hispanic or Latino	40	0.25

Race*	Population	%
African-American/Black (209)	308	1.89
Not Hispanic (206)	299	1.83
Hispanic (3)	9	0.06
American Indian/Alaska Native (10)	71	0.43
Not Hispanic (9)	67	0.41
Hispanic (1)	4	0.02
Blackfeet (1)	3	0.02
Central American Ind. (0)	1	0.01
Cherokee (1)	24	0.15
Chickasaw (1)	1	0.01
Chippewa (0)	4	0.02
Iroquois (0)	2	0.01
Mexican American Ind. (1)	1	0.01
Sioux (0)	3	0.02
Asian (152)	195	1.19
Not Hispanic (146)	177	1.08
Hispanic (6)	18	0.11
Chinese, ex. Taiwanese (23)	28	0.17
Filipino (26)	34	0.21
Indian (27)	37	0.23
Indonesian (1)	1	0.01
Japanese (18)	28	0.17
Korean (28)	31	0.19
Malaysian (1)	1	0.01
Nepalese (7)	10	0.06
Pakistani (6)	12	0.07
Sri Lankan (0)	2	0.01
Thai (5)	5	0.03
Vietnamese (1)	3	0.02
Hawaii Native/Pacific Islander (3)	13	0.08
Not Hispanic (3)	12	0.07
Hispanic (0)	1	0.01
Guamanian/Chamorro (3)	3	0.02
Native Hawaiian (0)	3	0.02
Samoan (0)	3	0.02
White (15,688)	15,865	97.18
Not Hispanic (15,529)	15,696	96.15
Hispanic (159)	169	1.04

Francisville

Place Type: CDP
County: Boone
Population: 7,944†

Ancestry‡	Population	%
American (563)	563	7.28
Austrian (0)	26	0.34
British (43)	71	0.92
Czech (14)	14	0.18
Dutch (0)	124	1.60
English (188)	739	9.55
European (209)	257	3.32
Finnish (14)	51	0.66
French, ex. Basque (10)	262	3.39
French Canadian (24)	32	0.41
German (1,085)	2,612	33.76
Iranian (0)	15	0.19
Irish (357)	1,499	19.37
Italian (103)	351	4.54
Latvian (33)	33	0.43

*Notes: † The Census 2010 population figure is used to calculate the percentages in the Hispanic Origin and Race categories. Ancestry percentages are based on the 2006-2010 American Community Survey population (not shown); ‡ Numbers in parentheses indicate the number of people reporting a single ancestry; * Numbers in parentheses indicate the number of persons reporting this race alone, not in combination with any other race; Please refer to the Explanation of Data for more information.*

New Zealander (0)	42	0.54
Northern European (63)	63	0.81
Norwegian (20)	55	0.71
Pennsylvania German (0)	42	0.54
Polish (73)	191	2.47
Russian (28)	61	0.79
Scotch-Irish (46)	75	0.97
Scottish (11)	180	2.33
Swedish (0)	80	1.03
Welsh (0)	109	1.41

Hispanic Origin	**Population**	**%**
Hispanic or Latino (of any race)	170	2.14
Central American, ex. Mexican	15	0.19
Costa Rican	1	0.01
Guatemalan	3	0.04
Honduran	5	0.06
Salvadoran	6	0.08
Cuban	6	0.08
Mexican	76	0.96
Puerto Rican	49	0.62
South American	14	0.18
Chilean	5	0.06
Colombian	4	0.05
Ecuadorian	1	0.01
Peruvian	3	0.04
Venezuelan	1	0.01
Other Hispanic or Latino	10	0.13

Race*	**Population**	**%**
African-American/Black (121)	150	1.89
Not Hispanic (119)	143	1.80
Hispanic (2)	7	0.09
American Indian/Alaska Native (4)	53	0.67
Not Hispanic (2)	48	0.60
Hispanic (2)	5	0.06
Blackfeet (0)	2	0.03
Cherokee (1)	18	0.23
Chippewa (0)	3	0.04
Choctaw (0)	1	0.01
Iroquois (1)	2	0.03
Mexican American Ind. (2)	2	0.03
Spanish American Ind. (0)	1	0.01
Asian (254)	326	4.10
Not Hispanic (250)	318	4.00
Hispanic (4)	8	0.10
Bangladeshi (1)	1	0.01
Cambodian (5)	6	0.08
Chinese, ex. Taiwanese (29)	42	0.53
Filipino (13)	34	0.43
Indian (68)	80	1.01
Japanese (73)	84	1.06
Korean (17)	27	0.34
Laotian (1)	1	0.01
Nepalese (4)	4	0.05
Sri Lankan (1)	3	0.04
Taiwanese (5)	5	0.06
Thai (1)	2	0.03
Vietnamese (19)	25	0.31
Hawaii Native/Pacific Islander (0)	5	0.06
Not Hispanic (0)	4	0.05
Hispanic (0)	1	0.01
White (7,360)	7,510	94.54
Not Hispanic (7,272)	7,390	93.03
Hispanic (88)	120	1.51

Frankfort

Place Type: City
County: Franklin
Population: 25,527†

Ancestry‡	**Population**	**%**
African, Sub-Saharan (67)	79	0.31
African (53)	65	0.25
Ghanaian (14)	14	0.05
American (3,992)	3,992	15.54
Arab (14)	24	0.09
Arab (14)	14	0.05
Lebanese (0)	10	0.04
Australian (10)	10	0.04
Austrian (0)	12	0.05
Belgian (16)	16	0.06
British (88)	305	1.19
Canadian (10)	10	0.04
Czech (13)	26	0.10
Dutch (214)	355	1.38
English (1,358)	3,131	12.19
European (200)	209	0.81
French, ex. Basque (144)	507	1.97
French Canadian (39)	97	0.38
German (943)	3,727	14.51
Hungarian (0)	37	0.14
Iranian (17)	17	0.07
Irish (1,339)	3,732	14.53
Italian (88)	476	1.85
Lithuanian (0)	12	0.05
Norwegian (17)	38	0.15
Polish (12)	140	0.55
Portuguese (12)	39	0.15
Russian (0)	70	0.27
Scandinavian (0)	12	0.05
Scotch-Irish (449)	783	3.05
Scottish (316)	726	2.83
Slovak (0)	10	0.04
Swedish (12)	35	0.14
Swiss (28)	28	0.11
Ukrainian (0)	13	0.05
Welsh (33)	190	0.74
West Indian, ex. Hispanic (14)	49	0.19
Barbadian (0)	12	0.05
Belizean (0)	12	0.05
Jamaican (14)	14	0.05
Other West Indian (0)	11	0.04

Hispanic Origin	**Population**	**%**
Hispanic or Latino (of any race)	961	3.76
Central American, ex. Mexican	164	0.64
Costa Rican	6	0.02
Guatemalan	30	0.12
Honduran	102	0.40
Nicaraguan	3	0.01
Panamanian	14	0.05
Salvadoran	6	0.02
Other Central American	3	0.01
Cuban	30	0.12
Dominican Republic	11	0.04
Mexican	604	2.37
Puerto Rican	52	0.20
South American	10	0.04
Chilean	2	0.01
Colombian	4	0.02
Peruvian	3	0.01
Venezuelan	1	<0.01
Other Hispanic or Latino	90	0.35

Race*	**Population**	**%**
African-American/Black (4,205)	4,740	18.57
Not Hispanic (4,163)	4,679	18.33
Hispanic (42)	61	0.24
American Indian/Alaska Native (72)	233	0.91
Not Hispanic (56)	202	0.79
Hispanic (16)	31	0.12
Apache (2)	6	0.02
Blackfeet (0)	17	0.07
Canadian/French Am. Ind. (4)	5	0.02
Cherokee (20)	66	0.26
Chippewa (4)	5	0.02
Choctaw (0)	2	0.01
Comanche (2)	2	0.01
Creek (0)	1	<0.01
Inupiat *(Alaska Native)* (0)	2	0.01
Iroquois (0)	1	<0.01
Lumbee (1)	2	0.01
Mexican American Ind. (5)	9	0.04
Navajo (2)	9	0.04
Pueblo (0)	1	<0.01
Sioux (3)	4	0.02
South American Ind. (0)	3	0.01
Asian (363)	416	1.63
Not Hispanic (353)	399	1.56
Hispanic (10)	17	0.07
Bangladeshi (2)	2	0.01
Cambodian (3)	3	0.01
Chinese, ex. Taiwanese (30)	36	0.14
Filipino (42)	49	0.19
Indian (195)	207	0.81
Indonesian (1)	2	0.01
Japanese (8)	17	0.07
Korean (19)	25	0.10
Nepalese (7)	7	0.03
Pakistani (11)	19	0.07
Thai (8)	13	0.05
Vietnamese (29)	31	0.12
Hawaii Native/Pacific Islander (5)	17	0.07
Not Hispanic (4)	16	0.06
Hispanic (1)	1	<0.01
Guamanian/Chamorro (1)	2	0.01
Native Hawaiian (1)	4	0.02
Samoan (1)	2	0.01
White (19,674)	20,370	79.80
Not Hispanic (19,287)	19,906	77.98
Hispanic (387)	464	1.82

Franklin

Place Type: City
County: Simpson
Population: 8,408†

Ancestry‡	**Population**	**%**
African, Sub-Saharan (22)	22	0.26
African (22)	22	0.26
American (1,028)	1,028	12.28
Assyrian/Chaldean/Syriac (9)	9	0.11
Canadian (0)	9	0.11
Dutch (35)	93	1.11
English (311)	775	9.26
French, ex. Basque (82)	214	2.56
German (201)	489	5.84
Irish (311)	772	9.23
Italian (25)	83	0.99
Norwegian (0)	14	0.17
Polish (14)	14	0.17
Scandinavian (0)	34	0.41
Scotch-Irish (16)	81	0.97
Scottish (13)	130	1.55
Swedish (17)	17	0.20
Welsh (18)	18	0.22

Hispanic Origin	**Population**	**%**
Hispanic or Latino (of any race)	199	2.37
Central American, ex. Mexican	24	0.29
Guatemalan	17	0.20
Honduran	3	0.04
Panamanian	1	0.01
Salvadoran	3	0.04
Cuban	3	0.04
Mexican	131	1.56
Puerto Rican	23	0.27
South American	7	0.08
Bolivian	3	0.04
Peruvian	4	0.05
Other Hispanic or Latino	11	0.13

Race*	**Population**	**%**
African-American/Black (1,228)	1,351	16.07
Not Hispanic (1,221)	1,341	15.95
Hispanic (7)	10	0.12
American Indian/Alaska Native (23)	80	0.95
Not Hispanic (20)	76	0.90
Hispanic (3)	4	0.05
Apache (0)	2	0.02
Arapaho (0)	1	0.01
Canadian/French Am. Ind. (1)	1	0.01
Cherokee (4)	35	0.42
Cheyenne (0)	1	0.01
Chippewa (1)	1	0.01
Choctaw (1)	4	0.05
Iroquois (1)	1	0.01

*Notes: † The Census 2010 population figure is used to calculate the percentages in the Hispanic Origin and Race categories. Ancestry percentages are based on the 2006-2010 American Community Survey population (not shown); ‡ Numbers in parentheses indicate the number of people reporting a single ancestry; * Numbers in parentheses indicate the number of persons reporting this race alone, not in combination with any other race; Please refer to the Explanation of Data for more information.*

Mexican American Ind. (1)	2	0.02
Navajo (0)	1	0.01
Asian (88)	106	1.26
Not Hispanic (88)	101	1.20
Hispanic (0)	5	0.06
Cambodian (2)	5	0.06
Chinese, ex. Taiwanese (14)	14	0.17
Filipino (16)	26	0.31
Indian (44)	45	0.54
Japanese (9)	12	0.14
Korean (2)	3	0.04
Vietnamese (1)	1	0.01
Hawaii Native/Pacific Islander (4)	4	0.05
Not Hispanic (4)	4	0.05
Native Hawaiian (1)	1	0.01
Samoan (3)	3	0.04
White (6,782)	6,972	82.92
Not Hispanic (6,693)	6,867	81.67
Hispanic (89)	105	1.25

Georgetown

Place Type: City
County: Scott
Population: 29,098†

Ancestry‡	Population	%
American (5,247)	5,247	19.24
Arab (0)	29	0.11
Egyptian (0)	29	0.11
Belgian (9)	9	0.03
British (49)	127	0.47
Croatian (0)	35	0.13
Czech (0)	22	0.08
Danish (0)	55	0.20
Dutch (67)	375	1.38
Eastern European (36)	36	0.13
English (1,152)	2,731	10.02
European (603)	621	2.28
Finnish (11)	11	0.04
French, ex. Basque (99)	517	1.90
French Canadian (10)	34	0.12
German (1,350)	3,906	14.32
Greek (46)	83	0.30
Hungarian (12)	115	0.42
Irish (1,532)	3,909	14.34
Israeli (0)	11	0.04
Italian (256)	762	2.79
Lithuanian (0)	8	0.03
Norwegian (19)	57	0.21
Pennsylvania German (0)	23	0.08
Polish (146)	510	1.87
Portuguese (25)	90	0.33
Romanian (11)	39	0.14
Russian (0)	23	0.08
Scotch-Irish (348)	617	2.26
Scottish (493)	766	2.81
Slovak (12)	58	0.21
Slovene (0)	10	0.04
Swedish (13)	191	0.70
Swiss (0)	104	0.38
Ukrainian (27)	63	0.23
Welsh (22)	117	0.43

Hispanic Origin	Population	%
Hispanic or Latino (of any race)	1,251	4.30
Central American, ex. Mexican	78	0.27
Costa Rican	2	0.01
Guatemalan	28	0.10
Honduran	25	0.09
Nicaraguan	10	0.03
Panamanian	5	0.02
Salvadoran	8	0.03
Cuban	11	0.04
Mexican	913	3.14
Puerto Rican	79	0.27
South American	42	0.14
Argentinean	6	0.02
Bolivian	2	0.01
Chilean	12	0.04
Colombian	7	0.02
Ecuadorian	1	<0.01
Paraguayan	1	<0.01
Peruvian	8	0.03
Venezuelan	5	0.02
Other Hispanic or Latino	128	0.44

Race*	Population	%
African-American/Black (2,024)	2,395	8.23
Not Hispanic (2,003)	2,352	8.08
Hispanic (21)	43	0.15
American Indian/Alaska Native (80)	194	0.67
Not Hispanic (61)	157	0.54
Hispanic (19)	37	0.13
Apache (0)	2	0.01
Blackfeet (0)	7	0.02
Central American Ind. (3)	3	0.01
Cherokee (17)	63	0.22
Cheyenne (0)	1	<0.01
Chickasaw (0)	1	<0.01
Choctaw (2)	2	0.01
Comanche (0)	1	<0.01
Cree (2)	2	0.01
Creek (5)	6	0.02
Crow (0)	2	0.01
Iroquois (3)	3	0.01
Lumbee (1)	6	0.02
Mexican American Ind. (7)	14	0.05
Navajo (0)	4	0.01
Osage (3)	3	0.01
Paiute (1)	1	<0.01
Sioux (2)	3	0.01
South American Ind. (1)	1	<0.01
Spanish American Ind. (4)	4	0.01
Asian (350)	438	1.51
Not Hispanic (346)	429	1.47
Hispanic (4)	9	0.03
Bangladeshi (2)	2	0.01
Burmese (2)	2	0.01
Cambodian (9)	9	0.03
Chinese, ex. Taiwanese (40)	47	0.16
Filipino (34)	54	0.19
Hmong (5)	5	0.02
Indian (97)	110	0.38
Indonesian (1)	1	<0.01
Japanese (72)	92	0.32
Korean (30)	49	0.17
Laotian (1)	1	<0.01
Malaysian (1)	1	<0.01
Nepalese (8)	8	0.03
Pakistani (4)	4	0.01
Taiwanese (1)	3	0.01
Thai (7)	7	0.02
Vietnamese (29)	36	0.12
Hawaii Native/Pacific Islander (8)	17	0.06
Not Hispanic (8)	16	0.05
Hispanic (0)	1	<0.01
Guamanian/Chamorro (4)	6	0.02
Native Hawaiian (4)	10	0.03
White (25,449)	26,043	89.50
Not Hispanic (24,864)	25,350	87.12
Hispanic (585)	693	2.38

Glasgow

Place Type: City
County: Barren
Population: 14,028†

Ancestry‡	Population	%
African, Sub-Saharan (0)	35	0.25
African (0)	35	0.25
American (3,358)	3,358	24.12
Armenian (8)	8	0.06
Austrian (0)	14	0.10
British (53)	61	0.44
Canadian (87)	87	0.62
Dutch (76)	372	2.67
English (665)	1,313	9.43
European (103)	103	0.74
Finnish (14)	14	0.10
French, ex. Basque (44)	160	1.15
French Canadian (52)	52	0.37
German (611)	1,609	11.56
Hungarian (14)	14	0.10
Irish (361)	1,124	8.07
Italian (60)	197	1.41
Polish (29)	165	1.19
Scotch-Irish (96)	346	2.48
Scottish (193)	469	3.37
Slovak (0)	10	0.07
Swedish (0)	34	0.24
Swiss (0)	32	0.23
Welsh (0)	26	0.19

Hispanic Origin	Population	%
Hispanic or Latino (of any race)	610	4.35
Central American, ex. Mexican	155	1.10
Guatemalan	133	0.95
Honduran	7	0.05
Panamanian	3	0.02
Salvadoran	8	0.06
Other Central American	4	0.03
Cuban	8	0.06
Dominican Republic	2	0.01
Mexican	300	2.14
Puerto Rican	45	0.32
South American	6	0.04
Colombian	6	0.04
Other Hispanic or Latino	94	0.67

Race*	Population	%
African-American/Black (1,120)	1,335	9.52
Not Hispanic (1,111)	1,307	9.32
Hispanic (9)	28	0.20
American Indian/Alaska Native (17)	122	0.87
Not Hispanic (14)	101	0.72
Hispanic (3)	21	0.15
Apache (0)	1	0.01
Blackfeet (0)	9	0.06
Central American Ind. (1)	1	0.01
Cherokee (4)	47	0.34
Cheyenne (1)	1	0.01
Chickasaw (0)	1	0.01
Chippewa (1)	1	0.01
Choctaw (2)	3	0.02
Creek (0)	1	0.01
Mexican American Ind. (0)	8	0.06
Sioux (0)	2	0.01
South American Ind. (1)	1	0.01
Asian (106)	134	0.96
Not Hispanic (106)	131	0.93
Hispanic (0)	3	0.02
Cambodian (6)	6	0.04
Chinese, ex. Taiwanese (13)	20	0.14
Filipino (13)	19	0.14
Indian (31)	36	0.26
Japanese (33)	39	0.28
Korean (0)	3	0.02
Thai (4)	4	0.03
Vietnamese (5)	6	0.04
Hawaii Native/Pacific Islander (27)	32	0.23
Not Hispanic (0)	3	0.02
Hispanic (27)	29	0.21
Guamanian/Chamorro (27)	30	0.21
Native Hawaiian (0)	1	0.01
White (12,080)	12,443	88.70
Not Hispanic (11,851)	12,151	86.62
Hispanic (229)	292	2.08

Harrodsburg

Place Type: City
County: Mercer
Population: 8,340†

Ancestry‡	Population	%
American (2,608)	2,608	31.35
British (15)	15	0.18
Dutch (60)	194	2.33

*Notes: † The Census 2010 population figure is used to calculate the percentages in the Hispanic Origin and Race categories. Ancestry percentages are based on the 2006-2010 American Community Survey population (not shown); ‡ Numbers in parentheses indicate the number of people reporting a single ancestry; * Numbers in parentheses indicate the number of persons reporting this race alone, not in combination with any other race; Please refer to the Explanation of Data for more information.*

SECTION TWO

English (425)	852	10.24
European (51)	85	1.02
French, ex. Basque (53)	183	2.20
French Canadian (14)	14	0.17
German (362)	950	11.42
Irish (529)	1,225	14.72
Italian (35)	119	1.43
Scotch-Irish (68)	172	2.07
Scottish (20)	75	0.90
Swedish (55)	55	0.66
Swiss (0)	10	0.12

Hispanic Origin	Population	%
Hispanic or Latino (of any race)	335	4.02
Central American, ex. Mexican	4	0.05
Guatemalan	2	0.02
Honduran	2	0.02
Cuban	2	0.02
Mexican	299	3.59
Puerto Rican	8	0.10
Other Hispanic or Latino	22	0.26

Race*	Population	%
African-American/Black (616)	781	9.36
Not Hispanic (604)	757	9.08
Hispanic (12)	24	0.29
American Indian/Alaska Native (15)	77	0.92
Not Hispanic (12)	70	0.84
Hispanic (3)	7	0.08
Apache (2)	2	0.02
Blackfeet (1)	6	0.07
Cherokee (5)	41	0.49
Choctaw (0)	2	0.02
Navajo (0)	4	0.05
Sioux (0)	1	0.01
Asian (55)	69	0.83
Not Hispanic (55)	69	0.83
Cambodian (12)	12	0.14
Chinese, ex. Taiwanese (9)	10	0.12
Filipino (8)	17	0.20
Indian (5)	5	0.06
Japanese (16)	20	0.24
Korean (4)	5	0.06
Taiwanese (1)	1	0.01
Hawaii Native/Pacific Islander (1)	7	0.08
Not Hispanic (1)	7	0.08
Native Hawaiian (1)	4	0.05
White (7,200)	7,434	89.14
Not Hispanic (7,104)	7,318	87.75
Hispanic (96)	116	1.39

Henderson

Place Type: City
County: Henderson
Population: 28,757†

Ancestry‡	Population	%
African, Sub-Saharan (56)	156	0.55
African (56)	156	0.55
American (3,748)	3,748	13.17
Arab (24)	40	0.14
Lebanese (24)	40	0.14
Australian (47)	47	0.17
Austrian (0)	43	0.15
British (38)	167	0.59
Canadian (0)	32	0.11
Danish (40)	112	0.39
Dutch (37)	359	1.26
Eastern European (0)	11	0.04
English (1,488)	2,923	10.27
European (130)	179	0.63
French, ex. Basque (69)	389	1.37
French Canadian (38)	62	0.22
German (1,842)	4,775	16.78
Greek (213)	242	0.85
Hungarian (17)	31	0.11
Irish (903)	3,363	11.81
Italian (207)	422	1.48
Norwegian (40)	119	0.42
Polish (92)	180	0.63
Russian (185)	234	0.82
Scotch-Irish (164)	454	1.59
Scottish (119)	386	1.36
Slovak (14)	14	0.05
Swedish (39)	72	0.25
Turkish (0)	12	0.04
Ukrainian (0)	12	0.04
Welsh (32)	100	0.35

Hispanic Origin	Population	%
Hispanic or Latino (of any race)	657	2.28
Central American, ex. Mexican	89	0.31
Costa Rican	2	0.01
Guatemalan	28	0.10
Honduran	30	0.10
Nicaraguan	5	0.02
Salvadoran	24	0.08
Cuban	14	0.05
Dominican Republic	12	0.04
Mexican	397	1.38
Puerto Rican	59	0.21
South American	20	0.07
Bolivian	1	<0.01
Colombian	12	0.04
Ecuadorian	4	0.01
Venezuelan	3	0.01
Other Hispanic or Latino	66	0.23

Race*	Population	%
African-American/Black (3,337)	3,774	13.12
Not Hispanic (3,316)	3,736	12.99
Hispanic (21)	38	0.13
American Indian/Alaska Native (61)	161	0.56
Not Hispanic (51)	133	0.46
Hispanic (10)	28	0.10
Apache (1)	4	0.01
Arapaho (1)	2	0.01
Blackfeet (3)	8	0.03
Cherokee (16)	42	0.15
Chippewa (0)	2	0.01
Choctaw (2)	5	0.02
Comanche (3)	3	0.01
Creek (0)	1	<0.01
Inupiat *(Alaska Native)* (0)	1	<0.01
Lumbee (1)	1	<0.01
Mexican American Ind. (7)	7	0.02
Navajo (1)	1	<0.01
Osage (2)	3	0.01
Paiute (1)	1	<0.01
Sioux (2)	4	0.01
South American Ind. (0)	1	<0.01
Asian (143)	209	0.73
Not Hispanic (141)	201	0.70
Hispanic (2)	8	0.03
Chinese, ex. Taiwanese (31)	44	0.15
Filipino (49)	84	0.29
Indian (24)	27	0.09
Indonesian (1)	2	0.01
Japanese (4)	8	0.03
Korean (9)	17	0.06
Sri Lankan (1)	1	<0.01
Taiwanese (3)	3	0.01
Thai (4)	6	0.02
Vietnamese (9)	10	0.03
Hawaii Native/Pacific Islander (11)	25	0.09
Not Hispanic (7)	20	0.07
Hispanic (4)	5	0.02
Guamanian/Chamorro (6)	11	0.04
Tongan (4)	5	0.02
White (24,298)	24,884	86.53
Not Hispanic (23,976)	24,510	85.23
Hispanic (322)	374	1.30

Hillview

Place Type: City
County: Bullitt
Population: 8,172†

Ancestry‡	Population	%
American (1,782)	1,782	22.10
Arab (10)	10	0.12
Lebanese (10)	10	0.12
Dutch (16)	185	2.29
English (452)	826	10.25
European (29)	38	0.47
Finnish (9)	9	0.11
French, ex. Basque (25)	129	1.60
French Canadian (9)	9	0.11
German (510)	1,288	15.98
Greek (10)	10	0.12
Irish (299)	1,098	13.62
Italian (6)	109	1.35
Lithuanian (0)	14	0.17
Norwegian (22)	46	0.57
Polish (6)	81	1.00
Portuguese (0)	12	0.15
Russian (0)	6	0.07
Scandinavian (22)	37	0.46
Scotch-Irish (51)	84	1.04
Scottish (68)	133	1.65
Swedish (8)	8	0.10
Welsh (0)	7	0.09
Yugoslavian (50)	50	0.62

Hispanic Origin	Population	%
Hispanic or Latino (of any race)	161	1.97
Central American, ex. Mexican	5	0.06
Guatemalan	4	0.05
Nicaraguan	1	0.01
Cuban	13	0.16
Dominican Republic	2	0.02
Mexican	93	1.14
Puerto Rican	16	0.20
South American	11	0.13
Argentinean	4	0.05
Colombian	7	0.09
Other Hispanic or Latino	21	0.26

Race*	Population	%
African-American/Black (92)	141	1.73
Not Hispanic (87)	136	1.66
Hispanic (5)	5	0.06
American Indian/Alaska Native (24)	59	0.72
Not Hispanic (24)	59	0.72
Central American Ind. (0)	3	0.04
Cherokee (15)	34	0.42
Choctaw (1)	1	0.01
Iroquois (2)	2	0.02
Asian (62)	100	1.22
Not Hispanic (62)	98	1.20
Hispanic (0)	2	0.02
Chinese, ex. Taiwanese (9)	11	0.13
Filipino (11)	22	0.27
Hmong (1)	3	0.04
Indian (8)	10	0.12
Indonesian (4)	4	0.05
Japanese (2)	5	0.06
Korean (16)	27	0.33
Laotian (9)	9	0.11
Thai (0)	1	0.01
Vietnamese (2)	3	0.04
Hawaii Native/Pacific Islander (2)	8	0.10
Not Hispanic (1)	3	0.04
Hispanic (1)	5	0.06
Guamanian/Chamorro (1)	2	0.02
Native Hawaiian (0)	2	0.02
White (7,845)	7,953	97.32
Not Hispanic (7,726)	7,823	95.73
Hispanic (119)	130	1.59

Hopkinsville

Place Type: City
County: Christian
Population: 31,577†

Ancestry‡	Population	%
African, Sub-Saharan (394)	425	1.38

*Notes: † The Census 2010 population figure is used to calculate the percentages in the Hispanic Origin and Race categories. Ancestry percentages are based on the 2006-2010 American Community Survey population (not shown); ‡ Numbers in parentheses indicate the number of people reporting a single ancestry; * Numbers in parentheses indicate the number of persons reporting this race alone, not in combination with any other race; Please refer to the Explanation of Data for more information.*

Ancestry (cont.)	Population	%
African (394)	425	1.38
American (4,986)	4,986	16.16
Arab (10)	36	0.12
Lebanese (10)	23	0.07
Syrian (0)	13	0.04
British (108)	151	0.49
Canadian (11)	68	0.22
Croatian (13)	25	0.08
Czech (0)	10	0.03
Dutch (99)	355	1.15
English (2,123)	3,380	10.95
European (119)	142	0.46
Finnish (7)	7	0.02
French, ex. Basque (99)	396	1.28
French Canadian (0)	29	0.09
German (855)	2,464	7.98
Greek (16)	16	0.05
Hungarian (25)	42	0.14
Irish (1,119)	2,954	9.57
Italian (230)	620	2.01
New Zealander (0)	36	0.12
Norwegian (0)	18	0.06
Polish (136)	316	1.02
Romanian (13)	89	0.29
Scotch-Irish (238)	572	1.85
Scottish (213)	359	1.16
Slavic (0)	7	0.02
Swedish (73)	181	0.59
Swiss (0)	16	0.05
Welsh (10)	102	0.33
West Indian, ex. Hispanic (9)	33	0.11
Jamaican (9)	33	0.11

Hispanic Origin	Population	%
Hispanic or Latino (of any race)	1,113	3.52
Central American, ex. Mexican	59	0.19
Costa Rican	1	<0.01
Guatemalan	39	0.12
Panamanian	9	0.03
Salvadoran	10	0.03
Cuban	11	0.03
Dominican Republic	14	0.04
Mexican	693	2.19
Puerto Rican	193	0.61
South American	38	0.12
Argentinean	2	0.01
Bolivian	3	0.01
Chilean	1	<0.01
Colombian	13	0.04
Ecuadorian	8	0.03
Peruvian	6	0.02
Uruguayan	1	<0.01
Venezuelan	4	0.01
Other Hispanic or Latino	105	0.33

Race*	Population	%
African-American/Black (10,076)	10,556	33.43
Not Hispanic (10,040)	10,476	33.18
Hispanic (36)	80	0.25
American Indian/Alaska Native (114)	325	1.03
Not Hispanic (80)	257	0.81
Hispanic (34)	68	0.22
Apache (11)	17	0.05
Arapaho (1)	1	<0.01
Blackfeet (0)	7	0.02
Canadian/French Am. Ind. (1)	1	<0.01
Cherokee (26)	88	0.28
Chickasaw (0)	1	<0.01
Chippewa (0)	3	0.01
Choctaw (5)	6	0.02
Comanche (1)	1	<0.01
Creek (1)	1	<0.01
Inupiat *(Alaska Native)* (3)	3	0.01
Iroquois (0)	2	0.01
Kiowa (1)	1	<0.01
Lumbee (5)	5	0.02
Mexican American Ind. (10)	15	0.05
Navajo (1)	4	0.01
Osage (1)	1	<0.01
Pueblo (0)	1	<0.01
Seminole (0)	4	0.01
Shoshone (0)	1	<0.01
Sioux (0)	8	0.03
South American Ind. (1)	7	0.02
Tsimshian *(Alaska Native)* (0)	3	0.01
Yaqui (0)	1	<0.01
Asian (356)	464	1.47
Not Hispanic (348)	441	1.40
Hispanic (8)	23	0.07
Cambodian (1)	2	0.01
Chinese, ex. Taiwanese (35)	42	0.13
Filipino (18)	47	0.15
Indian (113)	128	0.41
Japanese (76)	102	0.32
Korean (55)	76	0.24
Pakistani (14)	15	0.05
Taiwanese (2)	2	0.01
Thai (4)	10	0.03
Vietnamese (24)	31	0.10
Hawaii Native/Pacific Islander (30)	91	0.29
Not Hispanic (28)	79	0.25
Hispanic (2)	12	0.04
Fijian (1)	1	<0.01
Guamanian/Chamorro (3)	14	0.04
Native Hawaiian (15)	29	0.09
Samoan (6)	19	0.06
White (19,761)	20,447	64.75
Not Hispanic (19,279)	19,851	62.87
Hispanic (482)	596	1.89

Independence

Place Type: City
County: Kenton
Population: 24,757†

Ancestry‡	Population	%
African, Sub-Saharan (104)	104	0.45
African (104)	104	0.45
American (2,830)	2,830	12.32
Austrian (0)	9	0.04
Belgian (9)	9	0.04
British (8)	25	0.11
Canadian (11)	11	0.05
Croatian (107)	107	0.47
Czech (20)	20	0.09
Dutch (24)	370	1.61
Eastern European (13)	13	0.06
English (1,108)	2,435	10.60
European (151)	151	0.66
Finnish (9)	9	0.04
French, ex. Basque (46)	488	2.12
French Canadian (10)	80	0.35
German (3,224)	8,253	35.92
Greek (49)	102	0.44
Hungarian (43)	137	0.60
Irish (1,108)	4,700	20.46
Italian (282)	918	4.00
Lithuanian (29)	29	0.13
Norwegian (52)	122	0.53
Polish (98)	337	1.47
Russian (10)	55	0.24
Scandinavian (0)	6	0.03
Scotch-Irish (163)	355	1.55
Scottish (65)	224	0.97
Swedish (0)	55	0.24
Swiss (9)	47	0.20
Turkish (7)	7	0.03
Ukrainian (14)	14	0.06
Welsh (8)	55	0.24
West Indian, ex. Hispanic (9)	9	0.04
Trinidadian/Tobagonian (9)	9	0.04
Yugoslavian (44)	52	0.23

Hispanic Origin	Population	%
Hispanic or Latino (of any race)	447	1.81
Central American, ex. Mexican	35	0.14
Guatemalan	21	0.08
Honduran	10	0.04
Nicaraguan	1	<0.01
Salvadoran	2	0.01
Other Central American	1	<0.01
Cuban	24	0.10
Dominican Republic	7	0.03
Mexican	235	0.95
Puerto Rican	63	0.25
South American	33	0.13
Argentinean	1	<0.01
Bolivian	1	<0.01
Chilean	2	0.01
Colombian	14	0.06
Ecuadorian	7	0.03
Peruvian	5	0.02
Venezuelan	3	0.01
Other Hispanic or Latino	50	0.20

Race*	Population	%
African-American/Black (418)	580	2.34
Not Hispanic (417)	578	2.33
Hispanic (1)	2	0.01
American Indian/Alaska Native (39)	109	0.44
Not Hispanic (28)	92	0.37
Hispanic (11)	17	0.07
Apache (0)	1	<0.01
Blackfeet (0)	2	0.01
Cherokee (9)	29	0.12
Chippewa (3)	5	0.02
Inupiat *(Alaska Native)* (4)	4	0.02
Iroquois (1)	1	<0.01
Mexican American Ind. (8)	9	0.04
Navajo (0)	1	<0.01
Pueblo (1)	1	<0.01
Seminole (0)	2	0.01
Sioux (0)	3	0.01
Asian (204)	309	1.25
Not Hispanic (201)	304	1.23
Hispanic (3)	5	0.02
Bangladeshi (3)	4	0.02
Chinese, ex. Taiwanese (17)	37	0.15
Filipino (47)	77	0.31
Indian (54)	62	0.25
Indonesian (2)	2	0.01
Japanese (24)	48	0.19
Korean (22)	32	0.13
Laotian (12)	14	0.06
Pakistani (0)	2	0.01
Sri Lankan (4)	4	0.02
Taiwanese (1)	2	0.01
Thai (2)	10	0.04
Vietnamese (11)	21	0.08
Hawaii Native/Pacific Islander (14)	36	0.15
Not Hispanic (13)	35	0.14
Hispanic (1)	1	<0.01
Guamanian/Chamorro (2)	3	0.01
Native Hawaiian (7)	20	0.08
Samoan (4)	12	0.05
White (23,590)	23,935	96.68
Not Hispanic (23,294)	23,619	95.40
Hispanic (296)	316	1.28

Jeffersontown

Place Type: City
County: Jefferson
Population: 26,595†

Ancestry‡	Population	%
African, Sub-Saharan (165)	180	0.68
African (149)	164	0.62
Ethiopian (16)	16	0.06
American (3,351)	3,351	12.66
Arab (298)	344	1.30
Arab (70)	70	0.26
Jordanian (56)	56	0.21
Lebanese (99)	145	0.55
Palestinian (14)	14	0.05
Syrian (59)	59	0.22
Austrian (0)	32	0.12
British (113)	190	0.72
Bulgarian (0)	10	0.04

*Notes: † The Census 2010 population figure is used to calculate the percentages in the Hispanic Origin and Race categories. Ancestry percentages are based on the 2006-2010 American Community Survey population (not shown); ‡ Numbers in parentheses indicate the number of people reporting a single ancestry; * Numbers in parentheses indicate the number of persons reporting this race alone, not in combination with any other race; Please refer to the Explanation of Data for more information.*

Canadian (0)	9	0.03
Czech (28)	87	0.33
Dutch (123)	551	2.08
English (1,313)	3,256	12.31
European (144)	405	1.53
French, ex. Basque (97)	580	2.19
French Canadian (12)	12	0.05
German (1,884)	5,871	22.19
Greek (12)	12	0.05
Hungarian (16)	112	0.42
Irish (1,196)	4,245	16.04
Italian (319)	821	3.10
Norwegian (32)	65	0.25
Polish (14)	412	1.56
Portuguese (49)	57	0.22
Russian (44)	98	0.37
Scotch-Irish (231)	548	2.07
Scottish (165)	445	1.68
Slovak (27)	27	0.10
Swedish (26)	158	0.60
Swiss (34)	138	0.52
Ukrainian (130)	140	0.53
Welsh (17)	192	0.73
Yugoslavian (197)	197	0.74

Hispanic Origin	Population	%
Hispanic or Latino (of any race)	1,326	4.99
Central American, ex. Mexican	170	0.64
Costa Rican	6	0.02
Guatemalan	49	0.18
Honduran	10	0.04
Nicaraguan	5	0.02
Panamanian	12	0.05
Salvadoran	88	0.33
Cuban	103	0.39
Dominican Republic	9	0.03
Mexican	769	2.89
Puerto Rican	90	0.34
South American	78	0.29
Argentinean	6	0.02
Bolivian	3	0.01
Chilean	7	0.03
Colombian	24	0.09
Ecuadorian	6	0.02
Paraguayan	1	<0.01
Peruvian	21	0.08
Uruguayan	3	0.01
Venezuelan	6	0.02
Other South American	1	<0.01
Other Hispanic or Latino	107	0.40

Race*	Population	%
African-American/Black (2,956)	3,367	12.66
Not Hispanic (2,903)	3,283	12.34
Hispanic (53)	84	0.32
American Indian/Alaska Native (55)	180	0.68
Not Hispanic (34)	148	0.56
Hispanic (21)	32	0.12
Apache (1)	3	0.01
Blackfeet (1)	6	0.02
Central American Ind. (2)	2	0.01
Cherokee (8)	71	0.27
Chickasaw (0)	2	0.01
Chippewa (1)	4	0.02
Choctaw (3)	4	0.02
Creek (2)	3	0.01
Crow (2)	2	0.01
Iroquois (0)	3	0.01
Mexican American Ind. (1)	5	0.02
Paiute (1)	1	<0.01
Potawatomi (5)	5	0.02
Sioux (0)	1	<0.01
South American Ind. (1)	1	<0.01
Asian (484)	600	2.26
Not Hispanic (481)	587	2.21
Hispanic (3)	13	0.05
Bangladeshi (17)	17	0.06
Cambodian (7)	8	0.03
Chinese, ex. Taiwanese (73)	79	0.30
Filipino (95)	126	0.47
Hmong (3)	3	0.01
Indian (149)	165	0.62
Indonesian (1)	1	<0.01
Japanese (20)	34	0.13
Korean (54)	87	0.33
Laotian (6)	6	0.02
Malaysian (2)	2	0.01
Pakistani (1)	4	0.02
Taiwanese (6)	7	0.03
Thai (11)	15	0.06
Vietnamese (27)	29	0.11
Hawaii Native/Pacific Islander (19)	45	0.17
Not Hispanic (18)	40	0.15
Hispanic (1)	5	0.02
Guamanian/Chamorro (13)	17	0.06
Native Hawaiian (3)	16	0.06
Samoan (2)	9	0.03
White (21,864)	22,434	84.35
Not Hispanic (21,246)	21,735	81.73
Hispanic (618)	699	2.63

La Grange

Place Type: City
County: Oldham
Population: 8,082†

Ancestry‡	Population	%
African, Sub-Saharan (17)	17	0.22
Other Sub-Saharan African (17)	17	0.22
American (1,834)	1,834	23.63
Austrian (0)	15	0.19
British (18)	33	0.43
Croatian (0)	13	0.17
Dutch (0)	63	0.81
English (229)	427	5.50
European (45)	45	0.58
French, ex. Basque (71)	164	2.11
German (578)	1,247	16.07
Greek (41)	87	1.12
Irish (394)	1,044	13.45
Italian (6)	167	2.15
Norwegian (31)	140	1.80
Polish (23)	92	1.19
Portuguese (23)	23	0.30
Russian (18)	37	0.48
Scotch-Irish (111)	146	1.88
Scottish (133)	348	4.48
Swiss (0)	14	0.18
Welsh (24)	83	1.07
West Indian, ex. Hispanic (25)	25	0.32
Trinidadian/Tobagonian (25)	25	0.32
Yugoslavian (11)	30	0.39

Hispanic Origin	Population	%
Hispanic or Latino (of any race)	721	8.92
Central American, ex. Mexican	59	0.73
Guatemalan	41	0.51
Honduran	12	0.15
Panamanian	4	0.05
Salvadoran	2	0.02
Cuban	20	0.25
Mexican	500	6.19
Puerto Rican	67	0.83
South American	23	0.28
Bolivian	1	0.01
Chilean	7	0.09
Colombian	4	0.05
Ecuadorian	3	0.04
Peruvian	5	0.06
Venezuelan	3	0.04
Other Hispanic or Latino	52	0.64

Race*	Population	%
African-American/Black (383)	480	5.94
Not Hispanic (373)	465	5.75
Hispanic (10)	15	0.19
American Indian/Alaska Native (22)	78	0.97
Not Hispanic (17)	64	0.79
Hispanic (5)	14	0.17
Canadian/French Am. Ind. (0)	2	0.02
Cherokee (6)	29	0.36
Chippewa (3)	3	0.04
Mexican American Ind. (1)	1	0.01
Sioux (1)	1	0.01
South American Ind. (4)	4	0.05
Asian (51)	82	1.01
Not Hispanic (47)	74	0.92
Hispanic (4)	8	0.10
Chinese, ex. Taiwanese (10)	11	0.14
Filipino (19)	29	0.36
Indian (10)	17	0.21
Japanese (0)	3	0.04
Korean (3)	9	0.11
Malaysian (1)	1	0.01
Thai (1)	1	0.01
Vietnamese (6)	6	0.07
Hawaii Native/Pacific Islander (13)	13	0.16
Not Hispanic (5)	5	0.06
Hispanic (8)	8	0.10
Guamanian/Chamorro (8)	8	0.10
Samoan (1)	1	0.01
White (7,058)	7,227	89.42
Not Hispanic (6,752)	6,899	85.36
Hispanic (306)	328	4.06

Lawrenceburg

Place Type: City
County: Anderson
Population: 10,505†

Ancestry‡	Population	%
American (2,462)	2,462	24.12
Australian (39)	39	0.38
British (14)	14	0.14
Czech (0)	21	0.21
Danish (11)	11	0.11
Dutch (12)	166	1.63
English (694)	1,447	14.18
European (68)	68	0.67
French, ex. Basque (42)	225	2.20
German (455)	1,328	13.01
Hungarian (0)	36	0.35
Iranian (0)	11	0.11
Irish (555)	1,809	17.72
Italian (0)	382	3.74
Polish (0)	10	0.10
Russian (22)	136	1.33
Scotch-Irish (53)	79	0.77
Scottish (86)	124	1.21
Swedish (0)	14	0.14
Swiss (12)	12	0.12
Ukrainian (43)	43	0.42
Welsh (0)	34	0.33

Hispanic Origin	Population	%
Hispanic or Latino (of any race)	200	1.90
Central American, ex. Mexican	25	0.24
Guatemalan	2	0.02
Honduran	12	0.11
Nicaraguan	10	0.10
Salvadoran	1	0.01
Cuban	9	0.09
Mexican	139	1.32
Puerto Rican	8	0.08
South American	1	0.01
Colombian	1	0.01
Other Hispanic or Latino	18	0.17

Race*	Population	%
African-American/Black (340)	408	3.88
Not Hispanic (338)	406	3.86
Hispanic (2)	2	0.02
American Indian/Alaska Native (22)	75	0.71
Not Hispanic (21)	73	0.69
Hispanic (1)	2	0.02
Apache (0)	1	0.01
Canadian/French Am. Ind. (3)	3	0.03
Cherokee (3)	22	0.21

*Notes: † The Census 2010 population figure is used to calculate the percentages in the Hispanic Origin and Race categories. Ancestry percentages are based on the 2006-2010 American Community Survey population (not shown); ‡ Numbers in parentheses indicate the number of people reporting a single ancestry; * Numbers in parentheses indicate the number of persons reporting this race alone, not in combination with any other race; Please refer to the Explanation of Data for more information.*

Chippewa (1)	2	0.02
Choctaw (0)	1	0.01
Comanche (0)	1	0.01
Iroquois (0)	6	0.06
Lumbee (1)	1	0.01
Navajo (2)	3	0.03
Asian (79)	107	1.02
Not Hispanic (79)	107	1.02
Cambodian (3)	3	0.03
Chinese, ex. Taiwanese (15)	17	0.16
Filipino (9)	17	0.16
Hmong (1)	4	0.04
Indian (32)	33	0.31
Indonesian (2)	5	0.05
Japanese (5)	12	0.11
Korean (9)	11	0.10
Vietnamese (1)	2	0.02
Hawaii Native/Pacific Islander (4)	7	0.07
Not Hispanic (2)	5	0.05
Hispanic (2)	2	0.02
Guamanian/Chamorro (2)	2	0.02
Native Hawaiian (1)	1	0.01
Samoan (0)	1	0.01
White (9,806)	9,960	94.81
Not Hispanic (9,711)	9,852	93.78
Hispanic (95)	108	1.03

Lexington-Fayette

Place Type: Consolidated Government
County: Fayette
Population: 295,803†

Ancestry‡	Population	%
African, Sub-Saharan (1,592)	1,963	0.68
African (1,052)	1,383	0.48
Ethiopian (39)	39	0.01
Ghanaian (80)	80	0.03
Nigerian (64)	64	0.02
South African (22)	22	0.01
Ugandan (14)	14	<0.01
Zimbabwean (18)	18	0.01
Other Sub-Saharan African (303)	343	0.12
Albanian (192)	192	0.07
Alsatian (0)	20	0.01
American (35,561)	35,561	12.35
Arab (1,388)	1,875	0.65
Arab (521)	593	0.21
Egyptian (23)	23	0.01
Iraqi (32)	32	0.01
Jordanian (64)	77	0.03
Lebanese (310)	581	0.20
Moroccan (8)	30	0.01
Palestinian (228)	263	0.09
Syrian (52)	52	0.02
Other Arab (150)	224	0.08
Armenian (224)	288	0.10
Assyrian/Chaldean/Syriac (1)	1	<0.01
Australian (22)	249	0.09
Austrian (105)	368	0.13
Basque (16)	29	0.01
Belgian (151)	185	0.06
Brazilian (187)	187	0.06
British (1,008)	1,889	0.66
Bulgarian (135)	135	0.05
Cajun (12)	43	0.01
Canadian (207)	358	0.12
Celtic (13)	62	0.02
Croatian (62)	130	0.05
Czech (198)	480	0.17
Czechoslovakian (46)	113	0.04
Danish (377)	714	0.25
Dutch (1,107)	3,928	1.36
Eastern European (116)	184	0.06
English (16,364)	38,127	13.24
Estonian (34)	56	0.02
European (3,523)	4,060	1.41
Finnish (45)	200	0.07
French, ex. Basque (1,559)	6,600	2.29
French Canadian (797)	1,383	0.48
German (14,412)	42,920	14.90
Greek (394)	800	0.28
Guyanese (14)	14	<0.01
Hungarian (176)	661	0.23
Iranian (234)	297	0.10
Irish (14,394)	39,145	13.59
Italian (3,160)	7,961	2.76
Latvian (10)	60	0.02
Lithuanian (189)	423	0.15
Maltese (14)	26	0.01
Northern European (221)	230	0.08
Norwegian (777)	1,921	0.67
Pennsylvania German (15)	56	0.02
Polish (1,486)	4,181	1.45
Portuguese (96)	519	0.18
Romanian (339)	430	0.15
Russian (495)	1,244	0.43
Scandinavian (84)	279	0.10
Scotch-Irish (4,341)	8,882	3.08
Scottish (3,373)	8,625	2.99
Serbian (65)	74	0.03
Slavic (16)	27	0.01
Slovak (82)	287	0.10
Slovene (21)	46	0.02
Swedish (469)	2,030	0.70
Swiss (93)	708	0.25
Turkish (59)	106	0.04
Ukrainian (325)	478	0.17
Welsh (651)	2,350	0.82
West Indian, ex. Hispanic (272)	388	0.13
British West Indian (10)	10	<0.01
Dutch West Indian (0)	25	0.01
Haitian (67)	92	0.03
Jamaican (79)	112	0.04
Trinidadian/Tobagonian (74)	107	0.04
West Indian (42)	42	0.01
Yugoslavian (153)	179	0.06

Hispanic Origin	Population	%
Hispanic or Latino (of any race)	20,474	6.92
Central American, ex. Mexican	1,305	0.44
Costa Rican	50	0.02
Guatemalan	453	0.15
Honduran	387	0.13
Nicaraguan	75	0.03
Panamanian	97	0.03
Salvadoran	222	0.08
Other Central American	21	0.01
Cuban	488	0.16
Dominican Republic	171	0.06
Mexican	15,145	5.12
Puerto Rican	1,008	0.34
South American	1,027	0.35
Argentinean	112	0.04
Bolivian	31	0.01
Chilean	69	0.02
Colombian	296	0.10
Ecuadorian	84	0.03
Paraguayan	2	<0.01
Peruvian	246	0.08
Uruguayan	18	0.01
Venezuelan	161	0.05
Other South American	8	<0.01
Other Hispanic or Latino	1,330	0.45

Race*	Population	%
African-American/Black (42,972)	47,144	15.94
Not Hispanic (42,336)	46,163	15.61
Hispanic (636)	981	0.33
American Indian/Alaska Native (755)	2,287	0.77
Not Hispanic (599)	1,912	0.65
Hispanic (156)	375	0.13
Alaska Athabascan *(Ala. Nat.)* (7)	8	<0.01
Aleut *(Alaska Native)* (4)	5	<0.01
Apache (5)	21	0.01
Blackfeet (7)	47	0.02
Canadian/French Am. Ind. (6)	7	<0.01
Central American Ind. (2)	3	<0.01
Cherokee (165)	662	0.22
Cheyenne (3)	13	<0.01
Chickasaw (10)	17	0.01
Chippewa (17)	26	0.01
Choctaw (17)	41	0.01
Comanche (0)	1	<0.01
Cree (1)	2	<0.01
Creek (3)	13	<0.01
Crow (1)	2	<0.01
Delaware (3)	10	<0.01
Hopi (4)	7	<0.01
Houma (0)	1	<0.01
Inupiat *(Alaska Native)* (4)	5	<0.01
Iroquois (6)	20	0.01
Kiowa (1)	1	<0.01
Lumbee (13)	14	<0.01
Mexican American Ind. (60)	74	0.03
Navajo (10)	21	0.01
Osage (5)	9	<0.01
Ottawa (3)	4	<0.01
Pima (2)	2	<0.01
Potawatomi (5)	6	<0.01
Pueblo (2)	2	<0.01
Puget Sound Salish (5)	5	<0.01
Seminole (1)	3	<0.01
Sioux (17)	53	0.02
South American Ind. (6)	14	<0.01
Spanish American Ind. (5)	5	<0.01
Tlingit-Haida *(Alaska Native)* (0)	3	<0.01
Yaqui (4)	4	<0.01
Yup'ik *(Alaska Native)* (1)	4	<0.01
Asian (9,553)	11,331	3.83
Not Hispanic (9,506)	11,179	3.78
Hispanic (47)	152	0.05
Bangladeshi (55)	63	0.02
Bhutanese (44)	82	0.03
Burmese (38)	40	0.01
Cambodian (89)	97	0.03
Chinese, ex. Taiwanese (2,593)	2,812	0.95
Filipino (571)	886	0.30
Indian (2,574)	2,826	0.96
Indonesian (110)	138	0.05
Japanese (1,143)	1,413	0.48
Korean (726)	961	0.32
Laotian (11)	15	0.01
Malaysian (16)	26	0.01
Nepalese (226)	266	0.09
Pakistani (265)	290	0.10
Sri Lankan (60)	72	0.02
Taiwanese (125)	137	0.05
Thai (117)	166	0.06
Vietnamese (506)	632	0.21
Hawaii Native/Pacific Islander (141)	322	0.11
Not Hispanic (107)	261	0.09
Hispanic (34)	61	0.02
Fijian (3)	3	<0.01
Guamanian/Chamorro (44)	72	0.02
Marshallese (1)	1	<0.01
Native Hawaiian (41)	88	0.03
Samoan (22)	58	0.02
Tongan (0)	4	<0.01
White (223,999)	230,553	77.94
Not Hispanic (216,072)	221,623	74.92
Hispanic (7,927)	8,930	3.02

London

Place Type: City
County: Laurel
Population: 7,993†

Ancestry‡	Population	%
American (2,924)	2,924	36.88
Belgian (8)	8	0.10
British (7)	31	0.39
Danish (0)	28	0.35
Dutch (0)	34	0.43
English (569)	954	12.03
European (27)	27	0.34
French, ex. Basque (17)	41	0.52
French Canadian (0)	16	0.20
German (389)	895	11.29

*Notes: † The Census 2010 population figure is used to calculate the percentages in the Hispanic Origin and Race categories. Ancestry percentages are based on the 2006-2010 American Community Survey population (not shown); ‡ Numbers in parentheses indicate the number of people reporting a single ancestry; * Numbers in parentheses indicate the number of persons reporting this race alone, not in combination with any other race; Please refer to the Explanation of Data for more information.*

Irish (309)	1,012	12.76
Italian (68)	77	0.97
Norwegian (0)	60	0.76
Polish (34)	94	1.19
Scotch-Irish (19)	48	0.61
Scottish (9)	64	0.81
Swedish (19)	34	0.43
Swiss (30)	61	0.77
Welsh (12)	28	0.35
West Indian, ex. Hispanic (0)	10	0.13
Haitian (0)	10	0.13

Hispanic Origin	Population	%
Hispanic or Latino (of any race)	193	2.41
Central American, ex. Mexican	7	0.09
Guatemalan	7	0.09
Cuban	2	0.03
Dominican Republic	1	0.01
Mexican	129	1.61
Puerto Rican	37	0.46
Other Hispanic or Latino	17	0.21

Race*	Population	%
African-American/Black (139)	194	2.43
Not Hispanic (133)	187	2.34
Hispanic (6)	7	0.09
American Indian/Alaska Native (15)	73	0.91
Not Hispanic (14)	65	0.81
Hispanic (1)	8	0.10
Cherokee (4)	18	0.23
Choctaw (0)	3	0.04
Comanche (2)	4	0.05
Cree (0)	1	0.01
Crow (0)	2	0.03
Delaware (0)	1	0.01
Mexican American Ind. (1)	1	0.01
Sioux (0)	1	0.01
Asian (49)	63	0.79
Not Hispanic (49)	59	0.74
Hispanic (0)	4	0.05
Chinese, ex. Taiwanese (12)	12	0.15
Filipino (1)	3	0.04
Indian (16)	18	0.23
Japanese (4)	7	0.09
Korean (2)	5	0.06
Laotian (0)	2	0.03
Pakistani (9)	9	0.11
Vietnamese (4)	4	0.05
Hawaii Native/Pacific Islander (2)	3	0.04
Not Hispanic (1)	2	0.03
Hispanic (1)	1	0.01
Guamanian/Chamorro (2)	2	0.03
Native Hawaiian (0)	1	0.01
White (7,586)	7,697	96.30
Not Hispanic (7,494)	7,591	94.97
Hispanic (92)	106	1.33

Louisville-Jefferson County

Place Type: Metropolitan Government
County: Jefferson
Population: 597,337†

Ancestry‡	Population	%
Afghan (93)	146	0.02
African, Sub-Saharan (10,884)	12,401	2.11
African (8,781)	10,026	1.71
Cape Verdean (8)	8	<0.01
Ethiopian (274)	418	0.07
Kenyan (14)	14	<0.01
Liberian (327)	395	0.07
Nigerian (32)	50	0.01
Senegalese (39)	56	0.01
Sierra Leonean (10)	10	<0.01
Somalian (680)	680	0.12
South African (12)	20	<0.01
Sudanese (238)	245	0.04
Ugandan (26)	26	<0.01
Other Sub-Saharan African (443)	453	0.08
Albanian (145)	160	0.03
Alsatian (39)	39	0.01
American (61,150)	61,150	10.42
Arab (1,804)	2,417	0.41
Arab (583)	618	0.11
Egyptian (161)	161	0.03
Iraqi (229)	254	0.04
Jordanian (49)	108	0.02
Lebanese (318)	745	0.13
Moroccan (69)	69	0.01
Palestinian (149)	149	0.03
Syrian (108)	150	0.03
Other Arab (138)	163	0.03
Armenian (102)	217	0.04
Australian (37)	118	0.02
Austrian (421)	933	0.16
Basque (13)	60	0.01
Belgian (52)	197	0.03
Brazilian (99)	129	0.02
British (1,450)	2,671	0.46
Bulgarian (22)	40	0.01
Cajun (29)	84	0.01
Canadian (225)	502	0.09
Celtic (77)	77	0.01
Croatian (50)	149	0.03
Czech (234)	844	0.14
Czechoslovakian (89)	194	0.03
Danish (149)	625	0.11
Dutch (1,504)	8,249	1.41
Eastern European (365)	416	0.07
English (21,002)	54,761	9.33
Estonian (8)	58	0.01
European (4,033)	4,703	0.80
Finnish (59)	202	0.03
French, ex. Basque (2,684)	12,472	2.12
French Canadian (538)	1,114	0.19
German (41,735)	112,194	19.11
Greek (452)	1,023	0.17
Guyanese (34)	34	0.01
Hungarian (516)	1,283	0.22
Iranian (492)	573	0.10
Irish (23,836)	80,713	13.75
Israeli (0)	30	0.01
Italian (5,124)	15,482	2.64
Latvian (37)	171	0.03
Lithuanian (68)	303	0.05
Maltese (0)	15	<0.01
Northern European (128)	136	0.02
Norwegian (529)	1,362	0.23
Pennsylvania German (23)	87	0.01
Polish (2,322)	6,214	1.06
Portuguese (48)	489	0.08
Romanian (97)	305	0.05
Russian (1,410)	2,994	0.51
Scandinavian (209)	402	0.07
Scotch-Irish (4,776)	10,354	1.76
Scottish (3,232)	9,762	1.66
Serbian (10)	32	0.01
Slavic (55)	189	0.03
Slovak (207)	479	0.08
Slovene (70)	118	0.02
Swedish (747)	2,671	0.46
Swiss (326)	2,422	0.41
Turkish (296)	330	0.06
Ukrainian (331)	492	0.08
Welsh (861)	2,824	0.48
West Indian, ex. Hispanic (1,012)	1,677	0.29
Barbadian (197)	214	0.04
Belizean (19)	19	<0.01
British West Indian (0)	13	<0.01
Dutch West Indian (13)	24	<0.01
Haitian (419)	560	0.10
Jamaican (284)	554	0.09
Trinidadian/Tobagonian (31)	99	0.02
West Indian (49)	194	0.03
Yugoslavian (1,932)	2,040	0.35

Hispanic Origin	Population	%
Hispanic or Latino (of any race)	26,790	4.48
Central American, ex. Mexican	2,149	0.36
Costa Rican	32	0.01
Guatemalan	1,019	0.17
Honduran	313	0.05
Nicaraguan	112	0.02
Panamanian	246	0.04
Salvadoran	411	0.07
Other Central American	16	<0.01
Cuban	6,575	1.10
Dominican Republic	198	0.03
Mexican	12,537	2.10
Puerto Rican	2,112	0.35
South American	1,284	0.21
Argentinean	103	0.02
Bolivian	69	0.01
Chilean	78	0.01
Colombian	420	0.07
Ecuadorian	137	0.02
Paraguayan	19	<0.01
Peruvian	289	0.05
Uruguayan	28	<0.01
Venezuelan	132	0.02
Other South American	9	<0.01
Other Hispanic or Latino	1,935	0.32

Race*	Population	%
African-American/Black (136,705)	145,117	24.29
Not Hispanic (135,138)	142,817	23.91
Hispanic (1,567)	2,300	0.39
American Indian/Alaska Native (1,532)	4,772	0.80
Not Hispanic (1,289)	4,242	0.71
Hispanic (243)	530	0.09
Alaska Athabascan *(Ala. Nat.)* (5)	7	<0.01
Aleut *(Alaska Native)* (2)	4	<0.01
Apache (34)	61	0.01
Arapaho (2)	5	<0.01
Blackfeet (28)	162	0.03
Canadian/French Am. Ind. (3)	12	<0.01
Central American Ind. (2)	5	<0.01
Cherokee (348)	1,455	0.24
Cheyenne (3)	15	<0.01
Chickasaw (13)	19	<0.01
Chippewa (20)	42	0.01
Choctaw (20)	67	0.01
Comanche (5)	12	<0.01
Cree (0)	3	<0.01
Creek (11)	37	0.01
Crow (8)	17	<0.01
Delaware (4)	12	<0.01
Hopi (1)	3	<0.01
Inupiat *(Alaska Native)* (2)	2	<0.01
Iroquois (25)	59	0.01
Kiowa (1)	4	<0.01
Lumbee (9)	20	<0.01
Menominee (1)	1	<0.01
Mexican American Ind. (80)	119	0.02
Navajo (23)	48	0.01
Osage (3)	8	<0.01
Ottawa (4)	11	<0.01
Paiute (1)	5	<0.01
Potawatomi (8)	11	<0.01
Pueblo (11)	18	<0.01
Puget Sound Salish (1)	1	<0.01
Seminole (2)	24	<0.01
Shoshone (1)	5	<0.01
Sioux (42)	88	0.01
South American Ind. (4)	18	<0.01
Spanish American Ind. (0)	3	<0.01
Tlingit-Haida *(Alaska Native)* (1)	2	<0.01
Tohono O'Odham (2)	8	<0.01
Ute (6)	8	<0.01
Yaqui (1)	3	<0.01
Yuman (0)	2	<0.01
Asian (12,903)	15,676	2.62
Not Hispanic (12,764)	15,386	2.58
Hispanic (139)	290	0.05
Bangladeshi (24)	31	0.01
Bhutanese (145)	228	0.04
Burmese (492)	528	0.09
Cambodian (153)	193	0.03
Chinese, ex. Taiwanese (1,797)	2,131	0.36
Filipino (1,231)	1,869	0.31

*Notes: † The Census 2010 population figure is used to calculate the percentages in the Hispanic Origin and Race categories. Ancestry percentages are based on the 2006-2010 American Community Survey population (not shown); ‡ Numbers in parentheses indicate the number of people reporting a single ancestry; * Numbers in parentheses indicate the number of persons reporting this race alone, not in combination with any other race; Please refer to the Explanation of Data for more information.*

Hmong (16)	24	<0.01
Indian (3,257)	3,649	0.61
Indonesian (20)	28	<0.01
Japanese (319)	675	0.11
Korean (1,217)	1,673	0.28
Laotian (143)	179	0.03
Malaysian (12)	18	<0.01
Nepalese (218)	291	0.05
Pakistani (324)	352	0.06
Sri Lankan (59)	61	0.01
Taiwanese (55)	72	0.01
Thai (146)	236	0.04
Vietnamese (2,663)	2,914	0.49
Hawaii Native/Pacific Islander (398)	899	0.15
Not Hispanic (347)	753	0.13
Hispanic (51)	146	0.02
Fijian (3)	3	<0.01
Guamanian/Chamorro (85)	129	0.02
Marshallese (2)	6	<0.01
Native Hawaiian (120)	304	0.05
Samoan (93)	140	0.02
Tongan (1)	7	<0.01
White (421,439)	433,271	72.53
Not Hispanic (408,157)	418,417	70.05
Hispanic (13,282)	14,854	2.49

Lyndon

Place Type: City
County: Jefferson
Population: 11,002†

Ancestry‡	Population	%
African, Sub-Saharan (85)	101	0.94
African (52)	68	0.63
Senegalese (33)	33	0.31
American (1,037)	1,037	9.61
Arab (9)	9	0.08
Moroccan (9)	9	0.08
Armenian (0)	34	0.32
British (105)	119	1.10
Bulgarian (0)	68	0.63
Croatian (0)	48	0.45
Czech (18)	72	0.67
Danish (0)	14	0.13
Dutch (20)	80	0.74
English (691)	1,486	13.78
European (31)	31	0.29
French, ex. Basque (47)	360	3.34
French Canadian (0)	36	0.33
German (898)	2,336	21.66
Greek (0)	35	0.32
Hungarian (51)	132	1.22
Irish (547)	1,787	16.57
Italian (170)	350	3.24
Norwegian (14)	112	1.04
Pennsylvania German (0)	11	0.10
Polish (24)	154	1.43
Portuguese (0)	13	0.12
Romanian (0)	13	0.12
Russian (11)	138	1.28
Scandinavian (9)	9	0.08
Scotch-Irish (77)	194	1.80
Scottish (100)	196	1.82
Swedish (9)	9	0.08
Swiss (15)	103	0.95
Turkish (28)	28	0.26
Ukrainian (0)	11	0.10
Welsh (16)	66	0.61

Hispanic Origin	Population	%
Hispanic or Latino (of any race)	754	6.85
Central American, ex. Mexican	72	0.65
Costa Rican	4	0.04
Guatemalan	24	0.22
Honduran	8	0.07
Nicaraguan	2	0.02
Panamanian	3	0.03
Salvadoran	27	0.25
Other Central American	4	0.04
Cuban	47	0.43
Dominican Republic	4	0.04
Mexican	433	3.94
Puerto Rican	93	0.85
South American	48	0.44
Argentinean	5	0.05
Chilean	6	0.05
Colombian	11	0.10
Ecuadorian	7	0.06
Paraguayan	1	0.01
Peruvian	15	0.14
Venezuelan	3	0.03
Other Hispanic or Latino	57	0.52

Race*	Population	%
African-American/Black (1,254)	1,443	13.12
Not Hispanic (1,229)	1,401	12.73
Hispanic (25)	42	0.38
American Indian/Alaska Native (27)	81	0.74
Not Hispanic (23)	69	0.63
Hispanic (4)	12	0.11
Aleut *(Alaska Native)* (1)	7	0.06
Apache (0)	1	0.01
Cherokee (11)	21	0.19
Chickasaw (3)	3	0.03
Choctaw (1)	8	0.07
Comanche (0)	1	0.01
Creek (1)	1	0.01
Sioux (1)	1	0.01
Asian (230)	271	2.46
Not Hispanic (230)	270	2.45
Hispanic (0)	1	0.01
Cambodian (2)	2	0.02
Chinese, ex. Taiwanese (45)	50	0.45
Filipino (27)	42	0.38
Hmong (1)	3	0.03
Indian (71)	72	0.65
Japanese (9)	21	0.19
Korean (29)	33	0.30
Laotian (2)	3	0.03
Pakistani (5)	6	0.05
Taiwanese (7)	9	0.08
Thai (3)	4	0.04
Vietnamese (23)	24	0.22
Hawaii Native/Pacific Islander (3)	12	0.11
Not Hispanic (2)	9	0.08
Hispanic (1)	3	0.03
Native Hawaiian (2)	4	0.04
Samoan (1)	3	0.03
White (8,844)	9,094	82.66
Not Hispanic (8,515)	8,724	79.29
Hispanic (329)	370	3.36

Madisonville

Place Type: City
County: Hopkins
Population: 19,591†

Ancestry‡	Population	%
African, Sub-Saharan (111)	122	0.62
African (87)	98	0.50
South African (24)	24	0.12
American (3,294)	3,294	16.84
Arab (16)	16	0.08
Egyptian (16)	16	0.08
British (86)	152	0.78
Canadian (10)	40	0.20
Danish (10)	10	0.05
Dutch (51)	165	0.84
English (1,376)	2,493	12.75
European (100)	167	0.85
French, ex. Basque (45)	200	1.02
German (1,085)	2,620	13.40
Greek (13)	13	0.07
Irish (810)	1,835	9.38
Italian (201)	366	1.87
Northern European (9)	9	0.05
Norwegian (8)	68	0.35
Pennsylvania German (0)	22	0.11
Polish (38)	139	0.71
Russian (71)	103	0.53
Scotch-Irish (197)	350	1.79
Scottish (280)	629	3.22
Slovak (0)	14	0.07
Swedish (0)	24	0.12
Swiss (9)	9	0.05
Ukrainian (0)	17	0.09
Welsh (74)	107	0.55
West Indian, ex. Hispanic (0)	15	0.08
Dutch West Indian (0)	15	0.08

Hispanic Origin	Population	%
Hispanic or Latino (of any race)	435	2.22
Central American, ex. Mexican	26	0.13
Guatemalan	4	0.02
Honduran	10	0.05
Panamanian	2	0.01
Salvadoran	10	0.05
Cuban	5	0.03
Dominican Republic	3	0.02
Mexican	305	1.56
Puerto Rican	43	0.22
South American	7	0.04
Bolivian	1	0.01
Chilean	1	0.01
Colombian	1	0.01
Ecuadorian	2	0.01
Paraguayan	1	0.01
Venezuelan	1	0.01
Other Hispanic or Latino	46	0.23

Race*	Population	%
African-American/Black (2,385)	2,723	13.90
Not Hispanic (2,378)	2,697	13.77
Hispanic (7)	26	0.13
American Indian/Alaska Native (27)	105	0.54
Not Hispanic (24)	93	0.47
Hispanic (3)	12	0.06
Alaska Athabascan *(Ala. Nat.)* (1)	1	0.01
Blackfeet (3)	6	0.03
Cherokee (10)	51	0.26
Chickasaw (0)	1	0.01
Chippewa (1)	4	0.02
Choctaw (1)	1	0.01
Creek (0)	3	0.02
Iroquois (2)	4	0.02
Mexican American Ind. (0)	2	0.01
Osage (0)	1	0.01
Potawatomi (1)	1	0.01
Pueblo (3)	4	0.02
Sioux (0)	1	0.01
Asian (173)	212	1.08
Not Hispanic (172)	210	1.07
Hispanic (1)	2	0.01
Cambodian (5)	5	0.03
Chinese, ex. Taiwanese (40)	45	0.23
Filipino (14)	24	0.12
Indian (63)	66	0.34
Indonesian (1)	1	0.01
Japanese (12)	27	0.14
Korean (12)	15	0.08
Laotian (1)	1	0.01
Pakistani (4)	4	0.02
Taiwanese (1)	1	0.01
Thai (3)	3	0.02
Vietnamese (12)	12	0.06
Hawaii Native/Pacific Islander (15)	40	0.20
Not Hispanic (9)	31	0.16
Hispanic (6)	9	0.05
Guamanian/Chamorro (3)	11	0.06
Native Hawaiian (1)	4	0.02
Samoan (11)	19	0.10
White (16,317)	16,791	85.71
Not Hispanic (16,122)	16,544	84.45
Hispanic (195)	247	1.26

*Notes: † The Census 2010 population figure is used to calculate the percentages in the Hispanic Origin and Race categories. Ancestry percentages are based on the 2006-2010 American Community Survey population (not shown); ‡ Numbers in parentheses indicate the number of people reporting a single ancestry; * Numbers in parentheses indicate the number of persons reporting this race alone, not in combination with any other race; Please refer to the Explanation of Data for more information.*

Mayfield

Place Type: City
County: Graves
Population: 10,024†

Ancestry‡	Population	%
African, Sub-Saharan (11)	11	0.11
African (11)	11	0.11
American (1,208)	1,208	12.04
British (20)	26	0.26
Canadian (0)	7	0.07
Dutch (28)	114	1.14
English (475)	752	7.50
European (10)	10	0.10
French, ex. Basque (15)	93	0.93
French Canadian (0)	11	0.11
German (502)	1,149	11.45
Irish (387)	1,075	10.71
Italian (8)	73	0.73
Norwegian (8)	26	0.26
Polish (12)	12	0.12
Portuguese (12)	12	0.12
Scotch-Irish (30)	93	0.93
Scottish (94)	112	1.12
Swedish (0)	7	0.07
Swiss (0)	16	0.16
Ukrainian (19)	19	0.19
Welsh (7)	33	0.33
West Indian, ex. Hispanic (20)	20	0.20
West Indian (20)	20	0.20

Hispanic Origin	Population	%
Hispanic or Latino (of any race)	1,442	14.39
Central American, ex. Mexican	145	1.45
Guatemalan	135	1.35
Honduran	4	0.04
Salvadoran	5	0.05
Other Central American	1	0.01
Cuban	10	0.10
Mexican	1,175	11.72
Puerto Rican	35	0.35
South American	12	0.12
Colombian	9	0.09
Ecuadorian	1	0.01
Peruvian	2	0.02
Other Hispanic or Latino	65	0.65

Race*	Population	%
African-American/Black (1,285)	1,521	15.17
Not Hispanic (1,278)	1,501	14.97
Hispanic (7)	20	0.20
American Indian/Alaska Native (21)	86	0.86
Not Hispanic (16)	74	0.74
Hispanic (5)	12	0.12
Apache (2)	2	0.02
Blackfeet (1)	2	0.02
Cherokee (3)	26	0.26
Cheyenne (1)	1	0.01
Choctaw (1)	1	0.01
Comanche (0)	2	0.02
Mexican American Ind. (4)	4	0.04
Osage (0)	3	0.03
Sioux (0)	3	0.03
Asian (44)	60	0.60
Not Hispanic (44)	58	0.58
Hispanic (0)	2	0.02
Chinese, ex. Taiwanese (17)	18	0.18
Filipino (7)	8	0.08
Indian (5)	9	0.09
Japanese (0)	2	0.02
Korean (2)	2	0.02
Malaysian (0)	10	0.10
Thai (0)	10	0.10
Vietnamese (2)	5	0.05
Hawaii Native/Pacific Islander (15)	18	0.18
Not Hispanic (7)	10	0.10
Hispanic (8)	8	0.08
Fijian (0)	2	0.02
Guamanian/Chamorro (8)	8	0.08
Native Hawaiian (1)	1	0.01
Samoan (1)	1	0.01
White (7,608)	7,904	78.85
Not Hispanic (6,939)	7,204	71.87
Hispanic (669)	700	6.98

Maysville

Place Type: City
County: Mason
Population: 9,011†

Ancestry‡	Population	%
American (1,567)	1,567	17.40
Arab (0)	12	0.13
Lebanese (0)	12	0.13
Assyrian/Chaldean/Syriac (10)	32	0.36
Austrian (6)	20	0.22
British (26)	88	0.98
Cajun (0)	31	0.34
Dutch (74)	149	1.65
English (376)	954	10.60
European (0)	68	0.76
French, ex. Basque (8)	121	1.34
German (564)	1,714	19.04
Hungarian (10)	10	0.11
Irish (557)	1,297	14.40
Italian (50)	207	2.30
Polish (0)	20	0.22
Scandinavian (17)	25	0.28
Scotch-Irish (95)	232	2.58
Scottish (153)	268	2.98
Swiss (7)	7	0.08
Welsh (6)	25	0.28

Hispanic Origin	Population	%
Hispanic or Latino (of any race)	126	1.40
Central American, ex. Mexican	9	0.10
Costa Rican	1	0.01
Guatemalan	6	0.07
Panamanian	2	0.02
Cuban	5	0.06
Dominican Republic	1	0.01
Mexican	80	0.89
Puerto Rican	7	0.08
South American	1	0.01
Colombian	1	0.01
Other Hispanic or Latino	23	0.26

Race*	Population	%
African-American/Black (982)	1,144	12.70
Not Hispanic (979)	1,130	12.54
Hispanic (3)	14	0.16
American Indian/Alaska Native (22)	53	0.59
Not Hispanic (20)	45	0.50
Hispanic (2)	8	0.09
Cherokee (8)	14	0.16
Cheyenne (0)	1	0.01
Chickasaw (0)	1	0.01
Choctaw (0)	1	0.01
Navajo (0)	1	0.01
Osage (2)	2	0.02
Yaqui (3)	3	0.03
Asian (88)	105	1.17
Not Hispanic (86)	103	1.14
Hispanic (2)	2	0.02
Cambodian (9)	9	0.10
Chinese, ex. Taiwanese (13)	14	0.16
Filipino (1)	3	0.03
Indian (24)	31	0.34
Japanese (32)	35	0.39
Korean (2)	2	0.02
Taiwanese (1)	1	0.01
Thai (1)	1	0.01
Vietnamese (5)	6	0.07
Hawaii Native/Pacific Islander (0)	9	0.10
Not Hispanic (0)	9	0.10
Guamanian/Chamorro (0)	1	0.01
Native Hawaiian (0)	4	0.04
Samoan (0)	1	0.01
White (7,650)	7,856	87.18
Not Hispanic (7,592)	7,778	86.32
Hispanic (58)	78	0.87

Middlesborough

Place Type: City
County: Bell
Population: 10,334†

Ancestry‡	Population	%
African, Sub-Saharan (34)	34	0.33
African (34)	34	0.33
American (5,083)	5,083	48.85
Arab (154)	159	1.53
Egyptian (37)	37	0.36
Lebanese (117)	117	1.12
Syrian (0)	5	0.05
British (12)	12	0.12
Dutch (0)	83	0.80
English (788)	1,048	10.07
European (39)	55	0.53
French, ex. Basque (137)	149	1.43
German (165)	428	4.11
Greek (0)	52	0.50
Hungarian (16)	16	0.15
Irish (335)	682	6.55
Italian (66)	120	1.15
Polish (40)	58	0.56
Scotch-Irish (43)	78	0.75
Scottish (38)	38	0.37
Swedish (0)	44	0.42
Welsh (0)	21	0.20

Hispanic Origin	Population	%
Hispanic or Latino (of any race)	108	1.05
Central American, ex. Mexican	12	0.12
Guatemalan	11	0.11
Nicaraguan	1	0.01
Cuban	7	0.07
Mexican	54	0.52
Puerto Rican	10	0.10
South American	2	0.02
Ecuadorian	2	0.02
Other Hispanic or Latino	23	0.22

Race*	Population	%
African-American/Black (413)	527	5.10
Not Hispanic (405)	517	5.00
Hispanic (8)	10	0.10
American Indian/Alaska Native (16)	160	1.55
Not Hispanic (15)	159	1.54
Hispanic (1)	1	0.01
Apache (0)	1	0.01
Cherokee (7)	38	0.37
Choctaw (0)	2	0.02
Creek (0)	1	0.01
Delaware (1)	1	0.01
Mexican American Ind. (1)	1	0.01
Asian (50)	59	0.57
Not Hispanic (50)	57	0.55
Hispanic (0)	2	0.02
Chinese, ex. Taiwanese (8)	9	0.09
Filipino (20)	22	0.21
Indian (12)	16	0.15
Japanese (1)	1	0.01
Korean (1)	1	0.01
Thai (2)	2	0.02
Vietnamese (5)	5	0.05
Hawaii Native/Pacific Islander (10)	11	0.11
Not Hispanic (0)	1	0.01
Hispanic (10)	10	0.10
Guamanian/Chamorro (10)	10	0.10
White (9,541)	9,801	94.84
Not Hispanic (9,490)	9,739	94.24
Hispanic (51)	62	0.60

*Notes: † The Census 2010 population figure is used to calculate the percentages in the Hispanic Origin and Race categories. Ancestry percentages are based on the 2006-2010 American Community Survey population (not shown); ‡ Numbers in parentheses indicate the number of people reporting a single ancestry; * Numbers in parentheses indicate the number of persons reporting this race alone, not in combination with any other race; Please refer to the Explanation of Data for more information.*

Mount Washington

Place Type: City
County: Bullitt
Population: 9,117†

Ancestry‡	Population	%
American (2,710)	2,710	29.95
Australian (11)	11	0.12
Dutch (0)	89	0.98
English (410)	1,037	11.46
French, ex. Basque (39)	162	1.79
French Canadian (0)	16	0.18
German (626)	1,568	17.33
Irish (501)	1,152	12.73
Italian (304)	519	5.74
Norwegian (25)	35	0.39
Polish (11)	90	0.99
Scotch-Irish (61)	114	1.26
Scottish (121)	185	2.04
Swedish (16)	52	0.57
Swiss (0)	35	0.39
Welsh (0)	10	0.11

Hispanic Origin	Population	%
Hispanic or Latino (of any race)	147	1.61
Central American, ex. Mexican	15	0.16
Guatemalan	10	0.11
Nicaraguan	4	0.04
Salvadoran	1	0.01
Cuban	1	0.01
Dominican Republic	1	0.01
Mexican	86	0.94
Puerto Rican	14	0.15
South American	7	0.08
Colombian	5	0.05
Ecuadorian	1	0.01
Venezuelan	1	0.01
Other Hispanic or Latino	23	0.25

Race*	Population	%
African-American/Black (54)	80	0.88
Not Hispanic (54)	79	0.87
Hispanic (0)	1	0.01
American Indian/Alaska Native (11)	62	0.68
Not Hispanic (10)	58	0.64
Hispanic (1)	4	0.04
Alaska Athabascan *(Ala. Nat.)* (1)	1	0.01
Apache (0)	1	0.01
Blackfeet (1)	2	0.02
Cherokee (1)	27	0.30
Chippewa (0)	2	0.02
Creek (1)	3	0.03
Crow (0)	3	0.03
Inupiat *(Alaska Native)* (0)	1	0.01
Iroquois (1)	1	0.01
Pima (1)	1	0.01
Seminole (0)	1	0.01
Shoshone (0)	1	0.01
Asian (40)	65	0.71
Not Hispanic (40)	65	0.71
Chinese, ex. Taiwanese (10)	10	0.11
Filipino (7)	11	0.12
Indian (9)	13	0.14
Japanese (1)	4	0.04
Korean (3)	10	0.11
Thai (4)	7	0.08
Vietnamese (4)	4	0.04
Hawaii Native/Pacific Islander (6)	9	0.10
Not Hispanic (2)	5	0.05
Hispanic (4)	4	0.04
Guamanian/Chamorro (4)	4	0.04
Native Hawaiian (0)	2	0.02
Samoan (1)	1	0.01
White (8,849)	8,960	98.28
Not Hispanic (8,759)	8,855	97.13
Hispanic (90)	105	1.15

Murray

Place Type: City
County: Calloway
Population: 17,741†

Ancestry‡	Population	%
African, Sub-Saharan (35)	81	0.47
African (29)	55	0.32
Nigerian (6)	6	0.03
Other Sub-Saharan African (0)	20	0.12
American (2,384)	2,384	13.73
Arab (88)	88	0.51
Lebanese (64)	64	0.37
Syrian (11)	11	0.06
Other Arab (13)	13	0.07
Australian (12)	12	0.07
Austrian (12)	29	0.17
Belgian (0)	15	0.09
British (0)	54	0.31
Celtic (0)	9	0.05
Czechoslovakian (8)	8	0.05
Danish (0)	22	0.13
Dutch (16)	178	1.02
English (873)	1,843	10.61
European (92)	154	0.89
Finnish (13)	13	0.07
French, ex. Basque (117)	306	1.76
German (1,018)	2,593	14.93
German Russian (0)	14	0.08
Greek (0)	47	0.27
Hungarian (0)	35	0.20
Irish (1,117)	2,567	14.78
Italian (264)	460	2.65
Lithuanian (39)	67	0.39
Northern European (48)	48	0.28
Norwegian (0)	48	0.28
Pennsylvania German (0)	14	0.08
Polish (88)	301	1.73
Romanian (12)	12	0.07
Russian (0)	26	0.15
Scotch-Irish (416)	658	3.79
Scottish (180)	502	2.89
Serbian (0)	13	0.07
Slovak (32)	121	0.70
Swedish (70)	188	1.08
Swiss (7)	7	0.04
Welsh (11)	56	0.32
West Indian, ex. Hispanic (0)	32	0.18
Haitian (0)	17	0.10
West Indian (0)	15	0.09

Hispanic Origin	Population	%
Hispanic or Latino (of any race)	542	3.06
Central American, ex. Mexican	32	0.18
Guatemalan	10	0.06
Honduran	11	0.06
Panamanian	8	0.05
Salvadoran	3	0.02
Cuban	20	0.11
Mexican	397	2.24
Puerto Rican	25	0.14
South American	17	0.10
Argentinean	4	0.02
Chilean	2	0.01
Colombian	8	0.05
Peruvian	2	0.01
Uruguayan	1	0.01
Other Hispanic or Latino	51	0.29

Race*	Population	%
African-American/Black (1,204)	1,385	7.81
Not Hispanic (1,193)	1,365	7.69
Hispanic (11)	20	0.11
American Indian/Alaska Native (37)	112	0.63
Not Hispanic (20)	84	0.47
Hispanic (17)	28	0.16
Apache (1)	6	0.03
Blackfeet (0)	6	0.03
Canadian/French Am. Ind. (1)	1	0.01
Cherokee (5)	33	0.19
Cheyenne (0)	1	0.01
Chippewa (1)	3	0.02
Choctaw (1)	2	0.01
Cree (0)	1	0.01
Creek (2)	3	0.02
Delaware (0)	1	0.01
Iroquois (0)	2	0.01
Navajo (0)	1	0.01
Osage (1)	1	0.01
Potawatomi (0)	1	0.01
Seminole (1)	1	0.01
Sioux (1)	2	0.01
Tohono O'Odham (2)	2	0.01
Asian (587)	674	3.80
Not Hispanic (581)	664	3.74
Hispanic (6)	10	0.06
Chinese, ex. Taiwanese (262)	272	1.53
Filipino (8)	17	0.10
Indian (97)	100	0.56
Indonesian (9)	9	0.05
Japanese (20)	27	0.15
Korean (107)	122	0.69
Laotian (0)	2	0.01
Malaysian (7)	10	0.06
Nepalese (2)	2	0.01
Taiwanese (7)	7	0.04
Thai (19)	22	0.12
Vietnamese (24)	34	0.19
Hawaii Native/Pacific Islander (6)	16	0.09
Not Hispanic (5)	13	0.07
Hispanic (1)	3	0.02
Guamanian/Chamorro (2)	2	0.01
Native Hawaiian (1)	4	0.02
White (15,370)	15,686	88.42
Not Hispanic (15,073)	15,355	86.55
Hispanic (297)	331	1.87

Newport

Place Type: City
County: Campbell
Population: 15,273†

Ancestry‡	Population	%
African, Sub-Saharan (6)	41	0.27
African (6)	41	0.27
American (1,622)	1,622	10.53
Arab (7)	27	0.18
Egyptian (0)	20	0.13
Moroccan (7)	7	0.05
Armenian (16)	16	0.10
Austrian (0)	46	0.30
British (0)	34	0.22
Czech (13)	25	0.16
Dutch (0)	115	0.75
English (397)	1,153	7.49
European (91)	116	0.75
French, ex. Basque (48)	348	2.26
French Canadian (0)	52	0.34
German (1,519)	3,880	25.19
Greek (7)	120	0.78
Irish (521)	2,507	16.27
Italian (447)	974	6.32
Norwegian (0)	32	0.21
Polish (26)	55	0.36
Romanian (0)	27	0.18
Russian (0)	16	0.10
Scandinavian (21)	34	0.22
Scotch-Irish (257)	379	2.46
Scottish (168)	404	2.62
Serbian (0)	13	0.08
Swedish (11)	59	0.38
Swiss (0)	14	0.09
Ukrainian (40)	40	0.26
Welsh (35)	205	1.33
West Indian, ex. Hispanic (0)	10	0.06
Jamaican (0)	10	0.06
Yugoslavian (0)	21	0.14

SECTION TWO

*Notes: † The Census 2010 population figure is used to calculate the percentages in the Hispanic Origin and Race categories. Ancestry percentages are based on the 2006-2010 American Community Survey population (not shown); ‡ Numbers in parentheses indicate the number of people reporting a single ancestry; * Numbers in parentheses indicate the number of persons reporting this race alone, not in combination with any other race; Please refer to the Explanation of Data for more information.*

Hispanic Origin	Population	%
Hispanic or Latino (of any race)	621	4.07
Central American, ex. Mexican	174	1.14
Costa Rican	1	0.01
Guatemalan	159	1.04
Honduran	2	0.01
Panamanian	3	0.02
Salvadoran	8	0.05
Other Central American	1	0.01
Cuban	14	0.09
Dominican Republic	5	0.03
Mexican	303	1.98
Puerto Rican	38	0.25
South American	11	0.07
Bolivian	1	0.01
Colombian	7	0.05
Peruvian	3	0.02
Other Hispanic or Latino	76	0.50

Race*	Population	%
African-American/Black (1,166)	1,508	9.87
Not Hispanic (1,151)	1,478	9.68
Hispanic (15)	30	0.20
American Indian/Alaska Native (45)	146	0.96
Not Hispanic (25)	120	0.79
Hispanic (20)	26	0.17
Blackfeet (3)	12	0.08
Central American Ind. (1)	1	0.01
Cherokee (5)	39	0.26
Choctaw (0)	1	0.01
Creek (0)	1	0.01
Crow (0)	3	0.02
Delaware (0)	1	0.01
Iroquois (2)	2	0.01
Mexican American Ind. (17)	18	0.12
Potawatomi (1)	1	0.01
Sioux (2)	8	0.05
Tlingit-Haida *(Alaska Native)* (0)	1	0.01
Yuman (1)	1	0.01
Asian (112)	156	1.02
Not Hispanic (94)	135	0.88
Hispanic (18)	21	0.14
Cambodian (1)	5	0.03
Chinese, ex. Taiwanese (10)	15	0.10
Filipino (16)	30	0.20
Indian (52)	58	0.38
Japanese (5)	8	0.05
Korean (13)	27	0.18
Nepalese (1)	2	0.01
Thai (1)	1	0.01
Vietnamese (7)	10	0.07
Hawaii Native/Pacific Islander (5)	13	0.09
Not Hispanic (0)	3	0.02
Hispanic (5)	10	0.07
Guamanian/Chamorro (5)	10	0.07
Native Hawaiian (0)	1	0.01
White (13,176)	13,643	89.33
Not Hispanic (12,906)	13,327	87.26
Hispanic (270)	316	2.07

Nicholasville

Place Type: City
County: Jessamine
Population: 28,015†

Ancestry‡	Population	%
African, Sub-Saharan (23)	23	0.09
Other Sub-Saharan African (23)	23	0.09
Albanian (117)	117	0.44
American (6,445)	6,445	23.99
Arab (175)	175	0.65
Jordanian (167)	167	0.62
Syrian (8)	8	0.03
Austrian (0)	9	0.03
British (205)	276	1.03
Canadian (20)	20	0.07
Croatian (0)	13	0.05
Czech (34)	49	0.18
Dutch (41)	390	1.45
English (1,417)	2,691	10.02
European (147)	161	0.60
Finnish (8)	31	0.12
French, ex. Basque (205)	744	2.77
French Canadian (23)	87	0.32
German (1,439)	3,824	14.24
Greek (14)	40	0.15
Hungarian (11)	11	0.04
Irish (1,508)	4,490	16.72
Italian (179)	617	2.30
Northern European (15)	15	0.06
Norwegian (36)	91	0.34
Pennsylvania German (0)	40	0.15
Polish (34)	250	0.93
Portuguese (12)	12	0.04
Russian (0)	36	0.13
Scandinavian (0)	69	0.26
Scotch-Irish (252)	554	2.06
Scottish (181)	391	1.46
Slavic (6)	6	0.02
Swedish (13)	62	0.23
Swiss (0)	23	0.09
Ukrainian (137)	157	0.58
Welsh (31)	76	0.28

Hispanic Origin	Population	%
Hispanic or Latino (of any race)	991	3.54
Central American, ex. Mexican	43	0.15
Guatemalan	17	0.06
Honduran	6	0.02
Nicaraguan	5	0.02
Panamanian	6	0.02
Salvadoran	9	0.03
Cuban	25	0.09
Dominican Republic	8	0.03
Mexican	713	2.55
Puerto Rican	60	0.21
South American	58	0.21
Bolivian	10	0.04
Chilean	11	0.04
Colombian	17	0.06
Ecuadorian	2	0.01
Peruvian	10	0.04
Venezuelan	8	0.03
Other Hispanic or Latino	84	0.30

Race*	Population	%
African-American/Black (1,194)	1,543	5.51
Not Hispanic (1,185)	1,514	5.40
Hispanic (9)	29	0.10
American Indian/Alaska Native (69)	234	0.84
Not Hispanic (63)	216	0.77
Hispanic (6)	18	0.06
Apache (1)	2	0.01
Blackfeet (0)	7	0.02
Cherokee (20)	90	0.32
Chickasaw (0)	1	<0.01
Chippewa (7)	9	0.03
Choctaw (1)	4	0.01
Creek (0)	4	0.01
Iroquois (1)	2	0.01
Lumbee (1)	4	0.01
Mexican American Ind. (2)	2	0.01
Navajo (0)	1	<0.01
Pueblo (0)	1	<0.01
Seminole (1)	1	<0.01
Sioux (0)	1	<0.01
South American Ind. (0)	2	0.01
Spanish American Ind. (0)	3	0.01
Asian (153)	263	0.94
Not Hispanic (153)	255	0.91
Hispanic (0)	8	0.03
Bangladeshi (1)	1	<0.01
Burmese (1)	1	<0.01
Cambodian (13)	13	0.05
Chinese, ex. Taiwanese (48)	58	0.21
Filipino (18)	37	0.13
Indian (20)	35	0.12
Japanese (8)	23	0.08
Korean (27)	45	0.16
Malaysian (0)	5	0.02
Pakistani (0)	4	0.01
Thai (4)	13	0.05
Vietnamese (5)	10	0.04
Hawaii Native/Pacific Islander (17)	34	0.12
Not Hispanic (15)	28	0.10
Hispanic (2)	6	0.02
Guamanian/Chamorro (1)	2	0.01
Native Hawaiian (3)	12	0.04
Samoan (7)	9	0.03
Tongan (1)	1	<0.01
White (25,622)	26,223	93.60
Not Hispanic (25,031)	25,569	91.27
Hispanic (591)	654	2.33

Oakbrook

Place Type: CDP
County: Boone
Population: 9,036†

Ancestry‡	Population	%
American (522)	522	5.91
Arab (12)	32	0.36
Egyptian (12)	12	0.14
Syrian (0)	20	0.23
Austrian (0)	16	0.18
British (26)	50	0.57
Canadian (22)	22	0.25
Croatian (0)	11	0.12
Czech (16)	16	0.18
Dutch (10)	42	0.48
English (444)	1,086	12.29
European (93)	93	1.05
Finnish (0)	43	0.49
French, ex. Basque (25)	141	1.60
French Canadian (28)	28	0.32
German (1,908)	3,661	41.42
Greek (64)	95	1.07
Hungarian (26)	41	0.46
Irish (314)	1,454	16.45
Italian (119)	416	4.71
Lithuanian (0)	16	0.18
Macedonian (14)	14	0.16
Norwegian (24)	104	1.18
Polish (0)	77	0.87
Russian (20)	57	0.64
Scandinavian (14)	14	0.16
Scotch-Irish (78)	154	1.74
Scottish (118)	253	2.86
Serbian (14)	14	0.16
Slavic (0)	11	0.12
Slovak (0)	12	0.14
Swedish (14)	53	0.60
Swiss (12)	12	0.14
Ukrainian (0)	25	0.28
Welsh (0)	115	1.30

Hispanic Origin	Population	%
Hispanic or Latino (of any race)	184	2.04
Central American, ex. Mexican	15	0.17
Guatemalan	7	0.08
Honduran	5	0.06
Nicaraguan	1	0.01
Panamanian	1	0.01
Salvadoran	1	0.01
Cuban	1	0.01
Dominican Republic	4	0.04
Mexican	96	1.06
Puerto Rican	29	0.32
South American	22	0.24
Argentinean	3	0.03
Chilean	8	0.09
Colombian	6	0.07
Ecuadorian	4	0.04
Peruvian	1	0.01
Other Hispanic or Latino	17	0.19

Race*	Population	%
African-American/Black (179)	224	2.48

*Notes: † The Census 2010 population figure is used to calculate the percentages in the Hispanic Origin and Race categories. Ancestry percentages are based on the 2006-2010 American Community Survey population (not shown); ‡ Numbers in parentheses indicate the number of people reporting a single ancestry; * Numbers in parentheses indicate the number of persons reporting this race alone, not in combination with any other race; Please refer to the Explanation of Data for more information.*

Not Hispanic (175)	212	2.35
Hispanic (4)	12	0.13
American Indian/Alaska Native (10)	38	0.42
Not Hispanic (10)	33	0.37
Hispanic (0)	5	0.06
Alaska Athabascan *(Ala. Nat.)* (0)	1	0.01
Apache (0)	2	0.02
Cherokee (4)	17	0.19
Chickasaw (0)	1	0.01
Choctaw (1)	1	0.01
Cree (1)	1	0.01
Delaware (1)	1	0.01
Sioux (1)	1	0.01
Asian (203)	254	2.81
Not Hispanic (201)	246	2.72
Hispanic (2)	8	0.09
Chinese, ex. Taiwanese (28)	33	0.37
Filipino (14)	32	0.35
Hmong (4)	4	0.04
Indian (41)	52	0.58
Japanese (74)	89	0.98
Korean (14)	22	0.24
Laotian (1)	1	0.01
Taiwanese (2)	2	0.02
Thai (2)	3	0.03
Vietnamese (19)	20	0.22
Hawaii Native/Pacific Islander (3)	7	0.08
Not Hispanic (3)	6	0.07
Hispanic (0)	1	0.01
Native Hawaiian (3)	6	0.07
White (8,442)	8,575	94.90
Not Hispanic (8,334)	8,433	93.33
Hispanic (108)	142	1.57

Owensboro

Place Type: City
County: Daviess
Population: 57,265†

Ancestry‡	Population	%
African, Sub-Saharan (125)	142	0.25
African (93)	110	0.19
Liberian (8)	8	0.01
Other Sub-Saharan African (24)	24	0.04
American (15,563)	15,563	27.53
Arab (112)	112	0.20
Moroccan (9)	9	0.02
Other Arab (103)	103	0.18
Austrian (16)	36	0.06
Belgian (14)	26	0.05
British (109)	168	0.30
Canadian (8)	29	0.05
Celtic (7)	7	0.01
Czech (0)	45	0.08
Danish (8)	19	0.03
Dutch (120)	467	0.83
Eastern European (20)	26	0.05
English (3,245)	6,098	10.79
European (291)	334	0.59
Finnish (103)	103	0.18
French, ex. Basque (254)	1,094	1.93
French Canadian (29)	29	0.05
German (3,541)	7,560	13.37
Greek (118)	134	0.24
Hungarian (12)	24	0.04
Irish (2,733)	6,541	11.57
Italian (454)	825	1.46
Lithuanian (16)	16	0.03
Norwegian (28)	80	0.14
Pennsylvania German (10)	10	0.02
Polish (120)	240	0.42
Portuguese (0)	12	0.02
Russian (0)	18	0.03
Scandinavian (32)	32	0.06
Scotch-Irish (462)	875	1.55
Scottish (251)	913	1.61
Serbian (0)	22	0.04
Slovak (24)	30	0.05
Slovene (5)	20	0.04
Swedish (61)	163	0.29
Swiss (31)	166	0.29
Ukrainian (0)	13	0.02
Welsh (71)	240	0.42
West Indian, ex. Hispanic (12)	36	0.06
Jamaican (12)	12	0.02
West Indian (0)	24	0.04
Yugoslavian (44)	44	0.08

Hispanic Origin	Population	%
Hispanic or Latino (of any race)	1,842	3.22
Central American, ex. Mexican	160	0.28
Costa Rican	1	<0.01
Guatemalan	87	0.15
Honduran	24	0.04
Nicaraguan	8	0.01
Panamanian	5	0.01
Salvadoran	35	0.06
Cuban	29	0.05
Dominican Republic	10	0.02
Mexican	1,296	2.26
Puerto Rican	133	0.23
South American	56	0.10
Argentinean	4	0.01
Bolivian	12	0.02
Colombian	24	0.04
Ecuadorian	10	0.02
Paraguayan	1	<0.01
Peruvian	5	0.01
Other Hispanic or Latino	158	0.28

Race*	Population	%
African-American/Black (4,183)	5,194	9.07
Not Hispanic (4,162)	5,135	8.97
Hispanic (21)	59	0.10
American Indian/Alaska Native (79)	285	0.50
Not Hispanic (65)	256	0.45
Hispanic (14)	29	0.05
Apache (3)	5	0.01
Blackfeet (4)	13	0.02
Cherokee (20)	95	0.17
Chippewa (2)	7	0.01
Choctaw (0)	4	0.01
Creek (1)	2	<0.01
Iroquois (1)	2	<0.01
Kiowa (1)	1	<0.01
Mexican American Ind. (3)	3	0.01
Navajo (1)	8	0.01
Osage (0)	1	<0.01
Pueblo (0)	2	<0.01
Sioux (7)	9	0.02
Tlingit-Haida *(Alaska Native)* (1)	1	<0.01
Asian (503)	636	1.11
Not Hispanic (489)	610	1.07
Hispanic (14)	26	0.05
Burmese (30)	30	0.05
Cambodian (1)	3	0.01
Chinese, ex. Taiwanese (73)	83	0.14
Filipino (43)	80	0.14
Indian (195)	226	0.39
Indonesian (1)	1	<0.01
Japanese (36)	49	0.09
Korean (41)	58	0.10
Laotian (0)	1	<0.01
Nepalese (1)	1	<0.01
Pakistani (19)	24	0.04
Sri Lankan (6)	7	0.01
Taiwanese (3)	7	0.01
Thai (3)	8	0.01
Vietnamese (38)	41	0.07
Hawaii Native/Pacific Islander (44)	71	0.12
Not Hispanic (35)	52	0.09
Hispanic (9)	19	0.03
Guamanian/Chamorro (17)	23	0.04
Native Hawaiian (3)	18	0.03
Samoan (1)	8	0.01
White (50,122)	51,488	89.91
Not Hispanic (49,284)	50,494	88.18
Hispanic (838)	994	1.74

Paducah

Place Type: City
County: McCracken
Population: 25,024†

Ancestry‡	Population	%
African, Sub-Saharan (55)	83	0.33
African (55)	83	0.33
American (2,084)	2,084	8.30
Arab (25)	54	0.22
Arab (10)	10	0.04
Jordanian (15)	15	0.06
Lebanese (0)	19	0.08
Syrian (0)	10	0.04
Australian (15)	15	0.06
Brazilian (0)	15	0.06
British (14)	115	0.46
Canadian (12)	12	0.05
Celtic (0)	8	0.03
Czech (0)	26	0.10
Danish (0)	12	0.05
Dutch (60)	411	1.64
Eastern European (9)	19	0.08
English (1,086)	2,419	9.63
European (118)	232	0.92
Finnish (0)	26	0.10
French, ex. Basque (225)	918	3.66
French Canadian (16)	35	0.14
German (1,024)	2,978	11.86
German Russian (16)	16	0.06
Greek (0)	21	0.08
Hungarian (0)	52	0.21
Iranian (16)	16	0.06
Irish (649)	3,184	12.68
Italian (211)	635	2.53
Latvian (12)	12	0.05
Lithuanian (14)	14	0.06
Norwegian (37)	92	0.37
Pennsylvania German (0)	25	0.10
Polish (110)	384	1.53
Romanian (17)	17	0.07
Russian (28)	28	0.11
Scandinavian (37)	37	0.15
Scotch-Irish (277)	533	2.12
Scottish (139)	494	1.97
Slovak (0)	9	0.04
Slovene (0)	44	0.18
Swedish (23)	106	0.42
Swiss (11)	40	0.16
Welsh (45)	258	1.03
West Indian, ex. Hispanic (10)	23	0.09
Jamaican (10)	10	0.04
West Indian (0)	13	0.05

Hispanic Origin	Population	%
Hispanic or Latino (of any race)	671	2.68
Central American, ex. Mexican	35	0.14
Guatemalan	24	0.10
Honduran	4	0.02
Nicaraguan	2	0.01
Salvadoran	5	0.02
Cuban	21	0.08
Dominican Republic	8	0.03
Mexican	444	1.77
Puerto Rican	79	0.32
South American	28	0.11
Argentinean	4	0.02
Colombian	15	0.06
Peruvian	1	<0.01
Uruguayan	4	0.02
Venezuelan	4	0.02
Other Hispanic or Latino	56	0.22

Race*	Population	%
African-American/Black (5,925)	6,486	25.92
Not Hispanic (5,892)	6,433	25.71
Hispanic (33)	53	0.21
American Indian/Alaska Native (55)	245	0.98
Not Hispanic (50)	224	0.90

*Notes: † The Census 2010 population figure is used to calculate the percentages in the Hispanic Origin and Race categories. Ancestry percentages are based on the 2006-2010 American Community Survey population (not shown); ‡ Numbers in parentheses indicate the number of people reporting a single ancestry; * Numbers in parentheses indicate the number of persons reporting this race alone, not in combination with any other race; Please refer to the Explanation of Data for more information.*

Race* (continued)	Population	%
Hispanic (5)	21	0.08
Apache (2)	9	0.04
Blackfeet (2)	9	0.04
Cherokee (12)	60	0.24
Cheyenne (0)	1	<0.01
Chickasaw (1)	6	0.02
Chippewa (3)	11	0.04
Choctaw (2)	8	0.03
Creek (1)	1	<0.01
Iroquois (3)	4	0.02
Lumbee (1)	2	0.01
Mexican American Ind. (0)	5	0.02
Puget Sound Salish (0)	1	<0.01
Seminole (1)	1	<0.01
Sioux (1)	4	0.02
Asian (255)	313	1.25
Not Hispanic (250)	303	1.21
Hispanic (5)	10	0.04
Bangladeshi (1)	1	<0.01
Burmese (0)	2	0.01
Chinese, ex. Taiwanese (81)	89	0.36
Filipino (31)	45	0.18
Hmong (1)	1	<0.01
Indian (55)	59	0.24
Indonesian (3)	3	0.01
Japanese (9)	18	0.07
Korean (13)	24	0.10
Laotian (3)	4	0.02
Pakistani (19)	20	0.08
Thai (4)	4	0.02
Vietnamese (27)	38	0.15
Hawaii Native/Pacific Islander (4)	20	0.08
Not Hispanic (4)	19	0.08
Hispanic (0)	1	<0.01
Guamanian/Chamorro (0)	1	<0.01
Native Hawaiian (1)	11	0.04
Samoan (1)	3	0.01
White (17,765)	18,470	73.81
Not Hispanic (17,431)	18,085	72.27
Hispanic (334)	385	1.54

Paris

Place Type: City
County: Bourbon
Population: 8,553†

Ancestry‡	Population	%
American (2,344)	2,344	27.22
Austrian (10)	10	0.12
British (36)	36	0.42
Dutch (0)	102	1.18
English (396)	787	9.14
European (95)	95	1.10
French, ex. Basque (0)	58	0.67
German (279)	825	9.58
Irish (645)	1,168	13.56
Italian (98)	149	1.73
Pennsylvania German (20)	20	0.23
Polish (0)	77	0.89
Russian (0)	12	0.14
Scandinavian (0)	18	0.21
Scotch-Irish (19)	89	1.03
Scottish (45)	80	0.93
Swedish (0)	11	0.13
Swiss (0)	10	0.12
Welsh (0)	19	0.22

Hispanic Origin	Population	%
Hispanic or Latino (of any race)	571	6.68
Central American, ex. Mexican	16	0.19
Guatemalan	3	0.04
Honduran	9	0.11
Salvadoran	4	0.05
Cuban	6	0.07
Mexican	519	6.07
Puerto Rican	15	0.18
South American	2	0.02
Argentinean	1	0.01
Peruvian	1	0.01
Other Hispanic or Latino	13	0.15

Race*	Population	%
African-American/Black (985)	1,139	13.32
Not Hispanic (978)	1,126	13.16
Hispanic (7)	13	0.15
American Indian/Alaska Native (16)	50	0.58
Not Hispanic (14)	46	0.54
Hispanic (2)	4	0.05
Apache (0)	2	0.02
Cherokee (0)	9	0.11
Chickasaw (0)	2	0.02
Navajo (1)	3	0.04
Sioux (1)	1	0.01
Spanish American Ind. (0)	1	0.01
Yaqui (0)	1	0.01
Asian (34)	49	0.57
Not Hispanic (29)	40	0.47
Hispanic (5)	9	0.11
Cambodian (1)	1	0.01
Chinese, ex. Taiwanese (7)	9	0.11
Filipino (5)	9	0.11
Indian (10)	14	0.16
Japanese (5)	8	0.09
Korean (0)	2	0.02
Taiwanese (0)	1	0.01
Vietnamese (5)	5	0.06
Hawaii Native/Pacific Islander (0)	2	0.02
Not Hispanic (0)	2	0.02
Samoan (0)	2	0.02
White (6,939)	7,159	83.70
Not Hispanic (6,764)	6,941	81.15
Hispanic (175)	218	2.55

Radcliff

Place Type: City
County: Hardin
Population: 21,688†

Ancestry‡	Population	%
African, Sub-Saharan (701)	710	3.37
African (701)	710	3.37
American (2,232)	2,232	10.61
Arab (11)	22	0.10
Other Arab (11)	22	0.10
Australian (0)	14	0.07
Austrian (27)	37	0.18
British (54)	54	0.26
Cajun (10)	23	0.11
Croatian (0)	14	0.07
Czech (0)	14	0.07
Czechoslovakian (0)	8	0.04
Danish (0)	46	0.22
Dutch (31)	147	0.70
English (715)	1,568	7.45
European (163)	217	1.03
French, ex. Basque (140)	420	2.00
French Canadian (58)	96	0.46
German (1,173)	2,965	14.09
German Russian (12)	12	0.06
Greek (19)	89	0.42
Hungarian (0)	7	0.03
Iranian (12)	12	0.06
Irish (676)	2,021	9.61
Italian (163)	552	2.62
Lithuanian (30)	66	0.31
Norwegian (59)	145	0.69
Polish (155)	337	1.60
Romanian (22)	22	0.10
Scandinavian (11)	21	0.10
Scotch-Irish (164)	256	1.22
Scottish (165)	337	1.60
Slavic (23)	23	0.11
Slovene (0)	16	0.08
Swedish (0)	16	0.08
Swiss (0)	13	0.06
Welsh (0)	63	0.30
West Indian, ex. Hispanic (103)	156	0.74
Belizean (38)	38	0.18
Haitian (9)	9	0.04
Jamaican (47)	91	0.43
U.S. Virgin Islander (9)	9	0.04
West Indian (0)	9	0.04
Yugoslavian (0)	10	0.05

Hispanic Origin	Population	%
Hispanic or Latino (of any race)	1,802	8.31
Central American, ex. Mexican	169	0.78
Costa Rican	15	0.07
Guatemalan	19	0.09
Honduran	8	0.04
Nicaraguan	6	0.03
Panamanian	96	0.44
Salvadoran	25	0.12
Cuban	38	0.18
Dominican Republic	44	0.20
Mexican	701	3.23
Puerto Rican	706	3.26
South American	61	0.28
Colombian	30	0.14
Ecuadorian	13	0.06
Peruvian	7	0.03
Venezuelan	8	0.04
Other South American	3	0.01
Other Hispanic or Latino	83	0.38

Race*	Population	%
African-American/Black (5,471)	6,216	28.66
Not Hispanic (5,276)	5,913	27.26
Hispanic (195)	303	1.40
American Indian/Alaska Native (169)	436	2.01
Not Hispanic (148)	359	1.66
Hispanic (21)	77	0.36
Aleut *(Alaska Native)* (0)	2	0.01
Apache (2)	5	0.02
Blackfeet (2)	15	0.07
Central American Ind. (0)	2	0.01
Cherokee (47)	122	0.56
Chickasaw (0)	3	0.01
Chippewa (2)	6	0.03
Choctaw (4)	16	0.07
Comanche (0)	2	0.01
Cree (2)	3	0.01
Creek (3)	4	0.02
Iroquois (3)	9	0.04
Kiowa (4)	9	0.04
Mexican American Ind. (4)	4	0.02
Navajo (2)	7	0.03
Ottawa (1)	1	<0.01
Potawatomi (3)	3	0.01
Pueblo (0)	3	0.01
Seminole (2)	5	0.02
Shoshone (0)	1	<0.01
Sioux (10)	18	0.08
South American Ind. (2)	2	0.01
Tsimshian *(Alaska Native)* (1)	1	<0.01
Yakama (1)	1	<0.01
Asian (688)	1,096	5.05
Not Hispanic (685)	1,053	4.86
Hispanic (3)	43	0.20
Bangladeshi (1)	1	<0.01
Cambodian (8)	13	0.06
Chinese, ex. Taiwanese (51)	57	0.26
Filipino (149)	269	1.24
Indian (25)	36	0.17
Japanese (60)	117	0.54
Korean (335)	544	2.51
Laotian (3)	5	0.02
Taiwanese (1)	1	<0.01
Thai (21)	35	0.16
Vietnamese (16)	20	0.09
Hawaii Native/Pacific Islander (173)	278	1.28
Not Hispanic (165)	258	1.19
Hispanic (8)	20	0.09
Fijian (1)	1	<0.01
Guamanian/Chamorro (96)	139	0.64
Native Hawaiian (14)	39	0.18
Samoan (28)	65	0.30
Tongan (3)	3	0.01

*Notes: † The Census 2010 population figure is used to calculate the percentages in the Hispanic Origin and Race categories. Ancestry percentages are based on the 2006-2010 American Community Survey population (not shown); ‡ Numbers in parentheses indicate the number of people reporting a single ancestry; * Numbers in parentheses indicate the number of persons reporting this race alone, not in combination with any other race; Please refer to the Explanation of Data for more information.*

White (13,239)	14,353	66.18
Not Hispanic (12,418)	13,375	61.67
Hispanic (821)	978	4.51

Richmond

Place Type: City
County: Madison
Population: 31,364†

Ancestry‡	Population	%
African, Sub-Saharan (90)	105	0.34
African (54)	69	0.22
Kenyan (36)	36	0.12
American (4,539)	4,539	14.65
Arab (78)	143	0.46
Lebanese (13)	78	0.25
Syrian (65)	65	0.21
Armenian (0)	15	0.05
Belgian (11)	33	0.11
British (93)	189	0.61
Canadian (0)	25	0.08
Celtic (11)	11	0.04
Croatian (0)	16	0.05
Czech (0)	64	0.21
Czechoslovakian (0)	11	0.04
Dutch (70)	332	1.07
English (1,676)	3,490	11.26
European (310)	310	1.00
French, ex. Basque (93)	495	1.60
French Canadian (11)	22	0.07
German (1,617)	5,453	17.60
Greek (24)	24	0.08
Hungarian (28)	167	0.54
Irish (1,363)	5,414	17.47
Italian (279)	857	2.77
Lithuanian (0)	54	0.17
New Zealander (12)	12	0.04
Norwegian (126)	245	0.79
Polish (73)	506	1.63
Russian (5)	64	0.21
Scotch-Irish (640)	985	3.18
Scottish (245)	541	1.75
Swedish (18)	75	0.24
Swiss (82)	175	0.56
Ukrainian (68)	131	0.42
Welsh (58)	151	0.49
West Indian, ex. Hispanic (12)	23	0.07
Jamaican (12)	12	0.04
West Indian (0)	11	0.04

Hispanic Origin	Population	%
Hispanic or Latino (of any race)	858	2.74
Central American, ex. Mexican	48	0.15
Costa Rican	8	0.03
Guatemalan	9	0.03
Honduran	11	0.04
Nicaraguan	5	0.02
Panamanian	5	0.02
Salvadoran	10	0.03
Cuban	19	0.06
Dominican Republic	8	0.03
Mexican	578	1.84
Puerto Rican	84	0.27
South American	33	0.11
Argentinean	1	<0.01
Chilean	1	<0.01
Colombian	16	0.05
Ecuadorian	4	0.01
Peruvian	1	<0.01
Venezuelan	10	0.03
Other Hispanic or Latino	88	0.28

Race*	Population	%
African-American/Black (2,521)	2,973	9.48
Not Hispanic (2,493)	2,927	9.33
Hispanic (28)	46	0.15
American Indian/Alaska Native (86)	290	0.92
Not Hispanic (82)	268	0.85
Hispanic (4)	22	0.07
Apache (1)	1	<0.01
Blackfeet (1)	13	0.04
Central American Ind. (0)	3	0.01
Cherokee (26)	100	0.32
Cheyenne (0)	1	<0.01
Chippewa (1)	1	<0.01
Choctaw (0)	3	0.01
Creek (1)	1	<0.01
Delaware (0)	3	0.01
Iroquois (1)	1	<0.01
Lumbee (2)	2	0.01
Mexican American Ind. (2)	11	0.04
Navajo (1)	3	0.01
Potawatomi (0)	2	0.01
Seminole (0)	4	0.01
Sioux (2)	6	0.02
Asian (372)	496	1.58
Not Hispanic (370)	490	1.56
Hispanic (2)	6	0.02
Burmese (3)	3	0.01
Cambodian (1)	1	<0.01
Chinese, ex. Taiwanese (62)	72	0.23
Filipino (23)	43	0.14
Indian (109)	135	0.43
Indonesian (3)	9	0.03
Japanese (57)	73	0.23
Korean (32)	55	0.18
Malaysian (0)	2	0.01
Nepalese (13)	18	0.06
Pakistani (8)	13	0.04
Taiwanese (6)	7	0.02
Thai (1)	4	0.01
Vietnamese (21)	27	0.09
Hawaii Native/Pacific Islander (16)	34	0.11
Not Hispanic (13)	30	0.10
Hispanic (3)	4	0.01
Guamanian/Chamorro (3)	3	0.01
Native Hawaiian (3)	8	0.03
Samoan (4)	5	0.02
White (27,238)	27,976	89.20
Not Hispanic (26,791)	27,465	87.57
Hispanic (447)	511	1.63

Shelbyville

Place Type: City
County: Shelby
Population: 14,045†

Ancestry‡	Population	%
American (2,945)	2,945	21.97
Arab (0)	11	0.08
Lebanese (0)	11	0.08
Belgian (23)	23	0.17
British (13)	70	0.52
Dutch (11)	24	0.18
English (344)	932	6.95
European (113)	113	0.84
Finnish (8)	24	0.18
French, ex. Basque (29)	56	0.42
French Canadian (13)	68	0.51
German (697)	2,155	16.08
Greek (15)	15	0.11
Hungarian (20)	20	0.15
Irish (440)	1,815	13.54
Italian (70)	206	1.54
Lithuanian (0)	23	0.17
Northern European (17)	17	0.13
Polish (7)	165	1.23
Russian (26)	59	0.44
Scotch-Irish (62)	178	1.33
Scottish (57)	142	1.06
Swedish (13)	49	0.37
Swiss (0)	6	0.04
Ukrainian (0)	48	0.36
Welsh (52)	112	0.84

Hispanic Origin	Population	%
Hispanic or Latino (of any race)	2,494	17.76
Central American, ex. Mexican	568	4.04
Guatemalan	450	3.20
Honduran	66	0.47
Nicaraguan	2	0.01
Panamanian	9	0.06
Salvadoran	40	0.28
Other Central American	1	0.01
Cuban	28	0.20
Dominican Republic	12	0.09
Mexican	1,665	11.85
Puerto Rican	58	0.41
South American	30	0.21
Argentinean	2	0.01
Colombian	13	0.09
Ecuadorian	6	0.04
Peruvian	3	0.02
Venezuelan	1	0.01
Other South American	5	0.04
Other Hispanic or Latino	133	0.95

Race*	Population	%
African-American/Black (1,797)	2,070	14.74
Not Hispanic (1,718)	1,981	14.10
Hispanic (79)	89	0.63
American Indian/Alaska Native (66)	144	1.03
Not Hispanic (47)	106	0.75
Hispanic (19)	38	0.27
Apache (1)	3	0.02
Blackfeet (1)	1	0.01
Canadian/French Am. Ind. (1)	1	0.01
Cherokee (12)	29	0.21
Chippewa (2)	3	0.02
Choctaw (9)	9	0.06
Iroquois (1)	1	0.01
Mexican American Ind. (11)	14	0.10
Navajo (0)	1	0.01
Pima (1)	3	0.02
Seminole (2)	2	0.01
Sioux (6)	8	0.06
Asian (109)	157	1.12
Not Hispanic (103)	144	1.03
Hispanic (6)	13	0.09
Cambodian (3)	3	0.02
Chinese, ex. Taiwanese (27)	29	0.21
Filipino (15)	26	0.19
Indian (21)	23	0.16
Japanese (20)	30	0.21
Korean (5)	18	0.13
Laotian (1)	1	0.01
Pakistani (1)	1	0.01
Sri Lankan (1)	1	0.01
Taiwanese (6)	6	0.04
Thai (1)	4	0.03
Vietnamese (7)	8	0.06
Hawaii Native/Pacific Islander (24)	38	0.27
Not Hispanic (12)	19	0.14
Hispanic (12)	19	0.14
Guamanian/Chamorro (22)	28	0.20
Native Hawaiian (0)	3	0.02
Samoan (2)	6	0.04
White (10,465)	10,932	77.84
Not Hispanic (9,294)	9,640	68.64
Hispanic (1,171)	1,292	9.20

Shepherdsville

Place Type: City
County: Bullitt
Population: 11,222†

Ancestry‡	Population	%
American (3,107)	3,107	28.73
Arab (45)	67	0.62
Arab (45)	45	0.42
Lebanese (0)	22	0.20
British (0)	22	0.20
Dutch (12)	107	0.99
English (433)	896	8.29
European (59)	59	0.55
French, ex. Basque (24)	91	0.84
French Canadian (13)	32	0.30

*Notes: † The Census 2010 population figure is used to calculate the percentages in the Hispanic Origin and Race categories. Ancestry percentages are based on the 2006-2010 American Community Survey population (not shown); ‡ Numbers in parentheses indicate the number of people reporting a single ancestry; * Numbers in parentheses indicate the number of persons reporting this race alone, not in combination with any other race; Please refer to the Explanation of Data for more information.*

German (642)	1,761	16.29
Greek (92)	105	0.97
Irish (359)	1,356	12.54
Italian (135)	280	2.59
Norwegian (23)	23	0.21
Polish (116)	296	2.74
Portuguese (0)	19	0.18
Scotch-Irish (0)	68	0.63
Scottish (96)	191	1.77
Swedish (77)	278	2.57
Welsh (31)	31	0.29

Hispanic Origin	Population	%
Hispanic or Latino (of any race)	179	1.60
Central American, ex. Mexican	20	0.18
Honduran	1	0.01
Panamanian	7	0.06
Salvadoran	12	0.11
Cuban	4	0.04
Dominican Republic	4	0.04
Mexican	103	0.92
Puerto Rican	22	0.20
South American	9	0.08
Argentinean	1	0.01
Colombian	7	0.06
Venezuelan	1	0.01
Other Hispanic or Latino	17	0.15

Race*	Population	%
African-American/Black (111)	181	1.61
Not Hispanic (110)	174	1.55
Hispanic (1)	7	0.06
American Indian/Alaska Native (41)	115	1.02
Not Hispanic (41)	114	1.02
Hispanic (0)	1	0.01
Aleut *(Alaska Native)* (1)	1	0.01
Apache (1)	3	0.03
Blackfeet (0)	6	0.05
Cherokee (16)	37	0.33
Chickasaw (1)	1	0.01
Chippewa (1)	1	0.01
Choctaw (0)	3	0.03
Cree (0)	2	0.02
Iroquois (0)	1	0.01
Menominee (1)	1	0.01
Mexican American Ind. (1)	3	0.03
Navajo (1)	4	0.04
Pueblo (1)	1	0.01
Seminole (1)	4	0.04
Sioux (4)	5	0.04
Ute (0)	1	0.01
Asian (62)	87	0.78
Not Hispanic (62)	86	0.77
Hispanic (0)	1	0.01
Cambodian (1)	1	0.01
Chinese, ex. Taiwanese (8)	8	0.07
Filipino (15)	28	0.25
Indian (9)	10	0.09
Japanese (7)	11	0.10
Korean (5)	9	0.08
Laotian (13)	15	0.13
Thai (2)	2	0.02
Vietnamese (1)	2	0.02
Hawaii Native/Pacific Islander (3)	6	0.05
Not Hispanic (2)	5	0.04
Hispanic (1)	1	0.01
Guamanian/Chamorro (1)	1	0.01
Native Hawaiian (2)	5	0.04
White (10,754)	10,930	97.40
Not Hispanic (10,656)	10,816	96.38
Hispanic (98)	114	1.02

Shively

Place Type: City
County: Jefferson
Population: 15,264†

Ancestry‡	Population	%
African, Sub-Saharan (628)	789	5.21
African (628)	789	5.21
American (1,275)	1,275	8.42
Australian (0)	11	0.07
Austrian (11)	11	0.07
British (55)	55	0.36
Dutch (7)	220	1.45
English (429)	1,072	7.08
European (96)	120	0.79
French, ex. Basque (32)	562	3.71
French Canadian (11)	35	0.23
German (631)	1,730	11.43
Greek (39)	39	0.26
Hungarian (26)	32	0.21
Irish (559)	1,587	10.48
Italian (114)	157	1.04
Polish (11)	74	0.49
Scandinavian (0)	49	0.32
Scotch-Irish (117)	144	0.95
Scottish (11)	134	0.88
Ukrainian (12)	12	0.08
Welsh (11)	25	0.17
West Indian, ex. Hispanic (0)	9	0.06
West Indian (0)	9	0.06
Yugoslavian (36)	36	0.24

Hispanic Origin	Population	%
Hispanic or Latino (of any race)	541	3.54
Central American, ex. Mexican	65	0.43
Costa Rican	1	0.01
Guatemalan	19	0.12
Honduran	37	0.24
Nicaraguan	1	0.01
Salvadoran	7	0.05
Cuban	108	0.71
Mexican	279	1.83
Puerto Rican	34	0.22
South American	10	0.07
Bolivian	1	0.01
Colombian	5	0.03
Peruvian	1	0.01
Venezuelan	3	0.02
Other Hispanic or Latino	45	0.29

Race*	Population	%
African-American/Black (7,425)	7,708	50.50
Not Hispanic (7,385)	7,644	50.08
Hispanic (40)	64	0.42
American Indian/Alaska Native (30)	110	0.72
Not Hispanic (25)	101	0.66
Hispanic (5)	9	0.06
Apache (0)	1	0.01
Blackfeet (1)	5	0.03
Cherokee (10)	46	0.30
Choctaw (0)	1	0.01
Comanche (0)	3	0.02
Iroquois (0)	2	0.01
Lumbee (0)	1	0.01
Mexican American Ind. (5)	5	0.03
Navajo (0)	1	0.01
Sioux (1)	2	0.01
South American Ind. (0)	1	0.01
Yaqui (3)	3	0.02
Asian (106)	135	0.88
Not Hispanic (100)	126	0.83
Hispanic (6)	9	0.06
Chinese, ex. Taiwanese (23)	29	0.19
Filipino (13)	17	0.11
Indian (7)	8	0.05
Japanese (3)	10	0.07
Korean (7)	14	0.09
Laotian (5)	5	0.03
Thai (1)	1	0.01
Vietnamese (40)	49	0.32
Hawaii Native/Pacific Islander (12)	18	0.12
Not Hispanic (12)	18	0.12
Guamanian/Chamorro (2)	2	0.01
Native Hawaiian (1)	2	0.01
Samoan (7)	9	0.06
White (7,005)	7,345	48.12
Not Hispanic (6,835)	7,114	46.61
Hispanic (170)	231	1.51

Somerset

Place Type: City
County: Pulaski
Population: 11,196†

Ancestry‡	Population	%
American (2,908)	2,908	26.03
British (16)	16	0.14
Dutch (25)	83	0.74
English (960)	1,631	14.60
European (93)	120	1.07
French, ex. Basque (23)	142	1.27
German (343)	1,071	9.59
Irish (418)	1,590	14.23
Italian (57)	89	0.80
Polish (11)	33	0.30
Scandinavian (0)	21	0.19
Scotch-Irish (170)	302	2.70
Scottish (20)	141	1.26
Swedish (22)	63	0.56
Welsh (29)	83	0.74

Hispanic Origin	Population	%
Hispanic or Latino (of any race)	414	3.70
Central American, ex. Mexican	21	0.19
Guatemalan	8	0.07
Honduran	2	0.02
Nicaraguan	1	0.01
Panamanian	1	0.01
Salvadoran	4	0.04
Other Central American	5	0.04
Cuban	6	0.05
Dominican Republic	2	0.02
Mexican	343	3.06
Puerto Rican	10	0.09
South American	5	0.04
Chilean	1	0.01
Colombian	1	0.01
Ecuadorian	1	0.01
Peruvian	1	0.01
Venezuelan	1	0.01
Other Hispanic or Latino	27	0.24

Race*	Population	%
African-American/Black (389)	475	4.24
Not Hispanic (387)	469	4.19
Hispanic (2)	6	0.05
American Indian/Alaska Native (20)	83	0.74
Not Hispanic (20)	78	0.70
Hispanic (0)	5	0.04
Blackfeet (0)	1	0.01
Cherokee (6)	28	0.25
Choctaw (1)	1	0.01
Creek (2)	2	0.02
Mexican American Ind. (0)	1	0.01
Sioux (2)	2	0.02
Asian (76)	94	0.84
Not Hispanic (76)	93	0.83
Hispanic (0)	1	0.01
Burmese (1)	1	0.01
Chinese, ex. Taiwanese (15)	20	0.18
Filipino (5)	9	0.08
Indian (22)	25	0.22
Japanese (16)	22	0.20
Korean (0)	2	0.02
Pakistani (11)	11	0.10
Vietnamese (4)	5	0.04
Hawaii Native/Pacific Islander (6)	7	0.06
Not Hispanic (5)	6	0.05
Hispanic (1)	1	0.01
Guamanian/Chamorro (2)	2	0.02
Native Hawaiian (0)	1	0.01
Samoan (4)	4	0.04
White (10,329)	10,510	93.87
Not Hispanic (10,120)	10,277	91.79
Hispanic (209)	233	2.08

*Notes: † The Census 2010 population figure is used to calculate the percentages in the Hispanic Origin and Race categories. Ancestry percentages are based on the 2006-2010 American Community Survey population (not shown); ‡ Numbers in parentheses indicate the number of people reporting a single ancestry; * Numbers in parentheses indicate the number of persons reporting this race alone, not in combination with any other race; Please refer to the Explanation of Data for more information.*

St. Matthews

Place Type: City
County: Jefferson
Population: 17,472[†]

Ancestry[‡]	Population	%
American (3,644)	3,644	20.98
Arab (18)	103	0.59
Arab (0)	25	0.14
Lebanese (18)	78	0.45
Austrian (9)	48	0.28
British (83)	120	0.69
Cajun (0)	6	0.03
Canadian (7)	19	0.11
Croatian (0)	23	0.13
Czech (7)	66	0.38
Czechoslovakian (12)	12	0.07
Danish (0)	15	0.09
Dutch (57)	328	1.89
Eastern European (10)	10	0.06
English (632)	2,040	11.75
Estonian (11)	24	0.14
European (121)	149	0.86
Finnish (22)	37	0.21
French, ex. Basque (103)	274	1.58
German (2,015)	4,834	27.84
German Russian (0)	48	0.28
Greek (11)	93	0.54
Irish (689)	2,573	14.82
Italian (108)	457	2.63
Luxemburger (30)	47	0.27
Norwegian (7)	21	0.12
Pennsylvania German (8)	8	0.05
Polish (43)	152	0.88
Portuguese (0)	7	0.04
Russian (48)	102	0.59
Scandinavian (14)	14	0.08
Scotch-Irish (298)	587	3.38
Scottish (147)	535	3.08
Slavic (10)	30	0.17
Slovak (0)	16	0.09
Slovene (0)	24	0.14
Swedish (0)	130	0.75
Swiss (53)	320	1.84
Turkish (175)	175	1.01
Ukrainian (33)	33	0.19
Welsh (24)	156	0.90

Hispanic Origin	Population	%
Hispanic or Latino (of any race)	770	4.41
Central American, ex. Mexican	84	0.48
Guatemalan	32	0.18
Honduran	20	0.11
Nicaraguan	9	0.05
Panamanian	13	0.07
Salvadoran	10	0.06
Cuban	54	0.31
Dominican Republic	9	0.05
Mexican	412	2.36
Puerto Rican	62	0.35
South American	101	0.58
Argentinean	12	0.07
Bolivian	5	0.03
Chilean	11	0.06
Colombian	38	0.22
Ecuadorian	9	0.05
Paraguayan	1	0.01
Peruvian	16	0.09
Venezuelan	9	0.05
Other Hispanic or Latino	48	0.27

Race*	Population	%
African-American/Black (1,057)	1,204	6.89
Not Hispanic (1,045)	1,181	6.76
Hispanic (12)	23	0.13
American Indian/Alaska Native (33)	116	0.66
Not Hispanic (29)	104	0.60
Hispanic (4)	12	0.07
Apache (2)	4	0.02
Central American Ind. (0)	1	0.01
Cherokee (8)	37	0.21
Chickasaw (2)	2	0.01
Chippewa (1)	3	0.02
Choctaw (2)	4	0.02
Iroquois (0)	2	0.01
Mexican American Ind. (2)	2	0.01
Navajo (1)	2	0.01
Ottawa (0)	2	0.01
Pueblo (1)	1	0.01
Sioux (0)	1	0.01
Asian (455)	573	3.28
Not Hispanic (445)	559	3.20
Hispanic (10)	14	0.08
Burmese (18)	18	0.10
Cambodian (2)	2	0.01
Chinese, ex. Taiwanese (94)	100	0.57
Filipino (48)	72	0.41
Indian (137)	151	0.86
Indonesian (6)	7	0.04
Japanese (15)	30	0.17
Korean (51)	68	0.39
Laotian (2)	3	0.02
Malaysian (0)	1	0.01
Pakistani (21)	22	0.13
Taiwanese (9)	9	0.05
Thai (4)	5	0.03
Vietnamese (30)	32	0.18
Hawaii Native/Pacific Islander (4)	14	0.08
Not Hispanic (3)	12	0.07
Hispanic (1)	2	0.01
Native Hawaiian (4)	5	0.03
Samoan (0)	2	0.01
White (15,298)	15,601	89.29
Not Hispanic (14,866)	15,132	86.61
Hispanic (432)	469	2.68

Versailles

Place Type: City
County: Woodford
Population: 8,568[†]

Ancestry[‡]	Population	%
American (1,614)	1,614	19.13
British (39)	82	0.97
Celtic (0)	66	0.78
Danish (0)	7	0.08
Dutch (57)	166	1.97
English (425)	787	9.33
European (51)	51	0.60
Finnish (0)	20	0.24
French, ex. Basque (14)	169	2.00
French Canadian (28)	116	1.37
German (536)	1,255	14.87
Irish (266)	945	11.20
Italian (66)	88	1.04
Northern European (18)	18	0.21
Norwegian (29)	36	0.43
Polish (146)	183	2.17
Russian (0)	15	0.18
Scotch-Irish (188)	256	3.03
Scottish (50)	129	1.53
Welsh (7)	52	0.62

Hispanic Origin	Population	%
Hispanic or Latino (of any race)	1,018	11.88
Central American, ex. Mexican	52	0.61
Guatemalan	25	0.29
Honduran	24	0.28
Nicaraguan	2	0.02
Panamanian	1	0.01
Cuban	6	0.07
Dominican Republic	1	0.01
Mexican	893	10.42
Puerto Rican	14	0.16
South American	20	0.23
Chilean	1	0.01
Colombian	6	0.07
Peruvian	3	0.04
Uruguayan	1	0.01
Venezuelan	9	0.11
Other Hispanic or Latino	32	0.37

Race*	Population	%
African-American/Black (687)	799	9.33
Not Hispanic (677)	779	9.09
Hispanic (10)	20	0.23
American Indian/Alaska Native (23)	51	0.60
Not Hispanic (16)	41	0.48
Hispanic (7)	10	0.12
Cherokee (7)	20	0.23
Chippewa (1)	1	0.01
Mexican American Ind. (1)	1	0.01
Seminole (0)	1	0.01
Spanish American Ind. (1)	1	0.01
Tlingit-Haida *(Alaska Native)* (1)	1	0.01
Asian (41)	62	0.72
Not Hispanic (41)	54	0.63
Hispanic (0)	8	0.09
Cambodian (3)	3	0.04
Chinese, ex. Taiwanese (7)	7	0.08
Filipino (5)	13	0.15
Indian (8)	14	0.16
Japanese (2)	6	0.07
Korean (7)	9	0.11
Laotian (1)	1	0.01
Sri Lankan (2)	2	0.02
Taiwanese (1)	1	0.01
Thai (1)	1	0.01
Vietnamese (1)	1	0.01
Hawaii Native/Pacific Islander (2)	5	0.06
Not Hispanic (2)	4	0.05
Hispanic (0)	1	0.01
Native Hawaiian (2)	4	0.05
White (7,156)	7,342	85.69
Not Hispanic (6,671)	6,792	79.27
Hispanic (485)	550	6.42

Winchester

Place Type: City
County: Clark
Population: 18,368[†]

Ancestry[‡]	Population	%
African, Sub-Saharan (37)	37	0.20
African (37)	37	0.20
American (4,506)	4,506	24.85
Austrian (17)	17	0.09
British (53)	63	0.35
Czech (14)	14	0.08
Danish (0)	15	0.08
Dutch (32)	103	0.57
English (1,043)	1,726	9.52
European (104)	104	0.57
French, ex. Basque (65)	180	0.99
French Canadian (0)	33	0.18
German (427)	1,741	9.60
Hungarian (0)	10	0.06
Irish (857)	2,639	14.55
Italian (73)	272	1.50
Northern European (10)	10	0.06
Norwegian (35)	42	0.23
Polish (62)	361	1.99
Russian (2)	12	0.07
Scotch-Irish (249)	437	2.41
Scottish (157)	787	4.34
Swedish (0)	46	0.25
Swiss (12)	12	0.07
Welsh (41)	129	0.71

Hispanic Origin	Population	%
Hispanic or Latino (of any race)	605	3.29
Central American, ex. Mexican	21	0.11
Costa Rican	7	0.04
Guatemalan	3	0.02
Honduran	6	0.03
Panamanian	5	0.03
Cuban	4	0.02

SECTION TWO

*Notes: † The Census 2010 population figure is used to calculate the percentages in the Hispanic Origin and Race categories. Ancestry percentages are based on the 2006-2010 American Community Survey population (not shown); ‡ Numbers in parentheses indicate the number of people reporting a single ancestry; * Numbers in parentheses indicate the number of persons reporting this race alone, not in combination with any other race; Please refer to the Explanation of Data for more information.*

Dominican Republic	1	0.01
Mexican	479	2.61
Puerto Rican	40	0.22
South American	10	0.05
Chilean	1	0.01
Colombian	1	0.01
Ecuadorian	4	0.02
Venezuelan	4	0.02
Other Hispanic or Latino	50	0.27

Race*	Population	%
African-American/Black (1,502)	1,687	9.18
Not Hispanic (1,497)	1,672	9.10
Hispanic (5)	15	0.08
American Indian/Alaska Native (30)	112	0.61
Not Hispanic (27)	102	0.56
Hispanic (3)	10	0.05
Apache (3)	3	0.02
Blackfeet (0)	1	0.01
Cherokee (7)	39	0.21
Choctaw (2)	3	0.02
Comanche (0)	1	0.01
Crow (0)	1	0.01
Delaware (2)	2	0.01
Seminole (1)	6	0.03
Sioux (1)	1	0.01
Tlingit-Haida *(Alaska Native)* (1)	3	0.02
Asian (75)	126	0.69
Not Hispanic (75)	123	0.67
Hispanic (0)	3	0.02
Cambodian (6)	16	0.09
Chinese, ex. Taiwanese (26)	32	0.17
Filipino (8)	12	0.07
Indian (19)	24	0.13
Indonesian (1)	1	0.01
Japanese (2)	15	0.08
Korean (2)	4	0.02
Thai (3)	8	0.04
Vietnamese (2)	8	0.04
Hawaii Native/Pacific Islander (5)	13	0.07
Not Hispanic (3)	9	0.05
Hispanic (2)	4	0.02
Guamanian/Chamorro (3)	3	0.02
Native Hawaiian (2)	6	0.03
White (16,113)	16,451	89.56
Not Hispanic (15,857)	16,126	87.79
Hispanic (256)	325	1.77

*Notes: † The Census 2010 population figure is used to calculate the percentages in the Hispanic Origin and Race categories. Ancestry percentages are based on the 2006-2010 American Community Survey population (not shown); ‡ Numbers in parentheses indicate the number of people reporting a single ancestry; * Numbers in parentheses indicate the number of persons reporting this race alone, not in combination with any other race; Please refer to the Explanation of Data for more information.*

LOUISIANA

Place Type: State
Population: 4,533,372†

Ancestry‡	Population	%
Afghan (66)	92	<0.01
African, Sub-Saharan (29,933)	38,611	0.87
African (27,009)	35,140	0.79
Cape Verdean (50)	117	<0.01
Ethiopian (154)	181	<0.01
Ghanaian (38)	38	<0.01
Kenyan (121)	187	<0.01
Liberian (152)	152	<0.01
Nigerian (1,604)	1,717	0.04
Sierra Leonean (34)	34	<0.01
Somalian (103)	114	<0.01
South African (274)	403	0.01
Sudanese (7)	7	<0.01
Zimbabwean (38)	38	<0.01
Other Sub-Saharan African (349)	483	0.01
Albanian (45)	152	<0.01
Alsatian (58)	131	<0.01
American (406,029)	406,029	9.17
Arab (9,777)	15,274	0.34
Arab (3,007)	3,545	0.08
Egyptian (395)	618	0.01
Iraqi (588)	593	0.01
Jordanian (701)	771	0.02
Lebanese (2,795)	6,342	0.14
Moroccan (168)	168	<0.01
Palestinian (828)	872	0.02
Syrian (585)	1,362	0.03
Other Arab (710)	1,003	0.02
Armenian (236)	523	0.01
Australian (288)	552	0.01
Austrian (723)	2,926	0.07
Basque (83)	171	<0.01
Belgian (1,625)	4,531	0.10
Brazilian (1,748)	2,113	0.05
British (4,431)	9,341	0.21
Bulgarian (323)	416	0.01
Cajun (37,355)	49,469	1.12
Canadian (2,863)	5,310	0.12
Carpatho Rusyn (0)	12	<0.01
Celtic (178)	302	0.01
Croatian (1,609)	2,921	0.07
Cypriot (9)	13	<0.01
Czech (1,507)	5,251	0.12
Czechoslovakian (462)	1,277	0.03
Danish (1,123)	4,178	0.09
Dutch (5,732)	27,195	0.61
Eastern European (754)	1,015	0.02
English (141,305)	296,110	6.68
Estonian (51)	75	<0.01
European (16,531)	18,769	0.42
Finnish (434)	1,093	0.02
French, ex. Basque (317,731)	668,253	15.08
French Canadian (89,759)	112,549	2.54
German (103,067)	384,565	8.68
German Russian (20)	139	<0.01
Greek (2,445)	5,914	0.13
Guyanese (90)	115	<0.01
Hungarian (2,006)	5,280	0.12
Icelander (85)	226	0.01
Iranian (922)	1,249	0.03
Irish (104,088)	358,347	8.09
Israeli (365)	495	0.01
Italian (89,143)	224,434	5.07
Latvian (119)	265	0.01
Lithuanian (839)	1,888	0.04
Luxemburger (28)	42	<0.01
Macedonian (39)	58	<0.01
Maltese (24)	59	<0.01
New Zealander (25)	61	<0.01
Northern European (717)	767	0.02
Norwegian (3,703)	11,962	0.27
Pennsylvania German (182)	357	0.01
Polish (7,353)	22,235	0.50
Portuguese (1,717)	5,041	0.11
Romanian (1,108)	1,701	0.04
Russian (2,664)	7,899	0.18
Scandinavian (755)	1,776	0.04
Scotch-Irish (27,313)	57,163	1.29
Scottish (16,376)	45,283	1.02
Serbian (206)	526	0.01
Slavic (300)	690	0.02
Slovak (342)	1,187	0.03
Slovene (58)	190	<0.01
Swedish (3,582)	12,729	0.29
Swiss (818)	3,249	0.07
Turkish (525)	1,092	0.02
Ukrainian (1,120)	2,128	0.05
Welsh (2,705)	10,645	0.24
West Indian, ex. Hispanic (4,631)	7,057	0.16
Bahamian (92)	92	<0.01
Barbadian (3)	57	<0.01
Belizean (318)	628	0.01
Bermudan (47)	47	<0.01
British West Indian (342)	389	0.01
Dutch West Indian (240)	447	0.01
Haitian (1,330)	1,719	0.04
Jamaican (1,147)	2,140	0.05
Trinidadian/Tobagonian (694)	806	0.02
U.S. Virgin Islander (45)	55	<0.01
West Indian (344)	648	0.01
Other West Indian (29)	29	<0.01
Yugoslavian (942)	1,909	0.04

Hispanic Origin	Population	%
Hispanic or Latino (of any race)	192,560	4.25
Central American, ex. Mexican	51,722	1.14
Costa Rican	1,212	0.03
Guatemalan	6,660	0.15
Honduran	30,617	0.68
Nicaraguan	6,390	0.14
Panamanian	1,434	0.03
Salvadoran	5,120	0.11
Other Central American	289	0.01
Cuban	10,330	0.23
Dominican Republic	3,238	0.07
Mexican	78,643	1.73
Puerto Rican	11,603	0.26
South American	8,871	0.20
Argentinean	707	0.02
Bolivian	295	0.01
Chilean	548	0.01
Colombian	3,167	0.07
Ecuadorian	1,069	0.02
Paraguayan	68	<0.01
Peruvian	1,229	0.03
Uruguayan	109	<0.01
Venezuelan	1,591	0.04
Other South American	88	<0.01
Other Hispanic or Latino	28,153	0.62

Race*	Population	%
African-American/Black (1,452,396)	1,486,885	32.80
Not Hispanic (1,442,420)	1,472,789	32.49
Hispanic (9,976)	14,096	0.31
American Indian/Alaska Native (30,579)	55,079	1.21
Not Hispanic (28,092)	49,593	1.09
Hispanic (2,487)	5,486	0.12
Alaska Athabascan *(Ala. Nat.)* (39)	66	<0.01
Aleut *(Alaska Native)* (16)	32	<0.01
Apache (158)	486	0.01
Arapaho (11)	23	<0.01
Blackfeet (124)	650	0.01
Canadian/French Am. Ind. (75)	187	<0.01
Central American Ind. (135)	296	0.01
Cherokee (2,712)	7,631	0.17
Cheyenne (17)	65	<0.01
Chickasaw (155)	335	0.01
Chippewa (144)	232	0.01
Choctaw (1,644)	3,736	0.08
Colville (2)	5	<0.01
Comanche (61)	143	<0.01
Cree (11)	41	<0.01
Creek (323)	598	0.01
Crow (10)	45	<0.01
Delaware (27)	69	<0.01
Hopi (3)	18	<0.01
Houma (6,846)	8,666	0.19
Inupiat *(Alaska Native)* (15)	35	<0.01
Iroquois (94)	202	<0.01
Kiowa (21)	49	<0.01
Lumbee (71)	88	<0.01
Menominee (7)	10	<0.01
Mexican American Ind. (402)	675	0.01
Navajo (139)	277	0.01
Osage (41)	103	<0.01
Ottawa (35)	56	<0.01
Paiute (17)	34	<0.01
Pima (8)	13	<0.01
Potawatomi (78)	115	<0.01
Pueblo (36)	73	<0.01
Puget Sound Salish (3)	9	<0.01
Seminole (48)	150	<0.01
Shoshone (21)	42	<0.01
Sioux (223)	469	0.01
South American Ind. (40)	122	<0.01
Spanish American Ind. (69)	131	<0.01
Tlingit-Haida *(Alaska Native)* (17)	33	<0.01
Tohono O'Odham (4)	8	<0.01
Ute (3)	12	<0.01
Yakama (4)	6	<0.01
Yaqui (8)	23	<0.01
Yuman (6)	10	<0.01
Yup'ik *(Alaska Native)* (3)	6	<0.01
Asian (70,132)	84,335	1.86
Not Hispanic (69,327)	82,002	1.81
Hispanic (805)	2,333	0.05
Bangladeshi (375)	403	0.01
Bhutanese (12)	12	<0.01
Burmese (238)	270	0.01
Cambodian (589)	735	0.02
Chinese, ex. Taiwanese (9,412)	11,290	0.25
Filipino (6,416)	10,243	0.23
Hmong (30)	49	<0.01
Indian (11,174)	13,147	0.29
Indonesian (264)	394	0.01
Japanese (1,464)	3,117	0.07
Korean (3,367)	4,752	0.10
Laotian (1,636)	1,902	0.04
Malaysian (74)	129	<0.01
Nepalese (372)	396	0.01
Pakistani (1,776)	2,007	0.04
Sri Lankan (193)	204	<0.01
Taiwanese (586)	684	0.02
Thai (988)	1,466	0.03
Vietnamese (28,352)	30,202	0.67
Hawaii Native/Pacific Islander (1,963)	4,879	0.11
Not Hispanic (1,544)	3,859	0.09
Hispanic (419)	1,020	0.02
Fijian (19)	22	<0.01
Guamanian/Chamorro (738)	1,189	0.03
Marshallese (18)	28	<0.01
Native Hawaiian (466)	1,245	0.03
Samoan (252)	572	0.01
Tongan (22)	46	<0.01
White (2,836,192)	2,895,868	63.88
Not Hispanic (2,734,884)	2,782,654	61.38
Hispanic (101,308)	113,214	2.50

*Notes: † The Census 2010 population figure is used to calculate the percentages in the Hispanic Origin and Race categories. Ancestry percentages are based on the 2006-2010 American Community Survey population (not shown); ‡ Numbers in parentheses indicate the number of people reporting a single ancestry; * Numbers in parentheses indicate the number of persons reporting this race alone, not in combination with any other race; Please refer to the Explanation of Data for more information.*

Abbeville

Place Type: City
Parish: Vermilion
Population: 12,257†

Ancestry‡	Population	%
American (503)	503	4.11
Austrian (0)	12	0.10
Cajun (316)	420	3.44
Canadian (59)	59	0.48
Czech (0)	23	0.19
Danish (10)	10	0.08
English (248)	468	3.83
European (10)	10	0.08
French, ex. Basque (1,769)	2,269	18.56
French Canadian (822)	994	8.13
German (324)	604	4.94
Irish (115)	332	2.72
Italian (107)	293	2.40
Norwegian (14)	99	0.81
Polish (9)	18	0.15
Scotch-Irish (31)	90	0.74
Scottish (0)	10	0.08
Swedish (0)	10	0.08
Ukrainian (0)	38	0.31

Hispanic Origin	Population	%
Hispanic or Latino (of any race)	385	3.14
Central American, ex. Mexican	27	0.22
Guatemalan	12	0.10
Honduran	7	0.06
Nicaraguan	5	0.04
Panamanian	3	0.02
Cuban	8	0.07
Dominican Republic	5	0.04
Mexican	259	2.11
Puerto Rican	20	0.16
South American	13	0.11
Argentinean	1	0.01
Chilean	5	0.04
Colombian	3	0.02
Ecuadorian	2	0.02
Venezuelan	2	0.02
Other Hispanic or Latino	53	0.43

Race*	Population	%
African-American/Black (5,029)	5,174	42.21
Not Hispanic (5,007)	5,142	41.95
Hispanic (22)	32	0.26
American Indian/Alaska Native (32)	90	0.73
Not Hispanic (30)	86	0.70
Hispanic (2)	4	0.03
Blackfeet (1)	10	0.08
Cherokee (1)	11	0.09
Chickasaw (1)	2	0.02
Choctaw (0)	3	0.02
Houma (8)	13	0.11
Iroquois (2)	2	0.02
Navajo (1)	1	0.01
Sioux (0)	1	0.01
Asian (635)	674	5.50
Not Hispanic (629)	666	5.43
Hispanic (6)	8	0.07
Cambodian (1)	1	0.01
Chinese, ex. Taiwanese (18)	21	0.17
Filipino (4)	9	0.07
Indian (29)	35	0.29
Japanese (1)	3	0.02
Laotian (4)	5	0.04
Thai (1)	1	0.01
Vietnamese (572)	593	4.84
Hawaii Native/Pacific Islander (0)	10	0.08
Not Hispanic (0)	10	0.08
Fijian (0)	1	0.01
Native Hawaiian (0)	1	0.01
Samoan (0)	1	0.01
White (6,132)	6,343	51.75
Not Hispanic (5,987)	6,162	50.27
Hispanic (145)	181	1.48

Alexandria

Place Type: City
Parish: Rapides
Population: 47,723†

Ancestry‡	Population	%
African, Sub-Saharan (43)	152	0.32
African (43)	152	0.32
Albanian (0)	23	0.05
American (12,391)	12,391	26.05
Arab (93)	143	0.30
Lebanese (17)	59	0.12
Palestinian (65)	65	0.14
Syrian (11)	19	0.04
Armenian (23)	23	0.05
Austrian (13)	68	0.14
Belgian (108)	397	0.83
British (45)	103	0.22
Cajun (132)	223	0.47
Canadian (14)	28	0.06
Croatian (0)	20	0.04
Czech (37)	63	0.13
Czechoslovakian (0)	11	0.02
Danish (16)	35	0.07
Dutch (32)	147	0.31
English (802)	2,026	4.26
European (40)	84	0.18
Finnish (0)	9	0.02
French, ex. Basque (1,503)	3,476	7.31
French Canadian (310)	459	0.96
German (608)	1,822	3.83
Greek (0)	35	0.07
Hungarian (0)	43	0.09
Irish (574)	2,320	4.88
Italian (388)	1,564	3.29
Lithuanian (3)	3	0.01
Northern European (24)	24	0.05
Norwegian (34)	93	0.20
Polish (16)	109	0.23
Russian (8)	8	0.02
Scotch-Irish (325)	698	1.47
Scottish (58)	162	0.34
Slovak (0)	10	0.02
Swedish (50)	209	0.44
Swiss (0)	6	0.01
Turkish (15)	48	0.10
Welsh (13)	46	0.10
West Indian, ex. Hispanic (24)	61	0.13
Haitian (0)	37	0.08
Jamaican (12)	12	0.03
Trinidadian/Tobagonian (8)	8	0.02
West Indian (4)	4	0.01

Hispanic Origin	Population	%
Hispanic or Latino (of any race)	849	1.78
Central American, ex. Mexican	89	0.19
Costa Rican	8	0.02
Guatemalan	35	0.07
Honduran	19	0.04
Nicaraguan	15	0.03
Panamanian	7	0.01
Salvadoran	5	0.01
Cuban	36	0.08
Dominican Republic	6	0.01
Mexican	446	0.93
Puerto Rican	96	0.20
South American	38	0.08
Chilean	6	0.01
Colombian	9	0.02
Ecuadorian	17	0.04
Peruvian	2	<0.01
Venezuelan	4	0.01
Other Hispanic or Latino	138	0.29

Race*	Population	%
African-American/Black (27,322)	27,824	58.30
Not Hispanic (27,210)	27,670	57.98
Hispanic (112)	154	0.32
American Indian/Alaska Native (188)	452	0.95
Not Hispanic (171)	406	0.85
Hispanic (17)	46	0.10
Alaska Athabascan *(Ala. Nat.)* (0)	1	<0.01
Apache (0)	7	0.01
Blackfeet (0)	7	0.01
Canadian/French Am. Ind. (0)	7	0.01
Central American Ind. (3)	3	0.01
Cherokee (26)	90	0.19
Cheyenne (0)	1	<0.01
Chickasaw (0)	1	<0.01
Choctaw (16)	50	0.10
Comanche (0)	1	<0.01
Cree (0)	1	<0.01
Creek (7)	18	0.04
Crow (2)	4	0.01
Delaware (1)	1	<0.01
Hopi (1)	3	0.01
Houma (7)	11	0.02
Inupiat *(Alaska Native)* (4)	4	0.01
Iroquois (0)	4	0.01
Kiowa (0)	1	<0.01
Mexican American Ind. (1)	1	<0.01
Navajo (0)	5	0.01
Paiute (1)	1	<0.01
Pueblo (0)	4	0.01
Sioux (4)	7	0.01
Tohono O'Odham (1)	1	<0.01
Asian (873)	1,036	2.17
Not Hispanic (872)	1,031	2.16
Hispanic (1)	5	0.01
Bangladeshi (13)	13	0.03
Burmese (51)	56	0.12
Cambodian (12)	13	0.03
Chinese, ex. Taiwanese (85)	104	0.22
Filipino (127)	153	0.32
Indian (214)	233	0.49
Indonesian (1)	1	<0.01
Japanese (18)	38	0.08
Korean (25)	41	0.09
Laotian (5)	6	0.01
Malaysian (0)	1	<0.01
Nepalese (11)	11	0.02
Pakistani (39)	43	0.09
Taiwanese (8)	12	0.03
Thai (9)	18	0.04
Vietnamese (219)	234	0.49
Hawaii Native/Pacific Islander (8)	21	0.04
Not Hispanic (4)	15	0.03
Hispanic (4)	6	0.01
Guamanian/Chamorro (4)	6	0.01
Native Hawaiian (3)	4	0.01
Samoan (1)	5	0.01
White (18,288)	18,825	39.45
Not Hispanic (17,872)	18,353	38.46
Hispanic (416)	472	0.99

Baker

Place Type: City
Parish: East Baton Rouge
Population: 13,895†

Ancestry‡	Population	%
African, Sub-Saharan (121)	121	0.87
African (121)	121	0.87
American (1,272)	1,272	9.19
Arab (76)	76	0.55
Arab (76)	76	0.55
Cajun (0)	24	0.17
Canadian (8)	8	0.06
Czech (0)	16	0.12
Dutch (0)	11	0.08
English (164)	229	1.65
European (38)	38	0.27
French, ex. Basque (313)	734	5.30
French Canadian (20)	20	0.14
German (122)	476	3.44
Irish (90)	578	4.18
Italian (151)	253	1.83
Scotch-Irish (31)	59	0.43

*Notes: † The Census 2010 population figure is used to calculate the percentages in the Hispanic Origin and Race categories. Ancestry percentages are based on the 2006-2010 American Community Survey population (not shown); ‡ Numbers in parentheses indicate the number of people reporting a single ancestry; * Numbers in parentheses indicate the number of persons reporting this race alone, not in combination with any other race; Please refer to the Explanation of Data for more information.*

Ancestry	Population	%
Scottish (35)	72	0.52
Swedish (0)	10	0.07
Welsh (0)	12	0.09
West Indian, ex. Hispanic (0)	11	0.08
Trinidadian/Tobagonian (0)	11	0.08

Hispanic Origin	Population	%
Hispanic or Latino (of any race)	171	1.23
Central American, ex. Mexican	23	0.17
Costa Rican	1	0.01
Honduran	14	0.10
Nicaraguan	1	0.01
Salvadoran	3	0.02
Other Central American	4	0.03
Cuban	1	0.01
Dominican Republic	2	0.01
Mexican	82	0.59
Puerto Rican	18	0.13
Other Hispanic or Latino	45	0.32

Race*	Population	%
African-American/Black (10,739)	10,851	78.09
Not Hispanic (10,712)	10,813	77.82
Hispanic (27)	38	0.27
American Indian/Alaska Native (46)	100	0.72
Not Hispanic (44)	88	0.63
Hispanic (2)	12	0.09
Apache (0)	3	0.02
Blackfeet (1)	6	0.04
Cherokee (0)	8	0.06
Chickasaw (0)	2	0.01
Chippewa (0)	1	0.01
Choctaw (1)	3	0.02
Houma (4)	4	0.03
Mexican American Ind. (2)	4	0.03
Asian (25)	66	0.47
Not Hispanic (24)	63	0.45
Hispanic (1)	3	0.02
Chinese, ex. Taiwanese (2)	5	0.04
Filipino (20)	28	0.20
Indian (1)	4	0.03
Japanese (1)	9	0.06
Pakistani (0)	1	0.01
Vietnamese (1)	1	0.01
Hawaii Native/Pacific Islander (0)	7	0.05
Not Hispanic (0)	7	0.05
Native Hawaiian (0)	5	0.04
White (2,852)	2,970	21.37
Not Hispanic (2,781)	2,889	20.79
Hispanic (71)	81	0.58

Bastrop

Place Type: City
Parish: Morehouse
Population: 11,365†

Ancestry‡	Population	%
African, Sub-Saharan (15)	391	3.37
African (15)	391	3.37
American (733)	733	6.32
Canadian (10)	24	0.21
Dutch (10)	10	0.09
English (689)	808	6.96
European (35)	35	0.30
French, ex. Basque (54)	129	1.11
German (63)	218	1.88
Irish (193)	519	4.47
Italian (26)	26	0.22
Polish (8)	8	0.07
Scotch-Irish (62)	93	0.80
Scottish (17)	66	0.57
Swedish (21)	21	0.18
Welsh (0)	12	0.10

Hispanic Origin	Population	%
Hispanic or Latino (of any race)	86	0.76
Central American, ex. Mexican	1	0.01
Nicaraguan	1	0.01
Cuban	5	0.04
Mexican	42	0.37
Puerto Rican	15	0.13
Other Hispanic or Latino	23	0.20

Race*	Population	%
African-American/Black (8,236)	8,320	73.21
Not Hispanic (8,206)	8,276	72.82
Hispanic (30)	44	0.39
American Indian/Alaska Native (12)	52	0.46
Not Hispanic (12)	49	0.43
Hispanic (0)	3	0.03
Cherokee (0)	11	0.10
Choctaw (1)	8	0.07
Comanche (0)	1	0.01
Iroquois (1)	1	0.01
Potawatomi (4)	4	0.04
Seminole (0)	1	0.01
Sioux (0)	2	0.02
Asian (45)	66	0.58
Not Hispanic (45)	63	0.55
Hispanic (0)	3	0.03
Chinese, ex. Taiwanese (7)	7	0.06
Filipino (8)	16	0.14
Indian (14)	15	0.13
Japanese (2)	6	0.05
Korean (0)	1	0.01
Thai (2)	2	0.02
Vietnamese (11)	11	0.10
Hawaii Native/Pacific Islander (4)	8	0.07
Not Hispanic (3)	6	0.05
Hispanic (1)	2	0.02
Guamanian/Chamorro (3)	5	0.04
Native Hawaiian (1)	1	0.01
White (2,922)	3,017	26.55
Not Hispanic (2,906)	2,991	26.32
Hispanic (16)	26	0.23

Baton Rouge

Place Type: City
Parish: East Baton Rouge
Population: 229,493†

Ancestry‡	Population	%
African, Sub-Saharan (2,286)	2,652	1.16
African (1,650)	1,898	0.83
Ghanaian (9)	9	<0.01
Kenyan (65)	65	0.03
Liberian (19)	19	0.01
Nigerian (428)	509	0.22
Sierra Leonean (34)	34	0.01
South African (0)	37	0.02
Other Sub-Saharan African (81)	81	0.04
Albanian (20)	20	0.01
Alsatian (22)	22	0.01
American (11,516)	11,516	5.03
Arab (914)	1,263	0.55
Arab (501)	539	0.24
Egyptian (0)	11	<0.01
Iraqi (37)	37	0.02
Jordanian (39)	39	0.02
Lebanese (164)	362	0.16
Moroccan (19)	19	0.01
Palestinian (45)	72	0.03
Syrian (10)	58	0.03
Other Arab (99)	126	0.05
Armenian (54)	57	0.02
Australian (18)	18	0.01
Austrian (44)	301	0.13
Belgian (0)	120	0.05
Brazilian (83)	98	0.04
British (292)	614	0.27
Bulgarian (104)	104	0.05
Cajun (990)	1,586	0.69
Canadian (54)	101	0.04
Celtic (0)	11	<0.01
Croatian (26)	106	0.05
Czech (71)	262	0.11
Czechoslovakian (0)	132	0.06
Danish (102)	288	0.13
Dutch (163)	892	0.39
Eastern European (28)	32	0.01
English (5,930)	14,633	6.39
Estonian (8)	8	<0.01
European (1,021)	1,119	0.49
Finnish (7)	50	0.02
French, ex. Basque (7,001)	20,513	8.95
French Canadian (1,658)	2,470	1.08
German (3,212)	14,419	6.29
Greek (133)	355	0.15
Guyanese (11)	11	<0.01
Hungarian (35)	220	0.10
Iranian (193)	193	0.08
Irish (3,358)	12,594	5.50
Israeli (0)	20	0.01
Italian (4,271)	10,227	4.46
Latvian (0)	14	0.01
Lithuanian (36)	106	0.05
Luxemburger (0)	10	<0.01
New Zealander (13)	13	0.01
Northern European (49)	49	0.02
Norwegian (86)	490	0.21
Pennsylvania German (17)	43	0.02
Polish (470)	1,555	0.68
Portuguese (50)	130	0.06
Romanian (5)	39	0.02
Russian (214)	663	0.29
Scandinavian (53)	106	0.05
Scotch-Irish (1,630)	3,664	1.60
Scottish (1,125)	2,960	1.29
Serbian (71)	117	0.05
Slavic (0)	20	0.01
Slovak (10)	46	0.02
Slovene (25)	53	0.02
Swedish (170)	631	0.28
Swiss (64)	251	0.11
Turkish (99)	301	0.13
Ukrainian (83)	190	0.08
Welsh (75)	610	0.27
West Indian, ex. Hispanic (256)	551	0.24
Bahamian (24)	24	0.01
Haitian (17)	31	0.01
Jamaican (159)	419	0.18
Trinidadian/Tobagonian (19)	19	0.01
West Indian (37)	58	0.03
Yugoslavian (32)	48	0.02

Hispanic Origin	Population	%
Hispanic or Latino (of any race)	7,653	3.33
Central American, ex. Mexican	1,917	0.84
Costa Rican	75	0.03
Guatemalan	271	0.12
Honduran	730	0.32
Nicaraguan	130	0.06
Panamanian	57	0.02
Salvadoran	647	0.28
Other Central American	7	<0.01
Cuban	551	0.24
Dominican Republic	66	0.03
Mexican	3,070	1.34
Puerto Rican	489	0.21
South American	604	0.26
Argentinean	43	0.02
Bolivian	18	0.01
Chilean	33	0.01
Colombian	245	0.11
Ecuadorian	53	0.02
Paraguayan	2	<0.01
Peruvian	65	0.03
Uruguayan	6	<0.01
Venezuelan	139	0.06
Other Hispanic or Latino	956	0.42

Race*	Population	%
African-American/Black (125,155)	126,742	55.23
Not Hispanic (124,542)	125,944	54.88
Hispanic (613)	798	0.35
American Indian/Alaska Native (486)	1,351	0.59
Not Hispanic (397)	1,156	0.50
Hispanic (89)	195	0.08

*Notes: † The Census 2010 population figure is used to calculate the percentages in the Hispanic Origin and Race categories. Ancestry percentages are based on the 2006-2010 American Community Survey population (not shown); ‡ Numbers in parentheses indicate the number of people reporting a single ancestry; * Numbers in parentheses indicate the number of persons reporting this race alone, not in combination with any other race; Please refer to the Explanation of Data for more information.*

Apache (5)	9	<0.01
Blackfeet (0)	40	0.02
Canadian/French Am. Ind. (0)	3	<0.01
Central American Ind. (0)	11	<0.01
Cherokee (37)	186	0.08
Chickasaw (4)	15	0.01
Chippewa (6)	7	<0.01
Choctaw (17)	89	0.04
Comanche (4)	7	<0.01
Creek (11)	21	0.01
Delaware (4)	5	<0.01
Hopi (0)	1	<0.01
Houma (23)	41	0.02
Iroquois (3)	8	<0.01
Mexican American Ind. (12)	23	0.01
Navajo (4)	9	<0.01
Osage (0)	5	<0.01
Ottawa (0)	1	<0.01
Potawatomi (0)	6	<0.01
Pueblo (1)	1	<0.01
Seminole (0)	4	<0.01
Sioux (7)	16	0.01
South American Ind. (0)	5	<0.01
Spanish American Ind. (1)	1	<0.01
Ute (0)	1	<0.01
Yaqui (0)	1	<0.01
Yuman (0)	1	<0.01
Yup'ik *(Alaska Native)* (0)	1	<0.01
Asian (7,514)	8,300	3.62
Not Hispanic (7,469)	8,211	3.58
Hispanic (45)	89	0.04
Bangladeshi (67)	72	0.03
Bhutanese (12)	12	0.01
Burmese (37)	44	0.02
Cambodian (26)	33	0.01
Chinese, ex. Taiwanese (1,455)	1,589	0.69
Filipino (451)	576	0.25
Indian (1,354)	1,512	0.66
Indonesian (41)	45	0.02
Japanese (138)	219	0.10
Korean (315)	370	0.16
Laotian (67)	68	0.03
Malaysian (17)	25	0.01
Nepalese (118)	123	0.05
Pakistani (83)	90	0.04
Sri Lankan (70)	73	0.03
Taiwanese (126)	138	0.06
Thai (60)	94	0.04
Vietnamese (2,809)	2,913	1.27
Hawaii Native/Pacific Islander (81)	175	0.08
Not Hispanic (39)	121	0.05
Hispanic (42)	54	0.02
Fijian (1)	1	<0.01
Guamanian/Chamorro (43)	51	0.02
Native Hawaiian (16)	42	0.02
Samoan (5)	20	0.01
Tongan (0)	1	<0.01
White (90,348)	92,587	40.34
Not Hispanic (86,679)	88,470	38.55
Hispanic (3,669)	4,117	1.79

Bayou Blue

Place Type: CDP
Parish: Lafourche
Population: 12,352†

Ancestry‡	Population	%
American (2,032)	2,032	18.17
Arab (0)	22	0.20
Lebanese (0)	22	0.20
British (9)	9	0.08
Cajun (77)	120	1.07
English (256)	529	4.73
French, ex. Basque (1,920)	3,237	28.94
French Canadian (739)	825	7.38
German (284)	746	6.67
Irish (358)	886	7.92
Italian (103)	244	2.18
Lithuanian (0)	14	0.13
Norwegian (19)	40	0.36
Polish (0)	20	0.18
Portuguese (16)	101	0.90
Scottish (25)	76	0.68
Swedish (0)	32	0.29
Welsh (17)	17	0.15

Hispanic Origin	Population	%
Hispanic or Latino (of any race)	641	5.19
Central American, ex. Mexican	60	0.49
Guatemalan	20	0.16
Honduran	12	0.10
Nicaraguan	22	0.18
Panamanian	6	0.05
Cuban	2	0.02
Dominican Republic	1	0.01
Mexican	495	4.01
Puerto Rican	39	0.32
South American	12	0.10
Chilean	4	0.03
Colombian	1	0.01
Ecuadorian	1	0.01
Peruvian	1	0.01
Venezuelan	5	0.04
Other Hispanic or Latino	32	0.26

Race*	Population	%
African-American/Black (916)	1,045	8.46
Not Hispanic (908)	1,032	8.35
Hispanic (8)	13	0.11
American Indian/Alaska Native (700)	860	6.96
Not Hispanic (678)	835	6.76
Hispanic (22)	25	0.20
Apache (2)	4	0.03
Arapaho (1)	1	0.01
Blackfeet (1)	1	0.01
Cherokee (29)	48	0.39
Choctaw (21)	28	0.23
Comanche (0)	4	0.03
Creek (1)	3	0.02
Houma (275)	326	2.64
Iroquois (1)	1	0.01
Mexican American Ind. (1)	1	0.01
Seminole (0)	1	0.01
Sioux (1)	1	0.01
Asian (39)	64	0.52
Not Hispanic (39)	63	0.51
Hispanic (0)	1	0.01
Chinese, ex. Taiwanese (3)	3	0.02
Filipino (12)	19	0.15
Indian (4)	7	0.06
Indonesian (1)	1	0.01
Japanese (0)	2	0.02
Korean (1)	3	0.02
Pakistani (2)	5	0.04
Vietnamese (15)	23	0.19
Hawaii Native/Pacific Islander (2)	7	0.06
Not Hispanic (2)	7	0.06
Guamanian/Chamorro (2)	2	0.02
White (10,023)	10,304	83.42
Not Hispanic (9,784)	10,042	81.30
Hispanic (239)	262	2.12

Bayou Cane

Place Type: CDP
Parish: Terrebonne
Population: 19,355†

Ancestry‡	Population	%
African, Sub-Saharan (43)	51	0.26
African (43)	51	0.26
American (3,222)	3,222	16.22
Arab (0)	24	0.12
Lebanese (0)	24	0.12
Austrian (19)	19	0.10
Belgian (58)	58	0.29
British (10)	21	0.11
Cajun (355)	459	2.31
Canadian (67)	84	0.42
Czechoslovakian (22)	22	0.11
Dutch (26)	80	0.40
English (308)	1,203	6.05
European (28)	28	0.14
French, ex. Basque (2,417)	4,742	23.87
French Canadian (963)	1,068	5.38
German (265)	1,266	6.37
Irish (229)	1,395	7.02
Italian (213)	605	3.04
Norwegian (30)	39	0.20
Polish (16)	70	0.35
Portuguese (46)	55	0.28
Romanian (0)	14	0.07
Scotch-Irish (57)	77	0.39
Scottish (132)	250	1.26
Slovak (9)	19	0.10
Swedish (17)	17	0.09
Swiss (0)	8	0.04
Welsh (0)	33	0.17

Hispanic Origin	Population	%
Hispanic or Latino (of any race)	811	4.19
Central American, ex. Mexican	117	0.60
Costa Rican	9	0.05
Guatemalan	25	0.13
Honduran	44	0.23
Nicaraguan	9	0.05
Panamanian	9	0.05
Salvadoran	21	0.11
Cuban	46	0.24
Dominican Republic	7	0.04
Mexican	439	2.27
Puerto Rican	49	0.25
South American	39	0.20
Argentinean	2	0.01
Bolivian	10	0.05
Chilean	11	0.06
Colombian	11	0.06
Peruvian	3	0.02
Venezuelan	2	0.01
Other Hispanic or Latino	114	0.59

Race*	Population	%
African-American/Black (2,898)	3,061	15.82
Not Hispanic (2,877)	3,031	15.66
Hispanic (21)	30	0.15
American Indian/Alaska Native (536)	698	3.61
Not Hispanic (515)	661	3.42
Hispanic (21)	37	0.19
Blackfeet (1)	3	0.02
Central American Ind. (1)	1	0.01
Cherokee (4)	20	0.10
Chickasaw (0)	1	0.01
Choctaw (5)	11	0.06
Comanche (3)	3	0.02
Creek (4)	4	0.02
Houma (258)	307	1.59
Iroquois (0)	1	0.01
Mexican American Ind. (1)	1	0.01
Navajo (2)	2	0.01
Pueblo (0)	1	0.01
Seminole (1)	1	0.01
Shoshone (1)	4	0.02
Sioux (2)	5	0.03
South American Ind. (1)	1	0.01
Yuman (1)	1	0.01
Asian (242)	318	1.64
Not Hispanic (240)	309	1.60
Hispanic (2)	9	0.05
Bangladeshi (1)	1	0.01
Cambodian (0)	1	0.01
Chinese, ex. Taiwanese (61)	73	0.38
Filipino (29)	62	0.32
Indian (44)	49	0.25
Indonesian (4)	11	0.06
Japanese (4)	9	0.05
Korean (5)	10	0.05
Laotian (1)	1	0.01
Malaysian (2)	2	0.01
Thai (6)	6	0.03

*Notes: † The Census 2010 population figure is used to calculate the percentages in the Hispanic Origin and Race categories. Ancestry percentages are based on the 2006-2010 American Community Survey population (not shown); ‡ Numbers in parentheses indicate the number of people reporting a single ancestry; * Numbers in parentheses indicate the number of persons reporting this race alone, not in combination with any other race; Please refer to the Explanation of Data for more information.*

Vietnamese (81)	87	0.45
Hawaii Native/Pacific Islander (14)	41	0.21
Not Hispanic (6)	33	0.17
Hispanic (8)	8	0.04
Guamanian/Chamorro (8)	11	0.06
Native Hawaiian (1)	12	0.06
Samoan (2)	2	0.01
White (14,990)	15,300	79.05
Not Hispanic (14,568)	14,844	76.69
Hispanic (422)	456	2.36

Belle Chasse

Place Type: CDP
Parish: Plaquemines
Population: 12,679†

Ancestry‡	Population	%
African, Sub-Saharan (0)	23	0.15
African (0)	23	0.15
American (905)	905	6.07
Arab (5)	39	0.26
Lebanese (5)	39	0.26
British (41)	70	0.47
Cajun (39)	55	0.37
Canadian (0)	17	0.11
Croatian (289)	431	2.89
Danish (0)	50	0.34
Dutch (15)	98	0.66
English (633)	1,156	7.75
European (15)	15	0.10
French, ex. Basque (1,655)	3,227	21.63
French Canadian (251)	340	2.28
German (1,006)	2,133	14.30
Greek (125)	163	1.09
Hungarian (0)	42	0.28
Irish (395)	1,557	10.44
Italian (575)	1,436	9.62
Lithuanian (50)	50	0.34
Norwegian (35)	106	0.71
Polish (45)	62	0.42
Scotch-Irish (44)	108	0.72
Scottish (15)	152	1.02
Slavic (41)	41	0.27
Swedish (15)	61	0.41
Swiss (0)	36	0.24
Welsh (19)	57	0.38
West Indian, ex. Hispanic (156)	156	1.05
Jamaican (156)	156	1.05
Yugoslavian (120)	146	0.98

Hispanic Origin	Population	%
Hispanic or Latino (of any race)	800	6.31
Central American, ex. Mexican	145	1.14
Costa Rican	11	0.09
Guatemalan	26	0.21
Honduran	76	0.60
Nicaraguan	21	0.17
Panamanian	4	0.03
Salvadoran	7	0.06
Cuban	41	0.32
Dominican Republic	10	0.08
Mexican	378	2.98
Puerto Rican	102	0.80
South American	19	0.15
Argentinean	3	0.02
Chilean	2	0.02
Colombian	4	0.03
Ecuadorian	6	0.05
Venezuelan	4	0.03
Other Hispanic or Latino	105	0.83

Race*	Population	%
African-American/Black (1,003)	1,136	8.96
Not Hispanic (969)	1,075	8.48
Hispanic (34)	61	0.48
American Indian/Alaska Native (125)	251	1.98
Not Hispanic (110)	209	1.65
Hispanic (15)	42	0.33
Apache (0)	4	0.03
Blackfeet (0)	1	0.01
Central American Ind. (0)	1	0.01
Cherokee (9)	22	0.17
Chickasaw (2)	2	0.02
Choctaw (8)	20	0.16
Creek (3)	10	0.08
Delaware (4)	4	0.03
Houma (40)	47	0.37
Iroquois (0)	3	0.02
Mexican American Ind. (4)	4	0.03
Navajo (1)	4	0.03
Seminole (0)	3	0.02
Sioux (0)	3	0.02
Yaqui (0)	1	0.01
Asian (296)	367	2.89
Not Hispanic (292)	342	2.70
Hispanic (4)	25	0.20
Chinese, ex. Taiwanese (17)	34	0.27
Filipino (52)	93	0.73
Hmong (2)	2	0.02
Indian (11)	14	0.11
Indonesian (0)	1	0.01
Japanese (12)	22	0.17
Korean (13)	18	0.14
Laotian (3)	3	0.02
Malaysian (0)	1	0.01
Pakistani (6)	9	0.07
Thai (1)	4	0.03
Vietnamese (158)	177	1.40
Hawaii Native/Pacific Islander (29)	77	0.61
Not Hispanic (17)	63	0.50
Hispanic (12)	14	0.11
Guamanian/Chamorro (20)	37	0.29
Native Hawaiian (1)	21	0.17
Samoan (4)	11	0.09
Tongan (1)	1	0.01
White (10,666)	10,965	86.48
Not Hispanic (10,200)	10,426	82.23
Hispanic (466)	539	4.25

Bogalusa

Place Type: City
Parish: Washington
Population: 12,232†

Ancestry‡	Population	%
African, Sub-Saharan (11)	34	0.27
African (11)	34	0.27
American (1,382)	1,382	11.13
Arab (0)	44	0.35
Lebanese (0)	44	0.35
Cajun (11)	11	0.09
Danish (0)	29	0.23
Dutch (29)	58	0.47
English (409)	777	6.26
European (21)	21	0.17
French, ex. Basque (425)	805	6.48
French Canadian (0)	14	0.11
German (268)	993	8.00
Irish (335)	1,002	8.07
Italian (159)	421	3.39
Northern European (36)	36	0.29
Norwegian (12)	56	0.45
Polish (33)	82	0.66
Scotch-Irish (51)	172	1.39
Scottish (0)	60	0.48
Swedish (0)	24	0.19

Hispanic Origin	Population	%
Hispanic or Latino (of any race)	285	2.33
Central American, ex. Mexican	28	0.23
Costa Rican	3	0.02
Guatemalan	2	0.02
Honduran	19	0.16
Nicaraguan	1	0.01
Panamanian	2	0.02
Salvadoran	1	0.01
Cuban	2	0.02
Mexican	171	1.40
Puerto Rican	15	0.12
South American	2	0.02
Colombian	2	0.02
Other Hispanic or Latino	67	0.55

Race*	Population	%
African-American/Black (5,926)	6,043	49.40
Not Hispanic (5,889)	5,996	49.02
Hispanic (37)	47	0.38
American Indian/Alaska Native (23)	104	0.85
Not Hispanic (22)	100	0.82
Hispanic (1)	4	0.03
Apache (1)	1	0.01
Blackfeet (0)	3	0.02
Cherokee (1)	15	0.12
Choctaw (2)	12	0.10
Crow (0)	2	0.02
Delaware (0)	3	0.02
Houma (3)	3	0.02
Seminole (0)	1	0.01
Shoshone (0)	1	0.01
Sioux (0)	1	0.01
Asian (46)	66	0.54
Not Hispanic (46)	63	0.52
Hispanic (0)	3	0.02
Cambodian (7)	7	0.06
Chinese, ex. Taiwanese (9)	13	0.11
Filipino (2)	10	0.08
Indian (7)	13	0.11
Japanese (2)	2	0.02
Korean (2)	7	0.06
Vietnamese (17)	21	0.17
Hawaii Native/Pacific Islander (0)	11	0.09
Not Hispanic (0)	9	0.07
Hispanic (0)	2	0.02
Native Hawaiian (0)	2	0.02
Samoan (0)	4	0.03
White (5,935)	6,081	49.71
Not Hispanic (5,810)	5,940	48.56
Hispanic (125)	141	1.15

Bossier City

Place Type: City
Parish: Bossier
Population: 61,315†

Ancestry‡	Population	%
African, Sub-Saharan (147)	147	0.24
African (147)	147	0.24
American (7,802)	7,802	12.92
Arab (112)	153	0.25
Arab (25)	25	0.04
Egyptian (13)	39	0.06
Lebanese (12)	27	0.04
Palestinian (62)	62	0.10
Armenian (15)	15	0.02
Australian (0)	21	0.03
Austrian (0)	96	0.16
Belgian (26)	68	0.11
British (131)	306	0.51
Bulgarian (20)	20	0.03
Cajun (107)	152	0.25
Canadian (0)	16	0.03
Carpatho Rusyn (0)	12	0.02
Croatian (37)	73	0.12
Czech (16)	30	0.05
Czechoslovakian (9)	27	0.04
Danish (0)	48	0.08
Dutch (273)	1,015	1.68
English (1,695)	4,220	6.99
European (338)	356	0.59
Finnish (11)	11	0.02
French, ex. Basque (1,232)	3,532	5.85
French Canadian (122)	172	0.28
German (2,165)	6,413	10.62
Greek (41)	69	0.11
Hungarian (26)	52	0.09
Irish (2,772)	7,476	12.38
Italian (1,021)	2,201	3.64

*Notes: † The Census 2010 population figure is used to calculate the percentages in the Hispanic Origin and Race categories. Ancestry percentages are based on the 2006-2010 American Community Survey population (not shown); ‡ Numbers in parentheses indicate the number of people reporting a single ancestry; * Numbers in parentheses indicate the number of persons reporting this race alone, not in combination with any other race; Please refer to the Explanation of Data for more information.*

SECTION TWO

Lithuanian (10)	19	0.03
Northern European (19)	19	0.03
Norwegian (106)	209	0.35
Polish (139)	618	1.02
Portuguese (57)	96	0.16
Romanian (0)	7	0.01
Russian (16)	31	0.05
Scandinavian (12)	12	0.02
Scotch-Irish (720)	1,383	2.29
Scottish (357)	1,094	1.81
Slavic (11)	11	0.02
Slovak (0)	24	0.04
Swedish (169)	595	0.99
Swiss (0)	44	0.07
Ukrainian (0)	9	0.01
Welsh (124)	316	0.52
West Indian, ex. Hispanic (39)	74	0.12
Dutch West Indian (0)	35	0.06
West Indian (39)	39	0.06
Yugoslavian (4)	4	0.01

Hispanic Origin	Population	%
Hispanic or Latino (of any race)	4,955	8.08
Central American, ex. Mexican	399	0.65
Costa Rican	13	0.02
Guatemalan	72	0.12
Honduran	173	0.28
Nicaraguan	43	0.07
Panamanian	47	0.08
Salvadoran	51	0.08
Cuban	74	0.12
Dominican Republic	30	0.05
Mexican	3,477	5.67
Puerto Rican	339	0.55
South American	87	0.14
Argentinean	5	0.01
Bolivian	2	<0.01
Chilean	4	0.01
Colombian	29	0.05
Ecuadorian	13	0.02
Peruvian	22	0.04
Venezuelan	10	0.02
Other South American	2	<0.01
Other Hispanic or Latino	549	0.90

Race*	Population	%
African-American/Black (15,720)	16,557	27.00
Not Hispanic (15,545)	16,254	26.51
Hispanic (175)	303	0.49
American Indian/Alaska Native (336)	728	1.19
Not Hispanic (253)	577	0.94
Hispanic (83)	151	0.25
Apache (11)	14	0.02
Blackfeet (4)	31	0.05
Canadian/French Am. Ind. (1)	3	<0.01
Cherokee (41)	143	0.23
Cheyenne (0)	3	<0.01
Chickasaw (1)	2	<0.01
Chippewa (4)	5	0.01
Choctaw (39)	69	0.11
Comanche (1)	1	<0.01
Creek (6)	13	0.02
Crow (0)	1	<0.01
Delaware (0)	1	<0.01
Hopi (0)	2	<0.01
Houma (0)	1	<0.01
Iroquois (4)	7	0.01
Lumbee (2)	8	0.01
Mexican American Ind. (10)	23	0.04
Navajo (7)	10	0.02
Osage (0)	2	<0.01
Pima (1)	1	<0.01
Potawatomi (8)	8	0.01
Pueblo (1)	4	0.01
Seminole (2)	6	0.01
Shoshone (1)	1	<0.01
Sioux (9)	13	0.02
South American Ind. (0)	1	<0.01
Yaqui (1)	1	<0.01
Yup'ik *(Alaska Native)* (0)	2	<0.01
Asian (1,242)	1,797	2.93
Not Hispanic (1,205)	1,701	2.77
Hispanic (37)	96	0.16
Bangladeshi (3)	4	0.01
Burmese (47)	47	0.08
Cambodian (16)	23	0.04
Chinese, ex. Taiwanese (99)	150	0.24
Filipino (324)	546	0.89
Hmong (1)	3	<0.01
Indian (144)	162	0.26
Indonesian (6)	8	0.01
Japanese (86)	175	0.29
Korean (138)	227	0.37
Laotian (23)	26	0.04
Malaysian (1)	1	<0.01
Nepalese (2)	2	<0.01
Pakistani (8)	9	0.01
Taiwanese (3)	11	0.02
Thai (107)	150	0.24
Vietnamese (188)	195	0.32
Hawaii Native/Pacific Islander (122)	207	0.34
Not Hispanic (116)	189	0.31
Hispanic (6)	18	0.03
Fijian (7)	7	0.01
Guamanian/Chamorro (49)	74	0.12
Native Hawaiian (23)	59	0.10
Samoan (0)	15	0.02
Tongan (0)	1	<0.01
White (40,086)	41,455	67.61
Not Hispanic (37,838)	38,929	63.49
Hispanic (2,248)	2,526	4.12

Breaux Bridge

Place Type: City
Parish: St. Martin
Population: 8,139†

Ancestry‡	Population	%
American (558)	558	6.92
Austrian (0)	13	0.16
Cajun (129)	142	1.76
Canadian (32)	32	0.40
Czech (8)	8	0.10
Danish (18)	18	0.22
Dutch (0)	10	0.12
English (173)	204	2.53
French, ex. Basque (970)	1,415	17.55
French Canadian (335)	383	4.75
German (164)	410	5.08
Greek (0)	67	0.83
Irish (62)	264	3.27
Italian (64)	165	2.05
Polish (44)	74	0.92
Swedish (0)	14	0.17
West Indian, ex. Hispanic (0)	25	0.31
Dutch West Indian (0)	25	0.31

Hispanic Origin	Population	%
Hispanic or Latino (of any race)	104	1.28
Central American, ex. Mexican	10	0.12
Guatemalan	4	0.05
Honduran	6	0.07
Cuban	4	0.05
Mexican	55	0.68
Puerto Rican	7	0.09
South American	4	0.05
Colombian	1	0.01
Ecuadorian	2	0.02
Venezuelan	1	0.01
Other Hispanic or Latino	24	0.29

Race*	Population	%
African-American/Black (3,850)	3,918	48.14
Not Hispanic (3,836)	3,896	47.87
Hispanic (14)	22	0.27
American Indian/Alaska Native (35)	63	0.77
Not Hispanic (33)	56	0.69
Hispanic (2)	7	0.09
Cherokee (1)	4	0.05
Choctaw (0)	1	0.01
Houma (5)	8	0.10
Mexican American Ind. (1)	1	0.01
Navajo (2)	3	0.04
Seminole (0)	1	0.01
Asian (50)	63	0.77
Not Hispanic (50)	63	0.77
Bangladeshi (0)	4	0.05
Chinese, ex. Taiwanese (6)	6	0.07
Filipino (3)	7	0.09
Indian (12)	17	0.21
Korean (1)	4	0.05
Vietnamese (27)	27	0.33
Hawaii Native/Pacific Islander (0)	2	0.02
Not Hispanic (0)	2	0.02
Native Hawaiian (0)	2	0.02
White (4,067)	4,151	51.00
Not Hispanic (4,015)	4,091	50.26
Hispanic (52)	60	0.74

Bridge City

Place Type: CDP
Parish: Jefferson
Population: 7,706†

Ancestry‡	Population	%
African, Sub-Saharan (55)	55	0.60
African (55)	55	0.60
American (254)	254	2.78
Austrian (0)	10	0.11
British (0)	10	0.11
Cajun (42)	42	0.46
English (94)	317	3.47
French, ex. Basque (690)	1,749	19.14
French Canadian (66)	66	0.72
German (153)	550	6.02
Greek (0)	13	0.14
Irish (10)	472	5.17
Italian (147)	422	4.62
Norwegian (0)	11	0.12
Scotch-Irish (70)	70	0.77
Scottish (0)	13	0.14
West Indian, ex. Hispanic (67)	67	0.73
British West Indian (67)	67	0.73

Hispanic Origin	Population	%
Hispanic or Latino (of any race)	884	11.47
Central American, ex. Mexican	233	3.02
Costa Rican	6	0.08
Guatemalan	26	0.34
Honduran	157	2.04
Nicaraguan	23	0.30
Panamanian	4	0.05
Salvadoran	15	0.19
Other Central American	2	0.03
Cuban	40	0.52
Dominican Republic	180	2.34
Mexican	215	2.79
Puerto Rican	90	1.17
South American	25	0.32
Colombian	11	0.14
Ecuadorian	7	0.09
Peruvian	7	0.09
Other Hispanic or Latino	101	1.31

Race*	Population	%
African-American/Black (3,816)	3,874	50.27
Not Hispanic (3,701)	3,745	48.60
Hispanic (115)	129	1.67
American Indian/Alaska Native (44)	68	0.88
Not Hispanic (32)	53	0.69
Hispanic (12)	15	0.19
Cherokee (7)	9	0.12
Chickasaw (4)	4	0.05
Choctaw (0)	1	0.01
Houma (7)	14	0.18
Mexican American Ind. (1)	1	0.01
Sioux (1)	1	0.01
Asian (315)	342	4.44

*Notes: † The Census 2010 population figure is used to calculate the percentages in the Hispanic Origin and Race categories. Ancestry percentages are based on the 2006-2010 American Community Survey population (not shown); ‡ Numbers in parentheses indicate the number of people reporting a single ancestry; * Numbers in parentheses indicate the number of persons reporting this race alone, not in combination with any other race; Please refer to the Explanation of Data for more information.*

	Population	%
Not Hispanic (307)	326	4.23
Hispanic (8)	16	0.21
Chinese, ex. Taiwanese (3)	5	0.06
Filipino (10)	22	0.29
Indian (2)	7	0.09
Korean (2)	2	0.03
Laotian (1)	2	0.03
Taiwanese (2)	2	0.03
Thai (2)	2	0.03
Vietnamese (285)	301	3.91
Hawaii Native/Pacific Islander (2)	7	0.09
Not Hispanic (0)	2	0.03
Hispanic (2)	5	0.06
Guamanian/Chamorro (2)	2	0.03
Native Hawaiian (0)	2	0.03
White (3,028)	3,098	40.20
Not Hispanic (2,700)	2,756	35.76
Hispanic (328)	342	4.44

Broussard

Place Type: City
Parish: Lafayette
Population: 8,197†

Ancestry‡	Population	%
African, Sub-Saharan (28)	28	0.36
African (8)	8	0.10
South African (20)	20	0.26
American (671)	671	8.65
Arab (43)	72	0.93
Lebanese (43)	72	0.93
British (23)	142	1.83
Cajun (452)	463	5.97
Canadian (46)	46	0.59
English (245)	489	6.30
European (52)	52	0.67
French, ex. Basque (1,347)	2,400	30.92
French Canadian (322)	452	5.82
German (149)	457	5.89
Hungarian (0)	21	0.27
Irish (89)	389	5.01
Italian (81)	288	3.71
Norwegian (14)	41	0.53
Polish (0)	26	0.34
Scotch-Irish (0)	12	0.15
Scottish (0)	54	0.70
Swedish (10)	20	0.26
Welsh (0)	22	0.28

Hispanic Origin	Population	%
Hispanic or Latino (of any race)	221	2.70
Central American, ex. Mexican	38	0.46
Costa Rican	1	0.01
Guatemalan	9	0.11
Honduran	21	0.26
Nicaraguan	3	0.04
Panamanian	2	0.02
Salvadoran	2	0.02
Cuban	13	0.16
Dominican Republic	1	0.01
Mexican	89	1.09
Puerto Rican	7	0.09
South American	35	0.43
Argentinean	5	0.06
Bolivian	1	0.01
Chilean	3	0.04
Colombian	5	0.06
Peruvian	2	0.02
Venezuelan	19	0.23
Other Hispanic or Latino	38	0.46

Race*	Population	%
African-American/Black (1,300)	1,361	16.60
Not Hispanic (1,290)	1,345	16.41
Hispanic (10)	16	0.20
American Indian/Alaska Native (24)	54	0.66
Not Hispanic (21)	49	0.60
Hispanic (3)	5	0.06
Blackfeet (0)	1	0.01
Cherokee (0)	8	0.10
Chippewa (1)	1	0.01
Choctaw (0)	2	0.02
Creek (1)	1	0.01
Crow (0)	1	0.01
Houma (9)	13	0.16
Mexican American Ind. (1)	1	0.01
Asian (105)	126	1.54
Not Hispanic (103)	124	1.51
Hispanic (2)	2	0.02
Bangladeshi (3)	3	0.04
Cambodian (5)	5	0.06
Chinese, ex. Taiwanese (22)	22	0.27
Filipino (14)	18	0.22
Indian (10)	12	0.15
Indonesian (3)	3	0.04
Japanese (0)	4	0.05
Korean (2)	3	0.04
Laotian (9)	13	0.16
Malaysian (2)	2	0.02
Thai (6)	9	0.11
Vietnamese (22)	26	0.32
Hawaii Native/Pacific Islander (6)	10	0.12
Not Hispanic (6)	9	0.11
Hispanic (0)	1	0.01
Guamanian/Chamorro (2)	3	0.04
Native Hawaiian (4)	5	0.06
White (6,556)	6,654	81.18
Not Hispanic (6,443)	6,526	79.61
Hispanic (113)	128	1.56

Carencro

Place Type: City
Parish: Lafayette
Population: 7,526†

Ancestry‡	Population	%
African, Sub-Saharan (19)	19	0.26
African (19)	19	0.26
American (302)	302	4.11
Cajun (222)	367	4.99
Danish (0)	13	0.18
English (117)	176	2.39
French, ex. Basque (1,046)	1,669	22.69
French Canadian (404)	441	6.00
German (68)	322	4.38
Greek (0)	3	0.04
Hungarian (31)	31	0.42
Irish (57)	285	3.87
Italian (18)	74	1.01
Polish (0)	13	0.18
Scotch-Irish (9)	9	0.12
Scottish (72)	109	1.48
Swedish (0)	8	0.11

Hispanic Origin	Population	%
Hispanic or Latino (of any race)	382	5.08
Central American, ex. Mexican	55	0.73
Costa Rican	3	0.04
Guatemalan	23	0.31
Honduran	17	0.23
Nicaraguan	7	0.09
Panamanian	4	0.05
Other Central American	1	0.01
Mexican	210	2.79
Puerto Rican	21	0.28
South American	15	0.20
Chilean	1	0.01
Colombian	13	0.17
Ecuadorian	1	0.01
Other Hispanic or Latino	81	1.08

Race*	Population	%
African-American/Black (3,136)	3,194	42.44
Not Hispanic (3,121)	3,174	42.17
Hispanic (15)	20	0.27
American Indian/Alaska Native (42)	74	0.98
Not Hispanic (41)	70	0.93
Hispanic (1)	4	0.05
Apache (0)	1	0.01
Cherokee (3)	7	0.09
Chippewa (1)	1	0.01
Choctaw (1)	4	0.05
Houma (2)	2	0.03
Osage (0)	1	0.01
Puget Sound Salish (0)	2	0.03
Asian (49)	62	0.82
Not Hispanic (45)	57	0.76
Hispanic (4)	5	0.07
Cambodian (3)	3	0.04
Chinese, ex. Taiwanese (3)	5	0.07
Filipino (5)	10	0.13
Indian (9)	9	0.12
Japanese (1)	1	0.01
Korean (2)	2	0.03
Laotian (5)	5	0.07
Pakistani (3)	3	0.04
Thai (3)	4	0.05
Vietnamese (14)	16	0.21
Hawaii Native/Pacific Islander (1)	2	0.03
Not Hispanic (1)	2	0.03
Tongan (1)	1	0.01
White (4,024)	4,095	54.41
Not Hispanic (3,849)	3,917	52.05
Hispanic (175)	178	2.37

Central

Place Type: City
Parish: East Baton Rouge
Population: 26,864†

Ancestry‡	Population	%
African, Sub-Saharan (75)	153	0.57
African (75)	153	0.57
American (4,864)	4,864	18.09
Arab (31)	77	0.29
Lebanese (31)	77	0.29
Austrian (0)	50	0.19
Belgian (0)	11	0.04
British (52)	78	0.29
Cajun (367)	452	1.68
Canadian (12)	12	0.04
Czech (0)	41	0.15
Danish (25)	36	0.13
Dutch (40)	192	0.71
English (1,030)	2,948	10.96
European (170)	203	0.76
Finnish (10)	10	0.04
French, ex. Basque (1,848)	5,142	19.12
French Canadian (523)	559	2.08
German (657)	2,900	10.79
Greek (7)	7	0.03
Hungarian (27)	80	0.30
Irish (1,133)	3,511	13.06
Italian (803)	1,885	7.01
Norwegian (46)	121	0.45
Pennsylvania German (6)	6	0.02
Polish (75)	272	1.01
Portuguese (0)	16	0.06
Romanian (8)	8	0.03
Scandinavian (12)	22	0.08
Scotch-Irish (389)	858	3.19
Scottish (130)	303	1.13
Serbian (29)	29	0.11
Swedish (0)	53	0.20
Swiss (0)	14	0.05
Welsh (0)	56	0.21
West Indian, ex. Hispanic (0)	12	0.04
Jamaican (0)	12	0.04
Yugoslavian (29)	29	0.11

Hispanic Origin	Population	%
Hispanic or Latino (of any race)	433	1.61
Central American, ex. Mexican	68	0.25
Costa Rican	3	0.01
Guatemalan	20	0.07
Honduran	19	0.07
Nicaraguan	5	0.02

*Notes: † The Census 2010 population figure is used to calculate the percentages in the Hispanic Origin and Race categories. Ancestry percentages are based on the 2006-2010 American Community Survey population (not shown); ‡ Numbers in parentheses indicate the number of people reporting a single ancestry; * Numbers in parentheses indicate the number of persons reporting this race alone, not in combination with any other race; Please refer to the Explanation of Data for more information.*

Panamanian	3	0.01
Salvadoran	17	0.06
Other Central American	1	<0.01
Cuban	23	0.09
Dominican Republic	1	<0.01
Mexican	183	0.68
Puerto Rican	25	0.09
South American	29	0.11
Chilean	6	0.02
Colombian	10	0.04
Ecuadorian	1	<0.01
Peruvian	3	0.01
Venezuelan	9	0.03
Other Hispanic or Latino	104	0.39

Race*	Population	%
African-American/Black (2,241)	2,321	8.64
Not Hispanic (2,232)	2,309	8.60
Hispanic (9)	12	0.04
American Indian/Alaska Native (105)	241	0.90
Not Hispanic (97)	224	0.83
Hispanic (8)	17	0.06
Alaska Athabascan *(Ala. Nat.)* (2)	2	0.01
Blackfeet (0)	6	0.02
Central American Ind. (1)	2	0.01
Cherokee (19)	48	0.18
Chippewa (1)	1	<0.01
Choctaw (22)	37	0.14
Creek (1)	2	0.01
Crow (0)	1	<0.01
Houma (11)	17	0.06
Mexican American Ind. (1)	2	0.01
Osage (7)	7	0.03
Paiute (0)	1	<0.01
Potawatomi (0)	1	<0.01
Puget Sound Salish (0)	1	<0.01
Seminole (0)	1	<0.01
Spanish American Ind. (0)	1	<0.01
Asian (152)	199	0.74
Not Hispanic (147)	192	0.71
Hispanic (5)	7	0.03
Chinese, ex. Taiwanese (37)	42	0.16
Filipino (35)	48	0.18
Indian (1)	2	0.01
Indonesian (0)	1	<0.01
Japanese (1)	5	0.02
Korean (8)	15	0.06
Thai (6)	8	0.03
Vietnamese (62)	71	0.26
Hawaii Native/Pacific Islander (5)	19	0.07
Not Hispanic (4)	11	0.04
Hispanic (1)	8	0.03
Guamanian/Chamorro (3)	8	0.03
Native Hawaiian (0)	3	0.01
Samoan (2)	7	0.03
White (23,993)	24,232	90.20
Not Hispanic (23,706)	23,928	89.07
Hispanic (287)	304	1.13

Chalmette

Place Type: CDP
Parish: St. Bernard
Population: 16,751†

Ancestry‡	Population	%
African, Sub-Saharan (29)	29	0.23
African (29)	29	0.23
American (855)	855	6.87
Arab (48)	48	0.39
Palestinian (48)	48	0.39
Armenian (10)	10	0.08
Austrian (10)	36	0.29
Basque (12)	12	0.10
Brazilian (143)	143	1.15
Cajun (7)	56	0.45
Canadian (0)	41	0.33
Danish (0)	11	0.09
Dutch (0)	32	0.26
English (618)	840	6.75
European (10)	38	0.31
French, ex. Basque (1,298)	2,264	18.18
French Canadian (48)	67	0.54
German (1,325)	2,131	17.11
Greek (63)	63	0.51
Irish (119)	745	5.98
Italian (894)	1,850	14.86
Norwegian (113)	113	0.91
Polish (43)	51	0.41
Russian (8)	24	0.19
Scotch-Irish (9)	9	0.07
Scottish (7)	30	0.24

Hispanic Origin	Population	%
Hispanic or Latino (of any race)	1,726	10.30
Central American, ex. Mexican	596	3.56
Costa Rican	8	0.05
Guatemalan	42	0.25
Honduran	376	2.24
Nicaraguan	83	0.50
Panamanian	9	0.05
Salvadoran	73	0.44
Other Central American	5	0.03
Cuban	87	0.52
Dominican Republic	8	0.05
Mexican	522	3.12
Puerto Rican	79	0.47
South American	32	0.19
Argentinean	3	0.02
Bolivian	4	0.02
Chilean	1	0.01
Colombian	6	0.04
Ecuadorian	4	0.02
Peruvian	13	0.08
Venezuelan	1	0.01
Other Hispanic or Latino	402	2.40

Race*	Population	%
African-American/Black (2,207)	2,416	14.42
Not Hispanic (2,165)	2,333	13.93
Hispanic (42)	83	0.50
American Indian/Alaska Native (101)	240	1.43
Not Hispanic (62)	166	0.99
Hispanic (39)	74	0.44
Apache (1)	2	0.01
Arapaho (0)	2	0.01
Blackfeet (1)	7	0.04
Central American Ind. (7)	13	0.08
Cherokee (8)	49	0.29
Cheyenne (1)	1	0.01
Chickasaw (0)	1	0.01
Choctaw (6)	11	0.07
Comanche (0)	5	0.03
Creek (0)	1	0.01
Houma (20)	33	0.20
Lumbee (3)	3	0.02
Mexican American Ind. (0)	2	0.01
Potawatomi (1)	1	0.01
Pueblo (0)	1	0.01
Seminole (4)	4	0.02
Sioux (0)	4	0.02
South American Ind. (0)	1	0.01
Spanish American Ind. (0)	1	0.01
Asian (501)	620	3.70
Not Hispanic (493)	579	3.46
Hispanic (8)	41	0.24
Cambodian (2)	5	0.03
Chinese, ex. Taiwanese (42)	45	0.27
Filipino (132)	199	1.19
Indian (14)	28	0.17
Japanese (3)	6	0.04
Korean (2)	2	0.01
Pakistani (16)	16	0.10
Taiwanese (2)	2	0.01
Thai (1)	1	0.01
Vietnamese (273)	282	1.68
Hawaii Native/Pacific Islander (16)	28	0.17
Not Hispanic (8)	19	0.11
Hispanic (8)	9	0.05
Tongan (1)	1	0.01
White (12,727)	13,218	78.91
Not Hispanic (11,868)	12,180	72.71
Hispanic (859)	1,038	6.20

Claiborne

Place Type: CDP
Parish: Ouachita
Population: 11,507†

Ancestry‡	Population	%
African, Sub-Saharan (0)	21	0.18
African (0)	21	0.18
American (2,031)	2,031	17.49
British (56)	72	0.62
Cajun (18)	81	0.70
Canadian (0)	18	0.16
Dutch (0)	269	2.32
English (1,537)	2,420	20.84
European (85)	85	0.73
Finnish (0)	24	0.21
French, ex. Basque (122)	619	5.33
French Canadian (45)	89	0.77
German (382)	1,182	10.18
Irish (394)	1,730	14.90
Italian (149)	310	2.67
Norwegian (43)	43	0.37
Polish (160)	248	2.14
Romanian (0)	11	0.09
Scotch-Irish (124)	372	3.20
Scottish (93)	264	2.27
Swedish (0)	14	0.12
Ukrainian (31)	31	0.27
Welsh (17)	29	0.25
West Indian, ex. Hispanic (11)	11	0.09
Haitian (11)	11	0.09

Hispanic Origin	Population	%
Hispanic or Latino (of any race)	323	2.81
Central American, ex. Mexican	25	0.22
Costa Rican	1	0.01
Honduran	17	0.15
Nicaraguan	2	0.02
Salvadoran	5	0.04
Cuban	4	0.03
Mexican	223	1.94
Puerto Rican	14	0.12
South American	13	0.11
Argentinean	3	0.03
Chilean	1	0.01
Colombian	3	0.03
Ecuadorian	2	0.02
Peruvian	3	0.03
Venezuelan	1	0.01
Other Hispanic or Latino	44	0.38

Race*	Population	%
African-American/Black (347)	370	3.22
Not Hispanic (342)	363	3.15
Hispanic (5)	7	0.06
American Indian/Alaska Native (43)	99	0.86
Not Hispanic (40)	95	0.83
Hispanic (3)	4	0.03
Apache (1)	1	0.01
Cherokee (18)	30	0.26
Chickasaw (0)	2	0.02
Choctaw (8)	21	0.18
Creek (0)	2	0.02
Crow (0)	2	0.02
Inupiat *(Alaska Native)* (0)	1	0.01
Asian (166)	200	1.74
Not Hispanic (156)	190	1.65
Hispanic (10)	10	0.09
Chinese, ex. Taiwanese (32)	45	0.39
Filipino (20)	27	0.23
Indian (53)	61	0.53
Indonesian (1)	1	0.01
Japanese (2)	7	0.06
Korean (4)	5	0.04
Laotian (6)	6	0.05

*Notes: † The Census 2010 population figure is used to calculate the percentages in the Hispanic Origin and Race categories. Ancestry percentages are based on the 2006-2010 American Community Survey population (not shown); ‡ Numbers in parentheses indicate the number of people reporting a single ancestry; * Numbers in parentheses indicate the number of persons reporting this race alone, not in combination with any other race; Please refer to the Explanation of Data for more information.*

Nepalese (1)	1	0.01
Pakistani (22)	24	0.21
Thai (4)	7	0.06
Vietnamese (12)	18	0.16
Hawaii Native/Pacific Islander (4)	11	0.10
Not Hispanic (4)	7	0.06
Hispanic (0)	4	0.03
Native Hawaiian (3)	10	0.09
Samoan (0)	1	0.01
White (10,726)	10,841	94.21
Not Hispanic (10,529)	10,632	92.40
Hispanic (197)	209	1.82

Covington

Place Type: City
Parish: St. Tammany
Population: 8,765†

Ancestry‡	Population	%
African, Sub-Saharan (24)	24	0.27
African (24)	24	0.27
American (722)	722	8.08
Austrian (0)	8	0.09
Brazilian (9)	9	0.10
British (22)	34	0.38
Cajun (16)	34	0.38
Canadian (0)	60	0.67
Czech (0)	26	0.29
Dutch (33)	85	0.95
Eastern European (8)	17	0.19
English (329)	1,089	12.18
Finnish (0)	20	0.22
French, ex. Basque (395)	1,700	19.01
French Canadian (168)	285	3.19
German (386)	1,543	17.26
Greek (0)	22	0.25
Hungarian (7)	117	1.31
Irish (240)	1,058	11.83
Italian (197)	609	6.81
Latvian (0)	12	0.13
Norwegian (0)	104	1.16
Polish (7)	16	0.18
Portuguese (16)	35	0.39
Russian (0)	19	0.21
Scandinavian (0)	7	0.08
Scotch-Irish (74)	226	2.53
Scottish (0)	181	2.02
Swedish (0)	59	0.66
Welsh (7)	36	0.40

Hispanic Origin	Population	%
Hispanic or Latino (of any race)	320	3.65
Central American, ex. Mexican	95	1.08
Costa Rican	2	0.02
Guatemalan	24	0.27
Honduran	48	0.55
Nicaraguan	11	0.13
Panamanian	2	0.02
Salvadoran	8	0.09
Cuban	17	0.19
Dominican Republic	9	0.10
Mexican	66	0.75
Puerto Rican	42	0.48
South American	19	0.22
Argentinean	3	0.03
Chilean	1	0.01
Colombian	7	0.08
Ecuadorian	3	0.03
Peruvian	3	0.03
Venezuelan	2	0.02
Other Hispanic or Latino	72	0.82

Race*	Population	%
African-American/Black (1,666)	1,725	19.68
Not Hispanic (1,661)	1,715	19.57
Hispanic (5)	10	0.11
American Indian/Alaska Native (35)	90	1.03
Not Hispanic (35)	75	0.86
Hispanic (0)	15	0.17
Aleut *(Alaska Native)* (0)	1	0.01
Apache (0)	3	0.03
Canadian/French Am. Ind. (0)	1	0.01
Cherokee (8)	20	0.23
Chickasaw (0)	1	0.01
Chippewa (2)	4	0.05
Choctaw (1)	5	0.06
Creek (3)	3	0.03
Houma (3)	4	0.05
Mexican American Ind. (0)	5	0.06
Sioux (1)	4	0.05
Asian (55)	69	0.79
Not Hispanic (54)	66	0.75
Hispanic (1)	3	0.03
Chinese, ex. Taiwanese (24)	25	0.29
Filipino (6)	8	0.09
Indian (9)	10	0.11
Indonesian (1)	1	0.01
Japanese (1)	5	0.06
Korean (3)	6	0.07
Laotian (2)	3	0.03
Malaysian (1)	1	0.01
Thai (3)	3	0.03
Vietnamese (5)	5	0.06
Hawaii Native/Pacific Islander (4)	9	0.10
Not Hispanic (0)	3	0.03
Hispanic (4)	6	0.07
Guamanian/Chamorro (4)	5	0.06
Samoan (0)	1	0.01
White (6,816)	6,908	78.81
Not Hispanic (6,592)	6,666	76.05
Hispanic (224)	242	2.76

Crowley

Place Type: City
Parish: Acadia
Population: 13,265†

Ancestry‡	Population	%
African, Sub-Saharan (30)	30	0.22
African (30)	30	0.22
American (817)	817	6.09
Arab (38)	86	0.64
Lebanese (38)	86	0.64
Cajun (184)	237	1.77
Danish (0)	16	0.12
Dutch (37)	48	0.36
English (187)	597	4.45
French, ex. Basque (1,910)	3,483	25.95
French Canadian (727)	851	6.34
German (502)	1,518	11.31
Irish (69)	535	3.99
Italian (94)	291	2.17
Polish (0)	16	0.12
Russian (19)	30	0.22
Scotch-Irish (11)	11	0.08
Scottish (22)	73	0.54
Swiss (0)	14	0.10

Hispanic Origin	Population	%
Hispanic or Latino (of any race)	254	1.91
Central American, ex. Mexican	41	0.31
Guatemalan	3	0.02
Honduran	37	0.28
Salvadoran	1	0.01
Cuban	14	0.11
Dominican Republic	4	0.03
Mexican	133	1.00
Puerto Rican	12	0.09
South American	1	0.01
Colombian	1	0.01
Other Hispanic or Latino	49	0.37

Race*	Population	%
African-American/Black (4,317)	4,439	33.46
Not Hispanic (4,299)	4,402	33.19
Hispanic (18)	37	0.28
American Indian/Alaska Native (40)	102	0.77
Not Hispanic (37)	86	0.65
Hispanic (3)	16	0.12
Apache (3)	3	0.02
Canadian/French Am. Ind. (0)	3	0.02
Cherokee (11)	22	0.17
Chippewa (1)	1	0.01
Choctaw (1)	5	0.04
Creek (0)	1	0.01
Houma (1)	2	0.02
Inupiat *(Alaska Native)* (0)	1	0.01
Osage (1)	1	0.01
Sioux (0)	6	0.05
Asian (45)	78	0.59
Not Hispanic (45)	73	0.55
Hispanic (0)	5	0.04
Cambodian (5)	5	0.04
Chinese, ex. Taiwanese (15)	18	0.14
Filipino (1)	5	0.04
Indian (11)	17	0.13
Indonesian (1)	3	0.02
Japanese (1)	3	0.02
Korean (3)	4	0.03
Laotian (0)	4	0.03
Malaysian (2)	2	0.02
Vietnamese (6)	12	0.09
Hawaii Native/Pacific Islander (0)	2	0.02
Not Hispanic (0)	2	0.02
White (8,573)	8,742	65.90
Not Hispanic (8,460)	8,600	64.83
Hispanic (113)	142	1.07

DeRidder

Place Type: City
Parish: Beauregard
Population: 10,578†

Ancestry‡	Population	%
African, Sub-Saharan (17)	23	0.22
African (17)	23	0.22
American (605)	605	5.83
Arab (2)	16	0.15
Lebanese (2)	5	0.05
Syrian (0)	11	0.11
Austrian (3)	9	0.09
Belgian (0)	10	0.10
British (0)	3	0.03
Cajun (18)	30	0.29
Canadian (13)	13	0.13
Czech (0)	52	0.50
Czechoslovakian (0)	4	0.04
Danish (5)	9	0.09
Dutch (44)	162	1.56
English (467)	956	9.21
European (49)	58	0.56
Finnish (0)	5	0.05
French, ex. Basque (253)	801	7.72
French Canadian (123)	172	1.66
German (400)	1,038	10.00
Greek (4)	14	0.13
Hungarian (10)	34	0.33
Irish (363)	1,222	11.77
Italian (174)	357	3.44
Lithuanian (5)	5	0.05
Norwegian (24)	40	0.39
Polish (47)	94	0.91
Portuguese (5)	73	0.70
Russian (0)	14	0.13
Scotch-Irish (101)	199	1.92
Scottish (78)	182	1.75
Swedish (25)	66	0.64
Swiss (8)	19	0.18
Ukrainian (3)	8	0.08
Welsh (23)	50	0.48
West Indian, ex. Hispanic (24)	27	0.26
Dutch West Indian (0)	3	0.03
Jamaican (24)	24	0.23
Yugoslavian (2)	2	0.02

Hispanic Origin	Population	%
Hispanic or Latino (of any race)	474	4.48

*Notes: † The Census 2010 population figure is used to calculate the percentages in the Hispanic Origin and Race categories. Ancestry percentages are based on the 2006-2010 American Community Survey population (not shown); ‡ Numbers in parentheses indicate the number of people reporting a single ancestry; * Numbers in parentheses indicate the number of persons reporting this race alone, not in combination with any other race; Please refer to the Explanation of Data for more information.*

Central American, ex. Mexican	44	0.42
Costa Rican	1	0.01
Guatemalan	6	0.06
Honduran	11	0.10
Nicaraguan	3	0.03
Panamanian	20	0.19
Salvadoran	3	0.03
Cuban	13	0.12
Dominican Republic	2	0.02
Mexican	214	2.02
Puerto Rican	124	1.17
South American	24	0.23
Argentinean	1	0.01
Colombian	5	0.05
Peruvian	16	0.15
Uruguayan	1	0.01
Venezuelan	1	0.01
Other Hispanic or Latino	53	0.50

Race*	Population	%
African-American/Black (3,529)	3,755	35.50
Not Hispanic (3,487)	3,684	34.83
Hispanic (42)	71	0.67
American Indian/Alaska Native (93)	169	1.60
Not Hispanic (88)	146	1.38
Hispanic (5)	23	0.22
Aleut *(Alaska Native)* (0)	1	0.01
Blackfeet (0)	1	0.01
Canadian/French Am. Ind. (5)	5	0.05
Cherokee (23)	40	0.38
Chickasaw (0)	4	0.04
Chippewa (0)	3	0.03
Choctaw (7)	14	0.13
Creek (4)	4	0.04
Mexican American Ind. (1)	1	0.01
Navajo (4)	8	0.08
Seminole (0)	1	0.01
Sioux (2)	4	0.04
South American Ind. (0)	4	0.04
Yakama (3)	3	0.03
Asian (162)	237	2.24
Not Hispanic (156)	220	2.08
Hispanic (6)	17	0.16
Cambodian (4)	7	0.07
Chinese, ex. Taiwanese (30)	46	0.43
Filipino (27)	41	0.39
Indian (23)	26	0.25
Japanese (14)	26	0.25
Korean (32)	59	0.56
Taiwanese (1)	1	0.01
Thai (5)	6	0.06
Vietnamese (21)	26	0.25
Hawaii Native/Pacific Islander (14)	39	0.37
Not Hispanic (14)	34	0.32
Hispanic (0)	5	0.05
Guamanian/Chamorro (2)	2	0.02
Native Hawaiian (6)	20	0.19
Samoan (5)	6	0.06
White (6,306)	6,622	62.60
Not Hispanic (6,033)	6,285	59.42
Hispanic (273)	337	3.19

Denham Springs

Place Type: City
Parish: Livingston
Population: 10,215†

Ancestry‡	Population	%
American (868)	868	8.49
Armenian (0)	59	0.58
Austrian (13)	13	0.13
Bulgarian (29)	29	0.28
Cajun (57)	69	0.68
Czech (11)	90	0.88
Dutch (9)	125	1.22
English (1,116)	1,618	15.83
European (27)	63	0.62
French, ex. Basque (696)	1,534	15.01
French Canadian (88)	99	0.97
German (169)	867	8.48
Greek (13)	13	0.13
Hungarian (0)	16	0.16
Irish (342)	1,259	12.32
Italian (208)	399	3.90
Norwegian (13)	13	0.13
Polish (24)	55	0.54
Russian (71)	114	1.12
Scotch-Irish (50)	144	1.41
Scottish (59)	152	1.49
Swedish (14)	22	0.22
Ukrainian (12)	12	0.12
Welsh (15)	50	0.49

Hispanic Origin	Population	%
Hispanic or Latino (of any race)	422	4.13
Central American, ex. Mexican	63	0.62
Costa Rican	4	0.04
Guatemalan	11	0.11
Honduran	21	0.21
Nicaraguan	4	0.04
Salvadoran	23	0.23
Cuban	6	0.06
Mexican	242	2.37
Puerto Rican	28	0.27
South American	12	0.12
Chilean	1	0.01
Colombian	9	0.09
Peruvian	1	0.01
Venezuelan	1	0.01
Other Hispanic or Latino	71	0.70

Race*	Population	%
African-American/Black (1,525)	1,575	15.42
Not Hispanic (1,509)	1,552	15.19
Hispanic (16)	23	0.23
American Indian/Alaska Native (39)	66	0.65
Not Hispanic (36)	58	0.57
Hispanic (3)	8	0.08
Apache (1)	1	0.01
Cherokee (2)	16	0.16
Choctaw (3)	7	0.07
Houma (1)	2	0.02
Iroquois (1)	1	0.01
Mexican American Ind. (0)	1	0.01
Asian (54)	70	0.69
Not Hispanic (54)	68	0.67
Hispanic (0)	2	0.02
Chinese, ex. Taiwanese (12)	13	0.13
Filipino (5)	10	0.10
Indian (17)	18	0.18
Japanese (1)	3	0.03
Korean (2)	5	0.05
Pakistani (1)	1	0.01
Thai (1)	1	0.01
Vietnamese (14)	16	0.16
Hawaii Native/Pacific Islander (3)	5	0.05
Not Hispanic (3)	5	0.05
Guamanian/Chamorro (2)	3	0.03
Native Hawaiian (1)	2	0.02
White (8,306)	8,422	82.45
Not Hispanic (8,099)	8,181	80.09
Hispanic (207)	241	2.36

Destrehan

Place Type: CDP
Parish: St. Charles
Population: 11,535†

Ancestry‡	Population	%
African, Sub-Saharan (15)	67	0.59
African (15)	67	0.59
American (424)	424	3.71
Arab (26)	26	0.23
Lebanese (26)	26	0.23
Austrian (0)	6	0.05
British (0)	12	0.11
Cajun (56)	84	0.74
Croatian (11)	22	0.19
Czech (21)	21	0.18
Danish (0)	79	0.69
Dutch (25)	40	0.35
English (258)	574	5.03
European (113)	113	0.99
Finnish (15)	15	0.13
French, ex. Basque (1,077)	3,147	27.56
French Canadian (153)	218	1.91
German (245)	1,841	16.12
Greek (15)	45	0.39
Irish (357)	1,295	11.34
Italian (539)	1,374	12.03
Lithuanian (8)	8	0.07
Norwegian (9)	27	0.24
Polish (27)	67	0.59
Russian (0)	20	0.18
Scandinavian (16)	16	0.14
Scotch-Irish (38)	79	0.69
Scottish (31)	71	0.62
Swedish (0)	67	0.59
Welsh (13)	125	1.09

Hispanic Origin	Population	%
Hispanic or Latino (of any race)	734	6.36
Central American, ex. Mexican	327	2.83
Costa Rican	9	0.08
Guatemalan	36	0.31
Honduran	186	1.61
Nicaraguan	75	0.65
Panamanian	5	0.04
Salvadoran	15	0.13
Other Central American	1	0.01
Cuban	64	0.55
Dominican Republic	19	0.16
Mexican	119	1.03
Puerto Rican	46	0.40
South American	31	0.27
Argentinean	1	0.01
Chilean	3	0.03
Colombian	7	0.06
Peruvian	2	0.02
Uruguayan	1	0.01
Venezuelan	13	0.11
Other South American	4	0.03
Other Hispanic or Latino	128	1.11

Race*	Population	%
African-American/Black (1,891)	1,957	16.97
Not Hispanic (1,864)	1,922	16.66
Hispanic (27)	35	0.30
American Indian/Alaska Native (31)	71	0.62
Not Hispanic (29)	62	0.54
Hispanic (2)	9	0.08
Alaska Athabascan *(Ala. Nat.)* (0)	2	0.02
Blackfeet (1)	1	0.01
Canadian/French Am. Ind. (0)	2	0.02
Cherokee (1)	11	0.10
Chickasaw (0)	2	0.02
Choctaw (2)	12	0.10
Creek (0)	1	0.01
Houma (5)	8	0.07
Iroquois (1)	1	0.01
Mexican American Ind. (1)	1	0.01
Asian (141)	195	1.69
Not Hispanic (140)	189	1.64
Hispanic (1)	6	0.05
Bangladeshi (3)	3	0.03
Chinese, ex. Taiwanese (27)	39	0.34
Filipino (17)	32	0.28
Indian (57)	68	0.59
Indonesian (0)	1	0.01
Japanese (6)	9	0.08
Korean (3)	7	0.06
Taiwanese (2)	2	0.02
Thai (1)	2	0.02
Vietnamese (21)	30	0.26
Hawaii Native/Pacific Islander (9)	15	0.13
Not Hispanic (8)	14	0.12
Hispanic (1)	1	0.01
Guamanian/Chamorro (2)	2	0.02

*Notes: † The Census 2010 population figure is used to calculate the percentages in the Hispanic Origin and Race categories. Ancestry percentages are based on the 2006-2010 American Community Survey population (not shown); ‡ Numbers in parentheses indicate the number of people reporting a single ancestry; * Numbers in parentheses indicate the number of persons reporting this race alone, not in combination with any other race; Please refer to the Explanation of Data for more information.*

Native Hawaiian (0)	6	0.05
Samoan (0)	4	0.03
White (9,111)	9,281	80.46
Not Hispanic (8,604)	8,728	75.67
Hispanic (507)	553	4.79

Estelle

Place Type: CDP
Parish: Jefferson
Population: 16,377†

Ancestry‡	Population	%
African, Sub-Saharan (113)	113	0.67
African (113)	113	0.67
American (564)	564	3.33
Brazilian (54)	54	0.32
Cajun (221)	283	1.67
Croatian (12)	12	0.07
Dutch (0)	39	0.23
English (170)	567	3.35
European (30)	30	0.18
Finnish (17)	36	0.21
French, ex. Basque (2,029)	4,088	24.14
French Canadian (283)	348	2.05
German (368)	1,503	8.87
Hungarian (0)	6	0.04
Irish (386)	996	5.88
Italian (622)	1,752	10.34
Norwegian (8)	114	0.67
Polish (78)	154	0.91
Portuguese (0)	13	0.08
Russian (22)	22	0.13
Scotch-Irish (31)	40	0.24
Scottish (21)	58	0.34
Swedish (0)	35	0.21
Turkish (111)	111	0.66

Hispanic Origin	Population	%
Hispanic or Latino (of any race)	1,796	10.97
Central American, ex. Mexican	629	3.84
Costa Rican	17	0.10
Guatemalan	51	0.31
Honduran	477	2.91
Nicaraguan	37	0.23
Panamanian	2	0.01
Salvadoran	36	0.22
Other Central American	9	0.05
Cuban	121	0.74
Dominican Republic	45	0.27
Mexican	616	3.76
Puerto Rican	115	0.70
South American	61	0.37
Argentinean	1	0.01
Bolivian	1	0.01
Colombian	33	0.20
Ecuadorian	8	0.05
Peruvian	11	0.07
Venezuelan	5	0.03
Other South American	2	0.01
Other Hispanic or Latino	209	1.28

Race*	Population	%
African-American/Black (4,062)	4,190	25.58
Not Hispanic (3,988)	4,092	24.99
Hispanic (74)	98	0.60
American Indian/Alaska Native (154)	271	1.65
Not Hispanic (127)	224	1.37
Hispanic (27)	47	0.29
Apache (1)	5	0.03
Blackfeet (0)	3	0.02
Central American Ind. (1)	1	0.01
Cherokee (12)	19	0.12
Chippewa (0)	1	0.01
Choctaw (5)	15	0.09
Houma (62)	85	0.52
Iroquois (1)	1	0.01
Mexican American Ind. (5)	13	0.08
Osage (0)	1	0.01
Potawatomi (0)	1	0.01
South American Ind. (0)	3	0.02
Spanish American Ind. (4)	7	0.04
Asian (735)	807	4.93
Not Hispanic (734)	799	4.88
Hispanic (1)	8	0.05
Cambodian (1)	1	0.01
Chinese, ex. Taiwanese (27)	42	0.26
Filipino (74)	108	0.66
Indian (19)	24	0.15
Japanese (2)	4	0.02
Korean (17)	26	0.16
Pakistani (1)	2	0.01
Thai (2)	2	0.01
Vietnamese (570)	602	3.68
Hawaii Native/Pacific Islander (5)	13	0.08
Not Hispanic (4)	7	0.04
Hispanic (1)	6	0.04
Guamanian/Chamorro (4)	4	0.02
Native Hawaiian (1)	4	0.02
White (10,448)	10,787	65.87
Not Hispanic (9,466)	9,675	59.08
Hispanic (982)	1,112	6.79

Eunice

Place Type: City
Parish: St. Landry
Population: 10,398†

Ancestry‡	Population	%
African, Sub-Saharan (28)	118	1.14
African (28)	118	1.14
American (647)	647	6.25
Cajun (344)	439	4.24
Canadian (38)	99	0.96
Dutch (28)	54	0.52
English (365)	654	6.32
French, ex. Basque (2,395)	3,336	32.23
French Canadian (423)	481	4.65
German (63)	492	4.75
Irish (34)	269	2.60
Italian (90)	281	2.71
Portuguese (3)	3	0.03
Scotch-Irish (0)	33	0.32
Scottish (0)	14	0.14
Slovak (9)	9	0.09
Yugoslavian (0)	28	0.27

Hispanic Origin	Population	%
Hispanic or Latino (of any race)	240	2.31
Central American, ex. Mexican	7	0.07
Guatemalan	1	0.01
Honduran	3	0.03
Panamanian	1	0.01
Salvadoran	2	0.02
Cuban	5	0.05
Mexican	179	1.72
Puerto Rican	13	0.13
South American	1	0.01
Colombian	1	0.01
Other Hispanic or Latino	35	0.34

Race*	Population	%
African-American/Black (3,393)	3,487	33.54
Not Hispanic (3,380)	3,469	33.36
Hispanic (13)	18	0.17
American Indian/Alaska Native (26)	55	0.53
Not Hispanic (26)	50	0.48
Hispanic (0)	5	0.05
Cherokee (1)	5	0.05
Choctaw (2)	2	0.02
Cree (1)	1	0.01
Houma (3)	3	0.03
Asian (61)	71	0.68
Not Hispanic (59)	68	0.65
Hispanic (2)	3	0.03
Cambodian (7)	7	0.07
Chinese, ex. Taiwanese (9)	9	0.09
Filipino (6)	9	0.09
Indian (13)	14	0.13
Japanese (0)	4	0.04
Korean (1)	1	0.01
Thai (2)	3	0.03
Vietnamese (21)	22	0.21
Hawaii Native/Pacific Islander (0)	1	0.01
Not Hispanic (0)	1	0.01
White (6,664)	6,793	65.33
Not Hispanic (6,551)	6,670	64.15
Hispanic (113)	123	1.18

Fort Polk South

Place Type: CDP
Parish: Vernon
Population: 9,038†

Ancestry‡	Population	%
African, Sub-Saharan (0)	91	0.96
Cape Verdean (0)	67	0.71
Nigerian (0)	24	0.25
American (338)	338	3.58
Arab (23)	23	0.24
Arab (23)	23	0.24
British (45)	58	0.61
Czech (0)	5	0.05
Dutch (78)	162	1.71
English (172)	481	5.09
Finnish (20)	20	0.21
French, ex. Basque (230)	625	6.61
French Canadian (15)	87	0.92
German (419)	1,670	17.66
Greek (0)	20	0.21
Irish (380)	1,546	16.35
Israeli (0)	24	0.25
Italian (101)	442	4.68
Norwegian (0)	11	0.12
Polish (8)	70	0.74
Portuguese (0)	15	0.16
Russian (13)	33	0.35
Scotch-Irish (124)	233	2.46
Scottish (91)	120	1.27
Swedish (0)	18	0.19
Welsh (0)	59	0.62
West Indian, ex. Hispanic (9)	125	1.32
Jamaican (9)	125	1.32

Hispanic Origin	Population	%
Hispanic or Latino (of any race)	1,348	14.91
Central American, ex. Mexican	87	0.96
Guatemalan	13	0.14
Honduran	7	0.08
Nicaraguan	11	0.12
Panamanian	39	0.43
Salvadoran	17	0.19
Cuban	26	0.29
Dominican Republic	23	0.25
Mexican	739	8.18
Puerto Rican	301	3.33
South American	48	0.53
Chilean	4	0.04
Colombian	14	0.15
Ecuadorian	7	0.08
Peruvian	19	0.21
Uruguayan	1	0.01
Venezuelan	3	0.03
Other Hispanic or Latino	124	1.37

Race*	Population	%
African-American/Black (1,834)	2,141	23.69
Not Hispanic (1,775)	2,014	22.28
Hispanic (59)	127	1.41
American Indian/Alaska Native (77)	197	2.18
Not Hispanic (56)	150	1.66
Hispanic (21)	47	0.52
Apache (0)	2	0.02
Blackfeet (3)	12	0.13
Canadian/French Am. Ind. (0)	1	0.01
Cherokee (12)	44	0.49
Chippewa (5)	6	0.07
Choctaw (9)	18	0.20

SECTION TWO

*Notes: † The Census 2010 population figure is used to calculate the percentages in the Hispanic Origin and Race categories. Ancestry percentages are based on the 2006-2010 American Community Survey population (not shown); ‡ Numbers in parentheses indicate the number of people reporting a single ancestry; * Numbers in parentheses indicate the number of persons reporting this race alone, not in combination with any other race; Please refer to the Explanation of Data for more information.*

Creek (2)	6	0.07
Iroquois (1)	1	0.01
Lumbee (2)	2	0.02
Mexican American Ind. (2)	2	0.02
Navajo (7)	8	0.09
Seminole (0)	1	0.01
South American Ind. (0)	2	0.02
Tlingit-Haida *(Alaska Native)* (1)	1	0.01
Yaqui (0)	1	0.01
Yup'ik *(Alaska Native)* (1)	1	0.01
Asian (195)	401	4.44
Not Hispanic (186)	354	3.92
Hispanic (9)	47	0.52
Cambodian (8)	8	0.09
Chinese, ex. Taiwanese (10)	40	0.44
Filipino (66)	130	1.44
Indian (22)	40	0.44
Japanese (12)	43	0.48
Korean (57)	115	1.27
Laotian (0)	1	0.01
Malaysian (2)	2	0.02
Pakistani (0)	2	0.02
Thai (1)	8	0.09
Vietnamese (6)	10	0.11
Hawaii Native/Pacific Islander (79)	134	1.48
Not Hispanic (72)	107	1.18
Hispanic (7)	27	0.30
Guamanian/Chamorro (21)	30	0.33
Native Hawaiian (5)	27	0.30
Samoan (22)	30	0.33
White (5,720)	6,291	69.61
Not Hispanic (5,142)	5,541	61.31
Hispanic (578)	750	8.30

Franklin

Place Type: City
Parish: St. Mary
Population: 7,660†

Ancestry‡	Population	%
African, Sub-Saharan (117)	117	1.50
African (78)	78	1.00
Nigerian (14)	14	0.18
South African (25)	25	0.32
American (677)	677	8.70
Cajun (130)	218	2.80
Danish (14)	26	0.33
Dutch (10)	110	1.41
English (249)	364	4.68
French, ex. Basque (597)	1,027	13.20
French Canadian (198)	221	2.84
German (15)	120	1.54
Hungarian (0)	6	0.08
Irish (32)	264	3.39
Italian (27)	197	2.53
Polish (11)	24	0.31
Scotch-Irish (49)	57	0.73
Scottish (10)	10	0.13
Serbian (8)	8	0.10
Turkish (0)	11	0.14
Welsh (0)	6	0.08

Hispanic Origin	Population	%
Hispanic or Latino (of any race)	142	1.85
Central American, ex. Mexican	19	0.25
Guatemalan	1	0.01
Honduran	3	0.04
Panamanian	14	0.18
Salvadoran	1	0.01
Cuban	3	0.04
Dominican Republic	11	0.14
Mexican	48	0.63
Puerto Rican	33	0.43
Other Hispanic or Latino	28	0.37

Race*	Population	%
African-American/Black (4,305)	4,367	57.01
Not Hispanic (4,289)	4,346	56.74
Hispanic (16)	21	0.27
American Indian/Alaska Native (87)	117	1.53
Not Hispanic (81)	110	1.44
Hispanic (6)	7	0.09
Cherokee (1)	8	0.10
Chippewa (1)	1	0.01
Choctaw (2)	4	0.05
Houma (43)	45	0.59
Navajo (1)	1	0.01
Potawatomi (2)	2	0.03
Asian (53)	72	0.94
Not Hispanic (43)	58	0.76
Hispanic (10)	14	0.18
Chinese, ex. Taiwanese (6)	6	0.08
Filipino (13)	18	0.23
Indian (12)	15	0.20
Japanese (0)	1	0.01
Thai (0)	5	0.07
Vietnamese (22)	25	0.33
Hawaii Native/Pacific Islander (3)	4	0.05
Not Hispanic (3)	4	0.05
Guamanian/Chamorro (2)	2	0.03
Native Hawaiian (1)	1	0.01
White (3,070)	3,148	41.10
Not Hispanic (3,006)	3,070	40.08
Hispanic (64)	78	1.02

Galliano

Place Type: CDP
Parish: Lafourche
Population: 7,676†

Ancestry‡	Population	%
African, Sub-Saharan (9)	9	0.11
African (9)	9	0.11
American (1,154)	1,154	14.57
Austrian (11)	35	0.44
Cajun (341)	384	4.85
Canadian (19)	19	0.24
English (163)	265	3.35
French, ex. Basque (1,598)	2,419	30.54
French Canadian (1,187)	1,409	17.79
German (34)	221	2.79
Irish (23)	277	3.50
Italian (109)	380	4.80
Russian (0)	38	0.48
Swedish (0)	9	0.11
Welsh (16)	16	0.20

Hispanic Origin	Population	%
Hispanic or Latino (of any race)	582	7.58
Central American, ex. Mexican	106	1.38
Costa Rican	2	0.03
Guatemalan	13	0.17
Honduran	81	1.06
Nicaraguan	3	0.04
Panamanian	1	0.01
Salvadoran	5	0.07
Other Central American	1	0.01
Cuban	19	0.25
Mexican	380	4.95
Puerto Rican	1	0.01
South American	23	0.30
Bolivian	4	0.05
Colombian	1	0.01
Peruvian	18	0.23
Other Hispanic or Latino	53	0.69

Race*	Population	%
African-American/Black (131)	179	2.33
Not Hispanic (126)	171	2.23
Hispanic (5)	8	0.10
American Indian/Alaska Native (413)	549	7.15
Not Hispanic (395)	524	6.83
Hispanic (18)	25	0.33
Apache (0)	4	0.05
Blackfeet (0)	6	0.08
Cherokee (10)	29	0.38
Choctaw (1)	2	0.03
Comanche (0)	1	0.01
Houma (253)	320	4.17
Iroquois (1)	1	0.01
Kiowa (0)	1	0.01
Mexican American Ind. (5)	6	0.08
Navajo (1)	2	0.03
Seminole (0)	3	0.04
Sioux (2)	2	0.03
Spanish American Ind. (0)	2	0.03
Asian (39)	45	0.59
Not Hispanic (39)	42	0.55
Hispanic (0)	3	0.04
Chinese, ex. Taiwanese (5)	5	0.07
Filipino (6)	9	0.12
Indian (1)	1	0.01
Japanese (1)	2	0.03
Vietnamese (26)	27	0.35
Hawaii Native/Pacific Islander (6)	9	0.12
Not Hispanic (6)	7	0.09
Hispanic (0)	2	0.03
Guamanian/Chamorro (6)	6	0.08
Native Hawaiian (0)	1	0.01
White (6,526)	6,727	87.64
Not Hispanic (6,353)	6,523	84.98
Hispanic (173)	204	2.66

Gardere

Place Type: CDP
Parish: East Baton Rouge
Population: 10,580†

Ancestry‡	Population	%
African, Sub-Saharan (377)	377	3.59
African (331)	331	3.15
Nigerian (46)	46	0.44
American (655)	655	6.23
Armenian (12)	12	0.11
Cajun (13)	30	0.29
Croatian (9)	9	0.09
Dutch (9)	9	0.09
English (105)	201	1.91
French, ex. Basque (0)	353	3.36
French Canadian (0)	91	0.87
German (154)	343	3.26
Irish (15)	135	1.28
Italian (31)	147	1.40
Norwegian (11)	60	0.57
Scotch-Irish (9)	9	0.09
Scottish (59)	120	1.14
Welsh (0)	30	0.29
West Indian, ex. Hispanic (18)	18	0.17
Jamaican (18)	18	0.17

Hispanic Origin	Population	%
Hispanic or Latino (of any race)	1,463	13.83
Central American, ex. Mexican	633	5.98
Costa Rican	9	0.09
Guatemalan	68	0.64
Honduran	467	4.41
Nicaraguan	23	0.22
Panamanian	1	0.01
Salvadoran	63	0.60
Other Central American	2	0.02
Cuban	25	0.24
Dominican Republic	8	0.08
Mexican	576	5.44
Puerto Rican	43	0.41
South American	27	0.26
Argentinean	5	0.05
Chilean	3	0.03
Colombian	9	0.09
Ecuadorian	8	0.08
Venezuelan	2	0.02
Other Hispanic or Latino	151	1.43

Race*	Population	%
African-American/Black (6,744)	6,860	64.84
Not Hispanic (6,713)	6,813	64.40
Hispanic (31)	47	0.44
American Indian/Alaska Native (30)	55	0.52

*Notes: † The Census 2010 population figure is used to calculate the percentages in the Hispanic Origin and Race categories. Ancestry percentages are based on the 2006-2010 American Community Survey population (not shown); ‡ Numbers in parentheses indicate the number of people reporting a single ancestry; * Numbers in parentheses indicate the number of persons reporting this race alone, not in combination with any other race; Please refer to the Explanation of Data for more information.*

Not Hispanic (15)	35	0.33
Hispanic (15)	20	0.19
Aleut *(Alaska Native)* (0)	1	0.01
Blackfeet (0)	1	0.01
Cherokee (2)	6	0.06
Chickasaw (0)	1	0.01
Choctaw (0)	2	0.02
Houma (0)	2	0.02
Mexican American Ind. (1)	1	0.01
Spanish American Ind. (0)	1	0.01
Asian (183)	233	2.20
Not Hispanic (177)	227	2.15
Hispanic (6)	6	0.06
Cambodian (0)	3	0.03
Chinese, ex. Taiwanese (27)	30	0.28
Filipino (17)	20	0.19
Indian (47)	64	0.60
Indonesian (1)	1	0.01
Japanese (3)	8	0.08
Korean (14)	25	0.24
Laotian (6)	9	0.09
Pakistani (3)	3	0.03
Thai (1)	1	0.01
Vietnamese (52)	64	0.60
Hawaii Native/Pacific Islander (4)	9	0.09
Not Hispanic (2)	7	0.07
Hispanic (2)	2	0.02
Guamanian/Chamorro (0)	1	0.01
Native Hawaiian (3)	5	0.05
Samoan (1)	2	0.02
White (2,734)	2,919	27.59
Not Hispanic (2,045)	2,157	20.39
Hispanic (689)	762	7.20

Gonzales

Place Type: City
Parish: Ascension
Population: 9,781†

Ancestry‡	Population	%
African, Sub-Saharan (0)	63	0.66
African (0)	63	0.66
American (364)	364	3.79
Belgian (5)	5	0.05
British (13)	44	0.46
Cajun (67)	88	0.92
Canadian (12)	12	0.13
Croatian (7)	7	0.07
Danish (0)	18	0.19
English (29)	393	4.10
European (11)	11	0.11
French, ex. Basque (963)	1,695	17.66
French Canadian (184)	303	3.16
German (198)	833	8.68
Irish (180)	772	8.05
Italian (72)	340	3.54
Norwegian (0)	35	0.36
Polish (0)	12	0.13
Russian (19)	39	0.41
Scotch-Irish (27)	62	0.65
Scottish (39)	79	0.82
Swedish (7)	7	0.07
Welsh (6)	37	0.39

Hispanic Origin	Population	%
Hispanic or Latino (of any race)	824	8.42
Central American, ex. Mexican	82	0.84
Costa Rican	3	0.03
Guatemalan	22	0.22
Honduran	36	0.37
Nicaraguan	10	0.10
Panamanian	7	0.07
Salvadoran	4	0.04
Cuban	19	0.19
Dominican Republic	27	0.28
Mexican	578	5.91
Puerto Rican	57	0.58
South American	12	0.12
Argentinean	3	0.03
Colombian	9	0.09
Other Hispanic or Latino	49	0.50

Race*	Population	%
African-American/Black (4,324)	4,409	45.08
Not Hispanic (4,293)	4,369	44.67
Hispanic (31)	40	0.41
American Indian/Alaska Native (22)	75	0.77
Not Hispanic (15)	60	0.61
Hispanic (7)	15	0.15
Apache (0)	1	0.01
Blackfeet (0)	2	0.02
Central American Ind. (2)	2	0.02
Cherokee (2)	11	0.11
Creek (1)	1	0.01
Houma (2)	6	0.06
Mexican American Ind. (4)	4	0.04
Seminole (0)	1	0.01
South American Ind. (1)	1	0.01
Asian (110)	136	1.39
Not Hispanic (96)	119	1.22
Hispanic (14)	17	0.17
Chinese, ex. Taiwanese (38)	48	0.49
Filipino (33)	46	0.47
Indian (10)	12	0.12
Japanese (8)	10	0.10
Korean (1)	2	0.02
Thai (1)	3	0.03
Vietnamese (16)	18	0.18
Hawaii Native/Pacific Islander (7)	12	0.12
Not Hispanic (2)	6	0.06
Hispanic (5)	6	0.06
Native Hawaiian (0)	1	0.01
Samoan (7)	8	0.08
White (4,772)	4,900	50.10
Not Hispanic (4,420)	4,515	46.16
Hispanic (352)	385	3.94

Gretna

Place Type: City
Parish: Jefferson
Population: 17,736†

Ancestry‡	Population	%
African, Sub-Saharan (58)	58	0.33
African (11)	11	0.06
Nigerian (47)	47	0.27
American (627)	627	3.56
Arab (5)	5	0.03
Egyptian (5)	5	0.03
Austrian (0)	5	0.03
Brazilian (18)	18	0.10
British (0)	12	0.07
Cajun (32)	80	0.45
Croatian (0)	13	0.07
Czech (0)	10	0.06
Czechoslovakian (12)	25	0.14
Danish (0)	5	0.03
Dutch (24)	64	0.36
Eastern European (7)	23	0.13
English (188)	471	2.67
Estonian (15)	15	0.09
European (20)	33	0.19
French, ex. Basque (1,596)	2,993	16.98
French Canadian (73)	131	0.74
German (569)	1,763	10.00
Greek (0)	20	0.11
Hungarian (11)	29	0.16
Irish (374)	936	5.31
Italian (511)	1,302	7.39
Latvian (0)	12	0.07
New Zealander (0)	10	0.06
Norwegian (32)	32	0.18
Polish (5)	20	0.11
Portuguese (0)	15	0.09
Russian (14)	43	0.24
Scotch-Irish (19)	59	0.33
Scottish (36)	134	0.76
Slovene (11)	11	0.06
Swedish (0)	15	0.09
Swiss (0)	14	0.08
Ukrainian (0)	21	0.12
Welsh (0)	10	0.06
Yugoslavian (0)	8	0.05

Hispanic Origin	Population	%
Hispanic or Latino (of any race)	2,454	13.84
Central American, ex. Mexican	934	5.27
Costa Rican	13	0.07
Guatemalan	55	0.31
Honduran	762	4.30
Nicaraguan	28	0.16
Salvadoran	70	0.39
Other Central American	6	0.03
Cuban	120	0.68
Dominican Republic	204	1.15
Mexican	695	3.92
Puerto Rican	147	0.83
South American	58	0.33
Bolivian	2	0.01
Chilean	2	0.01
Colombian	31	0.17
Ecuadorian	7	0.04
Peruvian	5	0.03
Uruguayan	5	0.03
Venezuelan	5	0.03
Other South American	1	0.01
Other Hispanic or Latino	296	1.67

Race*	Population	%
African-American/Black (6,081)	6,253	35.26
Not Hispanic (5,961)	6,092	34.35
Hispanic (120)	161	0.91
American Indian/Alaska Native (89)	183	1.03
Not Hispanic (80)	151	0.85
Hispanic (9)	32	0.18
Apache (0)	1	0.01
Canadian/French Am. Ind. (0)	1	0.01
Cherokee (4)	12	0.07
Chickasaw (0)	4	0.02
Chippewa (4)	6	0.03
Choctaw (0)	5	0.03
Delaware (1)	1	0.01
Houma (24)	31	0.17
Iroquois (1)	1	0.01
Mexican American Ind. (1)	2	0.01
Sioux (1)	2	0.01
Asian (474)	550	3.10
Not Hispanic (467)	523	2.95
Hispanic (7)	27	0.15
Cambodian (1)	1	0.01
Chinese, ex. Taiwanese (28)	31	0.17
Filipino (37)	65	0.37
Indian (31)	37	0.21
Japanese (2)	4	0.02
Korean (7)	10	0.06
Laotian (3)	3	0.02
Pakistani (5)	8	0.05
Taiwanese (0)	1	0.01
Thai (3)	3	0.02
Vietnamese (347)	375	2.11
Hawaii Native/Pacific Islander (7)	21	0.12
Not Hispanic (5)	16	0.09
Hispanic (2)	5	0.03
Guamanian/Chamorro (5)	6	0.03
Native Hawaiian (1)	1	0.01
Samoan (0)	3	0.02
White (9,820)	10,124	57.08
Not Hispanic (8,505)	8,687	48.98
Hispanic (1,315)	1,437	8.10

Hammond

Place Type: City
Parish: Tangipahoa
Population: 20,019†

Ancestry‡	Population	%
African, Sub-Saharan (110)	110	0.56

*Notes: † The Census 2010 population figure is used to calculate the percentages in the Hispanic Origin and Race categories. Ancestry percentages are based on the 2006-2010 American Community Survey population (not shown); ‡ Numbers in parentheses indicate the number of people reporting a single ancestry; * Numbers in parentheses indicate the number of persons reporting this race alone, not in combination with any other race; Please refer to the Explanation of Data for more information.*

African (87)	87	0.44
Nigerian (23)	23	0.12
American (676)	676	3.42
Australian (0)	42	0.21
Brazilian (8)	8	0.04
British (0)	33	0.17
Cajun (25)	73	0.37
Czech (0)	38	0.19
Czechoslovakian (17)	17	0.09
Danish (0)	6	0.03
Dutch (0)	62	0.31
English (312)	839	4.25
European (87)	87	0.44
French, ex. Basque (743)	2,271	11.50
French Canadian (39)	48	0.24
German (173)	1,717	8.70
Greek (115)	121	0.61
Hungarian (43)	56	0.28
Irish (383)	1,211	6.13
Italian (795)	1,718	8.70
Lithuanian (0)	13	0.07
Norwegian (20)	65	0.33
Polish (59)	59	0.30
Russian (12)	66	0.33
Scandinavian (0)	6	0.03
Scotch-Irish (88)	209	1.06
Scottish (33)	143	0.72
Swedish (14)	41	0.21
Ukrainian (13)	21	0.11
Welsh (0)	23	0.12
West Indian, ex. Hispanic (19)	19	0.10
Jamaican (19)	19	0.10

Hispanic Origin	Population	%
Hispanic or Latino (of any race)	663	3.31
Central American, ex. Mexican	103	0.51
Costa Rican	11	0.05
Guatemalan	16	0.08
Honduran	49	0.24
Nicaraguan	9	0.04
Panamanian	3	0.01
Salvadoran	15	0.07
Cuban	15	0.07
Dominican Republic	1	<0.01
Mexican	346	1.73
Puerto Rican	33	0.16
South American	45	0.22
Argentinean	2	0.01
Chilean	1	<0.01
Colombian	23	0.11
Ecuadorian	2	0.01
Peruvian	9	0.04
Venezuelan	7	0.03
Other South American	1	<0.01
Other Hispanic or Latino	120	0.60

Race*	Population	%
African-American/Black (9,514)	9,632	48.11
Not Hispanic (9,468)	9,578	47.84
Hispanic (46)	54	0.27
American Indian/Alaska Native (47)	111	0.55
Not Hispanic (44)	106	0.53
Hispanic (3)	5	0.02
Blackfeet (2)	6	0.03
Cherokee (0)	12	0.06
Choctaw (1)	10	0.05
Cree (0)	4	0.02
Houma (3)	5	0.02
Lumbee (0)	1	<0.01
Mexican American Ind. (2)	2	0.01
Navajo (0)	1	<0.01
Osage (1)	1	<0.01
Potawatomi (1)	1	<0.01
Sioux (1)	6	0.03
Asian (294)	332	1.66
Not Hispanic (289)	326	1.63
Hispanic (5)	6	0.03
Burmese (1)	1	<0.01
Cambodian (3)	3	0.01
Chinese, ex. Taiwanese (62)	70	0.35
Filipino (31)	37	0.18
Indian (88)	95	0.47
Indonesian (0)	1	<0.01
Japanese (5)	9	0.04
Korean (3)	8	0.04
Malaysian (0)	1	<0.01
Nepalese (11)	11	0.05
Pakistani (7)	7	0.03
Sri Lankan (2)	2	0.01
Taiwanese (6)	6	0.03
Thai (10)	11	0.05
Vietnamese (46)	51	0.25
Hawaii Native/Pacific Islander (11)	22	0.11
Not Hispanic (11)	22	0.11
Guamanian/Chamorro (1)	2	0.01
Native Hawaiian (5)	6	0.03
Samoan (2)	6	0.03
White (9,724)	9,898	49.44
Not Hispanic (9,335)	9,480	47.36
Hispanic (389)	418	2.09

Harahan

Place Type: City
Parish: Jefferson
Population: 9,277†

Ancestry‡	Population	%
American (647)	647	6.98
British (10)	15	0.16
Cajun (68)	68	0.73
Danish (0)	23	0.25
Dutch (0)	61	0.66
Eastern European (44)	44	0.47
English (153)	692	7.46
European (12)	12	0.13
Finnish (0)	6	0.06
French, ex. Basque (1,130)	2,848	30.71
French Canadian (121)	231	2.49
German (603)	2,291	24.70
Greek (26)	26	0.28
Hungarian (6)	6	0.06
Icelander (16)	16	0.17
Irish (207)	1,234	13.30
Italian (678)	1,774	19.13
Norwegian (10)	47	0.51
Polish (31)	123	1.33
Portuguese (0)	20	0.22
Romanian (0)	9	0.10
Scotch-Irish (8)	45	0.49
Scottish (0)	23	0.25
Swedish (8)	34	0.37
Swiss (0)	19	0.20
Turkish (5)	5	0.05
Welsh (11)	11	0.12
West Indian, ex. Hispanic (0)	6	0.06
Haitian (0)	6	0.06

Hispanic Origin	Population	%
Hispanic or Latino (of any race)	405	4.37
Central American, ex. Mexican	119	1.28
Costa Rican	6	0.06
Guatemalan	17	0.18
Honduran	66	0.71
Nicaraguan	19	0.20
Panamanian	2	0.02
Salvadoran	8	0.09
Other Central American	1	0.01
Cuban	46	0.50
Dominican Republic	4	0.04
Mexican	103	1.11
Puerto Rican	24	0.26
South American	30	0.32
Argentinean	5	0.05
Bolivian	2	0.02
Chilean	5	0.05
Colombian	6	0.06
Ecuadorian	3	0.03
Peruvian	7	0.08
Venezuelan	2	0.02
Other Hispanic or Latino	79	0.85

Race*	Population	%
African-American/Black (203)	219	2.36
Not Hispanic (197)	212	2.29
Hispanic (6)	7	0.08
American Indian/Alaska Native (47)	74	0.80
Not Hispanic (42)	63	0.68
Hispanic (5)	11	0.12
Apache (0)	1	0.01
Blackfeet (0)	1	0.01
Cherokee (3)	6	0.06
Cheyenne (1)	3	0.03
Chickasaw (1)	1	0.01
Choctaw (0)	3	0.03
Comanche (0)	1	0.01
Creek (0)	2	0.02
Houma (20)	26	0.28
Lumbee (2)	2	0.02
Mexican American Ind. (1)	3	0.03
Seminole (0)	1	0.01
Sioux (1)	1	0.01
Asian (93)	116	1.25
Not Hispanic (93)	110	1.19
Hispanic (0)	6	0.06
Chinese, ex. Taiwanese (46)	52	0.56
Filipino (8)	16	0.17
Indian (18)	21	0.23
Japanese (0)	1	0.01
Korean (2)	6	0.06
Thai (2)	3	0.03
Vietnamese (9)	9	0.10
Hawaii Native/Pacific Islander (3)	4	0.04
Not Hispanic (3)	4	0.04
Samoan (0)	1	0.01
White (8,762)	8,841	95.30
Not Hispanic (8,468)	8,523	91.87
Hispanic (294)	318	3.43

Harvey

Place Type: CDP
Parish: Jefferson
Population: 20,348†

Ancestry‡	Population	%
African, Sub-Saharan (76)	88	0.44
African (76)	88	0.44
American (547)	547	2.75
Arab (44)	44	0.22
Arab (44)	44	0.22
Cajun (24)	38	0.19
Dutch (8)	59	0.30
English (141)	347	1.74
European (13)	13	0.07
French, ex. Basque (1,461)	3,261	16.37
French Canadian (124)	204	1.02
German (630)	1,679	8.43
Irish (329)	1,193	5.99
Italian (554)	1,480	7.43
Latvian (0)	9	0.05
Norwegian (0)	28	0.14
Portuguese (0)	14	0.07
Scotch-Irish (25)	60	0.30
Scottish (59)	86	0.43
Swedish (17)	17	0.09
Swiss (0)	8	0.04
Ukrainian (15)	32	0.16
West Indian, ex. Hispanic (197)	237	1.19
Belizean (0)	20	0.10
Haitian (51)	59	0.30
Jamaican (0)	12	0.06
Trinidadian/Tobagonian (50)	50	0.25
West Indian (75)	75	0.38
Other West Indian (21)	21	0.11

Hispanic Origin	Population	%
Hispanic or Latino (of any race)	2,732	13.43
Central American, ex. Mexican	1,119	5.50
Costa Rican	11	0.05

*Notes: † The Census 2010 population figure is used to calculate the percentages in the Hispanic Origin and Race categories. Ancestry percentages are based on the 2006-2010 American Community Survey population (not shown); ‡ Numbers in parentheses indicate the number of people reporting a single ancestry; * Numbers in parentheses indicate the number of persons reporting this race alone, not in combination with any other race; Please refer to the Explanation of Data for more information.*

Guatemalan	75	0.37
Honduran	862	4.24
Nicaraguan	87	0.43
Panamanian	7	0.03
Salvadoran	71	0.35
Other Central American	6	0.03
Cuban	155	0.76
Dominican Republic	210	1.03
Mexican	659	3.24
Puerto Rican	166	0.82
South American	57	0.28
Argentinean	4	0.02
Bolivian	1	<0.01
Chilean	4	0.02
Colombian	11	0.05
Ecuadorian	13	0.06
Paraguayan	7	0.03
Peruvian	1	<0.01
Venezuelan	16	0.08
Other Hispanic or Latino	366	1.80

Race*	Population	%
African-American/Black (8,360)	8,549	42.01
Not Hispanic (8,201)	8,342	41.00
Hispanic (159)	207	1.02
American Indian/Alaska Native (81)	206	1.01
Not Hispanic (64)	155	0.76
Hispanic (17)	51	0.25
Apache (1)	1	<0.01
Blackfeet (0)	1	<0.01
Canadian/French Am. Ind. (1)	1	<0.01
Cherokee (4)	21	0.10
Cheyenne (0)	1	<0.01
Chickasaw (1)	1	<0.01
Choctaw (3)	10	0.05
Creek (0)	1	<0.01
Houma (23)	34	0.17
Iroquois (1)	2	0.01
Mexican American Ind. (9)	12	0.06
Pueblo (0)	4	0.02
Shoshone (0)	3	0.01
Sioux (0)	1	<0.01
South American Ind. (1)	2	0.01
Tohono O'Odham (0)	3	0.01
Asian (1,378)	1,505	7.40
Not Hispanic (1,362)	1,468	7.21
Hispanic (16)	37	0.18
Cambodian (14)	16	0.08
Chinese, ex. Taiwanese (93)	103	0.51
Filipino (114)	158	0.78
Indian (30)	53	0.26
Japanese (3)	15	0.07
Korean (21)	31	0.15
Laotian (8)	9	0.04
Pakistani (7)	8	0.04
Thai (5)	8	0.04
Vietnamese (1,033)	1,081	5.31
Hawaii Native/Pacific Islander (17)	45	0.22
Not Hispanic (10)	25	0.12
Hispanic (7)	20	0.10
Guamanian/Chamorro (8)	11	0.05
Native Hawaiian (3)	9	0.04
Samoan (1)	2	0.01
White (8,860)	9,258	45.50
Not Hispanic (7,659)	7,885	38.75
Hispanic (1,201)	1,373	6.75

Houma

Place Type: City
Parish: Terrebonne
Population: 33,727†

Ancestry‡	Population	%
African, Sub-Saharan (352)	412	1.23
African (76)	136	0.40
Nigerian (276)	276	0.82
American (3,640)	3,640	10.82
Arab (31)	40	0.12
Lebanese (18)	27	0.08
Syrian (13)	13	0.04
Belgian (0)	16	0.05
British (0)	10	0.03
Cajun (434)	520	1.55
Canadian (17)	35	0.10
Czech (27)	98	0.29
Danish (0)	32	0.10
Dutch (12)	101	0.30
English (881)	1,589	4.72
European (80)	88	0.26
French, ex. Basque (4,664)	8,023	23.86
French Canadian (1,751)	2,267	6.74
German (608)	2,660	7.91
Greek (17)	65	0.19
Hungarian (39)	39	0.12
Irish (338)	1,146	3.41
Italian (434)	1,327	3.95
Norwegian (37)	69	0.21
Polish (20)	90	0.27
Portuguese (13)	69	0.21
Russian (0)	51	0.15
Scotch-Irish (73)	160	0.48
Scottish (28)	160	0.48
Serbian (0)	11	0.03
Slovak (0)	12	0.04
Swedish (0)	27	0.08
Swiss (0)	11	0.03
Welsh (0)	11	0.03
West Indian, ex. Hispanic (0)	43	0.13
Barbadian (0)	43	0.13

Hispanic Origin	Population	%
Hispanic or Latino (of any race)	1,626	4.82
Central American, ex. Mexican	301	0.89
Costa Rican	8	0.02
Guatemalan	73	0.22
Honduran	150	0.44
Nicaraguan	39	0.12
Panamanian	11	0.03
Salvadoran	16	0.05
Other Central American	4	0.01
Cuban	53	0.16
Dominican Republic	6	0.02
Mexican	973	2.88
Puerto Rican	77	0.23
South American	32	0.09
Argentinean	3	0.01
Bolivian	1	<0.01
Colombian	5	0.01
Paraguayan	3	0.01
Peruvian	10	0.03
Venezuelan	10	0.03
Other Hispanic or Latino	184	0.55

Race*	Population	%
African-American/Black (8,221)	8,521	25.26
Not Hispanic (8,196)	8,478	25.14
Hispanic (25)	43	0.13
American Indian/Alaska Native (1,341)	1,663	4.93
Not Hispanic (1,312)	1,619	4.80
Hispanic (29)	44	0.13
Alaska Athabascan *(Ala. Nat.)* (4)	4	0.01
Blackfeet (0)	3	0.01
Cherokee (23)	44	0.13
Chickasaw (2)	2	0.01
Choctaw (7)	11	0.03
Creek (2)	2	0.01
Houma (763)	885	2.62
Iroquois (1)	3	0.01
Mexican American Ind. (5)	5	0.01
Navajo (1)	1	<0.01
Seminole (3)	5	0.01
Sioux (4)	4	0.01
South American Ind. (2)	2	0.01
Spanish American Ind. (11)	11	0.03
Asian (346)	396	1.17
Not Hispanic (340)	384	1.14
Hispanic (6)	12	0.04
Burmese (1)	1	<0.01
Chinese, ex. Taiwanese (33)	41	0.12
Filipino (27)	40	0.12
Indian (81)	92	0.27
Japanese (5)	12	0.04
Korean (14)	17	0.05
Laotian (1)	2	0.01
Pakistani (16)	16	0.05
Taiwanese (2)	2	0.01
Thai (10)	10	0.03
Vietnamese (146)	150	0.44
Hawaii Native/Pacific Islander (24)	53	0.16
Not Hispanic (20)	42	0.12
Hispanic (4)	11	0.03
Guamanian/Chamorro (13)	19	0.06
Native Hawaiian (7)	15	0.04
Samoan (1)	4	0.01
White (22,245)	22,755	67.47
Not Hispanic (21,658)	22,102	65.53
Hispanic (587)	653	1.94

Jefferson

Place Type: CDP
Parish: Jefferson
Population: 11,193†

Ancestry‡	Population	%
African, Sub-Saharan (589)	652	5.41
African (589)	652	5.41
American (653)	653	5.42
Arab (5)	10	0.08
Arab (5)	5	0.04
Other Arab (0)	5	0.04
Armenian (0)	20	0.17
British (30)	40	0.33
Cajun (5)	31	0.26
Czechoslovakian (9)	9	0.07
Danish (4)	4	0.03
Dutch (7)	59	0.49
Eastern European (9)	9	0.07
English (127)	575	4.77
European (29)	29	0.24
French, ex. Basque (673)	2,573	21.36
French Canadian (78)	97	0.81
German (383)	2,086	17.32
Greek (5)	5	0.04
Irish (266)	1,337	11.10
Italian (372)	1,483	12.31
Norwegian (4)	4	0.03
Polish (17)	53	0.44
Portuguese (0)	17	0.14
Romanian (0)	15	0.12
Russian (14)	83	0.69
Scandinavian (0)	5	0.04
Scotch-Irish (29)	176	1.46
Scottish (11)	153	1.27
Swedish (0)	22	0.18
Swiss (28)	28	0.23
Turkish (0)	5	0.04
Welsh (0)	10	0.08
West Indian, ex. Hispanic (57)	86	0.71
Belizean (0)	29	0.24
British West Indian (48)	48	0.40
U.S. Virgin Islander (9)	9	0.07

Hispanic Origin	Population	%
Hispanic or Latino (of any race)	1,071	9.57
Central American, ex. Mexican	528	4.72
Costa Rican	16	0.14
Guatemalan	44	0.39
Honduran	274	2.45
Nicaraguan	72	0.64
Panamanian	8	0.07
Salvadoran	114	1.02
Cuban	56	0.50
Dominican Republic	9	0.08
Mexican	239	2.14
Puerto Rican	44	0.39
South American	56	0.50
Argentinean	5	0.04
Chilean	7	0.06

*Notes: † The Census 2010 population figure is used to calculate the percentages in the Hispanic Origin and Race categories. Ancestry percentages are based on the 2006-2010 American Community Survey population (not shown); ‡ Numbers in parentheses indicate the number of people reporting a single ancestry; * Numbers in parentheses indicate the number of persons reporting this race alone, not in combination with any other race; Please refer to the Explanation of Data for more information.*

Colombian	18	0.16
Ecuadorian	11	0.10
Peruvian	5	0.04
Uruguayan	2	0.02
Venezuelan	8	0.07
Other Hispanic or Latino	139	1.24

Race*	Population	%
African-American/Black (2,848)	2,909	25.99
Not Hispanic (2,811)	2,863	25.58
Hispanic (37)	46	0.41
American Indian/Alaska Native (40)	100	0.89
Not Hispanic (31)	75	0.67
Hispanic (9)	25	0.22
Apache (0)	1	0.01
Blackfeet (0)	1	0.01
Canadian/French Am. Ind. (0)	2	0.02
Central American Ind. (0)	6	0.05
Cherokee (5)	20	0.18
Chickasaw (0)	2	0.02
Chippewa (1)	1	0.01
Choctaw (0)	4	0.04
Creek (1)	1	0.01
Crow (1)	1	0.01
Houma (11)	13	0.12
Iroquois (3)	3	0.03
Lumbee (1)	1	0.01
Mexican American Ind. (3)	6	0.05
Sioux (1)	1	0.01
Asian (156)	192	1.72
Not Hispanic (150)	178	1.59
Hispanic (6)	14	0.13
Burmese (0)	2	0.02
Cambodian (5)	5	0.04
Chinese, ex. Taiwanese (23)	26	0.23
Filipino (45)	57	0.51
Indian (43)	49	0.44
Indonesian (1)	3	0.03
Japanese (7)	11	0.10
Korean (3)	4	0.04
Laotian (0)	4	0.04
Malaysian (2)	3	0.03
Pakistani (4)	4	0.04
Taiwanese (3)	3	0.03
Thai (6)	7	0.06
Vietnamese (13)	13	0.12
Hawaii Native/Pacific Islander (6)	18	0.16
Not Hispanic (6)	10	0.09
Hispanic (0)	8	0.07
Guamanian/Chamorro (2)	3	0.03
Native Hawaiian (4)	7	0.06
Samoan (0)	1	0.01
White (7,591)	7,747	69.21
Not Hispanic (6,995)	7,091	63.35
Hispanic (596)	656	5.86

Jennings

Place Type: City
Parish: Jefferson Davis
Population: 10,383†

Ancestry‡	Population	%
American (745)	745	7.12
British (36)	36	0.34
Cajun (358)	433	4.14
Canadian (22)	22	0.21
Dutch (0)	60	0.57
English (247)	539	5.15
European (105)	105	1.00
French, ex. Basque (1,210)	2,241	21.42
French Canadian (453)	555	5.30
German (288)	1,058	10.11
Irish (129)	416	3.98
Italian (18)	47	0.45
Norwegian (0)	16	0.15
Polish (48)	125	1.19
Scotch-Irish (40)	49	0.47
Scottish (12)	12	0.11
Swedish (16)	27	0.26

Hispanic Origin	Population	%
Hispanic or Latino (of any race)	200	1.93
Central American, ex. Mexican	15	0.14
Honduran	4	0.04
Nicaraguan	5	0.05
Salvadoran	6	0.06
Cuban	5	0.05
Dominican Republic	3	0.03
Mexican	119	1.15
Puerto Rican	23	0.22
South American	9	0.09
Colombian	1	0.01
Venezuelan	8	0.08
Other Hispanic or Latino	26	0.25

Race*	Population	%
African-American/Black (2,949)	3,076	29.63
Not Hispanic (2,943)	3,062	29.49
Hispanic (6)	14	0.13
American Indian/Alaska Native (32)	79	0.76
Not Hispanic (31)	74	0.71
Hispanic (1)	5	0.05
Aleut *(Alaska Native)* (0)	4	0.04
Apache (1)	1	0.01
Blackfeet (0)	1	0.01
Cherokee (7)	20	0.19
Cheyenne (0)	1	0.01
Choctaw (0)	2	0.02
Houma (2)	3	0.03
Kiowa (0)	1	0.01
Lumbee (0)	1	0.01
Asian (25)	39	0.38
Not Hispanic (25)	39	0.38
Bangladeshi (0)	2	0.02
Chinese, ex. Taiwanese (2)	5	0.05
Filipino (5)	7	0.07
Indian (9)	9	0.09
Japanese (0)	1	0.01
Korean (3)	9	0.09
Taiwanese (1)	1	0.01
Vietnamese (3)	6	0.06
Hawaii Native/Pacific Islander (2)	8	0.08
Not Hispanic (2)	7	0.07
Hispanic (0)	1	0.01
Native Hawaiian (2)	3	0.03
White (7,107)	7,295	70.26
Not Hispanic (7,006)	7,172	69.07
Hispanic (101)	123	1.18

Kenner

Place Type: City
Parish: Jefferson
Population: 66,702†

Ancestry‡	Population	%
African, Sub-Saharan (822)	951	1.43
African (734)	863	1.29
Kenyan (37)	37	0.06
Nigerian (51)	51	0.08
American (2,129)	2,129	3.19
Arab (786)	922	1.38
Arab (189)	238	0.36
Egyptian (36)	64	0.10
Iraqi (309)	309	0.46
Jordanian (123)	123	0.18
Lebanese (75)	89	0.13
Moroccan (22)	22	0.03
Palestinian (13)	13	0.02
Syrian (19)	64	0.10
Armenian (6)	6	0.01
Austrian (0)	28	0.04
Basque (0)	7	0.01
Belgian (0)	16	0.02
Brazilian (120)	151	0.23
British (42)	162	0.24
Cajun (374)	380	0.57
Canadian (25)	39	0.06
Croatian (33)	114	0.17
Czech (28)	61	0.09
Czechoslovakian (9)	92	0.14
Danish (27)	105	0.16
Dutch (84)	266	0.40
Eastern European (30)	30	0.05
English (1,170)	3,591	5.39
European (273)	299	0.45
Finnish (14)	14	0.02
French, ex. Basque (3,990)	11,139	16.71
French Canadian (306)	425	0.64
German (1,715)	7,313	10.97
Greek (21)	218	0.33
Hungarian (8)	123	0.18
Iranian (209)	282	0.42
Irish (1,440)	5,630	8.45
Israeli (12)	12	0.02
Italian (3,466)	8,342	12.52
Lithuanian (0)	10	0.02
Macedonian (16)	16	0.02
New Zealander (0)	14	0.02
Norwegian (33)	90	0.14
Polish (191)	256	0.38
Portuguese (0)	69	0.10
Romanian (0)	11	0.02
Russian (68)	268	0.40
Scotch-Irish (227)	512	0.77
Scottish (148)	350	0.53
Serbian (13)	13	0.02
Slavic (15)	24	0.04
Slovak (7)	33	0.05
Swedish (123)	273	0.41
Swiss (0)	53	0.08
Turkish (0)	86	0.13
Ukrainian (15)	25	0.04
Welsh (54)	131	0.20
West Indian, ex. Hispanic (200)	354	0.53
Belizean (48)	153	0.23
Haitian (152)	152	0.23
Jamaican (0)	49	0.07
Yugoslavian (15)	52	0.08

Hispanic Origin	Population	%
Hispanic or Latino (of any race)	14,918	22.37
Central American, ex. Mexican	8,641	12.95
Costa Rican	158	0.24
Guatemalan	844	1.27
Honduran	5,556	8.33
Nicaraguan	1,306	1.96
Panamanian	62	0.09
Salvadoran	679	1.02
Other Central American	36	0.05
Cuban	1,101	1.65
Dominican Republic	287	0.43
Mexican	2,214	3.32
Puerto Rican	617	0.93
South American	538	0.81
Argentinean	30	0.04
Bolivian	14	0.02
Chilean	27	0.04
Colombian	181	0.27
Ecuadorian	106	0.16
Paraguayan	1	<0.01
Peruvian	64	0.10
Uruguayan	14	0.02
Venezuelan	101	0.15
Other Hispanic or Latino	1,520	2.28

Race*	Population	%
African-American/Black (15,994)	16,468	24.69
Not Hispanic (15,650)	15,977	23.95
Hispanic (344)	491	0.74
American Indian/Alaska Native (248)	518	0.78
Not Hispanic (147)	313	0.47
Hispanic (101)	205	0.31
Apache (0)	6	0.01
Blackfeet (1)	2	<0.01
Canadian/French Am. Ind. (1)	1	<0.01
Central American Ind. (11)	23	0.03
Cherokee (24)	62	0.09
Chickasaw (4)	5	0.01
Chippewa (5)	6	0.01

*Notes: † The Census 2010 population figure is used to calculate the percentages in the Hispanic Origin and Race categories. Ancestry percentages are based on the 2006-2010 American Community Survey population (not shown); ‡ Numbers in parentheses indicate the number of people reporting a single ancestry; * Numbers in parentheses indicate the number of persons reporting this race alone, not in combination with any other race; Please refer to the Explanation of Data for more information.*

Choctaw (13)	29	0.04
Comanche (0)	1	<0.01
Creek (1)	1	<0.01
Crow (1)	4	0.01
Delaware (0)	3	<0.01
Houma (26)	38	0.06
Lumbee (1)	2	<0.01
Mexican American Ind. (10)	18	0.03
Navajo (5)	6	0.01
Potawatomi (0)	1	<0.01
Seminole (0)	5	0.01
Sioux (3)	6	0.01
South American Ind. (4)	5	0.01
Spanish American Ind. (13)	23	0.03
Tlingit-Haida *(Alaska Native)* (0)	1	<0.01
Ute (0)	1	<0.01
Asian (2,461)	2,864	4.29
Not Hispanic (2,434)	2,760	4.14
Hispanic (27)	104	0.16
Bangladeshi (45)	46	0.07
Burmese (6)	7	0.01
Cambodian (16)	22	0.03
Chinese, ex. Taiwanese (328)	376	0.56
Filipino (244)	331	0.50
Hmong (2)	2	<0.01
Indian (644)	722	1.08
Indonesian (8)	12	0.02
Japanese (30)	53	0.08
Korean (78)	98	0.15
Laotian (3)	4	0.01
Malaysian (1)	2	<0.01
Nepalese (1)	1	<0.01
Pakistani (363)	390	0.58
Sri Lankan (13)	16	0.02
Taiwanese (42)	43	0.06
Thai (9)	13	0.02
Vietnamese (531)	576	0.86
Hawaii Native/Pacific Islander (24)	75	0.11
Not Hispanic (15)	35	0.05
Hispanic (9)	40	0.06
Guamanian/Chamorro (10)	19	0.03
Native Hawaiian (12)	17	0.03
Samoan (0)	5	0.01
White (41,102)	42,519	63.74
Not Hispanic (32,564)	33,227	49.81
Hispanic (8,538)	9,292	13.93

Lacombe

Place Type: CDP
Parish: St. Tammany
Population: 8,679†

Ancestry‡	Population	%
African, Sub-Saharan (0)	224	2.89
African (0)	224	2.89
American (527)	527	6.79
Arab (0)	30	0.39
Lebanese (0)	30	0.39
British (51)	65	0.84
Bulgarian (18)	18	0.23
Cajun (145)	210	2.71
Canadian (0)	13	0.17
Czech (12)	12	0.15
Danish (42)	51	0.66
Dutch (0)	9	0.12
English (42)	204	2.63
French, ex. Basque (352)	1,522	19.61
French Canadian (178)	199	2.56
German (305)	1,108	14.27
Irish (220)	797	10.27
Italian (247)	777	10.01
Northern European (22)	22	0.28
Norwegian (23)	23	0.30
Polish (18)	61	0.79
Romanian (15)	15	0.19
Scotch-Irish (24)	95	1.22
Scottish (53)	63	0.81
Slavic (0)	9	0.12
Slovak (0)	13	0.17
Swedish (15)	15	0.19
Welsh (20)	42	0.54

Hispanic Origin	Population	%
Hispanic or Latino (of any race)	363	4.18
Central American, ex. Mexican	87	1.00
Costa Rican	6	0.07
Guatemalan	6	0.07
Honduran	58	0.67
Nicaraguan	3	0.03
Panamanian	3	0.03
Salvadoran	11	0.13
Cuban	34	0.39
Dominican Republic	2	0.02
Mexican	92	1.06
Puerto Rican	46	0.53
South American	10	0.12
Argentinean	2	0.02
Colombian	6	0.07
Peruvian	2	0.02
Other Hispanic or Latino	92	1.06

Race*	Population	%
African-American/Black (2,077)	2,225	25.64
Not Hispanic (2,054)	2,181	25.13
Hispanic (23)	44	0.51
American Indian/Alaska Native (80)	194	2.24
Not Hispanic (72)	174	2.00
Hispanic (8)	20	0.23
Apache (2)	2	0.02
Canadian/French Am. Ind. (4)	4	0.05
Cherokee (6)	33	0.38
Chickasaw (3)	3	0.03
Choctaw (9)	23	0.27
Comanche (3)	3	0.03
Creek (5)	8	0.09
Crow (0)	4	0.05
Houma (2)	4	0.05
Shoshone (0)	2	0.02
Sioux (2)	10	0.12
Asian (49)	70	0.81
Not Hispanic (48)	66	0.76
Hispanic (1)	4	0.05
Chinese, ex. Taiwanese (5)	6	0.07
Filipino (13)	26	0.30
Indian (13)	14	0.16
Japanese (2)	3	0.03
Korean (2)	2	0.02
Thai (2)	6	0.07
Vietnamese (12)	12	0.14
Hawaii Native/Pacific Islander (0)	6	0.07
Not Hispanic (0)	2	0.02
Hispanic (0)	4	0.05
Native Hawaiian (0)	2	0.02
White (5,997)	6,198	71.41
Not Hispanic (5,827)	5,986	68.97
Hispanic (170)	212	2.44

Lafayette

Place Type: City
Parish: Lafayette
Population: 120,623†

Ancestry‡	Population	%
African, Sub-Saharan (341)	421	0.35
African (182)	262	0.22
Liberian (50)	50	0.04
Nigerian (109)	109	0.09
American (6,934)	6,934	5.84
Arab (838)	1,481	1.25
Arab (142)	173	0.15
Egyptian (27)	55	0.05
Jordanian (49)	49	0.04
Lebanese (378)	897	0.76
Moroccan (12)	12	0.01
Syrian (119)	158	0.13
Other Arab (111)	137	0.12
Australian (28)	42	0.04
Austrian (42)	169	0.14
Basque (13)	28	0.02
Belgian (35)	148	0.12
Brazilian (43)	114	0.10
British (131)	227	0.19
Cajun (2,407)	3,304	2.78
Canadian (79)	161	0.14
Celtic (12)	12	0.01
Czech (103)	338	0.28
Czechoslovakian (54)	73	0.06
Danish (46)	115	0.10
Dutch (178)	751	0.63
Eastern European (14)	14	0.01
English (2,969)	7,464	6.28
European (531)	587	0.49
French, ex. Basque (14,942)	27,086	22.80
French Canadian (3,697)	4,911	4.13
German (2,878)	11,182	9.41
Greek (118)	327	0.28
Guyanese (0)	11	0.01
Hungarian (47)	143	0.12
Iranian (41)	117	0.10
Irish (1,623)	6,929	5.83
Israeli (21)	21	0.02
Italian (1,671)	4,893	4.12
Latvian (37)	37	0.03
Lithuanian (0)	134	0.11
Northern European (10)	10	0.01
Norwegian (92)	284	0.24
Polish (299)	822	0.69
Portuguese (34)	211	0.18
Romanian (11)	55	0.05
Russian (240)	486	0.41
Scandinavian (23)	33	0.03
Scotch-Irish (385)	1,061	0.89
Scottish (427)	1,284	1.08
Slavic (18)	38	0.03
Slovak (0)	21	0.02
Swedish (130)	592	0.50
Swiss (10)	54	0.05
Ukrainian (104)	104	0.09
Welsh (60)	298	0.25
West Indian, ex. Hispanic (46)	71	0.06
Barbadian (0)	11	0.01
Haitian (29)	29	0.02
Trinidadian/Tobagonian (0)	14	0.01
U.S. Virgin Islander (17)	17	0.01
Yugoslavian (29)	52	0.04

Hispanic Origin	Population	%
Hispanic or Latino (of any race)	4,531	3.76
Central American, ex. Mexican	727	0.60
Costa Rican	10	0.01
Guatemalan	191	0.16
Honduran	312	0.26
Nicaraguan	53	0.04
Panamanian	49	0.04
Salvadoran	108	0.09
Other Central American	4	<0.01
Cuban	444	0.37
Dominican Republic	55	0.05
Mexican	1,904	1.58
Puerto Rican	312	0.26
South American	416	0.34
Argentinean	29	0.02
Bolivian	12	0.01
Chilean	25	0.02
Colombian	126	0.10
Ecuadorian	25	0.02
Paraguayan	6	<0.01
Peruvian	57	0.05
Venezuelan	135	0.11
Other South American	1	<0.01
Other Hispanic or Latino	673	0.56

Race*	Population	%
African-American/Black (37,530)	38,528	31.94
Not Hispanic (37,255)	38,148	31.63
Hispanic (275)	380	0.32
American Indian/Alaska Native (389)	910	0.75
Not Hispanic (350)	787	0.65

*Notes: † The Census 2010 population figure is used to calculate the percentages in the Hispanic Origin and Race categories. Ancestry percentages are based on the 2006-2010 American Community Survey population (not shown); ‡ Numbers in parentheses indicate the number of people reporting a single ancestry; * Numbers in parentheses indicate the number of persons reporting this race alone, not in combination with any other race; Please refer to the Explanation of Data for more information.*

Hispanic (39)	123	0.10
Apache (5)	8	0.01
Arapaho (1)	1	<0.01
Blackfeet (2)	15	0.01
Canadian/French Am. Ind. (0)	1	<0.01
Cherokee (28)	108	0.09
Chickasaw (5)	8	0.01
Chippewa (6)	11	0.01
Choctaw (15)	61	0.05
Cree (0)	1	<0.01
Creek (14)	22	0.02
Delaware (2)	3	<0.01
Houma (64)	79	0.07
Iroquois (1)	4	<0.01
Menominee (1)	1	<0.01
Mexican American Ind. (1)	9	0.01
Navajo (6)	9	0.01
Osage (3)	8	0.01
Paiute (0)	1	<0.01
Potawatomi (3)	4	<0.01
Pueblo (3)	3	<0.01
Sioux (6)	18	0.01
South American Ind. (0)	3	<0.01
Tlingit-Haida *(Alaska Native)* (0)	3	<0.01
Yaqui (1)	1	<0.01
Asian (2,180)	2,580	2.14
Not Hispanic (2,162)	2,540	2.11
Hispanic (18)	40	0.03
Bangladeshi (17)	22	0.02
Burmese (6)	6	<0.01
Cambodian (7)	8	0.01
Chinese, ex. Taiwanese (399)	440	0.36
Filipino (144)	210	0.17
Hmong (3)	3	<0.01
Indian (536)	575	0.48
Indonesian (16)	34	0.03
Japanese (30)	79	0.07
Korean (69)	102	0.08
Laotian (38)	48	0.04
Malaysian (12)	16	0.01
Nepalese (26)	27	0.02
Pakistani (60)	66	0.05
Sri Lankan (1)	1	<0.01
Taiwanese (21)	25	0.02
Thai (28)	38	0.03
Vietnamese (663)	705	0.58
Hawaii Native/Pacific Islander (45)	124	0.10
Not Hispanic (29)	93	0.08
Hispanic (16)	31	0.03
Fijian (2)	2	<0.01
Guamanian/Chamorro (15)	30	0.02
Marshallese (0)	4	<0.01
Native Hawaiian (12)	35	0.03
Samoan (6)	11	0.01
White (76,937)	78,676	65.22
Not Hispanic (74,424)	75,835	62.87
Hispanic (2,513)	2,841	2.36

Lake Charles

Place Type: City
Parish: Calcasieu
Population: 71,993†

Ancestry‡	Population	%
African, Sub-Saharan (320)	498	0.70
African (275)	444	0.62
Kenyan (0)	9	0.01
Nigerian (16)	16	0.02
South African (29)	29	0.04
American (3,670)	3,670	5.15
Arab (115)	251	0.35
Arab (46)	46	0.06
Lebanese (49)	185	0.26
Syrian (20)	20	0.03
Austrian (0)	23	0.03
Belgian (0)	15	0.02
British (35)	121	0.17
Cajun (696)	1,050	1.47
Canadian (78)	165	0.23
Celtic (0)	37	0.05
Croatian (0)	10	0.01
Czech (27)	65	0.09
Danish (32)	46	0.06
Dutch (66)	504	0.71
English (1,794)	4,737	6.65
European (220)	266	0.37
French, ex. Basque (3,675)	8,608	12.09
French Canadian (1,902)	2,800	3.93
German (1,601)	4,851	6.81
Greek (49)	90	0.13
Hungarian (0)	32	0.04
Irish (1,500)	4,765	6.69
Italian (776)	2,363	3.32
Lithuanian (14)	49	0.07
Norwegian (61)	217	0.30
Polish (113)	197	0.28
Portuguese (85)	266	0.37
Romanian (66)	66	0.09
Russian (25)	62	0.09
Scandinavian (0)	23	0.03
Scotch-Irish (546)	1,157	1.62
Scottish (194)	658	0.92
Serbian (0)	21	0.03
Slavic (0)	6	0.01
Slovak (0)	20	0.03
Swedish (21)	130	0.18
Swiss (15)	28	0.04
Turkish (52)	52	0.07
Ukrainian (26)	38	0.05
Welsh (29)	122	0.17
West Indian, ex. Hispanic (138)	227	0.32
Dutch West Indian (13)	13	0.02
Jamaican (72)	146	0.20
Trinidadian/Tobagonian (36)	51	0.07
West Indian (17)	17	0.02

Hispanic Origin	Population	%
Hispanic or Latino (of any race)	2,069	2.87
Central American, ex. Mexican	217	0.30
Costa Rican	4	0.01
Guatemalan	36	0.05
Honduran	91	0.13
Nicaraguan	9	0.01
Panamanian	37	0.05
Salvadoran	38	0.05
Other Central American	2	<0.01
Cuban	78	0.11
Dominican Republic	9	0.01
Mexican	995	1.38
Puerto Rican	215	0.30
South American	204	0.28
Argentinean	5	0.01
Bolivian	13	0.02
Chilean	4	0.01
Colombian	76	0.11
Ecuadorian	24	0.03
Peruvian	40	0.06
Uruguayan	1	<0.01
Venezuelan	39	0.05
Other South American	2	<0.01
Other Hispanic or Latino	351	0.49

Race*	Population	%
African-American/Black (34,319)	35,336	49.08
Not Hispanic (34,120)	35,022	48.65
Hispanic (199)	314	0.44
American Indian/Alaska Native (294)	768	1.07
Not Hispanic (272)	681	0.95
Hispanic (22)	87	0.12
Alaska Athabascan *(Ala. Nat.)* (0)	2	<0.01
Apache (9)	12	0.02
Blackfeet (3)	18	0.03
Canadian/French Am. Ind. (1)	3	<0.01
Cherokee (30)	105	0.15
Chickasaw (4)	5	0.01
Chippewa (7)	7	0.01
Choctaw (22)	54	0.08
Cree (2)	2	<0.01
Creek (0)	4	0.01
Delaware (0)	1	<0.01
Houma (6)	10	0.01
Inupiat *(Alaska Native)* (1)	1	<0.01
Iroquois (1)	1	<0.01
Lumbee (2)	3	<0.01
Mexican American Ind. (12)	15	0.02
Navajo (8)	8	0.01
Ottawa (3)	3	<0.01
Potawatomi (0)	1	<0.01
Pueblo (1)	1	<0.01
Shoshone (0)	1	<0.01
Sioux (1)	3	<0.01
South American Ind. (1)	1	<0.01
Spanish American Ind. (1)	1	<0.01
Yaqui (1)	1	<0.01
Asian (1,193)	1,394	1.94
Not Hispanic (1,184)	1,364	1.89
Hispanic (9)	30	0.04
Bangladeshi (23)	24	0.03
Burmese (1)	1	<0.01
Cambodian (3)	3	<0.01
Chinese, ex. Taiwanese (206)	241	0.33
Filipino (85)	152	0.21
Indian (270)	291	0.40
Indonesian (23)	27	0.04
Japanese (16)	36	0.05
Korean (62)	81	0.11
Laotian (2)	4	0.01
Malaysian (1)	2	<0.01
Nepalese (19)	22	0.03
Pakistani (117)	120	0.17
Taiwanese (23)	23	0.03
Thai (20)	31	0.04
Vietnamese (255)	263	0.37
Hawaii Native/Pacific Islander (27)	89	0.12
Not Hispanic (21)	72	0.10
Hispanic (6)	17	0.02
Guamanian/Chamorro (14)	20	0.03
Marshallese (1)	1	<0.01
Native Hawaiian (11)	38	0.05
Samoan (1)	6	0.01
White (33,820)	34,856	48.42
Not Hispanic (32,793)	33,671	46.77
Hispanic (1,027)	1,185	1.65

Laplace

Place Type: CDP
Parish: St. John the Baptist
Population: 29,872†

Ancestry‡	Population	%
African, Sub-Saharan (476)	476	1.52
African (467)	467	1.49
Cape Verdean (9)	9	0.03
American (1,207)	1,207	3.85
Arab (0)	18	0.06
Lebanese (0)	18	0.06
British (0)	30	0.10
Cajun (94)	128	0.41
Canadian (0)	12	0.04
Croatian (12)	12	0.04
Czech (0)	26	0.08
Danish (5)	5	0.02
Dutch (51)	120	0.38
English (385)	933	2.98
European (67)	86	0.27
French, ex. Basque (1,724)	4,503	14.38
French Canadian (328)	405	1.29
German (836)	3,230	10.31
Greek (15)	15	0.05
Hungarian (142)	162	0.52
Irish (358)	1,295	4.13
Italian (646)	2,028	6.47
Luxemburger (14)	14	0.04
Norwegian (25)	54	0.17
Polish (13)	59	0.19
Portuguese (0)	52	0.17
Russian (0)	53	0.17
Scandinavian (0)	26	0.08

*Notes: † The Census 2010 population figure is used to calculate the percentages in the Hispanic Origin and Race categories. Ancestry percentages are based on the 2006-2010 American Community Survey population (not shown); ‡ Numbers in parentheses indicate the number of people reporting a single ancestry; * Numbers in parentheses indicate the number of persons reporting this race alone, not in combination with any other race; Please refer to the Explanation of Data for more information.*

Ancestry	Population	%
Scotch-Irish (153)	252	0.80
Scottish (22)	91	0.29
Slovak (30)	50	0.16
Swedish (20)	59	0.19
Swiss (0)	17	0.05
Ukrainian (6)	6	0.02
Welsh (11)	34	0.11
West Indian, ex. Hispanic (56)	56	0.18
Belizean (7)	7	0.02
British West Indian (11)	11	0.04
Jamaican (38)	38	0.12
Yugoslavian (12)	12	0.04

Hispanic Origin	Population	%
Hispanic or Latino (of any race)	1,829	6.12
Central American, ex. Mexican	678	2.27
Costa Rican	8	0.03
Guatemalan	110	0.37
Honduran	427	1.43
Nicaraguan	86	0.29
Panamanian	13	0.04
Salvadoran	32	0.11
Other Central American	2	0.01
Cuban	105	0.35
Dominican Republic	64	0.21
Mexican	531	1.78
Puerto Rican	126	0.42
South American	58	0.19
Argentinean	1	<0.01
Chilean	5	0.02
Colombian	21	0.07
Ecuadorian	1	<0.01
Peruvian	19	0.06
Venezuelan	11	0.04
Other Hispanic or Latino	267	0.89

Race*	Population	%
African-American/Black (14,303)	14,574	48.79
Not Hispanic (14,176)	14,392	48.18
Hispanic (127)	182	0.61
American Indian/Alaska Native (112)	227	0.76
Not Hispanic (91)	185	0.62
Hispanic (21)	42	0.14
Apache (1)	1	<0.01
Central American Ind. (1)	1	<0.01
Cherokee (11)	27	0.09
Choctaw (4)	10	0.03
Creek (3)	5	0.02
Houma (20)	35	0.12
Mexican American Ind. (3)	4	0.01
Navajo (3)	6	0.02
Potawatomi (1)	1	<0.01
Seminole (0)	1	<0.01
Sioux (0)	1	<0.01
Asian (284)	393	1.32
Not Hispanic (274)	365	1.22
Hispanic (10)	28	0.09
Cambodian (8)	8	0.03
Chinese, ex. Taiwanese (36)	58	0.19
Filipino (57)	85	0.28
Hmong (1)	1	<0.01
Indian (69)	96	0.32
Japanese (9)	19	0.06
Korean (10)	17	0.06
Laotian (5)	7	0.02
Pakistani (3)	4	0.01
Thai (1)	1	<0.01
Vietnamese (79)	82	0.27
Hawaii Native/Pacific Islander (18)	37	0.12
Not Hispanic (17)	30	0.10
Hispanic (1)	7	0.02
Guamanian/Chamorro (4)	8	0.03
Native Hawaiian (7)	12	0.04
Samoan (3)	9	0.03
Tongan (2)	2	0.01
White (14,041)	14,437	48.33
Not Hispanic (13,094)	13,390	44.82
Hispanic (947)	1,047	3.50

Luling

Place Type: CDP
Parish: St. Charles
Population: 12,119†

Ancestry‡	Population	%
American (743)	743	5.79
Arab (54)	54	0.42
Arab (7)	7	0.05
Egyptian (47)	47	0.37
Belgian (7)	7	0.05
Brazilian (0)	21	0.16
British (30)	37	0.29
Cajun (117)	117	0.91
Croatian (126)	126	0.98
Czech (11)	11	0.09
Danish (0)	16	0.12
Dutch (32)	86	0.67
English (360)	664	5.18
European (75)	75	0.58
French, ex. Basque (1,148)	3,245	25.30
French Canadian (235)	311	2.42
German (346)	1,750	13.64
Greek (0)	12	0.09
Irish (200)	822	6.41
Italian (459)	1,168	9.11
Norwegian (180)	207	1.61
Polish (35)	45	0.35
Portuguese (0)	12	0.09
Russian (0)	16	0.12
Scandinavian (16)	58	0.45
Scotch-Irish (61)	148	1.15
Scottish (100)	223	1.74
Slovak (11)	11	0.09
Swedish (21)	80	0.62
Welsh (0)	51	0.40

Hispanic Origin	Population	%
Hispanic or Latino (of any race)	533	4.40
Central American, ex. Mexican	104	0.86
Costa Rican	5	0.04
Guatemalan	11	0.09
Honduran	72	0.59
Nicaraguan	6	0.05
Panamanian	2	0.02
Salvadoran	8	0.07
Cuban	27	0.22
Dominican Republic	31	0.26
Mexican	214	1.77
Puerto Rican	50	0.41
South American	25	0.21
Argentinean	1	0.01
Colombian	8	0.07
Ecuadorian	9	0.07
Peruvian	3	0.02
Venezuelan	4	0.03
Other Hispanic or Latino	82	0.68

Race*	Population	%
African-American/Black (1,968)	2,069	17.07
Not Hispanic (1,949)	2,029	16.74
Hispanic (19)	40	0.33
American Indian/Alaska Native (34)	116	0.96
Not Hispanic (29)	92	0.76
Hispanic (5)	24	0.20
Apache (3)	3	0.02
Canadian/French Am. Ind. (0)	2	0.02
Cherokee (1)	7	0.06
Cheyenne (0)	1	0.01
Chickasaw (1)	2	0.02
Chippewa (0)	2	0.02
Choctaw (1)	10	0.08
Creek (2)	2	0.02
Houma (6)	19	0.16
Iroquois (1)	2	0.02
Kiowa (0)	1	0.01
Mexican American Ind. (0)	4	0.03
Osage (0)	1	0.01
Ottawa (0)	1	0.01
South American Ind. (0)	2	0.02
Tlingit-Haida *(Alaska Native)* (0)	1	0.01
Asian (113)	154	1.27
Not Hispanic (112)	147	1.21
Hispanic (1)	7	0.06
Chinese, ex. Taiwanese (30)	41	0.34
Filipino (14)	32	0.26
Hmong (1)	3	0.02
Indian (21)	27	0.22
Japanese (5)	10	0.08
Korean (7)	9	0.07
Pakistani (1)	1	0.01
Thai (2)	3	0.02
Vietnamese (25)	33	0.27
Hawaii Native/Pacific Islander (3)	6	0.05
Not Hispanic (1)	3	0.02
Hispanic (2)	3	0.02
Guamanian/Chamorro (1)	2	0.02
Native Hawaiian (2)	4	0.03
White (9,632)	9,844	81.23
Not Hispanic (9,329)	9,479	78.22
Hispanic (303)	365	3.01

Mandeville

Place Type: City
Parish: St. Tammany
Population: 11,560†

Ancestry‡	Population	%
Alsatian (18)	37	0.32
American (672)	672	5.85
Arab (0)	18	0.16
Lebanese (0)	9	0.08
Syrian (0)	9	0.08
British (40)	53	0.46
Cajun (14)	65	0.57
Canadian (19)	19	0.17
Czech (0)	14	0.12
Czechoslovakian (0)	15	0.13
Danish (0)	9	0.08
Dutch (92)	252	2.19
English (543)	1,624	14.14
European (156)	209	1.82
Finnish (0)	12	0.10
French, ex. Basque (411)	1,906	16.60
French Canadian (146)	296	2.58
German (602)	2,146	18.69
Irish (334)	1,762	15.34
Italian (381)	1,328	11.56
Lithuanian (0)	32	0.28
Northern European (17)	17	0.15
Norwegian (23)	88	0.77
Polish (13)	66	0.57
Portuguese (14)	14	0.12
Romanian (0)	12	0.10
Russian (20)	76	0.66
Scotch-Irish (140)	207	1.80
Scottish (89)	346	3.01
Swedish (19)	123	1.07
Swiss (0)	10	0.09
Welsh (14)	84	0.73
Yugoslavian (0)	86	0.75

Hispanic Origin	Population	%
Hispanic or Latino (of any race)	608	5.26
Central American, ex. Mexican	155	1.34
Costa Rican	4	0.03
Guatemalan	36	0.31
Honduran	91	0.79
Nicaraguan	20	0.17
Panamanian	1	0.01
Salvadoran	3	0.03
Cuban	44	0.38
Dominican Republic	3	0.03
Mexican	229	1.98
Puerto Rican	38	0.33
South American	43	0.37
Argentinean	3	0.03
Colombian	15	0.13

*Notes: † The Census 2010 population figure is used to calculate the percentages in the Hispanic Origin and Race categories. Ancestry percentages are based on the 2006-2010 American Community Survey population (not shown); ‡ Numbers in parentheses indicate the number of people reporting a single ancestry; * Numbers in parentheses indicate the number of persons reporting this race alone, not in combination with any other race; Please refer to the Explanation of Data for more information.*

Ecuadorian	9	0.08
Paraguayan	1	0.01
Peruvian	5	0.04
Venezuelan	10	0.09
Other Hispanic or Latino	96	0.83

Race*	Population	%
African-American/Black (509)	568	4.91
Not Hispanic (504)	552	4.78
Hispanic (5)	16	0.14
American Indian/Alaska Native (36)	98	0.85
Not Hispanic (30)	86	0.74
Hispanic (6)	12	0.10
Alaska Athabascan *(Ala. Nat.)* (1)	2	0.02
Blackfeet (0)	1	0.01
Cherokee (2)	13	0.11
Choctaw (2)	13	0.11
Comanche (1)	1	0.01
Creek (1)	3	0.03
Houma (3)	5	0.04
Kiowa (0)	3	0.03
Mexican American Ind. (1)	2	0.02
Osage (1)	1	0.01
Sioux (0)	3	0.03
South American Ind. (1)	1	0.01
Asian (223)	277	2.40
Not Hispanic (220)	267	2.31
Hispanic (3)	10	0.09
Burmese (21)	21	0.18
Cambodian (1)	2	0.02
Chinese, ex. Taiwanese (69)	74	0.64
Filipino (16)	39	0.34
Indian (56)	74	0.64
Indonesian (4)	4	0.03
Japanese (9)	14	0.12
Korean (6)	8	0.07
Pakistani (19)	28	0.24
Thai (3)	3	0.03
Vietnamese (9)	14	0.12
Hawaii Native/Pacific Islander (1)	10	0.09
Not Hispanic (0)	8	0.07
Hispanic (1)	2	0.02
Guamanian/Chamorro (0)	2	0.02
Native Hawaiian (0)	6	0.05
Samoan (1)	1	0.01
White (10,468)	10,644	92.08
Not Hispanic (10,039)	10,174	88.01
Hispanic (429)	470	4.07

Marrero

Place Type: CDP
Parish: Jefferson
Population: 33,141†

Ancestry‡	Population	%
African, Sub-Saharan (20)	67	0.20
African (20)	67	0.20
Albanian (0)	12	0.04
American (544)	544	1.65
Austrian (11)	11	0.03
British (0)	10	0.03
Cajun (85)	104	0.32
Czech (17)	17	0.05
Danish (8)	25	0.08
Dutch (0)	24	0.07
English (358)	713	2.17
European (37)	37	0.11
French, ex. Basque (4,028)	7,170	21.77
French Canadian (234)	299	0.91
German (370)	2,037	6.19
Greek (0)	20	0.06
Irish (225)	1,262	3.83
Italian (732)	2,061	6.26
Northern European (9)	9	0.03
Norwegian (43)	83	0.25
Polish (43)	54	0.16
Portuguese (8)	37	0.11
Russian (0)	22	0.07
Scotch-Irish (24)	70	0.21
Scottish (24)	114	0.35
Swedish (0)	56	0.17
Welsh (0)	43	0.13
West Indian, ex. Hispanic (276)	326	0.99
Belizean (9)	34	0.10
Jamaican (0)	25	0.08
Trinidadian/Tobagonian (250)	250	0.76
West Indian (17)	17	0.05
Yugoslavian (13)	13	0.04

Hispanic Origin	Population	%
Hispanic or Latino (of any race)	1,776	5.36
Central American, ex. Mexican	553	1.67
Costa Rican	16	0.05
Guatemalan	52	0.16
Honduran	371	1.12
Nicaraguan	66	0.20
Panamanian	14	0.04
Salvadoran	30	0.09
Other Central American	4	0.01
Cuban	142	0.43
Dominican Republic	100	0.30
Mexican	544	1.64
Puerto Rican	103	0.31
South American	51	0.15
Argentinean	2	0.01
Bolivian	1	<0.01
Chilean	2	0.01
Colombian	25	0.08
Ecuadorian	2	0.01
Peruvian	11	0.03
Venezuelan	8	0.02
Other Hispanic or Latino	283	0.85

Race*	Population	%
African-American/Black (16,303)	16,530	49.88
Not Hispanic (16,186)	16,360	49.36
Hispanic (117)	170	0.51
American Indian/Alaska Native (229)	379	1.14
Not Hispanic (206)	332	1.00
Hispanic (23)	47	0.14
Cherokee (19)	41	0.12
Cheyenne (0)	3	0.01
Chickasaw (3)	3	0.01
Chippewa (1)	3	0.01
Choctaw (16)	31	0.09
Comanche (0)	1	<0.01
Creek (1)	1	<0.01
Houma (94)	119	0.36
Mexican American Ind. (2)	2	0.01
Navajo (3)	3	0.01
Paiute (0)	1	<0.01
Sioux (1)	6	0.02
Spanish American Ind. (0)	1	<0.01
Asian (1,553)	1,660	5.01
Not Hispanic (1,545)	1,636	4.94
Hispanic (8)	24	0.07
Cambodian (6)	10	0.03
Chinese, ex. Taiwanese (49)	66	0.20
Filipino (40)	78	0.24
Indian (33)	53	0.16
Indonesian (1)	5	0.02
Japanese (7)	15	0.05
Korean (22)	26	0.08
Laotian (5)	6	0.02
Thai (11)	12	0.04
Vietnamese (1,341)	1,378	4.16
Hawaii Native/Pacific Islander (6)	23	0.07
Not Hispanic (2)	15	0.05
Hispanic (4)	8	0.02
Guamanian/Chamorro (1)	2	0.01
Native Hawaiian (1)	6	0.02
Samoan (0)	2	0.01
Tongan (0)	1	<0.01
White (13,939)	14,376	43.38
Not Hispanic (13,049)	13,348	40.28
Hispanic (890)	1,028	3.10

Merrydale

Place Type: CDP
Parish: East Baton Rouge
Population: 9,772†

Ancestry‡	Population	%
African, Sub-Saharan (42)	51	0.51
African (42)	51	0.51
American (453)	453	4.54
Cajun (22)	22	0.22
English (77)	119	1.19
European (3)	3	0.03
French, ex. Basque (12)	64	0.64
French Canadian (12)	12	0.12
German (0)	23	0.23
Irish (5)	5	0.05
Italian (12)	17	0.17
Scotch-Irish (4)	4	0.04
Scottish (44)	59	0.59

Hispanic Origin	Population	%
Hispanic or Latino (of any race)	142	1.45
Central American, ex. Mexican	60	0.61
Guatemalan	5	0.05
Honduran	16	0.16
Panamanian	4	0.04
Salvadoran	35	0.36
Cuban	5	0.05
Mexican	37	0.38
Puerto Rican	8	0.08
South American	1	0.01
Ecuadorian	1	0.01
Other Hispanic or Latino	31	0.32

Race*	Population	%
African-American/Black (9,169)	9,234	94.49
Not Hispanic (9,142)	9,200	94.15
Hispanic (27)	34	0.35
American Indian/Alaska Native (18)	43	0.44
Not Hispanic (18)	42	0.43
Hispanic (0)	1	0.01
Cherokee (0)	9	0.09
Choctaw (1)	1	0.01
Creek (0)	1	0.01
Sioux (3)	3	0.03
Asian (12)	26	0.27
Not Hispanic (12)	26	0.27
Chinese, ex. Taiwanese (0)	4	0.04
Filipino (2)	5	0.05
Indian (1)	2	0.02
Japanese (1)	1	0.01
Korean (0)	1	0.01
Laotian (5)	6	0.06
Vietnamese (3)	7	0.07
Hawaii Native/Pacific Islander (0)	4	0.04
Not Hispanic (0)	3	0.03
Hispanic (0)	1	0.01
Samoan (0)	3	0.03
White (448)	475	4.86
Not Hispanic (382)	403	4.12
Hispanic (66)	72	0.74

Metairie

Place Type: CDP
Parish: Jefferson
Population: 138,481†

Ancestry‡	Population	%
African, Sub-Saharan (1,063)	1,814	1.33
African (1,031)	1,782	1.31
Ethiopian (9)	9	0.01
Nigerian (23)	23	0.02
Albanian (13)	13	0.01
Alsatian (8)	20	0.01
American (7,156)	7,156	5.27
Arab (1,681)	1,998	1.47
Arab (294)	388	0.29
Egyptian (163)	173	0.13

*Notes: † The Census 2010 population figure is used to calculate the percentages in the Hispanic Origin and Race categories. Ancestry percentages are based on the 2006-2010 American Community Survey population (not shown); ‡ Numbers in parentheses indicate the number of people reporting a single ancestry; * Numbers in parentheses indicate the number of persons reporting this race alone, not in combination with any other race; Please refer to the Explanation of Data for more information.*

Iraqi (182)	182	0.13
Jordanian (384)	384	0.28
Lebanese (285)	364	0.27
Palestinian (26)	26	0.02
Syrian (50)	124	0.09
Other Arab (297)	357	0.26
Armenian (0)	23	0.02
Austrian (0)	162	0.12
Belgian (59)	121	0.09
Brazilian (456)	472	0.35
British (194)	523	0.38
Bulgarian (0)	45	0.03
Cajun (400)	651	0.48
Canadian (101)	269	0.20
Celtic (25)	36	0.03
Croatian (70)	256	0.19
Cypriot (6)	6	<0.01
Czech (57)	231	0.17
Czechoslovakian (12)	29	0.02
Danish (68)	259	0.19
Dutch (154)	882	0.65
Eastern European (72)	100	0.07
English (2,510)	9,516	7.00
European (867)	1,009	0.74
Finnish (22)	22	0.02
French, ex. Basque (8,586)	30,479	22.43
French Canadian (926)	1,433	1.05
German (6,058)	26,905	19.80
Greek (321)	457	0.34
Guyanese (13)	27	0.02
Hungarian (129)	234	0.17
Iranian (59)	110	0.08
Irish (3,662)	17,826	13.12
Italian (8,186)	22,255	16.38
Lithuanian (54)	74	0.05
Macedonian (11)	11	0.01
Northern European (73)	73	0.05
Norwegian (154)	589	0.43
Pennsylvania German (32)	32	0.02
Polish (345)	1,069	0.79
Portuguese (286)	611	0.45
Romanian (28)	41	0.03
Russian (166)	345	0.25
Scandinavian (0)	13	0.01
Scotch-Irish (875)	2,176	1.60
Scottish (308)	1,402	1.03
Serbian (25)	101	0.07
Slavic (32)	101	0.07
Slovak (11)	93	0.07
Slovene (6)	30	0.02
Swedish (136)	801	0.59
Swiss (117)	361	0.27
Ukrainian (106)	213	0.16
Welsh (109)	321	0.24
West Indian, ex. Hispanic (91)	132	0.10
Belizean (70)	107	0.08
Jamaican (21)	25	0.02
Yugoslavian (86)	123	0.09

Hispanic Origin	Population	%
Hispanic or Latino (of any race)	17,447	12.60
Central American, ex. Mexican	9,085	6.56
Costa Rican	200	0.14
Guatemalan	1,096	0.79
Honduran	5,611	4.05
Nicaraguan	1,462	1.06
Panamanian	92	0.07
Salvadoran	579	0.42
Other Central American	45	0.03
Cuban	1,396	1.01
Dominican Republic	267	0.19
Mexican	2,779	2.01
Puerto Rican	650	0.47
South American	1,062	0.77
Argentinean	100	0.07
Bolivian	34	0.02
Chilean	40	0.03
Colombian	331	0.24
Ecuadorian	179	0.13
Paraguayan	4	<0.01
Peruvian	186	0.13
Uruguayan	12	0.01
Venezuelan	158	0.11
Other South American	18	0.01
Other Hispanic or Latino	2,208	1.59

Race*	Population	%
African-American/Black (14,374)	15,157	10.95
Not Hispanic (14,020)	14,574	10.52
Hispanic (354)	583	0.42
American Indian/Alaska Native (418)	957	0.69
Not Hispanic (294)	679	0.49
Hispanic (124)	278	0.20
Apache (2)	8	0.01
Blackfeet (2)	14	0.01
Canadian/French Am. Ind. (0)	2	<0.01
Central American Ind. (13)	42	0.03
Cherokee (46)	149	0.11
Cheyenne (0)	1	<0.01
Chickasaw (6)	7	0.01
Chippewa (3)	7	0.01
Choctaw (20)	67	0.05
Creek (5)	13	0.01
Crow (1)	1	<0.01
Delaware (0)	1	<0.01
Houma (54)	72	0.05
Iroquois (1)	2	<0.01
Lumbee (2)	2	<0.01
Mexican American Ind. (31)	56	0.04
Navajo (0)	2	<0.01
Osage (0)	1	<0.01
Paiute (0)	1	<0.01
Pima (3)	3	<0.01
Potawatomi (4)	5	<0.01
Seminole (3)	5	<0.01
Sioux (9)	12	0.01
South American Ind. (3)	13	0.01
Spanish American Ind. (6)	15	0.01
Yaqui (1)	2	<0.01
Asian (4,507)	5,273	3.81
Not Hispanic (4,458)	5,095	3.68
Hispanic (49)	178	0.13
Bangladeshi (50)	51	0.04
Burmese (12)	12	0.01
Cambodian (20)	25	0.02
Chinese, ex. Taiwanese (1,363)	1,489	1.08
Filipino (310)	488	0.35
Indian (967)	1,088	0.79
Indonesian (20)	27	0.02
Japanese (108)	179	0.13
Korean (366)	425	0.31
Laotian (5)	5	<0.01
Malaysian (1)	11	0.01
Nepalese (12)	15	0.01
Pakistani (311)	341	0.25
Sri Lankan (31)	31	0.02
Taiwanese (82)	93	0.07
Thai (63)	69	0.05
Vietnamese (612)	682	0.49
Hawaii Native/Pacific Islander (65)	185	0.13
Not Hispanic (39)	120	0.09
Hispanic (26)	65	0.05
Guamanian/Chamorro (28)	41	0.03
Native Hawaiian (15)	32	0.02
Samoan (6)	7	0.01
White (110,827)	113,195	81.74
Not Hispanic (100,280)	101,649	73.40
Hispanic (10,547)	11,546	8.34

Minden

Place Type: City
Parish: Webster
Population: 13,082†

Ancestry‡	Population	%
African, Sub-Saharan (5)	20	0.15
African (5)	20	0.15
American (1,081)	1,081	8.24
British (17)	25	0.19
Cajun (26)	26	0.20
Canadian (0)	12	0.09
Czech (12)	49	0.37
Dutch (8)	119	0.91
English (472)	916	6.99
European (16)	26	0.20
French, ex. Basque (101)	305	2.33
French Canadian (11)	11	0.08
German (237)	913	6.96
Hungarian (0)	10	0.08
Irish (560)	1,342	10.23
Italian (116)	182	1.39
Norwegian (11)	49	0.37
Polish (16)	47	0.36
Scotch-Irish (89)	149	1.14
Scottish (69)	100	0.76
Swedish (17)	51	0.39
West Indian, ex. Hispanic (0)	4	0.03
Haitian (0)	4	0.03

Hispanic Origin	Population	%
Hispanic or Latino (of any race)	183	1.40
Central American, ex. Mexican	9	0.07
Guatemalan	2	0.02
Honduran	5	0.04
Nicaraguan	2	0.02
Cuban	10	0.08
Dominican Republic	1	0.01
Mexican	118	0.90
Puerto Rican	11	0.08
South American	9	0.07
Chilean	2	0.02
Ecuadorian	1	0.01
Peruvian	2	0.02
Venezuelan	4	0.03
Other Hispanic or Latino	25	0.19

Race*	Population	%
African-American/Black (6,761)	6,860	52.44
Not Hispanic (6,736)	6,831	52.22
Hispanic (25)	29	0.22
American Indian/Alaska Native (27)	82	0.63
Not Hispanic (25)	76	0.58
Hispanic (2)	6	0.05
Apache (0)	2	0.02
Cherokee (6)	13	0.10
Choctaw (2)	6	0.05
Crow (0)	1	0.01
Houma (1)	1	0.01
Iroquois (0)	1	0.01
Mexican American Ind. (1)	1	0.01
Sioux (2)	3	0.02
Spanish American Ind. (1)	1	0.01
Ute (0)	2	0.02
Asian (42)	73	0.56
Not Hispanic (42)	72	0.55
Hispanic (0)	1	0.01
Chinese, ex. Taiwanese (4)	4	0.03
Filipino (13)	17	0.13
Indian (7)	8	0.06
Japanese (2)	6	0.05
Korean (1)	3	0.02
Pakistani (0)	4	0.03
Thai (1)	3	0.02
Vietnamese (13)	15	0.11
Hawaii Native/Pacific Islander (1)	7	0.05
Not Hispanic (1)	7	0.05
Native Hawaiian (1)	5	0.04
White (6,041)	6,154	47.04
Not Hispanic (5,939)	6,041	46.18
Hispanic (102)	113	0.86

Monroe

Place Type: City
Parish: Ouachita
Population: 48,815†

Ancestry‡	Population	%
African, Sub-Saharan (321)	1,473	2.99

*Notes: † The Census 2010 population figure is used to calculate the percentages in the Hispanic Origin and Race categories. Ancestry percentages are based on the 2006-2010 American Community Survey population (not shown); ‡ Numbers in parentheses indicate the number of people reporting a single ancestry; * Numbers in parentheses indicate the number of persons reporting this race alone, not in combination with any other race; Please refer to the Explanation of Data for more information.*

SECTION TWO

African (321)	1,473	2.99
American (2,493)	2,493	5.06
Arab (23)	51	0.10
Lebanese (23)	42	0.09
Syrian (0)	9	0.02
Australian (0)	23	0.05
Austrian (0)	11	0.02
British (52)	88	0.18
Cajun (16)	80	0.16
Czech (16)	33	0.07
Czechoslovakian (5)	5	0.01
Danish (0)	10	0.02
Dutch (11)	190	0.39
English (2,357)	3,980	8.08
European (95)	95	0.19
French, ex. Basque (576)	1,875	3.81
French Canadian (71)	114	0.23
German (403)	1,435	2.91
Greek (46)	46	0.09
Hungarian (9)	62	0.13
Irish (1,034)	2,736	5.55
Israeli (12)	25	0.05
Italian (857)	1,255	2.55
Lithuanian (0)	36	0.07
Northern European (19)	19	0.04
Norwegian (108)	293	0.59
Polish (52)	151	0.31
Portuguese (10)	10	0.02
Scotch-Irish (443)	683	1.39
Scottish (163)	579	1.18
Swedish (27)	46	0.09
Swiss (9)	39	0.08
Welsh (19)	101	0.20
West Indian, ex. Hispanic (9)	50	0.10
Jamaican (9)	9	0.02
West Indian (0)	41	0.08
Yugoslavian (28)	28	0.06

Hispanic Origin	Population	%
Hispanic or Latino (of any race)	560	1.15
Central American, ex. Mexican	32	0.07
Guatemalan	2	<0.01
Honduran	13	0.03
Nicaraguan	6	0.01
Panamanian	6	0.01
Salvadoran	3	0.01
Other Central American	2	<0.01
Cuban	17	0.03
Dominican Republic	5	0.01
Mexican	296	0.61
Puerto Rican	31	0.06
South American	21	0.04
Chilean	1	<0.01
Colombian	9	0.02
Ecuadorian	1	<0.01
Peruvian	6	0.01
Venezuelan	4	0.01
Other Hispanic or Latino	158	0.32

Race*	Population	%
African-American/Black (31,189)	31,574	64.68
Not Hispanic (31,038)	31,404	64.33
Hispanic (151)	170	0.35
American Indian/Alaska Native (84)	241	0.49
Not Hispanic (76)	226	0.46
Hispanic (8)	15	0.03
Apache (0)	3	0.01
Blackfeet (0)	1	<0.01
Canadian/French Am. Ind. (0)	2	<0.01
Cherokee (6)	34	0.07
Chickasaw (4)	5	0.01
Choctaw (4)	30	0.06
Crow (0)	1	<0.01
Houma (6)	6	0.01
Kiowa (0)	1	<0.01
Mexican American Ind. (1)	2	<0.01
Sioux (0)	3	0.01
Asian (518)	647	1.33
Not Hispanic (508)	633	1.30
Hispanic (10)	14	0.03
Bangladeshi (1)	1	<0.01
Chinese, ex. Taiwanese (67)	91	0.19
Filipino (53)	78	0.16
Indian (183)	204	0.42
Indonesian (0)	1	<0.01
Japanese (3)	12	0.02
Korean (23)	34	0.07
Laotian (1)	1	<0.01
Malaysian (1)	1	<0.01
Nepalese (13)	16	0.03
Pakistani (19)	28	0.06
Taiwanese (3)	3	0.01
Thai (2)	3	0.01
Vietnamese (121)	131	0.27
Hawaii Native/Pacific Islander (25)	48	0.10
Not Hispanic (24)	45	0.09
Hispanic (1)	3	0.01
Guamanian/Chamorro (5)	11	0.02
Native Hawaiian (7)	7	0.01
Samoan (7)	9	0.02
Tongan (3)	3	0.01
White (16,312)	16,669	34.15
Not Hispanic (16,096)	16,426	33.65
Hispanic (216)	243	0.50

Morgan City

Place Type: City
Parish: St. Mary
Population: 12,404†

Ancestry‡	Population	%
African, Sub-Saharan (0)	19	0.15
African (0)	19	0.15
American (2,257)	2,257	18.15
Arab (11)	11	0.09
Lebanese (11)	11	0.09
Cajun (188)	207	1.66
Canadian (0)	34	0.27
Dutch (0)	10	0.08
English (289)	456	3.67
European (54)	54	0.43
French, ex. Basque (1,020)	2,117	17.03
French Canadian (229)	337	2.71
German (110)	702	5.65
Greek (0)	29	0.23
Irish (166)	550	4.42
Italian (500)	1,129	9.08
Norwegian (0)	24	0.19
Pennsylvania German (0)	12	0.10
Polish (12)	12	0.10
Portuguese (0)	9	0.07
Scotch-Irish (10)	105	0.84
Scottish (19)	68	0.55
Swedish (0)	30	0.24

Hispanic Origin	Population	%
Hispanic or Latino (of any race)	966	7.79
Central American, ex. Mexican	103	0.83
Costa Rican	1	0.01
Guatemalan	26	0.21
Honduran	55	0.44
Nicaraguan	8	0.06
Panamanian	2	0.02
Salvadoran	11	0.09
Cuban	84	0.68
Dominican Republic	26	0.21
Mexican	592	4.77
Puerto Rican	33	0.27
South American	37	0.30
Chilean	9	0.07
Colombian	13	0.10
Ecuadorian	3	0.02
Peruvian	3	0.02
Venezuelan	9	0.07
Other Hispanic or Latino	91	0.73

Race*	Population	%
African-American/Black (2,922)	3,030	24.43
Not Hispanic (2,888)	2,983	24.05
Hispanic (34)	47	0.38
American Indian/Alaska Native (143)	207	1.67
Not Hispanic (139)	195	1.57
Hispanic (4)	12	0.10
Aleut *(Alaska Native)* (2)	2	0.02
Apache (1)	3	0.02
Canadian/French Am. Ind. (0)	2	0.02
Cherokee (7)	12	0.10
Choctaw (5)	6	0.05
Creek (5)	5	0.04
Houma (73)	90	0.73
Mexican American Ind. (1)	1	0.01
Navajo (0)	2	0.02
Sioux (1)	5	0.04
Asian (224)	267	2.15
Not Hispanic (223)	263	2.12
Hispanic (1)	4	0.03
Burmese (2)	2	0.02
Chinese, ex. Taiwanese (5)	5	0.04
Filipino (5)	13	0.10
Hmong (0)	2	0.02
Indian (71)	75	0.60
Indonesian (1)	1	0.01
Japanese (2)	7	0.06
Korean (4)	4	0.03
Laotian (1)	1	0.01
Taiwanese (2)	2	0.02
Vietnamese (126)	148	1.19
Hawaii Native/Pacific Islander (15)	19	0.15
Not Hispanic (2)	4	0.03
Hispanic (13)	15	0.12
Guamanian/Chamorro (11)	12	0.10
Native Hawaiian (4)	6	0.05
White (8,348)	8,558	68.99
Not Hispanic (7,996)	8,154	65.74
Hispanic (352)	404	3.26

Moss Bluff

Place Type: CDP
Parish: Calcasieu
Population: 11,557†

Ancestry‡	Population	%
American (1,393)	1,393	11.92
Cajun (365)	554	4.74
Canadian (11)	27	0.23
Danish (11)	34	0.29
Dutch (11)	165	1.41
English (323)	841	7.20
European (41)	41	0.35
French, ex. Basque (1,214)	2,220	19.00
French Canadian (405)	520	4.45
German (468)	1,569	13.43
Irish (496)	1,600	13.69
Italian (158)	441	3.77
Norwegian (0)	54	0.46
Pennsylvania German (10)	10	0.09
Polish (22)	101	0.86
Scotch-Irish (26)	77	0.66
Scottish (51)	182	1.56
Slovak (10)	44	0.38
Swedish (0)	6	0.05
Welsh (8)	27	0.23

Hispanic Origin	Population	%
Hispanic or Latino (of any race)	340	2.94
Central American, ex. Mexican	19	0.16
Guatemalan	11	0.10
Honduran	1	0.01
Panamanian	4	0.03
Salvadoran	3	0.03
Cuban	7	0.06
Dominican Republic	1	0.01
Mexican	194	1.68
Puerto Rican	47	0.41
South American	23	0.20
Argentinean	1	0.01
Colombian	7	0.06
Uruguayan	1	0.01

*Notes: † The Census 2010 population figure is used to calculate the percentages in the Hispanic Origin and Race categories. Ancestry percentages are based on the 2006-2010 American Community Survey population (not shown); ‡ Numbers in parentheses indicate the number of people reporting a single ancestry; * Numbers in parentheses indicate the number of persons reporting this race alone, not in combination with any other race; Please refer to the Explanation of Data for more information.*

Venezuelan	14	0.12
Other Hispanic or Latino	49	0.42

Race*	Population	%
African-American/Black (699)	776	6.71
Not Hispanic (693)	767	6.64
Hispanic (6)	9	0.08
American Indian/Alaska Native (57)	116	1.00
Not Hispanic (52)	103	0.89
Hispanic (5)	13	0.11
Canadian/French Am. Ind. (1)	1	0.01
Central American Ind. (1)	1	0.01
Cherokee (10)	20	0.17
Chickasaw (0)	2	0.02
Choctaw (7)	15	0.13
Creek (1)	2	0.02
Delaware (1)	2	0.02
Hopi (0)	1	0.01
Houma (4)	5	0.04
Sioux (2)	3	0.03
Asian (119)	143	1.24
Not Hispanic (118)	142	1.23
Hispanic (1)	1	0.01
Chinese, ex. Taiwanese (18)	23	0.20
Filipino (5)	10	0.09
Indian (22)	26	0.22
Japanese (1)	2	0.02
Korean (2)	5	0.04
Laotian (5)	5	0.04
Pakistani (2)	2	0.02
Taiwanese (0)	1	0.01
Thai (0)	2	0.02
Vietnamese (63)	67	0.58
Hawaii Native/Pacific Islander (3)	13	0.11
Not Hispanic (1)	6	0.05
Hispanic (2)	7	0.06
Guamanian/Chamorro (2)	2	0.02
Native Hawaiian (1)	5	0.04
White (10,401)	10,566	91.43
Not Hispanic (10,187)	10,326	89.35
Hispanic (214)	240	2.08

Natchitoches

Place Type: City
Parish: Natchitoches
Population: 18,323†

Ancestry‡	Population	%
African, Sub-Saharan (72)	168	0.93
African (69)	165	0.91
Nigerian (3)	3	0.02
American (613)	613	3.39
Arab (7)	21	0.12
Lebanese (7)	13	0.07
Syrian (0)	5	0.03
Other Arab (0)	3	0.02
Austrian (0)	3	0.02
Belgian (19)	24	0.13
British (22)	40	0.22
Cajun (32)	38	0.21
Canadian (15)	47	0.26
Celtic (4)	4	0.02
Croatian (0)	7	0.04
Czech (36)	85	0.47
Danish (3)	32	0.18
Dutch (18)	100	0.55
English (427)	953	5.27
European (65)	78	0.43
Finnish (3)	19	0.11
French, ex. Basque (466)	1,317	7.28
French Canadian (62)	78	0.43
German (336)	986	5.45
Greek (14)	41	0.23
Irish (344)	1,203	6.65
Italian (90)	311	1.72
Latvian (3)	3	0.02
Luxemburger (0)	4	0.02
Northern European (3)	3	0.02
Norwegian (13)	16	0.09
Polish (33)	92	0.51
Portuguese (0)	7	0.04
Russian (0)	4	0.02
Scandinavian (0)	5	0.03
Scotch-Irish (130)	209	1.16
Scottish (59)	188	1.04
Swedish (12)	42	0.23
Swiss (4)	4	0.02
Welsh (11)	91	0.50
West Indian, ex. Hispanic (22)	26	0.14
Belizean (9)	9	0.05
Haitian (9)	9	0.05
Jamaican (4)	8	0.04

Hispanic Origin	Population	%
Hispanic or Latino (of any race)	309	1.69
Central American, ex. Mexican	13	0.07
Costa Rican	1	0.01
Guatemalan	2	0.01
Honduran	5	0.03
Nicaraguan	1	0.01
Panamanian	1	0.01
Salvadoran	3	0.02
Cuban	8	0.04
Mexican	178	0.97
Puerto Rican	26	0.14
South American	16	0.09
Bolivian	2	0.01
Chilean	3	0.02
Colombian	6	0.03
Ecuadorian	3	0.02
Venezuelan	1	0.01
Other South American	1	0.01
Other Hispanic or Latino	68	0.37

Race*	Population	%
African-American/Black (10,852)	11,054	60.33
Not Hispanic (10,807)	10,994	60.00
Hispanic (45)	60	0.33
American Indian/Alaska Native (86)	224	1.22
Not Hispanic (83)	210	1.15
Hispanic (3)	14	0.08
Blackfeet (1)	1	0.01
Canadian/French Am. Ind. (0)	1	0.01
Cherokee (10)	33	0.18
Cheyenne (1)	1	0.01
Chippewa (0)	3	0.02
Choctaw (5)	24	0.13
Comanche (0)	2	0.01
Creek (1)	3	0.02
Houma (0)	2	0.01
Inupiat *(Alaska Native)* (0)	1	0.01
Iroquois (3)	3	0.02
Mexican American Ind. (0)	2	0.01
Navajo (0)	1	0.01
Sioux (0)	4	0.02
Asian (103)	141	0.77
Not Hispanic (103)	140	0.76
Hispanic (0)	1	0.01
Bangladeshi (3)	4	0.02
Chinese, ex. Taiwanese (19)	32	0.17
Filipino (7)	13	0.07
Hmong (0)	1	0.01
Indian (27)	31	0.17
Indonesian (10)	10	0.05
Japanese (4)	7	0.04
Korean (20)	31	0.17
Thai (2)	2	0.01
Vietnamese (4)	4	0.02
Hawaii Native/Pacific Islander (2)	26	0.14
Not Hispanic (2)	25	0.14
Hispanic (0)	1	0.01
Guamanian/Chamorro (1)	6	0.03
Native Hawaiian (0)	6	0.03
Samoan (0)	1	0.01
White (6,824)	7,064	38.55
Not Hispanic (6,666)	6,881	37.55
Hispanic (158)	183	1.00

New Iberia

Place Type: City
Parish: Iberia
Population: 30,617†

Ancestry‡	Population	%
African, Sub-Saharan (117)	130	0.42
African (117)	130	0.42
American (3,268)	3,268	10.53
Arab (30)	77	0.25
Lebanese (23)	56	0.18
Syrian (7)	21	0.07
Austrian (14)	25	0.08
Belgian (0)	14	0.05
British (12)	24	0.08
Cajun (494)	575	1.85
Canadian (0)	98	0.32
Czech (8)	8	0.03
Danish (8)	8	0.03
Dutch (0)	83	0.27
English (698)	1,249	4.03
European (126)	148	0.48
French, ex. Basque (3,737)	6,165	19.87
French Canadian (1,164)	1,353	4.36
German (286)	1,768	5.70
Hungarian (6)	18	0.06
Irish (381)	1,381	4.45
Italian (208)	739	2.38
Norwegian (9)	62	0.20
Polish (4)	25	0.08
Portuguese (10)	23	0.07
Romanian (13)	30	0.10
Russian (23)	23	0.07
Scotch-Irish (20)	96	0.31
Scottish (15)	77	0.25
Swedish (69)	100	0.32
Welsh (0)	49	0.16
West Indian, ex. Hispanic (7)	7	0.02
British West Indian (7)	7	0.02

Hispanic Origin	Population	%
Hispanic or Latino (of any race)	956	3.12
Central American, ex. Mexican	115	0.38
Costa Rican	2	0.01
Guatemalan	16	0.05
Honduran	23	0.08
Nicaraguan	9	0.03
Panamanian	30	0.10
Salvadoran	33	0.11
Other Central American	2	0.01
Cuban	41	0.13
Dominican Republic	7	0.02
Mexican	570	1.86
Puerto Rican	39	0.13
South American	19	0.06
Argentinean	1	<0.01
Chilean	2	0.01
Colombian	10	0.03
Ecuadorian	1	<0.01
Venezuelan	5	0.02
Other Hispanic or Latino	165	0.54

Race*	Population	%
African-American/Black (12,694)	12,982	42.40
Not Hispanic (12,624)	12,891	42.10
Hispanic (70)	91	0.30
American Indian/Alaska Native (75)	160	0.52
Not Hispanic (70)	149	0.49
Hispanic (5)	11	0.04
Apache (0)	2	0.01
Canadian/French Am. Ind. (0)	3	0.01
Cherokee (9)	23	0.08
Chickasaw (0)	6	0.02
Chippewa (0)	1	<0.01
Choctaw (8)	13	0.04
Comanche (0)	2	0.01
Houma (14)	14	0.05
Iroquois (1)	1	<0.01
Menominee (1)	1	<0.01

*Notes: † The Census 2010 population figure is used to calculate the percentages in the Hispanic Origin and Race categories. Ancestry percentages are based on the 2006-2010 American Community Survey population (not shown); ‡ Numbers in parentheses indicate the number of people reporting a single ancestry; * Numbers in parentheses indicate the number of persons reporting this race alone, not in combination with any other race; Please refer to the Explanation of Data for more information.*

Mexican American Ind. (4)	4	0.01
Sioux (2)	3	0.01
Asian (821)	919	3.00
Not Hispanic (819)	910	2.97
Hispanic (2)	9	0.03
Burmese (1)	1	<0.01
Cambodian (7)	14	0.05
Chinese, ex. Taiwanese (42)	53	0.17
Filipino (30)	44	0.14
Indian (35)	59	0.19
Indonesian (1)	2	0.01
Japanese (2)	8	0.03
Korean (4)	9	0.03
Laotian (401)	443	1.45
Pakistani (0)	6	0.02
Thai (7)	16	0.05
Vietnamese (196)	217	0.71
Hawaii Native/Pacific Islander (9)	27	0.09
Not Hispanic (8)	25	0.08
Hispanic (1)	2	0.01
Guamanian/Chamorro (2)	2	0.01
Native Hawaiian (3)	5	0.02
Samoan (1)	1	<0.01
White (16,085)	16,473	53.80
Not Hispanic (15,691)	16,026	52.34
Hispanic (394)	447	1.46

New Orleans

Place Type: City
Parish: Orleans
Population: 343,829†

Ancestry‡	Population	%
Afghan (0)	18	0.01
African, Sub-Saharan (9,340)	10,425	3.53
African (8,901)	9,872	3.34
Ethiopian (107)	107	0.04
Ghanaian (8)	8	<0.01
Kenyan (19)	76	0.03
Liberian (83)	83	0.03
Nigerian (51)	51	0.02
South African (127)	127	0.04
Zimbabwean (24)	24	0.01
Other Sub-Saharan African (20)	77	0.03
Albanian (0)	58	0.02
Alsatian (10)	52	0.02
American (7,384)	7,384	2.50
Arab (516)	840	0.28
Arab (155)	155	0.05
Egyptian (17)	28	0.01
Iraqi (30)	30	0.01
Lebanese (166)	438	0.15
Moroccan (33)	33	0.01
Palestinian (0)	5	<0.01
Syrian (0)	17	0.01
Other Arab (115)	134	0.05
Armenian (38)	70	0.02
Australian (33)	54	0.02
Austrian (177)	572	0.19
Basque (17)	60	0.02
Belgian (48)	246	0.08
Brazilian (339)	385	0.13
British (505)	892	0.30
Bulgarian (46)	46	0.02
Cajun (506)	712	0.24
Canadian (60)	164	0.06
Celtic (32)	32	0.01
Croatian (167)	269	0.09
Czech (142)	436	0.15
Czechoslovakian (0)	90	0.03
Danish (128)	464	0.16
Dutch (297)	1,014	0.34
Eastern European (234)	367	0.12
English (5,015)	13,945	4.72
European (1,942)	2,260	0.77
Finnish (29)	127	0.04
French, ex. Basque (6,169)	19,655	6.66
French Canadian (794)	1,755	0.59
German (5,506)	20,406	6.91
Greek (157)	408	0.14
Guyanese (44)	44	0.01
Hungarian (119)	657	0.22
Icelander (0)	16	0.01
Iranian (132)	177	0.06
Irish (4,098)	16,645	5.64
Israeli (11)	20	0.01
Italian (3,862)	11,026	3.73
Latvian (20)	52	0.02
Lithuanian (53)	207	0.07
Maltese (11)	35	0.01
Northern European (131)	143	0.05
Norwegian (187)	621	0.21
Pennsylvania German (0)	17	0.01
Polish (677)	2,159	0.73
Portuguese (100)	252	0.09
Romanian (122)	200	0.07
Russian (605)	1,485	0.50
Scandinavian (99)	220	0.07
Scotch-Irish (947)	2,646	0.90
Scottish (916)	3,369	1.14
Serbian (26)	83	0.03
Slavic (18)	101	0.03
Slovak (25)	104	0.04
Slovene (0)	7	<0.01
Swedish (331)	1,099	0.37
Swiss (49)	383	0.13
Turkish (87)	137	0.05
Ukrainian (174)	354	0.12
Welsh (122)	738	0.25
West Indian, ex. Hispanic (746)	1,042	0.35
Belizean (141)	146	0.05
British West Indian (0)	7	<0.01
Haitian (217)	343	0.12
Jamaican (202)	320	0.11
Trinidadian/Tobagonian (156)	163	0.06
U.S. Virgin Islander (11)	11	<0.01
West Indian (19)	52	0.02
Yugoslavian (23)	129	0.04

Hispanic Origin	Population	%
Hispanic or Latino (of any race)	18,051	5.25
Central American, ex. Mexican	7,325	2.13
Costa Rican	135	0.04
Guatemalan	906	0.26
Honduran	4,572	1.33
Nicaraguan	976	0.28
Panamanian	165	0.05
Salvadoran	505	0.15
Other Central American	66	0.02
Cuban	1,285	0.37
Dominican Republic	244	0.07
Mexican	4,298	1.25
Puerto Rican	948	0.28
South American	1,352	0.39
Argentinean	165	0.05
Bolivian	65	0.02
Chilean	93	0.03
Colombian	459	0.13
Ecuadorian	194	0.06
Paraguayan	11	<0.01
Peruvian	166	0.05
Uruguayan	31	0.01
Venezuelan	154	0.04
Other South American	14	<0.01
Other Hispanic or Latino	2,599	0.76

Race*	Population	%
African-American/Black (206,871)	210,447	61.21
Not Hispanic (204,866)	207,691	60.41
Hispanic (2,005)	2,756	0.80
American Indian/Alaska Native (1,047)	2,792	0.81
Not Hispanic (827)	2,197	0.64
Hispanic (220)	595	0.17
Alaska Athabascan *(Ala. Nat.)* (2)	2	<0.01
Apache (10)	31	0.01
Arapaho (2)	2	<0.01
Blackfeet (11)	48	0.01
Canadian/French Am. Ind. (13)	18	0.01
Central American Ind. (53)	131	0.04
Cherokee (87)	349	0.10
Cheyenne (1)	1	<0.01
Chickasaw (8)	15	<0.01
Chippewa (15)	21	0.01
Choctaw (41)	161	0.05
Comanche (2)	9	<0.01
Cree (0)	7	<0.01
Creek (16)	35	0.01
Delaware (0)	1	<0.01
Houma (33)	66	0.02
Inupiat *(Alaska Native)* (0)	2	<0.01
Iroquois (6)	24	0.01
Kiowa (1)	2	<0.01
Lumbee (2)	3	<0.01
Menominee (1)	1	<0.01
Mexican American Ind. (43)	68	0.02
Navajo (3)	15	<0.01
Osage (1)	9	<0.01
Ottawa (0)	1	<0.01
Paiute (1)	1	<0.01
Pima (0)	3	<0.01
Potawatomi (0)	5	<0.01
Pueblo (5)	9	<0.01
Seminole (0)	12	<0.01
Shoshone (1)	1	<0.01
Sioux (11)	37	0.01
South American Ind. (6)	21	0.01
Spanish American Ind. (1)	5	<0.01
Tlingit-Haida *(Alaska Native)* (1)	5	<0.01
Ute (0)	1	<0.01
Yaqui (0)	5	<0.01
Yuman (1)	1	<0.01
Asian (9,970)	11,306	3.29
Not Hispanic (9,883)	11,072	3.22
Hispanic (87)	234	0.07
Bangladeshi (22)	24	0.01
Burmese (22)	25	0.01
Cambodian (15)	22	0.01
Chinese, ex. Taiwanese (1,113)	1,344	0.39
Filipino (452)	740	0.22
Hmong (1)	1	<0.01
Indian (1,153)	1,386	0.40
Indonesian (13)	23	0.01
Japanese (186)	377	0.11
Korean (368)	470	0.14
Laotian (67)	86	0.03
Malaysian (6)	10	<0.01
Nepalese (21)	23	0.01
Pakistani (93)	113	0.03
Sri Lankan (18)	20	0.01
Taiwanese (82)	90	0.03
Thai (57)	88	0.03
Vietnamese (5,994)	6,214	1.81
Hawaii Native/Pacific Islander (134)	339	0.10
Not Hispanic (105)	259	0.08
Hispanic (29)	80	0.02
Fijian (7)	7	<0.01
Guamanian/Chamorro (40)	74	0.02
Native Hawaiian (36)	68	0.02
Samoan (14)	37	0.01
Tongan (4)	8	<0.01
White (113,428)	117,460	34.16
Not Hispanic (104,770)	107,823	31.36
Hispanic (8,658)	9,637	2.80

Oak Hills Place

Place Type: CDP
Parish: East Baton Rouge
Population: 8,195†

Ancestry‡	Population	%
African, Sub-Saharan (0)	7	0.09
African (0)	7	0.09
American (924)	924	11.56
Arab (43)	124	1.55
Lebanese (43)	124	1.55
Austrian (0)	33	0.41
British (41)	41	0.51
Cajun (16)	29	0.36

*Notes: † The Census 2010 population figure is used to calculate the percentages in the Hispanic Origin and Race categories. Ancestry percentages are based on the 2006-2010 American Community Survey population (not shown); ‡ Numbers in parentheses indicate the number of people reporting a single ancestry; * Numbers in parentheses indicate the number of persons reporting this race alone, not in combination with any other race; Please refer to the Explanation of Data for more information.*

Croatian (0)	14	0.18
Czech (0)	13	0.16
Danish (0)	20	0.25
Dutch (82)	118	1.48
English (248)	1,004	12.56
European (45)	45	0.56
French, ex. Basque (340)	1,629	20.38
French Canadian (50)	75	0.94
German (213)	1,075	13.45
Irish (279)	1,079	13.50
Italian (241)	653	8.17
Norwegian (13)	13	0.16
Polish (17)	55	0.69
Romanian (0)	15	0.19
Russian (0)	25	0.31
Scotch-Irish (139)	285	3.57
Scottish (64)	197	2.46
Slavic (15)	30	0.38
Swedish (0)	43	0.54
Swiss (14)	14	0.18
Welsh (0)	51	0.64
West Indian, ex. Hispanic (15)	15	0.19
Jamaican (15)	15	0.19

Hispanic Origin	Population	%
Hispanic or Latino (of any race)	322	3.93
Central American, ex. Mexican	81	0.99
Costa Rican	4	0.05
Guatemalan	9	0.11
Honduran	32	0.39
Nicaraguan	24	0.29
Panamanian	4	0.05
Salvadoran	6	0.07
Other Central American	2	0.02
Cuban	29	0.35
Dominican Republic	3	0.04
Mexican	89	1.09
Puerto Rican	11	0.13
South American	54	0.66
Chilean	5	0.06
Colombian	37	0.45
Ecuadorian	1	0.01
Paraguayan	1	0.01
Peruvian	1	0.01
Venezuelan	9	0.11
Other Hispanic or Latino	55	0.67

Race*	Population	%
African-American/Black (1,301)	1,337	16.31
Not Hispanic (1,288)	1,322	16.13
Hispanic (13)	15	0.18
American Indian/Alaska Native (13)	38	0.46
Not Hispanic (13)	36	0.44
Hispanic (0)	2	0.02
Central American Ind. (0)	1	0.01
Cherokee (2)	5	0.06
Chickasaw (1)	1	0.01
Choctaw (0)	2	0.02
Delaware (0)	3	0.04
Lumbee (1)	1	0.01
Paiute (0)	1	0.01
Asian (390)	423	5.16
Not Hispanic (390)	419	5.11
Hispanic (0)	4	0.05
Burmese (3)	3	0.04
Cambodian (2)	4	0.05
Chinese, ex. Taiwanese (85)	92	1.12
Filipino (25)	29	0.35
Indian (139)	146	1.78
Indonesian (1)	1	0.01
Japanese (10)	16	0.20
Korean (48)	48	0.59
Pakistani (11)	11	0.13
Sri Lankan (1)	1	0.01
Taiwanese (7)	9	0.11
Vietnamese (52)	56	0.68
Hawaii Native/Pacific Islander (0)	6	0.07
Not Hispanic (0)	6	0.07
Guamanian/Chamorro (0)	5	0.06
White (6,339)	6,416	78.29
Not Hispanic (6,093)	6,151	75.06
Hispanic (246)	265	3.23

Oakdale

Place Type: City
Parish: Allen
Population: 7,780†

Ancestry‡	Population	%
African, Sub-Saharan (105)	105	1.33
African (85)	85	1.08
Cape Verdean (20)	20	0.25
American (425)	425	5.39
Arab (46)	57	0.72
Arab (22)	22	0.28
Lebanese (12)	16	0.20
Syrian (12)	19	0.24
Belgian (0)	14	0.18
Cajun (32)	32	0.41
Dutch (21)	25	0.32
English (296)	579	7.34
European (12)	12	0.15
French, ex. Basque (402)	1,013	12.84
French Canadian (33)	100	1.27
German (153)	516	6.54
Iranian (5)	5	0.06
Irish (287)	762	9.66
Italian (0)	77	0.98
Norwegian (0)	27	0.34
Polish (7)	17	0.22
Portuguese (9)	9	0.11
Scotch-Irish (31)	47	0.60
Scottish (42)	79	1.00
Ukrainian (3)	3	0.04
Welsh (0)	14	0.18
West Indian, ex. Hispanic (38)	77	0.98
Haitian (10)	10	0.13
Jamaican (19)	38	0.48
Trinidadian/Tobagonian (9)	19	0.24
U.S. Virgin Islander (0)	10	0.13

Hispanic Origin	Population	%
Hispanic or Latino (of any race)	63	0.81
Central American, ex. Mexican	4	0.05
Guatemalan	1	0.01
Panamanian	2	0.03
Salvadoran	1	0.01
Dominican Republic	2	0.03
Mexican	46	0.59
Puerto Rican	6	0.08
Other Hispanic or Latino	5	0.06

Race*	Population	%
African-American/Black (2,645)	2,695	34.64
Not Hispanic (2,640)	2,689	34.56
Hispanic (5)	6	0.08
American Indian/Alaska Native (97)	138	1.77
Not Hispanic (94)	133	1.71
Hispanic (3)	5	0.06
Central American Ind. (1)	2	0.03
Cherokee (49)	64	0.82
Choctaw (0)	3	0.04
Comanche (0)	1	0.01
Osage (2)	2	0.03
Asian (60)	72	0.93
Not Hispanic (60)	69	0.89
Hispanic (0)	3	0.04
Cambodian (17)	18	0.23
Chinese, ex. Taiwanese (1)	1	0.01
Filipino (6)	13	0.17
Indian (25)	26	0.33
Japanese (1)	1	0.01
Korean (1)	4	0.05
Vietnamese (3)	3	0.04
Hawaii Native/Pacific Islander (2)	3	0.04
Not Hispanic (1)	2	0.03
Hispanic (1)	1	0.01
Guamanian/Chamorro (1)	1	0.01
White (4,855)	4,927	63.33
Not Hispanic (4,831)	4,895	62.92
Hispanic (24)	32	0.41

Opelousas

Place Type: City
Parish: St. Landry
Population: 16,634†

Ancestry‡	Population	%
African, Sub-Saharan (21)	21	0.12
African (21)	21	0.12
American (375)	375	2.11
Arab (0)	3	0.02
Lebanese (0)	3	0.02
Cajun (55)	90	0.51
Canadian (11)	19	0.11
Czech (0)	14	0.08
Dutch (0)	80	0.45
English (281)	410	2.31
European (5)	5	0.03
French, ex. Basque (863)	1,292	7.27
French Canadian (754)	857	4.82
German (133)	382	2.15
Greek (8)	8	0.04
Irish (17)	147	0.83
Italian (100)	168	0.94
Scotch-Irish (0)	71	0.40
Scottish (25)	33	0.19
Swiss (0)	3	0.02

Hispanic Origin	Population	%
Hispanic or Latino (of any race)	192	1.15
Central American, ex. Mexican	19	0.11
Guatemalan	1	0.01
Honduran	12	0.07
Salvadoran	6	0.04
Cuban	6	0.04
Mexican	111	0.67
Puerto Rican	11	0.07
South American	8	0.05
Venezuelan	8	0.05
Other Hispanic or Latino	37	0.22

Race*	Population	%
African-American/Black (12,493)	12,647	76.03
Not Hispanic (12,450)	12,598	75.74
Hispanic (43)	49	0.29
American Indian/Alaska Native (58)	111	0.67
Not Hispanic (57)	108	0.65
Hispanic (1)	3	0.02
Apache (1)	4	0.02
Blackfeet (0)	4	0.02
Cherokee (1)	11	0.07
Choctaw (0)	1	0.01
Comanche (0)	4	0.02
Houma (3)	3	0.02
Seminole (0)	1	0.01
Yakama (1)	1	0.01
Asian (81)	88	0.53
Not Hispanic (80)	86	0.52
Hispanic (1)	2	0.01
Chinese, ex. Taiwanese (24)	26	0.16
Filipino (4)	6	0.04
Indian (7)	8	0.05
Indonesian (1)	1	0.01
Korean (1)	2	0.01
Vietnamese (42)	42	0.25
Hawaii Native/Pacific Islander (2)	7	0.04
Not Hispanic (2)	7	0.04
Guamanian/Chamorro (1)	1	0.01
Native Hawaiian (1)	4	0.02
White (3,707)	3,837	23.07
Not Hispanic (3,646)	3,772	22.68
Hispanic (61)	65	0.39

*Notes: † The Census 2010 population figure is used to calculate the percentages in the Hispanic Origin and Race categories. Ancestry percentages are based on the 2006-2010 American Community Survey population (not shown); ‡ Numbers in parentheses indicate the number of people reporting a single ancestry; * Numbers in parentheses indicate the number of persons reporting this race alone, not in combination with any other race; Please refer to the Explanation of Data for more information.*

Pineville

Place Type: City
Parish: Rapides
Population: 14,555†

Ancestry‡	Population	%
African, Sub-Saharan (60)	60	0.41
African (60)	60	0.41
American (1,869)	1,869	12.92
Arab (209)	220	1.52
Arab (148)	148	1.02
Iraqi (0)	5	0.03
Jordanian (7)	7	0.05
Lebanese (2)	2	0.01
Palestinian (52)	55	0.38
Syrian (0)	3	0.02
Australian (2)	2	0.01
Austrian (0)	11	0.08
Belgian (14)	47	0.32
British (16)	18	0.12
Cajun (52)	84	0.58
Canadian (8)	17	0.12
Czech (13)	18	0.12
Danish (11)	25	0.17
Dutch (18)	211	1.46
English (400)	918	6.35
European (123)	134	0.93
Finnish (0)	9	0.06
French, ex. Basque (636)	1,676	11.59
French Canadian (58)	128	0.89
German (240)	1,139	7.88
German Russian (0)	60	0.41
Greek (10)	33	0.23
Hungarian (0)	3	0.02
Iranian (0)	2	0.01
Irish (394)	1,301	9.00
Israeli (34)	37	0.26
Italian (126)	326	2.25
Lithuanian (2)	2	0.01
Northern European (23)	35	0.24
Norwegian (2)	21	0.15
Polish (11)	90	0.62
Portuguese (10)	72	0.50
Romanian (0)	3	0.02
Russian (6)	42	0.29
Scandinavian (0)	8	0.06
Scotch-Irish (86)	255	1.76
Scottish (33)	201	1.39
Slavic (0)	8	0.06
Swedish (5)	26	0.18
Swiss (0)	14	0.10
Ukrainian (0)	2	0.01
Welsh (4)	37	0.26
West Indian, ex. Hispanic (12)	12	0.08
Haitian (12)	12	0.08

Hispanic Origin	Population	%
Hispanic or Latino (of any race)	376	2.58
Central American, ex. Mexican	13	0.09
Guatemalan	4	0.03
Honduran	3	0.02
Panamanian	4	0.03
Salvadoran	1	0.01
Other Central American	1	0.01
Cuban	17	0.12
Dominican Republic	5	0.03
Mexican	230	1.58
Puerto Rican	30	0.21
South American	13	0.09
Argentinean	2	0.01
Bolivian	4	0.03
Colombian	4	0.03
Peruvian	3	0.02
Other Hispanic or Latino	68	0.47

Race*	Population	%
African-American/Black (4,483)	4,638	31.87
Not Hispanic (4,460)	4,609	31.67
Hispanic (23)	29	0.20
American Indian/Alaska Native (74)	176	1.21
Not Hispanic (71)	162	1.11
Hispanic (3)	14	0.10
Blackfeet (3)	10	0.07
Cherokee (11)	30	0.21
Cheyenne (1)	1	0.01
Chickasaw (1)	1	0.01
Choctaw (13)	28	0.19
Creek (0)	4	0.03
Delaware (0)	1	0.01
Houma (7)	10	0.07
Iroquois (0)	1	0.01
Mexican American Ind. (0)	1	0.01
Potawatomi (0)	1	0.01
Pueblo (1)	5	0.03
Asian (225)	283	1.94
Not Hispanic (221)	279	1.92
Hispanic (4)	4	0.03
Bangladeshi (8)	8	0.05
Cambodian (21)	33	0.23
Chinese, ex. Taiwanese (25)	30	0.21
Filipino (29)	37	0.25
Indian (38)	47	0.32
Indonesian (0)	1	0.01
Japanese (5)	12	0.08
Korean (16)	19	0.13
Laotian (0)	1	0.01
Nepalese (3)	3	0.02
Thai (1)	4	0.03
Vietnamese (68)	71	0.49
Hawaii Native/Pacific Islander (13)	18	0.12
Not Hispanic (12)	17	0.12
Hispanic (1)	1	0.01
Guamanian/Chamorro (3)	3	0.02
Native Hawaiian (7)	9	0.06
Samoan (0)	2	0.01
White (9,404)	9,637	66.21
Not Hispanic (9,149)	9,360	64.31
Hispanic (255)	277	1.90

Prairieville

Place Type: CDP
Parish: Ascension
Population: 26,895†

Ancestry‡	Population	%
African, Sub-Saharan (175)	209	0.80
African (72)	106	0.41
Somalian (103)	103	0.39
American (1,867)	1,867	7.14
Arab (35)	62	0.24
Arab (18)	34	0.13
Lebanese (17)	17	0.07
Syrian (0)	11	0.04
Austrian (0)	10	0.04
Brazilian (29)	43	0.16
British (28)	65	0.25
Cajun (152)	216	0.83
Canadian (29)	29	0.11
Croatian (0)	48	0.18
Czech (11)	35	0.13
Danish (24)	71	0.27
Dutch (53)	256	0.98
English (1,257)	2,787	10.67
Estonian (13)	13	0.05
European (162)	162	0.62
French, ex. Basque (2,819)	6,754	25.85
French Canadian (704)	866	3.31
German (1,041)	3,751	14.35
Hungarian (9)	9	0.03
Irish (757)	2,892	11.07
Italian (871)	3,281	12.56
Norwegian (18)	568	2.17
Polish (32)	157	0.60
Portuguese (0)	63	0.24
Russian (0)	66	0.25
Scotch-Irish (201)	431	1.65
Scottish (116)	347	1.33
Slovak (0)	13	0.05
Slovene (0)	16	0.06
Swedish (32)	138	0.53
Swiss (0)	14	0.05
Ukrainian (9)	9	0.03
Welsh (17)	39	0.15

Hispanic Origin	Population	%
Hispanic or Latino (of any race)	1,339	4.98
Central American, ex. Mexican	232	0.86
Costa Rican	13	0.05
Guatemalan	26	0.10
Honduran	103	0.38
Nicaraguan	30	0.11
Panamanian	12	0.04
Salvadoran	48	0.18
Cuban	64	0.24
Dominican Republic	12	0.04
Mexican	702	2.61
Puerto Rican	86	0.32
South American	70	0.26
Argentinean	4	0.01
Bolivian	1	<0.01
Chilean	4	0.01
Colombian	36	0.13
Ecuadorian	5	0.02
Peruvian	1	<0.01
Uruguayan	2	0.01
Venezuelan	17	0.06
Other Hispanic or Latino	173	0.64

Race*	Population	%
African-American/Black (3,315)	3,451	12.83
Not Hispanic (3,295)	3,404	12.66
Hispanic (20)	47	0.17
American Indian/Alaska Native (83)	169	0.63
Not Hispanic (79)	152	0.57
Hispanic (4)	17	0.06
Blackfeet (0)	3	0.01
Cherokee (9)	28	0.10
Chickasaw (4)	4	0.01
Chippewa (1)	1	<0.01
Choctaw (2)	10	0.04
Comanche (0)	1	<0.01
Creek (3)	4	0.01
Delaware (1)	1	<0.01
Houma (15)	18	0.07
Lumbee (1)	1	<0.01
Mexican American Ind. (0)	3	0.01
Paiute (0)	1	<0.01
Shoshone (2)	2	0.01
Sioux (0)	1	<0.01
Asian (484)	561	2.09
Not Hispanic (482)	554	2.06
Hispanic (2)	7	0.03
Burmese (3)	3	0.01
Cambodian (6)	6	0.02
Chinese, ex. Taiwanese (60)	64	0.24
Filipino (38)	72	0.27
Indian (76)	89	0.33
Japanese (12)	25	0.09
Korean (17)	19	0.07
Laotian (35)	39	0.15
Pakistani (6)	6	0.02
Thai (6)	7	0.03
Vietnamese (213)	229	0.85
Hawaii Native/Pacific Islander (24)	35	0.13
Not Hispanic (23)	34	0.13
Hispanic (1)	1	<0.01
Guamanian/Chamorro (7)	8	0.03
Marshallese (1)	1	<0.01
Native Hawaiian (2)	3	0.01
Samoan (3)	12	0.04
Tongan (0)	8	0.03
White (22,174)	22,489	83.62
Not Hispanic (21,390)	21,624	80.40
Hispanic (784)	865	3.22

*Notes: † The Census 2010 population figure is used to calculate the percentages in the Hispanic Origin and Race categories. Ancestry percentages are based on the 2006-2010 American Community Survey population (not shown); ‡ Numbers in parentheses indicate the number of people reporting a single ancestry; * Numbers in parentheses indicate the number of persons reporting this race alone, not in combination with any other race; Please refer to the Explanation of Data for more information.*

Prien

Place Type: CDP
Parish: Calcasieu
Population: 7,810†

Ancestry‡	Population	%
American (788)	788	11.02
Arab (72)	83	1.16
Egyptian (13)	13	0.18
Lebanese (0)	11	0.15
Syrian (59)	59	0.83
Cajun (247)	277	3.88
Canadian (13)	46	0.64
Czech (0)	20	0.28
Czechoslovakian (19)	19	0.27
Dutch (13)	115	1.61
Eastern European (12)	12	0.17
English (199)	594	8.31
European (10)	21	0.29
French, ex. Basque (603)	1,509	21.11
French Canadian (517)	708	9.90
German (247)	891	12.47
Greek (0)	32	0.45
Irish (152)	657	9.19
Italian (84)	477	6.67
Norwegian (0)	13	0.18
Portuguese (29)	29	0.41
Russian (0)	13	0.18
Scotch-Irish (71)	107	1.50
Scottish (58)	83	1.16
Swedish (12)	49	0.69
Swiss (0)	11	0.15
Welsh (12)	61	0.85

Hispanic Origin	Population	%
Hispanic or Latino (of any race)	169	2.16
Central American, ex. Mexican	24	0.31
Costa Rican	3	0.04
Guatemalan	10	0.13
Panamanian	7	0.09
Salvadoran	4	0.05
Cuban	9	0.12
Mexican	59	0.76
Puerto Rican	12	0.15
South American	26	0.33
Colombian	8	0.10
Peruvian	9	0.12
Venezuelan	9	0.12
Other Hispanic or Latino	39	0.50

Race*	Population	%
African-American/Black (581)	654	8.37
Not Hispanic (578)	643	8.23
Hispanic (3)	11	0.14
American Indian/Alaska Native (32)	93	1.19
Not Hispanic (32)	86	1.10
Hispanic (0)	7	0.09
Apache (3)	4	0.05
Canadian/French Am. Ind. (1)	1	0.01
Cherokee (6)	25	0.32
Chickasaw (0)	1	0.01
Choctaw (2)	2	0.03
Creek (1)	1	0.01
Iroquois (1)	3	0.04
Mexican American Ind. (0)	1	0.01
Potawatomi (0)	3	0.04
Sioux (1)	1	0.01
South American Ind. (0)	4	0.05
Asian (261)	305	3.91
Not Hispanic (259)	299	3.83
Hispanic (2)	6	0.08
Bangladeshi (8)	8	0.10
Cambodian (1)	1	0.01
Chinese, ex. Taiwanese (34)	44	0.56
Filipino (11)	20	0.26
Indian (36)	44	0.56
Indonesian (1)	3	0.04
Japanese (3)	7	0.09
Korean (3)	7	0.09
Laotian (2)	3	0.04
Pakistani (38)	38	0.49
Taiwanese (0)	4	0.05
Thai (14)	17	0.22
Vietnamese (99)	107	1.37
Hawaii Native/Pacific Islander (10)	19	0.24
Not Hispanic (9)	16	0.20
Hispanic (1)	3	0.04
Guamanian/Chamorro (6)	10	0.13
Native Hawaiian (4)	6	0.08
Samoan (0)	1	0.01
White (6,666)	6,816	87.27
Not Hispanic (6,571)	6,699	85.77
Hispanic (95)	117	1.50

Raceland

Place Type: CDP
Parish: Lafourche
Population: 10,193†

Ancestry‡	Population	%
African, Sub-Saharan (17)	17	0.16
African (17)	17	0.16
American (1,276)	1,276	11.96
British (13)	13	0.12
Cajun (205)	216	2.02
Canadian (0)	20	0.19
Dutch (15)	28	0.26
English (163)	314	2.94
European (17)	17	0.16
French, ex. Basque (902)	1,464	13.72
French Canadian (846)	1,039	9.74
German (217)	696	6.52
Irish (227)	388	3.64
Italian (187)	357	3.35
Polish (23)	47	0.44
Portuguese (16)	16	0.15
Scotch-Irish (13)	13	0.12
Scottish (0)	74	0.69
Swedish (0)	31	0.29
Swiss (0)	32	0.30

Hispanic Origin	Population	%
Hispanic or Latino (of any race)	282	2.77
Central American, ex. Mexican	29	0.28
Costa Rican	1	0.01
Guatemalan	1	0.01
Honduran	23	0.23
Nicaraguan	4	0.04
Cuban	2	0.02
Dominican Republic	4	0.04
Mexican	186	1.82
Puerto Rican	31	0.30
South American	3	0.03
Argentinean	3	0.03
Other Hispanic or Latino	27	0.26

Race*	Population	%
African-American/Black (2,909)	2,994	29.37
Not Hispanic (2,898)	2,980	29.24
Hispanic (11)	14	0.14
American Indian/Alaska Native (113)	173	1.70
Not Hispanic (111)	165	1.62
Hispanic (2)	8	0.08
Blackfeet (0)	1	0.01
Cherokee (9)	18	0.18
Choctaw (3)	5	0.05
Houma (57)	73	0.72
Asian (34)	46	0.45
Not Hispanic (33)	45	0.44
Hispanic (1)	1	0.01
Chinese, ex. Taiwanese (11)	12	0.12
Filipino (1)	4	0.04
Indian (2)	6	0.06
Japanese (3)	3	0.03
Korean (1)	3	0.03
Pakistani (11)	11	0.11
Thai (2)	3	0.03
Vietnamese (2)	4	0.04
Hawaii Native/Pacific Islander (4)	10	0.10
Not Hispanic (4)	10	0.10
Guamanian/Chamorro (0)	1	0.01
Native Hawaiian (1)	3	0.03
White (6,831)	6,966	68.34
Not Hispanic (6,729)	6,842	67.12
Hispanic (102)	124	1.22

Rayne

Place Type: City
Parish: Acadia
Population: 7,953†

Ancestry‡	Population	%
African, Sub-Saharan (53)	60	0.75
African (53)	60	0.75
American (648)	648	8.05
British (0)	8	0.10
Cajun (173)	190	2.36
Canadian (12)	12	0.15
Dutch (0)	16	0.20
English (237)	504	6.26
French, ex. Basque (1,555)	2,205	27.40
French Canadian (176)	176	2.19
German (86)	585	7.27
Irish (110)	347	4.31
Italian (24)	50	0.62
Pennsylvania German (0)	13	0.16
Scandinavian (10)	10	0.12
Scotch-Irish (0)	12	0.15
Scottish (0)	35	0.43
Ukrainian (0)	16	0.20
Welsh (0)	18	0.22

Hispanic Origin	Population	%
Hispanic or Latino (of any race)	118	1.48
Central American, ex. Mexican	3	0.04
Guatemalan	1	0.01
Honduran	1	0.01
Salvadoran	1	0.01
Cuban	9	0.11
Mexican	63	0.79
Puerto Rican	2	0.03
South American	9	0.11
Colombian	9	0.11
Other Hispanic or Latino	32	0.40

Race*	Population	%
African-American/Black (2,794)	2,899	36.45
Not Hispanic (2,780)	2,874	36.14
Hispanic (14)	25	0.31
American Indian/Alaska Native (23)	43	0.54
Not Hispanic (22)	37	0.47
Hispanic (1)	6	0.08
Cherokee (1)	4	0.05
Chickasaw (2)	2	0.03
Houma (1)	1	0.01
Navajo (0)	6	0.08
Asian (14)	19	0.24
Not Hispanic (14)	19	0.24
Cambodian (1)	1	0.01
Chinese, ex. Taiwanese (0)	1	0.01
Filipino (1)	1	0.01
Indian (2)	5	0.06
Japanese (1)	1	0.01
Vietnamese (8)	10	0.13
Hawaii Native/Pacific Islander (1)	2	0.03
Not Hispanic (0)	1	0.01
Hispanic (1)	1	0.01
Guamanian/Chamorro (1)	1	0.01
Samoan (0)	1	0.01
White (4,970)	5,087	63.96
Not Hispanic (4,900)	5,002	62.89
Hispanic (70)	85	1.07

*Notes: † The Census 2010 population figure is used to calculate the percentages in the Hispanic Origin and Race categories. Ancestry percentages are based on the 2006-2010 American Community Survey population (not shown); ‡ Numbers in parentheses indicate the number of people reporting a single ancestry; * Numbers in parentheses indicate the number of persons reporting this race alone, not in combination with any other race; Please refer to the Explanation of Data for more information.*

Reserve

Place Type: CDP
Parish: St. John the Baptist
Population: 9,766†

Ancestry‡	Population	%
African, Sub-Saharan (216)	216	2.28
African (216)	216	2.28
American (187)	187	1.97
Brazilian (0)	9	0.10
Cajun (128)	167	1.76
Dutch (0)	7	0.07
English (128)	170	1.79
European (21)	21	0.22
French, ex. Basque (419)	1,161	12.26
French Canadian (77)	101	1.07
German (217)	831	8.77
Greek (0)	18	0.19
Irish (41)	295	3.11
Italian (58)	284	3.00
Polish (16)	16	0.17
Scotch-Irish (0)	12	0.13
Scottish (0)	21	0.22
Welsh (9)	9	0.10
West Indian, ex. Hispanic (47)	47	0.50
Belizean (9)	9	0.10
West Indian (38)	38	0.40
Yugoslavian (29)	29	0.31

Hispanic Origin	Population	%
Hispanic or Latino (of any race)	280	2.87
Central American, ex. Mexican	107	1.10
Costa Rican	4	0.04
Guatemalan	15	0.15
Honduran	66	0.68
Nicaraguan	10	0.10
Panamanian	4	0.04
Salvadoran	8	0.08
Cuban	8	0.08
Dominican Republic	2	0.02
Mexican	97	0.99
Puerto Rican	22	0.23
South American	2	0.02
Chilean	1	0.01
Venezuelan	1	0.01
Other Hispanic or Latino	42	0.43

Race*	Population	%
African-American/Black (5,806)	5,876	60.17
Not Hispanic (5,772)	5,835	59.75
Hispanic (34)	41	0.42
American Indian/Alaska Native (22)	53	0.54
Not Hispanic (18)	49	0.50
Hispanic (4)	4	0.04
Apache (1)	2	0.02
Cherokee (0)	3	0.03
Chippewa (1)	1	0.01
Choctaw (0)	3	0.03
Cree (4)	4	0.04
Houma (1)	1	0.01
Sioux (1)	1	0.01
Asian (38)	49	0.50
Not Hispanic (38)	46	0.47
Hispanic (0)	3	0.03
Filipino (9)	11	0.11
Indian (3)	4	0.04
Japanese (0)	1	0.01
Korean (0)	4	0.04
Taiwanese (1)	1	0.01
Thai (1)	1	0.01
Vietnamese (24)	26	0.27
Hawaii Native/Pacific Islander (4)	8	0.08
Not Hispanic (4)	7	0.07
Hispanic (0)	1	0.01
Native Hawaiian (4)	7	0.07
White (3,712)	3,808	38.99
Not Hispanic (3,559)	3,636	37.23
Hispanic (153)	172	1.76

River Ridge

Place Type: CDP
Parish: Jefferson
Population: 13,494†

Ancestry‡	Population	%
African, Sub-Saharan (552)	552	4.12
African (552)	552	4.12
American (1,156)	1,156	8.62
Arab (16)	59	0.44
Iraqi (16)	16	0.12
Lebanese (0)	43	0.32
Armenian (33)	43	0.32
Austrian (0)	19	0.14
Belgian (9)	9	0.07
British (49)	117	0.87
Cajun (98)	145	1.08
Canadian (11)	22	0.16
Croatian (16)	132	0.98
Czech (28)	49	0.37
Czechoslovakian (0)	8	0.06
Danish (0)	21	0.16
Dutch (11)	95	0.71
English (459)	1,623	12.10
European (79)	79	0.59
Finnish (0)	9	0.07
French, ex. Basque (986)	3,331	24.84
French Canadian (100)	107	0.80
German (575)	2,521	18.80
Greek (16)	34	0.25
Hungarian (9)	9	0.07
Irish (345)	1,984	14.79
Italian (884)	2,165	16.14
Norwegian (0)	46	0.34
Pennsylvania German (0)	7	0.05
Polish (13)	63	0.47
Portuguese (0)	4	0.03
Russian (0)	32	0.24
Scotch-Irish (110)	257	1.92
Scottish (31)	255	1.90
Slovak (0)	30	0.22
Swedish (8)	62	0.46
Swiss (0)	26	0.19
Ukrainian (0)	10	0.07
Welsh (0)	45	0.34
West Indian, ex. Hispanic (6)	6	0.04
Belizean (6)	6	0.04
Yugoslavian (0)	21	0.16

Hispanic Origin	Population	%
Hispanic or Latino (of any race)	700	5.19
Central American, ex. Mexican	275	2.04
Costa Rican	18	0.13
Guatemalan	48	0.36
Honduran	139	1.03
Nicaraguan	35	0.26
Panamanian	6	0.04
Salvadoran	28	0.21
Other Central American	1	0.01
Cuban	88	0.65
Dominican Republic	9	0.07
Mexican	151	1.12
Puerto Rican	42	0.31
South American	50	0.37
Argentinean	8	0.06
Chilean	6	0.04
Colombian	20	0.15
Ecuadorian	3	0.02
Paraguayan	1	0.01
Peruvian	4	0.03
Uruguayan	2	0.01
Venezuelan	5	0.04
Other South American	1	0.01
Other Hispanic or Latino	85	0.63

Race*	Population	%
African-American/Black (1,639)	1,698	12.58
Not Hispanic (1,630)	1,680	12.45
Hispanic (9)	18	0.13
American Indian/Alaska Native (33)	96	0.71
Not Hispanic (30)	84	0.62
Hispanic (3)	12	0.09
Blackfeet (0)	2	0.01
Canadian/French Am. Ind. (0)	3	0.02
Central American Ind. (1)	1	0.01
Cherokee (2)	19	0.14
Chickasaw (1)	1	0.01
Choctaw (2)	13	0.10
Creek (2)	2	0.01
Houma (6)	10	0.07
Mexican American Ind. (1)	4	0.03
Sioux (2)	4	0.03
Spanish American Ind. (0)	2	0.01
Tlingit-Haida *(Alaska Native)* (1)	1	0.01
Asian (122)	163	1.21
Not Hispanic (122)	161	1.19
Hispanic (0)	2	0.01
Chinese, ex. Taiwanese (24)	27	0.20
Filipino (11)	23	0.17
Indian (29)	35	0.26
Indonesian (0)	4	0.03
Japanese (12)	18	0.13
Korean (10)	14	0.10
Laotian (1)	1	0.01
Thai (2)	3	0.02
Vietnamese (32)	34	0.25
Hawaii Native/Pacific Islander (4)	11	0.08
Not Hispanic (4)	6	0.04
Hispanic (0)	5	0.04
Guamanian/Chamorro (1)	4	0.03
Native Hawaiian (2)	3	0.02
Samoan (1)	2	0.01
White (11,369)	11,533	85.47
Not Hispanic (10,858)	10,982	81.38
Hispanic (511)	551	4.08

Ruston

Place Type: City
Parish: Lincoln
Population: 21,859†

Ancestry‡	Population	%
African, Sub-Saharan (343)	431	2.00
African (343)	431	2.00
American (1,064)	1,064	4.93
Arab (31)	110	0.51
Arab (23)	63	0.29
Lebanese (8)	31	0.14
Other Arab (0)	16	0.07
Armenian (0)	34	0.16
Australian (0)	12	0.06
Brazilian (3)	9	0.04
British (25)	49	0.23
Cajun (13)	69	0.32
Celtic (44)	44	0.20
Czech (6)	75	0.35
Czechoslovakian (0)	15	0.07
Danish (19)	19	0.09
Dutch (39)	223	1.03
English (1,067)	1,866	8.65
European (72)	87	0.40
Finnish (8)	8	0.04
French, ex. Basque (422)	1,270	5.89
French Canadian (106)	123	0.57
German (521)	1,624	7.53
Greek (10)	46	0.21
Irish (654)	2,109	9.77
Italian (141)	420	1.95
Lithuanian (12)	41	0.19
Norwegian (26)	31	0.14
Polish (21)	135	0.63
Portuguese (0)	28	0.13
Russian (0)	50	0.23
Scandinavian (0)	10	0.05
Scotch-Irish (348)	722	3.35
Scottish (127)	278	1.29
Slovak (0)	12	0.06
Swedish (0)	34	0.16

*Notes: † The Census 2010 population figure is used to calculate the percentages in the Hispanic Origin and Race categories. Ancestry percentages are based on the 2006-2010 American Community Survey population (not shown); ‡ Numbers in parentheses indicate the number of people reporting a single ancestry; * Numbers in parentheses indicate the number of persons reporting this race alone, not in combination with any other race; Please refer to the Explanation of Data for more information.*

Swiss (0)	11	0.05
Turkish (11)	11	0.05
Welsh (141)	184	0.85
West Indian, ex. Hispanic (0)	24	0.11
Dutch West Indian (0)	24	0.11
Yugoslavian (10)	10	0.05

Hispanic Origin	Population	%
Hispanic or Latino (of any race)	512	2.34
Central American, ex. Mexican	39	0.18
Costa Rican	1	<0.01
Guatemalan	14	0.06
Honduran	8	0.04
Nicaraguan	12	0.05
Panamanian	1	<0.01
Salvadoran	3	0.01
Cuban	22	0.10
Mexican	319	1.46
Puerto Rican	41	0.19
South American	37	0.17
Argentinean	13	0.06
Bolivian	1	<0.01
Chilean	1	<0.01
Colombian	6	0.03
Ecuadorian	4	0.02
Peruvian	1	<0.01
Venezuelan	11	0.05
Other Hispanic or Latino	54	0.25

Race*	Population	%
African-American/Black (9,180)	9,332	42.69
Not Hispanic (9,152)	9,293	42.51
Hispanic (28)	39	0.18
American Indian/Alaska Native (45)	139	0.64
Not Hispanic (39)	123	0.56
Hispanic (6)	16	0.07
Apache (0)	2	0.01
Blackfeet (1)	1	<0.01
Canadian/French Am. Ind. (0)	1	<0.01
Cherokee (8)	21	0.10
Cheyenne (0)	1	<0.01
Chickasaw (0)	2	0.01
Choctaw (1)	8	0.04
Comanche (3)	3	0.01
Creek (2)	4	0.02
Houma (1)	4	0.02
Mexican American Ind. (1)	2	0.01
Navajo (0)	1	<0.01
Sioux (0)	1	<0.01
Asian (691)	776	3.55
Not Hispanic (687)	766	3.50
Hispanic (4)	10	0.05
Bangladeshi (25)	26	0.12
Burmese (1)	1	<0.01
Chinese, ex. Taiwanese (134)	149	0.68
Filipino (26)	50	0.23
Indian (260)	278	1.27
Indonesian (1)	1	<0.01
Japanese (16)	21	0.10
Korean (37)	46	0.21
Laotian (3)	4	0.02
Nepalese (62)	63	0.29
Pakistani (24)	24	0.11
Sri Lankan (6)	6	0.03
Taiwanese (8)	9	0.04
Thai (14)	16	0.07
Vietnamese (55)	58	0.27
Hawaii Native/Pacific Islander (7)	26	0.12
Not Hispanic (6)	19	0.09
Hispanic (1)	7	0.03
Guamanian/Chamorro (1)	1	<0.01
Native Hawaiian (3)	6	0.03
Samoan (2)	4	0.02
White (11,436)	11,629	53.20
Not Hispanic (11,210)	11,381	52.07
Hispanic (226)	248	1.13

Scott

Place Type: City
Parish: Lafayette
Population: 8,614†

Ancestry‡	Population	%
African, Sub-Saharan (116)	116	1.38
African (116)	116	1.38
American (664)	664	7.88
Austrian (0)	42	0.50
British (11)	11	0.13
Cajun (481)	586	6.95
Dutch (6)	20	0.24
English (57)	275	3.26
French, ex. Basque (1,420)	2,258	26.78
French Canadian (391)	514	6.10
German (170)	958	11.36
Irish (129)	507	6.01
Italian (0)	70	0.83
Norwegian (38)	121	1.44
Polish (0)	16	0.19
Portuguese (105)	105	1.25
Russian (0)	43	0.51
Scotch-Irish (14)	29	0.34
Scottish (0)	38	0.45
Swiss (0)	13	0.15
West Indian, ex. Hispanic (0)	22	0.26
Jamaican (0)	22	0.26

Hispanic Origin	Population	%
Hispanic or Latino (of any race)	320	3.71
Central American, ex. Mexican	26	0.30
Guatemalan	8	0.09
Honduran	7	0.08
Panamanian	6	0.07
Salvadoran	5	0.06
Cuban	22	0.26
Mexican	189	2.19
Puerto Rican	16	0.19
South American	11	0.13
Colombian	4	0.05
Peruvian	2	0.02
Venezuelan	5	0.06
Other Hispanic or Latino	56	0.65

Race*	Population	%
African-American/Black (1,355)	1,433	16.64
Not Hispanic (1,334)	1,403	16.29
Hispanic (21)	30	0.35
American Indian/Alaska Native (41)	82	0.95
Not Hispanic (36)	71	0.82
Hispanic (5)	11	0.13
Blackfeet (0)	1	0.01
Central American Ind. (1)	3	0.03
Cherokee (3)	8	0.09
Choctaw (2)	5	0.06
Comanche (0)	1	0.01
Houma (5)	7	0.08
Mexican American Ind. (3)	4	0.05
Seminole (0)	3	0.03
Asian (143)	156	1.81
Not Hispanic (143)	155	1.80
Hispanic (0)	1	0.01
Chinese, ex. Taiwanese (15)	17	0.20
Filipino (4)	12	0.14
Indian (6)	6	0.07
Japanese (1)	1	0.01
Korean (0)	1	0.01
Laotian (1)	2	0.02
Pakistani (2)	2	0.02
Thai (4)	4	0.05
Vietnamese (106)	107	1.24
Hawaii Native/Pacific Islander (1)	6	0.07
Not Hispanic (1)	6	0.07
Guamanian/Chamorro (1)	2	0.02
White (6,778)	6,916	80.29
Not Hispanic (6,639)	6,762	78.50
Hispanic (139)	154	1.79

Shenandoah

Place Type: CDP
Parish: East Baton Rouge
Population: 18,399†

Ancestry‡	Population	%
African, Sub-Saharan (25)	25	0.14
African (25)	25	0.14
American (1,933)	1,933	10.56
Arab (136)	222	1.21
Lebanese (29)	91	0.50
Palestinian (79)	79	0.43
Other Arab (28)	52	0.28
Australian (84)	84	0.46
Austrian (21)	21	0.11
British (120)	214	1.17
Cajun (153)	269	1.47
Croatian (16)	16	0.09
Czech (0)	13	0.07
Danish (29)	80	0.44
Dutch (0)	81	0.44
English (742)	2,275	12.43
European (99)	99	0.54
French, ex. Basque (1,124)	3,535	19.32
French Canadian (235)	447	2.44
German (760)	2,927	16.00
Greek (0)	13	0.07
Hungarian (0)	96	0.52
Iranian (37)	37	0.20
Irish (648)	2,329	12.73
Italian (757)	1,686	9.21
Lithuanian (11)	11	0.06
Norwegian (0)	146	0.80
Polish (20)	284	1.55
Portuguese (0)	98	0.54
Russian (13)	47	0.26
Scotch-Irish (272)	664	3.63
Scottish (390)	709	3.87
Swedish (10)	107	0.58
Swiss (0)	21	0.11
Welsh (23)	80	0.44
West Indian, ex. Hispanic (7)	31	0.17
Trinidadian/Tobagonian (7)	31	0.17

Hispanic Origin	Population	%
Hispanic or Latino (of any race)	578	3.14
Central American, ex. Mexican	136	0.74
Costa Rican	3	0.02
Guatemalan	31	0.17
Honduran	70	0.38
Nicaraguan	15	0.08
Panamanian	2	0.01
Salvadoran	15	0.08
Cuban	54	0.29
Dominican Republic	16	0.09
Mexican	180	0.98
Puerto Rican	40	0.22
South American	75	0.41
Argentinean	4	0.02
Chilean	4	0.02
Colombian	27	0.15
Ecuadorian	4	0.02
Paraguayan	9	0.05
Peruvian	3	0.02
Venezuelan	24	0.13
Other Hispanic or Latino	77	0.42

Race*	Population	%
African-American/Black (2,063)	2,164	11.76
Not Hispanic (2,056)	2,145	11.66
Hispanic (7)	19	0.10
American Indian/Alaska Native (53)	104	0.57
Not Hispanic (49)	95	0.52
Hispanic (4)	9	0.05
Apache (1)	1	0.01
Cherokee (10)	25	0.14
Chippewa (2)	2	0.01
Choctaw (3)	6	0.03
Cree (0)	1	0.01

*Notes: † The Census 2010 population figure is used to calculate the percentages in the Hispanic Origin and Race categories. Ancestry percentages are based on the 2006-2010 American Community Survey population (not shown); ‡ Numbers in parentheses indicate the number of people reporting a single ancestry; * Numbers in parentheses indicate the number of persons reporting this race alone, not in combination with any other race; Please refer to the Explanation of Data for more information.*

Creek (1)	3	0.02
Crow (1)	1	0.01
Houma (5)	5	0.03
Asian (650)	730	3.97
Not Hispanic (643)	719	3.91
Hispanic (7)	11	0.06
Bangladeshi (5)	5	0.03
Chinese, ex. Taiwanese (89)	101	0.55
Filipino (35)	41	0.22
Indian (127)	140	0.76
Japanese (8)	12	0.07
Korean (26)	34	0.18
Laotian (17)	17	0.09
Pakistani (8)	9	0.05
Taiwanese (23)	26	0.14
Thai (2)	5	0.03
Vietnamese (290)	307	1.67
Hawaii Native/Pacific Islander (12)	33	0.18
Not Hispanic (12)	33	0.18
Guamanian/Chamorro (6)	9	0.05
Native Hawaiian (6)	12	0.07
Samoan (0)	3	0.02
White (15,238)	15,438	83.91
Not Hispanic (14,821)	14,991	81.48
Hispanic (417)	447	2.43

Shreveport

Place Type: City
Parish: Caddo
Population: 199,311†

Ancestry‡	Population	%
Afghan (66)	66	0.03
African, Sub-Saharan (3,462)	4,579	2.31
African (3,450)	4,567	2.30
Other Sub-Saharan African (12)	12	0.01
American (9,705)	9,705	4.89
Arab (451)	810	0.41
Egyptian (0)	7	<0.01
Jordanian (69)	139	0.07
Lebanese (269)	491	0.25
Palestinian (20)	20	0.01
Syrian (46)	78	0.04
Other Arab (47)	75	0.04
Austrian (40)	87	0.04
Belgian (69)	107	0.05
Brazilian (13)	13	0.01
British (208)	486	0.24
Cajun (291)	331	0.17
Canadian (123)	199	0.10
Celtic (13)	13	0.01
Croatian (13)	21	0.01
Czech (129)	253	0.13
Czechoslovakian (0)	12	0.01
Danish (55)	172	0.09
Dutch (621)	2,006	1.01
Eastern European (110)	127	0.06
English (5,970)	13,209	6.66
Estonian (0)	5	<0.01
European (773)	1,052	0.53
Finnish (12)	12	0.01
French, ex. Basque (3,028)	10,074	5.08
French Canadian (436)	638	0.32
German (3,537)	11,805	5.95
Greek (151)	375	0.19
Hungarian (29)	66	0.03
Iranian (85)	85	0.04
Irish (4,524)	12,778	6.44
Israeli (73)	73	0.04
Italian (1,924)	4,124	2.08
Latvian (0)	26	0.01
Lithuanian (15)	41	0.02
New Zealander (12)	12	0.01
Northern European (66)	82	0.04
Norwegian (211)	759	0.38
Pennsylvania German (0)	27	0.01
Polish (318)	874	0.44
Portuguese (52)	146	0.07
Romanian (88)	104	0.05
Russian (136)	395	0.20
Scandinavian (67)	85	0.04
Scotch-Irish (1,980)	3,479	1.75
Scottish (793)	2,268	1.14
Serbian (0)	13	0.01
Slavic (26)	37	0.02
Slovak (24)	57	0.03
Swedish (100)	499	0.25
Swiss (13)	95	0.05
Ukrainian (15)	70	0.04
Welsh (184)	835	0.42
West Indian, ex. Hispanic (77)	127	0.06
British West Indian (0)	13	0.01
Haitian (0)	14	0.01
Jamaican (77)	91	0.05
West Indian (0)	9	<0.01
Yugoslavian (0)	7	<0.01

Hispanic Origin	Population	%
Hispanic or Latino (of any race)	5,018	2.52
Central American, ex. Mexican	382	0.19
Costa Rican	14	0.01
Guatemalan	63	0.03
Honduran	105	0.05
Nicaraguan	67	0.03
Panamanian	52	0.03
Salvadoran	76	0.04
Other Central American	5	<0.01
Cuban	121	0.06
Dominican Republic	43	0.02
Mexican	3,182	1.60
Puerto Rican	365	0.18
South American	246	0.12
Argentinean	36	0.02
Bolivian	7	<0.01
Chilean	23	0.01
Colombian	83	0.04
Ecuadorian	22	0.01
Paraguayan	2	<0.01
Peruvian	40	0.02
Uruguayan	6	<0.01
Venezuelan	25	0.01
Other South American	2	<0.01
Other Hispanic or Latino	679	0.34

Race*	Population	%
African-American/Black (109,022)	110,693	55.54
Not Hispanic (108,535)	110,057	55.22
Hispanic (487)	636	0.32
American Indian/Alaska Native (725)	1,678	0.84
Not Hispanic (652)	1,523	0.76
Hispanic (73)	155	0.08
Alaska Athabascan *(Ala. Nat.)* (1)	6	<0.01
Aleut *(Alaska Native)* (1)	1	<0.01
Apache (4)	27	0.01
Arapaho (1)	1	<0.01
Blackfeet (5)	30	0.02
Canadian/French Am. Ind. (2)	12	0.01
Cherokee (87)	323	0.16
Cheyenne (2)	6	<0.01
Chickasaw (8)	18	0.01
Chippewa (5)	11	0.01
Choctaw (49)	127	0.06
Comanche (3)	9	<0.01
Creek (10)	19	0.01
Crow (0)	5	<0.01
Delaware (0)	4	<0.01
Houma (18)	24	0.01
Inupiat *(Alaska Native)* (0)	1	<0.01
Iroquois (2)	9	<0.01
Kiowa (4)	4	<0.01
Lumbee (5)	5	<0.01
Mexican American Ind. (9)	20	0.01
Navajo (7)	15	0.01
Osage (5)	8	<0.01
Ottawa (1)	2	<0.01
Paiute (0)	3	<0.01
Potawatomi (7)	10	0.01
Pueblo (4)	4	<0.01
Seminole (3)	8	<0.01
Sioux (9)	17	0.01
South American Ind. (0)	1	<0.01
Spanish American Ind. (0)	1	<0.01
Tohono O'Odham (1)	2	<0.01
Ute (1)	1	<0.01
Yuman (2)	3	<0.01
Asian (2,628)	3,303	1.66
Not Hispanic (2,600)	3,219	1.62
Hispanic (28)	84	0.04
Bangladeshi (9)	12	0.01
Burmese (6)	8	<0.01
Cambodian (35)	38	0.02
Chinese, ex. Taiwanese (495)	582	0.29
Filipino (383)	559	0.28
Hmong (0)	1	<0.01
Indian (730)	825	0.41
Indonesian (8)	19	0.01
Japanese (74)	160	0.08
Korean (180)	252	0.13
Laotian (28)	38	0.02
Malaysian (3)	3	<0.01
Nepalese (10)	10	0.01
Pakistani (77)	89	0.04
Sri Lankan (6)	7	<0.01
Taiwanese (23)	32	0.02
Thai (33)	73	0.04
Vietnamese (424)	462	0.23
Hawaii Native/Pacific Islander (97)	235	0.12
Not Hispanic (89)	211	0.11
Hispanic (8)	24	0.01
Guamanian/Chamorro (25)	49	0.02
Native Hawaiian (18)	53	0.03
Samoan (6)	31	0.02
Tongan (3)	4	<0.01
White (82,027)	84,302	42.30
Not Hispanic (79,693)	81,612	40.95
Hispanic (2,334)	2,690	1.35

Slidell

Place Type: City
Parish: St. Tammany
Population: 27,068†

Ancestry‡	Population	%
African, Sub-Saharan (34)	41	0.15
African (18)	25	0.09
Nigerian (16)	16	0.06
American (1,628)	1,628	6.01
Arab (10)	23	0.08
Lebanese (10)	23	0.08
Australian (0)	15	0.06
Austrian (0)	15	0.06
Belgian (59)	59	0.22
Brazilian (27)	27	0.10
British (30)	85	0.31
Bulgarian (0)	24	0.09
Cajun (41)	117	0.43
Croatian (0)	47	0.17
Czech (23)	33	0.12
Danish (11)	18	0.07
Dutch (0)	158	0.58
English (790)	2,248	8.31
European (140)	176	0.65
Finnish (13)	13	0.05
French, ex. Basque (1,254)	5,129	18.95
French Canadian (149)	300	1.11
German (992)	4,584	16.94
Greek (20)	20	0.07
Hungarian (0)	59	0.22
Irish (849)	3,793	14.01
Italian (1,411)	3,653	13.50
Lithuanian (29)	94	0.35
Northern European (9)	9	0.03
Norwegian (19)	129	0.48
Pennsylvania German (0)	11	0.04
Polish (127)	355	1.31
Portuguese (14)	74	0.27
Romanian (26)	26	0.10
Russian (14)	74	0.27

*Notes: † The Census 2010 population figure is used to calculate the percentages in the Hispanic Origin and Race categories. Ancestry percentages are based on the 2006-2010 American Community Survey population (not shown); ‡ Numbers in parentheses indicate the number of people reporting a single ancestry; * Numbers in parentheses indicate the number of persons reporting this race alone, not in combination with any other race; Please refer to the Explanation of Data for more information.*

Scandinavian (9)	57	0.21
Scotch-Irish (200)	482	1.78
Scottish (138)	523	1.93
Slovak (0)	7	0.03
Swedish (10)	124	0.46
Swiss (0)	32	0.12
Ukrainian (0)	19	0.07
Welsh (33)	124	0.46
West Indian, ex. Hispanic (0)	16	0.06
Haitian (0)	16	0.06
Yugoslavian (4)	8	0.03

Hispanic Origin	Population	%
Hispanic or Latino (of any race)	1,717	6.34
Central American, ex. Mexican	456	1.68
Costa Rican	4	0.01
Guatemalan	67	0.25
Honduran	254	0.94
Nicaraguan	81	0.30
Panamanian	18	0.07
Salvadoran	31	0.11
Other Central American	1	<0.01
Cuban	87	0.32
Dominican Republic	6	0.02
Mexican	703	2.60
Puerto Rican	123	0.45
South American	83	0.31
Argentinean	1	<0.01
Bolivian	1	<0.01
Chilean	4	0.01
Colombian	57	0.21
Ecuadorian	8	0.03
Peruvian	5	0.02
Uruguayan	2	0.01
Venezuelan	4	0.01
Other South American	1	<0.01
Other Hispanic or Latino	259	0.96

Race*	Population	%
African-American/Black (4,601)	4,882	18.04
Not Hispanic (4,568)	4,814	17.78
Hispanic (33)	68	0.25
American Indian/Alaska Native (127)	288	1.06
Not Hispanic (114)	237	0.88
Hispanic (13)	51	0.19
Aleut *(Alaska Native)* (1)	1	<0.01
Apache (0)	3	0.01
Blackfeet (1)	3	0.01
Central American Ind. (0)	1	<0.01
Cherokee (9)	40	0.15
Chickasaw (1)	1	<0.01
Choctaw (14)	46	0.17
Creek (8)	10	0.04
Houma (34)	44	0.16
Iroquois (2)	2	0.01
Lumbee (3)	4	0.01
Mexican American Ind. (2)	10	0.04
Potawatomi (4)	4	0.01
Seminole (1)	1	<0.01
Sioux (1)	2	0.01
Yaqui (0)	1	<0.01
Asian (423)	576	2.13
Not Hispanic (408)	531	1.96
Hispanic (15)	45	0.17
Bangladeshi (0)	1	<0.01
Chinese, ex. Taiwanese (80)	97	0.36
Filipino (59)	117	0.43
Indian (44)	53	0.20
Indonesian (8)	9	0.03
Japanese (23)	57	0.21
Korean (20)	31	0.11
Laotian (3)	6	0.02
Pakistani (13)	16	0.06
Taiwanese (0)	1	<0.01
Thai (13)	20	0.07
Vietnamese (134)	144	0.53
Hawaii Native/Pacific Islander (10)	41	0.15
Not Hispanic (10)	35	0.13
Hispanic (0)	6	0.02
Guamanian/Chamorro (2)	6	0.02
Native Hawaiian (1)	16	0.06
Samoan (1)	3	0.01
White (20,559)	21,056	77.79
Not Hispanic (19,714)	20,083	74.19
Hispanic (845)	973	3.59

St. Rose

Place Type: CDP
Parish: St. Charles
Population: 8,122†

Ancestry‡	Population	%
American (177)	177	2.12
Canadian (7)	7	0.08
Dutch (0)	59	0.71
English (432)	537	6.42
French, ex. Basque (142)	1,041	12.44
French Canadian (47)	81	0.97
German (177)	851	10.17
Hungarian (0)	11	0.13
Iranian (12)	12	0.14
Irish (72)	673	8.05
Italian (504)	902	10.78
Polish (0)	10	0.12
Scandinavian (0)	25	0.30
Scottish (0)	19	0.23

Hispanic Origin	Population	%
Hispanic or Latino (of any race)	768	9.46
Central American, ex. Mexican	391	4.81
Costa Rican	15	0.18
Guatemalan	15	0.18
Honduran	291	3.58
Nicaraguan	38	0.47
Panamanian	10	0.12
Salvadoran	22	0.27
Cuban	50	0.62
Dominican Republic	18	0.22
Mexican	150	1.85
Puerto Rican	20	0.25
South American	43	0.53
Colombian	15	0.18
Ecuadorian	23	0.28
Venezuelan	5	0.06
Other Hispanic or Latino	96	1.18

Race*	Population	%
African-American/Black (3,486)	3,540	43.59
Not Hispanic (3,439)	3,487	42.93
Hispanic (47)	53	0.65
American Indian/Alaska Native (14)	57	0.70
Not Hispanic (14)	47	0.58
Hispanic (0)	10	0.12
Alaska Athabascan *(Ala. Nat.)* (0)	1	0.01
Apache (1)	1	0.01
Blackfeet (0)	2	0.02
Cherokee (0)	4	0.05
Chippewa (1)	1	0.01
Choctaw (3)	8	0.10
Creek (0)	3	0.04
Houma (2)	5	0.06
Mexican American Ind. (0)	1	0.01
Spanish American Ind. (0)	1	0.01
Asian (107)	129	1.59
Not Hispanic (107)	123	1.51
Hispanic (0)	6	0.07
Cambodian (6)	6	0.07
Chinese, ex. Taiwanese (7)	7	0.09
Filipino (8)	15	0.18
Indian (26)	27	0.33
Japanese (1)	6	0.07
Korean (1)	2	0.02
Laotian (1)	1	0.01
Malaysian (1)	1	0.01
Pakistani (30)	31	0.38
Taiwanese (3)	3	0.04
Vietnamese (11)	13	0.16
Hawaii Native/Pacific Islander (1)	3	0.04
Not Hispanic (1)	3	0.04
White (4,094)	4,222	51.98
Not Hispanic (3,675)	3,757	46.26
Hispanic (419)	465	5.73

Sulphur

Place Type: City
Parish: Calcasieu
Population: 20,410†

Ancestry‡	Population	%
American (1,604)	1,604	7.93
Arab (62)	140	0.69
Arab (25)	25	0.12
Lebanese (37)	81	0.40
Syrian (0)	34	0.17
Belgian (0)	13	0.06
British (85)	178	0.88
Cajun (338)	486	2.40
Czech (0)	8	0.04
Czechoslovakian (25)	52	0.26
Danish (45)	45	0.22
Dutch (76)	343	1.70
English (1,338)	2,709	13.40
European (26)	35	0.17
French, ex. Basque (2,541)	5,782	28.60
French Canadian (953)	1,136	5.62
German (527)	2,556	12.64
Greek (26)	108	0.53
Hungarian (0)	33	0.16
Irish (593)	2,140	10.58
Italian (123)	782	3.87
Northern European (10)	10	0.05
Norwegian (104)	234	1.16
Polish (65)	145	0.72
Portuguese (12)	24	0.12
Scandinavian (0)	27	0.13
Scotch-Irish (189)	546	2.70
Scottish (114)	417	2.06
Slovak (13)	13	0.06
Swedish (18)	48	0.24
Swiss (0)	23	0.11
Welsh (40)	104	0.51
West Indian, ex. Hispanic (17)	41	0.20
Jamaican (17)	17	0.08
Trinidadian/Tobagonian (0)	24	0.12

Hispanic Origin	Population	%
Hispanic or Latino (of any race)	691	3.39
Central American, ex. Mexican	33	0.16
Guatemalan	7	0.03
Honduran	15	0.07
Nicaraguan	4	0.02
Panamanian	5	0.02
Salvadoran	1	<0.01
Other Central American	1	<0.01
Cuban	16	0.08
Dominican Republic	3	0.01
Mexican	452	2.21
Puerto Rican	57	0.28
South American	31	0.15
Bolivian	1	<0.01
Chilean	5	0.02
Colombian	11	0.05
Ecuadorian	2	0.01
Peruvian	6	0.03
Venezuelan	6	0.03
Other Hispanic or Latino	99	0.49

Race*	Population	%
African-American/Black (1,270)	1,419	6.95
Not Hispanic (1,240)	1,383	6.78
Hispanic (30)	36	0.18
American Indian/Alaska Native (85)	216	1.06
Not Hispanic (79)	194	0.95
Hispanic (6)	22	0.11
Apache (1)	2	0.01
Blackfeet (0)	4	0.02
Canadian/French Am. Ind. (0)	1	<0.01
Cherokee (15)	55	0.27

*Notes: † The Census 2010 population figure is used to calculate the percentages in the Hispanic Origin and Race categories. Ancestry percentages are based on the 2006-2010 American Community Survey population (not shown); ‡ Numbers in parentheses indicate the number of people reporting a single ancestry; * Numbers in parentheses indicate the number of persons reporting this race alone, not in combination with any other race; Please refer to the Explanation of Data for more information.*

Chickasaw (0)	1	<0.01
Chippewa (1)	1	<0.01
Choctaw (4)	10	0.05
Comanche (2)	2	0.01
Creek (2)	4	0.02
Houma (3)	13	0.06
Iroquois (0)	1	<0.01
Mexican American Ind. (3)	4	0.02
Osage (1)	1	<0.01
Shoshone (1)	2	0.01
Sioux (1)	2	0.01
Asian (156)	220	1.08
Not Hispanic (151)	208	1.02
Hispanic (5)	12	0.06
Bangladeshi (3)	3	0.01
Chinese, ex. Taiwanese (21)	26	0.13
Filipino (30)	49	0.24
Indian (54)	57	0.28
Indonesian (1)	1	<0.01
Japanese (2)	17	0.08
Korean (8)	17	0.08
Sri Lankan (2)	2	0.01
Thai (1)	1	<0.01
Vietnamese (19)	24	0.12
Hawaii Native/Pacific Islander (15)	36	0.18
Not Hispanic (14)	32	0.16
Hispanic (1)	4	0.02
Guamanian/Chamorro (1)	1	<0.01
Native Hawaiian (9)	19	0.09
Samoan (0)	1	<0.01
White (18,332)	18,662	91.44
Not Hispanic (17,895)	18,183	89.09
Hispanic (437)	479	2.35

Terrytown

Place Type: CDP
Parish: Jefferson
Population: 23,319†

Ancestry‡	Population	%
African, Sub-Saharan (139)	139	0.61
African (11)	11	0.05
Nigerian (128)	128	0.57
American (386)	386	1.71
Arab (624)	666	2.94
Arab (330)	330	1.46
Lebanese (89)	131	0.58
Palestinian (205)	205	0.91
Belgian (29)	29	0.13
British (35)	35	0.15
Bulgarian (39)	39	0.17
Cajun (50)	92	0.41
Croatian (40)	40	0.18
Danish (0)	21	0.09
Dutch (38)	101	0.45
Eastern European (22)	22	0.10
English (138)	475	2.10
European (137)	141	0.62
French, ex. Basque (1,120)	2,511	11.10
French Canadian (138)	160	0.71
German (435)	1,504	6.65
Irish (384)	1,281	5.66
Israeli (114)	114	0.50
Italian (776)	1,654	7.31
Northern European (29)	29	0.13
Norwegian (17)	105	0.46
Polish (0)	86	0.38
Portuguese (18)	18	0.08
Russian (0)	38	0.17
Scotch-Irish (36)	81	0.36
Scottish (55)	197	0.87
Swedish (0)	23	0.10
Swiss (16)	38	0.17
Turkish (14)	29	0.13
Ukrainian (20)	32	0.14
Welsh (17)	24	0.11
West Indian, ex. Hispanic (279)	295	1.30
Belizean (12)	28	0.12
Haitian (267)	267	1.18

Hispanic Origin	Population	%
Hispanic or Latino (of any race)	4,068	17.45
Central American, ex. Mexican	2,174	9.32
Costa Rican	19	0.08
Guatemalan	228	0.98
Honduran	1,528	6.55
Nicaraguan	234	1.00
Panamanian	17	0.07
Salvadoran	132	0.57
Other Central American	16	0.07
Cuban	162	0.69
Dominican Republic	324	1.39
Mexican	658	2.82
Puerto Rican	230	0.99
South American	120	0.51
Argentinean	9	0.04
Bolivian	5	0.02
Chilean	1	<0.01
Colombian	48	0.21
Ecuadorian	19	0.08
Peruvian	18	0.08
Uruguayan	1	<0.01
Venezuelan	19	0.08
Other Hispanic or Latino	400	1.72

Race*	Population	%
African-American/Black (9,278)	9,520	40.83
Not Hispanic (9,093)	9,266	39.74
Hispanic (185)	254	1.09
American Indian/Alaska Native (99)	248	1.06
Not Hispanic (77)	175	0.75
Hispanic (22)	73	0.31
Apache (1)	5	0.02
Blackfeet (3)	6	0.03
Canadian/French Am. Ind. (0)	1	<0.01
Central American Ind. (3)	3	0.01
Cherokee (1)	23	0.10
Chippewa (1)	3	0.01
Choctaw (7)	13	0.06
Comanche (1)	6	0.03
Creek (1)	1	<0.01
Houma (17)	36	0.15
Iroquois (1)	3	0.01
Lumbee (1)	1	<0.01
Mexican American Ind. (3)	3	0.01
Osage (2)	2	0.01
Potawatomi (0)	3	0.01
Pueblo (1)	1	<0.01
Seminole (0)	7	0.03
Sioux (3)	3	0.01
South American Ind. (0)	1	<0.01
Tlingit-Haida *(Alaska Native)* (3)	3	0.01
Asian (948)	1,112	4.77
Not Hispanic (941)	1,079	4.63
Hispanic (7)	33	0.14
Cambodian (13)	16	0.07
Chinese, ex. Taiwanese (38)	56	0.24
Filipino (90)	130	0.56
Indian (63)	93	0.40
Indonesian (2)	9	0.04
Japanese (10)	20	0.09
Korean (18)	25	0.11
Laotian (3)	3	0.01
Malaysian (1)	1	<0.01
Nepalese (4)	4	0.02
Pakistani (16)	21	0.09
Taiwanese (1)	1	<0.01
Thai (15)	17	0.07
Vietnamese (624)	669	2.87
Hawaii Native/Pacific Islander (14)	42	0.18
Not Hispanic (11)	25	0.11
Hispanic (3)	17	0.07
Guamanian/Chamorro (6)	8	0.03
Marshallese (0)	5	0.02
Native Hawaiian (2)	3	0.01
Samoan (1)	1	<0.01
White (10,444)	10,951	46.96
Not Hispanic (8,708)	8,968	38.46
Hispanic (1,736)	1,983	8.50

Thibodaux

Place Type: City
Parish: Lafourche
Population: 14,566†

Ancestry‡	Population	%
African, Sub-Saharan (23)	23	0.16
Nigerian (23)	23	0.16
American (1,341)	1,341	9.24
Belgian (13)	25	0.17
British (0)	14	0.10
Cajun (262)	336	2.32
Danish (0)	12	0.08
Dutch (42)	42	0.29
English (250)	434	2.99
European (61)	61	0.42
French, ex. Basque (1,754)	3,267	22.51
French Canadian (850)	967	6.66
German (204)	967	6.66
Greek (7)	7	0.05
Irish (181)	744	5.13
Italian (147)	703	4.84
Polish (36)	48	0.33
Portuguese (35)	35	0.24
Russian (9)	18	0.12
Scotch-Irish (35)	80	0.55
Scottish (0)	34	0.23
Swedish (0)	10	0.07
Swiss (0)	13	0.09
Welsh (0)	46	0.32
West Indian, ex. Hispanic (25)	47	0.32
Haitian (25)	25	0.17
Jamaican (0)	22	0.15

Hispanic Origin	Population	%
Hispanic or Latino (of any race)	290	1.99
Central American, ex. Mexican	55	0.38
Costa Rican	3	0.02
Guatemalan	10	0.07
Honduran	25	0.17
Nicaraguan	5	0.03
Panamanian	5	0.03
Salvadoran	7	0.05
Cuban	12	0.08
Dominican Republic	6	0.04
Mexican	107	0.73
Puerto Rican	26	0.18
South American	18	0.12
Argentinean	1	0.01
Bolivian	7	0.05
Colombian	9	0.06
Venezuelan	1	0.01
Other Hispanic or Latino	66	0.45

Race*	Population	%
African-American/Black (4,776)	4,873	33.45
Not Hispanic (4,753)	4,846	33.27
Hispanic (23)	27	0.19
American Indian/Alaska Native (81)	152	1.04
Not Hispanic (77)	146	1.00
Hispanic (4)	6	0.04
Alaska Athabascan *(Ala. Nat.)* (0)	3	0.02
Central American Ind. (0)	1	0.01
Cherokee (3)	8	0.05
Choctaw (7)	10	0.07
Creek (1)	1	0.01
Houma (27)	47	0.32
Mexican American Ind. (1)	1	0.01
Sioux (0)	2	0.01
Tlingit-Haida *(Alaska Native)* (1)	1	0.01
Ute (0)	1	0.01
Asian (152)	189	1.30
Not Hispanic (151)	184	1.26
Hispanic (1)	5	0.03
Bangladeshi (4)	4	0.03
Chinese, ex. Taiwanese (17)	20	0.14
Filipino (11)	25	0.17
Indian (33)	35	0.24
Indonesian (1)	2	0.01

*Notes: † The Census 2010 population figure is used to calculate the percentages in the Hispanic Origin and Race categories. Ancestry percentages are based on the 2006-2010 American Community Survey population (not shown); ‡ Numbers in parentheses indicate the number of people reporting a single ancestry; * Numbers in parentheses indicate the number of persons reporting this race alone, not in combination with any other race; Please refer to the Explanation of Data for more information.*

Japanese (5)	12	0.08
Korean (4)	7	0.05
Nepalese (16)	16	0.11
Vietnamese (54)	61	0.42
Hawaii Native/Pacific Islander (4)	12	0.08
Not Hispanic (4)	11	0.08
Hispanic (0)	1	0.01
Native Hawaiian (4)	6	0.04
Samoan (0)	2	0.01
White (9,285)	9,437	64.79
Not Hispanic (9,113)	9,244	63.46
Hispanic (172)	193	1.33

Timberlane

Place Type: CDP
Parish: Jefferson
Population: 10,243†

Ancestry‡	Population	%
African, Sub-Saharan (27)	27	0.28
African (27)	27	0.28
American (419)	419	4.34
Arab (185)	194	2.01
Arab (103)	103	1.07
Palestinian (82)	91	0.94
British (46)	57	0.59
Cajun (10)	10	0.10
Canadian (58)	58	0.60
Croatian (6)	6	0.06
Danish (15)	39	0.40
Dutch (9)	28	0.29
English (125)	270	2.80
European (36)	44	0.46
French, ex. Basque (866)	2,132	22.11
French Canadian (19)	28	0.29
German (137)	829	8.60
Greek (12)	41	0.43
Hungarian (26)	26	0.27
Irish (87)	418	4.33
Italian (177)	792	8.21
Norwegian (0)	12	0.12
Polish (27)	43	0.45
Romanian (0)	17	0.18
Russian (0)	17	0.18
Scandinavian (8)	19	0.20
Scotch-Irish (45)	65	0.67
Scottish (26)	36	0.37
Swedish (0)	37	0.38
Welsh (22)	22	0.23
Yugoslavian (17)	17	0.18

Hispanic Origin	Population	%
Hispanic or Latino (of any race)	1,185	11.57
Central American, ex. Mexican	499	4.87
Costa Rican	7	0.07
Guatemalan	51	0.50
Honduran	347	3.39
Nicaraguan	46	0.45
Panamanian	9	0.09
Salvadoran	34	0.33
Other Central American	5	0.05
Cuban	84	0.82
Dominican Republic	118	1.15
Mexican	250	2.44
Puerto Rican	34	0.33
South American	35	0.34
Bolivian	1	0.01
Chilean	1	0.01
Colombian	19	0.19
Ecuadorian	1	0.01
Peruvian	6	0.06
Uruguayan	1	0.01
Venezuelan	6	0.06
Other Hispanic or Latino	165	1.61

Race*	Population	%
African-American/Black (3,641)	3,751	36.62
Not Hispanic (3,551)	3,641	35.55
Hispanic (90)	110	1.07
American Indian/Alaska Native (51)	98	0.96
Not Hispanic (40)	75	0.73
Hispanic (11)	23	0.22
Canadian/French Am. Ind. (1)	1	0.01
Cherokee (2)	11	0.11
Chickasaw (2)	5	0.05
Chippewa (1)	1	0.01
Choctaw (1)	2	0.02
Creek (0)	1	0.01
Houma (7)	13	0.13
Iroquois (0)	1	0.01
Mexican American Ind. (0)	4	0.04
Pueblo (1)	1	0.01
Puget Sound Salish (0)	1	0.01
Seminole (0)	1	0.01
Sioux (2)	2	0.02
South American Ind. (4)	6	0.06
Spanish American Ind. (0)	1	0.01
Tlingit-Haida *(Alaska Native)* (3)	4	0.04
Asian (582)	688	6.72
Not Hispanic (581)	668	6.52
Hispanic (1)	20	0.20
Cambodian (2)	2	0.02
Chinese, ex. Taiwanese (27)	30	0.29
Filipino (45)	75	0.73
Indian (23)	30	0.29
Japanese (1)	7	0.07
Korean (10)	11	0.11
Pakistani (1)	1	0.01
Taiwanese (4)	7	0.07
Thai (5)	7	0.07
Vietnamese (453)	466	4.55
Hawaii Native/Pacific Islander (3)	19	0.19
Not Hispanic (3)	9	0.09
Hispanic (0)	10	0.10
Guamanian/Chamorro (3)	3	0.03
Native Hawaiian (0)	3	0.03
White (5,251)	5,488	53.58
Not Hispanic (4,656)	4,825	47.11
Hispanic (595)	663	6.47

Waggaman

Place Type: CDP
Parish: Jefferson
Population: 10,015†

Ancestry‡	Population	%
African, Sub-Saharan (29)	29	0.29
African (29)	29	0.29
American (504)	504	5.05
Cajun (0)	10	0.10
Dutch (0)	26	0.26
English (61)	122	1.22
European (8)	8	0.08
French, ex. Basque (688)	1,375	13.78
French Canadian (155)	200	2.00
German (136)	539	5.40
Hungarian (14)	25	0.25
Irish (86)	249	2.50
Italian (84)	241	2.42
Polish (137)	150	1.50
Scotch-Irish (0)	16	0.16
Scottish (0)	96	0.96
Welsh (0)	9	0.09

Hispanic Origin	Population	%
Hispanic or Latino (of any race)	572	5.71
Central American, ex. Mexican	212	2.12
Costa Rican	1	0.01
Guatemalan	45	0.45
Honduran	137	1.37
Nicaraguan	9	0.09
Salvadoran	19	0.19
Other Central American	1	0.01
Cuban	25	0.25
Dominican Republic	32	0.32
Mexican	127	1.27
Puerto Rican	58	0.58
South American	8	0.08
Argentinean	5	0.05
Colombian	3	0.03
Other Hispanic or Latino	110	1.10

Race*	Population	%
African-American/Black (6,364)	6,443	64.33
Not Hispanic (6,328)	6,401	63.91
Hispanic (36)	42	0.42
American Indian/Alaska Native (58)	91	0.91
Not Hispanic (55)	86	0.86
Hispanic (3)	5	0.05
Canadian/French Am. Ind. (1)	1	0.01
Central American Ind. (0)	1	0.01
Cherokee (4)	16	0.16
Choctaw (1)	9	0.09
Houma (12)	17	0.17
Lumbee (1)	1	0.01
Mexican American Ind. (0)	1	0.01
Sioux (1)	1	0.01
Asian (92)	115	1.15
Not Hispanic (90)	113	1.13
Hispanic (2)	2	0.02
Chinese, ex. Taiwanese (1)	5	0.05
Filipino (23)	38	0.38
Indian (0)	1	0.01
Japanese (1)	8	0.08
Korean (0)	1	0.01
Thai (0)	1	0.01
Vietnamese (60)	67	0.67
Hawaii Native/Pacific Islander (4)	5	0.05
Not Hispanic (3)	4	0.04
Hispanic (1)	1	0.01
Guamanian/Chamorro (3)	3	0.03
Native Hawaiian (0)	1	0.01
White (3,134)	3,252	32.47
Not Hispanic (2,852)	2,943	29.39
Hispanic (282)	309	3.09

West Monroe

Place Type: City
Parish: Ouachita
Population: 13,065†

Ancestry‡	Population	%
African, Sub-Saharan (67)	191	1.46
African (67)	191	1.46
American (1,673)	1,673	12.78
Arab (8)	47	0.36
Lebanese (8)	47	0.36
Australian (8)	8	0.06
British (40)	40	0.31
Cajun (42)	49	0.37
Czech (0)	12	0.09
Czechoslovakian (11)	11	0.08
Danish (0)	60	0.46
Dutch (20)	236	1.80
English (910)	1,889	14.43
European (13)	22	0.17
French, ex. Basque (173)	666	5.09
German (286)	1,226	9.37
Irish (316)	1,135	8.67
Italian (113)	382	2.92
Polish (12)	36	0.28
Russian (28)	51	0.39
Scotch-Irish (149)	391	2.99
Scottish (108)	281	2.15
Slovak (21)	21	0.16
Swiss (0)	10	0.08
Welsh (13)	35	0.27

Hispanic Origin	Population	%
Hispanic or Latino (of any race)	457	3.50
Central American, ex. Mexican	90	0.69
Guatemalan	3	0.02
Honduran	73	0.56
Nicaraguan	13	0.10
Salvadoran	1	0.01
Cuban	1	0.01
Dominican Republic	7	0.05

SECTION TWO

*Notes: † The Census 2010 population figure is used to calculate the percentages in the Hispanic Origin and Race categories. Ancestry percentages are based on the 2006-2010 American Community Survey population (not shown); ‡ Numbers in parentheses indicate the number of people reporting a single ancestry; * Numbers in parentheses indicate the number of persons reporting this race alone, not in combination with any other race; Please refer to the Explanation of Data for more information.*

	Population	%
Mexican	293	2.24
Puerto Rican	13	0.10
South American	6	0.05
Colombian	1	0.01
Ecuadorian	1	0.01
Peruvian	3	0.02
Venezuelan	1	0.01
Other Hispanic or Latino	47	0.36

Race*	Population	%
African-American/Black (4,386)	4,520	34.60
Not Hispanic (4,365)	4,493	34.39
Hispanic (21)	27	0.21
American Indian/Alaska Native (46)	92	0.70
Not Hispanic (37)	81	0.62
Hispanic (9)	11	0.08
Apache (1)	1	0.01
Blackfeet (1)	1	0.01
Cherokee (7)	15	0.11
Choctaw (4)	10	0.08
Creek (0)	4	0.03
Houma (2)	2	0.02
Inupiat *(Alaska Native)* (1)	1	0.01
Iroquois (0)	2	0.02
Mexican American Ind. (4)	4	0.03
Navajo (1)	1	0.01
Sioux (1)	2	0.02
Asian (105)	135	1.03
Not Hispanic (105)	134	1.03
Hispanic (0)	1	0.01
Chinese, ex. Taiwanese (26)	31	0.24
Filipino (7)	18	0.14
Indian (28)	33	0.25
Japanese (1)	2	0.02
Korean (1)	8	0.06
Laotian (1)	1	0.01
Nepalese (6)	6	0.05
Pakistani (3)	3	0.02
Thai (1)	1	0.01
Vietnamese (27)	27	0.21
Hawaii Native/Pacific Islander (5)	8	0.06
Not Hispanic (5)	8	0.06
Guamanian/Chamorro (5)	5	0.04
Native Hawaiian (0)	2	0.02
Samoan (0)	1	0.01
White (8,090)	8,271	63.31
Not Hispanic (7,908)	8,062	61.71
Hispanic (182)	209	1.60

Westwego

Place Type: City
Parish: Jefferson
Population: 8,534†

Ancestry‡	Population	%
African, Sub-Saharan (26)	26	0.29
African (12)	12	0.14
Zimbabwean (14)	14	0.16
American (391)	391	4.43
Arab (0)	51	0.58
Lebanese (0)	51	0.58
Australian (0)	13	0.15
British (15)	15	0.17
Cajun (166)	166	1.88
Dutch (0)	42	0.48
English (218)	490	5.55
French, ex. Basque (1,775)	3,186	36.12
French Canadian (113)	193	2.19
German (149)	693	7.86
Irish (97)	595	6.75
Italian (485)	954	10.82
Polish (2)	54	0.61
Scotch-Irish (19)	19	0.22
Scottish (0)	10	0.11
Slavic (0)	10	0.11
Swedish (0)	84	0.95
Swiss (0)	11	0.12
Welsh (0)	11	0.12
West Indian, ex. Hispanic (10)	10	0.11
British West Indian (10)	10	0.11

Hispanic Origin	Population	%
Hispanic or Latino (of any race)	530	6.21
Central American, ex. Mexican	141	1.65
Guatemalan	16	0.19
Honduran	105	1.23
Nicaraguan	6	0.07
Panamanian	6	0.07
Salvadoran	8	0.09
Cuban	35	0.41
Dominican Republic	28	0.33
Mexican	165	1.93
Puerto Rican	51	0.60
South American	38	0.45
Argentinean	3	0.04
Bolivian	13	0.15
Chilean	2	0.02
Colombian	11	0.13
Ecuadorian	5	0.06
Peruvian	3	0.04
Venezuelan	1	0.01
Other Hispanic or Latino	72	0.84

Race*	Population	%
African-American/Black (1,726)	1,796	21.05
Not Hispanic (1,708)	1,763	20.66
Hispanic (18)	33	0.39
American Indian/Alaska Native (113)	172	2.02
Not Hispanic (99)	157	1.84
Hispanic (14)	15	0.18
Apache (1)	2	0.02
Cherokee (12)	18	0.21
Choctaw (10)	19	0.22
Houma (51)	57	0.67
Iroquois (0)	2	0.02
Lumbee (2)	2	0.02
Mexican American Ind. (6)	6	0.07
Seminole (0)	2	0.02
Sioux (1)	2	0.02
Asian (64)	87	1.02
Not Hispanic (64)	81	0.95
Hispanic (0)	6	0.07
Chinese, ex. Taiwanese (3)	5	0.06
Filipino (17)	28	0.33
Indian (2)	8	0.09
Japanese (2)	3	0.04
Korean (1)	1	0.01
Thai (0)	1	0.01
Vietnamese (38)	39	0.46
Hawaii Native/Pacific Islander (1)	2	0.02
Not Hispanic (1)	2	0.02
Samoan (1)	1	0.01
White (6,319)	6,465	75.76
Not Hispanic (5,996)	6,111	71.61
Hispanic (323)	354	4.15

Woodmere

Place Type: CDP
Parish: Jefferson
Population: 12,080†

Ancestry‡	Population	%
African, Sub-Saharan (57)	60	0.52
African (57)	60	0.52
American (150)	150	1.29
Brazilian (6)	6	0.05
Czech (18)	29	0.25
Dutch (9)	23	0.20
English (56)	128	1.10
European (12)	12	0.10
French, ex. Basque (249)	582	5.01
French Canadian (40)	44	0.38
German (79)	372	3.20
Irish (46)	176	1.52
Italian (75)	208	1.79
Norwegian (8)	33	0.28
Scottish (10)	10	0.09
West Indian, ex. Hispanic (402)	402	3.46
Bahamian (68)	68	0.59
British West Indian (9)	9	0.08
Haitian (198)	198	1.71
Trinidadian/Tobagonian (127)	127	1.09

Hispanic Origin	Population	%
Hispanic or Latino (of any race)	703	5.82
Central American, ex. Mexican	235	1.95
Costa Rican	8	0.07
Guatemalan	16	0.13
Honduran	173	1.43
Nicaraguan	21	0.17
Panamanian	9	0.07
Salvadoran	8	0.07
Cuban	39	0.32
Dominican Republic	116	0.96
Mexican	120	0.99
Puerto Rican	75	0.62
South American	27	0.22
Colombian	18	0.15
Ecuadorian	3	0.02
Peruvian	2	0.02
Venezuelan	4	0.03
Other Hispanic or Latino	91	0.75

Race*	Population	%
African-American/Black (9,715)	9,864	81.66
Not Hispanic (9,602)	9,720	80.46
Hispanic (113)	144	1.19
American Indian/Alaska Native (38)	71	0.59
Not Hispanic (33)	62	0.51
Hispanic (5)	9	0.07
Cherokee (2)	5	0.04
Chippewa (0)	1	0.01
Houma (16)	17	0.14
Mexican American Ind. (1)	3	0.02
Navajo (3)	3	0.02
Asian (505)	550	4.55
Not Hispanic (504)	537	4.45
Hispanic (1)	13	0.11
Cambodian (6)	7	0.06
Chinese, ex. Taiwanese (12)	17	0.14
Filipino (34)	51	0.42
Indian (6)	11	0.09
Korean (10)	12	0.10
Laotian (1)	4	0.03
Malaysian (0)	4	0.03
Thai (2)	4	0.03
Vietnamese (424)	439	3.63
Hawaii Native/Pacific Islander (8)	19	0.16
Not Hispanic (1)	10	0.08
Hispanic (7)	9	0.07
Guamanian/Chamorro (1)	1	0.01
Native Hawaiian (5)	7	0.06
Samoan (0)	1	0.01
White (1,375)	1,514	12.53
Not Hispanic (1,081)	1,165	9.64
Hispanic (294)	349	2.89

Youngsville

Place Type: City
Parish: Lafayette
Population: 8,105†

Ancestry‡	Population	%
American (807)	807	11.00
Arab (24)	24	0.33
Lebanese (24)	24	0.33
Cajun (195)	289	3.94
Canadian (20)	20	0.27
Danish (16)	48	0.65
Dutch (21)	68	0.93
English (165)	430	5.86
European (162)	162	2.21
French, ex. Basque (1,086)	2,266	30.89
French Canadian (485)	508	6.92
German (190)	741	10.10
Hungarian (14)	14	0.19
Irish (250)	655	8.93

*Notes: † The Census 2010 population figure is used to calculate the percentages in the Hispanic Origin and Race categories. Ancestry percentages are based on the 2006-2010 American Community Survey population (not shown); ‡ Numbers in parentheses indicate the number of people reporting a single ancestry; * Numbers in parentheses indicate the number of persons reporting this race alone, not in combination with any other race; Please refer to the Explanation of Data for more information.*

Italian (158)	336	4.58
Norwegian (13)	13	0.18
Polish (14)	32	0.44
Russian (13)	13	0.18
Scotch-Irish (10)	10	0.14
Scottish (81)	202	2.75
Slovak (0)	20	0.27
Swiss (0)	18	0.25

Hispanic Origin	Population	%
Hispanic or Latino (of any race)	236	2.91
Central American, ex. Mexican	37	0.46
Guatemalan	9	0.11
Honduran	6	0.07
Nicaraguan	3	0.04
Panamanian	10	0.12
Salvadoran	9	0.11
Cuban	18	0.22
Dominican Republic	4	0.05
Mexican	86	1.06
Puerto Rican	16	0.20
South American	36	0.44
Colombian	8	0.10
Ecuadorian	3	0.04
Peruvian	4	0.05
Venezuelan	18	0.22
Other South American	3	0.04
Other Hispanic or Latino	39	0.48

Race*	Population	%
African-American/Black (550)	591	7.29
Not Hispanic (544)	580	7.16
Hispanic (6)	11	0.14
American Indian/Alaska Native (32)	54	0.67
Not Hispanic (26)	48	0.59
Hispanic (6)	6	0.07
Aleut *(Alaska Native)* (1)	1	0.01
Blackfeet (0)	1	0.01
Cherokee (2)	10	0.12
Chickasaw (0)	2	0.02
Chippewa (0)	1	0.01
Choctaw (3)	6	0.07
Houma (5)	8	0.10
Navajo (1)	1	0.01
Sioux (6)	6	0.07
Spanish American Ind. (0)	1	0.01
Asian (86)	110	1.36
Not Hispanic (85)	106	1.31
Hispanic (1)	4	0.05
Chinese, ex. Taiwanese (3)	9	0.11
Filipino (11)	18	0.22
Indian (0)	1	0.01
Indonesian (4)	4	0.05
Japanese (3)	10	0.12
Korean (2)	6	0.07
Laotian (20)	25	0.31
Pakistani (6)	6	0.07
Thai (2)	3	0.04
Vietnamese (25)	28	0.35
Hawaii Native/Pacific Islander (2)	3	0.04
Not Hispanic (1)	2	0.02
Hispanic (1)	1	0.01
Native Hawaiian (1)	1	0.01
White (7,276)	7,355	90.75
Not Hispanic (7,134)	7,195	88.77
Hispanic (142)	160	1.97

Zachary

Place Type: City
Parish: East Baton Rouge
Population: 14,960†

Ancestry‡	Population	%
African, Sub-Saharan (178)	178	1.25
African (90)	90	0.63
Nigerian (88)	88	0.62
American (1,943)	1,943	13.60
Arab (21)	21	0.15
Lebanese (21)	21	0.15
Armenian (0)	21	0.15
Austrian (0)	10	0.07
Brazilian (0)	33	0.23
Cajun (22)	132	0.92
Danish (0)	13	0.09
Dutch (0)	45	0.32
English (272)	948	6.64
European (91)	130	0.91
French, ex. Basque (365)	1,088	7.62
French Canadian (211)	350	2.45
German (281)	1,280	8.96
Irish (391)	1,257	8.80
Italian (76)	279	1.95
Norwegian (0)	34	0.24
Polish (16)	47	0.33
Portuguese (0)	76	0.53
Scotch-Irish (236)	377	2.64
Scottish (121)	414	2.90
Swedish (0)	28	0.20
Swiss (0)	19	0.13
Welsh (0)	55	0.39
West Indian, ex. Hispanic (75)	75	0.53
Dutch West Indian (75)	75	0.53

Hispanic Origin	Population	%
Hispanic or Latino (of any race)	221	1.48
Central American, ex. Mexican	17	0.11
Costa Rican	3	0.02
Guatemalan	3	0.02
Honduran	1	0.01
Nicaraguan	2	0.01
Panamanian	4	0.03
Salvadoran	4	0.03
Cuban	13	0.09
Dominican Republic	3	0.02
Mexican	106	0.71
Puerto Rican	18	0.12
South American	19	0.13
Argentinean	1	0.01
Colombian	1	0.01
Peruvian	3	0.02
Venezuelan	14	0.09
Other Hispanic or Latino	45	0.30

Race*	Population	%
African-American/Black (5,299)	5,399	36.09
Not Hispanic (5,283)	5,377	35.94
Hispanic (16)	22	0.15
American Indian/Alaska Native (47)	90	0.60
Not Hispanic (47)	90	0.60
Apache (2)	3	0.02
Canadian/French Am. Ind. (0)	2	0.01
Cherokee (4)	18	0.12
Chickasaw (1)	1	0.01
Choctaw (4)	5	0.03
Comanche (1)	3	0.02
Creek (2)	4	0.03
Houma (3)	3	0.02
Mexican American Ind. (2)	2	0.01
Asian (124)	170	1.14
Not Hispanic (124)	169	1.13
Hispanic (0)	1	0.01
Chinese, ex. Taiwanese (16)	19	0.13
Filipino (26)	41	0.27
Indian (17)	24	0.16
Japanese (2)	9	0.06
Korean (12)	13	0.09
Sri Lankan (9)	9	0.06
Thai (3)	4	0.03
Vietnamese (34)	38	0.25
Hawaii Native/Pacific Islander (1)	1	0.01
Not Hispanic (1)	1	0.01
Guamanian/Chamorro (1)	1	0.01
White (9,224)	9,402	62.85
Not Hispanic (9,088)	9,243	61.78
Hispanic (136)	159	1.06

SECTION TWO

*Notes: † The Census 2010 population figure is used to calculate the percentages in the Hispanic Origin and Race categories. Ancestry percentages are based on the 2006-2010 American Community Survey population (not shown); ‡ Numbers in parentheses indicate the number of people reporting a single ancestry; * Numbers in parentheses indicate the number of persons reporting this race alone, not in combination with any other race; Please refer to the Explanation of Data for more information.*

MAINE

Place Type: State
Population: 1,328,361†

Ancestry‡	Population	%
Afghan (183)	183	0.01
African, Sub-Saharan (5,368)	6,088	0.46
African (955)	1,309	0.10
Cape Verdean (104)	218	0.02
Ethiopian (420)	426	0.03
Ghanaian (15)	15	<0.01
Kenyan (79)	79	0.01
Nigerian (175)	208	0.02
Senegalese (72)	72	0.01
Somalian (2,406)	2,462	0.19
South African (23)	49	<0.01
Sudanese (788)	788	0.06
Other Sub-Saharan African (331)	462	0.03
Albanian (290)	854	0.06
Alsatian (0)	25	<0.01
American (92,362)	92,362	6.96
Arab (1,657)	3,422	0.26
Arab (343)	461	0.03
Egyptian (79)	79	0.01
Iraqi (35)	35	<0.01
Jordanian (0)	9	<0.01
Lebanese (896)	2,246	0.17
Moroccan (21)	42	<0.01
Palestinian (30)	44	<0.01
Syrian (212)	435	0.03
Other Arab (41)	71	0.01
Armenian (567)	1,384	0.10
Assyrian/Chaldean/Syriac (4)	28	<0.01
Australian (58)	333	0.03
Austrian (553)	2,418	0.18
Basque (47)	150	0.01
Belgian (359)	992	0.07
Brazilian (165)	236	0.02
British (4,055)	7,274	0.55
Bulgarian (266)	274	0.02
Cajun (795)	983	0.07
Canadian (9,627)	15,595	1.17
Celtic (221)	348	0.03
Croatian (110)	334	0.03
Cypriot (6)	9	<0.01
Czech (615)	2,259	0.17
Czechoslovakian (373)	947	0.07
Danish (1,647)	6,354	0.48
Dutch (3,046)	13,889	1.05
Eastern European (1,008)	1,166	0.09
English (125,478)	307,666	23.17
Estonian (61)	135	0.01
European (8,180)	9,177	0.69
Finnish (2,522)	7,205	0.54
French, ex. Basque (88,178)	232,390	17.50
French Canadian (66,730)	100,089	7.54
German (26,306)	111,073	8.37
German Russian (0)	12	<0.01
Greek (2,722)	6,702	0.50
Guyanese (16)	30	<0.01
Hungarian (1,123)	4,207	0.32
Icelander (35)	68	0.01
Iranian (93)	164	0.01
Irish (73,870)	237,955	17.92
Israeli (204)	237	0.02
Italian (23,706)	75,833	5.71
Latvian (131)	495	0.04
Lithuanian (1,594)	5,487	0.41
Luxemburger (0)	48	<0.01
Macedonian (47)	67	0.01
Maltese (23)	123	0.01
New Zealander (48)	76	0.01
Northern European (1,359)	1,466	0.11
Norwegian (3,377)	10,090	0.76
Pennsylvania German (162)	351	0.03
Polish (8,119)	30,427	2.29
Portuguese (2,423)	8,246	0.62
Romanian (413)	911	0.07
Russian (3,404)	9,751	0.73
Scandinavian (1,413)	2,909	0.22
Scotch-Irish (19,228)	49,422	3.72
Scottish (21,055)	74,329	5.60
Serbian (344)	470	0.04
Slavic (171)	640	0.05
Slovak (702)	1,960	0.15
Slovene (100)	226	0.02
Swedish (6,726)	25,098	1.89
Swiss (523)	2,496	0.19
Turkish (216)	278	0.02
Ukrainian (738)	2,222	0.17
Welsh (2,386)	11,608	0.87
West Indian, ex. Hispanic (958)	1,690	0.13
Bahamian (18)	35	<0.01
Barbadian (41)	55	<0.01
Bermudan (10)	10	<0.01
British West Indian (51)	51	<0.01
Dutch West Indian (3)	24	<0.01
Haitian (315)	364	0.03
Jamaican (482)	846	0.06
Trinidadian/Tobagonian (32)	150	0.01
U.S. Virgin Islander (0)	19	<0.01
West Indian (6)	136	0.01
Yugoslavian (279)	368	0.03

Hispanic Origin	Population	%
Hispanic or Latino (of any race)	16,935	1.27
Central American, ex. Mexican	1,708	0.13
Costa Rican	105	0.01
Guatemalan	457	0.03
Honduran	280	0.02
Nicaraguan	89	0.01
Panamanian	141	0.01
Salvadoran	618	0.05
Other Central American	18	<0.01
Cuban	783	0.06
Dominican Republic	610	0.05
Mexican	5,134	0.39
Puerto Rican	4,377	0.33
South American	1,515	0.11
Argentinean	149	0.01
Bolivian	52	<0.01
Chilean	166	0.01
Colombian	496	0.04
Ecuadorian	178	0.01
Paraguayan	25	<0.01
Peruvian	272	0.02
Uruguayan	11	<0.01
Venezuelan	146	0.01
Other South American	20	<0.01
Other Hispanic or Latino	2,808	0.21

Race*	Population	%
African-American/Black (15,707)	21,764	1.64
Not Hispanic (15,154)	20,645	1.55
Hispanic (553)	1,119	0.08
American Indian/Alaska Native (8,568)	18,482	1.39
Not Hispanic (8,210)	17,654	1.33
Hispanic (358)	828	0.06
Alaska Athabascan *(Ala. Nat.)* (7)	20	<0.01
Aleut *(Alaska Native)* (22)	34	<0.01
Apache (38)	113	0.01
Arapaho (2)	9	<0.01
Blackfeet (56)	370	0.03
Canadian/French Am. Ind. (139)	307	0.02
Central American Ind. (14)	22	<0.01
Cherokee (246)	1,230	0.09
Cheyenne (4)	15	<0.01
Chickasaw (15)	50	<0.01
Chippewa (81)	179	0.01
Choctaw (28)	102	0.01
Colville (1)	1	<0.01
Comanche (8)	17	<0.01
Cree (17)	47	<0.01
Creek (18)	61	<0.01
Crow (7)	27	<0.01
Delaware (15)	35	<0.01
Hopi (9)	16	<0.01
Houma (1)	1	<0.01
Inupiat *(Alaska Native)* (28)	46	<0.01
Iroquois (84)	282	0.02
Kiowa (5)	9	<0.01
Lumbee (19)	30	<0.01
Menominee (0)	2	<0.01
Mexican American Ind. (77)	116	0.01
Navajo (53)	106	0.01
Osage (6)	13	<0.01
Ottawa (3)	6	<0.01
Paiute (7)	14	<0.01
Pima (1)	4	<0.01
Potawatomi (15)	28	<0.01
Pueblo (9)	23	<0.01
Puget Sound Salish (2)	7	<0.01
Seminole (12)	50	<0.01
Shoshone (2)	15	<0.01
Sioux (86)	239	0.02
South American Ind. (34)	56	<0.01
Spanish American Ind. (7)	13	<0.01
Tlingit-Haida *(Alaska Native)* (6)	31	<0.01
Tohono O'Odham (3)	8	<0.01
Tsimshian *(Alaska Native)* (2)	15	<0.01
Ute (2)	2	<0.01
Yakama (3)	6	<0.01
Yaqui (2)	18	<0.01
Yup'ik *(Alaska Native)* (7)	12	<0.01
Asian (13,571)	18,333	1.38
Not Hispanic (13,442)	17,975	1.35
Hispanic (129)	358	0.03
Bangladeshi (38)	45	<0.01
Bhutanese (0)	1	<0.01
Burmese (62)	65	<0.01
Cambodian (1,456)	1,691	0.13
Chinese, ex. Taiwanese (3,429)	4,285	0.32
Filipino (1,639)	2,918	0.22
Hmong (7)	7	<0.01
Indian (1,959)	2,397	0.18
Indonesian (61)	109	0.01
Japanese (584)	1,181	0.09
Korean (1,144)	1,741	0.13
Laotian (103)	172	0.01
Malaysian (12)	33	<0.01
Nepalese (43)	51	<0.01
Pakistani (161)	192	0.01
Sri Lankan (30)	40	<0.01
Taiwanese (81)	109	0.01
Thai (367)	516	0.04
Vietnamese (1,713)	2,170	0.16
Hawaii Native/Pacific Islander (342)	988	0.07
Not Hispanic (313)	856	0.06
Hispanic (29)	132	0.01
Fijian (3)	4	<0.01
Guamanian/Chamorro (67)	152	0.01
Marshallese (9)	9	<0.01
Native Hawaiian (115)	350	0.03
Samoan (67)	126	0.01
Tongan (3)	6	<0.01
White (1,264,971)	1,284,877	96.73
Not Hispanic (1,254,297)	1,272,487	95.79
Hispanic (10,674)	12,390	0.93

*Notes: † The Census 2010 population figure is used to calculate the percentages in the Hispanic Origin and Race categories. Ancestry percentages are based on the 2006-2010 American Community Survey population (not shown); ‡ Numbers in parentheses indicate the number of people reporting a single ancestry; * Numbers in parentheses indicate the number of persons reporting this race alone, not in combination with any other race; Please refer to the Explanation of Data for more information.*

Auburn

Place Type: City
County: Androscoggin
Population: 23,055†

Ancestry‡	Population	%
African, Sub-Saharan (267)	277	1.19
African (23)	33	0.14
Nigerian (6)	6	0.03
Somalian (238)	238	1.02
American (1,054)	1,054	4.53
Arab (0)	15	0.06
Lebanese (0)	15	0.06
Austrian (18)	37	0.16
British (50)	108	0.46
Canadian (334)	518	2.23
Czech (26)	99	0.43
Czechoslovakian (13)	55	0.24
Danish (15)	108	0.46
Dutch (15)	216	0.93
English (1,846)	5,342	22.95
European (73)	97	0.42
Finnish (70)	171	0.73
French, ex. Basque (1,962)	4,460	19.16
French Canadian (3,221)	4,350	18.69
German (292)	1,759	7.56
Greek (34)	101	0.43
Hungarian (22)	38	0.16
Irish (870)	3,686	15.83
Italian (372)	1,268	5.45
Lithuanian (9)	131	0.56
Luxemburger (0)	18	0.08
Northern European (46)	46	0.20
Norwegian (25)	92	0.40
Pennsylvania German (0)	11	0.05
Polish (62)	493	2.12
Portuguese (11)	23	0.10
Romanian (13)	23	0.10
Russian (18)	88	0.38
Scandinavian (0)	20	0.09
Scotch-Irish (327)	841	3.61
Scottish (202)	820	3.52
Slovak (18)	18	0.08
Swedish (143)	370	1.59
Swiss (13)	60	0.26
Ukrainian (0)	53	0.23
Welsh (62)	225	0.97
West Indian, ex. Hispanic (94)	104	0.45
Barbadian (41)	41	0.18
Jamaican (53)	63	0.27
Yugoslavian (0)	11	0.05

Hispanic Origin	Population	%
Hispanic or Latino (of any race)	349	1.51
Central American, ex. Mexican	18	0.08
Costa Rican	1	<0.01
Guatemalan	3	0.01
Honduran	6	0.03
Nicaraguan	2	0.01
Panamanian	3	0.01
Salvadoran	3	0.01
Cuban	23	0.10
Dominican Republic	9	0.04
Mexican	111	0.48
Puerto Rican	108	0.47
South American	40	0.17
Argentinean	3	0.01
Chilean	5	0.02
Colombian	5	0.02
Ecuadorian	16	0.07
Peruvian	9	0.04
Venezuelan	2	0.01
Other Hispanic or Latino	40	0.17

Race*	Population	%
African-American/Black (570)	764	3.31
Not Hispanic (556)	736	3.19
Hispanic (14)	28	0.12
American Indian/Alaska Native (98)	271	1.18
Not Hispanic (92)	256	1.11
Hispanic (6)	15	0.07
Aleut *(Alaska Native)* (1)	1	<0.01
Apache (0)	2	0.01
Blackfeet (2)	10	0.04
Canadian/French Am. Ind. (4)	13	0.06
Cherokee (0)	5	0.02
Chickasaw (3)	3	0.01
Chippewa (1)	2	0.01
Hopi (2)	2	0.01
Inupiat *(Alaska Native)* (0)	1	<0.01
Iroquois (1)	5	0.02
Mexican American Ind. (1)	2	0.01
Navajo (1)	1	<0.01
Shoshone (0)	4	0.02
Sioux (1)	3	0.01
South American Ind. (0)	1	<0.01
Tlingit-Haida *(Alaska Native)* (1)	2	0.01
Yakama (1)	2	0.01
Yup'ik *(Alaska Native)* (1)	1	<0.01
Asian (218)	313	1.36
Not Hispanic (214)	305	1.32
Hispanic (4)	8	0.03
Cambodian (1)	3	0.01
Chinese, ex. Taiwanese (71)	81	0.35
Filipino (33)	57	0.25
Indian (41)	46	0.20
Indonesian (1)	3	0.01
Japanese (6)	18	0.08
Korean (8)	25	0.11
Laotian (5)	7	0.03
Malaysian (0)	1	<0.01
Nepalese (3)	3	0.01
Taiwanese (9)	9	0.04
Thai (6)	9	0.04
Vietnamese (23)	43	0.19
Hawaii Native/Pacific Islander (10)	24	0.10
Not Hispanic (10)	22	0.10
Hispanic (0)	2	0.01
Guamanian/Chamorro (4)	6	0.03
Native Hawaiian (1)	6	0.03
Samoan (0)	1	<0.01
White (21,604)	22,066	95.71
Not Hispanic (21,392)	21,808	94.59
Hispanic (212)	258	1.12

Augusta

Place Type: City
County: Kennebec
Population: 19,136†

Ancestry‡	Population	%
American (1,027)	1,027	5.36
Arab (33)	53	0.28
Arab (18)	18	0.09
Lebanese (15)	25	0.13
Palestinian (0)	10	0.05
Armenian (18)	18	0.09
Australian (0)	11	0.06
Austrian (0)	43	0.22
Brazilian (7)	7	0.04
British (37)	124	0.65
Canadian (134)	150	0.78
Croatian (9)	9	0.05
Danish (22)	60	0.31
Dutch (21)	32	0.17
Eastern European (13)	13	0.07
English (2,129)	4,115	21.49
European (214)	214	1.12
Finnish (0)	48	0.25
French, ex. Basque (1,813)	4,441	23.19
French Canadian (1,365)	1,986	10.37
German (454)	1,502	7.84
Greek (12)	38	0.20
Irish (748)	3,932	20.53
Italian (154)	782	4.08
Lithuanian (9)	114	0.60
Macedonian (0)	10	0.05
Maltese (0)	8	0.04
Northern European (70)	85	0.44
Norwegian (12)	77	0.40
Pennsylvania German (14)	14	0.07
Polish (79)	300	1.57
Portuguese (73)	145	0.76
Romanian (0)	10	0.05
Russian (41)	101	0.53
Scandinavian (15)	15	0.08
Scotch-Irish (278)	622	3.25
Scottish (319)	881	4.60
Slavic (0)	13	0.07
Slovak (111)	111	0.58
Swedish (56)	327	1.71
Swiss (0)	10	0.05
Ukrainian (26)	60	0.31
Welsh (0)	153	0.80
West Indian, ex. Hispanic (41)	41	0.21
Bermudan (10)	10	0.05
Haitian (19)	19	0.10
Jamaican (12)	12	0.06

Hispanic Origin	Population	%
Hispanic or Latino (of any race)	341	1.78
Central American, ex. Mexican	21	0.11
Costa Rican	5	0.03
Guatemalan	6	0.03
Honduran	6	0.03
Nicaraguan	1	0.01
Panamanian	1	0.01
Salvadoran	2	0.01
Cuban	12	0.06
Dominican Republic	10	0.05
Mexican	116	0.61
Puerto Rican	101	0.53
South American	22	0.11
Chilean	2	0.01
Colombian	11	0.06
Peruvian	2	0.01
Uruguayan	2	0.01
Venezuelan	4	0.02
Other South American	1	0.01
Other Hispanic or Latino	59	0.31

Race*	Population	%
African-American/Black (201)	346	1.81
Not Hispanic (189)	322	1.68
Hispanic (12)	24	0.13
American Indian/Alaska Native (127)	346	1.81
Not Hispanic (120)	324	1.69
Hispanic (7)	22	0.11
Apache (0)	6	0.03
Blackfeet (2)	10	0.05
Canadian/French Am. Ind. (5)	9	0.05
Cherokee (13)	36	0.19
Cheyenne (0)	1	0.01
Chickasaw (0)	1	0.01
Chippewa (0)	2	0.01
Cree (0)	1	0.01
Crow (1)	1	0.01
Iroquois (4)	8	0.04
Mexican American Ind. (1)	1	0.01
Navajo (2)	3	0.02
Sioux (1)	8	0.04
Spanish American Ind. (1)	1	0.01
Asian (291)	361	1.89
Not Hispanic (288)	355	1.86
Hispanic (3)	6	0.03
Bangladeshi (4)	4	0.02
Burmese (1)	1	0.01
Cambodian (22)	22	0.11
Chinese, ex. Taiwanese (67)	79	0.41
Filipino (13)	36	0.19
Indian (110)	117	0.61
Indonesian (2)	3	0.02
Japanese (7)	13	0.07
Korean (9)	17	0.09
Laotian (1)	2	0.01
Malaysian (1)	1	0.01
Nepalese (0)	1	0.01
Pakistani (4)	4	0.02

*Notes: † The Census 2010 population figure is used to calculate the percentages in the Hispanic Origin and Race categories. Ancestry percentages are based on the 2006-2010 American Community Survey population (not shown); ‡ Numbers in parentheses indicate the number of people reporting a single ancestry; * Numbers in parentheses indicate the number of persons reporting this race alone, not in combination with any other race; Please refer to the Explanation of Data for more information.*

Sri Lankan (1)	2	0.01
Thai (11)	13	0.07
Vietnamese (27)	38	0.20
Hawaii Native/Pacific Islander (10)	29	0.15
Not Hispanic (10)	28	0.15
Hispanic (0)	1	0.01
Guamanian/Chamorro (0)	5	0.03
Native Hawaiian (4)	11	0.06
Samoan (3)	6	0.03
White (18,001)	18,421	96.26
Not Hispanic (17,772)	18,158	94.89
Hispanic (229)	263	1.37

Bangor

Place Type: City
County: Penobscot
Population: 33,039†

Ancestry‡	Population	%
African, Sub-Saharan (56)	56	0.17
African (24)	24	0.07
Cape Verdean (32)	32	0.10
Albanian (26)	26	0.08
American (3,021)	3,021	9.18
Arab (29)	72	0.22
Jordanian (0)	9	0.03
Lebanese (29)	53	0.16
Syrian (0)	10	0.03
Austrian (11)	22	0.07
British (107)	196	0.60
Bulgarian (62)	62	0.19
Canadian (248)	393	1.19
Croatian (7)	7	0.02
Czech (0)	46	0.14
Czechoslovakian (12)	12	0.04
Danish (22)	121	0.37
Dutch (79)	212	0.64
Eastern European (24)	32	0.10
English (2,028)	6,348	19.30
European (322)	339	1.03
Finnish (27)	48	0.15
French, ex. Basque (1,313)	5,142	15.63
French Canadian (1,113)	2,026	6.16
German (471)	2,540	7.72
Greek (46)	87	0.26
Hungarian (15)	77	0.23
Irish (2,096)	6,382	19.40
Italian (566)	2,156	6.55
Latvian (3)	3	0.01
Lithuanian (45)	70	0.21
Norwegian (10)	143	0.43
Polish (271)	829	2.52
Portuguese (0)	129	0.39
Romanian (0)	14	0.04
Russian (75)	316	0.96
Scandinavian (20)	49	0.15
Scotch-Irish (695)	1,941	5.90
Scottish (383)	1,823	5.54
Slovak (8)	30	0.09
Swedish (176)	510	1.55
Swiss (26)	43	0.13
Welsh (107)	290	0.88
West Indian, ex. Hispanic (29)	80	0.24
Jamaican (29)	29	0.09
West Indian (0)	51	0.16

Hispanic Origin	Population	%
Hispanic or Latino (of any race)	491	1.49
Central American, ex. Mexican	42	0.13
Costa Rican	10	0.03
Guatemalan	4	0.01
Honduran	12	0.04
Nicaraguan	1	<0.01
Panamanian	8	0.02
Salvadoran	7	0.02
Cuban	25	0.08
Dominican Republic	25	0.08
Mexican	122	0.37
Puerto Rican	168	0.51
South American	44	0.13
Argentinean	8	0.02
Chilean	10	0.03
Colombian	12	0.04
Ecuadorian	2	0.01
Paraguayan	1	<0.01
Peruvian	10	0.03
Venezuelan	1	<0.01
Other Hispanic or Latino	65	0.20

Race*	Population	%
African-American/Black (558)	785	2.38
Not Hispanic (534)	736	2.23
Hispanic (24)	49	0.15
American Indian/Alaska Native (395)	701	2.12
Not Hispanic (387)	678	2.05
Hispanic (8)	23	0.07
Alaska Athabascan *(Ala. Nat.)* (1)	1	<0.01
Aleut *(Alaska Native)* (1)	1	<0.01
Apache (1)	2	0.01
Blackfeet (0)	8	0.02
Canadian/French Am. Ind. (0)	4	0.01
Cherokee (2)	33	0.10
Chickasaw (0)	2	0.01
Chippewa (3)	7	0.02
Choctaw (0)	1	<0.01
Cree (1)	2	0.01
Creek (0)	1	<0.01
Delaware (1)	1	<0.01
Inupiat *(Alaska Native)* (1)	1	<0.01
Iroquois (8)	17	0.05
Lumbee (0)	1	<0.01
Mexican American Ind. (3)	3	0.01
Navajo (2)	2	0.01
Paiute (0)	1	<0.01
Puget Sound Salish (1)	3	0.01
Seminole (0)	7	0.02
Sioux (4)	11	0.03
South American Ind. (4)	4	0.01
Spanish American Ind. (0)	1	<0.01
Yakama (0)	1	<0.01
Yaqui (0)	1	<0.01
Asian (549)	677	2.05
Not Hispanic (542)	667	2.02
Hispanic (7)	10	0.03
Burmese (2)	2	0.01
Cambodian (2)	2	0.01
Chinese, ex. Taiwanese (187)	205	0.62
Filipino (52)	89	0.27
Indian (91)	108	0.33
Indonesian (1)	1	<0.01
Japanese (22)	35	0.11
Korean (62)	76	0.23
Laotian (1)	4	0.01
Nepalese (2)	2	0.01
Pakistani (9)	9	0.03
Sri Lankan (1)	2	0.01
Taiwanese (1)	2	0.01
Thai (14)	19	0.06
Vietnamese (86)	98	0.30
Hawaii Native/Pacific Islander (16)	41	0.12
Not Hispanic (15)	37	0.11
Hispanic (1)	4	0.01
Guamanian/Chamorro (4)	9	0.03
Native Hawaiian (8)	18	0.05
Samoan (2)	3	0.01
White (30,764)	31,380	94.98
Not Hispanic (30,448)	31,021	93.89
Hispanic (316)	359	1.09

Bath

Place Type: City
County: Sagadahoc
Population: 8,514†

Ancestry‡	Population	%
African, Sub-Saharan (30)	30	0.34
African (30)	30	0.34
American (648)	648	7.40
Armenian (0)	10	0.11
Belgian (0)	14	0.16
British (14)	57	0.65
Canadian (22)	140	1.60
Czech (13)	24	0.27
Danish (0)	121	1.38
Dutch (49)	125	1.43
English (678)	1,965	22.43
European (10)	10	0.11
French, ex. Basque (222)	1,258	14.36
French Canadian (256)	440	5.02
German (233)	1,007	11.50
Greek (45)	45	0.51
Hungarian (0)	55	0.63
Irish (577)	1,640	18.72
Italian (267)	739	8.44
Lithuanian (0)	19	0.22
Norwegian (38)	160	1.83
Polish (70)	266	3.04
Portuguese (12)	86	0.98
Romanian (87)	137	1.56
Russian (31)	114	1.30
Scandinavian (0)	14	0.16
Scotch-Irish (81)	330	3.77
Scottish (121)	732	8.36
Slovak (0)	24	0.27
Swedish (83)	218	2.49
Swiss (0)	28	0.32
Turkish (13)	13	0.15
Welsh (18)	31	0.35
West Indian, ex. Hispanic (0)	38	0.43
Jamaican (0)	19	0.22
U.S. Virgin Islander (0)	19	0.22

Hispanic Origin	Population	%
Hispanic or Latino (of any race)	157	1.84
Central American, ex. Mexican	10	0.12
Guatemalan	4	0.05
Nicaraguan	3	0.04
Salvadoran	3	0.04
Cuban	8	0.09
Dominican Republic	2	0.02
Mexican	52	0.61
Puerto Rican	47	0.55
South American	23	0.27
Colombian	13	0.15
Ecuadorian	1	0.01
Peruvian	4	0.05
Venezuelan	5	0.06
Other Hispanic or Latino	15	0.18

Race*	Population	%
African-American/Black (102)	175	2.06
Not Hispanic (90)	155	1.82
Hispanic (12)	20	0.23
American Indian/Alaska Native (25)	97	1.14
Not Hispanic (22)	89	1.05
Hispanic (3)	8	0.09
Blackfeet (0)	1	0.01
Cherokee (0)	11	0.13
Choctaw (0)	3	0.04
Inupiat *(Alaska Native)* (0)	1	0.01
Iroquois (0)	2	0.02
Mexican American Ind. (0)	2	0.02
Paiute (1)	1	0.01
Pueblo (2)	2	0.02
South American Ind. (1)	1	0.01
Ute (1)	1	0.01
Asian (53)	105	1.23
Not Hispanic (50)	99	1.16
Hispanic (3)	6	0.07
Cambodian (3)	4	0.05
Chinese, ex. Taiwanese (7)	23	0.27
Filipino (14)	27	0.32
Indian (5)	10	0.12
Indonesian (0)	2	0.02
Japanese (4)	12	0.14
Korean (6)	16	0.19
Thai (4)	4	0.05
Vietnamese (5)	8	0.09

*Notes: † The Census 2010 population figure is used to calculate the percentages in the Hispanic Origin and Race categories. Ancestry percentages are based on the 2006-2010 American Community Survey population (not shown); ‡ Numbers in parentheses indicate the number of people reporting a single ancestry; * Numbers in parentheses indicate the number of persons reporting this race alone, not in combination with any other race; Please refer to the Explanation of Data for more information.*

Hawaii Native/Pacific Islander (2)	9	0.11
Not Hispanic (1)	6	0.07
Hispanic (1)	3	0.04
Native Hawaiian (2)	9	0.11
White (8,101)	8,292	97.39
Not Hispanic (8,008)	8,176	96.03
Hispanic (93)	116	1.36

Biddeford

Place Type: City
County: York
Population: 21,277†

Ancestry‡	Population	%
African, Sub-Saharan (22)	22	0.10
Ethiopian (22)	22	0.10
Albanian (12)	53	0.25
American (706)	706	3.29
Arab (18)	59	0.27
Egyptian (8)	8	0.04
Lebanese (0)	41	0.19
Other Arab (10)	10	0.05
Armenian (0)	25	0.12
Assyrian/Chaldean/Syriac (0)	10	0.05
Austrian (0)	5	0.02
British (10)	20	0.09
Cajun (0)	7	0.03
Canadian (230)	298	1.39
Czech (17)	17	0.08
Danish (0)	35	0.16
Dutch (8)	216	1.01
English (1,573)	3,797	17.67
European (65)	65	0.30
Finnish (58)	77	0.36
French, ex. Basque (2,839)	5,619	26.15
French Canadian (3,419)	4,022	18.72
German (280)	1,172	5.45
Greek (108)	346	1.61
Hungarian (0)	78	0.36
Irish (815)	2,983	13.88
Italian (331)	1,329	6.18
Latvian (22)	107	0.50
Lithuanian (67)	105	0.49
Norwegian (55)	147	0.68
Pennsylvania German (11)	11	0.05
Polish (173)	514	2.39
Portuguese (12)	53	0.25
Russian (16)	66	0.31
Scotch-Irish (220)	529	2.46
Scottish (241)	916	4.26
Slovak (0)	13	0.06
Slovene (0)	8	0.04
Swedish (23)	353	1.64
Swiss (0)	22	0.10
Ukrainian (0)	47	0.22
Welsh (47)	113	0.53

Hispanic Origin	Population	%
Hispanic or Latino (of any race)	352	1.65
Central American, ex. Mexican	44	0.21
Costa Rican	1	<0.01
Guatemalan	9	0.04
Nicaraguan	6	0.03
Panamanian	4	0.02
Salvadoran	24	0.11
Cuban	27	0.13
Dominican Republic	8	0.04
Mexican	111	0.52
Puerto Rican	100	0.47
South American	15	0.07
Argentinean	1	<0.01
Chilean	2	0.01
Colombian	10	0.05
Peruvian	2	0.01
Other Hispanic or Latino	47	0.22

Race*	Population	%
African-American/Black (207)	321	1.51
Not Hispanic (190)	294	1.38
Hispanic (17)	27	0.13
American Indian/Alaska Native (116)	265	1.25
Not Hispanic (102)	239	1.12
Hispanic (14)	26	0.12
Apache (2)	2	0.01
Blackfeet (0)	8	0.04
Canadian/French Am. Ind. (4)	6	0.03
Cherokee (2)	13	0.06
Cheyenne (0)	2	0.01
Chippewa (0)	1	<0.01
Choctaw (0)	1	<0.01
Comanche (1)	3	0.01
Creek (0)	1	<0.01
Crow (0)	1	<0.01
Hopi (1)	1	<0.01
Inupiat *(Alaska Native)* (1)	1	<0.01
Iroquois (1)	4	0.02
Mexican American Ind. (5)	6	0.03
Navajo (1)	1	<0.01
Sioux (11)	14	0.07
Tlingit-Haida *(Alaska Native)* (0)	1	<0.01
Tohono O'Odham (1)	1	<0.01
Asian (352)	435	2.04
Not Hispanic (350)	427	2.01
Hispanic (2)	8	0.04
Cambodian (64)	77	0.36
Chinese, ex. Taiwanese (96)	113	0.53
Filipino (22)	36	0.17
Indian (46)	50	0.23
Indonesian (0)	1	<0.01
Japanese (1)	12	0.06
Korean (23)	35	0.16
Laotian (6)	7	0.03
Thai (7)	11	0.05
Vietnamese (60)	68	0.32
Hawaii Native/Pacific Islander (8)	15	0.07
Not Hispanic (7)	13	0.06
Hispanic (1)	2	0.01
Guamanian/Chamorro (1)	1	<0.01
Native Hawaiian (1)	3	0.01
Samoan (3)	3	0.01
White (20,165)	20,510	96.40
Not Hispanic (19,956)	20,262	95.23
Hispanic (209)	248	1.17

Brewer

Place Type: City
County: Penobscot
Population: 9,482†

Ancestry‡	Population	%
Albanian (38)	38	0.40
American (957)	957	10.15
Arab (0)	15	0.16
Syrian (0)	15	0.16
Australian (0)	24	0.25
Belgian (10)	10	0.11
British (70)	100	1.06
Canadian (81)	97	1.03
Czech (0)	12	0.13
Danish (27)	39	0.41
Dutch (20)	43	0.46
English (695)	2,312	24.51
European (72)	86	0.91
French, ex. Basque (703)	1,598	16.94
French Canadian (415)	630	6.68
German (95)	748	7.93
Greek (0)	21	0.22
Hungarian (0)	29	0.31
Irish (809)	2,207	23.40
Italian (181)	502	5.32
Lithuanian (10)	22	0.23
Norwegian (44)	100	1.06
Polish (43)	160	1.70
Portuguese (5)	37	0.39
Russian (0)	40	0.42
Scandinavian (14)	26	0.28
Scotch-Irish (199)	369	3.91
Scottish (130)	659	6.99
Slovak (0)	21	0.22
Slovene (8)	8	0.08
Swedish (67)	156	1.65
Swiss (11)	11	0.12
Turkish (0)	10	0.11
Welsh (47)	102	1.08
West Indian, ex. Hispanic (0)	29	0.31
Jamaican (0)	29	0.31

Hispanic Origin	Population	%
Hispanic or Latino (of any race)	117	1.23
Central American, ex. Mexican	14	0.15
Costa Rican	1	0.01
Guatemalan	2	0.02
Honduran	5	0.05
Panamanian	4	0.04
Salvadoran	2	0.02
Cuban	7	0.07
Dominican Republic	9	0.09
Mexican	38	0.40
Puerto Rican	29	0.31
South American	10	0.11
Bolivian	4	0.04
Chilean	2	0.02
Colombian	2	0.02
Peruvian	1	0.01
Venezuelan	1	0.01
Other Hispanic or Latino	10	0.11

Race*	Population	%
African-American/Black (68)	123	1.30
Not Hispanic (61)	114	1.20
Hispanic (7)	9	0.09
American Indian/Alaska Native (74)	157	1.66
Not Hispanic (74)	149	1.57
Hispanic (0)	8	0.08
Apache (1)	2	0.02
Arapaho (1)	1	0.01
Blackfeet (0)	2	0.02
Cherokee (1)	15	0.16
Chippewa (4)	4	0.04
Cree (0)	1	0.01
Crow (0)	1	0.01
Inupiat *(Alaska Native)* (1)	2	0.02
Pueblo (2)	2	0.02
Sioux (4)	4	0.04
Tlingit-Haida *(Alaska Native)* (1)	1	0.01
Asian (99)	127	1.34
Not Hispanic (98)	126	1.33
Hispanic (1)	1	0.01
Bangladeshi (3)	3	0.03
Burmese (2)	2	0.02
Cambodian (1)	4	0.04
Chinese, ex. Taiwanese (37)	40	0.42
Filipino (10)	24	0.25
Indian (22)	22	0.23
Japanese (3)	4	0.04
Korean (4)	10	0.11
Pakistani (5)	5	0.05
Thai (3)	4	0.04
Vietnamese (2)	4	0.04
Hawaii Native/Pacific Islander (1)	4	0.04
Not Hispanic (1)	4	0.04
Guamanian/Chamorro (0)	2	0.02
Native Hawaiian (1)	2	0.02
White (9,045)	9,207	97.10
Not Hispanic (8,970)	9,120	96.18
Hispanic (75)	87	0.92

Brunswick

Place Type: CDP
County: Cumberland
Population: 15,175†

Ancestry‡	Population	%
African, Sub-Saharan (9)	23	0.16
African (0)	14	0.09
Ethiopian (9)	9	0.06
American (537)	537	3.62

*Notes: † The Census 2010 population figure is used to calculate the percentages in the Hispanic Origin and Race categories. Ancestry percentages are based on the 2006-2010 American Community Survey population (not shown); ‡ Numbers in parentheses indicate the number of people reporting a single ancestry; * Numbers in parentheses indicate the number of persons reporting this race alone, not in combination with any other race; Please refer to the Explanation of Data for more information.*

Ancestry	Population	%
Arab (0)	13	0.09
Lebanese (0)	13	0.09
Armenian (22)	22	0.15
Austrian (0)	31	0.21
Belgian (11)	22	0.15
Brazilian (0)	23	0.16
British (99)	179	1.21
Bulgarian (28)	28	0.19
Cajun (0)	33	0.22
Canadian (106)	143	0.96
Croatian (0)	11	0.07
Czech (10)	50	0.34
Danish (0)	91	0.61
Dutch (0)	112	0.76
Eastern European (16)	29	0.20
English (1,188)	3,657	24.67
European (137)	137	0.92
Finnish (25)	119	0.80
French, ex. Basque (588)	1,741	11.75
French Canadian (687)	1,123	7.58
German (241)	1,557	10.51
German Russian (0)	12	0.08
Greek (33)	202	1.36
Hungarian (22)	131	0.88
Irish (835)	2,503	16.89
Israeli (0)	8	0.05
Italian (268)	812	5.48
Latvian (13)	13	0.09
Lithuanian (15)	51	0.34
Northern European (56)	56	0.38
Norwegian (40)	202	1.36
Polish (63)	462	3.12
Portuguese (0)	125	0.84
Russian (16)	263	1.77
Scandinavian (0)	10	0.07
Scotch-Irish (157)	460	3.10
Scottish (277)	1,035	6.98
Serbian (11)	11	0.07
Slavic (0)	10	0.07
Slovak (14)	73	0.49
Slovene (9)	9	0.06
Swedish (64)	265	1.79
Swiss (28)	67	0.45
Turkish (7)	7	0.05
Ukrainian (10)	19	0.13
Welsh (38)	156	1.05
West Indian, ex. Hispanic (38)	51	0.34
British West Indian (38)	38	0.26
Dutch West Indian (0)	13	0.09

Hispanic Origin	Population	%
Hispanic or Latino (of any race)	424	2.79
Central American, ex. Mexican	31	0.20
Costa Rican	2	0.01
Guatemalan	8	0.05
Honduran	10	0.07
Nicaraguan	1	0.01
Panamanian	5	0.03
Salvadoran	5	0.03
Cuban	31	0.20
Dominican Republic	16	0.11
Mexican	147	0.97
Puerto Rican	83	0.55
South American	67	0.44
Argentinean	6	0.04
Bolivian	1	0.01
Chilean	6	0.04
Colombian	22	0.14
Ecuadorian	9	0.06
Paraguayan	1	0.01
Peruvian	9	0.06
Uruguayan	2	0.01
Venezuelan	11	0.07
Other Hispanic or Latino	49	0.32

Race*	Population	%
African-American/Black (227)	331	2.18
Not Hispanic (202)	298	1.96
Hispanic (25)	33	0.22
American Indian/Alaska Native (41)	143	0.94
Not Hispanic (37)	135	0.89
Hispanic (4)	8	0.05
Central American Ind. (1)	1	0.01
Cherokee (3)	16	0.11
Chickasaw (0)	2	0.01
Chippewa (1)	1	0.01
Choctaw (1)	2	0.01
Cree (1)	1	0.01
Creek (0)	4	0.03
Crow (1)	2	0.01
Delaware (2)	3	0.02
Inupiat *(Alaska Native)* (2)	3	0.02
Iroquois (2)	2	0.01
Mexican American Ind. (1)	3	0.02
Sioux (1)	2	0.01
South American Ind. (0)	2	0.01
Spanish American Ind. (0)	1	0.01
Tlingit-Haida *(Alaska Native)* (0)	1	0.01
Asian (372)	527	3.47
Not Hispanic (366)	514	3.39
Hispanic (6)	13	0.09
Bangladeshi (3)	4	0.03
Bhutanese (0)	1	0.01
Cambodian (14)	14	0.09
Chinese, ex. Taiwanese (111)	163	1.07
Filipino (50)	86	0.57
Indian (51)	67	0.44
Indonesian (1)	1	0.01
Japanese (19)	47	0.31
Korean (66)	83	0.55
Laotian (1)	1	0.01
Malaysian (1)	4	0.03
Nepalese (2)	2	0.01
Pakistani (5)	7	0.05
Sri Lankan (1)	1	0.01
Taiwanese (7)	8	0.05
Thai (13)	16	0.11
Vietnamese (17)	24	0.16
Hawaii Native/Pacific Islander (4)	15	0.10
Not Hispanic (4)	15	0.10
Native Hawaiian (1)	9	0.06
Samoan (1)	1	0.01
White (14,091)	14,430	95.09
Not Hispanic (13,806)	14,110	92.98
Hispanic (285)	320	2.11

Brunswick

Place Type: Town
County: Cumberland
Population: 20,278†

Ancestry‡	Population	%
African, Sub-Saharan (9)	32	0.16
African (0)	14	0.07
Ethiopian (9)	9	0.04
South African (0)	9	0.04
American (625)	625	3.04
Arab (0)	13	0.06
Lebanese (0)	13	0.06
Armenian (22)	22	0.11
Austrian (0)	46	0.22
Belgian (11)	22	0.11
Brazilian (0)	23	0.11
British (175)	263	1.28
Bulgarian (28)	28	0.14
Cajun (0)	33	0.16
Canadian (144)	219	1.07
Celtic (20)	20	0.10
Croatian (0)	11	0.05
Czech (27)	83	0.40
Danish (0)	103	0.50
Dutch (12)	146	0.71
Eastern European (39)	52	0.25
English (1,685)	4,834	23.52
European (229)	229	1.11
Finnish (25)	130	0.63
French, ex. Basque (927)	2,360	11.48
French Canadian (1,077)	1,693	8.24
German (442)	2,135	10.39
German Russian (0)	12	0.06
Greek (53)	222	1.08
Hungarian (42)	240	1.17
Irish (1,045)	3,415	16.61
Israeli (0)	8	0.04
Italian (576)	1,222	5.94
Latvian (13)	13	0.06
Lithuanian (24)	138	0.67
Northern European (56)	56	0.27
Norwegian (45)	256	1.25
Polish (118)	607	2.95
Portuguese (0)	125	0.61
Russian (50)	301	1.46
Scandinavian (0)	10	0.05
Scotch-Irish (220)	684	3.33
Scottish (312)	1,234	6.00
Serbian (11)	11	0.05
Slavic (0)	10	0.05
Slovak (14)	73	0.36
Slovene (9)	9	0.04
Swedish (75)	348	1.69
Swiss (28)	72	0.35
Turkish (7)	7	0.03
Ukrainian (10)	19	0.09
Welsh (62)	222	1.08
West Indian, ex. Hispanic (38)	51	0.25
British West Indian (38)	38	0.18
Dutch West Indian (0)	13	0.06

Hispanic Origin	Population	%
Hispanic or Latino (of any race)	597	2.94
Central American, ex. Mexican	48	0.24
Costa Rican	2	0.01
Guatemalan	13	0.06
Honduran	13	0.06
Nicaraguan	2	0.01
Panamanian	11	0.05
Salvadoran	7	0.03
Cuban	38	0.19
Dominican Republic	30	0.15
Mexican	215	1.06
Puerto Rican	128	0.63
South American	74	0.36
Argentinean	6	0.03
Bolivian	4	0.02
Chilean	6	0.03
Colombian	23	0.11
Ecuadorian	9	0.04
Paraguayan	1	<0.01
Peruvian	9	0.04
Uruguayan	2	0.01
Venezuelan	14	0.07
Other Hispanic or Latino	64	0.32

Race*	Population	%
African-American/Black (336)	491	2.42
Not Hispanic (294)	431	2.13
Hispanic (42)	60	0.30
American Indian/Alaska Native (56)	197	0.97
Not Hispanic (51)	186	0.92
Hispanic (5)	11	0.05
Blackfeet (1)	4	0.02
Canadian/French Am. Ind. (1)	9	0.04
Central American Ind. (1)	1	<0.01
Cherokee (4)	21	0.10
Chickasaw (0)	2	0.01
Chippewa (1)	1	<0.01
Choctaw (1)	2	0.01
Cree (1)	1	<0.01
Creek (0)	4	0.02
Crow (1)	3	0.01
Delaware (2)	3	0.01
Inupiat *(Alaska Native)* (2)	3	0.01
Iroquois (3)	4	0.02
Mexican American Ind. (1)	3	0.01
Navajo (1)	1	<0.01
Sioux (1)	2	0.01
South American Ind. (1)	3	0.01
Spanish American Ind. (0)	1	<0.01
Tlingit-Haida *(Alaska Native)* (0)	1	<0.01

SECTION TWO

*Notes: † The Census 2010 population figure is used to calculate the percentages in the Hispanic Origin and Race categories. Ancestry percentages are based on the 2006-2010 American Community Survey population (not shown); ‡ Numbers in parentheses indicate the number of people reporting a single ancestry; * Numbers in parentheses indicate the number of persons reporting this race alone, not in combination with any other race; Please refer to the Explanation of Data for more information.*

Asian (433)	641	3.16
Not Hispanic (426)	623	3.07
Hispanic (7)	18	0.09
Bangladeshi (3)	4	0.02
Bhutanese (0)	1	<0.01
Cambodian (14)	14	0.07
Chinese, ex. Taiwanese (117)	173	0.85
Filipino (62)	114	0.56
Indian (57)	79	0.39
Indonesian (3)	3	0.01
Japanese (26)	62	0.31
Korean (85)	114	0.56
Laotian (1)	1	<0.01
Malaysian (1)	4	0.02
Nepalese (2)	2	0.01
Pakistani (5)	7	0.03
Sri Lankan (1)	1	<0.01
Taiwanese (7)	8	0.04
Thai (13)	16	0.08
Vietnamese (23)	32	0.16
Hawaii Native/Pacific Islander (4)	18	0.09
Not Hispanic (4)	18	0.09
Native Hawaiian (1)	12	0.06
Samoan (1)	2	0.01
White (18,855)	19,318	95.27
Not Hispanic (18,448)	18,868	93.05
Hispanic (407)	450	2.22

Buxton

Place Type: Town
County: York
Population: 8,034†

Ancestry‡	Population	%
Albanian (0)	63	0.79
American (385)	385	4.80
Armenian (20)	60	0.75
Austrian (0)	6	0.07
Belgian (0)	26	0.32
British (20)	29	0.36
Canadian (54)	118	1.47
Czech (0)	59	0.74
Czechoslovakian (23)	23	0.29
Danish (0)	79	0.99
Dutch (41)	114	1.42
English (687)	2,136	26.64
European (20)	53	0.66
French, ex. Basque (316)	1,767	22.04
French Canadian (173)	349	4.35
German (78)	582	7.26
Greek (10)	68	0.85
Hungarian (19)	19	0.24
Irish (463)	1,773	22.12
Italian (149)	730	9.11
Lithuanian (0)	29	0.36
Norwegian (0)	143	1.78
Polish (7)	119	1.48
Portuguese (0)	56	0.70
Romanian (0)	42	0.52
Russian (0)	30	0.37
Scandinavian (16)	64	0.80
Scotch-Irish (129)	244	3.04
Scottish (145)	621	7.75
Swedish (109)	241	3.01
Swiss (0)	6	0.07
Ukrainian (20)	60	0.75
Welsh (0)	59	0.74

Hispanic Origin	Population	%
Hispanic or Latino (of any race)	54	0.67
Dominican Republic	6	0.07
Mexican	14	0.17
Puerto Rican	20	0.25
South American	4	0.05
Chilean	1	0.01
Ecuadorian	2	0.02
Paraguayan	1	0.01
Other Hispanic or Latino	10	0.12

Race*	Population	%
African-American/Black (45)	86	1.07
Not Hispanic (43)	82	1.02
Hispanic (2)	4	0.05
American Indian/Alaska Native (14)	92	1.15
Not Hispanic (14)	85	1.06
Hispanic (0)	7	0.09
Apache (0)	3	0.04
Blackfeet (0)	2	0.02
Cherokee (1)	2	0.02
Choctaw (0)	1	0.01
Iroquois (1)	2	0.02
Navajo (1)	2	0.02
Asian (72)	93	1.16
Not Hispanic (72)	92	1.15
Hispanic (0)	1	0.01
Cambodian (4)	6	0.07
Chinese, ex. Taiwanese (28)	35	0.44
Filipino (22)	27	0.34
Indian (2)	3	0.04
Japanese (2)	5	0.06
Korean (2)	2	0.02
Thai (0)	2	0.02
Vietnamese (7)	11	0.14
Hawaii Native/Pacific Islander (0)	1	0.01
Not Hispanic (0)	1	0.01
White (7,755)	7,887	98.17
Not Hispanic (7,729)	7,847	97.67
Hispanic (26)	40	0.50

Cape Elizabeth

Place Type: Town
County: Cumberland
Population: 9,015†

Ancestry‡	Population	%
Afghan (25)	25	0.28
African, Sub-Saharan (114)	114	1.26
Ethiopian (114)	114	1.26
Albanian (11)	21	0.23
American (215)	215	2.37
Arab (25)	25	0.28
Lebanese (25)	25	0.28
Austrian (22)	74	0.82
British (38)	55	0.61
Cajun (11)	11	0.12
Canadian (36)	72	0.80
Croatian (10)	10	0.11
Czech (8)	18	0.20
Czechoslovakian (0)	9	0.10
Danish (20)	95	1.05
Dutch (41)	170	1.88
Eastern European (33)	33	0.36
English (788)	2,277	25.14
European (141)	141	1.56
Finnish (23)	64	0.71
French, ex. Basque (297)	850	9.39
French Canadian (199)	362	4.00
German (352)	1,366	15.08
Greek (0)	32	0.35
Hungarian (9)	41	0.45
Iranian (9)	20	0.22
Irish (641)	2,291	25.30
Italian (351)	1,216	13.43
Lithuanian (0)	21	0.23
Luxemburger (0)	9	0.10
Northern European (12)	12	0.13
Norwegian (44)	108	1.19
Polish (77)	474	5.23
Portuguese (12)	44	0.49
Romanian (19)	19	0.21
Russian (8)	116	1.28
Scandinavian (14)	14	0.15
Scotch-Irish (181)	402	4.44
Scottish (126)	514	5.68
Slavic (0)	10	0.11
Slovak (0)	19	0.21
Slovene (0)	18	0.20
Swedish (95)	301	3.32
Swiss (0)	32	0.35
Ukrainian (21)	49	0.54
Welsh (0)	127	1.40
West Indian, ex. Hispanic (0)	12	0.13
West Indian (0)	12	0.13

Hispanic Origin	Population	%
Hispanic or Latino (of any race)	130	1.44
Central American, ex. Mexican	21	0.23
Costa Rican	5	0.06
Guatemalan	5	0.06
Honduran	5	0.06
Nicaraguan	5	0.06
Salvadoran	1	0.01
Cuban	11	0.12
Dominican Republic	4	0.04
Mexican	30	0.33
Puerto Rican	12	0.13
South American	15	0.17
Argentinean	2	0.02
Bolivian	1	0.01
Colombian	5	0.06
Paraguayan	1	0.01
Peruvian	2	0.02
Venezuelan	4	0.04
Other Hispanic or Latino	37	0.41

Race*	Population	%
African-American/Black (41)	59	0.65
Not Hispanic (38)	54	0.60
Hispanic (3)	5	0.06
American Indian/Alaska Native (17)	55	0.61
Not Hispanic (11)	49	0.54
Hispanic (6)	6	0.07
Blackfeet (0)	4	0.04
Cherokee (2)	6	0.07
Choctaw (0)	2	0.02
Cree (0)	2	0.02
Kiowa (1)	1	0.01
Mexican American Ind. (1)	1	0.01
Navajo (1)	3	0.03
South American Ind. (0)	1	0.01
Asian (128)	162	1.80
Not Hispanic (121)	155	1.72
Hispanic (7)	7	0.08
Cambodian (5)	5	0.06
Chinese, ex. Taiwanese (38)	42	0.47
Filipino (10)	20	0.22
Indian (29)	33	0.37
Japanese (8)	14	0.16
Korean (15)	22	0.24
Pakistani (8)	8	0.09
Thai (3)	4	0.04
Vietnamese (5)	7	0.08
Hawaii Native/Pacific Islander (5)	11	0.12
Not Hispanic (5)	11	0.12
Native Hawaiian (0)	1	0.01
Samoan (5)	5	0.06
White (8,711)	8,795	97.56
Not Hispanic (8,616)	8,698	96.48
Hispanic (95)	97	1.08

Caribou

Place Type: City
County: Aroostook
Population: 8,189†

Ancestry‡	Population	%
Albanian (0)	19	0.23
American (692)	692	8.40
Arab (4)	26	0.32
Arab (0)	7	0.09
Lebanese (4)	19	0.23
Armenian (5)	5	0.06
Austrian (2)	19	0.23
British (2)	2	0.02
Cajun (40)	40	0.49
Canadian (36)	57	0.69

*Notes: † The Census 2010 population figure is used to calculate the percentages in the Hispanic Origin and Race categories. Ancestry percentages are based on the 2006-2010 American Community Survey population (not shown); ‡ Numbers in parentheses indicate the number of people reporting a single ancestry; * Numbers in parentheses indicate the number of persons reporting this race alone, not in combination with any other race; Please refer to the Explanation of Data for more information.*

Ancestry	Population	%
Danish (11)	36	0.44
Dutch (14)	87	1.06
English (538)	1,803	21.89
Finnish (3)	3	0.04
French, ex. Basque (1,406)	2,579	31.32
French Canadian (494)	637	7.74
German (64)	407	4.94
Greek (0)	33	0.40
Hungarian (9)	32	0.39
Irish (523)	1,727	20.97
Italian (54)	243	2.95
Northern European (11)	11	0.13
Norwegian (21)	31	0.38
Polish (10)	84	1.02
Portuguese (0)	15	0.18
Russian (0)	11	0.13
Scandinavian (9)	18	0.22
Scotch-Irish (40)	190	2.31
Scottish (85)	285	3.46
Swedish (56)	436	5.29
Ukrainian (10)	10	0.12
Welsh (0)	35	0.43
West Indian, ex. Hispanic (0)	4	0.05
Dutch West Indian (0)	4	0.05

Hispanic Origin	Population	%
Hispanic or Latino (of any race)	67	0.82
Central American, ex. Mexican	3	0.04
Guatemalan	2	0.02
Honduran	1	0.01
Cuban	1	0.01
Mexican	24	0.29
Puerto Rican	29	0.35
South American	2	0.02
Colombian	2	0.02
Other Hispanic or Latino	8	0.10

Race*	Population	%
African-American/Black (35)	54	0.66
Not Hispanic (34)	49	0.60
Hispanic (1)	5	0.06
American Indian/Alaska Native (113)	172	2.10
Not Hispanic (111)	170	2.08
Hispanic (2)	2	0.02
Apache (0)	1	0.01
Blackfeet (0)	1	0.01
Cherokee (0)	1	0.01
Chippewa (1)	1	0.01
Delaware (3)	3	0.04
Inupiat *(Alaska Native)* (0)	1	0.01
Iroquois (0)	2	0.02
Navajo (1)	3	0.04
Spanish American Ind. (1)	1	0.01
Asian (56)	70	0.85
Not Hispanic (56)	70	0.85
Chinese, ex. Taiwanese (11)	11	0.13
Filipino (18)	25	0.31
Indian (5)	7	0.09
Japanese (5)	9	0.11
Korean (6)	7	0.09
Pakistani (3)	3	0.04
Sri Lankan (4)	5	0.06
Thai (3)	3	0.04
Vietnamese (0)	1	0.01
Hawaii Native/Pacific Islander (4)	5	0.06
Not Hispanic (4)	5	0.06
Native Hawaiian (3)	5	0.06
White (7,865)	7,961	97.22
Not Hispanic (7,826)	7,914	96.64
Hispanic (39)	47	0.57

Ellsworth

Place Type: City
County: Hancock
Population: 7,741†

Ancestry‡	Population	%
American (1,906)	1,906	25.23
Arab (11)	11	0.15
Lebanese (11)	11	0.15
British (49)	106	1.40
Bulgarian (16)	16	0.21
Canadian (39)	106	1.40
Czech (22)	106	1.40
Danish (0)	9	0.12
Dutch (21)	81	1.07
English (742)	1,346	17.82
European (13)	13	0.17
Finnish (0)	24	0.32
French, ex. Basque (219)	651	8.62
French Canadian (131)	230	3.04
German (146)	490	6.49
Greek (15)	25	0.33
Hungarian (14)	14	0.19
Irish (417)	1,269	16.80
Italian (278)	459	6.08
Northern European (21)	21	0.28
Norwegian (0)	67	0.89
Pennsylvania German (0)	23	0.30
Polish (25)	219	2.90
Portuguese (0)	65	0.86
Russian (23)	23	0.30
Scotch-Irish (90)	297	3.93
Scottish (123)	446	5.90
Swedish (7)	53	0.70
Ukrainian (11)	22	0.29
Welsh (14)	40	0.53

Hispanic Origin	Population	%
Hispanic or Latino (of any race)	108	1.40
Central American, ex. Mexican	13	0.17
Guatemalan	6	0.08
Panamanian	1	0.01
Salvadoran	3	0.04
Other Central American	3	0.04
Cuban	2	0.03
Mexican	28	0.36
Puerto Rican	26	0.34
South American	5	0.06
Argentinean	1	0.01
Bolivian	2	0.03
Ecuadorian	2	0.03
Other Hispanic or Latino	34	0.44

Race*	Population	%
African-American/Black (51)	73	0.94
Not Hispanic (43)	65	0.84
Hispanic (8)	8	0.10
American Indian/Alaska Native (34)	54	0.70
Not Hispanic (32)	50	0.65
Hispanic (2)	4	0.05
Canadian/French Am. Ind. (1)	1	0.01
Cherokee (2)	3	0.04
Lumbee (1)	1	0.01
Shoshone (1)	1	0.01
Sioux (1)	1	0.01
Asian (82)	108	1.40
Not Hispanic (82)	104	1.34
Hispanic (0)	4	0.05
Chinese, ex. Taiwanese (22)	30	0.39
Filipino (17)	24	0.31
Indian (4)	7	0.09
Indonesian (1)	3	0.04
Japanese (5)	7	0.09
Korean (4)	4	0.05
Taiwanese (1)	1	0.01
Thai (2)	2	0.03
Vietnamese (22)	24	0.31
Hawaii Native/Pacific Islander (4)	5	0.06
Not Hispanic (4)	4	0.05
Hispanic (0)	1	0.01
Native Hawaiian (1)	1	0.01
Samoan (1)	1	0.01
White (7,482)	7,544	97.46
Not Hispanic (7,410)	7,464	96.42
Hispanic (72)	80	1.03

Falmouth

Place Type: Town
County: Cumberland
Population: 11,185†

Ancestry‡	Population	%
Albanian (0)	24	0.22
Alsatian (0)	13	0.12
American (602)	602	5.43
Arab (37)	115	1.04
Lebanese (37)	115	1.04
Australian (11)	11	0.10
Austrian (30)	63	0.57
Belgian (51)	152	1.37
British (83)	161	1.45
Canadian (45)	227	2.05
Czech (0)	13	0.12
Danish (57)	131	1.18
Dutch (66)	207	1.87
Eastern European (57)	57	0.51
English (1,044)	2,905	26.20
Estonian (0)	12	0.11
European (187)	187	1.69
Finnish (18)	64	0.58
French, ex. Basque (181)	1,052	9.49
French Canadian (283)	574	5.18
German (264)	1,190	10.73
Greek (54)	200	1.80
Hungarian (0)	34	0.31
Irish (452)	1,711	15.43
Italian (552)	1,207	10.89
Latvian (11)	11	0.10
Lithuanian (13)	55	0.50
Norwegian (80)	159	1.43
Polish (107)	476	4.29
Portuguese (0)	41	0.37
Romanian (10)	23	0.21
Russian (46)	215	1.94
Scandinavian (18)	18	0.16
Scotch-Irish (79)	252	2.27
Scottish (265)	895	8.07
Slovak (0)	23	0.21
Swedish (74)	249	2.25
Swiss (21)	25	0.23
Ukrainian (0)	24	0.22
Welsh (39)	115	1.04

Hispanic Origin	Population	%
Hispanic or Latino (of any race)	145	1.30
Central American, ex. Mexican	14	0.13
Costa Rican	1	0.01
Guatemalan	10	0.09
Panamanian	1	0.01
Salvadoran	2	0.02
Cuban	5	0.04
Dominican Republic	6	0.05
Mexican	44	0.39
Puerto Rican	27	0.24
South American	19	0.17
Argentinean	1	0.01
Chilean	1	0.01
Colombian	3	0.03
Peruvian	10	0.09
Uruguayan	1	0.01
Venezuelan	3	0.03
Other Hispanic or Latino	30	0.27

Race*	Population	%
African-American/Black (55)	92	0.82
Not Hispanic (54)	88	0.79
Hispanic (1)	4	0.04
American Indian/Alaska Native (27)	56	0.50
Not Hispanic (22)	51	0.46
Hispanic (5)	5	0.04
Aleut *(Alaska Native)* (3)	3	0.03
Apache (1)	1	0.01
Blackfeet (0)	1	0.01
Central American Ind. (0)	3	0.03
Cherokee (1)	6	0.05

*Notes: † The Census 2010 population figure is used to calculate the percentages in the Hispanic Origin and Race categories. Ancestry percentages are based on the 2006-2010 American Community Survey population (not shown); ‡ Numbers in parentheses indicate the number of people reporting a single ancestry; * Numbers in parentheses indicate the number of persons reporting this race alone, not in combination with any other race; Please refer to the Explanation of Data for more information.*

Chippewa (1)	1	0.01
Mexican American Ind. (5)	5	0.04
Navajo (1)	1	0.01
Sioux (1)	2	0.02
Asian (252)	322	2.88
Not Hispanic (251)	320	2.86
Hispanic (1)	2	0.02
Cambodian (10)	10	0.09
Chinese, ex. Taiwanese (71)	94	0.84
Filipino (10)	15	0.13
Indian (77)	88	0.79
Indonesian (2)	2	0.02
Japanese (11)	14	0.13
Korean (47)	61	0.55
Pakistani (1)	1	0.01
Taiwanese (4)	4	0.04
Thai (2)	2	0.02
Vietnamese (8)	14	0.13
Hawaii Native/Pacific Islander (0)	5	0.04
Not Hispanic (0)	5	0.04
Native Hawaiian (0)	4	0.04
White (10,676)	10,803	96.58
Not Hispanic (10,569)	10,692	95.59
Hispanic (107)	111	0.99

Farmington

Place Type: Town
County: Franklin
Population: 7,760†

Ancestry‡	Population	%
African, Sub-Saharan (11)	11	0.14
Cape Verdean (11)	11	0.14
Albanian (0)	17	0.22
American (316)	316	4.09
Arab (14)	36	0.47
Lebanese (0)	22	0.28
Syrian (14)	14	0.18
Austrian (0)	46	0.60
Belgian (14)	29	0.38
British (0)	33	0.43
Canadian (16)	38	0.49
Czechoslovakian (0)	35	0.45
Danish (0)	10	0.13
Dutch (0)	38	0.49
English (836)	1,884	24.39
European (80)	94	1.22
Finnish (0)	24	0.31
French, ex. Basque (358)	1,132	14.65
French Canadian (260)	397	5.14
German (69)	545	7.05
Greek (23)	130	1.68
Irish (351)	1,301	16.84
Italian (65)	349	4.52
Lithuanian (0)	58	0.75
Norwegian (13)	33	0.43
Polish (95)	290	3.75
Portuguese (25)	153	1.98
Russian (0)	60	0.78
Scotch-Irish (45)	162	2.10
Scottish (113)	387	5.01
Serbian (0)	12	0.16
Swedish (0)	96	1.24
Welsh (36)	119	1.54

Hispanic Origin	Population	%
Hispanic or Latino (of any race)	100	1.29
Central American, ex. Mexican	10	0.13
Panamanian	10	0.13
Cuban	3	0.04
Dominican Republic	2	0.03
Mexican	27	0.35
Puerto Rican	30	0.39
South American	3	0.04
Argentinean	2	0.03
Peruvian	1	0.01
Other Hispanic or Latino	25	0.32

Race*	Population	%
African-American/Black (20)	44	0.57
Not Hispanic (20)	43	0.55
Hispanic (0)	1	0.01
American Indian/Alaska Native (32)	97	1.25
Not Hispanic (32)	93	1.20
Hispanic (0)	4	0.05
Apache (1)	2	0.03
Blackfeet (1)	5	0.06
Canadian/French Am. Ind. (3)	6	0.08
Cherokee (3)	7	0.09
Chippewa (0)	1	0.01
Creek (0)	1	0.01
Iroquois (0)	2	0.03
Lumbee (2)	2	0.03
Navajo (1)	1	0.01
Sioux (3)	5	0.06
Asian (27)	52	0.67
Not Hispanic (27)	51	0.66
Hispanic (0)	1	0.01
Bangladeshi (0)	1	0.01
Cambodian (2)	3	0.04
Chinese, ex. Taiwanese (9)	14	0.18
Filipino (3)	6	0.08
Indian (4)	4	0.05
Japanese (2)	6	0.08
Korean (4)	9	0.12
Malaysian (0)	1	0.01
Thai (0)	1	0.01
Vietnamese (0)	3	0.04
Hawaii Native/Pacific Islander (6)	12	0.15
Not Hispanic (6)	11	0.14
Hispanic (0)	1	0.01
Guamanian/Chamorro (1)	2	0.03
Native Hawaiian (1)	6	0.08
Samoan (0)	4	0.05
White (7,519)	7,649	98.57
Not Hispanic (7,463)	7,567	97.51
Hispanic (56)	82	1.06

Freeport

Place Type: Town
County: Cumberland
Population: 7,879†

Ancestry‡	Population	%
Albanian (0)	16	0.20
American (245)	245	3.10
Arab (0)	51	0.65
Lebanese (0)	51	0.65
Armenian (0)	63	0.80
Austrian (14)	23	0.29
Belgian (0)	9	0.11
British (15)	63	0.80
Canadian (21)	123	1.56
Danish (0)	99	1.25
Dutch (46)	128	1.62
Eastern European (11)	11	0.14
English (993)	2,754	34.90
European (69)	69	0.87
Finnish (11)	21	0.27
French, ex. Basque (244)	1,190	15.08
French Canadian (113)	447	5.66
German (236)	983	12.46
Greek (50)	50	0.63
Hungarian (0)	15	0.19
Irish (459)	1,546	19.59
Italian (42)	441	5.59
Latvian (0)	14	0.18
Lithuanian (8)	95	1.20
Northern European (14)	14	0.18
Norwegian (9)	44	0.56
Polish (10)	167	2.12
Portuguese (16)	231	2.93
Russian (41)	107	1.36
Scandinavian (0)	14	0.18
Scotch-Irish (122)	383	4.85
Scottish (118)	542	6.87
Slovene (0)	31	0.39
Swedish (64)	208	2.64
Swiss (0)	99	1.25
Ukrainian (0)	10	0.13
Welsh (15)	32	0.41

Hispanic Origin	Population	%
Hispanic or Latino (of any race)	83	1.05
Central American, ex. Mexican	4	0.05
Guatemalan	2	0.03
Panamanian	1	0.01
Other Central American	1	0.01
Cuban	10	0.13
Mexican	21	0.27
Puerto Rican	11	0.14
South American	16	0.20
Chilean	1	0.01
Colombian	8	0.10
Ecuadorian	1	0.01
Paraguayan	1	0.01
Peruvian	4	0.05
Venezuelan	1	0.01
Other Hispanic or Latino	21	0.27

Race*	Population	%
African-American/Black (45)	74	0.94
Not Hispanic (45)	74	0.94
American Indian/Alaska Native (28)	66	0.84
Not Hispanic (26)	64	0.81
Hispanic (2)	2	0.03
Blackfeet (0)	1	0.01
Canadian/French Am. Ind. (4)	4	0.05
Cherokee (1)	6	0.08
Choctaw (0)	1	0.01
Creek (0)	1	0.01
Crow (0)	1	0.01
Iroquois (2)	3	0.04
Mexican American Ind. (1)	1	0.01
Osage (1)	3	0.04
Seminole (0)	1	0.01
South American Ind. (1)	1	0.01
Asian (178)	218	2.77
Not Hispanic (174)	214	2.72
Hispanic (4)	4	0.05
Cambodian (7)	7	0.09
Chinese, ex. Taiwanese (115)	126	1.60
Filipino (10)	19	0.24
Indian (11)	17	0.22
Indonesian (0)	1	0.01
Japanese (9)	12	0.15
Korean (8)	12	0.15
Pakistani (1)	1	0.01
Thai (3)	3	0.04
Vietnamese (13)	19	0.24
Hawaii Native/Pacific Islander (1)	9	0.11
Not Hispanic (1)	8	0.10
Hispanic (0)	1	0.01
Native Hawaiian (0)	3	0.04
Samoan (1)	1	0.01
White (7,501)	7,599	96.45
Not Hispanic (7,440)	7,530	95.57
Hispanic (61)	69	0.88

Gorham

Place Type: Town
County: Cumberland
Population: 16,381†

Ancestry‡	Population	%
African, Sub-Saharan (39)	39	0.24
African (39)	39	0.24
American (816)	816	5.08
Austrian (40)	40	0.25
British (68)	122	0.76
Cajun (9)	9	0.06
Canadian (29)	96	0.60
Czech (0)	11	0.07
Danish (0)	15	0.09
Dutch (8)	77	0.48

*Notes: † The Census 2010 population figure is used to calculate the percentages in the Hispanic Origin and Race categories. Ancestry percentages are based on the 2006-2010 American Community Survey population (not shown); ‡ Numbers in parentheses indicate the number of people reporting a single ancestry; * Numbers in parentheses indicate the number of persons reporting this race alone, not in combination with any other race; Please refer to the Explanation of Data for more information.*

Eastern European (12)	25	0.16
English (1,364)	3,777	23.51
European (92)	137	0.85
Finnish (48)	98	0.61
French, ex. Basque (519)	2,148	13.37
French Canadian (637)	1,114	6.93
German (393)	1,602	9.97
Greek (0)	44	0.27
Hungarian (13)	36	0.22
Icelander (19)	19	0.12
Irish (1,073)	3,544	22.06
Italian (237)	1,177	7.33
Lithuanian (0)	108	0.67
Northern European (12)	12	0.07
Norwegian (0)	30	0.19
Pennsylvania German (0)	8	0.05
Polish (44)	440	2.74
Portuguese (25)	103	0.64
Russian (491)	550	3.42
Scotch-Irish (84)	523	3.26
Scottish (284)	1,173	7.30
Slavic (25)	127	0.79
Slovene (0)	11	0.07
Swedish (35)	218	1.36
Ukrainian (12)	31	0.19
Welsh (45)	236	1.47

Hispanic Origin	Population	%
Hispanic or Latino (of any race)	152	0.93
Central American, ex. Mexican	20	0.12
Costa Rican	3	0.02
Guatemalan	6	0.04
Honduran	4	0.02
Nicaraguan	1	0.01
Panamanian	3	0.02
Salvadoran	3	0.02
Mexican	64	0.39
Puerto Rican	36	0.22
South American	14	0.09
Argentinean	1	0.01
Chilean	1	0.01
Colombian	9	0.05
Ecuadorian	1	0.01
Peruvian	1	0.01
Uruguayan	1	0.01
Other Hispanic or Latino	18	0.11

Race*	Population	%
African-American/Black (110)	184	1.12
Not Hispanic (110)	180	1.10
Hispanic (0)	4	0.02
American Indian/Alaska Native (56)	127	0.78
Not Hispanic (55)	126	0.77
Hispanic (1)	1	0.01
Alaska Athabascan *(Ala. Nat.)* (1)	1	0.01
Blackfeet (1)	2	0.01
Canadian/French Am. Ind. (0)	1	0.01
Central American Ind. (1)	3	0.02
Cherokee (3)	6	0.04
Cheyenne (0)	1	0.01
Chippewa (0)	1	0.01
Choctaw (0)	1	0.01
Creek (4)	5	0.03
Iroquois (0)	4	0.02
Mexican American Ind. (1)	1	0.01
Tlingit-Haida *(Alaska Native)* (0)	2	0.01
Tsimshian *(Alaska Native)* (0)	2	0.01
Asian (155)	231	1.41
Not Hispanic (152)	228	1.39
Hispanic (3)	3	0.02
Burmese (1)	2	0.01
Cambodian (9)	9	0.05
Chinese, ex. Taiwanese (38)	51	0.31
Filipino (27)	50	0.31
Indian (23)	27	0.16
Indonesian (1)	1	0.01
Japanese (6)	13	0.08
Korean (19)	32	0.20
Laotian (2)	2	0.01
Taiwanese (3)	3	0.02
Vietnamese (25)	30	0.18
Hawaii Native/Pacific Islander (2)	4	0.02
Not Hispanic (2)	4	0.02
Fijian (1)	2	0.01
Guamanian/Chamorro (1)	1	0.01
Native Hawaiian (0)	1	0.01
White (15,806)	16,020	97.80
Not Hispanic (15,690)	15,894	97.03
Hispanic (116)	126	0.77

Gray

Place Type: Town
County: Cumberland
Population: 7,761†

Ancestry‡	Population	%
African, Sub-Saharan (24)	24	0.31
Ethiopian (24)	24	0.31
American (348)	348	4.56
Armenian (18)	18	0.24
British (10)	10	0.13
Canadian (39)	116	1.52
Czechoslovakian (0)	8	0.10
Danish (12)	46	0.60
Dutch (0)	16	0.21
English (642)	1,553	20.36
European (7)	19	0.25
Finnish (13)	13	0.17
French, ex. Basque (779)	1,480	19.40
French Canadian (246)	307	4.02
German (121)	437	5.73
Hungarian (0)	13	0.17
Irish (339)	1,135	14.88
Italian (307)	599	7.85
Norwegian (30)	127	1.66
Polish (77)	255	3.34
Russian (31)	36	0.47
Scotch-Irish (38)	99	1.30
Scottish (45)	255	3.34
Slovak (0)	6	0.08
Swedish (22)	142	1.86
Welsh (28)	35	0.46

Hispanic Origin	Population	%
Hispanic or Latino (of any race)	66	0.85
Central American, ex. Mexican	8	0.10
Costa Rican	3	0.04
Guatemalan	1	0.01
Honduran	2	0.03
Panamanian	2	0.03
Cuban	4	0.05
Mexican	23	0.30
Puerto Rican	13	0.17
South American	6	0.08
Bolivian	3	0.04
Chilean	3	0.04
Other Hispanic or Latino	12	0.15

Race*	Population	%
African-American/Black (53)	87	1.12
Not Hispanic (50)	79	1.02
Hispanic (3)	8	0.10
American Indian/Alaska Native (18)	58	0.75
Not Hispanic (18)	57	0.73
Hispanic (0)	1	0.01
Blackfeet (0)	2	0.03
Canadian/French Am. Ind. (2)	3	0.04
Cherokee (0)	1	0.01
Chippewa (0)	2	0.03
Comanche (2)	2	0.03
Potawatomi (0)	1	0.01
South American Ind. (0)	1	0.01
Asian (39)	55	0.71
Not Hispanic (38)	54	0.70
Hispanic (1)	1	0.01
Cambodian (8)	9	0.12
Chinese, ex. Taiwanese (12)	15	0.19
Filipino (8)	15	0.19
Indian (1)	1	0.01
Japanese (2)	3	0.04
Korean (2)	5	0.06
Thai (0)	1	0.01
Vietnamese (6)	6	0.08
Hawaii Native/Pacific Islander (5)	8	0.10
Not Hispanic (3)	6	0.08
Hispanic (2)	2	0.03
Guamanian/Chamorro (2)	2	0.03
Native Hawaiian (2)	4	0.05
Samoan (1)	1	0.01
White (7,541)	7,631	98.32
Not Hispanic (7,491)	7,575	97.60
Hispanic (50)	56	0.72

Kennebunk

Place Type: Town
County: York
Population: 10,798†

Ancestry‡	Population	%
African, Sub-Saharan (0)	9	0.08
South African (0)	9	0.08
American (605)	605	5.56
Arab (41)	57	0.52
Lebanese (30)	46	0.42
Syrian (11)	11	0.10
Armenian (14)	14	0.13
Austrian (41)	50	0.46
Belgian (11)	11	0.10
British (52)	173	1.59
Canadian (62)	158	1.45
Croatian (16)	16	0.15
Czech (0)	55	0.51
Czechoslovakian (26)	26	0.24
Danish (39)	39	0.36
Dutch (47)	104	0.96
English (973)	2,649	24.34
European (52)	52	0.48
Finnish (0)	17	0.16
French, ex. Basque (430)	1,146	10.53
French Canadian (370)	828	7.61
German (355)	1,343	12.34
Greek (40)	139	1.28
Hungarian (0)	53	0.49
Irish (1,059)	2,607	23.95
Italian (201)	793	7.29
Lithuanian (16)	122	1.12
Northern European (0)	23	0.21
Norwegian (29)	116	1.07
Polish (104)	382	3.51
Portuguese (0)	43	0.40
Russian (50)	120	1.10
Scotch-Irish (264)	650	5.97
Scottish (150)	784	7.20
Swedish (72)	371	3.41
Welsh (0)	39	0.36

Hispanic Origin	Population	%
Hispanic or Latino (of any race)	106	0.98
Central American, ex. Mexican	6	0.06
Costa Rican	1	0.01
Guatemalan	1	0.01
Salvadoran	4	0.04
Cuban	6	0.06
Dominican Republic	1	0.01
Mexican	35	0.32
Puerto Rican	23	0.21
South American	14	0.13
Argentinean	3	0.03
Colombian	7	0.06
Peruvian	4	0.04
Other Hispanic or Latino	21	0.19

Race*	Population	%
African-American/Black (43)	73	0.68
Not Hispanic (41)	70	0.65
Hispanic (2)	3	0.03
American Indian/Alaska Native (23)	83	0.77
Not Hispanic (23)	83	0.77

*Notes: † The Census 2010 population figure is used to calculate the percentages in the Hispanic Origin and Race categories. Ancestry percentages are based on the 2006-2010 American Community Survey population (not shown); ‡ Numbers in parentheses indicate the number of people reporting a single ancestry; * Numbers in parentheses indicate the number of persons reporting this race alone, not in combination with any other race; Please refer to the Explanation of Data for more information.*

Blackfeet (0)	5	0.05
Canadian/French Am. Ind. (1)	2	0.02
Cherokee (1)	8	0.07
Chickasaw (0)	3	0.03
Inupiat *(Alaska Native)* (1)	1	0.01
Iroquois (0)	3	0.03
Navajo (0)	1	0.01
Sioux (0)	1	0.01
Asian (112)	147	1.36
Not Hispanic (111)	146	1.35
Hispanic (1)	1	0.01
Cambodian (14)	14	0.13
Chinese, ex. Taiwanese (38)	50	0.46
Filipino (14)	20	0.19
Indian (1)	7	0.06
Indonesian (1)	3	0.03
Japanese (7)	15	0.14
Korean (5)	5	0.05
Taiwanese (2)	5	0.05
Vietnamese (25)	34	0.31
Hawaii Native/Pacific Islander (4)	10	0.09
Not Hispanic (4)	10	0.09
Native Hawaiian (2)	6	0.06
Samoan (2)	2	0.02
White (10,465)	10,582	98.00
Not Hispanic (10,385)	10,496	97.20
Hispanic (80)	86	0.80

Kittery

Place Type: Town
County: York
Population: 9,490†

Ancestry‡	Population	%
African, Sub-Saharan (79)	79	0.82
Nigerian (79)	79	0.82
American (820)	820	8.54
Arab (12)	32	0.33
Arab (0)	20	0.21
Lebanese (12)	12	0.12
Armenian (101)	101	1.05
Australian (0)	20	0.21
Austrian (11)	45	0.47
British (51)	106	1.10
Canadian (66)	98	1.02
Czech (15)	25	0.26
Czechoslovakian (22)	22	0.23
Danish (16)	52	0.54
Dutch (0)	39	0.41
Eastern European (10)	10	0.10
English (533)	1,780	18.53
European (111)	111	1.16
Finnish (41)	79	0.82
French, ex. Basque (236)	814	8.47
French Canadian (413)	737	7.67
German (194)	1,012	10.54
Greek (34)	84	0.87
Hungarian (10)	88	0.92
Irish (509)	1,750	18.22
Italian (371)	912	9.49
Lithuanian (32)	62	0.65
Norwegian (83)	112	1.17
Pennsylvania German (42)	42	0.44
Polish (75)	338	3.52
Portuguese (32)	96	1.00
Russian (30)	185	1.93
Scandinavian (63)	63	0.66
Scotch-Irish (147)	348	3.62
Scottish (184)	608	6.33
Swedish (48)	185	1.93
Ukrainian (15)	15	0.16
Welsh (38)	169	1.76

Hispanic Origin	Population	%
Hispanic or Latino (of any race)	251	2.64
Central American, ex. Mexican	10	0.11
Costa Rican	1	0.01
Guatemalan	5	0.05
Honduran	1	0.01
Salvadoran	3	0.03
Cuban	7	0.07
Dominican Republic	12	0.13
Mexican	116	1.22
Puerto Rican	50	0.53
South American	25	0.26
Bolivian	1	0.01
Chilean	7	0.07
Colombian	4	0.04
Ecuadorian	12	0.13
Peruvian	1	0.01
Other Hispanic or Latino	31	0.33

Race*	Population	%
African-American/Black (86)	127	1.34
Not Hispanic (85)	122	1.29
Hispanic (1)	5	0.05
American Indian/Alaska Native (14)	74	0.78
Not Hispanic (11)	62	0.65
Hispanic (3)	12	0.13
Blackfeet (0)	1	0.01
Canadian/French Am. Ind. (1)	2	0.02
Cherokee (0)	16	0.17
Iroquois (0)	7	0.07
Mexican American Ind. (1)	2	0.02
Navajo (0)	5	0.05
Osage (1)	2	0.02
Sioux (0)	1	0.01
South American Ind. (1)	2	0.02
Asian (103)	151	1.59
Not Hispanic (103)	147	1.55
Hispanic (0)	4	0.04
Cambodian (9)	9	0.09
Chinese, ex. Taiwanese (39)	46	0.48
Filipino (19)	38	0.40
Indian (16)	23	0.24
Indonesian (1)	2	0.02
Japanese (6)	13	0.14
Korean (2)	8	0.08
Nepalese (0)	2	0.02
Taiwanese (1)	1	0.01
Thai (6)	7	0.07
Vietnamese (2)	3	0.03
Hawaii Native/Pacific Islander (5)	14	0.15
Not Hispanic (4)	10	0.11
Hispanic (1)	4	0.04
Guamanian/Chamorro (1)	1	0.01
Native Hawaiian (2)	3	0.03
Samoan (1)	6	0.06
White (9,090)	9,226	97.22
Not Hispanic (8,905)	9,025	95.10
Hispanic (185)	201	2.12

Lewiston

Place Type: City
County: Androscoggin
Population: 36,592†

Ancestry‡	Population	%
African, Sub-Saharan (926)	957	2.61
African (9)	34	0.09
Cape Verdean (19)	19	0.05
Ethiopian (9)	9	0.02
Kenyan (47)	47	0.13
Nigerian (0)	6	0.02
Somalian (750)	750	2.04
Sudanese (92)	92	0.25
American (1,434)	1,434	3.91
Arab (58)	118	0.32
Lebanese (28)	54	0.15
Moroccan (0)	21	0.06
Palestinian (30)	30	0.08
Syrian (0)	13	0.04
Armenian (0)	13	0.04
Austrian (18)	78	0.21
Belgian (0)	7	0.02
British (36)	70	0.19
Canadian (517)	725	1.98
Czech (15)	92	0.25
Czechoslovakian (0)	62	0.17
Danish (13)	40	0.11
Dutch (146)	527	1.44
English (1,953)	5,352	14.59
European (8)	31	0.08
Finnish (110)	234	0.64
French, ex. Basque (4,506)	9,130	24.89
French Canadian (6,474)	8,580	23.39
German (431)	2,294	6.25
Greek (10)	106	0.29
Guyanese (0)	14	0.04
Hungarian (15)	76	0.21
Iranian (0)	15	0.04
Irish (1,384)	5,722	15.60
Italian (632)	1,684	4.59
Lithuanian (62)	76	0.21
Norwegian (22)	125	0.34
Polish (224)	695	1.89
Portuguese (21)	226	0.62
Romanian (0)	17	0.05
Russian (34)	156	0.43
Scandinavian (0)	58	0.16
Scotch-Irish (300)	980	2.67
Scottish (124)	697	1.90
Serbian (0)	10	0.03
Slovak (0)	53	0.14
Swedish (89)	479	1.31
Swiss (0)	86	0.23
Turkish (0)	12	0.03
Ukrainian (24)	24	0.07
Welsh (22)	206	0.56
West Indian, ex. Hispanic (4)	27	0.07
Haitian (0)	9	0.02
Jamaican (4)	18	0.05

Hispanic Origin	Population	%
Hispanic or Latino (of any race)	730	1.99
Central American, ex. Mexican	36	0.10
Costa Rican	1	<0.01
Guatemalan	12	0.03
Honduran	6	0.02
Nicaraguan	4	0.01
Panamanian	5	0.01
Salvadoran	8	0.02
Cuban	19	0.05
Dominican Republic	35	0.10
Mexican	273	0.75
Puerto Rican	232	0.63
South American	32	0.09
Chilean	2	0.01
Colombian	14	0.04
Ecuadorian	8	0.02
Peruvian	1	<0.01
Venezuelan	7	0.02
Other Hispanic or Latino	103	0.28

Race*	Population	%
African-American/Black (3,174)	3,664	10.01
Not Hispanic (3,129)	3,581	9.79
Hispanic (45)	83	0.23
American Indian/Alaska Native (156)	455	1.24
Not Hispanic (141)	418	1.14
Hispanic (15)	37	0.10
Apache (1)	3	0.01
Blackfeet (6)	12	0.03
Canadian/French Am. Ind. (9)	14	0.04
Cherokee (8)	44	0.12
Chickasaw (0)	3	0.01
Chippewa (1)	5	0.01
Cree (0)	1	<0.01
Creek (0)	2	0.01
Hopi (0)	1	<0.01
Inupiat *(Alaska Native)* (1)	1	<0.01
Iroquois (5)	10	0.03
Navajo (2)	6	0.02
Ottawa (1)	3	0.01
Paiute (1)	1	<0.01
Potawatomi (1)	3	0.01
Pueblo (1)	1	<0.01
Seminole (2)	5	0.01

*Notes: † The Census 2010 population figure is used to calculate the percentages in the Hispanic Origin and Race categories. Ancestry percentages are based on the 2006-2010 American Community Survey population (not shown); ‡ Numbers in parentheses indicate the number of people reporting a single ancestry; * Numbers in parentheses indicate the number of persons reporting this race alone, not in combination with any other race; Please refer to the Explanation of Data for more information.*

Sioux (2)	6	0.02
South American Ind. (2)	2	0.01
Spanish American Ind. (2)	2	0.01
Yaqui (0)	1	<0.01
Asian (384)	543	1.48
Not Hispanic (384)	538	1.47
Hispanic (0)	5	0.01
Bangladeshi (1)	1	<0.01
Burmese (0)	1	<0.01
Cambodian (8)	8	0.02
Chinese, ex. Taiwanese (154)	191	0.52
Filipino (68)	109	0.30
Indian (61)	84	0.23
Indonesian (0)	2	0.01
Japanese (15)	31	0.08
Korean (19)	39	0.11
Laotian (1)	2	0.01
Malaysian (0)	1	<0.01
Nepalese (2)	2	0.01
Sri Lankan (0)	1	<0.01
Taiwanese (2)	4	0.01
Thai (13)	15	0.04
Vietnamese (23)	43	0.12
Hawaii Native/Pacific Islander (14)	38	0.10
Not Hispanic (14)	37	0.10
Hispanic (0)	1	<0.01
Guamanian/Chamorro (2)	10	0.03
Native Hawaiian (6)	13	0.04
Samoan (5)	7	0.02
Tongan (1)	2	0.01
White (31,694)	32,560	88.98
Not Hispanic (31,273)	32,065	87.63
Hispanic (421)	495	1.35

Lisbon

Place Type: Town
County: Androscoggin
Population: 9,009†

Ancestry‡	Population	%
African, Sub-Saharan (0)	4	0.04
African (0)	4	0.04
Albanian (0)	16	0.18
American (604)	604	6.64
Arab (40)	40	0.44
Lebanese (40)	40	0.44
Austrian (15)	57	0.63
British (0)	9	0.10
Canadian (110)	137	1.51
Czech (0)	12	0.13
Danish (8)	25	0.27
Dutch (0)	73	0.80
English (661)	1,882	20.70
European (98)	98	1.08
Finnish (20)	39	0.43
French, ex. Basque (565)	1,446	15.90
French Canadian (1,203)	1,468	16.15
German (225)	908	9.99
Greek (0)	16	0.18
Irish (402)	1,489	16.38
Israeli (0)	9	0.10
Italian (56)	376	4.14
Lithuanian (9)	21	0.23
New Zealander (35)	44	0.48
Northern European (9)	9	0.10
Norwegian (30)	83	0.91
Pennsylvania German (15)	15	0.16
Polish (38)	119	1.31
Portuguese (34)	79	0.87
Russian (13)	48	0.53
Scandinavian (22)	22	0.24
Scotch-Irish (99)	286	3.15
Scottish (114)	401	4.41
Slovak (87)	168	1.85
Swedish (18)	162	1.78
Ukrainian (12)	12	0.13
Welsh (19)	79	0.87
Yugoslavian (32)	32	0.35

Hispanic Origin	Population	%
Hispanic or Latino (of any race)	94	1.04
Central American, ex. Mexican	7	0.08
Panamanian	6	0.07
Salvadoran	1	0.01
Cuban	3	0.03
Dominican Republic	4	0.04
Mexican	27	0.30
Puerto Rican	20	0.22
South American	7	0.08
Colombian	6	0.07
Ecuadorian	1	0.01
Other Hispanic or Latino	26	0.29

Race*	Population	%
African-American/Black (56)	103	1.14
Not Hispanic (53)	91	1.01
Hispanic (3)	12	0.13
American Indian/Alaska Native (41)	142	1.58
Not Hispanic (39)	136	1.51
Hispanic (2)	6	0.07
Blackfeet (2)	8	0.09
Canadian/French Am. Ind. (2)	3	0.03
Cherokee (1)	21	0.23
Cheyenne (0)	1	0.01
Chickasaw (1)	1	0.01
Chippewa (0)	4	0.04
Choctaw (0)	1	0.01
Cree (0)	1	0.01
Delaware (1)	4	0.04
Inupiat *(Alaska Native)* (1)	1	0.01
Iroquois (0)	2	0.02
Mexican American Ind. (1)	1	0.01
Ottawa (0)	1	0.01
Asian (47)	89	0.99
Not Hispanic (46)	84	0.93
Hispanic (1)	5	0.06
Chinese, ex. Taiwanese (10)	14	0.16
Filipino (15)	35	0.39
Indian (4)	11	0.12
Japanese (5)	8	0.09
Korean (7)	10	0.11
Taiwanese (1)	1	0.01
Vietnamese (4)	9	0.10
Hawaii Native/Pacific Islander (2)	2	0.02
Not Hispanic (2)	2	0.02
Native Hawaiian (1)	1	0.01
White (8,663)	8,833	98.05
Not Hispanic (8,602)	8,763	97.27
Hispanic (61)	70	0.78

Old Orchard Beach

Place Type: CDP/Town
County: York
Population: 8,624†

Ancestry‡	Population	%
African, Sub-Saharan (14)	14	0.16
African (14)	14	0.16
American (358)	358	4.09
Arab (18)	18	0.21
Lebanese (18)	18	0.21
Australian (0)	3	0.03
Austrian (20)	29	0.33
Belgian (0)	14	0.16
British (27)	27	0.31
Canadian (86)	171	1.95
Croatian (0)	26	0.30
Czech (0)	13	0.15
Danish (13)	27	0.31
Dutch (0)	171	1.95
English (504)	1,711	19.54
European (40)	49	0.56
Finnish (0)	54	0.62
French, ex. Basque (757)	1,862	21.26
French Canadian (666)	898	10.25
German (159)	892	10.19
Greek (29)	114	1.30
Irish (495)	2,061	23.54
Italian (278)	725	8.28
Lithuanian (0)	26	0.30
Norwegian (25)	53	0.61
Pennsylvania German (0)	15	0.17
Polish (53)	228	2.60
Portuguese (12)	12	0.14
Romanian (0)	9	0.10
Russian (10)	21	0.24
Scotch-Irish (276)	572	6.53
Scottish (198)	523	5.97
Slovak (0)	19	0.22
Swedish (23)	81	0.92
Swiss (0)	5	0.06
Welsh (0)	193	2.20
West Indian, ex. Hispanic (20)	20	0.23
Jamaican (20)	20	0.23

Hispanic Origin	Population	%
Hispanic or Latino (of any race)	147	1.70
Central American, ex. Mexican	8	0.09
Costa Rican	3	0.03
Nicaraguan	1	0.01
Salvadoran	4	0.05
Cuban	6	0.07
Dominican Republic	7	0.08
Mexican	46	0.53
Puerto Rican	36	0.42
South American	8	0.09
Argentinean	5	0.06
Chilean	1	0.01
Colombian	1	0.01
Ecuadorian	1	0.01
Other Hispanic or Latino	36	0.42

Race*	Population	%
African-American/Black (72)	104	1.21
Not Hispanic (66)	90	1.04
Hispanic (6)	14	0.16
American Indian/Alaska Native (37)	88	1.02
Not Hispanic (33)	80	0.93
Hispanic (4)	8	0.09
Apache (0)	1	0.01
Blackfeet (1)	2	0.02
Canadian/French Am. Ind. (5)	7	0.08
Cherokee (1)	8	0.09
Chippewa (1)	1	0.01
Inupiat *(Alaska Native)* (1)	3	0.03
Iroquois (0)	2	0.02
Navajo (1)	1	0.01
Sioux (0)	2	0.02
South American Ind. (1)	1	0.01
Asian (80)	108	1.25
Not Hispanic (80)	103	1.19
Hispanic (0)	5	0.06
Cambodian (7)	7	0.08
Chinese, ex. Taiwanese (8)	12	0.14
Filipino (23)	34	0.39
Indian (6)	8	0.09
Indonesian (4)	4	0.05
Japanese (2)	6	0.07
Korean (15)	15	0.17
Pakistani (1)	1	0.01
Thai (2)	3	0.03
Vietnamese (9)	12	0.14
Hawaii Native/Pacific Islander (1)	2	0.02
Not Hispanic (1)	1	0.01
Hispanic (0)	1	0.01
Tongan (1)	1	0.01
White (8,300)	8,401	97.41
Not Hispanic (8,201)	8,285	96.07
Hispanic (99)	116	1.35

Old Town

Place Type: City
County: Penobscot
Population: 7,840†

Ancestry‡	Population	%
African, Sub-Saharan (15)	24	0.30

*Notes: † The Census 2010 population figure is used to calculate the percentages in the Hispanic Origin and Race categories. Ancestry percentages are based on the 2006-2010 American Community Survey population (not shown); ‡ Numbers in parentheses indicate the number of people reporting a single ancestry; * Numbers in parentheses indicate the number of persons reporting this race alone, not in combination with any other race; Please refer to the Explanation of Data for more information.*

Cape Verdean (0)	9	0.11
Ghanaian (15)	15	0.19
American (314)	314	3.98
Arab (2)	27	0.34
Lebanese (2)	27	0.34
British (0)	14	0.18
Canadian (8)	19	0.24
Czechoslovakian (13)	13	0.16
Danish (0)	27	0.34
Dutch (17)	49	0.62
English (560)	1,631	20.68
European (92)	92	1.17
Finnish (0)	6	0.08
French, ex. Basque (1,089)	1,959	24.84
French Canadian (517)	711	9.02
German (135)	622	7.89
Hungarian (0)	9	0.11
Irish (400)	1,153	14.62
Italian (45)	227	2.88
Norwegian (18)	24	0.30
Polish (16)	129	1.64
Portuguese (36)	65	0.82
Scandinavian (100)	114	1.45
Scotch-Irish (113)	282	3.58
Scottish (39)	365	4.63
Slovak (0)	28	0.36
Swedish (75)	152	1.93
Welsh (0)	9	0.11

Hispanic Origin	Population	%
Hispanic or Latino (of any race)	102	1.30
Central American, ex. Mexican	8	0.10
Guatemalan	1	0.01
Honduran	4	0.05
Panamanian	3	0.04
Cuban	3	0.04
Dominican Republic	1	0.01
Mexican	30	0.38
Puerto Rican	19	0.24
South American	22	0.28
Argentinean	2	0.03
Bolivian	1	0.01
Chilean	5	0.06
Colombian	5	0.06
Ecuadorian	2	0.03
Paraguayan	1	0.01
Peruvian	1	0.01
Venezuelan	5	0.06
Other Hispanic or Latino	19	0.24

Race*	Population	%
African-American/Black (70)	109	1.39
Not Hispanic (70)	105	1.34
Hispanic (0)	4	0.05
American Indian/Alaska Native (129)	217	2.77
Not Hispanic (124)	209	2.67
Hispanic (5)	8	0.10
Apache (0)	2	0.03
Blackfeet (0)	1	0.01
Cherokee (2)	13	0.17
Chippewa (1)	1	0.01
Choctaw (1)	2	0.03
Cree (1)	1	0.01
Iroquois (4)	4	0.05
Lumbee (1)	2	0.03
Osage (1)	1	0.01
Seminole (0)	2	0.03
Sioux (1)	2	0.03
Asian (139)	182	2.32
Not Hispanic (139)	180	2.30
Hispanic (0)	2	0.03
Cambodian (1)	1	0.01
Chinese, ex. Taiwanese (57)	68	0.87
Filipino (3)	20	0.26
Indian (18)	21	0.27
Japanese (8)	10	0.13
Korean (25)	31	0.40
Laotian (1)	3	0.04
Nepalese (1)	1	0.01
Pakistani (1)	1	0.01
Sri Lankan (10)	10	0.13
Thai (2)	2	0.03
Vietnamese (1)	2	0.03
Hawaii Native/Pacific Islander (4)	4	0.05
Not Hispanic (3)	3	0.04
Hispanic (1)	1	0.01
Guamanian/Chamorro (1)	1	0.01
Samoan (3)	3	0.04
White (7,302)	7,460	95.15
Not Hispanic (7,247)	7,390	94.26
Hispanic (55)	70	0.89

Orono

Place Type: CDP
County: Penobscot
Population: 9,474†

Ancestry‡	Population	%
African, Sub-Saharan (25)	46	0.51
African (25)	25	0.28
Nigerian (0)	21	0.23
American (952)	952	10.65
Arab (0)	31	0.35
Lebanese (0)	16	0.18
Other Arab (0)	15	0.17
Australian (0)	16	0.18
Austrian (14)	43	0.48
British (0)	22	0.25
Bulgarian (12)	12	0.13
Canadian (73)	84	0.94
Danish (0)	19	0.21
Dutch (72)	187	2.09
English (276)	1,046	11.70
Estonian (15)	15	0.17
European (101)	101	1.13
French, ex. Basque (184)	919	10.28
French Canadian (391)	640	7.16
German (115)	849	9.49
Greek (22)	69	0.77
Hungarian (0)	19	0.21
Irish (374)	1,057	11.82
Italian (181)	417	4.66
Lithuanian (0)	19	0.21
Luxemburger (0)	21	0.23
Norwegian (15)	32	0.36
Polish (67)	273	3.05
Portuguese (23)	62	0.69
Russian (10)	132	1.48
Scandinavian (13)	26	0.29
Scotch-Irish (131)	290	3.24
Scottish (162)	389	4.35
Slovak (0)	24	0.27
Swedish (33)	226	2.53
Swiss (0)	32	0.36
Turkish (0)	20	0.22
Ukrainian (18)	49	0.55
Welsh (0)	39	0.44
West Indian, ex. Hispanic (0)	15	0.17
Trinidadian/Tobagonian (0)	15	0.17

Hispanic Origin	Population	%
Hispanic or Latino (of any race)	145	1.53
Central American, ex. Mexican	8	0.08
Costa Rican	4	0.04
Honduran	2	0.02
Salvadoran	2	0.02
Cuban	12	0.13
Dominican Republic	4	0.04
Mexican	36	0.38
Puerto Rican	37	0.39
South American	21	0.22
Argentinean	4	0.04
Bolivian	1	0.01
Chilean	2	0.02
Colombian	5	0.05
Ecuadorian	1	0.01
Paraguayan	1	0.01
Peruvian	3	0.03
Venezuelan	4	0.04
Other Hispanic or Latino	27	0.28

Race*	Population	%
African-American/Black (115)	159	1.68
Not Hispanic (112)	152	1.60
Hispanic (3)	7	0.07
American Indian/Alaska Native (102)	168	1.77
Not Hispanic (102)	162	1.71
Hispanic (0)	6	0.06
Alaska Athabascan *(Ala. Nat.)* (1)	1	0.01
Apache (2)	3	0.03
Blackfeet (0)	3	0.03
Canadian/French Am. Ind. (0)	3	0.03
Cherokee (2)	13	0.14
Chippewa (2)	2	0.02
Choctaw (0)	5	0.05
Cree (1)	1	0.01
Inupiat *(Alaska Native)* (1)	1	0.01
Iroquois (1)	2	0.02
Kiowa (1)	1	0.01
Lumbee (0)	2	0.02
Pueblo (0)	2	0.02
Sioux (1)	1	0.01
South American Ind. (1)	1	0.01
Yaqui (0)	1	0.01
Yup'ik *(Alaska Native)* (1)	1	0.01
Asian (187)	232	2.45
Not Hispanic (185)	230	2.43
Hispanic (2)	2	0.02
Cambodian (8)	9	0.09
Chinese, ex. Taiwanese (65)	76	0.80
Filipino (8)	13	0.14
Indian (26)	31	0.33
Indonesian (1)	1	0.01
Japanese (4)	8	0.08
Korean (21)	34	0.36
Laotian (0)	1	0.01
Nepalese (9)	9	0.09
Pakistani (19)	19	0.20
Sri Lankan (4)	5	0.05
Thai (3)	4	0.04
Vietnamese (5)	8	0.08
Hawaii Native/Pacific Islander (3)	6	0.06
Not Hispanic (3)	6	0.06
Native Hawaiian (2)	2	0.02
White (8,876)	9,023	95.24
Not Hispanic (8,772)	8,908	94.03
Hispanic (104)	115	1.21

Orono

Place Type: Town
County: Penobscot
Population: 10,362†

Ancestry‡	Population	%
African, Sub-Saharan (25)	46	0.45
African (25)	25	0.25
Nigerian (0)	21	0.21
American (1,058)	1,058	10.37
Arab (0)	31	0.30
Lebanese (0)	16	0.16
Other Arab (0)	15	0.15
Australian (0)	16	0.16
Austrian (14)	43	0.42
British (0)	22	0.22
Bulgarian (12)	12	0.12
Canadian (73)	96	0.94
Danish (0)	19	0.19
Dutch (86)	208	2.04
English (329)	1,318	12.92
Estonian (15)	15	0.15
European (109)	109	1.07
French, ex. Basque (189)	1,084	10.63
French Canadian (495)	786	7.71
German (123)	881	8.64
Greek (22)	69	0.68
Hungarian (0)	19	0.19
Irish (423)	1,345	13.19
Italian (181)	457	4.48

*Notes: † The Census 2010 population figure is used to calculate the percentages in the Hispanic Origin and Race categories. Ancestry percentages are based on the 2006-2010 American Community Survey population (not shown); ‡ Numbers in parentheses indicate the number of people reporting a single ancestry; * Numbers in parentheses indicate the number of persons reporting this race alone, not in combination with any other race; Please refer to the Explanation of Data for more information.*

Ancestry (continued)	Population	%
Lithuanian (0)	19	0.19
Luxemburger (0)	21	0.21
Norwegian (24)	41	0.40
Polish (67)	282	2.76
Portuguese (48)	87	0.85
Russian (10)	132	1.29
Scandinavian (13)	26	0.25
Scotch-Irish (160)	319	3.13
Scottish (180)	469	4.60
Slovak (0)	24	0.24
Swedish (33)	235	2.30
Swiss (0)	32	0.31
Turkish (0)	20	0.20
Ukrainian (18)	49	0.48
Welsh (0)	39	0.38
West Indian, ex. Hispanic (11)	26	0.25
Jamaican (11)	11	0.11
Trinidadian/Tobagonian (0)	15	0.15

Hispanic Origin	Population	%
Hispanic or Latino (of any race)	159	1.53
Central American, ex. Mexican	11	0.11
Costa Rican	4	0.04
Honduran	2	0.02
Panamanian	1	0.01
Salvadoran	4	0.04
Cuban	12	0.12
Dominican Republic	4	0.04
Mexican	38	0.37
Puerto Rican	39	0.38
South American	25	0.24
Argentinean	4	0.04
Bolivian	1	0.01
Chilean	2	0.02
Colombian	5	0.05
Ecuadorian	1	0.01
Paraguayan	1	0.01
Peruvian	3	0.03
Venezuelan	8	0.08
Other Hispanic or Latino	30	0.29

Race*	Population	%
African-American/Black (120)	167	1.61
Not Hispanic (117)	160	1.54
Hispanic (3)	7	0.07
American Indian/Alaska Native (110)	193	1.86
Not Hispanic (110)	187	1.80
Hispanic (0)	6	0.06
Alaska Athabascan *(Ala. Nat.)* (1)	1	0.01
Apache (2)	3	0.03
Blackfeet (0)	3	0.03
Canadian/French Am. Ind. (0)	3	0.03
Cherokee (2)	14	0.14
Chippewa (2)	2	0.02
Choctaw (0)	5	0.05
Cree (1)	1	0.01
Inupiat *(Alaska Native)* (1)	1	0.01
Iroquois (1)	2	0.02
Kiowa (1)	1	0.01
Lumbee (0)	2	0.02
Pueblo (0)	2	0.02
Seminole (1)	1	0.01
Sioux (1)	1	0.01
South American Ind. (1)	1	0.01
Yaqui (0)	1	0.01
Yup'ik *(Alaska Native)* (1)	1	0.01
Asian (196)	247	2.38
Not Hispanic (194)	245	2.36
Hispanic (2)	2	0.02
Cambodian (8)	9	0.09
Chinese, ex. Taiwanese (68)	79	0.76
Filipino (9)	14	0.14
Indian (26)	31	0.30
Indonesian (4)	4	0.04
Japanese (6)	12	0.12
Korean (21)	37	0.36
Laotian (0)	1	0.01
Nepalese (9)	9	0.09
Pakistani (19)	19	0.18
Sri Lankan (4)	5	0.05
Thai (3)	4	0.04
Vietnamese (5)	8	0.08
Hawaii Native/Pacific Islander (3)	6	0.06
Not Hispanic (3)	6	0.06
Native Hawaiian (2)	2	0.02
White (9,712)	9,888	95.43
Not Hispanic (9,594)	9,759	94.18
Hispanic (118)	129	1.24

Portland

Place Type: City
County: Cumberland
Population: 66,194†

Ancestry‡	Population	%
Afghan (158)	158	0.24
African, Sub-Saharan (2,356)	2,505	3.79
African (609)	688	1.04
Cape Verdean (23)	23	0.03
Ethiopian (170)	170	0.26
Kenyan (32)	32	0.05
Nigerian (9)	9	0.01
Senegalese (72)	72	0.11
Somalian (864)	920	1.39
Sudanese (416)	416	0.63
Other Sub-Saharan African (161)	175	0.26
Albanian (59)	91	0.14
American (2,110)	2,110	3.19
Arab (389)	475	0.72
Arab (295)	295	0.45
Lebanese (86)	151	0.23
Syrian (8)	29	0.04
Armenian (55)	170	0.26
Assyrian/Chaldean/Syriac (0)	14	0.02
Australian (25)	25	0.04
Austrian (30)	159	0.24
Belgian (0)	41	0.06
Brazilian (10)	10	0.02
British (129)	419	0.63
Bulgarian (74)	74	0.11
Cajun (0)	26	0.04
Canadian (218)	471	0.71
Celtic (0)	15	0.02
Croatian (24)	39	0.06
Czech (20)	109	0.16
Czechoslovakian (10)	42	0.06
Danish (108)	558	0.84
Dutch (130)	596	0.90
Eastern European (224)	269	0.41
English (4,088)	12,604	19.06
Estonian (10)	10	0.02
European (659)	694	1.05
Finnish (102)	401	0.61
French, ex. Basque (1,792)	7,416	11.21
French Canadian (1,535)	2,906	4.39
German (1,242)	5,432	8.21
Greek (174)	477	0.72
Hungarian (56)	260	0.39
Iranian (27)	35	0.05
Irish (5,075)	14,751	22.30
Italian (2,042)	5,974	9.03
Latvian (11)	24	0.04
Lithuanian (164)	399	0.60
Macedonian (17)	27	0.04
Northern European (34)	51	0.08
Norwegian (200)	613	0.93
Pennsylvania German (8)	8	0.01
Polish (551)	2,000	3.02
Portuguese (130)	451	0.68
Romanian (101)	161	0.24
Russian (370)	1,091	1.65
Scandinavian (137)	215	0.33
Scotch-Irish (995)	3,162	4.78
Scottish (1,105)	3,739	5.65
Serbian (247)	283	0.43
Slavic (36)	49	0.07
Slovak (7)	71	0.11
Swedish (253)	1,291	1.95
Swiss (19)	205	0.31
Turkish (7)	7	0.01
Ukrainian (45)	175	0.26
Welsh (47)	589	0.89
West Indian, ex. Hispanic (125)	218	0.33
Bahamian (10)	10	0.02
Haitian (24)	57	0.09
Jamaican (91)	151	0.23
Yugoslavian (119)	119	0.18

Hispanic Origin	Population	%
Hispanic or Latino (of any race)	1,998	3.02
Central American, ex. Mexican	602	0.91
Costa Rican	11	0.02
Guatemalan	123	0.19
Honduran	71	0.11
Nicaraguan	20	0.03
Panamanian	9	0.01
Salvadoran	363	0.55
Other Central American	5	0.01
Cuban	117	0.18
Dominican Republic	123	0.19
Mexican	381	0.58
Puerto Rican	352	0.53
South American	179	0.27
Argentinean	12	0.02
Bolivian	1	<0.01
Chilean	20	0.03
Colombian	64	0.10
Ecuadorian	13	0.02
Paraguayan	3	<0.01
Peruvian	53	0.08
Uruguayan	1	<0.01
Venezuelan	8	0.01
Other South American	4	0.01
Other Hispanic or Latino	244	0.37

Race*	Population	%
African-American/Black (4,684)	5,421	8.19
Not Hispanic (4,572)	5,249	7.93
Hispanic (112)	172	0.26
American Indian/Alaska Native (312)	769	1.16
Not Hispanic (272)	694	1.05
Hispanic (40)	75	0.11
Alaska Athabascan *(Ala. Nat.)* (0)	1	<0.01
Apache (5)	10	0.02
Arapaho (0)	1	<0.01
Blackfeet (2)	16	0.02
Canadian/French Am. Ind. (5)	7	0.01
Cherokee (18)	63	0.10
Chickasaw (2)	2	<0.01
Chippewa (4)	6	0.01
Choctaw (2)	9	0.01
Comanche (1)	1	<0.01
Cree (0)	1	<0.01
Creek (0)	1	<0.01
Delaware (0)	1	<0.01
Inupiat *(Alaska Native)* (1)	2	<0.01
Iroquois (0)	5	0.01
Kiowa (0)	2	<0.01
Lumbee (2)	3	<0.01
Mexican American Ind. (13)	18	0.03
Navajo (6)	17	0.03
Pueblo (0)	4	0.01
Seminole (1)	5	0.01
Shoshone (0)	1	<0.01
Sioux (10)	25	0.04
South American Ind. (4)	5	0.01
Asian (2,305)	2,867	4.33
Not Hispanic (2,288)	2,830	4.28
Hispanic (17)	37	0.06
Bangladeshi (12)	15	0.02
Burmese (34)	34	0.05
Cambodian (566)	647	0.98
Chinese, ex. Taiwanese (300)	392	0.59
Filipino (136)	239	0.36
Hmong (1)	1	<0.01
Indian (165)	233	0.35
Indonesian (1)	1	<0.01
Japanese (50)	101	0.15
Korean (112)	174	0.26

*Notes: † The Census 2010 population figure is used to calculate the percentages in the Hispanic Origin and Race categories. Ancestry percentages are based on the 2006-2010 American Community Survey population (not shown); ‡ Numbers in parentheses indicate the number of people reporting a single ancestry; * Numbers in parentheses indicate the number of persons reporting this race alone, not in combination with any other race; Please refer to the Explanation of Data for more information.*

Laotian (17)	29	0.04
Malaysian (2)	3	<0.01
Nepalese (1)	2	<0.01
Pakistani (8)	15	0.02
Sri Lankan (1)	2	<0.01
Taiwanese (6)	6	0.01
Thai (73)	88	0.13
Vietnamese (657)	750	1.13
Hawaii Native/Pacific Islander (28)	83	0.13
Not Hispanic (25)	69	0.10
Hispanic (3)	14	0.02
Guamanian/Chamorro (11)	21	0.03
Native Hawaiian (5)	19	0.03
Samoan (2)	4	0.01
Tongan (0)	1	<0.01
White (56,275)	57,834	87.37
Not Hispanic (55,336)	56,697	85.65
Hispanic (939)	1,137	1.72

Presque Isle

Place Type: City
County: Aroostook
Population: 9,692†

Ancestry‡	Population	%
African, Sub-Saharan (73)	73	0.75
Nigerian (73)	73	0.75
American (748)	748	7.73
Arab (13)	13	0.13
Egyptian (11)	11	0.11
Lebanese (2)	2	0.02
Armenian (0)	6	0.06
Australian (1)	1	0.01
Belgian (0)	10	0.10
British (2)	47	0.49
Cajun (10)	12	0.12
Canadian (125)	198	2.05
Celtic (0)	5	0.05
Czech (10)	10	0.10
Danish (3)	26	0.27
Dutch (4)	110	1.14
English (814)	1,877	19.40
European (37)	39	0.40
Finnish (6)	6	0.06
French, ex. Basque (886)	2,056	21.26
French Canadian (516)	606	6.26
German (229)	511	5.28
Greek (3)	11	0.11
Hungarian (0)	2	0.02
Irish (555)	1,344	13.89
Italian (65)	235	2.43
Lithuanian (34)	48	0.50
Northern European (0)	2	0.02
Norwegian (14)	43	0.44
Polish (100)	194	2.01
Portuguese (48)	94	0.97
Russian (1)	36	0.37
Scandinavian (4)	10	0.10
Scotch-Irish (135)	340	3.51
Scottish (188)	503	5.20
Slovak (0)	10	0.10
Swedish (51)	242	2.50
Swiss (0)	6	0.06
Ukrainian (3)	13	0.13
Welsh (35)	94	0.97

Hispanic Origin	Population	%
Hispanic or Latino (of any race)	127	1.31
Central American, ex. Mexican	16	0.17
Guatemalan	3	0.03
Honduran	4	0.04
Nicaraguan	8	0.08
Salvadoran	1	0.01
Cuban	1	0.01
Dominican Republic	5	0.05
Mexican	31	0.32
Puerto Rican	55	0.57
South American	3	0.03
Chilean	1	0.01
Colombian	1	0.01
Venezuelan	1	0.01
Other Hispanic or Latino	16	0.17

Race*	Population	%
African-American/Black (61)	103	1.06
Not Hispanic (58)	97	1.00
Hispanic (3)	6	0.06
American Indian/Alaska Native (232)	302	3.12
Not Hispanic (218)	284	2.93
Hispanic (14)	18	0.19
Apache (0)	1	0.01
Canadian/French Am. Ind. (2)	2	0.02
Cherokee (1)	6	0.06
Creek (0)	3	0.03
Iroquois (1)	2	0.02
Navajo (0)	2	0.02
Osage (0)	1	0.01
Pueblo (0)	1	0.01
Seminole (2)	2	0.02
Sioux (2)	3	0.03
South American Ind. (2)	2	0.02
Asian (85)	106	1.09
Not Hispanic (85)	105	1.08
Hispanic (0)	1	0.01
Chinese, ex. Taiwanese (35)	37	0.38
Filipino (10)	19	0.20
Indian (12)	14	0.14
Japanese (7)	9	0.09
Korean (3)	7	0.07
Nepalese (4)	6	0.06
Taiwanese (1)	1	0.01
Thai (5)	6	0.06
Vietnamese (7)	7	0.07
Hawaii Native/Pacific Islander (4)	6	0.06
Not Hispanic (4)	6	0.06
Samoan (1)	1	0.01
White (9,155)	9,281	95.76
Not Hispanic (9,077)	9,194	94.86
Hispanic (78)	87	0.90

Saco

Place Type: City
County: York
Population: 18,482†

Ancestry‡	Population	%
Albanian (0)	61	0.33
American (636)	636	3.46
Arab (88)	88	0.48
Iraqi (27)	27	0.15
Lebanese (43)	43	0.23
Syrian (18)	18	0.10
Armenian (56)	56	0.30
Austrian (0)	8	0.04
Belgian (26)	26	0.14
Brazilian (55)	85	0.46
British (11)	50	0.27
Cajun (11)	11	0.06
Canadian (141)	250	1.36
Croatian (0)	15	0.08
Czech (39)	76	0.41
Czechoslovakian (10)	10	0.05
Danish (22)	90	0.49
Dutch (86)	265	1.44
Eastern European (27)	27	0.15
English (1,147)	3,538	19.23
European (137)	137	0.74
Finnish (12)	37	0.20
French, ex. Basque (1,867)	4,676	25.42
French Canadian (1,586)	2,361	12.83
German (107)	1,015	5.52
Greek (232)	407	2.21
Hungarian (10)	24	0.13
Iranian (3)	8	0.04
Irish (945)	3,336	18.13
Italian (466)	1,460	7.94
Latvian (25)	25	0.14
Lithuanian (24)	47	0.26
Norwegian (26)	65	0.35
Polish (67)	473	2.57
Portuguese (0)	88	0.48
Russian (36)	133	0.72
Scandinavian (0)	53	0.29
Scotch-Irish (127)	786	4.27
Scottish (207)	856	4.65
Serbian (66)	66	0.36
Swedish (8)	274	1.49
Ukrainian (0)	18	0.10
Welsh (0)	95	0.52
Yugoslavian (13)	27	0.15

Hispanic Origin	Population	%
Hispanic or Latino (of any race)	237	1.28
Central American, ex. Mexican	23	0.12
Costa Rican	1	0.01
Guatemalan	8	0.04
Nicaraguan	2	0.01
Panamanian	2	0.01
Salvadoran	8	0.04
Other Central American	2	0.01
Cuban	14	0.08
Dominican Republic	6	0.03
Mexican	46	0.25
Puerto Rican	81	0.44
South American	34	0.18
Argentinean	1	0.01
Chilean	1	0.01
Colombian	17	0.09
Ecuadorian	3	0.02
Peruvian	9	0.05
Venezuelan	1	0.01
Other South American	2	0.01
Other Hispanic or Latino	33	0.18

Race*	Population	%
African-American/Black (125)	214	1.16
Not Hispanic (115)	196	1.06
Hispanic (10)	18	0.10
American Indian/Alaska Native (36)	126	0.68
Not Hispanic (34)	120	0.65
Hispanic (2)	6	0.03
Alaska Athabascan (*Ala. Nat.*) (0)	1	0.01
Blackfeet (0)	7	0.04
Canadian/French Am. Ind. (2)	5	0.03
Central American Ind. (2)	2	0.01
Cherokee (1)	9	0.05
Chickasaw (0)	1	0.01
Chippewa (0)	1	0.01
Choctaw (1)	1	0.01
Iroquois (1)	4	0.02
Lumbee (3)	4	0.02
Pueblo (1)	1	0.01
Sioux (0)	2	0.01
South American Ind. (0)	1	0.01
Asian (313)	385	2.08
Not Hispanic (312)	382	2.07
Hispanic (1)	3	0.02
Bangladeshi (5)	5	0.03
Cambodian (23)	31	0.17
Chinese, ex. Taiwanese (85)	95	0.51
Filipino (47)	73	0.39
Indian (31)	36	0.19
Indonesian (1)	1	0.01
Japanese (8)	16	0.09
Korean (14)	15	0.08
Nepalese (2)	2	0.01
Pakistani (6)	6	0.03
Taiwanese (1)	2	0.01
Thai (9)	15	0.08
Vietnamese (60)	69	0.37
Hawaii Native/Pacific Islander (4)	12	0.06
Not Hispanic (4)	7	0.04
Hispanic (0)	5	0.03
Native Hawaiian (3)	5	0.03
White (17,693)	17,936	97.05
Not Hispanic (17,552)	17,768	96.14
Hispanic (141)	168	0.91

*Notes: † The Census 2010 population figure is used to calculate the percentages in the Hispanic Origin and Race categories. Ancestry percentages are based on the 2006-2010 American Community Survey population (not shown); ‡ Numbers in parentheses indicate the number of people reporting a single ancestry; * Numbers in parentheses indicate the number of persons reporting this race alone, not in combination with any other race; Please refer to the Explanation of Data for more information.*

Sanford

Place Type: CDP
County: York
Population: 9,761†

Ancestry‡	Population	%
African, Sub-Saharan (0)	18	0.17
African (0)	18	0.17
Albanian (0)	12	0.11
American (474)	474	4.47
Arab (34)	62	0.59
Lebanese (8)	8	0.08
Syrian (26)	54	0.51
Austrian (7)	15	0.14
British (0)	29	0.27
Canadian (144)	172	1.62
Czechoslovakian (0)	8	0.08
Danish (0)	40	0.38
Dutch (0)	26	0.25
Eastern European (8)	8	0.08
English (790)	2,303	21.74
European (32)	32	0.30
Finnish (0)	30	0.28
French, ex. Basque (1,254)	2,990	28.22
French Canadian (1,025)	1,326	12.52
German (171)	608	5.74
Greek (28)	94	0.89
Hungarian (0)	25	0.24
Irish (487)	1,855	17.51
Italian (76)	712	6.72
Lithuanian (0)	19	0.18
Norwegian (20)	29	0.27
Polish (30)	271	2.56
Portuguese (42)	158	1.49
Russian (7)	45	0.42
Scandinavian (29)	29	0.27
Scotch-Irish (66)	219	2.07
Scottish (53)	374	3.53
Slavic (8)	8	0.08
Slovak (0)	16	0.15
Swedish (26)	93	0.88
Swiss (0)	73	0.69
Ukrainian (17)	17	0.16
Welsh (22)	22	0.21
West Indian, ex. Hispanic (21)	21	0.20
Jamaican (21)	21	0.20

Hispanic Origin	Population	%
Hispanic or Latino (of any race)	167	1.71
Central American, ex. Mexican	14	0.14
Guatemalan	4	0.04
Honduran	7	0.07
Panamanian	1	0.01
Salvadoran	1	0.01
Other Central American	1	0.01
Cuban	8	0.08
Dominican Republic	3	0.03
Mexican	47	0.48
Puerto Rican	56	0.57
South American	19	0.19
Argentinean	1	0.01
Chilean	3	0.03
Colombian	5	0.05
Ecuadorian	4	0.04
Paraguayan	2	0.02
Peruvian	4	0.04
Other Hispanic or Latino	20	0.20

Race*	Population	%
African-American/Black (81)	141	1.44
Not Hispanic (75)	128	1.31
Hispanic (6)	13	0.13
American Indian/Alaska Native (59)	170	1.74
Not Hispanic (49)	147	1.51
Hispanic (10)	23	0.24
Apache (0)	3	0.03
Blackfeet (1)	5	0.05
Canadian/French Am. Ind. (3)	8	0.08
Cherokee (4)	25	0.26
Chippewa (1)	4	0.04
Choctaw (0)	1	0.01
Crow (0)	1	0.01
Inupiat *(Alaska Native)* (4)	4	0.04
Iroquois (0)	1	0.01
Lumbee (1)	1	0.01
Seminole (0)	2	0.02
Sioux (0)	2	0.02
South American Ind. (0)	1	0.01
Spanish American Ind. (1)	1	0.01
Asian (203)	250	2.56
Not Hispanic (203)	249	2.55
Hispanic (0)	1	0.01
Cambodian (122)	137	1.40
Chinese, ex. Taiwanese (13)	25	0.26
Filipino (10)	26	0.27
Hmong (2)	2	0.02
Indian (16)	22	0.23
Japanese (0)	1	0.01
Korean (5)	7	0.07
Laotian (2)	17	0.17
Thai (2)	9	0.09
Vietnamese (17)	27	0.28
Hawaii Native/Pacific Islander (0)	1	0.01
Not Hispanic (0)	1	0.01
White (9,165)	9,376	96.06
Not Hispanic (9,071)	9,256	94.83
Hispanic (94)	120	1.23

Sanford

Place Type: Town
County: York
Population: 20,798†

Ancestry‡	Population	%
African, Sub-Saharan (0)	18	0.09
African (0)	18	0.09
Albanian (0)	23	0.11
American (966)	966	4.59
Arab (34)	62	0.29
Lebanese (8)	8	0.04
Syrian (26)	54	0.26
Austrian (14)	22	0.10
Brazilian (30)	30	0.14
British (50)	79	0.38
Canadian (282)	360	1.71
Czech (26)	26	0.12
Czechoslovakian (0)	8	0.04
Danish (0)	74	0.35
Dutch (14)	168	0.80
Eastern European (8)	8	0.04
English (1,495)	4,114	19.56
European (32)	32	0.15
Finnish (0)	30	0.14
French, ex. Basque (2,422)	5,617	26.70
French Canadian (1,920)	2,475	11.77
German (263)	1,339	6.37
Greek (58)	146	0.69
Hungarian (0)	38	0.18
Irish (1,015)	3,613	17.18
Italian (298)	1,237	5.88
Lithuanian (0)	68	0.32
Norwegian (20)	70	0.33
Polish (60)	407	1.93
Portuguese (60)	199	0.95
Romanian (0)	22	0.10
Russian (28)	122	0.58
Scandinavian (60)	60	0.29
Scotch-Irish (97)	648	3.08
Scottish (179)	826	3.93
Slavic (8)	8	0.04
Slovak (0)	16	0.08
Swedish (54)	208	0.99
Swiss (0)	102	0.48
Ukrainian (17)	17	0.08
Welsh (47)	123	0.58
West Indian, ex. Hispanic (21)	28	0.13
Jamaican (21)	28	0.13

Hispanic Origin	Population	%
Hispanic or Latino (of any race)	338	1.63
Central American, ex. Mexican	21	0.10
Costa Rican	2	0.01
Guatemalan	5	0.02
Honduran	8	0.04
Panamanian	4	0.02
Salvadoran	1	<0.01
Other Central American	1	<0.01
Cuban	16	0.08
Dominican Republic	8	0.04
Mexican	99	0.48
Puerto Rican	111	0.53
South American	41	0.20
Argentinean	5	0.02
Chilean	3	0.01
Colombian	14	0.07
Ecuadorian	6	0.03
Paraguayan	2	0.01
Peruvian	10	0.05
Venezuelan	1	<0.01
Other Hispanic or Latino	42	0.20

Race*	Population	%
African-American/Black (128)	254	1.22
Not Hispanic (119)	227	1.09
Hispanic (9)	27	0.13
American Indian/Alaska Native (91)	278	1.34
Not Hispanic (73)	243	1.17
Hispanic (18)	35	0.17
Apache (0)	3	0.01
Blackfeet (1)	11	0.05
Canadian/French Am. Ind. (5)	11	0.05
Cherokee (4)	28	0.13
Chippewa (1)	6	0.03
Choctaw (0)	1	<0.01
Cree (0)	1	<0.01
Crow (0)	1	<0.01
Hopi (5)	5	0.02
Inupiat *(Alaska Native)* (5)	5	0.02
Iroquois (1)	4	0.02
Lumbee (1)	1	<0.01
Mexican American Ind. (1)	1	<0.01
Seminole (0)	2	0.01
Sioux (0)	3	0.01
South American Ind. (0)	1	<0.01
Spanish American Ind. (1)	1	<0.01
Asian (420)	525	2.52
Not Hispanic (419)	523	2.51
Hispanic (1)	2	0.01
Cambodian (200)	223	1.07
Chinese, ex. Taiwanese (35)	60	0.29
Filipino (34)	69	0.33
Hmong (2)	2	0.01
Indian (48)	58	0.28
Indonesian (1)	1	<0.01
Japanese (2)	14	0.07
Korean (12)	20	0.10
Laotian (2)	19	0.09
Thai (6)	13	0.06
Vietnamese (49)	66	0.32
Hawaii Native/Pacific Islander (0)	4	0.02
Not Hispanic (0)	4	0.02
Native Hawaiian (0)	1	<0.01
White (19,687)	20,081	96.55
Not Hispanic (19,478)	19,829	95.34
Hispanic (209)	252	1.21

Scarborough

Place Type: Town
County: Cumberland
Population: 18,919†

Ancestry‡	Population	%
African, Sub-Saharan (142)	142	0.76
Other Sub-Saharan African (142)	142	0.76
Albanian (0)	12	0.06
American (969)	969	5.20
Arab (16)	144	0.77

*Notes: † The Census 2010 population figure is used to calculate the percentages in the Hispanic Origin and Race categories. Ancestry percentages are based on the 2006-2010 American Community Survey population (not shown); ‡ Numbers in parentheses indicate the number of people reporting a single ancestry; * Numbers in parentheses indicate the number of persons reporting this race alone, not in combination with any other race; Please refer to the Explanation of Data for more information.*

Ancestry	Population	%
Lebanese (0)	74	0.40
Syrian (16)	70	0.38
Armenian (43)	43	0.23
Austrian (0)	12	0.06
Belgian (0)	27	0.14
Brazilian (15)	15	0.08
British (36)	36	0.19
Canadian (121)	206	1.11
Croatian (0)	9	0.05
Danish (50)	219	1.18
Dutch (0)	100	0.54
English (1,716)	4,681	25.12
European (13)	13	0.07
Finnish (0)	59	0.32
French, ex. Basque (760)	2,768	14.85
French Canadian (586)	826	4.43
German (349)	1,761	9.45
Greek (100)	171	0.92
Hungarian (63)	175	0.94
Irish (1,563)	4,216	22.62
Italian (642)	2,034	10.91
Lithuanian (31)	136	0.73
Northern European (56)	56	0.30
Norwegian (28)	86	0.46
Pennsylvania German (0)	17	0.09
Polish (180)	871	4.67
Portuguese (11)	130	0.70
Romanian (0)	25	0.13
Russian (78)	243	1.30
Scandinavian (79)	105	0.56
Scotch-Irish (318)	886	4.75
Scottish (413)	1,064	5.71
Slovak (0)	29	0.16
Swedish (83)	313	1.68
Swiss (13)	13	0.07
Ukrainian (0)	26	0.14
Welsh (39)	74	0.40

Hispanic Origin	Population	%
Hispanic or Latino (of any race)	236	1.25
Central American, ex. Mexican	20	0.11
Guatemalan	9	0.05
Honduran	2	0.01
Nicaraguan	2	0.01
Salvadoran	7	0.04
Cuban	13	0.07
Dominican Republic	23	0.12
Mexican	66	0.35
Puerto Rican	46	0.24
South American	23	0.12
Argentinean	1	0.01
Bolivian	6	0.03
Chilean	2	0.01
Colombian	2	0.01
Ecuadorian	3	0.02
Peruvian	7	0.04
Venezuelan	2	0.01
Other Hispanic or Latino	45	0.24

Race*	Population	%
African-American/Black (101)	184	0.97
Not Hispanic (100)	158	0.84
Hispanic (1)	26	0.14
American Indian/Alaska Native (35)	112	0.59
Not Hispanic (33)	101	0.53
Hispanic (2)	11	0.06
Alaska Athabascan *(Ala. Nat.)* (0)	1	0.01
Blackfeet (1)	1	0.01
Cherokee (2)	8	0.04
Chippewa (1)	3	0.02
Iroquois (1)	1	0.01
Lumbee (1)	1	0.01
Mexican American Ind. (0)	2	0.01
Spanish American Ind. (0)	1	0.01
Asian (511)	642	3.39
Not Hispanic (504)	615	3.25
Hispanic (7)	27	0.14
Bangladeshi (0)	1	0.01
Burmese (2)	2	0.01
Cambodian (40)	49	0.26
Chinese, ex. Taiwanese (139)	171	0.90
Filipino (23)	57	0.30
Indian (175)	185	0.98
Indonesian (1)	1	0.01
Japanese (6)	19	0.10
Korean (26)	40	0.21
Laotian (0)	2	0.01
Nepalese (3)	4	0.02
Pakistani (5)	8	0.04
Taiwanese (6)	12	0.06
Thai (6)	13	0.07
Vietnamese (60)	69	0.36
Hawaii Native/Pacific Islander (1)	12	0.06
Not Hispanic (1)	7	0.04
Hispanic (0)	5	0.03
Native Hawaiian (0)	3	0.02
White (17,949)	18,187	96.13
Not Hispanic (17,798)	18,016	95.23
Hispanic (151)	171	0.90

Skowhegan

Place Type: Town
County: Somerset
Population: 8,589†

Ancestry‡	Population	%
African, Sub-Saharan (16)	16	0.18
Somalian (16)	16	0.18
American (350)	350	4.03
Arab (0)	11	0.13
Lebanese (0)	11	0.13
Belgian (0)	8	0.09
British (8)	18	0.21
Canadian (61)	118	1.36
Czech (0)	11	0.13
Czechoslovakian (12)	12	0.14
Dutch (0)	148	1.70
English (817)	1,698	19.56
European (39)	39	0.45
French, ex. Basque (1,316)	2,837	32.68
French Canadian (537)	661	7.61
German (208)	599	6.90
Irish (392)	1,239	14.27
Italian (75)	231	2.66
Lithuanian (17)	17	0.20
Pennsylvania German (0)	14	0.16
Polish (117)	202	2.33
Russian (0)	24	0.28
Scotch-Irish (173)	279	3.21
Scottish (77)	287	3.31
Slavic (0)	34	0.39
Slovak (22)	31	0.36
Swedish (57)	130	1.50
Ukrainian (25)	97	1.12
Welsh (37)	215	2.48

Hispanic Origin	Population	%
Hispanic or Latino (of any race)	44	0.51
Cuban	1	0.01
Mexican	17	0.20
Puerto Rican	15	0.17
Other Hispanic or Latino	11	0.13

Race*	Population	%
African-American/Black (31)	75	0.87
Not Hispanic (31)	68	0.79
Hispanic (0)	7	0.08
American Indian/Alaska Native (35)	106	1.23
Not Hispanic (34)	105	1.22
Hispanic (1)	1	0.01
Blackfeet (0)	2	0.02
Canadian/French Am. Ind. (0)	3	0.03
Cherokee (2)	5	0.06
Choctaw (0)	2	0.02
Cree (2)	2	0.02
Crow (1)	1	0.01
Iroquois (3)	3	0.03
Seminole (0)	1	0.01
Asian (59)	74	0.86
Not Hispanic (59)	74	0.86
Chinese, ex. Taiwanese (22)	30	0.35
Filipino (11)	21	0.24
Indian (11)	12	0.14
Japanese (1)	1	0.01
Korean (1)	3	0.03
Pakistani (4)	5	0.06
Thai (1)	1	0.01
Vietnamese (1)	1	0.01
Hawaii Native/Pacific Islander (1)	2	0.02
Not Hispanic (1)	2	0.02
Native Hawaiian (1)	1	0.01
White (8,327)	8,450	98.38
Not Hispanic (8,297)	8,412	97.94
Hispanic (30)	38	0.44

South Portland

Place Type: City
County: Cumberland
Population: 25,002†

Ancestry‡	Population	%
African, Sub-Saharan (634)	657	2.65
African (72)	95	0.38
Cape Verdean (7)	7	0.03
Somalian (258)	258	1.04
South African (17)	17	0.07
Sudanese (280)	280	1.13
Albanian (0)	21	0.08
American (1,383)	1,383	5.58
Arab (0)	9	0.04
Arab (0)	9	0.04
Armenian (12)	12	0.05
Austrian (0)	95	0.38
Belgian (0)	30	0.12
Brazilian (10)	10	0.04
British (67)	87	0.35
Bulgarian (30)	30	0.12
Canadian (197)	248	1.00
Croatian (11)	11	0.04
Czech (11)	76	0.31
Danish (61)	181	0.73
Dutch (85)	298	1.20
Eastern European (11)	11	0.04
English (1,877)	5,570	22.46
European (132)	142	0.57
Finnish (46)	57	0.23
French, ex. Basque (592)	3,037	12.24
French Canadian (939)	1,476	5.95
German (503)	1,841	7.42
Greek (197)	374	1.51
Hungarian (10)	74	0.30
Iranian (24)	24	0.10
Irish (2,344)	6,775	27.31
Italian (707)	2,546	10.26
Latvian (11)	42	0.17
Lithuanian (22)	119	0.48
Maltese (0)	34	0.14
Northern European (54)	54	0.22
Norwegian (71)	155	0.62
Polish (227)	874	3.52
Portuguese (98)	287	1.16
Russian (115)	327	1.32
Scandinavian (83)	198	0.80
Scotch-Irish (282)	930	3.75
Scottish (292)	1,505	6.07
Serbian (20)	31	0.12
Slovak (10)	19	0.08
Swedish (76)	376	1.52
Swiss (13)	78	0.31
Turkish (155)	155	0.62
Ukrainian (0)	8	0.03
Welsh (57)	252	1.02
West Indian, ex. Hispanic (39)	39	0.16
Haitian (39)	39	0.16
Yugoslavian (11)	11	0.04

Hispanic Origin	Population	%
Hispanic or Latino (of any race)	554	2.22

*Notes: † The Census 2010 population figure is used to calculate the percentages in the Hispanic Origin and Race categories. Ancestry percentages are based on the 2006-2010 American Community Survey population (not shown); ‡ Numbers in parentheses indicate the number of people reporting a single ancestry; * Numbers in parentheses indicate the number of persons reporting this race alone, not in combination with any other race; Please refer to the Explanation of Data for more information.*

Central American, ex. Mexican	60	0.24
Costa Rican	5	0.02
Guatemalan	13	0.05
Honduran	9	0.04
Nicaraguan	2	0.01
Panamanian	3	0.01
Salvadoran	28	0.11
Cuban	28	0.11
Dominican Republic	44	0.18
Mexican	122	0.49
Puerto Rican	109	0.44
South American	103	0.41
Argentinean	3	0.01
Bolivian	2	0.01
Chilean	2	0.01
Colombian	26	0.10
Ecuadorian	11	0.04
Peruvian	49	0.20
Venezuelan	8	0.03
Other South American	2	0.01
Other Hispanic or Latino	88	0.35

Race*	Population	%
African-American/Black (517)	696	2.78
Not Hispanic (497)	646	2.58
Hispanic (20)	50	0.20
American Indian/Alaska Native (74)	190	0.76
Not Hispanic (64)	175	0.70
Hispanic (10)	15	0.06
Blackfeet (0)	5	0.02
Canadian/French Am. Ind. (1)	3	0.01
Central American Ind. (1)	1	<0.01
Cherokee (3)	15	0.06
Chickasaw (2)	2	0.01
Chippewa (8)	15	0.06
Comanche (0)	1	<0.01
Creek (0)	2	0.01
Inupiat *(Alaska Native)* (0)	1	<0.01
Iroquois (0)	1	<0.01
Kiowa (0)	1	<0.01
Mexican American Ind. (1)	1	<0.01
Navajo (1)	1	<0.01
Seminole (0)	1	<0.01
Sioux (0)	1	<0.01
South American Ind. (3)	5	0.02
Asian (940)	1,109	4.44
Not Hispanic (929)	1,088	4.35
Hispanic (11)	21	0.08
Bangladeshi (9)	9	0.04
Cambodian (112)	127	0.51
Chinese, ex. Taiwanese (108)	140	0.56
Filipino (69)	104	0.42
Indian (340)	356	1.42
Indonesian (2)	2	0.01
Japanese (26)	46	0.18
Korean (55)	67	0.27
Laotian (25)	26	0.10
Nepalese (7)	7	0.03
Pakistani (18)	18	0.07
Sri Lankan (5)	5	0.02
Taiwanese (1)	3	0.01
Thai (12)	15	0.06
Vietnamese (127)	157	0.63
Hawaii Native/Pacific Islander (5)	23	0.09
Not Hispanic (5)	20	0.08
Hispanic (0)	3	0.01
Guamanian/Chamorro (0)	6	0.02
Native Hawaiian (3)	9	0.04
Samoan (1)	1	<0.01
White (22,767)	23,237	92.94
Not Hispanic (22,505)	22,916	91.66
Hispanic (262)	321	1.28

Standish

Place Type: Town
County: Cumberland
Population: 9,874†

Ancestry‡	Population	%
Albanian (0)	31	0.32
American (412)	412	4.20
Armenian (0)	24	0.24
British (13)	80	0.82
Canadian (0)	23	0.23
Czech (0)	16	0.16
Danish (44)	60	0.61
Dutch (14)	68	0.69
English (727)	2,291	23.34
European (126)	126	1.28
Finnish (19)	71	0.72
French, ex. Basque (359)	1,745	17.78
French Canadian (343)	568	5.79
German (261)	1,132	11.53
Greek (27)	27	0.28
Hungarian (0)	13	0.13
Irish (775)	2,171	22.12
Italian (198)	666	6.79
Lithuanian (23)	48	0.49
Northern European (58)	58	0.59
Norwegian (24)	79	0.80
Polish (59)	176	1.79
Portuguese (0)	80	0.82
Scotch-Irish (245)	510	5.20
Scottish (113)	662	6.74
Swedish (90)	289	2.94
Ukrainian (13)	53	0.54
Welsh (15)	45	0.46
West Indian, ex. Hispanic (12)	12	0.12
Jamaican (12)	12	0.12

Hispanic Origin	Population	%
Hispanic or Latino (of any race)	79	0.80
Central American, ex. Mexican	4	0.04
Honduran	1	0.01
Salvadoran	3	0.03
Cuban	2	0.02
Dominican Republic	4	0.04
Mexican	18	0.18
Puerto Rican	28	0.28
South American	4	0.04
Argentinean	1	0.01
Chilean	1	0.01
Colombian	2	0.02
Other Hispanic or Latino	19	0.19

Race*	Population	%
African-American/Black (46)	89	0.90
Not Hispanic (45)	83	0.84
Hispanic (1)	6	0.06
American Indian/Alaska Native (34)	85	0.86
Not Hispanic (34)	85	0.86
Blackfeet (0)	2	0.02
Canadian/French Am. Ind. (0)	1	0.01
Cherokee (5)	13	0.13
Chippewa (2)	2	0.02
Iroquois (1)	1	0.01
Asian (46)	78	0.79
Not Hispanic (45)	76	0.77
Hispanic (1)	2	0.02
Cambodian (10)	15	0.15
Chinese, ex. Taiwanese (5)	7	0.07
Filipino (15)	29	0.29
Indian (2)	3	0.03
Japanese (2)	5	0.05
Korean (0)	1	0.01
Pakistani (7)	7	0.07
Vietnamese (5)	5	0.05
Hawaii Native/Pacific Islander (2)	7	0.07
Not Hispanic (2)	7	0.07
Native Hawaiian (0)	1	0.01
White (9,608)	9,723	98.47
Not Hispanic (9,554)	9,665	97.88
Hispanic (54)	58	0.59

Topsham

Place Type: Town
County: Sagadahoc
Population: 8,784†

Ancestry‡	Population	%
African, Sub-Saharan (4)	4	0.04
Ethiopian (4)	4	0.04
American (450)	450	5.03
Australian (0)	6	0.07
Belgian (24)	24	0.27
Brazilian (0)	13	0.15
British (50)	87	0.97
Cajun (0)	10	0.11
Canadian (139)	221	2.47
Czech (0)	39	0.44
Czechoslovakian (29)	29	0.32
Danish (0)	7	0.08
Dutch (0)	103	1.15
English (872)	2,487	27.83
European (30)	53	0.59
Finnish (15)	84	0.94
French, ex. Basque (478)	1,406	15.73
French Canadian (716)	1,183	13.24
German (312)	1,102	12.33
Greek (46)	153	1.71
Guyanese (16)	16	0.18
Hungarian (0)	68	0.76
Irish (387)	1,588	17.77
Italian (92)	508	5.68
Lithuanian (0)	19	0.21
New Zealander (0)	6	0.07
Norwegian (35)	196	2.19
Polish (18)	102	1.14
Portuguese (85)	140	1.57
Romanian (0)	8	0.09
Russian (33)	49	0.55
Scandinavian (10)	21	0.23
Scotch-Irish (40)	373	4.17
Scottish (36)	455	5.09
Slovak (15)	15	0.17
Swedish (9)	212	2.37
Swiss (12)	12	0.13
Ukrainian (0)	27	0.30
Welsh (29)	97	1.09
West Indian, ex. Hispanic (11)	11	0.12
Haitian (11)	11	0.12

Hispanic Origin	Population	%
Hispanic or Latino (of any race)	142	1.62
Central American, ex. Mexican	6	0.07
Guatemalan	2	0.02
Honduran	1	0.01
Panamanian	3	0.03
Cuban	1	0.01
Dominican Republic	5	0.06
Mexican	41	0.47
Puerto Rican	57	0.65
South American	11	0.13
Chilean	2	0.02
Colombian	1	0.01
Ecuadorian	7	0.08
Peruvian	1	0.01
Other Hispanic or Latino	21	0.24

Race*	Population	%
African-American/Black (70)	109	1.24
Not Hispanic (67)	101	1.15
Hispanic (3)	8	0.09
American Indian/Alaska Native (28)	51	0.58
Not Hispanic (25)	48	0.55
Hispanic (3)	3	0.03
Blackfeet (0)	1	0.01
Canadian/French Am. Ind. (0)	3	0.03
Cherokee (0)	1	0.01
Creek (1)	1	0.01
Inupiat *(Alaska Native)* (1)	1	0.01
Iroquois (3)	7	0.08
Mexican American Ind. (2)	2	0.02

SECTION TWO

*Notes: † The Census 2010 population figure is used to calculate the percentages in the Hispanic Origin and Race categories. Ancestry percentages are based on the 2006-2010 American Community Survey population (not shown); ‡ Numbers in parentheses indicate the number of people reporting a single ancestry; * Numbers in parentheses indicate the number of persons reporting this race alone, not in combination with any other race; Please refer to the Explanation of Data for more information.*

Navajo (1)	1	0.01
Potawatomi (5)	5	0.06
Pueblo (0)	1	0.01
Puget Sound Salish (1)	1	0.01
Asian (118)	158	1.80
Not Hispanic (111)	151	1.72
Hispanic (7)	7	0.08
Burmese (4)	4	0.05
Cambodian (3)	4	0.05
Chinese, ex. Taiwanese (27)	41	0.47
Filipino (40)	63	0.72
Indian (6)	8	0.09
Indonesian (0)	2	0.02
Japanese (3)	5	0.06
Korean (7)	11	0.13
Taiwanese (3)	3	0.03
Vietnamese (15)	18	0.20
Hawaii Native/Pacific Islander (0)	9	0.10
Not Hispanic (0)	8	0.09
Hispanic (0)	1	0.01
Guamanian/Chamorro (0)	3	0.03
Native Hawaiian (0)	5	0.06
White (8,438)	8,542	97.24
Not Hispanic (8,336)	8,431	95.98
Hispanic (102)	111	1.26

Waterboro

Place Type: Town
County: York
Population: 7,693†

Ancestry‡	Population	%
Albanian (0)	17	0.23
American (456)	456	6.08
Armenian (8)	8	0.11
Australian (0)	18	0.24
Austrian (0)	18	0.24
Belgian (0)	16	0.21
British (45)	131	1.75
Canadian (51)	183	2.44
Czech (0)	13	0.17
Danish (0)	40	0.53
Dutch (12)	92	1.23
Eastern European (6)	12	0.16
English (545)	1,656	22.07
European (28)	28	0.37
Finnish (0)	60	0.80
French, ex. Basque (982)	2,469	32.91
French Canadian (385)	627	8.36
German (119)	672	8.96
Greek (14)	47	0.63
Hungarian (0)	46	0.61
Irish (199)	1,451	19.34
Italian (123)	371	4.95
Lithuanian (31)	31	0.41
Norwegian (31)	65	0.87
Pennsylvania German (0)	19	0.25
Polish (51)	251	3.35
Portuguese (10)	128	1.71
Russian (0)	9	0.12
Scandinavian (18)	29	0.39
Scotch-Irish (11)	341	4.55
Scottish (67)	303	4.04
Swedish (39)	185	2.47
Ukrainian (0)	42	0.56
Welsh (0)	25	0.33

Hispanic Origin	Population	%
Hispanic or Latino (of any race)	66	0.86
Central American, ex. Mexican	6	0.08
Guatemalan	4	0.05
Salvadoran	2	0.03
Cuban	2	0.03
Dominican Republic	2	0.03
Mexican	15	0.19
Puerto Rican	20	0.26
South American	3	0.04
Argentinean	1	0.01
Chilean	1	0.01
Other South American	1	0.01
Other Hispanic or Latino	18	0.23

Race*	Population	%
African-American/Black (34)	61	0.79
Not Hispanic (31)	48	0.62
Hispanic (3)	13	0.17
American Indian/Alaska Native (15)	58	0.75
Not Hispanic (14)	53	0.69
Hispanic (1)	5	0.06
Blackfeet (1)	2	0.03
Canadian/French Am. Ind. (0)	1	0.01
Cherokee (2)	3	0.04
Chippewa (0)	1	0.01
Crow (0)	1	0.01
Iroquois (0)	1	0.01
Tlingit-Haida *(Alaska Native)* (0)	1	0.01
Tsimshian *(Alaska Native)* (0)	1	0.01
Asian (50)	76	0.99
Not Hispanic (50)	76	0.99
Cambodian (15)	19	0.25
Chinese, ex. Taiwanese (10)	11	0.14
Filipino (5)	9	0.12
Indian (7)	9	0.12
Japanese (2)	7	0.09
Korean (4)	11	0.14
Laotian (0)	1	0.01
Thai (2)	2	0.03
Vietnamese (1)	6	0.08
Hawaii Native/Pacific Islander (3)	6	0.08
Not Hispanic (1)	4	0.05
Hispanic (2)	2	0.03
Fijian (1)	1	0.01
Guamanian/Chamorro (1)	1	0.01
Native Hawaiian (0)	1	0.01
White (7,487)	7,581	98.54
Not Hispanic (7,446)	7,526	97.83
Hispanic (41)	55	0.71

Waterville

Place Type: City
County: Kennebec
Population: 15,722†

Ancestry‡	Population	%
African, Sub-Saharan (11)	11	0.07
African (11)	11	0.07
American (681)	681	4.32
Arab (112)	201	1.27
Lebanese (112)	201	1.27
Armenian (15)	15	0.10
Austrian (0)	50	0.32
British (50)	87	0.55
Cajun (10)	10	0.06
Canadian (172)	260	1.65
Czech (0)	9	0.06
Danish (26)	41	0.26
Dutch (24)	57	0.36
English (1,865)	3,342	21.18
European (76)	93	0.59
Finnish (0)	38	0.24
French, ex. Basque (1,406)	2,836	17.98
French Canadian (842)	1,199	7.60
German (447)	1,331	8.44
Greek (0)	9	0.06
Hungarian (0)	37	0.23
Irish (833)	2,230	14.13
Italian (144)	509	3.23
Latvian (0)	14	0.09
Lithuanian (0)	25	0.16
Norwegian (44)	142	0.90
Pennsylvania German (16)	28	0.18
Polish (91)	344	2.18
Portuguese (54)	173	1.10
Russian (13)	227	1.44
Scotch-Irish (166)	510	3.23
Scottish (135)	502	3.18
Swedish (125)	247	1.57
Swiss (12)	31	0.20
Ukrainian (13)	25	0.16
Welsh (16)	159	1.01
West Indian, ex. Hispanic (80)	80	0.51
Haitian (80)	80	0.51

Hispanic Origin	Population	%
Hispanic or Latino (of any race)	374	2.38
Central American, ex. Mexican	18	0.11
Guatemalan	11	0.07
Honduran	5	0.03
Panamanian	1	0.01
Salvadoran	1	0.01
Cuban	15	0.10
Dominican Republic	5	0.03
Mexican	101	0.64
Puerto Rican	137	0.87
South American	28	0.18
Argentinean	11	0.07
Chilean	1	0.01
Colombian	8	0.05
Peruvian	1	0.01
Venezuelan	7	0.04
Other Hispanic or Latino	70	0.45

Race*	Population	%
African-American/Black (180)	303	1.93
Not Hispanic (164)	276	1.76
Hispanic (16)	27	0.17
American Indian/Alaska Native (88)	228	1.45
Not Hispanic (79)	208	1.32
Hispanic (9)	20	0.13
Apache (2)	2	0.01
Arapaho (1)	3	0.02
Blackfeet (1)	4	0.03
Canadian/French Am. Ind. (0)	5	0.03
Cherokee (7)	16	0.10
Chippewa (1)	3	0.02
Choctaw (4)	4	0.03
Creek (4)	4	0.03
Iroquois (0)	1	0.01
Mexican American Ind. (0)	1	0.01
Potawatomi (0)	2	0.01
Shoshone (0)	1	0.01
Sioux (2)	6	0.04
South American Ind. (1)	1	0.01
Tlingit-Haida *(Alaska Native)* (0)	6	0.04
Tsimshian *(Alaska Native)* (0)	6	0.04
Asian (189)	299	1.90
Not Hispanic (187)	291	1.85
Hispanic (2)	8	0.05
Cambodian (1)	1	0.01
Chinese, ex. Taiwanese (57)	88	0.56
Filipino (23)	46	0.29
Hmong (2)	2	0.01
Indian (48)	53	0.34
Japanese (11)	29	0.18
Korean (15)	22	0.14
Laotian (0)	2	0.01
Pakistani (8)	16	0.10
Sri Lankan (0)	1	0.01
Taiwanese (1)	1	0.01
Thai (5)	7	0.04
Vietnamese (14)	18	0.11
Hawaii Native/Pacific Islander (9)	16	0.10
Not Hispanic (9)	16	0.10
Native Hawaiian (1)	5	0.03
White (14,765)	15,112	96.12
Not Hispanic (14,554)	14,872	94.59
Hispanic (211)	240	1.53

Wells

Place Type: Town
County: York
Population: 9,589†

Ancestry‡	Population	%
African, Sub-Saharan (0)	8	0.08
South African (0)	8	0.08
American (911)	911	9.43

*Notes: † The Census 2010 population figure is used to calculate the percentages in the Hispanic Origin and Race categories. Ancestry percentages are based on the 2006-2010 American Community Survey population (not shown); ‡ Numbers in parentheses indicate the number of people reporting a single ancestry; * Numbers in parentheses indicate the number of persons reporting this race alone, not in combination with any other race; Please refer to the Explanation of Data for more information.*

Arab (59)	69	0.71
Lebanese (59)	69	0.71
Austrian (0)	44	0.46
British (111)	158	1.63
Bulgarian (19)	19	0.20
Cajun (34)	34	0.35
Canadian (106)	147	1.52
Czech (26)	26	0.27
Danish (23)	54	0.56
Dutch (0)	50	0.52
English (735)	2,063	21.35
European (9)	23	0.24
Finnish (7)	7	0.07
French, ex. Basque (701)	1,562	16.16
French Canadian (523)	792	8.20
German (265)	780	8.07
Greek (43)	99	1.02
Hungarian (8)	8	0.08
Irish (514)	1,939	20.06
Italian (321)	1,001	10.36
Lithuanian (30)	83	0.86
Norwegian (22)	136	1.41
Pennsylvania German (19)	19	0.20
Polish (104)	304	3.15
Portuguese (7)	33	0.34
Romanian (13)	13	0.13
Russian (48)	93	0.96
Scandinavian (15)	15	0.16
Scotch-Irish (162)	334	3.46
Scottish (226)	640	6.62
Swedish (61)	240	2.48
Ukrainian (52)	87	0.90
Welsh (0)	59	0.61
West Indian, ex. Hispanic (24)	24	0.25
Jamaican (24)	24	0.25

Hispanic Origin	Population	%
Hispanic or Latino (of any race)	111	1.16
Central American, ex. Mexican	12	0.13
Costa Rican	3	0.03
Guatemalan	5	0.05
Salvadoran	4	0.04
Cuban	7	0.07
Dominican Republic	2	0.02
Mexican	26	0.27
Puerto Rican	30	0.31
South American	9	0.09
Chilean	2	0.02
Colombian	3	0.03
Ecuadorian	1	0.01
Peruvian	1	0.01
Venezuelan	2	0.02
Other Hispanic or Latino	25	0.26

Race*	Population	%
African-American/Black (49)	80	0.83
Not Hispanic (43)	72	0.75
Hispanic (6)	8	0.08
American Indian/Alaska Native (15)	90	0.94
Not Hispanic (14)	81	0.84
Hispanic (1)	9	0.09
Apache (0)	1	0.01
Canadian/French Am. Ind. (0)	4	0.04
Cherokee (1)	9	0.09
Hopi (0)	2	0.02
Iroquois (0)	3	0.03
Navajo (1)	2	0.02
Sioux (0)	1	0.01
Tohono O'Odham (0)	4	0.04
Yup'ik *(Alaska Native)* (1)	1	0.01
Asian (59)	78	0.81
Not Hispanic (59)	78	0.81
Chinese, ex. Taiwanese (26)	31	0.32
Filipino (4)	6	0.06
Indian (6)	7	0.07
Indonesian (2)	2	0.02
Japanese (6)	7	0.07
Korean (2)	6	0.06
Laotian (1)	3	0.03
Malaysian (1)	1	0.01
Thai (10)	12	0.13
Vietnamese (1)	2	0.02
Hawaii Native/Pacific Islander (1)	2	0.02
Not Hispanic (1)	2	0.02
Native Hawaiian (1)	1	0.01
White (9,316)	9,442	98.47
Not Hispanic (9,244)	9,354	97.55
Hispanic (72)	88	0.92

Westbrook

Place Type: City
County: Cumberland
Population: 17,494†

Ancestry‡	Population	%
African, Sub-Saharan (329)	329	1.90
Ethiopian (49)	49	0.28
Somalian (280)	280	1.62
Albanian (36)	36	0.21
American (672)	672	3.88
Arab (20)	32	0.18
Egyptian (12)	12	0.07
Iraqi (8)	8	0.05
Other Arab (0)	12	0.07
Austrian (19)	19	0.11
Belgian (0)	9	0.05
Brazilian (11)	11	0.06
British (63)	91	0.53
Canadian (11)	105	0.61
Czech (0)	19	0.11
Danish (62)	187	1.08
Dutch (10)	122	0.70
English (1,095)	2,913	16.82
European (37)	37	0.21
Finnish (30)	69	0.40
French, ex. Basque (1,065)	2,759	15.94
French Canadian (866)	1,327	7.66
German (127)	856	4.94
Greek (72)	119	0.69
Irish (1,139)	3,562	20.57
Italian (624)	1,302	7.52
Lithuanian (11)	21	0.12
Northern European (42)	42	0.24
Norwegian (8)	53	0.31
Polish (143)	433	2.50
Portuguese (44)	91	0.53
Russian (210)	252	1.46
Scandinavian (52)	161	0.93
Scotch-Irish (233)	657	3.79
Scottish (209)	703	4.06
Swedish (45)	300	1.73
Swiss (0)	8	0.05
Ukrainian (0)	68	0.39
Welsh (23)	74	0.43
West Indian, ex. Hispanic (33)	67	0.39
Haitian (33)	33	0.19
West Indian (0)	34	0.20

Hispanic Origin	Population	%
Hispanic or Latino (of any race)	328	1.87
Central American, ex. Mexican	32	0.18
Guatemalan	13	0.07
Honduran	5	0.03
Panamanian	1	0.01
Salvadoran	13	0.07
Cuban	13	0.07
Dominican Republic	19	0.11
Mexican	100	0.57
Puerto Rican	97	0.55
South American	23	0.13
Argentinean	4	0.02
Chilean	9	0.05
Colombian	2	0.01
Ecuadorian	2	0.01
Peruvian	5	0.03
Other South American	1	0.01
Other Hispanic or Latino	44	0.25

Race*	Population	%
African-American/Black (406)	583	3.33
Not Hispanic (397)	554	3.17
Hispanic (9)	29	0.17
American Indian/Alaska Native (42)	183	1.05
Not Hispanic (40)	175	1.00
Hispanic (2)	8	0.05
Apache (1)	3	0.02
Blackfeet (0)	11	0.06
Canadian/French Am. Ind. (0)	1	0.01
Cherokee (0)	13	0.07
Chippewa (2)	5	0.03
Cree (1)	3	0.02
Crow (0)	3	0.02
Iroquois (0)	1	0.01
Mexican American Ind. (1)	1	0.01
Navajo (0)	2	0.01
Puget Sound Salish (0)	1	0.01
Sioux (1)	5	0.03
Asian (335)	482	2.76
Not Hispanic (331)	473	2.70
Hispanic (4)	9	0.05
Cambodian (84)	101	0.58
Chinese, ex. Taiwanese (45)	72	0.41
Filipino (57)	95	0.54
Indian (32)	39	0.22
Indonesian (6)	9	0.05
Japanese (8)	22	0.13
Korean (14)	23	0.13
Laotian (10)	16	0.09
Pakistani (1)	2	0.01
Thai (0)	2	0.01
Vietnamese (50)	66	0.38
Hawaii Native/Pacific Islander (12)	36	0.21
Not Hispanic (12)	36	0.21
Guamanian/Chamorro (0)	2	0.01
Native Hawaiian (2)	5	0.03
Samoan (10)	10	0.06
White (16,154)	16,561	94.67
Not Hispanic (15,963)	16,336	93.38
Hispanic (191)	225	1.29

Windham

Place Type: Town
County: Cumberland
Population: 17,001†

Ancestry‡	Population	%
African, Sub-Saharan (18)	37	0.22
African (6)	6	0.04
Cape Verdean (12)	31	0.19
Albanian (0)	35	0.21
American (785)	785	4.70
Arab (0)	26	0.16
Lebanese (0)	26	0.16
Belgian (11)	22	0.13
British (56)	77	0.46
Canadian (39)	107	0.64
Czech (0)	16	0.10
Danish (41)	125	0.75
Dutch (81)	159	0.95
Eastern European (51)	51	0.31
English (1,186)	2,903	17.39
Estonian (0)	7	0.04
European (103)	167	1.00
Finnish (0)	89	0.53
French, ex. Basque (938)	2,836	16.99
French Canadian (500)	814	4.88
German (486)	1,260	7.55
Greek (49)	65	0.39
Hungarian (0)	38	0.23
Irish (965)	2,820	16.89
Italian (413)	1,326	7.94
Latvian (0)	20	0.12
Lithuanian (21)	31	0.19
Norwegian (39)	135	0.81
Polish (46)	230	1.38
Portuguese (9)	9	0.05

SECTION TWO

*Notes: † The Census 2010 population figure is used to calculate the percentages in the Hispanic Origin and Race categories. Ancestry percentages are based on the 2006-2010 American Community Survey population (not shown); ‡ Numbers in parentheses indicate the number of people reporting a single ancestry; * Numbers in parentheses indicate the number of persons reporting this race alone, not in combination with any other race; Please refer to the Explanation of Data for more information.*

Ancestry	Population	%
Russian (86)	121	0.72
Scandinavian (23)	23	0.14
Scotch-Irish (79)	261	1.56
Scottish (189)	724	4.34
Swedish (31)	202	1.21
Swiss (21)	66	0.40
Welsh (48)	226	1.35
West Indian, ex. Hispanic (63)	72	0.43
British West Indian (10)	10	0.06
Jamaican (53)	62	0.37

Hispanic Origin	Population	%
Hispanic or Latino (of any race)	146	0.86
Central American, ex. Mexican	20	0.12
Guatemalan	16	0.09
Honduran	1	0.01
Salvadoran	3	0.02
Cuban	8	0.05
Dominican Republic	8	0.05
Mexican	28	0.16
Puerto Rican	37	0.22
South American	6	0.04
Argentinean	1	0.01
Colombian	2	0.01
Ecuadorian	1	0.01
Peruvian	2	0.01
Other Hispanic or Latino	39	0.23

Race*	Population	%
African-American/Black (162)	242	1.42
Not Hispanic (155)	230	1.35
Hispanic (7)	12	0.07
American Indian/Alaska Native (53)	148	0.87
Not Hispanic (52)	143	0.84
Hispanic (1)	5	0.03
Alaska Athabascan *(Ala. Nat.)* (0)	1	0.01
Aleut *(Alaska Native)* (0)	2	0.01
Blackfeet (2)	3	0.02
Canadian/French Am. Ind. (0)	1	0.01
Cherokee (3)	8	0.05
Chippewa (1)	5	0.03
Colville (1)	1	0.01
Inupiat *(Alaska Native)* (1)	2	0.01
Iroquois (1)	5	0.03
Mexican American Ind. (1)	1	0.01
Navajo (1)	2	0.01
Sioux (2)	2	0.01
South American Ind. (1)	2	0.01
Asian (109)	182	1.07
Not Hispanic (109)	182	1.07
Cambodian (12)	21	0.12
Chinese, ex. Taiwanese (18)	27	0.16
Filipino (11)	32	0.19
Indian (8)	9	0.05
Japanese (3)	8	0.05
Korean (14)	19	0.11
Laotian (1)	5	0.03
Malaysian (2)	2	0.01
Pakistani (2)	2	0.01
Taiwanese (1)	4	0.02
Thai (4)	9	0.05
Vietnamese (22)	27	0.16
Hawaii Native/Pacific Islander (6)	14	0.08
Not Hispanic (5)	11	0.06
Hispanic (1)	3	0.02
Guamanian/Chamorro (3)	8	0.05
Native Hawaiian (1)	1	0.01
Samoan (2)	2	0.01
White (16,382)	16,627	97.80
Not Hispanic (16,293)	16,520	97.17
Hispanic (89)	107	0.63

Winslow

Place Type: CDP/Town
County: Kennebec
Population: 7,794†

Ancestry‡	Population	%
American (529)	529	6.76
Arab (14)	39	0.50
Lebanese (14)	39	0.50
Armenian (7)	15	0.19
British (28)	28	0.36
Canadian (58)	73	0.93
Celtic (30)	30	0.38
Dutch (20)	81	1.04
English (620)	1,407	17.99
European (104)	122	1.56
Finnish (0)	28	0.36
French, ex. Basque (1,407)	2,176	27.82
French Canadian (936)	1,083	13.84
German (94)	324	4.14
Greek (0)	26	0.33
Irish (276)	965	12.34
Italian (85)	180	2.30
Lithuanian (0)	29	0.37
Northern European (30)	30	0.38
Norwegian (9)	41	0.52
Polish (50)	153	1.96
Portuguese (0)	88	1.12
Romanian (0)	12	0.15
Russian (0)	11	0.14
Scandinavian (0)	5	0.06
Scotch-Irish (34)	248	3.17
Scottish (95)	294	3.76
Swedish (55)	200	2.56
Welsh (16)	25	0.32

Hispanic Origin	Population	%
Hispanic or Latino (of any race)	84	1.08
Central American, ex. Mexican	6	0.08
Guatemalan	5	0.06
Panamanian	1	0.01
Cuban	5	0.06
Mexican	25	0.32
Puerto Rican	23	0.30
South American	5	0.06
Argentinean	1	0.01
Chilean	2	0.03
Peruvian	1	0.01
Venezuelan	1	0.01
Other Hispanic or Latino	20	0.26

Race*	Population	%
African-American/Black (31)	65	0.83
Not Hispanic (30)	60	0.77
Hispanic (1)	5	0.06
American Indian/Alaska Native (43)	163	2.09
Not Hispanic (39)	153	1.96
Hispanic (4)	10	0.13
Blackfeet (0)	1	0.01
Cherokee (8)	13	0.17
Chippewa (1)	3	0.04
Choctaw (1)	1	0.01
Inupiat *(Alaska Native)* (1)	1	0.01
Iroquois (1)	4	0.05
Mexican American Ind. (2)	5	0.06
Pueblo (0)	3	0.04
Sioux (1)	1	0.01
Tlingit-Haida *(Alaska Native)* (0)	1	0.01
Tsimshian *(Alaska Native)* (0)	1	0.01
Asian (43)	68	0.87
Not Hispanic (43)	65	0.83
Hispanic (0)	3	0.04
Cambodian (4)	4	0.05
Chinese, ex. Taiwanese (7)	11	0.14
Filipino (13)	20	0.26
Indian (4)	7	0.09
Indonesian (1)	4	0.05
Japanese (3)	5	0.06
Korean (4)	7	0.09
Laotian (1)	1	0.01
Thai (5)	5	0.06
Vietnamese (1)	3	0.04
Hawaii Native/Pacific Islander (0)	4	0.05
Not Hispanic (0)	4	0.05
White (7,480)	7,657	98.24
Not Hispanic (7,430)	7,590	97.38
Hispanic (50)	67	0.86

Yarmouth

Place Type: Town
County: Cumberland
Population: 8,349†

Ancestry‡	Population	%
American (451)	451	5.38
Arab (0)	33	0.39
Lebanese (0)	33	0.39
Australian (7)	7	0.08
Austrian (0)	22	0.26
British (0)	54	0.64
Canadian (66)	104	1.24
Czech (0)	21	0.25
Danish (18)	87	1.04
Dutch (61)	183	2.18
English (765)	2,196	26.17
European (164)	164	1.95
Finnish (0)	96	1.14
French, ex. Basque (117)	872	10.39
French Canadian (150)	267	3.18
German (283)	1,096	13.06
Greek (42)	50	0.60
Hungarian (0)	78	0.93
Irish (624)	2,033	24.23
Italian (256)	907	10.81
Lithuanian (0)	74	0.88
Norwegian (28)	40	0.48
Polish (49)	179	2.13
Portuguese (0)	6	0.07
Russian (69)	146	1.74
Scotch-Irish (66)	339	4.04
Scottish (129)	455	5.42
Swedish (45)	108	1.29
Swiss (0)	20	0.24
Ukrainian (0)	23	0.27
Welsh (19)	57	0.68
West Indian, ex. Hispanic (0)	47	0.56
Jamaican (0)	47	0.56

Hispanic Origin	Population	%
Hispanic or Latino (of any race)	104	1.25
Central American, ex. Mexican	7	0.08
Costa Rican	1	0.01
Guatemalan	4	0.05
Salvadoran	2	0.02
Cuban	3	0.04
Dominican Republic	7	0.08
Mexican	26	0.31
Puerto Rican	28	0.34
South American	19	0.23
Argentinean	2	0.02
Bolivian	6	0.07
Colombian	4	0.05
Ecuadorian	2	0.02
Peruvian	2	0.02
Venezuelan	3	0.04
Other Hispanic or Latino	14	0.17

Race*	Population	%
African-American/Black (44)	63	0.75
Not Hispanic (43)	61	0.73
Hispanic (1)	2	0.02
American Indian/Alaska Native (14)	40	0.48
Not Hispanic (12)	38	0.46
Hispanic (2)	2	0.02
Canadian/French Am. Ind. (0)	1	0.01
Central American Ind. (1)	1	0.01
Cherokee (0)	6	0.07
Chippewa (1)	2	0.02
Choctaw (1)	1	0.01
Cree (0)	2	0.02
Iroquois (1)	1	0.01
Navajo (1)	1	0.01
Sioux (1)	1	0.01
Asian (99)	142	1.70
Not Hispanic (99)	142	1.70
Cambodian (3)	4	0.05
Chinese, ex. Taiwanese (27)	32	0.38

*Notes: † The Census 2010 population figure is used to calculate the percentages in the Hispanic Origin and Race categories. Ancestry percentages are based on the 2006-2010 American Community Survey population (not shown); ‡ Numbers in parentheses indicate the number of people reporting a single ancestry; * Numbers in parentheses indicate the number of persons reporting this race alone, not in combination with any other race; Please refer to the Explanation of Data for more information.*

Filipino (4)	17	0.20
Indian (28)	32	0.38
Japanese (4)	7	0.08
Korean (15)	23	0.28
Pakistani (2)	2	0.02
Taiwanese (6)	8	0.10
Thai (0)	1	0.01
Vietnamese (5)	7	0.08
Hawaii Native/Pacific Islander (3)	6	0.07
Not Hispanic (3)	6	0.07
Native Hawaiian (0)	2	0.02
Samoan (3)	3	0.04
White (8,093)	8,164	97.78
Not Hispanic (8,004)	8,073	96.69
Hispanic (89)	91	1.09

York

Place Type: Town
County: York
Population: 12,529†

Ancestry‡	Population	%
Albanian (13)	24	0.19
American (1,024)	1,024	8.05
Arab (0)	12	0.09
Lebanese (0)	12	0.09
Armenian (35)	159	1.25
Austrian (11)	64	0.50
Basque (0)	11	0.09
Belgian (20)	66	0.52
British (96)	158	1.24
Canadian (25)	64	0.50
Czech (0)	20	0.16
Czechoslovakian (0)	7	0.06
Danish (15)	37	0.29
Dutch (0)	46	0.36
Eastern European (20)	20	0.16
English (985)	2,874	22.59
European (41)	103	0.81
Finnish (0)	10	0.08
French, ex. Basque (375)	1,785	14.03
French Canadian (448)	720	5.66
German (482)	1,276	10.03
Greek (96)	157	1.23
Hungarian (30)	120	0.94
Irish (898)	3,047	23.95
Israeli (51)	51	0.40
Italian (668)	1,514	11.90
Lithuanian (16)	74	0.58
Norwegian (57)	101	0.79
Polish (134)	570	4.48
Portuguese (51)	112	0.88
Russian (12)	176	1.38
Scandinavian (15)	41	0.32
Scotch-Irish (221)	478	3.76
Scottish (233)	871	6.85
Serbian (0)	44	0.35
Slovak (77)	77	0.61
Slovene (17)	17	0.13
Swedish (101)	256	2.01
Swiss (0)	74	0.58
Turkish (12)	12	0.09
Ukrainian (14)	29	0.23
Welsh (14)	33	0.26

Hispanic Origin	Population	%
Hispanic or Latino (of any race)	125	1.00
Central American, ex. Mexican	6	0.05
Guatemalan	2	0.02
Nicaraguan	1	0.01
Salvadoran	3	0.02
Cuban	9	0.07
Dominican Republic	11	0.09
Mexican	38	0.30
Puerto Rican	26	0.21
South American	10	0.08
Argentinean	1	0.01
Chilean	1	0.01
Colombian	5	0.04
Peruvian	2	0.02
Venezuelan	1	0.01
Other Hispanic or Latino	25	0.20

Race*	Population	%
African-American/Black (45)	68	0.54
Not Hispanic (43)	65	0.52
Hispanic (2)	3	0.02
American Indian/Alaska Native (17)	64	0.51
Not Hispanic (14)	56	0.45
Hispanic (3)	8	0.06
Apache (1)	1	0.01
Blackfeet (0)	1	0.01
Cherokee (0)	9	0.07
Creek (0)	1	0.01
Crow (1)	1	0.01
Iroquois (0)	1	0.01
Kiowa (0)	1	0.01
Mexican American Ind. (1)	2	0.02
Seminole (0)	1	0.01
South American Ind. (0)	1	0.01
Yup'ik *(Alaska Native)* (1)	1	0.01
Asian (102)	130	1.04
Not Hispanic (99)	127	1.01
Hispanic (3)	3	0.02
Cambodian (7)	8	0.06
Chinese, ex. Taiwanese (46)	51	0.41
Filipino (12)	23	0.18
Indian (8)	9	0.07
Japanese (5)	9	0.07
Korean (12)	17	0.14
Pakistani (0)	2	0.02
Thai (4)	7	0.06
Vietnamese (2)	2	0.02
Hawaii Native/Pacific Islander (0)	5	0.04
Not Hispanic (0)	5	0.04
Guamanian/Chamorro (0)	2	0.02
Native Hawaiian (0)	3	0.02
White (12,227)	12,328	98.40
Not Hispanic (12,140)	12,234	97.65
Hispanic (87)	94	0.75

*Notes: † The Census 2010 population figure is used to calculate the percentages in the Hispanic Origin and Race categories. Ancestry percentages are based on the 2006-2010 American Community Survey population (not shown); ‡ Numbers in parentheses indicate the number of people reporting a single ancestry; * Numbers in parentheses indicate the number of persons reporting this race alone, not in combination with any other race; Please refer to the Explanation of Data for more information.*

MARYLAND

Place Type: State
Population: 5,773,552†

Ancestry‡	Population	%
Afghan (936)	1,025	0.02
African, Sub-Saharan (150,032)	168,316	2.95
African (78,779)	90,411	1.59
Cape Verdean (498)	1,022	0.02
Ethiopian (15,795)	16,604	0.29
Ghanaian (6,857)	7,373	0.13
Kenyan (2,317)	2,458	0.04
Liberian (3,416)	4,007	0.07
Nigerian (23,193)	24,893	0.44
Senegalese (680)	782	0.01
Sierra Leonean (2,515)	2,915	0.05
Somalian (756)	765	0.01
South African (823)	1,076	0.02
Sudanese (595)	661	0.01
Ugandan (637)	671	0.01
Zimbabwean (226)	242	<0.01
Other Sub-Saharan African (12,945)	14,436	0.25
Albanian (976)	1,365	0.02
Alsatian (40)	213	<0.01
American (277,540)	277,540	4.87
Arab (16,073)	24,736	0.43
Arab (2,965)	4,108	0.07
Egyptian (3,117)	3,816	0.07
Iraqi (433)	553	0.01
Jordanian (463)	559	0.01
Lebanese (3,407)	6,284	0.11
Moroccan (1,628)	2,306	0.04
Palestinian (964)	1,434	0.03
Syrian (755)	2,004	0.04
Other Arab (2,341)	3,672	0.06
Armenian (2,764)	4,572	0.08
Assyrian/Chaldean/Syriac (92)	196	<0.01
Australian (616)	1,424	0.02
Austrian (3,793)	16,287	0.29
Basque (206)	463	0.01
Belgian (1,596)	3,928	0.07
Brazilian (4,884)	7,043	0.12
British (13,043)	27,502	0.48
Bulgarian (2,018)	2,338	0.04
Cajun (155)	404	0.01
Canadian (3,864)	8,086	0.14
Carpatho Rusyn (28)	126	<0.01
Celtic (505)	895	0.02
Croatian (1,091)	3,390	0.06
Cypriot (185)	201	<0.01
Czech (6,175)	23,982	0.42
Czechoslovakian (2,590)	5,207	0.09
Danish (3,020)	11,776	0.21
Dutch (12,211)	59,254	1.04
Eastern European (17,324)	19,110	0.34
English (155,369)	504,354	8.85
Estonian (511)	998	0.02
European (54,470)	61,268	1.08
Finnish (1,450)	4,905	0.09
French, ex. Basque (19,484)	108,376	1.90
French Canadian (7,658)	20,545	0.36
German (281,525)	924,581	16.23
German Russian (207)	412	0.01
Greek (18,705)	33,952	0.60
Guyanese (4,573)	5,981	0.10
Hungarian (8,423)	27,773	0.49
Icelander (209)	490	0.01
Iranian (13,217)	14,561	0.26
Irish (185,928)	693,953	12.18
Israeli (2,166)	3,268	0.06
Italian (107,378)	311,872	5.47
Latvian (1,444)	3,289	0.06
Lithuanian (6,612)	19,582	0.34
Luxemburger (128)	500	0.01
Macedonian (134)	195	<0.01
Maltese (57)	274	<0.01
New Zealander (254)	394	0.01
Northern European (4,003)	4,406	0.08
Norwegian (8,098)	29,174	0.51
Pennsylvania German (2,276)	4,035	0.07
Polish (64,239)	200,092	3.51
Portuguese (5,003)	11,577	0.20
Romanian (3,486)	8,183	0.14
Russian (37,967)	82,950	1.46
Scandinavian (2,316)	5,403	0.09
Scotch-Irish (30,258)	81,798	1.44
Scottish (27,696)	100,292	1.76
Serbian (1,036)	2,382	0.04
Slavic (1,201)	3,039	0.05
Slovak (4,278)	12,869	0.23
Slovene (675)	1,946	0.03
Soviet Union (0)	13	<0.01
Swedish (8,492)	37,285	0.65
Swiss (3,174)	13,369	0.23
Turkish (3,413)	5,049	0.09
Ukrainian (10,899)	21,727	0.38
Welsh (7,395)	41,924	0.74
West Indian, ex. Hispanic (51,641)	67,574	1.19
Bahamian (414)	766	0.01
Barbadian (737)	1,314	0.02
Belizean (148)	262	<0.01
Bermudan (200)	356	0.01
British West Indian (1,900)	2,637	0.05
Dutch West Indian (108)	145	<0.01
Haitian (8,885)	10,695	0.19
Jamaican (26,123)	32,252	0.57
Trinidadian/Tobagonian (7,331)	9,483	0.17
U.S. Virgin Islander (388)	534	0.01
West Indian (5,285)	8,974	0.16
Other West Indian (122)	156	<0.01
Yugoslavian (778)	2,087	0.04

Hispanic Origin	Population	%
Hispanic or Latino (of any race)	470,632	8.15
Central American, ex. Mexican	195,692	3.39
Costa Rican	2,304	0.04
Guatemalan	34,491	0.60
Honduran	20,576	0.36
Nicaraguan	8,196	0.14
Panamanian	5,341	0.09
Salvadoran	123,789	2.14
Other Central American	995	0.02
Cuban	10,366	0.18
Dominican Republic	14,873	0.26
Mexican	88,004	1.52
Puerto Rican	42,572	0.74
South American	61,400	1.06
Argentinean	5,138	0.09
Bolivian	7,496	0.13
Chilean	4,146	0.07
Colombian	12,990	0.22
Ecuadorian	7,076	0.12
Paraguayan	1,161	0.02
Peruvian	18,229	0.32
Uruguayan	1,282	0.02
Venezuelan	3,328	0.06
Other South American	554	0.01
Other Hispanic or Latino	57,725	1.00

Race*	Population	%
African-American/Black (1,700,298)	1,783,899	30.90
Not Hispanic (1,674,229)	1,745,599	30.23
Hispanic (26,069)	38,300	0.66
American Indian/Alaska Native (20,420)	58,657	1.02
Not Hispanic (13,815)	45,047	0.78
Hispanic (6,605)	13,610	0.24
Alaska Athabascan *(Ala. Nat.)* (23)	47	<0.01
Aleut *(Alaska Native)* (27)	49	<0.01
Apache (146)	495	0.01
Arapaho (11)	42	<0.01
Blackfeet (268)	2,099	0.04
Canadian/French Am. Ind. (40)	126	<0.01
Central American Ind. (410)	728	0.01
Cherokee (2,198)	11,055	0.19
Cheyenne (33)	108	<0.01
Chickasaw (50)	170	<0.01
Chippewa (228)	509	0.01
Choctaw (176)	701	0.01
Colville (2)	7	<0.01
Comanche (50)	125	<0.01
Cree (19)	93	<0.01
Creek (108)	349	0.01
Crow (29)	110	<0.01
Delaware (66)	239	<0.01
Hopi (13)	31	<0.01
Houma (9)	19	<0.01
Inupiat *(Alaska Native)* (49)	88	<0.01
Iroquois (246)	818	0.01
Kiowa (17)	44	<0.01
Lumbee (1,100)	1,715	0.03
Menominee (19)	47	<0.01
Mexican American Ind. (943)	1,495	0.03
Navajo (251)	520	0.01
Osage (33)	77	<0.01
Ottawa (33)	52	<0.01
Paiute (11)	15	<0.01
Pima (8)	13	<0.01
Potawatomi (55)	107	<0.01
Pueblo (82)	142	<0.01
Puget Sound Salish (10)	30	<0.01
Seminole (71)	340	0.01
Shoshone (8)	47	<0.01
Sioux (241)	819	0.01
South American Ind. (541)	1,325	0.02
Spanish American Ind. (211)	303	0.01
Tlingit-Haida *(Alaska Native)* (29)	53	<0.01
Tohono O'Odham (13)	26	<0.01
Tsimshian *(Alaska Native)* (8)	12	<0.01
Ute (19)	41	<0.01
Yakama (2)	7	<0.01
Yaqui (41)	64	<0.01
Yuman (3)	14	<0.01
Yup'ik *(Alaska Native)* (10)	18	<0.01
Asian (318,853)	370,044	6.41
Not Hispanic (316,694)	363,580	6.30
Hispanic (2,159)	6,464	0.11
Bangladeshi (3,127)	3,585	0.06
Bhutanese (252)	288	<0.01
Burmese (3,195)	3,450	0.06
Cambodian (2,587)	3,137	0.05
Chinese, ex. Taiwanese (64,487)	74,587	1.29
Filipino (43,923)	56,909	0.99
Hmong (53)	76	<0.01
Indian (79,051)	88,709	1.54
Indonesian (1,950)	2,495	0.04
Japanese (6,749)	12,826	0.22
Korean (48,592)	55,051	0.95
Laotian (1,061)	1,420	0.02
Malaysian (266)	482	0.01
Nepalese (3,109)	3,412	0.06
Pakistani (14,046)	15,600	0.27
Sri Lankan (2,478)	2,836	0.05
Taiwanese (4,571)	5,440	0.09
Thai (4,060)	5,513	0.10
Vietnamese (23,635)	26,605	0.46
Hawaii Native/Pacific Islander (3,157)	9,826	0.17
Not Hispanic (2,412)	7,746	0.13
Hispanic (745)	2,080	0.04
Fijian (51)	89	<0.01
Guamanian/Chamorro (1,319)	2,100	0.04
Marshallese (25)	34	<0.01
Native Hawaiian (634)	2,346	0.04
Samoan (308)	731	0.01
Tongan (26)	74	<0.01
White (3,359,284)	3,488,887	60.43
Not Hispanic (3,157,958)	3,257,918	56.43
Hispanic (201,326)	230,969	4.00

*Notes: † The Census 2010 population figure is used to calculate the percentages in the Hispanic Origin and Race categories. Ancestry percentages are based on the 2006-2010 American Community Survey population (not shown); ‡ Numbers in parentheses indicate the number of people reporting a single ancestry; * Numbers in parentheses indicate the number of persons reporting this race alone, not in combination with any other race; Please refer to the Explanation of Data for more information.*

Aberdeen

Place Type: City
County: Harford
Population: 14,959†

Ancestry‡	Population	%
African, Sub-Saharan (366)	551	3.69
African (205)	390	2.61
Ghanaian (161)	161	1.08
American (1,334)	1,334	8.94
Belgian (45)	76	0.51
Brazilian (13)	13	0.09
British (11)	20	0.13
Cajun (11)	11	0.07
Canadian (24)	24	0.16
Croatian (0)	8	0.05
Czech (28)	86	0.58
Czechoslovakian (0)	9	0.06
Dutch (14)	133	0.89
English (398)	866	5.80
European (112)	125	0.84
French, ex. Basque (55)	222	1.49
French Canadian (44)	152	1.02
German (1,027)	2,726	18.27
Greek (37)	37	0.25
Hungarian (0)	12	0.08
Irish (273)	1,362	9.13
Italian (241)	544	3.65
Lithuanian (0)	64	0.43
New Zealander (0)	20	0.13
Norwegian (21)	98	0.66
Polish (66)	234	1.57
Portuguese (0)	11	0.07
Russian (0)	30	0.20
Scandinavian (30)	30	0.20
Scotch-Irish (152)	252	1.69
Scottish (125)	217	1.45
Slavic (0)	11	0.07
Slovak (27)	27	0.18
Swedish (36)	36	0.24
Swiss (0)	12	0.08
Turkish (22)	22	0.15
Ukrainian (12)	18	0.12
Welsh (32)	46	0.31
West Indian, ex. Hispanic (67)	76	0.51
Haitian (44)	44	0.29
Jamaican (23)	23	0.15
West Indian (0)	9	0.06

Hispanic Origin	Population	%
Hispanic or Latino (of any race)	815	5.45
Central American, ex. Mexican	106	0.71
Costa Rican	7	0.05
Guatemalan	14	0.09
Honduran	28	0.19
Nicaraguan	1	0.01
Panamanian	25	0.17
Salvadoran	31	0.21
Cuban	15	0.10
Dominican Republic	23	0.15
Mexican	203	1.36
Puerto Rican	358	2.39
South American	39	0.26
Argentinean	3	0.02
Chilean	1	0.01
Colombian	19	0.13
Peruvian	10	0.07
Uruguayan	2	0.01
Venezuelan	3	0.02
Other South American	1	0.01
Other Hispanic or Latino	71	0.47

Race*	Population	%
African-American/Black (4,564)	5,097	34.07
Not Hispanic (4,462)	4,942	33.04
Hispanic (102)	155	1.04
American Indian/Alaska Native (59)	236	1.58
Not Hispanic (48)	201	1.34
Hispanic (11)	35	0.23
Alaska Athabascan *(Ala. Nat.)* (1)	1	0.01
Apache (2)	2	0.01
Blackfeet (2)	12	0.08
Cherokee (8)	55	0.37
Choctaw (0)	1	0.01
Comanche (0)	1	0.01
Creek (0)	1	0.01
Iroquois (1)	2	0.01
Lumbee (2)	4	0.03
Mexican American Ind. (1)	1	0.01
Osage (1)	1	0.01
Potawatomi (0)	1	0.01
Pueblo (2)	4	0.03
Sioux (1)	5	0.03
Asian (437)	631	4.22
Not Hispanic (431)	604	4.04
Hispanic (6)	27	0.18
Bangladeshi (0)	1	0.01
Cambodian (1)	1	0.01
Chinese, ex. Taiwanese (42)	61	0.41
Filipino (107)	158	1.06
Indian (125)	155	1.04
Indonesian (5)	5	0.03
Japanese (30)	63	0.42
Korean (81)	144	0.96
Nepalese (3)	3	0.02
Pakistani (8)	10	0.07
Thai (8)	13	0.09
Vietnamese (24)	26	0.17
Hawaii Native/Pacific Islander (52)	82	0.55
Not Hispanic (52)	78	0.52
Hispanic (0)	4	0.03
Guamanian/Chamorro (8)	12	0.08
Native Hawaiian (7)	21	0.14
Samoan (13)	17	0.11
White (8,815)	9,460	63.24
Not Hispanic (8,434)	9,004	60.19
Hispanic (381)	456	3.05

Accokeek

Place Type: CDP
County: Prince George's
Population: 10,573†

Ancestry‡	Population	%
African, Sub-Saharan (537)	594	5.65
African (381)	438	4.17
Kenyan (61)	61	0.58
Nigerian (49)	49	0.47
Sierra Leonean (46)	46	0.44
American (351)	351	3.34
Arab (0)	8	0.08
Moroccan (0)	8	0.08
Croatian (0)	16	0.15
Dutch (29)	38	0.36
Eastern European (42)	42	0.40
English (98)	269	2.56
European (32)	32	0.30
French, ex. Basque (29)	92	0.88
French Canadian (7)	15	0.14
German (173)	541	5.15
Irish (232)	531	5.05
Italian (30)	121	1.15
Polish (11)	52	0.49
Portuguese (9)	9	0.09
Russian (17)	30	0.29
Scotch-Irish (59)	140	1.33
Scottish (0)	60	0.57
Swedish (9)	9	0.09
Welsh (0)	17	0.16
West Indian, ex. Hispanic (143)	179	1.70
Belizean (17)	17	0.16
Haitian (20)	44	0.42
Jamaican (106)	118	1.12
Yugoslavian (21)	21	0.20

Hispanic Origin	Population	%
Hispanic or Latino (of any race)	497	4.70
Central American, ex. Mexican	197	1.86
Costa Rican	1	0.01
Guatemalan	13	0.12
Honduran	9	0.09
Nicaraguan	11	0.10
Panamanian	18	0.17
Salvadoran	145	1.37
Cuban	8	0.08
Dominican Republic	11	0.10
Mexican	95	0.90
Puerto Rican	102	0.96
South American	36	0.34
Argentinean	7	0.07
Bolivian	2	0.02
Chilean	2	0.02
Colombian	10	0.09
Ecuadorian	4	0.04
Peruvian	8	0.08
Venezuelan	1	0.01
Other South American	2	0.02
Other Hispanic or Latino	48	0.45

Race*	Population	%
African-American/Black (6,811)	7,047	66.65
Not Hispanic (6,706)	6,912	65.37
Hispanic (105)	135	1.28
American Indian/Alaska Native (49)	154	1.46
Not Hispanic (44)	138	1.31
Hispanic (5)	16	0.15
Apache (1)	1	0.01
Blackfeet (0)	8	0.08
Central American Ind. (0)	2	0.02
Cherokee (3)	21	0.20
Cheyenne (1)	5	0.05
Creek (1)	1	0.01
Inupiat *(Alaska Native)* (2)	2	0.02
Mexican American Ind. (1)	3	0.03
Seminole (0)	1	0.01
Sioux (2)	2	0.02
Yuman (0)	1	0.01
Asian (584)	650	6.15
Not Hispanic (579)	642	6.07
Hispanic (5)	8	0.08
Bangladeshi (1)	1	0.01
Cambodian (2)	4	0.04
Chinese, ex. Taiwanese (22)	25	0.24
Filipino (393)	425	4.02
Indian (80)	91	0.86
Japanese (7)	20	0.19
Korean (20)	26	0.25
Nepalese (1)	1	0.01
Pakistani (28)	29	0.27
Thai (12)	12	0.11
Vietnamese (3)	5	0.05
Hawaii Native/Pacific Islander (3)	14	0.13
Not Hispanic (3)	14	0.13
Guamanian/Chamorro (2)	4	0.04
Native Hawaiian (1)	4	0.04
White (2,630)	2,802	26.50
Not Hispanic (2,488)	2,640	24.97
Hispanic (142)	162	1.53

Adelphi

Place Type: CDP
County: Prince George's
Population: 15,086†

Ancestry‡	Population	%
African, Sub-Saharan (2,234)	2,244	14.92
African (781)	791	5.26
Ethiopian (430)	430	2.86
Ghanaian (88)	88	0.59
Liberian (32)	32	0.21
Nigerian (242)	242	1.61
Sierra Leonean (18)	18	0.12
Sudanese (6)	6	0.04
Other Sub-Saharan African (637)	637	4.24
American (419)	419	2.79
Arab (40)	46	0.31
Arab (19)	19	0.13

*Notes: † The Census 2010 population figure is used to calculate the percentages in the Hispanic Origin and Race categories. Ancestry percentages are based on the 2006-2010 American Community Survey population (not shown); ‡ Numbers in parentheses indicate the number of people reporting a single ancestry; * Numbers in parentheses indicate the number of persons reporting this race alone, not in combination with any other race; Please refer to the Explanation of Data for more information.*

Egyptian (0)	6	0.04
Lebanese (21)	21	0.14
Australian (10)	10	0.07
Austrian (0)	7	0.05
Brazilian (0)	13	0.09
British (7)	34	0.23
Bulgarian (56)	56	0.37
Czech (13)	31	0.21
Czechoslovakian (0)	30	0.20
Danish (0)	33	0.22
Dutch (8)	22	0.15
Eastern European (14)	14	0.09
English (25)	299	1.99
European (69)	93	0.62
French, ex. Basque (20)	43	0.29
French Canadian (15)	40	0.27
German (98)	521	3.46
Guyanese (10)	54	0.36
Hungarian (35)	41	0.27
Irish (39)	362	2.41
Italian (102)	226	1.50
Lithuanian (12)	12	0.08
Luxemburger (0)	10	0.07
Norwegian (0)	7	0.05
Polish (136)	307	2.04
Portuguese (0)	45	0.30
Russian (45)	59	0.39
Scotch-Irish (45)	65	0.43
Scottish (30)	81	0.54
Slovak (6)	6	0.04
Slovene (0)	31	0.21
Swedish (0)	34	0.23
Ukrainian (8)	40	0.27
Welsh (11)	50	0.33
West Indian, ex. Hispanic (786)	793	5.27
Haitian (243)	250	1.66
Jamaican (435)	435	2.89
Trinidadian/Tobagonian (74)	74	0.49
West Indian (34)	34	0.23

Hispanic Origin	Population	%
Hispanic or Latino (of any race)	6,345	42.06
Central American, ex. Mexican	4,080	27.04
Costa Rican	7	0.05
Guatemalan	761	5.04
Honduran	248	1.64
Nicaraguan	129	0.86
Panamanian	40	0.27
Salvadoran	2,884	19.12
Other Central American	11	0.07
Cuban	36	0.24
Dominican Republic	298	1.98
Mexican	421	2.79
Puerto Rican	88	0.58
South American	290	1.92
Argentinean	30	0.20
Bolivian	53	0.35
Chilean	13	0.09
Colombian	36	0.24
Ecuadorian	52	0.34
Paraguayan	3	0.02
Peruvian	79	0.52
Uruguayan	15	0.10
Venezuelan	8	0.05
Other South American	1	0.01
Other Hispanic or Latino	1,132	7.50

Race*	Population	%
African-American/Black (5,531)	5,752	38.13
Not Hispanic (5,291)	5,411	35.87
Hispanic (240)	341	2.26
American Indian/Alaska Native (208)	332	2.20
Not Hispanic (37)	90	0.60
Hispanic (171)	242	1.60
Arapaho (0)	2	0.01
Blackfeet (0)	3	0.02
Central American Ind. (11)	21	0.14
Cherokee (4)	11	0.07
Chippewa (1)	3	0.02
Choctaw (0)	2	0.01
Delaware (0)	3	0.02
Inupiat *(Alaska Native)* (3)	3	0.02
Iroquois (0)	2	0.01
Lumbee (8)	8	0.05
Mexican American Ind. (9)	11	0.07
Seminole (0)	1	0.01
Sioux (0)	1	0.01
South American Ind. (0)	1	0.01
Spanish American Ind. (6)	7	0.05
Asian (1,180)	1,276	8.46
Not Hispanic (1,168)	1,243	8.24
Hispanic (12)	33	0.22
Bangladeshi (17)	24	0.16
Burmese (2)	2	0.01
Cambodian (19)	20	0.13
Chinese, ex. Taiwanese (225)	241	1.60
Filipino (70)	78	0.52
Hmong (1)	2	0.01
Indian (484)	519	3.44
Indonesian (4)	4	0.03
Japanese (13)	22	0.15
Korean (51)	54	0.36
Laotian (21)	24	0.16
Malaysian (1)	1	0.01
Nepalese (13)	13	0.09
Pakistani (18)	23	0.15
Sri Lankan (1)	1	0.01
Taiwanese (12)	13	0.09
Thai (23)	28	0.19
Vietnamese (169)	178	1.18
Hawaii Native/Pacific Islander (7)	61	0.40
Not Hispanic (5)	30	0.20
Hispanic (2)	31	0.21
Guamanian/Chamorro (4)	4	0.03
Native Hawaiian (0)	5	0.03
White (3,834)	4,321	28.64
Not Hispanic (1,980)	2,110	13.99
Hispanic (1,854)	2,211	14.66

Annapolis Neck

Place Type: CDP
County: Anne Arundel
Population: 10,950†

Ancestry‡	Population	%
African, Sub-Saharan (74)	158	1.42
African (15)	15	0.14
Cape Verdean (25)	109	0.98
South African (34)	34	0.31
American (331)	331	2.98
Arab (15)	15	0.14
Lebanese (15)	15	0.14
Austrian (27)	92	0.83
Belgian (0)	11	0.10
British (122)	205	1.85
Canadian (22)	72	0.65
Croatian (0)	11	0.10
Czech (14)	29	0.26
Danish (37)	95	0.86
Dutch (18)	142	1.28
Eastern European (89)	89	0.80
English (560)	1,848	16.64
European (94)	126	1.13
Finnish (0)	42	0.38
French, ex. Basque (124)	374	3.37
French Canadian (0)	61	0.55
German (606)	2,170	19.54
Greek (176)	228	2.05
Hungarian (0)	72	0.65
Iranian (54)	72	0.65
Irish (643)	2,104	18.95
Italian (388)	911	8.20
Northern European (16)	16	0.14
Norwegian (35)	62	0.56
Polish (116)	376	3.39
Portuguese (69)	69	0.62
Russian (99)	242	2.18
Scandinavian (10)	10	0.09
Scotch-Irish (121)	298	2.68
Scottish (90)	403	3.63
Slavic (0)	22	0.20
Slovak (0)	16	0.14
Swedish (38)	154	1.39
Swiss (0)	22	0.20
Turkish (34)	34	0.31
Ukrainian (14)	28	0.25
Welsh (63)	157	1.41
West Indian, ex. Hispanic (0)	39	0.35
Jamaican (0)	29	0.26
West Indian (0)	10	0.09

Hispanic Origin	Population	%
Hispanic or Latino (of any race)	390	3.56
Central American, ex. Mexican	82	0.75
Costa Rican	1	0.01
Guatemalan	22	0.20
Honduran	12	0.11
Nicaraguan	3	0.03
Panamanian	3	0.03
Salvadoran	41	0.37
Cuban	21	0.19
Dominican Republic	5	0.05
Mexican	130	1.19
Puerto Rican	45	0.41
South American	64	0.58
Argentinean	9	0.08
Chilean	11	0.10
Colombian	18	0.16
Ecuadorian	11	0.10
Peruvian	3	0.03
Uruguayan	6	0.05
Venezuelan	6	0.05
Other Hispanic or Latino	43	0.39

Race*	Population	%
African-American/Black (803)	926	8.46
Not Hispanic (794)	915	8.36
Hispanic (9)	11	0.10
American Indian/Alaska Native (28)	85	0.78
Not Hispanic (19)	73	0.67
Hispanic (9)	12	0.11
Cherokee (8)	22	0.20
Choctaw (1)	3	0.03
Comanche (1)	1	0.01
Delaware (0)	7	0.06
Mexican American Ind. (8)	8	0.07
Sioux (2)	2	0.02
Asian (176)	271	2.47
Not Hispanic (170)	263	2.40
Hispanic (6)	8	0.07
Chinese, ex. Taiwanese (27)	45	0.41
Filipino (52)	72	0.66
Indian (29)	42	0.38
Indonesian (1)	2	0.02
Japanese (13)	27	0.25
Korean (21)	31	0.28
Pakistani (2)	2	0.02
Sri Lankan (4)	4	0.04
Taiwanese (2)	5	0.05
Thai (4)	9	0.08
Vietnamese (13)	25	0.23
Hawaii Native/Pacific Islander (5)	7	0.06
Not Hispanic (5)	7	0.06
Guamanian/Chamorro (3)	3	0.03
Native Hawaiian (1)	1	0.01
Samoan (1)	2	0.02
White (9,537)	9,751	89.05
Not Hispanic (9,321)	9,519	86.93
Hispanic (216)	232	2.12

Annapolis

Place Type: City
County: Anne Arundel
Population: 38,394†

Ancestry‡	Population	%
African, Sub-Saharan (218)	218	0.58
African (166)	166	0.44

*Notes: † The Census 2010 population figure is used to calculate the percentages in the Hispanic Origin and Race categories. Ancestry percentages are based on the 2006-2010 American Community Survey population (not shown); ‡ Numbers in parentheses indicate the number of people reporting a single ancestry; * Numbers in parentheses indicate the number of persons reporting this race alone, not in combination with any other race; Please refer to the Explanation of Data for more information.*

Nigerian (29)	29	0.08
Sierra Leonean (23)	23	0.06
Albanian (12)	12	0.03
American (940)	940	2.49
Arab (70)	141	0.37
Arab (0)	17	0.04
Egyptian (26)	40	0.11
Lebanese (36)	60	0.16
Palestinian (8)	8	0.02
Other Arab (0)	16	0.04
Armenian (12)	25	0.07
Austrian (79)	155	0.41
Basque (0)	12	0.03
Belgian (0)	6	0.02
Brazilian (0)	13	0.03
British (145)	228	0.60
Bulgarian (0)	15	0.04
Cajun (0)	21	0.06
Canadian (36)	51	0.13
Croatian (23)	34	0.09
Cypriot (16)	16	0.04
Czech (42)	131	0.35
Czechoslovakian (20)	30	0.08
Danish (66)	102	0.27
Dutch (43)	429	1.13
Eastern European (46)	64	0.17
English (999)	4,365	11.54
European (458)	479	1.27
Finnish (16)	30	0.08
French, ex. Basque (160)	1,142	3.02
French Canadian (42)	108	0.29
German (1,288)	5,353	14.15
Greek (311)	456	1.21
Hungarian (75)	284	0.75
Iranian (9)	23	0.06
Irish (1,996)	5,823	15.39
Israeli (0)	10	0.03
Italian (573)	2,063	5.45
Lithuanian (14)	105	0.28
Luxemburger (14)	14	0.04
Northern European (37)	37	0.10
Norwegian (66)	329	0.87
Polish (470)	1,234	3.26
Portuguese (0)	28	0.07
Romanian (13)	67	0.18
Russian (149)	332	0.88
Scandinavian (24)	77	0.20
Scotch-Irish (352)	731	1.93
Scottish (261)	929	2.46
Serbian (14)	14	0.04
Slavic (0)	74	0.20
Slovak (25)	59	0.16
Swedish (109)	407	1.08
Swiss (34)	152	0.40
Turkish (0)	15	0.04
Ukrainian (119)	210	0.56
Welsh (44)	387	1.02
West Indian, ex. Hispanic (54)	63	0.17
British West Indian (18)	18	0.05
Jamaican (0)	9	0.02
Trinidadian/Tobagonian (18)	18	0.05
West Indian (18)	18	0.05
Yugoslavian (13)	13	0.03

Hispanic Origin	Population	%
Hispanic or Latino (of any race)	6,448	16.79
Central American, ex. Mexican	3,181	8.29
Costa Rican	10	0.03
Guatemalan	190	0.49
Honduran	250	0.65
Nicaraguan	6	0.02
Panamanian	7	0.02
Salvadoran	2,708	7.05
Other Central American	10	0.03
Cuban	68	0.18
Dominican Republic	23	0.06
Mexican	2,015	5.25
Puerto Rican	196	0.51
South American	238	0.62
Argentinean	24	0.06
Bolivian	9	0.02
Chilean	24	0.06
Colombian	45	0.12
Ecuadorian	59	0.15
Paraguayan	1	<0.01
Peruvian	42	0.11
Uruguayan	8	0.02
Venezuelan	26	0.07
Other Hispanic or Latino	727	1.89

Race*	Population	%
African-American/Black (9,981)	10,432	27.17
Not Hispanic (9,854)	10,241	26.67
Hispanic (127)	191	0.50
American Indian/Alaska Native (97)	314	0.82
Not Hispanic (51)	221	0.58
Hispanic (46)	93	0.24
Alaska Athabascan *(Ala. Nat.)* (1)	1	<0.01
Aleut *(Alaska Native)* (1)	1	<0.01
Apache (1)	6	0.02
Blackfeet (0)	2	0.01
Central American Ind. (1)	3	0.01
Cherokee (4)	48	0.13
Cheyenne (1)	1	<0.01
Choctaw (3)	7	0.02
Colville (0)	1	<0.01
Delaware (0)	2	0.01
Iroquois (2)	12	0.03
Lumbee (2)	2	0.01
Mexican American Ind. (8)	12	0.03
Paiute (3)	3	0.01
Pima (1)	1	<0.01
Seminole (0)	1	<0.01
Sioux (4)	5	0.01
South American Ind. (0)	1	<0.01
Spanish American Ind. (1)	2	0.01
Asian (809)	1,036	2.70
Not Hispanic (789)	977	2.54
Hispanic (20)	59	0.15
Bangladeshi (13)	13	0.03
Burmese (1)	1	<0.01
Cambodian (1)	1	<0.01
Chinese, ex. Taiwanese (128)	162	0.42
Filipino (282)	356	0.93
Indian (109)	135	0.35
Indonesian (3)	3	0.01
Japanese (45)	87	0.23
Korean (65)	74	0.19
Laotian (8)	14	0.04
Malaysian (1)	1	<0.01
Nepalese (10)	10	0.03
Pakistani (43)	45	0.12
Sri Lankan (1)	2	0.01
Taiwanese (2)	2	0.01
Thai (14)	22	0.06
Vietnamese (54)	65	0.17
Hawaii Native/Pacific Islander (11)	49	0.13
Not Hispanic (9)	37	0.10
Hispanic (2)	12	0.03
Guamanian/Chamorro (4)	9	0.02
Native Hawaiian (4)	17	0.04
Samoan (1)	1	<0.01
Tongan (1)	5	0.01
White (23,073)	23,881	62.20
Not Hispanic (20,532)	21,061	54.85
Hispanic (2,541)	2,820	7.34

Arbutus

Place Type: CDP
County: Baltimore
Population: 20,483†

Ancestry‡	Population	%
African, Sub-Saharan (215)	215	1.05
African (194)	194	0.95
Other Sub-Saharan African (21)	21	0.10
American (1,088)	1,088	5.33
Arab (28)	79	0.39
Arab (12)	52	0.25
Egyptian (0)	11	0.05
Other Arab (16)	16	0.08
Armenian (0)	9	0.04
Assyrian/Chaldean/Syriac (16)	16	0.08
Austrian (16)	39	0.19
Belgian (0)	35	0.17
Brazilian (55)	55	0.27
British (115)	115	0.56
Canadian (30)	30	0.15
Czech (0)	70	0.34
Danish (89)	118	0.58
Dutch (100)	359	1.76
Eastern European (12)	12	0.06
English (360)	1,746	8.56
European (149)	166	0.81
French, ex. Basque (95)	463	2.27
French Canadian (81)	122	0.60
German (1,455)	4,961	24.31
Greek (126)	193	0.95
Guyanese (24)	24	0.12
Hungarian (31)	86	0.42
Iranian (13)	13	0.06
Irish (941)	3,859	18.91
Israeli (0)	21	0.10
Italian (498)	1,535	7.52
Latvian (0)	15	0.07
Lithuanian (142)	302	1.48
Luxemburger (0)	21	0.10
Northern European (25)	25	0.12
Pennsylvania German (11)	11	0.05
Polish (282)	884	4.33
Portuguese (24)	82	0.40
Russian (41)	135	0.66
Scandinavian (45)	45	0.22
Scotch-Irish (82)	211	1.03
Scottish (89)	282	1.38
Slovak (0)	19	0.09
Swedish (52)	93	0.46
Swiss (0)	32	0.16
Turkish (13)	13	0.06
Ukrainian (22)	34	0.17
Welsh (46)	205	1.00
West Indian, ex. Hispanic (50)	58	0.28
Barbadian (13)	13	0.06
Jamaican (37)	45	0.22
Yugoslavian (17)	17	0.08

Hispanic Origin	Population	%
Hispanic or Latino (of any race)	598	2.92
Central American, ex. Mexican	102	0.50
Costa Rican	3	0.01
Guatemalan	12	0.06
Honduran	23	0.11
Nicaraguan	9	0.04
Panamanian	2	0.01
Salvadoran	53	0.26
Cuban	34	0.17
Dominican Republic	14	0.07
Mexican	168	0.82
Puerto Rican	103	0.50
South American	110	0.54
Argentinean	5	0.02
Bolivian	1	<0.01
Chilean	15	0.07
Colombian	28	0.14
Ecuadorian	10	0.05
Paraguayan	1	<0.01
Peruvian	43	0.21
Uruguayan	2	0.01
Venezuelan	5	0.02
Other Hispanic or Latino	67	0.33

Race*	Population	%
African-American/Black (1,973)	2,164	10.56
Not Hispanic (1,946)	2,110	10.30
Hispanic (27)	54	0.26
American Indian/Alaska Native (48)	150	0.73
Not Hispanic (36)	113	0.55
Hispanic (12)	37	0.18
Apache (0)	1	<0.01

*Notes: † The Census 2010 population figure is used to calculate the percentages in the Hispanic Origin and Race categories. Ancestry percentages are based on the 2006-2010 American Community Survey population (not shown); ‡ Numbers in parentheses indicate the number of people reporting a single ancestry; * Numbers in parentheses indicate the number of persons reporting this race alone, not in combination with any other race; Please refer to the Explanation of Data for more information.*

Blackfeet (0)	3	0.01
Central American Ind. (1)	3	0.01
Cherokee (12)	37	0.18
Chickasaw (1)	1	<0.01
Choctaw (2)	2	0.01
Creek (0)	1	<0.01
Iroquois (1)	1	<0.01
Lumbee (2)	7	0.03
Mexican American Ind. (1)	6	0.03
Seminole (0)	1	<0.01
Sioux (1)	2	0.01
South American Ind. (1)	1	<0.01
Ute (1)	1	<0.01
Asian (1,768)	1,961	9.57
Not Hispanic (1,764)	1,940	9.47
Hispanic (4)	21	0.10
Bangladeshi (5)	6	0.03
Burmese (410)	423	2.07
Cambodian (2)	2	0.01
Chinese, ex. Taiwanese (368)	391	1.91
Filipino (147)	197	0.96
Hmong (1)	1	<0.01
Indian (436)	477	2.33
Indonesian (17)	19	0.09
Japanese (16)	26	0.13
Korean (112)	133	0.65
Malaysian (10)	14	0.07
Nepalese (26)	26	0.13
Pakistani (99)	110	0.54
Sri Lankan (15)	17	0.08
Taiwanese (10)	11	0.05
Thai (12)	15	0.07
Vietnamese (31)	45	0.22
Hawaii Native/Pacific Islander (16)	29	0.14
Not Hispanic (16)	27	0.13
Hispanic (0)	2	0.01
Guamanian/Chamorro (1)	2	0.01
Native Hawaiian (6)	12	0.06
Samoan (2)	2	0.01
White (15,983)	16,356	79.85
Not Hispanic (15,685)	15,999	78.11
Hispanic (298)	357	1.74

Arnold

Place Type: CDP
County: Anne Arundel
Population: 23,106†

Ancestry‡	Population	%
African, Sub-Saharan (58)	58	0.26
African (31)	31	0.14
Kenyan (17)	17	0.08
South African (10)	10	0.04
American (766)	766	3.41
Arab (21)	119	0.53
Egyptian (0)	20	0.09
Lebanese (0)	78	0.35
Syrian (21)	21	0.09
Austrian (32)	140	0.62
British (75)	119	0.53
Canadian (62)	81	0.36
Celtic (15)	25	0.11
Cypriot (16)	16	0.07
Czech (11)	141	0.63
Czechoslovakian (77)	112	0.50
Danish (93)	131	0.58
Dutch (122)	288	1.28
Eastern European (29)	29	0.13
English (1,287)	4,178	18.58
European (534)	560	2.49
French, ex. Basque (71)	912	4.06
French Canadian (22)	74	0.33
German (1,266)	5,123	22.79
Greek (100)	229	1.02
Guyanese (0)	14	0.06
Hungarian (57)	57	0.25
Irish (1,449)	5,451	24.24
Italian (739)	2,023	9.00
Lithuanian (15)	53	0.24
Northern European (38)	38	0.17
Norwegian (136)	282	1.25
Pennsylvania German (11)	20	0.09
Polish (282)	1,011	4.50
Portuguese (61)	217	0.97
Russian (84)	313	1.39
Scandinavian (0)	11	0.05
Scotch-Irish (248)	621	2.76
Scottish (256)	695	3.09
Serbian (0)	20	0.09
Slavic (0)	10	0.04
Slovak (15)	15	0.07
Swedish (114)	350	1.56
Swiss (50)	170	0.76
Ukrainian (111)	342	1.52
Welsh (38)	204	0.91
Yugoslavian (0)	9	0.04

Hispanic Origin	Population	%
Hispanic or Latino (of any race)	918	3.97
Central American, ex. Mexican	123	0.53
Guatemalan	28	0.12
Honduran	14	0.06
Nicaraguan	4	0.02
Panamanian	3	0.01
Salvadoran	74	0.32
Cuban	35	0.15
Dominican Republic	17	0.07
Mexican	254	1.10
Puerto Rican	130	0.56
South American	232	1.00
Argentinean	12	0.05
Bolivian	35	0.15
Chilean	14	0.06
Colombian	35	0.15
Ecuadorian	40	0.17
Paraguayan	5	0.02
Peruvian	71	0.31
Venezuelan	18	0.08
Other South American	2	0.01
Other Hispanic or Latino	127	0.55

Race*	Population	%
African-American/Black (1,208)	1,406	6.08
Not Hispanic (1,184)	1,356	5.87
Hispanic (24)	50	0.22
American Indian/Alaska Native (54)	167	0.72
Not Hispanic (41)	130	0.56
Hispanic (13)	37	0.16
Apache (1)	1	<0.01
Blackfeet (2)	6	0.03
Cherokee (13)	48	0.21
Chippewa (1)	1	<0.01
Choctaw (0)	2	0.01
Iroquois (1)	2	0.01
Lumbee (1)	2	0.01
Mexican American Ind. (3)	3	0.01
Navajo (1)	3	0.01
Osage (0)	2	0.01
Pueblo (0)	1	<0.01
Puget Sound Salish (1)	5	0.02
Seminole (0)	1	<0.01
South American Ind. (6)	9	0.04
Asian (558)	764	3.31
Not Hispanic (548)	735	3.18
Hispanic (10)	29	0.13
Bangladeshi (4)	7	0.03
Burmese (1)	1	<0.01
Cambodian (1)	1	<0.01
Chinese, ex. Taiwanese (90)	140	0.61
Filipino (136)	209	0.90
Indian (70)	91	0.39
Indonesian (1)	1	<0.01
Japanese (28)	46	0.20
Korean (76)	115	0.50
Laotian (0)	3	0.01
Pakistani (71)	86	0.37
Sri Lankan (0)	2	0.01
Taiwanese (6)	11	0.05
Thai (10)	18	0.08
Vietnamese (27)	38	0.16
Hawaii Native/Pacific Islander (6)	38	0.16
Not Hispanic (6)	33	0.14
Hispanic (0)	5	0.02
Fijian (0)	1	<0.01
Guamanian/Chamorro (1)	4	0.02
Native Hawaiian (1)	8	0.03
Samoan (3)	8	0.03
White (20,484)	20,960	90.71
Not Hispanic (19,938)	20,332	87.99
Hispanic (546)	628	2.72

Aspen Hill

Place Type: CDP
County: Montgomery
Population: 48,759†

Ancestry‡	Population	%
Afghan (53)	53	0.11
African, Sub-Saharan (2,880)	3,142	6.68
African (1,412)	1,657	3.52
Ethiopian (833)	833	1.77
Ghanaian (18)	18	0.04
Kenyan (19)	19	0.04
Liberian (101)	113	0.24
Nigerian (274)	274	0.58
Sierra Leonean (33)	33	0.07
Other Sub-Saharan African (190)	195	0.41
American (932)	932	1.98
Arab (472)	690	1.47
Arab (191)	206	0.44
Egyptian (33)	33	0.07
Lebanese (59)	99	0.21
Moroccan (37)	62	0.13
Palestinian (123)	261	0.56
Other Arab (29)	29	0.06
Armenian (18)	18	0.04
Austrian (71)	274	0.58
Basque (23)	23	0.05
Belgian (6)	23	0.05
Brazilian (288)	307	0.65
British (203)	257	0.55
Bulgarian (40)	40	0.09
Canadian (139)	148	0.31
Croatian (14)	14	0.03
Czech (66)	173	0.37
Czechoslovakian (28)	59	0.13
Danish (0)	200	0.43
Dutch (128)	292	0.62
Eastern European (226)	226	0.48
English (785)	3,501	7.45
European (426)	543	1.15
French, ex. Basque (69)	617	1.31
French Canadian (60)	106	0.23
German (754)	3,820	8.12
Greek (428)	452	0.96
Guyanese (13)	13	0.03
Hungarian (101)	175	0.37
Icelander (10)	39	0.08
Iranian (76)	76	0.16
Irish (876)	3,660	7.78
Israeli (125)	125	0.27
Italian (763)	2,126	4.52
Latvian (28)	51	0.11
Lithuanian (174)	257	0.55
Luxemburger (0)	16	0.03
Maltese (12)	30	0.06
Northern European (21)	31	0.07
Norwegian (107)	244	0.52
Pennsylvania German (0)	17	0.04
Polish (305)	910	1.94
Portuguese (280)	407	0.87
Romanian (164)	250	0.53
Russian (650)	1,137	2.42
Scandinavian (27)	76	0.16
Scotch-Irish (137)	508	1.08
Scottish (159)	908	1.93
Slavic (10)	20	0.04
Slovak (100)	111	0.24

*Notes: † The Census 2010 population figure is used to calculate the percentages in the Hispanic Origin and Race categories. Ancestry percentages are based on the 2006-2010 American Community Survey population (not shown); ‡ Numbers in parentheses indicate the number of people reporting a single ancestry; * Numbers in parentheses indicate the number of persons reporting this race alone, not in combination with any other race; Please refer to the Explanation of Data for more information.*

Slovene (14)	14	0.03
Swedish (183)	319	0.68
Swiss (24)	67	0.14
Turkish (35)	69	0.15
Ukrainian (85)	211	0.45
Welsh (32)	340	0.72
West Indian, ex. Hispanic (859)	953	2.03
Barbadian (12)	25	0.05
Haitian (215)	215	0.46
Jamaican (567)	578	1.23
Trinidadian/Tobagonian (18)	18	0.04
West Indian (34)	104	0.22
Other West Indian (13)	13	0.03

Hispanic Origin	Population	%
Hispanic or Latino (of any race)	13,593	27.88
Central American, ex. Mexican	7,037	14.43
Costa Rican	51	0.10
Guatemalan	712	1.46
Honduran	755	1.55
Nicaraguan	384	0.79
Panamanian	100	0.21
Salvadoran	5,023	10.30
Other Central American	12	0.02
Cuban	179	0.37
Dominican Republic	348	0.71
Mexican	1,084	2.22
Puerto Rican	379	0.78
South American	3,025	6.20
Argentinean	127	0.26
Bolivian	521	1.07
Chilean	212	0.43
Colombian	546	1.12
Ecuadorian	258	0.53
Paraguayan	77	0.16
Peruvian	1,144	2.35
Uruguayan	46	0.09
Venezuelan	69	0.14
Other South American	25	0.05
Other Hispanic or Latino	1,541	3.16

Race*	Population	%
African-American/Black (10,597)	11,335	23.25
Not Hispanic (10,200)	10,711	21.97
Hispanic (397)	624	1.28
American Indian/Alaska Native (290)	637	1.31
Not Hispanic (107)	297	0.61
Hispanic (183)	340	0.70
Aleut *(Alaska Native)* (2)	2	<0.01
Apache (2)	2	<0.01
Arapaho (1)	4	0.01
Blackfeet (3)	13	0.03
Central American Ind. (7)	11	0.02
Cherokee (8)	58	0.12
Cheyenne (1)	2	<0.01
Chickasaw (0)	1	<0.01
Chippewa (4)	6	0.01
Choctaw (8)	13	0.03
Colville (1)	1	<0.01
Comanche (1)	5	0.01
Creek (0)	6	0.01
Crow (1)	1	<0.01
Inupiat *(Alaska Native)* (1)	2	<0.01
Iroquois (0)	5	0.01
Lumbee (3)	3	0.01
Menominee (1)	1	<0.01
Mexican American Ind. (20)	28	0.06
Navajo (1)	1	<0.01
Osage (1)	1	<0.01
Pueblo (0)	1	<0.01
Seminole (2)	2	<0.01
Shoshone (1)	1	<0.01
Sioux (2)	7	0.01
South American Ind. (29)	56	0.11
Spanish American Ind. (9)	19	0.04
Asian (5,297)	5,922	12.15
Not Hispanic (5,241)	5,743	11.78
Hispanic (56)	179	0.37
Bangladeshi (18)	26	0.05
Burmese (89)	95	0.19
Cambodian (122)	135	0.28
Chinese, ex. Taiwanese (1,040)	1,232	2.53
Filipino (892)	1,060	2.17
Indian (673)	813	1.67
Indonesian (111)	122	0.25
Japanese (85)	150	0.31
Korean (813)	897	1.84
Laotian (17)	34	0.07
Malaysian (5)	6	0.01
Nepalese (76)	78	0.16
Pakistani (143)	162	0.33
Sri Lankan (178)	203	0.42
Taiwanese (56)	81	0.17
Thai (202)	227	0.47
Vietnamese (530)	584	1.20
Hawaii Native/Pacific Islander (18)	93	0.19
Not Hispanic (18)	71	0.15
Hispanic (0)	22	0.05
Guamanian/Chamorro (5)	10	0.02
Native Hawaiian (0)	12	0.02
Samoan (3)	3	0.01
Tongan (0)	2	<0.01
White (24,686)	26,448	54.24
Not Hispanic (18,145)	19,011	38.99
Hispanic (6,541)	7,437	15.25

Ballenger Creek

Place Type: CDP
County: Frederick
Population: 18,274[†]

Ancestry‡	Population	%
African, Sub-Saharan (161)	260	1.36
African (144)	243	1.27
Nigerian (10)	10	0.05
Other Sub-Saharan African (7)	7	0.04
American (793)	793	4.14
Arab (83)	150	0.78
Arab (34)	66	0.34
Egyptian (0)	9	0.05
Lebanese (49)	75	0.39
Armenian (15)	15	0.08
Assyrian/Chaldean/Syriac (16)	34	0.18
Belgian (12)	25	0.13
Brazilian (24)	24	0.13
British (56)	56	0.29
Canadian (0)	77	0.40
Czech (0)	46	0.24
Danish (0)	18	0.09
Dutch (42)	422	2.21
Eastern European (14)	14	0.07
English (279)	1,741	9.10
European (140)	152	0.79
French, ex. Basque (46)	466	2.44
French Canadian (0)	46	0.24
German (824)	3,759	19.64
Greek (36)	149	0.78
Guyanese (6)	12	0.06
Hungarian (0)	38	0.20
Iranian (118)	179	0.94
Irish (813)	3,214	16.79
Italian (543)	1,793	9.37
Lithuanian (0)	112	0.59
Norwegian (37)	139	0.73
Polish (172)	624	3.26
Romanian (10)	21	0.11
Russian (84)	143	0.75
Scandinavian (16)	32	0.17
Scotch-Irish (49)	392	2.05
Scottish (97)	401	2.10
Slavic (0)	31	0.16
Slovak (16)	16	0.08
Slovene (10)	10	0.05
Swedish (15)	128	0.67
Swiss (0)	24	0.13
Turkish (65)	65	0.34
Ukrainian (0)	85	0.44
Welsh (20)	151	0.79
West Indian, ex. Hispanic (68)	68	0.36
British West Indian (26)	26	0.14
Jamaican (35)	35	0.18
Trinidadian/Tobagonian (7)	7	0.04
Yugoslavian (0)	16	0.08

Hispanic Origin	Population	%
Hispanic or Latino (of any race)	1,851	10.13
Central American, ex. Mexican	591	3.23
Costa Rican	25	0.14
Guatemalan	94	0.51
Honduran	56	0.31
Nicaraguan	50	0.27
Panamanian	26	0.14
Salvadoran	326	1.78
Other Central American	14	0.08
Cuban	58	0.32
Dominican Republic	37	0.20
Mexican	342	1.87
Puerto Rican	232	1.27
South American	348	1.90
Argentinean	23	0.13
Bolivian	34	0.19
Chilean	23	0.13
Colombian	98	0.54
Ecuadorian	35	0.19
Paraguayan	2	0.01
Peruvian	108	0.59
Uruguayan	3	0.02
Venezuelan	21	0.11
Other South American	1	0.01
Other Hispanic or Latino	243	1.33

Race*	Population	%
African-American/Black (2,852)	3,256	17.82
Not Hispanic (2,764)	3,106	17.00
Hispanic (88)	150	0.82
American Indian/Alaska Native (76)	178	0.97
Not Hispanic (57)	133	0.73
Hispanic (19)	45	0.25
Apache (1)	8	0.04
Blackfeet (0)	6	0.03
Cherokee (13)	40	0.22
Chippewa (7)	13	0.07
Choctaw (1)	3	0.02
Comanche (2)	3	0.02
Creek (0)	5	0.03
Crow (1)	1	0.01
Iroquois (0)	2	0.01
Lumbee (0)	1	0.01
Menominee (1)	1	0.01
Mexican American Ind. (1)	3	0.02
Navajo (4)	4	0.02
Paiute (1)	1	0.01
Sioux (3)	3	0.02
South American Ind. (1)	7	0.04
Tlingit-Haida *(Alaska Native)* (1)	1	0.01
Asian (1,215)	1,445	7.91
Not Hispanic (1,213)	1,418	7.76
Hispanic (2)	27	0.15
Bangladeshi (14)	15	0.08
Burmese (76)	84	0.46
Cambodian (22)	26	0.14
Chinese, ex. Taiwanese (137)	168	0.92
Filipino (136)	197	1.08
Indian (384)	429	2.35
Indonesian (7)	10	0.05
Japanese (19)	47	0.26
Korean (84)	111	0.61
Laotian (28)	35	0.19
Malaysian (3)	3	0.02
Nepalese (13)	13	0.07
Pakistani (74)	82	0.45
Sri Lankan (11)	22	0.12
Taiwanese (12)	13	0.07
Thai (8)	19	0.10
Vietnamese (117)	131	0.72
Hawaii Native/Pacific Islander (18)	49	0.27
Not Hispanic (18)	44	0.24
Hispanic (0)	5	0.03
Guamanian/Chamorro (2)	5	0.03

*Notes: † The Census 2010 population figure is used to calculate the percentages in the Hispanic Origin and Race categories. Ancestry percentages are based on the 2006-2010 American Community Survey population (not shown); ‡ Numbers in parentheses indicate the number of people reporting a single ancestry; * Numbers in parentheses indicate the number of persons reporting this race alone, not in combination with any other race; Please refer to the Explanation of Data for more information.*

Native Hawaiian (4)	9	0.05
Samoan (2)	6	0.03
White (12,744)	13,430	73.49
Not Hispanic (11,735)	12,258	67.08
Hispanic (1,009)	1,172	6.41

Baltimore

Place Type: City
County: Baltimore city
Population: 620,961†

Ancestry‡	Population	%
African, Sub-Saharan (13,702)	15,989	2.58
African (9,444)	11,210	1.81
Cape Verdean (54)	73	0.01
Ethiopian (859)	965	0.16
Ghanaian (271)	303	0.05
Kenyan (245)	286	0.05
Liberian (61)	110	0.02
Nigerian (1,707)	1,814	0.29
Senegalese (222)	222	0.04
Sierra Leonean (101)	120	0.02
Somalian (22)	22	<0.01
South African (76)	86	0.01
Sudanese (164)	164	0.03
Ugandan (69)	69	0.01
Zimbabwean (44)	44	0.01
Other Sub-Saharan African (363)	501	0.08
Albanian (10)	10	<0.01
Alsatian (0)	9	<0.01
American (27,486)	27,486	4.43
Arab (1,361)	1,937	0.31
Arab (20)	99	0.02
Egyptian (86)	105	0.02
Iraqi (17)	25	<0.01
Jordanian (40)	61	0.01
Lebanese (108)	288	0.05
Moroccan (530)	564	0.09
Palestinian (48)	94	0.02
Syrian (73)	173	0.03
Other Arab (439)	528	0.09
Armenian (77)	128	0.02
Australian (52)	107	0.02
Austrian (267)	1,016	0.16
Basque (0)	15	<0.01
Belgian (129)	244	0.04
Brazilian (241)	350	0.06
British (839)	1,646	0.27
Bulgarian (51)	174	0.03
Cajun (46)	90	0.01
Canadian (222)	382	0.06
Carpatho Rusyn (0)	30	<0.01
Celtic (18)	36	0.01
Croatian (68)	237	0.04
Czech (393)	1,668	0.27
Czechoslovakian (164)	274	0.04
Danish (140)	457	0.07
Dutch (572)	2,727	0.44
Eastern European (1,266)	1,371	0.22
English (7,402)	23,236	3.74
Estonian (42)	55	0.01
European (2,666)	3,008	0.48
Finnish (21)	95	0.02
French, ex. Basque (966)	5,463	0.88
French Canadian (344)	877	0.14
German (12,396)	45,914	7.40
German Russian (59)	67	0.01
Greek (1,891)	2,621	0.42
Guyanese (289)	491	0.08
Hungarian (654)	2,050	0.33
Icelander (13)	31	<0.01
Iranian (729)	788	0.13
Irish (10,519)	39,501	6.37
Israeli (254)	355	0.06
Italian (6,351)	18,894	3.04
Latvian (75)	226	0.04
Lithuanian (452)	1,693	0.27
Luxemburger (11)	39	0.01
Maltese (0)	17	<0.01
New Zealander (55)	55	0.01
Northern European (229)	229	0.04
Norwegian (249)	1,303	0.21
Pennsylvania German (160)	160	0.03
Polish (5,919)	15,080	2.43
Portuguese (111)	600	0.10
Romanian (248)	634	0.10
Russian (2,774)	6,362	1.03
Scandinavian (72)	335	0.05
Scotch-Irish (1,285)	4,103	0.66
Scottish (1,141)	4,773	0.77
Serbian (116)	207	0.03
Slavic (46)	98	0.02
Slovak (156)	373	0.06
Slovene (19)	124	0.02
Swedish (256)	1,775	0.29
Swiss (128)	660	0.11
Turkish (281)	334	0.05
Ukrainian (969)	1,608	0.26
Welsh (403)	1,970	0.32
West Indian, ex. Hispanic (6,060)	8,122	1.31
Bahamian (37)	78	0.01
Barbadian (166)	199	0.03
Belizean (23)	23	<0.01
Bermudan (16)	48	0.01
British West Indian (131)	194	0.03
Dutch West Indian (0)	11	<0.01
Haitian (691)	953	0.15
Jamaican (3,135)	4,029	0.65
Trinidadian/Tobagonian (1,277)	1,502	0.24
U.S. Virgin Islander (30)	42	0.01
West Indian (554)	1,033	0.17
Other West Indian (0)	10	<0.01
Yugoslavian (18)	66	0.01

Hispanic Origin	Population	%
Hispanic or Latino (of any race)	25,960	4.18
Central American, ex. Mexican	6,921	1.11
Costa Rican	86	0.01
Guatemalan	1,246	0.20
Honduran	2,386	0.38
Nicaraguan	101	0.02
Panamanian	269	0.04
Salvadoran	2,796	0.45
Other Central American	37	0.01
Cuban	824	0.13
Dominican Republic	1,111	0.18
Mexican	7,855	1.26
Puerto Rican	3,137	0.51
South American	2,554	0.41
Argentinean	276	0.04
Bolivian	80	0.01
Chilean	111	0.02
Colombian	492	0.08
Ecuadorian	755	0.12
Paraguayan	24	<0.01
Peruvian	537	0.09
Uruguayan	59	0.01
Venezuelan	195	0.03
Other South American	25	<0.01
Other Hispanic or Latino	3,558	0.57

Race*	Population	%
African-American/Black (395,781)	403,998	65.06
Not Hispanic (392,938)	400,138	64.44
Hispanic (2,843)	3,860	0.62
American Indian/Alaska Native (2,270)	6,441	1.04
Not Hispanic (1,884)	5,370	0.86
Hispanic (386)	1,071	0.17
Aleut *(Alaska Native)* (1)	9	<0.01
Apache (12)	36	0.01
Arapaho (0)	2	<0.01
Blackfeet (38)	248	0.04
Canadian/French Am. Ind. (3)	14	<0.01
Central American Ind. (5)	28	<0.01
Cherokee (237)	1,131	0.18
Cheyenne (2)	8	<0.01
Chickasaw (3)	12	<0.01
Chippewa (6)	29	<0.01
Choctaw (11)	44	0.01
Comanche (3)	7	<0.01
Cree (1)	10	<0.01
Creek (3)	20	<0.01
Crow (0)	7	<0.01
Delaware (2)	10	<0.01
Hopi (0)	1	<0.01
Inupiat *(Alaska Native)* (3)	9	<0.01
Iroquois (18)	63	0.01
Lumbee (237)	335	0.05
Menominee (2)	4	<0.01
Mexican American Ind. (81)	108	0.02
Navajo (9)	34	0.01
Osage (5)	7	<0.01
Ottawa (0)	5	<0.01
Paiute (0)	1	<0.01
Potawatomi (3)	9	<0.01
Pueblo (1)	4	<0.01
Puget Sound Salish (0)	1	<0.01
Seminole (7)	35	0.01
Shoshone (0)	2	<0.01
Sioux (19)	69	0.01
South American Ind. (19)	76	0.01
Spanish American Ind. (15)	22	<0.01
Tlingit-Haida *(Alaska Native)* (0)	1	<0.01
Tohono O'Odham (1)	1	<0.01
Tsimshian *(Alaska Native)* (2)	5	<0.01
Ute (1)	2	<0.01
Yaqui (1)	1	<0.01
Yuman (0)	1	<0.01
Asian (14,548)	17,769	2.86
Not Hispanic (14,397)	17,372	2.80
Hispanic (151)	397	0.06
Bangladeshi (102)	121	0.02
Bhutanese (136)	165	0.03
Burmese (41)	42	0.01
Cambodian (25)	54	0.01
Chinese, ex. Taiwanese (3,228)	3,904	0.63
Filipino (2,290)	3,038	0.49
Hmong (3)	4	<0.01
Indian (3,358)	3,946	0.64
Indonesian (60)	83	0.01
Japanese (337)	758	0.12
Korean (1,990)	2,404	0.39
Laotian (148)	177	0.03
Malaysian (19)	27	<0.01
Nepalese (303)	347	0.06
Pakistani (402)	476	0.08
Sri Lankan (68)	85	0.01
Taiwanese (355)	406	0.07
Thai (145)	220	0.04
Vietnamese (670)	814	0.13
Hawaii Native/Pacific Islander (274)	864	0.14
Not Hispanic (192)	661	0.11
Hispanic (82)	203	0.03
Fijian (5)	8	<0.01
Guamanian/Chamorro (110)	164	0.03
Marshallese (1)	1	<0.01
Native Hawaiian (73)	224	0.04
Samoan (28)	80	0.01
White (183,830)	192,897	31.06
Not Hispanic (174,120)	181,450	29.22
Hispanic (9,710)	11,447	1.84

Bel Air North

Place Type: CDP
County: Harford
Population: 30,568†

Ancestry‡	Population	%
African, Sub-Saharan (9)	27	0.09
African (9)	27	0.09
Albanian (13)	13	0.04
American (1,478)	1,478	5.07
Arab (15)	76	0.26
Arab (15)	45	0.15
Lebanese (0)	31	0.11
Australian (0)	20	0.07
Austrian (0)	27	0.09
British (85)	229	0.78

*Notes: † The Census 2010 population figure is used to calculate the percentages in the Hispanic Origin and Race categories. Ancestry percentages are based on the 2006-2010 American Community Survey population (not shown); ‡ Numbers in parentheses indicate the number of people reporting a single ancestry; * Numbers in parentheses indicate the number of persons reporting this race alone, not in combination with any other race; Please refer to the Explanation of Data for more information.*

Canadian (11)	11	0.04
Croatian (0)	15	0.05
Czech (89)	366	1.25
Czechoslovakian (24)	24	0.08
Danish (0)	39	0.13
Dutch (146)	474	1.62
Eastern European (26)	26	0.09
English (1,042)	4,645	15.92
Estonian (0)	29	0.10
European (276)	318	1.09
French, ex. Basque (67)	638	2.19
French Canadian (48)	148	0.51
German (2,603)	9,936	34.06
German Russian (0)	36	0.12
Greek (80)	249	0.85
Hungarian (19)	205	0.70
Iranian (43)	43	0.15
Irish (1,455)	6,896	23.64
Italian (1,064)	3,826	13.12
Latvian (0)	12	0.04
Lithuanian (38)	129	0.44
Northern European (38)	38	0.13
Norwegian (150)	200	0.69
Pennsylvania German (26)	42	0.14
Polish (908)	2,975	10.20
Portuguese (0)	36	0.12
Romanian (13)	13	0.04
Russian (78)	414	1.42
Scandinavian (16)	58	0.20
Scotch-Irish (119)	497	1.70
Scottish (230)	836	2.87
Serbian (0)	30	0.10
Slavic (0)	45	0.15
Slovak (26)	133	0.46
Swedish (28)	392	1.34
Swiss (21)	118	0.40
Turkish (0)	12	0.04
Ukrainian (0)	41	0.14
Welsh (50)	375	1.29
West Indian, ex. Hispanic (0)	9	0.03
Trinidadian/Tobagonian (0)	9	0.03
Yugoslavian (23)	42	0.14

Hispanic Origin	Population	%
Hispanic or Latino (of any race)	724	2.37
Central American, ex. Mexican	100	0.33
Costa Rican	9	0.03
Guatemalan	43	0.14
Honduran	5	0.02
Nicaraguan	11	0.04
Panamanian	11	0.04
Salvadoran	21	0.07
Cuban	42	0.14
Dominican Republic	24	0.08
Mexican	188	0.62
Puerto Rican	170	0.56
South American	118	0.39
Argentinean	15	0.05
Bolivian	3	0.01
Chilean	9	0.03
Colombian	49	0.16
Ecuadorian	5	0.02
Peruvian	27	0.09
Uruguayan	3	0.01
Venezuelan	7	0.02
Other Hispanic or Latino	82	0.27

Race*	Population	%
African-American/Black (1,094)	1,289	4.22
Not Hispanic (1,068)	1,244	4.07
Hispanic (26)	45	0.15
American Indian/Alaska Native (34)	150	0.49
Not Hispanic (33)	138	0.45
Hispanic (1)	12	0.04
Apache (1)	3	0.01
Blackfeet (1)	10	0.03
Cherokee (8)	28	0.09
Chippewa (0)	3	0.01
Creek (0)	1	<0.01
Delaware (0)	4	0.01
Iroquois (1)	1	<0.01
Lumbee (10)	17	0.06
Navajo (0)	1	<0.01
Sioux (1)	6	0.02
Yaqui (1)	4	0.01
Asian (643)	831	2.72
Not Hispanic (640)	823	2.69
Hispanic (3)	8	0.03
Bangladeshi (3)	3	0.01
Cambodian (2)	4	0.01
Chinese, ex. Taiwanese (113)	136	0.44
Filipino (96)	151	0.49
Indian (129)	136	0.44
Japanese (16)	50	0.16
Korean (151)	188	0.62
Malaysian (1)	1	<0.01
Pakistani (30)	31	0.10
Sri Lankan (7)	7	0.02
Taiwanese (1)	1	<0.01
Thai (10)	11	0.04
Vietnamese (63)	70	0.23
Hawaii Native/Pacific Islander (2)	31	0.10
Not Hispanic (2)	27	0.09
Hispanic (0)	4	0.01
Guamanian/Chamorro (0)	1	<0.01
Native Hawaiian (1)	14	0.05
White (28,173)	28,581	93.50
Not Hispanic (27,650)	28,020	91.66
Hispanic (523)	561	1.84

Bel Air South

Place Type: CDP
County: Harford
Population: 47,709†

Ancestry‡	Population	%
African, Sub-Saharan (439)	460	1.01
African (324)	324	0.71
Liberian (0)	21	0.05
Nigerian (46)	46	0.10
Other Sub-Saharan African (69)	69	0.15
American (2,168)	2,168	4.74
Arab (0)	19	0.04
Lebanese (0)	6	0.01
Syrian (0)	13	0.03
Australian (6)	6	0.01
Austrian (0)	21	0.05
Belgian (8)	8	0.02
Brazilian (0)	12	0.03
British (86)	264	0.58
Bulgarian (11)	11	0.02
Canadian (18)	38	0.08
Czech (109)	420	0.92
Czechoslovakian (49)	69	0.15
Danish (28)	71	0.16
Dutch (148)	769	1.68
Eastern European (30)	30	0.07
English (1,331)	5,611	12.26
European (265)	304	0.66
Finnish (66)	66	0.14
French, ex. Basque (328)	1,590	3.47
French Canadian (87)	281	0.61
German (4,458)	14,781	32.29
Greek (175)	369	0.81
Hungarian (76)	383	0.84
Irish (2,425)	10,796	23.59
Italian (2,250)	5,867	12.82
Latvian (11)	33	0.07
Lithuanian (127)	214	0.47
Maltese (10)	20	0.04
Norwegian (83)	204	0.45
Pennsylvania German (58)	69	0.15
Polish (1,146)	3,905	8.53
Russian (240)	499	1.09
Scotch-Irish (236)	700	1.53
Scottish (362)	1,097	2.40
Serbian (10)	10	0.02
Slavic (22)	22	0.05
Slovak (27)	195	0.43
Swedish (14)	226	0.49
Swiss (25)	47	0.10
Ukrainian (106)	247	0.54
Welsh (78)	702	1.53
West Indian, ex. Hispanic (77)	122	0.27
Barbadian (9)	9	0.02
British West Indian (38)	38	0.08
Haitian (7)	7	0.02
Jamaican (23)	23	0.05
Trinidadian/Tobagonian (0)	45	0.10
Yugoslavian (0)	35	0.08

Hispanic Origin	Population	%
Hispanic or Latino (of any race)	1,629	3.41
Central American, ex. Mexican	186	0.39
Costa Rican	7	0.01
Guatemalan	54	0.11
Honduran	34	0.07
Nicaraguan	9	0.02
Panamanian	30	0.06
Salvadoran	52	0.11
Cuban	67	0.14
Dominican Republic	51	0.11
Mexican	337	0.71
Puerto Rican	522	1.09
South American	255	0.53
Argentinean	42	0.09
Bolivian	6	0.01
Chilean	10	0.02
Colombian	74	0.16
Ecuadorian	43	0.09
Paraguayan	1	<0.01
Peruvian	39	0.08
Uruguayan	15	0.03
Venezuelan	22	0.05
Other South American	3	0.01
Other Hispanic or Latino	211	0.44

Race*	Population	%
African-American/Black (3,374)	3,846	8.06
Not Hispanic (3,290)	3,705	7.77
Hispanic (84)	141	0.30
American Indian/Alaska Native (98)	303	0.64
Not Hispanic (74)	251	0.53
Hispanic (24)	52	0.11
Apache (6)	11	0.02
Blackfeet (1)	17	0.04
Cherokee (15)	76	0.16
Chippewa (0)	1	<0.01
Choctaw (0)	2	<0.01
Comanche (3)	4	0.01
Creek (0)	1	<0.01
Delaware (0)	1	<0.01
Inupiat *(Alaska Native)* (0)	3	0.01
Iroquois (0)	3	0.01
Lumbee (7)	13	0.03
Menominee (0)	1	<0.01
Mexican American Ind. (3)	6	0.01
Navajo (1)	1	<0.01
Puget Sound Salish (0)	2	<0.01
Seminole (5)	5	0.01
Sioux (1)	1	<0.01
South American Ind. (2)	2	<0.01
Ute (3)	3	0.01
Asian (1,868)	2,258	4.73
Not Hispanic (1,852)	2,216	4.64
Hispanic (16)	42	0.09
Bangladeshi (1)	2	<0.01
Burmese (9)	9	0.02
Cambodian (3)	5	0.01
Chinese, ex. Taiwanese (288)	371	0.78
Filipino (329)	450	0.94
Indian (524)	576	1.21
Japanese (32)	70	0.15
Korean (261)	332	0.70
Laotian (3)	4	0.01
Nepalese (12)	14	0.03
Pakistani (43)	44	0.09
Sri Lankan (3)	3	0.01
Taiwanese (7)	10	0.02

*Notes: † The Census 2010 population figure is used to calculate the percentages in the Hispanic Origin and Race categories. Ancestry percentages are based on the 2006-2010 American Community Survey population (not shown); ‡ Numbers in parentheses indicate the number of people reporting a single ancestry; * Numbers in parentheses indicate the number of persons reporting this race alone, not in combination with any other race; Please refer to the Explanation of Data for more information.*

	Population	%
Thai (34)	50	0.10
Vietnamese (272)	314	0.66
Hawaii Native/Pacific Islander (41)	92	0.19
Not Hispanic (33)	68	0.14
Hispanic (8)	24	0.05
Guamanian/Chamorro (25)	34	0.07
Native Hawaiian (7)	30	0.06
Samoan (1)	2	<0.01
White (40,945)	41,815	87.65
Not Hispanic (39,933)	40,686	85.28
Hispanic (1,012)	1,129	2.37

Bel Air

Place Type: Town
County: Harford
Population: 10,120†

Ancestry‡	Population	%
American (450)	450	4.43
Australian (0)	8	0.08
Austrian (0)	96	0.94
British (0)	29	0.29
Canadian (8)	16	0.16
Croatian (32)	51	0.50
Czech (61)	132	1.30
Danish (0)	82	0.81
Dutch (32)	197	1.94
English (607)	1,640	16.13
European (70)	90	0.89
Finnish (6)	20	0.20
French, ex. Basque (26)	331	3.26
French Canadian (30)	62	0.61
German (671)	2,361	23.22
Greek (0)	44	0.43
Guyanese (17)	17	0.17
Irish (623)	2,097	20.63
Italian (483)	986	9.70
Lithuanian (32)	50	0.49
Norwegian (11)	73	0.72
Pennsylvania German (16)	16	0.16
Polish (265)	633	6.23
Russian (0)	50	0.49
Scandinavian (0)	17	0.17
Scotch-Irish (90)	334	3.29
Scottish (105)	417	4.10
Slavic (22)	22	0.22
Slovak (15)	34	0.33
Swedish (8)	62	0.61
Ukrainian (33)	82	0.81
Welsh (0)	34	0.33

Hispanic Origin	Population	%
Hispanic or Latino (of any race)	439	4.34
Central American, ex. Mexican	100	0.99
Costa Rican	5	0.05
Guatemalan	12	0.12
Honduran	15	0.15
Nicaraguan	6	0.06
Panamanian	2	0.02
Salvadoran	55	0.54
Other Central American	5	0.05
Cuban	10	0.10
Dominican Republic	12	0.12
Mexican	199	1.97
Puerto Rican	60	0.59
South American	16	0.16
Argentinean	4	0.04
Chilean	2	0.02
Colombian	5	0.05
Ecuadorian	4	0.04
Venezuelan	1	0.01
Other Hispanic or Latino	42	0.42

Race*	Population	%
African-American/Black (448)	543	5.37
Not Hispanic (432)	518	5.12
Hispanic (16)	25	0.25
American Indian/Alaska Native (23)	63	0.62
Not Hispanic (14)	49	0.48
Hispanic (9)	14	0.14
Apache (1)	1	0.01
Blackfeet (1)	2	0.02
Central American Ind. (1)	1	0.01
Cherokee (2)	18	0.18
Iroquois (0)	5	0.05
Lumbee (2)	2	0.02
Mexican American Ind. (2)	4	0.04
Navajo (0)	2	0.02
Asian (182)	253	2.50
Not Hispanic (181)	252	2.49
Hispanic (1)	1	0.01
Bangladeshi (2)	2	0.02
Chinese, ex. Taiwanese (23)	29	0.29
Filipino (16)	31	0.31
Indian (50)	63	0.62
Japanese (4)	17	0.17
Korean (40)	45	0.44
Nepalese (3)	3	0.03
Pakistani (17)	17	0.17
Taiwanese (5)	6	0.06
Thai (5)	8	0.08
Vietnamese (15)	15	0.15
Hawaii Native/Pacific Islander (8)	20	0.20
Not Hispanic (5)	17	0.17
Hispanic (3)	3	0.03
Guamanian/Chamorro (6)	6	0.06
Native Hawaiian (2)	7	0.07
White (9,083)	9,258	91.48
Not Hispanic (8,868)	9,021	89.14
Hispanic (215)	237	2.34

Beltsville

Place Type: CDP
County: Prince George's
Population: 16,772†

Ancestry‡	Population	%
African, Sub-Saharan (1,010)	1,164	7.54
African (404)	467	3.02
Ethiopian (86)	118	0.76
Ghanaian (40)	51	0.33
Kenyan (24)	24	0.16
Nigerian (290)	327	2.12
Sierra Leonean (112)	112	0.73
Other Sub-Saharan African (54)	65	0.42
American (288)	288	1.86
Arab (22)	41	0.27
Arab (0)	9	0.06
Jordanian (10)	20	0.13
Lebanese (12)	12	0.08
Armenian (0)	23	0.15
Austrian (9)	28	0.18
Brazilian (23)	28	0.18
British (20)	29	0.19
Bulgarian (12)	12	0.08
Canadian (13)	13	0.08
Czech (9)	17	0.11
Czechoslovakian (9)	17	0.11
Danish (9)	38	0.25
Dutch (9)	47	0.30
Eastern European (11)	11	0.07
English (227)	1,164	7.54
European (136)	146	0.95
Finnish (15)	15	0.10
French, ex. Basque (0)	146	0.95
French Canadian (11)	40	0.26
German (423)	1,175	7.61
Greek (28)	28	0.18
Guyanese (47)	47	0.30
Irish (407)	1,279	8.28
Italian (192)	541	3.50
Latvian (14)	14	0.09
Lithuanian (4)	17	0.11
Norwegian (13)	24	0.16
Polish (64)	228	1.48
Portuguese (0)	14	0.09
Russian (10)	56	0.36
Scotch-Irish (40)	155	1.00
Scottish (57)	142	0.92
Slovak (24)	52	0.34
Swedish (76)	183	1.18
Swiss (0)	14	0.09
Welsh (0)	60	0.39
West Indian, ex. Hispanic (481)	559	3.62
Haitian (93)	105	0.68
Jamaican (207)	273	1.77
Trinidadian/Tobagonian (108)	108	0.70
West Indian (73)	73	0.47

Hispanic Origin	Population	%
Hispanic or Latino (of any race)	4,539	27.06
Central American, ex. Mexican	2,869	17.11
Costa Rican	9	0.05
Guatemalan	467	2.78
Honduran	166	0.99
Nicaraguan	107	0.64
Panamanian	26	0.16
Salvadoran	2,067	12.32
Other Central American	27	0.16
Cuban	38	0.23
Dominican Republic	287	1.71
Mexican	388	2.31
Puerto Rican	158	0.94
South American	320	1.91
Argentinean	8	0.05
Bolivian	48	0.29
Chilean	9	0.05
Colombian	79	0.47
Ecuadorian	22	0.13
Paraguayan	5	0.03
Peruvian	127	0.76
Uruguayan	15	0.09
Venezuelan	6	0.04
Other South American	1	0.01
Other Hispanic or Latino	479	2.86

Race*	Population	%
African-American/Black (5,846)	6,151	36.67
Not Hispanic (5,631)	5,843	34.84
Hispanic (215)	308	1.84
American Indian/Alaska Native (88)	261	1.56
Not Hispanic (34)	132	0.79
Hispanic (54)	129	0.77
Apache (0)	2	0.01
Blackfeet (0)	3	0.02
Central American Ind. (9)	13	0.08
Cherokee (4)	24	0.14
Chippewa (1)	1	0.01
Creek (0)	1	0.01
Iroquois (0)	2	0.01
Mexican American Ind. (0)	6	0.04
Navajo (0)	3	0.02
Shoshone (1)	1	0.01
Sioux (1)	1	0.01
South American Ind. (2)	6	0.04
Spanish American Ind. (8)	8	0.05
Yaqui (2)	2	0.01
Asian (1,593)	1,807	10.77
Not Hispanic (1,582)	1,783	10.63
Hispanic (11)	24	0.14
Bangladeshi (23)	44	0.26
Burmese (10)	10	0.06
Cambodian (27)	32	0.19
Chinese, ex. Taiwanese (292)	335	2.00
Filipino (171)	209	1.25
Indian (531)	628	3.74
Indonesian (4)	7	0.04
Japanese (12)	32	0.19
Korean (109)	127	0.76
Laotian (0)	2	0.01
Malaysian (3)	3	0.02
Nepalese (5)	5	0.03
Pakistani (55)	63	0.38
Sri Lankan (2)	3	0.02
Taiwanese (8)	9	0.05
Thai (15)	15	0.09
Vietnamese (259)	284	1.69
Hawaii Native/Pacific Islander (8)	54	0.32

*Notes: † The Census 2010 population figure is used to calculate the percentages in the Hispanic Origin and Race categories. Ancestry percentages are based on the 2006-2010 American Community Survey population (not shown); ‡ Numbers in parentheses indicate the number of people reporting a single ancestry; * Numbers in parentheses indicate the number of persons reporting this race alone, not in combination with any other race; Please refer to the Explanation of Data for more information.*

Not Hispanic (7)	31	0.18
Hispanic (1)	23	0.14
Native Hawaiian (1)	5	0.03
White (6,106)	6,550	39.05
Not Hispanic (4,508)	4,729	28.20
Hispanic (1,598)	1,821	10.86

Bensville

Place Type: CDP
County: Charles
Population: 11,923†

Ancestry‡	Population	%
African, Sub-Saharan (294)	313	2.68
African (294)	313	2.68
American (705)	705	6.03
Arab (0)	26	0.22
Arab (0)	13	0.11
Other Arab (0)	13	0.11
Austrian (0)	48	0.41
Canadian (0)	4	0.03
Croatian (0)	21	0.18
Czech (0)	41	0.35
Czechoslovakian (0)	18	0.15
Dutch (106)	142	1.21
English (302)	1,025	8.77
European (102)	102	0.87
Finnish (0)	26	0.22
French, ex. Basque (22)	517	4.42
French Canadian (16)	34	0.29
German (495)	1,678	14.35
Guyanese (71)	71	0.61
Hungarian (0)	135	1.15
Irish (412)	1,456	12.45
Israeli (32)	32	0.27
Italian (292)	793	6.78
Lithuanian (0)	7	0.06
Norwegian (32)	87	0.74
Polish (18)	105	0.90
Portuguese (51)	143	1.22
Scandinavian (34)	34	0.29
Scotch-Irish (75)	233	1.99
Scottish (110)	266	2.27
Slovak (0)	12	0.10
Swedish (15)	43	0.37
Swiss (0)	103	0.88
Ukrainian (139)	139	1.19
Welsh (0)	35	0.30
West Indian, ex. Hispanic (38)	220	1.88
Dutch West Indian (0)	11	0.09
Jamaican (38)	190	1.62
West Indian (0)	19	0.16

Hispanic Origin	Population	%
Hispanic or Latino (of any race)	519	4.35
Central American, ex. Mexican	93	0.78
Costa Rican	2	0.02
Guatemalan	7	0.06
Honduran	20	0.17
Nicaraguan	9	0.08
Panamanian	23	0.19
Salvadoran	32	0.27
Cuban	39	0.33
Dominican Republic	8	0.07
Mexican	129	1.08
Puerto Rican	135	1.13
South American	71	0.60
Bolivian	10	0.08
Colombian	18	0.15
Ecuadorian	1	0.01
Peruvian	27	0.23
Uruguayan	1	0.01
Venezuelan	10	0.08
Other South American	4	0.03
Other Hispanic or Latino	44	0.37

Race*	Population	%
African-American/Black (5,319)	5,642	47.32
Not Hispanic (5,238)	5,512	46.23
Hispanic (81)	130	1.09
American Indian/Alaska Native (67)	197	1.65
Not Hispanic (59)	180	1.51
Hispanic (8)	17	0.14
Blackfeet (1)	7	0.06
Cherokee (7)	49	0.41
Chickasaw (0)	2	0.02
Choctaw (0)	3	0.03
Comanche (0)	1	0.01
Inupiat *(Alaska Native)* (0)	2	0.02
Iroquois (0)	1	0.01
Mexican American Ind. (1)	1	0.01
Potawatomi (1)	1	0.01
Pueblo (3)	3	0.03
Sioux (0)	2	0.02
South American Ind. (3)	3	0.03
Asian (507)	696	5.84
Not Hispanic (496)	655	5.49
Hispanic (11)	41	0.34
Cambodian (2)	6	0.05
Chinese, ex. Taiwanese (47)	56	0.47
Filipino (257)	355	2.98
Indian (72)	97	0.81
Indonesian (0)	3	0.03
Japanese (11)	22	0.18
Korean (59)	83	0.70
Nepalese (3)	3	0.03
Pakistani (7)	7	0.06
Taiwanese (1)	3	0.03
Thai (3)	14	0.12
Vietnamese (31)	35	0.29
Hawaii Native/Pacific Islander (10)	33	0.28
Not Hispanic (10)	33	0.28
Guamanian/Chamorro (2)	4	0.03
Native Hawaiian (6)	8	0.07
Samoan (1)	2	0.02
White (5,370)	5,742	48.16
Not Hispanic (5,131)	5,454	45.74
Hispanic (239)	288	2.42

Bethesda

Place Type: CDP
County: Montgomery
Population: 60,858†

Ancestry‡	Population	%
African, Sub-Saharan (684)	915	1.56
African (384)	515	0.88
Ethiopian (124)	124	0.21
Ghanaian (33)	33	0.06
Nigerian (29)	29	0.05
Senegalese (0)	10	0.02
Other Sub-Saharan African (114)	204	0.35
Albanian (108)	108	0.18
Alsatian (17)	29	0.05
American (1,683)	1,683	2.88
Arab (600)	792	1.35
Arab (9)	9	0.02
Egyptian (145)	145	0.25
Iraqi (42)	42	0.07
Lebanese (244)	372	0.64
Moroccan (28)	28	0.05
Syrian (12)	24	0.04
Other Arab (120)	172	0.29
Armenian (124)	316	0.54
Assyrian/Chaldean/Syriac (0)	12	0.02
Australian (20)	57	0.10
Austrian (157)	619	1.06
Belgian (28)	187	0.32
Brazilian (200)	256	0.44
British (514)	1,028	1.76
Bulgarian (143)	154	0.26
Canadian (56)	136	0.23
Carpatho Rusyn (10)	10	0.02
Celtic (7)	7	0.01
Croatian (30)	91	0.16
Cypriot (10)	10	0.02
Czech (108)	268	0.46
Czechoslovakian (65)	104	0.18
Danish (76)	249	0.43
Dutch (214)	742	1.27
Eastern European (1,361)	1,513	2.58
English (1,852)	6,683	11.42
Estonian (25)	50	0.09
European (1,407)	1,661	2.84
Finnish (92)	146	0.25
French, ex. Basque (1,046)	2,624	4.48
French Canadian (85)	243	0.42
German (2,183)	8,234	14.07
Greek (331)	684	1.17
Guyanese (0)	23	0.04
Hungarian (179)	749	1.28
Iranian (713)	786	1.34
Irish (2,604)	8,142	13.91
Israeli (17)	130	0.22
Italian (1,437)	4,244	7.25
Latvian (11)	51	0.09
Lithuanian (283)	469	0.80
Luxemburger (0)	9	0.02
Macedonian (21)	21	0.04
Northern European (132)	162	0.28
Norwegian (213)	844	1.44
Pennsylvania German (11)	11	0.02
Polish (998)	3,121	5.33
Portuguese (153)	228	0.39
Romanian (188)	485	0.83
Russian (1,842)	4,117	7.03
Scandinavian (49)	164	0.28
Scotch-Irish (400)	1,105	1.89
Scottish (573)	2,176	3.72
Serbian (39)	96	0.16
Slavic (0)	28	0.05
Slovak (23)	169	0.29
Slovene (10)	17	0.03
Swedish (181)	738	1.26
Swiss (105)	349	0.60
Turkish (132)	142	0.24
Ukrainian (318)	596	1.02
Welsh (79)	429	0.73
West Indian, ex. Hispanic (276)	302	0.52
Barbadian (29)	29	0.05
Haitian (107)	118	0.20
Jamaican (10)	25	0.04
Trinidadian/Tobagonian (114)	114	0.19
West Indian (16)	16	0.03
Yugoslavian (67)	132	0.23

Hispanic Origin	Population	%
Hispanic or Latino (of any race)	4,144	6.81
Central American, ex. Mexican	563	0.93
Costa Rican	47	0.08
Guatemalan	120	0.20
Honduran	99	0.16
Nicaraguan	62	0.10
Panamanian	38	0.06
Salvadoran	193	0.32
Other Central American	4	0.01
Cuban	253	0.42
Dominican Republic	66	0.11
Mexican	609	1.00
Puerto Rican	230	0.38
South American	1,755	2.88
Argentinean	376	0.62
Bolivian	133	0.22
Chilean	183	0.30
Colombian	347	0.57
Ecuadorian	125	0.21
Paraguayan	53	0.09
Peruvian	313	0.51
Uruguayan	79	0.13
Venezuelan	137	0.23
Other South American	9	0.01
Other Hispanic or Latino	668	1.10

Race*	Population	%
African-American/Black (2,014)	2,374	3.90
Not Hispanic (1,944)	2,253	3.70
Hispanic (70)	121	0.20
American Indian/Alaska Native (82)	275	0.45

*Notes: † The Census 2010 population figure is used to calculate the percentages in the Hispanic Origin and Race categories. Ancestry percentages are based on the 2006-2010 American Community Survey population (not shown); ‡ Numbers in parentheses indicate the number of people reporting a single ancestry; * Numbers in parentheses indicate the number of persons reporting this race alone, not in combination with any other race; Please refer to the Explanation of Data for more information.*

	Population	%
Not Hispanic (59)	202	0.33
Hispanic (23)	73	0.12
Blackfeet (0)	5	0.01
Canadian/French Am. Ind. (1)	2	<0.01
Central American Ind. (2)	5	0.01
Cherokee (10)	41	0.07
Chickasaw (1)	7	0.01
Chippewa (0)	2	<0.01
Choctaw (1)	4	0.01
Colville (0)	1	<0.01
Comanche (5)	6	0.01
Creek (0)	3	<0.01
Delaware (2)	2	<0.01
Iroquois (2)	5	0.01
Lumbee (2)	2	<0.01
Mexican American Ind. (1)	3	<0.01
Navajo (5)	5	0.01
Osage (1)	2	<0.01
Ottawa (1)	2	<0.01
Paiute (1)	1	<0.01
Pima (1)	1	<0.01
Pueblo (1)	2	<0.01
Shoshone (0)	2	<0.01
Sioux (1)	3	<0.01
South American Ind. (8)	26	0.04
Spanish American Ind. (2)	2	<0.01
Tohono O'Odham (0)	1	<0.01
Asian (5,681)	6,828	11.22
Not Hispanic (5,647)	6,740	11.07
Hispanic (34)	88	0.14
Bangladeshi (62)	72	0.12
Bhutanese (1)	1	<0.01
Burmese (34)	35	0.06
Cambodian (16)	21	0.03
Chinese, ex. Taiwanese (1,512)	1,834	3.01
Filipino (475)	628	1.03
Indian (1,327)	1,573	2.58
Indonesian (87)	103	0.17
Japanese (658)	823	1.35
Korean (679)	789	1.30
Laotian (6)	14	0.02
Malaysian (10)	21	0.03
Nepalese (20)	26	0.04
Pakistani (114)	139	0.23
Sri Lankan (127)	145	0.24
Taiwanese (128)	170	0.28
Thai (95)	129	0.21
Vietnamese (122)	178	0.29
Hawaii Native/Pacific Islander (38)	100	0.16
Not Hispanic (37)	97	0.16
Hispanic (1)	3	<0.01
Fijian (0)	4	0.01
Guamanian/Chamorro (13)	28	0.05
Marshallese (2)	2	<0.01
Native Hawaiian (5)	19	0.03
Samoan (1)	8	0.01
Tongan (8)	8	0.01
White (50,642)	52,194	85.76
Not Hispanic (47,327)	48,679	79.99
Hispanic (3,315)	3,515	5.78

Bladensburg

Place Type: Town
County: Prince George's
Population: 9,148†

Ancestry‡	Population	%
African, Sub-Saharan (797)	905	10.15
African (297)	370	4.15
Ghanaian (249)	284	3.18
Nigerian (166)	166	1.86
Other Sub-Saharan African (85)	85	0.95
American (13)	13	0.15
Arab (21)	39	0.44
Egyptian (21)	21	0.24
Lebanese (0)	9	0.10
Palestinian (0)	9	0.10
Canadian (0)	12	0.13
Danish (0)	26	0.29
Dutch (0)	31	0.35
English (36)	109	1.22
European (10)	25	0.28
French, ex. Basque (27)	55	0.62
German (21)	97	1.09
Greek (15)	24	0.27
Guyanese (11)	59	0.66
Hungarian (0)	9	0.10
Irish (28)	155	1.74
Italian (35)	35	0.39
Polish (11)	11	0.12
Scotch-Irish (0)	11	0.12
Scottish (0)	12	0.13
Swiss (0)	21	0.24
West Indian, ex. Hispanic (225)	286	3.21
Barbadian (17)	30	0.34
Jamaican (78)	113	1.27
West Indian (130)	143	1.60

Hispanic Origin	Population	%
Hispanic or Latino (of any race)	2,463	26.92
Central American, ex. Mexican	1,043	11.40
Costa Rican	1	0.01
Guatemalan	146	1.60
Honduran	59	0.64
Nicaraguan	39	0.43
Panamanian	15	0.16
Salvadoran	775	8.47
Other Central American	8	0.09
Cuban	19	0.21
Dominican Republic	69	0.75
Mexican	903	9.87
Puerto Rican	66	0.72
South American	72	0.79
Argentinean	1	0.01
Bolivian	8	0.09
Chilean	3	0.03
Colombian	8	0.09
Ecuadorian	29	0.32
Peruvian	17	0.19
Venezuelan	5	0.05
Other South American	1	0.01
Other Hispanic or Latino	291	3.18

Race*	Population	%
African-American/Black (5,999)	6,132	67.03
Not Hispanic (5,885)	5,989	65.47
Hispanic (114)	143	1.56
American Indian/Alaska Native (50)	118	1.29
Not Hispanic (18)	56	0.61
Hispanic (32)	62	0.68
Blackfeet (0)	8	0.09
Central American Ind. (0)	2	0.02
Cherokee (7)	25	0.27
Cree (0)	1	0.01
Creek (0)	1	0.01
Lumbee (0)	1	0.01
Mexican American Ind. (11)	23	0.25
Osage (0)	2	0.02
Asian (187)	224	2.45
Not Hispanic (184)	212	2.32
Hispanic (3)	12	0.13
Bangladeshi (4)	4	0.04
Burmese (4)	4	0.04
Cambodian (21)	23	0.25
Chinese, ex. Taiwanese (15)	22	0.24
Filipino (48)	56	0.61
Hmong (1)	3	0.03
Indian (27)	34	0.37
Indonesian (0)	2	0.02
Japanese (1)	2	0.02
Korean (42)	44	0.48
Laotian (3)	3	0.03
Pakistani (7)	9	0.10
Thai (0)	2	0.02
Vietnamese (8)	8	0.09
Hawaii Native/Pacific Islander (2)	7	0.08
Not Hispanic (2)	7	0.08
Native Hawaiian (2)	2	0.02
White (1,149)	1,325	14.48
Not Hispanic (460)	532	5.82
Hispanic (689)	793	8.67

Bowie

Place Type: City
County: Prince George's
Population: 54,727†

Ancestry‡	Population	%
African, Sub-Saharan (3,193)	3,354	6.18
African (2,016)	2,095	3.86
Cape Verdean (68)	132	0.24
Ethiopian (74)	74	0.14
Ghanaian (19)	19	0.03
Kenyan (25)	25	0.05
Nigerian (851)	863	1.59
Sierra Leonean (36)	42	0.08
Other Sub-Saharan African (104)	104	0.19
Albanian (14)	14	0.03
American (1,360)	1,360	2.50
Arab (65)	202	0.37
Arab (21)	29	0.05
Iraqi (0)	57	0.10
Lebanese (9)	50	0.09
Moroccan (12)	12	0.02
Syrian (0)	31	0.06
Other Arab (23)	23	0.04
Armenian (0)	50	0.09
Australian (12)	12	0.02
Austrian (52)	196	0.36
Belgian (8)	30	0.06
Brazilian (30)	56	0.10
British (179)	503	0.93
Bulgarian (11)	11	0.02
Canadian (41)	144	0.27
Carpatho Rusyn (0)	8	0.01
Celtic (9)	38	0.07
Croatian (30)	30	0.06
Czech (0)	115	0.21
Czechoslovakian (27)	53	0.10
Danish (42)	90	0.17
Dutch (80)	414	0.76
Eastern European (28)	28	0.05
English (1,104)	4,129	7.60
Estonian (10)	10	0.02
European (542)	673	1.24
Finnish (7)	43	0.08
French, ex. Basque (169)	882	1.62
French Canadian (119)	333	0.61
German (1,469)	6,535	12.03
Greek (55)	196	0.36
Guyanese (22)	22	0.04
Hungarian (38)	266	0.49
Iranian (6)	10	0.02
Irish (1,763)	5,806	10.69
Italian (917)	2,531	4.66
Latvian (0)	11	0.02
Lithuanian (97)	271	0.50
Northern European (96)	107	0.20
Norwegian (56)	349	0.64
Polish (385)	1,325	2.44
Portuguese (39)	185	0.34
Romanian (18)	76	0.14
Russian (156)	505	0.93
Scandinavian (0)	8	0.01
Scotch-Irish (209)	795	1.46
Scottish (119)	651	1.20
Serbian (13)	22	0.04
Slavic (0)	33	0.06
Slovak (49)	150	0.28
Swedish (131)	558	1.03
Swiss (36)	68	0.13
Ukrainian (37)	77	0.14
Welsh (76)	388	0.71
West Indian, ex. Hispanic (1,000)	1,391	2.56
Bahamian (0)	19	0.03
Barbadian (13)	13	0.02
Bermudan (35)	35	0.06
British West Indian (7)	7	0.01

*Notes: † The Census 2010 population figure is used to calculate the percentages in the Hispanic Origin and Race categories. Ancestry percentages are based on the 2006-2010 American Community Survey population (not shown); ‡ Numbers in parentheses indicate the number of people reporting a single ancestry; * Numbers in parentheses indicate the number of persons reporting this race alone, not in combination with any other race; Please refer to the Explanation of Data for more information.*

Haitian (83)	128	0.24
Jamaican (700)	828	1.52
Trinidadian/Tobagonian (133)	255	0.47
West Indian (29)	106	0.20
Yugoslavian (0)	25	0.05

Hispanic Origin	Population	%
Hispanic or Latino (of any race)	3,086	5.64
Central American, ex. Mexican	916	1.67
Costa Rican	25	0.05
Guatemalan	120	0.22
Honduran	79	0.14
Nicaraguan	70	0.13
Panamanian	96	0.18
Salvadoran	519	0.95
Other Central American	7	0.01
Cuban	129	0.24
Dominican Republic	124	0.23
Mexican	651	1.19
Puerto Rican	506	0.92
South American	394	0.72
Argentinean	19	0.03
Bolivian	71	0.13
Chilean	26	0.05
Colombian	103	0.19
Ecuadorian	59	0.11
Paraguayan	9	0.02
Peruvian	74	0.14
Uruguayan	9	0.02
Venezuelan	22	0.04
Other South American	2	<0.01
Other Hispanic or Latino	366	0.67

Race*	Population	%
African-American/Black (26,632)	27,948	51.07
Not Hispanic (26,199)	27,364	50.00
Hispanic (433)	584	1.07
American Indian/Alaska Native (144)	658	1.20
Not Hispanic (115)	576	1.05
Hispanic (29)	82	0.15
Apache (2)	6	0.01
Blackfeet (2)	42	0.08
Central American Ind. (1)	14	0.03
Cherokee (16)	127	0.23
Cheyenne (0)	1	<0.01
Chickasaw (1)	7	0.01
Chippewa (1)	2	<0.01
Choctaw (1)	14	0.03
Comanche (0)	5	0.01
Creek (1)	13	0.02
Delaware (1)	2	<0.01
Iroquois (0)	3	0.01
Kiowa (2)	8	0.01
Lumbee (7)	9	0.02
Mexican American Ind. (2)	6	0.01
Navajo (0)	1	<0.01
Ottawa (1)	1	<0.01
Potawatomi (1)	1	<0.01
Puget Sound Salish (0)	1	<0.01
Seminole (0)	6	0.01
Sioux (0)	8	0.01
South American Ind. (1)	4	0.01
Spanish American Ind. (2)	3	0.01
Tlingit-Haida *(Alaska Native)* (2)	2	<0.01
Asian (2,265)	2,835	5.18
Not Hispanic (2,229)	2,767	5.06
Hispanic (36)	68	0.12
Bangladeshi (14)	14	0.03
Burmese (2)	2	<0.01
Cambodian (31)	38	0.07
Chinese, ex. Taiwanese (310)	420	0.77
Filipino (723)	873	1.60
Hmong (0)	1	<0.01
Indian (481)	608	1.11
Indonesian (8)	16	0.03
Japanese (57)	142	0.26
Korean (185)	260	0.48
Laotian (10)	24	0.04
Malaysian (1)	2	<0.01
Nepalese (4)	4	0.01
Pakistani (141)	155	0.28
Sri Lankan (4)	8	0.01
Taiwanese (7)	16	0.03
Thai (25)	63	0.12
Vietnamese (186)	222	0.41
Hawaii Native/Pacific Islander (36)	97	0.18
Not Hispanic (15)	65	0.12
Hispanic (21)	32	0.06
Guamanian/Chamorro (24)	34	0.06
Native Hawaiian (3)	21	0.04
Samoan (4)	7	0.01
White (22,659)	24,048	43.94
Not Hispanic (21,287)	22,488	41.09
Hispanic (1,372)	1,560	2.85

Brock Hall

Place Type: CDP
County: Prince George's
Population: 9,552[†]

Ancestry[‡]	Population	%
African, Sub-Saharan (584)	817	10.02
African (499)	513	6.29
Liberian (0)	114	1.40
Nigerian (48)	137	1.68
Sierra Leonean (0)	16	0.20
Other Sub-Saharan African (37)	37	0.45
American (182)	182	2.23
Czech (0)	12	0.15
Dutch (0)	28	0.34
English (27)	114	1.40
European (38)	38	0.47
French, ex. Basque (14)	41	0.50
German (74)	119	1.46
Guyanese (5)	5	0.06
Irish (43)	170	2.09
Italian (28)	156	1.91
Northern European (34)	34	0.42
Norwegian (0)	17	0.21
Polish (12)	28	0.34
Scottish (14)	40	0.49
Welsh (0)	11	0.13
West Indian, ex. Hispanic (89)	242	2.97
Bahamian (0)	8	0.10
Barbadian (0)	45	0.55
Haitian (15)	15	0.18
Jamaican (63)	140	1.72
Trinidadian/Tobagonian (0)	10	0.12
West Indian (11)	24	0.29

Hispanic Origin	Population	%
Hispanic or Latino (of any race)	192	2.01
Central American, ex. Mexican	77	0.81
Guatemalan	5	0.05
Honduran	3	0.03
Nicaraguan	4	0.04
Panamanian	30	0.31
Salvadoran	35	0.37
Cuban	13	0.14
Dominican Republic	2	0.02
Mexican	23	0.24
Puerto Rican	34	0.36
South American	21	0.22
Bolivian	5	0.05
Colombian	4	0.04
Ecuadorian	5	0.05
Peruvian	3	0.03
Venezuelan	4	0.04
Other Hispanic or Latino	22	0.23

Race*	Population	%
African-American/Black (8,503)	8,691	90.99
Not Hispanic (8,428)	8,600	90.03
Hispanic (75)	91	0.95
American Indian/Alaska Native (22)	89	0.93
Not Hispanic (20)	83	0.87
Hispanic (2)	6	0.06
Blackfeet (0)	3	0.03
Canadian/French Am. Ind. (0)	1	0.01
Central American Ind. (0)	2	0.02
Cherokee (0)	14	0.15
Choctaw (0)	2	0.02
Creek (0)	1	0.01
Lumbee (4)	4	0.04
Sioux (0)	1	0.01
Asian (185)	252	2.64
Not Hispanic (183)	250	2.62
Hispanic (2)	2	0.02
Burmese (1)	1	0.01
Chinese, ex. Taiwanese (7)	17	0.18
Filipino (86)	101	1.06
Indian (56)	82	0.86
Japanese (0)	5	0.05
Korean (13)	17	0.18
Laotian (1)	3	0.03
Pakistani (2)	7	0.07
Sri Lankan (1)	1	0.01
Thai (2)	4	0.04
Vietnamese (9)	10	0.10
Hawaii Native/Pacific Islander (2)	7	0.07
Not Hispanic (2)	7	0.07
Guamanian/Chamorro (1)	3	0.03
Native Hawaiian (0)	1	0.01
White (551)	657	6.88
Not Hispanic (509)	606	6.34
Hispanic (42)	51	0.53

Brooklyn Park

Place Type: CDP
County: Anne Arundel
Population: 14,373[†]

Ancestry[‡]	Population	%
African, Sub-Saharan (29)	59	0.42
African (0)	30	0.21
Other Sub-Saharan African (29)	29	0.20
American (812)	812	5.73
Arab (60)	237	1.67
Egyptian (44)	205	1.45
Other Arab (16)	32	0.23
Austrian (8)	17	0.12
British (8)	45	0.32
Czech (64)	145	1.02
Danish (0)	11	0.08
Dutch (11)	150	1.06
English (367)	1,126	7.94
Estonian (9)	19	0.13
European (34)	43	0.30
French, ex. Basque (107)	242	1.71
French Canadian (15)	30	0.21
German (1,132)	3,748	26.44
Greek (19)	36	0.25
Guyanese (19)	19	0.13
Hungarian (14)	69	0.49
Irish (458)	2,031	14.33
Italian (159)	551	3.89
Lithuanian (113)	189	1.33
Northern European (17)	17	0.12
Norwegian (9)	9	0.06
Pennsylvania German (0)	16	0.11
Polish (387)	1,194	8.42
Portuguese (0)	12	0.08
Russian (33)	50	0.35
Scotch-Irish (120)	241	1.70
Scottish (44)	168	1.18
Slovak (20)	33	0.23
Swedish (0)	12	0.08
Swiss (0)	17	0.12
Turkish (7)	7	0.05
Ukrainian (14)	32	0.23
Welsh (10)	70	0.49
West Indian, ex. Hispanic (0)	13	0.09
Bermudan (0)	13	0.09

Hispanic Origin	Population	%
Hispanic or Latino (of any race)	858	5.97
Central American, ex. Mexican	248	1.73
Guatemalan	66	0.46

*Notes: † The Census 2010 population figure is used to calculate the percentages in the Hispanic Origin and Race categories. Ancestry percentages are based on the 2006-2010 American Community Survey population (not shown); ‡ Numbers in parentheses indicate the number of people reporting a single ancestry; * Numbers in parentheses indicate the number of persons reporting this race alone, not in combination with any other race; Please refer to the Explanation of Data for more information.*

Honduran	47	0.33
Nicaraguan	8	0.06
Panamanian	10	0.07
Salvadoran	117	0.81
Cuban	18	0.13
Dominican Republic	13	0.09
Mexican	283	1.97
Puerto Rican	132	0.92
South American	87	0.61
Argentinean	1	0.01
Bolivian	10	0.07
Chilean	8	0.06
Colombian	12	0.08
Ecuadorian	20	0.14
Peruvian	31	0.22
Uruguayan	4	0.03
Venezuelan	1	0.01
Other Hispanic or Latino	77	0.54

Race*	Population	%
African-American/Black (2,398)	2,668	18.56
Not Hispanic (2,362)	2,604	18.12
Hispanic (36)	64	0.45
American Indian/Alaska Native (56)	175	1.22
Not Hispanic (50)	159	1.11
Hispanic (6)	16	0.11
Apache (0)	5	0.03
Blackfeet (1)	5	0.03
Cherokee (10)	45	0.31
Chippewa (3)	3	0.02
Choctaw (0)	1	0.01
Iroquois (1)	5	0.03
Lumbee (6)	10	0.07
Mexican American Ind. (1)	1	0.01
Ottawa (2)	2	0.01
Pueblo (3)	3	0.02
Sioux (1)	1	0.01
South American Ind. (1)	1	0.01
Asian (401)	494	3.44
Not Hispanic (400)	487	3.39
Hispanic (1)	7	0.05
Cambodian (2)	2	0.01
Chinese, ex. Taiwanese (87)	95	0.66
Filipino (180)	241	1.68
Indian (36)	46	0.32
Japanese (5)	10	0.07
Korean (29)	46	0.32
Laotian (6)	7	0.05
Pakistani (24)	24	0.17
Thai (2)	3	0.02
Vietnamese (21)	22	0.15
Hawaii Native/Pacific Islander (6)	34	0.24
Not Hispanic (5)	31	0.22
Hispanic (1)	3	0.02
Guamanian/Chamorro (3)	8	0.06
Native Hawaiian (1)	9	0.06
Samoan (2)	8	0.06
Tongan (0)	1	0.01
White (10,618)	11,035	76.78
Not Hispanic (10,282)	10,626	73.93
Hispanic (336)	409	2.85

Burtonsville

Place Type: CDP
County: Montgomery
Population: 8,323†

Ancestry‡	Population	%
African, Sub-Saharan (1,248)	1,271	13.77
African (288)	288	3.12
Ethiopian (167)	167	1.81
Ghanaian (160)	160	1.73
Kenyan (140)	140	1.52
Liberian (129)	129	1.40
Nigerian (276)	276	2.99
South African (18)	18	0.19
Ugandan (70)	70	0.76
Other Sub-Saharan African (0)	23	0.25
American (278)	278	3.01
Arab (104)	160	1.73
Arab (6)	6	0.06
Lebanese (82)	138	1.49
Moroccan (16)	16	0.17
Australian (9)	25	0.27
Brazilian (33)	33	0.36
British (0)	2	0.02
Czech (5)	12	0.13
Dutch (0)	55	0.60
English (96)	478	5.18
European (136)	171	1.85
French, ex. Basque (29)	117	1.27
German (140)	643	6.96
Guyanese (87)	87	0.94
Irish (213)	544	5.89
Italian (112)	349	3.78
Polish (0)	166	1.80
Romanian (14)	14	0.15
Russian (176)	217	2.35
Scandinavian (6)	6	0.06
Scotch-Irish (0)	34	0.37
Scottish (0)	70	0.76
Slavic (17)	25	0.27
Slovak (10)	10	0.11
Swiss (0)	31	0.34
Ukrainian (20)	20	0.22
Welsh (0)	11	0.12
West Indian, ex. Hispanic (218)	278	3.01
Haitian (32)	32	0.35
Jamaican (186)	246	2.66

Hispanic Origin	Population	%
Hispanic or Latino (of any race)	739	8.88
Central American, ex. Mexican	350	4.21
Costa Rican	4	0.05
Guatemalan	33	0.40
Honduran	17	0.20
Nicaraguan	41	0.49
Panamanian	15	0.18
Salvadoran	239	2.87
Other Central American	1	0.01
Cuban	31	0.37
Dominican Republic	29	0.35
Mexican	67	0.80
Puerto Rican	62	0.74
South American	118	1.42
Argentinean	7	0.08
Bolivian	17	0.20
Chilean	6	0.07
Colombian	19	0.23
Ecuadorian	5	0.06
Paraguayan	8	0.10
Peruvian	43	0.52
Uruguayan	6	0.07
Venezuelan	5	0.06
Other South American	2	0.02
Other Hispanic or Latino	82	0.99

Race*	Population	%
African-American/Black (3,190)	3,341	40.14
Not Hispanic (3,142)	3,270	39.29
Hispanic (48)	71	0.85
American Indian/Alaska Native (29)	88	1.06
Not Hispanic (13)	60	0.72
Hispanic (16)	28	0.34
Blackfeet (0)	8	0.10
Cherokee (0)	6	0.07
Creek (2)	2	0.02
Delaware (0)	1	0.01
Mexican American Ind. (8)	8	0.10
Navajo (0)	3	0.04
Seminole (0)	3	0.04
Asian (1,702)	1,828	21.96
Not Hispanic (1,688)	1,809	21.73
Hispanic (14)	19	0.23
Bangladeshi (26)	32	0.38
Burmese (1)	1	0.01
Cambodian (11)	11	0.13
Chinese, ex. Taiwanese (139)	154	1.85
Filipino (88)	101	1.21
Indian (797)	867	10.42
Indonesian (1)	2	0.02
Japanese (5)	12	0.14
Korean (233)	240	2.88
Malaysian (3)	8	0.10
Nepalese (29)	29	0.35
Pakistani (149)	160	1.92
Sri Lankan (6)	11	0.13
Taiwanese (10)	11	0.13
Thai (5)	8	0.10
Vietnamese (150)	157	1.89
Hawaii Native/Pacific Islander (2)	8	0.10
Not Hispanic (2)	6	0.07
Hispanic (0)	2	0.02
Native Hawaiian (2)	5	0.06
White (2,774)	2,980	35.80
Not Hispanic (2,468)	2,624	31.53
Hispanic (306)	356	4.28

California

Place Type: CDP
County: St. Mary's
Population: 11,857†

Ancestry‡	Population	%
African, Sub-Saharan (174)	209	1.75
African (12)	35	0.29
Nigerian (162)	174	1.45
American (1,001)	1,001	8.36
Arab (10)	18	0.15
Lebanese (10)	18	0.15
Armenian (0)	16	0.13
Austrian (0)	9	0.08
Belgian (11)	11	0.09
British (11)	50	0.42
Canadian (23)	32	0.27
Croatian (11)	21	0.18
Czech (14)	238	1.99
Dutch (37)	112	0.94
Eastern European (0)	8	0.07
English (1,054)	1,999	16.70
European (268)	268	2.24
Finnish (0)	18	0.15
French, ex. Basque (26)	187	1.56
French Canadian (76)	89	0.74
German (350)	1,932	16.14
Greek (8)	8	0.07
Hungarian (15)	27	0.23
Irish (333)	1,461	12.21
Italian (166)	335	2.80
Norwegian (14)	264	2.21
Pennsylvania German (14)	14	0.12
Polish (126)	321	2.68
Portuguese (57)	139	1.16
Russian (0)	42	0.35
Scandinavian (0)	7	0.06
Scotch-Irish (63)	165	1.38
Scottish (210)	433	3.62
Serbian (9)	9	0.08
Slavic (21)	21	0.18
Slovak (27)	54	0.45
Slovene (12)	21	0.18
Swedish (16)	134	1.12
Swiss (13)	21	0.18
Ukrainian (8)	8	0.07
Welsh (0)	99	0.83
West Indian, ex. Hispanic (65)	77	0.64
Jamaican (65)	77	0.64

Hispanic Origin	Population	%
Hispanic or Latino (of any race)	678	5.72
Central American, ex. Mexican	78	0.66
Costa Rican	6	0.05
Guatemalan	26	0.22
Honduran	2	0.02
Nicaraguan	6	0.05
Panamanian	13	0.11
Salvadoran	25	0.21
Cuban	18	0.15

*Notes: † The Census 2010 population figure is used to calculate the percentages in the Hispanic Origin and Race categories. Ancestry percentages are based on the 2006-2010 American Community Survey population (not shown); ‡ Numbers in parentheses indicate the number of people reporting a single ancestry; * Numbers in parentheses indicate the number of persons reporting this race alone, not in combination with any other race; Please refer to the Explanation of Data for more information.*

Dominican Republic	14	0.12
Mexican	227	1.91
Puerto Rican	192	1.62
South American	61	0.51
Argentinean	6	0.05
Bolivian	1	0.01
Chilean	4	0.03
Colombian	14	0.12
Ecuadorian	17	0.14
Peruvian	11	0.09
Venezuelan	4	0.03
Other South American	4	0.03
Other Hispanic or Latino	88	0.74

Race*	Population	%
African-American/Black (2,169)	2,413	20.35
Not Hispanic (2,121)	2,332	19.67
Hispanic (48)	81	0.68
American Indian/Alaska Native (54)	152	1.28
Not Hispanic (41)	123	1.04
Hispanic (13)	29	0.24
Apache (0)	1	0.01
Blackfeet (0)	2	0.02
Central American Ind. (5)	5	0.04
Cherokee (15)	34	0.29
Choctaw (0)	1	0.01
Comanche (0)	2	0.02
Creek (2)	2	0.02
Crow (0)	7	0.06
Delaware (0)	1	0.01
Iroquois (0)	6	0.05
Lumbee (2)	5	0.04
Mexican American Ind. (0)	1	0.01
Navajo (2)	4	0.03
Pima (2)	2	0.02
Potawatomi (1)	1	0.01
Sioux (0)	1	0.01
South American Ind. (0)	4	0.03
Tohono O'Odham (0)	1	0.01
Asian (543)	737	6.22
Not Hispanic (530)	714	6.02
Hispanic (13)	23	0.19
Bangladeshi (5)	5	0.04
Cambodian (4)	4	0.03
Chinese, ex. Taiwanese (51)	72	0.61
Filipino (236)	333	2.81
Indian (67)	73	0.62
Japanese (35)	65	0.55
Korean (52)	69	0.58
Laotian (2)	3	0.03
Nepalese (2)	2	0.02
Taiwanese (2)	2	0.02
Thai (7)	18	0.15
Vietnamese (66)	91	0.77
Hawaii Native/Pacific Islander (11)	31	0.26
Not Hispanic (7)	21	0.18
Hispanic (4)	10	0.08
Guamanian/Chamorro (7)	11	0.09
Native Hawaiian (3)	12	0.10
Samoan (0)	1	0.01
Tongan (1)	1	0.01
White (8,379)	8,806	74.27
Not Hispanic (8,046)	8,397	70.82
Hispanic (333)	409	3.45

Calverton

Place Type: CDP
County: Montgomery
Population: 17,724†

Ancestry‡	Population	%
African, Sub-Saharan (1,557)	1,581	8.88
African (386)	386	2.17
Ethiopian (404)	404	2.27
Ghanaian (369)	369	2.07
Nigerian (280)	304	1.71
Sierra Leonean (71)	71	0.40
Ugandan (30)	30	0.17
Other Sub-Saharan African (17)	17	0.10
American (389)	389	2.19
Australian (21)	21	0.12
Austrian (0)	49	0.28
Belgian (27)	36	0.20
British (47)	62	0.35
Croatian (0)	26	0.15
Czech (70)	150	0.84
Danish (12)	23	0.13
Dutch (38)	111	0.62
Eastern European (33)	33	0.19
English (420)	1,107	6.22
European (64)	97	0.54
Finnish (13)	13	0.07
French, ex. Basque (101)	232	1.30
French Canadian (43)	43	0.24
German (466)	1,430	8.03
Greek (13)	33	0.19
Guyanese (113)	113	0.63
Hungarian (31)	67	0.38
Iranian (49)	49	0.28
Irish (338)	1,163	6.53
Italian (321)	615	3.46
Lithuanian (28)	109	0.61
Norwegian (21)	53	0.30
Polish (75)	199	1.12
Portuguese (0)	19	0.11
Romanian (31)	45	0.25
Russian (106)	195	1.10
Scotch-Irish (128)	271	1.52
Scottish (73)	194	1.09
Serbian (0)	66	0.37
Slavic (0)	14	0.08
Slovak (22)	22	0.12
Swedish (11)	89	0.50
Swiss (24)	40	0.22
Turkish (0)	22	0.12
Ukrainian (34)	34	0.19
Welsh (0)	15	0.08
West Indian, ex. Hispanic (696)	869	4.88
Barbadian (11)	11	0.06
Haitian (380)	397	2.23
Jamaican (136)	182	1.02
Trinidadian/Tobagonian (111)	127	0.71
West Indian (58)	152	0.85
Yugoslavian (0)	15	0.08

Hispanic Origin	Population	%
Hispanic or Latino (of any race)	2,486	14.03
Central American, ex. Mexican	1,336	7.54
Costa Rican	6	0.03
Guatemalan	146	0.82
Honduran	84	0.47
Nicaraguan	112	0.63
Panamanian	36	0.20
Salvadoran	952	5.37
Cuban	39	0.22
Dominican Republic	126	0.71
Mexican	217	1.22
Puerto Rican	135	0.76
South American	347	1.96
Argentinean	27	0.15
Bolivian	66	0.37
Chilean	5	0.03
Colombian	68	0.38
Ecuadorian	23	0.13
Paraguayan	9	0.05
Peruvian	111	0.63
Uruguayan	5	0.03
Venezuelan	15	0.08
Other South American	18	0.10
Other Hispanic or Latino	286	1.61

Race*	Population	%
African-American/Black (6,642)	7,003	39.51
Not Hispanic (6,500)	6,780	38.25
Hispanic (142)	223	1.26
American Indian/Alaska Native (65)	211	1.19
Not Hispanic (27)	126	0.71
Hispanic (38)	85	0.48
Blackfeet (0)	4	0.02
Canadian/French Am. Ind. (0)	1	0.01
Central American Ind. (2)	9	0.05
Cherokee (3)	36	0.20
Choctaw (1)	4	0.02
Colville (0)	1	0.01
Creek (0)	3	0.02
Iroquois (1)	2	0.01
Lumbee (0)	2	0.01
Mexican American Ind. (3)	3	0.02
Sioux (0)	3	0.02
South American Ind. (4)	12	0.07
Asian (2,801)	3,044	17.17
Not Hispanic (2,787)	3,004	16.95
Hispanic (14)	40	0.23
Bangladeshi (54)	58	0.33
Burmese (3)	3	0.02
Cambodian (94)	100	0.56
Chinese, ex. Taiwanese (372)	421	2.38
Filipino (221)	269	1.52
Indian (838)	924	5.21
Indonesian (6)	6	0.03
Japanese (30)	49	0.28
Korean (331)	355	2.00
Laotian (5)	8	0.05
Malaysian (6)	10	0.06
Nepalese (4)	4	0.02
Pakistani (51)	68	0.38
Sri Lankan (11)	14	0.08
Taiwanese (20)	23	0.13
Thai (23)	29	0.16
Vietnamese (635)	689	3.89
Hawaii Native/Pacific Islander (9)	46	0.26
Not Hispanic (9)	43	0.24
Hispanic (0)	3	0.02
Fijian (5)	5	0.03
Guamanian/Chamorro (1)	4	0.02
Samoan (1)	1	0.01
White (6,417)	6,880	38.82
Not Hispanic (5,379)	5,686	32.08
Hispanic (1,038)	1,194	6.74

Cambridge

Place Type: City
County: Dorchester
Population: 12,326†

Ancestry‡	Population	%
African, Sub-Saharan (37)	37	0.31
African (37)	37	0.31
American (1,452)	1,452	11.99
Arab (8)	8	0.07
Syrian (8)	8	0.07
Austrian (0)	20	0.17
Brazilian (0)	54	0.45
British (47)	47	0.39
Canadian (0)	6	0.05
Czech (0)	13	0.11
Danish (0)	26	0.21
Dutch (18)	37	0.31
Eastern European (10)	10	0.08
English (455)	949	7.84
European (102)	102	0.84
French, ex. Basque (41)	229	1.89
French Canadian (0)	52	0.43
German (228)	779	6.43
Guyanese (0)	11	0.09
Icelander (11)	11	0.09
Irish (280)	1,077	8.89
Italian (158)	458	3.78
Lithuanian (9)	18	0.15
Norwegian (17)	54	0.45
Pennsylvania German (16)	16	0.13
Polish (41)	99	0.82
Russian (33)	67	0.55
Scandinavian (12)	12	0.10
Scotch-Irish (26)	83	0.69
Scottish (23)	119	0.98
Slovak (13)	13	0.11
Swedish (20)	54	0.45

*Notes: † The Census 2010 population figure is used to calculate the percentages in the Hispanic Origin and Race categories. Ancestry percentages are based on the 2006-2010 American Community Survey population (not shown); ‡ Numbers in parentheses indicate the number of people reporting a single ancestry; * Numbers in parentheses indicate the number of persons reporting this race alone, not in combination with any other race; Please refer to the Explanation of Data for more information.*

Swiss (19)	38	0.31
Ukrainian (9)	19	0.16
Welsh (0)	24	0.20
West Indian, ex. Hispanic (64)	89	0.73
Haitian (64)	89	0.73

Hispanic Origin	Population	%
Hispanic or Latino (of any race)	610	4.95
Central American, ex. Mexican	72	0.58
Costa Rican	1	0.01
Guatemalan	31	0.25
Honduran	15	0.12
Nicaraguan	1	0.01
Panamanian	2	0.02
Salvadoran	20	0.16
Other Central American	2	0.02
Cuban	8	0.06
Dominican Republic	16	0.13
Mexican	260	2.11
Puerto Rican	191	1.55
South American	22	0.18
Argentinean	2	0.02
Bolivian	1	0.01
Chilean	1	0.01
Colombian	5	0.04
Ecuadorian	6	0.05
Paraguayan	2	0.02
Peruvian	4	0.03
Venezuelan	1	0.01
Other Hispanic or Latino	41	0.33

Race*	Population	%
African-American/Black (5,899)	6,133	49.76
Not Hispanic (5,814)	6,032	48.94
Hispanic (85)	101	0.82
American Indian/Alaska Native (45)	117	0.95
Not Hispanic (33)	96	0.78
Hispanic (12)	21	0.17
Blackfeet (0)	1	0.01
Canadian/French Am. Ind. (1)	1	0.01
Central American Ind. (1)	1	0.01
Cherokee (1)	17	0.14
Choctaw (0)	1	0.01
Iroquois (1)	5	0.04
Lumbee (2)	2	0.02
Mexican American Ind. (2)	2	0.02
Seminole (8)	8	0.06
Sioux (2)	3	0.02
Asian (162)	193	1.57
Not Hispanic (162)	192	1.56
Hispanic (0)	1	0.01
Bangladeshi (2)	2	0.02
Cambodian (13)	13	0.11
Chinese, ex. Taiwanese (19)	24	0.19
Filipino (29)	36	0.29
Indian (28)	36	0.29
Korean (9)	12	0.10
Pakistani (28)	28	0.23
Taiwanese (2)	2	0.02
Thai (3)	6	0.05
Vietnamese (23)	27	0.22
Hawaii Native/Pacific Islander (5)	10	0.08
Not Hispanic (4)	8	0.06
Hispanic (1)	2	0.02
Guamanian/Chamorro (2)	3	0.02
Native Hawaiian (1)	2	0.02
Samoan (1)	1	0.01
White (5,657)	5,921	48.04
Not Hispanic (5,419)	5,647	45.81
Hispanic (238)	274	2.22

Camp Springs

Place Type: CDP
County: Prince George's
Population: 19,096†

Ancestry‡	Population	%
African, Sub-Saharan (544)	613	3.27
African (421)	479	2.55
Ethiopian (67)	67	0.36
Liberian (15)	15	0.08
Nigerian (30)	41	0.22
Zimbabwean (11)	11	0.06
American (377)	377	2.01
Arab (36)	36	0.19
Arab (10)	10	0.05
Egyptian (26)	26	0.14
Austrian (0)	11	0.06
British (0)	11	0.06
Dutch (0)	16	0.09
English (168)	564	3.00
European (16)	16	0.09
French, ex. Basque (12)	114	0.61
German (180)	794	4.23
Greek (0)	26	0.14
Guyanese (22)	34	0.18
Irish (148)	398	2.12
Italian (205)	338	1.80
Lithuanian (11)	11	0.06
Norwegian (16)	72	0.38
Polish (28)	81	0.43
Scotch-Irish (67)	141	0.75
Scottish (19)	59	0.31
Slavic (0)	16	0.09
Slovak (0)	12	0.06
Swedish (8)	20	0.11
Welsh (0)	17	0.09
West Indian, ex. Hispanic (188)	220	1.17
Bahamian (65)	65	0.35
British West Indian (0)	11	0.06
Jamaican (75)	84	0.45
Trinidadian/Tobagonian (39)	51	0.27
West Indian (9)	9	0.05

Hispanic Origin	Population	%
Hispanic or Latino (of any race)	1,573	8.24
Central American, ex. Mexican	736	3.85
Costa Rican	4	0.02
Guatemalan	100	0.52
Honduran	52	0.27
Nicaraguan	17	0.09
Panamanian	41	0.21
Salvadoran	514	2.69
Other Central American	8	0.04
Cuban	29	0.15
Dominican Republic	20	0.10
Mexican	474	2.48
Puerto Rican	82	0.43
South American	53	0.28
Argentinean	6	0.03
Bolivian	9	0.05
Chilean	1	0.01
Colombian	10	0.05
Ecuadorian	2	0.01
Peruvian	21	0.11
Venezuelan	4	0.02
Other Hispanic or Latino	179	0.94

Race*	Population	%
African-American/Black (15,051)	15,398	80.63
Not Hispanic (14,876)	15,184	79.51
Hispanic (175)	214	1.12
American Indian/Alaska Native (67)	248	1.30
Not Hispanic (45)	203	1.06
Hispanic (22)	45	0.24
Blackfeet (0)	12	0.06
Canadian/French Am. Ind. (0)	1	0.01
Central American Ind. (10)	10	0.05
Cherokee (12)	48	0.25
Chickasaw (0)	1	0.01
Choctaw (0)	2	0.01
Creek (0)	1	0.01
Iroquois (0)	9	0.05
Mexican American Ind. (4)	4	0.02
Seminole (0)	2	0.01
South American Ind. (0)	1	0.01
Tohono O'Odham (1)	1	0.01
Ute (1)	2	0.01
Asian (450)	536	2.81
Not Hispanic (441)	513	2.69
Hispanic (9)	23	0.12
Bangladeshi (3)	3	0.02
Cambodian (2)	2	0.01
Chinese, ex. Taiwanese (77)	89	0.47
Filipino (244)	283	1.48
Indian (19)	27	0.14
Indonesian (1)	2	0.01
Japanese (7)	15	0.08
Korean (33)	46	0.24
Laotian (5)	7	0.04
Nepalese (12)	12	0.06
Pakistani (12)	12	0.06
Thai (3)	5	0.03
Vietnamese (14)	15	0.08
Hawaii Native/Pacific Islander (14)	31	0.16
Not Hispanic (13)	23	0.12
Hispanic (1)	8	0.04
Guamanian/Chamorro (5)	8	0.04
Native Hawaiian (2)	3	0.02
Samoan (2)	6	0.03
White (2,123)	2,420	12.67
Not Hispanic (1,739)	1,963	10.28
Hispanic (384)	457	2.39

Cape St. Claire

Place Type: CDP
County: Anne Arundel
Population: 8,747†

Ancestry‡	Population	%
African, Sub-Saharan (0)	12	0.14
South African (0)	12	0.14
American (490)	490	5.65
Arab (13)	24	0.28
Arab (0)	11	0.13
Other Arab (13)	13	0.15
Armenian (0)	10	0.12
Austrian (13)	13	0.15
Basque (0)	42	0.48
Belgian (0)	8	0.09
British (9)	36	0.42
Croatian (0)	24	0.28
Czech (136)	198	2.28
Czechoslovakian (13)	31	0.36
Danish (30)	97	1.12
Dutch (51)	166	1.91
Eastern European (10)	10	0.12
English (532)	1,293	14.91
European (262)	324	3.74
French, ex. Basque (14)	224	2.58
French Canadian (39)	39	0.45
German (464)	1,656	19.10
Greek (21)	36	0.42
Hungarian (87)	172	1.98
Irish (584)	2,040	23.53
Italian (218)	640	7.38
Lithuanian (30)	40	0.46
Norwegian (28)	93	1.07
Pennsylvania German (12)	12	0.14
Polish (286)	624	7.20
Russian (13)	136	1.57
Scandinavian (48)	48	0.55
Scotch-Irish (155)	274	3.16
Scottish (81)	251	2.90
Slavic (0)	9	0.10
Slovak (0)	29	0.33
Swedish (37)	131	1.51
Swiss (39)	39	0.45
Ukrainian (24)	103	1.19
Welsh (0)	193	2.23

Hispanic Origin	Population	%
Hispanic or Latino (of any race)	393	4.49
Central American, ex. Mexican	73	0.83
Costa Rican	7	0.08
Guatemalan	5	0.06
Honduran	13	0.15
Nicaraguan	4	0.05

*Notes: † The Census 2010 population figure is used to calculate the percentages in the Hispanic Origin and Race categories. Ancestry percentages are based on the 2006-2010 American Community Survey population (not shown); ‡ Numbers in parentheses indicate the number of people reporting a single ancestry; * Numbers in parentheses indicate the number of persons reporting this race alone, not in combination with any other race; Please refer to the Explanation of Data for more information.*

Panamanian	6	0.07
Salvadoran	38	0.43
Cuban	26	0.30
Dominican Republic	4	0.05
Mexican	131	1.50
Puerto Rican	60	0.69
South American	62	0.71
Argentinean	2	0.02
Bolivian	9	0.10
Chilean	7	0.08
Colombian	18	0.21
Ecuadorian	13	0.15
Peruvian	10	0.11
Uruguayan	3	0.03
Other Hispanic or Latino	37	0.42

Race*	Population	%
African-American/Black (378)	456	5.21
Not Hispanic (372)	444	5.08
Hispanic (6)	12	0.14
American Indian/Alaska Native (24)	82	0.94
Not Hispanic (21)	69	0.79
Hispanic (3)	13	0.15
Apache (0)	1	0.01
Cherokee (9)	22	0.25
Chippewa (2)	6	0.07
Creek (0)	1	0.01
Crow (0)	1	0.01
Delaware (0)	3	0.03
Mexican American Ind. (0)	2	0.02
Navajo (4)	4	0.05
Potawatomi (2)	2	0.02
Asian (139)	227	2.60
Not Hispanic (135)	218	2.49
Hispanic (4)	9	0.10
Cambodian (4)	4	0.05
Chinese, ex. Taiwanese (16)	42	0.48
Filipino (58)	94	1.07
Indian (13)	19	0.22
Japanese (11)	22	0.25
Korean (17)	31	0.35
Nepalese (1)	1	0.01
Pakistani (3)	3	0.03
Thai (5)	8	0.09
Vietnamese (8)	9	0.10
Hawaii Native/Pacific Islander (3)	7	0.08
Not Hispanic (2)	2	0.02
Hispanic (1)	5	0.06
Guamanian/Chamorro (1)	4	0.05
White (7,938)	8,137	93.03
Not Hispanic (7,630)	7,803	89.21
Hispanic (308)	334	3.82

Carney

Place Type: CDP
County: Baltimore
Population: 29,941†

Ancestry‡	Population	%
African, Sub-Saharan (712)	712	2.58
African (699)	699	2.53
Ugandan (13)	13	0.05
Albanian (77)	77	0.28
American (1,877)	1,877	6.80
Arab (0)	9	0.03
Lebanese (0)	9	0.03
Austrian (22)	67	0.24
Brazilian (6)	6	0.02
British (18)	52	0.19
Bulgarian (62)	62	0.22
Croatian (0)	28	0.10
Czech (48)	168	0.61
Czechoslovakian (20)	32	0.12
Danish (14)	85	0.31
Dutch (67)	294	1.07
Eastern European (10)	10	0.04
English (592)	2,893	10.49
European (162)	173	0.63
Finnish (5)	42	0.15
French, ex. Basque (162)	528	1.91
French Canadian (12)	30	0.11
German (2,815)	7,592	27.52
German Russian (0)	7	0.03
Greek (92)	175	0.63
Guyanese (7)	7	0.03
Hungarian (90)	109	0.40
Iranian (39)	39	0.14
Irish (1,433)	5,598	20.30
Italian (1,265)	2,714	9.84
Lithuanian (15)	203	0.74
Norwegian (71)	122	0.44
Pennsylvania German (0)	21	0.08
Polish (673)	1,971	7.15
Romanian (27)	27	0.10
Russian (78)	187	0.68
Scotch-Irish (97)	243	0.88
Scottish (168)	587	2.13
Serbian (0)	15	0.05
Slavic (0)	24	0.09
Slovak (72)	93	0.34
Swedish (92)	211	0.76
Swiss (22)	98	0.36
Ukrainian (45)	129	0.47
Welsh (22)	367	1.33
West Indian, ex. Hispanic (207)	216	0.78
Bermudan (0)	9	0.03
Jamaican (181)	181	0.66
West Indian (26)	26	0.09
Yugoslavian (0)	11	0.04

Hispanic Origin	Population	%
Hispanic or Latino (of any race)	955	3.19
Central American, ex. Mexican	191	0.64
Costa Rican	9	0.03
Guatemalan	26	0.09
Honduran	31	0.10
Nicaraguan	5	0.02
Panamanian	13	0.04
Salvadoran	102	0.34
Other Central American	5	0.02
Cuban	30	0.10
Dominican Republic	41	0.14
Mexican	166	0.55
Puerto Rican	209	0.70
South American	210	0.70
Argentinean	16	0.05
Bolivian	5	0.02
Chilean	13	0.04
Colombian	51	0.17
Ecuadorian	23	0.08
Paraguayan	1	<0.01
Peruvian	87	0.29
Uruguayan	1	<0.01
Venezuelan	13	0.04
Other Hispanic or Latino	108	0.36

Race*	Population	%
African-American/Black (4,271)	4,594	15.34
Not Hispanic (4,198)	4,472	14.94
Hispanic (73)	122	0.41
American Indian/Alaska Native (70)	204	0.68
Not Hispanic (65)	188	0.63
Hispanic (5)	16	0.05
Apache (0)	1	<0.01
Blackfeet (0)	2	0.01
Canadian/French Am. Ind. (0)	1	<0.01
Central American Ind. (1)	1	<0.01
Cherokee (8)	45	0.15
Chippewa (2)	2	0.01
Choctaw (4)	7	0.02
Creek (0)	1	<0.01
Iroquois (1)	1	<0.01
Lumbee (16)	19	0.06
Menominee (0)	1	<0.01
Navajo (3)	3	0.01
Sioux (2)	3	0.01
Asian (2,095)	2,301	7.69
Not Hispanic (2,083)	2,275	7.60
Hispanic (12)	26	0.09
Bangladeshi (12)	12	0.04
Burmese (6)	6	0.02
Cambodian (6)	6	0.02
Chinese, ex. Taiwanese (331)	362	1.21
Filipino (428)	485	1.62
Indian (339)	389	1.30
Indonesian (15)	15	0.05
Japanese (22)	46	0.15
Korean (517)	548	1.83
Laotian (3)	4	0.01
Nepalese (100)	122	0.41
Pakistani (72)	78	0.26
Taiwanese (7)	7	0.02
Thai (12)	18	0.06
Vietnamese (144)	158	0.53
Hawaii Native/Pacific Islander (8)	24	0.08
Not Hispanic (7)	23	0.08
Hispanic (1)	1	<0.01
Guamanian/Chamorro (5)	9	0.03
Marshallese (1)	1	<0.01
Native Hawaiian (1)	2	0.01
White (22,571)	23,103	77.16
Not Hispanic (22,058)	22,510	75.18
Hispanic (513)	593	1.98

Catonsville

Place Type: CDP
County: Baltimore
Population: 41,567†

Ancestry‡	Population	%
African, Sub-Saharan (935)	976	2.33
African (491)	502	1.20
Ethiopian (228)	247	0.59
Ghanaian (99)	99	0.24
Nigerian (57)	57	0.14
Somalian (60)	60	0.14
Other Sub-Saharan African (0)	11	0.03
Alsatian (0)	14	0.03
American (2,859)	2,859	6.83
Arab (191)	191	0.46
Arab (101)	101	0.24
Lebanese (33)	33	0.08
Moroccan (10)	10	0.02
Syrian (12)	12	0.03
Other Arab (35)	35	0.08
Armenian (17)	24	0.06
Austrian (0)	48	0.11
Belgian (10)	32	0.08
Brazilian (0)	28	0.07
British (76)	258	0.62
Bulgarian (0)	10	0.02
Canadian (0)	37	0.09
Celtic (18)	18	0.04
Croatian (29)	51	0.12
Czech (58)	513	1.23
Czechoslovakian (26)	75	0.18
Danish (57)	70	0.17
Dutch (176)	784	1.87
Eastern European (76)	86	0.21
English (1,082)	5,232	12.50
Estonian (0)	11	0.03
European (329)	401	0.96
Finnish (12)	57	0.14
French, ex. Basque (139)	1,090	2.60
French Canadian (136)	376	0.90
German (3,436)	11,220	26.80
Greek (53)	113	0.27
Hungarian (25)	248	0.59
Iranian (100)	137	0.33
Irish (1,957)	8,763	20.93
Italian (929)	3,525	8.42
Latvian (0)	12	0.03
Lithuanian (75)	351	0.84
Luxemburger (0)	6	0.01
Northern European (35)	35	0.08
Norwegian (65)	237	0.57
Pennsylvania German (55)	103	0.25
Polish (559)	1,893	4.52

*Notes: † The Census 2010 population figure is used to calculate the percentages in the Hispanic Origin and Race categories. Ancestry percentages are based on the 2006-2010 American Community Survey population (not shown); ‡ Numbers in parentheses indicate the number of people reporting a single ancestry; * Numbers in parentheses indicate the number of persons reporting this race alone, not in combination with any other race; Please refer to the Explanation of Data for more information.*

Portuguese (16)	48	0.11
Romanian (30)	46	0.11
Russian (47)	337	0.80
Scandinavian (0)	41	0.10
Scotch-Irish (225)	677	1.62
Scottish (293)	975	2.33
Slavic (0)	33	0.08
Slovak (65)	120	0.29
Swedish (37)	290	0.69
Swiss (27)	101	0.24
Turkish (70)	137	0.33
Ukrainian (31)	105	0.25
Welsh (97)	421	1.01
West Indian, ex. Hispanic (277)	329	0.79
Belizean (12)	36	0.09
British West Indian (0)	17	0.04
Haitian (75)	75	0.18
Jamaican (110)	121	0.29
Trinidadian/Tobagonian (68)	68	0.16
U.S. Virgin Islander (12)	12	0.03
Yugoslavian (0)	8	0.02

Hispanic Origin	Population	%
Hispanic or Latino (of any race)	1,408	3.39
Central American, ex. Mexican	391	0.94
Costa Rican	11	0.03
Guatemalan	51	0.12
Honduran	73	0.18
Nicaraguan	22	0.05
Panamanian	21	0.05
Salvadoran	209	0.50
Other Central American	4	0.01
Cuban	69	0.17
Dominican Republic	32	0.08
Mexican	329	0.79
Puerto Rican	201	0.48
South American	232	0.56
Argentinean	14	0.03
Bolivian	15	0.04
Chilean	15	0.04
Colombian	69	0.17
Ecuadorian	35	0.08
Paraguayan	8	0.02
Peruvian	62	0.15
Uruguayan	4	0.01
Venezuelan	10	0.02
Other Hispanic or Latino	154	0.37

Race*	Population	%
African-American/Black (6,043)	6,513	15.67
Not Hispanic (5,954)	6,391	15.38
Hispanic (89)	122	0.29
American Indian/Alaska Native (118)	313	0.75
Not Hispanic (99)	272	0.65
Hispanic (19)	41	0.10
Apache (1)	3	0.01
Blackfeet (1)	14	0.03
Central American Ind. (0)	2	<0.01
Cherokee (17)	81	0.19
Cheyenne (1)	4	0.01
Choctaw (4)	4	0.01
Delaware (0)	1	<0.01
Iroquois (3)	5	0.01
Lumbee (3)	11	0.03
Mexican American Ind. (6)	6	0.01
Navajo (3)	9	0.02
Sioux (1)	4	0.01
South American Ind. (2)	6	0.01
Yaqui (1)	1	<0.01
Yuman (1)	1	<0.01
Asian (2,613)	3,028	7.28
Not Hispanic (2,598)	2,993	7.20
Hispanic (15)	35	0.08
Bangladeshi (3)	15	0.04
Burmese (22)	26	0.06
Cambodian (18)	22	0.05
Chinese, ex. Taiwanese (659)	743	1.79
Filipino (271)	370	0.89
Indian (760)	832	2.00
Indonesian (4)	8	0.02
Japanese (42)	95	0.23
Korean (308)	352	0.85
Laotian (11)	11	0.03
Malaysian (0)	3	0.01
Nepalese (24)	25	0.06
Pakistani (143)	159	0.38
Sri Lankan (18)	21	0.05
Taiwanese (36)	41	0.10
Thai (31)	52	0.13
Vietnamese (137)	155	0.37
Hawaii Native/Pacific Islander (27)	78	0.19
Not Hispanic (24)	74	0.18
Hispanic (3)	4	0.01
Fijian (0)	1	<0.01
Guamanian/Chamorro (12)	19	0.05
Native Hawaiian (9)	30	0.07
Samoan (1)	15	0.04
White (31,278)	32,145	77.33
Not Hispanic (30,514)	31,276	75.24
Hispanic (764)	869	2.09

Chesapeake Ranch Estates

Place Type: CDP
County: Calvert
Population: 10,519†

Ancestry‡	Population	%
African, Sub-Saharan (12)	59	0.61
African (12)	59	0.61
American (419)	419	4.30
Australian (0)	56	0.58
Austrian (0)	48	0.49
British (0)	55	0.56
Croatian (9)	9	0.09
Dutch (23)	259	2.66
English (233)	1,236	12.70
European (74)	102	1.05
Finnish (12)	12	0.12
French, ex. Basque (25)	266	2.73
French Canadian (74)	98	1.01
German (484)	2,275	23.37
Greek (42)	42	0.43
Hungarian (14)	47	0.48
Irish (431)	1,763	18.11
Italian (283)	865	8.89
Norwegian (44)	44	0.45
Pennsylvania German (26)	37	0.38
Polish (156)	648	6.66
Portuguese (21)	21	0.22
Romanian (68)	68	0.70
Russian (0)	30	0.31
Scotch-Irish (20)	132	1.36
Scottish (141)	531	5.45
Slovak (0)	9	0.09
Swedish (0)	81	0.83
Ukrainian (0)	29	0.30
Welsh (0)	41	0.42
West Indian, ex. Hispanic (0)	94	0.97
Jamaican (0)	94	0.97

Hispanic Origin	Population	%
Hispanic or Latino (of any race)	462	4.39
Central American, ex. Mexican	58	0.55
Costa Rican	4	0.04
Guatemalan	9	0.09
Honduran	3	0.03
Panamanian	9	0.09
Salvadoran	33	0.31
Cuban	11	0.10
Dominican Republic	20	0.19
Mexican	170	1.62
Puerto Rican	122	1.16
South American	48	0.46
Argentinean	17	0.16
Bolivian	4	0.04
Chilean	5	0.05
Colombian	10	0.10
Ecuadorian	4	0.04
Peruvian	5	0.05
Venezuelan	3	0.03
Other Hispanic or Latino	33	0.31

Race*	Population	%
African-American/Black (1,469)	1,671	15.89
Not Hispanic (1,443)	1,633	15.52
Hispanic (26)	38	0.36
American Indian/Alaska Native (49)	161	1.53
Not Hispanic (42)	153	1.45
Hispanic (7)	8	0.08
Blackfeet (1)	6	0.06
Central American Ind. (1)	1	0.01
Cherokee (10)	29	0.28
Chickasaw (4)	4	0.04
Chippewa (0)	2	0.02
Choctaw (3)	6	0.06
Cree (2)	2	0.02
Crow (1)	1	0.01
Delaware (2)	3	0.03
Iroquois (0)	3	0.03
Lumbee (1)	1	0.01
Osage (2)	2	0.02
Seminole (0)	7	0.07
Sioux (1)	7	0.07
South American Ind. (2)	2	0.02
Spanish American Ind. (0)	1	0.01
Ute (0)	1	0.01
Asian (129)	241	2.29
Not Hispanic (129)	233	2.22
Hispanic (0)	8	0.08
Burmese (1)	1	0.01
Cambodian (1)	2	0.02
Chinese, ex. Taiwanese (31)	42	0.40
Filipino (42)	82	0.78
Indian (9)	14	0.13
Indonesian (0)	1	0.01
Japanese (16)	40	0.38
Korean (3)	10	0.10
Malaysian (0)	1	0.01
Pakistani (5)	5	0.05
Taiwanese (2)	11	0.10
Thai (6)	7	0.07
Vietnamese (1)	13	0.12
Hawaii Native/Pacific Islander (11)	29	0.28
Not Hispanic (11)	27	0.26
Hispanic (0)	2	0.02
Guamanian/Chamorro (3)	9	0.09
Native Hawaiian (4)	8	0.08
Samoan (1)	2	0.02
White (8,337)	8,691	82.62
Not Hispanic (8,064)	8,394	79.80
Hispanic (273)	297	2.82

Chevy Chase

Place Type: CDP
County: Montgomery
Population: 9,545†

Ancestry‡	Population	%
African, Sub-Saharan (46)	46	0.47
African (46)	46	0.47
American (366)	366	3.76
Arab (177)	177	1.82
Arab (121)	121	1.24
Iraqi (37)	37	0.38
Lebanese (11)	11	0.11
Other Arab (8)	8	0.08
Armenian (30)	41	0.42
Austrian (10)	79	0.81
Belgian (0)	31	0.32
British (75)	146	1.50
Canadian (43)	43	0.44
Croatian (0)	12	0.12
Czech (12)	33	0.34
Czechoslovakian (0)	10	0.10
Danish (42)	133	1.37
Dutch (102)	150	1.54
Eastern European (206)	206	2.11
English (227)	1,118	11.48

*Notes: † The Census 2010 population figure is used to calculate the percentages in the Hispanic Origin and Race categories. Ancestry percentages are based on the 2006-2010 American Community Survey population (not shown); ‡ Numbers in parentheses indicate the number of people reporting a single ancestry; * Numbers in parentheses indicate the number of persons reporting this race alone, not in combination with any other race; Please refer to the Explanation of Data for more information.*

European (324)	367	3.77
Finnish (11)	20	0.21
French, ex. Basque (89)	261	2.68
French Canadian (0)	91	0.93
German (362)	1,545	15.86
Greek (71)	145	1.49
Hungarian (22)	94	0.96
Iranian (61)	71	0.73
Irish (549)	1,841	18.90
Israeli (10)	20	0.21
Italian (122)	538	5.52
Latvian (0)	10	0.10
Lithuanian (43)	86	0.88
New Zealander (10)	10	0.10
Northern European (43)	43	0.44
Norwegian (31)	92	0.94
Pennsylvania German (11)	11	0.11
Polish (97)	403	4.14
Romanian (0)	64	0.66
Russian (160)	458	4.70
Scandinavian (10)	10	0.10
Scotch-Irish (85)	183	1.88
Scottish (69)	250	2.57
Serbian (32)	32	0.33
Swedish (66)	187	1.92
Swiss (24)	68	0.70
Ukrainian (7)	67	0.69
Welsh (54)	180	1.85
West Indian, ex. Hispanic (67)	89	0.91
West Indian (67)	89	0.91

Hispanic Origin	Population	%
Hispanic or Latino (of any race)	528	5.53
Central American, ex. Mexican	88	0.92
Costa Rican	3	0.03
Guatemalan	10	0.10
Honduran	38	0.40
Nicaraguan	8	0.08
Panamanian	3	0.03
Salvadoran	26	0.27
Cuban	28	0.29
Dominican Republic	4	0.04
Mexican	78	0.82
Puerto Rican	49	0.51
South American	214	2.24
Argentinean	27	0.28
Bolivian	9	0.09
Chilean	13	0.14
Colombian	47	0.49
Ecuadorian	23	0.24
Paraguayan	5	0.05
Peruvian	55	0.58
Uruguayan	12	0.13
Venezuelan	23	0.24
Other Hispanic or Latino	67	0.70

Race*	Population	%
African-American/Black (456)	550	5.76
Not Hispanic (450)	533	5.58
Hispanic (6)	17	0.18
American Indian/Alaska Native (17)	52	0.54
Not Hispanic (14)	37	0.39
Hispanic (3)	15	0.16
Cherokee (3)	9	0.09
Chippewa (0)	1	0.01
Choctaw (4)	10	0.10
Mexican American Ind. (3)	3	0.03
Potawatomi (2)	2	0.02
Seminole (0)	4	0.04
South American Ind. (1)	7	0.07
Asian (406)	593	6.21
Not Hispanic (399)	570	5.97
Hispanic (7)	23	0.24
Burmese (1)	1	0.01
Chinese, ex. Taiwanese (116)	175	1.83
Filipino (34)	60	0.63
Indian (100)	131	1.37
Indonesian (8)	13	0.14
Japanese (32)	64	0.67
Korean (40)	52	0.54
Laotian (1)	1	0.01
Malaysian (0)	2	0.02
Nepalese (2)	6	0.06
Pakistani (5)	8	0.08
Sri Lankan (8)	10	0.10
Taiwanese (4)	10	0.10
Thai (14)	24	0.25
Vietnamese (17)	21	0.22
Hawaii Native/Pacific Islander (1)	8	0.08
Not Hispanic (0)	7	0.07
Hispanic (1)	1	0.01
Guamanian/Chamorro (0)	1	0.01
Native Hawaiian (0)	3	0.03
White (8,272)	8,525	89.31
Not Hispanic (7,870)	8,094	84.80
Hispanic (402)	431	4.52

Chillum

Place Type: CDP
County: Prince George's
Population: 33,513†

Ancestry‡	Population	%
African, Sub-Saharan (3,749)	3,842	10.97
African (1,796)	1,865	5.32
Ethiopian (497)	497	1.42
Ghanaian (49)	49	0.14
Kenyan (26)	26	0.07
Liberian (34)	34	0.10
Nigerian (341)	354	1.01
Sierra Leonean (52)	63	0.18
Other Sub-Saharan African (954)	954	2.72
American (479)	479	1.37
Belgian (0)	9	0.03
British (26)	63	0.18
Croatian (0)	9	0.03
Czech (0)	10	0.03
Dutch (17)	27	0.08
English (82)	128	0.37
European (8)	51	0.15
French, ex. Basque (34)	79	0.23
French Canadian (0)	21	0.06
German (106)	312	0.89
Greek (8)	8	0.02
Guyanese (145)	185	0.53
Hungarian (0)	10	0.03
Irish (32)	308	0.88
Italian (86)	182	0.52
Norwegian (0)	17	0.05
Polish (7)	69	0.20
Portuguese (0)	7	0.02
Russian (0)	33	0.09
Scotch-Irish (28)	46	0.13
Scottish (3)	19	0.05
Swedish (0)	7	0.02
West Indian, ex. Hispanic (1,599)	1,995	5.69
Belizean (0)	12	0.03
British West Indian (113)	113	0.32
Haitian (111)	166	0.47
Jamaican (1,122)	1,220	3.48
Trinidadian/Tobagonian (71)	85	0.24
U.S. Virgin Islander (65)	65	0.19
West Indian (117)	334	0.95

Hispanic Origin	Population	%
Hispanic or Latino (of any race)	14,099	42.07
Central American, ex. Mexican	9,869	29.45
Costa Rican	16	0.05
Guatemalan	1,569	4.68
Honduran	620	1.85
Nicaraguan	261	0.78
Panamanian	46	0.14
Salvadoran	7,315	21.83
Other Central American	42	0.13
Cuban	85	0.25
Dominican Republic	723	2.16
Mexican	993	2.96
Puerto Rican	179	0.53
South American	350	1.04
Argentinean	24	0.07
Bolivian	43	0.13
Chilean	15	0.04
Colombian	83	0.25
Ecuadorian	29	0.09
Paraguayan	11	0.03
Peruvian	111	0.33
Uruguayan	8	0.02
Venezuelan	17	0.05
Other South American	9	0.03
Other Hispanic or Latino	1,900	5.67

Race*	Population	%
African-American/Black (17,323)	17,890	53.38
Not Hispanic (16,700)	17,062	50.91
Hispanic (623)	828	2.47
American Indian/Alaska Native (321)	571	1.70
Not Hispanic (62)	201	0.60
Hispanic (259)	370	1.10
Alaska Athabascan *(Ala. Nat.)* (0)	1	<0.01
Apache (0)	4	0.01
Blackfeet (0)	12	0.04
Central American Ind. (10)	25	0.07
Cherokee (10)	34	0.10
Chippewa (0)	2	0.01
Comanche (0)	1	<0.01
Delaware (0)	1	<0.01
Iroquois (1)	2	0.01
Lumbee (3)	3	0.01
Menominee (0)	4	0.01
Mexican American Ind. (15)	33	0.10
Navajo (8)	9	0.03
Seminole (0)	3	0.01
Sioux (0)	1	<0.01
South American Ind. (21)	22	0.07
Spanish American Ind. (0)	4	0.01
Ute (1)	2	0.01
Asian (786)	968	2.89
Not Hispanic (758)	878	2.62
Hispanic (28)	90	0.27
Bangladeshi (4)	16	0.05
Bhutanese (5)	5	0.01
Cambodian (10)	17	0.05
Chinese, ex. Taiwanese (74)	104	0.31
Filipino (167)	184	0.55
Indian (209)	287	0.86
Indonesian (2)	4	0.01
Japanese (11)	20	0.06
Korean (13)	21	0.06
Laotian (19)	25	0.07
Nepalese (29)	33	0.10
Pakistani (41)	50	0.15
Taiwanese (0)	3	0.01
Thai (9)	12	0.04
Vietnamese (113)	121	0.36
Hawaii Native/Pacific Islander (44)	148	0.44
Not Hispanic (24)	88	0.26
Hispanic (20)	60	0.18
Guamanian/Chamorro (30)	38	0.11
Native Hawaiian (3)	11	0.03
Samoan (1)	3	0.01
White (4,531)	5,462	16.30
Not Hispanic (1,298)	1,521	4.54
Hispanic (3,233)	3,941	11.76

Clarksburg

Place Type: CDP
County: Montgomery
Population: 13,766†

Ancestry‡	Population	%
Afghan (44)	44	0.42
African, Sub-Saharan (379)	379	3.59
African (69)	69	0.65
Ethiopian (35)	35	0.33
Ghanaian (261)	261	2.48
Nigerian (14)	14	0.13
American (242)	242	2.30
Arab (35)	82	0.78

*Notes: † The Census 2010 population figure is used to calculate the percentages in the Hispanic Origin and Race categories. Ancestry percentages are based on the 2006-2010 American Community Survey population (not shown); ‡ Numbers in parentheses indicate the number of people reporting a single ancestry; * Numbers in parentheses indicate the number of persons reporting this race alone, not in combination with any other race; Please refer to the Explanation of Data for more information.*

Egyptian (35)	35	0.33
Lebanese (0)	47	0.45
Armenian (42)	42	0.40
Austrian (9)	29	0.28
Belgian (12)	12	0.11
British (0)	28	0.27
Canadian (34)	34	0.32
Carpatho Rusyn (0)	8	0.08
Czech (10)	69	0.65
Czechoslovakian (31)	42	0.40
Danish (0)	32	0.30
Dutch (0)	43	0.41
Eastern European (21)	21	0.20
English (160)	705	6.69
Estonian (26)	26	0.25
European (122)	139	1.32
Finnish (12)	12	0.11
French, ex. Basque (14)	245	2.32
French Canadian (20)	49	0.46
German (225)	1,227	11.64
Greek (27)	50	0.47
Guyanese (25)	25	0.24
Hungarian (36)	36	0.34
Iranian (150)	150	1.42
Irish (194)	719	6.82
Italian (314)	812	7.70
Latvian (0)	9	0.09
Lithuanian (14)	24	0.23
New Zealander (10)	10	0.09
Norwegian (11)	27	0.26
Polish (50)	265	2.51
Portuguese (24)	24	0.23
Russian (23)	136	1.29
Scandinavian (0)	10	0.09
Scotch-Irish (0)	85	0.81
Scottish (47)	155	1.47
Slovak (0)	7	0.07
Slovene (0)	39	0.37
Swedish (0)	56	0.53
Ukrainian (0)	16	0.15
Welsh (16)	41	0.39
West Indian, ex. Hispanic (85)	135	1.28
Jamaican (42)	42	0.40
Trinidadian/Tobagonian (24)	74	0.70
West Indian (19)	19	0.18

Hispanic Origin	Population	%
Hispanic or Latino (of any race)	1,348	9.79
Central American, ex. Mexican	422	3.07
Costa Rican	7	0.05
Guatemalan	61	0.44
Honduran	38	0.28
Nicaraguan	35	0.25
Panamanian	22	0.16
Salvadoran	249	1.81
Other Central American	10	0.07
Cuban	47	0.34
Dominican Republic	25	0.18
Mexican	138	1.00
Puerto Rican	147	1.07
South American	441	3.20
Argentinean	20	0.15
Bolivian	61	0.44
Chilean	16	0.12
Colombian	136	0.99
Ecuadorian	36	0.26
Paraguayan	2	0.01
Peruvian	129	0.94
Uruguayan	11	0.08
Venezuelan	30	0.22
Other Hispanic or Latino	128	0.93

Race*	Population	%
African-American/Black (2,027)	2,257	16.40
Not Hispanic (1,996)	2,185	15.87
Hispanic (31)	72	0.52
American Indian/Alaska Native (20)	103	0.75
Not Hispanic (11)	78	0.57
Hispanic (9)	25	0.18
Central American Ind. (0)	1	0.01
Cherokee (2)	31	0.23
Choctaw (1)	1	0.01
Creek (1)	3	0.02
Iroquois (1)	1	0.01
Sioux (0)	3	0.02
South American Ind. (2)	5	0.04
Asian (4,625)	4,923	35.76
Not Hispanic (4,612)	4,881	35.46
Hispanic (13)	42	0.31
Bangladeshi (56)	56	0.41
Burmese (4)	7	0.05
Cambodian (19)	31	0.23
Chinese, ex. Taiwanese (1,353)	1,481	10.76
Filipino (153)	218	1.58
Hmong (1)	7	0.05
Indian (1,389)	1,442	10.48
Indonesian (12)	15	0.11
Japanese (31)	55	0.40
Korean (769)	812	5.90
Laotian (15)	18	0.13
Malaysian (2)	7	0.05
Nepalese (6)	6	0.04
Pakistani (125)	135	0.98
Sri Lankan (25)	26	0.19
Taiwanese (43)	49	0.36
Thai (27)	45	0.33
Vietnamese (439)	491	3.57
Hawaii Native/Pacific Islander (15)	36	0.26
Not Hispanic (10)	29	0.21
Hispanic (5)	7	0.05
Guamanian/Chamorro (9)	15	0.11
Native Hawaiian (1)	6	0.04
White (6,065)	6,521	47.37
Not Hispanic (5,309)	5,667	41.17
Hispanic (756)	854	6.20

Clinton

Place Type: CDP
County: Prince George's
Population: 35,970†

Ancestry‡	Population	%
African, Sub-Saharan (936)	1,102	3.06
African (495)	630	1.75
Cape Verdean (0)	23	0.06
Ethiopian (185)	185	0.51
Nigerian (256)	264	0.73
American (1,389)	1,389	3.86
Arab (12)	12	0.03
Lebanese (12)	12	0.03
Armenian (18)	18	0.05
Australian (0)	11	0.03
Austrian (17)	30	0.08
British (0)	12	0.03
Czechoslovakian (11)	11	0.03
Dutch (27)	133	0.37
English (295)	778	2.16
European (44)	44	0.12
Finnish (40)	40	0.11
French, ex. Basque (99)	164	0.46
French Canadian (23)	23	0.06
German (304)	775	2.15
Guyanese (67)	147	0.41
Hungarian (10)	32	0.09
Iranian (14)	33	0.09
Irish (359)	1,245	3.46
Italian (309)	619	1.72
Lithuanian (11)	27	0.08
Norwegian (60)	60	0.17
Pennsylvania German (12)	12	0.03
Polish (28)	161	0.45
Portuguese (9)	20	0.06
Russian (19)	44	0.12
Scotch-Irish (18)	43	0.12
Scottish (36)	202	0.56
Ukrainian (20)	34	0.09
Welsh (17)	74	0.21
West Indian, ex. Hispanic (142)	319	0.89
British West Indian (11)	23	0.06
Jamaican (107)	225	0.63
West Indian (24)	71	0.20
Yugoslavian (21)	21	0.06

Hispanic Origin	Population	%
Hispanic or Latino (of any race)	1,865	5.18
Central American, ex. Mexican	679	1.89
Costa Rican	8	0.02
Guatemalan	91	0.25
Honduran	45	0.13
Nicaraguan	39	0.11
Panamanian	67	0.19
Salvadoran	422	1.17
Other Central American	7	0.02
Cuban	53	0.15
Dominican Republic	51	0.14
Mexican	539	1.50
Puerto Rican	194	0.54
South American	145	0.40
Argentinean	4	0.01
Bolivian	29	0.08
Chilean	4	0.01
Colombian	28	0.08
Ecuadorian	16	0.04
Paraguayan	9	0.03
Peruvian	46	0.13
Uruguayan	3	0.01
Venezuelan	2	0.01
Other South American	4	0.01
Other Hispanic or Latino	204	0.57

Race*	Population	%
African-American/Black (29,037)	29,771	82.77
Not Hispanic (28,784)	29,417	81.78
Hispanic (253)	354	0.98
American Indian/Alaska Native (123)	413	1.15
Not Hispanic (103)	353	0.98
Hispanic (20)	60	0.17
Blackfeet (0)	13	0.04
Central American Ind. (0)	2	0.01
Cherokee (3)	38	0.11
Cheyenne (0)	1	<0.01
Choctaw (0)	2	0.01
Iroquois (0)	2	0.01
Kiowa (0)	2	0.01
Lumbee (1)	2	0.01
Mexican American Ind. (0)	5	0.01
Navajo (3)	5	0.01
Seminole (0)	4	0.01
Sioux (0)	2	0.01
South American Ind. (0)	3	0.01
Spanish American Ind. (1)	1	<0.01
Ute (0)	1	<0.01
Asian (907)	1,103	3.07
Not Hispanic (903)	1,090	3.03
Hispanic (4)	13	0.04
Bangladeshi (6)	6	0.02
Burmese (1)	1	<0.01
Cambodian (4)	6	0.02
Chinese, ex. Taiwanese (144)	175	0.49
Filipino (473)	562	1.56
Indian (77)	100	0.28
Indonesian (2)	2	0.01
Japanese (19)	45	0.13
Korean (63)	75	0.21
Malaysian (1)	1	<0.01
Nepalese (2)	2	0.01
Pakistani (23)	29	0.08
Taiwanese (0)	1	<0.01
Thai (31)	47	0.13
Vietnamese (44)	51	0.14
Hawaii Native/Pacific Islander (15)	40	0.11
Not Hispanic (11)	35	0.10
Hispanic (4)	5	0.01
Guamanian/Chamorro (8)	13	0.04
Native Hawaiian (4)	11	0.03
Samoan (3)	3	0.01
White (4,081)	4,648	12.92
Not Hispanic (3,508)	3,975	11.05
Hispanic (573)	673	1.87

SECTION TWO

*Notes: † The Census 2010 population figure is used to calculate the percentages in the Hispanic Origin and Race categories. Ancestry percentages are based on the 2006-2010 American Community Survey population (not shown); ‡ Numbers in parentheses indicate the number of people reporting a single ancestry; * Numbers in parentheses indicate the number of persons reporting this race alone, not in combination with any other race; Please refer to the Explanation of Data for more information.*

Cloverly

Place Type: CDP
County: Montgomery
Population: 15,126†

Ancestry‡	Population	%
African, Sub-Saharan (731)	757	4.91
African (236)	262	1.70
Ethiopian (90)	90	0.58
Liberian (31)	31	0.20
Nigerian (186)	186	1.21
South African (47)	47	0.30
Ugandan (19)	19	0.12
Other Sub-Saharan African (122)	122	0.79
American (558)	558	3.62
Arab (165)	219	1.42
Arab (0)	26	0.17
Egyptian (22)	22	0.14
Lebanese (130)	130	0.84
Other Arab (13)	41	0.27
Austrian (47)	153	0.99
Brazilian (10)	20	0.13
British (54)	110	0.71
Cypriot (10)	10	0.06
Czech (9)	64	0.42
Czechoslovakian (13)	19	0.12
Danish (9)	71	0.46
Dutch (46)	125	0.81
Eastern European (117)	117	0.76
English (290)	1,181	7.66
European (226)	258	1.67
Finnish (6)	6	0.04
French, ex. Basque (58)	261	1.69
French Canadian (0)	41	0.27
German (296)	1,699	11.02
German Russian (26)	26	0.17
Greek (72)	199	1.29
Guyanese (9)	9	0.06
Hungarian (0)	41	0.27
Iranian (14)	28	0.18
Irish (430)	1,608	10.43
Israeli (16)	16	0.10
Italian (343)	755	4.90
Latvian (38)	38	0.25
Lithuanian (21)	40	0.26
Northern European (53)	53	0.34
Norwegian (118)	188	1.22
Polish (82)	456	2.96
Portuguese (67)	99	0.64
Russian (152)	281	1.82
Scandinavian (16)	16	0.10
Scotch-Irish (52)	159	1.03
Scottish (67)	219	1.42
Slovak (13)	13	0.08
Slovene (0)	13	0.08
Swedish (38)	105	0.68
Swiss (0)	9	0.06
Turkish (35)	35	0.23
Ukrainian (29)	91	0.59
Welsh (15)	84	0.54
West Indian, ex. Hispanic (179)	227	1.47
Haitian (29)	60	0.39
Jamaican (91)	108	0.70
Trinidadian/Tobagonian (16)	16	0.10
West Indian (43)	43	0.28
Yugoslavian (14)	14	0.09

Hispanic Origin	Population	%
Hispanic or Latino (of any race)	1,619	10.70
Central American, ex. Mexican	784	5.18
Costa Rican	4	0.03
Guatemalan	96	0.63
Honduran	45	0.30
Nicaraguan	60	0.40
Panamanian	12	0.08
Salvadoran	567	3.75
Cuban	52	0.34
Dominican Republic	44	0.29
Mexican	129	0.85
Puerto Rican	101	0.67
South American	329	2.18
Argentinean	21	0.14
Bolivian	96	0.63
Chilean	34	0.22
Colombian	52	0.34
Ecuadorian	32	0.21
Paraguayan	1	0.01
Peruvian	75	0.50
Uruguayan	5	0.03
Venezuelan	4	0.03
Other South American	9	0.06
Other Hispanic or Latino	180	1.19

Race*	Population	%
African-American/Black (3,848)	4,128	27.29
Not Hispanic (3,801)	4,031	26.65
Hispanic (47)	97	0.64
American Indian/Alaska Native (48)	148	0.98
Not Hispanic (31)	111	0.73
Hispanic (17)	37	0.24
Apache (0)	1	0.01
Blackfeet (0)	2	0.01
Central American Ind. (4)	5	0.03
Cherokee (4)	28	0.19
Chippewa (3)	4	0.03
Choctaw (0)	1	0.01
Creek (0)	1	0.01
Lumbee (8)	8	0.05
Mexican American Ind. (1)	3	0.02
Potawatomi (2)	2	0.01
South American Ind. (2)	3	0.02
Asian (2,745)	3,018	19.95
Not Hispanic (2,742)	2,989	19.76
Hispanic (3)	29	0.19
Bangladeshi (33)	44	0.29
Burmese (2)	2	0.01
Cambodian (75)	83	0.55
Chinese, ex. Taiwanese (385)	452	2.99
Filipino (172)	206	1.36
Indian (863)	984	6.51
Indonesian (4)	4	0.03
Japanese (19)	44	0.29
Korean (633)	660	4.36
Laotian (9)	16	0.11
Malaysian (1)	16	0.11
Nepalese (10)	12	0.08
Pakistani (126)	139	0.92
Sri Lankan (17)	19	0.13
Taiwanese (33)	35	0.23
Thai (37)	47	0.31
Vietnamese (224)	234	1.55
Hawaii Native/Pacific Islander (10)	20	0.13
Not Hispanic (9)	18	0.12
Hispanic (1)	2	0.01
Guamanian/Chamorro (3)	3	0.02
Native Hawaiian (0)	1	0.01
Samoan (4)	4	0.03
White (7,182)	7,660	50.64
Not Hispanic (6,392)	6,753	44.64
Hispanic (790)	907	6.00

Cockeysville

Place Type: CDP
County: Baltimore
Population: 20,776†

Ancestry‡	Population	%
Afghan (41)	76	0.38
African, Sub-Saharan (366)	411	2.07
African (49)	66	0.33
Ghanaian (140)	140	0.71
Nigerian (86)	86	0.43
Other Sub-Saharan African (91)	119	0.60
Albanian (128)	128	0.65
American (480)	480	2.42
Arab (203)	203	1.02
Arab (92)	92	0.46
Palestinian (41)	41	0.21
Other Arab (70)	70	0.35
Armenian (0)	14	0.07
Austrian (8)	53	0.27
British (35)	79	0.40
Bulgarian (231)	231	1.16
Canadian (0)	8	0.04
Czech (38)	95	0.48
Dutch (0)	188	0.95
Eastern European (18)	18	0.09
English (621)	2,204	11.11
European (155)	230	1.16
French, ex. Basque (71)	500	2.52
French Canadian (22)	33	0.17
German (1,051)	4,087	20.60
Greek (239)	297	1.50
Guyanese (41)	41	0.21
Hungarian (60)	141	0.71
Iranian (84)	114	0.57
Irish (665)	2,821	14.22
Israeli (14)	14	0.07
Italian (940)	2,225	11.21
Latvian (14)	29	0.15
Lithuanian (25)	65	0.33
Norwegian (56)	147	0.74
Pennsylvania German (13)	13	0.07
Polish (208)	1,137	5.73
Portuguese (0)	28	0.14
Romanian (34)	59	0.30
Russian (160)	375	1.89
Scandinavian (6)	6	0.03
Scotch-Irish (176)	440	2.22
Scottish (86)	188	0.95
Serbian (16)	16	0.08
Slovak (38)	59	0.30
Swedish (13)	86	0.43
Swiss (0)	86	0.43
Ukrainian (18)	18	0.09
Welsh (20)	191	0.96
West Indian, ex. Hispanic (151)	267	1.35
Belizean (15)	34	0.17
Haitian (0)	30	0.15
Jamaican (119)	152	0.77
Trinidadian/Tobagonian (17)	17	0.09
West Indian (0)	34	0.17
Yugoslavian (0)	17	0.09

Hispanic Origin	Population	%
Hispanic or Latino (of any race)	1,651	7.95
Central American, ex. Mexican	675	3.25
Costa Rican	11	0.05
Guatemalan	92	0.44
Honduran	79	0.38
Nicaraguan	13	0.06
Panamanian	8	0.04
Salvadoran	472	2.27
Cuban	28	0.13
Dominican Republic	38	0.18
Mexican	408	1.96
Puerto Rican	171	0.82
South American	148	0.71
Argentinean	4	0.02
Bolivian	1	<0.01
Chilean	12	0.06
Colombian	46	0.22
Ecuadorian	24	0.12
Paraguayan	5	0.02
Peruvian	39	0.19
Uruguayan	2	0.01
Venezuelan	15	0.07
Other Hispanic or Latino	183	0.88

Race*	Population	%
African-American/Black (3,796)	4,095	19.71
Not Hispanic (3,708)	3,966	19.09
Hispanic (88)	129	0.62
American Indian/Alaska Native (73)	180	0.87
Not Hispanic (50)	145	0.70
Hispanic (23)	35	0.17
Apache (2)	3	0.01
Blackfeet (0)	6	0.03

*Notes: † The Census 2010 population figure is used to calculate the percentages in the Hispanic Origin and Race categories. Ancestry percentages are based on the 2006-2010 American Community Survey population (not shown); ‡ Numbers in parentheses indicate the number of people reporting a single ancestry; * Numbers in parentheses indicate the number of persons reporting this race alone, not in combination with any other race; Please refer to the Explanation of Data for more information.*

Central American Ind. (0)	1	<0.01
Cherokee (1)	31	0.15
Chippewa (2)	2	0.01
Cree (1)	1	<0.01
Creek (0)	1	<0.01
Crow (0)	1	<0.01
Delaware (0)	1	<0.01
Iroquois (1)	5	0.02
Lumbee (3)	11	0.05
Mexican American Ind. (2)	4	0.02
Seminole (0)	1	<0.01
Sioux (1)	1	<0.01
South American Ind. (1)	3	0.01
Yuman (0)	2	0.01
Asian (2,616)	2,870	13.81
Not Hispanic (2,604)	2,845	13.69
Hispanic (12)	25	0.12
Bangladeshi (20)	20	0.10
Burmese (13)	13	0.06
Cambodian (1)	3	0.01
Chinese, ex. Taiwanese (553)	592	2.85
Filipino (155)	206	0.99
Indian (962)	1,035	4.98
Indonesian (10)	10	0.05
Japanese (36)	54	0.26
Korean (409)	443	2.13
Laotian (12)	14	0.07
Malaysian (0)	2	0.01
Nepalese (78)	88	0.42
Pakistani (99)	117	0.56
Sri Lankan (26)	30	0.14
Taiwanese (70)	75	0.36
Thai (12)	20	0.10
Vietnamese (47)	49	0.24
Hawaii Native/Pacific Islander (2)	20	0.10
Not Hispanic (2)	16	0.08
Hispanic (0)	4	0.02
Fijian (2)	2	0.01
Native Hawaiian (0)	2	0.01
Samoan (0)	2	0.01
White (12,865)	13,353	64.27
Not Hispanic (12,182)	12,580	60.55
Hispanic (683)	773	3.72

Colesville

Place Type: CDP
County: Montgomery
Population: 14,647†

Ancestry‡	Population	%
Afghan (18)	18	0.13
African, Sub-Saharan (768)	777	5.47
African (450)	459	3.23
Ethiopian (27)	27	0.19
Nigerian (159)	159	1.12
Senegalese (23)	23	0.16
Other Sub-Saharan African (109)	109	0.77
Albanian (26)	26	0.18
American (588)	588	4.14
Arab (150)	181	1.27
Arab (126)	126	0.89
Lebanese (0)	31	0.22
Syrian (9)	9	0.06
Other Arab (15)	15	0.11
Armenian (34)	34	0.24
Austrian (23)	54	0.38
Brazilian (71)	100	0.70
British (48)	137	0.96
Canadian (0)	6	0.04
Czech (0)	11	0.08
Danish (12)	53	0.37
Dutch (11)	153	1.08
Eastern European (39)	39	0.27
English (261)	1,198	8.44
European (64)	76	0.54
Finnish (5)	5	0.04
French, ex. Basque (67)	206	1.45
French Canadian (9)	48	0.34
German (273)	957	6.74
Greek (27)	27	0.19
Guyanese (26)	26	0.18
Hungarian (20)	85	0.60
Iranian (59)	66	0.46
Irish (218)	1,114	7.85
Italian (206)	614	4.32
Lithuanian (14)	33	0.23
Northern European (117)	127	0.89
Norwegian (0)	37	0.26
Polish (290)	488	3.44
Romanian (14)	121	0.85
Russian (115)	198	1.39
Scotch-Irish (153)	247	1.74
Scottish (0)	152	1.07
Slavic (0)	14	0.10
Slovak (0)	68	0.48
Slovene (0)	6	0.04
Swedish (26)	342	2.41
Swiss (0)	103	0.73
Turkish (0)	11	0.08
Ukrainian (36)	88	0.62
Welsh (49)	97	0.68
West Indian, ex. Hispanic (176)	246	1.73
Haitian (107)	107	0.75
Jamaican (69)	128	0.90
West Indian (0)	11	0.08

Hispanic Origin	Population	%
Hispanic or Latino (of any race)	2,176	14.86
Central American, ex. Mexican	1,009	6.89
Costa Rican	12	0.08
Guatemalan	140	0.96
Honduran	48	0.33
Nicaraguan	37	0.25
Panamanian	8	0.05
Salvadoran	756	5.16
Other Central American	8	0.05
Cuban	70	0.48
Dominican Republic	55	0.38
Mexican	168	1.15
Puerto Rican	112	0.76
South American	459	3.13
Argentinean	51	0.35
Bolivian	97	0.66
Chilean	19	0.13
Colombian	66	0.45
Ecuadorian	47	0.32
Paraguayan	15	0.10
Peruvian	132	0.90
Uruguayan	9	0.06
Venezuelan	19	0.13
Other South American	4	0.03
Other Hispanic or Latino	303	2.07

Race*	Population	%
African-American/Black (4,152)	4,421	30.18
Not Hispanic (4,060)	4,265	29.12
Hispanic (92)	156	1.07
American Indian/Alaska Native (43)	162	1.11
Not Hispanic (17)	99	0.68
Hispanic (26)	63	0.43
Blackfeet (1)	5	0.03
Canadian/French Am. Ind. (0)	1	0.01
Central American Ind. (2)	2	0.01
Cherokee (8)	32	0.22
Choctaw (0)	2	0.01
Creek (0)	2	0.01
Delaware (1)	3	0.02
Iroquois (1)	4	0.03
Lumbee (1)	3	0.02
Mexican American Ind. (4)	9	0.06
Pima (1)	1	0.01
Pueblo (1)	1	0.01
Seminole (0)	5	0.03
Sioux (0)	2	0.01
South American Ind. (3)	13	0.09
Spanish American Ind. (0)	1	0.01
Asian (2,357)	2,581	17.62
Not Hispanic (2,349)	2,551	17.42
Hispanic (8)	30	0.20
Bangladeshi (36)	39	0.27
Burmese (18)	24	0.16
Cambodian (72)	75	0.51
Chinese, ex. Taiwanese (390)	453	3.09
Filipino (166)	220	1.50
Indian (470)	527	3.60
Indonesian (1)	1	0.01
Japanese (12)	21	0.14
Korean (365)	390	2.66
Malaysian (0)	1	0.01
Nepalese (5)	5	0.03
Pakistani (77)	84	0.57
Sri Lankan (11)	11	0.08
Taiwanese (41)	44	0.30
Thai (34)	44	0.30
Vietnamese (576)	595	4.06
Hawaii Native/Pacific Islander (1)	17	0.12
Not Hispanic (1)	15	0.10
Hispanic (0)	2	0.01
Marshallese (1)	1	0.01
Native Hawaiian (0)	4	0.03
Samoan (0)	4	0.03
White (6,568)	6,976	47.63
Not Hispanic (5,598)	5,866	40.05
Hispanic (970)	1,110	7.58

College Park

Place Type: City
County: Prince George's
Population: 30,413†

Ancestry‡	Population	%
Afghan (18)	18	0.06
African, Sub-Saharan (573)	680	2.30
African (311)	323	1.09
Ethiopian (18)	18	0.06
Ghanaian (0)	17	0.06
Liberian (0)	12	0.04
Nigerian (203)	217	0.73
Sierra Leonean (0)	12	0.04
South African (0)	11	0.04
Sudanese (8)	8	0.03
Other Sub-Saharan African (33)	62	0.21
American (826)	826	2.79
Arab (95)	141	0.48
Arab (8)	8	0.03
Egyptian (17)	35	0.12
Lebanese (42)	42	0.14
Palestinian (23)	23	0.08
Syrian (5)	33	0.11
Armenian (26)	61	0.21
Australian (0)	18	0.06
Austrian (0)	148	0.50
Belgian (18)	41	0.14
Brazilian (12)	30	0.10
British (74)	245	0.83
Canadian (70)	70	0.24
Croatian (0)	29	0.10
Czech (0)	55	0.19
Czechoslovakian (0)	16	0.05
Danish (0)	27	0.09
Dutch (155)	228	0.77
Eastern European (104)	115	0.39
English (480)	1,930	6.52
European (678)	773	2.61
Finnish (18)	38	0.13
French, ex. Basque (55)	569	1.92
French Canadian (75)	144	0.49
German (666)	3,161	10.68
Greek (91)	301	1.02
Guyanese (0)	53	0.18
Hungarian (78)	433	1.46
Icelander (0)	10	0.03
Iranian (115)	165	0.56
Irish (707)	3,173	10.72
Israeli (104)	155	0.52
Italian (482)	2,244	7.58
Latvian (17)	70	0.24
Lithuanian (56)	106	0.36

*Notes: † The Census 2010 population figure is used to calculate the percentages in the Hispanic Origin and Race categories. Ancestry percentages are based on the 2006-2010 American Community Survey population (not shown); ‡ Numbers in parentheses indicate the number of people reporting a single ancestry; * Numbers in parentheses indicate the number of persons reporting this race alone, not in combination with any other race; Please refer to the Explanation of Data for more information.*

Ancestry	Population	%
Northern European (21)	21	0.07
Norwegian (0)	187	0.63
Pennsylvania German (2)	2	0.01
Polish (332)	1,526	5.16
Portuguese (9)	56	0.19
Romanian (22)	88	0.30
Russian (203)	775	2.62
Scandinavian (7)	14	0.05
Scotch-Irish (167)	390	1.32
Scottish (86)	331	1.12
Slavic (0)	48	0.16
Slovak (36)	146	0.49
Slovene (28)	28	0.09
Swedish (26)	226	0.76
Swiss (27)	88	0.30
Turkish (77)	77	0.26
Ukrainian (99)	215	0.73
Welsh (0)	137	0.46
West Indian, ex. Hispanic (312)	546	1.84
British West Indian (0)	18	0.06
Haitian (97)	97	0.33
Jamaican (68)	148	0.50
Trinidadian/Tobagonian (129)	215	0.73
West Indian (18)	68	0.23

Hispanic Origin	Population	%
Hispanic or Latino (of any race)	3,621	11.91
Central American, ex. Mexican	1,572	5.17
Costa Rican	15	0.05
Guatemalan	203	0.67
Honduran	99	0.33
Nicaraguan	67	0.22
Panamanian	23	0.08
Salvadoran	1,151	3.78
Other Central American	14	0.05
Cuban	107	0.35
Dominican Republic	102	0.34
Mexican	470	1.55
Puerto Rican	246	0.81
South American	422	1.39
Argentinean	65	0.21
Bolivian	49	0.16
Chilean	28	0.09
Colombian	100	0.33
Ecuadorian	47	0.15
Paraguayan	7	0.02
Peruvian	82	0.27
Uruguayan	12	0.04
Venezuelan	30	0.10
Other South American	2	0.01
Other Hispanic or Latino	702	2.31

Race*	Population	%
African-American/Black (4,349)	4,776	15.70
Not Hispanic (4,188)	4,518	14.86
Hispanic (161)	258	0.85
American Indian/Alaska Native (88)	243	0.80
Not Hispanic (50)	174	0.57
Hispanic (38)	69	0.23
Blackfeet (1)	8	0.03
Canadian/French Am. Ind. (2)	3	0.01
Central American Ind. (4)	5	0.02
Cherokee (4)	45	0.15
Cheyenne (1)	1	<0.01
Chickasaw (0)	2	0.01
Chippewa (1)	2	0.01
Choctaw (0)	1	<0.01
Creek (1)	1	<0.01
Crow (0)	1	<0.01
Delaware (1)	1	<0.01
Inupiat *(Alaska Native)* (1)	2	0.01
Iroquois (0)	1	<0.01
Kiowa (0)	1	<0.01
Lumbee (2)	3	0.01
Mexican American Ind. (9)	9	0.03
Navajo (0)	1	<0.01
Sioux (1)	1	<0.01
South American Ind. (3)	7	0.02
Spanish American Ind. (1)	1	<0.01
Asian (3,877)	4,383	14.41
Not Hispanic (3,853)	4,325	14.22
Hispanic (24)	58	0.19
Bangladeshi (46)	51	0.17
Burmese (24)	27	0.09
Cambodian (17)	21	0.07
Chinese, ex. Taiwanese (985)	1,115	3.67
Filipino (222)	305	1.00
Hmong (1)	1	<0.01
Indian (887)	961	3.16
Indonesian (27)	36	0.12
Japanese (47)	117	0.38
Korean (579)	649	2.13
Malaysian (7)	7	0.02
Nepalese (11)	14	0.05
Pakistani (102)	119	0.39
Sri Lankan (7)	13	0.04
Taiwanese (91)	97	0.32
Thai (29)	36	0.12
Vietnamese (151)	183	0.60
Hawaii Native/Pacific Islander (24)	48	0.16
Not Hispanic (18)	37	0.12
Hispanic (6)	11	0.04
Guamanian/Chamorro (8)	9	0.03
Native Hawaiian (2)	12	0.04
Samoan (4)	4	0.01
Tongan (2)	2	0.01
White (19,170)	20,081	66.03
Not Hispanic (17,691)	18,390	60.47
Hispanic (1,479)	1,691	5.56

Columbia

Place Type: CDP
County: Howard
Population: 99,615†

Ancestry‡	Population	%
Afghan (148)	148	0.15
African, Sub-Saharan (3,277)	4,023	4.09
African (1,541)	2,146	2.18
Cape Verdean (44)	44	0.04
Ethiopian (224)	243	0.25
Ghanaian (563)	563	0.57
Kenyan (135)	135	0.14
Liberian (85)	102	0.10
Nigerian (215)	275	0.28
Senegalese (22)	22	0.02
Sierra Leonean (35)	35	0.04
Somalian (58)	58	0.06
South African (14)	33	0.03
Other Sub-Saharan African (341)	367	0.37
Albanian (0)	12	0.01
American (4,031)	4,031	4.10
Arab (1,126)	1,362	1.38
Arab (309)	343	0.35
Egyptian (297)	297	0.30
Iraqi (30)	30	0.03
Jordanian (15)	15	0.02
Lebanese (205)	331	0.34
Moroccan (0)	13	0.01
Syrian (18)	69	0.07
Other Arab (252)	264	0.27
Armenian (4)	118	0.12
Australian (0)	39	0.04
Austrian (117)	547	0.56
Basque (0)	34	0.03
Belgian (12)	53	0.05
Brazilian (53)	149	0.15
British (294)	578	0.59
Bulgarian (78)	78	0.08
Canadian (83)	197	0.20
Croatian (20)	54	0.05
Czech (104)	440	0.45
Czechoslovakian (37)	136	0.14
Danish (127)	331	0.34
Dutch (213)	1,113	1.13
Eastern European (646)	676	0.69
English (2,539)	9,836	10.00
Estonian (0)	10	0.01
European (1,259)	1,419	1.44
Finnish (76)	183	0.19
French, ex. Basque (382)	2,082	2.12
French Canadian (238)	515	0.52
German (3,430)	14,345	14.58
Greek (159)	453	0.46
Guyanese (91)	91	0.09
Hungarian (187)	525	0.53
Icelander (0)	13	0.01
Iranian (575)	632	0.64
Irish (2,739)	11,112	11.30
Israeli (50)	112	0.11
Italian (1,817)	5,921	6.02
Latvian (9)	34	0.03
Lithuanian (109)	355	0.36
Luxemburger (7)	20	0.02
New Zealander (0)	17	0.02
Northern European (94)	184	0.19
Norwegian (193)	779	0.79
Pennsylvania German (24)	42	0.04
Polish (1,361)	4,217	4.29
Portuguese (86)	295	0.30
Romanian (67)	179	0.18
Russian (1,036)	2,500	2.54
Scandinavian (77)	131	0.13
Scotch-Irish (432)	1,172	1.19
Scottish (601)	1,852	1.88
Serbian (16)	16	0.02
Slavic (0)	46	0.05
Slovak (178)	342	0.35
Slovene (12)	12	0.01
Swedish (289)	1,086	1.10
Swiss (79)	213	0.22
Turkish (87)	115	0.12
Ukrainian (350)	515	0.52
Welsh (210)	1,012	1.03
West Indian, ex. Hispanic (1,322)	1,668	1.70
Barbadian (7)	29	0.03
Belizean (0)	13	0.01
Haitian (559)	585	0.59
Jamaican (583)	754	0.77
Trinidadian/Tobagonian (141)	201	0.20
U.S. Virgin Islander (0)	6	0.01
West Indian (21)	45	0.05
Other West Indian (11)	35	0.04
Yugoslavian (61)	61	0.06

Hispanic Origin	Population	%
Hispanic or Latino (of any race)	7,884	7.91
Central American, ex. Mexican	2,471	2.48
Costa Rican	28	0.03
Guatemalan	241	0.24
Honduran	507	0.51
Nicaraguan	125	0.13
Panamanian	153	0.15
Salvadoran	1,389	1.39
Other Central American	28	0.03
Cuban	220	0.22
Dominican Republic	254	0.25
Mexican	2,002	2.01
Puerto Rican	1,137	1.14
South American	1,007	1.01
Argentinean	97	0.10
Bolivian	104	0.10
Chilean	65	0.07
Colombian	283	0.28
Ecuadorian	108	0.11
Paraguayan	19	0.02
Peruvian	225	0.23
Uruguayan	18	0.02
Venezuelan	72	0.07
Other South American	16	0.02
Other Hispanic or Latino	793	0.80

Race*	Population	%
African-American/Black (25,231)	27,625	27.73
Not Hispanic (24,662)	26,741	26.84
Hispanic (569)	884	0.89
American Indian/Alaska Native (393)	1,314	1.32
Not Hispanic (181)	901	0.90
Hispanic (212)	413	0.41

*Notes: † The Census 2010 population figure is used to calculate the percentages in the Hispanic Origin and Race categories. Ancestry percentages are based on the 2006-2010 American Community Survey population (not shown); ‡ Numbers in parentheses indicate the number of people reporting a single ancestry; * Numbers in parentheses indicate the number of persons reporting this race alone, not in combination with any other race; Please refer to the Explanation of Data for more information.*

Alaska Athabascan *(Ala. Nat.)* (0)	1	<0.01
Aleut *(Alaska Native)* (2)	2	<0.01
Apache (4)	11	0.01
Arapaho (1)	2	<0.01
Blackfeet (4)	56	0.06
Canadian/French Am. Ind. (0)	2	<0.01
Central American Ind. (24)	32	0.03
Cherokee (32)	218	0.22
Chickasaw (1)	4	<0.01
Chippewa (9)	15	0.02
Choctaw (3)	26	0.03
Cree (0)	4	<0.01
Creek (1)	9	0.01
Delaware (0)	2	<0.01
Hopi (0)	1	<0.01
Houma (0)	4	<0.01
Inupiat *(Alaska Native)* (1)	2	<0.01
Iroquois (2)	16	0.02
Lumbee (5)	10	0.01
Menominee (0)	1	<0.01
Mexican American Ind. (8)	28	0.03
Navajo (7)	15	0.02
Osage (4)	7	0.01
Paiute (1)	1	<0.01
Pueblo (0)	6	0.01
Seminole (2)	8	0.01
Shoshone (0)	3	<0.01
Sioux (5)	24	0.02
South American Ind. (12)	41	0.04
Spanish American Ind. (0)	1	<0.01
Tlingit-Haida *(Alaska Native)* (2)	3	<0.01
Ute (0)	2	<0.01
Yaqui (2)	2	<0.01
Yup'ik *(Alaska Native)* (0)	1	<0.01
Asian (11,390)	13,090	13.14
Not Hispanic (11,352)	12,925	12.97
Hispanic (38)	165	0.17
Bangladeshi (107)	128	0.13
Burmese (94)	99	0.10
Cambodian (55)	69	0.07
Chinese, ex. Taiwanese (2,442)	2,821	2.83
Filipino (602)	886	0.89
Hmong (5)	5	0.01
Indian (3,288)	3,636	3.65
Indonesian (19)	28	0.03
Japanese (197)	408	0.41
Korean (2,759)	2,986	3.00
Laotian (15)	17	0.02
Malaysian (15)	25	0.03
Nepalese (60)	67	0.07
Pakistani (607)	668	0.67
Sri Lankan (48)	59	0.06
Taiwanese (165)	199	0.20
Thai (89)	130	0.13
Vietnamese (490)	577	0.58
Hawaii Native/Pacific Islander (44)	167	0.17
Not Hispanic (43)	150	0.15
Hispanic (1)	17	0.02
Guamanian/Chamorro (21)	35	0.04
Native Hawaiian (14)	58	0.06
Samoan (6)	10	0.01
White (55,322)	58,902	59.13
Not Hispanic (51,544)	54,498	54.71
Hispanic (3,778)	4,404	4.42

Coral Hills

Place Type: CDP
County: Prince George's
Population: 9,895†

Ancestry‡	Population	%
African, Sub-Saharan (536)	566	5.86
African (510)	540	5.59
Ghanaian (9)	9	0.09
Sierra Leonean (10)	10	0.10
Other Sub-Saharan African (7)	7	0.07
American (122)	122	1.26
British (14)	14	0.15
English (0)	39	0.40
European (18)	18	0.19
French, ex. Basque (0)	22	0.23
German (26)	79	0.82
Irish (0)	66	0.68
Scottish (17)	17	0.18
West Indian, ex. Hispanic (105)	126	1.31
Haitian (86)	86	0.89
Jamaican (8)	8	0.08
Trinidadian/Tobagonian (11)	32	0.33

Hispanic Origin	Population	%
Hispanic or Latino (of any race)	601	6.07
Central American, ex. Mexican	372	3.76
Guatemalan	36	0.36
Honduran	25	0.25
Nicaraguan	9	0.09
Panamanian	5	0.05
Salvadoran	292	2.95
Other Central American	5	0.05
Cuban	5	0.05
Dominican Republic	26	0.26
Mexican	77	0.78
Puerto Rican	28	0.28
South American	17	0.17
Argentinean	1	0.01
Bolivian	5	0.05
Colombian	3	0.03
Ecuadorian	2	0.02
Peruvian	1	0.01
Venezuelan	3	0.03
Other South American	2	0.02
Other Hispanic or Latino	76	0.77

Race*	Population	%
African-American/Black (8,914)	9,094	91.91
Not Hispanic (8,830)	8,989	90.84
Hispanic (84)	105	1.06
American Indian/Alaska Native (40)	136	1.37
Not Hispanic (29)	108	1.09
Hispanic (11)	28	0.28
Blackfeet (1)	13	0.13
Central American Ind. (1)	2	0.02
Cherokee (1)	13	0.13
Choctaw (0)	1	0.01
Iroquois (1)	2	0.02
Mexican American Ind. (1)	2	0.02
Seminole (0)	2	0.02
Sioux (0)	1	0.01
South American Ind. (0)	1	0.01
Asian (28)	53	0.54
Not Hispanic (27)	43	0.43
Hispanic (1)	10	0.10
Chinese, ex. Taiwanese (1)	4	0.04
Filipino (15)	25	0.25
Indian (1)	4	0.04
Japanese (4)	5	0.05
Korean (2)	3	0.03
Laotian (0)	1	0.01
Pakistani (0)	2	0.02
Thai (1)	1	0.01
Hawaii Native/Pacific Islander (2)	9	0.09
Not Hispanic (1)	6	0.06
Hispanic (1)	3	0.03
Guamanian/Chamorro (0)	3	0.03
Native Hawaiian (1)	1	0.01
Samoan (1)	2	0.02
White (359)	508	5.13
Not Hispanic (225)	308	3.11
Hispanic (134)	200	2.02

Crofton

Place Type: CDP
County: Anne Arundel
Population: 27,348†

Ancestry‡	Population	%
African, Sub-Saharan (134)	172	0.62
African (105)	143	0.52
Nigerian (29)	29	0.10
Albanian (41)	41	0.15
American (1,576)	1,576	5.71
Arab (146)	157	0.57
Arab (53)	53	0.19
Lebanese (69)	80	0.29
Palestinian (10)	10	0.04
Other Arab (14)	14	0.05
Armenian (36)	36	0.13
Australian (10)	42	0.15
Austrian (10)	194	0.70
Belgian (0)	42	0.15
Brazilian (15)	43	0.16
British (83)	117	0.42
Canadian (35)	79	0.29
Czech (35)	167	0.60
Czechoslovakian (17)	66	0.24
Danish (0)	34	0.12
Dutch (45)	283	1.02
Eastern European (26)	26	0.09
English (918)	3,380	12.24
European (399)	458	1.66
Finnish (12)	95	0.34
French, ex. Basque (234)	1,188	4.30
French Canadian (60)	178	0.64
German (1,592)	6,920	25.05
Greek (132)	311	1.13
Hungarian (25)	192	0.70
Iranian (21)	44	0.16
Irish (1,906)	6,039	21.86
Israeli (0)	46	0.17
Italian (832)	2,460	8.91
Latvian (0)	13	0.05
Lithuanian (14)	103	0.37
Norwegian (10)	148	0.54
Pennsylvania German (0)	7	0.03
Polish (313)	1,121	4.06
Portuguese (79)	204	0.74
Romanian (0)	83	0.30
Russian (145)	601	2.18
Scandinavian (9)	40	0.14
Scotch-Irish (193)	480	1.74
Scottish (385)	1,018	3.69
Slavic (0)	14	0.05
Slovak (35)	118	0.43
Swedish (128)	386	1.40
Swiss (0)	50	0.18
Turkish (108)	108	0.39
Ukrainian (56)	69	0.25
Welsh (99)	560	2.03
West Indian, ex. Hispanic (73)	149	0.54
Bahamian (12)	27	0.10
British West Indian (30)	91	0.33
Jamaican (15)	15	0.05
Trinidadian/Tobagonian (16)	16	0.06

Hispanic Origin	Population	%
Hispanic or Latino (of any race)	1,298	4.75
Central American, ex. Mexican	207	0.76
Costa Rican	6	0.02
Guatemalan	49	0.18
Honduran	26	0.10
Nicaraguan	26	0.10
Panamanian	21	0.08
Salvadoran	79	0.29
Cuban	74	0.27
Dominican Republic	22	0.08
Mexican	381	1.39
Puerto Rican	268	0.98
South American	214	0.78
Argentinean	13	0.05
Bolivian	33	0.12
Chilean	23	0.08
Colombian	45	0.16
Ecuadorian	34	0.12
Paraguayan	3	0.01
Peruvian	44	0.16
Uruguayan	1	<0.01
Venezuelan	18	0.07
Other Hispanic or Latino	132	0.48

*Notes: † The Census 2010 population figure is used to calculate the percentages in the Hispanic Origin and Race categories. Ancestry percentages are based on the 2006-2010 American Community Survey population (not shown); ‡ Numbers in parentheses indicate the number of people reporting a single ancestry; * Numbers in parentheses indicate the number of persons reporting this race alone, not in combination with any other race; Please refer to the Explanation of Data for more information.*

Race*	Population	%
African-American/Black (2,809)	3,211	11.74
Not Hispanic (2,718)	3,077	11.25
Hispanic (91)	134	0.49
American Indian/Alaska Native (45)	195	0.71
Not Hispanic (35)	169	0.62
Hispanic (10)	26	0.10
Aleut *(Alaska Native)* (1)	1	<0.01
Apache (0)	3	0.01
Arapaho (1)	3	0.01
Blackfeet (1)	8	0.03
Cherokee (6)	48	0.18
Chickasaw (0)	2	0.01
Chippewa (0)	4	0.01
Choctaw (0)	1	<0.01
Cree (0)	1	<0.01
Creek (0)	1	<0.01
Crow (0)	1	<0.01
Delaware (1)	2	0.01
Hopi (0)	1	<0.01
Iroquois (1)	7	0.03
Lumbee (2)	3	0.01
Mexican American Ind. (3)	5	0.02
Navajo (0)	2	0.01
Ottawa (2)	3	0.01
Seminole (0)	5	0.02
Sioux (4)	8	0.03
South American Ind. (1)	7	0.03
Asian (1,344)	1,702	6.22
Not Hispanic (1,338)	1,671	6.11
Hispanic (6)	31	0.11
Bangladeshi (23)	24	0.09
Bhutanese (1)	1	<0.01
Burmese (1)	1	<0.01
Cambodian (2)	3	0.01
Chinese, ex. Taiwanese (167)	220	0.80
Filipino (198)	305	1.12
Indian (386)	417	1.52
Japanese (32)	86	0.31
Korean (234)	291	1.06
Laotian (6)	7	0.03
Malaysian (0)	2	0.01
Nepalese (17)	23	0.08
Pakistani (135)	145	0.53
Sri Lankan (11)	14	0.05
Taiwanese (5)	7	0.03
Thai (9)	18	0.07
Vietnamese (82)	105	0.38
Hawaii Native/Pacific Islander (30)	70	0.26
Not Hispanic (28)	63	0.23
Hispanic (2)	7	0.03
Guamanian/Chamorro (6)	16	0.06
Native Hawaiian (14)	30	0.11
Samoan (1)	1	<0.01
White (21,831)	22,601	82.64
Not Hispanic (21,105)	21,775	79.62
Hispanic (726)	826	3.02

Cumberland

Place Type: City
County: Allegany
Population: 20,859†

Ancestry‡	Population	%
African, Sub-Saharan (87)	97	0.46
African (40)	40	0.19
Cape Verdean (38)	38	0.18
Ethiopian (4)	4	0.02
Other Sub-Saharan African (5)	15	0.07
American (2,348)	2,348	11.22
Austrian (8)	8	0.04
Brazilian (12)	12	0.06
British (8)	8	0.04
Canadian (10)	19	0.09
Czech (10)	40	0.19
Czechoslovakian (8)	8	0.04
Danish (0)	10	0.05
Dutch (64)	458	2.19
Eastern European (11)	11	0.05
English (878)	2,533	12.10
European (200)	255	1.22
French, ex. Basque (0)	320	1.53
French Canadian (37)	66	0.32
German (2,532)	6,899	32.97
Greek (33)	111	0.53
Guyanese (13)	13	0.06
Hungarian (0)	12	0.06
Irish (954)	3,498	16.72
Italian (383)	846	4.04
Luxemburger (0)	8	0.04
Norwegian (9)	51	0.24
Polish (172)	568	2.71
Romanian (15)	15	0.07
Russian (31)	59	0.28
Scandinavian (0)	13	0.06
Scotch-Irish (227)	473	2.26
Scottish (327)	897	4.29
Slavic (0)	13	0.06
Slovak (0)	8	0.04
Swedish (66)	175	0.84
Swiss (20)	63	0.30
Turkish (0)	13	0.06
Ukrainian (0)	37	0.18
Welsh (52)	270	1.29

Hispanic Origin	Population	%
Hispanic or Latino (of any race)	252	1.21
Central American, ex. Mexican	29	0.14
Costa Rican	2	0.01
Guatemalan	7	0.03
Honduran	4	0.02
Nicaraguan	4	0.02
Panamanian	2	0.01
Salvadoran	10	0.05
Cuban	10	0.05
Dominican Republic	4	0.02
Mexican	94	0.45
Puerto Rican	61	0.29
South American	20	0.10
Argentinean	5	0.02
Chilean	1	<0.01
Colombian	4	0.02
Ecuadorian	4	0.02
Peruvian	5	0.02
Venezuelan	1	<0.01
Other Hispanic or Latino	34	0.16

Race*	Population	%
African-American/Black (1,325)	1,766	8.47
Not Hispanic (1,300)	1,723	8.26
Hispanic (25)	43	0.21
American Indian/Alaska Native (47)	141	0.68
Not Hispanic (43)	130	0.62
Hispanic (4)	11	0.05
Apache (2)	2	0.01
Blackfeet (2)	3	0.01
Cherokee (13)	52	0.25
Cree (0)	1	<0.01
Iroquois (1)	2	0.01
Mexican American Ind. (1)	1	<0.01
Navajo (1)	2	0.01
Potawatomi (2)	2	0.01
Sioux (3)	13	0.06
South American Ind. (0)	1	<0.01
Tlingit-Haida *(Alaska Native)* (2)	2	0.01
Asian (184)	239	1.15
Not Hispanic (184)	237	1.14
Hispanic (0)	2	0.01
Chinese, ex. Taiwanese (23)	27	0.13
Filipino (36)	56	0.27
Indian (60)	66	0.32
Japanese (2)	9	0.04
Korean (24)	34	0.16
Pakistani (11)	11	0.05
Sri Lankan (0)	1	<0.01
Taiwanese (1)	2	0.01
Thai (1)	1	<0.01
Vietnamese (16)	21	0.10
Hawaii Native/Pacific Islander (15)	25	0.12
Not Hispanic (14)	24	0.12
Hispanic (1)	1	<0.01
Guamanian/Chamorro (1)	1	<0.01
Native Hawaiian (9)	12	0.06
Samoan (0)	1	<0.01
White (18,655)	19,207	92.08
Not Hispanic (18,501)	19,024	91.20
Hispanic (154)	183	0.88

Damascus

Place Type: CDP
County: Montgomery
Population: 15,257†

Ancestry‡	Population	%
Afghan (34)	34	0.22
African, Sub-Saharan (72)	72	0.46
African (72)	72	0.46
American (802)	802	5.17
Arab (40)	75	0.48
Lebanese (32)	32	0.21
Syrian (8)	8	0.05
Other Arab (0)	35	0.23
Armenian (36)	36	0.23
Austrian (0)	74	0.48
Belgian (13)	13	0.08
Brazilian (15)	43	0.28
British (92)	129	0.83
Celtic (64)	64	0.41
Croatian (0)	18	0.12
Czech (10)	58	0.37
Czechoslovakian (0)	13	0.08
Danish (8)	74	0.48
Dutch (50)	162	1.04
Eastern European (27)	27	0.17
English (465)	2,235	14.40
European (274)	300	1.93
Finnish (31)	44	0.28
French, ex. Basque (160)	649	4.18
French Canadian (29)	73	0.47
German (838)	3,272	21.08
Greek (99)	228	1.47
Hungarian (38)	113	0.73
Iranian (10)	28	0.18
Irish (465)	2,122	13.67
Italian (404)	1,236	7.96
Latvian (18)	18	0.12
Lithuanian (11)	92	0.59
Norwegian (19)	183	1.18
Pennsylvania German (0)	38	0.24
Polish (130)	513	3.31
Russian (23)	109	0.70
Scotch-Irish (53)	183	1.18
Scottish (80)	283	1.82
Serbian (0)	22	0.14
Slavic (0)	26	0.17
Slovak (11)	23	0.15
Swedish (20)	42	0.27
Swiss (0)	11	0.07
Turkish (0)	14	0.09
Ukrainian (37)	124	0.80
Welsh (66)	249	1.60
West Indian, ex. Hispanic (31)	31	0.20
Bahamian (3)	3	0.02
Jamaican (23)	23	0.15
West Indian (5)	5	0.03
Yugoslavian (8)	17	0.11

Hispanic Origin	Population	%
Hispanic or Latino (of any race)	1,769	11.59
Central American, ex. Mexican	713	4.67
Costa Rican	7	0.05
Guatemalan	98	0.64
Honduran	44	0.29
Nicaraguan	41	0.27
Panamanian	10	0.07
Salvadoran	513	3.36
Cuban	54	0.35

*Notes: † The Census 2010 population figure is used to calculate the percentages in the Hispanic Origin and Race categories. Ancestry percentages are based on the 2006-2010 American Community Survey population (not shown); ‡ Numbers in parentheses indicate the number of people reporting a single ancestry; * Numbers in parentheses indicate the number of persons reporting this race alone, not in combination with any other race; Please refer to the Explanation of Data for more information.*

Dominican Republic	25	0.16
Mexican	193	1.26
Puerto Rican	154	1.01
South American	409	2.68
Argentinean	26	0.17
Bolivian	36	0.24
Chilean	69	0.45
Colombian	103	0.68
Ecuadorian	25	0.16
Paraguayan	5	0.03
Peruvian	126	0.83
Uruguayan	3	0.02
Venezuelan	13	0.09
Other South American	3	0.02
Other Hispanic or Latino	221	1.45

Race*	Population	%
African-American/Black (1,216)	1,461	9.58
Not Hispanic (1,172)	1,389	9.10
Hispanic (44)	72	0.47
American Indian/Alaska Native (56)	144	0.94
Not Hispanic (32)	106	0.69
Hispanic (24)	38	0.25
Apache (1)	8	0.05
Cherokee (4)	31	0.20
Chippewa (1)	1	0.01
Choctaw (1)	2	0.01
Comanche (1)	1	0.01
Creek (3)	3	0.02
Iroquois (0)	1	0.01
Lumbee (1)	1	0.01
Mexican American Ind. (3)	3	0.02
Navajo (1)	1	0.01
Sioux (3)	4	0.03
South American Ind. (1)	5	0.03
Spanish American Ind. (11)	11	0.07
Asian (860)	1,004	6.58
Not Hispanic (855)	988	6.48
Hispanic (5)	16	0.10
Bangladeshi (9)	9	0.06
Burmese (3)	4	0.03
Cambodian (32)	35	0.23
Chinese, ex. Taiwanese (154)	189	1.24
Filipino (75)	98	0.64
Indian (260)	275	1.80
Indonesian (8)	8	0.05
Japanese (15)	33	0.22
Korean (100)	118	0.77
Nepalese (9)	9	0.06
Pakistani (37)	39	0.26
Sri Lankan (16)	16	0.10
Taiwanese (3)	5	0.03
Thai (22)	29	0.19
Vietnamese (89)	107	0.70
Hawaii Native/Pacific Islander (12)	30	0.20
Not Hispanic (8)	23	0.15
Hispanic (4)	7	0.05
Guamanian/Chamorro (4)	4	0.03
Native Hawaiian (0)	8	0.05
Samoan (0)	1	0.01
Tongan (0)	1	0.01
White (11,999)	12,457	81.65
Not Hispanic (11,020)	11,359	74.45
Hispanic (979)	1,098	7.20

Dundalk

Place Type: CDP
County: Baltimore
Population: 63,597†

Ancestry‡	Population	%
African, Sub-Saharan (623)	854	1.37
African (562)	767	1.23
Ethiopian (44)	44	0.07
Ghanaian (0)	12	0.02
Nigerian (17)	31	0.05
Albanian (14)	14	0.02
American (3,630)	3,630	5.81
Arab (37)	122	0.20
Arab (6)	6	0.01
Egyptian (22)	45	0.07
Lebanese (0)	36	0.06
Moroccan (9)	27	0.04
Other Arab (0)	8	0.01
Armenian (15)	15	0.02
Austrian (0)	51	0.08
Belgian (0)	60	0.10
Brazilian (53)	53	0.08
British (14)	128	0.20
Canadian (0)	13	0.02
Croatian (0)	105	0.17
Czech (161)	472	0.76
Czechoslovakian (123)	144	0.23
Danish (21)	108	0.17
Dutch (175)	1,372	2.20
Eastern European (8)	20	0.03
English (1,501)	5,931	9.50
European (227)	275	0.44
Finnish (43)	105	0.17
French, ex. Basque (117)	1,344	2.15
French Canadian (49)	140	0.22
German (5,623)	18,895	30.26
Greek (402)	689	1.10
Hungarian (69)	254	0.41
Iranian (0)	11	0.02
Irish (2,444)	12,443	19.93
Italian (2,438)	6,917	11.08
Latvian (0)	6	0.01
Lithuanian (26)	170	0.27
Northern European (47)	47	0.08
Norwegian (36)	168	0.27
Pennsylvania German (37)	145	0.23
Polish (2,786)	6,728	10.77
Portuguese (32)	78	0.12
Romanian (53)	53	0.08
Russian (81)	377	0.60
Scandinavian (11)	11	0.02
Scotch-Irish (384)	1,177	1.88
Scottish (135)	904	1.45
Serbian (0)	52	0.08
Slavic (0)	58	0.09
Slovak (53)	229	0.37
Slovene (0)	10	0.02
Swedish (32)	233	0.37
Swiss (9)	18	0.03
Ukrainian (224)	454	0.73
Welsh (79)	568	0.91
West Indian, ex. Hispanic (55)	161	0.26
British West Indian (0)	32	0.05
Trinidadian/Tobagonian (23)	49	0.08
West Indian (32)	80	0.13
Yugoslavian (39)	70	0.11

Hispanic Origin	Population	%
Hispanic or Latino (of any race)	3,158	4.97
Central American, ex. Mexican	891	1.40
Costa Rican	11	0.02
Guatemalan	60	0.09
Honduran	193	0.30
Nicaraguan	11	0.02
Panamanian	18	0.03
Salvadoran	591	0.93
Other Central American	7	0.01
Cuban	44	0.07
Dominican Republic	131	0.21
Mexican	837	1.32
Puerto Rican	682	1.07
South American	199	0.31
Argentinean	4	0.01
Bolivian	11	0.02
Chilean	8	0.01
Colombian	65	0.10
Ecuadorian	27	0.04
Peruvian	60	0.09
Uruguayan	7	0.01
Venezuelan	7	0.01
Other South American	10	0.02
Other Hispanic or Latino	374	0.59

Race*	Population	%
African-American/Black (7,014)	8,037	12.64
Not Hispanic (6,835)	7,770	12.22
Hispanic (179)	267	0.42
American Indian/Alaska Native (594)	1,263	1.99
Not Hispanic (519)	1,096	1.72
Hispanic (75)	167	0.26
Apache (2)	13	0.02
Blackfeet (10)	33	0.05
Canadian/French Am. Ind. (1)	1	<0.01
Central American Ind. (1)	3	<0.01
Cherokee (127)	311	0.49
Cheyenne (0)	1	<0.01
Chippewa (1)	4	0.01
Choctaw (1)	7	0.01
Inupiat *(Alaska Native)* (0)	2	<0.01
Iroquois (9)	27	0.04
Lumbee (139)	232	0.36
Mexican American Ind. (24)	25	0.04
Navajo (1)	3	<0.01
Osage (0)	1	<0.01
Potawatomi (1)	1	<0.01
Seminole (2)	9	0.01
Shoshone (0)	4	0.01
Sioux (8)	28	0.04
South American Ind. (3)	3	<0.01
Spanish American Ind. (4)	4	0.01
Yaqui (2)	2	<0.01
Asian (1,072)	1,338	2.10
Not Hispanic (1,058)	1,306	2.05
Hispanic (14)	32	0.05
Bangladeshi (13)	13	0.02
Burmese (26)	26	0.04
Cambodian (9)	10	0.02
Chinese, ex. Taiwanese (112)	132	0.21
Filipino (211)	302	0.47
Indian (411)	483	0.76
Japanese (21)	39	0.06
Korean (46)	85	0.13
Laotian (0)	4	0.01
Nepalese (15)	16	0.03
Pakistani (130)	144	0.23
Thai (3)	9	0.01
Vietnamese (33)	39	0.06
Hawaii Native/Pacific Islander (20)	103	0.16
Not Hispanic (11)	80	0.13
Hispanic (9)	23	0.04
Guamanian/Chamorro (3)	18	0.03
Native Hawaiian (7)	27	0.04
Samoan (0)	7	0.01
White (51,687)	53,301	83.81
Not Hispanic (50,347)	51,773	81.41
Hispanic (1,340)	1,528	2.40

East Riverdale

Place Type: CDP
County: Prince George's
Population: 15,509†

Ancestry‡	Population	%
African, Sub-Saharan (1,005)	1,104	7.05
African (384)	470	3.00
Ethiopian (33)	33	0.21
Ghanaian (8)	8	0.05
Nigerian (200)	200	1.28
Sierra Leonean (20)	33	0.21
Somalian (293)	293	1.87
Other Sub-Saharan African (67)	67	0.43
American (141)	141	0.90
Arab (70)	70	0.45
Iraqi (53)	53	0.34
Lebanese (17)	17	0.11
Brazilian (10)	10	0.06
British (10)	10	0.06
Dutch (7)	7	0.04
English (56)	99	0.63
European (13)	13	0.08
French, ex. Basque (7)	73	0.47

*Notes: † The Census 2010 population figure is used to calculate the percentages in the Hispanic Origin and Race categories. Ancestry percentages are based on the 2006-2010 American Community Survey population (not shown); ‡ Numbers in parentheses indicate the number of people reporting a single ancestry; * Numbers in parentheses indicate the number of persons reporting this race alone, not in combination with any other race; Please refer to the Explanation of Data for more information.*

French Canadian (0)	12	0.08
German (168)	334	2.13
Guyanese (38)	45	0.29
Hungarian (7)	17	0.11
Irish (109)	364	2.32
Italian (70)	128	0.82
Lithuanian (9)	9	0.06
Norwegian (10)	29	0.19
Polish (24)	24	0.15
Portuguese (0)	10	0.06
Scotch-Irish (15)	60	0.38
Scottish (0)	12	0.08
Slovak (0)	10	0.06
Slovene (0)	6	0.04
Swedish (7)	7	0.04
Swiss (0)	12	0.08
Turkish (0)	12	0.08
Ukrainian (0)	12	0.08
West Indian, ex. Hispanic (591)	723	4.61
British West Indian (19)	19	0.12
Haitian (76)	121	0.77
Jamaican (379)	416	2.65
Trinidadian/Tobagonian (81)	121	0.77
West Indian (36)	46	0.29

Hispanic Origin	Population	%
Hispanic or Latino (of any race)	8,273	53.34
Central American, ex. Mexican	3,238	20.88
Costa Rican	1	0.01
Guatemalan	530	3.42
Honduran	238	1.53
Nicaraguan	103	0.66
Panamanian	14	0.09
Salvadoran	2,352	15.17
Cuban	17	0.11
Dominican Republic	159	1.03
Mexican	3,871	24.96
Puerto Rican	63	0.41
South American	132	0.85
Argentinean	18	0.12
Bolivian	23	0.15
Chilean	3	0.02
Colombian	13	0.08
Ecuadorian	27	0.17
Paraguayan	3	0.02
Peruvian	44	0.28
Venezuelan	1	0.01
Other Hispanic or Latino	793	5.11

Race*	Population	%
African-American/Black (5,438)	5,697	36.73
Not Hispanic (5,198)	5,369	34.62
Hispanic (240)	328	2.11
American Indian/Alaska Native (181)	306	1.97
Not Hispanic (26)	101	0.65
Hispanic (155)	205	1.32
Apache (0)	1	0.01
Blackfeet (1)	9	0.06
Central American Ind. (7)	10	0.06
Cherokee (1)	22	0.14
Choctaw (0)	6	0.04
Comanche (0)	1	0.01
Iroquois (1)	6	0.04
Mexican American Ind. (28)	35	0.23
Sioux (1)	3	0.02
South American Ind. (2)	9	0.06
Spanish American Ind. (1)	5	0.03
Asian (412)	514	3.31
Not Hispanic (403)	482	3.11
Hispanic (9)	32	0.21
Bangladeshi (6)	6	0.04
Bhutanese (51)	51	0.33
Cambodian (18)	21	0.14
Chinese, ex. Taiwanese (30)	41	0.26
Filipino (83)	105	0.68
Indian (92)	113	0.73
Japanese (5)	9	0.06
Korean (8)	13	0.08
Laotian (2)	2	0.01
Nepalese (11)	11	0.07
Pakistani (19)	19	0.12
Thai (1)	6	0.04
Vietnamese (65)	66	0.43
Hawaii Native/Pacific Islander (5)	40	0.26
Not Hispanic (5)	23	0.15
Hispanic (0)	17	0.11
Guamanian/Chamorro (5)	5	0.03
Native Hawaiian (0)	1	0.01
White (3,628)	4,075	26.28
Not Hispanic (1,323)	1,466	9.45
Hispanic (2,305)	2,609	16.82

Easton

Place Type: Town
County: Talbot
Population: 15,945†

Ancestry‡	Population	%
African, Sub-Saharan (0)	16	0.10
African (0)	8	0.05
Other Sub-Saharan African (0)	8	0.05
American (1,079)	1,079	7.05
Arab (84)	84	0.55
Arab (17)	17	0.11
Egyptian (67)	67	0.44
Australian (18)	18	0.12
Austrian (20)	60	0.39
Belgian (18)	18	0.12
British (12)	49	0.32
Canadian (18)	41	0.27
Croatian (0)	9	0.06
Czech (8)	87	0.57
Danish (14)	101	0.66
Dutch (29)	221	1.44
Eastern European (36)	36	0.24
English (747)	2,335	15.25
European (208)	225	1.47
French, ex. Basque (39)	554	3.62
German (570)	2,571	16.79
Greek (10)	58	0.38
Hungarian (28)	36	0.24
Irish (1,079)	2,985	19.50
Italian (85)	567	3.70
Lithuanian (49)	70	0.46
Northern European (14)	14	0.09
Norwegian (11)	95	0.62
Polish (122)	284	1.85
Portuguese (12)	12	0.08
Russian (61)	191	1.25
Scandinavian (16)	16	0.10
Scotch-Irish (79)	362	2.36
Scottish (138)	411	2.68
Slovak (0)	35	0.23
Slovene (0)	13	0.08
Swedish (0)	118	0.77
Turkish (48)	48	0.31
Ukrainian (0)	26	0.17
Welsh (0)	168	1.10
West Indian, ex. Hispanic (0)	38	0.25
Jamaican (0)	38	0.25

Hispanic Origin	Population	%
Hispanic or Latino (of any race)	1,570	9.85
Central American, ex. Mexican	638	4.00
Costa Rican	8	0.05
Guatemalan	389	2.44
Honduran	95	0.60
Nicaraguan	1	0.01
Panamanian	3	0.02
Salvadoran	142	0.89
Cuban	13	0.08
Dominican Republic	21	0.13
Mexican	533	3.34
Puerto Rican	103	0.65
South American	66	0.41
Argentinean	16	0.10
Bolivian	1	0.01
Chilean	5	0.03
Colombian	5	0.03
Ecuadorian	16	0.10
Paraguayan	1	0.01
Peruvian	17	0.11
Uruguayan	3	0.02
Venezuelan	1	0.01
Other South American	1	0.01
Other Hispanic or Latino	196	1.23

Race*	Population	%
African-American/Black (2,742)	2,931	18.38
Not Hispanic (2,708)	2,870	18.00
Hispanic (34)	61	0.38
American Indian/Alaska Native (32)	113	0.71
Not Hispanic (25)	90	0.56
Hispanic (7)	23	0.14
Apache (1)	5	0.03
Blackfeet (0)	4	0.03
Canadian/French Am. Ind. (0)	5	0.03
Central American Ind. (2)	2	0.01
Cherokee (2)	17	0.11
Chickasaw (1)	1	0.01
Chippewa (1)	4	0.03
Choctaw (0)	1	0.01
Creek (1)	1	0.01
Delaware (1)	6	0.04
Iroquois (1)	4	0.03
Lumbee (2)	2	0.01
Mexican American Ind. (0)	4	0.03
Osage (0)	3	0.02
Seminole (3)	4	0.03
Sioux (1)	1	0.01
Asian (337)	410	2.57
Not Hispanic (329)	398	2.50
Hispanic (8)	12	0.08
Bangladeshi (5)	5	0.03
Burmese (4)	4	0.03
Cambodian (1)	2	0.01
Chinese, ex. Taiwanese (47)	53	0.33
Filipino (62)	87	0.55
Indian (77)	100	0.63
Indonesian (1)	1	0.01
Japanese (2)	2	0.01
Korean (36)	44	0.28
Nepalese (0)	4	0.03
Pakistani (65)	65	0.41
Thai (1)	1	0.01
Vietnamese (17)	22	0.14
Hawaii Native/Pacific Islander (8)	31	0.19
Not Hispanic (7)	28	0.18
Hispanic (1)	3	0.02
Guamanian/Chamorro (1)	2	0.01
Native Hawaiian (1)	13	0.08
White (11,657)	11,971	75.08
Not Hispanic (10,972)	11,238	70.48
Hispanic (685)	733	4.60

Edgemere

Place Type: CDP
County: Baltimore
Population: 8,669†

Ancestry‡	Population	%
American (616)	616	6.80
Arab (10)	10	0.11
Jordanian (10)	10	0.11
Austrian (19)	55	0.61
British (10)	19	0.21
Croatian (9)	9	0.10
Czech (10)	10	0.11
Czechoslovakian (9)	31	0.34
Dutch (18)	181	2.00
English (324)	1,020	11.27
European (11)	59	0.65
Finnish (30)	74	0.82
French, ex. Basque (48)	153	1.69
French Canadian (64)	64	0.71
German (776)	3,288	36.32
Greek (53)	80	0.88
Hungarian (0)	21	0.23

*Notes: † The Census 2010 population figure is used to calculate the percentages in the Hispanic Origin and Race categories. Ancestry percentages are based on the 2006-2010 American Community Survey population (not shown); ‡ Numbers in parentheses indicate the number of people reporting a single ancestry; * Numbers in parentheses indicate the number of persons reporting this race alone, not in combination with any other race; Please refer to the Explanation of Data for more information.*

Irish (633)	2,628	29.03
Italian (151)	828	9.15
Lithuanian (10)	19	0.21
Norwegian (20)	34	0.38
Polish (567)	975	10.77
Russian (39)	39	0.43
Scotch-Irish (137)	222	2.45
Scottish (47)	205	2.26
Slovak (42)	65	0.72
Swedish (25)	34	0.38
Ukrainian (0)	10	0.11
Welsh (9)	68	0.75
Yugoslavian (0)	11	0.12

Hispanic Origin	Population	%
Hispanic or Latino (of any race)	113	1.30
Central American, ex. Mexican	21	0.24
Guatemalan	10	0.12
Honduran	4	0.05
Nicaraguan	3	0.03
Salvadoran	4	0.05
Cuban	3	0.03
Dominican Republic	2	0.02
Mexican	41	0.47
Puerto Rican	22	0.25
South American	10	0.12
Argentinean	1	0.01
Chilean	3	0.03
Colombian	1	0.01
Peruvian	4	0.05
Uruguayan	1	0.01
Other Hispanic or Latino	14	0.16

Race*	Population	%
African-American/Black (342)	370	4.27
Not Hispanic (342)	369	4.26
Hispanic (0)	1	0.01
American Indian/Alaska Native (40)	106	1.22
Not Hispanic (38)	95	1.10
Hispanic (2)	11	0.13
Blackfeet (0)	1	0.01
Cherokee (8)	30	0.35
Cheyenne (0)	1	0.01
Creek (0)	2	0.02
Iroquois (1)	2	0.02
Lumbee (5)	9	0.10
Pueblo (0)	1	0.01
Sioux (1)	1	0.01
South American Ind. (2)	3	0.03
Asian (39)	54	0.62
Not Hispanic (37)	52	0.60
Hispanic (2)	2	0.02
Cambodian (1)	1	0.01
Chinese, ex. Taiwanese (7)	8	0.09
Filipino (5)	12	0.14
Indian (2)	2	0.02
Japanese (1)	7	0.08
Korean (8)	9	0.10
Nepalese (3)	3	0.03
Pakistani (5)	5	0.06
Vietnamese (7)	7	0.08
Hawaii Native/Pacific Islander (0)	6	0.07
Not Hispanic (0)	3	0.03
Hispanic (0)	3	0.03
Guamanian/Chamorro (0)	1	0.01
Native Hawaiian (0)	1	0.01
White (8,109)	8,206	94.66
Not Hispanic (8,041)	8,133	93.82
Hispanic (68)	73	0.84

Edgewater

Place Type: CDP
County: Anne Arundel
Population: 9,023†

Ancestry‡	Population	%
African, Sub-Saharan (22)	22	0.25
African (22)	22	0.25
American (547)	547	6.29
Arab (21)	42	0.48
Lebanese (21)	21	0.24
Syrian (0)	21	0.24
Austrian (7)	73	0.84
British (52)	71	0.82
Canadian (18)	18	0.21
Czech (0)	26	0.30
Danish (36)	57	0.66
Dutch (0)	117	1.35
Eastern European (55)	55	0.63
English (443)	1,261	14.51
European (83)	104	1.20
French, ex. Basque (8)	189	2.17
French Canadian (63)	137	1.58
German (615)	2,158	24.83
Greek (85)	128	1.47
Guyanese (8)	8	0.09
Hungarian (0)	48	0.55
Irish (626)	1,576	18.13
Italian (419)	933	10.73
Lithuanian (0)	24	0.28
Norwegian (38)	250	2.88
Polish (115)	412	4.74
Romanian (10)	10	0.12
Russian (10)	90	1.04
Scandinavian (15)	41	0.47
Scotch-Irish (13)	67	0.77
Scottish (49)	296	3.41
Slovak (12)	59	0.68
Swedish (36)	133	1.53
Swiss (0)	22	0.25
Turkish (0)	10	0.12
Ukrainian (0)	18	0.21
Welsh (14)	47	0.54
West Indian, ex. Hispanic (16)	16	0.18
Dutch West Indian (16)	16	0.18

Hispanic Origin	Population	%
Hispanic or Latino (of any race)	722	8.00
Central American, ex. Mexican	393	4.36
Costa Rican	4	0.04
Guatemalan	20	0.22
Honduran	21	0.23
Nicaraguan	17	0.19
Panamanian	1	0.01
Salvadoran	330	3.66
Cuban	26	0.29
Mexican	149	1.65
Puerto Rican	40	0.44
South American	48	0.53
Argentinean	9	0.10
Bolivian	6	0.07
Chilean	5	0.06
Colombian	10	0.11
Ecuadorian	1	0.01
Peruvian	9	0.10
Uruguayan	2	0.02
Venezuelan	4	0.04
Other South American	2	0.02
Other Hispanic or Latino	66	0.73

Race*	Population	%
African-American/Black (204)	274	3.04
Not Hispanic (203)	272	3.01
Hispanic (1)	2	0.02
American Indian/Alaska Native (38)	112	1.24
Not Hispanic (32)	97	1.08
Hispanic (6)	15	0.17
Apache (0)	1	0.01
Arapaho (0)	1	0.01
Cherokee (7)	30	0.33
Chippewa (3)	3	0.03
Iroquois (0)	1	0.01
Lumbee (2)	2	0.02
Mexican American Ind. (1)	2	0.02
Navajo (1)	1	0.01
Potawatomi (1)	2	0.02
Pueblo (0)	2	0.02
Seminole (0)	2	0.02
Sioux (2)	2	0.02
South American Ind. (1)	2	0.02
Asian (169)	238	2.64
Not Hispanic (168)	234	2.59
Hispanic (1)	4	0.04
Chinese, ex. Taiwanese (19)	32	0.35
Filipino (40)	64	0.71
Indian (34)	43	0.48
Indonesian (0)	1	0.01
Japanese (10)	27	0.30
Korean (11)	14	0.16
Laotian (1)	1	0.01
Nepalese (3)	3	0.03
Pakistani (3)	3	0.03
Taiwanese (2)	2	0.02
Thai (5)	10	0.11
Vietnamese (32)	36	0.40
Hawaii Native/Pacific Islander (2)	5	0.06
Not Hispanic (2)	5	0.06
Native Hawaiian (2)	4	0.04
White (8,013)	8,221	91.11
Not Hispanic (7,709)	7,870	87.22
Hispanic (304)	351	3.89

Edgewood

Place Type: CDP
County: Harford
Population: 25,562†

Ancestry‡	Population	%
African, Sub-Saharan (1,033)	1,053	4.15
African (584)	594	2.34
Cape Verdean (18)	18	0.07
Liberian (26)	36	0.14
Nigerian (405)	405	1.60
American (1,216)	1,216	4.79
Armenian (116)	116	0.46
Austrian (0)	13	0.05
Brazilian (21)	62	0.24
British (0)	65	0.26
Czech (15)	134	0.53
Czechoslovakian (0)	24	0.09
Danish (0)	76	0.30
Dutch (13)	403	1.59
Eastern European (10)	17	0.07
English (293)	1,093	4.30
European (50)	50	0.20
French, ex. Basque (73)	269	1.06
French Canadian (25)	28	0.11
German (1,202)	4,221	16.62
Greek (126)	163	0.64
Hungarian (18)	97	0.38
Irish (668)	2,683	10.57
Italian (632)	1,703	6.71
Lithuanian (6)	54	0.21
Norwegian (12)	44	0.17
Polish (219)	725	2.86
Portuguese (0)	57	0.22
Russian (106)	320	1.26
Scandinavian (20)	20	0.08
Scotch-Irish (199)	505	1.99
Scottish (169)	431	1.70
Slovak (12)	58	0.23
Swedish (18)	27	0.11
Swiss (11)	11	0.04
Turkish (14)	55	0.22
Ukrainian (0)	9	0.04
Welsh (57)	252	0.99
West Indian, ex. Hispanic (94)	194	0.76
Barbadian (13)	13	0.05
Haitian (81)	136	0.54
Jamaican (0)	45	0.18

Hispanic Origin	Population	%
Hispanic or Latino (of any race)	1,708	6.68
Central American, ex. Mexican	351	1.37
Costa Rican	8	0.03
Guatemalan	90	0.35
Honduran	49	0.19
Nicaraguan	3	0.01

SECTION TWO

*Notes: † The Census 2010 population figure is used to calculate the percentages in the Hispanic Origin and Race categories. Ancestry percentages are based on the 2006-2010 American Community Survey population (not shown); ‡ Numbers in parentheses indicate the number of people reporting a single ancestry; * Numbers in parentheses indicate the number of persons reporting this race alone, not in combination with any other race; Please refer to the Explanation of Data for more information.*

Panamanian	62	0.24
Salvadoran	126	0.49
Other Central American	13	0.05
Cuban	19	0.07
Dominican Republic	63	0.25
Mexican	358	1.40
Puerto Rican	633	2.48
South American	68	0.27
Argentinean	10	0.04
Chilean	8	0.03
Colombian	17	0.07
Ecuadorian	12	0.05
Peruvian	15	0.06
Venezuelan	4	0.02
Other South American	2	0.01
Other Hispanic or Latino	216	0.85

Race*	Population	%
African-American/Black (10,466)	11,266	44.07
Not Hispanic (10,275)	10,953	42.85
Hispanic (191)	313	1.22
American Indian/Alaska Native (74)	336	1.31
Not Hispanic (65)	281	1.10
Hispanic (9)	55	0.22
Aleut *(Alaska Native)* (1)	1	<0.01
Apache (0)	4	0.02
Blackfeet (1)	11	0.04
Cherokee (11)	73	0.29
Chippewa (5)	8	0.03
Choctaw (0)	4	0.02
Crow (0)	1	<0.01
Delaware (1)	2	0.01
Inupiat *(Alaska Native)* (1)	3	0.01
Iroquois (1)	6	0.02
Lumbee (7)	11	0.04
Navajo (3)	9	0.04
Seminole (2)	5	0.02
Sioux (0)	4	0.02
South American Ind. (0)	7	0.03
Ute (0)	1	<0.01
Asian (471)	680	2.66
Not Hispanic (471)	661	2.59
Hispanic (0)	19	0.07
Cambodian (5)	5	0.02
Chinese, ex. Taiwanese (35)	55	0.22
Filipino (140)	223	0.87
Indian (108)	151	0.59
Indonesian (1)	2	0.01
Japanese (7)	26	0.10
Korean (46)	83	0.32
Laotian (14)	14	0.05
Malaysian (1)	1	<0.01
Pakistani (21)	32	0.13
Thai (12)	20	0.08
Vietnamese (59)	79	0.31
Hawaii Native/Pacific Islander (42)	104	0.41
Not Hispanic (30)	75	0.29
Hispanic (12)	29	0.11
Guamanian/Chamorro (28)	38	0.15
Native Hawaiian (2)	15	0.06
Samoan (0)	2	0.01
White (12,732)	13,648	53.39
Not Hispanic (12,066)	12,835	50.21
Hispanic (666)	813	3.18

Eldersburg

Place Type: CDP
County: Carroll
Population: 30,531†

Ancestry‡	Population	%
African, Sub-Saharan (209)	209	0.66
African (166)	166	0.52
Kenyan (43)	43	0.14
Albanian (24)	24	0.08
American (1,984)	1,984	6.27
Arab (0)	18	0.06
Arab (0)	9	0.03
Other Arab (0)	9	0.03
Austrian (0)	43	0.14
Belgian (12)	34	0.11
Brazilian (8)	32	0.10
British (51)	121	0.38
Bulgarian (16)	16	0.05
Canadian (53)	117	0.37
Croatian (15)	21	0.07
Czech (130)	314	0.99
Czechoslovakian (0)	32	0.10
Danish (0)	55	0.17
Dutch (137)	736	2.33
Eastern European (50)	50	0.16
English (1,257)	4,926	15.57
European (691)	712	2.25
Finnish (0)	53	0.17
French, ex. Basque (122)	1,158	3.66
French Canadian (140)	301	0.95
German (3,103)	10,434	32.99
Greek (87)	289	0.91
Hungarian (52)	170	0.54
Icelander (0)	10	0.03
Iranian (17)	17	0.05
Irish (1,676)	7,340	23.20
Israeli (0)	12	0.04
Italian (1,061)	3,414	10.79
Lithuanian (85)	237	0.75
Norwegian (51)	191	0.60
Pennsylvania German (10)	10	0.03
Polish (500)	2,205	6.97
Portuguese (0)	36	0.11
Romanian (37)	91	0.29
Russian (137)	411	1.30
Scandinavian (28)	28	0.09
Scotch-Irish (219)	594	1.88
Scottish (187)	820	2.59
Serbian (8)	31	0.10
Slavic (8)	16	0.05
Slovak (18)	91	0.29
Slovene (14)	14	0.04
Swedish (40)	255	0.81
Swiss (0)	33	0.10
Ukrainian (48)	129	0.41
Welsh (34)	372	1.18
West Indian, ex. Hispanic (23)	23	0.07
Haitian (14)	14	0.04
West Indian (9)	9	0.03
Yugoslavian (0)	17	0.05

Hispanic Origin	Population	%
Hispanic or Latino (of any race)	681	2.23
Central American, ex. Mexican	80	0.26
Costa Rican	2	0.01
Guatemalan	24	0.08
Honduran	20	0.07
Nicaraguan	5	0.02
Panamanian	8	0.03
Salvadoran	20	0.07
Other Central American	1	<0.01
Cuban	58	0.19
Dominican Republic	8	0.03
Mexican	181	0.59
Puerto Rican	123	0.40
South American	117	0.38
Argentinean	9	0.03
Bolivian	5	0.02
Chilean	16	0.05
Colombian	32	0.10
Ecuadorian	16	0.05
Paraguayan	3	0.01
Peruvian	21	0.07
Venezuelan	14	0.05
Other South American	1	<0.01
Other Hispanic or Latino	114	0.37

Race*	Population	%
African-American/Black (1,045)	1,215	3.98
Not Hispanic (1,037)	1,188	3.89
Hispanic (8)	27	0.09
American Indian/Alaska Native (68)	165	0.54
Not Hispanic (56)	140	0.46
Hispanic (12)	25	0.08
Alaska Athabascan *(Ala. Nat.)* (0)	2	0.01
Blackfeet (0)	6	0.02
Cherokee (11)	44	0.14
Chickasaw (1)	1	<0.01
Chippewa (2)	4	0.01
Choctaw (1)	1	<0.01
Creek (1)	2	0.01
Crow (1)	1	<0.01
Hopi (5)	5	0.02
Inupiat *(Alaska Native)* (3)	3	0.01
Iroquois (1)	4	0.01
Lumbee (4)	7	0.02
Mexican American Ind. (2)	3	0.01
Navajo (1)	1	<0.01
Osage (1)	1	<0.01
Potawatomi (3)	3	0.01
Sioux (1)	2	0.01
South American Ind. (1)	1	<0.01
Tohono O'Odham (1)	1	<0.01
Asian (608)	814	2.67
Not Hispanic (605)	804	2.63
Hispanic (3)	10	0.03
Bangladeshi (6)	6	0.02
Burmese (3)	4	0.01
Cambodian (6)	7	0.02
Chinese, ex. Taiwanese (94)	121	0.40
Filipino (70)	138	0.45
Indian (137)	162	0.53
Indonesian (0)	1	<0.01
Japanese (14)	40	0.13
Korean (158)	187	0.61
Laotian (1)	7	0.02
Pakistani (10)	11	0.04
Taiwanese (4)	6	0.02
Thai (20)	28	0.09
Vietnamese (66)	74	0.24
Hawaii Native/Pacific Islander (2)	12	0.04
Not Hispanic (2)	11	0.04
Hispanic (0)	1	<0.01
Native Hawaiian (2)	4	0.01
Samoan (0)	1	<0.01
White (28,224)	28,643	93.82
Not Hispanic (27,714)	28,086	91.99
Hispanic (510)	557	1.82

Elkridge

Place Type: CDP
County: Howard
Population: 15,593†

Ancestry‡	Population	%
Afghan (16)	16	0.12
African, Sub-Saharan (461)	461	3.41
African (306)	306	2.26
Ghanaian (53)	53	0.39
Nigerian (40)	40	0.30
Other Sub-Saharan African (62)	62	0.46
American (616)	616	4.56
Arab (24)	54	0.40
Egyptian (0)	7	0.05
Lebanese (0)	17	0.13
Moroccan (24)	24	0.18
Syrian (0)	6	0.04
Austrian (0)	8	0.06
British (0)	42	0.31
Czech (7)	39	0.29
Czechoslovakian (32)	48	0.36
Danish (0)	7	0.05
Dutch (3)	127	0.94
Eastern European (23)	23	0.17
English (324)	1,392	10.30
European (129)	129	0.95
French, ex. Basque (7)	200	1.48
French Canadian (39)	228	1.69
German (810)	2,443	18.08
Greek (0)	15	0.11
Hungarian (9)	42	0.31
Irish (823)	2,335	17.28

*Notes: † The Census 2010 population figure is used to calculate the percentages in the Hispanic Origin and Race categories. Ancestry percentages are based on the 2006-2010 American Community Survey population (not shown); ‡ Numbers in parentheses indicate the number of people reporting a single ancestry; * Numbers in parentheses indicate the number of persons reporting this race alone, not in combination with any other race; Please refer to the Explanation of Data for more information.*

Italian (186)	730	5.40
Latvian (11)	18	0.13
Lithuanian (0)	58	0.43
Maltese (14)	14	0.10
Northern European (0)	17	0.13
Norwegian (16)	34	0.25
Polish (282)	566	4.19
Russian (55)	174	1.29
Scandinavian (19)	19	0.14
Scotch-Irish (40)	213	1.58
Scottish (130)	381	2.82
Slovak (7)	7	0.05
Swedish (25)	86	0.64
Swiss (9)	9	0.07
Turkish (0)	29	0.21
Ukrainian (55)	65	0.48
Welsh (0)	119	0.88
West Indian, ex. Hispanic (76)	96	0.71
Jamaican (69)	69	0.51
U.S. Virgin Islander (0)	20	0.15
West Indian (7)	7	0.05
Yugoslavian (0)	16	0.12

Hispanic Origin	Population	%
Hispanic or Latino (of any race)	981	6.29
Central American, ex. Mexican	342	2.19
Costa Rican	19	0.12
Guatemalan	45	0.29
Honduran	78	0.50
Nicaraguan	9	0.06
Panamanian	14	0.09
Salvadoran	177	1.14
Cuban	19	0.12
Dominican Republic	46	0.30
Mexican	185	1.19
Puerto Rican	154	0.99
South American	106	0.68
Argentinean	10	0.06
Bolivian	4	0.03
Chilean	7	0.04
Colombian	32	0.21
Ecuadorian	8	0.05
Peruvian	38	0.24
Venezuelan	7	0.04
Other Hispanic or Latino	129	0.83

Race*	Population	%
African-American/Black (3,084)	3,414	21.89
Not Hispanic (3,005)	3,292	21.11
Hispanic (79)	122	0.78
American Indian/Alaska Native (49)	167	1.07
Not Hispanic (37)	142	0.91
Hispanic (12)	25	0.16
Apache (1)	1	0.01
Blackfeet (0)	13	0.08
Cherokee (7)	33	0.21
Chippewa (1)	2	0.01
Comanche (0)	3	0.02
Cree (3)	4	0.03
Lumbee (2)	3	0.02
Menominee (0)	2	0.01
Mexican American Ind. (0)	7	0.04
Navajo (1)	3	0.02
Osage (0)	1	0.01
Puget Sound Salish (2)	5	0.03
Seminole (0)	4	0.03
Sioux (3)	4	0.03
South American Ind. (2)	3	0.02
Asian (1,900)	2,124	13.62
Not Hispanic (1,890)	2,104	13.49
Hispanic (10)	20	0.13
Bangladeshi (13)	15	0.10
Burmese (72)	72	0.46
Cambodian (13)	17	0.11
Chinese, ex. Taiwanese (229)	269	1.73
Filipino (188)	250	1.60
Indian (679)	725	4.65
Japanese (44)	74	0.47
Korean (356)	383	2.46
Laotian (1)	2	0.01
Malaysian (0)	2	0.01
Nepalese (15)	19	0.12
Pakistani (80)	83	0.53
Sri Lankan (13)	13	0.08
Taiwanese (12)	13	0.08
Thai (10)	21	0.13
Vietnamese (124)	138	0.89
Hawaii Native/Pacific Islander (8)	30	0.19
Not Hispanic (4)	21	0.13
Hispanic (4)	9	0.06
Guamanian/Chamorro (1)	8	0.05
Native Hawaiian (3)	9	0.06
White (9,602)	10,091	64.71
Not Hispanic (9,112)	9,533	61.14
Hispanic (490)	558	3.58

Elkton

Place Type: Town
County: Cecil
Population: 15,443†

Ancestry‡	Population	%
African, Sub-Saharan (44)	44	0.29
Kenyan (44)	44	0.29
American (691)	691	4.60
Austrian (0)	13	0.09
British (37)	73	0.49
Canadian (33)	86	0.57
Czech (0)	8	0.05
Danish (0)	57	0.38
Dutch (12)	165	1.10
Eastern European (0)	18	0.12
English (460)	1,353	9.00
European (62)	62	0.41
Finnish (0)	25	0.17
French, ex. Basque (31)	392	2.61
French Canadian (29)	70	0.47
German (421)	2,508	16.69
German Russian (55)	55	0.37
Greek (21)	60	0.40
Guyanese (162)	162	1.08
Hungarian (10)	68	0.45
Irish (800)	2,849	18.96
Italian (543)	1,656	11.02
Norwegian (17)	33	0.22
Pennsylvania German (0)	24	0.16
Polish (159)	723	4.81
Portuguese (0)	76	0.51
Romanian (13)	13	0.09
Russian (8)	58	0.39
Scandinavian (138)	138	0.92
Scotch-Irish (45)	221	1.47
Scottish (15)	77	0.51
Slovak (10)	37	0.25
Swedish (19)	178	1.18
Swiss (0)	15	0.10
Turkish (23)	23	0.15
Ukrainian (58)	188	1.25
Welsh (108)	387	2.58
West Indian, ex. Hispanic (98)	132	0.88
British West Indian (9)	26	0.17
Jamaican (89)	106	0.71

Hispanic Origin	Population	%
Hispanic or Latino (of any race)	913	5.91
Central American, ex. Mexican	51	0.33
Costa Rican	13	0.08
Guatemalan	7	0.05
Honduran	14	0.09
Panamanian	7	0.05
Salvadoran	6	0.04
Other Central American	4	0.03
Cuban	15	0.10
Dominican Republic	23	0.15
Mexican	385	2.49
Puerto Rican	304	1.97
South American	32	0.21
Argentinean	3	0.02
Chilean	1	0.01
Colombian	15	0.10
Ecuadorian	8	0.05
Peruvian	4	0.03
Other South American	1	0.01
Other Hispanic or Latino	103	0.67

Race*	Population	%
African-American/Black (2,337)	2,696	17.46
Not Hispanic (2,258)	2,589	16.76
Hispanic (79)	107	0.69
American Indian/Alaska Native (50)	173	1.12
Not Hispanic (39)	137	0.89
Hispanic (11)	36	0.23
Apache (0)	4	0.03
Blackfeet (3)	8	0.05
Canadian/French Am. Ind. (2)	2	0.01
Cherokee (10)	45	0.29
Chippewa (1)	1	0.01
Choctaw (0)	1	0.01
Cree (1)	2	0.01
Crow (0)	1	0.01
Delaware (1)	2	0.01
Iroquois (0)	2	0.01
Lumbee (2)	3	0.02
Mexican American Ind. (7)	9	0.06
Pueblo (0)	1	0.01
Sioux (0)	1	0.01
South American Ind. (0)	1	0.01
Spanish American Ind. (1)	1	0.01
Asian (407)	525	3.40
Not Hispanic (398)	500	3.24
Hispanic (9)	25	0.16
Cambodian (1)	1	0.01
Chinese, ex. Taiwanese (51)	67	0.43
Filipino (87)	108	0.70
Indian (124)	147	0.95
Japanese (9)	23	0.15
Korean (47)	63	0.41
Malaysian (1)	1	0.01
Pakistani (18)	21	0.14
Sri Lankan (10)	10	0.06
Thai (8)	20	0.13
Vietnamese (29)	34	0.22
Hawaii Native/Pacific Islander (11)	29	0.19
Not Hispanic (9)	27	0.17
Hispanic (2)	2	0.01
Guamanian/Chamorro (3)	9	0.06
Native Hawaiian (2)	5	0.03
Samoan (2)	4	0.03
White (11,738)	12,272	79.47
Not Hispanic (11,306)	11,772	76.23
Hispanic (432)	500	3.24

Ellicott City

Place Type: CDP
County: Howard
Population: 65,834†

Ancestry‡	Population	%
African, Sub-Saharan (810)	918	1.41
African (615)	688	1.06
Ethiopian (23)	23	0.04
Nigerian (132)	151	0.23
Sudanese (24)	24	0.04
Other Sub-Saharan African (16)	32	0.05
American (2,769)	2,769	4.26
Arab (184)	212	0.33
Arab (46)	65	0.10
Egyptian (87)	87	0.13
Lebanese (23)	23	0.04
Palestinian (0)	9	0.01
Syrian (28)	28	0.04
Armenian (10)	19	0.03
Australian (72)	72	0.11
Austrian (48)	446	0.69
Belgian (17)	80	0.12
Brazilian (55)	55	0.08
British (225)	467	0.72
Cajun (16)	16	0.02

*Notes: † The Census 2010 population figure is used to calculate the percentages in the Hispanic Origin and Race categories. Ancestry percentages are based on the 2006-2010 American Community Survey population (not shown); ‡ Numbers in parentheses indicate the number of people reporting a single ancestry; * Numbers in parentheses indicate the number of persons reporting this race alone, not in combination with any other race; Please refer to the Explanation of Data for more information.*

Canadian (39)	92	0.14
Croatian (30)	106	0.16
Czech (83)	263	0.40
Czechoslovakian (31)	51	0.08
Danish (51)	248	0.38
Dutch (124)	584	0.90
Eastern European (261)	293	0.45
English (1,783)	7,046	10.85
Estonian (25)	25	0.04
European (1,149)	1,232	1.90
Finnish (22)	151	0.23
French, ex. Basque (146)	1,185	1.82
French Canadian (167)	351	0.54
German (3,245)	12,282	18.90
Greek (343)	827	1.27
Guyanese (12)	25	0.04
Hungarian (252)	705	1.09
Iranian (207)	217	0.33
Irish (3,310)	10,339	15.91
Italian (1,788)	4,779	7.36
Latvian (24)	102	0.16
Lithuanian (77)	218	0.34
Luxemburger (15)	32	0.05
Northern European (100)	100	0.15
Norwegian (141)	619	0.95
Pennsylvania German (59)	59	0.09
Polish (960)	3,738	5.75
Portuguese (28)	75	0.12
Romanian (129)	172	0.26
Russian (627)	1,351	2.08
Scandinavian (75)	126	0.19
Scotch-Irish (380)	885	1.36
Scottish (353)	1,460	2.25
Serbian (0)	16	0.02
Slavic (49)	102	0.16
Slovak (96)	451	0.69
Swedish (166)	767	1.18
Swiss (28)	214	0.33
Turkish (265)	284	0.44
Ukrainian (49)	133	0.20
Welsh (73)	362	0.56
West Indian, ex. Hispanic (237)	360	0.55
Dutch West Indian (15)	22	0.03
Haitian (13)	33	0.05
Jamaican (186)	282	0.43
Trinidadian/Tobagonian (23)	23	0.04
Yugoslavian (0)	42	0.06

Hispanic Origin	Population	%
Hispanic or Latino (of any race)	2,323	3.53
Central American, ex. Mexican	469	0.71
Costa Rican	15	0.02
Guatemalan	36	0.05
Honduran	196	0.30
Nicaraguan	8	0.01
Panamanian	30	0.05
Salvadoran	179	0.27
Other Central American	5	0.01
Cuban	114	0.17
Dominican Republic	67	0.10
Mexican	576	0.87
Puerto Rican	377	0.57
South American	461	0.70
Argentinean	38	0.06
Bolivian	31	0.05
Chilean	53	0.08
Colombian	127	0.19
Ecuadorian	52	0.08
Paraguayan	5	0.01
Peruvian	109	0.17
Uruguayan	12	0.02
Venezuelan	33	0.05
Other South American	1	<0.01
Other Hispanic or Latino	259	0.39

Race*	Population	%
African-American/Black (5,585)	6,211	9.43
Not Hispanic (5,503)	6,060	9.20
Hispanic (82)	151	0.23
American Indian/Alaska Native (134)	429	0.65
Not Hispanic (87)	328	0.50
Hispanic (47)	101	0.15
Apache (3)	12	0.02
Blackfeet (5)	18	0.03
Canadian/French Am. Ind. (0)	2	<0.01
Central American Ind. (0)	4	0.01
Cherokee (11)	83	0.13
Cheyenne (0)	4	0.01
Chippewa (3)	4	0.01
Choctaw (3)	14	0.02
Comanche (0)	1	<0.01
Creek (1)	2	<0.01
Delaware (1)	2	<0.01
Iroquois (1)	8	0.01
Lumbee (8)	8	0.01
Mexican American Ind. (10)	15	0.02
Navajo (3)	8	0.01
Osage (0)	1	<0.01
Potawatomi (1)	2	<0.01
Seminole (0)	1	<0.01
Sioux (1)	8	0.01
South American Ind. (1)	5	0.01
Yaqui (1)	2	<0.01
Asian (15,056)	16,112	24.47
Not Hispanic (15,029)	16,045	24.37
Hispanic (27)	67	0.10
Bangladeshi (121)	127	0.19
Burmese (34)	36	0.05
Cambodian (14)	24	0.04
Chinese, ex. Taiwanese (3,124)	3,441	5.23
Filipino (256)	416	0.63
Indian (4,467)	4,712	7.16
Indonesian (7)	10	0.02
Japanese (110)	226	0.34
Korean (5,333)	5,531	8.40
Laotian (0)	2	<0.01
Malaysian (10)	12	0.02
Nepalese (45)	46	0.07
Pakistani (663)	710	1.08
Sri Lankan (42)	43	0.07
Taiwanese (168)	194	0.29
Thai (107)	119	0.18
Vietnamese (286)	334	0.51
Hawaii Native/Pacific Islander (24)	97	0.15
Not Hispanic (24)	90	0.14
Hispanic (0)	7	0.01
Guamanian/Chamorro (4)	10	0.02
Native Hawaiian (8)	29	0.04
Samoan (3)	8	0.01
Tongan (0)	6	0.01
White (42,452)	43,979	66.80
Not Hispanic (41,107)	42,459	64.49
Hispanic (1,345)	1,520	2.31

Essex

Place Type: CDP
County: Baltimore
Population: 39,262†

Ancestry‡	Population	%
African, Sub-Saharan (2,526)	2,745	7.08
African (1,572)	1,758	4.53
Ethiopian (166)	166	0.43
Kenyan (157)	157	0.40
Liberian (287)	287	0.74
Nigerian (243)	267	0.69
Sierra Leonean (35)	35	0.09
South African (22)	31	0.08
Other Sub-Saharan African (44)	44	0.11
American (1,928)	1,928	4.97
Arab (7)	28	0.07
Arab (7)	7	0.02
Egyptian (0)	9	0.02
Lebanese (0)	12	0.03
Armenian (0)	10	0.03
Austrian (0)	27	0.07
British (34)	47	0.12
Canadian (13)	26	0.07
Czech (165)	351	0.90
Czechoslovakian (19)	31	0.08
Danish (18)	38	0.10
Dutch (112)	596	1.54
Eastern European (11)	11	0.03
English (807)	2,910	7.50
European (83)	122	0.31
Finnish (0)	10	0.03
French, ex. Basque (143)	736	1.90
French Canadian (43)	190	0.49
German (3,157)	9,668	24.92
Greek (73)	151	0.39
Guyanese (189)	189	0.49
Hungarian (34)	111	0.29
Irish (1,125)	5,460	14.08
Italian (1,057)	2,772	7.15
Lithuanian (12)	56	0.14
Norwegian (8)	46	0.12
Pennsylvania German (10)	10	0.03
Polish (1,231)	2,721	7.01
Romanian (28)	28	0.07
Russian (42)	89	0.23
Scandinavian (14)	35	0.09
Scotch-Irish (216)	526	1.36
Scottish (82)	480	1.24
Slavic (42)	42	0.11
Slovak (34)	46	0.12
Swedish (20)	48	0.12
Swiss (0)	18	0.05
Ukrainian (11)	126	0.32
Welsh (38)	231	0.60
West Indian, ex. Hispanic (201)	405	1.04
Barbadian (0)	34	0.09
British West Indian (12)	46	0.12
Haitian (96)	96	0.25
Jamaican (68)	68	0.18
Trinidadian/Tobagonian (25)	25	0.06
West Indian (0)	136	0.35

Hispanic Origin	Population	%
Hispanic or Latino (of any race)	2,018	5.14
Central American, ex. Mexican	458	1.17
Costa Rican	12	0.03
Guatemalan	48	0.12
Honduran	130	0.33
Nicaraguan	1	<0.01
Panamanian	22	0.06
Salvadoran	240	0.61
Other Central American	5	0.01
Cuban	17	0.04
Dominican Republic	85	0.22
Mexican	671	1.71
Puerto Rican	460	1.17
South American	129	0.33
Argentinean	7	0.02
Bolivian	3	0.01
Chilean	8	0.02
Colombian	57	0.15
Ecuadorian	26	0.07
Peruvian	16	0.04
Venezuelan	8	0.02
Other South American	4	0.01
Other Hispanic or Latino	198	0.50

Race*	Population	%
African-American/Black (10,364)	11,128	28.34
Not Hispanic (10,187)	10,864	27.67
Hispanic (177)	264	0.67
American Indian/Alaska Native (204)	519	1.32
Not Hispanic (157)	428	1.09
Hispanic (47)	91	0.23
Apache (3)	7	0.02
Blackfeet (6)	16	0.04
Central American Ind. (0)	8	0.02
Cherokee (24)	96	0.24
Choctaw (0)	3	0.01
Cree (0)	4	0.01
Crow (0)	1	<0.01
Inupiat *(Alaska Native)* (1)	1	<0.01
Iroquois (3)	12	0.03
Lumbee (36)	66	0.17

*Notes: † The Census 2010 population figure is used to calculate the percentages in the Hispanic Origin and Race categories. Ancestry percentages are based on the 2006-2010 American Community Survey population (not shown); ‡ Numbers in parentheses indicate the number of people reporting a single ancestry; * Numbers in parentheses indicate the number of persons reporting this race alone, not in combination with any other race; Please refer to the Explanation of Data for more information.*

Menominee (1)	1	<0.01
Navajo (0)	3	0.01
Potawatomi (0)	1	<0.01
Sioux (0)	6	0.02
South American Ind. (7)	8	0.02
Ute (0)	2	0.01
Yaqui (3)	3	0.01
Asian (705)	877	2.23
Not Hispanic (702)	867	2.21
Hispanic (3)	10	0.03
Burmese (2)	2	0.01
Cambodian (6)	9	0.02
Chinese, ex. Taiwanese (93)	106	0.27
Filipino (169)	224	0.57
Indian (240)	288	0.73
Japanese (10)	25	0.06
Korean (39)	57	0.15
Laotian (12)	16	0.04
Malaysian (0)	1	<0.01
Nepalese (7)	7	0.02
Pakistani (41)	47	0.12
Sri Lankan (1)	1	<0.01
Thai (6)	13	0.03
Vietnamese (43)	50	0.13
Hawaii Native/Pacific Islander (10)	57	0.15
Not Hispanic (9)	47	0.12
Hispanic (1)	10	0.03
Guamanian/Chamorro (2)	9	0.02
Native Hawaiian (0)	4	0.01
Samoan (0)	2	0.01
White (26,072)	26,989	68.74
Not Hispanic (25,161)	25,912	66.00
Hispanic (911)	1,077	2.74

Fairland

Place Type: CDP
County: Montgomery
Population: 23,681†

Ancestry‡	Population	%
African, Sub-Saharan (2,757)	3,150	13.64
African (1,305)	1,444	6.25
Ethiopian (352)	432	1.87
Ghanaian (233)	291	1.26
Kenyan (33)	82	0.36
Liberian (107)	107	0.46
Nigerian (327)	327	1.42
Sierra Leonean (165)	214	0.93
Ugandan (96)	96	0.42
Other Sub-Saharan African (139)	157	0.68
American (318)	318	1.38
Arab (89)	197	0.85
Arab (9)	9	0.04
Egyptian (34)	81	0.35
Iraqi (0)	8	0.03
Jordanian (0)	6	0.03
Lebanese (27)	27	0.12
Syrian (19)	66	0.29
Austrian (70)	98	0.42
British (11)	11	0.05
Bulgarian (9)	9	0.04
Cajun (0)	9	0.04
Canadian (16)	27	0.12
Czech (37)	63	0.27
Czechoslovakian (0)	11	0.05
Danish (8)	8	0.03
Dutch (12)	33	0.14
Eastern European (20)	20	0.09
English (219)	982	4.25
European (36)	36	0.16
French, ex. Basque (36)	253	1.10
French Canadian (13)	13	0.06
German (415)	1,220	5.28
Greek (93)	143	0.62
Guyanese (10)	22	0.10
Hungarian (34)	34	0.15
Iranian (8)	8	0.03
Irish (314)	1,107	4.80
Italian (164)	604	2.62
Lithuanian (20)	20	0.09
Northern European (14)	14	0.06
Norwegian (10)	47	0.20
Pennsylvania German (13)	25	0.11
Polish (69)	196	0.85
Portuguese (28)	28	0.12
Russian (76)	95	0.41
Scotch-Irish (139)	270	1.17
Scottish (94)	254	1.10
Serbian (0)	10	0.04
Slovak (0)	44	0.19
Swedish (10)	50	0.22
Swiss (36)	83	0.36
Turkish (60)	60	0.26
Ukrainian (0)	12	0.05
Welsh (9)	86	0.37
West Indian, ex. Hispanic (989)	1,162	5.03
Barbadian (16)	96	0.42
British West Indian (27)	27	0.12
Haitian (232)	239	1.04
Jamaican (261)	329	1.43
Trinidadian/Tobagonian (167)	167	0.72
U.S. Virgin Islander (0)	11	0.05
West Indian (286)	293	1.27

Hispanic Origin	Population	%
Hispanic or Latino (of any race)	2,836	11.98
Central American, ex. Mexican	1,352	5.71
Costa Rican	14	0.06
Guatemalan	188	0.79
Honduran	88	0.37
Nicaraguan	104	0.44
Panamanian	73	0.31
Salvadoran	885	3.74
Cuban	80	0.34
Dominican Republic	198	0.84
Mexican	218	0.92
Puerto Rican	264	1.11
South American	407	1.72
Argentinean	21	0.09
Bolivian	37	0.16
Chilean	17	0.07
Colombian	107	0.45
Ecuadorian	35	0.15
Paraguayan	14	0.06
Peruvian	137	0.58
Uruguayan	11	0.05
Venezuelan	22	0.09
Other South American	6	0.03
Other Hispanic or Latino	317	1.34

Race*	Population	%
African-American/Black (12,280)	12,820	54.14
Not Hispanic (11,916)	12,360	52.19
Hispanic (364)	460	1.94
American Indian/Alaska Native (80)	230	0.97
Not Hispanic (43)	167	0.71
Hispanic (37)	63	0.27
Arapaho (0)	2	0.01
Blackfeet (0)	12	0.05
Canadian/French Am. Ind. (0)	2	0.01
Cherokee (4)	37	0.16
Chickasaw (0)	2	0.01
Chippewa (2)	3	0.01
Choctaw (0)	6	0.03
Creek (1)	1	<0.01
Inupiat *(Alaska Native)* (1)	1	<0.01
Iroquois (1)	4	0.02
Lumbee (0)	1	<0.01
Mexican American Ind. (12)	13	0.05
Navajo (0)	3	0.01
Puget Sound Salish (0)	2	0.01
Seminole (0)	2	0.01
Sioux (0)	1	<0.01
South American Ind. (1)	11	0.05
Asian (3,441)	3,773	15.93
Not Hispanic (3,415)	3,708	15.66
Hispanic (26)	65	0.27
Bangladeshi (52)	63	0.27
Burmese (22)	22	0.09
Cambodian (73)	83	0.35
Chinese, ex. Taiwanese (404)	477	2.01
Filipino (211)	274	1.16
Hmong (1)	1	<0.01
Indian (1,206)	1,339	5.65
Indonesian (6)	7	0.03
Japanese (28)	44	0.19
Korean (535)	560	2.36
Laotian (25)	26	0.11
Malaysian (7)	10	0.04
Nepalese (25)	25	0.11
Pakistani (166)	176	0.74
Sri Lankan (21)	25	0.11
Taiwanese (73)	75	0.32
Thai (43)	49	0.21
Vietnamese (437)	475	2.01
Hawaii Native/Pacific Islander (16)	60	0.25
Not Hispanic (14)	49	0.21
Hispanic (2)	11	0.05
Fijian (0)	1	<0.01
Guamanian/Chamorro (4)	11	0.05
Native Hawaiian (1)	3	0.01
Samoan (2)	10	0.04
White (5,801)	6,386	26.97
Not Hispanic (4,680)	5,096	21.52
Hispanic (1,121)	1,290	5.45

Fallston

Place Type: CDP
County: Harford
Population: 8,958†

Ancestry‡	Population	%
American (365)	365	4.53
Arab (6)	75	0.93
Egyptian (6)	13	0.16
Lebanese (0)	62	0.77
Armenian (0)	15	0.19
British (37)	37	0.46
Bulgarian (40)	40	0.50
Canadian (0)	31	0.38
Czech (14)	69	0.86
Dutch (21)	181	2.25
English (287)	1,324	16.42
European (113)	113	1.40
Finnish (0)	16	0.20
French, ex. Basque (14)	93	1.15
French Canadian (16)	70	0.87
German (899)	3,080	38.20
Greek (63)	63	0.78
Hungarian (0)	106	1.31
Irish (526)	2,586	32.08
Italian (472)	1,221	15.15
Lithuanian (12)	22	0.27
Norwegian (0)	66	0.82
Polish (172)	604	7.49
Portuguese (15)	15	0.19
Russian (32)	32	0.40
Scandinavian (0)	35	0.43
Scotch-Irish (70)	200	2.48
Scottish (8)	222	2.75
Slavic (16)	29	0.36
Swedish (0)	37	0.46
Swiss (0)	12	0.15
Ukrainian (0)	36	0.45
Welsh (30)	119	1.48

Hispanic Origin	Population	%
Hispanic or Latino (of any race)	125	1.40
Central American, ex. Mexican	5	0.06
Guatemalan	3	0.03
Honduran	1	0.01
Panamanian	1	0.01
Cuban	13	0.15
Dominican Republic	2	0.02
Mexican	21	0.23
Puerto Rican	22	0.25
South American	30	0.33
Argentinean	3	0.03

SECTION TWO

*Notes: † The Census 2010 population figure is used to calculate the percentages in the Hispanic Origin and Race categories. Ancestry percentages are based on the 2006-2010 American Community Survey population (not shown); ‡ Numbers in parentheses indicate the number of people reporting a single ancestry; * Numbers in parentheses indicate the number of persons reporting this race alone, not in combination with any other race; Please refer to the Explanation of Data for more information.*

Colombian	8	0.09
Ecuadorian	4	0.04
Peruvian	7	0.08
Venezuelan	8	0.09
Other Hispanic or Latino	32	0.36

Race*	Population	%
African-American/Black (106)	133	1.48
Not Hispanic (104)	120	1.34
Hispanic (2)	13	0.15
American Indian/Alaska Native (18)	39	0.44
Not Hispanic (17)	37	0.41
Hispanic (1)	2	0.02
Blackfeet (3)	3	0.03
Cherokee (5)	10	0.11
Cheyenne (0)	3	0.03
Choctaw (0)	3	0.03
Cree (0)	1	0.01
Lumbee (3)	3	0.03
Mexican American Ind. (0)	1	0.01
Spanish American Ind. (1)	1	0.01
Asian (149)	197	2.20
Not Hispanic (148)	192	2.14
Hispanic (1)	5	0.06
Chinese, ex. Taiwanese (23)	29	0.32
Filipino (23)	41	0.46
Indian (31)	37	0.41
Japanese (0)	3	0.03
Korean (35)	43	0.48
Taiwanese (2)	2	0.02
Vietnamese (35)	40	0.45
Hawaii Native/Pacific Islander (0)	2	0.02
Not Hispanic (0)	2	0.02
Guamanian/Chamorro (0)	1	0.01
White (8,564)	8,653	96.60
Not Hispanic (8,468)	8,543	95.37
Hispanic (96)	110	1.23

Ferndale

Place Type: CDP
County: Anne Arundel
Population: 16,746†

Ancestry‡	Population	%
African, Sub-Saharan (195)	334	1.95
African (139)	234	1.37
Nigerian (47)	91	0.53
Other Sub-Saharan African (9)	9	0.05
American (1,073)	1,073	6.27
Arab (44)	111	0.65
Egyptian (32)	72	0.42
Lebanese (12)	12	0.07
Syrian (0)	27	0.16
Austrian (0)	14	0.08
Belgian (0)	13	0.08
British (0)	55	0.32
Czech (99)	112	0.65
Czechoslovakian (0)	10	0.06
Dutch (22)	364	2.13
English (399)	1,338	7.82
European (25)	25	0.15
French, ex. Basque (111)	589	3.44
French Canadian (24)	51	0.30
German (1,454)	4,968	29.05
Greek (51)	67	0.39
Hungarian (109)	310	1.81
Irish (675)	3,270	19.12
Italian (649)	1,679	9.82
Lithuanian (0)	22	0.13
Norwegian (26)	78	0.46
Pennsylvania German (12)	12	0.07
Polish (177)	733	4.29
Portuguese (37)	45	0.26
Russian (21)	21	0.12
Scotch-Irish (35)	264	1.54
Scottish (63)	186	1.09
Slavic (0)	13	0.08
Slovak (31)	58	0.34
Swedish (44)	141	0.82
Swiss (0)	15	0.09
Ukrainian (13)	30	0.18
Welsh (46)	182	1.06
West Indian, ex. Hispanic (17)	17	0.10
Jamaican (17)	17	0.10

Hispanic Origin	Population	%
Hispanic or Latino (of any race)	1,355	8.09
Central American, ex. Mexican	523	3.12
Costa Rican	8	0.05
Guatemalan	197	1.18
Honduran	61	0.36
Nicaraguan	15	0.09
Panamanian	25	0.15
Salvadoran	199	1.19
Other Central American	18	0.11
Cuban	28	0.17
Dominican Republic	22	0.13
Mexican	420	2.51
Puerto Rican	174	1.04
South American	64	0.38
Argentinean	7	0.04
Bolivian	1	0.01
Chilean	4	0.02
Colombian	7	0.04
Ecuadorian	17	0.10
Peruvian	26	0.16
Venezuelan	2	0.01
Other Hispanic or Latino	124	0.74

Race*	Population	%
African-American/Black (3,023)	3,316	19.80
Not Hispanic (2,963)	3,220	19.23
Hispanic (60)	96	0.57
American Indian/Alaska Native (64)	198	1.18
Not Hispanic (53)	178	1.06
Hispanic (11)	20	0.12
Apache (0)	3	0.02
Blackfeet (1)	5	0.03
Cherokee (5)	25	0.15
Cheyenne (1)	1	0.01
Comanche (0)	1	0.01
Iroquois (0)	2	0.01
Lumbee (8)	13	0.08
Navajo (3)	3	0.02
Osage (0)	1	0.01
Sioux (1)	1	0.01
South American Ind. (0)	1	0.01
Spanish American Ind. (4)	4	0.02
Yaqui (3)	3	0.02
Asian (638)	770	4.60
Not Hispanic (638)	754	4.50
Hispanic (0)	16	0.10
Bangladeshi (1)	1	0.01
Burmese (15)	15	0.09
Cambodian (1)	1	0.01
Chinese, ex. Taiwanese (106)	115	0.69
Filipino (103)	158	0.94
Indian (174)	185	1.10
Indonesian (0)	1	0.01
Japanese (5)	23	0.14
Korean (111)	131	0.78
Laotian (2)	2	0.01
Malaysian (3)	3	0.02
Nepalese (4)	4	0.02
Pakistani (38)	43	0.26
Sri Lankan (14)	15	0.09
Taiwanese (8)	8	0.05
Thai (9)	12	0.07
Vietnamese (16)	17	0.10
Hawaii Native/Pacific Islander (9)	34	0.20
Not Hispanic (8)	32	0.19
Hispanic (1)	2	0.01
Guamanian/Chamorro (6)	11	0.07
Native Hawaiian (3)	13	0.08
Samoan (0)	8	0.05
White (11,822)	12,272	73.28
Not Hispanic (11,257)	11,623	69.41
Hispanic (565)	649	3.88

Forestville

Place Type: CDP
County: Prince George's
Population: 12,353†

Ancestry‡	Population	%
African, Sub-Saharan (358)	358	2.91
African (349)	349	2.84
Nigerian (9)	9	0.07
American (190)	190	1.55
Arab (8)	8	0.07
Moroccan (8)	8	0.07
British (24)	24	0.20
Czech (0)	8	0.07
Dutch (0)	5	0.04
English (61)	146	1.19
European (0)	10	0.08
French, ex. Basque (12)	38	0.31
French Canadian (0)	9	0.07
German (20)	157	1.28
Guyanese (125)	125	1.02
Hungarian (0)	4	0.03
Irish (9)	128	1.04
Lithuanian (0)	12	0.10
Luxemburger (0)	4	0.03
Polish (24)	36	0.29
Scotch-Irish (41)	51	0.41
Scottish (0)	8	0.07
Slovak (10)	27	0.22
Swedish (0)	13	0.11
Ukrainian (10)	10	0.08
West Indian, ex. Hispanic (162)	173	1.41
Jamaican (13)	13	0.11
Trinidadian/Tobagonian (119)	130	1.06
West Indian (30)	30	0.24

Hispanic Origin	Population	%
Hispanic or Latino (of any race)	703	5.69
Central American, ex. Mexican	375	3.04
Guatemalan	22	0.18
Honduran	44	0.36
Nicaraguan	7	0.06
Panamanian	15	0.12
Salvadoran	287	2.32
Cuban	23	0.19
Dominican Republic	12	0.10
Mexican	138	1.12
Puerto Rican	40	0.32
South American	51	0.41
Bolivian	12	0.10
Chilean	2	0.02
Colombian	3	0.02
Ecuadorian	8	0.06
Paraguayan	2	0.02
Peruvian	9	0.07
Uruguayan	1	0.01
Venezuelan	7	0.06
Other South American	7	0.06
Other Hispanic or Latino	64	0.52

Race*	Population	%
African-American/Black (10,864)	11,067	89.59
Not Hispanic (10,746)	10,917	88.38
Hispanic (118)	150	1.21
American Indian/Alaska Native (44)	132	1.07
Not Hispanic (27)	110	0.89
Hispanic (17)	22	0.18
Alaska Athabascan *(Ala. Nat.)* (1)	4	0.03
Apache (1)	1	0.01
Blackfeet (0)	7	0.06
Central American Ind. (1)	2	0.02
Cherokee (3)	23	0.19
Chippewa (0)	5	0.04
Choctaw (1)	3	0.02
Hopi (0)	1	0.01
Iroquois (0)	1	0.01
Navajo (0)	3	0.02
Potawatomi (0)	2	0.02
Sioux (1)	4	0.03

*Notes: † The Census 2010 population figure is used to calculate the percentages in the Hispanic Origin and Race categories. Ancestry percentages are based on the 2006-2010 American Community Survey population (not shown); ‡ Numbers in parentheses indicate the number of people reporting a single ancestry; * Numbers in parentheses indicate the number of persons reporting this race alone, not in combination with any other race; Please refer to the Explanation of Data for more information.*

South American Ind. (0)	3	0.02
Asian (87)	128	1.04
Not Hispanic (85)	114	0.92
Hispanic (2)	14	0.11
Bangladeshi (14)	14	0.11
Cambodian (1)	1	0.01
Chinese, ex. Taiwanese (16)	19	0.15
Filipino (25)	47	0.38
Indian (14)	20	0.16
Indonesian (1)	1	0.01
Japanese (4)	6	0.05
Korean (5)	8	0.06
Thai (2)	4	0.03
Vietnamese (1)	1	0.01
Hawaii Native/Pacific Islander (5)	13	0.11
Not Hispanic (5)	12	0.10
Hispanic (0)	1	0.01
Guamanian/Chamorro (5)	5	0.04
Native Hawaiian (0)	1	0.01
Samoan (0)	1	0.01
White (735)	878	7.11
Not Hispanic (577)	680	5.50
Hispanic (158)	198	1.60

Fort Meade

Place Type: CDP
County: Anne Arundel
Population: 9,327†

Ancestry‡	Population	%
African, Sub-Saharan (0)	13	0.12
Cape Verdean (0)	13	0.12
Alsatian (6)	6	0.05
American (246)	246	2.25
Arab (30)	64	0.59
Arab (30)	64	0.59
Austrian (0)	6	0.05
Belgian (0)	38	0.35
British (11)	21	0.19
Canadian (10)	42	0.38
Celtic (0)	9	0.08
Croatian (34)	89	0.82
Czech (9)	28	0.26
Danish (0)	10	0.09
Dutch (73)	237	2.17
English (110)	853	7.82
European (57)	63	0.58
French, ex. Basque (57)	248	2.27
French Canadian (17)	58	0.53
German (272)	1,521	13.94
Greek (0)	22	0.20
Guyanese (15)	15	0.14
Hungarian (0)	39	0.36
Irish (233)	1,601	14.67
Italian (305)	817	7.49
Norwegian (0)	56	0.51
Polish (65)	517	4.74
Portuguese (0)	36	0.33
Romanian (9)	9	0.08
Russian (4)	21	0.19
Scandinavian (19)	19	0.17
Scotch-Irish (25)	157	1.44
Scottish (183)	270	2.47
Swedish (16)	41	0.38
Ukrainian (65)	70	0.64
Welsh (0)	18	0.16
West Indian, ex. Hispanic (86)	164	1.50
Jamaican (86)	86	0.79
West Indian (0)	78	0.71

Hispanic Origin	Population	%
Hispanic or Latino (of any race)	1,179	12.64
Central American, ex. Mexican	60	0.64
Costa Rican	3	0.03
Guatemalan	4	0.04
Honduran	5	0.05
Nicaraguan	8	0.09
Panamanian	34	0.36
Salvadoran	6	0.06
Cuban	19	0.20
Dominican Republic	41	0.44
Mexican	479	5.14
Puerto Rican	417	4.47
South American	63	0.68
Argentinean	2	0.02
Bolivian	4	0.04
Colombian	21	0.23
Ecuadorian	7	0.08
Peruvian	21	0.23
Venezuelan	5	0.05
Other South American	3	0.03
Other Hispanic or Latino	100	1.07

Race*	Population	%
African-American/Black (2,227)	2,583	27.69
Not Hispanic (2,130)	2,406	25.80
Hispanic (97)	177	1.90
American Indian/Alaska Native (61)	196	2.10
Not Hispanic (49)	142	1.52
Hispanic (12)	54	0.58
Alaska Athabascan *(Ala. Nat.)* (0)	6	0.06
Apache (5)	9	0.10
Blackfeet (0)	3	0.03
Cherokee (8)	39	0.42
Chickasaw (1)	1	0.01
Chippewa (5)	5	0.05
Choctaw (1)	6	0.06
Cree (0)	4	0.04
Creek (3)	6	0.06
Delaware (0)	1	0.01
Inupiat *(Alaska Native)* (0)	1	0.01
Kiowa (1)	1	0.01
Lumbee (3)	7	0.08
Mexican American Ind. (2)	3	0.03
Navajo (0)	9	0.10
Seminole (0)	1	0.01
Sioux (0)	2	0.02
South American Ind. (0)	11	0.12
Tlingit-Haida *(Alaska Native)* (0)	3	0.03
Yakama (1)	1	0.01
Yup'ik *(Alaska Native)* (0)	1	0.01
Asian (267)	523	5.61
Not Hispanic (261)	491	5.26
Hispanic (6)	32	0.34
Chinese, ex. Taiwanese (25)	64	0.69
Filipino (112)	226	2.42
Hmong (1)	3	0.03
Indian (14)	32	0.34
Indonesian (0)	6	0.06
Japanese (15)	56	0.60
Korean (56)	95	1.02
Laotian (2)	2	0.02
Malaysian (0)	1	0.01
Nepalese (1)	1	0.01
Pakistani (7)	7	0.08
Taiwanese (3)	6	0.06
Thai (3)	20	0.21
Vietnamese (9)	30	0.32
Hawaii Native/Pacific Islander (31)	89	0.95
Not Hispanic (31)	78	0.84
Hispanic (0)	11	0.12
Guamanian/Chamorro (15)	25	0.27
Native Hawaiian (5)	37	0.40
Samoan (1)	8	0.09
Tongan (1)	1	0.01
White (5,781)	6,311	67.66
Not Hispanic (5,157)	5,556	59.57
Hispanic (624)	755	8.09

Fort Washington

Place Type: CDP
County: Prince George's
Population: 23,717†

Ancestry‡	Population	%
African, Sub-Saharan (864)	1,163	4.63
African (339)	400	1.59
Cape Verdean (7)	21	0.08
Ethiopian (112)	134	0.53
Ghanaian (109)	147	0.58
Nigerian (174)	240	0.95
Sudanese (73)	73	0.29
Other Sub-Saharan African (50)	148	0.59
American (203)	203	0.81
Arab (16)	60	0.24
Arab (9)	9	0.04
Lebanese (7)	43	0.17
Other Arab (0)	8	0.03
Austrian (0)	25	0.10
Brazilian (23)	23	0.09
British (7)	7	0.03
Canadian (16)	27	0.11
Croatian (0)	4	0.02
Czech (0)	9	0.04
Danish (0)	6	0.02
Dutch (31)	89	0.35
Eastern European (0)	8	0.03
English (192)	661	2.63
European (11)	67	0.27
French, ex. Basque (46)	134	0.53
French Canadian (20)	28	0.11
German (236)	976	3.88
Greek (11)	11	0.04
Guyanese (98)	98	0.39
Hungarian (0)	5	0.02
Iranian (13)	13	0.05
Irish (163)	938	3.73
Italian (65)	280	1.11
Norwegian (0)	18	0.07
Pennsylvania German (12)	12	0.05
Polish (46)	219	0.87
Portuguese (0)	9	0.04
Russian (24)	80	0.32
Scotch-Irish (70)	181	0.72
Scottish (9)	103	0.41
Slovak (30)	56	0.22
Slovene (0)	143	0.57
Swedish (0)	43	0.17
Swiss (11)	11	0.04
Turkish (0)	15	0.06
Ukrainian (26)	26	0.10
Welsh (0)	58	0.23
West Indian, ex. Hispanic (363)	595	2.37
Bahamian (16)	74	0.29
Barbadian (0)	25	0.10
British West Indian (42)	42	0.17
Haitian (106)	120	0.48
Jamaican (144)	234	0.93
Trinidadian/Tobagonian (20)	42	0.17
West Indian (35)	58	0.23

Hispanic Origin	Population	%
Hispanic or Latino (of any race)	1,565	6.60
Central American, ex. Mexican	778	3.28
Costa Rican	2	0.01
Guatemalan	61	0.26
Honduran	88	0.37
Nicaraguan	19	0.08
Panamanian	41	0.17
Salvadoran	562	2.37
Other Central American	5	0.02
Cuban	37	0.16
Dominican Republic	37	0.16
Mexican	217	0.91
Puerto Rican	155	0.65
South American	136	0.57
Argentinean	16	0.07
Bolivian	37	0.16
Chilean	1	<0.01
Colombian	19	0.08
Ecuadorian	4	0.02
Paraguayan	4	0.02
Peruvian	45	0.19
Uruguayan	5	0.02
Venezuelan	4	0.02
Other South American	1	<0.01
Other Hispanic or Latino	205	0.86

*Notes: † The Census 2010 population figure is used to calculate the percentages in the Hispanic Origin and Race categories. Ancestry percentages are based on the 2006-2010 American Community Survey population (not shown); ‡ Numbers in parentheses indicate the number of people reporting a single ancestry; * Numbers in parentheses indicate the number of persons reporting this race alone, not in combination with any other race; Please refer to the Explanation of Data for more information.*

Race*	Population	%
African-American/Black (16,742)	17,298	72.94
Not Hispanic (16,576)	17,045	71.87
Hispanic (166)	253	1.07
American Indian/Alaska Native (59)	272	1.15
Not Hispanic (51)	244	1.03
Hispanic (8)	28	0.12
Blackfeet (1)	11	0.05
Canadian/French Am. Ind. (3)	3	0.01
Central American Ind. (1)	1	<0.01
Cherokee (2)	63	0.27
Chippewa (3)	6	0.03
Choctaw (0)	2	0.01
Creek (1)	4	0.02
Delaware (3)	3	0.01
Iroquois (0)	1	<0.01
Lumbee (4)	7	0.03
Mexican American Ind. (0)	1	<0.01
Paiute (2)	2	0.01
Seminole (0)	5	0.02
Sioux (0)	2	0.01
South American Ind. (1)	8	0.03
Yup'ik *(Alaska Native)* (1)	1	<0.01
Asian (2,173)	2,425	10.22
Not Hispanic (2,154)	2,376	10.02
Hispanic (19)	49	0.21
Bangladeshi (0)	2	0.01
Cambodian (22)	22	0.09
Chinese, ex. Taiwanese (100)	142	0.60
Filipino (1,798)	1,963	8.28
Indian (41)	60	0.25
Indonesian (1)	3	0.01
Japanese (24)	40	0.17
Korean (62)	84	0.35
Laotian (5)	6	0.03
Malaysian (0)	3	0.01
Nepalese (2)	2	0.01
Pakistani (7)	7	0.03
Taiwanese (1)	1	<0.01
Thai (27)	32	0.13
Vietnamese (45)	61	0.26
Hawaii Native/Pacific Islander (8)	49	0.21
Not Hispanic (8)	47	0.20
Hispanic (0)	2	0.01
Fijian (1)	1	<0.01
Guamanian/Chamorro (3)	4	0.02
Native Hawaiian (0)	15	0.06
Samoan (2)	3	0.01
Tongan (0)	3	0.01
White (3,172)	3,648	15.38
Not Hispanic (2,690)	3,073	12.96
Hispanic (482)	575	2.42

Four Corners

Place Type: CDP
County: Montgomery
Population: 7,945†

Ancestry‡	Population	%
African, Sub-Saharan (106)	174	2.18
African (26)	70	0.88
Ethiopian (71)	71	0.89
Ghanaian (9)	33	0.41
American (184)	184	2.30
Arab (10)	50	0.63
Egyptian (10)	10	0.13
Lebanese (0)	28	0.35
Syrian (0)	12	0.15
Armenian (6)	25	0.31
Austrian (0)	29	0.36
British (23)	50	0.63
Czech (0)	35	0.44
Czechoslovakian (9)	9	0.11
Danish (0)	26	0.33
Dutch (89)	147	1.84
Eastern European (149)	149	1.86
English (196)	685	8.56
European (201)	236	2.95
Finnish (0)	25	0.31
French, ex. Basque (79)	209	2.61
French Canadian (7)	70	0.88
German (262)	1,034	12.93
Greek (26)	52	0.65
Guyanese (15)	30	0.38
Hungarian (0)	16	0.20
Irish (560)	1,178	14.73
Italian (262)	468	5.85
Northern European (7)	7	0.09
Norwegian (10)	33	0.41
Polish (79)	216	2.70
Portuguese (17)	34	0.43
Romanian (0)	75	0.94
Russian (131)	181	2.26
Scandinavian (0)	12	0.15
Scotch-Irish (70)	175	2.19
Scottish (47)	206	2.58
Slavic (0)	13	0.16
Slovene (0)	10	0.13
Swedish (20)	106	1.33
Swiss (0)	28	0.35
Turkish (0)	12	0.15
Ukrainian (18)	26	0.33
Welsh (0)	40	0.50
West Indian, ex. Hispanic (9)	41	0.51
West Indian (9)	41	0.51

Hispanic Origin	Population	%
Hispanic or Latino (of any race)	1,364	17.17
Central American, ex. Mexican	721	9.07
Costa Rican	8	0.10
Guatemalan	83	1.04
Honduran	28	0.35
Nicaraguan	37	0.47
Panamanian	11	0.14
Salvadoran	554	6.97
Cuban	34	0.43
Dominican Republic	54	0.68
Mexican	141	1.77
Puerto Rican	64	0.81
South American	240	3.02
Argentinean	19	0.24
Bolivian	67	0.84
Chilean	12	0.15
Colombian	49	0.62
Ecuadorian	37	0.47
Paraguayan	5	0.06
Peruvian	49	0.62
Venezuelan	1	0.01
Other South American	1	0.01
Other Hispanic or Latino	110	1.38

Race*	Population	%
African-American/Black (977)	1,074	13.52
Not Hispanic (926)	996	12.54
Hispanic (51)	78	0.98
American Indian/Alaska Native (29)	67	0.84
Not Hispanic (12)	37	0.47
Hispanic (17)	30	0.38
Blackfeet (0)	2	0.03
Central American Ind. (1)	1	0.01
Cherokee (0)	7	0.09
Cheyenne (0)	3	0.04
Comanche (3)	3	0.04
Crow (2)	2	0.03
Iroquois (0)	1	0.01
Lumbee (1)	2	0.03
Menominee (1)	1	0.01
Mexican American Ind. (4)	5	0.06
Spanish American Ind. (0)	1	0.01
Asian (463)	598	7.53
Not Hispanic (461)	576	7.25
Hispanic (2)	22	0.28
Burmese (3)	3	0.04
Cambodian (12)	18	0.23
Chinese, ex. Taiwanese (100)	125	1.57
Filipino (54)	81	1.02
Indian (84)	108	1.36
Indonesian (8)	10	0.13
Japanese (12)	34	0.43
Korean (29)	52	0.65
Malaysian (2)	4	0.05
Nepalese (6)	6	0.08
Pakistani (8)	9	0.11
Sri Lankan (2)	3	0.04
Taiwanese (1)	1	0.01
Thai (20)	30	0.38
Vietnamese (95)	110	1.38
Hawaii Native/Pacific Islander (4)	15	0.19
Not Hispanic (3)	11	0.14
Hispanic (1)	4	0.05
Fijian (1)	1	0.01
Guamanian/Chamorro (0)	3	0.04
Native Hawaiian (0)	2	0.03
White (5,516)	5,757	72.46
Not Hispanic (4,952)	5,118	64.42
Hispanic (564)	639	8.04

Frederick

Place Type: City
County: Frederick
Population: 65,239†

Ancestry‡	Population	%
Afghan (47)	47	0.07
African, Sub-Saharan (1,312)	1,377	2.16
African (756)	821	1.29
Ethiopian (106)	106	0.17
Ghanaian (155)	155	0.24
Liberian (123)	123	0.19
Nigerian (85)	85	0.13
Other Sub-Saharan African (87)	87	0.14
American (2,650)	2,650	4.16
Arab (81)	121	0.19
Arab (48)	59	0.09
Egyptian (0)	19	0.03
Lebanese (9)	9	0.01
Moroccan (24)	34	0.05
Armenian (0)	35	0.05
Australian (9)	25	0.04
Austrian (107)	430	0.67
Basque (0)	9	0.01
Belgian (33)	42	0.07
Brazilian (41)	58	0.09
British (125)	308	0.48
Cajun (20)	74	0.12
Canadian (46)	81	0.13
Celtic (18)	18	0.03
Croatian (0)	81	0.13
Czech (43)	265	0.42
Czechoslovakian (65)	111	0.17
Danish (50)	121	0.19
Dutch (273)	806	1.26
Eastern European (0)	78	0.12
English (1,740)	5,610	8.80
Estonian (17)	17	0.03
European (727)	792	1.24
Finnish (6)	111	0.17
French, ex. Basque (209)	1,853	2.91
French Canadian (188)	485	0.76
German (4,398)	13,045	20.47
Greek (77)	303	0.48
Hungarian (179)	531	0.83
Icelander (0)	13	0.02
Iranian (7)	35	0.05
Irish (2,569)	8,339	13.08
Italian (831)	3,134	4.92
Lithuanian (52)	256	0.40
New Zealander (8)	8	0.01
Northern European (9)	21	0.03
Norwegian (127)	375	0.59
Pennsylvania German (0)	33	0.05
Polish (367)	1,793	2.81
Portuguese (146)	280	0.44
Romanian (99)	159	0.25
Russian (326)	779	1.22
Scandinavian (53)	136	0.21
Scotch-Irish (595)	1,554	2.44

*Notes: † The Census 2010 population figure is used to calculate the percentages in the Hispanic Origin and Race categories. Ancestry percentages are based on the 2006-2010 American Community Survey population (not shown); ‡ Numbers in parentheses indicate the number of people reporting a single ancestry; * Numbers in parentheses indicate the number of persons reporting this race alone, not in combination with any other race; Please refer to the Explanation of Data for more information.*

Ancestry (cont.)	Population	%
Scottish (402)	1,302	2.04
Serbian (25)	83	0.13
Slavic (0)	25	0.04
Slovak (60)	168	0.26
Slovene (15)	44	0.07
Swedish (58)	509	0.80
Swiss (97)	293	0.46
Turkish (68)	68	0.11
Ukrainian (54)	140	0.22
Welsh (57)	531	0.83
West Indian, ex. Hispanic (506)	648	1.02
British West Indian (22)	70	0.11
Haitian (55)	84	0.13
Jamaican (274)	321	0.50
Trinidadian/Tobagonian (28)	46	0.07
West Indian (127)	127	0.20
Yugoslavian (0)	46	0.07

Hispanic Origin	Population	%
Hispanic or Latino (of any race)	9,402	14.41
Central American, ex. Mexican	4,321	6.62
Costa Rican	162	0.25
Guatemalan	935	1.43
Honduran	427	0.65
Nicaraguan	168	0.26
Panamanian	67	0.10
Salvadoran	2,494	3.82
Other Central American	68	0.10
Cuban	141	0.22
Dominican Republic	182	0.28
Mexican	1,891	2.90
Puerto Rican	749	1.15
South American	1,058	1.62
Argentinean	84	0.13
Bolivian	118	0.18
Chilean	85	0.13
Colombian	278	0.43
Ecuadorian	121	0.19
Paraguayan	8	0.01
Peruvian	282	0.43
Uruguayan	19	0.03
Venezuelan	62	0.10
Other South American	1	<0.01
Other Hispanic or Latino	1,060	1.62

Race*	Population	%
African-American/Black (12,144)	13,506	20.70
Not Hispanic (11,825)	13,000	19.93
Hispanic (319)	506	0.78
American Indian/Alaska Native (314)	755	1.16
Not Hispanic (185)	544	0.83
Hispanic (129)	211	0.32
Alaska Athabascan *(Ala. Nat.)* (1)	2	<0.01
Aleut *(Alaska Native)* (1)	1	<0.01
Apache (1)	3	<0.01
Blackfeet (3)	21	0.03
Central American Ind. (12)	18	0.03
Cherokee (23)	127	0.19
Chickasaw (1)	2	<0.01
Chippewa (11)	20	0.03
Choctaw (4)	8	0.01
Comanche (2)	2	<0.01
Creek (3)	4	0.01
Crow (5)	5	0.01
Delaware (2)	2	<0.01
Hopi (2)	2	<0.01
Inupiat *(Alaska Native)* (1)	1	<0.01
Iroquois (3)	13	0.02
Lumbee (6)	10	0.02
Menominee (0)	1	<0.01
Mexican American Ind. (13)	13	0.02
Navajo (4)	6	0.01
Osage (2)	2	<0.01
Pueblo (5)	5	0.01
Puget Sound Salish (0)	3	<0.01
Seminole (0)	2	<0.01
Shoshone (0)	1	<0.01
Sioux (6)	15	0.02
South American Ind. (8)	17	0.03
Spanish American Ind. (7)	7	0.01
Tlingit-Haida *(Alaska Native)* (0)	2	<0.01
Asian (3,800)	4,514	6.92
Not Hispanic (3,775)	4,413	6.76
Hispanic (25)	101	0.15
Bangladeshi (60)	66	0.10
Burmese (574)	621	0.95
Cambodian (45)	47	0.07
Chinese, ex. Taiwanese (585)	672	1.03
Filipino (369)	519	0.80
Hmong (4)	4	0.01
Indian (929)	1,088	1.67
Indonesian (26)	32	0.05
Japanese (54)	129	0.20
Korean (382)	486	0.74
Laotian (44)	47	0.07
Malaysian (1)	3	<0.01
Nepalese (50)	54	0.08
Pakistani (156)	197	0.30
Sri Lankan (27)	38	0.06
Taiwanese (23)	27	0.04
Thai (31)	49	0.08
Vietnamese (256)	293	0.45
Hawaii Native/Pacific Islander (54)	134	0.21
Not Hispanic (45)	102	0.16
Hispanic (9)	32	0.05
Guamanian/Chamorro (26)	39	0.06
Native Hawaiian (9)	26	0.04
Samoan (9)	13	0.02
White (41,681)	43,847	67.21
Not Hispanic (37,933)	39,548	60.62
Hispanic (3,748)	4,299	6.59

Friendly

Place Type: CDP
County: Prince George's
Population: 9,250†

Ancestry‡	Population	%
African, Sub-Saharan (602)	624	6.26
African (182)	204	2.05
Ethiopian (59)	59	0.59
Nigerian (361)	361	3.62
American (75)	75	0.75
Arab (18)	18	0.18
Lebanese (18)	18	0.18
Austrian (0)	10	0.10
Canadian (0)	22	0.22
Czech (0)	10	0.10
Dutch (0)	103	1.03
English (23)	92	0.92
European (17)	51	0.51
Finnish (0)	16	0.16
German (73)	217	2.18
Hungarian (10)	10	0.10
Irish (8)	95	0.95
Polish (20)	20	0.20
Scotch-Irish (10)	10	0.10
Swedish (0)	88	0.88
Welsh (0)	27	0.27
West Indian, ex. Hispanic (43)	84	0.84
Barbadian (0)	41	0.41
Jamaican (33)	33	0.33
Trinidadian/Tobagonian (10)	10	0.10
Yugoslavian (0)	22	0.22

Hispanic Origin	Population	%
Hispanic or Latino (of any race)	703	7.60
Central American, ex. Mexican	415	4.49
Costa Rican	4	0.04
Guatemalan	22	0.24
Honduran	37	0.40
Nicaraguan	9	0.10
Panamanian	14	0.15
Salvadoran	329	3.56
Cuban	1	0.01
Dominican Republic	21	0.23
Mexican	82	0.89
Puerto Rican	52	0.56
South American	57	0.62
Argentinean	6	0.06
Bolivian	13	0.14
Colombian	13	0.14
Ecuadorian	3	0.03
Peruvian	14	0.15
Uruguayan	2	0.02
Venezuelan	5	0.05
Other South American	1	0.01
Other Hispanic or Latino	75	0.81

Race*	Population	%
African-American/Black (7,362)	7,540	81.51
Not Hispanic (7,296)	7,454	80.58
Hispanic (66)	86	0.93
American Indian/Alaska Native (27)	112	1.21
Not Hispanic (24)	101	1.09
Hispanic (3)	11	0.12
Blackfeet (2)	10	0.11
Cherokee (4)	21	0.23
Choctaw (0)	7	0.08
Iroquois (0)	2	0.02
Navajo (0)	2	0.02
Seminole (0)	1	0.01
Sioux (0)	2	0.02
Spanish American Ind. (3)	3	0.03
Asian (439)	496	5.36
Not Hispanic (426)	479	5.18
Hispanic (13)	17	0.18
Chinese, ex. Taiwanese (16)	20	0.22
Filipino (359)	391	4.23
Indian (15)	22	0.24
Indonesian (1)	1	0.01
Japanese (5)	9	0.10
Korean (5)	6	0.06
Laotian (3)	3	0.03
Pakistani (11)	11	0.12
Taiwanese (1)	3	0.03
Thai (6)	7	0.08
Vietnamese (15)	18	0.19
Hawaii Native/Pacific Islander (4)	14	0.15
Not Hispanic (4)	14	0.15
Guamanian/Chamorro (1)	3	0.03
Native Hawaiian (3)	3	0.03
White (814)	928	10.03
Not Hispanic (589)	679	7.34
Hispanic (225)	249	2.69

Frostburg

Place Type: City
County: Allegany
Population: 9,002†

Ancestry‡	Population	%
African, Sub-Saharan (85)	85	0.97
African (67)	67	0.76
Nigerian (18)	18	0.20
American (736)	736	8.37
Austrian (13)	47	0.53
Belgian (0)	34	0.39
British (0)	64	0.73
Czech (0)	10	0.11
Czechoslovakian (34)	34	0.39
Danish (0)	17	0.19
Dutch (74)	244	2.78
Eastern European (0)	8	0.09
English (298)	897	10.20
European (26)	26	0.30
French, ex. Basque (96)	210	2.39
German (955)	2,597	29.54
Greek (32)	32	0.36
Hungarian (13)	34	0.39
Icelander (0)	14	0.16
Irish (526)	1,360	15.47
Italian (286)	759	8.63
Polish (155)	328	3.73
Portuguese (8)	8	0.09
Romanian (17)	17	0.19
Russian (19)	51	0.58
Scotch-Irish (209)	302	3.43

*Notes: † The Census 2010 population figure is used to calculate the percentages in the Hispanic Origin and Race categories. Ancestry percentages are based on the 2006-2010 American Community Survey population (not shown); ‡ Numbers in parentheses indicate the number of people reporting a single ancestry; * Numbers in parentheses indicate the number of persons reporting this race alone, not in combination with any other race; Please refer to the Explanation of Data for more information.*

Scottish (51)	206	2.34
Slovak (23)	23	0.26
Swedish (0)	54	0.61
Swiss (0)	39	0.44
Ukrainian (0)	14	0.16
Welsh (86)	273	3.11
West Indian, ex. Hispanic (18)	18	0.20
Jamaican (18)	18	0.20

Hispanic Origin	Population	%
Hispanic or Latino (of any race)	199	2.21
Central American, ex. Mexican	25	0.28
Costa Rican	3	0.03
Guatemalan	3	0.03
Honduran	8	0.09
Nicaraguan	1	0.01
Panamanian	6	0.07
Salvadoran	4	0.04
Cuban	5	0.06
Dominican Republic	3	0.03
Mexican	67	0.74
Puerto Rican	26	0.29
South American	15	0.17
Chilean	1	0.01
Colombian	8	0.09
Ecuadorian	1	0.01
Peruvian	5	0.06
Other Hispanic or Latino	58	0.64

Race*	Population	%
African-American/Black (1,124)	1,225	13.61
Not Hispanic (1,112)	1,207	13.41
Hispanic (12)	18	0.20
American Indian/Alaska Native (16)	55	0.61
Not Hispanic (11)	46	0.51
Hispanic (5)	9	0.10
Blackfeet (0)	1	0.01
Cherokee (1)	3	0.03
Yup'ik *(Alaska Native)* (1)	1	0.01
Asian (157)	194	2.16
Not Hispanic (156)	189	2.10
Hispanic (1)	5	0.06
Bangladeshi (2)	2	0.02
Burmese (0)	2	0.02
Chinese, ex. Taiwanese (41)	45	0.50
Filipino (9)	24	0.27
Indian (24)	27	0.30
Indonesian (4)	4	0.04
Japanese (0)	3	0.03
Korean (9)	19	0.21
Nepalese (1)	1	0.01
Pakistani (0)	1	0.01
Sri Lankan (2)	2	0.02
Thai (1)	1	0.01
Vietnamese (4)	4	0.04
Hawaii Native/Pacific Islander (7)	12	0.13
Not Hispanic (6)	11	0.12
Hispanic (1)	1	0.01
Samoan (3)	6	0.07
White (7,498)	7,638	84.85
Not Hispanic (7,369)	7,496	83.27
Hispanic (129)	142	1.58

Gaithersburg

Place Type: City
County: Montgomery
Population: 59,933†

Ancestry‡	Population	%
Afghan (26)	26	0.04
African, Sub-Saharan (2,036)	2,112	3.63
African (553)	593	1.02
Ethiopian (336)	372	0.64
Ghanaian (132)	132	0.23
Kenyan (50)	50	0.09
Liberian (109)	109	0.19
Senegalese (64)	64	0.11
Other Sub-Saharan African (792)	792	1.36
American (1,197)	1,197	2.06
Arab (145)	318	0.55
Arab (53)	71	0.12
Egyptian (0)	14	0.02
Lebanese (76)	76	0.13
Moroccan (0)	52	0.09
Palestinian (16)	16	0.03
Syrian (0)	27	0.05
Other Arab (0)	62	0.11
Armenian (171)	222	0.38
Assyrian/Chaldean/Syriac (16)	32	0.06
Australian (0)	31	0.05
Austrian (63)	175	0.30
Brazilian (86)	169	0.29
British (173)	417	0.72
Bulgarian (92)	108	0.19
Canadian (82)	149	0.26
Croatian (68)	137	0.24
Czech (23)	71	0.12
Czechoslovakian (78)	115	0.20
Danish (52)	393	0.68
Dutch (111)	357	0.61
Eastern European (295)	295	0.51
English (796)	3,813	6.56
Estonian (0)	56	0.10
European (763)	845	1.45
Finnish (24)	188	0.32
French, ex. Basque (282)	1,001	1.72
French Canadian (64)	149	0.26
German (1,564)	5,330	9.16
Greek (282)	310	0.53
Guyanese (43)	43	0.07
Hungarian (98)	316	0.54
Icelander (0)	19	0.03
Iranian (828)	893	1.54
Irish (1,334)	4,479	7.70
Israeli (22)	67	0.12
Italian (653)	1,955	3.36
Latvian (87)	164	0.28
Lithuanian (26)	167	0.29
Macedonian (16)	32	0.06
New Zealander (0)	14	0.02
Northern European (60)	60	0.10
Norwegian (80)	263	0.45
Polish (460)	1,189	2.04
Portuguese (11)	74	0.13
Romanian (51)	61	0.10
Russian (1,383)	1,868	3.21
Scandinavian (0)	77	0.13
Scotch-Irish (277)	810	1.39
Scottish (223)	882	1.52
Serbian (0)	48	0.08
Slavic (0)	23	0.04
Slovak (7)	123	0.21
Slovene (19)	86	0.15
Swedish (109)	531	0.91
Swiss (73)	110	0.19
Turkish (152)	152	0.26
Ukrainian (72)	237	0.41
Welsh (35)	266	0.46
West Indian, ex. Hispanic (365)	466	0.80
British West Indian (61)	84	0.14
Haitian (43)	73	0.13
Jamaican (184)	200	0.34
Trinidadian/Tobagonian (46)	78	0.13
West Indian (31)	31	0.05

Hispanic Origin	Population	%
Hispanic or Latino (of any race)	14,499	24.19
Central American, ex. Mexican	7,812	13.03
Costa Rican	60	0.10
Guatemalan	1,009	1.68
Honduran	1,211	2.02
Nicaraguan	415	0.69
Panamanian	100	0.17
Salvadoran	4,994	8.33
Other Central American	23	0.04
Cuban	154	0.26
Dominican Republic	328	0.55
Mexican	1,161	1.94
Puerto Rican	471	0.79
South American	2,870	4.79
Argentinean	112	0.19
Bolivian	443	0.74
Chilean	143	0.24
Colombian	456	0.76
Ecuadorian	280	0.47
Paraguayan	69	0.12
Peruvian	1,150	1.92
Uruguayan	69	0.12
Venezuelan	114	0.19
Other South American	34	0.06
Other Hispanic or Latino	1,703	2.84

Race*	Population	%
African-American/Black (9,752)	10,631	17.74
Not Hispanic (9,307)	10,012	16.71
Hispanic (445)	619	1.03
American Indian/Alaska Native (272)	678	1.13
Not Hispanic (129)	392	0.65
Hispanic (143)	286	0.48
Aleut *(Alaska Native)* (1)	1	<0.01
Apache (1)	2	<0.01
Arapaho (1)	1	<0.01
Blackfeet (0)	10	0.02
Central American Ind. (8)	18	0.03
Cherokee (8)	74	0.12
Chickasaw (0)	10	0.02
Chippewa (4)	7	0.01
Choctaw (5)	10	0.02
Comanche (5)	6	0.01
Creek (3)	10	0.02
Crow (1)	2	<0.01
Inupiat *(Alaska Native)* (1)	1	<0.01
Iroquois (1)	5	0.01
Lumbee (1)	1	<0.01
Menominee (3)	4	0.01
Mexican American Ind. (13)	24	0.04
Navajo (6)	9	0.02
Osage (0)	3	0.01
Pueblo (6)	9	0.02
Puget Sound Salish (3)	3	0.01
Seminole (3)	3	0.01
Shoshone (0)	2	<0.01
Sioux (4)	4	0.01
South American Ind. (32)	57	0.10
Spanish American Ind. (5)	5	0.01
Tlingit-Haida *(Alaska Native)* (0)	3	0.01
Ute (1)	1	<0.01
Asian (10,145)	11,174	18.64
Not Hispanic (10,099)	11,026	18.40
Hispanic (46)	148	0.25
Bangladeshi (114)	131	0.22
Burmese (64)	66	0.11
Cambodian (39)	54	0.09
Chinese, ex. Taiwanese (2,979)	3,245	5.41
Filipino (722)	896	1.50
Hmong (2)	2	<0.01
Indian (3,065)	3,302	5.51
Indonesian (119)	138	0.23
Japanese (126)	204	0.34
Korean (1,146)	1,275	2.13
Laotian (24)	31	0.05
Malaysian (18)	22	0.04
Nepalese (107)	113	0.19
Pakistani (251)	289	0.48
Sri Lankan (102)	117	0.20
Taiwanese (210)	243	0.41
Thai (111)	132	0.22
Vietnamese (604)	682	1.14
Hawaii Native/Pacific Islander (34)	124	0.21
Not Hispanic (28)	98	0.16
Hispanic (6)	26	0.04
Fijian (1)	5	0.01
Guamanian/Chamorro (10)	17	0.03
Native Hawaiian (7)	42	0.07
Samoan (1)	3	0.01
White (30,469)	32,764	54.67
Not Hispanic (23,961)	25,288	42.19
Hispanic (6,508)	7,476	12.47

*Notes: † The Census 2010 population figure is used to calculate the percentages in the Hispanic Origin and Race categories. Ancestry percentages are based on the 2006-2010 American Community Survey population (not shown); ‡ Numbers in parentheses indicate the number of people reporting a single ancestry; * Numbers in parentheses indicate the number of persons reporting this race alone, not in combination with any other race; Please refer to the Explanation of Data for more information.*

Garrison

Place Type: CDP
County: Baltimore
Population: 8,823†

Ancestry‡	Population	%
African, Sub-Saharan (111)	121	1.59
African (35)	45	0.59
South African (15)	15	0.20
Zimbabwean (61)	61	0.80
American (650)	650	8.53
Armenian (16)	16	0.21
Austrian (19)	98	1.29
Belgian (15)	15	0.20
British (39)	55	0.72
Czech (0)	12	0.16
Dutch (26)	76	1.00
Eastern European (134)	134	1.76
English (99)	424	5.56
Estonian (43)	43	0.56
European (95)	107	1.40
French, ex. Basque (0)	81	1.06
French Canadian (25)	45	0.59
German (159)	740	9.71
Greek (12)	12	0.16
Hungarian (59)	85	1.12
Iranian (95)	110	1.44
Irish (30)	475	6.23
Israeli (15)	15	0.20
Italian (113)	128	1.68
Lithuanian (62)	117	1.54
Norwegian (13)	13	0.17
Polish (302)	759	9.96
Portuguese (0)	17	0.22
Russian (722)	963	12.63
Scandinavian (49)	100	1.31
Scotch-Irish (0)	17	0.22
Scottish (12)	85	1.12
Slavic (22)	22	0.29
Swedish (10)	10	0.13
Swiss (0)	26	0.34
Turkish (25)	25	0.33
Ukrainian (44)	44	0.58
Welsh (0)	41	0.54
West Indian, ex. Hispanic (82)	82	1.08
Jamaican (63)	63	0.83
Trinidadian/Tobagonian (19)	19	0.25

Hispanic Origin	Population	%
Hispanic or Latino (of any race)	316	3.58
Central American, ex. Mexican	84	0.95
Guatemalan	23	0.26
Honduran	16	0.18
Nicaraguan	3	0.03
Panamanian	10	0.11
Salvadoran	32	0.36
Cuban	6	0.07
Dominican Republic	7	0.08
Mexican	50	0.57
Puerto Rican	57	0.65
South American	66	0.75
Argentinean	11	0.12
Bolivian	1	0.01
Colombian	13	0.15
Ecuadorian	1	0.01
Paraguayan	2	0.02
Peruvian	35	0.40
Uruguayan	3	0.03
Other Hispanic or Latino	46	0.52

Race*	Population	%
African-American/Black (2,647)	2,778	31.49
Not Hispanic (2,609)	2,719	30.82
Hispanic (38)	59	0.67
American Indian/Alaska Native (19)	81	0.92
Not Hispanic (19)	66	0.75
Hispanic (0)	15	0.17
Blackfeet (0)	7	0.08
Central American Ind. (0)	7	0.08
Cherokee (3)	21	0.24
Crow (0)	1	0.01
Inupiat *(Alaska Native)* (1)	1	0.01
Iroquois (0)	4	0.05
Lumbee (1)	3	0.03
Pueblo (1)	1	0.01
Sioux (1)	1	0.01
Spanish American Ind. (0)	1	0.01
Asian (381)	452	5.12
Not Hispanic (380)	450	5.10
Hispanic (1)	2	0.02
Cambodian (1)	1	0.01
Chinese, ex. Taiwanese (46)	66	0.75
Filipino (78)	97	1.10
Indian (100)	119	1.35
Indonesian (1)	1	0.01
Japanese (2)	3	0.03
Korean (42)	53	0.60
Laotian (6)	7	0.08
Nepalese (9)	9	0.10
Pakistani (31)	39	0.44
Taiwanese (9)	10	0.11
Thai (1)	6	0.07
Vietnamese (17)	19	0.22
Hawaii Native/Pacific Islander (1)	13	0.15
Not Hispanic (1)	13	0.15
Native Hawaiian (0)	9	0.10
Samoan (1)	1	0.01
White (5,466)	5,635	63.87
Not Hispanic (5,302)	5,423	61.46
Hispanic (164)	212	2.40

Germantown

Place Type: CDP
County: Montgomery
Population: 86,395†

Ancestry‡	Population	%
Afghan (0)	45	0.05
African, Sub-Saharan (4,884)	5,206	6.14
African (1,242)	1,429	1.68
Ethiopian (282)	282	0.33
Ghanaian (708)	708	0.83
Kenyan (113)	113	0.13
Liberian (574)	574	0.68
Nigerian (463)	492	0.58
Senegalese (0)	20	0.02
Sierra Leonean (24)	24	0.03
South African (11)	31	0.04
Sudanese (21)	44	0.05
Ugandan (59)	59	0.07
Other Sub-Saharan African (1,387)	1,430	1.69
American (2,141)	2,141	2.52
Arab (783)	895	1.05
Arab (69)	98	0.12
Egyptian (296)	304	0.36
Jordanian (9)	9	0.01
Lebanese (122)	134	0.16
Moroccan (30)	58	0.07
Palestinian (169)	169	0.20
Syrian (17)	52	0.06
Other Arab (71)	71	0.08
Armenian (104)	154	0.18
Austrian (33)	317	0.37
Belgian (14)	86	0.10
Brazilian (370)	509	0.60
British (279)	570	0.67
Bulgarian (139)	139	0.16
Canadian (77)	239	0.28
Celtic (15)	15	0.02
Croatian (0)	37	0.04
Czech (43)	199	0.23
Czechoslovakian (0)	15	0.02
Danish (19)	105	0.12
Dutch (226)	676	0.80
Eastern European (256)	256	0.30
English (1,145)	4,745	5.59
Estonian (2)	2	<0.01
European (1,119)	1,190	1.40
Finnish (15)	108	0.13
French, ex. Basque (97)	1,050	1.24
French Canadian (63)	235	0.28
German (2,024)	7,704	9.08
Greek (273)	393	0.46
Guyanese (48)	108	0.13
Hungarian (85)	315	0.37
Iranian (871)	902	1.06
Irish (1,492)	5,832	6.87
Israeli (25)	25	0.03
Italian (1,145)	3,539	4.17
Lithuanian (37)	118	0.14
Luxemburger (0)	37	0.04
Northern European (50)	80	0.09
Norwegian (60)	302	0.36
Polish (586)	2,023	2.38
Portuguese (305)	403	0.47
Romanian (0)	183	0.22
Russian (747)	1,690	1.99
Scandinavian (0)	108	0.13
Scotch-Irish (282)	632	0.74
Scottish (227)	1,168	1.38
Serbian (69)	69	0.08
Slavic (51)	79	0.09
Slovak (0)	107	0.13
Slovene (15)	126	0.15
Swedish (197)	781	0.92
Swiss (8)	130	0.15
Turkish (120)	120	0.14
Ukrainian (264)	463	0.55
Welsh (103)	420	0.50
West Indian, ex. Hispanic (1,145)	1,468	1.73
Bahamian (18)	90	0.11
Barbadian (19)	74	0.09
Haitian (285)	359	0.42
Jamaican (750)	798	0.94
Trinidadian/Tobagonian (32)	32	0.04
West Indian (41)	115	0.14
Yugoslavian (0)	18	0.02

Hispanic Origin	Population	%
Hispanic or Latino (of any race)	15,937	18.45
Central American, ex. Mexican	6,157	7.13
Costa Rican	112	0.13
Guatemalan	817	0.95
Honduran	519	0.60
Nicaraguan	537	0.62
Panamanian	163	0.19
Salvadoran	3,989	4.62
Other Central American	20	0.02
Cuban	264	0.31
Dominican Republic	488	0.56
Mexican	1,634	1.89
Puerto Rican	1,137	1.32
South American	4,441	5.14
Argentinean	162	0.19
Bolivian	545	0.63
Chilean	228	0.26
Colombian	1,077	1.25
Ecuadorian	388	0.45
Paraguayan	39	0.05
Peruvian	1,672	1.94
Uruguayan	63	0.07
Venezuelan	244	0.28
Other South American	23	0.03
Other Hispanic or Latino	1,816	2.10

Race*	Population	%
African-American/Black (19,469)	21,222	24.56
Not Hispanic (18,796)	20,150	23.32
Hispanic (673)	1,072	1.24
American Indian/Alaska Native (373)	966	1.12
Not Hispanic (189)	574	0.66
Hispanic (184)	392	0.45
Alaska Athabascan *(Ala. Nat.)* (0)	2	<0.01
Apache (3)	14	0.02
Blackfeet (4)	27	0.03
Canadian/French Am. Ind. (0)	1	<0.01
Central American Ind. (16)	30	0.03
Cherokee (9)	131	0.15

*Notes: † The Census 2010 population figure is used to calculate the percentages in the Hispanic Origin and Race categories. Ancestry percentages are based on the 2006-2010 American Community Survey population (not shown); ‡ Numbers in parentheses indicate the number of people reporting a single ancestry; * Numbers in parentheses indicate the number of persons reporting this race alone, not in combination with any other race; Please refer to the Explanation of Data for more information.*

Cheyenne (3)	5	0.01
Chickasaw (3)	7	0.01
Chippewa (10)	15	0.02
Choctaw (2)	9	0.01
Colville (0)	1	<0.01
Comanche (0)	3	<0.01
Cree (0)	2	<0.01
Creek (2)	5	0.01
Crow (2)	2	<0.01
Delaware (2)	3	<0.01
Houma (0)	1	<0.01
Iroquois (1)	4	<0.01
Kiowa (2)	4	<0.01
Lumbee (6)	13	0.02
Menominee (6)	7	0.01
Mexican American Ind. (4)	23	0.03
Navajo (15)	22	0.03
Osage (1)	1	<0.01
Pueblo (6)	6	0.01
Puget Sound Salish (0)	1	<0.01
Seminole (2)	5	0.01
Sioux (2)	14	0.02
South American Ind. (34)	76	0.09
Spanish American Ind. (6)	7	0.01
Yaqui (1)	2	<0.01
Yup'ik *(Alaska Native)* (0)	1	<0.01
Asian (17,090)	18,684	21.63
Not Hispanic (17,000)	18,470	21.38
Hispanic (90)	214	0.25
Bangladeshi (189)	209	0.24
Burmese (73)	81	0.09
Cambodian (127)	159	0.18
Chinese, ex. Taiwanese (4,070)	4,431	5.13
Filipino (1,340)	1,666	1.93
Hmong (1)	3	<0.01
Indian (5,581)	6,003	6.95
Indonesian (101)	116	0.13
Japanese (142)	292	0.34
Korean (1,887)	2,067	2.39
Laotian (48)	67	0.08
Malaysian (10)	22	0.03
Nepalese (144)	156	0.18
Pakistani (651)	722	0.84
Sri Lankan (188)	201	0.23
Taiwanese (240)	278	0.32
Thai (118)	142	0.16
Vietnamese (1,647)	1,803	2.09
Hawaii Native/Pacific Islander (36)	161	0.19
Not Hispanic (30)	130	0.15
Hispanic (6)	31	0.04
Fijian (0)	1	<0.01
Guamanian/Chamorro (10)	39	0.05
Native Hawaiian (7)	22	0.03
Samoan (1)	3	<0.01
Tongan (0)	1	<0.01
White (39,587)	42,915	49.67
Not Hispanic (31,341)	33,564	38.85
Hispanic (8,246)	9,351	10.82

Glassmanor

Place Type: CDP
County: Prince George's
Population: 17,295†

Ancestry‡	Population	%
African, Sub-Saharan (258)	258	1.47
African (125)	125	0.71
Ethiopian (84)	84	0.48
Kenyan (49)	49	0.28
American (113)	113	0.64
Dutch (0)	15	0.09
English (50)	50	0.29
European (5)	5	0.03
French, ex. Basque (0)	42	0.24
German (22)	43	0.25
Guyanese (28)	28	0.16
Irish (0)	112	0.64
Italian (26)	80	0.46
New Zealander (27)	27	0.15
West Indian, ex. Hispanic (69)	91	0.52
Haitian (9)	31	0.18
Trinidadian/Tobagonian (51)	51	0.29
West Indian (9)	9	0.05

Hispanic Origin	Population	%
Hispanic or Latino (of any race)	1,302	7.53
Central American, ex. Mexican	679	3.93
Guatemalan	52	0.30
Honduran	78	0.45
Nicaraguan	12	0.07
Panamanian	19	0.11
Salvadoran	511	2.95
Other Central American	7	0.04
Cuban	18	0.10
Dominican Republic	30	0.17
Mexican	188	1.09
Puerto Rican	108	0.62
South American	65	0.38
Argentinean	2	0.01
Bolivian	20	0.12
Chilean	2	0.01
Colombian	4	0.02
Ecuadorian	1	0.01
Peruvian	31	0.18
Other South American	5	0.03
Other Hispanic or Latino	214	1.24

Race*	Population	%
African-American/Black (15,433)	15,752	91.08
Not Hispanic (15,254)	15,513	89.70
Hispanic (179)	239	1.38
American Indian/Alaska Native (39)	180	1.04
Not Hispanic (24)	156	0.90
Hispanic (15)	24	0.14
Blackfeet (0)	8	0.05
Central American Ind. (0)	1	0.01
Cherokee (1)	11	0.06
Creek (1)	5	0.03
Iroquois (1)	1	0.01
Mexican American Ind. (1)	1	0.01
Seminole (0)	2	0.01
South American Ind. (1)	4	0.02
Asian (144)	227	1.31
Not Hispanic (126)	197	1.14
Hispanic (18)	30	0.17
Chinese, ex. Taiwanese (8)	13	0.08
Filipino (101)	134	0.77
Indian (14)	30	0.17
Indonesian (2)	2	0.01
Japanese (5)	12	0.07
Korean (2)	10	0.06
Sri Lankan (3)	3	0.02
Thai (2)	2	0.01
Vietnamese (5)	8	0.05
Hawaii Native/Pacific Islander (11)	18	0.10
Not Hispanic (5)	11	0.06
Hispanic (6)	7	0.04
Guamanian/Chamorro (2)	3	0.02
Native Hawaiian (5)	7	0.04
Samoan (2)	2	0.01
White (716)	969	5.60
Not Hispanic (275)	423	2.45
Hispanic (441)	546	3.16

Glen Burnie

Place Type: CDP
County: Anne Arundel
Population: 67,639†

Ancestry‡	Population	%
African, Sub-Saharan (479)	598	0.91
African (278)	382	0.58
Nigerian (111)	111	0.17
South African (90)	90	0.14
Other Sub-Saharan African (0)	15	0.02
American (2,799)	2,799	4.27
Arab (129)	223	0.34
Arab (38)	103	0.16
Egyptian (57)	57	0.09
Moroccan (8)	29	0.04
Syrian (0)	8	0.01
Other Arab (26)	26	0.04
Armenian (14)	45	0.07
Australian (25)	25	0.04
Austrian (61)	214	0.33
Belgian (20)	43	0.07
British (45)	75	0.11
Bulgarian (26)	26	0.04
Canadian (27)	78	0.12
Croatian (0)	21	0.03
Czech (89)	320	0.49
Czechoslovakian (5)	38	0.06
Danish (11)	131	0.20
Dutch (161)	1,026	1.57
Eastern European (19)	19	0.03
English (1,749)	5,669	8.65
European (574)	612	0.93
Finnish (0)	77	0.12
French, ex. Basque (135)	1,175	1.79
French Canadian (71)	229	0.35
German (4,894)	16,076	24.53
Greek (141)	311	0.47
Guyanese (29)	44	0.07
Hungarian (63)	260	0.40
Icelander (31)	31	0.05
Iranian (57)	57	0.09
Irish (2,931)	11,676	17.82
Italian (1,301)	4,578	6.99
Lithuanian (26)	326	0.50
Luxemburger (0)	13	0.02
Northern European (17)	17	0.03
Norwegian (102)	393	0.60
Pennsylvania German (14)	46	0.07
Polish (1,038)	3,035	4.63
Portuguese (15)	92	0.14
Romanian (54)	97	0.15
Russian (199)	459	0.70
Scotch-Irish (442)	1,098	1.68
Scottish (418)	1,177	1.80
Slavic (9)	59	0.09
Slovak (108)	178	0.27
Swedish (46)	244	0.37
Swiss (15)	93	0.14
Turkish (0)	18	0.03
Ukrainian (111)	268	0.41
Welsh (135)	586	0.89
West Indian, ex. Hispanic (230)	344	0.53
Bahamian (9)	9	0.01
Barbadian (31)	63	0.10
Jamaican (115)	185	0.28
Trinidadian/Tobagonian (34)	34	0.05
U.S. Virgin Islander (41)	41	0.06
West Indian (0)	12	0.02
Yugoslavian (0)	14	0.02

Hispanic Origin	Population	%
Hispanic or Latino (of any race)	5,368	7.94
Central American, ex. Mexican	1,889	2.79
Costa Rican	20	0.03
Guatemalan	788	1.17
Honduran	130	0.19
Nicaraguan	22	0.03
Panamanian	89	0.13
Salvadoran	835	1.23
Other Central American	5	0.01
Cuban	104	0.15
Dominican Republic	80	0.12
Mexican	1,531	2.26
Puerto Rican	807	1.19
South American	345	0.51
Argentinean	23	0.03
Bolivian	17	0.03
Chilean	30	0.04
Colombian	86	0.13
Ecuadorian	63	0.09
Paraguayan	1	<0.01
Peruvian	98	0.14
Uruguayan	1	<0.01

*Notes: † The Census 2010 population figure is used to calculate the percentages in the Hispanic Origin and Race categories. Ancestry percentages are based on the 2006-2010 American Community Survey population (not shown); ‡ Numbers in parentheses indicate the number of people reporting a single ancestry; * Numbers in parentheses indicate the number of persons reporting this race alone, not in combination with any other race; Please refer to the Explanation of Data for more information.*

Venezuelan	23	0.03
Other South American	3	<0.01
Other Hispanic or Latino	612	0.90

Race*	Population	%
African-American/Black (14,856)	16,186	23.93
Not Hispanic (14,544)	15,688	23.19
Hispanic (312)	498	0.74
American Indian/Alaska Native (260)	856	1.27
Not Hispanic (211)	725	1.07
Hispanic (49)	131	0.19
Alaska Athabascan *(Ala. Nat.)* (1)	1	<0.01
Aleut *(Alaska Native)* (1)	1	<0.01
Apache (4)	8	0.01
Blackfeet (7)	42	0.06
Canadian/French Am. Ind. (1)	1	<0.01
Central American Ind. (6)	7	0.01
Cherokee (38)	246	0.36
Chickasaw (1)	3	<0.01
Chippewa (3)	10	0.01
Choctaw (3)	11	0.02
Cree (0)	1	<0.01
Creek (1)	5	0.01
Crow (1)	1	<0.01
Delaware (1)	4	0.01
Hopi (1)	3	<0.01
Inupiat *(Alaska Native)* (0)	2	<0.01
Iroquois (3)	13	0.02
Lumbee (42)	45	0.07
Mexican American Ind. (7)	10	0.01
Navajo (2)	9	0.01
Pueblo (3)	3	<0.01
Seminole (2)	6	0.01
Sioux (3)	17	0.03
South American Ind. (4)	16	0.02
Spanish American Ind. (1)	1	<0.01
Ute (1)	1	<0.01
Yaqui (0)	1	<0.01
Asian (2,686)	3,309	4.89
Not Hispanic (2,664)	3,237	4.79
Hispanic (22)	72	0.11
Bangladeshi (1)	14	0.02
Burmese (1)	1	<0.01
Cambodian (7)	7	0.01
Chinese, ex. Taiwanese (232)	284	0.42
Filipino (669)	882	1.30
Indian (434)	505	0.75
Indonesian (1)	2	<0.01
Japanese (43)	121	0.18
Korean (744)	885	1.31
Laotian (7)	11	0.02
Nepalese (38)	41	0.06
Pakistani (183)	203	0.30
Sri Lankan (18)	20	0.03
Taiwanese (4)	5	0.01
Thai (40)	62	0.09
Vietnamese (177)	213	0.31
Hawaii Native/Pacific Islander (120)	247	0.37
Not Hispanic (75)	170	0.25
Hispanic (45)	77	0.11
Guamanian/Chamorro (88)	109	0.16
Native Hawaiian (18)	65	0.10
Samoan (6)	11	0.02
Tongan (1)	8	0.01
White (44,930)	46,934	69.39
Not Hispanic (42,734)	44,358	65.58
Hispanic (2,196)	2,576	3.81

Glenmont

Place Type: CDP
County: Montgomery
Population: 13,529†

Ancestry‡	Population	%
African, Sub-Saharan (1,741)	1,936	14.39
African (403)	420	3.12
Ethiopian (487)	487	3.62
Ghanaian (115)	115	0.85
Kenyan (13)	13	0.10
Nigerian (68)	68	0.51
Senegalese (0)	34	0.25
Sierra Leonean (15)	110	0.82
Ugandan (16)	16	0.12
Zimbabwean (42)	42	0.31
Other Sub-Saharan African (582)	631	4.69
American (132)	132	0.98
Arab (259)	274	2.04
Jordanian (87)	87	0.65
Lebanese (62)	62	0.46
Palestinian (13)	13	0.10
Syrian (14)	14	0.10
Other Arab (83)	98	0.73
Austrian (0)	30	0.22
British (0)	31	0.23
Canadian (0)	29	0.22
Czech (9)	9	0.07
Danish (0)	13	0.10
Dutch (17)	65	0.48
Eastern European (40)	40	0.30
English (101)	454	3.37
European (205)	243	1.81
French, ex. Basque (16)	190	1.41
French Canadian (0)	11	0.08
German (220)	943	7.01
Greek (41)	41	0.30
Guyanese (26)	26	0.19
Hungarian (26)	81	0.60
Iranian (39)	54	0.40
Irish (260)	817	6.07
Italian (133)	367	2.73
Lithuanian (33)	143	1.06
Macedonian (11)	11	0.08
Northern European (23)	23	0.17
Norwegian (0)	55	0.41
Pennsylvania German (11)	11	0.08
Polish (108)	225	1.67
Portuguese (25)	33	0.25
Russian (55)	129	0.96
Scotch-Irish (61)	174	1.29
Scottish (18)	128	0.95
Slavic (0)	10	0.07
Slovak (17)	52	0.39
Slovene (21)	21	0.16
Swedish (4)	53	0.39
Swiss (0)	13	0.10
Ukrainian (44)	44	0.33
Welsh (19)	69	0.51
West Indian, ex. Hispanic (45)	142	1.06
Haitian (7)	7	0.05
Jamaican (12)	12	0.09
Trinidadian/Tobagonian (26)	70	0.52
West Indian (0)	53	0.39
Yugoslavian (12)	12	0.09

Hispanic Origin	Population	%
Hispanic or Latino (of any race)	4,237	31.32
Central American, ex. Mexican	2,378	17.58
Costa Rican	13	0.10
Guatemalan	251	1.86
Honduran	218	1.61
Nicaraguan	148	1.09
Panamanian	27	0.20
Salvadoran	1,718	12.70
Other Central American	3	0.02
Cuban	39	0.29
Dominican Republic	148	1.09
Mexican	290	2.14
Puerto Rican	117	0.86
South American	792	5.85
Argentinean	37	0.27
Bolivian	146	1.08
Chilean	34	0.25
Colombian	205	1.52
Ecuadorian	74	0.55
Paraguayan	16	0.12
Peruvian	242	1.79
Uruguayan	10	0.07
Venezuelan	23	0.17
Other South American	5	0.04
Other Hispanic or Latino	473	3.50

Race*	Population	%
African-American/Black (3,102)	3,324	24.57
Not Hispanic (2,984)	3,159	23.35
Hispanic (118)	165	1.22
American Indian/Alaska Native (85)	202	1.49
Not Hispanic (31)	97	0.72
Hispanic (54)	105	0.78
Apache (0)	1	0.01
Blackfeet (2)	3	0.02
Central American Ind. (1)	2	0.01
Cherokee (2)	28	0.21
Comanche (1)	1	0.01
Creek (0)	2	0.01
Iroquois (1)	2	0.01
Mexican American Ind. (13)	13	0.10
Pueblo (4)	7	0.05
Seminole (0)	1	0.01
Sioux (0)	1	0.01
South American Ind. (3)	8	0.06
Spanish American Ind. (0)	1	0.01
Asian (1,939)	2,098	15.51
Not Hispanic (1,927)	2,065	15.26
Hispanic (12)	33	0.24
Bangladeshi (52)	59	0.44
Bhutanese (16)	17	0.13
Burmese (17)	18	0.13
Cambodian (22)	25	0.18
Chinese, ex. Taiwanese (339)	387	2.86
Filipino (287)	316	2.34
Indian (303)	350	2.59
Indonesian (79)	83	0.61
Japanese (23)	39	0.29
Korean (181)	192	1.42
Laotian (3)	4	0.03
Malaysian (2)	8	0.06
Nepalese (16)	16	0.12
Pakistani (22)	22	0.16
Sri Lankan (78)	88	0.65
Taiwanese (10)	19	0.14
Thai (113)	114	0.84
Vietnamese (306)	320	2.37
Hawaii Native/Pacific Islander (14)	36	0.27
Not Hispanic (14)	25	0.18
Hispanic (0)	11	0.08
Guamanian/Chamorro (1)	1	0.01
Native Hawaiian (1)	5	0.04
Samoan (7)	7	0.05
White (5,469)	5,928	43.82
Not Hispanic (3,954)	4,184	30.93
Hispanic (1,515)	1,744	12.89

Glenn Dale

Place Type: CDP
County: Prince George's
Population: 13,466†

Ancestry‡	Population	%
Afghan (184)	184	1.30
African, Sub-Saharan (1,350)	1,476	10.45
African (868)	876	6.20
Ghanaian (11)	11	0.08
Kenyan (10)	10	0.07
Nigerian (387)	387	2.74
Other Sub-Saharan African (74)	192	1.36
American (312)	312	2.21
Arab (13)	13	0.09
Lebanese (13)	13	0.09
Austrian (27)	39	0.28
Belgian (0)	12	0.08
Canadian (0)	46	0.33
Croatian (12)	12	0.08
Czech (27)	52	0.37
Czechoslovakian (0)	21	0.15
Dutch (0)	33	0.23
English (242)	596	4.22
European (89)	89	0.63
French, ex. Basque (50)	242	1.71

*Notes: † The Census 2010 population figure is used to calculate the percentages in the Hispanic Origin and Race categories. Ancestry percentages are based on the 2006-2010 American Community Survey population (not shown); ‡ Numbers in parentheses indicate the number of people reporting a single ancestry; * Numbers in parentheses indicate the number of persons reporting this race alone, not in combination with any other race; Please refer to the Explanation of Data for more information.*

French Canadian (23)	39	0.28
German (189)	1,003	7.10
Hungarian (11)	11	0.08
Irish (283)	863	6.11
Italian (150)	355	2.51
Lithuanian (0)	24	0.17
Polish (79)	201	1.42
Portuguese (48)	48	0.34
Russian (11)	32	0.23
Scotch-Irish (45)	92	0.65
Scottish (7)	48	0.34
Slavic (20)	20	0.14
Slovak (17)	17	0.12
Swedish (0)	61	0.43
Swiss (0)	52	0.37
Welsh (0)	62	0.44
West Indian, ex. Hispanic (337)	391	2.77
Barbadian (11)	11	0.08
British West Indian (15)	15	0.11
Jamaican (136)	148	1.05
Trinidadian/Tobagonian (135)	177	1.25
West Indian (40)	40	0.28

Hispanic Origin	Population	%
Hispanic or Latino (of any race)	1,050	7.80
Central American, ex. Mexican	461	3.42
Costa Rican	11	0.08
Guatemalan	53	0.39
Honduran	30	0.22
Nicaraguan	21	0.16
Panamanian	34	0.25
Salvadoran	312	2.32
Cuban	38	0.28
Dominican Republic	46	0.34
Mexican	255	1.89
Puerto Rican	73	0.54
South American	67	0.50
Argentinean	4	0.03
Bolivian	21	0.16
Chilean	1	0.01
Colombian	18	0.13
Ecuadorian	4	0.03
Peruvian	12	0.09
Uruguayan	3	0.02
Venezuelan	4	0.03
Other Hispanic or Latino	110	0.82

Race*	Population	%
African-American/Black (8,011)	8,277	61.47
Not Hispanic (7,941)	8,150	60.52
Hispanic (70)	127	0.94
American Indian/Alaska Native (70)	155	1.15
Not Hispanic (46)	119	0.88
Hispanic (24)	36	0.27
Apache (1)	1	0.01
Blackfeet (0)	4	0.03
Central American Ind. (1)	4	0.03
Cherokee (2)	24	0.18
Choctaw (1)	1	0.01
Creek (0)	1	0.01
Hopi (1)	1	0.01
Iroquois (0)	1	0.01
Lumbee (2)	2	0.01
Mexican American Ind. (16)	16	0.12
Navajo (1)	1	0.01
South American Ind. (0)	6	0.04
Spanish American Ind. (0)	2	0.01
Tlingit-Haida *(Alaska Native)* (0)	1	0.01
Asian (890)	1,013	7.52
Not Hispanic (881)	1,000	7.43
Hispanic (9)	13	0.10
Bangladeshi (6)	8	0.06
Burmese (0)	1	0.01
Cambodian (1)	1	0.01
Chinese, ex. Taiwanese (94)	115	0.85
Filipino (132)	159	1.18
Indian (377)	423	3.14
Indonesian (6)	9	0.07
Japanese (5)	22	0.16
Korean (106)	112	0.83
Malaysian (3)	4	0.03
Pakistani (57)	62	0.46
Sri Lankan (6)	7	0.05
Taiwanese (8)	8	0.06
Thai (2)	2	0.01
Vietnamese (68)	69	0.51
Hawaii Native/Pacific Islander (3)	16	0.12
Not Hispanic (3)	13	0.10
Hispanic (0)	3	0.02
Guamanian/Chamorro (0)	1	0.01
Native Hawaiian (0)	2	0.01
Samoan (2)	2	0.01
White (3,573)	3,809	28.29
Not Hispanic (3,193)	3,381	25.11
Hispanic (380)	428	3.18

Greenbelt

Place Type: City
County: Prince George's
Population: 23,068†

Ancestry‡	Population	%
African, Sub-Saharan (1,563)	1,743	7.64
African (764)	876	3.84
Ethiopian (82)	82	0.36
Ghanaian (71)	71	0.31
Kenyan (5)	5	0.02
Liberian (30)	30	0.13
Nigerian (223)	257	1.13
Ugandan (6)	6	0.03
Other Sub-Saharan African (382)	416	1.82
American (264)	264	1.16
Arab (32)	90	0.39
Arab (32)	32	0.14
Lebanese (0)	44	0.19
Palestinian (0)	14	0.06
Armenian (0)	6	0.03
Austrian (17)	55	0.24
Basque (21)	21	0.09
Brazilian (13)	13	0.06
British (49)	156	0.68
Canadian (13)	13	0.06
Celtic (18)	18	0.08
Czech (0)	40	0.18
Czechoslovakian (0)	14	0.06
Danish (0)	28	0.12
Dutch (100)	136	0.60
Eastern European (98)	131	0.57
English (384)	1,446	6.34
European (271)	271	1.19
French, ex. Basque (46)	261	1.14
French Canadian (23)	23	0.10
German (348)	1,845	8.09
Greek (5)	85	0.37
Guyanese (37)	37	0.16
Hungarian (43)	43	0.19
Iranian (18)	18	0.08
Irish (300)	1,634	7.16
Italian (190)	434	1.90
Latvian (13)	13	0.06
Lithuanian (0)	20	0.09
Northern European (23)	23	0.10
Norwegian (58)	272	1.19
Polish (29)	240	1.05
Portuguese (17)	42	0.18
Russian (146)	196	0.86
Scandinavian (0)	18	0.08
Scotch-Irish (90)	176	0.77
Scottish (96)	588	2.58
Serbian (0)	14	0.06
Slovak (26)	26	0.11
Swedish (30)	131	0.57
Swiss (0)	111	0.49
Turkish (36)	36	0.16
Ukrainian (17)	24	0.11
Welsh (50)	156	0.68
West Indian, ex. Hispanic (377)	429	1.88
Barbadian (0)	12	0.05
Jamaican (206)	246	1.08
Trinidadian/Tobagonian (16)	16	0.07
West Indian (155)	155	0.68

Hispanic Origin	Population	%
Hispanic or Latino (of any race)	3,301	14.31
Central American, ex. Mexican	1,556	6.75
Costa Rican	17	0.07
Guatemalan	236	1.02
Honduran	132	0.57
Nicaraguan	39	0.17
Panamanian	51	0.22
Salvadoran	1,081	4.69
Cuban	41	0.18
Dominican Republic	132	0.57
Mexican	712	3.09
Puerto Rican	178	0.77
South American	227	0.98
Argentinean	40	0.17
Bolivian	29	0.13
Chilean	12	0.05
Colombian	26	0.11
Ecuadorian	33	0.14
Paraguayan	4	0.02
Peruvian	57	0.25
Uruguayan	7	0.03
Venezuelan	17	0.07
Other South American	2	0.01
Other Hispanic or Latino	455	1.97

Race*	Population	%
African-American/Black (11,032)	11,494	49.83
Not Hispanic (10,852)	11,235	48.70
Hispanic (180)	259	1.12
American Indian/Alaska Native (74)	248	1.08
Not Hispanic (43)	185	0.80
Hispanic (31)	63	0.27
Blackfeet (2)	9	0.04
Central American Ind. (3)	5	0.02
Cherokee (3)	32	0.14
Choctaw (0)	2	0.01
Comanche (0)	1	<0.01
Creek (0)	1	<0.01
Delaware (0)	1	<0.01
Iroquois (1)	4	0.02
Lumbee (1)	1	<0.01
Mexican American Ind. (5)	6	0.03
Navajo (0)	1	<0.01
South American Ind. (3)	5	0.02
Spanish American Ind. (1)	1	<0.01
Tohono O'Odham (2)	3	0.01
Asian (2,239)	2,483	10.76
Not Hispanic (2,238)	2,467	10.69
Hispanic (1)	16	0.07
Bangladeshi (42)	44	0.19
Burmese (21)	21	0.09
Cambodian (20)	22	0.10
Chinese, ex. Taiwanese (626)	683	2.96
Filipino (167)	226	0.98
Indian (603)	673	2.92
Indonesian (11)	15	0.07
Japanese (43)	62	0.27
Korean (245)	265	1.15
Laotian (1)	2	0.01
Malaysian (4)	6	0.03
Nepalese (30)	31	0.13
Pakistani (131)	146	0.63
Sri Lankan (8)	10	0.04
Taiwanese (83)	87	0.38
Thai (10)	17	0.07
Vietnamese (126)	133	0.58
Hawaii Native/Pacific Islander (30)	63	0.27
Not Hispanic (18)	43	0.19
Hispanic (12)	20	0.09
Guamanian/Chamorro (21)	21	0.09
Native Hawaiian (4)	11	0.05
Samoan (0)	2	0.01
White (6,948)	7,431	32.21
Not Hispanic (5,974)	6,356	27.55
Hispanic (974)	1,075	4.66

*Notes: † The Census 2010 population figure is used to calculate the percentages in the Hispanic Origin and Race categories. Ancestry percentages are based on the 2006-2010 American Community Survey population (not shown); ‡ Numbers in parentheses indicate the number of people reporting a single ancestry; * Numbers in parentheses indicate the number of persons reporting this race alone, not in combination with any other race; Please refer to the Explanation of Data for more information.*

Hagerstown

Place Type: City
County: Washington
Population: 39,662†

Ancestry‡	Population	%
African, Sub-Saharan (819)	945	2.39
African (361)	453	1.15
Ghanaian (79)	79	0.20
Nigerian (207)	219	0.55
Sierra Leonean (37)	59	0.15
Other Sub-Saharan African (135)	135	0.34
American (2,967)	2,967	7.50
Arab (64)	93	0.24
Arab (0)	8	0.02
Egyptian (20)	20	0.05
Jordanian (7)	7	0.02
Lebanese (0)	11	0.03
Moroccan (37)	37	0.09
Other Arab (0)	10	0.03
Austrian (0)	17	0.04
Belgian (0)	82	0.21
Brazilian (24)	95	0.24
British (112)	203	0.51
Canadian (0)	27	0.07
Celtic (12)	12	0.03
Czech (17)	23	0.06
Czechoslovakian (8)	8	0.02
Danish (15)	78	0.20
Dutch (96)	683	1.73
Eastern European (53)	53	0.13
English (868)	2,905	7.35
European (187)	230	0.58
Finnish (8)	21	0.05
French, ex. Basque (122)	552	1.40
French Canadian (8)	49	0.12
German (4,248)	11,359	28.72
Greek (19)	55	0.14
Hungarian (25)	230	0.58
Irish (1,473)	5,591	14.14
Italian (355)	1,607	4.06
Latvian (0)	9	0.02
Lithuanian (0)	43	0.11
Northern European (24)	24	0.06
Norwegian (15)	87	0.22
Pennsylvania German (17)	32	0.08
Polish (334)	969	2.45
Portuguese (12)	18	0.05
Romanian (87)	138	0.35
Russian (31)	132	0.33
Scandinavian (9)	9	0.02
Scotch-Irish (172)	521	1.32
Scottish (171)	544	1.38
Slovak (0)	115	0.29
Slovene (42)	42	0.11
Swedish (88)	360	0.91
Swiss (0)	59	0.15
Turkish (132)	156	0.39
Ukrainian (29)	56	0.14
Welsh (30)	275	0.70
West Indian, ex. Hispanic (215)	267	0.68
Haitian (117)	117	0.30
Jamaican (53)	105	0.27
West Indian (45)	45	0.11
Yugoslavian (0)	21	0.05

Hispanic Origin	Population	%
Hispanic or Latino (of any race)	2,232	5.63
Central American, ex. Mexican	436	1.10
Costa Rican	18	0.05
Guatemalan	56	0.14
Honduran	70	0.18
Nicaraguan	22	0.06
Panamanian	15	0.04
Salvadoran	254	0.64
Other Central American	1	<0.01
Cuban	50	0.13
Dominican Republic	265	0.67
Mexican	523	1.32
Puerto Rican	545	1.37
South American	212	0.53
Argentinean	9	0.02
Bolivian	5	0.01
Chilean	27	0.07
Colombian	66	0.17
Ecuadorian	37	0.09
Paraguayan	1	<0.01
Peruvian	52	0.13
Venezuelan	14	0.04
Other South American	1	<0.01
Other Hispanic or Latino	201	0.51

Race*	Population	%
African-American/Black (6,140)	7,609	19.18
Not Hispanic (5,931)	7,261	18.31
Hispanic (209)	348	0.88
American Indian/Alaska Native (103)	393	0.99
Not Hispanic (74)	324	0.82
Hispanic (29)	69	0.17
Alaska Athabascan *(Ala. Nat.)* (1)	1	<0.01
Apache (3)	9	0.02
Blackfeet (0)	10	0.03
Cherokee (24)	92	0.23
Chickasaw (0)	1	<0.01
Chippewa (0)	5	0.01
Choctaw (0)	4	0.01
Comanche (1)	4	0.01
Creek (3)	3	0.01
Iroquois (4)	19	0.05
Lumbee (0)	1	<0.01
Mexican American Ind. (1)	3	0.01
Navajo (2)	3	0.01
Osage (1)	1	<0.01
Potawatomi (1)	1	<0.01
Seminole (3)	6	0.02
Sioux (0)	2	0.01
South American Ind. (1)	10	0.03
Spanish American Ind. (5)	6	0.02
Asian (504)	699	1.76
Not Hispanic (497)	668	1.68
Hispanic (7)	31	0.08
Bangladeshi (2)	2	0.01
Burmese (2)	2	0.01
Cambodian (7)	8	0.02
Chinese, ex. Taiwanese (100)	122	0.31
Filipino (96)	160	0.40
Indian (125)	155	0.39
Indonesian (5)	5	0.01
Japanese (14)	45	0.11
Korean (52)	77	0.19
Laotian (0)	1	<0.01
Pakistani (25)	29	0.07
Taiwanese (4)	7	0.02
Thai (8)	11	0.03
Vietnamese (36)	49	0.12
Hawaii Native/Pacific Islander (30)	71	0.18
Not Hispanic (27)	62	0.16
Hispanic (3)	9	0.02
Guamanian/Chamorro (6)	6	0.02
Native Hawaiian (10)	32	0.08
White (30,045)	31,881	80.38
Not Hispanic (29,119)	30,703	77.41
Hispanic (926)	1,178	2.97

Halfway

Place Type: CDP
County: Washington
Population: 10,701†

Ancestry‡	Population	%
American (951)	951	9.40
Austrian (0)	24	0.24
Czech (10)	18	0.18
Czechoslovakian (0)	21	0.21
Danish (53)	117	1.16
Dutch (6)	164	1.62
English (419)	1,248	12.33
European (173)	219	2.16
French, ex. Basque (17)	187	1.85
French Canadian (11)	31	0.31
German (1,522)	3,340	33.01
Greek (25)	25	0.25
Hungarian (47)	78	0.77
Irish (329)	1,364	13.48
Italian (210)	448	4.43
Lithuanian (0)	28	0.28
Norwegian (9)	60	0.59
Pennsylvania German (27)	27	0.27
Polish (50)	207	2.05
Romanian (26)	26	0.26
Russian (21)	42	0.42
Scotch-Irish (19)	97	0.96
Scottish (55)	240	2.37
Swedish (22)	64	0.63
Swiss (0)	29	0.29
Turkish (62)	62	0.61
Ukrainian (0)	18	0.18
Welsh (0)	10	0.10
West Indian, ex. Hispanic (0)	11	0.11
Jamaican (0)	11	0.11
Yugoslavian (58)	58	0.57

Hispanic Origin	Population	%
Hispanic or Latino (of any race)	349	3.26
Central American, ex. Mexican	82	0.77
Guatemalan	14	0.13
Honduran	18	0.17
Nicaraguan	1	0.01
Salvadoran	46	0.43
Other Central American	3	0.03
Cuban	6	0.06
Dominican Republic	20	0.19
Mexican	83	0.78
Puerto Rican	73	0.68
South American	43	0.40
Argentinean	1	0.01
Bolivian	3	0.03
Chilean	5	0.05
Colombian	15	0.14
Ecuadorian	1	0.01
Peruvian	11	0.10
Uruguayan	1	0.01
Venezuelan	5	0.05
Other South American	1	0.01
Other Hispanic or Latino	42	0.39

Race*	Population	%
African-American/Black (398)	542	5.06
Not Hispanic (386)	525	4.91
Hispanic (12)	17	0.16
American Indian/Alaska Native (22)	70	0.65
Not Hispanic (18)	60	0.56
Hispanic (4)	10	0.09
Blackfeet (1)	2	0.02
Cherokee (7)	17	0.16
Choctaw (1)	2	0.02
Lumbee (2)	2	0.02
Mexican American Ind. (1)	2	0.02
Navajo (3)	3	0.03
Sioux (1)	1	0.01
South American Ind. (0)	3	0.03
Spanish American Ind. (3)	3	0.03
Asian (190)	242	2.26
Not Hispanic (190)	242	2.26
Burmese (1)	3	0.03
Cambodian (7)	10	0.09
Chinese, ex. Taiwanese (27)	34	0.32
Filipino (27)	41	0.38
Indian (21)	26	0.24
Indonesian (3)	4	0.04
Japanese (9)	13	0.12
Korean (13)	18	0.17
Malaysian (0)	3	0.03
Nepalese (6)	6	0.06
Pakistani (8)	8	0.07
Taiwanese (1)	2	0.02
Thai (2)	4	0.04
Vietnamese (48)	51	0.48

*Notes: † The Census 2010 population figure is used to calculate the percentages in the Hispanic Origin and Race categories. Ancestry percentages are based on the 2006-2010 American Community Survey population (not shown); ‡ Numbers in parentheses indicate the number of people reporting a single ancestry; * Numbers in parentheses indicate the number of persons reporting this race alone, not in combination with any other race; Please refer to the Explanation of Data for more information.*

Hawaii Native/Pacific Islander (1)	19	0.18
Not Hispanic (1)	19	0.18
Guamanian/Chamorro (1)	5	0.05
Native Hawaiian (0)	8	0.07
White (9,708)	9,929	92.79
Not Hispanic (9,514)	9,724	90.87
Hispanic (194)	205	1.92

Havre de Grace

Place Type: City
County: Harford
Population: 12,952†

Ancestry‡	Population	%
African, Sub-Saharan (315)	315	2.46
African (170)	170	1.33
Ghanaian (145)	145	1.13
American (676)	676	5.28
Arab (0)	13	0.10
Syrian (0)	13	0.10
Austrian (14)	26	0.20
British (24)	67	0.52
Croatian (11)	11	0.09
Czech (36)	82	0.64
Danish (0)	42	0.33
Dutch (36)	241	1.88
Eastern European (9)	35	0.27
English (478)	1,609	12.58
European (91)	106	0.83
French, ex. Basque (54)	362	2.83
French Canadian (9)	22	0.17
German (782)	3,334	26.06
German Russian (0)	23	0.18
Greek (10)	29	0.23
Hungarian (60)	128	1.00
Irish (527)	2,433	19.02
Italian (420)	1,221	9.55
Latvian (11)	11	0.09
Lithuanian (22)	30	0.23
Norwegian (12)	42	0.33
Pennsylvania German (11)	32	0.25
Polish (163)	700	5.47
Portuguese (21)	21	0.16
Russian (22)	40	0.31
Scandinavian (24)	34	0.27
Scotch-Irish (131)	446	3.49
Scottish (41)	417	3.26
Slovak (13)	82	0.64
Slovene (0)	9	0.07
Swedish (34)	85	0.66
Swiss (10)	10	0.08
Ukrainian (11)	19	0.15
Welsh (17)	199	1.56

Hispanic Origin	Population	%
Hispanic or Latino (of any race)	608	4.69
Central American, ex. Mexican	39	0.30
Costa Rican	1	0.01
Guatemalan	7	0.05
Honduran	2	0.02
Nicaraguan	1	0.01
Panamanian	22	0.17
Salvadoran	6	0.05
Cuban	19	0.15
Dominican Republic	28	0.22
Mexican	140	1.08
Puerto Rican	291	2.25
South American	25	0.19
Argentinean	7	0.05
Bolivian	1	0.01
Chilean	2	0.02
Colombian	9	0.07
Peruvian	4	0.03
Uruguayan	1	0.01
Venezuelan	1	0.01
Other Hispanic or Latino	66	0.51

Race*	Population	%
African-American/Black (2,170)	2,447	18.89
Not Hispanic (2,074)	2,328	17.97
Hispanic (96)	119	0.92
American Indian/Alaska Native (36)	160	1.24
Not Hispanic (26)	136	1.05
Hispanic (10)	24	0.19
Apache (0)	4	0.03
Blackfeet (0)	8	0.06
Cherokee (15)	61	0.47
Chickasaw (2)	2	0.02
Choctaw (0)	2	0.02
Cree (0)	1	0.01
Creek (1)	1	0.01
Delaware (1)	3	0.02
Iroquois (1)	2	0.02
Lumbee (1)	7	0.05
Seminole (0)	2	0.02
Sioux (1)	9	0.07
Asian (310)	411	3.17
Not Hispanic (309)	405	3.13
Hispanic (1)	6	0.05
Bangladeshi (7)	10	0.08
Cambodian (1)	3	0.02
Chinese, ex. Taiwanese (33)	53	0.41
Filipino (62)	90	0.69
Indian (84)	97	0.75
Indonesian (2)	3	0.02
Japanese (12)	30	0.23
Korean (56)	88	0.68
Pakistani (21)	21	0.16
Taiwanese (2)	2	0.02
Thai (3)	8	0.06
Vietnamese (12)	23	0.18
Hawaii Native/Pacific Islander (14)	37	0.29
Not Hispanic (11)	28	0.22
Hispanic (3)	9	0.07
Guamanian/Chamorro (8)	13	0.10
Native Hawaiian (2)	9	0.07
White (9,809)	10,229	78.98
Not Hispanic (9,488)	9,867	76.18
Hispanic (321)	362	2.79

Hillcrest Heights

Place Type: CDP
County: Prince George's
Population: 16,469†

Ancestry‡	Population	%
African, Sub-Saharan (279)	279	1.75
African (152)	152	0.96
Ethiopian (98)	98	0.62
Nigerian (29)	29	0.18
American (144)	144	0.91
Arab (21)	21	0.13
Moroccan (21)	21	0.13
Austrian (0)	17	0.11
Czech (0)	10	0.06
Dutch (0)	65	0.41
English (27)	38	0.24
European (34)	34	0.21
French, ex. Basque (0)	34	0.21
German (107)	239	1.50
Hungarian (0)	26	0.16
Irish (28)	116	0.73
Italian (58)	69	0.43
Pennsylvania German (17)	17	0.11
Polish (9)	9	0.06
Scottish (0)	11	0.07
Swedish (0)	9	0.06
Turkish (0)	42	0.26
Welsh (4)	8	0.05
West Indian, ex. Hispanic (313)	321	2.02
Bahamian (10)	10	0.06
British West Indian (21)	21	0.13
Haitian (11)	11	0.07
Jamaican (7)	7	0.04
Trinidadian/Tobagonian (243)	243	1.53
West Indian (21)	29	0.18

Hispanic Origin	Population	%
Hispanic or Latino (of any race)	588	3.57
Central American, ex. Mexican	334	2.03
Costa Rican	1	0.01
Guatemalan	26	0.16
Honduran	35	0.21
Nicaraguan	1	0.01
Panamanian	22	0.13
Salvadoran	242	1.47
Other Central American	7	0.04
Cuban	19	0.12
Dominican Republic	17	0.10
Mexican	52	0.32
Puerto Rican	85	0.52
South American	14	0.09
Bolivian	1	0.01
Colombian	2	0.01
Ecuadorian	2	0.01
Paraguayan	6	0.04
Peruvian	2	0.01
Other South American	1	0.01
Other Hispanic or Latino	67	0.41

Race*	Population	%
African-American/Black (15,264)	15,544	94.38
Not Hispanic (15,167)	15,381	93.39
Hispanic (97)	163	0.99
American Indian/Alaska Native (46)	162	0.98
Not Hispanic (41)	135	0.82
Hispanic (5)	27	0.16
Blackfeet (2)	10	0.06
Cherokee (3)	41	0.25
Chippewa (1)	1	0.01
Cree (0)	3	0.02
Navajo (0)	1	0.01
Asian (74)	108	0.66
Not Hispanic (72)	103	0.63
Hispanic (2)	5	0.03
Bangladeshi (2)	2	0.01
Chinese, ex. Taiwanese (8)	12	0.07
Filipino (31)	39	0.24
Indian (9)	12	0.07
Japanese (2)	8	0.05
Korean (6)	8	0.05
Pakistani (1)	1	0.01
Thai (7)	8	0.05
Hawaii Native/Pacific Islander (3)	24	0.15
Not Hispanic (2)	19	0.12
Hispanic (1)	5	0.03
Guamanian/Chamorro (1)	2	0.01
Native Hawaiian (0)	1	0.01
Samoan (1)	3	0.02
White (481)	650	3.95
Not Hispanic (356)	481	2.92
Hispanic (125)	169	1.03

Hyattsville

Place Type: City
County: Prince George's
Population: 17,557†

Ancestry‡	Population	%
African, Sub-Saharan (1,311)	1,337	7.75
African (480)	506	2.93
Ethiopian (217)	217	1.26
Ghanaian (131)	131	0.76
Kenyan (21)	21	0.12
Nigerian (163)	163	0.94
Sierra Leonean (81)	81	0.47
Other Sub-Saharan African (218)	218	1.26
American (595)	595	3.45
Arab (34)	34	0.20
Lebanese (34)	34	0.20
Australian (0)	27	0.16
Austrian (11)	40	0.23
Belgian (0)	38	0.22
Brazilian (10)	10	0.06
British (17)	24	0.14
Canadian (20)	28	0.16

*Notes: † The Census 2010 population figure is used to calculate the percentages in the Hispanic Origin and Race categories. Ancestry percentages are based on the 2006-2010 American Community Survey population (not shown); ‡ Numbers in parentheses indicate the number of people reporting a single ancestry; * Numbers in parentheses indicate the number of persons reporting this race alone, not in combination with any other race; Please refer to the Explanation of Data for more information.*

Carpatho Rusyn (0)	8	0.05
Croatian (8)	8	0.05
Czech (0)	62	0.36
Dutch (0)	114	0.66
Eastern European (0)	5	0.03
English (225)	877	5.08
European (63)	77	0.45
French, ex. Basque (11)	284	1.65
French Canadian (0)	11	0.06
German (215)	884	5.12
Greek (54)	64	0.37
Guyanese (11)	11	0.06
Hungarian (6)	6	0.03
Irish (290)	1,156	6.70
Italian (191)	410	2.38
Lithuanian (21)	59	0.34
Northern European (9)	9	0.05
Norwegian (10)	36	0.21
Polish (76)	162	0.94
Russian (0)	146	0.85
Scandinavian (0)	5	0.03
Scotch-Irish (21)	75	0.43
Scottish (20)	137	0.79
Slavic (0)	4	0.02
Slovak (16)	23	0.13
Slovene (7)	7	0.04
Swedish (5)	88	0.51
Ukrainian (37)	95	0.55
Welsh (50)	86	0.50
West Indian, ex. Hispanic (514)	550	3.19
British West Indian (100)	108	0.63
Haitian (58)	58	0.34
Jamaican (281)	281	1.63
Trinidadian/Tobagonian (10)	18	0.10
West Indian (65)	85	0.49
Yugoslavian (10)	10	0.06

Hispanic Origin	Population	%
Hispanic or Latino (of any race)	5,972	34.01
Central American, ex. Mexican	3,805	21.67
Costa Rican	14	0.08
Guatemalan	541	3.08
Honduran	209	1.19
Nicaraguan	107	0.61
Panamanian	42	0.24
Salvadoran	2,876	16.38
Other Central American	16	0.09
Cuban	74	0.42
Dominican Republic	200	1.14
Mexican	723	4.12
Puerto Rican	147	0.84
South American	313	1.78
Argentinean	25	0.14
Bolivian	40	0.23
Chilean	9	0.05
Colombian	53	0.30
Ecuadorian	43	0.24
Peruvian	128	0.73
Uruguayan	3	0.02
Venezuelan	12	0.07
Other Hispanic or Latino	710	4.04

Race*	Population	%
African-American/Black (6,258)	6,651	37.88
Not Hispanic (6,076)	6,341	36.12
Hispanic (182)	310	1.77
American Indian/Alaska Native (139)	310	1.77
Not Hispanic (57)	152	0.87
Hispanic (82)	158	0.90
Apache (0)	5	0.03
Blackfeet (2)	8	0.05
Canadian/French Am. Ind. (0)	6	0.03
Central American Ind. (2)	4	0.02
Cherokee (2)	13	0.07
Chickasaw (0)	1	0.01
Chippewa (0)	1	0.01
Choctaw (3)	3	0.02
Creek (0)	1	0.01
Delaware (2)	2	0.01
Hopi (0)	1	0.01
Inupiat *(Alaska Native)* (6)	6	0.03
Iroquois (0)	2	0.01
Lumbee (1)	1	0.01
Mexican American Ind. (8)	18	0.10
Navajo (1)	1	0.01
Sioux (0)	2	0.01
South American Ind. (0)	6	0.03
Spanish American Ind. (1)	1	0.01
Asian (768)	944	5.38
Not Hispanic (757)	897	5.11
Hispanic (11)	47	0.27
Bangladeshi (20)	28	0.16
Bhutanese (25)	31	0.18
Cambodian (6)	11	0.06
Chinese, ex. Taiwanese (169)	195	1.11
Filipino (79)	109	0.62
Indian (217)	268	1.53
Indonesian (12)	17	0.10
Japanese (20)	55	0.31
Korean (31)	42	0.24
Laotian (13)	13	0.07
Malaysian (2)	2	0.01
Nepalese (26)	34	0.19
Pakistani (17)	21	0.12
Sri Lankan (10)	11	0.06
Taiwanese (4)	4	0.02
Thai (10)	11	0.06
Vietnamese (45)	45	0.26
Hawaii Native/Pacific Islander (9)	38	0.22
Not Hispanic (7)	32	0.18
Hispanic (2)	6	0.03
Guamanian/Chamorro (5)	6	0.03
Native Hawaiian (0)	2	0.01
Samoan (2)	2	0.01
White (5,826)	6,423	36.58
Not Hispanic (4,206)	4,489	25.57
Hispanic (1,620)	1,934	11.02

Ilchester

Place Type: CDP
County: Howard
Population: 23,476†

Ancestry‡	Population	%
African, Sub-Saharan (125)	153	0.67
African (75)	75	0.33
Ethiopian (37)	37	0.16
Ghanaian (0)	28	0.12
Kenyan (13)	13	0.06
Albanian (20)	98	0.43
American (1,060)	1,060	4.63
Armenian (15)	30	0.13
Brazilian (13)	13	0.06
British (27)	196	0.86
Czech (42)	174	0.76
Czechoslovakian (15)	15	0.07
Danish (0)	24	0.10
Dutch (108)	299	1.31
Eastern European (89)	153	0.67
English (797)	2,369	10.34
Estonian (0)	13	0.06
European (241)	254	1.11
Finnish (0)	13	0.06
French, ex. Basque (60)	393	1.72
French Canadian (42)	101	0.44
German (1,225)	4,904	21.41
Greek (13)	119	0.52
Guyanese (13)	13	0.06
Hungarian (4)	103	0.45
Iranian (11)	11	0.05
Irish (690)	3,075	13.42
Italian (803)	2,069	9.03
Lithuanian (13)	80	0.35
Norwegian (81)	367	1.60
Polish (318)	1,380	6.02
Portuguese (0)	16	0.07
Romanian (0)	71	0.31
Russian (151)	361	1.58
Scotch-Irish (75)	538	2.35
Scottish (200)	824	3.60
Slavic (77)	77	0.34
Slovak (30)	110	0.48
Slovene (0)	13	0.06
Swedish (0)	310	1.35
Swiss (37)	103	0.45
Ukrainian (33)	96	0.42
Welsh (59)	250	1.09

Hispanic Origin	Population	%
Hispanic or Latino (of any race)	1,075	4.58
Central American, ex. Mexican	263	1.12
Costa Rican	13	0.06
Guatemalan	40	0.17
Honduran	37	0.16
Nicaraguan	18	0.08
Panamanian	27	0.12
Salvadoran	124	0.53
Other Central American	4	0.02
Cuban	45	0.19
Dominican Republic	16	0.07
Mexican	235	1.00
Puerto Rican	198	0.84
South American	176	0.75
Argentinean	39	0.17
Bolivian	9	0.04
Chilean	16	0.07
Colombian	51	0.22
Ecuadorian	10	0.04
Paraguayan	1	<0.01
Peruvian	46	0.20
Uruguayan	1	<0.01
Venezuelan	1	<0.01
Other South American	2	0.01
Other Hispanic or Latino	142	0.60

Race*	Population	%
African-American/Black (2,712)	3,072	13.09
Not Hispanic (2,650)	2,958	12.60
Hispanic (62)	114	0.49
American Indian/Alaska Native (56)	191	0.81
Not Hispanic (39)	146	0.62
Hispanic (17)	45	0.19
Apache (0)	5	0.02
Blackfeet (0)	9	0.04
Canadian/French Am. Ind. (0)	4	0.02
Central American Ind. (4)	4	0.02
Cherokee (9)	36	0.15
Chippewa (1)	1	<0.01
Iroquois (2)	2	0.01
Lumbee (5)	11	0.05
Mexican American Ind. (3)	4	0.02
Navajo (0)	1	<0.01
Osage (0)	2	0.01
Pueblo (0)	4	0.02
Sioux (1)	2	0.01
South American Ind. (0)	3	0.01
Yaqui (1)	1	<0.01
Yuman (0)	1	<0.01
Asian (3,574)	3,975	16.93
Not Hispanic (3,570)	3,953	16.84
Hispanic (4)	22	0.09
Bangladeshi (6)	7	0.03
Burmese (24)	27	0.12
Cambodian (8)	13	0.06
Chinese, ex. Taiwanese (446)	511	2.18
Filipino (136)	209	0.89
Indian (1,332)	1,392	5.93
Indonesian (5)	5	0.02
Japanese (32)	85	0.36
Korean (1,114)	1,187	5.06
Laotian (13)	16	0.07
Nepalese (16)	16	0.07
Pakistani (137)	150	0.64
Sri Lankan (23)	26	0.11
Taiwanese (23)	25	0.11
Thai (34)	40	0.17
Vietnamese (150)	178	0.76
Hawaii Native/Pacific Islander (6)	27	0.12
Not Hispanic (5)	20	0.09

*Notes: † The Census 2010 population figure is used to calculate the percentages in the Hispanic Origin and Race categories. Ancestry percentages are based on the 2006-2010 American Community Survey population (not shown); ‡ Numbers in parentheses indicate the number of people reporting a single ancestry; * Numbers in parentheses indicate the number of persons reporting this race alone, not in combination with any other race; Please refer to the Explanation of Data for more information.*

SECTION TWO

Hispanic (1)	7	0.03
Guamanian/Chamorro (1)	1	<0.01
Native Hawaiian (3)	12	0.05
Samoan (1)	1	<0.01
White (15,978)	16,690	71.09
Not Hispanic (15,362)	15,977	68.06
Hispanic (616)	713	3.04

Joppatowne

Place Type: CDP
County: Harford
Population: 12,616†

Ancestry‡	Population	%
African, Sub-Saharan (231)	231	1.82
African (91)	91	0.72
Kenyan (38)	38	0.30
Nigerian (93)	93	0.73
Other Sub-Saharan African (9)	9	0.07
American (744)	744	5.88
Arab (0)	83	0.66
Other Arab (0)	83	0.66
Austrian (28)	41	0.32
British (37)	99	0.78
Canadian (27)	27	0.21
Czech (36)	114	0.90
Czechoslovakian (26)	72	0.57
Danish (0)	20	0.16
Dutch (0)	181	1.43
Eastern European (16)	16	0.13
English (411)	1,149	9.07
European (72)	155	1.22
French, ex. Basque (21)	443	3.50
French Canadian (33)	33	0.26
German (971)	3,189	25.19
Greek (60)	113	0.89
Hungarian (12)	57	0.45
Irish (828)	2,787	22.01
Italian (500)	1,209	9.55
Lithuanian (14)	28	0.22
Norwegian (0)	26	0.21
Pennsylvania German (10)	10	0.08
Polish (492)	1,164	9.19
Romanian (0)	12	0.09
Russian (23)	63	0.50
Scotch-Irish (54)	112	0.88
Scottish (58)	130	1.03
Slovak (15)	33	0.26
Swedish (12)	169	1.33
Ukrainian (11)	42	0.33
Welsh (22)	147	1.16
West Indian, ex. Hispanic (41)	41	0.32
Jamaican (41)	41	0.32
Yugoslavian (0)	19	0.15

Hispanic Origin	Population	%
Hispanic or Latino (of any race)	410	3.25
Central American, ex. Mexican	41	0.32
Costa Rican	5	0.04
Guatemalan	4	0.03
Honduran	2	0.02
Nicaraguan	3	0.02
Panamanian	14	0.11
Salvadoran	11	0.09
Other Central American	2	0.02
Cuban	15	0.12
Dominican Republic	13	0.10
Mexican	98	0.78
Puerto Rican	153	1.21
South American	29	0.23
Argentinean	5	0.04
Colombian	15	0.12
Ecuadorian	6	0.05
Peruvian	3	0.02
Other Hispanic or Latino	61	0.48

Race*	Population	%
African-American/Black (2,106)	2,268	17.98
Not Hispanic (2,054)	2,199	17.43
Hispanic (52)	69	0.55
American Indian/Alaska Native (37)	116	0.92
Not Hispanic (31)	96	0.76
Hispanic (6)	20	0.16
Apache (1)	1	0.01
Blackfeet (0)	5	0.04
Cherokee (9)	31	0.25
Chippewa (1)	5	0.04
Choctaw (0)	1	0.01
Delaware (1)	1	0.01
Iroquois (0)	1	0.01
Lumbee (4)	6	0.05
Mexican American Ind. (3)	4	0.03
Navajo (0)	1	0.01
Yaqui (0)	2	0.02
Asian (318)	394	3.12
Not Hispanic (314)	383	3.04
Hispanic (4)	11	0.09
Bangladeshi (15)	15	0.12
Chinese, ex. Taiwanese (23)	25	0.20
Filipino (119)	146	1.16
Indian (70)	89	0.71
Indonesian (2)	2	0.02
Japanese (11)	24	0.19
Korean (25)	40	0.32
Laotian (4)	4	0.03
Nepalese (2)	2	0.02
Pakistani (4)	5	0.04
Thai (3)	7	0.06
Vietnamese (29)	31	0.25
Hawaii Native/Pacific Islander (6)	16	0.13
Not Hispanic (4)	13	0.10
Hispanic (2)	3	0.02
Guamanian/Chamorro (4)	8	0.06
Native Hawaiian (2)	4	0.03
Samoan (0)	1	0.01
White (9,808)	10,039	79.57
Not Hispanic (9,547)	9,755	77.32
Hispanic (261)	284	2.25

Kemp Mill

Place Type: CDP
County: Montgomery
Population: 12,564†

Ancestry‡	Population	%
African, Sub-Saharan (560)	617	5.11
African (162)	177	1.46
Ethiopian (220)	220	1.82
Liberian (64)	85	0.70
Nigerian (54)	75	0.62
Sierra Leonean (44)	44	0.36
South African (16)	16	0.13
American (572)	572	4.73
Arab (43)	58	0.48
Lebanese (18)	18	0.15
Moroccan (25)	40	0.33
Armenian (10)	10	0.08
Austrian (34)	101	0.84
Basque (4)	8	0.07
Belgian (0)	10	0.08
Brazilian (9)	32	0.26
British (8)	48	0.40
Canadian (47)	61	0.50
Celtic (50)	50	0.41
Czech (12)	19	0.16
Czechoslovakian (12)	30	0.25
Danish (0)	13	0.11
Dutch (0)	47	0.39
Eastern European (416)	416	3.44
English (213)	655	5.42
European (412)	460	3.81
Finnish (11)	11	0.09
French, ex. Basque (39)	84	0.70
French Canadian (7)	39	0.32
German (352)	1,025	8.48
Greek (57)	76	0.63
Hungarian (26)	161	1.33
Iranian (95)	95	0.79
Irish (166)	699	5.78
Israeli (75)	75	0.62
Italian (133)	318	2.63
Lithuanian (16)	102	0.84
Macedonian (0)	9	0.07
Northern European (9)	9	0.07
Norwegian (46)	75	0.62
Polish (323)	835	6.91
Portuguese (15)	43	0.36
Romanian (21)	70	0.58
Russian (292)	744	6.16
Scotch-Irish (10)	85	0.70
Scottish (25)	161	1.33
Serbian (0)	10	0.08
Slavic (51)	60	0.50
Slovak (0)	36	0.30
Swedish (70)	91	0.75
Swiss (0)	31	0.26
Ukrainian (21)	30	0.25
Welsh (20)	39	0.32
West Indian, ex. Hispanic (337)	352	2.91
Haitian (154)	154	1.27
Jamaican (141)	141	1.17
Trinidadian/Tobagonian (0)	15	0.12
West Indian (42)	42	0.35

Hispanic Origin	Population	%
Hispanic or Latino (of any race)	2,066	16.44
Central American, ex. Mexican	1,120	8.91
Costa Rican	14	0.11
Guatemalan	129	1.03
Honduran	46	0.37
Nicaraguan	65	0.52
Panamanian	18	0.14
Salvadoran	846	6.73
Other Central American	2	0.02
Cuban	40	0.32
Dominican Republic	109	0.87
Mexican	159	1.27
Puerto Rican	92	0.73
South American	347	2.76
Argentinean	23	0.18
Bolivian	76	0.60
Chilean	22	0.18
Colombian	50	0.40
Ecuadorian	41	0.33
Paraguayan	23	0.18
Peruvian	93	0.74
Uruguayan	4	0.03
Venezuelan	15	0.12
Other Hispanic or Latino	199	1.58

Race*	Population	%
African-American/Black (2,082)	2,281	18.16
Not Hispanic (2,002)	2,165	17.23
Hispanic (80)	116	0.92
American Indian/Alaska Native (76)	150	1.19
Not Hispanic (19)	64	0.51
Hispanic (57)	86	0.68
Apache (1)	3	0.02
Blackfeet (0)	1	0.01
Central American Ind. (2)	4	0.03
Cherokee (2)	9	0.07
Chippewa (2)	2	0.02
Choctaw (0)	1	0.01
Creek (2)	3	0.02
Crow (0)	2	0.02
Iroquois (0)	1	0.01
Mexican American Ind. (8)	16	0.13
Sioux (2)	5	0.04
South American Ind. (1)	2	0.02
Asian (1,076)	1,264	10.06
Not Hispanic (1,068)	1,236	9.84
Hispanic (8)	28	0.22
Bangladeshi (1)	2	0.02
Burmese (2)	2	0.02
Cambodian (63)	68	0.54
Chinese, ex. Taiwanese (214)	268	2.13
Filipino (83)	116	0.92
Indian (168)	195	1.55

*Notes: † The Census 2010 population figure is used to calculate the percentages in the Hispanic Origin and Race categories. Ancestry percentages are based on the 2006-2010 American Community Survey population (not shown); ‡ Numbers in parentheses indicate the number of people reporting a single ancestry; * Numbers in parentheses indicate the number of persons reporting this race alone, not in combination with any other race; Please refer to the Explanation of Data for more information.*

Indonesian (8)	8	0.06
Japanese (14)	35	0.28
Korean (95)	106	0.84
Laotian (7)	9	0.07
Malaysian (0)	1	0.01
Nepalese (8)	10	0.08
Pakistani (24)	25	0.20
Sri Lankan (3)	5	0.04
Taiwanese (6)	8	0.06
Thai (67)	82	0.65
Vietnamese (246)	268	2.13
Hawaii Native/Pacific Islander (5)	25	0.20
Not Hispanic (5)	18	0.14
Hispanic (0)	7	0.06
Guamanian/Chamorro (0)	2	0.02
Marshallese (1)	1	0.01
Native Hawaiian (0)	5	0.04
Samoan (1)	6	0.05
White (7,916)	8,271	65.83
Not Hispanic (7,036)	7,285	57.98
Hispanic (880)	986	7.85

Kettering

Place Type: CDP
County: Prince George's
Population: 12,790†

Ancestry‡	Population	%
African, Sub-Saharan (1,135)	1,191	9.49
African (781)	811	6.46
Cape Verdean (11)	11	0.09
Nigerian (310)	310	2.47
Sierra Leonean (11)	11	0.09
South African (11)	32	0.26
Other Sub-Saharan African (11)	16	0.13
American (52)	52	0.41
Canadian (21)	21	0.17
English (26)	86	0.69
French, ex. Basque (0)	39	0.31
German (32)	108	0.86
Guyanese (16)	16	0.13
Irish (0)	31	0.25
Italian (7)	14	0.11
Polish (6)	6	0.05
Russian (1)	1	0.01
Scotch-Irish (0)	18	0.14
Slovak (6)	6	0.05
Swiss (0)	13	0.10
Welsh (11)	11	0.09
West Indian, ex. Hispanic (315)	315	2.51
Bermudan (14)	14	0.11
British West Indian (99)	99	0.79
Jamaican (181)	181	1.44
Trinidadian/Tobagonian (21)	21	0.17

Hispanic Origin	Population	%
Hispanic or Latino (of any race)	239	1.87
Central American, ex. Mexican	88	0.69
Costa Rican	3	0.02
Guatemalan	5	0.04
Honduran	4	0.03
Nicaraguan	9	0.07
Panamanian	31	0.24
Salvadoran	36	0.28
Cuban	19	0.15
Dominican Republic	11	0.09
Mexican	46	0.36
Puerto Rican	38	0.30
South American	27	0.21
Bolivian	1	0.01
Chilean	5	0.04
Colombian	7	0.05
Peruvian	11	0.09
Venezuelan	3	0.02
Other Hispanic or Latino	10	0.08

Race*	Population	%
African-American/Black (11,774)	12,001	93.83
Not Hispanic (11,675)	11,883	92.91
Hispanic (99)	118	0.92
American Indian/Alaska Native (18)	127	0.99
Not Hispanic (15)	116	0.91
Hispanic (3)	11	0.09
Blackfeet (1)	3	0.02
Canadian/French Am. Ind. (0)	1	0.01
Cherokee (1)	32	0.25
Creek (0)	1	0.01
Lumbee (1)	2	0.02
Navajo (0)	4	0.03
Seminole (0)	2	0.02
Sioux (0)	1	0.01
Ute (0)	1	0.01
Asian (241)	293	2.29
Not Hispanic (241)	288	2.25
Hispanic (0)	5	0.04
Chinese, ex. Taiwanese (18)	31	0.24
Filipino (153)	174	1.36
Indian (28)	41	0.32
Japanese (7)	11	0.09
Korean (15)	17	0.13
Pakistani (10)	10	0.08
Thai (1)	6	0.05
Vietnamese (2)	2	0.02
Hawaii Native/Pacific Islander (5)	12	0.09
Not Hispanic (5)	12	0.09
Fijian (1)	1	0.01
Guamanian/Chamorro (0)	3	0.02
White (411)	528	4.13
Not Hispanic (368)	474	3.71
Hispanic (43)	54	0.42

La Plata

Place Type: Town
County: Charles
Population: 8,753†

Ancestry‡	Population	%
African, Sub-Saharan (27)	27	0.32
African (27)	27	0.32
American (392)	392	4.61
Austrian (10)	45	0.53
Belgian (0)	18	0.21
British (21)	21	0.25
Canadian (0)	15	0.18
Czech (0)	24	0.28
Danish (0)	25	0.29
Dutch (0)	86	1.01
English (169)	765	9.00
European (56)	76	0.89
French, ex. Basque (48)	267	3.14
French Canadian (25)	104	1.22
German (450)	1,538	18.10
Greek (8)	24	0.28
Hungarian (0)	12	0.14
Irish (397)	1,298	15.28
Italian (231)	640	7.53
Latvian (0)	7	0.08
Lithuanian (0)	26	0.31
Northern European (30)	30	0.35
Norwegian (23)	42	0.49
Polish (14)	194	2.28
Russian (0)	25	0.29
Scotch-Irish (22)	211	2.48
Scottish (50)	210	2.47
Slovak (12)	27	0.32
Swedish (0)	62	0.73
Swiss (0)	12	0.14
Ukrainian (0)	40	0.47
West Indian, ex. Hispanic (14)	94	1.11
Dutch West Indian (0)	8	0.09
Jamaican (14)	44	0.52
West Indian (0)	42	0.49

Hispanic Origin	Population	%
Hispanic or Latino (of any race)	276	3.15
Central American, ex. Mexican	49	0.56
Guatemalan	13	0.15
Panamanian	5	0.06
Salvadoran	31	0.35
Cuban	15	0.17
Dominican Republic	2	0.02
Mexican	66	0.75
Puerto Rican	74	0.85
South American	20	0.23
Argentinean	2	0.02
Bolivian	3	0.03
Chilean	5	0.06
Colombian	3	0.03
Ecuadorian	1	0.01
Paraguayan	1	0.01
Peruvian	2	0.02
Uruguayan	2	0.02
Venezuelan	1	0.01
Other Hispanic or Latino	50	0.57

Race*	Population	%
African-American/Black (2,339)	2,473	28.25
Not Hispanic (2,319)	2,439	27.86
Hispanic (20)	34	0.39
American Indian/Alaska Native (47)	124	1.42
Not Hispanic (35)	105	1.20
Hispanic (12)	19	0.22
Apache (2)	3	0.03
Blackfeet (0)	2	0.02
Cherokee (5)	17	0.19
Kiowa (1)	1	0.01
Lumbee (2)	3	0.03
Mexican American Ind. (2)	2	0.02
Sioux (1)	1	0.01
Tohono O'Odham (1)	1	0.01
Ute (0)	3	0.03
Asian (233)	323	3.69
Not Hispanic (233)	312	3.56
Hispanic (0)	11	0.13
Bangladeshi (9)	9	0.10
Chinese, ex. Taiwanese (31)	47	0.54
Filipino (62)	105	1.20
Indian (53)	58	0.66
Japanese (10)	22	0.25
Korean (41)	48	0.55
Pakistani (3)	3	0.03
Taiwanese (3)	3	0.03
Thai (5)	6	0.07
Vietnamese (14)	19	0.22
Hawaii Native/Pacific Islander (10)	22	0.25
Not Hispanic (10)	20	0.23
Hispanic (0)	2	0.02
Guamanian/Chamorro (4)	5	0.06
Native Hawaiian (2)	3	0.03
Samoan (4)	10	0.11
White (5,800)	6,021	68.79
Not Hispanic (5,645)	5,844	66.77
Hispanic (155)	177	2.02

Lake Arbor

Place Type: CDP
County: Prince George's
Population: 9,776†

Ancestry‡	Population	%
African, Sub-Saharan (1,082)	1,227	11.90
African (448)	563	5.46
Cape Verdean (15)	15	0.15
Ghanaian (148)	148	1.44
Nigerian (226)	242	2.35
Sierra Leonean (201)	201	1.95
Other Sub-Saharan African (44)	58	0.56
American (104)	104	1.01
Dutch (0)	9	0.09
English (31)	118	1.14
French, ex. Basque (0)	16	0.16
German (9)	24	0.23
Greek (0)	12	0.12
Irish (46)	65	0.63
Italian (0)	38	0.37
Norwegian (0)	1	0.01
Polish (0)	1	0.01

SECTION TWO

*Notes: † The Census 2010 population figure is used to calculate the percentages in the Hispanic Origin and Race categories. Ancestry percentages are based on the 2006-2010 American Community Survey population (not shown); ‡ Numbers in parentheses indicate the number of people reporting a single ancestry; * Numbers in parentheses indicate the number of persons reporting this race alone, not in combination with any other race; Please refer to the Explanation of Data for more information.*

Russian (0)	1	0.01
Scotch-Irish (1)	15	0.15
Scottish (0)	16	0.16
Swedish (9)	9	0.09
West Indian, ex. Hispanic (73)	127	1.23
Haitian (23)	23	0.22
Jamaican (11)	65	0.63
Trinidadian/Tobagonian (39)	39	0.38

Hispanic Origin	Population	%
Hispanic or Latino (of any race)	240	2.45
Central American, ex. Mexican	65	0.66
Costa Rican	3	0.03
Guatemalan	9	0.09
Honduran	1	0.01
Nicaraguan	4	0.04
Panamanian	26	0.27
Salvadoran	22	0.23
Cuban	11	0.11
Dominican Republic	19	0.19
Mexican	43	0.44
Puerto Rican	82	0.84
South American	10	0.10
Chilean	7	0.07
Colombian	1	0.01
Ecuadorian	1	0.01
Other South American	1	0.01
Other Hispanic or Latino	10	0.10

Race*	Population	%
African-American/Black (9,058)	9,232	94.44
Not Hispanic (8,943)	9,092	93.00
Hispanic (115)	140	1.43
American Indian/Alaska Native (26)	97	0.99
Not Hispanic (24)	83	0.85
Hispanic (2)	14	0.14
Blackfeet (3)	4	0.04
Cherokee (11)	22	0.23
Creek (0)	2	0.02
Lumbee (0)	4	0.04
Asian (195)	251	2.57
Not Hispanic (195)	247	2.53
Hispanic (0)	4	0.04
Cambodian (8)	8	0.08
Chinese, ex. Taiwanese (5)	9	0.09
Filipino (98)	113	1.16
Indian (36)	60	0.61
Japanese (3)	8	0.08
Korean (15)	16	0.16
Malaysian (0)	1	0.01
Pakistani (5)	5	0.05
Thai (0)	1	0.01
Vietnamese (7)	14	0.14
Hawaii Native/Pacific Islander (2)	18	0.18
Not Hispanic (2)	16	0.16
Hispanic (0)	2	0.02
Fijian (0)	2	0.02
Guamanian/Chamorro (0)	1	0.01
Native Hawaiian (0)	7	0.07
Samoan (2)	4	0.04
White (250)	353	3.61
Not Hispanic (198)	281	2.87
Hispanic (52)	72	0.74

Lake Shore

Place Type: CDP
County: Anne Arundel
Population: 19,477†

Ancestry‡	Population	%
African, Sub-Saharan (4)	25	0.13
African (0)	21	0.11
Other Sub-Saharan African (4)	4	0.02
American (1,068)	1,068	5.66
Arab (38)	94	0.50
Egyptian (18)	18	0.10
Syrian (20)	76	0.40
Austrian (0)	42	0.22
Belgian (0)	15	0.08
Brazilian (16)	16	0.08
British (48)	141	0.75
Czech (30)	157	0.83
Danish (19)	40	0.21
Dutch (68)	275	1.46
Eastern European (54)	61	0.32
English (446)	2,698	14.29
Estonian (13)	13	0.07
European (44)	59	0.31
French, ex. Basque (160)	919	4.87
French Canadian (45)	115	0.61
German (2,255)	7,535	39.91
Greek (41)	90	0.48
Hungarian (0)	122	0.65
Irish (1,025)	4,408	23.35
Israeli (9)	28	0.15
Italian (744)	1,775	9.40
Latvian (15)	15	0.08
Lithuanian (62)	103	0.55
Norwegian (25)	130	0.69
Pennsylvania German (41)	41	0.22
Polish (506)	1,613	8.54
Portuguese (0)	7	0.04
Romanian (0)	13	0.07
Russian (40)	147	0.78
Scotch-Irish (56)	404	2.14
Scottish (87)	344	1.82
Slovak (0)	11	0.06
Swedish (22)	155	0.82
Welsh (13)	125	0.66

Hispanic Origin	Population	%
Hispanic or Latino (of any race)	428	2.20
Central American, ex. Mexican	68	0.35
Guatemalan	23	0.12
Honduran	6	0.03
Panamanian	8	0.04
Salvadoran	31	0.16
Cuban	19	0.10
Dominican Republic	19	0.10
Mexican	92	0.47
Puerto Rican	98	0.50
South American	71	0.36
Argentinean	9	0.05
Bolivian	3	0.02
Chilean	3	0.02
Colombian	17	0.09
Ecuadorian	9	0.05
Peruvian	18	0.09
Uruguayan	1	0.01
Venezuelan	11	0.06
Other Hispanic or Latino	61	0.31

Race*	Population	%
African-American/Black (712)	825	4.24
Not Hispanic (698)	793	4.07
Hispanic (14)	32	0.16
American Indian/Alaska Native (58)	186	0.95
Not Hispanic (55)	177	0.91
Hispanic (3)	9	0.05
Blackfeet (3)	8	0.04
Canadian/French Am. Ind. (2)	2	0.01
Cherokee (12)	46	0.24
Chickasaw (2)	3	0.02
Chippewa (1)	3	0.02
Choctaw (0)	1	0.01
Houma (3)	3	0.02
Iroquois (1)	2	0.01
Kiowa (1)	1	0.01
Lumbee (6)	14	0.07
Mexican American Ind. (2)	2	0.01
Sioux (0)	9	0.05
South American Ind. (0)	4	0.02
Asian (262)	392	2.01
Not Hispanic (260)	385	1.98
Hispanic (2)	7	0.04
Chinese, ex. Taiwanese (42)	62	0.32
Filipino (59)	105	0.54
Indian (35)	39	0.20
Japanese (13)	36	0.18
Korean (62)	80	0.41
Pakistani (13)	13	0.07
Taiwanese (1)	4	0.02
Thai (8)	15	0.08
Vietnamese (22)	26	0.13
Hawaii Native/Pacific Islander (17)	30	0.15
Not Hispanic (15)	28	0.14
Hispanic (2)	2	0.01
Guamanian/Chamorro (5)	10	0.05
Native Hawaiian (6)	9	0.05
Samoan (4)	4	0.02
White (17,945)	18,284	93.87
Not Hispanic (17,675)	17,977	92.30
Hispanic (270)	307	1.58

Landover

Place Type: CDP
County: Prince George's
Population: 23,078†

Ancestry‡	Population	%
African, Sub-Saharan (1,279)	1,417	6.02
African (633)	719	3.05
Ethiopian (0)	9	0.04
Ghanaian (0)	13	0.06
Liberian (29)	29	0.12
Nigerian (617)	647	2.75
American (159)	159	0.68
Canadian (0)	48	0.20
English (69)	160	0.68
French, ex. Basque (0)	19	0.08
French Canadian (0)	14	0.06
German (70)	230	0.98
Greek (39)	39	0.17
Guyanese (219)	254	1.08
Irish (44)	175	0.74
Italian (29)	172	0.73
Polish (9)	9	0.04
Portuguese (76)	76	0.32
Russian (0)	10	0.04
Scotch-Irish (9)	57	0.24
Scottish (4)	38	0.16
West Indian, ex. Hispanic (514)	702	2.98
British West Indian (72)	72	0.31
Dutch West Indian (40)	40	0.17
Haitian (34)	41	0.17
Jamaican (342)	408	1.73
Trinidadian/Tobagonian (0)	6	0.03
West Indian (26)	135	0.57

Hispanic Origin	Population	%
Hispanic or Latino (of any race)	3,359	14.55
Central American, ex. Mexican	1,643	7.12
Costa Rican	2	0.01
Guatemalan	231	1.00
Honduran	134	0.58
Nicaraguan	46	0.20
Panamanian	34	0.15
Salvadoran	1,194	5.17
Other Central American	2	0.01
Cuban	28	0.12
Dominican Republic	94	0.41
Mexican	816	3.54
Puerto Rican	112	0.49
South American	93	0.40
Argentinean	6	0.03
Bolivian	9	0.04
Chilean	4	0.02
Colombian	14	0.06
Ecuadorian	18	0.08
Peruvian	41	0.18
Other South American	1	<0.01
Other Hispanic or Latino	573	2.48

Race*	Population	%
African-American/Black (18,893)	19,279	83.54
Not Hispanic (18,671)	18,986	82.27
Hispanic (222)	293	1.27
American Indian/Alaska Native (95)	277	1.20

*Notes: † The Census 2010 population figure is used to calculate the percentages in the Hispanic Origin and Race categories. Ancestry percentages are based on the 2006-2010 American Community Survey population (not shown); ‡ Numbers in parentheses indicate the number of people reporting a single ancestry; * Numbers in parentheses indicate the number of persons reporting this race alone, not in combination with any other race; Please refer to the Explanation of Data for more information.*

Not Hispanic (59)	200	0.87
Hispanic (36)	77	0.33
Apache (0)	1	<0.01
Blackfeet (1)	22	0.10
Central American Ind. (5)	7	0.03
Cherokee (3)	38	0.16
Comanche (0)	2	0.01
Iroquois (0)	1	<0.01
Lumbee (0)	2	0.01
Mexican American Ind. (6)	6	0.03
South American Ind. (2)	9	0.04
Spanish American Ind. (1)	1	<0.01
Yuman (0)	1	<0.01
Asian (154)	211	0.91
Not Hispanic (151)	204	0.88
Hispanic (3)	7	0.03
Bangladeshi (0)	1	<0.01
Cambodian (5)	9	0.04
Chinese, ex. Taiwanese (27)	30	0.13
Filipino (47)	65	0.28
Indian (23)	29	0.13
Japanese (7)	12	0.05
Korean (0)	5	0.02
Malaysian (1)	3	0.01
Pakistani (4)	5	0.02
Taiwanese (1)	1	<0.01
Thai (4)	8	0.03
Vietnamese (31)	32	0.14
Hawaii Native/Pacific Islander (12)	53	0.23
Not Hispanic (7)	34	0.15
Hispanic (5)	19	0.08
Guamanian/Chamorro (8)	14	0.06
Native Hawaiian (2)	10	0.04
White (1,364)	1,701	7.37
Not Hispanic (450)	621	2.69
Hispanic (914)	1,080	4.68

Langley Park

Place Type: CDP
County: Prince George's
Population: 18,755†

Ancestry‡	Population	%
African, Sub-Saharan (469)	531	2.92
African (259)	321	1.77
Ethiopian (104)	104	0.57
Liberian (17)	17	0.09
Nigerian (11)	11	0.06
Other Sub-Saharan African (78)	78	0.43
American (56)	56	0.31
Canadian (0)	12	0.07
Croatian (0)	11	0.06
Czech (9)	19	0.10
Eastern European (49)	49	0.27
English (41)	96	0.53
European (38)	38	0.21
French, ex. Basque (7)	38	0.21
French Canadian (0)	6	0.03
German (60)	127	0.70
Greek (27)	46	0.25
Guyanese (53)	53	0.29
Iranian (34)	34	0.19
Irish (23)	88	0.48
Italian (38)	82	0.45
Norwegian (0)	13	0.07
Polish (0)	24	0.13
Portuguese (21)	21	0.12
Russian (8)	28	0.15
Scandinavian (0)	15	0.08
Scotch-Irish (10)	31	0.17
Scottish (9)	22	0.12
Serbian (0)	11	0.06
Swedish (0)	25	0.14
Welsh (0)	24	0.13
West Indian, ex. Hispanic (350)	409	2.25
Haitian (116)	116	0.64
Jamaican (224)	258	1.42
West Indian (10)	35	0.19

Hispanic Origin	Population	%
Hispanic or Latino (of any race)	14,359	76.56
Central American, ex. Mexican	10,197	54.37
Costa Rican	4	0.02
Guatemalan	5,029	26.81
Honduran	706	3.76
Nicaraguan	204	1.09
Panamanian	20	0.11
Salvadoran	4,217	22.48
Other Central American	17	0.09
Cuban	45	0.24
Dominican Republic	212	1.13
Mexican	1,101	5.87
Puerto Rican	152	0.81
South American	197	1.05
Argentinean	4	0.02
Bolivian	39	0.21
Chilean	4	0.02
Colombian	40	0.21
Ecuadorian	24	0.13
Paraguayan	5	0.03
Peruvian	65	0.35
Venezuelan	5	0.03
Other South American	11	0.06
Other Hispanic or Latino	2,455	13.09

Race*	Population	%
African-American/Black (3,084)	3,307	17.63
Not Hispanic (2,850)	2,942	15.69
Hispanic (234)	365	1.95
American Indian/Alaska Native (490)	667	3.56
Not Hispanic (39)	70	0.37
Hispanic (451)	597	3.18
Blackfeet (0)	5	0.03
Central American Ind. (46)	59	0.31
Cherokee (3)	7	0.04
Choctaw (0)	1	0.01
Delaware (0)	1	0.01
Mexican American Ind. (110)	144	0.77
Navajo (4)	4	0.02
Pueblo (2)	4	0.02
South American Ind. (8)	10	0.05
Spanish American Ind. (8)	18	0.10
Asian (548)	651	3.47
Not Hispanic (523)	584	3.11
Hispanic (25)	67	0.36
Bangladeshi (18)	19	0.10
Cambodian (16)	18	0.10
Chinese, ex. Taiwanese (132)	144	0.77
Filipino (82)	88	0.47
Indian (139)	175	0.93
Japanese (3)	10	0.05
Korean (25)	27	0.14
Laotian (1)	8	0.04
Nepalese (18)	18	0.10
Pakistani (5)	6	0.03
Sri Lankan (5)	5	0.03
Taiwanese (4)	6	0.03
Thai (3)	3	0.02
Vietnamese (78)	85	0.45
Hawaii Native/Pacific Islander (95)	241	1.28
Not Hispanic (9)	28	0.15
Hispanic (86)	213	1.14
Guamanian/Chamorro (94)	108	0.58
Native Hawaiian (0)	2	0.01
Samoan (1)	1	0.01
White (4,880)	5,966	31.81
Not Hispanic (779)	835	4.45
Hispanic (4,101)	5,131	27.36

Lanham

Place Type: CDP
County: Prince George's
Population: 10,157†

Ancestry‡	Population	%
African, Sub-Saharan (1,128)	1,301	14.57
African (659)	729	8.16
Ethiopian (26)	105	1.18
Liberian (15)	15	0.17
Nigerian (411)	411	4.60
Sierra Leonean (17)	41	0.46
American (264)	264	2.96
Czech (11)	24	0.27
English (74)	275	3.08
European (15)	15	0.17
French, ex. Basque (0)	161	1.80
German (80)	362	4.05
Guyanese (34)	61	0.68
Irish (26)	55	0.62
Italian (29)	59	0.66
Polish (0)	9	0.10
Russian (0)	12	0.13
Scottish (8)	8	0.09
West Indian, ex. Hispanic (352)	414	4.64
Bermudan (10)	10	0.11
Haitian (38)	38	0.43
Jamaican (183)	227	2.54
Trinidadian/Tobagonian (107)	107	1.20
West Indian (14)	32	0.36

Hispanic Origin	Population	%
Hispanic or Latino (of any race)	2,269	22.34
Central American, ex. Mexican	991	9.76
Costa Rican	7	0.07
Guatemalan	149	1.47
Honduran	74	0.73
Nicaraguan	27	0.27
Panamanian	17	0.17
Salvadoran	705	6.94
Other Central American	12	0.12
Cuban	14	0.14
Dominican Republic	44	0.43
Mexican	941	9.26
Puerto Rican	59	0.58
South American	68	0.67
Argentinean	8	0.08
Bolivian	7	0.07
Colombian	11	0.11
Ecuadorian	12	0.12
Paraguayan	2	0.02
Peruvian	19	0.19
Uruguayan	6	0.06
Venezuelan	3	0.03
Other Hispanic or Latino	152	1.50

Race*	Population	%
African-American/Black (6,661)	6,801	66.96
Not Hispanic (6,579)	6,684	65.81
Hispanic (82)	117	1.15
American Indian/Alaska Native (41)	105	1.03
Not Hispanic (16)	67	0.66
Hispanic (25)	38	0.37
Blackfeet (1)	6	0.06
Cherokee (5)	17	0.17
Mexican American Ind. (1)	2	0.02
Asian (319)	369	3.63
Not Hispanic (319)	363	3.57
Hispanic (0)	6	0.06
Cambodian (1)	1	0.01
Chinese, ex. Taiwanese (56)	63	0.62
Filipino (70)	89	0.88
Indian (48)	62	0.61
Indonesian (1)	1	0.01
Japanese (0)	7	0.07
Korean (9)	14	0.14
Malaysian (1)	1	0.01
Pakistani (9)	9	0.09
Taiwanese (1)	1	0.01
Thai (1)	1	0.01
Vietnamese (119)	121	1.19
Hawaii Native/Pacific Islander (6)	11	0.11
Not Hispanic (5)	8	0.08
Hispanic (1)	3	0.03
Guamanian/Chamorro (1)	3	0.03
Native Hawaiian (5)	6	0.06
Samoan (0)	1	0.01
White (1,417)	1,572	15.48
Not Hispanic (808)	880	8.66

*Notes: † The Census 2010 population figure is used to calculate the percentages in the Hispanic Origin and Race categories. Ancestry percentages are based on the 2006-2010 American Community Survey population (not shown); ‡ Numbers in parentheses indicate the number of people reporting a single ancestry; * Numbers in parentheses indicate the number of persons reporting this race alone, not in combination with any other race; Please refer to the Explanation of Data for more information.*

Hispanic (609)	692	6.81

Lansdowne

Place Type: CDP
County: Baltimore
Population: 8,409†

Ancestry‡	Population	%
African, Sub-Saharan (114)	137	1.59
African (114)	137	1.59
American (411)	411	4.76
British (42)	63	0.73
Czech (0)	28	0.32
Czechoslovakian (0)	8	0.09
Dutch (44)	268	3.11
English (164)	606	7.02
European (44)	44	0.51
French, ex. Basque (0)	96	1.11
German (421)	2,295	26.60
Greek (0)	10	0.12
Irish (327)	1,796	20.81
Italian (96)	360	4.17
Lithuanian (25)	38	0.44
Polish (42)	682	7.90
Scandinavian (0)	10	0.12
Scotch-Irish (43)	119	1.38
Scottish (0)	32	0.37
Swedish (0)	49	0.57
Swiss (0)	15	0.17
Ukrainian (0)	5	0.06
West Indian, ex. Hispanic (5)	9	0.10
Jamaican (5)	9	0.10

Hispanic Origin	Population	%
Hispanic or Latino (of any race)	650	7.73
Central American, ex. Mexican	206	2.45
Costa Rican	1	0.01
Guatemalan	53	0.63
Honduran	56	0.67
Panamanian	2	0.02
Salvadoran	86	1.02
Other Central American	8	0.10
Cuban	5	0.06
Dominican Republic	5	0.06
Mexican	261	3.10
Puerto Rican	33	0.39
South American	53	0.63
Argentinean	4	0.05
Colombian	6	0.07
Ecuadorian	23	0.27
Peruvian	8	0.10
Uruguayan	9	0.11
Venezuelan	3	0.04
Other Hispanic or Latino	87	1.03

Race*	Population	%
African-American/Black (2,012)	2,156	25.64
Not Hispanic (2,004)	2,136	25.40
Hispanic (8)	20	0.24
American Indian/Alaska Native (17)	74	0.88
Not Hispanic (17)	73	0.87
Hispanic (0)	1	0.01
Apache (0)	1	0.01
Blackfeet (0)	2	0.02
Cherokee (7)	9	0.11
Comanche (1)	1	0.01
Cree (0)	4	0.05
Creek (0)	2	0.02
Crow (0)	2	0.02
Delaware (0)	1	0.01
Iroquois (0)	1	0.01
Lumbee (1)	2	0.02
Navajo (0)	3	0.04
Pima (1)	1	0.01
Seminole (0)	2	0.02
Sioux (0)	1	0.01
Asian (175)	228	2.71
Not Hispanic (174)	221	2.63
Hispanic (1)	7	0.08
Burmese (8)	8	0.10
Cambodian (1)	6	0.07
Chinese, ex. Taiwanese (4)	9	0.11
Filipino (33)	64	0.76
Indian (46)	52	0.62
Japanese (6)	9	0.11
Korean (12)	13	0.15
Pakistani (26)	26	0.31
Thai (1)	1	0.01
Vietnamese (33)	34	0.40
Hawaii Native/Pacific Islander (0)	16	0.19
Not Hispanic (0)	12	0.14
Hispanic (0)	4	0.05
Native Hawaiian (0)	11	0.13
White (5,635)	5,853	69.60
Not Hispanic (5,340)	5,529	65.75
Hispanic (295)	324	3.85

Largo

Place Type: CDP
County: Prince George's
Population: 10,709†

Ancestry‡	Population	%
African, Sub-Saharan (1,332)	1,374	12.48
African (919)	943	8.56
Ethiopian (99)	99	0.90
Nigerian (314)	332	3.01
American (20)	20	0.18
Australian (0)	18	0.16
Basque (14)	14	0.13
British (0)	20	0.18
Dutch (24)	24	0.22
English (69)	116	1.05
French, ex. Basque (47)	47	0.43
French Canadian (17)	25	0.23
German (14)	90	0.82
Greek (25)	25	0.23
Guyanese (18)	18	0.16
Hungarian (14)	14	0.13
Irish (0)	97	0.88
Italian (0)	16	0.15
Norwegian (0)	12	0.11
Scotch-Irish (12)	12	0.11
Welsh (14)	14	0.13
West Indian, ex. Hispanic (271)	326	2.96
Haitian (11)	35	0.32
Jamaican (189)	207	1.88
Trinidadian/Tobagonian (30)	30	0.27
West Indian (41)	54	0.49

Hispanic Origin	Population	%
Hispanic or Latino (of any race)	277	2.59
Central American, ex. Mexican	100	0.93
Costa Rican	1	0.01
Guatemalan	5	0.05
Honduran	13	0.12
Nicaraguan	5	0.05
Panamanian	26	0.24
Salvadoran	50	0.47
Cuban	7	0.07
Dominican Republic	17	0.16
Mexican	32	0.30
Puerto Rican	58	0.54
South American	34	0.32
Argentinean	1	0.01
Bolivian	2	0.02
Chilean	2	0.02
Colombian	11	0.10
Ecuadorian	10	0.09
Paraguayan	1	0.01
Peruvian	4	0.04
Venezuelan	3	0.03
Other Hispanic or Latino	29	0.27

Race*	Population	%
African-American/Black (9,805)	10,004	93.42
Not Hispanic (9,691)	9,861	92.08
Hispanic (114)	143	1.34
American Indian/Alaska Native (33)	132	1.23
Not Hispanic (31)	120	1.12
Hispanic (2)	12	0.11
Apache (0)	2	0.02
Blackfeet (0)	10	0.09
Cherokee (5)	23	0.21
Choctaw (1)	2	0.02
Delaware (0)	1	0.01
Hopi (0)	2	0.02
Navajo (1)	1	0.01
Ottawa (3)	3	0.03
Seminole (0)	6	0.06
South American Ind. (1)	2	0.02
Tohono O'Odham (1)	3	0.03
Asian (195)	232	2.17
Not Hispanic (194)	227	2.12
Hispanic (1)	5	0.05
Cambodian (2)	2	0.02
Chinese, ex. Taiwanese (7)	15	0.14
Filipino (131)	142	1.33
Indian (21)	32	0.30
Indonesian (1)	1	0.01
Japanese (1)	7	0.07
Korean (5)	10	0.09
Pakistani (8)	15	0.14
Thai (12)	13	0.12
Hawaii Native/Pacific Islander (0)	9	0.08
Not Hispanic (0)	8	0.07
Hispanic (0)	1	0.01
Native Hawaiian (0)	1	0.01
White (374)	484	4.52
Not Hispanic (309)	408	3.81
Hispanic (65)	76	0.71

Laurel

Place Type: City
County: Prince George's
Population: 25,115†

Ancestry‡	Population	%
Afghan (9)	9	0.04
African, Sub-Saharan (1,639)	1,754	7.18
African (808)	923	3.78
Ethiopian (159)	159	0.65
Ghanaian (98)	98	0.40
Kenyan (13)	13	0.05
Liberian (92)	92	0.38
Nigerian (358)	358	1.47
Other Sub-Saharan African (111)	111	0.45
Albanian (0)	18	0.07
American (407)	407	1.67
Arab (206)	206	0.84
Arab (12)	12	0.05
Egyptian (63)	63	0.26
Jordanian (40)	40	0.16
Palestinian (47)	47	0.19
Other Arab (44)	44	0.18
Austrian (11)	72	0.29
Belgian (12)	24	0.10
Brazilian (19)	37	0.15
British (35)	101	0.41
Bulgarian (153)	153	0.63
Canadian (12)	19	0.08
Carpatho Rusyn (0)	11	0.05
Croatian (0)	12	0.05
Danish (0)	50	0.20
Dutch (16)	76	0.31
Eastern European (38)	38	0.16
English (322)	897	3.67
European (136)	171	0.70
Finnish (0)	9	0.04
French, ex. Basque (91)	380	1.56
French Canadian (36)	107	0.44
German (496)	1,504	6.16
Greek (46)	135	0.55
Guyanese (31)	56	0.23
Hungarian (41)	91	0.37
Iranian (178)	178	0.73
Irish (472)	1,204	4.93

*Notes: † The Census 2010 population figure is used to calculate the percentages in the Hispanic Origin and Race categories. Ancestry percentages are based on the 2006-2010 American Community Survey population (not shown); ‡ Numbers in parentheses indicate the number of people reporting a single ancestry; * Numbers in parentheses indicate the number of persons reporting this race alone, not in combination with any other race; Please refer to the Explanation of Data for more information.*

Ancestry	Population	%
Italian (140)	402	1.65
Lithuanian (0)	30	0.12
Macedonian (41)	41	0.17
Norwegian (19)	45	0.18
Pennsylvania German (26)	26	0.11
Polish (133)	347	1.42
Portuguese (0)	18	0.07
Russian (46)	66	0.27
Scandinavian (10)	10	0.04
Scotch-Irish (153)	355	1.45
Scottish (81)	271	1.11
Slavic (9)	27	0.11
Slovak (27)	39	0.16
Swedish (12)	38	0.16
Swiss (0)	16	0.07
Ukrainian (75)	85	0.35
Welsh (0)	46	0.19
West Indian, ex. Hispanic (622)	871	3.56
Bahamian (0)	42	0.17
Barbadian (24)	24	0.10
Belizean (11)	11	0.05
British West Indian (6)	6	0.02
Haitian (27)	27	0.11
Jamaican (338)	505	2.07
Trinidadian/Tobagonian (133)	155	0.63
West Indian (83)	101	0.41

Hispanic Origin	Population	%
Hispanic or Latino (of any race)	3,886	15.47
Central American, ex. Mexican	2,029	8.08
Costa Rican	10	0.04
Guatemalan	582	2.32
Honduran	145	0.58
Nicaraguan	46	0.18
Panamanian	76	0.30
Salvadoran	1,150	4.58
Other Central American	20	0.08
Cuban	78	0.31
Dominican Republic	175	0.70
Mexican	607	2.42
Puerto Rican	368	1.47
South American	273	1.09
Argentinean	16	0.06
Bolivian	19	0.08
Chilean	23	0.09
Colombian	74	0.29
Ecuadorian	31	0.12
Paraguayan	6	0.02
Peruvian	83	0.33
Uruguayan	2	0.01
Venezuelan	18	0.07
Other South American	1	<0.01
Other Hispanic or Latino	356	1.42

Race*	Population	%
African-American/Black (12,270)	12,868	51.24
Not Hispanic (12,009)	12,482	49.70
Hispanic (261)	386	1.54
American Indian/Alaska Native (108)	298	1.19
Not Hispanic (73)	231	0.92
Hispanic (35)	67	0.27
Aleut *(Alaska Native)* (0)	3	0.01
Apache (1)	1	<0.01
Blackfeet (1)	13	0.05
Central American Ind. (3)	5	0.02
Cherokee (14)	48	0.19
Cheyenne (0)	1	<0.01
Chippewa (0)	1	<0.01
Choctaw (0)	2	0.01
Cree (0)	1	<0.01
Delaware (0)	3	0.01
Inupiat *(Alaska Native)* (0)	1	<0.01
Iroquois (0)	3	0.01
Lumbee (1)	1	<0.01
Mexican American Ind. (8)	8	0.03
Navajo (5)	9	0.04
Seminole (0)	1	<0.01
Sioux (2)	4	0.02
South American Ind. (11)	16	0.06
Spanish American Ind. (1)	1	<0.01
Asian (2,300)	2,522	10.04
Not Hispanic (2,290)	2,483	9.89
Hispanic (10)	39	0.16
Bangladeshi (40)	44	0.18
Burmese (7)	9	0.04
Cambodian (11)	15	0.06
Chinese, ex. Taiwanese (155)	218	0.87
Filipino (278)	337	1.34
Indian (779)	847	3.37
Indonesian (4)	11	0.04
Japanese (13)	33	0.13
Korean (235)	251	1.00
Laotian (7)	8	0.03
Malaysian (2)	2	0.01
Nepalese (16)	19	0.08
Pakistani (298)	325	1.29
Sri Lankan (1)	2	0.01
Taiwanese (10)	16	0.06
Thai (9)	15	0.06
Vietnamese (341)	367	1.46
Hawaii Native/Pacific Islander (19)	43	0.17
Not Hispanic (14)	33	0.13
Hispanic (5)	10	0.04
Fijian (0)	2	0.01
Guamanian/Chamorro (15)	16	0.06
Native Hawaiian (1)	5	0.02
Samoan (2)	2	0.01
White (7,553)	8,240	32.81
Not Hispanic (6,116)	6,561	26.12
Hispanic (1,437)	1,679	6.69

Leisure World

Place Type: CDP
County: Montgomery
Population: 8,749†

Ancestry‡	Population	%
African, Sub-Saharan (80)	80	0.92
African (10)	10	0.12
Ethiopian (70)	70	0.81
American (458)	458	5.29
Arab (30)	43	0.50
Lebanese (14)	14	0.16
Syrian (0)	13	0.15
Other Arab (16)	16	0.18
Armenian (15)	15	0.17
Austrian (36)	89	1.03
British (44)	99	1.14
Celtic (0)	28	0.32
Czech (13)	40	0.46
Czechoslovakian (0)	28	0.32
Danish (13)	21	0.24
Dutch (40)	115	1.33
Eastern European (90)	90	1.04
English (393)	1,246	14.38
European (55)	55	0.63
Finnish (15)	15	0.17
French, ex. Basque (72)	294	3.39
French Canadian (13)	40	0.46
German (425)	1,057	12.20
Greek (58)	71	0.82
Hungarian (28)	80	0.92
Irish (408)	977	11.27
Israeli (11)	11	0.13
Italian (244)	338	3.90
Latvian (0)	13	0.15
Lithuanian (90)	134	1.55
Norwegian (0)	79	0.91
Polish (291)	535	6.17
Romanian (37)	50	0.58
Russian (376)	631	7.28
Scotch-Irish (147)	255	2.94
Scottish (51)	262	3.02
Slovak (0)	31	0.36
Slovene (16)	16	0.18
Swedish (14)	83	0.96
Swiss (16)	16	0.18
Ukrainian (28)	41	0.47
Welsh (16)	78	0.90
West Indian, ex. Hispanic (263)	263	3.03
Jamaican (202)	202	2.33
Trinidadian/Tobagonian (44)	44	0.51
West Indian (17)	17	0.20

Hispanic Origin	Population	%
Hispanic or Latino (of any race)	582	6.65
Central American, ex. Mexican	222	2.54
Costa Rican	3	0.03
Guatemalan	45	0.51
Honduran	27	0.31
Nicaraguan	19	0.22
Panamanian	11	0.13
Salvadoran	117	1.34
Cuban	31	0.35
Dominican Republic	22	0.25
Mexican	51	0.58
Puerto Rican	33	0.38
South American	150	1.71
Argentinean	18	0.21
Bolivian	23	0.26
Chilean	9	0.10
Colombian	27	0.31
Ecuadorian	20	0.23
Paraguayan	2	0.02
Peruvian	43	0.49
Uruguayan	1	0.01
Venezuelan	7	0.08
Other Hispanic or Latino	73	0.83

Race*	Population	%
African-American/Black (1,514)	1,576	18.01
Not Hispanic (1,498)	1,554	17.76
Hispanic (16)	22	0.25
American Indian/Alaska Native (8)	53	0.61
Not Hispanic (7)	45	0.51
Hispanic (1)	8	0.09
Blackfeet (0)	1	0.01
Cherokee (4)	13	0.15
Choctaw (0)	1	0.01
Creek (1)	4	0.05
Iroquois (0)	1	0.01
Navajo (0)	1	0.01
Pueblo (2)	2	0.02
Seminole (0)	2	0.02
Sioux (0)	1	0.01
South American Ind. (0)	2	0.02
Asian (333)	364	4.16
Not Hispanic (330)	357	4.08
Hispanic (3)	7	0.08
Burmese (1)	1	0.01
Cambodian (1)	1	0.01
Chinese, ex. Taiwanese (127)	130	1.49
Filipino (11)	15	0.17
Indian (36)	47	0.54
Indonesian (4)	5	0.06
Japanese (19)	22	0.25
Korean (72)	76	0.87
Malaysian (0)	2	0.02
Nepalese (9)	9	0.10
Pakistani (3)	5	0.06
Sri Lankan (8)	8	0.09
Taiwanese (4)	4	0.05
Thai (6)	6	0.07
Vietnamese (18)	19	0.22
Hawaii Native/Pacific Islander (5)	12	0.14
Not Hispanic (5)	11	0.13
Hispanic (0)	1	0.01
Guamanian/Chamorro (0)	1	0.01
Native Hawaiian (1)	4	0.05
Samoan (3)	3	0.03
White (6,556)	6,659	76.11
Not Hispanic (6,214)	6,279	71.77
Hispanic (342)	380	4.34

Lexington Park

Place Type: CDP
County: St. Mary's
Population: 11,626†

*Notes: † The Census 2010 population figure is used to calculate the percentages in the Hispanic Origin and Race categories. Ancestry percentages are based on the 2006-2010 American Community Survey population (not shown); ‡ Numbers in parentheses indicate the number of people reporting a single ancestry; * Numbers in parentheses indicate the number of persons reporting this race alone, not in combination with any other race; Please refer to the Explanation of Data for more information.*

Ancestry‡	Population	%
African, Sub-Saharan (19)	19	0.17
Nigerian (19)	19	0.17
American (782)	782	7.19
Arab (15)	20	0.18
Jordanian (15)	15	0.14
Lebanese (0)	5	0.05
Austrian (0)	22	0.20
Belgian (39)	39	0.36
British (44)	71	0.65
Celtic (0)	7	0.06
Czech (37)	58	0.53
Czechoslovakian (0)	12	0.11
Danish (0)	24	0.22
Dutch (10)	135	1.24
English (479)	978	8.99
European (52)	58	0.53
French, ex. Basque (12)	424	3.90
French Canadian (13)	142	1.30
German (287)	1,522	13.99
Greek (90)	145	1.33
Guyanese (34)	34	0.31
Hungarian (0)	14	0.13
Icelander (25)	71	0.65
Irish (227)	1,072	9.85
Italian (142)	499	4.59
Lithuanian (0)	36	0.33
Norwegian (46)	249	2.29
Pennsylvania German (7)	7	0.06
Polish (56)	231	2.12
Portuguese (0)	9	0.08
Romanian (0)	23	0.21
Russian (0)	58	0.53
Scandinavian (10)	10	0.09
Scotch-Irish (59)	228	2.10
Scottish (78)	199	1.83
Slovak (0)	64	0.59
Slovene (0)	16	0.15
Swedish (18)	112	1.03
Swiss (0)	15	0.14
Welsh (14)	26	0.24
West Indian, ex. Hispanic (35)	117	1.08
Haitian (18)	66	0.61
Jamaican (17)	51	0.47

Hispanic Origin	Population	%
Hispanic or Latino (of any race)	861	7.41
Central American, ex. Mexican	123	1.06
Costa Rican	1	0.01
Guatemalan	57	0.49
Honduran	7	0.06
Nicaraguan	7	0.06
Panamanian	6	0.05
Salvadoran	45	0.39
Cuban	31	0.27
Dominican Republic	17	0.15
Mexican	298	2.56
Puerto Rican	227	1.95
South American	68	0.58
Argentinean	1	0.01
Bolivian	7	0.06
Colombian	26	0.22
Ecuadorian	17	0.15
Peruvian	14	0.12
Uruguayan	1	0.01
Venezuelan	2	0.02
Other Hispanic or Latino	97	0.83

Race*	Population	%
African-American/Black (3,670)	4,072	35.02
Not Hispanic (3,626)	3,986	34.29
Hispanic (44)	86	0.74
American Indian/Alaska Native (72)	172	1.48
Not Hispanic (53)	137	1.18
Hispanic (19)	35	0.30
Apache (0)	1	0.01
Blackfeet (0)	12	0.10
Canadian/French Am. Ind. (1)	1	0.01
Cherokee (9)	45	0.39
Chippewa (2)	2	0.02
Choctaw (0)	5	0.04
Cree (0)	1	0.01
Creek (0)	2	0.02
Houma (3)	3	0.03
Iroquois (1)	1	0.01
Lumbee (2)	2	0.02
Mexican American Ind. (1)	1	0.01
Navajo (2)	2	0.02
Ottawa (3)	3	0.03
Potawatomi (6)	7	0.06
South American Ind. (0)	1	0.01
Spanish American Ind. (6)	6	0.05
Asian (508)	663	5.70
Not Hispanic (498)	626	5.38
Hispanic (10)	37	0.32
Bangladeshi (4)	4	0.03
Burmese (1)	1	0.01
Cambodian (4)	4	0.03
Chinese, ex. Taiwanese (55)	64	0.55
Filipino (239)	331	2.85
Indian (63)	76	0.65
Indonesian (2)	2	0.02
Japanese (30)	51	0.44
Korean (29)	57	0.49
Nepalese (2)	2	0.02
Pakistani (3)	4	0.03
Taiwanese (4)	4	0.03
Thai (9)	19	0.16
Vietnamese (33)	41	0.35
Hawaii Native/Pacific Islander (16)	29	0.25
Not Hispanic (16)	25	0.22
Hispanic (0)	4	0.03
Guamanian/Chamorro (10)	13	0.11
Native Hawaiian (2)	8	0.07
Samoan (2)	4	0.03
Tongan (2)	3	0.03
White (6,454)	6,966	59.92
Not Hispanic (6,047)	6,484	55.77
Hispanic (407)	482	4.15

Linganore

Place Type: CDP
County: Frederick
Population: 8,543†

Ancestry‡	Population	%
American (328)	328	3.95
Arab (55)	55	0.66
Jordanian (23)	23	0.28
Palestinian (32)	32	0.39
Armenian (12)	31	0.37
Brazilian (114)	114	1.37
British (9)	9	0.11
Canadian (0)	31	0.37
Czech (13)	36	0.43
Czechoslovakian (19)	26	0.31
Danish (10)	42	0.51
Dutch (10)	173	2.08
Eastern European (69)	81	0.97
English (468)	1,614	19.42
European (185)	216	2.60
French, ex. Basque (0)	106	1.28
French Canadian (83)	83	1.00
German (775)	2,354	28.33
Greek (73)	100	1.20
Hungarian (0)	29	0.35
Irish (425)	1,743	20.98
Italian (204)	468	5.63
Latvian (0)	8	0.10
Lithuanian (0)	13	0.16
Norwegian (81)	225	2.71
Pennsylvania German (0)	4	0.05
Polish (78)	378	4.55
Portuguese (12)	15	0.18
Romanian (0)	55	0.66
Russian (33)	85	1.02
Scotch-Irish (66)	184	2.21
Scottish (101)	369	4.44
Slavic (11)	11	0.13
Slovak (12)	100	1.20
Swedish (30)	174	2.09
Swiss (15)	75	0.90
Ukrainian (0)	8	0.10
Welsh (18)	210	2.53

Hispanic Origin	Population	%
Hispanic or Latino (of any race)	399	4.67
Central American, ex. Mexican	77	0.90
Costa Rican	7	0.08
Guatemalan	11	0.13
Honduran	5	0.06
Nicaraguan	16	0.19
Panamanian	2	0.02
Salvadoran	36	0.42
Cuban	27	0.32
Dominican Republic	19	0.22
Mexican	76	0.89
Puerto Rican	74	0.87
South American	75	0.88
Argentinean	3	0.04
Bolivian	5	0.06
Chilean	6	0.07
Colombian	16	0.19
Ecuadorian	11	0.13
Paraguayan	3	0.04
Peruvian	18	0.21
Uruguayan	4	0.05
Venezuelan	9	0.11
Other Hispanic or Latino	51	0.60

Race*	Population	%
African-American/Black (234)	310	3.63
Not Hispanic (228)	297	3.48
Hispanic (6)	13	0.15
American Indian/Alaska Native (12)	53	0.62
Not Hispanic (9)	45	0.53
Hispanic (3)	8	0.09
Blackfeet (0)	1	0.01
Central American Ind. (1)	1	0.01
Cherokee (0)	9	0.11
Chickasaw (0)	2	0.02
Choctaw (0)	2	0.02
Delaware (0)	3	0.04
Lumbee (1)	1	0.01
Mexican American Ind. (0)	2	0.02
Navajo (2)	2	0.02
Pueblo (3)	3	0.04
South American Ind. (1)	1	0.01
Yuman (0)	1	0.01
Asian (164)	248	2.90
Not Hispanic (164)	237	2.77
Hispanic (0)	11	0.13
Bangladeshi (2)	2	0.02
Chinese, ex. Taiwanese (40)	57	0.67
Filipino (27)	61	0.71
Indian (27)	38	0.44
Indonesian (3)	3	0.04
Japanese (2)	9	0.11
Korean (26)	30	0.35
Malaysian (1)	3	0.04
Pakistani (13)	14	0.16
Sri Lankan (2)	2	0.02
Thai (3)	7	0.08
Vietnamese (6)	8	0.09
Hawaii Native/Pacific Islander (1)	9	0.11
Not Hispanic (1)	9	0.11
Guamanian/Chamorro (1)	3	0.04
Native Hawaiian (0)	1	0.01
Samoan (0)	3	0.04
White (7,867)	8,063	94.38
Not Hispanic (7,562)	7,716	90.32
Hispanic (305)	347	4.06

Linthicum

Place Type: CDP
County: Anne Arundel
Population: 10,324†

*Notes: † The Census 2010 population figure is used to calculate the percentages in the Hispanic Origin and Race categories. Ancestry percentages are based on the 2006-2010 American Community Survey population (not shown); ‡ Numbers in parentheses indicate the number of people reporting a single ancestry; * Numbers in parentheses indicate the number of persons reporting this race alone, not in combination with any other race; Please refer to the Explanation of Data for more information.*

Ancestry‡	Population	%
American (297)	297	2.84
Arab (8)	23	0.22
Arab (8)	23	0.22
Armenian (37)	58	0.56
Austrian (8)	17	0.16
Belgian (0)	7	0.07
Brazilian (11)	11	0.11
British (9)	36	0.34
Canadian (9)	45	0.43
Celtic (0)	17	0.16
Czech (11)	25	0.24
Czechoslovakian (19)	19	0.18
Danish (0)	41	0.39
Dutch (35)	240	2.30
Eastern European (10)	10	0.10
English (516)	1,440	13.79
European (220)	220	2.11
French, ex. Basque (102)	273	2.61
French Canadian (0)	11	0.11
German (1,293)	3,543	33.92
Greek (146)	226	2.16
Hungarian (17)	51	0.49
Irish (477)	2,264	21.68
Italian (399)	892	8.54
Lithuanian (19)	86	0.82
Northern European (165)	178	1.70
Norwegian (11)	29	0.28
Pennsylvania German (13)	13	0.12
Polish (344)	819	7.84
Russian (35)	98	0.94
Scandinavian (0)	11	0.11
Scotch-Irish (53)	272	2.60
Scottish (34)	308	2.95
Slavic (0)	11	0.11
Slovene (9)	28	0.27
Swedish (0)	55	0.53
Swiss (0)	10	0.10
Ukrainian (0)	10	0.10
Welsh (0)	150	1.44
West Indian, ex. Hispanic (37)	37	0.35
U.S. Virgin Islander (37)	37	0.35

Hispanic Origin	Population	%
Hispanic or Latino (of any race)	276	2.67
Central American, ex. Mexican	57	0.55
Costa Rican	1	0.01
Guatemalan	10	0.10
Honduran	14	0.14
Nicaraguan	4	0.04
Panamanian	2	0.02
Salvadoran	26	0.25
Cuban	9	0.09
Dominican Republic	7	0.07
Mexican	82	0.79
Puerto Rican	53	0.51
South American	36	0.35
Argentinean	4	0.04
Chilean	1	0.01
Colombian	15	0.15
Ecuadorian	7	0.07
Peruvian	2	0.02
Venezuelan	7	0.07
Other Hispanic or Latino	32	0.31

Race*	Population	%
African-American/Black (377)	434	4.20
Not Hispanic (365)	417	4.04
Hispanic (12)	17	0.16
American Indian/Alaska Native (32)	74	0.72
Not Hispanic (29)	68	0.66
Hispanic (3)	6	0.06
Blackfeet (0)	3	0.03
Cherokee (3)	13	0.13
Choctaw (0)	1	0.01
Lumbee (2)	3	0.03
Mexican American Ind. (1)	2	0.02
Ottawa (1)	2	0.02
Sioux (0)	1	0.01
Asian (433)	506	4.90
Not Hispanic (432)	500	4.84
Hispanic (1)	6	0.06
Bangladeshi (21)	21	0.20
Burmese (1)	1	0.01
Cambodian (2)	2	0.02
Chinese, ex. Taiwanese (71)	81	0.78
Filipino (96)	120	1.16
Indian (102)	114	1.10
Indonesian (0)	1	0.01
Japanese (5)	14	0.14
Korean (51)	64	0.62
Nepalese (4)	4	0.04
Pakistani (42)	45	0.44
Sri Lankan (3)	3	0.03
Taiwanese (2)	6	0.06
Thai (1)	4	0.04
Vietnamese (19)	23	0.22
Hawaii Native/Pacific Islander (14)	23	0.22
Not Hispanic (14)	23	0.22
Guamanian/Chamorro (7)	7	0.07
Native Hawaiian (2)	6	0.06
Samoan (4)	9	0.09
White (9,184)	9,344	90.51
Not Hispanic (9,041)	9,188	89.00
Hispanic (143)	156	1.51

Lochearn

Place Type: CDP
County: Baltimore
Population: 25,333†

Ancestry‡	Population	%
African, Sub-Saharan (1,944)	2,010	7.81
African (1,259)	1,272	4.95
Ethiopian (46)	56	0.22
Ghanaian (51)	51	0.20
Liberian (89)	89	0.35
Nigerian (446)	489	1.90
Other Sub-Saharan African (53)	53	0.21
American (526)	526	2.05
Arab (28)	28	0.11
Arab (28)	28	0.11
Australian (7)	13	0.05
Austrian (0)	36	0.14
Brazilian (34)	34	0.13
British (0)	17	0.07
Canadian (4)	4	0.02
Croatian (0)	8	0.03
Danish (0)	11	0.04
Dutch (7)	16	0.06
Eastern European (57)	85	0.33
English (165)	375	1.46
European (40)	40	0.16
French, ex. Basque (3)	111	0.43
German (176)	665	2.59
German Russian (0)	39	0.15
Greek (7)	7	0.03
Guyanese (2)	2	0.01
Hungarian (25)	46	0.18
Irish (149)	532	2.07
Italian (121)	279	1.08
Latvian (0)	9	0.03
Lithuanian (26)	47	0.18
Polish (77)	171	0.66
Romanian (16)	47	0.18
Russian (93)	154	0.60
Scotch-Irish (39)	39	0.15
Scottish (11)	73	0.28
Swedish (45)	67	0.26
Swiss (10)	13	0.05
Ukrainian (19)	36	0.14
Welsh (0)	19	0.07
West Indian, ex. Hispanic (896)	961	3.74
Bahamian (12)	12	0.05
Bermudan (22)	22	0.09
Haitian (18)	18	0.07
Jamaican (503)	525	2.04
Trinidadian/Tobagonian (223)	223	0.87
U.S. Virgin Islander (31)	31	0.12
West Indian (87)	130	0.51

Hispanic Origin	Population	%
Hispanic or Latino (of any race)	900	3.55
Central American, ex. Mexican	289	1.14
Costa Rican	2	0.01
Guatemalan	69	0.27
Honduran	47	0.19
Nicaraguan	5	0.02
Panamanian	12	0.05
Salvadoran	150	0.59
Other Central American	4	0.02
Cuban	26	0.10
Dominican Republic	24	0.09
Mexican	230	0.91
Puerto Rican	141	0.56
South American	91	0.36
Argentinean	11	0.04
Bolivian	3	0.01
Chilean	13	0.05
Colombian	13	0.05
Ecuadorian	9	0.04
Paraguayan	3	0.01
Peruvian	34	0.13
Venezuelan	3	0.01
Other South American	2	0.01
Other Hispanic or Latino	99	0.39

Race*	Population	%
African-American/Black (20,448)	20,892	82.47
Not Hispanic (20,317)	20,708	81.74
Hispanic (131)	184	0.73
American Indian/Alaska Native (77)	255	1.01
Not Hispanic (66)	219	0.86
Hispanic (11)	36	0.14
Apache (0)	2	0.01
Arapaho (1)	2	0.01
Blackfeet (2)	15	0.06
Canadian/French Am. Ind. (0)	1	<0.01
Central American Ind. (1)	1	<0.01
Cherokee (8)	46	0.18
Chippewa (0)	3	0.01
Choctaw (0)	1	<0.01
Cree (1)	2	0.01
Creek (1)	1	<0.01
Iroquois (0)	4	0.02
Lumbee (3)	9	0.04
Mexican American Ind. (1)	1	<0.01
Navajo (0)	3	0.01
Seminole (0)	1	<0.01
Tlingit-Haida *(Alaska Native)* (2)	2	0.01
Asian (315)	450	1.78
Not Hispanic (315)	437	1.73
Hispanic (0)	13	0.05
Burmese (1)	1	<0.01
Cambodian (1)	1	<0.01
Chinese, ex. Taiwanese (29)	46	0.18
Filipino (57)	101	0.40
Indian (100)	117	0.46
Indonesian (8)	9	0.04
Japanese (4)	14	0.06
Korean (33)	38	0.15
Laotian (1)	3	0.01
Malaysian (0)	1	<0.01
Pakistani (12)	22	0.09
Sri Lankan (1)	1	<0.01
Thai (3)	6	0.02
Vietnamese (42)	50	0.20
Hawaii Native/Pacific Islander (14)	37	0.15
Not Hispanic (7)	28	0.11
Hispanic (7)	9	0.04
Guamanian/Chamorro (8)	10	0.04
Native Hawaiian (3)	8	0.03
Samoan (1)	1	<0.01
White (3,497)	3,818	15.07
Not Hispanic (3,200)	3,472	13.71
Hispanic (297)	346	1.37

*Notes: † The Census 2010 population figure is used to calculate the percentages in the Hispanic Origin and Race categories. Ancestry percentages are based on the 2006-2010 American Community Survey population (not shown); ‡ Numbers in parentheses indicate the number of people reporting a single ancestry; * Numbers in parentheses indicate the number of persons reporting this race alone, not in combination with any other race; Please refer to the Explanation of Data for more information.*

Marlboro Village

Place Type: CDP
County: Prince George's
Population: 9,438†

Ancestry‡	Population	%
African, Sub-Saharan (613)	649	6.93
African (458)	481	5.14
Liberian (13)	13	0.14
Nigerian (56)	69	0.74
Sierra Leonean (76)	76	0.81
Other Sub-Saharan African (10)	10	0.11
American (46)	46	0.49
Austrian (0)	14	0.15
British (0)	8	0.09
Czechoslovakian (0)	14	0.15
Dutch (0)	7	0.07
Eastern European (16)	16	0.17
English (55)	154	1.64
European (15)	15	0.16
French, ex. Basque (8)	31	0.33
German (43)	126	1.35
Guyanese (23)	23	0.25
Irish (28)	216	2.31
Italian (32)	94	1.00
Lithuanian (0)	20	0.21
Polish (0)	37	0.40
Portuguese (0)	18	0.19
Russian (0)	20	0.21
Scottish (13)	17	0.18
Swiss (9)	9	0.10
Ukrainian (10)	21	0.22
West Indian, ex. Hispanic (187)	281	3.00
British West Indian (15)	38	0.41
Haitian (25)	25	0.27
Jamaican (105)	148	1.58
Trinidadian/Tobagonian (0)	15	0.16
West Indian (42)	55	0.59

Hispanic Origin	Population	%
Hispanic or Latino (of any race)	366	3.88
Central American, ex. Mexican	128	1.36
Costa Rican	1	0.01
Guatemalan	34	0.36
Honduran	12	0.13
Nicaraguan	2	0.02
Panamanian	17	0.18
Salvadoran	62	0.66
Cuban	23	0.24
Dominican Republic	15	0.16
Mexican	82	0.87
Puerto Rican	71	0.75
South American	2	0.02
Colombian	2	0.02
Other Hispanic or Latino	45	0.48

Race*	Population	%
African-American/Black (8,278)	8,460	89.64
Not Hispanic (8,175)	8,333	88.29
Hispanic (103)	127	1.35
American Indian/Alaska Native (34)	102	1.08
Not Hispanic (29)	79	0.84
Hispanic (5)	23	0.24
Apache (1)	1	0.01
Blackfeet (1)	4	0.04
Cherokee (2)	22	0.23
Asian (86)	136	1.44
Not Hispanic (84)	126	1.34
Hispanic (2)	10	0.11
Cambodian (2)	2	0.02
Chinese, ex. Taiwanese (16)	22	0.23
Filipino (26)	46	0.49
Indian (19)	29	0.31
Japanese (0)	1	0.01
Korean (5)	14	0.15
Pakistani (10)	10	0.11
Taiwanese (0)	1	0.01
Thai (6)	9	0.10
Hawaii Native/Pacific Islander (4)	17	0.18
Not Hispanic (3)	11	0.12
Hispanic (1)	6	0.06
Guamanian/Chamorro (1)	3	0.03
Native Hawaiian (3)	5	0.05
Samoan (0)	1	0.01
White (659)	790	8.37
Not Hispanic (598)	708	7.50
Hispanic (61)	82	0.87

Marlton

Place Type: CDP
County: Prince George's
Population: 9,031†

Ancestry‡	Population	%
African, Sub-Saharan (165)	182	2.02
African (88)	105	1.17
Nigerian (77)	77	0.85
American (59)	59	0.65
Arab (11)	11	0.12
Arab (11)	11	0.12
British (0)	44	0.49
Dutch (15)	78	0.87
English (95)	212	2.35
European (83)	83	0.92
French, ex. Basque (0)	12	0.13
German (143)	312	3.46
Greek (25)	25	0.28
Hungarian (35)	35	0.39
Irish (285)	411	4.56
Italian (14)	83	0.92
Norwegian (0)	14	0.16
Pennsylvania German (11)	34	0.38
Polish (14)	27	0.30
Russian (19)	19	0.21
Scotch-Irish (15)	83	0.92
Scottish (0)	28	0.31
Swedish (16)	16	0.18
Turkish (21)	21	0.23
Welsh (0)	74	0.82
West Indian, ex. Hispanic (85)	187	2.08
Haitian (17)	34	0.38
Jamaican (68)	153	1.70

Hispanic Origin	Population	%
Hispanic or Latino (of any race)	234	2.59
Central American, ex. Mexican	67	0.74
Guatemalan	1	0.01
Honduran	6	0.07
Panamanian	25	0.28
Salvadoran	34	0.38
Other Central American	1	0.01
Cuban	13	0.14
Dominican Republic	19	0.21
Mexican	42	0.47
Puerto Rican	47	0.52
South American	25	0.28
Bolivian	1	0.01
Chilean	9	0.10
Colombian	9	0.10
Ecuadorian	4	0.04
Peruvian	1	0.01
Venezuelan	1	0.01
Other Hispanic or Latino	21	0.23

Race*	Population	%
African-American/Black (7,249)	7,531	83.39
Not Hispanic (7,187)	7,434	82.32
Hispanic (62)	97	1.07
American Indian/Alaska Native (53)	176	1.95
Not Hispanic (50)	161	1.78
Hispanic (3)	15	0.17
Arapaho (0)	1	0.01
Blackfeet (0)	11	0.12
Cherokee (2)	37	0.41
Chippewa (1)	1	0.01
Choctaw (1)	2	0.02
Lumbee (2)	2	0.02
Navajo (1)	1	0.01
Seminole (0)	2	0.02
Sioux (4)	4	0.04
South American Ind. (3)	3	0.03
Asian (139)	208	2.30
Not Hispanic (138)	203	2.25
Hispanic (1)	5	0.06
Cambodian (1)	1	0.01
Chinese, ex. Taiwanese (5)	16	0.18
Filipino (75)	100	1.11
Indian (24)	33	0.37
Japanese (3)	13	0.14
Korean (3)	14	0.16
Pakistani (7)	10	0.11
Thai (4)	6	0.07
Vietnamese (16)	17	0.19
Hawaii Native/Pacific Islander (5)	14	0.16
Not Hispanic (5)	14	0.16
Guamanian/Chamorro (2)	3	0.03
Native Hawaiian (3)	4	0.04
Samoan (0)	1	0.01
White (1,187)	1,384	15.32
Not Hispanic (1,122)	1,303	14.43
Hispanic (65)	81	0.90

Maryland City

Place Type: CDP
County: Anne Arundel
Population: 16,093†

Ancestry‡	Population	%
African, Sub-Saharan (624)	1,027	6.66
African (496)	821	5.32
Ghanaian (0)	19	0.12
Liberian (14)	33	0.21
Nigerian (114)	154	1.00
Albanian (0)	13	0.08
American (477)	477	3.09
Arab (36)	65	0.42
Arab (24)	24	0.16
Lebanese (12)	41	0.27
Austrian (0)	11	0.07
Belgian (0)	14	0.09
Brazilian (17)	17	0.11
British (0)	65	0.42
Czech (11)	11	0.07
Danish (0)	51	0.33
Dutch (0)	128	0.83
English (380)	1,333	8.64
European (192)	225	1.46
Finnish (0)	9	0.06
French, ex. Basque (99)	280	1.82
French Canadian (71)	153	0.99
German (441)	1,825	11.84
Greek (0)	11	0.07
Guyanese (12)	12	0.08
Hungarian (0)	43	0.28
Irish (163)	1,108	7.19
Italian (260)	667	4.33
Norwegian (17)	99	0.64
Pennsylvania German (0)	12	0.08
Polish (155)	656	4.25
Portuguese (11)	44	0.29
Romanian (34)	34	0.22
Russian (0)	83	0.54
Scandinavian (0)	9	0.06
Scotch-Irish (81)	183	1.19
Scottish (29)	230	1.49
Slavic (13)	13	0.08
Slovak (34)	34	0.22
Swedish (0)	15	0.10
Swiss (0)	11	0.07
Ukrainian (13)	33	0.21
Welsh (27)	154	1.00
West Indian, ex. Hispanic (655)	761	4.94
British West Indian (14)	37	0.24
Jamaican (599)	622	4.03
Trinidadian/Tobagonian (42)	82	0.53
West Indian (0)	20	0.13

*Notes: † The Census 2010 population figure is used to calculate the percentages in the Hispanic Origin and Race categories. Ancestry percentages are based on the 2006-2010 American Community Survey population (not shown); ‡ Numbers in parentheses indicate the number of people reporting a single ancestry; * Numbers in parentheses indicate the number of persons reporting this race alone, not in combination with any other race; Please refer to the Explanation of Data for more information.*

Hispanic Origin	Population	%
Hispanic or Latino (of any race)	2,151	13.37
Central American, ex. Mexican	930	5.78
Costa Rican	5	0.03
Guatemalan	232	1.44
Honduran	73	0.45
Nicaraguan	26	0.16
Panamanian	27	0.17
Salvadoran	565	3.51
Other Central American	2	0.01
Cuban	35	0.22
Dominican Republic	62	0.39
Mexican	484	3.01
Puerto Rican	227	1.41
South American	195	1.21
Argentinean	10	0.06
Bolivian	14	0.09
Chilean	34	0.21
Colombian	37	0.23
Ecuadorian	22	0.14
Paraguayan	3	0.02
Peruvian	44	0.27
Uruguayan	4	0.02
Venezuelan	22	0.14
Other South American	5	0.03
Other Hispanic or Latino	218	1.35

Race*	Population	%
African-American/Black (6,772)	7,139	44.36
Not Hispanic (6,626)	6,931	43.07
Hispanic (146)	208	1.29
American Indian/Alaska Native (40)	182	1.13
Not Hispanic (35)	135	0.84
Hispanic (5)	47	0.29
Apache (0)	3	0.02
Blackfeet (1)	3	0.02
Cherokee (5)	35	0.22
Chippewa (0)	1	0.01
Choctaw (1)	4	0.02
Creek (0)	4	0.02
Lumbee (5)	8	0.05
Mexican American Ind. (2)	7	0.04
Navajo (0)	1	0.01
Pueblo (1)	1	0.01
Seminole (0)	1	0.01
Sioux (0)	2	0.01
South American Ind. (1)	10	0.06
Spanish American Ind. (2)	2	0.01
Asian (1,333)	1,530	9.51
Not Hispanic (1,321)	1,498	9.31
Hispanic (12)	32	0.20
Bangladeshi (8)	9	0.06
Burmese (20)	20	0.12
Cambodian (11)	13	0.08
Chinese, ex. Taiwanese (102)	160	0.99
Filipino (153)	206	1.28
Indian (483)	523	3.25
Indonesian (9)	18	0.11
Japanese (15)	47	0.29
Korean (155)	192	1.19
Laotian (5)	10	0.06
Malaysian (1)	2	0.01
Nepalese (21)	21	0.13
Pakistani (126)	134	0.83
Taiwanese (10)	13	0.08
Thai (8)	20	0.12
Vietnamese (145)	163	1.01
Hawaii Native/Pacific Islander (8)	30	0.19
Not Hispanic (8)	28	0.17
Hispanic (0)	2	0.01
Guamanian/Chamorro (4)	8	0.05
Native Hawaiian (2)	7	0.04
Samoan (1)	3	0.02
White (6,272)	6,780	42.13
Not Hispanic (5,436)	5,797	36.02
Hispanic (836)	983	6.11

Mayo

Place Type: CDP
County: Anne Arundel
Population: 8,298†

Ancestry‡	Population	%
Alsatian (0)	21	0.27
American (479)	479	6.16
Arab (0)	32	0.41
Lebanese (0)	12	0.15
Syrian (0)	20	0.26
Armenian (12)	36	0.46
British (0)	103	1.32
Canadian (62)	62	0.80
Croatian (0)	12	0.15
Czech (17)	17	0.22
Czechoslovakian (34)	34	0.44
Danish (18)	35	0.45
Dutch (45)	159	2.04
Eastern European (10)	10	0.13
English (465)	1,845	23.73
Estonian (13)	13	0.17
European (189)	189	2.43
French, ex. Basque (134)	431	5.54
French Canadian (14)	14	0.18
German (395)	1,674	21.53
Greek (58)	102	1.31
Hungarian (9)	37	0.48
Iranian (18)	18	0.23
Irish (639)	1,906	24.51
Italian (234)	644	8.28
Norwegian (57)	78	1.00
Pennsylvania German (10)	10	0.13
Polish (32)	179	2.30
Portuguese (11)	26	0.33
Russian (0)	19	0.24
Scotch-Irish (76)	195	2.51
Scottish (123)	410	5.27
Slavic (30)	53	0.68
Slovak (0)	24	0.31
Swedish (0)	125	1.61
Swiss (0)	16	0.21
Ukrainian (54)	54	0.69
Welsh (20)	144	1.85

Hispanic Origin	Population	%
Hispanic or Latino (of any race)	266	3.21
Central American, ex. Mexican	76	0.92
Costa Rican	1	0.01
Guatemalan	6	0.07
Honduran	5	0.06
Nicaraguan	4	0.05
Panamanian	7	0.08
Salvadoran	53	0.64
Cuban	10	0.12
Dominican Republic	1	0.01
Mexican	59	0.71
Puerto Rican	64	0.77
South American	28	0.34
Argentinean	1	0.01
Bolivian	4	0.05
Chilean	6	0.07
Colombian	4	0.05
Ecuadorian	1	0.01
Peruvian	11	0.13
Venezuelan	1	0.01
Other Hispanic or Latino	28	0.34

Race*	Population	%
African-American/Black (144)	196	2.36
Not Hispanic (133)	177	2.13
Hispanic (11)	19	0.23
American Indian/Alaska Native (34)	78	0.94
Not Hispanic (31)	75	0.90
Hispanic (3)	3	0.04
Blackfeet (3)	3	0.04
Cherokee (1)	16	0.19
Chippewa (2)	4	0.05
Delaware (0)	2	0.02
Iroquois (0)	1	0.01
Lumbee (7)	8	0.10
Mexican American Ind. (1)	1	0.01
Sioux (0)	1	0.01
South American Ind. (1)	1	0.01
Asian (83)	155	1.87
Not Hispanic (83)	149	1.80
Hispanic (0)	6	0.07
Chinese, ex. Taiwanese (20)	42	0.51
Filipino (24)	45	0.54
Indian (6)	12	0.14
Indonesian (0)	1	0.01
Japanese (9)	20	0.24
Korean (13)	21	0.25
Malaysian (0)	1	0.01
Pakistani (1)	1	0.01
Vietnamese (3)	6	0.07
Hawaii Native/Pacific Islander (1)	5	0.06
Not Hispanic (0)	4	0.05
Hispanic (1)	1	0.01
Native Hawaiian (1)	2	0.02
White (7,790)	7,951	95.82
Not Hispanic (7,634)	7,777	93.72
Hispanic (156)	174	2.10

Mays Chapel

Place Type: CDP
County: Baltimore
Population: 11,420†

Ancestry‡	Population	%
African, Sub-Saharan (66)	66	0.55
African (66)	66	0.55
American (499)	499	4.17
Arab (58)	63	0.53
Egyptian (23)	23	0.19
Lebanese (35)	35	0.29
Palestinian (0)	5	0.04
Austrian (43)	49	0.41
Belgian (28)	28	0.23
British (66)	136	1.14
Canadian (13)	24	0.20
Croatian (7)	45	0.38
Czech (12)	66	0.55
Czechoslovakian (15)	15	0.13
Danish (0)	12	0.10
Dutch (19)	62	0.52
Eastern European (44)	44	0.37
English (703)	1,805	15.09
European (221)	221	1.85
Finnish (13)	13	0.11
French, ex. Basque (91)	433	3.62
French Canadian (0)	39	0.33
German (873)	2,949	24.65
Greek (98)	223	1.86
Hungarian (10)	47	0.39
Iranian (137)	137	1.15
Irish (554)	2,326	19.44
Italian (553)	1,276	10.66
Lithuanian (50)	84	0.70
Macedonian (14)	14	0.12
New Zealander (0)	11	0.09
Northern European (13)	40	0.33
Norwegian (12)	97	0.81
Pennsylvania German (0)	17	0.14
Polish (321)	750	6.27
Portuguese (0)	42	0.35
Romanian (0)	18	0.15
Russian (171)	281	2.35
Scotch-Irish (84)	201	1.68
Scottish (111)	347	2.90
Slavic (0)	14	0.12
Slovak (10)	23	0.19
Swedish (30)	131	1.09
Swiss (14)	14	0.12
Turkish (16)	16	0.13
Ukrainian (79)	114	0.95
Welsh (42)	190	1.59
West Indian, ex. Hispanic (0)	16	0.13

*Notes: † The Census 2010 population figure is used to calculate the percentages in the Hispanic Origin and Race categories. Ancestry percentages are based on the 2006-2010 American Community Survey population (not shown); ‡ Numbers in parentheses indicate the number of people reporting a single ancestry; * Numbers in parentheses indicate the number of persons reporting this race alone, not in combination with any other race; Please refer to the Explanation of Data for more information.*

Jamaican (0)	16	0.13

Hispanic Origin	Population	%
Hispanic or Latino (of any race)	273	2.39
Central American, ex. Mexican	31	0.27
Costa Rican	6	0.05
Guatemalan	13	0.11
Honduran	3	0.03
Nicaraguan	1	0.01
Salvadoran	8	0.07
Cuban	24	0.21
Dominican Republic	12	0.11
Mexican	28	0.25
Puerto Rican	30	0.26
South American	102	0.89
Argentinean	10	0.09
Chilean	4	0.04
Colombian	15	0.13
Ecuadorian	26	0.23
Peruvian	34	0.30
Uruguayan	5	0.04
Venezuelan	4	0.04
Other South American	4	0.04
Other Hispanic or Latino	46	0.40

Race*	Population	%
African-American/Black (208)	257	2.25
Not Hispanic (199)	239	2.09
Hispanic (9)	18	0.16
American Indian/Alaska Native (22)	34	0.30
Not Hispanic (22)	34	0.30
Arapaho (1)	1	0.01
Cherokee (2)	2	0.02
Creek (1)	1	0.01
Lumbee (2)	4	0.04
Mexican American Ind. (11)	11	0.10
Seminole (1)	1	0.01
Shoshone (1)	1	0.01
Asian (1,155)	1,245	10.90
Not Hispanic (1,151)	1,235	10.81
Hispanic (4)	10	0.09
Bangladeshi (7)	7	0.06
Burmese (18)	19	0.17
Cambodian (4)	4	0.04
Chinese, ex. Taiwanese (318)	362	3.17
Filipino (108)	145	1.27
Indian (173)	195	1.71
Indonesian (1)	1	0.01
Japanese (11)	15	0.13
Korean (397)	421	3.69
Pakistani (27)	36	0.32
Sri Lankan (4)	4	0.04
Taiwanese (15)	17	0.15
Thai (10)	12	0.11
Vietnamese (28)	33	0.29
Hawaii Native/Pacific Islander (8)	10	0.09
Not Hispanic (8)	10	0.09
Guamanian/Chamorro (0)	1	0.01
Native Hawaiian (4)	4	0.04
White (9,856)	9,981	87.40
Not Hispanic (9,636)	9,742	85.31
Hispanic (220)	239	2.09

Middle River

Place Type: CDP
County: Baltimore
Population: 25,191†

Ancestry‡	Population	%
African, Sub-Saharan (912)	1,015	4.26
African (768)	871	3.66
Nigerian (80)	80	0.34
Somalian (32)	32	0.13
Other Sub-Saharan African (32)	32	0.13
American (2,050)	2,050	8.61
Arab (164)	164	0.69
Arab (28)	28	0.12
Lebanese (13)	13	0.05
Palestinian (6)	6	0.03
Syrian (117)	117	0.49
Austrian (0)	9	0.04
Belgian (8)	8	0.03
Brazilian (0)	40	0.17
British (0)	46	0.19
Bulgarian (27)	27	0.11
Canadian (25)	35	0.15
Czech (100)	233	0.98
Czechoslovakian (7)	51	0.21
Dutch (27)	342	1.44
English (424)	1,515	6.37
European (40)	40	0.17
French, ex. Basque (76)	569	2.39
German (2,049)	5,464	22.96
Greek (64)	205	0.86
Hungarian (0)	25	0.11
Irish (1,084)	3,722	15.64
Italian (610)	1,831	7.69
Lithuanian (80)	127	0.53
Northern European (9)	9	0.04
Norwegian (10)	29	0.12
Pennsylvania German (14)	33	0.14
Polish (401)	1,220	5.13
Portuguese (0)	8	0.03
Russian (28)	81	0.34
Scotch-Irish (207)	427	1.79
Scottish (86)	290	1.22
Slovak (0)	56	0.24
Swedish (11)	156	0.66
Swiss (0)	14	0.06
Turkish (9)	9	0.04
Ukrainian (43)	72	0.30
Welsh (49)	143	0.60
West Indian, ex. Hispanic (258)	396	1.66
British West Indian (24)	24	0.10
Jamaican (37)	48	0.20
Trinidadian/Tobagonian (56)	56	0.24
West Indian (141)	268	1.13
Yugoslavian (0)	7	0.03

Hispanic Origin	Population	%
Hispanic or Latino (of any race)	1,572	6.24
Central American, ex. Mexican	645	2.56
Costa Rican	6	0.02
Guatemalan	23	0.09
Honduran	165	0.65
Nicaraguan	6	0.02
Panamanian	16	0.06
Salvadoran	424	1.68
Other Central American	5	0.02
Cuban	33	0.13
Dominican Republic	61	0.24
Mexican	219	0.87
Puerto Rican	355	1.41
South American	60	0.24
Argentinean	9	0.04
Bolivian	2	0.01
Chilean	3	0.01
Colombian	8	0.03
Ecuadorian	11	0.04
Peruvian	13	0.05
Uruguayan	1	<0.01
Venezuelan	5	0.02
Other South American	8	0.03
Other Hispanic or Latino	199	0.79

Race*	Population	%
African-American/Black (5,695)	6,259	24.85
Not Hispanic (5,557)	6,056	24.04
Hispanic (138)	203	0.81
American Indian/Alaska Native (167)	389	1.54
Not Hispanic (137)	309	1.23
Hispanic (30)	80	0.32
Apache (2)	2	0.01
Blackfeet (1)	12	0.05
Central American Ind. (8)	16	0.06
Cherokee (35)	95	0.38
Chippewa (1)	2	0.01
Choctaw (4)	4	0.02
Creek (1)	2	0.01
Iroquois (2)	7	0.03
Lumbee (33)	49	0.19
Mexican American Ind. (3)	5	0.02
Navajo (1)	2	0.01
Seminole (0)	1	<0.01
Sioux (0)	2	0.01
South American Ind. (7)	15	0.06
Asian (845)	1,014	4.03
Not Hispanic (832)	992	3.94
Hispanic (13)	22	0.09
Bangladeshi (4)	4	0.02
Burmese (2)	2	0.01
Chinese, ex. Taiwanese (64)	71	0.28
Filipino (375)	433	1.72
Indian (114)	148	0.59
Indonesian (1)	1	<0.01
Japanese (6)	12	0.05
Korean (73)	101	0.40
Laotian (36)	41	0.16
Nepalese (15)	15	0.06
Pakistani (71)	89	0.35
Taiwanese (4)	5	0.02
Thai (4)	6	0.02
Vietnamese (59)	68	0.27
Hawaii Native/Pacific Islander (10)	45	0.18
Not Hispanic (9)	36	0.14
Hispanic (1)	9	0.04
Guamanian/Chamorro (4)	11	0.04
Native Hawaiian (4)	12	0.05
Samoan (0)	1	<0.01
White (16,996)	17,724	70.36
Not Hispanic (16,356)	16,949	67.28
Hispanic (640)	775	3.08

Milford Mill

Place Type: CDP
County: Baltimore
Population: 29,042†

Ancestry‡	Population	%
African, Sub-Saharan (2,277)	2,633	9.15
African (1,398)	1,591	5.53
Ethiopian (173)	173	0.60
Ghanaian (251)	269	0.94
Liberian (67)	85	0.30
Nigerian (353)	480	1.67
Other Sub-Saharan African (35)	35	0.12
American (438)	438	1.52
Arab (59)	68	0.24
Arab (23)	23	0.08
Lebanese (0)	9	0.03
Moroccan (36)	36	0.13
Austrian (0)	16	0.06
British (20)	44	0.15
Czech (0)	26	0.09
Dutch (0)	21	0.07
Eastern European (14)	14	0.05
English (143)	340	1.18
European (32)	48	0.17
Finnish (0)	11	0.04
French, ex. Basque (0)	33	0.11
German (217)	826	2.87
Greek (30)	43	0.15
Guyanese (100)	100	0.35
Irish (37)	556	1.93
Italian (148)	214	0.74
Lithuanian (0)	21	0.07
New Zealander (7)	7	0.02
Polish (105)	205	0.71
Russian (57)	124	0.43
Scotch-Irish (8)	19	0.07
Scottish (13)	41	0.14
Slovak (24)	24	0.08
Slovene (12)	12	0.04
Swedish (12)	12	0.04
Ukrainian (12)	37	0.13
Welsh (0)	20	0.07
West Indian, ex. Hispanic (1,118)	1,373	4.77
Barbadian (30)	30	0.10

*Notes: † The Census 2010 population figure is used to calculate the percentages in the Hispanic Origin and Race categories. Ancestry percentages are based on the 2006-2010 American Community Survey population (not shown); ‡ Numbers in parentheses indicate the number of people reporting a single ancestry; * Numbers in parentheses indicate the number of persons reporting this race alone, not in combination with any other race; Please refer to the Explanation of Data for more information.*

Belizean (0)	12	0.04
Haitian (51)	51	0.18
Jamaican (637)	753	2.62
Trinidadian/Tobagonian (240)	342	1.19
West Indian (62)	87	0.30
Other West Indian (98)	98	0.34

Hispanic Origin	Population	%
Hispanic or Latino (of any race)	1,073	3.69
Central American, ex. Mexican	321	1.11
Guatemalan	26	0.09
Honduran	48	0.17
Nicaraguan	18	0.06
Panamanian	28	0.10
Salvadoran	186	0.64
Other Central American	15	0.05
Cuban	28	0.10
Dominican Republic	41	0.14
Mexican	222	0.76
Puerto Rican	231	0.80
South American	74	0.25
Argentinean	9	0.03
Bolivian	5	0.02
Chilean	4	0.01
Colombian	9	0.03
Ecuadorian	11	0.04
Paraguayan	1	<0.01
Peruvian	15	0.05
Uruguayan	17	0.06
Venezuelan	3	0.01
Other Hispanic or Latino	156	0.54

Race*	Population	%
African-American/Black (24,587)	25,172	86.67
Not Hispanic (24,333)	24,840	85.53
Hispanic (254)	332	1.14
American Indian/Alaska Native (72)	305	1.05
Not Hispanic (55)	252	0.87
Hispanic (17)	53	0.18
Blackfeet (1)	20	0.07
Cherokee (5)	50	0.17
Cheyenne (0)	2	0.01
Choctaw (0)	1	<0.01
Creek (0)	1	<0.01
Crow (0)	1	<0.01
Iroquois (0)	2	0.01
Lumbee (7)	10	0.03
Mexican American Ind. (7)	9	0.03
Potawatomi (1)	1	<0.01
Sioux (1)	4	0.01
Spanish American Ind. (1)	1	<0.01
Asian (696)	825	2.84
Not Hispanic (686)	811	2.79
Hispanic (10)	14	0.05
Bangladeshi (4)	4	0.01
Burmese (5)	5	0.02
Cambodian (1)	2	0.01
Chinese, ex. Taiwanese (42)	56	0.19
Filipino (105)	131	0.45
Indian (239)	275	0.95
Japanese (11)	22	0.08
Korean (44)	60	0.21
Laotian (4)	4	0.01
Malaysian (1)	1	<0.01
Nepalese (0)	1	<0.01
Pakistani (93)	102	0.35
Taiwanese (0)	1	<0.01
Thai (11)	18	0.06
Vietnamese (87)	97	0.33
Hawaii Native/Pacific Islander (6)	42	0.14
Not Hispanic (6)	39	0.13
Hispanic (0)	3	0.01
Fijian (0)	2	0.01
Guamanian/Chamorro (1)	2	0.01
Native Hawaiian (1)	7	0.02
White (2,533)	2,928	10.08
Not Hispanic (2,253)	2,583	8.89
Hispanic (280)	345	1.19

Mitchellville

Place Type: CDP
County: Prince George's
Population: 10,967†

Ancestry‡	Population	%
African, Sub-Saharan (1,528)	1,606	13.78
African (412)	438	3.76
Ethiopian (27)	27	0.23
Liberian (166)	166	1.42
Nigerian (724)	776	6.66
Senegalese (93)	93	0.80
Sierra Leonean (89)	89	0.76
Other Sub-Saharan African (17)	17	0.15
American (89)	89	0.76
Arab (44)	44	0.38
Other Arab (44)	44	0.38
Armenian (0)	11	0.09
Dutch (0)	22	0.19
English (33)	106	0.91
European (33)	50	0.43
French, ex. Basque (8)	32	0.27
French Canadian (0)	6	0.05
German (58)	209	1.79
Guyanese (102)	102	0.88
Iranian (17)	17	0.15
Irish (9)	27	0.23
Italian (22)	59	0.51
Polish (0)	14	0.12
Portuguese (21)	32	0.27
Scotch-Irish (25)	44	0.38
Scottish (0)	9	0.08
Slovak (6)	6	0.05
Swiss (0)	11	0.09
Welsh (0)	14	0.12
West Indian, ex. Hispanic (114)	133	1.14
Haitian (9)	28	0.24
Jamaican (54)	54	0.46
Trinidadian/Tobagonian (39)	39	0.33
West Indian (12)	12	0.10

Hispanic Origin	Population	%
Hispanic or Latino (of any race)	406	3.70
Central American, ex. Mexican	128	1.17
Costa Rican	6	0.05
Guatemalan	18	0.16
Honduran	2	0.02
Nicaraguan	13	0.12
Panamanian	8	0.07
Salvadoran	79	0.72
Other Central American	2	0.02
Cuban	10	0.09
Dominican Republic	39	0.36
Mexican	89	0.81
Puerto Rican	48	0.44
South American	37	0.34
Argentinean	2	0.02
Bolivian	4	0.04
Chilean	1	0.01
Colombian	16	0.15
Ecuadorian	4	0.04
Peruvian	5	0.05
Venezuelan	3	0.03
Other South American	2	0.02
Other Hispanic or Latino	55	0.50

Race*	Population	%
African-American/Black (9,371)	9,630	87.81
Not Hispanic (9,280)	9,510	86.71
Hispanic (91)	120	1.09
American Indian/Alaska Native (21)	133	1.21
Not Hispanic (21)	124	1.13
Hispanic (0)	9	0.08
Blackfeet (0)	7	0.06
Cherokee (0)	30	0.27
Choctaw (1)	1	0.01
Creek (1)	2	0.02
Lumbee (0)	2	0.02
Mexican American Ind. (1)	3	0.03
Seminole (0)	1	0.01
Sioux (1)	4	0.04
Tohono O'Odham (3)	3	0.03
Asian (353)	423	3.86
Not Hispanic (350)	419	3.82
Hispanic (3)	4	0.04
Cambodian (5)	5	0.05
Chinese, ex. Taiwanese (37)	44	0.40
Filipino (118)	138	1.26
Hmong (2)	3	0.03
Indian (116)	133	1.21
Indonesian (3)	5	0.05
Japanese (3)	14	0.13
Korean (9)	19	0.17
Pakistani (21)	21	0.19
Thai (3)	3	0.03
Vietnamese (24)	36	0.33
Hawaii Native/Pacific Islander (9)	19	0.17
Not Hispanic (4)	12	0.11
Hispanic (5)	7	0.06
Guamanian/Chamorro (0)	1	0.01
Native Hawaiian (1)	1	0.01
White (768)	900	8.21
Not Hispanic (635)	757	6.90
Hispanic (133)	143	1.30

Montgomery Village

Place Type: CDP
County: Montgomery
Population: 32,032†

Ancestry‡	Population	%
Afghan (26)	26	0.08
African, Sub-Saharan (1,773)	1,997	6.30
African (914)	993	3.13
Ethiopian (135)	135	0.43
Ghanaian (44)	44	0.14
Kenyan (51)	72	0.23
Liberian (156)	156	0.49
Nigerian (125)	196	0.62
Sierra Leonean (10)	42	0.13
Ugandan (13)	13	0.04
Other Sub-Saharan African (325)	346	1.09
American (987)	987	3.11
Arab (168)	221	0.70
Arab (10)	27	0.09
Egyptian (9)	9	0.03
Iraqi (35)	35	0.11
Lebanese (34)	34	0.11
Moroccan (49)	60	0.19
Palestinian (0)	25	0.08
Syrian (31)	31	0.10
Armenian (59)	59	0.19
Austrian (28)	142	0.45
Belgian (0)	9	0.03
Brazilian (70)	75	0.24
British (95)	133	0.42
Bulgarian (79)	79	0.25
Canadian (27)	35	0.11
Croatian (29)	36	0.11
Czech (26)	118	0.37
Danish (14)	60	0.19
Dutch (33)	236	0.74
Eastern European (117)	129	0.41
English (404)	2,048	6.46
Estonian (9)	9	0.03
European (250)	305	0.96
Finnish (0)	23	0.07
French, ex. Basque (90)	642	2.02
French Canadian (18)	96	0.30
German (948)	3,260	10.28
Greek (69)	100	0.32
Guyanese (23)	46	0.15
Hungarian (107)	154	0.49
Icelander (14)	21	0.07
Iranian (226)	226	0.71
Irish (554)	2,535	7.99
Israeli (26)	26	0.08
Italian (290)	1,148	3.62

*Notes: † The Census 2010 population figure is used to calculate the percentages in the Hispanic Origin and Race categories. Ancestry percentages are based on the 2006-2010 American Community Survey population (not shown); ‡ Numbers in parentheses indicate the number of people reporting a single ancestry; * Numbers in parentheses indicate the number of persons reporting this race alone, not in combination with any other race; Please refer to the Explanation of Data for more information.*

Lithuanian (76)	178	0.56
Northern European (60)	68	0.21
Norwegian (147)	387	1.22
Pennsylvania German (0)	14	0.04
Polish (344)	966	3.05
Portuguese (78)	127	0.40
Romanian (83)	91	0.29
Russian (274)	561	1.77
Scandinavian (12)	25	0.08
Scotch-Irish (203)	443	1.40
Scottish (129)	408	1.29
Serbian (122)	122	0.38
Slavic (0)	8	0.03
Slovak (13)	115	0.36
Slovene (19)	31	0.10
Swedish (9)	325	1.02
Swiss (0)	82	0.26
Turkish (41)	54	0.17
Ukrainian (53)	88	0.28
Welsh (0)	91	0.29
West Indian, ex. Hispanic (844)	1,633	5.15
Barbadian (0)	18	0.06
British West Indian (0)	147	0.46
Haitian (3)	3	0.01
Jamaican (609)	1,045	3.30
Trinidadian/Tobagonian (182)	348	1.10
West Indian (50)	72	0.23
Yugoslavian (11)	11	0.03

Hispanic Origin	Population	%
Hispanic or Latino (of any race)	7,812	24.39
Central American, ex. Mexican	3,662	11.43
Costa Rican	37	0.12
Guatemalan	461	1.44
Honduran	329	1.03
Nicaraguan	263	0.82
Panamanian	46	0.14
Salvadoran	2,522	7.87
Other Central American	4	0.01
Cuban	132	0.41
Dominican Republic	188	0.59
Mexican	597	1.86
Puerto Rican	377	1.18
South American	2,083	6.50
Argentinean	73	0.23
Bolivian	216	0.67
Chilean	108	0.34
Colombian	436	1.36
Ecuadorian	252	0.79
Paraguayan	40	0.12
Peruvian	842	2.63
Uruguayan	23	0.07
Venezuelan	88	0.27
Other South American	5	0.02
Other Hispanic or Latino	773	2.41

Race*	Population	%
African-American/Black (7,630)	8,289	25.88
Not Hispanic (7,419)	7,932	24.76
Hispanic (211)	357	1.11
American Indian/Alaska Native (125)	378	1.18
Not Hispanic (52)	233	0.73
Hispanic (73)	145	0.45
Apache (2)	3	0.01
Arapaho (1)	1	<0.01
Blackfeet (0)	11	0.03
Canadian/French Am. Ind. (0)	5	0.02
Central American Ind. (8)	14	0.04
Cherokee (7)	41	0.13
Cheyenne (0)	1	<0.01
Chickasaw (0)	1	<0.01
Chippewa (3)	5	0.02
Choctaw (0)	3	0.01
Cree (0)	1	<0.01
Creek (1)	3	0.01
Delaware (1)	9	0.03
Iroquois (1)	2	0.01
Kiowa (1)	1	<0.01
Lumbee (2)	3	0.01
Mexican American Ind. (5)	9	0.03
Navajo (7)	9	0.03
Osage (0)	1	<0.01
Potawatomi (1)	1	<0.01
Pueblo (1)	1	<0.01
Seminole (0)	6	0.02
Sioux (0)	1	<0.01
South American Ind. (5)	15	0.05
Spanish American Ind. (3)	3	0.01
Yaqui (0)	2	0.01
Asian (3,462)	3,969	12.39
Not Hispanic (3,434)	3,853	12.03
Hispanic (28)	116	0.36
Bangladeshi (95)	113	0.35
Burmese (45)	47	0.15
Cambodian (41)	49	0.15
Chinese, ex. Taiwanese (474)	573	1.79
Filipino (719)	820	2.56
Indian (924)	1,047	3.27
Indonesian (25)	38	0.12
Japanese (51)	104	0.32
Korean (212)	249	0.78
Laotian (9)	12	0.04
Malaysian (1)	10	0.03
Nepalese (151)	158	0.49
Pakistani (189)	220	0.69
Sri Lankan (89)	100	0.31
Taiwanese (29)	34	0.11
Thai (33)	50	0.16
Vietnamese (204)	250	0.78
Hawaii Native/Pacific Islander (20)	69	0.22
Not Hispanic (12)	44	0.14
Hispanic (8)	25	0.08
Guamanian/Chamorro (4)	10	0.03
Native Hawaiian (6)	24	0.07
Samoan (1)	1	<0.01
White (15,993)	17,179	53.63
Not Hispanic (12,200)	12,955	40.44
Hispanic (3,793)	4,224	13.19

Mount Airy

Place Type: Town
County: Carroll
Population: 9,288†

Ancestry‡	Population	%
American (396)	396	4.44
Arab (47)	102	1.14
Other Arab (47)	102	1.14
Armenian (10)	30	0.34
Australian (34)	34	0.38
Austrian (0)	7	0.08
Belgian (0)	15	0.17
Brazilian (32)	68	0.76
British (34)	137	1.54
Canadian (10)	10	0.11
Czech (0)	84	0.94
Danish (21)	42	0.47
Dutch (12)	139	1.56
English (446)	1,279	14.34
European (12)	12	0.13
French, ex. Basque (127)	516	5.78
French Canadian (26)	52	0.58
German (778)	2,982	33.43
Greek (52)	88	0.99
Hungarian (0)	90	1.01
Iranian (85)	105	1.18
Irish (316)	1,929	21.62
Italian (275)	863	9.67
Lithuanian (15)	15	0.17
Norwegian (55)	55	0.62
Pennsylvania German (0)	13	0.15
Polish (21)	329	3.69
Romanian (0)	16	0.18
Russian (46)	277	3.11
Scotch-Irish (69)	159	1.78
Scottish (58)	195	2.19
Serbian (0)	61	0.68
Slovak (11)	32	0.36
Slovene (0)	32	0.36
Swedish (0)	27	0.30
Swiss (0)	18	0.20
Turkish (22)	67	0.75
Ukrainian (9)	9	0.10
Welsh (48)	163	1.83
Yugoslavian (0)	11	0.12

Hispanic Origin	Population	%
Hispanic or Latino (of any race)	433	4.66
Central American, ex. Mexican	110	1.18
Costa Rican	8	0.09
Guatemalan	25	0.27
Honduran	9	0.10
Nicaraguan	8	0.09
Panamanian	3	0.03
Salvadoran	57	0.61
Cuban	26	0.28
Dominican Republic	11	0.12
Mexican	88	0.95
Puerto Rican	57	0.61
South American	85	0.92
Argentinean	6	0.06
Bolivian	10	0.11
Chilean	10	0.11
Colombian	7	0.08
Ecuadorian	15	0.16
Peruvian	22	0.24
Uruguayan	2	0.02
Venezuelan	9	0.10
Other South American	4	0.04
Other Hispanic or Latino	56	0.60

Race*	Population	%
African-American/Black (224)	292	3.14
Not Hispanic (216)	274	2.95
Hispanic (8)	18	0.19
American Indian/Alaska Native (18)	78	0.84
Not Hispanic (14)	64	0.69
Hispanic (4)	14	0.15
Blackfeet (0)	6	0.06
Cherokee (3)	17	0.18
Comanche (1)	1	0.01
Lumbee (4)	4	0.04
Mexican American Ind. (1)	1	0.01
Osage (0)	2	0.02
South American Ind. (0)	6	0.06
Asian (201)	273	2.94
Not Hispanic (200)	268	2.89
Hispanic (1)	5	0.05
Cambodian (9)	9	0.10
Chinese, ex. Taiwanese (22)	41	0.44
Filipino (37)	52	0.56
Indian (29)	44	0.47
Japanese (5)	20	0.22
Korean (39)	50	0.54
Malaysian (1)	1	0.01
Pakistani (5)	9	0.10
Taiwanese (3)	3	0.03
Thai (7)	8	0.09
Vietnamese (26)	31	0.33
Hawaii Native/Pacific Islander (4)	12	0.13
Not Hispanic (4)	12	0.13
Guamanian/Chamorro (0)	3	0.03
Native Hawaiian (0)	4	0.04
White (8,555)	8,740	94.10
Not Hispanic (8,262)	8,408	90.53
Hispanic (293)	332	3.57

Mount Rainier

Place Type: City
County: Prince George's
Population: 8,080†

Ancestry‡	Population	%
African, Sub-Saharan (376)	421	5.17
African (41)	86	1.06
Ethiopian (57)	57	0.70
Ghanaian (49)	49	0.60
Kenyan (25)	25	0.31

*Notes: † The Census 2010 population figure is used to calculate the percentages in the Hispanic Origin and Race categories. Ancestry percentages are based on the 2006-2010 American Community Survey population (not shown); ‡ Numbers in parentheses indicate the number of people reporting a single ancestry; * Numbers in parentheses indicate the number of persons reporting this race alone, not in combination with any other race; Please refer to the Explanation of Data for more information.*

Nigerian (83)	83	1.02
Senegalese (53)	53	0.65
Other Sub-Saharan African (68)	68	0.83
American (259)	259	3.18
Basque (7)	7	0.09
Brazilian (8)	8	0.10
British (22)	49	0.60
Canadian (0)	12	0.15
Dutch (0)	17	0.21
Eastern European (8)	22	0.27
English (13)	159	1.95
European (26)	35	0.43
French Canadian (8)	8	0.10
German (42)	215	2.64
Guyanese (51)	110	1.35
Hungarian (0)	10	0.12
Irish (83)	262	3.22
Italian (81)	213	2.61
Norwegian (0)	12	0.15
Polish (17)	54	0.66
Portuguese (0)	27	0.33
Russian (9)	9	0.11
Scotch-Irish (13)	47	0.58
Scottish (6)	38	0.47
Swedish (24)	49	0.60
West Indian, ex. Hispanic (347)	402	4.93
Bahamian (15)	15	0.18
British West Indian (43)	43	0.53
Haitian (46)	46	0.56
Jamaican (236)	248	3.04
West Indian (7)	50	0.61

Hispanic Origin	Population	%
Hispanic or Latino (of any race)	2,536	31.39
Central American, ex. Mexican	1,591	19.69
Costa Rican	1	0.01
Guatemalan	190	2.35
Honduran	137	1.70
Nicaraguan	55	0.68
Panamanian	26	0.32
Salvadoran	1,167	14.44
Other Central American	15	0.19
Cuban	14	0.17
Dominican Republic	117	1.45
Mexican	348	4.31
Puerto Rican	51	0.63
South American	83	1.03
Argentinean	5	0.06
Bolivian	16	0.20
Chilean	2	0.02
Colombian	10	0.12
Ecuadorian	14	0.17
Paraguayan	2	0.02
Peruvian	21	0.26
Uruguayan	3	0.04
Venezuelan	7	0.09
Other South American	3	0.04
Other Hispanic or Latino	332	4.11

Race*	Population	%
African-American/Black (4,263)	4,418	54.68
Not Hispanic (4,116)	4,220	52.23
Hispanic (147)	198	2.45
American Indian/Alaska Native (47)	136	1.68
Not Hispanic (27)	88	1.09
Hispanic (20)	48	0.59
Central American Ind. (0)	1	0.01
Cherokee (0)	17	0.21
Choctaw (0)	1	0.01
Cree (0)	1	0.01
Creek (0)	1	0.01
Delaware (1)	1	0.01
Mexican American Ind. (1)	2	0.02
Navajo (0)	5	0.06
Pueblo (6)	6	0.07
Seminole (0)	1	0.01
South American Ind. (0)	4	0.05
Yakama (0)	1	0.01
Asian (187)	223	2.76
Not Hispanic (187)	215	2.66
Hispanic (0)	8	0.10
Burmese (1)	1	0.01
Cambodian (1)	1	0.01
Chinese, ex. Taiwanese (61)	73	0.90
Filipino (56)	70	0.87
Indian (41)	52	0.64
Japanese (2)	6	0.07
Korean (2)	5	0.06
Laotian (1)	1	0.01
Pakistani (2)	4	0.05
Sri Lankan (3)	3	0.04
Taiwanese (3)	4	0.05
Thai (2)	2	0.02
Vietnamese (6)	6	0.07
Hawaii Native/Pacific Islander (4)	13	0.16
Not Hispanic (2)	8	0.10
Hispanic (2)	5	0.06
Guamanian/Chamorro (4)	4	0.05
White (1,606)	1,806	22.35
Not Hispanic (1,050)	1,119	13.85
Hispanic (556)	687	8.50

New Carrollton

Place Type: City
County: Prince George's
Population: 12,135†

Ancestry‡	Population	%
African, Sub-Saharan (1,637)	1,748	14.42
African (1,403)	1,461	12.05
Ethiopian (60)	60	0.49
Liberian (24)	24	0.20
Nigerian (107)	120	0.99
Sierra Leonean (0)	20	0.16
Other Sub-Saharan African (43)	63	0.52
American (130)	130	1.07
British (0)	20	0.16
Czech (14)	24	0.20
Czechoslovakian (0)	11	0.09
Dutch (0)	21	0.17
English (38)	121	1.00
European (24)	24	0.20
French, ex. Basque (83)	96	0.79
German (101)	241	1.99
German Russian (30)	30	0.25
Greek (23)	23	0.19
Hungarian (8)	8	0.07
Irish (152)	364	3.00
Italian (0)	110	0.91
Latvian (25)	25	0.21
Lithuanian (11)	11	0.09
Norwegian (6)	6	0.05
Polish (9)	43	0.35
Romanian (0)	7	0.06
Russian (8)	36	0.30
Scotch-Irish (38)	50	0.41
Scottish (11)	22	0.18
Welsh (0)	26	0.21
West Indian, ex. Hispanic (475)	493	4.07
British West Indian (68)	77	0.64
Haitian (12)	12	0.10
Jamaican (294)	303	2.50
Trinidadian/Tobagonian (57)	57	0.47
West Indian (44)	44	0.36

Hispanic Origin	Population	%
Hispanic or Latino (of any race)	3,207	26.43
Central American, ex. Mexican	1,559	12.85
Costa Rican	5	0.04
Guatemalan	187	1.54
Honduran	108	0.89
Nicaraguan	20	0.16
Panamanian	13	0.11
Salvadoran	1,224	10.09
Other Central American	2	0.02
Cuban	23	0.19
Dominican Republic	148	1.22
Mexican	938	7.73
Puerto Rican	82	0.68
South American	98	0.81
Argentinean	5	0.04
Bolivian	8	0.07
Chilean	4	0.03
Colombian	7	0.06
Ecuadorian	27	0.22
Paraguayan	2	0.02
Peruvian	32	0.26
Uruguayan	5	0.04
Venezuelan	8	0.07
Other Hispanic or Latino	359	2.96

Race*	Population	%
African-American/Black (7,220)	7,405	61.02
Not Hispanic (7,054)	7,198	59.32
Hispanic (166)	207	1.71
American Indian/Alaska Native (76)	158	1.30
Not Hispanic (12)	76	0.63
Hispanic (64)	82	0.68
Aleut *(Alaska Native)* (0)	1	0.01
Blackfeet (1)	7	0.06
Cherokee (1)	12	0.10
Creek (0)	1	0.01
Iroquois (0)	4	0.03
Seminole (0)	3	0.02
South American Ind. (0)	1	0.01
Asian (508)	553	4.56
Not Hispanic (506)	537	4.43
Hispanic (2)	16	0.13
Bangladeshi (8)	8	0.07
Cambodian (67)	72	0.59
Chinese, ex. Taiwanese (34)	38	0.31
Filipino (141)	150	1.24
Indian (87)	97	0.80
Indonesian (1)	1	0.01
Japanese (6)	9	0.07
Korean (19)	22	0.18
Laotian (12)	12	0.10
Nepalese (3)	3	0.02
Pakistani (22)	23	0.19
Taiwanese (1)	1	0.01
Thai (0)	3	0.02
Vietnamese (94)	105	0.87
Hawaii Native/Pacific Islander (3)	24	0.20
Not Hispanic (3)	19	0.16
Hispanic (0)	5	0.04
Native Hawaiian (0)	2	0.02
Tongan (3)	3	0.02
White (1,848)	2,037	16.79
Not Hispanic (1,139)	1,209	9.96
Hispanic (709)	828	6.82

North Bethesda

Place Type: CDP
County: Montgomery
Population: 43,828†

Ancestry‡	Population	%
African, Sub-Saharan (727)	831	2.05
African (299)	357	0.88
Ghanaian (0)	12	0.03
Kenyan (54)	54	0.13
Nigerian (19)	19	0.05
South African (49)	60	0.15
Ugandan (28)	51	0.13
Other Sub-Saharan African (278)	278	0.69
Alsatian (0)	9	0.02
American (912)	912	2.25
Arab (477)	789	1.95
Arab (42)	122	0.30
Egyptian (116)	116	0.29
Jordanian (60)	60	0.15
Lebanese (135)	195	0.48
Moroccan (11)	65	0.16
Palestinian (10)	25	0.06
Syrian (50)	75	0.19
Other Arab (53)	131	0.32
Armenian (145)	157	0.39
Austrian (21)	385	0.95

*Notes: † The Census 2010 population figure is used to calculate the percentages in the Hispanic Origin and Race categories. Ancestry percentages are based on the 2006-2010 American Community Survey population (not shown); ‡ Numbers in parentheses indicate the number of people reporting a single ancestry; * Numbers in parentheses indicate the number of persons reporting this race alone, not in combination with any other race; Please refer to the Explanation of Data for more information.*

SECTION TWO

Belgian (22)	35	0.09
Brazilian (87)	178	0.44
British (211)	332	0.82
Bulgarian (119)	119	0.29
Canadian (23)	43	0.11
Celtic (8)	8	0.02
Croatian (37)	53	0.13
Czech (38)	98	0.24
Czechoslovakian (12)	56	0.14
Danish (10)	69	0.17
Dutch (64)	311	0.77
Eastern European (599)	623	1.54
English (964)	3,460	8.55
Estonian (0)	8	0.02
European (853)	936	2.31
Finnish (41)	51	0.13
French, ex. Basque (388)	1,141	2.82
French Canadian (72)	212	0.52
German (1,188)	4,413	10.90
Greek (407)	488	1.21
Guyanese (5)	5	0.01
Hungarian (187)	400	0.99
Icelander (5)	13	0.03
Iranian (720)	732	1.81
Irish (931)	3,413	8.43
Israeli (231)	231	0.57
Italian (1,264)	3,089	7.63
Latvian (10)	94	0.23
Lithuanian (118)	351	0.87
Luxemburger (0)	28	0.07
New Zealander (21)	21	0.05
Northern European (65)	65	0.16
Norwegian (87)	298	0.74
Polish (551)	1,630	4.03
Portuguese (144)	333	0.82
Romanian (44)	196	0.48
Russian (1,515)	2,942	7.27
Scandinavian (7)	7	0.02
Scotch-Irish (147)	560	1.38
Scottish (170)	716	1.77
Serbian (18)	57	0.14
Slavic (0)	50	0.12
Slovak (39)	39	0.10
Slovene (0)	12	0.03
Swedish (64)	447	1.10
Swiss (14)	130	0.32
Turkish (12)	59	0.15
Ukrainian (370)	567	1.40
Welsh (51)	395	0.98
West Indian, ex. Hispanic (199)	328	0.81
Belizean (0)	15	0.04
Haitian (93)	93	0.23
Jamaican (21)	50	0.12
Trinidadian/Tobagonian (85)	156	0.39
West Indian (0)	14	0.03

Hispanic Origin	Population	%
Hispanic or Latino (of any race)	5,876	13.41
Central American, ex. Mexican	1,804	4.12
Costa Rican	65	0.15
Guatemalan	196	0.45
Honduran	374	0.85
Nicaraguan	129	0.29
Panamanian	41	0.09
Salvadoran	988	2.25
Other Central American	11	0.03
Cuban	179	0.41
Dominican Republic	144	0.33
Mexican	515	1.18
Puerto Rican	288	0.66
South American	2,291	5.23
Argentinean	297	0.68
Bolivian	337	0.77
Chilean	195	0.44
Colombian	444	1.01
Ecuadorian	152	0.35
Paraguayan	78	0.18
Peruvian	601	1.37
Uruguayan	64	0.15
Venezuelan	114	0.26
Other South American	9	0.02
Other Hispanic or Latino	655	1.49

Race*	Population	%
African-American/Black (3,040)	3,447	7.86
Not Hispanic (2,939)	3,249	7.41
Hispanic (101)	198	0.45
American Indian/Alaska Native (137)	340	0.78
Not Hispanic (82)	206	0.47
Hispanic (55)	134	0.31
Apache (1)	1	<0.01
Blackfeet (0)	7	0.02
Canadian/French Am. Ind. (1)	5	0.01
Central American Ind. (9)	13	0.03
Cherokee (13)	38	0.09
Chickasaw (2)	5	0.01
Chippewa (1)	2	<0.01
Choctaw (6)	8	0.02
Comanche (0)	1	<0.01
Creek (1)	4	0.01
Delaware (0)	3	0.01
Iroquois (1)	5	0.01
Lumbee (3)	6	0.01
Menominee (0)	2	<0.01
Mexican American Ind. (11)	23	0.05
Navajo (13)	15	0.03
Osage (1)	1	<0.01
Potawatomi (4)	5	0.01
Pueblo (1)	1	<0.01
Sioux (0)	1	<0.01
South American Ind. (12)	30	0.07
Spanish American Ind. (1)	2	<0.01
Tsimshian *(Alaska Native)* (1)	1	<0.01
Yakama (1)	1	<0.01
Asian (6,421)	7,268	16.58
Not Hispanic (6,399)	7,165	16.35
Hispanic (22)	103	0.24
Bangladeshi (91)	101	0.23
Burmese (91)	95	0.22
Cambodian (33)	39	0.09
Chinese, ex. Taiwanese (1,515)	1,708	3.90
Filipino (606)	743	1.70
Indian (1,387)	1,530	3.49
Indonesian (115)	136	0.31
Japanese (627)	733	1.67
Korean (988)	1,064	2.43
Laotian (7)	7	0.02
Malaysian (6)	10	0.02
Nepalese (80)	88	0.20
Pakistani (103)	120	0.27
Sri Lankan (86)	100	0.23
Taiwanese (146)	177	0.40
Thai (92)	107	0.24
Vietnamese (240)	288	0.66
Hawaii Native/Pacific Islander (30)	98	0.22
Not Hispanic (24)	80	0.18
Hispanic (6)	18	0.04
Fijian (1)	1	<0.01
Guamanian/Chamorro (5)	7	0.02
Native Hawaiian (4)	20	0.05
Samoan (1)	2	<0.01
White (30,707)	32,028	73.08
Not Hispanic (27,212)	28,182	64.30
Hispanic (3,495)	3,846	8.78

North Kensington

Place Type: CDP
County: Montgomery
Population: 9,514†

Ancestry‡	Population	%
African, Sub-Saharan (161)	192	2.00
African (35)	35	0.36
Ethiopian (91)	100	1.04
Kenyan (0)	10	0.10
Sierra Leonean (0)	12	0.12
Other Sub-Saharan African (35)	35	0.36
American (304)	304	3.16
Arab (0)	58	0.60
Egyptian (0)	22	0.23
Moroccan (0)	36	0.37
Austrian (9)	31	0.32
Belgian (0)	32	0.33
Brazilian (65)	86	0.89
British (5)	37	0.38
Canadian (0)	47	0.49
Czech (11)	32	0.33
Danish (0)	44	0.46
Dutch (20)	73	0.76
Eastern European (28)	28	0.29
English (209)	796	8.27
European (139)	163	1.69
Finnish (0)	14	0.15
French, ex. Basque (45)	200	2.08
French Canadian (0)	22	0.23
German (145)	1,180	12.26
Greek (88)	130	1.35
Hungarian (34)	56	0.58
Iranian (18)	42	0.44
Irish (356)	1,098	11.41
Italian (142)	466	4.84
Latvian (0)	19	0.20
Lithuanian (12)	20	0.21
Norwegian (52)	71	0.74
Pennsylvania German (11)	11	0.11
Polish (94)	202	2.10
Portuguese (43)	54	0.56
Russian (134)	246	2.56
Scandinavian (0)	9	0.09
Scotch-Irish (38)	133	1.38
Scottish (61)	222	2.31
Serbian (91)	91	0.95
Slovak (10)	52	0.54
Swedish (7)	71	0.74
Swiss (0)	61	0.63
Ukrainian (57)	57	0.59
Welsh (20)	64	0.67
West Indian, ex. Hispanic (143)	188	1.95
Bahamian (55)	55	0.57
Jamaican (88)	100	1.04
West Indian (0)	33	0.34

Hispanic Origin	Population	%
Hispanic or Latino (of any race)	2,100	22.07
Central American, ex. Mexican	1,040	10.93
Costa Rican	21	0.22
Guatemalan	189	1.99
Honduran	133	1.40
Nicaraguan	74	0.78
Panamanian	14	0.15
Salvadoran	609	6.40
Cuban	37	0.39
Dominican Republic	45	0.47
Mexican	191	2.01
Puerto Rican	84	0.88
South American	474	4.98
Argentinean	42	0.44
Bolivian	74	0.78
Chilean	60	0.63
Colombian	80	0.84
Ecuadorian	35	0.37
Paraguayan	13	0.14
Peruvian	153	1.61
Uruguayan	2	0.02
Venezuelan	15	0.16
Other Hispanic or Latino	229	2.41

Race*	Population	%
African-American/Black (1,191)	1,372	14.42
Not Hispanic (1,136)	1,257	13.21
Hispanic (55)	115	1.21
American Indian/Alaska Native (53)	155	1.63
Not Hispanic (25)	69	0.73
Hispanic (28)	86	0.90
Apache (2)	3	0.03
Cherokee (4)	22	0.23
Choctaw (0)	1	0.01
Creek (0)	1	0.01
Delaware (2)	2	0.02

*Notes: † The Census 2010 population figure is used to calculate the percentages in the Hispanic Origin and Race categories. Ancestry percentages are based on the 2006-2010 American Community Survey population (not shown); ‡ Numbers in parentheses indicate the number of people reporting a single ancestry; * Numbers in parentheses indicate the number of persons reporting this race alone, not in combination with any other race; Please refer to the Explanation of Data for more information.*

Hopi (0)	1	0.01
Iroquois (0)	1	0.01
Mexican American Ind. (0)	2	0.02
Navajo (0)	1	0.01
Pueblo (1)	2	0.02
Puget Sound Salish (0)	2	0.02
Seminole (0)	7	0.07
Sioux (0)	1	0.01
South American Ind. (3)	15	0.16
Spanish American Ind. (3)	5	0.05
Ute (0)	1	0.01
Asian (959)	1,131	11.89
Not Hispanic (947)	1,088	11.44
Hispanic (12)	43	0.45
Bangladeshi (3)	3	0.03
Burmese (0)	1	0.01
Cambodian (11)	12	0.13
Chinese, ex. Taiwanese (137)	176	1.85
Filipino (321)	366	3.85
Indian (141)	159	1.67
Indonesian (27)	37	0.39
Japanese (30)	50	0.53
Korean (44)	60	0.63
Laotian (5)	6	0.06
Malaysian (0)	3	0.03
Nepalese (24)	25	0.26
Pakistani (37)	39	0.41
Sri Lankan (29)	33	0.35
Taiwanese (8)	9	0.09
Thai (28)	36	0.38
Vietnamese (73)	77	0.81
Hawaii Native/Pacific Islander (2)	16	0.17
Not Hispanic (1)	8	0.08
Hispanic (1)	8	0.08
Guamanian/Chamorro (0)	1	0.01
Native Hawaiian (0)	2	0.02
White (5,939)	6,357	66.82
Not Hispanic (4,961)	5,206	54.72
Hispanic (978)	1,151	12.10

North Potomac

Place Type: CDP
County: Montgomery
Population: 24,410†

Ancestry‡	Population	%
African, Sub-Saharan (427)	437	1.75
African (118)	128	0.51
Ethiopian (153)	153	0.61
Ghanaian (156)	156	0.62
Albanian (0)	17	0.07
American (835)	835	3.34
Arab (281)	386	1.54
Arab (9)	9	0.04
Egyptian (7)	13	0.05
Lebanese (206)	272	1.09
Syrian (17)	17	0.07
Other Arab (42)	75	0.30
Armenian (56)	56	0.22
Austrian (0)	172	0.69
Basque (15)	15	0.06
Brazilian (19)	19	0.08
British (51)	175	0.70
Bulgarian (11)	11	0.04
Canadian (0)	106	0.42
Czech (0)	40	0.16
Czechoslovakian (10)	10	0.04
Danish (14)	54	0.22
Dutch (56)	126	0.50
Eastern European (372)	372	1.49
English (557)	1,832	7.32
European (429)	585	2.34
French, ex. Basque (19)	304	1.21
French Canadian (14)	43	0.17
German (411)	1,814	7.25
Greek (185)	360	1.44
Hungarian (50)	102	0.41
Icelander (44)	44	0.18
Iranian (699)	718	2.87
Irish (702)	2,102	8.40
Israeli (38)	38	0.15
Italian (586)	1,258	5.03
Latvian (17)	49	0.20
Lithuanian (26)	81	0.32
New Zealander (0)	6	0.02
Northern European (39)	39	0.16
Norwegian (13)	117	0.47
Polish (156)	619	2.47
Portuguese (25)	25	0.10
Romanian (132)	163	0.65
Russian (746)	1,270	5.07
Scandinavian (39)	107	0.43
Scotch-Irish (58)	171	0.68
Scottish (67)	467	1.87
Serbian (19)	19	0.08
Slavic (12)	12	0.05
Slovak (19)	30	0.12
Swedish (33)	152	0.61
Swiss (12)	73	0.29
Turkish (50)	125	0.50
Ukrainian (77)	177	0.71
Welsh (0)	99	0.40
West Indian, ex. Hispanic (90)	90	0.36
Jamaican (11)	11	0.04
Trinidadian/Tobagonian (79)	79	0.32
Yugoslavian (11)	11	0.04

Hispanic Origin	Population	%
Hispanic or Latino (of any race)	1,165	4.77
Central American, ex. Mexican	210	0.86
Costa Rican	10	0.04
Guatemalan	34	0.14
Honduran	23	0.09
Nicaraguan	18	0.07
Panamanian	9	0.04
Salvadoran	116	0.48
Cuban	64	0.26
Dominican Republic	38	0.16
Mexican	132	0.54
Puerto Rican	76	0.31
South American	497	2.04
Argentinean	48	0.20
Bolivian	42	0.17
Chilean	56	0.23
Colombian	107	0.44
Ecuadorian	53	0.22
Paraguayan	2	0.01
Peruvian	152	0.62
Uruguayan	14	0.06
Venezuelan	23	0.09
Other Hispanic or Latino	148	0.61

Race*	Population	%
African-American/Black (1,334)	1,502	6.15
Not Hispanic (1,300)	1,452	5.95
Hispanic (34)	50	0.20
American Indian/Alaska Native (39)	101	0.41
Not Hispanic (19)	62	0.25
Hispanic (20)	39	0.16
Central American Ind. (1)	3	0.01
Cherokee (2)	9	0.04
Chickasaw (5)	5	0.02
Choctaw (0)	3	0.01
Creek (0)	1	<0.01
Delaware (0)	2	0.01
Iroquois (0)	4	0.02
Mexican American Ind. (4)	8	0.03
Navajo (3)	4	0.02
Pueblo (1)	3	0.01
Sioux (0)	1	<0.01
South American Ind. (11)	12	0.05
Yaqui (1)	1	<0.01
Asian (8,281)	8,779	35.96
Not Hispanic (8,258)	8,741	35.81
Hispanic (23)	38	0.16
Bangladeshi (73)	79	0.32
Burmese (15)	17	0.07
Cambodian (12)	13	0.05
Chinese, ex. Taiwanese (3,995)	4,236	17.35
Filipino (121)	169	0.69
Indian (1,803)	1,904	7.80
Indonesian (23)	31	0.13
Japanese (72)	102	0.42
Korean (1,155)	1,226	5.02
Laotian (4)	4	0.02
Malaysian (1)	1	<0.01
Nepalese (4)	4	0.02
Pakistani (144)	154	0.63
Sri Lankan (26)	26	0.11
Taiwanese (459)	512	2.10
Thai (33)	47	0.19
Vietnamese (179)	217	0.89
Hawaii Native/Pacific Islander (3)	29	0.12
Not Hispanic (3)	25	0.10
Hispanic (0)	4	0.02
Guamanian/Chamorro (0)	1	<0.01
Native Hawaiian (0)	3	0.01
White (13,859)	14,462	59.25
Not Hispanic (13,003)	13,528	55.42
Hispanic (856)	934	3.83

Ocean Pines

Place Type: CDP
County: Worcester
Population: 11,710†

Ancestry‡	Population	%
American (419)	419	3.80
Arab (0)	8	0.07
Lebanese (0)	8	0.07
Australian (14)	14	0.13
Austrian (55)	153	1.39
Belgian (12)	12	0.11
Brazilian (14)	14	0.13
British (28)	41	0.37
Canadian (0)	29	0.26
Czech (22)	48	0.44
Dutch (65)	131	1.19
English (1,089)	2,422	21.97
European (65)	65	0.59
Finnish (0)	40	0.36
French, ex. Basque (127)	460	4.17
French Canadian (15)	25	0.23
German (1,103)	2,910	26.39
Greek (34)	46	0.42
Hungarian (18)	52	0.47
Irish (993)	2,697	24.46
Italian (586)	1,111	10.08
Lithuanian (63)	250	2.27
Northern European (11)	11	0.10
Norwegian (22)	65	0.59
Pennsylvania German (115)	129	1.17
Polish (228)	565	5.12
Portuguese (9)	19	0.17
Romanian (0)	13	0.12
Russian (75)	210	1.90
Scotch-Irish (156)	290	2.63
Scottish (111)	515	4.67
Slavic (0)	34	0.31
Slovak (23)	35	0.32
Swedish (46)	133	1.21
Swiss (0)	49	0.44
Ukrainian (6)	41	0.37
Welsh (46)	174	1.58
West Indian, ex. Hispanic (0)	9	0.08
Barbadian (0)	9	0.08

Hispanic Origin	Population	%
Hispanic or Latino (of any race)	276	2.36
Central American, ex. Mexican	24	0.20
Costa Rican	5	0.04
Guatemalan	5	0.04
Honduran	1	0.01
Nicaraguan	3	0.03
Salvadoran	10	0.09
Cuban	6	0.05
Dominican Republic	1	0.01
Mexican	109	0.93

*Notes: † The Census 2010 population figure is used to calculate the percentages in the Hispanic Origin and Race categories. Ancestry percentages are based on the 2006-2010 American Community Survey population (not shown); ‡ Numbers in parentheses indicate the number of people reporting a single ancestry; * Numbers in parentheses indicate the number of persons reporting this race alone, not in combination with any other race; Please refer to the Explanation of Data for more information.*

Puerto Rican	41	0.35
South American	60	0.51
Argentinean	12	0.10
Bolivian	10	0.09
Chilean	2	0.02
Colombian	8	0.07
Ecuadorian	7	0.06
Paraguayan	1	0.01
Peruvian	17	0.15
Uruguayan	2	0.02
Venezuelan	1	0.01
Other Hispanic or Latino	35	0.30

Race*	Population	%
African-American/Black (285)	362	3.09
Not Hispanic (281)	349	2.98
Hispanic (4)	13	0.11
American Indian/Alaska Native (22)	50	0.43
Not Hispanic (18)	45	0.38
Hispanic (4)	5	0.04
Apache (1)	2	0.02
Blackfeet (0)	4	0.03
Cherokee (4)	11	0.09
Chippewa (0)	1	0.01
Delaware (1)	1	0.01
Lumbee (0)	1	0.01
Pueblo (0)	1	0.01
Sioux (2)	3	0.03
Asian (104)	134	1.14
Not Hispanic (104)	134	1.14
Chinese, ex. Taiwanese (15)	17	0.15
Filipino (25)	34	0.29
Indian (17)	19	0.16
Japanese (9)	13	0.11
Korean (12)	13	0.11
Laotian (1)	4	0.03
Malaysian (1)	3	0.03
Pakistani (6)	6	0.05
Thai (4)	5	0.04
Vietnamese (12)	12	0.10
Hawaii Native/Pacific Islander (4)	9	0.08
Not Hispanic (4)	7	0.06
Hispanic (0)	2	0.02
Guamanian/Chamorro (1)	2	0.02
Native Hawaiian (1)	4	0.03
Samoan (2)	2	0.02
White (11,068)	11,201	95.65
Not Hispanic (10,900)	11,008	94.01
Hispanic (168)	193	1.65

Odenton

Place Type: CDP
County: Anne Arundel
Population: 37,132†

Ancestry‡	Population	%
African, Sub-Saharan (451)	660	1.86
African (215)	410	1.16
Nigerian (180)	194	0.55
Sierra Leonean (56)	56	0.16
Albanian (17)	17	0.05
American (1,394)	1,394	3.94
Arab (16)	221	0.62
Arab (0)	83	0.23
Jordanian (0)	15	0.04
Lebanese (16)	86	0.24
Palestinian (0)	15	0.04
Syrian (0)	22	0.06
Austrian (42)	181	0.51
Belgian (0)	27	0.08
Brazilian (43)	43	0.12
British (208)	411	1.16
Bulgarian (39)	39	0.11
Canadian (83)	97	0.27
Celtic (0)	12	0.03
Croatian (0)	10	0.03
Czech (42)	84	0.24
Czechoslovakian (14)	26	0.07
Danish (67)	100	0.28
Dutch (115)	420	1.19
Eastern European (93)	93	0.26
English (1,017)	3,748	10.59
European (260)	293	0.83
Finnish (20)	103	0.29
French, ex. Basque (137)	896	2.53
French Canadian (102)	371	1.05
German (1,872)	7,350	20.76
Greek (240)	581	1.64
Guyanese (18)	18	0.05
Hungarian (61)	453	1.28
Icelander (9)	9	0.03
Irish (1,292)	5,320	15.03
Italian (792)	2,388	6.75
Latvian (9)	9	0.03
Lithuanian (0)	66	0.19
Northern European (7)	7	0.02
Norwegian (93)	321	0.91
Pennsylvania German (16)	59	0.17
Polish (411)	1,624	4.59
Portuguese (34)	62	0.18
Russian (27)	245	0.69
Scandinavian (0)	18	0.05
Scotch-Irish (265)	628	1.77
Scottish (238)	695	1.96
Serbian (12)	25	0.07
Slavic (0)	16	0.05
Slovak (66)	217	0.61
Slovene (26)	26	0.07
Swedish (90)	280	0.79
Swiss (15)	34	0.10
Turkish (33)	49	0.14
Ukrainian (120)	237	0.67
Welsh (48)	261	0.74
West Indian, ex. Hispanic (275)	288	0.81
Haitian (103)	103	0.29
Jamaican (59)	72	0.20
Trinidadian/Tobagonian (88)	88	0.25
West Indian (25)	25	0.07
Yugoslavian (0)	55	0.16

Hispanic Origin	Population	%
Hispanic or Latino (of any race)	2,175	5.86
Central American, ex. Mexican	290	0.78
Costa Rican	13	0.04
Guatemalan	32	0.09
Honduran	34	0.09
Nicaraguan	20	0.05
Panamanian	104	0.28
Salvadoran	83	0.22
Other Central American	4	0.01
Cuban	59	0.16
Dominican Republic	73	0.20
Mexican	602	1.62
Puerto Rican	737	1.98
South American	185	0.50
Argentinean	20	0.05
Bolivian	15	0.04
Chilean	3	0.01
Colombian	80	0.22
Ecuadorian	26	0.07
Peruvian	23	0.06
Venezuelan	14	0.04
Other South American	4	0.01
Other Hispanic or Latino	229	0.62

Race*	Population	%
African-American/Black (8,548)	9,364	25.22
Not Hispanic (8,290)	8,968	24.15
Hispanic (258)	396	1.07
American Indian/Alaska Native (143)	431	1.16
Not Hispanic (122)	360	0.97
Hispanic (21)	71	0.19
Apache (0)	2	0.01
Blackfeet (8)	22	0.06
Cherokee (21)	108	0.29
Chickasaw (1)	7	0.02
Chippewa (0)	4	0.01
Choctaw (1)	7	0.02
Creek (0)	3	0.01
Houma (1)	1	<0.01
Iroquois (2)	12	0.03
Lumbee (8)	14	0.04
Mexican American Ind. (1)	1	<0.01
Navajo (1)	2	0.01
Potawatomi (0)	2	0.01
Seminole (0)	6	0.02
Sioux (0)	4	0.01
South American Ind. (6)	13	0.04
Spanish American Ind. (1)	1	<0.01
Tlingit-Haida *(Alaska Native)* (1)	1	<0.01
Ute (2)	5	0.01
Yup'ik *(Alaska Native)* (4)	4	0.01
Asian (2,035)	2,616	7.05
Not Hispanic (2,009)	2,547	6.86
Hispanic (26)	69	0.19
Bangladeshi (6)	6	0.02
Burmese (10)	11	0.03
Cambodian (29)	31	0.08
Chinese, ex. Taiwanese (304)	392	1.06
Filipino (305)	491	1.32
Hmong (1)	1	<0.01
Indian (470)	508	1.37
Indonesian (11)	18	0.05
Japanese (82)	196	0.53
Korean (408)	525	1.41
Laotian (8)	11	0.03
Malaysian (1)	2	0.01
Nepalese (23)	24	0.06
Pakistani (87)	95	0.26
Sri Lankan (3)	3	0.01
Taiwanese (6)	15	0.04
Thai (31)	52	0.14
Vietnamese (175)	202	0.54
Hawaii Native/Pacific Islander (50)	132	0.36
Not Hispanic (42)	111	0.30
Hispanic (8)	21	0.06
Guamanian/Chamorro (30)	40	0.11
Native Hawaiian (17)	52	0.14
Samoan (1)	17	0.05
Tongan (0)	2	0.01
White (24,241)	25,489	68.64
Not Hispanic (23,154)	24,187	65.14
Hispanic (1,087)	1,302	3.51

Olney

Place Type: CDP
County: Montgomery
Population: 33,844†

Ancestry‡	Population	%
African, Sub-Saharan (809)	1,053	3.17
African (241)	342	1.03
Ethiopian (364)	432	1.30
Ghanaian (108)	143	0.43
Liberian (23)	23	0.07
Sierra Leonean (3)	43	0.13
Ugandan (5)	5	0.02
Other Sub-Saharan African (65)	65	0.20
Albanian (0)	12	0.04
American (1,604)	1,604	4.84
Arab (253)	376	1.13
Arab (76)	76	0.23
Egyptian (91)	91	0.27
Lebanese (41)	132	0.40
Moroccan (45)	53	0.16
Syrian (0)	24	0.07
Armenian (46)	46	0.14
Australian (13)	13	0.04
Austrian (0)	79	0.24
Belgian (11)	33	0.10
Brazilian (30)	30	0.09
British (34)	201	0.61
Bulgarian (0)	11	0.03
Canadian (14)	62	0.19
Carpatho Rusyn (8)	8	0.02
Celtic (0)	29	0.09
Croatian (0)	48	0.14
Cypriot (40)	40	0.12

*Notes: † The Census 2010 population figure is used to calculate the percentages in the Hispanic Origin and Race categories. Ancestry percentages are based on the 2006-2010 American Community Survey population (not shown); ‡ Numbers in parentheses indicate the number of people reporting a single ancestry; * Numbers in parentheses indicate the number of persons reporting this race alone, not in combination with any other race; Please refer to the Explanation of Data for more information.*

Czech (0)	187	0.56
Czechoslovakian (9)	9	0.03
Danish (35)	80	0.24
Dutch (108)	530	1.60
Eastern European (345)	372	1.12
English (954)	3,525	10.63
European (728)	839	2.53
Finnish (18)	18	0.05
French, ex. Basque (62)	783	2.36
French Canadian (46)	180	0.54
German (1,074)	5,752	17.34
Greek (439)	744	2.24
Guyanese (54)	80	0.24
Hungarian (80)	368	1.11
Icelander (13)	13	0.04
Iranian (91)	91	0.27
Irish (1,575)	5,535	16.69
Israeli (15)	32	0.10
Italian (1,092)	2,935	8.85
Latvian (170)	170	0.51
Lithuanian (67)	265	0.80
Luxemburger (13)	13	0.04
Northern European (6)	6	0.02
Norwegian (60)	317	0.96
Polish (303)	1,135	3.42
Portuguese (175)	187	0.56
Romanian (0)	26	0.08
Russian (613)	1,271	3.83
Scandinavian (0)	9	0.03
Scotch-Irish (279)	657	1.98
Scottish (226)	699	2.11
Serbian (0)	32	0.10
Slavic (0)	12	0.04
Slovak (63)	262	0.79
Slovene (16)	84	0.25
Swedish (86)	328	0.99
Swiss (36)	101	0.30
Turkish (30)	48	0.14
Ukrainian (43)	198	0.60
Welsh (38)	194	0.58
West Indian, ex. Hispanic (191)	253	0.76
Belizean (34)	34	0.10
British West Indian (39)	39	0.12
Haitian (56)	56	0.17
Jamaican (46)	67	0.20
Trinidadian/Tobagonian (5)	5	0.02
West Indian (11)	52	0.16

Hispanic Origin	**Population**	**%**
Hispanic or Latino (of any race)	2,871	8.48
Central American, ex. Mexican	876	2.59
Costa Rican	16	0.05
Guatemalan	145	0.43
Honduran	62	0.18
Nicaraguan	100	0.30
Panamanian	20	0.06
Salvadoran	533	1.57
Cuban	137	0.40
Dominican Republic	62	0.18
Mexican	284	0.84
Puerto Rican	217	0.64
South American	964	2.85
Argentinean	61	0.18
Bolivian	175	0.52
Chilean	88	0.26
Colombian	194	0.57
Ecuadorian	77	0.23
Paraguayan	21	0.06
Peruvian	265	0.78
Uruguayan	6	0.02
Venezuelan	56	0.17
Other South American	21	0.06
Other Hispanic or Latino	331	0.98

Race*	**Population**	**%**
African-American/Black (3,691)	4,026	11.90
Not Hispanic (3,613)	3,912	11.56
Hispanic (78)	114	0.34
American Indian/Alaska Native (67)	180	0.53
Not Hispanic (34)	131	0.39
Hispanic (33)	49	0.14
Blackfeet (0)	4	0.01
Central American Ind. (10)	11	0.03
Cherokee (8)	31	0.09
Chickasaw (1)	2	0.01
Choctaw (0)	1	<0.01
Cree (1)	1	<0.01
Creek (0)	1	<0.01
Crow (1)	2	0.01
Delaware (2)	4	0.01
Iroquois (1)	2	0.01
Lumbee (1)	3	0.01
Mexican American Ind. (1)	6	0.02
Osage (4)	4	0.01
Pueblo (1)	1	<0.01
Sioux (0)	9	0.03
South American Ind. (3)	7	0.02
Spanish American Ind. (7)	7	0.02
Tohono O'Odham (0)	2	0.01
Tsimshian *(Alaska Native)* (3)	3	0.01
Asian (3,670)	4,077	12.05
Not Hispanic (3,654)	4,036	11.93
Hispanic (16)	41	0.12
Bangladeshi (17)	17	0.05
Burmese (10)	23	0.07
Cambodian (67)	76	0.22
Chinese, ex. Taiwanese (740)	838	2.48
Filipino (326)	401	1.18
Indian (813)	903	2.67
Indonesian (17)	20	0.06
Japanese (46)	108	0.32
Korean (871)	909	2.69
Laotian (14)	15	0.04
Malaysian (4)	4	0.01
Nepalese (21)	21	0.06
Pakistani (92)	110	0.33
Sri Lankan (82)	93	0.27
Taiwanese (25)	40	0.12
Thai (71)	79	0.23
Vietnamese (365)	386	1.14
Hawaii Native/Pacific Islander (6)	26	0.08
Not Hispanic (3)	20	0.06
Hispanic (3)	6	0.02
Guamanian/Chamorro (1)	3	0.01
Native Hawaiian (1)	4	0.01
Samoan (0)	1	<0.01
White (24,651)	25,402	75.06
Not Hispanic (22,872)	23,474	69.36
Hispanic (1,779)	1,928	5.70

Overlea

Place Type: CDP
County: Baltimore
Population: 12,275†

Ancestry‡	**Population**	**%**
African, Sub-Saharan (179)	179	1.41
African (126)	126	0.99
Ethiopian (50)	50	0.39
Nigerian (3)	3	0.02
Albanian (125)	125	0.99
American (738)	738	5.82
Arab (57)	57	0.45
Other Arab (57)	57	0.45
British (7)	12	0.09
Canadian (17)	17	0.13
Czech (28)	226	1.78
Czechoslovakian (3)	3	0.02
Danish (31)	56	0.44
Dutch (13)	127	1.00
English (323)	1,198	9.45
European (36)	36	0.28
French, ex. Basque (27)	258	2.04
French Canadian (25)	25	0.20
German (792)	3,123	24.64
Greek (67)	157	1.24
Hungarian (29)	53	0.42
Irish (492)	2,230	17.60
Italian (570)	1,800	14.20
Latvian (0)	26	0.21
Lithuanian (75)	131	1.03
Northern European (0)	12	0.09
Norwegian (22)	53	0.42
Polish (352)	1,081	8.53
Portuguese (0)	80	0.63
Romanian (106)	106	0.84
Russian (9)	77	0.61
Scotch-Irish (74)	356	2.81
Scottish (51)	159	1.25
Swedish (0)	14	0.11
Ukrainian (0)	8	0.06
Welsh (0)	80	0.63
West Indian, ex. Hispanic (33)	33	0.26
Trinidadian/Tobagonian (33)	33	0.26
Yugoslavian (0)	5	0.04

Hispanic Origin	**Population**	**%**
Hispanic or Latino (of any race)	379	3.09
Central American, ex. Mexican	67	0.55
Costa Rican	2	0.02
Guatemalan	5	0.04
Honduran	23	0.19
Panamanian	2	0.02
Salvadoran	35	0.29
Cuban	17	0.14
Dominican Republic	14	0.11
Mexican	82	0.67
Puerto Rican	70	0.57
South American	57	0.46
Argentinean	5	0.04
Chilean	8	0.07
Colombian	13	0.11
Ecuadorian	10	0.08
Peruvian	16	0.13
Uruguayan	1	0.01
Venezuelan	4	0.03
Other Hispanic or Latino	72	0.59

Race*	**Population**	**%**
African-American/Black (2,328)	2,466	20.09
Not Hispanic (2,307)	2,438	19.86
Hispanic (21)	28	0.23
American Indian/Alaska Native (27)	81	0.66
Not Hispanic (24)	74	0.60
Hispanic (3)	7	0.06
Blackfeet (1)	5	0.04
Central American Ind. (1)	1	0.01
Cherokee (2)	17	0.14
Choctaw (0)	1	0.01
Iroquois (1)	2	0.02
Lumbee (6)	8	0.07
Seminole (0)	1	0.01
Sioux (0)	5	0.04
Asian (395)	460	3.75
Not Hispanic (391)	452	3.68
Hispanic (4)	8	0.07
Burmese (1)	2	0.02
Chinese, ex. Taiwanese (40)	55	0.45
Filipino (161)	196	1.60
Indian (49)	66	0.54
Indonesian (1)	4	0.03
Japanese (11)	18	0.15
Korean (28)	29	0.24
Laotian (2)	2	0.02
Nepalese (13)	15	0.12
Pakistani (42)	50	0.41
Taiwanese (2)	3	0.02
Thai (4)	9	0.07
Vietnamese (22)	28	0.23
Hawaii Native/Pacific Islander (4)	14	0.11
Not Hispanic (4)	14	0.11
Guamanian/Chamorro (2)	2	0.02
Native Hawaiian (2)	5	0.04
White (9,168)	9,359	76.24
Not Hispanic (8,941)	9,118	74.28
Hispanic (227)	241	1.96

*Notes: † The Census 2010 population figure is used to calculate the percentages in the Hispanic Origin and Race categories. Ancestry percentages are based on the 2006-2010 American Community Survey population (not shown); ‡ Numbers in parentheses indicate the number of people reporting a single ancestry; * Numbers in parentheses indicate the number of persons reporting this race alone, not in combination with any other race; Please refer to the Explanation of Data for more information.*

Owings Mills

Place Type: CDP
County: Baltimore
Population: 30,622†

Ancestry‡	Population	%
African, Sub-Saharan (1,064)	1,163	3.91
African (605)	673	2.26
Ethiopian (38)	38	0.13
Ghanaian (72)	72	0.24
Kenyan (53)	53	0.18
Liberian (27)	27	0.09
Nigerian (28)	59	0.20
Sierra Leonean (44)	44	0.15
Other Sub-Saharan African (197)	197	0.66
Albanian (67)	67	0.23
American (1,168)	1,168	3.93
Arab (23)	93	0.31
Arab (9)	9	0.03
Egyptian (0)	12	0.04
Lebanese (14)	49	0.16
Syrian (0)	12	0.04
Other Arab (0)	11	0.04
Austrian (0)	13	0.04
Belgian (12)	12	0.04
Brazilian (16)	62	0.21
British (64)	77	0.26
Canadian (29)	29	0.10
Croatian (15)	39	0.13
Czech (0)	137	0.46
Danish (68)	158	0.53
Dutch (0)	151	0.51
Eastern European (98)	98	0.33
English (344)	920	3.09
European (151)	160	0.54
French, ex. Basque (0)	166	0.56
French Canadian (34)	47	0.16
German (1,025)	2,648	8.91
Greek (0)	21	0.07
Guyanese (62)	62	0.21
Hungarian (70)	176	0.59
Iranian (47)	47	0.16
Irish (445)	1,591	5.35
Italian (392)	1,156	3.89
Latvian (0)	19	0.06
Lithuanian (42)	77	0.26
Norwegian (12)	48	0.16
Pennsylvania German (9)	36	0.12
Polish (252)	800	2.69
Portuguese (11)	178	0.60
Romanian (9)	45	0.15
Russian (539)	907	3.05
Scandinavian (11)	11	0.04
Scotch-Irish (52)	148	0.50
Scottish (48)	212	0.71
Slavic (25)	25	0.08
Slovak (11)	42	0.14
Swedish (34)	64	0.22
Swiss (0)	16	0.05
Ukrainian (74)	74	0.25
Welsh (18)	79	0.27
West Indian, ex. Hispanic (355)	676	2.27
Barbadian (5)	5	0.02
Jamaican (264)	320	1.08
Trinidadian/Tobagonian (28)	66	0.22
West Indian (58)	285	0.96

Hispanic Origin	Population	%
Hispanic or Latino (of any race)	2,135	6.97
Central American, ex. Mexican	917	2.99
Costa Rican	14	0.05
Guatemalan	245	0.80
Honduran	206	0.67
Nicaraguan	12	0.04
Panamanian	40	0.13
Salvadoran	394	1.29
Other Central American	6	0.02
Cuban	27	0.09
Dominican Republic	68	0.22
Mexican	268	0.88
Puerto Rican	422	1.38
South American	203	0.66
Argentinean	17	0.06
Bolivian	3	0.01
Chilean	11	0.04
Colombian	56	0.18
Ecuadorian	22	0.07
Peruvian	56	0.18
Uruguayan	7	0.02
Venezuelan	29	0.09
Other South American	2	0.01
Other Hispanic or Latino	230	0.75

Race*	Population	%
African-American/Black (15,616)	16,262	53.11
Not Hispanic (15,374)	15,952	52.09
Hispanic (242)	310	1.01
American Indian/Alaska Native (91)	316	1.03
Not Hispanic (72)	264	0.86
Hispanic (19)	52	0.17
Apache (0)	1	<0.01
Blackfeet (0)	10	0.03
Central American Ind. (5)	5	0.02
Cherokee (7)	78	0.25
Chippewa (1)	1	<0.01
Choctaw (1)	4	0.01
Cree (0)	4	0.01
Creek (1)	1	<0.01
Delaware (1)	2	0.01
Inupiat *(Alaska Native)* (0)	1	<0.01
Iroquois (0)	1	<0.01
Lumbee (5)	7	0.02
Mexican American Ind. (13)	14	0.05
Sioux (0)	2	0.01
South American Ind. (0)	5	0.02
Spanish American Ind. (0)	4	0.01
Asian (2,395)	2,669	8.72
Not Hispanic (2,379)	2,635	8.60
Hispanic (16)	34	0.11
Bangladeshi (4)	4	0.01
Burmese (11)	11	0.04
Cambodian (3)	4	0.01
Chinese, ex. Taiwanese (171)	212	0.69
Filipino (298)	354	1.16
Hmong (1)	1	<0.01
Indian (1,208)	1,279	4.18
Indonesian (5)	7	0.02
Japanese (29)	58	0.19
Korean (215)	250	0.82
Laotian (3)	4	0.01
Malaysian (0)	1	<0.01
Nepalese (20)	21	0.07
Pakistani (218)	234	0.76
Sri Lankan (2)	3	0.01
Taiwanese (3)	11	0.04
Thai (19)	20	0.07
Vietnamese (130)	138	0.45
Hawaii Native/Pacific Islander (20)	51	0.17
Not Hispanic (11)	32	0.10
Hispanic (9)	19	0.06
Guamanian/Chamorro (14)	18	0.06
Native Hawaiian (1)	3	0.01
Samoan (0)	1	<0.01
White (10,490)	11,204	36.59
Not Hispanic (9,754)	10,326	33.72
Hispanic (736)	878	2.87

Oxon Hill

Place Type: CDP
County: Prince George's
Population: 17,722†

Ancestry‡	Population	%
African, Sub-Saharan (319)	374	2.03
African (104)	136	0.74
Ethiopian (79)	79	0.43
Ghanaian (28)	28	0.15
Nigerian (108)	131	0.71
American (187)	187	1.02
Austrian (10)	10	0.05
Canadian (0)	17	0.09
Czech (0)	8	0.04
Danish (0)	33	0.18
Dutch (8)	36	0.20
English (75)	336	1.82
European (83)	83	0.45
Finnish (0)	3	0.02
French, ex. Basque (15)	223	1.21
French Canadian (0)	16	0.09
German (58)	429	2.33
Greek (14)	14	0.08
Guyanese (13)	13	0.07
Hungarian (15)	18	0.10
Irish (130)	348	1.89
Italian (56)	137	0.74
Lithuanian (0)	15	0.08
Polish (20)	20	0.11
Portuguese (0)	46	0.25
Russian (0)	8	0.04
Scotch-Irish (0)	40	0.22
Scottish (14)	132	0.72
Welsh (0)	26	0.14
West Indian, ex. Hispanic (142)	192	1.04
Bahamian (0)	23	0.12
Barbadian (15)	15	0.08
Haitian (0)	14	0.08
Jamaican (59)	72	0.39
Trinidadian/Tobagonian (58)	58	0.31
West Indian (10)	10	0.05

Hispanic Origin	Population	%
Hispanic or Latino (of any race)	1,926	10.87
Central American, ex. Mexican	1,158	6.53
Costa Rican	3	0.02
Guatemalan	95	0.54
Honduran	154	0.87
Nicaraguan	19	0.11
Panamanian	31	0.17
Salvadoran	842	4.75
Other Central American	14	0.08
Cuban	14	0.08
Dominican Republic	18	0.10
Mexican	158	0.89
Puerto Rican	138	0.78
South American	115	0.65
Argentinean	7	0.04
Bolivian	35	0.20
Colombian	7	0.04
Peruvian	56	0.32
Uruguayan	1	0.01
Venezuelan	8	0.05
Other South American	1	0.01
Other Hispanic or Latino	325	1.83

Race*	Population	%
African-American/Black (13,377)	13,765	77.67
Not Hispanic (13,235)	13,570	76.57
Hispanic (142)	195	1.10
American Indian/Alaska Native (75)	262	1.48
Not Hispanic (58)	210	1.18
Hispanic (17)	52	0.29
Blackfeet (2)	12	0.07
Central American Ind. (1)	1	0.01
Cherokee (4)	21	0.12
Chippewa (1)	1	0.01
Choctaw (0)	2	0.01
Delaware (0)	5	0.03
Inupiat *(Alaska Native)* (0)	1	0.01
Iroquois (1)	3	0.02
Seminole (0)	1	0.01
Sioux (1)	2	0.01
South American Ind. (6)	10	0.06
Spanish American Ind. (5)	5	0.03
Asian (1,017)	1,130	6.38
Not Hispanic (1,006)	1,105	6.24
Hispanic (11)	25	0.14
Bangladeshi (7)	7	0.04
Cambodian (10)	10	0.06

*Notes: † The Census 2010 population figure is used to calculate the percentages in the Hispanic Origin and Race categories. Ancestry percentages are based on the 2006-2010 American Community Survey population (not shown); ‡ Numbers in parentheses indicate the number of people reporting a single ancestry; * Numbers in parentheses indicate the number of persons reporting this race alone, not in combination with any other race; Please refer to the Explanation of Data for more information.*

Chinese, ex. Taiwanese (28)	42	0.24
Filipino (854)	912	5.15
Indian (41)	61	0.34
Indonesian (3)	4	0.02
Japanese (4)	10	0.06
Korean (21)	34	0.19
Laotian (3)	5	0.03
Malaysian (1)	1	0.01
Pakistani (5)	8	0.05
Thai (6)	9	0.05
Vietnamese (11)	12	0.07
Hawaii Native/Pacific Islander (6)	27	0.15
Not Hispanic (6)	26	0.15
Hispanic (0)	1	0.01
Guamanian/Chamorro (5)	11	0.06
Native Hawaiian (1)	11	0.06
White (1,493)	1,807	10.20
Not Hispanic (1,073)	1,286	7.26
Hispanic (420)	521	2.94

Parkville

Place Type: CDP
County: Baltimore
Population: 30,734†

Ancestry‡	Population	%
African, Sub-Saharan (1,326)	1,499	4.97
African (818)	975	3.23
Cape Verdean (19)	19	0.06
Kenyan (57)	57	0.19
Nigerian (396)	412	1.37
South African (36)	36	0.12
American (1,537)	1,537	5.10
Arab (0)	80	0.27
Egyptian (0)	17	0.06
Syrian (0)	63	0.21
Austrian (0)	36	0.12
Brazilian (0)	11	0.04
British (72)	145	0.48
Canadian (34)	34	0.11
Czech (49)	163	0.54
Czechoslovakian (29)	63	0.21
Danish (0)	62	0.21
Dutch (42)	387	1.28
Eastern European (20)	20	0.07
English (814)	2,459	8.15
European (407)	407	1.35
Finnish (0)	7	0.02
French, ex. Basque (95)	526	1.74
French Canadian (7)	39	0.13
German (2,018)	7,231	23.98
Greek (51)	109	0.36
Hungarian (0)	150	0.50
Iranian (35)	56	0.19
Irish (1,201)	4,877	16.17
Israeli (0)	15	0.05
Italian (897)	2,764	9.17
Latvian (0)	8	0.03
Lithuanian (97)	174	0.58
Northern European (50)	50	0.17
Norwegian (26)	122	0.40
Pennsylvania German (14)	24	0.08
Polish (731)	1,655	5.49
Romanian (20)	33	0.11
Russian (71)	207	0.69
Scandinavian (11)	25	0.08
Scotch-Irish (134)	389	1.29
Scottish (72)	468	1.55
Slavic (0)	12	0.04
Slovak (9)	31	0.10
Swedish (30)	170	0.56
Swiss (0)	25	0.08
Ukrainian (0)	37	0.12
Welsh (96)	252	0.84
West Indian, ex. Hispanic (124)	187	0.62
Bermudan (0)	17	0.06
Jamaican (84)	130	0.43
Trinidadian/Tobagonian (40)	40	0.13

Hispanic Origin	Population	%
Hispanic or Latino (of any race)	1,158	3.77
Central American, ex. Mexican	349	1.14
Costa Rican	2	0.01
Guatemalan	45	0.15
Honduran	46	0.15
Nicaraguan	3	0.01
Panamanian	31	0.10
Salvadoran	219	0.71
Other Central American	3	0.01
Cuban	51	0.17
Dominican Republic	41	0.13
Mexican	234	0.76
Puerto Rican	192	0.62
South American	135	0.44
Argentinean	11	0.04
Bolivian	8	0.03
Chilean	7	0.02
Colombian	45	0.15
Ecuadorian	17	0.06
Paraguayan	3	0.01
Peruvian	34	0.11
Uruguayan	1	<0.01
Venezuelan	8	0.03
Other South American	1	<0.01
Other Hispanic or Latino	156	0.51

Race*	Population	%
African-American/Black (9,587)	10,068	32.76
Not Hispanic (9,459)	9,865	32.10
Hispanic (128)	203	0.66
American Indian/Alaska Native (74)	308	1.00
Not Hispanic (66)	274	0.89
Hispanic (8)	34	0.11
Apache (1)	3	0.01
Blackfeet (1)	9	0.03
Cherokee (13)	70	0.23
Chippewa (1)	2	0.01
Choctaw (1)	4	0.01
Comanche (0)	1	<0.01
Iroquois (3)	9	0.03
Lumbee (10)	17	0.06
Mexican American Ind. (2)	3	0.01
Navajo (2)	7	0.02
Ottawa (2)	2	0.01
Seminole (0)	2	0.01
Sioux (1)	4	0.01
South American Ind. (1)	2	0.01
Yaqui (1)	1	<0.01
Yuman (0)	1	<0.01
Asian (871)	1,068	3.47
Not Hispanic (865)	1,035	3.37
Hispanic (6)	33	0.11
Bangladeshi (3)	3	0.01
Burmese (10)	10	0.03
Cambodian (8)	8	0.03
Chinese, ex. Taiwanese (178)	205	0.67
Filipino (247)	321	1.04
Indian (139)	181	0.59
Indonesian (1)	2	0.01
Japanese (23)	50	0.16
Korean (56)	76	0.25
Laotian (6)	7	0.02
Malaysian (0)	6	0.02
Nepalese (57)	61	0.20
Pakistani (45)	51	0.17
Sri Lankan (1)	1	<0.01
Taiwanese (1)	1	<0.01
Thai (8)	8	0.03
Vietnamese (34)	43	0.14
Hawaii Native/Pacific Islander (14)	47	0.15
Not Hispanic (12)	44	0.14
Hispanic (2)	3	0.01
Guamanian/Chamorro (2)	7	0.02
Native Hawaiian (0)	11	0.04
White (19,038)	19,667	63.99
Not Hispanic (18,486)	19,009	61.85
Hispanic (552)	658	2.14

Parole

Place Type: CDP
County: Anne Arundel
Population: 15,922†

Ancestry‡	Population	%
Alsatian (0)	14	0.09
American (636)	636	4.27
Arab (67)	86	0.58
Iraqi (9)	9	0.06
Lebanese (58)	77	0.52
Armenian (26)	26	0.17
Australian (20)	33	0.22
Austrian (11)	82	0.55
Belgian (19)	34	0.23
British (93)	123	0.83
Canadian (0)	24	0.16
Czech (62)	102	0.68
Czechoslovakian (36)	60	0.40
Danish (0)	39	0.26
Dutch (42)	204	1.37
Eastern European (118)	118	0.79
English (963)	2,953	19.83
Estonian (48)	48	0.32
European (180)	180	1.21
Finnish (16)	31	0.21
French, ex. Basque (81)	369	2.48
French Canadian (45)	103	0.69
German (921)	3,843	25.80
Greek (128)	215	1.44
Hungarian (17)	140	0.94
Irish (815)	2,727	18.31
Italian (397)	1,058	7.10
Lithuanian (14)	75	0.50
Maltese (0)	49	0.33
Norwegian (61)	159	1.07
Pennsylvania German (0)	16	0.11
Polish (230)	627	4.21
Portuguese (0)	11	0.07
Romanian (0)	13	0.09
Russian (71)	214	1.44
Scotch-Irish (122)	366	2.46
Scottish (108)	476	3.20
Slovak (17)	65	0.44
Slovene (0)	11	0.07
Swedish (77)	296	1.99
Swiss (15)	46	0.31
Ukrainian (32)	49	0.33
Welsh (16)	76	0.51
West Indian, ex. Hispanic (13)	13	0.09
West Indian (13)	13	0.09

Hispanic Origin	Population	%
Hispanic or Latino (of any race)	535	3.36
Central American, ex. Mexican	95	0.60
Costa Rican	1	0.01
Guatemalan	22	0.14
Honduran	5	0.03
Nicaraguan	2	0.01
Panamanian	11	0.07
Salvadoran	54	0.34
Cuban	36	0.23
Dominican Republic	5	0.03
Mexican	128	0.80
Puerto Rican	89	0.56
South American	99	0.62
Argentinean	5	0.03
Bolivian	5	0.03
Chilean	3	0.02
Colombian	36	0.23
Ecuadorian	12	0.08
Peruvian	25	0.16
Venezuelan	13	0.08
Other Hispanic or Latino	83	0.52

Race*	Population	%
African-American/Black (1,056)	1,146	7.20
Not Hispanic (1,047)	1,130	7.10
Hispanic (9)	16	0.10

*Notes: † The Census 2010 population figure is used to calculate the percentages in the Hispanic Origin and Race categories. Ancestry percentages are based on the 2006-2010 American Community Survey population (not shown); ‡ Numbers in parentheses indicate the number of people reporting a single ancestry; * Numbers in parentheses indicate the number of persons reporting this race alone, not in combination with any other race; Please refer to the Explanation of Data for more information.*

American Indian/Alaska Native (32)	104	0.65
Not Hispanic (30)	95	0.60
Hispanic (2)	9	0.06
Apache (0)	1	0.01
Arapaho (1)	1	0.01
Cherokee (4)	31	0.19
Chickasaw (1)	3	0.02
Chippewa (0)	1	0.01
Choctaw (0)	2	0.01
Creek (0)	1	0.01
Crow (1)	1	0.01
Delaware (0)	1	0.01
Lumbee (1)	1	0.01
Mexican American Ind. (1)	3	0.02
Potawatomi (1)	5	0.03
Pueblo (0)	2	0.01
Sioux (1)	1	0.01
South American Ind. (1)	1	0.01
Asian (427)	510	3.20
Not Hispanic (425)	498	3.13
Hispanic (2)	12	0.08
Bangladeshi (9)	13	0.08
Cambodian (7)	7	0.04
Chinese, ex. Taiwanese (72)	91	0.57
Filipino (67)	96	0.60
Indian (127)	134	0.84
Indonesian (5)	5	0.03
Japanese (11)	18	0.11
Korean (50)	65	0.41
Nepalese (1)	1	0.01
Pakistani (10)	12	0.08
Sri Lankan (1)	1	0.01
Taiwanese (3)	5	0.03
Thai (9)	14	0.09
Vietnamese (36)	41	0.26
Hawaii Native/Pacific Islander (4)	11	0.07
Not Hispanic (4)	11	0.07
Native Hawaiian (4)	7	0.04
White (14,016)	14,223	89.33
Not Hispanic (13,658)	13,836	86.90
Hispanic (358)	387	2.43

Pasadena

Place Type: CDP
County: Anne Arundel
Population: 24,287†

Ancestry‡	Population	%
African, Sub-Saharan (51)	51	0.23
African (51)	51	0.23
American (1,054)	1,054	4.75
Arab (0)	35	0.16
Lebanese (0)	35	0.16
Armenian (0)	16	0.07
Austrian (29)	101	0.46
British (29)	81	0.37
Canadian (0)	21	0.09
Czech (15)	279	1.26
Czechoslovakian (0)	22	0.10
Dutch (60)	340	1.53
English (681)	2,688	12.11
European (214)	224	1.01
Finnish (0)	23	0.10
French, ex. Basque (185)	1,268	5.71
French Canadian (40)	197	0.89
German (1,879)	7,175	32.34
Greek (55)	185	0.83
Guyanese (0)	10	0.05
Hungarian (10)	62	0.28
Icelander (0)	11	0.05
Irish (1,323)	5,128	23.11
Italian (605)	1,908	8.60
Lithuanian (107)	131	0.59
Norwegian (13)	49	0.22
Pennsylvania German (0)	12	0.05
Polish (392)	1,257	5.66
Portuguese (0)	59	0.27
Romanian (0)	37	0.17
Russian (0)	49	0.22
Scotch-Irish (94)	416	1.87
Scottish (174)	628	2.83
Serbian (26)	26	0.12
Slavic (0)	25	0.11
Slovak (0)	65	0.29
Swedish (61)	191	0.86
Swiss (0)	40	0.18
Ukrainian (129)	249	1.12
Welsh (41)	239	1.08
West Indian, ex. Hispanic (0)	10	0.05
West Indian (0)	10	0.05
Yugoslavian (15)	44	0.20

Hispanic Origin	Population	%
Hispanic or Latino (of any race)	1,055	4.34
Central American, ex. Mexican	238	0.98
Costa Rican	5	0.02
Guatemalan	53	0.22
Honduran	29	0.12
Panamanian	19	0.08
Salvadoran	132	0.54
Cuban	22	0.09
Dominican Republic	19	0.08
Mexican	366	1.51
Puerto Rican	215	0.89
South American	91	0.37
Argentinean	10	0.04
Bolivian	8	0.03
Chilean	11	0.05
Colombian	12	0.05
Ecuadorian	14	0.06
Peruvian	19	0.08
Uruguayan	11	0.05
Venezuelan	5	0.02
Other South American	1	<0.01
Other Hispanic or Latino	104	0.43

Race*	Population	%
African-American/Black (1,677)	1,902	7.83
Not Hispanic (1,644)	1,851	7.62
Hispanic (33)	51	0.21
American Indian/Alaska Native (81)	234	0.96
Not Hispanic (65)	203	0.84
Hispanic (16)	31	0.13
Alaska Athabascan *(Ala. Nat.)* (3)	3	0.01
Aleut *(Alaska Native)* (1)	2	0.01
Arapaho (0)	1	<0.01
Blackfeet (0)	13	0.05
Cherokee (13)	74	0.30
Chickasaw (0)	2	0.01
Chippewa (0)	2	0.01
Choctaw (1)	3	0.01
Creek (1)	2	0.01
Delaware (1)	1	<0.01
Lumbee (12)	19	0.08
Osage (0)	1	<0.01
Sioux (3)	4	0.02
South American Ind. (0)	1	<0.01
Asian (628)	805	3.31
Not Hispanic (611)	769	3.17
Hispanic (17)	36	0.15
Burmese (1)	1	<0.01
Cambodian (1)	3	0.01
Chinese, ex. Taiwanese (152)	172	0.71
Filipino (157)	233	0.96
Indian (75)	95	0.39
Japanese (14)	43	0.18
Korean (119)	140	0.58
Laotian (2)	4	0.02
Nepalese (6)	6	0.02
Pakistani (33)	36	0.15
Taiwanese (5)	7	0.03
Thai (12)	14	0.06
Vietnamese (36)	44	0.18
Hawaii Native/Pacific Islander (23)	37	0.15
Not Hispanic (23)	36	0.15
Hispanic (0)	1	<0.01
Fijian (1)	1	<0.01
Guamanian/Chamorro (20)	26	0.11
Native Hawaiian (1)	6	0.02
Samoan (1)	4	0.02
White (20,935)	21,442	88.29
Not Hispanic (20,380)	20,823	85.74
Hispanic (555)	619	2.55

Perry Hall

Place Type: CDP
County: Baltimore
Population: 28,474†

Ancestry‡	Population	%
African, Sub-Saharan (254)	267	0.94
African (181)	181	0.64
Nigerian (73)	73	0.26
South African (0)	13	0.05
American (1,252)	1,252	4.41
Arab (265)	275	0.97
Egyptian (224)	224	0.79
Lebanese (0)	10	0.04
Palestinian (41)	41	0.14
Australian (0)	11	0.04
Austrian (21)	36	0.13
Brazilian (29)	29	0.10
British (23)	111	0.39
Cajun (0)	13	0.05
Canadian (63)	205	0.72
Czech (32)	329	1.16
Czechoslovakian (21)	49	0.17
Danish (0)	45	0.16
Dutch (41)	248	0.87
Eastern European (23)	23	0.08
English (740)	2,609	9.20
European (127)	155	0.55
Finnish (0)	56	0.20
French, ex. Basque (139)	515	1.82
French Canadian (11)	62	0.22
German (2,654)	8,037	28.33
Greek (190)	339	1.20
Hungarian (33)	173	0.61
Iranian (178)	178	0.63
Irish (1,484)	6,250	22.03
Italian (1,324)	3,689	13.00
Lithuanian (19)	61	0.22
Northern European (58)	58	0.20
Norwegian (65)	222	0.78
Pennsylvania German (13)	24	0.08
Polish (1,114)	3,110	10.96
Portuguese (11)	75	0.26
Russian (12)	296	1.04
Scandinavian (0)	12	0.04
Scotch-Irish (180)	355	1.25
Scottish (73)	412	1.45
Slavic (0)	25	0.09
Slovak (14)	123	0.43
Swedish (56)	261	0.92
Swiss (8)	20	0.07
Turkish (11)	69	0.24
Ukrainian (80)	149	0.53
Welsh (46)	241	0.85
West Indian, ex. Hispanic (171)	184	0.65
Dutch West Indian (21)	21	0.07
Jamaican (98)	98	0.35
U.S. Virgin Islander (16)	16	0.06
West Indian (36)	49	0.17
Yugoslavian (10)	10	0.04

Hispanic Origin	Population	%
Hispanic or Latino (of any race)	755	2.65
Central American, ex. Mexican	127	0.45
Costa Rican	7	0.02
Guatemalan	30	0.11
Honduran	11	0.04
Panamanian	16	0.06
Salvadoran	62	0.22
Other Central American	1	<0.01
Cuban	48	0.17
Dominican Republic	34	0.12
Mexican	134	0.47
Puerto Rican	192	0.67

*Notes: † The Census 2010 population figure is used to calculate the percentages in the Hispanic Origin and Race categories. Ancestry percentages are based on the 2006-2010 American Community Survey population (not shown); ‡ Numbers in parentheses indicate the number of people reporting a single ancestry; * Numbers in parentheses indicate the number of persons reporting this race alone, not in combination with any other race; Please refer to the Explanation of Data for more information.*

South American	127	0.45
Argentinean	18	0.06
Bolivian	3	0.01
Chilean	7	0.02
Colombian	38	0.13
Ecuadorian	6	0.02
Peruvian	38	0.13
Uruguayan	3	0.01
Venezuelan	14	0.05
Other Hispanic or Latino	93	0.33

Race*	Population	%
African-American/Black (2,731)	2,972	10.44
Not Hispanic (2,683)	2,890	10.15
Hispanic (48)	82	0.29
American Indian/Alaska Native (45)	152	0.53
Not Hispanic (40)	132	0.46
Hispanic (5)	20	0.07
Apache (0)	2	0.01
Blackfeet (1)	6	0.02
Cherokee (11)	48	0.17
Cheyenne (2)	2	0.01
Delaware (1)	1	<0.01
Iroquois (0)	4	0.01
Lumbee (0)	2	0.01
Mexican American Ind. (1)	1	<0.01
Navajo (1)	1	<0.01
Pueblo (2)	2	0.01
Seminole (0)	4	0.01
Sioux (0)	1	<0.01
South American Ind. (0)	6	0.02
Asian (2,327)	2,600	9.13
Not Hispanic (2,318)	2,578	9.05
Hispanic (9)	22	0.08
Bangladeshi (3)	3	0.01
Burmese (0)	1	<0.01
Cambodian (6)	6	0.02
Chinese, ex. Taiwanese (466)	508	1.78
Filipino (700)	781	2.74
Indian (429)	471	1.65
Indonesian (14)	16	0.06
Japanese (10)	38	0.13
Korean (393)	433	1.52
Laotian (7)	11	0.04
Nepalese (48)	55	0.19
Pakistani (93)	96	0.34
Taiwanese (7)	14	0.05
Thai (10)	18	0.06
Vietnamese (90)	101	0.35
Hawaii Native/Pacific Islander (7)	35	0.12
Not Hispanic (2)	27	0.09
Hispanic (5)	8	0.03
Guamanian/Chamorro (4)	5	0.02
Native Hawaiian (1)	5	0.02
Samoan (1)	1	<0.01
White (22,590)	23,104	81.14
Not Hispanic (22,127)	22,566	79.25
Hispanic (463)	538	1.89

Pikesville

Place Type: CDP
County: Baltimore
Population: 30,764†

Ancestry‡	Population	%
African, Sub-Saharan (162)	261	0.85
African (98)	161	0.52
Ethiopian (15)	15	0.05
Nigerian (34)	70	0.23
South African (15)	15	0.05
American (2,335)	2,335	7.60
Arab (126)	253	0.82
Arab (11)	11	0.04
Egyptian (0)	44	0.14
Iraqi (0)	8	0.03
Lebanese (29)	29	0.09
Moroccan (11)	11	0.04
Syrian (13)	28	0.09
Other Arab (62)	122	0.40
Austrian (36)	192	0.63
Belgian (21)	49	0.16
Brazilian (26)	26	0.08
British (23)	116	0.38
Bulgarian (29)	29	0.09
Canadian (8)	8	0.03
Celtic (0)	7	0.02
Czech (20)	65	0.21
Czechoslovakian (30)	45	0.15
Danish (10)	10	0.03
Dutch (79)	100	0.33
Eastern European (1,009)	1,085	3.53
English (438)	1,293	4.21
Estonian (11)	11	0.04
European (777)	802	2.61
French, ex. Basque (19)	117	0.38
French Canadian (7)	17	0.06
German (958)	2,453	7.99
Greek (28)	86	0.28
Hungarian (186)	524	1.71
Iranian (181)	195	0.63
Irish (423)	1,039	3.38
Israeli (239)	300	0.98
Italian (175)	450	1.46
Latvian (58)	121	0.39
Lithuanian (267)	541	1.76
Norwegian (16)	123	0.40
Polish (982)	2,369	7.71
Romanian (29)	156	0.51
Russian (3,376)	5,008	16.30
Scotch-Irish (60)	149	0.49
Scottish (11)	308	1.00
Slovak (10)	10	0.03
Swedish (15)	124	0.40
Swiss (0)	16	0.05
Ukrainian (663)	834	2.71
Welsh (22)	142	0.46
West Indian, ex. Hispanic (282)	330	1.07
Haitian (25)	49	0.16
Jamaican (139)	139	0.45
Trinidadian/Tobagonian (105)	129	0.42
West Indian (13)	13	0.04
Yugoslavian (26)	26	0.08

Hispanic Origin	Population	%
Hispanic or Latino (of any race)	832	2.70
Central American, ex. Mexican	267	0.87
Costa Rican	2	0.01
Guatemalan	90	0.29
Honduran	31	0.10
Nicaraguan	12	0.04
Panamanian	18	0.06
Salvadoran	112	0.36
Other Central American	2	0.01
Cuban	31	0.10
Dominican Republic	19	0.06
Mexican	173	0.56
Puerto Rican	72	0.23
South American	199	0.65
Argentinean	59	0.19
Bolivian	7	0.02
Chilean	15	0.05
Colombian	37	0.12
Ecuadorian	18	0.06
Peruvian	48	0.16
Uruguayan	6	0.02
Venezuelan	7	0.02
Other South American	2	0.01
Other Hispanic or Latino	71	0.23

Race*	Population	%
African-American/Black (4,452)	4,643	15.09
Not Hispanic (4,409)	4,572	14.86
Hispanic (43)	71	0.23
American Indian/Alaska Native (18)	103	0.33
Not Hispanic (10)	78	0.25
Hispanic (8)	25	0.08
Blackfeet (0)	8	0.03
Central American Ind. (0)	1	<0.01
Cherokee (2)	19	0.06
Chippewa (0)	1	<0.01
Choctaw (0)	2	0.01
Iroquois (1)	2	0.01
Lumbee (4)	4	0.01
Mexican American Ind. (0)	2	0.01
Navajo (0)	4	0.01
Seminole (0)	2	0.01
South American Ind. (0)	1	<0.01
Tlingit-Haida *(Alaska Native)* (1)	2	0.01
Asian (1,850)	2,089	6.79
Not Hispanic (1,845)	2,072	6.74
Hispanic (5)	17	0.06
Bangladeshi (7)	13	0.04
Burmese (9)	9	0.03
Chinese, ex. Taiwanese (182)	200	0.65
Filipino (723)	762	2.48
Hmong (1)	1	<0.01
Indian (356)	411	1.34
Indonesian (1)	1	<0.01
Japanese (143)	159	0.52
Korean (231)	248	0.81
Laotian (2)	5	0.02
Malaysian (1)	1	<0.01
Nepalese (11)	11	0.04
Pakistani (42)	46	0.15
Taiwanese (24)	27	0.09
Thai (17)	25	0.08
Vietnamese (30)	37	0.12
Hawaii Native/Pacific Islander (17)	38	0.12
Not Hispanic (14)	33	0.11
Hispanic (3)	5	0.02
Guamanian/Chamorro (4)	4	0.01
Native Hawaiian (2)	3	0.01
Samoan (2)	4	0.01
Tongan (1)	5	0.02
White (23,681)	24,079	78.27
Not Hispanic (23,179)	23,505	76.40
Hispanic (502)	574	1.87

Potomac

Place Type: CDP
County: Montgomery
Population: 44,965†

Ancestry‡	Population	%
African, Sub-Saharan (860)	1,010	2.26
African (355)	367	0.82
Cape Verdean (18)	35	0.08
Ethiopian (208)	208	0.46
Nigerian (37)	37	0.08
South African (34)	34	0.08
Other Sub-Saharan African (208)	329	0.73
Albanian (30)	30	0.07
Alsatian (0)	4	0.01
American (2,048)	2,048	4.57
Arab (448)	584	1.30
Arab (10)	10	0.02
Egyptian (22)	30	0.07
Iraqi (15)	15	0.03
Lebanese (223)	284	0.63
Moroccan (135)	202	0.45
Syrian (6)	6	0.01
Other Arab (37)	37	0.08
Armenian (97)	178	0.40
Australian (17)	17	0.04
Austrian (183)	569	1.27
Basque (12)	74	0.17
Belgian (153)	186	0.42
Brazilian (204)	287	0.64
British (163)	401	0.90
Canadian (143)	176	0.39
Croatian (10)	45	0.10
Czech (107)	299	0.67
Czechoslovakian (0)	9	0.02
Danish (29)	87	0.19
Dutch (127)	663	1.48
Eastern European (1,381)	1,483	3.31
English (945)	3,331	7.44
European (835)	1,000	2.23

*Notes: † The Census 2010 population figure is used to calculate the percentages in the Hispanic Origin and Race categories. Ancestry percentages are based on the 2006-2010 American Community Survey population (not shown); ‡ Numbers in parentheses indicate the number of people reporting a single ancestry; * Numbers in parentheses indicate the number of persons reporting this race alone, not in combination with any other race; Please refer to the Explanation of Data for more information.*

Finnish (17)	17	0.04
French, ex. Basque (346)	1,133	2.53
French Canadian (99)	229	0.51
German (1,395)	4,987	11.14
Greek (509)	555	1.24
Guyanese (11)	11	0.02
Hungarian (260)	641	1.43
Iranian (1,287)	1,336	2.98
Irish (1,137)	4,469	9.98
Israeli (348)	367	0.82
Italian (770)	2,417	5.40
Latvian (27)	72	0.16
Lithuanian (49)	228	0.51
Macedonian (0)	8	0.02
Northern European (96)	96	0.21
Norwegian (77)	292	0.65
Polish (729)	2,116	4.72
Portuguese (104)	198	0.44
Romanian (165)	388	0.87
Russian (1,952)	3,628	8.10
Scandinavian (20)	29	0.06
Scotch-Irish (194)	515	1.15
Scottish (120)	735	1.64
Serbian (0)	20	0.04
Slavic (18)	36	0.08
Slovak (71)	102	0.23
Slovene (91)	91	0.20
Swedish (98)	296	0.66
Swiss (63)	182	0.41
Turkish (41)	391	0.87
Ukrainian (238)	380	0.85
Welsh (47)	203	0.45
West Indian, ex. Hispanic (61)	112	0.25
Haitian (10)	31	0.07
Jamaican (51)	51	0.11
West Indian (0)	30	0.07
Yugoslavian (13)	47	0.10

Hispanic Origin	Population	%
Hispanic or Latino (of any race)	2,857	6.35
Central American, ex. Mexican	358	0.80
Costa Rican	20	0.04
Guatemalan	41	0.09
Honduran	58	0.13
Nicaraguan	53	0.12
Panamanian	26	0.06
Salvadoran	157	0.35
Other Central American	3	0.01
Cuban	175	0.39
Dominican Republic	70	0.16
Mexican	260	0.58
Puerto Rican	183	0.41
South American	1,482	3.30
Argentinean	321	0.71
Bolivian	95	0.21
Chilean	150	0.33
Colombian	300	0.67
Ecuadorian	104	0.23
Paraguayan	24	0.05
Peruvian	339	0.75
Uruguayan	59	0.13
Venezuelan	82	0.18
Other South American	8	0.02
Other Hispanic or Latino	329	0.73

Race*	Population	%
African-American/Black (2,076)	2,312	5.14
Not Hispanic (2,021)	2,225	4.95
Hispanic (55)	87	0.19
American Indian/Alaska Native (40)	141	0.31
Not Hispanic (20)	89	0.20
Hispanic (20)	52	0.12
Blackfeet (0)	1	<0.01
Central American Ind. (3)	8	0.02
Cherokee (2)	13	0.03
Chickasaw (0)	3	0.01
Chippewa (3)	3	0.01
Choctaw (0)	7	0.02
Delaware (0)	1	<0.01
Iroquois (1)	4	0.01
Kiowa (1)	1	<0.01
Lumbee (0)	4	0.01
Mexican American Ind. (0)	2	<0.01
Navajo (4)	4	0.01
Sioux (0)	1	<0.01
South American Ind. (10)	13	0.03
Asian (7,169)	7,958	17.70
Not Hispanic (7,159)	7,901	17.57
Hispanic (10)	57	0.13
Bangladeshi (43)	43	0.10
Burmese (20)	27	0.06
Cambodian (12)	19	0.04
Chinese, ex. Taiwanese (2,707)	2,972	6.61
Filipino (293)	351	0.78
Indian (1,556)	1,694	3.77
Indonesian (38)	47	0.10
Japanese (228)	297	0.66
Korean (1,247)	1,323	2.94
Laotian (1)	2	<0.01
Malaysian (2)	7	0.02
Nepalese (20)	20	0.04
Pakistani (184)	209	0.46
Sri Lankan (66)	80	0.18
Taiwanese (309)	354	0.79
Thai (70)	92	0.20
Vietnamese (184)	219	0.49
Hawaii Native/Pacific Islander (16)	50	0.11
Not Hispanic (16)	50	0.11
Fijian (1)	1	<0.01
Guamanian/Chamorro (3)	7	0.02
Native Hawaiian (5)	16	0.04
Samoan (1)	1	<0.01
Tongan (1)	1	<0.01
White (34,080)	35,108	78.08
Not Hispanic (31,770)	32,656	72.63
Hispanic (2,310)	2,452	5.45

Randallstown

Place Type: CDP
County: Baltimore
Population: 32,430†

Ancestry‡	Population	%
African, Sub-Saharan (1,374)	1,659	5.09
African (714)	977	3.00
Ethiopian (22)	22	0.07
Liberian (22)	22	0.07
Nigerian (490)	512	1.57
Other Sub-Saharan African (126)	126	0.39
American (624)	624	1.92
Arab (105)	105	0.32
Jordanian (95)	95	0.29
Moroccan (10)	10	0.03
Austrian (58)	66	0.20
Belgian (0)	7	0.02
British (0)	21	0.06
Canadian (28)	28	0.09
Czech (0)	14	0.04
Dutch (0)	71	0.22
Eastern European (86)	93	0.29
English (94)	595	1.83
European (45)	45	0.14
French, ex. Basque (0)	101	0.31
German (387)	1,452	4.46
Greek (0)	7	0.02
Guyanese (13)	39	0.12
Hungarian (12)	31	0.10
Irish (159)	925	2.84
Italian (111)	424	1.30
Latvian (10)	10	0.03
Lithuanian (25)	60	0.18
Norwegian (0)	11	0.03
Pennsylvania German (0)	10	0.03
Polish (148)	431	1.32
Romanian (0)	22	0.07
Russian (205)	414	1.27
Scotch-Irish (36)	80	0.25
Scottish (27)	152	0.47
Slovak (24)	24	0.07
Swedish (5)	48	0.15
Swiss (0)	19	0.06
Ukrainian (84)	98	0.30
Welsh (0)	77	0.24
West Indian, ex. Hispanic (872)	983	3.02
Barbadian (17)	17	0.05
Haitian (37)	49	0.15
Jamaican (609)	639	1.96
Trinidadian/Tobagonian (148)	148	0.45
West Indian (61)	130	0.40

Hispanic Origin	Population	%
Hispanic or Latino (of any race)	877	2.70
Central American, ex. Mexican	249	0.77
Costa Rican	2	0.01
Guatemalan	54	0.17
Honduran	53	0.16
Nicaraguan	2	0.01
Panamanian	55	0.17
Salvadoran	71	0.22
Other Central American	12	0.04
Cuban	46	0.14
Dominican Republic	36	0.11
Mexican	177	0.55
Puerto Rican	197	0.61
South American	81	0.25
Argentinean	6	0.02
Bolivian	4	0.01
Chilean	4	0.01
Colombian	17	0.05
Ecuadorian	9	0.03
Paraguayan	3	0.01
Peruvian	29	0.09
Uruguayan	4	0.01
Venezuelan	4	0.01
Other South American	1	<0.01
Other Hispanic or Latino	91	0.28

Race*	Population	%
African-American/Black (26,168)	26,807	82.66
Not Hispanic (25,943)	26,491	81.69
Hispanic (225)	316	0.97
American Indian/Alaska Native (68)	338	1.04
Not Hispanic (65)	301	0.93
Hispanic (3)	37	0.11
Apache (0)	1	<0.01
Arapaho (0)	1	<0.01
Blackfeet (2)	15	0.05
Cherokee (4)	81	0.25
Chickasaw (0)	1	<0.01
Chippewa (1)	1	<0.01
Choctaw (1)	4	0.01
Creek (0)	1	<0.01
Delaware (0)	3	0.01
Iroquois (3)	4	0.01
Lumbee (1)	5	0.02
Mexican American Ind. (1)	5	0.02
Navajo (0)	2	0.01
Sioux (0)	5	0.02
South American Ind. (0)	5	0.02
Asian (655)	812	2.50
Not Hispanic (651)	796	2.45
Hispanic (4)	16	0.05
Bangladeshi (0)	2	0.01
Burmese (5)	5	0.02
Cambodian (1)	1	<0.01
Chinese, ex. Taiwanese (86)	101	0.31
Filipino (90)	129	0.40
Hmong (0)	3	0.01
Indian (243)	298	0.92
Japanese (7)	17	0.05
Korean (48)	61	0.19
Pakistani (51)	58	0.18
Sri Lankan (3)	3	0.01
Taiwanese (8)	8	0.02
Thai (14)	15	0.05
Vietnamese (82)	89	0.27
Hawaii Native/Pacific Islander (15)	49	0.15
Not Hispanic (12)	43	0.13
Hispanic (3)	6	0.02

*Notes: † The Census 2010 population figure is used to calculate the percentages in the Hispanic Origin and Race categories. Ancestry percentages are based on the 2006-2010 American Community Survey population (not shown); ‡ Numbers in parentheses indicate the number of people reporting a single ancestry; * Numbers in parentheses indicate the number of persons reporting this race alone, not in combination with any other race; Please refer to the Explanation of Data for more information.*

Guamanian/Chamorro (0)	1	<0.01
Native Hawaiian (2)	11	0.03
Samoan (8)	9	0.03
White (4,389)	4,849	14.95
Not Hispanic (4,160)	4,552	14.04
Hispanic (229)	297	0.92

Redland

Place Type: CDP
County: Montgomery
Population: 17,242†

Ancestry‡	Population	%
African, Sub-Saharan (594)	662	3.91
African (343)	411	2.43
Ghanaian (136)	136	0.80
Kenyan (24)	24	0.14
Liberian (10)	10	0.06
Nigerian (51)	51	0.30
Sierra Leonean (5)	5	0.03
Other Sub-Saharan African (25)	25	0.15
American (442)	442	2.61
Arab (127)	167	0.99
Arab (50)	50	0.30
Egyptian (9)	9	0.05
Lebanese (25)	38	0.22
Palestinian (20)	20	0.12
Syrian (23)	37	0.22
Other Arab (0)	13	0.08
Assyrian/Chaldean/Syriac (0)	13	0.08
Austrian (0)	27	0.16
Brazilian (38)	48	0.28
British (65)	134	0.79
Bulgarian (31)	31	0.18
Canadian (11)	11	0.06
Croatian (0)	9	0.05
Czech (0)	18	0.11
Danish (11)	33	0.19
Dutch (10)	57	0.34
English (210)	1,145	6.76
European (261)	290	1.71
French, ex. Basque (27)	222	1.31
French Canadian (8)	49	0.29
German (402)	1,698	10.02
Greek (33)	127	0.75
Guyanese (18)	56	0.33
Hungarian (63)	75	0.44
Iranian (102)	109	0.64
Irish (314)	1,317	7.78
Israeli (43)	43	0.25
Italian (248)	763	4.50
Lithuanian (0)	47	0.28
New Zealander (0)	13	0.08
Northern European (19)	37	0.22
Norwegian (0)	82	0.48
Polish (240)	497	2.93
Portuguese (43)	51	0.30
Russian (129)	266	1.57
Scandinavian (15)	21	0.12
Scotch-Irish (80)	184	1.09
Scottish (79)	383	2.26
Serbian (0)	15	0.09
Slavic (9)	9	0.05
Slovak (23)	32	0.19
Slovene (11)	11	0.06
Swedish (35)	183	1.08
Swiss (19)	89	0.53
Turkish (11)	24	0.14
Ukrainian (87)	108	0.64
Welsh (10)	138	0.81
West Indian, ex. Hispanic (33)	92	0.54
Haitian (0)	9	0.05
Jamaican (18)	40	0.24
West Indian (15)	43	0.25
Yugoslavian (0)	33	0.19

Hispanic Origin	Population	%
Hispanic or Latino (of any race)	4,375	25.37
Central American, ex. Mexican	2,371	13.75
Costa Rican	20	0.12
Guatemalan	260	1.51
Honduran	235	1.36
Nicaraguan	80	0.46
Panamanian	19	0.11
Salvadoran	1,749	10.14
Other Central American	8	0.05
Cuban	57	0.33
Dominican Republic	169	0.98
Mexican	326	1.89
Puerto Rican	171	0.99
South American	848	4.92
Argentinean	54	0.31
Bolivian	149	0.86
Chilean	21	0.12
Colombian	116	0.67
Ecuadorian	95	0.55
Paraguayan	22	0.13
Peruvian	334	1.94
Uruguayan	12	0.07
Venezuelan	36	0.21
Other South American	9	0.05
Other Hispanic or Latino	433	2.51

Race*	Population	%
African-American/Black (2,652)	2,899	16.81
Not Hispanic (2,524)	2,709	15.71
Hispanic (128)	190	1.10
American Indian/Alaska Native (62)	144	0.84
Not Hispanic (31)	91	0.53
Hispanic (31)	53	0.31
Blackfeet (3)	7	0.04
Cherokee (3)	15	0.09
Chippewa (1)	4	0.02
Inupiat *(Alaska Native)* (2)	2	0.01
Iroquois (0)	2	0.01
Lumbee (1)	2	0.01
Mexican American Ind. (5)	11	0.06
Navajo (2)	6	0.03
Paiute (0)	1	0.01
Pueblo (2)	6	0.03
Sioux (1)	3	0.02
South American Ind. (7)	9	0.05
Spanish American Ind. (0)	1	0.01
Yaqui (1)	2	0.01
Asian (2,904)	3,226	18.71
Not Hispanic (2,881)	3,174	18.41
Hispanic (23)	52	0.30
Bangladeshi (45)	45	0.26
Burmese (48)	50	0.29
Cambodian (68)	69	0.40
Chinese, ex. Taiwanese (761)	829	4.81
Filipino (381)	436	2.53
Hmong (3)	3	0.02
Indian (570)	640	3.71
Indonesian (18)	25	0.14
Japanese (40)	77	0.45
Korean (298)	328	1.90
Laotian (6)	15	0.09
Malaysian (7)	7	0.04
Nepalese (30)	30	0.17
Pakistani (104)	110	0.64
Sri Lankan (79)	87	0.50
Taiwanese (54)	59	0.34
Thai (40)	56	0.32
Vietnamese (281)	303	1.76
Hawaii Native/Pacific Islander (14)	79	0.46
Not Hispanic (12)	53	0.31
Hispanic (2)	26	0.15
Guamanian/Chamorro (0)	3	0.02
Native Hawaiian (2)	27	0.16
Samoan (0)	8	0.05
Tongan (2)	2	0.01
White (9,029)	9,624	55.82
Not Hispanic (6,866)	7,244	42.01
Hispanic (2,163)	2,380	13.80

Reisterstown

Place Type: CDP
County: Baltimore
Population: 25,968†

Ancestry‡	Population	%
African, Sub-Saharan (77)	97	0.36
African (77)	97	0.36
American (994)	994	3.69
Arab (114)	218	0.81
Lebanese (34)	61	0.23
Moroccan (0)	77	0.29
Other Arab (80)	80	0.30
Armenian (7)	7	0.03
Austrian (25)	67	0.25
Brazilian (12)	12	0.04
British (0)	30	0.11
Canadian (0)	24	0.09
Celtic (10)	10	0.04
Croatian (24)	73	0.27
Cypriot (0)	13	0.05
Czech (17)	77	0.29
Czechoslovakian (26)	26	0.10
Danish (14)	44	0.16
Dutch (89)	259	0.96
Eastern European (86)	86	0.32
English (338)	1,613	5.99
European (299)	323	1.20
Finnish (0)	17	0.06
French, ex. Basque (42)	539	2.00
French Canadian (15)	67	0.25
German (1,241)	3,854	14.30
Greek (19)	19	0.07
Guyanese (25)	25	0.09
Hungarian (31)	102	0.38
Iranian (66)	66	0.24
Irish (720)	2,542	9.43
Israeli (12)	52	0.19
Italian (482)	1,190	4.42
Latvian (0)	24	0.09
Lithuanian (62)	155	0.58
New Zealander (27)	27	0.10
Northern European (46)	46	0.17
Norwegian (16)	55	0.20
Pennsylvania German (0)	26	0.10
Polish (342)	953	3.54
Romanian (10)	26	0.10
Russian (730)	1,185	4.40
Scandinavian (0)	15	0.06
Scotch-Irish (95)	323	1.20
Scottish (64)	292	1.08
Slavic (0)	8	0.03
Slovak (44)	82	0.30
Slovene (17)	17	0.06
Swedish (22)	117	0.43
Swiss (0)	65	0.24
Turkish (0)	13	0.05
Ukrainian (738)	803	2.98
Welsh (7)	69	0.26
West Indian, ex. Hispanic (244)	279	1.04
Jamaican (244)	279	1.04
Yugoslavian (0)	13	0.05

Hispanic Origin	Population	%
Hispanic or Latino (of any race)	2,322	8.94
Central American, ex. Mexican	1,063	4.09
Costa Rican	12	0.05
Guatemalan	309	1.19
Honduran	263	1.01
Nicaraguan	39	0.15
Panamanian	27	0.10
Salvadoran	406	1.56
Other Central American	7	0.03
Cuban	58	0.22
Dominican Republic	53	0.20
Mexican	397	1.53
Puerto Rican	160	0.62
South American	309	1.19
Argentinean	31	0.12

SECTION TWO

*Notes: † The Census 2010 population figure is used to calculate the percentages in the Hispanic Origin and Race categories. Ancestry percentages are based on the 2006-2010 American Community Survey population (not shown); ‡ Numbers in parentheses indicate the number of people reporting a single ancestry; * Numbers in parentheses indicate the number of persons reporting this race alone, not in combination with any other race; Please refer to the Explanation of Data for more information.*

Bolivian	3	0.01
Chilean	28	0.11
Colombian	83	0.32
Ecuadorian	9	0.03
Paraguayan	1	<0.01
Peruvian	142	0.55
Uruguayan	4	0.02
Venezuelan	8	0.03
Other Hispanic or Latino	282	1.09

Race*	Population	%
African-American/Black (7,609)	8,170	31.46
Not Hispanic (7,455)	7,970	30.69
Hispanic (154)	200	0.77
American Indian/Alaska Native (94)	289	1.11
Not Hispanic (46)	209	0.80
Hispanic (48)	80	0.31
Apache (1)	8	0.03
Blackfeet (1)	17	0.07
Central American Ind. (1)	3	0.01
Cherokee (11)	61	0.23
Choctaw (0)	5	0.02
Iroquois (2)	8	0.03
Lumbee (2)	6	0.02
Mexican American Ind. (0)	1	<0.01
Navajo (0)	2	0.01
Shoshone (0)	1	<0.01
Sioux (0)	4	0.02
South American Ind. (3)	8	0.03
Spanish American Ind. (0)	1	<0.01
Tohono O'Odham (1)	1	<0.01
Asian (1,627)	1,815	6.99
Not Hispanic (1,623)	1,799	6.93
Hispanic (4)	16	0.06
Bangladeshi (13)	22	0.08
Burmese (2)	2	0.01
Cambodian (9)	9	0.03
Chinese, ex. Taiwanese (220)	236	0.91
Filipino (267)	310	1.19
Indian (496)	542	2.09
Indonesian (3)	6	0.02
Japanese (8)	24	0.09
Korean (63)	84	0.32
Laotian (2)	2	0.01
Nepalese (24)	25	0.10
Pakistani (281)	302	1.16
Taiwanese (2)	2	0.01
Thai (21)	23	0.09
Vietnamese (150)	161	0.62
Hawaii Native/Pacific Islander (19)	38	0.15
Not Hispanic (16)	31	0.12
Hispanic (3)	7	0.03
Fijian (1)	1	<0.01
Guamanian/Chamorro (12)	12	0.05
Native Hawaiian (3)	4	0.02
Samoan (0)	3	0.01
White (14,842)	15,459	59.53
Not Hispanic (13,771)	14,281	54.99
Hispanic (1,071)	1,178	4.54

Riviera Beach

Place Type: CDP
County: Anne Arundel
Population: 12,677[†]

Ancestry[‡]	Population	%
African, Sub-Saharan (36)	36	0.30
African (15)	15	0.13
Sierra Leonean (21)	21	0.18
American (841)	841	7.12
Arab (0)	12	0.10
Syrian (0)	12	0.10
Armenian (0)	34	0.29
Austrian (0)	13	0.11
British (12)	33	0.28
Canadian (0)	12	0.10
Croatian (28)	41	0.35
Czech (66)	150	1.27
Danish (10)	10	0.08
Dutch (12)	149	1.26
English (399)	1,828	15.47
European (97)	97	0.82
French, ex. Basque (22)	436	3.69
French Canadian (14)	75	0.63
German (850)	3,452	29.22
Hungarian (11)	68	0.58
Irish (849)	2,934	24.84
Italian (564)	1,180	9.99
Lithuanian (12)	121	1.02
Norwegian (0)	103	0.87
Pennsylvania German (0)	14	0.12
Polish (396)	899	7.61
Romanian (0)	44	0.37
Russian (0)	143	1.21
Scandinavian (11)	11	0.09
Scotch-Irish (88)	258	2.18
Scottish (39)	156	1.32
Serbian (13)	23	0.19
Slavic (0)	20	0.17
Slovak (0)	21	0.18
Swedish (44)	162	1.37
Swiss (0)	41	0.35
Ukrainian (0)	14	0.12
Welsh (32)	95	0.80

Hispanic Origin	Population	%
Hispanic or Latino (of any race)	352	2.78
Central American, ex. Mexican	69	0.54
Costa Rican	3	0.02
Guatemalan	11	0.09
Honduran	5	0.04
Nicaraguan	2	0.02
Panamanian	3	0.02
Salvadoran	45	0.35
Cuban	11	0.09
Dominican Republic	13	0.10
Mexican	92	0.73
Puerto Rican	103	0.81
South American	34	0.27
Argentinean	3	0.02
Bolivian	1	0.01
Colombian	18	0.14
Ecuadorian	2	0.02
Peruvian	10	0.08
Other Hispanic or Latino	30	0.24

Race*	Population	%
African-American/Black (514)	653	5.15
Not Hispanic (499)	627	4.95
Hispanic (15)	26	0.21
American Indian/Alaska Native (31)	120	0.95
Not Hispanic (29)	108	0.85
Hispanic (2)	12	0.09
Apache (0)	2	0.02
Blackfeet (4)	9	0.07
Cherokee (4)	29	0.23
Chippewa (4)	4	0.03
Comanche (1)	1	0.01
Creek (0)	1	0.01
Iroquois (0)	2	0.02
Lumbee (7)	15	0.12
Ottawa (1)	1	0.01
Seminole (1)	1	0.01
Sioux (0)	4	0.03
South American Ind. (2)	3	0.02
Asian (137)	217	1.71
Not Hispanic (134)	211	1.66
Hispanic (3)	6	0.05
Chinese, ex. Taiwanese (33)	45	0.35
Filipino (39)	77	0.61
Indian (11)	16	0.13
Japanese (2)	15	0.12
Korean (19)	26	0.21
Nepalese (8)	8	0.06
Pakistani (0)	1	0.01
Thai (3)	4	0.03
Vietnamese (18)	20	0.16
Hawaii Native/Pacific Islander (3)	24	0.19
Not Hispanic (3)	19	0.15
Hispanic (0)	5	0.04
Guamanian/Chamorro (0)	1	0.01
Native Hawaiian (2)	3	0.02
Samoan (0)	1	0.01
White (11,613)	11,874	93.67
Not Hispanic (11,381)	11,615	91.62
Hispanic (232)	259	2.04

Rockville

Place Type: City
County: Montgomery
Population: 61,209[†]

Ancestry[‡]	Population	%
African, Sub-Saharan (1,150)	1,325	2.27
African (400)	495	0.85
Ethiopian (372)	372	0.64
Ghanaian (25)	84	0.14
Kenyan (95)	95	0.16
Nigerian (35)	35	0.06
South African (60)	60	0.10
Sudanese (16)	16	0.03
Ugandan (10)	10	0.02
Other Sub-Saharan African (137)	158	0.27
Albanian (67)	67	0.11
American (1,689)	1,689	2.90
Arab (280)	539	0.92
Arab (32)	60	0.10
Egyptian (16)	16	0.03
Lebanese (32)	117	0.20
Moroccan (53)	104	0.18
Palestinian (34)	79	0.14
Syrian (26)	48	0.08
Other Arab (87)	115	0.20
Armenian (271)	320	0.55
Austrian (11)	328	0.56
Belgian (10)	74	0.13
Brazilian (346)	477	0.82
British (144)	330	0.57
Bulgarian (22)	70	0.12
Canadian (52)	52	0.09
Celtic (0)	29	0.05
Croatian (29)	41	0.07
Czech (44)	200	0.34
Czechoslovakian (0)	25	0.04
Danish (27)	147	0.25
Dutch (157)	481	0.83
Eastern European (1,010)	1,196	2.05
English (974)	4,601	7.89
Estonian (32)	55	0.09
European (1,339)	1,464	2.51
Finnish (12)	48	0.08
French, ex. Basque (134)	1,057	1.81
French Canadian (63)	240	0.41
German (1,566)	5,929	10.17
Greek (355)	481	0.83
Guyanese (14)	14	0.02
Hungarian (133)	557	0.96
Iranian (1,136)	1,210	2.08
Irish (1,496)	5,725	9.82
Israeli (126)	189	0.32
Italian (756)	2,509	4.30
Latvian (25)	70	0.12
Lithuanian (99)	241	0.41
Macedonian (0)	11	0.02
Northern European (77)	92	0.16
Norwegian (112)	351	0.60
Pennsylvania German (0)	28	0.05
Polish (708)	2,047	3.51
Portuguese (115)	349	0.60
Romanian (80)	176	0.30
Russian (1,670)	2,935	5.03
Scandinavian (47)	105	0.18
Scotch-Irish (298)	1,082	1.86
Scottish (285)	1,159	1.99
Serbian (35)	153	0.26
Slavic (20)	38	0.07
Slovak (41)	169	0.29
Slovene (0)	17	0.03

*Notes: † The Census 2010 population figure is used to calculate the percentages in the Hispanic Origin and Race categories. Ancestry percentages are based on the 2006-2010 American Community Survey population (not shown); ‡ Numbers in parentheses indicate the number of people reporting a single ancestry; * Numbers in parentheses indicate the number of persons reporting this race alone, not in combination with any other race; Please refer to the Explanation of Data for more information.*

Swedish (89)	504	0.86
Swiss (18)	90	0.15
Turkish (70)	94	0.16
Ukrainian (320)	648	1.11
Welsh (57)	580	0.99
West Indian, ex. Hispanic (274)	359	0.62
Bahamian (14)	14	0.02
Barbadian (31)	31	0.05
British West Indian (9)	9	0.02
Haitian (34)	57	0.10
Jamaican (60)	74	0.13
Trinidadian/Tobagonian (28)	66	0.11
U.S. Virgin Islander (11)	11	0.02
West Indian (87)	97	0.17
Yugoslavian (0)	24	0.04

Hispanic Origin	Population	%
Hispanic or Latino (of any race)	8,781	14.35
Central American, ex. Mexican	3,396	5.55
Costa Rican	77	0.13
Guatemalan	355	0.58
Honduran	525	0.86
Nicaraguan	213	0.35
Panamanian	57	0.09
Salvadoran	2,135	3.49
Other Central American	34	0.06
Cuban	237	0.39
Dominican Republic	215	0.35
Mexican	758	1.24
Puerto Rican	373	0.61
South American	2,706	4.42
Argentinean	217	0.35
Bolivian	446	0.73
Chilean	198	0.32
Colombian	468	0.76
Ecuadorian	208	0.34
Paraguayan	101	0.17
Peruvian	850	1.39
Uruguayan	58	0.09
Venezuelan	150	0.25
Other South American	10	0.02
Other Hispanic or Latino	1,096	1.79

Race*	Population	%
African-American/Black (5,858)	6,529	10.67
Not Hispanic (5,570)	6,102	9.97
Hispanic (288)	427	0.70
American Indian/Alaska Native (205)	553	0.90
Not Hispanic (92)	305	0.50
Hispanic (113)	248	0.41
Alaska Athabascan *(Ala. Nat.)* (1)	1	<0.01
Apache (0)	3	<0.01
Blackfeet (1)	14	0.02
Canadian/French Am. Ind. (6)	8	0.01
Central American Ind. (3)	4	0.01
Cherokee (1)	64	0.10
Cheyenne (0)	1	<0.01
Chickasaw (0)	1	<0.01
Chippewa (4)	8	0.01
Choctaw (4)	9	0.01
Cree (0)	1	<0.01
Creek (1)	5	0.01
Crow (2)	2	<0.01
Delaware (1)	2	<0.01
Houma (0)	1	<0.01
Iroquois (2)	10	0.02
Lumbee (5)	5	0.01
Menominee (0)	4	0.01
Mexican American Ind. (23)	27	0.04
Navajo (14)	23	0.04
Pueblo (3)	8	0.01
Seminole (0)	1	<0.01
Sioux (8)	15	0.02
South American Ind. (21)	45	0.07
Tlingit-Haida *(Alaska Native)* (6)	7	0.01
Yakama (0)	4	0.01
Asian (12,582)	13,721	22.42
Not Hispanic (12,524)	13,574	22.18
Hispanic (58)	147	0.24
Bangladeshi (149)	154	0.25
Burmese (157)	165	0.27
Cambodian (12)	15	0.02
Chinese, ex. Taiwanese (4,809)	5,173	8.45
Filipino (1,107)	1,296	2.12
Hmong (2)	3	<0.01
Indian (2,106)	2,317	3.79
Indonesian (169)	188	0.31
Japanese (481)	602	0.98
Korean (1,662)	1,780	2.91
Laotian (14)	21	0.03
Malaysian (10)	22	0.04
Nepalese (88)	98	0.16
Pakistani (288)	308	0.50
Sri Lankan (153)	176	0.29
Taiwanese (436)	506	0.83
Thai (159)	193	0.32
Vietnamese (459)	525	0.86
Hawaii Native/Pacific Islander (27)	146	0.24
Not Hispanic (25)	119	0.19
Hispanic (2)	27	0.04
Fijian (0)	3	<0.01
Guamanian/Chamorro (3)	9	0.01
Native Hawaiian (8)	18	0.03
Samoan (6)	6	0.01
White (36,973)	38,897	63.55
Not Hispanic (32,344)	33,694	55.05
Hispanic (4,629)	5,203	8.50

Rosaryville

Place Type: CDP
County: Prince George's
Population: 10,697†

Ancestry‡	Population	%
African, Sub-Saharan (732)	732	6.38
African (685)	685	5.97
Ghanaian (47)	47	0.41
American (610)	610	5.31
Australian (0)	16	0.14
Austrian (13)	13	0.11
Danish (0)	16	0.14
Dutch (15)	15	0.13
English (39)	199	1.73
European (66)	66	0.57
French, ex. Basque (18)	18	0.16
German (164)	355	3.09
Greek (0)	81	0.71
Guyanese (41)	41	0.36
Irish (21)	138	1.20
Italian (59)	137	1.19
Norwegian (0)	46	0.40
Polish (15)	94	0.82
Russian (0)	28	0.24
Scandinavian (0)	12	0.10
Scotch-Irish (35)	50	0.44
Scottish (17)	50	0.44
Slovak (0)	15	0.13
Swedish (0)	51	0.44
Welsh (0)	33	0.29
West Indian, ex. Hispanic (157)	268	2.33
Bahamian (19)	31	0.27
British West Indian (16)	16	0.14
Haitian (28)	28	0.24
Jamaican (78)	135	1.18
Trinidadian/Tobagonian (16)	58	0.51

Hispanic Origin	Population	%
Hispanic or Latino (of any race)	319	2.98
Central American, ex. Mexican	110	1.03
Costa Rican	3	0.03
Guatemalan	12	0.11
Honduran	1	0.01
Nicaraguan	3	0.03
Panamanian	41	0.38
Salvadoran	50	0.47
Cuban	4	0.04
Dominican Republic	20	0.19
Mexican	70	0.65
Puerto Rican	54	0.50
South American	29	0.27
Argentinean	4	0.04
Bolivian	4	0.04
Chilean	6	0.06
Colombian	5	0.05
Peruvian	8	0.07
Venezuelan	2	0.02
Other Hispanic or Latino	32	0.30

Race*	Population	%
African-American/Black (8,756)	9,016	84.29
Not Hispanic (8,662)	8,899	83.19
Hispanic (94)	117	1.09
American Indian/Alaska Native (42)	191	1.79
Not Hispanic (42)	182	1.70
Hispanic (0)	9	0.08
Apache (0)	1	0.01
Blackfeet (0)	15	0.14
Central American Ind. (1)	3	0.03
Cherokee (1)	45	0.42
Chickasaw (0)	2	0.02
Chippewa (0)	3	0.03
Delaware (0)	4	0.04
Iroquois (0)	4	0.04
Seminole (0)	2	0.02
Sioux (4)	4	0.04
South American Ind. (0)	1	0.01
Asian (169)	226	2.11
Not Hispanic (168)	220	2.06
Hispanic (1)	6	0.06
Bangladeshi (1)	1	0.01
Cambodian (0)	1	0.01
Chinese, ex. Taiwanese (16)	23	0.22
Filipino (93)	114	1.07
Indian (17)	25	0.23
Indonesian (0)	1	0.01
Japanese (5)	11	0.10
Korean (11)	14	0.13
Laotian (9)	9	0.08
Pakistani (5)	5	0.05
Taiwanese (0)	1	0.01
Thai (8)	9	0.08
Vietnamese (4)	7	0.07
Hawaii Native/Pacific Islander (8)	19	0.18
Not Hispanic (8)	19	0.18
Guamanian/Chamorro (3)	12	0.11
Native Hawaiian (2)	2	0.02
Samoan (0)	1	0.01
White (1,309)	1,462	13.67
Not Hispanic (1,199)	1,338	12.51
Hispanic (110)	124	1.16

Rosedale

Place Type: CDP
County: Baltimore
Population: 19,257†

Ancestry‡	Population	%
African, Sub-Saharan (418)	482	2.53
African (72)	72	0.38
Ethiopian (23)	23	0.12
Kenyan (14)	14	0.07
Liberian (65)	65	0.34
Nigerian (211)	275	1.44
Other Sub-Saharan African (33)	33	0.17
American (1,217)	1,217	6.39
Arab (123)	154	0.81
Egyptian (14)	14	0.07
Lebanese (0)	21	0.11
Moroccan (109)	109	0.57
Syrian (0)	10	0.05
Belgian (0)	34	0.18
British (10)	10	0.05
Canadian (0)	21	0.11
Czech (111)	351	1.84
Czechoslovakian (18)	42	0.22
Danish (0)	12	0.06
Dutch (61)	247	1.30
English (516)	1,409	7.40

*Notes: † The Census 2010 population figure is used to calculate the percentages in the Hispanic Origin and Race categories. Ancestry percentages are based on the 2006-2010 American Community Survey population (not shown); ‡ Numbers in parentheses indicate the number of people reporting a single ancestry; * Numbers in parentheses indicate the number of persons reporting this race alone, not in combination with any other race; Please refer to the Explanation of Data for more information.*

Ancestry (cont.)	Population	%
Estonian (0)	12	0.06
European (22)	65	0.34
French, ex. Basque (74)	326	1.71
German (1,056)	3,682	19.33
Greek (218)	267	1.40
Hungarian (14)	14	0.07
Icelander (0)	32	0.17
Irish (612)	2,473	12.99
Italian (354)	1,210	6.35
Lithuanian (12)	24	0.13
Norwegian (25)	42	0.22
Pennsylvania German (21)	21	0.11
Polish (601)	1,522	7.99
Portuguese (35)	35	0.18
Russian (21)	44	0.23
Scotch-Irish (58)	117	0.61
Scottish (37)	159	0.83
Serbian (4)	4	0.02
Slavic (0)	14	0.07
Slovak (18)	40	0.21
Swedish (0)	61	0.32
Turkish (31)	31	0.16
Ukrainian (47)	111	0.58
Welsh (0)	20	0.11
West Indian, ex. Hispanic (169)	262	1.38
Haitian (9)	9	0.05
Jamaican (134)	227	1.19
Trinidadian/Tobagonian (26)	26	0.14
Yugoslavian (0)	8	0.04

Hispanic Origin	Population	%
Hispanic or Latino (of any race)	960	4.99
Central American, ex. Mexican	333	1.73
Costa Rican	10	0.05
Guatemalan	29	0.15
Honduran	61	0.32
Nicaraguan	4	0.02
Panamanian	12	0.06
Salvadoran	212	1.10
Other Central American	5	0.03
Cuban	24	0.12
Dominican Republic	115	0.60
Mexican	163	0.85
Puerto Rican	137	0.71
South American	61	0.32
Argentinean	4	0.02
Chilean	3	0.02
Colombian	22	0.11
Ecuadorian	9	0.05
Peruvian	19	0.10
Venezuelan	2	0.01
Other South American	2	0.01
Other Hispanic or Latino	127	0.66

Race*	Population	%
African-American/Black (6,346)	6,564	34.09
Not Hispanic (6,288)	6,492	33.71
Hispanic (58)	72	0.37
American Indian/Alaska Native (98)	237	1.23
Not Hispanic (76)	202	1.05
Hispanic (22)	35	0.18
Blackfeet (10)	12	0.06
Cherokee (12)	37	0.19
Choctaw (1)	2	0.01
Creek (1)	3	0.02
Iroquois (2)	2	0.01
Lumbee (8)	17	0.09
Mexican American Ind. (1)	1	0.01
Navajo (1)	5	0.03
Potawatomi (0)	1	0.01
Shoshone (0)	1	0.01
Sioux (1)	11	0.06
South American Ind. (4)	4	0.02
Spanish American Ind. (3)	3	0.02
Tlingit-Haida *(Alaska Native)* (1)	1	0.01
Asian (579)	643	3.34
Not Hispanic (578)	638	3.31
Hispanic (1)	5	0.03
Burmese (3)	3	0.02
Chinese, ex. Taiwanese (40)	42	0.22
Filipino (270)	297	1.54
Indian (73)	87	0.45
Japanese (2)	5	0.03
Korean (37)	47	0.24
Laotian (8)	12	0.06
Nepalese (6)	6	0.03
Pakistani (36)	38	0.20
Thai (3)	5	0.03
Vietnamese (80)	94	0.49
Hawaii Native/Pacific Islander (10)	24	0.12
Not Hispanic (10)	23	0.12
Hispanic (0)	1	0.01
Guamanian/Chamorro (7)	9	0.05
Samoan (0)	2	0.01
White (11,363)	11,649	60.49
Not Hispanic (10,978)	11,232	58.33
Hispanic (385)	417	2.17

Rossville

Place Type: CDP
County: Baltimore
Population: 15,147†

Ancestry‡	Population	%
African, Sub-Saharan (296)	390	2.59
African (89)	183	1.21
Nigerian (185)	185	1.23
Sierra Leonean (22)	22	0.15
American (491)	491	3.26
Arab (174)	192	1.27
Egyptian (71)	71	0.47
Lebanese (0)	9	0.06
Moroccan (93)	93	0.62
Syrian (10)	19	0.13
Armenian (8)	8	0.05
British (34)	48	0.32
Canadian (12)	12	0.08
Czech (49)	106	0.70
Danish (0)	15	0.10
Dutch (134)	203	1.35
Eastern European (14)	14	0.09
English (163)	973	6.46
European (54)	54	0.36
Finnish (0)	22	0.15
French, ex. Basque (14)	230	1.53
French Canadian (18)	85	0.56
German (856)	3,064	20.33
Greek (62)	122	0.81
Hungarian (26)	42	0.28
Iranian (10)	10	0.07
Irish (299)	2,112	14.01
Italian (1,004)	1,809	12.00
Lithuanian (0)	9	0.06
Norwegian (13)	112	0.74
Polish (316)	932	6.18
Romanian (0)	25	0.17
Russian (0)	165	1.09
Scandinavian (0)	33	0.22
Scotch-Irish (65)	132	0.88
Scottish (68)	231	1.53
Slovak (0)	21	0.14
Swedish (0)	22	0.15
Turkish (0)	17	0.11
Ukrainian (17)	52	0.35
Welsh (44)	98	0.65
West Indian, ex. Hispanic (164)	182	1.21
Barbadian (13)	13	0.09
Jamaican (133)	133	0.88
Trinidadian/Tobagonian (18)	36	0.24
Yugoslavian (12)	22	0.15

Hispanic Origin	Population	%
Hispanic or Latino (of any race)	1,042	6.88
Central American, ex. Mexican	366	2.42
Guatemalan	17	0.11
Honduran	64	0.42
Nicaraguan	13	0.09
Panamanian	18	0.12
Salvadoran	254	1.68
Cuban	17	0.11
Dominican Republic	55	0.36
Mexican	248	1.64
Puerto Rican	155	1.02
South American	83	0.55
Argentinean	7	0.05
Bolivian	9	0.06
Chilean	2	0.01
Colombian	22	0.15
Ecuadorian	16	0.11
Peruvian	19	0.13
Venezuelan	6	0.04
Other South American	2	0.01
Other Hispanic or Latino	118	0.78

Race*	Population	%
African-American/Black (4,690)	4,950	32.68
Not Hispanic (4,585)	4,817	31.80
Hispanic (105)	133	0.88
American Indian/Alaska Native (60)	148	0.98
Not Hispanic (57)	131	0.86
Hispanic (3)	17	0.11
Apache (1)	1	0.01
Blackfeet (2)	10	0.07
Cherokee (6)	32	0.21
Chippewa (1)	1	0.01
Choctaw (1)	1	0.01
Creek (1)	1	0.01
Crow (0)	1	0.01
Lumbee (10)	10	0.07
Mexican American Ind. (0)	1	0.01
Navajo (0)	1	0.01
Seminole (1)	5	0.03
Sioux (0)	1	0.01
South American Ind. (2)	3	0.02
Ute (1)	1	0.01
Yaqui (2)	2	0.01
Asian (1,593)	1,729	11.41
Not Hispanic (1,583)	1,711	11.30
Hispanic (10)	18	0.12
Bangladeshi (3)	4	0.03
Burmese (27)	28	0.18
Cambodian (1)	1	0.01
Chinese, ex. Taiwanese (103)	128	0.85
Filipino (531)	576	3.80
Indian (346)	387	2.55
Japanese (7)	8	0.05
Korean (184)	207	1.37
Laotian (13)	17	0.11
Nepalese (18)	26	0.17
Pakistani (116)	132	0.87
Sri Lankan (5)	5	0.03
Taiwanese (6)	9	0.06
Thai (16)	20	0.13
Vietnamese (140)	143	0.94
Hawaii Native/Pacific Islander (4)	26	0.17
Not Hispanic (4)	25	0.17
Hispanic (0)	1	0.01
Fijian (1)	1	0.01
Native Hawaiian (2)	2	0.01
Samoan (0)	4	0.03
White (7,852)	8,192	54.08
Not Hispanic (7,452)	7,739	51.09
Hispanic (400)	453	2.99

Salisbury

Place Type: City
County: Wicomico
Population: 30,343†

Ancestry‡	Population	%
African, Sub-Saharan (174)	205	0.70
African (100)	131	0.45
Ethiopian (22)	22	0.07
South African (35)	35	0.12
Other Sub-Saharan African (17)	17	0.06
Albanian (61)	61	0.21
American (1,133)	1,133	3.86
Arab (8)	143	0.49

*Notes: † The Census 2010 population figure is used to calculate the percentages in the Hispanic Origin and Race categories. Ancestry percentages are based on the 2006-2010 American Community Survey population (not shown); ‡ Numbers in parentheses indicate the number of people reporting a single ancestry; * Numbers in parentheses indicate the number of persons reporting this race alone, not in combination with any other race; Please refer to the Explanation of Data for more information.*

Arab (0)	62	0.21
Lebanese (8)	81	0.28
Australian (0)	18	0.06
Austrian (0)	30	0.10
Belgian (0)	31	0.11
Brazilian (121)	121	0.41
British (87)	184	0.63
Cajun (0)	13	0.04
Canadian (10)	50	0.17
Celtic (0)	23	0.08
Czech (56)	147	0.50
Czechoslovakian (8)	23	0.08
Danish (23)	48	0.16
Dutch (46)	252	0.86
Eastern European (10)	10	0.03
English (1,568)	3,261	11.11
European (68)	68	0.23
French, ex. Basque (126)	425	1.45
French Canadian (67)	98	0.33
German (1,507)	4,156	14.16
Greek (33)	168	0.57
Hungarian (93)	154	0.52
Iranian (8)	17	0.06
Irish (831)	3,288	11.21
Italian (496)	1,530	5.21
Lithuanian (13)	80	0.27
Northern European (48)	48	0.16
Norwegian (61)	209	0.71
Pennsylvania German (18)	18	0.06
Polish (237)	647	2.20
Portuguese (0)	16	0.05
Romanian (31)	31	0.11
Russian (52)	200	0.68
Scandinavian (0)	17	0.06
Scotch-Irish (197)	425	1.45
Scottish (105)	665	2.27
Slovak (0)	24	0.08
Swedish (56)	154	0.52
Swiss (0)	105	0.36
Ukrainian (59)	72	0.25
Welsh (20)	199	0.68
West Indian, ex. Hispanic (1,156)	1,305	4.45
Bermudan (24)	24	0.08
Haitian (963)	963	3.28
Jamaican (136)	189	0.64
Trinidadian/Tobagonian (33)	129	0.44

Hispanic Origin	Population	%
Hispanic or Latino (of any race)	2,128	7.01
Central American, ex. Mexican	308	1.02
Costa Rican	23	0.08
Guatemalan	169	0.56
Honduran	48	0.16
Nicaraguan	23	0.08
Panamanian	2	0.01
Salvadoran	43	0.14
Cuban	36	0.12
Dominican Republic	55	0.18
Mexican	990	3.26
Puerto Rican	382	1.26
South American	168	0.55
Argentinean	18	0.06
Bolivian	10	0.03
Chilean	20	0.07
Colombian	24	0.08
Ecuadorian	17	0.06
Peruvian	54	0.18
Uruguayan	4	0.01
Venezuelan	20	0.07
Other South American	1	<0.01
Other Hispanic or Latino	189	0.62

Race*	Population	%
African-American/Black (10,441)	11,100	36.58
Not Hispanic (10,278)	10,843	35.73
Hispanic (163)	257	0.85
American Indian/Alaska Native (81)	243	0.80
Not Hispanic (61)	200	0.66
Hispanic (20)	43	0.14
Aleut *(Alaska Native)* (0)	1	<0.01
Apache (1)	4	0.01
Blackfeet (1)	4	0.01
Canadian/French Am. Ind. (0)	2	0.01
Central American Ind. (1)	5	0.02
Cherokee (8)	46	0.15
Cheyenne (0)	1	<0.01
Creek (0)	1	<0.01
Inupiat *(Alaska Native)* (1)	4	0.01
Lumbee (3)	4	0.01
Mexican American Ind. (1)	1	<0.01
Navajo (3)	4	0.01
Ottawa (0)	1	<0.01
Pueblo (0)	2	0.01
Shoshone (1)	1	<0.01
Sioux (0)	1	<0.01
South American Ind. (0)	1	<0.01
Tlingit-Haida *(Alaska Native)* (1)	1	<0.01
Asian (964)	1,153	3.80
Not Hispanic (962)	1,139	3.75
Hispanic (2)	14	0.05
Bangladeshi (3)	3	0.01
Burmese (16)	16	0.05
Cambodian (1)	1	<0.01
Chinese, ex. Taiwanese (109)	144	0.47
Filipino (75)	110	0.36
Indian (329)	383	1.26
Indonesian (3)	11	0.04
Japanese (14)	42	0.14
Korean (245)	260	0.86
Laotian (0)	2	0.01
Malaysian (0)	1	<0.01
Nepalese (3)	3	0.01
Pakistani (102)	111	0.37
Taiwanese (2)	3	0.01
Thai (2)	2	0.01
Vietnamese (37)	42	0.14
Hawaii Native/Pacific Islander (21)	62	0.20
Not Hispanic (11)	44	0.15
Hispanic (10)	18	0.06
Guamanian/Chamorro (15)	18	0.06
Native Hawaiian (3)	10	0.03
Samoan (0)	4	0.01
White (16,911)	17,745	58.48
Not Hispanic (16,032)	16,699	55.03
Hispanic (879)	1,046	3.45

Scaggsville

Place Type: CDP
County: Howard
Population: 24,333†

Ancestry‡	Population	%
African, Sub-Saharan (734)	864	3.76
African (345)	475	2.07
Ethiopian (51)	51	0.22
Ghanaian (11)	11	0.05
Liberian (11)	11	0.05
Nigerian (267)	267	1.16
Sierra Leonean (49)	49	0.21
American (1,222)	1,222	5.31
Arab (28)	42	0.18
Egyptian (28)	28	0.12
Syrian (0)	14	0.06
Armenian (0)	13	0.06
Austrian (0)	73	0.32
Belgian (18)	32	0.14
Brazilian (310)	379	1.65
British (33)	83	0.36
Canadian (51)	125	0.54
Celtic (33)	33	0.14
Croatian (0)	33	0.14
Czech (20)	113	0.49
Czechoslovakian (75)	75	0.33
Danish (29)	29	0.13
Dutch (27)	233	1.01
Eastern European (33)	62	0.27
English (537)	2,057	8.95
Estonian (0)	63	0.27
European (122)	233	1.01
Finnish (0)	17	0.07
French, ex. Basque (105)	198	0.86
French Canadian (13)	164	0.71
German (497)	3,002	13.06
Greek (58)	70	0.30
Guyanese (98)	98	0.43
Hungarian (43)	125	0.54
Iranian (69)	69	0.30
Irish (545)	3,023	13.15
Israeli (0)	21	0.09
Italian (482)	1,638	7.12
Latvian (29)	85	0.37
Lithuanian (66)	66	0.29
Norwegian (48)	126	0.55
Polish (128)	622	2.70
Portuguese (48)	131	0.57
Romanian (14)	14	0.06
Russian (54)	339	1.47
Scotch-Irish (84)	344	1.50
Scottish (25)	268	1.17
Serbian (0)	13	0.06
Slavic (0)	10	0.04
Slovak (58)	127	0.55
Slovene (0)	95	0.41
Swedish (36)	172	0.75
Swiss (0)	27	0.12
Turkish (4)	56	0.24
Ukrainian (0)	16	0.07
Welsh (10)	123	0.53
West Indian, ex. Hispanic (863)	1,091	4.74
Barbadian (65)	65	0.28
Bermudan (0)	26	0.11
British West Indian (154)	154	0.67
Haitian (209)	248	1.08
Jamaican (200)	345	1.50
Trinidadian/Tobagonian (235)	235	1.02
West Indian (0)	18	0.08
Yugoslavian (54)	94	0.41

Hispanic Origin	Population	%
Hispanic or Latino (of any race)	2,088	8.58
Central American, ex. Mexican	740	3.04
Costa Rican	19	0.08
Guatemalan	130	0.53
Honduran	45	0.18
Nicaraguan	25	0.10
Panamanian	41	0.17
Salvadoran	474	1.95
Other Central American	6	0.02
Cuban	58	0.24
Dominican Republic	48	0.20
Mexican	422	1.73
Puerto Rican	272	1.12
South American	336	1.38
Argentinean	19	0.08
Bolivian	30	0.12
Chilean	50	0.21
Colombian	75	0.31
Ecuadorian	36	0.15
Paraguayan	7	0.03
Peruvian	55	0.23
Uruguayan	15	0.06
Venezuelan	46	0.19
Other South American	3	0.01
Other Hispanic or Latino	212	0.87

Race*	Population	%
African-American/Black (6,322)	6,855	28.17
Not Hispanic (6,184)	6,634	27.26
Hispanic (138)	221	0.91
American Indian/Alaska Native (79)	305	1.25
Not Hispanic (56)	234	0.96
Hispanic (23)	71	0.29
Apache (0)	4	0.02
Blackfeet (1)	22	0.09
Central American Ind. (1)	1	<0.01
Cherokee (7)	59	0.24
Chickasaw (0)	1	<0.01
Chippewa (0)	9	0.04
Choctaw (4)	5	0.02

*Notes: † The Census 2010 population figure is used to calculate the percentages in the Hispanic Origin and Race categories. Ancestry percentages are based on the 2006-2010 American Community Survey population (not shown); ‡ Numbers in parentheses indicate the number of people reporting a single ancestry; * Numbers in parentheses indicate the number of persons reporting this race alone, not in combination with any other race; Please refer to the Explanation of Data for more information.*

Cree (1)	2	0.01
Creek (0)	1	<0.01
Iroquois (0)	2	0.01
Lumbee (6)	6	0.02
Mexican American Ind. (1)	3	0.01
Navajo (0)	1	<0.01
Seminole (0)	1	<0.01
Shoshone (0)	1	<0.01
Sioux (2)	9	0.04
South American Ind. (0)	8	0.03
Ute (1)	1	<0.01
Yup'ik *(Alaska Native)* (1)	1	<0.01
Asian (3,318)	3,733	15.34
Not Hispanic (3,312)	3,680	15.12
Hispanic (6)	53	0.22
Bangladeshi (41)	46	0.19
Burmese (47)	49	0.20
Cambodian (6)	16	0.07
Chinese, ex. Taiwanese (475)	570	2.34
Filipino (187)	273	1.12
Indian (1,008)	1,124	4.62
Indonesian (13)	16	0.07
Japanese (43)	90	0.37
Korean (863)	924	3.80
Laotian (4)	4	0.02
Nepalese (18)	18	0.07
Pakistani (251)	269	1.11
Sri Lankan (4)	4	0.02
Taiwanese (15)	21	0.09
Thai (24)	34	0.14
Vietnamese (234)	274	1.13
Hawaii Native/Pacific Islander (12)	50	0.21
Not Hispanic (11)	47	0.19
Hispanic (1)	3	0.01
Guamanian/Chamorro (6)	12	0.05
Native Hawaiian (4)	13	0.05
Samoan (1)	1	<0.01
White (12,820)	13,626	56.00
Not Hispanic (11,787)	12,390	50.92
Hispanic (1,033)	1,236	5.08

Seabrook

Place Type: CDP
County: Prince George's
Population: 17,287†

Ancestry‡	Population	%
African, Sub-Saharan (1,681)	1,749	11.20
African (684)	717	4.59
Ghanaian (56)	56	0.36
Kenyan (17)	17	0.11
Liberian (15)	15	0.10
Nigerian (249)	261	1.67
Sierra Leonean (299)	311	1.99
Somalian (127)	127	0.81
South African (7)	7	0.04
Other Sub-Saharan African (227)	238	1.52
American (303)	303	1.94
Arab (118)	118	0.76
Iraqi (107)	107	0.69
Lebanese (11)	11	0.07
Austrian (0)	9	0.06
British (21)	31	0.20
Croatian (11)	11	0.07
Danish (0)	5	0.03
Dutch (32)	96	0.61
English (94)	220	1.41
Estonian (0)	46	0.29
European (44)	67	0.43
French, ex. Basque (24)	75	0.48
French Canadian (19)	19	0.12
German (139)	406	2.60
Greek (50)	50	0.32
Guyanese (23)	23	0.15
Irish (158)	308	1.97
Italian (39)	127	0.81
Northern European (11)	11	0.07
Norwegian (8)	8	0.05
Polish (54)	89	0.57
Portuguese (127)	127	0.81
Romanian (39)	39	0.25
Scandinavian (0)	10	0.06
Scotch-Irish (20)	62	0.40
Scottish (14)	86	0.55
Serbian (0)	10	0.06
Slovak (12)	12	0.08
Swedish (25)	36	0.23
Ukrainian (20)	20	0.13
Welsh (34)	82	0.52
West Indian, ex. Hispanic (528)	667	4.27
Bahamian (13)	13	0.08
Haitian (98)	98	0.63
Jamaican (190)	199	1.27
Trinidadian/Tobagonian (184)	235	1.50
West Indian (43)	122	0.78

Hispanic Origin	Population	%
Hispanic or Latino (of any race)	2,537	14.68
Central American, ex. Mexican	1,227	7.10
Costa Rican	10	0.06
Guatemalan	108	0.62
Honduran	86	0.50
Nicaraguan	56	0.32
Panamanian	38	0.22
Salvadoran	920	5.32
Other Central American	9	0.05
Cuban	20	0.12
Dominican Republic	56	0.32
Mexican	705	4.08
Puerto Rican	108	0.62
South American	80	0.46
Argentinean	10	0.06
Bolivian	7	0.04
Chilean	4	0.02
Colombian	8	0.05
Ecuadorian	2	0.01
Paraguayan	4	0.02
Peruvian	39	0.23
Uruguayan	2	0.01
Venezuelan	4	0.02
Other Hispanic or Latino	341	1.97

Race*	Population	%
African-American/Black (11,321)	11,681	67.57
Not Hispanic (11,175)	11,476	66.39
Hispanic (146)	205	1.19
American Indian/Alaska Native (46)	194	1.12
Not Hispanic (22)	145	0.84
Hispanic (24)	49	0.28
Alaska Athabascan *(Ala. Nat.)* (0)	1	0.01
Apache (0)	3	0.02
Blackfeet (0)	13	0.08
Central American Ind. (1)	1	0.01
Cherokee (2)	39	0.23
Choctaw (0)	5	0.03
Creek (0)	3	0.02
Delaware (0)	1	0.01
Iroquois (0)	1	0.01
Lumbee (0)	3	0.02
Mexican American Ind. (0)	6	0.03
Navajo (1)	1	0.01
Seminole (0)	1	0.01
South American Ind. (1)	1	0.01
Asian (1,027)	1,128	6.53
Not Hispanic (1,024)	1,119	6.47
Hispanic (3)	9	0.05
Bangladeshi (11)	16	0.09
Burmese (3)	3	0.02
Cambodian (12)	12	0.07
Chinese, ex. Taiwanese (125)	136	0.79
Filipino (204)	226	1.31
Indian (301)	331	1.91
Indonesian (0)	4	0.02
Japanese (8)	21	0.12
Korean (109)	123	0.71
Laotian (2)	2	0.01
Malaysian (0)	1	0.01
Nepalese (5)	5	0.03
Pakistani (73)	81	0.47
Sri Lankan (11)	11	0.06
Taiwanese (1)	4	0.02
Thai (4)	8	0.05
Vietnamese (141)	145	0.84
Hawaii Native/Pacific Islander (13)	38	0.22
Not Hispanic (12)	28	0.16
Hispanic (1)	10	0.06
Guamanian/Chamorro (4)	7	0.04
Native Hawaiian (2)	6	0.03
White (2,809)	3,146	18.20
Not Hispanic (2,098)	2,328	13.47
Hispanic (711)	818	4.73

Severn

Place Type: CDP
County: Anne Arundel
Population: 44,231†

Ancestry‡	Population	%
African, Sub-Saharan (940)	1,137	2.72
African (403)	577	1.38
Ghanaian (124)	124	0.30
Kenyan (80)	80	0.19
Liberian (102)	125	0.30
Nigerian (181)	181	0.43
Sierra Leonean (39)	39	0.09
Somalian (11)	11	0.03
Albanian (15)	15	0.04
American (1,294)	1,294	3.10
Arab (89)	102	0.24
Egyptian (68)	68	0.16
Syrian (10)	23	0.06
Other Arab (11)	11	0.03
Armenian (12)	12	0.03
Austrian (11)	74	0.18
Basque (0)	18	0.04
Belgian (48)	82	0.20
Brazilian (18)	18	0.04
British (106)	173	0.41
Canadian (38)	44	0.11
Celtic (12)	24	0.06
Croatian (0)	13	0.03
Czech (35)	143	0.34
Czechoslovakian (58)	89	0.21
Danish (13)	44	0.11
Dutch (26)	418	1.00
Eastern European (63)	94	0.23
English (1,009)	3,552	8.51
European (309)	332	0.80
Finnish (0)	20	0.05
French, ex. Basque (156)	766	1.83
French Canadian (86)	315	0.75
German (2,137)	7,044	16.87
Greek (148)	280	0.67
Guyanese (12)	44	0.11
Hungarian (52)	158	0.38
Iranian (54)	87	0.21
Irish (925)	4,909	11.76
Italian (584)	2,138	5.12
Lithuanian (16)	96	0.23
Northern European (41)	41	0.10
Norwegian (51)	181	0.43
Pennsylvania German (38)	38	0.09
Polish (473)	1,339	3.21
Portuguese (55)	114	0.27
Romanian (46)	46	0.11
Russian (51)	230	0.55
Scandinavian (27)	42	0.10
Scotch-Irish (192)	469	1.12
Scottish (209)	845	2.02
Serbian (17)	47	0.11
Slovak (30)	88	0.21
Slovene (27)	27	0.06
Swedish (14)	313	0.75
Swiss (7)	49	0.12
Turkish (35)	35	0.08
Ukrainian (64)	177	0.42
Welsh (75)	504	1.21
West Indian, ex. Hispanic (412)	503	1.20

*Notes: † The Census 2010 population figure is used to calculate the percentages in the Hispanic Origin and Race categories. Ancestry percentages are based on the 2006-2010 American Community Survey population (not shown); ‡ Numbers in parentheses indicate the number of people reporting a single ancestry; * Numbers in parentheses indicate the number of persons reporting this race alone, not in combination with any other race; Please refer to the Explanation of Data for more information.*

British West Indian (8)	8	0.02
Haitian (12)	77	0.18
Jamaican (283)	298	0.71
Trinidadian/Tobagonian (18)	18	0.04
U.S. Virgin Islander (79)	79	0.19
West Indian (12)	23	0.06

Hispanic Origin	Population	%
Hispanic or Latino (of any race)	2,775	6.27
Central American, ex. Mexican	675	1.53
Costa Rican	26	0.06
Guatemalan	101	0.23
Honduran	68	0.15
Nicaraguan	13	0.03
Panamanian	100	0.23
Salvadoran	360	0.81
Other Central American	7	0.02
Cuban	58	0.13
Dominican Republic	98	0.22
Mexican	606	1.37
Puerto Rican	767	1.73
South American	305	0.69
Argentinean	13	0.03
Bolivian	17	0.04
Chilean	31	0.07
Colombian	101	0.23
Ecuadorian	49	0.11
Paraguayan	2	<0.01
Peruvian	70	0.16
Venezuelan	19	0.04
Other South American	3	0.01
Other Hispanic or Latino	266	0.60

Race*	Population	%
African-American/Black (14,818)	15,893	35.93
Not Hispanic (14,524)	15,466	34.97
Hispanic (294)	427	0.97
American Indian/Alaska Native (136)	572	1.29
Not Hispanic (112)	504	1.14
Hispanic (24)	68	0.15
Alaska Athabascan *(Ala. Nat.)* (1)	2	<0.01
Apache (3)	3	0.01
Blackfeet (6)	32	0.07
Central American Ind. (1)	1	<0.01
Cherokee (19)	142	0.32
Cheyenne (0)	2	<0.01
Chippewa (5)	7	0.02
Choctaw (1)	4	0.01
Cree (0)	1	<0.01
Creek (0)	4	0.01
Crow (0)	1	<0.01
Delaware (0)	3	0.01
Inupiat *(Alaska Native)* (0)	1	<0.01
Iroquois (1)	5	0.01
Kiowa (1)	2	<0.01
Lumbee (7)	15	0.03
Mexican American Ind. (1)	4	0.01
Navajo (1)	7	0.02
Ottawa (4)	6	0.01
Paiute (1)	1	<0.01
Seminole (0)	8	0.02
Sioux (3)	9	0.02
South American Ind. (1)	4	0.01
Tlingit-Haida *(Alaska Native)* (0)	3	0.01
Asian (3,454)	4,194	9.48
Not Hispanic (3,429)	4,111	9.29
Hispanic (25)	83	0.19
Bangladeshi (22)	24	0.05
Burmese (6)	7	0.02
Cambodian (24)	29	0.07
Chinese, ex. Taiwanese (270)	354	0.80
Filipino (549)	803	1.82
Hmong (2)	2	<0.01
Indian (668)	727	1.64
Indonesian (1)	2	<0.01
Japanese (69)	172	0.39
Korean (1,022)	1,216	2.75
Laotian (8)	9	0.02
Malaysian (7)	7	0.02
Nepalese (38)	44	0.10
Pakistani (188)	210	0.47
Sri Lankan (11)	12	0.03
Taiwanese (33)	39	0.09
Thai (76)	106	0.24
Vietnamese (345)	392	0.89
Hawaii Native/Pacific Islander (71)	170	0.38
Not Hispanic (55)	146	0.33
Hispanic (16)	24	0.05
Fijian (6)	6	0.01
Guamanian/Chamorro (40)	61	0.14
Native Hawaiian (7)	40	0.09
Samoan (10)	16	0.04
White (22,943)	24,502	55.40
Not Hispanic (21,538)	22,900	51.77
Hispanic (1,405)	1,602	3.62

Severna Park

Place Type: CDP
County: Anne Arundel
Population: 37,634†

Ancestry‡	Population	%
African, Sub-Saharan (12)	25	0.07
African (0)	13	0.04
Ethiopian (12)	12	0.03
American (1,994)	1,994	5.38
Arab (37)	58	0.16
Egyptian (0)	21	0.06
Jordanian (37)	37	0.10
Armenian (28)	28	0.08
Australian (34)	67	0.18
Austrian (146)	242	0.65
Basque (0)	15	0.04
British (76)	265	0.71
Canadian (36)	130	0.35
Celtic (40)	40	0.11
Croatian (15)	52	0.14
Cypriot (19)	19	0.05
Czech (52)	181	0.49
Czechoslovakian (42)	57	0.15
Danish (0)	13	0.04
Dutch (115)	545	1.47
Eastern European (160)	169	0.46
English (1,801)	5,990	16.15
Estonian (14)	14	0.04
European (942)	976	2.63
Finnish (23)	89	0.24
French, ex. Basque (277)	1,192	3.21
French Canadian (71)	192	0.52
German (2,730)	10,986	29.63
Greek (187)	471	1.27
Hungarian (115)	354	0.95
Iranian (46)	46	0.12
Irish (2,090)	8,375	22.59
Italian (862)	3,015	8.13
Latvian (13)	13	0.04
Lithuanian (101)	169	0.46
Northern European (193)	193	0.52
Norwegian (109)	469	1.26
Polish (880)	2,684	7.24
Portuguese (0)	67	0.18
Romanian (0)	51	0.14
Russian (305)	585	1.58
Scandinavian (28)	42	0.11
Scotch-Irish (446)	1,214	3.27
Scottish (212)	1,048	2.83
Slovak (110)	256	0.69
Swedish (91)	325	0.88
Swiss (82)	331	0.89
Turkish (32)	32	0.09
Ukrainian (53)	89	0.24
Welsh (141)	430	1.16
Yugoslavian (0)	15	0.04

Hispanic Origin	Population	%
Hispanic or Latino (of any race)	889	2.36
Central American, ex. Mexican	180	0.48
Costa Rican	17	0.05
Guatemalan	54	0.14
Honduran	10	0.03
Nicaraguan	14	0.04
Panamanian	21	0.06
Salvadoran	64	0.17
Cuban	78	0.21
Dominican Republic	6	0.02
Mexican	258	0.69
Puerto Rican	139	0.37
South American	108	0.29
Argentinean	13	0.03
Bolivian	9	0.02
Chilean	6	0.02
Colombian	27	0.07
Ecuadorian	6	0.02
Paraguayan	1	<0.01
Peruvian	21	0.06
Uruguayan	3	0.01
Venezuelan	17	0.05
Other South American	5	0.01
Other Hispanic or Latino	120	0.32

Race*	Population	%
African-American/Black (1,629)	1,792	4.76
Not Hispanic (1,616)	1,766	4.69
Hispanic (13)	26	0.07
American Indian/Alaska Native (68)	205	0.54
Not Hispanic (56)	186	0.49
Hispanic (12)	19	0.05
Blackfeet (1)	9	0.02
Cherokee (15)	60	0.16
Cheyenne (0)	1	<0.01
Chippewa (4)	7	0.02
Choctaw (0)	4	0.01
Creek (0)	3	0.01
Crow (1)	2	0.01
Delaware (0)	1	<0.01
Hopi (2)	2	0.01
Inupiat *(Alaska Native)* (0)	2	0.01
Iroquois (5)	9	0.02
Kiowa (0)	3	0.01
Lumbee (6)	7	0.02
Mexican American Ind. (1)	1	<0.01
Ottawa (2)	2	0.01
Sioux (2)	2	0.01
South American Ind. (2)	2	0.01
Asian (1,064)	1,372	3.65
Not Hispanic (1,054)	1,340	3.56
Hispanic (10)	32	0.09
Bangladeshi (2)	2	0.01
Burmese (3)	8	0.02
Cambodian (8)	8	0.02
Chinese, ex. Taiwanese (184)	250	0.66
Filipino (174)	275	0.73
Indian (168)	205	0.54
Indonesian (5)	9	0.02
Japanese (34)	76	0.20
Korean (342)	384	1.02
Laotian (1)	1	<0.01
Pakistani (54)	55	0.15
Taiwanese (9)	10	0.03
Thai (14)	17	0.05
Vietnamese (37)	49	0.13
Hawaii Native/Pacific Islander (17)	58	0.15
Not Hispanic (10)	51	0.14
Hispanic (7)	7	0.02
Guamanian/Chamorro (5)	14	0.04
Native Hawaiian (7)	19	0.05
Samoan (3)	4	0.01
White (34,020)	34,617	91.98
Not Hispanic (33,417)	33,945	90.20
Hispanic (603)	672	1.79

Silver Spring

Place Type: CDP
County: Montgomery
Population: 71,452†

Ancestry‡	Population	%
Afghan (12)	12	0.02

*Notes: † The Census 2010 population figure is used to calculate the percentages in the Hispanic Origin and Race categories. Ancestry percentages are based on the 2006-2010 American Community Survey population (not shown); ‡ Numbers in parentheses indicate the number of people reporting a single ancestry; * Numbers in parentheses indicate the number of persons reporting this race alone, not in combination with any other race; Please refer to the Explanation of Data for more information.*

Ancestry	Population	%
African, Sub-Saharan (5,074)	5,328	7.61
African (1,713)	1,865	2.66
Cape Verdean (15)	55	0.08
Ethiopian (1,828)	1,854	2.65
Ghanaian (73)	73	0.10
Kenyan (247)	247	0.35
Liberian (85)	85	0.12
Nigerian (377)	377	0.54
Senegalese (78)	90	0.13
Sierra Leonean (34)	34	0.05
Somalian (35)	35	0.05
Sudanese (96)	96	0.14
Other Sub-Saharan African (493)	517	0.74
Albanian (0)	9	0.01
Alsatian (0)	11	0.02
American (859)	859	1.23
Arab (163)	462	0.66
Arab (0)	18	0.03
Egyptian (19)	19	0.03
Iraqi (15)	54	0.08
Lebanese (129)	228	0.33
Moroccan (0)	20	0.03
Syrian (0)	37	0.05
Other Arab (0)	86	0.12
Armenian (9)	20	0.03
Austrian (108)	282	0.40
Belgian (8)	69	0.10
Brazilian (117)	128	0.18
British (254)	581	0.83
Bulgarian (138)	138	0.20
Cajun (17)	44	0.06
Canadian (35)	53	0.08
Croatian (14)	14	0.02
Czech (53)	194	0.28
Danish (8)	95	0.14
Dutch (61)	373	0.53
Eastern European (722)	795	1.13
English (1,022)	3,633	5.19
Estonian (8)	8	0.01
European (995)	1,355	1.93
Finnish (14)	66	0.09
French, ex. Basque (123)	981	1.40
French Canadian (25)	175	0.25
German (1,193)	5,456	7.79
German Russian (0)	48	0.07
Greek (324)	574	0.82
Guyanese (75)	122	0.17
Hungarian (110)	281	0.40
Icelander (0)	9	0.01
Iranian (16)	27	0.04
Irish (1,528)	5,234	7.47
Israeli (0)	50	0.07
Italian (927)	2,632	3.76
Latvian (34)	34	0.05
Lithuanian (44)	194	0.28
Northern European (69)	79	0.11
Norwegian (64)	418	0.60
Pennsylvania German (0)	8	0.01
Polish (473)	1,892	2.70
Portuguese (32)	208	0.30
Romanian (0)	73	0.10
Russian (553)	1,472	2.10
Scandinavian (14)	14	0.02
Scotch-Irish (309)	677	0.97
Scottish (235)	1,129	1.61
Serbian (0)	9	0.01
Slavic (0)	28	0.04
Slovak (25)	104	0.15
Slovene (14)	14	0.02
Swedish (175)	714	1.02
Swiss (39)	173	0.25
Turkish (52)	71	0.10
Ukrainian (156)	345	0.49
Welsh (10)	177	0.25
West Indian, ex. Hispanic (1,811)	2,107	3.01
Bahamian (8)	8	0.01
Barbadian (0)	66	0.09
British West Indian (138)	146	0.21
Haitian (425)	443	0.63
Jamaican (665)	742	1.06
Trinidadian/Tobagonian (84)	211	0.30
West Indian (491)	491	0.70
Yugoslavian (10)	10	0.01

Hispanic Origin	Population	%
Hispanic or Latino (of any race)	18,759	26.25
Central American, ex. Mexican	11,474	16.06
Costa Rican	49	0.07
Guatemalan	2,360	3.30
Honduran	1,166	1.63
Nicaraguan	610	0.85
Panamanian	151	0.21
Salvadoran	7,103	9.94
Other Central American	35	0.05
Cuban	280	0.39
Dominican Republic	829	1.16
Mexican	1,887	2.64
Puerto Rican	564	0.79
South American	1,695	2.37
Argentinean	118	0.17
Bolivian	348	0.49
Chilean	96	0.13
Colombian	372	0.52
Ecuadorian	185	0.26
Paraguayan	27	0.04
Peruvian	446	0.62
Uruguayan	25	0.03
Venezuelan	65	0.09
Other South American	13	0.02
Other Hispanic or Latino	2,030	2.84

Race*	Population	%
African-American/Black (19,879)	21,333	29.86
Not Hispanic (19,120)	20,144	28.19
Hispanic (759)	1,189	1.66
American Indian/Alaska Native (413)	1,051	1.47
Not Hispanic (110)	488	0.68
Hispanic (303)	563	0.79
Apache (4)	7	0.01
Arapaho (0)	1	<0.01
Blackfeet (2)	26	0.04
Canadian/French Am. Ind. (1)	3	<0.01
Central American Ind. (41)	59	0.08
Cherokee (8)	122	0.17
Chickasaw (0)	1	<0.01
Chippewa (1)	6	0.01
Choctaw (1)	10	0.01
Comanche (1)	1	<0.01
Creek (7)	10	0.01
Delaware (2)	3	<0.01
Houma (0)	1	<0.01
Inupiat *(Alaska Native)* (2)	3	<0.01
Iroquois (1)	11	0.02
Kiowa (0)	1	<0.01
Lumbee (4)	6	0.01
Menominee (1)	1	<0.01
Mexican American Ind. (68)	110	0.15
Navajo (8)	10	0.01
Ottawa (2)	2	<0.01
Seminole (1)	10	0.01
Shoshone (0)	1	<0.01
Sioux (6)	17	0.02
South American Ind. (26)	69	0.10
Spanish American Ind. (18)	19	0.03
Tlingit-Haida *(Alaska Native)* (0)	2	<0.01
Tohono O'Odham (0)	1	<0.01
Ute (1)	2	<0.01
Yaqui (2)	3	<0.01
Yup'ik *(Alaska Native)* (2)	2	<0.01
Asian (5,637)	6,637	9.29
Not Hispanic (5,567)	6,462	9.04
Hispanic (70)	175	0.24
Bangladeshi (242)	273	0.38
Bhutanese (6)	6	0.01
Burmese (35)	41	0.06
Cambodian (176)	192	0.27
Chinese, ex. Taiwanese (731)	994	1.39
Filipino (632)	794	1.11
Hmong (3)	3	<0.01
Indian (1,336)	1,571	2.20
Indonesian (55)	68	0.10
Japanese (148)	282	0.39
Korean (390)	477	0.67
Laotian (44)	48	0.07
Malaysian (2)	7	0.01
Nepalese (92)	100	0.14
Pakistani (126)	153	0.21
Sri Lankan (64)	67	0.09
Taiwanese (55)	64	0.09
Thai (140)	164	0.23
Vietnamese (1,167)	1,262	1.77
Hawaii Native/Pacific Islander (49)	193	0.27
Not Hispanic (30)	126	0.18
Hispanic (19)	67	0.09
Fijian (3)	3	<0.01
Guamanian/Chamorro (13)	29	0.04
Marshallese (10)	10	0.01
Native Hawaiian (7)	36	0.05
Samoan (4)	11	0.02
Tongan (0)	1	<0.01
White (32,666)	35,234	49.31
Not Hispanic (25,702)	27,103	37.93
Hispanic (6,964)	8,131	11.38

South Kensington

Place Type: CDP
County: Montgomery
Population: 8,462†

Ancestry‡	Population	%
African, Sub-Saharan (9)	47	0.58
Ghanaian (0)	19	0.23
Senegalese (9)	28	0.34
American (332)	332	4.07
Arab (79)	126	1.55
Egyptian (8)	8	0.10
Lebanese (71)	82	1.01
Other Arab (0)	36	0.44
Armenian (15)	15	0.18
Australian (8)	16	0.20
Austrian (6)	52	0.64
British (67)	179	2.20
Canadian (10)	29	0.36
Czech (0)	19	0.23
Danish (10)	77	0.94
Dutch (44)	159	1.95
Eastern European (91)	91	1.12
English (217)	1,222	15.00
Estonian (10)	10	0.12
European (211)	211	2.59
Finnish (9)	9	0.11
French, ex. Basque (24)	275	3.37
French Canadian (12)	54	0.66
German (384)	1,855	22.76
Greek (47)	117	1.44
Guyanese (158)	158	1.94
Hungarian (10)	21	0.26
Iranian (21)	21	0.26
Irish (663)	1,925	23.62
Israeli (0)	11	0.13
Italian (237)	803	9.85
Latvian (9)	17	0.21
Lithuanian (16)	75	0.92
Norwegian (60)	162	1.99
Polish (135)	361	4.43
Portuguese (8)	8	0.10
Russian (96)	172	2.11
Scandinavian (10)	21	0.26
Scotch-Irish (167)	401	4.92
Scottish (37)	361	4.43
Slovak (8)	30	0.37
Swedish (7)	61	0.75
Swiss (10)	26	0.32
Turkish (0)	10	0.12
Ukrainian (20)	39	0.48
Welsh (0)	95	1.17
West Indian, ex. Hispanic (26)	41	0.50
Bermudan (26)	26	0.32
Jamaican (0)	15	0.18

*Notes: † The Census 2010 population figure is used to calculate the percentages in the Hispanic Origin and Race categories. Ancestry percentages are based on the 2006-2010 American Community Survey population (not shown); ‡ Numbers in parentheses indicate the number of people reporting a single ancestry; * Numbers in parentheses indicate the number of persons reporting this race alone, not in combination with any other race; Please refer to the Explanation of Data for more information.*

Hispanic Origin	Population	%
Hispanic or Latino (of any race)	554	6.55
Central American, ex. Mexican	104	1.23
Costa Rican	4	0.05
Guatemalan	16	0.19
Honduran	2	0.02
Nicaraguan	15	0.18
Panamanian	21	0.25
Salvadoran	45	0.53
Other Central American	1	0.01
Cuban	53	0.63
Dominican Republic	14	0.17
Mexican	78	0.92
Puerto Rican	43	0.51
South American	186	2.20
Argentinean	26	0.31
Bolivian	15	0.18
Chilean	19	0.22
Colombian	44	0.52
Ecuadorian	21	0.25
Paraguayan	12	0.14
Peruvian	30	0.35
Uruguayan	8	0.09
Venezuelan	7	0.08
Other South American	4	0.05
Other Hispanic or Latino	76	0.90

Race*	Population	%
African-American/Black (285)	360	4.25
Not Hispanic (270)	335	3.96
Hispanic (15)	25	0.30
American Indian/Alaska Native (22)	57	0.67
Not Hispanic (14)	39	0.46
Hispanic (8)	18	0.21
Blackfeet (0)	1	0.01
Canadian/French Am. Ind. (0)	5	0.06
Cherokee (1)	8	0.09
Chickasaw (1)	1	0.01
Chippewa (1)	1	0.01
Cree (0)	3	0.04
Iroquois (1)	1	0.01
Mexican American Ind. (2)	4	0.05
Navajo (7)	7	0.08
Sioux (2)	2	0.02
Spanish American Ind. (0)	1	0.01
Yaqui (1)	3	0.04
Asian (341)	467	5.52
Not Hispanic (336)	447	5.28
Hispanic (5)	20	0.24
Bangladeshi (11)	11	0.13
Burmese (1)	1	0.01
Cambodian (3)	5	0.06
Chinese, ex. Taiwanese (71)	109	1.29
Filipino (42)	64	0.76
Indian (71)	99	1.17
Indonesian (2)	4	0.05
Japanese (11)	34	0.40
Korean (43)	54	0.64
Laotian (2)	5	0.06
Pakistani (7)	7	0.08
Sri Lankan (3)	5	0.06
Taiwanese (14)	14	0.17
Thai (17)	24	0.28
Vietnamese (24)	33	0.39
Hawaii Native/Pacific Islander (0)	2	0.02
Not Hispanic (0)	2	0.02
Native Hawaiian (0)	1	0.01
Samoan (0)	2	0.02
White (7,456)	7,677	90.72
Not Hispanic (7,070)	7,251	85.69
Hispanic (386)	426	5.03

South Laurel

Place Type: CDP
County: Prince George's
Population: 26,112†

Ancestry‡	Population	%
African, Sub-Saharan (2,414)	2,720	10.57
African (965)	1,123	4.36
Cape Verdean (0)	44	0.17
Ghanaian (18)	35	0.14
Kenyan (21)	21	0.08
Liberian (24)	36	0.14
Nigerian (1,256)	1,307	5.08
Sierra Leonean (8)	16	0.06
Zimbabwean (17)	33	0.13
Other Sub-Saharan African (105)	105	0.41
Albanian (16)	16	0.06
American (400)	400	1.55
Arab (107)	136	0.53
Lebanese (0)	18	0.07
Moroccan (102)	102	0.40
Palestinian (5)	16	0.06
Brazilian (37)	37	0.14
British (53)	93	0.36
Cajun (0)	12	0.05
Canadian (20)	20	0.08
Croatian (0)	11	0.04
Czech (7)	24	0.09
Czechoslovakian (17)	26	0.10
Danish (0)	10	0.04
Dutch (61)	115	0.45
Eastern European (10)	10	0.04
English (403)	998	3.88
European (45)	100	0.39
Finnish (0)	8	0.03
French, ex. Basque (31)	400	1.55
French Canadian (8)	38	0.15
German (391)	1,662	6.46
Greek (58)	101	0.39
Hungarian (29)	46	0.18
Iranian (6)	6	0.02
Irish (209)	1,160	4.51
Italian (301)	904	3.51
Lithuanian (13)	22	0.09
Norwegian (15)	40	0.16
Polish (62)	187	0.73
Portuguese (17)	54	0.21
Russian (77)	104	0.40
Scotch-Irish (88)	153	0.59
Scottish (37)	239	0.93
Slovak (0)	100	0.39
Swedish (24)	203	0.79
Swiss (0)	49	0.19
Ukrainian (0)	10	0.04
Welsh (0)	57	0.22
West Indian, ex. Hispanic (718)	830	3.22
Barbadian (11)	11	0.04
British West Indian (11)	11	0.04
Haitian (85)	85	0.33
Jamaican (470)	548	2.13
Trinidadian/Tobagonian (48)	57	0.22
West Indian (93)	118	0.46

Hispanic Origin	Population	%
Hispanic or Latino (of any race)	3,535	13.54
Central American, ex. Mexican	1,722	6.59
Costa Rican	12	0.05
Guatemalan	400	1.53
Honduran	119	0.46
Nicaraguan	75	0.29
Panamanian	75	0.29
Salvadoran	1,030	3.94
Other Central American	11	0.04
Cuban	51	0.20
Dominican Republic	161	0.62
Mexican	728	2.79
Puerto Rican	293	1.12
South American	219	0.84
Argentinean	14	0.05
Bolivian	8	0.03
Chilean	17	0.07
Colombian	57	0.22
Ecuadorian	14	0.05
Paraguayan	3	0.01
Peruvian	89	0.34
Uruguayan	3	0.01
Venezuelan	10	0.04
Other South American	4	0.02
Other Hispanic or Latino	361	1.38

Race*	Population	%
African-American/Black (15,898)	16,576	63.48
Not Hispanic (15,586)	16,147	61.84
Hispanic (312)	429	1.64
American Indian/Alaska Native (81)	358	1.37
Not Hispanic (50)	279	1.07
Hispanic (31)	79	0.30
Alaska Athabascan *(Ala. Nat.)* (1)	1	<0.01
Aleut *(Alaska Native)* (0)	1	<0.01
Blackfeet (0)	9	0.03
Central American Ind. (0)	4	0.02
Cherokee (9)	50	0.19
Choctaw (0)	9	0.03
Cree (0)	1	<0.01
Creek (2)	2	0.01
Crow (0)	1	<0.01
Iroquois (0)	5	0.02
Lumbee (2)	8	0.03
Mexican American Ind. (4)	11	0.04
Navajo (2)	3	0.01
Sioux (1)	3	0.01
South American Ind. (3)	4	0.02
Spanish American Ind. (1)	3	0.01
Yaqui (1)	1	<0.01
Asian (1,353)	1,574	6.03
Not Hispanic (1,340)	1,536	5.88
Hispanic (13)	38	0.15
Bangladeshi (7)	7	0.03
Burmese (18)	22	0.08
Cambodian (28)	32	0.12
Chinese, ex. Taiwanese (126)	161	0.62
Filipino (216)	280	1.07
Indian (378)	430	1.65
Indonesian (5)	9	0.03
Japanese (23)	55	0.21
Korean (118)	145	0.56
Laotian (2)	2	0.01
Malaysian (3)	4	0.02
Nepalese (5)	5	0.02
Pakistani (163)	170	0.65
Sri Lankan (4)	4	0.02
Taiwanese (11)	12	0.05
Thai (7)	10	0.04
Vietnamese (210)	215	0.82
Hawaii Native/Pacific Islander (6)	47	0.18
Not Hispanic (6)	43	0.16
Hispanic (0)	4	0.02
Fijian (1)	4	0.02
Guamanian/Chamorro (1)	7	0.03
Native Hawaiian (0)	3	0.01
Samoan (0)	2	0.01
White (6,065)	6,707	25.69
Not Hispanic (4,798)	5,253	20.12
Hispanic (1,267)	1,454	5.57

Suitland

Place Type: CDP
County: Prince George's
Population: 25,825†

Ancestry‡	Population	%
African, Sub-Saharan (670)	772	3.06
African (540)	557	2.21
Cape Verdean (0)	36	0.14
Ethiopian (60)	60	0.24
Ghanaian (25)	25	0.10
Liberian (0)	49	0.19
Nigerian (45)	45	0.18
American (554)	554	2.19
Arab (0)	8	0.03
Other Arab (0)	8	0.03
British (11)	11	0.04
Canadian (11)	11	0.04
Czechoslovakian (9)	9	0.04
Danish (19)	19	0.08
Dutch (0)	20	0.08

*Notes: † The Census 2010 population figure is used to calculate the percentages in the Hispanic Origin and Race categories. Ancestry percentages are based on the 2006-2010 American Community Survey population (not shown); ‡ Numbers in parentheses indicate the number of people reporting a single ancestry; * Numbers in parentheses indicate the number of persons reporting this race alone, not in combination with any other race; Please refer to the Explanation of Data for more information.*

English (54)	120	0.48
German (64)	123	0.49
Guyanese (62)	62	0.25
Irish (9)	229	0.91
Italian (41)	89	0.35
Polish (0)	13	0.05
Portuguese (0)	36	0.14
Scotch-Irish (8)	8	0.03
Scottish (33)	43	0.17
Swedish (0)	21	0.08
Welsh (0)	12	0.05
West Indian, ex. Hispanic (159)	284	1.13
Bahamian (0)	33	0.13
Bermudan (47)	47	0.19
British West Indian (31)	31	0.12
Haitian (0)	23	0.09
Jamaican (66)	85	0.34
Trinidadian/Tobagonian (15)	15	0.06
West Indian (0)	50	0.20

Hispanic Origin	Population	%
Hispanic or Latino (of any race)	1,224	4.74
Central American, ex. Mexican	704	2.73
Guatemalan	33	0.13
Honduran	24	0.09
Nicaraguan	10	0.04
Panamanian	47	0.18
Salvadoran	590	2.28
Cuban	8	0.03
Dominican Republic	36	0.14
Mexican	120	0.46
Puerto Rican	111	0.43
South American	23	0.09
Argentinean	1	<0.01
Bolivian	9	0.03
Colombian	8	0.03
Ecuadorian	4	0.02
Paraguayan	1	<0.01
Other Hispanic or Latino	222	0.86

Race*	Population	%
African-American/Black (23,746)	24,160	93.55
Not Hispanic (23,569)	23,933	92.67
Hispanic (177)	227	0.88
American Indian/Alaska Native (104)	314	1.22
Not Hispanic (78)	247	0.96
Hispanic (26)	67	0.26
Blackfeet (1)	5	0.02
Cherokee (6)	47	0.18
Cheyenne (3)	6	0.02
Chickasaw (0)	1	<0.01
Choctaw (0)	1	<0.01
Crow (0)	2	0.01
Delaware (1)	2	0.01
Iroquois (0)	2	0.01
Mexican American Ind. (3)	14	0.05
Navajo (1)	4	0.02
Sioux (0)	1	<0.01
South American Ind. (0)	2	0.01
Spanish American Ind. (0)	1	<0.01
Asian (89)	156	0.60
Not Hispanic (88)	149	0.58
Hispanic (1)	7	0.03
Chinese, ex. Taiwanese (14)	25	0.10
Filipino (30)	54	0.21
Indian (14)	20	0.08
Indonesian (5)	9	0.03
Japanese (1)	5	0.02
Korean (6)	9	0.03
Laotian (9)	9	0.03
Taiwanese (0)	2	0.01
Thai (7)	8	0.03
Hawaii Native/Pacific Islander (12)	37	0.14
Not Hispanic (6)	26	0.10
Hispanic (6)	11	0.04
Guamanian/Chamorro (6)	6	0.02
Native Hawaiian (0)	6	0.02
Samoan (2)	5	0.02
White (663)	984	3.81
Not Hispanic (450)	659	2.55
Hispanic (213)	325	1.26

Summerfield

Place Type: CDP
County: Prince George's
Population: 10,898†

Ancestry‡	Population	%
African, Sub-Saharan (857)	923	8.29
African (447)	493	4.43
Liberian (36)	36	0.32
Nigerian (141)	141	1.27
Sierra Leonean (57)	57	0.51
Somalian (49)	58	0.52
Other Sub-Saharan African (127)	138	1.24
American (43)	43	0.39
Canadian (6)	6	0.05
English (40)	71	0.64
German (16)	42	0.38
Guyanese (67)	67	0.60
Irish (0)	27	0.24
West Indian, ex. Hispanic (193)	205	1.84
Jamaican (136)	148	1.33
Trinidadian/Tobagonian (57)	57	0.51

Hispanic Origin	Population	%
Hispanic or Latino (of any race)	493	4.52
Central American, ex. Mexican	221	2.03
Guatemalan	30	0.28
Honduran	20	0.18
Nicaraguan	10	0.09
Panamanian	32	0.29
Salvadoran	129	1.18
Cuban	12	0.11
Dominican Republic	44	0.40
Mexican	78	0.72
Puerto Rican	43	0.39
South American	17	0.16
Chilean	2	0.02
Colombian	2	0.02
Ecuadorian	2	0.02
Peruvian	7	0.06
Uruguayan	2	0.02
Venezuelan	1	0.01
Other South American	1	0.01
Other Hispanic or Latino	78	0.72

Race*	Population	%
African-American/Black (9,993)	10,201	93.60
Not Hispanic (9,861)	10,031	92.04
Hispanic (132)	170	1.56
American Indian/Alaska Native (29)	126	1.16
Not Hispanic (21)	101	0.93
Hispanic (8)	25	0.23
Blackfeet (0)	14	0.13
Cherokee (1)	27	0.25
Iroquois (0)	1	0.01
Mexican American Ind. (1)	1	0.01
Navajo (0)	5	0.05
Paiute (1)	1	0.01
Spanish American Ind. (0)	5	0.05
Asian (141)	182	1.67
Not Hispanic (141)	179	1.64
Hispanic (0)	3	0.03
Bangladeshi (6)	6	0.06
Cambodian (0)	1	0.01
Chinese, ex. Taiwanese (16)	21	0.19
Filipino (65)	77	0.71
Indian (14)	21	0.19
Indonesian (4)	4	0.04
Japanese (3)	9	0.08
Korean (1)	4	0.04
Nepalese (1)	1	0.01
Pakistani (5)	5	0.05
Thai (1)	6	0.06
Vietnamese (12)	12	0.11
Hawaii Native/Pacific Islander (3)	5	0.05
Not Hispanic (3)	5	0.05
Guamanian/Chamorro (0)	1	0.01
White (242)	379	3.48
Not Hispanic (178)	281	2.58
Hispanic (64)	98	0.90

Takoma Park

Place Type: City
County: Montgomery
Population: 16,715†

Ancestry‡	Population	%
Afghan (0)	9	0.05
African, Sub-Saharan (2,274)	2,750	16.32
African (754)	861	5.11
Cape Verdean (0)	12	0.07
Ethiopian (975)	1,072	6.36
Ghanaian (33)	44	0.26
Kenyan (7)	7	0.04
Liberian (38)	70	0.42
Nigerian (72)	111	0.66
Senegalese (37)	37	0.22
Sierra Leonean (204)	204	1.21
Zimbabwean (12)	12	0.07
Other Sub-Saharan African (142)	320	1.90
Albanian (0)	10	0.06
American (333)	333	1.98
Arab (11)	136	0.81
Arab (0)	49	0.29
Egyptian (11)	57	0.34
Lebanese (0)	12	0.07
Palestinian (0)	8	0.05
Other Arab (0)	10	0.06
Armenian (75)	102	0.61
Assyrian/Chaldean/Syriac (18)	18	0.11
Australian (0)	20	0.12
Austrian (23)	74	0.44
Belgian (61)	71	0.42
Brazilian (11)	54	0.32
British (67)	185	1.10
Canadian (10)	46	0.27
Croatian (0)	20	0.12
Czech (0)	56	0.33
Danish (0)	91	0.54
Dutch (47)	221	1.31
Eastern European (190)	210	1.25
English (354)	1,561	9.26
European (215)	263	1.56
Finnish (0)	15	0.09
French, ex. Basque (55)	505	3.00
French Canadian (0)	69	0.41
German (274)	2,252	13.36
Greek (38)	89	0.53
Guyanese (16)	36	0.21
Hungarian (0)	103	0.61
Iranian (0)	6	0.04
Irish (310)	1,692	10.04
Italian (220)	784	4.65
Latvian (0)	9	0.05
Lithuanian (0)	119	0.71
Northern European (5)	5	0.03
Norwegian (44)	144	0.85
Polish (95)	443	2.63
Portuguese (0)	80	0.47
Romanian (0)	55	0.33
Russian (172)	326	1.93
Scandinavian (0)	22	0.13
Scotch-Irish (69)	419	2.49
Scottish (111)	294	1.74
Slovak (27)	60	0.36
Swedish (16)	298	1.77
Swiss (43)	103	0.61
Turkish (20)	20	0.12
Ukrainian (34)	216	1.28
Welsh (17)	175	1.04
West Indian, ex. Hispanic (701)	866	5.14
Barbadian (11)	11	0.07
Bermudan (0)	16	0.09
British West Indian (0)	22	0.13
Haitian (66)	66	0.39
Jamaican (352)	443	2.63

*Notes: † The Census 2010 population figure is used to calculate the percentages in the Hispanic Origin and Race categories. Ancestry percentages are based on the 2006-2010 American Community Survey population (not shown); ‡ Numbers in parentheses indicate the number of people reporting a single ancestry; * Numbers in parentheses indicate the number of persons reporting this race alone, not in combination with any other race; Please refer to the Explanation of Data for more information.*

Trinidadian/Tobagonian (141)	177	1.05
West Indian (131)	131	0.78
Yugoslavian (30)	30	0.18

Hispanic Origin	Population	%
Hispanic or Latino (of any race)	2,417	14.46
Central American, ex. Mexican	1,259	7.53
Costa Rican	10	0.06
Guatemalan	285	1.71
Honduran	88	0.53
Nicaraguan	58	0.35
Panamanian	26	0.16
Salvadoran	787	4.71
Other Central American	5	0.03
Cuban	89	0.53
Dominican Republic	166	0.99
Mexican	231	1.38
Puerto Rican	91	0.54
South American	326	1.95
Argentinean	34	0.20
Bolivian	41	0.25
Chilean	18	0.11
Colombian	82	0.49
Ecuadorian	63	0.38
Paraguayan	6	0.04
Peruvian	59	0.35
Uruguayan	4	0.02
Venezuelan	16	0.10
Other South American	3	0.02
Other Hispanic or Latino	255	1.53

Race*	Population	%
African-American/Black (5,843)	6,225	37.24
Not Hispanic (5,685)	5,980	35.78
Hispanic (158)	245	1.47
American Indian/Alaska Native (45)	198	1.18
Not Hispanic (21)	123	0.74
Hispanic (24)	75	0.45
Blackfeet (1)	4	0.02
Central American Ind. (2)	7	0.04
Cherokee (4)	22	0.13
Chippewa (1)	1	0.01
Choctaw (0)	7	0.04
Iroquois (1)	2	0.01
Mexican American Ind. (4)	7	0.04
Navajo (2)	2	0.01
Osage (0)	1	0.01
Potawatomi (1)	1	0.01
Puget Sound Salish (1)	1	0.01
Seminole (0)	2	0.01
Shoshone (0)	1	0.01
Sioux (1)	3	0.02
South American Ind. (3)	10	0.06
Spanish American Ind. (0)	4	0.02
Tsimshian *(Alaska Native)* (2)	2	0.01
Asian (730)	1,016	6.08
Not Hispanic (727)	978	5.85
Hispanic (3)	38	0.23
Bangladeshi (6)	6	0.04
Burmese (2)	5	0.03
Cambodian (21)	27	0.16
Chinese, ex. Taiwanese (84)	124	0.74
Filipino (87)	143	0.86
Indian (329)	407	2.43
Indonesian (4)	4	0.02
Japanese (35)	63	0.38
Korean (49)	74	0.44
Laotian (0)	1	0.01
Nepalese (4)	4	0.02
Pakistani (11)	18	0.11
Sri Lankan (6)	6	0.04
Taiwanese (7)	14	0.08
Thai (8)	17	0.10
Vietnamese (43)	47	0.28
Hawaii Native/Pacific Islander (10)	42	0.25
Not Hispanic (10)	32	0.19
Hispanic (0)	10	0.06
Fijian (0)	1	0.01
Guamanian/Chamorro (1)	1	0.01
Native Hawaiian (0)	9	0.05
Samoan (3)	5	0.03
White (8,192)	8,814	52.73
Not Hispanic (7,244)	7,663	45.85
Hispanic (948)	1,151	6.89

Temple Hills

Place Type: CDP
County: Prince George's
Population: 7,852†

Ancestry‡	Population	%
African, Sub-Saharan (163)	163	2.13
African (73)	73	0.96
Ethiopian (59)	59	0.77
Nigerian (31)	31	0.41
American (302)	302	3.95
British (11)	11	0.14
Czech (0)	10	0.13
Dutch (7)	7	0.09
English (12)	31	0.41
European (16)	16	0.21
Finnish (0)	12	0.16
French, ex. Basque (12)	47	0.62
German (27)	69	0.90
German Russian (11)	11	0.14
Irish (25)	47	0.62
Italian (6)	16	0.21
Portuguese (0)	49	0.64
Scandinavian (5)	11	0.14
Scottish (30)	30	0.39
Swedish (12)	21	0.27
West Indian, ex. Hispanic (259)	277	3.63
Barbadian (0)	18	0.24
Jamaican (231)	231	3.02
Trinidadian/Tobagonian (12)	12	0.16
West Indian (16)	16	0.21

Hispanic Origin	Population	%
Hispanic or Latino (of any race)	484	6.16
Central American, ex. Mexican	210	2.67
Costa Rican	2	0.03
Guatemalan	38	0.48
Honduran	40	0.51
Nicaraguan	8	0.10
Panamanian	17	0.22
Salvadoran	105	1.34
Cuban	16	0.20
Dominican Republic	23	0.29
Mexican	115	1.46
Puerto Rican	48	0.61
South American	11	0.14
Bolivian	4	0.05
Colombian	2	0.03
Ecuadorian	1	0.01
Paraguayan	1	0.01
Peruvian	3	0.04
Other Hispanic or Latino	61	0.78

Race*	Population	%
African-American/Black (6,825)	6,996	89.10
Not Hispanic (6,748)	6,892	87.77
Hispanic (77)	104	1.32
American Indian/Alaska Native (28)	107	1.36
Not Hispanic (19)	86	1.10
Hispanic (9)	21	0.27
Blackfeet (0)	2	0.03
Cherokee (2)	8	0.10
Cheyenne (0)	3	0.04
Lumbee (0)	1	0.01
Seminole (0)	3	0.04
South American Ind. (1)	1	0.01
Asian (94)	142	1.81
Not Hispanic (94)	133	1.69
Hispanic (0)	9	0.11
Chinese, ex. Taiwanese (7)	15	0.19
Filipino (73)	90	1.15
Indian (5)	9	0.11
Japanese (1)	11	0.14
Korean (4)	14	0.18
Thai (2)	4	0.05
Vietnamese (1)	1	0.01
Hawaii Native/Pacific Islander (8)	16	0.20
Not Hispanic (2)	10	0.13
Hispanic (6)	6	0.08
Guamanian/Chamorro (8)	11	0.14
Samoan (0)	2	0.03
White (442)	545	6.94
Not Hispanic (332)	411	5.23
Hispanic (110)	134	1.71

Timonium

Place Type: CDP
County: Baltimore
Population: 9,925†

Ancestry‡	Population	%
African, Sub-Saharan (26)	26	0.27
African (26)	26	0.27
American (513)	513	5.25
Arab (80)	98	1.00
Arab (13)	13	0.13
Lebanese (23)	41	0.42
Other Arab (44)	44	0.45
Austrian (9)	9	0.09
British (20)	30	0.31
Canadian (0)	21	0.21
Croatian (0)	31	0.32
Czech (16)	70	0.72
Czechoslovakian (0)	31	0.32
Danish (0)	23	0.24
Dutch (27)	62	0.63
Eastern European (6)	6	0.06
English (457)	1,636	16.74
European (111)	111	1.14
French, ex. Basque (14)	310	3.17
French Canadian (0)	20	0.20
German (1,143)	2,815	28.80
Greek (269)	356	3.64
Hungarian (10)	83	0.85
Iranian (50)	50	0.51
Irish (588)	1,951	19.96
Italian (423)	1,052	10.76
Lithuanian (12)	81	0.83
Norwegian (33)	58	0.59
Polish (168)	564	5.77
Romanian (0)	43	0.44
Russian (56)	173	1.77
Scandinavian (12)	12	0.12
Scotch-Irish (36)	118	1.21
Scottish (99)	226	2.31
Serbian (13)	13	0.13
Slavic (0)	10	0.10
Slovak (0)	23	0.24
Swedish (13)	52	0.53
Swiss (0)	26	0.27
Ukrainian (80)	114	1.17
Welsh (0)	46	0.47
Yugoslavian (13)	13	0.13

Hispanic Origin	Population	%
Hispanic or Latino (of any race)	294	2.96
Central American, ex. Mexican	105	1.06
Guatemalan	16	0.16
Honduran	2	0.02
Nicaraguan	4	0.04
Panamanian	2	0.02
Salvadoran	81	0.82
Cuban	7	0.07
Dominican Republic	8	0.08
Mexican	47	0.47
Puerto Rican	31	0.31
South American	78	0.79
Argentinean	6	0.06
Bolivian	3	0.03
Chilean	6	0.06
Colombian	35	0.35
Ecuadorian	18	0.18
Paraguayan	7	0.07

*Notes: † The Census 2010 population figure is used to calculate the percentages in the Hispanic Origin and Race categories. Ancestry percentages are based on the 2006-2010 American Community Survey population (not shown); ‡ Numbers in parentheses indicate the number of people reporting a single ancestry; * Numbers in parentheses indicate the number of persons reporting this race alone, not in combination with any other race; Please refer to the Explanation of Data for more information.*

Peruvian	2	0.02
Venezuelan	1	0.01
Other Hispanic or Latino	18	0.18

Race*	Population	%
African-American/Black (337)	386	3.89
Not Hispanic (333)	375	3.78
Hispanic (4)	11	0.11
American Indian/Alaska Native (4)	33	0.33
Not Hispanic (4)	28	0.28
Hispanic (0)	5	0.05
Blackfeet (0)	3	0.03
Cherokee (1)	9	0.09
Choctaw (0)	1	0.01
Iroquois (0)	3	0.03
Mexican American Ind. (1)	3	0.03
Seminole (0)	4	0.04
Sioux (0)	2	0.02
South American Ind. (1)	1	0.01
Asian (770)	863	8.70
Not Hispanic (768)	861	8.68
Hispanic (2)	2	0.02
Bangladeshi (7)	9	0.09
Burmese (12)	12	0.12
Cambodian (1)	1	0.01
Chinese, ex. Taiwanese (232)	252	2.54
Filipino (112)	146	1.47
Indian (149)	168	1.69
Japanese (11)	21	0.21
Korean (171)	175	1.76
Malaysian (1)	1	0.01
Nepalese (3)	6	0.06
Pakistani (5)	6	0.06
Sri Lankan (2)	3	0.03
Taiwanese (28)	29	0.29
Thai (7)	9	0.09
Vietnamese (8)	11	0.11
Hawaii Native/Pacific Islander (5)	10	0.10
Not Hispanic (4)	6	0.06
Hispanic (1)	4	0.04
Native Hawaiian (1)	1	0.01
Samoan (2)	2	0.02
White (8,552)	8,699	87.65
Not Hispanic (8,360)	8,490	85.54
Hispanic (192)	209	2.11

Towson

Place Type: CDP
County: Baltimore
Population: 55,197†

Ancestry‡	Population	%
Afghan (24)	24	0.04
African, Sub-Saharan (418)	507	0.94
African (231)	297	0.55
Cape Verdean (14)	27	0.05
Ethiopian (52)	52	0.10
Ghanaian (31)	31	0.06
Nigerian (38)	38	0.07
Senegalese (33)	33	0.06
South African (0)	10	0.02
Other Sub-Saharan African (19)	19	0.04
Albanian (40)	71	0.13
Alsatian (0)	10	0.02
American (2,914)	2,914	5.39
Arab (226)	502	0.93
Arab (49)	118	0.22
Lebanese (54)	64	0.12
Moroccan (0)	12	0.02
Palestinian (43)	90	0.17
Syrian (80)	160	0.30
Other Arab (0)	58	0.11
Armenian (28)	78	0.14
Australian (32)	53	0.10
Austrian (61)	222	0.41
Belgian (34)	43	0.08
Brazilian (20)	20	0.04
British (212)	361	0.67
Canadian (128)	207	0.38
Celtic (20)	29	0.05
Croatian (15)	83	0.15
Czech (89)	527	0.97
Czechoslovakian (9)	77	0.14
Danish (35)	128	0.24
Dutch (153)	678	1.25
Eastern European (175)	175	0.32
English (2,186)	8,288	15.33
Estonian (13)	53	0.10
European (736)	854	1.58
Finnish (0)	33	0.06
French, ex. Basque (224)	1,724	3.19
French Canadian (42)	153	0.28
German (2,748)	10,586	19.58
Greek (190)	326	0.60
Guyanese (20)	20	0.04
Hungarian (134)	565	1.04
Icelander (0)	10	0.02
Iranian (39)	68	0.13
Irish (3,600)	10,515	19.45
Israeli (31)	43	0.08
Italian (1,630)	4,329	8.01
Latvian (30)	44	0.08
Lithuanian (96)	336	0.62
Macedonian (0)	6	0.01
New Zealander (41)	49	0.09
Northern European (140)	140	0.26
Norwegian (84)	452	0.84
Pennsylvania German (19)	28	0.05
Polish (816)	2,678	4.95
Portuguese (13)	51	0.09
Romanian (89)	154	0.28
Russian (563)	1,218	2.25
Scandinavian (36)	72	0.13
Scotch-Irish (628)	1,377	2.55
Scottish (418)	1,637	3.03
Serbian (53)	85	0.16
Slavic (11)	31	0.06
Slovak (44)	118	0.22
Slovene (0)	16	0.03
Swedish (108)	294	0.54
Swiss (20)	145	0.27
Turkish (237)	237	0.44
Ukrainian (194)	573	1.06
Welsh (163)	793	1.47
West Indian, ex. Hispanic (331)	407	0.75
Bermudan (0)	16	0.03
Haitian (31)	60	0.11
Jamaican (91)	122	0.23
Trinidadian/Tobagonian (16)	16	0.03
West Indian (193)	193	0.36
Yugoslavian (9)	9	0.02

Hispanic Origin	Population	%
Hispanic or Latino (of any race)	1,883	3.41
Central American, ex. Mexican	494	0.89
Costa Rican	20	0.04
Guatemalan	132	0.24
Honduran	120	0.22
Nicaraguan	22	0.04
Panamanian	53	0.10
Salvadoran	145	0.26
Other Central American	2	<0.01
Cuban	113	0.20
Dominican Republic	29	0.05
Mexican	373	0.68
Puerto Rican	297	0.54
South American	365	0.66
Argentinean	64	0.12
Bolivian	14	0.03
Chilean	35	0.06
Colombian	91	0.16
Ecuadorian	44	0.08
Paraguayan	6	0.01
Peruvian	84	0.15
Uruguayan	6	0.01
Venezuelan	20	0.04
Other South American	1	<0.01
Other Hispanic or Latino	212	0.38

Race*	Population	%
African-American/Black (6,062)	6,525	11.82
Not Hispanic (5,948)	6,374	11.55
Hispanic (114)	151	0.27
American Indian/Alaska Native (87)	301	0.55
Not Hispanic (73)	254	0.46
Hispanic (14)	47	0.09
Blackfeet (0)	7	0.01
Central American Ind. (0)	5	0.01
Cherokee (8)	50	0.09
Cheyenne (0)	1	<0.01
Chippewa (4)	12	0.02
Choctaw (1)	3	0.01
Comanche (0)	4	0.01
Creek (0)	2	<0.01
Crow (0)	1	<0.01
Iroquois (3)	5	0.01
Kiowa (1)	1	<0.01
Lumbee (9)	14	0.03
Mexican American Ind. (7)	8	0.01
Navajo (0)	1	<0.01
Potawatomi (0)	1	<0.01
Seminole (0)	4	0.01
Sioux (1)	4	0.01
South American Ind. (8)	13	0.02
Spanish American Ind. (0)	1	<0.01
Tohono O'Odham (0)	2	<0.01
Ute (0)	1	<0.01
Asian (2,835)	3,449	6.25
Not Hispanic (2,819)	3,411	6.18
Hispanic (16)	38	0.07
Bangladeshi (14)	17	0.03
Bhutanese (1)	1	<0.01
Burmese (7)	8	0.01
Cambodian (11)	20	0.04
Chinese, ex. Taiwanese (750)	879	1.59
Filipino (297)	441	0.80
Indian (681)	775	1.40
Indonesian (4)	7	0.01
Japanese (87)	199	0.36
Korean (333)	415	0.75
Laotian (7)	10	0.02
Malaysian (1)	5	0.01
Nepalese (250)	273	0.49
Pakistani (84)	95	0.17
Sri Lankan (5)	5	0.01
Taiwanese (50)	59	0.11
Thai (17)	26	0.05
Vietnamese (72)	104	0.19
Hawaii Native/Pacific Islander (20)	66	0.12
Not Hispanic (20)	55	0.10
Hispanic (0)	11	0.02
Fijian (1)	2	<0.01
Guamanian/Chamorro (5)	10	0.02
Native Hawaiian (5)	13	0.02
Samoan (4)	5	0.01
White (44,492)	45,485	82.40
Not Hispanic (43,301)	44,179	80.04
Hispanic (1,191)	1,306	2.37

Travilah

Place Type: CDP
County: Montgomery
Population: 12,159†

Ancestry‡	Population	%
Afghan (21)	21	0.17
African, Sub-Saharan (274)	300	2.49
Ethiopian (28)	28	0.23
Nigerian (205)	205	1.70
South African (13)	39	0.32
Zimbabwean (28)	28	0.23
American (412)	412	3.42
Arab (42)	42	0.35
Egyptian (30)	30	0.25
Lebanese (12)	12	0.10
Armenian (34)	64	0.53
Assyrian/Chaldean/Syriac (14)	14	0.12

*Notes: † The Census 2010 population figure is used to calculate the percentages in the Hispanic Origin and Race categories. Ancestry percentages are based on the 2006-2010 American Community Survey population (not shown); ‡ Numbers in parentheses indicate the number of people reporting a single ancestry; * Numbers in parentheses indicate the number of persons reporting this race alone, not in combination with any other race; Please refer to the Explanation of Data for more information.*

Ancestry	Population	%
Austrian (0)	40	0.33
Belgian (0)	37	0.31
British (74)	137	1.14
Canadian (0)	9	0.07
Czech (15)	62	0.51
Czechoslovakian (9)	9	0.07
Danish (14)	51	0.42
Dutch (12)	53	0.44
Eastern European (218)	260	2.16
English (316)	1,000	8.29
European (254)	282	2.34
French, ex. Basque (62)	240	1.99
French Canadian (0)	34	0.28
German (328)	1,213	10.06
Greek (134)	163	1.35
Hungarian (64)	195	1.62
Iranian (106)	163	1.35
Irish (292)	741	6.14
Israeli (11)	11	0.09
Italian (141)	354	2.93
Latvian (27)	54	0.45
Lithuanian (17)	40	0.33
Northern European (54)	54	0.45
Norwegian (30)	91	0.75
Polish (83)	387	3.21
Portuguese (38)	38	0.32
Romanian (13)	73	0.61
Russian (437)	625	5.18
Scandinavian (11)	24	0.20
Scotch-Irish (191)	345	2.86
Scottish (90)	330	2.74
Slovak (0)	17	0.14
Slovene (0)	11	0.09
Swedish (21)	116	0.96
Swiss (0)	21	0.17
Turkish (0)	32	0.27
Welsh (12)	49	0.41
West Indian, ex. Hispanic (16)	16	0.13
Bermudan (6)	6	0.05
Trinidadian/Tobagonian (10)	10	0.08

Hispanic Origin	Population	%
Hispanic or Latino (of any race)	439	3.61
Central American, ex. Mexican	57	0.47
Costa Rican	5	0.04
Guatemalan	9	0.07
Honduran	1	0.01
Nicaraguan	1	0.01
Panamanian	1	0.01
Salvadoran	36	0.30
Other Central American	4	0.03
Cuban	33	0.27
Dominican Republic	18	0.15
Mexican	82	0.67
Puerto Rican	32	0.26
South American	146	1.20
Argentinean	20	0.16
Bolivian	14	0.12
Chilean	13	0.11
Colombian	43	0.35
Ecuadorian	11	0.09
Paraguayan	3	0.02
Peruvian	24	0.20
Uruguayan	4	0.03
Venezuelan	12	0.10
Other South American	2	0.02
Other Hispanic or Latino	71	0.58

Race*	Population	%
African-American/Black (594)	642	5.28
Not Hispanic (571)	613	5.04
Hispanic (23)	29	0.24
American Indian/Alaska Native (11)	42	0.35
Not Hispanic (6)	32	0.26
Hispanic (5)	10	0.08
Cherokee (3)	6	0.05
Chippewa (0)	2	0.02
Choctaw (0)	1	0.01
Creek (0)	1	0.01
Mexican American Ind. (1)	6	0.05
South American Ind. (0)	3	0.02
Asian (3,610)	3,875	31.87
Not Hispanic (3,609)	3,872	31.84
Hispanic (1)	3	0.02
Bangladeshi (21)	30	0.25
Burmese (14)	15	0.12
Cambodian (2)	2	0.02
Chinese, ex. Taiwanese (1,500)	1,586	13.04
Filipino (56)	64	0.53
Indian (1,065)	1,140	9.38
Indonesian (3)	7	0.06
Japanese (16)	23	0.19
Korean (444)	468	3.85
Malaysian (3)	3	0.02
Nepalese (9)	9	0.07
Pakistani (87)	97	0.80
Sri Lankan (36)	38	0.31
Taiwanese (152)	185	1.52
Thai (6)	10	0.08
Vietnamese (101)	111	0.91
Hawaii Native/Pacific Islander (0)	20	0.16
Not Hispanic (0)	20	0.16
Native Hawaiian (0)	1	0.01
White (7,487)	7,767	63.88
Not Hispanic (7,167)	7,432	61.12
Hispanic (320)	335	2.76

Urbana

Place Type: CDP
County: Frederick
Population: 9,175[†]

Ancestry[‡]	Population	%
Afghan (45)	45	0.62
African, Sub-Saharan (107)	107	1.47
African (12)	12	0.16
Ghanaian (21)	21	0.29
Somalian (52)	52	0.71
Ugandan (22)	22	0.30
American (193)	193	2.65
Arab (12)	12	0.16
Egyptian (7)	7	0.10
Jordanian (5)	5	0.07
Australian (0)	5	0.07
Austrian (0)	37	0.51
Basque (0)	13	0.18
British (15)	20	0.27
Danish (0)	47	0.64
Dutch (0)	88	1.21
English (152)	784	10.75
European (86)	86	1.18
French, ex. Basque (0)	91	1.25
French Canadian (36)	54	0.74
German (345)	1,342	18.40
Greek (29)	29	0.40
Hungarian (66)	78	1.07
Iranian (31)	31	0.43
Irish (246)	1,005	13.78
Italian (125)	477	6.54
Lithuanian (0)	12	0.16
Northern European (12)	12	0.16
Norwegian (0)	31	0.43
Polish (33)	331	4.54
Portuguese (11)	19	0.26
Romanian (25)	25	0.34
Russian (82)	201	2.76
Scandinavian (0)	14	0.19
Scotch-Irish (15)	115	1.58
Scottish (82)	106	1.45
Slavic (0)	8	0.11
Slovak (28)	68	0.93
Slovene (11)	11	0.15
Swedish (0)	109	1.49
Turkish (34)	58	0.80
Ukrainian (9)	27	0.37
Welsh (0)	12	0.16
West Indian, ex. Hispanic (27)	107	1.47
Haitian (14)	14	0.19
Jamaican (13)	13	0.18
West Indian (0)	80	1.10

Hispanic Origin	Population	%
Hispanic or Latino (of any race)	924	10.07
Central American, ex. Mexican	230	2.51
Costa Rican	9	0.10
Guatemalan	38	0.41
Honduran	15	0.16
Nicaraguan	31	0.34
Panamanian	7	0.08
Salvadoran	129	1.41
Other Central American	1	0.01
Cuban	35	0.38
Dominican Republic	45	0.49
Mexican	89	0.97
Puerto Rican	132	1.44
South American	294	3.20
Argentinean	23	0.25
Bolivian	67	0.73
Chilean	21	0.23
Colombian	62	0.68
Ecuadorian	53	0.58
Paraguayan	3	0.03
Peruvian	61	0.66
Venezuelan	4	0.04
Other Hispanic or Latino	99	1.08

Race*	Population	%
African-American/Black (822)	936	10.20
Not Hispanic (796)	896	9.77
Hispanic (26)	40	0.44
American Indian/Alaska Native (23)	76	0.83
Not Hispanic (14)	54	0.59
Hispanic (9)	22	0.24
Apache (0)	1	0.01
Blackfeet (1)	1	0.01
Canadian/French Am. Ind. (0)	2	0.02
Central American Ind. (0)	1	0.01
Cherokee (4)	23	0.25
Chippewa (0)	1	0.01
Choctaw (0)	3	0.03
Lumbee (3)	6	0.07
Mexican American Ind. (2)	4	0.04
Pueblo (0)	2	0.02
Sioux (1)	1	0.01
South American Ind. (3)	4	0.04
Asian (1,602)	1,817	19.80
Not Hispanic (1,594)	1,802	19.64
Hispanic (8)	15	0.16
Bangladeshi (18)	22	0.24
Burmese (3)	3	0.03
Cambodian (21)	28	0.31
Chinese, ex. Taiwanese (341)	398	4.34
Filipino (117)	160	1.74
Indian (505)	540	5.89
Indonesian (4)	11	0.12
Japanese (12)	41	0.45
Korean (211)	248	2.70
Laotian (8)	15	0.16
Malaysian (2)	2	0.02
Nepalese (7)	11	0.12
Pakistani (61)	68	0.74
Sri Lankan (19)	25	0.27
Taiwanese (6)	15	0.16
Thai (6)	12	0.13
Vietnamese (195)	224	2.44
Hawaii Native/Pacific Islander (2)	16	0.17
Not Hispanic (2)	15	0.16
Hispanic (0)	1	0.01
Fijian (1)	1	0.01
Guamanian/Chamorro (0)	1	0.01
Native Hawaiian (0)	4	0.04
White (6,120)	6,451	70.31
Not Hispanic (5,479)	5,773	62.92
Hispanic (641)	678	7.39

*Notes: † The Census 2010 population figure is used to calculate the percentages in the Hispanic Origin and Race categories. Ancestry percentages are based on the 2006-2010 American Community Survey population (not shown); ‡ Numbers in parentheses indicate the number of people reporting a single ancestry; * Numbers in parentheses indicate the number of persons reporting this race alone, not in combination with any other race; Please refer to the Explanation of Data for more information.*

Waldorf

Place Type: CDP
County: Charles
Population: 67,752†

Ancestry‡	Population	%
African, Sub-Saharan (1,688)	1,782	2.65
African (1,114)	1,175	1.75
Ethiopian (38)	38	0.06
Liberian (19)	52	0.08
Nigerian (395)	395	0.59
Sierra Leonean (102)	102	0.15
Sudanese (20)	20	0.03
Albanian (0)	6	0.01
American (3,680)	3,680	5.48
Arab (112)	126	0.19
Arab (53)	67	0.10
Lebanese (59)	59	0.09
Armenian (0)	8	0.01
Austrian (10)	94	0.14
Belgian (11)	26	0.04
British (154)	235	0.35
Canadian (13)	27	0.04
Croatian (0)	43	0.06
Czech (14)	51	0.08
Czechoslovakian (12)	55	0.08
Danish (0)	34	0.05
Dutch (57)	288	0.43
Eastern European (11)	28	0.04
English (1,127)	3,769	5.61
European (301)	331	0.49
Finnish (0)	36	0.05
French, ex. Basque (303)	913	1.36
French Canadian (83)	254	0.38
German (2,362)	7,137	10.63
Greek (192)	351	0.52
Guyanese (37)	37	0.06
Hungarian (24)	131	0.20
Iranian (36)	36	0.05
Irish (1,376)	5,164	7.69
Italian (1,066)	3,053	4.55
Lithuanian (85)	226	0.34
Northern European (101)	101	0.15
Norwegian (59)	302	0.45
Pennsylvania German (15)	45	0.07
Polish (285)	1,350	2.01
Portuguese (106)	222	0.33
Romanian (16)	26	0.04
Russian (35)	203	0.30
Scandinavian (13)	48	0.07
Scotch-Irish (199)	643	0.96
Scottish (160)	651	0.97
Slavic (51)	84	0.13
Slovak (43)	188	0.28
Slovene (0)	21	0.03
Swedish (46)	287	0.43
Swiss (32)	135	0.20
Ukrainian (27)	122	0.18
Welsh (14)	336	0.50
West Indian, ex. Hispanic (567)	779	1.16
Bahamian (13)	13	0.02
British West Indian (0)	14	0.02
Haitian (19)	19	0.03
Jamaican (280)	377	0.56
Trinidadian/Tobagonian (30)	41	0.06
U.S. Virgin Islander (13)	13	0.02
West Indian (212)	302	0.45
Yugoslavian (57)	57	0.08

Hispanic Origin	Population	%
Hispanic or Latino (of any race)	3,972	5.86
Central American, ex. Mexican	1,016	1.50
Costa Rican	8	0.01
Guatemalan	200	0.30
Honduran	71	0.10
Nicaraguan	39	0.06
Panamanian	134	0.20
Salvadoran	558	0.82
Other Central American	6	0.01
Cuban	135	0.20
Dominican Republic	110	0.16
Mexican	991	1.46
Puerto Rican	974	1.44
South American	293	0.43
Argentinean	20	0.03
Bolivian	46	0.07
Chilean	15	0.02
Colombian	72	0.11
Ecuadorian	22	0.03
Paraguayan	1	<0.01
Peruvian	99	0.15
Uruguayan	2	<0.01
Venezuelan	11	0.02
Other South American	5	0.01
Other Hispanic or Latino	453	0.67

Race*	Population	%
African-American/Black (36,152)	38,259	56.47
Not Hispanic (35,559)	37,454	55.28
Hispanic (593)	805	1.19
American Indian/Alaska Native (363)	1,247	1.84
Not Hispanic (332)	1,097	1.62
Hispanic (31)	150	0.22
Apache (0)	7	0.01
Arapaho (1)	4	0.01
Blackfeet (10)	49	0.07
Canadian/French Am. Ind. (1)	5	0.01
Central American Ind. (0)	6	0.01
Cherokee (34)	208	0.31
Cheyenne (3)	3	<0.01
Chickasaw (0)	5	0.01
Chippewa (5)	7	0.01
Choctaw (5)	16	0.02
Comanche (2)	5	0.01
Cree (0)	2	<0.01
Creek (0)	10	0.01
Crow (0)	3	<0.01
Delaware (1)	1	<0.01
Inupiat *(Alaska Native)* (1)	1	<0.01
Iroquois (10)	15	0.02
Kiowa (2)	2	<0.01
Lumbee (4)	6	0.01
Menominee (0)	1	<0.01
Mexican American Ind. (4)	11	0.02
Navajo (1)	9	0.01
Potawatomi (3)	4	0.01
Pueblo (1)	1	<0.01
Seminole (1)	3	<0.01
Sioux (1)	21	0.03
South American Ind. (3)	10	0.01
Spanish American Ind. (0)	1	<0.01
Ute (0)	1	<0.01
Asian (2,664)	3,502	5.17
Not Hispanic (2,620)	3,371	4.98
Hispanic (44)	131	0.19
Bangladeshi (18)	18	0.03
Burmese (4)	6	0.01
Cambodian (11)	20	0.03
Chinese, ex. Taiwanese (231)	324	0.48
Filipino (1,199)	1,627	2.40
Indian (374)	432	0.64
Indonesian (9)	15	0.02
Japanese (62)	151	0.22
Korean (201)	315	0.46
Laotian (12)	18	0.03
Malaysian (0)	6	0.01
Nepalese (31)	31	0.05
Pakistani (169)	182	0.27
Sri Lankan (0)	1	<0.01
Taiwanese (3)	9	0.01
Thai (52)	106	0.16
Vietnamese (176)	211	0.31
Hawaii Native/Pacific Islander (61)	197	0.29
Not Hispanic (48)	162	0.24
Hispanic (13)	35	0.05
Guamanian/Chamorro (28)	61	0.09
Native Hawaiian (13)	54	0.08
Samoan (14)	22	0.03
White (24,052)	26,274	38.78
Not Hispanic (22,499)	24,403	36.02
Hispanic (1,553)	1,871	2.76

Walker Mill

Place Type: CDP
County: Prince George's
Population: 11,302†

Ancestry‡	Population	%
African, Sub-Saharan (437)	437	3.78
African (321)	321	2.77
Ethiopian (98)	98	0.85
Nigerian (18)	18	0.16
American (92)	92	0.79
Arab (0)	11	0.10
Arab (0)	11	0.10
Brazilian (0)	18	0.16
English (0)	6	0.05
French Canadian (0)	4	0.03
German (16)	76	0.66
Guyanese (0)	11	0.10
Irish (10)	28	0.24
Italian (14)	21	0.18
Polish (10)	19	0.16
Scotch-Irish (0)	6	0.05
West Indian, ex. Hispanic (122)	162	1.40
British West Indian (0)	18	0.16
Haitian (20)	20	0.17
Jamaican (102)	113	0.98
West Indian (0)	11	0.10

Hispanic Origin	Population	%
Hispanic or Latino (of any race)	284	2.51
Central American, ex. Mexican	135	1.19
Guatemalan	7	0.06
Honduran	2	0.02
Nicaraguan	3	0.03
Panamanian	21	0.19
Salvadoran	102	0.90
Cuban	12	0.11
Dominican Republic	20	0.18
Mexican	31	0.27
Puerto Rican	35	0.31
South American	9	0.08
Chilean	3	0.03
Ecuadorian	4	0.04
Venezuelan	2	0.02
Other Hispanic or Latino	42	0.37

Race*	Population	%
African-American/Black (10,710)	10,896	96.41
Not Hispanic (10,626)	10,791	95.48
Hispanic (84)	105	0.93
American Indian/Alaska Native (53)	129	1.14
Not Hispanic (46)	118	1.04
Hispanic (7)	11	0.10
Blackfeet (2)	17	0.15
Cherokee (5)	19	0.17
Choctaw (1)	1	0.01
Delaware (0)	1	0.01
Iroquois (0)	1	0.01
Mexican American Ind. (4)	4	0.04
Seminole (0)	1	0.01
Asian (42)	76	0.67
Not Hispanic (42)	75	0.66
Hispanic (0)	1	0.01
Cambodian (0)	1	0.01
Chinese, ex. Taiwanese (7)	8	0.07
Filipino (21)	32	0.28
Indian (2)	12	0.11
Japanese (5)	11	0.10
Korean (2)	2	0.02
Thai (1)	1	0.01
Vietnamese (2)	2	0.02
Hawaii Native/Pacific Islander (2)	8	0.07
Not Hispanic (2)	8	0.07
Guamanian/Chamorro (1)	2	0.02
Samoan (1)	3	0.03
White (159)	283	2.50

*Notes: † The Census 2010 population figure is used to calculate the percentages in the Hispanic Origin and Race categories. Ancestry percentages are based on the 2006-2010 American Community Survey population (not shown); ‡ Numbers in parentheses indicate the number of people reporting a single ancestry; * Numbers in parentheses indicate the number of persons reporting this race alone, not in combination with any other race; Please refer to the Explanation of Data for more information.*

Not Hispanic (129)	232	2.05
Hispanic (30)	51	0.45

Westminster

Place Type: City
County: Carroll
Population: 18,590†

Ancestry‡	Population	%
African, Sub-Saharan (68)	68	0.37
African (30)	30	0.16
Ghanaian (19)	19	0.10
Nigerian (19)	19	0.10
American (1,054)	1,054	5.67
Arab (195)	215	1.16
Arab (195)	195	1.05
Syrian (0)	20	0.11
Austrian (10)	29	0.16
British (49)	122	0.66
Canadian (19)	40	0.22
Czech (0)	103	0.55
Czechoslovakian (42)	42	0.23
Danish (27)	46	0.25
Dutch (156)	515	2.77
Eastern European (55)	63	0.34
English (529)	2,335	12.56
European (267)	301	1.62
French, ex. Basque (95)	398	2.14
French Canadian (13)	30	0.16
German (2,225)	6,039	32.48
Greek (0)	31	0.17
Hungarian (14)	83	0.45
Irish (752)	3,379	18.18
Italian (437)	1,403	7.55
Lithuanian (27)	80	0.43
New Zealander (25)	25	0.13
Norwegian (48)	98	0.53
Polish (231)	972	5.23
Portuguese (45)	83	0.45
Romanian (0)	10	0.05
Russian (69)	234	1.26
Scotch-Irish (121)	199	1.07
Scottish (115)	454	2.44
Slavic (0)	13	0.07
Slovak (12)	217	1.17
Swedish (35)	80	0.43
Swiss (0)	22	0.12
Turkish (0)	13	0.07
Ukrainian (0)	56	0.30
Welsh (91)	382	2.05
West Indian, ex. Hispanic (10)	19	0.10
West Indian (10)	19	0.10
Yugoslavian (11)	34	0.18

Hispanic Origin	Population	%
Hispanic or Latino (of any race)	1,123	6.04
Central American, ex. Mexican	234	1.26
Costa Rican	5	0.03
Guatemalan	30	0.16
Honduran	38	0.20
Nicaraguan	4	0.02
Panamanian	3	0.02
Salvadoran	146	0.79
Other Central American	8	0.04
Cuban	34	0.18
Dominican Republic	19	0.10
Mexican	446	2.40
Puerto Rican	177	0.95
South American	69	0.37
Argentinean	7	0.04
Chilean	4	0.02
Colombian	20	0.11
Ecuadorian	8	0.04
Paraguayan	3	0.02
Peruvian	21	0.11
Uruguayan	3	0.02
Venezuelan	3	0.02
Other Hispanic or Latino	144	0.77

Race*	Population	%
African-American/Black (1,303)	1,567	8.43
Not Hispanic (1,259)	1,509	8.12
Hispanic (44)	58	0.31
American Indian/Alaska Native (65)	146	0.79
Not Hispanic (52)	121	0.65
Hispanic (13)	25	0.13
Blackfeet (4)	7	0.04
Central American Ind. (0)	1	0.01
Cherokee (13)	36	0.19
Choctaw (0)	1	0.01
Crow (3)	3	0.02
Houma (0)	2	0.01
Inupiat *(Alaska Native)* (1)	1	0.01
Iroquois (3)	5	0.03
Lumbee (5)	8	0.04
Mexican American Ind. (9)	9	0.05
Navajo (1)	1	0.01
Potawatomi (0)	1	0.01
Sioux (3)	4	0.02
South American Ind. (0)	3	0.02
Spanish American Ind. (0)	1	0.01
Asian (415)	525	2.82
Not Hispanic (410)	517	2.78
Hispanic (5)	8	0.04
Burmese (4)	5	0.03
Chinese, ex. Taiwanese (73)	89	0.48
Filipino (40)	89	0.48
Indian (164)	182	0.98
Indonesian (1)	1	0.01
Japanese (5)	21	0.11
Korean (47)	57	0.31
Malaysian (0)	1	0.01
Nepalese (12)	12	0.06
Pakistani (32)	33	0.18
Taiwanese (0)	1	0.01
Thai (3)	6	0.03
Vietnamese (20)	24	0.13
Hawaii Native/Pacific Islander (5)	19	0.10
Not Hispanic (5)	16	0.09
Hispanic (0)	3	0.02
Guamanian/Chamorro (1)	2	0.01
Native Hawaiian (3)	5	0.03
Samoan (0)	1	0.01
Tongan (1)	1	0.01
White (15,990)	16,400	88.22
Not Hispanic (15,318)	15,674	84.31
Hispanic (672)	726	3.91

Wheaton

Place Type: CDP
County: Montgomery
Population: 48,284†

Ancestry‡	Population	%
African, Sub-Saharan (2,098)	2,184	4.84
African (535)	591	1.31
Ethiopian (1,145)	1,145	2.54
Ghanaian (56)	79	0.18
Liberian (69)	69	0.15
Nigerian (63)	63	0.14
Senegalese (26)	33	0.07
Zimbabwean (11)	11	0.02
Other Sub-Saharan African (193)	193	0.43
American (1,073)	1,073	2.38
Arab (271)	322	0.71
Arab (42)	42	0.09
Lebanese (4)	17	0.04
Moroccan (0)	28	0.06
Palestinian (142)	142	0.32
Syrian (0)	10	0.02
Other Arab (83)	83	0.18
Armenian (85)	85	0.19
Assyrian/Chaldean/Syriac (0)	12	0.03
Austrian (77)	163	0.36
Basque (0)	9	0.02
Brazilian (226)	277	0.61
British (54)	160	0.35
Canadian (14)	31	0.07
Cypriot (7)	7	0.02
Czech (9)	106	0.24
Czechoslovakian (12)	12	0.03
Danish (0)	92	0.20
Dutch (48)	184	0.41
Eastern European (54)	64	0.14
English (528)	1,811	4.02
Estonian (0)	8	0.02
European (341)	408	0.91
Finnish (66)	91	0.20
French, ex. Basque (44)	540	1.20
French Canadian (21)	53	0.12
German (530)	2,548	5.65
German Russian (0)	32	0.07
Greek (190)	224	0.50
Guyanese (31)	123	0.27
Hungarian (104)	186	0.41
Iranian (45)	57	0.13
Irish (676)	2,438	5.41
Israeli (10)	10	0.02
Italian (506)	1,343	2.98
Latvian (16)	31	0.07
Lithuanian (8)	91	0.20
Luxemburger (0)	13	0.03
New Zealander (12)	12	0.03
Northern European (91)	91	0.20
Norwegian (35)	166	0.37
Pennsylvania German (8)	8	0.02
Polish (176)	674	1.50
Portuguese (187)	284	0.63
Romanian (0)	20	0.04
Russian (183)	465	1.03
Scandinavian (0)	46	0.10
Scotch-Irish (160)	433	0.96
Scottish (115)	505	1.12
Slavic (0)	8	0.02
Slovak (0)	12	0.03
Slovene (14)	21	0.05
Swedish (33)	192	0.43
Swiss (48)	80	0.18
Turkish (14)	14	0.03
Ukrainian (51)	121	0.27
Welsh (0)	193	0.43
West Indian, ex. Hispanic (613)	761	1.69
British West Indian (99)	99	0.22
Haitian (56)	93	0.21
Jamaican (422)	461	1.02
Trinidadian/Tobagonian (29)	52	0.12
West Indian (7)	56	0.12
Yugoslavian (17)	17	0.04

Hispanic Origin	Population	%
Hispanic or Latino (of any race)	20,155	41.74
Central American, ex. Mexican	12,072	25.00
Costa Rican	44	0.09
Guatemalan	1,354	2.80
Honduran	1,101	2.28
Nicaraguan	561	1.16
Panamanian	83	0.17
Salvadoran	8,912	18.46
Other Central American	17	0.04
Cuban	168	0.35
Dominican Republic	626	1.30
Mexican	1,530	3.17
Puerto Rican	368	0.76
South American	2,789	5.78
Argentinean	122	0.25
Bolivian	476	0.99
Chilean	151	0.31
Colombian	411	0.85
Ecuadorian	319	0.66
Paraguayan	71	0.15
Peruvian	1,130	2.34
Uruguayan	41	0.08
Venezuelan	56	0.12
Other South American	12	0.02
Other Hispanic or Latino	2,602	5.39

*Notes: † The Census 2010 population figure is used to calculate the percentages in the Hispanic Origin and Race categories. Ancestry percentages are based on the 2006-2010 American Community Survey population (not shown); ‡ Numbers in parentheses indicate the number of people reporting a single ancestry; * Numbers in parentheses indicate the number of persons reporting this race alone, not in combination with any other race; Please refer to the Explanation of Data for more information.*

Race*	Population	%
African-American/Black (8,968)	9,713	20.12
Not Hispanic (8,499)	8,991	18.62
Hispanic (469)	722	1.50
American Indian/Alaska Native (390)	771	1.60
Not Hispanic (89)	270	0.56
Hispanic (301)	501	1.04
Apache (4)	6	0.01
Blackfeet (0)	10	0.02
Canadian/French Am. Ind. (4)	4	0.01
Central American Ind. (17)	30	0.06
Cherokee (13)	68	0.14
Chickasaw (0)	1	<0.01
Chippewa (1)	2	<0.01
Choctaw (6)	12	0.02
Comanche (1)	4	0.01
Creek (0)	2	<0.01
Crow (0)	2	<0.01
Delaware (0)	1	<0.01
Inupiat *(Alaska Native)* (2)	2	<0.01
Iroquois (2)	2	<0.01
Lumbee (2)	3	0.01
Menominee (2)	2	<0.01
Mexican American Ind. (44)	50	0.10
Navajo (3)	8	0.02
Pueblo (0)	1	<0.01
Seminole (0)	1	<0.01
Sioux (2)	4	0.01
South American Ind. (28)	45	0.09
Spanish American Ind. (23)	32	0.07
Ute (1)	2	<0.01
Yaqui (0)	1	<0.01
Asian (5,860)	6,528	13.52
Not Hispanic (5,782)	6,299	13.05
Hispanic (78)	229	0.47
Bangladeshi (42)	49	0.10
Bhutanese (8)	8	0.02
Burmese (68)	72	0.15
Cambodian (97)	118	0.24
Chinese, ex. Taiwanese (1,280)	1,417	2.93
Filipino (1,277)	1,433	2.97
Indian (525)	648	1.34
Indonesian (168)	208	0.43
Japanese (63)	132	0.27
Korean (356)	413	0.86
Laotian (30)	34	0.07
Malaysian (8)	10	0.02
Nepalese (69)	82	0.17
Pakistani (70)	81	0.17
Sri Lankan (133)	147	0.30
Taiwanese (31)	39	0.08
Thai (274)	300	0.62
Vietnamese (1,150)	1,215	2.52
Hawaii Native/Pacific Islander (49)	243	0.50
Not Hispanic (32)	184	0.38
Hispanic (17)	59	0.12
Guamanian/Chamorro (18)	22	0.05
Native Hawaiian (5)	24	0.05
Samoan (4)	11	0.02
White (20,389)	22,211	46.00
Not Hispanic (12,414)	13,151	27.24
Hispanic (7,975)	9,060	18.76

White Marsh

Place Type: CDP
County: Baltimore
Population: 9,513†

Ancestry‡	Population	%
African, Sub-Saharan (223)	292	3.07
African (0)	43	0.45
Cape Verdean (86)	86	0.90
Ghanaian (108)	108	1.13
Nigerian (29)	55	0.58
American (243)	243	2.55
Arab (109)	120	1.26
Arab (65)	65	0.68
Egyptian (44)	44	0.46
Lebanese (0)	11	0.12
Austrian (41)	80	0.84
Belgian (5)	5	0.05
British (14)	69	0.72
Czech (34)	166	1.74
Danish (15)	15	0.16
Dutch (42)	92	0.97
English (240)	902	9.47
European (97)	97	1.02
Finnish (0)	36	0.38
French, ex. Basque (77)	241	2.53
French Canadian (31)	101	1.06
German (760)	2,878	30.23
Greek (165)	241	2.53
Guyanese (25)	25	0.26
Hungarian (7)	31	0.33
Iranian (22)	22	0.23
Irish (572)	1,966	20.65
Italian (440)	1,368	14.37
Latvian (15)	15	0.16
Lithuanian (0)	54	0.57
Norwegian (9)	29	0.30
Polish (272)	800	8.40
Portuguese (0)	23	0.24
Romanian (23)	23	0.24
Russian (17)	97	1.02
Scotch-Irish (50)	251	2.64
Scottish (16)	168	1.76
Serbian (15)	15	0.16
Slovene (13)	13	0.14
Swedish (14)	26	0.27
Ukrainian (86)	105	1.10
Welsh (17)	92	0.97
West Indian, ex. Hispanic (75)	75	0.79
Jamaican (33)	33	0.35
West Indian (42)	42	0.44

Hispanic Origin	Population	%
Hispanic or Latino (of any race)	263	2.76
Central American, ex. Mexican	37	0.39
Costa Rican	2	0.02
Guatemalan	12	0.13
Honduran	5	0.05
Panamanian	4	0.04
Salvadoran	14	0.15
Cuban	6	0.06
Dominican Republic	18	0.19
Mexican	63	0.66
Puerto Rican	36	0.38
South American	68	0.71
Argentinean	4	0.04
Bolivian	8	0.08
Chilean	2	0.02
Colombian	21	0.22
Ecuadorian	13	0.14
Peruvian	17	0.18
Uruguayan	1	0.01
Venezuelan	2	0.02
Other Hispanic or Latino	35	0.37

Race*	Population	%
African-American/Black (968)	1,052	11.06
Not Hispanic (951)	1,027	10.80
Hispanic (17)	25	0.26
American Indian/Alaska Native (17)	47	0.49
Not Hispanic (16)	45	0.47
Hispanic (1)	2	0.02
Blackfeet (0)	3	0.03
Cherokee (3)	15	0.16
Delaware (0)	1	0.01
Lumbee (6)	6	0.06
Seminole (0)	1	0.01
Asian (976)	1,054	11.08
Not Hispanic (970)	1,045	10.98
Hispanic (6)	9	0.09
Cambodian (1)	1	0.01
Chinese, ex. Taiwanese (106)	121	1.27
Filipino (397)	425	4.47
Indian (196)	218	2.29
Indonesian (1)	1	0.01
Japanese (4)	13	0.14
Korean (100)	107	1.12
Laotian (7)	7	0.07
Nepalese (17)	20	0.21
Pakistani (29)	36	0.38
Sri Lankan (5)	6	0.06
Thai (4)	4	0.04
Vietnamese (68)	75	0.79
Hawaii Native/Pacific Islander (3)	7	0.07
Not Hispanic (2)	6	0.06
Hispanic (1)	1	0.01
Guamanian/Chamorro (1)	1	0.01
Native Hawaiian (1)	1	0.01
White (7,291)	7,439	78.20
Not Hispanic (7,120)	7,250	76.21
Hispanic (171)	189	1.99

White Oak

Place Type: CDP
County: Montgomery
Population: 17,403†

Ancestry‡	Population	%
Afghan (87)	87	0.52
African, Sub-Saharan (2,483)	2,643	15.87
African (968)	1,007	6.04
Ethiopian (727)	809	4.86
Ghanaian (29)	29	0.17
Kenyan (59)	59	0.35
Liberian (17)	33	0.20
Nigerian (36)	48	0.29
Sierra Leonean (14)	14	0.08
South African (92)	92	0.55
Sudanese (104)	104	0.62
Ugandan (0)	11	0.07
Other Sub-Saharan African (437)	437	2.62
American (615)	615	3.69
Arab (36)	36	0.22
Egyptian (36)	36	0.22
Armenian (16)	16	0.10
Austrian (9)	9	0.05
Basque (95)	95	0.57
Belgian (12)	12	0.07
Brazilian (35)	48	0.29
British (9)	94	0.56
Celtic (14)	14	0.08
Croatian (13)	29	0.17
Czech (0)	33	0.20
Danish (0)	45	0.27
Dutch (0)	75	0.45
Eastern European (10)	65	0.39
English (114)	375	2.25
European (35)	46	0.28
Finnish (0)	14	0.08
French, ex. Basque (70)	157	0.94
French Canadian (0)	10	0.06
German (143)	694	4.17
Greek (10)	67	0.40
Guyanese (10)	10	0.06
Hungarian (40)	81	0.49
Irish (242)	674	4.05
Italian (221)	431	2.59
Lithuanian (26)	37	0.22
Norwegian (0)	31	0.19
Polish (34)	266	1.60
Portuguese (0)	41	0.25
Romanian (45)	84	0.50
Russian (118)	206	1.24
Scandinavian (16)	16	0.10
Scotch-Irish (0)	52	0.31
Scottish (14)	144	0.86
Slovak (23)	23	0.14
Swedish (28)	65	0.39
Ukrainian (52)	113	0.68
Welsh (10)	19	0.11
West Indian, ex. Hispanic (551)	619	3.72
Haitian (350)	378	2.27
Jamaican (152)	179	1.07
Trinidadian/Tobagonian (34)	47	0.28

*Notes: † The Census 2010 population figure is used to calculate the percentages in the Hispanic Origin and Race categories. Ancestry percentages are based on the 2006-2010 American Community Survey population (not shown); ‡ Numbers in parentheses indicate the number of people reporting a single ancestry; * Numbers in parentheses indicate the number of persons reporting this race alone, not in combination with any other race; Please refer to the Explanation of Data for more information.*

West Indian (15)	15	0.09

Hispanic Origin	Population	%
Hispanic or Latino (of any race)	3,194	18.35
Central American, ex. Mexican	1,692	9.72
Costa Rican	9	0.05
Guatemalan	268	1.54
Honduran	138	0.79
Nicaraguan	104	0.60
Panamanian	52	0.30
Salvadoran	1,121	6.44
Cuban	39	0.22
Dominican Republic	293	1.68
Mexican	248	1.43
Puerto Rican	151	0.87
South American	382	2.20
Argentinean	21	0.12
Bolivian	74	0.43
Chilean	11	0.06
Colombian	74	0.43
Ecuadorian	40	0.23
Paraguayan	2	0.01
Peruvian	138	0.79
Uruguayan	9	0.05
Venezuelan	13	0.07
Other Hispanic or Latino	389	2.24

Race*	Population	%
African-American/Black (8,592)	9,007	51.76
Not Hispanic (8,314)	8,626	49.57
Hispanic (278)	381	2.19
American Indian/Alaska Native (66)	243	1.40
Not Hispanic (23)	153	0.88
Hispanic (43)	90	0.52
Blackfeet (0)	8	0.05
Central American Ind. (0)	6	0.03
Cherokee (4)	44	0.25
Choctaw (0)	3	0.02
Comanche (0)	3	0.02
Creek (0)	1	0.01
Hopi (0)	2	0.01
Mexican American Ind. (1)	1	0.01
Paiute (0)	1	0.01
Seminole (0)	1	0.01
Sioux (0)	1	0.01
South American Ind. (1)	9	0.05
Asian (1,554)	1,735	9.97
Not Hispanic (1,543)	1,704	9.79
Hispanic (11)	31	0.18
Bangladeshi (23)	23	0.13
Cambodian (8)	15	0.09
Chinese, ex. Taiwanese (282)	334	1.92
Filipino (95)	121	0.70
Hmong (0)	1	0.01
Indian (398)	434	2.49
Indonesian (5)	6	0.03
Japanese (16)	35	0.20
Korean (196)	211	1.21
Laotian (5)	7	0.04
Malaysian (2)	2	0.01
Nepalese (4)	6	0.03
Pakistani (20)	25	0.14
Sri Lankan (13)	15	0.09
Taiwanese (18)	18	0.10
Thai (5)	13	0.07
Vietnamese (428)	449	2.58
Hawaii Native/Pacific Islander (23)	46	0.26
Not Hispanic (23)	38	0.22
Hispanic (0)	8	0.05
Fijian (8)	8	0.05
Guamanian/Chamorro (2)	2	0.01
Native Hawaiian (1)	3	0.02
Samoan (5)	6	0.03
White (4,816)	5,370	30.86
Not Hispanic (3,766)	4,063	23.35
Hispanic (1,050)	1,307	7.51

Woodlawn

Place Type: CDP
County: Baltimore
Population: 37,879†

Ancestry‡	Population	%
Afghan (83)	83	0.22
African, Sub-Saharan (1,227)	1,294	3.41
African (683)	727	1.91
Cape Verdean (0)	23	0.06
Ethiopian (116)	116	0.31
Ghanaian (15)	15	0.04
Liberian (57)	57	0.15
Nigerian (299)	299	0.79
South African (21)	21	0.06
Other Sub-Saharan African (36)	36	0.09
American (620)	620	1.63
Arab (12)	68	0.18
Lebanese (0)	17	0.04
Syrian (0)	7	0.02
Other Arab (12)	44	0.12
Belgian (0)	35	0.09
British (46)	61	0.16
Bulgarian (14)	14	0.04
Canadian (32)	89	0.23
Croatian (30)	30	0.08
Czech (20)	111	0.29
Czechoslovakian (14)	35	0.09
Danish (0)	303	0.80
Dutch (69)	244	0.64
Eastern European (12)	12	0.03
English (397)	1,333	3.51
European (178)	200	0.53
French, ex. Basque (38)	268	0.71
French Canadian (46)	104	0.27
German (1,020)	2,781	7.32
Greek (30)	76	0.20
Guyanese (74)	96	0.25
Iranian (86)	86	0.23
Irish (475)	1,585	4.17
Italian (404)	1,043	2.75
Lithuanian (42)	110	0.29
Norwegian (41)	110	0.29
Pennsylvania German (10)	32	0.08
Polish (47)	527	1.39
Portuguese (18)	72	0.19
Romanian (0)	7	0.02
Russian (62)	161	0.42
Scandinavian (0)	5	0.01
Scotch-Irish (68)	381	1.00
Scottish (64)	358	0.94
Slovak (29)	44	0.12
Slovene (17)	17	0.04
Swedish (12)	45	0.12
Swiss (26)	148	0.39
Ukrainian (32)	42	0.11
Welsh (14)	226	0.60
West Indian, ex. Hispanic (705)	808	2.13
Bahamian (27)	27	0.07
Barbadian (21)	21	0.06
Belizean (0)	19	0.05
British West Indian (40)	40	0.11
Haitian (19)	19	0.05
Jamaican (439)	468	1.23
Trinidadian/Tobagonian (67)	101	0.27
West Indian (92)	113	0.30

Hispanic Origin	Population	%
Hispanic or Latino (of any race)	2,192	5.79
Central American, ex. Mexican	871	2.30
Costa Rican	4	0.01
Guatemalan	167	0.44
Honduran	117	0.31
Nicaraguan	19	0.05
Panamanian	37	0.10
Salvadoran	517	1.36
Other Central American	10	0.03
Cuban	35	0.09
Dominican Republic	52	0.14
Mexican	504	1.33
Puerto Rican	247	0.65
South American	151	0.40
Argentinean	7	0.02
Bolivian	1	<0.01
Chilean	7	0.02
Colombian	34	0.09
Ecuadorian	13	0.03
Paraguayan	4	0.01
Peruvian	59	0.16
Uruguayan	10	0.03
Venezuelan	10	0.03
Other South American	6	0.02
Other Hispanic or Latino	332	0.88

Race*	Population	%
African-American/Black (23,301)	24,023	63.42
Not Hispanic (23,048)	23,660	62.46
Hispanic (253)	363	0.96
American Indian/Alaska Native (140)	433	1.14
Not Hispanic (87)	329	0.87
Hispanic (53)	104	0.27
Apache (0)	5	0.01
Blackfeet (3)	28	0.07
Central American Ind. (1)	3	0.01
Cherokee (15)	69	0.18
Choctaw (0)	3	0.01
Creek (0)	6	0.02
Crow (1)	4	0.01
Delaware (0)	1	<0.01
Lumbee (10)	12	0.03
Mexican American Ind. (3)	9	0.02
Navajo (1)	4	0.01
Ottawa (3)	3	0.01
Seminole (0)	5	0.01
Shoshone (0)	4	0.01
Sioux (0)	4	0.01
South American Ind. (7)	17	0.04
Asian (3,387)	3,779	9.98
Not Hispanic (3,378)	3,752	9.91
Hispanic (9)	27	0.07
Bangladeshi (99)	124	0.33
Burmese (19)	29	0.08
Cambodian (3)	5	0.01
Chinese, ex. Taiwanese (177)	224	0.59
Filipino (189)	240	0.63
Indian (974)	1,099	2.90
Indonesian (13)	16	0.04
Japanese (8)	45	0.12
Korean (336)	364	0.96
Malaysian (2)	4	0.01
Nepalese (97)	105	0.28
Pakistani (986)	1,055	2.79
Sri Lankan (7)	11	0.03
Taiwanese (4)	5	0.01
Thai (46)	56	0.15
Vietnamese (279)	295	0.78
Hawaii Native/Pacific Islander (11)	60	0.16
Not Hispanic (8)	48	0.13
Hispanic (3)	12	0.03
Guamanian/Chamorro (8)	8	0.02
Native Hawaiian (2)	6	0.02
Samoan (0)	1	<0.01
White (8,829)	9,666	25.52
Not Hispanic (8,109)	8,768	23.15
Hispanic (720)	898	2.37

*Notes: † The Census 2010 population figure is used to calculate the percentages in the Hispanic Origin and Race categories. Ancestry percentages are based on the 2006-2010 American Community Survey population (not shown); ‡ Numbers in parentheses indicate the number of people reporting a single ancestry; * Numbers in parentheses indicate the number of persons reporting this race alone, not in combination with any other race; Please refer to the Explanation of Data for more information.*

MASSACHUSETTS

Place Type: State
Population: 6,547,629†

Ancestry‡	Population	%
Afghan (697)	723	0.01
African, Sub-Saharan (87,644)	109,092	1.68
African (19,869)	25,563	0.39
Cape Verdean (40,698)	53,174	0.82
Ethiopian (4,309)	4,593	0.07
Ghanaian (3,103)	3,276	0.05
Kenyan (3,709)	3,832	0.06
Liberian (1,476)	1,636	0.03
Nigerian (5,066)	5,678	0.09
Senegalese (367)	377	0.01
Sierra Leonean (660)	913	0.01
Somalian (2,653)	2,663	0.04
South African (822)	1,360	0.02
Sudanese (250)	483	0.01
Ugandan (1,892)	1,922	0.03
Zimbabwean (75)	103	<0.01
Other Sub-Saharan African (2,695)	3,519	0.05
Albanian (10,223)	15,095	0.23
Alsatian (50)	309	<0.01
American (211,558)	211,558	3.27
Arab (37,455)	63,448	0.98
Arab (3,507)	5,145	0.08
Egyptian (3,761)	4,335	0.07
Iraqi (1,090)	1,255	0.02
Jordanian (865)	1,005	0.02
Lebanese (16,223)	32,722	0.51
Moroccan (5,453)	6,471	0.10
Palestinian (693)	929	0.01
Syrian (2,233)	6,513	0.10
Other Arab (3,630)	5,073	0.08
Armenian (15,644)	28,471	0.44
Assyrian/Chaldean/Syriac (74)	223	<0.01
Australian (914)	1,992	0.03
Austrian (3,621)	17,069	0.26
Basque (45)	206	<0.01
Belgian (1,684)	5,453	0.08
Brazilian (58,344)	65,170	1.01
British (16,064)	29,647	0.46
Bulgarian (2,664)	3,166	0.05
Cajun (248)	585	0.01
Canadian (26,904)	59,793	0.92
Carpatho Rusyn (40)	40	<0.01
Celtic (1,070)	2,317	0.04
Croatian (1,158)	3,017	0.05
Cypriot (135)	267	<0.01
Czech (3,419)	13,668	0.21
Czechoslovakian (1,288)	3,825	0.06
Danish (3,296)	15,620	0.24
Dutch (9,979)	47,023	0.73
Eastern European (21,065)	23,919	0.37
English (195,255)	747,497	11.54
Estonian (297)	705	0.01
European (45,568)	50,608	0.78
Finnish (8,226)	26,973	0.42
French, ex. Basque (126,253)	544,113	8.40
French Canadian (122,864)	268,348	4.14
German (85,572)	436,061	6.73
German Russian (55)	55	<0.01
Greek (45,184)	85,195	1.32
Guyanese (1,085)	1,440	0.02
Hungarian (5,915)	21,035	0.32
Icelander (580)	1,058	0.02
Iranian (6,586)	7,989	0.12
Irish (563,577)	1,516,227	23.41
Israeli (3,325)	4,349	0.07
Italian (348,041)	902,713	13.94
Latvian (1,864)	4,706	0.07
Lithuanian (16,119)	53,895	0.83
Luxemburger (90)	269	<0.01
Macedonian (338)	618	0.01
Maltese (78)	379	0.01
New Zealander (297)	432	0.01
Northern European (5,007)	5,883	0.09
Norwegian (8,229)	33,943	0.52
Pennsylvania German (431)	901	0.01
Polish (108,509)	339,044	5.23
Portuguese (178,318)	312,022	4.82
Romanian (4,143)	8,711	0.13
Russian (57,435)	120,438	1.86
Scandinavian (3,417)	7,961	0.12
Scotch-Irish (47,149)	123,361	1.90
Scottish (42,881)	172,593	2.66
Serbian (906)	1,469	0.02
Slavic (481)	1,651	0.03
Slovak (2,499)	7,448	0.11
Slovene (393)	1,284	0.02
Soviet Union (90)	104	<0.01
Swedish (26,569)	122,801	1.90
Swiss (2,630)	12,578	0.19
Turkish (4,512)	5,933	0.09
Ukrainian (11,910)	23,908	0.37
Welsh (4,178)	26,359	0.41
West Indian, ex. Hispanic (93,876)	111,104	1.72
Bahamian (413)	740	0.01
Barbadian (3,539)	4,733	0.07
Belizean (242)	302	<0.01
Bermudan (190)	538	0.01
British West Indian (1,494)	2,076	0.03
Dutch West Indian (64)	130	<0.01
Haitian (59,394)	63,915	0.99
Jamaican (18,408)	23,772	0.37
Trinidadian/Tobagonian (3,722)	5,458	0.08
U.S. Virgin Islander (160)	433	0.01
West Indian (6,175)	8,779	0.14
Other West Indian (75)	228	<0.01
Yugoslavian (2,746)	4,342	0.07

Hispanic Origin	Population	%
Hispanic or Latino (of any race)	627,654	9.59
Central American, ex. Mexican	96,958	1.48
Costa Rican	2,951	0.05
Guatemalan	32,812	0.50
Honduran	12,533	0.19
Nicaraguan	1,722	0.03
Panamanian	2,436	0.04
Salvadoran	43,400	0.66
Other Central American	1,104	0.02
Cuban	11,306	0.17
Dominican Republic	103,292	1.58
Mexican	38,379	0.59
Puerto Rican	266,125	4.06
South American	54,398	0.83
Argentinean	4,022	0.06
Bolivian	1,401	0.02
Chilean	3,045	0.05
Colombian	23,843	0.36
Ecuadorian	7,592	0.12
Paraguayan	380	0.01
Peruvian	7,360	0.11
Uruguayan	2,317	0.04
Venezuelan	3,982	0.06
Other South American	456	0.01
Other Hispanic or Latino	57,196	0.87

Race*	Population	%
African-American/Black (434,398)	508,413	7.76
Not Hispanic (391,693)	446,991	6.83
Hispanic (42,705)	61,422	0.94
American Indian/Alaska Native (18,850)	50,705	0.77
Not Hispanic (10,778)	35,635	0.54
Hispanic (8,072)	15,070	0.23
Alaska Athabascan *(Ala. Nat.)* (16)	31	<0.01
Aleut *(Alaska Native)* (16)	40	<0.01
Apache (78)	334	0.01
Arapaho (1)	15	<0.01
Blackfeet (246)	1,645	0.03
Canadian/French Am. Ind. (162)	458	0.01
Central American Ind. (621)	967	0.01
Cherokee (787)	4,539	0.07
Cheyenne (11)	51	<0.01
Chickasaw (33)	116	<0.01
Chippewa (201)	450	0.01
Choctaw (91)	412	0.01
Colville (1)	4	<0.01
Comanche (24)	72	<0.01
Cree (27)	145	<0.01
Creek (50)	152	<0.01
Crow (6)	64	<0.01
Delaware (21)	98	<0.01
Hopi (17)	35	<0.01
Houma (15)	20	<0.01
Inupiat *(Alaska Native)* (28)	61	<0.01
Iroquois (413)	1,441	0.02
Kiowa (11)	21	<0.01
Lumbee (47)	103	<0.01
Menominee (9)	20	<0.01
Mexican American Ind. (1,100)	1,580	0.02
Navajo (158)	321	<0.01
Osage (19)	60	<0.01
Ottawa (4)	15	<0.01
Paiute (5)	14	<0.01
Pima (17)	20	<0.01
Potawatomi (48)	98	<0.01
Pueblo (89)	191	<0.01
Puget Sound Salish (9)	19	<0.01
Seminole (31)	227	<0.01
Shoshone (18)	50	<0.01
Sioux (171)	649	0.01
South American Ind. (799)	1,747	0.03
Spanish American Ind. (290)	459	0.01
Tlingit-Haida *(Alaska Native)* (27)	70	<0.01
Tohono O'Odham (11)	21	<0.01
Tsimshian *(Alaska Native)* (3)	3	<0.01
Ute (7)	26	<0.01
Yakama (2)	7	<0.01
Yaqui (12)	51	<0.01
Yuman (4)	14	<0.01
Yup'ik *(Alaska Native)* (11)	24	<0.01
Asian (349,768)	394,211	6.02
Not Hispanic (347,495)	388,293	5.93
Hispanic (2,273)	5,918	0.09
Bangladeshi (2,109)	2,387	0.04
Bhutanese (425)	544	0.01
Burmese (923)	1,072	0.02
Cambodian (25,387)	28,424	0.43
Chinese, ex. Taiwanese (118,164)	131,846	2.01
Filipino (12,309)	18,673	0.29
Hmong (992)	1,080	0.02
Indian (77,177)	85,441	1.30
Indonesian (847)	1,379	0.02
Japanese (9,224)	15,358	0.23
Korean (24,110)	28,904	0.44
Laotian (3,632)	4,530	0.07
Malaysian (357)	593	0.01
Nepalese (2,580)	2,865	0.04
Pakistani (6,205)	7,071	0.11
Sri Lankan (1,034)	1,254	0.02
Taiwanese (4,502)	5,353	0.08
Thai (3,529)	4,712	0.07
Vietnamese (42,915)	47,636	0.73
Hawaii Native/Pacific Islander (2,223)	10,257	0.16
Not Hispanic (1,467)	7,034	0.11
Hispanic (756)	3,223	0.05
Fijian (32)	65	<0.01
Guamanian/Chamorro (671)	1,179	0.02
Marshallese (22)	30	<0.01
Native Hawaiian (520)	1,780	0.03
Samoan (210)	511	0.01
Tongan (23)	64	<0.01
White (5,265,236)	5,400,458	82.48
Not Hispanic (4,984,800)	5,082,983	77.63
Hispanic (280,436)	317,475	4.85

*Notes: † The Census 2010 population figure is used to calculate the percentages in the Hispanic Origin and Race categories. Ancestry percentages are based on the 2006-2010 American Community Survey population (not shown); ‡ Numbers in parentheses indicate the number of people reporting a single ancestry; * Numbers in parentheses indicate the number of persons reporting this race alone, not in combination with any other race; Please refer to the Explanation of Data for more information.*

Abington

Place Type: CDP/Town
County: Plymouth
Population: 15,985†

Ancestry‡	Population	%
African, Sub-Saharan (24)	24	0.15
African (12)	12	0.08
Kenyan (12)	12	0.08
Albanian (8)	31	0.20
American (861)	861	5.48
Arab (81)	238	1.52
Lebanese (40)	127	0.81
Moroccan (41)	41	0.26
Syrian (0)	70	0.45
Armenian (32)	32	0.20
Belgian (8)	8	0.05
Brazilian (200)	200	1.27
British (26)	45	0.29
Canadian (79)	143	0.91
Croatian (0)	9	0.06
Czech (0)	28	0.18
Dutch (9)	48	0.31
English (488)	1,961	12.49
European (59)	59	0.38
Finnish (0)	25	0.16
French, ex. Basque (112)	865	5.51
French Canadian (109)	506	3.22
German (158)	1,270	8.09
Greek (96)	320	2.04
Hungarian (82)	100	0.64
Irish (2,837)	7,156	45.57
Italian (698)	3,206	20.42
Lithuanian (49)	188	1.20
Norwegian (31)	90	0.57
Polish (169)	591	3.76
Portuguese (144)	635	4.04
Romanian (0)	10	0.06
Russian (42)	195	1.24
Scotch-Irish (240)	723	4.60
Scottish (147)	465	2.96
Swedish (82)	429	2.73
Welsh (40)	111	0.71
West Indian, ex. Hispanic (194)	194	1.24
Haitian (194)	194	1.24
Yugoslavian (13)	13	0.08

Hispanic Origin	Population	%
Hispanic or Latino (of any race)	310	1.94
Central American, ex. Mexican	33	0.21
Costa Rican	1	0.01
Guatemalan	8	0.05
Honduran	11	0.07
Panamanian	2	0.01
Salvadoran	10	0.06
Other Central American	1	0.01
Cuban	16	0.10
Dominican Republic	19	0.12
Mexican	39	0.24
Puerto Rican	120	0.75
South American	31	0.19
Argentinean	2	0.01
Bolivian	1	0.01
Chilean	4	0.03
Colombian	10	0.06
Ecuadorian	4	0.03
Peruvian	5	0.03
Uruguayan	1	0.01
Venezuelan	4	0.03
Other Hispanic or Latino	52	0.33

Race*	Population	%
African-American/Black (342)	443	2.77
Not Hispanic (313)	408	2.55
Hispanic (29)	35	0.22
American Indian/Alaska Native (47)	92	0.58
Not Hispanic (41)	84	0.53
Hispanic (6)	8	0.05
Canadian/French Am. Ind. (0)	3	0.02
Cherokee (2)	4	0.03
Chippewa (0)	2	0.01
Delaware (0)	3	0.02
Iroquois (1)	9	0.06
Mexican American Ind. (1)	1	0.01
Navajo (0)	2	0.01
Potawatomi (5)	5	0.03
Tlingit-Haida *(Alaska Native)* (1)	1	0.01
Tohono O'Odham (1)	1	0.01
Asian (284)	340	2.13
Not Hispanic (282)	333	2.08
Hispanic (2)	7	0.04
Bangladeshi (4)	4	0.03
Cambodian (2)	4	0.03
Chinese, ex. Taiwanese (34)	53	0.33
Filipino (24)	41	0.26
Indian (113)	117	0.73
Indonesian (1)	1	0.01
Japanese (4)	14	0.09
Korean (16)	29	0.18
Laotian (3)	3	0.02
Pakistani (1)	1	0.01
Taiwanese (0)	2	0.01
Thai (1)	1	0.01
Vietnamese (62)	66	0.41
Hawaii Native/Pacific Islander (2)	5	0.03
Not Hispanic (2)	5	0.03
Guamanian/Chamorro (1)	1	0.01
Native Hawaiian (0)	1	0.01
White (14,788)	14,972	93.66
Not Hispanic (14,617)	14,782	92.47
Hispanic (171)	190	1.19

Acton

Place Type: Town
County: Middlesex
Population: 21,924†

Ancestry‡	Population	%
African, Sub-Saharan (70)	91	0.43
African (0)	13	0.06
Cape Verdean (40)	48	0.22
Nigerian (11)	11	0.05
South African (8)	8	0.04
Ugandan (11)	11	0.05
American (669)	669	3.13
Arab (172)	196	0.92
Arab (27)	27	0.13
Lebanese (133)	157	0.73
Syrian (12)	12	0.06
Armenian (32)	85	0.40
Austrian (87)	216	1.01
Belgian (0)	11	0.05
Brazilian (123)	213	1.00
British (91)	137	0.64
Bulgarian (46)	57	0.27
Canadian (64)	149	0.70
Croatian (9)	28	0.13
Czech (17)	96	0.45
Danish (26)	107	0.50
Dutch (56)	348	1.63
Eastern European (203)	203	0.95
English (631)	3,226	15.09
European (477)	487	2.28
Finnish (50)	111	0.52
French, ex. Basque (101)	1,117	5.23
French Canadian (200)	462	2.16
German (451)	2,424	11.34
Greek (86)	102	0.48
Hungarian (45)	99	0.46
Iranian (13)	37	0.17
Irish (1,351)	4,481	20.96
Israeli (26)	26	0.12
Italian (735)	2,057	9.62
Lithuanian (56)	360	1.68
Northern European (80)	80	0.37
Norwegian (55)	219	1.02
Polish (185)	833	3.90
Portuguese (97)	308	1.44
Romanian (0)	26	0.12
Russian (298)	657	3.07
Scandinavian (0)	25	0.12
Scotch-Irish (211)	571	2.67
Scottish (115)	637	2.98
Serbian (21)	73	0.34
Slavic (0)	13	0.06
Slovak (43)	98	0.46
Slovene (9)	31	0.15
Swedish (114)	514	2.40
Swiss (12)	122	0.57
Turkish (56)	56	0.26
Ukrainian (48)	142	0.66
Welsh (21)	186	0.87
West Indian, ex. Hispanic (54)	78	0.36
Haitian (42)	42	0.20
Jamaican (12)	24	0.11
Trinidadian/Tobagonian (0)	12	0.06
Yugoslavian (0)	10	0.05

Hispanic Origin	Population	%
Hispanic or Latino (of any race)	560	2.55
Central American, ex. Mexican	96	0.44
Costa Rican	6	0.03
Guatemalan	62	0.28
Honduran	4	0.02
Nicaraguan	2	0.01
Panamanian	8	0.04
Salvadoran	14	0.06
Cuban	24	0.11
Dominican Republic	17	0.08
Mexican	98	0.45
Puerto Rican	93	0.42
South American	154	0.70
Argentinean	16	0.07
Bolivian	1	<0.01
Chilean	5	0.02
Colombian	51	0.23
Ecuadorian	15	0.07
Paraguayan	8	0.04
Peruvian	33	0.15
Uruguayan	1	<0.01
Venezuelan	23	0.10
Other South American	1	<0.01
Other Hispanic or Latino	78	0.36

Race*	Population	%
African-American/Black (238)	327	1.49
Not Hispanic (232)	307	1.40
Hispanic (6)	20	0.09
American Indian/Alaska Native (18)	71	0.32
Not Hispanic (13)	53	0.24
Hispanic (5)	18	0.08
Blackfeet (0)	2	0.01
Canadian/French Am. Ind. (0)	1	<0.01
Cherokee (2)	10	0.05
Chickasaw (0)	1	<0.01
Chippewa (1)	1	<0.01
Choctaw (0)	1	<0.01
Creek (2)	2	0.01
Iroquois (1)	2	0.01
Sioux (2)	2	0.01
South American Ind. (1)	4	0.02
Asian (4,067)	4,296	19.59
Not Hispanic (4,062)	4,284	19.54
Hispanic (5)	12	0.05
Bangladeshi (12)	14	0.06
Burmese (3)	6	0.03
Cambodian (13)	13	0.06
Chinese, ex. Taiwanese (1,979)	2,063	9.41
Filipino (54)	67	0.31
Hmong (4)	4	0.02
Indian (1,438)	1,501	6.85
Indonesian (1)	4	0.02
Japanese (64)	101	0.46
Korean (261)	290	1.32
Laotian (2)	2	0.01
Malaysian (0)	2	0.01
Nepalese (11)	11	0.05
Pakistani (38)	38	0.17

*Notes: † The Census 2010 population figure is used to calculate the percentages in the Hispanic Origin and Race categories. Ancestry percentages are based on the 2006-2010 American Community Survey population (not shown); ‡ Numbers in parentheses indicate the number of people reporting a single ancestry; * Numbers in parentheses indicate the number of persons reporting this race alone, not in combination with any other race; Please refer to the Explanation of Data for more information.*

Sri Lankan (22)	25	0.11
Taiwanese (62)	70	0.32
Thai (12)	16	0.07
Vietnamese (35)	47	0.21
Hawaii Native/Pacific Islander (3)	20	0.09
Not Hispanic (3)	20	0.09
Native Hawaiian (0)	12	0.05
White (16,953)	17,293	78.88
Not Hispanic (16,555)	16,857	76.89
Hispanic (398)	436	1.99

Acushnet

Place Type: Town
County: Bristol
Population: 10,303†

Ancestry‡	Population	%
African, Sub-Saharan (90)	134	1.30
Cape Verdean (90)	134	1.30
American (518)	518	5.03
Arab (20)	20	0.19
Lebanese (20)	20	0.19
Brazilian (0)	9	0.09
British (51)	51	0.50
Cajun (13)	13	0.13
Canadian (56)	66	0.64
Croatian (0)	21	0.20
Czech (0)	13	0.13
Czechoslovakian (0)	13	0.13
Dutch (0)	56	0.54
English (242)	1,308	12.71
Finnish (0)	48	0.47
French, ex. Basque (584)	1,842	17.90
French Canadian (681)	1,095	10.64
German (23)	219	2.13
Greek (12)	12	0.12
Hungarian (0)	33	0.32
Iranian (12)	12	0.12
Irish (344)	1,566	15.22
Italian (80)	334	3.25
Lithuanian (20)	20	0.19
Norwegian (0)	12	0.12
Polish (209)	591	5.74
Portuguese (2,802)	4,606	44.77
Russian (12)	25	0.24
Scandinavian (5)	5	0.05
Scotch-Irish (10)	20	0.19
Scottish (50)	121	1.18
Slovak (0)	8	0.08
Slovene (23)	44	0.43
Swedish (0)	75	0.73

Hispanic Origin	Population	%
Hispanic or Latino (of any race)	119	1.16
Central American, ex. Mexican	7	0.07
Guatemalan	1	0.01
Honduran	1	0.01
Panamanian	1	0.01
Salvadoran	4	0.04
Cuban	3	0.03
Dominican Republic	3	0.03
Mexican	10	0.10
Puerto Rican	65	0.63
South American	10	0.10
Argentinean	6	0.06
Colombian	2	0.02
Ecuadorian	1	0.01
Peruvian	1	0.01
Other Hispanic or Latino	21	0.20

Race*	Population	%
African-American/Black (49)	88	0.85
Not Hispanic (48)	84	0.82
Hispanic (1)	4	0.04
American Indian/Alaska Native (16)	47	0.46
Not Hispanic (16)	47	0.46
Canadian/French Am. Ind. (1)	1	0.01
Cherokee (0)	8	0.08
Cheyenne (1)	1	0.01
Iroquois (0)	1	0.01
Seminole (1)	1	0.01
Sioux (0)	1	0.01
Asian (31)	52	0.50
Not Hispanic (31)	52	0.50
Chinese, ex. Taiwanese (12)	17	0.17
Filipino (2)	6	0.06
Indian (1)	1	0.01
Japanese (3)	7	0.07
Korean (6)	11	0.11
Pakistani (1)	1	0.01
Thai (1)	1	0.01
Vietnamese (5)	5	0.05
Hawaii Native/Pacific Islander (0)	6	0.06
Not Hispanic (0)	6	0.06
Native Hawaiian (0)	1	0.01
White (10,011)	10,119	98.21
Not Hispanic (9,919)	10,017	97.22
Hispanic (92)	102	0.99

Adams

Place Type: Town
County: Berkshire
Population: 8,485†

Ancestry‡	Population	%
African, Sub-Saharan (11)	19	0.22
African (11)	11	0.13
Cape Verdean (0)	8	0.09
Albanian (0)	10	0.12
American (327)	327	3.84
Arab (14)	89	1.04
Lebanese (14)	89	1.04
Australian (14)	14	0.16
Austrian (0)	30	0.35
Belgian (8)	8	0.09
British (0)	13	0.15
Canadian (51)	94	1.10
Czech (0)	6	0.07
Czechoslovakian (9)	9	0.11
Dutch (0)	31	0.36
Eastern European (7)	7	0.08
English (151)	835	9.80
European (20)	20	0.23
French, ex. Basque (550)	2,410	28.30
French Canadian (294)	665	7.81
German (156)	1,071	12.57
Greek (0)	44	0.52
Hungarian (0)	13	0.15
Irish (140)	1,247	14.64
Italian (174)	1,255	14.74
Norwegian (0)	64	0.75
Pennsylvania German (13)	13	0.15
Polish (807)	2,347	27.56
Portuguese (12)	41	0.48
Scandinavian (5)	5	0.06
Scotch-Irish (48)	153	1.80
Scottish (22)	554	6.50
Swedish (9)	104	1.22
Swiss (0)	8	0.09
Welsh (21)	46	0.54

Hispanic Origin	Population	%
Hispanic or Latino (of any race)	98	1.15
Central American, ex. Mexican	18	0.21
Costa Rican	3	0.04
Honduran	15	0.18
Cuban	6	0.07
Mexican	19	0.22
Puerto Rican	37	0.44
South American	8	0.09
Argentinean	1	0.01
Colombian	2	0.02
Ecuadorian	3	0.04
Other South American	2	0.02
Other Hispanic or Latino	10	0.12

Race*	Population	%
African-American/Black (56)	123	1.45
Not Hispanic (51)	111	1.31
Hispanic (5)	12	0.14
American Indian/Alaska Native (15)	60	0.71
Not Hispanic (8)	48	0.57
Hispanic (7)	12	0.14
Aleut *(Alaska Native)* (0)	1	0.01
Blackfeet (0)	3	0.04
Canadian/French Am. Ind. (0)	1	0.01
Central American Ind. (0)	1	0.01
Cherokee (1)	7	0.08
Choctaw (1)	2	0.02
Crow (0)	1	0.01
Iroquois (0)	6	0.07
Potawatomi (0)	1	0.01
Shoshone (0)	1	0.01
Asian (42)	62	0.73
Not Hispanic (40)	58	0.68
Hispanic (2)	4	0.05
Cambodian (2)	2	0.02
Chinese, ex. Taiwanese (6)	15	0.18
Filipino (4)	7	0.08
Indian (13)	16	0.19
Indonesian (0)	4	0.05
Japanese (0)	4	0.05
Korean (5)	11	0.13
Laotian (2)	3	0.04
Nepalese (1)	2	0.02
Vietnamese (3)	5	0.06
Hawaii Native/Pacific Islander (2)	8	0.09
Not Hispanic (2)	8	0.09
Guamanian/Chamorro (1)	3	0.04
Native Hawaiian (0)	3	0.04
White (8,226)	8,342	98.31
Not Hispanic (8,166)	8,273	97.50
Hispanic (60)	69	0.81

Agawam Town

Place Type: City
County: Hampden
Population: 28,438†

Ancestry‡	Population	%
African, Sub-Saharan (52)	52	0.18
African (25)	25	0.09
Nigerian (27)	27	0.10
American (925)	925	3.26
Arab (106)	168	0.59
Arab (12)	12	0.04
Egyptian (0)	12	0.04
Lebanese (81)	121	0.43
Syrian (13)	23	0.08
Armenian (31)	47	0.17
Assyrian/Chaldean/Syriac (0)	13	0.05
Austrian (31)	63	0.22
Belgian (0)	44	0.16
British (85)	119	0.42
Canadian (37)	109	0.38
Croatian (0)	76	0.27
Czech (0)	50	0.18
Czechoslovakian (10)	19	0.07
Danish (0)	25	0.09
Dutch (0)	131	0.46
Eastern European (10)	10	0.04
English (764)	3,526	12.42
European (51)	51	0.18
Finnish (0)	29	0.10
French, ex. Basque (979)	4,503	15.87
French Canadian (1,139)	2,448	8.62
German (586)	2,207	7.78
Greek (190)	419	1.48
Hungarian (0)	43	0.15
Iranian (0)	12	0.04
Irish (1,817)	6,984	24.61
Italian (2,564)	6,514	22.95
Latvian (11)	11	0.04
Lithuanian (47)	98	0.35
Norwegian (0)	52	0.18
Polish (1,277)	3,194	11.25
Portuguese (137)	275	0.97

*Notes: † The Census 2010 population figure is used to calculate the percentages in the Hispanic Origin and Race categories. Ancestry percentages are based on the 2006-2010 American Community Survey population (not shown); ‡ Numbers in parentheses indicate the number of people reporting a single ancestry; * Numbers in parentheses indicate the number of persons reporting this race alone, not in combination with any other race; Please refer to the Explanation of Data for more information.*

Romanian (16)	55	0.19
Russian (677)	1,079	3.80
Scotch-Irish (64)	325	1.15
Scottish (262)	1,084	3.82
Slavic (14)	27	0.10
Slovak (0)	10	0.04
Swedish (73)	342	1.20
Swiss (8)	76	0.27
Ukrainian (127)	228	0.80
Welsh (16)	80	0.28
West Indian, ex. Hispanic (75)	170	0.60
Barbadian (17)	17	0.06
Haitian (0)	12	0.04
Jamaican (58)	128	0.45
West Indian (0)	13	0.05

Hispanic Origin	Population	%
Hispanic or Latino (of any race)	940	3.31
Central American, ex. Mexican	25	0.09
Costa Rican	4	0.01
Guatemalan	2	0.01
Honduran	4	0.01
Nicaraguan	2	0.01
Salvadoran	13	0.05
Cuban	25	0.09
Dominican Republic	19	0.07
Mexican	62	0.22
Puerto Rican	663	2.33
South American	81	0.28
Argentinean	1	<0.01
Chilean	1	<0.01
Colombian	37	0.13
Ecuadorian	8	0.03
Paraguayan	2	0.01
Peruvian	19	0.07
Venezuelan	13	0.05
Other Hispanic or Latino	65	0.23

Race*	Population	%
African-American/Black (426)	562	1.98
Not Hispanic (383)	494	1.74
Hispanic (43)	68	0.24
American Indian/Alaska Native (45)	166	0.58
Not Hispanic (29)	125	0.44
Hispanic (16)	41	0.14
Apache (1)	2	0.01
Blackfeet (0)	8	0.03
Canadian/French Am. Ind. (3)	3	0.01
Cherokee (6)	14	0.05
Chippewa (4)	4	0.01
Choctaw (0)	1	<0.01
Creek (0)	1	<0.01
Iroquois (2)	7	0.02
Mexican American Ind. (0)	3	0.01
Sioux (0)	7	0.02
South American Ind. (7)	18	0.06
Spanish American Ind. (0)	8	0.03
Asian (502)	601	2.11
Not Hispanic (496)	584	2.05
Hispanic (6)	17	0.06
Chinese, ex. Taiwanese (89)	101	0.36
Filipino (34)	43	0.15
Indian (126)	149	0.52
Indonesian (4)	10	0.04
Japanese (18)	26	0.09
Korean (98)	123	0.43
Laotian (2)	4	0.01
Pakistani (50)	53	0.19
Taiwanese (1)	3	0.01
Thai (3)	5	0.02
Vietnamese (64)	83	0.29
Hawaii Native/Pacific Islander (0)	17	0.06
Not Hispanic (0)	16	0.06
Hispanic (0)	1	<0.01
Guamanian/Chamorro (0)	1	<0.01
Native Hawaiian (0)	5	0.02
Samoan (0)	3	0.01
White (26,899)	27,203	95.66
Not Hispanic (26,287)	26,536	93.31
Hispanic (612)	667	2.35

Amesbury Town

Place Type: City
County: Essex
Population: 16,283†

Ancestry‡	Population	%
African, Sub-Saharan (5)	5	0.03
Ethiopian (5)	5	0.03
Albanian (0)	15	0.09
American (780)	780	4.81
Arab (57)	105	0.65
Lebanese (57)	105	0.65
Armenian (9)	52	0.32
Austrian (0)	10	0.06
Belgian (0)	17	0.10
Brazilian (135)	141	0.87
British (36)	126	0.78
Canadian (185)	280	1.73
Czech (37)	48	0.30
Czechoslovakian (11)	22	0.14
Danish (0)	253	1.56
Dutch (8)	154	0.95
Eastern European (10)	10	0.06
English (673)	2,929	18.05
European (108)	108	0.67
Finnish (13)	36	0.22
French, ex. Basque (714)	2,601	16.03
French Canadian (718)	1,521	9.37
German (172)	1,411	8.70
Greek (63)	165	1.02
Hungarian (19)	19	0.12
Irish (1,590)	4,966	30.61
Italian (742)	2,429	14.97
Latvian (13)	13	0.08
Lithuanian (5)	80	0.49
Northern European (21)	21	0.13
Norwegian (7)	26	0.16
Polish (157)	788	4.86
Portuguese (22)	209	1.29
Romanian (27)	27	0.17
Russian (31)	234	1.44
Scandinavian (31)	31	0.19
Scotch-Irish (155)	441	2.72
Scottish (272)	854	5.26
Swedish (63)	491	3.03
Swiss (0)	27	0.17
Turkish (0)	10	0.06
Ukrainian (26)	120	0.74
Welsh (0)	21	0.13
West Indian, ex. Hispanic (14)	78	0.48
Haitian (14)	14	0.09
Jamaican (0)	64	0.39

Hispanic Origin	Population	%
Hispanic or Latino (of any race)	310	1.90
Central American, ex. Mexican	30	0.18
Costa Rican	2	0.01
Guatemalan	10	0.06
Honduran	7	0.04
Nicaraguan	2	0.01
Salvadoran	9	0.06
Cuban	23	0.14
Dominican Republic	38	0.23
Mexican	40	0.25
Puerto Rican	91	0.56
South American	44	0.27
Argentinean	3	0.02
Bolivian	5	0.03
Chilean	11	0.07
Colombian	11	0.07
Ecuadorian	4	0.02
Peruvian	6	0.04
Venezuelan	1	0.01
Other South American	3	0.02
Other Hispanic or Latino	44	0.27

Race*	Population	%
African-American/Black (120)	201	1.23
Not Hispanic (108)	176	1.08
Hispanic (12)	25	0.15
American Indian/Alaska Native (37)	121	0.74
Not Hispanic (30)	107	0.66
Hispanic (7)	14	0.09
Alaska Athabascan *(Ala. Nat.)* (3)	3	0.02
Aleut *(Alaska Native)* (1)	1	0.01
Apache (1)	6	0.04
Blackfeet (0)	1	0.01
Canadian/French Am. Ind. (0)	4	0.02
Cherokee (0)	11	0.07
Chippewa (3)	9	0.06
Creek (0)	1	0.01
Iroquois (0)	5	0.03
Mexican American Ind. (5)	7	0.04
Pueblo (0)	1	0.01
Sioux (0)	2	0.01
South American Ind. (0)	2	0.01
Tlingit-Haida *(Alaska Native)* (0)	1	0.01
Ute (0)	1	0.01
Yaqui (0)	3	0.02
Asian (106)	164	1.01
Not Hispanic (106)	164	1.01
Burmese (4)	4	0.02
Cambodian (5)	6	0.04
Chinese, ex. Taiwanese (21)	25	0.15
Filipino (10)	16	0.10
Indian (24)	28	0.17
Japanese (9)	33	0.20
Korean (11)	20	0.12
Nepalese (1)	2	0.01
Pakistani (6)	7	0.04
Taiwanese (1)	1	0.01
Thai (2)	2	0.01
Vietnamese (9)	12	0.07
Hawaii Native/Pacific Islander (7)	12	0.07
Not Hispanic (6)	11	0.07
Hispanic (1)	1	0.01
Guamanian/Chamorro (1)	1	0.01
Native Hawaiian (2)	2	0.01
White (15,688)	15,909	97.70
Not Hispanic (15,479)	15,676	96.27
Hispanic (209)	233	1.43

Amherst Center

Place Type: CDP
County: Hampshire
Population: 19,065†

Ancestry‡	Population	%
Afghan (15)	15	0.08
African, Sub-Saharan (172)	309	1.58
African (39)	72	0.37
Cape Verdean (43)	89	0.46
Ghanaian (33)	33	0.17
Kenyan (0)	26	0.13
Nigerian (12)	12	0.06
Sudanese (13)	13	0.07
Other Sub-Saharan African (32)	64	0.33
Albanian (43)	65	0.33
American (185)	185	0.95
Arab (63)	117	0.60
Lebanese (28)	65	0.33
Palestinian (15)	15	0.08
Syrian (6)	23	0.12
Other Arab (14)	14	0.07
Armenian (0)	134	0.69
Austrian (14)	14	0.07
Basque (0)	15	0.08
Brazilian (0)	63	0.32
British (27)	95	0.49
Bulgarian (0)	17	0.09
Canadian (0)	39	0.20
Croatian (0)	40	0.20
Czech (50)	121	0.62
Danish (37)	96	0.49
Dutch (45)	287	1.47
Eastern European (210)	224	1.15
English (313)	1,989	10.18
European (103)	130	0.67

*Notes: † The Census 2010 population figure is used to calculate the percentages in the Hispanic Origin and Race categories. Ancestry percentages are based on the 2006-2010 American Community Survey population (not shown); ‡ Numbers in parentheses indicate the number of people reporting a single ancestry; * Numbers in parentheses indicate the number of persons reporting this race alone, not in combination with any other race; Please refer to the Explanation of Data for more information.*

Finnish (11)	64	0.33
French, ex. Basque (125)	1,258	6.44
French Canadian (175)	681	3.49
German (121)	1,915	9.80
Greek (79)	253	1.30
Guyanese (16)	16	0.08
Hungarian (14)	91	0.47
Iranian (56)	131	0.67
Irish (1,004)	4,393	22.49
Italian (567)	2,260	11.57
Lithuanian (43)	210	1.07
Northern European (52)	52	0.27
Norwegian (29)	257	1.32
Polish (184)	1,402	7.18
Portuguese (162)	482	2.47
Romanian (42)	42	0.21
Russian (316)	848	4.34
Scandinavian (23)	74	0.38
Scotch-Irish (182)	606	3.10
Scottish (73)	608	3.11
Serbian (0)	35	0.18
Slavic (42)	42	0.21
Swedish (35)	468	2.40
Swiss (0)	73	0.37
Turkish (24)	38	0.19
Ukrainian (0)	51	0.26
Welsh (76)	310	1.59
West Indian, ex. Hispanic (206)	318	1.63
Barbadian (14)	35	0.18
British West Indian (17)	34	0.17
Haitian (144)	159	0.81
Jamaican (16)	75	0.38
West Indian (15)	15	0.08

Hispanic Origin	Population	%
Hispanic or Latino (of any race)	1,249	6.55
Central American, ex. Mexican	135	0.71
Costa Rican	10	0.05
Guatemalan	26	0.14
Honduran	18	0.09
Nicaraguan	8	0.04
Panamanian	7	0.04
Salvadoran	64	0.34
Other Central American	2	0.01
Cuban	89	0.47
Dominican Republic	145	0.76
Mexican	163	0.85
Puerto Rican	380	1.99
South American	202	1.06
Argentinean	34	0.18
Bolivian	7	0.04
Chilean	16	0.08
Colombian	66	0.35
Ecuadorian	27	0.14
Paraguayan	4	0.02
Peruvian	29	0.15
Uruguayan	5	0.03
Venezuelan	14	0.07
Other Hispanic or Latino	135	0.71

Race*	Population	%
African-American/Black (1,057)	1,360	7.13
Not Hispanic (921)	1,163	6.10
Hispanic (136)	197	1.03
American Indian/Alaska Native (38)	160	0.84
Not Hispanic (23)	119	0.62
Hispanic (15)	41	0.22
Alaska Athabascan *(Ala. Nat.)* (0)	1	0.01
Apache (1)	2	0.01
Blackfeet (0)	4	0.02
Canadian/French Am. Ind. (1)	1	0.01
Cherokee (1)	20	0.10
Chickasaw (1)	2	0.01
Chippewa (0)	2	0.01
Choctaw (0)	3	0.02
Cree (1)	2	0.01
Creek (0)	1	0.01
Inupiat *(Alaska Native)* (1)	1	0.01
Iroquois (6)	8	0.04
Mexican American Ind. (2)	2	0.01
Navajo (2)	3	0.02
Seminole (0)	2	0.01
Shoshone (0)	1	0.01
Sioux (0)	1	0.01
South American Ind. (2)	14	0.07
Yaqui (0)	1	0.01
Asian (1,817)	2,140	11.22
Not Hispanic (1,806)	2,100	11.01
Hispanic (11)	40	0.21
Bangladeshi (10)	11	0.06
Bhutanese (4)	4	0.02
Burmese (0)	3	0.02
Cambodian (46)	60	0.31
Chinese, ex. Taiwanese (781)	925	4.85
Filipino (47)	87	0.46
Indian (282)	335	1.76
Indonesian (2)	5	0.03
Japanese (73)	127	0.67
Korean (241)	285	1.49
Laotian (6)	9	0.05
Malaysian (2)	4	0.02
Nepalese (19)	19	0.10
Pakistani (40)	49	0.26
Sri Lankan (12)	13	0.07
Taiwanese (46)	59	0.31
Thai (10)	19	0.10
Vietnamese (108)	142	0.74
Hawaii Native/Pacific Islander (2)	25	0.13
Not Hispanic (2)	19	0.10
Hispanic (0)	6	0.03
Guamanian/Chamorro (0)	2	0.01
Native Hawaiian (1)	9	0.05
Samoan (0)	1	0.01
White (15,051)	15,693	82.31
Not Hispanic (14,416)	14,920	78.26
Hispanic (635)	773	4.05

Amherst

Place Type: Town
County: Hampshire
Population: 37,819†

Ancestry‡	Population	%
Afghan (15)	15	0.04
African, Sub-Saharan (424)	624	1.67
African (70)	166	0.44
Cape Verdean (78)	124	0.33
Ghanaian (52)	52	0.14
Kenyan (82)	108	0.29
Nigerian (44)	44	0.12
Sudanese (13)	13	0.03
Other Sub-Saharan African (85)	117	0.31
Albanian (43)	65	0.17
American (581)	581	1.55
Arab (122)	315	0.84
Egyptian (59)	59	0.16
Lebanese (28)	161	0.43
Palestinian (15)	15	0.04
Syrian (6)	34	0.09
Other Arab (14)	46	0.12
Armenian (35)	230	0.61
Australian (15)	15	0.04
Austrian (34)	177	0.47
Basque (0)	15	0.04
Belgian (11)	82	0.22
Brazilian (9)	72	0.19
British (97)	328	0.88
Bulgarian (0)	17	0.05
Canadian (0)	39	0.10
Croatian (20)	60	0.16
Czech (92)	212	0.57
Danish (37)	142	0.38
Dutch (92)	528	1.41
Eastern European (596)	731	1.95
English (934)	4,411	11.79
Estonian (0)	10	0.03
European (401)	428	1.14
Finnish (11)	76	0.20
French, ex. Basque (335)	2,200	5.88
French Canadian (295)	1,240	3.32
German (641)	3,959	10.58
Greek (110)	337	0.90
Guyanese (16)	16	0.04
Hungarian (58)	249	0.67
Iranian (145)	220	0.59
Irish (1,992)	7,649	20.45
Israeli (15)	29	0.08
Italian (1,023)	3,814	10.20
Latvian (0)	30	0.08
Lithuanian (61)	373	1.00
New Zealander (94)	94	0.25
Northern European (115)	129	0.34
Norwegian (61)	372	0.99
Pennsylvania German (0)	11	0.03
Polish (367)	2,419	6.47
Portuguese (226)	740	1.98
Romanian (71)	112	0.30
Russian (473)	1,450	3.88
Scandinavian (23)	74	0.20
Scotch-Irish (292)	970	2.59
Scottish (197)	1,282	3.43
Serbian (18)	53	0.14
Slavic (42)	42	0.11
Slovak (0)	15	0.04
Slovene (10)	10	0.03
Swedish (112)	909	2.43
Swiss (12)	149	0.40
Turkish (48)	76	0.20
Ukrainian (13)	173	0.46
Welsh (83)	418	1.12
West Indian, ex. Hispanic (247)	366	0.98
Barbadian (14)	35	0.09
British West Indian (17)	34	0.09
Haitian (157)	172	0.46
Jamaican (30)	89	0.24
West Indian (29)	36	0.10

Hispanic Origin	Population	%
Hispanic or Latino (of any race)	2,757	7.29
Central American, ex. Mexican	437	1.16
Costa Rican	21	0.06
Guatemalan	58	0.15
Honduran	26	0.07
Nicaraguan	16	0.04
Panamanian	19	0.05
Salvadoran	295	0.78
Other Central American	2	0.01
Cuban	139	0.37
Dominican Republic	223	0.59
Mexican	331	0.88
Puerto Rican	955	2.53
South American	428	1.13
Argentinean	66	0.17
Bolivian	12	0.03
Chilean	38	0.10
Colombian	135	0.36
Ecuadorian	75	0.20
Paraguayan	5	0.01
Peruvian	63	0.17
Uruguayan	8	0.02
Venezuelan	24	0.06
Other South American	2	0.01
Other Hispanic or Latino	244	0.65

Race*	Population	%
African-American/Black (2,044)	2,725	7.21
Not Hispanic (1,815)	2,340	6.19
Hispanic (229)	385	1.02
American Indian/Alaska Native (92)	363	0.96
Not Hispanic (47)	246	0.65
Hispanic (45)	117	0.31
Alaska Athabascan *(Ala. Nat.)* (0)	1	<0.01
Apache (2)	4	0.01
Blackfeet (1)	17	0.04
Canadian/French Am. Ind. (1)	2	0.01
Central American Ind. (0)	3	0.01
Cherokee (3)	36	0.10
Chickasaw (2)	4	0.01
Chippewa (1)	7	0.02

*Notes: † The Census 2010 population figure is used to calculate the percentages in the Hispanic Origin and Race categories. Ancestry percentages are based on the 2006-2010 American Community Survey population (not shown); ‡ Numbers in parentheses indicate the number of people reporting a single ancestry; * Numbers in parentheses indicate the number of persons reporting this race alone, not in combination with any other race; Please refer to the Explanation of Data for more information.*

Choctaw (0)	3	0.01
Cree (1)	2	0.01
Creek (0)	1	<0.01
Crow (0)	2	0.01
Delaware (0)	1	<0.01
Inupiat *(Alaska Native)* (1)	1	<0.01
Iroquois (6)	9	0.02
Kiowa (0)	3	0.01
Mexican American Ind. (8)	9	0.02
Navajo (2)	4	0.01
Ottawa (1)	1	<0.01
Potawatomi (0)	2	0.01
Seminole (0)	3	0.01
Shoshone (0)	1	<0.01
Sioux (0)	3	0.01
South American Ind. (7)	33	0.09
Yaqui (0)	3	0.01
Yuman (0)	1	<0.01
Asian (4,140)	4,829	12.77
Not Hispanic (4,109)	4,742	12.54
Hispanic (31)	87	0.23
Bangladeshi (21)	23	0.06
Bhutanese (5)	5	0.01
Burmese (2)	8	0.02
Cambodian (154)	188	0.50
Chinese, ex. Taiwanese (1,656)	1,917	5.07
Filipino (90)	162	0.43
Hmong (1)	1	<0.01
Indian (786)	899	2.38
Indonesian (8)	19	0.05
Japanese (155)	266	0.70
Korean (615)	694	1.84
Laotian (11)	19	0.05
Malaysian (4)	9	0.02
Nepalese (40)	41	0.11
Pakistani (74)	89	0.24
Sri Lankan (20)	22	0.06
Taiwanese (90)	107	0.28
Thai (23)	43	0.11
Vietnamese (208)	269	0.71
Hawaii Native/Pacific Islander (13)	54	0.14
Not Hispanic (11)	41	0.11
Hispanic (2)	13	0.03
Guamanian/Chamorro (0)	5	0.01
Native Hawaiian (3)	15	0.04
Samoan (2)	3	0.01
White (29,076)	30,396	80.37
Not Hispanic (27,717)	28,772	76.08
Hispanic (1,359)	1,624	4.29

Andover

Place Type: CDP
County: Essex
Population: 8,762†

Ancestry‡	Population	%
African, Sub-Saharan (56)	56	0.65
African (47)	47	0.55
South African (9)	9	0.10
American (270)	270	3.14
Arab (73)	114	1.33
Lebanese (56)	97	1.13
Moroccan (17)	17	0.20
Armenian (31)	42	0.49
Austrian (11)	20	0.23
Belgian (11)	20	0.23
British (60)	60	0.70
Bulgarian (16)	31	0.36
Canadian (12)	59	0.69
Celtic (11)	11	0.13
Croatian (0)	55	0.64
Czech (0)	31	0.36
Czechoslovakian (11)	19	0.22
Dutch (27)	105	1.22
Eastern European (68)	68	0.79
English (426)	1,448	16.86
European (111)	119	1.39
Finnish (19)	41	0.48
French, ex. Basque (183)	587	6.84
French Canadian (71)	259	3.02
German (149)	786	9.15
Greek (18)	63	0.73
Hungarian (8)	23	0.27
Iranian (8)	25	0.29
Irish (741)	2,290	26.67
Italian (559)	1,398	16.28
Latvian (8)	8	0.09
Lithuanian (36)	106	1.23
Luxemburger (11)	11	0.13
Northern European (10)	10	0.12
Norwegian (23)	153	1.78
Polish (79)	345	4.02
Portuguese (34)	198	2.31
Romanian (15)	37	0.43
Russian (131)	184	2.14
Scandinavian (0)	8	0.09
Scotch-Irish (36)	116	1.35
Scottish (79)	272	3.17
Slovak (12)	34	0.40
Swedish (39)	137	1.60
Swiss (0)	22	0.26
Ukrainian (13)	13	0.15
Welsh (22)	51	0.59
West Indian, ex. Hispanic (10)	66	0.77
U.S. Virgin Islander (10)	66	0.77

Hispanic Origin	Population	%
Hispanic or Latino (of any race)	375	4.28
Central American, ex. Mexican	18	0.21
Costa Rican	3	0.03
Guatemalan	3	0.03
Honduran	1	0.01
Nicaraguan	5	0.06
Panamanian	4	0.05
Salvadoran	2	0.02
Cuban	29	0.33
Dominican Republic	124	1.42
Mexican	31	0.35
Puerto Rican	96	1.10
South American	46	0.52
Argentinean	7	0.08
Bolivian	1	0.01
Chilean	4	0.05
Colombian	23	0.26
Ecuadorian	3	0.03
Peruvian	5	0.06
Venezuelan	3	0.03
Other Hispanic or Latino	31	0.35

Race*	Population	%
African-American/Black (153)	206	2.35
Not Hispanic (136)	179	2.04
Hispanic (17)	27	0.31
American Indian/Alaska Native (6)	38	0.43
Not Hispanic (6)	34	0.39
Hispanic (0)	4	0.05
Apache (0)	1	0.01
Blackfeet (0)	1	0.01
Cherokee (1)	7	0.08
Iroquois (0)	3	0.03
Mexican American Ind. (0)	1	0.01
Sioux (0)	1	0.01
South American Ind. (1)	1	0.01
Asian (448)	535	6.11
Not Hispanic (442)	517	5.90
Hispanic (6)	18	0.21
Bangladeshi (3)	3	0.03
Chinese, ex. Taiwanese (216)	238	2.72
Filipino (9)	28	0.32
Indian (85)	91	1.04
Indonesian (1)	1	0.01
Japanese (14)	34	0.39
Korean (78)	89	1.02
Nepalese (2)	2	0.02
Pakistani (1)	1	0.01
Taiwanese (5)	5	0.06
Thai (3)	6	0.07
Vietnamese (18)	25	0.29
Hawaii Native/Pacific Islander (9)	30	0.34
Not Hispanic (8)	15	0.17
Hispanic (1)	15	0.17
Native Hawaiian (1)	5	0.06
Samoan (4)	15	0.17
White (7,837)	7,986	91.14
Not Hispanic (7,633)	7,765	88.62
Hispanic (204)	221	2.52

Andover

Place Type: Town
County: Essex
Population: 33,201†

Ancestry‡	Population	%
African, Sub-Saharan (56)	72	0.22
African (47)	63	0.19
South African (9)	9	0.03
American (866)	866	2.65
Arab (236)	630	1.93
Egyptian (46)	46	0.14
Lebanese (148)	475	1.45
Moroccan (17)	17	0.05
Syrian (25)	92	0.28
Armenian (96)	143	0.44
Australian (38)	44	0.13
Austrian (25)	79	0.24
Belgian (26)	61	0.19
Brazilian (15)	15	0.05
British (124)	205	0.63
Bulgarian (16)	31	0.09
Canadian (101)	378	1.16
Celtic (24)	24	0.07
Croatian (14)	69	0.21
Czech (10)	180	0.55
Czechoslovakian (11)	63	0.19
Danish (12)	97	0.30
Dutch (46)	176	0.54
Eastern European (293)	293	0.90
English (1,203)	4,711	14.41
Estonian (0)	7	0.02
European (328)	363	1.11
Finnish (69)	169	0.52
French, ex. Basque (423)	1,994	6.10
French Canadian (349)	1,251	3.83
German (650)	3,346	10.23
Greek (300)	552	1.69
Hungarian (48)	169	0.52
Iranian (138)	155	0.47
Irish (3,198)	9,242	28.26
Italian (1,981)	5,229	15.99
Latvian (8)	38	0.12
Lithuanian (101)	420	1.28
Luxemburger (11)	11	0.03
Maltese (15)	15	0.05
Northern European (59)	59	0.18
Norwegian (56)	239	0.73
Polish (437)	1,725	5.28
Portuguese (171)	497	1.52
Romanian (54)	97	0.30
Russian (389)	706	2.16
Scandinavian (0)	8	0.02
Scotch-Irish (205)	468	1.43
Scottish (262)	1,147	3.51
Slovak (12)	78	0.24
Swedish (118)	686	2.10
Swiss (18)	207	0.63
Turkish (24)	24	0.07
Ukrainian (41)	89	0.27
Welsh (22)	154	0.47
West Indian, ex. Hispanic (24)	80	0.24
Barbadian (14)	14	0.04
U.S. Virgin Islander (10)	66	0.20

Hispanic Origin	Population	%
Hispanic or Latino (of any race)	1,196	3.60
Central American, ex. Mexican	74	0.22
Costa Rican	8	0.02
Guatemalan	22	0.07
Honduran	7	0.02

*Notes: † The Census 2010 population figure is used to calculate the percentages in the Hispanic Origin and Race categories. Ancestry percentages are based on the 2006-2010 American Community Survey population (not shown); ‡ Numbers in parentheses indicate the number of people reporting a single ancestry; * Numbers in parentheses indicate the number of persons reporting this race alone, not in combination with any other race; Please refer to the Explanation of Data for more information.*

Nicaraguan	7	0.02
Panamanian	9	0.03
Salvadoran	19	0.06
Other Central American	2	0.01
Cuban	90	0.27
Dominican Republic	329	0.99
Mexican	122	0.37
Puerto Rican	280	0.84
South American	171	0.52
Argentinean	27	0.08
Bolivian	2	0.01
Chilean	8	0.02
Colombian	85	0.26
Ecuadorian	17	0.05
Peruvian	18	0.05
Uruguayan	2	0.01
Venezuelan	12	0.04
Other Hispanic or Latino	130	0.39

Race*	Population	%
African-American/Black (391)	531	1.60
Not Hispanic (343)	458	1.38
Hispanic (48)	73	0.22
American Indian/Alaska Native (24)	111	0.33
Not Hispanic (15)	87	0.26
Hispanic (9)	24	0.07
Aleut *(Alaska Native)* (0)	1	<0.01
Apache (0)	1	<0.01
Blackfeet (0)	1	<0.01
Canadian/French Am. Ind. (1)	1	<0.01
Central American Ind. (0)	1	<0.01
Cherokee (1)	14	0.04
Chippewa (0)	1	<0.01
Iroquois (0)	3	0.01
Kiowa (1)	1	<0.01
Mexican American Ind. (2)	3	0.01
Potawatomi (0)	1	<0.01
Seminole (3)	3	0.01
Sioux (0)	2	0.01
South American Ind. (1)	1	<0.01
Yaqui (0)	1	<0.01
Asian (3,438)	3,741	11.27
Not Hispanic (3,415)	3,695	11.13
Hispanic (23)	46	0.14
Bangladeshi (36)	37	0.11
Burmese (1)	1	<0.01
Cambodian (5)	6	0.02
Chinese, ex. Taiwanese (1,445)	1,555	4.68
Filipino (50)	87	0.26
Indian (1,101)	1,146	3.45
Indonesian (4)	10	0.03
Japanese (89)	134	0.40
Korean (409)	459	1.38
Laotian (2)	2	0.01
Malaysian (1)	1	<0.01
Nepalese (2)	2	0.01
Pakistani (32)	37	0.11
Sri Lankan (2)	2	0.01
Taiwanese (81)	93	0.28
Thai (12)	17	0.05
Vietnamese (105)	130	0.39
Hawaii Native/Pacific Islander (11)	40	0.12
Not Hispanic (8)	20	0.06
Hispanic (3)	20	0.06
Guamanian/Chamorro (1)	2	0.01
Native Hawaiian (1)	9	0.03
Samoan (4)	16	0.05
White (28,360)	28,847	86.89
Not Hispanic (27,698)	28,103	84.65
Hispanic (662)	744	2.24

Arlington

Place Type: CDP/Town
County: Middlesex
Population: 42,844†

Ancestry‡	Population	%
African, Sub-Saharan (419)	459	1.09
African (227)	227	0.54
Cape Verdean (59)	81	0.19
Ethiopian (16)	16	0.04
Kenyan (23)	23	0.05
Nigerian (42)	60	0.14
South African (16)	16	0.04
Ugandan (36)	36	0.09
Albanian (43)	64	0.15
Alsatian (0)	10	0.02
American (1,015)	1,015	2.40
Arab (190)	417	0.99
Egyptian (131)	166	0.39
Lebanese (28)	191	0.45
Syrian (23)	36	0.09
Other Arab (8)	24	0.06
Armenian (375)	766	1.81
Austrian (12)	235	0.56
Belgian (12)	12	0.03
Brazilian (24)	33	0.08
British (195)	282	0.67
Canadian (356)	889	2.10
Celtic (36)	36	0.09
Croatian (0)	33	0.08
Czech (75)	136	0.32
Czechoslovakian (0)	16	0.04
Danish (0)	161	0.38
Dutch (219)	512	1.21
Eastern European (259)	318	0.75
English (1,155)	5,013	11.87
Estonian (10)	10	0.02
European (685)	770	1.82
Finnish (0)	116	0.27
French, ex. Basque (517)	1,619	3.83
French Canadian (425)	1,101	2.61
German (829)	3,632	8.60
Greek (986)	1,253	2.97
Hungarian (96)	291	0.69
Icelander (0)	53	0.13
Iranian (13)	57	0.13
Irish (5,289)	12,422	29.41
Italian (2,852)	6,567	15.55
Latvian (58)	90	0.21
Lithuanian (62)	350	0.83
Macedonian (0)	21	0.05
New Zealander (0)	10	0.02
Northern European (126)	126	0.30
Norwegian (142)	366	0.87
Pennsylvania German (13)	13	0.03
Polish (377)	1,919	4.54
Portuguese (436)	783	1.85
Romanian (69)	106	0.25
Russian (609)	1,332	3.15
Scandinavian (12)	12	0.03
Scotch-Irish (367)	902	2.14
Scottish (286)	1,179	2.79
Serbian (8)	8	0.02
Slavic (0)	14	0.03
Slovak (24)	42	0.10
Slovene (0)	15	0.04
Swedish (145)	809	1.92
Swiss (0)	80	0.19
Turkish (27)	78	0.18
Ukrainian (50)	174	0.41
Welsh (16)	141	0.33
West Indian, ex. Hispanic (113)	166	0.39
Haitian (83)	83	0.20
Jamaican (30)	83	0.20
Yugoslavian (77)	77	0.18

Hispanic Origin	Population	%
Hispanic or Latino (of any race)	1,395	3.26
Central American, ex. Mexican	222	0.52
Costa Rican	16	0.04
Guatemalan	78	0.18
Honduran	22	0.05
Nicaraguan	13	0.03
Panamanian	22	0.05
Salvadoran	69	0.16
Other Central American	2	<0.01
Cuban	70	0.16
Dominican Republic	78	0.18
Mexican	217	0.51
Puerto Rican	222	0.52
South American	399	0.93
Argentinean	49	0.11
Bolivian	13	0.03
Chilean	63	0.15
Colombian	116	0.27
Ecuadorian	46	0.11
Paraguayan	10	0.02
Peruvian	56	0.13
Uruguayan	4	0.01
Venezuelan	37	0.09
Other South American	5	0.01
Other Hispanic or Latino	187	0.44

Race*	Population	%
African-American/Black (1,040)	1,346	3.14
Not Hispanic (981)	1,230	2.87
Hispanic (59)	116	0.27
American Indian/Alaska Native (49)	191	0.45
Not Hispanic (29)	142	0.33
Hispanic (20)	49	0.11
Canadian/French Am. Ind. (0)	1	<0.01
Central American Ind. (1)	3	0.01
Cherokee (5)	26	0.06
Chickasaw (0)	2	<0.01
Chippewa (0)	2	<0.01
Choctaw (0)	2	<0.01
Creek (0)	2	<0.01
Delaware (4)	4	0.01
Iroquois (2)	15	0.04
Mexican American Ind. (13)	14	0.03
Navajo (2)	3	0.01
Seminole (0)	1	<0.01
South American Ind. (1)	4	0.01
Spanish American Ind. (1)	1	<0.01
Tlingit-Haida *(Alaska Native)* (0)	1	<0.01
Asian (3,550)	4,156	9.70
Not Hispanic (3,541)	4,116	9.61
Hispanic (9)	40	0.09
Bangladeshi (43)	44	0.10
Burmese (7)	8	0.02
Cambodian (12)	14	0.03
Chinese, ex. Taiwanese (1,270)	1,499	3.50
Filipino (103)	168	0.39
Indian (872)	997	2.33
Indonesian (5)	8	0.02
Japanese (344)	436	1.02
Korean (399)	464	1.08
Laotian (1)	1	<0.01
Malaysian (3)	7	0.02
Nepalese (174)	180	0.42
Pakistani (50)	58	0.14
Sri Lankan (9)	17	0.04
Taiwanese (39)	47	0.11
Thai (53)	63	0.15
Vietnamese (49)	73	0.17
Hawaii Native/Pacific Islander (8)	31	0.07
Not Hispanic (7)	22	0.05
Hispanic (1)	9	0.02
Guamanian/Chamorro (5)	9	0.02
Native Hawaiian (2)	8	0.02
Samoan (1)	1	<0.01
White (36,717)	37,703	88.00
Not Hispanic (35,804)	36,653	85.55
Hispanic (913)	1,050	2.45

Ashland

Place Type: Town
County: Middlesex
Population: 16,593†

Ancestry‡	Population	%
African, Sub-Saharan (48)	48	0.30
African (48)	48	0.30
Albanian (33)	101	0.63
American (600)	600	3.74
Arab (140)	238	1.48
Egyptian (61)	61	0.38

*Notes: † The Census 2010 population figure is used to calculate the percentages in the Hispanic Origin and Race categories. Ancestry percentages are based on the 2006-2010 American Community Survey population (not shown); ‡ Numbers in parentheses indicate the number of people reporting a single ancestry; * Numbers in parentheses indicate the number of persons reporting this race alone, not in combination with any other race; Please refer to the Explanation of Data for more information.*

Iraqi (17)	17	0.11
Lebanese (38)	38	0.24
Moroccan (12)	12	0.07
Syrian (0)	49	0.31
Other Arab (12)	61	0.38
Armenian (138)	179	1.12
Austrian (0)	109	0.68
Belgian (0)	9	0.06
Brazilian (131)	250	1.56
British (32)	66	0.41
Bulgarian (13)	13	0.08
Canadian (0)	95	0.59
Celtic (0)	153	0.95
Czech (0)	21	0.13
Danish (0)	37	0.23
Dutch (33)	294	1.83
Eastern European (331)	357	2.22
English (331)	1,978	12.32
European (132)	161	1.00
Finnish (31)	37	0.23
French, ex. Basque (124)	697	4.34
French Canadian (255)	595	3.71
German (293)	1,025	6.39
Greek (61)	159	0.99
Hungarian (20)	108	0.67
Irish (915)	3,371	21.00
Italian (1,209)	3,168	19.73
Latvian (30)	30	0.19
Lithuanian (32)	67	0.42
Norwegian (0)	19	0.12
Pennsylvania German (0)	16	0.10
Polish (501)	1,169	7.28
Portuguese (186)	570	3.55
Romanian (24)	24	0.15
Russian (436)	984	6.13
Scotch-Irish (94)	197	1.23
Scottish (26)	427	2.66
Slovak (0)	13	0.08
Swedish (25)	441	2.75
Ukrainian (65)	155	0.97
Welsh (25)	96	0.60
West Indian, ex. Hispanic (212)	212	1.32
Barbadian (13)	13	0.08
Dutch West Indian (15)	15	0.09
Haitian (112)	112	0.70
Jamaican (31)	31	0.19
Trinidadian/Tobagonian (16)	16	0.10
West Indian (25)	25	0.16
Yugoslavian (96)	96	0.60

Hispanic Origin	Population	%
Hispanic or Latino (of any race)	740	4.46
Central American, ex. Mexican	156	0.94
Costa Rican	2	0.01
Guatemalan	72	0.43
Honduran	4	0.02
Nicaraguan	2	0.01
Panamanian	5	0.03
Salvadoran	71	0.43
Cuban	22	0.13
Dominican Republic	33	0.20
Mexican	61	0.37
Puerto Rican	223	1.34
South American	118	0.71
Argentinean	15	0.09
Bolivian	11	0.07
Chilean	9	0.05
Colombian	44	0.27
Ecuadorian	5	0.03
Paraguayan	1	0.01
Peruvian	15	0.09
Uruguayan	5	0.03
Venezuelan	13	0.08
Other Hispanic or Latino	127	0.77

Race*	Population	%
African-American/Black (391)	467	2.81
Not Hispanic (369)	428	2.58
Hispanic (22)	39	0.24
American Indian/Alaska Native (23)	72	0.43
Not Hispanic (16)	57	0.34
Hispanic (7)	15	0.09
Blackfeet (0)	3	0.02
Cherokee (2)	8	0.05
Iroquois (0)	2	0.01
Lumbee (0)	1	0.01
Mexican American Ind. (1)	1	0.01
Osage (2)	2	0.01
South American Ind. (0)	1	0.01
Tlingit-Haida *(Alaska Native)* (0)	1	0.01
Asian (1,452)	1,577	9.50
Not Hispanic (1,450)	1,566	9.44
Hispanic (2)	11	0.07
Bangladeshi (5)	5	0.03
Cambodian (7)	9	0.05
Chinese, ex. Taiwanese (290)	318	1.92
Filipino (30)	47	0.28
Indian (932)	966	5.82
Japanese (18)	31	0.19
Korean (48)	60	0.36
Laotian (2)	2	0.01
Malaysian (2)	3	0.02
Nepalese (5)	8	0.05
Pakistani (52)	56	0.34
Taiwanese (9)	9	0.05
Thai (14)	22	0.13
Vietnamese (24)	30	0.18
Hawaii Native/Pacific Islander (3)	14	0.08
Not Hispanic (0)	7	0.04
Hispanic (3)	7	0.04
Guamanian/Chamorro (3)	3	0.02
White (13,978)	14,227	85.74
Not Hispanic (13,530)	13,743	82.82
Hispanic (448)	484	2.92

Athol

Place Type: CDP
County: Worcester
Population: 8,265†

Ancestry‡	Population	%
African, Sub-Saharan (0)	13	0.16
African (0)	13	0.16
American (360)	360	4.49
Arab (7)	7	0.09
Syrian (7)	7	0.09
Armenian (0)	34	0.42
Austrian (11)	11	0.14
Belgian (9)	18	0.22
Canadian (45)	76	0.95
Croatian (0)	13	0.16
Dutch (0)	35	0.44
English (566)	1,468	18.30
Estonian (29)	29	0.36
European (33)	46	0.57
Finnish (24)	152	1.90
French, ex. Basque (513)	1,696	21.15
French Canadian (361)	705	8.79
German (36)	445	5.55
Greek (51)	187	2.33
Irish (315)	1,273	15.87
Israeli (35)	35	0.44
Italian (282)	1,032	12.87
Lithuanian (148)	382	4.76
Northern European (49)	49	0.61
Norwegian (11)	19	0.24
Polish (178)	609	7.59
Portuguese (0)	8	0.10
Russian (0)	12	0.15
Scotch-Irish (130)	237	2.96
Scottish (110)	221	2.76
Swedish (11)	190	2.37
Ukrainian (0)	28	0.35
Welsh (0)	36	0.45
West Indian, ex. Hispanic (45)	97	1.21
Haitian (45)	87	1.08
Trinidadian/Tobagonian (0)	10	0.12

Hispanic Origin	Population	%
Hispanic or Latino (of any race)	326	3.94
Central American, ex. Mexican	13	0.16
Costa Rican	1	0.01
Guatemalan	4	0.05
Panamanian	2	0.02
Salvadoran	6	0.07
Cuban	8	0.10
Dominican Republic	27	0.33
Mexican	43	0.52
Puerto Rican	182	2.20
South American	25	0.30
Argentinean	7	0.08
Bolivian	3	0.04
Colombian	7	0.08
Ecuadorian	1	0.01
Peruvian	2	0.02
Uruguayan	4	0.05
Other South American	1	0.01
Other Hispanic or Latino	28	0.34

Race*	Population	%
African-American/Black (85)	159	1.92
Not Hispanic (72)	135	1.63
Hispanic (13)	24	0.29
American Indian/Alaska Native (23)	65	0.79
Not Hispanic (13)	46	0.56
Hispanic (10)	19	0.23
Apache (1)	1	0.01
Blackfeet (1)	9	0.11
Central American Ind. (2)	2	0.02
Chippewa (0)	2	0.02
Cree (0)	1	0.01
Creek (0)	1	0.01
Iroquois (0)	2	0.02
Lumbee (2)	2	0.02
Potawatomi (0)	1	0.01
Seminole (1)	2	0.02
Asian (78)	106	1.28
Not Hispanic (77)	105	1.27
Hispanic (1)	1	0.01
Cambodian (4)	4	0.05
Chinese, ex. Taiwanese (10)	19	0.23
Filipino (19)	22	0.27
Indian (13)	16	0.19
Japanese (2)	7	0.08
Korean (8)	20	0.24
Laotian (5)	7	0.08
Thai (1)	3	0.04
Vietnamese (8)	16	0.19
Hawaii Native/Pacific Islander (0)	3	0.04
Hispanic (0)	3	0.04
White (7,839)	7,984	96.60
Not Hispanic (7,639)	7,755	93.83
Hispanic (200)	229	2.77

Athol

Place Type: Town
County: Worcester
Population: 11,584†

Ancestry‡	Population	%
African, Sub-Saharan (0)	13	0.11
African (0)	13	0.11
American (515)	515	4.46
Arab (7)	7	0.06
Syrian (7)	7	0.06
Armenian (0)	34	0.29
Austrian (11)	52	0.45
Belgian (9)	64	0.55
Canadian (65)	96	0.83
Croatian (0)	13	0.11
Dutch (0)	35	0.30
English (841)	2,201	19.04
Estonian (29)	29	0.25
European (44)	57	0.49
Finnish (48)	246	2.13
French, ex. Basque (700)	2,357	20.39
French Canadian (538)	1,140	9.86

*Notes: † The Census 2010 population figure is used to calculate the percentages in the Hispanic Origin and Race categories. Ancestry percentages are based on the 2006-2010 American Community Survey population (not shown); ‡ Numbers in parentheses indicate the number of people reporting a single ancestry; * Numbers in parentheses indicate the number of persons reporting this race alone, not in combination with any other race; Please refer to the Explanation of Data for more information.*

German (78)	746	6.45
Greek (62)	198	1.71
Irish (461)	1,749	15.13
Israeli (35)	35	0.30
Italian (380)	1,394	12.06
Lithuanian (178)	480	4.15
Northern European (49)	49	0.42
Norwegian (11)	38	0.33
Polish (221)	774	6.70
Portuguese (79)	107	0.93
Russian (0)	12	0.10
Scandinavian (0)	11	0.10
Scotch-Irish (183)	409	3.54
Scottish (136)	337	2.92
Serbian (0)	9	0.08
Slavic (6)	6	0.05
Swedish (37)	357	3.09
Ukrainian (0)	38	0.33
Welsh (0)	36	0.31
West Indian, ex. Hispanic (45)	97	0.84
Haitian (45)	87	0.75
Trinidadian/Tobagonian (0)	10	0.09
Yugoslavian (0)	12	0.10

Hispanic Origin	Population	%
Hispanic or Latino (of any race)	413	3.57
Central American, ex. Mexican	18	0.16
Costa Rican	1	0.01
Guatemalan	7	0.06
Nicaraguan	1	0.01
Panamanian	2	0.02
Salvadoran	7	0.06
Cuban	11	0.09
Dominican Republic	41	0.35
Mexican	61	0.53
Puerto Rican	215	1.86
South American	26	0.22
Argentinean	7	0.06
Bolivian	3	0.03
Colombian	7	0.06
Ecuadorian	1	0.01
Peruvian	2	0.02
Uruguayan	5	0.04
Other South American	1	0.01
Other Hispanic or Latino	41	0.35

Race*	Population	%
African-American/Black (113)	205	1.77
Not Hispanic (95)	171	1.48
Hispanic (18)	34	0.29
American Indian/Alaska Native (29)	92	0.79
Not Hispanic (17)	65	0.56
Hispanic (12)	27	0.23
Apache (1)	1	0.01
Blackfeet (1)	10	0.09
Central American Ind. (2)	2	0.02
Chippewa (0)	2	0.02
Choctaw (1)	1	0.01
Cree (0)	1	0.01
Creek (0)	1	0.01
Delaware (1)	1	0.01
Iroquois (0)	3	0.03
Lumbee (2)	2	0.02
Mexican American Ind. (0)	3	0.03
Potawatomi (0)	1	0.01
Pueblo (1)	2	0.02
Seminole (1)	2	0.02
Asian (84)	121	1.04
Not Hispanic (83)	120	1.04
Hispanic (1)	1	0.01
Cambodian (4)	4	0.03
Chinese, ex. Taiwanese (10)	19	0.16
Filipino (19)	24	0.21
Hmong (1)	1	0.01
Indian (13)	16	0.14
Japanese (3)	12	0.10
Korean (11)	27	0.23
Laotian (5)	7	0.06
Thai (1)	3	0.03
Vietnamese (8)	19	0.16
Hawaii Native/Pacific Islander (0)	3	0.03
Hispanic (0)	3	0.03
White (11,040)	11,224	96.89
Not Hispanic (10,804)	10,949	94.52
Hispanic (236)	275	2.37

Attleboro

Place Type: City
County: Bristol
Population: 43,593†

Ancestry‡	Population	%
African, Sub-Saharan (335)	475	1.10
African (47)	47	0.11
Cape Verdean (173)	313	0.72
Kenyan (53)	53	0.12
Nigerian (62)	62	0.14
Albanian (8)	57	0.13
American (986)	986	2.27
Arab (275)	464	1.07
Arab (58)	58	0.13
Egyptian (25)	25	0.06
Jordanian (0)	11	0.03
Lebanese (132)	260	0.60
Moroccan (11)	41	0.09
Palestinian (38)	38	0.09
Syrian (11)	20	0.05
Other Arab (0)	11	0.03
Armenian (135)	262	0.60
Australian (6)	6	0.01
Austrian (0)	39	0.09
Belgian (10)	10	0.02
Brazilian (105)	141	0.33
British (47)	126	0.29
Canadian (293)	473	1.09
Croatian (0)	19	0.04
Czech (8)	34	0.08
Danish (0)	50	0.12
Dutch (40)	249	0.57
Eastern European (22)	22	0.05
English (1,138)	6,386	14.73
European (42)	51	0.12
Finnish (9)	60	0.14
French, ex. Basque (1,597)	5,966	13.76
French Canadian (1,483)	3,102	7.15
German (789)	3,724	8.59
Greek (92)	319	0.74
Hungarian (11)	58	0.13
Irish (3,355)	11,114	25.63
Italian (1,405)	5,312	12.25
Latvian (14)	14	0.03
Lithuanian (42)	215	0.50
Northern European (14)	14	0.03
Norwegian (14)	317	0.73
Polish (652)	2,331	5.38
Portuguese (2,624)	4,963	11.45
Romanian (9)	18	0.04
Russian (252)	398	0.92
Scandinavian (50)	62	0.14
Scotch-Irish (489)	1,018	2.35
Scottish (309)	1,623	3.74
Serbian (0)	33	0.08
Slavic (0)	42	0.10
Slovak (13)	25	0.06
Swedish (148)	945	2.18
Swiss (0)	74	0.17
Turkish (0)	14	0.03
Ukrainian (24)	84	0.19
Welsh (60)	153	0.35
West Indian, ex. Hispanic (289)	307	0.71
Barbadian (34)	34	0.08
Belizean (17)	35	0.08
Haitian (189)	189	0.44
Jamaican (49)	49	0.11
Yugoslavian (10)	10	0.02

Hispanic Origin	Population	%
Hispanic or Latino (of any race)	2,765	6.34
Central American, ex. Mexican	980	2.25
Costa Rican	14	0.03
Guatemalan	734	1.68
Honduran	40	0.09
Nicaraguan	8	0.02
Panamanian	7	0.02
Salvadoran	173	0.40
Other Central American	4	0.01
Cuban	49	0.11
Dominican Republic	120	0.28
Mexican	229	0.53
Puerto Rican	855	1.96
South American	195	0.45
Argentinean	11	0.03
Bolivian	12	0.03
Chilean	5	0.01
Colombian	102	0.23
Ecuadorian	12	0.03
Peruvian	34	0.08
Uruguayan	1	<0.01
Venezuelan	17	0.04
Other South American	1	<0.01
Other Hispanic or Latino	337	0.77

Race*	Population	%
African-American/Black (1,299)	1,682	3.86
Not Hispanic (1,247)	1,577	3.62
Hispanic (52)	105	0.24
American Indian/Alaska Native (98)	321	0.74
Not Hispanic (64)	268	0.61
Hispanic (34)	53	0.12
Blackfeet (3)	20	0.05
Canadian/French Am. Ind. (3)	8	0.02
Central American Ind. (1)	6	0.01
Cherokee (1)	24	0.06
Cheyenne (0)	3	0.01
Chippewa (1)	8	0.02
Creek (0)	1	<0.01
Iroquois (2)	7	0.02
Mexican American Ind. (9)	9	0.02
Potawatomi (1)	2	<0.01
Seminole (0)	3	0.01
Sioux (1)	7	0.02
South American Ind. (5)	5	0.01
Spanish American Ind. (1)	1	<0.01
Yup'ik *(Alaska Native)* (0)	1	<0.01
Asian (1,978)	2,238	5.13
Not Hispanic (1,973)	2,212	5.07
Hispanic (5)	26	0.06
Bangladeshi (9)	9	0.02
Cambodian (639)	708	1.62
Chinese, ex. Taiwanese (177)	226	0.52
Filipino (99)	143	0.33
Hmong (3)	4	0.01
Indian (556)	606	1.39
Indonesian (6)	8	0.02
Japanese (14)	39	0.09
Korean (64)	94	0.22
Laotian (16)	17	0.04
Malaysian (1)	1	<0.01
Nepalese (1)	1	<0.01
Pakistani (92)	101	0.23
Sri Lankan (7)	8	0.02
Taiwanese (3)	4	0.01
Thai (15)	31	0.07
Vietnamese (174)	192	0.44
Hawaii Native/Pacific Islander (39)	77	0.18
Not Hispanic (27)	51	0.12
Hispanic (12)	26	0.06
Fijian (3)	3	0.01
Guamanian/Chamorro (21)	23	0.05
Native Hawaiian (6)	11	0.03
White (37,975)	38,798	89.00
Not Hispanic (36,608)	37,237	85.42
Hispanic (1,367)	1,561	3.58

Auburn

Place Type: Town
County: Worcester
Population: 16,188†

*Notes: † The Census 2010 population figure is used to calculate the percentages in the Hispanic Origin and Race categories. Ancestry percentages are based on the 2006-2010 American Community Survey population (not shown); ‡ Numbers in parentheses indicate the number of people reporting a single ancestry; * Numbers in parentheses indicate the number of persons reporting this race alone, not in combination with any other race; Please refer to the Explanation of Data for more information.*

Ancestry‡	Population	%
African, Sub-Saharan (43)	43	0.27
African (36)	36	0.22
Cape Verdean (7)	7	0.04
Albanian (22)	31	0.19
American (768)	768	4.75
Arab (116)	408	2.52
Egyptian (55)	55	0.34
Lebanese (61)	319	1.97
Syrian (0)	34	0.21
Armenian (38)	81	0.50
Belgian (0)	8	0.05
Brazilian (176)	203	1.25
British (13)	104	0.64
Canadian (53)	73	0.45
Croatian (8)	8	0.05
Czech (0)	15	0.09
Danish (8)	34	0.21
Dutch (0)	31	0.19
Eastern European (0)	9	0.06
English (377)	1,875	11.58
Estonian (0)	140	0.86
European (30)	30	0.19
Finnish (22)	236	1.46
French, ex. Basque (656)	3,103	19.17
French Canadian (676)	1,008	6.23
German (184)	1,517	9.37
Greek (52)	177	1.09
Hungarian (7)	16	0.10
Iranian (8)	8	0.05
Irish (1,686)	5,301	32.75
Italian (720)	2,416	14.93
Lithuanian (123)	303	1.87
Norwegian (14)	89	0.55
Polish (587)	1,576	9.74
Portuguese (51)	113	0.70
Russian (58)	229	1.41
Scotch-Irish (85)	167	1.03
Scottish (52)	478	2.95
Slavic (0)	14	0.09
Slovak (0)	12	0.07
Swedish (409)	1,518	9.38
Swiss (0)	22	0.14
Turkish (0)	5	0.03
Ukrainian (0)	11	0.07
Welsh (0)	41	0.25
Yugoslavian (0)	8	0.05

Hispanic Origin	Population	%
Hispanic or Latino (of any race)	426	2.63
Central American, ex. Mexican	35	0.22
Guatemalan	4	0.02
Nicaraguan	2	0.01
Panamanian	2	0.01
Salvadoran	27	0.17
Cuban	11	0.07
Dominican Republic	38	0.23
Mexican	34	0.21
Puerto Rican	236	1.46
South American	58	0.36
Argentinean	11	0.07
Chilean	3	0.02
Colombian	26	0.16
Ecuadorian	8	0.05
Peruvian	6	0.04
Uruguayan	1	0.01
Venezuelan	3	0.02
Other Hispanic or Latino	14	0.09

Race*	Population	%
African-American/Black (178)	263	1.62
Not Hispanic (154)	225	1.39
Hispanic (24)	38	0.23
American Indian/Alaska Native (23)	77	0.48
Not Hispanic (21)	70	0.43
Hispanic (2)	7	0.04
Apache (0)	5	0.03
Canadian/French Am. Ind. (0)	2	0.01
Central American Ind. (0)	4	0.02
Cherokee (0)	12	0.07
Iroquois (0)	1	0.01
Mexican American Ind. (1)	1	0.01
Navajo (0)	4	0.02
Sioux (1)	3	0.02
Asian (299)	357	2.21
Not Hispanic (299)	356	2.20
Hispanic (0)	1	0.01
Cambodian (8)	13	0.08
Chinese, ex. Taiwanese (40)	50	0.31
Filipino (11)	18	0.11
Indian (58)	70	0.43
Indonesian (0)	1	0.01
Japanese (8)	15	0.09
Korean (21)	29	0.18
Laotian (3)	4	0.02
Pakistani (9)	13	0.08
Sri Lankan (2)	2	0.01
Thai (2)	4	0.02
Vietnamese (121)	135	0.83
Hawaii Native/Pacific Islander (3)	8	0.05
Not Hispanic (3)	8	0.05
Fijian (1)	1	0.01
Native Hawaiian (2)	3	0.02
White (15,366)	15,572	96.19
Not Hispanic (15,082)	15,252	94.22
Hispanic (284)	320	1.98

Barnstable Town

Place Type: City
County: Barnstable
Population: 45,193†

Ancestry‡	Population	%
African, Sub-Saharan (296)	398	0.87
African (21)	21	0.05
Cape Verdean (255)	317	0.69
Kenyan (0)	40	0.09
Other Sub-Saharan African (20)	20	0.04
Albanian (11)	11	0.02
American (4,118)	4,118	9.00
Arab (110)	187	0.41
Egyptian (0)	12	0.03
Lebanese (71)	136	0.30
Other Arab (39)	39	0.09
Armenian (260)	299	0.65
Austrian (18)	124	0.27
Belgian (9)	42	0.09
Brazilian (1,182)	1,214	2.65
British (115)	197	0.43
Bulgarian (52)	52	0.11
Canadian (167)	355	0.78
Celtic (0)	14	0.03
Czech (12)	69	0.15
Czechoslovakian (24)	24	0.05
Danish (39)	129	0.28
Dutch (95)	430	0.94
Eastern European (49)	49	0.11
English (2,550)	8,398	18.35
European (434)	474	1.04
Finnish (213)	548	1.20
French, ex. Basque (824)	3,060	6.68
French Canadian (548)	1,210	2.64
German (839)	3,774	8.24
Greek (574)	889	1.94
Hungarian (42)	149	0.33
Iranian (24)	24	0.05
Irish (4,672)	11,181	24.43
Italian (1,703)	5,242	11.45
Latvian (6)	18	0.04
Lithuanian (372)	596	1.30
New Zealander (0)	14	0.03
Northern European (75)	86	0.19
Norwegian (65)	306	0.67
Polish (567)	1,754	3.83
Portuguese (1,393)	2,172	4.74
Romanian (0)	29	0.06
Russian (359)	805	1.76
Scandinavian (10)	109	0.24
Scotch-Irish (427)	852	1.86
Scottish (571)	2,037	4.45
Slavic (13)	48	0.10
Slovak (11)	53	0.12
Swedish (359)	1,267	2.77
Swiss (22)	123	0.27
Ukrainian (191)	281	0.61
Welsh (129)	572	1.25
West Indian, ex. Hispanic (276)	299	0.65
Haitian (46)	46	0.10
Jamaican (230)	230	0.50
West Indian (0)	23	0.05

Hispanic Origin	Population	%
Hispanic or Latino (of any race)	1,418	3.14
Central American, ex. Mexican	186	0.41
Costa Rican	13	0.03
Guatemalan	22	0.05
Honduran	7	0.02
Nicaraguan	13	0.03
Panamanian	9	0.02
Salvadoran	121	0.27
Other Central American	1	<0.01
Cuban	39	0.09
Dominican Republic	151	0.33
Mexican	173	0.38
Puerto Rican	367	0.81
South American	238	0.53
Argentinean	15	0.03
Chilean	9	0.02
Colombian	30	0.07
Ecuadorian	136	0.30
Peruvian	24	0.05
Uruguayan	5	0.01
Venezuelan	10	0.02
Other South American	9	0.02
Other Hispanic or Latino	264	0.58

Race*	Population	%
African-American/Black (1,366)	1,943	4.30
Not Hispanic (1,291)	1,834	4.06
Hispanic (75)	109	0.24
American Indian/Alaska Native (280)	644	1.42
Not Hispanic (255)	587	1.30
Hispanic (25)	57	0.13
Apache (2)	7	0.02
Blackfeet (3)	22	0.05
Central American Ind. (1)	1	<0.01
Cherokee (10)	48	0.11
Chickasaw (0)	2	<0.01
Chippewa (3)	5	0.01
Cree (0)	1	<0.01
Delaware (0)	1	<0.01
Inupiat *(Alaska Native)* (4)	4	0.01
Iroquois (2)	6	0.01
Lumbee (0)	1	<0.01
Mexican American Ind. (2)	3	0.01
Navajo (1)	3	0.01
Puget Sound Salish (0)	4	0.01
Seminole (1)	6	0.01
Sioux (2)	5	0.01
South American Ind. (1)	3	0.01
Tlingit-Haida *(Alaska Native)* (2)	2	<0.01
Asian (562)	757	1.68
Not Hispanic (560)	745	1.65
Hispanic (2)	12	0.03
Burmese (0)	1	<0.01
Cambodian (6)	7	0.02
Chinese, ex. Taiwanese (145)	172	0.38
Filipino (49)	87	0.19
Indian (73)	124	0.27
Japanese (30)	65	0.14
Korean (35)	65	0.14
Laotian (8)	10	0.02
Malaysian (1)	1	<0.01
Nepalese (31)	37	0.08
Pakistani (60)	73	0.16
Sri Lankan (6)	7	0.02
Taiwanese (2)	5	0.01
Thai (27)	39	0.09
Vietnamese (44)	53	0.12

*Notes: † The Census 2010 population figure is used to calculate the percentages in the Hispanic Origin and Race categories. Ancestry percentages are based on the 2006-2010 American Community Survey population (not shown); ‡ Numbers in parentheses indicate the number of people reporting a single ancestry; * Numbers in parentheses indicate the number of persons reporting this race alone, not in combination with any other race; Please refer to the Explanation of Data for more information.*

Hawaii Native/Pacific Islander (27)	57	0.13
Not Hispanic (18)	38	0.08
Hispanic (9)	19	0.04
Guamanian/Chamorro (5)	8	0.02
Native Hawaiian (14)	20	0.04
Samoan (0)	2	<0.01
White (40,356)	41,485	91.80
Not Hispanic (39,512)	40,527	89.68
Hispanic (844)	958	2.12

Bedford

Place Type: Town
County: Middlesex
Population: 13,320†

Ancestry‡	Population	%
African, Sub-Saharan (22)	22	0.17
Cape Verdean (22)	22	0.17
American (393)	393	3.01
Arab (143)	215	1.64
Arab (82)	82	0.63
Jordanian (12)	35	0.27
Lebanese (28)	64	0.49
Syrian (13)	26	0.20
Other Arab (8)	8	0.06
Armenian (100)	206	1.58
Austrian (30)	73	0.56
British (68)	276	2.11
Canadian (100)	116	0.89
Croatian (0)	11	0.08
Czech (17)	44	0.34
Danish (44)	103	0.79
Dutch (44)	158	1.21
Eastern European (173)	173	1.32
English (464)	2,001	15.31
Estonian (16)	16	0.12
European (286)	286	2.19
French, ex. Basque (130)	587	4.49
French Canadian (174)	414	3.17
German (217)	1,153	8.82
Greek (65)	110	0.84
Hungarian (7)	7	0.05
Irish (1,124)	3,088	23.62
Italian (890)	2,208	16.89
Latvian (13)	20	0.15
Lithuanian (30)	155	1.19
Northern European (31)	31	0.24
Norwegian (23)	78	0.60
Polish (75)	497	3.80
Portuguese (74)	189	1.45
Russian (371)	553	4.23
Scandinavian (14)	95	0.73
Scotch-Irish (114)	397	3.04
Scottish (212)	464	3.55
Swedish (21)	213	1.63
Swiss (0)	12	0.09
Turkish (11)	11	0.08
Ukrainian (67)	132	1.01
Welsh (0)	57	0.44
West Indian, ex. Hispanic (22)	36	0.28
Haitian (0)	7	0.05
Jamaican (7)	7	0.05
West Indian (15)	22	0.17

Hispanic Origin	Population	%
Hispanic or Latino (of any race)	356	2.67
Central American, ex. Mexican	37	0.28
Costa Rican	2	0.02
Guatemalan	24	0.18
Honduran	5	0.04
Nicaraguan	3	0.02
Panamanian	2	0.02
Salvadoran	1	0.01
Cuban	23	0.17
Dominican Republic	25	0.19
Mexican	75	0.56
Puerto Rican	85	0.64
South American	82	0.62
Argentinean	20	0.15
Bolivian	2	0.02
Chilean	2	0.02
Colombian	24	0.18
Ecuadorian	6	0.05
Paraguayan	2	0.02
Peruvian	13	0.10
Uruguayan	1	0.01
Venezuelan	12	0.09
Other Hispanic or Latino	29	0.22

Race*	Population	%
African-American/Black (301)	404	3.03
Not Hispanic (282)	372	2.79
Hispanic (19)	32	0.24
American Indian/Alaska Native (19)	56	0.42
Not Hispanic (17)	47	0.35
Hispanic (2)	9	0.07
Blackfeet (1)	2	0.02
Canadian/French Am. Ind. (2)	2	0.02
Central American Ind. (1)	1	0.01
Cherokee (0)	4	0.03
Cheyenne (0)	1	0.01
Comanche (0)	1	0.01
Creek (1)	1	0.01
Iroquois (1)	1	0.01
Mexican American Ind. (0)	3	0.02
Sioux (1)	2	0.02
South American Ind. (8)	12	0.09
Asian (1,250)	1,362	10.23
Not Hispanic (1,250)	1,360	10.21
Hispanic (0)	2	0.02
Bangladeshi (3)	3	0.02
Cambodian (9)	14	0.11
Chinese, ex. Taiwanese (577)	631	4.74
Filipino (27)	50	0.38
Indian (312)	339	2.55
Indonesian (0)	1	0.01
Japanese (36)	64	0.48
Korean (162)	165	1.24
Laotian (3)	3	0.02
Nepalese (15)	16	0.12
Pakistani (4)	4	0.03
Taiwanese (28)	37	0.28
Thai (9)	10	0.08
Vietnamese (24)	26	0.20
Hawaii Native/Pacific Islander (7)	15	0.11
Not Hispanic (3)	7	0.05
Hispanic (4)	8	0.06
Guamanian/Chamorro (2)	6	0.05
Native Hawaiian (1)	5	0.04
White (11,443)	11,661	87.55
Not Hispanic (11,184)	11,376	85.41
Hispanic (259)	285	2.14

Belchertown

Place Type: Town
County: Hampshire
Population: 14,649†

Ancestry‡	Population	%
African, Sub-Saharan (15)	15	0.10
African (15)	15	0.10
Albanian (0)	13	0.09
American (852)	852	5.94
Arab (15)	47	0.33
Arab (15)	30	0.21
Lebanese (0)	17	0.12
Armenian (0)	9	0.06
Austrian (0)	50	0.35
British (67)	83	0.58
Cajun (0)	10	0.07
Canadian (75)	225	1.57
Czech (30)	46	0.32
Danish (30)	42	0.29
Dutch (0)	75	0.52
English (525)	2,183	15.21
European (74)	96	0.67
Finnish (0)	95	0.66
French, ex. Basque (830)	2,670	18.60
French Canadian (769)	1,250	8.71
German (239)	1,735	12.09
Greek (34)	151	1.05
Hungarian (8)	76	0.53
Irish (639)	3,369	23.47
Italian (268)	1,505	10.48
Latvian (0)	13	0.09
Lithuanian (0)	130	0.91
Northern European (65)	65	0.45
Norwegian (37)	48	0.33
Polish (857)	2,163	15.07
Portuguese (123)	266	1.85
Russian (38)	55	0.38
Scandinavian (14)	14	0.10
Scotch-Irish (69)	278	1.94
Scottish (85)	571	3.98
Slovak (0)	15	0.10
Swedish (48)	162	1.13
Swiss (9)	19	0.13
Ukrainian (0)	38	0.26
Welsh (0)	46	0.32
Yugoslavian (0)	18	0.13

Hispanic Origin	Population	%
Hispanic or Latino (of any race)	385	2.63
Central American, ex. Mexican	23	0.16
Guatemalan	9	0.06
Honduran	2	0.01
Panamanian	4	0.03
Salvadoran	8	0.05
Cuban	28	0.19
Dominican Republic	8	0.05
Mexican	26	0.18
Puerto Rican	235	1.60
South American	34	0.23
Argentinean	5	0.03
Bolivian	3	0.02
Chilean	1	0.01
Colombian	11	0.08
Ecuadorian	8	0.05
Peruvian	2	0.01
Uruguayan	2	0.01
Venezuelan	2	0.01
Other Hispanic or Latino	31	0.21

Race*	Population	%
African-American/Black (199)	318	2.17
Not Hispanic (190)	284	1.94
Hispanic (9)	34	0.23
American Indian/Alaska Native (21)	110	0.75
Not Hispanic (18)	100	0.68
Hispanic (3)	10	0.07
Blackfeet (1)	6	0.04
Canadian/French Am. Ind. (0)	1	0.01
Central American Ind. (1)	3	0.02
Cherokee (0)	6	0.04
Cree (2)	3	0.02
Iroquois (2)	10	0.07
Mexican American Ind. (2)	2	0.01
Navajo (1)	5	0.03
Pueblo (0)	4	0.03
Sioux (1)	1	0.01
South American Ind. (0)	3	0.02
Yaqui (0)	4	0.03
Asian (305)	371	2.53
Not Hispanic (304)	366	2.50
Hispanic (1)	5	0.03
Cambodian (58)	72	0.49
Chinese, ex. Taiwanese (81)	90	0.61
Filipino (20)	33	0.23
Indian (32)	51	0.35
Indonesian (3)	5	0.03
Japanese (7)	14	0.10
Korean (35)	39	0.27
Malaysian (1)	1	0.01
Nepalese (5)	5	0.03
Pakistani (14)	17	0.12
Sri Lankan (13)	13	0.09
Taiwanese (10)	12	0.08
Thai (2)	2	0.01

*Notes: † The Census 2010 population figure is used to calculate the percentages in the Hispanic Origin and Race categories. Ancestry percentages are based on the 2006-2010 American Community Survey population (not shown); ‡ Numbers in parentheses indicate the number of people reporting a single ancestry; * Numbers in parentheses indicate the number of persons reporting this race alone, not in combination with any other race; Please refer to the Explanation of Data for more information.*

	Population	%
Vietnamese (18)	20	0.14
Hawaii Native/Pacific Islander (8)	21	0.14
Not Hispanic (6)	18	0.12
Hispanic (2)	3	0.02
Native Hawaiian (3)	12	0.08
White (13,741)	13,977	95.41
Not Hispanic (13,504)	13,700	93.52
Hispanic (237)	277	1.89

Bellingham

Place Type: Town
County: Norfolk
Population: 16,332†

Ancestry‡	Population	%
Albanian (14)	65	0.41
American (324)	324	2.02
Arab (54)	140	0.87
Egyptian (33)	33	0.21
Lebanese (11)	84	0.52
Moroccan (10)	10	0.06
Syrian (0)	13	0.08
Armenian (14)	72	0.45
Austrian (54)	65	0.41
Belgian (18)	18	0.11
Brazilian (13)	42	0.26
British (0)	22	0.14
Canadian (146)	325	2.03
Danish (20)	36	0.22
Dutch (12)	95	0.59
Eastern European (82)	82	0.51
English (546)	2,284	14.26
European (71)	71	0.44
French, ex. Basque (442)	2,193	13.69
French Canadian (826)	1,355	8.46
German (161)	1,281	8.00
Greek (0)	53	0.33
Hungarian (12)	164	1.02
Irish (1,543)	4,893	30.55
Italian (878)	3,764	23.50
Latvian (15)	31	0.19
Lithuanian (15)	73	0.46
Northern European (14)	14	0.09
Norwegian (34)	90	0.56
Polish (537)	1,240	7.74
Portuguese (147)	318	1.99
Romanian (14)	33	0.21
Russian (197)	283	1.77
Scotch-Irish (175)	374	2.34
Scottish (102)	326	2.04
Swedish (35)	289	1.80
Swiss (0)	80	0.50
Turkish (58)	69	0.43
Ukrainian (93)	127	0.79
Welsh (0)	29	0.18
West Indian, ex. Hispanic (84)	272	1.70
Barbadian (35)	112	0.70
Jamaican (49)	126	0.79
West Indian (0)	34	0.21
Yugoslavian (0)	11	0.07

Hispanic Origin	Population	%
Hispanic or Latino (of any race)	409	2.50
Central American, ex. Mexican	47	0.29
Costa Rican	2	0.01
Guatemalan	17	0.10
Honduran	15	0.09
Salvadoran	13	0.08
Cuban	16	0.10
Dominican Republic	15	0.09
Mexican	54	0.33
Puerto Rican	171	1.05
South American	71	0.43
Argentinean	13	0.08
Bolivian	3	0.02
Chilean	5	0.03
Colombian	20	0.12
Ecuadorian	9	0.06
Peruvian	11	0.07
Uruguayan	1	0.01
Venezuelan	3	0.02
Other South American	6	0.04
Other Hispanic or Latino	35	0.21

Race*	Population	%
African-American/Black (235)	330	2.02
Not Hispanic (217)	298	1.82
Hispanic (18)	32	0.20
American Indian/Alaska Native (13)	65	0.40
Not Hispanic (10)	60	0.37
Hispanic (3)	5	0.03
Apache (0)	2	0.01
Blackfeet (0)	3	0.02
Cherokee (1)	5	0.03
Chippewa (1)	1	0.01
Creek (0)	1	0.01
Iroquois (2)	8	0.05
Mexican American Ind. (2)	2	0.01
Seminole (1)	1	0.01
South American Ind. (1)	1	0.01
Asian (476)	546	3.34
Not Hispanic (473)	540	3.31
Hispanic (3)	6	0.04
Bangladeshi (4)	4	0.02
Cambodian (14)	15	0.09
Chinese, ex. Taiwanese (54)	71	0.43
Filipino (21)	29	0.18
Indian (244)	251	1.54
Indonesian (2)	4	0.02
Japanese (14)	20	0.12
Korean (27)	34	0.21
Laotian (7)	15	0.09
Malaysian (0)	1	0.01
Nepalese (3)	3	0.02
Pakistani (29)	31	0.19
Sri Lankan (2)	2	0.01
Taiwanese (5)	6	0.04
Thai (2)	9	0.06
Vietnamese (34)	40	0.24
Hawaii Native/Pacific Islander (4)	6	0.04
Not Hispanic (3)	5	0.03
Hispanic (1)	1	0.01
Guamanian/Chamorro (2)	2	0.01
Native Hawaiian (1)	1	0.01
White (15,239)	15,433	94.50
Not Hispanic (14,985)	15,158	92.81
Hispanic (254)	275	1.68

Belmont

Place Type: CDP/Town
County: Middlesex
Population: 24,729†

Ancestry‡	Population	%
African, Sub-Saharan (52)	52	0.21
African (27)	27	0.11
Ugandan (13)	13	0.05
Other Sub-Saharan African (12)	12	0.05
Albanian (77)	77	0.32
American (786)	786	3.23
Arab (109)	305	1.25
Arab (10)	21	0.09
Lebanese (49)	152	0.62
Palestinian (0)	33	0.14
Syrian (34)	56	0.23
Other Arab (16)	43	0.18
Armenian (899)	1,126	4.62
Assyrian/Chaldean/Syriac (19)	19	0.08
Australian (34)	34	0.14
Austrian (70)	127	0.52
Belgian (11)	15	0.06
Brazilian (105)	118	0.48
British (125)	322	1.32
Canadian (50)	180	0.74
Croatian (0)	16	0.07
Czech (7)	74	0.30
Czechoslovakian (10)	21	0.09
Danish (10)	76	0.31
Dutch (34)	150	0.62
Eastern European (142)	155	0.64
English (733)	2,723	11.18
European (267)	296	1.22
Finnish (0)	49	0.20
French, ex. Basque (159)	837	3.44
French Canadian (281)	724	2.97
German (487)	1,720	7.06
Greek (493)	605	2.48
Hungarian (35)	63	0.26
Icelander (27)	35	0.14
Iranian (57)	75	0.31
Irish (2,662)	6,327	25.98
Israeli (57)	98	0.40
Italian (1,712)	3,822	15.69
Latvian (0)	12	0.05
Lithuanian (86)	129	0.53
Luxemburger (0)	10	0.04
Macedonian (8)	23	0.09
New Zealander (21)	30	0.12
Northern European (31)	31	0.13
Norwegian (14)	104	0.43
Polish (227)	784	3.22
Portuguese (48)	302	1.24
Romanian (30)	69	0.28
Russian (312)	760	3.12
Scandinavian (34)	136	0.56
Scotch-Irish (278)	543	2.23
Scottish (208)	892	3.66
Slavic (17)	17	0.07
Slovak (9)	9	0.04
Swedish (116)	580	2.38
Swiss (17)	110	0.45
Turkish (58)	58	0.24
Ukrainian (48)	69	0.28
Welsh (19)	154	0.63
West Indian, ex. Hispanic (143)	143	0.59
Barbadian (12)	12	0.05
Haitian (64)	64	0.26
Jamaican (6)	6	0.02
West Indian (61)	61	0.25

Hispanic Origin	Population	%
Hispanic or Latino (of any race)	754	3.05
Central American, ex. Mexican	105	0.42
Costa Rican	8	0.03
Guatemalan	42	0.17
Honduran	19	0.08
Nicaraguan	4	0.02
Panamanian	7	0.03
Salvadoran	24	0.10
Other Central American	1	<0.01
Cuban	39	0.16
Dominican Republic	18	0.07
Mexican	134	0.54
Puerto Rican	113	0.46
South American	223	0.90
Argentinean	39	0.16
Bolivian	14	0.06
Chilean	34	0.14
Colombian	66	0.27
Ecuadorian	10	0.04
Peruvian	25	0.10
Uruguayan	7	0.03
Venezuelan	28	0.11
Other Hispanic or Latino	122	0.49

Race*	Population	%
African-American/Black (455)	601	2.43
Not Hispanic (443)	567	2.29
Hispanic (12)	34	0.14
American Indian/Alaska Native (28)	119	0.48
Not Hispanic (18)	95	0.38
Hispanic (10)	24	0.10
Apache (2)	3	0.01
Blackfeet (1)	5	0.02
Cherokee (1)	17	0.07
Chippewa (0)	1	<0.01
Choctaw (0)	4	0.02
Iroquois (3)	5	0.02

*Notes: † The Census 2010 population figure is used to calculate the percentages in the Hispanic Origin and Race categories. Ancestry percentages are based on the 2006-2010 American Community Survey population (not shown); ‡ Numbers in parentheses indicate the number of people reporting a single ancestry; * Numbers in parentheses indicate the number of persons reporting this race alone, not in combination with any other race; Please refer to the Explanation of Data for more information.*

Mexican American Ind. (2)	8	0.03
Navajo (0)	5	0.02
Pima (1)	1	<0.01
Potawatomi (2)	2	0.01
Pueblo (0)	3	0.01
Sioux (2)	6	0.02
South American Ind. (1)	3	0.01
Ute (1)	1	<0.01
Asian (2,735)	3,155	12.76
Not Hispanic (2,724)	3,128	12.65
Hispanic (11)	27	0.11
Bangladeshi (3)	3	0.01
Cambodian (9)	9	0.04
Chinese, ex. Taiwanese (1,382)	1,553	6.28
Filipino (40)	92	0.37
Hmong (1)	1	<0.01
Indian (403)	486	1.97
Indonesian (15)	15	0.06
Japanese (187)	276	1.12
Korean (461)	517	2.09
Laotian (2)	12	0.05
Malaysian (2)	2	0.01
Nepalese (51)	61	0.25
Pakistani (24)	24	0.10
Sri Lankan (1)	4	0.02
Taiwanese (37)	45	0.18
Thai (19)	23	0.09
Vietnamese (22)	36	0.15
Hawaii Native/Pacific Islander (3)	20	0.08
Not Hispanic (3)	20	0.08
Guamanian/Chamorro (0)	2	0.01
Native Hawaiian (0)	1	<0.01
Samoan (2)	3	0.01
White (20,639)	21,256	85.96
Not Hispanic (20,118)	20,660	83.55
Hispanic (521)	596	2.41

Beverly

Place Type: City
County: Essex
Population: 39,502†

Ancestry‡	Population	%
African, Sub-Saharan (445)	445	1.13
African (383)	383	0.97
Ethiopian (11)	11	0.03
Nigerian (51)	51	0.13
Albanian (65)	97	0.25
American (1,473)	1,473	3.74
Arab (78)	178	0.45
Arab (26)	26	0.07
Egyptian (0)	22	0.06
Iraqi (0)	18	0.05
Jordanian (18)	18	0.05
Lebanese (15)	55	0.14
Moroccan (19)	30	0.08
Syrian (0)	9	0.02
Armenian (0)	15	0.04
Assyrian/Chaldean/Syriac (0)	10	0.03
Australian (18)	40	0.10
Austrian (0)	119	0.30
Belgian (35)	35	0.09
Brazilian (159)	173	0.44
British (237)	371	0.94
Bulgarian (41)	41	0.10
Canadian (125)	336	0.85
Celtic (41)	41	0.10
Croatian (0)	13	0.03
Czech (21)	100	0.25
Czechoslovakian (16)	16	0.04
Danish (11)	45	0.11
Dutch (71)	369	0.94
Eastern European (86)	86	0.22
English (1,895)	6,571	16.70
European (357)	408	1.04
Finnish (57)	155	0.39
French, ex. Basque (688)	3,091	7.85
French Canadian (706)	1,808	4.59
German (808)	3,679	9.35
Greek (563)	1,068	2.71
Hungarian (129)	235	0.60
Iranian (11)	11	0.03
Irish (3,539)	10,351	26.30
Italian (2,870)	7,066	17.96
Latvian (0)	27	0.07
Lithuanian (48)	241	0.61
Northern European (32)	32	0.08
Norwegian (67)	292	0.74
Polish (647)	2,253	5.73
Portuguese (557)	1,026	2.61
Romanian (37)	83	0.21
Russian (262)	664	1.69
Scandinavian (33)	71	0.18
Scotch-Irish (465)	1,195	3.04
Scottish (571)	1,770	4.50
Slovak (0)	19	0.05
Slovene (0)	44	0.11
Swedish (181)	925	2.35
Swiss (20)	64	0.16
Turkish (11)	11	0.03
Ukrainian (147)	228	0.58
Welsh (21)	189	0.48
West Indian, ex. Hispanic (363)	363	0.92
Haitian (146)	146	0.37
Jamaican (34)	34	0.09
Trinidadian/Tobagonian (183)	183	0.47
Yugoslavian (0)	71	0.18

Hispanic Origin	Population	%
Hispanic or Latino (of any race)	1,397	3.54
Central American, ex. Mexican	186	0.47
Costa Rican	18	0.05
Guatemalan	89	0.23
Honduran	23	0.06
Nicaraguan	4	0.01
Panamanian	10	0.03
Salvadoran	41	0.10
Other Central American	1	<0.01
Cuban	26	0.07
Dominican Republic	266	0.67
Mexican	151	0.38
Puerto Rican	393	0.99
South American	162	0.41
Argentinean	18	0.05
Bolivian	3	0.01
Chilean	20	0.05
Colombian	44	0.11
Ecuadorian	18	0.05
Peruvian	29	0.07
Uruguayan	17	0.04
Venezuelan	9	0.02
Other South American	4	0.01
Other Hispanic or Latino	213	0.54

Race*	Population	%
African-American/Black (647)	936	2.37
Not Hispanic (584)	813	2.06
Hispanic (63)	123	0.31
American Indian/Alaska Native (62)	222	0.56
Not Hispanic (42)	178	0.45
Hispanic (20)	44	0.11
Apache (1)	4	0.01
Blackfeet (1)	5	0.01
Canadian/French Am. Ind. (1)	1	<0.01
Central American Ind. (1)	3	0.01
Cherokee (7)	33	0.08
Chippewa (0)	1	<0.01
Cree (0)	1	<0.01
Inupiat *(Alaska Native)* (1)	1	<0.01
Iroquois (1)	4	0.01
Kiowa (2)	2	0.01
Lumbee (1)	2	0.01
Mexican American Ind. (2)	6	0.02
Navajo (1)	1	<0.01
Paiute (2)	3	0.01
Potawatomi (1)	2	0.01
Puget Sound Salish (0)	2	0.01
Seminole (1)	3	0.01
Sioux (0)	2	0.01
South American Ind. (0)	2	0.01
Spanish American Ind. (1)	1	<0.01
Ute (0)	1	<0.01
Asian (686)	837	2.12
Not Hispanic (677)	819	2.07
Hispanic (9)	18	0.05
Bangladeshi (12)	12	0.03
Cambodian (22)	23	0.06
Chinese, ex. Taiwanese (149)	191	0.48
Filipino (61)	101	0.26
Indian (127)	147	0.37
Japanese (29)	40	0.10
Korean (92)	112	0.28
Laotian (10)	15	0.04
Nepalese (26)	26	0.07
Pakistani (22)	22	0.06
Taiwanese (8)	8	0.02
Thai (24)	29	0.07
Vietnamese (58)	71	0.18
Hawaii Native/Pacific Islander (23)	54	0.14
Not Hispanic (23)	43	0.11
Hispanic (0)	11	0.03
Guamanian/Chamorro (2)	6	0.02
Native Hawaiian (4)	12	0.03
Samoan (4)	5	0.01
White (36,868)	37,435	94.77
Not Hispanic (36,105)	36,565	92.56
Hispanic (763)	870	2.20

Billerica

Place Type: Town
County: Middlesex
Population: 40,243†

Ancestry‡	Population	%
Afghan (11)	11	0.03
African, Sub-Saharan (57)	57	0.14
Cape Verdean (6)	6	0.02
Kenyan (37)	37	0.09
Nigerian (14)	14	0.04
Albanian (20)	20	0.05
American (1,303)	1,303	3.29
Arab (49)	92	0.23
Egyptian (41)	41	0.10
Lebanese (0)	43	0.11
Other Arab (8)	8	0.02
Armenian (254)	406	1.03
Australian (63)	63	0.16
Austrian (0)	36	0.09
Belgian (0)	13	0.03
Brazilian (193)	287	0.73
British (89)	129	0.33
Bulgarian (41)	41	0.10
Canadian (332)	704	1.78
Danish (0)	41	0.10
Dutch (31)	256	0.65
Eastern European (18)	39	0.10
English (1,449)	5,506	13.91
European (195)	195	0.49
Finnish (33)	92	0.23
French, ex. Basque (627)	2,898	7.32
French Canadian (674)	1,941	4.90
German (450)	2,529	6.39
Greek (173)	413	1.04
Hungarian (16)	134	0.34
Icelander (28)	55	0.14
Irish (4,683)	12,640	31.94
Italian (3,441)	9,368	23.67
Lithuanian (33)	176	0.44
Northern European (52)	52	0.13
Norwegian (30)	89	0.22
Polish (438)	1,431	3.62
Portuguese (768)	2,073	5.24
Romanian (0)	26	0.07
Russian (95)	309	0.78
Scandinavian (20)	20	0.05
Scotch-Irish (384)	936	2.37
Scottish (486)	1,380	3.49
Slavic (0)	16	0.04

SECTION TWO

*Notes: † The Census 2010 population figure is used to calculate the percentages in the Hispanic Origin and Race categories. Ancestry percentages are based on the 2006-2010 American Community Survey population (not shown); ‡ Numbers in parentheses indicate the number of people reporting a single ancestry; * Numbers in parentheses indicate the number of persons reporting this race alone, not in combination with any other race; Please refer to the Explanation of Data for more information.*

Swedish (281)	1,049	2.65
Swiss (12)	37	0.09
Turkish (19)	71	0.18
Ukrainian (0)	65	0.16
Welsh (23)	198	0.50
West Indian, ex. Hispanic (360)	443	1.12
Haitian (222)	252	0.64
Jamaican (138)	191	0.48
Yugoslavian (69)	69	0.17

Hispanic Origin	Population	%
Hispanic or Latino (of any race)	1,035	2.57
Central American, ex. Mexican	162	0.40
Costa Rican	5	0.01
Guatemalan	71	0.18
Honduran	11	0.03
Nicaraguan	2	<0.01
Panamanian	7	0.02
Salvadoran	66	0.16
Cuban	28	0.07
Dominican Republic	46	0.11
Mexican	149	0.37
Puerto Rican	296	0.74
South American	160	0.40
Argentinean	20	0.05
Chilean	1	<0.01
Colombian	66	0.16
Ecuadorian	19	0.05
Paraguayan	2	<0.01
Peruvian	32	0.08
Uruguayan	2	<0.01
Venezuelan	18	0.04
Other Hispanic or Latino	194	0.48

Race*	Population	%
African-American/Black (849)	1,003	2.49
Not Hispanic (826)	970	2.41
Hispanic (23)	33	0.08
American Indian/Alaska Native (59)	203	0.50
Not Hispanic (48)	173	0.43
Hispanic (11)	30	0.07
Apache (0)	3	0.01
Blackfeet (0)	2	<0.01
Canadian/French Am. Ind. (1)	1	<0.01
Cherokee (4)	20	0.05
Chippewa (3)	12	0.03
Choctaw (0)	2	<0.01
Iroquois (5)	9	0.02
Mexican American Ind. (0)	2	<0.01
Potawatomi (0)	7	0.02
Sioux (0)	2	<0.01
South American Ind. (1)	2	<0.01
Asian (2,194)	2,428	6.03
Not Hispanic (2,186)	2,416	6.00
Hispanic (8)	12	0.03
Bangladeshi (14)	25	0.06
Burmese (1)	1	<0.01
Cambodian (94)	111	0.28
Chinese, ex. Taiwanese (344)	386	0.96
Filipino (118)	167	0.41
Indian (1,245)	1,298	3.23
Indonesian (4)	11	0.03
Japanese (20)	45	0.11
Korean (85)	100	0.25
Laotian (20)	22	0.05
Malaysian (6)	6	0.01
Nepalese (8)	8	0.02
Pakistani (46)	46	0.11
Sri Lankan (5)	5	0.01
Taiwanese (19)	22	0.05
Thai (12)	21	0.05
Vietnamese (107)	123	0.31
Hawaii Native/Pacific Islander (8)	42	0.10
Not Hispanic (8)	39	0.10
Hispanic (0)	3	0.01
Fijian (0)	2	<0.01
Guamanian/Chamorro (2)	2	<0.01
Native Hawaiian (2)	11	0.03
Samoan (1)	3	0.01
Tongan (1)	1	<0.01
White (36,285)	36,774	91.38
Not Hispanic (35,568)	35,995	89.44
Hispanic (717)	779	1.94

Blackstone

Place Type: Town
County: Worcester
Population: 9,026†

Ancestry‡	Population	%
American (286)	286	3.18
Arab (332)	387	4.30
Egyptian (276)	276	3.07
Lebanese (18)	73	0.81
Syrian (38)	38	0.42
Armenian (6)	71	0.79
Brazilian (21)	21	0.23
Canadian (0)	17	0.19
Czechoslovakian (14)	14	0.16
Dutch (0)	90	1.00
English (381)	1,255	13.94
Finnish (20)	67	0.74
French, ex. Basque (1,063)	2,311	25.67
French Canadian (677)	1,337	14.85
German (37)	791	8.79
Greek (89)	203	2.25
Irish (297)	2,228	24.75
Italian (286)	1,368	15.19
Lithuanian (20)	58	0.64
Maltese (0)	24	0.27
Northern European (14)	14	0.16
Norwegian (16)	97	1.08
Polish (165)	719	7.99
Portuguese (82)	262	2.91
Russian (19)	76	0.84
Scotch-Irish (0)	93	1.03
Scottish (0)	263	2.92
Slovak (0)	30	0.33
Swedish (0)	136	1.51
Ukrainian (50)	100	1.11
Welsh (14)	141	1.57

Hispanic Origin	Population	%
Hispanic or Latino (of any race)	185	2.05
Central American, ex. Mexican	25	0.28
Costa Rican	1	0.01
Guatemalan	13	0.14
Panamanian	8	0.09
Salvadoran	3	0.03
Cuban	9	0.10
Dominican Republic	10	0.11
Mexican	25	0.28
Puerto Rican	81	0.90
South American	19	0.21
Bolivian	5	0.06
Colombian	4	0.04
Ecuadorian	3	0.03
Peruvian	1	0.01
Uruguayan	3	0.03
Venezuelan	3	0.03
Other Hispanic or Latino	16	0.18

Race*	Population	%
African-American/Black (82)	116	1.29
Not Hispanic (77)	108	1.20
Hispanic (5)	8	0.09
American Indian/Alaska Native (22)	56	0.62
Not Hispanic (21)	55	0.61
Hispanic (1)	1	0.01
Apache (1)	1	0.01
Canadian/French Am. Ind. (0)	1	0.01
Cherokee (5)	11	0.12
Chippewa (1)	3	0.03
Iroquois (0)	4	0.04
Seminole (0)	1	0.01
Sioux (0)	1	0.01
Asian (71)	98	1.09
Not Hispanic (71)	98	1.09
Cambodian (1)	6	0.07
Chinese, ex. Taiwanese (4)	7	0.08
Filipino (7)	16	0.18
Indian (13)	13	0.14
Indonesian (0)	1	0.01
Japanese (0)	1	0.01
Korean (13)	17	0.19
Laotian (15)	21	0.23
Pakistani (1)	2	0.02
Taiwanese (2)	2	0.02
Thai (2)	2	0.02
Vietnamese (6)	9	0.10
Hawaii Native/Pacific Islander (3)	5	0.06
Not Hispanic (3)	5	0.06
Guamanian/Chamorro (0)	1	0.01
Native Hawaiian (0)	1	0.01
Samoan (1)	1	0.01
White (8,704)	8,819	97.71
Not Hispanic (8,555)	8,663	95.98
Hispanic (149)	156	1.73

Boston

Place Type: City
County: Suffolk
Population: 617,594†

Ancestry‡	Population	%
Afghan (26)	37	0.01
African, Sub-Saharan (20,931)	24,343	4.04
African (5,651)	6,993	1.16
Cape Verdean (9,897)	11,284	1.87
Ethiopian (717)	786	0.13
Ghanaian (135)	135	0.02
Kenyan (45)	54	0.01
Liberian (390)	440	0.07
Nigerian (1,545)	1,775	0.29
Senegalese (101)	101	0.02
Sierra Leonean (277)	452	0.08
Somalian (1,186)	1,186	0.20
South African (95)	123	0.02
Sudanese (31)	31	0.01
Ugandan (183)	183	0.03
Zimbabwean (38)	50	0.01
Other Sub-Saharan African (640)	750	0.12
Albanian (1,628)	2,022	0.34
Alsatian (0)	9	<0.01
American (11,829)	11,829	1.96
Arab (4,345)	6,307	1.05
Arab (481)	609	0.10
Egyptian (171)	284	0.05
Iraqi (94)	119	0.02
Jordanian (79)	112	0.02
Lebanese (1,470)	2,304	0.38
Moroccan (1,005)	1,171	0.19
Palestinian (19)	32	0.01
Syrian (128)	540	0.09
Other Arab (898)	1,136	0.19
Armenian (667)	1,356	0.23
Australian (93)	176	0.03
Austrian (178)	1,039	0.17
Basque (5)	19	<0.01
Belgian (121)	293	0.05
Brazilian (4,984)	5,461	0.91
British (1,278)	2,755	0.46
Bulgarian (341)	453	0.08
Cajun (42)	54	0.01
Canadian (1,296)	2,864	0.48
Celtic (39)	88	0.01
Croatian (92)	327	0.05
Cypriot (43)	77	0.01
Czech (265)	1,167	0.19
Czechoslovakian (88)	307	0.05
Danish (149)	903	0.15
Dutch (861)	2,606	0.43
Eastern European (2,154)	2,474	0.41
English (8,484)	32,191	5.34
Estonian (7)	52	0.01
European (4,478)	4,962	0.82
Finnish (212)	757	0.13
French, ex. Basque (2,393)	13,866	2.30

*Notes: † The Census 2010 population figure is used to calculate the percentages in the Hispanic Origin and Race categories. Ancestry percentages are based on the 2006-2010 American Community Survey population (not shown); ‡ Numbers in parentheses indicate the number of people reporting a single ancestry; * Numbers in parentheses indicate the number of persons reporting this race alone, not in combination with any other race; Please refer to the Explanation of Data for more information.*

French Canadian (2,824)	7,407	1.23
German (6,728)	28,158	4.67
Greek (3,019)	4,794	0.80
Guyanese (438)	667	0.11
Hungarian (475)	1,882	0.31
Icelander (0)	79	0.01
Iranian (601)	739	0.12
Irish (49,183)	98,905	16.41
Israeli (399)	554	0.09
Italian (21,565)	49,847	8.27
Latvian (236)	694	0.12
Lithuanian (973)	2,722	0.45
Luxemburger (13)	66	0.01
Macedonian (10)	10	<0.01
Maltese (18)	27	<0.01
New Zealander (25)	32	0.01
Northern European (335)	383	0.06
Norwegian (580)	1,940	0.32
Pennsylvania German (11)	35	0.01
Polish (4,486)	15,708	2.61
Portuguese (2,015)	6,162	1.02
Romanian (374)	729	0.12
Russian (6,080)	11,209	1.86
Scandinavian (297)	551	0.09
Scotch-Irish (2,854)	6,305	1.05
Scottish (2,273)	8,580	1.42
Serbian (83)	93	0.02
Slavic (40)	119	0.02
Slovak (140)	457	0.08
Slovene (68)	130	0.02
Soviet Union (50)	50	0.01
Swedish (1,087)	5,313	0.88
Swiss (329)	1,406	0.23
Turkish (741)	876	0.15
Ukrainian (1,137)	2,138	0.35
Welsh (296)	2,022	0.34
West Indian, ex. Hispanic (33,004)	37,235	6.18
Bahamian (38)	52	0.01
Barbadian (1,721)	2,090	0.35
Belizean (23)	38	0.01
Bermudan (65)	157	0.03
British West Indian (666)	798	0.13
Dutch West Indian (32)	32	0.01
Haitian (18,720)	19,850	3.29
Jamaican (6,874)	7,904	1.31
Trinidadian/Tobagonian (2,302)	2,928	0.49
U.S. Virgin Islander (21)	68	0.01
West Indian (2,531)	3,307	0.55
Other West Indian (11)	11	<0.01
Yugoslavian (290)	507	0.08

Hispanic Origin	Population	%
Hispanic or Latino (of any race)	107,917	17.47
Central American, ex. Mexican	21,286	3.45
Costa Rican	652	0.11
Guatemalan	4,451	0.72
Honduran	4,017	0.65
Nicaraguan	397	0.06
Panamanian	737	0.12
Salvadoran	10,850	1.76
Other Central American	182	0.03
Cuban	2,319	0.38
Dominican Republic	25,648	4.15
Mexican	5,961	0.97
Puerto Rican	30,506	4.94
South American	11,184	1.81
Argentinean	631	0.10
Bolivian	263	0.04
Chilean	405	0.07
Colombian	6,649	1.08
Ecuadorian	732	0.12
Paraguayan	58	0.01
Peruvian	1,286	0.21
Uruguayan	77	0.01
Venezuelan	1,019	0.16
Other South American	64	0.01
Other Hispanic or Latino	11,013	1.78

Race*	Population	%
African-American/Black (150,437)	163,629	26.49
Not Hispanic (138,073)	147,088	23.82
Hispanic (12,364)	16,541	2.68
American Indian/Alaska Native (2,399)	6,529	1.06
Not Hispanic (1,227)	4,135	0.67
Hispanic (1,172)	2,394	0.39
Alaska Athabascan *(Ala. Nat.)* (2)	5	<0.01
Aleut *(Alaska Native)* (1)	5	<0.01
Apache (8)	31	0.01
Arapaho (0)	1	<0.01
Blackfeet (28)	212	0.03
Canadian/French Am. Ind. (12)	29	<0.01
Central American Ind. (85)	207	0.03
Cherokee (88)	645	0.10
Cheyenne (0)	4	<0.01
Chickasaw (0)	4	<0.01
Chippewa (11)	35	0.01
Choctaw (5)	53	0.01
Colville (1)	2	<0.01
Comanche (9)	12	<0.01
Cree (2)	10	<0.01
Creek (7)	17	<0.01
Crow (0)	5	<0.01
Delaware (0)	10	<0.01
Hopi (2)	7	<0.01
Houma (1)	1	<0.01
Inupiat *(Alaska Native)* (4)	9	<0.01
Iroquois (34)	99	0.02
Kiowa (1)	1	<0.01
Lumbee (8)	18	<0.01
Menominee (0)	1	<0.01
Mexican American Ind. (94)	189	0.03
Navajo (15)	26	<0.01
Osage (1)	5	<0.01
Ottawa (0)	1	<0.01
Potawatomi (4)	5	<0.01
Pueblo (31)	66	0.01
Seminole (0)	41	0.01
Shoshone (3)	3	<0.01
Sioux (20)	66	0.01
South American Ind. (126)	301	0.05
Spanish American Ind. (54)	80	0.01
Tlingit-Haida *(Alaska Native)* (2)	6	<0.01
Tohono O'Odham (7)	10	<0.01
Tsimshian *(Alaska Native)* (1)	1	<0.01
Yaqui (2)	3	<0.01
Yuman (1)	2	<0.01
Yup'ik *(Alaska Native)* (0)	3	<0.01
Asian (55,235)	60,712	9.83
Not Hispanic (54,846)	59,745	9.67
Hispanic (389)	967	0.16
Bangladeshi (306)	343	0.06
Bhutanese (22)	24	<0.01
Burmese (105)	124	0.02
Cambodian (616)	745	0.12
Chinese, ex. Taiwanese (23,998)	25,921	4.20
Filipino (1,722)	2,500	0.40
Hmong (13)	15	<0.01
Indian (7,461)	8,489	1.37
Indonesian (159)	218	0.04
Japanese (1,604)	2,376	0.38
Korean (4,040)	4,540	0.74
Laotian (103)	130	0.02
Malaysian (80)	124	0.02
Nepalese (199)	215	0.03
Pakistani (557)	659	0.11
Sri Lankan (82)	95	0.02
Taiwanese (867)	976	0.16
Thai (628)	762	0.12
Vietnamese (10,916)	11,670	1.89
Hawaii Native/Pacific Islander (265)	1,767	0.29
Not Hispanic (182)	1,202	0.19
Hispanic (83)	565	0.09
Fijian (3)	5	<0.01
Guamanian/Chamorro (60)	124	0.02
Marshallese (1)	1	<0.01
Native Hawaiian (54)	180	0.03
Samoan (45)	71	0.01
Tongan (1)	4	<0.01
White (333,033)	348,258	56.39
Not Hispanic (290,312)	299,393	48.48
Hispanic (42,721)	48,865	7.91

Bourne

Place Type: Town
County: Barnstable
Population: 19,754†

Ancestry‡	Population	%
African, Sub-Saharan (88)	88	0.45
African (59)	59	0.30
Cape Verdean (29)	29	0.15
American (2,822)	2,822	14.41
Arab (9)	55	0.28
Lebanese (9)	9	0.05
Palestinian (0)	23	0.12
Syrian (0)	23	0.12
Armenian (0)	7	0.04
Austrian (0)	24	0.12
British (162)	212	1.08
Canadian (68)	148	0.76
Celtic (11)	11	0.06
Croatian (11)	11	0.06
Czech (8)	44	0.22
Czechoslovakian (0)	7	0.04
Danish (8)	24	0.12
Dutch (19)	183	0.93
Eastern European (35)	35	0.18
English (1,606)	3,792	19.37
European (96)	96	0.49
Finnish (12)	51	0.26
French, ex. Basque (324)	1,111	5.68
French Canadian (259)	531	2.71
German (396)	1,387	7.08
Greek (118)	177	0.90
Hungarian (0)	49	0.25
Irish (2,867)	5,575	28.48
Italian (927)	2,418	12.35
Latvian (0)	15	0.08
Lithuanian (19)	112	0.57
New Zealander (0)	11	0.06
Northern European (18)	18	0.09
Norwegian (100)	171	0.87
Polish (237)	595	3.04
Portuguese (266)	632	3.23
Romanian (11)	11	0.06
Russian (96)	172	0.88
Scotch-Irish (229)	550	2.81
Scottish (188)	787	4.02
Slavic (0)	8	0.04
Slovene (0)	30	0.15
Swedish (147)	495	2.53
Swiss (12)	24	0.12
Ukrainian (29)	85	0.43
Welsh (10)	74	0.38
West Indian, ex. Hispanic (56)	56	0.29
Haitian (23)	23	0.12
Jamaican (33)	33	0.17

Hispanic Origin	Population	%
Hispanic or Latino (of any race)	356	1.80
Central American, ex. Mexican	31	0.16
Costa Rican	6	0.03
Guatemalan	9	0.05
Honduran	9	0.05
Nicaraguan	1	0.01
Panamanian	4	0.02
Salvadoran	2	0.01
Cuban	22	0.11
Dominican Republic	7	0.04
Mexican	78	0.39
Puerto Rican	127	0.64
South American	25	0.13
Argentinean	3	0.02
Chilean	2	0.01
Colombian	6	0.03
Ecuadorian	1	0.01
Peruvian	11	0.06
Venezuelan	2	0.01
Other Hispanic or Latino	66	0.33

*Notes: † The Census 2010 population figure is used to calculate the percentages in the Hispanic Origin and Race categories. Ancestry percentages are based on the 2006-2010 American Community Survey population (not shown); ‡ Numbers in parentheses indicate the number of people reporting a single ancestry; * Numbers in parentheses indicate the number of persons reporting this race alone, not in combination with any other race; Please refer to the Explanation of Data for more information.*

Race*	Population	%
African-American/Black (300)	472	2.39
Not Hispanic (287)	443	2.24
Hispanic (13)	29	0.15
American Indian/Alaska Native (106)	261	1.32
Not Hispanic (98)	247	1.25
Hispanic (8)	14	0.07
Blackfeet (0)	2	0.01
Cherokee (8)	37	0.19
Chickasaw (0)	4	0.02
Chippewa (3)	7	0.04
Choctaw (0)	1	0.01
Creek (0)	3	0.02
Iroquois (1)	7	0.04
Mexican American Ind. (1)	2	0.01
South American Ind. (3)	3	0.02
Asian (234)	320	1.62
Not Hispanic (232)	309	1.56
Hispanic (2)	11	0.06
Cambodian (9)	9	0.05
Chinese, ex. Taiwanese (67)	80	0.40
Filipino (22)	50	0.25
Indian (55)	63	0.32
Japanese (14)	28	0.14
Korean (23)	40	0.20
Laotian (1)	1	0.01
Pakistani (16)	16	0.08
Taiwanese (1)	1	0.01
Thai (5)	11	0.06
Vietnamese (15)	15	0.08
Hawaii Native/Pacific Islander (8)	29	0.15
Not Hispanic (6)	25	0.13
Hispanic (2)	4	0.02
Guamanian/Chamorro (6)	14	0.07
Native Hawaiian (0)	3	0.02
Samoan (0)	2	0.01
Tongan (1)	1	0.01
White (18,467)	18,828	95.31
Not Hispanic (18,261)	18,585	94.08
Hispanic (206)	243	1.23

Boxford

Place Type: Town
County: Essex
Population: 7,965†

Ancestry‡	Population	%
American (477)	477	6.03
Arab (29)	52	0.66
Lebanese (12)	35	0.44
Other Arab (17)	17	0.21
Austrian (0)	17	0.21
Belgian (16)	33	0.42
British (109)	228	2.88
Canadian (17)	114	1.44
Danish (23)	46	0.58
Dutch (56)	72	0.91
Eastern European (32)	32	0.40
English (531)	1,707	21.56
European (15)	15	0.19
French, ex. Basque (81)	597	7.54
French Canadian (317)	573	7.24
German (246)	936	11.82
Greek (187)	308	3.89
Iranian (22)	46	0.58
Irish (598)	2,037	25.73
Italian (866)	1,715	21.66
Lithuanian (18)	53	0.67
Northern European (21)	21	0.27
Polish (76)	187	2.36
Portuguese (21)	175	2.21
Russian (61)	96	1.21
Scotch-Irish (92)	197	2.49
Scottish (65)	254	3.21
Swedish (47)	113	1.43
Swiss (0)	37	0.47
Ukrainian (10)	10	0.13
Welsh (0)	194	2.45

Hispanic Origin	Population	%
Hispanic or Latino (of any race)	145	1.82
Central American, ex. Mexican	17	0.21
Costa Rican	3	0.04
Guatemalan	13	0.16
Honduran	1	0.01
Cuban	11	0.14
Dominican Republic	9	0.11
Mexican	31	0.39
Puerto Rican	29	0.36
South American	31	0.39
Argentinean	8	0.10
Chilean	2	0.03
Colombian	15	0.19
Peruvian	5	0.06
Venezuelan	1	0.01
Other Hispanic or Latino	17	0.21

Race*	Population	%
African-American/Black (41)	61	0.77
Not Hispanic (36)	50	0.63
Hispanic (5)	11	0.14
American Indian/Alaska Native (5)	29	0.36
Not Hispanic (2)	22	0.28
Hispanic (3)	7	0.09
Canadian/French Am. Ind. (0)	4	0.05
Central American Ind. (1)	1	0.01
Cherokee (1)	1	0.01
Cheyenne (0)	2	0.03
Creek (0)	1	0.01
Iroquois (1)	1	0.01
Mexican American Ind. (1)	1	0.01
South American Ind. (1)	1	0.01
Asian (123)	174	2.18
Not Hispanic (123)	174	2.18
Chinese, ex. Taiwanese (47)	63	0.79
Filipino (5)	15	0.19
Indian (19)	27	0.34
Indonesian (1)	2	0.03
Japanese (9)	19	0.24
Korean (23)	26	0.33
Pakistani (1)	1	0.01
Taiwanese (1)	1	0.01
Thai (3)	5	0.06
Vietnamese (3)	3	0.04
Hawaii Native/Pacific Islander (0)	1	0.01
Not Hispanic (0)	1	0.01
Native Hawaiian (0)	1	0.01
White (7,681)	7,772	97.58
Not Hispanic (7,570)	7,650	96.05
Hispanic (111)	122	1.53

Braintree Town

Place Type: City
County: Norfolk
Population: 35,744†

Ancestry‡	Population	%
African, Sub-Saharan (45)	68	0.19
African (9)	21	0.06
Cape Verdean (19)	30	0.09
Nigerian (17)	17	0.05
Albanian (301)	507	1.44
American (1,350)	1,350	3.84
Arab (197)	378	1.08
Egyptian (149)	149	0.42
Lebanese (26)	165	0.47
Moroccan (11)	22	0.06
Syrian (11)	42	0.12
Armenian (13)	163	0.46
Austrian (14)	72	0.20
Belgian (0)	52	0.15
Brazilian (58)	70	0.20
British (88)	123	0.35
Bulgarian (35)	35	0.10
Cajun (0)	11	0.03
Canadian (173)	653	1.86
Celtic (8)	8	0.02
Czech (0)	11	0.03
Danish (0)	48	0.14
Dutch (0)	177	0.50
Eastern European (86)	99	0.28
English (504)	3,996	11.38
European (44)	44	0.13
Finnish (0)	130	0.37
French, ex. Basque (188)	1,252	3.56
French Canadian (293)	786	2.24
German (138)	1,734	4.94
Greek (433)	655	1.86
Hungarian (0)	85	0.24
Iranian (15)	31	0.09
Irish (8,026)	15,564	44.31
Italian (2,940)	7,089	20.18
Latvian (9)	19	0.05
Lithuanian (163)	457	1.30
Northern European (16)	16	0.05
Norwegian (13)	66	0.19
Polish (433)	977	2.78
Portuguese (286)	642	1.83
Russian (140)	322	0.92
Scandinavian (30)	30	0.09
Scotch-Irish (453)	951	2.71
Scottish (423)	1,243	3.54
Serbian (16)	16	0.05
Slovak (25)	42	0.12
Swedish (205)	623	1.77
Swiss (0)	39	0.11
Turkish (64)	64	0.18
Ukrainian (50)	65	0.19
Welsh (0)	90	0.26
West Indian, ex. Hispanic (109)	206	0.59
Bahamian (109)	109	0.31
Jamaican (0)	26	0.07
West Indian (0)	12	0.03
Other West Indian (0)	59	0.17
Yugoslavian (26)	26	0.07

Hispanic Origin	Population	%
Hispanic or Latino (of any race)	890	2.49
Central American, ex. Mexican	80	0.22
Costa Rican	9	0.03
Guatemalan	32	0.09
Honduran	23	0.06
Nicaraguan	7	0.02
Panamanian	2	0.01
Salvadoran	7	0.02
Cuban	52	0.15
Dominican Republic	75	0.21
Mexican	70	0.20
Puerto Rican	327	0.91
South American	141	0.39
Argentinean	8	0.02
Bolivian	6	0.02
Chilean	12	0.03
Colombian	53	0.15
Ecuadorian	9	0.03
Paraguayan	3	0.01
Peruvian	35	0.10
Uruguayan	7	0.02
Venezuelan	8	0.02
Other Hispanic or Latino	145	0.41

Race*	Population	%
African-American/Black (972)	1,215	3.40
Not Hispanic (911)	1,127	3.15
Hispanic (61)	88	0.25
American Indian/Alaska Native (62)	162	0.45
Not Hispanic (46)	138	0.39
Hispanic (16)	24	0.07
Blackfeet (1)	8	0.02
Cherokee (2)	10	0.03
Chickasaw (0)	3	0.01
Choctaw (0)	2	0.01
Creek (0)	1	<0.01
Delaware (0)	1	<0.01
Houma (1)	1	<0.01
Iroquois (1)	7	0.02
Lumbee (0)	1	<0.01
Mexican American Ind. (2)	2	0.01

*Notes: † The Census 2010 population figure is used to calculate the percentages in the Hispanic Origin and Race categories. Ancestry percentages are based on the 2006-2010 American Community Survey population (not shown); ‡ Numbers in parentheses indicate the number of people reporting a single ancestry; * Numbers in parentheses indicate the number of persons reporting this race alone, not in combination with any other race; Please refer to the Explanation of Data for more information.*

Shoshone (0)	1	<0.01
Sioux (2)	4	0.01
South American Ind. (2)	2	0.01
Spanish American Ind. (1)	1	<0.01
Yaqui (1)	1	<0.01
Asian (2,701)	2,898	8.11
Not Hispanic (2,687)	2,871	8.03
Hispanic (14)	27	0.08
Bangladeshi (9)	10	0.03
Burmese (4)	5	0.01
Cambodian (28)	42	0.12
Chinese, ex. Taiwanese (1,476)	1,581	4.42
Filipino (126)	156	0.44
Indian (281)	325	0.91
Indonesian (1)	3	0.01
Japanese (26)	49	0.14
Korean (59)	88	0.25
Laotian (3)	6	0.02
Malaysian (18)	20	0.06
Pakistani (56)	58	0.16
Sri Lankan (10)	10	0.03
Taiwanese (19)	20	0.06
Thai (25)	29	0.08
Vietnamese (471)	501	1.40
Hawaii Native/Pacific Islander (12)	58	0.16
Not Hispanic (10)	45	0.13
Hispanic (2)	13	0.04
Guamanian/Chamorro (0)	7	0.02
Native Hawaiian (8)	13	0.04
Samoan (1)	2	0.01
White (30,976)	31,411	87.88
Not Hispanic (30,471)	30,840	86.28
Hispanic (505)	571	1.60

Brewster

Place Type: Town
County: Barnstable
Population: 9,820†

Ancestry‡	Population	%
American (1,271)	1,271	12.85
Arab (10)	10	0.10
Lebanese (10)	10	0.10
Armenian (41)	112	1.13
Austrian (25)	130	1.31
Belgian (0)	22	0.22
Brazilian (0)	25	0.25
British (31)	31	0.31
Canadian (38)	69	0.70
Czech (11)	35	0.35
Czechoslovakian (20)	32	0.32
Danish (23)	101	1.02
Dutch (27)	164	1.66
Eastern European (15)	15	0.15
English (746)	2,190	22.14
European (51)	51	0.52
Finnish (0)	49	0.50
French, ex. Basque (54)	569	5.75
French Canadian (109)	256	2.59
German (222)	1,233	12.47
Greek (63)	161	1.63
Hungarian (13)	82	0.83
Irish (926)	2,547	25.75
Italian (430)	1,206	12.19
Lithuanian (22)	44	0.44
Macedonian (59)	59	0.60
Norwegian (0)	147	1.49
Polish (159)	362	3.66
Portuguese (90)	295	2.98
Romanian (0)	16	0.16
Russian (32)	107	1.08
Scotch-Irish (31)	138	1.40
Scottish (169)	647	6.54
Slovak (0)	40	0.40
Swedish (67)	353	3.57
Swiss (14)	76	0.77
Ukrainian (21)	109	1.10
Welsh (0)	38	0.38
West Indian, ex. Hispanic (85)	85	0.86
Jamaican (85)	85	0.86

Hispanic Origin	Population	%
Hispanic or Latino (of any race)	166	1.69
Central American, ex. Mexican	12	0.12
Guatemalan	5	0.05
Honduran	2	0.02
Nicaraguan	1	0.01
Salvadoran	4	0.04
Cuban	9	0.09
Dominican Republic	16	0.16
Mexican	33	0.34
Puerto Rican	39	0.40
South American	32	0.33
Argentinean	1	0.01
Colombian	28	0.29
Ecuadorian	2	0.02
Peruvian	1	0.01
Other Hispanic or Latino	25	0.25

Race*	Population	%
African-American/Black (71)	117	1.19
Not Hispanic (67)	109	1.11
Hispanic (4)	8	0.08
American Indian/Alaska Native (15)	44	0.45
Not Hispanic (13)	42	0.43
Hispanic (2)	2	0.02
Apache (0)	2	0.02
Blackfeet (0)	9	0.09
Canadian/French Am. Ind. (0)	1	0.01
Cherokee (0)	3	0.03
Hopi (1)	1	0.01
Iroquois (0)	3	0.03
Mexican American Ind. (2)	2	0.02
Asian (88)	107	1.09
Not Hispanic (86)	104	1.06
Hispanic (2)	3	0.03
Cambodian (1)	1	0.01
Chinese, ex. Taiwanese (20)	29	0.30
Filipino (9)	13	0.13
Indian (19)	21	0.21
Indonesian (0)	2	0.02
Japanese (10)	15	0.15
Korean (5)	6	0.06
Pakistani (3)	3	0.03
Thai (3)	4	0.04
Vietnamese (12)	17	0.17
Hawaii Native/Pacific Islander (2)	3	0.03
Not Hispanic (0)	1	0.01
Hispanic (2)	2	0.02
Guamanian/Chamorro (1)	1	0.01
Native Hawaiian (1)	2	0.02
White (9,496)	9,589	97.65
Not Hispanic (9,370)	9,454	96.27
Hispanic (126)	135	1.37

Bridgewater

Place Type: CDP
County: Plymouth
Population: 7,841†

Ancestry‡	Population	%
African, Sub-Saharan (17)	117	1.60
African (0)	11	0.15
Cape Verdean (17)	81	1.11
Kenyan (0)	14	0.19
Other Sub-Saharan African (0)	11	0.15
American (118)	118	1.61
Arab (81)	97	1.32
Lebanese (81)	97	1.32
Armenian (0)	14	0.19
Brazilian (0)	12	0.16
British (15)	41	0.56
Bulgarian (17)	17	0.23
Canadian (10)	69	0.94
Celtic (0)	10	0.14
Dutch (0)	52	0.71
English (310)	1,230	16.78
French, ex. Basque (21)	595	8.12
French Canadian (88)	467	6.37
German (50)	351	4.79
Greek (40)	141	1.92
Irish (759)	2,500	34.12
Italian (335)	1,588	21.67
Lithuanian (42)	81	1.11
Macedonian (0)	13	0.18
Norwegian (13)	48	0.66
Polish (65)	473	6.45
Portuguese (391)	787	10.74
Russian (13)	37	0.50
Scandinavian (0)	17	0.23
Scotch-Irish (100)	197	2.69
Scottish (59)	420	5.73
Swedish (38)	316	4.31
Swiss (17)	25	0.34
Ukrainian (0)	14	0.19
Welsh (0)	27	0.37
West Indian, ex. Hispanic (27)	57	0.78
Haitian (13)	43	0.59
Jamaican (14)	14	0.19

Hispanic Origin	Population	%
Hispanic or Latino (of any race)	292	3.72
Central American, ex. Mexican	25	0.32
Costa Rican	2	0.03
Guatemalan	9	0.11
Honduran	8	0.10
Nicaraguan	1	0.01
Panamanian	1	0.01
Salvadoran	3	0.04
Other Central American	1	0.01
Cuban	13	0.17
Dominican Republic	34	0.43
Mexican	30	0.38
Puerto Rican	110	1.40
South American	52	0.66
Argentinean	1	0.01
Chilean	19	0.24
Colombian	18	0.23
Ecuadorian	2	0.03
Peruvian	8	0.10
Venezuelan	4	0.05
Other Hispanic or Latino	28	0.36

Race*	Population	%
African-American/Black (385)	490	6.25
Not Hispanic (360)	454	5.79
Hispanic (25)	36	0.46
American Indian/Alaska Native (12)	60	0.77
Not Hispanic (12)	57	0.73
Hispanic (0)	3	0.04
Blackfeet (0)	2	0.03
Cherokee (1)	9	0.11
Chippewa (1)	1	0.01
Sioux (2)	2	0.03
Asian (140)	182	2.32
Not Hispanic (138)	176	2.24
Hispanic (2)	6	0.08
Cambodian (13)	13	0.17
Chinese, ex. Taiwanese (35)	43	0.55
Filipino (12)	22	0.28
Hmong (1)	1	0.01
Indian (33)	45	0.57
Indonesian (0)	1	0.01
Japanese (11)	17	0.22
Korean (6)	13	0.17
Laotian (1)	1	0.01
Pakistani (9)	11	0.14
Taiwanese (1)	1	0.01
Thai (2)	5	0.06
Vietnamese (7)	8	0.10
Hawaii Native/Pacific Islander (0)	14	0.18
Not Hispanic (0)	10	0.13
Hispanic (0)	4	0.05
Native Hawaiian (0)	3	0.04
Samoan (0)	3	0.04
White (6,995)	7,141	91.07
Not Hispanic (6,837)	6,959	88.75
Hispanic (158)	182	2.32

*Notes: † The Census 2010 population figure is used to calculate the percentages in the Hispanic Origin and Race categories. Ancestry percentages are based on the 2006-2010 American Community Survey population (not shown); ‡ Numbers in parentheses indicate the number of people reporting a single ancestry; * Numbers in parentheses indicate the number of persons reporting this race alone, not in combination with any other race; Please refer to the Explanation of Data for more information.*

Bridgewater

Place Type: Town
County: Plymouth
Population: 26,563†

Ancestry‡	Population	%
African, Sub-Saharan (108)	263	1.00
African (3)	14	0.05
Cape Verdean (68)	159	0.60
Ethiopian (0)	10	0.04
Kenyan (0)	14	0.05
Nigerian (2)	2	0.01
South African (35)	53	0.20
Other Sub-Saharan African (0)	11	0.04
American (636)	636	2.41
Arab (128)	178	0.67
Lebanese (127)	177	0.67
Moroccan (1)	1	<0.01
Armenian (10)	34	0.13
Austrian (0)	26	0.10
Belgian (0)	17	0.06
Brazilian (0)	24	0.09
British (15)	59	0.22
Bulgarian (17)	17	0.06
Canadian (141)	458	1.74
Celtic (10)	41	0.16
Czech (0)	51	0.19
Danish (32)	102	0.39
Dutch (0)	276	1.05
English (920)	4,092	15.50
European (151)	164	0.62
Finnish (9)	37	0.14
French, ex. Basque (270)	2,303	8.72
French Canadian (401)	1,429	5.41
German (160)	1,592	6.03
Greek (109)	302	1.14
Irish (3,481)	10,084	38.20
Italian (1,587)	5,189	19.66
Lithuanian (161)	525	1.99
Macedonian (0)	13	0.05
Northern European (47)	47	0.18
Norwegian (38)	172	0.65
Polish (131)	955	3.62
Portuguese (807)	1,921	7.28
Romanian (10)	37	0.14
Russian (37)	194	0.73
Scandinavian (0)	17	0.06
Scotch-Irish (320)	982	3.72
Scottish (144)	1,119	4.24
Swedish (123)	969	3.67
Swiss (17)	34	0.13
Turkish (24)	42	0.16
Ukrainian (13)	148	0.56
Welsh (53)	136	0.52
West Indian, ex. Hispanic (151)	209	0.79
Haitian (13)	71	0.27
Jamaican (54)	54	0.20
Trinidadian/Tobagonian (16)	16	0.06
West Indian (68)	68	0.26
Yugoslavian (0)	39	0.15

Hispanic Origin	Population	%
Hispanic or Latino (of any race)	838	3.15
Central American, ex. Mexican	50	0.19
Costa Rican	3	0.01
Guatemalan	20	0.08
Honduran	10	0.04
Nicaraguan	5	0.02
Panamanian	4	0.02
Salvadoran	7	0.03
Other Central American	1	<0.01
Cuban	23	0.09
Dominican Republic	49	0.18
Mexican	77	0.29
Puerto Rican	232	0.87
South American	103	0.39
Argentinean	5	0.02
Chilean	26	0.10
Colombian	36	0.14
Ecuadorian	15	0.06
Peruvian	13	0.05
Venezuelan	8	0.03
Other Hispanic or Latino	304	1.14

Race*	Population	%
African-American/Black (1,292)	1,501	5.65
Not Hispanic (1,231)	1,424	5.36
Hispanic (61)	77	0.29
American Indian/Alaska Native (62)	169	0.64
Not Hispanic (55)	156	0.59
Hispanic (7)	13	0.05
Blackfeet (0)	3	0.01
Canadian/French Am. Ind. (0)	3	0.01
Cherokee (1)	14	0.05
Chickasaw (0)	1	<0.01
Chippewa (3)	3	0.01
Choctaw (0)	1	<0.01
Iroquois (0)	2	0.01
Mexican American Ind. (2)	4	0.02
Navajo (0)	2	0.01
Puget Sound Salish (1)	1	<0.01
Seminole (1)	1	<0.01
Sioux (2)	2	0.01
South American Ind. (0)	1	<0.01
Tlingit-Haida *(Alaska Native)* (0)	1	<0.01
Asian (328)	425	1.60
Not Hispanic (325)	418	1.57
Hispanic (3)	7	0.03
Burmese (0)	2	0.01
Cambodian (13)	13	0.05
Chinese, ex. Taiwanese (87)	107	0.40
Filipino (21)	46	0.17
Hmong (2)	7	0.03
Indian (88)	109	0.41
Indonesian (1)	2	0.01
Japanese (15)	30	0.11
Korean (17)	25	0.09
Laotian (1)	1	<0.01
Malaysian (1)	1	<0.01
Pakistani (24)	30	0.11
Taiwanese (6)	6	0.02
Thai (5)	9	0.03
Vietnamese (23)	25	0.09
Hawaii Native/Pacific Islander (0)	19	0.07
Not Hispanic (0)	13	0.05
Hispanic (0)	6	0.02
Native Hawaiian (0)	5	0.02
Samoan (0)	3	0.01
White (24,163)	24,514	92.29
Not Hispanic (23,622)	23,931	90.09
Hispanic (541)	583	2.19

Brockton

Place Type: City
County: Plymouth
Population: 93,810†

Ancestry‡	Population	%
African, Sub-Saharan (10,917)	13,116	13.97
African (598)	794	0.85
Cape Verdean (9,740)	11,709	12.47
Ghanaian (108)	108	0.12
Kenyan (66)	66	0.07
Liberian (111)	111	0.12
Nigerian (189)	189	0.20
South African (19)	19	0.02
Sudanese (57)	57	0.06
Other Sub-Saharan African (29)	63	0.07
Albanian (24)	63	0.07
American (1,594)	1,594	1.70
Arab (378)	755	0.80
Egyptian (13)	13	0.01
Lebanese (214)	529	0.56
Moroccan (151)	151	0.16
Syrian (0)	62	0.07
Armenian (70)	94	0.10
Austrian (48)	78	0.08
Belgian (10)	57	0.06
Brazilian (973)	1,238	1.32
British (77)	124	0.13
Bulgarian (71)	71	0.08
Canadian (488)	1,046	1.11
Carpatho Rusyn (21)	21	0.02
Czech (13)	20	0.02
Czechoslovakian (12)	52	0.06
Danish (35)	114	0.12
Dutch (21)	468	0.50
Eastern European (57)	57	0.06
English (1,388)	6,105	6.50
European (110)	169	0.18
Finnish (58)	216	0.23
French, ex. Basque (586)	3,909	4.16
French Canadian (665)	2,396	2.55
German (595)	2,957	3.15
Greek (565)	978	1.04
Guyanese (14)	44	0.05
Hungarian (36)	61	0.06
Irish (6,189)	16,949	18.06
Italian (3,159)	9,149	9.75
Latvian (16)	60	0.06
Lithuanian (697)	1,550	1.65
Norwegian (26)	206	0.22
Polish (498)	2,122	2.26
Portuguese (1,115)	4,006	4.27
Romanian (19)	47	0.05
Russian (217)	561	0.60
Scandinavian (15)	24	0.03
Scotch-Irish (562)	1,224	1.30
Scottish (311)	1,165	1.24
Slavic (9)	9	0.01
Slovak (0)	25	0.03
Swedish (352)	2,013	2.14
Turkish (57)	78	0.08
Ukrainian (31)	140	0.15
Welsh (61)	129	0.14
West Indian, ex. Hispanic (10,902)	12,651	13.48
Bahamian (9)	31	0.03
Barbadian (159)	305	0.32
Belizean (92)	92	0.10
British West Indian (136)	230	0.25
Haitian (9,254)	9,939	10.59
Jamaican (1,053)	1,424	1.52
Trinidadian/Tobagonian (123)	487	0.52
West Indian (76)	143	0.15

Hispanic Origin	Population	%
Hispanic or Latino (of any race)	9,357	9.97
Central American, ex. Mexican	1,093	1.17
Costa Rican	72	0.08
Guatemalan	309	0.33
Honduran	307	0.33
Nicaraguan	32	0.03
Panamanian	98	0.10
Salvadoran	263	0.28
Other Central American	12	0.01
Cuban	216	0.23
Dominican Republic	834	0.89
Mexican	470	0.50
Puerto Rican	5,154	5.49
South American	843	0.90
Argentinean	20	0.02
Bolivian	16	0.02
Chilean	65	0.07
Colombian	127	0.14
Ecuadorian	327	0.35
Paraguayan	11	0.01
Peruvian	234	0.25
Uruguayan	3	<0.01
Venezuelan	35	0.04
Other South American	5	0.01
Other Hispanic or Latino	747	0.80

Race*	Population	%
African-American/Black (29,276)	34,218	36.48
Not Hispanic (27,939)	32,364	34.50
Hispanic (1,337)	1,854	1.98
American Indian/Alaska Native (332)	1,023	1.09
Not Hispanic (253)	847	0.90

*Notes: † The Census 2010 population figure is used to calculate the percentages in the Hispanic Origin and Race categories. Ancestry percentages are based on the 2006-2010 American Community Survey population (not shown); ‡ Numbers in parentheses indicate the number of people reporting a single ancestry; * Numbers in parentheses indicate the number of persons reporting this race alone, not in combination with any other race; Please refer to the Explanation of Data for more information.*

Hispanic (79)	176	0.19
Apache (1)	16	0.02
Arapaho (0)	1	<0.01
Blackfeet (5)	29	0.03
Canadian/French Am. Ind. (1)	3	<0.01
Central American Ind. (5)	5	0.01
Cherokee (9)	107	0.11
Cheyenne (2)	4	<0.01
Chickasaw (0)	2	<0.01
Chippewa (2)	3	<0.01
Choctaw (3)	6	0.01
Comanche (0)	1	<0.01
Creek (0)	1	<0.01
Crow (0)	1	<0.01
Iroquois (6)	14	0.01
Kiowa (1)	3	<0.01
Lumbee (1)	1	<0.01
Mexican American Ind. (6)	10	0.01
Navajo (4)	13	0.01
Potawatomi (2)	3	<0.01
Pueblo (0)	1	<0.01
Seminole (0)	4	<0.01
Sioux (1)	16	0.02
South American Ind. (12)	37	0.04
Spanish American Ind. (3)	10	0.01
Tlingit-Haida *(Alaska Native)* (0)	5	0.01
Ute (0)	2	<0.01
Asian (2,151)	2,629	2.80
Not Hispanic (2,131)	2,564	2.73
Hispanic (20)	65	0.07
Bangladeshi (22)	22	0.02
Burmese (1)	2	<0.01
Cambodian (128)	154	0.16
Chinese, ex. Taiwanese (487)	611	0.65
Filipino (308)	395	0.42
Hmong (146)	157	0.17
Indian (174)	235	0.25
Indonesian (6)	14	0.01
Japanese (27)	56	0.06
Korean (42)	69	0.07
Laotian (39)	46	0.05
Nepalese (1)	1	<0.01
Pakistani (90)	104	0.11
Sri Lankan (4)	4	<0.01
Taiwanese (2)	7	0.01
Thai (16)	29	0.03
Vietnamese (516)	598	0.64
Hawaii Native/Pacific Islander (52)	519	0.55
Not Hispanic (37)	468	0.50
Hispanic (15)	51	0.05
Guamanian/Chamorro (9)	16	0.02
Marshallese (1)	1	<0.01
Native Hawaiian (9)	33	0.04
Samoan (6)	8	0.01
White (43,821)	46,505	49.57
Not Hispanic (40,268)	42,297	45.09
Hispanic (3,553)	4,208	4.49

Brookline

Place Type: CDP/Town
County: Norfolk
Population: 58,732†

Ancestry‡	Population	%
African, Sub-Saharan (268)	355	0.61
African (89)	95	0.16
Cape Verdean (56)	112	0.19
Ethiopian (72)	91	0.16
Ghanaian (19)	19	0.03
Nigerian (10)	10	0.02
South African (5)	11	0.02
Other Sub-Saharan African (17)	17	0.03
Albanian (57)	70	0.12
Alsatian (0)	8	0.01
American (1,792)	1,792	3.09
Arab (390)	622	1.07
Arab (0)	45	0.08
Egyptian (12)	28	0.05
Iraqi (0)	13	0.02
Jordanian (23)	37	0.06
Lebanese (235)	306	0.53
Moroccan (0)	21	0.04
Palestinian (18)	18	0.03
Syrian (9)	51	0.09
Other Arab (93)	103	0.18
Armenian (6)	64	0.11
Australian (0)	10	0.02
Austrian (104)	387	0.67
Belgian (8)	29	0.05
Brazilian (140)	167	0.29
British (261)	574	0.99
Bulgarian (100)	100	0.17
Canadian (167)	425	0.73
Celtic (0)	7	0.01
Croatian (0)	18	0.03
Cypriot (14)	27	0.05
Czech (169)	501	0.86
Czechoslovakian (9)	19	0.03
Danish (9)	85	0.15
Dutch (128)	459	0.79
Eastern European (1,262)	1,361	2.35
English (1,311)	5,017	8.66
Estonian (32)	32	0.06
European (1,074)	1,198	2.07
Finnish (139)	161	0.28
French, ex. Basque (266)	1,529	2.64
French Canadian (223)	487	0.84
German (1,529)	5,295	9.14
Greek (617)	1,082	1.87
Guyanese (16)	33	0.06
Hungarian (205)	461	0.80
Icelander (17)	33	0.06
Iranian (354)	441	0.76
Irish (3,077)	7,747	13.37
Israeli (432)	531	0.92
Italian (1,383)	4,415	7.62
Latvian (20)	51	0.09
Lithuanian (309)	697	1.20
Northern European (73)	173	0.30
Norwegian (96)	488	0.84
Polish (941)	3,111	5.37
Portuguese (134)	264	0.46
Romanian (88)	392	0.68
Russian (2,846)	4,869	8.40
Scandinavian (42)	65	0.11
Scotch-Irish (423)	1,046	1.80
Scottish (272)	1,185	2.04
Serbian (12)	57	0.10
Slavic (0)	46	0.08
Slovak (0)	186	0.32
Slovene (0)	11	0.02
Soviet Union (13)	13	0.02
Swedish (241)	900	1.55
Swiss (41)	261	0.45
Turkish (228)	239	0.41
Ukrainian (323)	465	0.80
Welsh (21)	278	0.48
West Indian, ex. Hispanic (195)	329	0.57
British West Indian (0)	11	0.02
Haitian (101)	101	0.17
Jamaican (73)	164	0.28
Trinidadian/Tobagonian (21)	21	0.04
West Indian (0)	32	0.06
Yugoslavian (79)	79	0.14

Hispanic Origin	Population	%
Hispanic or Latino (of any race)	2,964	5.05
Central American, ex. Mexican	309	0.53
Costa Rican	33	0.06
Guatemalan	90	0.15
Honduran	71	0.12
Nicaraguan	16	0.03
Panamanian	22	0.04
Salvadoran	77	0.13
Cuban	157	0.27
Dominican Republic	178	0.30
Mexican	502	0.85
Puerto Rican	481	0.82
South American	850	1.45
Argentinean	132	0.22
Bolivian	32	0.05
Chilean	100	0.17
Colombian	263	0.45
Ecuadorian	52	0.09
Paraguayan	17	0.03
Peruvian	98	0.17
Uruguayan	13	0.02
Venezuelan	134	0.23
Other South American	9	0.02
Other Hispanic or Latino	487	0.83

Race*	Population	%
African-American/Black (1,977)	2,443	4.16
Not Hispanic (1,828)	2,204	3.75
Hispanic (149)	239	0.41
American Indian/Alaska Native (67)	247	0.42
Not Hispanic (42)	178	0.30
Hispanic (25)	69	0.12
Arapaho (0)	1	<0.01
Blackfeet (2)	9	0.02
Canadian/French Am. Ind. (1)	1	<0.01
Central American Ind. (2)	2	<0.01
Cherokee (3)	34	0.06
Chickasaw (0)	3	0.01
Chippewa (3)	5	0.01
Choctaw (1)	2	<0.01
Comanche (0)	1	<0.01
Cree (0)	2	<0.01
Creek (2)	8	0.01
Inupiat *(Alaska Native)* (1)	2	<0.01
Iroquois (1)	5	0.01
Mexican American Ind. (10)	19	0.03
Navajo (3)	3	0.01
Potawatomi (0)	2	<0.01
Pueblo (1)	2	<0.01
Seminole (0)	1	<0.01
Sioux (0)	5	0.01
South American Ind. (6)	11	0.02
Yaqui (1)	4	0.01
Asian (9,183)	10,304	17.54
Not Hispanic (9,157)	10,231	17.42
Hispanic (26)	73	0.12
Bangladeshi (13)	15	0.03
Burmese (4)	4	0.01
Cambodian (31)	46	0.08
Chinese, ex. Taiwanese (3,942)	4,432	7.55
Filipino (179)	276	0.47
Hmong (1)	2	<0.01
Indian (1,517)	1,714	2.92
Indonesian (28)	42	0.07
Japanese (1,036)	1,203	2.05
Korean (1,360)	1,507	2.57
Laotian (3)	5	0.01
Malaysian (4)	12	0.02
Nepalese (30)	33	0.06
Pakistani (144)	157	0.27
Sri Lankan (22)	26	0.04
Taiwanese (355)	411	0.70
Thai (116)	137	0.23
Vietnamese (118)	158	0.27
Hawaii Native/Pacific Islander (14)	64	0.11
Not Hispanic (12)	60	0.10
Hispanic (2)	4	0.01
Guamanian/Chamorro (4)	6	0.01
Native Hawaiian (1)	15	0.03
Samoan (2)	4	0.01
Tongan (1)	1	<0.01
White (45,021)	46,552	79.26
Not Hispanic (43,040)	44,379	75.56
Hispanic (1,981)	2,173	3.70

Burlington

Place Type: CDP/Town
County: Middlesex
Population: 24,498†

Ancestry‡	Population	%
African, Sub-Saharan (243)	243	1.02

*Notes: † The Census 2010 population figure is used to calculate the percentages in the Hispanic Origin and Race categories. Ancestry percentages are based on the 2006-2010 American Community Survey population (not shown); ‡ Numbers in parentheses indicate the number of people reporting a single ancestry; * Numbers in parentheses indicate the number of persons reporting this race alone, not in combination with any other race; Please refer to the Explanation of Data for more information.*

Ancestry	Population	%
African (120)	120	0.50
Ghanaian (19)	19	0.08
Kenyan (14)	14	0.06
Ugandan (90)	90	0.38
Albanian (0)	42	0.18
American (631)	631	2.64
Arab (125)	239	1.00
Arab (7)	7	0.03
Egyptian (24)	24	0.10
Jordanian (29)	29	0.12
Lebanese (41)	155	0.65
Other Arab (24)	24	0.10
Armenian (249)	404	1.69
Austrian (17)	59	0.25
Belgian (27)	42	0.18
Brazilian (151)	151	0.63
British (30)	82	0.34
Bulgarian (13)	13	0.05
Canadian (143)	331	1.38
Celtic (15)	48	0.20
Czech (13)	13	0.05
Czechoslovakian (0)	21	0.09
Danish (222)	230	0.96
Dutch (14)	103	0.43
Eastern European (19)	19	0.08
English (516)	2,523	10.55
Estonian (16)	16	0.07
European (169)	169	0.71
Finnish (11)	53	0.22
French, ex. Basque (232)	1,379	5.76
French Canadian (185)	593	2.48
German (397)	1,992	8.33
Greek (206)	572	2.39
Hungarian (24)	73	0.31
Iranian (44)	90	0.38
Irish (3,123)	8,065	33.71
Israeli (26)	26	0.11
Italian (2,238)	4,344	18.16
Lithuanian (30)	183	0.76
Northern European (27)	27	0.11
Norwegian (12)	83	0.35
Polish (155)	669	2.80
Portuguese (195)	536	2.24
Romanian (21)	27	0.11
Russian (189)	604	2.52
Scandinavian (32)	32	0.13
Scotch-Irish (109)	207	0.87
Scottish (86)	377	1.58
Slavic (0)	38	0.16
Swedish (156)	548	2.29
Swiss (23)	46	0.19
Ukrainian (56)	104	0.43
Welsh (0)	45	0.19
West Indian, ex. Hispanic (78)	78	0.33
Haitian (78)	78	0.33

Hispanic Origin	Population	%
Hispanic or Latino (of any race)	578	2.36
Central American, ex. Mexican	70	0.29
Costa Rican	2	0.01
Guatemalan	27	0.11
Honduran	6	0.02
Nicaraguan	2	0.01
Panamanian	5	0.02
Salvadoran	27	0.11
Other Central American	1	<0.01
Cuban	19	0.08
Dominican Republic	46	0.19
Mexican	89	0.36
Puerto Rican	144	0.59
South American	147	0.60
Argentinean	14	0.06
Bolivian	6	0.02
Chilean	19	0.08
Colombian	50	0.20
Ecuadorian	28	0.11
Peruvian	14	0.06
Venezuelan	13	0.05
Other South American	3	0.01
Other Hispanic or Latino	63	0.26

Race*	Population	%
African-American/Black (801)	894	3.65
Not Hispanic (787)	869	3.55
Hispanic (14)	25	0.10
American Indian/Alaska Native (39)	104	0.42
Not Hispanic (32)	85	0.35
Hispanic (7)	19	0.08
Apache (2)	4	0.02
Blackfeet (3)	3	0.01
Canadian/French Am. Ind. (0)	2	0.01
Cherokee (3)	11	0.04
Cheyenne (0)	1	<0.01
Chickasaw (1)	3	0.01
Choctaw (0)	1	<0.01
Cree (1)	1	<0.01
Iroquois (1)	2	0.01
Lumbee (0)	3	0.01
Seminole (0)	1	<0.01
Sioux (1)	1	<0.01
South American Ind. (2)	5	0.02
Asian (3,271)	3,498	14.28
Not Hispanic (3,266)	3,483	14.22
Hispanic (5)	15	0.06
Bangladeshi (32)	35	0.14
Burmese (3)	4	0.02
Cambodian (9)	14	0.06
Chinese, ex. Taiwanese (520)	574	2.34
Filipino (41)	70	0.29
Indian (2,191)	2,276	9.29
Indonesian (8)	8	0.03
Japanese (48)	58	0.24
Korean (136)	157	0.64
Malaysian (2)	2	0.01
Nepalese (7)	7	0.03
Pakistani (60)	75	0.31
Sri Lankan (32)	32	0.13
Taiwanese (17)	21	0.09
Thai (13)	17	0.07
Vietnamese (104)	119	0.49
Hawaii Native/Pacific Islander (6)	14	0.06
Not Hispanic (5)	12	0.05
Hispanic (1)	2	0.01
Guamanian/Chamorro (2)	2	0.01
Native Hawaiian (0)	4	0.02
Tongan (4)	4	0.02
White (19,785)	20,063	81.90
Not Hispanic (19,392)	19,644	80.19
Hispanic (393)	419	1.71

Cambridge

Place Type: City
County: Middlesex
Population: 105,162†

Ancestry‡	Population	%
Afghan (10)	10	0.01
African, Sub-Saharan (3,406)	3,834	3.70
African (973)	1,246	1.20
Cape Verdean (309)	371	0.36
Ethiopian (1,462)	1,484	1.43
Ghanaian (23)	23	0.02
Kenyan (15)	15	0.01
Liberian (0)	11	0.01
Nigerian (167)	192	0.19
Somalian (287)	287	0.28
South African (70)	105	0.10
Sudanese (14)	14	0.01
Ugandan (48)	48	0.05
Other Sub-Saharan African (38)	38	0.04
Albanian (95)	129	0.12
Alsatian (15)	15	0.01
American (1,775)	1,775	1.71
Arab (1,051)	1,481	1.43
Arab (367)	432	0.42
Egyptian (38)	38	0.04
Iraqi (27)	38	0.04
Jordanian (25)	25	0.02
Lebanese (227)	416	0.40
Moroccan (160)	160	0.15
Palestinian (18)	28	0.03
Syrian (67)	125	0.12
Other Arab (122)	219	0.21
Armenian (392)	638	0.62
Australian (36)	108	0.10
Austrian (95)	528	0.51
Basque (13)	49	0.05
Belgian (205)	297	0.29
Brazilian (114)	193	0.19
British (669)	1,239	1.20
Bulgarian (174)	193	0.19
Cajun (14)	19	0.02
Canadian (198)	593	0.57
Celtic (38)	49	0.05
Croatian (51)	137	0.13
Cypriot (34)	46	0.04
Czech (167)	559	0.54
Czechoslovakian (30)	60	0.06
Danish (71)	503	0.49
Dutch (325)	1,152	1.11
Eastern European (1,155)	1,313	1.27
English (2,408)	10,331	9.98
Estonian (0)	31	0.03
European (2,228)	2,585	2.50
Finnish (23)	168	0.16
French, ex. Basque (791)	3,537	3.42
French Canadian (622)	1,695	1.64
German (2,398)	9,789	9.46
Greek (533)	1,020	0.99
Guyanese (16)	16	0.02
Hungarian (181)	577	0.56
Icelander (47)	47	0.05
Iranian (192)	279	0.27
Irish (5,039)	14,870	14.37
Israeli (285)	341	0.33
Italian (3,293)	8,974	8.67
Latvian (43)	126	0.12
Lithuanian (180)	792	0.77
Macedonian (0)	59	0.06
New Zealander (40)	65	0.06
Northern European (365)	420	0.41
Norwegian (314)	867	0.84
Pennsylvania German (23)	23	0.02
Polish (1,193)	4,283	4.14
Portuguese (1,425)	2,208	2.13
Romanian (276)	530	0.51
Russian (1,537)	3,852	3.72
Scandinavian (111)	251	0.24
Scotch-Irish (512)	1,780	1.72
Scottish (554)	2,939	2.84
Serbian (71)	71	0.07
Slavic (23)	23	0.02
Slovak (60)	184	0.18
Slovene (39)	93	0.09
Soviet Union (0)	14	0.01
Swedish (431)	1,743	1.68
Swiss (81)	418	0.40
Turkish (210)	267	0.26
Ukrainian (311)	775	0.75
Welsh (51)	608	0.59
West Indian, ex. Hispanic (3,252)	3,852	3.72
Barbadian (218)	338	0.33
Bermudan (0)	15	0.01
British West Indian (9)	9	0.01
Haitian (2,554)	2,816	2.72
Jamaican (257)	358	0.35
Trinidadian/Tobagonian (32)	49	0.05
U.S. Virgin Islander (0)	15	0.01
West Indian (182)	252	0.24
Yugoslavian (50)	64	0.06

Hispanic Origin	Population	%
Hispanic or Latino (of any race)	7,974	7.58
Central American, ex. Mexican	1,057	1.01
Costa Rican	90	0.09
Guatemalan	202	0.19
Honduran	112	0.11
Nicaraguan	53	0.05
Panamanian	86	0.08

*Notes: † The Census 2010 population figure is used to calculate the percentages in the Hispanic Origin and Race categories. Ancestry percentages are based on the 2006-2010 American Community Survey population (not shown); ‡ Numbers in parentheses indicate the number of people reporting a single ancestry; * Numbers in parentheses indicate the number of persons reporting this race alone, not in combination with any other race; Please refer to the Explanation of Data for more information.*

Salvadoran	506	0.48
Other Central American	8	0.01
Cuban	372	0.35
Dominican Republic	656	0.62
Mexican	1,446	1.38
Puerto Rican	1,667	1.59
South American	1,772	1.69
Argentinean	310	0.29
Bolivian	43	0.04
Chilean	275	0.26
Colombian	543	0.52
Ecuadorian	98	0.09
Paraguayan	19	0.02
Peruvian	218	0.21
Uruguayan	31	0.03
Venezuelan	232	0.22
Other South American	3	<0.01
Other Hispanic or Latino	1,004	0.95

Race*	Population	%
African-American/Black (12,253)	14,029	13.34
Not Hispanic (11,589)	13,040	12.40
Hispanic (664)	989	0.94
American Indian/Alaska Native (244)	927	0.88
Not Hispanic (159)	694	0.66
Hispanic (85)	233	0.22
Aleut *(Alaska Native)* (0)	1	<0.01
Apache (1)	11	0.01
Blackfeet (0)	10	0.01
Canadian/French Am. Ind. (5)	13	0.01
Central American Ind. (6)	15	0.01
Cherokee (14)	133	0.13
Chickasaw (1)	5	<0.01
Chippewa (2)	10	0.01
Choctaw (3)	16	0.02
Comanche (0)	1	<0.01
Cree (0)	3	<0.01
Creek (2)	5	<0.01
Crow (1)	1	<0.01
Delaware (1)	3	<0.01
Hopi (8)	8	0.01
Houma (1)	1	<0.01
Inupiat *(Alaska Native)* (1)	1	<0.01
Iroquois (2)	20	0.02
Lumbee (0)	1	<0.01
Mexican American Ind. (18)	37	0.04
Navajo (19)	23	0.02
Osage (1)	1	<0.01
Pima (4)	4	<0.01
Potawatomi (3)	6	0.01
Pueblo (4)	7	0.01
Puget Sound Salish (1)	1	<0.01
Seminole (1)	3	<0.01
Sioux (1)	17	0.02
South American Ind. (13)	46	0.04
Tlingit-Haida *(Alaska Native)* (0)	1	<0.01
Ute (0)	1	<0.01
Yaqui (1)	3	<0.01
Asian (15,879)	18,124	17.23
Not Hispanic (15,818)	17,944	17.06
Hispanic (61)	180	0.17
Bangladeshi (397)	455	0.43
Bhutanese (2)	2	<0.01
Burmese (10)	15	0.01
Cambodian (62)	80	0.08
Chinese, ex. Taiwanese (5,874)	6,693	6.36
Filipino (286)	499	0.47
Hmong (4)	8	0.01
Indian (3,650)	4,129	3.93
Indonesian (63)	103	0.10
Japanese (860)	1,267	1.20
Korean (2,299)	2,566	2.44
Laotian (10)	16	0.02
Malaysian (44)	63	0.06
Nepalese (205)	226	0.21
Pakistani (353)	400	0.38
Sri Lankan (56)	67	0.06
Taiwanese (628)	725	0.69
Thai (143)	169	0.16
Vietnamese (363)	442	0.42
Hawaii Native/Pacific Islander (38)	207	0.20
Not Hispanic (31)	185	0.18
Hispanic (7)	22	0.02
Guamanian/Chamorro (14)	23	0.02
Native Hawaiian (9)	56	0.05
Samoan (5)	21	0.02
Tongan (0)	5	<0.01
White (70,006)	73,788	70.17
Not Hispanic (65,259)	68,441	65.08
Hispanic (4,747)	5,347	5.08

Canton

Place Type: Town
County: Norfolk
Population: 21,561†

Ancestry‡	Population	%
African, Sub-Saharan (381)	415	1.95
African (156)	156	0.73
Cape Verdean (153)	187	0.88
Other Sub-Saharan African (72)	72	0.34
Albanian (13)	26	0.12
American (812)	812	3.82
Arab (256)	372	1.75
Egyptian (13)	52	0.24
Lebanese (117)	176	0.83
Syrian (89)	107	0.50
Other Arab (37)	37	0.17
Armenian (24)	127	0.60
Austrian (85)	98	0.46
Belgian (7)	7	0.03
Brazilian (13)	13	0.06
British (10)	40	0.19
Canadian (94)	233	1.10
Celtic (0)	20	0.09
Czech (0)	13	0.06
Czechoslovakian (14)	14	0.07
Dutch (16)	67	0.32
Eastern European (68)	94	0.44
English (409)	1,766	8.31
European (128)	128	0.60
Finnish (9)	45	0.21
French, ex. Basque (45)	473	2.23
French Canadian (100)	439	2.07
German (161)	1,356	6.38
Greek (235)	391	1.84
Hungarian (9)	54	0.25
Irish (3,671)	7,967	37.50
Israeli (86)	86	0.40
Italian (1,357)	3,962	18.65
Lithuanian (136)	235	1.11
Norwegian (39)	104	0.49
Polish (189)	761	3.58
Portuguese (253)	534	2.51
Romanian (0)	31	0.15
Russian (453)	887	4.17
Scotch-Irish (238)	452	2.13
Scottish (13)	331	1.56
Slovak (0)	24	0.11
Swedish (22)	454	2.14
Swiss (0)	45	0.21
Turkish (31)	31	0.15
Ukrainian (100)	145	0.68
Welsh (28)	54	0.25
West Indian, ex. Hispanic (268)	322	1.52
Barbadian (38)	38	0.18
Bermudan (0)	10	0.05
Haitian (214)	236	1.11
Jamaican (16)	16	0.08
Trinidadian/Tobagonian (0)	22	0.10

Hispanic Origin	Population	%
Hispanic or Latino (of any race)	596	2.76
Central American, ex. Mexican	64	0.30
Costa Rican	9	0.04
Guatemalan	26	0.12
Honduran	20	0.09
Nicaraguan	3	0.01
Salvadoran	5	0.02
Other Central American	1	<0.01
Cuban	28	0.13
Dominican Republic	63	0.29
Mexican	83	0.38
Puerto Rican	200	0.93
South American	101	0.47
Argentinean	6	0.03
Bolivian	1	<0.01
Chilean	13	0.06
Colombian	47	0.22
Ecuadorian	6	0.03
Peruvian	11	0.05
Uruguayan	1	<0.01
Venezuelan	16	0.07
Other Hispanic or Latino	57	0.26

Race*	Population	%
African-American/Black (1,363)	1,519	7.05
Not Hispanic (1,301)	1,432	6.64
Hispanic (62)	87	0.40
American Indian/Alaska Native (23)	92	0.43
Not Hispanic (17)	75	0.35
Hispanic (6)	17	0.08
Blackfeet (0)	3	0.01
Central American Ind. (2)	2	0.01
Cherokee (2)	15	0.07
Chickasaw (0)	2	0.01
Iroquois (2)	3	0.01
Mexican American Ind. (0)	1	<0.01
Navajo (0)	1	<0.01
Pima (1)	1	<0.01
Seminole (0)	1	<0.01
South American Ind. (4)	5	0.02
Spanish American Ind. (0)	1	<0.01
Asian (1,319)	1,451	6.73
Not Hispanic (1,312)	1,436	6.66
Hispanic (7)	15	0.07
Burmese (0)	1	<0.01
Cambodian (13)	15	0.07
Chinese, ex. Taiwanese (542)	616	2.86
Filipino (31)	57	0.26
Indian (332)	353	1.64
Indonesian (1)	4	0.02
Japanese (13)	18	0.08
Korean (91)	105	0.49
Laotian (1)	1	<0.01
Malaysian (4)	4	0.02
Pakistani (22)	24	0.11
Sri Lankan (8)	8	0.04
Taiwanese (34)	34	0.16
Thai (10)	15	0.07
Vietnamese (173)	193	0.90
Hawaii Native/Pacific Islander (2)	18	0.08
Not Hispanic (1)	15	0.07
Hispanic (1)	3	0.01
Fijian (0)	2	0.01
Native Hawaiian (1)	4	0.02
Samoan (1)	1	<0.01
White (18,273)	18,564	86.10
Not Hispanic (17,951)	18,191	84.37
Hispanic (322)	373	1.73

Carver

Place Type: Town
County: Plymouth
Population: 11,509†

Ancestry‡	Population	%
African, Sub-Saharan (232)	251	2.19
Cape Verdean (232)	251	2.19
Albanian (0)	21	0.18
American (730)	730	6.38
Arab (106)	121	1.06
Egyptian (92)	92	0.80
Lebanese (14)	14	0.12
Syrian (0)	15	0.13
Armenian (0)	44	0.38
Austrian (11)	11	0.10
British (35)	35	0.31

SECTION TWO

*Notes: † The Census 2010 population figure is used to calculate the percentages in the Hispanic Origin and Race categories. Ancestry percentages are based on the 2006-2010 American Community Survey population (not shown); ‡ Numbers in parentheses indicate the number of people reporting a single ancestry; * Numbers in parentheses indicate the number of persons reporting this race alone, not in combination with any other race; Please refer to the Explanation of Data for more information.*

Cajun (0)	12	0.10
Canadian (35)	182	1.59
Czechoslovakian (11)	11	0.10
Dutch (35)	92	0.80
English (891)	2,323	20.29
Finnish (119)	157	1.37
French, ex. Basque (205)	762	6.66
French Canadian (253)	511	4.46
German (75)	536	4.68
Hungarian (30)	82	0.72
Irish (1,695)	3,379	29.52
Italian (801)	1,833	16.01
Latvian (0)	40	0.35
Norwegian (0)	17	0.15
Polish (25)	124	1.08
Portuguese (343)	649	5.67
Romanian (0)	12	0.10
Russian (13)	55	0.48
Scandinavian (28)	28	0.24
Scotch-Irish (282)	496	4.33
Scottish (184)	520	4.54
Slovak (13)	13	0.11
Swedish (100)	235	2.05
Swiss (0)	19	0.17
Ukrainian (14)	14	0.12
Welsh (12)	25	0.22

Hispanic Origin	Population	%
Hispanic or Latino (of any race)	129	1.12
Central American, ex. Mexican	16	0.14
Costa Rican	4	0.03
Guatemalan	3	0.03
Salvadoran	9	0.08
Cuban	6	0.05
Dominican Republic	5	0.04
Mexican	23	0.20
Puerto Rican	61	0.53
South American	2	0.02
Colombian	2	0.02
Other Hispanic or Latino	16	0.14

Race*	Population	%
African-American/Black (136)	209	1.82
Not Hispanic (132)	204	1.77
Hispanic (4)	5	0.04
American Indian/Alaska Native (18)	69	0.60
Not Hispanic (18)	66	0.57
Hispanic (0)	3	0.03
Blackfeet (0)	1	0.01
Canadian/French Am. Ind. (0)	1	0.01
Cherokee (3)	4	0.03
Cree (0)	1	0.01
Iroquois (1)	2	0.02
Sioux (1)	2	0.02
Asian (46)	69	0.60
Not Hispanic (46)	68	0.59
Hispanic (0)	1	0.01
Chinese, ex. Taiwanese (5)	9	0.08
Filipino (14)	17	0.15
Indian (6)	6	0.05
Japanese (2)	10	0.09
Korean (5)	11	0.10
Taiwanese (1)	1	0.01
Thai (5)	6	0.05
Vietnamese (3)	3	0.03
Hawaii Native/Pacific Islander (1)	6	0.05
Not Hispanic (1)	6	0.05
Guamanian/Chamorro (1)	1	0.01
Native Hawaiian (0)	4	0.03
Samoan (0)	1	0.01
White (11,002)	11,168	97.04
Not Hispanic (10,922)	11,072	96.20
Hispanic (80)	96	0.83

Charlton

Place Type: Town
County: Worcester
Population: 12,981†

Ancestry‡	Population	%
American (397)	397	3.12
Arab (0)	31	0.24
Lebanese (0)	31	0.24
Armenian (23)	46	0.36
Austrian (0)	10	0.08
Brazilian (41)	41	0.32
Canadian (33)	95	0.75
Czech (0)	47	0.37
Czechoslovakian (0)	15	0.12
Danish (0)	41	0.32
Dutch (13)	60	0.47
Eastern European (13)	13	0.10
English (550)	2,019	15.89
European (114)	114	0.90
Finnish (31)	151	1.19
French, ex. Basque (758)	2,814	22.14
French Canadian (596)	1,336	10.51
German (117)	869	6.84
Greek (17)	142	1.12
Hungarian (28)	96	0.76
Icelander (31)	31	0.24
Irish (934)	3,271	25.74
Italian (562)	2,016	15.86
Latvian (0)	10	0.08
Lithuanian (0)	233	1.83
Northern European (41)	41	0.32
Norwegian (0)	34	0.27
Polish (442)	1,360	10.70
Portuguese (17)	126	0.99
Romanian (12)	12	0.09
Russian (19)	69	0.54
Scotch-Irish (71)	375	2.95
Scottish (54)	275	2.16
Slovak (0)	129	1.02
Swedish (100)	798	6.28
Swiss (0)	48	0.38
Ukrainian (0)	45	0.35
Welsh (0)	47	0.37

Hispanic Origin	Population	%
Hispanic or Latino (of any race)	374	2.88
Central American, ex. Mexican	20	0.15
Costa Rican	2	0.02
Guatemalan	10	0.08
Panamanian	2	0.02
Salvadoran	6	0.05
Cuban	8	0.06
Dominican Republic	13	0.10
Mexican	26	0.20
Puerto Rican	248	1.91
South American	37	0.29
Colombian	15	0.12
Ecuadorian	14	0.11
Peruvian	8	0.06
Other Hispanic or Latino	22	0.17

Race*	Population	%
African-American/Black (90)	135	1.04
Not Hispanic (75)	115	0.89
Hispanic (15)	20	0.15
American Indian/Alaska Native (23)	83	0.64
Not Hispanic (20)	78	0.60
Hispanic (3)	5	0.04
Apache (0)	2	0.02
Blackfeet (1)	3	0.02
Cherokee (6)	16	0.12
Chickasaw (0)	1	0.01
Chippewa (2)	2	0.02
Cree (0)	1	0.01
Creek (0)	1	0.01
Iroquois (0)	5	0.04
Sioux (0)	2	0.02
Asian (120)	173	1.33
Not Hispanic (114)	165	1.27
Hispanic (6)	8	0.06
Burmese (2)	2	0.02
Chinese, ex. Taiwanese (22)	33	0.25
Filipino (10)	31	0.24
Indian (41)	46	0.35
Japanese (2)	5	0.04
Korean (16)	20	0.15
Pakistani (13)	13	0.10
Sri Lankan (3)	3	0.02
Thai (3)	7	0.05
Vietnamese (7)	12	0.09
Hawaii Native/Pacific Islander (9)	11	0.08
Not Hispanic (8)	8	0.06
Hispanic (1)	3	0.02
Fijian (3)	3	0.02
Native Hawaiian (6)	7	0.05
White (12,488)	12,664	97.56
Not Hispanic (12,233)	12,375	95.33
Hispanic (255)	289	2.23

Chelmsford

Place Type: Town
County: Middlesex
Population: 33,802†

Ancestry‡	Population	%
African, Sub-Saharan (12)	12	0.04
Kenyan (12)	12	0.04
American (1,102)	1,102	3.30
Arab (205)	409	1.23
Lebanese (178)	256	0.77
Syrian (27)	153	0.46
Armenian (25)	73	0.22
Austrian (39)	120	0.36
Belgian (10)	40	0.12
Brazilian (93)	106	0.32
British (201)	370	1.11
Bulgarian (10)	10	0.03
Canadian (164)	446	1.34
Celtic (9)	9	0.03
Czech (0)	86	0.26
Czechoslovakian (0)	12	0.04
Danish (0)	124	0.37
Dutch (22)	163	0.49
Eastern European (55)	55	0.16
English (1,885)	6,123	18.35
European (235)	251	0.75
Finnish (36)	154	0.46
French, ex. Basque (675)	2,929	8.78
French Canadian (858)	2,133	6.39
German (388)	2,480	7.43
Greek (405)	765	2.29
Hungarian (9)	47	0.14
Iranian (83)	83	0.25
Irish (3,423)	10,488	31.43
Italian (1,715)	5,276	15.81
Latvian (23)	58	0.17
Lithuanian (44)	169	0.51
Norwegian (46)	227	0.68
Pennsylvania German (0)	27	0.08
Polish (487)	1,574	4.72
Portuguese (394)	1,154	3.46
Romanian (29)	53	0.16
Russian (236)	394	1.18
Scandinavian (20)	108	0.32
Scotch-Irish (265)	919	2.75
Scottish (361)	1,324	3.97
Slovak (42)	63	0.19
Swedish (109)	635	1.90
Swiss (9)	78	0.23
Turkish (28)	28	0.08
Ukrainian (17)	63	0.19
Welsh (65)	256	0.77

Hispanic Origin	Population	%
Hispanic or Latino (of any race)	686	2.03
Central American, ex. Mexican	29	0.09
Costa Rican	1	<0.01
Guatemalan	15	0.04
Honduran	2	0.01
Nicaraguan	3	0.01
Panamanian	2	0.01
Salvadoran	6	0.02
Cuban	44	0.13

*Notes: † The Census 2010 population figure is used to calculate the percentages in the Hispanic Origin and Race categories. Ancestry percentages are based on the 2006-2010 American Community Survey population (not shown); ‡ Numbers in parentheses indicate the number of people reporting a single ancestry; * Numbers in parentheses indicate the number of persons reporting this race alone, not in combination with any other race; Please refer to the Explanation of Data for more information.*

	Population	%
Dominican Republic	51	0.15
Mexican	108	0.32
Puerto Rican	233	0.69
South American	126	0.37
Argentinean	9	0.03
Bolivian	1	<0.01
Chilean	5	0.01
Colombian	80	0.24
Ecuadorian	12	0.04
Peruvian	9	0.03
Venezuelan	8	0.02
Other South American	2	0.01
Other Hispanic or Latino	95	0.28

Race*	Population	%
African-American/Black (358)	482	1.43
Not Hispanic (338)	443	1.31
Hispanic (20)	39	0.12
American Indian/Alaska Native (35)	120	0.36
Not Hispanic (30)	108	0.32
Hispanic (5)	12	0.04
Blackfeet (0)	4	0.01
Cherokee (2)	11	0.03
Chippewa (0)	1	<0.01
Choctaw (0)	1	<0.01
Comanche (0)	2	0.01
Creek (4)	4	0.01
Delaware (0)	4	0.01
Iroquois (0)	7	0.02
Mexican American Ind. (2)	2	0.01
Osage (0)	1	<0.01
Shoshone (1)	1	<0.01
Sioux (1)	1	<0.01
Asian (2,846)	3,105	9.19
Not Hispanic (2,837)	3,086	9.13
Hispanic (9)	19	0.06
Bangladeshi (9)	12	0.04
Burmese (8)	8	0.02
Cambodian (162)	184	0.54
Chinese, ex. Taiwanese (739)	826	2.44
Filipino (37)	66	0.20
Indian (1,376)	1,414	4.18
Indonesian (6)	7	0.02
Japanese (44)	82	0.24
Korean (116)	143	0.42
Laotian (28)	34	0.10
Malaysian (2)	6	0.02
Nepalese (1)	1	<0.01
Pakistani (64)	69	0.20
Sri Lankan (6)	7	0.02
Taiwanese (47)	64	0.19
Thai (9)	18	0.05
Vietnamese (136)	150	0.44
Hawaii Native/Pacific Islander (2)	23	0.07
Not Hispanic (2)	23	0.07
Guamanian/Chamorro (1)	1	<0.01
Marshallese (1)	1	<0.01
Native Hawaiian (0)	3	0.01
White (29,944)	30,361	89.82
Not Hispanic (29,455)	29,818	88.21
Hispanic (489)	543	1.61

Chelsea

Place Type: City
County: Suffolk
Population: 35,177†

Ancestry‡	Population	%
African, Sub-Saharan (1,030)	1,135	3.29
African (118)	154	0.45
Cape Verdean (365)	434	1.26
Ethiopian (415)	415	1.20
Kenyan (20)	20	0.06
Nigerian (23)	23	0.07
Somalian (53)	53	0.15
Sudanese (14)	14	0.04
Other Sub-Saharan African (22)	22	0.06
Albanian (43)	43	0.12
American (712)	712	2.06
Arab (400)	423	1.22
Arab (44)	52	0.15
Iraqi (7)	7	0.02
Moroccan (349)	364	1.05
Armenian (93)	106	0.31
Austrian (17)	17	0.05
Brazilian (435)	458	1.33
Canadian (74)	174	0.50
Czech (0)	19	0.06
Danish (15)	15	0.04
Dutch (0)	12	0.03
Eastern European (27)	27	0.08
English (166)	681	1.97
European (57)	90	0.26
French, ex. Basque (210)	500	1.45
French Canadian (144)	224	0.65
German (118)	270	0.78
Greek (37)	37	0.11
Hungarian (0)	19	0.06
Irish (1,040)	2,072	6.00
Italian (1,467)	2,228	6.45
Lithuanian (10)	115	0.33
Norwegian (0)	28	0.08
Polish (400)	1,053	3.05
Portuguese (39)	86	0.25
Romanian (0)	12	0.03
Russian (271)	407	1.18
Scandinavian (10)	10	0.03
Scotch-Irish (41)	115	0.33
Scottish (57)	195	0.56
Slovak (132)	132	0.38
Swedish (0)	7	0.02
Turkish (0)	56	0.16
Ukrainian (0)	36	0.10
Welsh (17)	42	0.12
West Indian, ex. Hispanic (911)	1,062	3.08
Barbadian (36)	36	0.10
British West Indian (0)	43	0.12
Haitian (341)	404	1.17
Jamaican (44)	44	0.13
West Indian (490)	535	1.55
Yugoslavian (231)	231	0.67

Hispanic Origin	Population	%
Hispanic or Latino (of any race)	21,855	62.13
Central American, ex. Mexican	12,682	36.05
Costa Rican	163	0.46
Guatemalan	2,553	7.26
Honduran	2,938	8.35
Nicaraguan	136	0.39
Panamanian	26	0.07
Salvadoran	6,391	18.17
Other Central American	475	1.35
Cuban	182	0.52
Dominican Republic	774	2.20
Mexican	997	2.83
Puerto Rican	4,458	12.67
South American	884	2.51
Argentinean	38	0.11
Bolivian	1	<0.01
Chilean	22	0.06
Colombian	554	1.57
Ecuadorian	50	0.14
Peruvian	170	0.48
Uruguayan	23	0.07
Venezuelan	20	0.06
Other South American	6	0.02
Other Hispanic or Latino	1,878	5.34

Race*	Population	%
African-American/Black (2,986)	3,551	10.09
Not Hispanic (2,341)	2,646	7.52
Hispanic (645)	905	2.57
American Indian/Alaska Native (370)	643	1.83
Not Hispanic (55)	150	0.43
Hispanic (315)	493	1.40
Apache (0)	5	0.01
Arapaho (0)	2	0.01
Blackfeet (2)	11	0.03
Central American Ind. (26)	33	0.09
Cherokee (5)	21	0.06
Chippewa (5)	5	0.01
Comanche (0)	1	<0.01
Crow (1)	1	<0.01
Delaware (0)	1	<0.01
Iroquois (3)	3	0.01
Mexican American Ind. (16)	38	0.11
Navajo (1)	1	<0.01
Pima (0)	1	<0.01
Seminole (0)	3	0.01
Sioux (7)	10	0.03
South American Ind. (13)	22	0.06
Spanish American Ind. (7)	15	0.04
Yaqui (0)	5	0.01
Asian (1,094)	1,324	3.76
Not Hispanic (1,052)	1,216	3.46
Hispanic (42)	108	0.31
Bangladeshi (2)	2	0.01
Bhutanese (0)	2	0.01
Burmese (6)	6	0.02
Cambodian (88)	109	0.31
Chinese, ex. Taiwanese (150)	172	0.49
Filipino (87)	111	0.32
Indian (119)	160	0.45
Indonesian (2)	4	0.01
Japanese (3)	6	0.02
Korean (47)	51	0.14
Laotian (6)	7	0.02
Malaysian (2)	2	0.01
Nepalese (27)	35	0.10
Pakistani (21)	24	0.07
Sri Lankan (1)	1	<0.01
Taiwanese (7)	15	0.04
Thai (6)	10	0.03
Vietnamese (465)	501	1.42
Hawaii Native/Pacific Islander (7)	140	0.40
Not Hispanic (2)	47	0.13
Hispanic (5)	93	0.26
Guamanian/Chamorro (0)	4	0.01
Native Hawaiian (2)	9	0.03
Samoan (0)	5	0.01
White (16,832)	18,462	52.48
Not Hispanic (8,882)	9,314	26.48
Hispanic (7,950)	9,148	26.01

Chicopee

Place Type: City
County: Hampden
Population: 55,298†

Ancestry‡	Population	%
African, Sub-Saharan (419)	428	0.78
African (23)	23	0.04
Cape Verdean (13)	22	0.04
Ghanaian (149)	149	0.27
Kenyan (62)	62	0.11
Other Sub-Saharan African (172)	172	0.31
Albanian (0)	79	0.14
American (1,395)	1,395	2.53
Arab (40)	107	0.19
Lebanese (40)	92	0.17
Other Arab (0)	15	0.03
Armenian (0)	17	0.03
Australian (0)	18	0.03
Austrian (0)	108	0.20
Brazilian (48)	73	0.13
British (16)	60	0.11
Canadian (277)	379	0.69
Czech (28)	96	0.17
Czechoslovakian (0)	59	0.11
Danish (10)	111	0.20
Dutch (30)	278	0.50
Eastern European (0)	28	0.05
English (1,260)	4,261	7.72
European (39)	75	0.14
Finnish (12)	103	0.19
French, ex. Basque (3,966)	12,103	21.94
French Canadian (3,404)	5,392	9.77
German (397)	2,512	4.55

*Notes: † The Census 2010 population figure is used to calculate the percentages in the Hispanic Origin and Race categories. Ancestry percentages are based on the 2006-2010 American Community Survey population (not shown); ‡ Numbers in parentheses indicate the number of people reporting a single ancestry; * Numbers in parentheses indicate the number of persons reporting this race alone, not in combination with any other race; Please refer to the Explanation of Data for more information.*

Greek (128)	509	0.92
Hungarian (71)	276	0.50
Irish (2,715)	8,739	15.84
Italian (1,099)	4,289	7.77
Lithuanian (25)	140	0.25
Northern European (10)	88	0.16
Norwegian (23)	231	0.42
Polish (6,002)	11,927	21.62
Portuguese (759)	1,417	2.57
Romanian (16)	16	0.03
Russian (396)	583	1.06
Scandinavian (21)	52	0.09
Scotch-Irish (200)	585	1.06
Scottish (133)	854	1.55
Slavic (0)	14	0.03
Slovak (8)	68	0.12
Swedish (92)	335	0.61
Swiss (0)	28	0.05
Turkish (63)	63	0.11
Ukrainian (190)	222	0.40
Welsh (159)	237	0.43
West Indian, ex. Hispanic (190)	238	0.43
Barbadian (12)	12	0.02
British West Indian (17)	17	0.03
Haitian (0)	9	0.02
Jamaican (161)	184	0.33
U.S. Virgin Islander (0)	16	0.03
Yugoslavian (0)	79	0.14

Hispanic Origin	Population	%
Hispanic or Latino (of any race)	8,196	14.82
Central American, ex. Mexican	77	0.14
Costa Rican	12	0.02
Guatemalan	6	0.01
Honduran	15	0.03
Nicaraguan	8	0.01
Panamanian	18	0.03
Salvadoran	18	0.03
Cuban	62	0.11
Dominican Republic	266	0.48
Mexican	208	0.38
Puerto Rican	7,097	12.83
South American	175	0.32
Argentinean	3	0.01
Chilean	2	<0.01
Colombian	87	0.16
Ecuadorian	47	0.08
Peruvian	21	0.04
Uruguayan	2	<0.01
Venezuelan	13	0.02
Other Hispanic or Latino	311	0.56

Race*	Population	%
African-American/Black (2,053)	2,629	4.75
Not Hispanic (1,525)	1,875	3.39
Hispanic (528)	754	1.36
American Indian/Alaska Native (204)	459	0.83
Not Hispanic (87)	269	0.49
Hispanic (117)	190	0.34
Aleut *(Alaska Native)* (0)	1	<0.01
Apache (1)	1	<0.01
Blackfeet (9)	16	0.03
Canadian/French Am. Ind. (1)	5	0.01
Central American Ind. (2)	2	<0.01
Cherokee (3)	30	0.05
Chickasaw (0)	1	<0.01
Chippewa (0)	1	<0.01
Choctaw (3)	7	0.01
Cree (0)	1	<0.01
Creek (0)	2	<0.01
Crow (0)	1	<0.01
Hopi (0)	1	<0.01
Iroquois (11)	22	0.04
Lumbee (3)	4	0.01
Menominee (1)	1	<0.01
Mexican American Ind. (5)	9	0.02
Navajo (3)	3	0.01
Potawatomi (0)	1	<0.01
Pueblo (2)	2	<0.01
Seminole (0)	2	<0.01
Sioux (0)	5	0.01
South American Ind. (12)	19	0.03
Asian (737)	934	1.69
Not Hispanic (722)	885	1.60
Hispanic (15)	49	0.09
Cambodian (75)	90	0.16
Chinese, ex. Taiwanese (167)	179	0.32
Filipino (45)	84	0.15
Indian (138)	155	0.28
Indonesian (8)	10	0.02
Japanese (47)	75	0.14
Korean (57)	83	0.15
Laotian (3)	4	0.01
Malaysian (0)	1	<0.01
Nepalese (20)	20	0.04
Pakistani (49)	54	0.10
Sri Lankan (13)	13	0.02
Taiwanese (4)	4	0.01
Thai (16)	20	0.04
Vietnamese (74)	87	0.16
Hawaii Native/Pacific Islander (36)	98	0.18
Not Hispanic (22)	68	0.12
Hispanic (14)	30	0.05
Fijian (0)	1	<0.01
Guamanian/Chamorro (6)	9	0.02
Native Hawaiian (8)	31	0.06
Samoan (15)	25	0.05
Tongan (2)	3	0.01
White (47,999)	49,076	88.75
Not Hispanic (43,938)	44,596	80.65
Hispanic (4,061)	4,480	8.10

Clinton

Place Type: Town
County: Worcester
Population: 13,606†

Ancestry‡	Population	%
Albanian (0)	15	0.11
American (477)	477	3.50
Arab (0)	11	0.08
Iraqi (0)	11	0.08
Armenian (0)	11	0.08
Austrian (0)	43	0.32
Belgian (7)	18	0.13
Brazilian (167)	198	1.45
British (22)	22	0.16
Canadian (41)	76	0.56
Czech (0)	26	0.19
Danish (14)	107	0.79
Dutch (21)	81	0.60
English (109)	1,105	8.12
European (23)	23	0.17
Finnish (0)	46	0.34
French, ex. Basque (304)	1,594	11.71
French Canadian (232)	626	4.60
German (328)	1,778	13.06
Greek (155)	205	1.51
Hungarian (18)	27	0.20
Irish (1,524)	4,313	31.69
Italian (512)	2,211	16.25
Latvian (0)	14	0.10
Lithuanian (23)	95	0.70
Maltese (0)	29	0.21
Northern European (14)	14	0.10
Norwegian (0)	42	0.31
Polish (438)	1,413	10.38
Portuguese (148)	316	2.32
Russian (22)	62	0.46
Scandinavian (49)	49	0.36
Scotch-Irish (92)	317	2.33
Scottish (109)	474	3.48
Slovene (0)	18	0.13
Swedish (83)	250	1.84
Swiss (0)	10	0.07
Ukrainian (11)	11	0.08
Welsh (0)	67	0.49
West Indian, ex. Hispanic (193)	193	1.42
Haitian (182)	182	1.34
West Indian (11)	11	0.08

Hispanic Origin	Population	%
Hispanic or Latino (of any race)	1,844	13.55
Central American, ex. Mexican	352	2.59
Costa Rican	9	0.07
Guatemalan	233	1.71
Honduran	41	0.30
Nicaraguan	7	0.05
Panamanian	6	0.04
Salvadoran	56	0.41
Cuban	11	0.08
Dominican Republic	362	2.66
Mexican	89	0.65
Puerto Rican	803	5.90
South American	85	0.62
Argentinean	4	0.03
Chilean	3	0.02
Colombian	20	0.15
Ecuadorian	14	0.10
Peruvian	18	0.13
Uruguayan	9	0.07
Venezuelan	17	0.12
Other Hispanic or Latino	142	1.04

Race*	Population	%
African-American/Black (470)	563	4.14
Not Hispanic (341)	406	2.98
Hispanic (129)	157	1.15
American Indian/Alaska Native (47)	117	0.86
Not Hispanic (25)	88	0.65
Hispanic (22)	29	0.21
Apache (1)	1	0.01
Blackfeet (1)	2	0.01
Canadian/French Am. Ind. (1)	10	0.07
Cherokee (0)	8	0.06
Chippewa (1)	1	0.01
Choctaw (0)	1	0.01
Houma (1)	1	0.01
Iroquois (1)	5	0.04
Mexican American Ind. (1)	1	0.01
Navajo (0)	1	0.01
Seminole (0)	3	0.02
Asian (182)	258	1.90
Not Hispanic (180)	250	1.84
Hispanic (2)	8	0.06
Bangladeshi (4)	4	0.03
Chinese, ex. Taiwanese (36)	49	0.36
Filipino (29)	38	0.28
Indian (59)	73	0.54
Japanese (14)	43	0.32
Korean (11)	19	0.14
Laotian (1)	1	0.01
Nepalese (1)	1	0.01
Pakistani (5)	5	0.04
Sri Lankan (3)	3	0.02
Taiwanese (2)	2	0.01
Thai (9)	9	0.07
Vietnamese (5)	5	0.04
Hawaii Native/Pacific Islander (5)	13	0.10
Not Hispanic (2)	9	0.07
Hispanic (3)	4	0.03
Guamanian/Chamorro (4)	4	0.03
Native Hawaiian (0)	6	0.04
White (11,845)	12,123	89.10
Not Hispanic (10,884)	11,064	81.32
Hispanic (961)	1,059	7.78

Cohasset

Place Type: Town
County: Norfolk
Population: 7,542†

Ancestry‡	Population	%
Albanian (0)	15	0.20
Alsatian (0)	13	0.17
American (201)	201	2.70
Arab (0)	67	0.90
Lebanese (0)	57	0.77

*Notes: † The Census 2010 population figure is used to calculate the percentages in the Hispanic Origin and Race categories. Ancestry percentages are based on the 2006-2010 American Community Survey population (not shown); ‡ Numbers in parentheses indicate the number of people reporting a single ancestry; * Numbers in parentheses indicate the number of persons reporting this race alone, not in combination with any other race; Please refer to the Explanation of Data for more information.*

Syrian (0)	10	0.13
Armenian (11)	11	0.15
Austrian (31)	214	2.88
British (29)	43	0.58
Canadian (37)	43	0.58
Croatian (0)	24	0.32
Danish (0)	25	0.34
Dutch (23)	81	1.09
English (304)	1,668	22.44
European (36)	36	0.48
Finnish (12)	12	0.16
French, ex. Basque (98)	892	12.00
French Canadian (0)	135	1.82
German (199)	1,178	15.85
Greek (37)	37	0.50
Hungarian (12)	46	0.62
Irish (946)	3,080	41.43
Italian (531)	1,468	19.75
Lithuanian (15)	67	0.90
Luxemburger (9)	9	0.12
Northern European (25)	25	0.34
Norwegian (0)	65	0.87
Polish (0)	185	2.49
Portuguese (49)	197	2.65
Romanian (0)	15	0.20
Russian (32)	311	4.18
Scotch-Irish (50)	191	2.57
Scottish (65)	299	4.02
Slovene (0)	42	0.56
Swedish (12)	67	0.90
Welsh (17)	83	1.12
West Indian, ex. Hispanic (0)	23	0.31
British West Indian (0)	23	0.31

Hispanic Origin	Population	%
Hispanic or Latino (of any race)	96	1.27
Central American, ex. Mexican	5	0.07
Guatemalan	3	0.04
Panamanian	1	0.01
Salvadoran	1	0.01
Cuban	9	0.12
Dominican Republic	6	0.08
Mexican	25	0.33
Puerto Rican	12	0.16
South American	16	0.21
Argentinean	2	0.03
Chilean	1	0.01
Colombian	6	0.08
Paraguayan	1	0.01
Peruvian	2	0.03
Venezuelan	3	0.04
Other South American	1	0.01
Other Hispanic or Latino	23	0.30

Race*	Population	%
African-American/Black (21)	31	0.41
Not Hispanic (20)	30	0.40
Hispanic (1)	1	0.01
American Indian/Alaska Native (11)	42	0.56
Not Hispanic (8)	37	0.49
Hispanic (3)	5	0.07
Cherokee (0)	9	0.12
Choctaw (0)	5	0.07
Creek (1)	1	0.01
Mexican American Ind. (1)	2	0.03
Potawatomi (0)	1	0.01
Seminole (0)	1	0.01
Sioux (0)	1	0.01
Ute (0)	1	0.01
Asian (75)	115	1.52
Not Hispanic (71)	111	1.47
Hispanic (4)	4	0.05
Cambodian (2)	2	0.03
Chinese, ex. Taiwanese (26)	42	0.56
Filipino (4)	8	0.11
Indian (4)	8	0.11
Indonesian (1)	2	0.03
Japanese (5)	6	0.08
Korean (22)	30	0.40
Laotian (0)	1	0.01
Sri Lankan (1)	1	0.01
Vietnamese (3)	11	0.15
Hawaii Native/Pacific Islander (1)	4	0.05
Not Hispanic (1)	4	0.05
Guamanian/Chamorro (0)	2	0.03
White (7,337)	7,419	98.37
Not Hispanic (7,254)	7,333	97.23
Hispanic (83)	86	1.14

Concord

Place Type: Town
County: Middlesex
Population: 17,668†

Ancestry‡	Population	%
African, Sub-Saharan (24)	24	0.14
Cape Verdean (24)	24	0.14
Albanian (14)	43	0.25
American (814)	814	4.69
Arab (74)	74	0.43
Lebanese (74)	74	0.43
Armenian (61)	91	0.52
Australian (11)	11	0.06
Austrian (23)	93	0.54
Belgian (0)	28	0.16
British (191)	333	1.92
Bulgarian (13)	13	0.07
Canadian (98)	218	1.25
Celtic (0)	13	0.07
Czech (0)	113	0.65
Czechoslovakian (0)	10	0.06
Danish (45)	110	0.63
Dutch (50)	337	1.94
Eastern European (240)	280	1.61
English (1,239)	3,608	20.77
European (224)	260	1.50
Finnish (28)	181	1.04
French, ex. Basque (101)	704	4.05
French Canadian (192)	353	2.03
German (473)	2,516	14.48
Greek (105)	127	0.73
Hungarian (34)	87	0.50
Iranian (27)	27	0.16
Irish (1,268)	3,702	21.31
Israeli (40)	40	0.23
Italian (714)	2,253	12.97
Latvian (11)	11	0.06
Lithuanian (40)	124	0.71
New Zealander (15)	15	0.09
Northern European (132)	132	0.76
Norwegian (42)	208	1.20
Pennsylvania German (0)	9	0.05
Polish (186)	630	3.63
Portuguese (33)	127	0.73
Romanian (0)	11	0.06
Russian (210)	414	2.38
Scandinavian (11)	39	0.22
Scotch-Irish (174)	597	3.44
Scottish (205)	825	4.75
Serbian (10)	10	0.06
Slovak (18)	66	0.38
Slovene (0)	12	0.07
Swedish (54)	408	2.35
Swiss (35)	52	0.30
Ukrainian (10)	55	0.32
Welsh (13)	197	1.13
West Indian, ex. Hispanic (28)	56	0.32
Barbadian (12)	12	0.07
Bermudan (0)	14	0.08
Haitian (0)	7	0.04
Jamaican (16)	16	0.09
U.S. Virgin Islander (0)	7	0.04
Yugoslavian (15)	15	0.09

Hispanic Origin	Population	%
Hispanic or Latino (of any race)	655	3.71
Central American, ex. Mexican	35	0.20
Costa Rican	2	0.01
Guatemalan	14	0.08
Honduran	3	0.02
Panamanian	9	0.05
Salvadoran	7	0.04
Cuban	32	0.18
Dominican Republic	16	0.09
Mexican	65	0.37
Puerto Rican	201	1.14
South American	67	0.38
Argentinean	21	0.12
Bolivian	1	0.01
Chilean	2	0.01
Colombian	17	0.10
Ecuadorian	2	0.01
Paraguayan	1	0.01
Peruvian	12	0.07
Uruguayan	2	0.01
Venezuelan	7	0.04
Other South American	2	0.01
Other Hispanic or Latino	239	1.35

Race*	Population	%
African-American/Black (673)	733	4.15
Not Hispanic (648)	703	3.98
Hispanic (25)	30	0.17
American Indian/Alaska Native (14)	59	0.33
Not Hispanic (8)	47	0.27
Hispanic (6)	12	0.07
Cherokee (2)	7	0.04
Choctaw (0)	1	0.01
Iroquois (0)	2	0.01
Mexican American Ind. (1)	1	0.01
Osage (0)	3	0.02
Sioux (0)	2	0.01
South American Ind. (2)	2	0.01
Asian (709)	850	4.81
Not Hispanic (708)	843	4.77
Hispanic (1)	7	0.04
Cambodian (8)	8	0.05
Chinese, ex. Taiwanese (384)	456	2.58
Filipino (14)	29	0.16
Indian (162)	179	1.01
Indonesian (2)	3	0.02
Japanese (28)	52	0.29
Korean (67)	83	0.47
Laotian (2)	4	0.02
Pakistani (6)	10	0.06
Taiwanese (3)	9	0.05
Thai (1)	1	0.01
Vietnamese (16)	22	0.12
Hawaii Native/Pacific Islander (0)	5	0.03
Not Hispanic (0)	4	0.02
Hispanic (0)	1	0.01
Guamanian/Chamorro (0)	2	0.01
White (15,850)	16,081	91.02
Not Hispanic (15,402)	15,597	88.28
Hispanic (448)	484	2.74

Danvers

Place Type: CDP/Town
County: Essex
Population: 26,493†

Ancestry‡	Population	%
Albanian (76)	107	0.41
American (813)	813	3.11
Arab (25)	92	0.35
Lebanese (0)	34	0.13
Syrian (25)	58	0.22
Armenian (15)	23	0.09
Austrian (15)	101	0.39
Belgian (0)	33	0.13
Brazilian (103)	110	0.42
British (99)	115	0.44
Canadian (107)	288	1.10
Celtic (0)	14	0.05
Croatian (0)	21	0.08
Czech (13)	13	0.05
Czechoslovakian (0)	8	0.03
Danish (0)	13	0.05

*Notes: † The Census 2010 population figure is used to calculate the percentages in the Hispanic Origin and Race categories. Ancestry percentages are based on the 2006-2010 American Community Survey population (not shown); ‡ Numbers in parentheses indicate the number of people reporting a single ancestry; * Numbers in parentheses indicate the number of persons reporting this race alone, not in combination with any other race; Please refer to the Explanation of Data for more information.*

Dutch (11)	71	0.27
Eastern European (102)	147	0.56
English (1,455)	4,565	17.48
European (364)	379	1.45
Finnish (55)	154	0.59
French, ex. Basque (627)	2,259	8.65
French Canadian (582)	1,502	5.75
German (422)	2,021	7.74
Greek (426)	937	3.59
Hungarian (0)	28	0.11
Irish (3,069)	6,908	26.45
Israeli (13)	13	0.05
Italian (2,206)	5,105	19.55
Latvian (0)	16	0.06
Lithuanian (33)	142	0.54
Northern European (13)	13	0.05
Norwegian (50)	124	0.47
Polish (500)	1,607	6.15
Portuguese (368)	597	2.29
Russian (290)	552	2.11
Scandinavian (0)	44	0.17
Scotch-Irish (495)	874	3.35
Scottish (319)	988	3.78
Serbian (16)	16	0.06
Slovak (0)	16	0.06
Swedish (130)	412	1.58
Swiss (0)	31	0.12
Turkish (0)	16	0.06
Ukrainian (56)	85	0.33
Welsh (0)	84	0.32
West Indian, ex. Hispanic (26)	50	0.19
Haitian (0)	24	0.09
Jamaican (26)	26	0.10
Yugoslavian (0)	154	0.59

Hispanic Origin	Population	%
Hispanic or Latino (of any race)	618	2.33
Central American, ex. Mexican	71	0.27
Costa Rican	11	0.04
Guatemalan	20	0.08
Honduran	13	0.05
Nicaraguan	3	0.01
Panamanian	9	0.03
Salvadoran	13	0.05
Other Central American	2	0.01
Cuban	12	0.05
Dominican Republic	167	0.63
Mexican	87	0.33
Puerto Rican	126	0.48
South American	60	0.23
Argentinean	4	0.02
Bolivian	2	0.01
Colombian	21	0.08
Ecuadorian	9	0.03
Paraguayan	4	0.02
Peruvian	13	0.05
Uruguayan	1	<0.01
Venezuelan	5	0.02
Other South American	1	<0.01
Other Hispanic or Latino	95	0.36

Race*	Population	%
African-American/Black (282)	399	1.51
Not Hispanic (253)	352	1.33
Hispanic (29)	47	0.18
American Indian/Alaska Native (30)	88	0.33
Not Hispanic (24)	72	0.27
Hispanic (6)	16	0.06
Apache (0)	1	<0.01
Blackfeet (1)	3	0.01
Canadian/French Am. Ind. (1)	1	<0.01
Cherokee (2)	8	0.03
Cheyenne (1)	1	<0.01
Choctaw (0)	1	<0.01
Kiowa (1)	1	<0.01
Lumbee (1)	1	<0.01
Navajo (1)	1	<0.01
Seminole (1)	1	<0.01
Sioux (0)	1	<0.01
South American Ind. (0)	4	0.02
Asian (500)	574	2.17
Not Hispanic (498)	568	2.14
Hispanic (2)	6	0.02
Cambodian (18)	21	0.08
Chinese, ex. Taiwanese (97)	123	0.46
Filipino (42)	59	0.22
Indian (152)	166	0.63
Indonesian (0)	2	0.01
Japanese (23)	29	0.11
Korean (43)	57	0.22
Laotian (1)	1	<0.01
Malaysian (1)	1	<0.01
Nepalese (0)	2	0.01
Pakistani (23)	23	0.09
Taiwanese (11)	14	0.05
Thai (3)	4	0.02
Vietnamese (64)	70	0.26
Hawaii Native/Pacific Islander (4)	11	0.04
Not Hispanic (4)	11	0.04
Guamanian/Chamorro (0)	1	<0.01
Native Hawaiian (4)	6	0.02
White (25,227)	25,481	96.18
Not Hispanic (24,839)	25,050	94.55
Hispanic (388)	431	1.63

Dartmouth

Place Type: Town
County: Bristol
Population: 34,032†

Ancestry‡	Population	%
African, Sub-Saharan (470)	644	1.92
African (40)	59	0.18
Cape Verdean (430)	585	1.75
Albanian (0)	16	0.05
American (758)	758	2.26
Arab (82)	149	0.44
Arab (7)	20	0.06
Egyptian (8)	8	0.02
Lebanese (67)	103	0.31
Moroccan (0)	18	0.05
Austrian (14)	69	0.21
Belgian (0)	29	0.09
British (19)	19	0.06
Cajun (0)	107	0.32
Canadian (63)	136	0.41
Croatian (0)	10	0.03
Czech (12)	26	0.08
Czechoslovakian (36)	36	0.11
Dutch (15)	42	0.13
Eastern European (53)	53	0.16
English (1,285)	4,950	14.77
European (344)	357	1.07
Finnish (43)	74	0.22
French, ex. Basque (1,133)	4,265	12.72
French Canadian (872)	1,696	5.06
German (248)	1,308	3.90
Greek (244)	332	0.99
Hungarian (20)	105	0.31
Irish (1,218)	4,969	14.83
Israeli (112)	112	0.33
Italian (558)	1,620	4.83
Latvian (11)	26	0.08
Lithuanian (0)	51	0.15
Maltese (0)	18	0.05
Norwegian (100)	264	0.79
Polish (426)	2,012	6.00
Portuguese (9,675)	13,152	39.24
Romanian (5)	34	0.10
Russian (186)	421	1.26
Scandinavian (0)	18	0.05
Scotch-Irish (47)	203	0.61
Scottish (148)	459	1.37
Swedish (0)	288	0.86
Swiss (111)	167	0.50
Ukrainian (32)	143	0.43
Welsh (31)	64	0.19
West Indian, ex. Hispanic (76)	94	0.28
Barbadian (10)	10	0.03
Haitian (39)	39	0.12
Jamaican (8)	8	0.02
West Indian (19)	37	0.11

Hispanic Origin	Population	%
Hispanic or Latino (of any race)	805	2.37
Central American, ex. Mexican	37	0.11
Costa Rican	1	<0.01
Guatemalan	16	0.05
Honduran	7	0.02
Nicaraguan	5	0.01
Panamanian	2	0.01
Salvadoran	5	0.01
Other Central American	1	<0.01
Cuban	17	0.05
Dominican Republic	68	0.20
Mexican	82	0.24
Puerto Rican	320	0.94
South American	66	0.19
Argentinean	14	0.04
Bolivian	2	0.01
Chilean	2	0.01
Colombian	32	0.09
Ecuadorian	2	0.01
Peruvian	10	0.03
Venezuelan	4	0.01
Other Hispanic or Latino	215	0.63

Race*	Population	%
African-American/Black (869)	1,147	3.37
Not Hispanic (824)	1,082	3.18
Hispanic (45)	65	0.19
American Indian/Alaska Native (61)	193	0.57
Not Hispanic (48)	175	0.51
Hispanic (13)	18	0.05
Apache (0)	1	<0.01
Blackfeet (2)	5	0.01
Canadian/French Am. Ind. (0)	5	0.01
Central American Ind. (2)	3	0.01
Cherokee (2)	15	0.04
Chippewa (1)	2	0.01
Comanche (1)	1	<0.01
Creek (1)	1	<0.01
Iroquois (5)	5	0.01
Lumbee (0)	1	<0.01
Mexican American Ind. (2)	2	0.01
Seminole (0)	4	0.01
South American Ind. (0)	3	0.01
Yakama (0)	1	<0.01
Asian (651)	779	2.29
Not Hispanic (642)	765	2.25
Hispanic (9)	14	0.04
Cambodian (15)	21	0.06
Chinese, ex. Taiwanese (267)	303	0.89
Filipino (61)	83	0.24
Indian (111)	119	0.35
Indonesian (3)	4	0.01
Japanese (18)	32	0.09
Korean (47)	59	0.17
Laotian (2)	3	0.01
Nepalese (3)	4	0.01
Pakistani (16)	19	0.06
Sri Lankan (2)	2	0.01
Taiwanese (4)	4	0.01
Thai (11)	16	0.05
Vietnamese (71)	85	0.25
Hawaii Native/Pacific Islander (6)	47	0.14
Not Hispanic (6)	44	0.13
Hispanic (0)	3	0.01
Guamanian/Chamorro (1)	2	0.01
Native Hawaiian (3)	9	0.03
Samoan (0)	2	0.01
White (31,323)	31,835	93.54
Not Hispanic (30,802)	31,271	91.89
Hispanic (521)	564	1.66

*Notes: † The Census 2010 population figure is used to calculate the percentages in the Hispanic Origin and Race categories. Ancestry percentages are based on the 2006-2010 American Community Survey population (not shown); ‡ Numbers in parentheses indicate the number of people reporting a single ancestry; * Numbers in parentheses indicate the number of persons reporting this race alone, not in combination with any other race; Please refer to the Explanation of Data for more information.*

Dedham

Place Type: CDP/Town
County: Norfolk
Population: 24,729†

Ancestry‡	Population	%
African, Sub-Saharan (147)	176	0.72
African (86)	86	0.35
Cape Verdean (14)	43	0.18
Other Sub-Saharan African (47)	47	0.19
Albanian (24)	85	0.35
American (671)	671	2.76
Arab (394)	722	2.97
Arab (16)	16	0.07
Lebanese (306)	592	2.43
Moroccan (37)	37	0.15
Syrian (0)	42	0.17
Other Arab (35)	35	0.14
Armenian (51)	82	0.34
Austrian (14)	25	0.10
Belgian (0)	25	0.10
Brazilian (0)	32	0.13
British (53)	102	0.42
Bulgarian (9)	27	0.11
Canadian (116)	380	1.56
Croatian (11)	29	0.12
Czech (0)	17	0.07
Danish (34)	52	0.21
Dutch (0)	91	0.37
Eastern European (18)	34	0.14
English (560)	2,581	10.61
European (385)	423	1.74
Finnish (9)	50	0.21
French, ex. Basque (120)	851	3.50
French Canadian (217)	634	2.61
German (217)	1,563	6.43
Greek (508)	668	2.75
Hungarian (20)	56	0.23
Iranian (0)	7	0.03
Irish (4,522)	9,299	38.23
Israeli (24)	24	0.10
Italian (1,882)	4,609	18.95
Latvian (172)	172	0.71
Lithuanian (89)	216	0.89
Northern European (14)	14	0.06
Norwegian (50)	145	0.60
Polish (118)	650	2.67
Portuguese (232)	338	1.39
Romanian (15)	29	0.12
Russian (234)	488	2.01
Scandinavian (14)	28	0.12
Scotch-Irish (237)	695	2.86
Scottish (241)	593	2.44
Slovak (0)	22	0.09
Slovene (7)	7	0.03
Swedish (68)	322	1.32
Swiss (38)	130	0.53
Turkish (7)	19	0.08
Ukrainian (59)	143	0.59
Welsh (42)	133	0.55
West Indian, ex. Hispanic (437)	479	1.97
Haitian (311)	311	1.28
Jamaican (59)	73	0.30
Trinidadian/Tobagonian (59)	87	0.36
West Indian (8)	8	0.03
Yugoslavian (0)	8	0.03

Hispanic Origin	Population	%
Hispanic or Latino (of any race)	1,353	5.47
Central American, ex. Mexican	165	0.67
Costa Rican	14	0.06
Guatemalan	66	0.27
Honduran	33	0.13
Nicaraguan	7	0.03
Panamanian	5	0.02
Salvadoran	40	0.16
Cuban	47	0.19
Dominican Republic	223	0.90
Mexican	166	0.67
Puerto Rican	423	1.71
South American	162	0.66
Argentinean	12	0.05
Bolivian	2	0.01
Chilean	6	0.02
Colombian	69	0.28
Ecuadorian	11	0.04
Paraguayan	2	0.01
Peruvian	33	0.13
Uruguayan	1	<0.01
Venezuelan	26	0.11
Other Hispanic or Latino	167	0.68

Race*	Population	%
African-American/Black (1,344)	1,490	6.03
Not Hispanic (1,268)	1,380	5.58
Hispanic (76)	110	0.44
American Indian/Alaska Native (65)	135	0.55
Not Hispanic (46)	103	0.42
Hispanic (19)	32	0.13
Apache (0)	5	0.02
Blackfeet (3)	4	0.02
Central American Ind. (0)	3	0.01
Cherokee (5)	16	0.06
Cheyenne (1)	1	<0.01
Chippewa (1)	1	<0.01
Iroquois (9)	11	0.04
Menominee (0)	1	<0.01
Mexican American Ind. (1)	2	0.01
Pueblo (1)	1	<0.01
Shoshone (0)	1	<0.01
Sioux (1)	1	<0.01
South American Ind. (1)	1	<0.01
Asian (640)	804	3.25
Not Hispanic (632)	785	3.17
Hispanic (8)	19	0.08
Bangladeshi (1)	1	<0.01
Cambodian (8)	19	0.08
Chinese, ex. Taiwanese (202)	250	1.01
Filipino (117)	154	0.62
Indian (113)	132	0.53
Indonesian (4)	4	0.02
Japanese (29)	41	0.17
Korean (53)	69	0.28
Laotian (8)	8	0.03
Pakistani (22)	24	0.10
Sri Lankan (4)	6	0.02
Taiwanese (3)	3	0.01
Thai (5)	11	0.04
Vietnamese (52)	60	0.24
Hawaii Native/Pacific Islander (4)	21	0.08
Not Hispanic (4)	17	0.07
Hispanic (0)	4	0.02
Guamanian/Chamorro (0)	5	0.02
Native Hawaiian (1)	6	0.02
Samoan (2)	2	0.01
White (21,858)	22,220	89.85
Not Hispanic (21,047)	21,312	86.18
Hispanic (811)	908	3.67

Dennis

Place Type: Town
County: Barnstable
Population: 14,207†

Ancestry‡	Population	%
African, Sub-Saharan (102)	246	1.69
Cape Verdean (102)	246	1.69
Albanian (0)	17	0.12
American (1,649)	1,649	11.33
Arab (7)	48	0.33
Lebanese (0)	9	0.06
Syrian (7)	39	0.27
Armenian (25)	25	0.17
Austrian (39)	76	0.52
Brazilian (46)	63	0.43
British (58)	87	0.60
Canadian (90)	118	0.81
Czech (0)	19	0.13
Danish (10)	33	0.23
Dutch (15)	151	1.04
Eastern European (34)	34	0.23
English (1,036)	3,100	21.30
European (67)	92	0.63
Finnish (26)	35	0.24
French, ex. Basque (101)	720	4.95
French Canadian (125)	347	2.38
German (331)	1,268	8.71
Greek (41)	46	0.32
Hungarian (12)	27	0.19
Irish (1,772)	4,057	27.87
Italian (816)	1,889	12.98
Latvian (8)	17	0.12
Lithuanian (34)	211	1.45
Northern European (8)	8	0.05
Norwegian (30)	77	0.53
Pennsylvania German (7)	7	0.05
Polish (229)	707	4.86
Portuguese (221)	582	4.00
Russian (97)	122	0.84
Scandinavian (0)	14	0.10
Scotch-Irish (192)	386	2.65
Scottish (164)	539	3.70
Slovak (25)	95	0.65
Swedish (111)	368	2.53
Swiss (8)	25	0.17
Ukrainian (12)	20	0.14
Welsh (16)	68	0.47
West Indian, ex. Hispanic (359)	363	2.49
Haitian (359)	363	2.49

Hispanic Origin	Population	%
Hispanic or Latino (of any race)	306	2.15
Central American, ex. Mexican	20	0.14
Guatemalan	10	0.07
Nicaraguan	1	0.01
Salvadoran	5	0.04
Other Central American	4	0.03
Cuban	9	0.06
Dominican Republic	25	0.18
Mexican	76	0.53
Puerto Rican	104	0.73
South American	37	0.26
Argentinean	2	0.01
Bolivian	2	0.01
Chilean	5	0.04
Colombian	8	0.06
Ecuadorian	4	0.03
Peruvian	9	0.06
Venezuelan	7	0.05
Other Hispanic or Latino	35	0.25

Race*	Population	%
African-American/Black (302)	430	3.03
Not Hispanic (279)	383	2.70
Hispanic (23)	47	0.33
American Indian/Alaska Native (69)	168	1.18
Not Hispanic (56)	142	1.00
Hispanic (13)	26	0.18
Apache (4)	5	0.04
Blackfeet (0)	1	0.01
Cherokee (3)	21	0.15
Chippewa (0)	4	0.03
Iroquois (2)	6	0.04
Lumbee (1)	2	0.01
Mexican American Ind. (9)	10	0.07
Sioux (2)	3	0.02
South American Ind. (1)	1	0.01
Asian (81)	103	0.72
Not Hispanic (81)	102	0.72
Hispanic (0)	1	0.01
Burmese (2)	2	0.01
Cambodian (1)	1	0.01
Chinese, ex. Taiwanese (18)	23	0.16
Filipino (12)	16	0.11
Indian (5)	7	0.05
Japanese (7)	9	0.06
Korean (9)	10	0.07
Nepalese (0)	2	0.01

*Notes: † The Census 2010 population figure is used to calculate the percentages in the Hispanic Origin and Race categories. Ancestry percentages are based on the 2006-2010 American Community Survey population (not shown); ‡ Numbers in parentheses indicate the number of people reporting a single ancestry; * Numbers in parentheses indicate the number of persons reporting this race alone, not in combination with any other race; Please refer to the Explanation of Data for more information.*

Thai (2)	5	0.04
Vietnamese (23)	24	0.17
Hawaii Native/Pacific Islander (12)	20	0.14
Not Hispanic (9)	17	0.12
Hispanic (3)	3	0.02
Guamanian/Chamorro (4)	6	0.04
Native Hawaiian (1)	2	0.01
Samoan (0)	1	0.01
White (13,289)	13,502	95.04
Not Hispanic (13,117)	13,302	93.63
Hispanic (172)	200	1.41

Douglas

Place Type: Town
County: Worcester
Population: 8,471†

Ancestry‡	Population	%
African, Sub-Saharan (31)	31	0.38
South African (31)	31	0.38
American (571)	571	6.93
Arab (0)	16	0.19
Lebanese (0)	16	0.19
Armenian (39)	172	2.09
Brazilian (67)	67	0.81
Canadian (18)	18	0.22
Czech (0)	24	0.29
Czechoslovakian (0)	54	0.66
Dutch (90)	364	4.42
English (389)	1,725	20.94
Finnish (0)	12	0.15
French, ex. Basque (113)	1,899	23.05
French Canadian (329)	542	6.58
German (113)	572	6.94
Greek (0)	47	0.57
Hungarian (0)	38	0.46
Irish (550)	2,052	24.91
Italian (280)	1,164	14.13
Lithuanian (27)	114	1.38
Norwegian (0)	83	1.01
Polish (164)	1,076	13.06
Portuguese (0)	80	0.97
Romanian (0)	22	0.27
Russian (0)	63	0.76
Scotch-Irish (97)	113	1.37
Scottish (68)	308	3.74
Slovak (56)	99	1.20
Swedish (42)	347	4.21
Ukrainian (16)	65	0.79
Welsh (0)	59	0.72
West Indian, ex. Hispanic (14)	14	0.17
Jamaican (14)	14	0.17

Hispanic Origin	Population	%
Hispanic or Latino (of any race)	139	1.64
Central American, ex. Mexican	12	0.14
Guatemalan	6	0.07
Panamanian	2	0.02
Salvadoran	3	0.04
Other Central American	1	0.01
Cuban	4	0.05
Dominican Republic	7	0.08
Mexican	25	0.30
Puerto Rican	54	0.64
South American	15	0.18
Argentinean	3	0.04
Bolivian	5	0.06
Colombian	2	0.02
Ecuadorian	1	0.01
Peruvian	3	0.04
Venezuelan	1	0.01
Other Hispanic or Latino	22	0.26

Race*	Population	%
African-American/Black (45)	71	0.84
Not Hispanic (35)	60	0.71
Hispanic (10)	11	0.13
American Indian/Alaska Native (15)	63	0.74
Not Hispanic (14)	61	0.72
Hispanic (1)	2	0.02
Apache (1)	1	0.01
Blackfeet (0)	3	0.04
Canadian/French Am. Ind. (1)	1	0.01
Cherokee (4)	5	0.06
Cheyenne (0)	1	0.01
Chickasaw (3)	3	0.04
Iroquois (2)	4	0.05
Asian (76)	116	1.37
Not Hispanic (75)	114	1.35
Hispanic (1)	2	0.02
Cambodian (3)	9	0.11
Chinese, ex. Taiwanese (15)	28	0.33
Filipino (10)	18	0.21
Indian (16)	19	0.22
Japanese (6)	11	0.13
Korean (10)	12	0.14
Laotian (4)	12	0.14
Pakistani (1)	1	0.01
Sri Lankan (3)	6	0.07
Thai (0)	3	0.04
Vietnamese (1)	4	0.05
Hawaii Native/Pacific Islander (3)	7	0.08
Not Hispanic (3)	7	0.08
Guamanian/Chamorro (0)	4	0.05
Marshallese (1)	1	0.01
Tongan (1)	1	0.01
White (8,181)	8,303	98.02
Not Hispanic (8,074)	8,188	96.66
Hispanic (107)	115	1.36

Dracut

Place Type: Town
County: Middlesex
Population: 29,457†

Ancestry‡	Population	%
African, Sub-Saharan (365)	365	1.26
African (191)	191	0.66
Ghanaian (13)	13	0.04
Kenyan (114)	114	0.39
Ugandan (47)	47	0.16
American (1,134)	1,134	3.92
Arab (52)	80	0.28
Lebanese (32)	49	0.17
Syrian (20)	31	0.11
Armenian (15)	126	0.44
Austrian (13)	43	0.15
Belgian (0)	38	0.13
British (16)	75	0.26
Canadian (144)	276	0.95
Czech (0)	27	0.09
Danish (0)	48	0.17
Dutch (33)	181	0.63
Eastern European (50)	50	0.17
English (516)	2,577	8.90
European (134)	153	0.53
Finnish (17)	26	0.09
French, ex. Basque (2,163)	5,859	20.23
French Canadian (2,224)	3,531	12.19
German (211)	940	3.25
Greek (392)	1,362	4.70
Hungarian (14)	97	0.33
Irish (2,891)	7,864	27.15
Italian (1,317)	4,269	14.74
Lithuanian (71)	195	0.67
Northern European (15)	15	0.05
Norwegian (16)	60	0.21
Polish (831)	2,147	7.41
Portuguese (788)	1,553	5.36
Russian (82)	127	0.44
Scandinavian (13)	152	0.52
Scotch-Irish (180)	521	1.80
Scottish (207)	988	3.41
Slavic (0)	8	0.03
Slovene (31)	75	0.26
Swedish (0)	537	1.85
Ukrainian (0)	41	0.14
Welsh (0)	91	0.31
West Indian, ex. Hispanic (66)	66	0.23
Haitian (37)	37	0.13
West Indian (29)	29	0.10

Hispanic Origin	Population	%
Hispanic or Latino (of any race)	1,149	3.90
Central American, ex. Mexican	42	0.14
Costa Rican	3	0.01
Guatemalan	19	0.06
Honduran	4	0.01
Panamanian	6	0.02
Salvadoran	10	0.03
Cuban	24	0.08
Dominican Republic	98	0.33
Mexican	81	0.27
Puerto Rican	602	2.04
South American	166	0.56
Argentinean	5	0.02
Bolivian	3	0.01
Chilean	2	0.01
Colombian	129	0.44
Ecuadorian	17	0.06
Peruvian	7	0.02
Venezuelan	3	0.01
Other Hispanic or Latino	136	0.46

Race*	Population	%
African-American/Black (737)	896	3.04
Not Hispanic (691)	825	2.80
Hispanic (46)	71	0.24
American Indian/Alaska Native (40)	111	0.38
Not Hispanic (32)	95	0.32
Hispanic (8)	16	0.05
Blackfeet (0)	2	0.01
Cherokee (2)	7	0.02
Chippewa (1)	1	<0.01
Choctaw (1)	4	0.01
Cree (0)	3	0.01
Iroquois (1)	3	0.01
Seminole (1)	1	<0.01
Shoshone (0)	3	0.01
Sioux (1)	1	<0.01
Asian (1,186)	1,345	4.57
Not Hispanic (1,176)	1,318	4.47
Hispanic (10)	27	0.09
Bangladeshi (11)	11	0.04
Cambodian (358)	409	1.39
Chinese, ex. Taiwanese (144)	183	0.62
Filipino (64)	83	0.28
Indian (318)	349	1.18
Indonesian (1)	2	0.01
Japanese (4)	17	0.06
Korean (69)	90	0.31
Laotian (25)	41	0.14
Malaysian (1)	2	0.01
Pakistani (0)	1	<0.01
Taiwanese (6)	11	0.04
Thai (4)	6	0.02
Vietnamese (115)	131	0.44
Hawaii Native/Pacific Islander (7)	24	0.08
Not Hispanic (3)	18	0.06
Hispanic (4)	6	0.02
Guamanian/Chamorro (4)	4	0.01
Native Hawaiian (2)	10	0.03
Samoan (1)	2	0.01
White (26,610)	27,027	91.75
Not Hispanic (25,965)	26,266	89.17
Hispanic (645)	761	2.58

Dudley

Place Type: Town
County: Worcester
Population: 11,390†

Ancestry‡	Population	%
African, Sub-Saharan (13)	25	0.22
Cape Verdean (0)	12	0.11
Kenyan (13)	13	0.12
American (725)	725	6.49

*Notes: † The Census 2010 population figure is used to calculate the percentages in the Hispanic Origin and Race categories. Ancestry percentages are based on the 2006-2010 American Community Survey population (not shown); ‡ Numbers in parentheses indicate the number of people reporting a single ancestry; * Numbers in parentheses indicate the number of persons reporting this race alone, not in combination with any other race; Please refer to the Explanation of Data for more information.*

Armenian (0)	17	0.15
Austrian (0)	15	0.13
Belgian (19)	19	0.17
British (0)	17	0.15
Canadian (55)	106	0.95
Czechoslovakian (0)	12	0.11
Danish (0)	9	0.08
Dutch (13)	71	0.64
English (267)	1,178	10.55
European (15)	15	0.13
Finnish (25)	78	0.70
French, ex. Basque (532)	2,447	21.90
French Canadian (508)	960	8.59
German (89)	788	7.05
Greek (72)	100	0.90
Hungarian (0)	25	0.22
Irish (464)	2,360	21.13
Italian (298)	1,385	12.40
Lithuanian (20)	173	1.55
Norwegian (21)	60	0.54
Polish (1,321)	2,727	24.41
Portuguese (81)	230	2.06
Romanian (0)	54	0.48
Russian (16)	121	1.08
Scotch-Irish (96)	241	2.16
Scottish (38)	215	1.92
Slovak (44)	89	0.80
Swedish (80)	436	3.90
Swiss (0)	12	0.11
West Indian, ex. Hispanic (26)	34	0.30
Barbadian (13)	13	0.12
Haitian (13)	21	0.19

Hispanic Origin	Population	%
Hispanic or Latino (of any race)	330	2.90
Central American, ex. Mexican	8	0.07
Costa Rican	1	0.01
Guatemalan	1	0.01
Nicaraguan	3	0.03
Panamanian	1	0.01
Salvadoran	2	0.02
Cuban	9	0.08
Dominican Republic	8	0.07
Mexican	43	0.38
Puerto Rican	233	2.05
South American	17	0.15
Bolivian	2	0.02
Colombian	8	0.07
Ecuadorian	6	0.05
Peruvian	1	0.01
Other Hispanic or Latino	12	0.11

Race*	Population	%
African-American/Black (136)	190	1.67
Not Hispanic (118)	168	1.47
Hispanic (18)	22	0.19
American Indian/Alaska Native (16)	51	0.45
Not Hispanic (13)	47	0.41
Hispanic (3)	4	0.04
Blackfeet (0)	3	0.03
Cherokee (0)	4	0.04
Mexican American Ind. (1)	1	0.01
Sioux (1)	4	0.04
Tsimshian *(Alaska Native)* (1)	1	0.01
Asian (95)	134	1.18
Not Hispanic (93)	131	1.15
Hispanic (2)	3	0.03
Cambodian (4)	5	0.04
Chinese, ex. Taiwanese (15)	19	0.17
Filipino (13)	23	0.20
Indian (17)	17	0.15
Japanese (0)	8	0.07
Korean (6)	10	0.09
Laotian (22)	23	0.20
Pakistani (1)	3	0.03
Thai (3)	4	0.04
Vietnamese (6)	11	0.10
Hawaii Native/Pacific Islander (1)	12	0.11
Not Hispanic (1)	12	0.11
Native Hawaiian (1)	7	0.06
Samoan (0)	3	0.03
White (10,876)	11,033	96.87
Not Hispanic (10,682)	10,810	94.91
Hispanic (194)	223	1.96

Duxbury

Place Type: Town
County: Plymouth
Population: 15,059†

Ancestry‡	Population	%
African, Sub-Saharan (10)	10	0.07
South African (10)	10	0.07
American (608)	608	4.08
Arab (19)	51	0.34
Lebanese (11)	43	0.29
Syrian (8)	8	0.05
Armenian (137)	137	0.92
Assyrian/Chaldean/Syriac (7)	22	0.15
Australian (0)	27	0.18
Austrian (0)	59	0.40
Basque (0)	16	0.11
Belgian (0)	56	0.38
British (217)	227	1.52
Canadian (28)	88	0.59
Celtic (0)	27	0.18
Croatian (8)	8	0.05
Czech (10)	53	0.36
Czechoslovakian (0)	8	0.05
Danish (48)	108	0.72
Dutch (58)	152	1.02
English (850)	3,020	20.27
European (338)	352	2.36
Finnish (35)	51	0.34
French, ex. Basque (134)	797	5.35
French Canadian (49)	247	1.66
German (236)	1,991	13.37
Greek (27)	136	0.91
Hungarian (12)	25	0.17
Irish (2,544)	6,141	41.22
Italian (720)	2,245	15.07
Lithuanian (0)	126	0.85
Northern European (28)	28	0.19
Norwegian (34)	177	1.19
Polish (142)	602	4.04
Portuguese (54)	200	1.34
Romanian (10)	37	0.25
Russian (80)	158	1.06
Scandinavian (0)	20	0.13
Scotch-Irish (139)	298	2.00
Scottish (165)	629	4.22
Slovak (12)	12	0.08
Swedish (110)	574	3.85
Swiss (8)	60	0.40
Turkish (72)	72	0.48
Ukrainian (0)	10	0.07
Welsh (10)	97	0.65

Hispanic Origin	Population	%
Hispanic or Latino (of any race)	184	1.22
Central American, ex. Mexican	9	0.06
Costa Rican	1	0.01
Guatemalan	6	0.04
Honduran	1	0.01
Salvadoran	1	0.01
Cuban	20	0.13
Dominican Republic	3	0.02
Mexican	53	0.35
Puerto Rican	18	0.12
South American	42	0.28
Argentinean	11	0.07
Chilean	1	0.01
Colombian	11	0.07
Ecuadorian	2	0.01
Paraguayan	3	0.02
Peruvian	5	0.03
Uruguayan	1	0.01
Venezuelan	4	0.03
Other South American	4	0.03
Other Hispanic or Latino	39	0.26

Race*	Population	%
African-American/Black (62)	95	0.63
Not Hispanic (59)	87	0.58
Hispanic (3)	8	0.05
American Indian/Alaska Native (16)	39	0.26
Not Hispanic (16)	32	0.21
Hispanic (0)	7	0.05
Cherokee (2)	6	0.04
Chippewa (1)	2	0.01
Houma (1)	1	0.01
Mexican American Ind. (1)	1	0.01
Navajo (1)	1	0.01
Osage (1)	1	0.01
Asian (149)	215	1.43
Not Hispanic (148)	212	1.41
Hispanic (1)	3	0.02
Cambodian (1)	1	0.01
Chinese, ex. Taiwanese (73)	108	0.72
Filipino (6)	12	0.08
Indian (10)	16	0.11
Japanese (8)	23	0.15
Korean (27)	43	0.29
Pakistani (5)	7	0.05
Taiwanese (4)	4	0.03
Thai (2)	3	0.02
Vietnamese (4)	8	0.05
Hawaii Native/Pacific Islander (2)	9	0.06
Not Hispanic (2)	9	0.06
Native Hawaiian (2)	7	0.05
White (14,649)	14,757	97.99
Not Hispanic (14,499)	14,599	96.95
Hispanic (150)	158	1.05

East Bridgewater

Place Type: Town
County: Plymouth
Population: 13,794†

Ancestry‡	Population	%
African, Sub-Saharan (0)	13	0.10
Cape Verdean (0)	13	0.10
Albanian (0)	45	0.33
American (445)	445	3.26
Arab (50)	129	0.95
Lebanese (50)	129	0.95
Australian (16)	16	0.12
Brazilian (22)	32	0.23
British (27)	27	0.20
Cajun (11)	11	0.08
Canadian (35)	78	0.57
Celtic (95)	287	2.10
Danish (15)	144	1.06
Dutch (0)	69	0.51
English (518)	2,766	20.28
European (94)	94	0.69
Finnish (0)	55	0.40
French, ex. Basque (133)	1,294	9.49
French Canadian (92)	473	3.47
German (41)	1,187	8.70
Greek (22)	158	1.16
Hungarian (0)	30	0.22
Irish (1,490)	4,521	33.15
Italian (708)	2,209	16.20
Latvian (33)	47	0.34
Lithuanian (79)	219	1.61
Norwegian (37)	119	0.87
Polish (191)	709	5.20
Portuguese (258)	603	4.42
Russian (65)	169	1.24
Scotch-Irish (307)	843	6.18
Scottish (86)	325	2.38
Slovak (0)	3	0.02
Slovene (0)	10	0.07
Swedish (169)	710	5.21
Ukrainian (22)	22	0.16
Welsh (0)	49	0.36
West Indian, ex. Hispanic (13)	22	0.16

*Notes: † The Census 2010 population figure is used to calculate the percentages in the Hispanic Origin and Race categories. Ancestry percentages are based on the 2006-2010 American Community Survey population (not shown); ‡ Numbers in parentheses indicate the number of people reporting a single ancestry; * Numbers in parentheses indicate the number of persons reporting this race alone, not in combination with any other race; Please refer to the Explanation of Data for more information.*

Haitian (13)	22	0.16

Hispanic Origin	Population	%
Hispanic or Latino (of any race)	204	1.48
Central American, ex. Mexican	20	0.14
Guatemalan	8	0.06
Honduran	4	0.03
Nicaraguan	3	0.02
Salvadoran	5	0.04
Cuban	19	0.14
Dominican Republic	13	0.09
Mexican	33	0.24
Puerto Rican	68	0.49
South American	28	0.20
Argentinean	1	0.01
Bolivian	1	0.01
Chilean	3	0.02
Colombian	13	0.09
Ecuadorian	1	0.01
Peruvian	6	0.04
Venezuelan	3	0.02
Other Hispanic or Latino	23	0.17

Race*	Population	%
African-American/Black (216)	298	2.16
Not Hispanic (209)	276	2.00
Hispanic (7)	22	0.16
American Indian/Alaska Native (28)	84	0.61
Not Hispanic (25)	66	0.48
Hispanic (3)	18	0.13
Apache (0)	1	0.01
Blackfeet (0)	1	0.01
Canadian/French Am. Ind. (0)	1	0.01
Cherokee (1)	10	0.07
Creek (0)	2	0.01
Iroquois (0)	1	0.01
Mexican American Ind. (1)	1	0.01
Navajo (1)	1	0.01
Sioux (1)	1	0.01
Yaqui (0)	1	0.01
Yuman (0)	1	0.01
Asian (117)	183	1.33
Not Hispanic (117)	175	1.27
Hispanic (0)	8	0.06
Cambodian (1)	1	0.01
Chinese, ex. Taiwanese (25)	39	0.28
Filipino (15)	23	0.17
Hmong (3)	3	0.02
Indian (28)	35	0.25
Indonesian (1)	1	0.01
Japanese (7)	23	0.17
Korean (2)	5	0.04
Malaysian (1)	1	0.01
Pakistani (3)	4	0.03
Thai (2)	4	0.03
Vietnamese (27)	35	0.25
Hawaii Native/Pacific Islander (0)	11	0.08
Not Hispanic (0)	2	0.01
Hispanic (0)	9	0.07
White (13,139)	13,328	96.62
Not Hispanic (13,004)	13,167	95.45
Hispanic (135)	161	1.17

East Longmeadow

Place Type: Town
County: Hampden
Population: 15,720†

Ancestry‡	Population	%
African, Sub-Saharan (9)	38	0.25
African (0)	9	0.06
Cape Verdean (9)	29	0.19
American (337)	337	2.18
Arab (103)	264	1.71
Jordanian (83)	83	0.54
Lebanese (20)	165	1.07
Syrian (0)	16	0.10
Armenian (27)	27	0.17
Assyrian/Chaldean/Syriac (0)	8	0.05
Austrian (9)	30	0.19
Belgian (0)	42	0.27
Brazilian (37)	37	0.24
British (5)	16	0.10
Canadian (70)	154	1.00
Croatian (0)	15	0.10
Czech (0)	34	0.22
Danish (5)	17	0.11
Dutch (0)	53	0.34
English (504)	1,911	12.37
European (114)	137	0.89
Finnish (17)	48	0.31
French, ex. Basque (388)	2,318	15.01
French Canadian (408)	937	6.07
German (292)	1,332	8.62
Greek (112)	213	1.38
Hungarian (0)	46	0.30
Irish (1,265)	4,300	27.84
Italian (1,585)	3,831	24.80
Lithuanian (15)	20	0.13
Northern European (0)	9	0.06
Norwegian (9)	50	0.32
Polish (617)	1,589	10.29
Portuguese (26)	119	0.77
Russian (84)	120	0.78
Scotch-Irish (44)	182	1.18
Scottish (78)	492	3.19
Slovak (13)	26	0.17
Swedish (91)	337	2.18
Swiss (0)	25	0.16
Ukrainian (36)	36	0.23
Welsh (12)	48	0.31
West Indian, ex. Hispanic (56)	134	0.87
Haitian (56)	56	0.36
Jamaican (0)	40	0.26
West Indian (0)	38	0.25
Yugoslavian (0)	6	0.04

Hispanic Origin	Population	%
Hispanic or Latino (of any race)	357	2.27
Central American, ex. Mexican	9	0.06
Costa Rican	3	0.02
Guatemalan	2	0.01
Panamanian	4	0.03
Cuban	30	0.19
Dominican Republic	23	0.15
Mexican	35	0.22
Puerto Rican	179	1.14
South American	47	0.30
Argentinean	5	0.03
Bolivian	2	0.01
Chilean	3	0.02
Colombian	10	0.06
Ecuadorian	7	0.04
Peruvian	17	0.11
Venezuelan	3	0.02
Other Hispanic or Latino	34	0.22

Race*	Population	%
African-American/Black (222)	296	1.88
Not Hispanic (212)	266	1.69
Hispanic (10)	30	0.19
American Indian/Alaska Native (11)	58	0.37
Not Hispanic (9)	46	0.29
Hispanic (2)	12	0.08
Apache (0)	1	0.01
Blackfeet (0)	3	0.02
Canadian/French Am. Ind. (2)	2	0.01
Cherokee (0)	9	0.06
Choctaw (0)	2	0.01
Iroquois (0)	2	0.01
Mexican American Ind. (1)	3	0.02
Sioux (0)	1	0.01
Asian (377)	440	2.80
Not Hispanic (376)	433	2.75
Hispanic (1)	7	0.04
Cambodian (6)	6	0.04
Chinese, ex. Taiwanese (103)	115	0.73
Filipino (27)	41	0.26
Indian (86)	103	0.66
Indonesian (6)	7	0.04
Japanese (7)	15	0.10
Korean (29)	36	0.23
Laotian (4)	4	0.03
Pakistani (35)	36	0.23
Taiwanese (2)	9	0.06
Thai (2)	2	0.01
Vietnamese (57)	60	0.38
Hawaii Native/Pacific Islander (0)	8	0.05
Not Hispanic (0)	6	0.04
Hispanic (0)	2	0.01
Guamanian/Chamorro (0)	2	0.01
Native Hawaiian (0)	1	0.01
White (14,858)	15,008	95.47
Not Hispanic (14,612)	14,735	93.73
Hispanic (246)	273	1.74

Easthampton Town

Place Type: City
County: Hampshire
Population: 16,053†

Ancestry‡	Population	%
African, Sub-Saharan (0)	16	0.10
Cape Verdean (0)	16	0.10
American (386)	386	2.40
Arab (12)	25	0.16
Moroccan (12)	12	0.07
Syrian (0)	13	0.08
Armenian (0)	18	0.11
Austrian (0)	10	0.06
Belgian (15)	15	0.09
British (38)	53	0.33
Canadian (164)	319	1.99
Celtic (0)	31	0.19
Croatian (241)	241	1.50
Czechoslovakian (27)	48	0.30
Danish (0)	83	0.52
Dutch (15)	238	1.48
Eastern European (48)	48	0.30
English (438)	1,658	10.33
Estonian (15)	15	0.09
European (123)	123	0.77
Finnish (0)	50	0.31
French, ex. Basque (618)	2,919	18.18
French Canadian (998)	1,748	10.89
German (375)	1,749	10.89
Greek (17)	55	0.34
Hungarian (0)	35	0.22
Iranian (15)	40	0.25
Irish (960)	3,614	22.51
Italian (292)	1,309	8.15
Lithuanian (15)	148	0.92
Norwegian (31)	47	0.29
Polish (1,395)	3,016	18.79
Portuguese (0)	31	0.19
Romanian (0)	34	0.21
Russian (158)	289	1.80
Scandinavian (0)	6	0.04
Scotch-Irish (196)	428	2.67
Scottish (123)	536	3.34
Slavic (11)	11	0.07
Slovak (14)	50	0.31
Swedish (14)	107	0.67
Swiss (0)	76	0.47
Ukrainian (83)	111	0.69
Welsh (10)	92	0.57
West Indian, ex. Hispanic (79)	102	0.64
Haitian (0)	23	0.14
Trinidadian/Tobagonian (79)	79	0.49
Yugoslavian (17)	17	0.11

Hispanic Origin	Population	%
Hispanic or Latino (of any race)	590	3.68
Central American, ex. Mexican	30	0.19
Guatemalan	5	0.03
Honduran	4	0.02
Panamanian	2	0.01
Salvadoran	19	0.12

*Notes: † The Census 2010 population figure is used to calculate the percentages in the Hispanic Origin and Race categories. Ancestry percentages are based on the 2006-2010 American Community Survey population (not shown); ‡ Numbers in parentheses indicate the number of people reporting a single ancestry; * Numbers in parentheses indicate the number of persons reporting this race alone, not in combination with any other race; Please refer to the Explanation of Data for more information.*

Cuban	10	0.06
Dominican Republic	14	0.09
Mexican	89	0.55
Puerto Rican	372	2.32
South American	31	0.19
Bolivian	1	0.01
Chilean	2	0.01
Colombian	10	0.06
Ecuadorian	11	0.07
Peruvian	6	0.04
Venezuelan	1	0.01
Other Hispanic or Latino	44	0.27

Race*	Population	%
African-American/Black (174)	265	1.65
Not Hispanic (160)	230	1.43
Hispanic (14)	35	0.22
American Indian/Alaska Native (31)	103	0.64
Not Hispanic (31)	96	0.60
Hispanic (0)	7	0.04
Blackfeet (0)	8	0.05
Canadian/French Am. Ind. (1)	1	0.01
Cherokee (1)	13	0.08
Choctaw (0)	2	0.01
Cree (0)	1	0.01
Iroquois (4)	10	0.06
Sioux (1)	2	0.01
South American Ind. (0)	1	0.01
Asian (380)	459	2.86
Not Hispanic (378)	453	2.82
Hispanic (2)	6	0.04
Cambodian (112)	114	0.71
Chinese, ex. Taiwanese (70)	88	0.55
Filipino (18)	28	0.17
Indian (76)	88	0.55
Indonesian (1)	3	0.02
Japanese (5)	12	0.07
Korean (29)	44	0.27
Malaysian (1)	1	0.01
Nepalese (1)	1	0.01
Pakistani (8)	17	0.11
Sri Lankan (2)	2	0.01
Thai (14)	15	0.09
Vietnamese (15)	25	0.16
Hawaii Native/Pacific Islander (4)	13	0.08
Not Hispanic (3)	10	0.06
Hispanic (1)	3	0.02
Native Hawaiian (4)	9	0.06
White (15,026)	15,250	95.00
Not Hispanic (14,677)	14,857	92.55
Hispanic (349)	393	2.45

Easton

Place Type: Town
County: Bristol
Population: 23,112†

Ancestry‡	Population	%
African, Sub-Saharan (101)	232	1.01
African (0)	14	0.06
Cape Verdean (101)	188	0.82
Liberian (0)	15	0.07
Other Sub-Saharan African (0)	15	0.07
Albanian (21)	21	0.09
American (858)	858	3.73
Arab (27)	244	1.06
Lebanese (27)	244	1.06
Armenian (18)	51	0.22
Austrian (9)	74	0.32
Belgian (15)	25	0.11
Brazilian (127)	155	0.67
British (56)	74	0.32
Canadian (36)	163	0.71
Croatian (0)	14	0.06
Czech (14)	14	0.06
Czechoslovakian (0)	44	0.19
Danish (24)	127	0.55
Dutch (9)	125	0.54
Eastern European (120)	120	0.52
English (638)	3,475	15.10
European (111)	111	0.48
Finnish (0)	66	0.29
French, ex. Basque (219)	1,412	6.13
French Canadian (390)	1,085	4.71
German (188)	1,697	7.37
Greek (239)	501	2.18
Guyanese (15)	15	0.07
Hungarian (13)	79	0.34
Icelander (21)	21	0.09
Irish (3,168)	8,252	35.85
Italian (1,209)	3,611	15.69
Latvian (13)	24	0.10
Lithuanian (65)	489	2.12
Luxemburger (13)	28	0.12
Norwegian (0)	85	0.37
Polish (175)	801	3.48
Portuguese (486)	913	3.97
Romanian (9)	46	0.20
Russian (284)	692	3.01
Scotch-Irish (189)	574	2.49
Scottish (171)	813	3.53
Serbian (26)	26	0.11
Slavic (0)	14	0.06
Slovak (15)	57	0.25
Swedish (251)	1,194	5.19
Swiss (10)	20	0.09
Ukrainian (34)	71	0.31
Welsh (21)	95	0.41
West Indian, ex. Hispanic (83)	83	0.36
Barbadian (12)	12	0.05
Haitian (40)	40	0.17
Jamaican (31)	31	0.13

Hispanic Origin	Population	%
Hispanic or Latino (of any race)	575	2.49
Central American, ex. Mexican	69	0.30
Costa Rican	12	0.05
Guatemalan	21	0.09
Honduran	6	0.03
Nicaraguan	6	0.03
Panamanian	8	0.03
Salvadoran	16	0.07
Cuban	33	0.14
Dominican Republic	49	0.21
Mexican	68	0.29
Puerto Rican	155	0.67
South American	109	0.47
Argentinean	5	0.02
Bolivian	2	0.01
Chilean	5	0.02
Colombian	42	0.18
Ecuadorian	5	0.02
Peruvian	27	0.12
Uruguayan	5	0.02
Venezuelan	18	0.08
Other Hispanic or Latino	92	0.40

Race*	Population	%
African-American/Black (745)	906	3.92
Not Hispanic (725)	867	3.75
Hispanic (20)	39	0.17
American Indian/Alaska Native (20)	80	0.35
Not Hispanic (17)	71	0.31
Hispanic (3)	9	0.04
Apache (1)	1	<0.01
Blackfeet (1)	5	0.02
Central American Ind. (0)	1	<0.01
Cherokee (3)	10	0.04
Choctaw (0)	1	<0.01
Cree (1)	2	0.01
Iroquois (0)	6	0.03
Mexican American Ind. (1)	3	0.01
Navajo (0)	1	<0.01
Seminole (0)	1	<0.01
South American Ind. (1)	2	0.01
Yup'ik *(Alaska Native)* (0)	1	<0.01
Asian (563)	708	3.06
Not Hispanic (561)	697	3.02
Hispanic (2)	11	0.05
Bangladeshi (19)	19	0.08
Cambodian (4)	5	0.02
Chinese, ex. Taiwanese (165)	197	0.85
Filipino (44)	65	0.28
Hmong (5)	5	0.02
Indian (118)	131	0.57
Indonesian (0)	3	0.01
Japanese (4)	25	0.11
Korean (69)	87	0.38
Laotian (1)	2	0.01
Malaysian (0)	1	<0.01
Pakistani (10)	11	0.05
Sri Lankan (2)	2	0.01
Taiwanese (7)	7	0.03
Thai (5)	7	0.03
Vietnamese (85)	98	0.42
Hawaii Native/Pacific Islander (5)	18	0.08
Not Hispanic (4)	16	0.07
Hispanic (1)	2	0.01
Guamanian/Chamorro (1)	5	0.02
Native Hawaiian (2)	4	0.02
Samoan (1)	1	<0.01
White (21,144)	21,493	92.99
Not Hispanic (20,785)	21,088	91.24
Hispanic (359)	405	1.75

Everett

Place Type: City
County: Middlesex
Population: 41,667†

Ancestry‡	Population	%
African, Sub-Saharan (585)	653	1.61
African (59)	91	0.22
Cape Verdean (219)	255	0.63
Ethiopian (55)	55	0.14
Ghanaian (30)	30	0.07
Nigerian (107)	107	0.26
Ugandan (115)	115	0.28
Albanian (227)	227	0.56
American (684)	684	1.69
Arab (382)	526	1.30
Arab (102)	221	0.54
Moroccan (203)	216	0.53
Syrian (0)	12	0.03
Other Arab (77)	77	0.19
Armenian (17)	29	0.07
Belgian (12)	73	0.18
Brazilian (3,052)	3,406	8.40
British (11)	23	0.06
Bulgarian (58)	58	0.14
Cajun (0)	18	0.04
Canadian (148)	523	1.29
Celtic (0)	115	0.28
Croatian (75)	75	0.18
Dutch (5)	61	0.15
English (350)	1,449	3.57
European (41)	41	0.10
Finnish (0)	24	0.06
French, ex. Basque (149)	1,604	3.95
French Canadian (379)	1,096	2.70
German (156)	1,197	2.95
Greek (85)	168	0.41
Hungarian (0)	16	0.04
Iranian (19)	19	0.05
Irish (2,088)	7,106	17.52
Italian (5,457)	10,105	24.91
Lithuanian (0)	178	0.44
Norwegian (15)	146	0.36
Polish (169)	767	1.89
Portuguese (1,670)	2,434	6.00
Romanian (12)	71	0.18
Russian (68)	303	0.75
Scotch-Irish (186)	511	1.26
Scottish (119)	467	1.15
Serbian (33)	33	0.08
Slovak (50)	63	0.16
Swedish (56)	187	0.46
Ukrainian (62)	72	0.18

SECTION TWO

*Notes: † The Census 2010 population figure is used to calculate the percentages in the Hispanic Origin and Race categories. Ancestry percentages are based on the 2006-2010 American Community Survey population (not shown); ‡ Numbers in parentheses indicate the number of people reporting a single ancestry; * Numbers in parentheses indicate the number of persons reporting this race alone, not in combination with any other race; Please refer to the Explanation of Data for more information.*

Welsh (26)	82	0.20
West Indian, ex. Hispanic (2,891)	3,103	7.65
Bahamian (123)	123	0.30
Barbadian (13)	25	0.06
Haitian (2,727)	2,888	7.12
Jamaican (28)	67	0.17
Yugoslavian (215)	215	0.53

Hispanic Origin	Population	%
Hispanic or Latino (of any race)	8,792	21.10
Central American, ex. Mexican	4,673	11.22
Costa Rican	46	0.11
Guatemalan	422	1.01
Honduran	241	0.58
Nicaraguan	34	0.08
Panamanian	8	0.02
Salvadoran	3,895	9.35
Other Central American	27	0.06
Cuban	98	0.24
Dominican Republic	462	1.11
Mexican	353	0.85
Puerto Rican	1,242	2.98
South American	833	2.00
Argentinean	44	0.11
Bolivian	5	0.01
Chilean	24	0.06
Colombian	478	1.15
Ecuadorian	30	0.07
Peruvian	181	0.43
Uruguayan	23	0.06
Venezuelan	34	0.08
Other South American	14	0.03
Other Hispanic or Latino	1,131	2.71

Race*	Population	%
African-American/Black (5,962)	6,491	15.58
Not Hispanic (5,652)	6,066	14.56
Hispanic (310)	425	1.02
American Indian/Alaska Native (162)	335	0.80
Not Hispanic (84)	198	0.48
Hispanic (78)	137	0.33
Blackfeet (0)	5	0.01
Canadian/French Am. Ind. (1)	1	<0.01
Central American Ind. (0)	3	0.01
Cherokee (4)	25	0.06
Chickasaw (0)	3	0.01
Choctaw (0)	1	<0.01
Creek (0)	1	<0.01
Hopi (0)	2	<0.01
Iroquois (3)	3	0.01
Mexican American Ind. (24)	26	0.06
Navajo (0)	2	<0.01
Pima (1)	1	<0.01
Seminole (0)	4	0.01
Sioux (1)	1	<0.01
South American Ind. (0)	8	0.02
Spanish American Ind. (1)	6	0.01
Tlingit-Haida *(Alaska Native)* (0)	2	<0.01
Tohono O'Odham (1)	1	<0.01
Ute (1)	1	<0.01
Yuman (0)	3	0.01
Yup'ik *(Alaska Native)* (1)	1	<0.01
Asian (2,005)	2,192	5.26
Not Hispanic (1,982)	2,131	5.11
Hispanic (23)	61	0.15
Bangladeshi (16)	26	0.06
Burmese (5)	5	0.01
Cambodian (46)	65	0.16
Chinese, ex. Taiwanese (259)	303	0.73
Filipino (96)	121	0.29
Hmong (2)	2	<0.01
Indian (292)	337	0.81
Indonesian (2)	2	<0.01
Japanese (12)	30	0.07
Korean (47)	60	0.14
Laotian (5)	8	0.02
Nepalese (23)	24	0.06
Pakistani (56)	61	0.15
Sri Lankan (15)	15	0.04
Taiwanese (9)	13	0.03
Thai (11)	22	0.05
Vietnamese (1,006)	1,051	2.52
Hawaii Native/Pacific Islander (18)	92	0.22
Not Hispanic (13)	69	0.17
Hispanic (5)	23	0.06
Guamanian/Chamorro (11)	11	0.03
Native Hawaiian (4)	17	0.04
White (26,177)	27,457	65.90
Not Hispanic (22,316)	23,124	55.50
Hispanic (3,861)	4,333	10.40

Fairhaven

Place Type: Town
County: Bristol
Population: 15,873†

Ancestry‡	Population	%
African, Sub-Saharan (116)	191	1.20
Cape Verdean (116)	191	1.20
Albanian (16)	16	0.10
American (761)	761	4.78
Arab (44)	232	1.46
Lebanese (20)	208	1.31
Syrian (24)	24	0.15
Australian (8)	8	0.05
Austrian (0)	9	0.06
Belgian (0)	26	0.16
British (40)	88	0.55
Cajun (0)	19	0.12
Canadian (90)	118	0.74
Danish (0)	12	0.08
Dutch (0)	54	0.34
English (661)	2,439	15.31
European (127)	127	0.80
Finnish (21)	72	0.45
French, ex. Basque (865)	2,810	17.64
French Canadian (632)	1,220	7.66
German (57)	703	4.41
Greek (0)	60	0.38
Irish (567)	2,687	16.86
Italian (366)	943	5.92
Latvian (7)	7	0.04
Lithuanian (12)	51	0.32
Northern European (11)	11	0.07
Norwegian (133)	275	1.73
Polish (403)	1,321	8.29
Portuguese (3,126)	5,225	32.79
Russian (0)	45	0.28
Scandinavian (12)	22	0.14
Scotch-Irish (53)	153	0.96
Scottish (52)	197	1.24
Swedish (26)	138	0.87
Swiss (0)	35	0.22
Ukrainian (0)	28	0.18
Welsh (9)	92	0.58

Hispanic Origin	Population	%
Hispanic or Latino (of any race)	198	1.25
Central American, ex. Mexican	26	0.16
Costa Rican	1	0.01
Guatemalan	21	0.13
Honduran	2	0.01
Nicaraguan	1	0.01
Salvadoran	1	0.01
Cuban	6	0.04
Dominican Republic	5	0.03
Mexican	23	0.14
Puerto Rican	91	0.57
South American	14	0.09
Argentinean	1	0.01
Bolivian	3	0.02
Colombian	3	0.02
Ecuadorian	3	0.02
Peruvian	2	0.01
Venezuelan	2	0.01
Other Hispanic or Latino	33	0.21

Race*	Population	%
African-American/Black (145)	233	1.47
Not Hispanic (140)	228	1.44
Hispanic (5)	5	0.03
American Indian/Alaska Native (25)	82	0.52
Not Hispanic (23)	73	0.46
Hispanic (2)	9	0.06
Blackfeet (0)	1	0.01
Canadian/French Am. Ind. (1)	1	0.01
Cherokee (0)	2	0.01
Cheyenne (0)	1	0.01
Chippewa (2)	3	0.02
Choctaw (0)	1	0.01
Iroquois (0)	3	0.02
Mexican American Ind. (0)	3	0.02
Asian (154)	174	1.10
Not Hispanic (152)	169	1.06
Hispanic (2)	5	0.03
Burmese (3)	3	0.02
Cambodian (2)	5	0.03
Chinese, ex. Taiwanese (75)	84	0.53
Filipino (10)	16	0.10
Hmong (4)	4	0.03
Indian (11)	13	0.08
Japanese (3)	4	0.03
Korean (5)	5	0.03
Malaysian (0)	1	0.01
Taiwanese (1)	1	0.01
Thai (2)	2	0.01
Vietnamese (29)	30	0.19
Hawaii Native/Pacific Islander (9)	13	0.08
Not Hispanic (9)	13	0.08
Guamanian/Chamorro (1)	1	0.01
Samoan (2)	4	0.03
White (15,166)	15,342	96.65
Not Hispanic (15,034)	15,199	95.75
Hispanic (132)	143	0.90

Fall River

Place Type: City
County: Bristol
Population: 88,857†

Ancestry‡	Population	%
African, Sub-Saharan (926)	1,945	2.17
African (131)	253	0.28
Cape Verdean (715)	1,574	1.76
Liberian (14)	14	0.02
Nigerian (35)	35	0.04
Other Sub-Saharan African (31)	69	0.08
Albanian (0)	13	0.01
American (1,386)	1,386	1.55
Arab (809)	1,258	1.41
Arab (0)	38	0.04
Lebanese (793)	1,149	1.28
Syrian (0)	38	0.04
Other Arab (16)	33	0.04
Armenian (0)	13	0.01
Austrian (42)	52	0.06
Belgian (0)	16	0.02
Brazilian (1,030)	1,197	1.34
British (79)	210	0.23
Canadian (112)	209	0.23
Celtic (14)	28	0.03
Czech (0)	19	0.02
Czechoslovakian (0)	39	0.04
Danish (0)	34	0.04
Dutch (24)	234	0.26
Eastern European (17)	17	0.02
English (2,180)	7,382	8.25
European (129)	129	0.14
Finnish (25)	81	0.09
French, ex. Basque (4,356)	14,459	16.16
French Canadian (2,353)	4,538	5.07
German (449)	2,761	3.09
Greek (105)	146	0.16
Hungarian (13)	13	0.01
Icelander (0)	38	0.04
Irish (2,288)	9,661	10.80
Italian (1,357)	5,669	6.34
Lithuanian (27)	99	0.11

*Notes: † The Census 2010 population figure is used to calculate the percentages in the Hispanic Origin and Race categories. Ancestry percentages are based on the 2006-2010 American Community Survey population (not shown); ‡ Numbers in parentheses indicate the number of people reporting a single ancestry; * Numbers in parentheses indicate the number of persons reporting this race alone, not in combination with any other race; Please refer to the Explanation of Data for more information.*

Ancestry (continued)	Population	%
Norwegian (0)	61	0.07
Polish (875)	3,401	3.80
Portuguese (28,622)	41,494	46.37
Romanian (45)	60	0.07
Russian (113)	274	0.31
Scandinavian (29)	42	0.05
Scotch-Irish (161)	418	0.47
Scottish (300)	1,223	1.37
Serbian (8)	8	0.01
Slavic (0)	8	0.01
Swedish (32)	327	0.37
Swiss (0)	53	0.06
Turkish (9)	9	0.01
Ukrainian (37)	95	0.11
Welsh (0)	134	0.15
West Indian, ex. Hispanic (247)	493	0.55
Bahamian (0)	126	0.14
Belizean (29)	29	0.03
Haitian (218)	218	0.24
Jamaican (0)	70	0.08
West Indian (0)	50	0.06

Hispanic Origin	Population	%
Hispanic or Latino (of any race)	6,562	7.38
Central American, ex. Mexican	358	0.40
Costa Rican	8	0.01
Guatemalan	84	0.09
Honduran	148	0.17
Nicaraguan	8	0.01
Panamanian	4	<0.01
Salvadoran	102	0.11
Other Central American	4	<0.01
Cuban	101	0.11
Dominican Republic	423	0.48
Mexican	321	0.36
Puerto Rican	4,401	4.95
South American	323	0.36
Argentinean	9	0.01
Bolivian	11	0.01
Chilean	7	0.01
Colombian	39	0.04
Ecuadorian	194	0.22
Paraguayan	2	<0.01
Peruvian	36	0.04
Uruguayan	2	<0.01
Venezuelan	16	0.02
Other South American	7	0.01
Other Hispanic or Latino	635	0.71

Race*	Population	%
African-American/Black (3,466)	4,739	5.33
Not Hispanic (3,016)	4,079	4.59
Hispanic (450)	660	0.74
American Indian/Alaska Native (250)	742	0.84
Not Hispanic (163)	581	0.65
Hispanic (87)	161	0.18
Apache (1)	7	0.01
Blackfeet (6)	16	0.02
Canadian/French Am. Ind. (1)	5	0.01
Central American Ind. (2)	2	<0.01
Cherokee (14)	59	0.07
Cheyenne (0)	1	<0.01
Chickasaw (0)	2	<0.01
Chippewa (2)	7	0.01
Choctaw (0)	7	0.01
Cree (0)	5	0.01
Creek (0)	3	<0.01
Crow (0)	2	<0.01
Hopi (0)	1	<0.01
Iroquois (4)	18	0.02
Menominee (4)	5	0.01
Mexican American Ind. (10)	11	0.01
Navajo (0)	3	<0.01
Paiute (0)	1	<0.01
Potawatomi (1)	1	<0.01
Pueblo (1)	1	<0.01
Seminole (1)	4	<0.01
Sioux (6)	8	0.01
South American Ind. (5)	13	0.01
Spanish American Ind. (2)	2	<0.01
Tlingit-Haida *(Alaska Native)* (0)	4	<0.01
Yup'ik *(Alaska Native)* (0)	1	<0.01
Asian (2,275)	2,617	2.95
Not Hispanic (2,249)	2,550	2.87
Hispanic (26)	67	0.08
Bangladeshi (13)	13	0.01
Burmese (4)	5	0.01
Cambodian (1,147)	1,241	1.40
Chinese, ex. Taiwanese (254)	317	0.36
Filipino (92)	168	0.19
Hmong (2)	2	<0.01
Indian (268)	332	0.37
Indonesian (3)	3	<0.01
Japanese (14)	52	0.06
Korean (43)	79	0.09
Laotian (21)	27	0.03
Malaysian (1)	2	<0.01
Nepalese (1)	1	<0.01
Pakistani (39)	44	0.05
Taiwanese (7)	8	0.01
Thai (22)	50	0.06
Vietnamese (147)	170	0.19
Hawaii Native/Pacific Islander (30)	195	0.22
Not Hispanic (10)	133	0.15
Hispanic (20)	62	0.07
Guamanian/Chamorro (7)	20	0.02
Native Hawaiian (8)	26	0.03
White (77,349)	79,442	89.40
Not Hispanic (74,107)	75,784	85.29
Hispanic (3,242)	3,658	4.12

Falmouth

Place Type: Town
County: Barnstable
Population: 31,531†

Ancestry‡	Population	%
African, Sub-Saharan (175)	287	0.90
African (0)	27	0.08
Cape Verdean (133)	218	0.69
Ethiopian (22)	22	0.07
South African (20)	20	0.06
Alsatian (0)	19	0.06
American (4,439)	4,439	13.96
Arab (60)	72	0.23
Lebanese (45)	57	0.18
Moroccan (15)	15	0.05
Armenian (96)	113	0.36
Austrian (38)	103	0.32
Belgian (0)	46	0.14
Brazilian (73)	73	0.23
British (218)	356	1.12
Bulgarian (0)	21	0.07
Canadian (168)	241	0.76
Celtic (14)	14	0.04
Croatian (9)	26	0.08
Czech (14)	147	0.46
Danish (47)	122	0.38
Dutch (65)	327	1.03
English (1,397)	4,939	15.53
European (243)	279	0.88
Finnish (76)	198	0.62
French, ex. Basque (332)	1,556	4.89
French Canadian (307)	918	2.89
German (669)	2,845	8.95
Greek (229)	419	1.32
Hungarian (0)	56	0.18
Icelander (10)	10	0.03
Iranian (47)	47	0.15
Irish (4,069)	8,834	27.78
Italian (835)	2,996	9.42
Latvian (44)	93	0.29
Lithuanian (156)	318	1.00
Maltese (0)	48	0.15
Northern European (40)	40	0.13
Norwegian (29)	229	0.72
Polish (492)	1,473	4.63
Portuguese (1,613)	2,589	8.14
Romanian (66)	93	0.29
Russian (297)	690	2.17
Scandinavian (0)	54	0.17
Scotch-Irish (248)	571	1.80
Scottish (348)	1,096	3.45
Slovak (11)	11	0.03
Slovene (0)	17	0.05
Swedish (221)	634	1.99
Swiss (28)	56	0.18
Ukrainian (12)	54	0.17
Welsh (61)	192	0.60
West Indian, ex. Hispanic (73)	158	0.50
Jamaican (60)	110	0.35
Trinidadian/Tobagonian (13)	29	0.09
West Indian (0)	19	0.06

Hispanic Origin	Population	%
Hispanic or Latino (of any race)	565	1.79
Central American, ex. Mexican	37	0.12
Costa Rican	6	0.02
Guatemalan	11	0.03
Honduran	5	0.02
Panamanian	10	0.03
Salvadoran	5	0.02
Cuban	28	0.09
Dominican Republic	15	0.05
Mexican	105	0.33
Puerto Rican	210	0.67
South American	62	0.20
Argentinean	14	0.04
Bolivian	4	0.01
Chilean	9	0.03
Colombian	19	0.06
Ecuadorian	2	0.01
Paraguayan	2	0.01
Peruvian	6	0.02
Uruguayan	1	<0.01
Venezuelan	5	0.02
Other Hispanic or Latino	108	0.34

Race*	Population	%
African-American/Black (594)	963	3.05
Not Hispanic (576)	927	2.94
Hispanic (18)	36	0.11
American Indian/Alaska Native (183)	450	1.43
Not Hispanic (163)	405	1.28
Hispanic (20)	45	0.14
Blackfeet (3)	19	0.06
Cherokee (7)	42	0.13
Choctaw (2)	3	0.01
Cree (0)	1	<0.01
Creek (0)	1	<0.01
Inupiat *(Alaska Native)* (1)	2	0.01
Iroquois (2)	7	0.02
Mexican American Ind. (3)	3	0.01
Osage (0)	2	0.01
Potawatomi (0)	1	<0.01
Seminole (0)	1	<0.01
Shoshone (0)	3	0.01
Sioux (0)	8	0.03
South American Ind. (2)	3	0.01
Spanish American Ind. (1)	1	<0.01
Yup'ik *(Alaska Native)* (1)	1	<0.01
Asian (409)	556	1.76
Not Hispanic (405)	549	1.74
Hispanic (4)	7	0.02
Burmese (1)	2	0.01
Cambodian (1)	4	0.01
Chinese, ex. Taiwanese (118)	158	0.50
Filipino (33)	71	0.23
Indian (84)	103	0.33
Indonesian (1)	1	<0.01
Japanese (39)	70	0.22
Korean (40)	54	0.17
Laotian (1)	1	<0.01
Pakistani (5)	5	0.02
Sri Lankan (3)	3	0.01
Taiwanese (15)	16	0.05
Thai (6)	7	0.02
Vietnamese (38)	48	0.15
Hawaii Native/Pacific Islander (12)	45	0.14

*Notes: † The Census 2010 population figure is used to calculate the percentages in the Hispanic Origin and Race categories. Ancestry percentages are based on the 2006-2010 American Community Survey population (not shown); ‡ Numbers in parentheses indicate the number of people reporting a single ancestry; * Numbers in parentheses indicate the number of persons reporting this race alone, not in combination with any other race; Please refer to the Explanation of Data for more information.*

Not Hispanic (12)	41	0.13
Hispanic (0)	4	0.01
Guamanian/Chamorro (1)	3	0.01
Native Hawaiian (1)	15	0.05
Samoan (0)	2	0.01
White (28,979)	29,691	94.16
Not Hispanic (28,612)	29,273	92.84
Hispanic (367)	418	1.33

Fitchburg

Place Type: City
County: Worcester
Population: 40,318†

Ancestry‡	Population	%
African, Sub-Saharan (519)	614	1.53
African (95)	132	0.33
Cape Verdean (49)	70	0.17
Ghanaian (0)	37	0.09
Kenyan (161)	161	0.40
Nigerian (139)	139	0.35
Other Sub-Saharan African (75)	75	0.19
Albanian (9)	47	0.12
American (836)	836	2.08
Arab (50)	78	0.19
Jordanian (18)	18	0.04
Lebanese (21)	49	0.12
Moroccan (11)	11	0.03
Armenian (0)	42	0.10
Austrian (13)	22	0.05
Brazilian (130)	130	0.32
British (63)	105	0.26
Cajun (35)	35	0.09
Canadian (393)	578	1.44
Cypriot (8)	8	0.02
Czech (0)	41	0.10
Czechoslovakian (8)	8	0.02
Danish (0)	101	0.25
Dutch (40)	301	0.75
Eastern European (22)	22	0.05
English (647)	3,599	8.95
European (55)	71	0.18
Finnish (399)	1,167	2.90
French, ex. Basque (2,177)	6,411	15.94
French Canadian (2,255)	4,262	10.60
German (604)	2,545	6.33
Greek (492)	859	2.14
Hungarian (47)	256	0.64
Iranian (0)	9	0.02
Irish (1,719)	6,707	16.68
Italian (1,841)	4,948	12.30
Lithuanian (13)	334	0.83
Norwegian (44)	106	0.26
Pennsylvania German (0)	44	0.11
Polish (225)	1,035	2.57
Portuguese (331)	580	1.44
Russian (65)	187	0.47
Scandinavian (26)	35	0.09
Scotch-Irish (187)	657	1.63
Scottish (250)	1,106	2.75
Serbian (31)	31	0.08
Slovak (0)	68	0.17
Swedish (142)	698	1.74
Swiss (0)	75	0.19
Ukrainian (19)	36	0.09
Welsh (42)	120	0.30
West Indian, ex. Hispanic (361)	426	1.06
British West Indian (0)	10	0.02
Haitian (340)	355	0.88
Jamaican (0)	28	0.07
West Indian (21)	33	0.08

Hispanic Origin	Population	%
Hispanic or Latino (of any race)	8,727	21.65
Central American, ex. Mexican	236	0.59
Costa Rican	17	0.04
Guatemalan	60	0.15
Honduran	66	0.16
Nicaraguan	12	0.03
Panamanian	21	0.05
Salvadoran	58	0.14
Other Central American	2	<0.01
Cuban	35	0.09
Dominican Republic	706	1.75
Mexican	551	1.37
Puerto Rican	5,871	14.56
South American	951	2.36
Argentinean	25	0.06
Bolivian	1	<0.01
Chilean	6	0.01
Colombian	85	0.21
Ecuadorian	106	0.26
Paraguayan	8	0.02
Peruvian	43	0.11
Uruguayan	650	1.61
Venezuelan	26	0.06
Other South American	1	<0.01
Other Hispanic or Latino	377	0.94

Race*	Population	%
African-American/Black (2,049)	2,742	6.80
Not Hispanic (1,614)	2,138	5.30
Hispanic (435)	604	1.50
American Indian/Alaska Native (133)	339	0.84
Not Hispanic (69)	235	0.58
Hispanic (64)	104	0.26
Apache (0)	3	0.01
Blackfeet (2)	22	0.05
Canadian/French Am. Ind. (1)	2	<0.01
Central American Ind. (1)	3	0.01
Cherokee (4)	30	0.07
Chickasaw (0)	1	<0.01
Chippewa (2)	2	<0.01
Choctaw (0)	2	<0.01
Comanche (0)	5	0.01
Iroquois (2)	13	0.03
Mexican American Ind. (5)	5	0.01
Navajo (2)	2	<0.01
Sioux (0)	1	<0.01
South American Ind. (2)	5	0.01
Asian (1,465)	1,722	4.27
Not Hispanic (1,451)	1,670	4.14
Hispanic (14)	52	0.13
Bangladeshi (1)	1	<0.01
Burmese (1)	1	<0.01
Cambodian (66)	77	0.19
Chinese, ex. Taiwanese (63)	89	0.22
Filipino (49)	83	0.21
Hmong (397)	412	1.02
Indian (100)	134	0.33
Indonesian (3)	4	0.01
Japanese (17)	56	0.14
Korean (49)	90	0.22
Laotian (300)	345	0.86
Nepalese (4)	4	0.01
Pakistani (52)	77	0.19
Taiwanese (0)	2	<0.01
Thai (16)	35	0.09
Vietnamese (224)	247	0.61
Hawaii Native/Pacific Islander (13)	47	0.12
Not Hispanic (7)	36	0.09
Hispanic (6)	11	0.03
Fijian (0)	1	<0.01
Guamanian/Chamorro (2)	6	0.01
Native Hawaiian (3)	9	0.02
Samoan (3)	5	0.01
White (31,529)	32,839	81.45
Not Hispanic (27,502)	28,288	70.16
Hispanic (4,027)	4,551	11.29

Foxborough

Place Type: Town
County: Norfolk
Population: 16,865†

Ancestry‡	Population	%
African, Sub-Saharan (22)	22	0.13
Cape Verdean (22)	22	0.13
American (551)	551	3.32
Arab (164)	315	1.90
Lebanese (106)	160	0.96
Syrian (44)	141	0.85
Other Arab (14)	14	0.08
Armenian (25)	57	0.34
Australian (0)	42	0.25
Austrian (0)	41	0.25
Brazilian (16)	16	0.10
British (11)	49	0.29
Canadian (33)	204	1.23
Croatian (0)	6	0.04
Czech (64)	64	0.39
Danish (14)	72	0.43
Dutch (39)	130	0.78
Eastern European (25)	25	0.15
English (531)	2,029	12.21
European (19)	29	0.17
Finnish (15)	76	0.46
French, ex. Basque (186)	1,383	8.32
French Canadian (229)	641	3.86
German (313)	1,183	7.12
Greek (79)	267	1.61
Hungarian (41)	185	1.11
Iranian (17)	17	0.10
Irish (2,756)	6,535	39.32
Italian (1,148)	3,148	18.94
Latvian (11)	57	0.34
Lithuanian (59)	192	1.16
Norwegian (38)	90	0.54
Pennsylvania German (15)	15	0.09
Polish (381)	1,043	6.28
Portuguese (96)	338	2.03
Romanian (0)	39	0.23
Russian (211)	467	2.81
Scandinavian (0)	8	0.05
Scotch-Irish (159)	441	2.65
Scottish (144)	500	3.01
Slovak (33)	49	0.29
Swedish (43)	290	1.74
Swiss (53)	68	0.41
Turkish (26)	26	0.16
Ukrainian (0)	12	0.07
Welsh (39)	95	0.57
West Indian, ex. Hispanic (56)	127	0.76
Haitian (37)	37	0.22
Jamaican (19)	90	0.54
Yugoslavian (0)	10	0.06

Hispanic Origin	Population	%
Hispanic or Latino (of any race)	309	1.83
Central American, ex. Mexican	31	0.18
Costa Rican	11	0.07
Guatemalan	9	0.05
Honduran	1	0.01
Nicaraguan	1	0.01
Panamanian	5	0.03
Salvadoran	4	0.02
Cuban	38	0.23
Dominican Republic	22	0.13
Mexican	53	0.31
Puerto Rican	78	0.46
South American	52	0.31
Argentinean	5	0.03
Bolivian	9	0.05
Chilean	2	0.01
Colombian	14	0.08
Ecuadorian	3	0.02
Paraguayan	1	0.01
Peruvian	16	0.09
Venezuelan	1	0.01
Other South American	1	0.01
Other Hispanic or Latino	35	0.21

Race*	Population	%
African-American/Black (324)	389	2.31
Not Hispanic (307)	362	2.15
Hispanic (17)	27	0.16
American Indian/Alaska Native (27)	90	0.53
Not Hispanic (25)	83	0.49

*Notes: † The Census 2010 population figure is used to calculate the percentages in the Hispanic Origin and Race categories. Ancestry percentages are based on the 2006-2010 American Community Survey population (not shown); ‡ Numbers in parentheses indicate the number of people reporting a single ancestry; * Numbers in parentheses indicate the number of persons reporting this race alone, not in combination with any other race; Please refer to the Explanation of Data for more information.*

Hispanic (2)	7	0.04
Apache (0)	1	0.01
Blackfeet (2)	3	0.02
Canadian/French Am. Ind. (0)	2	0.01
Cherokee (3)	6	0.04
Delaware (0)	1	0.01
Iroquois (0)	1	0.01
Mexican American Ind. (2)	2	0.01
Potawatomi (4)	4	0.02
Seminole (1)	6	0.04
Shoshone (2)	2	0.01
Sioux (0)	3	0.02
South American Ind. (0)	3	0.02
Asian (539)	615	3.65
Not Hispanic (539)	608	3.61
Hispanic (0)	7	0.04
Bangladeshi (6)	6	0.04
Cambodian (1)	1	0.01
Chinese, ex. Taiwanese (119)	131	0.78
Filipino (38)	62	0.37
Indian (202)	220	1.30
Indonesian (1)	3	0.02
Japanese (5)	13	0.08
Korean (30)	38	0.23
Laotian (7)	7	0.04
Pakistani (77)	81	0.48
Sri Lankan (1)	2	0.01
Thai (1)	2	0.01
Vietnamese (38)	38	0.23
Hawaii Native/Pacific Islander (4)	13	0.08
Not Hispanic (4)	11	0.07
Hispanic (0)	2	0.01
Native Hawaiian (4)	6	0.04
White (15,665)	15,840	93.92
Not Hispanic (15,465)	15,620	92.62
Hispanic (200)	220	1.30

Framingham

Place Type: CDP/Town
County: Middlesex
Population: 68,318†

Ancestry‡	Population	%
African, Sub-Saharan (591)	936	1.39
African (245)	356	0.53
Cape Verdean (90)	248	0.37
Ethiopian (46)	87	0.13
Ghanaian (58)	93	0.14
Nigerian (19)	19	0.03
Ugandan (52)	52	0.08
Other Sub-Saharan African (81)	81	0.12
Albanian (29)	53	0.08
American (2,004)	2,004	2.98
Arab (294)	487	0.72
Arab (18)	18	0.03
Egyptian (37)	53	0.08
Lebanese (211)	291	0.43
Moroccan (0)	17	0.03
Palestinian (10)	10	0.01
Syrian (0)	80	0.12
Other Arab (18)	18	0.03
Armenian (56)	116	0.17
Australian (0)	76	0.11
Austrian (28)	262	0.39
Belgian (11)	25	0.04
Brazilian (6,858)	7,030	10.44
British (166)	344	0.51
Bulgarian (60)	60	0.09
Canadian (209)	450	0.67
Croatian (14)	41	0.06
Czech (13)	62	0.09
Czechoslovakian (0)	24	0.04
Danish (14)	139	0.21
Dutch (115)	460	0.68
Eastern European (525)	538	0.80
English (1,284)	6,203	9.21
European (604)	803	1.19
Finnish (75)	198	0.29
French, ex. Basque (377)	2,651	3.94
French Canadian (838)	1,985	2.95
German (679)	3,600	5.35
Greek (454)	902	1.34
Hungarian (73)	289	0.43
Iranian (106)	130	0.19
Irish (3,983)	11,391	16.92
Israeli (53)	100	0.15
Italian (3,581)	8,873	13.18
Latvian (35)	44	0.07
Lithuanian (98)	348	0.52
Northern European (49)	71	0.11
Norwegian (163)	426	0.63
Pennsylvania German (17)	28	0.04
Polish (846)	2,724	4.05
Portuguese (962)	1,560	2.32
Romanian (65)	187	0.28
Russian (1,578)	3,180	4.72
Scandinavian (24)	24	0.04
Scotch-Irish (431)	1,023	1.52
Scottish (315)	1,485	2.21
Slovak (0)	27	0.04
Swedish (187)	1,066	1.58
Swiss (89)	202	0.30
Turkish (14)	14	0.02
Ukrainian (120)	201	0.30
Welsh (0)	173	0.26
West Indian, ex. Hispanic (463)	759	1.13
British West Indian (24)	24	0.04
Haitian (259)	315	0.47
Jamaican (78)	156	0.23
West Indian (102)	264	0.39

Hispanic Origin	Population	%
Hispanic or Latino (of any race)	9,161	13.41
Central American, ex. Mexican	2,497	3.65
Costa Rican	57	0.08
Guatemalan	1,247	1.83
Honduran	152	0.22
Nicaraguan	16	0.02
Panamanian	12	0.02
Salvadoran	1,007	1.47
Other Central American	6	0.01
Cuban	125	0.18
Dominican Republic	729	1.07
Mexican	592	0.87
Puerto Rican	3,179	4.65
South American	1,064	1.56
Argentinean	55	0.08
Bolivian	137	0.20
Chilean	61	0.09
Colombian	404	0.59
Ecuadorian	128	0.19
Paraguayan	4	0.01
Peruvian	188	0.28
Uruguayan	11	0.02
Venezuelan	67	0.10
Other South American	9	0.01
Other Hispanic or Latino	975	1.43

Race*	Population	%
African-American/Black (3,993)	4,712	6.90
Not Hispanic (3,446)	4,012	5.87
Hispanic (547)	700	1.02
American Indian/Alaska Native (205)	478	0.70
Not Hispanic (104)	305	0.45
Hispanic (101)	173	0.25
Apache (1)	1	<0.01
Blackfeet (0)	11	0.02
Canadian/French Am. Ind. (1)	2	<0.01
Central American Ind. (1)	2	<0.01
Cherokee (10)	55	0.08
Cheyenne (0)	1	<0.01
Chippewa (4)	4	0.01
Choctaw (4)	9	0.01
Creek (1)	1	<0.01
Crow (0)	2	<0.01
Delaware (2)	3	<0.01
Iroquois (4)	9	0.01
Kiowa (0)	1	<0.01
Lumbee (2)	2	<0.01
Menominee (0)	1	<0.01
Mexican American Ind. (12)	22	0.03
Potawatomi (2)	2	<0.01
Pueblo (0)	1	<0.01
Seminole (0)	1	<0.01
Sioux (3)	5	0.01
South American Ind. (1)	9	0.01
Spanish American Ind. (1)	3	<0.01
Yaqui (0)	2	<0.01
Asian (4,333)	4,808	7.04
Not Hispanic (4,302)	4,743	6.94
Hispanic (31)	65	0.10
Bangladeshi (6)	6	0.01
Burmese (11)	12	0.02
Cambodian (40)	52	0.08
Chinese, ex. Taiwanese (1,314)	1,467	2.15
Filipino (139)	205	0.30
Hmong (3)	3	<0.01
Indian (1,926)	2,018	2.95
Indonesian (10)	18	0.03
Japanese (88)	151	0.22
Korean (199)	235	0.34
Laotian (13)	21	0.03
Malaysian (3)	8	0.01
Nepalese (5)	6	0.01
Pakistani (133)	150	0.22
Sri Lankan (50)	60	0.09
Taiwanese (39)	40	0.06
Thai (40)	41	0.06
Vietnamese (193)	224	0.33
Hawaii Native/Pacific Islander (47)	115	0.17
Not Hispanic (18)	62	0.09
Hispanic (29)	53	0.08
Guamanian/Chamorro (15)	23	0.03
Native Hawaiian (7)	16	0.02
Samoan (0)	3	<0.01
White (49,122)	51,949	76.04
Not Hispanic (44,625)	46,993	68.79
Hispanic (4,497)	4,956	7.25

Franklin Town

Place Type: City
County: Norfolk
Population: 31,635†

Ancestry‡	Population	%
African, Sub-Saharan (7)	13	0.04
African (7)	13	0.04
Albanian (15)	56	0.18
American (1,228)	1,228	3.96
Arab (471)	542	1.75
Arab (28)	28	0.09
Egyptian (43)	43	0.14
Lebanese (385)	444	1.43
Palestinian (15)	15	0.05
Syrian (0)	12	0.04
Armenian (128)	331	1.07
Australian (0)	14	0.05
Austrian (45)	100	0.32
Belgian (20)	42	0.14
Brazilian (14)	82	0.26
British (120)	184	0.59
Bulgarian (152)	152	0.49
Canadian (98)	299	0.96
Celtic (0)	63	0.20
Czech (25)	105	0.34
Czechoslovakian (11)	31	0.10
Danish (21)	77	0.25
Dutch (39)	197	0.64
Eastern European (157)	173	0.56
English (718)	3,485	11.23
European (242)	279	0.90
Finnish (0)	105	0.34
French, ex. Basque (355)	2,291	7.38
French Canadian (406)	1,163	3.75
German (436)	2,637	8.50
Greek (93)	309	1.00
Hungarian (70)	156	0.50
Icelander (10)	10	0.03

*Notes: † The Census 2010 population figure is used to calculate the percentages in the Hispanic Origin and Race categories. Ancestry percentages are based on the 2006-2010 American Community Survey population (not shown); ‡ Numbers in parentheses indicate the number of people reporting a single ancestry; * Numbers in parentheses indicate the number of persons reporting this race alone, not in combination with any other race; Please refer to the Explanation of Data for more information.*

Iranian (100)	100	0.32
Irish (3,667)	9,826	31.67
Italian (2,597)	7,515	24.22
Lithuanian (151)	347	1.12
Luxemburger (34)	34	0.11
Macedonian (0)	11	0.04
Norwegian (13)	125	0.40
Polish (291)	1,589	5.12
Portuguese (281)	624	2.01
Romanian (13)	63	0.20
Russian (161)	444	1.43
Scandinavian (22)	55	0.18
Scotch-Irish (336)	1,033	3.33
Scottish (281)	1,147	3.70
Serbian (6)	6	0.02
Slovene (0)	8	0.03
Swedish (32)	469	1.51
Swiss (0)	35	0.11
Ukrainian (49)	151	0.49
Welsh (14)	190	0.61
West Indian, ex. Hispanic (63)	63	0.20
Haitian (16)	16	0.05
Trinidadian/Tobagonian (47)	47	0.15

Hispanic Origin	Population	%
Hispanic or Latino (of any race)	620	1.96
Central American, ex. Mexican	85	0.27
Costa Rican	8	0.03
Guatemalan	26	0.08
Honduran	9	0.03
Nicaraguan	4	0.01
Panamanian	3	0.01
Salvadoran	35	0.11
Cuban	47	0.15
Dominican Republic	34	0.11
Mexican	92	0.29
Puerto Rican	196	0.62
South American	92	0.29
Argentinean	9	0.03
Bolivian	7	0.02
Chilean	9	0.03
Colombian	43	0.14
Ecuadorian	7	0.02
Paraguayan	2	0.01
Peruvian	8	0.03
Uruguayan	3	0.01
Venezuelan	3	0.01
Other South American	1	<0.01
Other Hispanic or Latino	74	0.23

Race*	Population	%
African-American/Black (449)	588	1.86
Not Hispanic (416)	541	1.71
Hispanic (33)	47	0.15
American Indian/Alaska Native (45)	124	0.39
Not Hispanic (23)	94	0.30
Hispanic (22)	30	0.09
Apache (0)	5	0.02
Arapaho (0)	3	0.01
Blackfeet (0)	1	<0.01
Cherokee (2)	12	0.04
Chippewa (2)	3	0.01
Delaware (0)	1	<0.01
Iroquois (1)	4	0.01
Mexican American Ind. (4)	4	0.01
Sioux (0)	1	<0.01
South American Ind. (2)	2	0.01
Tlingit-Haida *(Alaska Native)* (1)	1	<0.01
Ute (0)	2	0.01
Asian (1,194)	1,417	4.48
Not Hispanic (1,193)	1,414	4.47
Hispanic (1)	3	0.01
Cambodian (3)	4	0.01
Chinese, ex. Taiwanese (367)	427	1.35
Filipino (28)	65	0.21
Hmong (1)	1	<0.01
Indian (585)	632	2.00
Indonesian (2)	13	0.04
Japanese (19)	52	0.16
Korean (62)	92	0.29
Laotian (17)	21	0.07
Nepalese (10)	10	0.03
Pakistani (9)	13	0.04
Sri Lankan (3)	3	0.01
Taiwanese (6)	12	0.04
Thai (17)	26	0.08
Vietnamese (36)	39	0.12
Hawaii Native/Pacific Islander (5)	25	0.08
Not Hispanic (4)	23	0.07
Hispanic (1)	2	0.01
Guamanian/Chamorro (3)	5	0.02
Native Hawaiian (0)	1	<0.01
Samoan (1)	2	0.01
White (29,350)	29,742	94.02
Not Hispanic (28,926)	29,286	92.57
Hispanic (424)	456	1.44

Freetown

Place Type: Town
County: Bristol
Population: 8,870†

Ancestry‡	Population	%
African, Sub-Saharan (75)	144	1.64
Cape Verdean (75)	144	1.64
American (199)	199	2.26
Arab (27)	45	0.51
Arab (0)	18	0.20
Lebanese (27)	27	0.31
Austrian (0)	12	0.14
Brazilian (0)	7	0.08
British (28)	39	0.44
Canadian (11)	47	0.53
Czech (15)	15	0.17
Danish (0)	12	0.14
Dutch (16)	54	0.61
English (431)	1,594	18.12
European (0)	49	0.56
French, ex. Basque (425)	1,197	13.61
French Canadian (565)	1,062	12.07
German (22)	351	3.99
Greek (24)	88	1.00
Irish (306)	1,519	17.27
Italian (188)	545	6.20
Lithuanian (27)	53	0.60
Pennsylvania German (7)	7	0.08
Polish (54)	508	5.78
Portuguese (1,958)	3,007	34.19
Russian (10)	77	0.88
Scandinavian (14)	14	0.16
Scotch-Irish (27)	103	1.17
Scottish (36)	259	2.94
Swedish (8)	51	0.58
Welsh (32)	86	0.98
West Indian, ex. Hispanic (114)	114	1.30
Haitian (114)	114	1.30

Hispanic Origin	Population	%
Hispanic or Latino (of any race)	109	1.23
Central American, ex. Mexican	4	0.05
Guatemalan	2	0.02
Salvadoran	2	0.02
Cuban	2	0.02
Dominican Republic	2	0.02
Mexican	22	0.25
Puerto Rican	51	0.57
South American	15	0.17
Bolivian	2	0.02
Chilean	4	0.05
Colombian	8	0.09
Peruvian	1	0.01
Other Hispanic or Latino	13	0.15

Race*	Population	%
African-American/Black (81)	117	1.32
Not Hispanic (77)	112	1.26
Hispanic (4)	5	0.06
American Indian/Alaska Native (13)	42	0.47
Not Hispanic (9)	35	0.39
Hispanic (4)	7	0.08
Apache (0)	1	0.01
Canadian/French Am. Ind. (1)	1	0.01
Cherokee (0)	2	0.02
Chippewa (1)	3	0.03
Navajo (0)	1	0.01
Pueblo (3)	3	0.03
Sioux (0)	3	0.03
Yup'ik *(Alaska Native)* (0)	1	0.01
Asian (55)	68	0.77
Not Hispanic (55)	67	0.76
Hispanic (0)	1	0.01
Cambodian (1)	1	0.01
Chinese, ex. Taiwanese (11)	12	0.14
Filipino (14)	22	0.25
Indian (19)	22	0.25
Japanese (0)	2	0.02
Korean (3)	3	0.03
Vietnamese (3)	4	0.05
White (8,550)	8,622	97.20
Not Hispanic (8,480)	8,548	96.37
Hispanic (70)	74	0.83

Gardner

Place Type: City
County: Worcester
Population: 20,228†

Ancestry‡	Population	%
African, Sub-Saharan (56)	69	0.34
African (25)	25	0.12
Cape Verdean (8)	21	0.10
Other Sub-Saharan African (23)	23	0.11
Albanian (0)	22	0.11
American (916)	916	4.49
Arab (54)	107	0.52
Lebanese (54)	107	0.52
Armenian (29)	114	0.56
Austrian (0)	100	0.49
Brazilian (36)	36	0.18
British (19)	25	0.12
Cajun (12)	47	0.23
Canadian (271)	293	1.44
Czech (0)	18	0.09
Danish (11)	31	0.15
Dutch (37)	64	0.31
English (425)	2,142	10.51
Estonian (18)	18	0.09
European (284)	301	1.48
Finnish (241)	886	4.35
French, ex. Basque (1,403)	4,170	20.46
French Canadian (1,719)	2,477	12.15
German (186)	1,367	6.71
Greek (26)	138	0.68
Hungarian (24)	75	0.37
Irish (901)	4,075	19.99
Israeli (0)	36	0.18
Italian (628)	1,813	8.89
Lithuanian (66)	357	1.75
New Zealander (8)	8	0.04
Norwegian (61)	156	0.77
Polish (343)	1,275	6.25
Portuguese (182)	395	1.94
Russian (78)	192	0.94
Scotch-Irish (66)	354	1.74
Scottish (76)	526	2.58
Swedish (186)	775	3.80
Swiss (11)	17	0.08
Turkish (0)	15	0.07
Welsh (55)	122	0.60
West Indian, ex. Hispanic (124)	171	0.84
Barbadian (106)	106	0.52
Haitian (0)	14	0.07
Jamaican (18)	39	0.19
Trinidadian/Tobagonian (0)	12	0.06
Yugoslavian (0)	12	0.06

Hispanic Origin	Population	%
Hispanic or Latino (of any race)	1,430	7.07

*Notes: † The Census 2010 population figure is used to calculate the percentages in the Hispanic Origin and Race categories. Ancestry percentages are based on the 2006-2010 American Community Survey population (not shown); ‡ Numbers in parentheses indicate the number of people reporting a single ancestry; * Numbers in parentheses indicate the number of persons reporting this race alone, not in combination with any other race; Please refer to the Explanation of Data for more information.*

Central American, ex. Mexican	95	0.47
Costa Rican	5	0.02
Guatemalan	19	0.09
Honduran	3	0.01
Nicaraguan	19	0.09
Panamanian	8	0.04
Salvadoran	39	0.19
Other Central American	2	0.01
Cuban	13	0.06
Dominican Republic	71	0.35
Mexican	159	0.79
Puerto Rican	676	3.34
South American	71	0.35
Argentinean	7	0.03
Bolivian	2	0.01
Chilean	15	0.07
Colombian	18	0.09
Ecuadorian	7	0.03
Peruvian	3	0.01
Uruguayan	19	0.09
Other Hispanic or Latino	345	1.71

Race*	Population	%
African-American/Black (568)	772	3.82
Not Hispanic (500)	671	3.32
Hispanic (68)	101	0.50
American Indian/Alaska Native (64)	189	0.93
Not Hispanic (44)	152	0.75
Hispanic (20)	37	0.18
Aleut *(Alaska Native)* (1)	1	<0.01
Apache (1)	8	0.04
Blackfeet (1)	2	0.01
Canadian/French Am. Ind. (0)	4	0.02
Central American Ind. (3)	3	0.01
Cherokee (1)	23	0.11
Chickasaw (0)	1	<0.01
Iroquois (2)	5	0.02
Lumbee (0)	3	0.01
Navajo (0)	1	<0.01
Paiute (0)	1	<0.01
Seminole (0)	2	0.01
Sioux (1)	3	0.01
South American Ind. (0)	1	<0.01
Tlingit-Haida *(Alaska Native)* (2)	3	0.01
Asian (293)	393	1.94
Not Hispanic (291)	376	1.86
Hispanic (2)	17	0.08
Bangladeshi (0)	4	0.02
Cambodian (1)	1	<0.01
Chinese, ex. Taiwanese (43)	49	0.24
Filipino (21)	37	0.18
Hmong (5)	5	0.02
Indian (28)	39	0.19
Indonesian (0)	1	<0.01
Japanese (9)	27	0.13
Korean (28)	48	0.24
Laotian (73)	91	0.45
Malaysian (1)	1	<0.01
Pakistani (12)	12	0.06
Sri Lankan (1)	1	<0.01
Thai (17)	24	0.12
Vietnamese (35)	37	0.18
Hawaii Native/Pacific Islander (10)	20	0.10
Not Hispanic (4)	10	0.05
Hispanic (6)	10	0.05
Guamanian/Chamorro (5)	6	0.03
Native Hawaiian (3)	7	0.03
Samoan (2)	3	0.01
White (18,496)	18,912	93.49
Not Hispanic (17,595)	17,918	88.58
Hispanic (901)	994	4.91

Georgetown

Place Type: Town
County: Essex
Population: 8,183†

Ancestry‡	Population	%
Albanian (0)	30	0.38
American (230)	230	2.88
Australian (0)	9	0.11
Austrian (0)	52	0.65
Belgian (0)	10	0.13
British (0)	41	0.51
Canadian (45)	100	1.25
Celtic (0)	7	0.09
Czech (7)	7	0.09
Danish (0)	36	0.45
Dutch (6)	145	1.81
Eastern European (8)	8	0.10
English (405)	1,669	20.88
European (106)	106	1.33
Finnish (0)	11	0.14
French, ex. Basque (234)	869	10.87
French Canadian (175)	513	6.42
German (114)	588	7.35
Greek (88)	185	2.31
Irish (800)	2,722	34.05
Italian (468)	1,760	22.01
Latvian (0)	15	0.19
Lithuanian (0)	25	0.31
Norwegian (10)	86	1.08
Polish (135)	500	6.25
Portuguese (26)	154	1.93
Russian (63)	168	2.10
Scotch-Irish (29)	141	1.76
Scottish (181)	528	6.60
Slavic (0)	16	0.20
Swedish (10)	218	2.73
Swiss (0)	7	0.09
Ukrainian (21)	51	0.64
Welsh (8)	58	0.73

Hispanic Origin	Population	%
Hispanic or Latino (of any race)	143	1.75
Central American, ex. Mexican	22	0.27
Costa Rican	2	0.02
Guatemalan	11	0.13
Salvadoran	9	0.11
Cuban	9	0.11
Dominican Republic	14	0.17
Mexican	22	0.27
Puerto Rican	47	0.57
South American	15	0.18
Argentinean	4	0.05
Colombian	3	0.04
Ecuadorian	4	0.05
Peruvian	4	0.05
Other Hispanic or Latino	14	0.17

Race*	Population	%
African-American/Black (38)	54	0.66
Not Hispanic (37)	47	0.57
Hispanic (1)	7	0.09
American Indian/Alaska Native (14)	41	0.50
Not Hispanic (7)	30	0.37
Hispanic (7)	11	0.13
Canadian/French Am. Ind. (0)	1	0.01
Cherokee (0)	5	0.06
Mexican American Ind. (3)	5	0.06
Shoshone (1)	1	0.01
Sioux (0)	6	0.07
South American Ind. (4)	5	0.06
Asian (77)	124	1.52
Not Hispanic (76)	120	1.47
Hispanic (1)	4	0.05
Cambodian (4)	5	0.06
Chinese, ex. Taiwanese (22)	34	0.42
Filipino (9)	18	0.22
Indian (19)	23	0.28
Indonesian (0)	4	0.05
Japanese (10)	21	0.26
Korean (11)	17	0.21
Pakistani (1)	2	0.02
Hawaii Native/Pacific Islander (0)	6	0.07
Not Hispanic (0)	3	0.04
Hispanic (0)	3	0.04
Guamanian/Chamorro (0)	4	0.05
White (7,927)	8,022	98.03
Not Hispanic (7,832)	7,914	96.71
Hispanic (95)	108	1.32

Gloucester

Place Type: City
County: Essex
Population: 28,789†

Ancestry‡	Population	%
African, Sub-Saharan (49)	49	0.17
African (23)	23	0.08
Cape Verdean (26)	26	0.09
Albanian (17)	17	0.06
American (1,467)	1,467	5.08
Arab (38)	170	0.59
Lebanese (38)	170	0.59
Armenian (54)	74	0.26
Australian (0)	48	0.17
Austrian (11)	147	0.51
Belgian (9)	9	0.03
Brazilian (281)	281	0.97
British (138)	211	0.73
Cajun (0)	17	0.06
Canadian (142)	339	1.17
Celtic (41)	41	0.14
Czech (38)	77	0.27
Danish (26)	140	0.48
Dutch (116)	408	1.41
Eastern European (108)	127	0.44
English (1,702)	5,047	17.47
European (213)	213	0.74
Finnish (105)	537	1.86
French, ex. Basque (540)	2,428	8.40
French Canadian (384)	895	3.10
German (436)	2,076	7.19
Greek (92)	350	1.21
Hungarian (0)	69	0.24
Irish (1,804)	5,648	19.55
Italian (3,902)	6,728	23.29
Lithuanian (21)	171	0.59
Northern European (11)	30	0.10
Norwegian (83)	276	0.96
Polish (182)	510	1.77
Portuguese (1,482)	2,840	9.83
Russian (187)	430	1.49
Scandinavian (49)	81	0.28
Scotch-Irish (370)	1,054	3.65
Scottish (133)	1,216	4.21
Slovak (93)	165	0.57
Slovene (0)	10	0.03
Swedish (116)	943	3.26
Swiss (0)	47	0.16
Ukrainian (12)	83	0.29
Welsh (57)	228	0.79
West Indian, ex. Hispanic (0)	26	0.09
Barbadian (0)	9	0.03
West Indian (0)	17	0.06
Yugoslavian (0)	14	0.05

Hispanic Origin	Population	%
Hispanic or Latino (of any race)	787	2.73
Central American, ex. Mexican	127	0.44
Costa Rican	1	<0.01
Guatemalan	73	0.25
Honduran	20	0.07
Nicaraguan	10	0.03
Panamanian	5	0.02
Salvadoran	18	0.06
Cuban	16	0.06
Dominican Republic	131	0.46
Mexican	133	0.46
Puerto Rican	166	0.58
South American	82	0.28
Argentinean	11	0.04
Bolivian	2	0.01
Chilean	7	0.02
Colombian	24	0.08
Ecuadorian	8	0.03
Paraguayan	2	0.01

*Notes: † The Census 2010 population figure is used to calculate the percentages in the Hispanic Origin and Race categories. Ancestry percentages are based on the 2006-2010 American Community Survey population (not shown); ‡ Numbers in parentheses indicate the number of people reporting a single ancestry; * Numbers in parentheses indicate the number of persons reporting this race alone, not in combination with any other race; Please refer to the Explanation of Data for more information.*

Peruvian	22	0.08
Venezuelan	4	0.01
Other South American	2	0.01
Other Hispanic or Latino	132	0.46

Race*	Population	%
African-American/Black (239)	364	1.26
Not Hispanic (199)	307	1.07
Hispanic (40)	57	0.20
American Indian/Alaska Native (40)	150	0.52
Not Hispanic (29)	129	0.45
Hispanic (11)	21	0.07
Aleut *(Alaska Native)* (3)	5	0.02
Apache (0)	4	0.01
Blackfeet (0)	9	0.03
Canadian/French Am. Ind. (1)	1	<0.01
Central American Ind. (2)	3	0.01
Cherokee (1)	9	0.03
Choctaw (1)	2	0.01
Cree (1)	7	0.02
Creek (0)	1	<0.01
Inupiat *(Alaska Native)* (0)	1	<0.01
Iroquois (0)	4	0.01
Mexican American Ind. (2)	2	0.01
Ottawa (0)	1	<0.01
Paiute (0)	2	0.01
Sioux (0)	1	<0.01
South American Ind. (2)	2	0.01
Spanish American Ind. (1)	1	<0.01
Yakama (0)	1	<0.01
Asian (258)	339	1.18
Not Hispanic (256)	334	1.16
Hispanic (2)	5	0.02
Cambodian (13)	19	0.07
Chinese, ex. Taiwanese (56)	67	0.23
Filipino (38)	62	0.22
Indian (44)	48	0.17
Indonesian (1)	1	<0.01
Japanese (33)	49	0.17
Korean (27)	33	0.11
Laotian (4)	4	0.01
Nepalese (2)	2	0.01
Pakistani (14)	17	0.06
Taiwanese (2)	2	0.01
Thai (4)	7	0.02
Vietnamese (12)	15	0.05
Hawaii Native/Pacific Islander (26)	35	0.12
Not Hispanic (16)	22	0.08
Hispanic (10)	13	0.05
Guamanian/Chamorro (5)	5	0.02
Native Hawaiian (4)	5	0.02
Samoan (0)	1	<0.01
White (27,548)	27,904	96.93
Not Hispanic (27,100)	27,391	95.14
Hispanic (448)	513	1.78

Grafton

Place Type: Town
County: Worcester
Population: 17,765†

Ancestry‡	Population	%
African, Sub-Saharan (114)	127	0.73
African (96)	96	0.56
Cape Verdean (18)	31	0.18
Albanian (10)	32	0.19
American (587)	587	3.40
Arab (47)	134	0.78
Lebanese (39)	96	0.56
Moroccan (8)	8	0.05
Syrian (0)	20	0.12
Other Arab (0)	10	0.06
Armenian (52)	113	0.65
Australian (0)	16	0.09
Austrian (0)	43	0.25
Belgian (0)	8	0.05
Brazilian (309)	331	1.92
British (18)	42	0.24
Cajun (0)	17	0.10
Canadian (111)	336	1.94
Czech (0)	36	0.21
Danish (14)	85	0.49
Dutch (176)	300	1.74
Eastern European (34)	34	0.20
English (322)	1,916	11.09
European (235)	235	1.36
Finnish (19)	43	0.25
French, ex. Basque (724)	2,409	13.94
French Canadian (606)	1,022	5.91
German (228)	1,253	7.25
Greek (57)	128	0.74
Hungarian (18)	18	0.10
Iranian (18)	18	0.10
Irish (1,292)	4,315	24.97
Italian (1,093)	2,931	16.96
Latvian (0)	37	0.21
Lithuanian (57)	318	1.84
Macedonian (0)	11	0.06
Norwegian (10)	52	0.30
Polish (338)	1,114	6.45
Portuguese (47)	137	0.79
Russian (119)	381	2.20
Scandinavian (30)	50	0.29
Scotch-Irish (128)	264	1.53
Scottish (120)	401	2.32
Slovak (0)	16	0.09
Swedish (76)	596	3.45
Ukrainian (42)	121	0.70
Welsh (0)	99	0.57
Yugoslavian (11)	48	0.28

Hispanic Origin	Population	%
Hispanic or Latino (of any race)	406	2.29
Central American, ex. Mexican	41	0.23
Costa Rican	5	0.03
Guatemalan	14	0.08
Honduran	3	0.02
Nicaraguan	1	0.01
Panamanian	3	0.02
Salvadoran	15	0.08
Cuban	28	0.16
Dominican Republic	9	0.05
Mexican	83	0.47
Puerto Rican	154	0.87
South American	58	0.33
Argentinean	4	0.02
Chilean	5	0.03
Colombian	17	0.10
Ecuadorian	10	0.06
Peruvian	9	0.05
Uruguayan	3	0.02
Venezuelan	8	0.05
Other South American	2	0.01
Other Hispanic or Latino	33	0.19

Race*	Population	%
African-American/Black (196)	295	1.66
Not Hispanic (184)	272	1.53
Hispanic (12)	23	0.13
American Indian/Alaska Native (25)	74	0.42
Not Hispanic (15)	63	0.35
Hispanic (10)	11	0.06
Blackfeet (0)	1	0.01
Canadian/French Am. Ind. (0)	1	0.01
Cherokee (0)	2	0.01
Chippewa (0)	1	0.01
Choctaw (0)	1	0.01
Creek (1)	1	0.01
Iroquois (2)	2	0.01
Mexican American Ind. (1)	2	0.01
Sioux (0)	1	0.01
Asian (1,370)	1,502	8.45
Not Hispanic (1,370)	1,493	8.40
Hispanic (0)	9	0.05
Bangladeshi (4)	4	0.02
Cambodian (14)	18	0.10
Chinese, ex. Taiwanese (204)	223	1.26
Filipino (35)	63	0.35
Indian (889)	921	5.18
Indonesian (9)	12	0.07
Japanese (13)	19	0.11
Korean (70)	95	0.53
Laotian (6)	6	0.03
Nepalese (5)	5	0.03
Pakistani (36)	39	0.22
Sri Lankan (8)	8	0.05
Taiwanese (20)	23	0.13
Thai (6)	7	0.04
Vietnamese (43)	46	0.26
Hawaii Native/Pacific Islander (2)	20	0.11
Not Hispanic (2)	15	0.08
Hispanic (0)	5	0.03
Guamanian/Chamorro (0)	4	0.02
Native Hawaiian (2)	5	0.03
White (15,748)	16,016	90.15
Not Hispanic (15,477)	15,719	88.48
Hispanic (271)	297	1.67

Greenfield Town

Place Type: City
County: Franklin
Population: 17,456†

Ancestry‡	Population	%
African, Sub-Saharan (0)	3	0.02
African (0)	3	0.02
American (662)	662	3.76
Arab (12)	12	0.07
Syrian (12)	12	0.07
Armenian (0)	23	0.13
Austrian (8)	139	0.79
Belgian (0)	3	0.02
Brazilian (18)	30	0.17
British (20)	70	0.40
Canadian (63)	174	0.99
Czech (8)	28	0.16
Danish (0)	64	0.36
Dutch (27)	186	1.06
Eastern European (19)	19	0.11
English (882)	3,419	19.42
European (194)	209	1.19
Finnish (0)	63	0.36
French, ex. Basque (422)	2,723	15.46
French Canadian (354)	968	5.50
German (298)	2,173	12.34
Greek (22)	34	0.19
Hungarian (61)	112	0.64
Icelander (23)	23	0.13
Irish (1,328)	3,841	21.81
Italian (444)	1,287	7.31
Latvian (0)	4	0.02
Lithuanian (8)	202	1.15
Maltese (0)	32	0.18
Northern European (12)	12	0.07
Norwegian (0)	77	0.44
Polish (814)	2,138	12.14
Portuguese (47)	292	1.66
Romanian (185)	185	1.05
Russian (152)	267	1.52
Scandinavian (24)	33	0.19
Scotch-Irish (183)	328	1.86
Scottish (178)	763	4.33
Slavic (11)	23	0.13
Swedish (35)	345	1.96
Swiss (0)	28	0.16
Ukrainian (38)	117	0.66
Welsh (18)	124	0.70
West Indian, ex. Hispanic (9)	9	0.05
West Indian (9)	9	0.05

Hispanic Origin	Population	%
Hispanic or Latino (of any race)	853	4.89
Central American, ex. Mexican	64	0.37
Costa Rican	9	0.05
Guatemalan	17	0.10
Honduran	4	0.02
Nicaraguan	3	0.02
Panamanian	5	0.03

*Notes: † The Census 2010 population figure is used to calculate the percentages in the Hispanic Origin and Race categories. Ancestry percentages are based on the 2006-2010 American Community Survey population (not shown); ‡ Numbers in parentheses indicate the number of people reporting a single ancestry; * Numbers in parentheses indicate the number of persons reporting this race alone, not in combination with any other race; Please refer to the Explanation of Data for more information.*

Salvadoran	25	0.14
Other Central American	1	0.01
Cuban	13	0.07
Dominican Republic	15	0.09
Mexican	67	0.38
Puerto Rican	608	3.48
South American	28	0.16
Argentinean	3	0.02
Chilean	4	0.02
Colombian	11	0.06
Ecuadorian	2	0.01
Peruvian	7	0.04
Venezuelan	1	0.01
Other Hispanic or Latino	58	0.33

Race*	Population	%
African-American/Black (297)	496	2.84
Not Hispanic (262)	423	2.42
Hispanic (35)	73	0.42
American Indian/Alaska Native (61)	225	1.29
Not Hispanic (52)	197	1.13
Hispanic (9)	28	0.16
Blackfeet (5)	22	0.13
Canadian/French Am. Ind. (2)	6	0.03
Central American Ind. (1)	1	0.01
Cherokee (5)	28	0.16
Cheyenne (0)	1	0.01
Chickasaw (0)	1	0.01
Chippewa (3)	6	0.03
Choctaw (0)	2	0.01
Creek (1)	1	0.01
Iroquois (5)	22	0.13
Lumbee (0)	1	0.01
Mexican American Ind. (2)	3	0.02
Navajo (0)	2	0.01
Potawatomi (0)	1	0.01
Sioux (0)	4	0.02
South American Ind. (0)	1	0.01
Spanish American Ind. (0)	1	0.01
Tlingit-Haida *(Alaska Native)* (1)	1	0.01
Yaqui (1)	1	0.01
Asian (239)	317	1.82
Not Hispanic (236)	310	1.78
Hispanic (3)	7	0.04
Bangladeshi (1)	1	0.01
Cambodian (6)	6	0.03
Chinese, ex. Taiwanese (79)	91	0.52
Filipino (24)	30	0.17
Hmong (0)	1	0.01
Indian (34)	50	0.29
Japanese (11)	22	0.13
Korean (24)	46	0.26
Laotian (1)	5	0.03
Malaysian (1)	6	0.03
Pakistani (2)	4	0.02
Taiwanese (0)	1	0.01
Thai (6)	9	0.05
Vietnamese (22)	29	0.17
Hawaii Native/Pacific Islander (5)	16	0.09
Not Hispanic (2)	5	0.03
Hispanic (3)	11	0.06
Native Hawaiian (5)	8	0.05
White (16,123)	16,523	94.66
Not Hispanic (15,675)	15,995	91.63
Hispanic (448)	528	3.02

Groton

Place Type: Town
County: Middlesex
Population: 10,646†

Ancestry‡	Population	%
Albanian (0)	32	0.31
American (382)	382	3.70
Arab (17)	29	0.28
Iraqi (0)	12	0.12
Lebanese (17)	17	0.16
Armenian (16)	29	0.28
Belgian (13)	13	0.13
Brazilian (16)	16	0.15
British (122)	198	1.92
Canadian (12)	112	1.08
Croatian (0)	13	0.13
Czech (0)	18	0.17
Danish (12)	41	0.40
Dutch (39)	156	1.51
Eastern European (13)	13	0.13
English (503)	1,900	18.40
European (153)	163	1.58
Finnish (18)	35	0.34
French, ex. Basque (112)	636	6.16
French Canadian (152)	398	3.85
German (259)	1,331	12.89
Greek (8)	64	0.62
Hungarian (49)	63	0.61
Iranian (54)	54	0.52
Irish (1,072)	3,226	31.24
Italian (384)	1,728	16.73
Lithuanian (16)	69	0.67
Northern European (53)	53	0.51
Norwegian (11)	125	1.21
Polish (130)	462	4.47
Portuguese (13)	87	0.84
Russian (82)	167	1.62
Scandinavian (0)	23	0.22
Scotch-Irish (243)	410	3.97
Scottish (69)	367	3.55
Swedish (27)	630	6.10
Turkish (0)	19	0.18
Welsh (0)	77	0.75
West Indian, ex. Hispanic (15)	15	0.15
Bermudan (15)	15	0.15
Yugoslavian (0)	18	0.17

Hispanic Origin	Population	%
Hispanic or Latino (of any race)	193	1.81
Central American, ex. Mexican	20	0.19
Guatemalan	17	0.16
Nicaraguan	3	0.03
Cuban	9	0.08
Dominican Republic	5	0.05
Mexican	37	0.35
Puerto Rican	40	0.38
South American	44	0.41
Argentinean	1	0.01
Bolivian	7	0.07
Chilean	10	0.09
Colombian	14	0.13
Ecuadorian	7	0.07
Paraguayan	1	0.01
Peruvian	3	0.03
Uruguayan	1	0.01
Other Hispanic or Latino	38	0.36

Race*	Population	%
African-American/Black (46)	80	0.75
Not Hispanic (45)	76	0.71
Hispanic (1)	4	0.04
American Indian/Alaska Native (7)	34	0.32
Not Hispanic (7)	33	0.31
Hispanic (0)	1	0.01
Blackfeet (0)	1	0.01
Cherokee (6)	10	0.09
Inupiat *(Alaska Native)* (1)	3	0.03
Iroquois (0)	1	0.01
Mexican American Ind. (0)	2	0.02
Sioux (0)	1	0.01
Asian (294)	375	3.52
Not Hispanic (293)	371	3.48
Hispanic (1)	4	0.04
Cambodian (1)	1	0.01
Chinese, ex. Taiwanese (91)	115	1.08
Filipino (11)	20	0.19
Indian (89)	95	0.89
Japanese (10)	29	0.27
Korean (55)	66	0.62
Laotian (4)	4	0.04
Pakistani (10)	10	0.09
Sri Lankan (2)	2	0.02
Taiwanese (5)	5	0.05
Thai (1)	1	0.01
Vietnamese (14)	21	0.20
Hawaii Native/Pacific Islander (1)	15	0.14
Not Hispanic (1)	13	0.12
Hispanic (0)	2	0.02
Guamanian/Chamorro (0)	1	0.01
Native Hawaiian (0)	10	0.09
Samoan (1)	4	0.04
White (10,111)	10,250	96.28
Not Hispanic (9,964)	10,089	94.77
Hispanic (147)	161	1.51

Halifax

Place Type: Town
County: Plymouth
Population: 7,518†

Ancestry‡	Population	%
African, Sub-Saharan (15)	15	0.20
Cape Verdean (15)	15	0.20
American (369)	369	4.91
Arab (66)	80	1.07
Lebanese (66)	80	1.07
Armenian (0)	12	0.16
Austrian (0)	14	0.19
Belgian (0)	24	0.32
British (18)	73	0.97
Canadian (15)	56	0.75
Celtic (13)	13	0.17
Dutch (0)	71	0.95
Eastern European (11)	11	0.15
English (151)	1,248	16.62
European (87)	87	1.16
French, ex. Basque (83)	603	8.03
French Canadian (40)	184	2.45
German (108)	534	7.11
Greek (13)	13	0.17
Hungarian (0)	17	0.23
Irish (1,073)	3,000	39.96
Italian (449)	1,872	24.93
Latvian (0)	12	0.16
Lithuanian (16)	162	2.16
Norwegian (14)	150	2.00
Polish (14)	99	1.32
Portuguese (55)	152	2.02
Russian (0)	70	0.93
Scotch-Irish (133)	264	3.52
Scottish (118)	367	4.89
Slovene (0)	28	0.37
Swedish (200)	415	5.53
Welsh (0)	32	0.43

Hispanic Origin	Population	%
Hispanic or Latino (of any race)	81	1.08
Central American, ex. Mexican	9	0.12
Costa Rican	1	0.01
Guatemalan	3	0.04
Honduran	2	0.03
Salvadoran	3	0.04
Cuban	4	0.05
Dominican Republic	2	0.03
Mexican	7	0.09
Puerto Rican	21	0.28
South American	16	0.21
Argentinean	1	0.01
Chilean	3	0.04
Colombian	7	0.09
Ecuadorian	1	0.01
Paraguayan	2	0.03
Peruvian	2	0.03
Other Hispanic or Latino	22	0.29

Race*	Population	%
African-American/Black (45)	76	1.01
Not Hispanic (45)	74	0.98
Hispanic (0)	2	0.03
American Indian/Alaska Native (6)	54	0.72
Not Hispanic (4)	44	0.59

*Notes: † The Census 2010 population figure is used to calculate the percentages in the Hispanic Origin and Race categories. Ancestry percentages are based on the 2006-2010 American Community Survey population (not shown); ‡ Numbers in parentheses indicate the number of people reporting a single ancestry; * Numbers in parentheses indicate the number of persons reporting this race alone, not in combination with any other race; Please refer to the Explanation of Data for more information.*

Hispanic (2)	10	0.13
Blackfeet (0)	3	0.04
Canadian/French Am. Ind. (0)	4	0.05
Central American Ind. (2)	5	0.07
Cherokee (0)	9	0.12
Iroquois (3)	3	0.04
Navajo (0)	1	0.01
Shoshone (1)	1	0.01
Sioux (0)	3	0.04
Asian (42)	65	0.86
Not Hispanic (42)	61	0.81
Hispanic (0)	4	0.05
Burmese (1)	1	0.01
Chinese, ex. Taiwanese (11)	16	0.21
Filipino (2)	3	0.04
Indian (15)	20	0.27
Japanese (1)	6	0.08
Korean (9)	14	0.19
Thai (0)	1	0.01
Vietnamese (1)	2	0.03
Hawaii Native/Pacific Islander (0)	9	0.12
Not Hispanic (0)	8	0.11
Hispanic (0)	1	0.01
Native Hawaiian (0)	4	0.05
White (7,291)	7,392	98.32
Not Hispanic (7,236)	7,322	97.39
Hispanic (55)	70	0.93

Hamilton

Place Type: Town
County: Essex
Population: 7,764†

Ancestry‡	Population	%
American (279)	279	3.57
Arab (6)	12	0.15
Arab (0)	6	0.08
Lebanese (6)	6	0.08
Armenian (18)	46	0.59
Austrian (20)	57	0.73
British (0)	19	0.24
Canadian (0)	28	0.36
Celtic (0)	65	0.83
Dutch (26)	184	2.35
Eastern European (43)	43	0.55
English (603)	1,967	25.14
European (64)	83	1.06
Finnish (16)	42	0.54
French, ex. Basque (46)	381	4.87
French Canadian (37)	230	2.94
German (177)	872	11.14
Greek (52)	197	2.52
Hungarian (0)	27	0.35
Irish (440)	1,797	22.96
Italian (542)	1,093	13.97
Lithuanian (0)	38	0.49
Norwegian (61)	95	1.21
Pennsylvania German (8)	8	0.10
Polish (50)	354	4.52
Portuguese (0)	106	1.35
Russian (40)	88	1.12
Scotch-Irish (196)	447	5.71
Scottish (219)	520	6.65
Slovak (0)	21	0.27
Swedish (53)	383	4.89
Swiss (0)	29	0.37
Ukrainian (10)	30	0.38
Welsh (12)	80	1.02

Hispanic Origin	Population	%
Hispanic or Latino (of any race)	121	1.56
Central American, ex. Mexican	14	0.18
Costa Rican	4	0.05
Guatemalan	7	0.09
Panamanian	1	0.01
Salvadoran	2	0.03
Cuban	9	0.12
Dominican Republic	6	0.08
Mexican	32	0.41
Puerto Rican	12	0.15
South American	28	0.36
Argentinean	4	0.05
Bolivian	1	0.01
Chilean	2	0.03
Colombian	12	0.15
Peruvian	4	0.05
Venezuelan	5	0.06
Other Hispanic or Latino	20	0.26

Race*	Population	%
African-American/Black (46)	73	0.94
Not Hispanic (42)	66	0.85
Hispanic (4)	7	0.09
American Indian/Alaska Native (14)	36	0.46
Not Hispanic (12)	34	0.44
Hispanic (2)	2	0.03
Cherokee (0)	4	0.05
Chippewa (0)	2	0.03
Iroquois (0)	2	0.03
Pima (3)	3	0.04
Sioux (0)	2	0.03
South American Ind. (2)	2	0.03
Asian (423)	462	5.95
Not Hispanic (420)	457	5.89
Hispanic (3)	5	0.06
Burmese (1)	3	0.04
Cambodian (6)	6	0.08
Chinese, ex. Taiwanese (101)	119	1.53
Filipino (7)	11	0.14
Indian (25)	29	0.37
Japanese (8)	11	0.14
Korean (263)	272	3.50
Malaysian (0)	3	0.04
Taiwanese (6)	6	0.08
Vietnamese (2)	5	0.06
Hawaii Native/Pacific Islander (0)	1	0.01
Not Hispanic (0)	1	0.01
Native Hawaiian (0)	1	0.01
White (7,175)	7,248	93.35
Not Hispanic (7,088)	7,155	92.16
Hispanic (87)	93	1.20

Hanover

Place Type: Town
County: Plymouth
Population: 13,879†

Ancestry‡	Population	%
African, Sub-Saharan (0)	34	0.25
African (0)	34	0.25
American (881)	881	6.41
Arab (27)	151	1.10
Lebanese (27)	125	0.91
Syrian (0)	26	0.19
Armenian (0)	23	0.17
Austrian (0)	14	0.10
Belgian (0)	12	0.09
British (13)	13	0.09
Canadian (25)	148	1.08
Czech (0)	13	0.09
Danish (14)	94	0.68
Dutch (71)	178	1.30
Eastern European (0)	18	0.13
English (486)	2,129	15.49
European (12)	25	0.18
Finnish (29)	108	0.79
French, ex. Basque (277)	785	5.71
French Canadian (178)	696	5.06
German (183)	957	6.96
Greek (78)	158	1.15
Hungarian (0)	85	0.62
Irish (2,451)	5,810	42.28
Italian (633)	2,232	16.24
Latvian (0)	27	0.20
Lithuanian (83)	340	2.47
Norwegian (89)	177	1.29
Polish (144)	486	3.54
Portuguese (65)	309	2.25
Romanian (0)	13	0.09
Russian (35)	67	0.49
Scandinavian (13)	27	0.20
Scotch-Irish (418)	619	4.50
Scottish (295)	554	4.03
Slovak (12)	12	0.09
Swedish (31)	483	3.51
Swiss (0)	16	0.12
Welsh (14)	26	0.19
West Indian, ex. Hispanic (17)	63	0.46
Jamaican (0)	46	0.33
West Indian (17)	17	0.12

Hispanic Origin	Population	%
Hispanic or Latino (of any race)	128	0.92
Central American, ex. Mexican	16	0.12
Costa Rican	5	0.04
Guatemalan	4	0.03
Nicaraguan	3	0.02
Panamanian	4	0.03
Cuban	11	0.08
Dominican Republic	3	0.02
Mexican	25	0.18
Puerto Rican	31	0.22
South American	21	0.15
Argentinean	4	0.03
Chilean	5	0.04
Colombian	4	0.03
Ecuadorian	1	0.01
Paraguayan	3	0.02
Venezuelan	3	0.02
Other South American	1	0.01
Other Hispanic or Latino	21	0.15

Race*	Population	%
African-American/Black (110)	132	0.95
Not Hispanic (106)	128	0.92
Hispanic (4)	4	0.03
American Indian/Alaska Native (15)	28	0.20
Not Hispanic (13)	26	0.19
Hispanic (2)	2	0.01
Aleut *(Alaska Native)* (1)	2	0.01
Cherokee (4)	5	0.04
Iroquois (0)	4	0.03
Mexican American Ind. (1)	1	0.01
Navajo (4)	4	0.03
Asian (161)	239	1.72
Not Hispanic (160)	238	1.71
Hispanic (1)	1	0.01
Chinese, ex. Taiwanese (53)	81	0.58
Filipino (5)	15	0.11
Indian (33)	49	0.35
Japanese (4)	7	0.05
Korean (25)	28	0.20
Pakistani (6)	6	0.04
Thai (1)	1	0.01
Vietnamese (31)	36	0.26
Hawaii Native/Pacific Islander (5)	7	0.05
Not Hispanic (4)	6	0.04
Hispanic (1)	1	0.01
Guamanian/Chamorro (2)	2	0.01
Native Hawaiian (2)	4	0.03
White (13,392)	13,516	97.38
Not Hispanic (13,300)	13,416	96.66
Hispanic (92)	100	0.72

Hanson

Place Type: Town
County: Plymouth
Population: 10,209†

Ancestry‡	Population	%
African, Sub-Saharan (205)	273	2.70
Cape Verdean (205)	273	2.70
Albanian (0)	60	0.59
American (422)	422	4.18
Armenian (0)	34	0.34
Austrian (10)	66	0.65
British (8)	37	0.37

*Notes: † The Census 2010 population figure is used to calculate the percentages in the Hispanic Origin and Race categories. Ancestry percentages are based on the 2006-2010 American Community Survey population (not shown); ‡ Numbers in parentheses indicate the number of people reporting a single ancestry; * Numbers in parentheses indicate the number of persons reporting this race alone, not in combination with any other race; Please refer to the Explanation of Data for more information.*

Canadian (41)	41	0.41
Czech (0)	24	0.24
Czechoslovakian (0)	22	0.22
Danish (12)	66	0.65
Dutch (0)	41	0.41
English (329)	1,477	14.63
European (56)	56	0.55
Finnish (11)	20	0.20
French, ex. Basque (59)	750	7.43
French Canadian (69)	349	3.46
German (195)	1,099	10.89
Greek (38)	97	0.96
Hungarian (7)	67	0.66
Irish (1,578)	4,150	41.11
Israeli (11)	32	0.32
Italian (466)	1,945	19.27
Lithuanian (41)	261	2.59
Northern European (0)	12	0.12
Norwegian (10)	87	0.86
Polish (89)	516	5.11
Portuguese (59)	161	1.60
Russian (16)	78	0.77
Scandinavian (12)	12	0.12
Scotch-Irish (157)	524	5.19
Scottish (113)	372	3.69
Slavic (0)	10	0.10
Swedish (51)	296	2.93
Swiss (0)	9	0.09
Ukrainian (11)	22	0.22
Welsh (0)	69	0.68

Hispanic Origin	Population	%
Hispanic or Latino (of any race)	95	0.93
Central American, ex. Mexican	9	0.09
Costa Rican	1	0.01
Guatemalan	5	0.05
Honduran	2	0.02
Salvadoran	1	0.01
Cuban	12	0.12
Dominican Republic	1	0.01
Mexican	15	0.15
Puerto Rican	30	0.29
South American	18	0.18
Bolivian	1	0.01
Chilean	1	0.01
Colombian	7	0.07
Ecuadorian	8	0.08
Venezuelan	1	0.01
Other Hispanic or Latino	10	0.10

Race*	Population	%
African-American/Black (104)	159	1.56
Not Hispanic (96)	149	1.46
Hispanic (8)	10	0.10
American Indian/Alaska Native (3)	39	0.38
Not Hispanic (2)	37	0.36
Hispanic (1)	2	0.02
Cherokee (0)	2	0.02
Mexican American Ind. (1)	1	0.01
Sioux (0)	4	0.04
Asian (48)	82	0.80
Not Hispanic (48)	81	0.79
Hispanic (0)	1	0.01
Cambodian (2)	3	0.03
Chinese, ex. Taiwanese (11)	21	0.21
Filipino (9)	15	0.15
Indian (13)	15	0.15
Indonesian (2)	3	0.03
Japanese (0)	1	0.01
Korean (8)	13	0.13
Thai (0)	1	0.01
Vietnamese (1)	8	0.08
Hawaii Native/Pacific Islander (1)	4	0.04
Not Hispanic (1)	4	0.04
Native Hawaiian (1)	1	0.01
White (9,850)	9,977	97.73
Not Hispanic (9,785)	9,906	97.03
Hispanic (65)	71	0.70

Harwich

Place Type: Town
County: Barnstable
Population: 12,243†

Ancestry‡	Population	%
African, Sub-Saharan (113)	121	0.98
Cape Verdean (113)	121	0.98
Albanian (43)	54	0.44
American (1,624)	1,624	13.21
Arab (11)	26	0.21
Lebanese (11)	26	0.21
Armenian (26)	26	0.21
Austrian (0)	58	0.47
Belgian (9)	9	0.07
Brazilian (0)	35	0.28
British (55)	61	0.50
Canadian (113)	145	1.18
Croatian (14)	35	0.28
Czech (0)	99	0.81
Danish (0)	35	0.28
Dutch (78)	163	1.33
Eastern European (24)	24	0.20
English (876)	2,574	20.94
European (36)	36	0.29
Finnish (42)	136	1.11
French, ex. Basque (134)	722	5.87
French Canadian (122)	323	2.63
German (186)	994	8.09
Greek (150)	204	1.66
Hungarian (0)	45	0.37
Irish (1,568)	3,347	27.23
Italian (435)	1,174	9.55
Lithuanian (61)	81	0.66
Northern European (14)	14	0.11
Norwegian (84)	207	1.68
Polish (209)	562	4.57
Portuguese (222)	530	4.31
Russian (52)	143	1.16
Scandinavian (12)	24	0.20
Scotch-Irish (71)	287	2.34
Scottish (266)	714	5.81
Slovak (33)	44	0.36
Swedish (95)	370	3.01
Swiss (8)	32	0.26
Ukrainian (22)	22	0.18
Welsh (13)	83	0.68
West Indian, ex. Hispanic (13)	13	0.11
Jamaican (13)	13	0.11

Hispanic Origin	Population	%
Hispanic or Latino (of any race)	178	1.45
Central American, ex. Mexican	4	0.03
Guatemalan	3	0.02
Salvadoran	1	0.01
Cuban	3	0.02
Dominican Republic	19	0.16
Mexican	24	0.20
Puerto Rican	49	0.40
South American	46	0.38
Argentinean	1	0.01
Chilean	5	0.04
Colombian	22	0.18
Peruvian	8	0.07
Venezuelan	3	0.02
Other South American	7	0.06
Other Hispanic or Latino	33	0.27

Race*	Population	%
African-American/Black (193)	293	2.39
Not Hispanic (188)	282	2.30
Hispanic (5)	11	0.09
American Indian/Alaska Native (52)	148	1.21
Not Hispanic (37)	125	1.02
Hispanic (15)	23	0.19
Aleut *(Alaska Native)* (1)	1	0.01
Apache (1)	1	0.01
Blackfeet (0)	2	0.02
Canadian/French Am. Ind. (1)	1	0.01
Cherokee (3)	25	0.20
Choctaw (0)	1	0.01
Iroquois (0)	5	0.04
Mexican American Ind. (2)	2	0.02
Shoshone (2)	2	0.02
Sioux (1)	6	0.05
Asian (83)	127	1.04
Not Hispanic (80)	124	1.01
Hispanic (3)	3	0.02
Cambodian (0)	2	0.02
Chinese, ex. Taiwanese (24)	30	0.25
Filipino (5)	13	0.11
Indian (16)	19	0.16
Indonesian (1)	6	0.05
Japanese (4)	10	0.08
Korean (11)	18	0.15
Nepalese (4)	4	0.03
Thai (0)	2	0.02
Vietnamese (16)	23	0.19
Hawaii Native/Pacific Islander (2)	7	0.06
Not Hispanic (2)	7	0.06
Native Hawaiian (0)	4	0.03
Samoan (1)	1	0.01
White (11,444)	11,635	95.03
Not Hispanic (11,347)	11,536	94.23
Hispanic (97)	99	0.81

Haverhill

Place Type: City
County: Essex
Population: 60,879†

Ancestry‡	Population	%
African, Sub-Saharan (328)	528	0.88
African (267)	467	0.78
Cape Verdean (9)	9	0.01
Kenyan (34)	34	0.06
Nigerian (3)	3	<0.01
Other Sub-Saharan African (15)	15	0.02
Albanian (112)	131	0.22
American (1,709)	1,709	2.84
Arab (411)	677	1.12
Egyptian (75)	75	0.12
Iraqi (156)	156	0.26
Lebanese (60)	291	0.48
Moroccan (51)	51	0.08
Palestinian (0)	8	0.01
Syrian (42)	59	0.10
Other Arab (27)	37	0.06
Armenian (243)	499	0.83
Austrian (9)	64	0.11
Belgian (0)	29	0.05
Brazilian (256)	284	0.47
British (114)	205	0.34
Canadian (305)	885	1.47
Czech (10)	32	0.05
Czechoslovakian (0)	21	0.03
Danish (8)	198	0.33
Dutch (62)	378	0.63
Eastern European (33)	33	0.05
English (1,418)	6,981	11.60
European (183)	193	0.32
Finnish (14)	108	0.18
French, ex. Basque (2,008)	8,478	14.08
French Canadian (1,925)	3,997	6.64
German (546)	3,496	5.81
Greek (791)	1,493	2.48
Hungarian (16)	66	0.11
Irish (4,364)	15,568	25.86
Italian (3,790)	10,559	17.54
Latvian (9)	26	0.04
Lithuanian (121)	682	1.13
Maltese (9)	9	0.01
Northern European (28)	28	0.05
Norwegian (66)	193	0.32
Pennsylvania German (0)	9	0.01
Polish (763)	2,607	4.33
Portuguese (457)	1,273	2.11
Romanian (30)	65	0.11

SECTION TWO

*Notes: † The Census 2010 population figure is used to calculate the percentages in the Hispanic Origin and Race categories. Ancestry percentages are based on the 2006-2010 American Community Survey population (not shown); ‡ Numbers in parentheses indicate the number of people reporting a single ancestry; * Numbers in parentheses indicate the number of persons reporting this race alone, not in combination with any other race; Please refer to the Explanation of Data for more information.*

Russian (129)	462	0.77
Scandinavian (0)	10	0.02
Scotch-Irish (302)	986	1.64
Scottish (463)	1,714	2.85
Serbian (42)	85	0.14
Slovak (12)	25	0.04
Swedish (228)	731	1.21
Swiss (0)	28	0.05
Turkish (0)	58	0.10
Ukrainian (8)	39	0.06
Welsh (33)	101	0.17
West Indian, ex. Hispanic (627)	958	1.59
Barbadian (0)	21	0.03
Bermudan (42)	42	0.07
British West Indian (0)	56	0.09
Haitian (518)	648	1.08
Jamaican (12)	12	0.02
Trinidadian/Tobagonian (42)	97	0.16
West Indian (13)	82	0.14

Hispanic Origin	Population	%
Hispanic or Latino (of any race)	8,831	14.51
Central American, ex. Mexican	612	1.01
Costa Rican	23	0.04
Guatemalan	288	0.47
Honduran	46	0.08
Nicaraguan	16	0.03
Panamanian	24	0.04
Salvadoran	208	0.34
Other Central American	7	0.01
Cuban	125	0.21
Dominican Republic	2,780	4.57
Mexican	564	0.93
Puerto Rican	3,555	5.84
South American	391	0.64
Argentinean	15	0.02
Bolivian	1	<0.01
Chilean	17	0.03
Colombian	198	0.33
Ecuadorian	84	0.14
Paraguayan	3	<0.01
Peruvian	43	0.07
Uruguayan	7	0.01
Venezuelan	20	0.03
Other South American	3	<0.01
Other Hispanic or Latino	804	1.32

Race*	Population	%
African-American/Black (2,042)	2,727	4.48
Not Hispanic (1,533)	1,951	3.20
Hispanic (509)	776	1.27
American Indian/Alaska Native (176)	470	0.77
Not Hispanic (82)	307	0.50
Hispanic (94)	163	0.27
Apache (1)	9	0.01
Blackfeet (4)	23	0.04
Canadian/French Am. Ind. (3)	7	0.01
Central American Ind. (6)	6	0.01
Cherokee (12)	51	0.08
Cheyenne (0)	2	<0.01
Chickasaw (1)	1	<0.01
Chippewa (0)	4	0.01
Choctaw (0)	6	0.01
Cree (1)	2	<0.01
Crow (0)	3	<0.01
Iroquois (5)	22	0.04
Menominee (1)	1	<0.01
Mexican American Ind. (5)	6	0.01
Navajo (1)	1	<0.01
Pueblo (2)	4	0.01
Seminole (0)	1	<0.01
Sioux (1)	9	0.01
South American Ind. (10)	21	0.03
Spanish American Ind. (3)	5	0.01
Tlingit-Haida *(Alaska Native)* (1)	1	<0.01
Asian (988)	1,298	2.13
Not Hispanic (971)	1,234	2.03
Hispanic (17)	64	0.11
Bangladeshi (6)	6	0.01
Cambodian (55)	74	0.12
Chinese, ex. Taiwanese (158)	214	0.35
Filipino (80)	137	0.23
Hmong (1)	1	<0.01
Indian (195)	238	0.39
Indonesian (8)	10	0.02
Japanese (17)	48	0.08
Korean (114)	155	0.25
Laotian (5)	6	0.01
Nepalese (0)	1	<0.01
Pakistani (20)	36	0.06
Taiwanese (7)	10	0.02
Thai (13)	20	0.03
Vietnamese (226)	290	0.48
Hawaii Native/Pacific Islander (17)	80	0.13
Not Hispanic (8)	45	0.07
Hispanic (9)	35	0.06
Guamanian/Chamorro (8)	14	0.02
Native Hawaiian (3)	23	0.04
Samoan (0)	1	<0.01
Tongan (0)	3	<0.01
White (52,381)	53,756	88.30
Not Hispanic (48,394)	49,233	80.87
Hispanic (3,987)	4,523	7.43

Hingham

Place Type: Town
County: Plymouth
Population: 22,157†

Ancestry‡	Population	%
African, Sub-Saharan (35)	66	0.30
Cape Verdean (35)	66	0.30
American (738)	738	3.40
Arab (54)	259	1.19
Lebanese (43)	211	0.97
Moroccan (11)	19	0.09
Syrian (0)	29	0.13
Armenian (76)	164	0.75
Australian (8)	61	0.28
Austrian (28)	138	0.64
Belgian (0)	21	0.10
British (106)	141	0.65
Canadian (161)	273	1.26
Czech (0)	92	0.42
Czechoslovakian (0)	9	0.04
Danish (9)	65	0.30
Dutch (31)	197	0.91
Eastern European (24)	24	0.11
English (888)	4,194	19.30
European (68)	68	0.31
Finnish (11)	113	0.52
French, ex. Basque (49)	1,159	5.33
French Canadian (156)	501	2.31
German (229)	2,063	9.49
Greek (109)	591	2.72
Hungarian (0)	58	0.27
Irish (3,908)	9,400	43.26
Italian (1,098)	3,481	16.02
Latvian (19)	49	0.23
Lithuanian (26)	146	0.67
Northern European (50)	50	0.23
Norwegian (90)	328	1.51
Polish (121)	743	3.42
Portuguese (75)	204	0.94
Romanian (0)	50	0.23
Russian (61)	371	1.71
Scandinavian (23)	40	0.18
Scotch-Irish (498)	842	3.87
Scottish (289)	1,082	4.98
Slovak (29)	39	0.18
Slovene (0)	12	0.06
Swedish (51)	562	2.59
Swiss (10)	161	0.74
Ukrainian (8)	51	0.23
Welsh (76)	211	0.97
West Indian, ex. Hispanic (0)	44	0.20
Barbadian (0)	26	0.12
West Indian (0)	18	0.08

Hispanic Origin	Population	%
Hispanic or Latino (of any race)	241	1.09
Central American, ex. Mexican	35	0.16
Guatemalan	17	0.08
Honduran	5	0.02
Nicaraguan	8	0.04
Panamanian	3	0.01
Salvadoran	2	0.01
Cuban	18	0.08
Dominican Republic	3	0.01
Mexican	40	0.18
Puerto Rican	36	0.16
South American	67	0.30
Argentinean	19	0.09
Bolivian	2	0.01
Chilean	11	0.05
Colombian	15	0.07
Ecuadorian	4	0.02
Paraguayan	2	0.01
Peruvian	9	0.04
Uruguayan	1	<0.01
Venezuelan	1	<0.01
Other South American	3	0.01
Other Hispanic or Latino	42	0.19

Race*	Population	%
African-American/Black (118)	175	0.79
Not Hispanic (109)	162	0.73
Hispanic (9)	13	0.06
American Indian/Alaska Native (34)	103	0.46
Not Hispanic (31)	99	0.45
Hispanic (3)	4	0.02
Apache (0)	1	<0.01
Blackfeet (0)	1	<0.01
Cherokee (2)	25	0.11
Choctaw (0)	4	0.02
Delaware (0)	1	<0.01
Lumbee (1)	1	<0.01
Mexican American Ind. (3)	3	0.01
Seminole (0)	2	0.01
Sioux (0)	1	<0.01
South American Ind. (0)	1	<0.01
Asian (343)	484	2.18
Not Hispanic (343)	475	2.14
Hispanic (0)	9	0.04
Cambodian (7)	9	0.04
Chinese, ex. Taiwanese (140)	193	0.87
Filipino (18)	52	0.23
Indian (55)	69	0.31
Indonesian (6)	9	0.04
Japanese (15)	30	0.14
Korean (43)	54	0.24
Pakistani (7)	10	0.05
Sri Lankan (1)	5	0.02
Taiwanese (3)	3	0.01
Thai (3)	7	0.03
Vietnamese (26)	40	0.18
Hawaii Native/Pacific Islander (8)	13	0.06
Not Hispanic (8)	13	0.06
Native Hawaiian (4)	8	0.04
White (21,325)	21,580	97.40
Not Hispanic (21,135)	21,375	96.47
Hispanic (190)	205	0.93

Holbrook

Place Type: CDP/Town
County: Norfolk
Population: 10,791†

Ancestry‡	Population	%
African, Sub-Saharan (186)	357	3.34
African (44)	191	1.79
Cape Verdean (142)	166	1.55
American (186)	186	1.74
Arab (75)	116	1.08
Arab (65)	65	0.61
Lebanese (10)	51	0.48
Austrian (20)	20	0.19
Brazilian (236)	236	2.21

*Notes: † The Census 2010 population figure is used to calculate the percentages in the Hispanic Origin and Race categories. Ancestry percentages are based on the 2006-2010 American Community Survey population (not shown); ‡ Numbers in parentheses indicate the number of people reporting a single ancestry; * Numbers in parentheses indicate the number of persons reporting this race alone, not in combination with any other race; Please refer to the Explanation of Data for more information.*

Bulgarian (49)	49	0.46
Canadian (50)	161	1.51
Czechoslovakian (66)	66	0.62
Danish (0)	50	0.47
Dutch (27)	78	0.73
Eastern European (24)	24	0.22
English (233)	1,238	11.58
Finnish (20)	48	0.45
French, ex. Basque (69)	549	5.13
French Canadian (164)	461	4.31
German (54)	838	7.84
Greek (32)	78	0.73
Hungarian (0)	28	0.26
Irish (1,493)	4,250	39.74
Italian (758)	2,198	20.55
Lithuanian (53)	66	0.62
Norwegian (11)	25	0.23
Pennsylvania German (0)	12	0.11
Polish (83)	514	4.81
Portuguese (23)	54	0.50
Russian (16)	61	0.57
Scotch-Irish (45)	110	1.03
Scottish (103)	400	3.74
Slovak (0)	25	0.23
Swedish (53)	150	1.40
Turkish (0)	8	0.07
Welsh (0)	30	0.28
West Indian, ex. Hispanic (325)	448	4.19
Haitian (179)	302	2.82
Jamaican (107)	107	1.00
Trinidadian/Tobagonian (39)	39	0.36

Hispanic Origin	Population	%
Hispanic or Latino (of any race)	474	4.39
Central American, ex. Mexican	48	0.44
Costa Rican	6	0.06
Guatemalan	12	0.11
Honduran	13	0.12
Panamanian	11	0.10
Salvadoran	2	0.02
Other Central American	4	0.04
Cuban	11	0.10
Dominican Republic	39	0.36
Mexican	34	0.32
Puerto Rican	139	1.29
South American	102	0.95
Argentinean	6	0.06
Chilean	10	0.09
Colombian	22	0.20
Peruvian	61	0.57
Uruguayan	2	0.02
Venezuelan	1	0.01
Other Hispanic or Latino	101	0.94

Race*	Population	%
African-American/Black (967)	1,132	10.49
Not Hispanic (918)	1,055	9.78
Hispanic (49)	77	0.71
American Indian/Alaska Native (28)	104	0.96
Not Hispanic (22)	88	0.82
Hispanic (6)	16	0.15
Apache (5)	5	0.05
Canadian/French Am. Ind. (0)	4	0.04
Cherokee (6)	21	0.19
Comanche (2)	2	0.02
Creek (0)	1	0.01
Iroquois (3)	3	0.03
Mexican American Ind. (1)	1	0.01
Sioux (0)	1	0.01
South American Ind. (2)	5	0.05
Asian (314)	368	3.41
Not Hispanic (310)	362	3.35
Hispanic (4)	6	0.06
Cambodian (6)	8	0.07
Chinese, ex. Taiwanese (60)	72	0.67
Filipino (66)	75	0.70
Hmong (0)	3	0.03
Indian (48)	49	0.45
Indonesian (0)	5	0.05
Japanese (10)	21	0.19
Korean (5)	8	0.07
Laotian (5)	5	0.05
Nepalese (1)	1	0.01
Pakistani (2)	2	0.02
Vietnamese (101)	104	0.96
Hawaii Native/Pacific Islander (3)	22	0.20
Not Hispanic (2)	19	0.18
Hispanic (1)	3	0.03
Guamanian/Chamorro (1)	2	0.02
Native Hawaiian (1)	7	0.06
Samoan (1)	3	0.03
White (8,935)	9,148	84.77
Not Hispanic (8,721)	8,897	82.45
Hispanic (214)	251	2.33

Holden

Place Type: Town
County: Worcester
Population: 17,346†

Ancestry‡	Population	%
African, Sub-Saharan (89)	89	0.52
African (39)	39	0.23
Ghanaian (50)	50	0.29
Albanian (84)	140	0.82
American (658)	658	3.85
Arab (218)	306	1.79
Arab (105)	105	0.62
Lebanese (113)	168	0.98
Syrian (0)	9	0.05
Other Arab (0)	24	0.14
Armenian (21)	67	0.39
Austrian (0)	33	0.19
British (73)	119	0.70
Canadian (70)	126	0.74
Czech (0)	18	0.11
Czechoslovakian (0)	7	0.04
Danish (15)	118	0.69
Dutch (10)	182	1.07
Eastern European (56)	56	0.33
English (766)	2,572	15.06
European (142)	142	0.83
Finnish (31)	135	0.79
French, ex. Basque (339)	2,054	12.03
French Canadian (256)	732	4.29
German (275)	1,694	9.92
Greek (157)	262	1.53
Hungarian (8)	57	0.33
Icelander (9)	9	0.05
Iranian (11)	33	0.19
Irish (1,404)	4,842	28.36
Italian (933)	2,819	16.51
Latvian (0)	27	0.16
Lithuanian (67)	340	1.99
Northern European (20)	20	0.12
Norwegian (28)	169	0.99
Polish (482)	1,243	7.28
Portuguese (41)	220	1.29
Russian (129)	288	1.69
Scandinavian (57)	70	0.41
Scotch-Irish (98)	335	1.96
Scottish (134)	528	3.09
Slovak (11)	33	0.19
Slovene (8)	17	0.10
Swedish (437)	1,221	7.15
Swiss (0)	7	0.04
Ukrainian (45)	131	0.77
Welsh (56)	135	0.79
West Indian, ex. Hispanic (13)	13	0.08
Trinidadian/Tobagonian (13)	13	0.08

Hispanic Origin	Population	%
Hispanic or Latino (of any race)	373	2.15
Central American, ex. Mexican	17	0.10
Guatemalan	1	0.01
Honduran	8	0.05
Panamanian	1	0.01
Salvadoran	7	0.04
Cuban	16	0.09
Dominican Republic	23	0.13
Mexican	57	0.33
Puerto Rican	149	0.86
South American	57	0.33
Argentinean	1	0.01
Chilean	4	0.02
Colombian	22	0.13
Ecuadorian	16	0.09
Peruvian	6	0.03
Uruguayan	4	0.02
Venezuelan	4	0.02
Other Hispanic or Latino	54	0.31

Race*	Population	%
African-American/Black (184)	253	1.46
Not Hispanic (163)	217	1.25
Hispanic (21)	36	0.21
American Indian/Alaska Native (11)	56	0.32
Not Hispanic (9)	48	0.28
Hispanic (2)	8	0.05
Blackfeet (1)	1	0.01
Canadian/French Am. Ind. (0)	1	0.01
Cherokee (0)	5	0.03
Comanche (0)	1	0.01
Creek (0)	1	0.01
Iroquois (1)	4	0.02
Mexican American Ind. (0)	1	0.01
Tlingit-Haida *(Alaska Native)* (0)	1	0.01
Ute (2)	2	0.01
Yaqui (1)	4	0.02
Asian (517)	610	3.52
Not Hispanic (513)	602	3.47
Hispanic (4)	8	0.05
Burmese (1)	1	0.01
Cambodian (10)	10	0.06
Chinese, ex. Taiwanese (142)	163	0.94
Filipino (36)	43	0.25
Indian (101)	115	0.66
Indonesian (2)	2	0.01
Japanese (36)	62	0.36
Korean (63)	81	0.47
Laotian (12)	14	0.08
Nepalese (3)	3	0.02
Pakistani (13)	14	0.08
Sri Lankan (2)	2	0.01
Taiwanese (7)	7	0.04
Thai (2)	2	0.01
Vietnamese (67)	81	0.47
Hawaii Native/Pacific Islander (2)	6	0.03
Not Hispanic (2)	6	0.03
Native Hawaiian (0)	2	0.01
Samoan (0)	2	0.01
White (16,320)	16,521	95.24
Not Hispanic (16,086)	16,249	93.68
Hispanic (234)	272	1.57

Holliston

Place Type: Town
County: Middlesex
Population: 13,547†

Ancestry‡	Population	%
African, Sub-Saharan (17)	17	0.13
African (17)	17	0.13
Albanian (16)	93	0.69
Alsatian (0)	36	0.27
American (804)	804	5.99
Arab (53)	119	0.89
Egyptian (44)	44	0.33
Lebanese (9)	47	0.35
Syrian (0)	28	0.21
Armenian (0)	73	0.54
Austrian (12)	47	0.35
Brazilian (38)	47	0.35
British (39)	108	0.80
Canadian (141)	236	1.76
Czech (12)	45	0.34
Czechoslovakian (8)	13	0.10
Danish (0)	74	0.55

*Notes: † The Census 2010 population figure is used to calculate the percentages in the Hispanic Origin and Race categories. Ancestry percentages are based on the 2006-2010 American Community Survey population (not shown); ‡ Numbers in parentheses indicate the number of people reporting a single ancestry; * Numbers in parentheses indicate the number of persons reporting this race alone, not in combination with any other race; Please refer to the Explanation of Data for more information.*

Dutch (8)	110	0.82
Eastern European (37)	37	0.28
English (650)	2,717	20.23
European (206)	206	1.53
Finnish (9)	34	0.25
French, ex. Basque (151)	674	5.02
French Canadian (148)	527	3.92
German (169)	1,280	9.53
Greek (0)	151	1.12
Hungarian (15)	46	0.34
Irish (1,398)	3,620	26.95
Italian (894)	2,309	17.19
Lithuanian (42)	104	0.77
Norwegian (9)	126	0.94
Polish (207)	1,064	7.92
Portuguese (82)	197	1.47
Romanian (0)	38	0.28
Russian (94)	264	1.97
Scandinavian (8)	20	0.15
Scotch-Irish (195)	385	2.87
Scottish (59)	656	4.88
Slovak (11)	11	0.08
Swedish (12)	266	1.98
Swiss (63)	76	0.57
Ukrainian (54)	92	0.68
Welsh (0)	105	0.78

Hispanic Origin	Population	%
Hispanic or Latino (of any race)	246	1.82
Central American, ex. Mexican	46	0.34
Costa Rican	3	0.02
Guatemalan	18	0.13
Honduran	4	0.03
Nicaraguan	2	0.01
Panamanian	1	0.01
Salvadoran	13	0.10
Other Central American	5	0.04
Cuban	15	0.11
Dominican Republic	4	0.03
Mexican	32	0.24
Puerto Rican	51	0.38
South American	62	0.46
Argentinean	1	0.01
Bolivian	12	0.09
Chilean	3	0.02
Colombian	36	0.27
Ecuadorian	1	0.01
Peruvian	4	0.03
Uruguayan	1	0.01
Venezuelan	4	0.03
Other Hispanic or Latino	36	0.27

Race*	Population	%
African-American/Black (118)	154	1.14
Not Hispanic (117)	153	1.13
Hispanic (1)	1	0.01
American Indian/Alaska Native (13)	33	0.24
Not Hispanic (12)	31	0.23
Hispanic (1)	2	0.01
Cherokee (0)	2	0.01
Chippewa (1)	1	0.01
Inupiat *(Alaska Native)* (5)	5	0.04
Iroquois (0)	7	0.05
Lumbee (2)	2	0.01
Asian (337)	415	3.06
Not Hispanic (331)	407	3.00
Hispanic (6)	8	0.06
Burmese (2)	2	0.01
Chinese, ex. Taiwanese (89)	117	0.86
Filipino (26)	39	0.29
Indian (125)	135	1.00
Japanese (18)	38	0.28
Korean (26)	36	0.27
Nepalese (2)	2	0.01
Pakistani (6)	6	0.04
Sri Lankan (1)	4	0.03
Taiwanese (11)	13	0.10
Thai (2)	4	0.03
Vietnamese (14)	22	0.16
Hawaii Native/Pacific Islander (2)	4	0.03
Not Hispanic (2)	3	0.02
Hispanic (0)	1	0.01
Guamanian/Chamorro (2)	3	0.02
White (12,825)	12,966	95.71
Not Hispanic (12,645)	12,772	94.28
Hispanic (180)	194	1.43

Holyoke

Place Type: City
County: Hampden
Population: 39,880†

Ancestry‡	Population	%
African, Sub-Saharan (72)	72	0.18
African (3)	3	0.01
Kenyan (28)	28	0.07
Sierra Leonean (41)	41	0.10
Albanian (23)	23	0.06
American (357)	357	0.90
Arab (49)	129	0.32
Lebanese (49)	79	0.20
Syrian (0)	25	0.06
Other Arab (0)	25	0.06
Austrian (0)	36	0.09
Belgian (0)	11	0.03
British (24)	53	0.13
Canadian (250)	322	0.81
Czech (14)	71	0.18
Czechoslovakian (13)	26	0.07
Danish (0)	31	0.08
Dutch (18)	150	0.38
Eastern European (53)	53	0.13
English (949)	2,217	5.56
European (97)	103	0.26
French, ex. Basque (1,126)	3,626	9.09
French Canadian (695)	1,342	3.36
German (578)	1,887	4.73
Greek (113)	172	0.43
Guyanese (11)	11	0.03
Hungarian (0)	44	0.11
Icelander (0)	6	0.02
Irish (2,740)	6,076	15.23
Italian (565)	1,609	4.03
Lithuanian (15)	51	0.13
Norwegian (0)	13	0.03
Polish (1,705)	3,379	8.47
Portuguese (153)	240	0.60
Russian (55)	134	0.34
Scandinavian (14)	14	0.04
Scotch-Irish (92)	339	0.85
Scottish (208)	431	1.08
Slovak (10)	38	0.10
Swedish (198)	318	0.80
Turkish (14)	14	0.04
Ukrainian (0)	38	0.10
Welsh (0)	70	0.18
West Indian, ex. Hispanic (78)	105	0.26
British West Indian (8)	8	0.02
Haitian (9)	9	0.02
Jamaican (61)	73	0.18
West Indian (0)	15	0.04
Yugoslavian (0)	6	0.02

Hispanic Origin	Population	%
Hispanic or Latino (of any race)	19,313	48.43
Central American, ex. Mexican	135	0.34
Costa Rican	7	0.02
Guatemalan	21	0.05
Honduran	18	0.05
Nicaraguan	8	0.02
Panamanian	13	0.03
Salvadoran	68	0.17
Cuban	70	0.18
Dominican Republic	349	0.88
Mexican	167	0.42
Puerto Rican	17,825	44.70
South American	297	0.74
Argentinean	2	0.01
Bolivian	1	<0.01
Colombian	202	0.51
Ecuadorian	40	0.10
Paraguayan	1	<0.01
Peruvian	17	0.04
Uruguayan	3	0.01
Venezuelan	25	0.06
Other South American	6	0.02
Other Hispanic or Latino	470	1.18

Race*	Population	%
African-American/Black (1,867)	2,466	6.18
Not Hispanic (961)	1,199	3.01
Hispanic (906)	1,267	3.18
American Indian/Alaska Native (301)	585	1.47
Not Hispanic (43)	181	0.45
Hispanic (258)	404	1.01
Apache (1)	4	0.01
Blackfeet (2)	19	0.05
Canadian/French Am. Ind. (1)	1	<0.01
Central American Ind. (6)	10	0.03
Cherokee (6)	26	0.07
Chippewa (0)	1	<0.01
Choctaw (1)	1	<0.01
Creek (0)	2	0.01
Houma (2)	2	0.01
Iroquois (3)	12	0.03
Menominee (1)	3	0.01
Mexican American Ind. (3)	5	0.01
Navajo (2)	2	0.01
Sioux (2)	5	0.01
South American Ind. (57)	67	0.17
Spanish American Ind. (0)	6	0.02
Asian (428)	574	1.44
Not Hispanic (402)	503	1.26
Hispanic (26)	71	0.18
Bangladeshi (3)	3	0.01
Cambodian (82)	96	0.24
Chinese, ex. Taiwanese (76)	99	0.25
Filipino (30)	43	0.11
Indian (99)	122	0.31
Indonesian (1)	3	0.01
Japanese (10)	21	0.05
Korean (28)	41	0.10
Laotian (3)	4	0.01
Nepalese (3)	3	0.01
Pakistani (18)	22	0.06
Taiwanese (2)	3	0.01
Thai (15)	19	0.05
Vietnamese (30)	33	0.08
Hawaii Native/Pacific Islander (27)	121	0.30
Not Hispanic (7)	16	0.04
Hispanic (20)	105	0.26
Guamanian/Chamorro (8)	11	0.03
Native Hawaiian (5)	13	0.03
Samoan (2)	7	0.02
White (26,329)	27,549	69.08
Not Hispanic (18,651)	19,045	47.76
Hispanic (7,678)	8,504	21.32

Hopkinton

Place Type: Town
County: Middlesex
Population: 14,925†

Ancestry‡	Population	%
Albanian (14)	28	0.19
American (550)	550	3.80
Arab (111)	173	1.20
Egyptian (111)	111	0.77
Lebanese (0)	62	0.43
Armenian (10)	62	0.43
Belgian (0)	23	0.16
Brazilian (12)	12	0.08
British (95)	95	0.66
Canadian (40)	173	1.20
Czech (0)	47	0.32
Czechoslovakian (0)	14	0.10
Danish (42)	114	0.79
Dutch (89)	181	1.25

*Notes: † The Census 2010 population figure is used to calculate the percentages in the Hispanic Origin and Race categories. Ancestry percentages are based on the 2006-2010 American Community Survey population (not shown); ‡ Numbers in parentheses indicate the number of people reporting a single ancestry; * Numbers in parentheses indicate the number of persons reporting this race alone, not in combination with any other race; Please refer to the Explanation of Data for more information.*

Ancestry	Population	%
Eastern European (46)	46	0.32
English (384)	2,217	15.32
Estonian (0)	10	0.07
European (94)	117	0.81
Finnish (0)	14	0.10
French, ex. Basque (90)	729	5.04
French Canadian (139)	680	4.70
German (309)	1,851	12.79
Greek (28)	189	1.31
Hungarian (9)	51	0.35
Irish (1,246)	4,899	33.85
Italian (1,189)	3,738	25.83
Latvian (0)	16	0.11
Lithuanian (0)	22	0.15
New Zealander (0)	16	0.11
Northern European (178)	178	1.23
Norwegian (27)	60	0.41
Polish (178)	728	5.03
Portuguese (59)	287	1.98
Romanian (45)	58	0.40
Russian (190)	318	2.20
Scandinavian (107)	134	0.93
Scotch-Irish (96)	287	1.98
Scottish (78)	362	2.50
Slovak (16)	25	0.17
Swedish (56)	260	1.80
Swiss (0)	21	0.15
Turkish (52)	52	0.36
Ukrainian (44)	44	0.30
Welsh (0)	60	0.41

Hispanic Origin	Population	%
Hispanic or Latino (of any race)	267	1.79
Central American, ex. Mexican	31	0.21
Costa Rican	2	0.01
Guatemalan	21	0.14
Nicaraguan	1	0.01
Salvadoran	4	0.03
Other Central American	3	0.02
Cuban	23	0.15
Dominican Republic	6	0.04
Mexican	53	0.36
Puerto Rican	70	0.47
South American	48	0.32
Argentinean	6	0.04
Chilean	6	0.04
Colombian	18	0.12
Ecuadorian	1	0.01
Paraguayan	1	0.01
Peruvian	8	0.05
Venezuelan	8	0.05
Other Hispanic or Latino	36	0.24

Race*	Population	%
African-American/Black (123)	154	1.03
Not Hispanic (122)	147	0.98
Hispanic (1)	7	0.05
American Indian/Alaska Native (11)	42	0.28
Not Hispanic (8)	34	0.23
Hispanic (3)	8	0.05
Blackfeet (0)	2	0.01
Cherokee (1)	6	0.04
Choctaw (0)	1	0.01
Cree (0)	2	0.01
Crow (1)	1	0.01
Iroquois (1)	1	0.01
Potawatomi (0)	1	0.01
South American Ind. (0)	5	0.03
Asian (655)	767	5.14
Not Hispanic (654)	763	5.11
Hispanic (1)	4	0.03
Bangladeshi (14)	14	0.09
Burmese (2)	2	0.01
Cambodian (1)	1	0.01
Chinese, ex. Taiwanese (174)	206	1.38
Filipino (21)	35	0.23
Indian (303)	328	2.20
Indonesian (2)	2	0.01
Japanese (19)	26	0.17
Korean (43)	59	0.40
Malaysian (0)	1	0.01
Nepalese (1)	3	0.02
Pakistani (31)	36	0.24
Taiwanese (10)	19	0.13
Thai (14)	17	0.11
Vietnamese (8)	11	0.07
Hawaii Native/Pacific Islander (0)	11	0.07
Not Hispanic (0)	10	0.07
Hispanic (0)	1	0.01
Guamanian/Chamorro (0)	6	0.04
Native Hawaiian (0)	1	0.01
White (13,902)	14,064	94.23
Not Hispanic (13,687)	13,830	92.66
Hispanic (215)	234	1.57

Hudson

Place Type: CDP
County: Middlesex
Population: 14,907[†]

Ancestry[‡]	Population	%
African, Sub-Saharan (8)	17	0.12
Other Sub-Saharan African (8)	17	0.12
Albanian (12)	22	0.15
American (466)	466	3.18
Arab (21)	77	0.53
Jordanian (21)	21	0.14
Lebanese (0)	18	0.12
Other Arab (0)	38	0.26
Armenian (66)	147	1.00
Assyrian/Chaldean/Syriac (0)	14	0.10
Austrian (54)	54	0.37
Brazilian (306)	306	2.09
British (50)	64	0.44
Canadian (12)	106	0.72
Czechoslovakian (0)	12	0.08
Danish (0)	68	0.46
Dutch (24)	89	0.61
Eastern European (29)	29	0.20
English (836)	1,925	13.14
European (138)	176	1.20
Finnish (10)	73	0.50
French, ex. Basque (196)	910	6.21
French Canadian (349)	790	5.39
German (357)	1,109	7.57
Greek (43)	117	0.80
Hungarian (8)	39	0.27
Irish (1,622)	3,718	25.37
Israeli (83)	83	0.57
Italian (603)	1,643	11.21
Latvian (29)	38	0.26
Lithuanian (46)	135	0.92
Norwegian (67)	155	1.06
Polish (147)	433	2.96
Portuguese (1,977)	2,337	15.95
Romanian (0)	9	0.06
Russian (108)	160	1.09
Scandinavian (18)	34	0.23
Scotch-Irish (167)	370	2.53
Scottish (85)	319	2.18
Slovene (9)	29	0.20
Swedish (79)	231	1.58
Swiss (16)	16	0.11
Ukrainian (12)	26	0.18
Welsh (0)	40	0.27
West Indian, ex. Hispanic (23)	23	0.16
Haitian (23)	23	0.16

Hispanic Origin	Population	%
Hispanic or Latino (of any race)	718	4.82
Central American, ex. Mexican	159	1.07
Costa Rican	5	0.03
Guatemalan	119	0.80
Honduran	6	0.04
Nicaraguan	7	0.05
Salvadoran	22	0.15
Cuban	5	0.03
Dominican Republic	29	0.19
Mexican	78	0.52
Puerto Rican	222	1.49
South American	128	0.86
Argentinean	10	0.07
Bolivian	5	0.03
Chilean	18	0.12
Colombian	32	0.21
Ecuadorian	24	0.16
Peruvian	27	0.18
Uruguayan	1	0.01
Venezuelan	3	0.02
Other South American	8	0.05
Other Hispanic or Latino	97	0.65

Race*	Population	%
African-American/Black (255)	360	2.41
Not Hispanic (243)	326	2.19
Hispanic (12)	34	0.23
American Indian/Alaska Native (25)	82	0.55
Not Hispanic (11)	58	0.39
Hispanic (14)	24	0.16
Blackfeet (3)	8	0.05
Cherokee (3)	5	0.03
Chippewa (0)	1	0.01
Creek (0)	2	0.01
Mexican American Ind. (1)	3	0.02
Navajo (1)	1	0.01
Pueblo (0)	1	0.01
Seminole (0)	1	0.01
South American Ind. (2)	6	0.04
Spanish American Ind. (4)	4	0.03
Yup'ik *(Alaska Native)* (0)	2	0.01
Asian (316)	388	2.60
Not Hispanic (311)	379	2.54
Hispanic (5)	9	0.06
Bangladeshi (3)	3	0.02
Cambodian (5)	12	0.08
Chinese, ex. Taiwanese (86)	99	0.66
Filipino (13)	17	0.11
Hmong (8)	8	0.05
Indian (123)	135	0.91
Japanese (10)	22	0.15
Korean (15)	22	0.15
Malaysian (2)	4	0.03
Pakistani (2)	3	0.02
Sri Lankan (1)	1	0.01
Taiwanese (6)	6	0.04
Thai (0)	1	0.01
Vietnamese (27)	33	0.22
Hawaii Native/Pacific Islander (0)	11	0.07
Not Hispanic (0)	11	0.07
Samoan (0)	2	0.01
White (13,548)	13,863	93.00
Not Hispanic (13,091)	13,353	89.58
Hispanic (457)	510	3.42

Hudson

Place Type: Town
County: Middlesex
Population: 19,063[†]

Ancestry[‡]	Population	%
African, Sub-Saharan (8)	17	0.09
Other Sub-Saharan African (8)	17	0.09
Albanian (12)	22	0.12
American (660)	660	3.54
Arab (21)	77	0.41
Jordanian (21)	21	0.11
Lebanese (0)	18	0.10
Other Arab (0)	38	0.20
Armenian (66)	147	0.79
Assyrian/Chaldean/Syriac (0)	14	0.08
Australian (0)	8	0.04
Austrian (54)	54	0.29
Brazilian (380)	380	2.04
British (101)	115	0.62
Canadian (49)	161	0.86
Czech (0)	32	0.17
Czechoslovakian (0)	19	0.10
Danish (0)	91	0.49

SECTION TWO

*Notes: † The Census 2010 population figure is used to calculate the percentages in the Hispanic Origin and Race categories. Ancestry percentages are based on the 2006-2010 American Community Survey population (not shown); ‡ Numbers in parentheses indicate the number of people reporting a single ancestry; * Numbers in parentheses indicate the number of persons reporting this race alone, not in combination with any other race; Please refer to the Explanation of Data for more information.*

Dutch (24)	95	0.51
Eastern European (29)	29	0.16
English (1,029)	2,550	13.68
European (151)	189	1.01
Finnish (48)	167	0.90
French, ex. Basque (224)	1,212	6.50
French Canadian (418)	930	4.99
German (481)	1,439	7.72
Greek (49)	131	0.70
Hungarian (8)	39	0.21
Irish (2,099)	4,874	26.14
Israeli (83)	83	0.45
Italian (846)	2,276	12.21
Latvian (29)	38	0.20
Lithuanian (59)	172	0.92
Norwegian (67)	176	0.94
Polish (275)	741	3.97
Portuguese (2,177)	2,576	13.82
Romanian (0)	26	0.14
Russian (119)	186	1.00
Scandinavian (18)	34	0.18
Scotch-Irish (238)	491	2.63
Scottish (176)	454	2.44
Slovene (9)	37	0.20
Swedish (100)	357	1.91
Swiss (16)	16	0.09
Ukrainian (20)	34	0.18
Welsh (0)	57	0.31
West Indian, ex. Hispanic (23)	23	0.12
Haitian (23)	23	0.12

Hispanic Origin	Population	%
Hispanic or Latino (of any race)	814	4.27
Central American, ex. Mexican	167	0.88
Costa Rican	6	0.03
Guatemalan	126	0.66
Honduran	6	0.03
Nicaraguan	7	0.04
Salvadoran	22	0.12
Cuban	9	0.05
Dominican Republic	30	0.16
Mexican	97	0.51
Puerto Rican	245	1.29
South American	146	0.77
Argentinean	10	0.05
Bolivian	6	0.03
Chilean	18	0.09
Colombian	42	0.22
Ecuadorian	25	0.13
Peruvian	33	0.17
Uruguayan	1	0.01
Venezuelan	3	0.02
Other South American	8	0.04
Other Hispanic or Latino	120	0.63

Race*	Population	%
African-American/Black (289)	404	2.12
Not Hispanic (276)	369	1.94
Hispanic (13)	35	0.18
American Indian/Alaska Native (27)	97	0.51
Not Hispanic (13)	72	0.38
Hispanic (14)	25	0.13
Blackfeet (3)	8	0.04
Cherokee (3)	7	0.04
Chippewa (0)	1	0.01
Creek (0)	2	0.01
Mexican American Ind. (1)	3	0.02
Navajo (1)	1	0.01
Pueblo (0)	1	0.01
Seminole (0)	1	0.01
South American Ind. (2)	6	0.03
Spanish American Ind. (4)	4	0.02
Yup'ik *(Alaska Native)* (0)	2	0.01
Asian (431)	522	2.74
Not Hispanic (426)	513	2.69
Hispanic (5)	9	0.05
Bangladeshi (3)	3	0.02
Cambodian (12)	19	0.10
Chinese, ex. Taiwanese (114)	135	0.71
Filipino (13)	17	0.09
Hmong (9)	10	0.05
Indian (174)	191	1.00
Japanese (14)	28	0.15
Korean (24)	33	0.17
Malaysian (2)	4	0.02
Pakistani (8)	9	0.05
Sri Lankan (1)	1	0.01
Taiwanese (7)	7	0.04
Thai (1)	2	0.01
Vietnamese (34)	41	0.22
Hawaii Native/Pacific Islander (0)	13	0.07
Not Hispanic (0)	13	0.07
Samoan (0)	2	0.01
White (17,474)	17,836	93.56
Not Hispanic (16,945)	17,252	90.50
Hispanic (529)	584	3.06

Hull

Place Type: CDP/Town
County: Plymouth
Population: 10,293†

Ancestry‡	Population	%
Albanian (51)	51	0.49
American (223)	223	2.14
Arab (0)	13	0.12
Lebanese (0)	13	0.12
Armenian (0)	12	0.12
Austrian (10)	33	0.32
Belgian (0)	9	0.09
Brazilian (36)	36	0.35
British (18)	42	0.40
Canadian (23)	68	0.65
Czech (13)	13	0.12
Czechoslovakian (13)	13	0.12
Danish (0)	53	0.51
Dutch (0)	76	0.73
Eastern European (13)	13	0.12
English (280)	1,236	11.86
European (52)	62	0.60
French, ex. Basque (63)	992	9.52
French Canadian (46)	146	1.40
German (95)	962	9.23
Greek (49)	177	1.70
Hungarian (10)	24	0.23
Irish (1,968)	4,949	47.50
Italian (579)	2,188	21.00
Lithuanian (38)	144	1.38
Norwegian (7)	32	0.31
Pennsylvania German (0)	21	0.20
Polish (49)	357	3.43
Portuguese (43)	436	4.18
Russian (158)	243	2.33
Scotch-Irish (150)	434	4.17
Scottish (94)	355	3.41
Slavic (9)	18	0.17
Slovak (16)	16	0.15
Swedish (78)	239	2.29
Swiss (0)	24	0.23
Ukrainian (28)	39	0.37
Welsh (0)	16	0.15
West Indian, ex. Hispanic (32)	32	0.31
Jamaican (32)	32	0.31

Hispanic Origin	Population	%
Hispanic or Latino (of any race)	173	1.68
Central American, ex. Mexican	19	0.18
Guatemalan	4	0.04
Honduran	2	0.02
Panamanian	3	0.03
Salvadoran	10	0.10
Cuban	14	0.14
Dominican Republic	5	0.05
Mexican	30	0.29
Puerto Rican	63	0.61
South American	19	0.18
Argentinean	1	0.01
Chilean	8	0.08
Colombian	4	0.04
Ecuadorian	1	0.01
Peruvian	4	0.04
Other South American	1	0.01
Other Hispanic or Latino	23	0.22

Race*	Population	%
African-American/Black (94)	155	1.51
Not Hispanic (88)	144	1.40
Hispanic (6)	11	0.11
American Indian/Alaska Native (52)	123	1.19
Not Hispanic (34)	98	0.95
Hispanic (18)	25	0.24
Blackfeet (0)	2	0.02
Canadian/French Am. Ind. (1)	1	0.01
Central American Ind. (3)	3	0.03
Cherokee (0)	9	0.09
Chippewa (3)	3	0.03
Choctaw (1)	2	0.02
Creek (3)	4	0.04
Inupiat *(Alaska Native)* (0)	1	0.01
Iroquois (1)	5	0.05
Menominee (0)	1	0.01
Mexican American Ind. (6)	9	0.09
Sioux (1)	6	0.06
Tlingit-Haida *(Alaska Native)* (1)	1	0.01
Asian (102)	129	1.25
Not Hispanic (100)	126	1.22
Hispanic (2)	3	0.03
Cambodian (13)	13	0.13
Chinese, ex. Taiwanese (27)	32	0.31
Filipino (3)	10	0.10
Hmong (3)	3	0.03
Indian (13)	19	0.18
Indonesian (5)	5	0.05
Japanese (3)	8	0.08
Korean (9)	13	0.13
Laotian (4)	4	0.04
Malaysian (0)	1	0.01
Thai (6)	6	0.06
Vietnamese (14)	15	0.15
Hawaii Native/Pacific Islander (5)	17	0.17
Not Hispanic (5)	17	0.17
Guamanian/Chamorro (0)	2	0.02
Marshallese (1)	2	0.02
Native Hawaiian (0)	5	0.05
Samoan (1)	6	0.06
White (9,802)	9,963	96.79
Not Hispanic (9,702)	9,842	95.62
Hispanic (100)	121	1.18

Ipswich

Place Type: Town
County: Essex
Population: 13,175†

Ancestry‡	Population	%
American (876)	876	6.70
Arab (10)	44	0.34
Lebanese (10)	18	0.14
Moroccan (0)	15	0.11
Syrian (0)	11	0.08
Austrian (28)	106	0.81
Belgian (24)	24	0.18
Brazilian (102)	102	0.78
British (98)	145	1.11
Canadian (164)	205	1.57
Czech (0)	70	0.54
Danish (12)	33	0.25
Dutch (28)	126	0.96
Eastern European (8)	8	0.06
English (997)	2,629	20.11
Finnish (32)	105	0.80
French, ex. Basque (323)	1,334	10.20
French Canadian (384)	864	6.61
German (255)	1,059	8.10
Greek (357)	780	5.97
Hungarian (14)	33	0.25
Irish (1,075)	3,244	24.81
Italian (783)	2,136	16.34

*Notes: † The Census 2010 population figure is used to calculate the percentages in the Hispanic Origin and Race categories. Ancestry percentages are based on the 2006-2010 American Community Survey population (not shown); ‡ Numbers in parentheses indicate the number of people reporting a single ancestry; * Numbers in parentheses indicate the number of persons reporting this race alone, not in combination with any other race; Please refer to the Explanation of Data for more information.*

Ancestry	Population	%
Latvian (13)	13	0.10
Lithuanian (19)	87	0.67
Luxemburger (0)	9	0.07
Maltese (0)	9	0.07
Northern European (33)	33	0.25
Norwegian (34)	120	0.92
Polish (363)	888	6.79
Portuguese (21)	214	1.64
Romanian (0)	9	0.07
Russian (80)	182	1.39
Scandinavian (61)	106	0.81
Scotch-Irish (189)	483	3.69
Scottish (185)	858	6.56
Swedish (48)	385	2.94
Swiss (0)	22	0.17
Ukrainian (0)	16	0.12
Welsh (0)	72	0.55

Hispanic Origin	Population	%
Hispanic or Latino (of any race)	232	1.76
Central American, ex. Mexican	29	0.22
Costa Rican	2	0.02
Guatemalan	11	0.08
Honduran	4	0.03
Nicaraguan	4	0.03
Panamanian	2	0.02
Salvadoran	5	0.04
Other Central American	1	0.01
Cuban	12	0.09
Dominican Republic	27	0.20
Mexican	45	0.34
Puerto Rican	54	0.41
South American	25	0.19
Argentinean	5	0.04
Chilean	3	0.02
Colombian	9	0.07
Ecuadorian	6	0.05
Peruvian	2	0.02
Other Hispanic or Latino	40	0.30

Race*	Population	%
African-American/Black (65)	115	0.87
Not Hispanic (61)	109	0.83
Hispanic (4)	6	0.05
American Indian/Alaska Native (20)	70	0.53
Not Hispanic (12)	62	0.47
Hispanic (8)	8	0.06
Apache (1)	1	0.01
Blackfeet (1)	1	0.01
Central American Ind. (0)	1	0.01
Cherokee (1)	6	0.05
Chickasaw (1)	1	0.01
Choctaw (0)	4	0.03
Cree (0)	3	0.02
Creek (1)	1	0.01
Houma (1)	1	0.01
Iroquois (0)	1	0.01
Navajo (0)	1	0.01
Potawatomi (0)	1	0.01
Pueblo (0)	1	0.01
Sioux (1)	2	0.02
South American Ind. (1)	1	0.01
Asian (174)	237	1.80
Not Hispanic (174)	235	1.78
Hispanic (0)	2	0.02
Cambodian (5)	5	0.04
Chinese, ex. Taiwanese (57)	68	0.52
Filipino (6)	14	0.11
Indian (24)	31	0.24
Indonesian (2)	3	0.02
Japanese (18)	29	0.22
Korean (38)	47	0.36
Laotian (5)	5	0.04
Sri Lankan (3)	3	0.02
Thai (5)	5	0.04
Vietnamese (7)	7	0.05
Hawaii Native/Pacific Islander (6)	15	0.11
Not Hispanic (6)	14	0.11
Hispanic (0)	1	0.01
Guamanian/Chamorro (4)	6	0.05
Native Hawaiian (0)	4	0.03
Samoan (1)	3	0.02
White (12,636)	12,803	97.18
Not Hispanic (12,471)	12,627	95.84
Hispanic (165)	176	1.34

Kingston

Place Type: Town
County: Plymouth
Population: 12,629†

Ancestry‡	Population	%
African, Sub-Saharan (59)	59	0.47
Cape Verdean (59)	59	0.47
American (351)	351	2.81
Arab (12)	29	0.23
Lebanese (12)	29	0.23
Armenian (45)	60	0.48
Austrian (0)	27	0.22
Belgian (8)	8	0.06
Brazilian (47)	47	0.38
British (17)	92	0.74
Canadian (60)	137	1.10
Czechoslovakian (0)	25	0.20
Danish (15)	28	0.22
Dutch (0)	210	1.68
Eastern European (0)	36	0.29
English (481)	1,926	15.45
European (16)	16	0.13
Finnish (19)	36	0.29
French, ex. Basque (228)	746	5.98
French Canadian (132)	363	2.91
German (429)	1,554	12.46
Greek (79)	107	0.86
Hungarian (0)	22	0.18
Irish (1,799)	4,543	36.43
Italian (1,093)	2,764	22.17
Lithuanian (30)	113	0.91
Northern European (22)	22	0.18
Norwegian (81)	121	0.97
Pennsylvania German (0)	11	0.09
Polish (97)	472	3.79
Portuguese (205)	430	3.45
Romanian (0)	72	0.58
Russian (0)	15	0.12
Scandinavian (0)	62	0.50
Scotch-Irish (208)	443	3.55
Scottish (52)	388	3.11
Swedish (90)	400	3.21
Swiss (0)	46	0.37
Ukrainian (0)	12	0.10
Welsh (0)	85	0.68
Yugoslavian (0)	23	0.18

Hispanic Origin	Population	%
Hispanic or Latino (of any race)	140	1.11
Central American, ex. Mexican	21	0.17
Costa Rican	3	0.02
Guatemalan	5	0.04
Honduran	3	0.02
Salvadoran	10	0.08
Cuban	7	0.06
Dominican Republic	6	0.05
Mexican	25	0.20
Puerto Rican	27	0.21
South American	26	0.21
Argentinean	6	0.05
Chilean	4	0.03
Colombian	5	0.04
Ecuadorian	2	0.02
Peruvian	6	0.05
Uruguayan	1	0.01
Venezuelan	1	0.01
Other South American	1	0.01
Other Hispanic or Latino	28	0.22

Race*	Population	%
African-American/Black (133)	189	1.50
Not Hispanic (129)	183	1.45
Hispanic (4)	6	0.05
American Indian/Alaska Native (14)	51	0.40
Not Hispanic (12)	44	0.35
Hispanic (2)	7	0.06
Cherokee (0)	5	0.04
Chickasaw (0)	1	0.01
Chippewa (5)	5	0.04
Iroquois (0)	3	0.02
Sioux (0)	1	0.01
South American Ind. (2)	7	0.06
Ute (0)	2	0.02
Asian (116)	170	1.35
Not Hispanic (116)	166	1.31
Hispanic (0)	4	0.03
Cambodian (1)	1	0.01
Chinese, ex. Taiwanese (38)	45	0.36
Filipino (14)	28	0.22
Indian (19)	23	0.18
Indonesian (1)	5	0.04
Japanese (6)	16	0.13
Korean (7)	18	0.14
Malaysian (1)	1	0.01
Pakistani (1)	1	0.01
Taiwanese (2)	2	0.02
Thai (9)	15	0.12
Vietnamese (1)	2	0.02
Hawaii Native/Pacific Islander (1)	7	0.06
Not Hispanic (1)	7	0.06
Guamanian/Chamorro (1)	3	0.02
White (12,137)	12,283	97.26
Not Hispanic (12,031)	12,163	96.31
Hispanic (106)	120	0.95

Lakeville

Place Type: Town
County: Plymouth
Population: 10,602†

Ancestry‡	Population	%
African, Sub-Saharan (131)	131	1.25
Cape Verdean (131)	131	1.25
Albanian (0)	199	1.90
American (318)	318	3.04
Arab (17)	117	1.12
Lebanese (0)	61	0.58
Other Arab (17)	56	0.54
Armenian (26)	52	0.50
Belgian (0)	23	0.22
Canadian (48)	140	1.34
Danish (20)	28	0.27
Dutch (34)	138	1.32
English (522)	2,090	19.98
European (56)	56	0.54
Finnish (6)	24	0.23
French, ex. Basque (335)	1,331	12.72
French Canadian (212)	635	6.07
German (312)	903	8.63
Greek (53)	189	1.81
Hungarian (2)	2	0.02
Irish (1,028)	3,001	28.68
Italian (487)	1,726	16.50
Latvian (13)	13	0.12
Lithuanian (23)	112	1.07
Northern European (15)	15	0.14
Norwegian (15)	58	0.55
Polish (114)	525	5.02
Portuguese (377)	967	9.24
Romanian (18)	18	0.17
Russian (34)	132	1.26
Scandinavian (6)	17	0.16
Scotch-Irish (0)	112	1.07
Scottish (47)	275	2.63
Slovak (0)	12	0.11
Swedish (80)	270	2.58
Swiss (0)	8	0.08
Welsh (0)	22	0.21

Hispanic Origin	Population	%
Hispanic or Latino (of any race)	92	0.87

*Notes: † The Census 2010 population figure is used to calculate the percentages in the Hispanic Origin and Race categories. Ancestry percentages are based on the 2006-2010 American Community Survey population (not shown); ‡ Numbers in parentheses indicate the number of people reporting a single ancestry; * Numbers in parentheses indicate the number of persons reporting this race alone, not in combination with any other race; Please refer to the Explanation of Data for more information.*

Central American, ex. Mexican	9	0.08
Costa Rican	1	0.01
Guatemalan	8	0.08
Cuban	9	0.08
Dominican Republic	1	0.01
Mexican	23	0.22
Puerto Rican	22	0.21
South American	13	0.12
Colombian	7	0.07
Ecuadorian	3	0.03
Peruvian	3	0.03
Other Hispanic or Latino	15	0.14

Race*	Population	%
African-American/Black (80)	109	1.03
Not Hispanic (78)	104	0.98
Hispanic (2)	5	0.05
American Indian/Alaska Native (13)	55	0.52
Not Hispanic (13)	54	0.51
Hispanic (0)	1	0.01
Blackfeet (0)	2	0.02
Cherokee (0)	2	0.02
Chippewa (4)	4	0.04
Seminole (3)	3	0.03
Sioux (0)	3	0.03
Yakama (0)	2	0.02
Asian (86)	129	1.22
Not Hispanic (86)	126	1.19
Hispanic (0)	3	0.03
Cambodian (1)	2	0.02
Chinese, ex. Taiwanese (32)	36	0.34
Filipino (12)	19	0.18
Indian (9)	14	0.13
Indonesian (1)	1	0.01
Japanese (6)	17	0.16
Korean (7)	14	0.13
Pakistani (6)	7	0.07
Thai (0)	3	0.03
Vietnamese (11)	12	0.11
Hawaii Native/Pacific Islander (1)	1	0.01
Not Hispanic (1)	1	0.01
White (10,262)	10,363	97.75
Not Hispanic (10,187)	10,282	96.98
Hispanic (75)	81	0.76

Lancaster

Place Type: Town
County: Worcester
Population: 8,055†

Ancestry‡	Population	%
African, Sub-Saharan (15)	25	0.32
African (0)	10	0.13
Cape Verdean (15)	15	0.19
American (238)	238	3.06
Armenian (0)	57	0.73
Belgian (0)	8	0.10
Brazilian (5)	11	0.14
British (0)	63	0.81
Canadian (30)	163	2.10
Dutch (0)	13	0.17
English (191)	1,083	13.93
Estonian (14)	14	0.18
European (105)	105	1.35
Finnish (172)	196	2.52
French, ex. Basque (106)	766	9.85
French Canadian (187)	396	5.09
German (144)	990	12.73
Greek (31)	83	1.07
Irish (690)	2,186	28.11
Italian (195)	1,148	14.76
Latvian (0)	21	0.27
Lithuanian (12)	57	0.73
Northern European (13)	13	0.17
Norwegian (9)	9	0.12
Polish (205)	486	6.25
Portuguese (80)	195	2.51
Russian (40)	106	1.36
Scotch-Irish (37)	96	1.23
Scottish (36)	198	2.55
Swedish (22)	115	1.48
Ukrainian (55)	55	0.71
Welsh (25)	147	1.89
West Indian, ex. Hispanic (255)	329	4.23
Bermudan (0)	38	0.49
British West Indian (22)	32	0.41
Haitian (223)	223	2.87
Jamaican (10)	30	0.39
Trinidadian/Tobagonian (0)	6	0.08

Hispanic Origin	Population	%
Hispanic or Latino (of any race)	655	8.13
Central American, ex. Mexican	35	0.43
Costa Rican	11	0.14
Guatemalan	6	0.07
Honduran	11	0.14
Panamanian	4	0.05
Salvadoran	3	0.04
Cuban	16	0.20
Dominican Republic	53	0.66
Mexican	29	0.36
Puerto Rican	390	4.84
South American	37	0.46
Argentinean	1	0.01
Chilean	3	0.04
Colombian	3	0.04
Ecuadorian	9	0.11
Peruvian	6	0.07
Uruguayan	4	0.05
Venezuelan	11	0.14
Other Hispanic or Latino	95	1.18

Race*	Population	%
African-American/Black (624)	683	8.48
Not Hispanic (572)	605	7.51
Hispanic (52)	78	0.97
American Indian/Alaska Native (7)	36	0.45
Not Hispanic (5)	27	0.34
Hispanic (2)	9	0.11
Cherokee (0)	1	0.01
Chippewa (0)	2	0.02
Mexican American Ind. (1)	5	0.06
Asian (140)	172	2.14
Not Hispanic (140)	169	2.10
Hispanic (0)	3	0.04
Cambodian (1)	2	0.02
Chinese, ex. Taiwanese (35)	37	0.46
Filipino (15)	18	0.22
Hmong (1)	1	0.01
Indian (41)	47	0.58
Japanese (9)	20	0.25
Korean (21)	30	0.37
Nepalese (1)	1	0.01
Vietnamese (10)	13	0.16
White (6,959)	7,062	87.67
Not Hispanic (6,568)	6,648	82.53
Hispanic (391)	414	5.14

Lawrence

Place Type: City
County: Essex
Population: 76,377†

Ancestry‡	Population	%
African, Sub-Saharan (239)	349	0.46
African (112)	222	0.30
Cape Verdean (27)	27	0.04
Ghanaian (16)	16	0.02
Kenyan (37)	37	0.05
Nigerian (29)	29	0.04
Other Sub-Saharan African (18)	18	0.02
American (2,870)	2,870	3.82
Arab (354)	452	0.60
Lebanese (259)	354	0.47
Syrian (36)	39	0.05
Other Arab (59)	59	0.08
Armenian (12)	72	0.10
Austrian (12)	23	0.03
Belgian (34)	47	0.06
Brazilian (81)	141	0.19
British (0)	11	0.01
Cajun (5)	5	0.01
Canadian (137)	224	0.30
Croatian (12)	12	0.02
Czech (0)	17	0.02
Danish (15)	61	0.08
Dutch (16)	124	0.16
Eastern European (26)	26	0.03
English (458)	1,625	2.16
European (132)	144	0.19
Finnish (0)	8	0.01
French, ex. Basque (759)	2,215	2.95
French Canadian (1,026)	1,858	2.47
German (257)	1,109	1.48
Greek (42)	76	0.10
Hungarian (20)	22	0.03
Irish (1,200)	3,413	4.54
Italian (1,805)	3,422	4.55
Latvian (30)	38	0.05
Lithuanian (150)	262	0.35
Norwegian (23)	49	0.07
Polish (214)	661	0.88
Portuguese (598)	969	1.29
Russian (95)	186	0.25
Scandinavian (0)	20	0.03
Scotch-Irish (56)	140	0.19
Scottish (18)	223	0.30
Serbian (8)	8	0.01
Slavic (0)	11	0.01
Swedish (12)	120	0.16
Swiss (35)	35	0.05
Turkish (45)	45	0.06
Ukrainian (39)	78	0.10
Welsh (13)	54	0.07
West Indian, ex. Hispanic (96)	211	0.28
British West Indian (16)	16	0.02
Dutch West Indian (0)	11	0.01
Haitian (58)	83	0.11
Jamaican (0)	70	0.09
Trinidadian/Tobagonian (22)	22	0.03
West Indian (0)	9	0.01

Hispanic Origin	Population	%
Hispanic or Latino (of any race)	56,363	73.80
Central American, ex. Mexican	3,052	4.00
Costa Rican	63	0.08
Guatemalan	2,262	2.96
Honduran	155	0.20
Nicaraguan	46	0.06
Panamanian	23	0.03
Salvadoran	495	0.65
Other Central American	8	0.01
Cuban	369	0.48
Dominican Republic	30,243	39.60
Mexican	551	0.72
Puerto Rican	16,953	22.20
South American	1,185	1.55
Argentinean	28	0.04
Bolivian	11	0.01
Chilean	14	0.02
Colombian	335	0.44
Ecuadorian	597	0.78
Paraguayan	4	0.01
Peruvian	100	0.13
Uruguayan	13	0.02
Venezuelan	81	0.11
Other South American	2	<0.01
Other Hispanic or Latino	4,010	5.25

Race*	Population	%
African-American/Black (5,788)	7,826	10.25
Not Hispanic (1,722)	1,954	2.56
Hispanic (4,066)	5,872	7.69
American Indian/Alaska Native (957)	1,641	2.15
Not Hispanic (130)	234	0.31
Hispanic (827)	1,407	1.84
Blackfeet (3)	10	0.01
Canadian/French Am. Ind. (4)	4	0.01

*Notes: † The Census 2010 population figure is used to calculate the percentages in the Hispanic Origin and Race categories. Ancestry percentages are based on the 2006-2010 American Community Survey population (not shown); ‡ Numbers in parentheses indicate the number of people reporting a single ancestry; * Numbers in parentheses indicate the number of persons reporting this race alone, not in combination with any other race; Please refer to the Explanation of Data for more information.*

Central American Ind. (54)	80	0.10
Cherokee (14)	35	0.05
Cheyenne (0)	1	<0.01
Choctaw (1)	1	<0.01
Colville (0)	1	<0.01
Comanche (0)	2	<0.01
Cree (4)	4	0.01
Hopi (0)	3	<0.01
Iroquois (4)	4	0.01
Mexican American Ind. (36)	50	0.07
Navajo (1)	3	<0.01
Osage (1)	4	0.01
Pueblo (3)	13	0.02
South American Ind. (61)	113	0.15
Spanish American Ind. (77)	141	0.18
Asian (1,895)	2,247	2.94
Not Hispanic (1,756)	1,912	2.50
Hispanic (139)	335	0.44
Burmese (0)	1	<0.01
Cambodian (606)	636	0.83
Chinese, ex. Taiwanese (152)	224	0.29
Filipino (29)	48	0.06
Indian (278)	368	0.48
Indonesian (5)	5	0.01
Japanese (8)	19	0.02
Korean (54)	67	0.09
Laotian (1)	4	0.01
Malaysian (2)	2	<0.01
Pakistani (12)	18	0.02
Sri Lankan (1)	3	<0.01
Taiwanese (5)	6	0.01
Thai (10)	13	0.02
Vietnamese (630)	702	0.92
Hawaii Native/Pacific Islander (57)	364	0.48
Not Hispanic (2)	27	0.04
Hispanic (55)	337	0.44
Guamanian/Chamorro (6)	9	0.01
Native Hawaiian (10)	22	0.03
Samoan (2)	4	0.01
White (32,704)	36,253	47.47
Not Hispanic (15,637)	16,054	21.02
Hispanic (17,067)	20,199	26.45

Leicester

Place Type: Town
County: Worcester
Population: 10,970†

Ancestry‡	Population	%
African, Sub-Saharan (78)	78	0.71
African (78)	78	0.71
Albanian (24)	49	0.45
American (408)	408	3.74
Arab (117)	256	2.35
Egyptian (8)	8	0.07
Lebanese (0)	50	0.46
Syrian (109)	198	1.81
Armenian (85)	104	0.95
Austrian (0)	21	0.19
Brazilian (33)	33	0.30
British (24)	24	0.22
Canadian (25)	81	0.74
Danish (55)	55	0.50
Dutch (11)	75	0.69
English (349)	1,402	12.85
European (132)	132	1.21
Finnish (16)	39	0.36
French, ex. Basque (709)	2,420	22.18
French Canadian (377)	858	7.86
German (87)	499	4.57
Greek (137)	150	1.37
Hungarian (0)	16	0.15
Irish (901)	2,542	23.30
Italian (369)	1,480	13.56
Lithuanian (149)	272	2.49
Norwegian (8)	18	0.16
Polish (240)	941	8.62
Portuguese (0)	28	0.26
Romanian (0)	36	0.33
Russian (0)	78	0.71
Scandinavian (0)	25	0.23
Scotch-Irish (13)	117	1.07
Scottish (29)	236	2.16
Swedish (122)	554	5.08
Welsh (13)	143	1.31
West Indian, ex. Hispanic (16)	16	0.15
Haitian (16)	16	0.15

Hispanic Origin	Population	%
Hispanic or Latino (of any race)	414	3.77
Central American, ex. Mexican	60	0.55
Costa Rican	5	0.05
Guatemalan	14	0.13
Nicaraguan	1	0.01
Panamanian	1	0.01
Salvadoran	39	0.36
Cuban	12	0.11
Dominican Republic	5	0.05
Mexican	39	0.36
Puerto Rican	246	2.24
South American	31	0.28
Argentinean	5	0.05
Chilean	1	0.01
Colombian	16	0.15
Ecuadorian	6	0.05
Peruvian	3	0.03
Other Hispanic or Latino	21	0.19

Race*	Population	%
African-American/Black (228)	281	2.56
Not Hispanic (213)	256	2.33
Hispanic (15)	25	0.23
American Indian/Alaska Native (31)	105	0.96
Not Hispanic (31)	98	0.89
Hispanic (0)	7	0.06
Blackfeet (2)	4	0.04
Canadian/French Am. Ind. (2)	4	0.04
Cherokee (5)	10	0.09
Iroquois (0)	9	0.08
Lumbee (0)	1	0.01
Navajo (0)	3	0.03
Asian (181)	228	2.08
Not Hispanic (181)	223	2.03
Hispanic (0)	5	0.05
Burmese (2)	2	0.02
Cambodian (2)	3	0.03
Chinese, ex. Taiwanese (10)	11	0.10
Filipino (19)	24	0.22
Indian (21)	24	0.22
Indonesian (1)	1	0.01
Japanese (4)	10	0.09
Korean (5)	12	0.11
Laotian (3)	3	0.03
Malaysian (1)	1	0.01
Taiwanese (2)	2	0.02
Thai (0)	1	0.01
Vietnamese (103)	109	0.99
Hawaii Native/Pacific Islander (7)	19	0.17
Not Hispanic (6)	18	0.16
Hispanic (1)	1	0.01
Guamanian/Chamorro (1)	7	0.06
Native Hawaiian (0)	1	0.01
White (10,205)	10,374	94.57
Not Hispanic (9,961)	10,096	92.03
Hispanic (244)	278	2.53

Leominster

Place Type: City
County: Worcester
Population: 40,759†

Ancestry‡	Population	%
African, Sub-Saharan (510)	522	1.28
African (113)	113	0.28
Cape Verdean (88)	100	0.24
Ethiopian (36)	36	0.09
Ghanaian (104)	104	0.25
Kenyan (17)	17	0.04
Nigerian (113)	113	0.28
Other Sub-Saharan African (39)	39	0.10
Albanian (11)	11	0.03
American (918)	918	2.24
Arab (23)	98	0.24
Egyptian (10)	10	0.02
Iraqi (0)	11	0.03
Lebanese (13)	35	0.09
Syrian (0)	42	0.10
Armenian (12)	71	0.17
Austrian (0)	45	0.11
Belgian (11)	26	0.06
Brazilian (1,205)	1,390	3.40
British (24)	91	0.22
Canadian (461)	612	1.49
Croatian (0)	15	0.04
Czech (18)	50	0.12
Czechoslovakian (0)	15	0.04
Danish (15)	38	0.09
Dutch (10)	270	0.66
English (1,482)	4,317	10.54
European (202)	229	0.56
Finnish (139)	616	1.50
French, ex. Basque (2,141)	6,262	15.30
French Canadian (2,715)	4,102	10.02
German (727)	2,569	6.27
Greek (141)	514	1.26
Hungarian (17)	72	0.18
Irish (2,441)	7,503	18.33
Italian (3,234)	7,568	18.49
Lithuanian (47)	231	0.56
Northern European (18)	18	0.04
Norwegian (14)	94	0.23
Pennsylvania German (28)	28	0.07
Polish (402)	1,390	3.40
Portuguese (473)	725	1.77
Russian (187)	389	0.95
Scandinavian (42)	42	0.10
Scotch-Irish (199)	637	1.56
Scottish (167)	750	1.83
Slavic (5)	5	0.01
Slovak (0)	11	0.03
Swedish (125)	592	1.45
Ukrainian (68)	78	0.19
Welsh (28)	46	0.11
West Indian, ex. Hispanic (431)	488	1.19
Haitian (431)	431	1.05
Jamaican (0)	57	0.14

Hispanic Origin	Population	%
Hispanic or Latino (of any race)	5,900	14.48
Central American, ex. Mexican	321	0.79
Costa Rican	12	0.03
Guatemalan	105	0.26
Honduran	57	0.14
Nicaraguan	12	0.03
Panamanian	44	0.11
Salvadoran	90	0.22
Other Central American	1	<0.01
Cuban	33	0.08
Dominican Republic	454	1.11
Mexican	285	0.70
Puerto Rican	3,237	7.94
South American	1,157	2.84
Argentinean	33	0.08
Bolivian	12	0.03
Chilean	9	0.02
Colombian	104	0.26
Ecuadorian	75	0.18
Paraguayan	2	<0.01
Peruvian	36	0.09
Uruguayan	824	2.02
Venezuelan	61	0.15
Other South American	1	<0.01
Other Hispanic or Latino	413	1.01

Race*	Population	%
African-American/Black (2,060)	2,563	6.29
Not Hispanic (1,826)	2,194	5.38
Hispanic (234)	369	0.91

SECTION TWO

*Notes: † The Census 2010 population figure is used to calculate the percentages in the Hispanic Origin and Race categories. Ancestry percentages are based on the 2006-2010 American Community Survey population (not shown); ‡ Numbers in parentheses indicate the number of people reporting a single ancestry; * Numbers in parentheses indicate the number of persons reporting this race alone, not in combination with any other race; Please refer to the Explanation of Data for more information.*

American Indian/Alaska Native (73)	273	0.67
Not Hispanic (49)	206	0.51
Hispanic (24)	67	0.16
Apache (1)	2	<0.01
Blackfeet (1)	11	0.03
Canadian/French Am. Ind. (0)	3	0.01
Central American Ind. (5)	5	0.01
Cherokee (5)	38	0.09
Chickasaw (0)	2	<0.01
Chippewa (3)	4	0.01
Choctaw (2)	7	0.02
Crow (0)	1	<0.01
Iroquois (4)	13	0.03
Navajo (0)	2	<0.01
Potawatomi (0)	1	<0.01
Seminole (0)	1	<0.01
Sioux (2)	3	0.01
South American Ind. (5)	19	0.05
Spanish American Ind. (1)	1	<0.01
Asian (1,124)	1,390	3.41
Not Hispanic (1,104)	1,345	3.30
Hispanic (20)	45	0.11
Bangladeshi (12)	14	0.03
Burmese (8)	8	0.02
Cambodian (45)	53	0.13
Chinese, ex. Taiwanese (96)	128	0.31
Filipino (77)	103	0.25
Hmong (159)	170	0.42
Indian (137)	177	0.43
Indonesian (4)	4	0.01
Japanese (21)	71	0.17
Korean (137)	205	0.50
Laotian (138)	163	0.40
Pakistani (35)	46	0.11
Sri Lankan (0)	4	0.01
Taiwanese (4)	4	0.01
Thai (30)	43	0.11
Vietnamese (152)	170	0.42
Hawaii Native/Pacific Islander (23)	57	0.14
Not Hispanic (16)	47	0.12
Hispanic (7)	10	0.02
Fijian (0)	1	<0.01
Guamanian/Chamorro (15)	19	0.05
Native Hawaiian (5)	9	0.02
Samoan (1)	2	<0.01
White (34,175)	35,192	86.34
Not Hispanic (30,745)	31,425	77.10
Hispanic (3,430)	3,767	9.24

Lexington

Place Type: CDP/Town
County: Middlesex
Population: 31,394†

Ancestry‡	Population	%
African, Sub-Saharan (56)	78	0.25
Ethiopian (56)	56	0.18
South African (0)	22	0.07
Albanian (28)	66	0.21
American (673)	673	2.18
Arab (169)	224	0.73
Arab (39)	65	0.21
Egyptian (74)	74	0.24
Lebanese (24)	53	0.17
Syrian (32)	32	0.10
Armenian (563)	801	2.60
Australian (59)	76	0.25
Austrian (35)	131	0.42
Brazilian (0)	11	0.04
British (229)	525	1.70
Bulgarian (0)	16	0.05
Canadian (95)	217	0.70
Celtic (17)	17	0.06
Croatian (0)	12	0.04
Czech (94)	296	0.96
Czechoslovakian (0)	23	0.07
Danish (73)	173	0.56
Dutch (156)	251	0.81
Eastern European (430)	494	1.60
English (1,052)	3,873	12.55
European (575)	628	2.03
Finnish (47)	109	0.35
French, ex. Basque (426)	1,126	3.65
French Canadian (115)	611	1.98
German (625)	2,727	8.84
Greek (287)	446	1.45
Hungarian (13)	278	0.90
Iranian (167)	167	0.54
Irish (1,913)	5,741	18.60
Israeli (146)	146	0.47
Italian (1,484)	3,796	12.30
Latvian (10)	88	0.29
Lithuanian (50)	273	0.88
Northern European (91)	109	0.35
Norwegian (50)	206	0.67
Polish (394)	1,243	4.03
Portuguese (130)	348	1.13
Romanian (11)	39	0.13
Russian (638)	1,312	4.25
Scandinavian (34)	116	0.38
Scotch-Irish (227)	614	1.99
Scottish (188)	825	2.67
Slovak (17)	67	0.22
Slovene (30)	30	0.10
Swedish (200)	585	1.90
Swiss (0)	152	0.49
Turkish (23)	36	0.12
Ukrainian (112)	258	0.84
Welsh (0)	200	0.65
West Indian, ex. Hispanic (9)	69	0.22
British West Indian (9)	9	0.03
Trinidadian/Tobagonian (0)	60	0.19
Yugoslavian (0)	16	0.05

Hispanic Origin	Population	%
Hispanic or Latino (of any race)	713	2.27
Central American, ex. Mexican	67	0.21
Costa Rican	5	0.02
Guatemalan	34	0.11
Honduran	4	0.01
Nicaraguan	6	0.02
Panamanian	3	0.01
Salvadoran	15	0.05
Cuban	31	0.10
Dominican Republic	26	0.08
Mexican	162	0.52
Puerto Rican	107	0.34
South American	206	0.66
Argentinean	60	0.19
Bolivian	1	<0.01
Chilean	28	0.09
Colombian	51	0.16
Ecuadorian	8	0.03
Paraguayan	4	0.01
Peruvian	12	0.04
Uruguayan	11	0.04
Venezuelan	31	0.10
Other Hispanic or Latino	114	0.36

Race*	Population	%
African-American/Black (473)	650	2.07
Not Hispanic (457)	614	1.96
Hispanic (16)	36	0.11
American Indian/Alaska Native (25)	104	0.33
Not Hispanic (21)	89	0.28
Hispanic (4)	15	0.05
Blackfeet (0)	8	0.03
Canadian/French Am. Ind. (0)	1	<0.01
Cherokee (1)	13	0.04
Chippewa (2)	2	0.01
Choctaw (1)	2	0.01
Cree (0)	1	<0.01
Creek (0)	1	<0.01
Iroquois (0)	2	0.01
Mexican American Ind. (3)	3	0.01
Navajo (1)	1	<0.01
Potawatomi (0)	1	<0.01
Sioux (1)	8	0.03
South American Ind. (0)	1	<0.01
Asian (6,240)	6,836	21.77
Not Hispanic (6,239)	6,815	21.71
Hispanic (1)	21	0.07
Bangladeshi (59)	70	0.22
Burmese (2)	3	0.01
Cambodian (20)	23	0.07
Chinese, ex. Taiwanese (2,721)	2,984	9.51
Filipino (88)	130	0.41
Indian (1,514)	1,643	5.23
Indonesian (19)	32	0.10
Japanese (247)	364	1.16
Korean (1,019)	1,088	3.47
Malaysian (3)	4	0.01
Nepalese (7)	7	0.02
Pakistani (45)	54	0.17
Sri Lankan (40)	44	0.14
Taiwanese (203)	248	0.79
Thai (36)	40	0.13
Vietnamese (59)	75	0.24
Hawaii Native/Pacific Islander (3)	33	0.11
Not Hispanic (3)	31	0.10
Hispanic (0)	2	0.01
Native Hawaiian (2)	4	0.01
Samoan (0)	1	<0.01
White (23,705)	24,399	77.72
Not Hispanic (23,138)	23,786	75.77
Hispanic (567)	613	1.95

Littleton

Place Type: Town
County: Middlesex
Population: 8,924†

Ancestry‡	Population	%
African, Sub-Saharan (15)	15	0.17
South African (15)	15	0.17
American (386)	386	4.44
Arab (11)	11	0.13
Syrian (11)	11	0.13
Armenian (11)	32	0.37
Austrian (0)	13	0.15
Belgian (16)	16	0.18
Brazilian (18)	51	0.59
British (31)	66	0.76
Canadian (109)	224	2.58
Czech (16)	78	0.90
Danish (10)	60	0.69
Dutch (66)	94	1.08
Eastern European (54)	54	0.62
English (585)	1,606	18.47
European (138)	138	1.59
Finnish (30)	58	0.67
French, ex. Basque (19)	488	5.61
French Canadian (137)	398	4.58
German (68)	838	9.64
Greek (48)	171	1.97
Hungarian (14)	43	0.49
Irish (1,042)	2,658	30.56
Israeli (0)	15	0.17
Italian (357)	1,008	11.59
Latvian (10)	10	0.11
Lithuanian (13)	83	0.95
Northern European (25)	25	0.29
Norwegian (11)	84	0.97
Polish (102)	490	5.63
Portuguese (15)	107	1.23
Romanian (0)	13	0.15
Russian (41)	213	2.45
Scandinavian (26)	34	0.39
Scotch-Irish (49)	190	2.18
Scottish (46)	379	4.36
Slavic (0)	29	0.33
Slovak (0)	29	0.33
Slovene (0)	15	0.17
Swedish (107)	368	4.23
Swiss (0)	28	0.32
Ukrainian (18)	63	0.72
Welsh (0)	142	1.63
West Indian, ex. Hispanic (0)	42	0.48

*Notes: † The Census 2010 population figure is used to calculate the percentages in the Hispanic Origin and Race categories. Ancestry percentages are based on the 2006-2010 American Community Survey population (not shown); ‡ Numbers in parentheses indicate the number of people reporting a single ancestry; * Numbers in parentheses indicate the number of persons reporting this race alone, not in combination with any other race; Please refer to the Explanation of Data for more information.*

Jamaican (0)	42	0.48

Hispanic Origin	Population	%
Hispanic or Latino (of any race)	121	1.36
Central American, ex. Mexican	12	0.13
Costa Rican	1	0.01
Guatemalan	2	0.02
Honduran	2	0.02
Salvadoran	7	0.08
Cuban	7	0.08
Dominican Republic	1	0.01
Mexican	30	0.34
Puerto Rican	34	0.38
South American	27	0.30
Argentinean	1	0.01
Chilean	4	0.04
Colombian	11	0.12
Ecuadorian	4	0.04
Peruvian	1	0.01
Venezuelan	6	0.07
Other Hispanic or Latino	10	0.11

Race*	Population	%
African-American/Black (54)	87	0.97
Not Hispanic (46)	75	0.84
Hispanic (8)	12	0.13
American Indian/Alaska Native (10)	64	0.72
Not Hispanic (6)	59	0.66
Hispanic (4)	5	0.06
Alaska Athabascan *(Ala. Nat.)* (1)	1	0.01
Blackfeet (1)	1	0.01
Canadian/French Am. Ind. (0)	5	0.06
Cherokee (0)	6	0.07
Cree (0)	1	0.01
Iroquois (0)	4	0.04
Lumbee (0)	2	0.02
Navajo (0)	2	0.02
Osage (0)	1	0.01
Puget Sound Salish (3)	3	0.03
South American Ind. (0)	4	0.04
Asian (352)	431	4.83
Not Hispanic (350)	423	4.74
Hispanic (2)	8	0.09
Burmese (4)	6	0.07
Cambodian (6)	8	0.09
Chinese, ex. Taiwanese (102)	119	1.33
Filipino (7)	12	0.13
Indian (144)	160	1.79
Indonesian (1)	2	0.02
Japanese (20)	36	0.40
Korean (25)	38	0.43
Laotian (2)	2	0.02
Malaysian (1)	1	0.01
Nepalese (1)	3	0.03
Pakistani (6)	6	0.07
Taiwanese (13)	13	0.15
Thai (3)	6	0.07
Vietnamese (10)	16	0.18
White (8,328)	8,478	95.00
Not Hispanic (8,239)	8,379	93.89
Hispanic (89)	99	1.11

Longmeadow

Place Type: CDP/Town
County: Hampden
Population: 15,784†

Ancestry‡	Population	%
African, Sub-Saharan (0)	15	0.10
African (0)	15	0.10
American (545)	545	3.46
Arab (65)	169	1.07
Iraqi (10)	10	0.06
Lebanese (55)	141	0.89
Syrian (0)	18	0.11
Armenian (16)	16	0.10
Austrian (44)	130	0.82
Belgian (16)	16	0.10
British (21)	90	0.57
Canadian (54)	112	0.71
Croatian (14)	14	0.09
Czech (0)	13	0.08
Danish (9)	46	0.29
Dutch (55)	281	1.78
Eastern European (140)	171	1.09
English (288)	1,856	11.78
European (27)	27	0.17
French, ex. Basque (62)	1,078	6.84
French Canadian (352)	856	5.43
German (333)	1,860	11.80
Greek (161)	356	2.26
Hungarian (0)	36	0.23
Iranian (42)	42	0.27
Irish (1,262)	4,125	26.18
Israeli (0)	13	0.08
Italian (807)	2,393	15.18
Latvian (6)	6	0.04
Lithuanian (73)	169	1.07
Luxemburger (0)	5	0.03
Norwegian (0)	174	1.10
Polish (250)	1,107	7.02
Portuguese (158)	232	1.47
Romanian (13)	13	0.08
Russian (587)	916	5.81
Scotch-Irish (49)	205	1.30
Scottish (62)	673	4.27
Slovak (24)	192	1.22
Swedish (4)	278	1.76
Swiss (13)	18	0.11
Ukrainian (83)	83	0.53
Welsh (0)	94	0.60
West Indian, ex. Hispanic (15)	15	0.10
Barbadian (15)	15	0.10

Hispanic Origin	Population	%
Hispanic or Latino (of any race)	370	2.34
Central American, ex. Mexican	26	0.16
Costa Rican	3	0.02
Guatemalan	12	0.08
Panamanian	1	0.01
Salvadoran	10	0.06
Cuban	22	0.14
Dominican Republic	15	0.10
Mexican	41	0.26
Puerto Rican	141	0.89
South American	64	0.41
Argentinean	6	0.04
Chilean	11	0.07
Colombian	22	0.14
Ecuadorian	13	0.08
Paraguayan	3	0.02
Peruvian	9	0.06
Other Hispanic or Latino	61	0.39

Race*	Population	%
African-American/Black (167)	227	1.44
Not Hispanic (155)	202	1.28
Hispanic (12)	25	0.16
American Indian/Alaska Native (5)	41	0.26
Not Hispanic (4)	27	0.17
Hispanic (1)	14	0.09
Canadian/French Am. Ind. (1)	1	0.01
Cherokee (2)	4	0.03
Chippewa (0)	1	0.01
Delaware (0)	1	0.01
Iroquois (0)	2	0.01
Mexican American Ind. (1)	5	0.03
Navajo (0)	1	0.01
Pueblo (0)	2	0.01
South American Ind. (0)	2	0.01
Asian (745)	855	5.42
Not Hispanic (743)	851	5.39
Hispanic (2)	4	0.03
Bangladeshi (9)	9	0.06
Chinese, ex. Taiwanese (228)	255	1.62
Filipino (50)	76	0.48
Indian (176)	194	1.23
Indonesian (0)	1	0.01
Japanese (11)	28	0.18
Korean (118)	135	0.86
Laotian (1)	1	0.01
Nepalese (1)	1	0.01
Pakistani (41)	43	0.27
Taiwanese (24)	26	0.16
Thai (12)	15	0.10
Vietnamese (40)	45	0.29
Hawaii Native/Pacific Islander (3)	14	0.09
Not Hispanic (3)	14	0.09
Guamanian/Chamorro (2)	3	0.02
Native Hawaiian (1)	3	0.02
Samoan (0)	1	0.01
White (14,587)	14,772	93.59
Not Hispanic (14,322)	14,482	91.75
Hispanic (265)	290	1.84

Lowell

Place Type: City
County: Middlesex
Population: 106,519†

Ancestry‡	Population	%
African, Sub-Saharan (3,205)	3,805	3.62
African (1,150)	1,552	1.48
Cape Verdean (60)	183	0.17
Ethiopian (69)	69	0.07
Ghanaian (188)	204	0.19
Kenyan (1,292)	1,309	1.25
Liberian (99)	99	0.09
Nigerian (148)	148	0.14
Sierra Leonean (52)	52	0.05
Ugandan (46)	46	0.04
Other Sub-Saharan African (101)	143	0.14
Albanian (48)	63	0.06
American (2,278)	2,278	2.17
Arab (297)	529	0.50
Arab (0)	14	0.01
Egyptian (67)	67	0.06
Jordanian (13)	27	0.03
Lebanese (127)	276	0.26
Syrian (28)	83	0.08
Other Arab (62)	62	0.06
Armenian (208)	366	0.35
Austrian (10)	113	0.11
Brazilian (2,455)	2,774	2.64
British (15)	37	0.04
Bulgarian (11)	11	0.01
Cajun (12)	12	0.01
Canadian (461)	840	0.80
Celtic (0)	28	0.03
Croatian (5)	40	0.04
Czech (10)	10	0.01
Danish (46)	113	0.11
Dutch (17)	272	0.26
English (1,225)	6,079	5.78
European (191)	207	0.20
Finnish (10)	103	0.10
French, ex. Basque (3,026)	9,625	9.16
French Canadian (3,806)	5,733	5.46
German (431)	3,370	3.21
Greek (1,990)	2,821	2.68
Guyanese (27)	27	0.03
Hungarian (29)	165	0.16
Iranian (31)	81	0.08
Irish (6,725)	18,066	17.19
Italian (2,003)	6,891	6.56
Lithuanian (105)	497	0.47
Maltese (0)	46	0.04
Norwegian (45)	254	0.24
Polish (929)	3,363	3.20
Portuguese (3,623)	6,158	5.86
Romanian (0)	10	0.01
Russian (78)	455	0.43
Scandinavian (9)	47	0.04
Scotch-Irish (424)	1,111	1.06
Scottish (279)	1,065	1.01
Slavic (0)	66	0.06
Swedish (70)	766	0.73
Swiss (0)	133	0.13

SECTION TWO

*Notes: † The Census 2010 population figure is used to calculate the percentages in the Hispanic Origin and Race categories. Ancestry percentages are based on the 2006-2010 American Community Survey population (not shown); ‡ Numbers in parentheses indicate the number of people reporting a single ancestry; * Numbers in parentheses indicate the number of persons reporting this race alone, not in combination with any other race; Please refer to the Explanation of Data for more information.*

Ukrainian (23)	171	0.16
Welsh (24)	223	0.21
West Indian, ex. Hispanic (1,115)	1,193	1.14
British West Indian (27)	27	0.03
Haitian (858)	881	0.84
Jamaican (173)	188	0.18
Trinidadian/Tobagonian (0)	40	0.04
West Indian (34)	34	0.03
Other West Indian (23)	23	0.02
Yugoslavian (11)	44	0.04

Hispanic Origin	Population	%
Hispanic or Latino (of any race)	18,396	17.27
Central American, ex. Mexican	621	0.58
Costa Rican	23	0.02
Guatemalan	203	0.19
Honduran	79	0.07
Nicaraguan	24	0.02
Panamanian	43	0.04
Salvadoran	239	0.22
Other Central American	10	0.01
Cuban	128	0.12
Dominican Republic	2,008	1.89
Mexican	511	0.48
Puerto Rican	12,079	11.34
South American	1,927	1.81
Argentinean	23	0.02
Bolivian	11	0.01
Chilean	22	0.02
Colombian	1,575	1.48
Ecuadorian	122	0.11
Paraguayan	4	<0.01
Peruvian	93	0.09
Uruguayan	15	0.01
Venezuelan	58	0.05
Other South American	4	<0.01
Other Hispanic or Latino	1,122	1.05

Race*	Population	%
African-American/Black (7,238)	8,440	7.92
Not Hispanic (6,367)	7,155	6.72
Hispanic (871)	1,285	1.21
American Indian/Alaska Native (292)	706	0.66
Not Hispanic (137)	424	0.40
Hispanic (155)	282	0.26
Apache (2)	5	<0.01
Blackfeet (5)	24	0.02
Canadian/French Am. Ind. (0)	6	0.01
Central American Ind. (10)	19	0.02
Cherokee (17)	60	0.06
Cheyenne (0)	2	<0.01
Chickasaw (0)	1	<0.01
Chippewa (1)	2	<0.01
Choctaw (4)	7	0.01
Comanche (2)	2	<0.01
Creek (0)	1	<0.01
Inupiat *(Alaska Native)* (0)	1	<0.01
Iroquois (3)	14	0.01
Mexican American Ind. (7)	8	0.01
Navajo (1)	1	<0.01
Pima (2)	2	<0.01
Potawatomi (1)	1	<0.01
Pueblo (3)	12	0.01
Seminole (0)	3	<0.01
Shoshone (0)	1	<0.01
Sioux (8)	11	0.01
South American Ind. (20)	50	0.05
Spanish American Ind. (1)	4	<0.01
Tlingit-Haida *(Alaska Native)* (3)	3	<0.01
Asian (21,513)	22,764	21.37
Not Hispanic (21,337)	22,459	21.08
Hispanic (176)	305	0.29
Bangladeshi (38)	43	0.04
Bhutanese (47)	65	0.06
Burmese (113)	114	0.11
Cambodian (13,319)	14,470	13.58
Chinese, ex. Taiwanese (581)	851	0.80
Filipino (225)	322	0.30
Hmong (10)	12	0.01
Indian (2,130)	2,472	2.32
Indonesian (11)	18	0.02
Japanese (32)	73	0.07
Korean (85)	111	0.10
Laotian (1,480)	1,765	1.66
Malaysian (3)	6	0.01
Nepalese (20)	36	0.03
Pakistani (49)	50	0.05
Sri Lankan (7)	9	0.01
Taiwanese (10)	14	0.01
Thai (104)	200	0.19
Vietnamese (1,828)	2,057	1.93
Hawaii Native/Pacific Islander (44)	273	0.26
Not Hispanic (34)	171	0.16
Hispanic (10)	102	0.10
Guamanian/Chamorro (8)	9	0.01
Marshallese (2)	3	<0.01
Native Hawaiian (7)	27	0.03
Samoan (6)	12	0.01
White (64,240)	67,249	63.13
Not Hispanic (56,280)	58,178	54.62
Hispanic (7,960)	9,071	8.52

Ludlow

Place Type: Town
County: Hampden
Population: 21,103†

Ancestry‡	Population	%
African, Sub-Saharan (93)	113	0.53
African (8)	28	0.13
Cape Verdean (8)	8	0.04
Kenyan (77)	77	0.36
American (465)	465	2.20
Arab (124)	212	1.00
Iraqi (112)	112	0.53
Lebanese (12)	95	0.45
Syrian (0)	5	0.02
Austrian (0)	33	0.16
Brazilian (63)	84	0.40
British (26)	41	0.19
Canadian (63)	223	1.05
Czech (40)	99	0.47
Czechoslovakian (16)	57	0.27
Dutch (0)	178	0.84
English (336)	1,861	8.80
European (0)	11	0.05
Finnish (0)	30	0.14
French, ex. Basque (1,145)	3,889	18.38
French Canadian (729)	1,579	7.46
German (231)	960	4.54
Greek (83)	235	1.11
Hungarian (17)	17	0.08
Irish (814)	3,505	16.57
Italian (691)	2,748	12.99
Lithuanian (5)	25	0.12
Macedonian (8)	8	0.04
Norwegian (14)	30	0.14
Polish (1,496)	3,723	17.60
Portuguese (3,180)	4,330	20.47
Romanian (16)	16	0.08
Russian (22)	95	0.45
Scotch-Irish (155)	371	1.75
Scottish (174)	681	3.22
Slavic (0)	10	0.05
Swedish (0)	112	0.53
Turkish (150)	150	0.71
Ukrainian (57)	70	0.33
Welsh (25)	77	0.36
West Indian, ex. Hispanic (31)	55	0.26
Barbadian (5)	5	0.02
Haitian (5)	5	0.02
Jamaican (21)	36	0.17
West Indian (0)	9	0.04
Yugoslavian (0)	15	0.07

Hispanic Origin	Population	%
Hispanic or Latino (of any race)	1,183	5.61
Central American, ex. Mexican	28	0.13
Costa Rican	5	0.02
Guatemalan	9	0.04
Honduran	1	<0.01
Nicaraguan	4	0.02
Panamanian	6	0.03
Salvadoran	3	0.01
Cuban	14	0.07
Dominican Republic	33	0.16
Mexican	60	0.28
Puerto Rican	894	4.24
South American	60	0.28
Argentinean	12	0.06
Bolivian	1	<0.01
Chilean	1	<0.01
Colombian	24	0.11
Ecuadorian	2	0.01
Peruvian	2	0.01
Uruguayan	6	0.03
Venezuelan	11	0.05
Other South American	1	<0.01
Other Hispanic or Latino	94	0.45

Race*	Population	%
African-American/Black (514)	601	2.85
Not Hispanic (485)	564	2.67
Hispanic (29)	37	0.18
American Indian/Alaska Native (25)	82	0.39
Not Hispanic (14)	68	0.32
Hispanic (11)	14	0.07
Blackfeet (1)	2	0.01
Canadian/French Am. Ind. (2)	5	0.02
Central American Ind. (1)	1	<0.01
Cherokee (0)	2	0.01
Chippewa (0)	4	0.02
Choctaw (0)	2	0.01
Iroquois (0)	6	0.03
Navajo (3)	3	0.01
Pueblo (1)	1	<0.01
Sioux (4)	4	0.02
Spanish American Ind. (1)	1	<0.01
Asian (171)	242	1.15
Not Hispanic (170)	233	1.10
Hispanic (1)	9	0.04
Cambodian (3)	5	0.02
Chinese, ex. Taiwanese (43)	46	0.22
Filipino (35)	52	0.25
Indian (19)	24	0.11
Indonesian (1)	1	<0.01
Japanese (5)	7	0.03
Korean (21)	27	0.13
Pakistani (4)	4	0.02
Thai (4)	7	0.03
Vietnamese (26)	30	0.14
Hawaii Native/Pacific Islander (8)	24	0.11
Not Hispanic (8)	22	0.10
Hispanic (0)	2	0.01
Guamanian/Chamorro (1)	2	0.01
Samoan (1)	2	0.01
White (19,828)	20,096	95.23
Not Hispanic (18,963)	19,192	90.94
Hispanic (865)	904	4.28

Lunenburg

Place Type: Town
County: Worcester
Population: 10,086†

Ancestry‡	Population	%
Albanian (13)	13	0.13
American (431)	431	4.32
Arab (5)	19	0.19
Lebanese (5)	19	0.19
Armenian (0)	11	0.11
Austrian (0)	29	0.29
British (0)	35	0.35
Canadian (81)	137	1.37
Czech (0)	11	0.11
Czechoslovakian (41)	41	0.41
Danish (0)	81	0.81
Dutch (32)	164	1.64

*Notes: † The Census 2010 population figure is used to calculate the percentages in the Hispanic Origin and Race categories. Ancestry percentages are based on the 2006-2010 American Community Survey population (not shown); ‡ Numbers in parentheses indicate the number of people reporting a single ancestry; * Numbers in parentheses indicate the number of persons reporting this race alone, not in combination with any other race; Please refer to the Explanation of Data for more information.*

Ancestry	Population	%
Eastern European (11)	11	0.11
English (524)	2,290	22.93
European (40)	52	0.52
Finnish (155)	316	3.16
French, ex. Basque (493)	1,995	19.98
French Canadian (470)	819	8.20
German (239)	986	9.87
Greek (15)	44	0.44
Hungarian (0)	9	0.09
Irish (970)	2,603	26.07
Italian (522)	1,667	16.70
Lithuanian (13)	115	1.15
Norwegian (9)	29	0.29
Pennsylvania German (14)	14	0.14
Polish (31)	353	3.54
Portuguese (69)	200	2.00
Russian (14)	142	1.42
Scotch-Irish (98)	332	3.32
Scottish (40)	314	3.14
Swedish (37)	187	1.87
Turkish (9)	9	0.09
Ukrainian (13)	96	0.96
Welsh (13)	119	1.19

Hispanic Origin	Population	%
Hispanic or Latino (of any race)	240	2.38
Central American, ex. Mexican	14	0.14
Costa Rican	3	0.03
Guatemalan	8	0.08
Panamanian	2	0.02
Salvadoran	1	0.01
Cuban	19	0.19
Dominican Republic	11	0.11
Mexican	38	0.38
Puerto Rican	73	0.72
South American	66	0.65
Argentinean	5	0.05
Bolivian	2	0.02
Chilean	1	0.01
Colombian	9	0.09
Ecuadorian	14	0.14
Paraguayan	1	0.01
Uruguayan	30	0.30
Venezuelan	4	0.04
Other Hispanic or Latino	19	0.19

Race*	Population	%
African-American/Black (90)	149	1.48
Not Hispanic (79)	127	1.26
Hispanic (11)	22	0.22
American Indian/Alaska Native (17)	42	0.42
Not Hispanic (16)	36	0.36
Hispanic (1)	6	0.06
Apache (0)	1	0.01
Blackfeet (0)	2	0.02
Canadian/French Am. Ind. (0)	4	0.04
Cherokee (1)	2	0.02
Sioux (0)	1	0.01
Asian (157)	225	2.23
Not Hispanic (153)	219	2.17
Hispanic (4)	6	0.06
Bangladeshi (3)	3	0.03
Cambodian (11)	11	0.11
Chinese, ex. Taiwanese (16)	31	0.31
Filipino (17)	37	0.37
Indian (16)	20	0.20
Japanese (7)	12	0.12
Korean (40)	51	0.51
Laotian (1)	1	0.01
Pakistani (12)	14	0.14
Sri Lankan (1)	1	0.01
Taiwanese (0)	2	0.02
Thai (7)	10	0.10
Vietnamese (19)	22	0.22
Hawaii Native/Pacific Islander (0)	4	0.04
Not Hispanic (0)	4	0.04
Samoan (0)	3	0.03
White (9,600)	9,749	96.66
Not Hispanic (9,451)	9,577	94.95
Hispanic (149)	172	1.71

Lynn

Place Type: City
County: Essex
Population: 90,329†

Ancestry‡	Population	%
Afghan (47)	47	0.05
African, Sub-Saharan (2,243)	2,732	3.05
African (714)	955	1.07
Cape Verdean (100)	215	0.24
Ethiopian (57)	57	0.06
Ghanaian (51)	51	0.06
Kenyan (135)	135	0.15
Liberian (252)	263	0.29
Nigerian (445)	445	0.50
Senegalese (103)	103	0.11
Somalian (195)	195	0.22
Sudanese (74)	183	0.20
Other Sub-Saharan African (117)	130	0.15
Albanian (190)	289	0.32
American (3,732)	3,732	4.16
Arab (280)	352	0.39
Arab (52)	75	0.08
Iraqi (28)	28	0.03
Lebanese (55)	68	0.08
Moroccan (118)	118	0.13
Syrian (0)	36	0.04
Other Arab (27)	27	0.03
Armenian (110)	149	0.17
Austrian (0)	107	0.12
Belgian (21)	21	0.02
Brazilian (442)	520	0.58
British (142)	159	0.18
Bulgarian (35)	35	0.04
Canadian (647)	1,312	1.46
Croatian (117)	153	0.17
Czech (7)	55	0.06
Czechoslovakian (0)	23	0.03
Danish (4)	81	0.09
Dutch (41)	322	0.36
Eastern European (4)	4	<0.01
English (1,405)	5,883	6.56
European (190)	214	0.24
Finnish (77)	200	0.22
French, ex. Basque (1,307)	6,087	6.79
French Canadian (997)	2,232	2.49
German (596)	2,353	2.63
Greek (1,954)	2,729	3.04
Guyanese (0)	13	0.01
Hungarian (111)	215	0.24
Iranian (63)	69	0.08
Irish (6,519)	15,863	17.70
Italian (4,490)	11,161	12.45
Latvian (65)	65	0.07
Lithuanian (185)	343	0.38
Norwegian (55)	180	0.20
Pennsylvania German (10)	19	0.02
Polish (800)	2,330	2.60
Portuguese (646)	1,262	1.41
Russian (970)	1,201	1.34
Scandinavian (20)	45	0.05
Scotch-Irish (418)	1,044	1.16
Scottish (436)	1,239	1.38
Serbian (53)	112	0.12
Slavic (0)	6	0.01
Swedish (259)	710	0.79
Swiss (19)	90	0.10
Ukrainian (86)	176	0.20
Welsh (29)	155	0.17
West Indian, ex. Hispanic (2,082)	2,618	2.92
Barbadian (65)	79	0.09
British West Indian (47)	47	0.05
Haitian (1,516)	1,623	1.81
Jamaican (209)	405	0.45
Trinidadian/Tobagonian (14)	30	0.03
U.S. Virgin Islander (22)	22	0.02
West Indian (209)	412	0.46
Yugoslavian (264)	274	0.31

Hispanic Origin	Population	%
Hispanic or Latino (of any race)	29,013	32.12
Central American, ex. Mexican	9,049	10.02
Costa Rican	115	0.13
Guatemalan	5,715	6.33
Honduran	523	0.58
Nicaraguan	83	0.09
Panamanian	37	0.04
Salvadoran	2,509	2.78
Other Central American	67	0.07
Cuban	179	0.20
Dominican Republic	9,528	10.55
Mexican	1,519	1.68
Puerto Rican	4,894	5.42
South American	878	0.97
Argentinean	38	0.04
Bolivian	26	0.03
Chilean	77	0.09
Colombian	387	0.43
Ecuadorian	45	0.05
Peruvian	204	0.23
Uruguayan	28	0.03
Venezuelan	68	0.08
Other South American	5	0.01
Other Hispanic or Latino	2,966	3.28

Race*	Population	%
African-American/Black (11,540)	13,760	15.23
Not Hispanic (9,494)	10,784	11.94
Hispanic (2,046)	2,976	3.29
American Indian/Alaska Native (659)	1,363	1.51
Not Hispanic (178)	536	0.59
Hispanic (481)	827	0.92
Aleut *(Alaska Native)* (0)	2	<0.01
Apache (3)	7	0.01
Blackfeet (4)	59	0.07
Canadian/French Am. Ind. (3)	5	0.01
Central American Ind. (26)	29	0.03
Cherokee (14)	74	0.08
Chickasaw (0)	1	<0.01
Chippewa (1)	2	<0.01
Choctaw (2)	5	0.01
Cree (0)	1	<0.01
Creek (0)	6	0.01
Hopi (0)	1	<0.01
Inupiat *(Alaska Native)* (0)	1	<0.01
Iroquois (11)	24	0.03
Mexican American Ind. (100)	134	0.15
Navajo (2)	3	<0.01
Pueblo (5)	6	0.01
Seminole (1)	2	<0.01
Shoshone (0)	1	<0.01
Sioux (1)	11	0.01
South American Ind. (16)	36	0.04
Spanish American Ind. (16)	18	0.02
Yaqui (0)	1	<0.01
Yuman (2)	2	<0.01
Asian (6,292)	6,946	7.69
Not Hispanic (6,210)	6,707	7.43
Hispanic (82)	239	0.26
Bangladeshi (99)	120	0.13
Bhutanese (61)	66	0.07
Burmese (85)	88	0.10
Cambodian (3,489)	3,899	4.32
Chinese, ex. Taiwanese (232)	362	0.40
Filipino (114)	231	0.26
Indian (332)	519	0.57
Indonesian (6)	10	0.01
Japanese (34)	78	0.09
Korean (35)	67	0.07
Laotian (189)	242	0.27
Malaysian (6)	11	0.01
Nepalese (26)	31	0.03
Pakistani (23)	26	0.03
Taiwanese (8)	8	0.01
Thai (23)	51	0.06
Vietnamese (942)	1,117	1.24
Hawaii Native/Pacific Islander (82)	291	0.32
Not Hispanic (37)	117	0.13
Hispanic (45)	174	0.19

*Notes: † The Census 2010 population figure is used to calculate the percentages in the Hispanic Origin and Race categories. Ancestry percentages are based on the 2006-2010 American Community Survey population (not shown); ‡ Numbers in parentheses indicate the number of people reporting a single ancestry; * Numbers in parentheses indicate the number of persons reporting this race alone, not in combination with any other race; Please refer to the Explanation of Data for more information.*

Guamanian/Chamorro (60)	85	0.09
Native Hawaiian (7)	19	0.02
Samoan (2)	9	0.01
Tongan (2)	2	<0.01
White (52,019)	55,576	61.53
Not Hispanic (42,969)	44,657	49.44
Hispanic (9,050)	10,919	12.09

Lynnfield

Place Type: CDP/Town
County: Essex
Population: 11,596†

Ancestry‡	Population	%
African, Sub-Saharan (14)	49	0.43
South African (14)	14	0.12
Other Sub-Saharan African (0)	35	0.30
Albanian (0)	26	0.23
American (182)	182	1.58
Arab (18)	119	1.04
Arab (18)	84	0.73
Syrian (0)	35	0.30
Armenian (145)	273	2.38
Australian (0)	11	0.10
Austrian (0)	32	0.28
British (0)	22	0.19
Canadian (30)	99	0.86
Danish (0)	186	1.62
English (455)	1,563	13.61
Finnish (0)	45	0.39
French, ex. Basque (28)	473	4.12
French Canadian (105)	270	2.35
German (184)	665	5.79
Greek (265)	493	4.29
Hungarian (0)	28	0.24
Iranian (39)	39	0.34
Irish (1,406)	3,776	32.87
Israeli (42)	42	0.37
Italian (1,715)	3,582	31.18
Lithuanian (29)	72	0.63
Northern European (27)	27	0.24
Norwegian (0)	15	0.13
Polish (93)	465	4.05
Portuguese (12)	39	0.34
Russian (167)	317	2.76
Scotch-Irish (146)	309	2.69
Scottish (255)	435	3.79
Slovak (30)	30	0.26
Swedish (23)	190	1.65
Swiss (75)	156	1.36
Turkish (27)	27	0.24
Ukrainian (67)	142	1.24
Welsh (0)	25	0.22

Hispanic Origin	Population	%
Hispanic or Latino (of any race)	202	1.74
Central American, ex. Mexican	24	0.21
Costa Rican	3	0.03
Guatemalan	10	0.09
Honduran	2	0.02
Nicaraguan	2	0.02
Salvadoran	7	0.06
Cuban	8	0.07
Dominican Republic	21	0.18
Mexican	34	0.29
Puerto Rican	53	0.46
South American	43	0.37
Chilean	1	0.01
Colombian	25	0.22
Ecuadorian	8	0.07
Paraguayan	1	0.01
Peruvian	4	0.03
Uruguayan	1	0.01
Venezuelan	1	0.01
Other South American	2	0.02
Other Hispanic or Latino	19	0.16

Race*	Population	%
African-American/Black (58)	89	0.77
Not Hispanic (48)	74	0.64
Hispanic (10)	15	0.13
American Indian/Alaska Native (5)	8	0.07
Not Hispanic (5)	7	0.06
Hispanic (0)	1	0.01
Blackfeet (1)	2	0.02
Cherokee (0)	1	0.01
Lumbee (1)	1	0.01
Asian (379)	440	3.79
Not Hispanic (379)	438	3.78
Hispanic (0)	2	0.02
Cambodian (4)	6	0.05
Chinese, ex. Taiwanese (113)	131	1.13
Filipino (12)	24	0.21
Indian (114)	121	1.04
Japanese (11)	21	0.18
Korean (37)	50	0.43
Malaysian (1)	1	0.01
Nepalese (2)	2	0.02
Pakistani (4)	4	0.03
Sri Lankan (0)	3	0.03
Taiwanese (6)	6	0.05
Vietnamese (54)	55	0.47
Hawaii Native/Pacific Islander (0)	4	0.03
Not Hispanic (0)	4	0.03
Native Hawaiian (0)	1	0.01
Samoan (0)	3	0.03
White (10,986)	11,096	95.69
Not Hispanic (10,838)	10,926	94.22
Hispanic (148)	170	1.47

Malden

Place Type: City
County: Middlesex
Population: 59,450†

Ancestry‡	Population	%
Afghan (165)	180	0.31
African, Sub-Saharan (1,794)	1,878	3.23
African (707)	750	1.29
Cape Verdean (217)	249	0.43
Ethiopian (180)	189	0.32
Kenyan (118)	118	0.20
Liberian (18)	18	0.03
Nigerian (59)	59	0.10
Ugandan (481)	481	0.83
Other Sub-Saharan African (14)	14	0.02
Albanian (222)	241	0.41
American (1,093)	1,093	1.88
Arab (1,330)	1,671	2.87
Arab (212)	259	0.45
Egyptian (46)	46	0.08
Lebanese (78)	260	0.45
Moroccan (630)	671	1.15
Palestinian (106)	106	0.18
Syrian (0)	13	0.02
Other Arab (258)	316	0.54
Armenian (0)	43	0.07
Austrian (14)	51	0.09
Belgian (14)	81	0.14
Brazilian (2,871)	3,303	5.68
British (64)	100	0.17
Bulgarian (10)	10	0.02
Canadian (298)	527	0.91
Croatian (19)	19	0.03
Cypriot (10)	30	0.05
Czech (45)	112	0.19
Danish (0)	53	0.09
Dutch (14)	189	0.32
Eastern European (81)	94	0.16
English (569)	2,794	4.80
Estonian (19)	19	0.03
European (93)	117	0.20
Finnish (0)	14	0.02
French, ex. Basque (302)	1,367	2.35
French Canadian (512)	1,158	1.99
German (499)	1,981	3.40
Greek (133)	342	0.59
Hungarian (43)	117	0.20
Iranian (431)	448	0.77
Irish (2,962)	9,599	16.50
Italian (5,122)	10,187	17.51
Latvian (14)	81	0.14
Lithuanian (64)	274	0.47
Northern European (48)	48	0.08
Norwegian (0)	79	0.14
Pennsylvania German (0)	11	0.02
Polish (309)	1,219	2.10
Portuguese (744)	1,655	2.84
Romanian (21)	21	0.04
Russian (334)	791	1.36
Scandinavian (0)	26	0.04
Scotch-Irish (207)	636	1.09
Scottish (200)	919	1.58
Slovak (14)	40	0.07
Swedish (120)	475	0.82
Swiss (0)	17	0.03
Ukrainian (79)	126	0.22
Welsh (15)	57	0.10
West Indian, ex. Hispanic (3,274)	3,580	6.15
Barbadian (56)	99	0.17
Bermudan (15)	15	0.03
British West Indian (11)	11	0.02
Haitian (2,846)	2,927	5.03
Jamaican (203)	324	0.56
Trinidadian/Tobagonian (21)	69	0.12
West Indian (122)	135	0.23
Yugoslavian (222)	246	0.42

Hispanic Origin	Population	%
Hispanic or Latino (of any race)	4,992	8.40
Central American, ex. Mexican	1,345	2.26
Costa Rican	39	0.07
Guatemalan	216	0.36
Honduran	112	0.19
Nicaraguan	27	0.05
Panamanian	28	0.05
Salvadoran	909	1.53
Other Central American	14	0.02
Cuban	139	0.23
Dominican Republic	416	0.70
Mexican	309	0.52
Puerto Rican	1,061	1.78
South American	1,091	1.84
Argentinean	58	0.10
Bolivian	31	0.05
Chilean	114	0.19
Colombian	560	0.94
Ecuadorian	42	0.07
Paraguayan	2	<0.01
Peruvian	228	0.38
Uruguayan	14	0.02
Venezuelan	36	0.06
Other South American	6	0.01
Other Hispanic or Latino	631	1.06

Race*	Population	%
African-American/Black (8,796)	9,589	16.13
Not Hispanic (8,483)	9,149	15.39
Hispanic (313)	440	0.74
American Indian/Alaska Native (104)	355	0.60
Not Hispanic (76)	276	0.46
Hispanic (28)	79	0.13
Alaska Athabascan *(Ala. Nat.)* (1)	3	0.01
Apache (0)	1	<0.01
Blackfeet (0)	3	0.01
Canadian/French Am. Ind. (0)	1	<0.01
Central American Ind. (2)	2	<0.01
Cherokee (8)	48	0.08
Cheyenne (0)	1	<0.01
Chippewa (2)	6	0.01
Choctaw (0)	4	0.01
Cree (0)	1	<0.01
Iroquois (0)	1	<0.01
Lumbee (0)	1	<0.01
Mexican American Ind. (6)	6	0.01
Navajo (0)	3	0.01
Pueblo (0)	2	<0.01
Seminole (0)	1	<0.01

*Notes: † The Census 2010 population figure is used to calculate the percentages in the Hispanic Origin and Race categories. Ancestry percentages are based on the 2006-2010 American Community Survey population (not shown); ‡ Numbers in parentheses indicate the number of people reporting a single ancestry; * Numbers in parentheses indicate the number of persons reporting this race alone, not in combination with any other race; Please refer to the Explanation of Data for more information.*

Sioux (2)	4	0.01
South American Ind. (3)	17	0.03
Spanish American Ind. (0)	1	<0.01
Tlingit-Haida *(Alaska Native)* (2)	4	0.01
Yaqui (0)	2	<0.01
Asian (11,971)	12,448	20.94
Not Hispanic (11,898)	12,343	20.76
Hispanic (73)	105	0.18
Bangladeshi (76)	79	0.13
Burmese (24)	24	0.04
Cambodian (197)	246	0.41
Chinese, ex. Taiwanese (6,626)	6,926	11.65
Filipino (237)	303	0.51
Indian (1,893)	1,985	3.34
Indonesian (21)	27	0.05
Japanese (88)	137	0.23
Korean (298)	341	0.57
Laotian (37)	51	0.09
Malaysian (3)	6	0.01
Nepalese (65)	65	0.11
Pakistani (146)	160	0.27
Sri Lankan (37)	42	0.07
Taiwanese (50)	61	0.10
Thai (111)	124	0.21
Vietnamese (1,678)	1,874	3.15
Hawaii Native/Pacific Islander (16)	111	0.19
Not Hispanic (14)	92	0.15
Hispanic (2)	19	0.03
Fijian (1)	2	<0.01
Guamanian/Chamorro (6)	7	0.01
Marshallese (0)	1	<0.01
Native Hawaiian (2)	13	0.02
Samoan (2)	8	0.01
Tongan (0)	2	<0.01
White (33,691)	35,221	59.24
Not Hispanic (31,211)	32,436	54.56
Hispanic (2,480)	2,785	4.68

Mansfield

Place Type: Town
County: Bristol
Population: 23,184†

Ancestry‡	Population	%
African, Sub-Saharan (155)	261	1.13
African (0)	24	0.10
Cape Verdean (116)	198	0.86
Nigerian (39)	39	0.17
Albanian (17)	28	0.12
American (759)	759	3.29
Arab (29)	140	0.61
Lebanese (17)	115	0.50
Syrian (12)	25	0.11
Armenian (36)	60	0.26
Austrian (14)	55	0.24
British (62)	182	0.79
Canadian (134)	353	1.53
Czech (17)	22	0.10
Danish (23)	60	0.26
Dutch (48)	205	0.89
Eastern European (63)	94	0.41
English (761)	3,044	13.21
European (105)	149	0.65
Finnish (8)	8	0.03
French, ex. Basque (240)	1,375	5.97
French Canadian (348)	947	4.11
German (538)	2,371	10.29
Greek (70)	170	0.74
Hungarian (13)	85	0.37
Iranian (56)	56	0.24
Irish (3,093)	8,373	36.32
Italian (1,405)	5,151	22.35
Lithuanian (13)	245	1.06
Northern European (13)	13	0.06
Norwegian (76)	130	0.56
Polish (269)	853	3.70
Portuguese (503)	1,106	4.80
Russian (185)	486	2.11
Scandinavian (0)	10	0.04
Scotch-Irish (202)	501	2.17
Scottish (76)	425	1.84
Serbian (7)	15	0.07
Slovak (0)	15	0.07
Slovene (19)	19	0.08
Swedish (192)	585	2.54
Swiss (11)	39	0.17
Welsh (11)	43	0.19
West Indian, ex. Hispanic (30)	54	0.23
Haitian (18)	42	0.18
Trinidadian/Tobagonian (12)	12	0.05
Yugoslavian (25)	25	0.11

Hispanic Origin	Population	%
Hispanic or Latino (of any race)	487	2.10
Central American, ex. Mexican	57	0.25
Costa Rican	9	0.04
Guatemalan	26	0.11
Honduran	12	0.05
Nicaraguan	2	0.01
Panamanian	2	0.01
Salvadoran	6	0.03
Cuban	37	0.16
Dominican Republic	33	0.14
Mexican	63	0.27
Puerto Rican	160	0.69
South American	80	0.35
Argentinean	14	0.06
Bolivian	8	0.03
Chilean	9	0.04
Colombian	17	0.07
Ecuadorian	11	0.05
Peruvian	19	0.08
Venezuelan	2	0.01
Other Hispanic or Latino	57	0.25

Race*	Population	%
African-American/Black (634)	748	3.23
Not Hispanic (601)	696	3.00
Hispanic (33)	52	0.22
American Indian/Alaska Native (59)	114	0.49
Not Hispanic (59)	105	0.45
Hispanic (0)	9	0.04
Apache (0)	3	0.01
Blackfeet (2)	3	0.01
Cherokee (2)	9	0.04
Chippewa (3)	3	0.01
Crow (0)	1	<0.01
Delaware (0)	1	<0.01
Inupiat *(Alaska Native)* (1)	1	<0.01
Iroquois (0)	2	0.01
Sioux (2)	2	0.01
South American Ind. (0)	4	0.02
Asian (793)	933	4.02
Not Hispanic (791)	929	4.01
Hispanic (2)	4	0.02
Bangladeshi (14)	14	0.06
Burmese (6)	6	0.03
Cambodian (2)	2	0.01
Chinese, ex. Taiwanese (167)	199	0.86
Filipino (33)	69	0.30
Indian (444)	475	2.05
Japanese (7)	19	0.08
Korean (36)	44	0.19
Laotian (1)	3	0.01
Pakistani (17)	21	0.09
Sri Lankan (12)	12	0.05
Taiwanese (1)	1	<0.01
Thai (13)	19	0.08
Vietnamese (30)	39	0.17
Hawaii Native/Pacific Islander (8)	24	0.10
Not Hispanic (4)	18	0.08
Hispanic (4)	6	0.03
Guamanian/Chamorro (4)	6	0.03
Native Hawaiian (4)	5	0.02
White (21,227)	21,501	92.74
Not Hispanic (20,899)	21,148	91.22
Hispanic (328)	353	1.52

Marblehead

Place Type: CDP/Town
County: Essex
Population: 19,808†

Ancestry‡	Population	%
Albanian (37)	37	0.19
American (1,245)	1,245	6.29
Arab (24)	75	0.38
Egyptian (12)	12	0.06
Lebanese (12)	28	0.14
Palestinian (0)	10	0.05
Syrian (0)	25	0.13
Armenian (12)	12	0.06
Australian (0)	38	0.19
Austrian (0)	138	0.70
Belgian (10)	40	0.20
Brazilian (35)	47	0.24
British (127)	145	0.73
Canadian (83)	187	0.94
Celtic (12)	26	0.13
Czech (10)	78	0.39
Czechoslovakian (20)	55	0.28
Danish (13)	28	0.14
Dutch (43)	132	0.67
Eastern European (225)	249	1.26
English (1,360)	4,103	20.73
Estonian (0)	14	0.07
European (391)	432	2.18
Finnish (67)	96	0.48
French, ex. Basque (270)	1,233	6.23
French Canadian (261)	759	3.83
German (648)	2,403	12.14
Greek (164)	256	1.29
Hungarian (44)	79	0.40
Irish (2,077)	4,969	25.10
Israeli (10)	10	0.05
Italian (701)	2,020	10.20
Latvian (16)	107	0.54
Lithuanian (57)	187	0.94
Northern European (58)	69	0.35
Norwegian (46)	148	0.75
Polish (293)	843	4.26
Portuguese (12)	47	0.24
Romanian (26)	41	0.21
Russian (582)	1,198	6.05
Scandinavian (142)	186	0.94
Scotch-Irish (156)	543	2.74
Scottish (202)	1,014	5.12
Serbian (11)	11	0.06
Slovak (0)	34	0.17
Swedish (101)	494	2.50
Swiss (29)	64	0.32
Turkish (54)	54	0.27
Ukrainian (137)	173	0.87
Welsh (58)	273	1.38
West Indian, ex. Hispanic (0)	11	0.06
Haitian (0)	11	0.06
Yugoslavian (10)	41	0.21

Hispanic Origin	Population	%
Hispanic or Latino (of any race)	417	2.11
Central American, ex. Mexican	35	0.18
Costa Rican	7	0.04
Guatemalan	13	0.07
Honduran	9	0.05
Nicaraguan	3	0.02
Panamanian	1	0.01
Salvadoran	2	0.01
Cuban	25	0.13
Dominican Republic	53	0.27
Mexican	57	0.29
Puerto Rican	106	0.54
South American	96	0.48
Argentinean	9	0.05
Bolivian	8	0.04
Chilean	13	0.07
Colombian	36	0.18
Ecuadorian	3	0.02

*Notes: † The Census 2010 population figure is used to calculate the percentages in the Hispanic Origin and Race categories. Ancestry percentages are based on the 2006-2010 American Community Survey population (not shown); ‡ Numbers in parentheses indicate the number of people reporting a single ancestry; * Numbers in parentheses indicate the number of persons reporting this race alone, not in combination with any other race; Please refer to the Explanation of Data for more information.*

Paraguayan	1	0.01
Peruvian	14	0.07
Uruguayan	2	0.01
Venezuelan	9	0.05
Other South American	1	0.01
Other Hispanic or Latino	45	0.23

Race*	Population	%
African-American/Black (151)	205	1.03
Not Hispanic (131)	177	0.89
Hispanic (20)	28	0.14
American Indian/Alaska Native (22)	64	0.32
Not Hispanic (12)	47	0.24
Hispanic (10)	17	0.09
Central American Ind. (0)	2	0.01
Cherokee (1)	3	0.02
Iroquois (3)	4	0.02
Mexican American Ind. (2)	2	0.01
Osage (0)	3	0.02
Seminole (0)	2	0.01
South American Ind. (1)	1	0.01
Spanish American Ind. (2)	2	0.01
Asian (202)	332	1.68
Not Hispanic (198)	325	1.64
Hispanic (4)	7	0.04
Cambodian (5)	8	0.04
Chinese, ex. Taiwanese (71)	103	0.52
Filipino (22)	48	0.24
Indian (31)	45	0.23
Indonesian (1)	7	0.04
Japanese (12)	37	0.19
Korean (36)	57	0.29
Laotian (1)	2	0.01
Pakistani (3)	3	0.02
Taiwanese (2)	2	0.01
Thai (3)	7	0.04
Vietnamese (8)	13	0.07
Hawaii Native/Pacific Islander (1)	7	0.04
Not Hispanic (1)	6	0.03
Hispanic (0)	1	0.01
Fijian (1)	1	0.01
White (19,087)	19,307	97.47
Not Hispanic (18,818)	19,012	95.98
Hispanic (269)	295	1.49

Marlborough

Place Type: City
County: Middlesex
Population: 38,499†

Ancestry‡	Population	%
African, Sub-Saharan (137)	173	0.46
African (128)	164	0.44
Ghanaian (9)	9	0.02
Albanian (26)	52	0.14
American (881)	881	2.34
Arab (408)	596	1.58
Arab (39)	39	0.10
Egyptian (0)	9	0.02
Jordanian (32)	32	0.08
Lebanese (315)	483	1.28
Moroccan (22)	22	0.06
Syrian (0)	11	0.03
Armenian (18)	18	0.05
Austrian (21)	46	0.12
Belgian (12)	12	0.03
Brazilian (1,200)	1,412	3.75
British (121)	176	0.47
Bulgarian (27)	27	0.07
Canadian (153)	299	0.79
Croatian (16)	33	0.09
Czech (0)	29	0.08
Czechoslovakian (0)	15	0.04
Danish (16)	97	0.26
Dutch (27)	131	0.35
Eastern European (114)	114	0.30
English (1,204)	4,475	11.88
European (236)	335	0.89
Finnish (27)	66	0.18
French, ex. Basque (829)	2,896	7.69
French Canadian (793)	1,899	5.04
German (705)	2,901	7.70
Greek (143)	787	2.09
Hungarian (0)	76	0.20
Iranian (115)	115	0.31
Irish (2,531)	7,753	20.58
Italian (2,577)	5,616	14.91
Latvian (10)	24	0.06
Lithuanian (84)	402	1.07
Luxemburger (0)	13	0.03
Northern European (12)	12	0.03
Norwegian (45)	225	0.60
Pennsylvania German (24)	24	0.06
Polish (327)	1,425	3.78
Portuguese (1,711)	2,192	5.82
Romanian (38)	38	0.10
Russian (255)	508	1.35
Scandinavian (0)	26	0.07
Scotch-Irish (394)	1,051	2.79
Scottish (349)	1,072	2.85
Serbian (0)	12	0.03
Slovene (0)	21	0.06
Swedish (41)	451	1.20
Swiss (25)	149	0.40
Ukrainian (45)	114	0.30
Welsh (14)	97	0.26
West Indian, ex. Hispanic (60)	104	0.28
Haitian (12)	12	0.03
Jamaican (11)	11	0.03
West Indian (37)	81	0.22

Hispanic Origin	Population	%
Hispanic or Latino (of any race)	4,174	10.84
Central American, ex. Mexican	1,353	3.51
Costa Rican	14	0.04
Guatemalan	1,060	2.75
Honduran	53	0.14
Nicaraguan	6	0.02
Panamanian	1	<0.01
Salvadoran	204	0.53
Other Central American	15	0.04
Cuban	45	0.12
Dominican Republic	168	0.44
Mexican	635	1.65
Puerto Rican	1,014	2.63
South American	379	0.98
Argentinean	28	0.07
Bolivian	35	0.09
Chilean	50	0.13
Colombian	122	0.32
Ecuadorian	52	0.14
Paraguayan	2	0.01
Peruvian	53	0.14
Uruguayan	2	0.01
Venezuelan	33	0.09
Other South American	2	0.01
Other Hispanic or Latino	580	1.51

Race*	Population	%
African-American/Black (1,061)	1,504	3.91
Not Hispanic (981)	1,327	3.45
Hispanic (80)	177	0.46
American Indian/Alaska Native (91)	250	0.65
Not Hispanic (52)	174	0.45
Hispanic (39)	76	0.20
Blackfeet (3)	12	0.03
Central American Ind. (12)	12	0.03
Cherokee (4)	18	0.05
Chippewa (2)	3	0.01
Choctaw (3)	5	0.01
Delaware (1)	1	<0.01
Iroquois (1)	5	0.01
Lumbee (1)	3	0.01
Mexican American Ind. (5)	7	0.02
Navajo (1)	1	<0.01
Potawatomi (3)	5	0.01
Sioux (0)	2	0.01
South American Ind. (8)	17	0.04
Tohono O'Odham (1)	1	<0.01
Asian (1,933)	2,184	5.67
Not Hispanic (1,927)	2,165	5.62
Hispanic (6)	19	0.05
Bangladeshi (11)	11	0.03
Burmese (6)	6	0.02
Cambodian (12)	12	0.03
Chinese, ex. Taiwanese (348)	406	1.05
Filipino (72)	108	0.28
Indian (1,150)	1,208	3.14
Indonesian (3)	3	0.01
Japanese (48)	96	0.25
Korean (52)	82	0.21
Laotian (7)	9	0.02
Malaysian (3)	4	0.01
Nepalese (12)	12	0.03
Pakistani (20)	20	0.05
Sri Lankan (20)	20	0.05
Taiwanese (14)	25	0.06
Thai (20)	23	0.06
Vietnamese (104)	115	0.30
Hawaii Native/Pacific Islander (25)	75	0.19
Not Hispanic (16)	54	0.14
Hispanic (9)	21	0.05
Guamanian/Chamorro (21)	26	0.07
Native Hawaiian (3)	9	0.02
Samoan (1)	2	0.01
White (31,147)	32,286	83.86
Not Hispanic (28,953)	29,868	77.58
Hispanic (2,194)	2,418	6.28

Marshfield

Place Type: Town
County: Plymouth
Population: 25,132†

Ancestry‡	Population	%
African, Sub-Saharan (119)	119	0.48
African (13)	13	0.05
Cape Verdean (106)	106	0.42
Albanian (14)	43	0.17
American (996)	996	3.99
Arab (45)	134	0.54
Arab (21)	21	0.08
Lebanese (13)	102	0.41
Syrian (11)	11	0.04
Armenian (0)	39	0.16
Australian (0)	10	0.04
Austrian (0)	110	0.44
Belgian (10)	71	0.28
Brazilian (128)	128	0.51
British (23)	69	0.28
Canadian (132)	458	1.83
Czech (26)	86	0.34
Danish (22)	66	0.26
Dutch (10)	131	0.52
Eastern European (11)	11	0.04
English (1,178)	4,171	16.70
European (19)	29	0.12
Finnish (19)	59	0.24
French, ex. Basque (105)	1,181	4.73
French Canadian (124)	648	2.60
German (337)	2,312	9.26
Greek (23)	307	1.23
Hungarian (0)	72	0.29
Irish (4,941)	11,111	44.50
Israeli (14)	14	0.06
Italian (1,394)	4,407	17.65
Lithuanian (91)	402	1.61
Maltese (0)	32	0.13
Northern European (32)	32	0.13
Norwegian (48)	217	0.87
Polish (99)	896	3.59
Portuguese (180)	560	2.24
Russian (87)	291	1.17
Scandinavian (0)	104	0.42
Scotch-Irish (539)	1,047	4.19
Scottish (363)	966	3.87
Slovak (0)	34	0.14
Swedish (135)	806	3.23

*Notes: † The Census 2010 population figure is used to calculate the percentages in the Hispanic Origin and Race categories. Ancestry percentages are based on the 2006-2010 American Community Survey population (not shown); ‡ Numbers in parentheses indicate the number of people reporting a single ancestry; * Numbers in parentheses indicate the number of persons reporting this race alone, not in combination with any other race; Please refer to the Explanation of Data for more information.*

Ancestry (continued)	Population	%
Swiss (30)	173	0.69
Turkish (7)	7	0.03
Ukrainian (55)	173	0.69
Welsh (0)	127	0.51
West Indian, ex. Hispanic (15)	30	0.12
Jamaican (0)	15	0.06
Trinidadian/Tobagonian (15)	15	0.06

Hispanic Origin	Population	%
Hispanic or Latino (of any race)	315	1.25
Central American, ex. Mexican	24	0.10
Costa Rican	4	0.02
Guatemalan	12	0.05
Nicaraguan	6	0.02
Panamanian	2	0.01
Cuban	12	0.05
Dominican Republic	8	0.03
Mexican	71	0.28
Puerto Rican	84	0.33
South American	74	0.29
Argentinean	3	0.01
Bolivian	4	0.02
Colombian	29	0.12
Ecuadorian	12	0.05
Paraguayan	1	<0.01
Peruvian	15	0.06
Venezuelan	10	0.04
Other Hispanic or Latino	42	0.17

Race*	Population	%
African-American/Black (112)	192	0.76
Not Hispanic (110)	183	0.73
Hispanic (2)	9	0.04
American Indian/Alaska Native (38)	125	0.50
Not Hispanic (35)	117	0.47
Hispanic (3)	8	0.03
Blackfeet (0)	1	<0.01
Canadian/French Am. Ind. (0)	2	0.01
Cherokee (2)	11	0.04
Chickasaw (3)	3	0.01
Choctaw (0)	8	0.03
Cree (0)	4	0.02
Houma (2)	2	0.01
Iroquois (1)	4	0.02
Lumbee (2)	2	0.01
Mexican American Ind. (1)	1	<0.01
Navajo (0)	6	0.02
Osage (2)	2	0.01
Pueblo (0)	1	<0.01
Sioux (2)	2	0.01
South American Ind. (0)	1	<0.01
Asian (178)	252	1.00
Not Hispanic (178)	239	0.95
Hispanic (0)	13	0.05
Burmese (0)	3	0.01
Cambodian (4)	4	0.02
Chinese, ex. Taiwanese (49)	76	0.30
Filipino (18)	32	0.13
Indian (38)	47	0.19
Indonesian (0)	5	0.02
Japanese (5)	9	0.04
Korean (31)	45	0.18
Laotian (1)	3	0.01
Sri Lankan (1)	1	<0.01
Taiwanese (4)	6	0.02
Thai (6)	8	0.03
Vietnamese (8)	12	0.05
Hawaii Native/Pacific Islander (4)	21	0.08
Not Hispanic (4)	21	0.08
Guamanian/Chamorro (1)	7	0.03
Marshallese (1)	1	<0.01
Native Hawaiian (2)	6	0.02
Samoan (0)	1	<0.01
White (24,336)	24,582	97.81
Not Hispanic (24,127)	24,345	96.87
Hispanic (209)	237	0.94

Mashpee

Place Type: Town
County: Barnstable
Population: 14,006†

Ancestry‡	Population	%
African, Sub-Saharan (311)	421	3.04
African (16)	16	0.12
Cape Verdean (280)	377	2.72
Other Sub-Saharan African (15)	28	0.20
Albanian (8)	8	0.06
American (1,591)	1,591	11.49
Arab (13)	15	0.11
Lebanese (13)	15	0.11
Armenian (0)	21	0.15
Austrian (14)	29	0.21
Belgian (0)	37	0.27
Brazilian (269)	269	1.94
British (93)	136	0.98
Canadian (41)	104	0.75
Celtic (0)	30	0.22
Croatian (0)	15	0.11
Czechoslovakian (0)	2	0.01
Danish (14)	23	0.17
Dutch (99)	160	1.16
Eastern European (17)	17	0.12
English (617)	2,142	15.47
European (49)	49	0.35
Finnish (13)	62	0.45
French, ex. Basque (223)	1,175	8.48
French Canadian (92)	468	3.38
German (157)	1,026	7.41
Greek (80)	324	2.34
Hungarian (9)	78	0.56
Iranian (12)	12	0.09
Irish (1,447)	3,760	27.15
Italian (755)	1,688	12.19
Latvian (0)	10	0.07
Lithuanian (80)	103	0.74
Norwegian (56)	97	0.70
Polish (259)	832	6.01
Portuguese (239)	592	4.27
Russian (98)	296	2.14
Scandinavian (0)	21	0.15
Scotch-Irish (72)	251	1.81
Scottish (213)	578	4.17
Slavic (0)	21	0.15
Slovak (0)	24	0.17
Slovene (0)	13	0.09
Swedish (152)	418	3.02
Swiss (0)	12	0.09
Turkish (49)	164	1.18
Ukrainian (0)	11	0.08
Welsh (19)	37	0.27
West Indian, ex. Hispanic (0)	14	0.10
Haitian (0)	14	0.10

Hispanic Origin	Population	%
Hispanic or Latino (of any race)	315	2.25
Central American, ex. Mexican	30	0.21
Costa Rican	11	0.08
Guatemalan	8	0.06
Honduran	3	0.02
Panamanian	1	0.01
Salvadoran	7	0.05
Cuban	24	0.17
Dominican Republic	5	0.04
Mexican	44	0.31
Puerto Rican	125	0.89
South American	52	0.37
Bolivian	4	0.03
Chilean	6	0.04
Colombian	14	0.10
Ecuadorian	15	0.11
Peruvian	5	0.04
Uruguayan	1	0.01
Venezuelan	4	0.03
Other South American	3	0.02
Other Hispanic or Latino	35	0.25

Race*	Population	%
African-American/Black (320)	533	3.81
Not Hispanic (312)	518	3.70
Hispanic (8)	15	0.11
American Indian/Alaska Native (432)	588	4.20
Not Hispanic (405)	557	3.98
Hispanic (27)	31	0.22
Alaska Athabascan *(Ala. Nat.)* (0)	1	0.01
Aleut *(Alaska Native)* (0)	4	0.03
Apache (0)	1	0.01
Blackfeet (3)	6	0.04
Canadian/French Am. Ind. (1)	1	0.01
Cherokee (8)	12	0.09
Chippewa (0)	1	0.01
Choctaw (1)	3	0.02
Inupiat *(Alaska Native)* (0)	1	0.01
Iroquois (2)	3	0.02
Mexican American Ind. (7)	7	0.05
Navajo (0)	3	0.02
Seminole (0)	2	0.01
Sioux (0)	3	0.02
South American Ind. (2)	3	0.02
Asian (171)	218	1.56
Not Hispanic (168)	211	1.51
Hispanic (3)	7	0.05
Burmese (5)	5	0.04
Chinese, ex. Taiwanese (33)	41	0.29
Filipino (37)	43	0.31
Indian (20)	42	0.30
Indonesian (0)	3	0.02
Japanese (9)	15	0.11
Korean (13)	16	0.11
Nepalese (4)	4	0.03
Pakistani (20)	33	0.24
Sri Lankan (3)	3	0.02
Thai (0)	5	0.04
Vietnamese (15)	19	0.14
Hawaii Native/Pacific Islander (9)	23	0.16
Not Hispanic (9)	18	0.13
Hispanic (0)	5	0.04
Native Hawaiian (6)	15	0.11
Samoan (0)	6	0.04
White (12,484)	12,807	91.44
Not Hispanic (12,281)	12,578	89.80
Hispanic (203)	229	1.64

Maynard

Place Type: CDP/Town
County: Middlesex
Population: 10,106†

Ancestry‡	Population	%
Albanian (32)	52	0.52
American (308)	308	3.07
Arab (44)	72	0.72
Lebanese (13)	13	0.13
Moroccan (31)	31	0.31
Syrian (0)	28	0.28
Armenian (0)	11	0.11
Austrian (0)	25	0.25
Brazilian (81)	81	0.81
British (93)	121	1.21
Canadian (38)	64	0.64
Danish (13)	38	0.38
Dutch (14)	102	1.02
Eastern European (32)	65	0.65
English (547)	2,044	20.37
European (59)	59	0.59
Finnish (105)	310	3.09
French, ex. Basque (61)	534	5.32
French Canadian (257)	472	4.70
German (125)	936	9.33
Greek (158)	302	3.01
Hungarian (0)	19	0.19
Irish (993)	3,103	30.92
Italian (415)	1,548	15.42
Latvian (14)	41	0.41
Lithuanian (53)	113	1.13

*Notes: † The Census 2010 population figure is used to calculate the percentages in the Hispanic Origin and Race categories. Ancestry percentages are based on the 2006-2010 American Community Survey population (not shown); ‡ Numbers in parentheses indicate the number of people reporting a single ancestry; * Numbers in parentheses indicate the number of persons reporting this race alone, not in combination with any other race; Please refer to the Explanation of Data for more information.*

Northern European (14)	14	0.14
Norwegian (0)	244	2.43
Pennsylvania German (0)	15	0.15
Polish (227)	642	6.40
Portuguese (13)	98	0.98
Romanian (15)	95	0.95
Russian (38)	191	1.90
Scandinavian (18)	70	0.70
Scotch-Irish (45)	239	2.38
Scottish (32)	333	3.32
Swedish (53)	323	3.22
Swiss (0)	32	0.32
Turkish (15)	15	0.15
Ukrainian (12)	24	0.24
Welsh (0)	48	0.48
West Indian, ex. Hispanic (41)	41	0.41
Bahamian (14)	14	0.14
Haitian (27)	27	0.27

Hispanic Origin	Population	%
Hispanic or Latino (of any race)	377	3.73
Central American, ex. Mexican	61	0.60
Costa Rican	5	0.05
Guatemalan	30	0.30
Honduran	5	0.05
Nicaraguan	9	0.09
Salvadoran	11	0.11
Other Central American	1	0.01
Cuban	5	0.05
Dominican Republic	8	0.08
Mexican	76	0.75
Puerto Rican	122	1.21
South American	72	0.71
Argentinean	3	0.03
Bolivian	1	0.01
Chilean	6	0.06
Colombian	39	0.39
Peruvian	16	0.16
Uruguayan	4	0.04
Venezuelan	3	0.03
Other Hispanic or Latino	33	0.33

Race*	Population	%
African-American/Black (170)	215	2.13
Not Hispanic (159)	195	1.93
Hispanic (11)	20	0.20
American Indian/Alaska Native (13)	43	0.43
Not Hispanic (12)	37	0.37
Hispanic (1)	6	0.06
Apache (0)	1	0.01
Blackfeet (0)	1	0.01
Cherokee (2)	7	0.07
Creek (1)	1	0.01
Lumbee (1)	1	0.01
Mexican American Ind. (1)	2	0.02
Sioux (1)	4	0.04
Asian (275)	326	3.23
Not Hispanic (274)	320	3.17
Hispanic (1)	6	0.06
Bangladeshi (0)	1	0.01
Cambodian (5)	5	0.05
Chinese, ex. Taiwanese (85)	102	1.01
Filipino (29)	33	0.33
Indian (78)	88	0.87
Indonesian (2)	3	0.03
Japanese (3)	6	0.06
Korean (22)	38	0.38
Laotian (9)	9	0.09
Pakistani (6)	8	0.08
Sri Lankan (0)	2	0.02
Taiwanese (6)	6	0.06
Thai (14)	15	0.15
Vietnamese (11)	12	0.12
Hawaii Native/Pacific Islander (1)	6	0.06
Not Hispanic (1)	4	0.04
Hispanic (0)	2	0.02
Marshallese (1)	1	0.01
Native Hawaiian (0)	2	0.02
White (9,365)	9,507	94.07
Not Hispanic (9,110)	9,229	91.32
Hispanic (255)	278	2.75

Medfield

Place Type: Town
County: Norfolk
Population: 12,024†

Ancestry‡	Population	%
Albanian (0)	23	0.19
Alsatian (17)	73	0.61
American (550)	550	4.59
Arab (94)	150	1.25
Egyptian (16)	24	0.20
Lebanese (78)	126	1.05
Armenian (13)	26	0.22
Austrian (6)	32	0.27
British (57)	83	0.69
Canadian (82)	202	1.69
Celtic (15)	30	0.25
Czech (25)	82	0.68
Czechoslovakian (0)	12	0.10
Dutch (11)	187	1.56
Eastern European (35)	35	0.29
English (481)	1,790	14.95
European (316)	316	2.64
Finnish (18)	38	0.32
French, ex. Basque (16)	448	3.74
French Canadian (92)	342	2.86
German (267)	1,316	10.99
Greek (51)	211	1.76
Hungarian (7)	43	0.36
Icelander (0)	48	0.40
Irish (2,060)	4,228	35.30
Italian (672)	1,679	14.02
Latvian (10)	10	0.08
Lithuanian (38)	95	0.79
Northern European (74)	74	0.62
Norwegian (83)	236	1.97
Polish (54)	415	3.47
Portuguese (0)	63	0.53
Romanian (51)	80	0.67
Russian (183)	414	3.46
Scandinavian (12)	12	0.10
Scotch-Irish (262)	377	3.15
Scottish (66)	533	4.45
Swedish (87)	387	3.23
Swiss (0)	14	0.12
Ukrainian (9)	29	0.24
Welsh (0)	23	0.19
West Indian, ex. Hispanic (25)	34	0.28
Haitian (25)	34	0.28

Hispanic Origin	Population	%
Hispanic or Latino (of any race)	180	1.50
Central American, ex. Mexican	19	0.16
Costa Rican	3	0.02
Guatemalan	13	0.11
Salvadoran	3	0.02
Cuban	21	0.17
Dominican Republic	6	0.05
Mexican	39	0.32
Puerto Rican	36	0.30
South American	46	0.38
Argentinean	5	0.04
Chilean	1	0.01
Colombian	16	0.13
Ecuadorian	10	0.08
Paraguayan	4	0.03
Peruvian	7	0.06
Venezuelan	3	0.02
Other Hispanic or Latino	13	0.11

Race*	Population	%
African-American/Black (74)	117	0.97
Not Hispanic (72)	113	0.94
Hispanic (2)	4	0.03
American Indian/Alaska Native (9)	27	0.22
Not Hispanic (8)	26	0.22
Hispanic (1)	1	0.01
Cherokee (1)	4	0.03
Chickasaw (3)	3	0.02
Chippewa (0)	1	0.01
Crow (0)	1	0.01
Seminole (0)	2	0.02
South American Ind. (1)	1	0.01
Asian (325)	401	3.33
Not Hispanic (325)	401	3.33
Bangladeshi (2)	2	0.02
Chinese, ex. Taiwanese (153)	183	1.52
Filipino (14)	33	0.27
Hmong (1)	3	0.02
Indian (85)	97	0.81
Indonesian (0)	1	0.01
Japanese (7)	18	0.15
Korean (29)	32	0.27
Nepalese (6)	9	0.07
Sri Lankan (4)	4	0.03
Taiwanese (8)	8	0.07
Thai (3)	3	0.02
Vietnamese (4)	11	0.09
Hawaii Native/Pacific Islander (0)	5	0.04
Not Hispanic (0)	5	0.04
White (11,435)	11,561	96.15
Not Hispanic (11,293)	11,411	94.90
Hispanic (142)	150	1.25

Medford

Place Type: City
County: Middlesex
Population: 56,173†

Ancestry‡	Population	%
African, Sub-Saharan (678)	917	1.65
African (175)	232	0.42
Cape Verdean (14)	165	0.30
Ethiopian (275)	275	0.50
Kenyan (16)	16	0.03
Liberian (72)	72	0.13
Nigerian (35)	35	0.06
Somalian (23)	23	0.04
Sudanese (0)	9	0.02
Zimbabwean (6)	6	0.01
Other Sub-Saharan African (62)	84	0.15
Albanian (110)	190	0.34
Alsatian (0)	25	0.05
American (960)	960	1.73
Arab (618)	856	1.54
Arab (0)	28	0.05
Egyptian (124)	133	0.24
Jordanian (146)	172	0.31
Lebanese (15)	64	0.12
Moroccan (176)	176	0.32
Syrian (36)	72	0.13
Other Arab (121)	211	0.38
Armenian (181)	198	0.36
Australian (0)	27	0.05
Austrian (55)	182	0.33
Belgian (40)	82	0.15
Brazilian (1,112)	1,180	2.13
British (73)	155	0.28
Bulgarian (38)	51	0.09
Canadian (224)	625	1.13
Croatian (0)	18	0.03
Czech (31)	83	0.15
Czechoslovakian (0)	28	0.05
Danish (27)	106	0.19
Dutch (83)	326	0.59
Eastern European (110)	162	0.29
English (758)	4,210	7.59
Estonian (0)	17	0.03
European (480)	561	1.01
Finnish (11)	42	0.08
French, ex. Basque (524)	2,187	3.94
French Canadian (468)	1,608	2.90
German (505)	3,051	5.50
Greek (388)	687	1.24
Hungarian (58)	162	0.29
Irish (5,028)	13,212	23.83

*Notes: † The Census 2010 population figure is used to calculate the percentages in the Hispanic Origin and Race categories. Ancestry percentages are based on the 2006-2010 American Community Survey population (not shown); ‡ Numbers in parentheses indicate the number of people reporting a single ancestry; * Numbers in parentheses indicate the number of persons reporting this race alone, not in combination with any other race; Please refer to the Explanation of Data for more information.*

Ancestry	Population	%
Israeli (0)	9	0.02
Italian (8,279)	13,886	25.04
Latvian (5)	5	0.01
Lithuanian (92)	437	0.79
Macedonian (0)	9	0.02
Northern European (71)	71	0.13
Norwegian (39)	383	0.69
Polish (397)	2,079	3.75
Portuguese (1,263)	1,853	3.34
Romanian (134)	188	0.34
Russian (261)	850	1.53
Scandinavian (1)	12	0.02
Scotch-Irish (279)	803	1.45
Scottish (198)	949	1.71
Slovak (26)	38	0.07
Swedish (100)	372	0.67
Swiss (13)	24	0.04
Turkish (155)	191	0.34
Ukrainian (73)	104	0.19
Welsh (17)	251	0.45
West Indian, ex. Hispanic (1,987)	2,180	3.93
Barbadian (24)	33	0.06
Bermudan (14)	14	0.03
Haitian (1,674)	1,690	3.05
Jamaican (77)	174	0.31
Trinidadian/Tobagonian (98)	98	0.18
West Indian (100)	171	0.31
Yugoslavian (8)	23	0.04

Hispanic Origin	Population	%
Hispanic or Latino (of any race)	2,447	4.36
Central American, ex. Mexican	562	1.00
Costa Rican	21	0.04
Guatemalan	97	0.17
Honduran	39	0.07
Nicaraguan	17	0.03
Panamanian	26	0.05
Salvadoran	355	0.63
Other Central American	7	0.01
Cuban	112	0.20
Dominican Republic	184	0.33
Mexican	294	0.52
Puerto Rican	480	0.85
South American	512	0.91
Argentinean	46	0.08
Bolivian	32	0.06
Chilean	62	0.11
Colombian	180	0.32
Ecuadorian	34	0.06
Paraguayan	1	<0.01
Peruvian	66	0.12
Uruguayan	10	0.02
Venezuelan	72	0.13
Other South American	9	0.02
Other Hispanic or Latino	303	0.54

Race*	Population	%
African-American/Black (4,939)	5,583	9.94
Not Hispanic (4,787)	5,343	9.51
Hispanic (152)	240	0.43
American Indian/Alaska Native (124)	338	0.60
Not Hispanic (81)	256	0.46
Hispanic (43)	82	0.15
Apache (0)	1	<0.01
Blackfeet (1)	10	0.02
Canadian/French Am. Ind. (8)	13	0.02
Central American Ind. (0)	1	<0.01
Cherokee (4)	24	0.04
Cheyenne (0)	1	<0.01
Chickasaw (0)	3	0.01
Chippewa (1)	3	0.01
Choctaw (2)	4	0.01
Cree (0)	1	<0.01
Creek (0)	1	<0.01
Iroquois (1)	10	0.02
Mexican American Ind. (8)	10	0.02
Navajo (2)	3	0.01
Seminole (1)	5	0.01
Shoshone (1)	2	<0.01
Sioux (1)	7	0.01
South American Ind. (7)	19	0.03
Spanish American Ind. (10)	10	0.02
Yaqui (0)	1	<0.01
Asian (3,865)	4,303	7.66
Not Hispanic (3,856)	4,273	7.61
Hispanic (9)	30	0.05
Bangladeshi (78)	86	0.15
Burmese (0)	1	<0.01
Cambodian (16)	21	0.04
Chinese, ex. Taiwanese (1,556)	1,742	3.10
Filipino (133)	186	0.33
Indian (888)	998	1.78
Indonesian (10)	12	0.02
Japanese (81)	145	0.26
Korean (225)	269	0.48
Laotian (9)	13	0.02
Malaysian (7)	7	0.01
Nepalese (68)	71	0.13
Pakistani (51)	58	0.10
Sri Lankan (26)	36	0.06
Taiwanese (57)	70	0.12
Thai (37)	41	0.07
Vietnamese (457)	516	0.92
Hawaii Native/Pacific Islander (8)	62	0.11
Not Hispanic (7)	54	0.10
Hispanic (1)	8	0.01
Guamanian/Chamorro (0)	2	<0.01
Native Hawaiian (6)	23	0.04
Samoan (0)	1	<0.01
White (44,133)	45,400	80.82
Not Hispanic (42,789)	43,844	78.05
Hispanic (1,344)	1,556	2.77

Medway

Place Type: Town
County: Norfolk
Population: 12,752†

Ancestry‡	Population	%
Albanian (0)	9	0.07
American (375)	375	2.98
Arab (30)	86	0.68
Lebanese (30)	80	0.64
Syrian (0)	6	0.05
Armenian (77)	155	1.23
Austrian (0)	22	0.17
Brazilian (26)	26	0.21
British (52)	110	0.87
Canadian (57)	95	0.75
Croatian (11)	22	0.17
Czech (0)	45	0.36
Czechoslovakian (0)	16	0.13
Danish (0)	20	0.16
Dutch (15)	72	0.57
Eastern European (35)	35	0.28
English (655)	2,659	21.11
European (174)	182	1.44
Finnish (51)	85	0.67
French, ex. Basque (162)	665	5.28
French Canadian (106)	278	2.21
German (135)	1,434	11.38
Greek (238)	323	2.56
Hungarian (24)	112	0.89
Irish (1,167)	3,839	30.48
Italian (807)	2,443	19.39
Latvian (0)	29	0.23
Lithuanian (34)	180	1.43
Northern European (31)	31	0.25
Norwegian (33)	188	1.49
Polish (109)	933	7.41
Portuguese (112)	333	2.64
Romanian (13)	60	0.48
Russian (125)	343	2.72
Scandinavian (10)	81	0.64
Scotch-Irish (39)	232	1.84
Scottish (82)	451	3.58
Slavic (0)	16	0.13
Slovak (0)	23	0.18
Swedish (91)	341	2.71
Swiss (8)	16	0.13
Turkish (11)	51	0.40
Ukrainian (24)	59	0.47
Welsh (0)	32	0.25

Hispanic Origin	Population	%
Hispanic or Latino (of any race)	250	1.96
Central American, ex. Mexican	29	0.23
Costa Rican	6	0.05
Guatemalan	4	0.03
Honduran	4	0.03
Nicaraguan	3	0.02
Panamanian	1	0.01
Salvadoran	11	0.09
Cuban	23	0.18
Dominican Republic	6	0.05
Mexican	50	0.39
Puerto Rican	63	0.49
South American	40	0.31
Argentinean	8	0.06
Bolivian	6	0.05
Chilean	7	0.05
Colombian	9	0.07
Ecuadorian	8	0.06
Peruvian	2	0.02
Other Hispanic or Latino	39	0.31

Race*	Population	%
African-American/Black (131)	177	1.39
Not Hispanic (124)	169	1.33
Hispanic (7)	8	0.06
American Indian/Alaska Native (30)	75	0.59
Not Hispanic (20)	65	0.51
Hispanic (10)	10	0.08
Central American Ind. (1)	1	0.01
Cherokee (1)	6	0.05
Choctaw (1)	1	0.01
Iroquois (1)	3	0.02
Mexican American Ind. (1)	1	0.01
Navajo (2)	2	0.02
Osage (0)	1	0.01
Sioux (0)	1	0.01
South American Ind. (1)	1	0.01
Asian (280)	345	2.71
Not Hispanic (277)	336	2.63
Hispanic (3)	9	0.07
Bangladeshi (1)	3	0.02
Chinese, ex. Taiwanese (78)	100	0.78
Filipino (18)	33	0.26
Indian (113)	118	0.93
Japanese (12)	28	0.22
Korean (9)	22	0.17
Nepalese (2)	2	0.02
Pakistani (19)	19	0.15
Sri Lankan (0)	3	0.02
Taiwanese (5)	6	0.05
Thai (6)	6	0.05
Vietnamese (8)	9	0.07
Hawaii Native/Pacific Islander (1)	8	0.06
Not Hispanic (1)	8	0.06
Guamanian/Chamorro (1)	3	0.02
Native Hawaiian (0)	4	0.03
White (12,109)	12,259	96.13
Not Hispanic (11,924)	12,059	94.57
Hispanic (185)	200	1.57

Melrose

Place Type: City
County: Middlesex
Population: 26,983†

Ancestry‡	Population	%
African, Sub-Saharan (323)	323	1.21
African (47)	47	0.18
Cape Verdean (13)	13	0.05
Ethiopian (56)	56	0.21
Kenyan (33)	33	0.12
Ugandan (174)	174	0.65
Albanian (71)	81	0.30

*Notes: † The Census 2010 population figure is used to calculate the percentages in the Hispanic Origin and Race categories. Ancestry percentages are based on the 2006-2010 American Community Survey population (not shown); ‡ Numbers in parentheses indicate the number of people reporting a single ancestry; * Numbers in parentheses indicate the number of persons reporting this race alone, not in combination with any other race; Please refer to the Explanation of Data for more information.*

Alsatian (0)	14	0.05
American (506)	506	1.89
Arab (191)	278	1.04
Lebanese (27)	69	0.26
Moroccan (132)	132	0.49
Syrian (0)	30	0.11
Other Arab (32)	47	0.18
Armenian (127)	234	0.88
Assyrian/Chaldean/Syriac (0)	15	0.06
Austrian (26)	51	0.19
Belgian (0)	37	0.14
Brazilian (434)	451	1.69
British (64)	115	0.43
Canadian (58)	463	1.73
Croatian (12)	12	0.04
Czech (0)	13	0.05
Czechoslovakian (0)	74	0.28
Danish (29)	63	0.24
Dutch (38)	200	0.75
Eastern European (210)	210	0.79
English (778)	3,769	14.11
European (302)	346	1.30
Finnish (25)	107	0.40
French, ex. Basque (155)	1,684	6.31
French Canadian (269)	791	2.96
German (282)	1,877	7.03
Greek (237)	395	1.48
Hungarian (0)	60	0.22
Iranian (8)	23	0.09
Irish (3,136)	9,118	34.14
Italian (2,958)	6,639	24.86
Lithuanian (0)	43	0.16
Northern European (12)	12	0.04
Norwegian (23)	157	0.59
Polish (194)	890	3.33
Portuguese (181)	640	2.40
Romanian (119)	119	0.45
Russian (156)	252	0.94
Scandinavian (11)	25	0.09
Scotch-Irish (223)	733	2.74
Scottish (177)	713	2.67
Slovak (11)	11	0.04
Swedish (62)	396	1.48
Swiss (24)	94	0.35
Turkish (212)	212	0.79
Ukrainian (14)	85	0.32
Welsh (11)	118	0.44
West Indian, ex. Hispanic (69)	87	0.33
Haitian (69)	87	0.33
Yugoslavian (68)	68	0.25

Hispanic Origin	Population	%
Hispanic or Latino (of any race)	663	2.46
Central American, ex. Mexican	102	0.38
Costa Rican	5	0.02
Guatemalan	32	0.12
Honduran	12	0.04
Nicaraguan	2	0.01
Panamanian	2	0.01
Salvadoran	45	0.17
Other Central American	4	0.01
Cuban	22	0.08
Dominican Republic	37	0.14
Mexican	96	0.36
Puerto Rican	146	0.54
South American	163	0.60
Argentinean	6	0.02
Bolivian	2	0.01
Chilean	17	0.06
Colombian	73	0.27
Ecuadorian	19	0.07
Paraguayan	1	<0.01
Peruvian	24	0.09
Uruguayan	7	0.03
Venezuelan	11	0.04
Other South American	3	0.01
Other Hispanic or Latino	97	0.36

Race*	Population	%
African-American/Black (656)	795	2.95
Not Hispanic (625)	750	2.78
Hispanic (31)	45	0.17
American Indian/Alaska Native (22)	91	0.34
Not Hispanic (11)	71	0.26
Hispanic (11)	20	0.07
Alaska Athabascan (*Ala. Nat.*) (1)	1	<0.01
Blackfeet (0)	5	0.02
Canadian/French Am. Ind. (0)	2	0.01
Cherokee (0)	8	0.03
Choctaw (0)	5	0.02
Iroquois (0)	5	0.02
Lumbee (1)	6	0.02
Menominee (1)	1	<0.01
South American Ind. (4)	5	0.02
Asian (1,022)	1,222	4.53
Not Hispanic (1,020)	1,213	4.50
Hispanic (2)	9	0.03
Bangladeshi (6)	6	0.02
Burmese (0)	1	<0.01
Cambodian (14)	20	0.07
Chinese, ex. Taiwanese (460)	513	1.90
Filipino (82)	128	0.47
Indian (168)	192	0.71
Indonesian (2)	5	0.02
Japanese (30)	49	0.18
Korean (68)	97	0.36
Laotian (0)	1	<0.01
Malaysian (0)	3	0.01
Nepalese (5)	9	0.03
Pakistani (10)	12	0.04
Sri Lankan (6)	6	0.02
Taiwanese (10)	13	0.05
Thai (15)	20	0.07
Vietnamese (125)	147	0.54
Hawaii Native/Pacific Islander (5)	17	0.06
Not Hispanic (1)	10	0.04
Hispanic (4)	7	0.03
Guamanian/Chamorro (4)	7	0.03
Native Hawaiian (1)	6	0.02
White (24,594)	25,002	92.66
Not Hispanic (24,161)	24,529	90.91
Hispanic (433)	473	1.75

Methuen Town

Place Type: City
County: Essex
Population: 47,255†

Ancestry‡	Population	%
African, Sub-Saharan (334)	476	1.03
African (102)	102	0.22
Cape Verdean (50)	50	0.11
Kenyan (12)	12	0.03
Liberian (9)	9	0.02
Nigerian (113)	255	0.55
Other Sub-Saharan African (48)	48	0.10
Alsatian (18)	18	0.04
American (1,250)	1,250	2.69
Arab (1,077)	1,897	4.09
Arab (22)	22	0.05
Lebanese (966)	1,776	3.83
Moroccan (28)	28	0.06
Palestinian (19)	19	0.04
Syrian (37)	47	0.10
Other Arab (5)	5	0.01
Armenian (153)	225	0.48
Austrian (19)	37	0.08
Belgian (52)	120	0.26
Brazilian (23)	30	0.06
British (57)	148	0.32
Canadian (271)	487	1.05
Celtic (158)	158	0.34
Czech (25)	36	0.08
Czechoslovakian (14)	49	0.11
Danish (10)	20	0.04
Dutch (114)	244	0.53
English (1,152)	4,134	8.91
European (193)	238	0.51
Finnish (0)	59	0.13
French, ex. Basque (1,597)	5,483	11.82
French Canadian (1,463)	3,038	6.55
German (466)	2,366	5.10
Greek (363)	909	1.96
Hungarian (0)	16	0.03
Iranian (9)	15	0.03
Irish (3,102)	10,000	21.55
Italian (4,752)	9,956	21.46
Latvian (12)	18	0.04
Lithuanian (120)	532	1.15
Norwegian (8)	92	0.20
Pennsylvania German (18)	35	0.08
Polish (571)	1,994	4.30
Portuguese (416)	838	1.81
Romanian (12)	12	0.03
Russian (57)	308	0.66
Scandinavian (0)	14	0.03
Scotch-Irish (202)	714	1.54
Scottish (169)	828	1.78
Serbian (12)	23	0.05
Slovene (0)	16	0.03
Swedish (91)	388	0.84
Swiss (27)	35	0.08
Turkish (210)	253	0.55
Ukrainian (16)	74	0.16
Welsh (11)	31	0.07
West Indian, ex. Hispanic (152)	186	0.40
Barbadian (51)	51	0.11
Haitian (81)	81	0.17
Jamaican (20)	54	0.12
Yugoslavian (0)	16	0.03

Hispanic Origin	Population	%
Hispanic or Latino (of any race)	8,531	18.05
Central American, ex. Mexican	458	0.97
Costa Rican	20	0.04
Guatemalan	286	0.61
Honduran	33	0.07
Nicaraguan	6	0.01
Panamanian	7	0.01
Salvadoran	103	0.22
Other Central American	3	0.01
Cuban	122	0.26
Dominican Republic	3,953	8.37
Mexican	154	0.33
Puerto Rican	2,695	5.70
South American	357	0.76
Argentinean	13	0.03
Bolivian	3	0.01
Chilean	7	0.01
Colombian	112	0.24
Ecuadorian	164	0.35
Peruvian	41	0.09
Venezuelan	17	0.04
Other Hispanic or Latino	792	1.68

Race*	Population	%
African-American/Black (1,476)	1,847	3.91
Not Hispanic (935)	1,102	2.33
Hispanic (541)	745	1.58
American Indian/Alaska Native (160)	369	0.78
Not Hispanic (68)	135	0.29
Hispanic (92)	234	0.50
Blackfeet (0)	6	0.01
Canadian/French Am. Ind. (2)	2	<0.01
Central American Ind. (1)	7	0.01
Cherokee (6)	18	0.04
Chippewa (1)	1	<0.01
Cree (0)	1	<0.01
Creek (0)	1	<0.01
Iroquois (4)	4	0.01
Mexican American Ind. (1)	1	<0.01
Potawatomi (3)	3	0.01
Pueblo (3)	3	0.01
Shoshone (0)	2	<0.01
Sioux (2)	5	0.01
South American Ind. (14)	20	0.04
Spanish American Ind. (9)	10	0.02
Asian (1,767)	2,031	4.30
Not Hispanic (1,741)	1,964	4.16

*Notes: † The Census 2010 population figure is used to calculate the percentages in the Hispanic Origin and Race categories. Ancestry percentages are based on the 2006-2010 American Community Survey population (not shown); ‡ Numbers in parentheses indicate the number of people reporting a single ancestry; * Numbers in parentheses indicate the number of persons reporting this race alone, not in combination with any other race; Please refer to the Explanation of Data for more information.*

Hispanic (26)	67	0.14
Bangladeshi (4)	4	0.01
Burmese (2)	2	<0.01
Cambodian (127)	157	0.33
Chinese, ex. Taiwanese (232)	275	0.58
Filipino (59)	88	0.19
Indian (402)	441	0.93
Indonesian (3)	3	0.01
Japanese (34)	56	0.12
Korean (176)	205	0.43
Laotian (7)	13	0.03
Malaysian (2)	2	<0.01
Nepalese (1)	1	<0.01
Pakistani (64)	69	0.15
Sri Lankan (11)	11	0.02
Taiwanese (2)	2	<0.01
Thai (25)	29	0.06
Vietnamese (528)	573	1.21
Hawaii Native/Pacific Islander (10)	86	0.18
Not Hispanic (1)	39	0.08
Hispanic (9)	47	0.10
Guamanian/Chamorro (5)	10	0.02
Native Hawaiian (4)	4	0.01
White (38,762)	39,602	83.80
Not Hispanic (35,387)	35,805	75.77
Hispanic (3,375)	3,797	8.04

Hispanic Origin	Population	%
Hispanic or Latino (of any race)	367	1.59
Central American, ex. Mexican	36	0.16
Costa Rican	4	0.02
Guatemalan	11	0.05
Honduran	2	0.01
Salvadoran	19	0.08
Cuban	16	0.07
Dominican Republic	13	0.06
Mexican	58	0.25
Puerto Rican	166	0.72
South American	30	0.13
Argentinean	10	0.04
Chilean	3	0.01
Colombian	10	0.04
Ecuadorian	3	0.01
Peruvian	2	0.01
Venezuelan	1	<0.01
Other South American	1	<0.01
Other Hispanic or Latino	48	0.21

Race*	Population	%
African-American/Black (361)	524	2.27
Not Hispanic (342)	491	2.12
Hispanic (19)	33	0.14
American Indian/Alaska Native (56)	165	0.71
Not Hispanic (48)	151	0.65
Hispanic (8)	14	0.06
Blackfeet (0)	3	0.01
Cherokee (4)	12	0.05
Chippewa (0)	2	0.01
Choctaw (0)	2	0.01
Comanche (1)	1	<0.01
Iroquois (0)	2	0.01
Navajo (5)	5	0.02
Potawatomi (1)	1	<0.01
Sioux (0)	2	0.01
South American Ind. (1)	6	0.03
Asian (170)	249	1.08
Not Hispanic (168)	246	1.06
Hispanic (2)	3	0.01
Cambodian (1)	4	0.02
Chinese, ex. Taiwanese (35)	53	0.23
Filipino (33)	61	0.26
Indian (24)	28	0.12
Indonesian (4)	4	0.02
Japanese (8)	27	0.12
Korean (17)	19	0.08
Laotian (2)	4	0.02
Nepalese (8)	8	0.03
Pakistani (0)	4	0.02
Sri Lankan (0)	1	<0.01
Thai (3)	4	0.02
Vietnamese (18)	20	0.09
Hawaii Native/Pacific Islander (4)	24	0.10
Not Hispanic (2)	22	0.10
Hispanic (2)	2	0.01
Fijian (1)	3	0.01
Guamanian/Chamorro (2)	5	0.02
Native Hawaiian (1)	3	0.01
White (22,010)	22,316	96.54
Not Hispanic (21,730)	22,014	95.23
Hispanic (280)	302	1.31

Middleborough

Place Type: Town
County: Plymouth
Population: 23,116†

Ancestry‡	Population	%
African, Sub-Saharan (183)	279	1.24
Cape Verdean (147)	243	1.08
Ethiopian (36)	36	0.16
American (965)	965	4.28
Arab (15)	105	0.47
Lebanese (8)	98	0.43
Palestinian (7)	7	0.03
Armenian (22)	127	0.56
Austrian (0)	75	0.33
Belgian (0)	11	0.05
Brazilian (49)	252	1.12
British (0)	30	0.13
Bulgarian (0)	13	0.06
Canadian (155)	358	1.59
Danish (0)	12	0.05
Dutch (0)	79	0.35
Eastern European (15)	15	0.07
English (1,155)	3,675	16.31
European (157)	192	0.85
Finnish (111)	191	0.85
French, ex. Basque (240)	1,694	7.52
French Canadian (421)	956	4.24
German (280)	1,148	5.09
Greek (46)	84	0.37
Hungarian (0)	14	0.06
Icelander (0)	8	0.04
Irish (2,797)	6,795	30.15
Italian (1,042)	3,549	15.75
Latvian (0)	11	0.05
Lithuanian (306)	472	2.09
Northern European (48)	48	0.21
Norwegian (91)	209	0.93
Polish (197)	866	3.84
Portuguese (921)	2,040	9.05
Russian (113)	248	1.10
Scandinavian (9)	9	0.04
Scotch-Irish (153)	513	2.28
Scottish (262)	782	3.47
Slavic (0)	29	0.13
Swedish (278)	811	3.60
Swiss (0)	17	0.08
Welsh (8)	41	0.18
West Indian, ex. Hispanic (10)	22	0.10
Bermudan (10)	10	0.04
Jamaican (0)	12	0.05
Syrian (49)	103	1.18
Armenian (46)	92	1.06
Australian (0)	16	0.18
Austrian (0)	16	0.18
British (42)	57	0.65
Canadian (75)	91	1.04
Danish (0)	27	0.31
Dutch (0)	7	0.08
English (264)	1,217	13.96
European (12)	12	0.14
French, ex. Basque (190)	702	8.05
French Canadian (96)	291	3.34
German (101)	684	7.85
Greek (150)	313	3.59
Irish (795)	2,436	27.95
Italian (1,072)	2,019	23.16
Lithuanian (0)	17	0.20
Maltese (8)	8	0.09
Polish (223)	516	5.92
Portuguese (163)	431	4.94
Russian (102)	161	1.85
Scotch-Irish (29)	222	2.55
Scottish (27)	254	2.91
Swedish (15)	73	0.84
Swiss (0)	31	0.36
Ukrainian (0)	12	0.14
Welsh (0)	29	0.33

Hispanic Origin	Population	%
Hispanic or Latino (of any race)	640	7.12
Central American, ex. Mexican	45	0.50
Costa Rican	7	0.08
Guatemalan	16	0.18
Honduran	1	0.01
Nicaraguan	2	0.02
Panamanian	3	0.03
Salvadoran	16	0.18
Cuban	20	0.22
Dominican Republic	127	1.41
Mexican	34	0.38
Puerto Rican	320	3.56
South American	32	0.36
Argentinean	1	0.01
Bolivian	1	0.01
Chilean	3	0.03
Colombian	18	0.20
Ecuadorian	1	0.01
Peruvian	6	0.07
Other South American	2	0.02
Other Hispanic or Latino	62	0.69

Race*	Population	%
African-American/Black (204)	252	2.80
Not Hispanic (153)	179	1.99
Hispanic (51)	73	0.81
American Indian/Alaska Native (43)	107	1.19
Not Hispanic (13)	65	0.72
Hispanic (30)	42	0.47
Apache (0)	5	0.06
Blackfeet (0)	3	0.03
Canadian/French Am. Ind. (0)	1	0.01
Central American Ind. (1)	1	0.01
Cherokee (2)	10	0.11
Chippewa (1)	1	0.01
Choctaw (0)	2	0.02
Cree (0)	1	0.01
Crow (0)	3	0.03
Inupiat *(Alaska Native)* (1)	1	0.01
Mexican American Ind. (1)	1	0.01
South American Ind. (1)	1	0.01
Tohono O'Odham (1)	1	0.01
Asian (204)	251	2.79
Not Hispanic (202)	247	2.75
Hispanic (2)	4	0.04
Bangladeshi (2)	2	0.02
Burmese (2)	2	0.02
Cambodian (13)	18	0.20
Chinese, ex. Taiwanese (58)	62	0.69
Filipino (15)	19	0.21
Indian (39)	49	0.55

Middleton

Place Type: Town
County: Essex
Population: 8,987†

Ancestry‡	Population	%
African, Sub-Saharan (32)	32	0.37
African (25)	25	0.29
Cape Verdean (7)	7	0.08
Albanian (0)	33	0.38
American (389)	389	4.46
Arab (83)	259	2.97
Arab (0)	92	1.06
Jordanian (16)	16	0.18
Lebanese (18)	48	0.55

*Notes: † The Census 2010 population figure is used to calculate the percentages in the Hispanic Origin and Race categories. Ancestry percentages are based on the 2006-2010 American Community Survey population (not shown); ‡ Numbers in parentheses indicate the number of people reporting a single ancestry; * Numbers in parentheses indicate the number of persons reporting this race alone, not in combination with any other race; Please refer to the Explanation of Data for more information.*

Japanese (21)	28	0.31
Korean (26)	38	0.42
Laotian (3)	4	0.04
Malaysian (1)	2	0.02
Taiwanese (5)	5	0.06
Thai (3)	4	0.04
Vietnamese (4)	7	0.08
Hawaii Native/Pacific Islander (3)	13	0.14
Not Hispanic (0)	7	0.08
Hispanic (3)	6	0.07
Native Hawaiian (0)	2	0.02
Samoan (1)	1	0.01
White (8,063)	8,198	91.22
Not Hispanic (7,845)	7,954	88.51
Hispanic (218)	244	2.72

Milford

Place Type: CDP
County: Worcester
Population: 25,055†

Ancestry‡	Population	%
African, Sub-Saharan (9)	62	0.25
Cape Verdean (9)	32	0.13
Other Sub-Saharan African (0)	30	0.12
Albanian (47)	93	0.37
American (577)	577	2.31
Arab (145)	205	0.82
Arab (27)	27	0.11
Egyptian (100)	100	0.40
Moroccan (0)	60	0.24
Syrian (18)	18	0.07
Armenian (91)	245	0.98
Austrian (13)	42	0.17
Belgian (9)	19	0.08
Brazilian (2,169)	2,230	8.94
British (55)	73	0.29
Bulgarian (29)	29	0.12
Canadian (35)	146	0.59
Croatian (8)	8	0.03
Czech (48)	68	0.27
Danish (22)	96	0.38
Dutch (88)	165	0.66
Eastern European (29)	123	0.49
English (777)	2,487	9.97
European (144)	144	0.58
Finnish (13)	77	0.31
French, ex. Basque (272)	1,572	6.30
French Canadian (339)	697	2.79
German (355)	1,257	5.04
Greek (77)	253	1.01
Guyanese (0)	5	0.02
Hungarian (12)	38	0.15
Irish (1,733)	5,585	22.39
Italian (2,702)	6,200	24.85
Lithuanian (33)	126	0.51
Norwegian (0)	80	0.32
Pennsylvania German (0)	11	0.04
Polish (194)	1,016	4.07
Portuguese (1,442)	1,691	6.78
Russian (177)	288	1.15
Scotch-Irish (171)	390	1.56
Scottish (180)	550	2.20
Serbian (0)	11	0.04
Slavic (0)	16	0.06
Slovak (0)	21	0.08
Swedish (35)	351	1.41
Ukrainian (0)	16	0.06
Welsh (11)	62	0.25
West Indian, ex. Hispanic (0)	19	0.08
Jamaican (0)	19	0.08

Hispanic Origin	Population	%
Hispanic or Latino (of any race)	2,249	8.98
Central American, ex. Mexican	217	0.87
Costa Rican	6	0.02
Guatemalan	92	0.37
Honduran	24	0.10
Nicaraguan	2	0.01
Panamanian	13	0.05
Salvadoran	80	0.32
Cuban	18	0.07
Dominican Republic	131	0.52
Mexican	166	0.66
Puerto Rican	791	3.16
South American	673	2.69
Argentinean	13	0.05
Bolivian	10	0.04
Chilean	6	0.02
Colombian	68	0.27
Ecuadorian	509	2.03
Paraguayan	1	<0.01
Peruvian	45	0.18
Uruguayan	2	0.01
Venezuelan	19	0.08
Other Hispanic or Latino	253	1.01

Race*	Population	%
African-American/Black (584)	801	3.20
Not Hispanic (509)	686	2.74
Hispanic (75)	115	0.46
American Indian/Alaska Native (68)	140	0.56
Not Hispanic (32)	91	0.36
Hispanic (36)	49	0.20
Apache (0)	1	<0.01
Blackfeet (0)	1	<0.01
Canadian/French Am. Ind. (0)	1	<0.01
Cherokee (5)	12	0.05
Chickasaw (0)	1	<0.01
Iroquois (1)	2	0.01
Mexican American Ind. (1)	2	0.01
Navajo (1)	1	<0.01
Pueblo (0)	1	<0.01
Sioux (0)	1	<0.01
South American Ind. (25)	30	0.12
Asian (584)	691	2.76
Not Hispanic (577)	677	2.70
Hispanic (7)	14	0.06
Bangladeshi (15)	15	0.06
Cambodian (3)	5	0.02
Chinese, ex. Taiwanese (80)	103	0.41
Filipino (53)	82	0.33
Indian (276)	298	1.19
Indonesian (0)	3	0.01
Japanese (17)	29	0.12
Korean (47)	59	0.24
Laotian (1)	3	0.01
Nepalese (2)	2	0.01
Pakistani (15)	18	0.07
Sri Lankan (6)	6	0.02
Taiwanese (4)	4	0.02
Thai (12)	14	0.06
Vietnamese (34)	41	0.16
Hawaii Native/Pacific Islander (5)	26	0.10
Not Hispanic (1)	15	0.06
Hispanic (4)	11	0.04
Guamanian/Chamorro (4)	5	0.02
Native Hawaiian (0)	2	0.01
Samoan (1)	2	0.01
White (21,621)	22,298	89.00
Not Hispanic (20,390)	20,936	83.56
Hispanic (1,231)	1,362	5.44

Milford

Place Type: Town
County: Worcester
Population: 27,999†

Ancestry‡	Population	%
African, Sub-Saharan (9)	62	0.22
Cape Verdean (9)	32	0.11
Other Sub-Saharan African (0)	30	0.11
Albanian (47)	93	0.33
American (647)	647	2.32
Arab (162)	354	1.27
Arab (27)	27	0.10
Egyptian (100)	100	0.36
Lebanese (17)	149	0.53
Moroccan (0)	60	0.22
Syrian (18)	18	0.06
Armenian (106)	260	0.93
Austrian (13)	42	0.15
Belgian (9)	19	0.07
Brazilian (2,210)	2,271	8.15
British (55)	105	0.38
Bulgarian (29)	29	0.10
Canadian (35)	146	0.52
Croatian (8)	8	0.03
Czech (48)	92	0.33
Danish (22)	96	0.34
Dutch (88)	174	0.62
Eastern European (29)	123	0.44
English (870)	2,743	9.85
European (155)	155	0.56
Finnish (13)	77	0.28
French, ex. Basque (272)	1,734	6.23
French Canadian (376)	813	2.92
German (401)	1,480	5.31
Greek (109)	349	1.25
Guyanese (0)	5	0.02
Hungarian (12)	38	0.14
Irish (2,078)	6,415	23.03
Italian (2,960)	6,960	24.99
Lithuanian (47)	140	0.50
Norwegian (0)	92	0.33
Pennsylvania German (0)	11	0.04
Polish (232)	1,160	4.16
Portuguese (1,587)	1,977	7.10
Russian (177)	288	1.03
Scotch-Irish (255)	505	1.81
Scottish (209)	635	2.28
Serbian (9)	20	0.07
Slavic (0)	16	0.06
Slovak (15)	36	0.13
Swedish (45)	463	1.66
Swiss (0)	14	0.05
Turkish (0)	15	0.05
Ukrainian (0)	16	0.06
Welsh (47)	121	0.43
West Indian, ex. Hispanic (0)	19	0.07
Jamaican (0)	19	0.07

Hispanic Origin	Population	%
Hispanic or Latino (of any race)	2,315	8.27
Central American, ex. Mexican	229	0.82
Costa Rican	8	0.03
Guatemalan	97	0.35
Honduran	26	0.09
Nicaraguan	2	0.01
Panamanian	13	0.05
Salvadoran	83	0.30
Cuban	21	0.08
Dominican Republic	132	0.47
Mexican	174	0.62
Puerto Rican	819	2.93
South American	683	2.44
Argentinean	13	0.05
Bolivian	10	0.04
Chilean	6	0.02
Colombian	73	0.26
Ecuadorian	509	1.82
Paraguayan	1	<0.01
Peruvian	50	0.18
Uruguayan	2	0.01
Venezuelan	19	0.07
Other Hispanic or Latino	257	0.92

Race*	Population	%
African-American/Black (611)	836	2.99
Not Hispanic (535)	719	2.57
Hispanic (76)	117	0.42
American Indian/Alaska Native (69)	150	0.54
Not Hispanic (33)	98	0.35
Hispanic (36)	52	0.19
Apache (0)	1	<0.01
Blackfeet (0)	1	<0.01
Canadian/French Am. Ind. (0)	1	<0.01
Cherokee (5)	12	0.04

*Notes: † The Census 2010 population figure is used to calculate the percentages in the Hispanic Origin and Race categories. Ancestry percentages are based on the 2006-2010 American Community Survey population (not shown); ‡ Numbers in parentheses indicate the number of people reporting a single ancestry; * Numbers in parentheses indicate the number of persons reporting this race alone, not in combination with any other race; Please refer to the Explanation of Data for more information.*

Chickasaw (0)	1	<0.01
Iroquois (1)	2	0.01
Mexican American Ind. (1)	2	0.01
Navajo (1)	1	<0.01
Pueblo (0)	1	<0.01
Sioux (0)	1	<0.01
South American Ind. (25)	30	0.11
Asian (681)	801	2.86
Not Hispanic (674)	787	2.81
Hispanic (7)	14	0.05
Bangladeshi (16)	16	0.06
Cambodian (3)	5	0.02
Chinese, ex. Taiwanese (98)	124	0.44
Filipino (55)	86	0.31
Indian (317)	339	1.21
Indonesian (0)	3	0.01
Japanese (19)	33	0.12
Korean (59)	75	0.27
Laotian (2)	5	0.02
Nepalese (2)	2	0.01
Pakistani (26)	29	0.10
Sri Lankan (6)	6	0.02
Taiwanese (7)	7	0.03
Thai (13)	18	0.06
Vietnamese (38)	45	0.16
Hawaii Native/Pacific Islander (6)	27	0.10
Not Hispanic (2)	16	0.06
Hispanic (4)	11	0.04
Guamanian/Chamorro (4)	5	0.02
Native Hawaiian (1)	3	0.01
Samoan (1)	2	0.01
White (24,393)	25,106	89.67
Not Hispanic (23,104)	23,684	84.59
Hispanic (1,289)	1,422	5.08

Millbury

Place Type: Town
County: Worcester
Population: 13,261†

Ancestry‡	Population	%
African, Sub-Saharan (0)	17	0.13
Kenyan (0)	17	0.13
Albanian (13)	49	0.37
American (217)	217	1.64
Arab (153)	217	1.64
Iraqi (71)	71	0.54
Lebanese (82)	137	1.04
Syrian (0)	9	0.07
Armenian (29)	60	0.45
Austrian (31)	133	1.01
Brazilian (41)	41	0.31
British (13)	38	0.29
Canadian (100)	202	1.53
Celtic (10)	10	0.08
Czech (0)	17	0.13
Danish (0)	28	0.21
Dutch (13)	44	0.33
Eastern European (18)	18	0.14
English (427)	1,731	13.09
European (127)	127	0.96
Finnish (27)	210	1.59
French, ex. Basque (754)	2,878	21.77
French Canadian (515)	946	7.16
German (175)	1,229	9.30
Greek (39)	98	0.74
Hungarian (0)	21	0.16
Irish (1,001)	3,416	25.84
Italian (535)	1,761	13.32
Lithuanian (203)	473	3.58
Norwegian (12)	49	0.37
Polish (307)	1,071	8.10
Portuguese (65)	143	1.08
Romanian (13)	26	0.20
Russian (52)	136	1.03
Scandinavian (13)	13	0.10
Scotch-Irish (68)	240	1.82
Scottish (64)	212	1.60
Slavic (0)	15	0.11
Slovak (13)	13	0.10
Swedish (95)	515	3.90
Ukrainian (0)	26	0.20
Welsh (0)	42	0.32

Hispanic Origin	Population	%
Hispanic or Latino (of any race)	306	2.31
Central American, ex. Mexican	28	0.21
Costa Rican	3	0.02
Guatemalan	16	0.12
Honduran	6	0.05
Salvadoran	3	0.02
Cuban	21	0.16
Dominican Republic	25	0.19
Mexican	32	0.24
Puerto Rican	142	1.07
South American	44	0.33
Bolivian	7	0.05
Chilean	6	0.05
Colombian	13	0.10
Ecuadorian	1	0.01
Peruvian	11	0.08
Venezuelan	2	0.02
Other South American	4	0.03
Other Hispanic or Latino	14	0.11

Race*	Population	%
African-American/Black (177)	239	1.80
Not Hispanic (165)	219	1.65
Hispanic (12)	20	0.15
American Indian/Alaska Native (26)	97	0.73
Not Hispanic (20)	88	0.66
Hispanic (6)	9	0.07
Blackfeet (2)	5	0.04
Canadian/French Am. Ind. (1)	4	0.03
Cherokee (1)	13	0.10
Chippewa (1)	1	0.01
Choctaw (0)	1	0.01
Cree (0)	2	0.02
Iroquois (1)	5	0.04
Potawatomi (1)	1	0.01
Shoshone (3)	3	0.02
Sioux (0)	3	0.02
Asian (248)	303	2.28
Not Hispanic (248)	302	2.28
Hispanic (0)	1	0.01
Bangladeshi (1)	1	0.01
Burmese (1)	1	0.01
Cambodian (3)	3	0.02
Chinese, ex. Taiwanese (27)	36	0.27
Filipino (24)	38	0.29
Hmong (6)	6	0.05
Indian (81)	88	0.66
Indonesian (0)	1	0.01
Japanese (7)	18	0.14
Korean (17)	24	0.18
Laotian (1)	1	0.01
Pakistani (3)	3	0.02
Taiwanese (1)	1	0.01
Thai (10)	11	0.08
Vietnamese (56)	65	0.49
Hawaii Native/Pacific Islander (9)	11	0.08
Not Hispanic (8)	10	0.08
Hispanic (1)	1	0.01
Native Hawaiian (8)	10	0.08
White (12,497)	12,700	95.77
Not Hispanic (12,309)	12,479	94.10
Hispanic (188)	221	1.67

Millis

Place Type: Town
County: Norfolk
Population: 7,891†

Ancestry‡	Population	%
Albanian (0)	47	0.60
American (369)	369	4.72
Arab (0)	100	1.28
Lebanese (0)	100	1.28
Armenian (55)	100	1.28
Austrian (0)	42	0.54
Bulgarian (10)	15	0.19
Canadian (75)	90	1.15
Czech (0)	11	0.14
Czechoslovakian (0)	13	0.17
Danish (0)	10	0.13
Dutch (0)	13	0.17
Eastern European (21)	21	0.27
English (503)	1,014	12.96
European (171)	190	2.43
Finnish (12)	50	0.64
French, ex. Basque (67)	348	4.45
French Canadian (43)	135	1.73
German (113)	755	9.65
Greek (82)	207	2.65
Irish (1,029)	2,585	33.04
Italian (727)	1,883	24.07
Lithuanian (14)	28	0.36
New Zealander (27)	27	0.35
Norwegian (0)	44	0.56
Polish (24)	303	3.87
Portuguese (11)	93	1.19
Russian (16)	133	1.70
Scandinavian (23)	23	0.29
Scotch-Irish (170)	296	3.78
Scottish (65)	204	2.61
Slavic (87)	87	1.11
Swedish (67)	179	2.29
Swiss (0)	14	0.18
Ukrainian (0)	15	0.19
Welsh (0)	69	0.88

Hispanic Origin	Population	%
Hispanic or Latino (of any race)	136	1.72
Central American, ex. Mexican	15	0.19
Costa Rican	2	0.03
Guatemalan	5	0.06
Panamanian	3	0.04
Salvadoran	5	0.06
Cuban	16	0.20
Dominican Republic	12	0.15
Mexican	25	0.32
Puerto Rican	23	0.29
South American	31	0.39
Argentinean	3	0.04
Bolivian	2	0.03
Chilean	4	0.05
Colombian	8	0.10
Peruvian	9	0.11
Venezuelan	5	0.06
Other Hispanic or Latino	14	0.18

Race*	Population	%
African-American/Black (60)	96	1.22
Not Hispanic (57)	93	1.18
Hispanic (3)	3	0.04
American Indian/Alaska Native (22)	42	0.53
Not Hispanic (21)	41	0.52
Hispanic (1)	1	0.01
Blackfeet (0)	3	0.04
Chickasaw (0)	1	0.01
Choctaw (2)	6	0.08
Delaware (4)	4	0.05
Iroquois (0)	1	0.01
Navajo (3)	3	0.04
Sioux (0)	1	0.01
Asian (238)	284	3.60
Not Hispanic (238)	284	3.60
Bangladeshi (5)	5	0.06
Burmese (4)	4	0.05
Cambodian (1)	3	0.04
Chinese, ex. Taiwanese (64)	68	0.86
Filipino (28)	35	0.44
Indian (94)	106	1.34
Japanese (5)	14	0.18
Korean (16)	25	0.32
Laotian (1)	1	0.01
Nepalese (1)	1	0.01
Pakistani (1)	1	0.01

*Notes: † The Census 2010 population figure is used to calculate the percentages in the Hispanic Origin and Race categories. Ancestry percentages are based on the 2006-2010 American Community Survey population (not shown); ‡ Numbers in parentheses indicate the number of people reporting a single ancestry; * Numbers in parentheses indicate the number of persons reporting this race alone, not in combination with any other race; Please refer to the Explanation of Data for more information.*

Taiwanese (4)	4	0.05
Thai (2)	4	0.05
Vietnamese (8)	8	0.10
Hawaii Native/Pacific Islander (1)	3	0.04
Not Hispanic (0)	2	0.03
Hispanic (1)	1	0.01
Guamanian/Chamorro (1)	1	0.01
White (7,430)	7,524	95.35
Not Hispanic (7,315)	7,407	93.87
Hispanic (115)	117	1.48

Milton

Place Type: CDP/Town
County: Norfolk
Population: 27,003†

Ancestry‡	Population	%
African, Sub-Saharan (468)	521	1.95
African (48)	87	0.33
Cape Verdean (293)	307	1.15
Nigerian (117)	117	0.44
South African (10)	10	0.04
Albanian (44)	44	0.16
American (328)	328	1.23
Arab (224)	292	1.09
Arab (40)	69	0.26
Egyptian (15)	15	0.06
Lebanese (42)	61	0.23
Syrian (127)	147	0.55
Armenian (96)	140	0.52
Australian (17)	17	0.06
Austrian (29)	100	0.37
Belgian (0)	72	0.27
Brazilian (0)	31	0.12
British (92)	106	0.40
Bulgarian (10)	10	0.04
Canadian (142)	322	1.21
Czech (0)	32	0.12
Czechoslovakian (0)	26	0.10
Danish (0)	87	0.33
Dutch (7)	58	0.22
Eastern European (114)	129	0.48
English (336)	2,793	10.47
European (302)	349	1.31
Finnish (12)	192	0.72
French, ex. Basque (90)	664	2.49
French Canadian (218)	896	3.36
German (143)	1,228	4.60
Greek (375)	507	1.90
Hungarian (90)	166	0.62
Icelander (0)	53	0.20
Irish (7,103)	11,589	43.46
Italian (1,181)	3,117	11.69
Latvian (11)	11	0.04
Lithuanian (155)	269	1.01
Norwegian (20)	79	0.30
Polish (218)	1,079	4.05
Portuguese (146)	228	0.85
Romanian (0)	12	0.04
Russian (168)	510	1.91
Scandinavian (0)	20	0.07
Scotch-Irish (290)	656	2.46
Scottish (116)	595	2.23
Serbian (24)	24	0.09
Slovak (0)	16	0.06
Swedish (30)	431	1.62
Swiss (0)	104	0.39
Ukrainian (150)	179	0.67
Welsh (11)	85	0.32
West Indian, ex. Hispanic (1,280)	1,310	4.91
Barbadian (27)	27	0.10
British West Indian (15)	15	0.06
Haitian (956)	956	3.58
Jamaican (103)	103	0.39
Trinidadian/Tobagonian (30)	43	0.16
U.S. Virgin Islander (58)	58	0.22
West Indian (91)	108	0.40

Hispanic Origin	Population	%
Hispanic or Latino (of any race)	881	3.26
Central American, ex. Mexican	135	0.50
Costa Rican	19	0.07
Guatemalan	35	0.13
Honduran	50	0.19
Nicaraguan	8	0.03
Panamanian	5	0.02
Salvadoran	16	0.06
Other Central American	2	0.01
Cuban	63	0.23
Dominican Republic	134	0.50
Mexican	77	0.29
Puerto Rican	252	0.93
South American	141	0.52
Argentinean	22	0.08
Bolivian	4	0.01
Chilean	15	0.06
Colombian	48	0.18
Ecuadorian	13	0.05
Paraguayan	3	0.01
Peruvian	19	0.07
Venezuelan	17	0.06
Other Hispanic or Latino	79	0.29

Race*	Population	%
African-American/Black (3,872)	4,281	15.85
Not Hispanic (3,705)	4,063	15.05
Hispanic (167)	218	0.81
American Indian/Alaska Native (39)	160	0.59
Not Hispanic (30)	136	0.50
Hispanic (9)	24	0.09
Blackfeet (0)	4	0.01
Canadian/French Am. Ind. (1)	7	0.03
Central American Ind. (4)	4	0.01
Cherokee (4)	9	0.03
Iroquois (0)	2	0.01
Seminole (0)	1	<0.01
South American Ind. (1)	5	0.02
Asian (1,118)	1,363	5.05
Not Hispanic (1,111)	1,343	4.97
Hispanic (7)	20	0.07
Bangladeshi (10)	10	0.04
Burmese (0)	3	0.01
Cambodian (8)	16	0.06
Chinese, ex. Taiwanese (571)	677	2.51
Filipino (27)	50	0.19
Indian (101)	139	0.51
Indonesian (0)	2	0.01
Japanese (11)	59	0.22
Korean (39)	78	0.29
Laotian (1)	3	0.01
Malaysian (0)	7	0.03
Nepalese (3)	3	0.01
Pakistani (8)	8	0.03
Sri Lankan (1)	2	0.01
Taiwanese (5)	8	0.03
Thai (3)	4	0.01
Vietnamese (288)	304	1.13
Hawaii Native/Pacific Islander (5)	52	0.19
Not Hispanic (5)	49	0.18
Hispanic (0)	3	0.01
Guamanian/Chamorro (2)	9	0.03
Native Hawaiian (0)	9	0.03
Samoan (1)	1	<0.01
White (20,901)	21,409	79.28
Not Hispanic (20,489)	20,944	77.56
Hispanic (412)	465	1.72

Monson

Place Type: Town
County: Hampden
Population: 8,560†

Ancestry‡	Population	%
American (240)	240	2.81
Arab (0)	13	0.15
Lebanese (0)	13	0.15
Armenian (14)	14	0.16
Austrian (0)	11	0.13
Belgian (0)	13	0.15
British (20)	48	0.56
Canadian (23)	50	0.59
Czech (0)	54	0.63
Czechoslovakian (0)	33	0.39
Danish (0)	29	0.34
Dutch (14)	114	1.34
English (397)	1,099	12.88
European (74)	74	0.87
French, ex. Basque (394)	1,832	21.47
French Canadian (610)	961	11.26
German (146)	770	9.02
Greek (25)	59	0.69
Irish (359)	1,831	21.46
Italian (364)	1,251	14.66
Norwegian (0)	119	1.39
Polish (391)	1,309	15.34
Portuguese (15)	125	1.46
Russian (33)	102	1.20
Scandinavian (0)	18	0.21
Scotch-Irish (83)	194	2.27
Scottish (48)	207	2.43
Swedish (13)	385	4.51
Swiss (0)	14	0.16
Ukrainian (0)	15	0.18
Welsh (0)	14	0.16
West Indian, ex. Hispanic (38)	38	0.45
Jamaican (38)	38	0.45

Hispanic Origin	Population	%
Hispanic or Latino (of any race)	153	1.79
Central American, ex. Mexican	5	0.06
Guatemalan	4	0.05
Panamanian	1	0.01
Cuban	10	0.12
Dominican Republic	1	0.01
Mexican	15	0.18
Puerto Rican	87	1.02
South American	12	0.14
Colombian	4	0.05
Ecuadorian	1	0.01
Peruvian	5	0.06
Other South American	2	0.02
Other Hispanic or Latino	23	0.27

Race*	Population	%
African-American/Black (73)	120	1.40
Not Hispanic (65)	111	1.30
Hispanic (8)	9	0.11
American Indian/Alaska Native (18)	47	0.55
Not Hispanic (18)	41	0.48
Hispanic (0)	6	0.07
Blackfeet (1)	4	0.05
Cherokee (1)	2	0.02
Chippewa (1)	1	0.01
Comanche (0)	1	0.01
Creek (4)	4	0.05
Hopi (0)	1	0.01
Iroquois (1)	3	0.04
Mexican American Ind. (0)	2	0.02
Sioux (1)	1	0.01
Asian (52)	79	0.92
Not Hispanic (52)	75	0.88
Hispanic (0)	4	0.05
Cambodian (2)	5	0.06
Chinese, ex. Taiwanese (17)	23	0.27
Filipino (5)	8	0.09
Japanese (6)	10	0.12
Korean (7)	19	0.22
Laotian (1)	1	0.01
Malaysian (1)	2	0.02
Pakistani (5)	5	0.06
Thai (1)	1	0.01
Vietnamese (0)	1	0.01
Hawaii Native/Pacific Islander (0)	4	0.05
Not Hispanic (0)	4	0.05
White (8,287)	8,395	98.07
Not Hispanic (8,172)	8,262	96.52
Hispanic (115)	133	1.55

*Notes: † The Census 2010 population figure is used to calculate the percentages in the Hispanic Origin and Race categories. Ancestry percentages are based on the 2006-2010 American Community Survey population (not shown); ‡ Numbers in parentheses indicate the number of people reporting a single ancestry; * Numbers in parentheses indicate the number of persons reporting this race alone, not in combination with any other race; Please refer to the Explanation of Data for more information.*

Montague

Place Type: Town
County: Franklin
Population: 8,437†

Ancestry‡	Population	%
American (380)	380	4.49
Arab (0)	7	0.08
Other Arab (0)	7	0.08
Armenian (0)	34	0.40
Australian (0)	19	0.22
Austrian (10)	20	0.24
Belgian (0)	8	0.09
British (0)	13	0.15
Cajun (0)	14	0.17
Canadian (11)	31	0.37
Czech (22)	63	0.75
Czechoslovakian (0)	10	0.12
Danish (0)	23	0.27
Dutch (0)	47	0.56
Eastern European (13)	13	0.15
English (306)	996	11.78
European (0)	13	0.15
French, ex. Basque (394)	1,822	21.55
French Canadian (304)	721	8.53
German (75)	1,000	11.83
Greek (6)	6	0.07
Hungarian (0)	18	0.21
Iranian (50)	50	0.59
Irish (228)	1,519	17.97
Italian (308)	1,223	14.47
Lithuanian (54)	145	1.72
Norwegian (0)	58	0.69
Polish (439)	1,264	14.95
Portuguese (10)	96	1.14
Romanian (56)	66	0.78
Russian (10)	50	0.59
Scandinavian (5)	15	0.18
Scotch-Irish (17)	48	0.57
Scottish (89)	292	3.45
Slavic (0)	10	0.12
Slovak (0)	12	0.14
Swedish (10)	124	1.47
Ukrainian (0)	10	0.12
Welsh (10)	80	0.95

Hispanic Origin	Population	%
Hispanic or Latino (of any race)	438	5.19
Central American, ex. Mexican	47	0.56
Guatemalan	35	0.41
Honduran	2	0.02
Nicaraguan	1	0.01
Panamanian	2	0.02
Salvadoran	7	0.08
Cuban	5	0.06
Dominican Republic	6	0.07
Mexican	110	1.30
Puerto Rican	227	2.69
South American	15	0.18
Argentinean	2	0.02
Chilean	2	0.02
Colombian	3	0.04
Ecuadorian	7	0.08
Venezuelan	1	0.01
Other Hispanic or Latino	28	0.33

Race*	Population	%
African-American/Black (101)	194	2.30
Not Hispanic (81)	157	1.86
Hispanic (20)	37	0.44
American Indian/Alaska Native (25)	117	1.39
Not Hispanic (15)	102	1.21
Hispanic (10)	15	0.18
Aleut *(Alaska Native)* (1)	1	0.01
Apache (1)	1	0.01
Blackfeet (0)	18	0.21
Canadian/French Am. Ind. (0)	1	0.01
Central American Ind. (1)	1	0.01
Cherokee (1)	14	0.17
Chippewa (2)	2	0.02
Choctaw (0)	1	0.01
Cree (1)	2	0.02
Inupiat *(Alaska Native)* (1)	2	0.02
Iroquois (1)	7	0.08
Lumbee (1)	2	0.02
Mexican American Ind. (0)	1	0.01
Navajo (1)	1	0.01
Seminole (0)	2	0.02
Sioux (0)	3	0.04
South American Ind. (1)	1	0.01
Asian (67)	120	1.42
Not Hispanic (67)	119	1.41
Hispanic (0)	1	0.01
Cambodian (6)	6	0.07
Chinese, ex. Taiwanese (19)	27	0.32
Filipino (7)	10	0.12
Indian (6)	9	0.11
Indonesian (2)	3	0.04
Japanese (3)	11	0.13
Korean (10)	22	0.26
Laotian (7)	8	0.09
Sri Lankan (0)	1	0.01
Thai (1)	13	0.15
Vietnamese (4)	5	0.06
Hawaii Native/Pacific Islander (2)	15	0.18
Not Hispanic (1)	4	0.05
Hispanic (1)	11	0.13
Guamanian/Chamorro (0)	5	0.06
Native Hawaiian (1)	4	0.05
White (7,823)	8,051	95.42
Not Hispanic (7,621)	7,806	92.52
Hispanic (202)	245	2.90

Nantucket

Place Type: Town
County: Nantucket
Population: 10,172†

Ancestry‡	Population	%
African, Sub-Saharan (82)	97	0.96
African (68)	68	0.68
South African (14)	29	0.29
American (1,155)	1,155	11.47
Arab (29)	54	0.54
Lebanese (29)	54	0.54
Armenian (19)	19	0.19
Austrian (6)	6	0.06
Belgian (0)	9	0.09
Brazilian (36)	44	0.44
British (38)	77	0.76
Bulgarian (121)	137	1.36
Canadian (61)	110	1.09
Danish (0)	50	0.50
Dutch (28)	231	2.29
Eastern European (10)	10	0.10
English (619)	2,102	20.88
European (75)	90	0.89
Finnish (0)	38	0.38
French, ex. Basque (140)	574	5.70
French Canadian (37)	73	0.72
German (258)	1,102	10.94
Greek (0)	16	0.16
Hungarian (0)	11	0.11
Irish (621)	1,894	18.81
Italian (231)	641	6.37
Latvian (9)	17	0.17
Lithuanian (0)	79	0.78
Northern European (45)	45	0.45
Norwegian (15)	113	1.12
Polish (175)	319	3.17
Portuguese (144)	473	4.70
Russian (10)	121	1.20
Scandinavian (0)	11	0.11
Scotch-Irish (132)	293	2.91
Scottish (107)	456	4.53
Swedish (92)	313	3.11
Swiss (5)	14	0.14
Ukrainian (0)	15	0.15
Welsh (0)	87	0.86
West Indian, ex. Hispanic (588)	597	5.93
Barbadian (44)	44	0.44
Jamaican (544)	553	5.49

Hispanic Origin	Population	%
Hispanic or Latino (of any race)	957	9.41
Central American, ex. Mexican	645	6.34
Costa Rican	30	0.29
Guatemalan	40	0.39
Honduran	10	0.10
Nicaraguan	3	0.03
Salvadoran	559	5.50
Other Central American	3	0.03
Cuban	5	0.05
Dominican Republic	78	0.77
Mexican	114	1.12
Puerto Rican	20	0.20
South American	37	0.36
Argentinean	4	0.04
Bolivian	1	0.01
Chilean	5	0.05
Colombian	13	0.13
Ecuadorian	4	0.04
Uruguayan	2	0.02
Venezuelan	8	0.08
Other Hispanic or Latino	58	0.57

Race*	Population	%
African-American/Black (688)	774	7.61
Not Hispanic (664)	745	7.32
Hispanic (24)	29	0.29
American Indian/Alaska Native (6)	42	0.41
Not Hispanic (6)	41	0.40
Hispanic (0)	1	0.01
Blackfeet (1)	2	0.02
Cherokee (1)	5	0.05
Chippewa (0)	2	0.02
Cree (0)	1	0.01
Iroquois (1)	2	0.02
Asian (118)	159	1.56
Not Hispanic (118)	156	1.53
Hispanic (0)	3	0.03
Bangladeshi (1)	1	0.01
Cambodian (1)	1	0.01
Chinese, ex. Taiwanese (18)	22	0.22
Filipino (14)	25	0.25
Indian (25)	32	0.31
Indonesian (1)	1	0.01
Japanese (4)	12	0.12
Korean (3)	6	0.06
Nepalese (18)	21	0.21
Pakistani (4)	4	0.04
Sri Lankan (1)	1	0.01
Thai (23)	28	0.28
Vietnamese (2)	4	0.04
Hawaii Native/Pacific Islander (1)	5	0.05
Not Hispanic (1)	5	0.05
Native Hawaiian (1)	3	0.03
Samoan (0)	1	0.01
White (8,913)	9,081	89.27
Not Hispanic (8,192)	8,332	81.91
Hispanic (721)	749	7.36

Natick

Place Type: Town
County: Middlesex
Population: 33,006†

Ancestry‡	Population	%
Afghan (13)	13	0.04
African, Sub-Saharan (93)	123	0.38
African (41)	41	0.13
Nigerian (29)	29	0.09
South African (23)	53	0.16
Albanian (158)	226	0.70
American (1,183)	1,183	3.65
Arab (169)	262	0.81
Arab (71)	71	0.22

*Notes: † The Census 2010 population figure is used to calculate the percentages in the Hispanic Origin and Race categories. Ancestry percentages are based on the 2006-2010 American Community Survey population (not shown); ‡ Numbers in parentheses indicate the number of people reporting a single ancestry; * Numbers in parentheses indicate the number of persons reporting this race alone, not in combination with any other race; Please refer to the Explanation of Data for more information.*

Iraqi (45)	45	0.14
Lebanese (11)	54	0.17
Moroccan (29)	41	0.13
Syrian (13)	51	0.16
Armenian (41)	110	0.34
Australian (0)	28	0.09
Austrian (22)	89	0.27
Belgian (29)	76	0.23
Brazilian (253)	299	0.92
British (144)	199	0.61
Canadian (157)	345	1.06
Celtic (22)	22	0.07
Croatian (9)	28	0.09
Cypriot (8)	8	0.02
Czech (282)	300	0.92
Czechoslovakian (8)	28	0.09
Danish (35)	86	0.27
Dutch (51)	253	0.78
Eastern European (389)	442	1.36
English (1,034)	4,188	12.91
European (332)	373	1.15
Finnish (28)	95	0.29
French, ex. Basque (212)	1,542	4.75
French Canadian (470)	792	2.44
German (487)	3,196	9.85
Greek (181)	273	0.84
Guyanese (7)	7	0.02
Hungarian (84)	198	0.61
Iranian (38)	38	0.12
Irish (3,924)	8,632	26.61
Israeli (25)	37	0.11
Italian (1,686)	4,430	13.65
Latvian (40)	81	0.25
Lithuanian (48)	364	1.12
Northern European (43)	43	0.13
Norwegian (32)	117	0.36
Polish (374)	1,403	4.32
Portuguese (136)	359	1.11
Romanian (56)	105	0.32
Russian (727)	1,447	4.46
Scandinavian (19)	71	0.22
Scotch-Irish (282)	983	3.03
Scottish (209)	888	2.74
Slavic (0)	37	0.11
Slovak (27)	37	0.11
Swedish (107)	700	2.16
Swiss (27)	68	0.21
Turkish (0)	15	0.05
Ukrainian (45)	176	0.54
Welsh (63)	155	0.48
West Indian, ex. Hispanic (194)	507	1.56
Bermudan (0)	132	0.41
Haitian (39)	57	0.18
Jamaican (143)	275	0.85
West Indian (12)	43	0.13
Yugoslavian (0)	8	0.02

Hispanic Origin	Population	%
Hispanic or Latino (of any race)	994	3.01
Central American, ex. Mexican	109	0.33
Costa Rican	11	0.03
Guatemalan	50	0.15
Honduran	6	0.02
Nicaraguan	10	0.03
Panamanian	11	0.03
Salvadoran	21	0.06
Cuban	62	0.19
Dominican Republic	44	0.13
Mexican	149	0.45
Puerto Rican	301	0.91
South American	237	0.72
Argentinean	28	0.08
Bolivian	12	0.04
Chilean	18	0.05
Colombian	80	0.24
Ecuadorian	24	0.07
Paraguayan	3	0.01
Peruvian	41	0.12
Venezuelan	30	0.09
Other South American	1	<0.01
Other Hispanic or Latino	92	0.28

Race*	Population	%
African-American/Black (692)	877	2.66
Not Hispanic (647)	806	2.44
Hispanic (45)	71	0.22
American Indian/Alaska Native (42)	135	0.41
Not Hispanic (28)	109	0.33
Hispanic (14)	26	0.08
Apache (0)	1	<0.01
Blackfeet (1)	2	0.01
Central American Ind. (1)	1	<0.01
Cherokee (2)	21	0.06
Choctaw (1)	1	<0.01
Iroquois (1)	4	0.01
Mexican American Ind. (3)	4	0.01
Osage (0)	3	0.01
Sioux (1)	2	0.01
South American Ind. (3)	5	0.02
Asian (2,386)	2,730	8.27
Not Hispanic (2,375)	2,711	8.21
Hispanic (11)	19	0.06
Bangladeshi (7)	7	0.02
Burmese (0)	4	0.01
Cambodian (15)	17	0.05
Chinese, ex. Taiwanese (878)	1,029	3.12
Filipino (113)	149	0.45
Hmong (1)	2	0.01
Indian (815)	880	2.67
Indonesian (9)	18	0.05
Japanese (94)	146	0.44
Korean (155)	194	0.59
Laotian (1)	1	<0.01
Malaysian (1)	5	0.02
Nepalese (26)	26	0.08
Pakistani (36)	39	0.12
Sri Lankan (4)	8	0.02
Taiwanese (31)	43	0.13
Thai (33)	39	0.12
Vietnamese (86)	115	0.35
Hawaii Native/Pacific Islander (10)	36	0.11
Not Hispanic (9)	32	0.10
Hispanic (1)	4	0.01
Guamanian/Chamorro (1)	4	0.01
Native Hawaiian (8)	18	0.05
White (28,822)	29,421	89.14
Not Hispanic (28,189)	28,723	87.02
Hispanic (633)	698	2.11

Needham

Place Type: CDP/Town
County: Norfolk
Population: 28,886†

Ancestry‡	Population	%
African, Sub-Saharan (16)	16	0.06
South African (16)	16	0.06
Albanian (0)	30	0.10
American (1,120)	1,120	3.90
Arab (145)	359	1.25
Arab (81)	129	0.45
Iraqi (0)	14	0.05
Lebanese (55)	166	0.58
Moroccan (0)	27	0.09
Syrian (9)	23	0.08
Armenian (149)	191	0.67
Austrian (34)	180	0.63
Belgian (20)	20	0.07
Brazilian (9)	23	0.08
British (182)	298	1.04
Canadian (136)	350	1.22
Czech (8)	112	0.39
Danish (70)	124	0.43
Dutch (53)	166	0.58
Eastern European (568)	618	2.15
English (1,244)	3,625	12.64
European (518)	528	1.84
French, ex. Basque (223)	988	3.44
French Canadian (131)	358	1.25
German (537)	2,616	9.12
Greek (98)	234	0.82
Hungarian (0)	106	0.37
Icelander (44)	44	0.15
Iranian (31)	31	0.11
Irish (3,227)	7,249	25.27
Israeli (99)	99	0.35
Italian (1,722)	3,733	13.01
Latvian (0)	28	0.10
Lithuanian (142)	372	1.30
Macedonian (18)	53	0.18
Maltese (0)	9	0.03
Northern European (37)	37	0.13
Norwegian (42)	180	0.63
Polish (361)	1,474	5.14
Portuguese (57)	152	0.53
Romanian (44)	65	0.23
Russian (1,630)	2,587	9.02
Scandinavian (4)	19	0.07
Scotch-Irish (385)	762	2.66
Scottish (119)	787	2.74
Swedish (218)	549	1.91
Swiss (26)	178	0.62
Turkish (62)	62	0.22
Ukrainian (138)	209	0.73
Welsh (53)	202	0.70
West Indian, ex. Hispanic (221)	221	0.77
Jamaican (16)	16	0.06
West Indian (205)	205	0.71
Yugoslavian (9)	21	0.07

Hispanic Origin	Population	%
Hispanic or Latino (of any race)	618	2.14
Central American, ex. Mexican	66	0.23
Costa Rican	8	0.03
Guatemalan	34	0.12
Honduran	9	0.03
Nicaraguan	4	0.01
Panamanian	1	<0.01
Salvadoran	10	0.03
Cuban	48	0.17
Dominican Republic	30	0.10
Mexican	126	0.44
Puerto Rican	95	0.33
South American	177	0.61
Argentinean	35	0.12
Bolivian	6	0.02
Chilean	11	0.04
Colombian	61	0.21
Ecuadorian	20	0.07
Paraguayan	2	0.01
Peruvian	31	0.11
Uruguayan	1	<0.01
Venezuelan	10	0.03
Other Hispanic or Latino	76	0.26

Race*	Population	%
African-American/Black (288)	395	1.37
Not Hispanic (275)	368	1.27
Hispanic (13)	27	0.09
American Indian/Alaska Native (11)	66	0.23
Not Hispanic (10)	57	0.20
Hispanic (1)	9	0.03
Blackfeet (0)	2	0.01
Cherokee (3)	9	0.03
Delaware (0)	1	<0.01
Iroquois (0)	4	0.01
Mexican American Ind. (1)	3	0.01
Navajo (0)	1	<0.01
Pueblo (0)	1	<0.01
Shoshone (1)	1	<0.01
South American Ind. (1)	5	0.02
Tlingit-Haida *(Alaska Native)* (0)	1	<0.01
Asian (1,759)	2,065	7.15
Not Hispanic (1,753)	2,053	7.11
Hispanic (6)	12	0.04
Burmese (4)	9	0.03
Cambodian (9)	12	0.04
Chinese, ex. Taiwanese (968)	1,099	3.80
Filipino (50)	81	0.28

*Notes: † The Census 2010 population figure is used to calculate the percentages in the Hispanic Origin and Race categories. Ancestry percentages are based on the 2006-2010 American Community Survey population (not shown); ‡ Numbers in parentheses indicate the number of people reporting a single ancestry; * Numbers in parentheses indicate the number of persons reporting this race alone, not in combination with any other race; Please refer to the Explanation of Data for more information.*

Indian (359)	415	1.44
Indonesian (9)	12	0.04
Japanese (59)	102	0.35
Korean (129)	179	0.62
Laotian (7)	8	0.03
Pakistani (17)	22	0.08
Sri Lankan (3)	5	0.02
Taiwanese (49)	64	0.22
Thai (10)	11	0.04
Vietnamese (29)	36	0.12
Hawaii Native/Pacific Islander (8)	27	0.09
Not Hispanic (8)	27	0.09
Guamanian/Chamorro (5)	5	0.02
Native Hawaiian (2)	12	0.04
White (26,227)	26,658	92.29
Not Hispanic (25,730)	26,138	90.49
Hispanic (497)	520	1.80

New Bedford

Place Type: City
County: Bristol
Population: 95,072†

Ancestry‡	Population	%
African, Sub-Saharan (8,054)	10,738	11.31
African (351)	476	0.50
Cape Verdean (7,703)	10,262	10.81
Albanian (8)	23	0.02
American (1,176)	1,176	1.24
Arab (232)	460	0.48
Arab (13)	38	0.04
Lebanese (211)	353	0.37
Moroccan (8)	8	0.01
Other Arab (0)	61	0.06
Armenian (22)	110	0.12
Austrian (8)	53	0.06
Belgian (17)	31	0.03
Brazilian (678)	997	1.05
British (8)	72	0.08
Canadian (202)	434	0.46
Croatian (9)	18	0.02
Czech (0)	24	0.03
Czechoslovakian (0)	9	0.01
Danish (0)	11	0.01
Dutch (60)	424	0.45
Eastern European (60)	60	0.06
English (2,385)	7,026	7.40
European (165)	173	0.18
Finnish (8)	27	0.03
French, ex. Basque (2,256)	9,256	9.75
French Canadian (2,217)	3,628	3.82
German (669)	2,257	2.38
Greek (211)	315	0.33
Hungarian (32)	86	0.09
Iranian (24)	35	0.04
Irish (1,888)	7,693	8.10
Israeli (0)	58	0.06
Italian (808)	3,587	3.78
Latvian (8)	8	0.01
Lithuanian (5)	39	0.04
Norwegian (162)	435	0.46
Pennsylvania German (0)	27	0.03
Polish (831)	3,165	3.33
Portuguese (27,792)	38,632	40.69
Russian (81)	130	0.14
Scandinavian (21)	33	0.03
Scotch-Irish (91)	394	0.41
Scottish (31)	478	0.50
Serbian (15)	27	0.03
Slovak (0)	10	0.01
Swedish (19)	231	0.24
Swiss (0)	58	0.06
Turkish (52)	63	0.07
Welsh (32)	162	0.17
West Indian, ex. Hispanic (95)	219	0.23
Haitian (19)	74	0.08
Jamaican (11)	30	0.03
West Indian (65)	115	0.12

Hispanic Origin	Population	%
Hispanic or Latino (of any race)	15,916	16.74
Central American, ex. Mexican	2,960	3.11
Costa Rican	27	0.03
Guatemalan	1,532	1.61
Honduran	532	0.56
Nicaraguan	4	<0.01
Panamanian	26	0.03
Salvadoran	780	0.82
Other Central American	59	0.06
Cuban	129	0.14
Dominican Republic	902	0.95
Mexican	734	0.77
Puerto Rican	9,554	10.05
South American	278	0.29
Argentinean	17	0.02
Bolivian	5	0.01
Chilean	14	0.01
Colombian	114	0.12
Ecuadorian	38	0.04
Paraguayan	1	<0.01
Peruvian	26	0.03
Uruguayan	30	0.03
Venezuelan	31	0.03
Other South American	2	<0.01
Other Hispanic or Latino	1,359	1.43

Race*	Population	%
African-American/Black (6,083)	9,122	9.59
Not Hispanic (4,919)	7,486	7.87
Hispanic (1,164)	1,636	1.72
American Indian/Alaska Native (1,220)	2,167	2.28
Not Hispanic (409)	1,129	1.19
Hispanic (811)	1,038	1.09
Apache (1)	8	0.01
Arapaho (1)	2	<0.01
Blackfeet (10)	45	0.05
Canadian/French Am. Ind. (1)	7	0.01
Central American Ind. (228)	265	0.28
Cherokee (17)	85	0.09
Chippewa (11)	19	0.02
Choctaw (0)	2	<0.01
Comanche (0)	2	<0.01
Cree (0)	1	<0.01
Delaware (0)	1	<0.01
Inupiat *(Alaska Native)* (0)	2	<0.01
Iroquois (4)	22	0.02
Kiowa (2)	4	<0.01
Mexican American Ind. (372)	430	0.45
Navajo (4)	5	0.01
Potawatomi (1)	1	<0.01
Seminole (0)	1	<0.01
Shoshone (0)	1	<0.01
Sioux (1)	8	0.01
South American Ind. (9)	29	0.03
Spanish American Ind. (13)	17	0.02
Tlingit-Haida *(Alaska Native)* (1)	2	<0.01
Tohono O'Odham (0)	5	0.01
Yup'ik *(Alaska Native)* (2)	3	<0.01
Asian (893)	1,231	1.29
Not Hispanic (879)	1,181	1.24
Hispanic (14)	50	0.05
Bangladeshi (14)	14	0.01
Burmese (1)	1	<0.01
Cambodian (41)	45	0.05
Chinese, ex. Taiwanese (222)	264	0.28
Filipino (131)	218	0.23
Hmong (2)	3	<0.01
Indian (182)	216	0.23
Indonesian (2)	4	<0.01
Japanese (19)	63	0.07
Korean (50)	96	0.10
Laotian (7)	12	0.01
Malaysian (1)	1	<0.01
Nepalese (14)	14	0.01
Pakistani (15)	23	0.02
Sri Lankan (1)	3	<0.01
Thai (14)	16	0.02
Vietnamese (155)	165	0.17
Hawaii Native/Pacific Islander (50)	341	0.36
Not Hispanic (15)	256	0.27
Hispanic (35)	85	0.09
Guamanian/Chamorro (37)	44	0.05
Native Hawaiian (6)	21	0.02
Samoan (0)	2	<0.01
White (70,799)	74,175	78.02
Not Hispanic (64,598)	67,049	70.52
Hispanic (6,201)	7,126	7.50

Newburyport

Place Type: City
County: Essex
Population: 17,416†

Ancestry‡	Population	%
African, Sub-Saharan (24)	24	0.14
Ethiopian (24)	24	0.14
Albanian (0)	10	0.06
American (726)	726	4.20
Arab (112)	181	1.05
Egyptian (88)	88	0.51
Lebanese (24)	84	0.49
Syrian (0)	9	0.05
Armenian (60)	60	0.35
Austrian (14)	42	0.24
Belgian (0)	9	0.05
Brazilian (34)	179	1.04
British (82)	82	0.47
Canadian (60)	140	0.81
Celtic (0)	7	0.04
Croatian (0)	22	0.13
Czech (0)	90	0.52
Czechoslovakian (0)	9	0.05
Danish (0)	12	0.07
Dutch (64)	342	1.98
Eastern European (52)	82	0.47
English (1,113)	3,445	19.93
European (70)	133	0.77
Finnish (11)	20	0.12
French, ex. Basque (137)	1,318	7.62
French Canadian (411)	944	5.46
German (373)	1,280	7.40
Greek (190)	442	2.56
Hungarian (12)	26	0.15
Iranian (26)	26	0.15
Irish (1,818)	5,514	31.89
Italian (802)	2,980	17.24
Lithuanian (35)	137	0.79
New Zealander (0)	33	0.19
Norwegian (33)	191	1.10
Polish (267)	955	5.52
Portuguese (236)	485	2.81
Russian (147)	314	1.82
Scandinavian (21)	45	0.26
Scotch-Irish (110)	272	1.57
Scottish (461)	1,200	6.94
Slovak (0)	11	0.06
Swedish (68)	325	1.88
Swiss (30)	43	0.25
Ukrainian (51)	112	0.65
Welsh (24)	78	0.45

Hispanic Origin	Population	%
Hispanic or Latino (of any race)	291	1.67
Central American, ex. Mexican	27	0.16
Guatemalan	17	0.10
Honduran	6	0.03
Nicaraguan	2	0.01
Panamanian	1	0.01
Salvadoran	1	0.01
Cuban	17	0.10
Dominican Republic	13	0.07
Mexican	60	0.34
Puerto Rican	74	0.42
South American	63	0.36
Argentinean	11	0.06
Chilean	2	0.01
Colombian	20	0.11
Ecuadorian	3	0.02

*Notes: † The Census 2010 population figure is used to calculate the percentages in the Hispanic Origin and Race categories. Ancestry percentages are based on the 2006-2010 American Community Survey population (not shown); ‡ Numbers in parentheses indicate the number of people reporting a single ancestry; * Numbers in parentheses indicate the number of persons reporting this race alone, not in combination with any other race; Please refer to the Explanation of Data for more information.*

	Population	%
Paraguayan	4	0.02
Peruvian	8	0.05
Venezuelan	9	0.05
Other South American	6	0.03
Other Hispanic or Latino	37	0.21

Race*	Population	%
African-American/Black (98)	147	0.84
Not Hispanic (95)	142	0.82
Hispanic (3)	5	0.03
American Indian/Alaska Native (24)	88	0.51
Not Hispanic (17)	77	0.44
Hispanic (7)	11	0.06
Blackfeet (0)	3	0.02
Cherokee (1)	10	0.06
Chippewa (2)	6	0.03
Iroquois (4)	4	0.02
Mexican American Ind. (6)	9	0.05
Paiute (0)	3	0.02
Asian (195)	276	1.58
Not Hispanic (194)	275	1.58
Hispanic (1)	1	0.01
Cambodian (2)	2	0.01
Chinese, ex. Taiwanese (72)	84	0.48
Filipino (14)	18	0.10
Indian (27)	34	0.20
Japanese (10)	25	0.14
Korean (38)	56	0.32
Laotian (7)	9	0.05
Pakistani (6)	6	0.03
Taiwanese (1)	2	0.01
Thai (7)	7	0.04
Vietnamese (8)	10	0.06
Hawaii Native/Pacific Islander (1)	7	0.04
Not Hispanic (1)	7	0.04
Native Hawaiian (0)	3	0.02
White (16,788)	16,992	97.57
Not Hispanic (16,574)	16,758	96.22
Hispanic (214)	234	1.34

Newton

Place Type: City
County: Middlesex
Population: 85,146†

Ancestry‡	Population	%
African, Sub-Saharan (445)	575	0.68
African (59)	59	0.07
Cape Verdean (222)	345	0.41
Ethiopian (15)	15	0.02
South African (85)	92	0.11
Ugandan (36)	36	0.04
Other Sub-Saharan African (28)	28	0.03
Albanian (273)	295	0.35
American (2,612)	2,612	3.11
Arab (382)	566	0.67
Arab (109)	109	0.13
Egyptian (54)	54	0.06
Iraqi (20)	20	0.02
Lebanese (48)	108	0.13
Moroccan (27)	98	0.12
Palestinian (13)	24	0.03
Syrian (0)	8	0.01
Other Arab (111)	145	0.17
Armenian (329)	356	0.42
Assyrian/Chaldean/Syriac (24)	24	0.03
Austrian (80)	650	0.77
Belgian (55)	89	0.11
Brazilian (132)	132	0.16
British (389)	666	0.79
Bulgarian (52)	52	0.06
Canadian (355)	636	0.76
Carpatho Rusyn (13)	13	0.02
Celtic (0)	18	0.02
Croatian (18)	37	0.04
Czech (52)	148	0.18
Czechoslovakian (10)	58	0.07
Danish (22)	121	0.14
Dutch (196)	540	0.64
Eastern European (2,117)	2,236	2.66
English (1,923)	7,304	8.70
Estonian (0)	32	0.04
European (2,108)	2,164	2.58
Finnish (37)	159	0.19
French, ex. Basque (430)	2,154	2.57
French Canadian (342)	766	0.91
German (1,393)	6,065	7.22
Greek (614)	1,056	1.26
Hungarian (209)	718	0.86
Icelander (122)	155	0.18
Iranian (718)	788	0.94
Irish (6,567)	13,724	16.35
Israeli (557)	651	0.78
Italian (4,440)	8,709	10.37
Latvian (81)	281	0.33
Lithuanian (253)	866	1.03
Macedonian (45)	56	0.07
Northern European (131)	188	0.22
Norwegian (90)	481	0.57
Pennsylvania German (8)	8	0.01
Polish (1,311)	4,496	5.36
Portuguese (316)	712	0.85
Romanian (191)	378	0.45
Russian (4,277)	7,389	8.80
Scandinavian (144)	263	0.31
Scotch-Irish (524)	1,097	1.31
Scottish (273)	1,653	1.97
Serbian (41)	52	0.06
Slovak (44)	74	0.09
Slovene (10)	27	0.03
Swedish (139)	832	0.99
Swiss (35)	154	0.18
Turkish (65)	98	0.12
Ukrainian (573)	903	1.08
Welsh (58)	414	0.49
West Indian, ex. Hispanic (201)	220	0.26
Barbadian (4)	4	<0.01
British West Indian (8)	8	0.01
Haitian (153)	153	0.18
Jamaican (35)	43	0.05
West Indian (1)	12	0.01
Yugoslavian (0)	12	0.01

Hispanic Origin	Population	%
Hispanic or Latino (of any race)	3,476	4.08
Central American, ex. Mexican	463	0.54
Costa Rican	27	0.03
Guatemalan	250	0.29
Honduran	48	0.06
Nicaraguan	30	0.04
Panamanian	24	0.03
Salvadoran	84	0.10
Cuban	201	0.24
Dominican Republic	205	0.24
Mexican	488	0.57
Puerto Rican	582	0.68
South American	1,085	1.27
Argentinean	219	0.26
Bolivian	20	0.02
Chilean	76	0.09
Colombian	309	0.36
Ecuadorian	91	0.11
Paraguayan	16	0.02
Peruvian	159	0.19
Uruguayan	15	0.02
Venezuelan	167	0.20
Other South American	13	0.02
Other Hispanic or Latino	452	0.53

Race*	Population	%
African-American/Black (2,160)	2,658	3.12
Not Hispanic (2,008)	2,428	2.85
Hispanic (152)	230	0.27
American Indian/Alaska Native (91)	346	0.41
Not Hispanic (56)	252	0.30
Hispanic (35)	94	0.11
Apache (1)	4	<0.01
Blackfeet (5)	13	0.02
Central American Ind. (1)	4	<0.01
Cherokee (4)	40	0.05
Chickasaw (0)	3	<0.01
Chippewa (1)	1	<0.01
Choctaw (0)	4	<0.01
Comanche (1)	1	<0.01
Creek (0)	1	<0.01
Crow (0)	1	<0.01
Delaware (0)	4	<0.01
Hopi (2)	3	<0.01
Inupiat *(Alaska Native)* (0)	2	<0.01
Iroquois (1)	3	<0.01
Mexican American Ind. (12)	25	0.03
Navajo (0)	3	<0.01
Osage (0)	1	<0.01
Ottawa (1)	1	<0.01
Pueblo (1)	4	<0.01
Seminole (0)	7	0.01
Shoshone (1)	4	<0.01
Sioux (0)	4	<0.01
South American Ind. (6)	11	0.01
Asian (9,790)	10,999	12.92
Not Hispanic (9,759)	10,919	12.82
Hispanic (31)	80	0.09
Bangladeshi (22)	22	0.03
Burmese (11)	13	0.02
Cambodian (41)	52	0.06
Chinese, ex. Taiwanese (5,522)	6,040	7.09
Filipino (184)	301	0.35
Hmong (2)	7	0.01
Indian (1,391)	1,588	1.87
Indonesian (22)	31	0.04
Japanese (342)	527	0.62
Korean (1,132)	1,280	1.50
Laotian (11)	13	0.02
Malaysian (9)	17	0.02
Nepalese (32)	33	0.04
Pakistani (161)	167	0.20
Sri Lankan (35)	47	0.06
Taiwanese (284)	338	0.40
Thai (56)	60	0.07
Vietnamese (254)	347	0.41
Hawaii Native/Pacific Islander (19)	95	0.11
Not Hispanic (18)	83	0.10
Hispanic (1)	12	0.01
Fijian (0)	1	<0.01
Guamanian/Chamorro (1)	6	0.01
Marshallese (3)	3	<0.01
Native Hawaiian (3)	28	0.03
Samoan (3)	7	0.01
White (70,074)	71,893	84.43
Not Hispanic (67,801)	69,382	81.49
Hispanic (2,273)	2,511	2.95

Norfolk

Place Type: Town
County: Norfolk
Population: 11,227†

Ancestry‡	Population	%
African, Sub-Saharan (73)	74	0.67
African (24)	25	0.23
Cape Verdean (38)	38	0.34
Nigerian (11)	11	0.10
Albanian (33)	66	0.60
American (486)	486	4.40
Arab (66)	199	1.80
Lebanese (50)	90	0.81
Syrian (16)	109	0.99
Armenian (12)	68	0.62
Austrian (24)	36	0.33
Belgian (7)	30	0.27
Brazilian (3)	3	0.03
British (80)	80	0.72
Canadian (26)	51	0.46
Czech (11)	21	0.19
Czechoslovakian (0)	9	0.08
Danish (0)	23	0.21
Dutch (34)	66	0.60
Eastern European (10)	28	0.25

*Notes: † The Census 2010 population figure is used to calculate the percentages in the Hispanic Origin and Race categories. Ancestry percentages are based on the 2006-2010 American Community Survey population (not shown); ‡ Numbers in parentheses indicate the number of people reporting a single ancestry; * Numbers in parentheses indicate the number of persons reporting this race alone, not in combination with any other race; Please refer to the Explanation of Data for more information.*

English (416)	1,741	15.75
European (241)	241	2.18
Finnish (17)	42	0.38
French, ex. Basque (273)	837	7.57
French Canadian (130)	401	3.63
German (98)	723	6.54
Greek (39)	191	1.73
Hungarian (0)	8	0.07
Iranian (41)	71	0.64
Irish (1,356)	3,395	30.71
Italian (578)	1,614	14.60
Lithuanian (77)	123	1.11
Northern European (11)	11	0.10
Norwegian (8)	60	0.54
Polish (160)	511	4.62
Portuguese (63)	204	1.85
Russian (110)	265	2.40
Scandinavian (12)	32	0.29
Scotch-Irish (185)	285	2.58
Scottish (115)	545	4.93
Slavic (11)	11	0.10
Slovak (0)	28	0.25
Swedish (85)	313	2.83
Swiss (0)	18	0.16
Ukrainian (7)	7	0.06
Welsh (0)	49	0.44
West Indian, ex. Hispanic (147)	156	1.41
Barbadian (9)	9	0.08
Haitian (9)	9	0.08
Jamaican (65)	74	0.67
West Indian (64)	64	0.58

Hispanic Origin	Population	%
Hispanic or Latino (of any race)	802	7.14
Central American, ex. Mexican	14	0.12
Costa Rican	2	0.02
Guatemalan	7	0.06
Honduran	1	0.01
Panamanian	1	0.01
Salvadoran	3	0.03
Cuban	11	0.10
Dominican Republic	2	0.02
Mexican	105	0.94
Puerto Rican	19	0.17
South American	19	0.17
Argentinean	8	0.07
Chilean	3	0.03
Colombian	3	0.03
Ecuadorian	1	0.01
Paraguayan	1	0.01
Peruvian	2	0.02
Venezuelan	1	0.01
Other Hispanic or Latino	632	5.63

Race*	Population	%
African-American/Black (720)	741	6.60
Not Hispanic (666)	679	6.05
Hispanic (54)	62	0.55
American Indian/Alaska Native (32)	43	0.38
Not Hispanic (21)	32	0.29
Hispanic (11)	11	0.10
Blackfeet (0)	1	0.01
Cherokee (1)	3	0.03
Chippewa (0)	1	0.01
Creek (0)	2	0.02
Navajo (1)	1	0.01
Asian (174)	224	2.00
Not Hispanic (169)	218	1.94
Hispanic (5)	6	0.05
Burmese (1)	3	0.03
Cambodian (1)	1	0.01
Chinese, ex. Taiwanese (35)	45	0.40
Filipino (12)	12	0.11
Indian (38)	47	0.42
Indonesian (1)	1	0.01
Japanese (5)	11	0.10
Korean (15)	24	0.21
Malaysian (0)	1	0.01
Nepalese (1)	1	0.01
Pakistani (5)	6	0.05
Taiwanese (2)	2	0.02
Thai (3)	9	0.08
Vietnamese (5)	5	0.04
White (10,023)	10,112	90.07
Not Hispanic (9,493)	9,562	85.17
Hispanic (530)	550	4.90

North Adams

Place Type: City
County: Berkshire
Population: 13,708†

Ancestry‡	Population	%
African, Sub-Saharan (27)	69	0.50
African (27)	69	0.50
American (467)	467	3.37
Arab (95)	152	1.10
Lebanese (95)	130	0.94
Syrian (0)	22	0.16
Austrian (9)	36	0.26
British (26)	26	0.19
Canadian (61)	111	0.80
Czech (0)	11	0.08
Danish (0)	14	0.10
Dutch (39)	196	1.42
Eastern European (9)	20	0.14
English (353)	1,338	9.66
European (39)	39	0.28
Finnish (8)	8	0.06
French, ex. Basque (879)	3,416	24.66
French Canadian (481)	936	6.76
German (167)	1,035	7.47
Greek (22)	64	0.46
Hungarian (0)	75	0.54
Irish (438)	2,378	17.17
Italian (651)	2,523	18.22
Lithuanian (0)	19	0.14
Norwegian (10)	16	0.12
Polish (115)	946	6.83
Portuguese (38)	175	1.26
Romanian (8)	8	0.06
Russian (30)	167	1.21
Scandinavian (0)	10	0.07
Scotch-Irish (73)	196	1.42
Scottish (30)	454	3.28
Slovak (10)	18	0.13
Swedish (43)	106	0.77
Welsh (6)	59	0.43
West Indian, ex. Hispanic (93)	93	0.67
Haitian (41)	41	0.30
Jamaican (52)	52	0.38

Hispanic Origin	Population	%
Hispanic or Latino (of any race)	476	3.47
Central American, ex. Mexican	95	0.69
Guatemalan	14	0.10
Honduran	71	0.52
Nicaraguan	1	0.01
Panamanian	3	0.02
Salvadoran	6	0.04
Cuban	21	0.15
Dominican Republic	24	0.18
Mexican	58	0.42
Puerto Rican	193	1.41
South American	28	0.20
Chilean	2	0.01
Colombian	10	0.07
Ecuadorian	6	0.04
Peruvian	6	0.04
Other South American	4	0.03
Other Hispanic or Latino	57	0.42

Race*	Population	%
African-American/Black (310)	501	3.65
Not Hispanic (279)	443	3.23
Hispanic (31)	58	0.42
American Indian/Alaska Native (43)	160	1.17
Not Hispanic (39)	138	1.01
Hispanic (4)	22	0.16
Aleut *(Alaska Native)* (0)	1	0.01
Apache (0)	1	0.01
Blackfeet (4)	18	0.13
Central American Ind. (0)	1	0.01
Cherokee (3)	19	0.14
Chickasaw (1)	1	0.01
Choctaw (4)	8	0.06
Houma (2)	2	0.01
Iroquois (4)	16	0.12
Mexican American Ind. (0)	2	0.01
Navajo (0)	3	0.02
Ottawa (0)	1	0.01
Pima (1)	2	0.01
Seminole (0)	1	0.01
Sioux (1)	2	0.01
South American Ind. (2)	2	0.01
Asian (100)	140	1.02
Not Hispanic (97)	136	0.99
Hispanic (3)	4	0.03
Cambodian (8)	9	0.07
Chinese, ex. Taiwanese (30)	42	0.31
Filipino (3)	11	0.08
Indian (21)	26	0.19
Indonesian (0)	4	0.03
Japanese (4)	6	0.04
Korean (19)	26	0.19
Laotian (1)	1	0.01
Malaysian (0)	1	0.01
Pakistani (1)	1	0.01
Thai (2)	3	0.02
Vietnamese (6)	8	0.06
Hawaii Native/Pacific Islander (8)	26	0.19
Not Hispanic (8)	25	0.18
Hispanic (0)	1	0.01
Fijian (1)	1	0.01
Guamanian/Chamorro (2)	6	0.04
Native Hawaiian (3)	7	0.05
Samoan (0)	7	0.05
Tongan (0)	2	0.01
White (12,744)	13,069	95.34
Not Hispanic (12,498)	12,785	93.27
Hispanic (246)	284	2.07

North Andover

Place Type: Town
County: Essex
Population: 28,352†

Ancestry‡	Population	%
African, Sub-Saharan (170)	212	0.76
African (23)	23	0.08
Cape Verdean (0)	42	0.15
Other Sub-Saharan African (147)	147	0.53
American (726)	726	2.60
Arab (198)	609	2.18
Arab (0)	10	0.04
Egyptian (48)	145	0.52
Lebanese (144)	350	1.25
Moroccan (6)	6	0.02
Syrian (0)	27	0.10
Other Arab (0)	71	0.25
Armenian (129)	136	0.49
Austrian (31)	187	0.67
Basque (0)	28	0.10
Belgian (52)	52	0.19
British (138)	192	0.69
Cajun (0)	27	0.10
Canadian (200)	412	1.47
Croatian (7)	31	0.11
Czech (18)	136	0.49
Czechoslovakian (9)	17	0.06
Danish (27)	103	0.37
Dutch (49)	236	0.84
Eastern European (90)	104	0.37
English (652)	3,804	13.60
Estonian (18)	18	0.06
European (81)	92	0.33
Finnish (18)	59	0.21
French, ex. Basque (405)	2,528	9.04

SECTION TWO

*Notes: † The Census 2010 population figure is used to calculate the percentages in the Hispanic Origin and Race categories. Ancestry percentages are based on the 2006-2010 American Community Survey population (not shown); ‡ Numbers in parentheses indicate the number of people reporting a single ancestry; * Numbers in parentheses indicate the number of persons reporting this race alone, not in combination with any other race; Please refer to the Explanation of Data for more information.*

French Canadian (497)	1,419	5.07
German (545)	2,541	9.09
Greek (176)	480	1.72
Hungarian (35)	133	0.48
Iranian (36)	62	0.22
Irish (2,854)	9,039	32.32
Israeli (0)	15	0.05
Italian (2,322)	6,205	22.19
Latvian (14)	47	0.17
Lithuanian (111)	331	1.18
Luxemburger (10)	10	0.04
Northern European (28)	47	0.17
Norwegian (52)	163	0.58
Pennsylvania German (0)	8	0.03
Polish (288)	1,613	5.77
Portuguese (116)	299	1.07
Romanian (10)	69	0.25
Russian (221)	583	2.08
Scandinavian (0)	8	0.03
Scotch-Irish (223)	637	2.28
Scottish (324)	1,022	3.65
Serbian (0)	7	0.03
Slovak (86)	158	0.56
Swedish (14)	589	2.11
Swiss (0)	38	0.14
Turkish (68)	68	0.24
Ukrainian (30)	110	0.39
Welsh (0)	151	0.54
West Indian, ex. Hispanic (47)	73	0.26
Haitian (36)	36	0.13
Jamaican (11)	37	0.13

Hispanic Origin	Population	%
Hispanic or Latino (of any race)	1,398	4.93
Central American, ex. Mexican	99	0.35
Costa Rican	28	0.10
Guatemalan	30	0.11
Honduran	7	0.02
Nicaraguan	10	0.04
Panamanian	4	0.01
Salvadoran	20	0.07
Cuban	52	0.18
Dominican Republic	418	1.47
Mexican	133	0.47
Puerto Rican	363	1.28
South American	224	0.79
Argentinean	23	0.08
Bolivian	3	0.01
Chilean	12	0.04
Colombian	106	0.37
Ecuadorian	34	0.12
Paraguayan	3	0.01
Peruvian	32	0.11
Uruguayan	2	0.01
Venezuelan	8	0.03
Other South American	1	<0.01
Other Hispanic or Latino	109	0.38

Race*	Population	%
African-American/Black (506)	600	2.12
Not Hispanic (427)	496	1.75
Hispanic (79)	104	0.37
American Indian/Alaska Native (28)	99	0.35
Not Hispanic (22)	81	0.29
Hispanic (6)	18	0.06
Apache (0)	1	<0.01
Blackfeet (0)	2	0.01
Cherokee (5)	17	0.06
Chickasaw (0)	2	0.01
Chippewa (0)	3	0.01
Cree (0)	1	<0.01
Creek (2)	3	0.01
Iroquois (4)	4	0.01
Mexican American Ind. (1)	2	0.01
Potawatomi (0)	1	<0.01
South American Ind. (4)	7	0.02
Asian (1,787)	1,990	7.02
Not Hispanic (1,783)	1,981	6.99
Hispanic (4)	9	0.03
Bangladeshi (12)	16	0.06
Burmese (4)	4	0.01
Cambodian (27)	29	0.10
Chinese, ex. Taiwanese (463)	543	1.92
Filipino (48)	88	0.31
Indian (726)	757	2.67
Indonesian (2)	7	0.02
Japanese (42)	72	0.25
Korean (218)	237	0.84
Laotian (2)	3	0.01
Malaysian (0)	1	<0.01
Pakistani (33)	40	0.14
Sri Lankan (1)	1	<0.01
Taiwanese (18)	27	0.10
Thai (5)	8	0.03
Vietnamese (124)	153	0.54
Hawaii Native/Pacific Islander (4)	18	0.06
Not Hispanic (3)	13	0.05
Hispanic (1)	5	0.02
Guamanian/Chamorro (4)	4	0.01
Native Hawaiian (0)	4	0.01
White (25,144)	25,531	90.05
Not Hispanic (24,355)	24,665	87.00
Hispanic (789)	866	3.05

North Attleborough

Place Type: Town
County: Bristol
Population: 28,712†

Ancestry‡	Population	%
African, Sub-Saharan (98)	125	0.44
African (28)	28	0.10
Cape Verdean (58)	85	0.30
Nigerian (12)	12	0.04
American (1,014)	1,014	3.56
Arab (256)	416	1.46
Egyptian (58)	58	0.20
Lebanese (47)	124	0.44
Moroccan (109)	109	0.38
Syrian (15)	98	0.34
Other Arab (27)	27	0.09
Armenian (45)	214	0.75
Austrian (15)	15	0.05
Belgian (3)	37	0.13
Brazilian (0)	64	0.22
British (80)	125	0.44
Canadian (54)	208	0.73
Czech (0)	45	0.16
Czechoslovakian (10)	10	0.04
Danish (12)	62	0.22
Dutch (75)	237	0.83
Eastern European (72)	72	0.25
English (998)	5,558	19.51
European (259)	259	0.91
Finnish (19)	82	0.29
French, ex. Basque (1,002)	3,766	13.22
French Canadian (1,144)	2,258	7.93
German (608)	2,819	9.90
Greek (242)	356	1.25
Hungarian (0)	121	0.42
Icelander (0)	7	0.02
Iranian (15)	15	0.05
Irish (2,638)	8,500	29.84
Italian (1,373)	4,480	15.73
Lithuanian (12)	27	0.09
Northern European (14)	29	0.10
Norwegian (33)	228	0.80
Polish (242)	1,432	5.03
Portuguese (596)	1,694	5.95
Romanian (0)	17	0.06
Russian (107)	314	1.10
Scandinavian (16)	16	0.06
Scotch-Irish (379)	1,142	4.01
Scottish (316)	970	3.41
Slovak (12)	12	0.04
Swedish (127)	542	1.90
Swiss (0)	44	0.15
Ukrainian (0)	52	0.18
Welsh (0)	164	0.58

Hispanic Origin	Population	%
Hispanic or Latino (of any race)	675	2.35
Central American, ex. Mexican	144	0.50
Costa Rican	3	0.01
Guatemalan	65	0.23
Honduran	9	0.03
Nicaraguan	3	0.01
Salvadoran	64	0.22
Cuban	34	0.12
Dominican Republic	30	0.10
Mexican	92	0.32
Puerto Rican	182	0.63
South American	109	0.38
Argentinean	3	0.01
Bolivian	2	0.01
Chilean	5	0.02
Colombian	58	0.20
Ecuadorian	20	0.07
Peruvian	12	0.04
Venezuelan	9	0.03
Other Hispanic or Latino	84	0.29

Race*	Population	%
African-American/Black (427)	584	2.03
Not Hispanic (417)	547	1.91
Hispanic (10)	37	0.13
American Indian/Alaska Native (51)	188	0.65
Not Hispanic (32)	150	0.52
Hispanic (19)	38	0.13
Blackfeet (1)	9	0.03
Canadian/French Am. Ind. (0)	2	0.01
Central American Ind. (1)	1	<0.01
Cherokee (2)	19	0.07
Choctaw (0)	2	0.01
Comanche (0)	1	<0.01
Creek (0)	1	<0.01
Delaware (2)	2	0.01
Iroquois (0)	11	0.04
Mexican American Ind. (4)	5	0.02
Pueblo (4)	6	0.02
Seminole (0)	4	0.01
Sioux (0)	2	0.01
South American Ind. (3)	4	0.01
Spanish American Ind. (1)	1	<0.01
Asian (1,008)	1,159	4.04
Not Hispanic (1,001)	1,146	3.99
Hispanic (7)	13	0.05
Bangladeshi (14)	14	0.05
Cambodian (56)	63	0.22
Chinese, ex. Taiwanese (244)	284	0.99
Filipino (41)	67	0.23
Hmong (2)	2	0.01
Indian (454)	484	1.69
Japanese (11)	27	0.09
Korean (36)	58	0.20
Malaysian (4)	4	0.01
Nepalese (2)	2	0.01
Pakistani (31)	34	0.12
Sri Lankan (6)	10	0.03
Taiwanese (6)	6	0.02
Thai (11)	13	0.05
Vietnamese (70)	79	0.28
Hawaii Native/Pacific Islander (7)	19	0.07
Not Hispanic (7)	18	0.06
Hispanic (0)	1	<0.01
Fijian (4)	4	0.01
Guamanian/Chamorro (0)	1	<0.01
Native Hawaiian (3)	5	0.02
White (26,547)	26,944	93.84
Not Hispanic (26,129)	26,484	92.24
Hispanic (418)	460	1.60

North Reading

Place Type: Town
County: Middlesex
Population: 14,892†

Ancestry‡	Population	%
African, Sub-Saharan (0)	18	0.12

*Notes: † The Census 2010 population figure is used to calculate the percentages in the Hispanic Origin and Race categories. Ancestry percentages are based on the 2006-2010 American Community Survey population (not shown); ‡ Numbers in parentheses indicate the number of people reporting a single ancestry; * Numbers in parentheses indicate the number of persons reporting this race alone, not in combination with any other race; Please refer to the Explanation of Data for more information.*

Cape Verdean (0)	18	0.12
American (769)	769	5.29
Arab (0)	29	0.20
Lebanese (0)	9	0.06
Syrian (0)	20	0.14
Armenian (100)	170	1.17
Brazilian (16)	16	0.11
British (35)	96	0.66
Canadian (114)	212	1.46
Croatian (0)	11	0.08
Czechoslovakian (0)	18	0.12
Danish (0)	22	0.15
Dutch (29)	87	0.60
English (647)	2,278	15.67
European (108)	141	0.97
Finnish (0)	32	0.22
French, ex. Basque (83)	826	5.68
French Canadian (240)	635	4.37
German (200)	1,173	8.07
Greek (218)	470	3.23
Hungarian (13)	79	0.54
Irish (2,096)	5,114	35.18
Italian (1,617)	3,701	25.46
Latvian (0)	43	0.30
Lithuanian (41)	248	1.71
Northern European (0)	28	0.19
Norwegian (0)	67	0.46
Polish (71)	552	3.80
Portuguese (78)	271	1.86
Russian (10)	139	0.96
Scandinavian (0)	34	0.23
Scotch-Irish (114)	298	2.05
Scottish (56)	331	2.28
Swedish (95)	424	2.92
Swiss (9)	23	0.16
Ukrainian (7)	21	0.14
Welsh (0)	22	0.15
West Indian, ex. Hispanic (21)	41	0.28
Jamaican (21)	41	0.28
Yugoslavian (31)	44	0.30

Hispanic Origin	Population	%
Hispanic or Latino (of any race)	231	1.55
Central American, ex. Mexican	14	0.09
Costa Rican	3	0.02
Guatemalan	6	0.04
Honduran	2	0.01
Salvadoran	3	0.02
Cuban	9	0.06
Dominican Republic	13	0.09
Mexican	54	0.36
Puerto Rican	44	0.30
South American	63	0.42
Argentinean	6	0.04
Bolivian	2	0.01
Chilean	9	0.06
Colombian	31	0.21
Ecuadorian	9	0.06
Peruvian	3	0.02
Venezuelan	3	0.02
Other Hispanic or Latino	34	0.23

Race*	Population	%
African-American/Black (84)	115	0.77
Not Hispanic (84)	110	0.74
Hispanic (0)	5	0.03
American Indian/Alaska Native (23)	72	0.48
Not Hispanic (16)	62	0.42
Hispanic (7)	10	0.07
Canadian/French Am. Ind. (2)	3	0.02
Cherokee (5)	7	0.05
Cree (0)	1	0.01
Iroquois (0)	2	0.01
Navajo (0)	1	0.01
Osage (0)	2	0.01
Pueblo (1)	1	0.01
Shoshone (0)	1	0.01
Sioux (1)	12	0.08
South American Ind. (2)	5	0.03
Asian (397)	469	3.15
Not Hispanic (397)	468	3.14
Hispanic (0)	1	0.01
Bangladeshi (9)	9	0.06
Cambodian (4)	4	0.03
Chinese, ex. Taiwanese (172)	193	1.30
Filipino (23)	39	0.26
Indian (110)	118	0.79
Japanese (10)	12	0.08
Korean (29)	45	0.30
Pakistani (1)	3	0.02
Taiwanese (1)	3	0.02
Thai (2)	6	0.04
Vietnamese (22)	29	0.19
Hawaii Native/Pacific Islander (0)	4	0.03
Not Hispanic (0)	4	0.03
Samoan (0)	1	0.01
Tongan (0)	3	0.02
White (14,174)	14,331	96.23
Not Hispanic (13,991)	14,137	94.93
Hispanic (183)	194	1.30

Northampton

Place Type: City
County: Hampshire
Population: 28,549[†]

Ancestry[‡]	Population	%
African, Sub-Saharan (68)	195	0.68
African (19)	66	0.23
Cape Verdean (0)	50	0.17
Ghanaian (15)	30	0.10
Nigerian (0)	15	0.05
Sierra Leonean (14)	14	0.05
South African (5)	5	0.02
Other Sub-Saharan African (15)	15	0.05
Albanian (38)	38	0.13
Alsatian (0)	18	0.06
American (763)	763	2.66
Arab (72)	170	0.59
Lebanese (11)	60	0.21
Moroccan (34)	34	0.12
Syrian (13)	62	0.22
Other Arab (14)	14	0.05
Armenian (9)	9	0.03
Austrian (52)	142	0.49
Belgian (0)	10	0.03
Brazilian (16)	32	0.11
British (85)	276	0.96
Bulgarian (38)	38	0.13
Canadian (99)	171	0.60
Czech (147)	281	0.98
Czechoslovakian (0)	33	0.11
Danish (13)	60	0.21
Dutch (13)	181	0.63
Eastern European (340)	461	1.61
English (662)	4,021	14.01
European (318)	328	1.14
Finnish (0)	66	0.23
French, ex. Basque (549)	2,913	10.15
French Canadian (540)	1,222	4.26
German (562)	3,327	11.59
Greek (47)	165	0.57
Hungarian (29)	139	0.48
Iranian (11)	36	0.13
Irish (1,313)	6,325	22.03
Israeli (0)	23	0.08
Italian (729)	2,826	9.84
Latvian (0)	14	0.05
Lithuanian (108)	311	1.08
New Zealander (12)	12	0.04
Northern European (50)	64	0.22
Norwegian (17)	190	0.66
Pennsylvania German (9)	9	0.03
Polish (1,343)	3,377	11.76
Portuguese (47)	226	0.79
Romanian (0)	77	0.27
Russian (281)	1,003	3.49
Scandinavian (17)	17	0.06
Scotch-Irish (228)	637	2.22
Scottish (214)	953	3.32
Slovak (33)	112	0.39
Slovene (0)	14	0.05
Swedish (81)	484	1.69
Swiss (15)	113	0.39
Turkish (14)	14	0.05
Ukrainian (32)	74	0.26
Welsh (34)	187	0.65
West Indian, ex. Hispanic (131)	186	0.65
Barbadian (6)	19	0.07
Belizean (70)	85	0.30
Haitian (14)	14	0.05
Jamaican (0)	15	0.05
Trinidadian/Tobagonian (0)	12	0.04
West Indian (41)	41	0.14
Yugoslavian (0)	24	0.08

Hispanic Origin	Population	%
Hispanic or Latino (of any race)	1,928	6.75
Central American, ex. Mexican	124	0.43
Costa Rican	9	0.03
Guatemalan	47	0.16
Honduran	6	0.02
Nicaraguan	12	0.04
Panamanian	4	0.01
Salvadoran	46	0.16
Cuban	58	0.20
Dominican Republic	52	0.18
Mexican	158	0.55
Puerto Rican	1,193	4.18
South American	221	0.77
Argentinean	24	0.08
Bolivian	4	0.01
Chilean	20	0.07
Colombian	53	0.19
Ecuadorian	77	0.27
Paraguayan	3	0.01
Peruvian	24	0.08
Uruguayan	4	0.01
Venezuelan	7	0.02
Other South American	5	0.02
Other Hispanic or Latino	122	0.43

Race*	Population	%
African-American/Black (776)	1,059	3.71
Not Hispanic (700)	907	3.18
Hispanic (76)	152	0.53
American Indian/Alaska Native (83)	281	0.98
Not Hispanic (59)	212	0.74
Hispanic (24)	69	0.24
Aleut *(Alaska Native)* (0)	1	<0.01
Apache (0)	2	0.01
Blackfeet (1)	8	0.03
Canadian/French Am. Ind. (0)	5	0.02
Central American Ind. (1)	6	0.02
Cherokee (6)	42	0.15
Cheyenne (0)	2	0.01
Chippewa (2)	4	0.01
Choctaw (1)	8	0.03
Creek (1)	2	0.01
Inupiat *(Alaska Native)* (1)	1	<0.01
Iroquois (5)	13	0.05
Mexican American Ind. (7)	10	0.04
Navajo (1)	1	<0.01
Ottawa (0)	1	<0.01
Potawatomi (0)	1	<0.01
Pueblo (1)	1	<0.01
Seminole (0)	2	0.01
Sioux (1)	7	0.02
South American Ind. (10)	21	0.07
Spanish American Ind. (1)	2	0.01
Tlingit-Haida *(Alaska Native)* (2)	2	0.01
Yakama (1)	1	<0.01
Asian (1,162)	1,448	5.07
Not Hispanic (1,148)	1,415	4.96
Hispanic (14)	33	0.12
Bangladeshi (8)	11	0.04
Burmese (2)	2	0.01
Cambodian (97)	105	0.37
Chinese, ex. Taiwanese (300)	379	1.33

*Notes: † The Census 2010 population figure is used to calculate the percentages in the Hispanic Origin and Race categories. Ancestry percentages are based on the 2006-2010 American Community Survey population (not shown); ‡ Numbers in parentheses indicate the number of people reporting a single ancestry; * Numbers in parentheses indicate the number of persons reporting this race alone, not in combination with any other race; Please refer to the Explanation of Data for more information.*

Filipino (36)	67	0.23
Hmong (2)	2	0.01
Indian (254)	315	1.10
Indonesian (0)	3	0.01
Japanese (48)	119	0.42
Korean (169)	202	0.71
Laotian (0)	2	0.01
Malaysian (0)	3	0.01
Nepalese (10)	11	0.04
Pakistani (41)	50	0.18
Sri Lankan (5)	7	0.02
Taiwanese (15)	21	0.07
Thai (33)	38	0.13
Vietnamese (78)	102	0.36
Hawaii Native/Pacific Islander (14)	43	0.15
Not Hispanic (7)	25	0.09
Hispanic (7)	18	0.06
Guamanian/Chamorro (4)	4	0.01
Native Hawaiian (4)	14	0.05
Samoan (0)	3	0.01
Tongan (2)	2	0.01
White (25,025)	25,715	90.07
Not Hispanic (24,030)	24,565	86.05
Hispanic (995)	1,150	4.03

Northborough

Place Type: Town
County: Worcester
Population: 14,155†

Ancestry‡	Population	%
African, Sub-Saharan (0)	106	0.75
African (0)	32	0.23
South African (0)	74	0.52
Albanian (16)	35	0.25
American (591)	591	4.17
Arab (17)	69	0.49
Lebanese (17)	69	0.49
Armenian (67)	89	0.63
Assyrian/Chaldean/Syriac (9)	9	0.06
Australian (20)	20	0.14
Austrian (0)	22	0.16
Brazilian (166)	281	1.98
British (48)	118	0.83
Canadian (70)	101	0.71
Czechoslovakian (10)	20	0.14
Danish (0)	65	0.46
Dutch (52)	259	1.83
Eastern European (61)	91	0.64
English (848)	2,252	15.90
European (15)	47	0.33
Finnish (0)	83	0.59
French, ex. Basque (229)	1,206	8.52
French Canadian (177)	619	4.37
German (364)	1,255	8.86
Greek (171)	223	1.57
Hungarian (11)	41	0.29
Iranian (10)	10	0.07
Irish (1,088)	3,415	24.12
Italian (676)	2,374	16.76
Lithuanian (49)	300	2.12
Northern European (33)	33	0.23
Norwegian (14)	129	0.91
Polish (124)	694	4.90
Portuguese (37)	191	1.35
Romanian (12)	24	0.17
Russian (218)	408	2.88
Scandinavian (14)	25	0.18
Scotch-Irish (55)	389	2.75
Scottish (130)	516	3.64
Slovak (0)	87	0.61
Swedish (176)	672	4.75
Swiss (0)	115	0.81
Ukrainian (35)	82	0.58
Welsh (17)	103	0.73
West Indian, ex. Hispanic (11)	11	0.08
Barbadian (11)	11	0.08

Hispanic Origin	Population	%
Hispanic or Latino (of any race)	381	2.69
Central American, ex. Mexican	76	0.54
Guatemalan	57	0.40
Honduran	3	0.02
Nicaraguan	1	0.01
Panamanian	1	0.01
Salvadoran	14	0.10
Cuban	30	0.21
Dominican Republic	9	0.06
Mexican	58	0.41
Puerto Rican	88	0.62
South American	62	0.44
Argentinean	6	0.04
Bolivian	5	0.04
Chilean	3	0.02
Colombian	24	0.17
Ecuadorian	6	0.04
Paraguayan	4	0.03
Peruvian	8	0.06
Venezuelan	6	0.04
Other Hispanic or Latino	58	0.41

Race*	Population	%
African-American/Black (142)	219	1.55
Not Hispanic (127)	191	1.35
Hispanic (15)	28	0.20
American Indian/Alaska Native (16)	67	0.47
Not Hispanic (10)	57	0.40
Hispanic (6)	10	0.07
Apache (0)	3	0.02
Canadian/French Am. Ind. (0)	2	0.01
Cherokee (0)	4	0.03
Creek (0)	1	0.01
Inupiat *(Alaska Native)* (0)	2	0.01
Iroquois (0)	4	0.03
Lumbee (0)	5	0.04
Menominee (0)	1	0.01
Mexican American Ind. (2)	6	0.04
Sioux (0)	1	0.01
South American Ind. (0)	3	0.02
Asian (1,158)	1,319	9.32
Not Hispanic (1,153)	1,312	9.27
Hispanic (5)	7	0.05
Bangladeshi (6)	6	0.04
Burmese (9)	9	0.06
Cambodian (7)	7	0.05
Chinese, ex. Taiwanese (461)	526	3.72
Filipino (15)	27	0.19
Indian (422)	461	3.26
Indonesian (9)	11	0.08
Japanese (18)	38	0.27
Korean (99)	115	0.81
Laotian (0)	3	0.02
Malaysian (0)	1	0.01
Nepalese (7)	7	0.05
Pakistani (22)	26	0.18
Sri Lankan (13)	13	0.09
Taiwanese (17)	27	0.19
Thai (8)	10	0.07
Vietnamese (23)	27	0.19
Hawaii Native/Pacific Islander (3)	11	0.08
Not Hispanic (2)	10	0.07
Hispanic (1)	1	0.01
Guamanian/Chamorro (1)	3	0.02
Samoan (2)	3	0.02
White (12,405)	12,658	89.42
Not Hispanic (12,160)	12,390	87.53
Hispanic (245)	268	1.89

Northbridge

Place Type: Town
County: Worcester
Population: 15,707†

Ancestry‡	Population	%
African, Sub-Saharan (29)	66	0.43
Cape Verdean (0)	37	0.24
Ethiopian (29)	29	0.19
Albanian (0)	25	0.16
American (734)	734	4.80
Arab (0)	70	0.46
Lebanese (0)	70	0.46
Armenian (101)	113	0.74
Austrian (9)	9	0.06
Brazilian (0)	29	0.19
British (57)	69	0.45
Canadian (93)	194	1.27
Czech (4)	47	0.31
Danish (0)	22	0.14
Dutch (465)	761	4.98
Eastern European (16)	31	0.20
English (396)	2,082	13.62
European (106)	106	0.69
Finnish (11)	31	0.20
French, ex. Basque (627)	2,634	17.23
French Canadian (842)	1,787	11.69
German (72)	921	6.02
Greek (23)	178	1.16
Hungarian (26)	41	0.27
Iranian (14)	22	0.14
Irish (1,028)	3,490	22.83
Italian (698)	2,412	15.78
Lithuanian (72)	286	1.87
Northern European (14)	14	0.09
Norwegian (21)	72	0.47
Polish (221)	1,161	7.59
Portuguese (77)	279	1.83
Russian (176)	261	1.71
Scandinavian (16)	16	0.10
Scotch-Irish (112)	755	4.94
Scottish (82)	502	3.28
Slovak (10)	59	0.39
Swedish (90)	541	3.54
Ukrainian (0)	33	0.22
Welsh (12)	68	0.44
West Indian, ex. Hispanic (12)	39	0.26
Trinidadian/Tobagonian (12)	39	0.26

Hispanic Origin	Population	%
Hispanic or Latino (of any race)	491	3.13
Central American, ex. Mexican	39	0.25
Guatemalan	14	0.09
Honduran	1	0.01
Panamanian	3	0.02
Salvadoran	21	0.13
Cuban	9	0.06
Dominican Republic	48	0.31
Mexican	53	0.34
Puerto Rican	221	1.41
South American	45	0.29
Argentinean	3	0.02
Bolivian	5	0.03
Chilean	2	0.01
Colombian	17	0.11
Ecuadorian	5	0.03
Peruvian	5	0.03
Venezuelan	4	0.03
Other South American	4	0.03
Other Hispanic or Latino	76	0.48

Race*	Population	%
African-American/Black (112)	192	1.22
Not Hispanic (96)	168	1.07
Hispanic (16)	24	0.15
American Indian/Alaska Native (23)	92	0.59
Not Hispanic (22)	91	0.58
Hispanic (1)	1	0.01
Blackfeet (2)	9	0.06
Canadian/French Am. Ind. (1)	1	0.01
Cherokee (0)	8	0.05
Choctaw (0)	1	0.01
Comanche (0)	5	0.03
Delaware (0)	1	0.01
Iroquois (3)	7	0.04
Seminole (0)	2	0.01
Asian (159)	222	1.41
Not Hispanic (159)	214	1.36
Hispanic (0)	8	0.05

*Notes: † The Census 2010 population figure is used to calculate the percentages in the Hispanic Origin and Race categories. Ancestry percentages are based on the 2006-2010 American Community Survey population (not shown); ‡ Numbers in parentheses indicate the number of people reporting a single ancestry; * Numbers in parentheses indicate the number of persons reporting this race alone, not in combination with any other race; Please refer to the Explanation of Data for more information.*

Cambodian (8)	10	0.06
Chinese, ex. Taiwanese (20)	39	0.25
Filipino (14)	21	0.13
Indian (51)	53	0.34
Japanese (2)	10	0.06
Korean (16)	27	0.17
Laotian (20)	23	0.15
Pakistani (5)	5	0.03
Thai (7)	13	0.08
Vietnamese (8)	12	0.08
Hawaii Native/Pacific Islander (1)	10	0.06
Not Hispanic (1)	9	0.06
Hispanic (0)	1	0.01
Native Hawaiian (0)	3	0.02
Samoan (1)	4	0.03
White (15,071)	15,298	97.40
Not Hispanic (14,720)	14,916	94.96
Hispanic (351)	382	2.43

Norton

Place Type: Town
County: Bristol
Population: 19,031†

Ancestry‡	Population	%
African, Sub-Saharan (6)	20	0.11
Cape Verdean (6)	20	0.11
Albanian (0)	14	0.07
American (618)	618	3.27
Arab (32)	128	0.68
Lebanese (6)	77	0.41
Syrian (26)	51	0.27
Armenian (0)	54	0.29
Austrian (0)	93	0.49
British (6)	65	0.34
Canadian (88)	311	1.65
Czech (11)	24	0.13
Danish (0)	48	0.25
Dutch (20)	199	1.05
Eastern European (50)	50	0.26
English (714)	3,263	17.28
European (73)	87	0.46
Finnish (17)	101	0.53
French, ex. Basque (173)	1,918	10.16
French Canadian (425)	818	4.33
German (256)	1,619	8.58
Greek (33)	83	0.44
Guyanese (14)	14	0.07
Hungarian (0)	100	0.53
Irish (1,842)	6,063	32.11
Italian (1,168)	3,601	19.07
Lithuanian (44)	167	0.88
Macedonian (0)	13	0.07
Norwegian (32)	94	0.50
Polish (259)	1,214	6.43
Portuguese (349)	1,094	5.79
Romanian (10)	38	0.20
Russian (141)	308	1.63
Scandinavian (7)	21	0.11
Scotch-Irish (166)	518	2.74
Scottish (148)	744	3.94
Slovak (31)	59	0.31
Swedish (168)	520	2.75
Swiss (0)	38	0.20
Turkish (0)	38	0.20
Ukrainian (13)	45	0.24
Welsh (0)	14	0.07
West Indian, ex. Hispanic (312)	398	2.11
Barbadian (0)	14	0.07
Bermudan (0)	10	0.05
British West Indian (0)	28	0.15
Haitian (253)	253	1.34
Jamaican (27)	47	0.25
Trinidadian/Tobagonian (32)	32	0.17
U.S. Virgin Islander (0)	14	0.07
Yugoslavian (0)	10	0.05

Hispanic Origin	Population	%
Hispanic or Latino (of any race)	374	1.97
Central American, ex. Mexican	43	0.23
Costa Rican	4	0.02
Guatemalan	24	0.13
Honduran	7	0.04
Panamanian	3	0.02
Salvadoran	5	0.03
Cuban	11	0.06
Dominican Republic	27	0.14
Mexican	65	0.34
Puerto Rican	133	0.70
South American	48	0.25
Argentinean	14	0.07
Colombian	12	0.06
Ecuadorian	8	0.04
Paraguayan	1	0.01
Peruvian	7	0.04
Venezuelan	6	0.03
Other Hispanic or Latino	47	0.25

Race*	Population	%
African-American/Black (349)	474	2.49
Not Hispanic (318)	427	2.24
Hispanic (31)	47	0.25
American Indian/Alaska Native (27)	93	0.49
Not Hispanic (21)	81	0.43
Hispanic (6)	12	0.06
Blackfeet (0)	3	0.02
Canadian/French Am. Ind. (1)	2	0.01
Central American Ind. (2)	6	0.03
Cherokee (4)	18	0.09
Chippewa (1)	4	0.02
Choctaw (1)	1	0.01
Cree (0)	1	0.01
Creek (1)	1	0.01
Iroquois (1)	1	0.01
Mexican American Ind. (1)	1	0.01
Sioux (1)	1	0.01
Asian (344)	443	2.33
Not Hispanic (338)	430	2.26
Hispanic (6)	13	0.07
Bhutanese (4)	4	0.02
Burmese (2)	2	0.01
Cambodian (6)	10	0.05
Chinese, ex. Taiwanese (89)	126	0.66
Filipino (41)	62	0.33
Hmong (5)	7	0.04
Indian (76)	87	0.46
Indonesian (0)	5	0.03
Japanese (27)	43	0.23
Korean (33)	49	0.26
Malaysian (0)	2	0.01
Pakistani (7)	8	0.04
Sri Lankan (1)	3	0.02
Taiwanese (1)	2	0.01
Thai (6)	13	0.07
Vietnamese (30)	38	0.20
Hawaii Native/Pacific Islander (12)	25	0.13
Not Hispanic (6)	15	0.08
Hispanic (6)	10	0.05
Native Hawaiian (0)	6	0.03
Samoan (0)	1	0.01
White (17,885)	18,151	95.38
Not Hispanic (17,669)	17,907	94.09
Hispanic (216)	244	1.28

Norwell

Place Type: Town
County: Plymouth
Population: 10,506†

Ancestry‡	Population	%
African, Sub-Saharan (71)	77	0.74
Cape Verdean (0)	6	0.06
Nigerian (71)	71	0.68
Albanian (23)	92	0.89
American (462)	462	4.46
Arab (0)	36	0.35
Lebanese (0)	36	0.35
Armenian (9)	31	0.30
Austrian (0)	10	0.10
Belgian (10)	10	0.10
British (22)	68	0.66
Canadian (57)	107	1.03
Czech (0)	22	0.21
Danish (0)	47	0.45
Dutch (11)	76	0.73
Eastern European (13)	35	0.34
English (541)	2,075	20.01
European (59)	59	0.57
Finnish (9)	41	0.40
French, ex. Basque (82)	666	6.42
French Canadian (73)	212	2.04
German (113)	847	8.17
Greek (141)	214	2.06
Hungarian (22)	45	0.43
Irish (1,611)	4,309	41.55
Israeli (28)	28	0.27
Italian (691)	1,999	19.28
Lithuanian (56)	176	1.70
Norwegian (44)	85	0.82
Polish (84)	251	2.42
Portuguese (28)	189	1.82
Russian (30)	73	0.70
Scandinavian (36)	36	0.35
Scotch-Irish (82)	386	3.72
Scottish (59)	389	3.75
Swedish (44)	501	4.83
Swiss (0)	10	0.10
Welsh (0)	13	0.13

Hispanic Origin	Population	%
Hispanic or Latino (of any race)	128	1.22
Central American, ex. Mexican	8	0.08
Costa Rican	2	0.02
Guatemalan	3	0.03
Honduran	2	0.02
Panamanian	1	0.01
Cuban	19	0.18
Dominican Republic	2	0.02
Mexican	29	0.28
Puerto Rican	22	0.21
South American	33	0.31
Argentinean	1	0.01
Chilean	1	0.01
Colombian	20	0.19
Ecuadorian	6	0.06
Paraguayan	2	0.02
Peruvian	1	0.01
Venezuelan	2	0.02
Other Hispanic or Latino	15	0.14

Race*	Population	%
African-American/Black (64)	92	0.88
Not Hispanic (63)	89	0.85
Hispanic (1)	3	0.03
American Indian/Alaska Native (8)	38	0.36
Not Hispanic (8)	37	0.35
Hispanic (0)	1	0.01
Apache (1)	1	0.01
Cherokee (0)	4	0.04
Choctaw (0)	1	0.01
Iroquois (2)	2	0.02
Asian (181)	241	2.29
Not Hispanic (181)	236	2.25
Hispanic (0)	5	0.05
Cambodian (2)	4	0.04
Chinese, ex. Taiwanese (72)	91	0.87
Filipino (26)	39	0.37
Indian (31)	36	0.34
Japanese (8)	22	0.21
Korean (28)	38	0.36
Malaysian (0)	4	0.04
Pakistani (1)	1	0.01
Taiwanese (1)	1	0.01
Thai (0)	3	0.03
Vietnamese (4)	13	0.12
White (10,114)	10,217	97.25
Not Hispanic (10,011)	10,103	96.16
Hispanic (103)	114	1.09

*Notes: † The Census 2010 population figure is used to calculate the percentages in the Hispanic Origin and Race categories. Ancestry percentages are based on the 2006-2010 American Community Survey population (not shown); ‡ Numbers in parentheses indicate the number of people reporting a single ancestry; * Numbers in parentheses indicate the number of persons reporting this race alone, not in combination with any other race; Please refer to the Explanation of Data for more information.*

Norwood

Place Type: CDP/Town
County: Norfolk
Population: 28,602†

Ancestry‡	Population	%
African, Sub-Saharan (292)	300	1.06
African (278)	286	1.01
Nigerian (14)	14	0.05
Albanian (192)	220	0.78
American (595)	595	2.10
Arab (730)	1,066	3.76
Arab (78)	117	0.41
Egyptian (30)	30	0.11
Lebanese (577)	742	2.61
Palestinian (0)	57	0.20
Syrian (31)	92	0.32
Other Arab (14)	28	0.10
Armenian (0)	31	0.11
Australian (0)	9	0.03
Austrian (0)	27	0.10
Brazilian (495)	558	1.97
British (42)	101	0.36
Canadian (82)	283	1.00
Celtic (40)	40	0.14
Croatian (0)	17	0.06
Czech (0)	74	0.26
Danish (11)	82	0.29
Dutch (0)	97	0.34
Eastern European (121)	121	0.43
English (545)	2,554	9.00
European (158)	184	0.65
Finnish (68)	81	0.29
French, ex. Basque (92)	1,147	4.04
French Canadian (219)	729	2.57
German (538)	1,705	6.01
German Russian (55)	55	0.19
Greek (355)	513	1.81
Hungarian (0)	16	0.06
Irish (5,063)	10,354	36.49
Italian (2,008)	4,934	17.39
Lithuanian (253)	584	2.06
Northern European (13)	13	0.05
Norwegian (29)	137	0.48
Polish (251)	793	2.79
Portuguese (854)	1,192	4.20
Romanian (0)	48	0.17
Russian (226)	453	1.60
Scandinavian (8)	43	0.15
Scotch-Irish (255)	675	2.38
Scottish (245)	827	2.91
Slovak (16)	27	0.10
Swedish (263)	665	2.34
Swiss (0)	33	0.12
Ukrainian (24)	80	0.28
Welsh (0)	19	0.07
West Indian, ex. Hispanic (249)	280	0.99
British West Indian (15)	15	0.05
Haitian (155)	186	0.66
Jamaican (56)	56	0.20
West Indian (23)	23	0.08

Hispanic Origin	Population	%
Hispanic or Latino (of any race)	1,227	4.29
Central American, ex. Mexican	223	0.78
Costa Rican	10	0.03
Guatemalan	70	0.24
Honduran	44	0.15
Nicaraguan	2	0.01
Panamanian	6	0.02
Salvadoran	88	0.31
Other Central American	3	0.01
Cuban	51	0.18
Dominican Republic	130	0.45
Mexican	131	0.46
Puerto Rican	416	1.45
South American	134	0.47
Argentinean	3	0.01
Bolivian	4	0.01
Chilean	7	0.02
Colombian	53	0.19
Ecuadorian	21	0.07
Paraguayan	1	<0.01
Peruvian	25	0.09
Venezuelan	18	0.06
Other South American	2	0.01
Other Hispanic or Latino	142	0.50

Race*	Population	%
African-American/Black (1,483)	1,666	5.82
Not Hispanic (1,392)	1,528	5.34
Hispanic (91)	138	0.48
American Indian/Alaska Native (51)	133	0.47
Not Hispanic (41)	109	0.38
Hispanic (10)	24	0.08
Blackfeet (0)	2	0.01
Cherokee (1)	7	0.02
Chippewa (3)	3	0.01
Choctaw (0)	1	<0.01
Iroquois (0)	3	0.01
Kiowa (0)	1	<0.01
Mexican American Ind. (3)	3	0.01
Sioux (0)	2	0.01
South American Ind. (2)	2	0.01
Asian (1,698)	1,879	6.57
Not Hispanic (1,695)	1,866	6.52
Hispanic (3)	13	0.05
Bangladeshi (8)	10	0.03
Burmese (7)	7	0.02
Cambodian (4)	4	0.01
Chinese, ex. Taiwanese (244)	296	1.03
Filipino (82)	110	0.38
Indian (1,121)	1,149	4.02
Indonesian (0)	1	<0.01
Japanese (12)	21	0.07
Korean (69)	81	0.28
Laotian (12)	12	0.04
Malaysian (0)	2	0.01
Nepalese (16)	16	0.06
Pakistani (17)	18	0.06
Sri Lankan (3)	5	0.02
Taiwanese (7)	10	0.03
Thai (10)	14	0.05
Vietnamese (57)	66	0.23
Hawaii Native/Pacific Islander (8)	34	0.12
Not Hispanic (5)	28	0.10
Hispanic (3)	6	0.02
Guamanian/Chamorro (2)	3	0.01
Native Hawaiian (4)	10	0.03
Samoan (0)	1	<0.01
White (24,345)	24,759	86.56
Not Hispanic (23,642)	23,980	83.84
Hispanic (703)	779	2.72

Orange

Place Type: Town
County: Franklin
Population: 7,839†

Ancestry‡	Population	%
African, Sub-Saharan (25)	25	0.32
Ghanaian (25)	25	0.32
American (497)	497	6.38
Armenian (0)	14	0.18
Belgian (0)	12	0.15
Brazilian (28)	28	0.36
British (0)	32	0.41
Canadian (40)	81	1.04
Czechoslovakian (0)	12	0.15
Danish (0)	11	0.14
Dutch (33)	248	3.18
Eastern European (14)	14	0.18
English (448)	1,562	20.04
European (89)	89	1.14
Finnish (14)	45	0.58
French, ex. Basque (482)	1,813	23.26
French Canadian (277)	484	6.21
German (100)	747	9.58
Greek (12)	12	0.15
Irish (432)	1,844	23.66
Italian (88)	912	11.70
Lithuanian (82)	128	1.64
Norwegian (0)	87	1.12
Polish (106)	361	4.63
Portuguese (27)	99	1.27
Scotch-Irish (13)	74	0.95
Scottish (146)	357	4.58
Swedish (65)	267	3.43
Welsh (13)	13	0.17

Hispanic Origin	Population	%
Hispanic or Latino (of any race)	222	2.83
Central American, ex. Mexican	7	0.09
Costa Rican	1	0.01
Guatemalan	5	0.06
Honduran	1	0.01
Cuban	17	0.22
Dominican Republic	10	0.13
Mexican	25	0.32
Puerto Rican	140	1.79
South American	7	0.09
Argentinean	3	0.04
Ecuadorian	1	0.01
Venezuelan	3	0.04
Other Hispanic or Latino	16	0.20

Race*	Population	%
African-American/Black (81)	139	1.77
Not Hispanic (75)	123	1.57
Hispanic (6)	16	0.20
American Indian/Alaska Native (31)	77	0.98
Not Hispanic (29)	73	0.93
Hispanic (2)	4	0.05
Blackfeet (1)	6	0.08
Canadian/French Am. Ind. (6)	6	0.08
Cherokee (1)	4	0.05
Iroquois (5)	9	0.11
Mexican American Ind. (1)	3	0.04
Asian (74)	87	1.11
Not Hispanic (74)	87	1.11
Cambodian (4)	11	0.14
Chinese, ex. Taiwanese (6)	7	0.09
Filipino (6)	13	0.17
Indian (19)	19	0.24
Indonesian (1)	1	0.01
Japanese (3)	5	0.06
Korean (5)	6	0.08
Laotian (1)	1	0.01
Nepalese (8)	8	0.10
Pakistani (9)	9	0.11
Thai (1)	4	0.05
Vietnamese (2)	10	0.13
Hawaii Native/Pacific Islander (1)	12	0.15
Not Hispanic (1)	12	0.15
Guamanian/Chamorro (1)	9	0.11
Native Hawaiian (0)	1	0.01
Samoan (0)	1	0.01
White (7,461)	7,591	96.84
Not Hispanic (7,309)	7,421	94.67
Hispanic (152)	170	2.17

Oxford

Place Type: Town
County: Worcester
Population: 13,709†

Ancestry‡	Population	%
African, Sub-Saharan (0)	40	0.29
African (0)	20	0.15
Ugandan (0)	20	0.15
American (504)	504	3.68
Arab (46)	161	1.18
Lebanese (30)	70	0.51
Syrian (16)	91	0.66
Armenian (35)	111	0.81
Austrian (16)	16	0.12
Brazilian (0)	51	0.37

*Notes: † The Census 2010 population figure is used to calculate the percentages in the Hispanic Origin and Race categories. Ancestry percentages are based on the 2006-2010 American Community Survey population (not shown); ‡ Numbers in parentheses indicate the number of people reporting a single ancestry; * Numbers in parentheses indicate the number of persons reporting this race alone, not in combination with any other race; Please refer to the Explanation of Data for more information.*

British (0)	80	0.58
Canadian (20)	62	0.45
Croatian (0)	18	0.13
Czech (0)	30	0.22
Czechoslovakian (10)	10	0.07
Danish (16)	53	0.39
Dutch (10)	119	0.87
English (333)	2,160	15.78
European (127)	127	0.93
Finnish (34)	94	0.69
French, ex. Basque (775)	3,917	28.61
French Canadian (421)	880	6.43
German (76)	869	6.35
Greek (174)	329	2.40
Guyanese (7)	7	0.05
Hungarian (26)	40	0.29
Irish (626)	3,649	26.65
Italian (517)	1,902	13.89
Lithuanian (115)	343	2.51
Norwegian (0)	67	0.49
Polish (439)	1,619	11.83
Portuguese (113)	349	2.55
Romanian (0)	14	0.10
Russian (14)	45	0.33
Scotch-Irish (160)	298	2.18
Scottish (10)	429	3.13
Slavic (0)	13	0.09
Slovak (0)	16	0.12
Swedish (139)	788	5.76
Swiss (0)	14	0.10
Ukrainian (0)	26	0.19
Welsh (12)	81	0.59
West Indian, ex. Hispanic (8)	8	0.06
West Indian (8)	8	0.06

Hispanic Origin	Population	%
Hispanic or Latino (of any race)	464	3.38
Central American, ex. Mexican	15	0.11
Costa Rican	4	0.03
Guatemalan	2	0.01
Salvadoran	9	0.07
Cuban	7	0.05
Dominican Republic	15	0.11
Mexican	32	0.23
Puerto Rican	323	2.36
South American	40	0.29
Argentinean	2	0.01
Bolivian	2	0.01
Chilean	4	0.03
Colombian	14	0.10
Ecuadorian	13	0.09
Peruvian	4	0.03
Venezuelan	1	0.01
Other Hispanic or Latino	32	0.23

Race*	Population	%
African-American/Black (143)	219	1.60
Not Hispanic (134)	199	1.45
Hispanic (9)	20	0.15
American Indian/Alaska Native (21)	81	0.59
Not Hispanic (16)	70	0.51
Hispanic (5)	11	0.08
Blackfeet (2)	6	0.04
Cherokee (0)	5	0.04
Choctaw (0)	1	0.01
Cree (0)	2	0.01
Iroquois (3)	4	0.03
Seminole (0)	1	0.01
Shoshone (0)	3	0.02
Asian (142)	181	1.32
Not Hispanic (141)	180	1.31
Hispanic (1)	1	0.01
Cambodian (3)	3	0.02
Chinese, ex. Taiwanese (26)	32	0.23
Filipino (9)	25	0.18
Indian (23)	30	0.22
Japanese (2)	4	0.03
Korean (7)	14	0.10
Laotian (7)	10	0.07
Pakistani (6)	7	0.05
Sri Lankan (1)	1	0.01
Thai (1)	4	0.03
Vietnamese (44)	48	0.35
Hawaii Native/Pacific Islander (3)	13	0.09
Not Hispanic (2)	6	0.04
Hispanic (1)	7	0.05
Guamanian/Chamorro (2)	2	0.01
Native Hawaiian (1)	2	0.01
Tongan (0)	1	0.01
White (13,066)	13,239	96.57
Not Hispanic (12,791)	12,934	94.35
Hispanic (275)	305	2.22

Palmer Town

Place Type: City
County: Hampden
Population: 12,140†

Ancestry‡	Population	%
Albanian (12)	26	0.21
American (316)	316	2.59
Arab (27)	43	0.35
Egyptian (27)	27	0.22
Lebanese (0)	16	0.13
Armenian (0)	61	0.50
Austrian (6)	6	0.05
British (23)	218	1.79
Canadian (127)	159	1.30
Croatian (18)	18	0.15
Czech (0)	127	1.04
Czechoslovakian (15)	44	0.36
Danish (18)	59	0.48
Dutch (0)	55	0.45
English (327)	1,354	11.10
European (10)	10	0.08
Finnish (0)	43	0.35
French, ex. Basque (712)	2,673	21.92
French Canadian (407)	914	7.49
German (171)	1,270	10.41
Greek (24)	78	0.64
Hungarian (0)	16	0.13
Irish (790)	2,630	21.56
Italian (418)	1,194	9.79
Lithuanian (21)	70	0.57
Pennsylvania German (0)	14	0.11
Polish (1,594)	3,106	25.47
Portuguese (164)	397	3.26
Romanian (0)	7	0.06
Russian (0)	57	0.47
Scandinavian (0)	28	0.23
Scotch-Irish (100)	300	2.46
Scottish (55)	304	2.49
Swedish (6)	193	1.58
Turkish (0)	16	0.13
Ukrainian (0)	14	0.11

Hispanic Origin	Population	%
Hispanic or Latino (of any race)	291	2.40
Central American, ex. Mexican	15	0.12
Costa Rican	1	0.01
Guatemalan	2	0.02
Honduran	2	0.02
Nicaraguan	2	0.02
Panamanian	2	0.02
Salvadoran	6	0.05
Cuban	9	0.07
Mexican	23	0.19
Puerto Rican	202	1.66
South American	12	0.10
Argentinean	3	0.02
Colombian	9	0.07
Other Hispanic or Latino	30	0.25

Race*	Population	%
African-American/Black (137)	213	1.75
Not Hispanic (122)	186	1.53
Hispanic (15)	27	0.22
American Indian/Alaska Native (24)	93	0.77
Not Hispanic (20)	82	0.68
Hispanic (4)	11	0.09
Apache (0)	1	0.01
Blackfeet (0)	18	0.15
Canadian/French Am. Ind. (0)	3	0.02
Cherokee (5)	10	0.08
Chippewa (0)	2	0.02
Creek (0)	1	0.01
Iroquois (0)	1	0.01
Spanish American Ind. (1)	1	0.01
Asian (107)	135	1.11
Not Hispanic (107)	134	1.10
Hispanic (0)	1	0.01
Cambodian (9)	9	0.07
Chinese, ex. Taiwanese (44)	53	0.44
Filipino (5)	9	0.07
Indian (21)	28	0.23
Japanese (3)	12	0.10
Korean (3)	7	0.06
Laotian (1)	3	0.02
Pakistani (14)	16	0.13
Vietnamese (2)	4	0.03
Hawaii Native/Pacific Islander (0)	5	0.04
Not Hispanic (0)	2	0.02
Hispanic (0)	3	0.02
Guamanian/Chamorro (0)	1	0.01
Native Hawaiian (0)	3	0.02
Samoan (0)	1	0.01
White (11,599)	11,798	97.18
Not Hispanic (11,446)	11,591	95.48
Hispanic (153)	207	1.71

Peabody

Place Type: City
County: Essex
Population: 51,251†

Ancestry‡	Population	%
African, Sub-Saharan (120)	120	0.24
Ethiopian (18)	18	0.04
Kenyan (102)	102	0.20
Albanian (109)	148	0.29
American (1,457)	1,457	2.89
Arab (109)	339	0.67
Egyptian (10)	37	0.07
Jordanian (49)	49	0.10
Lebanese (44)	209	0.41
Moroccan (0)	12	0.02
Other Arab (6)	32	0.06
Armenian (73)	151	0.30
Australian (17)	20	0.04
Austrian (52)	202	0.40
Belgian (11)	36	0.07
Brazilian (1,436)	1,505	2.98
British (72)	112	0.22
Canadian (221)	475	0.94
Celtic (0)	11	0.02
Czech (14)	52	0.10
Danish (11)	62	0.12
Dutch (77)	183	0.36
Eastern European (130)	130	0.26
English (1,345)	5,203	10.31
European (218)	218	0.43
Finnish (86)	276	0.55
French, ex. Basque (614)	3,579	7.09
French Canadian (1,065)	2,268	4.50
German (286)	1,800	3.57
Greek (2,426)	3,419	6.78
Hungarian (14)	149	0.30
Irish (4,805)	13,085	25.93
Italian (4,672)	11,616	23.02
Latvian (9)	20	0.04
Lithuanian (146)	509	1.01
Norwegian (16)	127	0.25
Polish (1,328)	3,221	6.38
Portuguese (2,150)	3,541	7.02
Romanian (13)	54	0.11
Russian (505)	999	1.98
Scotch-Irish (427)	1,083	2.15
Scottish (326)	1,562	3.10

*Notes: † The Census 2010 population figure is used to calculate the percentages in the Hispanic Origin and Race categories. Ancestry percentages are based on the 2006-2010 American Community Survey population (not shown); ‡ Numbers in parentheses indicate the number of people reporting a single ancestry; * Numbers in parentheses indicate the number of persons reporting this race alone, not in combination with any other race; Please refer to the Explanation of Data for more information.*

Ancestry (continued)	Population	%
Slovak (11)	11	0.02
Swedish (213)	725	1.44
Swiss (0)	84	0.17
Ukrainian (200)	263	0.52
Welsh (0)	86	0.17
West Indian, ex. Hispanic (143)	159	0.32
Barbadian (20)	20	0.04
British West Indian (10)	10	0.02
Haitian (72)	72	0.14
Jamaican (20)	36	0.07
West Indian (21)	21	0.04
Yugoslavian (50)	50	0.10

Hispanic Origin	Population	%
Hispanic or Latino (of any race)	3,212	6.27
Central American, ex. Mexican	170	0.33
Costa Rican	20	0.04
Guatemalan	71	0.14
Honduran	39	0.08
Nicaraguan	4	0.01
Panamanian	6	0.01
Salvadoran	28	0.05
Other Central American	2	<0.01
Cuban	61	0.12
Dominican Republic	1,405	2.74
Mexican	147	0.29
Puerto Rican	686	1.34
South American	222	0.43
Argentinean	12	0.02
Bolivian	2	<0.01
Chilean	21	0.04
Colombian	92	0.18
Ecuadorian	36	0.07
Paraguayan	2	<0.01
Peruvian	33	0.06
Uruguayan	3	0.01
Venezuelan	14	0.03
Other South American	7	0.01
Other Hispanic or Latino	521	1.02

Race*	Population	%
African-American/Black (1,206)	1,529	2.98
Not Hispanic (970)	1,210	2.36
Hispanic (236)	319	0.62
American Indian/Alaska Native (91)	199	0.39
Not Hispanic (45)	135	0.26
Hispanic (46)	64	0.12
Apache (0)	1	<0.01
Blackfeet (0)	5	0.01
Canadian/French Am. Ind. (1)	1	<0.01
Central American Ind. (0)	1	<0.01
Cherokee (7)	22	0.04
Chippewa (4)	7	0.01
Creek (0)	2	<0.01
Iroquois (4)	6	0.01
Lumbee (1)	1	<0.01
Mexican American Ind. (6)	6	0.01
Osage (0)	2	<0.01
South American Ind. (4)	10	0.02
Asian (956)	1,120	2.19
Not Hispanic (940)	1,088	2.12
Hispanic (16)	32	0.06
Bangladeshi (11)	11	0.02
Cambodian (80)	100	0.20
Chinese, ex. Taiwanese (194)	251	0.49
Filipino (133)	176	0.34
Indian (204)	234	0.46
Indonesian (3)	8	0.02
Japanese (38)	52	0.10
Korean (77)	103	0.20
Laotian (11)	12	0.02
Malaysian (6)	8	0.02
Nepalese (4)	4	0.01
Pakistani (17)	17	0.03
Sri Lankan (3)	4	0.01
Taiwanese (3)	4	0.01
Thai (19)	22	0.04
Vietnamese (104)	121	0.24
Hawaii Native/Pacific Islander (5)	54	0.11
Not Hispanic (5)	26	0.05
Hispanic (0)	28	0.05
Guamanian/Chamorro (2)	4	0.01
Native Hawaiian (0)	4	0.01
Samoan (0)	2	<0.01
White (46,318)	47,049	91.80
Not Hispanic (44,934)	45,475	88.73
Hispanic (1,384)	1,574	3.07

Pembroke

Place Type: Town
County: Plymouth
Population: 17,837†

Ancestry‡	Population	%
African, Sub-Saharan (0)	140	0.79
African (0)	140	0.79
Albanian (0)	79	0.45
American (639)	639	3.62
Arab (86)	151	0.86
Egyptian (10)	10	0.06
Lebanese (19)	68	0.39
Moroccan (17)	33	0.19
Other Arab (40)	40	0.23
Armenian (53)	175	0.99
Austrian (0)	20	0.11
Belgian (0)	29	0.16
Brazilian (12)	12	0.07
British (56)	101	0.57
Bulgarian (0)	10	0.06
Canadian (66)	342	1.94
Czech (0)	42	0.24
Czechoslovakian (12)	41	0.23
Danish (13)	24	0.14
Dutch (44)	181	1.02
Eastern European (0)	11	0.06
English (540)	2,683	15.19
European (59)	75	0.42
Finnish (63)	340	1.93
French, ex. Basque (102)	1,114	6.31
French Canadian (144)	682	3.86
German (399)	1,785	10.11
Greek (28)	76	0.43
Hungarian (19)	33	0.19
Iranian (6)	13	0.07
Irish (2,846)	7,836	44.37
Italian (834)	3,292	18.64
Latvian (0)	23	0.13
Lithuanian (81)	337	1.91
Northern European (17)	17	0.10
Norwegian (51)	122	0.69
Polish (177)	766	4.34
Portuguese (73)	443	2.51
Russian (90)	267	1.51
Scandinavian (12)	51	0.29
Scotch-Irish (360)	958	5.42
Scottish (221)	711	4.03
Swedish (62)	538	3.05
Swiss (0)	11	0.06
Ukrainian (9)	9	0.05
Welsh (60)	220	1.25
West Indian, ex. Hispanic (16)	156	0.88
Haitian (0)	140	0.79
West Indian (16)	16	0.09

Hispanic Origin	Population	%
Hispanic or Latino (of any race)	193	1.08
Central American, ex. Mexican	21	0.12
Costa Rican	5	0.03
Guatemalan	7	0.04
Honduran	2	0.01
Panamanian	2	0.01
Salvadoran	5	0.03
Cuban	5	0.03
Dominican Republic	14	0.08
Mexican	38	0.21
Puerto Rican	41	0.23
South American	40	0.22
Argentinean	9	0.05
Chilean	1	0.01
Colombian	10	0.06
Ecuadorian	10	0.06
Paraguayan	1	0.01
Peruvian	6	0.03
Venezuelan	3	0.02
Other Hispanic or Latino	34	0.19

Race*	Population	%
African-American/Black (109)	170	0.95
Not Hispanic (105)	163	0.91
Hispanic (4)	7	0.04
American Indian/Alaska Native (29)	95	0.53
Not Hispanic (24)	86	0.48
Hispanic (5)	9	0.05
Apache (0)	1	0.01
Blackfeet (0)	9	0.05
Cherokee (0)	6	0.03
Chickasaw (0)	1	0.01
Iroquois (0)	5	0.03
Mexican American Ind. (1)	3	0.02
Navajo (1)	1	0.01
Potawatomi (0)	2	0.01
Pueblo (0)	3	0.02
Seminole (0)	2	0.01
Sioux (1)	1	0.01
Yaqui (0)	3	0.02
Asian (170)	214	1.20
Not Hispanic (167)	209	1.17
Hispanic (3)	5	0.03
Cambodian (1)	5	0.03
Chinese, ex. Taiwanese (55)	65	0.36
Filipino (8)	16	0.09
Indian (38)	48	0.27
Japanese (7)	12	0.07
Korean (11)	22	0.12
Laotian (2)	3	0.02
Pakistani (0)	2	0.01
Taiwanese (1)	1	0.01
Thai (10)	10	0.06
Vietnamese (24)	26	0.15
Hawaii Native/Pacific Islander (3)	3	0.02
Not Hispanic (3)	3	0.02
Guamanian/Chamorro (2)	2	0.01
Native Hawaiian (1)	1	0.01
White (17,274)	17,429	97.71
Not Hispanic (17,138)	17,287	96.92
Hispanic (136)	142	0.80

Pepperell

Place Type: Town
County: Middlesex
Population: 11,497†

Ancestry‡	Population	%
American (358)	358	3.17
Arab (0)	8	0.07
Syrian (0)	8	0.07
Armenian (8)	8	0.07
Austrian (0)	98	0.87
Basque (0)	10	0.09
Belgian (0)	11	0.10
British (40)	94	0.83
Canadian (48)	144	1.27
Czech (0)	23	0.20
Czechoslovakian (13)	61	0.54
Danish (7)	116	1.03
Dutch (34)	116	1.03
Eastern European (11)	11	0.10
English (517)	2,526	22.36
European (151)	159	1.41
Finnish (9)	54	0.48
French, ex. Basque (208)	1,283	11.35
French Canadian (287)	850	7.52
German (127)	932	8.25
Greek (114)	114	1.01
Hungarian (10)	34	0.30
Irish (1,093)	3,690	32.66
Italian (527)	1,854	16.41
Lithuanian (34)	234	2.07

*Notes: † The Census 2010 population figure is used to calculate the percentages in the Hispanic Origin and Race categories. Ancestry percentages are based on the 2006-2010 American Community Survey population (not shown); ‡ Numbers in parentheses indicate the number of people reporting a single ancestry; * Numbers in parentheses indicate the number of persons reporting this race alone, not in combination with any other race; Please refer to the Explanation of Data for more information.*

Norwegian (41)	137	1.21
Polish (137)	430	3.81
Portuguese (73)	159	1.41
Russian (42)	133	1.18
Scandinavian (0)	11	0.10
Scotch-Irish (226)	418	3.70
Scottish (106)	435	3.85
Slavic (0)	42	0.37
Swedish (107)	386	3.42
Swiss (23)	33	0.29
Ukrainian (31)	41	0.36
Welsh (10)	77	0.68
West Indian, ex. Hispanic (8)	15	0.13
Haitian (0)	7	0.06
Jamaican (8)	8	0.07
Yugoslavian (0)	35	0.31

Hispanic Origin	Population	%
Hispanic or Latino (of any race)	194	1.69
Central American, ex. Mexican	11	0.10
Guatemalan	3	0.03
Nicaraguan	1	0.01
Salvadoran	7	0.06
Cuban	10	0.09
Dominican Republic	10	0.09
Mexican	41	0.36
Puerto Rican	81	0.70
South American	25	0.22
Argentinean	2	0.02
Bolivian	9	0.08
Colombian	6	0.05
Paraguayan	4	0.03
Peruvian	2	0.02
Venezuelan	2	0.02
Other Hispanic or Latino	16	0.14

Race*	Population	%
African-American/Black (60)	104	0.90
Not Hispanic (50)	93	0.81
Hispanic (10)	11	0.10
American Indian/Alaska Native (20)	63	0.55
Not Hispanic (14)	53	0.46
Hispanic (6)	10	0.09
Blackfeet (0)	1	0.01
Cherokee (1)	4	0.03
Choctaw (0)	1	0.01
Iroquois (4)	4	0.03
Navajo (3)	5	0.04
Seminole (0)	1	0.01
Asian (134)	199	1.73
Not Hispanic (133)	196	1.70
Hispanic (1)	3	0.03
Cambodian (10)	16	0.14
Chinese, ex. Taiwanese (31)	47	0.41
Filipino (12)	32	0.28
Indian (29)	35	0.30
Indonesian (1)	1	0.01
Japanese (12)	38	0.33
Korean (7)	8	0.07
Laotian (6)	6	0.05
Nepalese (1)	2	0.02
Pakistani (5)	5	0.04
Thai (3)	6	0.05
Vietnamese (7)	14	0.12
Hawaii Native/Pacific Islander (2)	2	0.02
Hispanic (2)	2	0.02
Guamanian/Chamorro (2)	2	0.02
White (11,082)	11,231	97.69
Not Hispanic (10,946)	11,080	96.37
Hispanic (136)	151	1.31

Pittsfield

Place Type: City
County: Berkshire
Population: 44,737†

Ancestry‡	Population	%
African, Sub-Saharan (291)	407	0.91
African (196)	285	0.64
Cape Verdean (18)	45	0.10
Ghanaian (54)	54	0.12
Other Sub-Saharan African (23)	23	0.05
Albanian (0)	25	0.06
American (1,030)	1,030	2.30
Arab (221)	383	0.86
Lebanese (206)	333	0.74
Palestinian (0)	13	0.03
Syrian (9)	31	0.07
Other Arab (6)	6	0.01
Armenian (17)	89	0.20
Austrian (12)	113	0.25
Belgian (0)	6	0.01
Brazilian (149)	149	0.33
British (43)	83	0.19
Canadian (92)	229	0.51
Celtic (0)	17	0.04
Czech (18)	84	0.19
Danish (10)	146	0.33
Dutch (63)	813	1.82
Eastern European (70)	82	0.18
English (1,359)	6,239	13.93
European (106)	161	0.36
Finnish (64)	142	0.32
French, ex. Basque (993)	6,960	15.54
French Canadian (854)	2,303	5.14
German (979)	4,957	11.07
Greek (82)	264	0.59
Hungarian (39)	144	0.32
Irish (3,233)	12,239	27.33
Israeli (20)	54	0.12
Italian (3,367)	8,571	19.14
Lithuanian (23)	145	0.32
Norwegian (29)	177	0.40
Polish (1,189)	3,501	7.82
Portuguese (165)	668	1.49
Romanian (0)	11	0.02
Russian (232)	647	1.44
Scandinavian (43)	61	0.14
Scotch-Irish (176)	827	1.85
Scottish (208)	1,156	2.58
Slavic (0)	44	0.10
Slovak (0)	75	0.17
Swedish (69)	575	1.28
Swiss (176)	238	0.53
Turkish (32)	32	0.07
Ukrainian (88)	306	0.68
Welsh (29)	208	0.46
West Indian, ex. Hispanic (251)	473	1.06
Bahamian (0)	144	0.32
Haitian (9)	9	0.02
Jamaican (125)	203	0.45
Trinidadian/Tobagonian (117)	117	0.26
Yugoslavian (0)	10	0.02

Hispanic Origin	Population	%
Hispanic or Latino (of any race)	2,225	4.97
Central American, ex. Mexican	266	0.59
Costa Rican	4	0.01
Guatemalan	43	0.10
Honduran	21	0.05
Nicaraguan	5	0.01
Panamanian	14	0.03
Salvadoran	178	0.40
Other Central American	1	<0.01
Cuban	64	0.14
Dominican Republic	68	0.15
Mexican	315	0.70
Puerto Rican	881	1.97
South American	391	0.87
Argentinean	10	0.02
Bolivian	5	0.01
Chilean	6	0.01
Colombian	120	0.27
Ecuadorian	191	0.43
Paraguayan	2	<0.01
Peruvian	53	0.12
Venezuelan	1	<0.01
Other South American	3	0.01
Other Hispanic or Latino	240	0.54

Race*	Population	%
African-American/Black (2,369)	3,286	7.35
Not Hispanic (2,214)	3,028	6.77
Hispanic (155)	258	0.58
American Indian/Alaska Native (90)	313	0.70
Not Hispanic (77)	286	0.64
Hispanic (13)	27	0.06
Apache (1)	7	0.02
Blackfeet (5)	22	0.05
Canadian/French Am. Ind. (4)	6	0.01
Central American Ind. (3)	6	0.01
Cherokee (5)	47	0.11
Cheyenne (1)	1	<0.01
Chippewa (0)	1	<0.01
Choctaw (0)	3	0.01
Comanche (0)	5	0.01
Cree (2)	5	0.01
Delaware (1)	2	<0.01
Iroquois (3)	15	0.03
Navajo (5)	5	0.01
Seminole (1)	1	<0.01
Sioux (3)	12	0.03
South American Ind. (1)	3	0.01
Spanish American Ind. (0)	1	<0.01
Asian (550)	727	1.63
Not Hispanic (550)	715	1.60
Hispanic (0)	12	0.03
Bangladeshi (1)	1	<0.01
Cambodian (19)	23	0.05
Chinese, ex. Taiwanese (125)	169	0.38
Filipino (38)	58	0.13
Indian (156)	186	0.42
Indonesian (7)	11	0.02
Japanese (13)	25	0.06
Korean (47)	60	0.13
Laotian (0)	2	<0.01
Malaysian (5)	5	0.01
Nepalese (1)	2	<0.01
Pakistani (37)	37	0.08
Sri Lankan (7)	7	0.02
Taiwanese (1)	3	0.01
Thai (14)	30	0.07
Vietnamese (61)	84	0.19
Hawaii Native/Pacific Islander (7)	48	0.11
Not Hispanic (4)	33	0.07
Hispanic (3)	15	0.03
Fijian (1)	2	<0.01
Guamanian/Chamorro (1)	1	<0.01
Native Hawaiian (3)	14	0.03
Samoan (0)	4	0.01
White (39,516)	40,747	91.08
Not Hispanic (38,437)	39,490	88.27
Hispanic (1,079)	1,257	2.81

Plainville

Place Type: Town
County: Norfolk
Population: 8,264†

Ancestry‡	Population	%
African, Sub-Saharan (45)	45	0.56
Cape Verdean (14)	14	0.17
Zimbabwean (31)	31	0.38
American (372)	372	4.60
Arab (152)	246	3.04
Egyptian (36)	36	0.44
Lebanese (116)	173	2.14
Syrian (0)	37	0.46
Austrian (0)	33	0.41
Canadian (31)	80	0.99
Czech (41)	120	1.48
Danish (0)	42	0.52
Dutch (0)	10	0.12
English (420)	1,270	15.70
European (12)	12	0.15
Finnish (0)	43	0.53
French, ex. Basque (135)	973	12.03
French Canadian (397)	618	7.64

SECTION TWO

*Notes: † The Census 2010 population figure is used to calculate the percentages in the Hispanic Origin and Race categories. Ancestry percentages are based on the 2006-2010 American Community Survey population (not shown); ‡ Numbers in parentheses indicate the number of people reporting a single ancestry; * Numbers in parentheses indicate the number of persons reporting this race alone, not in combination with any other race; Please refer to the Explanation of Data for more information.*

German (226)	978	12.09
Greek (25)	114	1.41
Irish (751)	2,342	28.95
Italian (360)	1,594	19.70
Lithuanian (0)	69	0.85
Norwegian (14)	53	0.66
Polish (73)	326	4.03
Portuguese (52)	91	1.12
Russian (23)	95	1.17
Scotch-Irish (176)	290	3.58
Scottish (37)	355	4.39
Slovak (0)	14	0.17
Swedish (0)	135	1.67
Ukrainian (0)	11	0.14
Welsh (0)	57	0.70
West Indian, ex. Hispanic (34)	44	0.54
Haitian (18)	18	0.22
Jamaican (16)	26	0.32
Yugoslavian (0)	15	0.19

Hispanic Origin	Population	%
Hispanic or Latino (of any race)	147	1.78
Central American, ex. Mexican	19	0.23
Guatemalan	8	0.10
Honduran	2	0.02
Panamanian	2	0.02
Salvadoran	7	0.08
Cuban	7	0.08
Dominican Republic	9	0.11
Mexican	28	0.34
Puerto Rican	39	0.47
South American	23	0.28
Argentinean	2	0.02
Chilean	1	0.01
Colombian	13	0.16
Ecuadorian	1	0.01
Paraguayan	1	0.01
Venezuelan	5	0.06
Other Hispanic or Latino	22	0.27

Race*	Population	%
African-American/Black (88)	115	1.39
Not Hispanic (80)	104	1.26
Hispanic (8)	11	0.13
American Indian/Alaska Native (12)	36	0.44
Not Hispanic (9)	31	0.38
Hispanic (3)	5	0.06
Blackfeet (0)	1	0.01
Cherokee (0)	4	0.05
Choctaw (1)	1	0.01
Iroquois (0)	4	0.05
Navajo (1)	1	0.01
Sioux (0)	1	0.01
Ute (0)	1	0.01
Asian (258)	281	3.40
Not Hispanic (257)	280	3.39
Hispanic (1)	1	0.01
Bangladeshi (4)	4	0.05
Chinese, ex. Taiwanese (59)	60	0.73
Filipino (9)	9	0.11
Indian (146)	152	1.84
Indonesian (6)	6	0.07
Japanese (2)	6	0.07
Korean (8)	11	0.13
Malaysian (5)	5	0.06
Pakistani (0)	1	0.01
Taiwanese (1)	2	0.02
Thai (4)	13	0.16
Vietnamese (9)	10	0.12
White (7,785)	7,868	95.21
Not Hispanic (7,691)	7,763	93.94
Hispanic (94)	105	1.27

Plymouth

Place Type: Town
County: Plymouth
Population: 56,468†

Ancestry‡	Population	%
African, Sub-Saharan (461)	761	1.37
African (125)	180	0.32
Cape Verdean (329)	574	1.03
Other Sub-Saharan African (7)	7	0.01
Albanian (38)	53	0.10
American (2,693)	2,693	4.84
Arab (214)	404	0.73
Arab (38)	38	0.07
Egyptian (41)	55	0.10
Lebanese (65)	203	0.37
Syrian (61)	87	0.16
Other Arab (9)	21	0.04
Armenian (63)	149	0.27
Austrian (0)	76	0.14
Brazilian (698)	698	1.26
British (133)	223	0.40
Bulgarian (0)	24	0.04
Canadian (234)	555	1.00
Celtic (8)	8	0.01
Croatian (0)	35	0.06
Czech (19)	121	0.22
Czechoslovakian (9)	89	0.16
Danish (0)	142	0.26
Dutch (55)	494	0.89
Eastern European (87)	87	0.16
English (3,570)	10,868	19.54
European (150)	150	0.27
Finnish (131)	394	0.71
French, ex. Basque (916)	3,698	6.65
French Canadian (556)	2,035	3.66
German (857)	4,777	8.59
Greek (183)	405	0.73
Hungarian (20)	161	0.29
Irish (7,955)	18,408	33.10
Italian (3,947)	9,953	17.90
Latvian (12)	49	0.09
Lithuanian (71)	294	0.53
Northern European (86)	86	0.15
Norwegian (238)	441	0.79
Pennsylvania German (13)	13	0.02
Polish (533)	1,988	3.58
Portuguese (1,440)	3,065	5.51
Romanian (30)	78	0.14
Russian (153)	377	0.68
Scandinavian (52)	103	0.19
Scotch-Irish (536)	1,787	3.21
Scottish (563)	1,951	3.51
Serbian (0)	7	0.01
Slovak (0)	14	0.03
Slovene (0)	7	0.01
Swedish (309)	1,468	2.64
Swiss (22)	131	0.24
Ukrainian (113)	151	0.27
Welsh (0)	113	0.20
West Indian, ex. Hispanic (134)	144	0.26
Bahamian (0)	10	0.02
British West Indian (9)	9	0.02
Haitian (93)	93	0.17
Jamaican (25)	25	0.04
West Indian (7)	7	0.01

Hispanic Origin	Population	%
Hispanic or Latino (of any race)	1,030	1.82
Central American, ex. Mexican	63	0.11
Costa Rican	13	0.02
Guatemalan	23	0.04
Honduran	6	0.01
Nicaraguan	6	0.01
Panamanian	4	0.01
Salvadoran	10	0.02
Other Central American	1	<0.01
Cuban	36	0.06
Dominican Republic	42	0.07
Mexican	299	0.53
Puerto Rican	322	0.57
South American	123	0.22
Argentinean	10	0.02
Bolivian	3	0.01
Chilean	17	0.03
Colombian	62	0.11
Ecuadorian	10	0.02
Paraguayan	1	<0.01
Peruvian	9	0.02
Uruguayan	1	<0.01
Venezuelan	4	0.01
Other South American	6	0.01
Other Hispanic or Latino	145	0.26

Race*	Population	%
African-American/Black (1,147)	1,513	2.68
Not Hispanic (1,106)	1,453	2.57
Hispanic (41)	60	0.11
American Indian/Alaska Native (193)	457	0.81
Not Hispanic (175)	421	0.75
Hispanic (18)	36	0.06
Apache (0)	2	<0.01
Blackfeet (2)	12	0.02
Canadian/French Am. Ind. (3)	6	0.01
Cherokee (15)	51	0.09
Chickasaw (0)	1	<0.01
Chippewa (0)	4	0.01
Choctaw (4)	4	0.01
Comanche (2)	2	<0.01
Cree (1)	1	<0.01
Creek (1)	1	<0.01
Hopi (1)	1	<0.01
Iroquois (7)	28	0.05
Lumbee (2)	3	0.01
Mexican American Ind. (0)	1	<0.01
Navajo (0)	4	0.01
Osage (1)	2	<0.01
Seminole (1)	4	0.01
Shoshone (0)	3	0.01
Sioux (3)	8	0.01
South American Ind. (0)	4	0.01
Ute (0)	1	<0.01
Yaqui (0)	1	<0.01
Asian (516)	753	1.33
Not Hispanic (514)	735	1.30
Hispanic (2)	18	0.03
Bangladeshi (2)	2	<0.01
Cambodian (3)	5	0.01
Chinese, ex. Taiwanese (109)	164	0.29
Filipino (77)	127	0.22
Indian (85)	103	0.18
Indonesian (3)	6	0.01
Japanese (22)	62	0.11
Korean (64)	96	0.17
Laotian (12)	17	0.03
Nepalese (20)	22	0.04
Pakistani (18)	19	0.03
Taiwanese (0)	3	0.01
Thai (15)	24	0.04
Vietnamese (53)	71	0.13
Hawaii Native/Pacific Islander (22)	51	0.09
Not Hispanic (22)	47	0.08
Hispanic (0)	4	0.01
Fijian (1)	1	<0.01
Guamanian/Chamorro (7)	8	0.01
Marshallese (2)	3	0.01
Native Hawaiian (4)	14	0.02
Samoan (0)	5	0.01
White (52,955)	53,824	95.32
Not Hispanic (52,238)	53,048	93.94
Hispanic (717)	776	1.37

Quincy

Place Type: City
County: Norfolk
Population: 92,271†

Ancestry‡	Population	%
African, Sub-Saharan (523)	659	0.73
African (109)	148	0.16
Cape Verdean (189)	262	0.29
Ethiopian (15)	15	0.02
Kenyan (17)	17	0.02
Nigerian (46)	46	0.05

*Notes: † The Census 2010 population figure is used to calculate the percentages in the Hispanic Origin and Race categories. Ancestry percentages are based on the 2006-2010 American Community Survey population (not shown); ‡ Numbers in parentheses indicate the number of people reporting a single ancestry; * Numbers in parentheses indicate the number of persons reporting this race alone, not in combination with any other race; Please refer to the Explanation of Data for more information.*

Ancestry	Population	%
Somalian (125)	125	0.14
South African (0)	24	0.03
Other Sub-Saharan African (22)	22	0.02
Albanian (873)	958	1.06
American (1,497)	1,497	1.65
Arab (1,283)	1,614	1.78
Arab (0)	43	0.05
Egyptian (248)	248	0.27
Iraqi (58)	58	0.06
Jordanian (37)	37	0.04
Lebanese (243)	428	0.47
Moroccan (438)	465	0.51
Palestinian (14)	14	0.02
Syrian (15)	42	0.05
Other Arab (230)	279	0.31
Armenian (51)	252	0.28
Assyrian/Chaldean/Syriac (0)	9	0.01
Australian (0)	29	0.03
Austrian (83)	202	0.22
Belgian (63)	187	0.21
Brazilian (924)	949	1.05
British (130)	224	0.25
Canadian (260)	1,024	1.13
Celtic (11)	11	0.01
Croatian (0)	12	0.01
Czech (22)	144	0.16
Czechoslovakian (11)	16	0.02
Danish (24)	68	0.07
Dutch (41)	312	0.34
Eastern European (29)	29	0.03
English (1,252)	6,902	7.60
European (443)	476	0.52
Finnish (124)	357	0.39
French, ex. Basque (669)	3,585	3.95
French Canadian (659)	2,249	2.48
German (726)	4,508	4.97
Greek (457)	816	0.90
Guyanese (7)	7	0.01
Hungarian (31)	136	0.15
Iranian (14)	49	0.05
Irish (15,784)	29,819	32.85
Israeli (0)	14	0.02
Italian (4,703)	11,127	12.26
Latvian (29)	49	0.05
Lithuanian (148)	564	0.62
Northern European (10)	20	0.02
Norwegian (117)	394	0.43
Pennsylvania German (5)	5	0.01
Polish (1,024)	2,747	3.03
Portuguese (658)	1,409	1.55
Romanian (169)	224	0.25
Russian (546)	1,225	1.35
Scandinavian (35)	55	0.06
Scotch-Irish (918)	2,103	2.32
Scottish (396)	2,065	2.27
Slavic (30)	30	0.03
Slovak (29)	56	0.06
Slovene (0)	18	0.02
Swedish (264)	1,503	1.66
Swiss (0)	66	0.07
Turkish (180)	275	0.30
Ukrainian (95)	198	0.22
Welsh (0)	268	0.30
West Indian, ex. Hispanic (714)	820	0.90
British West Indian (15)	15	0.02
Haitian (516)	533	0.59
Jamaican (112)	159	0.18
Trinidadian/Tobagonian (15)	41	0.05
West Indian (56)	72	0.08
Yugoslavian (31)	31	0.03

Hispanic Origin	Population	%
Hispanic or Latino (of any race)	3,089	3.35
Central American, ex. Mexican	421	0.46
Costa Rican	15	0.02
Guatemalan	190	0.21
Honduran	87	0.09
Nicaraguan	9	0.01
Panamanian	37	0.04
Salvadoran	82	0.09
Other Central American	1	<0.01
Cuban	119	0.13
Dominican Republic	319	0.35
Mexican	282	0.31
Puerto Rican	1,068	1.16
South American	513	0.56
Argentinean	63	0.07
Bolivian	9	0.01
Chilean	52	0.06
Colombian	164	0.18
Ecuadorian	42	0.05
Paraguayan	4	<0.01
Peruvian	112	0.12
Uruguayan	12	0.01
Venezuelan	49	0.05
Other South American	6	0.01
Other Hispanic or Latino	367	0.40

Race*	Population	%
African-American/Black (4,248)	5,024	5.44
Not Hispanic (3,998)	4,683	5.08
Hispanic (250)	341	0.37
American Indian/Alaska Native (177)	493	0.53
Not Hispanic (137)	423	0.46
Hispanic (40)	70	0.08
Apache (3)	6	0.01
Blackfeet (0)	18	0.02
Canadian/French Am. Ind. (0)	1	<0.01
Central American Ind. (4)	9	0.01
Cherokee (10)	45	0.05
Chippewa (3)	7	0.01
Choctaw (3)	6	0.01
Cree (0)	1	<0.01
Creek (2)	3	<0.01
Crow (0)	5	0.01
Iroquois (3)	15	0.02
Lumbee (1)	1	<0.01
Mexican American Ind. (6)	10	0.01
Navajo (3)	5	0.01
Osage (0)	1	<0.01
Ottawa (1)	1	<0.01
Puget Sound Salish (2)	2	<0.01
Shoshone (0)	1	<0.01
Sioux (1)	11	0.01
South American Ind. (5)	8	0.01
Spanish American Ind. (0)	1	<0.01
Tlingit-Haida *(Alaska Native)* (1)	2	<0.01
Ute (0)	3	<0.01
Yakama (0)	1	<0.01
Yuman (0)	1	<0.01
Yup'ik *(Alaska Native)* (3)	3	<0.01
Asian (22,174)	22,968	24.89
Not Hispanic (22,124)	22,870	24.79
Hispanic (50)	98	0.11
Bangladeshi (21)	23	0.02
Burmese (79)	100	0.11
Cambodian (81)	101	0.11
Chinese, ex. Taiwanese (14,444)	14,979	16.23
Filipino (651)	788	0.85
Hmong (10)	12	0.01
Indian (2,404)	2,550	2.76
Indonesian (15)	24	0.03
Japanese (128)	201	0.22
Korean (271)	323	0.35
Laotian (12)	16	0.02
Malaysian (14)	22	0.02
Nepalese (35)	39	0.04
Pakistani (98)	113	0.12
Sri Lankan (11)	11	0.01
Taiwanese (65)	82	0.09
Thai (245)	262	0.28
Vietnamese (2,979)	3,297	3.57
Hawaii Native/Pacific Islander (21)	108	0.12
Not Hispanic (21)	96	0.10
Hispanic (0)	12	0.01
Fijian (0)	1	<0.01
Guamanian/Chamorro (2)	8	0.01
Native Hawaiian (6)	20	0.02
Samoan (6)	9	0.01
White (62,098)	63,594	68.92
Not Hispanic (60,448)	61,749	66.92
Hispanic (1,650)	1,845	2.00

Randolph

Place Type: CDP/Town
County: Norfolk
Population: 32,112†

Ancestry‡	Population	%
African, Sub-Saharan (1,578)	2,078	6.56
African (96)	105	0.33
Cape Verdean (663)	968	3.06
Ethiopian (51)	83	0.26
Ghanaian (17)	17	0.05
Nigerian (434)	434	1.37
Sierra Leonean (238)	316	1.00
Somalian (53)	53	0.17
South African (0)	32	0.10
Other Sub-Saharan African (26)	70	0.22
Albanian (16)	47	0.15
American (705)	705	2.23
Arab (184)	284	0.90
Arab (7)	7	0.02
Lebanese (177)	268	0.85
Syrian (0)	9	0.03
Australian (10)	10	0.03
Austrian (6)	52	0.16
Brazilian (531)	562	1.78
British (19)	66	0.21
Canadian (164)	449	1.42
Dutch (30)	130	0.41
Eastern European (34)	34	0.11
English (242)	1,565	4.94
European (177)	177	0.56
Finnish (14)	36	0.11
French, ex. Basque (111)	697	2.20
French Canadian (138)	491	1.55
German (111)	627	1.98
Greek (159)	252	0.80
Guyanese (10)	10	0.03
Hungarian (15)	28	0.09
Irish (2,222)	4,927	15.56
Italian (1,128)	2,555	8.07
Lithuanian (83)	218	0.69
Norwegian (65)	124	0.39
Polish (283)	633	2.00
Portuguese (81)	478	1.51
Russian (267)	484	1.53
Scotch-Irish (189)	363	1.15
Scottish (175)	543	1.72
Slovak (0)	14	0.04
Swedish (17)	190	0.60
Swiss (0)	13	0.04
Ukrainian (86)	117	0.37
Welsh (10)	38	0.12
West Indian, ex. Hispanic (5,646)	6,103	19.28
Barbadian (158)	179	0.57
British West Indian (65)	114	0.36
Haitian (3,992)	4,214	13.31
Jamaican (1,143)	1,304	4.12
Trinidadian/Tobagonian (49)	49	0.15
West Indian (239)	243	0.77

Hispanic Origin	Population	%
Hispanic or Latino (of any race)	2,057	6.41
Central American, ex. Mexican	316	0.98
Costa Rican	19	0.06
Guatemalan	124	0.39
Honduran	93	0.29
Nicaraguan	1	<0.01
Panamanian	39	0.12
Salvadoran	39	0.12
Other Central American	1	<0.01
Cuban	75	0.23
Dominican Republic	242	0.75
Mexican	99	0.31
Puerto Rican	818	2.55
South American	261	0.81
Argentinean	15	0.05

SECTION TWO

*Notes: † The Census 2010 population figure is used to calculate the percentages in the Hispanic Origin and Race categories. Ancestry percentages are based on the 2006-2010 American Community Survey population (not shown); ‡ Numbers in parentheses indicate the number of people reporting a single ancestry; * Numbers in parentheses indicate the number of persons reporting this race alone, not in combination with any other race; Please refer to the Explanation of Data for more information.*

Chilean	14	0.04
Colombian	80	0.25
Ecuadorian	20	0.06
Peruvian	118	0.37
Uruguayan	1	<0.01
Venezuelan	11	0.03
Other South American	2	0.01
Other Hispanic or Latino	246	0.77

Race*	Population	%
African-American/Black (12,308)	13,090	40.76
Not Hispanic (11,918)	12,553	39.09
Hispanic (390)	537	1.67
American Indian/Alaska Native (108)	331	1.03
Not Hispanic (69)	262	0.82
Hispanic (39)	69	0.21
Aleut *(Alaska Native)* (1)	1	<0.01
Apache (0)	1	<0.01
Blackfeet (7)	18	0.06
Canadian/French Am. Ind. (1)	4	0.01
Central American Ind. (5)	5	0.02
Cherokee (2)	36	0.11
Cheyenne (0)	1	<0.01
Chickasaw (0)	1	<0.01
Choctaw (0)	2	0.01
Cree (0)	1	<0.01
Iroquois (0)	3	0.01
Mexican American Ind. (2)	10	0.03
Navajo (1)	4	0.01
Potawatomi (0)	2	0.01
Pueblo (0)	2	0.01
Puget Sound Salish (0)	1	<0.01
Seminole (0)	1	<0.01
Sioux (0)	7	0.02
South American Ind. (3)	9	0.03
Asian (3,998)	4,222	13.15
Not Hispanic (3,989)	4,192	13.05
Hispanic (9)	30	0.09
Bangladeshi (9)	9	0.03
Burmese (8)	8	0.02
Cambodian (38)	52	0.16
Chinese, ex. Taiwanese (1,058)	1,186	3.69
Filipino (297)	342	1.07
Hmong (1)	2	0.01
Indian (252)	312	0.97
Indonesian (1)	7	0.02
Japanese (39)	50	0.16
Korean (27)	38	0.12
Laotian (31)	37	0.12
Malaysian (1)	1	<0.01
Nepalese (4)	4	0.01
Pakistani (26)	34	0.11
Taiwanese (3)	6	0.02
Thai (15)	19	0.06
Vietnamese (2,034)	2,150	6.70
Hawaii Native/Pacific Islander (4)	93	0.29
Not Hispanic (3)	87	0.27
Hispanic (1)	6	0.02
Guamanian/Chamorro (1)	2	0.01
Native Hawaiian (0)	1	<0.01
White (13,362)	13,966	43.49
Not Hispanic (12,553)	13,048	40.63
Hispanic (809)	918	2.86

Raynham

Place Type: Town
County: Bristol
Population: 13,383†

Ancestry‡	Population	%
African, Sub-Saharan (89)	126	0.96
African (0)	18	0.14
Cape Verdean (89)	108	0.83
American (374)	374	2.86
Arab (47)	140	1.07
Arab (0)	10	0.08
Lebanese (47)	130	0.99
Armenian (0)	55	0.42
Belgian (0)	30	0.23
Brazilian (147)	154	1.18
British (10)	10	0.08
Canadian (112)	322	2.46
Czech (0)	12	0.09
Czechoslovakian (0)	68	0.52
Danish (0)	35	0.27
Dutch (0)	156	1.19
English (481)	2,453	18.75
European (38)	49	0.37
French, ex. Basque (141)	1,052	8.04
French Canadian (262)	610	4.66
German (225)	1,343	10.26
Greek (10)	71	0.54
Irish (1,835)	5,096	38.95
Italian (402)	1,726	13.19
Lithuanian (33)	95	0.73
Norwegian (38)	120	0.92
Polish (126)	551	4.21
Portuguese (534)	1,437	10.98
Romanian (0)	23	0.18
Russian (82)	205	1.57
Scandinavian (8)	17	0.13
Scotch-Irish (81)	295	2.25
Scottish (87)	548	4.19
Slovak (24)	24	0.18
Swedish (54)	465	3.55
Ukrainian (0)	18	0.14
Welsh (0)	33	0.25

Hispanic Origin	Population	%
Hispanic or Latino (of any race)	247	1.85
Central American, ex. Mexican	28	0.21
Guatemalan	15	0.11
Honduran	6	0.04
Nicaraguan	1	0.01
Panamanian	5	0.04
Salvadoran	1	0.01
Cuban	8	0.06
Dominican Republic	7	0.05
Mexican	24	0.18
Puerto Rican	127	0.95
South American	11	0.08
Argentinean	2	0.01
Colombian	5	0.04
Ecuadorian	1	0.01
Peruvian	1	0.01
Other South American	2	0.01
Other Hispanic or Latino	42	0.31

Race*	Population	%
African-American/Black (350)	459	3.43
Not Hispanic (344)	440	3.29
Hispanic (6)	19	0.14
American Indian/Alaska Native (27)	61	0.46
Not Hispanic (23)	55	0.41
Hispanic (4)	6	0.04
Apache (0)	1	0.01
Blackfeet (2)	2	0.01
Cherokee (3)	7	0.05
Iroquois (2)	3	0.02
Mexican American Ind. (1)	1	0.01
South American Ind. (3)	3	0.02
Asian (217)	257	1.92
Not Hispanic (209)	248	1.85
Hispanic (8)	9	0.07
Bangladeshi (0)	1	0.01
Cambodian (9)	14	0.10
Chinese, ex. Taiwanese (50)	71	0.53
Filipino (22)	29	0.22
Indian (52)	62	0.46
Japanese (7)	12	0.09
Korean (21)	21	0.16
Nepalese (0)	3	0.02
Pakistani (3)	4	0.03
Thai (8)	11	0.08
Vietnamese (25)	32	0.24
Hawaii Native/Pacific Islander (0)	11	0.08
Not Hispanic (0)	7	0.05
Hispanic (0)	4	0.03
White (12,473)	12,637	94.43
Not Hispanic (12,319)	12,469	93.17
Hispanic (154)	168	1.26

Reading

Place Type: CDP/Town
County: Middlesex
Population: 24,747†

Ancestry‡	Population	%
African, Sub-Saharan (13)	13	0.05
South African (13)	13	0.05
Albanian (0)	11	0.05
American (794)	794	3.27
Arab (90)	156	0.64
Lebanese (10)	28	0.12
Syrian (17)	65	0.27
Other Arab (63)	63	0.26
Armenian (38)	106	0.44
Austrian (0)	74	0.31
Belgian (0)	63	0.26
Brazilian (37)	48	0.20
British (128)	152	0.63
Bulgarian (0)	11	0.05
Canadian (56)	240	0.99
Celtic (9)	30	0.12
Czech (0)	51	0.21
Danish (21)	73	0.30
Dutch (30)	110	0.45
English (1,086)	4,377	18.04
European (77)	86	0.35
French, ex. Basque (225)	1,218	5.02
French Canadian (297)	1,063	4.38
German (147)	1,675	6.90
Greek (170)	322	1.33
Hungarian (37)	101	0.42
Iranian (0)	13	0.05
Irish (2,574)	8,574	35.34
Italian (2,631)	6,389	26.33
Lithuanian (0)	124	0.51
Northern European (15)	15	0.06
Norwegian (20)	190	0.78
Polish (267)	1,131	4.66
Portuguese (130)	503	2.07
Romanian (15)	56	0.23
Russian (231)	545	2.25
Scandinavian (0)	14	0.06
Scotch-Irish (231)	730	3.01
Scottish (230)	965	3.98
Slovene (0)	28	0.12
Swedish (244)	1,021	4.21
Swiss (14)	58	0.24
Ukrainian (18)	69	0.28
Welsh (64)	148	0.61
West Indian, ex. Hispanic (40)	40	0.16
Haitian (40)	40	0.16

Hispanic Origin	Population	%
Hispanic or Latino (of any race)	378	1.53
Central American, ex. Mexican	39	0.16
Costa Rican	1	<0.01
Guatemalan	11	0.04
Honduran	7	0.03
Nicaraguan	2	0.01
Panamanian	2	0.01
Salvadoran	16	0.06
Cuban	21	0.08
Dominican Republic	43	0.17
Mexican	72	0.29
Puerto Rican	63	0.25
South American	80	0.32
Argentinean	7	0.03
Bolivian	5	0.02
Chilean	2	0.01
Colombian	34	0.14
Ecuadorian	15	0.06
Paraguayan	2	0.01
Peruvian	7	0.03
Uruguayan	1	<0.01
Venezuelan	5	0.02

*Notes: † The Census 2010 population figure is used to calculate the percentages in the Hispanic Origin and Race categories. Ancestry percentages are based on the 2006-2010 American Community Survey population (not shown); ‡ Numbers in parentheses indicate the number of people reporting a single ancestry; * Numbers in parentheses indicate the number of persons reporting this race alone, not in combination with any other race; Please refer to the Explanation of Data for more information.*

Other South American	2	0.01
Other Hispanic or Latino	60	0.24

Race*	Population	%
African-American/Black (188)	268	1.08
Not Hispanic (183)	248	1.00
Hispanic (5)	20	0.08
American Indian/Alaska Native (18)	66	0.27
Not Hispanic (10)	53	0.21
Hispanic (8)	13	0.05
Canadian/French Am. Ind. (0)	3	0.01
Cherokee (0)	1	<0.01
Choctaw (0)	1	<0.01
Delaware (0)	2	0.01
Iroquois (2)	7	0.03
Mexican American Ind. (3)	5	0.02
Shoshone (1)	1	<0.01
Sioux (1)	2	0.01
South American Ind. (1)	2	0.01
Asian (1,031)	1,179	4.76
Not Hispanic (1,029)	1,172	4.74
Hispanic (2)	7	0.03
Bangladeshi (3)	3	0.01
Burmese (6)	6	0.02
Cambodian (3)	4	0.02
Chinese, ex. Taiwanese (373)	411	1.66
Filipino (27)	47	0.19
Indian (309)	336	1.36
Japanese (33)	60	0.24
Korean (105)	122	0.49
Laotian (3)	3	0.01
Malaysian (2)	3	0.01
Nepalese (4)	4	0.02
Pakistani (29)	32	0.13
Sri Lankan (38)	45	0.18
Taiwanese (15)	15	0.06
Thai (7)	12	0.05
Vietnamese (57)	64	0.26
Hawaii Native/Pacific Islander (6)	16	0.06
Not Hispanic (6)	10	0.04
Hispanic (0)	6	0.02
Native Hawaiian (0)	5	0.02
White (23,141)	23,373	94.45
Not Hispanic (22,877)	23,084	93.28
Hispanic (264)	289	1.17

Rehoboth

Place Type: Town
County: Bristol
Population: 11,608†

Ancestry‡	Population	%
African, Sub-Saharan (20)	20	0.18
Cape Verdean (20)	20	0.18
American (257)	257	2.26
Arab (15)	123	1.08
Lebanese (15)	101	0.89
Syrian (0)	22	0.19
Armenian (32)	85	0.75
Austrian (0)	29	0.26
British (11)	11	0.10
Canadian (131)	277	2.44
Czech (11)	48	0.42
Dutch (12)	50	0.44
English (577)	2,324	20.48
European (133)	133	1.17
Finnish (0)	9	0.08
French, ex. Basque (312)	1,383	12.19
French Canadian (419)	950	8.37
German (105)	784	6.91
Greek (78)	280	2.47
Hungarian (9)	19	0.17
Irish (569)	2,394	21.09
Italian (516)	1,442	12.71
Lithuanian (0)	35	0.31
Norwegian (15)	83	0.73
Polish (203)	471	4.15
Portuguese (1,057)	2,161	19.04
Romanian (8)	8	0.07
Russian (77)	216	1.90
Scandinavian (11)	11	0.10
Scotch-Irish (69)	238	2.10
Scottish (33)	440	3.88
Slovak (0)	83	0.73
Swedish (69)	248	2.19
Swiss (0)	47	0.41
Turkish (14)	24	0.21
Ukrainian (0)	8	0.07
Welsh (10)	19	0.17

Hispanic Origin	Population	%
Hispanic or Latino (of any race)	183	1.58
Central American, ex. Mexican	19	0.16
Guatemalan	19	0.16
Cuban	6	0.05
Dominican Republic	11	0.09
Mexican	29	0.25
Puerto Rican	59	0.51
South American	37	0.32
Argentinean	1	0.01
Bolivian	2	0.02
Colombian	28	0.24
Ecuadorian	2	0.02
Venezuelan	2	0.02
Other South American	2	0.02
Other Hispanic or Latino	22	0.19

Race*	Population	%
African-American/Black (60)	94	0.81
Not Hispanic (56)	89	0.77
Hispanic (4)	5	0.04
American Indian/Alaska Native (22)	57	0.49
Not Hispanic (22)	56	0.48
Hispanic (0)	1	0.01
Canadian/French Am. Ind. (0)	3	0.03
Cherokee (1)	2	0.02
Chippewa (2)	2	0.02
Cree (1)	1	0.01
Delaware (0)	2	0.02
Iroquois (0)	5	0.04
Asian (117)	161	1.39
Not Hispanic (115)	157	1.35
Hispanic (2)	4	0.03
Cambodian (3)	3	0.03
Chinese, ex. Taiwanese (29)	39	0.34
Filipino (5)	11	0.09
Indian (19)	23	0.20
Japanese (2)	14	0.12
Korean (18)	24	0.21
Laotian (2)	2	0.02
Pakistani (2)	5	0.04
Thai (1)	1	0.01
Vietnamese (26)	32	0.28
Hawaii Native/Pacific Islander (5)	8	0.07
Not Hispanic (4)	7	0.06
Hispanic (1)	1	0.01
Guamanian/Chamorro (1)	1	0.01
Native Hawaiian (2)	5	0.04
White (11,204)	11,325	97.56
Not Hispanic (11,084)	11,186	96.36
Hispanic (120)	139	1.20

Revere

Place Type: City
County: Suffolk
Population: 51,755†

Ancestry‡	Population	%
African, Sub-Saharan (569)	668	1.34
African (460)	546	1.09
Cape Verdean (83)	96	0.19
Ugandan (11)	11	0.02
Other Sub-Saharan African (15)	15	0.03
Albanian (201)	279	0.56
American (714)	714	1.43
Arab (2,037)	2,310	4.62
Arab (447)	578	1.16
Egyptian (300)	316	0.63
Lebanese (0)	12	0.02
Moroccan (773)	792	1.58
Syrian (20)	20	0.04
Other Arab (497)	592	1.18
Armenian (45)	85	0.17
Australian (9)	25	0.05
Austrian (0)	53	0.11
Brazilian (1,511)	1,616	3.23
British (23)	44	0.09
Canadian (92)	204	0.41
Croatian (10)	21	0.04
Czech (11)	11	0.02
Czechoslovakian (39)	39	0.08
Danish (0)	48	0.10
Dutch (0)	8	0.02
Eastern European (10)	10	0.02
English (353)	2,158	4.32
European (100)	114	0.23
Finnish (16)	112	0.22
French, ex. Basque (220)	2,065	4.13
French Canadian (257)	1,072	2.14
German (177)	998	2.00
Greek (133)	278	0.56
Guyanese (11)	11	0.02
Hungarian (21)	63	0.13
Irish (2,251)	8,125	16.25
Italian (9,478)	15,677	31.35
Lithuanian (8)	205	0.41
Macedonian (0)	14	0.03
Norwegian (13)	72	0.14
Polish (245)	861	1.72
Portuguese (425)	1,151	2.30
Romanian (45)	45	0.09
Russian (386)	799	1.60
Scotch-Irish (152)	403	0.81
Scottish (182)	487	0.97
Slavic (0)	12	0.02
Slovak (147)	147	0.29
Slovene (0)	15	0.03
Swedish (83)	392	0.78
Swiss (0)	35	0.07
Ukrainian (37)	117	0.23
Welsh (0)	25	0.05
West Indian, ex. Hispanic (302)	328	0.66
Barbadian (50)	50	0.10
Belizean (0)	12	0.02
Haitian (60)	74	0.15
Jamaican (76)	76	0.15
Trinidadian/Tobagonian (34)	34	0.07
West Indian (82)	82	0.16
Yugoslavian (245)	264	0.53

Hispanic Origin	Population	%
Hispanic or Latino (of any race)	12,617	24.38
Central American, ex. Mexican	4,457	8.61
Costa Rican	66	0.13
Guatemalan	769	1.49
Honduran	505	0.98
Nicaraguan	46	0.09
Panamanian	13	0.03
Salvadoran	3,024	5.84
Other Central American	34	0.07
Cuban	138	0.27
Dominican Republic	661	1.28
Mexican	966	1.87
Puerto Rican	1,897	3.67
South American	3,184	6.15
Argentinean	67	0.13
Bolivian	34	0.07
Chilean	74	0.14
Colombian	2,520	4.87
Ecuadorian	95	0.18
Paraguayan	1	<0.01
Peruvian	325	0.63
Uruguayan	9	0.02
Venezuelan	49	0.09
Other South American	10	0.02
Other Hispanic or Latino	1,314	2.54

SECTION TWO

*Notes: † The Census 2010 population figure is used to calculate the percentages in the Hispanic Origin and Race categories. Ancestry percentages are based on the 2006-2010 American Community Survey population (not shown); ‡ Numbers in parentheses indicate the number of people reporting a single ancestry; * Numbers in parentheses indicate the number of persons reporting this race alone, not in combination with any other race; Please refer to the Explanation of Data for more information.*

Race*	Population	%
African-American/Black (2,518)	3,129	6.05
Not Hispanic (2,237)	2,667	5.15
Hispanic (281)	462	0.89
American Indian/Alaska Native (186)	412	0.80
Not Hispanic (66)	203	0.39
Hispanic (120)	209	0.40
Aleut *(Alaska Native)* (0)	1	<0.01
Blackfeet (1)	6	0.01
Canadian/French Am. Ind. (1)	3	0.01
Central American Ind. (11)	13	0.03
Cherokee (4)	21	0.04
Choctaw (0)	2	<0.01
Creek (1)	1	<0.01
Iroquois (1)	2	<0.01
Mexican American Ind. (21)	28	0.05
Navajo (1)	1	<0.01
Osage (4)	4	0.01
Potawatomi (2)	2	<0.01
Puget Sound Salish (1)	1	<0.01
Seminole (0)	4	0.01
Sioux (3)	3	0.01
South American Ind. (13)	26	0.05
Spanish American Ind. (9)	9	0.02
Asian (2,888)	3,139	6.07
Not Hispanic (2,856)	3,053	5.90
Hispanic (32)	86	0.17
Bangladeshi (16)	24	0.05
Cambodian (898)	974	1.88
Chinese, ex. Taiwanese (311)	390	0.75
Filipino (86)	123	0.24
Indian (353)	430	0.83
Indonesian (4)	6	0.01
Japanese (21)	45	0.09
Korean (72)	92	0.18
Laotian (5)	17	0.03
Malaysian (2)	5	0.01
Nepalese (20)	22	0.04
Pakistani (172)	185	0.36
Sri Lankan (9)	10	0.02
Taiwanese (5)	6	0.01
Thai (25)	38	0.07
Vietnamese (703)	750	1.45
Hawaii Native/Pacific Islander (13)	60	0.12
Not Hispanic (6)	33	0.06
Hispanic (7)	27	0.05
Guamanian/Chamorro (1)	3	0.01
Native Hawaiian (4)	11	0.02
Samoan (0)	1	<0.01
White (38,349)	39,805	76.91
Not Hispanic (32,299)	33,074	63.90
Hispanic (6,050)	6,731	13.01

Rockland

Place Type: Town
County: Plymouth
Population: 17,489†

Ancestry‡	Population	%
Albanian (16)	16	0.09
American (937)	937	5.35
Arab (138)	227	1.30
Arab (0)	15	0.09
Lebanese (138)	201	1.15
Syrian (0)	11	0.06
Armenian (0)	96	0.55
Australian (0)	47	0.27
Belgian (0)	15	0.09
Brazilian (216)	230	1.31
British (58)	74	0.42
Canadian (154)	386	2.20
Danish (121)	134	0.77
Dutch (48)	98	0.56
English (742)	2,500	14.28
European (45)	45	0.26
Finnish (15)	49	0.28
French, ex. Basque (79)	851	4.86
French Canadian (199)	789	4.51
German (168)	972	5.55
Greek (31)	49	0.28
Guyanese (0)	38	0.22
Irish (2,984)	6,511	37.18
Italian (1,030)	2,768	15.81
Lithuanian (45)	158	0.90
Macedonian (11)	11	0.06
Norwegian (0)	34	0.19
Pennsylvania German (8)	8	0.05
Polish (227)	520	2.97
Portuguese (132)	643	3.67
Russian (33)	44	0.25
Scotch-Irish (443)	710	4.05
Scottish (336)	904	5.16
Slovak (12)	12	0.07
Swedish (79)	511	2.92
Welsh (18)	58	0.33
West Indian, ex. Hispanic (212)	249	1.42
Haitian (171)	171	0.98
Jamaican (41)	78	0.45

Hispanic Origin	Population	%
Hispanic or Latino (of any race)	348	1.99
Central American, ex. Mexican	20	0.11
Guatemalan	7	0.04
Honduran	5	0.03
Panamanian	2	0.01
Salvadoran	6	0.03
Cuban	17	0.10
Dominican Republic	40	0.23
Mexican	40	0.23
Puerto Rican	136	0.78
South American	40	0.23
Argentinean	6	0.03
Bolivian	5	0.03
Chilean	2	0.01
Colombian	14	0.08
Ecuadorian	5	0.03
Uruguayan	1	0.01
Venezuelan	6	0.03
Other South American	1	0.01
Other Hispanic or Latino	55	0.31

Race*	Population	%
African-American/Black (452)	601	3.44
Not Hispanic (431)	561	3.21
Hispanic (21)	40	0.23
American Indian/Alaska Native (27)	125	0.71
Not Hispanic (22)	115	0.66
Hispanic (5)	10	0.06
Blackfeet (0)	2	0.01
Canadian/French Am. Ind. (0)	1	0.01
Cherokee (2)	22	0.13
Comanche (1)	1	0.01
Cree (0)	3	0.02
Iroquois (0)	3	0.02
Mexican American Ind. (3)	3	0.02
Sioux (0)	1	0.01
Asian (192)	247	1.41
Not Hispanic (192)	247	1.41
Cambodian (1)	1	0.01
Chinese, ex. Taiwanese (34)	49	0.28
Filipino (11)	26	0.15
Hmong (7)	7	0.04
Indian (32)	48	0.27
Indonesian (3)	4	0.02
Japanese (1)	4	0.02
Korean (7)	9	0.05
Pakistani (3)	3	0.02
Thai (10)	10	0.06
Vietnamese (77)	83	0.47
Hawaii Native/Pacific Islander (5)	15	0.09
Not Hispanic (5)	15	0.09
Fijian (2)	2	0.01
Guamanian/Chamorro (1)	2	0.01
Native Hawaiian (1)	1	0.01
Samoan (0)	1	0.01
White (16,095)	16,396	93.75
Not Hispanic (15,879)	16,148	92.33
Hispanic (216)	248	1.42

Rutland

Place Type: Town
County: Worcester
Population: 7,973†

Ancestry‡	Population	%
African, Sub-Saharan (39)	39	0.51
African (39)	39	0.51
American (196)	196	2.55
Arab (15)	48	0.62
Arab (15)	15	0.19
Lebanese (0)	33	0.43
Armenian (10)	91	1.18
Austrian (8)	27	0.35
Belgian (0)	45	0.58
Canadian (0)	22	0.29
Dutch (0)	23	0.30
English (297)	1,133	14.71
European (67)	94	1.22
Finnish (65)	97	1.26
French, ex. Basque (382)	1,553	20.17
French Canadian (360)	548	7.12
German (26)	731	9.49
Greek (15)	40	0.52
Irish (480)	2,071	26.90
Italian (294)	1,183	15.36
Latvian (0)	16	0.21
Lithuanian (39)	168	2.18
Norwegian (0)	16	0.21
Polish (142)	456	5.92
Portuguese (64)	99	1.29
Russian (0)	69	0.90
Scandinavian (14)	69	0.90
Scotch-Irish (23)	150	1.95
Scottish (96)	245	3.18
Swedish (116)	597	7.75
Swiss (0)	10	0.13
Ukrainian (0)	15	0.19
Welsh (0)	11	0.14
West Indian, ex. Hispanic (31)	31	0.40
Haitian (31)	31	0.40

Hispanic Origin	Population	%
Hispanic or Latino (of any race)	146	1.83
Central American, ex. Mexican	20	0.25
Costa Rican	2	0.03
Guatemalan	1	0.01
Nicaraguan	9	0.11
Panamanian	1	0.01
Salvadoran	7	0.09
Cuban	6	0.08
Dominican Republic	6	0.08
Mexican	14	0.18
Puerto Rican	61	0.77
South American	27	0.34
Argentinean	1	0.01
Colombian	12	0.15
Ecuadorian	7	0.09
Peruvian	7	0.09
Other Hispanic or Latino	12	0.15

Race*	Population	%
African-American/Black (92)	125	1.57
Not Hispanic (91)	122	1.53
Hispanic (1)	3	0.04
American Indian/Alaska Native (6)	24	0.30
Not Hispanic (6)	23	0.29
Hispanic (0)	1	0.01
Blackfeet (0)	3	0.04
Canadian/French Am. Ind. (0)	1	0.01
Chippewa (1)	1	0.01
Iroquois (0)	2	0.03
Sioux (0)	1	0.01
South American Ind. (0)	1	0.01
Asian (126)	163	2.04
Not Hispanic (126)	159	1.99
Hispanic (0)	4	0.05
Cambodian (3)	7	0.09
Chinese, ex. Taiwanese (44)	49	0.61

*Notes: † The Census 2010 population figure is used to calculate the percentages in the Hispanic Origin and Race categories. Ancestry percentages are based on the 2006-2010 American Community Survey population (not shown); ‡ Numbers in parentheses indicate the number of people reporting a single ancestry; * Numbers in parentheses indicate the number of persons reporting this race alone, not in combination with any other race; Please refer to the Explanation of Data for more information.*

Filipino (14)	22	0.28
Hmong (1)	1	0.01
Indian (20)	20	0.25
Japanese (4)	17	0.21
Korean (12)	15	0.19
Malaysian (0)	1	0.01
Nepalese (1)	1	0.01
Pakistani (6)	6	0.08
Thai (1)	1	0.01
Vietnamese (16)	22	0.28
Hawaii Native/Pacific Islander (1)	4	0.05
Not Hispanic (1)	4	0.05
Native Hawaiian (1)	4	0.05
White (7,625)	7,712	96.73
Not Hispanic (7,510)	7,588	95.17
Hispanic (115)	124	1.56

Salem

Place Type: City
County: Essex
Population: 41,340†

Ancestry‡	Population	%
African, Sub-Saharan (409)	549	1.34
African (320)	389	0.95
Cape Verdean (15)	27	0.07
Liberian (0)	43	0.10
Nigerian (0)	16	0.04
Ugandan (16)	16	0.04
Other Sub-Saharan African (58)	58	0.14
Albanian (206)	206	0.50
American (777)	777	1.90
Arab (218)	256	0.62
Jordanian (43)	43	0.10
Lebanese (44)	75	0.18
Moroccan (118)	118	0.29
Syrian (0)	7	0.02
Other Arab (13)	13	0.03
Armenian (28)	83	0.20
Australian (14)	22	0.05
Austrian (68)	172	0.42
Belgian (9)	22	0.05
Brazilian (455)	511	1.25
British (194)	328	0.80
Canadian (111)	336	0.82
Celtic (0)	89	0.22
Croatian (11)	11	0.03
Czech (68)	136	0.33
Czechoslovakian (0)	26	0.06
Danish (12)	129	0.31
Dutch (55)	170	0.41
Eastern European (89)	99	0.24
English (939)	3,974	9.70
European (553)	585	1.43
Finnish (11)	33	0.08
French, ex. Basque (1,009)	3,723	9.09
French Canadian (1,425)	2,603	6.35
German (329)	2,275	5.55
Greek (752)	1,400	3.42
Hungarian (24)	102	0.25
Iranian (27)	41	0.10
Irish (3,569)	10,127	24.72
Israeli (0)	25	0.06
Italian (2,135)	6,365	15.54
Lithuanian (25)	104	0.25
Northern European (65)	65	0.16
Norwegian (105)	268	0.65
Polish (784)	2,162	5.28
Portuguese (553)	1,429	3.49
Romanian (11)	60	0.15
Russian (498)	1,034	2.52
Scotch-Irish (158)	547	1.34
Scottish (172)	840	2.05
Slavic (0)	12	0.03
Slovak (21)	46	0.11
Slovene (0)	15	0.04
Swedish (31)	464	1.13
Swiss (23)	87	0.21
Turkish (10)	10	0.02
Ukrainian (48)	124	0.30
Welsh (12)	141	0.34
West Indian, ex. Hispanic (151)	277	0.68
Bahamian (0)	11	0.03
Barbadian (29)	29	0.07
British West Indian (57)	68	0.17
Haitian (37)	77	0.19
Trinidadian/Tobagonian (28)	92	0.22

Hispanic Origin	Population	%
Hispanic or Latino (of any race)	6,465	15.64
Central American, ex. Mexican	342	0.83
Costa Rican	29	0.07
Guatemalan	119	0.29
Honduran	83	0.20
Nicaraguan	14	0.03
Panamanian	12	0.03
Salvadoran	85	0.21
Cuban	73	0.18
Dominican Republic	3,749	9.07
Mexican	224	0.54
Puerto Rican	1,191	2.88
South American	239	0.58
Argentinean	32	0.08
Bolivian	9	0.02
Chilean	29	0.07
Colombian	72	0.17
Ecuadorian	27	0.07
Paraguayan	6	0.01
Peruvian	33	0.08
Uruguayan	5	0.01
Venezuelan	22	0.05
Other South American	4	0.01
Other Hispanic or Latino	647	1.57

Race*	Population	%
African-American/Black (2,040)	2,694	6.52
Not Hispanic (1,450)	1,805	4.37
Hispanic (590)	889	2.15
American Indian/Alaska Native (173)	434	1.05
Not Hispanic (66)	224	0.54
Hispanic (107)	210	0.51
Apache (1)	6	0.01
Blackfeet (4)	14	0.03
Canadian/French Am. Ind. (1)	2	<0.01
Central American Ind. (8)	10	0.02
Cherokee (3)	27	0.07
Chippewa (3)	4	0.01
Choctaw (0)	4	0.01
Crow (0)	3	0.01
Inupiat *(Alaska Native)* (0)	3	0.01
Iroquois (1)	10	0.02
Mexican American Ind. (11)	15	0.04
Navajo (1)	7	0.02
Osage (0)	1	<0.01
Potawatomi (0)	2	<0.01
Pueblo (6)	7	0.02
Seminole (0)	1	<0.01
Sioux (1)	4	0.01
South American Ind. (6)	8	0.02
Spanish American Ind. (4)	4	0.01
Asian (1,095)	1,344	3.25
Not Hispanic (1,083)	1,300	3.14
Hispanic (12)	44	0.11
Bangladeshi (6)	8	0.02
Cambodian (44)	55	0.13
Chinese, ex. Taiwanese (231)	291	0.70
Filipino (282)	341	0.82
Indian (144)	181	0.44
Indonesian (3)	8	0.02
Japanese (65)	105	0.25
Korean (47)	80	0.19
Laotian (12)	12	0.03
Nepalese (6)	9	0.02
Pakistani (16)	21	0.05
Sri Lankan (1)	1	<0.01
Taiwanese (7)	9	0.02
Thai (22)	33	0.08
Vietnamese (170)	196	0.47
Hawaii Native/Pacific Islander (21)	97	0.23
Not Hispanic (17)	41	0.10
Hispanic (4)	56	0.14
Fijian (1)	1	<0.01
Guamanian/Chamorro (4)	7	0.02
Native Hawaiian (6)	20	0.05
Samoan (3)	3	0.01
White (33,694)	34,826	84.24
Not Hispanic (31,377)	32,021	77.46
Hispanic (2,317)	2,805	6.79

Salisbury

Place Type: Town
County: Essex
Population: 8,283†

Ancestry‡	Population	%
Albanian (0)	18	0.22
American (307)	307	3.76
Arab (38)	57	0.70
Lebanese (38)	57	0.70
Armenian (26)	41	0.50
Austrian (0)	34	0.42
Belgian (0)	9	0.11
British (10)	10	0.12
Canadian (24)	129	1.58
Danish (37)	64	0.78
Dutch (29)	29	0.36
English (425)	1,569	19.24
European (48)	68	0.83
Finnish (10)	58	0.71
French, ex. Basque (347)	1,415	17.35
French Canadian (111)	388	4.76
German (42)	480	5.88
Greek (166)	290	3.56
Irish (952)	2,375	29.12
Italian (697)	1,453	17.81
Norwegian (9)	9	0.11
Polish (48)	363	4.45
Portuguese (46)	95	1.16
Russian (36)	73	0.89
Scandinavian (0)	6	0.07
Scotch-Irish (143)	185	2.27
Scottish (193)	516	6.33
Swedish (0)	236	2.89
Turkish (0)	22	0.27
Ukrainian (0)	9	0.11
Welsh (10)	10	0.12
West Indian, ex. Hispanic (22)	32	0.39
Haitian (0)	10	0.12
Jamaican (22)	22	0.27
Yugoslavian (0)	11	0.13

Hispanic Origin	Population	%
Hispanic or Latino (of any race)	128	1.55
Central American, ex. Mexican	11	0.13
Guatemalan	3	0.04
Panamanian	1	0.01
Salvadoran	7	0.08
Cuban	5	0.06
Dominican Republic	14	0.17
Mexican	26	0.31
Puerto Rican	47	0.57
South American	12	0.14
Argentinean	1	0.01
Chilean	3	0.04
Colombian	4	0.05
Ecuadorian	1	0.01
Peruvian	2	0.02
Venezuelan	1	0.01
Other Hispanic or Latino	13	0.16

Race*	Population	%
African-American/Black (38)	76	0.92
Not Hispanic (35)	71	0.86
Hispanic (3)	5	0.06
American Indian/Alaska Native (19)	61	0.74
Not Hispanic (18)	60	0.72
Hispanic (1)	1	0.01
Apache (0)	1	0.01

*Notes: † The Census 2010 population figure is used to calculate the percentages in the Hispanic Origin and Race categories. Ancestry percentages are based on the 2006-2010 American Community Survey population (not shown); ‡ Numbers in parentheses indicate the number of people reporting a single ancestry; * Numbers in parentheses indicate the number of persons reporting this race alone, not in combination with any other race; Please refer to the Explanation of Data for more information.*

Blackfeet (2)	4	0.05
Cherokee (1)	1	0.01
Cheyenne (0)	2	0.02
Chippewa (0)	2	0.02
Choctaw (4)	4	0.05
Delaware (1)	1	0.01
Iroquois (0)	2	0.02
Navajo (0)	2	0.02
Asian (98)	123	1.48
Not Hispanic (97)	120	1.45
Hispanic (1)	3	0.04
Bangladeshi (4)	4	0.05
Cambodian (1)	2	0.02
Chinese, ex. Taiwanese (7)	7	0.08
Filipino (3)	9	0.11
Indian (20)	22	0.27
Japanese (6)	12	0.14
Korean (6)	15	0.18
Laotian (0)	2	0.02
Thai (2)	3	0.04
Vietnamese (44)	48	0.58
Hawaii Native/Pacific Islander (1)	7	0.08
Not Hispanic (1)	7	0.08
Native Hawaiian (1)	4	0.05
Samoan (0)	2	0.02
White (7,978)	8,094	97.72
Not Hispanic (7,884)	7,987	96.43
Hispanic (94)	107	1.29

Sandwich

Place Type: Town
County: Barnstable
Population: 20,675†

Ancestry‡	Population	%
African, Sub-Saharan (99)	128	0.62
African (27)	27	0.13
Cape Verdean (72)	92	0.45
South African (0)	9	0.04
American (1,560)	1,560	7.56
Arab (33)	114	0.55
Lebanese (33)	114	0.55
Armenian (6)	12	0.06
Australian (0)	15	0.07
Austrian (0)	65	0.32
Belgian (28)	37	0.18
Brazilian (25)	25	0.12
British (28)	63	0.31
Bulgarian (50)	58	0.28
Canadian (97)	240	1.16
Croatian (28)	28	0.14
Czech (31)	56	0.27
Czechoslovakian (0)	41	0.20
Danish (19)	47	0.23
Dutch (26)	253	1.23
Eastern European (24)	24	0.12
English (1,060)	3,564	17.28
European (179)	179	0.87
Finnish (63)	274	1.33
French, ex. Basque (161)	1,425	6.91
French Canadian (309)	630	3.05
German (293)	2,217	10.75
Greek (388)	543	2.63
Hungarian (13)	80	0.39
Irish (2,503)	6,794	32.94
Italian (949)	3,220	15.61
Latvian (0)	14	0.07
Lithuanian (26)	129	0.63
Luxemburger (0)	10	0.05
Northern European (0)	22	0.11
Norwegian (0)	143	0.69
Polish (227)	1,071	5.19
Portuguese (210)	592	2.87
Russian (43)	308	1.49
Scandinavian (8)	58	0.28
Scotch-Irish (242)	490	2.38
Scottish (146)	808	3.92
Serbian (29)	59	0.29
Slovak (10)	30	0.15
Slovene (0)	13	0.06
Swedish (263)	879	4.26
Swiss (7)	43	0.21
Ukrainian (49)	140	0.68
Welsh (48)	169	0.82
West Indian, ex. Hispanic (31)	31	0.15
Jamaican (31)	31	0.15

Hispanic Origin	Population	%
Hispanic or Latino (of any race)	274	1.33
Central American, ex. Mexican	20	0.10
Costa Rican	2	0.01
Guatemalan	3	0.01
Honduran	6	0.03
Nicaraguan	1	<0.01
Panamanian	1	<0.01
Salvadoran	7	0.03
Cuban	11	0.05
Dominican Republic	12	0.06
Mexican	66	0.32
Puerto Rican	63	0.30
South American	48	0.23
Argentinean	1	<0.01
Bolivian	2	0.01
Chilean	1	<0.01
Colombian	23	0.11
Ecuadorian	4	0.02
Paraguayan	3	0.01
Peruvian	4	0.02
Uruguayan	1	<0.01
Venezuelan	9	0.04
Other Hispanic or Latino	54	0.26

Race*	Population	%
African-American/Black (78)	133	0.64
Not Hispanic (70)	115	0.56
Hispanic (8)	18	0.09
American Indian/Alaska Native (51)	123	0.59
Not Hispanic (44)	101	0.49
Hispanic (7)	22	0.11
Apache (1)	1	<0.01
Blackfeet (1)	5	0.02
Cherokee (4)	11	0.05
Chippewa (0)	1	<0.01
Comanche (0)	1	<0.01
Creek (1)	1	<0.01
Iroquois (0)	4	0.02
Mexican American Ind. (0)	1	<0.01
Asian (246)	322	1.56
Not Hispanic (244)	312	1.51
Hispanic (2)	10	0.05
Chinese, ex. Taiwanese (41)	60	0.29
Filipino (27)	48	0.23
Indian (41)	54	0.26
Indonesian (1)	1	<0.01
Japanese (13)	25	0.12
Korean (31)	50	0.24
Laotian (1)	3	0.01
Malaysian (0)	5	0.02
Nepalese (4)	5	0.02
Pakistani (40)	42	0.20
Sri Lankan (3)	3	0.01
Taiwanese (5)	6	0.03
Thai (2)	5	0.02
Vietnamese (10)	10	0.05
Hawaii Native/Pacific Islander (5)	25	0.12
Not Hispanic (5)	21	0.10
Hispanic (0)	4	0.02
Guamanian/Chamorro (0)	4	0.02
Native Hawaiian (2)	8	0.04
Samoan (2)	2	0.01
White (19,997)	20,191	97.66
Not Hispanic (19,817)	19,982	96.65
Hispanic (180)	209	1.01

Saugus

Place Type: CDP/Town
County: Essex
Population: 26,628†

Ancestry‡	Population	%
African, Sub-Saharan (59)	59	0.22
African (8)	8	0.03
Ethiopian (51)	51	0.19
Albanian (154)	154	0.58
American (486)	486	1.84
Arab (61)	84	0.32
Arab (52)	52	0.20
Lebanese (9)	9	0.03
Syrian (0)	23	0.09
Armenian (41)	86	0.33
Austrian (26)	63	0.24
Brazilian (383)	383	1.45
British (70)	70	0.27
Canadian (116)	217	0.82
Celtic (13)	23	0.09
Czech (0)	91	0.34
Czechoslovakian (23)	23	0.09
Danish (8)	8	0.03
Dutch (0)	37	0.14
English (873)	2,878	10.90
European (114)	114	0.43
Finnish (0)	51	0.19
French, ex. Basque (538)	1,907	7.23
French Canadian (181)	659	2.50
German (228)	941	3.57
Greek (276)	438	1.66
Hungarian (25)	38	0.14
Irish (2,931)	7,434	28.17
Italian (4,989)	9,094	34.46
Latvian (0)	11	0.04
Lithuanian (25)	63	0.24
Norwegian (56)	147	0.56
Polish (377)	1,601	6.07
Portuguese (322)	640	2.42
Russian (140)	258	0.98
Scotch-Irish (200)	640	2.42
Scottish (278)	777	2.94
Swedish (138)	731	2.77
Swiss (0)	26	0.10
Ukrainian (10)	83	0.31
Welsh (0)	47	0.18
West Indian, ex. Hispanic (91)	126	0.48
Barbadian (0)	35	0.13
Haitian (63)	63	0.24
West Indian (28)	28	0.11
Yugoslavian (97)	97	0.37

Hispanic Origin	Population	%
Hispanic or Latino (of any race)	1,066	4.00
Central American, ex. Mexican	236	0.89
Costa Rican	20	0.08
Guatemalan	70	0.26
Honduran	10	0.04
Nicaraguan	1	<0.01
Panamanian	6	0.02
Salvadoran	129	0.48
Cuban	23	0.09
Dominican Republic	79	0.30
Mexican	103	0.39
Puerto Rican	266	1.00
South American	211	0.79
Argentinean	23	0.09
Chilean	8	0.03
Colombian	87	0.33
Ecuadorian	21	0.08
Peruvian	53	0.20
Uruguayan	12	0.05
Venezuelan	3	0.01
Other South American	4	0.02
Other Hispanic or Latino	148	0.56

Race*	Population	%
African-American/Black (552)	724	2.72
Not Hispanic (525)	650	2.44
Hispanic (27)	74	0.28
American Indian/Alaska Native (39)	124	0.47
Not Hispanic (28)	100	0.38
Hispanic (11)	24	0.09
Aleut *(Alaska Native)* (0)	2	0.01

*Notes: † The Census 2010 population figure is used to calculate the percentages in the Hispanic Origin and Race categories. Ancestry percentages are based on the 2006-2010 American Community Survey population (not shown); ‡ Numbers in parentheses indicate the number of people reporting a single ancestry; * Numbers in parentheses indicate the number of persons reporting this race alone, not in combination with any other race; Please refer to the Explanation of Data for more information.*

Apache (0)	1	<0.01
Blackfeet (1)	2	0.01
Canadian/French Am. Ind. (0)	2	0.01
Cherokee (1)	18	0.07
Chickasaw (5)	5	0.02
Chippewa (0)	4	0.02
Choctaw (1)	1	<0.01
Cree (1)	2	0.01
Iroquois (0)	3	0.01
Mexican American Ind. (1)	1	<0.01
Seminole (0)	1	<0.01
Shoshone (0)	1	<0.01
Sioux (0)	3	0.01
South American Ind. (1)	9	0.03
Spanish American Ind. (2)	2	0.01
Asian (712)	814	3.06
Not Hispanic (708)	801	3.01
Hispanic (4)	13	0.05
Bangladeshi (9)	9	0.03
Cambodian (139)	160	0.60
Chinese, ex. Taiwanese (149)	197	0.74
Filipino (21)	41	0.15
Indian (91)	104	0.39
Japanese (8)	24	0.09
Korean (25)	31	0.12
Laotian (4)	9	0.03
Malaysian (1)	2	0.01
Pakistani (18)	18	0.07
Taiwanese (3)	3	0.01
Thai (15)	18	0.07
Vietnamese (167)	204	0.77
Hawaii Native/Pacific Islander (3)	18	0.07
Not Hispanic (1)	10	0.04
Hispanic (2)	8	0.03
Guamanian/Chamorro (0)	1	<0.01
Native Hawaiian (2)	5	0.02
Samoan (0)	1	<0.01
White (24,479)	24,845	93.30
Not Hispanic (23,860)	24,135	90.64
Hispanic (619)	710	2.67

Scituate

Place Type: Town
County: Plymouth
Population: 18,133†

Ancestry‡	Population	%
African, Sub-Saharan (243)	268	1.48
Cape Verdean (243)	268	1.48
American (540)	540	2.99
Arab (53)	76	0.42
Lebanese (53)	65	0.36
Syrian (0)	11	0.06
Armenian (31)	44	0.24
Austrian (0)	102	0.56
Belgian (22)	118	0.65
Brazilian (140)	156	0.86
British (61)	84	0.46
Cajun (16)	16	0.09
Canadian (106)	208	1.15
Croatian (0)	42	0.23
Czech (0)	8	0.04
Danish (0)	28	0.15
Dutch (131)	293	1.62
Eastern European (59)	59	0.33
English (874)	3,425	18.95
European (113)	170	0.94
Finnish (23)	76	0.42
French, ex. Basque (123)	811	4.49
French Canadian (46)	349	1.93
German (304)	1,928	10.67
Greek (97)	193	1.07
Hungarian (0)	15	0.08
Irish (3,954)	8,427	46.62
Italian (678)	2,435	13.47
Latvian (14)	58	0.32
Lithuanian (11)	240	1.33
Maltese (0)	8	0.04
Norwegian (75)	264	1.46
Polish (275)	834	4.61
Portuguese (79)	201	1.11
Russian (74)	346	1.91
Scandinavian (25)	68	0.38
Scotch-Irish (215)	449	2.48
Scottish (181)	832	4.60
Slovak (15)	29	0.16
Slovene (0)	31	0.17
Swedish (35)	535	2.96
Swiss (38)	117	0.65
Turkish (15)	15	0.08
Ukrainian (12)	65	0.36
Welsh (0)	199	1.10
West Indian, ex. Hispanic (0)	17	0.09
Jamaican (0)	17	0.09
Yugoslavian (0)	14	0.08

Hispanic Origin	Population	%
Hispanic or Latino (of any race)	191	1.05
Central American, ex. Mexican	14	0.08
Costa Rican	4	0.02
Guatemalan	7	0.04
Honduran	1	0.01
Panamanian	1	0.01
Salvadoran	1	0.01
Cuban	28	0.15
Dominican Republic	10	0.06
Mexican	23	0.13
Puerto Rican	45	0.25
South American	40	0.22
Argentinean	11	0.06
Chilean	7	0.04
Colombian	13	0.07
Ecuadorian	4	0.02
Peruvian	4	0.02
Venezuelan	1	0.01
Other Hispanic or Latino	31	0.17

Race*	Population	%
African-American/Black (104)	195	1.08
Not Hispanic (98)	184	1.01
Hispanic (6)	11	0.06
American Indian/Alaska Native (14)	65	0.36
Not Hispanic (13)	56	0.31
Hispanic (1)	9	0.05
Blackfeet (0)	3	0.02
Canadian/French Am. Ind. (0)	1	0.01
Cherokee (0)	2	0.01
Hopi (1)	1	0.01
Iroquois (0)	5	0.03
Mexican American Ind. (1)	2	0.01
Sioux (1)	1	0.01
Asian (136)	208	1.15
Not Hispanic (132)	202	1.11
Hispanic (4)	6	0.03
Bangladeshi (2)	5	0.03
Cambodian (0)	3	0.02
Chinese, ex. Taiwanese (49)	56	0.31
Filipino (17)	46	0.25
Indian (27)	42	0.23
Japanese (6)	9	0.05
Korean (20)	34	0.19
Pakistani (3)	4	0.02
Thai (2)	7	0.04
Vietnamese (3)	4	0.02
Hawaii Native/Pacific Islander (7)	24	0.13
Not Hispanic (7)	23	0.13
Hispanic (0)	1	0.01
Fijian (0)	1	0.01
Marshallese (2)	2	0.01
Native Hawaiian (1)	4	0.02
White (17,425)	17,609	97.11
Not Hispanic (17,277)	17,450	96.23
Hispanic (148)	159	0.88

Seekonk

Place Type: Town
County: Bristol
Population: 13,722†

Ancestry‡	Population	%
African, Sub-Saharan (161)	372	2.72
African (51)	51	0.37
Cape Verdean (52)	186	1.36
Ethiopian (24)	40	0.29
Sudanese (34)	95	0.69
Albanian (0)	15	0.11
American (429)	429	3.13
Arab (11)	119	0.87
Arab (0)	36	0.26
Lebanese (11)	36	0.26
Syrian (0)	47	0.34
Armenian (39)	89	0.65
Austrian (0)	37	0.27
British (54)	102	0.75
Canadian (38)	71	0.52
Dutch (0)	74	0.54
English (552)	1,882	13.75
European (13)	13	0.09
Finnish (74)	74	0.54
French, ex. Basque (440)	2,269	16.58
French Canadian (565)	903	6.60
German (98)	772	5.64
Greek (32)	87	0.64
Hungarian (15)	15	0.11
Irish (816)	3,307	24.16
Italian (547)	1,987	14.52
Lithuanian (0)	23	0.17
Norwegian (0)	45	0.33
Polish (176)	790	5.77
Portuguese (1,946)	3,784	27.65
Russian (0)	86	0.63
Scandinavian (0)	11	0.08
Scotch-Irish (70)	185	1.35
Scottish (36)	275	2.01
Swedish (99)	448	3.27
Swiss (0)	33	0.24
Ukrainian (0)	28	0.20
Welsh (0)	27	0.20
West Indian, ex. Hispanic (51)	51	0.37
Jamaican (38)	38	0.28
West Indian (13)	13	0.09

Hispanic Origin	Population	%
Hispanic or Latino (of any race)	251	1.83
Central American, ex. Mexican	25	0.18
Costa Rican	1	0.01
Guatemalan	17	0.12
Salvadoran	7	0.05
Cuban	7	0.05
Dominican Republic	29	0.21
Mexican	37	0.27
Puerto Rican	78	0.57
South American	49	0.36
Bolivian	4	0.03
Colombian	36	0.26
Ecuadorian	2	0.01
Paraguayan	2	0.01
Peruvian	5	0.04
Other Hispanic or Latino	26	0.19

Race*	Population	%
African-American/Black (147)	215	1.57
Not Hispanic (137)	199	1.45
Hispanic (10)	16	0.12
American Indian/Alaska Native (30)	88	0.64
Not Hispanic (23)	80	0.58
Hispanic (7)	8	0.06
Cherokee (1)	6	0.04
Chickasaw (0)	1	0.01
Choctaw (0)	1	0.01
Iroquois (0)	5	0.04
Seminole (0)	1	0.01
Sioux (0)	1	0.01
Spanish American Ind. (5)	5	0.04
Yup'ik *(Alaska Native)* (0)	1	0.01
Asian (166)	212	1.54
Not Hispanic (166)	212	1.54
Cambodian (6)	7	0.05
Chinese, ex. Taiwanese (58)	70	0.51

*Notes: † The Census 2010 population figure is used to calculate the percentages in the Hispanic Origin and Race categories. Ancestry percentages are based on the 2006-2010 American Community Survey population (not shown); ‡ Numbers in parentheses indicate the number of people reporting a single ancestry; * Numbers in parentheses indicate the number of persons reporting this race alone, not in combination with any other race; Please refer to the Explanation of Data for more information.*

Filipino (6)	10	0.07
Indian (37)	42	0.31
Japanese (5)	10	0.07
Korean (19)	30	0.22
Laotian (2)	2	0.01
Pakistani (10)	10	0.07
Thai (6)	6	0.04
Vietnamese (12)	14	0.10
Hawaii Native/Pacific Islander (2)	20	0.15
Not Hispanic (2)	18	0.13
Hispanic (0)	2	0.01
Guamanian/Chamorro (1)	4	0.03
Native Hawaiian (1)	5	0.04
White (13,058)	13,226	96.39
Not Hispanic (12,898)	13,051	95.11
Hispanic (160)	175	1.28

Sharon

Place Type: Town
County: Norfolk
Population: 17,612†

Ancestry‡	Population	%
African, Sub-Saharan (125)	171	0.98
African (0)	12	0.07
Cape Verdean (12)	46	0.26
Nigerian (58)	58	0.33
South African (55)	55	0.32
American (967)	967	5.55
Arab (128)	166	0.95
Arab (14)	29	0.17
Egyptian (46)	60	0.34
Lebanese (0)	9	0.05
Moroccan (14)	14	0.08
Syrian (54)	54	0.31
Armenian (0)	42	0.24
Austrian (15)	68	0.39
Belgian (14)	14	0.08
Brazilian (41)	50	0.29
British (13)	13	0.07
Canadian (24)	53	0.30
Celtic (0)	12	0.07
Croatian (24)	72	0.41
Czech (11)	33	0.19
Czechoslovakian (15)	26	0.15
Danish (0)	105	0.60
Dutch (27)	64	0.37
Eastern European (732)	742	4.26
English (290)	1,240	7.11
European (233)	260	1.49
Finnish (0)	18	0.10
French, ex. Basque (29)	489	2.80
French Canadian (147)	401	2.30
German (268)	1,080	6.19
Greek (45)	120	0.69
Hungarian (61)	94	0.54
Iranian (30)	49	0.28
Irish (898)	2,497	14.32
Israeli (10)	23	0.13
Italian (502)	1,548	8.88
Latvian (9)	48	0.28
Lithuanian (58)	175	1.00
Norwegian (0)	103	0.59
Polish (407)	1,348	7.73
Portuguese (35)	158	0.91
Romanian (100)	112	0.64
Russian (1,558)	2,498	14.33
Scandinavian (16)	63	0.36
Scotch-Irish (43)	146	0.84
Scottish (10)	192	1.10
Serbian (0)	8	0.05
Swedish (14)	221	1.27
Swiss (21)	36	0.21
Ukrainian (74)	126	0.72
Welsh (0)	58	0.33
West Indian, ex. Hispanic (421)	481	2.76
Haitian (182)	192	1.10
Jamaican (64)	114	0.65
West Indian (175)	175	1.00

Hispanic Origin	Population	%
Hispanic or Latino (of any race)	373	2.12
Central American, ex. Mexican	29	0.16
Guatemalan	13	0.07
Honduran	4	0.02
Panamanian	5	0.03
Salvadoran	7	0.04
Cuban	32	0.18
Dominican Republic	13	0.07
Mexican	59	0.33
Puerto Rican	93	0.53
South American	98	0.56
Argentinean	29	0.16
Bolivian	7	0.04
Chilean	8	0.05
Colombian	31	0.18
Ecuadorian	2	0.01
Paraguayan	1	0.01
Peruvian	11	0.06
Venezuelan	9	0.05
Other Hispanic or Latino	49	0.28

Race*	Population	%
African-American/Black (746)	862	4.89
Not Hispanic (701)	806	4.58
Hispanic (45)	56	0.32
American Indian/Alaska Native (15)	60	0.34
Not Hispanic (9)	48	0.27
Hispanic (6)	12	0.07
Blackfeet (0)	3	0.02
Cherokee (0)	3	0.02
Chickasaw (0)	1	0.01
Choctaw (0)	1	0.01
Comanche (0)	2	0.01
Cree (0)	2	0.01
Iroquois (1)	1	0.01
Seminole (0)	1	0.01
Sioux (1)	3	0.02
South American Ind. (0)	1	0.01
Asian (1,922)	2,072	11.76
Not Hispanic (1,920)	2,066	11.73
Hispanic (2)	6	0.03
Bangladeshi (20)	24	0.14
Cambodian (17)	27	0.15
Chinese, ex. Taiwanese (717)	766	4.35
Filipino (38)	51	0.29
Indian (779)	826	4.69
Indonesian (2)	4	0.02
Japanese (15)	32	0.18
Korean (111)	130	0.74
Pakistani (56)	69	0.39
Sri Lankan (13)	18	0.10
Taiwanese (28)	29	0.16
Thai (10)	10	0.06
Vietnamese (64)	75	0.43
Hawaii Native/Pacific Islander (6)	12	0.07
Not Hispanic (6)	9	0.05
Hispanic (0)	3	0.02
White (14,497)	14,777	83.90
Not Hispanic (14,271)	14,523	82.46
Hispanic (226)	254	1.44

Shrewsbury

Place Type: Town
County: Worcester
Population: 35,608†

Ancestry‡	Population	%
African, Sub-Saharan (11)	11	0.03
African (11)	11	0.03
Albanian (52)	148	0.42
American (1,005)	1,005	2.87
Arab (390)	710	2.03
Arab (28)	43	0.12
Egyptian (32)	32	0.09
Lebanese (172)	433	1.24
Palestinian (15)	15	0.04
Syrian (8)	52	0.15
Other Arab (135)	135	0.39
Armenian (224)	432	1.23
Austrian (0)	11	0.03
Belgian (16)	30	0.09
Brazilian (543)	575	1.64
British (70)	112	0.32
Bulgarian (27)	27	0.08
Canadian (288)	459	1.31
Celtic (70)	79	0.23
Croatian (11)	33	0.09
Czech (11)	41	0.12
Czechoslovakian (23)	23	0.07
Danish (17)	92	0.26
Dutch (44)	217	0.62
Eastern European (96)	96	0.27
English (941)	3,582	10.23
Estonian (12)	25	0.07
European (237)	261	0.75
Finnish (13)	75	0.21
French, ex. Basque (777)	3,570	10.20
French Canadian (619)	1,685	4.81
German (416)	2,412	6.89
Greek (157)	322	0.92
Guyanese (68)	68	0.19
Hungarian (104)	209	0.60
Iranian (251)	269	0.77
Irish (2,747)	8,452	24.15
Italian (2,181)	6,148	17.57
Latvian (0)	33	0.09
Lithuanian (118)	694	1.98
Luxemburger (0)	35	0.10
Norwegian (38)	135	0.39
Polish (642)	1,929	5.51
Portuguese (88)	547	1.56
Romanian (9)	50	0.14
Russian (311)	607	1.73
Scandinavian (65)	97	0.28
Scotch-Irish (170)	478	1.37
Scottish (283)	729	2.08
Serbian (48)	48	0.14
Slovak (24)	114	0.33
Slovene (0)	12	0.03
Swedish (385)	1,297	3.71
Swiss (50)	94	0.27
Ukrainian (43)	96	0.27
Welsh (40)	143	0.41
West Indian, ex. Hispanic (121)	121	0.35
Haitian (68)	68	0.19
Jamaican (53)	53	0.15

Hispanic Origin	Population	%
Hispanic or Latino (of any race)	961	2.70
Central American, ex. Mexican	71	0.20
Costa Rican	6	0.02
Guatemalan	30	0.08
Honduran	2	0.01
Nicaraguan	6	0.02
Panamanian	3	0.01
Salvadoran	24	0.07
Cuban	40	0.11
Dominican Republic	54	0.15
Mexican	171	0.48
Puerto Rican	316	0.89
South American	162	0.45
Argentinean	27	0.08
Bolivian	2	0.01
Chilean	6	0.02
Colombian	57	0.16
Ecuadorian	18	0.05
Paraguayan	1	<0.01
Peruvian	15	0.04
Uruguayan	2	0.01
Venezuelan	27	0.08
Other South American	7	0.02
Other Hispanic or Latino	147	0.41

Race*	Population	%
African-American/Black (752)	874	2.45
Not Hispanic (717)	816	2.29
Hispanic (35)	58	0.16
American Indian/Alaska Native (33)	113	0.32

*Notes: † The Census 2010 population figure is used to calculate the percentages in the Hispanic Origin and Race categories. Ancestry percentages are based on the 2006-2010 American Community Survey population (not shown); ‡ Numbers in parentheses indicate the number of people reporting a single ancestry; * Numbers in parentheses indicate the number of persons reporting this race alone, not in combination with any other race; Please refer to the Explanation of Data for more information.*

Not Hispanic (27)	94	0.26
Hispanic (6)	19	0.05
Apache (0)	1	<0.01
Blackfeet (0)	6	0.02
Canadian/French Am. Ind. (0)	1	<0.01
Central American Ind. (0)	3	0.01
Cherokee (1)	8	0.02
Crow (0)	2	0.01
Inupiat *(Alaska Native)* (1)	1	<0.01
Iroquois (0)	2	0.01
Mexican American Ind. (1)	1	<0.01
Sioux (1)	3	0.01
South American Ind. (0)	2	0.01
Spanish American Ind. (1)	1	<0.01
Yaqui (0)	1	<0.01
Asian (5,451)	5,817	16.34
Not Hispanic (5,447)	5,807	16.31
Hispanic (4)	10	0.03
Bangladeshi (24)	25	0.07
Burmese (5)	5	0.01
Cambodian (32)	37	0.10
Chinese, ex. Taiwanese (1,268)	1,358	3.81
Filipino (108)	147	0.41
Hmong (5)	5	0.01
Indian (3,137)	3,261	9.16
Indonesian (2)	3	0.01
Japanese (75)	128	0.36
Korean (191)	208	0.58
Laotian (3)	6	0.02
Malaysian (4)	7	0.02
Nepalese (6)	7	0.02
Pakistani (151)	170	0.48
Sri Lankan (24)	29	0.08
Taiwanese (38)	43	0.12
Thai (9)	18	0.05
Vietnamese (260)	281	0.79
Hawaii Native/Pacific Islander (5)	15	0.04
Not Hispanic (5)	13	0.04
Hispanic (0)	2	0.01
Native Hawaiian (1)	7	0.02
Samoan (4)	5	0.01
White (28,187)	28,720	80.66
Not Hispanic (27,534)	28,014	78.67
Hispanic (653)	706	1.98

Somerset

Place Type: CDP/Town
County: Bristol
Population: 18,165†

Ancestry‡	Population	%
African, Sub-Saharan (58)	58	0.32
Cape Verdean (14)	14	0.08
South African (44)	44	0.24
American (429)	429	2.36
Arab (134)	478	2.63
Lebanese (134)	454	2.50
Syrian (0)	24	0.13
Armenian (11)	11	0.06
Cajun (15)	15	0.08
Canadian (37)	84	0.46
Croatian (0)	27	0.15
Czech (0)	9	0.05
Danish (0)	20	0.11
Dutch (0)	40	0.22
English (479)	2,274	12.50
European (59)	59	0.32
Finnish (17)	17	0.09
French, ex. Basque (846)	3,687	20.27
French Canadian (938)	1,550	8.52
German (60)	446	2.45
Greek (0)	44	0.24
Hungarian (0)	30	0.16
Irish (979)	3,392	18.65
Italian (228)	1,102	6.06
Lithuanian (0)	53	0.29
Norwegian (0)	40	0.22
Polish (241)	730	4.01
Portuguese (4,450)	7,714	42.42
Russian (12)	58	0.32
Scotch-Irish (16)	63	0.35
Scottish (138)	285	1.57
Swedish (36)	76	0.42
Swiss (0)	36	0.20
Ukrainian (62)	97	0.53
Welsh (16)	84	0.46
West Indian, ex. Hispanic (31)	31	0.17
Haitian (10)	10	0.05
Jamaican (21)	21	0.12

Hispanic Origin	Population	%
Hispanic or Latino (of any race)	191	1.05
Central American, ex. Mexican	24	0.13
Guatemalan	9	0.05
Honduran	11	0.06
Panamanian	1	0.01
Salvadoran	3	0.02
Cuban	2	0.01
Dominican Republic	10	0.06
Mexican	49	0.27
Puerto Rican	55	0.30
South American	17	0.09
Bolivian	1	0.01
Colombian	10	0.06
Paraguayan	1	0.01
Peruvian	3	0.02
Uruguayan	1	0.01
Venezuelan	1	0.01
Other Hispanic or Latino	34	0.19

Race*	Population	%
African-American/Black (68)	132	0.73
Not Hispanic (66)	125	0.69
Hispanic (2)	7	0.04
American Indian/Alaska Native (20)	77	0.42
Not Hispanic (20)	77	0.42
Blackfeet (0)	2	0.01
Canadian/French Am. Ind. (3)	5	0.03
Cherokee (0)	9	0.05
Chippewa (3)	8	0.04
Choctaw (0)	3	0.02
Cree (0)	4	0.02
Iroquois (0)	2	0.01
Sioux (0)	2	0.01
Asian (148)	190	1.05
Not Hispanic (148)	186	1.02
Hispanic (0)	4	0.02
Cambodian (2)	2	0.01
Chinese, ex. Taiwanese (48)	52	0.29
Filipino (21)	44	0.24
Indian (46)	49	0.27
Indonesian (1)	1	0.01
Japanese (3)	5	0.03
Korean (11)	13	0.07
Pakistani (10)	10	0.06
Thai (6)	7	0.04
Hawaii Native/Pacific Islander (1)	7	0.04
Not Hispanic (1)	7	0.04
Native Hawaiian (1)	1	0.01
Samoan (0)	1	0.01
White (17,700)	17,865	98.35
Not Hispanic (17,555)	17,705	97.47
Hispanic (145)	160	0.88

Somerville

Place Type: City
County: Middlesex
Population: 75,754†

Ancestry‡	Population	%
Afghan (69)	69	0.09
African, Sub-Saharan (668)	761	1.01
African (213)	244	0.32
Cape Verdean (260)	282	0.37
Ethiopian (53)	64	0.09
Ghanaian (41)	41	0.05
Nigerian (17)	17	0.02
Somalian (40)	40	0.05
South African (0)	17	0.02
Ugandan (44)	44	0.06
Other Sub-Saharan African (0)	12	0.02
Albanian (52)	52	0.07
American (3,958)	3,958	5.26
Arab (385)	649	0.86
Arab (83)	83	0.11
Egyptian (58)	69	0.09
Jordanian (14)	14	0.02
Lebanese (82)	284	0.38
Moroccan (35)	70	0.09
Palestinian (12)	12	0.02
Syrian (12)	28	0.04
Other Arab (89)	89	0.12
Armenian (75)	138	0.18
Assyrian/Chaldean/Syriac (0)	10	0.01
Australian (76)	76	0.10
Austrian (0)	230	0.31
Belgian (11)	95	0.13
Brazilian (3,345)	3,547	4.72
British (221)	543	0.72
Canadian (439)	731	0.97
Croatian (0)	40	0.05
Czech (22)	68	0.09
Czechoslovakian (0)	11	0.01
Danish (48)	116	0.15
Dutch (139)	619	0.82
Eastern European (543)	666	0.89
English (1,030)	5,232	6.96
European (1,287)	1,410	1.87
Finnish (62)	123	0.16
French, ex. Basque (509)	2,270	3.02
French Canadian (805)	1,800	2.39
German (738)	4,557	6.06
Greek (705)	1,054	1.40
Guyanese (50)	50	0.07
Hungarian (48)	225	0.30
Icelander (12)	24	0.03
Iranian (64)	105	0.14
Irish (5,369)	12,778	16.99
Israeli (28)	41	0.05
Italian (3,911)	8,540	11.35
Latvian (11)	37	0.05
Lithuanian (101)	359	0.48
Northern European (53)	84	0.11
Norwegian (69)	412	0.55
Pennsylvania German (0)	4	0.01
Polish (502)	2,789	3.71
Portuguese (3,243)	4,650	6.18
Romanian (136)	185	0.25
Russian (515)	1,542	2.05
Scandinavian (39)	152	0.20
Scotch-Irish (479)	1,241	1.65
Scottish (258)	1,431	1.90
Serbian (92)	92	0.12
Slovak (0)	38	0.05
Slovene (7)	17	0.02
Swedish (208)	874	1.16
Swiss (82)	184	0.24
Turkish (111)	188	0.25
Ukrainian (182)	334	0.44
Welsh (0)	306	0.41
West Indian, ex. Hispanic (1,365)	1,790	2.38
Bahamian (92)	92	0.12
Barbadian (11)	25	0.03
Belizean (11)	11	0.01
Haitian (975)	1,094	1.45
Jamaican (204)	340	0.45
Trinidadian/Tobagonian (14)	14	0.02
West Indian (32)	94	0.12
Other West Indian (26)	120	0.16
Yugoslavian (13)	25	0.03

Hispanic Origin	Population	%
Hispanic or Latino (of any race)	8,017	10.58
Central American, ex. Mexican	3,962	5.23
Costa Rican	52	0.07
Guatemalan	408	0.54
Honduran	170	0.22
Nicaraguan	82	0.11

*Notes: † The Census 2010 population figure is used to calculate the percentages in the Hispanic Origin and Race categories. Ancestry percentages are based on the 2006-2010 American Community Survey population (not shown); ‡ Numbers in parentheses indicate the number of people reporting a single ancestry; * Numbers in parentheses indicate the number of persons reporting this race alone, not in combination with any other race; Please refer to the Explanation of Data for more information.*

Panamanian	24	0.03
Salvadoran	3,211	4.24
Other Central American	15	0.02
Cuban	186	0.25
Dominican Republic	336	0.44
Mexican	737	0.97
Puerto Rican	907	1.20
South American	835	1.10
Argentinean	93	0.12
Bolivian	26	0.03
Chilean	55	0.07
Colombian	277	0.37
Ecuadorian	75	0.10
Paraguayan	6	0.01
Peruvian	171	0.23
Uruguayan	20	0.03
Venezuelan	93	0.12
Other South American	19	0.03
Other Hispanic or Latino	1,054	1.39

Race*	Population	%
African-American/Black (5,161)	6,033	7.96
Not Hispanic (4,869)	5,587	7.38
Hispanic (292)	446	0.59
American Indian/Alaska Native (198)	606	0.80
Not Hispanic (90)	416	0.55
Hispanic (108)	190	0.25
Apache (2)	7	0.01
Blackfeet (1)	10	0.01
Canadian/French Am. Ind. (3)	8	0.01
Central American Ind. (9)	11	0.01
Cherokee (9)	54	0.07
Chickasaw (1)	1	<0.01
Chippewa (1)	5	0.01
Choctaw (1)	11	0.01
Cree (0)	2	<0.01
Creek (1)	3	<0.01
Delaware (0)	3	<0.01
Inupiat *(Alaska Native)* (1)	1	<0.01
Iroquois (6)	14	0.02
Lumbee (0)	1	<0.01
Mexican American Ind. (10)	19	0.03
Navajo (3)	8	0.01
Osage (1)	1	<0.01
Ottawa (0)	1	<0.01
Potawatomi (1)	5	0.01
Seminole (1)	5	0.01
Shoshone (0)	1	<0.01
Sioux (2)	9	0.01
South American Ind. (14)	28	0.04
Spanish American Ind. (4)	4	0.01
Tlingit-Haida *(Alaska Native)* (0)	2	<0.01
Yup'ik *(Alaska Native)* (1)	1	<0.01
Asian (6,606)	7,545	9.96
Not Hispanic (6,578)	7,434	9.81
Hispanic (28)	111	0.15
Bangladeshi (98)	109	0.14
Bhutanese (5)	6	0.01
Burmese (4)	6	0.01
Cambodian (39)	54	0.07
Chinese, ex. Taiwanese (2,096)	2,422	3.20
Filipino (189)	304	0.40
Hmong (2)	2	<0.01
Indian (1,775)	2,023	2.67
Indonesian (31)	42	0.06
Japanese (263)	432	0.57
Korean (486)	580	0.77
Laotian (11)	18	0.02
Malaysian (13)	18	0.02
Nepalese (752)	792	1.05
Pakistani (87)	107	0.14
Sri Lankan (20)	31	0.04
Taiwanese (134)	159	0.21
Thai (57)	75	0.10
Vietnamese (255)	333	0.44
Hawaii Native/Pacific Islander (31)	152	0.20
Not Hispanic (16)	123	0.16
Hispanic (15)	29	0.04
Guamanian/Chamorro (15)	21	0.03
Native Hawaiian (2)	23	0.03
Samoan (3)	9	0.01
Tongan (0)	1	<0.01
White (55,994)	58,260	76.91
Not Hispanic (52,359)	54,145	71.47
Hispanic (3,635)	4,115	5.43

South Hadley

Place Type: Town
County: Hampshire
Population: 17,514†

Ancestry‡	Population	%
African, Sub-Saharan (100)	107	0.61
African (28)	35	0.20
Ghanaian (38)	38	0.22
Senegalese (16)	16	0.09
Somalian (18)	18	0.10
American (298)	298	1.70
Arab (34)	49	0.28
Lebanese (34)	34	0.19
Syrian (0)	15	0.09
Armenian (13)	76	0.43
Austrian (73)	198	1.13
Belgian (9)	9	0.05
British (88)	162	0.93
Bulgarian (30)	30	0.17
Canadian (44)	121	0.69
Czech (0)	111	0.63
Czechoslovakian (12)	24	0.14
Danish (0)	76	0.43
Dutch (0)	183	1.05
Eastern European (24)	24	0.14
English (553)	2,377	13.59
European (118)	147	0.84
Finnish (11)	35	0.20
French, ex. Basque (783)	3,237	18.50
French Canadian (738)	1,364	7.80
German (270)	1,560	8.92
Greek (27)	27	0.15
Guyanese (16)	16	0.09
Hungarian (30)	185	1.06
Iranian (18)	18	0.10
Irish (1,290)	4,608	26.34
Italian (244)	1,262	7.21
Lithuanian (12)	105	0.60
Norwegian (21)	131	0.75
Polish (1,143)	2,838	16.22
Portuguese (187)	390	2.23
Romanian (16)	16	0.09
Russian (42)	162	0.93
Scandinavian (26)	43	0.25
Scotch-Irish (154)	408	2.33
Scottish (115)	589	3.37
Slavic (0)	7	0.04
Slovak (15)	33	0.19
Swedish (25)	295	1.69
Swiss (0)	28	0.16
Ukrainian (21)	44	0.25
Welsh (25)	117	0.67
West Indian, ex. Hispanic (13)	13	0.07
Jamaican (13)	13	0.07

Hispanic Origin	Population	%
Hispanic or Latino (of any race)	753	4.30
Central American, ex. Mexican	56	0.32
Costa Rican	11	0.06
Guatemalan	4	0.02
Honduran	4	0.02
Nicaraguan	1	0.01
Panamanian	10	0.06
Salvadoran	26	0.15
Cuban	26	0.15
Dominican Republic	32	0.18
Mexican	87	0.50
Puerto Rican	405	2.31
South American	58	0.33
Argentinean	3	0.02
Bolivian	1	0.01
Chilean	6	0.03
Colombian	26	0.15
Ecuadorian	12	0.07
Paraguayan	1	0.01
Peruvian	5	0.03
Uruguayan	2	0.01
Venezuelan	1	0.01
Other South American	1	0.01
Other Hispanic or Latino	89	0.51

Race*	Population	%
African-American/Black (393)	560	3.20
Not Hispanic (368)	504	2.88
Hispanic (25)	56	0.32
American Indian/Alaska Native (23)	109	0.62
Not Hispanic (20)	91	0.52
Hispanic (3)	18	0.10
Blackfeet (0)	2	0.01
Canadian/French Am. Ind. (0)	1	0.01
Cherokee (3)	17	0.10
Chippewa (2)	4	0.02
Choctaw (0)	1	0.01
Cree (0)	1	0.01
Iroquois (0)	3	0.02
Navajo (1)	2	0.01
Ottawa (0)	3	0.02
Pueblo (0)	1	0.01
Sioux (1)	3	0.02
South American Ind. (0)	2	0.01
Yup'ik *(Alaska Native)* (1)	1	0.01
Asian (706)	882	5.04
Not Hispanic (701)	856	4.89
Hispanic (5)	26	0.15
Bangladeshi (18)	18	0.10
Bhutanese (4)	4	0.02
Burmese (4)	4	0.02
Cambodian (28)	29	0.17
Chinese, ex. Taiwanese (213)	256	1.46
Filipino (37)	71	0.41
Hmong (2)	2	0.01
Indian (102)	131	0.75
Indonesian (0)	1	0.01
Japanese (22)	55	0.31
Korean (63)	80	0.46
Laotian (1)	2	0.01
Malaysian (5)	8	0.05
Nepalese (23)	25	0.14
Pakistani (63)	70	0.40
Sri Lankan (10)	10	0.06
Taiwanese (5)	8	0.05
Thai (6)	11	0.06
Vietnamese (51)	62	0.35
Hawaii Native/Pacific Islander (9)	20	0.11
Not Hispanic (9)	15	0.09
Hispanic (0)	5	0.03
Fijian (0)	1	0.01
Guamanian/Chamorro (1)	1	0.01
Native Hawaiian (0)	2	0.01
Samoan (0)	3	0.02
White (15,770)	16,103	91.94
Not Hispanic (15,308)	15,593	89.03
Hispanic (462)	510	2.91

South Yarmouth

Place Type: CDP
County: Barnstable
Population: 11,092†

Ancestry‡	Population	%
African, Sub-Saharan (72)	102	0.89
Cape Verdean (72)	102	0.89
Albanian (15)	15	0.13
American (1,330)	1,330	11.60
Arab (43)	153	1.33
Arab (43)	43	0.37
Lebanese (0)	88	0.77
Moroccan (0)	22	0.19
Armenian (44)	44	0.38
Brazilian (432)	432	3.77
British (104)	143	1.25

*Notes: † The Census 2010 population figure is used to calculate the percentages in the Hispanic Origin and Race categories. Ancestry percentages are based on the 2006-2010 American Community Survey population (not shown); ‡ Numbers in parentheses indicate the number of people reporting a single ancestry; * Numbers in parentheses indicate the number of persons reporting this race alone, not in combination with any other race; Please refer to the Explanation of Data for more information.*

Ancestry (cont.)	Population	%
Bulgarian (24)	24	0.21
Canadian (92)	163	1.42
Czechoslovakian (25)	25	0.22
Danish (27)	66	0.58
Dutch (13)	84	0.73
Eastern European (18)	38	0.33
English (727)	2,088	18.21
European (30)	30	0.26
Finnish (34)	141	1.23
French, ex. Basque (170)	1,207	10.52
French Canadian (109)	223	1.94
German (261)	968	8.44
Greek (27)	27	0.24
Hungarian (67)	105	0.92
Irish (1,545)	3,270	28.51
Italian (785)	1,450	12.64
Lithuanian (28)	50	0.44
Norwegian (0)	12	0.10
Polish (157)	753	6.57
Portuguese (111)	365	3.18
Russian (0)	11	0.10
Scotch-Irish (76)	369	3.22
Scottish (90)	263	2.29
Slovak (0)	25	0.22
Slovene (0)	12	0.10
Swedish (72)	378	3.30
Swiss (17)	30	0.26
Welsh (0)	48	0.42
West Indian, ex. Hispanic (38)	38	0.33
Haitian (12)	12	0.10
Jamaican (26)	26	0.23

Hispanic Origin	Population	%
Hispanic or Latino (of any race)	318	2.87
Central American, ex. Mexican	8	0.07
Guatemalan	2	0.02
Honduran	4	0.04
Salvadoran	2	0.02
Cuban	10	0.09
Dominican Republic	26	0.23
Mexican	42	0.38
Puerto Rican	131	1.18
South American	52	0.47
Argentinean	3	0.03
Chilean	9	0.08
Colombian	7	0.06
Ecuadorian	21	0.19
Paraguayan	1	0.01
Peruvian	11	0.10
Other Hispanic or Latino	49	0.44

Race*	Population	%
African-American/Black (267)	356	3.21
Not Hispanic (245)	317	2.86
Hispanic (22)	39	0.35
American Indian/Alaska Native (39)	97	0.87
Not Hispanic (31)	85	0.77
Hispanic (8)	12	0.11
Blackfeet (1)	6	0.05
Cherokee (4)	7	0.06
Chippewa (1)	3	0.03
Cree (0)	1	0.01
Iroquois (1)	3	0.03
Sioux (2)	3	0.03
South American Ind. (1)	1	0.01
Asian (141)	180	1.62
Not Hispanic (139)	175	1.58
Hispanic (2)	5	0.05
Cambodian (1)	2	0.02
Chinese, ex. Taiwanese (47)	54	0.49
Filipino (17)	28	0.25
Indian (23)	30	0.27
Indonesian (0)	1	0.01
Japanese (3)	12	0.11
Korean (4)	5	0.05
Laotian (1)	3	0.03
Nepalese (0)	2	0.02
Pakistani (25)	25	0.23
Thai (3)	5	0.05
Vietnamese (12)	13	0.12
Hawaii Native/Pacific Islander (1)	10	0.09
Not Hispanic (1)	9	0.08
Hispanic (0)	1	0.01
Native Hawaiian (0)	1	0.01
White (10,218)	10,404	93.80
Not Hispanic (10,056)	10,203	91.99
Hispanic (162)	201	1.81

Southborough

Place Type: Town
County: Worcester
Population: 9,767†

Ancestry‡	Population	%
Albanian (13)	13	0.14
American (324)	324	3.37
Arab (69)	114	1.19
Egyptian (35)	35	0.36
Lebanese (24)	69	0.72
Syrian (10)	10	0.10
Armenian (23)	36	0.37
Austrian (14)	34	0.35
Brazilian (12)	12	0.12
British (37)	37	0.38
Canadian (18)	148	1.54
Croatian (0)	11	0.11
Czech (88)	132	1.37
Danish (0)	11	0.11
Dutch (17)	17	0.18
Eastern European (130)	130	1.35
English (339)	1,541	16.02
European (209)	209	2.17
French, ex. Basque (191)	748	7.78
French Canadian (145)	288	2.99
German (150)	822	8.55
Greek (164)	361	3.75
Hungarian (16)	27	0.28
Iranian (0)	12	0.12
Irish (1,213)	3,176	33.02
Israeli (22)	57	0.59
Italian (660)	1,606	16.70
Latvian (11)	11	0.11
Lithuanian (12)	91	0.95
Northern European (12)	12	0.12
Norwegian (19)	151	1.57
Polish (20)	157	1.63
Portuguese (65)	117	1.22
Russian (173)	289	3.01
Scotch-Irish (42)	205	2.13
Scottish (49)	185	1.92
Slovak (0)	29	0.30
Swedish (81)	236	2.45
Welsh (12)	39	0.41

Hispanic Origin	Population	%
Hispanic or Latino (of any race)	272	2.78
Central American, ex. Mexican	34	0.35
Costa Rican	1	0.01
Guatemalan	18	0.18
Honduran	1	0.01
Panamanian	3	0.03
Salvadoran	11	0.11
Cuban	32	0.33
Dominican Republic	10	0.10
Mexican	62	0.63
Puerto Rican	36	0.37
South American	64	0.66
Argentinean	11	0.11
Bolivian	4	0.04
Chilean	3	0.03
Colombian	22	0.23
Ecuadorian	7	0.07
Peruvian	12	0.12
Venezuelan	5	0.05
Other Hispanic or Latino	34	0.35

Race*	Population	%
African-American/Black (89)	116	1.19
Not Hispanic (80)	100	1.02
Hispanic (9)	16	0.16
American Indian/Alaska Native (16)	48	0.49
Not Hispanic (13)	37	0.38
Hispanic (3)	11	0.11
Blackfeet (0)	4	0.04
Cherokee (0)	4	0.04
Mexican American Ind. (1)	4	0.04
South American Ind. (2)	2	0.02
Asian (815)	932	9.54
Not Hispanic (813)	921	9.43
Hispanic (2)	11	0.11
Cambodian (6)	8	0.08
Chinese, ex. Taiwanese (358)	400	4.10
Filipino (19)	30	0.31
Indian (288)	323	3.31
Japanese (21)	31	0.32
Korean (50)	58	0.59
Malaysian (1)	2	0.02
Pakistani (21)	21	0.22
Sri Lankan (5)	6	0.06
Taiwanese (13)	21	0.22
Thai (4)	5	0.05
Vietnamese (13)	22	0.23
Hawaii Native/Pacific Islander (1)	7	0.07
Not Hispanic (0)	5	0.05
Hispanic (1)	2	0.02
Guamanian/Chamorro (1)	1	0.01
Native Hawaiian (0)	5	0.05
Samoan (0)	1	0.01
White (8,605)	8,750	89.59
Not Hispanic (8,405)	8,525	87.28
Hispanic (200)	225	2.30

Southbridge Town

Place Type: City
County: Worcester
Population: 16,719†

Ancestry‡	Population	%
African, Sub-Saharan (86)	99	0.59
Cape Verdean (33)	46	0.27
Kenyan (53)	53	0.31
Albanian (84)	121	0.72
American (514)	514	3.05
Armenian (8)	8	0.05
Austrian (19)	27	0.16
British (17)	36	0.21
Canadian (75)	149	0.88
Czech (0)	20	0.12
Czechoslovakian (0)	3	0.02
Danish (8)	8	0.05
Dutch (9)	78	0.46
English (263)	1,065	6.32
European (18)	28	0.17
French, ex. Basque (1,072)	3,697	21.94
French Canadian (1,182)	2,005	11.90
German (111)	945	5.61
Greek (65)	134	0.80
Hungarian (8)	66	0.39
Irish (463)	2,529	15.01
Italian (438)	2,212	13.13
Latvian (4)	4	0.02
Lithuanian (8)	36	0.21
Norwegian (28)	35	0.21
Polish (397)	1,231	7.31
Portuguese (25)	266	1.58
Romanian (8)	8	0.05
Russian (0)	7	0.04
Scandinavian (0)	8	0.05
Scotch-Irish (63)	247	1.47
Scottish (42)	189	1.12
Slovak (0)	10	0.06
Swedish (29)	185	1.10
Welsh (0)	42	0.25

Hispanic Origin	Population	%
Hispanic or Latino (of any race)	4,452	26.63
Central American, ex. Mexican	69	0.41
Costa Rican	8	0.05

*Notes: † The Census 2010 population figure is used to calculate the percentages in the Hispanic Origin and Race categories. Ancestry percentages are based on the 2006-2010 American Community Survey population (not shown); ‡ Numbers in parentheses indicate the number of people reporting a single ancestry; * Numbers in parentheses indicate the number of persons reporting this race alone, not in combination with any other race; Please refer to the Explanation of Data for more information.*

Guatemalan	16	0.10
Honduran	14	0.08
Panamanian	7	0.04
Salvadoran	23	0.14
Other Central American	1	0.01
Cuban	18	0.11
Dominican Republic	176	1.05
Mexican	104	0.62
Puerto Rican	3,858	23.08
South American	83	0.50
Argentinean	2	0.01
Bolivian	2	0.01
Chilean	3	0.02
Colombian	35	0.21
Ecuadorian	22	0.13
Peruvian	11	0.07
Uruguayan	1	0.01
Venezuelan	7	0.04
Other Hispanic or Latino	144	0.86

Race*	Population	%
African-American/Black (431)	606	3.62
Not Hispanic (236)	324	1.94
Hispanic (195)	282	1.69
American Indian/Alaska Native (88)	193	1.15
Not Hispanic (58)	130	0.78
Hispanic (30)	63	0.38
Apache (0)	2	0.01
Blackfeet (1)	4	0.02
Canadian/French Am. Ind. (0)	3	0.02
Central American Ind. (2)	6	0.04
Cherokee (7)	17	0.10
Cheyenne (1)	1	0.01
Cree (0)	1	0.01
Iroquois (0)	4	0.02
Navajo (4)	4	0.02
South American Ind. (2)	2	0.01
Spanish American Ind. (1)	5	0.03
Asian (310)	359	2.15
Not Hispanic (296)	326	1.95
Hispanic (14)	33	0.20
Burmese (1)	1	0.01
Cambodian (5)	9	0.05
Chinese, ex. Taiwanese (35)	44	0.26
Filipino (22)	29	0.17
Indian (58)	75	0.45
Indonesian (1)	2	0.01
Japanese (4)	9	0.05
Korean (8)	10	0.06
Laotian (112)	130	0.78
Nepalese (3)	3	0.02
Pakistani (10)	21	0.13
Thai (1)	3	0.02
Vietnamese (12)	14	0.08
Hawaii Native/Pacific Islander (3)	12	0.07
Not Hispanic (3)	6	0.04
Hispanic (0)	6	0.04
Native Hawaiian (3)	7	0.04
White (13,580)	13,981	83.62
Not Hispanic (11,465)	11,641	69.63
Hispanic (2,115)	2,340	14.00

Southwick

Place Type: Town
County: Hampden
Population: 9,502†

Ancestry‡	Population	%
American (429)	429	4.57
Arab (35)	307	3.27
Lebanese (0)	166	1.77
Moroccan (35)	141	1.50
Armenian (0)	76	0.81
Austrian (0)	16	0.17
British (29)	29	0.31
Canadian (15)	44	0.47
Czech (0)	31	0.33
Czechoslovakian (0)	33	0.35
Dutch (179)	307	3.27
Eastern European (47)	47	0.50
English (423)	1,457	15.54
European (50)	50	0.53
French, ex. Basque (350)	1,429	15.24
French Canadian (272)	506	5.40
German (150)	1,030	10.98
Greek (39)	139	1.48
Hungarian (12)	12	0.13
Irish (605)	2,106	22.46
Italian (413)	1,765	18.82
Lithuanian (28)	28	0.30
Northern European (44)	44	0.47
Polish (830)	1,438	15.33
Portuguese (53)	146	1.56
Russian (16)	216	2.30
Scotch-Irish (124)	311	3.32
Scottish (53)	267	2.85
Slovak (16)	85	0.91
Slovene (10)	10	0.11
Swedish (30)	212	2.26
Ukrainian (23)	162	1.73
Welsh (0)	54	0.58

Hispanic Origin	Population	%
Hispanic or Latino (of any race)	198	2.08
Central American, ex. Mexican	6	0.06
Costa Rican	3	0.03
Guatemalan	2	0.02
Salvadoran	1	0.01
Cuban	1	0.01
Dominican Republic	4	0.04
Mexican	29	0.31
Puerto Rican	97	1.02
South American	34	0.36
Colombian	22	0.23
Ecuadorian	3	0.03
Peruvian	3	0.03
Venezuelan	5	0.05
Other South American	1	0.01
Other Hispanic or Latino	27	0.28

Race*	Population	%
African-American/Black (85)	113	1.19
Not Hispanic (79)	105	1.11
Hispanic (6)	8	0.08
American Indian/Alaska Native (24)	63	0.66
Not Hispanic (23)	58	0.61
Hispanic (1)	5	0.05
Apache (1)	1	0.01
Blackfeet (0)	4	0.04
Canadian/French Am. Ind. (3)	3	0.03
Cherokee (3)	9	0.09
Chippewa (0)	2	0.02
Delaware (1)	1	0.01
Iroquois (0)	1	0.01
Shoshone (0)	1	0.01
Sioux (0)	2	0.02
South American Ind. (0)	1	0.01
Asian (77)	105	1.11
Not Hispanic (77)	104	1.09
Hispanic (0)	1	0.01
Chinese, ex. Taiwanese (16)	21	0.22
Filipino (9)	14	0.15
Indian (12)	16	0.17
Japanese (4)	11	0.12
Korean (10)	13	0.14
Laotian (5)	5	0.05
Pakistani (4)	5	0.05
Taiwanese (1)	3	0.03
Thai (0)	1	0.01
Vietnamese (6)	7	0.07
Hawaii Native/Pacific Islander (3)	12	0.13
Not Hispanic (3)	10	0.11
Hispanic (0)	2	0.02
Guamanian/Chamorro (0)	4	0.04
Native Hawaiian (0)	4	0.04
White (9,157)	9,270	97.56
Not Hispanic (9,028)	9,119	95.97
Hispanic (129)	151	1.59

Spencer

Place Type: Town
County: Worcester
Population: 11,688†

Ancestry‡	Population	%
African, Sub-Saharan (51)	51	0.44
Cape Verdean (18)	18	0.15
Ghanaian (33)	33	0.28
Albanian (17)	32	0.27
American (406)	406	3.46
Arab (0)	50	0.43
Lebanese (0)	42	0.36
Syrian (0)	8	0.07
Armenian (0)	15	0.13
British (19)	19	0.16
Canadian (58)	103	0.88
Czech (17)	47	0.40
Danish (0)	55	0.47
Dutch (63)	226	1.93
English (505)	1,778	15.17
European (24)	24	0.20
Finnish (14)	75	0.64
French, ex. Basque (891)	3,456	29.48
French Canadian (915)	1,346	11.48
German (41)	476	4.06
Greek (119)	142	1.21
Hungarian (0)	14	0.12
Irish (587)	2,929	24.98
Italian (222)	1,186	10.12
Lithuanian (108)	205	1.75
Norwegian (16)	47	0.40
Polish (454)	1,229	10.48
Portuguese (0)	180	1.54
Russian (15)	32	0.27
Scotch-Irish (39)	139	1.19
Scottish (82)	341	2.91
Swedish (109)	394	3.36
Welsh (0)	14	0.12
Yugoslavian (0)	14	0.12

Hispanic Origin	Population	%
Hispanic or Latino (of any race)	335	2.87
Central American, ex. Mexican	25	0.21
Costa Rican	1	0.01
Guatemalan	2	0.02
Honduran	5	0.04
Panamanian	1	0.01
Salvadoran	16	0.14
Cuban	8	0.07
Dominican Republic	33	0.28
Mexican	26	0.22
Puerto Rican	187	1.60
South American	35	0.30
Argentinean	10	0.09
Chilean	2	0.02
Colombian	14	0.12
Ecuadorian	4	0.03
Peruvian	5	0.04
Other Hispanic or Latino	21	0.18

Race*	Population	%
African-American/Black (74)	122	1.04
Not Hispanic (61)	98	0.84
Hispanic (13)	24	0.21
American Indian/Alaska Native (26)	72	0.62
Not Hispanic (20)	64	0.55
Hispanic (6)	8	0.07
Blackfeet (0)	7	0.06
Canadian/French Am. Ind. (8)	8	0.07
Crow (1)	2	0.02
Iroquois (2)	2	0.02
Mexican American Ind. (1)	1	0.01
Navajo (1)	1	0.01
Pueblo (1)	1	0.01
Sioux (2)	2	0.02
South American Ind. (1)	1	0.01
Asian (84)	124	1.06
Not Hispanic (79)	117	1.00

*Notes: † The Census 2010 population figure is used to calculate the percentages in the Hispanic Origin and Race categories. Ancestry percentages are based on the 2006-2010 American Community Survey population (not shown); ‡ Numbers in parentheses indicate the number of people reporting a single ancestry; * Numbers in parentheses indicate the number of persons reporting this race alone, not in combination with any other race; Please refer to the Explanation of Data for more information.*

Hispanic (5)	7	0.06
Cambodian (4)	4	0.03
Chinese, ex. Taiwanese (8)	10	0.09
Filipino (7)	15	0.13
Indian (12)	12	0.10
Japanese (1)	4	0.03
Korean (10)	16	0.14
Laotian (10)	12	0.10
Thai (1)	1	0.01
Vietnamese (21)	24	0.21
Hawaii Native/Pacific Islander (8)	13	0.11
Not Hispanic (5)	10	0.09
Hispanic (3)	3	0.03
Guamanian/Chamorro (3)	5	0.04
Marshallese (1)	2	0.02
Native Hawaiian (4)	4	0.03
White (11,249)	11,385	97.41
Not Hispanic (11,061)	11,172	95.59
Hispanic (188)	213	1.82

Springfield

Place Type: City
County: Hampden
Population: 153,060†

Ancestry‡	Population	%
African, Sub-Saharan (2,038)	2,648	1.73
African (805)	1,166	0.76
Cape Verdean (101)	153	0.10
Ethiopian (181)	187	0.12
Ghanaian (101)	101	0.07
Kenyan (46)	46	0.03
Nigerian (95)	222	0.15
Senegalese (143)	143	0.09
Somalian (542)	542	0.35
Sudanese (0)	54	0.04
Ugandan (0)	10	0.01
Other Sub-Saharan African (24)	24	0.02
Albanian (21)	64	0.04
American (2,989)	2,989	1.95
Arab (401)	578	0.38
Arab (19)	43	0.03
Iraqi (0)	17	0.01
Jordanian (34)	34	0.02
Lebanese (206)	302	0.20
Moroccan (9)	17	0.01
Palestinian (123)	123	0.08
Syrian (0)	32	0.02
Other Arab (10)	10	0.01
Armenian (84)	122	0.08
Austrian (26)	99	0.06
Belgian (18)	18	0.01
Brazilian (89)	94	0.06
British (83)	124	0.08
Canadian (218)	422	0.28
Celtic (11)	11	0.01
Czech (0)	29	0.02
Czechoslovakian (11)	11	0.01
Danish (19)	73	0.05
Dutch (163)	755	0.49
Eastern European (43)	43	0.03
English (2,102)	7,085	4.63
European (303)	335	0.22
Finnish (39)	88	0.06
French, ex. Basque (3,038)	11,383	7.44
French Canadian (1,922)	3,965	2.59
German (869)	4,635	3.03
Greek (489)	775	0.51
Hungarian (66)	176	0.12
Iranian (49)	69	0.05
Irish (5,923)	17,440	11.41
Italian (4,356)	10,876	7.11
Lithuanian (57)	311	0.20
Macedonian (17)	43	0.03
Norwegian (43)	217	0.14
Pennsylvania German (14)	14	0.01
Polish (2,893)	7,121	4.66
Portuguese (681)	1,678	1.10
Romanian (55)	82	0.05
Russian (371)	840	0.55
Scandinavian (39)	39	0.03
Scotch-Irish (509)	1,250	0.82
Scottish (397)	1,787	1.17
Slavic (0)	45	0.03
Slovak (10)	60	0.04
Swedish (208)	1,073	0.70
Swiss (12)	53	0.03
Turkish (73)	89	0.06
Ukrainian (204)	238	0.16
Welsh (28)	137	0.09
West Indian, ex. Hispanic (3,985)	5,251	3.43
Bahamian (21)	21	0.01
Barbadian (197)	234	0.15
British West Indian (162)	176	0.12
Haitian (455)	526	0.34
Jamaican (2,869)	3,692	2.41
Trinidadian/Tobagonian (59)	106	0.07
U.S. Virgin Islander (25)	143	0.09
West Indian (182)	338	0.22
Other West Indian (15)	15	0.01
Yugoslavian (39)	113	0.07

Hispanic Origin	Population	%
Hispanic or Latino (of any race)	59,451	38.84
Central American, ex. Mexican	1,399	0.91
Costa Rican	122	0.08
Guatemalan	727	0.47
Honduran	121	0.08
Nicaraguan	18	0.01
Panamanian	157	0.10
Salvadoran	234	0.15
Other Central American	20	0.01
Cuban	384	0.25
Dominican Republic	2,649	1.73
Mexican	1,514	0.99
Puerto Rican	50,798	33.19
South American	893	0.58
Argentinean	27	0.02
Bolivian	10	0.01
Chilean	17	0.01
Colombian	375	0.25
Ecuadorian	193	0.13
Paraguayan	7	<0.01
Peruvian	196	0.13
Uruguayan	19	0.01
Venezuelan	46	0.03
Other South American	3	<0.01
Other Hispanic or Latino	1,814	1.19

Race*	Population	%
African-American/Black (34,073)	38,318	25.03
Not Hispanic (29,934)	32,328	21.12
Hispanic (4,139)	5,990	3.91
American Indian/Alaska Native (987)	2,553	1.67
Not Hispanic (329)	1,220	0.80
Hispanic (658)	1,333	0.87
Alaska Athabascan *(Ala. Nat.)* (5)	5	<0.01
Apache (3)	7	<0.01
Blackfeet (9)	95	0.06
Canadian/French Am. Ind. (7)	23	0.02
Central American Ind. (19)	22	0.01
Cherokee (22)	179	0.12
Cheyenne (1)	2	<0.01
Chickasaw (0)	1	<0.01
Chippewa (2)	5	<0.01
Choctaw (8)	17	0.01
Comanche (1)	1	<0.01
Cree (3)	8	0.01
Creek (3)	9	0.01
Crow (0)	1	<0.01
Delaware (0)	3	<0.01
Houma (2)	3	<0.01
Inupiat *(Alaska Native)* (0)	1	<0.01
Iroquois (24)	88	0.06
Lumbee (1)	1	<0.01
Mexican American Ind. (24)	35	0.02
Navajo (3)	15	0.01
Ottawa (0)	1	<0.01
Pueblo (7)	7	<0.01
Seminole (3)	10	0.01
Shoshone (1)	2	<0.01
Sioux (1)	15	0.01
South American Ind. (83)	196	0.13
Spanish American Ind. (12)	26	0.02
Tlingit-Haida *(Alaska Native)* (1)	1	<0.01
Asian (3,728)	4,462	2.92
Not Hispanic (3,615)	4,146	2.71
Hispanic (113)	316	0.21
Bangladeshi (8)	8	0.01
Bhutanese (52)	66	0.04
Burmese (31)	32	0.02
Cambodian (153)	200	0.13
Chinese, ex. Taiwanese (407)	516	0.34
Filipino (142)	247	0.16
Hmong (78)	80	0.05
Indian (291)	418	0.27
Indonesian (9)	21	0.01
Japanese (43)	146	0.10
Korean (116)	164	0.11
Laotian (102)	129	0.08
Malaysian (9)	13	0.01
Nepalese (33)	47	0.03
Pakistani (118)	136	0.09
Sri Lankan (8)	10	0.01
Taiwanese (10)	11	0.01
Thai (51)	74	0.05
Vietnamese (1,865)	1,997	1.30
Hawaii Native/Pacific Islander (128)	554	0.36
Not Hispanic (47)	243	0.16
Hispanic (81)	311	0.20
Fijian (1)	1	<0.01
Guamanian/Chamorro (28)	60	0.04
Native Hawaiian (38)	92	0.06
Samoan (18)	33	0.02
Tongan (2)	10	0.01
White (79,335)	84,628	55.29
Not Hispanic (56,248)	58,780	38.40
Hispanic (23,087)	25,848	16.89

Sterling

Place Type: Town
County: Worcester
Population: 7,808†

Ancestry‡	Population	%
Albanian (18)	32	0.41
Alsatian (0)	20	0.26
American (464)	464	6.01
Arab (52)	73	0.95
Egyptian (52)	52	0.67
Lebanese (0)	21	0.27
Armenian (0)	35	0.45
Assyrian/Chaldean/Syriac (0)	10	0.13
Australian (0)	12	0.16
Austrian (18)	66	0.86
Brazilian (0)	22	0.29
British (15)	15	0.19
Canadian (44)	55	0.71
Celtic (12)	36	0.47
Danish (0)	63	0.82
Dutch (51)	75	0.97
English (349)	1,012	13.11
European (147)	147	1.90
Finnish (72)	235	3.04
French, ex. Basque (118)	746	9.66
French Canadian (299)	605	7.84
German (318)	828	10.73
Greek (0)	25	0.32
Hungarian (20)	53	0.69
Irish (675)	2,155	27.92
Italian (429)	1,568	20.31
Lithuanian (26)	87	1.13
Norwegian (0)	24	0.31
Polish (211)	871	11.28
Portuguese (46)	206	2.67
Scotch-Irish (25)	141	1.83
Scottish (49)	233	3.02
Slovene (24)	24	0.31

*Notes: † The Census 2010 population figure is used to calculate the percentages in the Hispanic Origin and Race categories. Ancestry percentages are based on the 2006-2010 American Community Survey population (not shown); ‡ Numbers in parentheses indicate the number of people reporting a single ancestry; * Numbers in parentheses indicate the number of persons reporting this race alone, not in combination with any other race; Please refer to the Explanation of Data for more information.*

Swedish (37)	215	2.79
Swiss (41)	41	0.53
Ukrainian (0)	50	0.65
Welsh (0)	26	0.34

Hispanic Origin	Population	%
Hispanic or Latino (of any race)	158	2.02
Central American, ex. Mexican	11	0.14
Guatemalan	6	0.08
Honduran	4	0.05
Panamanian	1	0.01
Cuban	2	0.03
Dominican Republic	6	0.08
Mexican	19	0.24
Puerto Rican	66	0.85
South American	32	0.41
Argentinean	1	0.01
Colombian	13	0.17
Ecuadorian	4	0.05
Peruvian	5	0.06
Uruguayan	1	0.01
Other South American	8	0.10
Other Hispanic or Latino	22	0.28

Race*	Population	%
African-American/Black (55)	81	1.04
Not Hispanic (52)	76	0.97
Hispanic (3)	5	0.06
American Indian/Alaska Native (14)	38	0.49
Not Hispanic (13)	37	0.47
Hispanic (1)	1	0.01
Apache (1)	1	0.01
Canadian/French Am. Ind. (1)	1	0.01
Cherokee (0)	4	0.05
Iroquois (0)	1	0.01
Sioux (3)	3	0.04
Asian (68)	88	1.13
Not Hispanic (67)	87	1.11
Hispanic (1)	1	0.01
Cambodian (2)	2	0.03
Chinese, ex. Taiwanese (25)	27	0.35
Filipino (2)	4	0.05
Indian (11)	17	0.22
Japanese (0)	2	0.03
Korean (13)	19	0.24
Laotian (8)	8	0.10
Taiwanese (2)	2	0.03
Thai (1)	1	0.01
Vietnamese (3)	4	0.05
Hawaii Native/Pacific Islander (5)	8	0.10
Not Hispanic (5)	8	0.10
Guamanian/Chamorro (5)	6	0.08
Native Hawaiian (0)	2	0.03
White (7,571)	7,642	97.87
Not Hispanic (7,441)	7,508	96.16
Hispanic (130)	134	1.72

Stoneham

Place Type: CDP/Town
County: Middlesex
Population: 21,437†

Ancestry‡	Population	%
African, Sub-Saharan (0)	41	0.19
African (0)	41	0.19
Albanian (45)	117	0.55
American (448)	448	2.10
Arab (79)	156	0.73
Egyptian (22)	22	0.10
Lebanese (46)	74	0.35
Syrian (11)	60	0.28
Armenian (92)	285	1.34
Austrian (8)	38	0.18
Brazilian (60)	60	0.28
British (0)	14	0.07
Bulgarian (31)	31	0.15
Cajun (14)	14	0.07
Canadian (43)	291	1.36
Celtic (13)	13	0.06
Croatian (0)	12	0.06
Cypriot (13)	55	0.26
Czech (0)	62	0.29
Czechoslovakian (164)	213	1.00
Dutch (46)	140	0.66
Eastern European (29)	29	0.14
English (650)	2,898	13.59
European (125)	186	0.87
Finnish (19)	45	0.21
French, ex. Basque (172)	1,162	5.45
French Canadian (155)	522	2.45
German (135)	1,260	5.91
Greek (175)	483	2.27
Hungarian (17)	32	0.15
Icelander (57)	57	0.27
Iranian (55)	78	0.37
Irish (2,686)	6,398	30.01
Italian (4,505)	7,672	35.98
Lithuanian (10)	49	0.23
Norwegian (0)	57	0.27
Polish (224)	560	2.63
Portuguese (489)	736	3.45
Romanian (7)	15	0.07
Russian (58)	129	0.61
Scotch-Irish (89)	446	2.09
Scottish (185)	617	2.89
Slovak (10)	10	0.05
Swedish (37)	232	1.09
Swiss (0)	35	0.16
Ukrainian (12)	37	0.17
Welsh (0)	45	0.21
West Indian, ex. Hispanic (22)	79	0.37
Haitian (22)	22	0.10
Jamaican (0)	45	0.21
Trinidadian/Tobagonian (0)	12	0.06
Yugoslavian (0)	14	0.07

Hispanic Origin	Population	%
Hispanic or Latino (of any race)	634	2.96
Central American, ex. Mexican	141	0.66
Costa Rican	22	0.10
Guatemalan	46	0.21
Honduran	8	0.04
Nicaraguan	2	0.01
Panamanian	1	<0.01
Salvadoran	59	0.28
Other Central American	3	0.01
Cuban	26	0.12
Dominican Republic	37	0.17
Mexican	91	0.42
Puerto Rican	165	0.77
South American	107	0.50
Argentinean	17	0.08
Chilean	7	0.03
Colombian	35	0.16
Ecuadorian	24	0.11
Peruvian	19	0.09
Venezuelan	5	0.02
Other Hispanic or Latino	67	0.31

Race*	Population	%
African-American/Black (379)	482	2.25
Not Hispanic (339)	426	1.99
Hispanic (40)	56	0.26
American Indian/Alaska Native (26)	93	0.43
Not Hispanic (18)	71	0.33
Hispanic (8)	22	0.10
Alaska Athabascan *(Ala. Nat.)* (0)	2	0.01
Blackfeet (0)	5	0.02
Canadian/French Am. Ind. (0)	3	0.01
Cherokee (6)	17	0.08
Chippewa (1)	1	<0.01
Iroquois (0)	1	<0.01
Mexican American Ind. (0)	2	0.01
Navajo (3)	3	0.01
Sioux (0)	4	0.02
South American Ind. (1)	1	<0.01
Spanish American Ind. (2)	2	0.01
Asian (727)	821	3.83
Not Hispanic (723)	798	3.72
Hispanic (4)	23	0.11
Bangladeshi (3)	3	0.01
Cambodian (16)	18	0.08
Chinese, ex. Taiwanese (290)	329	1.53
Filipino (26)	46	0.21
Indian (192)	208	0.97
Indonesian (1)	1	<0.01
Japanese (21)	29	0.14
Korean (53)	62	0.29
Laotian (1)	1	<0.01
Nepalese (2)	2	0.01
Pakistani (15)	18	0.08
Sri Lankan (6)	6	0.03
Taiwanese (3)	7	0.03
Thai (9)	13	0.06
Vietnamese (59)	68	0.32
Hawaii Native/Pacific Islander (5)	27	0.13
Not Hispanic (5)	21	0.10
Hispanic (0)	6	0.03
Guamanian/Chamorro (2)	2	0.01
Native Hawaiian (1)	8	0.04
White (19,767)	20,026	93.42
Not Hispanic (19,404)	19,611	91.48
Hispanic (363)	415	1.94

Stoughton

Place Type: Town
County: Norfolk
Population: 26,962†

Ancestry‡	Population	%
African, Sub-Saharan (268)	492	1.84
African (163)	200	0.75
Cape Verdean (78)	265	0.99
South African (27)	27	0.10
Albanian (0)	83	0.31
American (880)	880	3.29
Arab (84)	184	0.69
Arab (7)	11	0.04
Egyptian (9)	29	0.11
Lebanese (50)	111	0.41
Moroccan (9)	9	0.03
Syrian (0)	11	0.04
Other Arab (9)	13	0.05
Armenian (33)	189	0.71
Austrian (37)	49	0.18
Brazilian (1,177)	1,177	4.39
British (10)	19	0.07
Canadian (114)	235	0.88
Czech (0)	33	0.12
Danish (0)	26	0.10
Dutch (22)	177	0.66
Eastern European (51)	101	0.38
English (462)	2,033	7.59
European (243)	253	0.94
Finnish (0)	54	0.20
French, ex. Basque (132)	1,262	4.71
French Canadian (280)	758	2.83
German (228)	1,178	4.40
Greek (124)	297	1.11
Hungarian (13)	46	0.17
Irish (3,049)	6,675	24.92
Italian (1,507)	4,229	15.79
Lithuanian (167)	377	1.41
Northern European (0)	31	0.12
Norwegian (11)	51	0.19
Polish (487)	1,553	5.80
Portuguese (2,057)	2,721	10.16
Romanian (0)	13	0.05
Russian (532)	1,228	4.59
Scandinavian (26)	26	0.10
Scotch-Irish (283)	513	1.92
Scottish (235)	592	2.21
Serbian (9)	9	0.03
Swedish (72)	329	1.23
Swiss (0)	22	0.08
Ukrainian (108)	171	0.64
Welsh (0)	43	0.16
West Indian, ex. Hispanic (878)	966	3.61

*Notes: † The Census 2010 population figure is used to calculate the percentages in the Hispanic Origin and Race categories. Ancestry percentages are based on the 2006-2010 American Community Survey population (not shown); ‡ Numbers in parentheses indicate the number of people reporting a single ancestry; * Numbers in parentheses indicate the number of persons reporting this race alone, not in combination with any other race; Please refer to the Explanation of Data for more information.*

Barbadian (58)	58	0.22
Bermudan (13)	13	0.05
Haitian (732)	761	2.84
Jamaican (1)	36	0.13
Trinidadian/Tobagonian (50)	74	0.28
U.S. Virgin Islander (24)	24	0.09
Yugoslavian (24)	24	0.09

Hispanic Origin	Population	%
Hispanic or Latino (of any race)	876	3.25
Central American, ex. Mexican	80	0.30
Costa Rican	4	0.01
Guatemalan	37	0.14
Honduran	12	0.04
Panamanian	10	0.04
Salvadoran	16	0.06
Other Central American	1	<0.01
Cuban	61	0.23
Dominican Republic	84	0.31
Mexican	75	0.28
Puerto Rican	329	1.22
South American	126	0.47
Argentinean	9	0.03
Chilean	9	0.03
Colombian	45	0.17
Ecuadorian	26	0.10
Peruvian	13	0.05
Venezuelan	17	0.06
Other South American	7	0.03
Other Hispanic or Latino	121	0.45

Race*	Population	%
African-American/Black (2,984)	3,356	12.45
Not Hispanic (2,878)	3,205	11.89
Hispanic (106)	151	0.56
American Indian/Alaska Native (46)	165	0.61
Not Hispanic (35)	138	0.51
Hispanic (11)	27	0.10
Apache (0)	1	<0.01
Blackfeet (0)	6	0.02
Canadian/French Am. Ind. (1)	3	0.01
Central American Ind. (1)	1	<0.01
Cherokee (5)	15	0.06
Chippewa (0)	3	0.01
Choctaw (0)	1	<0.01
Iroquois (2)	2	0.01
Navajo (0)	5	0.02
Paiute (0)	1	<0.01
Seminole (1)	6	0.02
Sioux (0)	2	0.01
South American Ind. (0)	3	0.01
Spanish American Ind. (1)	1	<0.01
Asian (971)	1,157	4.29
Not Hispanic (970)	1,151	4.27
Hispanic (1)	6	0.02
Burmese (1)	1	<0.01
Cambodian (15)	16	0.06
Chinese, ex. Taiwanese (279)	326	1.21
Filipino (88)	132	0.49
Hmong (5)	7	0.03
Indian (254)	283	1.05
Indonesian (4)	4	0.01
Japanese (14)	28	0.10
Korean (44)	56	0.21
Laotian (3)	8	0.03
Malaysian (2)	7	0.03
Nepalese (7)	11	0.04
Pakistani (19)	20	0.07
Taiwanese (3)	3	0.01
Thai (12)	16	0.06
Vietnamese (192)	217	0.80
Hawaii Native/Pacific Islander (2)	41	0.15
Not Hispanic (2)	29	0.11
Hispanic (0)	12	0.04
Native Hawaiian (1)	4	0.01
Samoan (1)	2	0.01
White (21,634)	22,142	82.12
Not Hispanic (21,140)	21,589	80.07
Hispanic (494)	553	2.05

Sturbridge

Place Type: Town
County: Worcester
Population: 9,268†

Ancestry‡	Population	%
Albanian (20)	20	0.22
American (423)	423	4.68
Arab (68)	102	1.13
Lebanese (68)	102	1.13
Armenian (0)	42	0.46
British (23)	23	0.25
Canadian (45)	96	1.06
Danish (0)	27	0.30
Dutch (0)	70	0.77
Eastern European (37)	37	0.41
English (279)	1,404	15.54
Finnish (0)	60	0.66
French, ex. Basque (653)	1,924	21.29
French Canadian (656)	943	10.43
German (246)	989	10.94
Greek (0)	47	0.52
Hungarian (0)	52	0.58
Irish (618)	2,481	27.45
Italian (342)	1,027	11.36
Lithuanian (27)	114	1.26
Norwegian (0)	55	0.61
Polish (225)	992	10.98
Portuguese (24)	37	0.41
Romanian (15)	15	0.17
Russian (14)	36	0.40
Scandinavian (0)	13	0.14
Scotch-Irish (44)	366	4.05
Scottish (119)	434	4.80
Serbian (0)	19	0.21
Slovak (0)	14	0.15
Swedish (25)	284	3.14
Swiss (8)	8	0.09
Welsh (7)	55	0.61
Yugoslavian (14)	14	0.15

Hispanic Origin	Population	%
Hispanic or Latino (of any race)	231	2.49
Central American, ex. Mexican	6	0.06
Costa Rican	2	0.02
Guatemalan	3	0.03
Honduran	1	0.01
Cuban	4	0.04
Dominican Republic	6	0.06
Mexican	31	0.33
Puerto Rican	141	1.52
South American	25	0.27
Chilean	6	0.06
Colombian	11	0.12
Ecuadorian	4	0.04
Peruvian	3	0.03
Uruguayan	1	0.01
Other Hispanic or Latino	18	0.19

Race*	Population	%
African-American/Black (56)	88	0.95
Not Hispanic (56)	87	0.94
Hispanic (0)	1	0.01
American Indian/Alaska Native (25)	56	0.60
Not Hispanic (23)	51	0.55
Hispanic (2)	5	0.05
Apache (0)	1	0.01
Cherokee (1)	2	0.02
Chippewa (4)	5	0.05
Iroquois (5)	6	0.06
Sioux (0)	4	0.04
South American Ind. (0)	3	0.03
Asian (184)	230	2.48
Not Hispanic (184)	226	2.44
Hispanic (0)	4	0.04
Cambodian (1)	1	0.01
Chinese, ex. Taiwanese (46)	57	0.62
Filipino (15)	25	0.27
Indian (61)	70	0.76
Indonesian (1)	1	0.01
Japanese (1)	4	0.04
Korean (8)	10	0.11
Laotian (24)	27	0.29
Pakistani (9)	10	0.11
Thai (4)	7	0.08
Vietnamese (8)	8	0.09
Hawaii Native/Pacific Islander (0)	5	0.05
Not Hispanic (0)	5	0.05
Guamanian/Chamorro (0)	2	0.02
Native Hawaiian (0)	1	0.01
White (8,816)	8,925	96.30
Not Hispanic (8,665)	8,758	94.50
Hispanic (151)	167	1.80

Sudbury

Place Type: Town
County: Middlesex
Population: 17,659†

Ancestry‡	Population	%
African, Sub-Saharan (0)	7	0.04
African (0)	7	0.04
American (729)	729	4.21
Arab (148)	222	1.28
Egyptian (50)	50	0.29
Lebanese (29)	82	0.47
Syrian (59)	59	0.34
Other Arab (10)	31	0.18
Armenian (227)	263	1.52
Australian (29)	29	0.17
Austrian (9)	165	0.95
Brazilian (94)	118	0.68
British (78)	78	0.45
Bulgarian (0)	20	0.12
Canadian (147)	208	1.20
Czech (39)	168	0.97
Danish (49)	95	0.55
Dutch (14)	63	0.36
Eastern European (289)	311	1.80
English (824)	2,625	15.17
Estonian (0)	11	0.06
European (261)	313	1.81
Finnish (59)	77	0.44
French, ex. Basque (56)	483	2.79
French Canadian (119)	363	2.10
German (359)	1,779	10.28
Greek (193)	273	1.58
Hungarian (139)	359	2.07
Iranian (29)	29	0.17
Irish (1,949)	4,302	24.86
Italian (792)	2,214	12.79
Latvian (0)	22	0.13
Lithuanian (0)	66	0.38
Northern European (46)	46	0.27
Norwegian (19)	75	0.43
Polish (219)	927	5.36
Portuguese (0)	63	0.36
Romanian (47)	54	0.31
Russian (581)	943	5.45
Scandinavian (0)	10	0.06
Scotch-Irish (226)	441	2.55
Scottish (132)	703	4.06
Slavic (0)	20	0.12
Slovak (0)	18	0.10
Slovene (0)	14	0.08
Swedish (42)	330	1.91
Swiss (10)	77	0.44
Turkish (9)	25	0.14
Ukrainian (51)	95	0.55
Welsh (26)	145	0.84
Yugoslavian (9)	9	0.05

Hispanic Origin	Population	%
Hispanic or Latino (of any race)	350	1.98
Central American, ex. Mexican	28	0.16
Costa Rican	1	0.01
Guatemalan	12	0.07
Honduran	7	0.04

SECTION TWO

*Notes: † The Census 2010 population figure is used to calculate the percentages in the Hispanic Origin and Race categories. Ancestry percentages are based on the 2006-2010 American Community Survey population (not shown); ‡ Numbers in parentheses indicate the number of people reporting a single ancestry; * Numbers in parentheses indicate the number of persons reporting this race alone, not in combination with any other race; Please refer to the Explanation of Data for more information.*

Nicaraguan	1	0.01
Panamanian	2	0.01
Salvadoran	5	0.03
Cuban	39	0.22
Dominican Republic	13	0.07
Mexican	65	0.37
Puerto Rican	63	0.36
South American	81	0.46
Argentinean	12	0.07
Bolivian	4	0.02
Chilean	6	0.03
Colombian	25	0.14
Ecuadorian	6	0.03
Peruvian	17	0.10
Uruguayan	2	0.01
Venezuelan	9	0.05
Other Hispanic or Latino	61	0.35

Race*	Population	%
African-American/Black (149)	199	1.13
Not Hispanic (137)	176	1.00
Hispanic (12)	23	0.13
American Indian/Alaska Native (9)	37	0.21
Not Hispanic (6)	24	0.14
Hispanic (3)	13	0.07
Blackfeet (0)	3	0.02
Central American Ind. (0)	1	0.01
Cherokee (2)	9	0.05
Creek (0)	1	0.01
Mexican American Ind. (1)	1	0.01
Navajo (0)	5	0.03
Sioux (1)	2	0.01
Spanish American Ind. (1)	1	0.01
Asian (1,041)	1,280	7.25
Not Hispanic (1,040)	1,270	7.19
Hispanic (1)	10	0.06
Bangladeshi (1)	6	0.03
Burmese (7)	7	0.04
Cambodian (9)	12	0.07
Chinese, ex. Taiwanese (524)	619	3.51
Filipino (31)	53	0.30
Indian (286)	336	1.90
Indonesian (1)	3	0.02
Japanese (26)	51	0.29
Korean (80)	110	0.62
Pakistani (11)	12	0.07
Sri Lankan (1)	2	0.01
Taiwanese (16)	23	0.13
Thai (18)	21	0.12
Vietnamese (8)	13	0.07
Hawaii Native/Pacific Islander (9)	22	0.12
Not Hispanic (6)	19	0.11
Hispanic (3)	3	0.02
Guamanian/Chamorro (3)	5	0.03
Native Hawaiian (0)	3	0.02
Samoan (1)	1	0.01
White (16,036)	16,324	92.44
Not Hispanic (15,779)	16,044	90.85
Hispanic (257)	280	1.59

Sutton

Place Type: Town
County: Worcester
Population: 8,963†

Ancestry‡	Population	%
African, Sub-Saharan (76)	76	0.86
South African (76)	76	0.86
Albanian (0)	26	0.29
American (359)	359	4.05
Arab (148)	172	1.94
Egyptian (75)	75	0.85
Lebanese (58)	71	0.80
Moroccan (15)	26	0.29
Austrian (0)	14	0.16
Belgian (19)	37	0.42
British (18)	80	0.90
Canadian (59)	74	0.83
Czech (19)	32	0.36
Czechoslovakian (18)	18	0.20
Danish (0)	28	0.32
Dutch (16)	170	1.92
English (110)	1,067	12.03
European (122)	122	1.38
Finnish (18)	82	0.92
French, ex. Basque (392)	1,741	19.63
French Canadian (283)	671	7.57
German (49)	578	6.52
Greek (76)	207	2.33
Iranian (18)	37	0.42
Irish (524)	2,513	28.33
Italian (410)	1,537	17.33
Lithuanian (83)	305	3.44
Norwegian (29)	93	1.05
Polish (178)	936	10.55
Portuguese (0)	71	0.80
Russian (14)	102	1.15
Scandinavian (0)	10	0.11
Scotch-Irish (69)	216	2.44
Scottish (36)	240	2.71
Slovak (0)	3	0.03
Swedish (248)	667	7.52
Ukrainian (14)	29	0.33
Welsh (0)	30	0.34

Hispanic Origin	Population	%
Hispanic or Latino (of any race)	115	1.28
Central American, ex. Mexican	4	0.04
Guatemalan	1	0.01
Honduran	1	0.01
Salvadoran	2	0.02
Cuban	5	0.06
Dominican Republic	5	0.06
Mexican	25	0.28
Puerto Rican	47	0.52
South American	17	0.19
Chilean	2	0.02
Colombian	7	0.08
Ecuadorian	2	0.02
Peruvian	1	0.01
Venezuelan	5	0.06
Other Hispanic or Latino	12	0.13

Race*	Population	%
African-American/Black (39)	67	0.75
Not Hispanic (38)	63	0.70
Hispanic (1)	4	0.04
American Indian/Alaska Native (12)	62	0.69
Not Hispanic (3)	49	0.55
Hispanic (9)	13	0.15
Blackfeet (0)	2	0.02
Canadian/French Am. Ind. (2)	2	0.02
Cherokee (0)	6	0.07
Houma (0)	3	0.03
Iroquois (4)	4	0.04
Lumbee (0)	1	0.01
Mexican American Ind. (1)	2	0.02
Seminole (0)	1	0.01
South American Ind. (0)	3	0.03
Asian (84)	117	1.31
Not Hispanic (84)	117	1.31
Cambodian (2)	2	0.02
Chinese, ex. Taiwanese (18)	25	0.28
Filipino (4)	17	0.19
Indian (30)	41	0.46
Japanese (8)	9	0.10
Korean (3)	8	0.09
Taiwanese (1)	1	0.01
Vietnamese (13)	16	0.18
Hawaii Native/Pacific Islander (8)	13	0.15
Not Hispanic (8)	12	0.13
Hispanic (0)	1	0.01
Fijian (1)	1	0.01
Guamanian/Chamorro (1)	1	0.01
Native Hawaiian (6)	10	0.11
White (8,691)	8,797	98.15
Not Hispanic (8,604)	8,706	97.13
Hispanic (87)	91	1.02

Swampscott

Place Type: CDP/Town
County: Essex
Population: 13,787†

Ancestry‡	Population	%
Albanian (16)	16	0.12
Alsatian (0)	11	0.08
American (779)	779	5.64
Arab (18)	54	0.39
Lebanese (0)	27	0.20
Other Arab (18)	27	0.20
Armenian (58)	79	0.57
Austrian (31)	124	0.90
Brazilian (97)	97	0.70
British (90)	90	0.65
Canadian (74)	114	0.82
Croatian (16)	23	0.17
Czech (23)	71	0.51
Danish (8)	8	0.06
Dutch (0)	82	0.59
Eastern European (118)	134	0.97
English (558)	1,987	14.38
European (87)	105	0.76
French, ex. Basque (123)	703	5.09
French Canadian (144)	389	2.81
German (282)	1,024	7.41
Greek (146)	167	1.21
Hungarian (19)	70	0.51
Irish (1,232)	3,690	26.70
Israeli (15)	22	0.16
Italian (1,200)	2,902	21.00
Latvian (12)	23	0.17
Lithuanian (42)	70	0.51
Norwegian (25)	124	0.90
Polish (178)	716	5.18
Portuguese (12)	56	0.41
Romanian (27)	27	0.20
Russian (804)	1,085	7.85
Scandinavian (0)	13	0.09
Scotch-Irish (73)	231	1.67
Scottish (141)	489	3.54
Slovene (0)	15	0.11
Swedish (26)	78	0.56
Swiss (0)	30	0.22
Ukrainian (283)	385	2.79
Welsh (31)	147	1.06
West Indian, ex. Hispanic (36)	55	0.40
Barbadian (15)	15	0.11
Haitian (21)	21	0.15
West Indian (0)	19	0.14

Hispanic Origin	Population	%
Hispanic or Latino (of any race)	355	2.57
Central American, ex. Mexican	34	0.25
Costa Rican	4	0.03
Guatemalan	15	0.11
Honduran	3	0.02
Panamanian	1	0.01
Salvadoran	11	0.08
Cuban	25	0.18
Dominican Republic	68	0.49
Mexican	34	0.25
Puerto Rican	67	0.49
South American	77	0.56
Argentinean	13	0.09
Bolivian	3	0.02
Chilean	13	0.09
Colombian	21	0.15
Ecuadorian	4	0.03
Paraguayan	1	0.01
Peruvian	17	0.12
Uruguayan	4	0.03
Venezuelan	1	0.01
Other Hispanic or Latino	50	0.36

Race*	Population	%
African-American/Black (165)	233	1.69
Not Hispanic (157)	213	1.54

*Notes: † The Census 2010 population figure is used to calculate the percentages in the Hispanic Origin and Race categories. Ancestry percentages are based on the 2006-2010 American Community Survey population (not shown); ‡ Numbers in parentheses indicate the number of people reporting a single ancestry; * Numbers in parentheses indicate the number of persons reporting this race alone, not in combination with any other race; Please refer to the Explanation of Data for more information.*

Hispanic (8)	20	0.15
American Indian/Alaska Native (13)	32	0.23
Not Hispanic (7)	21	0.15
Hispanic (6)	11	0.08
Blackfeet (0)	1	0.01
Iroquois (1)	2	0.01
Mexican American Ind. (2)	3	0.02
Navajo (1)	1	0.01
South American Ind. (0)	2	0.01
Asian (265)	362	2.63
Not Hispanic (264)	348	2.52
Hispanic (1)	14	0.10
Cambodian (18)	27	0.20
Chinese, ex. Taiwanese (65)	86	0.62
Filipino (14)	29	0.21
Indian (71)	89	0.65
Japanese (14)	37	0.27
Korean (21)	26	0.19
Laotian (2)	3	0.02
Pakistani (8)	8	0.06
Thai (1)	3	0.02
Vietnamese (38)	41	0.30
Hawaii Native/Pacific Islander (4)	10	0.07
Not Hispanic (4)	10	0.07
Guamanian/Chamorro (3)	3	0.02
Native Hawaiian (1)	2	0.01
White (13,048)	13,215	95.85
Not Hispanic (12,824)	12,961	94.01
Hispanic (224)	254	1.84

Swansea

Place Type: Town
County: Bristol
Population: 15,865†

Ancestry‡	Population	%
African, Sub-Saharan (0)	76	0.48
Cape Verdean (0)	76	0.48
American (552)	552	3.47
Arab (0)	112	0.70
Lebanese (0)	112	0.70
Austrian (0)	40	0.25
British (47)	64	0.40
Canadian (41)	92	0.58
Czech (10)	10	0.06
Dutch (9)	48	0.30
English (501)	1,664	10.47
European (38)	38	0.24
Finnish (0)	6	0.04
French, ex. Basque (804)	3,407	21.43
French Canadian (964)	1,342	8.44
German (92)	485	3.05
Greek (43)	163	1.03
Hungarian (13)	32	0.20
Irish (623)	2,610	16.42
Italian (625)	2,007	12.62
Lithuanian (0)	17	0.11
Polish (145)	500	3.14
Portuguese (3,191)	5,981	37.62
Romanian (0)	15	0.09
Russian (0)	25	0.16
Scotch-Irish (118)	154	0.97
Scottish (39)	158	0.99
Slovak (11)	11	0.07
Swedish (11)	159	1.00
Ukrainian (0)	18	0.11

Hispanic Origin	Population	%
Hispanic or Latino (of any race)	173	1.09
Central American, ex. Mexican	7	0.04
Guatemalan	5	0.03
Panamanian	1	0.01
Salvadoran	1	0.01
Cuban	16	0.10
Dominican Republic	9	0.06
Mexican	33	0.21
Puerto Rican	69	0.43
South American	15	0.09
Argentinean	1	0.01
Colombian	8	0.05
Ecuadorian	1	0.01
Paraguayan	3	0.02
Peruvian	2	0.01
Other Hispanic or Latino	24	0.15

Race*	Population	%
African-American/Black (101)	166	1.05
Not Hispanic (95)	158	1.00
Hispanic (6)	8	0.05
American Indian/Alaska Native (13)	74	0.47
Not Hispanic (9)	69	0.43
Hispanic (4)	5	0.03
Apache (1)	1	0.01
Canadian/French Am. Ind. (0)	1	0.01
Cherokee (1)	9	0.06
Iroquois (0)	2	0.01
Pueblo (0)	1	0.01
Sioux (0)	2	0.01
South American Ind. (1)	1	0.01
Asian (110)	163	1.03
Not Hispanic (109)	162	1.02
Hispanic (1)	1	0.01
Cambodian (5)	13	0.08
Chinese, ex. Taiwanese (32)	45	0.28
Filipino (21)	41	0.26
Indian (10)	16	0.10
Indonesian (2)	2	0.01
Japanese (8)	19	0.12
Korean (12)	21	0.13
Sri Lankan (0)	1	0.01
Thai (4)	4	0.03
Vietnamese (7)	8	0.05
Hawaii Native/Pacific Islander (1)	15	0.09
Not Hispanic (1)	14	0.09
Hispanic (0)	1	0.01
Guamanian/Chamorro (1)	2	0.01
Native Hawaiian (0)	8	0.05
White (15,429)	15,586	98.24
Not Hispanic (15,287)	15,431	97.26
Hispanic (142)	155	0.98

Taunton

Place Type: City
County: Bristol
Population: 55,874†

Ancestry‡	Population	%
African, Sub-Saharan (1,479)	2,026	3.62
African (0)	25	0.04
Cape Verdean (1,330)	1,852	3.31
Ethiopian (30)	30	0.05
Kenyan (32)	32	0.06
Nigerian (45)	45	0.08
South African (42)	42	0.08
Albanian (0)	16	0.03
American (1,553)	1,553	2.78
Arab (268)	769	1.37
Arab (0)	98	0.18
Egyptian (141)	141	0.25
Lebanese (113)	464	0.83
Syrian (14)	66	0.12
Armenian (14)	14	0.03
Austrian (7)	7	0.01
Basque (27)	27	0.05
Brazilian (382)	669	1.20
British (20)	35	0.06
Canadian (317)	688	1.23
Czech (25)	130	0.23
Czechoslovakian (9)	9	0.02
Danish (0)	71	0.13
Dutch (19)	186	0.33
Eastern European (52)	52	0.09
English (1,625)	6,378	11.40
European (85)	85	0.15
Finnish (71)	177	0.32
French, ex. Basque (1,194)	6,431	11.49
French Canadian (928)	2,377	4.25
German (339)	2,163	3.87
Greek (148)	469	0.84
Guyanese (176)	176	0.31
Hungarian (7)	59	0.11
Iranian (22)	22	0.04
Irish (4,071)	12,379	22.12
Israeli (56)	68	0.12
Italian (1,220)	5,293	9.46
Latvian (26)	26	0.05
Lithuanian (56)	247	0.44
Norwegian (7)	51	0.09
Polish (545)	2,207	3.94
Portuguese (10,422)	17,002	30.39
Russian (198)	272	0.49
Scandinavian (10)	21	0.04
Scotch-Irish (226)	773	1.38
Scottish (286)	1,250	2.23
Slovak (11)	11	0.02
Swedish (222)	943	1.69
Swiss (12)	46	0.08
Ukrainian (0)	39	0.07
Welsh (11)	124	0.22
West Indian, ex. Hispanic (779)	902	1.61
British West Indian (58)	90	0.16
Haitian (478)	498	0.89
Jamaican (172)	172	0.31
Trinidadian/Tobagonian (11)	11	0.02
West Indian (60)	131	0.23

Hispanic Origin	Population	%
Hispanic or Latino (of any race)	3,058	5.47
Central American, ex. Mexican	179	0.32
Costa Rican	28	0.05
Guatemalan	76	0.14
Honduran	12	0.02
Nicaraguan	7	0.01
Panamanian	10	0.02
Salvadoran	46	0.08
Cuban	53	0.09
Dominican Republic	184	0.33
Mexican	172	0.31
Puerto Rican	2,000	3.58
South American	149	0.27
Argentinean	8	0.01
Bolivian	4	0.01
Chilean	11	0.02
Colombian	55	0.10
Ecuadorian	20	0.04
Peruvian	31	0.06
Uruguayan	6	0.01
Venezuelan	12	0.02
Other South American	2	<0.01
Other Hispanic or Latino	321	0.57

Race*	Population	%
African-American/Black (2,773)	3,835	6.86
Not Hispanic (2,529)	3,433	6.14
Hispanic (244)	402	0.72
American Indian/Alaska Native (142)	467	0.84
Not Hispanic (108)	397	0.71
Hispanic (34)	70	0.13
Apache (0)	2	<0.01
Blackfeet (0)	21	0.04
Canadian/French Am. Ind. (1)	4	0.01
Central American Ind. (3)	3	0.01
Cherokee (8)	53	0.09
Cheyenne (0)	1	<0.01
Chippewa (2)	4	0.01
Choctaw (1)	1	<0.01
Comanche (0)	2	<0.01
Delaware (0)	2	<0.01
Iroquois (6)	17	0.03
Lumbee (0)	1	<0.01
Mexican American Ind. (5)	6	0.01
Navajo (3)	5	0.01
Ottawa (1)	1	<0.01
Sioux (2)	8	0.01
South American Ind. (4)	5	0.01
Asian (560)	760	1.36
Not Hispanic (546)	733	1.31
Hispanic (14)	27	0.05

*Notes: † The Census 2010 population figure is used to calculate the percentages in the Hispanic Origin and Race categories. Ancestry percentages are based on the 2006-2010 American Community Survey population (not shown); ‡ Numbers in parentheses indicate the number of people reporting a single ancestry; * Numbers in parentheses indicate the number of persons reporting this race alone, not in combination with any other race; Please refer to the Explanation of Data for more information.*

	Population	%
Bangladeshi (18)	25	0.04
Cambodian (10)	14	0.03
Chinese, ex. Taiwanese (146)	166	0.30
Filipino (81)	126	0.23
Hmong (7)	7	0.01
Indian (99)	136	0.24
Indonesian (8)	10	0.02
Japanese (17)	49	0.09
Korean (32)	46	0.08
Laotian (7)	8	0.01
Malaysian (6)	6	0.01
Pakistani (19)	24	0.04
Sri Lankan (1)	1	<0.01
Thai (9)	15	0.03
Vietnamese (63)	87	0.16
Hawaii Native/Pacific Islander (25)	109	0.20
Not Hispanic (18)	93	0.17
Hispanic (7)	16	0.03
Guamanian/Chamorro (8)	16	0.03
Native Hawaiian (5)	12	0.02
Samoan (3)	9	0.02
Tongan (1)	2	<0.01
White (48,742)	50,089	89.65
Not Hispanic (47,221)	48,304	86.45
Hispanic (1,521)	1,785	3.19

Templeton

Place Type: Town
County: Worcester
Population: 8,013†

Ancestry‡	Population	%
African, Sub-Saharan (14)	14	0.18
African (14)	14	0.18
American (159)	159	2.04
Austrian (0)	28	0.36
Brazilian (114)	114	1.46
Canadian (55)	107	1.37
Czech (0)	10	0.13
Danish (15)	15	0.19
Dutch (0)	30	0.38
Eastern European (15)	15	0.19
English (114)	847	10.86
European (20)	20	0.26
Finnish (190)	508	6.51
French, ex. Basque (716)	1,912	24.51
French Canadian (493)	814	10.43
German (62)	526	6.74
Iranian (57)	57	0.73
Irish (422)	1,604	20.56
Italian (160)	809	10.37
Lithuanian (31)	308	3.95
Norwegian (47)	85	1.09
Polish (219)	616	7.90
Portuguese (101)	216	2.77
Russian (29)	50	0.64
Scandinavian (15)	15	0.19
Scotch-Irish (114)	229	2.94
Scottish (151)	304	3.90
Slovak (0)	14	0.18
Swedish (139)	347	4.45
West Indian, ex. Hispanic (12)	12	0.15
West Indian (12)	12	0.15

Hispanic Origin	Population	%
Hispanic or Latino (of any race)	153	1.91
Central American, ex. Mexican	8	0.10
Costa Rican	4	0.05
Honduran	2	0.02
Salvadoran	2	0.02
Cuban	2	0.02
Dominican Republic	5	0.06
Mexican	16	0.20
Puerto Rican	72	0.90
South American	24	0.30
Colombian	7	0.09
Ecuadorian	4	0.05
Peruvian	6	0.07
Uruguayan	7	0.09
Other Hispanic or Latino	26	0.32

Race*	Population	%
African-American/Black (58)	98	1.22
Not Hispanic (52)	87	1.09
Hispanic (6)	11	0.14
American Indian/Alaska Native (10)	48	0.60
Not Hispanic (7)	43	0.54
Hispanic (3)	5	0.06
Apache (0)	3	0.04
Cherokee (1)	3	0.04
Chippewa (0)	1	0.01
Crow (0)	3	0.04
Lumbee (0)	4	0.05
Seminole (0)	2	0.02
South American Ind. (1)	1	0.01
Yaqui (0)	1	0.01
Asian (42)	75	0.94
Not Hispanic (42)	73	0.91
Hispanic (0)	2	0.02
Chinese, ex. Taiwanese (13)	15	0.19
Filipino (3)	6	0.07
Hmong (9)	9	0.11
Indian (5)	6	0.07
Japanese (1)	12	0.15
Korean (8)	17	0.21
Thai (1)	5	0.06
Vietnamese (1)	1	0.01
Hawaii Native/Pacific Islander (0)	1	0.01
Hispanic (0)	1	0.01
Guamanian/Chamorro (0)	1	0.01
White (7,752)	7,871	98.23
Not Hispanic (7,656)	7,754	96.77
Hispanic (96)	117	1.46

Tewksbury

Place Type: Town
County: Middlesex
Population: 28,961†

Ancestry‡	Population	%
African, Sub-Saharan (274)	290	1.01
Kenyan (274)	274	0.96
South African (0)	16	0.06
Albanian (43)	53	0.19
American (988)	988	3.45
Arab (86)	153	0.53
Lebanese (73)	126	0.44
Syrian (13)	27	0.09
Armenian (21)	118	0.41
Austrian (0)	136	0.48
Belgian (0)	14	0.05
Brazilian (24)	24	0.08
British (49)	120	0.42
Canadian (126)	359	1.25
Celtic (32)	32	0.11
Croatian (0)	11	0.04
Czech (0)	35	0.12
Danish (0)	56	0.20
Dutch (33)	117	0.41
Eastern European (0)	9	0.03
English (873)	3,700	12.93
European (116)	125	0.44
Finnish (0)	199	0.70
French, ex. Basque (512)	2,365	8.26
French Canadian (650)	1,611	5.63
German (322)	1,609	5.62
Greek (182)	381	1.33
Hungarian (62)	83	0.29
Irish (4,161)	10,258	35.84
Italian (2,724)	7,243	25.31
Lithuanian (11)	78	0.27
Northern European (35)	59	0.21
Norwegian (23)	109	0.38
Polish (352)	1,070	3.74
Portuguese (683)	1,386	4.84
Romanian (12)	12	0.04
Russian (80)	217	0.76
Scandinavian (30)	30	0.10
Scotch-Irish (458)	1,095	3.83
Scottish (427)	1,309	4.57
Swedish (72)	598	2.09
Swiss (10)	78	0.27
Ukrainian (58)	68	0.24
Welsh (0)	41	0.14
West Indian, ex. Hispanic (0)	31	0.11
Trinidadian/Tobagonian (0)	16	0.06
West Indian (0)	15	0.05

Hispanic Origin	Population	%
Hispanic or Latino (of any race)	602	2.08
Central American, ex. Mexican	75	0.26
Costa Rican	10	0.03
Guatemalan	11	0.04
Honduran	10	0.03
Nicaraguan	1	<0.01
Panamanian	4	0.01
Salvadoran	38	0.13
Other Central American	1	<0.01
Cuban	33	0.11
Dominican Republic	55	0.19
Mexican	47	0.16
Puerto Rican	221	0.76
South American	100	0.35
Argentinean	10	0.03
Bolivian	3	0.01
Chilean	8	0.03
Colombian	48	0.17
Ecuadorian	13	0.04
Peruvian	9	0.03
Venezuelan	5	0.02
Other South American	4	0.01
Other Hispanic or Latino	71	0.25

Race*	Population	%
African-American/Black (321)	417	1.44
Not Hispanic (307)	401	1.38
Hispanic (14)	16	0.06
American Indian/Alaska Native (32)	141	0.49
Not Hispanic (27)	135	0.47
Hispanic (5)	6	0.02
Blackfeet (1)	6	0.02
Cherokee (0)	14	0.05
Chickasaw (0)	2	0.01
Chippewa (0)	2	0.01
Choctaw (3)	4	0.01
Iroquois (0)	7	0.02
Mexican American Ind. (2)	2	0.01
Osage (0)	3	0.01
Potawatomi (3)	3	0.01
South American Ind. (1)	1	<0.01
Asian (786)	889	3.07
Not Hispanic (785)	884	3.05
Hispanic (1)	5	0.02
Bangladeshi (4)	4	0.01
Cambodian (36)	52	0.18
Chinese, ex. Taiwanese (157)	178	0.61
Filipino (35)	56	0.19
Indian (312)	333	1.15
Indonesian (1)	4	0.01
Japanese (12)	23	0.08
Korean (57)	73	0.25
Laotian (5)	9	0.03
Malaysian (1)	1	<0.01
Nepalese (5)	5	0.02
Pakistani (31)	32	0.11
Taiwanese (10)	10	0.03
Thai (4)	7	0.02
Vietnamese (89)	93	0.32
Hawaii Native/Pacific Islander (1)	12	0.04
Not Hispanic (1)	11	0.04
Hispanic (0)	1	<0.01
Fijian (1)	1	<0.01
Guamanian/Chamorro (0)	1	<0.01
Native Hawaiian (0)	7	0.02
Samoan (0)	1	<0.01
White (27,327)	27,634	95.42
Not Hispanic (26,886)	27,156	93.77
Hispanic (441)	478	1.65

*Notes: † The Census 2010 population figure is used to calculate the percentages in the Hispanic Origin and Race categories. Ancestry percentages are based on the 2006-2010 American Community Survey population (not shown); ‡ Numbers in parentheses indicate the number of people reporting a single ancestry; * Numbers in parentheses indicate the number of persons reporting this race alone, not in combination with any other race; Please refer to the Explanation of Data for more information.*

Townsend

Place Type: Town
County: Middlesex
Population: 8,926†

Ancestry‡	Population	%
African, Sub-Saharan (10)	29	0.33
Cape Verdean (10)	29	0.33
American (287)	287	3.24
Arab (0)	28	0.32
Lebanese (0)	28	0.32
Armenian (0)	7	0.08
Austrian (13)	31	0.35
Belgian (0)	8	0.09
British (45)	65	0.73
Canadian (69)	125	1.41
Danish (0)	11	0.12
Dutch (11)	83	0.94
Eastern European (33)	33	0.37
English (588)	1,777	20.03
European (120)	143	1.61
Finnish (56)	119	1.34
French, ex. Basque (421)	1,278	14.41
French Canadian (273)	588	6.63
German (299)	1,078	12.15
Greek (29)	40	0.45
Irish (710)	2,554	28.79
Italian (363)	1,528	17.22
Lithuanian (24)	43	0.48
Norwegian (0)	40	0.45
Polish (10)	266	3.00
Portuguese (83)	306	3.45
Romanian (0)	22	0.25
Russian (79)	155	1.75
Scotch-Irish (158)	266	3.00
Scottish (57)	419	4.72
Slavic (0)	11	0.12
Slovak (0)	15	0.17
Swedish (35)	167	1.88
Welsh (28)	78	0.88

Hispanic Origin	Population	%
Hispanic or Latino (of any race)	163	1.83
Central American, ex. Mexican	10	0.11
Costa Rican	1	0.01
Guatemalan	5	0.06
Honduran	1	0.01
Panamanian	3	0.03
Cuban	5	0.06
Dominican Republic	6	0.07
Mexican	26	0.29
Puerto Rican	90	1.01
South American	19	0.21
Argentinean	3	0.03
Bolivian	1	0.01
Colombian	2	0.02
Ecuadorian	4	0.04
Peruvian	9	0.10
Other Hispanic or Latino	7	0.08

Race*	Population	%
African-American/Black (56)	89	1.00
Not Hispanic (54)	87	0.97
Hispanic (2)	2	0.02
American Indian/Alaska Native (18)	57	0.64
Not Hispanic (17)	54	0.60
Hispanic (1)	3	0.03
Blackfeet (0)	6	0.07
Canadian/French Am. Ind. (2)	3	0.03
Cherokee (2)	9	0.10
Cheyenne (0)	3	0.03
Chippewa (5)	5	0.06
Crow (0)	7	0.08
Iroquois (4)	5	0.06
Sioux (0)	2	0.02
Asian (75)	108	1.21
Not Hispanic (74)	104	1.17
Hispanic (1)	4	0.04
Cambodian (8)	10	0.11
Chinese, ex. Taiwanese (10)	15	0.17
Filipino (1)	3	0.03
Hmong (0)	3	0.03
Indian (20)	22	0.25
Indonesian (1)	1	0.01
Japanese (4)	7	0.08
Korean (9)	24	0.27
Laotian (5)	8	0.09
Pakistani (9)	9	0.10
Taiwanese (1)	5	0.06
Thai (1)	3	0.03
Vietnamese (1)	1	0.01
Hawaii Native/Pacific Islander (0)	8	0.09
Not Hispanic (0)	8	0.09
Native Hawaiian (0)	3	0.03
White (8,624)	8,741	97.93
Not Hispanic (8,506)	8,609	96.45
Hispanic (118)	132	1.48

Tyngsborough

Place Type: Town
County: Middlesex
Population: 11,292†

Ancestry‡	Population	%
American (240)	240	2.16
Arab (101)	189	1.70
Arab (18)	18	0.16
Egyptian (0)	13	0.12
Lebanese (56)	75	0.67
Syrian (27)	83	0.75
Armenian (9)	46	0.41
Austrian (0)	61	0.55
Belgian (0)	28	0.25
Brazilian (38)	38	0.34
British (51)	73	0.66
Canadian (96)	121	1.09
Czech (0)	83	0.75
Danish (0)	81	0.73
Dutch (0)	86	0.77
Eastern European (10)	10	0.09
English (300)	1,406	12.64
European (18)	46	0.41
Finnish (0)	13	0.12
French, ex. Basque (428)	1,416	12.73
French Canadian (408)	848	7.62
German (116)	721	6.48
Greek (207)	419	3.77
Hungarian (0)	10	0.09
Irish (1,734)	3,612	32.47
Italian (347)	1,526	13.72
Lithuanian (18)	100	0.90
Northern European (10)	10	0.09
Norwegian (0)	58	0.52
Polish (228)	844	7.59
Portuguese (100)	322	2.89
Russian (50)	189	1.70
Scotch-Irish (241)	483	4.34
Scottish (154)	400	3.60
Swedish (21)	143	1.29
Ukrainian (10)	26	0.23
Welsh (0)	26	0.23

Hispanic Origin	Population	%
Hispanic or Latino (of any race)	265	2.35
Central American, ex. Mexican	15	0.13
Guatemalan	10	0.09
Honduran	1	0.01
Nicaraguan	1	0.01
Panamanian	1	0.01
Salvadoran	2	0.02
Cuban	18	0.16
Dominican Republic	11	0.10
Mexican	39	0.35
Puerto Rican	108	0.96
South American	53	0.47
Argentinean	2	0.02
Bolivian	1	0.01
Chilean	2	0.02
Colombian	27	0.24
Paraguayan	1	0.01
Peruvian	12	0.11
Venezuelan	7	0.06
Other South American	1	0.01
Other Hispanic or Latino	21	0.19

Race*	Population	%
African-American/Black (120)	157	1.39
Not Hispanic (118)	148	1.31
Hispanic (2)	9	0.08
American Indian/Alaska Native (14)	44	0.39
Not Hispanic (9)	33	0.29
Hispanic (5)	11	0.10
Apache (1)	1	0.01
Blackfeet (0)	1	0.01
Cherokee (0)	4	0.04
Iroquois (1)	4	0.04
Mexican American Ind. (1)	1	0.01
Navajo (0)	4	0.04
Paiute (1)	1	0.01
Potawatomi (0)	1	0.01
Sioux (0)	1	0.01
Asian (535)	599	5.30
Not Hispanic (531)	594	5.26
Hispanic (4)	5	0.04
Cambodian (90)	105	0.93
Chinese, ex. Taiwanese (79)	94	0.83
Filipino (18)	26	0.23
Hmong (3)	3	0.03
Indian (202)	216	1.91
Indonesian (0)	1	0.01
Japanese (3)	7	0.06
Korean (32)	43	0.38
Laotian (10)	22	0.19
Malaysian (1)	1	0.01
Pakistani (13)	23	0.20
Taiwanese (0)	1	0.01
Thai (11)	12	0.11
Vietnamese (28)	31	0.27
Hawaii Native/Pacific Islander (0)	5	0.04
Not Hispanic (0)	3	0.03
Hispanic (0)	2	0.02
Guamanian/Chamorro (0)	1	0.01
Native Hawaiian (0)	3	0.03
White (10,390)	10,539	93.33
Not Hispanic (10,237)	10,352	91.68
Hispanic (153)	187	1.66

Upton

Place Type: Town
County: Worcester
Population: 7,542†

Ancestry‡	Population	%
American (434)	434	6.00
Arab (54)	66	0.91
Egyptian (42)	42	0.58
Lebanese (0)	12	0.17
Syrian (12)	12	0.17
Armenian (0)	26	0.36
Belgian (0)	34	0.47
British (101)	101	1.40
Canadian (23)	57	0.79
Czech (15)	15	0.21
Czechoslovakian (23)	59	0.82
Dutch (13)	68	0.94
Eastern European (32)	32	0.44
English (283)	1,536	21.24
European (114)	159	2.20
Finnish (15)	69	0.95
French, ex. Basque (55)	866	11.98
French Canadian (155)	279	3.86
German (112)	700	9.68
Greek (82)	93	1.29
Hungarian (0)	98	1.36
Irish (425)	2,189	30.27
Italian (303)	1,285	17.77
Latvian (0)	12	0.17

*Notes: † The Census 2010 population figure is used to calculate the percentages in the Hispanic Origin and Race categories. Ancestry percentages are based on the 2006-2010 American Community Survey population (not shown); ‡ Numbers in parentheses indicate the number of people reporting a single ancestry; * Numbers in parentheses indicate the number of persons reporting this race alone, not in combination with any other race; Please refer to the Explanation of Data for more information.*

Lithuanian (38)	99	1.37
Northern European (32)	32	0.44
Norwegian (29)	105	1.45
Polish (118)	753	10.41
Portuguese (44)	147	2.03
Russian (8)	98	1.36
Scotch-Irish (55)	194	2.68
Scottish (110)	278	3.84
Swedish (63)	200	2.77
Ukrainian (0)	14	0.19
Welsh (0)	24	0.33

Hispanic Origin	Population	%
Hispanic or Latino (of any race)	119	1.58
Central American, ex. Mexican	16	0.21
Costa Rican	2	0.03
Guatemalan	5	0.07
Panamanian	7	0.09
Salvadoran	2	0.03
Cuban	10	0.13
Dominican Republic	4	0.05
Mexican	17	0.23
Puerto Rican	38	0.50
South American	22	0.29
Argentinean	2	0.03
Bolivian	2	0.03
Colombian	11	0.15
Ecuadorian	3	0.04
Uruguayan	1	0.01
Venezuelan	3	0.04
Other Hispanic or Latino	12	0.16

Race*	Population	%
African-American/Black (57)	78	1.03
Not Hispanic (52)	70	0.93
Hispanic (5)	8	0.11
American Indian/Alaska Native (12)	35	0.46
Not Hispanic (4)	22	0.29
Hispanic (8)	13	0.17
Blackfeet (0)	4	0.05
Cherokee (0)	5	0.07
South American Ind. (2)	2	0.03
Ute (1)	3	0.04
Asian (162)	212	2.81
Not Hispanic (162)	211	2.80
Hispanic (0)	1	0.01
Chinese, ex. Taiwanese (58)	70	0.93
Filipino (9)	21	0.28
Indian (64)	70	0.93
Japanese (7)	15	0.20
Korean (14)	20	0.27
Laotian (1)	2	0.03
Pakistani (3)	3	0.04
Taiwanese (1)	1	0.01
Vietnamese (4)	8	0.11
Hawaii Native/Pacific Islander (1)	8	0.11
Not Hispanic (1)	7	0.09
Hispanic (0)	1	0.01
Guamanian/Chamorro (0)	1	0.01
Tongan (1)	6	0.08
White (7,188)	7,290	96.66
Not Hispanic (7,105)	7,198	95.44
Hispanic (83)	92	1.22

Uxbridge

Place Type: Town
County: Worcester
Population: 13,457†

Ancestry‡	Population	%
African, Sub-Saharan (52)	67	0.51
African (39)	39	0.30
Cape Verdean (13)	28	0.21
American (472)	472	3.61
Arab (43)	120	0.92
Arab (0)	13	0.10
Egyptian (32)	32	0.24
Lebanese (11)	34	0.26
Syrian (0)	41	0.31
Armenian (13)	13	0.10
Austrian (23)	23	0.18
Belgian (0)	12	0.09
British (24)	46	0.35
Canadian (15)	51	0.39
Celtic (36)	36	0.28
Czech (0)	41	0.31
Danish (30)	30	0.23
Dutch (114)	413	3.16
English (406)	2,207	16.87
Estonian (0)	13	0.10
European (57)	57	0.44
Finnish (0)	59	0.45
French, ex. Basque (708)	2,478	18.94
French Canadian (635)	1,181	9.03
German (92)	1,179	9.01
Greek (50)	256	1.96
Hungarian (0)	83	0.63
Irish (1,101)	3,447	26.35
Italian (633)	2,424	18.53
Lithuanian (0)	70	0.54
Northern European (14)	14	0.11
Norwegian (15)	93	0.71
Polish (192)	869	6.64
Portuguese (101)	234	1.79
Russian (28)	117	0.89
Scandinavian (16)	76	0.58
Scotch-Irish (282)	619	4.73
Scottish (174)	388	2.97
Slovak (38)	107	0.82
Slovene (0)	17	0.13
Swedish (58)	372	2.84
Swiss (0)	50	0.38
Ukrainian (22)	70	0.54
Welsh (20)	32	0.24
Yugoslavian (10)	10	0.08

Hispanic Origin	Population	%
Hispanic or Latino (of any race)	257	1.91
Central American, ex. Mexican	18	0.13
Costa Rican	4	0.03
Guatemalan	6	0.04
Honduran	3	0.02
Panamanian	1	0.01
Salvadoran	4	0.03
Cuban	20	0.15
Dominican Republic	17	0.13
Mexican	45	0.33
Puerto Rican	83	0.62
South American	49	0.36
Argentinean	11	0.08
Bolivian	4	0.03
Colombian	10	0.07
Ecuadorian	12	0.09
Peruvian	11	0.08
Venezuelan	1	0.01
Other Hispanic or Latino	25	0.19

Race*	Population	%
African-American/Black (111)	180	1.34
Not Hispanic (101)	167	1.24
Hispanic (10)	13	0.10
American Indian/Alaska Native (19)	73	0.54
Not Hispanic (7)	59	0.44
Hispanic (12)	14	0.10
Apache (0)	1	0.01
Blackfeet (2)	12	0.09
Canadian/French Am. Ind. (0)	2	0.01
Cherokee (0)	5	0.04
Chickasaw (0)	1	0.01
Chippewa (1)	7	0.05
Cree (0)	2	0.01
Crow (0)	1	0.01
Delaware (0)	1	0.01
Iroquois (1)	5	0.04
Mexican American Ind. (1)	3	0.02
Navajo (1)	1	0.01
South American Ind. (8)	9	0.07
Asian (140)	186	1.38
Not Hispanic (140)	185	1.37
Hispanic (0)	1	0.01
Bangladeshi (4)	5	0.04
Cambodian (1)	1	0.01
Chinese, ex. Taiwanese (20)	30	0.22
Filipino (18)	25	0.19
Hmong (12)	12	0.09
Indian (41)	44	0.33
Indonesian (0)	4	0.03
Japanese (2)	9	0.07
Korean (15)	27	0.20
Laotian (2)	2	0.01
Pakistani (1)	1	0.01
Taiwanese (2)	2	0.01
Thai (3)	3	0.02
Vietnamese (6)	8	0.06
Hawaii Native/Pacific Islander (2)	19	0.14
Not Hispanic (2)	18	0.13
Hispanic (0)	1	0.01
Native Hawaiian (1)	6	0.04
Samoan (1)	3	0.02
White (12,934)	13,113	97.44
Not Hispanic (12,756)	12,918	95.99
Hispanic (178)	195	1.45

Wakefield

Place Type: CDP/Town
County: Middlesex
Population: 24,932†

Ancestry‡	Population	%
American (931)	931	3.78
Arab (136)	303	1.23
Arab (20)	20	0.08
Lebanese (61)	153	0.62
Moroccan (26)	26	0.11
Palestinian (21)	50	0.20
Syrian (0)	46	0.19
Other Arab (8)	8	0.03
Armenian (39)	140	0.57
Austrian (0)	71	0.29
Belgian (36)	56	0.23
Brazilian (36)	60	0.24
British (114)	172	0.70
Canadian (109)	306	1.24
Czech (30)	70	0.28
Czechoslovakian (30)	47	0.19
Danish (29)	85	0.35
Dutch (46)	247	1.00
Eastern European (26)	26	0.11
English (871)	3,453	14.03
Estonian (16)	16	0.06
European (67)	112	0.45
Finnish (30)	49	0.20
French, ex. Basque (195)	1,352	5.49
French Canadian (686)	1,425	5.79
German (298)	1,775	7.21
Greek (241)	282	1.15
Hungarian (10)	98	0.40
Iranian (0)	30	0.12
Irish (2,977)	8,078	32.81
Italian (3,056)	7,217	29.31
Latvian (42)	42	0.17
Lithuanian (0)	84	0.34
Norwegian (14)	133	0.54
Pennsylvania German (19)	19	0.08
Polish (351)	1,095	4.45
Portuguese (236)	637	2.59
Romanian (0)	50	0.20
Russian (138)	298	1.21
Scandinavian (28)	61	0.25
Scotch-Irish (394)	917	3.72
Scottish (274)	899	3.65
Serbian (0)	32	0.13
Slovak (16)	16	0.06
Swedish (63)	681	2.77
Swiss (15)	35	0.14
Ukrainian (21)	21	0.09
Welsh (13)	64	0.26
West Indian, ex. Hispanic (32)	32	0.13

*Notes: † The Census 2010 population figure is used to calculate the percentages in the Hispanic Origin and Race categories. Ancestry percentages are based on the 2006-2010 American Community Survey population (not shown); ‡ Numbers in parentheses indicate the number of people reporting a single ancestry; * Numbers in parentheses indicate the number of persons reporting this race alone, not in combination with any other race; Please refer to the Explanation of Data for more information.*

Haitian (32)	32	0.13
Yugoslavian (29)	39	0.16

Hispanic Origin	Population	%
Hispanic or Latino (of any race)	575	2.31
Central American, ex. Mexican	144	0.58
Costa Rican	8	0.03
Guatemalan	74	0.30
Honduran	6	0.02
Nicaraguan	1	<0.01
Panamanian	4	0.02
Salvadoran	50	0.20
Other Central American	1	<0.01
Cuban	20	0.08
Dominican Republic	31	0.12
Mexican	97	0.39
Puerto Rican	124	0.50
South American	109	0.44
Argentinean	18	0.07
Bolivian	2	0.01
Chilean	4	0.02
Colombian	44	0.18
Ecuadorian	15	0.06
Paraguayan	2	0.01
Peruvian	10	0.04
Venezuelan	14	0.06
Other Hispanic or Latino	50	0.20

Race*	Population	%
African-American/Black (229)	320	1.28
Not Hispanic (214)	291	1.17
Hispanic (15)	29	0.12
American Indian/Alaska Native (30)	91	0.36
Not Hispanic (22)	79	0.32
Hispanic (8)	12	0.05
Alaska Athabascan *(Ala. Nat.)* (0)	1	<0.01
Blackfeet (0)	1	<0.01
Canadian/French Am. Ind. (1)	1	<0.01
Cherokee (6)	18	0.07
Choctaw (4)	4	0.02
Cree (0)	1	<0.01
Inupiat *(Alaska Native)* (0)	1	<0.01
Mexican American Ind. (5)	6	0.02
Sioux (1)	2	0.01
South American Ind. (2)	2	0.01
Yuman (0)	3	0.01
Yup'ik *(Alaska Native)* (1)	1	<0.01
Asian (660)	775	3.11
Not Hispanic (659)	772	3.10
Hispanic (1)	3	0.01
Bangladeshi (4)	6	0.02
Cambodian (14)	17	0.07
Chinese, ex. Taiwanese (259)	306	1.23
Filipino (28)	48	0.19
Indian (174)	199	0.80
Indonesian (0)	4	0.02
Japanese (15)	39	0.16
Korean (43)	47	0.19
Laotian (3)	4	0.02
Nepalese (4)	4	0.02
Pakistani (24)	25	0.10
Sri Lankan (3)	4	0.02
Taiwanese (8)	10	0.04
Thai (16)	18	0.07
Vietnamese (38)	45	0.18
Hawaii Native/Pacific Islander (0)	8	0.03
Not Hispanic (0)	8	0.03
Guamanian/Chamorro (0)	1	<0.01
Native Hawaiian (0)	5	0.02
White (23,573)	23,852	95.67
Not Hispanic (23,181)	23,426	93.96
Hispanic (392)	426	1.71

Walpole

Place Type: Town
County: Norfolk
Population: 24,070[†]

Ancestry[‡]	Population	%
African, Sub-Saharan (43)	101	0.43
African (0)	44	0.19
Cape Verdean (34)	48	0.20
Ugandan (9)	9	0.04
Albanian (16)	16	0.07
American (997)	997	4.21
Arab (264)	415	1.75
Arab (33)	33	0.14
Lebanese (156)	265	1.12
Syrian (75)	117	0.49
Armenian (22)	82	0.35
Austrian (10)	37	0.16
Belgian (0)	15	0.06
British (45)	115	0.49
Canadian (67)	159	0.67
Czech (0)	29	0.12
Danish (0)	39	0.16
Dutch (7)	198	0.84
English (509)	2,934	12.39
European (234)	234	0.99
Finnish (13)	68	0.29
French, ex. Basque (115)	1,108	4.68
French Canadian (156)	575	2.43
German (447)	1,799	7.60
Greek (172)	304	1.28
Hungarian (40)	122	0.52
Irish (5,349)	10,722	45.29
Italian (1,623)	4,719	19.93
Latvian (0)	15	0.06
Lithuanian (102)	243	1.03
Norwegian (45)	248	1.05
Polish (133)	1,061	4.48
Portuguese (147)	490	2.07
Russian (389)	554	2.34
Scandinavian (10)	52	0.22
Scotch-Irish (223)	469	1.98
Scottish (177)	632	2.67
Slavic (17)	17	0.07
Slovak (25)	25	0.11
Swedish (38)	351	1.48
Turkish (51)	51	0.22
Ukrainian (19)	70	0.30
Welsh (6)	117	0.49
West Indian, ex. Hispanic (192)	203	0.86
Haitian (187)	187	0.79
Trinidadian/Tobagonian (5)	16	0.07
Yugoslavian (0)	24	0.10

Hispanic Origin	Population	%
Hispanic or Latino (of any race)	651	2.70
Central American, ex. Mexican	64	0.27
Costa Rican	4	0.02
Guatemalan	27	0.11
Honduran	9	0.04
Nicaraguan	2	0.01
Panamanian	2	0.01
Salvadoran	20	0.08
Cuban	35	0.15
Dominican Republic	37	0.15
Mexican	95	0.39
Puerto Rican	131	0.54
South American	99	0.41
Argentinean	6	0.02
Bolivian	20	0.08
Chilean	3	0.01
Colombian	36	0.15
Ecuadorian	2	0.01
Peruvian	21	0.09
Uruguayan	1	<0.01
Venezuelan	10	0.04
Other Hispanic or Latino	190	0.79

Race*	Population	%
African-American/Black (604)	662	2.75
Not Hispanic (569)	608	2.53
Hispanic (35)	54	0.22
American Indian/Alaska Native (30)	64	0.27
Not Hispanic (26)	53	0.22
Hispanic (4)	11	0.05
Blackfeet (0)	1	<0.01
Central American Ind. (0)	1	<0.01
Cherokee (3)	7	0.03
Chickasaw (4)	4	0.02
Chippewa (1)	1	<0.01
Iroquois (1)	6	0.02
Mexican American Ind. (3)	4	0.02
Pima (1)	1	<0.01
Potawatomi (4)	4	0.02
Asian (725)	846	3.51
Not Hispanic (723)	840	3.49
Hispanic (2)	6	0.02
Bangladeshi (4)	4	0.02
Cambodian (3)	5	0.02
Chinese, ex. Taiwanese (235)	268	1.11
Filipino (39)	53	0.22
Hmong (0)	1	<0.01
Indian (304)	316	1.31
Indonesian (1)	7	0.03
Japanese (10)	20	0.08
Korean (61)	82	0.34
Laotian (1)	5	0.02
Pakistani (13)	13	0.05
Sri Lankan (1)	1	<0.01
Taiwanese (2)	5	0.02
Thai (1)	2	0.01
Vietnamese (33)	35	0.15
Hawaii Native/Pacific Islander (1)	15	0.06
Not Hispanic (1)	14	0.06
Hispanic (0)	1	<0.01
Native Hawaiian (1)	5	0.02
White (22,293)	22,513	93.53
Not Hispanic (21,848)	22,034	91.54
Hispanic (445)	479	1.99

Waltham

Place Type: City
County: Middlesex
Population: 60,632[†]

Ancestry[‡]	Population	%
African, Sub-Saharan (932)	1,144	1.91
African (301)	327	0.55
Cape Verdean (18)	18	0.03
Ethiopian (171)	171	0.29
Ghanaian (47)	47	0.08
Nigerian (81)	81	0.14
Somalian (23)	33	0.06
South African (2)	141	0.24
Ugandan (279)	279	0.47
Zimbabwean (0)	16	0.03
Other Sub-Saharan African (10)	31	0.05
Albanian (27)	108	0.18
American (1,178)	1,178	1.97
Arab (339)	617	1.03
Arab (40)	40	0.07
Iraqi (0)	22	0.04
Jordanian (83)	83	0.14
Lebanese (39)	234	0.39
Moroccan (104)	104	0.17
Syrian (31)	81	0.14
Other Arab (42)	53	0.09
Armenian (1,005)	1,267	2.12
Australian (73)	73	0.12
Austrian (48)	144	0.24
Belgian (14)	38	0.06
Brazilian (197)	225	0.38
British (81)	185	0.31
Bulgarian (36)	36	0.06
Canadian (569)	908	1.52
Croatian (10)	61	0.10
Czech (34)	130	0.22
Czechoslovakian (0)	9	0.02
Danish (50)	194	0.32
Dutch (107)	428	0.72
Eastern European (126)	126	0.21
English (1,377)	4,753	7.95
European (277)	305	0.51
Finnish (7)	113	0.19

*Notes: † The Census 2010 population figure is used to calculate the percentages in the Hispanic Origin and Race categories. Ancestry percentages are based on the 2006-2010 American Community Survey population (not shown); ‡ Numbers in parentheses indicate the number of people reporting a single ancestry; * Numbers in parentheses indicate the number of persons reporting this race alone, not in combination with any other race; Please refer to the Explanation of Data for more information.*

French, ex. Basque (987)	2,877	4.81
French Canadian (1,035)	2,192	3.67
German (615)	3,585	6.00
Greek (392)	777	1.30
Guyanese (27)	50	0.08
Hungarian (120)	326	0.55
Iranian (277)	282	0.47
Irish (4,819)	12,493	20.90
Israeli (125)	152	0.25
Italian (4,378)	9,299	15.56
Latvian (34)	47	0.08
Lithuanian (72)	323	0.54
New Zealander (13)	13	0.02
Norwegian (88)	288	0.48
Polish (515)	2,059	3.44
Portuguese (474)	1,002	1.68
Romanian (27)	167	0.28
Russian (622)	1,725	2.89
Scandinavian (11)	41	0.07
Scotch-Irish (343)	922	1.54
Scottish (595)	1,534	2.57
Slavic (11)	11	0.02
Slovak (10)	65	0.11
Slovene (15)	15	0.03
Swedish (114)	892	1.49
Swiss (24)	48	0.08
Turkish (92)	92	0.15
Ukrainian (159)	434	0.73
Welsh (20)	218	0.36
West Indian, ex. Hispanic (806)	957	1.60
Barbadian (47)	52	0.09
British West Indian (0)	23	0.04
Haitian (496)	496	0.83
Jamaican (218)	311	0.52
Trinidadian/Tobagonian (16)	24	0.04
West Indian (29)	51	0.09

Hispanic Origin	Population	%
Hispanic or Latino (of any race)	8,280	13.66
Central American, ex. Mexican	3,816	6.29
Costa Rican	38	0.06
Guatemalan	3,252	5.36
Honduran	92	0.15
Nicaraguan	19	0.03
Panamanian	27	0.04
Salvadoran	373	0.62
Other Central American	15	0.02
Cuban	119	0.20
Dominican Republic	258	0.43
Mexican	991	1.63
Puerto Rican	1,188	1.96
South American	1,000	1.65
Argentinean	121	0.20
Bolivian	94	0.16
Chilean	63	0.10
Colombian	207	0.34
Ecuadorian	208	0.34
Paraguayan	3	<0.01
Peruvian	199	0.33
Uruguayan	24	0.04
Venezuelan	79	0.13
Other South American	2	<0.01
Other Hispanic or Latino	908	1.50

Race*	Population	%
African-American/Black (3,651)	4,106	6.77
Not Hispanic (3,459)	3,809	6.28
Hispanic (192)	297	0.49
American Indian/Alaska Native (139)	336	0.55
Not Hispanic (66)	207	0.34
Hispanic (73)	129	0.21
Blackfeet (2)	12	0.02
Central American Ind. (11)	14	0.02
Cherokee (5)	29	0.05
Chickasaw (0)	1	<0.01
Chippewa (1)	5	0.01
Comanche (0)	1	<0.01
Delaware (0)	4	0.01
Houma (1)	1	<0.01
Iroquois (3)	16	0.03
Menominee (1)	1	<0.01
Mexican American Ind. (8)	14	0.02
Navajo (0)	2	<0.01
Osage (0)	1	<0.01
Potawatomi (0)	2	<0.01
Pueblo (4)	4	0.01
Seminole (0)	2	<0.01
Sioux (5)	9	0.01
South American Ind. (6)	15	0.02
Spanish American Ind. (1)	1	<0.01
Tohono O'Odham (0)	2	<0.01
Ute (1)	1	<0.01
Asian (5,860)	6,427	10.60
Not Hispanic (5,834)	6,361	10.49
Hispanic (26)	66	0.11
Bangladeshi (33)	37	0.06
Bhutanese (5)	5	0.01
Burmese (19)	19	0.03
Cambodian (35)	45	0.07
Chinese, ex. Taiwanese (1,827)	2,012	3.32
Filipino (153)	229	0.38
Hmong (1)	1	<0.01
Indian (2,284)	2,405	3.97
Indonesian (16)	28	0.05
Japanese (124)	173	0.29
Korean (428)	470	0.78
Laotian (48)	60	0.10
Malaysian (7)	13	0.02
Nepalese (72)	74	0.12
Pakistani (107)	120	0.20
Sri Lankan (14)	18	0.03
Taiwanese (100)	106	0.17
Thai (106)	124	0.20
Vietnamese (281)	330	0.54
Hawaii Native/Pacific Islander (73)	159	0.26
Not Hispanic (31)	81	0.13
Hispanic (42)	78	0.13
Fijian (2)	3	<0.01
Guamanian/Chamorro (51)	73	0.12
Native Hawaiian (3)	12	0.02
Tongan (2)	2	<0.01
White (45,697)	46,906	77.36
Not Hispanic (41,678)	42,492	70.08
Hispanic (4,019)	4,414	7.28

Ware

Place Type: Town
County: Hampshire
Population: 9,872[†]

Ancestry‡	Population	%
African, Sub-Saharan (10)	30	0.30
Cape Verdean (10)	30	0.30
American (224)	224	2.27
Arab (26)	26	0.26
Lebanese (26)	26	0.26
Australian (0)	8	0.08
Belgian (0)	16	0.16
British (17)	57	0.58
Canadian (13)	13	0.13
Danish (0)	12	0.12
Dutch (0)	13	0.13
English (313)	1,240	12.58
European (35)	35	0.35
French, ex. Basque (659)	3,010	30.53
French Canadian (632)	1,115	11.31
German (137)	778	7.89
Greek (0)	114	1.16
Hungarian (17)	41	0.42
Irish (354)	1,965	19.93
Italian (148)	781	7.92
Lithuanian (8)	74	0.75
Norwegian (0)	7	0.07
Polish (1,452)	2,803	28.43
Portuguese (37)	67	0.68
Scotch-Irish (22)	154	1.56
Scottish (50)	260	2.64
Slovak (0)	13	0.13
Swedish (50)	153	1.55
Ukrainian (0)	20	0.20
Welsh (0)	8	0.08

Hispanic Origin	Population	%
Hispanic or Latino (of any race)	389	3.94
Central American, ex. Mexican	12	0.12
Costa Rican	3	0.03
Guatemalan	2	0.02
Panamanian	1	0.01
Salvadoran	6	0.06
Cuban	10	0.10
Dominican Republic	8	0.08
Mexican	38	0.38
Puerto Rican	250	2.53
South American	26	0.26
Chilean	3	0.03
Colombian	2	0.02
Ecuadorian	11	0.11
Peruvian	9	0.09
Uruguayan	1	0.01
Other Hispanic or Latino	45	0.46

Race*	Population	%
African-American/Black (102)	217	2.20
Not Hispanic (95)	194	1.97
Hispanic (7)	23	0.23
American Indian/Alaska Native (30)	86	0.87
Not Hispanic (25)	78	0.79
Hispanic (5)	8	0.08
Apache (0)	6	0.06
Blackfeet (2)	7	0.07
Cherokee (6)	14	0.14
Cheyenne (0)	1	0.01
Mexican American Ind. (1)	1	0.01
Sioux (2)	5	0.05
Asian (71)	114	1.15
Not Hispanic (68)	105	1.06
Hispanic (3)	9	0.09
Chinese, ex. Taiwanese (16)	22	0.22
Filipino (25)	44	0.45
Indian (12)	20	0.20
Indonesian (0)	2	0.02
Japanese (7)	11	0.11
Korean (5)	9	0.09
Pakistani (0)	1	0.01
Taiwanese (1)	1	0.01
Thai (1)	3	0.03
Vietnamese (4)	4	0.04
Hawaii Native/Pacific Islander (0)	18	0.18
Not Hispanic (0)	14	0.14
Hispanic (0)	4	0.04
Native Hawaiian (0)	6	0.06
Samoan (0)	2	0.02
White (9,292)	9,507	96.30
Not Hispanic (9,101)	9,270	93.90
Hispanic (191)	237	2.40

Wareham

Place Type: Town
County: Plymouth
Population: 21,822[†]

Ancestry‡	Population	%
African, Sub-Saharan (977)	1,225	5.69
African (0)	12	0.06
Cape Verdean (977)	1,184	5.50
Other Sub-Saharan African (0)	29	0.13
American (1,108)	1,108	5.14
Arab (109)	172	0.80
Lebanese (109)	134	0.62
Syrian (0)	38	0.18
Austrian (0)	34	0.16
Brazilian (9)	9	0.04
British (45)	45	0.21
Canadian (84)	216	1.00
Czech (0)	34	0.16
Czechoslovakian (16)	16	0.07
Danish (13)	30	0.14
Dutch (0)	19	0.09

*Notes: † The Census 2010 population figure is used to calculate the percentages in the Hispanic Origin and Race categories. Ancestry percentages are based on the 2006-2010 American Community Survey population (not shown); ‡ Numbers in parentheses indicate the number of people reporting a single ancestry; * Numbers in parentheses indicate the number of persons reporting this race alone, not in combination with any other race; Please refer to the Explanation of Data for more information.*

English (1,235)	3,582	16.63
European (126)	153	0.71
Finnish (55)	181	0.84
French, ex. Basque (343)	1,672	7.76
French Canadian (407)	814	3.78
German (478)	1,177	5.47
Greek (135)	211	0.98
Hungarian (0)	22	0.10
Iranian (42)	42	0.20
Irish (3,147)	6,202	28.80
Italian (1,224)	2,949	13.69
Latvian (0)	31	0.14
Lithuanian (120)	370	1.72
Northern European (51)	51	0.24
Norwegian (37)	184	0.85
Polish (248)	766	3.56
Portuguese (985)	1,752	8.14
Romanian (0)	22	0.10
Russian (21)	144	0.67
Scotch-Irish (178)	436	2.02
Scottish (130)	398	1.85
Slovene (15)	15	0.07
Swedish (310)	555	2.58
Swiss (0)	39	0.18
Ukrainian (16)	16	0.07
Welsh (11)	127	0.59
West Indian, ex. Hispanic (17)	79	0.37
Haitian (17)	51	0.24
Jamaican (0)	28	0.13

Hispanic Origin	Population	%
Hispanic or Latino (of any race)	502	2.30
Central American, ex. Mexican	32	0.15
Costa Rican	1	<0.01
Guatemalan	10	0.05
Honduran	8	0.04
Panamanian	1	<0.01
Salvadoran	12	0.05
Cuban	11	0.05
Dominican Republic	23	0.11
Mexican	87	0.40
Puerto Rican	260	1.19
South American	24	0.11
Argentinean	11	0.05
Chilean	1	<0.01
Colombian	4	0.02
Ecuadorian	2	0.01
Peruvian	2	0.01
Uruguayan	1	<0.01
Venezuelan	2	0.01
Other South American	1	<0.01
Other Hispanic or Latino	65	0.30

Race*	Population	%
African-American/Black (769)	1,243	5.70
Not Hispanic (728)	1,175	5.38
Hispanic (41)	68	0.31
American Indian/Alaska Native (141)	350	1.60
Not Hispanic (125)	322	1.48
Hispanic (16)	28	0.13
Blackfeet (1)	5	0.02
Canadian/French Am. Ind. (1)	2	0.01
Cherokee (12)	29	0.13
Choctaw (1)	2	0.01
Comanche (1)	3	0.01
Cree (0)	1	<0.01
Creek (1)	3	0.01
Delaware (1)	2	0.01
Iroquois (1)	6	0.03
Lumbee (1)	2	0.01
Mexican American Ind. (1)	1	<0.01
Seminole (0)	2	0.01
Shoshone (0)	1	<0.01
Sioux (1)	3	0.01
Spanish American Ind. (4)	4	0.02
Tsimshian *(Alaska Native)* (1)	1	<0.01
Asian (150)	229	1.05
Not Hispanic (147)	221	1.01
Hispanic (3)	8	0.04
Cambodian (1)	2	0.01
Chinese, ex. Taiwanese (33)	47	0.22
Filipino (15)	32	0.15
Indian (28)	36	0.16
Indonesian (1)	1	<0.01
Japanese (17)	35	0.16
Korean (10)	19	0.09
Laotian (9)	11	0.05
Thai (3)	12	0.05
Vietnamese (26)	31	0.14
Hawaii Native/Pacific Islander (5)	33	0.15
Not Hispanic (5)	33	0.15
Guamanian/Chamorro (4)	6	0.03
Native Hawaiian (1)	10	0.05
White (18,874)	19,564	89.65
Not Hispanic (18,594)	19,235	88.14
Hispanic (280)	329	1.51

Watertown Town

Place Type: City
County: Middlesex
Population: 31,915[†]

Ancestry[‡]	Population	%
African, Sub-Saharan (423)	613	1.94
African (56)	56	0.18
Kenyan (61)	61	0.19
Nigerian (54)	71	0.22
Ugandan (110)	110	0.35
Other Sub-Saharan African (142)	315	1.00
Albanian (35)	143	0.45
American (643)	643	2.04
Arab (988)	1,151	3.64
Arab (31)	63	0.20
Egyptian (20)	31	0.10
Jordanian (45)	45	0.14
Lebanese (762)	811	2.57
Moroccan (11)	11	0.03
Palestinian (7)	22	0.07
Syrian (97)	124	0.39
Other Arab (15)	44	0.14
Armenian (1,907)	2,036	6.44
Austrian (8)	31	0.10
Belgian (20)	57	0.18
Brazilian (427)	459	1.45
British (85)	218	0.69
Bulgarian (67)	67	0.21
Cajun (0)	19	0.06
Canadian (261)	377	1.19
Celtic (19)	19	0.06
Czech (0)	103	0.33
Czechoslovakian (0)	24	0.08
Danish (0)	108	0.34
Dutch (9)	228	0.72
Eastern European (114)	155	0.49
English (574)	2,715	8.59
Estonian (0)	5	0.02
European (342)	374	1.18
Finnish (52)	185	0.59
French, ex. Basque (282)	1,449	4.59
French Canadian (261)	815	2.58
German (288)	1,831	5.80
Greek (629)	805	2.55
Hungarian (59)	177	0.56
Iranian (272)	316	1.00
Irish (2,408)	6,638	21.01
Israeli (14)	28	0.09
Italian (3,341)	6,157	19.49
Latvian (27)	56	0.18
Lithuanian (78)	178	0.56
Macedonian (0)	16	0.05
New Zealander (18)	18	0.06
Northern European (24)	97	0.31
Norwegian (44)	185	0.59
Polish (135)	955	3.02
Portuguese (301)	466	1.48
Romanian (201)	284	0.90
Russian (553)	1,277	4.04
Scandinavian (73)	85	0.27
Scotch-Irish (206)	461	1.46
Scottish (288)	846	2.68
Serbian (13)	13	0.04
Slovak (0)	21	0.07
Slovene (0)	16	0.05
Swedish (99)	539	1.71
Swiss (32)	88	0.28
Turkish (50)	50	0.16
Ukrainian (9)	80	0.25
Welsh (10)	117	0.37
West Indian, ex. Hispanic (135)	151	0.48
Haitian (92)	92	0.29
Jamaican (12)	12	0.04
Trinidadian/Tobagonian (14)	30	0.09
West Indian (17)	17	0.05
Yugoslavian (15)	15	0.05

Hispanic Origin	Population	%
Hispanic or Latino (of any race)	1,688	5.29
Central American, ex. Mexican	391	1.23
Costa Rican	15	0.05
Guatemalan	182	0.57
Honduran	38	0.12
Nicaraguan	2	0.01
Panamanian	14	0.04
Salvadoran	140	0.44
Cuban	60	0.19
Dominican Republic	67	0.21
Mexican	211	0.66
Puerto Rican	263	0.82
South American	447	1.40
Argentinean	61	0.19
Bolivian	15	0.05
Chilean	40	0.13
Colombian	109	0.34
Ecuadorian	86	0.27
Paraguayan	4	0.01
Peruvian	72	0.23
Uruguayan	4	0.01
Venezuelan	52	0.16
Other South American	4	0.01
Other Hispanic or Latino	249	0.78

Race*	Population	%
African-American/Black (950)	1,205	3.78
Not Hispanic (883)	1,102	3.45
Hispanic (67)	103	0.32
American Indian/Alaska Native (40)	140	0.44
Not Hispanic (25)	105	0.33
Hispanic (15)	35	0.11
Alaska Athabascan *(Ala. Nat.)* (0)	1	<0.01
Apache (0)	2	0.01
Blackfeet (0)	6	0.02
Canadian/French Am. Ind. (0)	1	<0.01
Cherokee (3)	21	0.07
Choctaw (0)	3	0.01
Delaware (0)	1	<0.01
Inupiat *(Alaska Native)* (0)	1	<0.01
Iroquois (0)	4	0.01
Kiowa (0)	1	<0.01
Mexican American Ind. (2)	3	0.01
Navajo (0)	2	0.01
Osage (0)	3	0.01
Paiute (1)	1	<0.01
Seminole (0)	2	0.01
South American Ind. (8)	14	0.04
Tlingit-Haida *(Alaska Native)* (1)	1	<0.01
Yakama (1)	1	<0.01
Yup'ik *(Alaska Native)* (1)	1	<0.01
Asian (2,304)	2,697	8.45
Not Hispanic (2,286)	2,663	8.34
Hispanic (18)	34	0.11
Bangladeshi (16)	16	0.05
Burmese (1)	1	<0.01
Cambodian (29)	31	0.10
Chinese, ex. Taiwanese (743)	822	2.58
Filipino (81)	116	0.36
Indian (506)	585	1.83
Indonesian (36)	44	0.14
Japanese (87)	138	0.43
Korean (215)	238	0.75

SECTION TWO

*Notes: † The Census 2010 population figure is used to calculate the percentages in the Hispanic Origin and Race categories. Ancestry percentages are based on the 2006-2010 American Community Survey population (not shown); ‡ Numbers in parentheses indicate the number of people reporting a single ancestry; * Numbers in parentheses indicate the number of persons reporting this race alone, not in combination with any other race; Please refer to the Explanation of Data for more information.*

Laotian (9)	10	0.03
Malaysian (1)	2	0.01
Nepalese (43)	48	0.15
Pakistani (177)	213	0.67
Sri Lankan (15)	17	0.05
Taiwanese (40)	43	0.13
Thai (119)	127	0.40
Vietnamese (107)	123	0.39
Hawaii Native/Pacific Islander (14)	42	0.13
Not Hispanic (10)	33	0.10
Hispanic (4)	9	0.03
Fijian (0)	1	<0.01
Guamanian/Chamorro (7)	12	0.04
Native Hawaiian (1)	5	0.02
Samoan (1)	3	0.01
White (27,091)	27,858	87.29
Not Hispanic (26,065)	26,710	83.69
Hispanic (1,026)	1,148	3.60

Wayland

Place Type: Town
County: Middlesex
Population: 12,994†

Ancestry‡	Population	%
African, Sub-Saharan (9)	9	0.07
South African (9)	9	0.07
Albanian (15)	15	0.12
American (336)	336	2.61
Arab (43)	92	0.72
Lebanese (18)	37	0.29
Moroccan (13)	13	0.10
Syrian (12)	42	0.33
Armenian (23)	64	0.50
Australian (13)	50	0.39
Austrian (0)	135	1.05
Basque (0)	7	0.05
Brazilian (13)	37	0.29
British (81)	169	1.31
Bulgarian (12)	12	0.09
Canadian (63)	105	0.82
Czech (18)	49	0.38
Danish (0)	9	0.07
Dutch (21)	187	1.45
Eastern European (220)	363	2.82
English (531)	2,033	15.80
European (198)	254	1.97
Finnish (0)	13	0.10
French, ex. Basque (77)	458	3.56
French Canadian (14)	175	1.36
German (492)	1,801	14.00
Greek (59)	258	2.01
Hungarian (19)	102	0.79
Iranian (14)	14	0.11
Irish (1,030)	3,111	24.18
Israeli (40)	40	0.31
Italian (462)	1,550	12.05
Latvian (10)	10	0.08
Lithuanian (57)	202	1.57
Northern European (39)	93	0.72
Norwegian (0)	183	1.42
Polish (209)	661	5.14
Portuguese (0)	34	0.26
Romanian (13)	63	0.49
Russian (527)	1,061	8.25
Scotch-Irish (154)	369	2.87
Scottish (60)	425	3.30
Slovak (0)	16	0.12
Slovene (17)	17	0.13
Swedish (80)	251	1.95
Swiss (8)	149	1.16
Turkish (13)	13	0.10
Ukrainian (0)	21	0.16
Welsh (0)	116	0.90
West Indian, ex. Hispanic (49)	49	0.38
Barbadian (49)	49	0.38

Hispanic Origin	Population	%
Hispanic or Latino (of any race)	315	2.42
Central American, ex. Mexican	18	0.14
Costa Rican	1	0.01
Guatemalan	14	0.11
Honduran	2	0.02
Salvadoran	1	0.01
Cuban	27	0.21
Dominican Republic	24	0.18
Mexican	52	0.40
Puerto Rican	59	0.45
South American	77	0.59
Argentinean	14	0.11
Bolivian	1	0.01
Chilean	3	0.02
Colombian	36	0.28
Ecuadorian	4	0.03
Paraguayan	8	0.06
Peruvian	9	0.07
Venezuelan	2	0.02
Other Hispanic or Latino	58	0.45

Race*	Population	%
African-American/Black (113)	148	1.14
Not Hispanic (101)	128	0.99
Hispanic (12)	20	0.15
American Indian/Alaska Native (4)	27	0.21
Not Hispanic (4)	19	0.15
Hispanic (0)	8	0.06
Blackfeet (0)	1	0.01
Chippewa (1)	2	0.02
Sioux (0)	1	0.01
Asian (1,286)	1,431	11.01
Not Hispanic (1,284)	1,422	10.94
Hispanic (2)	9	0.07
Bangladeshi (5)	5	0.04
Cambodian (3)	3	0.02
Chinese, ex. Taiwanese (746)	814	6.26
Filipino (19)	30	0.23
Indian (255)	277	2.13
Indonesian (1)	7	0.05
Japanese (35)	64	0.49
Korean (105)	130	1.00
Malaysian (3)	6	0.05
Pakistani (6)	10	0.08
Taiwanese (46)	53	0.41
Thai (16)	18	0.14
Vietnamese (16)	23	0.18
Hawaii Native/Pacific Islander (2)	13	0.10
Not Hispanic (2)	12	0.09
Hispanic (0)	1	0.01
Guamanian/Chamorro (1)	1	0.01
Native Hawaiian (1)	1	0.01
Samoan (0)	2	0.02
White (11,330)	11,528	88.72
Not Hispanic (11,082)	11,258	86.64
Hispanic (248)	270	2.08

Webster

Place Type: CDP
County: Worcester
Population: 11,412†

Ancestry‡	Population	%
African, Sub-Saharan (145)	145	1.27
African (20)	20	0.18
Cape Verdean (103)	103	0.90
Ghanaian (22)	22	0.19
Albanian (0)	25	0.22
American (505)	505	4.43
Arab (47)	67	0.59
Lebanese (47)	47	0.41
Other Arab (0)	20	0.18
Armenian (0)	28	0.25
Austrian (0)	13	0.11
British (11)	11	0.10
Cajun (10)	10	0.09
Canadian (0)	14	0.12
Czech (8)	36	0.32
Czechoslovakian (0)	63	0.55
Dutch (0)	20	0.18
English (232)	924	8.11
European (7)	7	0.06
Finnish (0)	9	0.08
French, ex. Basque (818)	3,296	28.93
French Canadian (498)	855	7.50
German (87)	674	5.92
Greek (98)	132	1.16
Hungarian (0)	57	0.50
Irish (562)	2,294	20.14
Italian (223)	732	6.42
Lithuanian (0)	186	1.63
Macedonian (35)	35	0.31
Northern European (33)	33	0.29
Norwegian (10)	10	0.09
Polish (874)	2,330	20.45
Portuguese (30)	164	1.44
Romanian (0)	9	0.08
Russian (0)	62	0.54
Scandinavian (0)	12	0.11
Scotch-Irish (44)	190	1.67
Scottish (48)	245	2.15
Slovak (64)	128	1.12
Swedish (58)	270	2.37
Swiss (0)	4	0.04
Turkish (11)	11	0.10
Ukrainian (0)	9	0.08
Welsh (0)	65	0.57
Yugoslavian (9)	9	0.08

Hispanic Origin	Population	%
Hispanic or Latino (of any race)	1,012	8.87
Central American, ex. Mexican	43	0.38
Costa Rican	7	0.06
Guatemalan	9	0.08
Honduran	2	0.02
Nicaraguan	3	0.03
Panamanian	7	0.06
Salvadoran	14	0.12
Other Central American	1	0.01
Cuban	14	0.12
Dominican Republic	32	0.28
Mexican	44	0.39
Puerto Rican	759	6.65
South American	57	0.50
Argentinean	3	0.03
Bolivian	9	0.08
Chilean	3	0.03
Colombian	34	0.30
Ecuadorian	6	0.05
Peruvian	2	0.02
Other Hispanic or Latino	63	0.55

Race*	Population	%
African-American/Black (438)	548	4.80
Not Hispanic (379)	466	4.08
Hispanic (59)	82	0.72
American Indian/Alaska Native (41)	135	1.18
Not Hispanic (38)	129	1.13
Hispanic (3)	6	0.05
Blackfeet (1)	6	0.05
Canadian/French Am. Ind. (1)	2	0.02
Cherokee (3)	20	0.18
Chippewa (2)	6	0.05
Choctaw (0)	2	0.02
Iroquois (2)	5	0.04
Mexican American Ind. (1)	1	0.01
Seminole (0)	1	0.01
Sioux (0)	1	0.01
Asian (115)	168	1.47
Not Hispanic (111)	161	1.41
Hispanic (4)	7	0.06
Cambodian (2)	5	0.04
Chinese, ex. Taiwanese (16)	25	0.22
Filipino (11)	31	0.27
Indian (13)	26	0.23
Japanese (3)	8	0.07
Korean (5)	10	0.09
Laotian (10)	13	0.11
Nepalese (1)	1	0.01
Pakistani (13)	13	0.11

*Notes: † The Census 2010 population figure is used to calculate the percentages in the Hispanic Origin and Race categories. Ancestry percentages are based on the 2006-2010 American Community Survey population (not shown); ‡ Numbers in parentheses indicate the number of people reporting a single ancestry; * Numbers in parentheses indicate the number of persons reporting this race alone, not in combination with any other race; Please refer to the Explanation of Data for more information.*

Taiwanese (1)	1	0.01
Thai (4)	6	0.05
Vietnamese (19)	23	0.20
Hawaii Native/Pacific Islander (0)	14	0.12
Not Hispanic (0)	9	0.08
Hispanic (0)	5	0.04
Guamanian/Chamorro (0)	1	0.01
Native Hawaiian (0)	3	0.03
White (10,170)	10,437	91.46
Not Hispanic (9,612)	9,816	86.01
Hispanic (558)	621	5.44

Webster

Place Type: Town
County: Worcester
Population: 16,767†

Ancestry‡	Population	%
African, Sub-Saharan (145)	145	0.87
African (20)	20	0.12
Cape Verdean (103)	103	0.62
Ghanaian (22)	22	0.13
Albanian (0)	25	0.15
American (649)	649	3.88
Arab (78)	145	0.87
Lebanese (47)	61	0.36
Syrian (17)	50	0.30
Other Arab (14)	34	0.20
Armenian (15)	143	0.85
Austrian (0)	13	0.08
British (11)	11	0.07
Cajun (10)	10	0.06
Canadian (15)	81	0.48
Czech (29)	57	0.34
Czechoslovakian (0)	63	0.38
Dutch (0)	106	0.63
English (300)	1,394	8.32
European (7)	7	0.04
Finnish (0)	9	0.05
French, ex. Basque (1,214)	4,615	27.56
French Canadian (864)	1,502	8.97
German (227)	967	5.77
Greek (110)	218	1.30
Hungarian (0)	57	0.34
Irish (767)	3,531	21.09
Italian (535)	1,622	9.69
Lithuanian (23)	236	1.41
Macedonian (35)	35	0.21
Northern European (33)	33	0.20
Norwegian (10)	24	0.14
Polish (1,349)	3,370	20.13
Portuguese (85)	318	1.90
Romanian (0)	9	0.05
Russian (0)	62	0.37
Scandinavian (0)	12	0.07
Scotch-Irish (62)	228	1.36
Scottish (48)	344	2.05
Slovak (117)	212	1.27
Swedish (125)	385	2.30
Swiss (0)	4	0.02
Turkish (11)	11	0.07
Ukrainian (0)	33	0.20
Welsh (12)	107	0.64
Yugoslavian (9)	9	0.05

Hispanic Origin	Population	%
Hispanic or Latino (of any race)	1,148	6.85
Central American, ex. Mexican	54	0.32
Costa Rican	7	0.04
Guatemalan	9	0.05
Honduran	3	0.02
Nicaraguan	3	0.02
Panamanian	13	0.08
Salvadoran	18	0.11
Other Central American	1	0.01
Cuban	17	0.10
Dominican Republic	34	0.20
Mexican	57	0.34
Puerto Rican	819	4.88
South American	85	0.51
Argentinean	4	0.02
Bolivian	9	0.05
Chilean	3	0.02
Colombian	42	0.25
Ecuadorian	17	0.10
Peruvian	4	0.02
Uruguayan	2	0.01
Venezuelan	3	0.02
Other South American	1	0.01
Other Hispanic or Latino	82	0.49

Race*	Population	%
African-American/Black (482)	617	3.68
Not Hispanic (420)	532	3.17
Hispanic (62)	85	0.51
American Indian/Alaska Native (50)	168	1.00
Not Hispanic (46)	157	0.94
Hispanic (4)	11	0.07
Blackfeet (1)	9	0.05
Canadian/French Am. Ind. (1)	2	0.01
Central American Ind. (1)	3	0.02
Cherokee (3)	20	0.12
Chippewa (2)	6	0.04
Choctaw (0)	2	0.01
Iroquois (2)	5	0.03
Lumbee (3)	3	0.02
Mexican American Ind. (1)	1	0.01
Seminole (0)	1	0.01
Sioux (0)	2	0.01
Asian (184)	253	1.51
Not Hispanic (178)	244	1.46
Hispanic (6)	9	0.05
Cambodian (5)	8	0.05
Chinese, ex. Taiwanese (27)	38	0.23
Filipino (17)	40	0.24
Indian (24)	41	0.24
Indonesian (1)	1	0.01
Japanese (4)	12	0.07
Korean (13)	18	0.11
Laotian (15)	20	0.12
Nepalese (1)	1	0.01
Pakistani (13)	13	0.08
Taiwanese (2)	4	0.02
Thai (4)	6	0.04
Vietnamese (40)	44	0.26
Hawaii Native/Pacific Islander (0)	16	0.10
Not Hispanic (0)	11	0.07
Hispanic (0)	5	0.03
Guamanian/Chamorro (0)	1	0.01
Native Hawaiian (0)	3	0.02
White (15,293)	15,620	93.16
Not Hispanic (14,658)	14,904	88.89
Hispanic (635)	716	4.27

Wellesley

Place Type: CDP/Town
County: Norfolk
Population: 27,982†

Ancestry‡	Population	%
African, Sub-Saharan (88)	123	0.45
African (14)	28	0.10
Ethiopian (0)	13	0.05
Ghanaian (14)	14	0.05
Nigerian (15)	15	0.05
South African (32)	40	0.14
Ugandan (13)	13	0.05
Albanian (10)	18	0.07
American (1,010)	1,010	3.66
Arab (103)	216	0.78
Arab (16)	23	0.08
Egyptian (25)	25	0.09
Lebanese (42)	121	0.44
Moroccan (0)	16	0.06
Syrian (20)	31	0.11
Armenian (121)	191	0.69
Australian (88)	110	0.40
Austrian (0)	192	0.70
Belgian (9)	9	0.03
Brazilian (73)	90	0.33
British (188)	319	1.15
Bulgarian (19)	42	0.15
Canadian (185)	392	1.42
Croatian (11)	53	0.19
Czech (34)	173	0.63
Czechoslovakian (14)	28	0.10
Danish (23)	113	0.41
Dutch (118)	578	2.09
Eastern European (193)	208	0.75
English (954)	3,909	14.15
Estonian (0)	12	0.04
European (495)	532	1.93
Finnish (45)	129	0.47
French, ex. Basque (235)	1,383	5.01
French Canadian (75)	359	1.30
German (565)	3,003	10.87
Greek (107)	190	0.69
Guyanese (47)	47	0.17
Hungarian (36)	183	0.66
Iranian (112)	133	0.48
Irish (2,323)	6,178	22.37
Israeli (60)	74	0.27
Italian (1,461)	3,700	13.39
Latvian (0)	10	0.04
Lithuanian (7)	113	0.41
Macedonian (14)	14	0.05
New Zealander (11)	11	0.04
Northern European (43)	43	0.16
Norwegian (127)	284	1.03
Polish (142)	955	3.46
Portuguese (66)	181	0.66
Romanian (0)	34	0.12
Russian (470)	983	3.56
Scandinavian (25)	104	0.38
Scotch-Irish (183)	660	2.39
Scottish (132)	791	2.86
Serbian (0)	15	0.05
Slovak (0)	28	0.10
Swedish (212)	530	1.92
Swiss (5)	191	0.69
Turkish (22)	43	0.16
Ukrainian (56)	107	0.39
Welsh (43)	186	0.67
West Indian, ex. Hispanic (44)	83	0.30
Haitian (10)	41	0.15
Jamaican (19)	27	0.10
West Indian (15)	15	0.05
Yugoslavian (8)	8	0.03

Hispanic Origin	Population	%
Hispanic or Latino (of any race)	1,020	3.65
Central American, ex. Mexican	102	0.36
Costa Rican	10	0.04
Guatemalan	52	0.19
Honduran	8	0.03
Nicaraguan	14	0.05
Panamanian	7	0.03
Salvadoran	11	0.04
Cuban	89	0.32
Dominican Republic	51	0.18
Mexican	233	0.83
Puerto Rican	121	0.43
South American	300	1.07
Argentinean	49	0.18
Bolivian	8	0.03
Chilean	29	0.10
Colombian	98	0.35
Ecuadorian	30	0.11
Paraguayan	7	0.03
Peruvian	35	0.13
Uruguayan	7	0.03
Venezuelan	33	0.12
Other South American	4	0.01
Other Hispanic or Latino	124	0.44

Race*	Population	%
African-American/Black (571)	679	2.43
Not Hispanic (546)	643	2.30

*Notes: † The Census 2010 population figure is used to calculate the percentages in the Hispanic Origin and Race categories. Ancestry percentages are based on the 2006-2010 American Community Survey population (not shown); ‡ Numbers in parentheses indicate the number of people reporting a single ancestry; * Numbers in parentheses indicate the number of persons reporting this race alone, not in combination with any other race; Please refer to the Explanation of Data for more information.*

SECTION TWO

Hispanic (25)	36	0.13
American Indian/Alaska Native (36)	90	0.32
Not Hispanic (22)	66	0.24
Hispanic (14)	24	0.09
Blackfeet (0)	8	0.03
Central American Ind. (1)	1	<0.01
Cherokee (7)	20	0.07
Cheyenne (1)	1	<0.01
Chippewa (2)	2	0.01
Choctaw (0)	1	<0.01
Creek (0)	2	0.01
Mexican American Ind. (3)	3	0.01
Potawatomi (0)	1	<0.01
Pueblo (1)	1	<0.01
Sioux (2)	2	0.01
South American Ind. (0)	2	0.01
Spanish American Ind. (7)	7	0.03
Yaqui (0)	1	<0.01
Asian (2,756)	3,191	11.40
Not Hispanic (2,742)	3,159	11.29
Hispanic (14)	32	0.11
Bangladeshi (7)	10	0.04
Burmese (4)	15	0.05
Cambodian (5)	17	0.06
Chinese, ex. Taiwanese (1,413)	1,609	5.75
Filipino (48)	99	0.35
Hmong (2)	2	0.01
Indian (458)	533	1.90
Indonesian (8)	13	0.05
Japanese (96)	162	0.58
Korean (418)	478	1.71
Laotian (1)	4	0.01
Malaysian (6)	7	0.03
Nepalese (4)	4	0.01
Pakistani (51)	53	0.19
Sri Lankan (3)	7	0.03
Taiwanese (75)	105	0.38
Thai (28)	31	0.11
Vietnamese (37)	65	0.23
Hawaii Native/Pacific Islander (7)	30	0.11
Not Hispanic (1)	20	0.07
Hispanic (6)	10	0.04
Guamanian/Chamorro (2)	4	0.01
Native Hawaiian (0)	7	0.03
White (23,817)	24,347	87.01
Not Hispanic (23,061)	23,549	84.16
Hispanic (756)	798	2.85

West Boylston

Place Type: Town
County: Worcester
Population: 7,669†

Ancestry‡	Population	%
African, Sub-Saharan (30)	30	0.39
African (30)	30	0.39
Albanian (53)	53	0.69
American (115)	115	1.50
Arab (32)	64	0.84
Arab (0)	5	0.07
Egyptian (12)	24	0.31
Lebanese (12)	12	0.16
Syrian (8)	23	0.30
Armenian (46)	88	1.15
Austrian (0)	32	0.42
British (20)	20	0.26
Canadian (34)	73	0.95
Danish (13)	13	0.17
Dutch (36)	76	0.99
Eastern European (7)	19	0.25
English (202)	803	10.49
European (38)	38	0.50
Finnish (14)	37	0.48
French, ex. Basque (111)	786	10.27
French Canadian (89)	236	3.08
German (70)	248	3.24
Greek (104)	104	1.36
Irish (943)	2,083	27.20
Italian (440)	1,029	13.44
Latvian (0)	10	0.13
Lithuanian (22)	92	1.20
Norwegian (20)	61	0.80
Polish (136)	297	3.88
Portuguese (115)	167	2.18
Russian (40)	64	0.84
Scandinavian (44)	56	0.73
Scotch-Irish (59)	97	1.27
Scottish (58)	184	2.40
Serbian (9)	19	0.25
Swedish (103)	461	6.02
Welsh (7)	37	0.48
West Indian, ex. Hispanic (52)	60	0.78
Haitian (40)	40	0.52
Jamaican (12)	12	0.16
Trinidadian/Tobagonian (0)	8	0.10

Hispanic Origin	Population	%
Hispanic or Latino (of any race)	404	5.27
Central American, ex. Mexican	9	0.12
Guatemalan	5	0.07
Honduran	1	0.01
Salvadoran	3	0.04
Cuban	7	0.09
Dominican Republic	12	0.16
Mexican	27	0.35
Puerto Rican	95	1.24
South American	26	0.34
Argentinean	1	0.01
Bolivian	1	0.01
Chilean	2	0.03
Colombian	9	0.12
Ecuadorian	8	0.10
Paraguayan	2	0.03
Peruvian	1	0.01
Uruguayan	1	0.01
Venezuelan	1	0.01
Other Hispanic or Latino	228	2.97

Race*	Population	%
African-American/Black (323)	335	4.37
Not Hispanic (321)	332	4.33
Hispanic (2)	3	0.04
American Indian/Alaska Native (17)	26	0.34
Not Hispanic (17)	26	0.34
Blackfeet (1)	1	0.01
Canadian/French Am. Ind. (0)	2	0.03
Cherokee (0)	3	0.04
Asian (52)	76	0.99
Not Hispanic (52)	74	0.96
Hispanic (0)	2	0.03
Chinese, ex. Taiwanese (30)	30	0.39
Filipino (2)	6	0.08
Indian (7)	8	0.10
Japanese (4)	10	0.13
Korean (5)	8	0.10
Laotian (1)	3	0.04
Pakistani (0)	1	0.01
Taiwanese (1)	1	0.01
Thai (1)	2	0.03
Vietnamese (1)	4	0.05
Hawaii Native/Pacific Islander (2)	6	0.08
Not Hispanic (2)	5	0.07
Hispanic (0)	1	0.01
Native Hawaiian (2)	5	0.07
White (7,158)	7,206	93.96
Not Hispanic (6,817)	6,858	89.42
Hispanic (341)	348	4.54

West Springfield Town

Place Type: City
County: Hampden
Population: 28,391†

Ancestry‡	Population	%
African, Sub-Saharan (170)	191	0.68
African (0)	21	0.07
Cape Verdean (102)	102	0.36
Ethiopian (11)	11	0.04
Ugandan (10)	10	0.04
Other Sub-Saharan African (47)	47	0.17
Albanian (69)	69	0.24
American (688)	688	2.43
Arab (244)	375	1.33
Iraqi (69)	69	0.24
Jordanian (16)	33	0.12
Lebanese (159)	273	0.97
Armenian (15)	15	0.05
Australian (0)	14	0.05
Austrian (46)	75	0.27
Belgian (0)	38	0.13
British (28)	82	0.29
Bulgarian (50)	50	0.18
Cajun (12)	12	0.04
Canadian (223)	314	1.11
Czech (0)	122	0.43
Czechoslovakian (23)	38	0.13
Dutch (65)	170	0.60
English (985)	2,638	9.33
European (148)	170	0.60
Finnish (0)	15	0.05
French, ex. Basque (1,023)	3,256	11.51
French Canadian (858)	1,848	6.53
German (449)	1,912	6.76
Greek (332)	597	2.11
Hungarian (41)	71	0.25
Iranian (28)	28	0.10
Irish (2,398)	5,276	18.65
Italian (1,946)	4,188	14.81
Lithuanian (21)	84	0.30
Macedonian (82)	82	0.29
Northern European (15)	15	0.05
Norwegian (0)	44	0.16
Polish (1,279)	2,662	9.41
Portuguese (66)	200	0.71
Romanian (115)	115	0.41
Russian (1,260)	1,571	5.55
Scandinavian (0)	13	0.05
Scotch-Irish (142)	552	1.95
Scottish (205)	607	2.15
Swedish (33)	147	0.52
Turkish (290)	290	1.03
Ukrainian (870)	1,111	3.93
Welsh (0)	99	0.35
West Indian, ex. Hispanic (79)	135	0.48
Jamaican (79)	135	0.48
Yugoslavian (117)	126	0.45

Hispanic Origin	Population	%
Hispanic or Latino (of any race)	2,471	8.70
Central American, ex. Mexican	159	0.56
Costa Rican	2	0.01
Guatemalan	24	0.08
Honduran	6	0.02
Nicaraguan	2	0.01
Panamanian	14	0.05
Salvadoran	110	0.39
Other Central American	1	<0.01
Cuban	13	0.05
Dominican Republic	53	0.19
Mexican	108	0.38
Puerto Rican	1,863	6.56
South American	149	0.52
Argentinean	4	0.01
Bolivian	2	0.01
Chilean	2	0.01
Colombian	61	0.21
Ecuadorian	29	0.10
Paraguayan	1	<0.01
Peruvian	39	0.14
Uruguayan	4	0.01
Venezuelan	6	0.02
Other South American	1	<0.01
Other Hispanic or Latino	126	0.44

Race*	Population	%
African-American/Black (939)	1,180	4.16
Not Hispanic (841)	1,005	3.54
Hispanic (98)	175	0.62

*Notes: † The Census 2010 population figure is used to calculate the percentages in the Hispanic Origin and Race categories. Ancestry percentages are based on the 2006-2010 American Community Survey population (not shown); ‡ Numbers in parentheses indicate the number of people reporting a single ancestry; * Numbers in parentheses indicate the number of persons reporting this race alone, not in combination with any other race; Please refer to the Explanation of Data for more information.*

American Indian/Alaska Native (65)	180	0.63
Not Hispanic (34)	128	0.45
Hispanic (31)	52	0.18
Apache (1)	1	<0.01
Blackfeet (2)	6	0.02
Canadian/French Am. Ind. (0)	2	0.01
Cherokee (3)	11	0.04
Chippewa (1)	2	0.01
Choctaw (1)	1	<0.01
Crow (0)	3	0.01
Iroquois (4)	19	0.07
Ottawa (0)	2	0.01
Sioux (1)	8	0.03
South American Ind. (1)	4	0.01
Asian (1,253)	1,454	5.12
Not Hispanic (1,245)	1,429	5.03
Hispanic (8)	25	0.09
Bangladeshi (5)	5	0.02
Bhutanese (34)	48	0.17
Burmese (80)	83	0.29
Cambodian (21)	25	0.09
Chinese, ex. Taiwanese (141)	165	0.58
Filipino (93)	110	0.39
Hmong (1)	1	<0.01
Indian (352)	387	1.36
Indonesian (4)	7	0.02
Japanese (7)	15	0.05
Korean (41)	60	0.21
Laotian (21)	23	0.08
Nepalese (49)	66	0.23
Pakistani (110)	115	0.41
Sri Lankan (1)	1	<0.01
Taiwanese (2)	2	0.01
Thai (20)	26	0.09
Vietnamese (201)	217	0.76
Hawaii Native/Pacific Islander (14)	46	0.16
Not Hispanic (14)	36	0.13
Hispanic (0)	10	0.04
Native Hawaiian (4)	10	0.04
Samoan (3)	3	0.01
White (24,508)	25,059	88.26
Not Hispanic (23,306)	23,712	83.52
Hispanic (1,202)	1,347	4.74

Westborough

Place Type: Town
County: Worcester
Population: 18,272†

Ancestry‡	Population	%
African, Sub-Saharan (122)	146	0.80
African (110)	110	0.60
Cape Verdean (12)	36	0.20
Albanian (0)	13	0.07
American (719)	719	3.93
Arab (31)	212	1.16
Arab (0)	22	0.12
Lebanese (8)	50	0.27
Moroccan (6)	83	0.45
Syrian (17)	57	0.31
Armenian (25)	49	0.27
Australian (0)	18	0.10
Austrian (0)	35	0.19
Belgian (10)	23	0.13
Brazilian (224)	238	1.30
British (93)	120	0.66
Canadian (52)	68	0.37
Celtic (0)	15	0.08
Danish (32)	112	0.61
Dutch (38)	191	1.05
Eastern European (130)	130	0.71
English (735)	2,348	12.85
Estonian (0)	11	0.06
European (273)	273	1.49
Finnish (10)	31	0.17
French, ex. Basque (111)	893	4.89
French Canadian (256)	530	2.90
German (412)	1,585	8.67
Greek (5)	61	0.33
Hungarian (40)	78	0.43
Irish (1,203)	3,521	19.27
Italian (658)	1,731	9.47
Lithuanian (44)	172	0.94
Luxemburger (0)	8	0.04
Maltese (19)	37	0.20
Northern European (11)	22	0.12
Norwegian (83)	198	1.08
Pennsylvania German (14)	14	0.08
Polish (165)	757	4.14
Portuguese (244)	404	2.21
Romanian (7)	17	0.09
Russian (285)	628	3.44
Scotch-Irish (80)	203	1.11
Scottish (167)	603	3.30
Slovak (0)	24	0.13
Swedish (160)	541	2.96
Swiss (13)	38	0.21
Turkish (35)	35	0.19
Ukrainian (9)	9	0.05
Welsh (15)	64	0.35
West Indian, ex. Hispanic (353)	369	2.02
Haitian (336)	352	1.93
Jamaican (17)	17	0.09

Hispanic Origin	Population	%
Hispanic or Latino (of any race)	717	3.92
Central American, ex. Mexican	227	1.24
Costa Rican	1	0.01
Guatemalan	197	1.08
Honduran	3	0.02
Nicaraguan	1	0.01
Panamanian	5	0.03
Salvadoran	18	0.10
Other Central American	2	0.01
Cuban	23	0.13
Dominican Republic	16	0.09
Mexican	133	0.73
Puerto Rican	123	0.67
South American	122	0.67
Argentinean	21	0.11
Bolivian	4	0.02
Chilean	4	0.02
Colombian	27	0.15
Ecuadorian	24	0.13
Paraguayan	3	0.02
Peruvian	23	0.13
Uruguayan	3	0.02
Venezuelan	12	0.07
Other South American	1	0.01
Other Hispanic or Latino	73	0.40

Race*	Population	%
African-American/Black (273)	340	1.86
Not Hispanic (231)	285	1.56
Hispanic (42)	55	0.30
American Indian/Alaska Native (30)	72	0.39
Not Hispanic (26)	66	0.36
Hispanic (4)	6	0.03
Canadian/French Am. Ind. (1)	1	0.01
Central American Ind. (1)	1	0.01
Cherokee (1)	7	0.04
Chippewa (0)	1	0.01
Crow (1)	1	0.01
Iroquois (0)	4	0.02
Mexican American Ind. (1)	1	0.01
Seminole (1)	1	0.01
Asian (3,188)	3,390	18.55
Not Hispanic (3,181)	3,379	18.49
Hispanic (7)	11	0.06
Bangladeshi (8)	8	0.04
Burmese (2)	2	0.01
Cambodian (4)	4	0.02
Chinese, ex. Taiwanese (584)	629	3.44
Filipino (23)	50	0.27
Indian (2,160)	2,229	12.20
Indonesian (5)	5	0.03
Japanese (13)	28	0.15
Korean (173)	191	1.05
Laotian (1)	1	0.01
Nepalese (3)	3	0.02
Pakistani (86)	114	0.62
Sri Lankan (7)	9	0.05
Taiwanese (25)	34	0.19
Thai (8)	12	0.07
Vietnamese (39)	49	0.27
Hawaii Native/Pacific Islander (4)	14	0.08
Not Hispanic (4)	13	0.07
Hispanic (0)	1	0.01
Fijian (1)	1	0.01
Guamanian/Chamorro (0)	2	0.01
Samoan (0)	1	0.01
White (14,143)	14,436	79.01
Not Hispanic (13,723)	13,976	76.49
Hispanic (420)	460	2.52

Westfield

Place Type: City
County: Hampden
Population: 41,094†

Ancestry‡	Population	%
African, Sub-Saharan (27)	51	0.12
Cape Verdean (0)	15	0.04
South African (0)	9	0.02
Other Sub-Saharan African (27)	27	0.07
Albanian (8)	8	0.02
Alsatian (0)	14	0.03
American (1,903)	1,903	4.64
Arab (96)	161	0.39
Arab (35)	35	0.09
Lebanese (49)	93	0.23
Syrian (12)	33	0.08
Armenian (99)	125	0.31
Austrian (0)	21	0.05
Brazilian (18)	18	0.04
British (41)	74	0.18
Canadian (151)	254	0.62
Croatian (0)	30	0.07
Czech (53)	149	0.36
Czechoslovakian (0)	79	0.19
Danish (0)	70	0.17
Dutch (117)	366	0.89
Eastern European (164)	164	0.40
English (1,779)	4,685	11.43
European (189)	189	0.46
Finnish (25)	67	0.16
French, ex. Basque (1,657)	5,147	12.56
French Canadian (1,148)	2,134	5.21
German (1,108)	3,381	8.25
Greek (166)	370	0.90
Hungarian (11)	101	0.25
Iranian (66)	66	0.16
Irish (3,556)	9,002	21.97
Italian (2,038)	4,578	11.17
Lithuanian (118)	248	0.61
Northern European (60)	60	0.15
Norwegian (36)	235	0.57
Pennsylvania German (0)	21	0.05
Polish (2,490)	5,371	13.11
Portuguese (195)	388	0.95
Romanian (18)	18	0.04
Russian (1,026)	1,137	2.77
Scotch-Irish (148)	501	1.22
Scottish (269)	780	1.90
Slavic (17)	28	0.07
Slovak (148)	349	0.85
Swedish (192)	557	1.36
Swiss (0)	43	0.10
Turkish (54)	54	0.13
Ukrainian (990)	1,111	2.71
Welsh (0)	118	0.29
West Indian, ex. Hispanic (58)	89	0.22
Barbadian (15)	15	0.04
Haitian (43)	60	0.15
Jamaican (0)	14	0.03

Hispanic Origin	Population	%
Hispanic or Latino (of any race)	3,097	7.54

*Notes: † The Census 2010 population figure is used to calculate the percentages in the Hispanic Origin and Race categories. Ancestry percentages are based on the 2006-2010 American Community Survey population (not shown); ‡ Numbers in parentheses indicate the number of people reporting a single ancestry; * Numbers in parentheses indicate the number of persons reporting this race alone, not in combination with any other race; Please refer to the Explanation of Data for more information.*

Central American, ex. Mexican	60	0.15
Costa Rican	4	0.01
Guatemalan	9	0.02
Honduran	11	0.03
Nicaraguan	2	<0.01
Panamanian	7	0.02
Salvadoran	26	0.06
Other Central American	1	<0.01
Cuban	21	0.05
Dominican Republic	38	0.09
Mexican	133	0.32
Puerto Rican	2,504	6.09
South American	94	0.23
Argentinean	3	0.01
Chilean	5	0.01
Colombian	48	0.12
Ecuadorian	17	0.04
Paraguayan	1	<0.01
Peruvian	18	0.04
Venezuelan	1	<0.01
Other South American	1	<0.01
Other Hispanic or Latino	247	0.60

Race*	Population	%
African-American/Black (663)	975	2.37
Not Hispanic (543)	756	1.84
Hispanic (120)	219	0.53
American Indian/Alaska Native (103)	324	0.79
Not Hispanic (56)	246	0.60
Hispanic (47)	78	0.19
Aleut *(Alaska Native)* (1)	1	<0.01
Apache (3)	3	0.01
Blackfeet (9)	25	0.06
Canadian/French Am. Ind. (2)	3	0.01
Central American Ind. (1)	7	0.02
Cherokee (5)	41	0.10
Chickasaw (2)	7	0.02
Choctaw (0)	5	0.01
Comanche (0)	1	<0.01
Cree (0)	1	<0.01
Creek (0)	2	<0.01
Inupiat *(Alaska Native)* (0)	4	0.01
Iroquois (10)	20	0.05
Lumbee (0)	1	<0.01
Navajo (1)	3	0.01
Potawatomi (0)	1	<0.01
Sioux (1)	4	0.01
South American Ind. (15)	18	0.04
Spanish American Ind. (1)	2	<0.01
Asian (534)	688	1.67
Not Hispanic (526)	653	1.59
Hispanic (8)	35	0.09
Bangladeshi (7)	7	0.02
Bhutanese (5)	23	0.06
Cambodian (6)	12	0.03
Chinese, ex. Taiwanese (90)	123	0.30
Filipino (73)	105	0.26
Hmong (2)	2	<0.01
Indian (85)	111	0.27
Indonesian (1)	5	0.01
Japanese (12)	41	0.10
Korean (69)	84	0.20
Laotian (0)	2	<0.01
Malaysian (2)	2	<0.01
Nepalese (9)	26	0.06
Pakistani (53)	61	0.15
Sri Lankan (8)	9	0.02
Taiwanese (4)	4	0.01
Thai (7)	10	0.02
Vietnamese (34)	44	0.11
Hawaii Native/Pacific Islander (10)	49	0.12
Not Hispanic (8)	26	0.06
Hispanic (2)	23	0.06
Guamanian/Chamorro (1)	5	0.01
Marshallese (2)	2	<0.01
Native Hawaiian (5)	13	0.03
Samoan (0)	3	0.01
White (38,122)	38,817	94.46
Not Hispanic (36,330)	36,827	89.62
Hispanic (1,792)	1,990	4.84

Westford

Place Type: Town
County: Middlesex
Population: 21,951†

Ancestry‡	Population	%
African, Sub-Saharan (6)	6	0.03
African (6)	6	0.03
Albanian (0)	13	0.06
American (686)	686	3.19
Arab (0)	90	0.42
Arab (0)	80	0.37
Lebanese (0)	10	0.05
Armenian (53)	86	0.40
Australian (40)	156	0.73
Austrian (23)	106	0.49
Brazilian (12)	29	0.13
British (62)	141	0.66
Canadian (86)	311	1.45
Croatian (0)	40	0.19
Czech (0)	33	0.15
Danish (21)	95	0.44
Dutch (68)	169	0.79
Eastern European (72)	72	0.34
English (960)	3,523	16.40
European (116)	168	0.78
Finnish (52)	88	0.41
French, ex. Basque (360)	1,696	7.89
French Canadian (518)	1,037	4.83
German (434)	2,248	10.46
Greek (106)	222	1.03
Hungarian (69)	129	0.60
Irish (1,885)	5,975	27.81
Italian (980)	3,669	17.08
Latvian (10)	10	0.05
Lithuanian (185)	332	1.55
Northern European (120)	120	0.56
Norwegian (11)	110	0.51
Polish (227)	1,032	4.80
Portuguese (124)	325	1.51
Russian (96)	295	1.37
Scandinavian (41)	52	0.24
Scotch-Irish (268)	408	1.90
Scottish (269)	1,004	4.67
Slavic (0)	9	0.04
Slovak (0)	64	0.30
Swedish (108)	563	2.62
Swiss (6)	6	0.03
Ukrainian (62)	163	0.76
Welsh (28)	251	1.17

Hispanic Origin	Population	%
Hispanic or Latino (of any race)	333	1.52
Central American, ex. Mexican	38	0.17
Costa Rican	4	0.02
Guatemalan	30	0.14
Honduran	1	<0.01
Panamanian	3	0.01
Cuban	33	0.15
Dominican Republic	10	0.05
Mexican	58	0.26
Puerto Rican	90	0.41
South American	68	0.31
Argentinean	12	0.05
Bolivian	1	<0.01
Chilean	7	0.03
Colombian	31	0.14
Ecuadorian	6	0.03
Paraguayan	1	<0.01
Peruvian	1	<0.01
Uruguayan	2	0.01
Venezuelan	7	0.03
Other Hispanic or Latino	36	0.16

Race*	Population	%
African-American/Black (83)	150	0.68
Not Hispanic (74)	136	0.62
Hispanic (9)	14	0.06
American Indian/Alaska Native (18)	70	0.32
Not Hispanic (12)	61	0.28
Hispanic (6)	9	0.04
Canadian/French Am. Ind. (0)	2	0.01
Central American Ind. (2)	3	0.01
Creek (1)	1	<0.01
Iroquois (1)	2	0.01
Mexican American Ind. (1)	2	0.01
Osage (0)	1	<0.01
Sioux (1)	2	0.01
Asian (2,762)	2,982	13.58
Not Hispanic (2,761)	2,978	13.57
Hispanic (1)	4	0.02
Bangladeshi (11)	11	0.05
Cambodian (60)	73	0.33
Chinese, ex. Taiwanese (1,088)	1,180	5.38
Filipino (22)	46	0.21
Indian (1,259)	1,318	6.00
Indonesian (0)	6	0.03
Japanese (38)	67	0.31
Korean (134)	147	0.67
Laotian (8)	9	0.04
Malaysian (2)	2	0.01
Pakistani (12)	12	0.05
Sri Lankan (5)	6	0.03
Taiwanese (38)	42	0.19
Thai (6)	10	0.05
Vietnamese (39)	49	0.22
Hawaii Native/Pacific Islander (1)	11	0.05
Not Hispanic (1)	11	0.05
Guamanian/Chamorro (1)	1	<0.01
Native Hawaiian (0)	7	0.03
White (18,678)	18,975	86.44
Not Hispanic (18,425)	18,700	85.19
Hispanic (253)	275	1.25

Weston

Place Type: Town
County: Middlesex
Population: 11,261†

Ancestry‡	Population	%
African, Sub-Saharan (21)	61	0.55
Cape Verdean (21)	61	0.55
Albanian (0)	65	0.58
Alsatian (0)	6	0.05
American (490)	490	4.38
Arab (86)	175	1.56
Iraqi (75)	75	0.67
Lebanese (11)	87	0.78
Syrian (0)	13	0.12
Armenian (115)	139	1.24
Austrian (36)	100	0.89
Belgian (0)	24	0.21
Brazilian (31)	51	0.46
British (66)	83	0.74
Canadian (60)	60	0.54
Celtic (31)	42	0.38
Croatian (14)	55	0.49
Czech (37)	37	0.33
Czechoslovakian (13)	26	0.23
Danish (0)	14	0.13
Dutch (49)	140	1.25
Eastern European (203)	215	1.92
English (466)	1,489	13.31
European (223)	223	1.99
Finnish (14)	22	0.20
French, ex. Basque (45)	484	4.32
French Canadian (80)	113	1.01
German (183)	1,414	12.64
Greek (226)	311	2.78
Hungarian (11)	78	0.70
Iranian (142)	142	1.27
Irish (1,308)	2,679	23.94
Italian (477)	1,314	11.74
Latvian (0)	41	0.37
Lithuanian (65)	178	1.59
Norwegian (11)	239	2.14
Polish (34)	270	2.41
Portuguese (0)	113	1.01

*Notes: † The Census 2010 population figure is used to calculate the percentages in the Hispanic Origin and Race categories. Ancestry percentages are based on the 2006-2010 American Community Survey population (not shown); ‡ Numbers in parentheses indicate the number of people reporting a single ancestry; * Numbers in parentheses indicate the number of persons reporting this race alone, not in combination with any other race; Please refer to the Explanation of Data for more information.*

Romanian (11)	41	0.37
Russian (255)	597	5.33
Scotch-Irish (78)	234	2.09
Scottish (87)	307	2.74
Soviet Union (27)	27	0.24
Swedish (12)	101	0.90
Swiss (0)	40	0.36
Ukrainian (39)	115	1.03
Welsh (22)	111	0.99
West Indian, ex. Hispanic (118)	134	1.20
Haitian (109)	117	1.05
Jamaican (0)	8	0.07
West Indian (9)	9	0.08
Yugoslavian (14)	14	0.13

Hispanic Origin	Population	%
Hispanic or Latino (of any race)	294	2.61
Central American, ex. Mexican	37	0.33
Costa Rican	2	0.02
Guatemalan	14	0.12
Honduran	1	0.01
Nicaraguan	8	0.07
Panamanian	1	0.01
Salvadoran	10	0.09
Other Central American	1	0.01
Cuban	30	0.27
Dominican Republic	21	0.19
Mexican	41	0.36
Puerto Rican	43	0.38
South American	79	0.70
Argentinean	5	0.04
Chilean	8	0.07
Colombian	37	0.33
Ecuadorian	6	0.05
Paraguayan	1	0.01
Peruvian	7	0.06
Uruguayan	4	0.04
Venezuelan	11	0.10
Other Hispanic or Latino	43	0.38

Race*	Population	%
African-American/Black (230)	258	2.29
Not Hispanic (209)	234	2.08
Hispanic (21)	24	0.21
American Indian/Alaska Native (8)	28	0.25
Not Hispanic (5)	25	0.22
Hispanic (3)	3	0.03
Canadian/French Am. Ind. (0)	1	0.01
Central American Ind. (2)	2	0.02
Creek (0)	4	0.04
Iroquois (1)	1	0.01
Mexican American Ind. (1)	1	0.01
Sioux (0)	1	0.01
Asian (1,114)	1,284	11.40
Not Hispanic (1,114)	1,279	11.36
Hispanic (0)	5	0.04
Bangladeshi (6)	6	0.05
Cambodian (3)	4	0.04
Chinese, ex. Taiwanese (517)	575	5.11
Filipino (26)	41	0.36
Indian (280)	324	2.88
Japanese (25)	38	0.34
Korean (151)	173	1.54
Pakistani (20)	26	0.23
Sri Lankan (4)	5	0.04
Taiwanese (13)	14	0.12
Thai (6)	6	0.05
Vietnamese (29)	36	0.32
Hawaii Native/Pacific Islander (0)	1	0.01
Hispanic (0)	1	0.01
White (9,611)	9,819	87.19
Not Hispanic (9,393)	9,588	85.14
Hispanic (218)	231	2.05

Westport

Place Type: Town
County: Bristol
Population: 15,532†

Ancestry‡	Population	%
African, Sub-Saharan (134)	217	1.42
Cape Verdean (75)	158	1.03
Kenyan (59)	59	0.39
American (164)	164	1.07
Arab (83)	171	1.12
Lebanese (83)	154	1.01
Syrian (0)	17	0.11
Armenian (17)	17	0.11
Belgian (0)	16	0.10
Brazilian (56)	118	0.77
British (47)	197	1.29
Canadian (52)	52	0.34
Danish (14)	41	0.27
Dutch (0)	71	0.46
Eastern European (16)	16	0.10
English (666)	2,595	16.96
Estonian (32)	32	0.21
European (58)	58	0.38
Finnish (0)	15	0.10
French, ex. Basque (808)	2,757	18.02
French Canadian (879)	1,415	9.25
German (73)	448	2.93
Greek (27)	145	0.95
Hungarian (0)	40	0.26
Irish (373)	2,339	15.29
Italian (110)	850	5.56
Lithuanian (0)	81	0.53
Norwegian (15)	96	0.63
Polish (236)	1,077	7.04
Portuguese (3,708)	6,339	41.44
Russian (8)	24	0.16
Scandinavian (0)	16	0.10
Scotch-Irish (103)	218	1.43
Scottish (53)	197	1.29
Slovene (0)	16	0.10
Swedish (0)	197	1.29
Swiss (25)	32	0.21
Ukrainian (0)	25	0.16
Welsh (0)	46	0.30

Hispanic Origin	Population	%
Hispanic or Latino (of any race)	138	0.89
Central American, ex. Mexican	7	0.05
Guatemalan	7	0.05
Cuban	6	0.04
Dominican Republic	5	0.03
Mexican	21	0.14
Puerto Rican	50	0.32
South American	17	0.11
Argentinean	3	0.02
Chilean	2	0.01
Colombian	4	0.03
Venezuelan	8	0.05
Other Hispanic or Latino	32	0.21

Race*	Population	%
African-American/Black (72)	114	0.73
Not Hispanic (67)	105	0.68
Hispanic (5)	9	0.06
American Indian/Alaska Native (7)	51	0.33
Not Hispanic (5)	46	0.30
Hispanic (2)	5	0.03
Blackfeet (0)	1	0.01
Cherokee (0)	11	0.07
Delaware (0)	3	0.02
Sioux (0)	2	0.01
Asian (103)	132	0.85
Not Hispanic (103)	132	0.85
Burmese (2)	5	0.03
Cambodian (8)	9	0.06
Chinese, ex. Taiwanese (29)	35	0.23
Filipino (12)	20	0.13
Indian (23)	27	0.17
Japanese (6)	7	0.05
Korean (8)	18	0.12
Malaysian (1)	1	0.01
Nepalese (2)	2	0.01
Sri Lankan (2)	2	0.01
Vietnamese (2)	2	0.01
Hawaii Native/Pacific Islander (4)	11	0.07
Not Hispanic (4)	11	0.07
Samoan (0)	1	0.01
White (15,170)	15,289	98.44
Not Hispanic (15,056)	15,168	97.66
Hispanic (114)	121	0.78

Westwood

Place Type: Town
County: Norfolk
Population: 14,618†

Ancestry‡	Population	%
American (432)	432	3.00
Arab (207)	329	2.28
Arab (8)	17	0.12
Egyptian (0)	15	0.10
Lebanese (199)	266	1.85
Palestinian (0)	12	0.08
Syrian (0)	19	0.13
Armenian (79)	159	1.10
Austrian (47)	127	0.88
British (76)	93	0.65
Canadian (28)	184	1.28
Czech (0)	54	0.37
Danish (0)	39	0.27
Dutch (0)	52	0.36
Eastern European (52)	88	0.61
English (448)	1,740	12.08
European (238)	238	1.65
Finnish (0)	13	0.09
French, ex. Basque (24)	399	2.77
French Canadian (107)	306	2.12
German (247)	1,043	7.24
Greek (436)	527	3.66
Hungarian (46)	158	1.10
Icelander (16)	47	0.33
Iranian (212)	227	1.58
Irish (2,793)	5,188	36.02
Italian (1,041)	2,510	17.42
Latvian (75)	83	0.58
Lithuanian (71)	246	1.71
Northern European (10)	10	0.07
Norwegian (11)	11	0.08
Polish (53)	305	2.12
Portuguese (19)	101	0.70
Romanian (7)	48	0.33
Russian (242)	401	2.78
Scandinavian (15)	28	0.19
Scotch-Irish (158)	448	3.11
Scottish (146)	412	2.86
Slovak (0)	21	0.15
Swedish (138)	341	2.37
Swiss (0)	75	0.52
Ukrainian (22)	65	0.45
Welsh (0)	122	0.85
West Indian, ex. Hispanic (0)	10	0.07
Haitian (0)	10	0.07

Hispanic Origin	Population	%
Hispanic or Latino (of any race)	237	1.62
Central American, ex. Mexican	42	0.29
Costa Rican	5	0.03
Guatemalan	16	0.11
Honduran	8	0.05
Nicaraguan	4	0.03
Panamanian	4	0.03
Salvadoran	5	0.03
Cuban	9	0.06
Dominican Republic	11	0.08
Mexican	40	0.27
Puerto Rican	43	0.29
South American	62	0.42
Argentinean	8	0.05
Bolivian	1	0.01
Chilean	4	0.03
Colombian	16	0.11
Ecuadorian	2	0.01
Paraguayan	1	0.01

SECTION TWO

*Notes: † The Census 2010 population figure is used to calculate the percentages in the Hispanic Origin and Race categories. Ancestry percentages are based on the 2006-2010 American Community Survey population (not shown); ‡ Numbers in parentheses indicate the number of people reporting a single ancestry; * Numbers in parentheses indicate the number of persons reporting this race alone, not in combination with any other race; Please refer to the Explanation of Data for more information.*

Peruvian	10	0.07
Uruguayan	1	0.01
Venezuelan	19	0.13
Other Hispanic or Latino	30	0.21

Race*	Population	%
African-American/Black (136)	169	1.16
Not Hispanic (127)	155	1.06
Hispanic (9)	14	0.10
American Indian/Alaska Native (5)	20	0.14
Not Hispanic (3)	14	0.10
Hispanic (2)	6	0.04
Arapaho (0)	2	0.01
Blackfeet (0)	1	0.01
Cherokee (1)	1	0.01
Mexican American Ind. (0)	1	0.01
South American Ind. (0)	1	0.01
Asian (726)	819	5.60
Not Hispanic (725)	811	5.55
Hispanic (1)	8	0.05
Chinese, ex. Taiwanese (421)	454	3.11
Filipino (22)	32	0.22
Indian (144)	157	1.07
Japanese (10)	18	0.12
Korean (60)	69	0.47
Nepalese (2)	2	0.01
Pakistani (21)	22	0.15
Sri Lankan (1)	1	0.01
Taiwanese (11)	11	0.08
Thai (3)	4	0.03
Vietnamese (13)	23	0.16
Hawaii Native/Pacific Islander (0)	1	0.01
Not Hispanic (0)	1	0.01
White (13,555)	13,688	93.64
Not Hispanic (13,381)	13,494	92.31
Hispanic (174)	194	1.33

Weymouth Town

Place Type: City
County: Norfolk
Population: 53,743†

Ancestry‡	Population	%
African, Sub-Saharan (786)	841	1.58
African (155)	198	0.37
Cape Verdean (583)	595	1.12
Ghanaian (11)	11	0.02
South African (12)	12	0.02
Other Sub-Saharan African (25)	25	0.05
Albanian (37)	72	0.13
American (2,057)	2,057	3.86
Arab (295)	572	1.07
Arab (11)	11	0.02
Egyptian (21)	41	0.08
Lebanese (196)	288	0.54
Moroccan (0)	28	0.05
Palestinian (10)	10	0.02
Syrian (17)	126	0.24
Other Arab (40)	68	0.13
Armenian (76)	160	0.30
Australian (13)	24	0.04
Austrian (11)	52	0.10
Belgian (13)	177	0.33
Brazilian (859)	907	1.70
British (25)	44	0.08
Bulgarian (82)	82	0.15
Canadian (284)	785	1.47
Celtic (32)	51	0.10
Czech (0)	12	0.02
Czechoslovakian (0)	6	0.01
Danish (65)	134	0.25
Dutch (76)	320	0.60
English (1,436)	6,936	13.00
Estonian (9)	9	0.02
European (258)	279	0.52
Finnish (47)	271	0.51
French, ex. Basque (356)	2,529	4.74
French Canadian (430)	1,549	2.90
German (430)	3,047	5.71
Greek (115)	366	0.69
Hungarian (0)	42	0.08
Icelander (106)	106	0.20
Irish (11,198)	23,257	43.60
Italian (3,427)	9,833	18.43
Latvian (12)	24	0.04
Lithuanian (312)	714	1.34
Norwegian (31)	217	0.41
Pennsylvania German (25)	41	0.08
Polish (507)	1,614	3.03
Portuguese (184)	750	1.41
Romanian (0)	71	0.13
Russian (192)	469	0.88
Scandinavian (30)	115	0.22
Scotch-Irish (783)	1,706	3.20
Scottish (746)	2,443	4.58
Serbian (10)	10	0.02
Slavic (0)	12	0.02
Slovak (7)	100	0.19
Slovene (9)	23	0.04
Swedish (486)	1,469	2.75
Swiss (0)	55	0.10
Turkish (36)	36	0.07
Ukrainian (0)	17	0.03
Welsh (0)	99	0.19
West Indian, ex. Hispanic (287)	305	0.57
Barbadian (30)	30	0.06
Haitian (212)	212	0.40
Jamaican (11)	11	0.02
Trinidadian/Tobagonian (16)	16	0.03
West Indian (18)	36	0.07

Hispanic Origin	Population	%
Hispanic or Latino (of any race)	1,412	2.63
Central American, ex. Mexican	137	0.25
Costa Rican	12	0.02
Guatemalan	61	0.11
Honduran	19	0.04
Nicaraguan	5	0.01
Panamanian	7	0.01
Salvadoran	28	0.05
Other Central American	5	0.01
Cuban	70	0.13
Dominican Republic	101	0.19
Mexican	187	0.35
Puerto Rican	534	0.99
South American	186	0.35
Argentinean	38	0.07
Bolivian	6	0.01
Chilean	13	0.02
Colombian	55	0.10
Ecuadorian	18	0.03
Peruvian	44	0.08
Uruguayan	1	<0.01
Venezuelan	10	0.02
Other South American	1	<0.01
Other Hispanic or Latino	197	0.37

Race*	Population	%
African-American/Black (1,651)	2,037	3.79
Not Hispanic (1,527)	1,872	3.48
Hispanic (124)	165	0.31
American Indian/Alaska Native (96)	284	0.53
Not Hispanic (87)	262	0.49
Hispanic (9)	22	0.04
Alaska Athabascan *(Ala. Nat.)* (0)	1	<0.01
Blackfeet (1)	12	0.02
Canadian/French Am. Ind. (2)	3	0.01
Central American Ind. (0)	3	0.01
Cherokee (5)	18	0.03
Chippewa (0)	2	<0.01
Choctaw (0)	1	<0.01
Creek (0)	1	<0.01
Crow (1)	1	<0.01
Hopi (1)	1	<0.01
Iroquois (1)	11	0.02
Lumbee (3)	3	0.01
Mexican American Ind. (2)	2	<0.01
Potawatomi (1)	1	<0.01
Puget Sound Salish (1)	1	<0.01
Seminole (1)	2	<0.01
Sioux (1)	2	<0.01
South American Ind. (2)	8	0.01
Asian (1,720)	1,952	3.63
Not Hispanic (1,716)	1,938	3.61
Hispanic (4)	14	0.03
Burmese (2)	5	0.01
Cambodian (16)	23	0.04
Chinese, ex. Taiwanese (456)	534	0.99
Filipino (150)	186	0.35
Indian (565)	610	1.14
Indonesian (7)	13	0.02
Japanese (21)	43	0.08
Korean (68)	95	0.18
Laotian (3)	3	0.01
Malaysian (3)	5	0.01
Nepalese (4)	4	0.01
Pakistani (70)	78	0.15
Sri Lankan (3)	5	0.01
Taiwanese (7)	7	0.01
Thai (20)	29	0.05
Vietnamese (264)	302	0.56
Hawaii Native/Pacific Islander (12)	47	0.09
Not Hispanic (10)	41	0.08
Hispanic (2)	6	0.01
Fijian (0)	1	<0.01
Guamanian/Chamorro (1)	1	<0.01
Native Hawaiian (2)	14	0.03
Samoan (3)	6	0.01
White (48,230)	49,057	91.28
Not Hispanic (47,364)	48,090	89.48
Hispanic (866)	967	1.80

Whitman

Place Type: Town
County: Plymouth
Population: 14,489†

Ancestry‡	Population	%
African, Sub-Saharan (110)	157	1.09
African (52)	64	0.45
Cape Verdean (58)	82	0.57
Other Sub-Saharan African (0)	11	0.08
Albanian (0)	9	0.06
American (559)	559	3.89
Arab (11)	132	0.92
Lebanese (0)	99	0.69
Other Arab (11)	33	0.23
Belgian (0)	71	0.49
Brazilian (194)	222	1.54
Canadian (17)	195	1.36
Czech (7)	39	0.27
Danish (54)	80	0.56
Dutch (6)	82	0.57
English (313)	1,974	13.74
Finnish (9)	93	0.65
French, ex. Basque (83)	983	6.84
French Canadian (215)	769	5.35
German (192)	1,179	8.20
Greek (41)	65	0.45
Hungarian (11)	57	0.40
Irish (2,169)	6,041	42.04
Italian (919)	3,058	21.28
Lithuanian (71)	203	1.41
Norwegian (54)	99	0.69
Polish (154)	602	4.19
Portuguese (90)	443	3.08
Russian (31)	43	0.30
Scandinavian (0)	14	0.10
Scotch-Irish (143)	448	3.12
Scottish (226)	807	5.62
Slovak (0)	10	0.07
Swedish (30)	304	2.12
Ukrainian (0)	11	0.08
Welsh (42)	89	0.62
West Indian, ex. Hispanic (163)	175	1.22
Haitian (154)	154	1.07
Jamaican (9)	9	0.06
West Indian (0)	12	0.08

*Notes: † The Census 2010 population figure is used to calculate the percentages in the Hispanic Origin and Race categories. Ancestry percentages are based on the 2006-2010 American Community Survey population (not shown); ‡ Numbers in parentheses indicate the number of people reporting a single ancestry; * Numbers in parentheses indicate the number of persons reporting this race alone, not in combination with any other race; Please refer to the Explanation of Data for more information.*

Yugoslavian (0)	8	0.06

Hispanic Origin	Population	%
Hispanic or Latino (of any race)	267	1.84
Central American, ex. Mexican	25	0.17
Costa Rican	5	0.03
Guatemalan	10	0.07
Nicaraguan	1	0.01
Panamanian	4	0.03
Salvadoran	5	0.03
Cuban	15	0.10
Dominican Republic	14	0.10
Mexican	40	0.28
Puerto Rican	110	0.76
South American	28	0.19
Argentinean	3	0.02
Bolivian	2	0.01
Chilean	1	0.01
Colombian	4	0.03
Ecuadorian	11	0.08
Peruvian	5	0.03
Uruguayan	2	0.01
Other Hispanic or Latino	35	0.24

Race*	Population	%
African-American/Black (180)	287	1.98
Not Hispanic (176)	272	1.88
Hispanic (4)	15	0.10
American Indian/Alaska Native (35)	89	0.61
Not Hispanic (32)	83	0.57
Hispanic (3)	6	0.04
Blackfeet (0)	3	0.02
Canadian/French Am. Ind. (1)	1	0.01
Cherokee (4)	10	0.07
Chippewa (3)	3	0.02
Comanche (0)	2	0.01
Delaware (0)	2	0.01
Iroquois (0)	3	0.02
Lumbee (1)	1	0.01
Mexican American Ind. (0)	1	0.01
Tlingit-Haida *(Alaska Native)* (0)	2	0.01
Asian (111)	161	1.11
Not Hispanic (108)	154	1.06
Hispanic (3)	7	0.05
Cambodian (4)	7	0.05
Chinese, ex. Taiwanese (24)	31	0.21
Filipino (16)	37	0.26
Indian (14)	16	0.11
Indonesian (1)	3	0.02
Japanese (2)	4	0.03
Korean (13)	18	0.12
Laotian (1)	3	0.02
Thai (4)	7	0.05
Vietnamese (30)	35	0.24
Hawaii Native/Pacific Islander (5)	9	0.06
Not Hispanic (5)	9	0.06
Native Hawaiian (4)	6	0.04
White (13,768)	13,968	96.40
Not Hispanic (13,603)	13,772	95.05
Hispanic (165)	196	1.35

Wilbraham

Place Type: Town
County: Hampden
Population: 14,219†

Ancestry‡	Population	%
African, Sub-Saharan (101)	101	0.72
Cape Verdean (29)	29	0.21
Ghanaian (23)	23	0.16
Kenyan (49)	49	0.35
American (457)	457	3.24
Arab (58)	132	0.94
Lebanese (58)	132	0.94
Armenian (13)	13	0.09
Austrian (0)	52	0.37
Belgian (0)	11	0.08
British (18)	114	0.81
Czech (0)	61	0.43
Czechoslovakian (0)	27	0.19
Danish (0)	15	0.11
Dutch (15)	126	0.89
Eastern European (12)	33	0.23
English (665)	2,265	16.08
European (48)	48	0.34
Finnish (0)	25	0.18
French, ex. Basque (408)	1,910	13.56
French Canadian (238)	739	5.25
German (273)	1,403	9.96
Greek (79)	123	0.87
Hungarian (42)	133	0.94
Icelander (0)	10	0.07
Iranian (49)	49	0.35
Irish (1,274)	3,699	26.25
Italian (1,134)	2,315	16.43
Latvian (10)	10	0.07
Lithuanian (18)	76	0.54
Norwegian (0)	29	0.21
Polish (969)	2,388	16.95
Portuguese (186)	309	2.19
Russian (84)	280	1.99
Scotch-Irish (142)	447	3.17
Scottish (61)	433	3.07
Swedish (76)	251	1.78
Swiss (0)	14	0.10
Ukrainian (33)	115	0.82
Welsh (0)	39	0.28

Hispanic Origin	Population	%
Hispanic or Latino (of any race)	393	2.76
Central American, ex. Mexican	8	0.06
Costa Rican	3	0.02
Nicaraguan	3	0.02
Panamanian	2	0.01
Cuban	6	0.04
Dominican Republic	7	0.05
Mexican	68	0.48
Puerto Rican	238	1.67
South American	39	0.27
Argentinean	1	0.01
Bolivian	3	0.02
Chilean	2	0.01
Colombian	18	0.13
Ecuadorian	2	0.01
Peruvian	8	0.06
Uruguayan	2	0.01
Venezuelan	3	0.02
Other Hispanic or Latino	27	0.19

Race*	Population	%
African-American/Black (307)	369	2.60
Not Hispanic (277)	333	2.34
Hispanic (30)	36	0.25
American Indian/Alaska Native (10)	49	0.34
Not Hispanic (4)	35	0.25
Hispanic (6)	14	0.10
Blackfeet (1)	1	0.01
Cherokee (0)	11	0.08
Creek (0)	1	0.01
Iroquois (0)	1	0.01
Mexican American Ind. (0)	1	0.01
Sioux (0)	6	0.04
South American Ind. (3)	4	0.03
Asian (286)	351	2.47
Not Hispanic (285)	342	2.41
Hispanic (1)	9	0.06
Bangladeshi (4)	4	0.03
Cambodian (2)	4	0.03
Chinese, ex. Taiwanese (124)	143	1.01
Filipino (15)	20	0.14
Indian (52)	61	0.43
Japanese (7)	20	0.14
Korean (43)	51	0.36
Laotian (2)	2	0.01
Pakistani (15)	15	0.11
Taiwanese (1)	1	0.01
Thai (1)	1	0.01
Vietnamese (11)	15	0.11
Hawaii Native/Pacific Islander (1)	9	0.06
Not Hispanic (1)	6	0.04
Hispanic (0)	3	0.02
Guamanian/Chamorro (1)	3	0.02
Native Hawaiian (0)	2	0.01
Samoan (0)	1	0.01
White (13,367)	13,509	95.01
Not Hispanic (13,108)	13,225	93.01
Hispanic (259)	284	2.00

Williamstown

Place Type: Town
County: Berkshire
Population: 7,754†

Ancestry‡	Population	%
African, Sub-Saharan (37)	49	0.62
African (13)	13	0.16
Liberian (12)	12	0.15
South African (0)	12	0.15
Other Sub-Saharan African (12)	12	0.15
American (146)	146	1.85
Arab (13)	93	1.18
Arab (0)	80	1.02
Egyptian (13)	13	0.16
Armenian (13)	23	0.29
Austrian (10)	87	1.10
Belgian (0)	28	0.36
British (73)	116	1.47
Canadian (0)	66	0.84
Croatian (0)	36	0.46
Czech (27)	45	0.57
Danish (0)	34	0.43
Dutch (0)	118	1.50
Eastern European (14)	14	0.18
English (529)	1,461	18.54
European (38)	38	0.48
French, ex. Basque (33)	398	5.05
French Canadian (187)	323	4.10
German (211)	939	11.92
Greek (15)	15	0.19
Hungarian (0)	28	0.36
Irish (490)	1,387	17.60
Italian (94)	562	7.13
Latvian (0)	36	0.46
Lithuanian (13)	100	1.27
Northern European (51)	51	0.65
Norwegian (82)	154	1.95
Polish (183)	528	6.70
Portuguese (27)	90	1.14
Romanian (0)	27	0.34
Russian (68)	181	2.30
Scandinavian (11)	43	0.55
Scotch-Irish (116)	246	3.12
Scottish (84)	435	5.52
Swedish (34)	211	2.68
Swiss (9)	24	0.30
Ukrainian (25)	35	0.44
Welsh (43)	88	1.12

Hispanic Origin	Population	%
Hispanic or Latino (of any race)	320	4.13
Central American, ex. Mexican	54	0.70
Costa Rican	5	0.06
Guatemalan	20	0.26
Honduran	10	0.13
Panamanian	4	0.05
Salvadoran	14	0.18
Other Central American	1	0.01
Cuban	18	0.23
Dominican Republic	10	0.13
Mexican	77	0.99
Puerto Rican	70	0.90
South American	51	0.66
Argentinean	10	0.13
Bolivian	1	0.01
Chilean	5	0.06
Colombian	14	0.18
Ecuadorian	8	0.10
Peruvian	7	0.09

*Notes: † The Census 2010 population figure is used to calculate the percentages in the Hispanic Origin and Race categories. Ancestry percentages are based on the 2006-2010 American Community Survey population (not shown); ‡ Numbers in parentheses indicate the number of people reporting a single ancestry; * Numbers in parentheses indicate the number of persons reporting this race alone, not in combination with any other race; Please refer to the Explanation of Data for more information.*

	Population	%
Uruguayan	1	0.01
Venezuelan	5	0.06
Other Hispanic or Latino	40	0.52

Race*	Population	%
African-American/Black (224)	333	4.29
Not Hispanic (212)	299	3.86
Hispanic (12)	34	0.44
American Indian/Alaska Native (8)	52	0.67
Not Hispanic (6)	38	0.49
Hispanic (2)	14	0.18
Cherokee (0)	9	0.12
Choctaw (0)	1	0.01
Houma (0)	1	0.01
Iroquois (0)	2	0.03
Mexican American Ind. (1)	3	0.04
Navajo (0)	1	0.01
Sioux (2)	2	0.03
South American Ind. (1)	1	0.01
Asian (400)	515	6.64
Not Hispanic (398)	508	6.55
Hispanic (2)	7	0.09
Bangladeshi (5)	6	0.08
Burmese (5)	5	0.06
Cambodian (7)	7	0.09
Chinese, ex. Taiwanese (143)	183	2.36
Filipino (10)	24	0.31
Indian (52)	70	0.90
Indonesian (1)	1	0.01
Japanese (22)	51	0.66
Korean (87)	96	1.24
Nepalese (5)	5	0.06
Pakistani (8)	9	0.12
Taiwanese (8)	9	0.12
Thai (10)	13	0.17
Vietnamese (16)	18	0.23
Hawaii Native/Pacific Islander (4)	8	0.10
Not Hispanic (1)	4	0.05
Hispanic (3)	4	0.05
Guamanian/Chamorro (3)	3	0.04
Native Hawaiian (1)	4	0.05
White (6,782)	7,019	90.52
Not Hispanic (6,587)	6,789	87.55
Hispanic (195)	230	2.97

Wilmington

Place Type: CDP/Town
County: Middlesex
Population: 22,325†

Ancestry‡	Population	%
African, Sub-Saharan (45)	77	0.35
African (45)	45	0.21
Cape Verdean (0)	32	0.15
Albanian (0)	31	0.14
American (642)	642	2.93
Arab (25)	105	0.48
Lebanese (9)	57	0.26
Moroccan (16)	48	0.22
Armenian (117)	196	0.90
Austrian (0)	16	0.07
Belgian (9)	24	0.11
Brazilian (0)	30	0.14
British (0)	32	0.15
Bulgarian (10)	19	0.09
Canadian (93)	505	2.31
Czech (0)	30	0.14
Czechoslovakian (0)	12	0.05
Danish (25)	181	0.83
Dutch (11)	147	0.67
Eastern European (15)	15	0.07
English (794)	3,223	14.72
European (61)	97	0.44
Finnish (7)	164	0.75
French, ex. Basque (177)	1,456	6.65
French Canadian (305)	870	3.97
German (267)	1,388	6.34
Greek (151)	531	2.43
Hungarian (27)	77	0.35
Irish (2,822)	8,301	37.92
Israeli (64)	64	0.29
Italian (2,237)	5,861	26.77
Latvian (11)	11	0.05
Lithuanian (14)	107	0.49
Norwegian (0)	156	0.71
Polish (247)	925	4.23
Portuguese (213)	675	3.08
Russian (123)	276	1.26
Scandinavian (6)	6	0.03
Scotch-Irish (263)	555	2.54
Scottish (112)	641	2.93
Slavic (0)	11	0.05
Slovak (0)	8	0.04
Swedish (62)	500	2.28
Turkish (12)	12	0.05
Ukrainian (22)	22	0.10
Welsh (0)	51	0.23
West Indian, ex. Hispanic (59)	59	0.27
Haitian (49)	49	0.22
Trinidadian/Tobagonian (10)	10	0.05

Hispanic Origin	Population	%
Hispanic or Latino (of any race)	403	1.81
Central American, ex. Mexican	49	0.22
Costa Rican	6	0.03
Guatemalan	13	0.06
Honduran	10	0.04
Salvadoran	20	0.09
Cuban	18	0.08
Dominican Republic	17	0.08
Mexican	68	0.30
Puerto Rican	132	0.59
South American	63	0.28
Argentinean	2	0.01
Chilean	8	0.04
Colombian	16	0.07
Ecuadorian	12	0.05
Peruvian	14	0.06
Uruguayan	1	<0.01
Venezuelan	10	0.04
Other Hispanic or Latino	56	0.25

Race*	Population	%
African-American/Black (174)	268	1.20
Not Hispanic (162)	240	1.08
Hispanic (12)	28	0.13
American Indian/Alaska Native (18)	71	0.32
Not Hispanic (15)	62	0.28
Hispanic (3)	9	0.04
Blackfeet (2)	8	0.04
Cherokee (0)	5	0.02
Choctaw (0)	1	<0.01
Navajo (3)	3	0.01
South American Ind. (0)	1	<0.01
Asian (831)	971	4.35
Not Hispanic (831)	970	4.34
Hispanic (0)	1	<0.01
Bangladeshi (4)	4	0.02
Cambodian (11)	15	0.07
Chinese, ex. Taiwanese (210)	251	1.12
Filipino (52)	92	0.41
Hmong (2)	2	0.01
Indian (291)	310	1.39
Indonesian (4)	8	0.04
Japanese (16)	35	0.16
Korean (38)	47	0.21
Laotian (1)	4	0.02
Pakistani (15)	15	0.07
Sri Lankan (6)	6	0.03
Taiwanese (2)	2	0.01
Thai (5)	8	0.04
Vietnamese (152)	166	0.74
Hawaii Native/Pacific Islander (13)	22	0.10
Not Hispanic (12)	21	0.09
Hispanic (1)	1	<0.01
Guamanian/Chamorro (5)	5	0.02
Samoan (0)	1	<0.01
White (20,869)	21,151	94.74
Not Hispanic (20,600)	20,842	93.36
Hispanic (269)	309	1.38

Winchendon

Place Type: Town
County: Worcester
Population: 10,300†

Ancestry‡	Population	%
American (362)	362	3.54
Arab (15)	41	0.40
Lebanese (15)	41	0.40
Armenian (0)	5	0.05
Belgian (12)	63	0.62
Brazilian (8)	8	0.08
Bulgarian (31)	31	0.30
Canadian (124)	174	1.70
Czech (0)	51	0.50
Dutch (0)	95	0.93
English (481)	1,356	13.28
Estonian (15)	15	0.15
European (15)	29	0.28
Finnish (23)	488	4.78
French, ex. Basque (870)	2,514	24.62
French Canadian (536)	1,008	9.87
German (192)	853	8.35
Greek (17)	38	0.37
Hungarian (22)	65	0.64
Irish (814)	2,204	21.58
Italian (404)	1,120	10.97
Lithuanian (47)	212	2.08
Norwegian (9)	41	0.40
Pennsylvania German (37)	37	0.36
Polish (237)	850	8.32
Portuguese (117)	183	1.79
Romanian (0)	52	0.51
Russian (0)	28	0.27
Scotch-Irish (32)	205	2.01
Scottish (81)	294	2.88
Swedish (31)	327	3.20
Swiss (0)	16	0.16
Ukrainian (49)	49	0.48
West Indian, ex. Hispanic (0)	12	0.12
Jamaican (0)	12	0.12

Hispanic Origin	Population	%
Hispanic or Latino (of any race)	351	3.41
Central American, ex. Mexican	34	0.33
Costa Rican	3	0.03
Guatemalan	5	0.05
Honduran	6	0.06
Panamanian	9	0.09
Salvadoran	11	0.11
Dominican Republic	13	0.13
Mexican	42	0.41
Puerto Rican	218	2.12
South American	19	0.18
Chilean	2	0.02
Colombian	2	0.02
Ecuadorian	1	0.01
Peruvian	6	0.06
Uruguayan	8	0.08
Other Hispanic or Latino	25	0.24

Race*	Population	%
African-American/Black (154)	206	2.00
Not Hispanic (133)	182	1.77
Hispanic (21)	24	0.23
American Indian/Alaska Native (17)	61	0.59
Not Hispanic (13)	50	0.49
Hispanic (4)	11	0.11
Apache (0)	3	0.03
Blackfeet (1)	2	0.02
Canadian/French Am. Ind. (1)	1	0.01
Cherokee (0)	3	0.03
Choctaw (1)	1	0.01
Cree (1)	2	0.02
Iroquois (0)	5	0.05
Navajo (0)	1	0.01
Osage (0)	2	0.02

*Notes: † The Census 2010 population figure is used to calculate the percentages in the Hispanic Origin and Race categories. Ancestry percentages are based on the 2006-2010 American Community Survey population (not shown); ‡ Numbers in parentheses indicate the number of people reporting a single ancestry; * Numbers in parentheses indicate the number of persons reporting this race alone, not in combination with any other race; Please refer to the Explanation of Data for more information.*

South American Ind. (1)	1	0.01
Asian (190)	237	2.30
Not Hispanic (189)	234	2.27
Hispanic (1)	3	0.03
Burmese (1)	4	0.04
Cambodian (6)	6	0.06
Chinese, ex. Taiwanese (68)	79	0.77
Filipino (11)	16	0.16
Hmong (2)	2	0.02
Indian (9)	9	0.09
Indonesian (1)	1	0.01
Japanese (9)	21	0.20
Korean (26)	32	0.31
Laotian (21)	30	0.29
Malaysian (1)	1	0.01
Pakistani (3)	3	0.03
Taiwanese (6)	6	0.06
Thai (5)	8	0.08
Vietnamese (9)	12	0.12
Hawaii Native/Pacific Islander (0)	6	0.06
Not Hispanic (0)	3	0.03
Hispanic (0)	3	0.03
Native Hawaiian (0)	3	0.03
White (9,672)	9,838	95.51
Not Hispanic (9,476)	9,603	93.23
Hispanic (196)	235	2.28

Winchester

Place Type: CDP/Town
County: Middlesex
Population: 21,374†

Ancestry‡	Population	%
Afghan (10)	10	0.05
African, Sub-Saharan (0)	49	0.23
African (0)	14	0.07
Ethiopian (0)	11	0.05
South African (0)	24	0.11
Albanian (44)	68	0.32
American (644)	644	3.06
Arab (64)	102	0.49
Arab (7)	7	0.03
Egyptian (13)	13	0.06
Lebanese (44)	82	0.39
Armenian (121)	265	1.26
Australian (10)	10	0.05
Austrian (53)	63	0.30
Belgian (0)	14	0.07
Brazilian (0)	27	0.13
British (101)	148	0.70
Canadian (50)	106	0.50
Croatian (14)	61	0.29
Czech (8)	44	0.21
Danish (8)	39	0.19
Dutch (22)	206	0.98
Eastern European (49)	49	0.23
English (638)	3,268	15.55
European (304)	304	1.45
Finnish (21)	69	0.33
French, ex. Basque (209)	925	4.40
French Canadian (143)	658	3.13
German (345)	1,981	9.43
Greek (181)	576	2.74
Hungarian (86)	202	0.96
Iranian (120)	120	0.57
Irish (2,649)	6,677	31.77
Israeli (0)	9	0.04
Italian (2,048)	4,216	20.06
Latvian (33)	33	0.16
Lithuanian (20)	98	0.47
Northern European (26)	26	0.12
Norwegian (0)	251	1.19
Polish (265)	1,030	4.90
Portuguese (60)	166	0.79
Romanian (17)	38	0.18
Russian (195)	634	3.02
Scandinavian (0)	62	0.30
Scotch-Irish (119)	448	2.13
Scottish (142)	699	3.33
Serbian (50)	78	0.37
Slavic (0)	23	0.11
Slovak (10)	37	0.18
Swedish (55)	587	2.79
Swiss (82)	93	0.44
Turkish (33)	100	0.48
Ukrainian (67)	159	0.76
Welsh (32)	157	0.75
West Indian, ex. Hispanic (0)	16	0.08
Haitian (0)	16	0.08
Yugoslavian (0)	23	0.11

Hispanic Origin	Population	%
Hispanic or Latino (of any race)	405	1.89
Central American, ex. Mexican	44	0.21
Costa Rican	8	0.04
Guatemalan	12	0.06
Honduran	7	0.03
Panamanian	4	0.02
Salvadoran	12	0.06
Other Central American	1	<0.01
Cuban	23	0.11
Dominican Republic	25	0.12
Mexican	60	0.28
Puerto Rican	79	0.37
South American	120	0.56
Argentinean	13	0.06
Bolivian	3	0.01
Chilean	16	0.07
Colombian	48	0.22
Paraguayan	2	0.01
Peruvian	8	0.04
Uruguayan	1	<0.01
Venezuelan	29	0.14
Other Hispanic or Latino	54	0.25

Race*	Population	%
African-American/Black (221)	306	1.43
Not Hispanic (213)	285	1.33
Hispanic (8)	21	0.10
American Indian/Alaska Native (17)	69	0.32
Not Hispanic (12)	58	0.27
Hispanic (5)	11	0.05
Alaska Athabascan *(Ala. Nat.)* (0)	1	<0.01
Apache (0)	1	<0.01
Blackfeet (3)	3	0.01
Cherokee (0)	10	0.05
Chippewa (5)	5	0.02
Choctaw (0)	6	0.03
Iroquois (0)	1	<0.01
Mexican American Ind. (1)	1	<0.01
Sioux (1)	4	0.02
South American Ind. (0)	4	0.02
Asian (1,998)	2,297	10.75
Not Hispanic (1,992)	2,281	10.67
Hispanic (6)	16	0.07
Bangladeshi (13)	13	0.06
Burmese (3)	4	0.02
Cambodian (7)	19	0.09
Chinese, ex. Taiwanese (1,101)	1,249	5.84
Filipino (30)	43	0.20
Indian (385)	451	2.11
Indonesian (6)	7	0.03
Japanese (67)	117	0.55
Korean (140)	164	0.77
Laotian (1)	12	0.06
Malaysian (0)	1	<0.01
Nepalese (1)	1	<0.01
Pakistani (36)	44	0.21
Sri Lankan (52)	60	0.28
Taiwanese (38)	50	0.23
Thai (11)	22	0.10
Vietnamese (36)	46	0.22
Hawaii Native/Pacific Islander (9)	21	0.10
Not Hispanic (8)	20	0.09
Hispanic (1)	1	<0.01
Guamanian/Chamorro (1)	1	<0.01
Native Hawaiian (7)	9	0.04
White (18,625)	18,996	88.87
Not Hispanic (18,309)	18,653	87.27
Hispanic (316)	343	1.60

Winthrop Town

Place Type: City
County: Suffolk
Population: 17,497†

Ancestry‡	Population	%
African, Sub-Saharan (350)	361	2.09
African (240)	251	1.45
Kenyan (4)	4	0.02
Nigerian (106)	106	0.61
Albanian (280)	280	1.62
American (676)	676	3.91
Arab (159)	229	1.32
Lebanese (47)	54	0.31
Moroccan (94)	121	0.70
Syrian (18)	18	0.10
Other Arab (0)	36	0.21
Armenian (8)	78	0.45
Australian (0)	14	0.08
Austrian (21)	34	0.20
Belgian (0)	51	0.29
Brazilian (69)	100	0.58
British (12)	19	0.11
Canadian (86)	294	1.70
Celtic (10)	10	0.06
Croatian (0)	15	0.09
Czechoslovakian (0)	14	0.08
Danish (0)	8	0.05
Dutch (10)	35	0.20
Eastern European (19)	19	0.11
English (299)	1,594	9.21
European (127)	229	1.32
Finnish (0)	44	0.25
French, ex. Basque (122)	1,053	6.08
French Canadian (146)	465	2.69
German (63)	761	4.40
Greek (142)	179	1.03
Hungarian (8)	55	0.32
Irish (2,071)	6,534	37.74
Italian (2,925)	5,847	33.78
Lithuanian (55)	296	1.71
Norwegian (0)	27	0.16
Polish (120)	536	3.10
Portuguese (24)	228	1.32
Romanian (14)	14	0.08
Russian (171)	375	2.17
Scandinavian (0)	22	0.13
Scotch-Irish (192)	509	2.94
Scottish (127)	310	1.79
Slavic (7)	21	0.12
Swedish (30)	140	0.81
Ukrainian (0)	86	0.50
Welsh (0)	62	0.36
West Indian, ex. Hispanic (43)	66	0.38
Barbadian (0)	14	0.08
Haitian (43)	43	0.25
West Indian (0)	9	0.05
Yugoslavian (12)	12	0.07

Hispanic Origin	Population	%
Hispanic or Latino (of any race)	1,066	6.09
Central American, ex. Mexican	210	1.20
Costa Rican	21	0.12
Guatemalan	54	0.31
Honduran	25	0.14
Nicaraguan	9	0.05
Panamanian	1	0.01
Salvadoran	96	0.55
Other Central American	4	0.02
Cuban	29	0.17
Dominican Republic	52	0.30
Mexican	104	0.59
Puerto Rican	231	1.32
South American	302	1.73
Argentinean	12	0.07
Bolivian	5	0.03
Chilean	18	0.10

SECTION TWO

*Notes: † The Census 2010 population figure is used to calculate the percentages in the Hispanic Origin and Race categories. Ancestry percentages are based on the 2006-2010 American Community Survey population (not shown); ‡ Numbers in parentheses indicate the number of people reporting a single ancestry; * Numbers in parentheses indicate the number of persons reporting this race alone, not in combination with any other race; Please refer to the Explanation of Data for more information.*

Colombian	200	1.14
Ecuadorian	3	0.02
Paraguayan	2	0.01
Peruvian	48	0.27
Uruguayan	3	0.02
Venezuelan	6	0.03
Other South American	5	0.03
Other Hispanic or Latino	138	0.79

Race*	Population	%
African-American/Black (351)	486	2.78
Not Hispanic (329)	438	2.50
Hispanic (22)	48	0.27
American Indian/Alaska Native (29)	111	0.63
Not Hispanic (19)	86	0.49
Hispanic (10)	25	0.14
Aleut *(Alaska Native)* (1)	3	0.02
Blackfeet (0)	2	0.01
Cherokee (0)	3	0.02
Chippewa (1)	1	0.01
Comanche (0)	1	0.01
Iroquois (0)	5	0.03
Mexican American Ind. (1)	2	0.01
Seminole (0)	1	0.01
South American Ind. (1)	2	0.01
Tlingit-Haida *(Alaska Native)* (0)	4	0.02
Asian (212)	279	1.59
Not Hispanic (209)	273	1.56
Hispanic (3)	6	0.03
Cambodian (19)	25	0.14
Chinese, ex. Taiwanese (54)	68	0.39
Filipino (16)	35	0.20
Indian (28)	40	0.23
Indonesian (4)	4	0.02
Japanese (18)	31	0.18
Korean (13)	14	0.08
Laotian (4)	5	0.03
Malaysian (1)	2	0.01
Pakistani (1)	3	0.02
Sri Lankan (2)	3	0.02
Thai (6)	6	0.03
Vietnamese (25)	30	0.17
Hawaii Native/Pacific Islander (7)	15	0.09
Not Hispanic (6)	12	0.07
Hispanic (1)	3	0.02
Guamanian/Chamorro (1)	3	0.02
Native Hawaiian (3)	6	0.03
Samoan (0)	1	0.01
Tongan (1)	3	0.02
White (16,055)	16,354	93.47
Not Hispanic (15,486)	15,706	89.76
Hispanic (569)	648	3.70

Woburn

Place Type: City
County: Middlesex
Population: 38,120†

Ancestry‡	Population	%
African, Sub-Saharan (303)	424	1.13
African (133)	171	0.46
Cape Verdean (46)	129	0.34
Kenyan (76)	76	0.20
Ugandan (34)	34	0.09
Other Sub-Saharan African (14)	14	0.04
Albanian (117)	181	0.48
American (1,198)	1,198	3.19
Arab (201)	241	0.64
Lebanese (89)	89	0.24
Syrian (47)	47	0.13
Other Arab (65)	105	0.28
Armenian (177)	284	0.76
Austrian (0)	11	0.03
Belgian (0)	15	0.04
Brazilian (506)	517	1.38
British (90)	106	0.28
Bulgarian (353)	429	1.14
Canadian (287)	615	1.64
Celtic (0)	11	0.03
Croatian (63)	63	0.17
Czech (0)	22	0.06
Danish (23)	153	0.41
Dutch (31)	294	0.78
Eastern European (34)	34	0.09
English (746)	3,792	10.10
European (94)	119	0.32
Finnish (49)	140	0.37
French, ex. Basque (334)	2,396	6.38
French Canadian (347)	1,350	3.60
German (263)	1,776	4.73
Greek (386)	787	2.10
Hungarian (30)	61	0.16
Irish (4,988)	12,938	34.47
Italian (4,080)	9,069	24.16
Lithuanian (22)	103	0.27
Northern European (24)	24	0.06
Norwegian (28)	142	0.38
Polish (130)	1,092	2.91
Portuguese (825)	1,522	4.05
Romanian (14)	25	0.07
Russian (102)	326	0.87
Scandinavian (17)	132	0.35
Scotch-Irish (319)	801	2.13
Scottish (221)	827	2.20
Serbian (0)	41	0.11
Slovak (0)	23	0.06
Swedish (108)	850	2.26
Swiss (14)	102	0.27
Turkish (39)	57	0.15
Ukrainian (52)	150	0.40
Welsh (0)	18	0.05
West Indian, ex. Hispanic (523)	627	1.67
Barbadian (0)	89	0.24
Haitian (383)	383	1.02
Jamaican (8)	23	0.06
West Indian (132)	132	0.35

Hispanic Origin	Population	%
Hispanic or Latino (of any race)	1,724	4.52
Central American, ex. Mexican	371	0.97
Costa Rican	8	0.02
Guatemalan	122	0.32
Honduran	72	0.19
Nicaraguan	10	0.03
Panamanian	4	0.01
Salvadoran	154	0.40
Other Central American	1	<0.01
Cuban	38	0.10
Dominican Republic	109	0.29
Mexican	172	0.45
Puerto Rican	611	1.60
South American	270	0.71
Argentinean	54	0.14
Bolivian	15	0.04
Chilean	16	0.04
Colombian	83	0.22
Ecuadorian	29	0.08
Paraguayan	1	<0.01
Peruvian	37	0.10
Uruguayan	4	0.01
Venezuelan	24	0.06
Other South American	7	0.02
Other Hispanic or Latino	153	0.40

Race*	Population	%
African-American/Black (1,592)	1,831	4.80
Not Hispanic (1,537)	1,720	4.51
Hispanic (55)	111	0.29
American Indian/Alaska Native (61)	174	0.46
Not Hispanic (46)	132	0.35
Hispanic (15)	42	0.11
Apache (0)	4	0.01
Blackfeet (2)	6	0.02
Canadian/French Am. Ind. (3)	6	0.02
Central American Ind. (1)	1	<0.01
Cherokee (2)	17	0.04
Cheyenne (0)	3	0.01
Chippewa (3)	4	0.01
Choctaw (0)	2	0.01
Hopi (1)	1	<0.01
Iroquois (2)	8	0.02
Mexican American Ind. (2)	4	0.01
Navajo (3)	3	0.01
Potawatomi (1)	1	<0.01
Seminole (0)	2	0.01
Sioux (1)	2	0.01
South American Ind. (1)	4	0.01
Ute (0)	1	<0.01
Asian (2,775)	2,988	7.84
Not Hispanic (2,770)	2,967	7.78
Hispanic (5)	21	0.06
Bangladeshi (12)	13	0.03
Burmese (2)	2	0.01
Cambodian (25)	34	0.09
Chinese, ex. Taiwanese (376)	409	1.07
Filipino (80)	113	0.30
Hmong (3)	3	0.01
Indian (1,733)	1,792	4.70
Indonesian (4)	7	0.02
Japanese (35)	57	0.15
Korean (130)	138	0.36
Laotian (4)	9	0.02
Nepalese (37)	37	0.10
Pakistani (51)	53	0.14
Sri Lankan (14)	22	0.06
Taiwanese (20)	24	0.06
Thai (19)	30	0.08
Vietnamese (183)	206	0.54
Hawaii Native/Pacific Islander (2)	22	0.06
Not Hispanic (2)	18	0.05
Hispanic (0)	4	0.01
Guamanian/Chamorro (0)	2	0.01
Native Hawaiian (0)	6	0.02
Samoan (0)	4	0.01
White (32,107)	32,718	85.83
Not Hispanic (31,130)	31,614	82.93
Hispanic (977)	1,104	2.90

Worcester

Place Type: City
County: Worcester
Population: 181,045†

Ancestry‡	Population	%
Afghan (291)	291	0.16
African, Sub-Saharan (4,787)	5,301	2.95
African (1,415)	1,614	0.90
Cape Verdean (73)	184	0.10
Ethiopian (50)	69	0.04
Ghanaian (1,614)	1,681	0.93
Kenyan (408)	408	0.23
Liberian (499)	529	0.29
Nigerian (332)	354	0.20
Sierra Leonean (23)	23	0.01
Somalian (108)	108	0.06
Sudanese (13)	13	0.01
Other Sub-Saharan African (252)	318	0.18
Albanian (2,318)	2,568	1.43
American (3,364)	3,364	1.87
Arab (1,932)	2,701	1.50
Arab (122)	199	0.11
Egyptian (69)	69	0.04
Iraqi (301)	312	0.17
Jordanian (29)	29	0.02
Lebanese (885)	1,347	0.75
Moroccan (208)	244	0.14
Palestinian (206)	206	0.11
Syrian (86)	259	0.14
Other Arab (26)	36	0.02
Armenian (813)	1,417	0.79
Assyrian/Chaldean/Syriac (0)	29	0.02
Australian (13)	13	0.01
Austrian (69)	302	0.17
Belgian (17)	37	0.02
Brazilian (3,250)	3,363	1.87
British (262)	432	0.24
Canadian (327)	527	0.29
Celtic (8)	8	<0.01

*Notes: † The Census 2010 population figure is used to calculate the percentages in the Hispanic Origin and Race categories. Ancestry percentages are based on the 2006-2010 American Community Survey population (not shown); ‡ Numbers in parentheses indicate the number of people reporting a single ancestry; * Numbers in parentheses indicate the number of persons reporting this race alone, not in combination with any other race; Please refer to the Explanation of Data for more information.*

Croatian (51)	51	0.03
Czech (105)	303	0.17
Czechoslovakian (0)	17	0.01
Danish (0)	217	0.12
Dutch (157)	1,039	0.58
Eastern European (283)	299	0.17
English (2,333)	10,881	6.05
European (458)	464	0.26
Finnish (263)	1,066	0.59
French, ex. Basque (4,086)	17,457	9.70
French Canadian (2,514)	5,259	2.92
German (1,019)	6,474	3.60
Greek (1,329)	2,240	1.24
Guyanese (92)	92	0.05
Hungarian (143)	609	0.34
Icelander (0)	7	<0.01
Iranian (250)	265	0.15
Irish (11,455)	31,857	17.70
Israeli (79)	89	0.05
Italian (9,490)	21,873	12.15
Lithuanian (1,559)	3,290	1.83
Northern European (31)	43	0.02
Norwegian (261)	748	0.42
Pennsylvania German (14)	26	0.01
Polish (3,868)	9,684	5.38
Portuguese (703)	1,480	0.82
Romanian (45)	149	0.08
Russian (1,084)	2,321	1.29
Scandinavian (103)	202	0.11
Scotch-Irish (481)	1,705	0.95
Scottish (824)	2,755	1.53
Slavic (22)	22	0.01
Slovak (34)	48	0.03
Slovene (0)	10	0.01
Swedish (1,495)	4,756	2.64
Swiss (13)	88	0.05
Turkish (125)	138	0.08
Ukrainian (154)	315	0.18
Welsh (149)	365	0.20
West Indian, ex. Hispanic (1,977)	2,360	1.31
Barbadian (47)	106	0.06
Bermudan (16)	45	0.03
British West Indian (52)	63	0.04
Dutch West Indian (0)	38	0.02
Haitian (885)	957	0.53
Jamaican (685)	734	0.41
Trinidadian/Tobagonian (29)	94	0.05
West Indian (263)	323	0.18
Yugoslavian (134)	200	0.11

Hispanic Origin	Population	%
Hispanic or Latino (of any race)	37,818	20.89
Central American, ex. Mexican	3,792	2.09
Costa Rican	116	0.06
Guatemalan	474	0.26
Honduran	206	0.11
Nicaraguan	66	0.04
Panamanian	129	0.07
Salvadoran	2,776	1.53
Other Central American	25	0.01
Cuban	490	0.27
Dominican Republic	4,221	2.33
Mexican	1,356	0.75
Puerto Rican	23,074	12.74
South American	2,351	1.30
Argentinean	62	0.03
Bolivian	23	0.01
Chilean	102	0.06
Colombian	769	0.42
Ecuadorian	953	0.53
Paraguayan	3	<0.01
Peruvian	252	0.14
Uruguayan	63	0.03
Venezuelan	109	0.06
Other South American	15	0.01
Other Hispanic or Latino	2,534	1.40

Race*	Population	%
African-American/Black (21,056)	24,631	13.60
Not Hispanic (18,501)	20,873	11.53
Hispanic (2,555)	3,758	2.08
American Indian/Alaska Native (755)	2,062	1.14
Not Hispanic (427)	1,407	0.78
Hispanic (328)	655	0.36
Alaska Athabascan *(Ala. Nat.)* (3)	3	<0.01
Apache (1)	6	<0.01
Arapaho (0)	1	<0.01
Blackfeet (8)	52	0.03
Canadian/French Am. Ind. (6)	21	0.01
Central American Ind. (14)	30	0.02
Cherokee (39)	153	0.08
Cheyenne (1)	1	<0.01
Chickasaw (0)	5	<0.01
Chippewa (4)	9	<0.01
Choctaw (0)	4	<0.01
Colville (0)	1	<0.01
Comanche (2)	3	<0.01
Cree (0)	1	<0.01
Creek (0)	1	<0.01
Crow (0)	3	<0.01
Delaware (0)	3	<0.01
Inupiat *(Alaska Native)* (3)	3	<0.01
Iroquois (21)	56	0.03
Kiowa (3)	3	<0.01
Lumbee (0)	1	<0.01
Mexican American Ind. (16)	22	0.01
Navajo (4)	6	<0.01
Pueblo (0)	7	<0.01
Seminole (0)	3	<0.01
Sioux (2)	14	0.01
South American Ind. (36)	67	0.04
Spanish American Ind. (14)	20	0.01
Tlingit-Haida *(Alaska Native)* (0)	2	<0.01
Yaqui (3)	3	<0.01
Yuman (1)	1	<0.01
Yup'ik *(Alaska Native)* (0)	1	<0.01
Asian (11,034)	12,228	6.75
Not Hispanic (10,927)	11,960	6.61
Hispanic (107)	268	0.15
Bangladeshi (35)	56	0.03
Bhutanese (178)	222	0.12
Burmese (148)	171	0.09
Cambodian (370)	433	0.24
Chinese, ex. Taiwanese (1,625)	1,913	1.06
Filipino (255)	390	0.22
Hmong (14)	15	0.01
Indian (1,482)	1,677	0.93
Indonesian (29)	40	0.02
Japanese (166)	292	0.16
Korean (266)	348	0.19
Laotian (163)	193	0.11
Malaysian (8)	11	0.01
Nepalese (76)	109	0.06
Pakistani (140)	150	0.08
Sri Lankan (25)	26	0.01
Taiwanese (66)	77	0.04
Thai (51)	71	0.04
Vietnamese (5,392)	5,759	3.18
Hawaii Native/Pacific Islander (85)	378	0.21
Not Hispanic (52)	198	0.11
Hispanic (33)	180	0.10
Fijian (0)	7	<0.01
Guamanian/Chamorro (17)	44	0.02
Marshallese (1)	1	<0.01
Native Hawaiian (30)	69	0.04
Samoan (12)	21	0.01
Tongan (0)	2	<0.01
White (125,706)	131,504	72.64
Not Hispanic (107,814)	111,403	61.53
Hispanic (17,892)	20,101	11.10

Wrentham

Place Type: Town
County: Norfolk
Population: 10,955†

Ancestry‡	Population	%
African, Sub-Saharan (0)	10	0.09
Cape Verdean (0)	10	0.09
American (393)	393	3.63
Armenian (34)	164	1.52
Austrian (11)	47	0.43
Belgian (0)	11	0.10
British (68)	86	0.80
Canadian (15)	43	0.40
Croatian (0)	11	0.10
Czech (0)	64	0.59
Czechoslovakian (10)	36	0.33
Danish (0)	69	0.64
Dutch (0)	29	0.27
Eastern European (7)	7	0.06
English (662)	2,203	20.38
European (61)	61	0.56
Finnish (36)	50	0.46
French, ex. Basque (234)	797	7.37
French Canadian (140)	410	3.79
German (200)	1,262	11.67
Greek (34)	95	0.88
Hungarian (11)	33	0.31
Iranian (0)	9	0.08
Irish (1,080)	3,476	32.15
Italian (552)	1,973	18.25
Lithuanian (59)	190	1.76
Norwegian (20)	90	0.83
Polish (368)	961	8.89
Portuguese (77)	209	1.93
Russian (34)	99	0.92
Scotch-Irish (40)	232	2.15
Scottish (91)	218	2.02
Slavic (11)	11	0.10
Swedish (125)	454	4.20
Swiss (0)	26	0.24
Ukrainian (11)	11	0.10
Welsh (0)	23	0.21
West Indian, ex. Hispanic (0)	28	0.26
Haitian (0)	28	0.26
Yugoslavian (0)	9	0.08

Hispanic Origin	Population	%
Hispanic or Latino (of any race)	133	1.21
Central American, ex. Mexican	25	0.23
Costa Rican	1	0.01
Guatemalan	9	0.08
Nicaraguan	8	0.07
Panamanian	1	0.01
Salvadoran	6	0.05
Cuban	3	0.03
Dominican Republic	5	0.05
Mexican	29	0.26
Puerto Rican	19	0.17
South American	31	0.28
Argentinean	2	0.02
Bolivian	3	0.03
Chilean	1	0.01
Colombian	16	0.15
Ecuadorian	2	0.02
Peruvian	5	0.05
Venezuelan	2	0.02
Other Hispanic or Latino	21	0.19

Race*	Population	%
African-American/Black (61)	91	0.83
Not Hispanic (60)	85	0.78
Hispanic (1)	6	0.05
American Indian/Alaska Native (19)	55	0.50
Not Hispanic (16)	45	0.41
Hispanic (3)	10	0.09
Canadian/French Am. Ind. (0)	2	0.02
Central American Ind. (0)	5	0.05
Cherokee (0)	5	0.05
Chippewa (0)	1	0.01
Iroquois (5)	7	0.06
Mexican American Ind. (1)	1	0.01
South American Ind. (2)	3	0.03
Asian (112)	148	1.35
Not Hispanic (112)	147	1.34
Hispanic (0)	1	0.01
Cambodian (5)	5	0.05
Chinese, ex. Taiwanese (36)	45	0.41

SECTION TWO

*Notes: † The Census 2010 population figure is used to calculate the percentages in the Hispanic Origin and Race categories. Ancestry percentages are based on the 2006-2010 American Community Survey population (not shown); ‡ Numbers in parentheses indicate the number of people reporting a single ancestry; * Numbers in parentheses indicate the number of persons reporting this race alone, not in combination with any other race; Please refer to the Explanation of Data for more information.*

Filipino (5)	8	0.07
Indian (23)	34	0.31
Indonesian (4)	5	0.05
Japanese (4)	7	0.06
Korean (25)	32	0.29
Laotian (1)	1	0.01
Taiwanese (0)	1	0.01
Thai (2)	4	0.04
Vietnamese (6)	6	0.05
Hawaii Native/Pacific Islander (0)	4	0.04
Not Hispanic (0)	4	0.04
White (10,634)	10,735	97.99
Not Hispanic (10,541)	10,627	97.01
Hispanic (93)	108	0.99

Yarmouth

Place Type: Town
County: Barnstable
Population: 23,793†

Ancestry‡	Population	%
African, Sub-Saharan (86)	260	1.08
Cape Verdean (86)	208	0.87
Other Sub-Saharan African (0)	52	0.22
Albanian (15)	45	0.19
American (2,660)	2,660	11.06
Arab (148)	258	1.07
Arab (43)	43	0.18
Lebanese (105)	193	0.80
Moroccan (0)	22	0.09
Armenian (70)	139	0.58
Assyrian/Chaldean/Syriac (15)	15	0.06
Australian (13)	13	0.05
Brazilian (608)	608	2.53
British (140)	179	0.74
Bulgarian (68)	68	0.28
Cajun (14)	14	0.06
Canadian (158)	294	1.22
Croatian (0)	12	0.05
Czech (22)	22	0.09
Czechoslovakian (38)	38	0.16
Danish (27)	66	0.27
Dutch (39)	251	1.04
Eastern European (37)	57	0.24
English (1,437)	4,952	20.60
European (51)	68	0.28
Finnish (104)	310	1.29
French, ex. Basque (426)	2,215	9.21
French Canadian (242)	621	2.58
German (433)	2,148	8.94
Greek (216)	250	1.04
Hungarian (77)	115	0.48
Irish (2,978)	6,643	27.63
Italian (1,280)	2,533	10.54
Latvian (30)	30	0.12
Lithuanian (54)	116	0.48
Luxemburger (0)	14	0.06
Norwegian (16)	120	0.50
Polish (380)	1,327	5.52
Portuguese (353)	832	3.46
Russian (11)	103	0.43
Scandinavian (12)	12	0.05
Scotch-Irish (183)	708	2.95
Scottish (161)	831	3.46
Slavic (0)	11	0.05
Slovak (0)	58	0.24
Slovene (0)	12	0.05
Swedish (180)	707	2.94
Swiss (17)	30	0.12
Welsh (41)	116	0.48
West Indian, ex. Hispanic (92)	110	0.46
British West Indian (0)	18	0.07
Haitian (12)	12	0.05
Jamaican (80)	80	0.33

Hispanic Origin	Population	%
Hispanic or Latino (of any race)	621	2.61
Central American, ex. Mexican	19	0.08
Costa Rican	5	0.02
Guatemalan	2	0.01
Honduran	6	0.03
Panamanian	1	<0.01
Salvadoran	5	0.02
Cuban	15	0.06
Dominican Republic	58	0.24
Mexican	88	0.37
Puerto Rican	216	0.91
South American	113	0.47
Argentinean	5	0.02
Chilean	11	0.05
Colombian	20	0.08
Ecuadorian	48	0.20
Paraguayan	1	<0.01
Peruvian	16	0.07
Venezuelan	4	0.02
Other South American	8	0.03
Other Hispanic or Latino	112	0.47

Race*	Population	%
African-American/Black (486)	686	2.88
Not Hispanic (448)	620	2.61
Hispanic (38)	66	0.28
American Indian/Alaska Native (72)	193	0.81
Not Hispanic (59)	176	0.74
Hispanic (13)	17	0.07
Apache (1)	1	<0.01
Blackfeet (1)	7	0.03
Cherokee (5)	14	0.06
Chippewa (1)	3	0.01
Choctaw (1)	3	0.01
Cree (0)	2	0.01
Creek (2)	2	0.01
Delaware (1)	1	<0.01
Iroquois (1)	4	0.02
Mexican American Ind. (1)	1	<0.01
Sioux (2)	3	0.01
South American Ind. (2)	2	0.01
Tlingit-Haida *(Alaska Native)* (3)	7	0.03
Asian (262)	340	1.43
Not Hispanic (258)	329	1.38
Hispanic (4)	11	0.05
Cambodian (1)	2	0.01
Chinese, ex. Taiwanese (82)	97	0.41
Filipino (38)	57	0.24
Indian (34)	44	0.18
Indonesian (1)	3	0.01
Japanese (5)	23	0.10
Korean (13)	22	0.09
Laotian (1)	3	0.01
Nepalese (8)	12	0.05
Pakistani (38)	39	0.16
Taiwanese (5)	5	0.02
Thai (4)	6	0.03
Vietnamese (18)	21	0.09
Hawaii Native/Pacific Islander (3)	28	0.12
Not Hispanic (3)	25	0.11
Hispanic (0)	3	0.01
Native Hawaiian (2)	7	0.03
White (22,031)	22,466	94.42
Not Hispanic (21,698)	22,071	92.76
Hispanic (333)	395	1.66

*Notes: † The Census 2010 population figure is used to calculate the percentages in the Hispanic Origin and Race categories. Ancestry percentages are based on the 2006-2010 American Community Survey population (not shown); ‡ Numbers in parentheses indicate the number of people reporting a single ancestry; * Numbers in parentheses indicate the number of persons reporting this race alone, not in combination with any other race; Please refer to the Explanation of Data for more information.*

MICHIGAN

Place Type: State
Population: 9,883,640†

Ancestry‡	Population	%
Afghan (108)	174	<0.01
African, Sub-Saharan (43,840)	54,355	0.55
African (31,011)	39,842	0.40
Cape Verdean (124)	177	<0.01
Ethiopian (1,455)	1,696	0.02
Ghanaian (513)	563	0.01
Kenyan (849)	876	0.01
Liberian (780)	830	0.01
Nigerian (3,981)	4,487	0.05
Senegalese (323)	396	<0.01
Sierra Leonean (23)	23	<0.01
Somalian (936)	981	0.01
South African (763)	1,042	0.01
Sudanese (812)	846	0.01
Ugandan (101)	129	<0.01
Zimbabwean (437)	446	<0.01
Other Sub-Saharan African (1,732)	2,021	0.02
Albanian (21,347)	22,903	0.23
Alsatian (17)	147	<0.01
American (473,397)	473,397	4.76
Arab (118,517)	152,212	1.53
Arab (30,035)	34,741	0.35
Egyptian (2,685)	3,275	0.03
Iraqi (16,327)	19,942	0.20
Jordanian (3,332)	3,841	0.04
Lebanese (40,452)	57,876	0.58
Moroccan (1,268)	1,643	0.02
Palestinian (3,810)	4,576	0.05
Syrian (4,118)	8,240	0.08
Other Arab (16,490)	18,078	0.18
Armenian (9,378)	17,345	0.17
Assyrian/Chaldean/Syriac (27,439)	33,051	0.33
Australian (1,225)	2,822	0.03
Austrian (4,829)	22,990	0.23
Basque (59)	301	<0.01
Belgian (13,825)	56,212	0.56
Brazilian (1,520)	2,563	0.03
British (15,371)	33,670	0.34
Bulgarian (1,869)	3,473	0.03
Cajun (260)	547	0.01
Canadian (21,090)	50,490	0.51
Carpatho Rusyn (54)	269	<0.01
Celtic (800)	1,510	0.02
Croatian (6,713)	20,547	0.21
Cypriot (53)	82	<0.01
Czech (12,666)	52,092	0.52
Czechoslovakian (7,065)	16,698	0.17
Danish (10,543)	44,243	0.44
Dutch (210,571)	515,229	5.18
Eastern European (7,249)	8,444	0.08
English (287,286)	1,034,184	10.39
Estonian (292)	461	<0.01
European (76,047)	86,424	0.87
Finnish (42,350)	111,010	1.12
French, ex. Basque (74,075)	509,548	5.12
French Canadian (60,597)	177,875	1.79
German (672,071)	2,254,107	22.65
German Russian (176)	417	<0.01
Greek (19,573)	46,165	0.46
Guyanese (142)	366	<0.01
Hungarian (31,666)	104,987	1.05
Icelander (221)	1,022	0.01
Iranian (3,448)	4,305	0.04
Irish (260,092)	1,186,068	11.92
Israeli (1,469)	1,908	0.02
Italian (167,367)	478,974	4.81
Latvian (2,240)	4,265	0.04
Lithuanian (10,723)	31,966	0.32
Luxemburger (265)	781	0.01
Macedonian (6,976)	10,155	0.10
Maltese (5,113)	12,447	0.13
New Zealander (228)	286	<0.01
Northern European (4,876)	5,448	0.05
Norwegian (22,747)	87,020	0.87
Pennsylvania German (5,245)	9,478	0.10
Polish (326,853)	900,446	9.05
Portuguese (1,989)	6,093	0.06
Romanian (17,284)	30,320	0.30
Russian (26,497)	78,153	0.79
Scandinavian (5,797)	14,042	0.14
Scotch-Irish (52,590)	156,935	1.58
Scottish (61,687)	245,563	2.47
Serbian (4,264)	9,458	0.10
Slavic (1,896)	6,334	0.06
Slovak (9,078)	27,400	0.28
Slovene (1,407)	4,617	0.05
Soviet Union (52)	52	<0.01
Swedish (39,339)	172,043	1.73
Swiss (4,874)	24,617	0.25
Turkish (1,774)	2,589	0.03
Ukrainian (16,914)	41,842	0.42
Welsh (7,900)	51,799	0.52
West Indian, ex. Hispanic (7,948)	13,682	0.14
Bahamian (221)	326	<0.01
Barbadian (176)	356	<0.01
Belizean (133)	188	<0.01
Bermudan (50)	153	<0.01
British West Indian (177)	301	<0.01
Dutch West Indian (127)	284	<0.01
Haitian (1,351)	2,376	0.02
Jamaican (4,598)	7,188	0.07
Trinidadian/Tobagonian (509)	980	0.01
U.S. Virgin Islander (32)	108	<0.01
West Indian (553)	1,380	0.01
Other West Indian (21)	42	<0.01
Yugoslavian (12,894)	20,532	0.21

Hispanic Origin	Population	%
Hispanic or Latino (of any race)	436,358	4.41
Central American, ex. Mexican	17,785	0.18
Costa Rican	903	0.01
Guatemalan	8,428	0.09
Honduran	2,694	0.03
Nicaraguan	870	0.01
Panamanian	1,359	0.01
Salvadoran	3,401	0.03
Other Central American	130	<0.01
Cuban	9,922	0.10
Dominican Republic	5,012	0.05
Mexican	317,903	3.22
Puerto Rican	37,267	0.38
South American	13,243	0.13
Argentinean	2,113	0.02
Bolivian	512	0.01
Chilean	1,160	0.01
Colombian	3,991	0.04
Ecuadorian	1,312	0.01
Paraguayan	225	<0.01
Peruvian	2,040	0.02
Uruguayan	224	<0.01
Venezuelan	1,496	0.02
Other South American	170	<0.01
Other Hispanic or Latino	35,226	0.36

Race*	Population	%
African-American/Black (1,400,362)	1,505,514	15.23
Not Hispanic (1,383,756)	1,477,071	14.94
Hispanic (16,606)	28,443	0.29
American Indian/Alaska Native (62,007)	139,095	1.41
Not Hispanic (54,665)	123,267	1.25
Hispanic (7,342)	15,828	0.16
Alaska Athabascan *(Ala. Nat.)* (64)	113	<0.01
Aleut *(Alaska Native)* (54)	107	<0.01
Apache (379)	1,246	0.01
Arapaho (28)	67	<0.01
Blackfeet (496)	3,911	0.04
Canadian/French Am. Ind. (683)	1,366	0.01
Central American Ind. (137)	194	<0.01
Cherokee (3,396)	17,821	0.18
Cheyenne (39)	175	<0.01
Chickasaw (92)	261	<0.01
Chippewa (23,564)	36,296	0.37
Choctaw (366)	1,463	0.01
Colville (7)	15	<0.01
Comanche (94)	214	<0.01
Cree (82)	358	<0.01
Creek (238)	620	0.01
Crow (18)	169	<0.01
Delaware (127)	308	<0.01
Hopi (21)	66	<0.01
Houma (9)	15	<0.01
Inupiat *(Alaska Native)* (50)	150	<0.01
Iroquois (1,260)	2,803	0.03
Kiowa (15)	44	<0.01
Lumbee (629)	1,130	0.01
Menominee (103)	212	<0.01
Mexican American Ind. (1,402)	2,219	0.02
Navajo (292)	646	0.01
Osage (30)	110	<0.01
Ottawa (4,297)	7,499	0.08
Paiute (10)	41	<0.01
Pima (18)	36	<0.01
Potawatomi (2,881)	4,901	0.05
Pueblo (78)	150	<0.01
Puget Sound Salish (32)	46	<0.01
Seminole (58)	375	<0.01
Shoshone (29)	77	<0.01
Sioux (614)	1,856	0.02
South American Ind. (141)	348	<0.01
Spanish American Ind. (93)	143	<0.01
Tlingit-Haida *(Alaska Native)* (67)	123	<0.01
Tohono O'Odham (13)	22	<0.01
Tsimshian *(Alaska Native)* (10)	22	<0.01
Ute (17)	43	<0.01
Yakama (6)	17	<0.01
Yaqui (61)	119	<0.01
Yuman (5)	22	<0.01
Yup'ik *(Alaska Native)* (36)	62	<0.01
Asian (238,199)	289,607	2.93
Not Hispanic (236,490)	284,695	2.88
Hispanic (1,709)	4,912	0.05
Bangladeshi (7,965)	8,730	0.09
Bhutanese (360)	443	<0.01
Burmese (1,652)	1,856	0.02
Cambodian (1,658)	2,219	0.02
Chinese, ex. Taiwanese (41,451)	48,302	0.49
Filipino (22,047)	32,324	0.33
Hmong (5,580)	5,924	0.06
Indian (77,132)	84,750	0.86
Indonesian (641)	1,148	0.01
Japanese (10,911)	17,412	0.18
Korean (24,186)	30,292	0.31
Laotian (2,646)	3,380	0.03
Malaysian (447)	629	0.01
Nepalese (722)	847	0.01
Pakistani (9,931)	11,056	0.11
Sri Lankan (757)	887	0.01
Taiwanese (2,926)	3,347	0.03
Thai (1,972)	3,212	0.03
Vietnamese (16,787)	19,456	0.20
Hawaii Native/Pacific Islander (2,604)	9,348	0.09
Not Hispanic (2,170)	7,917	0.08
Hispanic (434)	1,431	0.01
Fijian (36)	77	<0.01
Guamanian/Chamorro (521)	1,072	0.01
Marshallese (28)	47	<0.01
Native Hawaiian (753)	2,708	0.03
Samoan (359)	848	0.01
Tongan (54)	108	<0.01
White (7,803,120)	8,006,969	81.01
Not Hispanic (7,569,939)	7,740,156	78.31
Hispanic (233,181)	266,813	2.70

*Notes: † The Census 2010 population figure is used to calculate the percentages in the Hispanic Origin and Race categories. Ancestry percentages are based on the 2006-2010 American Community Survey population (not shown); ‡ Numbers in parentheses indicate the number of people reporting a single ancestry; * Numbers in parentheses indicate the number of persons reporting this race alone, not in combination with any other race; Please refer to the Explanation of Data for more information.*

Ada

Place Type: Township
County: Kent
Population: 13,142†

Ancestry‡	Population	%
African, Sub-Saharan (18)	18	0.14
Ethiopian (18)	18	0.14
Albanian (30)	30	0.24
American (485)	485	3.85
Arab (66)	126	1.00
Lebanese (40)	48	0.38
Other Arab (26)	78	0.62
Armenian (0)	10	0.08
Austrian (13)	68	0.54
Belgian (26)	64	0.51
Brazilian (15)	15	0.12
British (90)	139	1.10
Cajun (0)	9	0.07
Canadian (29)	39	0.31
Croatian (0)	33	0.26
Czech (8)	32	0.25
Czechoslovakian (32)	42	0.33
Danish (11)	60	0.48
Dutch (1,330)	2,744	21.79
English (497)	1,834	14.56
European (338)	338	2.68
Finnish (0)	8	0.06
French, ex. Basque (23)	590	4.69
French Canadian (42)	140	1.11
German (900)	3,382	26.86
Greek (19)	30	0.24
Hungarian (46)	207	1.64
Icelander (10)	10	0.08
Irish (314)	1,772	14.07
Italian (263)	600	4.76
Lithuanian (30)	62	0.49
Norwegian (96)	329	2.61
Polish (236)	819	6.50
Romanian (0)	8	0.06
Russian (17)	124	0.98
Scotch-Irish (97)	277	2.20
Scottish (72)	394	3.13
Slovak (18)	56	0.44
Swedish (85)	335	2.66
Swiss (8)	67	0.53
Ukrainian (38)	52	0.41
Welsh (0)	102	0.81
Yugoslavian (26)	26	0.21

Hispanic Origin	Population	%
Hispanic or Latino (of any race)	225	1.71
Central American, ex. Mexican	30	0.23
Costa Rican	2	0.02
Guatemalan	17	0.13
Nicaraguan	9	0.07
Panamanian	1	0.01
Salvadoran	1	0.01
Cuban	3	0.02
Dominican Republic	3	0.02
Mexican	98	0.75
Puerto Rican	28	0.21
South American	33	0.25
Argentinean	1	0.01
Chilean	5	0.04
Colombian	16	0.12
Paraguayan	4	0.03
Peruvian	6	0.05
Other South American	1	0.01
Other Hispanic or Latino	30	0.23

Race*	Population	%
African-American/Black (129)	189	1.44
Not Hispanic (127)	183	1.39
Hispanic (2)	6	0.05
American Indian/Alaska Native (26)	62	0.47
Not Hispanic (21)	56	0.43
Hispanic (5)	6	0.05
Central American Ind. (1)	1	0.01
Cherokee (1)	3	0.02
Chippewa (7)	9	0.07
Choctaw (0)	1	0.01
Cree (0)	4	0.03
Creek (0)	2	0.02
Iroquois (1)	4	0.03
Mexican American Ind. (4)	4	0.03
Ottawa (2)	5	0.04
Sioux (1)	3	0.02
Asian (478)	575	4.38
Not Hispanic (477)	570	4.34
Hispanic (1)	5	0.04
Burmese (2)	2	0.02
Chinese, ex. Taiwanese (175)	202	1.54
Filipino (29)	49	0.37
Hmong (16)	17	0.13
Indian (100)	118	0.90
Indonesian (0)	1	0.01
Japanese (15)	23	0.18
Korean (59)	62	0.47
Malaysian (2)	2	0.02
Pakistani (21)	23	0.18
Taiwanese (5)	7	0.05
Thai (5)	12	0.09
Vietnamese (30)	38	0.29
Hawaii Native/Pacific Islander (1)	4	0.03
Not Hispanic (1)	4	0.03
White (12,262)	12,451	94.74
Not Hispanic (12,095)	12,265	93.33
Hispanic (167)	186	1.42

Adrian

Place Type: City
County: Lenawee
Population: 21,133†

Ancestry‡	Population	%
African, Sub-Saharan (109)	129	0.60
African (22)	42	0.19
Kenyan (87)	87	0.40
American (1,266)	1,266	5.87
Arab (44)	102	0.47
Arab (31)	46	0.21
Lebanese (13)	41	0.19
Syrian (0)	15	0.07
Armenian (0)	40	0.19
Australian (0)	7	0.03
Belgian (33)	33	0.15
British (32)	61	0.28
Bulgarian (0)	14	0.06
Canadian (28)	51	0.24
Czech (126)	211	0.98
Czechoslovakian (46)	46	0.21
Danish (20)	47	0.22
Dutch (153)	968	4.49
Eastern European (15)	15	0.07
English (1,053)	2,713	12.59
European (136)	156	0.72
Finnish (10)	60	0.28
French, ex. Basque (165)	985	4.57
French Canadian (53)	359	1.67
German (1,586)	5,092	23.62
Greek (44)	115	0.53
Hungarian (12)	165	0.77
Irish (637)	2,831	13.13
Italian (290)	528	2.45
Luxemburger (9)	9	0.04
Norwegian (35)	35	0.16
Pennsylvania German (29)	52	0.24
Polish (213)	1,028	4.77
Portuguese (0)	17	0.08
Russian (40)	64	0.30
Scotch-Irish (129)	225	1.04
Scottish (77)	412	1.91
Slavic (0)	9	0.04
Slovak (12)	25	0.12
Swedish (38)	106	0.49
Swiss (29)	85	0.39
Ukrainian (10)	60	0.28
Welsh (32)	143	0.66
West Indian, ex. Hispanic (0)	12	0.06
Jamaican (0)	12	0.06
Yugoslavian (0)	10	0.05

Hispanic Origin	Population	%
Hispanic or Latino (of any race)	3,983	18.85
Central American, ex. Mexican	26	0.12
Costa Rican	2	0.01
Guatemalan	18	0.09
Honduran	1	<0.01
Panamanian	1	<0.01
Salvadoran	4	0.02
Cuban	17	0.08
Dominican Republic	12	0.06
Mexican	3,345	15.83
Puerto Rican	254	1.20
South American	49	0.23
Argentinean	4	0.02
Bolivian	4	0.02
Chilean	9	0.04
Colombian	15	0.07
Ecuadorian	3	0.01
Paraguayan	7	0.03
Peruvian	2	0.01
Venezuelan	2	0.01
Other South American	3	0.01
Other Hispanic or Latino	280	1.32

Race*	Population	%
African-American/Black (926)	1,380	6.53
Not Hispanic (809)	1,144	5.41
Hispanic (117)	236	1.12
American Indian/Alaska Native (123)	290	1.37
Not Hispanic (81)	214	1.01
Hispanic (42)	76	0.36
Alaska Athabascan *(Ala. Nat.)* (0)	1	<0.01
Apache (2)	8	0.04
Blackfeet (0)	8	0.04
Cherokee (13)	52	0.25
Chickasaw (0)	2	0.01
Chippewa (17)	22	0.10
Choctaw (6)	12	0.06
Iroquois (5)	12	0.06
Mexican American Ind. (9)	12	0.06
Ottawa (2)	4	0.02
Potawatomi (2)	3	0.01
Sioux (2)	9	0.04
South American Ind. (1)	1	<0.01
Spanish American Ind. (0)	1	<0.01
Yaqui (0)	2	0.01
Yup'ik *(Alaska Native)* (1)	1	<0.01
Asian (199)	278	1.32
Not Hispanic (187)	255	1.21
Hispanic (12)	23	0.11
Bangladeshi (2)	2	0.01
Chinese, ex. Taiwanese (16)	32	0.15
Filipino (33)	59	0.28
Indian (72)	77	0.36
Indonesian (1)	5	0.02
Japanese (13)	23	0.11
Korean (26)	38	0.18
Pakistani (8)	9	0.04
Taiwanese (0)	2	0.01
Thai (0)	5	0.02
Vietnamese (19)	24	0.11
Hawaii Native/Pacific Islander (3)	15	0.07
Not Hispanic (2)	13	0.06
Hispanic (1)	2	0.01
Guamanian/Chamorro (1)	1	<0.01
Native Hawaiian (1)	6	0.03
Samoan (1)	1	<0.01
Tongan (0)	1	<0.01
White (17,782)	18,572	87.88
Not Hispanic (15,548)	16,037	75.89
Hispanic (2,234)	2,535	12.00

*Notes: † The Census 2010 population figure is used to calculate the percentages in the Hispanic Origin and Race categories. Ancestry percentages are based on the 2006-2010 American Community Survey population (not shown); ‡ Numbers in parentheses indicate the number of people reporting a single ancestry; * Numbers in parentheses indicate the number of persons reporting this race alone, not in combination with any other race; Please refer to the Explanation of Data for more information.*

Albion

Place Type: City
County: Calhoun
Population: 8,616†

Ancestry‡	Population	%
African, Sub-Saharan (6)	6	0.07
African (6)	6	0.07
American (260)	260	2.97
Arab (18)	18	0.21
Arab (18)	18	0.21
Austrian (8)	8	0.09
Belgian (0)	31	0.35
Danish (0)	40	0.46
Dutch (100)	112	1.28
English (312)	857	9.79
European (151)	151	1.73
Finnish (10)	59	0.67
French, ex. Basque (12)	155	1.77
French Canadian (9)	39	0.45
German (771)	1,648	18.83
Greek (8)	8	0.09
Hungarian (8)	53	0.61
Irish (348)	938	10.72
Italian (96)	265	3.03
Lithuanian (69)	69	0.79
Norwegian (0)	46	0.53
Polish (126)	371	4.24
Russian (19)	78	0.89
Scotch-Irish (42)	147	1.68
Scottish (28)	104	1.19
Swedish (6)	124	1.42
Swiss (0)	8	0.09
Ukrainian (0)	12	0.14
Welsh (0)	10	0.11
West Indian, ex. Hispanic (6)	6	0.07
Barbadian (6)	6	0.07

Hispanic Origin	Population	%
Hispanic or Latino (of any race)	500	5.80
Central American, ex. Mexican	5	0.06
Costa Rican	3	0.03
Honduran	2	0.02
Cuban	11	0.13
Dominican Republic	1	0.01
Mexican	388	4.50
Puerto Rican	41	0.48
South American	15	0.17
Argentinean	4	0.05
Bolivian	1	0.01
Chilean	1	0.01
Colombian	1	0.01
Peruvian	4	0.05
Venezuelan	4	0.05
Other Hispanic or Latino	39	0.45

Race*	Population	%
African-American/Black (2,579)	2,823	32.76
Not Hispanic (2,533)	2,751	31.93
Hispanic (46)	72	0.84
American Indian/Alaska Native (29)	105	1.22
Not Hispanic (25)	93	1.08
Hispanic (4)	12	0.14
Apache (0)	1	0.01
Blackfeet (0)	2	0.02
Canadian/French Am. Ind. (0)	1	0.01
Cherokee (6)	23	0.27
Cheyenne (0)	2	0.02
Chickasaw (0)	1	0.01
Chippewa (1)	3	0.03
Choctaw (0)	1	0.01
Ottawa (2)	4	0.05
Potawatomi (0)	2	0.02
Asian (91)	130	1.51
Not Hispanic (89)	125	1.45
Hispanic (2)	5	0.06
Burmese (2)	2	0.02
Chinese, ex. Taiwanese (40)	48	0.56
Filipino (3)	8	0.09
Indian (21)	25	0.29
Indonesian (0)	1	0.01
Japanese (8)	19	0.22
Korean (8)	14	0.16
Nepalese (3)	3	0.03
Taiwanese (1)	1	0.01
Vietnamese (0)	4	0.05
Hawaii Native/Pacific Islander (17)	25	0.29
Not Hispanic (7)	14	0.16
Hispanic (10)	11	0.13
Fijian (0)	1	0.01
Native Hawaiian (3)	9	0.10
White (5,477)	5,775	67.03
Not Hispanic (5,176)	5,431	63.03
Hispanic (301)	344	3.99

Algoma

Place Type: Township
County: Kent
Population: 9,932†

Ancestry‡	Population	%
American (411)	411	4.31
Arab (13)	13	0.14
Lebanese (13)	13	0.14
Armenian (0)	87	0.91
Australian (0)	14	0.15
Austrian (0)	45	0.47
Belgian (0)	48	0.50
British (11)	77	0.81
Canadian (11)	32	0.34
Croatian (0)	60	0.63
Czech (0)	52	0.55
Danish (12)	61	0.64
Dutch (951)	2,022	21.19
English (473)	1,684	17.65
European (160)	160	1.68
Finnish (74)	84	0.88
French, ex. Basque (25)	505	5.29
French Canadian (45)	65	0.68
German (784)	2,970	31.13
Greek (0)	76	0.80
Hungarian (0)	26	0.27
Irish (118)	1,246	13.06
Italian (36)	334	3.50
Lithuanian (9)	35	0.37
Norwegian (20)	136	1.43
Pennsylvania German (0)	11	0.12
Polish (271)	891	9.34
Portuguese (0)	58	0.61
Russian (8)	68	0.71
Scandinavian (10)	66	0.69
Scotch-Irish (30)	159	1.67
Scottish (11)	38	0.40
Slovak (12)	43	0.45
Swedish (10)	254	2.66
Swiss (0)	68	0.71
Ukrainian (0)	11	0.12
Welsh (0)	24	0.25

Hispanic Origin	Population	%
Hispanic or Latino (of any race)	202	2.03
Central American, ex. Mexican	7	0.07
Costa Rican	4	0.04
Guatemalan	1	0.01
Panamanian	2	0.02
Cuban	9	0.09
Dominican Republic	12	0.12
Mexican	138	1.39
Puerto Rican	16	0.16
South American	3	0.03
Argentinean	1	0.01
Bolivian	1	0.01
Chilean	1	0.01
Other Hispanic or Latino	17	0.17

Race*	Population	%
African-American/Black (43)	80	0.81
Not Hispanic (41)	76	0.77
Hispanic (2)	4	0.04
American Indian/Alaska Native (22)	77	0.78
Not Hispanic (18)	68	0.68
Hispanic (4)	9	0.09
Apache (5)	6	0.06
Canadian/French Am. Ind. (1)	2	0.02
Cherokee (0)	2	0.02
Chippewa (5)	18	0.18
Choctaw (1)	1	0.01
Cree (0)	1	0.01
Delaware (0)	4	0.04
Inupiat *(Alaska Native)* (1)	3	0.03
Iroquois (0)	2	0.02
Mexican American Ind. (1)	2	0.02
Navajo (1)	2	0.02
Ottawa (2)	4	0.04
Potawatomi (1)	7	0.07
South American Ind. (1)	1	0.01
Asian (73)	99	1.00
Not Hispanic (73)	96	0.97
Hispanic (0)	3	0.03
Chinese, ex. Taiwanese (15)	16	0.16
Filipino (18)	21	0.21
Indian (6)	6	0.06
Japanese (7)	14	0.14
Korean (9)	17	0.17
Pakistani (2)	3	0.03
Vietnamese (15)	15	0.15
Hawaii Native/Pacific Islander (2)	5	0.05
Not Hispanic (2)	4	0.04
Hispanic (0)	1	0.01
Guamanian/Chamorro (1)	1	0.01
Native Hawaiian (0)	2	0.02
White (9,617)	9,735	98.02
Not Hispanic (9,469)	9,579	96.45
Hispanic (148)	156	1.57

Allen Park

Place Type: City
County: Wayne
Population: 28,210†

Ancestry‡	Population	%
African, Sub-Saharan (28)	47	0.16
African (28)	47	0.16
Albanian (123)	123	0.43
American (984)	984	3.45
Arab (242)	357	1.25
Arab (11)	46	0.16
Egyptian (21)	21	0.07
Iraqi (0)	27	0.09
Lebanese (27)	44	0.15
Syrian (183)	219	0.77
Armenian (237)	281	0.98
Assyrian/Chaldean/Syriac (0)	27	0.09
Austrian (22)	96	0.34
Belgian (11)	78	0.27
British (0)	20	0.07
Bulgarian (0)	5	0.02
Canadian (102)	227	0.80
Croatian (22)	50	0.18
Czech (0)	94	0.33
Czechoslovakian (5)	52	0.18
Danish (14)	73	0.26
Dutch (229)	632	2.21
Eastern European (0)	6	0.02
English (643)	2,707	9.48
European (245)	253	0.89
Finnish (90)	166	0.58
French, ex. Basque (226)	1,621	5.68
French Canadian (194)	738	2.59
German (1,232)	6,656	23.32
Greek (91)	134	0.47
Hungarian (459)	1,456	5.10
Irish (1,183)	4,184	14.66
Italian (1,297)	3,129	10.96
Lithuanian (61)	138	0.48
Macedonian (77)	77	0.27
Maltese (121)	232	0.81

Notes: † The Census 2010 population figure is used to calculate the percentages in the Hispanic Origin and Race categories. Ancestry percentages are based on the 2006-2010 American Community Survey population (not shown); ‡ Numbers in parentheses indicate the number of people reporting a single ancestry; * Numbers in parentheses indicate the number of persons reporting this race alone, not in combination with any other race; Please refer to the Explanation of Data for more information.

Ancestry	Population	%
Northern European (18)	18	0.06
Norwegian (0)	117	0.41
Pennsylvania German (0)	10	0.04
Polish (1,709)	5,275	18.48
Romanian (75)	231	0.81
Russian (147)	302	1.06
Scandinavian (11)	11	0.04
Scotch-Irish (224)	842	2.95
Scottish (138)	861	3.02
Serbian (11)	45	0.16
Slavic (7)	79	0.28
Slovak (136)	238	0.83
Swedish (50)	267	0.94
Swiss (0)	44	0.15
Turkish (19)	19	0.07
Ukrainian (66)	103	0.36
Welsh (10)	79	0.28
West Indian, ex. Hispanic (0)	5	0.02
Dutch West Indian (0)	5	0.02
Yugoslavian (46)	61	0.21

Hispanic Origin	Population	%
Hispanic or Latino (of any race)	2,274	8.06
Central American, ex. Mexican	13	0.05
Costa Rican	1	<0.01
Guatemalan	6	0.02
Honduran	2	0.01
Nicaraguan	2	0.01
Salvadoran	2	0.01
Cuban	42	0.15
Dominican Republic	4	0.01
Mexican	1,864	6.61
Puerto Rican	199	0.71
South American	31	0.11
Argentinean	3	0.01
Chilean	7	0.02
Colombian	11	0.04
Ecuadorian	4	0.01
Peruvian	3	0.01
Venezuelan	1	<0.01
Other South American	2	0.01
Other Hispanic or Latino	121	0.43

Race*	Population	%
African-American/Black (604)	728	2.58
Not Hispanic (588)	696	2.47
Hispanic (16)	32	0.11
American Indian/Alaska Native (147)	307	1.09
Not Hispanic (120)	254	0.90
Hispanic (27)	53	0.19
Apache (6)	6	0.02
Blackfeet (0)	3	0.01
Canadian/French Am. Ind. (2)	5	0.02
Cherokee (20)	63	0.22
Chippewa (31)	49	0.17
Choctaw (9)	9	0.03
Creek (0)	3	0.01
Delaware (0)	1	<0.01
Iroquois (17)	28	0.10
Lumbee (6)	12	0.04
Menominee (0)	1	<0.01
Mexican American Ind. (0)	2	0.01
Navajo (1)	1	<0.01
Ottawa (5)	5	0.02
Potawatomi (0)	1	<0.01
Pueblo (2)	2	0.01
Sioux (1)	7	0.02
South American Ind. (1)	1	<0.01
Spanish American Ind. (1)	2	0.01
Asian (228)	326	1.16
Not Hispanic (223)	315	1.12
Hispanic (5)	11	0.04
Cambodian (0)	1	<0.01
Chinese, ex. Taiwanese (21)	36	0.13
Filipino (65)	89	0.32
Hmong (5)	5	0.02
Indian (49)	61	0.22
Japanese (23)	39	0.14
Korean (13)	18	0.06
Pakistani (8)	8	0.03
Thai (6)	9	0.03
Vietnamese (30)	41	0.15
Hawaii Native/Pacific Islander (9)	22	0.08
Not Hispanic (7)	17	0.06
Hispanic (2)	5	0.02
Guamanian/Chamorro (0)	2	0.01
Native Hawaiian (3)	7	0.02
Samoan (5)	6	0.02
White (26,204)	26,631	94.40
Not Hispanic (24,643)	24,963	88.49
Hispanic (1,561)	1,668	5.91

Allendale

Place Type: CDP
County: Ottawa
Population: 17,579†

Ancestry‡	Population	%
African, Sub-Saharan (0)	29	0.17
African (0)	29	0.17
American (492)	492	2.95
Arab (65)	130	0.78
Lebanese (65)	102	0.61
Palestinian (0)	15	0.09
Other Arab (0)	13	0.08
Australian (0)	14	0.08
Belgian (29)	50	0.30
Brazilian (10)	10	0.06
British (12)	43	0.26
Canadian (23)	71	0.43
Croatian (13)	27	0.16
Czech (0)	66	0.40
Czechoslovakian (0)	51	0.31
Danish (15)	83	0.50
Dutch (2,316)	4,184	25.13
Eastern European (11)	11	0.07
English (164)	1,552	9.32
European (202)	266	1.60
Finnish (46)	238	1.43
French, ex. Basque (77)	617	3.71
French Canadian (71)	297	1.78
German (803)	4,573	27.46
Greek (0)	27	0.16
Hungarian (54)	217	1.30
Iranian (16)	16	0.10
Irish (241)	1,917	11.51
Italian (89)	688	4.13
Latvian (0)	3	0.02
Lithuanian (26)	107	0.64
Norwegian (21)	184	1.10
Polish (508)	2,019	12.12
Portuguese (0)	25	0.15
Romanian (0)	27	0.16
Russian (14)	145	0.87
Scandinavian (11)	41	0.25
Scotch-Irish (59)	144	0.86
Scottish (0)	455	2.73
Slovak (0)	12	0.07
Swedish (74)	388	2.33
Swiss (0)	69	0.41
Turkish (34)	34	0.20
Ukrainian (0)	39	0.23
Welsh (24)	80	0.48
West Indian, ex. Hispanic (0)	27	0.16
Jamaican (0)	13	0.08
West Indian (0)	14	0.08
Yugoslavian (10)	23	0.14

Hispanic Origin	Population	%
Hispanic or Latino (of any race)	839	4.77
Central American, ex. Mexican	41	0.23
Costa Rican	3	0.02
Guatemalan	18	0.10
Honduran	13	0.07
Nicaraguan	1	0.01
Panamanian	3	0.02
Salvadoran	3	0.02
Cuban	38	0.22
Dominican Republic	8	0.05
Mexican	620	3.53
Puerto Rican	41	0.23
South American	29	0.16
Argentinean	4	0.02
Bolivian	2	0.01
Chilean	3	0.02
Colombian	7	0.04
Ecuadorian	2	0.01
Paraguayan	3	0.02
Peruvian	5	0.03
Venezuelan	3	0.02
Other Hispanic or Latino	62	0.35

Race*	Population	%
African-American/Black (574)	715	4.07
Not Hispanic (562)	689	3.92
Hispanic (12)	26	0.15
American Indian/Alaska Native (75)	191	1.09
Not Hispanic (53)	152	0.86
Hispanic (22)	39	0.22
Blackfeet (0)	2	0.01
Cherokee (1)	13	0.07
Chippewa (8)	21	0.12
Choctaw (5)	14	0.08
Colville (1)	1	0.01
Iroquois (1)	4	0.02
Lumbee (2)	2	0.01
Mexican American Ind. (1)	1	0.01
Ottawa (2)	11	0.06
Potawatomi (2)	11	0.06
Sioux (3)	7	0.04
South American Ind. (1)	1	0.01
Asian (255)	382	2.17
Not Hispanic (252)	372	2.12
Hispanic (3)	10	0.06
Bangladeshi (1)	2	0.01
Cambodian (4)	5	0.03
Chinese, ex. Taiwanese (50)	79	0.45
Filipino (27)	48	0.27
Hmong (6)	6	0.03
Indian (21)	28	0.16
Indonesian (1)	2	0.01
Japanese (9)	31	0.18
Korean (87)	108	0.61
Laotian (8)	10	0.06
Pakistani (0)	1	0.01
Sri Lankan (0)	1	0.01
Taiwanese (1)	1	0.01
Thai (2)	9	0.05
Vietnamese (26)	36	0.20
Hawaii Native/Pacific Islander (7)	18	0.10
Not Hispanic (7)	16	0.09
Hispanic (0)	2	0.01
Guamanian/Chamorro (1)	1	0.01
Marshallese (1)	1	0.01
Native Hawaiian (1)	9	0.05
White (15,937)	16,325	92.87
Not Hispanic (15,523)	15,839	90.10
Hispanic (414)	486	2.76

Allendale

Place Type: Charter Township
County: Ottawa
Population: 20,708†

Ancestry‡	Population	%
African, Sub-Saharan (0)	29	0.15
African (0)	29	0.15
American (560)	560	2.87
Arab (106)	171	0.88
Lebanese (65)	102	0.52
Palestinian (41)	56	0.29
Other Arab (0)	13	0.07
Australian (0)	14	0.07
Belgian (29)	65	0.33
Brazilian (10)	10	0.05
British (12)	43	0.22
Canadian (23)	71	0.36
Croatian (13)	27	0.14

*Notes: † The Census 2010 population figure is used to calculate the percentages in the Hispanic Origin and Race categories. Ancestry percentages are based on the 2006-2010 American Community Survey population (not shown); ‡ Numbers in parentheses indicate the number of people reporting a single ancestry; * Numbers in parentheses indicate the number of persons reporting this race alone, not in combination with any other race; Please refer to the Explanation of Data for more information.*

Ancestry	Population	%
Czech (0)	66	0.34
Czechoslovakian (0)	51	0.26
Danish (15)	83	0.43
Dutch (2,783)	4,973	25.50
Eastern European (11)	11	0.06
English (219)	1,759	9.02
European (202)	282	1.45
Finnish (46)	253	1.30
French, ex. Basque (102)	678	3.48
French Canadian (71)	297	1.52
German (928)	5,056	25.93
Greek (0)	27	0.14
Hungarian (54)	217	1.11
Iranian (16)	16	0.08
Irish (241)	2,132	10.93
Italian (135)	748	3.84
Latvian (0)	3	0.02
Lithuanian (26)	119	0.61
Norwegian (21)	184	0.94
Polish (517)	2,213	11.35
Portuguese (0)	25	0.13
Romanian (0)	27	0.14
Russian (14)	145	0.74
Scandinavian (11)	41	0.21
Scotch-Irish (71)	174	0.89
Scottish (0)	494	2.53
Slovak (0)	12	0.06
Swedish (74)	421	2.16
Swiss (0)	69	0.35
Turkish (34)	34	0.17
Ukrainian (0)	39	0.20
Welsh (24)	80	0.41
West Indian, ex. Hispanic (0)	27	0.14
Jamaican (0)	13	0.07
West Indian (0)	14	0.07
Yugoslavian (10)	23	0.12

Hispanic Origin	Population	%
Hispanic or Latino (of any race)	947	4.57
Central American, ex. Mexican	42	0.20
Costa Rican	3	0.01
Guatemalan	19	0.09
Honduran	13	0.06
Nicaraguan	1	<0.01
Panamanian	3	0.01
Salvadoran	3	0.01
Cuban	43	0.21
Dominican Republic	13	0.06
Mexican	696	3.36
Puerto Rican	50	0.24
South American	34	0.16
Argentinean	4	0.02
Bolivian	2	0.01
Chilean	3	0.01
Colombian	10	0.05
Ecuadorian	2	0.01
Paraguayan	3	0.01
Peruvian	7	0.03
Venezuelan	3	0.01
Other Hispanic or Latino	69	0.33

Race*	Population	%
African-American/Black (637)	792	3.82
Not Hispanic (625)	764	3.69
Hispanic (12)	28	0.14
American Indian/Alaska Native (84)	208	1.00
Not Hispanic (60)	167	0.81
Hispanic (24)	41	0.20
Blackfeet (0)	2	0.01
Cherokee (1)	15	0.07
Chippewa (9)	28	0.14
Choctaw (5)	14	0.07
Colville (1)	1	<0.01
Iroquois (1)	4	0.02
Lumbee (2)	2	0.01
Mexican American Ind. (3)	3	0.01
Ottawa (4)	13	0.06
Potawatomi (3)	12	0.06
Sioux (3)	8	0.04
South American Ind. (1)	1	<0.01
Asian (297)	446	2.15
Not Hispanic (289)	428	2.07
Hispanic (8)	18	0.09
Bangladeshi (1)	2	0.01
Cambodian (5)	6	0.03
Chinese, ex. Taiwanese (52)	85	0.41
Filipino (36)	62	0.30
Hmong (6)	6	0.03
Indian (23)	30	0.14
Indonesian (1)	3	0.01
Japanese (11)	34	0.16
Korean (112)	135	0.65
Laotian (9)	13	0.06
Pakistani (0)	1	<0.01
Sri Lankan (0)	1	<0.01
Taiwanese (1)	7	0.03
Thai (2)	9	0.04
Vietnamese (26)	36	0.17
Hawaii Native/Pacific Islander (7)	20	0.10
Not Hispanic (7)	18	0.09
Hispanic (0)	2	0.01
Guamanian/Chamorro (1)	1	<0.01
Marshallese (1)	1	<0.01
Native Hawaiian (1)	9	0.04
White (18,873)	19,301	93.21
Not Hispanic (18,399)	18,744	90.52
Hispanic (474)	557	2.69

Alma

Place Type: City
County: Gratiot
Population: 9,383†

Ancestry‡	Population	%
African, Sub-Saharan (4)	4	0.04
Nigerian (4)	4	0.04
Alsatian (0)	7	0.07
American (583)	583	6.21
Belgian (7)	44	0.47
British (8)	19	0.20
Canadian (10)	21	0.22
Czech (9)	33	0.35
Czechoslovakian (51)	67	0.71
Danish (7)	32	0.34
Dutch (141)	339	3.61
English (469)	1,105	11.78
European (103)	103	1.10
Finnish (0)	10	0.11
French, ex. Basque (77)	235	2.50
French Canadian (25)	46	0.49
German (896)	2,225	23.71
Greek (0)	51	0.54
Hungarian (25)	55	0.59
Irish (358)	971	10.35
Italian (51)	185	1.97
Norwegian (0)	58	0.62
Polish (174)	682	7.27
Romanian (27)	27	0.29
Russian (0)	11	0.12
Scandinavian (14)	67	0.71
Scotch-Irish (12)	52	0.55
Scottish (119)	290	3.09
Slavic (0)	10	0.11
Slovak (0)	12	0.13
Swedish (31)	112	1.19
Swiss (0)	51	0.54
Ukrainian (7)	35	0.37
Welsh (8)	43	0.46

Hispanic Origin	Population	%
Hispanic or Latino (of any race)	763	8.13
Central American, ex. Mexican	7	0.07
Costa Rican	1	0.01
Guatemalan	3	0.03
Nicaraguan	1	0.01
Salvadoran	2	0.02
Cuban	2	0.02
Mexican	652	6.95
Puerto Rican	26	0.28
South American	14	0.15
Argentinean	1	0.01
Chilean	2	0.02
Colombian	3	0.03
Ecuadorian	3	0.03
Peruvian	4	0.04
Uruguayan	1	0.01
Other Hispanic or Latino	62	0.66

Race*	Population	%
African-American/Black (81)	133	1.42
Not Hispanic (75)	115	1.23
Hispanic (6)	18	0.19
American Indian/Alaska Native (54)	129	1.37
Not Hispanic (48)	106	1.13
Hispanic (6)	23	0.25
Apache (0)	1	0.01
Blackfeet (0)	3	0.03
Canadian/French Am. Ind. (1)	2	0.02
Cherokee (3)	6	0.06
Chippewa (16)	31	0.33
Creek (6)	6	0.06
Iroquois (1)	6	0.06
Mexican American Ind. (3)	6	0.06
Potawatomi (0)	2	0.02
Sioux (0)	1	0.01
Ute (0)	1	0.01
Asian (71)	99	1.06
Not Hispanic (70)	91	0.97
Hispanic (1)	8	0.09
Bangladeshi (1)	1	0.01
Chinese, ex. Taiwanese (20)	21	0.22
Filipino (8)	16	0.17
Indian (20)	22	0.23
Indonesian (1)	1	0.01
Japanese (3)	14	0.15
Korean (12)	17	0.18
Vietnamese (6)	6	0.06
Hawaii Native/Pacific Islander (2)	10	0.11
Not Hispanic (2)	5	0.05
Hispanic (0)	5	0.05
Guamanian/Chamorro (0)	1	0.01
Native Hawaiian (0)	7	0.07
Samoan (1)	1	0.01
White (8,707)	8,903	94.88
Not Hispanic (8,303)	8,419	89.73
Hispanic (404)	484	5.16

Alpena

Place Type: City
County: Alpena
Population: 10,483†

Ancestry‡	Population	%
American (509)	509	4.78
Arab (0)	9	0.08
Lebanese (0)	9	0.08
Austrian (82)	102	0.96
British (0)	31	0.29
Canadian (78)	101	0.95
Croatian (8)	8	0.08
Czech (23)	73	0.69
Czechoslovakian (16)	16	0.15
Danish (0)	9	0.08
Dutch (8)	138	1.30
Eastern European (8)	8	0.08
English (378)	1,512	14.20
European (22)	42	0.39
Finnish (137)	226	2.12
French, ex. Basque (264)	1,327	12.46
French Canadian (93)	270	2.54
German (1,156)	3,410	32.02
Greek (0)	24	0.23
Hungarian (0)	6	0.06
Irish (267)	1,162	10.91
Italian (31)	325	3.05
Lithuanian (5)	31	0.29
Norwegian (213)	372	3.49
Polish (1,160)	2,416	22.69

SECTION TWO

*Notes: † The Census 2010 population figure is used to calculate the percentages in the Hispanic Origin and Race categories. Ancestry percentages are based on the 2006-2010 American Community Survey population (not shown); ‡ Numbers in parentheses indicate the number of people reporting a single ancestry; * Numbers in parentheses indicate the number of persons reporting this race alone, not in combination with any other race; Please refer to the Explanation of Data for more information.*

Russian (33)	87	0.82
Scandinavian (7)	7	0.07
Scotch-Irish (18)	150	1.41
Scottish (52)	197	1.85
Slavic (8)	17	0.16
Slovak (0)	8	0.08
Swedish (0)	106	1.00
Swiss (0)	9	0.08
Ukrainian (7)	7	0.07
Welsh (10)	40	0.38

Hispanic Origin	Population	%
Hispanic or Latino (of any race)	109	1.04
Central American, ex. Mexican	1	0.01
Guatemalan	1	0.01
Cuban	1	0.01
Dominican Republic	1	0.01
Mexican	71	0.68
Puerto Rican	13	0.12
South American	3	0.03
Chilean	1	0.01
Peruvian	2	0.02
Other Hispanic or Latino	19	0.18

Race*	Population	%
African-American/Black (48)	104	0.99
Not Hispanic (47)	103	0.98
Hispanic (1)	1	0.01
American Indian/Alaska Native (42)	108	1.03
Not Hispanic (39)	105	1.00
Hispanic (3)	3	0.03
Apache (1)	1	0.01
Canadian/French Am. Ind. (0)	1	0.01
Cherokee (4)	15	0.14
Chippewa (13)	29	0.28
Comanche (0)	4	0.04
Cree (0)	1	0.01
Delaware (0)	1	0.01
Mexican American Ind. (2)	2	0.02
Navajo (1)	1	0.01
Ottawa (6)	8	0.08
Potawatomi (1)	4	0.04
Sioux (1)	4	0.04
Asian (76)	100	0.95
Not Hispanic (76)	100	0.95
Chinese, ex. Taiwanese (25)	26	0.25
Filipino (24)	30	0.29
Indian (14)	22	0.21
Japanese (3)	9	0.09
Korean (5)	9	0.09
Thai (1)	1	0.01
Vietnamese (4)	6	0.06
Hawaii Native/Pacific Islander (7)	7	0.07
Not Hispanic (4)	4	0.04
Hispanic (3)	3	0.03
Guamanian/Chamorro (2)	2	0.02
Native Hawaiian (3)	3	0.03
White (10,147)	10,291	98.17
Not Hispanic (10,066)	10,203	97.33
Hispanic (81)	88	0.84

Alpena

Place Type: Township
County: Alpena
Population: 9,060†

Ancestry‡	Population	%
Albanian (13)	13	0.14
American (507)	507	5.51
Arab (0)	11	0.12
Lebanese (0)	11	0.12
Belgian (0)	34	0.37
British (16)	27	0.29
Canadian (7)	95	1.03
Czech (0)	9	0.10
Dutch (29)	108	1.17
English (284)	1,234	13.41
European (24)	24	0.26
Finnish (38)	67	0.73
French, ex. Basque (289)	1,308	14.21
French Canadian (130)	225	2.45
German (909)	3,018	32.80
Greek (20)	20	0.22
Hungarian (0)	13	0.14
Irish (222)	811	8.81
Italian (52)	328	3.56
Latvian (0)	10	0.11
Lithuanian (0)	12	0.13
Norwegian (73)	427	4.64
Pennsylvania German (0)	55	0.60
Polish (1,121)	2,473	26.87
Russian (22)	40	0.43
Scotch-Irish (40)	112	1.22
Scottish (35)	315	3.42
Swedish (16)	128	1.39
Swiss (0)	18	0.20
Ukrainian (0)	37	0.40
Welsh (0)	24	0.26

Hispanic Origin	Population	%
Hispanic or Latino (of any race)	92	1.02
Central American, ex. Mexican	1	0.01
Costa Rican	1	0.01
Cuban	4	0.04
Mexican	66	0.73
Puerto Rican	5	0.06
South American	7	0.08
Bolivian	2	0.02
Peruvian	2	0.02
Venezuelan	3	0.03
Other Hispanic or Latino	9	0.10

Race*	Population	%
African-American/Black (16)	31	0.34
Not Hispanic (16)	31	0.34
American Indian/Alaska Native (51)	118	1.30
Not Hispanic (49)	110	1.21
Hispanic (2)	8	0.09
Apache (0)	1	0.01
Cherokee (3)	8	0.09
Chippewa (21)	45	0.50
Inupiat *(Alaska Native)* (0)	4	0.04
Navajo (0)	2	0.02
Ottawa (4)	8	0.09
Potawatomi (5)	8	0.09
Puget Sound Salish (0)	1	0.01
Sioux (0)	6	0.07
Asian (52)	63	0.70
Not Hispanic (52)	61	0.67
Hispanic (0)	2	0.02
Chinese, ex. Taiwanese (5)	6	0.07
Filipino (14)	20	0.22
Hmong (8)	8	0.09
Indian (9)	9	0.10
Japanese (3)	5	0.06
Korean (6)	6	0.07
Malaysian (1)	1	0.01
Taiwanese (1)	1	0.01
Vietnamese (3)	3	0.03
Hawaii Native/Pacific Islander (3)	6	0.07
Not Hispanic (3)	6	0.07
Native Hawaiian (2)	2	0.02
White (8,828)	8,929	98.55
Not Hispanic (8,758)	8,845	97.63
Hispanic (70)	84	0.93

Alpine

Place Type: Township
County: Kent
Population: 13,336†

Ancestry‡	Population	%
African, Sub-Saharan (64)	64	0.47
African (64)	64	0.47
American (623)	623	4.62
Arab (10)	24	0.18
Lebanese (0)	14	0.10
Other Arab (10)	10	0.07
Armenian (76)	84	0.62
Austrian (0)	33	0.24
Belgian (15)	151	1.12
British (0)	14	0.10
Canadian (0)	41	0.30
Croatian (8)	34	0.25
Czech (0)	10	0.07
Danish (33)	89	0.66
Dutch (837)	1,999	14.82
English (262)	1,343	9.95
European (100)	100	0.74
Finnish (24)	69	0.51
French, ex. Basque (27)	365	2.71
French Canadian (41)	50	0.37
German (974)	2,969	22.01
Hungarian (12)	12	0.09
Irish (490)	1,991	14.76
Italian (69)	456	3.38
Lithuanian (37)	93	0.69
Norwegian (40)	91	0.67
Pennsylvania German (0)	32	0.24
Polish (467)	1,499	11.11
Russian (0)	64	0.47
Scotch-Irish (125)	336	2.49
Scottish (56)	146	1.08
Slovak (11)	11	0.08
Swedish (39)	372	2.76
Swiss (0)	52	0.39
Ukrainian (0)	15	0.11
Welsh (14)	38	0.28

Hispanic Origin	Population	%
Hispanic or Latino (of any race)	1,735	13.01
Central American, ex. Mexican	70	0.52
Costa Rican	3	0.02
Guatemalan	51	0.38
Honduran	11	0.08
Salvadoran	5	0.04
Cuban	29	0.22
Dominican Republic	13	0.10
Mexican	1,294	9.70
Puerto Rican	157	1.18
South American	10	0.07
Chilean	1	0.01
Ecuadorian	7	0.05
Venezuelan	2	0.01
Other Hispanic or Latino	162	1.21

Race*	Population	%
African-American/Black (824)	1,065	7.99
Not Hispanic (794)	983	7.37
Hispanic (30)	82	0.61
American Indian/Alaska Native (82)	217	1.63
Not Hispanic (46)	155	1.16
Hispanic (36)	62	0.46
Blackfeet (0)	8	0.06
Canadian/French Am. Ind. (1)	1	0.01
Cherokee (3)	16	0.12
Cheyenne (0)	1	0.01
Chippewa (11)	22	0.16
Inupiat *(Alaska Native)* (0)	2	0.01
Iroquois (0)	2	0.01
Mexican American Ind. (3)	3	0.02
Ottawa (13)	27	0.20
Potawatomi (8)	16	0.12
Seminole (0)	4	0.03
Sioux (0)	2	0.01
Yaqui (1)	1	0.01
Asian (135)	204	1.53
Not Hispanic (133)	192	1.44
Hispanic (2)	12	0.09
Burmese (0)	1	0.01
Chinese, ex. Taiwanese (9)	17	0.13
Filipino (18)	46	0.34
Hmong (3)	3	0.02
Indian (16)	19	0.14
Japanese (1)	8	0.06
Korean (21)	35	0.26
Laotian (3)	4	0.03
Malaysian (0)	1	0.01

*Notes: † The Census 2010 population figure is used to calculate the percentages in the Hispanic Origin and Race categories. Ancestry percentages are based on the 2006-2010 American Community Survey population (not shown); ‡ Numbers in parentheses indicate the number of people reporting a single ancestry; * Numbers in parentheses indicate the number of persons reporting this race alone, not in combination with any other race; Please refer to the Explanation of Data for more information.*

Nepalese (3)	3	0.02
Pakistani (7)	8	0.06
Thai (0)	1	0.01
Vietnamese (45)	54	0.40
Hawaii Native/Pacific Islander (5)	25	0.19
Not Hispanic (5)	15	0.11
Hispanic (0)	10	0.07
Fijian (1)	1	0.01
Guamanian/Chamorro (3)	7	0.05
Native Hawaiian (1)	7	0.05
White (10,927)	11,348	85.09
Not Hispanic (10,308)	10,586	79.38
Hispanic (619)	762	5.71

Ann Arbor

Place Type: City
County: Washtenaw
Population: 113,934†

Ancestry‡	Population	%
Afghan (13)	23	0.02
African, Sub-Saharan (1,060)	1,399	1.21
African (535)	809	0.70
Ethiopian (12)	59	0.05
Ghanaian (48)	48	0.04
Nigerian (338)	338	0.29
Somalian (2)	2	<0.01
South African (114)	123	0.11
Zimbabwean (0)	9	0.01
Other Sub-Saharan African (11)	11	0.01
Albanian (132)	162	0.14
Alsatian (0)	13	0.01
American (3,530)	3,530	3.06
Arab (1,620)	2,158	1.87
Arab (300)	327	0.28
Egyptian (166)	189	0.16
Iraqi (42)	67	0.06
Jordanian (104)	104	0.09
Lebanese (195)	367	0.32
Palestinian (353)	410	0.36
Syrian (10)	172	0.15
Other Arab (450)	522	0.45
Armenian (137)	274	0.24
Assyrian/Chaldean/Syriac (60)	60	0.05
Australian (33)	95	0.08
Austrian (154)	484	0.42
Basque (0)	12	0.01
Belgian (105)	605	0.53
Brazilian (120)	174	0.15
British (642)	1,287	1.12
Bulgarian (26)	32	0.03
Cajun (32)	32	0.03
Canadian (326)	638	0.55
Celtic (5)	24	0.02
Croatian (102)	216	0.19
Czech (194)	842	0.73
Czechoslovakian (9)	58	0.05
Danish (158)	721	0.63
Dutch (624)	2,277	1.98
Eastern European (649)	719	0.62
English (3,270)	13,447	11.67
Estonian (36)	36	0.03
European (2,470)	2,664	2.31
Finnish (173)	786	0.68
French, ex. Basque (597)	3,984	3.46
French Canadian (247)	1,281	1.11
German (6,586)	22,916	19.89
German Russian (0)	37	0.03
Greek (661)	1,161	1.01
Guyanese (9)	9	0.01
Hungarian (287)	1,847	1.60
Icelander (11)	78	0.07
Iranian (274)	336	0.29
Irish (3,015)	12,142	10.54
Israeli (73)	147	0.13
Italian (1,591)	5,212	4.52
Latvian (48)	136	0.12
Lithuanian (133)	450	0.39
Luxemburger (11)	26	0.02
Macedonian (24)	40	0.03
Maltese (39)	92	0.08
New Zealander (24)	24	0.02
Northern European (188)	203	0.18
Norwegian (308)	1,312	1.14
Pennsylvania German (44)	62	0.05
Polish (2,298)	7,858	6.82
Portuguese (22)	88	0.08
Romanian (364)	650	0.56
Russian (1,168)	3,214	2.79
Scandinavian (92)	229	0.20
Scotch-Irish (549)	2,326	2.02
Scottish (652)	3,574	3.10
Serbian (106)	166	0.14
Slavic (7)	64	0.06
Slovak (136)	270	0.23
Slovene (19)	67	0.06
Swedish (523)	2,065	1.79
Swiss (62)	537	0.47
Turkish (278)	373	0.32
Ukrainian (223)	607	0.53
Welsh (112)	1,064	0.92
West Indian, ex. Hispanic (228)	380	0.33
Bahamian (12)	12	0.01
Barbadian (0)	16	0.01
British West Indian (11)	35	0.03
Haitian (4)	14	0.01
Jamaican (121)	181	0.16
Trinidadian/Tobagonian (25)	58	0.05
West Indian (55)	64	0.06
Yugoslavian (60)	112	0.10

Hispanic Origin	Population	%
Hispanic or Latino (of any race)	4,666	4.10
Central American, ex. Mexican	394	0.35
Costa Rican	43	0.04
Guatemalan	130	0.11
Honduran	54	0.05
Nicaraguan	41	0.04
Panamanian	52	0.05
Salvadoran	74	0.06
Cuban	226	0.20
Dominican Republic	78	0.07
Mexican	2,056	1.80
Puerto Rican	466	0.41
South American	963	0.85
Argentinean	169	0.15
Bolivian	46	0.04
Chilean	87	0.08
Colombian	292	0.26
Ecuadorian	73	0.06
Paraguayan	4	<0.01
Peruvian	162	0.14
Uruguayan	19	0.02
Venezuelan	108	0.09
Other South American	3	<0.01
Other Hispanic or Latino	483	0.42

Race*	Population	%
African-American/Black (8,804)	10,363	9.10
Not Hispanic (8,658)	10,057	8.83
Hispanic (146)	306	0.27
American Indian/Alaska Native (301)	1,110	0.97
Not Hispanic (224)	885	0.78
Hispanic (77)	225	0.20
Alaska Athabascan *(Ala. Nat.)* (3)	4	<0.01
Apache (3)	12	0.01
Arapaho (0)	2	<0.01
Blackfeet (8)	36	0.03
Canadian/French Am. Ind. (6)	16	0.01
Central American Ind. (0)	1	<0.01
Cherokee (9)	161	0.14
Chickasaw (1)	6	0.01
Chippewa (46)	125	0.11
Choctaw (8)	12	0.01
Comanche (1)	4	<0.01
Cree (2)	14	0.01
Creek (7)	21	0.02
Crow (0)	3	<0.01
Delaware (1)	3	<0.01
Hopi (0)	1	<0.01
Inupiat *(Alaska Native)* (0)	3	<0.01
Iroquois (10)	23	0.02
Lumbee (4)	14	0.01
Menominee (3)	4	<0.01
Mexican American Ind. (26)	48	0.04
Navajo (6)	8	0.01
Ottawa (8)	18	0.02
Paiute (1)	1	<0.01
Potawatomi (11)	17	0.01
Pueblo (1)	1	<0.01
Puget Sound Salish (4)	4	<0.01
Seminole (0)	3	<0.01
Shoshone (4)	4	<0.01
Sioux (6)	19	0.02
South American Ind. (6)	22	0.02
Tlingit-Haida *(Alaska Native)* (0)	1	<0.01
Tohono O'Odham (1)	1	<0.01
Yaqui (0)	1	<0.01
Yup'ik *(Alaska Native)* (0)	1	<0.01
Asian (16,353)	18,345	16.10
Not Hispanic (16,293)	18,205	15.98
Hispanic (60)	140	0.12
Bangladeshi (90)	102	0.09
Burmese (9)	16	0.01
Cambodian (19)	29	0.03
Chinese, ex. Taiwanese (5,938)	6,555	5.75
Filipino (341)	580	0.51
Hmong (17)	17	0.01
Indian (3,826)	4,216	3.70
Indonesian (57)	83	0.07
Japanese (1,048)	1,428	1.25
Korean (2,924)	3,159	2.77
Laotian (7)	12	0.01
Malaysian (65)	81	0.07
Nepalese (25)	29	0.03
Pakistani (283)	324	0.28
Sri Lankan (66)	77	0.07
Taiwanese (788)	858	0.75
Thai (124)	168	0.15
Vietnamese (320)	395	0.35
Hawaii Native/Pacific Islander (38)	144	0.13
Not Hispanic (34)	126	0.11
Hispanic (4)	18	0.02
Fijian (1)	2	<0.01
Guamanian/Chamorro (10)	21	0.02
Marshallese (2)	8	0.01
Native Hawaiian (8)	36	0.03
Samoan (6)	9	0.01
Tongan (5)	6	0.01
White (83,171)	86,809	76.19
Not Hispanic (80,158)	83,380	73.18
Hispanic (3,013)	3,429	3.01

Antwerp

Place Type: Township
County: Van Buren
Population: 12,182†

Ancestry‡	Population	%
African, Sub-Saharan (0)	13	0.11
African (0)	13	0.11
American (1,088)	1,088	9.07
Arab (33)	64	0.53
Arab (0)	31	0.26
Lebanese (33)	33	0.28
Austrian (0)	15	0.13
Belgian (0)	9	0.08
Canadian (50)	92	0.77
Croatian (32)	75	0.63
Czech (23)	36	0.30
Czechoslovakian (4)	8	0.07
Danish (11)	67	0.56
Dutch (463)	1,481	12.35
English (337)	1,498	12.49
European (194)	194	1.62
Finnish (14)	58	0.48
French, ex. Basque (11)	370	3.09
French Canadian (74)	194	1.62

*Notes: † The Census 2010 population figure is used to calculate the percentages in the Hispanic Origin and Race categories. Ancestry percentages are based on the 2006-2010 American Community Survey population (not shown); ‡ Numbers in parentheses indicate the number of people reporting a single ancestry; * Numbers in parentheses indicate the number of persons reporting this race alone, not in combination with any other race; Please refer to the Explanation of Data for more information.*

Ancestry	Population	%
German (984)	3,726	31.07
Greek (30)	61	0.51
Hungarian (3)	85	0.71
Irish (421)	1,988	16.58
Italian (128)	486	4.05
Latvian (6)	6	0.05
Lithuanian (12)	34	0.28
Macedonian (24)	24	0.20
Northern European (13)	13	0.11
Norwegian (25)	84	0.70
Pennsylvania German (38)	38	0.32
Polish (284)	889	7.41
Russian (3)	3	0.03
Scandinavian (9)	56	0.47
Scotch-Irish (61)	186	1.55
Scottish (82)	385	3.21
Slovak (22)	64	0.53
Swedish (25)	197	1.64
Swiss (17)	42	0.35
Ukrainian (4)	69	0.58
Welsh (10)	39	0.33
Yugoslavian (3)	3	0.03

Hispanic Origin	Population	%
Hispanic or Latino (of any race)	630	5.17
Central American, ex. Mexican	14	0.11
Guatemalan	7	0.06
Honduran	1	0.01
Panamanian	5	0.04
Salvadoran	1	0.01
Cuban	8	0.07
Dominican Republic	3	0.02
Mexican	547	4.49
Puerto Rican	19	0.16
South American	2	0.02
Chilean	1	0.01
Colombian	1	0.01
Other Hispanic or Latino	37	0.30

Race*	Population	%
African-American/Black (129)	227	1.86
Not Hispanic (122)	215	1.76
Hispanic (7)	12	0.10
American Indian/Alaska Native (55)	138	1.13
Not Hispanic (40)	118	0.97
Hispanic (15)	20	0.16
Alaska Athabascan *(Ala. Nat.)* (0)	2	0.02
Blackfeet (1)	2	0.02
Cherokee (6)	28	0.23
Chippewa (10)	22	0.18
Comanche (0)	1	0.01
Creek (0)	2	0.02
Crow (0)	1	0.01
Mexican American Ind. (6)	6	0.05
Ottawa (6)	7	0.06
Potawatomi (12)	25	0.21
Sioux (1)	1	0.01
Spanish American Ind. (1)	1	0.01
Asian (50)	108	0.89
Not Hispanic (48)	101	0.83
Hispanic (2)	7	0.06
Bangladeshi (2)	2	0.02
Chinese, ex. Taiwanese (7)	13	0.11
Filipino (3)	17	0.14
Indian (11)	13	0.11
Indonesian (0)	1	0.01
Japanese (3)	11	0.09
Korean (15)	30	0.25
Pakistani (0)	2	0.02
Taiwanese (2)	2	0.02
Thai (0)	6	0.05
Vietnamese (3)	6	0.05
Hawaii Native/Pacific Islander (2)	6	0.05
Not Hispanic (2)	6	0.05
Native Hawaiian (1)	1	0.01
Samoan (1)	3	0.02
White (11,450)	11,696	96.01
Not Hispanic (11,123)	11,332	93.02
Hispanic (327)	364	2.99

Ash

Place Type: Township
County: Monroe
Population: 7,783†

Ancestry‡	Population	%
American (513)	513	6.53
Arab (7)	14	0.18
Syrian (7)	14	0.18
Armenian (18)	18	0.23
Australian (0)	6	0.08
Austrian (0)	11	0.14
Belgian (0)	16	0.20
Brazilian (0)	13	0.17
British (10)	21	0.27
Canadian (0)	6	0.08
Celtic (6)	6	0.08
Croatian (0)	28	0.36
Czech (9)	21	0.27
Czechoslovakian (9)	9	0.11
Dutch (49)	135	1.72
English (276)	729	9.29
European (13)	13	0.17
Finnish (21)	135	1.72
French, ex. Basque (79)	724	9.22
French Canadian (271)	441	5.62
German (457)	1,991	25.36
Greek (55)	55	0.70
Hungarian (148)	312	3.97
Irish (110)	858	10.93
Italian (190)	408	5.20
Lithuanian (0)	40	0.51
Maltese (11)	22	0.28
Norwegian (0)	26	0.33
Polish (247)	981	12.50
Romanian (10)	26	0.33
Russian (9)	31	0.39
Scotch-Irish (88)	230	2.93
Scottish (95)	324	4.13
Serbian (11)	39	0.50
Swedish (10)	141	1.80
Swiss (0)	25	0.32
Ukrainian (0)	59	0.75
Welsh (0)	19	0.24
West Indian, ex. Hispanic (0)	10	0.13
Dutch West Indian (0)	10	0.13
Yugoslavian (0)	10	0.13

Hispanic Origin	Population	%
Hispanic or Latino (of any race)	158	2.03
Central American, ex. Mexican	3	0.04
Guatemalan	2	0.03
Honduran	1	0.01
Mexican	125	1.61
Puerto Rican	11	0.14
South American	1	0.01
Argentinean	1	0.01
Other Hispanic or Latino	18	0.23

Race*	Population	%
African-American/Black (55)	92	1.18
Not Hispanic (55)	91	1.17
Hispanic (0)	1	0.01
American Indian/Alaska Native (23)	78	1.00
Not Hispanic (19)	70	0.90
Hispanic (4)	8	0.10
Blackfeet (0)	3	0.04
Cherokee (4)	21	0.27
Chickasaw (1)	1	0.01
Chippewa (4)	9	0.12
Creek (0)	1	0.01
Iroquois (3)	3	0.04
Lumbee (2)	3	0.04
Mexican American Ind. (3)	3	0.04
Ottawa (0)	3	0.04
Sioux (2)	2	0.03
Asian (29)	41	0.53
Not Hispanic (29)	41	0.53
Chinese, ex. Taiwanese (10)	10	0.13
Filipino (7)	16	0.21
Japanese (1)	2	0.03
Korean (6)	8	0.10
Thai (1)	1	0.01
Vietnamese (2)	2	0.03
Hawaii Native/Pacific Islander (2)	3	0.04
Not Hispanic (2)	3	0.04
Guamanian/Chamorro (2)	2	0.03
Samoan (0)	1	0.01
White (7,548)	7,657	98.38
Not Hispanic (7,416)	7,516	96.57
Hispanic (132)	141	1.81

Atlas

Place Type: Township
County: Genesee
Population: 7,993†

Ancestry‡	Population	%
American (643)	643	8.09
Arab (56)	56	0.70
Palestinian (56)	56	0.70
Assyrian/Chaldean/Syriac (16)	16	0.20
Austrian (0)	3	0.04
Belgian (3)	68	0.86
British (19)	41	0.52
Canadian (31)	31	0.39
Czech (0)	19	0.24
Danish (5)	28	0.35
Dutch (115)	186	2.34
English (286)	1,037	13.05
European (69)	69	0.87
Finnish (7)	48	0.60
French, ex. Basque (22)	342	4.30
French Canadian (35)	169	2.13
German (355)	1,809	22.76
Greek (18)	18	0.23
Hungarian (9)	60	0.75
Irish (275)	1,173	14.76
Italian (97)	283	3.56
Lithuanian (0)	72	0.91
Norwegian (88)	135	1.70
Polish (232)	743	9.35
Romanian (4)	21	0.26
Russian (52)	95	1.20
Scotch-Irish (48)	202	2.54
Scottish (37)	288	3.62
Serbian (0)	6	0.08
Slovak (7)	28	0.35
Swedish (3)	29	0.36
Swiss (0)	79	0.99
Ukrainian (0)	14	0.18
Welsh (0)	26	0.33

Hispanic Origin	Population	%
Hispanic or Latino (of any race)	166	2.08
Central American, ex. Mexican	7	0.09
Guatemalan	2	0.03
Honduran	5	0.06
Cuban	4	0.05
Mexican	110	1.38
Puerto Rican	22	0.28
South American	10	0.13
Argentinean	2	0.03
Paraguayan	1	0.01
Venezuelan	7	0.09
Other Hispanic or Latino	13	0.16

Race*	Population	%
African-American/Black (53)	77	0.96
Not Hispanic (53)	68	0.85
Hispanic (0)	9	0.11
American Indian/Alaska Native (17)	42	0.53
Not Hispanic (17)	42	0.53
Blackfeet (0)	1	0.01
Cherokee (3)	16	0.20
Chippewa (9)	11	0.14
Choctaw (0)	1	0.01
Iroquois (1)	2	0.03

*Notes: † The Census 2010 population figure is used to calculate the percentages in the Hispanic Origin and Race categories. Ancestry percentages are based on the 2006-2010 American Community Survey population (not shown); ‡ Numbers in parentheses indicate the number of people reporting a single ancestry; * Numbers in parentheses indicate the number of persons reporting this race alone, not in combination with any other race; Please refer to the Explanation of Data for more information.*

Lumbee (1)	1	0.01
Ottawa (0)	1	0.01
Asian (59)	84	1.05
Not Hispanic (58)	80	1.00
Hispanic (1)	4	0.05
Chinese, ex. Taiwanese (4)	5	0.06
Filipino (14)	20	0.25
Hmong (7)	8	0.10
Indian (23)	26	0.33
Japanese (1)	7	0.09
Korean (9)	14	0.18
Pakistani (0)	3	0.04
Thai (1)	1	0.01
White (7,760)	7,823	97.87
Not Hispanic (7,640)	7,695	96.27
Hispanic (120)	128	1.60

Auburn Hills

Place Type: City
County: Oakland
Population: 21,412†

Ancestry‡	Population	%
African, Sub-Saharan (17)	28	0.13
African (17)	28	0.13
Albanian (16)	16	0.08
American (620)	620	2.93
Arab (106)	262	1.24
Arab (27)	27	0.13
Egyptian (22)	44	0.21
Jordanian (29)	110	0.52
Lebanese (28)	81	0.38
Armenian (9)	9	0.04
Assyrian/Chaldean/Syriac (26)	28	0.13
Australian (1)	1	<0.01
Austrian (0)	21	0.10
Belgian (38)	171	0.81
British (0)	29	0.14
Canadian (33)	138	0.65
Croatian (10)	40	0.19
Czech (0)	21	0.10
Danish (0)	31	0.15
Dutch (193)	570	2.69
English (510)	1,776	8.39
European (123)	157	0.74
Finnish (63)	178	0.84
French, ex. Basque (219)	896	4.23
French Canadian (88)	346	1.64
German (1,083)	4,310	20.37
Greek (39)	157	0.74
Hungarian (41)	99	0.47
Icelander (0)	20	0.09
Iranian (20)	20	0.09
Irish (408)	2,206	10.42
Italian (487)	1,261	5.96
Lithuanian (9)	107	0.51
Macedonian (11)	11	0.05
Norwegian (33)	53	0.25
Polish (791)	2,025	9.57
Portuguese (10)	27	0.13
Romanian (104)	171	0.81
Russian (30)	95	0.45
Scandinavian (0)	35	0.17
Scotch-Irish (148)	295	1.39
Scottish (106)	454	2.15
Slavic (43)	43	0.20
Slovak (0)	19	0.09
Slovene (0)	28	0.13
Swedish (0)	163	0.77
Swiss (0)	10	0.05
Ukrainian (7)	60	0.28
Welsh (46)	172	0.81
West Indian, ex. Hispanic (38)	104	0.49
Haitian (15)	15	0.07
Jamaican (23)	89	0.42
Yugoslavian (0)	27	0.13

Hispanic Origin	Population	%
Hispanic or Latino (of any race)	1,676	7.83
Central American, ex. Mexican	59	0.28
Costa Rican	3	0.01
Guatemalan	6	0.03
Honduran	13	0.06
Nicaraguan	3	0.01
Panamanian	1	<0.01
Salvadoran	33	0.15
Cuban	12	0.06
Dominican Republic	3	0.01
Mexican	1,232	5.75
Puerto Rican	228	1.06
South American	49	0.23
Argentinean	14	0.07
Chilean	2	0.01
Colombian	13	0.06
Ecuadorian	7	0.03
Peruvian	10	0.05
Venezuelan	3	0.01
Other Hispanic or Latino	93	0.43

Race*	Population	%
African-American/Black (3,959)	4,350	20.32
Not Hispanic (3,881)	4,229	19.75
Hispanic (78)	121	0.57
American Indian/Alaska Native (60)	226	1.06
Not Hispanic (54)	196	0.92
Hispanic (6)	30	0.14
Blackfeet (3)	8	0.04
Canadian/French Am. Ind. (1)	3	0.01
Cherokee (3)	32	0.15
Chippewa (16)	28	0.13
Choctaw (1)	3	0.01
Cree (0)	10	0.05
Creek (0)	1	<0.01
Crow (0)	1	<0.01
Inupiat *(Alaska Native)* (0)	1	<0.01
Iroquois (3)	4	0.02
Lumbee (0)	1	<0.01
Mexican American Ind. (1)	2	0.01
Navajo (0)	3	0.01
Osage (1)	1	<0.01
Ottawa (1)	7	0.03
Potawatomi (5)	5	0.02
Sioux (0)	2	0.01
South American Ind. (1)	2	0.01
Yaqui (1)	3	0.01
Asian (1,896)	2,116	9.88
Not Hispanic (1,888)	2,092	9.77
Hispanic (8)	24	0.11
Bangladeshi (12)	12	0.06
Burmese (2)	2	0.01
Cambodian (3)	4	0.02
Chinese, ex. Taiwanese (206)	234	1.09
Filipino (122)	176	0.82
Hmong (36)	42	0.20
Indian (1,250)	1,275	5.95
Indonesian (1)	1	<0.01
Japanese (20)	47	0.22
Korean (92)	111	0.52
Laotian (8)	12	0.06
Malaysian (1)	1	<0.01
Nepalese (9)	9	0.04
Pakistani (54)	58	0.27
Sri Lankan (2)	2	0.01
Taiwanese (13)	14	0.07
Thai (0)	3	0.01
Vietnamese (28)	35	0.16
Hawaii Native/Pacific Islander (8)	26	0.12
Not Hispanic (8)	23	0.11
Hispanic (0)	3	0.01
Native Hawaiian (2)	12	0.06
Samoan (0)	1	<0.01
White (14,196)	14,787	69.06
Not Hispanic (13,279)	13,770	64.31
Hispanic (917)	1,017	4.75

Bangor

Place Type: Charter Township
County: Bay
Population: 14,641†

Ancestry‡	Population	%
American (757)	757	5.11
Arab (11)	30	0.20
Egyptian (0)	12	0.08
Lebanese (11)	18	0.12
Austrian (7)	25	0.17
Belgian (0)	11	0.07
British (27)	78	0.53
Bulgarian (0)	8	0.05
Canadian (47)	104	0.70
Croatian (17)	28	0.19
Czech (0)	69	0.47
Czechoslovakian (46)	46	0.31
Dutch (139)	409	2.76
English (341)	1,230	8.31
Finnish (10)	102	0.69
French, ex. Basque (332)	2,012	13.59
French Canadian (321)	701	4.74
German (2,039)	4,899	33.09
Hungarian (17)	91	0.61
Irish (571)	1,807	12.21
Italian (51)	203	1.37
Lithuanian (10)	10	0.07
Norwegian (6)	112	0.76
Pennsylvania German (12)	12	0.08
Polish (1,272)	2,815	19.02
Romanian (0)	10	0.07
Russian (11)	77	0.52
Scandinavian (36)	36	0.24
Scotch-Irish (150)	318	2.15
Scottish (128)	354	2.39
Serbian (0)	12	0.08
Slovak (0)	10	0.07
Slovene (0)	11	0.07
Swedish (40)	234	1.58
Swiss (0)	37	0.25
Ukrainian (0)	11	0.07
Welsh (10)	51	0.34
Yugoslavian (3)	3	0.02

Hispanic Origin	Population	%
Hispanic or Latino (of any race)	567	3.87
Central American, ex. Mexican	7	0.05
Costa Rican	2	0.01
Guatemalan	1	0.01
Honduran	1	0.01
Panamanian	2	0.01
Salvadoran	1	0.01
Cuban	5	0.03
Dominican Republic	1	0.01
Mexican	469	3.20
Puerto Rican	11	0.08
South American	9	0.06
Argentinean	1	0.01
Chilean	5	0.03
Colombian	1	0.01
Peruvian	1	0.01
Venezuelan	1	0.01
Other Hispanic or Latino	65	0.44

Race*	Population	%
African-American/Black (129)	223	1.52
Not Hispanic (120)	201	1.37
Hispanic (9)	22	0.15
American Indian/Alaska Native (81)	174	1.19
Not Hispanic (73)	144	0.98
Hispanic (8)	30	0.20
Apache (0)	1	0.01
Blackfeet (1)	2	0.01
Canadian/French Am. Ind. (4)	7	0.05
Cherokee (2)	12	0.08
Cheyenne (0)	1	0.01
Chippewa (26)	48	0.33
Choctaw (0)	4	0.03

SECTION TWO

*Notes: † The Census 2010 population figure is used to calculate the percentages in the Hispanic Origin and Race categories. Ancestry percentages are based on the 2006-2010 American Community Survey population (not shown); ‡ Numbers in parentheses indicate the number of people reporting a single ancestry; * Numbers in parentheses indicate the number of persons reporting this race alone, not in combination with any other race; Please refer to the Explanation of Data for more information.*

Cree (0)	2	0.01
Hopi (2)	3	0.02
Iroquois (4)	4	0.03
Kiowa (0)	4	0.03
Mexican American Ind. (0)	3	0.02
Navajo (0)	1	0.01
Ottawa (6)	13	0.09
Potawatomi (2)	2	0.01
Asian (116)	144	0.98
Not Hispanic (116)	141	0.96
Hispanic (0)	3	0.02
Chinese, ex. Taiwanese (20)	22	0.15
Filipino (17)	25	0.17
Hmong (6)	6	0.04
Indian (15)	15	0.10
Indonesian (1)	2	0.01
Japanese (5)	11	0.08
Korean (9)	14	0.10
Nepalese (2)	2	0.01
Pakistani (13)	13	0.09
Thai (1)	1	0.01
Vietnamese (27)	28	0.19
Hawaii Native/Pacific Islander (2)	5	0.03
Not Hispanic (2)	5	0.03
Native Hawaiian (1)	1	0.01
Samoan (1)	1	0.01
White (13,933)	14,181	96.86
Not Hispanic (13,580)	13,754	93.94
Hispanic (353)	427	2.92

Bath

Place Type: Charter Township
County: Clinton
Population: 11,598†

Ancestry‡	Population	%
African, Sub-Saharan (0)	54	0.49
African (0)	54	0.49
American (1,467)	1,467	13.36
Arab (0)	100	0.91
Lebanese (0)	70	0.64
Syrian (0)	30	0.27
Armenian (11)	11	0.10
Australian (0)	45	0.41
Austrian (12)	23	0.21
Belgian (0)	11	0.10
British (10)	32	0.29
Canadian (0)	13	0.12
Croatian (0)	11	0.10
Czech (12)	93	0.85
Czechoslovakian (0)	26	0.24
Danish (12)	98	0.89
Dutch (136)	501	4.56
English (352)	1,472	13.41
European (59)	105	0.96
Finnish (46)	112	1.02
French, ex. Basque (24)	271	2.47
French Canadian (37)	99	0.90
German (816)	3,340	30.43
Greek (0)	10	0.09
Hungarian (38)	148	1.35
Irish (406)	1,887	17.19
Italian (161)	487	4.44
Lithuanian (0)	22	0.20
Northern European (23)	23	0.21
Norwegian (65)	141	1.28
Polish (258)	742	6.76
Russian (25)	135	1.23
Scotch-Irish (30)	324	2.95
Scottish (35)	297	2.71
Swedish (24)	234	2.13
Swiss (0)	206	1.88
Welsh (12)	127	1.16
Yugoslavian (11)	11	0.10

Hispanic Origin	Population	%
Hispanic or Latino (of any race)	391	3.37
Central American, ex. Mexican	11	0.09
Costa Rican	1	0.01
Guatemalan	6	0.05
Nicaraguan	3	0.03
Panamanian	1	0.01
Cuban	16	0.14
Dominican Republic	4	0.03
Mexican	274	2.36
Puerto Rican	17	0.15
South American	26	0.22
Argentinean	12	0.10
Chilean	1	0.01
Colombian	4	0.03
Ecuadorian	4	0.03
Peruvian	2	0.02
Venezuelan	3	0.03
Other Hispanic or Latino	43	0.37

Race*	Population	%
African-American/Black (606)	704	6.07
Not Hispanic (601)	695	5.99
Hispanic (5)	9	0.08
American Indian/Alaska Native (46)	107	0.92
Not Hispanic (45)	102	0.88
Hispanic (1)	5	0.04
Cherokee (6)	18	0.16
Cheyenne (0)	2	0.02
Chippewa (16)	22	0.19
Inupiat *(Alaska Native)* (1)	1	0.01
Iroquois (0)	1	0.01
Ottawa (10)	13	0.11
Pima (1)	1	0.01
South American Ind. (0)	2	0.02
Tlingit-Haida *(Alaska Native)* (2)	2	0.02
Asian (414)	508	4.38
Not Hispanic (413)	506	4.36
Hispanic (1)	2	0.02
Chinese, ex. Taiwanese (133)	147	1.27
Filipino (21)	49	0.42
Hmong (19)	19	0.16
Indian (82)	96	0.83
Indonesian (0)	1	0.01
Japanese (12)	22	0.19
Korean (104)	120	1.03
Malaysian (1)	3	0.03
Pakistani (5)	5	0.04
Sri Lankan (3)	3	0.03
Taiwanese (1)	2	0.02
Thai (2)	3	0.03
Vietnamese (18)	22	0.19
Hawaii Native/Pacific Islander (3)	4	0.03
Not Hispanic (3)	4	0.03
Native Hawaiian (1)	1	0.01
White (10,146)	10,399	89.66
Not Hispanic (9,900)	10,118	87.24
Hispanic (246)	281	2.42

Battle Creek

Place Type: City
County: Calhoun
Population: 52,347†

Ancestry‡	Population	%
African, Sub-Saharan (76)	138	0.26
African (35)	97	0.18
Kenyan (9)	9	0.02
Ugandan (9)	9	0.02
Zimbabwean (23)	23	0.04
Albanian (9)	9	0.02
American (3,106)	3,106	5.89
Arab (50)	50	0.09
Arab (41)	41	0.08
Moroccan (9)	9	0.02
Australian (0)	13	0.02
Austrian (0)	18	0.03
Basque (10)	10	0.02
Belgian (9)	19	0.04
Brazilian (24)	24	0.05
British (84)	179	0.34
Bulgarian (43)	43	0.08
Canadian (83)	182	0.34
Celtic (6)	6	0.01
Croatian (29)	44	0.08
Czech (23)	112	0.21
Czechoslovakian (0)	18	0.03
Danish (10)	122	0.23
Dutch (532)	1,828	3.46
English (2,259)	6,221	11.79
European (276)	319	0.60
Finnish (79)	178	0.34
French, ex. Basque (255)	1,741	3.30
French Canadian (261)	513	0.97
German (4,195)	10,192	19.32
Greek (69)	130	0.25
Hungarian (101)	265	0.50
Iranian (6)	6	0.01
Irish (1,611)	5,662	10.73
Italian (381)	942	1.79
Latvian (11)	34	0.06
Lithuanian (0)	92	0.17
Macedonian (100)	194	0.37
Maltese (0)	37	0.07
Norwegian (167)	311	0.59
Pennsylvania German (13)	81	0.15
Polish (452)	1,512	2.87
Portuguese (93)	101	0.19
Russian (56)	171	0.32
Scandinavian (50)	106	0.20
Scotch-Irish (280)	661	1.25
Scottish (186)	754	1.43
Serbian (0)	28	0.05
Slavic (0)	9	0.02
Slovak (0)	165	0.31
Swedish (136)	455	0.86
Swiss (58)	73	0.14
Turkish (12)	12	0.02
Ukrainian (34)	47	0.09
Welsh (22)	207	0.39
West Indian, ex. Hispanic (101)	109	0.21
Barbadian (51)	51	0.10
Jamaican (0)	8	0.02
Trinidadian/Tobagonian (50)	50	0.09
Yugoslavian (56)	70	0.13

Hispanic Origin	Population	%
Hispanic or Latino (of any race)	3,517	6.72
Central American, ex. Mexican	37	0.07
Costa Rican	8	0.02
Guatemalan	12	0.02
Honduran	3	0.01
Panamanian	12	0.02
Salvadoran	2	<0.01
Cuban	52	0.10
Dominican Republic	26	0.05
Mexican	2,713	5.18
Puerto Rican	245	0.47
South American	68	0.13
Argentinean	1	<0.01
Chilean	1	<0.01
Colombian	34	0.06
Ecuadorian	4	0.01
Peruvian	24	0.05
Venezuelan	4	0.01
Other Hispanic or Latino	376	0.72

Race*	Population	%
African-American/Black (9,502)	11,026	21.06
Not Hispanic (9,347)	10,733	20.50
Hispanic (155)	293	0.56
American Indian/Alaska Native (377)	941	1.80
Not Hispanic (292)	796	1.52
Hispanic (85)	145	0.28
Alaska Athabascan *(Ala. Nat.)* (5)	6	0.01
Aleut *(Alaska Native)* (0)	2	<0.01
Apache (6)	19	0.04
Blackfeet (5)	55	0.11
Canadian/French Am. Ind. (1)	3	0.01
Cherokee (26)	165	0.32
Cheyenne (0)	2	<0.01
Chippewa (46)	77	0.15
Choctaw (0)	4	0.01

*Notes: † The Census 2010 population figure is used to calculate the percentages in the Hispanic Origin and Race categories. Ancestry percentages are based on the 2006-2010 American Community Survey population (not shown); ‡ Numbers in parentheses indicate the number of people reporting a single ancestry; * Numbers in parentheses indicate the number of persons reporting this race alone, not in combination with any other race; Please refer to the Explanation of Data for more information.*

Comanche (0)	1	<0.01
Cree (0)	4	0.01
Creek (0)	3	0.01
Crow (0)	6	0.01
Hopi (1)	2	<0.01
Houma (1)	1	<0.01
Iroquois (3)	9	0.02
Lumbee (1)	2	<0.01
Mexican American Ind. (9)	15	0.03
Navajo (4)	7	0.01
Ottawa (32)	42	0.08
Potawatomi (43)	81	0.15
Pueblo (0)	1	<0.01
Puget Sound Salish (3)	3	0.01
Seminole (0)	1	<0.01
Sioux (6)	18	0.03
South American Ind. (2)	3	0.01
Tlingit-Haida *(Alaska Native)* (0)	1	<0.01
Ute (1)	1	<0.01
Yaqui (5)	5	0.01
Asian (1,271)	1,518	2.90
Not Hispanic (1,254)	1,482	2.83
Hispanic (17)	36	0.07
Bangladeshi (5)	5	0.01
Burmese (285)	301	0.58
Cambodian (1)	1	<0.01
Chinese, ex. Taiwanese (120)	143	0.27
Filipino (112)	159	0.30
Indian (279)	325	0.62
Indonesian (8)	21	0.04
Japanese (254)	313	0.60
Korean (82)	120	0.23
Laotian (1)	2	<0.01
Pakistani (2)	2	<0.01
Taiwanese (2)	2	<0.01
Thai (10)	21	0.04
Vietnamese (49)	57	0.11
Hawaii Native/Pacific Islander (16)	83	0.16
Not Hispanic (15)	68	0.13
Hispanic (1)	15	0.03
Guamanian/Chamorro (6)	14	0.03
Native Hawaiian (2)	19	0.04
Samoan (3)	15	0.03
White (37,522)	39,558	75.57
Not Hispanic (35,911)	37,693	72.01
Hispanic (1,611)	1,865	3.56

Bay City

Place Type: City
County: Bay
Population: 34,932†

Ancestry‡	Population	%
African, Sub-Saharan (157)	217	0.62
African (96)	156	0.44
Ethiopian (9)	9	0.03
Kenyan (52)	52	0.15
Albanian (18)	33	0.09
American (1,195)	1,195	3.39
Arab (47)	105	0.30
Arab (47)	57	0.16
Lebanese (0)	48	0.14
Armenian (53)	64	0.18
Australian (0)	15	0.04
Austrian (21)	70	0.20
Belgian (0)	80	0.23
British (12)	48	0.14
Bulgarian (29)	38	0.11
Canadian (255)	382	1.08
Croatian (11)	35	0.10
Czech (19)	206	0.58
Czechoslovakian (0)	8	0.02
Danish (13)	49	0.14
Dutch (282)	1,153	3.27
Eastern European (0)	11	0.03
English (927)	3,106	8.82
European (108)	108	0.31
Finnish (67)	105	0.30
French, ex. Basque (879)	4,212	11.95
French Canadian (555)	1,289	3.66
German (3,584)	9,482	26.91
German Russian (11)	11	0.03
Greek (45)	247	0.70
Hungarian (169)	503	1.43
Irish (1,410)	4,315	12.25
Italian (529)	1,250	3.55
Lithuanian (10)	22	0.06
Northern European (16)	16	0.05
Norwegian (47)	115	0.33
Pennsylvania German (0)	12	0.03
Polish (3,235)	7,089	20.12
Portuguese (10)	10	0.03
Russian (26)	116	0.33
Scandinavian (0)	16	0.05
Scotch-Irish (170)	552	1.57
Scottish (208)	734	2.08
Slovak (9)	16	0.05
Slovene (0)	12	0.03
Swedish (21)	199	0.56
Swiss (23)	134	0.38
Ukrainian (27)	79	0.22
Welsh (19)	148	0.42
Yugoslavian (12)	12	0.03

Hispanic Origin	Population	%
Hispanic or Latino (of any race)	2,970	8.50
Central American, ex. Mexican	15	0.04
Costa Rican	3	0.01
Guatemalan	6	0.02
Honduran	2	0.01
Panamanian	3	0.01
Salvadoran	1	<0.01
Cuban	19	0.05
Dominican Republic	6	0.02
Mexican	2,603	7.45
Puerto Rican	53	0.15
South American	13	0.04
Argentinean	1	<0.01
Colombian	6	0.02
Ecuadorian	2	0.01
Paraguayan	2	0.01
Venezuelan	2	0.01
Other Hispanic or Latino	261	0.75

Race*	Population	%
African-American/Black (1,222)	1,908	5.46
Not Hispanic (1,117)	1,712	4.90
Hispanic (105)	196	0.56
American Indian/Alaska Native (224)	647	1.85
Not Hispanic (172)	501	1.43
Hispanic (52)	146	0.42
Aleut *(Alaska Native)* (1)	4	0.01
Apache (0)	7	0.02
Blackfeet (1)	17	0.05
Canadian/French Am. Ind. (1)	8	0.02
Cherokee (16)	65	0.19
Chickasaw (0)	3	0.01
Chippewa (93)	212	0.61
Choctaw (1)	3	0.01
Comanche (0)	3	0.01
Cree (1)	1	<0.01
Hopi (0)	3	0.01
Iroquois (2)	8	0.02
Lumbee (0)	3	0.01
Menominee (1)	1	<0.01
Mexican American Ind. (8)	11	0.03
Navajo (1)	3	0.01
Ottawa (5)	25	0.07
Potawatomi (3)	6	0.02
Pueblo (0)	5	0.01
Sioux (1)	7	0.02
Asian (159)	260	0.74
Not Hispanic (156)	237	0.68
Hispanic (3)	23	0.07
Cambodian (6)	6	0.02
Chinese, ex. Taiwanese (33)	41	0.12
Filipino (21)	44	0.13
Hmong (4)	5	0.01
Indian (12)	20	0.06
Indonesian (3)	5	0.01
Japanese (3)	12	0.03
Korean (31)	55	0.16
Laotian (10)	13	0.04
Nepalese (1)	3	0.01
Pakistani (2)	3	0.01
Thai (7)	16	0.05
Vietnamese (18)	24	0.07
Hawaii Native/Pacific Islander (5)	12	0.03
Not Hispanic (4)	8	0.02
Hispanic (1)	4	0.01
Native Hawaiian (2)	5	0.01
Samoan (2)	5	0.01
White (31,319)	32,639	93.44
Not Hispanic (29,532)	30,468	87.22
Hispanic (1,787)	2,171	6.21

Bedford

Place Type: Charter Township
County: Calhoun
Population: 9,357†

Ancestry‡	Population	%
Albanian (11)	11	0.12
American (871)	871	9.22
Arab (73)	80	0.85
Arab (0)	7	0.07
Lebanese (73)	73	0.77
Australian (0)	60	0.63
Austrian (0)	22	0.23
Belgian (0)	103	1.09
British (9)	19	0.20
Croatian (0)	9	0.10
Czech (0)	23	0.24
Danish (21)	50	0.53
Dutch (337)	684	7.24
English (315)	1,098	11.62
French, ex. Basque (44)	350	3.70
French Canadian (21)	101	1.07
German (730)	2,033	21.52
Greek (48)	48	0.51
Hungarian (20)	31	0.33
Irish (265)	907	9.60
Italian (138)	271	2.87
Macedonian (0)	17	0.18
Northern European (19)	19	0.20
Norwegian (12)	47	0.50
Pennsylvania German (0)	9	0.10
Polish (140)	405	4.29
Russian (25)	25	0.26
Scotch-Irish (68)	164	1.74
Scottish (31)	309	3.27
Swedish (108)	161	1.70
Swiss (0)	20	0.21
Welsh (34)	142	1.50
Yugoslavian (12)	28	0.30

Hispanic Origin	Population	%
Hispanic or Latino (of any race)	287	3.07
Central American, ex. Mexican	2	0.02
Salvadoran	2	0.02
Dominican Republic	4	0.04
Mexican	200	2.14
Puerto Rican	48	0.51
South American	1	0.01
Colombian	1	0.01
Other Hispanic or Latino	32	0.34

Race*	Population	%
African-American/Black (1,018)	1,165	12.45
Not Hispanic (1,012)	1,151	12.30
Hispanic (6)	14	0.15
American Indian/Alaska Native (45)	165	1.76
Not Hispanic (41)	152	1.62
Hispanic (4)	13	0.14
Blackfeet (0)	7	0.07
Cherokee (5)	38	0.41
Chippewa (12)	14	0.15
Choctaw (0)	1	0.01

*Notes: † The Census 2010 population figure is used to calculate the percentages in the Hispanic Origin and Race categories. Ancestry percentages are based on the 2006-2010 American Community Survey population (not shown); ‡ Numbers in parentheses indicate the number of people reporting a single ancestry; * Numbers in parentheses indicate the number of persons reporting this race alone, not in combination with any other race; Please refer to the Explanation of Data for more information.*

SECTION TWO

Iroquois (0)	2	0.02
Mexican American Ind. (2)	2	0.02
Ottawa (1)	1	0.01
Potawatomi (2)	10	0.11
Seminole (0)	1	0.01
Sioux (1)	8	0.09
Spanish American Ind. (0)	1	0.01
Asian (40)	75	0.80
Not Hispanic (40)	75	0.80
Burmese (0)	4	0.04
Chinese, ex. Taiwanese (0)	1	0.01
Filipino (11)	25	0.27
Indian (11)	14	0.15
Japanese (9)	15	0.16
Korean (5)	8	0.09
Laotian (0)	3	0.03
Thai (2)	2	0.02
Vietnamese (1)	1	0.01
Hawaii Native/Pacific Islander (5)	17	0.18
Not Hispanic (5)	17	0.18
Native Hawaiian (0)	3	0.03
Samoan (0)	1	0.01
White (7,848)	8,109	86.66
Not Hispanic (7,691)	7,931	84.76
Hispanic (157)	178	1.90

Bedford

Place Type: Township
County: Monroe
Population: 31,085†

Ancestry‡	Population	%
African, Sub-Saharan (0)	37	0.12
African (0)	37	0.12
Alsatian (0)	12	0.04
American (1,120)	1,120	3.60
Arab (199)	334	1.07
Arab (43)	54	0.17
Iraqi (68)	68	0.22
Jordanian (13)	13	0.04
Lebanese (64)	143	0.46
Syrian (11)	56	0.18
Austrian (0)	27	0.09
Belgian (31)	76	0.24
British (63)	265	0.85
Bulgarian (19)	51	0.16
Canadian (45)	89	0.29
Czech (16)	93	0.30
Czechoslovakian (43)	83	0.27
Danish (35)	55	0.18
Dutch (172)	796	2.56
English (728)	3,212	10.33
Estonian (0)	15	0.05
European (309)	318	1.02
Finnish (45)	132	0.42
French, ex. Basque (483)	3,123	10.04
French Canadian (61)	519	1.67
German (3,982)	12,816	41.22
Greek (50)	181	0.58
Hungarian (257)	780	2.51
Irish (928)	5,456	17.55
Israeli (49)	49	0.16
Italian (535)	1,948	6.27
Lithuanian (16)	16	0.05
Macedonian (17)	38	0.12
Norwegian (104)	178	0.57
Pennsylvania German (16)	16	0.05
Polish (1,844)	4,992	16.06
Romanian (33)	42	0.14
Russian (43)	199	0.64
Scandinavian (20)	59	0.19
Scotch-Irish (185)	430	1.38
Scottish (185)	674	2.17
Serbian (9)	20	0.06
Slovak (15)	101	0.32
Slovene (0)	13	0.04
Swedish (21)	224	0.72
Swiss (0)	137	0.44
Ukrainian (10)	36	0.12
Welsh (44)	174	0.56
West Indian, ex. Hispanic (0)	37	0.12
Jamaican (0)	37	0.12
Yugoslavian (11)	62	0.20

Hispanic Origin	Population	%
Hispanic or Latino (of any race)	787	2.53
Central American, ex. Mexican	22	0.07
Costa Rican	5	0.02
Guatemalan	9	0.03
Nicaraguan	1	<0.01
Panamanian	6	0.02
Salvadoran	1	<0.01
Cuban	25	0.08
Mexican	602	1.94
Puerto Rican	45	0.14
South American	16	0.05
Argentinean	2	0.01
Bolivian	2	0.01
Chilean	1	<0.01
Colombian	2	0.01
Paraguayan	1	<0.01
Peruvian	4	0.01
Venezuelan	4	0.01
Other Hispanic or Latino	77	0.25

Race*	Population	%
African-American/Black (159)	262	0.84
Not Hispanic (155)	247	0.79
Hispanic (4)	15	0.05
American Indian/Alaska Native (72)	211	0.68
Not Hispanic (56)	179	0.58
Hispanic (16)	32	0.10
Apache (5)	8	0.03
Blackfeet (1)	5	0.02
Canadian/French Am. Ind. (1)	3	0.01
Cherokee (14)	68	0.22
Chippewa (10)	18	0.06
Comanche (0)	2	0.01
Cree (0)	1	<0.01
Crow (0)	1	<0.01
Iroquois (1)	3	0.01
Kiowa (1)	3	0.01
Lumbee (1)	3	0.01
Menominee (0)	1	<0.01
Mexican American Ind. (2)	6	0.02
Navajo (0)	2	0.01
Ottawa (4)	6	0.02
Potawatomi (0)	2	0.01
Seminole (2)	2	0.01
Sioux (2)	4	0.01
South American Ind. (0)	1	<0.01
Asian (256)	329	1.06
Not Hispanic (254)	326	1.05
Hispanic (2)	3	0.01
Cambodian (2)	2	0.01
Chinese, ex. Taiwanese (48)	53	0.17
Filipino (39)	59	0.19
Indian (63)	74	0.24
Indonesian (3)	4	0.01
Japanese (8)	20	0.06
Korean (50)	61	0.20
Laotian (1)	2	0.01
Malaysian (4)	4	0.01
Pakistani (1)	1	<0.01
Taiwanese (4)	4	0.01
Thai (3)	4	0.01
Vietnamese (19)	20	0.06
Hawaii Native/Pacific Islander (7)	20	0.06
Not Hispanic (7)	20	0.06
Native Hawaiian (1)	3	0.01
Samoan (2)	8	0.03
White (30,010)	30,372	97.71
Not Hispanic (29,507)	29,794	95.85
Hispanic (503)	578	1.86

Beecher

Place Type: CDP
County: Genesee
Population: 10,232†

Ancestry‡	Population	%
African, Sub-Saharan (166)	166	1.40
African (166)	166	1.40
American (356)	356	3.01
Arab (0)	31	0.26
Arab (0)	31	0.26
Canadian (9)	28	0.24
Dutch (15)	48	0.41
English (51)	249	2.10
European (8)	8	0.07
French, ex. Basque (0)	124	1.05
French Canadian (14)	45	0.38
German (147)	379	3.20
Irish (185)	539	4.55
Italian (55)	200	1.69
Norwegian (0)	11	0.09
Polish (7)	66	0.56
Scandinavian (0)	9	0.08
Scotch-Irish (39)	51	0.43
Scottish (28)	68	0.57
Slovak (0)	8	0.07
West Indian, ex. Hispanic (0)	53	0.45
Haitian (0)	27	0.23
Jamaican (0)	26	0.22

Hispanic Origin	Population	%
Hispanic or Latino (of any race)	362	3.54
Central American, ex. Mexican	1	0.01
Panamanian	1	0.01
Cuban	9	0.09
Mexican	290	2.83
Puerto Rican	26	0.25
South American	5	0.05
Colombian	5	0.05
Other Hispanic or Latino	31	0.30

Race*	Population	%
African-American/Black (7,071)	7,346	71.79
Not Hispanic (7,011)	7,264	70.99
Hispanic (60)	82	0.80
American Indian/Alaska Native (85)	201	1.96
Not Hispanic (74)	181	1.77
Hispanic (11)	20	0.20
Blackfeet (0)	9	0.09
Cherokee (8)	36	0.35
Chickasaw (0)	4	0.04
Chippewa (15)	21	0.21
Choctaw (1)	1	0.01
Cree (0)	3	0.03
Creek (0)	4	0.04
Inupiat *(Alaska Native)* (1)	1	0.01
Iroquois (1)	2	0.02
Mexican American Ind. (5)	8	0.08
Navajo (1)	2	0.02
Ottawa (3)	6	0.06
Potawatomi (1)	3	0.03
Seminole (0)	1	0.01
Sioux (1)	2	0.02
Spanish American Ind. (1)	3	0.03
Asian (12)	27	0.26
Not Hispanic (12)	26	0.25
Hispanic (0)	1	0.01
Chinese, ex. Taiwanese (2)	6	0.06
Filipino (0)	1	0.01
Indian (4)	11	0.11
Japanese (1)	2	0.02
Korean (0)	1	0.01
Thai (4)	4	0.04
Vietnamese (1)	1	0.01
Hawaii Native/Pacific Islander (1)	7	0.07
Not Hispanic (1)	7	0.07
Native Hawaiian (1)	6	0.06
White (2,592)	2,870	28.05
Not Hispanic (2,428)	2,686	26.25

*Notes: † The Census 2010 population figure is used to calculate the percentages in the Hispanic Origin and Race categories. Ancestry percentages are based on the 2006-2010 American Community Survey population (not shown); ‡ Numbers in parentheses indicate the number of people reporting a single ancestry; * Numbers in parentheses indicate the number of persons reporting this race alone, not in combination with any other race; Please refer to the Explanation of Data for more information.*

Hispanic (164)	184	1.80

Benton Harbor

Place Type: City
County: Berrien
Population: 10,038†

Ancestry‡	Population	%
African, Sub-Saharan (121)	121	1.18
African (121)	121	1.18
American (52)	52	0.51
Dutch (0)	89	0.87
English (66)	174	1.70
French, ex. Basque (0)	24	0.23
French Canadian (4)	14	0.14
German (242)	504	4.91
Irish (0)	46	0.45
Polish (19)	19	0.19
Russian (0)	11	0.11
Scotch-Irish (34)	48	0.47
Swedish (0)	11	0.11
West Indian, ex. Hispanic (0)	54	0.53
Jamaican (0)	54	0.53

Hispanic Origin	Population	%
Hispanic or Latino (of any race)	220	2.19
Cuban	4	0.04
Dominican Republic	1	0.01
Mexican	169	1.68
Puerto Rican	14	0.14
South American	1	0.01
Argentinean	1	0.01
Other Hispanic or Latino	31	0.31

Race*	Population	%
African-American/Black (8,952)	9,170	91.35
Not Hispanic (8,899)	9,101	90.67
Hispanic (53)	69	0.69
American Indian/Alaska Native (32)	126	1.26
Not Hispanic (30)	119	1.19
Hispanic (2)	7	0.07
Blackfeet (0)	1	0.01
Cherokee (1)	23	0.23
Chickasaw (0)	1	0.01
Chippewa (2)	2	0.02
Choctaw (0)	12	0.12
Ottawa (1)	2	0.02
Potawatomi (13)	14	0.14
Asian (6)	32	0.32
Not Hispanic (6)	30	0.30
Hispanic (0)	2	0.02
Filipino (1)	1	0.01
Indian (0)	7	0.07
Japanese (1)	7	0.07
Korean (4)	4	0.04
Hawaii Native/Pacific Islander (5)	9	0.09
Not Hispanic (4)	7	0.07
Hispanic (1)	2	0.02
Native Hawaiian (1)	3	0.03
Samoan (0)	1	0.01
Tongan (4)	4	0.04
White (701)	889	8.86
Not Hispanic (641)	801	7.98
Hispanic (60)	88	0.88

Benton

Place Type: Charter Township
County: Berrien
Population: 14,749†

Ancestry‡	Population	%
African, Sub-Saharan (129)	144	0.96
African (109)	124	0.83
Zimbabwean (8)	8	0.05
Other Sub-Saharan African (12)	12	0.08
American (539)	539	3.60
Armenian (12)	12	0.08
Austrian (0)	7	0.05
Belgian (0)	10	0.07
Canadian (19)	25	0.17
Czech (14)	72	0.48
Danish (0)	11	0.07
Dutch (94)	423	2.83
English (138)	486	3.25
European (52)	52	0.35
Finnish (9)	76	0.51
French, ex. Basque (20)	179	1.20
French Canadian (30)	59	0.39
German (1,143)	2,512	16.80
Greek (26)	26	0.17
Hungarian (35)	58	0.39
Irish (183)	1,432	9.58
Italian (105)	393	2.63
Lithuanian (12)	12	0.08
Maltese (12)	12	0.08
Norwegian (10)	10	0.07
Pennsylvania German (0)	21	0.14
Polish (99)	286	1.91
Romanian (8)	16	0.11
Russian (5)	14	0.09
Scotch-Irish (36)	49	0.33
Scottish (16)	178	1.19
Slovene (30)	30	0.20
Swedish (31)	50	0.33
Ukrainian (13)	25	0.17
Welsh (0)	50	0.33
West Indian, ex. Hispanic (11)	11	0.07
Jamaican (11)	11	0.07

Hispanic Origin	Population	%
Hispanic or Latino (of any race)	882	5.98
Central American, ex. Mexican	21	0.14
Costa Rican	1	0.01
Guatemalan	4	0.03
Honduran	6	0.04
Panamanian	4	0.03
Salvadoran	6	0.04
Cuban	17	0.12
Dominican Republic	1	0.01
Mexican	720	4.88
Puerto Rican	42	0.28
South American	9	0.06
Colombian	2	0.01
Peruvian	6	0.04
Uruguayan	1	0.01
Other Hispanic or Latino	72	0.49

Race*	Population	%
African-American/Black (7,625)	7,902	53.58
Not Hispanic (7,566)	7,819	53.01
Hispanic (59)	83	0.56
American Indian/Alaska Native (76)	194	1.32
Not Hispanic (71)	176	1.19
Hispanic (5)	18	0.12
Apache (1)	1	0.01
Blackfeet (0)	6	0.04
Cherokee (8)	31	0.21
Chippewa (5)	9	0.06
Choctaw (3)	3	0.02
Houma (1)	1	0.01
Iroquois (1)	1	0.01
Ottawa (0)	1	0.01
Potawatomi (25)	42	0.28
Sioux (1)	1	0.01
South American Ind. (4)	4	0.03
Asian (58)	98	0.66
Not Hispanic (47)	68	0.46
Hispanic (11)	30	0.20
Bangladeshi (5)	5	0.03
Chinese, ex. Taiwanese (5)	11	0.07
Filipino (15)	26	0.18
Indian (17)	24	0.16
Japanese (2)	8	0.05
Korean (3)	4	0.03
Laotian (0)	1	0.01
Pakistani (1)	1	0.01
Thai (1)	1	0.01
Vietnamese (8)	10	0.07
Hawaii Native/Pacific Islander (0)	21	0.14
Not Hispanic (0)	9	0.06
Hispanic (0)	12	0.08
Fijian (0)	1	0.01
Guamanian/Chamorro (0)	2	0.01
Native Hawaiian (0)	9	0.06
White (6,189)	6,486	43.98
Not Hispanic (5,858)	6,109	41.42
Hispanic (331)	377	2.56

Berkley

Place Type: City
County: Oakland
Population: 14,970†

Ancestry‡	Population	%
African, Sub-Saharan (30)	30	0.20
African (30)	30	0.20
Albanian (0)	11	0.07
American (474)	474	3.15
Arab (59)	97	0.64
Arab (0)	9	0.06
Lebanese (59)	76	0.50
Other Arab (0)	12	0.08
Armenian (56)	84	0.56
Assyrian/Chaldean/Syriac (73)	73	0.48
Austrian (23)	108	0.72
Belgian (24)	88	0.58
Brazilian (0)	8	0.05
British (7)	39	0.26
Bulgarian (11)	11	0.07
Canadian (92)	105	0.70
Croatian (13)	54	0.36
Czech (11)	60	0.40
Czechoslovakian (19)	19	0.13
Danish (57)	156	1.04
Dutch (14)	324	2.15
Eastern European (38)	38	0.25
English (877)	2,415	16.03
European (182)	218	1.45
Finnish (53)	360	2.39
French, ex. Basque (103)	864	5.74
French Canadian (173)	483	3.21
German (919)	4,549	30.20
Greek (21)	65	0.43
Hungarian (25)	159	1.06
Icelander (11)	32	0.21
Irish (791)	2,677	17.77
Italian (320)	1,501	9.96
Lithuanian (41)	52	0.35
Macedonian (0)	9	0.06
Maltese (21)	30	0.20
Northern European (0)	29	0.19
Norwegian (42)	121	0.80
Polish (657)	2,246	14.91
Portuguese (22)	30	0.20
Romanian (57)	103	0.68
Russian (83)	310	2.06
Scandinavian (21)	70	0.46
Scotch-Irish (122)	464	3.08
Scottish (90)	573	3.80
Serbian (10)	10	0.07
Slavic (14)	14	0.09
Slovak (9)	51	0.34
Swedish (38)	255	1.69
Swiss (9)	19	0.13
Ukrainian (26)	48	0.32
Welsh (0)	176	1.17
Yugoslavian (0)	57	0.38

Hispanic Origin	Population	%
Hispanic or Latino (of any race)	275	1.84
Central American, ex. Mexican	16	0.11
Costa Rican	6	0.04
Guatemalan	7	0.05
Nicaraguan	1	0.01
Panamanian	2	0.01
Cuban	15	0.10
Mexican	167	1.12

*Notes: † The Census 2010 population figure is used to calculate the percentages in the Hispanic Origin and Race categories. Ancestry percentages are based on the 2006-2010 American Community Survey population (not shown); ‡ Numbers in parentheses indicate the number of people reporting a single ancestry; * Numbers in parentheses indicate the number of persons reporting this race alone, not in combination with any other race; Please refer to the Explanation of Data for more information.*

	Population	%
Puerto Rican	21	0.14
South American	21	0.14
Argentinean	5	0.03
Colombian	12	0.08
Ecuadorian	1	0.01
Paraguayan	2	0.01
Peruvian	1	0.01
Other Hispanic or Latino	35	0.23

Race*	Population	%
African-American/Black (453)	565	3.77
Not Hispanic (439)	544	3.63
Hispanic (14)	21	0.14
American Indian/Alaska Native (39)	121	0.81
Not Hispanic (39)	113	0.75
Hispanic (0)	8	0.05
Canadian/French Am. Ind. (2)	4	0.03
Central American Ind. (0)	2	0.01
Cherokee (0)	19	0.13
Chippewa (14)	26	0.17
Choctaw (1)	3	0.02
Comanche (0)	1	0.01
Creek (1)	1	0.01
Delaware (0)	1	0.01
Inupiat *(Alaska Native)* (0)	1	0.01
Iroquois (5)	10	0.07
Lumbee (0)	1	0.01
Mexican American Ind. (0)	2	0.01
Ottawa (1)	1	0.01
Potawatomi (1)	2	0.01
Shoshone (0)	2	0.01
Sioux (1)	1	0.01
Spanish American Ind. (0)	2	0.01
Asian (196)	291	1.94
Not Hispanic (190)	285	1.90
Hispanic (6)	6	0.04
Bangladeshi (5)	5	0.03
Cambodian (5)	6	0.04
Chinese, ex. Taiwanese (36)	51	0.34
Filipino (35)	59	0.39
Indian (29)	38	0.25
Indonesian (0)	1	0.01
Japanese (16)	30	0.20
Korean (27)	44	0.29
Pakistani (14)	14	0.09
Taiwanese (5)	6	0.04
Thai (5)	5	0.03
Vietnamese (11)	12	0.08
Hawaii Native/Pacific Islander (13)	21	0.14
Not Hispanic (8)	16	0.11
Hispanic (5)	5	0.03
Fijian (1)	1	0.01
Guamanian/Chamorro (5)	5	0.03
Native Hawaiian (2)	4	0.03
Samoan (2)	2	0.01
White (13,960)	14,202	94.87
Not Hispanic (13,757)	13,980	93.39
Hispanic (203)	222	1.48

Berlin

Place Type: Charter Township
County: Monroe
Population: 9,299†

Ancestry‡	Population	%
American (541)	541	6.02
Arab (3)	11	0.12
Lebanese (3)	3	0.03
Syrian (0)	8	0.09
Austrian (0)	39	0.43
Belgian (9)	24	0.27
Cajun (7)	7	0.08
Canadian (7)	45	0.50
Croatian (0)	3	0.03
Czech (31)	38	0.42
Czechoslovakian (0)	15	0.17
Danish (7)	9	0.10
Dutch (16)	117	1.30
English (174)	556	6.19
European (101)	113	1.26
Finnish (15)	15	0.17
French, ex. Basque (377)	1,421	15.82
French Canadian (102)	273	3.04
German (525)	2,405	26.78
Greek (51)	71	0.79
Hungarian (117)	392	4.37
Irish (195)	1,377	15.33
Italian (175)	425	4.73
Lithuanian (15)	30	0.33
Maltese (19)	21	0.23
Norwegian (28)	76	0.85
Pennsylvania German (0)	10	0.11
Polish (258)	787	8.76
Portuguese (0)	10	0.11
Romanian (3)	33	0.37
Russian (2)	36	0.40
Scandinavian (5)	7	0.08
Scotch-Irish (62)	208	2.32
Scottish (132)	312	3.47
Serbian (8)	42	0.47
Slavic (0)	3	0.03
Slovak (8)	95	1.06
Swedish (20)	148	1.65
Turkish (0)	21	0.23
Ukrainian (0)	7	0.08
Welsh (0)	31	0.35
Yugoslavian (0)	26	0.29

Hispanic Origin	Population	%
Hispanic or Latino (of any race)	298	3.20
Central American, ex. Mexican	1	0.01
Costa Rican	1	0.01
Cuban	3	0.03
Mexican	253	2.72
Puerto Rican	12	0.13
South American	2	0.02
Paraguayan	2	0.02
Other Hispanic or Latino	27	0.29

Race*	Population	%
African-American/Black (125)	160	1.72
Not Hispanic (125)	159	1.71
Hispanic (0)	1	0.01
American Indian/Alaska Native (21)	74	0.80
Not Hispanic (17)	58	0.62
Hispanic (4)	16	0.17
Apache (3)	6	0.06
Canadian/French Am. Ind. (0)	1	0.01
Cherokee (0)	4	0.04
Chippewa (7)	11	0.12
Creek (0)	1	0.01
Menominee (1)	1	0.01
Mexican American Ind. (0)	3	0.03
Ottawa (0)	2	0.02
Potawatomi (3)	3	0.03
Asian (25)	44	0.47
Not Hispanic (25)	42	0.45
Hispanic (0)	2	0.02
Chinese, ex. Taiwanese (2)	6	0.06
Filipino (4)	9	0.10
Indian (6)	7	0.08
Japanese (4)	10	0.11
Korean (6)	6	0.06
Pakistani (2)	2	0.02
Vietnamese (0)	4	0.04
Hawaii Native/Pacific Islander (0)	1	0.01
Not Hispanic (0)	1	0.01
Native Hawaiian (0)	1	0.01
White (8,953)	9,067	97.51
Not Hispanic (8,742)	8,827	94.92
Hispanic (211)	240	2.58

Beverly Hills

Place Type: Village
County: Oakland
Population: 10,267†

Ancestry‡	Population	%
Albanian (21)	62	0.60
American (393)	393	3.82
Arab (58)	129	1.25
Lebanese (39)	59	0.57
Syrian (0)	36	0.35
Other Arab (19)	34	0.33
Armenian (244)	307	2.99
Assyrian/Chaldean/Syriac (41)	41	0.40
Austrian (0)	125	1.22
Belgian (0)	21	0.20
Brazilian (13)	37	0.36
British (72)	81	0.79
Canadian (31)	78	0.76
Croatian (16)	37	0.36
Czech (0)	25	0.24
Danish (7)	27	0.26
Dutch (67)	357	3.47
Eastern European (63)	63	0.61
English (462)	1,485	14.44
European (177)	185	1.80
Finnish (50)	164	1.59
French, ex. Basque (58)	496	4.82
French Canadian (27)	104	1.01
German (501)	2,309	22.45
Greek (76)	189	1.84
Hungarian (57)	198	1.93
Iranian (12)	12	0.12
Irish (650)	2,116	20.58
Italian (184)	772	7.51
Lithuanian (7)	53	0.52
Maltese (0)	21	0.20
Norwegian (11)	95	0.92
Pennsylvania German (12)	12	0.12
Polish (486)	1,146	11.14
Romanian (19)	38	0.37
Russian (108)	175	1.70
Scotch-Irish (139)	351	3.41
Scottish (94)	447	4.35
Serbian (12)	12	0.12
Slovak (14)	22	0.21
Slovene (7)	27	0.26
Swedish (29)	322	3.13
Swiss (8)	31	0.30
Turkish (10)	10	0.10
Ukrainian (29)	102	0.99
Welsh (10)	65	0.63
West Indian, ex. Hispanic (11)	42	0.41
Jamaican (11)	11	0.11
West Indian (0)	31	0.30

Hispanic Origin	Population	%
Hispanic or Latino (of any race)	172	1.68
Central American, ex. Mexican	12	0.12
Costa Rican	1	0.01
Guatemalan	9	0.09
Honduran	1	0.01
Panamanian	1	0.01
Cuban	2	0.02
Dominican Republic	1	0.01
Mexican	94	0.92
Puerto Rican	13	0.13
South American	31	0.30
Argentinean	16	0.16
Bolivian	3	0.03
Chilean	3	0.03
Colombian	4	0.04
Ecuadorian	1	0.01
Paraguayan	1	0.01
Peruvian	3	0.03
Other Hispanic or Latino	19	0.19

Race*	Population	%
African-American/Black (678)	752	7.32
Not Hispanic (677)	746	7.27
Hispanic (1)	6	0.06
American Indian/Alaska Native (20)	67	0.65
Not Hispanic (18)	61	0.59
Hispanic (2)	6	0.06
Cherokee (1)	15	0.15

*Notes: † The Census 2010 population figure is used to calculate the percentages in the Hispanic Origin and Race categories. Ancestry percentages are based on the 2006-2010 American Community Survey population (not shown); ‡ Numbers in parentheses indicate the number of people reporting a single ancestry; * Numbers in parentheses indicate the number of persons reporting this race alone, not in combination with any other race; Please refer to the Explanation of Data for more information.*

Chippewa (8)	14	0.14
Iroquois (0)	1	0.01
Mexican American Ind. (1)	1	0.01
Potawatomi (0)	3	0.03
Sioux (3)	3	0.03
Spanish American Ind. (1)	1	0.01
Asian (210)	275	2.68
Not Hispanic (206)	266	2.59
Hispanic (4)	9	0.09
Chinese, ex. Taiwanese (46)	59	0.57
Filipino (26)	42	0.41
Indian (76)	89	0.87
Indonesian (1)	1	0.01
Japanese (11)	21	0.20
Korean (17)	25	0.24
Laotian (0)	2	0.02
Pakistani (2)	2	0.02
Sri Lankan (5)	5	0.05
Taiwanese (0)	1	0.01
Vietnamese (15)	17	0.17
Hawaii Native/Pacific Islander (2)	14	0.14
Not Hispanic (2)	14	0.14
Native Hawaiian (2)	3	0.03
White (9,155)	9,302	90.60
Not Hispanic (9,025)	9,165	89.27
Hispanic (130)	137	1.33

Big Rapids

Place Type: City
County: Mecosta
Population: 10,601†

Ancestry‡	Population	%
African, Sub-Saharan (0)	13	0.12
African (0)	13	0.12
Albanian (5)	5	0.05
American (302)	302	2.82
Arab (146)	164	1.53
Arab (70)	70	0.65
Lebanese (42)	51	0.48
Palestinian (5)	5	0.05
Syrian (12)	21	0.20
Other Arab (17)	17	0.16
Austrian (0)	43	0.40
Belgian (0)	18	0.17
British (42)	82	0.77
Bulgarian (35)	35	0.33
Canadian (9)	27	0.25
Croatian (30)	30	0.28
Czech (23)	42	0.39
Czechoslovakian (50)	93	0.87
Danish (36)	126	1.18
Dutch (271)	856	8.00
English (237)	874	8.17
European (5)	5	0.05
Finnish (7)	76	0.71
French, ex. Basque (140)	567	5.30
French Canadian (66)	165	1.54
German (993)	3,262	30.50
Greek (10)	36	0.34
Hungarian (62)	143	1.34
Irish (284)	1,538	14.38
Italian (97)	488	4.56
Lithuanian (0)	8	0.07
Northern European (11)	11	0.10
Norwegian (12)	127	1.19
Polish (292)	1,143	10.69
Russian (0)	116	1.08
Scotch-Irish (46)	83	0.78
Scottish (78)	184	1.72
Slovak (0)	7	0.07
Slovene (0)	14	0.13
Swedish (45)	302	2.82
Swiss (0)	7	0.07
Turkish (13)	13	0.12
Welsh (19)	42	0.39

Hispanic Origin	Population	%
Hispanic or Latino (of any race)	252	2.38
Central American, ex. Mexican	8	0.08
Costa Rican	1	0.01
Guatemalan	4	0.04
Honduran	2	0.02
Salvadoran	1	0.01
Cuban	15	0.14
Dominican Republic	6	0.06
Mexican	153	1.44
Puerto Rican	25	0.24
South American	15	0.14
Argentinean	2	0.02
Bolivian	1	0.01
Colombian	6	0.06
Peruvian	2	0.02
Venezuelan	4	0.04
Other Hispanic or Latino	30	0.28

Race*	Population	%
African-American/Black (716)	863	8.14
Not Hispanic (706)	851	8.03
Hispanic (10)	12	0.11
American Indian/Alaska Native (74)	164	1.55
Not Hispanic (65)	146	1.38
Hispanic (9)	18	0.17
Apache (0)	2	0.02
Blackfeet (0)	7	0.07
Canadian/French Am. Ind. (0)	2	0.02
Cherokee (1)	16	0.15
Chickasaw (0)	1	0.01
Chippewa (22)	29	0.27
Iroquois (0)	3	0.03
Mexican American Ind. (2)	6	0.06
Navajo (1)	1	0.01
Ottawa (5)	13	0.12
Potawatomi (0)	2	0.02
Seminole (0)	3	0.03
Sioux (1)	3	0.03
Asian (156)	196	1.85
Not Hispanic (155)	193	1.82
Hispanic (1)	3	0.03
Cambodian (1)	3	0.03
Chinese, ex. Taiwanese (18)	26	0.25
Filipino (7)	13	0.12
Hmong (20)	23	0.22
Indian (34)	46	0.43
Indonesian (0)	1	0.01
Japanese (6)	16	0.15
Korean (30)	32	0.30
Laotian (4)	4	0.04
Malaysian (0)	1	0.01
Thai (2)	2	0.02
Vietnamese (26)	30	0.28
Hawaii Native/Pacific Islander (2)	7	0.07
Not Hispanic (0)	5	0.05
Hispanic (2)	2	0.02
Guamanian/Chamorro (0)	2	0.02
Samoan (0)	2	0.02
White (9,326)	9,580	90.37
Not Hispanic (9,169)	9,403	88.70
Hispanic (157)	177	1.67

Birmingham

Place Type: City
County: Oakland
Population: 20,103†

Ancestry‡	Population	%
African, Sub-Saharan (8)	8	0.04
African (8)	8	0.04
Albanian (131)	173	0.87
Alsatian (0)	10	0.05
American (710)	710	3.56
Arab (110)	420	2.10
Arab (32)	41	0.21
Egyptian (23)	55	0.28
Jordanian (7)	69	0.35
Lebanese (48)	240	1.20
Moroccan (0)	15	0.08
Armenian (81)	195	0.98
Assyrian/Chaldean/Syriac (32)	32	0.16
Australian (12)	50	0.25
Austrian (0)	51	0.26
Belgian (41)	248	1.24
British (155)	194	0.97
Bulgarian (13)	13	0.07
Canadian (74)	159	0.80
Croatian (10)	53	0.27
Czech (45)	169	0.85
Czechoslovakian (0)	14	0.07
Danish (0)	49	0.25
Dutch (154)	592	2.97
Eastern European (146)	174	0.87
English (615)	3,092	15.49
European (506)	530	2.66
Finnish (20)	184	0.92
French, ex. Basque (9)	712	3.57
French Canadian (102)	361	1.81
German (1,394)	5,008	25.09
Greek (131)	196	0.98
Hungarian (80)	197	0.99
Icelander (0)	8	0.04
Iranian (10)	10	0.05
Irish (879)	3,286	16.46
Italian (728)	1,578	7.91
Latvian (0)	54	0.27
Lithuanian (49)	119	0.60
Macedonian (0)	10	0.05
Maltese (13)	13	0.07
Northern European (8)	8	0.04
Norwegian (86)	314	1.57
Polish (490)	1,675	8.39
Portuguese (0)	15	0.08
Romanian (27)	150	0.75
Russian (424)	692	3.47
Scandinavian (0)	29	0.15
Scotch-Irish (166)	439	2.20
Scottish (316)	921	4.61
Serbian (26)	34	0.17
Slovak (43)	97	0.49
Slovene (0)	13	0.07
Swedish (61)	501	2.51
Swiss (10)	156	0.78
Turkish (13)	26	0.13
Ukrainian (33)	92	0.46
Welsh (57)	332	1.66
West Indian, ex. Hispanic (11)	61	0.31
Jamaican (11)	61	0.31
Yugoslavian (27)	75	0.38

Hispanic Origin	Population	%
Hispanic or Latino (of any race)	419	2.08
Central American, ex. Mexican	9	0.04
Guatemalan	4	0.02
Nicaraguan	1	<0.01
Panamanian	1	<0.01
Salvadoran	3	0.01
Cuban	17	0.08
Dominican Republic	5	0.02
Mexican	230	1.14
Puerto Rican	30	0.15
South American	78	0.39
Argentinean	20	0.10
Bolivian	3	0.01
Chilean	6	0.03
Colombian	21	0.10
Ecuadorian	14	0.07
Paraguayan	3	0.01
Peruvian	4	0.02
Venezuelan	7	0.03
Other Hispanic or Latino	50	0.25

Race*	Population	%
African-American/Black (612)	716	3.56
Not Hispanic (601)	691	3.44
Hispanic (11)	25	0.12
American Indian/Alaska Native (30)	126	0.63
Not Hispanic (26)	96	0.48
Hispanic (4)	30	0.15
Apache (0)	3	0.01

SECTION TWO

*Notes: † The Census 2010 population figure is used to calculate the percentages in the Hispanic Origin and Race categories. Ancestry percentages are based on the 2006-2010 American Community Survey population (not shown); ‡ Numbers in parentheses indicate the number of people reporting a single ancestry; * Numbers in parentheses indicate the number of persons reporting this race alone, not in combination with any other race; Please refer to the Explanation of Data for more information.*

Blackfeet (0)	1	<0.01
Canadian/French Am. Ind. (0)	1	<0.01
Cherokee (4)	14	0.07
Chippewa (6)	12	0.06
Choctaw (1)	1	<0.01
Creek (0)	3	0.01
Iroquois (2)	8	0.04
Lumbee (3)	3	0.01
Mexican American Ind. (1)	6	0.03
Ottawa (0)	4	0.02
Potawatomi (0)	1	<0.01
Seminole (0)	1	<0.01
South American Ind. (0)	3	0.01
Ute (0)	3	0.01
Asian (504)	680	3.38
Not Hispanic (500)	659	3.28
Hispanic (4)	21	0.10
Bangladeshi (5)	8	0.04
Cambodian (2)	3	0.01
Chinese, ex. Taiwanese (117)	149	0.74
Filipino (79)	119	0.59
Indian (129)	174	0.87
Indonesian (0)	5	0.02
Japanese (30)	54	0.27
Korean (73)	106	0.53
Pakistani (6)	9	0.04
Sri Lankan (5)	6	0.03
Taiwanese (6)	7	0.03
Thai (5)	11	0.05
Vietnamese (25)	30	0.15
Hawaii Native/Pacific Islander (1)	13	0.06
Not Hispanic (1)	10	0.05
Hispanic (0)	3	0.01
Guamanian/Chamorro (0)	2	0.01
Native Hawaiian (1)	2	0.01
Samoan (0)	1	<0.01
White (18,556)	18,854	93.79
Not Hispanic (18,243)	18,504	92.05
Hispanic (313)	350	1.74

Blackman

Place Type: Charter Township
County: Jackson
Population: 24,051†

Ancestry‡	Population	%
African, Sub-Saharan (18)	24	0.10
African (18)	24	0.10
American (1,380)	1,380	5.70
Arab (107)	158	0.65
Arab (0)	18	0.07
Iraqi (9)	9	0.04
Lebanese (26)	42	0.17
Moroccan (72)	72	0.30
Syrian (0)	17	0.07
Austrian (19)	28	0.12
Belgian (52)	85	0.35
Bulgarian (7)	7	0.03
Canadian (60)	95	0.39
Celtic (0)	10	0.04
Czech (7)	25	0.10
Czechoslovakian (8)	31	0.13
Danish (25)	94	0.39
Dutch (111)	739	3.05
English (1,244)	3,360	13.87
European (160)	166	0.69
Finnish (49)	105	0.43
French, ex. Basque (166)	861	3.55
French Canadian (53)	80	0.33
German (2,058)	5,963	24.61
Greek (10)	39	0.16
Hungarian (20)	75	0.31
Irish (736)	3,215	13.27
Italian (208)	764	3.15
Lithuanian (11)	11	0.05
Macedonian (43)	126	0.52
Norwegian (16)	172	0.71
Pennsylvania German (52)	59	0.24
Polish (1,030)	2,064	8.52
Russian (49)	118	0.49
Scandinavian (10)	10	0.04
Scotch-Irish (136)	353	1.46
Scottish (125)	428	1.77
Serbian (11)	32	0.13
Slovak (10)	10	0.04
Swedish (35)	205	0.85
Swiss (0)	20	0.08
Ukrainian (14)	45	0.19
Welsh (22)	104	0.43
West Indian, ex. Hispanic (9)	9	0.04
Jamaican (9)	9	0.04

Hispanic Origin	Population	%
Hispanic or Latino (of any race)	862	3.58
Central American, ex. Mexican	14	0.06
Costa Rican	1	<0.01
Guatemalan	9	0.04
Honduran	3	0.01
Panamanian	1	<0.01
Cuban	2	0.01
Dominican Republic	2	0.01
Mexican	588	2.44
Puerto Rican	67	0.28
South American	19	0.08
Chilean	1	<0.01
Colombian	4	0.02
Peruvian	7	0.03
Venezuelan	1	<0.01
Other South American	6	0.02
Other Hispanic or Latino	170	0.71

Race*	Population	%
African-American/Black (3,984)	4,267	17.74
Not Hispanic (3,961)	4,220	17.55
Hispanic (23)	47	0.20
American Indian/Alaska Native (125)	255	1.06
Not Hispanic (110)	230	0.96
Hispanic (15)	25	0.10
Aleut *(Alaska Native)* (0)	1	<0.01
Apache (1)	1	<0.01
Blackfeet (4)	13	0.05
Canadian/French Am. Ind. (2)	2	0.01
Cherokee (11)	47	0.20
Chippewa (8)	24	0.10
Choctaw (1)	2	0.01
Creek (1)	1	<0.01
Iroquois (1)	1	<0.01
Mexican American Ind. (1)	1	<0.01
Ottawa (2)	2	0.01
Potawatomi (0)	2	0.01
Seminole (0)	1	<0.01
Shoshone (0)	1	<0.01
Sioux (0)	1	<0.01
Tlingit-Haida *(Alaska Native)* (1)	1	<0.01
Asian (232)	290	1.21
Not Hispanic (231)	287	1.19
Hispanic (1)	3	0.01
Chinese, ex. Taiwanese (10)	11	0.05
Filipino (24)	37	0.15
Indian (117)	122	0.51
Japanese (13)	19	0.08
Korean (16)	40	0.17
Malaysian (1)	1	<0.01
Nepalese (2)	2	0.01
Pakistani (14)	14	0.06
Sri Lankan (3)	3	0.01
Thai (5)	5	0.02
Vietnamese (10)	17	0.07
Hawaii Native/Pacific Islander (1)	8	0.03
Not Hispanic (1)	8	0.03
Guamanian/Chamorro (1)	1	<0.01
White (19,036)	19,452	80.88
Not Hispanic (18,462)	18,834	78.31
Hispanic (574)	618	2.57

Blair

Place Type: Township
County: Grand Traverse
Population: 8,209†

Ancestry‡	Population	%
American (760)	760	9.55
Armenian (16)	16	0.20
Austrian (0)	16	0.20
Belgian (0)	12	0.15
British (34)	34	0.43
Canadian (10)	35	0.44
Czech (26)	114	1.43
Danish (18)	76	0.96
Dutch (164)	350	4.40
English (208)	711	8.94
European (55)	68	0.85
Finnish (38)	147	1.85
French, ex. Basque (66)	373	4.69
French Canadian (75)	198	2.49
German (832)	2,381	29.93
Hungarian (16)	39	0.49
Irish (130)	865	10.87
Italian (54)	261	3.28
Latvian (0)	11	0.14
Lithuanian (7)	38	0.48
Norwegian (29)	105	1.32
Polish (196)	866	10.88
Romanian (10)	10	0.13
Russian (0)	75	0.94
Scandinavian (17)	17	0.21
Scotch-Irish (82)	159	2.00
Scottish (37)	149	1.87
Swedish (39)	150	1.89
Swiss (0)	22	0.28
Ukrainian (106)	106	1.33
Welsh (0)	16	0.20

Hispanic Origin	Population	%
Hispanic or Latino (of any race)	290	3.53
Central American, ex. Mexican	3	0.04
Costa Rican	2	0.02
Guatemalan	1	0.01
Cuban	6	0.07
Mexican	215	2.62
Puerto Rican	16	0.19
South American	11	0.13
Colombian	6	0.07
Ecuadorian	1	0.01
Paraguayan	1	0.01
Venezuelan	3	0.04
Other Hispanic or Latino	39	0.48

Race*	Population	%
African-American/Black (31)	75	0.91
Not Hispanic (30)	69	0.84
Hispanic (1)	6	0.07
American Indian/Alaska Native (154)	255	3.11
Not Hispanic (149)	247	3.01
Hispanic (5)	8	0.10
Alaska Athabascan *(Ala. Nat.)* (0)	1	0.01
Apache (0)	1	0.01
Blackfeet (0)	6	0.07
Canadian/French Am. Ind. (0)	5	0.06
Central American Ind. (1)	1	0.01
Cherokee (1)	3	0.04
Chippewa (99)	143	1.74
Navajo (6)	7	0.09
Ottawa (10)	31	0.38
Potawatomi (0)	1	0.01
Shoshone (0)	1	0.01
Sioux (2)	5	0.06
South American Ind. (1)	1	0.01
Yup'ik *(Alaska Native)* (1)	1	0.01
Asian (78)	118	1.44
Not Hispanic (77)	112	1.36
Hispanic (1)	6	0.07
Chinese, ex. Taiwanese (20)	25	0.30
Filipino (16)	28	0.34

*Notes: † The Census 2010 population figure is used to calculate the percentages in the Hispanic Origin and Race categories. Ancestry percentages are based on the 2006-2010 American Community Survey population (not shown); ‡ Numbers in parentheses indicate the number of people reporting a single ancestry; * Numbers in parentheses indicate the number of persons reporting this race alone, not in combination with any other race; Please refer to the Explanation of Data for more information.*

Indian (5)	7	0.09
Japanese (2)	9	0.11
Korean (14)	18	0.22
Laotian (11)	18	0.22
Thai (0)	10	0.12
Vietnamese (5)	6	0.07
Hawaii Native/Pacific Islander (6)	10	0.12
Not Hispanic (6)	9	0.11
Hispanic (0)	1	0.01
Fijian (1)	2	0.02
Guamanian/Chamorro (0)	1	0.01
Native Hawaiian (0)	1	0.01
White (7,645)	7,833	95.42
Not Hispanic (7,484)	7,641	93.08
Hispanic (161)	192	2.34

Bloomfield

Place Type: Charter Township
County: Oakland
Population: 41,070†

Ancestry‡	Population	%
African, Sub-Saharan (87)	121	0.29
African (47)	55	0.13
Ethiopian (30)	30	0.07
South African (0)	26	0.06
Other Sub-Saharan African (10)	10	0.02
Albanian (181)	197	0.48
American (2,001)	2,001	4.83
Arab (1,026)	1,477	3.56
Arab (240)	264	0.64
Iraqi (158)	256	0.62
Jordanian (12)	12	0.03
Lebanese (408)	654	1.58
Palestinian (39)	67	0.16
Syrian (144)	191	0.46
Other Arab (25)	33	0.08
Armenian (460)	583	1.41
Assyrian/Chaldean/Syriac (309)	367	0.89
Austrian (49)	190	0.46
Basque (0)	59	0.14
Belgian (69)	138	0.33
Brazilian (31)	31	0.07
British (150)	371	0.90
Bulgarian (34)	34	0.08
Canadian (214)	437	1.05
Croatian (78)	118	0.28
Czech (54)	250	0.60
Czechoslovakian (50)	91	0.22
Danish (13)	102	0.25
Dutch (214)	731	1.76
Eastern European (278)	313	0.76
English (1,287)	4,905	11.84
European (673)	681	1.64
Finnish (42)	362	0.87
French, ex. Basque (344)	1,779	4.29
French Canadian (231)	623	1.50
German (2,558)	8,689	20.97
Greek (285)	521	1.26
Hungarian (214)	801	1.93
Iranian (34)	68	0.16
Irish (1,752)	6,502	15.69
Israeli (25)	63	0.15
Italian (831)	2,475	5.97
Latvian (74)	84	0.20
Lithuanian (83)	179	0.43
Macedonian (15)	32	0.08
Maltese (22)	95	0.23
Northern European (53)	53	0.13
Norwegian (66)	308	0.74
Pennsylvania German (0)	18	0.04
Polish (1,077)	3,708	8.95
Portuguese (22)	65	0.16
Romanian (105)	270	0.65
Russian (992)	2,201	5.31
Scandinavian (10)	74	0.18
Scotch-Irish (188)	768	1.85
Scottish (253)	1,167	2.82
Serbian (8)	47	0.11
Slavic (0)	9	0.02
Slovak (25)	50	0.12
Slovene (9)	37	0.09
Swedish (283)	1,215	2.93
Swiss (37)	300	0.72
Ukrainian (232)	450	1.09
Welsh (59)	364	0.88
West Indian, ex. Hispanic (19)	27	0.07
Jamaican (11)	11	0.03
Trinidadian/Tobagonian (8)	8	0.02
West Indian (0)	8	0.02
Yugoslavian (8)	8	0.02

Hispanic Origin	Population	%
Hispanic or Latino (of any race)	740	1.80
Central American, ex. Mexican	35	0.09
Costa Rican	3	0.01
Guatemalan	15	0.04
Honduran	6	0.01
Nicaraguan	5	0.01
Panamanian	4	0.01
Salvadoran	2	<0.01
Cuban	41	0.10
Dominican Republic	12	0.03
Mexican	392	0.95
Puerto Rican	47	0.11
South American	125	0.30
Argentinean	39	0.09
Bolivian	1	<0.01
Chilean	11	0.03
Colombian	31	0.08
Ecuadorian	7	0.02
Paraguayan	6	0.01
Peruvian	23	0.06
Venezuelan	5	0.01
Other South American	2	<0.01
Other Hispanic or Latino	88	0.21

Race*	Population	%
African-American/Black (2,751)	2,994	7.29
Not Hispanic (2,732)	2,947	7.18
Hispanic (19)	47	0.11
American Indian/Alaska Native (41)	178	0.43
Not Hispanic (38)	163	0.40
Hispanic (3)	15	0.04
Apache (0)	1	<0.01
Blackfeet (0)	6	0.01
Canadian/French Am. Ind. (1)	3	0.01
Cherokee (5)	48	0.12
Chippewa (12)	25	0.06
Choctaw (0)	9	0.02
Delaware (1)	1	<0.01
Lumbee (3)	3	0.01
Ottawa (0)	1	<0.01
Potawatomi (0)	3	0.01
Seminole (0)	1	<0.01
Sioux (0)	3	0.01
Asian (2,974)	3,439	8.37
Not Hispanic (2,968)	3,411	8.31
Hispanic (6)	28	0.07
Bangladeshi (35)	38	0.09
Burmese (9)	9	0.02
Cambodian (2)	2	<0.01
Chinese, ex. Taiwanese (406)	488	1.19
Filipino (235)	316	0.77
Hmong (11)	11	0.03
Indian (1,428)	1,539	3.75
Indonesian (2)	4	0.01
Japanese (106)	156	0.38
Korean (369)	403	0.98
Malaysian (1)	9	0.02
Pakistani (222)	247	0.60
Sri Lankan (29)	33	0.08
Taiwanese (34)	39	0.09
Thai (18)	21	0.05
Vietnamese (16)	26	0.06
Hawaii Native/Pacific Islander (10)	41	0.10
Not Hispanic (6)	36	0.09
Hispanic (4)	5	0.01
Guamanian/Chamorro (1)	2	<0.01
Native Hawaiian (7)	9	0.02
Samoan (1)	2	<0.01
White (34,359)	35,014	85.25
Not Hispanic (33,797)	34,384	83.72
Hispanic (562)	630	1.53

Brandon

Place Type: Charter Township
County: Oakland
Population: 15,175†

Ancestry‡	Population	%
American (537)	537	3.55
Arab (48)	70	0.46
Jordanian (22)	22	0.15
Lebanese (0)	22	0.15
Syrian (26)	26	0.17
Armenian (20)	63	0.42
Assyrian/Chaldean/Syriac (0)	27	0.18
Austrian (0)	8	0.05
Belgian (9)	164	1.09
British (25)	50	0.33
Canadian (117)	241	1.60
Croatian (19)	19	0.13
Czech (39)	172	1.14
Czechoslovakian (9)	9	0.06
Danish (0)	48	0.32
Dutch (50)	289	1.91
English (457)	1,885	12.48
European (80)	80	0.53
Finnish (40)	179	1.18
French, ex. Basque (147)	1,330	8.80
French Canadian (169)	484	3.20
German (987)	3,874	25.65
Greek (54)	89	0.59
Hungarian (42)	222	1.47
Icelander (3)	3	0.02
Irish (493)	2,456	16.26
Italian (356)	1,390	9.20
Lithuanian (9)	28	0.19
Macedonian (9)	9	0.06
Maltese (13)	39	0.26
Norwegian (35)	272	1.80
Pennsylvania German (0)	83	0.55
Polish (595)	1,846	12.22
Portuguese (0)	10	0.07
Romanian (24)	87	0.58
Russian (11)	45	0.30
Scotch-Irish (67)	499	3.30
Scottish (224)	716	4.74
Serbian (10)	25	0.17
Slovak (39)	55	0.36
Slovene (3)	23	0.15
Swedish (59)	128	0.85
Swiss (0)	48	0.32
Ukrainian (2)	50	0.33
Welsh (28)	151	1.00
Yugoslavian (0)	24	0.16

Hispanic Origin	Population	%
Hispanic or Latino (of any race)	464	3.06
Central American, ex. Mexican	16	0.11
Guatemalan	7	0.05
Honduran	4	0.03
Nicaraguan	1	0.01
Salvadoran	4	0.03
Cuban	1	0.01
Dominican Republic	1	0.01
Mexican	318	2.10
Puerto Rican	64	0.42
South American	10	0.07
Argentinean	1	0.01
Chilean	1	0.01
Colombian	2	0.01
Ecuadorian	5	0.03
Venezuelan	1	0.01
Other Hispanic or Latino	54	0.36

*Notes: † The Census 2010 population figure is used to calculate the percentages in the Hispanic Origin and Race categories. Ancestry percentages are based on the 2006-2010 American Community Survey population (not shown); ‡ Numbers in parentheses indicate the number of people reporting a single ancestry; * Numbers in parentheses indicate the number of persons reporting this race alone, not in combination with any other race; Please refer to the Explanation of Data for more information.*

Race*	Population	%
African-American/Black (127)	197	1.30
Not Hispanic (123)	191	1.26
Hispanic (4)	6	0.04
American Indian/Alaska Native (60)	162	1.07
Not Hispanic (50)	140	0.92
Hispanic (10)	22	0.14
Apache (1)	2	0.01
Blackfeet (0)	5	0.03
Canadian/French Am. Ind. (1)	2	0.01
Cherokee (11)	42	0.28
Chippewa (28)	47	0.31
Choctaw (3)	4	0.03
Cree (0)	4	0.03
Hopi (0)	1	0.01
Iroquois (0)	5	0.03
Mexican American Ind. (0)	4	0.03
Ottawa (1)	1	0.01
Potawatomi (0)	1	0.01
Sioux (0)	1	0.01
Tlingit-Haida *(Alaska Native)* (0)	1	0.01
Asian (131)	166	1.09
Not Hispanic (131)	166	1.09
Chinese, ex. Taiwanese (8)	17	0.11
Filipino (21)	34	0.22
Hmong (54)	61	0.40
Indian (7)	7	0.05
Indonesian (0)	1	0.01
Japanese (5)	11	0.07
Korean (13)	16	0.11
Malaysian (1)	4	0.03
Thai (3)	5	0.03
Vietnamese (7)	10	0.07
Hawaii Native/Pacific Islander (4)	8	0.05
Not Hispanic (4)	8	0.05
Fijian (1)	1	0.01
Guamanian/Chamorro (1)	1	0.01
Native Hawaiian (0)	3	0.02
White (14,565)	14,754	97.23
Not Hispanic (14,212)	14,383	94.78
Hispanic (353)	371	2.44

Bridgeport

Place Type: Charter Township
County: Saginaw
Population: 10,514†

Ancestry‡	Population	%
African, Sub-Saharan (24)	24	0.22
African (24)	24	0.22
American (398)	398	3.71
Arab (17)	17	0.16
Lebanese (17)	17	0.16
Austrian (0)	37	0.34
Belgian (0)	38	0.35
Canadian (15)	23	0.21
Czech (50)	56	0.52
Danish (36)	208	1.94
Dutch (0)	213	1.98
English (104)	732	6.82
European (8)	8	0.07
Finnish (0)	84	0.78
French, ex. Basque (68)	635	5.92
French Canadian (45)	214	1.99
German (1,177)	3,415	31.82
Hungarian (9)	43	0.40
Irish (212)	812	7.57
Italian (20)	58	0.54
Lithuanian (0)	60	0.56
Norwegian (11)	64	0.60
Polish (262)	900	8.39
Russian (0)	88	0.82
Scotch-Irish (192)	278	2.59
Scottish (40)	195	1.82
Serbian (0)	47	0.44
Slavic (6)	30	0.28
Slovak (0)	31	0.29
Swedish (22)	92	0.86
Ukrainian (22)	51	0.48
Welsh (35)	49	0.46

Hispanic Origin	Population	%
Hispanic or Latino (of any race)	1,040	9.89
Central American, ex. Mexican	6	0.06
Honduran	1	0.01
Panamanian	5	0.05
Cuban	1	0.01
Dominican Republic	3	0.03
Mexican	920	8.75
Puerto Rican	23	0.22
South American	2	0.02
Chilean	1	0.01
Peruvian	1	0.01
Other Hispanic or Latino	85	0.81

Race*	Population	%
African-American/Black (2,675)	2,836	26.97
Not Hispanic (2,609)	2,735	26.01
Hispanic (66)	101	0.96
American Indian/Alaska Native (57)	120	1.14
Not Hispanic (46)	96	0.91
Hispanic (11)	24	0.23
Apache (4)	8	0.08
Blackfeet (0)	2	0.02
Canadian/French Am. Ind. (0)	1	0.01
Cherokee (0)	8	0.08
Chippewa (32)	50	0.48
Choctaw (0)	4	0.04
Comanche (0)	1	0.01
Iroquois (0)	1	0.01
Mexican American Ind. (4)	6	0.06
Navajo (1)	4	0.04
Ottawa (0)	1	0.01
Potawatomi (0)	1	0.01
Sioux (1)	1	0.01
Asian (38)	60	0.57
Not Hispanic (33)	44	0.42
Hispanic (5)	16	0.15
Chinese, ex. Taiwanese (1)	3	0.03
Filipino (23)	28	0.27
Hmong (6)	6	0.06
Indian (2)	2	0.02
Japanese (1)	4	0.04
Korean (4)	14	0.13
Thai (1)	1	0.01
Hawaii Native/Pacific Islander (1)	3	0.03
Not Hispanic (0)	1	0.01
Hispanic (1)	2	0.02
Guamanian/Chamorro (1)	2	0.02
Native Hawaiian (0)	1	0.01
White (7,139)	7,399	70.37
Not Hispanic (6,599)	6,763	64.32
Hispanic (540)	636	6.05

Brighton

Place Type: Township
County: Livingston
Population: 17,791†

Ancestry‡	Population	%
Albanian (41)	41	0.22
American (1,309)	1,309	7.17
Arab (117)	186	1.02
Arab (24)	24	0.13
Lebanese (47)	95	0.52
Palestinian (0)	12	0.07
Syrian (46)	55	0.30
Armenian (29)	69	0.38
Australian (0)	14	0.08
Austrian (0)	98	0.54
Belgian (12)	133	0.73
British (86)	104	0.57
Cajun (8)	8	0.04
Canadian (76)	162	0.89
Celtic (5)	5	0.03
Croatian (33)	42	0.23
Czech (31)	105	0.58
Czechoslovakian (29)	69	0.38
Danish (0)	16	0.09
Dutch (82)	472	2.59
Eastern European (7)	7	0.04
English (810)	2,802	15.36
European (239)	250	1.37
Finnish (269)	512	2.81
French, ex. Basque (100)	980	5.37
French Canadian (110)	415	2.27
German (1,349)	5,071	27.79
Greek (67)	156	0.86
Hungarian (107)	297	1.63
Irish (618)	3,145	17.24
Italian (361)	1,531	8.39
Lithuanian (28)	74	0.41
Macedonian (37)	49	0.27
Maltese (0)	113	0.62
Northern European (52)	52	0.29
Norwegian (62)	235	1.29
Pennsylvania German (0)	13	0.07
Polish (919)	2,434	13.34
Romanian (120)	145	0.79
Russian (30)	229	1.26
Scandinavian (21)	21	0.12
Scotch-Irish (158)	418	2.29
Scottish (222)	633	3.47
Serbian (0)	40	0.22
Slovak (12)	119	0.65
Swedish (43)	291	1.59
Swiss (34)	75	0.41
Turkish (7)	7	0.04
Ukrainian (47)	199	1.09
Welsh (0)	171	0.94
Yugoslavian (0)	18	0.10

Hispanic Origin	Population	%
Hispanic or Latino (of any race)	301	1.69
Central American, ex. Mexican	13	0.07
Costa Rican	1	0.01
Guatemalan	9	0.05
Honduran	1	0.01
Salvadoran	2	0.01
Cuban	8	0.04
Mexican	193	1.08
Puerto Rican	25	0.14
South American	23	0.13
Argentinean	6	0.03
Chilean	4	0.02
Colombian	10	0.06
Peruvian	1	0.01
Venezuelan	2	0.01
Other Hispanic or Latino	39	0.22

Race*	Population	%
African-American/Black (111)	144	0.81
Not Hispanic (106)	129	0.73
Hispanic (5)	15	0.08
American Indian/Alaska Native (45)	122	0.69
Not Hispanic (43)	104	0.58
Hispanic (2)	18	0.10
Apache (1)	1	0.01
Canadian/French Am. Ind. (0)	1	0.01
Central American Ind. (2)	2	0.01
Cherokee (2)	8	0.04
Chickasaw (2)	3	0.02
Chippewa (8)	31	0.17
Choctaw (0)	1	0.01
Creek (1)	3	0.02
Iroquois (1)	6	0.03
Lumbee (5)	6	0.03
Menominee (1)	1	0.01
Navajo (2)	2	0.01
Ottawa (1)	1	0.01
Sioux (1)	4	0.02
Asian (161)	225	1.26
Not Hispanic (160)	220	1.24
Hispanic (1)	5	0.03
Chinese, ex. Taiwanese (39)	53	0.30
Filipino (16)	34	0.19
Hmong (1)	1	0.01

*Notes: † The Census 2010 population figure is used to calculate the percentages in the Hispanic Origin and Race categories. Ancestry percentages are based on the 2006-2010 American Community Survey population (not shown); ‡ Numbers in parentheses indicate the number of people reporting a single ancestry; * Numbers in parentheses indicate the number of persons reporting this race alone, not in combination with any other race; Please refer to the Explanation of Data for more information.*

Indian (31)	36	0.20
Indonesian (0)	3	0.02
Japanese (18)	30	0.17
Korean (29)	36	0.20
Malaysian (1)	1	0.01
Taiwanese (1)	1	0.01
Thai (8)	10	0.06
Vietnamese (13)	13	0.07
Hawaii Native/Pacific Islander (6)	20	0.11
Not Hispanic (6)	16	0.09
Hispanic (0)	4	0.02
Guamanian/Chamorro (2)	2	0.01
Native Hawaiian (1)	9	0.05
Samoan (0)	2	0.01
White (17,256)	17,420	97.91
Not Hispanic (17,020)	17,165	96.48
Hispanic (236)	255	1.43

Brownstown

Place Type: Charter Township
County: Wayne
Population: 30,627†

Ancestry‡	Population	%
African, Sub-Saharan (174)	199	0.68
African (174)	199	0.68
American (1,007)	1,007	3.43
Arab (452)	525	1.79
Arab (61)	90	0.31
Iraqi (20)	28	0.10
Jordanian (179)	179	0.61
Lebanese (153)	189	0.64
Palestinian (30)	30	0.10
Other Arab (9)	9	0.03
Armenian (47)	94	0.32
Austrian (9)	59	0.20
Belgian (53)	90	0.31
Brazilian (41)	77	0.26
British (19)	65	0.22
Canadian (105)	178	0.61
Croatian (30)	70	0.24
Czech (35)	147	0.50
Czechoslovakian (0)	27	0.09
Danish (0)	28	0.10
Dutch (241)	687	2.34
English (857)	2,997	10.21
European (216)	241	0.82
Finnish (18)	113	0.38
French, ex. Basque (280)	1,993	6.79
French Canadian (181)	473	1.61
German (1,250)	6,198	21.12
Greek (152)	215	0.73
Hungarian (457)	1,529	5.21
Iranian (0)	26	0.09
Irish (629)	3,623	12.34
Italian (928)	2,094	7.13
Latvian (0)	8	0.03
Lithuanian (40)	140	0.48
Macedonian (0)	9	0.03
Maltese (30)	110	0.37
Norwegian (47)	216	0.74
Polish (1,467)	3,634	12.38
Portuguese (13)	70	0.24
Romanian (80)	124	0.42
Russian (18)	179	0.61
Scandinavian (7)	7	0.02
Scotch-Irish (122)	322	1.10
Scottish (121)	779	2.65
Slavic (11)	11	0.04
Slovak (8)	157	0.53
Slovene (9)	44	0.15
Swedish (10)	283	0.96
Swiss (8)	19	0.06
Ukrainian (79)	124	0.42
Welsh (7)	40	0.14
West Indian, ex. Hispanic (8)	37	0.13
Bahamian (0)	29	0.10
Jamaican (8)	8	0.03
Yugoslavian (28)	35	0.12

Hispanic Origin	Population	%
Hispanic or Latino (of any race)	1,593	5.20
Central American, ex. Mexican	18	0.06
Guatemalan	4	0.01
Honduran	5	0.02
Panamanian	4	0.01
Salvadoran	4	0.01
Other Central American	1	<0.01
Cuban	28	0.09
Dominican Republic	5	0.02
Mexican	1,251	4.08
Puerto Rican	154	0.50
South American	36	0.12
Argentinean	14	0.05
Chilean	1	<0.01
Colombian	10	0.03
Ecuadorian	4	0.01
Peruvian	4	0.01
Uruguayan	3	0.01
Other Hispanic or Latino	101	0.33

Race*	Population	%
African-American/Black (2,640)	2,886	9.42
Not Hispanic (2,615)	2,838	9.27
Hispanic (25)	48	0.16
American Indian/Alaska Native (133)	316	1.03
Not Hispanic (98)	263	0.86
Hispanic (35)	53	0.17
Apache (2)	5	0.02
Blackfeet (2)	7	0.02
Canadian/French Am. Ind. (0)	3	0.01
Central American Ind. (0)	2	0.01
Cherokee (15)	64	0.21
Chippewa (32)	51	0.17
Choctaw (2)	3	0.01
Cree (0)	1	<0.01
Creek (0)	3	0.01
Delaware (0)	4	0.01
Iroquois (12)	22	0.07
Lumbee (6)	8	0.03
Menominee (1)	1	<0.01
Mexican American Ind. (6)	7	0.02
Navajo (0)	1	<0.01
Ottawa (4)	7	0.02
Potawatomi (3)	3	0.01
Pueblo (1)	1	<0.01
Sioux (0)	7	0.02
South American Ind. (2)	5	0.02
Asian (1,589)	1,772	5.79
Not Hispanic (1,578)	1,755	5.73
Hispanic (11)	17	0.06
Bangladeshi (16)	18	0.06
Cambodian (0)	1	<0.01
Chinese, ex. Taiwanese (82)	91	0.30
Filipino (317)	344	1.12
Indian (402)	470	1.53
Japanese (13)	42	0.14
Korean (29)	46	0.15
Pakistani (519)	579	1.89
Sri Lankan (2)	2	0.01
Taiwanese (1)	2	0.01
Thai (5)	5	0.02
Vietnamese (91)	103	0.34
Hawaii Native/Pacific Islander (3)	24	0.08
Not Hispanic (3)	21	0.07
Hispanic (0)	3	0.01
Native Hawaiian (2)	13	0.04
Samoan (1)	1	<0.01
White (25,224)	25,757	84.10
Not Hispanic (24,181)	24,628	80.41
Hispanic (1,043)	1,129	3.69

Bruce

Place Type: Township
County: Macomb
Population: 8,700†

Ancestry‡	Population	%
Albanian (281)	281	3.24
American (205)	205	2.37
Arab (11)	11	0.13
Lebanese (11)	11	0.13
Austrian (10)	30	0.35
Belgian (96)	507	5.85
Brazilian (12)	34	0.39
British (0)	15	0.17
Canadian (13)	48	0.55
Croatian (15)	65	0.75
Czech (18)	57	0.66
Czechoslovakian (0)	26	0.30
Danish (0)	40	0.46
Dutch (55)	206	2.38
English (163)	1,142	13.18
European (17)	17	0.20
Finnish (19)	96	1.11
French, ex. Basque (24)	561	6.47
French Canadian (46)	168	1.94
German (808)	2,755	31.79
Greek (11)	21	0.24
Hungarian (37)	148	1.71
Irish (230)	1,133	13.07
Italian (273)	755	8.71
Lithuanian (22)	55	0.63
Macedonian (32)	32	0.37
Maltese (0)	27	0.31
Norwegian (10)	43	0.50
Polish (490)	1,309	15.11
Portuguese (0)	22	0.25
Romanian (46)	46	0.53
Russian (13)	92	1.06
Scotch-Irish (85)	245	2.83
Scottish (52)	261	3.01
Serbian (3)	3	0.03
Slovak (8)	57	0.66
Slovene (7)	19	0.22
Swedish (63)	127	1.47
Swiss (0)	51	0.59
Ukrainian (7)	18	0.21
Welsh (0)	71	0.82
Yugoslavian (0)	4	0.05

Hispanic Origin	Population	%
Hispanic or Latino (of any race)	415	4.77
Central American, ex. Mexican	11	0.13
Costa Rican	1	0.01
Guatemalan	10	0.11
Cuban	7	0.08
Dominican Republic	1	0.01
Mexican	346	3.98
Puerto Rican	14	0.16
South American	7	0.08
Colombian	7	0.08
Other Hispanic or Latino	29	0.33

Race*	Population	%
African-American/Black (139)	179	2.06
Not Hispanic (134)	172	1.98
Hispanic (5)	7	0.08
American Indian/Alaska Native (21)	83	0.95
Not Hispanic (21)	79	0.91
Hispanic (0)	4	0.05
Apache (0)	1	0.01
Cherokee (3)	11	0.13
Chickasaw (0)	1	0.01
Chippewa (7)	23	0.26
Choctaw (1)	1	0.01
Iroquois (1)	3	0.03
Navajo (0)	3	0.03
Ottawa (1)	3	0.03
Potawatomi (4)	4	0.05
Yup'ik *(Alaska Native)* (2)	5	0.06
Asian (40)	59	0.68
Not Hispanic (37)	56	0.64
Hispanic (3)	3	0.03
Chinese, ex. Taiwanese (7)	10	0.11
Filipino (9)	14	0.16
Indonesian (0)	4	0.05
Japanese (3)	5	0.06
Korean (10)	14	0.16

*Notes: † The Census 2010 population figure is used to calculate the percentages in the Hispanic Origin and Race categories. Ancestry percentages are based on the 2006-2010 American Community Survey population (not shown); ‡ Numbers in parentheses indicate the number of people reporting a single ancestry; * Numbers in parentheses indicate the number of persons reporting this race alone, not in combination with any other race; Please refer to the Explanation of Data for more information.*

SECTION TWO

Pakistani (2)	5	0.06
Thai (4)	5	0.06
Vietnamese (2)	4	0.05
Hawaii Native/Pacific Islander (0)	7	0.08
Not Hispanic (0)	7	0.08
White (8,273)	8,396	96.51
Not Hispanic (7,982)	8,087	92.95
Hispanic (291)	309	3.55

Buena Vista

Place Type: Charter Township
County: Saginaw
Population: 8,676†

Ancestry‡	Population	%
African, Sub-Saharan (209)	311	3.46
African (140)	242	2.69
Ghanaian (55)	55	0.61
Senegalese (14)	14	0.16
American (432)	432	4.81
Belgian (0)	12	0.13
Czech (0)	47	0.52
Dutch (10)	85	0.95
English (9)	90	1.00
European (6)	6	0.07
Finnish (64)	64	0.71
French, ex. Basque (14)	246	2.74
French Canadian (0)	23	0.26
German (483)	879	9.78
Hungarian (62)	131	1.46
Irish (44)	150	1.67
Italian (12)	25	0.28
Norwegian (12)	66	0.73
Pennsylvania German (0)	11	0.12
Polish (267)	413	4.59
Russian (0)	23	0.26
Scandinavian (0)	39	0.43
Scotch-Irish (0)	120	1.33
Scottish (0)	36	0.40
Slavic (0)	24	0.27
Slovak (12)	12	0.13
Swedish (0)	12	0.13
Ukrainian (13)	13	0.14

Hispanic Origin	Population	%
Hispanic or Latino (of any race)	803	9.26
Mexican	720	8.30
Puerto Rican	12	0.14
South American	1	0.01
Colombian	1	0.01
Other Hispanic or Latino	70	0.81

Race*	Population	%
African-American/Black (5,299)	5,501	63.40
Not Hispanic (5,206)	5,362	61.80
Hispanic (93)	139	1.60
American Indian/Alaska Native (55)	140	1.61
Not Hispanic (33)	105	1.21
Hispanic (22)	35	0.40
Blackfeet (0)	2	0.02
Cherokee (4)	10	0.12
Chippewa (17)	35	0.40
Crow (0)	1	0.01
Iroquois (0)	1	0.01
Lumbee (1)	1	0.01
Mexican American Ind. (9)	15	0.17
Navajo (0)	3	0.03
Ottawa (1)	5	0.06
Spanish American Ind. (0)	1	0.01
Yaqui (3)	4	0.05
Asian (26)	45	0.52
Not Hispanic (25)	38	0.44
Hispanic (1)	7	0.08
Chinese, ex. Taiwanese (6)	9	0.10
Filipino (3)	8	0.09
Indian (9)	11	0.13
Japanese (0)	1	0.01
Korean (2)	7	0.08
Malaysian (0)	1	0.01
Pakistani (1)	1	0.01
Thai (0)	1	0.01
Vietnamese (1)	1	0.01
Hawaii Native/Pacific Islander (2)	8	0.09
Not Hispanic (1)	3	0.03
Hispanic (1)	5	0.06
Guamanian/Chamorro (2)	2	0.02
Tongan (0)	1	0.01
White (2,730)	2,924	33.70
Not Hispanic (2,407)	2,558	29.48
Hispanic (323)	366	4.22

Burton

Place Type: City
County: Genesee
Population: 29,999†

Ancestry‡	Population	%
African, Sub-Saharan (140)	140	0.46
African (129)	129	0.42
Nigerian (11)	11	0.04
American (2,116)	2,116	6.95
Arab (73)	247	0.81
Arab (12)	36	0.12
Lebanese (44)	171	0.56
Palestinian (17)	40	0.13
Assyrian/Chaldean/Syriac (103)	125	0.41
Austrian (0)	29	0.10
Belgian (31)	114	0.37
British (0)	62	0.20
Bulgarian (9)	18	0.06
Canadian (102)	176	0.58
Croatian (15)	37	0.12
Czech (45)	198	0.65
Czechoslovakian (47)	58	0.19
Danish (12)	58	0.19
Dutch (165)	897	2.95
Eastern European (9)	9	0.03
English (871)	2,896	9.51
European (282)	325	1.07
Finnish (24)	149	0.49
French, ex. Basque (361)	1,817	5.97
French Canadian (356)	1,161	3.81
German (1,369)	5,361	17.61
Greek (111)	136	0.45
Hungarian (220)	434	1.43
Irish (620)	2,995	9.84
Italian (465)	1,244	4.09
Latvian (0)	5	0.02
Maltese (0)	30	0.10
Northern European (21)	21	0.07
Norwegian (49)	402	1.32
Pennsylvania German (0)	16	0.05
Polish (707)	1,762	5.79
Portuguese (0)	13	0.04
Romanian (22)	22	0.07
Russian (0)	55	0.18
Scandinavian (22)	41	0.13
Scotch-Irish (201)	522	1.71
Scottish (145)	941	3.09
Slovak (24)	36	0.12
Slovene (0)	9	0.03
Swedish (87)	339	1.11
Ukrainian (119)	194	0.64
Welsh (53)	139	0.46
Yugoslavian (101)	162	0.53

Hispanic Origin	Population	%
Hispanic or Latino (of any race)	930	3.10
Central American, ex. Mexican	26	0.09
Costa Rican	8	0.03
Guatemalan	8	0.03
Honduran	3	0.01
Nicaraguan	1	<0.01
Panamanian	4	0.01
Salvadoran	2	0.01
Cuban	14	0.05
Dominican Republic	1	<0.01
Mexican	752	2.51
Puerto Rican	58	0.19
South American	14	0.05
Argentinean	2	0.01
Chilean	2	0.01
Colombian	3	0.01
Ecuadorian	2	0.01
Paraguayan	1	<0.01
Peruvian	2	0.01
Venezuelan	2	0.01
Other Hispanic or Latino	65	0.22

Race*	Population	%
African-American/Black (2,203)	2,528	8.43
Not Hispanic (2,164)	2,475	8.25
Hispanic (39)	53	0.18
American Indian/Alaska Native (192)	495	1.65
Not Hispanic (176)	458	1.53
Hispanic (16)	37	0.12
Aleut *(Alaska Native)* (1)	2	0.01
Apache (4)	9	0.03
Blackfeet (2)	12	0.04
Canadian/French Am. Ind. (0)	1	<0.01
Central American Ind. (2)	3	0.01
Cherokee (45)	103	0.34
Cheyenne (2)	2	0.01
Chickasaw (0)	1	<0.01
Chippewa (56)	111	0.37
Choctaw (0)	4	0.01
Crow (0)	4	0.01
Inupiat *(Alaska Native)* (0)	2	0.01
Iroquois (6)	8	0.03
Mexican American Ind. (0)	4	0.01
Osage (0)	1	<0.01
Ottawa (5)	8	0.03
Potawatomi (1)	2	0.01
Seminole (1)	3	0.01
Sioux (3)	3	0.01
Asian (177)	296	0.99
Not Hispanic (174)	285	0.95
Hispanic (3)	11	0.04
Chinese, ex. Taiwanese (43)	61	0.20
Filipino (29)	45	0.15
Hmong (5)	5	0.02
Indian (17)	23	0.08
Indonesian (0)	2	0.01
Japanese (9)	28	0.09
Korean (25)	56	0.19
Laotian (2)	8	0.03
Malaysian (1)	4	0.01
Taiwanese (2)	3	0.01
Thai (7)	16	0.05
Vietnamese (23)	37	0.12
Hawaii Native/Pacific Islander (7)	36	0.12
Not Hispanic (7)	32	0.11
Hispanic (0)	4	0.01
Fijian (2)	6	0.02
Guamanian/Chamorro (2)	9	0.03
Native Hawaiian (2)	11	0.04
Samoan (0)	2	0.01
White (26,442)	27,156	90.52
Not Hispanic (25,868)	26,501	88.34
Hispanic (574)	655	2.18

Byron

Place Type: Township
County: Kent
Population: 20,317†

Ancestry‡	Population	%
African, Sub-Saharan (52)	75	0.38
African (52)	75	0.38
American (1,271)	1,271	6.40
Austrian (0)	12	0.06
Belgian (0)	8	0.04
British (10)	26	0.13
Canadian (31)	44	0.22
Czech (14)	29	0.15
Danish (0)	142	0.71
Dutch (4,806)	7,207	36.27

*Notes: † The Census 2010 population figure is used to calculate the percentages in the Hispanic Origin and Race categories. Ancestry percentages are based on the 2006-2010 American Community Survey population (not shown); ‡ Numbers in parentheses indicate the number of people reporting a single ancestry; * Numbers in parentheses indicate the number of persons reporting this race alone, not in combination with any other race; Please refer to the Explanation of Data for more information.*

English (544)	2,206	11.10
European (91)	91	0.46
Finnish (50)	138	0.69
French, ex. Basque (25)	686	3.45
French Canadian (9)	77	0.39
German (1,063)	4,980	25.06
Greek (27)	98	0.49
Hungarian (29)	90	0.45
Icelander (16)	16	0.08
Irish (446)	2,427	12.22
Italian (93)	567	2.85
Lithuanian (15)	44	0.22
Norwegian (43)	123	0.62
Polish (310)	1,078	5.43
Portuguese (0)	13	0.07
Russian (0)	74	0.37
Scandinavian (16)	16	0.08
Scotch-Irish (17)	280	1.41
Scottish (53)	234	1.18
Slavic (17)	33	0.17
Swedish (53)	321	1.62
Ukrainian (12)	12	0.06
Welsh (24)	65	0.33
West Indian, ex. Hispanic (12)	34	0.17
Dutch West Indian (12)	12	0.06
West Indian (0)	22	0.11
Yugoslavian (8)	30	0.15

Hispanic Origin	Population	%
Hispanic or Latino (of any race)	844	4.15
Central American, ex. Mexican	57	0.28
Guatemalan	36	0.18
Honduran	8	0.04
Nicaraguan	1	<0.01
Panamanian	2	0.01
Salvadoran	9	0.04
Other Central American	1	<0.01
Cuban	34	0.17
Dominican Republic	6	0.03
Mexican	585	2.88
Puerto Rican	94	0.46
South American	27	0.13
Argentinean	4	0.02
Bolivian	1	<0.01
Chilean	4	0.02
Colombian	6	0.03
Ecuadorian	3	0.01
Paraguayan	1	<0.01
Peruvian	5	0.02
Venezuelan	3	0.01
Other Hispanic or Latino	41	0.20

Race*	Population	%
African-American/Black (329)	490	2.41
Not Hispanic (322)	464	2.28
Hispanic (7)	26	0.13
American Indian/Alaska Native (104)	195	0.96
Not Hispanic (92)	170	0.84
Hispanic (12)	25	0.12
Blackfeet (2)	4	0.02
Canadian/French Am. Ind. (2)	2	0.01
Cherokee (6)	16	0.08
Chippewa (28)	38	0.19
Mexican American Ind. (2)	6	0.03
Navajo (1)	1	<0.01
Ottawa (8)	16	0.08
Potawatomi (13)	19	0.09
Sioux (1)	4	0.02
South American Ind. (0)	1	<0.01
Tlingit-Haida *(Alaska Native)* (1)	1	<0.01
Asian (330)	412	2.03
Not Hispanic (329)	406	2.00
Hispanic (1)	6	0.03
Cambodian (6)	11	0.05
Chinese, ex. Taiwanese (42)	60	0.30
Filipino (11)	25	0.12
Indian (6)	13	0.06
Indonesian (3)	12	0.06
Japanese (4)	10	0.05
Korean (67)	88	0.43
Laotian (0)	1	<0.01
Pakistani (1)	1	<0.01
Thai (0)	2	0.01
Vietnamese (172)	193	0.95
Hawaii Native/Pacific Islander (4)	18	0.09
Not Hispanic (3)	17	0.08
Hispanic (1)	1	<0.01
Guamanian/Chamorro (2)	2	0.01
Native Hawaiian (1)	6	0.03
Samoan (0)	2	0.01
White (18,854)	19,221	94.61
Not Hispanic (18,411)	18,704	92.06
Hispanic (443)	517	2.54

Cadillac

Place Type: City
County: Wexford
Population: 10,355†

Ancestry‡	Population	%
American (546)	546	5.26
Arab (22)	22	0.21
Other Arab (22)	22	0.21
Austrian (0)	39	0.38
Belgian (0)	22	0.21
British (23)	23	0.22
Canadian (8)	37	0.36
Croatian (0)	16	0.15
Czech (0)	10	0.10
Danish (0)	84	0.81
Dutch (356)	878	8.46
English (296)	950	9.15
Finnish (36)	83	0.80
French, ex. Basque (84)	538	5.18
French Canadian (79)	198	1.91
German (927)	3,042	29.30
Greek (11)	19	0.18
Hungarian (52)	144	1.39
Icelander (15)	31	0.30
Irish (603)	1,937	18.65
Italian (124)	456	4.39
Lithuanian (0)	9	0.09
Norwegian (31)	305	2.94
Polish (212)	851	8.20
Russian (0)	9	0.09
Scotch-Irish (100)	165	1.59
Scottish (55)	208	2.00
Slovene (10)	10	0.10
Swedish (241)	673	6.48
Swiss (0)	7	0.07
Ukrainian (13)	13	0.13
Welsh (27)	51	0.49
Yugoslavian (0)	17	0.16

Hispanic Origin	Population	%
Hispanic or Latino (of any race)	185	1.79
Central American, ex. Mexican	2	0.02
Guatemalan	1	0.01
Honduran	1	0.01
Cuban	4	0.04
Dominican Republic	1	0.01
Mexican	142	1.37
Puerto Rican	19	0.18
South American	3	0.03
Colombian	2	0.02
Ecuadorian	1	0.01
Other Hispanic or Latino	14	0.14

Race*	Population	%
African-American/Black (53)	117	1.13
Not Hispanic (50)	109	1.05
Hispanic (3)	8	0.08
American Indian/Alaska Native (61)	157	1.52
Not Hispanic (60)	147	1.42
Hispanic (1)	10	0.10
Apache (0)	1	0.01
Blackfeet (1)	5	0.05
Canadian/French Am. Ind. (0)	3	0.03
Cherokee (1)	15	0.14
Chippewa (13)	33	0.32
Choctaw (3)	6	0.06
Cree (0)	1	0.01
Iroquois (1)	3	0.03
Lumbee (2)	2	0.02
Menominee (0)	1	0.01
Mexican American Ind. (0)	3	0.03
Ottawa (6)	18	0.17
Potawatomi (3)	7	0.07
Sioux (0)	2	0.02
Asian (106)	130	1.26
Not Hispanic (106)	130	1.26
Bangladeshi (2)	2	0.02
Chinese, ex. Taiwanese (12)	12	0.12
Filipino (17)	29	0.28
Indian (33)	34	0.33
Japanese (3)	3	0.03
Korean (8)	15	0.14
Laotian (4)	6	0.06
Taiwanese (1)	2	0.02
Thai (1)	1	0.01
Vietnamese (21)	24	0.23
Hawaii Native/Pacific Islander (1)	5	0.05
Not Hispanic (1)	5	0.05
Samoan (1)	1	0.01
White (9,902)	10,086	97.40
Not Hispanic (9,782)	9,948	96.07
Hispanic (120)	138	1.33

Caledonia

Place Type: Township
County: Kent
Population: 12,332†

Ancestry‡	Population	%
American (475)	475	4.04
Arab (14)	23	0.20
Lebanese (0)	9	0.08
Other Arab (14)	14	0.12
Austrian (6)	9	0.08
Belgian (15)	32	0.27
British (10)	24	0.20
Bulgarian (11)	11	0.09
Cajun (0)	11	0.09
Canadian (22)	42	0.36
Croatian (50)	91	0.77
Czech (0)	24	0.20
Danish (0)	46	0.39
Dutch (1,617)	2,846	24.18
Eastern European (33)	33	0.28
English (486)	1,656	14.07
European (42)	60	0.51
Finnish (27)	85	0.72
French, ex. Basque (50)	467	3.97
French Canadian (3)	55	0.47
German (844)	3,683	31.29
Greek (10)	36	0.31
Hungarian (0)	56	0.48
Iranian (17)	17	0.14
Irish (247)	1,753	14.89
Italian (181)	522	4.44
Latvian (14)	65	0.55
Lithuanian (24)	49	0.42
Maltese (11)	11	0.09
Northern European (73)	73	0.62
Norwegian (42)	212	1.80
Pennsylvania German (0)	9	0.08
Polish (252)	935	7.94
Portuguese (0)	14	0.12
Romanian (38)	56	0.48
Russian (21)	140	1.19
Scandinavian (3)	13	0.11
Scotch-Irish (50)	162	1.38
Scottish (17)	216	1.84
Slovak (11)	11	0.09
Swedish (110)	373	3.17
Swiss (0)	5	0.04
Welsh (0)	95	0.81
Yugoslavian (28)	54	0.46

*Notes: † The Census 2010 population figure is used to calculate the percentages in the Hispanic Origin and Race categories. Ancestry percentages are based on the 2006-2010 American Community Survey population (not shown); ‡ Numbers in parentheses indicate the number of people reporting a single ancestry; * Numbers in parentheses indicate the number of persons reporting this race alone, not in combination with any other race; Please refer to the Explanation of Data for more information.*

Hispanic Origin	Population	%
Hispanic or Latino (of any race)	280	2.27
Central American, ex. Mexican	25	0.20
Guatemalan	21	0.17
Nicaraguan	3	0.02
Salvadoran	1	0.01
Cuban	28	0.23
Dominican Republic	10	0.08
Mexican	110	0.89
Puerto Rican	47	0.38
South American	13	0.11
Chilean	3	0.02
Colombian	3	0.02
Ecuadorian	3	0.02
Peruvian	2	0.02
Venezuelan	2	0.02
Other Hispanic or Latino	47	0.38

Race*	Population	%
African-American/Black (151)	203	1.65
Not Hispanic (147)	196	1.59
Hispanic (4)	7	0.06
American Indian/Alaska Native (33)	101	0.82
Not Hispanic (25)	89	0.72
Hispanic (8)	12	0.10
Apache (0)	1	0.01
Blackfeet (0)	7	0.06
Canadian/French Am. Ind. (0)	1	0.01
Cherokee (1)	13	0.11
Cheyenne (0)	1	0.01
Chippewa (7)	25	0.20
Creek (0)	1	0.01
Inupiat *(Alaska Native)* (2)	2	0.02
Iroquois (0)	1	0.01
Lumbee (1)	4	0.03
Menominee (0)	1	0.01
Mexican American Ind. (4)	6	0.05
Ottawa (4)	10	0.08
Potawatomi (0)	1	0.01
Puget Sound Salish (1)	1	0.01
Sioux (0)	1	0.01
Asian (146)	217	1.76
Not Hispanic (146)	207	1.68
Hispanic (0)	10	0.08
Cambodian (2)	2	0.02
Chinese, ex. Taiwanese (27)	36	0.29
Filipino (11)	33	0.27
Indian (18)	26	0.21
Indonesian (4)	6	0.05
Japanese (3)	12	0.10
Korean (40)	61	0.49
Laotian (1)	2	0.02
Pakistani (5)	5	0.04
Thai (2)	4	0.03
Vietnamese (26)	34	0.28
Hawaii Native/Pacific Islander (2)	23	0.19
Not Hispanic (2)	17	0.14
Hispanic (0)	6	0.05
Guamanian/Chamorro (0)	1	0.01
Native Hawaiian (2)	15	0.12
White (11,741)	11,920	96.66
Not Hispanic (11,546)	11,704	94.91
Hispanic (195)	216	1.75

Cannon

Place Type: Township
County: Kent
Population: 13,336†

Ancestry‡	Population	%
American (608)	608	4.63
Arab (0)	7	0.05
Syrian (0)	7	0.05
Armenian (10)	29	0.22
Austrian (0)	37	0.28
Belgian (0)	55	0.42
British (0)	39	0.30
Canadian (31)	53	0.40
Croatian (13)	40	0.30
Czech (10)	45	0.34
Czechoslovakian (14)	14	0.11
Danish (30)	278	2.12
Dutch (1,086)	2,469	18.79
English (450)	2,499	19.02
European (347)	347	2.64
Finnish (0)	38	0.29
French, ex. Basque (69)	342	2.60
French Canadian (55)	356	2.71
German (883)	4,181	31.82
Greek (14)	29	0.22
Hungarian (11)	81	0.62
Icelander (0)	13	0.10
Irish (391)	1,902	14.47
Italian (53)	218	1.66
Latvian (20)	43	0.33
Lithuanian (30)	96	0.73
Northern European (38)	38	0.29
Norwegian (88)	340	2.59
Polish (442)	1,249	9.50
Romanian (23)	23	0.18
Russian (54)	128	0.97
Scandinavian (0)	33	0.25
Scotch-Irish (65)	323	2.46
Scottish (236)	713	5.43
Slavic (8)	32	0.24
Slovak (0)	19	0.14
Swedish (83)	499	3.80
Swiss (11)	21	0.16
Ukrainian (7)	66	0.50
Welsh (66)	133	1.01

Hispanic Origin	Population	%
Hispanic or Latino (of any race)	244	1.83
Central American, ex. Mexican	29	0.22
Guatemalan	23	0.17
Honduran	2	0.01
Nicaraguan	4	0.03
Cuban	11	0.08
Dominican Republic	3	0.02
Mexican	153	1.15
Puerto Rican	14	0.10
South American	13	0.10
Argentinean	1	0.01
Chilean	5	0.04
Colombian	6	0.04
Peruvian	1	0.01
Other Hispanic or Latino	21	0.16

Race*	Population	%
African-American/Black (97)	170	1.27
Not Hispanic (97)	168	1.26
Hispanic (0)	2	0.01
American Indian/Alaska Native (23)	86	0.64
Not Hispanic (18)	77	0.58
Hispanic (5)	9	0.07
Apache (0)	2	0.01
Arapaho (1)	1	0.01
Cherokee (2)	21	0.16
Chippewa (6)	24	0.18
Choctaw (0)	1	0.01
Iroquois (0)	1	0.01
Mexican American Ind. (5)	5	0.04
Ottawa (2)	7	0.05
Potawatomi (0)	3	0.02
Sioux (0)	1	0.01
Asian (112)	182	1.36
Not Hispanic (112)	180	1.35
Hispanic (0)	2	0.01
Chinese, ex. Taiwanese (52)	65	0.49
Filipino (5)	21	0.16
Indian (7)	10	0.07
Indonesian (0)	3	0.02
Japanese (1)	19	0.14
Korean (31)	43	0.32
Laotian (0)	2	0.01
Malaysian (0)	1	0.01
Thai (4)	6	0.04
Vietnamese (6)	14	0.10
Hawaii Native/Pacific Islander (8)	17	0.13
Not Hispanic (8)	17	0.13
Native Hawaiian (0)	4	0.03
White (12,845)	13,036	97.75
Not Hispanic (12,659)	12,838	96.27
Hispanic (186)	198	1.48

Canton

Place Type: Charter Township
County: Wayne
Population: 90,173†

Ancestry‡	Population	%
African, Sub-Saharan (500)	664	0.75
African (170)	279	0.32
Ethiopian (135)	135	0.15
Nigerian (195)	233	0.26
Ugandan (0)	17	0.02
Albanian (213)	213	0.24
American (4,185)	4,185	4.76
Arab (1,878)	2,465	2.80
Arab (664)	709	0.81
Egyptian (19)	27	0.03
Iraqi (57)	126	0.14
Jordanian (23)	23	0.03
Lebanese (694)	969	1.10
Palestinian (236)	255	0.29
Syrian (57)	173	0.20
Other Arab (128)	183	0.21
Armenian (174)	376	0.43
Assyrian/Chaldean/Syriac (113)	113	0.13
Australian (0)	9	0.01
Austrian (0)	165	0.19
Basque (0)	8	0.01
Belgian (63)	329	0.37
Brazilian (9)	30	0.03
British (320)	468	0.53
Bulgarian (27)	27	0.03
Canadian (266)	572	0.65
Croatian (43)	200	0.23
Czech (40)	457	0.52
Czechoslovakian (34)	93	0.11
Danish (37)	144	0.16
Dutch (356)	1,514	1.72
Eastern European (29)	49	0.06
English (2,244)	8,145	9.26
European (988)	1,228	1.40
Finnish (86)	547	0.62
French, ex. Basque (522)	4,267	4.85
French Canadian (347)	1,371	1.56
German (4,399)	17,180	19.53
Greek (259)	537	0.61
Guyanese (0)	16	0.02
Hungarian (326)	927	1.05
Iranian (61)	72	0.08
Irish (2,118)	9,745	11.08
Italian (1,808)	5,771	6.56
Lithuanian (109)	364	0.41
Macedonian (103)	113	0.13
Maltese (151)	366	0.42
Northern European (8)	8	0.01
Norwegian (178)	675	0.77
Pennsylvania German (7)	32	0.04
Polish (4,503)	11,542	13.12
Portuguese (10)	33	0.04
Romanian (506)	699	0.79
Russian (222)	728	0.83
Scandinavian (20)	119	0.14
Scotch-Irish (546)	1,393	1.58
Scottish (672)	2,402	2.73
Serbian (72)	161	0.18
Slavic (65)	154	0.18
Slovak (118)	323	0.37
Slovene (19)	44	0.05
Swedish (189)	1,022	1.16
Swiss (82)	254	0.29
Turkish (133)	142	0.16
Ukrainian (190)	582	0.66
Welsh (127)	444	0.50
West Indian, ex. Hispanic (117)	211	0.24

*Notes: † The Census 2010 population figure is used to calculate the percentages in the Hispanic Origin and Race categories. Ancestry percentages are based on the 2006-2010 American Community Survey population (not shown); ‡ Numbers in parentheses indicate the number of people reporting a single ancestry; * Numbers in parentheses indicate the number of persons reporting this race alone, not in combination with any other race; Please refer to the Explanation of Data for more information.*

Haitian (10)	31	0.04
Jamaican (107)	180	0.20
Yugoslavian (46)	182	0.21

Hispanic Origin	Population	%
Hispanic or Latino (of any race)	2,822	3.13
Central American, ex. Mexican	120	0.13
Costa Rican	13	0.01
Guatemalan	39	0.04
Honduran	28	0.03
Nicaraguan	5	0.01
Panamanian	23	0.03
Salvadoran	10	0.01
Other Central American	2	<0.01
Cuban	98	0.11
Dominican Republic	27	0.03
Mexican	1,837	2.04
Puerto Rican	266	0.29
South American	196	0.22
Argentinean	35	0.04
Bolivian	7	0.01
Chilean	5	0.01
Colombian	79	0.09
Ecuadorian	27	0.03
Paraguayan	6	0.01
Peruvian	14	0.02
Uruguayan	1	<0.01
Venezuelan	21	0.02
Other South American	1	<0.01
Other Hispanic or Latino	278	0.31

Race*	Population	%
African-American/Black (9,176)	9,984	11.07
Not Hispanic (9,070)	9,812	10.88
Hispanic (106)	172	0.19
American Indian/Alaska Native (224)	702	0.78
Not Hispanic (206)	649	0.72
Hispanic (18)	53	0.06
Apache (2)	3	<0.01
Arapaho (2)	2	<0.01
Blackfeet (2)	31	0.03
Canadian/French Am. Ind. (4)	9	0.01
Cherokee (22)	124	0.14
Chickasaw (0)	2	<0.01
Chippewa (46)	98	0.11
Choctaw (1)	14	0.02
Comanche (0)	1	<0.01
Cree (0)	1	<0.01
Creek (4)	7	0.01
Delaware (4)	5	0.01
Inupiat *(Alaska Native)* (0)	3	<0.01
Iroquois (11)	22	0.02
Lumbee (4)	12	0.01
Mexican American Ind. (3)	5	0.01
Navajo (4)	4	<0.01
Osage (0)	2	<0.01
Ottawa (13)	22	0.02
Potawatomi (1)	3	<0.01
Pueblo (1)	1	<0.01
Puget Sound Salish (0)	1	<0.01
Sioux (0)	3	<0.01
South American Ind. (1)	10	0.01
Asian (12,739)	13,875	15.39
Not Hispanic (12,720)	13,816	15.32
Hispanic (19)	59	0.07
Bangladeshi (122)	125	0.14
Burmese (0)	1	<0.01
Cambodian (7)	10	0.01
Chinese, ex. Taiwanese (1,849)	2,022	2.24
Filipino (646)	849	0.94
Hmong (6)	6	0.01
Indian (7,174)	7,546	8.37
Indonesian (24)	34	0.04
Japanese (307)	435	0.48
Korean (404)	481	0.53
Laotian (8)	16	0.02
Malaysian (2)	11	0.01
Nepalese (28)	30	0.03
Pakistani (1,396)	1,479	1.64
Sri Lankan (31)	31	0.03
Taiwanese (95)	100	0.11
Thai (39)	45	0.05
Vietnamese (288)	347	0.38
Hawaii Native/Pacific Islander (27)	83	0.09
Not Hispanic (21)	73	0.08
Hispanic (6)	10	0.01
Guamanian/Chamorro (8)	15	0.02
Marshallese (2)	2	<0.01
Native Hawaiian (4)	17	0.02
Samoan (1)	4	<0.01
White (65,140)	66,962	74.26
Not Hispanic (63,165)	64,802	71.86
Hispanic (1,975)	2,160	2.40

Cascade

Place Type: Charter Township
County: Kent
Population: 17,134†

Ancestry‡	Population	%
American (949)	949	5.64
Arab (203)	281	1.67
Lebanese (203)	281	1.67
Assyrian/Chaldean/Syriac (35)	81	0.48
Austrian (13)	13	0.08
Belgian (16)	73	0.43
British (23)	74	0.44
Bulgarian (42)	42	0.25
Canadian (8)	49	0.29
Croatian (19)	32	0.19
Czech (44)	97	0.58
Czechoslovakian (84)	108	0.64
Danish (0)	64	0.38
Dutch (1,328)	2,786	16.56
English (754)	2,838	16.87
European (336)	382	2.27
Finnish (23)	68	0.40
French, ex. Basque (65)	596	3.54
French Canadian (87)	281	1.67
German (793)	4,591	27.30
Greek (26)	26	0.15
Hungarian (0)	54	0.32
Irish (747)	2,850	16.95
Italian (271)	748	4.45
Latvian (22)	75	0.45
Lithuanian (92)	216	1.28
Northern European (0)	11	0.07
Norwegian (38)	273	1.62
Pennsylvania German (15)	15	0.09
Polish (505)	1,481	8.81
Portuguese (0)	34	0.20
Romanian (8)	37	0.22
Russian (20)	64	0.38
Scandinavian (21)	30	0.18
Scotch-Irish (127)	477	2.84
Scottish (125)	816	4.85
Slavic (13)	26	0.15
Slovak (25)	41	0.24
Swedish (120)	878	5.22
Swiss (7)	68	0.40
Turkish (7)	7	0.04
Ukrainian (63)	132	0.78
Welsh (25)	96	0.57
West Indian, ex. Hispanic (0)	13	0.08
Jamaican (0)	13	0.08

Hispanic Origin	Population	%
Hispanic or Latino (of any race)	333	1.94
Central American, ex. Mexican	14	0.08
Costa Rican	1	0.01
Guatemalan	8	0.05
Honduran	2	0.01
Nicaraguan	1	0.01
Panamanian	1	0.01
Salvadoran	1	0.01
Cuban	17	0.10
Dominican Republic	12	0.07
Mexican	173	1.01
Puerto Rican	52	0.30
South American	31	0.18
Argentinean	1	0.01
Chilean	7	0.04
Colombian	12	0.07
Ecuadorian	2	0.01
Peruvian	4	0.02
Venezuelan	5	0.03
Other Hispanic or Latino	34	0.20

Race*	Population	%
African-American/Black (256)	319	1.86
Not Hispanic (248)	309	1.80
Hispanic (8)	10	0.06
American Indian/Alaska Native (38)	76	0.44
Not Hispanic (29)	61	0.36
Hispanic (9)	15	0.09
Arapaho (1)	1	0.01
Blackfeet (0)	1	0.01
Canadian/French Am. Ind. (1)	1	0.01
Cherokee (2)	9	0.05
Cheyenne (0)	1	0.01
Chippewa (10)	15	0.09
Comanche (0)	1	0.01
Creek (1)	3	0.02
Iroquois (4)	4	0.02
Mexican American Ind. (2)	5	0.03
Ottawa (1)	2	0.01
Potawatomi (4)	4	0.02
Sioux (1)	1	0.01
Asian (526)	648	3.78
Not Hispanic (518)	638	3.72
Hispanic (8)	10	0.06
Cambodian (0)	2	0.01
Chinese, ex. Taiwanese (127)	161	0.94
Filipino (40)	58	0.34
Indian (153)	170	0.99
Indonesian (2)	2	0.01
Japanese (21)	37	0.22
Korean (66)	87	0.51
Pakistani (37)	41	0.24
Sri Lankan (2)	4	0.02
Taiwanese (4)	4	0.02
Thai (8)	13	0.08
Vietnamese (54)	61	0.36
Hawaii Native/Pacific Islander (3)	14	0.08
Not Hispanic (1)	10	0.06
Hispanic (2)	4	0.02
Native Hawaiian (1)	3	0.02
Samoan (1)	4	0.02
Tongan (1)	1	0.01
White (16,020)	16,219	94.66
Not Hispanic (15,785)	15,960	93.15
Hispanic (235)	259	1.51

Center Line

Place Type: City
County: Macomb
Population: 8,257†

Ancestry‡	Population	%
African, Sub-Saharan (55)	120	1.43
African (55)	120	1.43
Albanian (62)	62	0.74
American (345)	345	4.12
Arab (90)	96	1.15
Egyptian (76)	76	0.91
Iraqi (14)	14	0.17
Lebanese (0)	6	0.07
Belgian (7)	63	0.75
British (0)	12	0.14
Canadian (21)	58	0.69
Celtic (17)	17	0.20
Croatian (0)	36	0.43
Czech (13)	25	0.30
Danish (10)	42	0.50
Dutch (114)	234	2.79
English (68)	641	7.65
European (15)	15	0.18
Finnish (0)	13	0.16

*Notes: † The Census 2010 population figure is used to calculate the percentages in the Hispanic Origin and Race categories. Ancestry percentages are based on the 2006-2010 American Community Survey population (not shown); ‡ Numbers in parentheses indicate the number of people reporting a single ancestry; * Numbers in parentheses indicate the number of persons reporting this race alone, not in combination with any other race; Please refer to the Explanation of Data for more information.*

French, ex. Basque (55)	340	4.06
French Canadian (117)	220	2.63
German (455)	2,117	25.28
Greek (11)	21	0.25
Hungarian (99)	136	1.62
Irish (358)	1,267	15.13
Italian (148)	495	5.91
Lithuanian (12)	26	0.31
Norwegian (10)	73	0.87
Polish (778)	1,767	21.10
Romanian (16)	16	0.19
Russian (49)	69	0.82
Scotch-Irish (45)	160	1.91
Scottish (78)	244	2.91
Serbian (0)	21	0.25
Slavic (20)	20	0.24
Slovak (0)	15	0.18
Swedish (13)	23	0.27
Ukrainian (38)	104	1.24
Welsh (0)	14	0.17
Yugoslavian (18)	88	1.05

Hispanic Origin	Population	%
Hispanic or Latino (of any race)	140	1.70
Central American, ex. Mexican	4	0.05
Panamanian	1	0.01
Salvadoran	3	0.04
Cuban	10	0.12
Dominican Republic	5	0.06
Mexican	86	1.04
Puerto Rican	25	0.30
South American	4	0.05
Colombian	3	0.04
Ecuadorian	1	0.01
Other Hispanic or Latino	6	0.07

Race*	Population	%
African-American/Black (992)	1,107	13.41
Not Hispanic (983)	1,093	13.24
Hispanic (9)	14	0.17
American Indian/Alaska Native (29)	91	1.10
Not Hispanic (27)	85	1.03
Hispanic (2)	6	0.07
Blackfeet (4)	5	0.06
Canadian/French Am. Ind. (1)	2	0.02
Cherokee (7)	28	0.34
Chippewa (8)	8	0.10
Creek (0)	2	0.02
Iroquois (1)	2	0.02
Lumbee (0)	2	0.02
Navajo (1)	1	0.01
Ottawa (1)	1	0.01
Pima (1)	1	0.01
Asian (205)	252	3.05
Not Hispanic (200)	246	2.98
Hispanic (5)	6	0.07
Bangladeshi (41)	42	0.51
Chinese, ex. Taiwanese (14)	19	0.23
Filipino (30)	41	0.50
Hmong (35)	41	0.50
Indian (15)	22	0.27
Indonesian (2)	4	0.05
Japanese (2)	7	0.08
Korean (8)	8	0.10
Pakistani (19)	24	0.29
Taiwanese (4)	4	0.05
Thai (3)	3	0.04
Vietnamese (11)	17	0.21
Hawaii Native/Pacific Islander (3)	10	0.12
Not Hispanic (3)	10	0.12
Native Hawaiian (1)	1	0.01
White (6,812)	6,992	84.68
Not Hispanic (6,710)	6,882	83.35
Hispanic (102)	110	1.33

Charlotte

Place Type: City
County: Eaton
Population: 9,074†

Ancestry‡	Population	%
American (554)	554	6.07
Armenian (0)	16	0.18
Australian (0)	25	0.27
Austrian (0)	11	0.12
British (14)	42	0.46
Canadian (7)	23	0.25
Czech (0)	41	0.45
Danish (0)	30	0.33
Dutch (108)	522	5.72
Eastern European (12)	12	0.13
English (946)	1,696	18.58
European (65)	79	0.87
Finnish (25)	74	0.81
French, ex. Basque (46)	320	3.51
French Canadian (70)	156	1.71
German (683)	2,168	23.76
Hungarian (44)	72	0.79
Irish (265)	1,041	11.41
Italian (160)	476	5.22
Lithuanian (0)	29	0.32
Northern European (45)	45	0.49
Norwegian (11)	95	1.04
Pennsylvania German (42)	73	0.80
Polish (61)	376	4.12
Russian (12)	28	0.31
Scotch-Irish (81)	154	1.69
Scottish (82)	208	2.28
Slavic (0)	41	0.45
Swedish (56)	132	1.45
Swiss (0)	25	0.27
Ukrainian (19)	74	0.81
Welsh (0)	11	0.12

Hispanic Origin	Population	%
Hispanic or Latino (of any race)	421	4.64
Central American, ex. Mexican	21	0.23
Costa Rican	3	0.03
Guatemalan	1	0.01
Honduran	4	0.04
Nicaraguan	1	0.01
Panamanian	12	0.13
Cuban	7	0.08
Mexican	339	3.74
Puerto Rican	19	0.21
South American	5	0.06
Argentinean	1	0.01
Colombian	2	0.02
Ecuadorian	1	0.01
Peruvian	1	0.01
Other Hispanic or Latino	30	0.33

Race*	Population	%
African-American/Black (106)	165	1.82
Not Hispanic (106)	162	1.79
Hispanic (0)	3	0.03
American Indian/Alaska Native (37)	98	1.08
Not Hispanic (30)	79	0.87
Hispanic (7)	19	0.21
Arapaho (1)	1	0.01
Blackfeet (4)	5	0.06
Canadian/French Am. Ind. (1)	2	0.02
Cherokee (3)	13	0.14
Chippewa (14)	18	0.20
Iroquois (0)	1	0.01
Menominee (1)	1	0.01
Mexican American Ind. (3)	3	0.03
Ottawa (4)	8	0.09
Potawatomi (0)	3	0.03
Sioux (1)	11	0.12
Asian (43)	79	0.87
Not Hispanic (43)	73	0.80
Hispanic (0)	6	0.07
Chinese, ex. Taiwanese (17)	27	0.30
Filipino (5)	11	0.12
Indian (6)	9	0.10
Japanese (2)	9	0.10
Korean (6)	13	0.14
Thai (1)	3	0.03
Vietnamese (4)	13	0.14
Hawaii Native/Pacific Islander (0)	3	0.03
Not Hispanic (0)	3	0.03
Native Hawaiian (0)	1	0.01
White (8,627)	8,802	97.00
Not Hispanic (8,346)	8,466	93.30
Hispanic (281)	336	3.70

Chesterfield

Place Type: Township
County: Macomb
Population: 43,381†

Ancestry‡	Population	%
African, Sub-Saharan (47)	118	0.28
African (47)	104	0.24
South African (0)	14	0.03
Albanian (209)	255	0.60
American (1,705)	1,705	4.00
Arab (139)	650	1.53
Arab (12)	96	0.23
Iraqi (6)	6	0.01
Jordanian (0)	8	0.02
Lebanese (112)	418	0.98
Syrian (0)	102	0.24
Other Arab (9)	20	0.05
Armenian (19)	144	0.34
Assyrian/Chaldean/Syriac (0)	14	0.03
Australian (167)	218	0.51
Belgian (269)	1,276	2.99
British (29)	209	0.49
Bulgarian (0)	9	0.02
Canadian (152)	217	0.51
Carpatho Rusyn (0)	11	0.03
Celtic (10)	10	0.02
Croatian (22)	182	0.43
Czech (10)	69	0.16
Czechoslovakian (0)	35	0.08
Danish (33)	148	0.35
Dutch (113)	475	1.11
English (631)	2,941	6.90
European (286)	308	0.72
Finnish (56)	388	0.91
French, ex. Basque (247)	2,613	6.13
French Canadian (378)	1,138	2.67
German (3,032)	12,043	28.26
Greek (155)	364	0.85
Hungarian (172)	586	1.38
Icelander (0)	14	0.03
Irish (1,281)	5,662	13.29
Israeli (16)	16	0.04
Italian (2,394)	6,132	14.39
Latvian (0)	14	0.03
Lithuanian (52)	195	0.46
Luxemburger (0)	14	0.03
Macedonian (146)	146	0.34
Maltese (11)	115	0.27
Northern European (17)	17	0.04
Norwegian (34)	149	0.35
Pennsylvania German (0)	38	0.09
Polish (2,909)	9,296	21.81
Portuguese (35)	47	0.11
Romanian (90)	170	0.40
Russian (70)	368	0.86
Scotch-Irish (128)	600	1.41
Scottish (212)	1,029	2.41
Serbian (71)	133	0.31
Slavic (7)	36	0.08
Slovak (75)	366	0.86
Slovene (14)	28	0.07
Swedish (55)	293	0.69
Swiss (0)	12	0.03
Turkish (8)	8	0.02
Ukrainian (44)	192	0.45
Welsh (39)	197	0.46
West Indian, ex. Hispanic (14)	14	0.03
Jamaican (14)	14	0.03
Yugoslavian (32)	100	0.23

*Notes: † The Census 2010 population figure is used to calculate the percentages in the Hispanic Origin and Race categories. Ancestry percentages are based on the 2006-2010 American Community Survey population (not shown); ‡ Numbers in parentheses indicate the number of people reporting a single ancestry; * Numbers in parentheses indicate the number of persons reporting this race alone, not in combination with any other race; Please refer to the Explanation of Data for more information.*

Hispanic Origin	Population	%
Hispanic or Latino (of any race)	1,038	2.39
Central American, ex. Mexican	35	0.08
Costa Rican	2	<0.01
Guatemalan	8	0.02
Honduran	5	0.01
Panamanian	5	0.01
Salvadoran	15	0.03
Cuban	25	0.06
Dominican Republic	3	0.01
Mexican	745	1.72
Puerto Rican	112	0.26
South American	27	0.06
Argentinean	1	<0.01
Colombian	6	0.01
Ecuadorian	1	<0.01
Peruvian	5	0.01
Uruguayan	7	0.02
Venezuelan	5	0.01
Other South American	2	<0.01
Other Hispanic or Latino	91	0.21

Race*	Population	%
African-American/Black (2,285)	2,653	6.12
Not Hispanic (2,245)	2,593	5.98
Hispanic (40)	60	0.14
American Indian/Alaska Native (159)	367	0.85
Not Hispanic (141)	336	0.77
Hispanic (18)	31	0.07
Arapaho (0)	1	<0.01
Blackfeet (2)	14	0.03
Canadian/French Am. Ind. (3)	5	0.01
Cherokee (19)	97	0.22
Cheyenne (1)	1	<0.01
Chippewa (21)	45	0.10
Choctaw (0)	7	0.02
Comanche (2)	2	<0.01
Cree (0)	4	0.01
Creek (1)	1	<0.01
Crow (1)	2	<0.01
Inupiat *(Alaska Native)* (0)	1	<0.01
Iroquois (24)	39	0.09
Lumbee (7)	12	0.03
Mexican American Ind. (7)	13	0.03
Ottawa (5)	8	0.02
Paiute (0)	2	<0.01
Potawatomi (0)	2	<0.01
Sioux (1)	2	<0.01
South American Ind. (2)	3	0.01
Tlingit-Haida *(Alaska Native)* (0)	1	<0.01
Asian (415)	593	1.37
Not Hispanic (410)	570	1.31
Hispanic (5)	23	0.05
Bangladeshi (2)	2	<0.01
Cambodian (5)	12	0.03
Chinese, ex. Taiwanese (60)	87	0.20
Filipino (94)	149	0.34
Hmong (12)	14	0.03
Indian (49)	75	0.17
Indonesian (5)	5	0.01
Japanese (17)	34	0.08
Korean (57)	90	0.21
Laotian (3)	7	0.02
Pakistani (28)	31	0.07
Sri Lankan (0)	1	<0.01
Thai (11)	22	0.05
Vietnamese (43)	56	0.13
Hawaii Native/Pacific Islander (15)	51	0.12
Not Hispanic (15)	44	0.10
Hispanic (0)	7	0.02
Guamanian/Chamorro (2)	6	0.01
Native Hawaiian (9)	23	0.05
Samoan (1)	4	0.01
White (39,411)	40,130	92.51
Not Hispanic (38,809)	39,446	90.93
Hispanic (602)	684	1.58

Clawson

Place Type: City
County: Oakland
Population: 11,825†

Ancestry‡	Population	%
African, Sub-Saharan (10)	10	0.08
African (10)	10	0.08
Albanian (180)	180	1.50
American (682)	682	5.69
Arab (58)	83	0.69
Arab (11)	11	0.09
Iraqi (11)	11	0.09
Lebanese (27)	43	0.36
Syrian (9)	9	0.08
Other Arab (0)	9	0.08
Armenian (29)	55	0.46
Assyrian/Chaldean/Syriac (27)	46	0.38
Austrian (0)	11	0.09
Belgian (0)	18	0.15
British (36)	86	0.72
Bulgarian (22)	22	0.18
Canadian (117)	252	2.10
Croatian (18)	69	0.58
Czech (0)	79	0.66
Czechoslovakian (14)	56	0.47
Danish (0)	34	0.28
Dutch (20)	302	2.52
Eastern European (0)	12	0.10
English (318)	1,664	13.87
European (130)	149	1.24
Finnish (45)	145	1.21
French, ex. Basque (167)	828	6.90
French Canadian (132)	519	4.33
German (742)	3,101	25.85
Greek (136)	228	1.90
Hungarian (77)	172	1.43
Icelander (20)	20	0.17
Irish (442)	2,170	18.09
Italian (287)	884	7.37
Lithuanian (11)	47	0.39
Northern European (7)	7	0.06
Norwegian (48)	98	0.82
Pennsylvania German (0)	9	0.08
Polish (659)	1,795	14.96
Portuguese (0)	10	0.08
Romanian (0)	19	0.16
Russian (21)	88	0.73
Scotch-Irish (188)	505	4.21
Scottish (134)	529	4.41
Serbian (20)	20	0.17
Slovak (0)	27	0.23
Swedish (36)	216	1.80
Swiss (0)	56	0.47
Turkish (24)	33	0.28
Ukrainian (9)	29	0.24
Welsh (15)	119	0.99
Yugoslavian (100)	100	0.83

Hispanic Origin	Population	%
Hispanic or Latino (of any race)	254	2.15
Central American, ex. Mexican	48	0.41
Guatemalan	9	0.08
Nicaraguan	2	0.02
Salvadoran	37	0.31
Cuban	15	0.13
Dominican Republic	2	0.02
Mexican	136	1.15
Puerto Rican	25	0.21
South American	11	0.09
Argentinean	2	0.02
Chilean	2	0.02
Colombian	1	0.01
Ecuadorian	1	0.01
Peruvian	4	0.03
Venezuelan	1	0.01
Other Hispanic or Latino	17	0.14

Race*	Population	%
African-American/Black (223)	293	2.48
Not Hispanic (220)	287	2.43
Hispanic (3)	6	0.05
American Indian/Alaska Native (32)	110	0.93
Not Hispanic (24)	99	0.84
Hispanic (8)	11	0.09
Apache (0)	5	0.04
Blackfeet (0)	1	0.01
Cherokee (7)	27	0.23
Cheyenne (0)	3	0.03
Chippewa (7)	13	0.11
Creek (0)	1	0.01
Delaware (1)	1	0.01
Iroquois (2)	4	0.03
Lumbee (0)	1	0.01
Mexican American Ind. (2)	3	0.03
Sioux (0)	3	0.03
Yaqui (1)	1	0.01
Asian (241)	316	2.67
Not Hispanic (241)	314	2.66
Hispanic (0)	2	0.02
Cambodian (1)	2	0.02
Chinese, ex. Taiwanese (40)	49	0.41
Filipino (38)	70	0.59
Hmong (1)	4	0.03
Indian (60)	72	0.61
Indonesian (3)	4	0.03
Japanese (20)	32	0.27
Korean (30)	39	0.33
Laotian (2)	2	0.02
Malaysian (1)	3	0.03
Nepalese (4)	4	0.03
Pakistani (5)	5	0.04
Taiwanese (1)	1	0.01
Thai (10)	10	0.08
Vietnamese (18)	22	0.19
Hawaii Native/Pacific Islander (4)	10	0.08
Not Hispanic (3)	9	0.08
Hispanic (1)	1	0.01
Guamanian/Chamorro (1)	1	0.01
Native Hawaiian (1)	6	0.05
Tongan (1)	1	0.01
White (11,049)	11,257	95.20
Not Hispanic (10,870)	11,057	93.51
Hispanic (179)	200	1.69

Clay

Place Type: Township
County: St. Clair
Population: 9,066†

Ancestry‡	Population	%
Albanian (10)	10	0.11
American (520)	520	5.56
Arab (64)	247	2.64
Lebanese (64)	186	1.99
Syrian (0)	61	0.65
Armenian (10)	10	0.11
Austrian (11)	38	0.41
Belgian (66)	212	2.27
British (8)	29	0.31
Canadian (50)	90	0.96
Croatian (0)	23	0.25
Czech (7)	7	0.07
Danish (0)	55	0.59
Dutch (15)	101	1.08
English (172)	938	10.03
European (9)	17	0.18
Finnish (22)	164	1.75
French, ex. Basque (205)	940	10.05
French Canadian (113)	226	2.42
German (910)	2,959	31.63
Greek (51)	57	0.61
Hungarian (69)	137	1.46
Irish (371)	1,491	15.94
Italian (232)	791	8.45
Lithuanian (26)	110	1.18

SECTION TWO

*Notes: † The Census 2010 population figure is used to calculate the percentages in the Hispanic Origin and Race categories. Ancestry percentages are based on the 2006-2010 American Community Survey population (not shown); ‡ Numbers in parentheses indicate the number of people reporting a single ancestry; * Numbers in parentheses indicate the number of persons reporting this race alone, not in combination with any other race; Please refer to the Explanation of Data for more information.*

Macedonian (0)	10	0.11
Norwegian (0)	36	0.38
Pennsylvania German (10)	10	0.11
Polish (674)	1,781	19.04
Romanian (0)	52	0.56
Russian (14)	37	0.40
Scandinavian (53)	64	0.68
Scotch-Irish (77)	242	2.59
Scottish (84)	332	3.55
Serbian (0)	20	0.21
Slovak (11)	46	0.49
Swedish (30)	178	1.90
Swiss (0)	14	0.15
Ukrainian (49)	139	1.49
Welsh (7)	18	0.19
Yugoslavian (0)	11	0.12

Hispanic Origin	Population	%
Hispanic or Latino (of any race)	97	1.07
Cuban	1	0.01
Mexican	50	0.55
Puerto Rican	21	0.23
South American	4	0.04
Colombian	3	0.03
Uruguayan	1	0.01
Other Hispanic or Latino	21	0.23

Race*	Population	%
African-American/Black (13)	31	0.34
Not Hispanic (13)	31	0.34
American Indian/Alaska Native (44)	120	1.32
Not Hispanic (42)	116	1.28
Hispanic (2)	4	0.04
Canadian/French Am. Ind. (8)	9	0.10
Cherokee (5)	13	0.14
Chickasaw (0)	13	0.14
Chippewa (4)	11	0.12
Delaware (1)	3	0.03
Iroquois (1)	2	0.02
Lumbee (1)	5	0.06
Ottawa (1)	4	0.04
Potawatomi (2)	6	0.07
Sioux (4)	5	0.06
Spanish American Ind. (1)	1	0.01
Asian (27)	37	0.41
Not Hispanic (27)	37	0.41
Chinese, ex. Taiwanese (8)	8	0.09
Filipino (5)	8	0.09
Indian (3)	3	0.03
Japanese (4)	4	0.04
Korean (6)	11	0.12
Taiwanese (1)	1	0.01
Hawaii Native/Pacific Islander (3)	3	0.03
Not Hispanic (3)	3	0.03
Native Hawaiian (3)	3	0.03
White (8,864)	8,968	98.92
Not Hispanic (8,786)	8,884	97.99
Hispanic (78)	84	0.93

Clayton

Place Type: Charter Township
County: Genesee
Population: 7,581[†]

Ancestry[‡]	Population	%
African, Sub-Saharan (0)	13	0.17
African (0)	13	0.17
American (507)	507	6.60
Arab (25)	81	1.06
Arab (7)	7	0.09
Lebanese (9)	23	0.30
Syrian (9)	37	0.48
Other Arab (0)	14	0.18
Assyrian/Chaldean/Syriac (68)	68	0.89
Belgian (14)	43	0.56
British (11)	16	0.21
Canadian (6)	72	0.94
Croatian (0)	38	0.49
Czech (51)	108	1.41
Czechoslovakian (13)	21	0.27
Danish (0)	80	1.04
Dutch (32)	211	2.75
Eastern European (6)	19	0.25
English (308)	1,389	18.09
European (75)	75	0.98
Finnish (9)	16	0.21
French, ex. Basque (62)	553	7.20
French Canadian (67)	244	3.18
German (520)	2,238	29.15
Hungarian (13)	97	1.26
Iranian (34)	34	0.44
Irish (269)	1,322	17.22
Italian (141)	280	3.65
Luxemburger (0)	10	0.13
Northern European (25)	25	0.33
Norwegian (9)	81	1.06
Polish (139)	470	6.12
Romanian (16)	16	0.21
Scandinavian (0)	11	0.14
Scotch-Irish (16)	71	0.92
Scottish (94)	289	3.76
Serbian (0)	2	0.03
Slovak (56)	134	1.75
Swedish (30)	118	1.54
Welsh (7)	32	0.42
Yugoslavian (0)	13	0.17

Hispanic Origin	Population	%
Hispanic or Latino (of any race)	215	2.84
Central American, ex. Mexican	4	0.05
Guatemalan	1	0.01
Panamanian	1	0.01
Salvadoran	2	0.03
Cuban	3	0.04
Dominican Republic	2	0.03
Mexican	162	2.14
Puerto Rican	24	0.32
South American	9	0.12
Argentinean	3	0.04
Colombian	2	0.03
Ecuadorian	1	0.01
Peruvian	3	0.04
Other Hispanic or Latino	11	0.15

Race*	Population	%
African-American/Black (244)	284	3.75
Not Hispanic (244)	278	3.67
Hispanic (0)	6	0.08
American Indian/Alaska Native (39)	79	1.04
Not Hispanic (26)	62	0.82
Hispanic (13)	17	0.22
Apache (6)	6	0.08
Cherokee (2)	8	0.11
Chippewa (8)	19	0.25
Choctaw (0)	3	0.04
Comanche (1)	1	0.01
Crow (0)	1	0.01
Iroquois (1)	1	0.01
Menominee (0)	5	0.07
Mexican American Ind. (1)	1	0.01
Navajo (0)	1	0.01
Ottawa (1)	1	0.01
Potawatomi (1)	1	0.01
Shoshone (0)	1	0.01
Sioux (1)	1	0.01
South American Ind. (2)	2	0.03
Asian (52)	79	1.04
Not Hispanic (52)	77	1.02
Hispanic (0)	2	0.03
Chinese, ex. Taiwanese (9)	9	0.12
Filipino (9)	18	0.24
Hmong (4)	4	0.05
Indian (12)	17	0.22
Japanese (3)	3	0.04
Korean (6)	14	0.18
Thai (8)	8	0.11
Vietnamese (1)	1	0.01
Hawaii Native/Pacific Islander (4)	6	0.08
Not Hispanic (4)	6	0.08
Fijian (4)	4	0.05
White (7,068)	7,176	94.66
Not Hispanic (6,947)	7,038	92.84
Hispanic (121)	138	1.82

Clinton

Place Type: Charter Township
County: Macomb
Population: 96,796[†]

Ancestry[‡]	Population	%
African, Sub-Saharan (614)	614	0.63
African (414)	414	0.43
Ghanaian (110)	110	0.11
Nigerian (90)	90	0.09
Albanian (746)	757	0.78
Alsatian (0)	10	0.01
American (4,195)	4,195	4.31
Arab (862)	1,873	1.93
Arab (192)	312	0.32
Iraqi (92)	95	0.10
Jordanian (44)	44	0.05
Lebanese (450)	1,184	1.22
Moroccan (0)	41	0.04
Syrian (41)	154	0.16
Other Arab (43)	43	0.04
Armenian (39)	132	0.14
Austrian (64)	259	0.27
Belgian (457)	1,840	1.89
Brazilian (6)	13	0.01
British (153)	353	0.36
Bulgarian (0)	10	0.01
Canadian (278)	612	0.63
Croatian (73)	334	0.34
Czech (56)	637	0.65
Czechoslovakian (45)	218	0.22
Danish (32)	176	0.18
Dutch (228)	1,146	1.18
English (1,558)	6,730	6.92
European (331)	403	0.41
Finnish (131)	585	0.60
French, ex. Basque (535)	4,802	4.94
French Canadian (518)	1,822	1.87
German (5,962)	21,482	22.08
Greek (276)	705	0.72
Guyanese (15)	15	0.02
Hungarian (233)	958	0.98
Icelander (0)	14	0.01
Iranian (22)	22	0.02
Irish (1,963)	10,861	11.16
Israeli (0)	11	0.01
Italian (6,881)	14,389	14.79
Lithuanian (108)	331	0.34
Luxemburger (8)	8	0.01
Macedonian (214)	242	0.25
Maltese (37)	183	0.19
Northern European (19)	53	0.05
Norwegian (56)	371	0.38
Pennsylvania German (0)	10	0.01
Polish (7,011)	17,913	18.41
Portuguese (0)	16	0.02
Romanian (527)	810	0.83
Russian (74)	654	0.67
Scandinavian (7)	68	0.07
Scotch-Irish (312)	1,119	1.15
Scottish (367)	2,496	2.57
Serbian (136)	246	0.25
Slavic (8)	60	0.06
Slovak (140)	493	0.51
Slovene (35)	45	0.05
Swedish (213)	762	0.78
Swiss (9)	87	0.09
Turkish (14)	14	0.01
Ukrainian (164)	598	0.61
Welsh (52)	484	0.50
West Indian, ex. Hispanic (13)	25	0.03
Bahamian (13)	13	0.01
Jamaican (0)	12	0.01
Yugoslavian (825)	850	0.87

*Notes: † The Census 2010 population figure is used to calculate the percentages in the Hispanic Origin and Race categories. Ancestry percentages are based on the 2006-2010 American Community Survey population (not shown); ‡ Numbers in parentheses indicate the number of people reporting a single ancestry; * Numbers in parentheses indicate the number of persons reporting this race alone, not in combination with any other race; Please refer to the Explanation of Data for more information.*

Hispanic Origin	Population	%
Hispanic or Latino (of any race)	2,290	2.37
Central American, ex. Mexican	75	0.08
Costa Rican	6	0.01
Guatemalan	24	0.02
Honduran	5	0.01
Nicaraguan	5	0.01
Panamanian	9	0.01
Salvadoran	26	0.03
Cuban	72	0.07
Dominican Republic	14	0.01
Mexican	1,534	1.58
Puerto Rican	210	0.22
South American	128	0.13
Argentinean	17	0.02
Bolivian	3	<0.01
Chilean	2	<0.01
Colombian	36	0.04
Ecuadorian	29	0.03
Peruvian	7	0.01
Uruguayan	13	0.01
Venezuelan	21	0.02
Other Hispanic or Latino	257	0.27

Race*	Population	%
African-American/Black (12,623)	13,832	14.29
Not Hispanic (12,509)	13,614	14.06
Hispanic (114)	218	0.23
American Indian/Alaska Native (267)	893	0.92
Not Hispanic (230)	798	0.82
Hispanic (37)	95	0.10
Apache (3)	11	0.01
Blackfeet (5)	45	0.05
Canadian/French Am. Ind. (3)	12	0.01
Central American Ind. (1)	2	<0.01
Cherokee (33)	209	0.22
Chippewa (47)	111	0.11
Choctaw (3)	11	0.01
Comanche (1)	4	<0.01
Creek (0)	1	<0.01
Inupiat *(Alaska Native)* (2)	5	0.01
Iroquois (8)	32	0.03
Lumbee (12)	18	0.02
Mexican American Ind. (5)	11	0.01
Navajo (1)	1	<0.01
Osage (0)	1	<0.01
Ottawa (5)	16	0.02
Potawatomi (1)	10	0.01
Pueblo (0)	2	<0.01
Seminole (3)	7	0.01
Sioux (2)	13	0.01
Asian (1,737)	2,266	2.34
Not Hispanic (1,723)	2,220	2.29
Hispanic (14)	46	0.05
Bangladeshi (8)	10	0.01
Burmese (0)	3	<0.01
Cambodian (20)	25	0.03
Chinese, ex. Taiwanese (246)	336	0.35
Filipino (383)	531	0.55
Hmong (100)	101	0.10
Indian (409)	501	0.52
Indonesian (1)	4	<0.01
Japanese (55)	115	0.12
Korean (152)	224	0.23
Laotian (17)	17	0.02
Malaysian (1)	2	<0.01
Nepalese (4)	4	<0.01
Pakistani (85)	108	0.11
Sri Lankan (1)	3	<0.01
Taiwanese (1)	1	<0.01
Thai (13)	20	0.02
Vietnamese (143)	164	0.17
Hawaii Native/Pacific Islander (31)	74	0.08
Not Hispanic (29)	66	0.07
Hispanic (2)	8	0.01
Guamanian/Chamorro (0)	2	<0.01
Native Hawaiian (5)	21	0.02
Samoan (5)	5	0.01
White (79,447)	81,257	83.95
Not Hispanic (78,062)	79,688	82.33
Hispanic (1,385)	1,569	1.62

Coldwater

Place Type: City
County: Branch
Population: 10,945†

Ancestry‡	Population	%
American (1,124)	1,124	10.24
Arab (775)	775	7.06
Arab (218)	218	1.99
Other Arab (557)	557	5.07
Armenian (12)	12	0.11
British (0)	14	0.13
Canadian (17)	35	0.32
Czech (0)	18	0.16
Danish (0)	15	0.14
Dutch (147)	387	3.52
English (587)	1,290	11.75
European (104)	104	0.95
Finnish (0)	45	0.41
French, ex. Basque (101)	458	4.17
French Canadian (51)	85	0.77
German (1,146)	2,866	26.10
Greek (0)	14	0.13
Hungarian (45)	73	0.66
Irish (274)	1,262	11.49
Italian (122)	519	4.73
Norwegian (11)	37	0.34
Pennsylvania German (9)	9	0.08
Polish (188)	848	7.72
Romanian (0)	9	0.08
Russian (0)	63	0.57
Scandinavian (0)	14	0.13
Scotch-Irish (112)	248	2.26
Scottish (59)	223	2.03
Slovak (12)	12	0.11
Swedish (62)	185	1.69
Swiss (0)	12	0.11
Ukrainian (0)	34	0.31
Welsh (34)	100	0.91

Hispanic Origin	Population	%
Hispanic or Latino (of any race)	725	6.62
Central American, ex. Mexican	18	0.16
Guatemalan	1	0.01
Honduran	2	0.02
Panamanian	7	0.06
Salvadoran	8	0.07
Cuban	1	0.01
Dominican Republic	1	0.01
Mexican	610	5.57
Puerto Rican	40	0.37
South American	3	0.03
Colombian	1	0.01
Peruvian	2	0.02
Other Hispanic or Latino	52	0.48

Race*	Population	%
African-American/Black (62)	119	1.09
Not Hispanic (61)	118	1.08
Hispanic (1)	1	0.01
American Indian/Alaska Native (21)	90	0.82
Not Hispanic (15)	75	0.69
Hispanic (6)	15	0.14
Apache (0)	2	0.02
Blackfeet (0)	14	0.13
Cherokee (3)	20	0.18
Chippewa (6)	9	0.08
Menominee (0)	2	0.02
Mexican American Ind. (0)	1	0.01
Navajo (0)	1	0.01
Potawatomi (2)	6	0.05
Asian (88)	222	2.03
Not Hispanic (88)	219	2.00
Hispanic (0)	3	0.03
Cambodian (0)	5	0.05
Chinese, ex. Taiwanese (12)	19	0.17
Filipino (13)	26	0.24
Indian (17)	18	0.16
Japanese (16)	26	0.24
Korean (2)	10	0.09
Nepalese (3)	3	0.03
Thai (1)	4	0.04
Vietnamese (6)	6	0.05
Hawaii Native/Pacific Islander (1)	21	0.19
Not Hispanic (1)	17	0.16
Hispanic (0)	4	0.04
Guamanian/Chamorro (0)	4	0.04
Native Hawaiian (1)	5	0.05
Samoan (0)	3	0.03
White (10,124)	10,416	95.17
Not Hispanic (9,791)	10,041	91.74
Hispanic (333)	375	3.43

Commerce

Place Type: Charter Township
County: Oakland
Population: 40,186†

Ancestry‡	Population	%
African, Sub-Saharan (0)	17	0.04
African (0)	17	0.04
Albanian (257)	257	0.65
American (1,934)	1,934	4.93
Arab (486)	885	2.25
Arab (131)	142	0.36
Iraqi (175)	399	1.02
Lebanese (55)	153	0.39
Palestinian (7)	7	0.02
Syrian (39)	105	0.27
Other Arab (79)	79	0.20
Armenian (137)	251	0.64
Assyrian/Chaldean/Syriac (875)	1,119	2.85
Austrian (53)	85	0.22
Belgian (63)	208	0.53
British (97)	328	0.84
Bulgarian (19)	19	0.05
Canadian (178)	440	1.12
Croatian (37)	79	0.20
Czech (55)	424	1.08
Czechoslovakian (37)	114	0.29
Danish (44)	278	0.71
Dutch (160)	1,058	2.70
Eastern European (78)	78	0.20
English (1,112)	5,454	13.90
European (384)	482	1.23
Finnish (162)	635	1.62
French, ex. Basque (256)	2,191	5.58
French Canadian (237)	913	2.33
German (2,272)	10,181	25.94
Greek (162)	512	1.30
Hungarian (113)	521	1.33
Iranian (0)	12	0.03
Irish (1,379)	6,901	17.58
Italian (1,151)	3,282	8.36
Latvian (17)	57	0.15
Lithuanian (67)	136	0.35
Luxemburger (0)	32	0.08
Macedonian (60)	174	0.44
Maltese (93)	178	0.45
Northern European (13)	13	0.03
Norwegian (132)	476	1.21
Pennsylvania German (0)	20	0.05
Polish (1,565)	5,246	13.37
Portuguese (12)	32	0.08
Romanian (85)	249	0.63
Russian (520)	1,003	2.56
Scandinavian (17)	26	0.07
Scotch-Irish (247)	674	1.72
Scottish (389)	1,568	4.00
Serbian (14)	29	0.07
Slavic (11)	25	0.06
Slovak (10)	126	0.32
Slovene (0)	36	0.09
Swedish (218)	996	2.54
Swiss (7)	111	0.28
Turkish (20)	20	0.05

*Notes: † The Census 2010 population figure is used to calculate the percentages in the Hispanic Origin and Race categories. Ancestry percentages are based on the 2006-2010 American Community Survey population (not shown); ‡ Numbers in parentheses indicate the number of people reporting a single ancestry; * Numbers in parentheses indicate the number of persons reporting this race alone, not in combination with any other race; Please refer to the Explanation of Data for more information.*

Ukrainian (69)	335	0.85
Welsh (52)	373	0.95
Yugoslavian (38)	160	0.41

Hispanic Origin	Population	%
Hispanic or Latino (of any race)	1,042	2.59
Central American, ex. Mexican	78	0.19
Costa Rican	4	0.01
Guatemalan	42	0.10
Honduran	3	0.01
Nicaraguan	2	<0.01
Panamanian	12	0.03
Salvadoran	15	0.04
Cuban	29	0.07
Dominican Republic	11	0.03
Mexican	637	1.59
Puerto Rican	63	0.16
South American	116	0.29
Argentinean	30	0.07
Bolivian	6	0.01
Chilean	14	0.03
Colombian	39	0.10
Ecuadorian	11	0.03
Peruvian	10	0.02
Venezuelan	5	0.01
Other South American	1	<0.01
Other Hispanic or Latino	108	0.27

Race*	Population	%
African-American/Black (654)	783	1.95
Not Hispanic (637)	756	1.88
Hispanic (17)	27	0.07
American Indian/Alaska Native (101)	284	0.71
Not Hispanic (89)	262	0.65
Hispanic (12)	22	0.05
Apache (1)	5	0.01
Blackfeet (0)	7	0.02
Canadian/French Am. Ind. (0)	1	<0.01
Cherokee (7)	46	0.11
Cheyenne (0)	1	<0.01
Chippewa (43)	68	0.17
Choctaw (1)	11	0.03
Cree (0)	1	<0.01
Creek (1)	2	<0.01
Crow (1)	1	<0.01
Iroquois (12)	29	0.07
Lumbee (0)	1	<0.01
Menominee (0)	1	<0.01
Mexican American Ind. (4)	4	0.01
Navajo (2)	2	<0.01
Ottawa (3)	5	0.01
Potawatomi (0)	1	<0.01
Sioux (0)	3	0.01
South American Ind. (1)	4	0.01
Ute (0)	3	0.01
Asian (983)	1,253	3.12
Not Hispanic (982)	1,250	3.11
Hispanic (1)	3	0.01
Bangladeshi (0)	1	<0.01
Cambodian (2)	2	<0.01
Chinese, ex. Taiwanese (142)	177	0.44
Filipino (87)	131	0.33
Hmong (2)	3	0.01
Indian (280)	323	0.80
Indonesian (5)	9	0.02
Japanese (235)	289	0.72
Korean (108)	142	0.35
Laotian (5)	7	0.02
Pakistani (29)	37	0.09
Taiwanese (1)	2	<0.01
Thai (5)	11	0.03
Vietnamese (46)	52	0.13
Hawaii Native/Pacific Islander (5)	28	0.07
Not Hispanic (5)	26	0.06
Hispanic (0)	2	<0.01
Guamanian/Chamorro (3)	4	0.01
Native Hawaiian (1)	2	<0.01
White (37,599)	38,203	95.07
Not Hispanic (36,837)	37,377	93.01
Hispanic (762)	826	2.06

Comstock Park

Place Type: CDP
County: Kent
Population: 10,088†

Ancestry‡	Population	%
African, Sub-Saharan (64)	64	0.62
African (64)	64	0.62
American (438)	438	4.24
Arab (10)	24	0.23
Lebanese (0)	14	0.14
Other Arab (10)	10	0.10
Armenian (56)	64	0.62
Belgian (0)	117	1.13
Canadian (0)	22	0.21
Croatian (0)	17	0.16
Czech (0)	10	0.10
Danish (20)	51	0.49
Dutch (637)	1,609	15.59
English (128)	884	8.57
European (100)	100	0.97
Finnish (24)	69	0.67
French, ex. Basque (32)	302	2.93
French Canadian (12)	30	0.29
German (657)	2,070	20.06
Hungarian (12)	12	0.12
Irish (284)	1,525	14.78
Italian (36)	366	3.55
Lithuanian (23)	61	0.59
Northern European (11)	11	0.11
Norwegian (11)	36	0.35
Polish (354)	1,153	11.17
Russian (0)	33	0.32
Scotch-Irish (51)	273	2.65
Scottish (33)	72	0.70
Swedish (49)	302	2.93
Swiss (0)	62	0.60
Ukrainian (0)	15	0.15

Hispanic Origin	Population	%
Hispanic or Latino (of any race)	1,444	14.31
Central American, ex. Mexican	63	0.62
Costa Rican	3	0.03
Guatemalan	45	0.45
Honduran	11	0.11
Salvadoran	4	0.04
Cuban	21	0.21
Dominican Republic	14	0.14
Mexican	1,055	10.46
Puerto Rican	141	1.40
South American	10	0.10
Chilean	1	0.01
Ecuadorian	7	0.07
Venezuelan	2	0.02
Other Hispanic or Latino	140	1.39

Race*	Population	%
African-American/Black (804)	1,013	10.04
Not Hispanic (770)	930	9.22
Hispanic (34)	83	0.82
American Indian/Alaska Native (75)	194	1.92
Not Hispanic (39)	134	1.33
Hispanic (36)	60	0.59
Blackfeet (0)	8	0.08
Cherokee (2)	11	0.11
Chippewa (11)	20	0.20
Choctaw (1)	1	0.01
Inupiat *(Alaska Native)* (0)	2	0.02
Mexican American Ind. (3)	3	0.03
Ottawa (11)	25	0.25
Potawatomi (5)	11	0.11
Seminole (0)	4	0.04
Shoshone (1)	1	0.01
Sioux (0)	2	0.02
Yaqui (1)	1	0.01
Asian (118)	176	1.74
Not Hispanic (116)	165	1.64
Hispanic (2)	11	0.11
Burmese (0)	1	0.01
Chinese, ex. Taiwanese (9)	16	0.16
Filipino (15)	42	0.42
Hmong (3)	3	0.03
Indian (16)	19	0.19
Japanese (1)	6	0.06
Korean (20)	31	0.31
Laotian (3)	4	0.04
Malaysian (0)	1	0.01
Nepalese (3)	3	0.03
Pakistani (5)	5	0.05
Thai (0)	1	0.01
Vietnamese (34)	39	0.39
Hawaii Native/Pacific Islander (5)	19	0.19
Not Hispanic (5)	13	0.13
Hispanic (0)	6	0.06
Fijian (1)	1	0.01
Guamanian/Chamorro (3)	3	0.03
Native Hawaiian (1)	7	0.07
White (7,938)	8,291	82.19
Not Hispanic (7,455)	7,680	76.13
Hispanic (483)	611	6.06

Comstock

Place Type: Charter Township
County: Kalamazoo
Population: 14,854†

Ancestry‡	Population	%
African, Sub-Saharan (210)	225	1.54
African (35)	50	0.34
Zimbabwean (175)	175	1.20
American (813)	813	5.56
Arab (25)	35	0.24
Lebanese (25)	35	0.24
Armenian (0)	10	0.07
Austrian (18)	24	0.16
Belgian (27)	36	0.25
British (12)	76	0.52
Canadian (9)	27	0.18
Croatian (0)	17	0.12
Czech (19)	30	0.21
Danish (7)	59	0.40
Dutch (1,018)	2,519	17.21
Eastern European (35)	35	0.24
English (631)	2,179	14.89
European (41)	51	0.35
Finnish (0)	50	0.34
French, ex. Basque (110)	671	4.59
French Canadian (68)	208	1.42
German (1,159)	3,580	24.47
Greek (37)	78	0.53
Hungarian (55)	195	1.33
Irish (457)	2,127	14.54
Israeli (10)	10	0.07
Italian (72)	408	2.79
Latvian (45)	45	0.31
Lithuanian (0)	27	0.18
Luxemburger (15)	15	0.10
Norwegian (6)	71	0.49
Pennsylvania German (54)	54	0.37
Polish (309)	818	5.59
Russian (0)	14	0.10
Scandinavian (0)	47	0.32
Scotch-Irish (93)	225	1.54
Scottish (102)	493	3.37
Slovak (24)	24	0.16
Slovene (15)	15	0.10
Swedish (118)	204	1.39
Swiss (24)	33	0.23
Turkish (7)	7	0.05
Ukrainian (0)	13	0.09
Welsh (0)	95	0.65
West Indian, ex. Hispanic (0)	7	0.05
Belizean (0)	7	0.05
Yugoslavian (0)	10	0.07

Hispanic Origin	Population	%
Hispanic or Latino (of any race)	441	2.97
Central American, ex. Mexican	17	0.11

*Notes: † The Census 2010 population figure is used to calculate the percentages in the Hispanic Origin and Race categories. Ancestry percentages are based on the 2006-2010 American Community Survey population (not shown); ‡ Numbers in parentheses indicate the number of people reporting a single ancestry; * Numbers in parentheses indicate the number of persons reporting this race alone, not in combination with any other race; Please refer to the Explanation of Data for more information.*

Costa Rican	3	0.02
Guatemalan	7	0.05
Honduran	2	0.01
Panamanian	5	0.03
Cuban	13	0.09
Dominican Republic	7	0.05
Mexican	308	2.07
Puerto Rican	24	0.16
South American	8	0.05
Bolivian	1	0.01
Colombian	2	0.01
Ecuadorian	3	0.02
Peruvian	2	0.01
Other Hispanic or Latino	64	0.43

Race*	Population	%
African-American/Black (830)	1,031	6.94
Not Hispanic (817)	993	6.69
Hispanic (13)	38	0.26
American Indian/Alaska Native (71)	194	1.31
Not Hispanic (66)	175	1.18
Hispanic (5)	19	0.13
Apache (1)	3	0.02
Blackfeet (3)	6	0.04
Cherokee (8)	31	0.21
Chippewa (6)	17	0.11
Comanche (0)	1	0.01
Crow (0)	1	0.01
Kiowa (0)	1	0.01
Mexican American Ind. (2)	8	0.05
Navajo (1)	2	0.01
Ottawa (6)	7	0.05
Potawatomi (9)	12	0.08
Pueblo (0)	3	0.02
Seminole (0)	2	0.01
Sioux (3)	4	0.03
Tlingit-Haida *(Alaska Native)* (3)	3	0.02
Asian (276)	381	2.56
Not Hispanic (275)	373	2.51
Hispanic (1)	8	0.05
Bangladeshi (1)	5	0.03
Chinese, ex. Taiwanese (35)	49	0.33
Filipino (25)	30	0.20
Hmong (5)	5	0.03
Indian (114)	138	0.93
Indonesian (0)	1	0.01
Japanese (21)	39	0.26
Korean (21)	31	0.21
Laotian (2)	7	0.05
Malaysian (0)	1	0.01
Nepalese (2)	3	0.02
Pakistani (9)	11	0.07
Sri Lankan (1)	1	0.01
Taiwanese (3)	3	0.02
Thai (4)	9	0.06
Vietnamese (17)	22	0.15
Hawaii Native/Pacific Islander (13)	21	0.14
Not Hispanic (13)	21	0.14
Guamanian/Chamorro (0)	1	0.01
Native Hawaiian (0)	3	0.02
Samoan (2)	3	0.02
White (13,080)	13,482	90.76
Not Hispanic (12,866)	13,193	88.82
Hispanic (214)	289	1.95

Cooper

Place Type: Charter Township
County: Kalamazoo
Population: 10,111†

Ancestry‡	Population	%
African, Sub-Saharan (35)	35	0.36
African (35)	35	0.36
Albanian (0)	9	0.09
American (503)	503	5.11
Belgian (0)	12	0.12
British (14)	43	0.44
Canadian (13)	13	0.13
Croatian (0)	12	0.12
Czech (14)	49	0.50
Czechoslovakian (9)	9	0.09
Danish (0)	52	0.53
Dutch (881)	1,815	18.45
English (291)	1,483	15.08
European (131)	131	1.33
Finnish (0)	11	0.11
French, ex. Basque (13)	444	4.51
French Canadian (7)	43	0.44
German (786)	2,519	25.61
Greek (0)	8	0.08
Hungarian (40)	49	0.50
Irish (243)	1,054	10.72
Italian (168)	357	3.63
Lithuanian (15)	48	0.49
Northern European (30)	30	0.31
Norwegian (29)	133	1.35
Polish (150)	621	6.31
Russian (0)	38	0.39
Scotch-Irish (96)	305	3.10
Scottish (97)	271	2.76
Slovak (20)	20	0.20
Swedish (29)	102	1.04
Swiss (12)	12	0.12
Welsh (0)	72	0.73
Yugoslavian (12)	12	0.12

Hispanic Origin	Population	%
Hispanic or Latino (of any race)	157	1.55
Central American, ex. Mexican	4	0.04
Guatemalan	1	0.01
Nicaraguan	1	0.01
Panamanian	1	0.01
Salvadoran	1	0.01
Cuban	1	0.01
Dominican Republic	2	0.02
Mexican	124	1.23
Puerto Rican	4	0.04
South American	12	0.12
Argentinean	1	0.01
Chilean	1	0.01
Colombian	6	0.06
Ecuadorian	1	0.01
Paraguayan	1	0.01
Peruvian	2	0.02
Other Hispanic or Latino	10	0.10

Race*	Population	%
African-American/Black (308)	403	3.99
Not Hispanic (307)	390	3.86
Hispanic (1)	13	0.13
American Indian/Alaska Native (39)	131	1.30
Not Hispanic (37)	124	1.23
Hispanic (2)	7	0.07
Blackfeet (1)	6	0.06
Cherokee (4)	22	0.22
Chippewa (16)	21	0.21
Iroquois (1)	1	0.01
Mexican American Ind. (0)	1	0.01
Ottawa (4)	5	0.05
Potawatomi (6)	7	0.07
Seminole (0)	1	0.01
Sioux (0)	3	0.03
Asian (97)	133	1.32
Not Hispanic (95)	128	1.27
Hispanic (2)	5	0.05
Chinese, ex. Taiwanese (7)	9	0.09
Filipino (19)	32	0.32
Indian (24)	29	0.29
Japanese (3)	7	0.07
Korean (19)	22	0.22
Laotian (3)	3	0.03
Malaysian (2)	3	0.03
Pakistani (7)	8	0.08
Vietnamese (10)	13	0.13
Hawaii Native/Pacific Islander (1)	1	0.01
Not Hispanic (1)	1	0.01
Native Hawaiian (1)	1	0.01
White (9,424)	9,635	95.29
Not Hispanic (9,314)	9,504	94.00
Hispanic (110)	131	1.30

Courtland

Place Type: Township
County: Kent
Population: 7,678†

Ancestry‡	Population	%
American (463)	463	6.27
Armenian (0)	18	0.24
Belgian (0)	13	0.18
British (0)	26	0.35
Canadian (0)	15	0.20
Czech (14)	124	1.68
Danish (15)	79	1.07
Dutch (540)	1,346	18.24
English (227)	1,138	15.42
European (138)	138	1.87
Finnish (8)	93	1.26
French, ex. Basque (15)	286	3.88
French Canadian (57)	137	1.86
German (628)	2,127	28.82
Greek (0)	18	0.24
Hungarian (7)	27	0.37
Irish (154)	898	12.17
Italian (88)	344	4.66
Lithuanian (15)	112	1.52
Luxemburger (13)	13	0.18
Norwegian (56)	165	2.24
Polish (248)	924	12.52
Russian (0)	32	0.43
Scandinavian (0)	44	0.60
Scotch-Irish (12)	144	1.95
Scottish (27)	297	4.02
Slovak (8)	8	0.11
Swedish (18)	230	3.12
Swiss (0)	36	0.49
Welsh (6)	44	0.60
Yugoslavian (0)	7	0.09

Hispanic Origin	Population	%
Hispanic or Latino (of any race)	124	1.62
Central American, ex. Mexican	14	0.18
Guatemalan	9	0.12
Panamanian	3	0.04
Salvadoran	2	0.03
Cuban	6	0.08
Mexican	79	1.03
Puerto Rican	11	0.14
South American	5	0.07
Colombian	1	0.01
Peruvian	4	0.05
Other Hispanic or Latino	9	0.12

Race*	Population	%
African-American/Black (22)	50	0.65
Not Hispanic (22)	49	0.64
Hispanic (0)	1	0.01
American Indian/Alaska Native (23)	48	0.63
Not Hispanic (21)	46	0.60
Hispanic (2)	2	0.03
Apache (0)	1	0.01
Blackfeet (3)	3	0.04
Chippewa (12)	19	0.25
Mexican American Ind. (1)	1	0.01
Ottawa (1)	4	0.05
Potawatomi (1)	2	0.03
Asian (81)	100	1.30
Not Hispanic (81)	100	1.30
Burmese (1)	1	0.01
Chinese, ex. Taiwanese (29)	34	0.44
Filipino (9)	13	0.17
Hmong (11)	11	0.14
Indian (7)	8	0.10
Indonesian (1)	1	0.01
Japanese (0)	5	0.07
Korean (17)	20	0.26
Taiwanese (1)	1	0.01
Thai (4)	4	0.05

SECTION TWO

*Notes: † The Census 2010 population figure is used to calculate the percentages in the Hispanic Origin and Race categories. Ancestry percentages are based on the 2006-2010 American Community Survey population (not shown); ‡ Numbers in parentheses indicate the number of people reporting a single ancestry; * Numbers in parentheses indicate the number of persons reporting this race alone, not in combination with any other race; Please refer to the Explanation of Data for more information.*

Vietnamese (1)	1	0.01
Hawaii Native/Pacific Islander (1)	8	0.10
Not Hispanic (1)	8	0.10
Native Hawaiian (1)	6	0.08
White (7,425)	7,509	97.80
Not Hispanic (7,348)	7,420	96.64
Hispanic (77)	89	1.16

Cutlerville

Place Type: CDP
County: Kent
Population: 14,370†

Ancestry‡	Population	%
African, Sub-Saharan (0)	23	0.16
African (0)	23	0.16
American (590)	590	4.22
Arab (45)	45	0.32
Arab (45)	45	0.32
Austrian (0)	12	0.09
British (10)	26	0.19
Canadian (0)	13	0.09
Czech (36)	87	0.62
Czechoslovakian (12)	12	0.09
Danish (0)	88	0.63
Dutch (2,671)	3,950	28.25
English (257)	1,005	7.19
European (107)	107	0.77
Finnish (74)	162	1.16
French, ex. Basque (45)	386	2.76
French Canadian (44)	133	0.95
German (854)	3,217	23.01
Greek (0)	24	0.17
Hungarian (21)	53	0.38
Icelander (16)	16	0.11
Irish (172)	1,453	10.39
Italian (56)	374	2.67
Lithuanian (27)	27	0.19
Norwegian (21)	33	0.24
Pennsylvania German (11)	24	0.17
Polish (256)	823	5.89
Portuguese (0)	13	0.09
Romanian (34)	34	0.24
Russian (10)	84	0.60
Scotch-Irish (28)	163	1.17
Scottish (44)	91	0.65
Slovak (0)	36	0.26
Swedish (44)	178	1.27
Ukrainian (32)	43	0.31
Welsh (0)	14	0.10
Yugoslavian (24)	24	0.17

Hispanic Origin	Population	%
Hispanic or Latino (of any race)	1,175	8.18
Central American, ex. Mexican	98	0.68
Costa Rican	2	0.01
Guatemalan	50	0.35
Honduran	13	0.09
Nicaraguan	4	0.03
Panamanian	6	0.04
Salvadoran	22	0.15
Other Central American	1	0.01
Cuban	42	0.29
Dominican Republic	19	0.13
Mexican	818	5.69
Puerto Rican	133	0.93
South American	22	0.15
Argentinean	4	0.03
Bolivian	1	0.01
Chilean	3	0.02
Colombian	6	0.04
Paraguayan	1	0.01
Peruvian	7	0.05
Other Hispanic or Latino	43	0.30

Race*	Population	%
African-American/Black (1,033)	1,235	8.59
Not Hispanic (1,007)	1,182	8.23
Hispanic (26)	53	0.37
American Indian/Alaska Native (115)	235	1.64
Not Hispanic (99)	192	1.34
Hispanic (16)	43	0.30
Blackfeet (0)	1	0.01
Canadian/French Am. Ind. (2)	5	0.03
Cherokee (7)	23	0.16
Chickasaw (1)	3	0.02
Chippewa (24)	45	0.31
Mexican American Ind. (6)	12	0.08
Navajo (4)	4	0.03
Ottawa (11)	18	0.13
Potawatomi (26)	38	0.26
Sioux (1)	4	0.03
South American Ind. (0)	1	0.01
Asian (425)	489	3.40
Not Hispanic (425)	481	3.35
Hispanic (0)	8	0.06
Burmese (2)	2	0.01
Cambodian (5)	6	0.04
Chinese, ex. Taiwanese (26)	44	0.31
Filipino (11)	26	0.18
Hmong (1)	3	0.02
Indian (4)	9	0.06
Indonesian (2)	2	0.01
Japanese (3)	9	0.06
Korean (37)	55	0.38
Nepalese (1)	1	0.01
Thai (0)	1	0.01
Vietnamese (312)	332	2.31
Hawaii Native/Pacific Islander (3)	17	0.12
Not Hispanic (3)	14	0.10
Hispanic (0)	3	0.02
Native Hawaiian (1)	8	0.06
Samoan (0)	2	0.01
White (11,814)	12,222	85.05
Not Hispanic (11,314)	11,627	80.91
Hispanic (500)	595	4.14

Dalton

Place Type: Township
County: Muskegon
Population: 9,300†

Ancestry‡	Population	%
African, Sub-Saharan (3)	3	0.03
African (3)	3	0.03
American (305)	305	3.33
Austrian (0)	8	0.09
Belgian (10)	13	0.14
Brazilian (0)	2	0.02
British (8)	30	0.33
Canadian (11)	21	0.23
Croatian (10)	21	0.23
Czech (0)	17	0.19
Czechoslovakian (4)	19	0.21
Danish (3)	51	0.56
Dutch (322)	1,278	13.97
Eastern European (7)	7	0.08
English (328)	1,041	11.38
European (127)	127	1.39
Finnish (11)	18	0.20
French, ex. Basque (97)	490	5.36
French Canadian (36)	204	2.23
German (736)	2,526	27.62
German Russian (0)	8	0.09
Greek (15)	15	0.16
Hungarian (12)	43	0.47
Irish (105)	1,230	13.45
Italian (78)	174	1.90
Lithuanian (10)	56	0.61
Northern European (19)	19	0.21
Norwegian (14)	153	1.67
Polish (153)	726	7.94
Russian (0)	17	0.19
Scandinavian (0)	7	0.08
Scotch-Irish (0)	65	0.71
Scottish (30)	139	1.52
Slavic (0)	3	0.03
Slovak (22)	31	0.34
Swedish (104)	266	2.91
Ukrainian (0)	57	0.62
Welsh (0)	10	0.11
Yugoslavian (9)	74	0.81

Hispanic Origin	Population	%
Hispanic or Latino (of any race)	314	3.38
Central American, ex. Mexican	9	0.10
Costa Rican	4	0.04
Guatemalan	3	0.03
Nicaraguan	1	0.01
Panamanian	1	0.01
Cuban	3	0.03
Dominican Republic	1	0.01
Mexican	232	2.49
Puerto Rican	28	0.30
South American	8	0.09
Bolivian	1	0.01
Chilean	1	0.01
Colombian	5	0.05
Peruvian	1	0.01
Other Hispanic or Latino	33	0.35

Race*	Population	%
African-American/Black (169)	247	2.66
Not Hispanic (161)	230	2.47
Hispanic (8)	17	0.18
American Indian/Alaska Native (84)	183	1.97
Not Hispanic (83)	172	1.85
Hispanic (1)	11	0.12
Alaska Athabascan *(Ala. Nat.)* (3)	3	0.03
Blackfeet (0)	2	0.02
Cherokee (2)	9	0.10
Chippewa (21)	30	0.32
Choctaw (0)	1	0.01
Iroquois (0)	1	0.01
Lumbee (1)	5	0.05
Mexican American Ind. (0)	1	0.01
Ottawa (35)	51	0.55
Potawatomi (4)	4	0.04
Sioux (0)	3	0.03
Asian (20)	31	0.33
Not Hispanic (20)	30	0.32
Hispanic (0)	1	0.01
Chinese, ex. Taiwanese (5)	6	0.06
Filipino (0)	2	0.02
Korean (10)	17	0.18
Laotian (3)	3	0.03
Pakistani (0)	1	0.01
Vietnamese (1)	1	0.01
Hawaii Native/Pacific Islander (1)	1	0.01
Not Hispanic (1)	1	0.01
Samoan (1)	1	0.01
White (8,754)	8,955	96.29
Not Hispanic (8,561)	8,719	93.75
Hispanic (193)	236	2.54

Davison

Place Type: Township
County: Genesee
Population: 19,575†

Ancestry‡	Population	%
African, Sub-Saharan (31)	31	0.16
African (31)	31	0.16
American (1,211)	1,211	6.22
Arab (52)	52	0.27
Lebanese (52)	52	0.27
Armenian (0)	29	0.15
Austrian (14)	81	0.42
Belgian (27)	37	0.19
British (93)	176	0.90
Canadian (153)	232	1.19
Celtic (11)	11	0.06
Czech (92)	238	1.22
Czechoslovakian (0)	63	0.32
Danish (34)	92	0.47
Dutch (115)	485	2.49
English (767)	2,694	13.84

*Notes: † The Census 2010 population figure is used to calculate the percentages in the Hispanic Origin and Race categories. Ancestry percentages are based on the 2006-2010 American Community Survey population (not shown); ‡ Numbers in parentheses indicate the number of people reporting a single ancestry; * Numbers in parentheses indicate the number of persons reporting this race alone, not in combination with any other race; Please refer to the Explanation of Data for more information.*

European (176)	226	1.16
Finnish (78)	174	0.89
French, ex. Basque (145)	861	4.42
French Canadian (277)	555	2.85
German (1,080)	4,071	20.91
Greek (24)	74	0.38
Hungarian (91)	284	1.46
Irish (643)	2,853	14.65
Italian (59)	423	2.17
Lithuanian (33)	59	0.30
Macedonian (16)	16	0.08
Maltese (24)	39	0.20
Norwegian (21)	51	0.26
Polish (524)	1,425	7.32
Romanian (9)	21	0.11
Russian (23)	170	0.87
Scandinavian (0)	13	0.07
Scotch-Irish (126)	343	1.76
Scottish (255)	575	2.95
Slovak (18)	155	0.80
Swedish (50)	260	1.34
Ukrainian (25)	36	0.18
Welsh (35)	108	0.55
Yugoslavian (10)	10	0.05

Hispanic Origin	Population	%
Hispanic or Latino (of any race)	628	3.21
Central American, ex. Mexican	10	0.05
Guatemalan	4	0.02
Panamanian	4	0.02
Salvadoran	2	0.01
Cuban	11	0.06
Mexican	499	2.55
Puerto Rican	43	0.22
South American	12	0.06
Colombian	4	0.02
Ecuadorian	1	0.01
Paraguayan	1	0.01
Peruvian	6	0.03
Other Hispanic or Latino	53	0.27

Race*	Population	%
African-American/Black (562)	704	3.60
Not Hispanic (552)	679	3.47
Hispanic (10)	25	0.13
American Indian/Alaska Native (119)	272	1.39
Not Hispanic (100)	239	1.22
Hispanic (19)	33	0.17
Alaska Athabascan *(Ala. Nat.)* (1)	3	0.02
Apache (4)	7	0.04
Blackfeet (1)	11	0.06
Canadian/French Am. Ind. (1)	3	0.02
Central American Ind. (1)	1	0.01
Cherokee (17)	48	0.25
Chippewa (40)	60	0.31
Choctaw (6)	8	0.04
Creek (0)	3	0.02
Iroquois (3)	5	0.03
Lumbee (2)	2	0.01
Mexican American Ind. (3)	4	0.02
Ottawa (8)	12	0.06
Paiute (0)	2	0.01
Potawatomi (2)	4	0.02
Seminole (0)	3	0.02
Shoshone (0)	1	0.01
Sioux (0)	1	0.01
South American Ind. (0)	1	0.01
Asian (151)	205	1.05
Not Hispanic (151)	203	1.04
Hispanic (0)	2	0.01
Cambodian (1)	1	0.01
Chinese, ex. Taiwanese (27)	35	0.18
Filipino (25)	41	0.21
Indian (21)	27	0.14
Japanese (5)	19	0.10
Korean (23)	36	0.18
Pakistani (1)	2	0.01
Thai (3)	3	0.02
Vietnamese (37)	39	0.20
Hawaii Native/Pacific Islander (5)	14	0.07
Not Hispanic (5)	12	0.06
Hispanic (0)	2	0.01
Fijian (0)	1	0.01
Guamanian/Chamorro (1)	3	0.02
Native Hawaiian (3)	7	0.04
Samoan (1)	2	0.01
White (18,256)	18,625	95.15
Not Hispanic (17,801)	18,110	92.52
Hispanic (455)	515	2.63

DeWitt

Place Type: Charter Township
County: Clinton
Population: 14,321†

Ancestry‡	Population	%
American (1,812)	1,812	12.88
Arab (13)	13	0.09
Lebanese (13)	13	0.09
Armenian (22)	29	0.21
Austrian (12)	48	0.34
Belgian (7)	41	0.29
British (8)	16	0.11
Canadian (39)	98	0.70
Croatian (14)	66	0.47
Czech (0)	67	0.48
Czechoslovakian (29)	82	0.58
Danish (0)	42	0.30
Dutch (115)	450	3.20
Eastern European (9)	9	0.06
English (665)	2,244	15.95
European (65)	65	0.46
Finnish (21)	115	0.82
French, ex. Basque (80)	546	3.88
French Canadian (122)	297	2.11
German (1,443)	4,489	31.91
Greek (40)	88	0.63
Hungarian (13)	159	1.13
Irish (414)	1,917	13.63
Italian (219)	477	3.39
Latvian (12)	37	0.26
Lithuanian (19)	49	0.35
Macedonian (14)	14	0.10
Maltese (0)	17	0.12
Norwegian (37)	188	1.34
Polish (164)	723	5.14
Portuguese (14)	14	0.10
Romanian (0)	8	0.06
Russian (21)	21	0.15
Scandinavian (0)	9	0.06
Scotch-Irish (31)	230	1.64
Scottish (5)	363	2.58
Serbian (13)	58	0.41
Slavic (0)	19	0.14
Slovak (14)	24	0.17
Swedish (30)	311	2.21
Swiss (9)	25	0.18
Ukrainian (10)	29	0.21
Welsh (38)	178	1.27
Yugoslavian (0)	6	0.04

Hispanic Origin	Population	%
Hispanic or Latino (of any race)	878	6.13
Central American, ex. Mexican	28	0.20
Costa Rican	5	0.03
Guatemalan	11	0.08
Honduran	10	0.07
Panamanian	1	0.01
Salvadoran	1	0.01
Cuban	49	0.34
Mexican	678	4.73
Puerto Rican	26	0.18
South American	14	0.10
Colombian	2	0.01
Paraguayan	2	0.01
Uruguayan	2	0.01
Venezuelan	4	0.03
Other South American	4	0.03
Other Hispanic or Latino	83	0.58

Race*	Population	%
African-American/Black (377)	559	3.90
Not Hispanic (367)	514	3.59
Hispanic (10)	45	0.31
American Indian/Alaska Native (85)	215	1.50
Not Hispanic (78)	202	1.41
Hispanic (7)	13	0.09
Blackfeet (0)	2	0.01
Canadian/French Am. Ind. (3)	9	0.06
Cherokee (7)	29	0.20
Chippewa (29)	53	0.37
Iroquois (4)	10	0.07
Menominee (1)	1	0.01
Mexican American Ind. (1)	3	0.02
Ottawa (7)	23	0.16
Potawatomi (3)	3	0.02
Sioux (0)	3	0.02
Asian (196)	258	1.80
Not Hispanic (192)	252	1.76
Hispanic (4)	6	0.04
Burmese (11)	11	0.08
Chinese, ex. Taiwanese (36)	43	0.30
Filipino (22)	39	0.27
Hmong (26)	26	0.18
Indian (28)	33	0.23
Japanese (5)	13	0.09
Korean (21)	35	0.24
Laotian (8)	10	0.07
Malaysian (0)	4	0.03
Pakistani (8)	8	0.06
Sri Lankan (1)	1	0.01
Taiwanese (1)	1	0.01
Thai (3)	4	0.03
Vietnamese (13)	18	0.13
Hawaii Native/Pacific Islander (3)	7	0.05
Not Hispanic (1)	5	0.03
Hispanic (2)	2	0.01
Guamanian/Chamorro (1)	1	0.01
Native Hawaiian (0)	3	0.02
White (13,001)	13,368	93.35
Not Hispanic (12,488)	12,785	89.27
Hispanic (513)	583	4.07

Dearborn Heights

Place Type: City
County: Wayne
Population: 57,774†

Ancestry‡	Population	%
African, Sub-Saharan (98)	119	0.20
African (92)	113	0.19
Other Sub-Saharan African (6)	6	0.01
Albanian (50)	61	0.11
American (1,967)	1,967	3.39
Arab (9,307)	10,397	17.91
Arab (858)	1,002	1.73
Egyptian (27)	27	0.05
Iraqi (524)	578	1.00
Jordanian (226)	265	0.46
Lebanese (6,743)	7,446	12.82
Palestinian (166)	196	0.34
Syrian (430)	512	0.88
Other Arab (333)	371	0.64
Armenian (115)	303	0.52
Assyrian/Chaldean/Syriac (48)	48	0.08
Austrian (45)	198	0.34
Belgian (61)	97	0.17
Brazilian (11)	23	0.04
British (61)	102	0.18
Bulgarian (0)	28	0.05
Canadian (95)	250	0.43
Croatian (11)	60	0.10
Czech (41)	231	0.40
Czechoslovakian (112)	181	0.31
Danish (25)	121	0.21
Dutch (205)	762	1.31
Eastern European (63)	63	0.11
English (1,445)	5,091	8.77

*Notes: † The Census 2010 population figure is used to calculate the percentages in the Hispanic Origin and Race categories. Ancestry percentages are based on the 2006-2010 American Community Survey population (not shown); ‡ Numbers in parentheses indicate the number of people reporting a single ancestry; * Numbers in parentheses indicate the number of persons reporting this race alone, not in combination with any other race; Please refer to the Explanation of Data for more information.*

European (387)	409	0.70
Finnish (190)	417	0.72
French, ex. Basque (166)	2,147	3.70
French Canadian (388)	1,102	1.90
German (1,883)	8,682	14.95
Greek (164)	408	0.70
Guyanese (0)	5	0.01
Hungarian (263)	952	1.64
Irish (1,282)	6,820	11.75
Israeli (0)	9	0.02
Italian (1,793)	4,117	7.09
Lithuanian (160)	272	0.47
Macedonian (298)	393	0.68
Maltese (236)	286	0.49
Northern European (21)	39	0.07
Norwegian (35)	204	0.35
Polish (4,862)	9,260	15.95
Portuguese (5)	13	0.02
Romanian (456)	560	0.96
Russian (33)	343	0.59
Scandinavian (20)	33	0.06
Scotch-Irish (323)	931	1.60
Scottish (225)	1,474	2.54
Serbian (0)	54	0.09
Slavic (16)	16	0.03
Slovak (44)	175	0.30
Slovene (13)	13	0.02
Swedish (138)	569	0.98
Swiss (0)	113	0.19
Turkish (24)	39	0.07
Ukrainian (162)	456	0.79
Welsh (20)	194	0.33
West Indian, ex. Hispanic (61)	75	0.13
Jamaican (61)	75	0.13
Yugoslavian (199)	279	0.48

Hispanic Origin	Population	%
Hispanic or Latino (of any race)	2,712	4.69
Central American, ex. Mexican	87	0.15
Costa Rican	11	0.02
Guatemalan	14	0.02
Honduran	10	0.02
Nicaraguan	16	0.03
Panamanian	8	0.01
Salvadoran	28	0.05
Cuban	60	0.10
Dominican Republic	18	0.03
Mexican	1,861	3.22
Puerto Rican	352	0.61
South American	100	0.17
Argentinean	23	0.04
Chilean	1	<0.01
Colombian	33	0.06
Ecuadorian	11	0.02
Paraguayan	2	<0.01
Peruvian	3	0.01
Venezuelan	24	0.04
Other South American	3	0.01
Other Hispanic or Latino	234	0.41

Race*	Population	%
African-American/Black (4,546)	5,011	8.67
Not Hispanic (4,490)	4,892	8.47
Hispanic (56)	119	0.21
American Indian/Alaska Native (237)	561	0.97
Not Hispanic (196)	472	0.82
Hispanic (41)	89	0.15
Alaska Athabascan *(Ala. Nat.)* (1)	1	<0.01
Apache (2)	5	0.01
Blackfeet (0)	15	0.03
Canadian/French Am. Ind. (7)	9	0.02
Cherokee (25)	101	0.17
Chickasaw (3)	3	0.01
Chippewa (49)	78	0.14
Choctaw (3)	4	0.01
Comanche (2)	3	0.01
Cree (1)	1	<0.01
Creek (0)	1	<0.01
Delaware (0)	1	<0.01
Hopi (0)	1	<0.01
Iroquois (37)	61	0.11
Kiowa (0)	1	<0.01
Lumbee (7)	8	0.01
Menominee (2)	2	<0.01
Mexican American Ind. (0)	6	0.01
Navajo (3)	4	0.01
Ottawa (3)	15	0.03
Paiute (2)	2	<0.01
Potawatomi (0)	3	0.01
Seminole (0)	3	0.01
Sioux (0)	7	0.01
South American Ind. (1)	1	<0.01
Asian (999)	1,696	2.94
Not Hispanic (995)	1,673	2.90
Hispanic (4)	23	0.04
Bangladeshi (0)	1	<0.01
Cambodian (4)	9	0.02
Chinese, ex. Taiwanese (137)	157	0.27
Filipino (132)	199	0.34
Indian (288)	317	0.55
Indonesian (3)	3	0.01
Japanese (16)	45	0.08
Korean (37)	59	0.10
Pakistani (89)	99	0.17
Sri Lankan (2)	2	<0.01
Taiwanese (3)	3	0.01
Thai (9)	22	0.04
Vietnamese (214)	219	0.38
Hawaii Native/Pacific Islander (12)	73	0.13
Not Hispanic (9)	69	0.12
Hispanic (3)	4	0.01
Guamanian/Chamorro (1)	7	0.01
Native Hawaiian (3)	10	0.02
Samoan (7)	8	0.01
White (49,772)	51,263	88.73
Not Hispanic (47,943)	49,214	85.18
Hispanic (1,829)	2,049	3.55

Dearborn

Place Type: City
County: Wayne
Population: 98,153†

Ancestry‡	Population	%
Afghan (42)	42	0.04
African, Sub-Saharan (141)	351	0.36
African (46)	183	0.19
Nigerian (3)	3	<0.01
Somalian (41)	41	0.04
Other Sub-Saharan African (51)	124	0.13
Albanian (591)	666	0.68
Alsatian (0)	11	0.01
American (1,835)	1,835	1.86
Arab (35,960)	38,503	39.13
Arab (7,455)	8,134	8.27
Egyptian (328)	356	0.36
Iraqi (2,618)	2,820	2.87
Jordanian (785)	805	0.82
Lebanese (17,582)	18,812	19.12
Moroccan (60)	121	0.12
Palestinian (680)	792	0.80
Syrian (249)	309	0.31
Other Arab (6,203)	6,354	6.46
Armenian (345)	542	0.55
Assyrian/Chaldean/Syriac (13)	33	0.03
Australian (12)	26	0.03
Austrian (63)	218	0.22
Basque (11)	11	0.01
Belgian (41)	339	0.34
Brazilian (60)	77	0.08
British (122)	276	0.28
Bulgarian (23)	55	0.06
Canadian (173)	417	0.42
Celtic (16)	22	0.02
Croatian (45)	147	0.15
Czech (128)	398	0.40
Czechoslovakian (16)	91	0.09
Danish (29)	162	0.16
Dutch (167)	911	0.93
Eastern European (120)	176	0.18
English (1,336)	5,649	5.74
European (638)	688	0.70
Finnish (190)	458	0.47
French, ex. Basque (238)	2,748	2.79
French Canadian (520)	1,773	1.80
German (2,855)	12,189	12.39
Greek (226)	399	0.41
Hungarian (593)	1,569	1.59
Iranian (33)	43	0.04
Irish (1,894)	9,225	9.38
Israeli (32)	32	0.03
Italian (2,319)	4,907	4.99
Latvian (25)	25	0.03
Lithuanian (137)	528	0.54
Luxemburger (0)	11	0.01
Macedonian (138)	165	0.17
Maltese (326)	662	0.67
Northern European (92)	92	0.09
Norwegian (35)	413	0.42
Pennsylvania German (9)	9	0.01
Polish (4,194)	10,629	10.80
Portuguese (32)	32	0.03
Romanian (779)	916	0.93
Russian (143)	534	0.54
Scandinavian (9)	9	0.01
Scotch-Irish (464)	1,388	1.41
Scottish (482)	1,516	1.54
Serbian (36)	93	0.09
Slavic (15)	68	0.07
Slovak (78)	236	0.24
Slovene (8)	48	0.05
Swedish (154)	954	0.97
Swiss (5)	75	0.08
Turkish (12)	35	0.04
Ukrainian (424)	988	1.00
Welsh (82)	353	0.36
West Indian, ex. Hispanic (45)	180	0.18
Haitian (0)	25	0.03
Trinidadian/Tobagonian (45)	155	0.16
Yugoslavian (29)	233	0.24

Hispanic Origin	Population	%
Hispanic or Latino (of any race)	3,386	3.45
Central American, ex. Mexican	97	0.10
Guatemalan	38	0.04
Honduran	9	0.01
Nicaraguan	10	0.01
Panamanian	11	0.01
Salvadoran	29	0.03
Cuban	72	0.07
Dominican Republic	33	0.03
Mexican	2,320	2.36
Puerto Rican	383	0.39
South American	141	0.14
Argentinean	21	0.02
Bolivian	1	<0.01
Chilean	13	0.01
Colombian	42	0.04
Ecuadorian	9	0.01
Paraguayan	3	<0.01
Peruvian	7	0.01
Venezuelan	43	0.04
Other South American	2	<0.01
Other Hispanic or Latino	340	0.35

Race*	Population	%
African-American/Black (3,965)	4,413	4.50
Not Hispanic (3,895)	4,296	4.38
Hispanic (70)	117	0.12
American Indian/Alaska Native (220)	555	0.57
Not Hispanic (166)	450	0.46
Hispanic (54)	105	0.11
Apache (0)	2	<0.01
Blackfeet (2)	9	0.01
Canadian/French Am. Ind. (4)	5	0.01
Central American Ind. (0)	1	<0.01
Cherokee (17)	92	0.09
Cheyenne (0)	1	<0.01
Chippewa (42)	69	0.07

*Notes: † The Census 2010 population figure is used to calculate the percentages in the Hispanic Origin and Race categories. Ancestry percentages are based on the 2006-2010 American Community Survey population (not shown); ‡ Numbers in parentheses indicate the number of people reporting a single ancestry; * Numbers in parentheses indicate the number of persons reporting this race alone, not in combination with any other race; Please refer to the Explanation of Data for more information.*

Choctaw (2)	17	0.02
Comanche (0)	2	<0.01
Cree (0)	2	<0.01
Creek (1)	4	<0.01
Delaware (1)	1	<0.01
Inupiat *(Alaska Native)* (0)	6	0.01
Iroquois (30)	39	0.04
Lumbee (3)	6	0.01
Menominee (0)	1	<0.01
Mexican American Ind. (9)	15	0.02
Navajo (2)	3	<0.01
Osage (0)	1	<0.01
Ottawa (3)	3	<0.01
Potawatomi (2)	9	0.01
Shoshone (1)	1	<0.01
Sioux (1)	5	0.01
South American Ind. (5)	12	0.01
Tlingit-Haida *(Alaska Native)* (1)	1	<0.01
Yaqui (5)	9	0.01
Asian (1,706)	4,603	4.69
Not Hispanic (1,696)	4,522	4.61
Hispanic (10)	81	0.08
Bangladeshi (7)	7	0.01
Cambodian (8)	13	0.01
Chinese, ex. Taiwanese (176)	236	0.24
Filipino (172)	269	0.27
Hmong (1)	1	<0.01
Indian (547)	695	0.71
Indonesian (6)	8	0.01
Japanese (17)	64	0.07
Korean (74)	104	0.11
Laotian (2)	2	<0.01
Malaysian (4)	7	0.01
Nepalese (6)	7	0.01
Pakistani (346)	379	0.39
Sri Lankan (0)	1	<0.01
Taiwanese (16)	17	0.02
Thai (8)	13	0.01
Vietnamese (131)	157	0.16
Hawaii Native/Pacific Islander (32)	208	0.21
Not Hispanic (31)	201	0.20
Hispanic (1)	7	0.01
Guamanian/Chamorro (0)	2	<0.01
Native Hawaiian (4)	16	0.02
Samoan (16)	18	0.02
Tongan (1)	5	0.01
White (87,454)	91,285	93.00
Not Hispanic (85,116)	88,708	90.38
Hispanic (2,338)	2,577	2.63

Delhi

Place Type: Charter Township
County: Ingham
Population: 25,877†

Ancestry‡	Population	%
African, Sub-Saharan (35)	98	0.39
African (17)	72	0.28
Ghanaian (18)	18	0.07
Nigerian (0)	8	0.03
Albanian (102)	102	0.40
American (2,050)	2,050	8.09
Arab (96)	107	0.42
Lebanese (96)	107	0.42
Australian (77)	77	0.30
Austrian (0)	38	0.15
Belgian (12)	119	0.47
British (54)	99	0.39
Canadian (68)	212	0.84
Celtic (0)	24	0.09
Croatian (136)	136	0.54
Czech (22)	257	1.01
Czechoslovakian (9)	72	0.28
Danish (26)	102	0.40
Dutch (264)	1,381	5.45
English (894)	3,462	13.66
European (172)	195	0.77
Finnish (51)	212	0.84
French, ex. Basque (279)	1,305	5.15
French Canadian (125)	459	1.81
German (1,977)	7,233	28.54
Greek (0)	62	0.24
Hungarian (47)	171	0.67
Irish (575)	3,139	12.39
Italian (253)	895	3.53
Lithuanian (11)	32	0.13
Macedonian (13)	13	0.05
Maltese (0)	44	0.17
Norwegian (166)	362	1.43
Pennsylvania German (12)	34	0.13
Polish (464)	1,527	6.03
Romanian (0)	36	0.14
Russian (81)	199	0.79
Scotch-Irish (189)	429	1.69
Scottish (300)	799	3.15
Slavic (0)	12	0.05
Slovak (22)	22	0.09
Swedish (77)	463	1.83
Swiss (19)	70	0.28
Ukrainian (12)	79	0.31
Welsh (14)	183	0.72
West Indian, ex. Hispanic (19)	19	0.07
Belizean (11)	11	0.04
Haitian (8)	8	0.03

Hispanic Origin	Population	%
Hispanic or Latino (of any race)	1,381	5.34
Central American, ex. Mexican	45	0.17
Costa Rican	3	0.01
Guatemalan	16	0.06
Honduran	4	0.02
Nicaraguan	11	0.04
Panamanian	4	0.02
Salvadoran	4	0.02
Other Central American	3	0.01
Cuban	50	0.19
Dominican Republic	4	0.02
Mexican	1,021	3.95
Puerto Rican	94	0.36
South American	28	0.11
Argentinean	4	0.02
Chilean	3	0.01
Colombian	11	0.04
Ecuadorian	2	0.01
Peruvian	4	0.02
Uruguayan	1	<0.01
Venezuelan	3	0.01
Other Hispanic or Latino	139	0.54

Race*	Population	%
African-American/Black (1,350)	1,754	6.78
Not Hispanic (1,296)	1,631	6.30
Hispanic (54)	123	0.48
American Indian/Alaska Native (128)	330	1.28
Not Hispanic (116)	299	1.16
Hispanic (12)	31	0.12
Blackfeet (2)	20	0.08
Canadian/French Am. Ind. (1)	5	0.02
Cherokee (8)	43	0.17
Chippewa (40)	61	0.24
Choctaw (2)	2	0.01
Comanche (2)	2	0.01
Cree (1)	1	<0.01
Creek (3)	3	0.01
Crow (0)	2	0.01
Iroquois (3)	7	0.03
Lumbee (0)	1	<0.01
Mexican American Ind. (6)	7	0.03
Navajo (0)	6	0.02
Osage (0)	2	0.01
Ottawa (12)	22	0.09
Potawatomi (5)	15	0.06
Seminole (1)	4	0.02
Sioux (1)	9	0.03
South American Ind. (0)	3	0.01
Spanish American Ind. (1)	1	<0.01
Asian (759)	922	3.56
Not Hispanic (753)	910	3.52
Hispanic (6)	12	0.05
Bangladeshi (2)	4	0.02
Cambodian (2)	3	0.01
Chinese, ex. Taiwanese (57)	67	0.26
Filipino (44)	87	0.34
Hmong (49)	51	0.20
Indian (157)	177	0.68
Indonesian (5)	8	0.03
Japanese (26)	64	0.25
Korean (95)	112	0.43
Laotian (2)	7	0.03
Malaysian (0)	1	<0.01
Pakistani (13)	16	0.06
Taiwanese (1)	1	<0.01
Thai (4)	5	0.02
Vietnamese (279)	296	1.14
Hawaii Native/Pacific Islander (9)	29	0.11
Not Hispanic (8)	28	0.11
Hispanic (1)	1	<0.01
Fijian (1)	1	<0.01
Guamanian/Chamorro (1)	2	0.01
Native Hawaiian (4)	13	0.05
Samoan (0)	5	0.02
White (22,472)	23,200	89.65
Not Hispanic (21,658)	22,248	85.98
Hispanic (814)	952	3.68

Delta

Place Type: Charter Township
County: Eaton
Population: 32,408†

Ancestry‡	Population	%
African, Sub-Saharan (122)	122	0.38
African (63)	63	0.20
Ethiopian (59)	59	0.18
Albanian (179)	179	0.56
American (1,134)	1,134	3.52
Arab (197)	376	1.17
Lebanese (189)	351	1.09
Palestinian (8)	8	0.02
Other Arab (0)	17	0.05
Armenian (0)	39	0.12
Austrian (11)	40	0.12
Belgian (9)	59	0.18
British (88)	114	0.35
Canadian (10)	35	0.11
Celtic (0)	17	0.05
Croatian (22)	29	0.09
Czech (57)	388	1.20
Czechoslovakian (46)	66	0.20
Danish (35)	231	0.72
Dutch (227)	1,354	4.20
Eastern European (12)	51	0.16
English (1,295)	4,711	14.62
European (420)	459	1.42
Finnish (108)	225	0.70
French, ex. Basque (134)	1,452	4.51
French Canadian (137)	566	1.76
German (2,612)	8,821	27.38
Greek (96)	156	0.48
Guyanese (0)	8	0.02
Hungarian (34)	142	0.44
Irish (733)	4,879	15.14
Italian (638)	1,625	5.04
Lithuanian (52)	99	0.31
Macedonian (16)	16	0.05
Northern European (58)	58	0.18
Norwegian (94)	420	1.30
Pennsylvania German (0)	10	0.03
Polish (563)	1,912	5.93
Portuguese (49)	49	0.15
Romanian (0)	46	0.14
Russian (29)	154	0.48
Scandinavian (0)	18	0.06
Scotch-Irish (238)	611	1.90
Scottish (300)	929	2.88
Serbian (0)	13	0.04
Slavic (0)	143	0.44
Slovak (27)	204	0.63

*Notes: † The Census 2010 population figure is used to calculate the percentages in the Hispanic Origin and Race categories. Ancestry percentages are based on the 2006-2010 American Community Survey population (not shown); ‡ Numbers in parentheses indicate the number of people reporting a single ancestry; * Numbers in parentheses indicate the number of persons reporting this race alone, not in combination with any other race; Please refer to the Explanation of Data for more information.*

Slovene (0)	13	0.04
Swedish (126)	1,047	3.25
Swiss (0)	97	0.30
Turkish (7)	7	0.02
Ukrainian (29)	46	0.14
Welsh (29)	189	0.59
West Indian, ex. Hispanic (28)	28	0.09
Jamaican (28)	28	0.09
Yugoslavian (96)	96	0.30

Hispanic Origin	Population	%
Hispanic or Latino (of any race)	1,996	6.16
Central American, ex. Mexican	54	0.17
Costa Rican	5	0.02
Guatemalan	27	0.08
Honduran	3	0.01
Nicaraguan	7	0.02
Panamanian	7	0.02
Salvadoran	5	0.02
Cuban	167	0.52
Dominican Republic	11	0.03
Mexican	1,441	4.45
Puerto Rican	106	0.33
South American	65	0.20
Argentinean	11	0.03
Bolivian	11	0.03
Chilean	2	0.01
Colombian	14	0.04
Ecuadorian	15	0.05
Peruvian	3	0.01
Uruguayan	1	<0.01
Venezuelan	5	0.02
Other South American	3	0.01
Other Hispanic or Latino	152	0.47

Race*	Population	%
African-American/Black (3,754)	4,378	13.51
Not Hispanic (3,680)	4,217	13.01
Hispanic (74)	161	0.50
American Indian/Alaska Native (174)	474	1.46
Not Hispanic (154)	423	1.31
Hispanic (20)	51	0.16
Apache (1)	2	0.01
Blackfeet (1)	17	0.05
Canadian/French Am. Ind. (4)	6	0.02
Central American Ind. (2)	2	0.01
Cherokee (6)	70	0.22
Chippewa (39)	82	0.25
Choctaw (2)	6	0.02
Creek (1)	6	0.02
Crow (0)	1	<0.01
Delaware (4)	4	0.01
Iroquois (4)	14	0.04
Menominee (0)	7	0.02
Mexican American Ind. (3)	4	0.01
Navajo (2)	3	0.01
Osage (0)	1	<0.01
Ottawa (29)	47	0.15
Potawatomi (2)	6	0.02
Sioux (2)	3	0.01
Tlingit-Haida *(Alaska Native)* (1)	1	<0.01
Tohono O'Odham (0)	1	<0.01
Asian (1,242)	1,460	4.51
Not Hispanic (1,234)	1,447	4.46
Hispanic (8)	13	0.04
Burmese (5)	5	0.02
Cambodian (2)	4	0.01
Chinese, ex. Taiwanese (122)	147	0.45
Filipino (44)	75	0.23
Hmong (27)	40	0.12
Indian (552)	602	1.86
Indonesian (4)	7	0.02
Japanese (11)	30	0.09
Korean (71)	101	0.31
Laotian (12)	17	0.05
Nepalese (1)	2	0.01
Pakistani (56)	63	0.19
Sri Lankan (6)	8	0.02
Taiwanese (1)	4	0.01
Thai (3)	9	0.03
Vietnamese (284)	302	0.93
Hawaii Native/Pacific Islander (3)	26	0.08
Not Hispanic (3)	18	0.06
Hispanic (0)	8	0.02
Guamanian/Chamorro (1)	2	0.01
Native Hawaiian (1)	3	0.01
Samoan (1)	2	0.01
White (25,461)	26,468	81.67
Not Hispanic (24,366)	25,170	77.67
Hispanic (1,095)	1,298	4.01

Detroit

Place Type: City
County: Wayne
Population: 713,777†

Ancestry‡	Population	%
African, Sub-Saharan (9,758)	12,021	1.58
African (7,657)	9,726	1.28
Cape Verdean (16)	16	<0.01
Ethiopian (43)	106	0.01
Ghanaian (0)	28	<0.01
Kenyan (286)	286	0.04
Liberian (81)	81	0.01
Nigerian (1,207)	1,282	0.17
Senegalese (28)	28	<0.01
Somalian (87)	97	0.01
South African (75)	75	0.01
Sudanese (37)	37	<0.01
Other Sub-Saharan African (241)	259	0.03
Albanian (214)	233	0.03
American (7,086)	7,086	0.93
Arab (8,077)	8,642	1.14
Arab (4,276)	4,349	0.57
Egyptian (20)	92	0.01
Iraqi (1,072)	1,125	0.15
Jordanian (106)	117	0.02
Lebanese (362)	566	0.07
Moroccan (313)	398	0.05
Palestinian (121)	132	0.02
Syrian (9)	26	<0.01
Other Arab (1,798)	1,837	0.24
Armenian (139)	234	0.03
Assyrian/Chaldean/Syriac (630)	656	0.09
Australian (50)	129	0.02
Austrian (19)	157	0.02
Basque (13)	13	<0.01
Belgian (80)	422	0.06
British (323)	405	0.05
Bulgarian (44)	53	0.01
Cajun (41)	62	0.01
Canadian (371)	743	0.10
Celtic (0)	9	<0.01
Croatian (64)	216	0.03
Czech (60)	326	0.04
Czechoslovakian (14)	52	0.01
Danish (80)	230	0.03
Dutch (327)	1,226	0.16
Eastern European (49)	61	0.01
English (2,251)	5,767	0.76
Estonian (7)	7	<0.01
European (349)	736	0.10
Finnish (238)	624	0.08
French, ex. Basque (691)	3,837	0.51
French Canadian (243)	906	0.12
German (2,715)	11,126	1.47
German Russian (83)	119	0.02
Greek (171)	451	0.06
Hungarian (340)	1,137	0.15
Iranian (10)	10	<0.01
Irish (2,594)	10,866	1.43
Italian (1,909)	4,785	0.63
Latvian (8)	8	<0.01
Lithuanian (149)	261	0.03
Luxemburger (0)	9	<0.01
Macedonian (17)	17	<0.01
Maltese (118)	266	0.04
Northern European (25)	25	<0.01
Norwegian (106)	292	0.04
Pennsylvania German (17)	78	0.01
Polish (5,452)	10,573	1.39
Portuguese (9)	42	0.01
Romanian (515)	608	0.08
Russian (211)	635	0.08
Scandinavian (84)	94	0.01
Scotch-Irish (486)	1,253	0.17
Scottish (377)	1,309	0.17
Serbian (40)	111	0.01
Slavic (53)	89	0.01
Slovak (96)	378	0.05
Slovene (0)	9	<0.01
Swedish (115)	717	0.09
Swiss (25)	149	0.02
Turkish (31)	40	0.01
Ukrainian (272)	647	0.09
Welsh (64)	317	0.04
West Indian, ex. Hispanic (1,859)	2,609	0.34
Bahamian (59)	59	0.01
Barbadian (18)	29	<0.01
Belizean (11)	11	<0.01
Bermudan (0)	10	<0.01
Haitian (149)	199	0.03
Jamaican (1,412)	1,946	0.26
Trinidadian/Tobagonian (100)	119	0.02
U.S. Virgin Islander (15)	15	<0.01
West Indian (95)	221	0.03
Yugoslavian (31)	45	0.01

Hispanic Origin	Population	%
Hispanic or Latino (of any race)	48,679	6.82
Central American, ex. Mexican	1,813	0.25
Costa Rican	33	<0.01
Guatemalan	542	0.08
Honduran	566	0.08
Nicaraguan	69	0.01
Panamanian	124	0.02
Salvadoran	451	0.06
Other Central American	28	<0.01
Cuban	773	0.11
Dominican Republic	688	0.10
Mexican	36,452	5.11
Puerto Rican	5,783	0.81
South American	337	0.05
Argentinean	41	0.01
Bolivian	3	<0.01
Chilean	24	<0.01
Colombian	101	0.01
Ecuadorian	38	0.01
Peruvian	77	0.01
Uruguayan	7	<0.01
Venezuelan	38	0.01
Other South American	8	<0.01
Other Hispanic or Latino	2,833	0.40

Race*	Population	%
African-American/Black (590,226)	601,988	84.34
Not Hispanic (586,573)	596,963	83.63
Hispanic (3,653)	5,025	0.70
American Indian/Alaska Native (2,636)	8,448	1.18
Not Hispanic (1,927)	6,965	0.98
Hispanic (709)	1,483	0.21
Alaska Athabascan *(Ala. Nat.)* (0)	1	<0.01
Aleut *(Alaska Native)* (0)	1	<0.01
Apache (15)	59	0.01
Arapaho (1)	4	<0.01
Blackfeet (43)	441	0.06
Canadian/French Am. Ind. (23)	45	0.01
Central American Ind. (7)	15	<0.01
Cherokee (158)	1,321	0.19
Cheyenne (0)	6	<0.01
Chickasaw (3)	19	<0.01
Chippewa (126)	285	0.04
Choctaw (32)	193	0.03
Comanche (7)	16	<0.01
Cree (1)	32	<0.01
Creek (14)	71	0.01
Crow (2)	17	<0.01
Delaware (6)	28	<0.01
Hopi (1)	8	<0.01

*Notes: † The Census 2010 population figure is used to calculate the percentages in the Hispanic Origin and Race categories. Ancestry percentages are based on the 2006-2010 American Community Survey population (not shown); ‡ Numbers in parentheses indicate the number of people reporting a single ancestry; * Numbers in parentheses indicate the number of persons reporting this race alone, not in combination with any other race; Please refer to the Explanation of Data for more information.*

Race* (continued)	Population	%
Inupiat *(Alaska Native)* (0)	3	<0.01
Iroquois (65)	140	0.02
Kiowa (0)	1	<0.01
Lumbee (15)	48	0.01
Menominee (3)	15	<0.01
Mexican American Ind. (170)	238	0.03
Navajo (15)	46	0.01
Osage (0)	1	<0.01
Ottawa (34)	59	0.01
Paiute (0)	1	<0.01
Potawatomi (22)	61	0.01
Pueblo (5)	5	<0.01
Puget Sound Salish (4)	5	<0.01
Seminole (12)	63	0.01
Shoshone (0)	4	<0.01
Sioux (27)	68	0.01
South American Ind. (7)	29	<0.01
Spanish American Ind. (10)	10	<0.01
Tlingit-Haida *(Alaska Native)* (1)	3	<0.01
Tohono O'Odham (0)	2	<0.01
Ute (7)	7	<0.01
Yakama (2)	3	<0.01
Yaqui (1)	2	<0.01
Yuman (0)	2	<0.01
Yup'ik *(Alaska Native)* (2)	2	<0.01
Asian (7,559)	9,925	1.39
Not Hispanic (7,436)	9,598	1.34
Hispanic (123)	327	0.05
Bangladeshi (2,597)	2,825	0.40
Burmese (3)	3	<0.01
Cambodian (9)	13	<0.01
Chinese, ex. Taiwanese (597)	852	0.12
Filipino (538)	875	0.12
Hmong (545)	578	0.08
Indian (1,959)	2,588	0.36
Indonesian (5)	12	<0.01
Japanese (107)	307	0.04
Korean (203)	341	0.05
Laotian (82)	112	0.02
Malaysian (5)	8	<0.01
Nepalese (17)	17	<0.01
Pakistani (86)	124	0.02
Sri Lankan (39)	46	0.01
Taiwanese (30)	38	0.01
Thai (41)	96	0.01
Vietnamese (127)	182	0.03
Hawaii Native/Pacific Islander (129)	673	0.09
Not Hispanic (82)	503	0.07
Hispanic (47)	170	0.02
Fijian (0)	2	<0.01
Guamanian/Chamorro (49)	117	0.02
Native Hawaiian (30)	130	0.02
Samoan (18)	71	0.01
Tongan (0)	4	<0.01
White (75,758)	86,039	12.05
Not Hispanic (55,604)	63,384	8.88
Hispanic (20,154)	22,655	3.17

East Bay

Place Type: Township
County: Grand Traverse
Population: 10,663†

Ancestry‡	Population	%
African, Sub-Saharan (0)	18	0.17
South African (0)	18	0.17
American (823)	823	7.75
Belgian (0)	171	1.61
British (15)	44	0.41
Bulgarian (21)	21	0.20
Canadian (8)	51	0.48
Croatian (0)	8	0.08
Czech (50)	173	1.63
Czechoslovakian (0)	9	0.08
Danish (24)	102	0.96
Dutch (309)	790	7.44
English (305)	1,334	12.56
European (119)	129	1.22
Finnish (42)	184	1.73
French, ex. Basque (100)	719	6.77
French Canadian (71)	570	5.37
German (763)	3,210	30.23
Greek (0)	31	0.29
Hungarian (9)	31	0.29
Irish (264)	1,395	13.14
Italian (147)	597	5.62
Lithuanian (24)	47	0.44
Norwegian (21)	200	1.88
Pennsylvania German (22)	22	0.21
Polish (228)	741	6.98
Russian (12)	23	0.22
Scandinavian (8)	60	0.57
Scotch-Irish (27)	298	2.81
Scottish (68)	422	3.97
Serbian (0)	9	0.08
Slovene (9)	9	0.08
Swedish (40)	222	2.09
Swiss (12)	67	0.63
Ukrainian (12)	22	0.21
Welsh (8)	102	0.96
Yugoslavian (0)	10	0.09

Hispanic Origin	Population	%
Hispanic or Latino (of any race)	175	1.64
Central American, ex. Mexican	6	0.06
Guatemalan	4	0.04
Honduran	1	0.01
Panamanian	1	0.01
Cuban	8	0.08
Mexican	105	0.98
Puerto Rican	17	0.16
South American	9	0.08
Chilean	1	0.01
Colombian	5	0.05
Ecuadorian	3	0.03
Other Hispanic or Latino	30	0.28

Race*	Population	%
African-American/Black (33)	80	0.75
Not Hispanic (33)	76	0.71
Hispanic (0)	4	0.04
American Indian/Alaska Native (104)	183	1.72
Not Hispanic (93)	168	1.58
Hispanic (11)	15	0.14
Blackfeet (0)	1	0.01
Canadian/French Am. Ind. (4)	6	0.06
Cherokee (0)	4	0.04
Chippewa (48)	79	0.74
Creek (1)	1	0.01
Delaware (2)	2	0.02
Mexican American Ind. (3)	4	0.04
Navajo (1)	3	0.03
Ottawa (13)	40	0.38
Potawatomi (5)	8	0.08
Asian (71)	97	0.91
Not Hispanic (69)	92	0.86
Hispanic (2)	5	0.05
Chinese, ex. Taiwanese (8)	12	0.11
Filipino (10)	23	0.22
Hmong (7)	7	0.07
Indian (4)	7	0.07
Japanese (4)	9	0.08
Korean (9)	10	0.09
Laotian (21)	22	0.21
Vietnamese (0)	1	0.01
Hawaii Native/Pacific Islander (4)	10	0.09
Not Hispanic (4)	10	0.09
Native Hawaiian (2)	6	0.06
White (10,249)	10,401	97.54
Not Hispanic (10,140)	10,279	96.40
Hispanic (109)	122	1.14

East Grand Rapids

Place Type: City
County: Kent
Population: 10,694†

Ancestry‡	Population	%
American (244)	244	2.27
Arab (30)	41	0.38
Arab (0)	11	0.10
Lebanese (21)	21	0.20
Syrian (9)	9	0.08
Austrian (11)	45	0.42
Belgian (0)	29	0.27
British (43)	104	0.97
Canadian (66)	99	0.92
Croatian (0)	14	0.13
Czech (0)	36	0.34
Czechoslovakian (0)	22	0.20
Danish (8)	77	0.72
Dutch (957)	1,985	18.49
Eastern European (12)	12	0.11
English (366)	2,118	19.73
European (226)	265	2.47
Finnish (0)	54	0.50
French, ex. Basque (58)	569	5.30
French Canadian (21)	120	1.12
German (556)	2,816	26.23
Greek (102)	137	1.28
Hungarian (8)	51	0.48
Iranian (0)	10	0.09
Irish (597)	2,126	19.81
Italian (209)	752	7.01
Latvian (17)	17	0.16
Luxemburger (30)	30	0.28
Northern European (21)	26	0.24
Norwegian (21)	159	1.48
Polish (136)	857	7.98
Romanian (9)	45	0.42
Russian (34)	72	0.67
Scandinavian (63)	81	0.75
Scotch-Irish (129)	241	2.25
Scottish (123)	561	5.23
Serbian (10)	10	0.09
Slovak (0)	17	0.16
Swedish (185)	439	4.09
Swiss (0)	59	0.55
Welsh (38)	286	2.66

Hispanic Origin	Population	%
Hispanic or Latino (of any race)	158	1.48
Central American, ex. Mexican	12	0.11
Guatemalan	8	0.07
Honduran	1	0.01
Salvadoran	3	0.03
Cuban	9	0.08
Mexican	76	0.71
Puerto Rican	14	0.13
South American	25	0.23
Argentinean	9	0.08
Chilean	9	0.08
Colombian	4	0.04
Ecuadorian	1	0.01
Peruvian	1	0.01
Uruguayan	1	0.01
Other Hispanic or Latino	22	0.21

Race*	Population	%
African-American/Black (113)	161	1.51
Not Hispanic (107)	149	1.39
Hispanic (6)	12	0.11
American Indian/Alaska Native (16)	53	0.50
Not Hispanic (13)	47	0.44
Hispanic (3)	6	0.06
Cherokee (0)	4	0.04
Chippewa (1)	16	0.15
Iroquois (1)	1	0.01
Mexican American Ind. (1)	3	0.03
Navajo (1)	2	0.02
Potawatomi (4)	5	0.05
Tlingit-Haida *(Alaska Native)* (0)	1	0.01
Asian (160)	237	2.22
Not Hispanic (160)	236	2.21
Hispanic (0)	1	0.01
Bangladeshi (1)	3	0.03
Chinese, ex. Taiwanese (45)	72	0.67

*Notes: † The Census 2010 population figure is used to calculate the percentages in the Hispanic Origin and Race categories. Ancestry percentages are based on the 2006-2010 American Community Survey population (not shown); ‡ Numbers in parentheses indicate the number of people reporting a single ancestry; * Numbers in parentheses indicate the number of persons reporting this race alone, not in combination with any other race; Please refer to the Explanation of Data for more information.*

Filipino (19)	23	0.22
Indian (32)	42	0.39
Indonesian (0)	2	0.02
Japanese (20)	36	0.34
Korean (36)	40	0.37
Pakistani (0)	1	0.01
Taiwanese (0)	2	0.02
Thai (2)	8	0.07
Vietnamese (2)	8	0.07
Hawaii Native/Pacific Islander (5)	15	0.14
Not Hispanic (5)	15	0.14
Guamanian/Chamorro (0)	2	0.02
Native Hawaiian (1)	7	0.07
White (10,204)	10,369	96.96
Not Hispanic (10,088)	10,237	95.73
Hispanic (116)	132	1.23

East Lansing

Place Type: City
County: Ingham
Population: 46,610†

Ancestry‡	Population	%
African, Sub-Saharan (833)	968	2.07
African (428)	563	1.20
Ethiopian (39)	39	0.08
Ghanaian (5)	5	0.01
Kenyan (44)	44	0.09
Nigerian (143)	143	0.31
Somalian (32)	32	0.07
South African (28)	28	0.06
Sudanese (58)	58	0.12
Zimbabwean (20)	20	0.04
Other Sub-Saharan African (36)	36	0.08
Albanian (92)	101	0.22
American (2,968)	2,968	6.35
Arab (394)	731	1.56
Arab (47)	47	0.10
Egyptian (63)	63	0.13
Iraqi (31)	44	0.09
Lebanese (90)	331	0.71
Palestinian (29)	61	0.13
Syrian (22)	60	0.13
Other Arab (112)	125	0.27
Armenian (217)	287	0.61
Assyrian/Chaldean/Syriac (31)	41	0.09
Australian (43)	43	0.09
Austrian (11)	143	0.31
Belgian (13)	280	0.60
Brazilian (0)	35	0.07
British (125)	454	0.97
Bulgarian (36)	61	0.13
Canadian (25)	168	0.36
Croatian (30)	117	0.25
Czech (77)	323	0.69
Czechoslovakian (54)	104	0.22
Danish (132)	283	0.61
Dutch (766)	1,774	3.80
Eastern European (53)	65	0.14
English (970)	4,633	9.91
European (576)	624	1.34
Finnish (159)	361	0.77
French, ex. Basque (317)	2,160	4.62
French Canadian (137)	442	0.95
German (3,252)	11,000	23.54
Greek (173)	286	0.61
Hungarian (244)	675	1.44
Iranian (51)	64	0.14
Irish (1,685)	7,901	16.91
Italian (1,069)	3,736	7.99
Latvian (27)	61	0.13
Lithuanian (45)	204	0.44
Macedonian (22)	50	0.11
Maltese (23)	132	0.28
Northern European (40)	40	0.09
Norwegian (151)	551	1.18
Polish (1,311)	4,293	9.19
Portuguese (7)	7	0.01
Romanian (148)	293	0.63
Russian (323)	927	1.98
Scandinavian (16)	99	0.21
Scotch-Irish (221)	788	1.69
Scottish (279)	1,140	2.44
Serbian (60)	78	0.17
Slavic (26)	34	0.07
Slovak (50)	220	0.47
Slovene (15)	78	0.17
Swedish (131)	933	2.00
Swiss (38)	194	0.42
Turkish (29)	43	0.09
Ukrainian (48)	243	0.52
Welsh (28)	424	0.91
West Indian, ex. Hispanic (74)	139	0.30
Jamaican (32)	48	0.10
Trinidadian/Tobagonian (29)	29	0.06
West Indian (13)	62	0.13
Yugoslavian (36)	116	0.25

Hispanic Origin	Population	%
Hispanic or Latino (of any race)	1,566	3.36
Central American, ex. Mexican	69	0.15
Costa Rican	8	0.02
Guatemalan	29	0.06
Honduran	8	0.02
Nicaraguan	5	0.01
Panamanian	4	0.01
Salvadoran	15	0.03
Cuban	84	0.18
Dominican Republic	29	0.06
Mexican	912	1.96
Puerto Rican	123	0.26
South American	183	0.39
Argentinean	26	0.06
Bolivian	6	0.01
Chilean	10	0.02
Colombian	64	0.14
Ecuadorian	23	0.05
Paraguayan	4	0.01
Peruvian	30	0.06
Uruguayan	2	<0.01
Venezuelan	18	0.04
Other Hispanic or Latino	166	0.36

Race*	Population	%
African-American/Black (3,118)	3,645	7.82
Not Hispanic (3,069)	3,547	7.61
Hispanic (49)	98	0.21
American Indian/Alaska Native (146)	414	0.89
Not Hispanic (120)	356	0.76
Hispanic (26)	58	0.12
Arapaho (1)	1	<0.01
Blackfeet (1)	9	0.02
Canadian/French Am. Ind. (1)	2	<0.01
Cherokee (7)	53	0.11
Chickasaw (3)	4	0.01
Chippewa (54)	111	0.24
Choctaw (1)	1	<0.01
Creek (0)	1	<0.01
Hopi (1)	1	<0.01
Inupiat *(Alaska Native)* (1)	1	<0.01
Iroquois (5)	15	0.03
Lumbee (1)	3	0.01
Mexican American Ind. (10)	15	0.03
Navajo (0)	1	<0.01
Ottawa (15)	27	0.06
Paiute (0)	1	<0.01
Potawatomi (3)	9	0.02
Pueblo (1)	1	<0.01
Seminole (0)	2	<0.01
Shoshone (2)	4	0.01
Sioux (0)	6	0.01
South American Ind. (1)	2	<0.01
Spanish American Ind. (0)	1	<0.01
Yaqui (0)	3	0.01
Asian (4,877)	5,473	11.74
Not Hispanic (4,860)	5,440	11.67
Hispanic (17)	33	0.07
Bangladeshi (19)	19	0.04
Burmese (5)	7	0.02
Cambodian (9)	9	0.02
Chinese, ex. Taiwanese (1,859)	1,978	4.24
Filipino (127)	221	0.47
Hmong (28)	32	0.07
Indian (898)	986	2.12
Indonesian (43)	47	0.10
Japanese (158)	243	0.52
Korean (894)	955	2.05
Laotian (5)	9	0.02
Malaysian (62)	65	0.14
Nepalese (28)	32	0.07
Pakistani (185)	207	0.44
Sri Lankan (17)	20	0.04
Taiwanese (167)	185	0.40
Thai (77)	84	0.18
Vietnamese (139)	159	0.34
Hawaii Native/Pacific Islander (22)	65	0.14
Not Hispanic (20)	57	0.12
Hispanic (2)	8	0.02
Fijian (1)	1	<0.01
Guamanian/Chamorro (2)	3	0.01
Native Hawaiian (6)	14	0.03
Samoan (3)	6	0.01
White (36,653)	37,829	81.16
Not Hispanic (35,717)	36,746	78.84
Hispanic (936)	1,083	2.32

East Lansing

Place Type: City
County: Ingham
Population: 48,579†

Ancestry‡	Population	%
African, Sub-Saharan (1,011)	1,223	2.54
African (606)	782	1.62
Ethiopian (39)	39	0.08
Ghanaian (5)	5	0.01
Kenyan (44)	44	0.09
Nigerian (143)	143	0.30
Somalian (32)	32	0.07
South African (28)	64	0.13
Sudanese (58)	58	0.12
Zimbabwean (20)	20	0.04
Other Sub-Saharan African (36)	36	0.07
Albanian (92)	101	0.21
American (3,169)	3,169	6.57
Arab (423)	784	1.63
Arab (47)	47	0.10
Egyptian (63)	63	0.13
Iraqi (46)	71	0.15
Lebanese (90)	331	0.69
Palestinian (29)	61	0.13
Syrian (36)	86	0.18
Other Arab (112)	125	0.26
Armenian (217)	287	0.60
Assyrian/Chaldean/Syriac (38)	48	0.10
Australian (43)	43	0.09
Austrian (11)	147	0.30
Belgian (13)	287	0.60
Brazilian (0)	35	0.07
British (125)	454	0.94
Bulgarian (36)	61	0.13
Canadian (25)	197	0.41
Croatian (30)	117	0.24
Czech (89)	344	0.71
Czechoslovakian (54)	104	0.22
Danish (132)	283	0.59
Dutch (766)	1,820	3.77
Eastern European (53)	65	0.13
English (999)	4,801	9.96
European (623)	671	1.39
Finnish (159)	361	0.75
French, ex. Basque (317)	2,219	4.60
French Canadian (148)	453	0.94
German (3,287)	11,149	23.12
Greek (173)	293	0.61
Hungarian (244)	675	1.40
Iranian (51)	64	0.13
Irish (1,724)	7,985	16.56

*Notes: † The Census 2010 population figure is used to calculate the percentages in the Hispanic Origin and Race categories. Ancestry percentages are based on the 2006-2010 American Community Survey population (not shown); ‡ Numbers in parentheses indicate the number of people reporting a single ancestry; * Numbers in parentheses indicate the number of persons reporting this race alone, not in combination with any other race; Please refer to the Explanation of Data for more information.*

Italian (1,080)	3,754	7.79
Latvian (27)	61	0.13
Lithuanian (45)	211	0.44
Macedonian (22)	50	0.10
Maltese (23)	132	0.27
Northern European (40)	40	0.08
Norwegian (151)	567	1.18
Polish (1,311)	4,338	9.00
Portuguese (7)	7	0.01
Romanian (148)	293	0.61
Russian (323)	927	1.92
Scandinavian (16)	116	0.24
Scotch-Irish (221)	797	1.65
Scottish (279)	1,166	2.42
Serbian (60)	78	0.16
Slavic (26)	34	0.07
Slovak (50)	224	0.46
Slovene (15)	78	0.16
Swedish (131)	940	1.95
Swiss (38)	194	0.40
Turkish (29)	43	0.09
Ukrainian (48)	243	0.50
Welsh (28)	424	0.88
West Indian, ex. Hispanic (74)	157	0.33
Jamaican (32)	66	0.14
Trinidadian/Tobagonian (29)	29	0.06
West Indian (13)	62	0.13
Yugoslavian (36)	116	0.24

Hispanic Origin	Population	%
Hispanic or Latino (of any race)	1,643	3.38
Central American, ex. Mexican	73	0.15
Costa Rican	8	0.02
Guatemalan	30	0.06
Honduran	9	0.02
Nicaraguan	5	0.01
Panamanian	4	0.01
Salvadoran	17	0.03
Cuban	86	0.18
Dominican Republic	30	0.06
Mexican	951	1.96
Puerto Rican	128	0.26
South American	194	0.40
Argentinean	26	0.05
Bolivian	6	0.01
Chilean	11	0.02
Colombian	70	0.14
Ecuadorian	23	0.05
Paraguayan	4	0.01
Peruvian	33	0.07
Uruguayan	3	0.01
Venezuelan	18	0.04
Other Hispanic or Latino	181	0.37

Race*	Population	%
African-American/Black (3,303)	3,867	7.96
Not Hispanic (3,249)	3,761	7.74
Hispanic (54)	106	0.22
American Indian/Alaska Native (148)	421	0.87
Not Hispanic (121)	361	0.74
Hispanic (27)	60	0.12
Arapaho (1)	1	<0.01
Blackfeet (1)	9	0.02
Canadian/French Am. Ind. (1)	2	<0.01
Cherokee (7)	53	0.11
Chickasaw (3)	4	0.01
Chippewa (55)	114	0.23
Choctaw (1)	2	<0.01
Creek (0)	1	<0.01
Hopi (1)	1	<0.01
Inupiat *(Alaska Native)* (1)	1	<0.01
Iroquois (5)	15	0.03
Lumbee (1)	3	0.01
Mexican American Ind. (10)	15	0.03
Navajo (0)	1	<0.01
Ottawa (16)	28	0.06
Paiute (0)	1	<0.01
Potawatomi (3)	9	0.02
Pueblo (1)	1	<0.01
Seminole (0)	2	<0.01
Shoshone (2)	4	0.01
Sioux (0)	6	0.01
South American Ind. (1)	2	<0.01
Spanish American Ind. (0)	1	<0.01
Yaqui (0)	3	0.01
Asian (5,135)	5,765	11.87
Not Hispanic (5,118)	5,732	11.80
Hispanic (17)	33	0.07
Bangladeshi (19)	19	0.04
Burmese (5)	7	0.01
Cambodian (9)	9	0.02
Chinese, ex. Taiwanese (1,998)	2,124	4.37
Filipino (134)	235	0.48
Hmong (29)	33	0.07
Indian (946)	1,037	2.13
Indonesian (43)	47	0.10
Japanese (161)	249	0.51
Korean (939)	1,007	2.07
Laotian (5)	9	0.02
Malaysian (62)	65	0.13
Nepalese (31)	35	0.07
Pakistani (185)	212	0.44
Sri Lankan (17)	20	0.04
Taiwanese (171)	192	0.40
Thai (78)	85	0.17
Vietnamese (142)	163	0.34
Hawaii Native/Pacific Islander (22)	66	0.14
Not Hispanic (20)	58	0.12
Hispanic (2)	8	0.02
Fijian (1)	1	<0.01
Guamanian/Chamorro (2)	3	0.01
Native Hawaiian (6)	14	0.03
Samoan (3)	6	0.01
White (38,072)	39,313	80.93
Not Hispanic (37,086)	38,177	78.59
Hispanic (986)	1,136	2.34

Eastpointe

Place Type: City
County: Macomb
Population: 32,442†

Ancestry‡	Population	%
African, Sub-Saharan (133)	289	0.88
African (100)	256	0.78
Nigerian (13)	13	0.04
South African (20)	20	0.06
Albanian (126)	175	0.53
American (971)	971	2.95
Arab (83)	217	0.66
Arab (45)	83	0.25
Iraqi (1)	1	<0.01
Lebanese (37)	133	0.40
Armenian (0)	57	0.17
Australian (0)	35	0.11
Austrian (0)	57	0.17
Belgian (87)	432	1.31
British (9)	24	0.07
Canadian (58)	269	0.82
Croatian (32)	45	0.14
Czech (32)	128	0.39
Czechoslovakian (0)	10	0.03
Danish (9)	9	0.03
Dutch (68)	316	0.96
Eastern European (16)	16	0.05
English (559)	1,781	5.41
European (113)	188	0.57
Finnish (43)	269	0.82
French, ex. Basque (275)	1,505	4.57
French Canadian (179)	877	2.66
German (1,918)	6,752	20.50
Greek (143)	171	0.52
Hungarian (26)	151	0.46
Irish (644)	3,351	10.17
Italian (1,389)	3,697	11.22
Lithuanian (16)	64	0.19
Maltese (11)	32	0.10
Northern European (13)	13	0.04
Norwegian (0)	101	0.31
Polish (1,718)	4,519	13.72
Romanian (0)	55	0.17
Russian (50)	206	0.63
Scandinavian (6)	6	0.02
Scotch-Irish (134)	393	1.19
Scottish (170)	796	2.42
Serbian (20)	57	0.17
Slavic (16)	29	0.09
Slovak (27)	53	0.16
Swedish (34)	169	0.51
Swiss (0)	42	0.13
Ukrainian (111)	226	0.69
Welsh (0)	122	0.37
West Indian, ex. Hispanic (41)	61	0.19
Haitian (41)	41	0.12
Jamaican (0)	20	0.06
Yugoslavian (8)	19	0.06

Hispanic Origin	Population	%
Hispanic or Latino (of any race)	677	2.09
Central American, ex. Mexican	22	0.07
Costa Rican	1	<0.01
Guatemalan	10	0.03
Honduran	4	0.01
Panamanian	6	0.02
Salvadoran	1	<0.01
Cuban	29	0.09
Dominican Republic	4	0.01
Mexican	432	1.33
Puerto Rican	106	0.33
South American	32	0.10
Argentinean	4	0.01
Chilean	3	0.01
Colombian	11	0.03
Ecuadorian	4	0.01
Peruvian	4	0.01
Uruguayan	4	0.01
Venezuelan	2	0.01
Other Hispanic or Latino	52	0.16

Race*	Population	%
African-American/Black (9,575)	10,094	31.11
Not Hispanic (9,503)	9,990	30.79
Hispanic (72)	104	0.32
American Indian/Alaska Native (130)	520	1.60
Not Hispanic (114)	458	1.41
Hispanic (16)	62	0.19
Alaska Athabascan *(Ala. Nat.)* (0)	1	<0.01
Apache (1)	5	0.02
Blackfeet (2)	30	0.09
Canadian/French Am. Ind. (3)	12	0.04
Cherokee (17)	128	0.39
Cheyenne (0)	1	<0.01
Chippewa (22)	56	0.17
Choctaw (3)	4	0.01
Comanche (0)	1	<0.01
Cree (0)	5	0.02
Creek (1)	2	0.01
Delaware (2)	2	0.01
Iroquois (13)	22	0.07
Lumbee (8)	19	0.06
Menominee (1)	1	<0.01
Mexican American Ind. (3)	4	0.01
Navajo (0)	1	<0.01
Osage (0)	1	<0.01
Ottawa (4)	12	0.04
Paiute (0)	2	0.01
Potawatomi (0)	2	0.01
Sioux (0)	10	0.03
Yakama (0)	1	<0.01
Asian (353)	500	1.54
Not Hispanic (346)	484	1.49
Hispanic (7)	16	0.05
Bangladeshi (5)	5	0.02
Cambodian (24)	31	0.10
Chinese, ex. Taiwanese (31)	55	0.17
Filipino (52)	100	0.31
Hmong (104)	106	0.33
Indian (41)	61	0.19
Indonesian (2)	2	0.01

*Notes: † The Census 2010 population figure is used to calculate the percentages in the Hispanic Origin and Race categories. Ancestry percentages are based on the 2006-2010 American Community Survey population (not shown); ‡ Numbers in parentheses indicate the number of people reporting a single ancestry; * Numbers in parentheses indicate the number of persons reporting this race alone, not in combination with any other race; Please refer to the Explanation of Data for more information.*

Japanese (11)	26	0.08
Korean (20)	40	0.12
Laotian (14)	20	0.06
Pakistani (9)	19	0.06
Thai (7)	13	0.04
Vietnamese (18)	34	0.10
Hawaii Native/Pacific Islander (5)	34	0.10
Not Hispanic (4)	31	0.10
Hispanic (1)	3	0.01
Fijian (0)	1	<0.01
Guamanian/Chamorro (5)	14	0.04
Native Hawaiian (0)	3	0.01
Samoan (0)	1	<0.01
White (21,297)	22,123	68.19
Not Hispanic (20,898)	21,649	66.73
Hispanic (399)	474	1.46

Ecorse

Place Type: City
County: Wayne
Population: 9,512†

Ancestry‡	Population	%
African, Sub-Saharan (0)	11	0.11
African (0)	11	0.11
American (126)	126	1.28
Belgian (0)	24	0.24
Czechoslovakian (18)	45	0.46
Danish (0)	18	0.18
Dutch (0)	107	1.09
English (116)	386	3.92
European (0)	33	0.34
Finnish (63)	105	1.07
French, ex. Basque (12)	372	3.78
French Canadian (18)	179	1.82
German (114)	586	5.95
Greek (27)	49	0.50
Hungarian (40)	141	1.43
Irish (69)	448	4.55
Italian (46)	357	3.63
Norwegian (0)	11	0.11
Polish (150)	600	6.09
Romanian (23)	45	0.46
Russian (0)	43	0.44
Scotch-Irish (57)	75	0.76
Scottish (14)	62	0.63
Serbian (0)	11	0.11
Slovak (9)	9	0.09
Swedish (0)	58	0.59
Ukrainian (13)	40	0.41
Welsh (0)	52	0.53

Hispanic Origin	Population	%
Hispanic or Latino (of any race)	1,278	13.44
Central American, ex. Mexican	27	0.28
Guatemalan	7	0.07
Honduran	1	0.01
Panamanian	1	0.01
Salvadoran	18	0.19
Cuban	4	0.04
Dominican Republic	7	0.07
Mexican	1,042	10.95
Puerto Rican	85	0.89
South American	1	0.01
Argentinean	1	0.01
Other Hispanic or Latino	112	1.18

Race*	Population	%
African-American/Black (4,415)	4,627	48.64
Not Hispanic (4,375)	4,554	47.88
Hispanic (40)	73	0.77
American Indian/Alaska Native (74)	199	2.09
Not Hispanic (58)	150	1.58
Hispanic (16)	49	0.52
Apache (0)	1	0.01
Blackfeet (0)	12	0.13
Canadian/French Am. Ind. (6)	6	0.06
Cherokee (9)	35	0.37
Chippewa (6)	10	0.11
Choctaw (0)	2	0.02
Creek (0)	6	0.06
Iroquois (0)	1	0.01
Lumbee (0)	2	0.02
Mexican American Ind. (6)	7	0.07
Navajo (1)	1	0.01
Ottawa (0)	2	0.02
Potawatomi (3)	5	0.05
Sioux (1)	1	0.01
Yup'ik *(Alaska Native)* (1)	1	0.01
Asian (27)	65	0.68
Not Hispanic (27)	60	0.63
Hispanic (0)	5	0.05
Chinese, ex. Taiwanese (0)	1	0.01
Filipino (14)	24	0.25
Indian (2)	7	0.07
Japanese (1)	8	0.08
Korean (0)	6	0.06
Pakistani (2)	2	0.02
Thai (1)	1	0.01
Hawaii Native/Pacific Islander (1)	9	0.09
Not Hispanic (1)	6	0.06
Hispanic (0)	3	0.03
Guamanian/Chamorro (1)	1	0.01
Samoan (0)	4	0.04
White (4,186)	4,564	47.98
Not Hispanic (3,476)	3,727	39.18
Hispanic (710)	837	8.80

Egelston

Place Type: Township
County: Muskegon
Population: 9,909†

Ancestry‡	Population	%
American (649)	649	6.55
Armenian (0)	16	0.16
Belgian (38)	38	0.38
British (31)	31	0.31
Czech (0)	40	0.40
Czechoslovakian (14)	30	0.30
Danish (0)	14	0.14
Dutch (106)	701	7.07
English (212)	963	9.72
European (102)	102	1.03
Finnish (187)	226	2.28
French, ex. Basque (79)	756	7.63
French Canadian (73)	242	2.44
German (737)	2,626	26.49
Greek (0)	49	0.49
Hungarian (50)	124	1.25
Irish (300)	1,217	12.28
Italian (35)	84	0.85
Lithuanian (26)	60	0.61
Norwegian (39)	155	1.56
Polish (153)	410	4.14
Scotch-Irish (55)	135	1.36
Scottish (31)	293	2.96
Slovak (0)	8	0.08
Swedish (8)	188	1.90
Turkish (0)	10	0.10
Welsh (0)	26	0.26

Hispanic Origin	Population	%
Hispanic or Latino (of any race)	514	5.19
Central American, ex. Mexican	16	0.16
Costa Rican	4	0.04
Guatemalan	8	0.08
Panamanian	2	0.02
Salvadoran	2	0.02
Cuban	3	0.03
Mexican	426	4.30
Puerto Rican	26	0.26
South American	8	0.08
Chilean	4	0.04
Colombian	3	0.03
Peruvian	1	0.01
Other Hispanic or Latino	35	0.35

Race*	Population	%
African-American/Black (120)	206	2.08
Not Hispanic (117)	194	1.96
Hispanic (3)	12	0.12
American Indian/Alaska Native (106)	227	2.29
Not Hispanic (95)	197	1.99
Hispanic (11)	30	0.30
Blackfeet (4)	6	0.06
Cherokee (1)	15	0.15
Chippewa (15)	40	0.40
Crow (0)	1	0.01
Inupiat *(Alaska Native)* (3)	3	0.03
Iroquois (1)	1	0.01
Mexican American Ind. (3)	5	0.05
Ottawa (38)	64	0.65
Pima (1)	1	0.01
Potawatomi (15)	22	0.22
Pueblo (1)	1	0.01
Asian (35)	80	0.81
Not Hispanic (34)	79	0.80
Hispanic (1)	1	0.01
Chinese, ex. Taiwanese (13)	26	0.26
Filipino (9)	19	0.19
Indonesian (1)	1	0.01
Japanese (2)	7	0.07
Korean (6)	14	0.14
Malaysian (1)	1	0.01
Pakistani (1)	1	0.01
Thai (0)	3	0.03
Vietnamese (2)	8	0.08
Hawaii Native/Pacific Islander (1)	11	0.11
Not Hispanic (1)	10	0.10
Hispanic (0)	1	0.01
Guamanian/Chamorro (0)	4	0.04
Native Hawaiian (0)	2	0.02
Samoan (1)	1	0.01
White (9,224)	9,516	96.03
Not Hispanic (8,919)	9,137	92.21
Hispanic (305)	379	3.82

Emmett

Place Type: Charter Township
County: Calhoun
Population: 11,770†

Ancestry‡	Population	%
American (969)	969	8.17
Arab (10)	36	0.30
Arab (0)	14	0.12
Palestinian (10)	22	0.19
Armenian (0)	14	0.12
Belgian (10)	21	0.18
Brazilian (10)	10	0.08
British (29)	46	0.39
Bulgarian (0)	8	0.07
Canadian (101)	110	0.93
Croatian (14)	38	0.32
Czech (0)	20	0.17
Danish (11)	30	0.25
Dutch (128)	704	5.94
English (817)	1,967	16.58
European (198)	198	1.67
Finnish (0)	83	0.70
French, ex. Basque (128)	346	2.92
French Canadian (45)	108	0.91
German (894)	2,937	24.76
Hungarian (11)	86	0.73
Irish (282)	1,331	11.22
Italian (87)	420	3.54
Lithuanian (0)	14	0.12
Macedonian (50)	57	0.48
Norwegian (10)	129	1.09
Pennsylvania German (0)	14	0.12
Polish (190)	384	3.24
Portuguese (37)	37	0.31
Russian (20)	64	0.54
Scandinavian (16)	25	0.21
Scotch-Irish (56)	197	1.66

*Notes: † The Census 2010 population figure is used to calculate the percentages in the Hispanic Origin and Race categories. Ancestry percentages are based on the 2006-2010 American Community Survey population (not shown); ‡ Numbers in parentheses indicate the number of people reporting a single ancestry; * Numbers in parentheses indicate the number of persons reporting this race alone, not in combination with any other race; Please refer to the Explanation of Data for more information.*

Ancestry	Population	%
Scottish (56)	306	2.58
Serbian (22)	22	0.19
Swedish (35)	288	2.43
Swiss (0)	12	0.10
Ukrainian (0)	22	0.19
Welsh (23)	93	0.78

Hispanic Origin	Population	%
Hispanic or Latino (of any race)	456	3.87
Central American, ex. Mexican	12	0.10
Guatemalan	1	0.01
Honduran	1	0.01
Panamanian	4	0.03
Salvadoran	5	0.04
Other Central American	1	0.01
Cuban	14	0.12
Mexican	358	3.04
Puerto Rican	33	0.28
South American	7	0.06
Colombian	6	0.05
Paraguayan	1	0.01
Other Hispanic or Latino	32	0.27

Race*	Population	%
African-American/Black (369)	513	4.36
Not Hispanic (364)	498	4.23
Hispanic (5)	15	0.13
American Indian/Alaska Native (69)	178	1.51
Not Hispanic (68)	171	1.45
Hispanic (1)	7	0.06
Blackfeet (1)	12	0.10
Canadian/French Am. Ind. (1)	4	0.03
Cherokee (5)	26	0.22
Chippewa (16)	21	0.18
Choctaw (0)	2	0.02
Iroquois (0)	1	0.01
Lumbee (1)	3	0.03
Mexican American Ind. (1)	1	0.01
Ottawa (5)	11	0.09
Potawatomi (13)	37	0.31
Sioux (1)	1	0.01
Asian (141)	183	1.55
Not Hispanic (139)	181	1.54
Hispanic (2)	2	0.02
Burmese (2)	2	0.02
Chinese, ex. Taiwanese (7)	8	0.07
Filipino (19)	35	0.30
Indian (78)	83	0.71
Japanese (11)	14	0.12
Korean (16)	30	0.25
Nepalese (3)	3	0.03
Pakistani (0)	1	0.01
Thai (3)	3	0.03
Vietnamese (1)	1	0.01
Hawaii Native/Pacific Islander (1)	1	0.01
Not Hispanic (1)	1	0.01
Native Hawaiian (1)	1	0.01
White (10,762)	11,032	93.73
Not Hispanic (10,478)	10,713	91.02
Hispanic (284)	319	2.71

Escanaba

Place Type: City
County: Delta
Population: 12,616†

Ancestry‡	Population	%
American (249)	249	1.96
Arab (0)	103	0.81
Arab (0)	10	0.08
Lebanese (0)	93	0.73
Armenian (9)	9	0.07
Australian (23)	23	0.18
Austrian (0)	25	0.20
Belgian (42)	275	2.16
Brazilian (0)	9	0.07
Canadian (8)	56	0.44
Croatian (144)	244	1.92
Czech (22)	75	0.59
Danish (7)	65	0.51
Dutch (31)	221	1.74
English (222)	975	7.66
European (60)	69	0.54
Finnish (155)	681	5.35
French, ex. Basque (609)	2,458	19.30
French Canadian (605)	995	7.81
German (734)	2,845	22.34
Greek (35)	62	0.49
Hungarian (32)	38	0.30
Irish (178)	1,534	12.05
Italian (61)	423	3.32
Lithuanian (0)	9	0.07
Luxemburger (0)	31	0.24
Northern European (30)	30	0.24
Norwegian (102)	428	3.36
Polish (207)	747	5.87
Portuguese (0)	14	0.11
Romanian (56)	66	0.52
Russian (0)	38	0.30
Scandinavian (32)	67	0.53
Scotch-Irish (9)	129	1.01
Scottish (20)	131	1.03
Slavic (0)	11	0.09
Slovak (8)	25	0.20
Swedish (321)	1,359	10.67
Swiss (0)	40	0.31
Ukrainian (17)	33	0.26
Welsh (25)	74	0.58

Hispanic Origin	Population	%
Hispanic or Latino (of any race)	154	1.22
Central American, ex. Mexican	2	0.02
Guatemalan	1	0.01
Honduran	1	0.01
Cuban	5	0.04
Mexican	99	0.78
Puerto Rican	25	0.20
South American	4	0.03
Colombian	1	0.01
Peruvian	1	0.01
Venezuelan	2	0.02
Other Hispanic or Latino	19	0.15

Race*	Population	%
African-American/Black (53)	119	0.94
Not Hispanic (49)	110	0.87
Hispanic (4)	9	0.07
American Indian/Alaska Native (328)	572	4.53
Not Hispanic (321)	557	4.42
Hispanic (7)	15	0.12
Alaska Athabascan *(Ala. Nat.)* (1)	1	0.01
Apache (3)	8	0.06
Blackfeet (2)	3	0.02
Cherokee (2)	18	0.14
Cheyenne (1)	5	0.04
Chippewa (139)	243	1.93
Delaware (0)	1	0.01
Inupiat *(Alaska Native)* (0)	3	0.02
Iroquois (0)	1	0.01
Ottawa (15)	29	0.23
Potawatomi (48)	84	0.67
Sioux (16)	21	0.17
Asian (74)	112	0.89
Not Hispanic (73)	107	0.85
Hispanic (1)	5	0.04
Bangladeshi (1)	1	0.01
Chinese, ex. Taiwanese (24)	27	0.21
Filipino (13)	24	0.19
Indian (14)	14	0.11
Japanese (2)	14	0.11
Korean (11)	17	0.13
Sri Lankan (1)	1	0.01
Thai (0)	1	0.01
Vietnamese (7)	8	0.06
Hawaii Native/Pacific Islander (0)	2	0.02
Not Hispanic (0)	1	0.01
Hispanic (0)	1	0.01
Native Hawaiian (0)	1	0.01
White (11,790)	12,125	96.11
Not Hispanic (11,696)	12,012	95.21
Hispanic (94)	113	0.90

Fair Plain

Place Type: CDP
County: Berrien
Population: 7,631†

Ancestry‡	Population	%
African, Sub-Saharan (96)	96	1.28
African (76)	76	1.02
Zimbabwean (8)	8	0.11
Other Sub-Saharan African (12)	12	0.16
American (324)	324	4.33
Armenian (12)	12	0.16
Belgian (0)	10	0.13
Canadian (16)	22	0.29
Croatian (11)	11	0.15
Czech (0)	24	0.32
Danish (13)	13	0.17
Dutch (83)	185	2.47
English (84)	320	4.27
European (10)	15	0.20
Finnish (7)	16	0.21
French, ex. Basque (25)	72	0.96
French Canadian (31)	60	0.80
German (488)	1,249	16.68
Greek (24)	24	0.32
Hungarian (4)	42	0.56
Irish (120)	747	9.98
Italian (145)	394	5.26
Norwegian (0)	11	0.15
Pennsylvania German (0)	5	0.07
Polish (59)	139	1.86
Romanian (0)	8	0.11
Russian (10)	18	0.24
Scotch-Irish (31)	51	0.68
Scottish (0)	60	0.80
Slovene (8)	8	0.11
Swedish (34)	48	0.64
Ukrainian (0)	12	0.16
Welsh (16)	16	0.21

Hispanic Origin	Population	%
Hispanic or Latino (of any race)	249	3.26
Central American, ex. Mexican	7	0.09
Guatemalan	4	0.05
Salvadoran	3	0.04
Cuban	13	0.17
Dominican Republic	4	0.05
Mexican	171	2.24
Puerto Rican	30	0.39
South American	3	0.04
Argentinean	1	0.01
Colombian	1	0.01
Peruvian	1	0.01
Other Hispanic or Latino	21	0.28

Race*	Population	%
African-American/Black (3,943)	4,073	53.37
Not Hispanic (3,924)	4,044	52.99
Hispanic (19)	29	0.38
American Indian/Alaska Native (27)	89	1.17
Not Hispanic (23)	78	1.02
Hispanic (4)	11	0.14
Apache (1)	2	0.03
Blackfeet (0)	2	0.03
Cherokee (4)	15	0.20
Chippewa (2)	10	0.13
Iroquois (1)	1	0.01
Mexican American Ind. (1)	1	0.01
Potawatomi (4)	10	0.13
Sioux (0)	1	0.01
Asian (64)	93	1.22
Not Hispanic (64)	83	1.09
Hispanic (0)	10	0.13
Bangladeshi (5)	5	0.07
Cambodian (1)	1	0.01
Chinese, ex. Taiwanese (8)	11	0.14

*Notes: † The Census 2010 population figure is used to calculate the percentages in the Hispanic Origin and Race categories. Ancestry percentages are based on the 2006-2010 American Community Survey population (not shown); ‡ Numbers in parentheses indicate the number of people reporting a single ancestry; * Numbers in parentheses indicate the number of persons reporting this race alone, not in combination with any other race; Please refer to the Explanation of Data for more information.*

Filipino (4)	7	0.09
Indian (28)	36	0.47
Japanese (4)	12	0.16
Korean (7)	8	0.10
Pakistani (1)	1	0.01
Vietnamese (4)	6	0.08
Hawaii Native/Pacific Islander (0)	12	0.16
Not Hispanic (0)	7	0.09
Hispanic (0)	5	0.07
Guamanian/Chamorro (0)	2	0.03
Native Hawaiian (0)	3	0.04
White (3,318)	3,480	45.60
Not Hispanic (3,194)	3,336	43.72
Hispanic (124)	144	1.89

Farmington Hills

Place Type: City
County: Oakland
Population: 79,740†

Ancestry‡	Population	%
African, Sub-Saharan (639)	871	1.09
African (255)	395	0.49
Ethiopian (26)	26	0.03
Ghanaian (22)	22	0.03
Kenyan (15)	15	0.02
Nigerian (236)	269	0.34
South African (43)	69	0.09
Zimbabwean (16)	16	0.02
Other Sub-Saharan African (26)	59	0.07
Albanian (856)	866	1.08
American (3,057)	3,057	3.81
Arab (2,121)	2,505	3.12
Arab (553)	587	0.73
Egyptian (12)	12	0.01
Iraqi (657)	777	0.97
Lebanese (221)	451	0.56
Palestinian (92)	92	0.11
Syrian (174)	174	0.22
Other Arab (412)	412	0.51
Armenian (476)	564	0.70
Assyrian/Chaldean/Syriac (1,094)	1,226	1.53
Australian (0)	78	0.10
Austrian (93)	268	0.33
Belgian (44)	225	0.28
Brazilian (94)	106	0.13
British (207)	340	0.42
Bulgarian (18)	18	0.02
Cajun (0)	32	0.04
Canadian (166)	435	0.54
Celtic (11)	11	0.01
Croatian (38)	190	0.24
Czech (72)	328	0.41
Czechoslovakian (72)	178	0.22
Danish (115)	386	0.48
Dutch (231)	938	1.17
Eastern European (481)	501	0.62
English (1,625)	6,565	8.19
Estonian (9)	9	0.01
European (602)	794	0.99
Finnish (215)	779	0.97
French, ex. Basque (459)	2,726	3.40
French Canadian (296)	1,026	1.28
German (3,204)	12,353	15.40
Greek (242)	466	0.58
Hungarian (659)	1,546	1.93
Icelander (11)	11	0.01
Iranian (76)	101	0.13
Irish (1,871)	7,439	9.28
Israeli (75)	78	0.10
Italian (1,526)	3,683	4.59
Latvian (11)	62	0.08
Lithuanian (308)	584	0.73
Macedonian (0)	11	0.01
Maltese (115)	220	0.27
New Zealander (0)	17	0.02
Northern European (48)	48	0.06
Norwegian (136)	503	0.63
Polish (3,391)	8,787	10.96
Portuguese (17)	81	0.10
Romanian (505)	794	0.99
Russian (2,025)	3,395	4.23
Scandinavian (41)	181	0.23
Scotch-Irish (363)	1,146	1.43
Scottish (324)	1,821	2.27
Serbian (179)	195	0.24
Slavic (28)	37	0.05
Slovak (124)	298	0.37
Slovene (40)	185	0.23
Swedish (156)	656	0.82
Swiss (0)	233	0.29
Turkish (51)	61	0.08
Ukrainian (633)	1,053	1.31
Welsh (73)	372	0.46
West Indian, ex. Hispanic (165)	254	0.32
Barbadian (22)	22	0.03
British West Indian (20)	47	0.06
Haitian (38)	46	0.06
Jamaican (85)	100	0.12
Trinidadian/Tobagonian (0)	29	0.04
West Indian (0)	10	0.01
Yugoslavian (288)	374	0.47

Hispanic Origin	Population	%
Hispanic or Latino (of any race)	1,544	1.94
Central American, ex. Mexican	93	0.12
Costa Rican	5	0.01
Guatemalan	35	0.04
Honduran	11	0.01
Nicaraguan	12	0.02
Panamanian	11	0.01
Salvadoran	18	0.02
Other Central American	1	<0.01
Cuban	60	0.08
Dominican Republic	22	0.03
Mexican	796	1.00
Puerto Rican	148	0.19
South American	204	0.26
Argentinean	60	0.08
Bolivian	10	0.01
Chilean	10	0.01
Colombian	60	0.08
Ecuadorian	14	0.02
Paraguayan	15	0.02
Peruvian	15	0.02
Uruguayan	7	0.01
Venezuelan	13	0.02
Other Hispanic or Latino	221	0.28

Race*	Population	%
African-American/Black (13,848)	14,574	18.28
Not Hispanic (13,768)	14,436	18.10
Hispanic (80)	138	0.17
American Indian/Alaska Native (157)	567	0.71
Not Hispanic (139)	498	0.62
Hispanic (18)	69	0.09
Apache (1)	7	0.01
Blackfeet (0)	19	0.02
Canadian/French Am. Ind. (3)	4	0.01
Central American Ind. (0)	2	<0.01
Cherokee (14)	126	0.16
Chickasaw (3)	8	0.01
Chippewa (29)	60	0.08
Choctaw (1)	20	0.03
Cree (0)	3	<0.01
Creek (0)	4	0.01
Delaware (0)	3	<0.01
Houma (1)	2	<0.01
Iroquois (2)	10	0.01
Lumbee (3)	3	<0.01
Menominee (0)	1	<0.01
Mexican American Ind. (9)	9	0.01
Ottawa (2)	4	0.01
Potawatomi (0)	4	0.01
Seminole (0)	2	<0.01
Sioux (0)	3	<0.01
South American Ind. (0)	3	<0.01
Tlingit-Haida *(Alaska Native)* (1)	2	<0.01
Yuman (1)	1	<0.01
Asian (8,072)	8,910	11.17
Not Hispanic (8,063)	8,868	11.12
Hispanic (9)	42	0.05
Bangladeshi (16)	17	0.02
Burmese (1)	1	<0.01
Cambodian (2)	8	0.01
Chinese, ex. Taiwanese (776)	864	1.08
Filipino (357)	468	0.59
Hmong (7)	10	0.01
Indian (5,037)	5,216	6.54
Indonesian (6)	9	0.01
Japanese (542)	643	0.81
Korean (533)	580	0.73
Laotian (5)	10	0.01
Malaysian (5)	7	0.01
Nepalese (17)	19	0.02
Pakistani (447)	500	0.63
Sri Lankan (41)	51	0.06
Taiwanese (37)	51	0.06
Thai (18)	24	0.03
Vietnamese (100)	131	0.16
Hawaii Native/Pacific Islander (13)	85	0.11
Not Hispanic (12)	77	0.10
Hispanic (1)	8	0.01
Guamanian/Chamorro (1)	6	0.01
Marshallese (1)	1	<0.01
Native Hawaiian (2)	19	0.02
Samoan (1)	5	0.01
White (55,539)	56,938	71.40
Not Hispanic (54,466)	55,749	69.91
Hispanic (1,073)	1,189	1.49

Farmington

Place Type: City
County: Oakland
Population: 10,372†

Ancestry‡	Population	%
American (309)	309	2.98
Arab (146)	391	3.77
Arab (10)	29	0.28
Egyptian (28)	28	0.27
Iraqi (33)	44	0.42
Lebanese (75)	176	1.70
Syrian (0)	114	1.10
Armenian (29)	29	0.28
Assyrian/Chaldean/Syriac (41)	52	0.50
Austrian (22)	48	0.46
Belgian (8)	27	0.26
British (39)	106	1.02
Bulgarian (28)	28	0.27
Canadian (26)	95	0.92
Croatian (0)	25	0.24
Czech (0)	19	0.18
Czechoslovakian (0)	9	0.09
Dutch (88)	246	2.37
Eastern European (7)	7	0.07
English (246)	1,314	12.66
Estonian (11)	11	0.11
European (103)	103	0.99
Finnish (18)	196	1.89
French, ex. Basque (9)	557	5.37
French Canadian (86)	238	2.29
German (467)	1,889	18.20
Greek (55)	195	1.88
Hungarian (24)	105	1.01
Irish (288)	1,330	12.81
Italian (217)	640	6.17
Lithuanian (26)	84	0.81
Macedonian (19)	19	0.18
Maltese (0)	16	0.15
Norwegian (24)	117	1.13
Polish (264)	864	8.32
Romanian (21)	63	0.61
Russian (19)	69	0.66
Scandinavian (0)	6	0.06
Scotch-Irish (34)	257	2.48
Scottish (187)	416	4.01
Serbian (0)	10	0.10

*Notes: † The Census 2010 population figure is used to calculate the percentages in the Hispanic Origin and Race categories. Ancestry percentages are based on the 2006-2010 American Community Survey population (not shown); ‡ Numbers in parentheses indicate the number of people reporting a single ancestry; * Numbers in parentheses indicate the number of persons reporting this race alone, not in combination with any other race; Please refer to the Explanation of Data for more information.*

Slavic (0)	44	0.42
Slovak (23)	51	0.49
Slovene (12)	20	0.19
Swedish (34)	236	2.27
Swiss (0)	12	0.12
Ukrainian (35)	81	0.78
Welsh (24)	127	1.22
West Indian, ex. Hispanic (44)	100	0.96
British West Indian (0)	33	0.32
Jamaican (44)	55	0.53
West Indian (0)	12	0.12
Yugoslavian (0)	35	0.34

Hispanic Origin	Population	%
Hispanic or Latino (of any race)	215	2.07
Central American, ex. Mexican	15	0.14
Costa Rican	1	0.01
Guatemalan	3	0.03
Honduran	4	0.04
Salvadoran	7	0.07
Cuban	5	0.05
Mexican	114	1.10
Puerto Rican	30	0.29
South American	24	0.23
Argentinean	4	0.04
Bolivian	2	0.02
Chilean	2	0.02
Colombian	5	0.05
Ecuadorian	5	0.05
Peruvian	3	0.03
Venezuelan	3	0.03
Other Hispanic or Latino	27	0.26

Race*	Population	%
African-American/Black (1,186)	1,279	12.33
Not Hispanic (1,171)	1,259	12.14
Hispanic (15)	20	0.19
American Indian/Alaska Native (41)	116	1.12
Not Hispanic (36)	106	1.02
Hispanic (5)	10	0.10
Aleut *(Alaska Native)* (0)	1	0.01
Blackfeet (0)	1	0.01
Cherokee (1)	15	0.14
Chippewa (10)	16	0.15
Cree (0)	2	0.02
Iroquois (1)	2	0.02
Mexican American Ind. (1)	2	0.02
Navajo (0)	1	0.01
Ottawa (0)	1	0.01
Sioux (1)	2	0.02
South American Ind. (2)	2	0.02
Yaqui (1)	2	0.02
Asian (1,440)	1,549	14.93
Not Hispanic (1,437)	1,542	14.87
Hispanic (3)	7	0.07
Bangladeshi (1)	1	0.01
Chinese, ex. Taiwanese (65)	80	0.77
Filipino (59)	83	0.80
Hmong (7)	7	0.07
Indian (1,206)	1,240	11.96
Japanese (20)	32	0.31
Korean (26)	30	0.29
Malaysian (0)	1	0.01
Nepalese (5)	11	0.11
Pakistani (16)	17	0.16
Sri Lankan (9)	9	0.09
Taiwanese (1)	1	0.01
Thai (1)	2	0.02
Vietnamese (6)	6	0.06
Hawaii Native/Pacific Islander (7)	17	0.16
Not Hispanic (7)	17	0.16
Native Hawaiian (0)	5	0.05
Samoan (1)	1	0.01
White (7,415)	7,584	73.12
Not Hispanic (7,274)	7,429	71.63
Hispanic (141)	155	1.49

Fenton

Place Type: Charter Township
County: Genesee
Population: 15,552[†]

Ancestry[‡]	Population	%
American (870)	870	5.69
Arab (161)	325	2.13
Arab (11)	25	0.16
Lebanese (150)	272	1.78
Other Arab (0)	28	0.18
Assyrian/Chaldean/Syriac (10)	10	0.07
Australian (8)	51	0.33
Austrian (12)	80	0.52
Belgian (26)	164	1.07
British (32)	54	0.35
Canadian (14)	41	0.27
Carpatho Rusyn (0)	36	0.24
Croatian (0)	11	0.07
Czech (0)	135	0.88
Czechoslovakian (24)	46	0.30
Danish (26)	54	0.35
Dutch (152)	453	2.96
Eastern European (29)	29	0.19
English (634)	2,098	13.73
European (177)	204	1.34
Finnish (167)	335	2.19
French, ex. Basque (153)	966	6.32
French Canadian (121)	443	2.90
German (1,199)	4,500	29.45
Greek (56)	123	0.81
Hungarian (109)	356	2.33
Icelander (14)	29	0.19
Iranian (59)	59	0.39
Irish (440)	2,105	13.78
Italian (228)	861	5.64
Lithuanian (0)	13	0.09
Macedonian (15)	60	0.39
Maltese (12)	21	0.14
New Zealander (17)	17	0.11
Norwegian (21)	86	0.56
Pennsylvania German (10)	24	0.16
Polish (534)	1,685	11.03
Romanian (16)	30	0.20
Russian (12)	138	0.90
Scotch-Irish (42)	281	1.84
Scottish (62)	736	4.82
Slavic (11)	25	0.16
Slovak (24)	50	0.33
Swedish (16)	209	1.37
Swiss (0)	20	0.13
Ukrainian (37)	80	0.52
Welsh (9)	106	0.69
Yugoslavian (13)	13	0.09

Hispanic Origin	Population	%
Hispanic or Latino (of any race)	285	1.83
Central American, ex. Mexican	14	0.09
Costa Rican	1	0.01
Guatemalan	6	0.04
Salvadoran	7	0.05
Cuban	5	0.03
Mexican	181	1.16
Puerto Rican	29	0.19
South American	12	0.08
Argentinean	1	0.01
Chilean	1	0.01
Colombian	2	0.01
Peruvian	5	0.03
Venezuelan	3	0.02
Other Hispanic or Latino	44	0.28

Race*	Population	%
African-American/Black (68)	103	0.66
Not Hispanic (65)	98	0.63
Hispanic (3)	5	0.03
American Indian/Alaska Native (59)	164	1.05
Not Hispanic (56)	161	1.04
Hispanic (3)	3	0.02
Aleut *(Alaska Native)* (2)	2	0.01
Apache (2)	2	0.01
Blackfeet (0)	6	0.04
Cherokee (9)	35	0.23
Chippewa (20)	45	0.29
Choctaw (0)	4	0.03
Cree (0)	1	0.01
Menominee (1)	1	0.01
Navajo (1)	1	0.01
Ottawa (1)	6	0.04
Potawatomi (0)	1	0.01
Sioux (0)	3	0.02
Yakama (0)	1	0.01
Asian (149)	211	1.36
Not Hispanic (148)	206	1.32
Hispanic (1)	5	0.03
Chinese, ex. Taiwanese (25)	33	0.21
Filipino (29)	46	0.30
Hmong (12)	16	0.10
Indian (49)	51	0.33
Japanese (4)	13	0.08
Korean (16)	21	0.14
Pakistani (1)	1	0.01
Taiwanese (5)	8	0.05
Thai (5)	7	0.05
Vietnamese (1)	5	0.03
Hawaii Native/Pacific Islander (4)	11	0.07
Not Hispanic (3)	10	0.06
Hispanic (1)	1	0.01
Guamanian/Chamorro (2)	2	0.01
Native Hawaiian (1)	5	0.03
White (15,007)	15,212	97.81
Not Hispanic (14,793)	14,978	96.31
Hispanic (214)	234	1.50

Fenton

Place Type: City
County: Genesee
Population: 11,746[†]

Ancestry[‡]	Population	%
American (528)	528	4.52
Arab (29)	106	0.91
Lebanese (29)	106	0.91
Austrian (0)	13	0.11
Brazilian (15)	15	0.13
British (0)	6	0.05
Canadian (26)	59	0.51
Czech (0)	71	0.61
Czechoslovakian (0)	12	0.10
Danish (0)	34	0.29
Dutch (69)	230	1.97
Eastern European (0)	7	0.06
English (276)	1,397	11.97
European (149)	149	1.28
Finnish (113)	163	1.40
French, ex. Basque (98)	757	6.48
French Canadian (88)	170	1.46
German (903)	3,006	25.75
Greek (0)	70	0.60
Hungarian (14)	58	0.50
Irish (512)	1,536	13.16
Italian (242)	694	5.94
Lithuanian (0)	31	0.27
Macedonian (0)	16	0.14
Norwegian (13)	99	0.85
Polish (279)	1,032	8.84
Russian (75)	111	0.95
Scotch-Irish (57)	140	1.20
Scottish (230)	416	3.56
Serbian (0)	32	0.27
Slovak (0)	17	0.15
Slovene (0)	14	0.12
Swedish (42)	184	1.58
Swiss (16)	75	0.64
Ukrainian (33)	46	0.39
Welsh (0)	46	0.39
West Indian, ex. Hispanic (0)	20	0.17
Haitian (0)	10	0.09

*Notes: † The Census 2010 population figure is used to calculate the percentages in the Hispanic Origin and Race categories. Ancestry percentages are based on the 2006-2010 American Community Survey population (not shown); ‡ Numbers in parentheses indicate the number of people reporting a single ancestry; * Numbers in parentheses indicate the number of persons reporting this race alone, not in combination with any other race; Please refer to the Explanation of Data for more information.*

Jamaican (0)	10	0.09

Hispanic Origin	Population	%
Hispanic or Latino (of any race)	293	2.49
Central American, ex. Mexican	2	0.02
Guatemalan	1	0.01
Salvadoran	1	0.01
Cuban	11	0.09
Mexican	213	1.81
Puerto Rican	20	0.17
South American	17	0.14
Argentinean	3	0.03
Chilean	1	0.01
Colombian	7	0.06
Peruvian	2	0.02
Venezuelan	4	0.03
Other Hispanic or Latino	30	0.26

Race*	Population	%
African-American/Black (151)	228	1.94
Not Hispanic (147)	221	1.88
Hispanic (4)	7	0.06
American Indian/Alaska Native (40)	128	1.09
Not Hispanic (36)	117	1.00
Hispanic (4)	11	0.09
Blackfeet (0)	4	0.03
Cherokee (6)	32	0.27
Chippewa (21)	43	0.37
Choctaw (0)	1	0.01
Cree (0)	2	0.02
Creek (0)	1	0.01
Crow (0)	1	0.01
Houma (1)	1	0.01
Iroquois (1)	6	0.05
Lumbee (1)	1	0.01
Mexican American Ind. (1)	2	0.02
Navajo (2)	2	0.02
Osage (1)	2	0.02
Ottawa (1)	8	0.07
Potawatomi (1)	2	0.02
Sioux (0)	1	0.01
Tlingit-Haida *(Alaska Native)* (0)	1	0.01
Asian (88)	145	1.23
Not Hispanic (86)	139	1.18
Hispanic (2)	6	0.05
Cambodian (2)	2	0.02
Chinese, ex. Taiwanese (12)	18	0.15
Filipino (16)	23	0.20
Hmong (9)	10	0.09
Indian (5)	15	0.13
Japanese (1)	6	0.05
Korean (19)	37	0.32
Laotian (2)	2	0.02
Pakistani (0)	4	0.03
Thai (1)	3	0.03
Vietnamese (8)	9	0.08
Hawaii Native/Pacific Islander (2)	6	0.05
Not Hispanic (2)	6	0.05
Native Hawaiian (2)	3	0.03
White (11,172)	11,401	97.06
Not Hispanic (10,982)	11,169	95.09
Hispanic (190)	232	1.98

Fenton

Place Type: City
County: Genesee
Population: 11,756†

Ancestry‡	Population	%
American (528)	528	4.52
Arab (29)	106	0.91
Lebanese (29)	106	0.91
Austrian (0)	13	0.11
Brazilian (15)	15	0.13
British (0)	6	0.05
Canadian (26)	59	0.51
Czech (0)	71	0.61
Czechoslovakian (0)	12	0.10
Danish (0)	34	0.29
Dutch (69)	230	1.97
Eastern European (0)	7	0.06
English (276)	1,397	11.97
European (149)	149	1.28
Finnish (113)	163	1.40
French, ex. Basque (98)	757	6.48
French Canadian (88)	170	1.46
German (903)	3,006	25.75
Greek (0)	70	0.60
Hungarian (14)	58	0.50
Irish (512)	1,536	13.16
Italian (242)	694	5.94
Lithuanian (0)	31	0.27
Macedonian (0)	16	0.14
Norwegian (13)	99	0.85
Polish (279)	1,032	8.84
Russian (75)	111	0.95
Scotch-Irish (57)	140	1.20
Scottish (230)	416	3.56
Serbian (0)	32	0.27
Slovak (0)	17	0.15
Slovene (0)	14	0.12
Swedish (42)	184	1.58
Swiss (16)	75	0.64
Ukrainian (33)	46	0.39
Welsh (0)	46	0.39
West Indian, ex. Hispanic (0)	20	0.17
Haitian (0)	10	0.09
Jamaican (0)	10	0.09

Hispanic Origin	Population	%
Hispanic or Latino (of any race)	293	2.49
Central American, ex. Mexican	2	0.02
Guatemalan	1	0.01
Salvadoran	1	0.01
Cuban	11	0.09
Mexican	213	1.81
Puerto Rican	20	0.17
South American	17	0.14
Argentinean	3	0.03
Chilean	1	0.01
Colombian	7	0.06
Peruvian	2	0.02
Venezuelan	4	0.03
Other Hispanic or Latino	30	0.26

Race*	Population	%
African-American/Black (151)	228	1.94
Not Hispanic (147)	221	1.88
Hispanic (4)	7	0.06
American Indian/Alaska Native (40)	128	1.09
Not Hispanic (36)	117	1.00
Hispanic (4)	11	0.09
Blackfeet (0)	4	0.03
Cherokee (6)	32	0.27
Chippewa (21)	43	0.37
Choctaw (0)	1	0.01
Cree (0)	2	0.02
Creek (0)	1	0.01
Crow (0)	1	0.01
Houma (1)	1	0.01
Iroquois (1)	6	0.05
Lumbee (1)	1	0.01
Mexican American Ind. (1)	2	0.02
Navajo (2)	2	0.02
Osage (1)	2	0.02
Ottawa (1)	8	0.07
Potawatomi (1)	2	0.02
Sioux (0)	1	0.01
Tlingit-Haida *(Alaska Native)* (0)	1	0.01
Asian (88)	145	1.23
Not Hispanic (86)	139	1.18
Hispanic (2)	6	0.05
Cambodian (2)	2	0.02
Chinese, ex. Taiwanese (12)	18	0.15
Filipino (16)	23	0.20
Hmong (9)	10	0.09
Indian (5)	15	0.13
Japanese (1)	6	0.05
Korean (19)	37	0.31
Laotian (2)	2	0.02
Pakistani (0)	4	0.03
Thai (1)	3	0.03
Vietnamese (8)	9	0.08
Hawaii Native/Pacific Islander (2)	6	0.05
Not Hispanic (2)	6	0.05
Native Hawaiian (2)	3	0.03
White (11,182)	11,411	97.07
Not Hispanic (10,992)	11,179	95.09
Hispanic (190)	232	1.97

Ferndale

Place Type: City
County: Oakland
Population: 19,900†

Ancestry‡	Population	%
African, Sub-Saharan (11)	42	0.21
African (11)	42	0.21
Albanian (93)	93	0.46
American (777)	777	3.83
Arab (60)	179	0.88
Egyptian (0)	23	0.11
Lebanese (27)	82	0.40
Moroccan (14)	14	0.07
Palestinian (0)	26	0.13
Syrian (19)	34	0.17
Armenian (20)	32	0.16
Assyrian/Chaldean/Syriac (62)	62	0.31
Austrian (26)	75	0.37
Belgian (36)	89	0.44
British (32)	46	0.23
Bulgarian (0)	17	0.08
Canadian (43)	109	0.54
Celtic (14)	14	0.07
Croatian (8)	33	0.16
Czech (0)	302	1.49
Czechoslovakian (11)	11	0.05
Danish (63)	147	0.72
Dutch (90)	385	1.90
Eastern European (45)	45	0.22
English (489)	2,271	11.19
European (466)	580	2.86
Finnish (133)	234	1.15
French, ex. Basque (79)	1,223	6.03
French Canadian (285)	729	3.59
German (981)	4,601	22.68
Greek (273)	427	2.10
Hungarian (59)	205	1.01
Irish (714)	3,913	19.29
Israeli (0)	23	0.11
Italian (309)	1,019	5.02
Lithuanian (56)	155	0.76
Macedonian (27)	27	0.13
Northern European (9)	9	0.04
Norwegian (51)	265	1.31
Polish (847)	2,339	11.53
Portuguese (9)	9	0.04
Romanian (28)	83	0.41
Russian (153)	550	2.71
Scandinavian (0)	46	0.23
Scotch-Irish (134)	319	1.57
Scottish (124)	713	3.51
Serbian (0)	9	0.04
Slavic (0)	22	0.11
Slovak (31)	77	0.38
Slovene (0)	25	0.12
Swedish (36)	355	1.75
Swiss (15)	49	0.24
Ukrainian (118)	244	1.20
Welsh (52)	139	0.69
West Indian, ex. Hispanic (32)	75	0.37
British West Indian (0)	7	0.03
Jamaican (32)	68	0.34
Yugoslavian (0)	33	0.16

Hispanic Origin	Population	%
Hispanic or Latino (of any race)	554	2.78
Central American, ex. Mexican	25	0.13

*Notes: † The Census 2010 population figure is used to calculate the percentages in the Hispanic Origin and Race categories. Ancestry percentages are based on the 2006-2010 American Community Survey population (not shown); ‡ Numbers in parentheses indicate the number of people reporting a single ancestry; * Numbers in parentheses indicate the number of persons reporting this race alone, not in combination with any other race; Please refer to the Explanation of Data for more information.*

Costa Rican	8	0.04
Guatemalan	6	0.03
Honduran	2	0.01
Nicaraguan	2	0.01
Panamanian	7	0.04
Cuban	20	0.10
Dominican Republic	8	0.04
Mexican	346	1.74
Puerto Rican	66	0.33
South American	29	0.15
Argentinean	6	0.03
Bolivian	1	0.01
Chilean	1	0.01
Colombian	7	0.04
Ecuadorian	6	0.03
Peruvian	3	0.02
Venezuelan	5	0.03
Other Hispanic or Latino	60	0.30

Race*	Population	%
African-American/Black (1,901)	2,251	11.31
Not Hispanic (1,871)	2,200	11.06
Hispanic (30)	51	0.26
American Indian/Alaska Native (96)	326	1.64
Not Hispanic (89)	299	1.50
Hispanic (7)	27	0.14
Apache (0)	1	0.01
Blackfeet (0)	12	0.06
Canadian/French Am. Ind. (3)	7	0.04
Cherokee (10)	68	0.34
Chickasaw (0)	1	0.01
Chippewa (27)	45	0.23
Choctaw (0)	7	0.04
Comanche (2)	3	0.02
Hopi (0)	1	0.01
Iroquois (6)	13	0.07
Lumbee (1)	2	0.01
Mexican American Ind. (2)	6	0.03
Navajo (1)	1	0.01
Osage (0)	2	0.01
Ottawa (8)	13	0.07
Potawatomi (0)	4	0.02
Seminole (0)	1	0.01
Sioux (0)	5	0.03
Asian (266)	436	2.19
Not Hispanic (261)	427	2.15
Hispanic (5)	9	0.05
Bangladeshi (0)	3	0.02
Cambodian (1)	1	0.01
Chinese, ex. Taiwanese (67)	94	0.47
Filipino (64)	110	0.55
Hmong (8)	13	0.07
Indian (31)	46	0.23
Indonesian (0)	4	0.02
Japanese (12)	47	0.24
Korean (37)	56	0.28
Pakistani (3)	6	0.03
Taiwanese (4)	5	0.03
Thai (8)	21	0.11
Vietnamese (11)	17	0.09
Hawaii Native/Pacific Islander (12)	27	0.14
Not Hispanic (12)	26	0.13
Hispanic (0)	1	0.01
Guamanian/Chamorro (3)	4	0.02
Native Hawaiian (4)	10	0.05
Samoan (2)	2	0.01
White (16,854)	17,453	87.70
Not Hispanic (16,477)	17,025	85.55
Hispanic (377)	428	2.15

Flat Rock

Place Type: City
County: Wayne
Population: 9,878†

Ancestry‡	Population	%
American (651)	651	6.73
Arab (25)	76	0.79
Lebanese (25)	76	0.79
Armenian (9)	23	0.24
Austrian (0)	16	0.17
Belgian (0)	8	0.08
British (16)	24	0.25
Canadian (0)	50	0.52
Croatian (0)	99	1.02
Czech (0)	12	0.12
Czechoslovakian (9)	18	0.19
Danish (0)	9	0.09
Dutch (30)	190	1.97
English (511)	1,106	11.44
European (56)	56	0.58
Finnish (9)	46	0.48
French, ex. Basque (156)	995	10.29
French Canadian (82)	195	2.02
German (760)	2,009	20.78
Greek (0)	138	1.43
Hungarian (49)	329	3.40
Irish (414)	1,446	14.96
Italian (265)	683	7.07
Lithuanian (0)	19	0.20
Maltese (21)	21	0.22
Norwegian (0)	32	0.33
Polish (275)	1,262	13.06
Romanian (83)	171	1.77
Russian (0)	8	0.08
Scotch-Irish (119)	235	2.43
Scottish (50)	196	2.03
Slovak (0)	17	0.18
Slovene (0)	8	0.08
Swedish (14)	144	1.49
Turkish (0)	9	0.09
Ukrainian (8)	25	0.26
Welsh (9)	69	0.71
Yugoslavian (8)	8	0.08

Hispanic Origin	Population	%
Hispanic or Latino (of any race)	436	4.41
Central American, ex. Mexican	3	0.03
Costa Rican	3	0.03
Cuban	5	0.05
Mexican	350	3.54
Puerto Rican	33	0.33
South American	14	0.14
Bolivian	4	0.04
Colombian	8	0.08
Venezuelan	1	0.01
Other South American	1	0.01
Other Hispanic or Latino	31	0.31

Race*	Population	%
African-American/Black (404)	522	5.28
Not Hispanic (400)	509	5.15
Hispanic (4)	13	0.13
American Indian/Alaska Native (45)	165	1.67
Not Hispanic (38)	139	1.41
Hispanic (7)	26	0.26
Apache (0)	9	0.09
Blackfeet (1)	6	0.06
Canadian/French Am. Ind. (0)	1	0.01
Cherokee (3)	38	0.38
Chippewa (6)	21	0.21
Comanche (0)	1	0.01
Creek (1)	3	0.03
Inupiat *(Alaska Native)* (0)	1	0.01
Iroquois (6)	11	0.11
Lumbee (3)	10	0.10
Mexican American Ind. (1)	4	0.04
Ottawa (3)	5	0.05
Potawatomi (0)	3	0.03
Pueblo (2)	2	0.02
Seminole (0)	2	0.02
Sioux (0)	1	0.01
Asian (83)	135	1.37
Not Hispanic (83)	134	1.36
Hispanic (0)	1	0.01
Chinese, ex. Taiwanese (7)	16	0.16
Filipino (21)	38	0.38
Indian (26)	28	0.28
Japanese (5)	7	0.07
Korean (5)	18	0.18
Pakistani (9)	9	0.09
Thai (2)	2	0.02
Vietnamese (8)	13	0.13
Hawaii Native/Pacific Islander (1)	6	0.06
Not Hispanic (1)	6	0.06
Native Hawaiian (1)	3	0.03
White (9,000)	9,277	93.92
Not Hispanic (8,671)	8,906	90.16
Hispanic (329)	371	3.76

Flint

Place Type: Charter Township
County: Genesee
Population: 31,929†

Ancestry‡	Population	%
African, Sub-Saharan (260)	300	0.92
African (177)	217	0.66
South African (52)	52	0.16
Sudanese (31)	31	0.09
Alsatian (0)	9	0.03
American (1,474)	1,474	4.51
Arab (671)	686	2.10
Arab (201)	201	0.62
Lebanese (122)	137	0.42
Moroccan (14)	14	0.04
Syrian (267)	267	0.82
Other Arab (67)	67	0.21
Assyrian/Chaldean/Syriac (17)	17	0.05
Austrian (20)	45	0.14
Basque (0)	11	0.03
Belgian (11)	62	0.19
British (35)	75	0.23
Bulgarian (0)	42	0.13
Cajun (38)	38	0.12
Canadian (24)	47	0.14
Celtic (31)	109	0.33
Croatian (8)	23	0.07
Czech (35)	194	0.59
Czechoslovakian (54)	220	0.67
Danish (0)	81	0.25
Dutch (67)	859	2.63
English (1,390)	3,682	11.27
European (146)	212	0.65
Finnish (12)	84	0.26
French, ex. Basque (286)	1,679	5.14
French Canadian (186)	418	1.28
German (1,582)	5,273	16.14
Greek (43)	148	0.45
Hungarian (89)	273	0.84
Irish (952)	3,475	10.64
Israeli (192)	192	0.59
Italian (245)	657	2.01
Latvian (24)	24	0.07
Lithuanian (10)	66	0.20
Maltese (16)	16	0.05
Northern European (47)	47	0.14
Norwegian (149)	340	1.04
Pennsylvania German (0)	14	0.04
Polish (486)	1,495	4.58
Romanian (28)	58	0.18
Russian (40)	151	0.46
Scandinavian (14)	14	0.04
Scotch-Irish (101)	401	1.23
Scottish (158)	703	2.15
Serbian (0)	32	0.10
Slavic (33)	41	0.13
Slovak (44)	173	0.53
Swedish (109)	322	0.99
Swiss (23)	97	0.30
Ukrainian (26)	34	0.10
Welsh (11)	217	0.66
West Indian, ex. Hispanic (15)	15	0.05
Haitian (15)	15	0.05

Hispanic Origin	Population	%
Hispanic or Latino (of any race)	927	2.90
Central American, ex. Mexican	19	0.06

*Notes: † The Census 2010 population figure is used to calculate the percentages in the Hispanic Origin and Race categories. Ancestry percentages are based on the 2006-2010 American Community Survey population (not shown); ‡ Numbers in parentheses indicate the number of people reporting a single ancestry; * Numbers in parentheses indicate the number of persons reporting this race alone, not in combination with any other race; Please refer to the Explanation of Data for more information.*

Guatemalan	14	0.04
Honduran	1	<0.01
Nicaraguan	2	0.01
Panamanian	1	<0.01
Salvadoran	1	<0.01
Cuban	11	0.03
Dominican Republic	2	0.01
Mexican	705	2.21
Puerto Rican	65	0.20
South American	25	0.08
Bolivian	8	0.03
Colombian	6	0.02
Ecuadorian	2	0.01
Peruvian	9	0.03
Other Hispanic or Latino	100	0.31

Race*	Population	%
African-American/Black (8,209)	8,772	27.47
Not Hispanic (8,154)	8,685	27.20
Hispanic (55)	87	0.27
American Indian/Alaska Native (175)	511	1.60
Not Hispanic (164)	480	1.50
Hispanic (11)	31	0.10
Apache (1)	14	0.04
Blackfeet (7)	22	0.07
Cherokee (20)	96	0.30
Chickasaw (1)	1	<0.01
Chippewa (58)	89	0.28
Choctaw (0)	7	0.02
Comanche (1)	2	0.01
Cree (2)	8	0.03
Crow (0)	6	0.02
Iroquois (0)	4	0.01
Lumbee (2)	6	0.02
Mexican American Ind. (1)	5	0.02
Ottawa (8)	17	0.05
Potawatomi (1)	8	0.03
Puget Sound Salish (6)	6	0.02
Seminole (1)	8	0.03
Sioux (1)	5	0.02
South American Ind. (1)	1	<0.01
Tlingit-Haida *(Alaska Native)* (0)	1	<0.01
Asian (604)	795	2.49
Not Hispanic (602)	780	2.44
Hispanic (2)	15	0.05
Bangladeshi (9)	11	0.03
Chinese, ex. Taiwanese (34)	47	0.15
Filipino (66)	91	0.29
Hmong (10)	10	0.03
Indian (324)	341	1.07
Indonesian (0)	1	<0.01
Japanese (5)	22	0.07
Korean (33)	57	0.18
Pakistani (55)	66	0.21
Sri Lankan (12)	12	0.04
Taiwanese (1)	2	0.01
Thai (6)	14	0.04
Vietnamese (34)	37	0.12
Hawaii Native/Pacific Islander (6)	30	0.09
Not Hispanic (5)	23	0.07
Hispanic (1)	7	0.02
Fijian (0)	1	<0.01
Guamanian/Chamorro (1)	6	0.02
Native Hawaiian (2)	6	0.02
White (21,700)	22,598	70.78
Not Hispanic (21,136)	21,944	68.73
Hispanic (564)	654	2.05

Flint

Place Type: City
County: Genesee
Population: 102,434†

Ancestry‡	Population	%
African, Sub-Saharan (1,391)	1,740	1.61
African (1,189)	1,515	1.41
Ethiopian (38)	38	0.04
Nigerian (115)	138	0.13
Other Sub-Saharan African (49)	49	0.05
American (3,644)	3,644	3.38
Arab (358)	492	0.46
Arab (76)	89	0.08
Egyptian (15)	15	0.01
Iraqi (20)	39	0.04
Lebanese (145)	236	0.22
Moroccan (49)	49	0.05
Palestinian (11)	11	0.01
Syrian (42)	53	0.05
Armenian (9)	9	0.01
Assyrian/Chaldean/Syriac (258)	277	0.26
Belgian (0)	111	0.10
British (38)	92	0.09
Canadian (149)	378	0.35
Czech (59)	147	0.14
Czechoslovakian (46)	70	0.06
Danish (34)	83	0.08
Dutch (251)	1,046	0.97
English (2,165)	5,391	5.00
European (372)	496	0.46
Finnish (75)	249	0.23
French, ex. Basque (315)	2,105	1.95
French Canadian (557)	1,300	1.21
German (2,242)	7,597	7.05
German Russian (0)	6	0.01
Greek (33)	126	0.12
Guyanese (0)	58	0.05
Hungarian (165)	310	0.29
Irish (1,309)	5,535	5.13
Italian (395)	1,379	1.28
Latvian (0)	14	0.01
Lithuanian (19)	44	0.04
Macedonian (27)	41	0.04
Maltese (12)	12	0.01
Norwegian (173)	411	0.38
Pennsylvania German (23)	23	0.02
Polish (628)	1,732	1.61
Portuguese (40)	55	0.05
Romanian (18)	29	0.03
Russian (82)	201	0.19
Scandinavian (11)	101	0.09
Scotch-Irish (288)	601	0.56
Scottish (262)	1,116	1.04
Serbian (36)	36	0.03
Slovak (39)	62	0.06
Swedish (105)	487	0.45
Swiss (25)	50	0.05
Turkish (11)	11	0.01
Ukrainian (69)	118	0.11
Welsh (26)	258	0.24
West Indian, ex. Hispanic (105)	219	0.20
Bahamian (7)	7	0.01
Dutch West Indian (0)	23	0.02
Jamaican (32)	89	0.08
Trinidadian/Tobagonian (55)	76	0.07
West Indian (11)	24	0.02
Yugoslavian (0)	14	0.01

Hispanic Origin	Population	%
Hispanic or Latino (of any race)	3,976	3.88
Central American, ex. Mexican	65	0.06
Costa Rican	4	<0.01
Guatemalan	11	0.01
Honduran	14	0.01
Nicaraguan	4	<0.01
Panamanian	18	0.02
Salvadoran	14	0.01
Cuban	59	0.06
Dominican Republic	13	0.01
Mexican	3,087	3.01
Puerto Rican	324	0.32
South American	50	0.05
Argentinean	3	<0.01
Chilean	2	<0.01
Colombian	29	0.03
Ecuadorian	3	<0.01
Peruvian	10	0.01
Uruguayan	3	<0.01
Other Hispanic or Latino	378	0.37

Race*	Population	%
African-American/Black (57,939)	60,928	59.48
Not Hispanic (57,451)	60,166	58.74
Hispanic (488)	762	0.74
American Indian/Alaska Native (550)	1,950	1.90
Not Hispanic (455)	1,724	1.68
Hispanic (95)	226	0.22
Alaska Athabascan *(Ala. Nat.)* (1)	1	<0.01
Apache (11)	36	0.04
Arapaho (0)	3	<0.01
Blackfeet (17)	141	0.14
Canadian/French Am. Ind. (3)	11	0.01
Central American Ind. (0)	1	<0.01
Cherokee (51)	423	0.41
Cheyenne (3)	12	0.01
Chickasaw (4)	14	0.01
Chippewa (123)	231	0.23
Choctaw (8)	51	0.05
Comanche (0)	2	<0.01
Cree (1)	3	<0.01
Creek (6)	16	0.02
Crow (1)	3	<0.01
Delaware (0)	2	<0.01
Inupiat *(Alaska Native)* (0)	4	<0.01
Iroquois (5)	25	0.02
Menominee (1)	1	<0.01
Mexican American Ind. (17)	40	0.04
Navajo (2)	11	0.01
Osage (1)	2	<0.01
Ottawa (20)	41	0.04
Pima (1)	1	<0.01
Potawatomi (4)	16	0.02
Pueblo (1)	1	<0.01
Puget Sound Salish (1)	2	<0.01
Seminole (0)	4	<0.01
Shoshone (1)	1	<0.01
Sioux (9)	26	0.03
South American Ind. (0)	2	<0.01
Tohono O'Odham (0)	1	<0.01
Asian (464)	746	0.73
Not Hispanic (450)	700	0.68
Hispanic (14)	46	0.04
Cambodian (11)	16	0.02
Chinese, ex. Taiwanese (117)	153	0.15
Filipino (75)	148	0.14
Hmong (15)	18	0.02
Indian (91)	145	0.14
Indonesian (1)	2	<0.01
Japanese (20)	56	0.05
Korean (51)	84	0.08
Laotian (6)	11	0.01
Nepalese (9)	9	0.01
Pakistani (6)	9	0.01
Taiwanese (2)	9	0.01
Thai (9)	13	0.01
Vietnamese (15)	27	0.03
Hawaii Native/Pacific Islander (16)	72	0.07
Not Hispanic (14)	63	0.06
Hispanic (2)	9	0.01
Fijian (1)	1	<0.01
Guamanian/Chamorro (2)	12	0.01
Native Hawaiian (6)	25	0.02
Samoan (2)	7	0.01
White (38,328)	41,527	40.54
Not Hispanic (36,537)	39,292	38.36
Hispanic (1,791)	2,235	2.18

Flushing

Place Type: Charter Township
County: Genesee
Population: 10,640†

Ancestry‡	Population	%
American (509)	509	4.76
Arab (67)	78	0.73
Arab (14)	14	0.13
Lebanese (12)	12	0.11
Syrian (0)	11	0.10

*Notes: † The Census 2010 population figure is used to calculate the percentages in the Hispanic Origin and Race categories. Ancestry percentages are based on the 2006-2010 American Community Survey population (not shown); ‡ Numbers in parentheses indicate the number of people reporting a single ancestry; * Numbers in parentheses indicate the number of persons reporting this race alone, not in combination with any other race; Please refer to the Explanation of Data for more information.*

Other Arab (41)	41	0.38
Austrian (11)	16	0.15
British (0)	36	0.34
Canadian (32)	152	1.42
Croatian (9)	47	0.44
Czech (84)	103	0.96
Czechoslovakian (11)	37	0.35
Danish (0)	67	0.63
Dutch (38)	127	1.19
Eastern European (15)	30	0.28
English (523)	1,724	16.11
European (46)	46	0.43
Finnish (27)	195	1.82
French, ex. Basque (129)	796	7.44
French Canadian (117)	385	3.60
German (1,239)	3,238	30.25
Greek (14)	14	0.13
Hungarian (34)	198	1.85
Irish (656)	1,729	16.15
Italian (109)	340	3.18
Norwegian (22)	182	1.70
Polish (211)	813	7.60
Russian (0)	48	0.45
Scandinavian (39)	76	0.71
Scotch-Irish (93)	486	4.54
Scottish (57)	403	3.76
Serbian (0)	51	0.48
Slavic (0)	42	0.39
Slovak (34)	45	0.42
Swedish (9)	54	0.50
Swiss (16)	25	0.23
Ukrainian (10)	40	0.37
Welsh (0)	15	0.14
Yugoslavian (0)	17	0.16

Hispanic Origin	Population	%
Hispanic or Latino (of any race)	255	2.40
Central American, ex. Mexican	13	0.12
Guatemalan	3	0.03
Panamanian	6	0.06
Salvadoran	4	0.04
Cuban	9	0.08
Mexican	199	1.87
Puerto Rican	16	0.15
South American	9	0.08
Chilean	1	0.01
Colombian	8	0.08
Other Hispanic or Latino	9	0.08

Race*	Population	%
African-American/Black (227)	290	2.73
Not Hispanic (226)	288	2.71
Hispanic (1)	2	0.02
American Indian/Alaska Native (68)	130	1.22
Not Hispanic (67)	129	1.21
Hispanic (1)	1	0.01
Apache (1)	1	0.01
Blackfeet (0)	6	0.06
Cherokee (3)	13	0.12
Chippewa (29)	36	0.34
Iroquois (2)	7	0.07
Lumbee (5)	5	0.05
Mexican American Ind. (1)	1	0.01
Potawatomi (2)	9	0.08
Shoshone (1)	1	0.01
Asian (83)	113	1.06
Not Hispanic (83)	112	1.05
Hispanic (0)	1	0.01
Chinese, ex. Taiwanese (21)	27	0.25
Filipino (8)	13	0.12
Indian (9)	16	0.15
Indonesian (0)	2	0.02
Japanese (6)	10	0.09
Korean (13)	14	0.13
Pakistani (8)	11	0.10
Thai (1)	3	0.03
Vietnamese (11)	13	0.12
Hawaii Native/Pacific Islander (3)	7	0.07
Not Hispanic (3)	6	0.06
Hispanic (0)	1	0.01
Native Hawaiian (2)	6	0.06
Samoan (1)	1	0.01
White (10,045)	10,206	95.92
Not Hispanic (9,858)	9,993	93.92
Hispanic (187)	213	2.00

Flushing

Place Type: City
County: Genesee
Population: 8,389†

Ancestry‡	Population	%
African, Sub-Saharan (13)	13	0.15
Sierra Leonean (13)	13	0.15
American (450)	450	5.31
Arab (49)	63	0.74
Egyptian (12)	12	0.14
Lebanese (23)	23	0.27
Syrian (14)	28	0.33
Assyrian/Chaldean/Syriac (90)	115	1.36
Austrian (7)	60	0.71
Belgian (12)	34	0.40
British (19)	19	0.22
Bulgarian (0)	11	0.13
Canadian (0)	15	0.18
Carpatho Rusyn (0)	57	0.67
Croatian (0)	42	0.50
Czech (12)	25	0.29
Czechoslovakian (26)	38	0.45
Dutch (80)	279	3.29
Eastern European (11)	26	0.31
English (569)	1,214	14.32
European (118)	118	1.39
Finnish (47)	82	0.97
French, ex. Basque (50)	560	6.60
French Canadian (44)	293	3.46
German (729)	2,232	26.32
Hungarian (90)	201	2.37
Irish (212)	1,335	15.74
Italian (134)	332	3.92
Lithuanian (0)	26	0.31
Luxemburger (35)	35	0.41
Maltese (0)	12	0.14
Norwegian (25)	84	0.99
Polish (192)	854	10.07
Russian (0)	125	1.47
Scandinavian (11)	16	0.19
Scotch-Irish (58)	112	1.32
Scottish (0)	301	3.55
Slovak (22)	22	0.26
Swedish (126)	183	2.16
Swiss (0)	76	0.90
Ukrainian (15)	104	1.23
Welsh (0)	70	0.83
Yugoslavian (12)	12	0.14

Hispanic Origin	Population	%
Hispanic or Latino (of any race)	181	2.16
Central American, ex. Mexican	8	0.10
Guatemalan	2	0.02
Honduran	6	0.07
Cuban	6	0.07
Dominican Republic	1	0.01
Mexican	134	1.60
Puerto Rican	18	0.21
South American	4	0.05
Chilean	2	0.02
Ecuadorian	2	0.02
Other Hispanic or Latino	10	0.12

Race*	Population	%
African-American/Black (198)	235	2.80
Not Hispanic (196)	233	2.78
Hispanic (2)	2	0.02
American Indian/Alaska Native (31)	81	0.97
Not Hispanic (29)	78	0.93
Hispanic (2)	3	0.04
Apache (0)	3	0.04
Blackfeet (0)	1	0.01
Cherokee (3)	11	0.13
Chippewa (6)	10	0.12
Choctaw (0)	2	0.02
Iroquois (1)	2	0.02
Ottawa (10)	12	0.14
Potawatomi (2)	3	0.04
Sioux (0)	1	0.01
Tlingit-Haida *(Alaska Native)* (0)	1	0.01
Yup'ik *(Alaska Native)* (0)	3	0.04
Asian (37)	72	0.86
Not Hispanic (37)	72	0.86
Chinese, ex. Taiwanese (4)	8	0.10
Filipino (7)	14	0.17
Indian (1)	2	0.02
Japanese (2)	2	0.02
Korean (18)	21	0.25
Pakistani (3)	3	0.04
Thai (1)	1	0.01
Vietnamese (1)	5	0.06
Hawaii Native/Pacific Islander (2)	7	0.08
Not Hispanic (2)	7	0.08
White (7,956)	8,088	96.41
Not Hispanic (7,813)	7,936	94.60
Hispanic (143)	152	1.81

Forest Hills

Place Type: CDP
County: Kent
Population: 25,867†

Ancestry‡	Population	%
African, Sub-Saharan (18)	18	0.07
Ethiopian (18)	18	0.07
Albanian (30)	30	0.12
American (1,162)	1,162	4.57
Arab (269)	407	1.60
Lebanese (243)	329	1.29
Other Arab (26)	78	0.31
Armenian (0)	10	0.04
Assyrian/Chaldean/Syriac (0)	46	0.18
Austrian (26)	81	0.32
Belgian (42)	128	0.50
Brazilian (15)	15	0.06
British (102)	181	0.71
Bulgarian (42)	42	0.17
Cajun (0)	9	0.04
Canadian (29)	80	0.31
Croatian (19)	65	0.26
Czech (42)	119	0.47
Czechoslovakian (116)	150	0.59
Danish (11)	124	0.49
Dutch (2,207)	4,743	18.65
English (1,191)	4,213	16.57
European (645)	677	2.66
Finnish (15)	50	0.20
French, ex. Basque (35)	1,010	3.97
French Canadian (85)	309	1.22
German (1,367)	6,922	27.22
Greek (35)	46	0.18
Hungarian (46)	250	0.98
Icelander (10)	10	0.04
Irish (839)	3,962	15.58
Italian (486)	1,182	4.65
Latvian (10)	63	0.25
Lithuanian (105)	246	0.97
Norwegian (123)	538	2.12
Pennsylvania German (15)	15	0.06
Polish (683)	1,915	7.53
Portuguese (0)	34	0.13
Romanian (0)	21	0.08
Russian (29)	156	0.61
Scandinavian (21)	21	0.08
Scotch-Irish (216)	689	2.71
Scottish (144)	1,079	4.24
Slavic (13)	26	0.10
Slovak (33)	87	0.34
Swedish (173)	1,055	4.15
Swiss (15)	128	0.50
Turkish (7)	7	0.03

SECTION TWO

*Notes: † The Census 2010 population figure is used to calculate the percentages in the Hispanic Origin and Race categories. Ancestry percentages are based on the 2006-2010 American Community Survey population (not shown); ‡ Numbers in parentheses indicate the number of people reporting a single ancestry; * Numbers in parentheses indicate the number of persons reporting this race alone, not in combination with any other race; Please refer to the Explanation of Data for more information.*

Ukrainian (74)	157	0.62
Welsh (13)	176	0.69
West Indian, ex. Hispanic (0)	13	0.05
Jamaican (0)	13	0.05
Yugoslavian (26)	26	0.10

Hispanic Origin	Population	%
Hispanic or Latino (of any race)	439	1.70
Central American, ex. Mexican	40	0.15
Costa Rican	2	0.01
Guatemalan	23	0.09
Honduran	2	0.01
Nicaraguan	10	0.04
Panamanian	1	<0.01
Salvadoran	2	0.01
Cuban	13	0.05
Dominican Republic	15	0.06
Mexican	207	0.80
Puerto Rican	61	0.24
South American	56	0.22
Argentinean	1	<0.01
Chilean	10	0.04
Colombian	26	0.10
Paraguayan	4	0.02
Peruvian	10	0.04
Venezuelan	4	0.02
Other South American	1	<0.01
Other Hispanic or Latino	47	0.18

Race*	Population	%
African-American/Black (318)	409	1.58
Not Hispanic (312)	398	1.54
Hispanic (6)	11	0.04
American Indian/Alaska Native (56)	115	0.44
Not Hispanic (46)	98	0.38
Hispanic (10)	17	0.07
Arapaho (1)	1	<0.01
Blackfeet (0)	1	<0.01
Canadian/French Am. Ind. (1)	1	<0.01
Central American Ind. (1)	1	<0.01
Cherokee (3)	8	0.03
Cheyenne (0)	1	<0.01
Chippewa (14)	19	0.07
Choctaw (0)	1	<0.01
Comanche (0)	1	<0.01
Cree (0)	4	0.02
Creek (1)	5	0.02
Iroquois (5)	8	0.03
Mexican American Ind. (6)	9	0.03
Ottawa (3)	7	0.03
Potawatomi (4)	4	0.02
Sioux (2)	4	0.02
Asian (883)	1,073	4.15
Not Hispanic (879)	1,066	4.12
Hispanic (4)	7	0.03
Burmese (2)	2	0.01
Chinese, ex. Taiwanese (270)	322	1.24
Filipino (65)	100	0.39
Hmong (16)	17	0.07
Indian (207)	239	0.92
Indonesian (2)	3	0.01
Japanese (33)	53	0.20
Korean (110)	132	0.51
Malaysian (2)	2	0.01
Pakistani (55)	60	0.23
Sri Lankan (2)	4	0.02
Taiwanese (6)	8	0.03
Thai (11)	21	0.08
Vietnamese (74)	89	0.34
Hawaii Native/Pacific Islander (4)	17	0.07
Not Hispanic (2)	13	0.05
Hispanic (2)	4	0.02
Native Hawaiian (1)	2	0.01
Samoan (1)	4	0.02
Tongan (1)	1	<0.01
White (24,170)	24,491	94.68
Not Hispanic (23,838)	24,132	93.29
Hispanic (332)	359	1.39

Fort Gratiot

Place Type: Charter Township
County: St. Clair
Population: 11,108†

Ancestry‡	Population	%
American (620)	620	5.53
Arab (23)	55	0.49
Egyptian (10)	28	0.25
Iraqi (3)	3	0.03
Lebanese (10)	24	0.21
Australian (0)	11	0.10
Austrian (20)	44	0.39
Belgian (9)	231	2.06
British (7)	61	0.54
Canadian (87)	341	3.04
Croatian (0)	56	0.50
Czech (0)	114	1.02
Czechoslovakian (0)	49	0.44
Dutch (71)	283	2.53
English (425)	1,818	16.23
European (141)	141	1.26
Finnish (21)	87	0.78
French, ex. Basque (122)	685	6.11
French Canadian (142)	245	2.19
German (1,164)	3,601	32.15
Greek (13)	13	0.12
Hungarian (51)	88	0.79
Iranian (12)	12	0.11
Irish (558)	1,842	16.44
Italian (221)	479	4.28
Latvian (13)	50	0.45
Lithuanian (30)	88	0.79
Northern European (34)	34	0.30
Norwegian (0)	20	0.18
Polish (310)	749	6.69
Portuguese (17)	59	0.53
Romanian (12)	26	0.23
Russian (12)	183	1.63
Scandinavian (20)	35	0.31
Scotch-Irish (77)	298	2.66
Scottish (333)	635	5.67
Serbian (9)	9	0.08
Slovak (11)	25	0.22
Swedish (87)	326	2.91
Swiss (17)	25	0.22
Ukrainian (13)	75	0.67
Welsh (47)	101	0.90

Hispanic Origin	Population	%
Hispanic or Latino (of any race)	278	2.50
Central American, ex. Mexican	10	0.09
Guatemalan	2	0.02
Honduran	4	0.04
Panamanian	3	0.03
Salvadoran	1	0.01
Cuban	7	0.06
Dominican Republic	1	0.01
Mexican	198	1.78
Puerto Rican	26	0.23
South American	11	0.10
Bolivian	1	0.01
Colombian	6	0.05
Ecuadorian	4	0.04
Other Hispanic or Latino	25	0.23

Race*	Population	%
African-American/Black (181)	251	2.26
Not Hispanic (180)	246	2.21
Hispanic (1)	5	0.05
American Indian/Alaska Native (29)	92	0.83
Not Hispanic (25)	87	0.78
Hispanic (4)	5	0.05
Apache (1)	1	0.01
Canadian/French Am. Ind. (2)	3	0.03
Cherokee (2)	10	0.09
Chippewa (7)	28	0.25
Choctaw (1)	1	0.01
Comanche (1)	1	0.01
Cree (0)	2	0.02
Delaware (1)	1	0.01
Iroquois (3)	3	0.03
Mexican American Ind. (1)	1	0.01
Potawatomi (0)	3	0.03
Sioux (1)	1	0.01
Asian (150)	195	1.76
Not Hispanic (148)	192	1.73
Hispanic (2)	3	0.03
Bangladeshi (8)	8	0.07
Chinese, ex. Taiwanese (17)	23	0.21
Filipino (22)	36	0.32
Indian (65)	71	0.64
Indonesian (1)	1	0.01
Japanese (7)	8	0.07
Korean (8)	12	0.11
Laotian (4)	4	0.04
Pakistani (10)	10	0.09
Sri Lankan (0)	1	0.01
Vietnamese (7)	8	0.07
Hawaii Native/Pacific Islander (2)	3	0.03
Not Hispanic (2)	3	0.03
Native Hawaiian (1)	1	0.01
Samoan (1)	2	0.02
White (10,503)	10,687	96.21
Not Hispanic (10,301)	10,463	94.19
Hispanic (202)	224	2.02

Fraser

Place Type: City
County: Macomb
Population: 14,480†

Ancestry‡	Population	%
African, Sub-Saharan (136)	136	0.92
Other Sub-Saharan African (136)	136	0.92
Albanian (0)	37	0.25
American (551)	551	3.74
Arab (109)	182	1.23
Egyptian (8)	8	0.05
Iraqi (25)	25	0.17
Jordanian (0)	11	0.07
Lebanese (58)	120	0.81
Syrian (9)	9	0.06
Other Arab (9)	9	0.06
Austrian (10)	140	0.95
Belgian (92)	420	2.85
British (19)	47	0.32
Canadian (36)	99	0.67
Croatian (0)	42	0.28
Czech (50)	182	1.23
Czechoslovakian (29)	29	0.20
Danish (0)	39	0.26
Dutch (41)	154	1.04
English (334)	1,443	9.79
European (28)	61	0.41
Finnish (11)	83	0.56
French, ex. Basque (49)	808	5.48
French Canadian (62)	388	2.63
German (1,316)	4,229	28.69
Greek (27)	103	0.70
Hungarian (0)	143	0.97
Irish (433)	2,136	14.49
Italian (1,046)	2,584	17.53
Lithuanian (17)	53	0.36
Maltese (13)	40	0.27
Norwegian (23)	48	0.33
Polish (1,258)	3,109	21.09
Portuguese (0)	13	0.09
Romanian (7)	112	0.76
Russian (33)	112	0.76
Scotch-Irish (92)	232	1.57
Scottish (109)	237	1.61
Serbian (0)	23	0.16
Slavic (0)	60	0.41
Slovak (42)	117	0.79
Slovene (0)	9	0.06
Swedish (0)	41	0.28
Swiss (9)	18	0.12

*Notes: † The Census 2010 population figure is used to calculate the percentages in the Hispanic Origin and Race categories. Ancestry percentages are based on the 2006-2010 American Community Survey population (not shown); ‡ Numbers in parentheses indicate the number of people reporting a single ancestry; * Numbers in parentheses indicate the number of persons reporting this race alone, not in combination with any other race; Please refer to the Explanation of Data for more information.*

Ukrainian (33)	99	0.67
Welsh (0)	47	0.32
Yugoslavian (71)	98	0.66

Hispanic Origin	Population	%
Hispanic or Latino (of any race)	297	2.05
Central American, ex. Mexican	9	0.06
Guatemalan	4	0.03
Salvadoran	5	0.03
Cuban	7	0.05
Dominican Republic	4	0.03
Mexican	214	1.48
Puerto Rican	20	0.14
South American	8	0.06
Argentinean	1	0.01
Colombian	6	0.04
Ecuadorian	1	0.01
Other Hispanic or Latino	35	0.24

Race*	Population	%
African-American/Black (566)	686	4.74
Not Hispanic (562)	675	4.66
Hispanic (4)	11	0.08
American Indian/Alaska Native (74)	155	1.07
Not Hispanic (61)	137	0.95
Hispanic (13)	18	0.12
Apache (1)	1	0.01
Blackfeet (0)	9	0.06
Canadian/French Am. Ind. (5)	8	0.06
Cherokee (3)	23	0.16
Chippewa (22)	36	0.25
Choctaw (1)	1	0.01
Comanche (3)	3	0.02
Iroquois (3)	3	0.02
Lumbee (11)	12	0.08
Mexican American Ind. (1)	1	0.01
Ottawa (4)	4	0.03
Potawatomi (1)	4	0.03
Sioux (1)	4	0.03
Tsimshian *(Alaska Native)* (1)	2	0.01
Asian (211)	287	1.98
Not Hispanic (210)	280	1.93
Hispanic (1)	7	0.05
Cambodian (3)	5	0.03
Chinese, ex. Taiwanese (44)	51	0.35
Filipino (38)	56	0.39
Hmong (7)	7	0.05
Indian (57)	61	0.42
Japanese (7)	20	0.14
Korean (15)	24	0.17
Laotian (3)	5	0.03
Pakistani (6)	6	0.04
Sri Lankan (1)	1	0.01
Taiwanese (1)	1	0.01
Thai (1)	6	0.04
Vietnamese (15)	18	0.12
Hawaii Native/Pacific Islander (1)	8	0.06
Not Hispanic (1)	8	0.06
Guamanian/Chamorro (1)	2	0.01
Native Hawaiian (0)	6	0.04
White (13,319)	13,566	93.69
Not Hispanic (13,099)	13,325	92.02
Hispanic (220)	241	1.66

Frenchtown

Place Type: Township
County: Monroe
Population: 20,428†

Ancestry‡	Population	%
African, Sub-Saharan (16)	60	0.29
African (16)	60	0.29
Albanian (86)	86	0.41
American (785)	785	3.78
Arab (83)	182	0.88
Arab (68)	127	0.61
Lebanese (0)	27	0.13
Syrian (15)	28	0.13
Armenian (0)	28	0.13
Austrian (0)	28	0.13
Belgian (7)	272	1.31
British (20)	96	0.46
Bulgarian (0)	15	0.07
Canadian (16)	147	0.71
Croatian (11)	19	0.09
Czech (0)	94	0.45
Danish (0)	12	0.06
Dutch (104)	513	2.47
Eastern European (31)	31	0.15
English (350)	1,874	9.02
European (96)	96	0.46
Finnish (0)	47	0.23
French, ex. Basque (423)	2,744	13.21
French Canadian (127)	387	1.86
German (2,122)	6,940	33.41
Greek (24)	42	0.20
Hungarian (249)	555	2.67
Irish (869)	3,392	16.33
Italian (457)	1,096	5.28
Lithuanian (0)	50	0.24
Maltese (0)	12	0.06
Norwegian (12)	23	0.11
Pennsylvania German (18)	18	0.09
Polish (690)	1,547	7.45
Romanian (9)	116	0.56
Russian (10)	89	0.43
Scotch-Irish (96)	351	1.69
Scottish (129)	876	4.22
Serbian (61)	136	0.65
Slavic (0)	13	0.06
Slovak (10)	41	0.20
Slovene (12)	29	0.14
Swedish (14)	124	0.60
Swiss (0)	23	0.11
Ukrainian (16)	40	0.19
Welsh (0)	43	0.21
Yugoslavian (38)	114	0.55

Hispanic Origin	Population	%
Hispanic or Latino (of any race)	847	4.15
Central American, ex. Mexican	15	0.07
Guatemalan	5	0.02
Honduran	3	0.01
Nicaraguan	6	0.03
Salvadoran	1	<0.01
Cuban	9	0.04
Dominican Republic	1	<0.01
Mexican	677	3.31
Puerto Rican	87	0.43
South American	5	0.02
Bolivian	1	<0.01
Ecuadorian	1	<0.01
Paraguayan	1	<0.01
Peruvian	2	0.01
Other Hispanic or Latino	53	0.26

Race*	Population	%
African-American/Black (428)	600	2.94
Not Hispanic (415)	570	2.79
Hispanic (13)	30	0.15
American Indian/Alaska Native (69)	291	1.42
Not Hispanic (61)	263	1.29
Hispanic (8)	28	0.14
Apache (0)	1	<0.01
Blackfeet (3)	19	0.09
Canadian/French Am. Ind. (1)	2	0.01
Cherokee (8)	83	0.41
Chippewa (16)	34	0.17
Choctaw (0)	2	0.01
Cree (1)	1	<0.01
Delaware (1)	1	<0.01
Iroquois (7)	9	0.04
Kiowa (1)	1	<0.01
Lumbee (0)	1	<0.01
Menominee (3)	7	0.03
Ottawa (3)	11	0.05
Potawatomi (1)	1	<0.01
Shoshone (0)	1	<0.01
Sioux (1)	6	0.03
Tlingit-Haida *(Alaska Native)* (1)	1	<0.01
Asian (129)	159	0.78
Not Hispanic (129)	157	0.77
Hispanic (0)	2	0.01
Bangladeshi (1)	1	<0.01
Chinese, ex. Taiwanese (12)	16	0.08
Filipino (8)	17	0.08
Indian (62)	65	0.32
Indonesian (1)	2	0.01
Japanese (5)	8	0.04
Korean (11)	14	0.07
Thai (3)	7	0.03
Vietnamese (13)	15	0.07
Hawaii Native/Pacific Islander (3)	7	0.03
Not Hispanic (2)	4	0.02
Hispanic (1)	3	0.01
Guamanian/Chamorro (1)	1	<0.01
Native Hawaiian (2)	6	0.03
White (19,087)	19,502	95.47
Not Hispanic (18,598)	18,948	92.76
Hispanic (489)	554	2.71

Fruitport

Place Type: Charter Township
County: Muskegon
Population: 13,598†

Ancestry‡	Population	%
American (447)	447	3.31
Arab (4)	8	0.06
Arab (4)	8	0.06
Armenian (4)	4	0.03
Australian (0)	16	0.12
Austrian (0)	17	0.13
Belgian (9)	17	0.13
Canadian (38)	56	0.41
Croatian (0)	4	0.03
Czech (14)	161	1.19
Danish (11)	102	0.75
Dutch (833)	2,383	17.63
English (315)	1,436	10.62
European (114)	114	0.84
Finnish (19)	55	0.41
French, ex. Basque (116)	952	7.04
French Canadian (139)	238	1.76
German (882)	3,398	25.14
Hungarian (53)	116	0.86
Irish (367)	1,605	11.87
Italian (116)	498	3.68
Latvian (3)	10	0.07
Lithuanian (29)	103	0.76
Maltese (9)	9	0.07
Northern European (8)	8	0.06
Norwegian (114)	262	1.94
Pennsylvania German (21)	23	0.17
Polish (279)	1,068	7.90
Romanian (10)	10	0.07
Russian (8)	18	0.13
Scandinavian (23)	37	0.27
Scotch-Irish (58)	279	2.06
Scottish (38)	252	1.86
Slovak (40)	137	1.01
Swedish (114)	600	4.44
Swiss (12)	109	0.81
Ukrainian (41)	71	0.53
Welsh (9)	30	0.22
West Indian, ex. Hispanic (0)	3	0.02
Jamaican (0)	3	0.02
Yugoslavian (3)	6	0.04

Hispanic Origin	Population	%
Hispanic or Latino (of any race)	429	3.15
Central American, ex. Mexican	22	0.16
Guatemalan	7	0.05
Honduran	7	0.05
Panamanian	2	0.01
Salvadoran	6	0.04
Mexican	340	2.50
Puerto Rican	36	0.26

*Notes: † The Census 2010 population figure is used to calculate the percentages in the Hispanic Origin and Race categories. Ancestry percentages are based on the 2006-2010 American Community Survey population (not shown); ‡ Numbers in parentheses indicate the number of people reporting a single ancestry; * Numbers in parentheses indicate the number of persons reporting this race alone, not in combination with any other race; Please refer to the Explanation of Data for more information.*

South American	5	0.04
Colombian	2	0.01
Peruvian	2	0.01
Venezuelan	1	0.01
Other Hispanic or Latino	26	0.19

Race*	Population	%
African-American/Black (173)	232	1.71
Not Hispanic (172)	230	1.69
Hispanic (1)	2	0.01
American Indian/Alaska Native (91)	198	1.46
Not Hispanic (83)	172	1.26
Hispanic (8)	26	0.19
Blackfeet (0)	3	0.02
Central American Ind. (2)	2	0.01
Cherokee (2)	22	0.16
Chickasaw (0)	2	0.01
Chippewa (19)	33	0.24
Choctaw (0)	1	0.01
Cree (0)	1	0.01
Lumbee (0)	1	0.01
Menominee (2)	2	0.01
Ottawa (28)	51	0.38
Potawatomi (11)	13	0.10
Seminole (0)	2	0.01
Sioux (1)	1	0.01
Asian (110)	155	1.14
Not Hispanic (107)	147	1.08
Hispanic (3)	8	0.06
Cambodian (5)	6	0.04
Chinese, ex. Taiwanese (29)	36	0.26
Filipino (13)	29	0.21
Indian (16)	18	0.13
Japanese (4)	13	0.10
Korean (29)	41	0.30
Taiwanese (1)	1	0.01
Thai (2)	2	0.01
Vietnamese (9)	9	0.07
Hawaii Native/Pacific Islander (0)	2	0.01
Not Hispanic (0)	2	0.01
Guamanian/Chamorro (0)	1	0.01
Native Hawaiian (0)	1	0.01
White (12,878)	13,098	96.32
Not Hispanic (12,606)	12,793	94.08
Hispanic (272)	305	2.24

Gaines

Place Type: Charter Township
County: Kent
Population: 25,146†

Ancestry‡	Population	%
African, Sub-Saharan (53)	67	0.28
African (33)	33	0.14
Ethiopian (8)	22	0.09
Zimbabwean (12)	12	0.05
American (928)	928	3.82
Arab (145)	389	1.60
Arab (45)	45	0.19
Jordanian (84)	84	0.35
Lebanese (0)	110	0.45
Syrian (16)	150	0.62
Austrian (16)	44	0.18
Belgian (11)	26	0.11
British (17)	38	0.16
Canadian (77)	162	0.67
Croatian (26)	44	0.18
Czech (22)	66	0.27
Czechoslovakian (44)	87	0.36
Danish (32)	212	0.87
Dutch (4,401)	6,541	26.89
English (731)	2,332	9.59
European (220)	268	1.10
Finnish (24)	63	0.26
French, ex. Basque (179)	816	3.35
French Canadian (84)	274	1.13
German (1,430)	4,772	19.62
Greek (0)	41	0.17
Hungarian (31)	123	0.51
Irish (229)	2,004	8.24
Italian (254)	674	2.77
Latvian (6)	17	0.07
Lithuanian (44)	83	0.34
Macedonian (8)	8	0.03
Maltese (7)	7	0.03
Norwegian (51)	137	0.56
Pennsylvania German (11)	24	0.10
Polish (485)	1,574	6.47
Portuguese (0)	38	0.16
Romanian (34)	34	0.14
Russian (51)	70	0.29
Scandinavian (0)	10	0.04
Scotch-Irish (156)	359	1.48
Scottish (75)	304	1.25
Serbian (16)	23	0.09
Slovak (0)	45	0.19
Slovene (0)	8	0.03
Swedish (43)	217	0.89
Swiss (5)	31	0.13
Ukrainian (47)	77	0.32
Welsh (8)	55	0.23
West Indian, ex. Hispanic (0)	6	0.02
West Indian (0)	6	0.02
Yugoslavian (122)	139	0.57

Hispanic Origin	Population	%
Hispanic or Latino (of any race)	1,532	6.09
Central American, ex. Mexican	113	0.45
Costa Rican	6	0.02
Guatemalan	64	0.25
Honduran	14	0.06
Nicaraguan	4	0.02
Panamanian	4	0.02
Salvadoran	21	0.08
Cuban	103	0.41
Dominican Republic	41	0.16
Mexican	993	3.95
Puerto Rican	175	0.70
South American	45	0.18
Argentinean	2	0.01
Bolivian	8	0.03
Chilean	6	0.02
Colombian	11	0.04
Ecuadorian	1	<0.01
Peruvian	14	0.06
Venezuelan	3	0.01
Other Hispanic or Latino	62	0.25

Race*	Population	%
African-American/Black (2,338)	2,685	10.68
Not Hispanic (2,275)	2,570	10.22
Hispanic (63)	115	0.46
American Indian/Alaska Native (119)	272	1.08
Not Hispanic (107)	228	0.91
Hispanic (12)	44	0.17
Blackfeet (0)	1	<0.01
Canadian/French Am. Ind. (2)	8	0.03
Central American Ind. (1)	1	<0.01
Cherokee (5)	35	0.14
Chickasaw (1)	4	0.02
Chippewa (30)	60	0.24
Choctaw (1)	2	0.01
Creek (0)	2	0.01
Iroquois (0)	4	0.02
Mexican American Ind. (9)	15	0.06
Navajo (4)	4	0.02
Ottawa (24)	35	0.14
Potawatomi (20)	28	0.11
Seminole (0)	2	0.01
South American Ind. (0)	3	0.01
Asian (1,169)	1,303	5.18
Not Hispanic (1,168)	1,293	5.14
Hispanic (1)	10	0.04
Burmese (6)	6	0.02
Cambodian (3)	6	0.02
Chinese, ex. Taiwanese (89)	102	0.41
Filipino (27)	55	0.22
Hmong (10)	13	0.05
Indian (118)	127	0.51
Indonesian (1)	7	0.03
Japanese (12)	28	0.11
Korean (105)	141	0.56
Laotian (10)	14	0.06
Nepalese (1)	1	<0.01
Pakistani (16)	17	0.07
Sri Lankan (1)	1	<0.01
Taiwanese (3)	3	0.01
Thai (3)	10	0.04
Vietnamese (734)	773	3.07
Hawaii Native/Pacific Islander (8)	37	0.15
Not Hispanic (8)	30	0.12
Hispanic (0)	7	0.03
Fijian (0)	1	<0.01
Native Hawaiian (1)	12	0.05
Samoan (1)	2	0.01
White (20,236)	20,836	82.86
Not Hispanic (19,498)	19,974	79.43
Hispanic (738)	862	3.43

Garden City

Place Type: City
County: Wayne
Population: 27,692†

Ancestry‡	Population	%
African, Sub-Saharan (0)	60	0.21
African (0)	60	0.21
Albanian (36)	36	0.13
American (1,160)	1,160	4.11
Arab (124)	276	0.98
Arab (12)	32	0.11
Lebanese (39)	76	0.27
Palestinian (43)	138	0.49
Other Arab (30)	30	0.11
Armenian (16)	180	0.64
Austrian (26)	41	0.15
Belgian (11)	97	0.34
British (58)	220	0.78
Bulgarian (0)	10	0.04
Canadian (97)	188	0.67
Croatian (0)	10	0.04
Czech (9)	109	0.39
Czechoslovakian (0)	43	0.15
Danish (7)	100	0.35
Dutch (70)	534	1.89
Eastern European (13)	13	0.05
English (636)	2,915	10.34
European (52)	75	0.27
Finnish (87)	353	1.25
French, ex. Basque (123)	1,616	5.73
French Canadian (335)	1,138	4.04
German (1,409)	6,855	24.31
Greek (24)	119	0.42
Hungarian (175)	454	1.61
Irish (838)	4,549	16.13
Italian (810)	2,691	9.54
Lithuanian (85)	112	0.40
Macedonian (23)	23	0.08
Maltese (65)	228	0.81
Northern European (11)	11	0.04
Norwegian (26)	208	0.74
Polish (1,795)	5,657	20.06
Portuguese (34)	59	0.21
Romanian (265)	356	1.26
Russian (61)	260	0.92
Scandinavian (12)	23	0.08
Scotch-Irish (249)	809	2.87
Scottish (327)	1,016	3.60
Serbian (0)	16	0.06
Slavic (0)	24	0.09
Slovak (19)	50	0.18
Slovene (0)	5	0.02
Swedish (73)	381	1.35
Swiss (0)	35	0.12
Ukrainian (78)	118	0.42
Welsh (23)	166	0.59
West Indian, ex. Hispanic (9)	9	0.03
U.S. Virgin Islander (9)	9	0.03

*Notes: † The Census 2010 population figure is used to calculate the percentages in the Hispanic Origin and Race categories. Ancestry percentages are based on the 2006-2010 American Community Survey population (not shown); ‡ Numbers in parentheses indicate the number of people reporting a single ancestry; * Numbers in parentheses indicate the number of persons reporting this race alone, not in combination with any other race; Please refer to the Explanation of Data for more information.*

Yugoslavian (0)	7	0.02

Hispanic Origin	Population	%
Hispanic or Latino (of any race)	903	3.26
Central American, ex. Mexican	19	0.07
Guatemalan	5	0.02
Honduran	2	0.01
Nicaraguan	2	0.01
Panamanian	1	<0.01
Salvadoran	9	0.03
Cuban	14	0.05
Dominican Republic	5	0.02
Mexican	691	2.50
Puerto Rican	71	0.26
South American	24	0.09
Argentinean	6	0.02
Chilean	3	0.01
Colombian	4	0.01
Ecuadorian	6	0.02
Peruvian	4	0.01
Uruguayan	1	<0.01
Other Hispanic or Latino	79	0.29

Race*	Population	%
African-American/Black (934)	1,145	4.13
Not Hispanic (928)	1,133	4.09
Hispanic (6)	12	0.04
American Indian/Alaska Native (115)	326	1.18
Not Hispanic (113)	306	1.11
Hispanic (2)	20	0.07
Aleut *(Alaska Native)* (0)	1	<0.01
Apache (0)	8	0.03
Blackfeet (1)	5	0.02
Canadian/French Am. Ind. (5)	5	0.02
Cherokee (18)	76	0.27
Chippewa (19)	47	0.17
Choctaw (0)	3	0.01
Cree (0)	1	<0.01
Creek (2)	3	0.01
Crow (0)	1	<0.01
Delaware (4)	6	0.02
Inupiat *(Alaska Native)* (1)	1	<0.01
Iroquois (9)	21	0.08
Mexican American Ind. (1)	2	0.01
Navajo (6)	9	0.03
Osage (1)	7	0.03
Ottawa (7)	8	0.03
Potawatomi (0)	2	0.01
Sioux (2)	5	0.02
Yuman (0)	1	<0.01
Asian (234)	347	1.25
Not Hispanic (232)	340	1.23
Hispanic (2)	7	0.03
Cambodian (2)	3	0.01
Chinese, ex. Taiwanese (35)	41	0.15
Filipino (71)	97	0.35
Indian (29)	34	0.12
Indonesian (2)	2	0.01
Japanese (14)	33	0.12
Korean (13)	34	0.12
Pakistani (16)	18	0.07
Sri Lankan (0)	1	<0.01
Thai (2)	3	0.01
Vietnamese (37)	41	0.15
Hawaii Native/Pacific Islander (4)	18	0.07
Not Hispanic (4)	15	0.05
Hispanic (0)	3	0.01
Guamanian/Chamorro (1)	2	0.01
Native Hawaiian (2)	5	0.02
Samoan (1)	3	0.01
White (25,602)	26,155	94.45
Not Hispanic (24,977)	25,444	91.88
Hispanic (625)	711	2.57

Garfield

Place Type: Charter Township
County: Grand Traverse
Population: 16,256†

Ancestry‡	Population	%
African, Sub-Saharan (286)	286	1.79
African (286)	286	1.79
American (1,172)	1,172	7.35
Arab (16)	44	0.28
Iraqi (16)	44	0.28
Armenian (0)	35	0.22
Austrian (14)	96	0.60
Belgian (0)	10	0.06
British (70)	128	0.80
Canadian (12)	120	0.75
Croatian (14)	70	0.44
Czech (17)	403	2.53
Czechoslovakian (32)	56	0.35
Danish (23)	208	1.30
Dutch (228)	808	5.07
Eastern European (12)	26	0.16
English (616)	2,442	15.32
European (169)	169	1.06
Finnish (9)	70	0.44
French, ex. Basque (189)	1,429	8.97
French Canadian (127)	253	1.59
German (1,690)	4,998	31.36
Greek (0)	75	0.47
Hungarian (0)	87	0.55
Irish (746)	2,409	15.11
Italian (166)	564	3.54
Lithuanian (0)	26	0.16
Maltese (14)	14	0.09
Norwegian (89)	330	2.07
Pennsylvania German (0)	12	0.08
Polish (434)	1,210	7.59
Russian (13)	31	0.19
Scandinavian (0)	30	0.19
Scotch-Irish (68)	275	1.73
Scottish (182)	601	3.77
Serbian (0)	45	0.28
Slavic (12)	12	0.08
Swedish (48)	550	3.45
Swiss (15)	43	0.27
Ukrainian (25)	36	0.23
Welsh (0)	132	0.83

Hispanic Origin	Population	%
Hispanic or Latino (of any race)	398	2.45
Central American, ex. Mexican	20	0.12
Costa Rican	1	0.01
Guatemalan	4	0.02
Honduran	1	0.01
Nicaraguan	2	0.01
Salvadoran	12	0.07
Cuban	3	0.02
Dominican Republic	1	0.01
Mexican	262	1.61
Puerto Rican	29	0.18
South American	13	0.08
Argentinean	4	0.02
Bolivian	1	0.01
Colombian	5	0.03
Paraguayan	1	0.01
Peruvian	1	0.01
Venezuelan	1	0.01
Other Hispanic or Latino	70	0.43

Race*	Population	%
African-American/Black (130)	256	1.57
Not Hispanic (129)	252	1.55
Hispanic (1)	4	0.02
American Indian/Alaska Native (192)	381	2.34
Not Hispanic (182)	355	2.18
Hispanic (10)	26	0.16
Apache (0)	3	0.02
Arapaho (0)	4	0.02
Blackfeet (1)	9	0.06
Canadian/French Am. Ind. (4)	4	0.02
Cherokee (3)	19	0.12
Chickasaw (1)	1	0.01
Chippewa (91)	169	1.04
Choctaw (0)	8	0.05
Comanche (0)	2	0.01
Delaware (2)	3	0.02
Iroquois (3)	3	0.02
Mexican American Ind. (1)	1	0.01
Ottawa (26)	67	0.41
Pima (2)	2	0.01
Potawatomi (3)	5	0.03
Sioux (3)	6	0.04
South American Ind. (1)	1	0.01
Asian (173)	256	1.57
Not Hispanic (170)	249	1.53
Hispanic (3)	7	0.04
Chinese, ex. Taiwanese (48)	69	0.42
Filipino (21)	43	0.26
Hmong (8)	10	0.06
Indian (13)	17	0.10
Indonesian (0)	1	0.01
Japanese (2)	8	0.05
Korean (11)	26	0.16
Laotian (15)	16	0.10
Nepalese (0)	1	0.01
Pakistani (3)	3	0.02
Taiwanese (3)	3	0.02
Thai (2)	2	0.01
Vietnamese (41)	44	0.27
Hawaii Native/Pacific Islander (7)	27	0.17
Not Hispanic (1)	21	0.13
Hispanic (6)	6	0.04
Guamanian/Chamorro (1)	2	0.01
Native Hawaiian (5)	12	0.07
Samoan (1)	1	0.01
Tongan (0)	1	0.01
White (15,259)	15,631	96.16
Not Hispanic (15,016)	15,356	94.46
Hispanic (243)	275	1.69

Genesee

Place Type: Charter Township
County: Genesee
Population: 21,581†

Ancestry‡	Population	%
African, Sub-Saharan (44)	44	0.20
African (44)	44	0.20
American (1,878)	1,878	8.42
Arab (143)	241	1.08
Arab (133)	162	0.73
Lebanese (10)	39	0.17
Moroccan (0)	30	0.13
Syrian (0)	10	0.04
Australian (11)	25	0.11
Austrian (0)	29	0.13
Belgian (22)	45	0.20
British (36)	72	0.32
Canadian (38)	136	0.61
Czech (18)	74	0.33
Czechoslovakian (34)	34	0.15
Danish (0)	21	0.09
Dutch (132)	586	2.63
English (880)	2,732	12.25
European (164)	193	0.87
Finnish (11)	101	0.45
French, ex. Basque (318)	1,659	7.44
French Canadian (484)	875	3.92
German (1,446)	4,436	19.89
Greek (0)	47	0.21
Hungarian (60)	281	1.26
Irish (562)	3,217	14.42
Israeli (26)	26	0.12
Italian (177)	568	2.55
Lithuanian (0)	10	0.04
Northern European (0)	10	0.04
Norwegian (12)	133	0.60
Polish (384)	1,007	4.51
Romanian (13)	13	0.06
Russian (13)	87	0.39
Scandinavian (0)	10	0.04
Scotch-Irish (194)	471	2.11
Scottish (197)	453	2.03
Slovak (8)	37	0.17

*Notes: † The Census 2010 population figure is used to calculate the percentages in the Hispanic Origin and Race categories. Ancestry percentages are based on the 2006-2010 American Community Survey population (not shown); ‡ Numbers in parentheses indicate the number of people reporting a single ancestry; * Numbers in parentheses indicate the number of persons reporting this race alone, not in combination with any other race; Please refer to the Explanation of Data for more information.*

Swedish (28)	147	0.66
Swiss (6)	6	0.03
Ukrainian (9)	126	0.56
Welsh (0)	24	0.11
Yugoslavian (16)	16	0.07

Hispanic Origin	Population	%
Hispanic or Latino (of any race)	810	3.75
Central American, ex. Mexican	9	0.04
Costa Rican	5	0.02
Honduran	3	0.01
Panamanian	1	<0.01
Cuban	11	0.05
Dominican Republic	1	<0.01
Mexican	640	2.97
Puerto Rican	47	0.22
South American	12	0.06
Colombian	10	0.05
Peruvian	2	0.01
Other Hispanic or Latino	90	0.42

Race*	Population	%
African-American/Black (1,851)	2,112	9.79
Not Hispanic (1,834)	2,065	9.57
Hispanic (17)	47	0.22
American Indian/Alaska Native (181)	404	1.87
Not Hispanic (154)	354	1.64
Hispanic (27)	50	0.23
Aleut *(Alaska Native)* (1)	1	<0.01
Apache (3)	6	0.03
Blackfeet (3)	22	0.10
Canadian/French Am. Ind. (0)	1	<0.01
Cherokee (26)	100	0.46
Chickasaw (1)	1	<0.01
Chippewa (40)	67	0.31
Choctaw (3)	7	0.03
Comanche (0)	2	0.01
Cree (0)	3	0.01
Creek (0)	2	0.01
Crow (0)	2	0.01
Iroquois (0)	4	0.02
Mexican American Ind. (0)	3	0.01
Ottawa (6)	11	0.05
Pueblo (1)	4	0.02
Sioux (3)	4	0.02
South American Ind. (0)	3	0.01
Tlingit-Haida *(Alaska Native)* (0)	1	<0.01
Asian (49)	83	0.38
Not Hispanic (48)	81	0.38
Hispanic (1)	2	0.01
Chinese, ex. Taiwanese (2)	2	0.01
Filipino (7)	17	0.08
Indian (14)	20	0.09
Japanese (5)	9	0.04
Korean (10)	22	0.10
Thai (2)	7	0.03
Vietnamese (4)	6	0.03
Hawaii Native/Pacific Islander (1)	14	0.06
Not Hispanic (1)	13	0.06
Hispanic (0)	1	<0.01
Guamanian/Chamorro (0)	4	0.02
Native Hawaiian (1)	3	0.01
Samoan (0)	3	0.01
White (18,826)	19,313	89.49
Not Hispanic (18,274)	18,681	86.56
Hispanic (552)	632	2.93

Genoa

Place Type: Township
County: Livingston
Population: 19,821†

Ancestry‡	Population	%
African, Sub-Saharan (11)	11	0.06
South African (11)	11	0.06
American (1,023)	1,023	5.20
Arab (23)	87	0.44
Lebanese (23)	78	0.40
Syrian (0)	9	0.05
Armenian (38)	200	1.02
Australian (0)	11	0.06
Austrian (50)	83	0.42
Belgian (30)	112	0.57
Brazilian (25)	25	0.13
British (44)	103	0.52
Canadian (27)	148	0.75
Croatian (9)	70	0.36
Czech (58)	198	1.01
Czechoslovakian (22)	60	0.31
Danish (56)	175	0.89
Dutch (117)	433	2.20
English (929)	2,869	14.59
European (154)	162	0.82
Finnish (113)	347	1.76
French, ex. Basque (146)	1,457	7.41
French Canadian (128)	643	3.27
German (1,561)	5,843	29.72
Greek (40)	173	0.88
Hungarian (65)	287	1.46
Irish (939)	3,496	17.78
Italian (403)	1,503	7.64
Latvian (9)	17	0.09
Lithuanian (73)	238	1.21
Macedonian (0)	75	0.38
Maltese (56)	96	0.49
Northern European (8)	8	0.04
Norwegian (85)	177	0.90
Polish (964)	2,766	14.07
Portuguese (24)	89	0.45
Romanian (36)	72	0.37
Russian (61)	190	0.97
Scandinavian (11)	11	0.06
Scotch-Irish (137)	330	1.68
Scottish (198)	782	3.98
Serbian (8)	38	0.19
Slavic (0)	8	0.04
Slovak (18)	146	0.74
Slovene (0)	9	0.05
Swedish (80)	384	1.95
Swiss (0)	24	0.12
Turkish (0)	11	0.06
Ukrainian (5)	47	0.24
Welsh (37)	171	0.87
West Indian, ex. Hispanic (14)	14	0.07
Trinidadian/Tobagonian (14)	14	0.07
Yugoslavian (0)	62	0.32

Hispanic Origin	Population	%
Hispanic or Latino (of any race)	423	2.13
Central American, ex. Mexican	20	0.10
Guatemalan	14	0.07
Honduran	1	0.01
Panamanian	1	0.01
Salvadoran	4	0.02
Cuban	23	0.12
Mexican	275	1.39
Puerto Rican	34	0.17
South American	27	0.14
Argentinean	11	0.06
Chilean	1	0.01
Colombian	7	0.04
Ecuadorian	3	0.02
Peruvian	2	0.01
Venezuelan	3	0.02
Other Hispanic or Latino	44	0.22

Race*	Population	%
African-American/Black (127)	188	0.95
Not Hispanic (121)	172	0.87
Hispanic (6)	16	0.08
American Indian/Alaska Native (70)	167	0.84
Not Hispanic (65)	151	0.76
Hispanic (5)	16	0.08
Aleut *(Alaska Native)* (0)	3	0.02
Apache (2)	3	0.02
Blackfeet (0)	1	0.01
Canadian/French Am. Ind. (1)	3	0.02
Cherokee (7)	21	0.11
Chippewa (24)	41	0.21
Creek (1)	1	0.01
Iroquois (6)	6	0.03
Lumbee (1)	1	0.01
Mexican American Ind. (3)	7	0.04
Navajo (3)	3	0.02
Osage (0)	1	0.01
Ottawa (3)	3	0.02
Potawatomi (1)	3	0.02
Sioux (1)	1	0.01
Asian (207)	318	1.60
Not Hispanic (203)	308	1.55
Hispanic (4)	10	0.05
Chinese, ex. Taiwanese (45)	74	0.37
Filipino (28)	46	0.23
Hmong (4)	5	0.03
Indian (37)	45	0.23
Indonesian (0)	2	0.01
Japanese (16)	33	0.17
Korean (47)	62	0.31
Malaysian (1)	1	0.01
Nepalese (0)	2	0.01
Pakistani (1)	3	0.02
Taiwanese (4)	6	0.03
Thai (3)	3	0.02
Vietnamese (14)	22	0.11
Hawaii Native/Pacific Islander (7)	18	0.09
Not Hispanic (5)	16	0.08
Hispanic (2)	2	0.01
Guamanian/Chamorro (2)	2	0.01
Native Hawaiian (1)	2	0.01
Samoan (0)	1	0.01
White (19,044)	19,303	97.39
Not Hispanic (18,758)	18,983	95.77
Hispanic (286)	320	1.61

Georgetown

Place Type: Charter Township
County: Ottawa
Population: 46,985†

Ancestry‡	Population	%
African, Sub-Saharan (18)	18	0.04
Ethiopian (18)	18	0.04
American (2,284)	2,284	4.92
Arab (42)	106	0.23
Lebanese (42)	85	0.18
Syrian (0)	11	0.02
Other Arab (0)	10	0.02
Austrian (5)	148	0.32
Belgian (27)	126	0.27
Brazilian (17)	37	0.08
British (176)	214	0.46
Canadian (43)	189	0.41
Croatian (19)	36	0.08
Czech (33)	238	0.51
Czechoslovakian (10)	35	0.08
Danish (23)	153	0.33
Dutch (12,995)	19,742	42.55
Eastern European (16)	16	0.03
English (1,374)	4,687	10.10
European (585)	690	1.49
Finnish (49)	175	0.38
French, ex. Basque (144)	1,600	3.45
French Canadian (101)	336	0.72
German (2,102)	10,831	23.34
Greek (47)	210	0.45
Hungarian (102)	203	0.44
Icelander (0)	15	0.03
Irish (890)	4,954	10.68
Italian (238)	1,286	2.77
Lithuanian (54)	283	0.61
Norwegian (91)	474	1.02
Pennsylvania German (16)	30	0.06
Polish (619)	2,420	5.22
Romanian (24)	48	0.10
Russian (86)	203	0.44
Scandinavian (15)	26	0.06
Scotch-Irish (202)	533	1.15
Scottish (95)	763	1.64

*Notes: † The Census 2010 population figure is used to calculate the percentages in the Hispanic Origin and Race categories. Ancestry percentages are based on the 2006-2010 American Community Survey population (not shown); ‡ Numbers in parentheses indicate the number of people reporting a single ancestry; * Numbers in parentheses indicate the number of persons reporting this race alone, not in combination with any other race; Please refer to the Explanation of Data for more information.*

Serbian (0)	13	0.03
Slovene (15)	25	0.05
Swedish (213)	1,090	2.35
Swiss (33)	65	0.14
Ukrainian (0)	10	0.02
Welsh (0)	151	0.33
West Indian, ex. Hispanic (0)	18	0.04
Bermudan (0)	18	0.04
Yugoslavian (0)	20	0.04

Hispanic Origin	Population	%
Hispanic or Latino (of any race)	1,279	2.72
Central American, ex. Mexican	86	0.18
Costa Rican	8	0.02
Guatemalan	46	0.10
Honduran	16	0.03
Panamanian	6	0.01
Salvadoran	10	0.02
Cuban	92	0.20
Dominican Republic	23	0.05
Mexican	792	1.69
Puerto Rican	123	0.26
South American	40	0.09
Argentinean	5	0.01
Bolivian	4	0.01
Chilean	5	0.01
Colombian	9	0.02
Ecuadorian	3	0.01
Peruvian	9	0.02
Uruguayan	1	<0.01
Venezuelan	1	<0.01
Other South American	3	0.01
Other Hispanic or Latino	123	0.26

Race*	Population	%
African-American/Black (455)	713	1.52
Not Hispanic (432)	663	1.41
Hispanic (23)	50	0.11
American Indian/Alaska Native (118)	302	0.64
Not Hispanic (98)	263	0.56
Hispanic (20)	39	0.08
Apache (0)	3	0.01
Canadian/French Am. Ind. (1)	2	<0.01
Central American Ind. (2)	2	<0.01
Cherokee (9)	32	0.07
Chippewa (27)	46	0.10
Choctaw (0)	4	0.01
Iroquois (1)	3	0.01
Mexican American Ind. (11)	15	0.03
Navajo (3)	6	0.01
Ottawa (18)	27	0.06
Potawatomi (15)	42	0.09
Sioux (1)	7	0.01
Asian (610)	846	1.80
Not Hispanic (602)	828	1.76
Hispanic (8)	18	0.04
Bangladeshi (3)	3	0.01
Bhutanese (0)	9	0.02
Burmese (3)	5	0.01
Cambodian (14)	17	0.04
Chinese, ex. Taiwanese (121)	149	0.32
Filipino (48)	92	0.20
Hmong (6)	6	0.01
Indian (78)	91	0.19
Indonesian (4)	18	0.04
Japanese (10)	32	0.07
Korean (154)	230	0.49
Laotian (4)	9	0.02
Malaysian (1)	1	<0.01
Nepalese (0)	9	0.02
Pakistani (1)	1	<0.01
Taiwanese (1)	1	<0.01
Thai (5)	10	0.02
Vietnamese (118)	150	0.32
Hawaii Native/Pacific Islander (6)	27	0.06
Not Hispanic (6)	26	0.06
Hispanic (0)	1	<0.01
Guamanian/Chamorro (0)	1	<0.01
Native Hawaiian (3)	8	0.02
Samoan (1)	1	<0.01
White (44,774)	45,454	96.74
Not Hispanic (43,940)	44,515	94.74
Hispanic (834)	939	2.00

Grand Blanc

Place Type: Charter Township
County: Genesee
Population: 37,508†

Ancestry‡	Population	%
African, Sub-Saharan (142)	142	0.39
African (122)	122	0.33
Nigerian (20)	20	0.05
Albanian (15)	15	0.04
American (1,738)	1,738	4.76
Arab (675)	726	1.99
Arab (0)	19	0.05
Iraqi (48)	48	0.13
Lebanese (250)	272	0.74
Palestinian (134)	134	0.37
Syrian (117)	117	0.32
Other Arab (126)	136	0.37
Armenian (10)	39	0.11
Assyrian/Chaldean/Syriac (213)	262	0.72
Australian (10)	10	0.03
Austrian (19)	95	0.26
Belgian (20)	57	0.16
British (239)	325	0.89
Bulgarian (11)	11	0.03
Canadian (113)	186	0.51
Croatian (15)	65	0.18
Czech (91)	260	0.71
Czechoslovakian (28)	38	0.10
Danish (44)	144	0.39
Dutch (147)	692	1.89
Eastern European (15)	27	0.07
English (1,110)	4,222	11.56
European (447)	460	1.26
Finnish (62)	347	0.95
French, ex. Basque (191)	1,564	4.28
French Canadian (216)	619	1.69
German (1,991)	7,813	21.39
Greek (149)	197	0.54
Hungarian (153)	474	1.30
Iranian (11)	11	0.03
Irish (818)	4,256	11.65
Israeli (145)	145	0.40
Italian (412)	1,610	4.41
Lithuanian (0)	10	0.03
Macedonian (43)	80	0.22
Maltese (19)	19	0.05
Norwegian (106)	355	0.97
Polish (986)	2,742	7.51
Romanian (51)	93	0.25
Russian (135)	356	0.97
Scandinavian (158)	204	0.56
Scotch-Irish (191)	707	1.94
Scottish (215)	950	2.60
Serbian (54)	54	0.15
Slavic (11)	30	0.08
Slovak (35)	175	0.48
Slovene (10)	19	0.05
Swedish (189)	621	1.70
Swiss (0)	79	0.22
Ukrainian (49)	120	0.33
Welsh (22)	66	0.18
Yugoslavian (19)	26	0.07

Hispanic Origin	Population	%
Hispanic or Latino (of any race)	1,149	3.06
Central American, ex. Mexican	33	0.09
Costa Rican	1	<0.01
Guatemalan	18	0.05
Honduran	1	<0.01
Nicaraguan	3	0.01
Panamanian	7	0.02
Salvadoran	3	0.01
Cuban	39	0.10
Dominican Republic	7	0.02
Mexican	843	2.25
Puerto Rican	86	0.23
South American	55	0.15
Argentinean	2	0.01
Bolivian	5	0.01
Chilean	1	<0.01
Colombian	27	0.07
Ecuadorian	4	0.01
Peruvian	8	0.02
Venezuelan	8	0.02
Other Hispanic or Latino	86	0.23

Race*	Population	%
African-American/Black (4,009)	4,425	11.80
Not Hispanic (3,964)	4,349	11.59
Hispanic (45)	76	0.20
American Indian/Alaska Native (162)	381	1.02
Not Hispanic (141)	342	0.91
Hispanic (21)	39	0.10
Aleut *(Alaska Native)* (1)	1	<0.01
Apache (2)	4	0.01
Blackfeet (0)	18	0.05
Canadian/French Am. Ind. (2)	3	0.01
Central American Ind. (0)	1	<0.01
Cherokee (23)	84	0.22
Cheyenne (0)	4	0.01
Chippewa (56)	78	0.21
Choctaw (4)	10	0.03
Creek (6)	6	0.02
Crow (0)	1	<0.01
Hopi (0)	1	<0.01
Iroquois (4)	8	0.02
Kiowa (3)	3	0.01
Lumbee (0)	2	0.01
Mexican American Ind. (2)	6	0.02
Navajo (2)	3	0.01
Ottawa (4)	10	0.03
Potawatomi (4)	7	0.02
Seminole (0)	2	0.01
Sioux (4)	5	0.01
Ute (1)	1	<0.01
Yaqui (0)	1	<0.01
Yuman (0)	1	<0.01
Asian (1,270)	1,533	4.09
Not Hispanic (1,256)	1,504	4.01
Hispanic (14)	29	0.08
Bangladeshi (13)	13	0.03
Burmese (0)	1	<0.01
Chinese, ex. Taiwanese (146)	184	0.49
Filipino (145)	196	0.52
Indian (612)	643	1.71
Indonesian (1)	5	0.01
Japanese (18)	36	0.10
Korean (136)	159	0.42
Nepalese (9)	9	0.02
Pakistani (62)	68	0.18
Sri Lankan (2)	4	0.01
Taiwanese (9)	9	0.02
Thai (5)	17	0.05
Vietnamese (82)	95	0.25
Hawaii Native/Pacific Islander (10)	33	0.09
Not Hispanic (10)	33	0.09
Fijian (0)	1	<0.01
Guamanian/Chamorro (1)	1	<0.01
Native Hawaiian (7)	16	0.04
Samoan (1)	4	0.01
White (30,981)	31,744	84.63
Not Hispanic (30,196)	30,859	82.27
Hispanic (785)	885	2.36

Grand Blanc

Place Type: City
County: Genesee
Population: 8,276†

Ancestry‡	Population	%
African, Sub-Saharan (18)	18	0.21
Nigerian (18)	18	0.21
American (374)	374	4.46

*Notes: † The Census 2010 population figure is used to calculate the percentages in the Hispanic Origin and Race categories. Ancestry percentages are based on the 2006-2010 American Community Survey population (not shown); ‡ Numbers in parentheses indicate the number of people reporting a single ancestry; * Numbers in parentheses indicate the number of persons reporting this race alone, not in combination with any other race; Please refer to the Explanation of Data for more information.*

Arab (110)	110	1.31
Egyptian (17)	17	0.20
Lebanese (81)	81	0.96
Other Arab (12)	12	0.14
Armenian (16)	16	0.19
Austrian (0)	14	0.17
British (0)	26	0.31
Canadian (41)	52	0.62
Croatian (16)	33	0.39
Czech (15)	32	0.38
Czechoslovakian (64)	77	0.92
Danish (0)	34	0.41
Dutch (47)	187	2.23
English (256)	942	11.22
European (114)	126	1.50
Finnish (28)	78	0.93
French, ex. Basque (120)	578	6.89
French Canadian (0)	13	0.15
German (552)	1,602	19.08
Greek (54)	62	0.74
Hungarian (15)	15	0.18
Iranian (0)	8	0.10
Irish (349)	1,144	13.63
Italian (181)	283	3.37
Macedonian (0)	51	0.61
Northern European (31)	65	0.77
Norwegian (97)	165	1.97
Polish (204)	666	7.93
Russian (30)	61	0.73
Scandinavian (0)	11	0.13
Scotch-Irish (70)	178	2.12
Scottish (147)	347	4.13
Swedish (27)	170	2.03
Ukrainian (0)	42	0.50
Welsh (23)	52	0.62

Hispanic Origin	Population	%
Hispanic or Latino (of any race)	216	2.61
Central American, ex. Mexican	3	0.04
Guatemalan	1	0.01
Panamanian	2	0.02
Cuban	15	0.18
Mexican	163	1.97
Puerto Rican	18	0.22
South American	10	0.12
Colombian	4	0.05
Paraguayan	2	0.02
Peruvian	3	0.04
Venezuelan	1	0.01
Other Hispanic or Latino	7	0.08

Race*	Population	%
African-American/Black (918)	1,039	12.55
Not Hispanic (908)	1,025	12.39
Hispanic (10)	14	0.17
American Indian/Alaska Native (29)	90	1.09
Not Hispanic (22)	73	0.88
Hispanic (7)	17	0.21
Blackfeet (0)	5	0.06
Cherokee (4)	18	0.22
Chippewa (1)	9	0.11
Choctaw (0)	4	0.05
Iroquois (0)	3	0.04
Mexican American Ind. (3)	4	0.05
Osage (0)	1	0.01
Ottawa (2)	3	0.04
Sioux (0)	1	0.01
Asian (228)	300	3.62
Not Hispanic (228)	293	3.54
Hispanic (0)	7	0.08
Burmese (4)	4	0.05
Chinese, ex. Taiwanese (59)	64	0.77
Filipino (16)	29	0.35
Indian (111)	120	1.45
Japanese (1)	11	0.13
Korean (20)	28	0.34
Laotian (1)	1	0.01
Taiwanese (2)	3	0.04
Thai (1)	2	0.02
Vietnamese (11)	13	0.16
Hawaii Native/Pacific Islander (0)	9	0.11
Not Hispanic (0)	6	0.07
Hispanic (0)	3	0.04
Native Hawaiian (0)	7	0.08
White (6,826)	7,042	85.09
Not Hispanic (6,688)	6,875	83.07
Hispanic (138)	167	2.02

Grand Haven

Place Type: Charter Township
County: Ottawa
Population: 15,178†

Ancestry‡	Population	%
American (385)	385	2.57
Austrian (0)	14	0.09
Brazilian (44)	44	0.29
British (12)	39	0.26
Canadian (16)	119	0.80
Croatian (0)	29	0.19
Czech (0)	45	0.30
Czechoslovakian (18)	32	0.21
Danish (31)	174	1.16
Dutch (1,440)	3,354	22.42
English (365)	1,792	11.98
European (115)	115	0.77
Finnish (14)	90	0.60
French, ex. Basque (53)	719	4.81
French Canadian (179)	320	2.14
German (1,025)	3,810	25.46
Greek (0)	15	0.10
Hungarian (27)	117	0.78
Iranian (13)	13	0.09
Irish (481)	1,820	12.16
Italian (65)	473	3.16
Latvian (53)	74	0.49
Lithuanian (40)	138	0.92
Norwegian (36)	317	2.12
Polish (600)	1,360	9.09
Romanian (13)	13	0.09
Russian (13)	42	0.28
Scotch-Irish (30)	308	2.06
Scottish (49)	334	2.23
Serbian (0)	16	0.11
Slovak (11)	100	0.67
Slovene (0)	26	0.17
Swedish (59)	478	3.19
Swiss (14)	89	0.59
Ukrainian (14)	26	0.17
Welsh (18)	129	0.86
West Indian, ex. Hispanic (34)	34	0.23
Haitian (34)	34	0.23

Hispanic Origin	Population	%
Hispanic or Latino (of any race)	446	2.94
Central American, ex. Mexican	19	0.13
Guatemalan	5	0.03
Honduran	6	0.04
Panamanian	8	0.05
Cuban	4	0.03
Mexican	348	2.29
Puerto Rican	13	0.09
South American	14	0.09
Colombian	4	0.03
Ecuadorian	1	0.01
Venezuelan	9	0.06
Other Hispanic or Latino	48	0.32

Race*	Population	%
African-American/Black (43)	95	0.63
Not Hispanic (43)	93	0.61
Hispanic (0)	2	0.01
American Indian/Alaska Native (83)	173	1.14
Not Hispanic (68)	150	0.99
Hispanic (15)	23	0.15
Blackfeet (0)	1	0.01
Canadian/French Am. Ind. (5)	8	0.05
Central American Ind. (0)	1	0.01
Cherokee (5)	11	0.07
Chickasaw (1)	2	0.01
Chippewa (16)	38	0.25
Delaware (1)	1	0.01
Iroquois (0)	2	0.01
Mexican American Ind. (4)	4	0.03
Ottawa (8)	16	0.11
Potawatomi (23)	40	0.26
Sioux (2)	3	0.02
Asian (149)	224	1.48
Not Hispanic (149)	223	1.47
Hispanic (0)	1	0.01
Burmese (2)	3	0.02
Cambodian (2)	2	0.01
Chinese, ex. Taiwanese (39)	40	0.26
Filipino (17)	33	0.22
Indian (31)	36	0.24
Indonesian (1)	4	0.03
Japanese (3)	14	0.09
Korean (35)	57	0.38
Laotian (1)	1	0.01
Malaysian (4)	4	0.03
Pakistani (1)	1	0.01
Sri Lankan (0)	3	0.02
Thai (1)	2	0.01
Vietnamese (12)	21	0.14
Hawaii Native/Pacific Islander (1)	9	0.06
Not Hispanic (1)	9	0.06
Native Hawaiian (0)	1	0.01
Samoan (1)	5	0.03
White (14,537)	14,772	97.33
Not Hispanic (14,263)	14,461	95.28
Hispanic (274)	311	2.05

Grand Haven

Place Type: City
County: Ottawa
Population: 10,412†

Ancestry‡	Population	%
African, Sub-Saharan (14)	34	0.32
African (14)	34	0.32
American (405)	405	3.81
Arab (14)	52	0.49
Lebanese (0)	25	0.23
Syrian (0)	13	0.12
Other Arab (14)	14	0.13
Belgian (17)	28	0.26
British (71)	86	0.81
Canadian (12)	46	0.43
Croatian (16)	31	0.29
Czech (31)	120	1.13
Czechoslovakian (17)	17	0.16
Danish (0)	60	0.56
Dutch (1,265)	2,413	22.68
English (297)	1,155	10.86
European (106)	106	1.00
Finnish (58)	204	1.92
French, ex. Basque (109)	480	4.51
French Canadian (24)	233	2.19
German (798)	2,454	23.06
Greek (56)	56	0.53
Hungarian (13)	70	0.66
Iranian (15)	29	0.27
Irish (260)	1,362	12.80
Italian (104)	294	2.76
Lithuanian (0)	13	0.12
Maltese (11)	22	0.21
Northern European (59)	59	0.55
Norwegian (11)	113	1.06
Pennsylvania German (27)	40	0.38
Polish (202)	578	5.43
Russian (0)	37	0.35
Scandinavian (0)	13	0.12
Scotch-Irish (75)	163	1.53
Scottish (108)	275	2.58
Serbian (19)	19	0.18
Slavic (11)	23	0.22
Slovak (23)	48	0.45
Slovene (0)	42	0.39

*Notes: † The Census 2010 population figure is used to calculate the percentages in the Hispanic Origin and Race categories. Ancestry percentages are based on the 2006-2010 American Community Survey population (not shown); ‡ Numbers in parentheses indicate the number of people reporting a single ancestry; * Numbers in parentheses indicate the number of persons reporting this race alone, not in combination with any other race; Please refer to the Explanation of Data for more information.*

Swedish (153)	374	3.52
Swiss (13)	29	0.27
Ukrainian (68)	95	0.89
Welsh (12)	24	0.23

Hispanic Origin	Population	%
Hispanic or Latino (of any race)	249	2.39
Central American, ex. Mexican	13	0.12
Guatemalan	2	0.02
Honduran	4	0.04
Panamanian	2	0.02
Salvadoran	5	0.05
Cuban	4	0.04
Mexican	169	1.62
Puerto Rican	29	0.28
South American	11	0.11
Colombian	4	0.04
Ecuadorian	3	0.03
Peruvian	2	0.02
Venezuelan	2	0.02
Other Hispanic or Latino	23	0.22

Race*	Population	%
African-American/Black (75)	155	1.49
Not Hispanic (65)	143	1.37
Hispanic (10)	12	0.12
American Indian/Alaska Native (91)	166	1.59
Not Hispanic (76)	143	1.37
Hispanic (15)	23	0.22
Alaska Athabascan *(Ala. Nat.)* (1)	2	0.02
Apache (6)	6	0.06
Blackfeet (0)	4	0.04
Canadian/French Am. Ind. (5)	6	0.06
Cherokee (2)	9	0.09
Chippewa (20)	32	0.31
Lumbee (1)	1	0.01
Mexican American Ind. (4)	6	0.06
Navajo (0)	1	0.01
Ottawa (14)	31	0.30
Potawatomi (13)	19	0.18
Seminole (0)	3	0.03
Yup'ik *(Alaska Native)* (0)	1	0.01
Asian (104)	137	1.32
Not Hispanic (104)	134	1.29
Hispanic (0)	3	0.03
Bhutanese (18)	18	0.17
Burmese (2)	2	0.02
Chinese, ex. Taiwanese (21)	25	0.24
Filipino (3)	5	0.05
Indian (4)	5	0.05
Japanese (5)	9	0.09
Korean (20)	33	0.32
Laotian (3)	3	0.03
Nepalese (4)	4	0.04
Taiwanese (0)	1	0.01
Thai (1)	1	0.01
Vietnamese (15)	18	0.17
Hawaii Native/Pacific Islander (3)	8	0.08
Not Hispanic (3)	8	0.08
Guamanian/Chamorro (0)	1	0.01
Native Hawaiian (1)	3	0.03
Samoan (1)	3	0.03
Tongan (1)	1	0.01
White (9,891)	10,086	96.87
Not Hispanic (9,745)	9,907	95.15
Hispanic (146)	179	1.72

Grand Ledge

Place Type: City
County: Eaton
Population: 7,784†

Ancestry‡	Population	%
African, Sub-Saharan (0)	25	0.32
African (0)	25	0.32
American (360)	360	4.58
Austrian (0)	40	0.51
Belgian (0)	11	0.14
British (8)	32	0.41
Canadian (13)	28	0.36
Croatian (15)	38	0.48
Czech (0)	30	0.38
Danish (0)	83	1.06
Dutch (32)	336	4.28
English (382)	1,362	17.35
European (52)	52	0.66
Finnish (0)	19	0.24
French, ex. Basque (46)	657	8.37
French Canadian (53)	122	1.55
German (884)	3,062	39.00
Hungarian (0)	24	0.31
Irish (267)	1,477	18.81
Italian (52)	287	3.66
Lithuanian (0)	9	0.11
Norwegian (70)	176	2.24
Pennsylvania German (0)	12	0.15
Polish (132)	520	6.62
Russian (0)	61	0.78
Scandinavian (40)	78	0.99
Scotch-Irish (63)	225	2.87
Scottish (15)	205	2.61
Slavic (53)	53	0.67
Swedish (44)	147	1.87
Swiss (10)	10	0.13
Turkish (0)	20	0.25
Ukrainian (0)	15	0.19
Welsh (0)	107	1.36

Hispanic Origin	Population	%
Hispanic or Latino (of any race)	358	4.60
Central American, ex. Mexican	3	0.04
Guatemalan	1	0.01
Panamanian	1	0.01
Salvadoran	1	0.01
Cuban	14	0.18
Dominican Republic	1	0.01
Mexican	277	3.56
Puerto Rican	11	0.14
South American	9	0.12
Bolivian	2	0.03
Colombian	2	0.03
Peruvian	1	0.01
Venezuelan	4	0.05
Other Hispanic or Latino	43	0.55

Race*	Population	%
African-American/Black (68)	160	2.06
Not Hispanic (66)	142	1.82
Hispanic (2)	18	0.23
American Indian/Alaska Native (39)	114	1.46
Not Hispanic (32)	94	1.21
Hispanic (7)	20	0.26
Apache (1)	1	0.01
Blackfeet (1)	3	0.04
Cherokee (0)	4	0.05
Chippewa (13)	25	0.32
Choctaw (1)	2	0.03
Cree (1)	6	0.08
Creek (0)	1	0.01
Iroquois (3)	5	0.06
Mexican American Ind. (1)	2	0.03
Ottawa (7)	10	0.13
Sioux (0)	1	0.01
Asian (59)	77	0.99
Not Hispanic (56)	73	0.94
Hispanic (3)	4	0.05
Chinese, ex. Taiwanese (13)	19	0.24
Filipino (5)	9	0.12
Indian (7)	8	0.10
Japanese (1)	4	0.05
Korean (12)	14	0.18
Laotian (2)	2	0.03
Malaysian (1)	1	0.01
Pakistani (4)	4	0.05
Vietnamese (14)	15	0.19
Hawaii Native/Pacific Islander (6)	10	0.13
Not Hispanic (4)	4	0.05
Hispanic (2)	6	0.08
Guamanian/Chamorro (2)	6	0.08
White (7,351)	7,541	96.88
Not Hispanic (7,116)	7,266	93.35
Hispanic (235)	275	3.53

Grand Ledge

Place Type: City
County: Eaton
Population: 7,786†

Ancestry‡	Population	%
African, Sub-Saharan (0)	25	0.32
African (0)	25	0.32
American (360)	360	4.58
Austrian (0)	40	0.51
Belgian (0)	11	0.14
British (8)	32	0.41
Canadian (13)	28	0.36
Croatian (15)	38	0.48
Czech (0)	30	0.38
Danish (0)	83	1.06
Dutch (32)	336	4.28
English (382)	1,362	17.35
European (52)	52	0.66
Finnish (0)	19	0.24
French, ex. Basque (46)	657	8.37
French Canadian (53)	122	1.55
German (884)	3,062	39.00
Hungarian (0)	24	0.31
Irish (267)	1,477	18.81
Italian (52)	287	3.66
Lithuanian (0)	9	0.11
Norwegian (70)	176	2.24
Pennsylvania German (0)	12	0.15
Polish (132)	520	6.62
Russian (0)	61	0.78
Scandinavian (40)	78	0.99
Scotch-Irish (63)	225	2.87
Scottish (15)	205	2.61
Slavic (53)	53	0.67
Swedish (44)	147	1.87
Swiss (10)	10	0.13
Turkish (0)	20	0.25
Ukrainian (0)	15	0.19
Welsh (0)	107	1.36

Hispanic Origin	Population	%
Hispanic or Latino (of any race)	358	4.60
Central American, ex. Mexican	3	0.04
Guatemalan	1	0.01
Panamanian	1	0.01
Salvadoran	1	0.01
Cuban	14	0.18
Dominican Republic	1	0.01
Mexican	277	3.56
Puerto Rican	11	0.14
South American	9	0.12
Bolivian	2	0.03
Colombian	2	0.03
Peruvian	1	0.01
Venezuelan	4	0.05
Other Hispanic or Latino	43	0.55

Race*	Population	%
African-American/Black (68)	160	2.05
Not Hispanic (66)	142	1.82
Hispanic (2)	18	0.23
American Indian/Alaska Native (39)	114	1.46
Not Hispanic (32)	94	1.21
Hispanic (7)	20	0.26
Apache (1)	1	0.01
Blackfeet (1)	3	0.04
Cherokee (0)	4	0.05
Chippewa (13)	25	0.32
Choctaw (1)	2	0.03
Cree (1)	6	0.08
Creek (0)	1	0.01
Iroquois (3)	5	0.06
Mexican American Ind. (1)	2	0.03
Ottawa (7)	10	0.13

*Notes: † The Census 2010 population figure is used to calculate the percentages in the Hispanic Origin and Race categories. Ancestry percentages are based on the 2006-2010 American Community Survey population (not shown); ‡ Numbers in parentheses indicate the number of people reporting a single ancestry; * Numbers in parentheses indicate the number of persons reporting this race alone, not in combination with any other race; Please refer to the Explanation of Data for more information.*

Sioux (0)	1	0.01
Asian (59)	77	0.99
Not Hispanic (56)	73	0.94
Hispanic (3)	4	0.05
Chinese, ex. Taiwanese (13)	19	0.24
Filipino (5)	9	0.12
Indian (7)	8	0.10
Japanese (1)	4	0.05
Korean (12)	14	0.18
Laotian (2)	2	0.03
Malaysian (1)	1	0.01
Pakistani (4)	4	0.05
Vietnamese (14)	15	0.19
Hawaii Native/Pacific Islander (6)	10	0.13
Not Hispanic (4)	4	0.05
Hispanic (2)	6	0.08
Guamanian/Chamorro (2)	6	0.08
White (7,353)	7,543	96.88
Not Hispanic (7,118)	7,268	93.35
Hispanic (235)	275	3.53

Grand Rapids

Place Type: Charter Township
County: Kent
Population: 16,661†

Ancestry‡	Population	%
African, Sub-Saharan (23)	77	0.47
African (0)	54	0.33
Liberian (23)	23	0.14
American (641)	641	3.95
Arab (30)	70	0.43
Jordanian (12)	12	0.07
Lebanese (18)	34	0.21
Syrian (0)	24	0.15
Austrian (0)	39	0.24
Belgian (6)	70	0.43
British (79)	146	0.90
Canadian (50)	97	0.60
Czech (0)	28	0.17
Czechoslovakian (29)	38	0.23
Danish (103)	388	2.39
Dutch (1,805)	3,169	19.51
Eastern European (37)	37	0.23
English (821)	2,686	16.54
European (206)	206	1.27
Finnish (0)	91	0.56
French, ex. Basque (32)	459	2.83
French Canadian (46)	244	1.50
German (907)	4,050	24.94
Greek (32)	80	0.49
Hungarian (40)	132	0.81
Iranian (0)	11	0.07
Irish (466)	2,338	14.40
Italian (192)	706	4.35
Lithuanian (61)	228	1.40
Luxemburger (0)	6	0.04
Northern European (27)	27	0.17
Norwegian (138)	330	2.03
Polish (441)	1,687	10.39
Russian (0)	94	0.58
Scandinavian (13)	100	0.62
Scotch-Irish (108)	326	2.01
Scottish (46)	430	2.65
Slavic (0)	10	0.06
Slovak (33)	33	0.20
Swedish (71)	547	3.37
Swiss (8)	69	0.42
Ukrainian (0)	107	0.66
Welsh (33)	154	0.95
Yugoslavian (0)	77	0.47

Hispanic Origin	Population	%
Hispanic or Latino (of any race)	341	2.05
Central American, ex. Mexican	16	0.10
Guatemalan	14	0.08
Nicaraguan	2	0.01
Cuban	15	0.09
Dominican Republic	16	0.10
Mexican	189	1.13
Puerto Rican	32	0.19
South American	39	0.23
Argentinean	2	0.01
Bolivian	6	0.04
Chilean	2	0.01
Colombian	17	0.10
Ecuadorian	1	0.01
Paraguayan	1	0.01
Peruvian	5	0.03
Venezuelan	5	0.03
Other Hispanic or Latino	34	0.20

Race*	Population	%
African-American/Black (294)	380	2.28
Not Hispanic (290)	371	2.23
Hispanic (4)	9	0.05
American Indian/Alaska Native (28)	83	0.50
Not Hispanic (26)	76	0.46
Hispanic (2)	7	0.04
Cherokee (4)	10	0.06
Chippewa (4)	21	0.13
Creek (3)	6	0.04
Iroquois (0)	1	0.01
Mexican American Ind. (1)	3	0.02
Ottawa (3)	12	0.07
Shoshone (0)	1	0.01
Asian (727)	866	5.20
Not Hispanic (724)	857	5.14
Hispanic (3)	9	0.05
Bangladeshi (16)	16	0.10
Burmese (4)	4	0.02
Chinese, ex. Taiwanese (128)	153	0.92
Filipino (38)	56	0.34
Indian (290)	319	1.91
Indonesian (5)	10	0.06
Japanese (18)	33	0.20
Korean (98)	128	0.77
Malaysian (1)	3	0.02
Nepalese (8)	8	0.05
Pakistani (33)	38	0.23
Sri Lankan (1)	3	0.02
Taiwanese (4)	4	0.02
Thai (3)	4	0.02
Vietnamese (56)	67	0.40
Hawaii Native/Pacific Islander (2)	8	0.05
Not Hispanic (1)	7	0.04
Hispanic (1)	1	0.01
Guamanian/Chamorro (2)	3	0.02
Samoan (0)	1	0.01
White (15,249)	15,505	93.06
Not Hispanic (15,011)	15,243	91.49
Hispanic (238)	262	1.57

Grand Rapids

Place Type: City
County: Kent
Population: 188,040†

Ancestry‡	Population	%
African, Sub-Saharan (2,279)	2,553	1.34
African (1,099)	1,313	0.69
Cape Verdean (72)	72	0.04
Ethiopian (306)	335	0.18
Kenyan (17)	34	0.02
Liberian (309)	309	0.16
Nigerian (18)	18	0.01
Somalian (68)	68	0.04
South African (53)	67	0.04
Sudanese (285)	285	0.15
Other Sub-Saharan African (52)	52	0.03
Albanian (28)	65	0.03
American (3,510)	3,510	1.84
Arab (465)	894	0.47
Arab (137)	242	0.13
Jordanian (0)	12	0.01
Lebanese (207)	379	0.20
Palestinian (43)	43	0.02
Syrian (17)	89	0.05
Other Arab (61)	129	0.07
Armenian (37)	37	0.02
Australian (33)	86	0.05
Austrian (56)	357	0.19
Belgian (153)	335	0.18
Brazilian (42)	96	0.05
British (208)	667	0.35
Bulgarian (9)	9	<0.01
Canadian (315)	649	0.34
Celtic (0)	14	0.01
Croatian (96)	296	0.16
Czech (150)	666	0.35
Czechoslovakian (90)	217	0.11
Danish (200)	1,324	0.70
Dutch (16,182)	29,229	15.35
Eastern European (78)	108	0.06
English (3,152)	14,001	7.35
Estonian (10)	10	0.01
European (1,621)	2,054	1.08
Finnish (116)	703	0.37
French, ex. Basque (643)	5,485	2.88
French Canadian (566)	1,455	0.76
German (6,681)	30,522	16.03
Greek (82)	378	0.20
Hungarian (128)	603	0.32
Iranian (70)	116	0.06
Irish (3,359)	18,575	9.75
Israeli (13)	13	0.01
Italian (1,636)	5,060	2.66
Latvian (110)	204	0.11
Lithuanian (383)	1,236	0.65
Luxemburger (16)	49	0.03
Macedonian (11)	46	0.02
Maltese (19)	35	0.02
Northern European (87)	87	0.05
Norwegian (206)	1,190	0.62
Pennsylvania German (14)	76	0.04
Polish (6,048)	15,189	7.98
Portuguese (43)	89	0.05
Romanian (302)	399	0.21
Russian (386)	989	0.52
Scandinavian (30)	138	0.07
Scotch-Irish (633)	2,161	1.13
Scottish (544)	2,430	1.28
Serbian (0)	11	0.01
Slavic (26)	91	0.05
Slovak (30)	169	0.09
Slovene (0)	27	0.01
Swedish (857)	3,385	1.78
Swiss (47)	639	0.34
Turkish (0)	11	0.01
Ukrainian (96)	351	0.18
Welsh (119)	743	0.39
West Indian, ex. Hispanic (169)	352	0.18
Barbadian (14)	14	0.01
Bermudan (0)	12	0.01
Dutch West Indian (14)	14	0.01
Haitian (42)	42	0.02
Jamaican (68)	160	0.08
U.S. Virgin Islander (0)	11	0.01
West Indian (22)	90	0.05
Other West Indian (9)	9	<0.01
Yugoslavian (394)	492	0.26

Hispanic Origin	Population	%
Hispanic or Latino (of any race)	29,261	15.56
Central American, ex. Mexican	4,051	2.15
Costa Rican	20	0.01
Guatemalan	3,372	1.79
Honduran	197	0.10
Nicaraguan	45	0.02
Panamanian	35	0.02
Salvadoran	348	0.19
Other Central American	34	0.02
Cuban	417	0.22
Dominican Republic	1,342	0.71
Mexican	18,698	9.94
Puerto Rican	2,712	1.44
South American	337	0.18
Argentinean	41	0.02

*Notes: † The Census 2010 population figure is used to calculate the percentages in the Hispanic Origin and Race categories. Ancestry percentages are based on the 2006-2010 American Community Survey population (not shown); ‡ Numbers in parentheses indicate the number of people reporting a single ancestry; * Numbers in parentheses indicate the number of persons reporting this race alone, not in combination with any other race; Please refer to the Explanation of Data for more information.*

	Population	%
Bolivian	21	0.01
Chilean	25	0.01
Colombian	99	0.05
Ecuadorian	41	0.02
Paraguayan	6	<0.01
Peruvian	65	0.03
Uruguayan	2	<0.01
Venezuelan	35	0.02
Other South American	2	<0.01
Other Hispanic or Latino	1,704	0.91

Race*	Population	%
African-American/Black (39,251)	44,032	23.42
Not Hispanic (37,890)	41,741	22.20
Hispanic (1,361)	2,291	1.22
American Indian/Alaska Native (1,390)	3,327	1.77
Not Hispanic (788)	2,337	1.24
Hispanic (602)	990	0.53
Alaska Athabascan *(Ala. Nat.)* (2)	3	<0.01
Apache (6)	30	0.02
Arapaho (1)	1	<0.01
Blackfeet (8)	104	0.06
Canadian/French Am. Ind. (14)	17	0.01
Central American Ind. (73)	77	0.04
Cherokee (31)	269	0.14
Cheyenne (1)	5	<0.01
Chickasaw (3)	4	<0.01
Chippewa (229)	436	0.23
Choctaw (0)	15	0.01
Colville (0)	1	<0.01
Comanche (2)	9	<0.01
Cree (1)	4	<0.01
Creek (5)	12	0.01
Crow (0)	3	<0.01
Inupiat *(Alaska Native)* (1)	4	<0.01
Iroquois (2)	20	0.01
Lumbee (7)	15	0.01
Mexican American Ind. (131)	166	0.09
Navajo (10)	26	0.01
Osage (0)	1	<0.01
Ottawa (148)	286	0.15
Potawatomi (84)	166	0.09
Pueblo (0)	2	<0.01
Puget Sound Salish (0)	1	<0.01
Seminole (0)	16	0.01
Sioux (10)	43	0.02
South American Ind. (14)	25	0.01
Spanish American Ind. (12)	16	0.01
Tlingit-Haida *(Alaska Native)* (3)	4	<0.01
Tohono O'Odham (0)	1	<0.01
Ute (0)	1	<0.01
Yaqui (2)	3	<0.01
Yuman (1)	1	<0.01
Asian (3,495)	4,532	2.41
Not Hispanic (3,445)	4,365	2.32
Hispanic (50)	167	0.09
Bangladeshi (42)	45	0.02
Bhutanese (86)	98	0.05
Burmese (398)	424	0.23
Cambodian (17)	26	0.01
Chinese, ex. Taiwanese (356)	511	0.27
Filipino (244)	451	0.24
Hmong (16)	19	0.01
Indian (344)	474	0.25
Indonesian (30)	59	0.03
Japanese (60)	173	0.09
Korean (641)	821	0.44
Laotian (24)	33	0.02
Malaysian (5)	5	<0.01
Nepalese (29)	41	0.02
Pakistani (21)	27	0.01
Sri Lankan (15)	23	0.01
Taiwanese (21)	27	0.01
Thai (24)	59	0.03
Vietnamese (967)	1,090	0.58
Hawaii Native/Pacific Islander (116)	314	0.17
Not Hispanic (58)	208	0.11
Hispanic (58)	106	0.06
Fijian (3)	9	<0.01
Guamanian/Chamorro (53)	73	0.04
Marshallese (1)	4	<0.01
Native Hawaiian (30)	81	0.04
Samoan (5)	10	0.01
White (121,411)	128,050	68.10
Not Hispanic (110,890)	115,639	61.50
Hispanic (10,521)	12,411	6.60

Grandville

Place Type: City
County: Kent
Population: 15,378†

Ancestry‡	Population	%
African, Sub-Saharan (86)	115	0.74
African (16)	45	0.29
Kenyan (70)	70	0.45
Albanian (0)	15	0.10
American (421)	421	2.70
Arab (12)	55	0.35
Lebanese (0)	15	0.10
Syrian (12)	40	0.26
Austrian (0)	46	0.29
Belgian (11)	26	0.17
British (12)	36	0.23
Bulgarian (12)	43	0.28
Canadian (0)	14	0.09
Czech (18)	99	0.63
Czechoslovakian (0)	107	0.69
Danish (52)	80	0.51
Dutch (3,144)	5,342	34.25
Eastern European (40)	81	0.52
English (429)	1,912	12.26
European (69)	124	0.79
Finnish (0)	9	0.06
French, ex. Basque (45)	393	2.52
French Canadian (14)	84	0.54
German (906)	4,265	27.34
Hungarian (27)	89	0.57
Irish (517)	2,101	13.47
Italian (250)	758	4.86
Latvian (0)	13	0.08
Lithuanian (0)	40	0.26
Norwegian (10)	110	0.71
Pennsylvania German (15)	15	0.10
Polish (297)	1,300	8.33
Russian (23)	65	0.42
Scotch-Irish (64)	195	1.25
Scottish (47)	287	1.84
Serbian (10)	10	0.06
Slavic (0)	21	0.13
Slovak (0)	24	0.15
Swedish (152)	371	2.38
Swiss (37)	56	0.36
Welsh (32)	79	0.51

Hispanic Origin	Population	%
Hispanic or Latino (of any race)	960	6.24
Central American, ex. Mexican	55	0.36
Costa Rican	4	0.03
Guatemalan	19	0.12
Honduran	18	0.12
Nicaraguan	5	0.03
Panamanian	3	0.02
Salvadoran	6	0.04
Cuban	99	0.64
Dominican Republic	39	0.25
Mexican	627	4.08
Puerto Rican	64	0.42
South American	20	0.13
Argentinean	1	0.01
Bolivian	2	0.01
Colombian	3	0.02
Ecuadorian	1	0.01
Paraguayan	3	0.02
Peruvian	7	0.05
Venezuelan	3	0.02
Other Hispanic or Latino	56	0.36

Race*	Population	%
African-American/Black (332)	499	3.24
Not Hispanic (314)	447	2.91
Hispanic (18)	52	0.34
American Indian/Alaska Native (32)	122	0.79
Not Hispanic (21)	98	0.64
Hispanic (11)	24	0.16
Alaska Athabascan *(Ala. Nat.)* (1)	2	0.01
Apache (1)	1	0.01
Blackfeet (0)	3	0.02
Cherokee (1)	12	0.08
Cheyenne (0)	4	0.03
Chippewa (10)	15	0.10
Crow (0)	1	0.01
Iroquois (0)	1	0.01
Mexican American Ind. (3)	5	0.03
Ottawa (5)	13	0.08
Potawatomi (2)	12	0.08
Pueblo (1)	3	0.02
Seminole (0)	1	0.01
Sioux (0)	6	0.04
Spanish American Ind. (0)	1	0.01
Asian (223)	302	1.96
Not Hispanic (222)	297	1.93
Hispanic (1)	5	0.03
Bhutanese (7)	7	0.05
Burmese (5)	5	0.03
Chinese, ex. Taiwanese (28)	38	0.25
Filipino (18)	37	0.24
Indian (20)	31	0.20
Indonesian (0)	3	0.02
Japanese (6)	10	0.07
Korean (39)	57	0.37
Pakistani (6)	6	0.04
Taiwanese (3)	3	0.02
Vietnamese (87)	99	0.64
Hawaii Native/Pacific Islander (3)	19	0.12
Not Hispanic (3)	13	0.08
Hispanic (0)	6	0.04
Native Hawaiian (2)	6	0.04
Samoan (1)	1	0.01
White (14,151)	14,492	94.24
Not Hispanic (13,581)	13,839	89.99
Hispanic (570)	653	4.25

Green Oak

Place Type: Township
County: Livingston
Population: 17,476†

Ancestry‡	Population	%
American (1,256)	1,256	7.13
Arab (39)	127	0.72
Arab (18)	18	0.10
Lebanese (0)	42	0.24
Palestinian (12)	49	0.28
Syrian (9)	18	0.10
Armenian (9)	58	0.33
Assyrian/Chaldean/Syriac (16)	62	0.35
Australian (13)	39	0.22
Austrian (8)	42	0.24
Belgian (29)	78	0.44
British (20)	32	0.18
Canadian (37)	137	0.78
Croatian (24)	69	0.39
Czech (22)	109	0.62
Czechoslovakian (15)	28	0.16
Danish (7)	58	0.33
Dutch (103)	553	3.14
English (771)	2,679	15.22
European (241)	287	1.63
Finnish (98)	378	2.15
French, ex. Basque (202)	1,088	6.18
French Canadian (119)	385	2.19
German (1,123)	4,456	25.31
Greek (61)	100	0.57
Hungarian (93)	224	1.27
Irish (891)	3,014	17.12

*Notes: † The Census 2010 population figure is used to calculate the percentages in the Hispanic Origin and Race categories. Ancestry percentages are based on the 2006-2010 American Community Survey population (not shown); ‡ Numbers in parentheses indicate the number of people reporting a single ancestry; * Numbers in parentheses indicate the number of persons reporting this race alone, not in combination with any other race; Please refer to the Explanation of Data for more information.*

Italian (408)	1,366	7.76
Lithuanian (19)	67	0.38
Macedonian (24)	112	0.64
Maltese (68)	176	1.00
Northern European (14)	55	0.31
Norwegian (98)	270	1.53
Pennsylvania German (9)	29	0.16
Polish (911)	2,307	13.10
Portuguese (0)	12	0.07
Romanian (0)	11	0.06
Russian (104)	104	0.59
Scandinavian (48)	48	0.27
Scotch-Irish (324)	617	3.50
Scottish (245)	772	4.38
Serbian (18)	18	0.10
Slovak (21)	127	0.72
Slovene (9)	29	0.16
Swedish (67)	351	1.99
Swiss (0)	12	0.07
Turkish (0)	42	0.24
Ukrainian (46)	175	0.99
Welsh (0)	59	0.34
Yugoslavian (18)	38	0.22

Hispanic Origin	Population	%
Hispanic or Latino (of any race)	335	1.92
Central American, ex. Mexican	12	0.07
Costa Rican	4	0.02
Guatemalan	3	0.02
Honduran	1	0.01
Nicaraguan	2	0.01
Panamanian	1	0.01
Salvadoran	1	0.01
Cuban	25	0.14
Dominican Republic	1	0.01
Mexican	204	1.17
Puerto Rican	38	0.22
South American	18	0.10
Argentinean	4	0.02
Chilean	4	0.02
Colombian	8	0.05
Ecuadorian	1	0.01
Other South American	1	0.01
Other Hispanic or Latino	37	0.21

Race*	Population	%
African-American/Black (118)	153	0.88
Not Hispanic (114)	148	0.85
Hispanic (4)	5	0.03
American Indian/Alaska Native (82)	160	0.92
Not Hispanic (77)	146	0.84
Hispanic (5)	14	0.08
Aleut *(Alaska Native)* (1)	1	0.01
Apache (5)	8	0.05
Blackfeet (0)	3	0.02
Cherokee (8)	38	0.22
Chippewa (25)	38	0.22
Choctaw (3)	4	0.02
Hopi (1)	5	0.03
Iroquois (1)	5	0.03
Lumbee (7)	7	0.04
Ottawa (2)	2	0.01
Sioux (1)	2	0.01
Yup'ik *(Alaska Native)* (2)	2	0.01
Asian (150)	218	1.25
Not Hispanic (150)	211	1.21
Hispanic (0)	7	0.04
Chinese, ex. Taiwanese (46)	61	0.35
Filipino (16)	40	0.23
Hmong (2)	2	0.01
Indian (28)	40	0.23
Japanese (8)	17	0.10
Korean (26)	29	0.17
Pakistani (6)	6	0.03
Sri Lankan (3)	3	0.02
Thai (6)	9	0.05
Vietnamese (6)	7	0.04
Hawaii Native/Pacific Islander (0)	4	0.02
Not Hispanic (0)	4	0.02
White (16,888)	17,067	97.66
Not Hispanic (16,619)	16,778	96.01
Hispanic (269)	289	1.65

Greenville

Place Type: City
County: Montcalm
Population: 8,481†

Ancestry‡	Population	%
American (355)	355	4.19
Arab (0)	9	0.11
Syrian (0)	9	0.11
Assyrian/Chaldean/Syriac (18)	55	0.65
Canadian (25)	25	0.30
Czech (0)	10	0.12
Czechoslovakian (0)	28	0.33
Danish (179)	419	4.95
Dutch (431)	853	10.07
English (338)	1,053	12.43
European (15)	15	0.18
Finnish (79)	136	1.61
French, ex. Basque (76)	414	4.89
French Canadian (23)	128	1.51
German (1,040)	2,848	33.62
Greek (60)	60	0.71
Irish (209)	1,176	13.88
Italian (12)	235	2.77
Lithuanian (10)	10	0.12
Norwegian (16)	39	0.46
Polish (171)	346	4.09
Russian (0)	28	0.33
Scandinavian (0)	15	0.18
Scotch-Irish (0)	106	1.25
Scottish (0)	49	0.58
Serbian (37)	37	0.44
Slovak (0)	40	0.47
Swedish (0)	189	2.23
Swiss (0)	19	0.22
Welsh (165)	241	2.85
Yugoslavian (0)	10	0.12

Hispanic Origin	Population	%
Hispanic or Latino (of any race)	413	4.87
Central American, ex. Mexican	12	0.14
Costa Rican	3	0.04
Guatemalan	4	0.05
Honduran	3	0.04
Salvadoran	2	0.02
Cuban	6	0.07
Dominican Republic	5	0.06
Mexican	326	3.84
Puerto Rican	22	0.26
South American	3	0.04
Bolivian	1	0.01
Chilean	1	0.01
Colombian	1	0.01
Other Hispanic or Latino	39	0.46

Race*	Population	%
African-American/Black (27)	86	1.01
Not Hispanic (27)	78	0.92
Hispanic (0)	8	0.09
American Indian/Alaska Native (40)	145	1.71
Not Hispanic (32)	117	1.38
Hispanic (8)	28	0.33
Aleut *(Alaska Native)* (1)	1	0.01
Apache (1)	3	0.04
Blackfeet (0)	2	0.02
Cherokee (4)	16	0.19
Chippewa (3)	22	0.26
Creek (1)	4	0.05
Mexican American Ind. (3)	6	0.07
Navajo (0)	2	0.02
Ottawa (6)	14	0.17
South American Ind. (0)	1	0.01
Asian (57)	80	0.94
Not Hispanic (57)	76	0.90
Hispanic (0)	4	0.05
Chinese, ex. Taiwanese (13)	16	0.19
Filipino (5)	11	0.13
Indian (16)	17	0.20
Indonesian (1)	2	0.02
Japanese (4)	8	0.09
Korean (13)	21	0.25
Malaysian (0)	1	0.01
Thai (1)	1	0.01
Vietnamese (2)	3	0.04
Hawaii Native/Pacific Islander (5)	15	0.18
Not Hispanic (5)	15	0.18
Native Hawaiian (1)	7	0.08
White (7,997)	8,192	96.59
Not Hispanic (7,787)	7,940	93.62
Hispanic (210)	252	2.97

Grosse Ile

Place Type: Township
County: Wayne
Population: 10,371†

Ancestry‡	Population	%
American (350)	350	3.33
Arab (156)	183	1.74
Arab (107)	107	1.02
Lebanese (42)	69	0.66
Syrian (7)	7	0.07
Armenian (13)	25	0.24
Assyrian/Chaldean/Syriac (0)	14	0.13
Austrian (0)	26	0.25
Belgian (0)	41	0.39
British (8)	20	0.19
Cajun (0)	8	0.08
Canadian (149)	234	2.23
Croatian (0)	16	0.15
Czech (0)	35	0.33
Czechoslovakian (12)	26	0.25
Danish (8)	141	1.34
Dutch (51)	222	2.11
Eastern European (70)	70	0.67
English (455)	1,606	15.29
European (153)	153	1.46
Finnish (86)	147	1.40
French, ex. Basque (53)	857	8.16
French Canadian (70)	261	2.48
German (798)	2,891	27.52
Greek (47)	209	1.99
Hungarian (179)	457	4.35
Irish (373)	1,426	13.58
Italian (278)	984	9.37
Lithuanian (17)	33	0.31
Macedonian (0)	5	0.05
Maltese (25)	115	1.09
Northern European (44)	44	0.42
Norwegian (29)	134	1.28
Pennsylvania German (0)	15	0.14
Polish (374)	1,242	11.82
Romanian (0)	56	0.53
Russian (19)	104	0.99
Scandinavian (12)	12	0.11
Scotch-Irish (90)	255	2.43
Scottish (52)	403	3.84
Serbian (34)	34	0.32
Slavic (0)	22	0.21
Slovak (77)	113	1.08
Slovene (11)	11	0.10
Swedish (25)	128	1.22
Swiss (15)	27	0.26
Turkish (35)	35	0.33
Ukrainian (16)	65	0.62
Welsh (43)	221	2.10
Yugoslavian (22)	22	0.21

Hispanic Origin	Population	%
Hispanic or Latino (of any race)	272	2.62
Central American, ex. Mexican	9	0.09
Guatemalan	6	0.06
Honduran	2	0.02
Salvadoran	1	0.01
Cuban	11	0.11

*Notes: † The Census 2010 population figure is used to calculate the percentages in the Hispanic Origin and Race categories. Ancestry percentages are based on the 2006-2010 American Community Survey population (not shown); ‡ Numbers in parentheses indicate the number of people reporting a single ancestry; * Numbers in parentheses indicate the number of persons reporting this race alone, not in combination with any other race; Please refer to the Explanation of Data for more information.*

Mexican	164	1.58
Puerto Rican	9	0.09
South American	33	0.32
Argentinean	4	0.04
Chilean	8	0.08
Colombian	8	0.08
Ecuadorian	7	0.07
Peruvian	3	0.03
Venezuelan	2	0.02
Other South American	1	0.01
Other Hispanic or Latino	46	0.44

Race*	Population	%
African-American/Black (41)	59	0.57
Not Hispanic (39)	53	0.51
Hispanic (2)	6	0.06
American Indian/Alaska Native (38)	76	0.73
Not Hispanic (34)	63	0.61
Hispanic (4)	13	0.13
Apache (0)	2	0.02
Canadian/French Am. Ind. (0)	2	0.02
Cherokee (2)	18	0.17
Chickasaw (0)	1	0.01
Chippewa (3)	4	0.04
Choctaw (0)	1	0.01
Iroquois (12)	17	0.16
Kiowa (0)	1	0.01
Lumbee (2)	2	0.02
Mexican American Ind. (1)	5	0.05
Navajo (1)	1	0.01
Ottawa (2)	2	0.02
Sioux (1)	4	0.04
Asian (247)	300	2.89
Not Hispanic (246)	295	2.84
Hispanic (1)	5	0.05
Cambodian (3)	3	0.03
Chinese, ex. Taiwanese (61)	63	0.61
Filipino (26)	46	0.44
Indian (72)	83	0.80
Indonesian (1)	1	0.01
Japanese (10)	15	0.14
Korean (26)	34	0.33
Pakistani (24)	25	0.24
Taiwanese (0)	1	0.01
Thai (11)	11	0.11
Vietnamese (3)	3	0.03
Hawaii Native/Pacific Islander (0)	3	0.03
Not Hispanic (0)	3	0.03
White (9,907)	10,013	96.55
Not Hispanic (9,686)	9,775	94.25
Hispanic (221)	238	2.29

Grosse Pointe Farms

Place Type: City
County: Wayne
Population: 9,479†

Ancestry‡	Population	%
American (228)	228	2.38
Arab (73)	205	2.14
Egyptian (0)	14	0.15
Lebanese (73)	162	1.69
Syrian (0)	29	0.30
Armenian (7)	18	0.19
Austrian (13)	20	0.21
Belgian (70)	217	2.27
British (8)	30	0.31
Canadian (15)	120	1.26
Croatian (10)	42	0.44
Czech (0)	44	0.46
Danish (0)	61	0.64
Dutch (91)	263	2.75
Eastern European (14)	14	0.15
English (318)	1,304	13.64
European (285)	285	2.98
Finnish (14)	36	0.38
French, ex. Basque (69)	552	5.77
French Canadian (27)	124	1.30
German (450)	2,383	24.92
Greek (97)	182	1.90
Hungarian (20)	68	0.71
Icelander (0)	55	0.58
Iranian (13)	28	0.29
Irish (477)	1,959	20.49
Italian (364)	1,082	11.32
Lithuanian (0)	88	0.92
Luxemburger (0)	9	0.09
Norwegian (37)	101	1.06
Polish (540)	1,034	10.81
Romanian (12)	12	0.13
Russian (66)	119	1.24
Scandinavian (3)	10	0.10
Scotch-Irish (158)	249	2.60
Scottish (114)	512	5.36
Serbian (0)	12	0.13
Slovak (50)	89	0.93
Swedish (49)	210	2.20
Swiss (0)	23	0.24
Ukrainian (10)	63	0.66
Welsh (20)	82	0.86

Hispanic Origin	Population	%
Hispanic or Latino (of any race)	188	1.98
Central American, ex. Mexican	14	0.15
Costa Rican	1	0.01
Guatemalan	9	0.09
Honduran	1	0.01
Nicaraguan	1	0.01
Panamanian	2	0.02
Cuban	12	0.13
Mexican	71	0.75
Puerto Rican	34	0.36
South American	31	0.33
Argentinean	4	0.04
Chilean	1	0.01
Colombian	8	0.08
Ecuadorian	8	0.08
Paraguayan	1	0.01
Peruvian	3	0.03
Venezuelan	5	0.05
Other South American	1	0.01
Other Hispanic or Latino	26	0.27

Race*	Population	%
African-American/Black (169)	211	2.23
Not Hispanic (164)	199	2.10
Hispanic (5)	12	0.13
American Indian/Alaska Native (16)	28	0.30
Not Hispanic (16)	28	0.30
Canadian/French Am. Ind. (0)	1	0.01
Cherokee (4)	8	0.08
Chippewa (9)	13	0.14
Iroquois (0)	1	0.01
Asian (119)	157	1.66
Not Hispanic (117)	153	1.61
Hispanic (2)	4	0.04
Chinese, ex. Taiwanese (25)	31	0.33
Filipino (17)	22	0.23
Indian (24)	28	0.30
Japanese (2)	9	0.09
Korean (33)	40	0.42
Pakistani (6)	6	0.06
Thai (1)	1	0.01
Vietnamese (5)	8	0.08
Hawaii Native/Pacific Islander (1)	9	0.09
Not Hispanic (1)	9	0.09
Guamanian/Chamorro (1)	4	0.04
White (9,046)	9,129	96.31
Not Hispanic (8,905)	8,979	94.73
Hispanic (141)	150	1.58

Grosse Pointe Park

Place Type: City
County: Wayne
Population: 11,555†

Ancestry‡	Population	%
African, Sub-Saharan (29)	29	0.25
African (29)	29	0.25
Albanian (472)	472	4.02
Alsatian (0)	16	0.14
American (156)	156	1.33
Arab (19)	204	1.74
Arab (10)	32	0.27
Lebanese (9)	141	1.20
Syrian (0)	31	0.26
Armenian (23)	63	0.54
Austrian (0)	49	0.42
Belgian (11)	210	1.79
British (34)	53	0.45
Canadian (42)	109	0.93
Croatian (52)	214	1.82
Czech (0)	12	0.10
Czechoslovakian (0)	9	0.08
Danish (13)	91	0.77
Dutch (78)	230	1.96
Eastern European (6)	6	0.05
English (454)	1,373	11.68
European (148)	148	1.26
Finnish (15)	75	0.64
French, ex. Basque (43)	489	4.16
French Canadian (39)	168	1.43
German (725)	2,986	25.40
Greek (109)	201	1.71
Hungarian (37)	202	1.72
Irish (502)	1,928	16.40
Italian (182)	930	7.91
Latvian (9)	9	0.08
Lithuanian (51)	74	0.63
Norwegian (22)	145	1.23
Pennsylvania German (12)	12	0.10
Polish (510)	1,534	13.05
Portuguese (15)	44	0.37
Romanian (12)	24	0.20
Russian (81)	144	1.23
Scandinavian (9)	18	0.15
Scotch-Irish (170)	418	3.56
Scottish (31)	514	4.37
Serbian (0)	7	0.06
Slavic (0)	33	0.28
Slovak (9)	58	0.49
Slovene (0)	33	0.28
Swedish (7)	122	1.04
Swiss (9)	106	0.90
Turkish (50)	50	0.43
Ukrainian (13)	20	0.17
Welsh (18)	112	0.95
West Indian, ex. Hispanic (7)	7	0.06
Haitian (7)	7	0.06
Yugoslavian (0)	19	0.16

Hispanic Origin	Population	%
Hispanic or Latino (of any race)	291	2.52
Central American, ex. Mexican	17	0.15
Costa Rican	7	0.06
Guatemalan	2	0.02
Honduran	4	0.03
Panamanian	3	0.03
Salvadoran	1	0.01
Cuban	7	0.06
Mexican	150	1.30
Puerto Rican	10	0.09
South American	73	0.63
Argentinean	18	0.16
Chilean	19	0.16
Colombian	20	0.17
Ecuadorian	3	0.03
Peruvian	5	0.04
Venezuelan	8	0.07
Other Hispanic or Latino	34	0.29

Race*	Population	%
African-American/Black (1,219)	1,327	11.48
Not Hispanic (1,210)	1,313	11.36
Hispanic (9)	14	0.12
American Indian/Alaska Native (21)	78	0.68
Not Hispanic (18)	70	0.61
Hispanic (3)	8	0.07

*Notes: † The Census 2010 population figure is used to calculate the percentages in the Hispanic Origin and Race categories. Ancestry percentages are based on the 2006-2010 American Community Survey population (not shown); ‡ Numbers in parentheses indicate the number of people reporting a single ancestry; * Numbers in parentheses indicate the number of persons reporting this race alone, not in combination with any other race; Please refer to the Explanation of Data for more information.*

Blackfeet (1)	5	0.04
Cherokee (0)	30	0.26
Chippewa (2)	8	0.07
Iroquois (0)	5	0.04
Lumbee (1)	4	0.03
Mexican American Ind. (1)	1	0.01
Ottawa (1)	1	0.01
Potawatomi (5)	5	0.04
South American Ind. (1)	1	0.01
Asian (210)	289	2.50
Not Hispanic (206)	281	2.43
Hispanic (4)	8	0.07
Bangladeshi (11)	11	0.10
Chinese, ex. Taiwanese (60)	79	0.68
Filipino (40)	58	0.50
Indian (53)	73	0.63
Japanese (5)	23	0.20
Korean (20)	27	0.23
Laotian (0)	1	0.01
Pakistani (2)	5	0.04
Thai (4)	4	0.03
Vietnamese (4)	6	0.05
Hawaii Native/Pacific Islander (3)	12	0.10
Not Hispanic (2)	9	0.08
Hispanic (1)	3	0.03
Guamanian/Chamorro (0)	2	0.02
Native Hawaiian (0)	1	0.01
Samoan (1)	1	0.01
White (9,818)	10,013	86.66
Not Hispanic (9,596)	9,774	84.59
Hispanic (222)	239	2.07

Grosse Pointe Woods

Place Type: City
County: Wayne
Population: 16,135†

Ancestry‡	Population	%
Albanian (175)	175	1.07
American (688)	688	4.21
Arab (329)	604	3.69
Arab (68)	91	0.56
Egyptian (10)	10	0.06
Lebanese (109)	355	2.17
Syrian (142)	148	0.90
Austrian (0)	81	0.50
Belgian (220)	776	4.74
British (14)	58	0.35
Canadian (82)	136	0.83
Croatian (0)	24	0.15
Cypriot (7)	27	0.17
Czech (12)	110	0.67
Czechoslovakian (10)	18	0.11
Danish (0)	11	0.07
Dutch (45)	369	2.26
English (369)	2,018	12.34
European (158)	158	0.97
Finnish (17)	34	0.21
French, ex. Basque (77)	1,188	7.26
French Canadian (71)	317	1.94
German (947)	4,396	26.88
Greek (253)	325	1.99
Hungarian (50)	211	1.29
Iranian (12)	12	0.07
Irish (398)	2,682	16.40
Israeli (0)	33	0.20
Italian (1,020)	2,377	14.53
Lithuanian (18)	40	0.24
Macedonian (17)	28	0.17
Northern European (40)	40	0.24
Norwegian (27)	75	0.46
Polish (597)	2,140	13.08
Romanian (71)	129	0.79
Russian (0)	99	0.61
Scotch-Irish (113)	424	2.59
Scottish (150)	641	3.92
Serbian (0)	39	0.24
Slavic (0)	19	0.12
Slovak (24)	125	0.76
Slovene (6)	14	0.09
Swedish (20)	276	1.69
Swiss (24)	104	0.64
Ukrainian (120)	245	1.50
Welsh (18)	167	1.02
Yugoslavian (22)	22	0.13

Hispanic Origin	Population	%
Hispanic or Latino (of any race)	270	1.67
Central American, ex. Mexican	15	0.09
Costa Rican	4	0.02
Guatemalan	5	0.03
Honduran	1	0.01
Nicaraguan	3	0.02
Salvadoran	2	0.01
Cuban	6	0.04
Dominican Republic	1	0.01
Mexican	132	0.82
Puerto Rican	19	0.12
South American	60	0.37
Argentinean	18	0.11
Chilean	3	0.02
Colombian	14	0.09
Ecuadorian	8	0.05
Paraguayan	1	0.01
Peruvian	8	0.05
Uruguayan	1	0.01
Venezuelan	7	0.04
Other Hispanic or Latino	37	0.23

Race*	Population	%
African-American/Black (726)	794	4.92
Not Hispanic (725)	791	4.90
Hispanic (1)	3	0.02
American Indian/Alaska Native (18)	78	0.48
Not Hispanic (14)	71	0.44
Hispanic (4)	7	0.04
Blackfeet (0)	3	0.02
Cherokee (1)	21	0.13
Chippewa (4)	6	0.04
Choctaw (1)	2	0.01
Cree (0)	1	0.01
Iroquois (1)	3	0.02
Lumbee (1)	6	0.04
Potawatomi (0)	1	0.01
Sioux (0)	3	0.02
Asian (392)	477	2.96
Not Hispanic (389)	472	2.93
Hispanic (3)	5	0.03
Bangladeshi (5)	5	0.03
Cambodian (5)	5	0.03
Chinese, ex. Taiwanese (55)	62	0.38
Filipino (84)	115	0.71
Indian (156)	168	1.04
Indonesian (4)	4	0.02
Japanese (14)	29	0.18
Korean (34)	42	0.26
Pakistani (8)	11	0.07
Sri Lankan (5)	5	0.03
Taiwanese (1)	1	0.01
Thai (2)	4	0.02
Vietnamese (10)	11	0.07
Hawaii Native/Pacific Islander (1)	11	0.07
Not Hispanic (0)	10	0.06
Hispanic (1)	1	0.01
Guamanian/Chamorro (0)	1	0.01
Native Hawaiian (0)	2	0.01
White (14,741)	14,927	92.51
Not Hispanic (14,525)	14,702	91.12
Hispanic (216)	225	1.39

Hamburg

Place Type: Township
County: Livingston
Population: 21,165†

Ancestry‡	Population	%
African, Sub-Saharan (0)	14	0.06
African (0)	14	0.06
Albanian (0)	55	0.25
American (1,069)	1,069	4.94
Arab (81)	176	0.81
Arab (10)	10	0.05
Iraqi (10)	22	0.10
Lebanese (48)	131	0.61
Syrian (13)	13	0.06
Armenian (10)	42	0.19
Assyrian/Chaldean/Syriac (0)	12	0.06
Austrian (28)	136	0.63
Belgian (26)	165	0.76
Brazilian (0)	12	0.06
British (97)	179	0.83
Canadian (73)	236	1.09
Celtic (18)	18	0.08
Croatian (7)	41	0.19
Czech (9)	160	0.74
Czechoslovakian (18)	47	0.22
Danish (9)	51	0.24
Dutch (194)	808	3.73
Eastern European (11)	11	0.05
English (1,149)	3,472	16.05
European (245)	265	1.22
Finnish (306)	587	2.71
French, ex. Basque (157)	1,413	6.53
French Canadian (138)	562	2.60
German (1,745)	6,607	30.54
Greek (21)	94	0.43
Hungarian (107)	312	1.44
Iranian (11)	11	0.05
Irish (862)	3,985	18.42
Italian (443)	1,575	7.28
Lithuanian (8)	88	0.41
Macedonian (32)	32	0.15
Maltese (38)	58	0.27
Northern European (14)	14	0.06
Norwegian (52)	173	0.80
Pennsylvania German (20)	20	0.09
Polish (988)	2,825	13.06
Romanian (17)	40	0.18
Russian (30)	140	0.65
Scandinavian (21)	21	0.10
Scotch-Irish (313)	607	2.81
Scottish (401)	1,074	4.96
Slavic (27)	35	0.16
Slovak (23)	66	0.31
Slovene (0)	29	0.13
Swedish (149)	367	1.70
Swiss (56)	118	0.55
Ukrainian (118)	151	0.70
Welsh (29)	120	0.55
Yugoslavian (0)	9	0.04

Hispanic Origin	Population	%
Hispanic or Latino (of any race)	279	1.32
Central American, ex. Mexican	12	0.06
Costa Rican	1	<0.01
Guatemalan	6	0.03
Honduran	1	<0.01
Panamanian	4	0.02
Cuban	15	0.07
Dominican Republic	3	0.01
Mexican	154	0.73
Puerto Rican	21	0.10
South American	21	0.10
Argentinean	3	0.01
Bolivian	1	<0.01
Chilean	2	0.01
Colombian	2	0.01
Ecuadorian	2	0.01
Peruvian	9	0.04
Venezuelan	2	0.01
Other Hispanic or Latino	53	0.25

Race*	Population	%
African-American/Black (69)	119	0.56
Not Hispanic (66)	111	0.52
Hispanic (3)	8	0.04
American Indian/Alaska Native (72)	182	0.86
Not Hispanic (67)	161	0.76

*Notes: † The Census 2010 population figure is used to calculate the percentages in the Hispanic Origin and Race categories. Ancestry percentages are based on the 2006-2010 American Community Survey population (not shown); ‡ Numbers in parentheses indicate the number of people reporting a single ancestry; * Numbers in parentheses indicate the number of persons reporting this race alone, not in combination with any other race; Please refer to the Explanation of Data for more information.*

Hispanic (5)	21	0.10
Apache (0)	5	0.02
Blackfeet (0)	5	0.02
Cherokee (22)	48	0.23
Chippewa (17)	42	0.20
Choctaw (2)	3	0.01
Creek (1)	1	<0.01
Crow (0)	2	0.01
Delaware (1)	1	<0.01
Iroquois (2)	3	0.01
Lumbee (3)	3	0.01
Mexican American Ind. (1)	2	0.01
Ottawa (3)	14	0.07
Paiute (1)	1	<0.01
Potawatomi (1)	1	<0.01
Sioux (1)	1	<0.01
Asian (123)	233	1.10
Not Hispanic (122)	224	1.06
Hispanic (1)	9	0.04
Burmese (0)	1	<0.01
Chinese, ex. Taiwanese (33)	48	0.23
Filipino (21)	49	0.23
Indian (9)	19	0.09
Indonesian (0)	5	0.02
Japanese (20)	47	0.22
Korean (20)	32	0.15
Taiwanese (5)	6	0.03
Thai (2)	5	0.02
Vietnamese (9)	13	0.06
Hawaii Native/Pacific Islander (6)	23	0.11
Not Hispanic (6)	22	0.10
Hispanic (0)	1	<0.01
Guamanian/Chamorro (0)	1	<0.01
Native Hawaiian (4)	15	0.07
Tongan (1)	1	<0.01
White (20,577)	20,834	98.44
Not Hispanic (20,367)	20,601	97.34
Hispanic (210)	233	1.10

Hampton

Place Type: Charter Township
County: Bay
Population: 9,652†

Ancestry‡	Population	%
American (366)	366	3.77
Arab (87)	95	0.98
Arab (17)	25	0.26
Lebanese (62)	62	0.64
Other Arab (8)	8	0.08
Assyrian/Chaldean/Syriac (2)	2	0.02
Austrian (13)	42	0.43
Belgian (36)	113	1.16
British (0)	13	0.13
Canadian (13)	13	0.13
Czech (44)	82	0.85
Czechoslovakian (0)	13	0.13
Danish (0)	16	0.16
Dutch (114)	353	3.64
Eastern European (13)	13	0.13
English (202)	613	6.32
Estonian (13)	13	0.13
European (28)	45	0.46
Finnish (48)	69	0.71
French, ex. Basque (359)	1,150	11.85
French Canadian (66)	295	3.04
German (1,221)	2,841	29.28
Hungarian (146)	242	2.49
Irish (633)	1,626	16.76
Italian (70)	226	2.33
Lithuanian (55)	67	0.69
Polish (1,072)	1,963	20.23
Romanian (10)	29	0.30
Russian (43)	59	0.61
Scotch-Irish (48)	141	1.45
Scottish (38)	80	0.82
Slovene (13)	13	0.13
Swedish (45)	45	0.46
Swiss (0)	20	0.21
Ukrainian (0)	33	0.34
Welsh (7)	7	0.07

Hispanic Origin	Population	%
Hispanic or Latino (of any race)	345	3.57
Central American, ex. Mexican	4	0.04
Honduran	1	0.01
Panamanian	1	0.01
Salvadoran	2	0.02
Cuban	4	0.04
Dominican Republic	5	0.05
Mexican	299	3.10
Puerto Rican	10	0.10
South American	4	0.04
Chilean	1	0.01
Ecuadorian	3	0.03
Other Hispanic or Latino	19	0.20

Race*	Population	%
African-American/Black (141)	237	2.46
Not Hispanic (131)	217	2.25
Hispanic (10)	20	0.21
American Indian/Alaska Native (30)	100	1.04
Not Hispanic (27)	86	0.89
Hispanic (3)	14	0.15
Apache (0)	2	0.02
Blackfeet (0)	1	0.01
Cherokee (1)	12	0.12
Chippewa (18)	41	0.42
Choctaw (0)	1	0.01
Iroquois (4)	4	0.04
Mexican American Ind. (1)	1	0.01
Ottawa (0)	1	0.01
Seminole (0)	1	0.01
Asian (62)	83	0.86
Not Hispanic (60)	77	0.80
Hispanic (2)	6	0.06
Chinese, ex. Taiwanese (2)	12	0.12
Filipino (8)	13	0.13
Indian (29)	30	0.31
Japanese (5)	6	0.06
Korean (6)	9	0.09
Malaysian (1)	1	0.01
Pakistani (5)	5	0.05
Vietnamese (6)	6	0.06
Hawaii Native/Pacific Islander (0)	4	0.04
Not Hispanic (0)	4	0.04
Native Hawaiian (0)	3	0.03
White (9,149)	9,346	96.83
Not Hispanic (8,919)	9,077	94.04
Hispanic (230)	269	2.79

Hamtramck

Place Type: City
County: Wayne
Population: 22,423†

Ancestry‡	Population	%
African, Sub-Saharan (173)	180	0.80
African (76)	83	0.37
Liberian (97)	97	0.43
Albanian (205)	205	0.91
American (241)	241	1.07
Arab (4,141)	4,285	18.97
Arab (2,217)	2,280	10.09
Lebanese (4)	13	0.06
Moroccan (10)	10	0.04
Syrian (0)	9	0.04
Other Arab (1,910)	1,973	8.73
Australian (20)	20	0.09
Austrian (0)	9	0.04
British (0)	22	0.10
Cajun (0)	9	0.04
Canadian (24)	45	0.20
Croatian (24)	70	0.31
Czech (0)	19	0.08
Czechoslovakian (6)	6	0.03
Danish (14)	28	0.12
Dutch (10)	97	0.43
English (40)	228	1.01
European (89)	109	0.48
Finnish (11)	42	0.19
French, ex. Basque (19)	147	0.65
French Canadian (46)	91	0.40
German (168)	643	2.85
Greek (0)	31	0.14
Hungarian (0)	11	0.05
Irish (181)	506	2.24
Italian (43)	141	0.62
Lithuanian (23)	93	0.41
Maltese (0)	10	0.04
Norwegian (0)	27	0.12
Polish (2,613)	3,265	14.45
Portuguese (9)	9	0.04
Romanian (17)	86	0.38
Russian (58)	116	0.51
Scotch-Irish (26)	30	0.13
Scottish (25)	64	0.28
Serbian (32)	78	0.35
Slavic (0)	28	0.12
Slovak (0)	21	0.09
Swedish (13)	62	0.27
Swiss (0)	13	0.06
Turkish (21)	21	0.09
Ukrainian (226)	343	1.52
West Indian, ex. Hispanic (7)	27	0.12
Jamaican (7)	27	0.12
Yugoslavian (1,141)	1,162	5.14

Hispanic Origin	Population	%
Hispanic or Latino (of any race)	328	1.46
Central American, ex. Mexican	6	0.03
Honduran	1	<0.01
Nicaraguan	2	0.01
Panamanian	2	0.01
Salvadoran	1	<0.01
Cuban	17	0.08
Dominican Republic	3	0.01
Mexican	139	0.62
Puerto Rican	67	0.30
South American	9	0.04
Colombian	2	0.01
Ecuadorian	4	0.02
Peruvian	2	0.01
Venezuelan	1	<0.01
Other Hispanic or Latino	87	0.39

Race*	Population	%
African-American/Black (4,317)	4,572	20.39
Not Hispanic (4,285)	4,521	20.16
Hispanic (32)	51	0.23
American Indian/Alaska Native (64)	206	0.92
Not Hispanic (58)	184	0.82
Hispanic (6)	22	0.10
Blackfeet (0)	5	0.02
Canadian/French Am. Ind. (1)	3	0.01
Central American Ind. (0)	3	0.01
Cherokee (4)	20	0.09
Cheyenne (0)	3	0.01
Chippewa (4)	7	0.03
Creek (0)	6	0.03
Iroquois (4)	6	0.03
Navajo (1)	1	<0.01
Ottawa (1)	2	0.01
Potawatomi (0)	1	<0.01
Sioux (1)	1	<0.01
Asian (4,831)	5,539	24.70
Not Hispanic (4,806)	5,495	24.51
Hispanic (25)	44	0.20
Bangladeshi (2,795)	3,083	13.75
Chinese, ex. Taiwanese (16)	18	0.08
Filipino (48)	55	0.25
Indian (1,397)	1,751	7.81
Indonesian (0)	1	<0.01
Japanese (1)	5	0.02
Korean (2)	3	0.01
Pakistani (155)	160	0.71
Taiwanese (1)	1	<0.01
Hawaii Native/Pacific Islander (2)	37	0.17

*Notes: † The Census 2010 population figure is used to calculate the percentages in the Hispanic Origin and Race categories. Ancestry percentages are based on the 2006-2010 American Community Survey population (not shown); ‡ Numbers in parentheses indicate the number of people reporting a single ancestry; * Numbers in parentheses indicate the number of persons reporting this race alone, not in combination with any other race; Please refer to the Explanation of Data for more information.*

	Population	%
Not Hispanic (2)	32	0.14
Hispanic (0)	5	0.02
Guamanian/Chamorro (0)	1	<0.01
Native Hawaiian (2)	5	0.02
White (12,009)	12,954	57.77
Not Hispanic (11,876)	12,775	56.97
Hispanic (133)	179	0.80

Handy

Place Type: Township
County: Livingston
Population: 8,006†

Ancestry‡	Population	%
American (680)	680	8.47
Arab (0)	54	0.67
Lebanese (0)	27	0.34
Syrian (0)	27	0.34
Armenian (0)	8	0.10
Belgian (9)	20	0.25
British (21)	51	0.64
Canadian (13)	23	0.29
Croatian (85)	85	1.06
Czech (0)	10	0.12
Czechoslovakian (0)	8	0.10
Danish (0)	81	1.01
Dutch (59)	194	2.42
English (304)	1,261	15.72
European (57)	69	0.86
Finnish (36)	78	0.97
French, ex. Basque (63)	537	6.69
French Canadian (72)	120	1.50
German (670)	2,337	29.13
Greek (168)	253	3.15
Hungarian (0)	58	0.72
Irish (389)	1,295	16.14
Italian (202)	435	5.42
Lithuanian (0)	7	0.09
Maltese (28)	38	0.47
Norwegian (13)	49	0.61
Pennsylvania German (7)	7	0.09
Polish (243)	867	10.81
Russian (42)	84	1.05
Scotch-Irish (28)	130	1.62
Scottish (70)	186	2.32
Slovene (24)	24	0.30
Swedish (67)	118	1.47
Swiss (0)	42	0.52
Ukrainian (41)	67	0.83
Welsh (25)	49	0.61
Yugoslavian (0)	8	0.10

Hispanic Origin	Population	%
Hispanic or Latino (of any race)	176	2.20
Central American, ex. Mexican	12	0.15
Guatemalan	5	0.06
Honduran	5	0.06
Nicaraguan	2	0.02
Cuban	7	0.09
Mexican	106	1.32
Puerto Rican	1	0.01
South American	36	0.45
Argentinean	6	0.07
Chilean	4	0.05
Colombian	3	0.04
Ecuadorian	1	0.01
Peruvian	15	0.19
Venezuelan	3	0.04
Other South American	4	0.05
Other Hispanic or Latino	14	0.17

Race*	Population	%
African-American/Black (32)	57	0.71
Not Hispanic (32)	57	0.71
American Indian/Alaska Native (39)	100	1.25
Not Hispanic (38)	89	1.11
Hispanic (1)	11	0.14
Blackfeet (0)	4	0.05
Canadian/French Am. Ind. (0)	2	0.02
Cherokee (4)	23	0.29
Chippewa (20)	26	0.32
Iroquois (1)	1	0.01
Mexican American Ind. (0)	1	0.01
Navajo (0)	1	0.01
Ottawa (4)	4	0.05
Potawatomi (1)	1	0.01
Sioux (0)	2	0.02
Asian (36)	44	0.55
Not Hispanic (36)	44	0.55
Burmese (3)	3	0.04
Chinese, ex. Taiwanese (6)	8	0.10
Filipino (8)	8	0.10
Hmong (5)	5	0.06
Indian (8)	11	0.14
Japanese (1)	3	0.04
Korean (1)	3	0.04
Malaysian (0)	1	0.01
Taiwanese (1)	1	0.01
Thai (1)	1	0.01
Hawaii Native/Pacific Islander (0)	2	0.02
Not Hispanic (0)	2	0.02
White (7,761)	7,869	98.29
Not Hispanic (7,635)	7,719	96.42
Hispanic (126)	150	1.87

Harper Woods

Place Type: City
County: Wayne
Population: 14,236†

Ancestry‡	Population	%
African, Sub-Saharan (101)	101	0.71
African (92)	92	0.64
Nigerian (9)	9	0.06
Albanian (103)	103	0.72
American (70)	70	0.49
Arab (69)	129	0.90
Egyptian (7)	24	0.17
Lebanese (38)	65	0.45
Syrian (24)	40	0.28
Austrian (0)	19	0.13
Belgian (92)	255	1.78
Brazilian (22)	22	0.15
British (11)	62	0.43
Canadian (19)	50	0.35
Croatian (0)	40	0.28
Czech (8)	30	0.21
Czechoslovakian (22)	22	0.15
Danish (0)	19	0.13
Dutch (43)	149	1.04
English (161)	656	4.59
European (74)	74	0.52
Finnish (11)	46	0.32
French, ex. Basque (31)	571	3.99
French Canadian (33)	184	1.29
German (545)	2,523	17.65
Greek (131)	203	1.42
Hungarian (17)	73	0.51
Irish (400)	1,512	10.58
Italian (606)	1,493	10.44
Lithuanian (0)	12	0.08
Macedonian (37)	69	0.48
Maltese (0)	12	0.08
Norwegian (0)	11	0.08
Polish (736)	1,820	12.73
Romanian (7)	18	0.13
Russian (62)	91	0.64
Scotch-Irish (100)	336	2.35
Scottish (125)	352	2.46
Serbian (11)	11	0.08
Slovak (27)	50	0.35
Slovene (0)	31	0.22
Swedish (42)	129	0.90
Swiss (0)	33	0.23
Turkish (0)	12	0.08
Ukrainian (29)	94	0.66
Welsh (0)	42	0.29

Hispanic Origin	Population	%
Hispanic or Latino (of any race)	281	1.97
Central American, ex. Mexican	21	0.15
Costa Rican	1	0.01
Guatemalan	3	0.02
Honduran	3	0.02
Panamanian	5	0.04
Salvadoran	9	0.06
Cuban	7	0.05
Dominican Republic	6	0.04
Mexican	138	0.97
Puerto Rican	42	0.30
South American	39	0.27
Argentinean	6	0.04
Bolivian	5	0.04
Chilean	9	0.06
Colombian	6	0.04
Ecuadorian	1	0.01
Peruvian	2	0.01
Venezuelan	8	0.06
Other South American	2	0.01
Other Hispanic or Latino	28	0.20

Race*	Population	%
African-American/Black (6,488)	6,779	47.62
Not Hispanic (6,451)	6,711	47.14
Hispanic (37)	68	0.48
American Indian/Alaska Native (34)	142	1.00
Not Hispanic (31)	126	0.89
Hispanic (3)	16	0.11
Apache (0)	1	0.01
Blackfeet (0)	3	0.02
Canadian/French Am. Ind. (1)	3	0.02
Cherokee (3)	23	0.16
Chippewa (6)	19	0.13
Choctaw (0)	7	0.05
Delaware (1)	1	0.01
Iroquois (1)	5	0.04
Lumbee (1)	1	0.01
Mexican American Ind. (2)	2	0.01
Navajo (1)	1	0.01
Ottawa (4)	7	0.05
Sioux (0)	3	0.02
Asian (209)	268	1.88
Not Hispanic (204)	262	1.84
Hispanic (5)	6	0.04
Burmese (2)	2	0.01
Chinese, ex. Taiwanese (24)	27	0.19
Filipino (80)	97	0.68
Hmong (3)	3	0.02
Indian (35)	36	0.25
Indonesian (3)	7	0.05
Japanese (4)	13	0.09
Korean (17)	21	0.15
Pakistani (16)	23	0.16
Thai (4)	5	0.04
Vietnamese (18)	24	0.17
Hawaii Native/Pacific Islander (2)	3	0.02
Not Hispanic (2)	3	0.02
Native Hawaiian (1)	1	0.01
Samoan (0)	1	0.01
White (7,061)	7,374	51.80
Not Hispanic (6,909)	7,192	50.52
Hispanic (152)	182	1.28

Harrison

Place Type: Charter Township
County: Macomb
Population: 24,587†

Ancestry‡	Population	%
African, Sub-Saharan (68)	68	0.27
African (59)	59	0.24
Ghanaian (9)	9	0.04
American (1,219)	1,219	4.93
Arab (175)	491	1.98
Arab (64)	108	0.44
Jordanian (0)	8	0.03
Lebanese (78)	293	1.18

*Notes: † The Census 2010 population figure is used to calculate the percentages in the Hispanic Origin and Race categories. Ancestry percentages are based on the 2006-2010 American Community Survey population (not shown); ‡ Numbers in parentheses indicate the number of people reporting a single ancestry; * Numbers in parentheses indicate the number of persons reporting this race alone, not in combination with any other race; Please refer to the Explanation of Data for more information.*

Moroccan (0)	17	0.07
Palestinian (0)	16	0.06
Other Arab (33)	49	0.20
Armenian (12)	12	0.05
Austrian (46)	73	0.30
Belgian (231)	553	2.24
British (35)	48	0.19
Canadian (28)	58	0.23
Croatian (45)	58	0.23
Czech (14)	138	0.56
Czechoslovakian (9)	9	0.04
Danish (14)	78	0.32
Dutch (131)	408	1.65
Eastern European (14)	14	0.06
English (521)	2,294	9.27
European (289)	289	1.17
Finnish (11)	99	0.40
French, ex. Basque (320)	1,694	6.85
French Canadian (258)	669	2.70
German (1,883)	6,921	27.98
Greek (51)	127	0.51
Guyanese (0)	5	0.02
Hungarian (42)	312	1.26
Irish (776)	3,268	13.21
Italian (1,047)	2,830	11.44
Lithuanian (27)	143	0.58
Macedonian (15)	15	0.06
Maltese (13)	85	0.34
New Zealander (0)	16	0.06
Norwegian (94)	225	0.91
Pennsylvania German (0)	52	0.21
Polish (1,852)	4,305	17.40
Romanian (63)	170	0.69
Russian (62)	241	0.97
Scandinavian (17)	28	0.11
Scotch-Irish (182)	370	1.50
Scottish (110)	549	2.22
Serbian (9)	35	0.14
Slavic (0)	15	0.06
Slovak (0)	88	0.36
Slovene (15)	63	0.25
Swedish (73)	276	1.12
Swiss (6)	20	0.08
Ukrainian (52)	251	1.01
Welsh (29)	101	0.41
Yugoslavian (346)	373	1.51

Hispanic Origin	Population	%
Hispanic or Latino (of any race)	627	2.55
Central American, ex. Mexican	20	0.08
Costa Rican	4	0.02
Guatemalan	11	0.04
Panamanian	5	0.02
Cuban	14	0.06
Dominican Republic	5	0.02
Mexican	432	1.76
Puerto Rican	81	0.33
South American	30	0.12
Argentinean	7	0.03
Colombian	8	0.03
Peruvian	6	0.02
Venezuelan	8	0.03
Other South American	1	<0.01
Other Hispanic or Latino	45	0.18

Race*	Population	%
African-American/Black (1,824)	2,033	8.27
Not Hispanic (1,811)	2,002	8.14
Hispanic (13)	31	0.13
American Indian/Alaska Native (84)	238	0.97
Not Hispanic (76)	218	0.89
Hispanic (8)	20	0.08
Aleut *(Alaska Native)* (1)	1	<0.01
Apache (0)	4	0.02
Blackfeet (4)	10	0.04
Canadian/French Am. Ind. (3)	6	0.02
Cherokee (9)	52	0.21
Cheyenne (0)	1	<0.01
Chippewa (12)	28	0.11
Crow (0)	1	<0.01
Inupiat *(Alaska Native)* (2)	2	0.01
Iroquois (6)	8	0.03
Lumbee (7)	10	0.04
Mexican American Ind. (6)	7	0.03
Navajo (0)	1	<0.01
Ottawa (3)	3	0.01
Pima (0)	1	<0.01
Potawatomi (0)	4	0.02
Sioux (0)	4	0.02
Spanish American Ind. (1)	1	<0.01
Tohono O'Odham (1)	2	0.01
Ute (0)	1	<0.01
Asian (170)	248	1.01
Not Hispanic (164)	237	0.96
Hispanic (6)	11	0.04
Burmese (6)	6	0.02
Chinese, ex. Taiwanese (40)	55	0.22
Filipino (45)	68	0.28
Hmong (9)	9	0.04
Indian (22)	27	0.11
Indonesian (0)	3	0.01
Japanese (13)	23	0.09
Korean (19)	36	0.15
Laotian (1)	1	<0.01
Pakistani (4)	7	0.03
Vietnamese (7)	8	0.03
Hawaii Native/Pacific Islander (4)	16	0.07
Not Hispanic (3)	15	0.06
Hispanic (1)	1	<0.01
Guamanian/Chamorro (2)	5	0.02
Native Hawaiian (0)	4	0.02
Samoan (1)	1	<0.01
White (21,883)	22,291	90.66
Not Hispanic (21,481)	21,859	88.90
Hispanic (402)	432	1.76

Hartland

Place Type: Township
County: Livingston
Population: 14,663†

Ancestry‡	Population	%
African, Sub-Saharan (56)	56	0.39
South African (56)	56	0.39
Albanian (25)	25	0.17
American (851)	851	5.92
Arab (19)	154	1.07
Arab (9)	9	0.06
Jordanian (0)	8	0.06
Lebanese (0)	12	0.08
Moroccan (10)	10	0.07
Syrian (0)	115	0.80
Armenian (0)	9	0.06
Austrian (0)	10	0.07
Belgian (6)	48	0.33
Brazilian (0)	7	0.05
British (0)	81	0.56
Canadian (42)	127	0.88
Croatian (0)	44	0.31
Czech (51)	80	0.56
Danish (66)	117	0.81
Dutch (54)	587	4.08
English (457)	1,982	13.79
European (57)	100	0.70
Finnish (313)	475	3.30
French, ex. Basque (119)	1,060	7.37
French Canadian (146)	556	3.87
German (1,069)	4,021	27.97
Greek (0)	29	0.20
Hungarian (161)	332	2.31
Irish (446)	2,418	16.82
Italian (261)	1,067	7.42
Latvian (7)	7	0.05
Lithuanian (6)	71	0.49
Maltese (20)	66	0.46
Norwegian (14)	63	0.44
Pennsylvania German (21)	21	0.15
Polish (981)	2,235	15.55
Portuguese (14)	32	0.22
Romanian (11)	26	0.18
Russian (0)	209	1.45
Scandinavian (12)	23	0.16
Scotch-Irish (43)	209	1.45
Scottish (131)	569	3.96
Serbian (0)	23	0.16
Slavic (0)	32	0.22
Slovak (12)	40	0.28
Swedish (95)	368	2.56
Swiss (0)	45	0.31
Turkish (0)	4	0.03
Ukrainian (45)	102	0.71
Welsh (10)	72	0.50

Hispanic Origin	Population	%
Hispanic or Latino (of any race)	338	2.31
Central American, ex. Mexican	14	0.10
Guatemalan	13	0.09
Salvadoran	1	0.01
Cuban	6	0.04
Dominican Republic	4	0.03
Mexican	202	1.38
Puerto Rican	36	0.25
South American	31	0.21
Argentinean	6	0.04
Chilean	3	0.02
Colombian	14	0.10
Peruvian	3	0.02
Venezuelan	5	0.03
Other Hispanic or Latino	45	0.31

Race*	Population	%
African-American/Black (67)	99	0.68
Not Hispanic (65)	90	0.61
Hispanic (2)	9	0.06
American Indian/Alaska Native (39)	120	0.82
Not Hispanic (31)	109	0.74
Hispanic (8)	11	0.08
Aleut *(Alaska Native)* (0)	2	0.01
Blackfeet (0)	1	0.01
Canadian/French Am. Ind. (0)	3	0.02
Central American Ind. (1)	1	0.01
Cherokee (4)	19	0.13
Chippewa (17)	27	0.18
Colville (1)	5	0.03
Comanche (1)	1	0.01
Iroquois (1)	5	0.03
Mexican American Ind. (3)	3	0.02
Sioux (0)	4	0.03
Asian (145)	206	1.40
Not Hispanic (141)	196	1.34
Hispanic (4)	10	0.07
Chinese, ex. Taiwanese (27)	34	0.23
Filipino (25)	45	0.31
Hmong (2)	2	0.01
Indian (10)	18	0.12
Indonesian (0)	3	0.02
Japanese (20)	25	0.17
Korean (11)	16	0.11
Laotian (15)	22	0.15
Malaysian (5)	5	0.03
Pakistani (6)	8	0.05
Taiwanese (2)	2	0.01
Vietnamese (14)	22	0.15
Hawaii Native/Pacific Islander (3)	10	0.07
Not Hispanic (3)	7	0.05
Hispanic (0)	3	0.02
Native Hawaiian (2)	6	0.04
White (14,165)	14,346	97.84
Not Hispanic (13,920)	14,070	95.96
Hispanic (245)	276	1.88

Haslett

Place Type: CDP
County: Ingham
Population: 19,220†

Ancestry‡	Population	%
African, Sub-Saharan (205)	255	1.29

*Notes: † The Census 2010 population figure is used to calculate the percentages in the Hispanic Origin and Race categories. Ancestry percentages are based on the 2006-2010 American Community Survey population (not shown); ‡ Numbers in parentheses indicate the number of people reporting a single ancestry; * Numbers in parentheses indicate the number of persons reporting this race alone, not in combination with any other race; Please refer to the Explanation of Data for more information.*

African (38)	88	0.45
Kenyan (53)	53	0.27
Nigerian (30)	30	0.15
Senegalese (84)	84	0.43
American (1,315)	1,315	6.67
Arab (161)	218	1.11
Arab (36)	54	0.27
Egyptian (30)	30	0.15
Lebanese (42)	42	0.21
Moroccan (0)	14	0.07
Syrian (53)	64	0.32
Other Arab (0)	14	0.07
Armenian (10)	10	0.05
Assyrian/Chaldean/Syriac (11)	11	0.06
Austrian (0)	50	0.25
Belgian (25)	141	0.72
Brazilian (16)	50	0.25
British (51)	197	1.00
Canadian (35)	90	0.46
Croatian (5)	104	0.53
Czech (31)	126	0.64
Danish (8)	152	0.77
Dutch (138)	696	3.53
Eastern European (29)	29	0.15
English (787)	2,891	14.66
Estonian (0)	12	0.06
European (376)	419	2.13
Finnish (44)	261	1.32
French, ex. Basque (80)	764	3.88
French Canadian (33)	233	1.18
German (1,418)	4,818	24.44
Greek (46)	232	1.18
Hungarian (57)	222	1.13
Iranian (90)	100	0.51
Irish (596)	2,786	14.13
Italian (274)	729	3.70
Latvian (0)	20	0.10
Lithuanian (87)	140	0.71
Luxemburger (0)	12	0.06
Macedonian (21)	21	0.11
Maltese (0)	13	0.07
Northern European (16)	16	0.08
Norwegian (55)	342	1.73
Polish (377)	1,154	5.85
Portuguese (27)	68	0.34
Romanian (13)	22	0.11
Russian (145)	299	1.52
Scandinavian (0)	76	0.39
Scotch-Irish (149)	536	2.72
Scottish (158)	567	2.88
Slavic (0)	10	0.05
Slovak (17)	60	0.30
Slovene (9)	9	0.05
Swedish (178)	548	2.78
Swiss (11)	38	0.19
Turkish (56)	56	0.28
Ukrainian (118)	155	0.79
Welsh (10)	153	0.78

Hispanic Origin	Population	%
Hispanic or Latino (of any race)	822	4.28
Central American, ex. Mexican	22	0.11
Costa Rican	3	0.02
Guatemalan	7	0.04
Nicaraguan	1	0.01
Panamanian	3	0.02
Salvadoran	6	0.03
Other Central American	2	0.01
Cuban	38	0.20
Dominican Republic	11	0.06
Mexican	579	3.01
Puerto Rican	60	0.31
South American	55	0.29
Argentinean	6	0.03
Bolivian	6	0.03
Chilean	6	0.03
Colombian	9	0.05
Ecuadorian	5	0.03
Paraguayan	1	0.01
Peruvian	13	0.07
Venezuelan	9	0.05
Other Hispanic or Latino	57	0.30

Race*	Population	%
African-American/Black (850)	1,098	5.71
Not Hispanic (813)	1,027	5.34
Hispanic (37)	71	0.37
American Indian/Alaska Native (77)	230	1.20
Not Hispanic (60)	190	0.99
Hispanic (17)	40	0.21
Apache (1)	2	0.01
Blackfeet (1)	3	0.02
Canadian/French Am. Ind. (1)	7	0.04
Cherokee (8)	41	0.21
Chickasaw (0)	1	0.01
Chippewa (15)	39	0.20
Choctaw (0)	1	0.01
Creek (4)	5	0.03
Crow (0)	1	0.01
Delaware (0)	1	0.01
Inupiat *(Alaska Native)* (0)	1	0.01
Iroquois (0)	2	0.01
Mexican American Ind. (2)	5	0.03
Ottawa (3)	5	0.03
Potawatomi (2)	2	0.01
Pueblo (2)	2	0.01
Sioux (1)	5	0.03
South American Ind. (2)	3	0.02
Spanish American Ind. (1)	1	0.01
Asian (1,256)	1,451	7.55
Not Hispanic (1,251)	1,436	7.47
Hispanic (5)	15	0.08
Bangladeshi (1)	2	0.01
Burmese (10)	10	0.05
Cambodian (1)	1	0.01
Chinese, ex. Taiwanese (257)	303	1.58
Filipino (37)	68	0.35
Hmong (8)	9	0.05
Indian (404)	437	2.27
Indonesian (13)	15	0.08
Japanese (26)	53	0.28
Korean (322)	345	1.80
Laotian (1)	3	0.02
Malaysian (8)	8	0.04
Nepalese (3)	3	0.02
Pakistani (41)	43	0.22
Sri Lankan (4)	9	0.05
Taiwanese (31)	35	0.18
Thai (11)	15	0.08
Vietnamese (50)	56	0.29
Hawaii Native/Pacific Islander (5)	26	0.14
Not Hispanic (4)	25	0.13
Hispanic (1)	1	0.01
Guamanian/Chamorro (0)	6	0.03
Native Hawaiian (3)	11	0.06
Samoan (1)	3	0.02
White (16,279)	16,782	87.32
Not Hispanic (15,780)	16,186	84.21
Hispanic (499)	596	3.10

Hazel Park

Place Type: City
County: Oakland
Population: 16,422†

Ancestry‡	Population	%
African, Sub-Saharan (13)	13	0.08
Other Sub-Saharan African (13)	13	0.08
Albanian (12)	12	0.07
American (1,036)	1,036	6.14
Arab (326)	454	2.69
Arab (0)	54	0.32
Egyptian (0)	9	0.05
Iraqi (264)	277	1.64
Lebanese (0)	52	0.31
Palestinian (52)	52	0.31
Other Arab (10)	10	0.06
Armenian (26)	42	0.25
Assyrian/Chaldean/Syriac (514)	561	3.32
Austrian (0)	46	0.27
Belgian (0)	57	0.34
Brazilian (0)	21	0.12
British (12)	22	0.13
Bulgarian (0)	9	0.05
Canadian (137)	320	1.90
Croatian (0)	41	0.24
Czech (30)	63	0.37
Czechoslovakian (20)	24	0.14
Danish (25)	286	1.69
Dutch (59)	181	1.07
English (449)	1,497	8.87
European (0)	164	0.97
Finnish (28)	129	0.76
French, ex. Basque (107)	619	3.67
French Canadian (116)	251	1.49
German (811)	2,971	17.60
Greek (0)	21	0.12
Hungarian (8)	72	0.43
Irish (630)	2,756	16.33
Israeli (11)	11	0.07
Italian (230)	963	5.71
Lithuanian (6)	63	0.37
Macedonian (0)	4	0.02
Maltese (0)	25	0.15
Northern European (20)	20	0.12
Norwegian (22)	129	0.76
Polish (618)	1,360	8.06
Portuguese (0)	25	0.15
Romanian (35)	95	0.56
Russian (56)	310	1.84
Scandinavian (0)	23	0.14
Scotch-Irish (220)	415	2.46
Scottish (483)	788	4.67
Serbian (0)	56	0.33
Slavic (23)	23	0.14
Slovak (32)	32	0.19
Slovene (15)	15	0.09
Swedish (13)	291	1.72
Ukrainian (8)	35	0.21
Welsh (40)	125	0.74
Yugoslavian (0)	12	0.07

Hispanic Origin	Population	%
Hispanic or Latino (of any race)	446	2.72
Central American, ex. Mexican	11	0.07
Guatemalan	4	0.02
Honduran	1	0.01
Nicaraguan	1	0.01
Salvadoran	5	0.03
Cuban	11	0.07
Dominican Republic	3	0.02
Mexican	260	1.58
Puerto Rican	69	0.42
South American	20	0.12
Argentinean	2	0.01
Chilean	1	0.01
Ecuadorian	6	0.04
Peruvian	3	0.02
Uruguayan	4	0.02
Venezuelan	4	0.02
Other Hispanic or Latino	72	0.44

Race*	Population	%
African-American/Black (1,608)	2,005	12.21
Not Hispanic (1,586)	1,954	11.90
Hispanic (22)	51	0.31
American Indian/Alaska Native (140)	429	2.61
Not Hispanic (132)	400	2.44
Hispanic (8)	29	0.18
Aleut *(Alaska Native)* (1)	1	0.01
Arapaho (0)	1	0.01
Blackfeet (1)	9	0.05
Canadian/French Am. Ind. (3)	4	0.02
Cherokee (14)	102	0.62
Chickasaw (0)	1	0.01
Chippewa (34)	77	0.47
Choctaw (2)	3	0.02
Creek (0)	3	0.02
Crow (0)	2	0.01

*Notes: † The Census 2010 population figure is used to calculate the percentages in the Hispanic Origin and Race categories. Ancestry percentages are based on the 2006-2010 American Community Survey population (not shown); ‡ Numbers in parentheses indicate the number of people reporting a single ancestry; * Numbers in parentheses indicate the number of persons reporting this race alone, not in combination with any other race; Please refer to the Explanation of Data for more information.*

Iroquois (12)	21	0.13
Lumbee (14)	23	0.14
Mexican American Ind. (0)	1	0.01
Navajo (0)	1	0.01
Ottawa (2)	4	0.02
Potawatomi (8)	13	0.08
Seminole (0)	1	0.01
Sioux (3)	9	0.05
South American Ind. (0)	3	0.02
Ute (1)	1	0.01
Asian (243)	389	2.37
Not Hispanic (239)	376	2.29
Hispanic (4)	13	0.08
Bangladeshi (1)	1	0.01
Cambodian (1)	2	0.01
Chinese, ex. Taiwanese (22)	30	0.18
Filipino (68)	111	0.68
Hmong (41)	42	0.26
Indian (15)	21	0.13
Japanese (18)	32	0.19
Korean (7)	15	0.09
Laotian (6)	8	0.05
Pakistani (2)	2	0.01
Taiwanese (1)	1	0.01
Thai (21)	23	0.14
Vietnamese (35)	41	0.25
Hawaii Native/Pacific Islander (4)	16	0.10
Not Hispanic (2)	12	0.07
Hispanic (2)	4	0.02
Guamanian/Chamorro (2)	2	0.01
Native Hawaiian (2)	6	0.04
White (13,599)	14,289	87.01
Not Hispanic (13,312)	13,946	84.92
Hispanic (287)	343	2.09

Highland Park

Place Type: City
County: Wayne
Population: 11,776†

Ancestry‡	Population	%
African, Sub-Saharan (328)	352	2.77
African (317)	341	2.68
Kenyan (11)	11	0.09
American (191)	191	1.50
Arab (16)	16	0.13
Arab (16)	16	0.13
Dutch (9)	27	0.21
English (0)	24	0.19
European (4)	4	0.03
German (47)	165	1.30
Greek (0)	13	0.10
Hungarian (16)	32	0.25
Irish (19)	112	0.88
Italian (16)	41	0.32
Norwegian (12)	12	0.09
Polish (0)	30	0.24
Russian (0)	26	0.20
Scotch-Irish (0)	61	0.48
Scottish (0)	26	0.20
Swedish (10)	10	0.08
Swiss (0)	10	0.08
Welsh (0)	11	0.09
West Indian, ex. Hispanic (89)	89	0.70
Haitian (16)	16	0.13
Jamaican (73)	73	0.57
Yugoslavian (9)	9	0.07

Hispanic Origin	Population	%
Hispanic or Latino (of any race)	156	1.32
Central American, ex. Mexican	10	0.08
Guatemalan	1	0.01
Honduran	3	0.03
Nicaraguan	1	0.01
Panamanian	2	0.02
Salvadoran	3	0.03
Cuban	19	0.16
Dominican Republic	4	0.03
Mexican	65	0.55
Puerto Rican	35	0.30
Other Hispanic or Latino	23	0.20

Race*	Population	%
African-American/Black (11,012)	11,258	95.60
Not Hispanic (10,955)	11,172	94.87
Hispanic (57)	86	0.73
American Indian/Alaska Native (31)	144	1.22
Not Hispanic (26)	131	1.11
Hispanic (5)	13	0.11
Blackfeet (0)	14	0.12
Canadian/French Am. Ind. (0)	2	0.02
Cherokee (3)	23	0.20
Chippewa (2)	4	0.03
Choctaw (0)	3	0.03
Creek (0)	3	0.03
Mexican American Ind. (2)	3	0.03
Sioux (0)	1	0.01
Yup'ik *(Alaska Native)* (0)	1	0.01
Asian (47)	74	0.63
Not Hispanic (46)	67	0.57
Hispanic (1)	7	0.06
Bangladeshi (20)	20	0.17
Cambodian (2)	8	0.07
Chinese, ex. Taiwanese (2)	9	0.08
Filipino (11)	14	0.12
Indian (1)	6	0.05
Pakistani (0)	3	0.03
Vietnamese (10)	11	0.09
Hawaii Native/Pacific Islander (3)	6	0.05
Not Hispanic (3)	5	0.04
Hispanic (0)	1	0.01
Native Hawaiian (3)	3	0.03
White (374)	514	4.36
Not Hispanic (347)	474	4.03
Hispanic (27)	40	0.34

Highland

Place Type: Charter Township
County: Oakland
Population: 19,202†

Ancestry‡	Population	%
Albanian (61)	61	0.32
American (1,374)	1,374	7.15
Arab (132)	181	0.94
Arab (8)	8	0.04
Lebanese (111)	123	0.64
Syrian (13)	50	0.26
Armenian (33)	33	0.17
Assyrian/Chaldean/Syriac (21)	21	0.11
Austrian (15)	74	0.39
Belgian (72)	183	0.95
British (57)	102	0.53
Canadian (44)	196	1.02
Celtic (0)	9	0.05
Croatian (0)	49	0.25
Czech (0)	18	0.09
Czechoslovakian (10)	18	0.09
Danish (11)	42	0.22
Dutch (89)	713	3.71
English (832)	3,064	15.95
European (102)	142	0.74
Finnish (62)	352	1.83
French, ex. Basque (263)	1,781	9.27
French Canadian (159)	537	2.79
German (1,294)	4,530	23.57
Greek (12)	62	0.32
Hungarian (62)	190	0.99
Icelander (0)	15	0.08
Irish (787)	3,360	17.49
Italian (597)	1,595	8.30
Lithuanian (39)	91	0.47
Macedonian (0)	20	0.10
Maltese (6)	12	0.06
Northern European (19)	19	0.10
Norwegian (73)	220	1.14
Polish (668)	2,094	10.90
Portuguese (28)	65	0.34
Romanian (20)	20	0.10
Russian (29)	213	1.11
Scandinavian (9)	96	0.50
Scotch-Irish (107)	359	1.87
Scottish (132)	598	3.11
Serbian (0)	21	0.11
Slavic (0)	9	0.05
Slovak (30)	122	0.63
Slovene (0)	30	0.16
Swedish (331)	615	3.20
Swiss (11)	46	0.24
Ukrainian (21)	117	0.61
Welsh (10)	201	1.05

Hispanic Origin	Population	%
Hispanic or Latino (of any race)	371	1.93
Central American, ex. Mexican	13	0.07
Guatemalan	3	0.02
Honduran	8	0.04
Nicaraguan	1	0.01
Salvadoran	1	0.01
Cuban	5	0.03
Dominican Republic	2	0.01
Mexican	255	1.33
Puerto Rican	50	0.26
South American	15	0.08
Chilean	4	0.02
Colombian	1	0.01
Ecuadorian	5	0.03
Peruvian	5	0.03
Other Hispanic or Latino	31	0.16

Race*	Population	%
African-American/Black (76)	138	0.72
Not Hispanic (74)	135	0.70
Hispanic (2)	3	0.02
American Indian/Alaska Native (57)	184	0.96
Not Hispanic (51)	167	0.87
Hispanic (6)	17	0.09
Aleut *(Alaska Native)* (2)	5	0.03
Blackfeet (1)	7	0.04
Cherokee (5)	48	0.25
Chippewa (9)	21	0.11
Creek (0)	1	0.01
Iroquois (1)	6	0.03
Lumbee (0)	1	0.01
Mexican American Ind. (1)	7	0.04
Navajo (0)	1	0.01
Osage (0)	1	0.01
Ottawa (2)	6	0.03
Potawatomi (2)	5	0.03
Seminole (1)	2	0.01
Sioux (1)	4	0.02
Tlingit-Haida *(Alaska Native)* (2)	3	0.02
Asian (97)	170	0.89
Not Hispanic (89)	162	0.84
Hispanic (8)	8	0.04
Chinese, ex. Taiwanese (25)	32	0.17
Filipino (10)	30	0.16
Indian (14)	18	0.09
Japanese (11)	24	0.12
Korean (22)	34	0.18
Thai (4)	6	0.03
Vietnamese (8)	8	0.04
Hawaii Native/Pacific Islander (0)	3	0.02
Not Hispanic (0)	3	0.02
White (18,649)	18,907	98.46
Not Hispanic (18,370)	18,605	96.89
Hispanic (279)	302	1.57

Hillsdale

Place Type: City
County: Hillsdale
Population: 8,305†

Ancestry‡	Population	%
American (570)	570	6.82
Austrian (0)	9	0.11
Basque (0)	14	0.17

SECTION TWO

*Notes: † The Census 2010 population figure is used to calculate the percentages in the Hispanic Origin and Race categories. Ancestry percentages are based on the 2006-2010 American Community Survey population (not shown); ‡ Numbers in parentheses indicate the number of people reporting a single ancestry; * Numbers in parentheses indicate the number of persons reporting this race alone, not in combination with any other race; Please refer to the Explanation of Data for more information.*

British (10)	31	0.37
Canadian (10)	10	0.12
Croatian (14)	40	0.48
Czech (0)	31	0.37
Dutch (70)	180	2.16
English (402)	1,189	14.24
European (39)	50	0.60
French, ex. Basque (44)	487	5.83
French Canadian (58)	71	0.85
German (1,165)	3,170	37.95
Greek (0)	27	0.32
Hungarian (0)	36	0.43
Irish (409)	1,520	18.20
Italian (49)	285	3.41
Lithuanian (12)	12	0.14
Northern European (43)	43	0.51
Norwegian (13)	42	0.50
Pennsylvania German (53)	53	0.63
Polish (70)	182	2.18
Portuguese (11)	11	0.13
Scandinavian (13)	13	0.16
Scotch-Irish (23)	150	1.80
Scottish (33)	227	2.72
Swedish (41)	105	1.26
Swiss (0)	24	0.29
Ukrainian (0)	27	0.32
Welsh (7)	100	1.20
West Indian, ex. Hispanic (10)	10	0.12
Trinidadian/Tobagonian (10)	10	0.12

Hispanic Origin	Population	%
Hispanic or Latino (of any race)	190	2.29
Central American, ex. Mexican	6	0.07
Costa Rican	5	0.06
Salvadoran	1	0.01
Cuban	7	0.08
Mexican	132	1.59
Puerto Rican	15	0.18
South American	8	0.10
Argentinean	3	0.04
Colombian	4	0.05
Venezuelan	1	0.01
Other Hispanic or Latino	22	0.26

Race*	Population	%
African-American/Black (59)	105	1.26
Not Hispanic (57)	103	1.24
Hispanic (2)	2	0.02
American Indian/Alaska Native (33)	114	1.37
Not Hispanic (30)	108	1.30
Hispanic (3)	6	0.07
Apache (2)	2	0.02
Blackfeet (1)	10	0.12
Canadian/French Am. Ind. (0)	3	0.04
Cherokee (5)	36	0.43
Chippewa (4)	11	0.13
Choctaw (0)	1	0.01
Lumbee (2)	3	0.04
Mexican American Ind. (1)	2	0.02
Navajo (0)	1	0.01
Ottawa (2)	3	0.04
Potawatomi (0)	3	0.04
Seminole (0)	3	0.04
Sioux (0)	1	0.01
Tlingit-Haida *(Alaska Native)* (1)	1	0.01
Yakama (1)	1	0.01
Asian (59)	94	1.13
Not Hispanic (59)	93	1.12
Hispanic (0)	1	0.01
Chinese, ex. Taiwanese (14)	17	0.20
Filipino (9)	22	0.26
Indian (9)	10	0.12
Indonesian (1)	1	0.01
Japanese (3)	11	0.13
Korean (9)	11	0.13
Thai (1)	1	0.01
Vietnamese (7)	9	0.11
Hawaii Native/Pacific Islander (2)	5	0.06
Not Hispanic (2)	5	0.06
Guamanian/Chamorro (1)	1	0.01
Samoan (1)	1	0.01
White (7,959)	8,122	97.80
Not Hispanic (7,807)	7,956	95.80
Hispanic (152)	166	2.00

Holland

Place Type: Charter Township
County: Ottawa
Population: 35,636†

Ancestry‡	Population	%
African, Sub-Saharan (15)	15	0.04
Senegalese (15)	15	0.04
Albanian (64)	64	0.18
American (1,226)	1,226	3.53
Arab (49)	132	0.38
Arab (0)	9	0.03
Lebanese (9)	83	0.24
Other Arab (40)	40	0.12
Armenian (0)	18	0.05
Austrian (0)	75	0.22
Belgian (0)	20	0.06
British (58)	140	0.40
Canadian (10)	10	0.03
Czech (0)	115	0.33
Czechoslovakian (15)	48	0.14
Danish (42)	158	0.46
Dutch (6,374)	9,456	27.26
English (277)	1,828	5.27
European (180)	251	0.72
Finnish (26)	206	0.59
French, ex. Basque (69)	980	2.83
French Canadian (121)	292	0.84
German (1,264)	5,696	16.42
Greek (0)	33	0.10
Hungarian (73)	180	0.52
Irish (434)	2,517	7.26
Italian (160)	701	2.02
Latvian (0)	9	0.03
Lithuanian (43)	112	0.32
Maltese (0)	22	0.06
Norwegian (18)	112	0.32
Pennsylvania German (50)	84	0.24
Polish (183)	959	2.76
Portuguese (22)	33	0.10
Russian (52)	114	0.33
Scandinavian (0)	31	0.09
Scotch-Irish (126)	402	1.16
Scottish (226)	702	2.02
Slavic (0)	17	0.05
Slovak (0)	16	0.05
Swedish (165)	966	2.79
Swiss (15)	45	0.13
Welsh (0)	38	0.11
West Indian, ex. Hispanic (14)	14	0.04
Jamaican (14)	14	0.04
Yugoslavian (79)	79	0.23

Hispanic Origin	Population	%
Hispanic or Latino (of any race)	8,347	23.42
Central American, ex. Mexican	171	0.48
Costa Rican	3	0.01
Guatemalan	49	0.14
Honduran	24	0.07
Nicaraguan	33	0.09
Panamanian	4	0.01
Salvadoran	58	0.16
Cuban	123	0.35
Dominican Republic	16	0.04
Mexican	6,950	19.50
Puerto Rican	340	0.95
South American	134	0.38
Argentinean	9	0.03
Bolivian	4	0.01
Chilean	43	0.12
Colombian	17	0.05
Ecuadorian	12	0.03
Peruvian	26	0.07
Venezuelan	23	0.06
Other Hispanic or Latino	613	1.72

Race*	Population	%
African-American/Black (930)	1,311	3.68
Not Hispanic (814)	1,094	3.07
Hispanic (116)	217	0.61
American Indian/Alaska Native (186)	396	1.11
Not Hispanic (91)	248	0.70
Hispanic (95)	148	0.42
Apache (5)	9	0.03
Blackfeet (0)	11	0.03
Canadian/French Am. Ind. (0)	1	<0.01
Cherokee (4)	45	0.13
Chippewa (21)	52	0.15
Choctaw (4)	6	0.02
Comanche (1)	4	0.01
Iroquois (1)	3	0.01
Mexican American Ind. (24)	41	0.12
Navajo (7)	7	0.02
Ottawa (14)	32	0.09
Potawatomi (19)	23	0.06
Sioux (1)	7	0.02
South American Ind. (1)	2	0.01
Asian (3,346)	3,744	10.51
Not Hispanic (3,276)	3,601	10.10
Hispanic (70)	143	0.40
Bangladeshi (6)	6	0.02
Burmese (5)	5	0.01
Cambodian (610)	749	2.10
Chinese, ex. Taiwanese (194)	278	0.78
Filipino (103)	163	0.46
Hmong (10)	12	0.03
Indian (355)	391	1.10
Indonesian (2)	6	0.02
Japanese (22)	37	0.10
Korean (90)	127	0.36
Laotian (1,056)	1,250	3.51
Pakistani (8)	8	0.02
Sri Lankan (6)	6	0.02
Taiwanese (8)	9	0.03
Thai (45)	85	0.24
Vietnamese (549)	633	1.78
Hawaii Native/Pacific Islander (8)	39	0.11
Not Hispanic (4)	32	0.09
Hispanic (4)	7	0.02
Guamanian/Chamorro (1)	1	<0.01
Native Hawaiian (7)	14	0.04
Tongan (0)	1	<0.01
White (26,180)	27,192	76.30
Not Hispanic (22,353)	22,974	64.47
Hispanic (3,827)	4,218	11.84

Holland

Place Type: City
County: Ottawa
Population: 26,035†

Ancestry‡	Population	%
African, Sub-Saharan (0)	12	0.05
Ethiopian (0)	12	0.05
American (530)	530	1.99
Arab (14)	84	0.32
Arab (0)	12	0.05
Lebanese (14)	72	0.27
Armenian (0)	13	0.05
Assyrian/Chaldean/Syriac (0)	14	0.05
Austrian (0)	36	0.14
Belgian (0)	25	0.09
Brazilian (0)	13	0.05
British (66)	79	0.30
Canadian (10)	50	0.19
Croatian (0)	59	0.22
Czech (55)	123	0.46
Czechoslovakian (13)	40	0.15
Danish (19)	179	0.67
Dutch (3,736)	6,776	25.45
Eastern European (13)	13	0.05
English (498)	2,173	8.16
European (171)	273	1.03

*Notes: † The Census 2010 population figure is used to calculate the percentages in the Hispanic Origin and Race categories. Ancestry percentages are based on the 2006-2010 American Community Survey population (not shown); ‡ Numbers in parentheses indicate the number of people reporting a single ancestry; * Numbers in parentheses indicate the number of persons reporting this race alone, not in combination with any other race; Please refer to the Explanation of Data for more information.*

Ancestry	Population	%
Finnish (12)	315	1.18
French, ex. Basque (187)	1,054	3.96
French Canadian (27)	106	0.40
German (1,070)	5,120	19.23
Greek (37)	48	0.18
Hungarian (24)	146	0.55
Iranian (33)	33	0.12
Irish (349)	2,104	7.90
Italian (224)	812	3.05
Lithuanian (0)	53	0.20
Macedonian (0)	35	0.13
Maltese (10)	10	0.04
Northern European (54)	54	0.20
Norwegian (68)	262	0.98
Pennsylvania German (0)	28	0.11
Polish (219)	968	3.64
Romanian (0)	21	0.08
Russian (40)	105	0.39
Scandinavian (14)	48	0.18
Scotch-Irish (56)	349	1.31
Scottish (151)	592	2.22
Serbian (0)	25	0.09
Slavic (0)	25	0.09
Slovak (0)	8	0.03
Swedish (127)	734	2.76
Swiss (0)	23	0.09
Ukrainian (45)	110	0.41
Welsh (13)	131	0.49
Yugoslavian (86)	120	0.45

Hispanic Origin	Population	%
Hispanic or Latino (of any race)	6,114	23.48
Central American, ex. Mexican	88	0.34
Costa Rican	2	0.01
Guatemalan	23	0.09
Honduran	22	0.08
Nicaraguan	15	0.06
Panamanian	6	0.02
Salvadoran	20	0.08
Cuban	76	0.29
Dominican Republic	12	0.05
Mexican	5,070	19.47
Puerto Rican	342	1.31
South American	76	0.29
Argentinean	1	<0.01
Chilean	36	0.14
Colombian	15	0.06
Ecuadorian	3	0.01
Peruvian	17	0.07
Venezuelan	4	0.02
Other Hispanic or Latino	450	1.73

Race*	Population	%
African-American/Black (908)	1,235	4.74
Not Hispanic (816)	1,041	4.00
Hispanic (92)	194	0.75
American Indian/Alaska Native (155)	300	1.15
Not Hispanic (72)	180	0.69
Hispanic (83)	120	0.46
Aleut *(Alaska Native)* (0)	1	<0.01
Apache (7)	12	0.05
Blackfeet (0)	6	0.02
Canadian/French Am. Ind. (2)	2	0.01
Cherokee (9)	27	0.10
Chippewa (19)	33	0.13
Choctaw (5)	7	0.03
Inupiat *(Alaska Native)* (0)	1	<0.01
Iroquois (3)	6	0.02
Lumbee (0)	1	<0.01
Mexican American Ind. (23)	29	0.11
Navajo (2)	4	0.02
Ottawa (18)	25	0.10
Potawatomi (2)	4	0.02
Pueblo (1)	2	0.01
Sioux (3)	4	0.02
Spanish American Ind. (3)	3	0.01
Tlingit-Haida *(Alaska Native)* (1)	3	0.01
Yaqui (1)	1	<0.01
Asian (866)	1,047	4.02
Not Hispanic (824)	968	3.72
Hispanic (42)	79	0.30
Burmese (5)	5	0.02
Cambodian (217)	264	1.01
Chinese, ex. Taiwanese (88)	135	0.52
Filipino (38)	61	0.23
Hmong (1)	3	0.01
Indian (113)	135	0.52
Indonesian (2)	10	0.04
Japanese (8)	30	0.12
Korean (79)	104	0.40
Laotian (101)	131	0.50
Pakistani (3)	3	0.01
Thai (5)	17	0.07
Vietnamese (104)	136	0.52
Hawaii Native/Pacific Islander (27)	59	0.23
Not Hispanic (24)	44	0.17
Hispanic (3)	15	0.06
Guamanian/Chamorro (0)	2	0.01
Native Hawaiian (3)	7	0.03
Samoan (4)	5	0.02
White (20,591)	21,408	82.23
Not Hispanic (17,698)	18,140	69.68
Hispanic (2,893)	3,268	12.55

Holland

Place Type: City
County: Ottawa
Population: 33,051†

Ancestry‡	Population	%
African, Sub-Saharan (36)	48	0.14
African (36)	36	0.11
Ethiopian (0)	12	0.04
American (702)	702	2.08
Arab (14)	84	0.25
Arab (0)	12	0.04
Lebanese (14)	72	0.21
Armenian (0)	13	0.04
Assyrian/Chaldean/Syriac (0)	14	0.04
Austrian (0)	78	0.23
Belgian (0)	25	0.07
Brazilian (0)	13	0.04
British (66)	79	0.23
Canadian (19)	59	0.18
Croatian (0)	74	0.22
Czech (55)	138	0.41
Czechoslovakian (13)	40	0.12
Danish (19)	179	0.53
Dutch (5,387)	9,167	27.20
Eastern European (13)	13	0.04
English (523)	2,500	7.42
European (171)	273	0.81
Finnish (24)	370	1.10
French, ex. Basque (243)	1,207	3.58
French Canadian (27)	106	0.31
German (1,322)	6,137	18.21
Greek (37)	48	0.14
Hungarian (24)	208	0.62
Iranian (33)	33	0.10
Irish (435)	2,632	7.81
Italian (249)	986	2.93
Lithuanian (0)	53	0.16
Macedonian (0)	35	0.10
Maltese (10)	10	0.03
Northern European (54)	54	0.16
Norwegian (89)	312	0.93
Pennsylvania German (0)	37	0.11
Polish (349)	1,355	4.02
Romanian (0)	21	0.06
Russian (40)	120	0.36
Scandinavian (14)	48	0.14
Scotch-Irish (68)	384	1.14
Scottish (187)	703	2.09
Serbian (0)	25	0.07
Slavic (0)	40	0.12
Slovak (0)	21	0.06
Swedish (157)	904	2.68
Swiss (0)	35	0.10
Ukrainian (45)	132	0.39
Welsh (13)	131	0.39
Yugoslavian (86)	120	0.36

Hispanic Origin	Population	%
Hispanic or Latino (of any race)	7,512	22.73
Central American, ex. Mexican	125	0.38
Costa Rican	2	0.01
Guatemalan	31	0.09
Honduran	46	0.14
Nicaraguan	18	0.05
Panamanian	6	0.02
Salvadoran	22	0.07
Cuban	85	0.26
Dominican Republic	15	0.05
Mexican	6,241	18.88
Puerto Rican	450	1.36
South American	87	0.26
Argentinean	1	<0.01
Chilean	36	0.11
Colombian	20	0.06
Ecuadorian	6	0.02
Paraguayan	2	0.01
Peruvian	17	0.05
Uruguayan	1	<0.01
Venezuelan	4	0.01
Other Hispanic or Latino	509	1.54

Race*	Population	%
African-American/Black (1,187)	1,600	4.84
Not Hispanic (1,068)	1,363	4.12
Hispanic (119)	237	0.72
American Indian/Alaska Native (212)	394	1.19
Not Hispanic (94)	222	0.67
Hispanic (118)	172	0.52
Aleut *(Alaska Native)* (0)	1	<0.01
Apache (7)	14	0.04
Blackfeet (0)	6	0.02
Canadian/French Am. Ind. (2)	3	0.01
Central American Ind. (1)	1	<0.01
Cherokee (13)	45	0.14
Cheyenne (1)	1	<0.01
Chickasaw (1)	1	<0.01
Chippewa (37)	54	0.16
Choctaw (5)	7	0.02
Inupiat *(Alaska Native)* (0)	1	<0.01
Iroquois (3)	6	0.02
Lumbee (0)	1	<0.01
Mexican American Ind. (24)	30	0.09
Navajo (2)	6	0.02
Osage (0)	1	<0.01
Ottawa (22)	32	0.10
Potawatomi (2)	7	0.02
Pueblo (1)	2	0.01
Sioux (8)	9	0.03
Spanish American Ind. (3)	3	0.01
Tlingit-Haida *(Alaska Native)* (1)	3	0.01
Yaqui (1)	1	<0.01
Asian (996)	1,219	3.69
Not Hispanic (944)	1,124	3.40
Hispanic (52)	95	0.29
Burmese (7)	7	0.02
Cambodian (247)	295	0.89
Chinese, ex. Taiwanese (97)	146	0.44
Filipino (42)	67	0.20
Hmong (1)	3	0.01
Indian (116)	141	0.43
Indonesian (2)	10	0.03
Japanese (9)	36	0.11
Korean (96)	129	0.39
Laotian (120)	156	0.47
Pakistani (3)	3	0.01
Thai (13)	31	0.09
Vietnamese (132)	168	0.51
Hawaii Native/Pacific Islander (32)	73	0.22
Not Hispanic (29)	54	0.16
Hispanic (3)	19	0.06
Guamanian/Chamorro (0)	2	0.01
Native Hawaiian (7)	15	0.05
Samoan (4)	6	0.02
White (26,457)	27,462	83.09

*Notes: † The Census 2010 population figure is used to calculate the percentages in the Hispanic Origin and Race categories. Ancestry percentages are based on the 2006-2010 American Community Survey population (not shown); ‡ Numbers in parentheses indicate the number of people reporting a single ancestry; * Numbers in parentheses indicate the number of persons reporting this race alone, not in combination with any other race; Please refer to the Explanation of Data for more information.*

	Population	%
Not Hispanic (22,778)	23,338	70.61
Hispanic (3,679)	4,124	12.48

Holly

Place Type: Township
County: Oakland
Population: 11,362†

Ancestry‡	Population	%
African, Sub-Saharan (62)	62	0.56
African (62)	62	0.56
Albanian (134)	134	1.21
American (565)	565	5.08
Arab (59)	59	0.53
Iraqi (26)	26	0.23
Other Arab (33)	33	0.30
Armenian (0)	13	0.12
Assyrian/Chaldean/Syriac (13)	13	0.12
Austrian (0)	8	0.07
Belgian (21)	46	0.41
Brazilian (0)	17	0.15
British (0)	11	0.10
Canadian (148)	181	1.63
Croatian (0)	17	0.15
Czech (21)	21	0.19
Danish (0)	11	0.10
Dutch (61)	317	2.85
Eastern European (7)	7	0.06
English (437)	1,463	13.16
Estonian (6)	6	0.05
European (45)	72	0.65
Finnish (29)	100	0.90
French, ex. Basque (166)	648	5.83
French Canadian (45)	164	1.48
German (1,015)	2,982	26.82
Greek (15)	15	0.13
Hungarian (22)	39	0.35
Irish (663)	1,932	17.38
Italian (218)	700	6.30
Lithuanian (0)	6	0.05
Luxemburger (6)	6	0.05
Maltese (8)	22	0.20
Norwegian (22)	93	0.84
Polish (269)	784	7.05
Romanian (11)	123	1.11
Russian (14)	43	0.39
Scandinavian (0)	18	0.16
Scotch-Irish (159)	349	3.14
Scottish (132)	402	3.62
Serbian (0)	40	0.36
Slavic (0)	33	0.30
Slovak (0)	13	0.12
Swedish (49)	216	1.94
Ukrainian (7)	7	0.06
Welsh (28)	83	0.75

Hispanic Origin	Population	%
Hispanic or Latino (of any race)	368	3.24
Central American, ex. Mexican	5	0.04
Nicaraguan	1	0.01
Panamanian	4	0.04
Cuban	7	0.06
Mexican	249	2.19
Puerto Rican	41	0.36
South American	34	0.30
Argentinean	6	0.05
Chilean	3	0.03
Colombian	16	0.14
Ecuadorian	2	0.02
Peruvian	3	0.03
Venezuelan	4	0.04
Other Hispanic or Latino	32	0.28

Race*	Population	%
African-American/Black (238)	304	2.68
Not Hispanic (234)	295	2.60
Hispanic (4)	9	0.08
American Indian/Alaska Native (65)	162	1.43
Not Hispanic (63)	145	1.28
Hispanic (2)	17	0.15
Apache (1)	2	0.02
Blackfeet (4)	7	0.06
Canadian/French Am. Ind. (1)	1	0.01
Cherokee (4)	25	0.22
Chippewa (11)	21	0.18
Choctaw (8)	8	0.07
Iroquois (1)	1	0.01
Lumbee (3)	4	0.04
Menominee (1)	4	0.04
Mexican American Ind. (2)	2	0.02
Ottawa (1)	4	0.04
Potawatomi (0)	1	0.01
Sioux (2)	2	0.02
South American Ind. (0)	2	0.02
Asian (128)	167	1.47
Not Hispanic (128)	158	1.39
Hispanic (0)	9	0.08
Chinese, ex. Taiwanese (18)	21	0.18
Filipino (13)	26	0.23
Hmong (25)	25	0.22
Indian (20)	22	0.19
Japanese (5)	15	0.13
Korean (20)	27	0.24
Laotian (1)	1	0.01
Sri Lankan (3)	3	0.03
Taiwanese (2)	2	0.02
Vietnamese (17)	18	0.16
Hawaii Native/Pacific Islander (9)	15	0.13
Not Hispanic (8)	14	0.12
Hispanic (1)	1	0.01
Guamanian/Chamorro (2)	4	0.04
Native Hawaiian (3)	3	0.03
White (10,630)	10,841	95.41
Not Hispanic (10,384)	10,549	92.84
Hispanic (246)	292	2.57

Holt

Place Type: CDP
County: Ingham
Population: 23,973†

Ancestry‡	Population	%
African, Sub-Saharan (35)	98	0.42
African (17)	72	0.31
Ghanaian (18)	18	0.08
Nigerian (0)	8	0.03
Albanian (102)	102	0.43
American (1,788)	1,788	7.58
Arab (96)	107	0.45
Lebanese (96)	107	0.45
Australian (77)	77	0.33
Austrian (0)	38	0.16
Belgian (12)	109	0.46
British (54)	99	0.42
Canadian (11)	155	0.66
Celtic (0)	24	0.10
Croatian (136)	136	0.58
Czech (22)	257	1.09
Czechoslovakian (9)	61	0.26
Danish (26)	95	0.40
Dutch (264)	1,328	5.63
English (769)	3,128	13.26
European (112)	135	0.57
Finnish (51)	201	0.85
French, ex. Basque (193)	1,169	4.95
French Canadian (125)	438	1.86
German (1,768)	6,780	28.73
Greek (0)	62	0.26
Hungarian (47)	171	0.72
Irish (564)	2,998	12.71
Italian (253)	873	3.70
Lithuanian (11)	32	0.14
Macedonian (13)	13	0.06
Maltese (0)	44	0.19
Norwegian (166)	362	1.53
Pennsylvania German (12)	34	0.14
Polish (415)	1,478	6.26
Romanian (0)	36	0.15
Russian (81)	199	0.84
Scotch-Irish (181)	391	1.66
Scottish (281)	751	3.18
Slavic (0)	12	0.05
Slovak (22)	22	0.09
Swedish (77)	463	1.96
Swiss (19)	70	0.30
Ukrainian (12)	79	0.33
Welsh (14)	183	0.78
West Indian, ex. Hispanic (19)	19	0.08
Belizean (11)	11	0.05
Haitian (8)	8	0.03

Hispanic Origin	Population	%
Hispanic or Latino (of any race)	1,290	5.38
Central American, ex. Mexican	36	0.15
Costa Rican	3	0.01
Guatemalan	13	0.05
Honduran	2	0.01
Nicaraguan	8	0.03
Panamanian	3	0.01
Salvadoran	4	0.02
Other Central American	3	0.01
Cuban	46	0.19
Dominican Republic	4	0.02
Mexican	951	3.97
Puerto Rican	88	0.37
South American	27	0.11
Argentinean	4	0.02
Chilean	3	0.01
Colombian	10	0.04
Ecuadorian	2	0.01
Peruvian	4	0.02
Uruguayan	1	<0.01
Venezuelan	3	0.01
Other Hispanic or Latino	138	0.58

Race*	Population	%
African-American/Black (1,340)	1,731	7.22
Not Hispanic (1,287)	1,612	6.72
Hispanic (53)	119	0.50
American Indian/Alaska Native (115)	303	1.26
Not Hispanic (104)	273	1.14
Hispanic (11)	30	0.13
Blackfeet (2)	20	0.08
Canadian/French Am. Ind. (1)	5	0.02
Cherokee (8)	39	0.16
Chippewa (39)	55	0.23
Choctaw (2)	2	0.01
Comanche (2)	2	0.01
Cree (1)	1	<0.01
Creek (3)	3	0.01
Crow (0)	2	0.01
Iroquois (3)	7	0.03
Lumbee (0)	1	<0.01
Mexican American Ind. (5)	6	0.03
Navajo (0)	6	0.03
Osage (0)	2	0.01
Ottawa (12)	22	0.09
Potawatomi (2)	12	0.05
Seminole (1)	4	0.02
Sioux (1)	9	0.04
South American Ind. (0)	3	0.01
Spanish American Ind. (1)	1	<0.01
Asian (743)	893	3.73
Not Hispanic (737)	884	3.69
Hispanic (6)	9	0.04
Bangladeshi (1)	1	<0.01
Cambodian (2)	3	0.01
Chinese, ex. Taiwanese (54)	64	0.27
Filipino (44)	83	0.35
Hmong (49)	51	0.21
Indian (157)	177	0.74
Indonesian (5)	8	0.03
Japanese (25)	60	0.25
Korean (94)	110	0.46
Laotian (2)	7	0.03
Malaysian (0)	1	<0.01
Pakistani (13)	16	0.07
Taiwanese (1)	1	<0.01

*Notes: † The Census 2010 population figure is used to calculate the percentages in the Hispanic Origin and Race categories. Ancestry percentages are based on the 2006-2010 American Community Survey population (not shown); ‡ Numbers in parentheses indicate the number of people reporting a single ancestry; * Numbers in parentheses indicate the number of persons reporting this race alone, not in combination with any other race; Please refer to the Explanation of Data for more information.*

Thai (2)	3	0.01
Vietnamese (271)	288	1.20
Hawaii Native/Pacific Islander (9)	25	0.10
Not Hispanic (8)	24	0.10
Hispanic (1)	1	<0.01
Fijian (1)	1	<0.01
Guamanian/Chamorro (1)	2	0.01
Native Hawaiian (4)	11	0.05
Samoan (0)	5	0.02
White (20,683)	21,366	89.13
Not Hispanic (19,918)	20,474	85.40
Hispanic (765)	892	3.72

Houghton

Place Type: City
County: Houghton
Population: 7,708†

Ancestry‡	Population	%
African, Sub-Saharan (34)	34	0.45
Ethiopian (16)	16	0.21
Nigerian (16)	16	0.21
Sudanese (2)	2	0.03
American (204)	204	2.69
Arab (115)	115	1.52
Egyptian (24)	24	0.32
Other Arab (91)	91	1.20
Austrian (0)	17	0.22
Belgian (23)	85	1.12
British (17)	107	1.41
Canadian (15)	29	0.38
Croatian (0)	138	1.82
Czech (20)	91	1.20
Czechoslovakian (83)	83	1.10
Danish (0)	19	0.25
Dutch (96)	207	2.73
English (149)	1,008	13.31
European (39)	47	0.62
Finnish (351)	762	10.06
French, ex. Basque (47)	494	6.52
French Canadian (31)	146	1.93
German (324)	1,906	25.17
Greek (17)	53	0.70
Hungarian (43)	78	1.03
Iranian (32)	32	0.42
Irish (229)	1,156	15.26
Italian (49)	508	6.71
Lithuanian (0)	28	0.37
Maltese (0)	18	0.24
Norwegian (44)	196	2.59
Polish (152)	651	8.60
Romanian (41)	41	0.54
Russian (8)	47	0.62
Scandinavian (7)	32	0.42
Scotch-Irish (54)	174	2.30
Scottish (0)	227	3.00
Slavic (15)	21	0.28
Slovak (0)	7	0.09
Slovene (0)	30	0.40
Swedish (49)	244	3.22
Swiss (16)	25	0.33
Turkish (1)	1	0.01
Welsh (0)	39	0.51
West Indian, ex. Hispanic (12)	12	0.16
Trinidadian/Tobagonian (12)	12	0.16
Yugoslavian (0)	44	0.58

Hispanic Origin	Population	%
Hispanic or Latino (of any race)	142	1.84
Central American, ex. Mexican	2	0.03
Guatemalan	1	0.01
Other Central American	1	0.01
Cuban	4	0.05
Dominican Republic	1	0.01
Mexican	79	1.02
Puerto Rican	15	0.19
South American	25	0.32
Argentinean	6	0.08
Bolivian	2	0.03
Chilean	3	0.04
Colombian	12	0.16
Venezuelan	2	0.03
Other Hispanic or Latino	16	0.21

Race*	Population	%
African-American/Black (78)	100	1.30
Not Hispanic (77)	98	1.27
Hispanic (1)	2	0.03
American Indian/Alaska Native (30)	77	1.00
Not Hispanic (26)	69	0.90
Hispanic (4)	8	0.10
Canadian/French Am. Ind. (2)	2	0.03
Cherokee (0)	4	0.05
Chippewa (7)	24	0.31
Iroquois (1)	1	0.01
Lumbee (1)	1	0.01
Mexican American Ind. (1)	2	0.03
Osage (0)	1	0.01
Ottawa (0)	3	0.04
Potawatomi (3)	4	0.05
Asian (864)	923	11.97
Not Hispanic (862)	920	11.94
Hispanic (2)	3	0.04
Bangladeshi (1)	1	0.01
Chinese, ex. Taiwanese (499)	510	6.62
Filipino (6)	19	0.25
Hmong (6)	6	0.08
Indian (252)	260	3.37
Indonesian (2)	3	0.04
Japanese (4)	8	0.10
Korean (47)	48	0.62
Malaysian (1)	3	0.04
Nepalese (7)	7	0.09
Pakistani (14)	14	0.18
Sri Lankan (2)	2	0.03
Taiwanese (5)	5	0.06
Thai (9)	9	0.12
Vietnamese (3)	7	0.09
Hawaii Native/Pacific Islander (4)	17	0.22
Not Hispanic (4)	14	0.18
Hispanic (0)	3	0.04
Guamanian/Chamorro (3)	3	0.04
Native Hawaiian (1)	10	0.13
White (6,565)	6,687	86.75
Not Hispanic (6,467)	6,575	85.30
Hispanic (98)	112	1.45

Howell

Place Type: City
County: Livingston
Population: 9,489†

Ancestry‡	Population	%
American (283)	283	2.92
Arab (15)	68	0.70
Lebanese (15)	56	0.58
Syrian (0)	12	0.12
Armenian (0)	43	0.44
Belgian (0)	41	0.42
British (38)	72	0.74
Canadian (16)	116	1.20
Croatian (0)	20	0.21
Czech (0)	59	0.61
Czechoslovakian (12)	24	0.25
Danish (59)	86	0.89
Dutch (59)	224	2.31
English (704)	1,846	19.06
European (30)	46	0.47
Finnish (59)	123	1.27
French, ex. Basque (57)	581	6.00
French Canadian (36)	176	1.82
German (871)	2,815	29.07
Greek (0)	26	0.27
Hungarian (59)	121	1.25
Icelander (0)	14	0.14
Irish (449)	1,534	15.84
Italian (95)	358	3.70
Latvian (0)	14	0.14
Lithuanian (79)	86	0.89
Maltese (9)	9	0.09
Northern European (57)	57	0.59
Norwegian (13)	40	0.41
Pennsylvania German (11)	11	0.11
Polish (302)	681	7.03
Romanian (14)	27	0.28
Russian (0)	34	0.35
Scotch-Irish (90)	326	3.37
Scottish (99)	484	5.00
Swedish (58)	217	2.24
Swiss (0)	13	0.13
Ukrainian (25)	48	0.50
Welsh (28)	104	1.07

Hispanic Origin	Population	%
Hispanic or Latino (of any race)	331	3.49
Central American, ex. Mexican	9	0.09
Costa Rican	2	0.02
Guatemalan	3	0.03
Honduran	3	0.03
Nicaraguan	1	0.01
Cuban	13	0.14
Mexican	261	2.75
Puerto Rican	13	0.14
South American	9	0.09
Argentinean	1	0.01
Colombian	1	0.01
Peruvian	7	0.07
Other Hispanic or Latino	26	0.27

Race*	Population	%
African-American/Black (40)	69	0.73
Not Hispanic (38)	67	0.71
Hispanic (2)	2	0.02
American Indian/Alaska Native (68)	128	1.35
Not Hispanic (56)	115	1.21
Hispanic (12)	13	0.14
Arapaho (1)	1	0.01
Blackfeet (1)	3	0.03
Central American Ind. (1)	1	0.01
Cherokee (4)	10	0.11
Chippewa (13)	25	0.26
Colville (1)	1	0.01
Inupiat *(Alaska Native)* (1)	1	0.01
Iroquois (2)	3	0.03
Lumbee (4)	6	0.06
Mexican American Ind. (2)	2	0.02
Navajo (1)	1	0.01
Osage (1)	1	0.01
Potawatomi (0)	1	0.01
Sioux (4)	5	0.05
Asian (109)	137	1.44
Not Hispanic (107)	134	1.41
Hispanic (2)	3	0.03
Chinese, ex. Taiwanese (17)	19	0.20
Filipino (28)	39	0.41
Hmong (8)	8	0.08
Indian (14)	19	0.20
Japanese (9)	14	0.15
Korean (6)	12	0.13
Laotian (1)	1	0.01
Pakistani (2)	7	0.07
Thai (1)	1	0.01
Vietnamese (16)	17	0.18
Hawaii Native/Pacific Islander (32)	39	0.41
Not Hispanic (32)	39	0.41
Guamanian/Chamorro (0)	1	0.01
Marshallese (1)	1	0.01
Native Hawaiian (5)	6	0.06
White (8,992)	9,116	96.07
Not Hispanic (8,800)	8,913	93.93
Hispanic (192)	203	2.14

Huron

Place Type: Charter Township
County: Wayne
Population: 15,879†

*Notes: † The Census 2010 population figure is used to calculate the percentages in the Hispanic Origin and Race categories. Ancestry percentages are based on the 2006-2010 American Community Survey population (not shown); ‡ Numbers in parentheses indicate the number of people reporting a single ancestry; * Numbers in parentheses indicate the number of persons reporting this race alone, not in combination with any other race; Please refer to the Explanation of Data for more information.*

Ancestry‡	Population	%
African, Sub-Saharan (13)	80	0.52
African (13)	80	0.52
American (817)	817	5.26
Arab (0)	103	0.66
Arab (0)	9	0.06
Jordanian (0)	10	0.06
Lebanese (0)	58	0.37
Syrian (0)	17	0.11
Other Arab (0)	9	0.06
Armenian (20)	32	0.21
Australian (0)	9	0.06
Austrian (0)	25	0.16
Belgian (60)	88	0.57
Canadian (29)	65	0.42
Czech (28)	114	0.73
Czechoslovakian (11)	32	0.21
Danish (0)	46	0.30
Dutch (67)	418	2.69
English (292)	1,828	11.77
European (77)	77	0.50
Finnish (23)	153	0.99
French, ex. Basque (169)	1,367	8.80
French Canadian (33)	169	1.09
German (1,059)	4,034	25.97
Greek (17)	17	0.11
Hungarian (295)	727	4.68
Irish (455)	2,500	16.10
Italian (339)	1,413	9.10
Macedonian (10)	10	0.06
Maltese (60)	70	0.45
Norwegian (54)	143	0.92
Polish (863)	2,572	16.56
Portuguese (0)	17	0.11
Romanian (63)	114	0.73
Russian (0)	92	0.59
Scotch-Irish (134)	377	2.43
Scottish (21)	430	2.77
Slavic (0)	14	0.09
Slovak (11)	71	0.46
Swedish (16)	289	1.86
Swiss (12)	36	0.23
Ukrainian (22)	77	0.50
Welsh (0)	55	0.35

Hispanic Origin	Population	%
Hispanic or Latino (of any race)	502	3.16
Central American, ex. Mexican	17	0.11
Costa Rican	1	0.01
Guatemalan	4	0.03
Nicaraguan	3	0.02
Panamanian	7	0.04
Salvadoran	2	0.01
Cuban	19	0.12
Mexican	319	2.01
Puerto Rican	30	0.19
South American	10	0.06
Argentinean	4	0.03
Colombian	5	0.03
Paraguayan	1	0.01
Other Hispanic or Latino	107	0.67

Race*	Population	%
African-American/Black (402)	524	3.30
Not Hispanic (398)	516	3.25
Hispanic (4)	8	0.05
American Indian/Alaska Native (110)	294	1.85
Not Hispanic (102)	275	1.73
Hispanic (8)	19	0.12
Alaska Athabascan *(Ala. Nat.)* (1)	1	0.01
Apache (1)	2	0.01
Blackfeet (4)	19	0.12
Canadian/French Am. Ind. (0)	3	0.02
Cherokee (14)	91	0.57
Cheyenne (2)	2	0.01
Chickasaw (2)	2	0.01
Chippewa (25)	44	0.28
Choctaw (1)	2	0.01
Creek (10)	10	0.06
Delaware (0)	1	0.01
Inupiat *(Alaska Native)* (0)	1	0.01
Iroquois (4)	12	0.08
Lumbee (1)	1	0.01
Menominee (0)	2	0.01
Mexican American Ind. (5)	6	0.04
Ottawa (1)	6	0.04
Potawatomi (0)	3	0.02
Pueblo (1)	5	0.03
Shoshone (0)	2	0.01
Sioux (0)	4	0.03
South American Ind. (0)	1	0.01
Yaqui (0)	2	0.01
Asian (116)	189	1.19
Not Hispanic (114)	184	1.16
Hispanic (2)	5	0.03
Cambodian (2)	2	0.01
Chinese, ex. Taiwanese (11)	20	0.13
Filipino (31)	59	0.37
Indian (22)	29	0.18
Indonesian (0)	1	0.01
Japanese (6)	11	0.07
Korean (9)	16	0.10
Malaysian (1)	1	0.01
Pakistani (20)	31	0.20
Thai (1)	4	0.03
Vietnamese (12)	15	0.09
Hawaii Native/Pacific Islander (1)	8	0.05
Not Hispanic (1)	7	0.04
Hispanic (0)	1	0.01
Native Hawaiian (1)	5	0.03
White (14,777)	15,131	95.29
Not Hispanic (14,415)	14,722	92.71
Hispanic (362)	409	2.58

Independence

Place Type: Charter Township
County: Oakland
Population: 34,681†

Ancestry‡	Population	%
African, Sub-Saharan (27)	58	0.17
African (27)	38	0.11
South African (0)	20	0.06
Albanian (0)	9	0.03
American (1,967)	1,967	5.74
Arab (92)	233	0.68
Arab (9)	33	0.10
Iraqi (0)	23	0.07
Lebanese (61)	132	0.38
Other Arab (22)	45	0.13
Armenian (94)	132	0.38
Assyrian/Chaldean/Syriac (20)	75	0.22
Austrian (10)	120	0.35
Basque (0)	14	0.04
Belgian (24)	117	0.34
British (296)	450	1.31
Canadian (192)	362	1.06
Celtic (0)	13	0.04
Croatian (54)	162	0.47
Czech (0)	212	0.62
Czechoslovakian (35)	47	0.14
Danish (8)	121	0.35
Dutch (108)	806	2.35
Eastern European (8)	8	0.02
English (1,342)	4,971	14.50
European (379)	449	1.31
Finnish (95)	213	0.62
French, ex. Basque (296)	2,299	6.71
French Canadian (308)	972	2.83
German (2,467)	9,089	26.51
Greek (22)	297	0.87
Hungarian (61)	241	0.70
Icelander (0)	24	0.07
Irish (1,600)	6,521	19.02
Italian (712)	2,444	7.13
Latvian (0)	14	0.04
Lithuanian (55)	119	0.35
Macedonian (10)	21	0.06
Maltese (18)	60	0.17
Norwegian (76)	456	1.33
Pennsylvania German (12)	23	0.07
Polish (1,230)	3,671	10.71
Portuguese (12)	34	0.10
Romanian (48)	132	0.38
Russian (102)	345	1.01
Scandinavian (19)	62	0.18
Scotch-Irish (149)	582	1.70
Scottish (315)	1,474	4.30
Serbian (0)	20	0.06
Slavic (32)	174	0.51
Slovak (90)	214	0.62
Slovene (11)	11	0.03
Swedish (134)	512	1.49
Swiss (0)	91	0.27
Ukrainian (115)	354	1.03
Welsh (14)	285	0.83
Yugoslavian (68)	250	0.73

Hispanic Origin	Population	%
Hispanic or Latino (of any race)	1,551	4.47
Central American, ex. Mexican	72	0.21
Costa Rican	3	0.01
Guatemalan	25	0.07
Honduran	8	0.02
Nicaraguan	3	0.01
Panamanian	7	0.02
Salvadoran	26	0.07
Cuban	13	0.04
Dominican Republic	7	0.02
Mexican	1,145	3.30
Puerto Rican	145	0.42
South American	58	0.17
Argentinean	10	0.03
Bolivian	2	0.01
Chilean	7	0.02
Colombian	14	0.04
Ecuadorian	7	0.02
Paraguayan	2	0.01
Peruvian	5	0.01
Venezuelan	5	0.01
Other South American	6	0.02
Other Hispanic or Latino	111	0.32

Race*	Population	%
African-American/Black (653)	840	2.42
Not Hispanic (630)	793	2.29
Hispanic (23)	47	0.14
American Indian/Alaska Native (96)	324	0.93
Not Hispanic (75)	283	0.82
Hispanic (21)	41	0.12
Alaska Athabascan *(Ala. Nat.)* (0)	1	<0.01
Apache (2)	4	0.01
Blackfeet (2)	12	0.03
Canadian/French Am. Ind. (1)	6	0.02
Cherokee (3)	64	0.18
Chickasaw (1)	1	<0.01
Chippewa (32)	64	0.18
Choctaw (1)	3	0.01
Cree (0)	3	0.01
Iroquois (2)	5	0.01
Lumbee (8)	9	0.03
Mexican American Ind. (6)	11	0.03
Navajo (1)	3	0.01
Ottawa (1)	3	0.01
Potawatomi (6)	12	0.03
Shoshone (1)	1	<0.01
Sioux (2)	4	0.01
Asian (523)	775	2.23
Not Hispanic (506)	742	2.14
Hispanic (17)	33	0.10
Bangladeshi (1)	2	0.01
Burmese (1)	1	<0.01
Chinese, ex. Taiwanese (112)	141	0.41
Filipino (78)	142	0.41
Hmong (17)	19	0.05
Indian (127)	152	0.44
Indonesian (1)	6	0.02
Japanese (19)	73	0.21
Korean (105)	130	0.37

*Notes: † The Census 2010 population figure is used to calculate the percentages in the Hispanic Origin and Race categories. Ancestry percentages are based on the 2006-2010 American Community Survey population (not shown); ‡ Numbers in parentheses indicate the number of people reporting a single ancestry; * Numbers in parentheses indicate the number of persons reporting this race alone, not in combination with any other race; Please refer to the Explanation of Data for more information.*

	Population	%
Laotian (1)	3	0.01
Nepalese (1)	1	<0.01
Pakistani (4)	5	0.01
Sri Lankan (2)	2	0.01
Taiwanese (2)	3	0.01
Thai (13)	20	0.06
Vietnamese (24)	43	0.12
Hawaii Native/Pacific Islander (10)	46	0.13
Not Hispanic (6)	36	0.10
Hispanic (4)	10	0.03
Guamanian/Chamorro (5)	6	0.02
Native Hawaiian (1)	23	0.07
Samoan (1)	6	0.02
White (32,249)	32,905	94.88
Not Hispanic (31,311)	31,867	91.89
Hispanic (938)	1,038	2.99

Inkster

Place Type: City
County: Wayne
Population: 25,369†

Ancestry‡	Population	%
African, Sub-Saharan (612)	676	2.57
African (247)	311	1.18
Liberian (61)	61	0.23
Nigerian (232)	232	0.88
Sudanese (59)	59	0.22
Other Sub-Saharan African (13)	13	0.05
American (302)	302	1.15
Arab (392)	399	1.52
Arab (223)	223	0.85
Iraqi (68)	68	0.26
Lebanese (53)	60	0.23
Moroccan (14)	14	0.05
Palestinian (34)	34	0.13
Armenian (0)	50	0.19
Belgian (0)	9	0.03
British (0)	8	0.03
Cajun (5)	5	0.02
Canadian (10)	31	0.12
Czech (20)	20	0.08
Dutch (15)	121	0.46
English (111)	366	1.39
Estonian (0)	26	0.10
European (4)	11	0.04
Finnish (0)	83	0.32
French, ex. Basque (36)	183	0.70
French Canadian (19)	74	0.28
German (259)	991	3.77
Greek (9)	9	0.03
Hungarian (0)	32	0.12
Iranian (7)	7	0.03
Irish (227)	694	2.64
Italian (94)	351	1.33
Lithuanian (9)	55	0.21
Norwegian (13)	13	0.05
Polish (225)	576	2.19
Russian (20)	34	0.13
Scotch-Irish (26)	134	0.51
Scottish (35)	173	0.66
Serbian (21)	21	0.08
Slovak (13)	13	0.05
Slovene (0)	13	0.05
Swedish (14)	24	0.09
Welsh (0)	24	0.09
West Indian, ex. Hispanic (132)	149	0.57
Barbadian (11)	11	0.04
Belizean (50)	50	0.19
Jamaican (61)	70	0.27
West Indian (10)	18	0.07

Hispanic Origin	Population	%
Hispanic or Latino (of any race)	653	2.57
Central American, ex. Mexican	19	0.07
Guatemalan	1	<0.01
Honduran	5	0.02
Nicaraguan	1	<0.01
Panamanian	10	0.04
Salvadoran	2	0.01
Cuban	26	0.10
Dominican Republic	4	0.02
Mexican	374	1.47
Puerto Rican	134	0.53
South American	6	0.02
Chilean	3	0.01
Colombian	2	0.01
Peruvian	1	<0.01
Other Hispanic or Latino	90	0.35

Race*	Population	%
African-American/Black (18,569)	19,324	76.17
Not Hispanic (18,413)	19,106	75.31
Hispanic (156)	218	0.86
American Indian/Alaska Native (81)	384	1.51
Not Hispanic (70)	348	1.37
Hispanic (11)	36	0.14
Apache (0)	3	0.01
Blackfeet (3)	25	0.10
Canadian/French Am. Ind. (1)	1	<0.01
Cherokee (8)	86	0.34
Chippewa (8)	15	0.06
Choctaw (0)	5	0.02
Cree (1)	1	<0.01
Creek (0)	1	<0.01
Delaware (2)	2	0.01
Iroquois (2)	5	0.02
Mexican American Ind. (2)	2	0.01
Navajo (0)	2	0.01
Osage (0)	1	<0.01
Ottawa (0)	3	0.01
Seminole (0)	2	0.01
Shoshone (0)	1	<0.01
Sioux (1)	4	0.02
Asian (413)	519	2.05
Not Hispanic (409)	504	1.99
Hispanic (4)	15	0.06
Cambodian (1)	1	<0.01
Chinese, ex. Taiwanese (29)	35	0.14
Filipino (35)	57	0.22
Hmong (1)	1	<0.01
Indian (305)	315	1.24
Japanese (3)	9	0.04
Korean (6)	15	0.06
Malaysian (4)	4	0.02
Pakistani (9)	9	0.04
Sri Lankan (4)	4	0.02
Thai (1)	1	<0.01
Vietnamese (3)	4	0.02
Hawaii Native/Pacific Islander (14)	33	0.13
Not Hispanic (4)	16	0.06
Hispanic (10)	17	0.07
Guamanian/Chamorro (10)	12	0.05
Native Hawaiian (0)	3	0.01
Samoan (1)	1	<0.01
White (5,194)	5,866	23.12
Not Hispanic (4,959)	5,565	21.94
Hispanic (235)	301	1.19

Ionia

Place Type: City
County: Ionia
Population: 11,394†

Ancestry‡	Population	%
African, Sub-Saharan (118)	118	0.98
African (118)	118	0.98
American (752)	752	6.25
Arab (119)	133	1.11
Arab (0)	14	0.12
Egyptian (13)	13	0.11
Iraqi (9)	9	0.07
Lebanese (25)	25	0.21
Moroccan (72)	72	0.60
Australian (0)	9	0.07
Canadian (0)	29	0.24
Czech (22)	66	0.55
Czechoslovakian (25)	25	0.21
Danish (0)	20	0.17
Dutch (168)	575	4.78
English (214)	885	7.36
European (55)	55	0.46
Finnish (12)	12	0.10
French, ex. Basque (203)	651	5.41
French Canadian (36)	162	1.35
German (836)	2,507	20.84
Greek (0)	8	0.07
Hungarian (11)	24	0.20
Irish (227)	1,461	12.14
Italian (143)	369	3.07
Lithuanian (37)	81	0.67
Maltese (0)	9	0.07
Norwegian (15)	44	0.37
Pennsylvania German (0)	15	0.12
Polish (145)	783	6.51
Russian (35)	82	0.68
Scotch-Irish (17)	40	0.33
Scottish (86)	208	1.73
Serbian (8)	8	0.07
Slovak (0)	10	0.08
Swedish (18)	96	0.80
Swiss (14)	14	0.12
Welsh (0)	16	0.13
West Indian, ex. Hispanic (12)	21	0.17
Jamaican (12)	21	0.17
Yugoslavian (9)	9	0.07

Hispanic Origin	Population	%
Hispanic or Latino (of any race)	879	7.71
Central American, ex. Mexican	17	0.15
Costa Rican	1	0.01
Guatemalan	7	0.06
Honduran	6	0.05
Salvadoran	3	0.03
Cuban	12	0.11
Dominican Republic	11	0.10
Mexican	597	5.24
Puerto Rican	45	0.39
South American	2	0.02
Colombian	1	0.01
Ecuadorian	1	0.01
Other Hispanic or Latino	195	1.71

Race*	Population	%
African-American/Black (2,846)	2,905	25.50
Not Hispanic (2,795)	2,843	24.95
Hispanic (51)	62	0.54
American Indian/Alaska Native (80)	136	1.19
Not Hispanic (58)	109	0.96
Hispanic (22)	27	0.24
Apache (0)	2	0.02
Blackfeet (0)	3	0.03
Canadian/French Am. Ind. (1)	1	0.01
Cherokee (0)	4	0.04
Chippewa (8)	16	0.14
Choctaw (0)	1	0.01
Cree (1)	1	0.01
Lumbee (1)	1	0.01
Mexican American Ind. (2)	2	0.02
Ottawa (1)	4	0.04
Potawatomi (0)	6	0.05
Sioux (0)	5	0.04
Asian (46)	68	0.60
Not Hispanic (40)	61	0.54
Hispanic (6)	7	0.06
Chinese, ex. Taiwanese (2)	4	0.04
Filipino (2)	9	0.08
Indian (24)	25	0.22
Japanese (1)	1	0.01
Korean (7)	15	0.13
Taiwanese (1)	3	0.03
Vietnamese (0)	1	0.01
Hawaii Native/Pacific Islander (2)	9	0.08
Not Hispanic (2)	7	0.06
Hispanic (0)	2	0.02
Guamanian/Chamorro (1)	1	0.01
Native Hawaiian (0)	4	0.04
White (8,079)	8,237	72.29

*Notes: † The Census 2010 population figure is used to calculate the percentages in the Hispanic Origin and Race categories. Ancestry percentages are based on the 2006-2010 American Community Survey population (not shown); ‡ Numbers in parentheses indicate the number of people reporting a single ancestry; * Numbers in parentheses indicate the number of persons reporting this race alone, not in combination with any other race; Please refer to the Explanation of Data for more information.*

Not Hispanic (7,504)	7,612	66.81
Hispanic (575)	625	5.49

Iron Mountain

Place Type: City
County: Dickinson
Population: 7,624†

Ancestry‡	Population	%
Alsatian (0)	10	0.13
American (138)	138	1.77
Arab (11)	11	0.14
Other Arab (11)	11	0.14
Austrian (25)	95	1.22
Belgian (0)	114	1.46
Bulgarian (0)	9	0.12
Canadian (0)	21	0.27
Croatian (32)	53	0.68
Czech (16)	90	1.16
Czechoslovakian (22)	102	1.31
Danish (0)	20	0.26
Dutch (76)	190	2.44
English (156)	1,006	12.92
Finnish (261)	697	8.95
French, ex. Basque (167)	1,028	13.20
French Canadian (130)	400	5.14
German (433)	2,121	27.24
Hungarian (0)	55	0.71
Irish (179)	874	11.22
Italian (323)	1,252	16.08
Northern European (9)	24	0.31
Norwegian (41)	262	3.36
Polish (104)	623	8.00
Romanian (9)	9	0.12
Russian (15)	34	0.44
Scotch-Irish (25)	121	1.55
Scottish (25)	158	2.03
Slovak (0)	14	0.18
Slovene (11)	21	0.27
Swedish (369)	1,082	13.89
Swiss (0)	28	0.36
Welsh (10)	10	0.13

Hispanic Origin	Population	%
Hispanic or Latino (of any race)	122	1.60
Central American, ex. Mexican	8	0.10
Guatemalan	1	0.01
Salvadoran	7	0.09
Cuban	2	0.03
Dominican Republic	4	0.05
Mexican	66	0.87
Puerto Rican	23	0.30
South American	7	0.09
Colombian	4	0.05
Paraguayan	1	0.01
Peruvian	2	0.03
Other Hispanic or Latino	12	0.16

Race*	Population	%
African-American/Black (35)	70	0.92
Not Hispanic (34)	69	0.91
Hispanic (1)	1	0.01
American Indian/Alaska Native (48)	108	1.42
Not Hispanic (45)	92	1.21
Hispanic (3)	16	0.21
Apache (3)	3	0.04
Blackfeet (1)	1	0.01
Cherokee (5)	7	0.09
Chippewa (13)	30	0.39
Comanche (0)	1	0.01
Iroquois (1)	4	0.05
Menominee (0)	1	0.01
Mexican American Ind. (0)	2	0.03
Navajo (1)	2	0.03
Ottawa (5)	6	0.08
Potawatomi (1)	2	0.03
Seminole (0)	1	0.01
Sioux (3)	9	0.12
South American Ind. (0)	1	0.01
Asian (50)	69	0.91
Not Hispanic (50)	69	0.91
Chinese, ex. Taiwanese (26)	35	0.46
Filipino (3)	4	0.05
Indian (4)	6	0.08
Japanese (1)	2	0.03
Korean (9)	11	0.14
Thai (1)	1	0.01
Vietnamese (5)	5	0.07
Hawaii Native/Pacific Islander (2)	4	0.05
Not Hispanic (2)	3	0.04
Hispanic (0)	1	0.01
Guamanian/Chamorro (1)	2	0.03
White (7,343)	7,463	97.89
Not Hispanic (7,272)	7,366	96.62
Hispanic (71)	97	1.27

Jackson

Place Type: City
County: Jackson
Population: 33,534†

Ancestry‡	Population	%
African, Sub-Saharan (1,508)	1,671	4.86
African (1,484)	1,634	4.76
Ethiopian (24)	24	0.07
Senegalese (0)	13	0.04
American (2,829)	2,829	8.24
Arab (13)	13	0.04
Lebanese (13)	13	0.04
Armenian (17)	25	0.07
Austrian (0)	20	0.06
Belgian (39)	156	0.45
British (46)	163	0.47
Canadian (71)	94	0.27
Croatian (62)	62	0.18
Czech (78)	132	0.38
Danish (0)	19	0.06
Dutch (133)	735	2.14
Eastern European (18)	18	0.05
English (2,541)	5,182	15.09
European (200)	247	0.72
Finnish (7)	57	0.17
French, ex. Basque (107)	1,232	3.59
French Canadian (167)	212	0.62
German (1,792)	6,642	19.34
Greek (38)	148	0.43
Hungarian (26)	260	0.76
Irish (693)	4,423	12.88
Israeli (31)	59	0.17
Italian (284)	718	2.09
Lithuanian (66)	108	0.31
Maltese (0)	9	0.03
Northern European (38)	38	0.11
Norwegian (18)	136	0.40
Pennsylvania German (0)	56	0.16
Polish (749)	2,059	5.99
Portuguese (11)	102	0.30
Romanian (11)	21	0.06
Russian (46)	156	0.45
Scandinavian (48)	87	0.25
Scotch-Irish (421)	984	2.86
Scottish (115)	580	1.69
Slovak (11)	36	0.10
Swedish (75)	241	0.70
Swiss (10)	159	0.46
Turkish (0)	9	0.03
Ukrainian (15)	52	0.15
Welsh (53)	190	0.55
West Indian, ex. Hispanic (53)	143	0.42
Barbadian (0)	14	0.04
Haitian (13)	32	0.09
Jamaican (40)	97	0.28
Yugoslavian (17)	17	0.05

Hispanic Origin	Population	%
Hispanic or Latino (of any race)	1,769	5.28
Central American, ex. Mexican	24	0.07
Costa Rican	2	0.01
Guatemalan	5	0.01
Honduran	6	0.02
Nicaraguan	6	0.02
Panamanian	4	0.01
Salvadoran	1	<0.01
Cuban	15	0.04
Dominican Republic	2	0.01
Mexican	1,401	4.18
Puerto Rican	168	0.50
South American	25	0.07
Argentinean	2	0.01
Bolivian	6	0.02
Colombian	9	0.03
Peruvian	8	0.02
Other Hispanic or Latino	134	0.40

Race*	Population	%
African-American/Black (6,857)	8,297	24.74
Not Hispanic (6,727)	8,036	23.96
Hispanic (130)	261	0.78
American Indian/Alaska Native (120)	535	1.60
Not Hispanic (107)	463	1.38
Hispanic (13)	72	0.21
Apache (0)	2	0.01
Blackfeet (3)	25	0.07
Canadian/French Am. Ind. (5)	9	0.03
Cherokee (12)	133	0.40
Cheyenne (0)	3	0.01
Chippewa (16)	43	0.13
Choctaw (0)	4	0.01
Comanche (2)	2	0.01
Creek (0)	2	0.01
Crow (0)	2	0.01
Delaware (0)	1	<0.01
Iroquois (1)	5	0.01
Lumbee (2)	2	0.01
Mexican American Ind. (3)	8	0.02
Ottawa (7)	9	0.03
Potawatomi (9)	31	0.09
Seminole (0)	4	0.01
Sioux (1)	9	0.03
South American Ind. (0)	6	0.02
Yaqui (0)	1	<0.01
Asian (240)	319	0.95
Not Hispanic (235)	304	0.91
Hispanic (5)	15	0.04
Chinese, ex. Taiwanese (37)	39	0.12
Filipino (25)	45	0.13
Indian (67)	77	0.23
Indonesian (1)	1	<0.01
Japanese (10)	32	0.10
Korean (21)	30	0.09
Laotian (4)	4	0.01
Pakistani (19)	22	0.07
Taiwanese (1)	1	<0.01
Thai (1)	3	0.01
Vietnamese (42)	48	0.14
Hawaii Native/Pacific Islander (7)	31	0.09
Not Hispanic (7)	22	0.07
Hispanic (0)	9	0.03
Guamanian/Chamorro (1)	1	<0.01
Native Hawaiian (4)	6	0.02
Samoan (1)	4	0.01
Tongan (0)	3	0.01
White (23,947)	25,620	76.40
Not Hispanic (23,062)	24,521	73.12
Hispanic (885)	1,099	3.28

Jenison

Place Type: CDP
County: Ottawa
Population: 16,538†

Ancestry‡	Population	%
American (1,031)	1,031	5.98
Arab (14)	54	0.31
Lebanese (14)	43	0.25
Syrian (0)	11	0.06
Austrian (5)	37	0.21

*Notes: † The Census 2010 population figure is used to calculate the percentages in the Hispanic Origin and Race categories. Ancestry percentages are based on the 2006-2010 American Community Survey population (not shown); ‡ Numbers in parentheses indicate the number of people reporting a single ancestry; * Numbers in parentheses indicate the number of persons reporting this race alone, not in combination with any other race; Please refer to the Explanation of Data for more information.*

Ancestry	Population	%
Belgian (0)	31	0.18
British (71)	82	0.48
Canadian (0)	63	0.37
Croatian (19)	19	0.11
Czech (0)	21	0.12
Czechoslovakian (0)	16	0.09
Danish (0)	78	0.45
Dutch (4,519)	7,138	41.41
English (493)	1,922	11.15
European (263)	277	1.61
Finnish (0)	10	0.06
French, ex. Basque (51)	667	3.87
French Canadian (57)	207	1.20
German (887)	4,046	23.47
Greek (10)	82	0.48
Hungarian (27)	99	0.57
Irish (322)	1,970	11.43
Italian (56)	284	1.65
Lithuanian (14)	69	0.40
Norwegian (18)	165	0.96
Pennsylvania German (16)	30	0.17
Polish (261)	850	4.93
Romanian (24)	48	0.28
Russian (20)	128	0.74
Scotch-Irish (68)	196	1.14
Scottish (10)	323	1.87
Slovene (15)	25	0.15
Swedish (81)	285	1.65
Swiss (0)	17	0.10
Welsh (0)	76	0.44
West Indian, ex. Hispanic (0)	18	0.10
Bermudan (0)	18	0.10
Yugoslavian (0)	20	0.12

Hispanic Origin	Population	%
Hispanic or Latino (of any race)	416	2.52
Central American, ex. Mexican	28	0.17
Costa Rican	7	0.04
Guatemalan	10	0.06
Honduran	3	0.02
Salvadoran	8	0.05
Cuban	29	0.18
Dominican Republic	9	0.05
Mexican	262	1.58
Puerto Rican	42	0.25
South American	8	0.05
Bolivian	2	0.01
Chilean	4	0.02
Colombian	1	0.01
Peruvian	1	0.01
Other Hispanic or Latino	38	0.23

Race*	Population	%
African-American/Black (126)	214	1.29
Not Hispanic (113)	188	1.14
Hispanic (13)	26	0.16
American Indian/Alaska Native (44)	125	0.76
Not Hispanic (38)	109	0.66
Hispanic (6)	16	0.10
Apache (0)	3	0.02
Canadian/French Am. Ind. (1)	2	0.01
Cherokee (1)	6	0.04
Chippewa (5)	9	0.05
Choctaw (0)	4	0.02
Iroquois (1)	3	0.02
Mexican American Ind. (6)	7	0.04
Navajo (2)	2	0.01
Ottawa (6)	9	0.05
Potawatomi (7)	19	0.11
Sioux (1)	7	0.04
Asian (143)	199	1.20
Not Hispanic (143)	194	1.17
Hispanic (0)	5	0.03
Burmese (1)	1	0.01
Cambodian (4)	5	0.03
Chinese, ex. Taiwanese (16)	23	0.14
Filipino (12)	29	0.18
Hmong (1)	1	0.01
Indian (11)	14	0.08
Indonesian (1)	2	0.01
Japanese (3)	7	0.04
Korean (39)	57	0.34
Laotian (0)	2	0.01
Thai (4)	6	0.04
Vietnamese (43)	54	0.33
Hawaii Native/Pacific Islander (2)	7	0.04
Not Hispanic (2)	7	0.04
Native Hawaiian (1)	4	0.02
Samoan (1)	1	0.01
White (15,878)	16,114	97.44
Not Hispanic (15,626)	15,814	95.62
Hispanic (252)	300	1.81

Kalamazoo

Place Type: Charter Township
County: Kalamazoo
Population: 21,918†

Ancestry‡	Population	%
African, Sub-Saharan (264)	291	1.34
African (233)	244	1.12
Ghanaian (7)	15	0.07
Nigerian (8)	16	0.07
South African (16)	16	0.07
American (963)	963	4.42
Arab (31)	40	0.18
Arab (9)	18	0.08
Egyptian (11)	11	0.05
Lebanese (11)	11	0.05
Armenian (0)	34	0.16
Austrian (12)	12	0.06
Belgian (9)	169	0.78
Brazilian (9)	18	0.08
British (40)	108	0.50
Cajun (17)	41	0.19
Canadian (15)	39	0.18
Celtic (0)	16	0.07
Croatian (39)	68	0.31
Czech (45)	159	0.73
Czechoslovakian (14)	38	0.17
Danish (19)	82	0.38
Dutch (1,563)	2,979	13.67
Eastern European (36)	36	0.17
English (1,067)	2,915	13.38
European (115)	132	0.61
Finnish (65)	197	0.90
French, ex. Basque (39)	687	3.15
French Canadian (63)	214	0.98
German (1,107)	4,159	19.09
Greek (49)	113	0.52
Hungarian (0)	96	0.44
Irish (541)	2,901	13.31
Israeli (111)	111	0.51
Italian (235)	858	3.94
Latvian (47)	101	0.46
Lithuanian (0)	53	0.24
Macedonian (10)	26	0.12
Northern European (11)	11	0.05
Norwegian (22)	129	0.59
Pennsylvania German (8)	33	0.15
Polish (297)	1,028	4.72
Romanian (19)	19	0.09
Russian (12)	80	0.37
Scandinavian (0)	14	0.06
Scotch-Irish (101)	352	1.62
Scottish (225)	659	3.02
Slovak (0)	11	0.05
Slovene (12)	12	0.06
Swedish (126)	536	2.46
Swiss (0)	30	0.14
Ukrainian (13)	13	0.06
Welsh (66)	163	0.75
West Indian, ex. Hispanic (14)	24	0.11
British West Indian (0)	10	0.05
Trinidadian/Tobagonian (14)	14	0.06
Yugoslavian (0)	17	0.08

Hispanic Origin	Population	%
Hispanic or Latino (of any race)	1,004	4.58
Central American, ex. Mexican	42	0.19
Costa Rican	5	0.02
Guatemalan	21	0.10
Honduran	6	0.03
Nicaraguan	1	<0.01
Panamanian	6	0.03
Salvadoran	3	0.01
Cuban	28	0.13
Dominican Republic	9	0.04
Mexican	748	3.41
Puerto Rican	61	0.28
South American	18	0.08
Argentinean	2	0.01
Colombian	8	0.04
Ecuadorian	2	0.01
Peruvian	2	0.01
Venezuelan	4	0.02
Other Hispanic or Latino	98	0.45

Race*	Population	%
African-American/Black (3,605)	4,210	19.21
Not Hispanic (3,547)	4,102	18.72
Hispanic (58)	108	0.49
American Indian/Alaska Native (90)	348	1.59
Not Hispanic (81)	314	1.43
Hispanic (9)	34	0.16
Apache (0)	1	<0.01
Arapaho (3)	3	0.01
Blackfeet (3)	18	0.08
Canadian/French Am. Ind. (1)	1	<0.01
Central American Ind. (2)	5	0.02
Cherokee (8)	54	0.25
Cheyenne (1)	1	<0.01
Chippewa (17)	32	0.15
Choctaw (0)	10	0.05
Delaware (0)	4	0.02
Hopi (1)	1	<0.01
Inupiat *(Alaska Native)* (1)	1	<0.01
Iroquois (2)	9	0.04
Lumbee (1)	1	<0.01
Menominee (0)	2	0.01
Mexican American Ind. (3)	5	0.02
Ottawa (13)	24	0.11
Potawatomi (9)	18	0.08
Pueblo (0)	1	<0.01
Seminole (0)	4	0.02
Shoshone (0)	1	<0.01
Sioux (1)	2	0.01
South American Ind. (0)	1	<0.01
Asian (289)	425	1.94
Not Hispanic (288)	413	1.88
Hispanic (1)	12	0.05
Bangladeshi (3)	3	0.01
Burmese (0)	2	0.01
Chinese, ex. Taiwanese (39)	51	0.23
Filipino (66)	90	0.41
Indian (51)	68	0.31
Indonesian (1)	1	<0.01
Japanese (17)	52	0.24
Korean (36)	49	0.22
Laotian (4)	5	0.02
Malaysian (5)	6	0.03
Nepalese (4)	4	0.02
Pakistani (6)	6	0.03
Taiwanese (0)	1	<0.01
Thai (10)	19	0.09
Vietnamese (31)	35	0.16
Hawaii Native/Pacific Islander (3)	25	0.11
Not Hispanic (3)	23	0.10
Hispanic (0)	2	0.01
Guamanian/Chamorro (2)	3	0.01
Native Hawaiian (1)	8	0.04
Samoan (0)	2	0.01
White (16,589)	17,408	79.42
Not Hispanic (16,140)	16,868	76.96
Hispanic (449)	540	2.46

SECTION TWO

*Notes: † The Census 2010 population figure is used to calculate the percentages in the Hispanic Origin and Race categories. Ancestry percentages are based on the 2006-2010 American Community Survey population (not shown); ‡ Numbers in parentheses indicate the number of people reporting a single ancestry; * Numbers in parentheses indicate the number of persons reporting this race alone, not in combination with any other race; Please refer to the Explanation of Data for more information.*

Kalamazoo

Place Type: City
County: Kalamazoo
Population: 74,262†

Ancestry‡	Population	%
African, Sub-Saharan (389)	447	0.60
African (222)	280	0.38
Kenyan (23)	23	0.03
South African (37)	37	0.05
Ugandan (61)	61	0.08
Zimbabwean (46)	46	0.06
Albanian (17)	17	0.02
American (1,987)	1,987	2.67
Arab (475)	503	0.68
Arab (210)	217	0.29
Iraqi (59)	59	0.08
Lebanese (74)	95	0.13
Other Arab (132)	132	0.18
Armenian (37)	114	0.15
Assyrian/Chaldean/Syriac (26)	40	0.05
Australian (0)	35	0.05
Austrian (86)	315	0.42
Belgian (13)	193	0.26
British (180)	308	0.41
Bulgarian (0)	55	0.07
Cajun (0)	9	0.01
Canadian (69)	228	0.31
Celtic (47)	47	0.06
Croatian (59)	85	0.11
Czech (128)	400	0.54
Czechoslovakian (68)	123	0.17
Danish (46)	223	0.30
Dutch (2,297)	6,165	8.30
Eastern European (172)	180	0.24
English (2,037)	7,733	10.41
European (629)	758	1.02
Finnish (55)	307	0.41
French, ex. Basque (287)	2,458	3.31
French Canadian (185)	938	1.26
German (4,772)	15,282	20.56
Greek (95)	193	0.26
Hungarian (128)	506	0.68
Icelander (25)	65	0.09
Iranian (33)	44	0.06
Irish (1,856)	8,753	11.78
Israeli (14)	14	0.02
Italian (787)	2,422	3.26
Latvian (76)	146	0.20
Lithuanian (32)	226	0.30
Luxemburger (0)	24	0.03
Macedonian (40)	40	0.05
Northern European (0)	5	0.01
Norwegian (240)	843	1.13
Pennsylvania German (13)	51	0.07
Polish (1,130)	4,217	5.67
Portuguese (0)	37	0.05
Romanian (49)	91	0.12
Russian (44)	327	0.44
Scandinavian (82)	135	0.18
Scotch-Irish (385)	1,279	1.72
Scottish (528)	1,932	2.60
Serbian (2)	19	0.03
Slavic (21)	21	0.03
Slovak (46)	138	0.19
Slovene (0)	29	0.04
Swedish (260)	1,224	1.65
Swiss (23)	122	0.16
Ukrainian (49)	173	0.23
Welsh (134)	534	0.72
West Indian, ex. Hispanic (0)	26	0.03
Jamaican (0)	26	0.03
Yugoslavian (30)	91	0.12

Hispanic Origin	Population	%
Hispanic or Latino (of any race)	4,736	6.38
Central American, ex. Mexican	160	0.22
Costa Rican	5	0.01
Guatemalan	73	0.10
Honduran	18	0.02
Nicaraguan	5	0.01
Panamanian	27	0.04
Salvadoran	32	0.04
Cuban	108	0.15
Dominican Republic	189	0.25
Mexican	3,430	4.62
Puerto Rican	340	0.46
South American	138	0.19
Argentinean	42	0.06
Bolivian	7	0.01
Chilean	7	0.01
Colombian	27	0.04
Ecuadorian	19	0.03
Paraguayan	1	<0.01
Peruvian	11	0.01
Uruguayan	1	<0.01
Venezuelan	22	0.03
Other South American	1	<0.01
Other Hispanic or Latino	371	0.50

Race*	Population	%
African-American/Black (16,460)	18,823	25.35
Not Hispanic (16,117)	18,255	24.58
Hispanic (343)	568	0.76
American Indian/Alaska Native (384)	1,341	1.81
Not Hispanic (312)	1,134	1.53
Hispanic (72)	207	0.28
Alaska Athabascan *(Ala. Nat.)* (1)	2	<0.01
Aleut *(Alaska Native)* (1)	1	<0.01
Apache (3)	14	0.02
Blackfeet (8)	40	0.05
Canadian/French Am. Ind. (2)	5	0.01
Central American Ind. (1)	1	<0.01
Cherokee (30)	202	0.27
Cheyenne (0)	2	<0.01
Chickasaw (0)	1	<0.01
Chippewa (63)	116	0.16
Choctaw (4)	23	0.03
Comanche (2)	4	0.01
Cree (1)	2	<0.01
Creek (2)	11	0.01
Crow (2)	2	<0.01
Delaware (0)	2	<0.01
Iroquois (6)	17	0.02
Lumbee (1)	1	<0.01
Mexican American Ind. (13)	25	0.03
Navajo (7)	9	0.01
Ottawa (20)	23	0.03
Potawatomi (34)	81	0.11
Pueblo (4)	4	0.01
Seminole (0)	2	<0.01
Shoshone (1)	1	<0.01
Sioux (7)	17	0.02
South American Ind. (1)	2	<0.01
Spanish American Ind. (0)	1	<0.01
Tlingit-Haida *(Alaska Native)* (0)	2	<0.01
Yaqui (6)	10	0.01
Asian (1,279)	1,766	2.38
Not Hispanic (1,266)	1,708	2.30
Hispanic (13)	58	0.08
Bangladeshi (12)	12	0.02
Burmese (0)	1	<0.01
Cambodian (10)	22	0.03
Chinese, ex. Taiwanese (270)	325	0.44
Filipino (80)	178	0.24
Hmong (6)	6	0.01
Indian (396)	466	0.63
Indonesian (10)	20	0.03
Japanese (76)	125	0.17
Korean (161)	222	0.30
Laotian (6)	13	0.02
Malaysian (36)	43	0.06
Nepalese (10)	11	0.01
Pakistani (44)	51	0.07
Sri Lankan (2)	3	<0.01
Taiwanese (21)	22	0.03
Thai (21)	60	0.08
Vietnamese (72)	94	0.13
Hawaii Native/Pacific Islander (27)	123	0.17
Not Hispanic (20)	91	0.12
Hispanic (7)	32	0.04
Fijian (1)	1	<0.01
Guamanian/Chamorro (5)	6	0.01
Native Hawaiian (8)	28	0.04
Samoan (4)	15	0.02
Tongan (0)	1	<0.01
White (50,604)	53,580	72.15
Not Hispanic (48,752)	51,354	69.15
Hispanic (1,852)	2,226	3.00

Kentwood

Place Type: City
County: Kent
Population: 48,707†

Ancestry‡	Population	%
African, Sub-Saharan (441)	552	1.14
African (236)	290	0.60
Ethiopian (92)	104	0.22
Ghanaian (2)	2	<0.01
Liberian (2)	38	0.08
Somalian (18)	18	0.04
Other Sub-Saharan African (91)	100	0.21
Albanian (25)	25	0.05
American (1,314)	1,314	2.72
Arab (315)	474	0.98
Arab (142)	142	0.29
Jordanian (26)	26	0.05
Lebanese (53)	129	0.27
Syrian (39)	122	0.25
Other Arab (55)	55	0.11
Armenian (0)	12	0.02
Assyrian/Chaldean/Syriac (48)	48	0.10
Australian (10)	21	0.04
Austrian (0)	101	0.21
Belgian (32)	201	0.42
British (53)	85	0.18
Bulgarian (0)	11	0.02
Canadian (42)	141	0.29
Croatian (33)	49	0.10
Czech (7)	112	0.23
Czechoslovakian (57)	162	0.34
Danish (25)	280	0.58
Dutch (5,010)	8,913	18.48
Eastern European (46)	46	0.10
English (989)	4,385	9.09
European (450)	497	1.03
Finnish (31)	206	0.43
French, ex. Basque (166)	1,724	3.57
French Canadian (171)	437	0.91
German (2,324)	9,092	18.85
Greek (53)	116	0.24
Hungarian (22)	172	0.36
Irish (952)	4,346	9.01
Italian (282)	887	1.84
Latvian (51)	64	0.13
Lithuanian (82)	194	0.40
Northern European (10)	10	0.02
Norwegian (180)	517	1.07
Pennsylvania German (34)	54	0.11
Polish (674)	2,328	4.83
Portuguese (0)	14	0.03
Romanian (20)	20	0.04
Russian (155)	266	0.55
Scandinavian (67)	109	0.23
Scotch-Irish (280)	603	1.25
Scottish (288)	1,095	2.27
Serbian (18)	74	0.15
Slavic (0)	10	0.02
Slovak (0)	7	0.01
Swedish (125)	832	1.72
Swiss (6)	135	0.28
Ukrainian (20)	31	0.06
Welsh (0)	156	0.32
West Indian, ex. Hispanic (57)	57	0.12
Bahamian (13)	13	0.03
Haitian (10)	10	0.02
Jamaican (34)	34	0.07

*Notes: † The Census 2010 population figure is used to calculate the percentages in the Hispanic Origin and Race categories. Ancestry percentages are based on the 2006-2010 American Community Survey population (not shown); ‡ Numbers in parentheses indicate the number of people reporting a single ancestry; * Numbers in parentheses indicate the number of persons reporting this race alone, not in combination with any other race; Please refer to the Explanation of Data for more information.*

Yugoslavian (1,345)	1,378	2.86

Hispanic Origin	Population	%
Hispanic or Latino (of any race)	4,120	8.46
Central American, ex. Mexican	273	0.56
Costa Rican	5	0.01
Guatemalan	102	0.21
Honduran	58	0.12
Nicaraguan	9	0.02
Panamanian	8	0.02
Salvadoran	88	0.18
Other Central American	3	0.01
Cuban	151	0.31
Dominican Republic	308	0.63
Mexican	2,450	5.03
Puerto Rican	532	1.09
South American	187	0.38
Argentinean	8	0.02
Bolivian	19	0.04
Chilean	19	0.04
Colombian	41	0.08
Ecuadorian	21	0.04
Paraguayan	6	0.01
Peruvian	60	0.12
Uruguayan	1	<0.01
Venezuelan	12	0.02
Other Hispanic or Latino	219	0.45

Race*	Population	%
African-American/Black (7,516)	8,712	17.89
Not Hispanic (7,283)	8,303	17.05
Hispanic (233)	409	0.84
American Indian/Alaska Native (199)	605	1.24
Not Hispanic (172)	529	1.09
Hispanic (27)	76	0.16
Apache (3)	4	0.01
Blackfeet (1)	18	0.04
Canadian/French Am. Ind. (0)	3	0.01
Central American Ind. (0)	1	<0.01
Cherokee (14)	73	0.15
Chickasaw (3)	6	0.01
Chippewa (47)	94	0.19
Choctaw (1)	7	0.01
Colville (1)	2	<0.01
Cree (0)	1	<0.01
Crow (0)	1	<0.01
Delaware (0)	2	<0.01
Iroquois (0)	2	<0.01
Lumbee (0)	1	<0.01
Mexican American Ind. (9)	16	0.03
Navajo (2)	3	0.01
Osage (0)	2	<0.01
Ottawa (17)	36	0.07
Potawatomi (17)	33	0.07
Pueblo (2)	5	0.01
Seminole (0)	3	0.01
Sioux (3)	18	0.04
South American Ind. (2)	3	0.01
Ute (0)	1	<0.01
Asian (3,227)	3,602	7.40
Not Hispanic (3,215)	3,559	7.31
Hispanic (12)	43	0.09
Bangladeshi (7)	7	0.01
Bhutanese (12)	12	0.02
Burmese (32)	36	0.07
Cambodian (5)	7	0.01
Chinese, ex. Taiwanese (314)	422	0.87
Filipino (123)	184	0.38
Hmong (11)	12	0.02
Indian (498)	538	1.10
Indonesian (7)	12	0.02
Japanese (57)	106	0.22
Korean (286)	353	0.72
Laotian (5)	7	0.01
Malaysian (5)	6	0.01
Nepalese (7)	9	0.02
Pakistani (58)	73	0.15
Sri Lankan (9)	11	0.02
Taiwanese (8)	11	0.02
Thai (17)	35	0.07
Vietnamese (1,671)	1,786	3.67
Hawaii Native/Pacific Islander (25)	64	0.13
Not Hispanic (15)	46	0.09
Hispanic (10)	18	0.04
Guamanian/Chamorro (8)	12	0.02
Marshallese (0)	2	<0.01
Native Hawaiian (7)	20	0.04
Samoan (5)	8	0.02
Tongan (0)	1	<0.01
White (34,152)	35,753	73.40
Not Hispanic (32,315)	33,585	68.95
Hispanic (1,837)	2,168	4.45

Kimball

Place Type: Township
County: St. Clair
Population: 9,358†

Ancestry‡	Population	%
American (426)	426	4.56
Arab (0)	28	0.30
Lebanese (0)	28	0.30
Austrian (0)	9	0.10
Belgian (23)	102	1.09
British (0)	29	0.31
Canadian (28)	59	0.63
Czech (0)	36	0.38
Czechoslovakian (0)	51	0.55
Dutch (12)	164	1.75
English (285)	1,570	16.79
European (36)	36	0.38
Finnish (0)	14	0.15
French, ex. Basque (53)	614	6.57
French Canadian (50)	331	3.54
German (757)	3,094	33.09
Greek (22)	44	0.47
Hungarian (0)	81	0.87
Irish (342)	1,876	20.06
Italian (112)	665	7.11
Macedonian (17)	17	0.18
Norwegian (16)	133	1.42
Pennsylvania German (0)	16	0.17
Polish (404)	1,136	12.15
Romanian (0)	18	0.19
Russian (64)	156	1.67
Scandinavian (0)	13	0.14
Scotch-Irish (43)	228	2.44
Scottish (39)	377	4.03
Serbian (0)	20	0.21
Swedish (36)	69	0.74
Swiss (0)	19	0.20
Ukrainian (0)	11	0.12
Welsh (0)	7	0.07

Hispanic Origin	Population	%
Hispanic or Latino (of any race)	202	2.16
Central American, ex. Mexican	3	0.03
Guatemalan	3	0.03
Cuban	1	0.01
Mexican	181	1.93
Puerto Rican	3	0.03
South American	5	0.05
Colombian	1	0.01
Ecuadorian	1	0.01
Peruvian	3	0.03
Other Hispanic or Latino	9	0.10

Race*	Population	%
African-American/Black (112)	163	1.74
Not Hispanic (112)	161	1.72
Hispanic (0)	2	0.02
American Indian/Alaska Native (41)	115	1.23
Not Hispanic (37)	109	1.16
Hispanic (4)	6	0.06
Blackfeet (2)	4	0.04
Canadian/French Am. Ind. (1)	3	0.03
Cherokee (2)	7	0.07
Cheyenne (0)	6	0.06
Chippewa (8)	22	0.24
Choctaw (1)	1	0.01
Iroquois (2)	5	0.05
Ottawa (0)	1	0.01
Sioux (0)	1	0.01
Asian (21)	45	0.48
Not Hispanic (21)	40	0.43
Hispanic (0)	5	0.05
Chinese, ex. Taiwanese (5)	10	0.11
Filipino (6)	12	0.13
Indian (1)	4	0.04
Japanese (2)	3	0.03
Korean (2)	6	0.06
Pakistani (0)	1	0.01
Taiwanese (1)	1	0.01
Thai (3)	5	0.05
White (8,995)	9,153	97.81
Not Hispanic (8,842)	8,980	95.96
Hispanic (153)	173	1.85

Kinross

Place Type: Charter Township
County: Chippewa
Population: 7,561†

Ancestry‡	Population	%
African, Sub-Saharan (286)	319	3.97
African (236)	269	3.34
Other Sub-Saharan African (50)	50	0.62
American (166)	166	2.06
Arab (167)	173	2.15
Arab (9)	9	0.11
Lebanese (6)	12	0.15
Moroccan (152)	152	1.89
Austrian (0)	4	0.05
Brazilian (8)	8	0.10
British (7)	7	0.09
Cajun (20)	45	0.56
Canadian (48)	69	0.86
Croatian (0)	10	0.12
Czech (9)	30	0.37
Czechoslovakian (13)	13	0.16
Dutch (35)	130	1.62
English (130)	681	8.47
European (41)	55	0.68
Finnish (69)	149	1.85
French, ex. Basque (119)	439	5.46
French Canadian (75)	129	1.60
German (415)	1,295	16.10
Greek (3)	3	0.04
Irish (211)	725	9.01
Italian (105)	232	2.88
Latvian (0)	9	0.11
Norwegian (0)	91	1.13
Polish (66)	284	3.53
Romanian (11)	24	0.30
Russian (11)	46	0.57
Scandinavian (9)	31	0.39
Scotch-Irish (28)	113	1.40
Scottish (16)	121	1.50
Swedish (55)	98	1.22
Ukrainian (12)	21	0.26
Welsh (0)	27	0.34
West Indian, ex. Hispanic (0)	35	0.44
British West Indian (0)	12	0.15
Haitian (0)	12	0.15
Jamaican (0)	11	0.14
Yugoslavian (11)	11	0.14

Hispanic Origin	Population	%
Hispanic or Latino (of any race)	135	1.79
Central American, ex. Mexican	2	0.03
Honduran	1	0.01
Panamanian	1	0.01
Cuban	5	0.07
Mexican	90	1.19
Puerto Rican	17	0.22
South American	2	0.03
Colombian	1	0.01
Peruvian	1	0.01

*Notes: † The Census 2010 population figure is used to calculate the percentages in the Hispanic Origin and Race categories. Ancestry percentages are based on the 2006-2010 American Community Survey population (not shown); ‡ Numbers in parentheses indicate the number of people reporting a single ancestry; * Numbers in parentheses indicate the number of persons reporting this race alone, not in combination with any other race; Please refer to the Explanation of Data for more information.*

Other Hispanic or Latino	19	0.25

Race*	Population	%
African-American/Black (2,372)	2,395	31.68
Not Hispanic (2,368)	2,390	31.61
Hispanic (4)	5	0.07
American Indian/Alaska Native (845)	1,077	14.24
Not Hispanic (822)	1,044	13.81
Hispanic (23)	33	0.44
Apache (1)	2	0.03
Blackfeet (0)	1	0.01
Canadian/French Am. Ind. (6)	7	0.09
Cherokee (5)	6	0.08
Chippewa (669)	826	10.92
Creek (1)	1	0.01
Crow (0)	3	0.04
Inupiat *(Alaska Native)* (1)	1	0.01
Iroquois (0)	2	0.03
Lumbee (1)	1	0.01
Mexican American Ind. (3)	3	0.04
Ottawa (16)	20	0.26
Potawatomi (14)	18	0.24
Sioux (0)	2	0.03
Yup'ik *(Alaska Native)* (0)	1	0.01
Asian (36)	69	0.91
Not Hispanic (36)	69	0.91
Chinese, ex. Taiwanese (3)	10	0.13
Filipino (11)	21	0.28
Indian (6)	8	0.11
Japanese (2)	9	0.12
Korean (3)	7	0.09
Vietnamese (0)	3	0.04
Hawaii Native/Pacific Islander (1)	21	0.28
Not Hispanic (1)	21	0.28
Native Hawaiian (1)	10	0.13
Samoan (0)	3	0.04
White (4,021)	4,277	56.57
Not Hispanic (3,941)	4,184	55.34
Hispanic (80)	93	1.23

Laketon

Place Type: Township
County: Muskegon
Population: 7,563†

Ancestry‡	Population	%
African, Sub-Saharan (0)	5	0.07
Nigerian (0)	5	0.07
American (358)	358	4.71
Arab (9)	9	0.12
Lebanese (9)	9	0.12
Belgian (11)	25	0.33
Brazilian (0)	5	0.07
British (0)	11	0.14
Canadian (0)	11	0.14
Croatian (8)	8	0.11
Czech (0)	8	0.11
Czechoslovakian (12)	25	0.33
Danish (32)	77	1.01
Dutch (355)	927	12.20
English (185)	817	10.76
European (38)	38	0.50
Finnish (9)	27	0.36
French, ex. Basque (64)	550	7.24
French Canadian (35)	72	0.95
German (575)	1,996	26.28
Greek (0)	45	0.59
Hungarian (18)	107	1.41
Irish (295)	1,028	13.53
Italian (36)	307	4.04
Lithuanian (16)	16	0.21
Maltese (0)	21	0.28
Northern European (28)	28	0.37
Norwegian (42)	83	1.09
Pennsylvania German (0)	16	0.21
Polish (271)	820	10.80
Romanian (0)	8	0.11
Russian (20)	60	0.79
Scandinavian (14)	14	0.18
Scotch-Irish (25)	52	0.68
Scottish (36)	176	2.32
Slovak (19)	53	0.70
Slovene (33)	33	0.43
Swedish (210)	541	7.12
Swiss (0)	10	0.13
Ukrainian (13)	13	0.17
Welsh (10)	40	0.53
West Indian, ex. Hispanic (0)	9	0.12
West Indian (0)	9	0.12
Yugoslavian (0)	12	0.16

Hispanic Origin	Population	%
Hispanic or Latino (of any race)	192	2.54
Central American, ex. Mexican	4	0.05
Honduran	3	0.04
Salvadoran	1	0.01
Cuban	2	0.03
Mexican	151	2.00
Puerto Rican	17	0.22
South American	2	0.03
Peruvian	2	0.03
Other Hispanic or Latino	16	0.21

Race*	Population	%
African-American/Black (145)	204	2.70
Not Hispanic (145)	197	2.60
Hispanic (0)	7	0.09
American Indian/Alaska Native (38)	101	1.34
Not Hispanic (29)	83	1.10
Hispanic (9)	18	0.24
Blackfeet (0)	4	0.05
Cherokee (0)	1	0.01
Chippewa (9)	18	0.24
Choctaw (2)	3	0.04
Navajo (3)	3	0.04
Ottawa (13)	15	0.20
Potawatomi (3)	8	0.11
Asian (47)	87	1.15
Not Hispanic (47)	84	1.11
Hispanic (0)	3	0.04
Chinese, ex. Taiwanese (11)	17	0.22
Filipino (9)	20	0.26
Indian (8)	10	0.13
Japanese (1)	5	0.07
Korean (12)	17	0.22
Taiwanese (0)	1	0.01
Thai (1)	8	0.11
Vietnamese (4)	11	0.15
Hawaii Native/Pacific Islander (0)	9	0.12
Not Hispanic (0)	8	0.11
Hispanic (0)	1	0.01
Native Hawaiian (0)	3	0.04
White (7,154)	7,309	96.64
Not Hispanic (7,022)	7,145	94.47
Hispanic (132)	164	2.17

Lambertville

Place Type: CDP
County: Monroe
Population: 9,953†

Ancestry‡	Population	%
Alsatian (0)	12	0.12
American (390)	390	3.81
Arab (43)	104	1.01
Arab (43)	43	0.42
Lebanese (0)	16	0.16
Syrian (0)	45	0.44
Austrian (0)	17	0.17
Belgian (10)	10	0.10
British (0)	96	0.94
Canadian (38)	59	0.58
Czech (0)	11	0.11
Czechoslovakian (13)	13	0.13
Danish (24)	44	0.43
Dutch (58)	283	2.76
English (155)	899	8.77
Estonian (0)	15	0.15
European (93)	93	0.91
Finnish (33)	97	0.95
French, ex. Basque (187)	1,106	10.79
French Canadian (0)	159	1.55
German (1,337)	4,264	41.61
Greek (41)	105	1.02
Hungarian (77)	374	3.65
Irish (233)	1,752	17.10
Italian (296)	628	6.13
Macedonian (17)	38	0.37
Norwegian (75)	104	1.01
Polish (543)	1,524	14.87
Romanian (13)	13	0.13
Russian (33)	65	0.63
Scandinavian (0)	19	0.19
Scotch-Irish (57)	185	1.81
Scottish (64)	206	2.01
Serbian (0)	11	0.11
Slovak (15)	27	0.26
Swedish (0)	109	1.06
Swiss (0)	82	0.80
Ukrainian (0)	17	0.17
Welsh (0)	67	0.65
Yugoslavian (11)	62	0.60

Hispanic Origin	Population	%
Hispanic or Latino (of any race)	224	2.25
Central American, ex. Mexican	4	0.04
Guatemalan	3	0.03
Panamanian	1	0.01
Cuban	3	0.03
Mexican	172	1.73
Puerto Rican	13	0.13
South American	7	0.07
Bolivian	2	0.02
Chilean	1	0.01
Paraguayan	1	0.01
Venezuelan	3	0.03
Other Hispanic or Latino	25	0.25

Race*	Population	%
African-American/Black (39)	70	0.70
Not Hispanic (39)	65	0.65
Hispanic (0)	5	0.05
American Indian/Alaska Native (25)	59	0.59
Not Hispanic (15)	46	0.46
Hispanic (10)	13	0.13
Blackfeet (0)	2	0.02
Cherokee (3)	20	0.20
Chippewa (7)	13	0.13
Cree (0)	1	0.01
Mexican American Ind. (0)	4	0.04
Sioux (2)	3	0.03
South American Ind. (0)	1	0.01
Asian (86)	113	1.14
Not Hispanic (86)	113	1.14
Cambodian (2)	2	0.02
Chinese, ex. Taiwanese (13)	13	0.13
Filipino (13)	18	0.18
Indian (17)	20	0.20
Indonesian (2)	3	0.03
Japanese (0)	6	0.06
Korean (26)	29	0.29
Taiwanese (4)	4	0.04
Thai (1)	1	0.01
Vietnamese (5)	5	0.05
Hawaii Native/Pacific Islander (4)	6	0.06
Not Hispanic (4)	6	0.06
Native Hawaiian (1)	3	0.03
Samoan (1)	1	0.01
White (9,641)	9,739	97.85
Not Hispanic (9,499)	9,581	96.26
Hispanic (142)	158	1.59

Lansing

Place Type: Charter Township
County: Ingham
Population: 8,126†

*Notes: † The Census 2010 population figure is used to calculate the percentages in the Hispanic Origin and Race categories. Ancestry percentages are based on the 2006-2010 American Community Survey population (not shown); ‡ Numbers in parentheses indicate the number of people reporting a single ancestry; * Numbers in parentheses indicate the number of persons reporting this race alone, not in combination with any other race; Please refer to the Explanation of Data for more information.*

Ancestry‡	Population	%
African, Sub-Saharan (95)	101	1.23
African (85)	91	1.11
Nigerian (10)	10	0.12
American (405)	405	4.93
Arab (49)	78	0.95
Arab (12)	12	0.15
Lebanese (25)	39	0.47
Other Arab (12)	27	0.33
Austrian (11)	11	0.13
Basque (13)	13	0.16
Belgian (4)	14	0.17
Brazilian (0)	23	0.28
British (38)	57	0.69
Canadian (0)	10	0.12
Czech (30)	83	1.01
Czechoslovakian (20)	28	0.34
Danish (19)	89	1.08
Dutch (78)	275	3.35
English (171)	795	9.68
European (27)	41	0.50
Finnish (18)	75	0.91
French, ex. Basque (72)	422	5.14
French Canadian (28)	80	0.97
German (392)	1,859	22.64
Greek (9)	48	0.58
Hungarian (39)	49	0.60
Iranian (10)	10	0.12
Irish (186)	1,053	12.82
Italian (119)	423	5.15
Macedonian (10)	10	0.12
Northern European (10)	10	0.12
Norwegian (0)	78	0.95
Polish (87)	397	4.83
Russian (9)	30	0.37
Scotch-Irish (72)	238	2.90
Scottish (67)	300	3.65
Slovak (20)	26	0.32
Swedish (0)	70	0.85
Swiss (0)	32	0.39
Ukrainian (25)	45	0.55
Welsh (11)	69	0.84
West Indian, ex. Hispanic (13)	74	0.90
British West Indian (13)	13	0.16
West Indian (0)	61	0.74

Hispanic Origin	Population	%
Hispanic or Latino (of any race)	883	10.87
Central American, ex. Mexican	18	0.22
Costa Rican	1	0.01
Guatemalan	11	0.14
Honduran	1	0.01
Panamanian	2	0.02
Salvadoran	3	0.04
Cuban	97	1.19
Dominican Republic	1	0.01
Mexican	653	8.04
Puerto Rican	30	0.37
South American	31	0.38
Argentinean	5	0.06
Chilean	1	0.01
Colombian	14	0.17
Ecuadorian	3	0.04
Venezuelan	3	0.04
Other South American	5	0.06
Other Hispanic or Latino	53	0.65

Race*	Population	%
African-American/Black (1,012)	1,239	15.25
Not Hispanic (973)	1,165	14.34
Hispanic (39)	74	0.91
American Indian/Alaska Native (38)	148	1.82
Not Hispanic (29)	116	1.43
Hispanic (9)	32	0.39
Apache (5)	12	0.15
Blackfeet (0)	5	0.06
Cherokee (1)	18	0.22
Chippewa (7)	18	0.22
Creek (0)	3	0.04
Iroquois (0)	1	0.01
Mexican American Ind. (3)	3	0.04
Ottawa (3)	9	0.11
Potawatomi (0)	7	0.09
Sioux (0)	2	0.02
South American Ind. (0)	1	0.01
Asian (215)	258	3.17
Not Hispanic (212)	247	3.04
Hispanic (3)	11	0.14
Bhutanese (7)	7	0.09
Burmese (1)	1	0.01
Chinese, ex. Taiwanese (41)	56	0.69
Filipino (8)	9	0.11
Hmong (24)	27	0.33
Indian (45)	47	0.58
Japanese (7)	13	0.16
Korean (28)	36	0.44
Pakistani (1)	2	0.02
Sri Lankan (0)	2	0.02
Taiwanese (8)	8	0.10
Thai (5)	5	0.06
Vietnamese (23)	34	0.42
Hawaii Native/Pacific Islander (0)	6	0.07
Not Hispanic (0)	5	0.06
Hispanic (0)	1	0.01
Guamanian/Chamorro (0)	1	0.01
Native Hawaiian (0)	4	0.05
White (6,200)	6,530	80.36
Not Hispanic (5,749)	5,999	73.82
Hispanic (451)	531	6.53

Lansing

Place Type: City
County: Ingham
Population: 109,563†

Ancestry‡	Population	%
African, Sub-Saharan (1,575)	1,797	1.62
African (594)	798	0.72
Ethiopian (107)	107	0.10
Nigerian (41)	41	0.04
Somalian (305)	316	0.29
South African (0)	7	0.01
Sudanese (239)	239	0.22
Other Sub-Saharan African (289)	289	0.26
American (6,886)	6,886	6.22
Arab (737)	986	0.89
Arab (77)	110	0.10
Egyptian (28)	28	0.03
Iraqi (246)	246	0.22
Lebanese (368)	565	0.51
Syrian (10)	10	0.01
Other Arab (8)	27	0.02
Armenian (15)	54	0.05
Australian (13)	13	0.01
Austrian (13)	150	0.14
Belgian (48)	326	0.29
Brazilian (10)	19	0.02
British (190)	441	0.40
Bulgarian (31)	77	0.07
Canadian (76)	276	0.25
Celtic (15)	24	0.02
Croatian (106)	255	0.23
Cypriot (9)	9	0.01
Czech (47)	371	0.34
Czechoslovakian (63)	140	0.13
Danish (10)	203	0.18
Dutch (908)	3,759	3.39
Eastern European (45)	65	0.06
English (2,695)	10,508	9.49
Estonian (0)	11	0.01
European (938)	1,222	1.10
Finnish (115)	436	0.39
French, ex. Basque (311)	3,198	2.89
French Canadian (246)	1,302	1.18
German (5,187)	20,812	18.80
German Russian (6)	6	0.01
Greek (237)	465	0.42
Hungarian (178)	732	0.66
Iranian (7)	26	0.02
Irish (2,599)	12,034	10.87
Italian (1,032)	3,383	3.06
Latvian (31)	41	0.04
Lithuanian (120)	241	0.22
Macedonian (11)	33	0.03
Maltese (0)	9	0.01
New Zealander (0)	9	0.01
Northern European (77)	106	0.10
Norwegian (156)	774	0.70
Pennsylvania German (41)	83	0.07
Polish (1,130)	4,254	3.84
Portuguese (23)	41	0.04
Romanian (11)	115	0.10
Russian (101)	609	0.55
Scandinavian (57)	128	0.12
Scotch-Irish (542)	1,369	1.24
Scottish (415)	2,365	2.14
Serbian (46)	66	0.06
Slavic (9)	35	0.03
Slovak (101)	164	0.15
Slovene (21)	31	0.03
Swedish (248)	1,391	1.26
Swiss (0)	146	0.13
Turkish (22)	22	0.02
Ukrainian (126)	369	0.33
Welsh (83)	606	0.55
West Indian, ex. Hispanic (468)	601	0.54
Barbadian (0)	37	0.03
Haitian (312)	336	0.30
Jamaican (138)	194	0.18
Trinidadian/Tobagonian (18)	18	0.02
Other West Indian (0)	16	0.01
Yugoslavian (94)	145	0.13

Hispanic Origin	Population	%
Hispanic or Latino (of any race)	13,753	12.55
Central American, ex. Mexican	198	0.18
Costa Rican	16	0.01
Guatemalan	86	0.08
Honduran	31	0.03
Nicaraguan	10	0.01
Panamanian	26	0.02
Salvadoran	25	0.02
Other Central American	4	<0.01
Cuban	1,144	1.04
Dominican Republic	52	0.05
Mexican	10,468	9.55
Puerto Rican	682	0.62
South American	244	0.22
Argentinean	37	0.03
Bolivian	12	0.01
Chilean	16	0.01
Colombian	76	0.07
Ecuadorian	38	0.03
Paraguayan	8	0.01
Peruvian	29	0.03
Uruguayan	3	<0.01
Venezuelan	25	0.02
Other Hispanic or Latino	965	0.88

Race*	Population	%
African-American/Black (24,870)	29,313	26.75
Not Hispanic (23,969)	27,626	25.21
Hispanic (901)	1,687	1.54
American Indian/Alaska Native (861)	2,480	2.26
Not Hispanic (663)	1,948	1.78
Hispanic (198)	532	0.49
Alaska Athabascan *(Ala. Nat.)* (0)	1	<0.01
Aleut *(Alaska Native)* (0)	2	<0.01
Apache (13)	39	0.04
Arapaho (0)	1	<0.01
Blackfeet (18)	142	0.13
Canadian/French Am. Ind. (20)	29	0.03
Central American Ind. (2)	2	<0.01
Cherokee (36)	214	0.20
Cheyenne (1)	3	<0.01
Chickasaw (1)	3	<0.01
Chippewa (176)	376	0.34
Choctaw (7)	34	0.03
Comanche (1)	3	<0.01

*Notes: † The Census 2010 population figure is used to calculate the percentages in the Hispanic Origin and Race categories. Ancestry percentages are based on the 2006-2010 American Community Survey population (not shown); ‡ Numbers in parentheses indicate the number of people reporting a single ancestry; * Numbers in parentheses indicate the number of persons reporting this race alone, not in combination with any other race; Please refer to the Explanation of Data for more information.*

Cree (0)	6	0.01
Creek (0)	6	0.01
Delaware (2)	2	<0.01
Hopi (1)	1	<0.01
Houma (1)	1	<0.01
Inupiat *(Alaska Native)* (2)	3	<0.01
Iroquois (19)	49	0.04
Lumbee (0)	3	<0.01
Menominee (2)	4	<0.01
Mexican American Ind. (46)	91	0.08
Navajo (5)	8	0.01
Osage (0)	1	<0.01
Ottawa (106)	181	0.17
Paiute (1)	2	<0.01
Potawatomi (26)	50	0.05
Pueblo (2)	2	<0.01
Seminole (1)	13	0.01
Shoshone (0)	1	<0.01
Sioux (8)	43	0.04
South American Ind. (4)	7	0.01
Spanish American Ind. (1)	1	<0.01
Tlingit-Haida *(Alaska Native)* (4)	5	<0.01
Tohono O'Odham (1)	2	<0.01
Ute (0)	1	<0.01
Yaqui (1)	4	<0.01
Yup'ik *(Alaska Native)* (3)	3	<0.01
Asian (4,077)	4,846	4.42
Not Hispanic (4,025)	4,717	4.31
Hispanic (52)	129	0.12
Bangladeshi (6)	6	0.01
Bhutanese (219)	281	0.26
Burmese (343)	373	0.34
Cambodian (7)	9	0.01
Chinese, ex. Taiwanese (558)	679	0.62
Filipino (144)	263	0.24
Hmong (518)	549	0.50
Indian (564)	657	0.60
Indonesian (16)	21	0.02
Japanese (53)	151	0.14
Korean (315)	390	0.36
Laotian (45)	60	0.05
Malaysian (17)	19	0.02
Nepalese (70)	113	0.10
Pakistani (39)	57	0.05
Sri Lankan (18)	21	0.02
Taiwanese (18)	21	0.02
Thai (42)	59	0.05
Vietnamese (895)	960	0.88
Hawaii Native/Pacific Islander (54)	190	0.17
Not Hispanic (38)	145	0.13
Hispanic (16)	45	0.04
Guamanian/Chamorro (13)	22	0.02
Marshallese (2)	2	<0.01
Native Hawaiian (15)	74	0.07
Samoan (10)	34	0.03
Tongan (1)	1	<0.01
White (68,261)	74,131	67.66
Not Hispanic (61,887)	66,437	60.64
Hispanic (6,374)	7,694	7.02

Lansing

Place Type: City
County: Ingham
Population: 114,297†

Ancestry‡	Population	%
African, Sub-Saharan (1,615)	1,905	1.65
African (634)	906	0.78
Ethiopian (107)	107	0.09
Nigerian (41)	41	0.04
Somalian (305)	316	0.27
South African (0)	7	0.01
Sudanese (239)	239	0.21
Other Sub-Saharan African (289)	289	0.25
American (6,973)	6,973	6.03
Arab (751)	1,000	0.86
Arab (77)	110	0.10
Egyptian (28)	28	0.02
Iraqi (246)	246	0.21
Lebanese (382)	579	0.50
Syrian (10)	10	0.01
Other Arab (8)	27	0.02
Armenian (15)	54	0.05
Australian (13)	13	0.01
Austrian (13)	179	0.15
Belgian (48)	326	0.28
Brazilian (10)	19	0.02
British (200)	451	0.39
Bulgarian (31)	77	0.07
Canadian (76)	276	0.24
Celtic (15)	24	0.02
Croatian (106)	255	0.22
Cypriot (9)	9	0.01
Czech (47)	431	0.37
Czechoslovakian (63)	140	0.12
Danish (10)	223	0.19
Dutch (908)	3,759	3.25
Eastern European (45)	65	0.06
English (2,707)	10,696	9.25
Estonian (0)	11	0.01
European (955)	1,260	1.09
Finnish (115)	462	0.40
French, ex. Basque (311)	3,355	2.90
French Canadian (246)	1,314	1.14
German (5,318)	21,220	18.35
German Russian (6)	6	0.01
Greek (237)	465	0.40
Hungarian (178)	805	0.70
Iranian (7)	26	0.02
Irish (2,924)	12,586	10.88
Italian (1,066)	3,473	3.00
Latvian (31)	41	0.04
Lithuanian (120)	241	0.21
Macedonian (11)	33	0.03
Maltese (0)	9	0.01
New Zealander (0)	9	0.01
Northern European (77)	106	0.09
Norwegian (156)	774	0.67
Pennsylvania German (41)	83	0.07
Polish (1,141)	4,385	3.79
Portuguese (23)	41	0.04
Romanian (11)	115	0.10
Russian (101)	626	0.54
Scandinavian (57)	128	0.11
Scotch-Irish (542)	1,369	1.18
Scottish (415)	2,375	2.05
Serbian (46)	73	0.06
Slavic (9)	35	0.03
Slovak (101)	164	0.14
Slovene (21)	31	0.03
Swedish (277)	1,420	1.23
Swiss (17)	187	0.16
Turkish (22)	22	0.02
Ukrainian (126)	369	0.32
Welsh (83)	606	0.52
West Indian, ex. Hispanic (468)	601	0.52
Barbadian (0)	37	0.03
Haitian (312)	336	0.29
Jamaican (138)	194	0.17
Trinidadian/Tobagonian (18)	18	0.02
Other West Indian (0)	16	0.01
Yugoslavian (94)	145	0.13

Hispanic Origin	Population	%
Hispanic or Latino (of any race)	14,292	12.50
Central American, ex. Mexican	211	0.18
Costa Rican	19	0.02
Guatemalan	86	0.08
Honduran	39	0.03
Nicaraguan	10	0.01
Panamanian	26	0.02
Salvadoran	27	0.02
Other Central American	4	<0.01
Cuban	1,193	1.04
Dominican Republic	56	0.05
Mexican	10,870	9.51
Puerto Rican	701	0.61
South American	251	0.22
Argentinean	37	0.03
Bolivian	12	0.01
Chilean	17	0.01
Colombian	78	0.07
Ecuadorian	39	0.03
Paraguayan	8	0.01
Peruvian	29	0.03
Uruguayan	6	0.01
Venezuelan	25	0.02
Other Hispanic or Latino	1,010	0.88

Race*	Population	%
African-American/Black (27,138)	31,830	27.85
Not Hispanic (26,194)	30,058	26.30
Hispanic (944)	1,772	1.55
American Indian/Alaska Native (882)	2,601	2.28
Not Hispanic (681)	2,048	1.79
Hispanic (201)	553	0.48
Alaska Athabascan *(Ala. Nat.)* (0)	1	<0.01
Aleut *(Alaska Native)* (0)	2	<0.01
Apache (14)	40	0.03
Arapaho (0)	1	<0.01
Blackfeet (18)	147	0.13
Canadian/French Am. Ind. (20)	29	0.03
Central American Ind. (2)	2	<0.01
Cherokee (39)	241	0.21
Cheyenne (1)	3	<0.01
Chickasaw (1)	3	<0.01
Chippewa (179)	381	0.33
Choctaw (7)	36	0.03
Comanche (1)	3	<0.01
Cree (0)	6	0.01
Creek (0)	6	0.01
Delaware (2)	2	<0.01
Hopi (1)	1	<0.01
Houma (1)	1	<0.01
Inupiat *(Alaska Native)* (2)	3	<0.01
Iroquois (19)	49	0.04
Lumbee (0)	3	<0.01
Menominee (2)	4	<0.01
Mexican American Ind. (46)	91	0.08
Navajo (5)	8	0.01
Osage (0)	1	<0.01
Ottawa (110)	191	0.17
Paiute (1)	2	<0.01
Potawatomi (26)	51	0.04
Pueblo (2)	2	<0.01
Seminole (1)	13	0.01
Shoshone (0)	1	<0.01
Sioux (8)	43	0.04
South American Ind. (4)	8	0.01
Spanish American Ind. (1)	1	<0.01
Tlingit-Haida *(Alaska Native)* (4)	5	<0.01
Tohono O'Odham (1)	2	<0.01
Ute (0)	1	<0.01
Yaqui (1)	4	<0.01
Yup'ik *(Alaska Native)* (3)	3	<0.01
Asian (4,256)	5,060	4.43
Not Hispanic (4,202)	4,924	4.31
Hispanic (54)	136	0.12
Bangladeshi (6)	6	0.01
Bhutanese (219)	281	0.25
Burmese (353)	383	0.34
Cambodian (11)	17	0.01
Chinese, ex. Taiwanese (565)	689	0.60
Filipino (149)	272	0.24
Hmong (604)	643	0.56
Indian (576)	674	0.59
Indonesian (19)	25	0.02
Japanese (56)	157	0.14
Korean (321)	404	0.35
Laotian (45)	60	0.05
Malaysian (18)	20	0.02
Nepalese (70)	113	0.10
Pakistani (39)	57	0.05
Sri Lankan (18)	21	0.02
Taiwanese (18)	21	0.02
Thai (43)	60	0.05
Vietnamese (928)	993	0.87
Hawaii Native/Pacific Islander (54)	194	0.17
Not Hispanic (38)	148	0.13

*Notes: † The Census 2010 population figure is used to calculate the percentages in the Hispanic Origin and Race categories. Ancestry percentages are based on the 2006-2010 American Community Survey population (not shown); ‡ Numbers in parentheses indicate the number of people reporting a single ancestry; * Numbers in parentheses indicate the number of persons reporting this race alone, not in combination with any other race; Please refer to the Explanation of Data for more information.*

	Population	%
Hispanic (16)	46	0.04
Guamanian/Chamorro (13)	22	0.02
Marshallese (2)	2	<0.01
Native Hawaiian (15)	77	0.07
Samoan (10)	34	0.03
Tongan (1)	1	<0.01
White (69,983)	76,134	66.61
Not Hispanic (63,381)	68,146	59.62
Hispanic (6,602)	7,988	6.99

Lapeer

Place Type: City
County: Lapeer
Population: 8,841†

Ancestry‡	Population	%
Albanian (9)	9	0.10
American (765)	765	8.43
Arab (138)	138	1.52
Iraqi (9)	9	0.10
Lebanese (102)	102	1.12
Moroccan (27)	27	0.30
Armenian (6)	6	0.07
Austrian (0)	23	0.25
Belgian (0)	8	0.09
British (29)	29	0.32
Canadian (0)	35	0.39
Croatian (49)	49	0.54
Czech (33)	33	0.36
Dutch (36)	190	2.09
English (379)	1,040	11.46
European (52)	65	0.72
Finnish (0)	17	0.19
French, ex. Basque (10)	360	3.97
French Canadian (63)	208	2.29
German (753)	2,035	22.42
Greek (20)	32	0.35
Hungarian (9)	33	0.36
Icelander (0)	10	0.11
Irish (584)	1,503	16.56
Italian (75)	273	3.01
Latvian (30)	30	0.33
Lithuanian (37)	66	0.73
Maltese (0)	24	0.26
Norwegian (8)	69	0.76
Pennsylvania German (9)	9	0.10
Polish (125)	395	4.35
Russian (0)	11	0.12
Scotch-Irish (24)	66	0.73
Scottish (83)	434	4.78
Slovak (9)	9	0.10
Slovene (8)	31	0.34
Swedish (6)	215	2.37
Swiss (0)	20	0.22
Ukrainian (10)	10	0.11
Welsh (9)	70	0.77
West Indian, ex. Hispanic (0)	14	0.15
Barbadian (0)	14	0.15

Hispanic Origin	Population	%
Hispanic or Latino (of any race)	345	3.90
Central American, ex. Mexican	3	0.03
Guatemalan	2	0.02
Salvadoran	1	0.01
Cuban	1	0.01
Mexican	278	3.14
Puerto Rican	41	0.46
South American	6	0.07
Chilean	1	0.01
Colombian	2	0.02
Venezuelan	3	0.03
Other Hispanic or Latino	16	0.18

Race*	Population	%
African-American/Black (669)	719	8.13
Not Hispanic (666)	714	8.08
Hispanic (3)	5	0.06
American Indian/Alaska Native (57)	138	1.56
Not Hispanic (52)	126	1.43
Hispanic (5)	12	0.14
Blackfeet (0)	8	0.09
Cherokee (2)	23	0.26
Chickasaw (4)	4	0.05
Chippewa (20)	40	0.45
Choctaw (0)	1	0.01
Iroquois (0)	2	0.02
Mexican American Ind. (0)	1	0.01
Navajo (0)	2	0.02
Ottawa (2)	4	0.05
Potawatomi (2)	3	0.03
Asian (73)	93	1.05
Not Hispanic (73)	88	1.00
Hispanic (0)	5	0.06
Cambodian (0)	3	0.03
Chinese, ex. Taiwanese (14)	18	0.20
Filipino (18)	27	0.31
Indian (20)	23	0.26
Korean (4)	9	0.10
Laotian (0)	1	0.01
Pakistani (2)	2	0.02
Thai (1)	1	0.01
Vietnamese (10)	10	0.11
Hawaii Native/Pacific Islander (1)	4	0.05
Not Hispanic (1)	4	0.05
Native Hawaiian (1)	3	0.03
White (7,837)	7,988	90.35
Not Hispanic (7,572)	7,700	87.09
Hispanic (265)	288	3.26

Lenox

Place Type: Township
County: Macomb
Population: 10,470†

Ancestry‡	Population	%
African, Sub-Saharan (89)	142	1.40
African (89)	142	1.40
Albanian (9)	9	0.09
American (482)	482	4.74
Arab (59)	77	0.76
Arab (9)	9	0.09
Iraqi (12)	12	0.12
Lebanese (10)	19	0.19
Moroccan (28)	28	0.28
Syrian (0)	9	0.09
Australian (11)	11	0.11
Austrian (0)	9	0.09
Belgian (56)	461	4.54
Canadian (12)	78	0.77
Croatian (11)	11	0.11
Czechoslovakian (0)	22	0.22
Dutch (0)	118	1.16
English (290)	1,217	11.98
European (20)	20	0.20
Finnish (8)	29	0.29
French, ex. Basque (47)	693	6.82
French Canadian (32)	96	0.94
German (572)	2,712	26.69
Greek (21)	33	0.32
Hungarian (28)	157	1.55
Irish (151)	1,287	12.67
Italian (242)	793	7.81
Lithuanian (11)	11	0.11
Macedonian (9)	9	0.09
Maltese (0)	9	0.09
Norwegian (0)	66	0.65
Pennsylvania German (11)	11	0.11
Polish (612)	1,919	18.89
Portuguese (0)	26	0.26
Russian (9)	31	0.31
Scandinavian (9)	17	0.17
Scotch-Irish (47)	205	2.02
Scottish (25)	187	1.84
Slovak (34)	46	0.45
Swedish (9)	19	0.19
Swiss (0)	40	0.39
Ukrainian (57)	155	1.53
Welsh (20)	20	0.20
Yugoslavian (19)	19	0.19

Hispanic Origin	Population	%
Hispanic or Latino (of any race)	398	3.80
Central American, ex. Mexican	8	0.08
Costa Rican	3	0.03
Panamanian	2	0.02
Salvadoran	3	0.03
Cuban	6	0.06
Mexican	276	2.64
Puerto Rican	27	0.26
South American	9	0.09
Argentinean	3	0.03
Chilean	1	0.01
Colombian	1	0.01
Peruvian	1	0.01
Venezuelan	3	0.03
Other Hispanic or Latino	72	0.69

Race*	Population	%
African-American/Black (1,521)	1,710	16.33
Not Hispanic (1,506)	1,684	16.08
Hispanic (15)	26	0.25
American Indian/Alaska Native (57)	145	1.38
Not Hispanic (54)	134	1.28
Hispanic (3)	11	0.11
Alaska Athabascan *(Ala. Nat.)* (0)	1	0.01
Apache (1)	9	0.09
Blackfeet (0)	5	0.05
Cherokee (4)	33	0.32
Chippewa (14)	23	0.22
Choctaw (0)	2	0.02
Creek (0)	4	0.04
Iroquois (5)	9	0.09
Lumbee (2)	3	0.03
Navajo (0)	1	0.01
Ottawa (1)	1	0.01
Potawatomi (3)	4	0.04
Sioux (1)	8	0.08
Asian (51)	73	0.70
Not Hispanic (48)	70	0.67
Hispanic (3)	3	0.03
Cambodian (1)	2	0.02
Chinese, ex. Taiwanese (7)	13	0.12
Filipino (11)	17	0.16
Hmong (2)	4	0.04
Indian (5)	7	0.07
Indonesian (0)	1	0.01
Japanese (2)	6	0.06
Korean (8)	11	0.11
Pakistani (4)	4	0.04
Vietnamese (6)	6	0.06
Hawaii Native/Pacific Islander (3)	9	0.09
Not Hispanic (3)	5	0.05
Hispanic (0)	4	0.04
Native Hawaiian (0)	3	0.03
White (8,479)	8,737	83.45
Not Hispanic (8,203)	8,439	80.60
Hispanic (276)	298	2.85

Leoni

Place Type: Township
County: Jackson
Population: 13,807†

Ancestry‡	Population	%
American (1,182)	1,182	8.52
Arab (12)	16	0.12
Lebanese (12)	16	0.12
Australian (0)	10	0.07
Austrian (0)	11	0.08
Belgian (53)	53	0.38
British (0)	11	0.08
Bulgarian (34)	34	0.25
Canadian (12)	58	0.42
Celtic (0)	28	0.20
Czech (9)	98	0.71
Czechoslovakian (0)	26	0.19
Danish (0)	10	0.07

*Notes: † The Census 2010 population figure is used to calculate the percentages in the Hispanic Origin and Race categories. Ancestry percentages are based on the 2006-2010 American Community Survey population (not shown); ‡ Numbers in parentheses indicate the number of people reporting a single ancestry; * Numbers in parentheses indicate the number of persons reporting this race alone, not in combination with any other race; Please refer to the Explanation of Data for more information.*

SECTION TWO

Dutch (162)	598	4.31
English (802)	2,314	16.69
European (70)	70	0.50
Finnish (29)	68	0.49
French, ex. Basque (10)	424	3.06
French Canadian (59)	124	0.89
German (1,653)	4,081	29.43
Greek (116)	116	0.84
Hungarian (30)	103	0.74
Irish (762)	2,715	19.58
Italian (145)	257	1.85
Lithuanian (0)	16	0.12
Maltese (0)	9	0.06
Norwegian (31)	55	0.40
Polish (564)	1,338	9.65
Romanian (44)	157	1.13
Russian (0)	40	0.29
Scandinavian (39)	39	0.28
Scotch-Irish (26)	81	0.58
Scottish (90)	433	3.12
Slovak (0)	39	0.28
Swedish (8)	201	1.45
Swiss (0)	42	0.30
Ukrainian (34)	34	0.25
Welsh (12)	25	0.18

Hispanic Origin	Population	%
Hispanic or Latino (of any race)	325	2.35
Central American, ex. Mexican	6	0.04
Costa Rican	1	0.01
Guatemalan	2	0.01
Honduran	1	0.01
Panamanian	2	0.01
Cuban	15	0.11
Dominican Republic	1	0.01
Mexican	230	1.67
Puerto Rican	20	0.14
South American	7	0.05
Argentinean	1	0.01
Chilean	2	0.01
Colombian	3	0.02
Peruvian	1	0.01
Other Hispanic or Latino	46	0.33

Race*	Population	%
African-American/Black (170)	294	2.13
Not Hispanic (170)	288	2.09
Hispanic (0)	6	0.04
American Indian/Alaska Native (56)	165	1.20
Not Hispanic (45)	143	1.04
Hispanic (11)	22	0.16
Apache (0)	1	0.01
Blackfeet (1)	4	0.03
Cherokee (8)	30	0.22
Chippewa (14)	34	0.25
Choctaw (1)	1	0.01
Comanche (2)	2	0.01
Crow (0)	1	0.01
Iroquois (0)	1	0.01
Menominee (0)	1	0.01
Navajo (2)	2	0.01
Ottawa (2)	3	0.02
Potawatomi (1)	4	0.03
Shoshone (1)	1	0.01
Sioux (1)	2	0.01
Asian (63)	97	0.70
Not Hispanic (63)	94	0.68
Hispanic (0)	3	0.02
Chinese, ex. Taiwanese (23)	31	0.22
Filipino (11)	27	0.20
Indian (1)	4	0.03
Japanese (2)	8	0.06
Korean (14)	16	0.12
Thai (1)	1	0.01
Vietnamese (4)	5	0.04
Hawaii Native/Pacific Islander (3)	7	0.05
Not Hispanic (3)	6	0.04
Hispanic (0)	1	0.01
Guamanian/Chamorro (1)	1	0.01
Native Hawaiian (0)	2	0.01
White (13,154)	13,433	97.29
Not Hispanic (12,944)	13,187	95.51
Hispanic (210)	246	1.78

Lincoln Park

Place Type: City
County: Wayne
Population: 38,144†

Ancestry‡	Population	%
African, Sub-Saharan (103)	137	0.35
African (60)	60	0.16
South African (13)	13	0.03
Sudanese (30)	64	0.17
Albanian (6)	6	0.02
American (1,510)	1,510	3.91
Arab (192)	257	0.67
Egyptian (0)	12	0.03
Lebanese (186)	239	0.62
Other Arab (6)	6	0.02
Armenian (63)	74	0.19
Assyrian/Chaldean/Syriac (10)	10	0.03
Austrian (26)	87	0.23
Belgian (61)	147	0.38
British (57)	86	0.22
Canadian (89)	205	0.53
Croatian (32)	223	0.58
Czech (21)	181	0.47
Czechoslovakian (90)	280	0.73
Danish (0)	9	0.02
Dutch (66)	614	1.59
Eastern European (19)	19	0.05
English (721)	3,273	8.48
European (174)	231	0.60
Finnish (18)	139	0.36
French, ex. Basque (202)	2,693	6.98
French Canadian (260)	884	2.29
German (1,591)	7,496	19.42
Greek (67)	242	0.63
Hungarian (838)	2,225	5.76
Irish (1,005)	5,733	14.85
Italian (1,315)	3,802	9.85
Lithuanian (93)	215	0.56
Macedonian (0)	53	0.14
Maltese (41)	101	0.26
Norwegian (0)	143	0.37
Pennsylvania German (14)	14	0.04
Polish (1,904)	5,260	13.63
Portuguese (11)	25	0.06
Romanian (221)	319	0.83
Russian (7)	81	0.21
Scotch-Irish (376)	902	2.34
Scottish (164)	801	2.08
Serbian (10)	10	0.03
Slavic (22)	31	0.08
Slovak (32)	148	0.38
Swedish (24)	317	0.82
Ukrainian (111)	186	0.48
Welsh (20)	228	0.59
Yugoslavian (66)	107	0.28

Hispanic Origin	Population	%
Hispanic or Latino (of any race)	5,676	14.88
Central American, ex. Mexican	79	0.21
Guatemalan	13	0.03
Honduran	15	0.04
Nicaraguan	6	0.02
Panamanian	6	0.02
Salvadoran	39	0.10
Cuban	31	0.08
Dominican Republic	65	0.17
Mexican	4,696	12.31
Puerto Rican	514	1.35
South American	29	0.08
Argentinean	2	0.01
Colombian	9	0.02
Ecuadorian	11	0.03
Peruvian	2	0.01
Venezuelan	3	0.01
Other South American	2	0.01
Other Hispanic or Latino	262	0.69

Race*	Population	%
African-American/Black (2,260)	2,726	7.15
Not Hispanic (2,172)	2,577	6.76
Hispanic (88)	149	0.39
American Indian/Alaska Native (269)	615	1.61
Not Hispanic (205)	507	1.33
Hispanic (64)	108	0.28
Alaska Athabascan *(Ala. Nat.)* (1)	2	0.01
Apache (1)	1	<0.01
Blackfeet (4)	27	0.07
Canadian/French Am. Ind. (12)	18	0.05
Cherokee (33)	132	0.35
Cheyenne (0)	1	<0.01
Chippewa (43)	75	0.20
Choctaw (0)	1	<0.01
Comanche (0)	1	<0.01
Cree (0)	1	<0.01
Crow (0)	1	<0.01
Delaware (2)	2	0.01
Iroquois (13)	28	0.07
Lumbee (13)	32	0.08
Menominee (3)	3	0.01
Mexican American Ind. (6)	9	0.02
Navajo (2)	3	0.01
Osage (3)	6	0.02
Ottawa (9)	11	0.03
Potawatomi (3)	10	0.03
Pueblo (2)	2	0.01
Sioux (2)	6	0.02
Spanish American Ind. (1)	1	<0.01
Asian (193)	308	0.81
Not Hispanic (183)	279	0.73
Hispanic (10)	29	0.08
Cambodian (6)	6	0.02
Chinese, ex. Taiwanese (10)	32	0.08
Filipino (95)	145	0.38
Indian (23)	34	0.09
Japanese (2)	15	0.04
Korean (12)	20	0.05
Laotian (3)	6	0.02
Pakistani (15)	15	0.04
Taiwanese (0)	4	0.01
Thai (17)	24	0.06
Vietnamese (2)	6	0.02
Hawaii Native/Pacific Islander (13)	47	0.12
Not Hispanic (8)	28	0.07
Hispanic (5)	19	0.05
Guamanian/Chamorro (2)	3	0.01
Native Hawaiian (4)	25	0.07
Samoan (4)	4	0.01
White (32,126)	33,284	87.26
Not Hispanic (29,102)	29,833	78.21
Hispanic (3,024)	3,451	9.05

Lincoln

Place Type: Charter Township
County: Berrien
Population: 14,691†

Ancestry‡	Population	%
African, Sub-Saharan (99)	99	0.68
African (97)	97	0.67
Other Sub-Saharan African (2)	2	0.01
American (965)	965	6.65
Arab (8)	28	0.19
Arab (0)	20	0.14
Iraqi (8)	8	0.06
Assyrian/Chaldean/Syriac (43)	43	0.30
Austrian (12)	12	0.08
Belgian (65)	151	1.04
British (61)	108	0.74
Canadian (24)	49	0.34
Croatian (0)	28	0.19
Czech (61)	103	0.71
Czechoslovakian (18)	18	0.12
Danish (80)	255	1.76

*Notes: † The Census 2010 population figure is used to calculate the percentages in the Hispanic Origin and Race categories. Ancestry percentages are based on the 2006-2010 American Community Survey population (not shown); ‡ Numbers in parentheses indicate the number of people reporting a single ancestry; * Numbers in parentheses indicate the number of persons reporting this race alone, not in combination with any other race; Please refer to the Explanation of Data for more information.*

Dutch (314)	925	6.37
Eastern European (11)	11	0.08
English (413)	1,557	10.73
European (195)	195	1.34
Finnish (0)	50	0.34
French, ex. Basque (110)	630	4.34
French Canadian (35)	120	0.83
German (2,551)	6,154	42.41
Greek (35)	86	0.59
Hungarian (48)	208	1.43
Iranian (3)	3	0.02
Irish (406)	2,225	15.33
Israeli (6)	18	0.12
Italian (283)	910	6.27
Latvian (0)	6	0.04
Lithuanian (17)	39	0.27
Northern European (16)	16	0.11
Norwegian (22)	201	1.39
Pennsylvania German (8)	17	0.12
Polish (259)	1,069	7.37
Russian (0)	81	0.56
Scandinavian (16)	29	0.20
Scotch-Irish (118)	220	1.52
Scottish (95)	271	1.87
Slovak (16)	35	0.24
Slovene (9)	9	0.06
Swedish (106)	386	2.66
Swiss (2)	41	0.28
Ukrainian (40)	147	1.01
Welsh (0)	88	0.61
Yugoslavian (50)	64	0.44

Hispanic Origin	Population	%
Hispanic or Latino (of any race)	405	2.76
Central American, ex. Mexican	14	0.10
Guatemalan	9	0.06
Honduran	1	0.01
Salvadoran	4	0.03
Cuban	11	0.07
Dominican Republic	1	0.01
Mexican	293	1.99
Puerto Rican	24	0.16
South American	37	0.25
Argentinean	6	0.04
Chilean	6	0.04
Colombian	9	0.06
Ecuadorian	3	0.02
Venezuelan	13	0.09
Other Hispanic or Latino	25	0.17

Race*	Population	%
African-American/Black (326)	408	2.78
Not Hispanic (324)	404	2.75
Hispanic (2)	4	0.03
American Indian/Alaska Native (44)	111	0.76
Not Hispanic (43)	107	0.73
Hispanic (1)	4	0.03
Blackfeet (0)	9	0.06
Canadian/French Am. Ind. (0)	3	0.02
Cherokee (4)	24	0.16
Chippewa (12)	15	0.10
Menominee (1)	1	0.01
Mexican American Ind. (0)	1	0.01
Ottawa (0)	3	0.02
Potawatomi (13)	18	0.12
Seminole (0)	2	0.01
Sioux (0)	4	0.03
Asian (357)	458	3.12
Not Hispanic (355)	455	3.10
Hispanic (2)	3	0.02
Bangladeshi (4)	4	0.03
Chinese, ex. Taiwanese (74)	96	0.65
Filipino (24)	56	0.38
Indian (180)	200	1.36
Indonesian (1)	2	0.01
Japanese (4)	25	0.17
Korean (49)	58	0.39
Laotian (2)	3	0.02
Pakistani (6)	6	0.04
Taiwanese (1)	1	0.01
Vietnamese (6)	7	0.05
Hawaii Native/Pacific Islander (7)	21	0.14
Not Hispanic (7)	20	0.14
Hispanic (0)	1	0.01
Guamanian/Chamorro (2)	4	0.03
Native Hawaiian (1)	12	0.08
Tongan (4)	4	0.03
White (13,571)	13,816	94.04
Not Hispanic (13,316)	13,533	92.12
Hispanic (255)	283	1.93

Livonia

Place Type: City
County: Wayne
Population: 96,942†

Ancestry‡	Population	%
African, Sub-Saharan (232)	255	0.26
African (54)	77	0.08
Nigerian (37)	37	0.04
South African (27)	27	0.03
Other Sub-Saharan African (114)	114	0.12
Albanian (381)	420	0.43
American (5,356)	5,356	5.47
Arab (1,779)	2,374	2.42
Arab (904)	1,013	1.03
Egyptian (0)	15	0.02
Iraqi (50)	50	0.05
Jordanian (152)	216	0.22
Lebanese (268)	668	0.68
Palestinian (220)	220	0.22
Syrian (92)	99	0.10
Other Arab (93)	93	0.09
Armenian (358)	580	0.59
Assyrian/Chaldean/Syriac (65)	95	0.10
Australian (0)	10	0.01
Austrian (54)	432	0.44
Belgian (55)	314	0.32
British (345)	652	0.67
Bulgarian (49)	60	0.06
Canadian (359)	885	0.90
Celtic (44)	51	0.05
Croatian (101)	301	0.31
Czech (100)	428	0.44
Czechoslovakian (51)	174	0.18
Danish (142)	494	0.50
Dutch (255)	1,539	1.57
Eastern European (98)	133	0.14
English (2,521)	11,053	11.29
Estonian (8)	8	0.01
European (747)	832	0.85
Finnish (749)	2,019	2.06
French, ex. Basque (644)	5,107	5.22
French Canadian (925)	2,931	2.99
German (5,336)	22,261	22.74
Greek (695)	1,272	1.30
Hungarian (596)	1,923	1.96
Icelander (0)	11	0.01
Iranian (76)	76	0.08
Irish (3,587)	16,361	16.71
Italian (3,212)	8,822	9.01
Latvian (45)	65	0.07
Lithuanian (348)	637	0.65
Macedonian (225)	293	0.30
Maltese (305)	845	0.86
New Zealander (10)	10	0.01
Northern European (126)	126	0.13
Norwegian (173)	789	0.81
Pennsylvania German (0)	47	0.05
Polish (7,033)	17,428	17.80
Portuguese (21)	71	0.07
Romanian (322)	524	0.54
Russian (340)	1,101	1.12
Scandinavian (51)	104	0.11
Scotch-Irish (783)	2,368	2.42
Scottish (1,086)	4,098	4.19
Serbian (172)	253	0.26
Slavic (8)	95	0.10
Slovak (199)	667	0.68
Slovene (25)	72	0.07
Swedish (158)	1,449	1.48
Swiss (11)	174	0.18
Turkish (26)	49	0.05
Ukrainian (374)	1,041	1.06
Welsh (39)	873	0.89
West Indian, ex. Hispanic (27)	32	0.03
Barbadian (12)	12	0.01
Jamaican (15)	15	0.02
Trinidadian/Tobagonian (0)	5	0.01
Yugoslavian (83)	343	0.35

Hispanic Origin	Population	%
Hispanic or Latino (of any race)	2,399	2.47
Central American, ex. Mexican	104	0.11
Costa Rican	1	<0.01
Guatemalan	49	0.05
Honduran	11	0.01
Nicaraguan	4	<0.01
Panamanian	12	0.01
Salvadoran	26	0.03
Other Central American	1	<0.01
Cuban	90	0.09
Dominican Republic	21	0.02
Mexican	1,542	1.59
Puerto Rican	203	0.21
South American	179	0.18
Argentinean	51	0.05
Bolivian	9	0.01
Chilean	11	0.01
Colombian	40	0.04
Ecuadorian	17	0.02
Paraguayan	12	0.01
Peruvian	31	0.03
Uruguayan	3	<0.01
Venezuelan	3	<0.01
Other South American	2	<0.01
Other Hispanic or Latino	260	0.27

Race*	Population	%
African-American/Black (3,309)	3,691	3.81
Not Hispanic (3,264)	3,609	3.72
Hispanic (45)	82	0.08
American Indian/Alaska Native (237)	632	0.65
Not Hispanic (204)	561	0.58
Hispanic (33)	71	0.07
Apache (0)	1	<0.01
Blackfeet (5)	13	0.01
Canadian/French Am. Ind. (2)	11	0.01
Central American Ind. (2)	2	<0.01
Cherokee (10)	84	0.09
Chippewa (50)	116	0.12
Choctaw (3)	10	0.01
Colville (0)	1	<0.01
Cree (0)	3	<0.01
Creek (4)	7	0.01
Crow (0)	2	<0.01
Delaware (3)	4	<0.01
Inupiat *(Alaska Native)* (0)	1	<0.01
Iroquois (27)	48	0.05
Lumbee (13)	20	0.02
Menominee (3)	7	0.01
Mexican American Ind. (20)	28	0.03
Navajo (3)	3	<0.01
Osage (0)	1	<0.01
Ottawa (8)	18	0.02
Paiute (1)	3	<0.01
Potawatomi (4)	4	<0.01
Pueblo (3)	6	0.01
Puget Sound Salish (0)	1	<0.01
Sioux (2)	14	0.01
Asian (2,459)	3,022	3.12
Not Hispanic (2,441)	2,980	3.07
Hispanic (18)	42	0.04
Bangladeshi (11)	11	0.01
Cambodian (11)	11	0.01
Chinese, ex. Taiwanese (509)	597	0.62
Filipino (433)	566	0.58
Hmong (1)	3	<0.01
Indian (882)	930	0.96

SECTION TWO

*Notes: † The Census 2010 population figure is used to calculate the percentages in the Hispanic Origin and Race categories. Ancestry percentages are based on the 2006-2010 American Community Survey population (not shown); ‡ Numbers in parentheses indicate the number of people reporting a single ancestry; * Numbers in parentheses indicate the number of persons reporting this race alone, not in combination with any other race; Please refer to the Explanation of Data for more information.*

Indonesian (4)	10	0.01
Japanese (95)	175	0.18
Korean (166)	227	0.23
Laotian (3)	5	0.01
Malaysian (3)	5	0.01
Nepalese (2)	2	<0.01
Pakistani (70)	81	0.08
Sri Lankan (6)	8	0.01
Taiwanese (11)	19	0.02
Thai (15)	27	0.03
Vietnamese (193)	208	0.21
Hawaii Native/Pacific Islander (12)	60	0.06
Not Hispanic (11)	55	0.06
Hispanic (1)	5	0.01
Guamanian/Chamorro (1)	5	0.01
Native Hawaiian (2)	21	0.02
Samoan (2)	3	<0.01
White (89,159)	90,446	93.30
Not Hispanic (87,332)	88,468	91.26
Hispanic (1,827)	1,978	2.04

Long Lake

Place Type: Township
County: Grand Traverse
Population: 8,662[†]

Ancestry[‡]	Population	%
American (623)	623	7.27
Armenian (17)	17	0.20
Belgian (0)	119	1.39
British (0)	30	0.35
Canadian (18)	36	0.42
Czech (13)	113	1.32
Danish (0)	15	0.18
Dutch (213)	508	5.93
English (420)	989	11.55
European (18)	18	0.21
Finnish (93)	140	1.63
French, ex. Basque (44)	677	7.90
French Canadian (39)	180	2.10
German (900)	2,884	33.67
Hungarian (27)	27	0.32
Irish (302)	1,110	12.96
Italian (73)	373	4.35
Norwegian (78)	223	2.60
Pennsylvania German (0)	11	0.13
Polish (213)	1,073	12.53
Portuguese (0)	13	0.15
Russian (0)	13	0.15
Scandinavian (44)	44	0.51
Scotch-Irish (54)	128	1.49
Scottish (104)	299	3.49
Soviet Union (52)	52	0.61
Swedish (43)	165	1.93
Swiss (32)	46	0.54
Ukrainian (13)	13	0.15
Welsh (0)	43	0.50
Yugoslavian (0)	9	0.11

Hispanic Origin	Population	%
Hispanic or Latino (of any race)	172	1.99
Central American, ex. Mexican	2	0.02
Guatemalan	2	0.02
Cuban	3	0.03
Mexican	121	1.40
Puerto Rican	8	0.09
South American	15	0.17
Bolivian	1	0.01
Colombian	4	0.05
Ecuadorian	5	0.06
Peruvian	2	0.02
Venezuelan	3	0.03
Other Hispanic or Latino	23	0.27

Race*	Population	%
African-American/Black (15)	43	0.50
Not Hispanic (15)	42	0.48
Hispanic (0)	1	0.01
American Indian/Alaska Native (76)	123	1.42
Not Hispanic (68)	113	1.30
Hispanic (8)	10	0.12
Aleut *(Alaska Native)* (0)	1	0.01
Apache (0)	2	0.02
Blackfeet (3)	3	0.03
Canadian/French Am. Ind. (1)	2	0.02
Cherokee (0)	6	0.07
Chippewa (30)	54	0.62
Cree (0)	1	0.01
Creek (1)	1	0.01
Iroquois (2)	2	0.02
Menominee (1)	1	0.01
Ottawa (2)	8	0.09
Potawatomi (5)	6	0.07
Sioux (2)	7	0.08
Spanish American Ind. (2)	2	0.02
Asian (39)	65	0.75
Not Hispanic (35)	61	0.70
Hispanic (4)	4	0.05
Chinese, ex. Taiwanese (3)	5	0.06
Filipino (4)	9	0.10
Indian (3)	6	0.07
Japanese (3)	15	0.17
Korean (12)	17	0.20
Laotian (3)	3	0.03
Pakistani (1)	1	0.01
Thai (1)	1	0.01
Vietnamese (3)	8	0.09
Hawaii Native/Pacific Islander (2)	11	0.13
Not Hispanic (2)	11	0.13
Guamanian/Chamorro (0)	1	0.01
Native Hawaiian (1)	7	0.08
White (8,374)	8,484	97.95
Not Hispanic (8,265)	8,367	96.59
Hispanic (109)	117	1.35

Ludington

Place Type: City
County: Mason
Population: 8,076[†]

Ancestry[‡]	Population	%
African, Sub-Saharan (29)	29	0.36
African (29)	29	0.36
American (290)	290	3.55
Austrian (11)	11	0.13
Belgian (7)	40	0.49
British (0)	70	0.86
Canadian (11)	11	0.13
Croatian (15)	15	0.18
Czech (0)	26	0.32
Czechoslovakian (0)	25	0.31
Danish (97)	431	5.28
Dutch (193)	572	7.00
English (183)	1,011	12.38
European (9)	9	0.11
Finnish (0)	67	0.82
French, ex. Basque (42)	499	6.11
French Canadian (47)	127	1.56
German (844)	2,592	31.74
Greek (51)	51	0.62
Hungarian (0)	152	1.86
Irish (177)	1,074	13.15
Italian (66)	234	2.87
Lithuanian (30)	108	1.32
Norwegian (20)	214	2.62
Polish (293)	912	11.17
Portuguese (0)	8	0.10
Russian (24)	34	0.42
Scandinavian (0)	38	0.47
Scotch-Irish (30)	158	1.93
Scottish (41)	341	4.18
Swedish (74)	429	5.25
Welsh (0)	89	1.09

Hispanic Origin	Population	%
Hispanic or Latino (of any race)	512	6.34
Central American, ex. Mexican	3	0.04
Guatemalan	2	0.02
Nicaraguan	1	0.01
Cuban	1	0.01
Dominican Republic	4	0.05
Mexican	429	5.31
Puerto Rican	5	0.06
South American	6	0.07
Chilean	2	0.02
Colombian	2	0.02
Venezuelan	1	0.01
Other South American	1	0.01
Other Hispanic or Latino	64	0.79

Race*	Population	%
African-American/Black (92)	158	1.96
Not Hispanic (79)	134	1.66
Hispanic (13)	24	0.30
American Indian/Alaska Native (113)	201	2.49
Not Hispanic (90)	166	2.06
Hispanic (23)	35	0.43
Apache (0)	1	0.01
Canadian/French Am. Ind. (0)	2	0.02
Cherokee (8)	16	0.20
Chippewa (20)	34	0.42
Choctaw (1)	3	0.04
Crow (0)	1	0.01
Delaware (0)	1	0.01
Iroquois (1)	1	0.01
Menominee (1)	1	0.01
Ottawa (41)	62	0.77
Potawatomi (1)	2	0.02
Sioux (3)	4	0.05
South American Ind. (6)	6	0.07
Spanish American Ind. (0)	2	0.02
Asian (52)	72	0.89
Not Hispanic (51)	71	0.88
Hispanic (1)	1	0.01
Chinese, ex. Taiwanese (17)	17	0.21
Filipino (5)	9	0.11
Indian (18)	22	0.27
Japanese (1)	3	0.04
Korean (11)	18	0.22
Vietnamese (0)	3	0.04
Hawaii Native/Pacific Islander (0)	1	0.01
Hispanic (0)	1	0.01
White (7,448)	7,652	94.75
Not Hispanic (7,194)	7,337	90.85
Hispanic (254)	315	3.90

Lyon

Place Type: Charter Township
County: Oakland
Population: 14,545[†]

Ancestry[‡]	Population	%
African, Sub-Saharan (12)	12	0.09
African (12)	12	0.09
Albanian (108)	108	0.77
American (778)	778	5.58
Arab (15)	84	0.60
Arab (0)	8	0.06
Lebanese (7)	52	0.37
Palestinian (8)	24	0.17
Armenian (10)	31	0.22
Assyrian/Chaldean/Syriac (0)	33	0.24
Australian (0)	25	0.18
Austrian (24)	34	0.24
Belgian (0)	39	0.28
British (11)	11	0.08
Canadian (38)	109	0.78
Czech (40)	180	1.29
Danish (0)	33	0.24
Dutch (98)	358	2.57
English (345)	1,653	11.85
European (110)	110	0.79
Finnish (50)	233	1.67
French, ex. Basque (85)	600	4.30
French Canadian (210)	585	4.20
German (971)	3,819	27.39
Greek (38)	120	0.86

*Notes: † The Census 2010 population figure is used to calculate the percentages in the Hispanic Origin and Race categories. Ancestry percentages are based on the 2006-2010 American Community Survey population (not shown); ‡ Numbers in parentheses indicate the number of people reporting a single ancestry; * Numbers in parentheses indicate the number of persons reporting this race alone, not in combination with any other race; Please refer to the Explanation of Data for more information.*

Hungarian (49)	212	1.52
Iranian (35)	35	0.25
Irish (633)	2,500	17.93
Italian (438)	1,640	11.76
Latvian (0)	10	0.07
Lithuanian (42)	66	0.47
Macedonian (7)	15	0.11
Maltese (0)	54	0.39
Northern European (27)	27	0.19
Norwegian (33)	166	1.19
Polish (606)	2,076	14.89
Romanian (60)	108	0.77
Russian (31)	142	1.02
Scotch-Irish (29)	160	1.15
Scottish (66)	515	3.69
Slavic (24)	123	0.88
Slovak (30)	30	0.22
Slovene (0)	38	0.27
Swedish (24)	202	1.45
Swiss (0)	9	0.06
Ukrainian (22)	92	0.66
Welsh (10)	161	1.15
West Indian, ex. Hispanic (0)	11	0.08
West Indian (0)	11	0.08
Yugoslavian (59)	81	0.58

Hispanic Origin	Population	%
Hispanic or Latino (of any race)	419	2.88
Central American, ex. Mexican	14	0.10
Guatemalan	11	0.08
Salvadoran	3	0.02
Cuban	9	0.06
Dominican Republic	1	0.01
Mexican	302	2.08
Puerto Rican	18	0.12
South American	33	0.23
Argentinean	5	0.03
Bolivian	4	0.03
Chilean	1	0.01
Colombian	9	0.06
Ecuadorian	5	0.03
Paraguayan	4	0.03
Peruvian	4	0.03
Venezuelan	1	0.01
Other Hispanic or Latino	42	0.29

Race*	Population	%
African-American/Black (210)	270	1.86
Not Hispanic (206)	265	1.82
Hispanic (4)	5	0.03
American Indian/Alaska Native (40)	137	0.94
Not Hispanic (37)	131	0.90
Hispanic (3)	6	0.04
Blackfeet (1)	2	0.01
Canadian/French Am. Ind. (0)	1	0.01
Cherokee (6)	31	0.21
Chickasaw (0)	2	0.01
Chippewa (10)	20	0.14
Choctaw (0)	1	0.01
Delaware (1)	7	0.05
Iroquois (4)	7	0.05
Lumbee (3)	7	0.05
Mexican American Ind. (2)	2	0.01
Navajo (0)	1	0.01
Sioux (1)	1	0.01
Asian (225)	308	2.12
Not Hispanic (223)	303	2.08
Hispanic (2)	5	0.03
Bangladeshi (4)	4	0.03
Cambodian (0)	4	0.03
Chinese, ex. Taiwanese (34)	42	0.29
Filipino (23)	46	0.32
Indian (72)	76	0.52
Japanese (34)	57	0.39
Korean (32)	47	0.32
Sri Lankan (4)	4	0.03
Taiwanese (4)	4	0.03
Thai (4)	7	0.05
Vietnamese (8)	8	0.06
Hawaii Native/Pacific Islander (3)	8	0.06
Not Hispanic (3)	8	0.06
Guamanian/Chamorro (0)	2	0.01
Marshallese (2)	2	0.01
Native Hawaiian (1)	2	0.01
White (13,758)	14,006	96.29
Not Hispanic (13,426)	13,650	93.85
Hispanic (332)	356	2.45

Macomb

Place Type: Township
County: Macomb
Population: 79,580†

Ancestry‡	Population	%
African, Sub-Saharan (527)	527	0.70
African (454)	454	0.61
Liberian (19)	19	0.03
Nigerian (28)	28	0.04
South African (26)	26	0.03
Albanian (1,820)	2,016	2.69
American (3,167)	3,167	4.23
Arab (874)	1,625	2.17
Arab (203)	260	0.35
Egyptian (0)	7	0.01
Iraqi (86)	124	0.17
Jordanian (48)	95	0.13
Lebanese (348)	808	1.08
Palestinian (19)	35	0.05
Syrian (54)	169	0.23
Other Arab (116)	127	0.17
Armenian (97)	262	0.35
Assyrian/Chaldean/Syriac (346)	430	0.57
Austrian (27)	99	0.13
Belgian (514)	1,860	2.48
British (52)	90	0.12
Bulgarian (0)	53	0.07
Canadian (203)	571	0.76
Carpatho Rusyn (0)	12	0.02
Celtic (36)	36	0.05
Croatian (139)	220	0.29
Czech (79)	412	0.55
Czechoslovakian (29)	119	0.16
Danish (35)	69	0.09
Dutch (290)	1,243	1.66
Eastern European (47)	55	0.07
English (886)	4,987	6.66
European (303)	315	0.42
Finnish (60)	458	0.61
French, ex. Basque (499)	4,292	5.73
French Canadian (482)	1,401	1.87
German (4,199)	17,908	23.92
German Russian (0)	28	0.04
Greek (240)	664	0.89
Hungarian (119)	884	1.18
Icelander (0)	16	0.02
Irish (1,605)	7,998	10.68
Italian (5,997)	13,499	18.03
Lithuanian (20)	186	0.25
Macedonian (964)	1,123	1.50
Maltese (108)	192	0.26
Norwegian (46)	336	0.45
Pennsylvania German (0)	14	0.02
Polish (5,644)	15,670	20.93
Portuguese (7)	40	0.05
Romanian (378)	621	0.83
Russian (94)	533	0.71
Scandinavian (0)	11	0.01
Scotch-Irish (299)	861	1.15
Scottish (227)	1,376	1.84
Serbian (83)	268	0.36
Slavic (126)	204	0.27
Slovak (70)	190	0.25
Slovene (0)	58	0.08
Swedish (291)	841	1.12
Swiss (31)	217	0.29
Turkish (36)	48	0.06
Ukrainian (147)	528	0.71
Welsh (18)	342	0.46
West Indian, ex. Hispanic (7)	7	0.01
West Indian (7)	7	0.01
Yugoslavian (782)	1,041	1.39

Hispanic Origin	Population	%
Hispanic or Latino (of any race)	1,803	2.27
Central American, ex. Mexican	74	0.09
Costa Rican	5	0.01
Guatemalan	43	0.05
Honduran	1	<0.01
Panamanian	17	0.02
Salvadoran	8	0.01
Cuban	51	0.06
Dominican Republic	14	0.02
Mexican	1,182	1.49
Puerto Rican	122	0.15
South American	113	0.14
Argentinean	21	0.03
Chilean	6	0.01
Colombian	32	0.04
Ecuadorian	16	0.02
Peruvian	16	0.02
Uruguayan	4	0.01
Venezuelan	18	0.02
Other Hispanic or Latino	247	0.31

Race*	Population	%
African-American/Black (3,131)	3,522	4.43
Not Hispanic (3,096)	3,450	4.34
Hispanic (35)	72	0.09
American Indian/Alaska Native (161)	465	0.58
Not Hispanic (136)	409	0.51
Hispanic (25)	56	0.07
Apache (1)	6	0.01
Blackfeet (1)	13	0.02
Canadian/French Am. Ind. (3)	8	0.01
Cherokee (15)	91	0.11
Chickasaw (0)	1	<0.01
Chippewa (53)	78	0.10
Choctaw (3)	10	0.01
Comanche (0)	1	<0.01
Delaware (0)	2	<0.01
Iroquois (20)	29	0.04
Lumbee (5)	18	0.02
Mexican American Ind. (8)	10	0.01
Navajo (0)	3	<0.01
Osage (2)	6	0.01
Ottawa (8)	15	0.02
Potawatomi (0)	1	<0.01
Pueblo (1)	1	<0.01
Seminole (0)	1	<0.01
Sioux (0)	2	<0.01
Yup'ik *(Alaska Native)* (1)	4	0.01
Asian (2,462)	2,957	3.72
Not Hispanic (2,446)	2,929	3.68
Hispanic (16)	28	0.04
Bangladeshi (17)	17	0.02
Burmese (0)	2	<0.01
Cambodian (12)	18	0.02
Chinese, ex. Taiwanese (361)	421	0.53
Filipino (602)	774	0.97
Hmong (84)	86	0.11
Indian (657)	714	0.90
Indonesian (7)	7	0.01
Japanese (36)	82	0.10
Korean (192)	268	0.34
Laotian (18)	18	0.02
Malaysian (2)	2	<0.01
Nepalese (8)	8	0.01
Pakistani (114)	134	0.17
Sri Lankan (4)	4	0.01
Taiwanese (8)	11	0.01
Thai (7)	14	0.02
Vietnamese (238)	273	0.34
Hawaii Native/Pacific Islander (17)	68	0.09
Not Hispanic (15)	64	0.08
Hispanic (2)	4	0.01
Guamanian/Chamorro (5)	13	0.02
Native Hawaiian (2)	11	0.01
Samoan (1)	4	0.01
White (72,050)	73,177	91.95

*Notes: † The Census 2010 population figure is used to calculate the percentages in the Hispanic Origin and Race categories. Ancestry percentages are based on the 2006-2010 American Community Survey population (not shown); ‡ Numbers in parentheses indicate the number of people reporting a single ancestry; * Numbers in parentheses indicate the number of persons reporting this race alone, not in combination with any other race; Please refer to the Explanation of Data for more information.*

Not Hispanic (70,906)	71,917	90.37
Hispanic (1,144)	1,260	1.58

Madison Heights

Place Type: City
County: Oakland
Population: 29,694†

Ancestry‡	Population	%
African, Sub-Saharan (40)	57	0.19
African (40)	57	0.19
Albanian (514)	514	1.72
American (1,203)	1,203	4.02
Arab (1,152)	1,463	4.88
Arab (479)	503	1.68
Egyptian (172)	172	0.57
Iraqi (277)	424	1.42
Lebanese (85)	225	0.75
Palestinian (55)	55	0.18
Syrian (60)	60	0.20
Other Arab (24)	24	0.08
Armenian (119)	221	0.74
Assyrian/Chaldean/Syriac (1,177)	1,310	4.37
Austrian (14)	127	0.42
Belgian (21)	236	0.79
Brazilian (63)	63	0.21
British (40)	102	0.34
Bulgarian (41)	41	0.14
Canadian (90)	281	0.94
Croatian (76)	108	0.36
Czech (0)	49	0.16
Czechoslovakian (0)	14	0.05
Danish (29)	57	0.19
Dutch (176)	479	1.60
Eastern European (16)	16	0.05
English (615)	2,934	9.80
European (259)	274	0.91
Finnish (162)	571	1.91
French, ex. Basque (128)	1,637	5.47
French Canadian (227)	729	2.43
German (1,178)	6,435	21.48
Greek (54)	295	0.98
Hungarian (31)	176	0.59
Iranian (0)	14	0.05
Irish (636)	3,963	13.23
Italian (399)	1,936	6.46
Lithuanian (27)	38	0.13
Northern European (18)	18	0.06
Norwegian (31)	145	0.48
Polish (1,542)	3,746	12.51
Portuguese (14)	39	0.13
Romanian (453)	522	1.74
Russian (93)	416	1.39
Scotch-Irish (105)	375	1.25
Scottish (318)	1,243	4.15
Serbian (18)	39	0.13
Slovak (0)	75	0.25
Slovene (11)	29	0.10
Swedish (72)	428	1.43
Swiss (0)	50	0.17
Ukrainian (112)	266	0.89
Welsh (37)	163	0.54
Yugoslavian (25)	25	0.08

Hispanic Origin	Population	%
Hispanic or Latino (of any race)	756	2.55
Central American, ex. Mexican	73	0.25
Costa Rican	12	0.04
Guatemalan	3	0.01
Nicaraguan	2	0.01
Panamanian	12	0.04
Salvadoran	44	0.15
Cuban	19	0.06
Dominican Republic	17	0.06
Mexican	435	1.46
Puerto Rican	74	0.25
South American	26	0.09
Argentinean	5	0.02
Bolivian	2	0.01
Chilean	1	<0.01
Colombian	6	0.02
Paraguayan	4	0.01
Peruvian	5	0.02
Venezuelan	3	0.01
Other Hispanic or Latino	112	0.38

Race*	Population	%
African-American/Black (1,897)	2,202	7.42
Not Hispanic (1,870)	2,158	7.27
Hispanic (27)	44	0.15
American Indian/Alaska Native (136)	314	1.06
Not Hispanic (132)	295	0.99
Hispanic (4)	19	0.06
Apache (0)	1	<0.01
Blackfeet (1)	11	0.04
Canadian/French Am. Ind. (9)	12	0.04
Cherokee (6)	57	0.19
Cheyenne (0)	1	<0.01
Chickasaw (1)	1	<0.01
Chippewa (38)	50	0.17
Choctaw (0)	1	<0.01
Creek (1)	5	0.02
Iroquois (8)	10	0.03
Lumbee (6)	9	0.03
Mexican American Ind. (2)	5	0.02
Ottawa (2)	4	0.01
Potawatomi (0)	2	0.01
Pueblo (0)	1	<0.01
Seminole (3)	3	0.01
Shoshone (2)	2	0.01
Sioux (2)	5	0.02
Spanish American Ind. (1)	1	<0.01
Tlingit-Haida *(Alaska Native)* (1)	1	<0.01
Asian (1,725)	2,045	6.89
Not Hispanic (1,711)	2,022	6.81
Hispanic (14)	23	0.08
Bangladeshi (87)	95	0.32
Cambodian (14)	14	0.05
Chinese, ex. Taiwanese (382)	408	1.37
Filipino (333)	400	1.35
Hmong (5)	6	0.02
Indian (436)	480	1.62
Japanese (16)	46	0.15
Korean (53)	81	0.27
Laotian (17)	18	0.06
Nepalese (26)	27	0.09
Pakistani (34)	45	0.15
Taiwanese (7)	7	0.02
Thai (18)	19	0.06
Vietnamese (227)	240	0.81
Hawaii Native/Pacific Islander (19)	59	0.20
Not Hispanic (19)	56	0.19
Hispanic (0)	3	0.01
Guamanian/Chamorro (3)	4	0.01
Native Hawaiian (5)	14	0.05
Samoan (0)	2	0.01
White (24,909)	25,652	86.39
Not Hispanic (24,444)	25,133	84.64
Hispanic (465)	519	1.75

Madison

Place Type: Charter Township
County: Lenawee
Population: 8,621†

Ancestry‡	Population	%
African, Sub-Saharan (12)	26	0.31
African (12)	26	0.31
American (609)	609	7.18
Arab (9)	9	0.11
Moroccan (9)	9	0.11
British (43)	43	0.51
Canadian (0)	22	0.26
Czechoslovakian (0)	10	0.12
Dutch (41)	260	3.07
English (427)	1,057	12.46
European (0)	12	0.14
Finnish (10)	23	0.27
French, ex. Basque (74)	258	3.04
French Canadian (138)	418	4.93
German (943)	2,430	28.65
Hungarian (34)	64	0.75
Irish (324)	1,046	12.33
Italian (53)	205	2.42
Maltese (18)	60	0.71
Norwegian (17)	107	1.26
Pennsylvania German (0)	13	0.15
Polish (147)	454	5.35
Russian (0)	33	0.39
Scandinavian (12)	12	0.14
Scotch-Irish (23)	40	0.47
Scottish (23)	96	1.13
Slavic (34)	34	0.40
Slovak (0)	16	0.19
Swedish (12)	76	0.90
Swiss (15)	52	0.61
Welsh (0)	33	0.39

Hispanic Origin	Population	%
Hispanic or Latino (of any race)	731	8.48
Central American, ex. Mexican	2	0.02
Nicaraguan	1	0.01
Salvadoran	1	0.01
Cuban	2	0.02
Mexican	621	7.20
Puerto Rican	31	0.36
South American	9	0.10
Colombian	8	0.09
Peruvian	1	0.01
Other Hispanic or Latino	66	0.77

Race*	Population	%
African-American/Black (1,174)	1,245	14.44
Not Hispanic (1,165)	1,222	14.17
Hispanic (9)	23	0.27
American Indian/Alaska Native (55)	113	1.31
Not Hispanic (40)	90	1.04
Hispanic (15)	23	0.27
Apache (0)	1	0.01
Blackfeet (4)	12	0.14
Central American Ind. (1)	1	0.01
Cherokee (2)	13	0.15
Chippewa (6)	11	0.13
Choctaw (2)	2	0.02
Delaware (1)	1	0.01
Inupiat *(Alaska Native)* (1)	1	0.01
Mexican American Ind. (3)	3	0.03
Ottawa (1)	1	0.01
Sioux (0)	1	0.01
Asian (34)	53	0.61
Not Hispanic (34)	49	0.57
Hispanic (0)	4	0.05
Chinese, ex. Taiwanese (2)	2	0.02
Filipino (6)	14	0.16
Indian (1)	7	0.08
Japanese (7)	9	0.10
Korean (4)	8	0.09
Malaysian (0)	3	0.03
Pakistani (2)	3	0.03
Vietnamese (3)	3	0.03
Hawaii Native/Pacific Islander (0)	1	0.01
Not Hispanic (0)	1	0.01
Native Hawaiian (0)	1	0.01
White (6,997)	7,158	83.03
Not Hispanic (6,534)	6,645	77.08
Hispanic (463)	513	5.95

Marion

Place Type: Township
County: Livingston
Population: 9,996†

Ancestry‡	Population	%
American (482)	482	4.99
Arab (5)	15	0.16
Lebanese (5)	15	0.16
Austrian (0)	16	0.17

*Notes: † The Census 2010 population figure is used to calculate the percentages in the Hispanic Origin and Race categories. Ancestry percentages are based on the 2006-2010 American Community Survey population (not shown); ‡ Numbers in parentheses indicate the number of people reporting a single ancestry; * Numbers in parentheses indicate the number of persons reporting this race alone, not in combination with any other race; Please refer to the Explanation of Data for more information.*

Ancestry	Population	%
Belgian (23)	41	0.42
British (40)	64	0.66
Canadian (21)	70	0.72
Czech (0)	41	0.42
Czechoslovakian (0)	10	0.10
Danish (0)	51	0.53
Dutch (66)	159	1.64
Eastern European (27)	27	0.28
English (456)	1,409	14.58
European (48)	48	0.50
Finnish (208)	243	2.51
French, ex. Basque (106)	566	5.86
French Canadian (28)	342	3.54
German (616)	2,665	27.57
Greek (35)	35	0.36
Hungarian (0)	59	0.61
Irish (705)	2,322	24.02
Italian (228)	649	6.71
Lithuanian (9)	9	0.09
Northern European (10)	10	0.10
Norwegian (104)	216	2.23
Pennsylvania German (7)	7	0.07
Polish (483)	1,279	13.23
Romanian (25)	52	0.54
Russian (9)	32	0.33
Scandinavian (0)	30	0.31
Scotch-Irish (70)	364	3.77
Scottish (139)	456	4.72
Slavic (0)	10	0.10
Slovak (17)	25	0.26
Swedish (47)	180	1.86
Swiss (60)	90	0.93
Ukrainian (41)	80	0.83
Welsh (8)	68	0.70

Hispanic Origin	Population	%
Hispanic or Latino (of any race)	161	1.61
Central American, ex. Mexican	3	0.03
Nicaraguan	3	0.03
Cuban	7	0.07
Dominican Republic	1	0.01
Mexican	100	1.00
Puerto Rican	4	0.04
South American	22	0.22
Argentinean	2	0.02
Chilean	4	0.04
Colombian	11	0.11
Ecuadorian	1	0.01
Peruvian	4	0.04
Other Hispanic or Latino	24	0.24

Race*	Population	%
African-American/Black (12)	29	0.29
Not Hispanic (12)	27	0.27
Hispanic (0)	2	0.02
American Indian/Alaska Native (35)	93	0.93
Not Hispanic (34)	91	0.91
Hispanic (1)	2	0.02
Cherokee (4)	8	0.08
Chippewa (19)	38	0.38
Inupiat *(Alaska Native)* (0)	3	0.03
Iroquois (0)	2	0.02
Ottawa (2)	7	0.07
Sioux (1)	1	0.01
Asian (75)	111	1.11
Not Hispanic (75)	111	1.11
Bangladeshi (3)	3	0.03
Chinese, ex. Taiwanese (13)	20	0.20
Filipino (13)	23	0.23
Indian (13)	15	0.15
Japanese (3)	9	0.09
Korean (10)	20	0.20
Malaysian (1)	1	0.01
Pakistani (1)	1	0.01
Taiwanese (3)	3	0.03
Vietnamese (15)	15	0.15
Hawaii Native/Pacific Islander (3)	11	0.11
Not Hispanic (3)	11	0.11
Guamanian/Chamorro (3)	3	0.03
Native Hawaiian (0)	4	0.04
White (9,726)	9,839	98.43
Not Hispanic (9,600)	9,706	97.10
Hispanic (126)	133	1.33

Marquette

Place Type: City
County: Marquette
Population: 21,355†

Ancestry‡	Population	%
African, Sub-Saharan (9)	9	0.04
African (9)	9	0.04
American (397)	397	1.87
Arab (88)	104	0.49
Arab (9)	9	0.04
Lebanese (12)	28	0.13
Moroccan (10)	10	0.05
Palestinian (30)	30	0.14
Syrian (27)	27	0.13
Armenian (0)	10	0.05
Assyrian/Chaldean/Syriac (14)	14	0.07
Austrian (12)	89	0.42
Belgian (137)	351	1.65
British (52)	85	0.40
Canadian (97)	106	0.50
Croatian (39)	232	1.09
Czech (12)	178	0.84
Czechoslovakian (15)	28	0.13
Danish (22)	234	1.10
Dutch (112)	637	3.00
Eastern European (36)	36	0.17
English (385)	2,735	12.87
Estonian (12)	12	0.06
European (411)	425	2.00
Finnish (966)	2,593	12.20
French, ex. Basque (234)	2,274	10.70
French Canadian (212)	568	2.67
German (1,055)	4,719	22.21
Greek (141)	236	1.11
Hungarian (33)	148	0.70
Irish (353)	2,803	13.19
Italian (472)	1,800	8.47
Latvian (0)	16	0.08
Lithuanian (0)	110	0.52
Norwegian (125)	537	2.53
Polish (317)	1,395	6.57
Portuguese (0)	41	0.19
Romanian (0)	39	0.18
Russian (10)	165	0.78
Scandinavian (51)	101	0.48
Scotch-Irish (128)	499	2.35
Scottish (31)	567	2.67
Serbian (0)	13	0.06
Slovak (0)	11	0.05
Slovene (0)	10	0.05
Swedish (459)	1,868	8.79
Swiss (0)	26	0.12
Turkish (32)	32	0.15
Ukrainian (12)	76	0.36
Welsh (39)	189	0.89
West Indian, ex. Hispanic (0)	14	0.07
Jamaican (0)	14	0.07
Yugoslavian (11)	11	0.05

Hispanic Origin	Population	%
Hispanic or Latino (of any race)	309	1.45
Central American, ex. Mexican	28	0.13
Guatemalan	19	0.09
Honduran	2	0.01
Panamanian	5	0.02
Salvadoran	2	0.01
Cuban	26	0.12
Mexican	165	0.77
Puerto Rican	36	0.17
South American	13	0.06
Argentinean	1	<0.01
Chilean	5	0.02
Colombian	1	<0.01
Ecuadorian	1	<0.01
Peruvian	3	0.01
Venezuelan	2	0.01
Other Hispanic or Latino	41	0.19

Race*	Population	%
African-American/Black (946)	1,057	4.95
Not Hispanic (934)	1,034	4.84
Hispanic (12)	23	0.11
American Indian/Alaska Native (316)	504	2.36
Not Hispanic (310)	490	2.29
Hispanic (6)	14	0.07
Apache (1)	1	<0.01
Blackfeet (1)	5	0.02
Canadian/French Am. Ind. (0)	1	<0.01
Central American Ind. (0)	3	0.01
Cherokee (2)	13	0.06
Chippewa (192)	292	1.37
Iroquois (5)	7	0.03
Menominee (0)	1	<0.01
Ottawa (11)	15	0.07
Potawatomi (4)	8	0.04
Puget Sound Salish (0)	1	<0.01
Sioux (1)	5	0.02
Asian (188)	277	1.30
Not Hispanic (188)	264	1.24
Hispanic (0)	13	0.06
Chinese, ex. Taiwanese (37)	59	0.28
Filipino (24)	49	0.23
Indian (39)	48	0.22
Indonesian (0)	1	<0.01
Japanese (13)	25	0.12
Korean (30)	46	0.22
Malaysian (0)	2	0.01
Nepalese (1)	1	<0.01
Pakistani (12)	12	0.06
Taiwanese (4)	6	0.03
Thai (9)	11	0.05
Vietnamese (5)	9	0.04
Hawaii Native/Pacific Islander (6)	19	0.09
Not Hispanic (5)	13	0.06
Hispanic (1)	6	0.03
Guamanian/Chamorro (2)	6	0.03
Marshallese (0)	2	0.01
Native Hawaiian (3)	5	0.02
Samoan (0)	3	0.01
White (19,455)	19,823	92.83
Not Hispanic (19,255)	19,589	91.73
Hispanic (200)	234	1.10

Marysville

Place Type: City
County: St. Clair
Population: 9,959†

Ancestry‡	Population	%
American (551)	551	5.48
Arab (53)	64	0.64
Arab (20)	31	0.31
Lebanese (33)	33	0.33
Armenian (0)	25	0.25
Assyrian/Chaldean/Syriac (75)	75	0.75
Austrian (0)	28	0.28
Belgian (26)	35	0.35
British (16)	16	0.16
Canadian (33)	98	0.97
Czech (24)	33	0.33
Czechoslovakian (10)	10	0.10
Danish (8)	66	0.66
Dutch (56)	220	2.19
English (454)	1,226	12.19
European (174)	174	1.73
Finnish (24)	57	0.57
French, ex. Basque (111)	766	7.62
French Canadian (85)	287	2.85
German (1,120)	3,288	32.69
Greek (21)	95	0.94
Hungarian (48)	174	1.73
Irish (490)	1,480	14.72
Italian (242)	736	7.32

*Notes: † The Census 2010 population figure is used to calculate the percentages in the Hispanic Origin and Race categories. Ancestry percentages are based on the 2006-2010 American Community Survey population (not shown); ‡ Numbers in parentheses indicate the number of people reporting a single ancestry; * Numbers in parentheses indicate the number of persons reporting this race alone, not in combination with any other race; Please refer to the Explanation of Data for more information.*

Ancestry	Population	%
Lithuanian (0)	9	0.09
Norwegian (38)	141	1.40
Pennsylvania German (20)	20	0.20
Polish (305)	1,113	11.07
Portuguese (9)	9	0.09
Romanian (0)	79	0.79
Russian (27)	88	0.88
Scotch-Irish (48)	339	3.37
Scottish (102)	467	4.64
Slovak (18)	18	0.18
Swedish (20)	88	0.88
Swiss (0)	6	0.06
Welsh (0)	26	0.26
West Indian, ex. Hispanic (0)	10	0.10
Dutch West Indian (0)	10	0.10
Yugoslavian (0)	28	0.28

Hispanic Origin	Population	%
Hispanic or Latino (of any race)	177	1.78
Central American, ex. Mexican	13	0.13
Guatemalan	9	0.09
Honduran	3	0.03
Panamanian	1	0.01
Cuban	9	0.09
Mexican	107	1.07
Puerto Rican	7	0.07
South American	7	0.07
Argentinean	3	0.03
Colombian	4	0.04
Other Hispanic or Latino	34	0.34

Race*	Population	%
African-American/Black (34)	52	0.52
Not Hispanic (34)	51	0.51
Hispanic (0)	1	0.01
American Indian/Alaska Native (24)	55	0.55
Not Hispanic (21)	46	0.46
Hispanic (3)	9	0.09
Blackfeet (2)	4	0.04
Canadian/French Am. Ind. (1)	1	0.01
Cherokee (1)	3	0.03
Chippewa (6)	6	0.06
Choctaw (0)	4	0.04
Iroquois (4)	4	0.04
Mexican American Ind. (2)	3	0.03
Osage (0)	1	0.01
Ottawa (0)	1	0.01
Potawatomi (0)	2	0.02
Sioux (1)	1	0.01
Yuman (1)	1	0.01
Asian (62)	85	0.85
Not Hispanic (62)	84	0.84
Hispanic (0)	1	0.01
Chinese, ex. Taiwanese (8)	9	0.09
Filipino (21)	29	0.29
Hmong (14)	14	0.14
Indian (3)	3	0.03
Japanese (2)	4	0.04
Korean (13)	13	0.13
Thai (1)	1	0.01
Hawaii Native/Pacific Islander (2)	6	0.06
Not Hispanic (2)	6	0.06
Native Hawaiian (1)	3	0.03
Samoan (0)	5	0.05
White (9,708)	9,792	98.32
Not Hispanic (9,595)	9,663	97.03
Hispanic (113)	129	1.30

Mason

Place Type: City
County: Ingham
Population: 8,252†

Ancestry‡	Population	%
Albanian (73)	73	0.90
American (576)	576	7.13
Arab (0)	27	0.33
Arab (0)	9	0.11
Lebanese (0)	18	0.22
Austrian (20)	30	0.37
Belgian (12)	12	0.15
British (82)	151	1.87
Canadian (0)	23	0.28
Croatian (0)	29	0.36
Danish (24)	38	0.47
Dutch (68)	322	3.99
English (570)	1,747	21.64
European (42)	42	0.52
Finnish (37)	68	0.84
French, ex. Basque (45)	380	4.71
French Canadian (78)	144	1.78
German (474)	2,254	27.92
Greek (14)	23	0.28
Hungarian (26)	36	0.45
Irish (448)	1,495	18.52
Italian (18)	158	1.96
Lithuanian (0)	14	0.17
Macedonian (0)	9	0.11
Polish (55)	307	3.80
Scandinavian (13)	39	0.48
Scotch-Irish (31)	95	1.18
Scottish (97)	287	3.55
Swedish (9)	105	1.30
Swiss (0)	34	0.42
Ukrainian (40)	84	1.04
Welsh (10)	84	1.04
Yugoslavian (0)	8	0.10

Hispanic Origin	Population	%
Hispanic or Latino (of any race)	309	3.74
Central American, ex. Mexican	5	0.06
Guatemalan	2	0.02
Honduran	2	0.02
Panamanian	1	0.01
Cuban	16	0.19
Mexican	246	2.98
Puerto Rican	17	0.21
South American	6	0.07
Colombian	3	0.04
Peruvian	3	0.04
Other Hispanic or Latino	19	0.23

Race*	Population	%
African-American/Black (483)	548	6.64
Not Hispanic (479)	542	6.57
Hispanic (4)	6	0.07
American Indian/Alaska Native (36)	95	1.15
Not Hispanic (31)	87	1.05
Hispanic (5)	8	0.10
Blackfeet (1)	4	0.05
Canadian/French Am. Ind. (0)	1	0.01
Cherokee (4)	11	0.13
Chippewa (14)	34	0.41
Iroquois (0)	1	0.01
Menominee (1)	1	0.01
Mexican American Ind. (1)	2	0.02
Ottawa (2)	4	0.05
Potawatomi (1)	1	0.01
Sioux (0)	1	0.01
Asian (73)	88	1.07
Not Hispanic (72)	87	1.05
Hispanic (1)	1	0.01
Bangladeshi (3)	3	0.04
Chinese, ex. Taiwanese (13)	15	0.18
Filipino (10)	12	0.15
Indian (14)	14	0.17
Indonesian (1)	1	0.01
Japanese (3)	5	0.06
Korean (12)	16	0.19
Thai (1)	1	0.01
Vietnamese (16)	18	0.22
Hawaii Native/Pacific Islander (4)	7	0.08
Not Hispanic (4)	7	0.08
Native Hawaiian (2)	4	0.05
White (7,447)	7,585	91.92
Not Hispanic (7,220)	7,346	89.02
Hispanic (227)	239	2.90

Mayfield

Place Type: Township
County: Lapeer
Population: 7,955†

Ancestry‡	Population	%
American (632)	632	7.86
Arab (32)	32	0.40
Lebanese (17)	17	0.21
Syrian (15)	15	0.19
Armenian (0)	12	0.15
Austrian (0)	34	0.42
Belgian (0)	12	0.15
British (10)	29	0.36
Bulgarian (16)	16	0.20
Canadian (38)	38	0.47
Croatian (7)	25	0.31
Czech (45)	60	0.75
Czechoslovakian (39)	39	0.48
Dutch (58)	149	1.85
English (275)	971	12.07
European (125)	128	1.59
Finnish (38)	54	0.67
French, ex. Basque (67)	503	6.25
French Canadian (133)	372	4.62
German (604)	2,033	25.27
Hungarian (13)	32	0.40
Irish (277)	969	12.05
Italian (150)	318	3.95
Lithuanian (11)	11	0.14
Norwegian (25)	124	1.54
Pennsylvania German (0)	13	0.16
Polish (316)	785	9.76
Russian (10)	33	0.41
Scotch-Irish (161)	282	3.51
Scottish (197)	462	5.74
Slovak (30)	49	0.61
Swedish (39)	119	1.48
Swiss (0)	14	0.17
Ukrainian (15)	15	0.19
Welsh (0)	23	0.29

Hispanic Origin	Population	%
Hispanic or Latino (of any race)	218	2.74
Central American, ex. Mexican	2	0.03
Guatemalan	1	0.01
Panamanian	1	0.01
Cuban	7	0.09
Mexican	154	1.94
Puerto Rican	31	0.39
South American	4	0.05
Argentinean	1	0.01
Colombian	3	0.04
Other Hispanic or Latino	20	0.25

Race*	Population	%
African-American/Black (24)	47	0.59
Not Hispanic (21)	42	0.53
Hispanic (3)	5	0.06
American Indian/Alaska Native (48)	91	1.14
Not Hispanic (40)	80	1.01
Hispanic (8)	11	0.14
Blackfeet (1)	6	0.08
Canadian/French Am. Ind. (2)	2	0.03
Cherokee (2)	15	0.19
Chippewa (18)	22	0.28
Choctaw (3)	5	0.06
Creek (0)	1	0.01
Crow (0)	1	0.01
Iroquois (0)	2	0.03
Kiowa (1)	1	0.01
Ottawa (6)	7	0.09
Potawatomi (1)	1	0.01
Pueblo (1)	1	0.01
Yup'ik *(Alaska Native)* (1)	1	0.01
Asian (14)	39	0.49
Not Hispanic (14)	37	0.47
Hispanic (0)	2	0.03
Chinese, ex. Taiwanese (1)	5	0.06

*Notes: † The Census 2010 population figure is used to calculate the percentages in the Hispanic Origin and Race categories. Ancestry percentages are based on the 2006-2010 American Community Survey population (not shown); ‡ Numbers in parentheses indicate the number of people reporting a single ancestry; * Numbers in parentheses indicate the number of persons reporting this race alone, not in combination with any other race; Please refer to the Explanation of Data for more information.*

Filipino (4)	10	0.13
Indian (1)	1	0.01
Indonesian (2)	2	0.03
Japanese (1)	2	0.03
Korean (3)	8	0.10
Laotian (0)	1	0.01
Pakistani (0)	2	0.03
Thai (1)	2	0.03
Vietnamese (1)	2	0.03
Hawaii Native/Pacific Islander (2)	2	0.03
Not Hispanic (2)	2	0.03
White (7,746)	7,831	98.44
Not Hispanic (7,577)	7,657	96.25
Hispanic (169)	174	2.19

Melvindale

Place Type: City
County: Wayne
Population: 10,715[†]

Ancestry[‡]	Population	%
African, Sub-Saharan (0)	15	0.14
African (0)	15	0.14
American (339)	339	3.15
Arab (685)	685	6.37
Arab (329)	329	3.06
Iraqi (55)	55	0.51
Lebanese (9)	9	0.08
Other Arab (292)	292	2.71
Armenian (37)	61	0.57
Belgian (0)	33	0.31
British (8)	41	0.38
Canadian (41)	63	0.59
Croatian (12)	12	0.11
Czech (0)	24	0.22
Dutch (34)	80	0.74
Eastern European (0)	13	0.12
English (181)	600	5.58
European (32)	32	0.30
Finnish (20)	59	0.55
French, ex. Basque (108)	446	4.15
French Canadian (202)	299	2.78
German (472)	1,885	17.52
Greek (13)	13	0.12
Hungarian (79)	154	1.43
Irish (318)	1,272	11.82
Italian (225)	587	5.46
Maltese (62)	62	0.58
Norwegian (117)	117	1.09
Polish (272)	915	8.50
Russian (0)	17	0.16
Scotch-Irish (26)	89	0.83
Scottish (69)	261	2.43
Slovak (0)	35	0.33
Swedish (0)	42	0.39
Ukrainian (19)	70	0.65
Welsh (0)	13	0.12
West Indian, ex. Hispanic (13)	13	0.12
British West Indian (13)	13	0.12

Hispanic Origin	Population	%
Hispanic or Latino (of any race)	1,958	18.27
Central American, ex. Mexican	27	0.25
Guatemalan	3	0.03
Honduran	8	0.07
Nicaraguan	1	0.01
Panamanian	2	0.02
Salvadoran	13	0.12
Cuban	16	0.15
Dominican Republic	42	0.39
Mexican	1,527	14.25
Puerto Rican	243	2.27
South American	17	0.16
Argentinean	5	0.05
Colombian	5	0.05
Peruvian	6	0.06
Venezuelan	1	0.01
Other Hispanic or Latino	86	0.80

Race*	Population	%
African-American/Black (1,207)	1,331	12.42
Not Hispanic (1,156)	1,260	11.76
Hispanic (51)	71	0.66
American Indian/Alaska Native (79)	245	2.29
Not Hispanic (64)	201	1.88
Hispanic (15)	44	0.41
Aleut *(Alaska Native)* (1)	2	0.02
Apache (1)	1	0.01
Blackfeet (0)	12	0.11
Canadian/French Am. Ind. (2)	4	0.04
Cherokee (12)	41	0.38
Cheyenne (0)	1	0.01
Chippewa (13)	25	0.23
Choctaw (1)	2	0.02
Creek (0)	1	0.01
Delaware (1)	1	0.01
Iroquois (4)	13	0.12
Menominee (0)	3	0.03
Mexican American Ind. (7)	8	0.07
Ottawa (4)	5	0.05
Potawatomi (5)	8	0.07
South American Ind. (0)	2	0.02
Asian (90)	186	1.74
Not Hispanic (83)	176	1.64
Hispanic (7)	10	0.09
Burmese (3)	3	0.03
Chinese, ex. Taiwanese (9)	10	0.09
Filipino (24)	43	0.40
Hmong (2)	3	0.03
Indian (16)	26	0.24
Japanese (4)	5	0.05
Korean (4)	4	0.04
Malaysian (2)	2	0.02
Pakistani (16)	18	0.17
Vietnamese (8)	8	0.07
Hawaii Native/Pacific Islander (3)	7	0.07
Not Hispanic (1)	2	0.02
Hispanic (2)	5	0.05
Native Hawaiian (2)	4	0.04
White (8,231)	8,609	80.35
Not Hispanic (7,135)	7,411	69.16
Hispanic (1,096)	1,198	11.18

Menominee

Place Type: City
County: Menominee
Population: 8,599[†]

Ancestry[‡]	Population	%
American (266)	266	3.06
Austrian (10)	32	0.37
Belgian (20)	242	2.79
British (9)	9	0.10
Bulgarian (0)	29	0.33
Canadian (8)	18	0.21
Czech (34)	214	2.46
Czechoslovakian (44)	44	0.51
Danish (42)	197	2.27
Dutch (18)	151	1.74
English (115)	421	4.85
European (66)	113	1.30
Finnish (59)	210	2.42
French, ex. Basque (178)	1,167	13.43
French Canadian (126)	382	4.40
German (1,173)	3,578	41.18
Hungarian (101)	217	2.50
Irish (107)	616	7.09
Italian (18)	250	2.88
Lithuanian (0)	11	0.13
Norwegian (82)	327	3.76
Polish (390)	1,173	13.50
Russian (0)	56	0.64
Scandinavian (68)	117	1.35
Scotch-Irish (0)	80	0.92
Scottish (38)	149	1.71
Swedish (119)	653	7.52
Ukrainian (119)	128	1.47
Yugoslavian (13)	45	0.52

Hispanic Origin	Population	%
Hispanic or Latino (of any race)	122	1.42
Central American, ex. Mexican	5	0.06
Guatemalan	3	0.03
Honduran	2	0.02
Cuban	1	0.01
Dominican Republic	3	0.03
Mexican	74	0.86
Puerto Rican	19	0.22
South American	5	0.06
Colombian	1	0.01
Ecuadorian	1	0.01
Peruvian	2	0.02
Venezuelan	1	0.01
Other Hispanic or Latino	15	0.17

Race*	Population	%
African-American/Black (37)	73	0.85
Not Hispanic (34)	70	0.81
Hispanic (3)	3	0.03
American Indian/Alaska Native (80)	128	1.49
Not Hispanic (66)	109	1.27
Hispanic (14)	19	0.22
Blackfeet (1)	1	0.01
Central American Ind. (0)	1	0.01
Cherokee (2)	10	0.12
Chippewa (20)	29	0.34
Creek (0)	1	0.01
Iroquois (2)	2	0.02
Menominee (7)	7	0.08
Mexican American Ind. (2)	2	0.02
Navajo (0)	3	0.03
Ottawa (3)	5	0.06
Potawatomi (6)	10	0.12
Sioux (0)	2	0.02
Asian (41)	55	0.64
Not Hispanic (41)	53	0.62
Hispanic (0)	2	0.02
Chinese, ex. Taiwanese (16)	18	0.21
Filipino (11)	12	0.14
Indian (5)	6	0.07
Japanese (1)	4	0.05
Korean (7)	11	0.13
Malaysian (0)	1	0.01
Taiwanese (1)	1	0.01
Vietnamese (0)	2	0.02
Hawaii Native/Pacific Islander (1)	4	0.05
Not Hispanic (1)	3	0.03
Hispanic (0)	1	0.01
Guamanian/Chamorro (0)	1	0.01
Samoan (1)	1	0.01
White (8,314)	8,415	97.86
Not Hispanic (8,237)	8,329	96.86
Hispanic (77)	86	1.00

Meridian

Place Type: Charter Township
County: Ingham
Population: 39,688[†]

Ancestry[‡]	Population	%
African, Sub-Saharan (310)	404	1.02
African (67)	161	0.41
Kenyan (53)	53	0.13
Nigerian (30)	30	0.08
Senegalese (84)	84	0.21
Somalian (13)	13	0.03
South African (15)	15	0.04
Zimbabwean (48)	48	0.12
American (2,753)	2,753	6.94
Arab (379)	436	1.10
Arab (72)	90	0.23
Egyptian (30)	30	0.08
Lebanese (121)	121	0.31
Moroccan (0)	14	0.04
Palestinian (16)	16	0.04
Syrian (53)	64	0.16

*Notes: † The Census 2010 population figure is used to calculate the percentages in the Hispanic Origin and Race categories. Ancestry percentages are based on the 2006-2010 American Community Survey population (not shown); ‡ Numbers in parentheses indicate the number of people reporting a single ancestry; * Numbers in parentheses indicate the number of persons reporting this race alone, not in combination with any other race; Please refer to the Explanation of Data for more information.*

Ancestry	Population	%
Other Arab (87)	101	0.25
Armenian (109)	138	0.35
Assyrian/Chaldean/Syriac (11)	11	0.03
Australian (0)	15	0.04
Austrian (0)	98	0.25
Belgian (48)	263	0.66
Brazilian (16)	50	0.13
British (57)	260	0.66
Bulgarian (57)	57	0.14
Canadian (50)	131	0.33
Carpatho Rusyn (0)	15	0.04
Croatian (5)	184	0.46
Czech (76)	271	0.68
Czechoslovakian (13)	13	0.03
Danish (39)	356	0.90
Dutch (381)	1,251	3.15
Eastern European (156)	156	0.39
English (1,450)	5,298	13.36
Estonian (0)	12	0.03
European (868)	953	2.40
Finnish (69)	446	1.12
French, ex. Basque (207)	1,464	3.69
French Canadian (70)	387	0.98
German (2,677)	9,431	23.77
Greek (69)	286	0.72
Hungarian (100)	411	1.04
Iranian (90)	100	0.25
Irish (1,030)	5,007	12.62
Israeli (14)	14	0.04
Italian (638)	1,433	3.61
Latvian (24)	44	0.11
Lithuanian (95)	198	0.50
Luxemburger (0)	12	0.03
Macedonian (34)	34	0.09
Maltese (0)	34	0.09
Northern European (33)	48	0.12
Norwegian (117)	664	1.67
Pennsylvania German (14)	14	0.04
Polish (744)	2,320	5.85
Portuguese (27)	72	0.18
Romanian (13)	37	0.09
Russian (360)	763	1.92
Scandinavian (0)	162	0.41
Scotch-Irish (252)	863	2.18
Scottish (459)	1,228	3.10
Serbian (38)	38	0.10
Slavic (0)	10	0.03
Slovak (49)	102	0.26
Slovene (25)	67	0.17
Swedish (230)	997	2.51
Swiss (23)	146	0.37
Turkish (138)	138	0.35
Ukrainian (108)	210	0.53
Welsh (10)	234	0.59
West Indian, ex. Hispanic (0)	10	0.03
Belizean (0)	10	0.03
Yugoslavian (15)	15	0.04

Hispanic Origin	Population	%
Hispanic or Latino (of any race)	1,524	3.84
Central American, ex. Mexican	73	0.18
Costa Rican	6	0.02
Guatemalan	38	0.10
Honduran	6	0.02
Nicaraguan	7	0.02
Panamanian	7	0.02
Salvadoran	7	0.02
Other Central American	2	0.01
Cuban	60	0.15
Dominican Republic	17	0.04
Mexican	955	2.41
Puerto Rican	125	0.31
South American	134	0.34
Argentinean	12	0.03
Bolivian	8	0.02
Chilean	8	0.02
Colombian	49	0.12
Ecuadorian	6	0.02
Paraguayan	5	0.01
Peruvian	23	0.06
Uruguayan	2	0.01
Venezuelan	20	0.05
Other South American	1	<0.01
Other Hispanic or Latino	160	0.40

Race*	Population	%
African-American/Black (1,926)	2,351	5.92
Not Hispanic (1,872)	2,243	5.65
Hispanic (54)	108	0.27
American Indian/Alaska Native (145)	399	1.01
Not Hispanic (106)	318	0.80
Hispanic (39)	81	0.20
Apache (1)	4	0.01
Blackfeet (1)	7	0.02
Canadian/French Am. Ind. (1)	7	0.02
Cherokee (12)	62	0.16
Cheyenne (0)	1	<0.01
Chickasaw (0)	1	<0.01
Chippewa (28)	64	0.16
Choctaw (1)	2	0.01
Cree (0)	3	0.01
Creek (4)	6	0.02
Crow (0)	1	<0.01
Delaware (0)	1	<0.01
Inupiat *(Alaska Native)* (1)	2	0.01
Iroquois (0)	4	0.01
Mexican American Ind. (10)	20	0.05
Navajo (0)	2	0.01
Ottawa (3)	9	0.02
Potawatomi (3)	6	0.02
Pueblo (2)	2	0.01
Sioux (1)	6	0.02
South American Ind. (3)	4	0.01
Spanish American Ind. (4)	4	0.01
Asian (4,333)	4,809	12.12
Not Hispanic (4,317)	4,776	12.03
Hispanic (16)	33	0.08
Bangladeshi (10)	13	0.03
Burmese (16)	17	0.04
Cambodian (1)	4	0.01
Chinese, ex. Taiwanese (1,036)	1,138	2.87
Filipino (118)	203	0.51
Hmong (31)	35	0.09
Indian (1,566)	1,665	4.20
Indonesian (17)	22	0.06
Japanese (99)	159	0.40
Korean (921)	996	2.51
Laotian (1)	3	0.01
Malaysian (14)	14	0.04
Nepalese (11)	12	0.03
Pakistani (103)	115	0.29
Sri Lankan (29)	37	0.09
Taiwanese (106)	119	0.30
Thai (31)	37	0.09
Vietnamese (129)	143	0.36
Hawaii Native/Pacific Islander (17)	59	0.15
Not Hispanic (16)	56	0.14
Hispanic (1)	3	0.01
Guamanian/Chamorro (1)	7	0.02
Native Hawaiian (5)	22	0.06
Samoan (4)	7	0.02
White (31,749)	32,727	82.46
Not Hispanic (30,822)	31,658	79.77
Hispanic (927)	1,069	2.69

Midland

Place Type: City
County: Midland
Population: 41,706†

Ancestry‡	Population	%
African, Sub-Saharan (32)	32	0.08
African (19)	19	0.05
South African (11)	11	0.03
Other Sub-Saharan African (2)	2	<0.01
Albanian (12)	12	0.03
American (2,185)	2,185	5.24
Arab (34)	84	0.20
Egyptian (34)	34	0.08
Lebanese (0)	14	0.03
Syrian (0)	36	0.09
Armenian (15)	52	0.12
Austrian (21)	97	0.23
Belgian (54)	105	0.25
Brazilian (12)	35	0.08
British (146)	415	0.99
Canadian (180)	387	0.93
Celtic (33)	33	0.08
Croatian (14)	26	0.06
Czech (207)	571	1.37
Czechoslovakian (17)	81	0.19
Danish (68)	308	0.74
Dutch (278)	1,276	3.06
Eastern European (24)	39	0.09
English (1,570)	5,552	13.30
European (549)	569	1.36
Finnish (74)	429	1.03
French, ex. Basque (431)	2,884	6.91
French Canadian (373)	994	2.38
German (4,705)	13,588	32.56
Greek (49)	145	0.35
Guyanese (6)	6	0.01
Hungarian (103)	409	0.98
Iranian (7)	7	0.02
Irish (1,089)	5,824	13.96
Italian (368)	1,488	3.57
Latvian (12)	12	0.03
Lithuanian (0)	26	0.06
Luxemburger (15)	15	0.04
Maltese (0)	19	0.05
Northern European (70)	108	0.26
Norwegian (232)	1,021	2.45
Pennsylvania German (0)	8	0.02
Polish (907)	3,860	9.25
Portuguese (0)	40	0.10
Romanian (0)	13	0.03
Russian (89)	276	0.66
Scandinavian (33)	120	0.29
Scotch-Irish (356)	949	2.27
Scottish (260)	1,364	3.27
Slavic (0)	35	0.08
Slovak (60)	131	0.31
Slovene (11)	91	0.22
Swedish (381)	1,005	2.41
Swiss (30)	186	0.45
Turkish (0)	20	0.05
Ukrainian (68)	184	0.44
Welsh (30)	212	0.51
Yugoslavian (15)	15	0.04

Hispanic Origin	Population	%
Hispanic or Latino (of any race)	1,011	2.42
Central American, ex. Mexican	39	0.09
Costa Rican	5	0.01
Guatemalan	14	0.03
Honduran	3	0.01
Nicaraguan	10	0.02
Panamanian	7	0.02
Cuban	24	0.06
Dominican Republic	6	0.01
Mexican	622	1.49
Puerto Rican	91	0.22
South American	130	0.31
Argentinean	46	0.11
Bolivian	1	<0.01
Chilean	6	0.01
Colombian	47	0.11
Ecuadorian	11	0.03
Peruvian	7	0.02
Uruguayan	3	0.01
Venezuelan	7	0.02
Other South American	2	<0.01
Other Hispanic or Latino	99	0.24

Race*	Population	%
African-American/Black (846)	1,137	2.73
Not Hispanic (823)	1,094	2.62
Hispanic (23)	43	0.10
American Indian/Alaska Native (146)	350	0.84

*Notes: † The Census 2010 population figure is used to calculate the percentages in the Hispanic Origin and Race categories. Ancestry percentages are based on the 2006-2010 American Community Survey population (not shown); ‡ Numbers in parentheses indicate the number of people reporting a single ancestry; * Numbers in parentheses indicate the number of persons reporting this race alone, not in combination with any other race; Please refer to the Explanation of Data for more information.*

Race* (continued)	Population	%
Not Hispanic (128)	309	0.74
Hispanic (18)	41	0.10
Aleut *(Alaska Native)* (1)	1	<0.01
Apache (2)	3	0.01
Blackfeet (0)	4	0.01
Canadian/French Am. Ind. (2)	2	<0.01
Cherokee (4)	16	0.04
Cheyenne (0)	1	<0.01
Chickasaw (1)	1	<0.01
Chippewa (56)	104	0.25
Choctaw (0)	4	0.01
Comanche (0)	2	<0.01
Cree (0)	1	<0.01
Creek (1)	3	0.01
Delaware (0)	1	<0.01
Inupiat *(Alaska Native)* (2)	2	<0.01
Iroquois (4)	8	0.02
Mexican American Ind. (4)	5	0.01
Osage (0)	1	<0.01
Ottawa (9)	18	0.04
Potawatomi (11)	16	0.04
Puget Sound Salish (0)	1	<0.01
Seminole (0)	1	<0.01
Sioux (3)	7	0.02
Asian (1,368)	1,573	3.77
Not Hispanic (1,367)	1,567	3.76
Hispanic (1)	6	0.01
Bangladeshi (6)	6	0.01
Cambodian (3)	6	0.01
Chinese, ex. Taiwanese (462)	494	1.18
Filipino (71)	104	0.25
Hmong (5)	5	0.01
Indian (436)	458	1.10
Indonesian (1)	2	<0.01
Japanese (77)	120	0.29
Korean (135)	168	0.40
Laotian (2)	4	0.01
Malaysian (4)	5	0.01
Pakistani (43)	55	0.13
Sri Lankan (2)	4	0.01
Taiwanese (24)	25	0.06
Thai (16)	24	0.06
Vietnamese (54)	60	0.14
Hawaii Native/Pacific Islander (44)	59	0.14
Not Hispanic (44)	59	0.14
Guamanian/Chamorro (3)	3	0.01
Native Hawaiian (17)	20	0.05
Samoan (1)	2	<0.01
Tongan (2)	4	0.01
White (38,353)	39,029	93.58
Not Hispanic (37,650)	38,231	91.67
Hispanic (703)	798	1.91

Midland

Place Type: City
County: Midland
Population: 41,863†

Ancestry‡	Population	%
African, Sub-Saharan (32)	32	0.08
African (19)	19	0.05
South African (11)	11	0.03
Other Sub-Saharan African (2)	2	<0.01
Albanian (12)	12	0.03
American (2,185)	2,185	5.21
Arab (34)	84	0.20
Egyptian (34)	34	0.08
Lebanese (0)	14	0.03
Syrian (0)	36	0.09
Armenian (15)	52	0.12
Austrian (21)	97	0.23
Belgian (54)	105	0.25
Brazilian (12)	35	0.08
British (146)	415	0.99
Canadian (180)	387	0.92
Celtic (33)	33	0.08
Croatian (14)	26	0.06
Czech (207)	571	1.36
Czechoslovakian (17)	81	0.19
Danish (68)	308	0.73
Dutch (278)	1,276	3.04
Eastern European (24)	39	0.09
English (1,582)	5,577	13.29
European (549)	569	1.36
Finnish (74)	429	1.02
French, ex. Basque (431)	2,897	6.90
French Canadian (373)	994	2.37
German (4,734)	13,745	32.76
Greek (49)	145	0.35
Guyanese (6)	6	0.01
Hungarian (103)	409	0.97
Iranian (7)	7	0.02
Irish (1,089)	5,824	13.88
Italian (368)	1,488	3.55
Latvian (12)	12	0.03
Lithuanian (0)	26	0.06
Luxemburger (15)	15	0.04
Maltese (0)	19	0.05
Northern European (70)	108	0.26
Norwegian (232)	1,021	2.43
Pennsylvania German (0)	8	0.02
Polish (907)	3,860	9.20
Portuguese (0)	40	0.10
Romanian (0)	13	0.03
Russian (89)	276	0.66
Scandinavian (33)	120	0.29
Scotch-Irish (356)	949	2.26
Scottish (260)	1,364	3.25
Slavic (0)	35	0.08
Slovak (60)	131	0.31
Slovene (11)	91	0.22
Swedish (381)	1,005	2.40
Swiss (30)	186	0.44
Turkish (0)	20	0.05
Ukrainian (68)	184	0.44
Welsh (30)	212	0.51
Yugoslavian (15)	15	0.04

Hispanic Origin	Population	%
Hispanic or Latino (of any race)	1,015	2.42
Central American, ex. Mexican	39	0.09
Costa Rican	5	0.01
Guatemalan	14	0.03
Honduran	3	0.01
Nicaraguan	10	0.02
Panamanian	7	0.02
Cuban	24	0.06
Dominican Republic	6	0.01
Mexican	625	1.49
Puerto Rican	91	0.22
South American	130	0.31
Argentinean	46	0.11
Bolivian	1	<0.01
Chilean	6	0.01
Colombian	47	0.11
Ecuadorian	11	0.03
Peruvian	7	0.02
Uruguayan	3	0.01
Venezuelan	7	0.02
Other South American	2	<0.01
Other Hispanic or Latino	100	0.24

Race*	Population	%
African-American/Black (846)	1,138	2.72
Not Hispanic (823)	1,095	2.62
Hispanic (23)	43	0.10
American Indian/Alaska Native (146)	350	0.84
Not Hispanic (128)	309	0.74
Hispanic (18)	41	0.10
Aleut *(Alaska Native)* (1)	1	<0.01
Apache (2)	3	0.01
Blackfeet (0)	4	0.01
Canadian/French Am. Ind. (2)	2	<0.01
Cherokee (4)	16	0.04
Cheyenne (0)	1	<0.01
Chickasaw (1)	1	<0.01
Chippewa (56)	104	0.25
Choctaw (0)	4	0.01
Comanche (0)	2	<0.01
Cree (0)	1	<0.01
Creek (1)	3	0.01
Delaware (0)	1	<0.01
Inupiat *(Alaska Native)* (2)	2	<0.01
Iroquois (4)	8	0.02
Mexican American Ind. (4)	5	0.01
Osage (0)	1	<0.01
Ottawa (9)	18	0.04
Potawatomi (11)	16	0.04
Puget Sound Salish (0)	1	<0.01
Seminole (0)	1	<0.01
Sioux (3)	7	0.02
Asian (1,368)	1,573	3.76
Not Hispanic (1,367)	1,567	3.74
Hispanic (1)	6	0.01
Bangladeshi (6)	6	0.01
Cambodian (3)	6	0.01
Chinese, ex. Taiwanese (462)	494	1.18
Filipino (71)	104	0.25
Hmong (5)	5	0.01
Indian (436)	458	1.09
Indonesian (1)	2	<0.01
Japanese (77)	120	0.29
Korean (135)	168	0.40
Laotian (2)	4	0.01
Malaysian (4)	5	0.01
Pakistani (43)	55	0.13
Sri Lankan (2)	4	0.01
Taiwanese (24)	25	0.06
Thai (16)	24	0.06
Vietnamese (54)	60	0.14
Hawaii Native/Pacific Islander (44)	59	0.14
Not Hispanic (44)	59	0.14
Guamanian/Chamorro (3)	3	0.01
Native Hawaiian (17)	20	0.05
Samoan (1)	2	<0.01
Tongan (2)	4	0.01
White (38,508)	39,185	93.60
Not Hispanic (37,802)	38,384	91.69
Hispanic (706)	801	1.91

Milford

Place Type: Charter Township
County: Oakland
Population: 15,736†

Ancestry‡	Population	%
Albanian (190)	190	1.22
American (840)	840	5.37
Arab (0)	7	0.04
Lebanese (0)	7	0.04
Armenian (16)	47	0.30
Assyrian/Chaldean/Syriac (32)	32	0.20
Austrian (30)	120	0.77
Belgian (66)	92	0.59
British (97)	134	0.86
Canadian (108)	230	1.47
Croatian (0)	27	0.17
Czech (4)	65	0.42
Czechoslovakian (33)	44	0.28
Danish (0)	15	0.10
Dutch (78)	315	2.02
Eastern European (25)	25	0.16
English (489)	2,697	17.26
European (641)	641	4.10
Finnish (122)	315	2.02
French, ex. Basque (90)	798	5.11
French Canadian (56)	358	2.29
German (1,208)	4,298	27.50
Greek (106)	114	0.73
Hungarian (34)	187	1.20
Irish (646)	2,538	16.24
Italian (432)	1,047	6.70
Lithuanian (74)	110	0.70
Maltese (0)	53	0.34
Norwegian (10)	95	0.61
Pennsylvania German (0)	24	0.15
Polish (856)	2,482	15.88
Romanian (11)	19	0.12

*Notes: † The Census 2010 population figure is used to calculate the percentages in the Hispanic Origin and Race categories. Ancestry percentages are based on the 2006-2010 American Community Survey population (not shown); ‡ Numbers in parentheses indicate the number of people reporting a single ancestry; * Numbers in parentheses indicate the number of persons reporting this race alone, not in combination with any other race; Please refer to the Explanation of Data for more information.*

	Population	%
Russian (42)	232	1.48
Scandinavian (16)	93	0.60
Scotch-Irish (117)	397	2.54
Scottish (139)	635	4.06
Slovak (18)	79	0.51
Swedish (40)	250	1.60
Swiss (0)	53	0.34
Ukrainian (8)	66	0.42
Welsh (8)	154	0.99
West Indian, ex. Hispanic (0)	27	0.17
West Indian (0)	27	0.17
Yugoslavian (0)	8	0.05

Hispanic Origin	Population	%
Hispanic or Latino (of any race)	345	2.19
Central American, ex. Mexican	30	0.19
Costa Rican	8	0.05
Guatemalan	13	0.08
Honduran	3	0.02
Panamanian	2	0.01
Salvadoran	4	0.03
Cuban	13	0.08
Dominican Republic	5	0.03
Mexican	209	1.33
Puerto Rican	27	0.17
South American	21	0.13
Argentinean	4	0.03
Chilean	4	0.03
Colombian	8	0.05
Peruvian	2	0.01
Other South American	3	0.02
Other Hispanic or Latino	40	0.25

Race*	Population	%
African-American/Black (146)	199	1.26
Not Hispanic (137)	186	1.18
Hispanic (9)	13	0.08
American Indian/Alaska Native (54)	156	0.99
Not Hispanic (48)	142	0.90
Hispanic (6)	14	0.09
Blackfeet (1)	5	0.03
Canadian/French Am. Ind. (1)	1	0.01
Central American Ind. (1)	1	0.01
Cherokee (0)	28	0.18
Chippewa (24)	32	0.20
Choctaw (0)	2	0.01
Comanche (0)	3	0.02
Iroquois (1)	14	0.09
Kiowa (0)	1	0.01
Menominee (1)	1	0.01
Mexican American Ind. (3)	3	0.02
Ottawa (0)	2	0.01
Paiute (0)	4	0.03
Potawatomi (2)	2	0.01
Sioux (1)	3	0.02
South American Ind. (1)	1	0.01
Asian (171)	256	1.63
Not Hispanic (170)	253	1.61
Hispanic (1)	3	0.02
Cambodian (3)	5	0.03
Chinese, ex. Taiwanese (40)	46	0.29
Filipino (22)	50	0.32
Hmong (8)	8	0.05
Indian (36)	41	0.26
Indonesian (2)	2	0.01
Japanese (7)	19	0.12
Korean (28)	42	0.27
Laotian (3)	6	0.04
Pakistani (1)	1	0.01
Thai (5)	11	0.07
Vietnamese (13)	16	0.10
Hawaii Native/Pacific Islander (4)	7	0.04
Not Hispanic (4)	7	0.04
Native Hawaiian (4)	7	0.04
White (15,000)	15,241	96.85
Not Hispanic (14,781)	14,988	95.25
Hispanic (219)	253	1.61

Monitor

Place Type: Charter Township
County: Bay
Population: 10,735†

Ancestry‡	Population	%
American (281)	281	2.65
Arab (0)	8	0.08
Syrian (0)	8	0.08
British (13)	13	0.12
Canadian (0)	27	0.25
Czech (0)	66	0.62
Czechoslovakian (8)	8	0.08
Danish (12)	12	0.11
Dutch (21)	273	2.57
English (189)	1,021	9.62
Finnish (0)	37	0.35
French, ex. Basque (274)	1,660	15.65
French Canadian (109)	237	2.23
German (1,685)	4,440	41.85
Greek (0)	16	0.15
Hungarian (0)	116	1.09
Irish (236)	1,224	11.54
Italian (157)	241	2.27
Lithuanian (13)	31	0.29
Norwegian (0)	39	0.37
Pennsylvania German (0)	22	0.21
Polish (1,151)	2,612	24.62
Russian (44)	115	1.08
Scandinavian (0)	13	0.12
Scotch-Irish (26)	115	1.08
Scottish (106)	321	3.03
Slovak (0)	13	0.12
Swedish (47)	238	2.24
Swiss (23)	96	0.90
Ukrainian (0)	20	0.19
Welsh (57)	101	0.95
Yugoslavian (0)	14	0.13

Hispanic Origin	Population	%
Hispanic or Latino (of any race)	257	2.39
Central American, ex. Mexican	4	0.04
Honduran	1	0.01
Nicaraguan	2	0.02
Panamanian	1	0.01
Cuban	4	0.04
Mexican	204	1.90
Puerto Rican	7	0.07
South American	6	0.06
Chilean	1	0.01
Colombian	3	0.03
Peruvian	2	0.02
Other Hispanic or Latino	32	0.30

Race*	Population	%
African-American/Black (40)	92	0.86
Not Hispanic (40)	89	0.83
Hispanic (0)	3	0.03
American Indian/Alaska Native (31)	76	0.71
Not Hispanic (30)	71	0.66
Hispanic (1)	5	0.05
Apache (1)	1	0.01
Arapaho (0)	1	0.01
Cherokee (0)	4	0.04
Chippewa (16)	34	0.32
Crow (1)	2	0.02
Iroquois (0)	2	0.02
Ottawa (0)	3	0.03
Sioux (3)	3	0.03
Asian (62)	90	0.84
Not Hispanic (62)	88	0.82
Hispanic (0)	2	0.02
Cambodian (1)	1	0.01
Chinese, ex. Taiwanese (4)	4	0.04
Filipino (14)	24	0.22
Hmong (14)	15	0.14
Indian (9)	12	0.11
Japanese (1)	8	0.07
Korean (6)	12	0.11
Nepalese (1)	1	0.01
Pakistani (4)	4	0.04
Vietnamese (1)	1	0.01
Hawaii Native/Pacific Islander (2)	7	0.07
Not Hispanic (2)	7	0.07
Samoan (0)	3	0.03
White (10,419)	10,566	98.43
Not Hispanic (10,220)	10,337	96.29
Hispanic (199)	229	2.13

Monroe

Place Type: Charter Township
County: Monroe
Population: 14,568†

Ancestry‡	Population	%
African, Sub-Saharan (29)	29	0.20
African (29)	29	0.20
American (851)	851	5.84
Arab (0)	24	0.16
Arab (0)	14	0.10
Lebanese (0)	10	0.07
Armenian (16)	64	0.44
Belgian (77)	322	2.21
British (9)	22	0.15
Bulgarian (0)	9	0.06
Canadian (26)	74	0.51
Croatian (19)	19	0.13
Czech (20)	91	0.62
Czechoslovakian (0)	18	0.12
Dutch (155)	613	4.21
English (325)	1,169	8.03
European (141)	141	0.97
Finnish (0)	23	0.16
French, ex. Basque (405)	2,182	14.99
French Canadian (162)	237	1.63
German (1,550)	4,899	33.64
Greek (46)	140	0.96
Hungarian (114)	420	2.88
Irish (523)	2,147	14.74
Italian (331)	1,020	7.01
Lithuanian (10)	10	0.07
Norwegian (25)	96	0.66
Polish (97)	777	5.34
Romanian (0)	9	0.06
Russian (22)	137	0.94
Scotch-Irish (65)	187	1.28
Scottish (94)	436	2.99
Serbian (69)	69	0.47
Slavic (8)	8	0.05
Slovak (11)	29	0.20
Slovene (13)	13	0.09
Swedish (23)	99	0.68
Swiss (0)	98	0.67
Ukrainian (89)	101	0.69
Welsh (0)	104	0.71

Hispanic Origin	Population	%
Hispanic or Latino (of any race)	587	4.03
Central American, ex. Mexican	11	0.08
Guatemalan	11	0.08
Cuban	3	0.02
Mexican	441	3.03
Puerto Rican	70	0.48
South American	11	0.08
Chilean	4	0.03
Ecuadorian	3	0.02
Peruvian	3	0.02
Other South American	1	0.01
Other Hispanic or Latino	51	0.35

Race*	Population	%
African-American/Black (371)	526	3.61
Not Hispanic (356)	496	3.40
Hispanic (15)	30	0.21
American Indian/Alaska Native (27)	125	0.86
Not Hispanic (22)	113	0.78
Hispanic (5)	12	0.08
Blackfeet (2)	6	0.04

*Notes: † The Census 2010 population figure is used to calculate the percentages in the Hispanic Origin and Race categories. Ancestry percentages are based on the 2006-2010 American Community Survey population (not shown); ‡ Numbers in parentheses indicate the number of people reporting a single ancestry; * Numbers in parentheses indicate the number of persons reporting this race alone, not in combination with any other race; Please refer to the Explanation of Data for more information.*

Canadian/French Am. Ind. (0)	1	0.01
Cherokee (2)	35	0.24
Cheyenne (1)	1	0.01
Chippewa (5)	17	0.12
Choctaw (0)	1	0.01
Crow (0)	1	0.01
Iroquois (1)	1	0.01
Mexican American Ind. (0)	1	0.01
Ottawa (3)	3	0.02
Potawatomi (1)	2	0.01
Sioux (0)	1	0.01
South American Ind. (1)	2	0.01
Spanish American Ind. (0)	1	0.01
Asian (108)	149	1.02
Not Hispanic (108)	148	1.02
Hispanic (0)	1	0.01
Bangladeshi (1)	1	0.01
Chinese, ex. Taiwanese (23)	24	0.16
Filipino (10)	12	0.08
Indian (39)	41	0.28
Japanese (3)	13	0.09
Korean (9)	16	0.11
Pakistani (16)	16	0.11
Thai (0)	3	0.02
Vietnamese (5)	6	0.04
Hawaii Native/Pacific Islander (1)	7	0.05
Not Hispanic (1)	4	0.03
Hispanic (0)	3	0.02
Native Hawaiian (0)	1	0.01
Samoan (1)	1	0.01
White (13,538)	13,863	95.16
Not Hispanic (13,224)	13,490	92.60
Hispanic (314)	373	2.56

Monroe

Place Type: City
County: Monroe
Population: 20,733†

Ancestry‡	Population	%
African, Sub-Saharan (7)	7	0.03
African (7)	7	0.03
American (841)	841	3.97
Arab (124)	132	0.62
Iraqi (33)	33	0.16
Lebanese (45)	45	0.21
Syrian (0)	8	0.04
Other Arab (46)	46	0.22
Armenian (27)	78	0.37
Australian (70)	70	0.33
Austrian (0)	63	0.30
Belgian (27)	198	0.93
British (61)	94	0.44
Bulgarian (18)	25	0.12
Canadian (8)	52	0.25
Croatian (5)	5	0.02
Cypriot (18)	18	0.08
Czech (49)	199	0.94
Czechoslovakian (35)	123	0.58
Danish (0)	23	0.11
Dutch (97)	373	1.76
Eastern European (9)	9	0.04
English (486)	1,805	8.52
European (45)	51	0.24
Finnish (0)	28	0.13
French, ex. Basque (344)	2,165	10.22
French Canadian (87)	214	1.01
German (1,760)	5,701	26.92
Greek (39)	242	1.14
Hungarian (109)	531	2.51
Irish (756)	2,916	13.77
Italian (817)	1,938	9.15
Lithuanian (18)	36	0.17
Maltese (14)	14	0.07
Norwegian (25)	226	1.07
Pennsylvania German (0)	8	0.04
Polish (487)	1,533	7.24
Romanian (0)	10	0.05
Russian (50)	138	0.65
Scotch-Irish (96)	451	2.13
Scottish (147)	548	2.59
Serbian (45)	66	0.31
Slavic (12)	12	0.06
Slovak (13)	26	0.12
Swedish (10)	333	1.57
Swiss (64)	86	0.41
Ukrainian (21)	84	0.40
Welsh (9)	84	0.40
West Indian, ex. Hispanic (0)	28	0.13
Haitian (0)	28	0.13
Yugoslavian (0)	11	0.05

Hispanic Origin	Population	%
Hispanic or Latino (of any race)	860	4.15
Central American, ex. Mexican	9	0.04
Guatemalan	5	0.02
Nicaraguan	1	<0.01
Panamanian	3	0.01
Cuban	10	0.05
Mexican	646	3.12
Puerto Rican	125	0.60
South American	12	0.06
Argentinean	2	0.01
Colombian	1	<0.01
Ecuadorian	6	0.03
Peruvian	2	0.01
Other South American	1	<0.01
Other Hispanic or Latino	58	0.28

Race*	Population	%
African-American/Black (1,293)	1,664	8.03
Not Hispanic (1,251)	1,585	7.64
Hispanic (42)	79	0.38
American Indian/Alaska Native (91)	270	1.30
Not Hispanic (81)	236	1.14
Hispanic (10)	34	0.16
Apache (0)	1	<0.01
Blackfeet (0)	4	0.02
Canadian/French Am. Ind. (2)	2	0.01
Cherokee (15)	52	0.25
Chickasaw (1)	3	0.01
Chippewa (14)	33	0.16
Choctaw (2)	4	0.02
Comanche (4)	4	0.02
Creek (0)	1	<0.01
Iroquois (2)	10	0.05
Kiowa (1)	3	0.01
Lumbee (1)	4	0.02
Menominee (0)	1	<0.01
Mexican American Ind. (1)	5	0.02
Ottawa (8)	9	0.04
Potawatomi (0)	4	0.02
Seminole (0)	2	0.01
Sioux (2)	6	0.03
South American Ind. (1)	1	<0.01
Yaqui (1)	1	<0.01
Asian (142)	205	0.99
Not Hispanic (140)	198	0.95
Hispanic (2)	7	0.03
Chinese, ex. Taiwanese (14)	18	0.09
Filipino (20)	34	0.16
Indian (40)	50	0.24
Indonesian (1)	1	<0.01
Japanese (20)	28	0.14
Korean (16)	28	0.14
Malaysian (1)	1	<0.01
Pakistani (7)	12	0.06
Sri Lankan (1)	1	<0.01
Taiwanese (1)	1	<0.01
Thai (6)	8	0.04
Vietnamese (8)	11	0.05
Hawaii Native/Pacific Islander (6)	15	0.07
Not Hispanic (5)	11	0.05
Hispanic (1)	4	0.02
Guamanian/Chamorro (1)	1	<0.01
Native Hawaiian (1)	4	0.02
Samoan (1)	3	0.01
White (18,335)	18,916	91.24
Not Hispanic (17,855)	18,361	88.56
Hispanic (480)	555	2.68

Mount Clemens

Place Type: City
County: Macomb
Population: 16,314†

Ancestry‡	Population	%
African, Sub-Saharan (40)	58	0.35
African (40)	49	0.29
Cape Verdean (0)	9	0.05
Albanian (10)	10	0.06
American (783)	783	4.71
Arab (73)	129	0.78
Arab (0)	13	0.08
Iraqi (10)	10	0.06
Lebanese (9)	43	0.26
Moroccan (29)	29	0.17
Syrian (25)	34	0.20
Australian (15)	15	0.09
Austrian (16)	16	0.10
Belgian (34)	235	1.41
British (18)	59	0.36
Canadian (34)	68	0.41
Czech (5)	47	0.28
Czechoslovakian (10)	10	0.06
Dutch (6)	156	0.94
English (277)	1,181	7.11
European (134)	134	0.81
Finnish (170)	210	1.26
French, ex. Basque (101)	1,138	6.85
French Canadian (164)	397	2.39
German (1,020)	3,737	22.49
Greek (121)	189	1.14
Hungarian (112)	182	1.10
Irish (394)	1,888	11.36
Italian (329)	1,206	7.26
Lithuanian (17)	39	0.23
Macedonian (34)	34	0.20
Norwegian (0)	40	0.24
Polish (428)	1,299	7.82
Portuguese (0)	28	0.17
Romanian (14)	55	0.33
Russian (82)	177	1.07
Scandinavian (43)	57	0.34
Scotch-Irish (149)	256	1.54
Scottish (100)	271	1.63
Serbian (28)	81	0.49
Slavic (0)	7	0.04
Slovak (20)	20	0.12
Swedish (16)	105	0.63
Swiss (33)	33	0.20
Ukrainian (30)	116	0.70
Welsh (11)	169	1.02
West Indian, ex. Hispanic (0)	41	0.25
West Indian (0)	41	0.25
Yugoslavian (9)	25	0.15

Hispanic Origin	Population	%
Hispanic or Latino (of any race)	477	2.92
Central American, ex. Mexican	19	0.12
Guatemalan	1	0.01
Honduran	1	0.01
Nicaraguan	1	0.01
Panamanian	14	0.09
Salvadoran	2	0.01
Cuban	5	0.03
Dominican Republic	11	0.07
Mexican	323	1.98
Puerto Rican	75	0.46
South American	16	0.10
Argentinean	4	0.02
Chilean	3	0.02
Colombian	1	0.01
Peruvian	7	0.04
Other South American	1	0.01
Other Hispanic or Latino	28	0.17

*Notes: † The Census 2010 population figure is used to calculate the percentages in the Hispanic Origin and Race categories. Ancestry percentages are based on the 2006-2010 American Community Survey population (not shown); ‡ Numbers in parentheses indicate the number of people reporting a single ancestry; * Numbers in parentheses indicate the number of persons reporting this race alone, not in combination with any other race; Please refer to the Explanation of Data for more information.*

Race*	Population	%
African-American/Black (4,038)	4,449	27.27
Not Hispanic (3,993)	4,375	26.82
Hispanic (45)	74	0.45
American Indian/Alaska Native (57)	251	1.54
Not Hispanic (44)	224	1.37
Hispanic (13)	27	0.17
Apache (0)	7	0.04
Blackfeet (2)	15	0.09
Canadian/French Am. Ind. (2)	2	0.01
Cherokee (4)	57	0.35
Chippewa (13)	33	0.20
Choctaw (0)	4	0.02
Comanche (2)	2	0.01
Delaware (2)	2	0.01
Iroquois (2)	3	0.02
Mexican American Ind. (0)	1	0.01
Navajo (1)	1	0.01
Osage (0)	1	0.01
Ottawa (1)	2	0.01
Potawatomi (0)	1	0.01
Pueblo (0)	1	0.01
Seminole (0)	1	0.01
Shoshone (0)	1	0.01
Sioux (1)	4	0.02
Tlingit-Haida *(Alaska Native)* (1)	1	0.01
Asian (82)	140	0.86
Not Hispanic (79)	136	0.83
Hispanic (3)	4	0.02
Bangladeshi (2)	2	0.01
Chinese, ex. Taiwanese (17)	22	0.13
Filipino (21)	37	0.23
Hmong (2)	2	0.01
Indian (13)	15	0.09
Indonesian (0)	2	0.01
Japanese (3)	13	0.08
Korean (14)	28	0.17
Pakistani (1)	2	0.01
Thai (1)	2	0.01
Vietnamese (5)	10	0.06
Hawaii Native/Pacific Islander (5)	17	0.10
Not Hispanic (5)	16	0.10
Hispanic (0)	1	0.01
Native Hawaiian (1)	5	0.03
Samoan (4)	4	0.02
White (11,417)	11,935	73.16
Not Hispanic (11,150)	11,621	71.23
Hispanic (267)	314	1.92

Mount Morris

Place Type: Township
County: Genesee
Population: 21,501†

Ancestry‡	Population	%
African, Sub-Saharan (193)	193	0.87
African (136)	136	0.61
Ethiopian (57)	57	0.26
American (963)	963	4.33
Arab (87)	130	0.58
Arab (24)	67	0.30
Lebanese (63)	63	0.28
Assyrian/Chaldean/Syriac (0)	26	0.12
Belgian (7)	16	0.07
British (0)	32	0.14
Canadian (69)	132	0.59
Croatian (0)	55	0.25
Czech (43)	76	0.34
Czechoslovakian (11)	50	0.22
Danish (0)	11	0.05
Dutch (20)	306	1.38
Eastern European (11)	11	0.05
English (635)	1,591	7.16
European (6)	6	0.03
Finnish (115)	140	0.63
French, ex. Basque (63)	665	2.99
French Canadian (188)	497	2.24
German (772)	2,303	10.36
Greek (35)	35	0.16
Hungarian (64)	162	0.73
Irish (258)	1,627	7.32
Italian (208)	426	1.92
Macedonian (7)	7	0.03
Norwegian (47)	84	0.38
Polish (291)	812	3.65
Romanian (8)	31	0.14
Russian (13)	102	0.46
Scandinavian (0)	9	0.04
Scotch-Irish (29)	259	1.17
Scottish (123)	447	2.01
Slavic (10)	10	0.04
Slovak (26)	41	0.18
Swedish (7)	126	0.57
Swiss (14)	34	0.15
Ukrainian (0)	66	0.30
Welsh (16)	93	0.42
West Indian, ex. Hispanic (13)	66	0.30
Haitian (0)	27	0.12
Jamaican (13)	39	0.18

Hispanic Origin	Population	%
Hispanic or Latino (of any race)	711	3.31
Central American, ex. Mexican	17	0.08
Guatemalan	1	<0.01
Honduran	8	0.04
Panamanian	2	0.01
Salvadoran	6	0.03
Cuban	9	0.04
Dominican Republic	3	0.01
Mexican	582	2.71
Puerto Rican	38	0.18
South American	3	0.01
Colombian	1	<0.01
Other South American	2	0.01
Other Hispanic or Latino	59	0.27

Race*	Population	%
African-American/Black (9,212)	9,693	45.08
Not Hispanic (9,130)	9,568	44.50
Hispanic (82)	125	0.58
American Indian/Alaska Native (154)	396	1.84
Not Hispanic (136)	356	1.66
Hispanic (18)	40	0.19
Apache (1)	1	<0.01
Blackfeet (2)	20	0.09
Canadian/French Am. Ind. (1)	2	0.01
Cherokee (11)	58	0.27
Chickasaw (0)	4	0.02
Chippewa (39)	66	0.31
Choctaw (2)	3	0.01
Cree (0)	3	0.01
Creek (0)	3	0.01
Inupiat *(Alaska Native)* (1)	1	<0.01
Iroquois (2)	3	0.01
Lumbee (1)	1	<0.01
Mexican American Ind. (6)	9	0.04
Navajo (1)	2	0.01
Ottawa (10)	14	0.07
Potawatomi (7)	12	0.06
Seminole (0)	1	<0.01
Sioux (1)	4	0.02
Spanish American Ind. (1)	3	0.01
Tlingit-Haida *(Alaska Native)* (0)	1	<0.01
Yakama (0)	1	<0.01
Asian (69)	151	0.70
Not Hispanic (68)	145	0.67
Hispanic (1)	6	0.03
Chinese, ex. Taiwanese (8)	23	0.11
Filipino (11)	17	0.08
Indian (19)	34	0.16
Indonesian (0)	3	0.01
Japanese (6)	19	0.09
Korean (11)	22	0.10
Pakistani (0)	1	<0.01
Thai (8)	10	0.05
Vietnamese (1)	1	<0.01
Hawaii Native/Pacific Islander (2)	32	0.15
Not Hispanic (2)	32	0.15
Guamanian/Chamorro (1)	4	0.02
Native Hawaiian (1)	19	0.09
White (11,112)	11,742	54.61
Not Hispanic (10,775)	11,330	52.70
Hispanic (337)	412	1.92

Mount Pleasant

Place Type: City
County: Isabella
Population: 26,016†

Ancestry‡	Population	%
African, Sub-Saharan (136)	190	0.73
African (106)	135	0.52
Ghanaian (14)	14	0.05
Other Sub-Saharan African (16)	41	0.16
Albanian (3)	3	0.01
Alsatian (0)	3	0.01
American (554)	554	2.12
Arab (48)	183	0.70
Arab (48)	48	0.18
Lebanese (0)	86	0.33
Syrian (0)	49	0.19
Armenian (47)	69	0.26
Assyrian/Chaldean/Syriac (3)	3	0.01
Austrian (2)	81	0.31
Belgian (61)	128	0.49
Brazilian (12)	12	0.05
British (22)	107	0.41
Bulgarian (3)	3	0.01
Canadian (25)	97	0.37
Celtic (3)	3	0.01
Croatian (0)	16	0.06
Czech (40)	156	0.60
Czechoslovakian (25)	62	0.24
Danish (24)	153	0.59
Dutch (225)	977	3.74
English (1,161)	3,279	12.55
European (155)	159	0.61
Finnish (58)	230	0.88
French, ex. Basque (287)	1,437	5.50
French Canadian (175)	571	2.19
German (2,225)	7,521	28.80
Greek (102)	146	0.56
Hungarian (96)	208	0.80
Iranian (40)	40	0.15
Irish (1,317)	4,562	17.47
Italian (398)	1,279	4.90
Lithuanian (13)	44	0.17
Macedonian (12)	12	0.05
Maltese (0)	2	0.01
Northern European (34)	34	0.13
Norwegian (62)	317	1.21
Pennsylvania German (0)	19	0.07
Polish (701)	2,351	9.00
Portuguese (11)	11	0.04
Romanian (13)	100	0.38
Russian (177)	342	1.31
Scandinavian (30)	48	0.18
Scotch-Irish (190)	585	2.24
Scottish (332)	1,099	4.21
Serbian (4)	4	0.02
Slavic (0)	9	0.03
Slovak (6)	29	0.11
Swedish (142)	383	1.47
Swiss (3)	76	0.29
Turkish (0)	3	0.01
Ukrainian (3)	87	0.33
Welsh (8)	139	0.53
West Indian, ex. Hispanic (60)	60	0.23
Jamaican (60)	60	0.23
Yugoslavian (9)	37	0.14

Hispanic Origin	Population	%
Hispanic or Latino (of any race)	857	3.29
Central American, ex. Mexican	38	0.15
Costa Rican	6	0.02
Guatemalan	4	0.02
Honduran	12	0.05

*Notes: † The Census 2010 population figure is used to calculate the percentages in the Hispanic Origin and Race categories. Ancestry percentages are based on the 2006-2010 American Community Survey population (not shown); ‡ Numbers in parentheses indicate the number of people reporting a single ancestry; * Numbers in parentheses indicate the number of persons reporting this race alone, not in combination with any other race; Please refer to the Explanation of Data for more information.*

Nicaraguan	3	0.01
Panamanian	3	0.01
Salvadoran	10	0.04
Cuban	15	0.06
Dominican Republic	4	0.02
Mexican	594	2.28
Puerto Rican	63	0.24
South American	57	0.22
Argentinean	16	0.06
Chilean	10	0.04
Colombian	10	0.04
Ecuadorian	4	0.02
Paraguayan	1	<0.01
Peruvian	10	0.04
Uruguayan	1	<0.01
Venezuelan	4	0.02
Other South American	1	<0.01
Other Hispanic or Latino	86	0.33

Race*	Population	%
African-American/Black (1,020)	1,313	5.05
Not Hispanic (1,006)	1,276	4.90
Hispanic (14)	37	0.14
American Indian/Alaska Native (528)	799	3.07
Not Hispanic (460)	690	2.65
Hispanic (68)	109	0.42
Aleut *(Alaska Native)* (0)	1	<0.01
Apache (0)	1	<0.01
Blackfeet (0)	4	0.02
Canadian/French Am. Ind. (6)	11	0.04
Cherokee (4)	21	0.08
Chippewa (284)	380	1.46
Choctaw (0)	2	0.01
Crow (1)	1	<0.01
Houma (1)	1	<0.01
Inupiat *(Alaska Native)* (0)	1	<0.01
Iroquois (6)	11	0.04
Menominee (3)	4	0.02
Mexican American Ind. (2)	2	0.01
Navajo (3)	5	0.02
Osage (0)	1	<0.01
Ottawa (32)	44	0.17
Potawatomi (14)	22	0.08
Sioux (0)	1	<0.01
South American Ind. (1)	1	<0.01
Spanish American Ind. (0)	1	<0.01
Tlingit-Haida *(Alaska Native)* (0)	1	<0.01
Ute (1)	1	<0.01
Yup'ik *(Alaska Native)* (0)	1	<0.01
Asian (785)	950	3.65
Not Hispanic (780)	938	3.61
Hispanic (5)	12	0.05
Bangladeshi (4)	5	0.02
Cambodian (7)	8	0.03
Chinese, ex. Taiwanese (282)	301	1.16
Filipino (41)	64	0.25
Hmong (6)	7	0.03
Indian (194)	229	0.88
Indonesian (1)	3	0.01
Japanese (53)	79	0.30
Korean (101)	120	0.46
Laotian (1)	1	<0.01
Malaysian (0)	2	0.01
Nepalese (8)	8	0.03
Pakistani (10)	17	0.07
Sri Lankan (13)	14	0.05
Taiwanese (13)	13	0.05
Thai (2)	17	0.07
Vietnamese (22)	28	0.11
Hawaii Native/Pacific Islander (10)	43	0.17
Not Hispanic (6)	36	0.14
Hispanic (4)	7	0.03
Guamanian/Chamorro (3)	8	0.03
Native Hawaiian (6)	11	0.04
Samoan (0)	12	0.05
Tongan (0)	1	<0.01
White (22,788)	23,426	90.04
Not Hispanic (22,258)	22,818	87.71
Hispanic (530)	608	2.34

Mundy

Place Type: Township
County: Genesee
Population: 15,082†

Ancestry‡	Population	%
African, Sub-Saharan (0)	49	0.33
African (0)	49	0.33
American (1,040)	1,040	7.06
Arab (192)	328	2.23
Arab (76)	109	0.74
Egyptian (23)	23	0.16
Lebanese (93)	184	1.25
Syrian (0)	12	0.08
Austrian (0)	32	0.22
Belgian (13)	39	0.26
British (70)	99	0.67
Canadian (13)	29	0.20
Croatian (15)	86	0.58
Czech (50)	107	0.73
Czechoslovakian (39)	102	0.69
Danish (39)	102	0.69
Dutch (62)	213	1.45
Eastern European (12)	12	0.08
English (554)	1,979	13.43
European (248)	263	1.78
Finnish (33)	71	0.48
French, ex. Basque (233)	760	5.16
French Canadian (136)	401	2.72
German (872)	3,341	22.67
Greek (21)	21	0.14
Hungarian (72)	181	1.23
Irish (423)	1,844	12.51
Italian (268)	594	4.03
Lithuanian (41)	112	0.76
Norwegian (49)	170	1.15
Pennsylvania German (27)	56	0.38
Polish (267)	945	6.41
Portuguese (28)	28	0.19
Romanian (10)	10	0.07
Russian (15)	112	0.76
Scotch-Irish (55)	272	1.85
Scottish (110)	474	3.22
Serbian (10)	30	0.20
Slovak (14)	56	0.38
Swedish (63)	232	1.57
Swiss (0)	23	0.16
Ukrainian (12)	24	0.16
Welsh (20)	258	1.75

Hispanic Origin	Population	%
Hispanic or Latino (of any race)	360	2.39
Central American, ex. Mexican	11	0.07
Costa Rican	1	0.01
Guatemalan	3	0.02
Honduran	4	0.03
Nicaraguan	2	0.01
Salvadoran	1	0.01
Cuban	16	0.11
Mexican	265	1.76
Puerto Rican	16	0.11
South American	19	0.13
Argentinean	1	0.01
Colombian	4	0.03
Ecuadorian	3	0.02
Peruvian	3	0.02
Venezuelan	8	0.05
Other Hispanic or Latino	33	0.22

Race*	Population	%
African-American/Black (655)	751	4.98
Not Hispanic (651)	739	4.90
Hispanic (4)	12	0.08
American Indian/Alaska Native (45)	153	1.01
Not Hispanic (42)	139	0.92
Hispanic (3)	14	0.09
Blackfeet (0)	5	0.03
Canadian/French Am. Ind. (1)	5	0.03
Cherokee (6)	26	0.17
Chippewa (15)	41	0.27
Choctaw (5)	7	0.05
Creek (2)	2	0.01
Houma (1)	1	0.01
Iroquois (1)	3	0.02
Mexican American Ind. (1)	2	0.01
Osage (0)	3	0.02
Ottawa (0)	1	0.01
Potawatomi (0)	1	0.01
Yup'ik *(Alaska Native)* (0)	1	0.01
Asian (153)	221	1.47
Not Hispanic (151)	216	1.43
Hispanic (2)	5	0.03
Chinese, ex. Taiwanese (12)	20	0.13
Filipino (18)	24	0.16
Hmong (29)	30	0.20
Indian (34)	39	0.26
Indonesian (1)	2	0.01
Japanese (4)	15	0.10
Korean (28)	39	0.26
Laotian (0)	1	0.01
Malaysian (1)	1	0.01
Taiwanese (0)	2	0.01
Thai (6)	11	0.07
Vietnamese (9)	9	0.06
Hawaii Native/Pacific Islander (8)	16	0.11
Not Hispanic (8)	16	0.11
Guamanian/Chamorro (3)	3	0.02
Native Hawaiian (3)	5	0.03
White (13,887)	14,141	93.76
Not Hispanic (13,619)	13,848	91.82
Hispanic (268)	293	1.94

Muskegon Heights

Place Type: City
County: Muskegon
Population: 10,856†

Ancestry‡	Population	%
African, Sub-Saharan (113)	179	1.60
African (113)	179	1.60
American (220)	220	1.97
Canadian (0)	8	0.07
Croatian (12)	12	0.11
Danish (12)	26	0.23
Dutch (15)	138	1.24
English (35)	201	1.80
Finnish (0)	13	0.12
French, ex. Basque (30)	183	1.64
French Canadian (0)	23	0.21
German (106)	370	3.32
Greek (0)	25	0.22
Hungarian (0)	51	0.46
Irish (177)	520	4.66
Italian (21)	113	1.01
Norwegian (8)	16	0.14
Polish (57)	128	1.15
Russian (0)	12	0.11
Scotch-Irish (22)	22	0.20
Scottish (39)	39	0.35
Swedish (8)	61	0.55
Welsh (0)	22	0.20
West Indian, ex. Hispanic (38)	66	0.59
Jamaican (38)	66	0.59

Hispanic Origin	Population	%
Hispanic or Latino (of any race)	451	4.15
Central American, ex. Mexican	5	0.05
Panamanian	5	0.05
Cuban	4	0.04
Dominican Republic	1	0.01
Mexican	352	3.24
Puerto Rican	40	0.37
Other Hispanic or Latino	49	0.45

Race*	Population	%
African-American/Black (8,501)	8,828	81.32
Not Hispanic (8,434)	8,731	80.43
Hispanic (67)	97	0.89

*Notes: † The Census 2010 population figure is used to calculate the percentages in the Hispanic Origin and Race categories. Ancestry percentages are based on the 2006-2010 American Community Survey population (not shown); ‡ Numbers in parentheses indicate the number of people reporting a single ancestry; * Numbers in parentheses indicate the number of persons reporting this race alone, not in combination with any other race; Please refer to the Explanation of Data for more information.*

	Population	%
American Indian/Alaska Native (33)	173	1.59
Not Hispanic (29)	157	1.45
Hispanic (4)	16	0.15
Apache (3)	4	0.04
Blackfeet (0)	12	0.11
Canadian/French Am. Ind. (0)	2	0.02
Cherokee (1)	19	0.18
Chippewa (2)	4	0.04
Choctaw (1)	5	0.05
Crow (0)	3	0.03
Navajo (0)	1	0.01
Ottawa (9)	25	0.23
Asian (14)	38	0.35
Not Hispanic (13)	36	0.33
Hispanic (1)	2	0.02
Chinese, ex. Taiwanese (0)	2	0.02
Filipino (1)	10	0.09
Indian (11)	13	0.12
Japanese (0)	2	0.02
Korean (1)	7	0.06
Pakistani (0)	1	0.01
Thai (1)	3	0.03
Hawaii Native/Pacific Islander (0)	3	0.03
Not Hispanic (0)	3	0.03
Native Hawaiian (0)	3	0.03
White (1,739)	2,081	19.17
Not Hispanic (1,564)	1,857	17.11
Hispanic (175)	224	2.06

Muskegon

Place Type: Charter Township
County: Muskegon
Population: 17,840†

Ancestry‡	Population	%
American (1,000)	1,000	5.57
Arab (16)	16	0.09
Lebanese (16)	16	0.09
Belgian (10)	45	0.25
British (0)	7	0.04
Bulgarian (0)	11	0.06
Canadian (5)	26	0.14
Croatian (12)	12	0.07
Czech (31)	68	0.38
Czechoslovakian (0)	29	0.16
Danish (67)	111	0.62
Dutch (638)	1,891	10.53
Eastern European (14)	14	0.08
English (331)	1,357	7.55
European (51)	51	0.28
Finnish (64)	91	0.51
French, ex. Basque (107)	948	5.28
French Canadian (94)	314	1.75
German (1,068)	4,081	22.72
Greek (25)	77	0.43
Hungarian (33)	160	0.89
Irish (287)	1,847	10.28
Italian (210)	600	3.34
Lithuanian (0)	7	0.04
Norwegian (83)	209	1.16
Pennsylvania German (32)	40	0.22
Polish (442)	1,493	8.31
Portuguese (10)	32	0.18
Russian (0)	92	0.51
Scandinavian (23)	48	0.27
Scotch-Irish (48)	262	1.46
Scottish (51)	235	1.31
Slavic (0)	21	0.12
Slovak (24)	61	0.34
Swedish (89)	658	3.66
Swiss (0)	8	0.04
Ukrainian (26)	37	0.21
Welsh (0)	96	0.53

Hispanic Origin	Population	%
Hispanic or Latino (of any race)	903	5.06
Central American, ex. Mexican	18	0.10
Costa Rican	8	0.04
Guatemalan	1	0.01
Honduran	5	0.03
Nicaraguan	1	0.01
Panamanian	3	0.02
Cuban	8	0.04
Mexican	739	4.14
Puerto Rican	64	0.36
South American	9	0.05
Argentinean	1	0.01
Colombian	7	0.04
Other South American	1	0.01
Other Hispanic or Latino	65	0.36

Race*	Population	%
African-American/Black (1,086)	1,351	7.57
Not Hispanic (1,072)	1,301	7.29
Hispanic (14)	50	0.28
American Indian/Alaska Native (193)	403	2.26
Not Hispanic (174)	353	1.98
Hispanic (19)	50	0.28
Blackfeet (3)	7	0.04
Canadian/French Am. Ind. (2)	2	0.01
Cherokee (7)	21	0.12
Chippewa (34)	53	0.30
Choctaw (0)	5	0.03
Crow (0)	1	0.01
Iroquois (4)	4	0.02
Lumbee (5)	6	0.03
Mexican American Ind. (1)	3	0.02
Navajo (1)	1	0.01
Ottawa (74)	137	0.77
Potawatomi (14)	22	0.12
Sioux (2)	8	0.04
Asian (79)	144	0.81
Not Hispanic (77)	134	0.75
Hispanic (2)	10	0.06
Cambodian (0)	1	0.01
Chinese, ex. Taiwanese (8)	13	0.07
Filipino (13)	28	0.16
Indian (11)	18	0.10
Indonesian (3)	3	0.02
Japanese (6)	16	0.09
Korean (13)	24	0.13
Laotian (2)	7	0.04
Thai (2)	6	0.03
Vietnamese (15)	19	0.11
Hawaii Native/Pacific Islander (6)	19	0.11
Not Hispanic (3)	11	0.06
Hispanic (3)	8	0.04
Guamanian/Chamorro (1)	2	0.01
Marshallese (0)	1	0.01
Native Hawaiian (3)	9	0.05
White (15,675)	16,213	90.88
Not Hispanic (15,155)	15,576	87.31
Hispanic (520)	637	3.57

Muskegon

Place Type: City
County: Muskegon
Population: 38,401†

Ancestry‡	Population	%
African, Sub-Saharan (74)	86	0.22
African (74)	86	0.22
American (909)	909	2.33
Arab (127)	140	0.36
Arab (9)	18	0.05
Iraqi (63)	63	0.16
Lebanese (0)	4	0.01
Moroccan (46)	46	0.12
Other Arab (9)	9	0.02
Armenian (0)	13	0.03
Assyrian/Chaldean/Syriac (9)	9	0.02
Austrian (27)	106	0.27
Belgian (54)	171	0.44
British (13)	36	0.09
Canadian (21)	41	0.11
Croatian (0)	30	0.08
Czech (41)	208	0.53
Czechoslovakian (0)	10	0.03
Danish (13)	232	0.59
Dutch (969)	2,594	6.65
English (496)	2,269	5.81
Estonian (10)	10	0.03
European (87)	87	0.22
Finnish (121)	201	0.52
French, ex. Basque (120)	1,202	3.08
French Canadian (250)	649	1.66
German (1,306)	5,105	13.08
German Russian (8)	8	0.02
Greek (24)	45	0.12
Hungarian (58)	165	0.42
Irish (619)	3,065	7.85
Italian (216)	706	1.81
Lithuanian (41)	104	0.27
Norwegian (85)	406	1.04
Pennsylvania German (20)	37	0.09
Polish (561)	1,899	4.87
Portuguese (0)	31	0.08
Romanian (0)	64	0.16
Russian (24)	153	0.39
Scandinavian (17)	27	0.07
Scotch-Irish (151)	498	1.28
Scottish (78)	307	0.79
Serbian (35)	35	0.09
Slavic (11)	11	0.03
Slovak (9)	121	0.31
Swedish (257)	896	2.30
Swiss (0)	7	0.02
Turkish (8)	8	0.02
Ukrainian (15)	35	0.09
Welsh (19)	91	0.23
West Indian, ex. Hispanic (56)	100	0.26
Haitian (19)	28	0.07
Jamaican (37)	72	0.18
Yugoslavian (59)	71	0.18

Hispanic Origin	Population	%
Hispanic or Latino (of any race)	3,157	8.22
Central American, ex. Mexican	17	0.04
Guatemalan	7	0.02
Honduran	1	<0.01
Panamanian	4	0.01
Salvadoran	5	0.01
Cuban	16	0.04
Dominican Republic	7	0.02
Mexican	2,718	7.08
Puerto Rican	203	0.53
South American	16	0.04
Argentinean	2	0.01
Colombian	4	0.01
Ecuadorian	2	0.01
Peruvian	8	0.02
Other Hispanic or Latino	180	0.47

Race*	Population	%
African-American/Black (13,241)	14,348	37.36
Not Hispanic (13,079)	14,059	36.61
Hispanic (162)	289	0.75
American Indian/Alaska Native (361)	909	2.37
Not Hispanic (307)	753	1.96
Hispanic (54)	156	0.41
Apache (6)	16	0.04
Blackfeet (6)	26	0.07
Canadian/French Am. Ind. (4)	8	0.02
Cherokee (19)	86	0.22
Chickasaw (1)	1	<0.01
Chippewa (50)	86	0.22
Choctaw (2)	11	0.03
Cree (2)	2	0.01
Creek (3)	6	0.02
Delaware (1)	1	<0.01
Inupiat *(Alaska Native)* (1)	1	<0.01
Iroquois (0)	8	0.02
Kiowa (0)	1	<0.01
Mexican American Ind. (2)	11	0.03
Navajo (2)	7	0.02
Ottawa (95)	181	0.47
Potawatomi (20)	27	0.07
Sioux (2)	7	0.02

*Notes: † The Census 2010 population figure is used to calculate the percentages in the Hispanic Origin and Race categories. Ancestry percentages are based on the 2006-2010 American Community Survey population (not shown); ‡ Numbers in parentheses indicate the number of people reporting a single ancestry; * Numbers in parentheses indicate the number of persons reporting this race alone, not in combination with any other race; Please refer to the Explanation of Data for more information.*

	Population	%
South American Ind. (1)	3	0.01
Tlingit-Haida *(Alaska Native)* (1)	2	0.01
Asian (148)	257	0.67
Not Hispanic (142)	240	0.62
Hispanic (6)	17	0.04
Burmese (2)	2	0.01
Cambodian (1)	4	0.01
Chinese, ex. Taiwanese (37)	48	0.12
Filipino (20)	43	0.11
Indian (16)	30	0.08
Indonesian (2)	4	0.01
Japanese (17)	35	0.09
Korean (22)	46	0.12
Laotian (1)	1	<0.01
Pakistani (2)	2	0.01
Thai (2)	11	0.03
Vietnamese (8)	16	0.04
Hawaii Native/Pacific Islander (5)	29	0.08
Not Hispanic (2)	17	0.04
Hispanic (3)	12	0.03
Fijian (0)	2	0.01
Guamanian/Chamorro (0)	4	0.01
Native Hawaiian (3)	9	0.02
Samoan (0)	3	0.01
Tongan (0)	2	0.01
White (21,906)	23,468	61.11
Not Hispanic (20,317)	21,548	56.11
Hispanic (1,589)	1,920	5.00

New Baltimore

Place Type: City
County: Macomb
Population: 12,084†

Ancestry‡	Population	%
Albanian (18)	18	0.16
American (491)	491	4.33
Arab (8)	96	0.85
Iraqi (0)	37	0.33
Lebanese (8)	46	0.41
Syrian (0)	13	0.11
Armenian (27)	27	0.24
Assyrian/Chaldean/Syriac (17)	70	0.62
Austrian (0)	10	0.09
Belgian (87)	532	4.70
British (13)	24	0.21
Bulgarian (16)	16	0.14
Canadian (26)	93	0.82
Croatian (34)	52	0.46
Czech (0)	83	0.73
Czechoslovakian (0)	44	0.39
Danish (16)	37	0.33
Dutch (40)	273	2.41
English (226)	1,314	11.60
European (106)	146	1.29
Finnish (0)	54	0.48
French, ex. Basque (43)	796	7.03
French Canadian (27)	185	1.63
German (552)	2,798	24.70
Greek (0)	116	1.02
Hungarian (0)	67	0.59
Icelander (0)	14	0.12
Irish (239)	1,581	13.96
Italian (373)	1,535	13.55
Latvian (0)	10	0.09
Lithuanian (0)	27	0.24
Macedonian (93)	126	1.11
Maltese (22)	31	0.27
Norwegian (4)	52	0.46
Polish (684)	2,241	19.78
Portuguese (17)	21	0.19
Romanian (10)	108	0.95
Russian (17)	65	0.57
Scandinavian (9)	33	0.29
Scotch-Irish (30)	134	1.18
Scottish (40)	263	2.32
Serbian (16)	16	0.14
Slavic (0)	21	0.19
Slovak (44)	68	0.60
Slovene (12)	12	0.11
Swedish (80)	162	1.43
Swiss (0)	8	0.07
Turkish (27)	38	0.34
Ukrainian (12)	143	1.26
Welsh (6)	70	0.62
West Indian, ex. Hispanic (0)	5	0.04
Jamaican (0)	5	0.04
Yugoslavian (0)	134	1.18

Hispanic Origin	Population	%
Hispanic or Latino (of any race)	221	1.83
Central American, ex. Mexican	5	0.04
Guatemalan	1	0.01
Honduran	1	0.01
Panamanian	3	0.02
Cuban	1	0.01
Mexican	152	1.26
Puerto Rican	19	0.16
South American	18	0.15
Argentinean	3	0.02
Colombian	4	0.03
Ecuadorian	7	0.06
Peruvian	1	0.01
Uruguayan	2	0.02
Venezuelan	1	0.01
Other Hispanic or Latino	26	0.22

Race*	Population	%
African-American/Black (332)	381	3.15
Not Hispanic (329)	376	3.11
Hispanic (3)	5	0.04
American Indian/Alaska Native (49)	108	0.89
Not Hispanic (49)	106	0.88
Hispanic (0)	2	0.02
Arapaho (1)	1	0.01
Blackfeet (0)	5	0.04
Cherokee (2)	16	0.13
Chippewa (11)	25	0.21
Choctaw (0)	4	0.03
Creek (4)	4	0.03
Crow (0)	1	0.01
Iroquois (12)	15	0.12
Lumbee (9)	10	0.08
Potawatomi (0)	7	0.06
Shoshone (0)	2	0.02
Sioux (0)	3	0.02
Asian (104)	155	1.28
Not Hispanic (104)	154	1.27
Hispanic (0)	1	0.01
Chinese, ex. Taiwanese (16)	24	0.20
Filipino (29)	45	0.37
Hmong (2)	2	0.02
Indian (7)	9	0.07
Indonesian (5)	5	0.04
Japanese (4)	18	0.15
Korean (13)	26	0.22
Pakistani (7)	8	0.07
Thai (5)	11	0.09
Vietnamese (10)	12	0.10
Hawaii Native/Pacific Islander (2)	6	0.05
Not Hispanic (2)	6	0.05
Native Hawaiian (1)	4	0.03
White (11,402)	11,562	95.68
Not Hispanic (11,224)	11,370	94.09
Hispanic (178)	192	1.59

Niles

Place Type: City
County: Berrien
Population: 11,599†

Ancestry‡	Population	%
African, Sub-Saharan (19)	62	0.53
African (8)	51	0.44
Ghanaian (11)	11	0.09
American (1,040)	1,040	8.92
Arab (32)	32	0.27
Arab (6)	6	0.05
Egyptian (5)	5	0.04
Jordanian (21)	21	0.18
Australian (3)	3	0.03
Austrian (0)	37	0.32
Belgian (20)	46	0.39
British (40)	40	0.34
Canadian (3)	32	0.27
Croatian (0)	12	0.10
Czech (6)	37	0.32
Czechoslovakian (4)	22	0.19
Danish (11)	47	0.40
Dutch (70)	521	4.47
English (281)	992	8.51
European (40)	43	0.37
Finnish (8)	25	0.21
French, ex. Basque (57)	399	3.42
French Canadian (15)	33	0.28
German (1,139)	3,178	27.27
Greek (16)	29	0.25
Hungarian (64)	160	1.37
Irish (394)	1,730	14.84
Italian (131)	367	3.15
Lithuanian (28)	54	0.46
Luxemburger (0)	2	0.02
Northern European (3)	3	0.03
Norwegian (32)	93	0.80
Pennsylvania German (13)	16	0.14
Polish (240)	687	5.89
Portuguese (2)	4	0.03
Russian (23)	70	0.60
Scandinavian (2)	6	0.05
Scotch-Irish (38)	211	1.81
Scottish (33)	230	1.97
Serbian (2)	2	0.02
Slavic (3)	9	0.08
Slovak (4)	8	0.07
Slovene (0)	28	0.24
Swedish (45)	178	1.53
Swiss (12)	21	0.18
Ukrainian (0)	17	0.15
Welsh (3)	20	0.17
West Indian, ex. Hispanic (2)	18	0.15
Barbadian (0)	2	0.02
Belizean (0)	3	0.03
Haitian (2)	2	0.02
Jamaican (0)	3	0.03
West Indian (0)	8	0.07
Yugoslavian (0)	9	0.08

Hispanic Origin	Population	%
Hispanic or Latino (of any race)	665	5.73
Central American, ex. Mexican	20	0.17
Costa Rican	2	0.02
Guatemalan	3	0.03
Honduran	1	0.01
Nicaraguan	3	0.03
Panamanian	8	0.07
Salvadoran	3	0.03
Cuban	12	0.10
Mexican	418	3.60
Puerto Rican	154	1.33
South American	20	0.17
Argentinean	9	0.08
Chilean	1	0.01
Colombian	3	0.03
Ecuadorian	4	0.03
Peruvian	1	0.01
Uruguayan	1	0.01
Venezuelan	1	0.01
Other Hispanic or Latino	41	0.35

Race*	Population	%
African-American/Black (1,440)	1,764	15.21
Not Hispanic (1,402)	1,694	14.60
Hispanic (38)	70	0.60
American Indian/Alaska Native (72)	206	1.78
Not Hispanic (71)	195	1.68
Hispanic (1)	11	0.09
Apache (0)	1	0.01
Blackfeet (1)	14	0.12

*Notes: † The Census 2010 population figure is used to calculate the percentages in the Hispanic Origin and Race categories. Ancestry percentages are based on the 2006-2010 American Community Survey population (not shown); ‡ Numbers in parentheses indicate the number of people reporting a single ancestry; * Numbers in parentheses indicate the number of persons reporting this race alone, not in combination with any other race; Please refer to the Explanation of Data for more information.*

Cherokee (6)	49	0.42
Chippewa (11)	16	0.14
Comanche (5)	5	0.04
Cree (0)	2	0.02
Creek (1)	1	0.01
Iroquois (0)	3	0.03
Mexican American Ind. (0)	1	0.01
Ottawa (2)	4	0.03
Potawatomi (29)	50	0.43
Puget Sound Salish (0)	1	0.01
Seminole (0)	1	0.01
Sioux (1)	3	0.03
Asian (69)	120	1.03
Not Hispanic (69)	107	0.92
Hispanic (0)	13	0.11
Bangladeshi (14)	16	0.14
Chinese, ex. Taiwanese (7)	15	0.13
Filipino (6)	16	0.14
Indian (10)	22	0.19
Indonesian (2)	2	0.02
Japanese (8)	16	0.14
Korean (12)	19	0.16
Laotian (1)	1	0.01
Malaysian (1)	1	0.01
Taiwanese (1)	1	0.01
Thai (4)	5	0.04
Vietnamese (1)	4	0.03
Hawaii Native/Pacific Islander (6)	8	0.07
Not Hispanic (6)	8	0.07
Native Hawaiian (4)	4	0.03
Samoan (1)	2	0.02
Tongan (1)	1	0.01
White (9,314)	9,792	84.42
Not Hispanic (8,963)	9,357	80.67
Hispanic (351)	435	3.75

Niles

Place Type: City
County: Berrien
Population: 11,600†

Ancestry‡	Population	%
African, Sub-Saharan (19)	62	0.53
African (8)	51	0.44
Ghanaian (11)	11	0.09
American (1,040)	1,040	8.92
Arab (32)	32	0.27
Arab (6)	6	0.05
Egyptian (5)	5	0.04
Jordanian (21)	21	0.18
Australian (3)	3	0.03
Austrian (0)	37	0.32
Belgian (20)	46	0.39
British (40)	40	0.34
Canadian (3)	32	0.27
Croatian (0)	12	0.10
Czech (6)	37	0.32
Czechoslovakian (4)	22	0.19
Danish (11)	47	0.40
Dutch (70)	521	4.47
English (281)	992	8.51
European (40)	43	0.37
Finnish (8)	25	0.21
French, ex. Basque (57)	399	3.42
French Canadian (15)	33	0.28
German (1,139)	3,178	27.27
Greek (16)	29	0.25
Hungarian (64)	160	1.37
Irish (394)	1,730	14.84
Italian (131)	367	3.15
Lithuanian (28)	54	0.46
Luxemburger (0)	2	0.02
Northern European (3)	3	0.03
Norwegian (32)	93	0.80
Pennsylvania German (13)	16	0.14
Polish (240)	687	5.89
Portuguese (2)	4	0.03
Russian (23)	70	0.60
Scandinavian (2)	6	0.05
Scotch-Irish (38)	211	1.81
Scottish (33)	230	1.97
Serbian (2)	2	0.02
Slavic (3)	9	0.08
Slovak (4)	8	0.07
Slovene (0)	28	0.24
Swedish (45)	178	1.53
Swiss (12)	21	0.18
Ukrainian (0)	17	0.15
Welsh (3)	20	0.17
West Indian, ex. Hispanic (2)	18	0.15
Barbadian (0)	2	0.02
Belizean (0)	3	0.03
Haitian (2)	2	0.02
Jamaican (0)	3	0.03
West Indian (0)	8	0.07
Yugoslavian (0)	9	0.08

Hispanic Origin	Population	%
Hispanic or Latino (of any race)	665	5.73
Central American, ex. Mexican	20	0.17
Costa Rican	2	0.02
Guatemalan	3	0.03
Honduran	1	0.01
Nicaraguan	3	0.03
Panamanian	8	0.07
Salvadoran	3	0.03
Cuban	12	0.10
Mexican	418	3.60
Puerto Rican	154	1.33
South American	20	0.17
Argentinean	9	0.08
Chilean	1	0.01
Colombian	3	0.03
Ecuadorian	4	0.03
Peruvian	1	0.01
Uruguayan	1	0.01
Venezuelan	1	0.01
Other Hispanic or Latino	41	0.35

Race*	Population	%
African-American/Black (1,440)	1,764	15.21
Not Hispanic (1,402)	1,694	14.60
Hispanic (38)	70	0.60
American Indian/Alaska Native (72)	207	1.78
Not Hispanic (71)	196	1.69
Hispanic (1)	11	0.09
Apache (0)	1	0.01
Blackfeet (1)	14	0.12
Cherokee (6)	49	0.42
Chippewa (11)	16	0.14
Comanche (5)	5	0.04
Cree (0)	2	0.02
Creek (1)	1	0.01
Iroquois (0)	3	0.03
Mexican American Ind. (0)	1	0.01
Ottawa (2)	4	0.03
Potawatomi (29)	50	0.43
Puget Sound Salish (0)	1	0.01
Seminole (0)	1	0.01
Sioux (1)	3	0.03
Asian (69)	120	1.03
Not Hispanic (69)	107	0.92
Hispanic (0)	13	0.11
Bangladeshi (14)	16	0.14
Chinese, ex. Taiwanese (7)	15	0.13
Filipino (6)	16	0.14
Indian (10)	22	0.19
Indonesian (2)	2	0.02
Japanese (8)	16	0.14
Korean (12)	19	0.16
Laotian (1)	1	0.01
Malaysian (1)	1	0.01
Taiwanese (1)	1	0.01
Thai (4)	5	0.04
Vietnamese (1)	4	0.03
Hawaii Native/Pacific Islander (6)	8	0.07
Not Hispanic (6)	8	0.07
Native Hawaiian (4)	4	0.03
Samoan (1)	2	0.02
Tongan (1)	1	0.01
White (9,314)	9,793	84.42
Not Hispanic (8,963)	9,358	80.67
Hispanic (351)	435	3.75

Niles

Place Type: Township
County: Berrien
Population: 14,164†

Ancestry‡	Population	%
African, Sub-Saharan (28)	28	0.20
African (28)	28	0.20
American (844)	844	6.04
Arab (7)	7	0.05
Egyptian (7)	7	0.05
Austrian (4)	53	0.38
Belgian (15)	93	0.67
Brazilian (36)	36	0.26
British (11)	14	0.10
Canadian (4)	7	0.05
Celtic (0)	10	0.07
Croatian (2)	27	0.19
Czech (39)	106	0.76
Czechoslovakian (10)	44	0.31
Danish (3)	40	0.29
Dutch (96)	864	6.18
English (470)	1,529	10.94
Estonian (25)	25	0.18
European (123)	134	0.96
Finnish (0)	52	0.37
French, ex. Basque (64)	496	3.55
French Canadian (57)	158	1.13
German (1,639)	4,727	33.81
German Russian (0)	3	0.02
Greek (4)	5	0.04
Hungarian (61)	188	1.34
Irish (476)	2,401	17.17
Italian (79)	355	2.54
Lithuanian (18)	54	0.39
Northern European (0)	8	0.06
Norwegian (43)	90	0.64
Pennsylvania German (15)	44	0.31
Polish (317)	775	5.54
Portuguese (3)	3	0.02
Romanian (5)	10	0.07
Russian (14)	60	0.43
Scandinavian (0)	27	0.19
Scotch-Irish (22)	125	0.89
Scottish (32)	233	1.67
Serbian (7)	7	0.05
Slovak (13)	23	0.16
Swedish (59)	335	2.40
Swiss (24)	55	0.39
Ukrainian (23)	37	0.26
Welsh (0)	54	0.39
West Indian, ex. Hispanic (3)	8	0.06
U.S. Virgin Islander (0)	5	0.04
Other West Indian (3)	3	0.02
Yugoslavian (0)	9	0.06

Hispanic Origin	Population	%
Hispanic or Latino (of any race)	642	4.53
Central American, ex. Mexican	7	0.05
Nicaraguan	1	0.01
Panamanian	6	0.04
Cuban	18	0.13
Dominican Republic	2	0.01
Mexican	468	3.30
Puerto Rican	89	0.63
South American	23	0.16
Argentinean	8	0.06
Chilean	3	0.02
Colombian	1	0.01
Ecuadorian	1	0.01
Peruvian	6	0.04
Uruguayan	1	0.01
Venezuelan	3	0.02
Other Hispanic or Latino	35	0.25

*Notes: † The Census 2010 population figure is used to calculate the percentages in the Hispanic Origin and Race categories. Ancestry percentages are based on the 2006-2010 American Community Survey population (not shown); ‡ Numbers in parentheses indicate the number of people reporting a single ancestry; * Numbers in parentheses indicate the number of persons reporting this race alone, not in combination with any other race; Please refer to the Explanation of Data for more information.*

Race*	Population	%
African-American/Black (517)	674	4.76
Not Hispanic (509)	660	4.66
Hispanic (8)	14	0.10
American Indian/Alaska Native (102)	272	1.92
Not Hispanic (94)	257	1.81
Hispanic (8)	15	0.11
Apache (0)	2	0.01
Blackfeet (0)	10	0.07
Canadian/French Am. Ind. (1)	1	0.01
Cherokee (6)	69	0.49
Chippewa (12)	25	0.18
Choctaw (1)	2	0.01
Cree (0)	1	0.01
Crow (0)	1	0.01
Delaware (0)	1	0.01
Iroquois (1)	2	0.01
Mexican American Ind. (3)	3	0.02
Ottawa (3)	5	0.04
Potawatomi (38)	58	0.41
Puget Sound Salish (0)	4	0.03
Sioux (0)	7	0.05
Asian (104)	159	1.12
Not Hispanic (99)	151	1.07
Hispanic (5)	8	0.06
Chinese, ex. Taiwanese (15)	26	0.18
Filipino (26)	42	0.30
Indian (18)	22	0.16
Indonesian (0)	1	0.01
Japanese (4)	18	0.13
Korean (18)	32	0.23
Malaysian (5)	5	0.04
Pakistani (7)	7	0.05
Taiwanese (2)	2	0.01
Thai (1)	1	0.01
Vietnamese (4)	7	0.05
Hawaii Native/Pacific Islander (5)	15	0.11
Not Hispanic (5)	14	0.10
Hispanic (0)	1	0.01
Fijian (2)	2	0.01
Native Hawaiian (3)	6	0.04
Samoan (0)	5	0.04
White (12,753)	13,116	92.60
Not Hispanic (12,458)	12,800	90.37
Hispanic (295)	316	2.23

Northfield

Place Type: Township
County: Washtenaw
Population: 8,245†

Ancestry‡	Population	%
American (524)	524	6.30
Arab (18)	90	1.08
Lebanese (18)	90	1.08
Armenian (30)	63	0.76
Austrian (0)	5	0.06
Belgian (0)	108	1.30
Brazilian (14)	21	0.25
British (62)	81	0.97
Canadian (18)	54	0.65
Czech (0)	41	0.49
Danish (0)	19	0.23
Dutch (72)	361	4.34
English (403)	1,044	12.56
European (236)	236	2.84
Finnish (10)	94	1.13
French, ex. Basque (143)	680	8.18
French Canadian (116)	351	4.22
German (631)	1,981	23.83
Greek (20)	30	0.36
Hungarian (20)	86	1.03
Irish (486)	1,360	16.36
Italian (172)	473	5.69
Latvian (47)	47	0.57
Lithuanian (22)	22	0.26
Maltese (0)	12	0.14
Northern European (0)	37	0.45
Norwegian (0)	13	0.16
Polish (360)	1,024	12.32
Portuguese (0)	18	0.22
Romanian (10)	44	0.53
Russian (42)	190	2.29
Scotch-Irish (89)	131	1.58
Scottish (153)	335	4.03
Serbian (0)	9	0.11
Slavic (0)	11	0.13
Slovak (12)	33	0.40
Swedish (31)	67	0.81
Swiss (0)	6	0.07
Ukrainian (0)	6	0.07
Welsh (13)	107	1.29
Yugoslavian (7)	21	0.25

Hispanic Origin	Population	%
Hispanic or Latino (of any race)	190	2.30
Central American, ex. Mexican	12	0.15
Costa Rican	3	0.04
Guatemalan	5	0.06
Honduran	3	0.04
Salvadoran	1	0.01
Cuban	3	0.04
Mexican	116	1.41
Puerto Rican	22	0.27
South American	12	0.15
Argentinean	2	0.02
Colombian	5	0.06
Ecuadorian	2	0.02
Peruvian	2	0.02
Venezuelan	1	0.01
Other Hispanic or Latino	25	0.30

Race*	Population	%
African-American/Black (83)	132	1.60
Not Hispanic (82)	130	1.58
Hispanic (1)	2	0.02
American Indian/Alaska Native (32)	91	1.10
Not Hispanic (31)	89	1.08
Hispanic (1)	2	0.02
Blackfeet (2)	6	0.07
Canadian/French Am. Ind. (2)	3	0.04
Cherokee (5)	18	0.22
Chippewa (1)	3	0.04
Choctaw (0)	1	0.01
Creek (0)	1	0.01
Iroquois (2)	10	0.12
Menominee (5)	7	0.08
Mexican American Ind. (1)	1	0.01
Navajo (0)	1	0.01
Ottawa (0)	1	0.01
Potawatomi (0)	1	0.01
South American Ind. (0)	1	0.01
Asian (74)	112	1.36
Not Hispanic (74)	108	1.31
Hispanic (0)	4	0.05
Cambodian (2)	2	0.02
Chinese, ex. Taiwanese (12)	18	0.22
Filipino (12)	26	0.32
Indian (10)	14	0.17
Japanese (5)	8	0.10
Korean (12)	18	0.22
Laotian (1)	1	0.01
Pakistani (0)	2	0.02
Taiwanese (3)	4	0.05
Thai (3)	5	0.06
Vietnamese (2)	2	0.02
Hawaii Native/Pacific Islander (1)	5	0.06
Not Hispanic (0)	3	0.04
Hispanic (1)	2	0.02
Guamanian/Chamorro (1)	1	0.01
Native Hawaiian (0)	1	0.01
White (7,866)	7,999	97.02
Not Hispanic (7,717)	7,845	95.15
Hispanic (149)	154	1.87

Northview

Place Type: CDP
County: Kent
Population: 14,541†

Ancestry‡	Population	%
African, Sub-Saharan (0)	11	0.08
Ugandan (0)	11	0.08
American (313)	313	2.17
Arab (17)	110	0.76
Syrian (17)	110	0.76
Austrian (9)	26	0.18
British (10)	10	0.07
Canadian (9)	19	0.13
Celtic (9)	9	0.06
Czech (19)	113	0.78
Czechoslovakian (10)	31	0.21
Danish (55)	228	1.58
Dutch (1,106)	2,401	16.64
Eastern European (14)	14	0.10
English (534)	1,896	13.14
European (262)	262	1.82
Finnish (61)	126	0.87
French, ex. Basque (109)	908	6.29
French Canadian (224)	414	2.87
German (958)	4,119	28.55
Greek (115)	172	1.19
Hungarian (16)	104	0.72
Iranian (15)	15	0.10
Irish (242)	2,296	15.92
Italian (153)	327	2.27
Latvian (47)	47	0.33
Lithuanian (71)	141	0.98
New Zealander (7)	7	0.05
Norwegian (82)	273	1.89
Pennsylvania German (8)	8	0.06
Polish (555)	1,282	8.89
Portuguese (0)	9	0.06
Russian (10)	45	0.31
Scotch-Irish (40)	250	1.73
Scottish (90)	314	2.18
Swedish (106)	345	2.39
Swiss (15)	142	0.98
Ukrainian (13)	13	0.09
Welsh (17)	64	0.44
Yugoslavian (0)	20	0.14

Hispanic Origin	Population	%
Hispanic or Latino (of any race)	416	2.86
Central American, ex. Mexican	16	0.11
Guatemalan	10	0.07
Honduran	1	0.01
Panamanian	1	0.01
Salvadoran	4	0.03
Cuban	23	0.16
Dominican Republic	3	0.02
Mexican	259	1.78
Puerto Rican	43	0.30
South American	25	0.17
Argentinean	4	0.03
Bolivian	5	0.03
Chilean	3	0.02
Colombian	12	0.08
Venezuelan	1	0.01
Other Hispanic or Latino	47	0.32

Race*	Population	%
African-American/Black (525)	723	4.97
Not Hispanic (509)	690	4.75
Hispanic (16)	33	0.23
American Indian/Alaska Native (42)	145	1.00
Not Hispanic (34)	127	0.87
Hispanic (8)	18	0.12
Apache (0)	1	0.01
Blackfeet (0)	2	0.01
Canadian/French Am. Ind. (1)	5	0.03
Cherokee (2)	15	0.10
Chippewa (19)	39	0.27
Comanche (0)	1	0.01

SECTION TWO

*Notes: † The Census 2010 population figure is used to calculate the percentages in the Hispanic Origin and Race categories. Ancestry percentages are based on the 2006-2010 American Community Survey population (not shown); ‡ Numbers in parentheses indicate the number of people reporting a single ancestry; * Numbers in parentheses indicate the number of persons reporting this race alone, not in combination with any other race; Please refer to the Explanation of Data for more information.*

Iroquois (1)	1	0.01
Ottawa (4)	13	0.09
Potawatomi (2)	8	0.06
Sioux (0)	1	0.01
South American Ind. (0)	4	0.03
Asian (183)	264	1.82
Not Hispanic (181)	254	1.75
Hispanic (2)	10	0.07
Bangladeshi (8)	8	0.06
Burmese (0)	1	0.01
Cambodian (0)	1	0.01
Chinese, ex. Taiwanese (46)	49	0.34
Filipino (18)	43	0.30
Indian (17)	23	0.16
Indonesian (1)	6	0.04
Japanese (8)	18	0.12
Korean (45)	64	0.44
Laotian (2)	2	0.01
Nepalese (3)	3	0.02
Pakistani (1)	1	0.01
Sri Lankan (2)	4	0.03
Taiwanese (1)	1	0.01
Thai (2)	9	0.06
Vietnamese (21)	24	0.17
Hawaii Native/Pacific Islander (8)	13	0.09
Not Hispanic (6)	11	0.08
Hispanic (2)	2	0.01
Guamanian/Chamorro (2)	2	0.01
Native Hawaiian (3)	5	0.03
Samoan (3)	3	0.02
White (13,303)	13,663	93.96
Not Hispanic (13,053)	13,365	91.91
Hispanic (250)	298	2.05

Northville

Place Type: Township
County: Wayne
Population: 28,497†

Ancestry‡	Population	%
African, Sub-Saharan (16)	25	0.09
African (0)	9	0.03
Nigerian (16)	16	0.06
Albanian (7)	7	0.03
American (1,068)	1,068	3.92
Arab (797)	1,008	3.70
Arab (90)	114	0.42
Iraqi (97)	122	0.45
Jordanian (20)	20	0.07
Lebanese (378)	468	1.72
Palestinian (46)	72	0.26
Syrian (60)	94	0.35
Other Arab (106)	118	0.43
Armenian (97)	159	0.58
Assyrian/Chaldean/Syriac (153)	214	0.79
Austrian (32)	126	0.46
Belgian (19)	118	0.43
British (190)	306	1.12
Bulgarian (0)	40	0.15
Canadian (53)	188	0.69
Croatian (20)	132	0.48
Czech (65)	254	0.93
Czechoslovakian (17)	77	0.28
Danish (16)	137	0.50
Dutch (45)	278	1.02
English (1,087)	3,175	11.65
European (344)	385	1.41
Finnish (39)	311	1.14
French, ex. Basque (272)	1,338	4.91
French Canadian (161)	424	1.56
German (1,231)	5,220	19.16
Greek (138)	485	1.78
Hungarian (159)	369	1.35
Icelander (0)	20	0.07
Iranian (74)	74	0.27
Irish (842)	3,861	14.17
Italian (717)	1,806	6.63
Latvian (20)	20	0.07
Lithuanian (69)	100	0.37
Macedonian (145)	145	0.53
Maltese (29)	185	0.68
Norwegian (172)	405	1.49
Polish (1,406)	3,514	12.90
Romanian (116)	332	1.22
Russian (78)	296	1.09
Scandinavian (0)	47	0.17
Scotch-Irish (140)	407	1.49
Scottish (271)	856	3.14
Serbian (9)	17	0.06
Slovak (50)	192	0.70
Slovene (0)	39	0.14
Swedish (48)	341	1.25
Swiss (27)	115	0.42
Turkish (0)	14	0.05
Ukrainian (71)	220	0.81
Welsh (18)	168	0.62
Yugoslavian (0)	25	0.09

Hispanic Origin	Population	%
Hispanic or Latino (of any race)	671	2.35
Central American, ex. Mexican	22	0.08
Costa Rican	2	0.01
Guatemalan	13	0.05
Honduran	3	0.01
Nicaraguan	4	0.01
Cuban	31	0.11
Mexican	357	1.25
Puerto Rican	62	0.22
South American	115	0.40
Argentinean	13	0.05
Bolivian	13	0.05
Chilean	9	0.03
Colombian	28	0.10
Ecuadorian	10	0.04
Paraguayan	3	0.01
Peruvian	18	0.06
Venezuelan	15	0.05
Other South American	6	0.02
Other Hispanic or Latino	84	0.29

Race*	Population	%
African-American/Black (1,035)	1,184	4.15
Not Hispanic (1,021)	1,154	4.05
Hispanic (14)	30	0.11
American Indian/Alaska Native (35)	102	0.36
Not Hispanic (32)	92	0.32
Hispanic (3)	10	0.04
Apache (1)	1	<0.01
Blackfeet (0)	2	0.01
Canadian/French Am. Ind. (0)	3	0.01
Cherokee (5)	17	0.06
Chickasaw (0)	1	<0.01
Chippewa (12)	19	0.07
Choctaw (2)	2	0.01
Iroquois (1)	1	<0.01
Lumbee (0)	3	0.01
Mexican American Ind. (1)	2	0.01
Ottawa (1)	1	<0.01
Potawatomi (1)	3	0.01
Seminole (0)	3	0.01
Asian (3,212)	3,520	12.35
Not Hispanic (3,205)	3,501	12.29
Hispanic (7)	19	0.07
Bangladeshi (9)	9	0.03
Chinese, ex. Taiwanese (735)	797	2.80
Filipino (83)	126	0.44
Hmong (2)	3	0.01
Indian (1,594)	1,660	5.83
Indonesian (2)	3	0.01
Japanese (262)	293	1.03
Korean (316)	342	1.20
Malaysian (0)	1	<0.01
Nepalese (6)	6	0.02
Pakistani (68)	73	0.26
Sri Lankan (6)	6	0.02
Taiwanese (45)	48	0.17
Thai (1)	2	0.01
Vietnamese (42)	53	0.19
Hawaii Native/Pacific Islander (10)	16	0.06
Not Hispanic (9)	15	0.05
Hispanic (1)	1	<0.01
Fijian (0)	1	<0.01
Guamanian/Chamorro (3)	3	0.01
Native Hawaiian (0)	2	0.01
Samoan (1)	1	<0.01
White (23,580)	24,018	84.28
Not Hispanic (23,049)	23,446	82.28
Hispanic (531)	572	2.01

Norton Shores

Place Type: City
County: Muskegon
Population: 23,994†

Ancestry‡	Population	%
African, Sub-Saharan (0)	54	0.23
African (0)	54	0.23
American (937)	937	3.92
Arab (195)	276	1.15
Arab (0)	28	0.12
Iraqi (181)	181	0.76
Lebanese (14)	67	0.28
Austrian (38)	122	0.51
Belgian (14)	115	0.48
British (15)	73	0.31
Bulgarian (15)	15	0.06
Canadian (0)	29	0.12
Croatian (0)	31	0.13
Czech (24)	132	0.55
Czechoslovakian (14)	86	0.36
Danish (23)	140	0.59
Dutch (1,269)	3,547	14.83
English (496)	3,115	13.02
Estonian (19)	19	0.08
European (131)	204	0.85
Finnish (24)	108	0.45
French, ex. Basque (135)	1,797	7.51
French Canadian (127)	495	2.07
German (1,411)	6,202	25.93
Greek (70)	104	0.43
Hungarian (71)	311	1.30
Irish (446)	2,937	12.28
Italian (291)	1,282	5.36
Lithuanian (0)	105	0.44
Norwegian (153)	573	2.40
Pennsylvania German (0)	12	0.05
Polish (587)	2,087	8.73
Romanian (26)	26	0.11
Russian (66)	106	0.44
Scandinavian (42)	155	0.65
Scotch-Irish (134)	397	1.66
Scottish (75)	423	1.77
Serbian (10)	21	0.09
Slovak (112)	199	0.83
Slovene (37)	90	0.38
Swedish (271)	1,521	6.36
Swiss (13)	22	0.09
Turkish (0)	3	0.01
Ukrainian (30)	67	0.28
Welsh (15)	100	0.42
West Indian, ex. Hispanic (12)	12	0.05
Haitian (12)	12	0.05
Yugoslavian (24)	33	0.14

Hispanic Origin	Population	%
Hispanic or Latino (of any race)	911	3.80
Central American, ex. Mexican	23	0.10
Costa Rican	2	0.01
Guatemalan	11	0.05
Nicaraguan	1	<0.01
Panamanian	8	0.03
Salvadoran	1	<0.01
Cuban	15	0.06
Dominican Republic	7	0.03
Mexican	708	2.95
Puerto Rican	72	0.30
South American	25	0.10
Argentinean	2	0.01

*Notes: † The Census 2010 population figure is used to calculate the percentages in the Hispanic Origin and Race categories. Ancestry percentages are based on the 2006-2010 American Community Survey population (not shown); ‡ Numbers in parentheses indicate the number of people reporting a single ancestry; * Numbers in parentheses indicate the number of persons reporting this race alone, not in combination with any other race; Please refer to the Explanation of Data for more information.*

Bolivian	3	0.01
Chilean	8	0.03
Colombian	5	0.02
Ecuadorian	1	<0.01
Paraguayan	1	<0.01
Peruvian	5	0.02
Other Hispanic or Latino	61	0.25

Race*	Population	%
African-American/Black (759)	951	3.96
Not Hispanic (740)	916	3.82
Hispanic (19)	35	0.15
American Indian/Alaska Native (188)	347	1.45
Not Hispanic (167)	302	1.26
Hispanic (21)	45	0.19
Apache (0)	1	<0.01
Blackfeet (2)	4	0.02
Canadian/French Am. Ind. (0)	3	0.01
Cherokee (4)	18	0.08
Chickasaw (0)	1	<0.01
Chippewa (22)	57	0.24
Cree (0)	1	<0.01
Menominee (1)	1	<0.01
Mexican American Ind. (0)	4	0.02
Osage (0)	1	<0.01
Ottawa (70)	101	0.42
Potawatomi (20)	25	0.10
Sioux (0)	1	<0.01
South American Ind. (3)	3	0.01
Tsimshian *(Alaska Native)* (1)	2	0.01
Asian (294)	381	1.59
Not Hispanic (292)	377	1.57
Hispanic (2)	4	0.02
Chinese, ex. Taiwanese (50)	56	0.23
Filipino (29)	54	0.23
Indian (111)	126	0.53
Japanese (11)	21	0.09
Korean (52)	64	0.27
Laotian (2)	2	0.01
Pakistani (8)	9	0.04
Thai (5)	5	0.02
Vietnamese (17)	24	0.10
Hawaii Native/Pacific Islander (8)	20	0.08
Not Hispanic (4)	15	0.06
Hispanic (4)	5	0.02
Guamanian/Chamorro (4)	8	0.03
Native Hawaiian (2)	7	0.03
Samoan (1)	1	<0.01
White (22,027)	22,480	93.69
Not Hispanic (21,467)	21,842	91.03
Hispanic (560)	638	2.66

Novi

Place Type: City
County: Oakland
Population: 55,224†

Ancestry‡	Population	%
African, Sub-Saharan (89)	171	0.32
African (89)	102	0.19
Nigerian (0)	32	0.06
Other Sub-Saharan African (0)	37	0.07
Albanian (240)	240	0.45
American (1,895)	1,895	3.52
Arab (973)	1,215	2.26
Arab (392)	392	0.73
Iraqi (110)	208	0.39
Jordanian (38)	48	0.09
Lebanese (265)	374	0.69
Palestinian (38)	38	0.07
Syrian (104)	104	0.19
Other Arab (26)	51	0.09
Armenian (202)	432	0.80
Assyrian/Chaldean/Syriac (373)	450	0.84
Australian (55)	72	0.13
Austrian (14)	91	0.17
Belgian (63)	295	0.55
Brazilian (27)	35	0.07
British (177)	390	0.72
Bulgarian (64)	84	0.16
Canadian (149)	466	0.87
Croatian (9)	95	0.18
Czech (46)	242	0.45
Czechoslovakian (34)	50	0.09
Danish (28)	129	0.24
Dutch (180)	662	1.23
Eastern European (24)	36	0.07
English (1,271)	5,566	10.34
European (640)	725	1.35
Finnish (100)	894	1.66
French, ex. Basque (173)	2,240	4.16
French Canadian (399)	1,132	2.10
German (2,366)	10,119	18.80
Greek (277)	677	1.26
Guyanese (12)	12	0.02
Hungarian (150)	692	1.29
Icelander (0)	69	0.13
Iranian (52)	120	0.22
Irish (1,697)	6,629	12.32
Israeli (33)	70	0.13
Italian (1,496)	4,511	8.38
Latvian (0)	10	0.02
Lithuanian (21)	128	0.24
Macedonian (46)	57	0.11
Maltese (79)	120	0.22
Northern European (67)	77	0.14
Norwegian (263)	598	1.11
Pennsylvania German (0)	35	0.07
Polish (2,207)	5,841	10.85
Portuguese (17)	17	0.03
Romanian (136)	227	0.42
Russian (236)	770	1.43
Scandinavian (17)	140	0.26
Scotch-Irish (504)	1,175	2.18
Scottish (583)	2,051	3.81
Serbian (75)	142	0.26
Slavic (0)	16	0.03
Slovak (19)	196	0.36
Slovene (10)	31	0.06
Swedish (138)	1,111	2.06
Swiss (17)	96	0.18
Ukrainian (101)	398	0.74
Welsh (101)	490	0.91
West Indian, ex. Hispanic (17)	17	0.03
Haitian (17)	17	0.03
Yugoslavian (0)	47	0.09

Hispanic Origin	Population	%
Hispanic or Latino (of any race)	1,634	2.96
Central American, ex. Mexican	141	0.26
Costa Rican	3	0.01
Guatemalan	92	0.17
Honduran	13	0.02
Nicaraguan	5	0.01
Panamanian	5	0.01
Salvadoran	17	0.03
Other Central American	6	0.01
Cuban	53	0.10
Dominican Republic	22	0.04
Mexican	1,003	1.82
Puerto Rican	113	0.20
South American	131	0.24
Argentinean	14	0.03
Bolivian	3	0.01
Chilean	9	0.02
Colombian	40	0.07
Ecuadorian	2	<0.01
Paraguayan	3	0.01
Peruvian	30	0.05
Venezuelan	30	0.05
Other Hispanic or Latino	171	0.31

Race*	Population	%
African-American/Black (4,482)	4,848	8.78
Not Hispanic (4,451)	4,785	8.66
Hispanic (31)	63	0.11
American Indian/Alaska Native (111)	338	0.61
Not Hispanic (96)	299	0.54
Hispanic (15)	39	0.07
Apache (1)	4	0.01
Blackfeet (1)	5	0.01
Canadian/French Am. Ind. (2)	6	0.01
Central American Ind. (0)	2	<0.01
Cherokee (12)	64	0.12
Cheyenne (1)	1	<0.01
Chickasaw (0)	1	<0.01
Chippewa (22)	41	0.07
Choctaw (1)	4	0.01
Comanche (5)	5	0.01
Cree (0)	2	<0.01
Creek (1)	4	0.01
Inupiat *(Alaska Native)* (0)	4	0.01
Iroquois (3)	7	0.01
Lumbee (2)	4	0.01
Mexican American Ind. (2)	2	<0.01
Navajo (1)	4	0.01
Ottawa (9)	10	0.02
Paiute (0)	1	<0.01
Potawatomi (0)	4	0.01
Shoshone (1)	1	<0.01
Sioux (1)	2	<0.01
South American Ind. (1)	2	<0.01
Tlingit-Haida *(Alaska Native)* (0)	5	0.01
Asian (8,767)	9,354	16.94
Not Hispanic (8,756)	9,318	16.87
Hispanic (11)	36	0.07
Bangladeshi (20)	23	0.04
Cambodian (1)	1	<0.01
Chinese, ex. Taiwanese (1,637)	1,745	3.16
Filipino (225)	324	0.59
Hmong (7)	7	0.01
Indian (3,542)	3,657	6.62
Indonesian (11)	18	0.03
Japanese (1,984)	2,120	3.84
Korean (829)	893	1.62
Laotian (3)	4	0.01
Malaysian (6)	10	0.02
Nepalese (11)	11	0.02
Pakistani (89)	100	0.18
Sri Lankan (15)	15	0.03
Taiwanese (114)	131	0.24
Thai (14)	16	0.03
Vietnamese (146)	161	0.29
Hawaii Native/Pacific Islander (5)	51	0.09
Not Hispanic (2)	46	0.08
Hispanic (3)	5	0.01
Guamanian/Chamorro (2)	9	0.02
Native Hawaiian (2)	15	0.03
Samoan (0)	3	0.01
White (40,313)	41,290	74.77
Not Hispanic (39,228)	40,098	72.61
Hispanic (1,085)	1,192	2.16

Oak Park

Place Type: City
County: Oakland
Population: 29,319†

Ancestry‡	Population	%
African, Sub-Saharan (630)	771	2.58
African (512)	653	2.18
Ethiopian (88)	88	0.29
Kenyan (17)	17	0.06
Other Sub-Saharan African (13)	13	0.04
Albanian (61)	61	0.20
American (607)	607	2.03
Arab (476)	537	1.80
Arab (152)	197	0.66
Iraqi (201)	209	0.70
Lebanese (46)	54	0.18
Moroccan (5)	5	0.02
Other Arab (72)	72	0.24
Armenian (133)	185	0.62
Assyrian/Chaldean/Syriac (605)	706	2.36
Austrian (11)	43	0.14
Belgian (0)	83	0.28
Canadian (68)	174	0.58
Croatian (8)	8	0.03

*Notes: † The Census 2010 population figure is used to calculate the percentages in the Hispanic Origin and Race categories. Ancestry percentages are based on the 2006-2010 American Community Survey population (not shown); ‡ Numbers in parentheses indicate the number of people reporting a single ancestry; * Numbers in parentheses indicate the number of persons reporting this race alone, not in combination with any other race; Please refer to the Explanation of Data for more information.*

SECTION TWO

Ancestry	Population	%
Czech (0)	82	0.27
Czechoslovakian (12)	23	0.08
Danish (0)	10	0.03
Dutch (56)	266	0.89
Eastern European (199)	199	0.67
English (228)	828	2.77
European (935)	935	3.13
Finnish (33)	94	0.31
French, ex. Basque (34)	386	1.29
French Canadian (23)	202	0.68
German (474)	2,008	6.72
Greek (83)	115	0.38
Hungarian (67)	210	0.70
Irish (242)	1,361	4.55
Israeli (42)	42	0.14
Italian (271)	510	1.71
Latvian (0)	11	0.04
Lithuanian (111)	179	0.60
Northern European (0)	9	0.03
Norwegian (9)	41	0.14
Polish (500)	1,476	4.94
Romanian (74)	197	0.66
Russian (823)	1,391	4.65
Scandinavian (34)	34	0.11
Scotch-Irish (20)	246	0.82
Scottish (126)	305	1.02
Slovak (0)	22	0.07
Swedish (0)	16	0.05
Swiss (0)	24	0.08
Turkish (0)	50	0.17
Ukrainian (225)	268	0.90
Welsh (7)	55	0.18
West Indian, ex. Hispanic (76)	142	0.48
Jamaican (76)	142	0.48
Yugoslavian (0)	12	0.04

Hispanic Origin	Population	%
Hispanic or Latino (of any race)	423	1.44
Central American, ex. Mexican	16	0.05
Costa Rican	1	<0.01
Guatemalan	5	0.02
Honduran	2	0.01
Nicaraguan	1	<0.01
Panamanian	7	0.02
Cuban	27	0.09
Dominican Republic	15	0.05
Mexican	200	0.68
Puerto Rican	65	0.22
South American	32	0.11
Argentinean	4	0.01
Chilean	9	0.03
Colombian	5	0.02
Ecuadorian	3	0.01
Peruvian	4	0.01
Uruguayan	1	<0.01
Other South American	6	0.02
Other Hispanic or Latino	68	0.23

Race*	Population	%
African-American/Black (16,842)	17,464	59.57
Not Hispanic (16,748)	17,321	59.08
Hispanic (94)	143	0.49
American Indian/Alaska Native (64)	324	1.11
Not Hispanic (54)	282	0.96
Hispanic (10)	42	0.14
Apache (2)	2	0.01
Blackfeet (2)	21	0.07
Canadian/French Am. Ind. (6)	8	0.03
Central American Ind. (2)	2	0.01
Cherokee (6)	73	0.25
Cheyenne (0)	1	<0.01
Chippewa (5)	12	0.04
Choctaw (0)	5	0.02
Comanche (1)	1	<0.01
Cree (0)	1	<0.01
Creek (1)	4	0.01
Iroquois (1)	3	0.01
Lumbee (1)	1	<0.01
Menominee (1)	1	<0.01
Mexican American Ind. (1)	2	0.01
Ottawa (0)	2	0.01
Seminole (1)	6	0.02
Sioux (3)	13	0.04
Asian (419)	662	2.26
Not Hispanic (417)	646	2.20
Hispanic (2)	16	0.05
Cambodian (2)	3	0.01
Chinese, ex. Taiwanese (73)	103	0.35
Filipino (193)	245	0.84
Hmong (2)	2	0.01
Indian (39)	62	0.21
Indonesian (1)	1	<0.01
Japanese (14)	39	0.13
Korean (21)	44	0.15
Laotian (0)	1	<0.01
Malaysian (1)	1	<0.01
Nepalese (1)	1	<0.01
Pakistani (6)	8	0.03
Sri Lankan (19)	22	0.08
Taiwanese (0)	1	<0.01
Thai (2)	7	0.02
Vietnamese (22)	23	0.08
Hawaii Native/Pacific Islander (3)	40	0.14
Not Hispanic (3)	39	0.13
Hispanic (0)	1	<0.01
Native Hawaiian (3)	11	0.04
Samoan (0)	2	0.01
White (10,962)	11,647	39.73
Not Hispanic (10,806)	11,437	39.01
Hispanic (156)	210	0.72

Oakland

Place Type: Charter Township
County: Oakland
Population: 16,779†

Ancestry‡	Population	%
African, Sub-Saharan (17)	17	0.11
African (7)	7	0.04
South African (10)	10	0.06
Albanian (467)	467	2.90
American (450)	450	2.79
Arab (176)	290	1.80
Arab (17)	17	0.11
Egyptian (62)	62	0.38
Iraqi (68)	68	0.42
Lebanese (19)	133	0.83
Syrian (10)	10	0.06
Armenian (19)	68	0.42
Assyrian/Chaldean/Syriac (80)	120	0.74
Australian (0)	22	0.14
Austrian (21)	60	0.37
Basque (10)	32	0.20
Belgian (35)	151	0.94
Brazilian (0)	6	0.04
British (104)	176	1.09
Canadian (132)	248	1.54
Croatian (25)	122	0.76
Czech (0)	68	0.42
Czechoslovakian (0)	7	0.04
Danish (12)	93	0.58
Dutch (33)	162	1.01
English (475)	2,261	14.04
Estonian (11)	24	0.15
European (123)	123	0.76
Finnish (22)	94	0.58
French, ex. Basque (63)	925	5.74
French Canadian (8)	123	0.76
German (1,049)	4,444	27.59
Greek (39)	75	0.47
Hungarian (42)	174	1.08
Iranian (16)	32	0.20
Irish (515)	2,093	12.99
Italian (522)	1,859	11.54
Lithuanian (19)	47	0.29
Macedonian (79)	116	0.72
Maltese (0)	10	0.06
Norwegian (0)	131	0.81
Pennsylvania German (0)	13	0.08
Polish (661)	2,347	14.57
Portuguese (0)	16	0.10
Romanian (12)	148	0.92
Russian (92)	155	0.96
Scandinavian (0)	47	0.29
Scotch-Irish (102)	303	1.88
Scottish (119)	610	3.79
Slavic (0)	11	0.07
Slovak (101)	204	1.27
Slovene (0)	13	0.08
Swedish (62)	421	2.61
Swiss (17)	77	0.48
Ukrainian (107)	274	1.70
Welsh (33)	126	0.78
Yugoslavian (0)	11	0.07

Hispanic Origin	Population	%
Hispanic or Latino (of any race)	344	2.05
Central American, ex. Mexican	17	0.10
Costa Rican	2	0.01
Guatemalan	5	0.03
Honduran	1	0.01
Nicaraguan	1	0.01
Panamanian	7	0.04
Salvadoran	1	0.01
Cuban	9	0.05
Dominican Republic	5	0.03
Mexican	211	1.26
Puerto Rican	24	0.14
South American	45	0.27
Argentinean	27	0.16
Chilean	1	0.01
Colombian	12	0.07
Ecuadorian	3	0.02
Peruvian	2	0.01
Other Hispanic or Latino	33	0.20

Race*	Population	%
African-American/Black (402)	458	2.73
Not Hispanic (392)	438	2.61
Hispanic (10)	20	0.12
American Indian/Alaska Native (37)	90	0.54
Not Hispanic (35)	82	0.49
Hispanic (2)	8	0.05
Apache (0)	1	0.01
Cherokee (3)	19	0.11
Chippewa (12)	27	0.16
Iroquois (8)	11	0.07
Lumbee (2)	3	0.02
Mexican American Ind. (1)	2	0.01
Ottawa (0)	1	0.01
Potawatomi (1)	1	0.01
Asian (901)	1,025	6.11
Not Hispanic (897)	1,020	6.08
Hispanic (4)	5	0.03
Bangladeshi (16)	16	0.10
Chinese, ex. Taiwanese (159)	182	1.08
Filipino (69)	109	0.65
Hmong (1)	1	0.01
Indian (408)	440	2.62
Japanese (28)	47	0.28
Korean (136)	150	0.89
Malaysian (0)	4	0.02
Pakistani (10)	13	0.08
Sri Lankan (10)	10	0.06
Taiwanese (24)	27	0.16
Thai (3)	3	0.02
Vietnamese (10)	15	0.09
Hawaii Native/Pacific Islander (1)	2	0.01
Not Hispanic (1)	2	0.01
Guamanian/Chamorro (1)	1	0.01
Native Hawaiian (0)	1	0.01
White (15,158)	15,370	91.60
Not Hispanic (14,872)	15,063	89.77
Hispanic (286)	307	1.83

*Notes: † The Census 2010 population figure is used to calculate the percentages in the Hispanic Origin and Race categories. Ancestry percentages are based on the 2006-2010 American Community Survey population (not shown); ‡ Numbers in parentheses indicate the number of people reporting a single ancestry; * Numbers in parentheses indicate the number of persons reporting this race alone, not in combination with any other race; Please refer to the Explanation of Data for more information.*

Oceola

Place Type: Township
County: Livingston
Population: 11,936†

Ancestry‡	Population	%
American (802)	802	6.93
Arab (15)	34	0.29
Arab (7)	14	0.12
Lebanese (8)	20	0.17
Australian (8)	8	0.07
Austrian (11)	67	0.58
Belgian (0)	33	0.29
British (43)	113	0.98
Canadian (95)	148	1.28
Croatian (0)	8	0.07
Czech (0)	34	0.29
Czechoslovakian (0)	30	0.26
Danish (13)	107	0.93
Dutch (63)	270	2.33
English (393)	1,474	12.75
European (157)	157	1.36
Finnish (44)	327	2.83
French, ex. Basque (102)	675	5.84
French Canadian (55)	312	2.70
German (798)	3,252	28.12
Greek (22)	22	0.19
Hungarian (39)	93	0.80
Irish (354)	2,113	18.27
Italian (208)	636	5.50
Latvian (0)	18	0.16
Lithuanian (15)	40	0.35
Maltese (16)	20	0.17
Northern European (41)	41	0.35
Norwegian (16)	94	0.81
Pennsylvania German (10)	20	0.17
Polish (710)	2,036	17.60
Romanian (0)	27	0.23
Russian (68)	118	1.02
Scandinavian (34)	34	0.29
Scotch-Irish (93)	246	2.13
Scottish (126)	527	4.56
Slavic (0)	42	0.36
Slovak (19)	34	0.29
Slovene (12)	35	0.30
Swedish (56)	376	3.25
Ukrainian (80)	122	1.05
Welsh (51)	51	0.44
Yugoslavian (0)	12	0.10

Hispanic Origin	Population	%
Hispanic or Latino (of any race)	228	1.91
Central American, ex. Mexican	7	0.06
Guatemalan	3	0.03
Honduran	4	0.03
Cuban	5	0.04
Dominican Republic	1	0.01
Mexican	142	1.19
Puerto Rican	37	0.31
South American	19	0.16
Argentinean	6	0.05
Colombian	4	0.03
Ecuadorian	1	0.01
Peruvian	1	0.01
Venezuelan	7	0.06
Other Hispanic or Latino	17	0.14

Race*	Population	%
African-American/Black (48)	72	0.60
Not Hispanic (47)	71	0.59
Hispanic (1)	1	0.01
American Indian/Alaska Native (42)	113	0.95
Not Hispanic (40)	101	0.85
Hispanic (2)	12	0.10
Blackfeet (0)	2	0.02
Cherokee (3)	9	0.08
Chickasaw (0)	1	0.01
Chippewa (13)	27	0.23
Choctaw (1)	1	0.01
Iroquois (0)	3	0.03
Lumbee (1)	3	0.03
Ottawa (7)	7	0.06
Potawatomi (0)	3	0.03
Sioux (6)	6	0.05
Tlingit-Haida *(Alaska Native)* (2)	2	0.02
Ute (1)	1	0.01
Yup'ik *(Alaska Native)* (0)	1	0.01
Asian (105)	155	1.30
Not Hispanic (105)	154	1.29
Hispanic (0)	1	0.01
Chinese, ex. Taiwanese (32)	36	0.30
Filipino (13)	24	0.20
Indian (7)	9	0.08
Japanese (10)	26	0.22
Korean (13)	20	0.17
Taiwanese (5)	5	0.04
Vietnamese (23)	30	0.25
Hawaii Native/Pacific Islander (6)	21	0.18
Not Hispanic (5)	20	0.17
Hispanic (1)	1	0.01
Guamanian/Chamorro (1)	1	0.01
Native Hawaiian (5)	16	0.13
White (11,540)	11,710	98.11
Not Hispanic (11,361)	11,502	96.36
Hispanic (179)	208	1.74

Okemos

Place Type: CDP
County: Ingham
Population: 21,369†

Ancestry‡	Population	%
African, Sub-Saharan (105)	149	0.71
African (29)	73	0.35
Somalian (13)	13	0.06
South African (15)	15	0.07
Zimbabwean (48)	48	0.23
American (1,387)	1,387	6.60
Arab (218)	218	1.04
Arab (36)	36	0.17
Lebanese (79)	79	0.38
Palestinian (16)	16	0.08
Other Arab (87)	87	0.41
Armenian (99)	128	0.61
Australian (0)	15	0.07
Austrian (0)	48	0.23
Belgian (23)	150	0.71
British (15)	72	0.34
Bulgarian (57)	57	0.27
Canadian (15)	41	0.20
Carpatho Rusyn (0)	15	0.07
Croatian (0)	80	0.38
Czech (45)	155	0.74
Czechoslovakian (13)	13	0.06
Danish (31)	237	1.13
Dutch (256)	568	2.70
Eastern European (127)	127	0.60
English (757)	2,719	12.93
European (501)	543	2.58
Finnish (25)	175	0.83
French, ex. Basque (127)	793	3.77
French Canadian (37)	144	0.68
German (1,349)	4,928	23.44
Greek (23)	66	0.31
Hungarian (43)	189	0.90
Irish (430)	2,594	12.34
Israeli (14)	14	0.07
Italian (375)	726	3.45
Latvian (24)	24	0.11
Lithuanian (20)	70	0.33
Macedonian (13)	13	0.06
Maltese (0)	21	0.10
Northern European (17)	32	0.15
Norwegian (72)	347	1.65
Pennsylvania German (14)	14	0.07
Polish (404)	1,399	6.65
Portuguese (0)	4	0.02
Romanian (0)	15	0.07
Russian (225)	482	2.29
Scandinavian (0)	86	0.41
Scotch-Irish (103)	350	1.66
Scottish (342)	736	3.50
Serbian (38)	38	0.18
Slovak (32)	42	0.20
Slovene (16)	58	0.28
Swedish (71)	483	2.30
Swiss (12)	141	0.67
Turkish (82)	82	0.39
Ukrainian (0)	53	0.25
Welsh (0)	110	0.52
West Indian, ex. Hispanic (0)	10	0.05
Belizean (0)	10	0.05
Yugoslavian (15)	15	0.07

Hispanic Origin	Population	%
Hispanic or Latino (of any race)	701	3.28
Central American, ex. Mexican	42	0.20
Costa Rican	3	0.01
Guatemalan	22	0.10
Honduran	6	0.03
Nicaraguan	6	0.03
Panamanian	4	0.02
Salvadoran	1	<0.01
Cuban	23	0.11
Dominican Republic	6	0.03
Mexican	381	1.78
Puerto Rican	65	0.30
South American	80	0.37
Argentinean	6	0.03
Bolivian	2	0.01
Chilean	2	0.01
Colombian	40	0.19
Ecuadorian	1	<0.01
Paraguayan	4	0.02
Peruvian	10	0.05
Uruguayan	2	0.01
Venezuelan	12	0.06
Other South American	1	<0.01
Other Hispanic or Latino	104	0.49

Race*	Population	%
African-American/Black (1,092)	1,276	5.97
Not Hispanic (1,075)	1,239	5.80
Hispanic (17)	37	0.17
American Indian/Alaska Native (70)	170	0.80
Not Hispanic (48)	129	0.60
Hispanic (22)	41	0.19
Apache (0)	2	0.01
Blackfeet (0)	4	0.02
Cherokee (3)	20	0.09
Cheyenne (0)	1	<0.01
Chippewa (17)	30	0.14
Choctaw (1)	1	<0.01
Cree (0)	3	0.01
Creek (0)	1	<0.01
Inupiat *(Alaska Native)* (1)	1	<0.01
Iroquois (1)	3	0.01
Mexican American Ind. (8)	15	0.07
Navajo (0)	2	0.01
Ottawa (0)	4	0.02
Potawatomi (1)	4	0.02
Sioux (0)	1	<0.01
South American Ind. (1)	1	<0.01
Spanish American Ind. (3)	3	0.01
Asian (3,076)	3,358	15.71
Not Hispanic (3,065)	3,340	15.63
Hispanic (11)	18	0.08
Bangladeshi (9)	11	0.05
Burmese (6)	7	0.03
Cambodian (0)	3	0.01
Chinese, ex. Taiwanese (784)	841	3.94
Filipino (84)	138	0.65
Hmong (14)	17	0.08
Indian (1,152)	1,217	5.70
Indonesian (4)	7	0.03
Japanese (75)	109	0.51
Korean (603)	655	3.07
Malaysian (6)	6	0.03

*Notes: † The Census 2010 population figure is used to calculate the percentages in the Hispanic Origin and Race categories. Ancestry percentages are based on the 2006-2010 American Community Survey population (not shown); ‡ Numbers in parentheses indicate the number of people reporting a single ancestry; * Numbers in parentheses indicate the number of persons reporting this race alone, not in combination with any other race; Please refer to the Explanation of Data for more information.*

Nepalese (9)	10	0.05
Pakistani (62)	72	0.34
Sri Lankan (25)	28	0.13
Taiwanese (77)	86	0.40
Thai (20)	22	0.10
Vietnamese (79)	87	0.41
Hawaii Native/Pacific Islander (12)	33	0.15
Not Hispanic (12)	31	0.15
Hispanic (0)	2	0.01
Guamanian/Chamorro (1)	1	<0.01
Native Hawaiian (2)	11	0.05
Samoan (3)	4	0.02
White (16,345)	16,831	78.76
Not Hispanic (15,918)	16,358	76.55
Hispanic (427)	473	2.21

Orion

Place Type: Charter Township
County: Oakland
Population: 35,394†

Ancestry‡	Population	%
African, Sub-Saharan (10)	10	0.03
Ethiopian (10)	10	0.03
Albanian (64)	134	0.38
American (1,484)	1,484	4.23
Arab (112)	453	1.29
Arab (31)	106	0.30
Lebanese (45)	288	0.82
Moroccan (16)	16	0.05
Syrian (20)	43	0.12
Armenian (11)	67	0.19
Austrian (30)	195	0.56
Belgian (35)	382	1.09
British (43)	170	0.48
Bulgarian (0)	21	0.06
Canadian (111)	251	0.72
Celtic (0)	24	0.07
Croatian (50)	234	0.67
Czech (60)	310	0.88
Czechoslovakian (46)	115	0.33
Danish (60)	288	0.82
Dutch (293)	946	2.70
Eastern European (18)	40	0.11
English (1,144)	4,323	12.33
European (409)	423	1.21
Finnish (64)	389	1.11
French, ex. Basque (195)	1,617	4.61
French Canadian (341)	903	2.58
German (2,417)	9,039	25.78
Greek (28)	159	0.45
Hungarian (93)	333	0.95
Icelander (0)	10	0.03
Iranian (0)	13	0.04
Irish (1,283)	6,345	18.09
Italian (970)	3,126	8.91
Latvian (8)	8	0.02
Lithuanian (13)	156	0.44
Macedonian (0)	11	0.03
Maltese (19)	85	0.24
New Zealander (0)	6	0.02
Northern European (40)	49	0.14
Norwegian (154)	485	1.38
Pennsylvania German (7)	40	0.11
Polish (1,513)	4,282	12.21
Portuguese (9)	47	0.13
Romanian (23)	58	0.17
Russian (60)	233	0.66
Scandinavian (25)	80	0.23
Scotch-Irish (266)	650	1.85
Scottish (389)	1,334	3.80
Serbian (61)	61	0.17
Slavic (12)	50	0.14
Slovak (32)	143	0.41
Slovene (12)	50	0.14
Swedish (358)	864	2.46
Swiss (17)	78	0.22
Turkish (8)	8	0.02
Ukrainian (36)	336	0.96
Welsh (19)	309	0.88
Yugoslavian (0)	24	0.07

Hispanic Origin	Population	%
Hispanic or Latino (of any race)	1,433	4.05
Central American, ex. Mexican	63	0.18
Costa Rican	4	0.01
Guatemalan	17	0.05
Honduran	21	0.06
Nicaraguan	1	<0.01
Panamanian	3	0.01
Salvadoran	17	0.05
Cuban	19	0.05
Dominican Republic	6	0.02
Mexican	988	2.79
Puerto Rican	182	0.51
South American	73	0.21
Argentinean	6	0.02
Chilean	2	0.01
Colombian	31	0.09
Ecuadorian	4	0.01
Paraguayan	3	0.01
Peruvian	16	0.05
Venezuelan	11	0.03
Other Hispanic or Latino	102	0.29

Race*	Population	%
African-American/Black (937)	1,170	3.31
Not Hispanic (915)	1,103	3.12
Hispanic (22)	67	0.19
American Indian/Alaska Native (114)	276	0.78
Not Hispanic (84)	224	0.63
Hispanic (30)	52	0.15
Apache (1)	3	0.01
Blackfeet (0)	3	0.01
Canadian/French Am. Ind. (2)	4	0.01
Central American Ind. (1)	1	<0.01
Cherokee (16)	42	0.12
Chippewa (30)	50	0.14
Choctaw (1)	3	0.01
Creek (1)	2	0.01
Delaware (1)	1	<0.01
Iroquois (7)	10	0.03
Lumbee (0)	1	<0.01
Mexican American Ind. (8)	19	0.05
Ottawa (2)	5	0.01
Potawatomi (2)	3	0.01
Seminole (0)	4	0.01
Sioux (1)	1	<0.01
Asian (759)	970	2.74
Not Hispanic (754)	953	2.69
Hispanic (5)	17	0.05
Chinese, ex. Taiwanese (135)	158	0.45
Filipino (111)	183	0.52
Hmong (36)	40	0.11
Indian (214)	232	0.66
Indonesian (5)	8	0.02
Japanese (45)	77	0.22
Korean (86)	122	0.34
Laotian (5)	7	0.02
Malaysian (1)	8	0.02
Pakistani (12)	16	0.05
Sri Lankan (11)	11	0.03
Taiwanese (2)	2	0.01
Thai (12)	17	0.05
Vietnamese (50)	65	0.18
Hawaii Native/Pacific Islander (6)	17	0.05
Not Hispanic (6)	16	0.05
Hispanic (0)	1	<0.01
Native Hawaiian (1)	3	0.01
Samoan (3)	3	0.01
White (32,565)	33,148	93.65
Not Hispanic (31,677)	32,150	90.83
Hispanic (888)	998	2.82

Oronoko

Place Type: Charter Township
County: Berrien
Population: 9,193†

Ancestry‡	Population	%
African, Sub-Saharan (296)	459	4.97
African (272)	414	4.49
Nigerian (0)	15	0.16
South African (9)	9	0.10
Other Sub-Saharan African (15)	21	0.23
American (485)	485	5.26
Arab (0)	25	0.27
Arab (0)	25	0.27
Austrian (73)	144	1.56
Brazilian (47)	107	1.16
British (9)	20	0.22
Bulgarian (11)	11	0.12
Canadian (53)	89	0.96
Croatian (19)	19	0.21
Czech (14)	25	0.27
Czechoslovakian (0)	11	0.12
Danish (39)	74	0.80
Dutch (44)	155	1.68
English (255)	860	9.32
European (26)	60	0.65
Finnish (3)	7	0.08
French, ex. Basque (116)	320	3.47
French Canadian (0)	24	0.26
German (1,208)	2,533	27.45
Guyanese (0)	11	0.12
Hungarian (49)	49	0.53
Icelander (0)	6	0.07
Irish (163)	857	9.29
Italian (87)	217	2.35
Lithuanian (0)	27	0.29
Luxemburger (0)	11	0.12
Norwegian (30)	80	0.87
Pennsylvania German (14)	14	0.15
Polish (58)	303	3.28
Portuguese (6)	23	0.25
Romanian (30)	42	0.46
Russian (18)	45	0.49
Scandinavian (21)	21	0.23
Scotch-Irish (7)	120	1.30
Scottish (61)	230	2.49
Serbian (15)	15	0.16
Slovak (8)	8	0.09
Slovene (0)	9	0.10
Swedish (45)	128	1.39
Ukrainian (38)	59	0.64
Welsh (0)	36	0.39
West Indian, ex. Hispanic (502)	678	7.35
Bahamian (0)	13	0.14
Barbadian (11)	11	0.12
Belizean (15)	15	0.16
British West Indian (51)	62	0.67
Haitian (198)	213	2.31
Jamaican (162)	253	2.74
Trinidadian/Tobagonian (16)	57	0.62
West Indian (40)	45	0.49
Other West Indian (9)	9	0.10

Hispanic Origin	Population	%
Hispanic or Latino (of any race)	1,058	11.51
Central American, ex. Mexican	109	1.19
Costa Rican	16	0.17
Guatemalan	13	0.14
Honduran	12	0.13
Nicaraguan	23	0.25
Panamanian	22	0.24
Salvadoran	23	0.25
Cuban	46	0.50
Dominican Republic	97	1.06
Mexican	355	3.86
Puerto Rican	152	1.65
South American	205	2.23
Argentinean	24	0.26
Bolivian	8	0.09
Chilean	31	0.34
Colombian	55	0.60
Ecuadorian	21	0.23
Paraguayan	1	0.01
Peruvian	34	0.37
Uruguayan	6	0.07

*Notes: † The Census 2010 population figure is used to calculate the percentages in the Hispanic Origin and Race categories. Ancestry percentages are based on the 2006-2010 American Community Survey population (not shown); ‡ Numbers in parentheses indicate the number of people reporting a single ancestry; * Numbers in parentheses indicate the number of persons reporting this race alone, not in combination with any other race; Please refer to the Explanation of Data for more information.*

Venezuelan	22	0.24
Other South American	3	0.03
Other Hispanic or Latino	94	1.02

Race*	Population	%
African-American/Black (1,702)	1,875	20.40
Not Hispanic (1,641)	1,772	19.28
Hispanic (61)	103	1.12
American Indian/Alaska Native (45)	146	1.59
Not Hispanic (37)	113	1.23
Hispanic (8)	33	0.36
Blackfeet (1)	1	0.01
Canadian/French Am. Ind. (2)	2	0.02
Cherokee (2)	27	0.29
Chickasaw (1)	1	0.01
Chippewa (4)	6	0.07
Choctaw (2)	3	0.03
Mexican American Ind. (0)	3	0.03
Ottawa (2)	5	0.05
Potawatomi (7)	10	0.11
Sioux (0)	3	0.03
South American Ind. (0)	1	0.01
Spanish American Ind. (1)	1	0.01
Asian (737)	888	9.66
Not Hispanic (730)	858	9.33
Hispanic (7)	30	0.33
Bangladeshi (22)	25	0.27
Burmese (2)	7	0.08
Chinese, ex. Taiwanese (51)	83	0.90
Filipino (103)	128	1.39
Hmong (5)	5	0.05
Indian (75)	122	1.33
Indonesian (52)	62	0.67
Japanese (18)	34	0.37
Korean (363)	380	4.13
Malaysian (14)	21	0.23
Nepalese (0)	1	0.01
Pakistani (5)	7	0.08
Sri Lankan (0)	4	0.04
Taiwanese (2)	3	0.03
Thai (3)	6	0.07
Vietnamese (2)	3	0.03
Hawaii Native/Pacific Islander (74)	101	1.10
Not Hispanic (74)	95	1.03
Hispanic (0)	6	0.07
Fijian (1)	6	0.07
Native Hawaiian (1)	13	0.14
Samoan (58)	68	0.74
Tongan (10)	10	0.11
White (5,828)	6,168	67.09
Not Hispanic (5,336)	5,567	60.56
Hispanic (492)	601	6.54

Oshtemo

Place Type: Charter Township
County: Kalamazoo
Population: 21,705†

Ancestry‡	Population	%
Afghan (0)	32	0.15
African, Sub-Saharan (207)	207	1.00
African (183)	183	0.88
Ghanaian (14)	14	0.07
Nigerian (10)	10	0.05
American (807)	807	3.88
Arab (71)	71	0.34
Jordanian (41)	41	0.20
Lebanese (16)	16	0.08
Other Arab (14)	14	0.07
Austrian (0)	81	0.39
Belgian (0)	22	0.11
British (113)	148	0.71
Canadian (22)	42	0.20
Celtic (27)	27	0.13
Croatian (22)	45	0.22
Czech (69)	91	0.44
Czechoslovakian (0)	57	0.27
Danish (27)	63	0.30
Dutch (1,259)	2,665	12.82
English (516)	2,582	12.42
European (373)	420	2.02
Finnish (27)	228	1.10
French, ex. Basque (80)	707	3.40
French Canadian (14)	119	0.57
German (1,860)	5,622	27.04
Greek (22)	63	0.30
Hungarian (83)	213	1.02
Iranian (29)	59	0.28
Irish (469)	2,657	12.78
Italian (254)	774	3.72
Latvian (56)	69	0.33
Lithuanian (13)	175	0.84
Macedonian (9)	9	0.04
Norwegian (87)	301	1.45
Pennsylvania German (17)	39	0.19
Polish (399)	1,388	6.68
Russian (25)	154	0.74
Scotch-Irish (106)	422	2.03
Scottish (167)	644	3.10
Serbian (11)	20	0.10
Slavic (0)	16	0.08
Slovak (0)	175	0.84
Swedish (61)	420	2.02
Swiss (29)	69	0.33
Ukrainian (32)	72	0.35
Welsh (41)	200	0.96
Yugoslavian (0)	25	0.12

Hispanic Origin	Population	%
Hispanic or Latino (of any race)	877	4.04
Central American, ex. Mexican	24	0.11
Guatemalan	5	0.02
Honduran	7	0.03
Nicaraguan	1	<0.01
Panamanian	5	0.02
Salvadoran	6	0.03
Cuban	19	0.09
Dominican Republic	26	0.12
Mexican	560	2.58
Puerto Rican	105	0.48
South American	66	0.30
Argentinean	4	0.02
Bolivian	7	0.03
Colombian	23	0.11
Ecuadorian	5	0.02
Peruvian	9	0.04
Venezuelan	15	0.07
Other South American	3	0.01
Other Hispanic or Latino	77	0.35

Race*	Population	%
African-American/Black (2,645)	3,077	14.18
Not Hispanic (2,564)	2,941	13.55
Hispanic (81)	136	0.63
American Indian/Alaska Native (68)	283	1.30
Not Hispanic (58)	242	1.11
Hispanic (10)	41	0.19
Apache (1)	3	0.01
Arapaho (1)	1	<0.01
Blackfeet (1)	19	0.09
Cherokee (4)	49	0.23
Chickasaw (2)	2	0.01
Chippewa (11)	20	0.09
Choctaw (0)	1	<0.01
Comanche (0)	2	0.01
Cree (1)	1	<0.01
Creek (0)	1	<0.01
Delaware (0)	1	<0.01
Iroquois (0)	6	0.03
Menominee (1)	1	<0.01
Mexican American Ind. (0)	7	0.03
Navajo (0)	3	0.01
Ottawa (6)	8	0.04
Potawatomi (6)	33	0.15
Seminole (2)	2	0.01
Sioux (2)	9	0.04
Asian (602)	760	3.50
Not Hispanic (600)	748	3.45
Hispanic (2)	12	0.06
Bangladeshi (1)	1	<0.01
Burmese (2)	4	0.02
Cambodian (2)	2	0.01
Chinese, ex. Taiwanese (127)	147	0.68
Filipino (54)	80	0.37
Hmong (1)	1	<0.01
Indian (178)	203	0.94
Indonesian (3)	7	0.03
Japanese (26)	40	0.18
Korean (68)	82	0.38
Laotian (5)	6	0.03
Malaysian (19)	19	0.09
Nepalese (17)	19	0.09
Pakistani (14)	16	0.07
Sri Lankan (15)	15	0.07
Taiwanese (9)	14	0.06
Thai (0)	1	<0.01
Vietnamese (34)	41	0.19
Hawaii Native/Pacific Islander (8)	22	0.10
Not Hispanic (7)	20	0.09
Hispanic (1)	2	0.01
Guamanian/Chamorro (2)	2	0.01
Native Hawaiian (4)	10	0.05
White (17,357)	17,992	82.89
Not Hispanic (16,944)	17,484	80.55
Hispanic (413)	508	2.34

Owosso

Place Type: City
County: Shiawassee
Population: 15,194†

Ancestry‡	Population	%
American (1,191)	1,191	7.71
Arab (0)	19	0.12
Lebanese (0)	19	0.12
Australian (17)	17	0.11
Austrian (0)	30	0.19
Belgian (12)	70	0.45
British (12)	162	1.05
Canadian (123)	206	1.33
Croatian (0)	10	0.06
Czech (273)	816	5.28
Czechoslovakian (43)	114	0.74
Danish (10)	51	0.33
Dutch (94)	542	3.51
Eastern European (7)	17	0.11
English (720)	2,155	13.95
European (29)	67	0.43
Finnish (53)	77	0.50
French, ex. Basque (111)	1,084	7.02
French Canadian (96)	235	1.52
German (1,222)	4,430	28.67
Greek (10)	61	0.39
Hungarian (26)	124	0.80
Irish (374)	1,950	12.62
Italian (56)	237	1.53
Macedonian (25)	25	0.16
Norwegian (10)	76	0.49
Pennsylvania German (0)	10	0.06
Polish (172)	743	4.81
Romanian (0)	29	0.19
Russian (130)	198	1.28
Scotch-Irish (101)	271	1.75
Scottish (138)	315	2.04
Slovak (55)	77	0.50
Swedish (18)	92	0.60
Swiss (24)	36	0.23
Ukrainian (20)	43	0.28
Welsh (35)	89	0.58
West Indian, ex. Hispanic (0)	8	0.05
Bahamian (0)	8	0.05

Hispanic Origin	Population	%
Hispanic or Latino (of any race)	592	3.90
Central American, ex. Mexican	9	0.06
Guatemalan	2	0.01
Panamanian	3	0.02
Salvadoran	4	0.03

*Notes: † The Census 2010 population figure is used to calculate the percentages in the Hispanic Origin and Race categories. Ancestry percentages are based on the 2006-2010 American Community Survey population (not shown); ‡ Numbers in parentheses indicate the number of people reporting a single ancestry; * Numbers in parentheses indicate the number of persons reporting this race alone, not in combination with any other race; Please refer to the Explanation of Data for more information.*

Cuban	3	0.02
Mexican	463	3.05
Puerto Rican	36	0.24
South American	22	0.14
Argentinean	6	0.04
Colombian	10	0.07
Ecuadorian	1	0.01
Uruguayan	5	0.03
Other Hispanic or Latino	59	0.39

Race*	Population	%
African-American/Black (117)	227	1.49
Not Hispanic (108)	207	1.36
Hispanic (9)	20	0.13
American Indian/Alaska Native (78)	205	1.35
Not Hispanic (60)	159	1.05
Hispanic (18)	46	0.30
Apache (2)	5	0.03
Blackfeet (1)	3	0.02
Canadian/French Am. Ind. (1)	1	0.01
Cherokee (3)	22	0.14
Chippewa (22)	44	0.29
Choctaw (1)	2	0.01
Iroquois (2)	6	0.04
Lumbee (1)	2	0.01
Mexican American Ind. (4)	5	0.03
Navajo (1)	2	0.01
Ottawa (7)	14	0.09
Potawatomi (1)	2	0.01
Sioux (3)	5	0.03
South American Ind. (0)	3	0.02
Spanish American Ind. (1)	1	0.01
Asian (47)	88	0.58
Not Hispanic (46)	79	0.52
Hispanic (1)	9	0.06
Chinese, ex. Taiwanese (21)	25	0.16
Filipino (12)	22	0.14
Indian (3)	3	0.02
Japanese (3)	12	0.08
Korean (4)	11	0.07
Laotian (0)	1	0.01
Pakistani (2)	2	0.01
Thai (2)	3	0.02
Vietnamese (0)	1	0.01
Hawaii Native/Pacific Islander (3)	13	0.09
Not Hispanic (3)	10	0.07
Hispanic (0)	3	0.02
Native Hawaiian (2)	6	0.04
Tongan (1)	1	0.01
White (14,540)	14,846	97.71
Not Hispanic (14,151)	14,373	94.60
Hispanic (389)	473	3.11

Oxford

Place Type: Charter Township
County: Oakland
Population: 20,526†

Ancestry‡	Population	%
African, Sub-Saharan (20)	20	0.10
African (20)	20	0.10
American (1,084)	1,084	5.49
Arab (13)	90	0.46
Lebanese (13)	79	0.40
Syrian (0)	11	0.06
Armenian (30)	47	0.24
Assyrian/Chaldean/Syriac (44)	44	0.22
Austrian (21)	31	0.16
Belgian (41)	110	0.56
British (41)	144	0.73
Bulgarian (0)	11	0.06
Canadian (23)	190	0.96
Croatian (19)	128	0.65
Czech (11)	57	0.29
Czechoslovakian (12)	25	0.13
Danish (13)	54	0.27
Dutch (98)	575	2.91
English (747)	2,957	14.99
European (119)	119	0.60
Finnish (35)	233	1.18
French, ex. Basque (134)	1,017	5.15
French Canadian (199)	403	2.04
German (1,559)	5,439	27.56
Greek (48)	135	0.68
Hungarian (172)	358	1.81
Iranian (7)	7	0.04
Irish (784)	3,342	16.94
Italian (398)	996	5.05
Maltese (0)	38	0.19
Norwegian (74)	247	1.25
Polish (702)	2,328	11.80
Romanian (37)	58	0.29
Russian (11)	169	0.86
Scandinavian (0)	37	0.19
Scotch-Irish (34)	377	1.91
Scottish (307)	601	3.05
Slovak (48)	159	0.81
Slovene (0)	15	0.08
Swedish (56)	475	2.41
Swiss (0)	53	0.27
Ukrainian (26)	75	0.38
Welsh (77)	183	0.93
West Indian, ex. Hispanic (0)	6	0.03
Belizean (0)	6	0.03
Yugoslavian (47)	124	0.63

Hispanic Origin	Population	%
Hispanic or Latino (of any race)	633	3.08
Central American, ex. Mexican	16	0.08
Costa Rican	2	0.01
Guatemalan	4	0.02
Nicaraguan	2	0.01
Panamanian	7	0.03
Salvadoran	1	<0.01
Cuban	12	0.06
Mexican	473	2.30
Puerto Rican	52	0.25
South American	24	0.12
Argentinean	7	0.03
Chilean	3	0.01
Colombian	4	0.02
Ecuadorian	7	0.03
Peruvian	3	0.01
Other Hispanic or Latino	56	0.27

Race*	Population	%
African-American/Black (278)	362	1.76
Not Hispanic (271)	344	1.68
Hispanic (7)	18	0.09
American Indian/Alaska Native (71)	187	0.91
Not Hispanic (53)	148	0.72
Hispanic (18)	39	0.19
Blackfeet (3)	7	0.03
Canadian/French Am. Ind. (1)	2	0.01
Cherokee (7)	34	0.17
Chippewa (12)	22	0.11
Choctaw (0)	9	0.04
Comanche (2)	2	0.01
Iroquois (2)	4	0.02
Lumbee (0)	1	<0.01
Mexican American Ind. (11)	11	0.05
Navajo (5)	5	0.02
Ottawa (1)	8	0.04
Potawatomi (2)	2	0.01
Sioux (2)	3	0.01
Yakama (0)	1	<0.01
Asian (237)	331	1.61
Not Hispanic (237)	328	1.60
Hispanic (0)	3	0.01
Chinese, ex. Taiwanese (39)	56	0.27
Filipino (48)	88	0.43
Hmong (18)	18	0.09
Indian (58)	73	0.36
Indonesian (1)	1	<0.01
Japanese (6)	17	0.08
Korean (33)	45	0.22
Laotian (1)	2	0.01
Pakistani (10)	10	0.05
Thai (7)	9	0.04
Vietnamese (12)	15	0.07
Hawaii Native/Pacific Islander (11)	21	0.10
Not Hispanic (10)	13	0.06
Hispanic (1)	8	0.04
Guamanian/Chamorro (1)	1	<0.01
Native Hawaiian (2)	3	0.01
Samoan (3)	6	0.03
White (19,472)	19,784	96.39
Not Hispanic (19,049)	19,298	94.02
Hispanic (423)	486	2.37

Park

Place Type: Township
County: Ottawa
Population: 17,802†

Ancestry‡	Population	%
American (483)	483	2.70
Arab (0)	14	0.08
Lebanese (0)	14	0.08
Austrian (12)	26	0.15
Belgian (0)	96	0.54
British (95)	139	0.78
Canadian (45)	81	0.45
Czech (11)	149	0.83
Czechoslovakian (14)	14	0.08
Danish (22)	99	0.55
Dutch (3,574)	5,929	33.10
Eastern European (0)	14	0.08
English (495)	2,054	11.47
European (179)	255	1.42
Finnish (87)	173	0.97
French, ex. Basque (195)	856	4.78
French Canadian (74)	188	1.05
German (1,252)	4,382	24.46
Greek (0)	78	0.44
Hungarian (70)	112	0.63
Irish (432)	1,942	10.84
Italian (233)	802	4.48
Latvian (12)	12	0.07
Lithuanian (13)	68	0.38
Luxemburger (0)	11	0.06
Northern European (34)	34	0.19
Norwegian (18)	169	0.94
Polish (171)	661	3.69
Portuguese (13)	13	0.07
Romanian (24)	24	0.13
Russian (0)	60	0.33
Scandinavian (17)	50	0.28
Scotch-Irish (77)	181	1.01
Scottish (141)	414	2.31
Serbian (0)	14	0.08
Slavic (0)	13	0.07
Slovak (27)	27	0.15
Slovene (8)	8	0.04
Swedish (106)	479	2.67
Swiss (36)	36	0.20
Ukrainian (84)	95	0.53
Welsh (28)	124	0.69
West Indian, ex. Hispanic (65)	76	0.42
Jamaican (65)	76	0.42
Yugoslavian (0)	14	0.08

Hispanic Origin	Population	%
Hispanic or Latino (of any race)	1,430	8.03
Central American, ex. Mexican	44	0.25
Costa Rican	3	0.02
Guatemalan	13	0.07
Honduran	11	0.06
Nicaraguan	2	0.01
Panamanian	7	0.04
Salvadoran	8	0.04
Cuban	33	0.19
Dominican Republic	3	0.02
Mexican	1,148	6.45
Puerto Rican	56	0.31
South American	48	0.27
Argentinean	4	0.02
Bolivian	7	0.04

*Notes: † The Census 2010 population figure is used to calculate the percentages in the Hispanic Origin and Race categories. Ancestry percentages are based on the 2006-2010 American Community Survey population (not shown); ‡ Numbers in parentheses indicate the number of people reporting a single ancestry; * Numbers in parentheses indicate the number of persons reporting this race alone, not in combination with any other race; Please refer to the Explanation of Data for more information.*

Chilean	7	0.04
Colombian	7	0.04
Ecuadorian	5	0.03
Peruvian	15	0.08
Venezuelan	3	0.02
Other Hispanic or Latino	98	0.55

Race*	Population	%
African-American/Black (160)	253	1.42
Not Hispanic (136)	218	1.22
Hispanic (24)	35	0.20
American Indian/Alaska Native (32)	78	0.44
Not Hispanic (27)	62	0.35
Hispanic (5)	16	0.09
Aleut *(Alaska Native)* (1)	3	0.02
Apache (0)	2	0.01
Blackfeet (0)	4	0.02
Central American Ind. (1)	1	0.01
Cherokee (2)	9	0.05
Chickasaw (0)	1	0.01
Chippewa (10)	21	0.12
Choctaw (0)	1	0.01
Ottawa (3)	5	0.03
Potawatomi (3)	4	0.02
Ute (0)	1	0.01
Asian (384)	498	2.80
Not Hispanic (371)	471	2.65
Hispanic (13)	27	0.15
Bangladeshi (3)	3	0.02
Cambodian (45)	77	0.43
Chinese, ex. Taiwanese (36)	56	0.31
Filipino (20)	36	0.20
Indian (19)	26	0.15
Indonesian (0)	6	0.03
Japanese (12)	24	0.13
Korean (51)	66	0.37
Laotian (117)	150	0.84
Pakistani (5)	7	0.04
Taiwanese (2)	2	0.01
Thai (4)	14	0.08
Vietnamese (31)	50	0.28
Hawaii Native/Pacific Islander (5)	18	0.10
Not Hispanic (4)	15	0.08
Hispanic (1)	3	0.02
Guamanian/Chamorro (2)	3	0.02
Native Hawaiian (1)	7	0.04
Samoan (1)	1	0.01
White (16,421)	16,713	93.88
Not Hispanic (15,592)	15,797	88.74
Hispanic (829)	916	5.15

Pennfield

Place Type: Charter Township
County: Calhoun
Population: 9,001†

Ancestry‡	Population	%
African, Sub-Saharan (41)	41	0.45
African (10)	10	0.11
South African (31)	31	0.34
American (1,124)	1,124	12.44
Arab (0)	10	0.11
Lebanese (0)	10	0.11
Belgian (0)	54	0.60
British (12)	21	0.23
Canadian (0)	13	0.14
Croatian (0)	9	0.10
Czech (0)	11	0.12
Czechoslovakian (0)	9	0.10
Danish (10)	30	0.33
Dutch (191)	535	5.92
English (370)	1,062	11.76
European (130)	130	1.44
French, ex. Basque (113)	486	5.38
French Canadian (60)	101	1.12
German (859)	2,332	25.82
Greek (0)	10	0.11
Hungarian (31)	61	0.68
Irish (348)	1,092	12.09
Italian (54)	161	1.78
Macedonian (0)	7	0.08
Northern European (10)	26	0.29
Norwegian (68)	123	1.36
Polish (152)	439	4.86
Portuguese (0)	21	0.23
Russian (0)	10	0.11
Scandinavian (0)	35	0.39
Scotch-Irish (117)	217	2.40
Scottish (54)	225	2.49
Serbian (0)	19	0.21
Swedish (57)	101	1.12
Swiss (0)	7	0.08
Welsh (0)	154	1.71
West Indian, ex. Hispanic (32)	32	0.35
Jamaican (32)	32	0.35
Yugoslavian (0)	27	0.30

Hispanic Origin	Population	%
Hispanic or Latino (of any race)	256	2.84
Central American, ex. Mexican	11	0.12
Costa Rican	5	0.06
Guatemalan	3	0.03
Honduran	1	0.01
Panamanian	1	0.01
Salvadoran	1	0.01
Cuban	3	0.03
Dominican Republic	4	0.04
Mexican	173	1.92
Puerto Rican	24	0.27
South American	10	0.11
Argentinean	1	0.01
Colombian	4	0.04
Ecuadorian	1	0.01
Paraguayan	1	0.01
Peruvian	3	0.03
Other Hispanic or Latino	31	0.34

Race*	Population	%
African-American/Black (502)	620	6.89
Not Hispanic (498)	603	6.70
Hispanic (4)	17	0.19
American Indian/Alaska Native (50)	133	1.48
Not Hispanic (47)	122	1.36
Hispanic (3)	11	0.12
Alaska Athabascan *(Ala. Nat.)* (2)	5	0.06
Aleut *(Alaska Native)* (0)	1	0.01
Apache (0)	2	0.02
Blackfeet (0)	5	0.06
Cherokee (4)	33	0.37
Chippewa (7)	15	0.17
Choctaw (2)	2	0.02
Iroquois (0)	1	0.01
Navajo (3)	3	0.03
Osage (2)	2	0.02
Ottawa (3)	3	0.03
Potawatomi (6)	9	0.10
Asian (57)	96	1.07
Not Hispanic (57)	95	1.06
Hispanic (0)	1	0.01
Burmese (4)	8	0.09
Chinese, ex. Taiwanese (7)	15	0.17
Filipino (8)	15	0.17
Indian (20)	25	0.28
Japanese (2)	8	0.09
Korean (11)	23	0.26
Laotian (0)	1	0.01
Pakistani (3)	3	0.03
Thai (0)	3	0.03
Vietnamese (0)	3	0.03
Hawaii Native/Pacific Islander (6)	8	0.09
Not Hispanic (6)	8	0.09
Guamanian/Chamorro (1)	2	0.02
Samoan (1)	1	0.01
White (8,097)	8,296	92.17
Not Hispanic (7,940)	8,115	90.16
Hispanic (157)	181	2.01

Pittsfield

Place Type: Charter Township
County: Washtenaw
Population: 34,663†

Ancestry‡	Population	%
African, Sub-Saharan (443)	481	1.41
African (221)	231	0.68
Ethiopian (9)	9	0.03
Nigerian (127)	155	0.45
Somalian (73)	73	0.21
Other Sub-Saharan African (13)	13	0.04
Albanian (34)	70	0.21
American (1,526)	1,526	4.48
Arab (1,184)	1,249	3.66
Arab (582)	582	1.71
Egyptian (29)	29	0.09
Iraqi (50)	59	0.17
Jordanian (92)	92	0.27
Lebanese (7)	49	0.14
Palestinian (336)	336	0.99
Syrian (0)	14	0.04
Other Arab (88)	88	0.26
Armenian (88)	163	0.48
Assyrian/Chaldean/Syriac (0)	10	0.03
Australian (0)	22	0.06
Austrian (9)	81	0.24
Belgian (0)	86	0.25
Brazilian (0)	13	0.04
British (137)	178	0.52
Bulgarian (32)	32	0.09
Canadian (131)	169	0.50
Celtic (0)	10	0.03
Croatian (16)	50	0.15
Czech (23)	273	0.80
Czechoslovakian (54)	86	0.25
Danish (14)	100	0.29
Dutch (159)	691	2.03
Eastern European (100)	150	0.44
English (901)	3,348	9.82
European (476)	553	1.62
Finnish (116)	304	0.89
French, ex. Basque (102)	727	2.13
French Canadian (185)	419	1.23
German (1,884)	6,467	18.97
Greek (158)	272	0.80
Hungarian (126)	523	1.53
Icelander (23)	23	0.07
Iranian (135)	145	0.43
Irish (719)	3,239	9.50
Israeli (37)	37	0.11
Italian (510)	1,384	4.06
Latvian (18)	18	0.05
Lithuanian (15)	60	0.18
Macedonian (18)	26	0.08
Maltese (11)	24	0.07
Northern European (14)	14	0.04
Norwegian (29)	208	0.61
Polish (658)	1,938	5.68
Portuguese (0)	39	0.11
Romanian (99)	99	0.29
Russian (221)	424	1.24
Scandinavian (33)	59	0.17
Scotch-Irish (323)	697	2.04
Scottish (123)	888	2.60
Serbian (25)	39	0.11
Slavic (22)	83	0.24
Slovak (11)	50	0.15
Slovene (6)	22	0.06
Swedish (130)	623	1.83
Swiss (22)	90	0.26
Turkish (22)	39	0.11
Ukrainian (78)	182	0.53
Welsh (43)	215	0.63
West Indian, ex. Hispanic (148)	208	0.61
Bahamian (96)	96	0.28
British West Indian (20)	20	0.06
Haitian (12)	12	0.04

*Notes: † The Census 2010 population figure is used to calculate the percentages in the Hispanic Origin and Race categories. Ancestry percentages are based on the 2006-2010 American Community Survey population (not shown); ‡ Numbers in parentheses indicate the number of people reporting a single ancestry; * Numbers in parentheses indicate the number of persons reporting this race alone, not in combination with any other race; Please refer to the Explanation of Data for more information.*

Jamaican (20)	52	0.15
Trinidadian/Tobagonian (0)	28	0.08
Yugoslavian (11)	23	0.07

Hispanic Origin	Population	%
Hispanic or Latino (of any race)	2,270	6.55
Central American, ex. Mexican	345	1.00
Costa Rican	50	0.14
Guatemalan	68	0.20
Honduran	123	0.35
Nicaraguan	17	0.05
Panamanian	17	0.05
Salvadoran	64	0.18
Other Central American	6	0.02
Cuban	46	0.13
Dominican Republic	13	0.04
Mexican	1,240	3.58
Puerto Rican	194	0.56
South American	216	0.62
Argentinean	30	0.09
Bolivian	6	0.02
Chilean	19	0.05
Colombian	72	0.21
Ecuadorian	20	0.06
Paraguayan	1	<0.01
Peruvian	28	0.08
Uruguayan	2	0.01
Venezuelan	38	0.11
Other Hispanic or Latino	216	0.62

Race*	Population	%
African-American/Black (4,579)	5,207	15.02
Not Hispanic (4,501)	5,050	14.57
Hispanic (78)	157	0.45
American Indian/Alaska Native (133)	377	1.09
Not Hispanic (103)	318	0.92
Hispanic (30)	59	0.17
Aleut *(Alaska Native)* (2)	2	0.01
Apache (0)	3	0.01
Blackfeet (0)	7	0.02
Canadian/French Am. Ind. (4)	5	0.01
Central American Ind. (4)	4	0.01
Cherokee (7)	41	0.12
Chippewa (16)	46	0.13
Choctaw (3)	6	0.02
Cree (0)	4	0.01
Creek (1)	8	0.02
Crow (0)	1	<0.01
Delaware (0)	2	0.01
Houma (0)	1	<0.01
Iroquois (4)	10	0.03
Lumbee (2)	2	0.01
Menominee (2)	2	0.01
Mexican American Ind. (9)	12	0.03
Navajo (2)	6	0.02
Ottawa (3)	19	0.05
Potawatomi (2)	7	0.02
Seminole (0)	4	0.01
Shoshone (0)	2	0.01
Sioux (4)	10	0.03
Spanish American Ind. (0)	1	<0.01
Yup'ik *(Alaska Native)* (1)	3	0.01
Asian (4,710)	5,273	15.21
Not Hispanic (4,700)	5,233	15.10
Hispanic (10)	40	0.12
Bangladeshi (29)	30	0.09
Burmese (2)	2	0.01
Cambodian (19)	19	0.05
Chinese, ex. Taiwanese (1,315)	1,441	4.16
Filipino (212)	280	0.81
Hmong (11)	12	0.03
Indian (1,442)	1,565	4.51
Indonesian (11)	12	0.03
Japanese (231)	290	0.84
Korean (602)	661	1.91
Laotian (17)	25	0.07
Malaysian (7)	8	0.02
Nepalese (9)	9	0.03
Pakistani (292)	308	0.89
Sri Lankan (25)	34	0.10
Taiwanese (108)	123	0.35
Thai (42)	55	0.16
Vietnamese (200)	236	0.68
Hawaii Native/Pacific Islander (9)	47	0.14
Not Hispanic (8)	42	0.12
Hispanic (1)	5	0.01
Fijian (0)	3	0.01
Guamanian/Chamorro (2)	3	0.01
Native Hawaiian (1)	7	0.02
Samoan (1)	7	0.02
White (22,928)	24,129	69.61
Not Hispanic (21,805)	22,823	65.84
Hispanic (1,123)	1,306	3.77

Plainfield

Place Type: Charter Township
County: Kent
Population: 30,952†

Ancestry‡	Population	%
African, Sub-Saharan (34)	45	0.15
African (9)	9	0.03
Ethiopian (25)	25	0.08
Ugandan (0)	11	0.04
American (969)	969	3.13
Arab (29)	191	0.62
Arab (0)	25	0.08
Lebanese (0)	33	0.11
Syrian (29)	122	0.39
Other Arab (0)	11	0.04
Armenian (0)	33	0.11
Austrian (24)	73	0.24
Belgian (0)	40	0.13
British (21)	33	0.11
Canadian (28)	129	0.42
Celtic (9)	9	0.03
Czech (30)	226	0.73
Czechoslovakian (10)	43	0.14
Danish (83)	405	1.31
Dutch (2,178)	6,200	20.05
Eastern European (14)	14	0.05
English (974)	4,358	14.09
European (443)	477	1.54
Finnish (113)	226	0.73
French, ex. Basque (167)	1,722	5.57
French Canadian (326)	734	2.37
German (2,093)	8,633	27.92
Greek (115)	213	0.69
Guyanese (0)	7	0.02
Hungarian (47)	254	0.82
Iranian (15)	15	0.05
Irish (801)	5,253	16.99
Italian (270)	999	3.23
Latvian (47)	47	0.15
Lithuanian (101)	221	0.71
Maltese (0)	12	0.04
New Zealander (7)	7	0.02
Northern European (11)	11	0.04
Norwegian (244)	650	2.10
Pennsylvania German (23)	45	0.15
Polish (1,033)	3,180	10.28
Portuguese (0)	34	0.11
Romanian (38)	94	0.30
Russian (19)	156	0.50
Scandinavian (30)	40	0.13
Scotch-Irish (117)	535	1.73
Scottish (182)	611	1.98
Slovak (12)	77	0.25
Swedish (240)	1,021	3.30
Swiss (23)	195	0.63
Ukrainian (45)	51	0.16
Welsh (17)	74	0.24
Yugoslavian (26)	46	0.15

Hispanic Origin	Population	%
Hispanic or Latino (of any race)	810	2.62
Central American, ex. Mexican	33	0.11
Costa Rican	3	0.01
Guatemalan	22	0.07
Honduran	3	0.01
Panamanian	1	<0.01
Salvadoran	4	0.01
Cuban	33	0.11
Dominican Republic	4	0.01
Mexican	529	1.71
Puerto Rican	81	0.26
South American	42	0.14
Argentinean	4	0.01
Bolivian	10	0.03
Chilean	4	0.01
Colombian	20	0.06
Venezuelan	4	0.01
Other Hispanic or Latino	88	0.28

Race*	Population	%
African-American/Black (647)	954	3.08
Not Hispanic (623)	897	2.90
Hispanic (24)	57	0.18
American Indian/Alaska Native (96)	282	0.91
Not Hispanic (78)	243	0.79
Hispanic (18)	39	0.13
Apache (0)	2	0.01
Blackfeet (0)	3	0.01
Canadian/French Am. Ind. (2)	6	0.02
Cherokee (6)	37	0.12
Chippewa (34)	63	0.20
Choctaw (2)	5	0.02
Comanche (0)	1	<0.01
Inupiat *(Alaska Native)* (1)	1	<0.01
Iroquois (1)	3	0.01
Lumbee (1)	1	<0.01
Mexican American Ind. (2)	7	0.02
Ottawa (7)	21	0.07
Potawatomi (3)	10	0.03
Shoshone (1)	1	<0.01
Sioux (0)	8	0.03
South American Ind. (0)	4	0.01
Asian (361)	498	1.61
Not Hispanic (356)	480	1.55
Hispanic (5)	18	0.06
Bangladeshi (8)	8	0.03
Burmese (2)	3	0.01
Cambodian (0)	1	<0.01
Chinese, ex. Taiwanese (83)	98	0.32
Filipino (36)	76	0.25
Hmong (7)	7	0.02
Indian (36)	46	0.15
Indonesian (1)	8	0.03
Japanese (25)	42	0.14
Korean (78)	113	0.37
Laotian (2)	2	0.01
Malaysian (1)	1	<0.01
Nepalese (3)	3	0.01
Pakistani (1)	1	<0.01
Sri Lankan (2)	4	0.01
Taiwanese (4)	4	0.01
Thai (4)	11	0.04
Vietnamese (54)	63	0.20
Hawaii Native/Pacific Islander (9)	15	0.05
Not Hispanic (7)	12	0.04
Hispanic (2)	3	0.01
Guamanian/Chamorro (2)	2	0.01
Native Hawaiian (4)	6	0.02
Samoan (3)	3	0.01
White (29,006)	29,608	95.66
Not Hispanic (28,513)	29,028	93.78
Hispanic (493)	580	1.87

Plymouth

Place Type: Charter Township
County: Wayne
Population: 27,524†

Ancestry‡	Population	%
African, Sub-Saharan (21)	21	0.08
African (10)	10	0.04
Sudanese (11)	11	0.04
Albanian (19)	19	0.07

*Notes: † The Census 2010 population figure is used to calculate the percentages in the Hispanic Origin and Race categories. Ancestry percentages are based on the 2006-2010 American Community Survey population (not shown); ‡ Numbers in parentheses indicate the number of people reporting a single ancestry; * Numbers in parentheses indicate the number of persons reporting this race alone, not in combination with any other race; Please refer to the Explanation of Data for more information.*

American (1,654)	1,654	5.98
Arab (274)	498	1.80
Arab (28)	37	0.13
Jordanian (135)	147	0.53
Lebanese (104)	244	0.88
Palestinian (0)	2	0.01
Syrian (0)	24	0.09
Other Arab (7)	44	0.16
Armenian (22)	120	0.43
Australian (16)	16	0.06
Austrian (13)	58	0.21
Belgian (13)	146	0.53
British (21)	155	0.56
Bulgarian (11)	23	0.08
Canadian (122)	224	0.81
Croatian (16)	108	0.39
Czech (39)	172	0.62
Czechoslovakian (12)	28	0.10
Danish (0)	48	0.17
Dutch (419)	1,018	3.68
Eastern European (53)	53	0.19
English (811)	3,838	13.88
European (289)	304	1.10
Finnish (83)	373	1.35
French, ex. Basque (209)	1,592	5.76
French Canadian (105)	392	1.42
German (1,579)	7,100	25.67
Greek (120)	168	0.61
Hungarian (132)	548	1.98
Irish (1,030)	4,727	17.09
Italian (807)	2,530	9.15
Lithuanian (53)	221	0.80
Macedonian (89)	126	0.46
Maltese (49)	81	0.29
Norwegian (71)	425	1.54
Pennsylvania German (17)	17	0.06
Polish (1,591)	4,122	14.90
Portuguese (10)	21	0.08
Romanian (95)	242	0.87
Russian (18)	251	0.91
Scandinavian (0)	14	0.05
Scotch-Irish (255)	786	2.84
Scottish (330)	1,218	4.40
Serbian (12)	50	0.18
Slavic (16)	25	0.09
Slovak (37)	142	0.51
Slovene (15)	15	0.05
Swedish (102)	445	1.61
Swiss (0)	48	0.17
Ukrainian (218)	437	1.58
Welsh (31)	257	0.93
Yugoslavian (45)	210	0.76

Hispanic Origin	Population	%
Hispanic or Latino (of any race)	658	2.39
Central American, ex. Mexican	39	0.14
Costa Rican	8	0.03
Guatemalan	14	0.05
Honduran	5	0.02
Nicaraguan	4	0.01
Panamanian	6	0.02
Salvadoran	2	0.01
Cuban	21	0.08
Dominican Republic	1	<0.01
Mexican	428	1.56
Puerto Rican	59	0.21
South American	43	0.16
Argentinean	8	0.03
Bolivian	3	0.01
Chilean	1	<0.01
Colombian	16	0.06
Ecuadorian	4	0.01
Peruvian	8	0.03
Venezuelan	3	0.01
Other Hispanic or Latino	67	0.24

Race*	Population	%
African-American/Black (594)	694	2.52
Not Hispanic (589)	678	2.46
Hispanic (5)	16	0.06
American Indian/Alaska Native (74)	178	0.65
Not Hispanic (68)	159	0.58
Hispanic (6)	19	0.07
Apache (5)	5	0.02
Blackfeet (0)	12	0.04
Canadian/French Am. Ind. (1)	2	0.01
Cherokee (3)	12	0.04
Chickasaw (0)	1	<0.01
Chippewa (30)	48	0.17
Choctaw (0)	2	0.01
Comanche (1)	1	<0.01
Creek (1)	1	<0.01
Iroquois (6)	12	0.04
Lumbee (2)	2	0.01
Mexican American Ind. (2)	2	0.01
Navajo (0)	1	<0.01
Ottawa (1)	2	0.01
Potawatomi (2)	3	0.01
Sioux (0)	1	<0.01
South American Ind. (0)	6	0.02
Asian (962)	1,161	4.22
Not Hispanic (957)	1,153	4.19
Hispanic (5)	8	0.03
Cambodian (0)	1	<0.01
Chinese, ex. Taiwanese (140)	171	0.62
Filipino (101)	155	0.56
Indian (424)	464	1.69
Indonesian (10)	11	0.04
Japanese (49)	76	0.28
Korean (83)	111	0.40
Malaysian (1)	2	0.01
Nepalese (5)	5	0.02
Pakistani (64)	70	0.25
Taiwanese (18)	19	0.07
Thai (4)	8	0.03
Vietnamese (39)	42	0.15
Hawaii Native/Pacific Islander (4)	8	0.03
Not Hispanic (4)	8	0.03
Samoan (1)	1	<0.01
White (25,356)	25,711	93.41
Not Hispanic (24,872)	25,183	91.49
Hispanic (484)	528	1.92

Plymouth

Place Type: City
County: Wayne
Population: 9,132†

Ancestry‡	Population	%
American (607)	607	6.64
Arab (0)	59	0.65
Arab (0)	32	0.35
Lebanese (0)	27	0.30
Armenian (18)	44	0.48
Belgian (9)	59	0.65
British (34)	109	1.19
Canadian (34)	55	0.60
Carpatho Rusyn (0)	14	0.15
Croatian (46)	92	1.01
Czech (0)	74	0.81
Czechoslovakian (9)	9	0.10
Danish (0)	9	0.10
Dutch (65)	236	2.58
Eastern European (0)	8	0.09
English (411)	1,681	18.40
European (153)	153	1.67
Finnish (38)	126	1.38
French, ex. Basque (58)	703	7.69
French Canadian (63)	401	4.39
German (528)	2,223	24.33
Greek (21)	42	0.46
Hungarian (26)	184	2.01
Iranian (32)	32	0.35
Irish (546)	1,645	18.01
Italian (218)	675	7.39
Lithuanian (26)	38	0.42
Macedonian (0)	39	0.43
Maltese (36)	49	0.54
Northern European (21)	21	0.23
Norwegian (37)	115	1.26
Pennsylvania German (8)	8	0.09
Polish (465)	1,078	11.80
Romanian (28)	95	1.04
Russian (57)	90	0.99
Scandinavian (25)	25	0.27
Scotch-Irish (63)	298	3.26
Scottish (121)	297	3.25
Serbian (25)	61	0.67
Slovak (0)	28	0.31
Swedish (25)	129	1.41
Swiss (20)	66	0.72
Ukrainian (90)	151	1.65
Welsh (0)	67	0.73
Yugoslavian (4)	4	0.04

Hispanic Origin	Population	%
Hispanic or Latino (of any race)	163	1.78
Central American, ex. Mexican	13	0.14
Guatemalan	6	0.07
Honduran	1	0.01
Nicaraguan	2	0.02
Panamanian	4	0.04
Cuban	5	0.05
Dominican Republic	1	0.01
Mexican	91	1.00
Puerto Rican	15	0.16
South American	13	0.14
Chilean	4	0.04
Colombian	8	0.09
Peruvian	1	0.01
Other Hispanic or Latino	25	0.27

Race*	Population	%
African-American/Black (146)	174	1.91
Not Hispanic (144)	171	1.87
Hispanic (2)	3	0.03
American Indian/Alaska Native (24)	60	0.66
Not Hispanic (22)	57	0.62
Hispanic (2)	3	0.03
Cherokee (3)	11	0.12
Cheyenne (0)	1	0.01
Chickasaw (0)	1	0.01
Chippewa (8)	15	0.16
Choctaw (1)	1	0.01
Iroquois (5)	6	0.07
Lumbee (1)	1	0.01
Mexican American Ind. (1)	1	0.01
Ottawa (0)	1	0.01
Seminole (0)	2	0.02
Spanish American Ind. (0)	1	0.01
Asian (199)	260	2.85
Not Hispanic (199)	257	2.81
Hispanic (0)	3	0.03
Chinese, ex. Taiwanese (19)	34	0.37
Filipino (24)	38	0.42
Indian (107)	114	1.25
Indonesian (0)	1	0.01
Japanese (17)	21	0.23
Korean (22)	34	0.37
Thai (1)	4	0.04
Vietnamese (5)	7	0.08
Hawaii Native/Pacific Islander (2)	4	0.04
Not Hispanic (2)	3	0.03
Hispanic (0)	1	0.01
Native Hawaiian (1)	1	0.01
White (8,598)	8,723	95.52
Not Hispanic (8,469)	8,588	94.04
Hispanic (129)	135	1.48

Pontiac

Place Type: City
County: Oakland
Population: 59,515†

Ancestry‡	Population	%
African, Sub-Saharan (569)	776	1.27
African (389)	580	0.95
Ethiopian (39)	39	0.06

*Notes: † The Census 2010 population figure is used to calculate the percentages in the Hispanic Origin and Race categories. Ancestry percentages are based on the 2006-2010 American Community Survey population (not shown); ‡ Numbers in parentheses indicate the number of people reporting a single ancestry; * Numbers in parentheses indicate the number of persons reporting this race alone, not in combination with any other race; Please refer to the Explanation of Data for more information.*

Ancestry	Population	%
Liberian (62)	62	0.10
Nigerian (15)	31	0.05
Senegalese (50)	50	0.08
Other Sub-Saharan African (14)	14	0.02
Albanian (20)	20	0.03
American (1,737)	1,737	2.85
Arab (50)	135	0.22
Arab (17)	17	0.03
Lebanese (9)	72	0.12
Moroccan (9)	9	0.01
Other Arab (15)	37	0.06
Armenian (43)	52	0.09
Assyrian/Chaldean/Syriac (0)	9	0.01
Austrian (0)	57	0.09
Belgian (0)	20	0.03
Brazilian (0)	9	0.01
British (60)	118	0.19
Canadian (28)	148	0.24
Croatian (27)	81	0.13
Czech (9)	86	0.14
Czechoslovakian (16)	24	0.04
Danish (0)	7	0.01
Dutch (66)	620	1.02
English (691)	2,250	3.69
European (84)	115	0.19
Finnish (40)	143	0.23
French, ex. Basque (37)	906	1.49
French Canadian (218)	687	1.13
German (890)	3,983	6.53
Greek (46)	286	0.47
Hungarian (78)	321	0.53
Irish (851)	2,896	4.75
Italian (263)	1,003	1.64
Macedonian (7)	35	0.06
Maltese (13)	13	0.02
Norwegian (77)	115	0.19
Pennsylvania German (4)	4	0.01
Polish (739)	1,458	2.39
Portuguese (0)	92	0.15
Romanian (47)	56	0.09
Russian (26)	192	0.31
Scotch-Irish (219)	499	0.82
Scottish (150)	531	0.87
Slavic (6)	6	0.01
Slovak (12)	42	0.07
Swedish (53)	174	0.29
Turkish (0)	28	0.05
Ukrainian (0)	41	0.07
Welsh (28)	191	0.31
West Indian, ex. Hispanic (129)	814	1.33
Bermudan (50)	89	0.15
Haitian (10)	502	0.82
Jamaican (63)	120	0.20
Trinidadian/Tobagonian (0)	77	0.13
U.S. Virgin Islander (0)	20	0.03
West Indian (6)	6	0.01
Yugoslavian (16)	16	0.03

Hispanic Origin	Population	%
Hispanic or Latino (of any race)	9,835	16.53
Central American, ex. Mexican	457	0.77
Costa Rican	2	<0.01
Guatemalan	20	0.03
Honduran	147	0.25
Nicaraguan	2	<0.01
Panamanian	20	0.03
Salvadoran	266	0.45
Cuban	50	0.08
Dominican Republic	25	0.04
Mexican	6,605	11.10
Puerto Rican	2,309	3.88
South American	41	0.07
Argentinean	2	<0.01
Bolivian	3	0.01
Chilean	1	<0.01
Colombian	8	0.01
Ecuadorian	12	0.02
Peruvian	3	0.01
Venezuelan	10	0.02
Other South American	2	<0.01
Other Hispanic or Latino	348	0.58

Race*	Population	%
African-American/Black (30,988)	32,910	55.30
Not Hispanic (30,384)	31,897	53.59
Hispanic (604)	1,013	1.70
American Indian/Alaska Native (350)	990	1.66
Not Hispanic (242)	775	1.30
Hispanic (108)	215	0.36
Alaska Athabascan *(Ala. Nat.)* (1)	1	<0.01
Apache (2)	13	0.02
Arapaho (0)	1	<0.01
Blackfeet (3)	44	0.07
Canadian/French Am. Ind. (3)	4	0.01
Central American Ind. (1)	1	<0.01
Cherokee (40)	186	0.31
Chickasaw (0)	1	<0.01
Chippewa (65)	102	0.17
Choctaw (2)	10	0.02
Cree (0)	1	<0.01
Creek (1)	3	0.01
Crow (0)	7	0.01
Iroquois (5)	8	0.01
Kiowa (0)	1	<0.01
Lumbee (7)	10	0.02
Mexican American Ind. (26)	36	0.06
Navajo (2)	4	0.01
Ottawa (12)	16	0.03
Potawatomi (6)	15	0.03
Seminole (0)	6	0.01
Sioux (4)	14	0.02
Spanish American Ind. (3)	3	0.01
Yaqui (3)	6	0.01
Asian (1,372)	1,615	2.71
Not Hispanic (1,359)	1,564	2.63
Hispanic (13)	51	0.09
Bangladeshi (1)	2	<0.01
Cambodian (34)	44	0.07
Chinese, ex. Taiwanese (186)	205	0.34
Filipino (93)	164	0.28
Hmong (675)	695	1.17
Indian (138)	171	0.29
Indonesian (2)	4	0.01
Japanese (9)	35	0.06
Korean (22)	44	0.07
Laotian (39)	47	0.08
Malaysian (1)	1	<0.01
Pakistani (7)	9	0.02
Taiwanese (4)	4	0.01
Thai (27)	31	0.05
Vietnamese (49)	67	0.11
Hawaii Native/Pacific Islander (12)	86	0.14
Not Hispanic (2)	46	0.08
Hispanic (10)	40	0.07
Guamanian/Chamorro (5)	8	0.01
Native Hawaiian (7)	27	0.05
Samoan (0)	1	<0.01
Tongan (0)	1	<0.01
White (20,466)	22,597	37.97
Not Hispanic (15,815)	17,293	29.06
Hispanic (4,651)	5,304	8.91

Port Huron

Place Type: Charter Township
County: St. Clair
Population: 10,654†

Ancestry‡	Population	%
American (707)	707	6.76
Arab (28)	66	0.63
Lebanese (28)	66	0.63
Austrian (9)	50	0.48
Belgian (65)	161	1.54
Brazilian (0)	12	0.11
British (48)	48	0.46
Canadian (8)	79	0.76
Czech (17)	64	0.61
Danish (13)	25	0.24
Dutch (16)	169	1.62
English (366)	1,454	13.91
European (0)	19	0.18
Finnish (36)	36	0.34
French, ex. Basque (134)	717	6.86
French Canadian (86)	142	1.36
German (1,104)	3,310	31.66
Greek (17)	99	0.95
Hungarian (58)	182	1.74
Irish (457)	1,588	15.19
Italian (88)	164	1.57
Norwegian (55)	178	1.70
Polish (361)	1,106	10.58
Romanian (0)	53	0.51
Russian (50)	101	0.97
Scotch-Irish (77)	165	1.58
Scottish (78)	643	6.15
Slovak (13)	13	0.12
Swedish (15)	51	0.49
Swiss (6)	6	0.06
Ukrainian (13)	46	0.44
Welsh (0)	66	0.63

Hispanic Origin	Population	%
Hispanic or Latino (of any race)	403	3.78
Central American, ex. Mexican	11	0.10
Guatemalan	2	0.02
Honduran	4	0.04
Nicaraguan	3	0.03
Panamanian	1	0.01
Salvadoran	1	0.01
Cuban	2	0.02
Dominican Republic	2	0.02
Mexican	316	2.97
Puerto Rican	10	0.09
South American	4	0.04
Colombian	1	0.01
Ecuadorian	2	0.02
Venezuelan	1	0.01
Other Hispanic or Latino	58	0.54

Race*	Population	%
African-American/Black (478)	658	6.18
Not Hispanic (468)	622	5.84
Hispanic (10)	36	0.34
American Indian/Alaska Native (73)	171	1.61
Not Hispanic (64)	141	1.32
Hispanic (9)	30	0.28
Blackfeet (0)	7	0.07
Canadian/French Am. Ind. (4)	5	0.05
Cherokee (7)	14	0.13
Chippewa (25)	41	0.38
Choctaw (0)	1	0.01
Creek (1)	3	0.03
Crow (0)	1	0.01
Iroquois (3)	7	0.07
Mexican American Ind. (5)	5	0.05
Ottawa (2)	3	0.03
Pima (0)	2	0.02
Potawatomi (0)	2	0.02
Sioux (0)	2	0.02
Asian (39)	69	0.65
Not Hispanic (39)	69	0.65
Bangladeshi (3)	3	0.03
Chinese, ex. Taiwanese (3)	6	0.06
Filipino (15)	26	0.24
Hmong (1)	1	0.01
Indian (4)	8	0.08
Japanese (2)	9	0.08
Korean (7)	15	0.14
Pakistani (1)	1	0.01
Thai (1)	1	0.01
Vietnamese (1)	2	0.02
Hawaii Native/Pacific Islander (5)	9	0.08
Not Hispanic (5)	9	0.08
Guamanian/Chamorro (2)	2	0.02
Native Hawaiian (2)	6	0.06
Samoan (1)	1	0.01
White (9,686)	9,976	93.64
Not Hispanic (9,412)	9,666	90.73
Hispanic (274)	310	2.91

*Notes: † The Census 2010 population figure is used to calculate the percentages in the Hispanic Origin and Race categories. Ancestry percentages are based on the 2006-2010 American Community Survey population (not shown); ‡ Numbers in parentheses indicate the number of people reporting a single ancestry; * Numbers in parentheses indicate the number of persons reporting this race alone, not in combination with any other race; Please refer to the Explanation of Data for more information.*

Port Huron

Place Type: City
County: St. Clair
Population: 30,184†

Ancestry‡	Population	%
African, Sub-Saharan (92)	103	0.33
African (92)	103	0.33
American (1,556)	1,556	5.02
Arab (109)	194	0.63
Arab (0)	76	0.24
Egyptian (11)	11	0.04
Lebanese (58)	58	0.19
Syrian (40)	49	0.16
Armenian (21)	21	0.07
Australian (0)	13	0.04
Austrian (10)	31	0.10
Belgian (34)	194	0.63
British (77)	157	0.51
Bulgarian (80)	80	0.26
Canadian (201)	485	1.56
Croatian (39)	152	0.49
Czech (37)	71	0.23
Czechoslovakian (67)	96	0.31
Danish (9)	50	0.16
Dutch (171)	729	2.35
Eastern European (12)	12	0.04
English (951)	3,143	10.13
European (216)	226	0.73
Finnish (90)	196	0.63
French, ex. Basque (234)	1,916	6.18
French Canadian (307)	1,181	3.81
German (2,636)	8,121	26.18
Greek (61)	147	0.47
Hungarian (30)	154	0.50
Iranian (27)	27	0.09
Irish (1,229)	4,243	13.68
Israeli (11)	11	0.04
Italian (224)	1,038	3.35
Lithuanian (12)	64	0.21
Maltese (60)	60	0.19
Northern European (0)	14	0.05
Norwegian (42)	225	0.73
Polish (448)	1,647	5.31
Portuguese (0)	10	0.03
Romanian (25)	33	0.11
Russian (43)	378	1.22
Scandinavian (4)	7	0.02
Scotch-Irish (142)	461	1.49
Scottish (303)	1,067	3.44
Serbian (88)	88	0.28
Slavic (0)	3	0.01
Slovak (13)	13	0.04
Slovene (11)	11	0.04
Swedish (76)	346	1.12
Swiss (0)	11	0.04
Turkish (24)	24	0.08
Ukrainian (106)	109	0.35
Welsh (9)	144	0.46
West Indian, ex. Hispanic (36)	49	0.16
Jamaican (36)	49	0.16
Yugoslavian (57)	57	0.18

Hispanic Origin	Population	%
Hispanic or Latino (of any race)	1,634	5.41
Central American, ex. Mexican	31	0.10
Guatemalan	1	<0.01
Honduran	3	0.01
Nicaraguan	13	0.04
Panamanian	10	0.03
Salvadoran	2	0.01
Other Central American	2	0.01
Cuban	20	0.07
Dominican Republic	4	0.01
Mexican	1,249	4.14
Puerto Rican	133	0.44
South American	25	0.08
Argentinean	2	0.01
Colombian	10	0.03
Ecuadorian	2	0.01
Peruvian	2	0.01
Uruguayan	4	0.01
Other South American	5	0.02
Other Hispanic or Latino	172	0.57

Race*	Population	%
African-American/Black (2,736)	3,567	11.82
Not Hispanic (2,654)	3,387	11.22
Hispanic (82)	180	0.60
American Indian/Alaska Native (198)	608	2.01
Not Hispanic (169)	522	1.73
Hispanic (29)	86	0.28
Apache (0)	9	0.03
Arapaho (0)	1	<0.01
Blackfeet (2)	22	0.07
Canadian/French Am. Ind. (14)	23	0.08
Cherokee (21)	101	0.33
Chickasaw (0)	5	0.02
Chippewa (49)	98	0.32
Choctaw (0)	7	0.02
Comanche (1)	1	<0.01
Cree (1)	1	<0.01
Crow (0)	3	0.01
Delaware (0)	1	<0.01
Hopi (0)	1	<0.01
Iroquois (8)	14	0.05
Lumbee (2)	3	0.01
Menominee (0)	2	0.01
Mexican American Ind. (8)	14	0.05
Navajo (0)	2	0.01
Ottawa (8)	22	0.07
Pima (0)	1	<0.01
Potawatomi (1)	2	0.01
Seminole (0)	4	0.01
Sioux (1)	12	0.04
Spanish American Ind. (1)	1	<0.01
Yaqui (0)	1	<0.01
Asian (172)	267	0.88
Not Hispanic (166)	240	0.80
Hispanic (6)	27	0.09
Cambodian (5)	5	0.02
Chinese, ex. Taiwanese (38)	47	0.16
Filipino (41)	75	0.25
Indian (27)	40	0.13
Indonesian (5)	5	0.02
Japanese (4)	16	0.05
Korean (14)	22	0.07
Laotian (4)	5	0.02
Pakistani (7)	9	0.03
Thai (6)	13	0.04
Vietnamese (9)	10	0.03
Hawaii Native/Pacific Islander (4)	28	0.09
Not Hispanic (3)	20	0.07
Hispanic (1)	8	0.03
Guamanian/Chamorro (1)	3	0.01
Native Hawaiian (3)	14	0.05
White (25,342)	26,612	88.17
Not Hispanic (24,465)	25,481	84.42
Hispanic (877)	1,131	3.75

Portage

Place Type: City
County: Kalamazoo
Population: 46,292†

Ancestry‡	Population	%
African, Sub-Saharan (172)	187	0.41
African (172)	187	0.41
Albanian (0)	25	0.05
American (2,097)	2,097	4.57
Arab (64)	159	0.35
Arab (0)	41	0.09
Iraqi (23)	33	0.07
Lebanese (25)	43	0.09
Syrian (0)	9	0.02
Other Arab (16)	33	0.07
Assyrian/Chaldean/Syriac (18)	18	0.04
Australian (7)	31	0.07
Austrian (23)	94	0.20
Belgian (16)	153	0.33
Brazilian (31)	31	0.07
British (50)	214	0.47
Bulgarian (29)	29	0.06
Canadian (122)	305	0.66
Celtic (11)	11	0.02
Croatian (11)	99	0.22
Czech (60)	223	0.49
Czechoslovakian (60)	97	0.21
Danish (59)	222	0.48
Dutch (2,286)	5,214	11.36
Eastern European (7)	7	0.02
English (2,080)	6,708	14.61
European (412)	501	1.09
Finnish (71)	213	0.46
French, ex. Basque (181)	2,082	4.53
French Canadian (164)	727	1.58
German (3,520)	12,728	27.72
German Russian (11)	11	0.02
Greek (41)	293	0.64
Hungarian (195)	475	1.03
Iranian (0)	8	0.02
Irish (1,536)	6,382	13.90
Israeli (10)	10	0.02
Italian (401)	1,745	3.80
Latvian (41)	115	0.25
Lithuanian (31)	123	0.27
Luxemburger (13)	13	0.03
Maltese (23)	43	0.09
Northern European (44)	44	0.10
Norwegian (212)	835	1.82
Pennsylvania German (44)	70	0.15
Polish (894)	3,094	6.74
Portuguese (8)	8	0.02
Romanian (11)	20	0.04
Russian (85)	271	0.59
Scandinavian (27)	38	0.08
Scotch-Irish (324)	738	1.61
Scottish (414)	1,416	3.08
Slavic (0)	25	0.05
Slovak (41)	148	0.32
Slovene (0)	38	0.08
Swedish (274)	1,064	2.32
Swiss (20)	220	0.48
Turkish (10)	29	0.06
Ukrainian (0)	161	0.35
Welsh (49)	218	0.47
Yugoslavian (28)	80	0.17

Hispanic Origin	Population	%
Hispanic or Latino (of any race)	1,413	3.05
Central American, ex. Mexican	78	0.17
Costa Rican	2	<0.01
Guatemalan	37	0.08
Honduran	3	0.01
Nicaraguan	9	0.02
Panamanian	16	0.03
Salvadoran	11	0.02
Cuban	58	0.13
Dominican Republic	9	0.02
Mexican	906	1.96
Puerto Rican	129	0.28
South American	111	0.24
Argentinean	11	0.02
Bolivian	1	<0.01
Chilean	17	0.04
Colombian	35	0.08
Ecuadorian	10	0.02
Peruvian	5	0.01
Uruguayan	1	<0.01
Venezuelan	31	0.07
Other Hispanic or Latino	122	0.26

Race*	Population	%
African-American/Black (2,252)	2,921	6.31
Not Hispanic (2,195)	2,815	6.08
Hispanic (57)	106	0.23
American Indian/Alaska Native (202)	534	1.15
Not Hispanic (183)	485	1.05

SECTION TWO

*Notes: † The Census 2010 population figure is used to calculate the percentages in the Hispanic Origin and Race categories. Ancestry percentages are based on the 2006-2010 American Community Survey population (not shown); ‡ Numbers in parentheses indicate the number of people reporting a single ancestry; * Numbers in parentheses indicate the number of persons reporting this race alone, not in combination with any other race; Please refer to the Explanation of Data for more information.*

Hispanic (19)	49	0.11
Apache (2)	7	0.02
Blackfeet (3)	21	0.05
Canadian/French Am. Ind. (0)	4	0.01
Cherokee (29)	110	0.24
Chickasaw (5)	5	0.01
Chippewa (39)	79	0.17
Choctaw (1)	8	0.02
Creek (1)	1	<0.01
Iroquois (7)	9	0.02
Lumbee (0)	1	<0.01
Mexican American Ind. (9)	10	0.02
Navajo (0)	3	0.01
Ottawa (18)	26	0.06
Potawatomi (27)	49	0.11
Sioux (3)	7	0.02
South American Ind. (1)	1	<0.01
Yaqui (2)	2	<0.01
Asian (1,763)	2,179	4.71
Not Hispanic (1,761)	2,158	4.66
Hispanic (2)	21	0.05
Bangladeshi (3)	5	0.01
Burmese (8)	12	0.03
Cambodian (8)	11	0.02
Chinese, ex. Taiwanese (275)	347	0.75
Filipino (104)	174	0.38
Hmong (1)	3	0.01
Indian (693)	753	1.63
Indonesian (4)	14	0.03
Japanese (38)	108	0.23
Korean (204)	272	0.59
Laotian (2)	5	0.01
Malaysian (2)	6	0.01
Nepalese (19)	20	0.04
Pakistani (111)	116	0.25
Sri Lankan (15)	15	0.03
Taiwanese (27)	32	0.07
Thai (18)	33	0.07
Vietnamese (169)	188	0.41
Hawaii Native/Pacific Islander (21)	54	0.12
Not Hispanic (17)	48	0.10
Hispanic (4)	6	0.01
Guamanian/Chamorro (5)	7	0.02
Marshallese (4)	4	0.01
Native Hawaiian (6)	15	0.03
Samoan (1)	3	0.01
White (40,217)	41,469	89.58
Not Hispanic (39,427)	40,545	87.59
Hispanic (790)	924	2.00

Putnam

Place Type: Township
County: Livingston
Population: 8,248†

Ancestry‡	Population	%
American (631)	631	7.57
Arab (0)	40	0.48
Arab (0)	8	0.10
Lebanese (0)	32	0.38
Austrian (16)	40	0.48
Belgian (0)	82	0.98
British (16)	16	0.19
Canadian (6)	82	0.98
Croatian (0)	12	0.14
Czech (3)	46	0.55
Czechoslovakian (6)	54	0.65
Danish (0)	40	0.48
Dutch (87)	259	3.11
English (392)	1,132	13.59
European (220)	260	3.12
Finnish (24)	91	1.09
French, ex. Basque (101)	439	5.27
French Canadian (45)	206	2.47
German (696)	2,473	29.68
Greek (44)	80	0.96
Hungarian (55)	194	2.33
Irish (272)	1,177	14.13
Italian (81)	349	4.19
Lithuanian (19)	65	0.78
Northern European (20)	20	0.24
Norwegian (31)	107	1.28
Polish (244)	1,067	12.81
Portuguese (9)	9	0.11
Russian (0)	21	0.25
Scandinavian (0)	35	0.42
Scotch-Irish (87)	164	1.97
Scottish (124)	346	4.15
Serbian (0)	13	0.16
Slovak (4)	24	0.29
Swedish (114)	312	3.74
Swiss (0)	11	0.13
Ukrainian (4)	14	0.17
Welsh (4)	23	0.28
Yugoslavian (6)	6	0.07

Hispanic Origin	Population	%
Hispanic or Latino (of any race)	117	1.42
Central American, ex. Mexican	10	0.12
Guatemalan	7	0.08
Honduran	1	0.01
Salvadoran	2	0.02
Cuban	5	0.06
Dominican Republic	4	0.05
Mexican	67	0.81
Puerto Rican	3	0.04
South American	7	0.08
Argentinean	1	0.01
Colombian	2	0.02
Peruvian	3	0.04
Venezuelan	1	0.01
Other Hispanic or Latino	21	0.25

Race*	Population	%
African-American/Black (24)	40	0.48
Not Hispanic (24)	40	0.48
American Indian/Alaska Native (12)	57	0.69
Not Hispanic (10)	54	0.65
Hispanic (2)	3	0.04
Apache (0)	3	0.04
Blackfeet (0)	1	0.01
Cherokee (1)	6	0.07
Chippewa (4)	6	0.07
Cree (1)	1	0.01
Iroquois (0)	3	0.04
Mexican American Ind. (2)	2	0.02
Navajo (0)	3	0.04
Ottawa (0)	1	0.01
Shoshone (0)	1	0.01
Sioux (1)	2	0.02
Ute (0)	4	0.05
Yup'ik *(Alaska Native)* (1)	1	0.01
Asian (33)	61	0.74
Not Hispanic (33)	60	0.73
Hispanic (0)	1	0.01
Chinese, ex. Taiwanese (6)	10	0.12
Filipino (9)	14	0.17
Indian (3)	6	0.07
Indonesian (0)	2	0.02
Japanese (5)	15	0.18
Korean (8)	12	0.15
Hawaii Native/Pacific Islander (0)	9	0.11
Not Hispanic (0)	9	0.11
Native Hawaiian (0)	5	0.06
White (8,062)	8,161	98.95
Not Hispanic (7,974)	8,062	97.74
Hispanic (88)	99	1.20

Raisin

Place Type: Township
County: Lenawee
Population: 7,559†

Ancestry‡	Population	%
African, Sub-Saharan (141)	141	1.89
African (141)	141	1.89
American (622)	622	8.34
Arab (143)	158	2.12
Lebanese (143)	158	2.12
Belgian (0)	14	0.19
British (14)	14	0.19
Canadian (102)	116	1.56
Czech (0)	15	0.20
Czechoslovakian (0)	16	0.21
Danish (0)	16	0.21
Dutch (0)	89	1.19
English (169)	813	10.91
European (31)	31	0.42
Finnish (0)	8	0.11
French, ex. Basque (57)	604	8.10
French Canadian (40)	152	2.04
German (1,030)	2,467	33.09
Greek (0)	14	0.19
Hungarian (18)	83	1.11
Irish (248)	1,026	13.76
Italian (206)	301	4.04
Lithuanian (18)	44	0.59
Norwegian (0)	46	0.62
Pennsylvania German (13)	24	0.32
Polish (84)	382	5.12
Russian (0)	14	0.19
Scotch-Irish (29)	214	2.87
Scottish (31)	219	2.94
Slovak (0)	25	0.34
Swedish (44)	80	1.07
Ukrainian (0)	65	0.87
Welsh (0)	47	0.63

Hispanic Origin	Population	%
Hispanic or Latino (of any race)	404	5.34
Central American, ex. Mexican	5	0.07
Guatemalan	2	0.03
Nicaraguan	1	0.01
Panamanian	1	0.01
Salvadoran	1	0.01
Dominican Republic	3	0.04
Mexican	310	4.10
Puerto Rican	23	0.30
South American	8	0.11
Ecuadorian	5	0.07
Peruvian	2	0.03
Venezuelan	1	0.01
Other Hispanic or Latino	55	0.73

Race*	Population	%
African-American/Black (54)	83	1.10
Not Hispanic (53)	79	1.05
Hispanic (1)	4	0.05
American Indian/Alaska Native (33)	90	1.19
Not Hispanic (28)	83	1.10
Hispanic (5)	7	0.09
Blackfeet (0)	4	0.05
Cherokee (2)	5	0.07
Chippewa (10)	22	0.29
Houma (0)	1	0.01
Lumbee (2)	3	0.04
Navajo (0)	4	0.05
Potawatomi (0)	1	0.01
Sioux (0)	1	0.01
Asian (42)	66	0.87
Not Hispanic (37)	61	0.81
Hispanic (5)	5	0.07
Chinese, ex. Taiwanese (5)	12	0.16
Filipino (6)	13	0.17
Indian (3)	3	0.04
Indonesian (1)	1	0.01
Japanese (8)	13	0.17
Korean (7)	10	0.13
Thai (3)	4	0.05
Vietnamese (8)	8	0.11
Hawaii Native/Pacific Islander (2)	2	0.03
Not Hispanic (2)	2	0.03
White (7,184)	7,317	96.80
Not Hispanic (6,925)	7,019	92.86
Hispanic (259)	298	3.94

*Notes: † The Census 2010 population figure is used to calculate the percentages in the Hispanic Origin and Race categories. Ancestry percentages are based on the 2006-2010 American Community Survey population (not shown); ‡ Numbers in parentheses indicate the number of people reporting a single ancestry; * Numbers in parentheses indicate the number of persons reporting this race alone, not in combination with any other race; Please refer to the Explanation of Data for more information.*

Redford

Place Type: Charter Township
County: Wayne
Population: 48,362†

Ancestry‡	Population	%
African, Sub-Saharan (332)	518	1.05
African (257)	443	0.90
Nigerian (64)	64	0.13
South African (11)	11	0.02
Albanian (19)	19	0.04
American (2,039)	2,039	4.15
Arab (146)	284	0.58
Arab (17)	53	0.11
Lebanese (80)	104	0.21
Palestinian (12)	12	0.02
Syrian (7)	57	0.12
Other Arab (30)	58	0.12
Armenian (52)	246	0.50
Assyrian/Chaldean/Syriac (20)	20	0.04
Austrian (18)	102	0.21
Belgian (16)	88	0.18
Brazilian (0)	44	0.09
British (16)	127	0.26
Canadian (55)	205	0.42
Croatian (0)	21	0.04
Czech (33)	191	0.39
Czechoslovakian (54)	95	0.19
Danish (37)	227	0.46
Dutch (166)	835	1.70
Eastern European (78)	85	0.17
English (812)	4,263	8.68
European (266)	294	0.60
Finnish (278)	665	1.35
French, ex. Basque (266)	2,237	4.55
French Canadian (266)	936	1.91
German (2,081)	9,114	18.55
Greek (183)	431	0.88
Guyanese (25)	35	0.07
Hungarian (199)	572	1.16
Icelander (0)	29	0.06
Irish (1,861)	6,807	13.86
Italian (903)	3,354	6.83
Latvian (58)	71	0.14
Lithuanian (108)	208	0.42
Luxemburger (0)	5	0.01
Maltese (250)	432	0.88
Norwegian (20)	249	0.51
Pennsylvania German (0)	8	0.02
Polish (2,553)	6,762	13.77
Romanian (38)	195	0.40
Russian (65)	246	0.50
Scandinavian (0)	99	0.20
Scotch-Irish (251)	928	1.89
Scottish (270)	1,620	3.30
Serbian (21)	74	0.15
Slavic (6)	31	0.06
Slovak (40)	95	0.19
Slovene (0)	74	0.15
Swedish (39)	402	0.82
Swiss (0)	67	0.14
Turkish (0)	19	0.04
Ukrainian (148)	408	0.83
Welsh (38)	270	0.55
West Indian, ex. Hispanic (10)	31	0.06
Jamaican (10)	20	0.04
West Indian (0)	11	0.02
Yugoslavian (48)	119	0.24

Hispanic Origin	Population	%
Hispanic or Latino (of any race)	1,420	2.94
Central American, ex. Mexican	60	0.12
Costa Rican	1	<0.01
Guatemalan	12	0.02
Honduran	25	0.05
Nicaraguan	2	<0.01
Panamanian	7	0.01
Salvadoran	13	0.03
Cuban	38	0.08
Dominican Republic	11	0.02
Mexican	1,003	2.07
Puerto Rican	148	0.31
South American	49	0.10
Argentinean	6	0.01
Bolivian	4	0.01
Colombian	22	0.05
Peruvian	10	0.02
Uruguayan	1	<0.01
Venezuelan	6	0.01
Other Hispanic or Latino	111	0.23

Race*	Population	%
African-American/Black (13,982)	14,769	30.54
Not Hispanic (13,891)	14,637	30.27
Hispanic (91)	132	0.27
American Indian/Alaska Native (239)	663	1.37
Not Hispanic (206)	583	1.21
Hispanic (33)	80	0.17
Apache (3)	8	0.02
Arapaho (0)	1	<0.01
Blackfeet (3)	13	0.03
Canadian/French Am. Ind. (11)	16	0.03
Cherokee (14)	101	0.21
Cheyenne (0)	1	<0.01
Chippewa (64)	97	0.20
Choctaw (2)	12	0.02
Creek (1)	1	<0.01
Delaware (2)	3	0.01
Inupiat *(Alaska Native)* (0)	1	<0.01
Iroquois (17)	45	0.09
Kiowa (1)	1	<0.01
Lumbee (5)	12	0.02
Mexican American Ind. (7)	9	0.02
Navajo (0)	2	<0.01
Ottawa (1)	7	0.01
Pima (1)	4	0.01
Potawatomi (5)	8	0.02
Seminole (1)	1	<0.01
Sioux (4)	5	0.01
South American Ind. (0)	4	0.01
Spanish American Ind. (1)	1	<0.01
Yup'ik *(Alaska Native)* (0)	1	<0.01
Asian (399)	610	1.26
Not Hispanic (399)	595	1.23
Hispanic (0)	15	0.03
Burmese (1)	3	0.01
Cambodian (4)	7	0.01
Chinese, ex. Taiwanese (48)	93	0.19
Filipino (113)	157	0.32
Hmong (5)	7	0.01
Indian (91)	128	0.26
Indonesian (0)	4	0.01
Japanese (28)	56	0.12
Korean (27)	63	0.13
Laotian (6)	6	0.01
Malaysian (1)	1	<0.01
Pakistani (22)	29	0.06
Sri Lankan (3)	3	0.01
Taiwanese (1)	1	<0.01
Thai (0)	13	0.03
Vietnamese (24)	35	0.07
Hawaii Native/Pacific Islander (9)	17	0.04
Not Hispanic (5)	13	0.03
Hispanic (4)	4	0.01
Guamanian/Chamorro (0)	2	<0.01
Native Hawaiian (3)	6	0.01
Samoan (1)	2	<0.01
Tongan (1)	1	<0.01
White (32,120)	33,153	68.55
Not Hispanic (31,292)	32,228	66.64
Hispanic (828)	925	1.91

Richfield

Place Type: Township
County: Genesee
Population: 8,730†

Ancestry‡	Population	%
American (616)	616	7.05
Arab (108)	108	1.24
Arab (108)	108	1.24
Austrian (9)	9	0.10
Belgian (0)	34	0.39
British (24)	61	0.70
Canadian (10)	48	0.55
Croatian (0)	24	0.27
Czech (0)	36	0.41
Czechoslovakian (10)	19	0.22
Danish (8)	55	0.63
Dutch (11)	276	3.16
English (640)	1,487	17.03
European (19)	41	0.47
Finnish (10)	19	0.22
French, ex. Basque (76)	647	7.41
French Canadian (82)	209	2.39
German (635)	2,227	25.50
Greek (3)	36	0.41
Hungarian (110)	220	2.52
Irish (334)	1,273	14.58
Italian (184)	327	3.74
Lithuanian (12)	12	0.14
Maltese (35)	35	0.40
Norwegian (21)	67	0.77
Polish (194)	708	8.11
Romanian (48)	48	0.55
Scotch-Irish (27)	177	2.03
Scottish (34)	93	1.06
Serbian (0)	9	0.10
Slavic (11)	11	0.13
Slovak (0)	13	0.15
Swedish (15)	93	1.06
Ukrainian (0)	109	1.25
Welsh (0)	10	0.11

Hispanic Origin	Population	%
Hispanic or Latino (of any race)	231	2.65
Central American, ex. Mexican	3	0.03
Guatemalan	2	0.02
Salvadoran	1	0.01
Cuban	4	0.05
Dominican Republic	8	0.09
Mexican	182	2.08
Puerto Rican	20	0.23
South American	2	0.02
Argentinean	1	0.01
Other South American	1	0.01
Other Hispanic or Latino	12	0.14

Race*	Population	%
African-American/Black (186)	240	2.75
Not Hispanic (185)	235	2.69
Hispanic (1)	5	0.06
American Indian/Alaska Native (42)	110	1.26
Not Hispanic (36)	102	1.17
Hispanic (6)	8	0.09
Apache (0)	2	0.02
Blackfeet (0)	3	0.03
Cherokee (6)	21	0.24
Chippewa (8)	29	0.33
Choctaw (0)	2	0.02
Creek (0)	3	0.03
Osage (0)	1	0.01
Ottawa (3)	3	0.03
Potawatomi (1)	1	0.01
Sioux (2)	3	0.03
South American Ind. (1)	3	0.03
Yaqui (4)	4	0.05
Asian (40)	83	0.95
Not Hispanic (39)	73	0.84
Hispanic (1)	10	0.11
Chinese, ex. Taiwanese (6)	8	0.09
Filipino (6)	16	0.18
Hmong (1)	1	0.01
Indian (1)	11	0.13
Japanese (5)	16	0.18
Korean (8)	11	0.13
Pakistani (7)	7	0.08

*Notes: † The Census 2010 population figure is used to calculate the percentages in the Hispanic Origin and Race categories. Ancestry percentages are based on the 2006-2010 American Community Survey population (not shown); ‡ Numbers in parentheses indicate the number of people reporting a single ancestry; * Numbers in parentheses indicate the number of persons reporting this race alone, not in combination with any other race; Please refer to the Explanation of Data for more information.*

Thai (1)	1	0.01
Vietnamese (4)	9	0.10
Hawaii Native/Pacific Islander (0)	8	0.09
Not Hispanic (0)	6	0.07
Hispanic (0)	2	0.02
Guamanian/Chamorro (0)	5	0.06
Native Hawaiian (0)	6	0.07
Samoan (0)	5	0.06
White (8,261)	8,410	96.33
Not Hispanic (8,104)	8,231	94.28
Hispanic (157)	179	2.05

Richland

Place Type: Township
County: Kalamazoo
Population: 7,580†

Ancestry‡	Population	%
American (536)	536	7.27
Arab (0)	10	0.14
Lebanese (0)	10	0.14
Assyrian/Chaldean/Syriac (32)	32	0.43
Austrian (3)	19	0.26
Belgian (0)	7	0.10
British (3)	6	0.08
Czech (0)	26	0.35
Czechoslovakian (0)	4	0.05
Danish (24)	37	0.50
Dutch (439)	1,022	13.87
English (432)	1,248	16.94
European (128)	154	2.09
Finnish (0)	23	0.31
French, ex. Basque (45)	308	4.18
French Canadian (14)	33	0.45
German (361)	1,892	25.68
Greek (18)	45	0.61
Hungarian (34)	62	0.84
Irish (159)	1,177	15.97
Italian (35)	310	4.21
Latvian (13)	13	0.18
Luxemburger (0)	13	0.18
Northern European (81)	81	1.10
Norwegian (45)	85	1.15
Polish (60)	329	4.47
Romanian (0)	14	0.19
Russian (12)	41	0.56
Scandinavian (0)	55	0.75
Scotch-Irish (49)	143	1.94
Scottish (18)	158	2.14
Serbian (0)	3	0.04
Slavic (0)	16	0.22
Swedish (3)	86	1.17
Swiss (0)	12	0.16
Ukrainian (0)	17	0.23
Welsh (0)	15	0.20

Hispanic Origin	Population	%
Hispanic or Latino (of any race)	226	2.98
Central American, ex. Mexican	14	0.18
Guatemalan	12	0.16
Salvadoran	2	0.03
Cuban	6	0.08
Mexican	161	2.12
Puerto Rican	13	0.17
South American	9	0.12
Bolivian	1	0.01
Colombian	6	0.08
Ecuadorian	1	0.01
Venezuelan	1	0.01
Other Hispanic or Latino	23	0.30

Race*	Population	%
African-American/Black (299)	350	4.62
Not Hispanic (291)	336	4.43
Hispanic (8)	14	0.18
American Indian/Alaska Native (21)	73	0.96
Not Hispanic (20)	72	0.95
Hispanic (1)	1	0.01
Cherokee (0)	7	0.09
Chippewa (2)	20	0.26
Choctaw (1)	1	0.01
Creek (0)	1	0.01
Iroquois (1)	3	0.04
Mexican American Ind. (1)	1	0.01
Ottawa (1)	1	0.01
Potawatomi (7)	13	0.17
Asian (95)	138	1.82
Not Hispanic (94)	136	1.79
Hispanic (1)	2	0.03
Cambodian (1)	4	0.05
Chinese, ex. Taiwanese (21)	25	0.33
Filipino (10)	14	0.18
Indian (20)	30	0.40
Japanese (7)	11	0.15
Korean (22)	30	0.40
Pakistani (0)	1	0.01
Taiwanese (2)	2	0.03
Thai (1)	6	0.08
Vietnamese (8)	15	0.20
Hawaii Native/Pacific Islander (7)	9	0.12
Not Hispanic (6)	7	0.09
Hispanic (1)	2	0.03
Guamanian/Chamorro (1)	2	0.03
Native Hawaiian (1)	1	0.01
Samoan (1)	2	0.03
White (6,940)	7,062	93.17
Not Hispanic (6,806)	6,918	91.27
Hispanic (134)	144	1.90

River Rouge

Place Type: City
County: Wayne
Population: 7,903†

Ancestry‡	Population	%
African, Sub-Saharan (83)	83	1.00
African (83)	83	1.00
American (81)	81	0.98
Armenian (0)	32	0.39
Belgian (0)	20	0.24
British (0)	25	0.30
Croatian (9)	9	0.11
Czech (0)	13	0.16
Danish (23)	23	0.28
Dutch (0)	117	1.41
Eastern European (9)	9	0.11
English (25)	219	2.64
European (8)	8	0.10
Finnish (44)	104	1.25
French, ex. Basque (118)	442	5.33
French Canadian (178)	243	2.93
German (300)	975	11.75
Greek (6)	6	0.07
Hungarian (22)	144	1.74
Irish (404)	968	11.66
Italian (16)	89	1.07
Lithuanian (30)	91	1.10
Norwegian (24)	40	0.48
Polish (152)	552	6.65
Scotch-Irish (29)	29	0.35
Scottish (0)	30	0.36
Serbian (30)	30	0.36
Slovak (11)	28	0.34
Slovene (0)	13	0.16
Swedish (0)	8	0.10
Welsh (0)	15	0.18
West Indian, ex. Hispanic (0)	87	1.05
Haitian (0)	68	0.82
Trinidadian/Tobagonian (0)	19	0.23

Hispanic Origin	Population	%
Hispanic or Latino (of any race)	884	11.19
Central American, ex. Mexican	14	0.18
Guatemalan	1	0.01
Honduran	2	0.03
Nicaraguan	3	0.04
Panamanian	4	0.05
Salvadoran	4	0.05
Cuban	8	0.10
Dominican Republic	11	0.14
Mexican	692	8.76
Puerto Rican	86	1.09
Other Hispanic or Latino	73	0.92

Race*	Population	%
African-American/Black (3,994)	4,252	53.80
Not Hispanic (3,933)	4,152	52.54
Hispanic (61)	100	1.27
American Indian/Alaska Native (48)	158	2.00
Not Hispanic (38)	129	1.63
Hispanic (10)	29	0.37
Blackfeet (1)	5	0.06
Canadian/French Am. Ind. (1)	3	0.04
Cherokee (10)	42	0.53
Chippewa (10)	17	0.22
Iroquois (0)	2	0.03
Mexican American Ind. (3)	6	0.08
Ottawa (0)	1	0.01
Seminole (0)	1	0.01
Asian (17)	47	0.59
Not Hispanic (17)	36	0.46
Hispanic (0)	11	0.14
Chinese, ex. Taiwanese (0)	12	0.15
Filipino (4)	26	0.33
Indian (9)	11	0.14
Japanese (1)	9	0.11
Laotian (0)	3	0.04
Vietnamese (1)	2	0.03
Hawaii Native/Pacific Islander (10)	25	0.32
Not Hispanic (2)	4	0.05
Hispanic (8)	21	0.27
Guamanian/Chamorro (1)	5	0.06
Native Hawaiian (7)	18	0.23
Tongan (1)	1	0.01
White (3,111)	3,430	43.40
Not Hispanic (2,751)	2,976	37.66
Hispanic (360)	454	5.74

Riverview

Place Type: City
County: Wayne
Population: 12,486†

Ancestry‡	Population	%
African, Sub-Saharan (37)	37	0.29
Nigerian (37)	37	0.29
Albanian (47)	47	0.37
American (546)	546	4.32
Arab (126)	148	1.17
Arab (19)	19	0.15
Lebanese (73)	95	0.75
Palestinian (34)	34	0.27
Armenian (0)	9	0.07
Austrian (9)	42	0.33
Belgian (18)	29	0.23
British (0)	12	0.09
Canadian (28)	49	0.39
Celtic (12)	24	0.19
Croatian (8)	88	0.70
Czech (20)	52	0.41
Czechoslovakian (28)	65	0.51
Danish (0)	46	0.36
Dutch (23)	222	1.76
Eastern European (41)	41	0.32
English (376)	1,289	10.20
European (128)	138	1.09
Finnish (17)	43	0.34
French, ex. Basque (178)	1,169	9.25
French Canadian (109)	257	2.03
German (556)	2,703	21.38
Greek (143)	166	1.31
Hungarian (119)	653	5.17
Irish (339)	1,950	15.43
Israeli (0)	38	0.30
Italian (404)	938	7.42
Lithuanian (11)	48	0.38
Maltese (34)	177	1.40

*Notes: † The Census 2010 population figure is used to calculate the percentages in the Hispanic Origin and Race categories. Ancestry percentages are based on the 2006-2010 American Community Survey population (not shown); ‡ Numbers in parentheses indicate the number of people reporting a single ancestry; * Numbers in parentheses indicate the number of persons reporting this race alone, not in combination with any other race; Please refer to the Explanation of Data for more information.*

Norwegian (35)	121	0.96
Polish (862)	1,815	14.36
Portuguese (0)	9	0.07
Romanian (7)	21	0.17
Russian (29)	124	0.98
Scotch-Irish (135)	261	2.06
Scottish (172)	462	3.66
Serbian (0)	24	0.19
Slavic (24)	24	0.19
Slovak (0)	63	0.50
Slovene (17)	17	0.13
Swedish (25)	40	0.32
Swiss (6)	48	0.38
Ukrainian (12)	25	0.20
Welsh (0)	113	0.89
West Indian, ex. Hispanic (29)	29	0.23
West Indian (29)	29	0.23
Yugoslavian (48)	85	0.67

Hispanic Origin	Population	%
Hispanic or Latino (of any race)	512	4.10
Central American, ex. Mexican	3	0.02
Guatemalan	1	0.01
Nicaraguan	1	0.01
Panamanian	1	0.01
Cuban	14	0.11
Dominican Republic	1	0.01
Mexican	381	3.05
Puerto Rican	48	0.38
South American	9	0.07
Chilean	4	0.03
Colombian	5	0.04
Other Hispanic or Latino	56	0.45

Race*	Population	%
African-American/Black (389)	443	3.55
Not Hispanic (380)	418	3.35
Hispanic (9)	25	0.20
American Indian/Alaska Native (56)	114	0.91
Not Hispanic (48)	90	0.72
Hispanic (8)	24	0.19
Blackfeet (4)	4	0.03
Cherokee (11)	21	0.17
Chippewa (14)	16	0.13
Choctaw (0)	1	0.01
Iroquois (1)	4	0.03
Lumbee (4)	5	0.04
Navajo (1)	1	0.01
Ottawa (0)	4	0.03
Sioux (2)	3	0.02
Asian (196)	234	1.87
Not Hispanic (192)	230	1.84
Hispanic (4)	4	0.03
Bangladeshi (2)	2	0.02
Chinese, ex. Taiwanese (13)	16	0.13
Filipino (66)	74	0.59
Indian (58)	63	0.50
Japanese (9)	16	0.13
Korean (18)	23	0.18
Laotian (1)	1	0.01
Pakistani (19)	24	0.19
Taiwanese (2)	4	0.03
Thai (4)	4	0.03
Vietnamese (1)	1	0.01
Hawaii Native/Pacific Islander (5)	14	0.11
Not Hispanic (5)	14	0.11
Guamanian/Chamorro (1)	1	0.01
Native Hawaiian (1)	5	0.04
Samoan (1)	1	0.01
White (11,613)	11,761	94.19
Not Hispanic (11,233)	11,341	90.83
Hispanic (380)	420	3.36

Rochester Hills

Place Type: City
County: Oakland
Population: 70,995†

Ancestry‡	Population	%
African, Sub-Saharan (146)	219	0.31
African (40)	68	0.10
Nigerian (12)	12	0.02
South African (0)	45	0.06
Zimbabwean (20)	20	0.03
Other Sub-Saharan African (74)	74	0.10
Albanian (821)	831	1.18
Alsatian (9)	9	0.01
American (2,436)	2,436	3.45
Arab (1,294)	1,483	2.10
Arab (248)	248	0.35
Egyptian (204)	213	0.30
Iraqi (280)	331	0.47
Jordanian (8)	8	0.01
Lebanese (259)	351	0.50
Syrian (134)	171	0.24
Other Arab (161)	161	0.23
Armenian (50)	86	0.12
Assyrian/Chaldean/Syriac (357)	500	0.71
Australian (9)	9	0.01
Austrian (89)	268	0.38
Belgian (131)	586	0.83
Brazilian (64)	75	0.11
British (213)	398	0.56
Bulgarian (12)	12	0.02
Canadian (362)	733	1.04
Celtic (11)	11	0.02
Croatian (18)	141	0.20
Czech (182)	497	0.70
Czechoslovakian (38)	107	0.15
Danish (100)	353	0.50
Dutch (294)	1,469	2.08
Eastern European (70)	83	0.12
English (1,857)	7,261	10.28
European (747)	806	1.14
Finnish (145)	550	0.78
French, ex. Basque (757)	3,842	5.44
French Canadian (420)	1,183	1.68
German (4,207)	15,757	22.32
Greek (356)	722	1.02
Hungarian (180)	738	1.05
Iranian (189)	206	0.29
Irish (1,714)	9,197	13.03
Italian (1,939)	5,615	7.95
Latvian (0)	21	0.03
Lithuanian (131)	350	0.50
Macedonian (136)	217	0.31
Maltese (52)	221	0.31
Northern European (51)	51	0.07
Norwegian (153)	647	0.92
Pennsylvania German (0)	7	0.01
Polish (2,749)	7,882	11.16
Portuguese (87)	128	0.18
Romanian (496)	642	0.91
Russian (212)	647	0.92
Scandinavian (39)	57	0.08
Scotch-Irish (475)	1,248	1.77
Scottish (699)	2,398	3.40
Serbian (240)	382	0.54
Slavic (0)	45	0.06
Slovak (168)	480	0.68
Slovene (11)	46	0.07
Swedish (237)	1,031	1.46
Swiss (59)	213	0.30
Turkish (0)	8	0.01
Ukrainian (459)	1,108	1.57
Welsh (114)	671	0.95
West Indian, ex. Hispanic (81)	173	0.25
Belizean (8)	8	0.01
Haitian (21)	60	0.08
Jamaican (44)	44	0.06
U.S. Virgin Islander (8)	8	0.01
West Indian (0)	53	0.08
Yugoslavian (22)	119	0.17

Hispanic Origin	Population	%
Hispanic or Latino (of any race)	2,183	3.07
Central American, ex. Mexican	92	0.13
Costa Rican	11	0.02
Guatemalan	36	0.05
Honduran	15	0.02
Nicaraguan	9	0.01
Panamanian	10	0.01
Salvadoran	11	0.02
Cuban	49	0.07
Dominican Republic	2	<0.01
Mexican	1,331	1.87
Puerto Rican	229	0.32
South American	319	0.45
Argentinean	132	0.19
Bolivian	4	0.01
Chilean	31	0.04
Colombian	60	0.08
Ecuadorian	9	0.01
Paraguayan	3	<0.01
Peruvian	25	0.04
Uruguayan	4	0.01
Venezuelan	46	0.06
Other South American	5	0.01
Other Hispanic or Latino	161	0.23

Race*	Population	%
African-American/Black (3,228)	3,606	5.08
Not Hispanic (3,177)	3,516	4.95
Hispanic (51)	90	0.13
American Indian/Alaska Native (132)	425	0.60
Not Hispanic (108)	371	0.52
Hispanic (24)	54	0.08
Apache (0)	4	0.01
Blackfeet (0)	7	0.01
Canadian/French Am. Ind. (1)	6	0.01
Central American Ind. (1)	1	<0.01
Cherokee (18)	103	0.15
Chickasaw (2)	5	0.01
Chippewa (30)	67	0.09
Choctaw (0)	4	0.01
Comanche (1)	1	<0.01
Cree (0)	4	0.01
Creek (0)	3	<0.01
Inupiat *(Alaska Native)* (2)	2	<0.01
Iroquois (3)	16	0.02
Lumbee (4)	7	0.01
Mexican American Ind. (9)	10	0.01
Navajo (0)	2	<0.01
Osage (1)	1	<0.01
Ottawa (1)	4	0.01
Potawatomi (3)	10	0.01
Seminole (1)	5	0.01
Sioux (0)	6	0.01
South American Ind. (1)	1	<0.01
Tsimshian *(Alaska Native)* (1)	1	<0.01
Asian (7,458)	8,144	11.47
Not Hispanic (7,447)	8,104	11.41
Hispanic (11)	40	0.06
Bangladeshi (74)	80	0.11
Burmese (4)	4	0.01
Cambodian (7)	12	0.02
Chinese, ex. Taiwanese (1,367)	1,487	2.09
Filipino (504)	655	0.92
Hmong (67)	70	0.10
Indian (3,337)	3,470	4.89
Indonesian (14)	17	0.02
Japanese (211)	299	0.42
Korean (847)	891	1.26
Laotian (6)	10	0.01
Malaysian (9)	18	0.03
Nepalese (15)	15	0.02
Pakistani (498)	522	0.74
Sri Lankan (36)	36	0.05
Taiwanese (124)	133	0.19
Thai (40)	50	0.07
Vietnamese (169)	208	0.29
Hawaii Native/Pacific Islander (9)	31	0.04
Not Hispanic (6)	27	0.04
Hispanic (3)	4	0.01
Guamanian/Chamorro (1)	1	<0.01
Native Hawaiian (8)	15	0.02
Samoan (0)	1	<0.01
White (58,309)	59,497	83.80

*Notes: † The Census 2010 population figure is used to calculate the percentages in the Hispanic Origin and Race categories. Ancestry percentages are based on the 2006-2010 American Community Survey population (not shown); ‡ Numbers in parentheses indicate the number of people reporting a single ancestry; * Numbers in parentheses indicate the number of persons reporting this race alone, not in combination with any other race; Please refer to the Explanation of Data for more information.*

Not Hispanic (56,818)	57,852	81.49
Hispanic (1,491)	1,645	2.32

Rochester

Place Type: City
County: Oakland
Population: 12,711†

Ancestry‡	Population	%
African, Sub-Saharan (42)	42	0.34
African (42)	42	0.34
Albanian (14)	14	0.11
American (312)	312	2.53
Arab (13)	88	0.71
Egyptian (0)	10	0.08
Lebanese (13)	78	0.63
Armenian (14)	41	0.33
Assyrian/Chaldean/Syriac (28)	60	0.49
Australian (0)	49	0.40
Austrian (27)	64	0.52
Belgian (34)	182	1.48
British (30)	66	0.54
Bulgarian (71)	71	0.58
Canadian (112)	181	1.47
Croatian (11)	20	0.16
Czech (23)	91	0.74
Danish (34)	66	0.54
Dutch (66)	294	2.39
English (376)	1,554	12.62
Estonian (16)	16	0.13
European (199)	212	1.72
Finnish (14)	105	0.85
French, ex. Basque (61)	523	4.25
French Canadian (121)	282	2.29
German (840)	2,908	23.62
Greek (48)	136	1.10
Hungarian (36)	151	1.23
Irish (357)	1,960	15.92
Italian (503)	1,586	12.88
Lithuanian (25)	126	1.02
Macedonian (77)	77	0.63
Norwegian (26)	141	1.15
Pennsylvania German (15)	60	0.49
Polish (489)	1,986	16.13
Romanian (45)	80	0.65
Russian (74)	169	1.37
Scandinavian (0)	13	0.11
Scotch-Irish (73)	303	2.46
Scottish (160)	502	4.08
Serbian (18)	36	0.29
Slavic (15)	42	0.34
Slovak (0)	20	0.16
Slovene (0)	14	0.11
Swedish (39)	284	2.31
Swiss (11)	25	0.20
Turkish (15)	15	0.12
Ukrainian (11)	106	0.86
Welsh (0)	40	0.32
Yugoslavian (23)	36	0.29

Hispanic Origin	Population	%
Hispanic or Latino (of any race)	342	2.69
Central American, ex. Mexican	18	0.14
Costa Rican	1	0.01
Guatemalan	9	0.07
Nicaraguan	3	0.02
Panamanian	1	0.01
Salvadoran	4	0.03
Cuban	12	0.09
Dominican Republic	1	0.01
Mexican	186	1.46
Puerto Rican	50	0.39
South American	42	0.33
Argentinean	14	0.11
Chilean	5	0.04
Colombian	10	0.08
Ecuadorian	4	0.03
Peruvian	4	0.03
Venezuelan	5	0.04
Other Hispanic or Latino	33	0.26

Race*	Population	%
African-American/Black (466)	519	4.08
Not Hispanic (458)	507	3.99
Hispanic (8)	12	0.09
American Indian/Alaska Native (26)	85	0.67
Not Hispanic (19)	66	0.52
Hispanic (7)	19	0.15
Apache (3)	5	0.04
Blackfeet (0)	8	0.06
Canadian/French Am. Ind. (1)	1	0.01
Cherokee (1)	13	0.10
Cheyenne (0)	6	0.05
Chippewa (0)	9	0.07
Choctaw (0)	1	0.01
Iroquois (2)	2	0.02
Navajo (1)	2	0.02
Ottawa (0)	1	0.01
Pueblo (0)	1	0.01
Seminole (0)	1	0.01
Sioux (1)	6	0.05
Asian (701)	775	6.10
Not Hispanic (700)	770	6.06
Hispanic (1)	5	0.04
Chinese, ex. Taiwanese (129)	144	1.13
Filipino (42)	55	0.43
Indian (286)	303	2.38
Indonesian (1)	1	0.01
Japanese (30)	41	0.32
Korean (156)	168	1.32
Malaysian (0)	2	0.02
Nepalese (4)	4	0.03
Pakistani (21)	25	0.20
Taiwanese (5)	5	0.04
Thai (3)	7	0.06
Vietnamese (12)	19	0.15
Hawaii Native/Pacific Islander (0)	5	0.04
Not Hispanic (0)	2	0.02
Hispanic (0)	3	0.02
Native Hawaiian (0)	4	0.03
White (11,262)	11,435	89.96
Not Hispanic (11,037)	11,181	87.96
Hispanic (225)	254	2.00

Romulus

Place Type: City
County: Wayne
Population: 23,989†

Ancestry‡	Population	%
African, Sub-Saharan (510)	588	2.46
African (370)	448	1.88
Liberian (47)	47	0.20
Nigerian (30)	30	0.13
Senegalese (50)	50	0.21
Sudanese (13)	13	0.05
American (628)	628	2.63
Arab (92)	101	0.42
Arab (40)	49	0.21
Iraqi (10)	10	0.04
Jordanian (42)	42	0.18
Armenian (0)	16	0.07
Assyrian/Chaldean/Syriac (0)	9	0.04
Austrian (0)	22	0.09
Belgian (0)	39	0.16
Brazilian (75)	75	0.31
British (17)	28	0.12
Canadian (115)	202	0.85
Croatian (10)	66	0.28
Czechoslovakian (0)	8	0.03
Dutch (0)	231	0.97
English (260)	1,056	4.42
European (23)	83	0.35
Finnish (0)	74	0.31
French, ex. Basque (108)	880	3.69
French Canadian (146)	388	1.63
German (866)	3,309	13.86
German Russian (0)	10	0.04
Greek (0)	55	0.23
Hungarian (127)	331	1.39
Irish (705)	2,574	10.78
Italian (360)	1,165	4.88
Lithuanian (21)	64	0.27
Maltese (59)	94	0.39
Norwegian (10)	54	0.23
Polish (819)	2,005	8.40
Romanian (5)	18	0.08
Russian (17)	272	1.14
Scandinavian (0)	11	0.05
Scotch-Irish (145)	403	1.69
Scottish (52)	345	1.45
Slavic (0)	26	0.11
Slovak (0)	12	0.05
Swedish (0)	90	0.38
Ukrainian (46)	86	0.36
Welsh (16)	135	0.57
West Indian, ex. Hispanic (36)	69	0.29
Bahamian (7)	7	0.03
Haitian (7)	7	0.03
Jamaican (22)	55	0.23
Yugoslavian (25)	25	0.10

Hispanic Origin	Population	%
Hispanic or Latino (of any race)	730	3.04
Central American, ex. Mexican	8	0.03
Guatemalan	2	0.01
Panamanian	2	0.01
Salvadoran	3	0.01
Other Central American	1	<0.01
Cuban	14	0.06
Dominican Republic	7	0.03
Mexican	487	2.03
Puerto Rican	113	0.47
South American	20	0.08
Argentinean	5	0.02
Colombian	3	0.01
Ecuadorian	3	0.01
Peruvian	2	0.01
Venezuelan	7	0.03
Other Hispanic or Latino	81	0.34

Race*	Population	%
African-American/Black (10,327)	10,980	45.77
Not Hispanic (10,251)	10,857	45.26
Hispanic (76)	123	0.51
American Indian/Alaska Native (124)	431	1.80
Not Hispanic (118)	404	1.68
Hispanic (6)	27	0.11
Apache (2)	5	0.02
Blackfeet (1)	25	0.10
Canadian/French Am. Ind. (1)	2	0.01
Cherokee (20)	123	0.51
Cheyenne (0)	1	<0.01
Chickasaw (2)	2	0.01
Chippewa (16)	24	0.10
Choctaw (1)	8	0.03
Cree (0)	2	0.01
Creek (3)	5	0.02
Crow (0)	1	<0.01
Delaware (0)	1	<0.01
Iroquois (5)	8	0.03
Lumbee (3)	5	0.02
Mexican American Ind. (0)	3	0.01
Navajo (0)	1	<0.01
Ottawa (6)	9	0.04
Seminole (0)	1	<0.01
Sioux (0)	3	0.01
Asian (259)	395	1.65
Not Hispanic (256)	378	1.58
Hispanic (3)	17	0.07
Cambodian (1)	1	<0.01
Chinese, ex. Taiwanese (32)	41	0.17
Filipino (61)	106	0.44
Hmong (0)	1	<0.01
Indian (54)	65	0.27
Indonesian (1)	2	0.01
Japanese (17)	53	0.22
Korean (12)	22	0.09

*Notes: † The Census 2010 population figure is used to calculate the percentages in the Hispanic Origin and Race categories. Ancestry percentages are based on the 2006-2010 American Community Survey population (not shown); ‡ Numbers in parentheses indicate the number of people reporting a single ancestry; * Numbers in parentheses indicate the number of persons reporting this race alone, not in combination with any other race; Please refer to the Explanation of Data for more information.*

Malaysian (0)	4	0.02
Pakistani (55)	60	0.25
Taiwanese (4)	4	0.02
Thai (2)	7	0.03
Vietnamese (6)	10	0.04
Hawaii Native/Pacific Islander (14)	43	0.18
Not Hispanic (12)	37	0.15
Hispanic (2)	6	0.03
Guamanian/Chamorro (1)	4	0.02
Native Hawaiian (9)	19	0.08
Samoan (1)	7	0.03
White (12,107)	12,896	53.76
Not Hispanic (11,752)	12,445	51.88
Hispanic (355)	451	1.88

Roseville

Place Type: City
County: Macomb
Population: 47,299†

Ancestry‡	Population	%
African, Sub-Saharan (211)	302	0.63
African (211)	302	0.63
Albanian (28)	28	0.06
American (3,017)	3,017	6.31
Arab (283)	671	1.40
Arab (35)	82	0.17
Egyptian (43)	43	0.09
Jordanian (12)	12	0.03
Lebanese (154)	440	0.92
Syrian (33)	77	0.16
Other Arab (6)	17	0.04
Armenian (0)	35	0.07
Assyrian/Chaldean/Syriac (9)	9	0.02
Austrian (25)	128	0.27
Belgian (321)	978	2.04
British (1)	31	0.06
Bulgarian (33)	50	0.10
Canadian (79)	168	0.35
Croatian (51)	176	0.37
Czech (3)	39	0.08
Czechoslovakian (25)	58	0.12
Danish (24)	114	0.24
Dutch (99)	490	1.02
Eastern European (0)	55	0.11
English (880)	4,003	8.37
European (497)	497	1.04
Finnish (87)	299	0.63
French, ex. Basque (379)	2,737	5.72
French Canadian (403)	1,389	2.90
German (3,089)	11,362	23.75
Greek (199)	441	0.92
Hungarian (107)	652	1.36
Icelander (10)	10	0.02
Irish (1,320)	6,538	13.67
Italian (2,765)	6,401	13.38
Lithuanian (0)	32	0.07
Macedonian (13)	23	0.05
Maltese (37)	120	0.25
Northern European (0)	14	0.03
Norwegian (50)	243	0.51
Pennsylvania German (24)	51	0.11
Polish (3,195)	8,671	18.13
Portuguese (0)	27	0.06
Romanian (76)	209	0.44
Russian (88)	493	1.03
Scandinavian (0)	9	0.02
Scotch-Irish (250)	921	1.93
Scottish (283)	1,254	2.62
Serbian (39)	94	0.20
Slavic (11)	11	0.02
Slovak (0)	106	0.22
Slovene (0)	10	0.02
Swedish (82)	413	0.86
Swiss (0)	33	0.07
Ukrainian (89)	262	0.55
Welsh (34)	272	0.57
Yugoslavian (61)	145	0.30

Hispanic Origin	Population	%
Hispanic or Latino (of any race)	951	2.01
Central American, ex. Mexican	30	0.06
Costa Rican	2	<0.01
Guatemalan	16	0.03
Honduran	9	0.02
Nicaraguan	1	<0.01
Panamanian	1	<0.01
Salvadoran	1	<0.01
Cuban	43	0.09
Dominican Republic	5	0.01
Mexican	622	1.32
Puerto Rican	120	0.25
South American	31	0.07
Argentinean	3	0.01
Bolivian	1	<0.01
Colombian	9	0.02
Ecuadorian	9	0.02
Peruvian	4	0.01
Uruguayan	1	<0.01
Venezuelan	1	<0.01
Other South American	3	0.01
Other Hispanic or Latino	100	0.21

Race*	Population	%
African-American/Black (5,583)	6,248	13.21
Not Hispanic (5,551)	6,165	13.03
Hispanic (32)	83	0.18
American Indian/Alaska Native (201)	688	1.45
Not Hispanic (177)	611	1.29
Hispanic (24)	77	0.16
Aleut *(Alaska Native)* (1)	1	<0.01
Apache (4)	8	0.02
Arapaho (0)	3	0.01
Blackfeet (1)	33	0.07
Canadian/French Am. Ind. (3)	7	0.01
Cherokee (22)	160	0.34
Cheyenne (0)	5	0.01
Chippewa (42)	108	0.23
Choctaw (1)	7	0.01
Comanche (3)	3	0.01
Cree (0)	6	0.01
Creek (1)	2	<0.01
Crow (0)	1	<0.01
Iroquois (13)	25	0.05
Lumbee (8)	20	0.04
Mexican American Ind. (5)	5	0.01
Navajo (1)	7	0.01
Ottawa (1)	9	0.02
Potawatomi (1)	6	0.01
Pueblo (5)	5	0.01
Seminole (0)	2	<0.01
Sioux (3)	6	0.01
South American Ind. (3)	3	0.01
Asian (758)	952	2.01
Not Hispanic (755)	941	1.99
Hispanic (3)	11	0.02
Bangladeshi (2)	2	<0.01
Cambodian (21)	27	0.06
Chinese, ex. Taiwanese (87)	112	0.24
Filipino (131)	187	0.40
Hmong (107)	108	0.23
Indian (217)	234	0.49
Indonesian (2)	10	0.02
Japanese (13)	39	0.08
Korean (27)	55	0.12
Laotian (21)	22	0.05
Malaysian (0)	2	<0.01
Pakistani (30)	41	0.09
Thai (16)	17	0.04
Vietnamese (52)	61	0.13
Hawaii Native/Pacific Islander (5)	44	0.09
Not Hispanic (5)	41	0.09
Hispanic (0)	3	0.01
Guamanian/Chamorro (0)	9	0.02
Native Hawaiian (3)	15	0.03
Samoan (1)	3	0.01
White (39,311)	40,440	85.50
Not Hispanic (38,686)	39,713	83.96
Hispanic (625)	727	1.54

Royal Oak

Place Type: City
County: Oakland
Population: 57,236†

Ancestry‡	Population	%
African, Sub-Saharan (33)	58	0.10
African (20)	45	0.08
Ethiopian (13)	13	0.02
Albanian (238)	238	0.41
American (2,007)	2,007	3.48
Arab (477)	910	1.58
Arab (42)	94	0.16
Egyptian (0)	17	0.03
Iraqi (124)	181	0.31
Jordanian (16)	16	0.03
Lebanese (162)	411	0.71
Syrian (10)	68	0.12
Other Arab (123)	123	0.21
Armenian (139)	351	0.61
Assyrian/Chaldean/Syriac (59)	116	0.20
Australian (0)	19	0.03
Austrian (98)	466	0.81
Belgian (122)	424	0.73
Brazilian (12)	26	0.05
British (206)	445	0.77
Bulgarian (0)	22	0.04
Canadian (269)	559	0.97
Carpatho Rusyn (7)	39	0.07
Celtic (0)	13	0.02
Croatian (66)	154	0.27
Cypriot (10)	10	0.02
Czech (92)	449	0.78
Czechoslovakian (54)	103	0.18
Danish (60)	247	0.43
Dutch (260)	1,581	2.74
Eastern European (160)	181	0.31
English (2,238)	8,727	15.11
European (802)	865	1.50
Finnish (277)	747	1.29
French, ex. Basque (277)	2,993	5.18
French Canadian (411)	1,318	2.28
German (3,817)	14,457	25.04
Greek (341)	654	1.13
Guyanese (20)	20	0.03
Hungarian (223)	882	1.53
Iranian (18)	18	0.03
Irish (2,282)	9,767	16.92
Italian (1,353)	4,293	7.43
Latvian (34)	51	0.09
Lithuanian (84)	353	0.61
Luxemburger (0)	16	0.03
Macedonian (0)	43	0.07
Maltese (59)	88	0.15
New Zealander (43)	43	0.07
Northern European (123)	123	0.21
Norwegian (129)	596	1.03
Pennsylvania German (0)	10	0.02
Polish (2,827)	7,841	13.58
Portuguese (46)	46	0.08
Romanian (44)	310	0.54
Russian (414)	1,263	2.19
Scandinavian (28)	80	0.14
Scotch-Irish (468)	1,472	2.55
Scottish (735)	2,460	4.26
Serbian (98)	264	0.46
Slavic (13)	59	0.10
Slovak (79)	191	0.33
Slovene (57)	110	0.19
Swedish (231)	1,302	2.25
Swiss (38)	228	0.39
Turkish (41)	41	0.07
Ukrainian (95)	603	1.04
Welsh (124)	492	0.85
West Indian, ex. Hispanic (11)	88	0.15
Bahamian (11)	11	0.02
Barbadian (0)	64	0.11
Jamaican (0)	7	0.01

SECTION TWO

*Notes: † The Census 2010 population figure is used to calculate the percentages in the Hispanic Origin and Race categories. Ancestry percentages are based on the 2006-2010 American Community Survey population (not shown); ‡ Numbers in parentheses indicate the number of people reporting a single ancestry; * Numbers in parentheses indicate the number of persons reporting this race alone, not in combination with any other race; Please refer to the Explanation of Data for more information.*

Ancestry	Population	%
Trinidadian/Tobagonian (0)	6	0.01
Yugoslavian (21)	44	0.08

Hispanic Origin	Population	%
Hispanic or Latino (of any race)	1,340	2.34
Central American, ex. Mexican	66	0.12
Costa Rican	4	0.01
Guatemalan	17	0.03
Honduran	12	0.02
Nicaraguan	9	0.02
Panamanian	8	0.01
Salvadoran	15	0.03
Other Central American	1	<0.01
Cuban	68	0.12
Dominican Republic	11	0.02
Mexican	741	1.29
Puerto Rican	111	0.19
South American	168	0.29
Argentinean	33	0.06
Bolivian	3	0.01
Chilean	14	0.02
Colombian	49	0.09
Ecuadorian	21	0.04
Paraguayan	1	<0.01
Peruvian	20	0.03
Uruguayan	3	0.01
Venezuelan	24	0.04
Other Hispanic or Latino	175	0.31

Race*	Population	%
African-American/Black (2,435)	2,866	5.01
Not Hispanic (2,399)	2,795	4.88
Hispanic (36)	71	0.12
American Indian/Alaska Native (153)	453	0.79
Not Hispanic (127)	403	0.70
Hispanic (26)	50	0.09
Apache (4)	11	0.02
Blackfeet (6)	24	0.04
Canadian/French Am. Ind. (2)	10	0.02
Central American Ind. (1)	1	<0.01
Cherokee (21)	75	0.13
Cheyenne (0)	1	<0.01
Chickasaw (0)	1	<0.01
Chippewa (41)	84	0.15
Choctaw (2)	8	0.01
Creek (2)	4	0.01
Delaware (0)	1	<0.01
Hopi (1)	1	<0.01
Iroquois (15)	20	0.03
Lumbee (5)	11	0.02
Mexican American Ind. (2)	6	0.01
Navajo (1)	1	<0.01
Osage (0)	2	<0.01
Ottawa (4)	23	0.04
Potawatomi (2)	5	0.01
Pueblo (1)	1	<0.01
Seminole (0)	3	0.01
Sioux (3)	8	0.01
Spanish American Ind. (1)	1	<0.01
Tlingit-Haida *(Alaska Native)* (1)	1	<0.01
Asian (1,359)	1,759	3.07
Not Hispanic (1,339)	1,719	3.00
Hispanic (20)	40	0.07
Bangladeshi (7)	7	0.01
Burmese (2)	2	<0.01
Cambodian (10)	17	0.03
Chinese, ex. Taiwanese (286)	354	0.62
Filipino (258)	378	0.66
Hmong (4)	6	0.01
Indian (382)	442	0.77
Indonesian (3)	10	0.02
Japanese (60)	128	0.22
Korean (161)	219	0.38
Laotian (3)	8	0.01
Malaysian (2)	5	0.01
Nepalese (11)	11	0.02
Pakistani (28)	36	0.06
Sri Lankan (5)	5	0.01
Taiwanese (8)	12	0.02
Thai (17)	23	0.04
Vietnamese (57)	77	0.13
Hawaii Native/Pacific Islander (23)	62	0.11
Not Hispanic (22)	56	0.10
Hispanic (1)	6	0.01
Guamanian/Chamorro (11)	12	0.02
Native Hawaiian (1)	19	0.03
Samoan (3)	10	0.02
White (51,941)	52,915	92.45
Not Hispanic (50,975)	51,861	90.61
Hispanic (966)	1,054	1.84

Saginaw

Place Type: Charter Township
County: Saginaw
Population: 40,840†

Ancestry‡	Population	%
African, Sub-Saharan (67)	119	0.29
African (40)	92	0.23
South African (16)	16	0.04
Zimbabwean (11)	11	0.03
American (1,305)	1,305	3.21
Arab (302)	372	0.91
Arab (65)	65	0.16
Lebanese (144)	194	0.48
Palestinian (70)	70	0.17
Other Arab (23)	43	0.11
Armenian (14)	29	0.07
Assyrian/Chaldean/Syriac (56)	56	0.14
Austrian (9)	125	0.31
Belgian (88)	198	0.49
British (96)	183	0.45
Bulgarian (0)	16	0.04
Canadian (61)	94	0.23
Croatian (0)	9	0.02
Czech (82)	292	0.72
Czechoslovakian (71)	237	0.58
Danish (0)	182	0.45
Dutch (151)	815	2.00
English (1,291)	4,283	10.53
European (262)	262	0.64
Finnish (62)	141	0.35
French, ex. Basque (410)	3,056	7.51
French Canadian (281)	784	1.93
German (5,097)	13,906	34.17
Greek (164)	260	0.64
Hungarian (153)	483	1.19
Icelander (0)	11	0.03
Iranian (66)	66	0.16
Irish (1,218)	4,875	11.98
Italian (653)	1,783	4.38
Latvian (92)	92	0.23
Lithuanian (74)	301	0.74
Macedonian (0)	16	0.04
Maltese (11)	11	0.03
Norwegian (77)	321	0.79
Pennsylvania German (0)	13	0.03
Polish (1,409)	4,530	11.13
Portuguese (10)	10	0.02
Romanian (28)	79	0.19
Russian (40)	292	0.72
Scotch-Irish (147)	500	1.23
Scottish (318)	1,154	2.84
Serbian (0)	22	0.05
Slavic (0)	9	0.02
Slovak (23)	141	0.35
Swedish (102)	613	1.51
Swiss (34)	123	0.30
Turkish (23)	23	0.06
Ukrainian (41)	125	0.31
Welsh (46)	217	0.53
West Indian, ex. Hispanic (55)	55	0.14
Barbadian (31)	31	0.08
Trinidadian/Tobagonian (24)	24	0.06

Hispanic Origin	Population	%
Hispanic or Latino (of any race)	2,608	6.39
Central American, ex. Mexican	43	0.11
Costa Rican	4	0.01
Guatemalan	15	0.04
Honduran	4	0.01
Nicaraguan	5	0.01
Panamanian	6	0.01
Salvadoran	9	0.02
Cuban	20	0.05
Dominican Republic	2	<0.01
Mexican	2,235	5.47
Puerto Rican	79	0.19
South American	57	0.14
Argentinean	3	0.01
Bolivian	9	0.02
Chilean	4	0.01
Colombian	17	0.04
Ecuadorian	2	<0.01
Peruvian	12	0.03
Uruguayan	5	0.01
Venezuelan	5	0.01
Other Hispanic or Latino	172	0.42

Race*	Population	%
African-American/Black (3,586)	3,998	9.79
Not Hispanic (3,501)	3,832	9.38
Hispanic (85)	166	0.41
American Indian/Alaska Native (114)	302	0.74
Not Hispanic (77)	243	0.60
Hispanic (37)	59	0.14
Blackfeet (0)	1	<0.01
Canadian/French Am. Ind. (0)	5	0.01
Cherokee (4)	44	0.11
Chickasaw (0)	1	<0.01
Chippewa (38)	85	0.21
Choctaw (0)	3	0.01
Crow (1)	1	<0.01
Delaware (0)	1	<0.01
Iroquois (3)	6	0.01
Lumbee (3)	5	0.01
Mexican American Ind. (6)	8	0.02
Navajo (2)	2	<0.01
Ottawa (5)	12	0.03
Paiute (1)	1	<0.01
Potawatomi (8)	8	0.02
Seminole (0)	2	<0.01
Sioux (0)	1	<0.01
Yaqui (0)	1	<0.01
Asian (1,389)	1,570	3.84
Not Hispanic (1,385)	1,557	3.81
Hispanic (4)	13	0.03
Bangladeshi (17)	17	0.04
Cambodian (1)	1	<0.01
Chinese, ex. Taiwanese (201)	226	0.55
Filipino (148)	180	0.44
Hmong (6)	6	0.01
Indian (601)	633	1.55
Indonesian (5)	6	0.01
Japanese (9)	19	0.05
Korean (120)	143	0.35
Laotian (2)	5	0.01
Malaysian (0)	3	0.01
Nepalese (5)	6	0.01
Pakistani (136)	142	0.35
Sri Lankan (6)	6	0.01
Taiwanese (11)	12	0.03
Thai (17)	25	0.06
Vietnamese (69)	74	0.18
Hawaii Native/Pacific Islander (31)	57	0.14
Not Hispanic (29)	54	0.13
Hispanic (2)	3	0.01
Guamanian/Chamorro (3)	5	0.01
Marshallese (1)	1	<0.01
Native Hawaiian (8)	11	0.03
Samoan (2)	3	0.01
White (34,215)	35,012	85.73
Not Hispanic (32,534)	33,125	81.11
Hispanic (1,681)	1,887	4.62

*Notes: † The Census 2010 population figure is used to calculate the percentages in the Hispanic Origin and Race categories. Ancestry percentages are based on the 2006-2010 American Community Survey population (not shown); ‡ Numbers in parentheses indicate the number of people reporting a single ancestry; * Numbers in parentheses indicate the number of persons reporting this race alone, not in combination with any other race; Please refer to the Explanation of Data for more information.*

Saginaw

Place Type: City
County: Saginaw
Population: 51,508†

Ancestry‡	Population	%
African, Sub-Saharan (164)	164	0.31
African (151)	151	0.28
Liberian (13)	13	0.02
American (1,372)	1,372	2.57
Arab (46)	109	0.20
Moroccan (12)	12	0.02
Other Arab (34)	97	0.18
Armenian (0)	22	0.04
Assyrian/Chaldean/Syriac (21)	21	0.04
Austrian (24)	106	0.20
Belgian (16)	64	0.12
British (31)	124	0.23
Cajun (0)	7	0.01
Canadian (52)	114	0.21
Czech (9)	139	0.26
Czechoslovakian (7)	98	0.18
Danish (11)	51	0.10
Dutch (43)	483	0.90
Eastern European (9)	9	0.02
English (713)	2,717	5.08
European (215)	290	0.54
Finnish (25)	51	0.10
French, ex. Basque (233)	2,179	4.08
French Canadian (320)	945	1.77
German (3,172)	8,373	15.66
Greek (41)	51	0.10
Hungarian (34)	297	0.56
Irish (648)	3,068	5.74
Italian (473)	926	1.73
Latvian (19)	35	0.07
Lithuanian (33)	90	0.17
Norwegian (13)	242	0.45
Pennsylvania German (2)	2	<0.01
Polish (860)	2,887	5.40
Romanian (0)	40	0.07
Russian (72)	327	0.61
Scotch-Irish (56)	446	0.83
Scottish (188)	711	1.33
Slovak (0)	87	0.16
Slovene (0)	7	0.01
Swedish (21)	125	0.23
Swiss (0)	69	0.13
Turkish (0)	6	0.01
Ukrainian (0)	44	0.08
Welsh (9)	102	0.19
West Indian, ex. Hispanic (71)	117	0.22
British West Indian (16)	16	0.03
Haitian (4)	4	0.01
Jamaican (2)	48	0.09
Trinidadian/Tobagonian (39)	39	0.07
West Indian (10)	10	0.02
Yugoslavian (16)	16	0.03

Hispanic Origin	Population	%
Hispanic or Latino (of any race)	7,344	14.26
Central American, ex. Mexican	47	0.09
Costa Rican	1	<0.01
Guatemalan	17	0.03
Honduran	9	0.02
Nicaraguan	2	<0.01
Panamanian	10	0.02
Salvadoran	8	0.02
Cuban	35	0.07
Dominican Republic	3	0.01
Mexican	6,487	12.59
Puerto Rican	162	0.31
South American	29	0.06
Argentinean	7	0.01
Bolivian	3	0.01
Chilean	4	0.01
Colombian	11	0.02
Peruvian	1	<0.01
Uruguayan	2	<0.01
Venezuelan	1	<0.01
Other Hispanic or Latino	581	1.13

Race*	Population	%
African-American/Black (23,721)	25,266	49.05
Not Hispanic (23,127)	24,231	47.04
Hispanic (594)	1,035	2.01
American Indian/Alaska Native (268)	657	1.28
Not Hispanic (180)	490	0.95
Hispanic (88)	167	0.32
Apache (3)	4	0.01
Blackfeet (5)	21	0.04
Canadian/French Am. Ind. (2)	5	0.01
Cherokee (6)	73	0.14
Cheyenne (1)	1	<0.01
Chippewa (46)	102	0.20
Choctaw (1)	5	0.01
Comanche (3)	3	0.01
Cree (0)	3	0.01
Iroquois (2)	11	0.02
Lumbee (4)	4	0.01
Mexican American Ind. (11)	14	0.03
Ottawa (2)	6	0.01
Potawatomi (8)	12	0.02
Seminole (1)	5	0.01
Sioux (2)	5	0.01
Spanish American Ind. (1)	3	0.01
Ute (2)	2	<0.01
Yuman (1)	3	0.01
Asian (165)	298	0.58
Not Hispanic (145)	244	0.47
Hispanic (20)	54	0.10
Chinese, ex. Taiwanese (28)	48	0.09
Filipino (29)	72	0.14
Hmong (31)	35	0.07
Indian (21)	36	0.07
Japanese (14)	27	0.05
Korean (30)	42	0.08
Laotian (1)	5	0.01
Malaysian (0)	1	<0.01
Pakistani (2)	3	0.01
Taiwanese (3)	3	0.01
Thai (1)	2	<0.01
Vietnamese (3)	7	0.01
Hawaii Native/Pacific Islander (15)	56	0.11
Not Hispanic (10)	31	0.06
Hispanic (5)	25	0.05
Fijian (3)	3	0.01
Guamanian/Chamorro (8)	17	0.03
Marshallese (0)	1	<0.01
Native Hawaiian (2)	10	0.02
Samoan (0)	1	<0.01
White (22,401)	24,229	47.04
Not Hispanic (19,310)	20,468	39.74
Hispanic (3,091)	3,761	7.30

Saline

Place Type: City
County: Washtenaw
Population: 8,810†

Ancestry‡	Population	%
American (478)	478	5.47
Arab (19)	36	0.41
Arab (19)	19	0.22
Syrian (0)	17	0.19
Belgian (54)	86	0.98
British (7)	19	0.22
Canadian (18)	72	0.82
Croatian (12)	47	0.54
Czech (10)	107	1.22
Danish (0)	41	0.47
Dutch (85)	392	4.48
English (430)	1,532	17.52
European (227)	257	2.94
Finnish (9)	59	0.67
French, ex. Basque (16)	392	4.48
French Canadian (18)	144	1.65
German (962)	2,721	31.12
Greek (39)	39	0.45
Hungarian (48)	68	0.78
Irish (137)	1,303	14.90
Italian (113)	354	4.05
Lithuanian (13)	42	0.48
Northern European (14)	14	0.16
Norwegian (54)	219	2.50
Polish (248)	776	8.87
Portuguese (8)	31	0.35
Romanian (16)	16	0.18
Russian (7)	55	0.63
Scandinavian (9)	20	0.23
Scotch-Irish (60)	157	1.80
Scottish (118)	505	5.78
Serbian (13)	25	0.29
Slavic (0)	11	0.13
Slovak (13)	13	0.15
Swedish (46)	141	1.61
Swiss (0)	8	0.09
Ukrainian (91)	105	1.20
Welsh (36)	81	0.93

Hispanic Origin	Population	%
Hispanic or Latino (of any race)	225	2.55
Central American, ex. Mexican	14	0.16
Costa Rican	2	0.02
Guatemalan	7	0.08
Honduran	2	0.02
Nicaraguan	2	0.02
Panamanian	1	0.01
Cuban	14	0.16
Mexican	143	1.62
Puerto Rican	15	0.17
South American	25	0.28
Bolivian	3	0.03
Chilean	3	0.03
Colombian	13	0.15
Peruvian	2	0.02
Venezuelan	4	0.05
Other Hispanic or Latino	14	0.16

Race*	Population	%
African-American/Black (121)	177	2.01
Not Hispanic (119)	170	1.93
Hispanic (2)	7	0.08
American Indian/Alaska Native (20)	67	0.76
Not Hispanic (19)	54	0.61
Hispanic (1)	13	0.15
Blackfeet (0)	2	0.02
Cherokee (6)	21	0.24
Chippewa (1)	7	0.08
Choctaw (0)	2	0.02
Crow (0)	2	0.02
Iroquois (0)	1	0.01
Lumbee (0)	1	0.01
Menominee (1)	1	0.01
Mexican American Ind. (0)	9	0.10
Osage (3)	3	0.03
Seminole (3)	3	0.03
Ute (0)	5	0.06
Asian (218)	270	3.06
Not Hispanic (215)	262	2.97
Hispanic (3)	8	0.09
Chinese, ex. Taiwanese (36)	51	0.58
Filipino (32)	40	0.45
Indian (70)	73	0.83
Indonesian (2)	2	0.02
Japanese (9)	28	0.32
Korean (32)	38	0.43
Pakistani (3)	3	0.03
Sri Lankan (6)	6	0.07
Taiwanese (3)	3	0.03
Thai (2)	2	0.02
Vietnamese (15)	16	0.18
Hawaii Native/Pacific Islander (4)	5	0.06
Not Hispanic (4)	5	0.06
Fijian (1)	1	0.01
Native Hawaiian (2)	2	0.02
White (8,249)	8,403	95.38
Not Hispanic (8,083)	8,207	93.16

*Notes: † The Census 2010 population figure is used to calculate the percentages in the Hispanic Origin and Race categories. Ancestry percentages are based on the 2006-2010 American Community Survey population (not shown); ‡ Numbers in parentheses indicate the number of people reporting a single ancestry; * Numbers in parentheses indicate the number of persons reporting this race alone, not in combination with any other race; Please refer to the Explanation of Data for more information.*

Hispanic (166)	196	2.22

Sault Ste. Marie

Place Type: City
County: Chippewa
Population: 14,144†

Ancestry‡	Population	%
African, Sub-Saharan (0)	32	0.22
African (0)	32	0.22
American (433)	433	3.01
Arab (63)	96	0.67
Lebanese (63)	96	0.67
Austrian (6)	34	0.24
Belgian (80)	96	0.67
British (41)	56	0.39
Canadian (35)	139	0.97
Croatian (0)	22	0.15
Czech (21)	84	0.58
Czechoslovakian (15)	19	0.13
Danish (0)	23	0.16
Dutch (112)	412	2.86
English (405)	2,007	13.95
European (9)	9	0.06
Finnish (159)	618	4.30
French, ex. Basque (242)	1,348	9.37
French Canadian (113)	239	1.66
German (986)	3,177	22.09
Greek (0)	113	0.79
Hungarian (0)	32	0.22
Irish (358)	2,115	14.71
Italian (290)	1,021	7.10
Lithuanian (20)	32	0.22
Luxemburger (8)	8	0.06
Northern European (32)	32	0.22
Norwegian (21)	96	0.67
Pennsylvania German (0)	42	0.29
Polish (363)	1,001	6.96
Romanian (0)	11	0.08
Russian (7)	79	0.55
Scandinavian (7)	7	0.05
Scotch-Irish (134)	428	2.98
Scottish (82)	569	3.96
Slovak (12)	24	0.17
Swedish (55)	304	2.11
Swiss (0)	9	0.06
Ukrainian (42)	63	0.44
Welsh (17)	52	0.36
Yugoslavian (9)	9	0.06

Hispanic Origin	Population	%
Hispanic or Latino (of any race)	217	1.53
Central American, ex. Mexican	5	0.04
Nicaraguan	3	0.02
Panamanian	2	0.01
Cuban	12	0.08
Mexican	134	0.95
Puerto Rican	39	0.28
South American	1	0.01
Paraguayan	1	0.01
Other Hispanic or Latino	26	0.18

Race*	Population	%
African-American/Black (99)	179	1.27
Not Hispanic (99)	177	1.25
Hispanic (0)	2	0.01
American Indian/Alaska Native (2,506)	3,167	22.39
Not Hispanic (2,482)	3,137	22.18
Hispanic (24)	30	0.21
Blackfeet (0)	6	0.04
Canadian/French Am. Ind. (30)	40	0.28
Cherokee (14)	33	0.23
Chickasaw (0)	1	0.01
Chippewa (2,076)	2,558	18.09
Choctaw (0)	3	0.02
Comanche (0)	1	0.01
Delaware (0)	2	0.01
Inupiat *(Alaska Native)* (0)	1	0.01
Iroquois (4)	6	0.04
Navajo (2)	3	0.02
Ottawa (19)	27	0.19
Potawatomi (21)	22	0.16
Seminole (3)	4	0.03
Sioux (4)	9	0.06
Tlingit-Haida *(Alaska Native)* (1)	1	0.01
Yup'ik *(Alaska Native)* (4)	6	0.04
Asian (130)	207	1.46
Not Hispanic (129)	201	1.42
Hispanic (1)	6	0.04
Bangladeshi (6)	6	0.04
Burmese (34)	34	0.24
Chinese, ex. Taiwanese (14)	14	0.10
Filipino (16)	32	0.23
Hmong (5)	5	0.04
Indian (12)	26	0.18
Japanese (3)	14	0.10
Korean (12)	16	0.11
Nepalese (4)	4	0.03
Pakistani (7)	7	0.05
Sri Lankan (0)	3	0.02
Thai (4)	4	0.03
Vietnamese (10)	11	0.08
Hawaii Native/Pacific Islander (13)	29	0.21
Not Hispanic (10)	20	0.14
Hispanic (3)	9	0.06
Guamanian/Chamorro (4)	6	0.04
Native Hawaiian (3)	6	0.04
White (10,576)	11,322	80.05
Not Hispanic (10,435)	11,167	78.95
Hispanic (141)	155	1.10

Schoolcraft

Place Type: Township
County: Kalamazoo
Population: 8,214†

Ancestry‡	Population	%
African, Sub-Saharan (17)	17	0.21
Other Sub-Saharan African (17)	17	0.21
American (642)	642	8.00
Austrian (0)	16	0.20
Belgian (0)	21	0.26
British (4)	7	0.09
Canadian (2)	26	0.32
Croatian (32)	37	0.46
Czech (10)	79	0.98
Czechoslovakian (11)	14	0.17
Danish (9)	41	0.51
Dutch (450)	1,299	16.18
English (477)	1,351	16.83
European (8)	8	0.10
Finnish (0)	16	0.20
French, ex. Basque (35)	398	4.96
French Canadian (24)	70	0.87
German (698)	2,402	29.92
Hungarian (3)	14	0.17
Irish (298)	1,270	15.82
Italian (68)	158	1.97
Northern European (3)	3	0.04
Norwegian (14)	47	0.59
Pennsylvania German (24)	48	0.60
Polish (106)	494	6.15
Portuguese (0)	8	0.10
Romanian (31)	31	0.39
Russian (30)	101	1.26
Scotch-Irish (120)	222	2.76
Scottish (62)	240	2.99
Serbian (0)	8	0.10
Slavic (0)	10	0.12
Slovak (0)	3	0.04
Swedish (6)	156	1.94
Swiss (0)	14	0.17
Turkish (12)	24	0.30
Ukrainian (11)	11	0.14
Welsh (4)	60	0.75
Yugoslavian (74)	74	0.92

Hispanic Origin	Population	%
Hispanic or Latino (of any race)	178	2.17
Central American, ex. Mexican	5	0.06
Costa Rican	2	0.02
Guatemalan	1	0.01
Salvadoran	2	0.02
Cuban	7	0.09
Dominican Republic	1	0.01
Mexican	131	1.59
Puerto Rican	11	0.13
South American	5	0.06
Argentinean	1	0.01
Bolivian	1	0.01
Chilean	1	0.01
Ecuadorian	1	0.01
Peruvian	1	0.01
Other Hispanic or Latino	18	0.22

Race*	Population	%
African-American/Black (59)	128	1.56
Not Hispanic (55)	112	1.36
Hispanic (4)	16	0.19
American Indian/Alaska Native (38)	104	1.27
Not Hispanic (34)	97	1.18
Hispanic (4)	7	0.09
Blackfeet (0)	5	0.06
Cherokee (6)	9	0.11
Chippewa (7)	15	0.18
Choctaw (0)	1	0.01
Creek (1)	1	0.01
Mexican American Ind. (0)	2	0.02
Navajo (1)	1	0.01
Ottawa (1)	2	0.02
Potawatomi (3)	13	0.16
Pueblo (3)	3	0.04
Sioux (2)	5	0.06
Tohono O'Odham (1)	1	0.01
Asian (45)	70	0.85
Not Hispanic (44)	66	0.80
Hispanic (1)	4	0.05
Chinese, ex. Taiwanese (6)	9	0.11
Filipino (9)	14	0.17
Indian (4)	11	0.13
Japanese (2)	9	0.11
Korean (11)	12	0.15
Laotian (4)	4	0.05
Pakistani (3)	3	0.04
Vietnamese (6)	7	0.09
Hawaii Native/Pacific Islander (0)	2	0.02
Hispanic (0)	2	0.02
White (7,873)	8,019	97.63
Not Hispanic (7,777)	7,895	96.12
Hispanic (96)	124	1.51

Scio

Place Type: Township
County: Washtenaw
Population: 20,081†

Ancestry‡	Population	%
African, Sub-Saharan (73)	82	0.42
African (35)	44	0.23
Ethiopian (38)	38	0.20
Albanian (10)	10	0.05
American (892)	892	4.58
Arab (117)	193	0.99
Iraqi (45)	45	0.23
Lebanese (13)	32	0.16
Palestinian (46)	46	0.24
Syrian (0)	30	0.15
Other Arab (13)	40	0.21
Armenian (0)	42	0.22
Australian (10)	20	0.10
Austrian (35)	53	0.27
Belgian (18)	72	0.37
British (132)	185	0.95
Canadian (116)	146	0.75
Croatian (0)	28	0.14
Czech (9)	129	0.66

*Notes: † The Census 2010 population figure is used to calculate the percentages in the Hispanic Origin and Race categories. Ancestry percentages are based on the 2006-2010 American Community Survey population (not shown); ‡ Numbers in parentheses indicate the number of people reporting a single ancestry; * Numbers in parentheses indicate the number of persons reporting this race alone, not in combination with any other race; Please refer to the Explanation of Data for more information.*

Czechoslovakian (0)	45	0.23
Danish (41)	246	1.26
Dutch (195)	750	3.85
Eastern European (79)	107	0.55
English (743)	2,817	14.47
European (290)	290	1.49
Finnish (44)	214	1.10
French, ex. Basque (122)	891	4.58
French Canadian (44)	235	1.21
German (1,339)	5,410	27.80
Greek (171)	235	1.21
Guyanese (0)	23	0.12
Hungarian (29)	151	0.78
Iranian (9)	9	0.05
Irish (573)	2,985	15.34
Israeli (39)	39	0.20
Italian (277)	871	4.48
Latvian (74)	87	0.45
Lithuanian (26)	94	0.48
Luxemburger (0)	11	0.06
Maltese (7)	21	0.11
Northern European (21)	31	0.16
Norwegian (70)	295	1.52
Polish (298)	1,359	6.98
Portuguese (0)	34	0.17
Romanian (8)	37	0.19
Russian (126)	345	1.77
Scandinavian (35)	42	0.22
Scotch-Irish (134)	617	3.17
Scottish (114)	734	3.77
Serbian (23)	48	0.25
Slovak (0)	12	0.06
Swedish (36)	347	1.78
Swiss (31)	89	0.46
Turkish (34)	34	0.17
Ukrainian (32)	79	0.41
Welsh (28)	207	1.06
Yugoslavian (6)	29	0.15

Hispanic Origin	Population	%
Hispanic or Latino (of any race)	715	3.56
Central American, ex. Mexican	70	0.35
Costa Rican	8	0.04
Guatemalan	29	0.14
Honduran	17	0.08
Nicaraguan	6	0.03
Panamanian	8	0.04
Salvadoran	2	0.01
Cuban	22	0.11
Mexican	352	1.75
Puerto Rican	60	0.30
South American	159	0.79
Argentinean	20	0.10
Bolivian	10	0.05
Chilean	16	0.08
Colombian	62	0.31
Ecuadorian	14	0.07
Peruvian	7	0.03
Uruguayan	2	0.01
Venezuelan	28	0.14
Other Hispanic or Latino	52	0.26

Race*	Population	%
African-American/Black (865)	1,119	5.57
Not Hispanic (840)	1,067	5.31
Hispanic (25)	52	0.26
American Indian/Alaska Native (58)	214	1.07
Not Hispanic (48)	179	0.89
Hispanic (10)	35	0.17
Apache (0)	1	<0.01
Blackfeet (1)	2	0.01
Canadian/French Am. Ind. (2)	4	0.02
Cherokee (2)	34	0.17
Chickasaw (0)	2	0.01
Chippewa (17)	35	0.17
Choctaw (3)	3	0.01
Cree (0)	1	<0.01
Creek (1)	4	0.02
Inupiat *(Alaska Native)* (0)	1	<0.01
Iroquois (0)	4	0.02
Mexican American Ind. (7)	8	0.04
Navajo (0)	3	0.01
Ottawa (3)	6	0.03
Seminole (0)	3	0.01
Sioux (2)	6	0.03
South American Ind. (3)	10	0.05
Tsimshian *(Alaska Native)* (0)	2	0.01
Asian (1,719)	2,038	10.15
Not Hispanic (1,715)	2,021	10.06
Hispanic (4)	17	0.08
Bangladeshi (7)	8	0.04
Burmese (1)	3	0.01
Cambodian (0)	1	<0.01
Chinese, ex. Taiwanese (646)	745	3.71
Filipino (52)	94	0.47
Indian (400)	453	2.26
Indonesian (2)	3	0.01
Japanese (137)	194	0.97
Korean (291)	339	1.69
Laotian (4)	4	0.02
Malaysian (8)	9	0.04
Nepalese (3)	4	0.02
Pakistani (57)	58	0.29
Sri Lankan (11)	12	0.06
Taiwanese (31)	42	0.21
Thai (12)	28	0.14
Vietnamese (17)	32	0.16
Hawaii Native/Pacific Islander (8)	28	0.14
Not Hispanic (8)	28	0.14
Guamanian/Chamorro (2)	5	0.02
Native Hawaiian (4)	7	0.03
Samoan (0)	3	0.01
Tongan (1)	3	0.01
White (16,572)	17,178	85.54
Not Hispanic (16,114)	16,668	83.00
Hispanic (458)	510	2.54

Shelby

Place Type: Charter Township
County: Macomb
Population: 73,804†

Ancestry‡	Population	%
African, Sub-Saharan (408)	438	0.60
African (390)	390	0.54
South African (0)	30	0.04
Zimbabwean (18)	18	0.02
Albanian (1,484)	1,549	2.13
American (3,530)	3,530	4.85
Arab (1,351)	2,092	2.87
Arab (244)	397	0.55
Egyptian (134)	134	0.18
Iraqi (522)	639	0.88
Jordanian (29)	40	0.05
Lebanese (342)	686	0.94
Syrian (60)	176	0.24
Other Arab (20)	20	0.03
Armenian (97)	276	0.38
Assyrian/Chaldean/Syriac (1,179)	1,454	2.00
Austrian (69)	231	0.32
Basque (0)	10	0.01
Belgian (307)	1,336	1.84
British (134)	325	0.45
Bulgarian (60)	174	0.24
Canadian (197)	597	0.82
Croatian (82)	197	0.27
Czech (69)	458	0.63
Czechoslovakian (66)	158	0.22
Danish (59)	266	0.37
Dutch (208)	1,077	1.48
English (1,941)	7,589	10.43
European (520)	544	0.75
Finnish (83)	685	0.94
French, ex. Basque (346)	3,667	5.04
French Canadian (411)	1,199	1.65
German (4,734)	17,369	23.87
Greek (504)	996	1.37
Guyanese (17)	17	0.02
Hungarian (223)	781	1.07
Iranian (0)	13	0.02
Irish (1,519)	8,159	11.21
Italian (5,130)	10,823	14.87
Lithuanian (90)	257	0.35
Macedonian (537)	639	0.88
Maltese (25)	65	0.09
Northern European (47)	47	0.06
Norwegian (119)	493	0.68
Pennsylvania German (8)	44	0.06
Polish (4,995)	12,829	17.63
Portuguese (32)	49	0.07
Romanian (478)	728	1.00
Russian (109)	549	0.75
Scandinavian (22)	57	0.08
Scotch-Irish (290)	1,108	1.52
Scottish (525)	1,845	2.54
Serbian (168)	265	0.36
Slavic (10)	64	0.09
Slovak (194)	669	0.92
Slovene (15)	34	0.05
Swedish (78)	743	1.02
Swiss (14)	169	0.23
Ukrainian (233)	517	0.71
Welsh (76)	419	0.58
West Indian, ex. Hispanic (29)	37	0.05
Jamaican (0)	8	0.01
West Indian (29)	29	0.04
Yugoslavian (402)	638	0.88

Hispanic Origin	Population	%
Hispanic or Latino (of any race)	1,777	2.41
Central American, ex. Mexican	54	0.07
Costa Rican	5	0.01
Guatemalan	22	0.03
Honduran	4	0.01
Nicaraguan	7	0.01
Panamanian	8	0.01
Salvadoran	7	0.01
Other Central American	1	<0.01
Cuban	54	0.07
Dominican Republic	13	0.02
Mexican	1,186	1.61
Puerto Rican	131	0.18
South American	163	0.22
Argentinean	37	0.05
Bolivian	2	<0.01
Chilean	14	0.02
Colombian	40	0.05
Ecuadorian	25	0.03
Paraguayan	2	<0.01
Peruvian	22	0.03
Venezuelan	21	0.03
Other Hispanic or Latino	176	0.24

Race*	Population	%
African-American/Black (2,331)	2,706	3.67
Not Hispanic (2,287)	2,634	3.57
Hispanic (44)	72	0.10
American Indian/Alaska Native (194)	536	0.73
Not Hispanic (171)	488	0.66
Hispanic (23)	48	0.07
Apache (2)	3	<0.01
Arapaho (2)	2	<0.01
Blackfeet (3)	12	0.02
Canadian/French Am. Ind. (1)	3	<0.01
Cherokee (22)	117	0.16
Chippewa (42)	79	0.11
Choctaw (2)	6	0.01
Comanche (0)	1	<0.01
Cree (2)	7	0.01
Creek (0)	2	<0.01
Iroquois (30)	35	0.05
Lumbee (11)	25	0.03
Menominee (0)	1	<0.01
Mexican American Ind. (10)	10	0.01
Navajo (2)	9	0.01
Ottawa (6)	9	0.01
Potawatomi (2)	6	0.01
Pueblo (3)	3	<0.01
Seminole (7)	16	0.02

*Notes: † The Census 2010 population figure is used to calculate the percentages in the Hispanic Origin and Race categories. Ancestry percentages are based on the 2006-2010 American Community Survey population (not shown); ‡ Numbers in parentheses indicate the number of people reporting a single ancestry; * Numbers in parentheses indicate the number of persons reporting this race alone, not in combination with any other race; Please refer to the Explanation of Data for more information.*

Sioux (2)	12	0.02
Yaqui (0)	1	<0.01
Asian (2,411)	2,909	3.94
Not Hispanic (2,403)	2,889	3.91
Hispanic (8)	20	0.03
Bangladeshi (48)	48	0.07
Burmese (4)	7	0.01
Cambodian (3)	8	0.01
Chinese, ex. Taiwanese (237)	269	0.36
Filipino (337)	444	0.60
Hmong (37)	48	0.07
Indian (1,009)	1,064	1.44
Indonesian (0)	5	0.01
Japanese (40)	76	0.10
Korean (292)	359	0.49
Laotian (6)	14	0.02
Nepalese (2)	2	<0.01
Pakistani (155)	163	0.22
Taiwanese (11)	13	0.02
Thai (14)	27	0.04
Vietnamese (151)	161	0.22
Hawaii Native/Pacific Islander (14)	75	0.10
Not Hispanic (14)	75	0.10
Fijian (3)	4	0.01
Guamanian/Chamorro (2)	4	0.01
Native Hawaiian (0)	6	0.01
Samoan (1)	11	0.01
White (67,121)	68,257	92.48
Not Hispanic (65,966)	67,019	90.81
Hispanic (1,155)	1,238	1.68

South Lyon

Place Type: City
County: Oakland
Population: 11,327†

Ancestry‡	Population	%
Albanian (13)	13	0.12
American (663)	663	5.99
Arab (152)	165	1.49
Lebanese (152)	165	1.49
Armenian (30)	110	0.99
Austrian (16)	51	0.46
Belgian (0)	64	0.58
British (27)	54	0.49
Canadian (120)	261	2.36
Croatian (0)	20	0.18
Czech (7)	15	0.14
Czechoslovakian (0)	8	0.07
Danish (14)	40	0.36
Dutch (53)	214	1.93
English (359)	1,738	15.70
Estonian (0)	14	0.13
European (172)	183	1.65
Finnish (63)	212	1.91
French, ex. Basque (13)	493	4.45
French Canadian (108)	262	2.37
German (683)	3,115	28.13
Greek (20)	52	0.47
Hungarian (30)	151	1.36
Irish (421)	1,724	15.57
Italian (298)	1,050	9.48
Lithuanian (16)	16	0.14
Macedonian (0)	8	0.07
Maltese (57)	95	0.86
Norwegian (45)	127	1.15
Polish (335)	1,694	15.30
Romanian (0)	14	0.13
Russian (39)	143	1.29
Scandinavian (8)	32	0.29
Scotch-Irish (151)	436	3.94
Scottish (91)	600	5.42
Slovak (0)	10	0.09
Swedish (22)	137	1.24
Swiss (0)	15	0.14
Ukrainian (17)	72	0.65
Welsh (13)	103	0.93
Yugoslavian (0)	73	0.66

Hispanic Origin	Population	%
Hispanic or Latino (of any race)	309	2.73
Central American, ex. Mexican	5	0.04
Costa Rican	3	0.03
Guatemalan	1	0.01
Salvadoran	1	0.01
Cuban	11	0.10
Dominican Republic	3	0.03
Mexican	217	1.92
Puerto Rican	26	0.23
South American	13	0.11
Argentinean	3	0.03
Chilean	2	0.02
Colombian	1	0.01
Peruvian	2	0.02
Venezuelan	5	0.04
Other Hispanic or Latino	34	0.30

Race*	Population	%
African-American/Black (95)	150	1.32
Not Hispanic (91)	145	1.28
Hispanic (4)	5	0.04
American Indian/Alaska Native (32)	84	0.74
Not Hispanic (25)	66	0.58
Hispanic (7)	18	0.16
Alaska Athabascan *(Ala. Nat.)* (1)	1	0.01
Apache (1)	1	0.01
Blackfeet (1)	1	0.01
Canadian/French Am. Ind. (1)	4	0.04
Cherokee (2)	16	0.14
Chippewa (8)	17	0.15
Cree (1)	1	0.01
Iroquois (1)	6	0.05
Navajo (0)	6	0.05
Potawatomi (1)	1	0.01
Seminole (1)	1	0.01
Sioux (2)	2	0.02
Asian (188)	249	2.20
Not Hispanic (188)	247	2.18
Hispanic (0)	2	0.02
Burmese (0)	1	0.01
Cambodian (2)	2	0.02
Chinese, ex. Taiwanese (43)	56	0.49
Filipino (15)	36	0.32
Indian (68)	78	0.69
Japanese (24)	35	0.31
Korean (10)	17	0.15
Pakistani (1)	1	0.01
Sri Lankan (4)	4	0.04
Taiwanese (4)	4	0.04
Thai (2)	2	0.02
Vietnamese (11)	13	0.11
Hawaii Native/Pacific Islander (2)	7	0.06
Not Hispanic (2)	7	0.06
Guamanian/Chamorro (0)	1	0.01
Native Hawaiian (1)	3	0.03
Samoan (0)	1	0.01
White (10,778)	10,950	96.67
Not Hispanic (10,547)	10,695	94.42
Hispanic (231)	255	2.25

Southfield

Place Type: City
County: Oakland
Population: 71,739†

Ancestry‡	Population	%
African, Sub-Saharan (1,677)	2,102	2.88
African (1,243)	1,632	2.24
Ethiopian (99)	121	0.17
Ghanaian (0)	14	0.02
Kenyan (10)	10	0.01
Nigerian (248)	248	0.34
Senegalese (19)	19	0.03
Zimbabwean (12)	12	0.02
Other Sub-Saharan African (46)	46	0.06
Albanian (88)	88	0.12
American (1,357)	1,357	1.86
Arab (1,441)	1,650	2.26
Arab (299)	299	0.41
Egyptian (0)	13	0.02
Iraqi (983)	1,164	1.60
Jordanian (10)	10	0.01
Lebanese (18)	18	0.02
Moroccan (27)	42	0.06
Palestinian (11)	11	0.02
Syrian (18)	18	0.02
Other Arab (75)	75	0.10
Armenian (230)	241	0.33
Assyrian/Chaldean/Syriac (662)	863	1.18
Austrian (88)	203	0.28
Belgian (0)	27	0.04
Brazilian (6)	14	0.02
British (49)	145	0.20
Cajun (12)	12	0.02
Canadian (152)	332	0.46
Croatian (17)	68	0.09
Czech (36)	288	0.39
Czechoslovakian (18)	39	0.05
Danish (0)	64	0.09
Dutch (76)	371	0.51
Eastern European (173)	173	0.24
English (485)	1,861	2.55
European (431)	478	0.66
Finnish (61)	173	0.24
French, ex. Basque (137)	831	1.14
French Canadian (93)	326	0.45
German (728)	3,332	4.57
Greek (108)	170	0.23
Hungarian (341)	594	0.81
Iranian (17)	51	0.07
Irish (461)	2,274	3.12
Israeli (51)	60	0.08
Italian (334)	794	1.09
Lithuanian (186)	269	0.37
Macedonian (0)	6	0.01
Maltese (0)	33	0.05
Norwegian (33)	168	0.23
Polish (972)	2,791	3.83
Portuguese (0)	14	0.02
Romanian (123)	262	0.36
Russian (1,274)	1,961	2.69
Scandinavian (7)	17	0.02
Scotch-Irish (162)	494	0.68
Scottish (200)	734	1.01
Slavic (11)	11	0.02
Slovak (52)	87	0.12
Slovene (17)	25	0.03
Swedish (67)	266	0.36
Swiss (40)	64	0.09
Turkish (26)	26	0.04
Ukrainian (211)	287	0.39
Welsh (23)	250	0.34
West Indian, ex. Hispanic (464)	726	1.00
Bahamian (0)	9	0.01
Belizean (10)	10	0.01
Dutch West Indian (0)	20	0.03
Haitian (23)	55	0.08
Jamaican (362)	461	0.63
Trinidadian/Tobagonian (11)	26	0.04
U.S. Virgin Islander (0)	24	0.03
West Indian (58)	121	0.17

Hispanic Origin	Population	%
Hispanic or Latino (of any race)	957	1.33
Central American, ex. Mexican	53	0.07
Costa Rican	2	<0.01
Guatemalan	5	0.01
Honduran	7	0.01
Nicaraguan	5	0.01
Panamanian	20	0.03
Salvadoran	14	0.02
Cuban	54	0.08
Dominican Republic	21	0.03
Mexican	443	0.62
Puerto Rican	168	0.23
South American	82	0.11
Argentinean	17	0.02
Bolivian	1	<0.01

*Notes: † The Census 2010 population figure is used to calculate the percentages in the Hispanic Origin and Race categories. Ancestry percentages are based on the 2006-2010 American Community Survey population (not shown); ‡ Numbers in parentheses indicate the number of people reporting a single ancestry; * Numbers in parentheses indicate the number of persons reporting this race alone, not in combination with any other race; Please refer to the Explanation of Data for more information.*

	Population	%
Chilean	5	0.01
Colombian	27	0.04
Ecuadorian	6	0.01
Peruvian	15	0.02
Venezuelan	7	0.01
Other South American	4	0.01
Other Hispanic or Latino	136	0.19

Race*	Population	%
African-American/Black (50,432)	51,817	72.23
Not Hispanic (50,181)	51,445	71.71
Hispanic (251)	372	0.52
American Indian/Alaska Native (143)	689	0.96
Not Hispanic (135)	645	0.90
Hispanic (8)	44	0.06
Apache (0)	9	0.01
Blackfeet (0)	28	0.04
Canadian/French Am. Ind. (5)	10	0.01
Cherokee (11)	119	0.17
Cheyenne (0)	2	<0.01
Chickasaw (0)	2	<0.01
Chippewa (13)	26	0.04
Choctaw (2)	14	0.02
Comanche (0)	1	<0.01
Cree (0)	6	0.01
Creek (0)	9	0.01
Crow (0)	1	<0.01
Delaware (2)	6	0.01
Hopi (0)	1	<0.01
Iroquois (2)	5	0.01
Kiowa (0)	1	<0.01
Lumbee (1)	1	<0.01
Mexican American Ind. (1)	1	<0.01
Ottawa (2)	4	0.01
Potawatomi (2)	7	0.01
Seminole (0)	6	0.01
Shoshone (0)	1	<0.01
Sioux (1)	3	<0.01
South American Ind. (0)	1	<0.01
Spanish American Ind. (0)	1	<0.01
Asian (1,233)	1,602	2.23
Not Hispanic (1,217)	1,554	2.17
Hispanic (16)	48	0.07
Bangladeshi (4)	8	0.01
Burmese (2)	2	<0.01
Cambodian (4)	7	0.01
Chinese, ex. Taiwanese (179)	225	0.31
Filipino (263)	365	0.51
Hmong (22)	24	0.03
Indian (406)	461	0.64
Indonesian (2)	5	0.01
Japanese (29)	56	0.08
Korean (75)	88	0.12
Laotian (8)	10	0.01
Malaysian (2)	3	<0.01
Nepalese (3)	3	<0.01
Pakistani (56)	72	0.10
Sri Lankan (25)	28	0.04
Taiwanese (5)	5	0.01
Thai (23)	28	0.04
Vietnamese (71)	88	0.12
Hawaii Native/Pacific Islander (17)	74	0.10
Not Hispanic (16)	69	0.10
Hispanic (1)	5	0.01
Guamanian/Chamorro (0)	3	<0.01
Native Hawaiian (4)	15	0.02
Samoan (2)	4	0.01
Tongan (1)	1	<0.01
White (17,876)	19,077	26.59
Not Hispanic (17,537)	18,613	25.95
Hispanic (339)	464	0.65

Southfield

Place Type: Township
County: Oakland
Population: 14,547†

Ancestry‡	Population	%
African, Sub-Saharan (27)	36	0.25
African (27)	36	0.25
Albanian (26)	67	0.46
American (529)	529	3.64
Arab (77)	158	1.09
Arab (7)	10	0.07
Lebanese (46)	70	0.48
Palestinian (0)	3	0.02
Syrian (5)	41	0.28
Other Arab (19)	34	0.23
Armenian (271)	356	2.45
Assyrian/Chaldean/Syriac (72)	78	0.54
Austrian (3)	188	1.30
Belgian (0)	26	0.18
Brazilian (13)	37	0.25
British (100)	109	0.75
Canadian (33)	108	0.74
Croatian (23)	52	0.36
Czech (14)	46	0.32
Czechoslovakian (7)	7	0.05
Danish (10)	38	0.26
Dutch (70)	404	2.78
Eastern European (222)	222	1.53
English (557)	1,930	13.30
European (257)	301	2.07
Finnish (53)	181	1.25
French, ex. Basque (69)	611	4.21
French Canadian (33)	116	0.80
German (734)	3,069	21.14
Greek (97)	216	1.49
Hungarian (72)	259	1.78
Iranian (57)	64	0.44
Irish (746)	2,477	17.07
Italian (258)	979	6.74
Latvian (0)	8	0.06
Lithuanian (40)	110	0.76
Macedonian (11)	17	0.12
Maltese (0)	21	0.14
Norwegian (11)	120	0.83
Pennsylvania German (12)	12	0.08
Polish (637)	1,611	11.10
Romanian (25)	72	0.50
Russian (300)	512	3.53
Scandinavian (4)	4	0.03
Scotch-Irish (157)	409	2.82
Scottish (101)	534	3.68
Serbian (12)	12	0.08
Slavic (0)	4	0.03
Slovak (14)	22	0.15
Slovene (7)	27	0.19
Swedish (36)	359	2.47
Swiss (13)	47	0.32
Turkish (31)	31	0.21
Ukrainian (33)	116	0.80
Welsh (16)	107	0.74
West Indian, ex. Hispanic (11)	42	0.29
Jamaican (11)	11	0.08
West Indian (0)	31	0.21

Hispanic Origin	Population	%
Hispanic or Latino (of any race)	224	1.54
Central American, ex. Mexican	22	0.15
Costa Rican	1	0.01
Guatemalan	13	0.09
Honduran	1	0.01
Panamanian	1	0.01
Salvadoran	6	0.04
Cuban	7	0.05
Dominican Republic	3	0.02
Mexican	116	0.80
Puerto Rican	14	0.10
South American	37	0.25
Argentinean	17	0.12
Bolivian	3	0.02
Chilean	3	0.02
Colombian	6	0.04
Ecuadorian	2	0.01
Paraguayan	1	0.01
Peruvian	5	0.03
Other Hispanic or Latino	25	0.17

Race*	Population	%
African-American/Black (971)	1,066	7.33
Not Hispanic (969)	1,058	7.27
Hispanic (2)	8	0.05
American Indian/Alaska Native (24)	81	0.56
Not Hispanic (22)	73	0.50
Hispanic (2)	8	0.05
Blackfeet (0)	1	0.01
Cherokee (1)	15	0.10
Chippewa (8)	14	0.10
Iroquois (0)	2	0.01
Lumbee (0)	1	0.01
Mexican American Ind. (1)	1	0.01
Potawatomi (0)	3	0.02
Sioux (3)	3	0.02
Spanish American Ind. (1)	1	0.01
Asian (411)	515	3.54
Not Hispanic (407)	505	3.47
Hispanic (4)	10	0.07
Bangladeshi (1)	2	0.01
Chinese, ex. Taiwanese (78)	99	0.68
Filipino (43)	60	0.41
Hmong (3)	3	0.02
Indian (166)	194	1.33
Indonesian (1)	1	0.01
Japanese (18)	35	0.24
Korean (27)	35	0.24
Laotian (0)	2	0.01
Malaysian (1)	1	0.01
Pakistani (15)	15	0.10
Sri Lankan (7)	7	0.05
Taiwanese (0)	1	0.01
Thai (6)	6	0.04
Vietnamese (34)	36	0.25
Hawaii Native/Pacific Islander (5)	20	0.14
Not Hispanic (5)	20	0.14
Native Hawaiian (2)	3	0.02
White (12,836)	13,046	89.68
Not Hispanic (12,670)	12,867	88.45
Hispanic (166)	179	1.23

Southgate

Place Type: City
County: Wayne
Population: 30,047†

Ancestry‡	Population	%
African, Sub-Saharan (52)	64	0.21
African (45)	57	0.19
Ugandan (7)	7	0.02
Albanian (386)	386	1.28
American (1,128)	1,128	3.74
Arab (32)	90	0.30
Arab (13)	13	0.04
Lebanese (6)	47	0.16
Syrian (13)	22	0.07
Other Arab (0)	8	0.03
Armenian (78)	100	0.33
Austrian (7)	97	0.32
Belgian (17)	93	0.31
Brazilian (0)	41	0.14
British (6)	56	0.19
Bulgarian (0)	18	0.06
Canadian (140)	198	0.66
Croatian (28)	79	0.26
Czech (23)	179	0.59
Czechoslovakian (20)	84	0.28
Danish (0)	202	0.67
Dutch (111)	703	2.33
Eastern European (10)	10	0.03
English (951)	3,419	11.34
European (175)	194	0.64
Finnish (41)	143	0.47
French, ex. Basque (283)	2,124	7.04
French Canadian (225)	886	2.94
German (1,513)	6,719	22.28
German Russian (0)	49	0.16
Greek (175)	236	0.78

*Notes: † The Census 2010 population figure is used to calculate the percentages in the Hispanic Origin and Race categories. Ancestry percentages are based on the 2006-2010 American Community Survey population (not shown); ‡ Numbers in parentheses indicate the number of people reporting a single ancestry; * Numbers in parentheses indicate the number of persons reporting this race alone, not in combination with any other race; Please refer to the Explanation of Data for more information.*

Hungarian (595)	1,630	5.40
Irish (905)	4,532	15.03
Italian (1,165)	2,487	8.25
Latvian (14)	14	0.05
Lithuanian (57)	357	1.18
Macedonian (35)	59	0.20
Maltese (9)	19	0.06
Northern European (13)	13	0.04
Norwegian (18)	201	0.67
Pennsylvania German (6)	48	0.16
Polish (1,558)	4,665	15.47
Romanian (102)	250	0.83
Russian (54)	290	0.96
Scandinavian (19)	29	0.10
Scotch-Irish (240)	722	2.39
Scottish (258)	739	2.45
Serbian (28)	68	0.23
Slovak (56)	147	0.49
Swedish (80)	462	1.53
Swiss (12)	12	0.04
Ukrainian (78)	188	0.62
Welsh (40)	188	0.62
West Indian, ex. Hispanic (42)	42	0.14
Jamaican (42)	42	0.14
Yugoslavian (34)	123	0.41

Hispanic Origin	Population	%
Hispanic or Latino (of any race)	1,956	6.51
Central American, ex. Mexican	22	0.07
Costa Rican	4	0.01
Guatemalan	8	0.03
Honduran	3	0.01
Nicaraguan	3	0.01
Panamanian	2	0.01
Salvadoran	2	0.01
Cuban	24	0.08
Dominican Republic	2	0.01
Mexican	1,536	5.11
Puerto Rican	187	0.62
South American	49	0.16
Argentinean	14	0.05
Bolivian	1	<0.01
Chilean	3	0.01
Colombian	18	0.06
Ecuadorian	3	0.01
Peruvian	2	0.01
Uruguayan	1	<0.01
Venezuelan	7	0.02
Other Hispanic or Latino	136	0.45

Race*	Population	%
African-American/Black (1,666)	1,890	6.29
Not Hispanic (1,635)	1,843	6.13
Hispanic (31)	47	0.16
American Indian/Alaska Native (148)	339	1.13
Not Hispanic (116)	275	0.92
Hispanic (32)	64	0.21
Apache (0)	1	<0.01
Blackfeet (4)	14	0.05
Canadian/French Am. Ind. (1)	9	0.03
Central American Ind. (1)	1	<0.01
Cherokee (18)	62	0.21
Cheyenne (0)	2	0.01
Chippewa (26)	53	0.18
Choctaw (1)	3	0.01
Cree (0)	1	<0.01
Creek (0)	1	<0.01
Crow (0)	1	<0.01
Delaware (2)	6	0.02
Iroquois (15)	20	0.07
Lumbee (10)	15	0.05
Menominee (6)	7	0.02
Mexican American Ind. (5)	8	0.03
Navajo (1)	2	0.01
Ottawa (5)	6	0.02
Paiute (0)	1	<0.01
Potawatomi (2)	4	0.01
Sioux (2)	6	0.02
Tlingit-Haida *(Alaska Native)* (0)	2	0.01
Asian (493)	608	2.02
Not Hispanic (488)	592	1.97
Hispanic (5)	16	0.05
Cambodian (8)	8	0.03
Chinese, ex. Taiwanese (74)	84	0.28
Filipino (124)	172	0.57
Hmong (1)	2	0.01
Indian (143)	155	0.52
Indonesian (4)	6	0.02
Japanese (10)	24	0.08
Korean (28)	41	0.14
Laotian (1)	6	0.02
Pakistani (30)	30	0.10
Thai (3)	4	0.01
Vietnamese (61)	66	0.22
Hawaii Native/Pacific Islander (5)	24	0.08
Not Hispanic (5)	24	0.08
Fijian (0)	1	<0.01
Native Hawaiian (4)	13	0.04
Samoan (1)	2	0.01
White (26,644)	27,192	90.50
Not Hispanic (25,389)	25,793	85.84
Hispanic (1,255)	1,399	4.66

Sparta

Place Type: Township
County: Kent
Population: 9,110†

Ancestry‡	Population	%
American (434)	434	4.76
Armenian (10)	10	0.11
Canadian (0)	30	0.33
Croatian (0)	9	0.10
Czech (0)	58	0.64
Czechoslovakian (0)	9	0.10
Danish (0)	14	0.15
Dutch (530)	1,313	14.41
English (322)	1,108	12.16
European (131)	131	1.44
Finnish (17)	59	0.65
French, ex. Basque (75)	319	3.50
French Canadian (83)	187	2.05
German (1,053)	2,737	30.04
Irish (169)	1,157	12.70
Italian (33)	123	1.35
Lithuanian (7)	39	0.43
Norwegian (16)	108	1.19
Pennsylvania German (11)	11	0.12
Polish (120)	692	7.60
Portuguese (11)	22	0.24
Russian (0)	58	0.64
Scandinavian (7)	7	0.08
Scotch-Irish (32)	122	1.34
Scottish (49)	163	1.79
Slavic (10)	10	0.11
Slovak (0)	37	0.41
Swedish (128)	299	3.28
Ukrainian (0)	9	0.10
Welsh (0)	25	0.27

Hispanic Origin	Population	%
Hispanic or Latino (of any race)	482	5.29
Central American, ex. Mexican	5	0.05
Guatemalan	4	0.04
Salvadoran	1	0.01
Cuban	7	0.08
Mexican	413	4.53
Puerto Rican	13	0.14
South American	2	0.02
Other South American	2	0.02
Other Hispanic or Latino	42	0.46

Race*	Population	%
African-American/Black (62)	111	1.22
Not Hispanic (60)	106	1.16
Hispanic (2)	5	0.05
American Indian/Alaska Native (30)	80	0.88
Not Hispanic (25)	69	0.76
Hispanic (5)	11	0.12
Apache (0)	5	0.05
Blackfeet (2)	7	0.08
Cherokee (0)	12	0.13
Chippewa (7)	17	0.19
Choctaw (0)	4	0.04
Creek (1)	1	0.01
Mexican American Ind. (0)	1	0.01
Osage (0)	1	0.01
Ottawa (7)	15	0.16
Potawatomi (1)	5	0.05
Sioux (4)	4	0.04
Tlingit-Haida *(Alaska Native)* (1)	1	0.01
Asian (35)	65	0.71
Not Hispanic (35)	63	0.69
Hispanic (0)	2	0.02
Chinese, ex. Taiwanese (8)	14	0.15
Filipino (11)	23	0.25
Indian (1)	1	0.01
Japanese (0)	12	0.13
Korean (7)	12	0.13
Taiwanese (1)	1	0.01
Thai (2)	2	0.02
Vietnamese (3)	7	0.08
Hawaii Native/Pacific Islander (0)	2	0.02
Not Hispanic (0)	2	0.02
Native Hawaiian (0)	2	0.02
White (8,610)	8,766	96.22
Not Hispanic (8,380)	8,502	93.33
Hispanic (230)	264	2.90

Spring Arbor

Place Type: Township
County: Jackson
Population: 8,267†

Ancestry‡	Population	%
American (503)	503	6.11
Arab (2)	2	0.02
Lebanese (2)	2	0.02
Armenian (0)	15	0.18
Belgian (39)	52	0.63
British (0)	28	0.34
Canadian (27)	41	0.50
Croatian (0)	52	0.63
Czech (12)	28	0.34
Dutch (66)	542	6.58
Eastern European (0)	9	0.11
English (868)	1,889	22.94
European (30)	30	0.36
Finnish (12)	12	0.15
French, ex. Basque (27)	299	3.63
French Canadian (84)	119	1.44
German (749)	2,304	27.97
Greek (0)	56	0.68
Hungarian (0)	68	0.83
Irish (290)	1,261	15.31
Italian (92)	248	3.01
Macedonian (11)	50	0.61
Northern European (32)	32	0.39
Norwegian (25)	52	0.63
Polish (155)	379	4.60
Russian (0)	28	0.34
Scandinavian (0)	13	0.16
Scotch-Irish (29)	187	2.27
Scottish (39)	191	2.32
Slavic (17)	17	0.21
Slovak (0)	28	0.34
Swedish (28)	71	0.86
Swiss (0)	15	0.18
Welsh (38)	89	1.08
West Indian, ex. Hispanic (0)	13	0.16
U.S. Virgin Islander (0)	13	0.16

Hispanic Origin	Population	%
Hispanic or Latino (of any race)	142	1.72
Central American, ex. Mexican	2	0.02
Guatemalan	2	0.02
Cuban	6	0.07
Dominican Republic	4	0.05

*Notes: † The Census 2010 population figure is used to calculate the percentages in the Hispanic Origin and Race categories. Ancestry percentages are based on the 2006-2010 American Community Survey population (not shown); ‡ Numbers in parentheses indicate the number of people reporting a single ancestry; * Numbers in parentheses indicate the number of persons reporting this race alone, not in combination with any other race; Please refer to the Explanation of Data for more information.*

Mexican	105	1.27
Puerto Rican	8	0.10
South American	1	0.01
Argentinean	1	0.01
Other Hispanic or Latino	16	0.19

Race*	Population	%
African-American/Black (123)	170	2.06
Not Hispanic (120)	164	1.98
Hispanic (3)	6	0.07
American Indian/Alaska Native (21)	70	0.85
Not Hispanic (19)	61	0.74
Hispanic (2)	9	0.11
Apache (0)	1	0.01
Blackfeet (1)	1	0.01
Canadian/French Am. Ind. (0)	1	0.01
Cherokee (0)	7	0.08
Cheyenne (1)	1	0.01
Chippewa (9)	13	0.16
Choctaw (0)	2	0.02
Crow (0)	1	0.01
Lumbee (2)	2	0.02
Ottawa (1)	1	0.01
Potawatomi (0)	4	0.05
Sioux (0)	5	0.06
Ute (1)	1	0.01
Asian (73)	96	1.16
Not Hispanic (73)	96	1.16
Chinese, ex. Taiwanese (23)	25	0.30
Filipino (2)	3	0.04
Hmong (6)	6	0.07
Indian (18)	20	0.24
Japanese (11)	16	0.19
Korean (8)	14	0.17
Thai (1)	4	0.05
Vietnamese (2)	4	0.05
Hawaii Native/Pacific Islander (2)	3	0.04
Not Hispanic (2)	3	0.04
Samoan (1)	1	0.01
White (7,894)	8,014	96.94
Not Hispanic (7,796)	7,901	95.57
Hispanic (98)	113	1.37

Spring Lake

Place Type: Township
County: Ottawa
Population: 14,300†

Ancestry‡	Population	%
American (432)	432	3.04
Arab (0)	47	0.33
Syrian (0)	47	0.33
Australian (0)	20	0.14
Austrian (46)	74	0.52
Belgian (27)	58	0.41
British (102)	109	0.77
Canadian (42)	85	0.60
Croatian (0)	85	0.60
Czech (42)	75	0.53
Czechoslovakian (0)	27	0.19
Danish (7)	90	0.63
Dutch (1,529)	3,279	23.09
Eastern European (5)	5	0.04
English (532)	1,921	13.53
European (229)	239	1.68
Finnish (27)	201	1.42
French, ex. Basque (90)	537	3.78
French Canadian (44)	260	1.83
German (1,068)	3,698	26.04
Greek (56)	139	0.98
Hungarian (75)	149	1.05
Irish (301)	1,740	12.25
Italian (249)	655	4.61
Lithuanian (0)	74	0.52
Northern European (25)	25	0.18
Norwegian (46)	233	1.64
Pennsylvania German (0)	7	0.05
Polish (429)	1,105	7.78
Portuguese (0)	22	0.15
Romanian (23)	23	0.16
Russian (25)	86	0.61
Scandinavian (0)	107	0.75
Scotch-Irish (55)	176	1.24
Scottish (34)	302	2.13
Slavic (27)	43	0.30
Slovak (21)	99	0.70
Slovene (7)	7	0.05
Swedish (126)	537	3.78
Swiss (12)	29	0.20
Turkish (32)	32	0.23
Ukrainian (28)	28	0.20
Welsh (20)	144	1.01
West Indian, ex. Hispanic (0)	11	0.08
Jamaican (0)	11	0.08

Hispanic Origin	Population	%
Hispanic or Latino (of any race)	307	2.15
Central American, ex. Mexican	7	0.05
Costa Rican	2	0.01
Honduran	2	0.01
Nicaraguan	2	0.01
Salvadoran	1	0.01
Cuban	12	0.08
Mexican	225	1.57
Puerto Rican	24	0.17
South American	13	0.09
Argentinean	1	0.01
Colombian	1	0.01
Peruvian	8	0.06
Uruguayan	3	0.02
Other Hispanic or Latino	26	0.18

Race*	Population	%
African-American/Black (79)	145	1.01
Not Hispanic (67)	128	0.90
Hispanic (12)	17	0.12
American Indian/Alaska Native (78)	169	1.18
Not Hispanic (71)	151	1.06
Hispanic (7)	18	0.13
Apache (1)	2	0.01
Blackfeet (0)	1	0.01
Canadian/French Am. Ind. (2)	2	0.01
Cherokee (2)	14	0.10
Chippewa (22)	34	0.24
Inupiat *(Alaska Native)* (0)	3	0.02
Iroquois (0)	1	0.01
Mexican American Ind. (0)	3	0.02
Ottawa (19)	29	0.20
Potawatomi (7)	17	0.12
Pueblo (1)	2	0.01
Sioux (1)	3	0.02
Asian (118)	170	1.19
Not Hispanic (116)	164	1.15
Hispanic (2)	6	0.04
Bhutanese (5)	5	0.03
Cambodian (2)	2	0.01
Chinese, ex. Taiwanese (29)	38	0.27
Filipino (12)	22	0.15
Indian (24)	28	0.20
Indonesian (0)	1	0.01
Japanese (3)	10	0.07
Korean (26)	41	0.29
Pakistani (5)	6	0.04
Taiwanese (4)	4	0.03
Thai (4)	6	0.04
Vietnamese (2)	2	0.01
Hawaii Native/Pacific Islander (7)	13	0.09
Not Hispanic (7)	12	0.08
Hispanic (0)	1	0.01
Guamanian/Chamorro (2)	2	0.01
Native Hawaiian (1)	4	0.03
White (13,734)	13,938	97.47
Not Hispanic (13,542)	13,717	95.92
Hispanic (192)	221	1.55

Springfield

Place Type: Charter Township
County: Oakland
Population: 13,940†

Ancestry‡	Population	%
Albanian (11)	65	0.47
American (1,061)	1,061	7.67
Arab (44)	83	0.60
Arab (26)	26	0.19
Lebanese (18)	57	0.41
Armenian (19)	35	0.25
Austrian (27)	96	0.69
Belgian (44)	102	0.74
Brazilian (12)	29	0.21
British (55)	246	1.78
Bulgarian (0)	13	0.09
Canadian (84)	130	0.94
Croatian (11)	37	0.27
Czech (33)	167	1.21
Czechoslovakian (17)	44	0.32
Danish (7)	76	0.55
Dutch (113)	460	3.32
Eastern European (10)	10	0.07
English (789)	2,187	15.81
European (78)	177	1.28
Finnish (100)	189	1.37
French, ex. Basque (111)	786	5.68
French Canadian (142)	526	3.80
German (977)	3,547	25.63
Greek (34)	172	1.24
Hungarian (52)	274	1.98
Irish (504)	2,056	14.86
Italian (394)	1,102	7.96
Latvian (0)	12	0.09
Lithuanian (5)	55	0.40
Macedonian (0)	38	0.27
Maltese (7)	7	0.05
Norwegian (45)	270	1.95
Polish (333)	1,248	9.02
Portuguese (0)	9	0.07
Romanian (32)	43	0.31
Russian (46)	209	1.51
Scandinavian (22)	55	0.40
Scotch-Irish (52)	274	1.98
Scottish (160)	486	3.51
Serbian (11)	11	0.08
Slavic (0)	54	0.39
Slovak (16)	38	0.27
Swedish (114)	304	2.20
Swiss (13)	38	0.27
Ukrainian (40)	142	1.03
Welsh (8)	181	1.31
West Indian, ex. Hispanic (0)	21	0.15
West Indian (0)	21	0.15
Yugoslavian (0)	5	0.04

Hispanic Origin	Population	%
Hispanic or Latino (of any race)	403	2.89
Central American, ex. Mexican	15	0.11
Costa Rican	5	0.04
Guatemalan	5	0.04
Panamanian	3	0.02
Salvadoran	2	0.01
Cuban	7	0.05
Mexican	312	2.24
Puerto Rican	13	0.09
South American	22	0.16
Argentinean	4	0.03
Colombian	1	0.01
Ecuadorian	4	0.03
Peruvian	11	0.08
Venezuelan	1	0.01
Other South American	1	0.01
Other Hispanic or Latino	34	0.24

Race*	Population	%
African-American/Black (157)	205	1.47
Not Hispanic (151)	191	1.37

SECTION TWO

*Notes: † The Census 2010 population figure is used to calculate the percentages in the Hispanic Origin and Race categories. Ancestry percentages are based on the 2006-2010 American Community Survey population (not shown); ‡ Numbers in parentheses indicate the number of people reporting a single ancestry; * Numbers in parentheses indicate the number of persons reporting this race alone, not in combination with any other race; Please refer to the Explanation of Data for more information.*

Hispanic (6)	14	0.10
American Indian/Alaska Native (54)	137	0.98
Not Hispanic (46)	116	0.83
Hispanic (8)	21	0.15
Blackfeet (0)	3	0.02
Cherokee (8)	30	0.22
Chickasaw (0)	1	0.01
Chippewa (23)	42	0.30
Choctaw (0)	2	0.01
Cree (1)	1	0.01
Creek (1)	5	0.04
Iroquois (1)	1	0.01
Mexican American Ind. (4)	4	0.03
Navajo (1)	1	0.01
Osage (1)	3	0.02
Ottawa (1)	4	0.03
Potawatomi (7)	8	0.06
Sioux (0)	1	0.01
Asian (135)	185	1.33
Not Hispanic (125)	171	1.23
Hispanic (10)	14	0.10
Chinese, ex. Taiwanese (31)	42	0.30
Filipino (36)	53	0.38
Hmong (20)	20	0.14
Indian (3)	4	0.03
Japanese (11)	25	0.18
Korean (22)	25	0.18
Nepalese (1)	1	0.01
Pakistani (1)	1	0.01
Vietnamese (4)	5	0.04
Hawaii Native/Pacific Islander (3)	4	0.03
Not Hispanic (3)	4	0.03
Guamanian/Chamorro (1)	1	0.01
Samoan (2)	2	0.01
White (13,303)	13,485	96.74
Not Hispanic (13,055)	13,199	94.68
Hispanic (248)	286	2.05

St. Clair Shores

Place Type: City
County: Macomb
Population: 59,715†

Ancestry‡	Population	%
African, Sub-Saharan (127)	161	0.26
African (116)	126	0.21
Cape Verdean (11)	35	0.06
Albanian (351)	351	0.58
American (2,044)	2,044	3.36
Arab (625)	992	1.63
Arab (152)	222	0.37
Egyptian (90)	90	0.15
Iraqi (12)	12	0.02
Lebanese (284)	558	0.92
Palestinian (9)	9	0.01
Syrian (78)	101	0.17
Armenian (49)	79	0.13
Assyrian/Chaldean/Syriac (0)	50	0.08
Austrian (30)	311	0.51
Belgian (716)	2,178	3.58
Brazilian (15)	15	0.02
British (49)	109	0.18
Canadian (471)	716	1.18
Croatian (157)	334	0.55
Czech (41)	290	0.48
Czechoslovakian (37)	102	0.17
Danish (0)	60	0.10
Dutch (123)	917	1.51
Eastern European (30)	30	0.05
English (1,276)	5,786	9.52
European (333)	398	0.65
Finnish (80)	312	0.51
French, ex. Basque (426)	4,772	7.85
French Canadian (523)	1,601	2.63
German (3,950)	16,348	26.90
Greek (343)	617	1.02
Hungarian (201)	586	0.96
Irish (1,817)	9,621	15.83
Italian (3,208)	8,779	14.44
Lithuanian (119)	324	0.53
Macedonian (28)	84	0.14
Maltese (106)	191	0.31
Northern European (19)	19	0.03
Norwegian (147)	473	0.78
Pennsylvania German (0)	14	0.02
Polish (4,818)	12,345	20.31
Portuguese (10)	80	0.13
Romanian (147)	223	0.37
Russian (80)	460	0.76
Scandinavian (10)	25	0.04
Scotch-Irish (628)	1,611	2.65
Scottish (734)	2,269	3.73
Serbian (20)	86	0.14
Slavic (8)	44	0.07
Slovak (127)	475	0.78
Slovene (7)	7	0.01
Swedish (152)	576	0.95
Swiss (25)	96	0.16
Ukrainian (220)	599	0.99
Welsh (37)	192	0.32
Yugoslavian (4)	91	0.15

Hispanic Origin	Population	%
Hispanic or Latino (of any race)	1,040	1.74
Central American, ex. Mexican	40	0.07
Costa Rican	6	0.01
Guatemalan	13	0.02
Honduran	7	0.01
Nicaraguan	1	<0.01
Panamanian	8	0.01
Salvadoran	5	0.01
Cuban	35	0.06
Dominican Republic	15	0.03
Mexican	672	1.13
Puerto Rican	84	0.14
South American	61	0.10
Argentinean	19	0.03
Chilean	1	<0.01
Colombian	17	0.03
Ecuadorian	9	0.02
Peruvian	9	0.02
Uruguayan	1	<0.01
Venezuelan	4	0.01
Other South American	1	<0.01
Other Hispanic or Latino	133	0.22

Race*	Population	%
African-American/Black (2,350)	2,719	4.55
Not Hispanic (2,333)	2,678	4.48
Hispanic (17)	41	0.07
American Indian/Alaska Native (188)	601	1.01
Not Hispanic (169)	536	0.90
Hispanic (19)	65	0.11
Apache (2)	9	0.02
Blackfeet (5)	26	0.04
Canadian/French Am. Ind. (1)	9	0.02
Central American Ind. (1)	1	<0.01
Cherokee (16)	139	0.23
Chickasaw (0)	1	<0.01
Chippewa (43)	86	0.14
Choctaw (0)	7	0.01
Comanche (0)	2	<0.01
Cree (1)	1	<0.01
Delaware (1)	4	0.01
Hopi (0)	4	0.01
Iroquois (11)	24	0.04
Lumbee (20)	28	0.05
Mexican American Ind. (2)	2	<0.01
Navajo (1)	7	0.01
Osage (0)	7	0.01
Ottawa (6)	10	0.02
Paiute (0)	2	<0.01
Potawatomi (2)	2	<0.01
Pueblo (0)	1	<0.01
Seminole (0)	1	<0.01
Shoshone (0)	1	<0.01
Sioux (1)	13	0.02
Asian (614)	913	1.53
Not Hispanic (611)	888	1.49
Hispanic (3)	25	0.04
Bangladeshi (0)	2	<0.01
Cambodian (1)	4	0.01
Chinese, ex. Taiwanese (107)	144	0.24
Filipino (227)	332	0.56
Hmong (14)	16	0.03
Indian (87)	105	0.18
Indonesian (0)	1	<0.01
Japanese (27)	71	0.12
Korean (66)	130	0.22
Laotian (2)	6	0.01
Pakistani (9)	12	0.02
Taiwanese (1)	4	0.01
Thai (15)	20	0.03
Vietnamese (38)	51	0.09
Hawaii Native/Pacific Islander (9)	31	0.05
Not Hispanic (9)	31	0.05
Fijian (1)	1	<0.01
Guamanian/Chamorro (4)	9	0.02
Native Hawaiian (2)	10	0.02
White (55,373)	56,353	94.37
Not Hispanic (54,575)	55,454	92.86
Hispanic (798)	899	1.51

St. Johns

Place Type: City
County: Clinton
Population: 7,865†

Ancestry‡	Population	%
African, Sub-Saharan (16)	16	0.20
African (16)	16	0.20
American (893)	893	11.28
Armenian (21)	21	0.27
Assyrian/Chaldean/Syriac (18)	18	0.23
Austrian (0)	29	0.37
Belgian (17)	17	0.21
British (22)	40	0.51
Canadian (24)	119	1.50
Czech (39)	268	3.38
Czechoslovakian (39)	101	1.28
Danish (0)	55	0.69
Dutch (39)	283	3.57
English (215)	1,059	13.37
Finnish (9)	59	0.74
French, ex. Basque (33)	486	6.14
French Canadian (13)	104	1.31
German (1,155)	2,779	35.09
Hungarian (42)	124	1.57
Irish (217)	938	11.84
Italian (189)	300	3.79
Lithuanian (0)	11	0.14
Norwegian (31)	57	0.72
Polish (112)	475	6.00
Russian (0)	9	0.11
Scandinavian (10)	10	0.13
Scotch-Irish (25)	109	1.38
Scottish (106)	334	4.22
Slovak (29)	104	1.31
Swedish (2)	182	2.30
Swiss (0)	40	0.51
Welsh (0)	34	0.43

Hispanic Origin	Population	%
Hispanic or Latino (of any race)	358	4.55
Central American, ex. Mexican	3	0.04
Nicaraguan	1	0.01
Salvadoran	2	0.03
Cuban	7	0.09
Mexican	293	3.73
Puerto Rican	20	0.25
South American	3	0.04
Colombian	2	0.03
Ecuadorian	1	0.01
Other Hispanic or Latino	32	0.41

Race*	Population	%
African-American/Black (111)	180	2.29
Not Hispanic (99)	160	2.03

*Notes: † The Census 2010 population figure is used to calculate the percentages in the Hispanic Origin and Race categories. Ancestry percentages are based on the 2006-2010 American Community Survey population (not shown); ‡ Numbers in parentheses indicate the number of people reporting a single ancestry; * Numbers in parentheses indicate the number of persons reporting this race alone, not in combination with any other race; Please refer to the Explanation of Data for more information.*

Hispanic (12)	20	0.25
American Indian/Alaska Native (49)	122	1.55
Not Hispanic (47)	114	1.45
Hispanic (2)	8	0.10
Apache (0)	2	0.03
Blackfeet (0)	1	0.01
Canadian/French Am. Ind. (0)	1	0.01
Cherokee (1)	9	0.11
Chippewa (24)	35	0.45
Comanche (1)	1	0.01
Iroquois (4)	5	0.06
Kiowa (0)	4	0.05
Lumbee (0)	1	0.01
Mexican American Ind. (0)	1	0.01
Navajo (0)	1	0.01
Ottawa (13)	14	0.18
Potawatomi (0)	5	0.06
Asian (42)	57	0.72
Not Hispanic (41)	53	0.67
Hispanic (1)	4	0.05
Chinese, ex. Taiwanese (15)	17	0.22
Filipino (7)	16	0.20
Hmong (1)	1	0.01
Indian (4)	5	0.06
Japanese (0)	2	0.03
Korean (9)	12	0.15
Pakistani (3)	3	0.04
Vietnamese (2)	2	0.03
Hawaii Native/Pacific Islander (4)	12	0.15
Not Hispanic (4)	11	0.14
Hispanic (0)	1	0.01
Native Hawaiian (1)	4	0.05
Samoan (3)	8	0.10
White (7,389)	7,554	96.05
Not Hispanic (7,176)	7,302	92.84
Hispanic (213)	252	3.20

St. Joseph

Place Type: Charter Township
County: Berrien
Population: 10,028†

Ancestry‡	Population	%
American (341)	341	3.41
Australian (0)	8	0.08
Austrian (0)	22	0.22
Belgian (9)	9	0.09
Brazilian (8)	8	0.08
British (3)	19	0.19
Canadian (33)	52	0.52
Croatian (22)	72	0.72
Czech (37)	100	1.00
Danish (13)	20	0.20
Dutch (85)	421	4.21
English (326)	1,361	13.60
European (38)	45	0.45
Finnish (16)	59	0.59
French, ex. Basque (34)	290	2.90
French Canadian (40)	124	1.24
German (1,700)	3,480	34.78
German Russian (9)	9	0.09
Greek (26)	45	0.45
Hungarian (16)	146	1.46
Irish (318)	1,477	14.76
Italian (254)	798	7.97
Latvian (0)	31	0.31
Lithuanian (20)	37	0.37
Norwegian (8)	34	0.34
Pennsylvania German (0)	14	0.14
Polish (207)	648	6.48
Romanian (3)	6	0.06
Russian (30)	173	1.73
Scandinavian (9)	46	0.46
Scotch-Irish (38)	97	0.97
Scottish (68)	304	3.04
Serbian (2)	2	0.02
Slovak (0)	23	0.23
Slovene (8)	8	0.08
Swedish (31)	176	1.76
Swiss (0)	30	0.30
Ukrainian (0)	10	0.10
Welsh (16)	67	0.67
Yugoslavian (0)	4	0.04

Hispanic Origin	Population	%
Hispanic or Latino (of any race)	244	2.43
Central American, ex. Mexican	10	0.10
Costa Rican	2	0.02
Guatemalan	1	0.01
Nicaraguan	2	0.02
Panamanian	4	0.04
Salvadoran	1	0.01
Cuban	9	0.09
Dominican Republic	9	0.09
Mexican	123	1.23
Puerto Rican	18	0.18
South American	35	0.35
Argentinean	5	0.05
Chilean	11	0.11
Colombian	8	0.08
Paraguayan	2	0.02
Peruvian	5	0.05
Venezuelan	3	0.03
Other South American	1	0.01
Other Hispanic or Latino	40	0.40

Race*	Population	%
African-American/Black (1,334)	1,395	13.91
Not Hispanic (1,326)	1,382	13.78
Hispanic (8)	13	0.13
American Indian/Alaska Native (27)	68	0.68
Not Hispanic (22)	59	0.59
Hispanic (5)	9	0.09
Apache (0)	1	0.01
Cherokee (4)	17	0.17
Chippewa (1)	6	0.06
Lumbee (0)	1	0.01
Mexican American Ind. (1)	1	0.01
Ottawa (1)	1	0.01
Potawatomi (9)	17	0.17
Pueblo (1)	1	0.01
Sioux (1)	2	0.02
Asian (263)	306	3.05
Not Hispanic (262)	304	3.03
Hispanic (1)	2	0.02
Cambodian (1)	1	0.01
Chinese, ex. Taiwanese (38)	39	0.39
Filipino (30)	45	0.45
Indian (119)	122	1.22
Japanese (4)	13	0.13
Korean (28)	34	0.34
Laotian (12)	12	0.12
Pakistani (12)	12	0.12
Thai (1)	1	0.01
Vietnamese (11)	14	0.14
Hawaii Native/Pacific Islander (1)	9	0.09
Not Hispanic (1)	9	0.09
Guamanian/Chamorro (0)	1	0.01
Native Hawaiian (1)	3	0.03
Samoan (0)	4	0.04
White (8,179)	8,327	83.04
Not Hispanic (8,030)	8,158	81.35
Hispanic (149)	169	1.69

St. Joseph

Place Type: City
County: Berrien
Population: 8,365†

Ancestry‡	Population	%
African, Sub-Saharan (83)	83	0.99
African (83)	83	0.99
American (283)	283	3.37
Arab (0)	19	0.23
Lebanese (0)	13	0.15
Syrian (0)	6	0.07
Australian (126)	138	1.64
Austrian (0)	59	0.70
Belgian (0)	6	0.07
Brazilian (0)	16	0.19
British (43)	87	1.04
Canadian (27)	49	0.58
Croatian (10)	111	1.32
Czech (33)	61	0.73
Czechoslovakian (0)	11	0.13
Danish (53)	71	0.85
Dutch (231)	742	8.84
English (294)	1,009	12.02
European (76)	91	1.08
French, ex. Basque (39)	236	2.81
French Canadian (27)	37	0.44
German (1,638)	3,332	39.70
Greek (0)	23	0.27
Hungarian (53)	94	1.12
Irish (191)	1,143	13.62
Italian (145)	442	5.27
Lithuanian (12)	29	0.35
Macedonian (0)	8	0.10
Norwegian (15)	115	1.37
Pennsylvania German (31)	50	0.60
Polish (106)	360	4.29
Romanian (17)	17	0.20
Russian (44)	132	1.57
Scandinavian (24)	37	0.44
Scotch-Irish (82)	132	1.57
Scottish (125)	196	2.34
Serbian (27)	59	0.70
Slovak (11)	11	0.13
Swedish (73)	143	1.70
Swiss (0)	15	0.18
Ukrainian (19)	29	0.35
Welsh (21)	75	0.89
Yugoslavian (0)	14	0.17

Hispanic Origin	Population	%
Hispanic or Latino (of any race)	235	2.81
Central American, ex. Mexican	6	0.07
Guatemalan	2	0.02
Honduran	2	0.02
Salvadoran	2	0.02
Cuban	3	0.04
Dominican Republic	5	0.06
Mexican	158	1.89
Puerto Rican	13	0.16
South American	28	0.33
Colombian	21	0.25
Ecuadorian	3	0.04
Uruguayan	1	0.01
Venezuelan	2	0.02
Other South American	1	0.01
Other Hispanic or Latino	22	0.26

Race*	Population	%
African-American/Black (446)	503	6.01
Not Hispanic (444)	501	5.99
Hispanic (2)	2	0.02
American Indian/Alaska Native (28)	81	0.97
Not Hispanic (24)	68	0.81
Hispanic (4)	13	0.16
Blackfeet (0)	1	0.01
Cherokee (6)	13	0.16
Chippewa (6)	9	0.11
Choctaw (0)	1	0.01
Houma (0)	1	0.01
Menominee (0)	2	0.02
Ottawa (3)	4	0.05
Potawatomi (3)	12	0.14
Pueblo (1)	2	0.02
Sioux (0)	1	0.01
Asian (284)	339	4.05
Not Hispanic (281)	330	3.95
Hispanic (3)	9	0.11
Burmese (3)	3	0.04
Chinese, ex. Taiwanese (67)	73	0.87
Filipino (15)	29	0.35
Indian (155)	162	1.94
Indonesian (1)	1	0.01
Japanese (3)	18	0.22

*Notes: † The Census 2010 population figure is used to calculate the percentages in the Hispanic Origin and Race categories. Ancestry percentages are based on the 2006-2010 American Community Survey population (not shown); ‡ Numbers in parentheses indicate the number of people reporting a single ancestry; * Numbers in parentheses indicate the number of persons reporting this race alone, not in combination with any other race; Please refer to the Explanation of Data for more information.*

Korean (20)	26	0.31
Laotian (2)	2	0.02
Nepalese (1)	1	0.01
Pakistani (1)	1	0.01
Thai (6)	7	0.08
Vietnamese (6)	12	0.14
Hawaii Native/Pacific Islander (0)	3	0.04
Not Hispanic (0)	1	0.01
Hispanic (0)	2	0.02
White (7,371)	7,521	89.91
Not Hispanic (7,227)	7,354	87.91
Hispanic (144)	167	2.00

Sterling Heights

Place Type: City
County: Macomb
Population: 129,699†

Ancestry‡	Population	%
Afghan (41)	41	0.03
African, Sub-Saharan (932)	966	0.74
African (782)	802	0.62
Cape Verdean (0)	14	0.01
Nigerian (33)	33	0.03
Somalian (75)	75	0.06
Other Sub-Saharan African (42)	42	0.03
Albanian (3,206)	3,414	2.63
American (4,311)	4,311	3.32
Arab (7,011)	8,488	6.54
Arab (1,807)	1,888	1.46
Egyptian (252)	283	0.22
Iraqi (3,473)	4,199	3.24
Jordanian (113)	161	0.12
Lebanese (994)	1,441	1.11
Palestinian (0)	29	0.02
Syrian (119)	187	0.14
Other Arab (253)	300	0.23
Armenian (282)	288	0.22
Assyrian/Chaldean/Syriac (6,987)	8,026	6.19
Australian (9)	18	0.01
Austrian (90)	526	0.41
Belgian (450)	1,835	1.41
Brazilian (57)	57	0.04
British (59)	163	0.13
Bulgarian (12)	24	0.02
Canadian (265)	604	0.47
Celtic (20)	20	0.02
Croatian (151)	347	0.27
Czech (106)	463	0.36
Czechoslovakian (185)	456	0.35
Danish (35)	261	0.20
Dutch (209)	1,216	0.94
Eastern European (40)	53	0.04
English (2,422)	8,908	6.87
European (481)	516	0.40
Finnish (133)	854	0.66
French, ex. Basque (669)	6,116	4.72
French Canadian (669)	1,986	1.53
German (6,203)	23,659	18.24
Greek (728)	1,148	0.89
Guyanese (0)	9	0.01
Hungarian (206)	1,195	0.92
Icelander (0)	10	0.01
Iranian (135)	163	0.13
Irish (2,457)	11,759	9.07
Israeli (17)	17	0.01
Italian (6,769)	15,325	11.82
Latvian (10)	39	0.03
Lithuanian (120)	310	0.24
Macedonian (1,264)	1,382	1.07
Maltese (103)	235	0.18
Northern European (115)	115	0.09
Norwegian (159)	712	0.55
Polish (11,674)	23,071	17.79
Portuguese (35)	94	0.07
Romanian (1,447)	1,620	1.25
Russian (418)	1,070	0.83
Scandinavian (0)	12	0.01
Scotch-Irish (596)	1,593	1.23
Scottish (535)	2,501	1.93
Serbian (301)	369	0.28
Slavic (24)	69	0.05
Slovak (297)	1,027	0.79
Slovene (0)	32	0.02
Swedish (207)	899	0.69
Swiss (11)	93	0.07
Turkish (14)	14	0.01
Ukrainian (791)	1,410	1.09
Welsh (46)	398	0.31
West Indian, ex. Hispanic (11)	20	0.02
Bahamian (0)	9	0.01
Jamaican (11)	11	0.01
Yugoslavian (1,357)	1,665	1.28

Hispanic Origin	Population	%
Hispanic or Latino (of any race)	2,523	1.95
Central American, ex. Mexican	55	0.04
Costa Rican	13	0.01
Guatemalan	12	0.01
Honduran	9	0.01
Nicaraguan	1	<0.01
Panamanian	11	0.01
Salvadoran	9	0.01
Cuban	69	0.05
Dominican Republic	33	0.03
Mexican	1,537	1.19
Puerto Rican	301	0.23
South American	192	0.15
Argentinean	36	0.03
Bolivian	9	0.01
Chilean	16	0.01
Colombian	59	0.05
Ecuadorian	16	0.01
Peruvian	22	0.02
Venezuelan	31	0.02
Other South American	3	<0.01
Other Hispanic or Latino	336	0.26

Race*	Population	%
African-American/Black (6,697)	7,313	5.64
Not Hispanic (6,638)	7,213	5.56
Hispanic (59)	100	0.08
American Indian/Alaska Native (281)	832	0.64
Not Hispanic (246)	735	0.57
Hispanic (35)	97	0.07
Apache (2)	10	0.01
Arapaho (0)	1	<0.01
Blackfeet (6)	30	0.02
Canadian/French Am. Ind. (2)	5	<0.01
Cherokee (27)	164	0.13
Chickasaw (0)	2	<0.01
Chippewa (59)	104	0.08
Choctaw (1)	15	0.01
Cree (6)	6	<0.01
Creek (0)	2	<0.01
Delaware (4)	7	0.01
Iroquois (8)	23	0.02
Lumbee (12)	20	0.02
Menominee (0)	1	<0.01
Mexican American Ind. (4)	11	0.01
Navajo (5)	9	0.01
Ottawa (10)	19	0.01
Potawatomi (5)	7	0.01
Seminole (1)	2	<0.01
Shoshone (1)	1	<0.01
Sioux (6)	13	0.01
South American Ind. (1)	3	<0.01
Asian (8,742)	10,282	7.93
Not Hispanic (8,713)	10,193	7.86
Hispanic (29)	89	0.07
Bangladeshi (205)	223	0.17
Burmese (5)	5	<0.01
Cambodian (20)	25	0.02
Chinese, ex. Taiwanese (929)	1,023	0.79
Filipino (1,733)	1,981	1.53
Hmong (171)	175	0.13
Indian (3,340)	3,551	2.74
Indonesian (8)	14	0.01
Japanese (98)	170	0.13
Korean (406)	489	0.38
Laotian (31)	47	0.04
Malaysian (11)	15	0.01
Nepalese (5)	7	0.01
Pakistani (454)	501	0.39
Sri Lankan (11)	11	0.01
Taiwanese (34)	36	0.03
Thai (37)	46	0.04
Vietnamese (961)	1,027	0.79
Hawaii Native/Pacific Islander (19)	320	0.25
Not Hispanic (16)	306	0.24
Hispanic (3)	14	0.01
Guamanian/Chamorro (7)	12	0.01
Native Hawaiian (7)	17	0.01
Samoan (3)	10	0.01
White (110,426)	112,990	87.12
Not Hispanic (108,750)	111,121	85.68
Hispanic (1,676)	1,869	1.44

Sturgis

Place Type: City
County: St. Joseph
Population: 10,994†

Ancestry‡	Population	%
American (1,580)	1,580	14.23
Belgian (0)	43	0.39
Canadian (0)	11	0.10
Croatian (0)	9	0.08
Dutch (57)	467	4.21
English (457)	1,069	9.63
European (181)	181	1.63
French, ex. Basque (32)	275	2.48
French Canadian (13)	62	0.56
German (1,494)	3,163	28.49
Greek (22)	59	0.53
Hungarian (0)	15	0.14
Irish (375)	1,066	9.60
Italian (55)	221	1.99
Northern European (11)	11	0.10
Norwegian (49)	187	1.68
Pennsylvania German (67)	74	0.67
Polish (58)	391	3.52
Romanian (63)	63	0.57
Russian (0)	45	0.41
Scandinavian (0)	11	0.10
Scotch-Irish (53)	177	1.59
Scottish (22)	184	1.66
Serbian (10)	10	0.09
Slovak (0)	13	0.12
Swedish (14)	76	0.68
Swiss (11)	19	0.17
Ukrainian (0)	11	0.10
Welsh (0)	14	0.13

Hispanic Origin	Population	%
Hispanic or Latino (of any race)	2,510	22.83
Central American, ex. Mexican	18	0.16
Honduran	10	0.09
Nicaraguan	1	0.01
Panamanian	5	0.05
Salvadoran	2	0.02
Cuban	19	0.17
Dominican Republic	3	0.03
Mexican	2,385	21.69
Puerto Rican	50	0.45
South American	1	0.01
Colombian	1	0.01
Other Hispanic or Latino	34	0.31

Race*	Population	%
African-American/Black (156)	277	2.52
Not Hispanic (144)	250	2.27
Hispanic (12)	27	0.25
American Indian/Alaska Native (37)	126	1.15
Not Hispanic (21)	103	0.94
Hispanic (16)	23	0.21
Apache (2)	6	0.05
Arapaho (0)	1	0.01

*Notes: † The Census 2010 population figure is used to calculate the percentages in the Hispanic Origin and Race categories. Ancestry percentages are based on the 2006-2010 American Community Survey population (not shown); ‡ Numbers in parentheses indicate the number of people reporting a single ancestry; * Numbers in parentheses indicate the number of persons reporting this race alone, not in combination with any other race; Please refer to the Explanation of Data for more information.*

Blackfeet (0)	7	0.06
Cherokee (2)	26	0.24
Chippewa (8)	9	0.08
Comanche (1)	1	0.01
Delaware (0)	1	0.01
Iroquois (2)	4	0.04
Lumbee (0)	1	0.01
Mexican American Ind. (6)	7	0.06
Ottawa (1)	3	0.03
Paiute (0)	2	0.02
Potawatomi (0)	1	0.01
Sioux (0)	4	0.04
South American Ind. (0)	1	0.01
Asian (96)	139	1.26
Not Hispanic (96)	126	1.15
Hispanic (0)	13	0.12
Burmese (2)	2	0.02
Cambodian (0)	1	0.01
Chinese, ex. Taiwanese (12)	15	0.14
Filipino (28)	42	0.38
Hmong (0)	2	0.02
Indian (28)	40	0.36
Japanese (5)	11	0.10
Korean (7)	7	0.06
Laotian (1)	2	0.02
Pakistani (0)	2	0.02
Thai (2)	5	0.05
Vietnamese (6)	7	0.06
Hawaii Native/Pacific Islander (1)	11	0.10
Not Hispanic (1)	11	0.10
Native Hawaiian (0)	6	0.05
Tongan (1)	5	0.05
White (8,856)	9,199	83.67
Not Hispanic (7,977)	8,201	74.60
Hispanic (879)	998	9.08

Summit

Place Type: Township
County: Jackson
Population: 22,508†

Ancestry‡	Population	%
African, Sub-Saharan (213)	213	0.95
African (213)	213	0.95
American (1,478)	1,478	6.56
Arab (46)	81	0.36
Lebanese (16)	51	0.23
Other Arab (30)	30	0.13
Austrian (10)	51	0.23
Belgian (42)	183	0.81
Brazilian (19)	19	0.08
British (50)	50	0.22
Bulgarian (10)	22	0.10
Canadian (18)	61	0.27
Croatian (29)	93	0.41
Czech (31)	109	0.48
Czechoslovakian (0)	83	0.37
Danish (0)	37	0.16
Dutch (114)	870	3.86
English (1,627)	4,325	19.20
European (166)	166	0.74
Finnish (78)	108	0.48
French, ex. Basque (195)	894	3.97
French Canadian (127)	394	1.75
German (1,682)	5,398	23.97
Greek (24)	87	0.39
Hungarian (23)	28	0.12
Irish (1,061)	4,070	18.07
Italian (315)	720	3.20
Lithuanian (14)	66	0.29
Macedonian (29)	66	0.29
Northern European (31)	31	0.14
Norwegian (53)	311	1.38
Pennsylvania German (0)	9	0.04
Polish (525)	1,627	7.22
Portuguese (12)	47	0.21
Romanian (20)	20	0.09
Russian (20)	137	0.61
Scandinavian (13)	57	0.25
Scotch-Irish (120)	362	1.61
Scottish (260)	725	3.22
Slovak (12)	70	0.31
Slovene (0)	9	0.04
Swedish (118)	317	1.41
Swiss (0)	89	0.40
Ukrainian (11)	16	0.07
Welsh (58)	191	0.85
Yugoslavian (0)	11	0.05

Hispanic Origin	Population	%
Hispanic or Latino (of any race)	609	2.71
Central American, ex. Mexican	24	0.11
Costa Rican	2	0.01
Guatemalan	10	0.04
Honduran	3	0.01
Nicaraguan	1	<0.01
Panamanian	8	0.04
Cuban	4	0.02
Dominican Republic	1	<0.01
Mexican	451	2.00
Puerto Rican	47	0.21
South American	17	0.08
Bolivian	3	0.01
Chilean	2	0.01
Colombian	5	0.02
Peruvian	3	0.01
Venezuelan	4	0.02
Other Hispanic or Latino	65	0.29

Race*	Population	%
African-American/Black (1,188)	1,503	6.68
Not Hispanic (1,169)	1,459	6.48
Hispanic (19)	44	0.20
American Indian/Alaska Native (65)	253	1.12
Not Hispanic (52)	220	0.98
Hispanic (13)	33	0.15
Apache (2)	6	0.03
Blackfeet (3)	17	0.08
Canadian/French Am. Ind. (0)	1	<0.01
Cherokee (4)	46	0.20
Chippewa (13)	28	0.12
Choctaw (0)	4	0.02
Comanche (0)	1	<0.01
Cree (0)	1	<0.01
Creek (0)	1	<0.01
Crow (0)	2	0.01
Delaware (0)	4	0.02
Hopi (1)	1	<0.01
Iroquois (2)	9	0.04
Lumbee (2)	7	0.03
Mexican American Ind. (3)	8	0.04
Navajo (1)	1	<0.01
Ottawa (2)	11	0.05
Potawatomi (0)	2	0.01
Pueblo (0)	4	0.02
Seminole (0)	1	<0.01
Sioux (1)	3	0.01
South American Ind. (1)	2	0.01
Asian (346)	401	1.78
Not Hispanic (340)	392	1.74
Hispanic (6)	9	0.04
Bangladeshi (2)	2	0.01
Cambodian (2)	2	0.01
Chinese, ex. Taiwanese (32)	35	0.16
Filipino (22)	38	0.17
Indian (122)	130	0.58
Indonesian (3)	3	0.01
Japanese (45)	58	0.26
Korean (25)	34	0.15
Pakistani (37)	37	0.16
Taiwanese (2)	2	0.01
Thai (6)	9	0.04
Vietnamese (26)	29	0.13
Hawaii Native/Pacific Islander (12)	23	0.10
Not Hispanic (9)	19	0.08
Hispanic (3)	4	0.02
Guamanian/Chamorro (2)	3	0.01
Native Hawaiian (7)	13	0.06
Tongan (3)	6	0.03
White (20,176)	20,709	92.01
Not Hispanic (19,833)	20,287	90.13
Hispanic (343)	422	1.87

Sumpter

Place Type: Township
County: Wayne
Population: 9,549†

Ancestry‡	Population	%
American (589)	589	5.89
Austrian (0)	27	0.27
Belgian (14)	21	0.21
Brazilian (8)	26	0.26
British (58)	96	0.96
Canadian (7)	7	0.07
Croatian (0)	36	0.36
Czech (0)	45	0.45
Danish (0)	27	0.27
Dutch (28)	126	1.26
English (213)	1,106	11.05
European (172)	172	1.72
Finnish (11)	58	0.58
French, ex. Basque (132)	827	8.27
French Canadian (146)	344	3.44
German (476)	2,303	23.02
Greek (22)	66	0.66
Hungarian (51)	293	2.93
Irish (377)	1,519	15.18
Italian (67)	184	1.84
Lithuanian (9)	23	0.23
Maltese (0)	10	0.10
Norwegian (7)	39	0.39
Polish (414)	1,033	10.32
Portuguese (0)	15	0.15
Romanian (12)	12	0.12
Russian (15)	32	0.32
Scotch-Irish (130)	237	2.37
Scottish (19)	201	2.01
Slovak (14)	68	0.68
Slovene (0)	11	0.11
Swedish (20)	40	0.40
Ukrainian (27)	38	0.38
Welsh (0)	82	0.82

Hispanic Origin	Population	%
Hispanic or Latino (of any race)	251	2.63
Central American, ex. Mexican	10	0.10
Costa Rican	1	0.01
Guatemalan	1	0.01
Nicaraguan	1	0.01
Panamanian	2	0.02
Salvadoran	5	0.05
Cuban	14	0.15
Mexican	170	1.78
Puerto Rican	37	0.39
Other Hispanic or Latino	20	0.21

Race*	Population	%
African-American/Black (1,147)	1,267	13.27
Not Hispanic (1,133)	1,239	12.98
Hispanic (14)	28	0.29
American Indian/Alaska Native (53)	153	1.60
Not Hispanic (41)	139	1.46
Hispanic (12)	14	0.15
Apache (0)	2	0.02
Blackfeet (1)	9	0.09
Canadian/French Am. Ind. (1)	1	0.01
Cherokee (12)	38	0.40
Chippewa (6)	12	0.13
Choctaw (1)	1	0.01
Creek (5)	5	0.05
Iroquois (3)	3	0.03
Lumbee (1)	2	0.02
Mexican American Ind. (1)	1	0.01
Navajo (0)	1	0.01
Ottawa (1)	2	0.02
Potawatomi (2)	2	0.02
Pueblo (3)	3	0.03

*Notes: † The Census 2010 population figure is used to calculate the percentages in the Hispanic Origin and Race categories. Ancestry percentages are based on the 2006-2010 American Community Survey population (not shown); ‡ Numbers in parentheses indicate the number of people reporting a single ancestry; * Numbers in parentheses indicate the number of persons reporting this race alone, not in combination with any other race; Please refer to the Explanation of Data for more information.*

Race*	Population	%
Shoshone (1)	1	0.01
Sioux (1)	7	0.07
Asian (26)	77	0.81
Not Hispanic (23)	73	0.76
Hispanic (3)	4	0.04
Chinese, ex. Taiwanese (4)	11	0.12
Filipino (10)	19	0.20
Indian (1)	2	0.02
Japanese (0)	11	0.12
Korean (9)	17	0.18
Laotian (1)	2	0.02
Vietnamese (1)	3	0.03
Hawaii Native/Pacific Islander (0)	11	0.12
Not Hispanic (0)	11	0.12
Native Hawaiian (0)	10	0.10
Samoan (0)	1	0.01
White (8,006)	8,267	86.57
Not Hispanic (7,839)	8,075	84.56
Hispanic (167)	192	2.01

Superior

Place Type: Charter Township
County: Washtenaw
Population: 13,058†

Ancestry‡	Population	%
African, Sub-Saharan (186)	219	1.72
African (164)	197	1.55
Nigerian (9)	9	0.07
Ugandan (13)	13	0.10
American (722)	722	5.66
Arab (276)	320	2.51
Arab (103)	103	0.81
Lebanese (32)	54	0.42
Syrian (11)	11	0.09
Other Arab (130)	152	1.19
Armenian (10)	10	0.08
Australian (6)	6	0.05
Austrian (0)	9	0.07
Belgian (12)	20	0.16
British (10)	10	0.08
Cajun (0)	6	0.05
Canadian (0)	8	0.06
Croatian (15)	31	0.24
Czech (0)	46	0.36
Czechoslovakian (17)	34	0.27
Danish (19)	50	0.39
Dutch (38)	299	2.35
Eastern European (13)	24	0.19
English (227)	1,259	9.88
European (80)	120	0.94
Finnish (62)	114	0.89
French, ex. Basque (46)	336	2.64
French Canadian (29)	94	0.74
German (506)	1,864	14.62
Greek (35)	54	0.42
Hungarian (20)	107	0.84
Iranian (11)	32	0.25
Irish (195)	1,208	9.48
Italian (164)	547	4.29
Lithuanian (5)	5	0.04
Maltese (0)	13	0.10
Northern European (9)	9	0.07
Norwegian (18)	54	0.42
Polish (382)	945	7.41
Portuguese (0)	26	0.20
Romanian (116)	126	0.99
Russian (55)	120	0.94
Scandinavian (0)	30	0.24
Scotch-Irish (71)	230	1.80
Scottish (15)	247	1.94
Serbian (10)	19	0.15
Slovak (11)	85	0.67
Slovene (0)	9	0.07
Swedish (20)	148	1.16
Swiss (8)	35	0.27
Ukrainian (0)	19	0.15
Welsh (0)	20	0.16
West Indian, ex. Hispanic (0)	19	0.15
Jamaican (0)	12	0.09
Trinidadian/Tobagonian (0)	7	0.05

Hispanic Origin	Population	%
Hispanic or Latino (of any race)	495	3.79
Central American, ex. Mexican	100	0.77
Costa Rican	5	0.04
Guatemalan	15	0.11
Honduran	30	0.23
Nicaraguan	4	0.03
Panamanian	3	0.02
Salvadoran	43	0.33
Cuban	11	0.08
Dominican Republic	7	0.05
Mexican	236	1.81
Puerto Rican	52	0.40
South American	39	0.30
Argentinean	6	0.05
Bolivian	2	0.02
Colombian	15	0.11
Ecuadorian	4	0.03
Peruvian	6	0.05
Venezuelan	5	0.04
Other South American	1	0.01
Other Hispanic or Latino	50	0.38

Race*	Population	%
African-American/Black (3,929)	4,229	32.39
Not Hispanic (3,894)	4,180	32.01
Hispanic (35)	49	0.38
American Indian/Alaska Native (31)	146	1.12
Not Hispanic (28)	135	1.03
Hispanic (3)	11	0.08
Blackfeet (0)	9	0.07
Canadian/French Am. Ind. (0)	2	0.02
Cherokee (4)	37	0.28
Chippewa (3)	8	0.06
Creek (1)	1	0.01
Delaware (1)	4	0.03
Iroquois (1)	1	0.01
Lumbee (0)	1	0.01
Mexican American Ind. (1)	1	0.01
Ottawa (0)	2	0.02
Potawatomi (4)	7	0.05
Sioux (0)	2	0.02
Spanish American Ind. (0)	1	0.01
Asian (746)	856	6.56
Not Hispanic (741)	847	6.49
Hispanic (5)	9	0.07
Bangladeshi (6)	8	0.06
Chinese, ex. Taiwanese (180)	201	1.54
Filipino (60)	72	0.55
Hmong (4)	5	0.04
Indian (265)	290	2.22
Indonesian (1)	1	0.01
Japanese (14)	36	0.28
Korean (74)	84	0.64
Laotian (10)	10	0.08
Malaysian (1)	1	0.01
Nepalese (5)	7	0.05
Pakistani (52)	56	0.43
Sri Lankan (8)	8	0.06
Taiwanese (19)	28	0.21
Thai (8)	8	0.06
Vietnamese (19)	19	0.15
Hawaii Native/Pacific Islander (1)	18	0.14
Not Hispanic (1)	18	0.14
Native Hawaiian (1)	11	0.08
White (7,704)	8,111	62.12
Not Hispanic (7,441)	7,805	59.77
Hispanic (263)	306	2.34

Tallmadge

Place Type: Charter Township
County: Ottawa
Population: 7,575†

Ancestry‡	Population	%
American (373)	373	4.97
Arab (13)	23	0.31
Lebanese (13)	13	0.17
Syrian (0)	10	0.13
Czech (0)	12	0.16
Danish (44)	44	0.59
Dutch (1,497)	2,517	33.52
English (151)	628	8.36
European (75)	95	1.26
Finnish (0)	24	0.32
French, ex. Basque (0)	230	3.06
French Canadian (28)	38	0.51
German (359)	1,850	24.63
Hungarian (19)	19	0.25
Irish (208)	769	10.24
Italian (97)	289	3.85
Lithuanian (24)	62	0.83
Norwegian (28)	53	0.71
Polish (338)	791	10.53
Russian (23)	36	0.48
Scandinavian (0)	11	0.15
Scotch-Irish (12)	47	0.63
Scottish (10)	89	1.19
Swedish (0)	238	3.17
Welsh (28)	28	0.37

Hispanic Origin	Population	%
Hispanic or Latino (of any race)	148	1.95
Central American, ex. Mexican	5	0.07
Guatemalan	4	0.05
Panamanian	1	0.01
Cuban	7	0.09
Dominican Republic	5	0.07
Mexican	98	1.29
Puerto Rican	17	0.22
South American	2	0.03
Chilean	1	0.01
Colombian	1	0.01
Other Hispanic or Latino	14	0.18

Race*	Population	%
African-American/Black (36)	62	0.82
Not Hispanic (35)	60	0.79
Hispanic (1)	2	0.03
American Indian/Alaska Native (39)	82	1.08
Not Hispanic (32)	73	0.96
Hispanic (7)	9	0.12
Blackfeet (1)	3	0.04
Canadian/French Am. Ind. (0)	1	0.01
Cherokee (6)	12	0.16
Cheyenne (0)	1	0.01
Chippewa (5)	16	0.21
Cree (1)	1	0.01
Lumbee (4)	4	0.05
Navajo (0)	1	0.01
Ottawa (0)	7	0.09
Potawatomi (4)	5	0.07
Sioux (0)	1	0.01
Asian (51)	64	0.84
Not Hispanic (51)	63	0.83
Hispanic (0)	1	0.01
Cambodian (0)	2	0.03
Chinese, ex. Taiwanese (14)	14	0.18
Filipino (4)	10	0.13
Indian (6)	8	0.11
Japanese (2)	2	0.03
Korean (18)	19	0.25
Vietnamese (7)	8	0.11
Hawaii Native/Pacific Islander (0)	5	0.07
Not Hispanic (0)	1	0.01
Hispanic (0)	4	0.05
White (7,318)	7,405	97.76
Not Hispanic (7,228)	7,304	96.42
Hispanic (90)	101	1.33

Taylor

Place Type: City
County: Wayne
Population: 63,131†

*Notes: † The Census 2010 population figure is used to calculate the percentages in the Hispanic Origin and Race categories. Ancestry percentages are based on the 2006-2010 American Community Survey population (not shown); ‡ Numbers in parentheses indicate the number of people reporting a single ancestry; * Numbers in parentheses indicate the number of persons reporting this race alone, not in combination with any other race; Please refer to the Explanation of Data for more information.*

Ancestry‡	Population	%
African, Sub-Saharan (274)	305	0.48
African (218)	249	0.39
Ghanaian (56)	56	0.09
Albanian (385)	385	0.60
American (2,291)	2,291	3.59
Arab (172)	356	0.56
Arab (51)	111	0.17
Lebanese (51)	145	0.23
Palestinian (7)	7	0.01
Syrian (63)	93	0.15
Armenian (70)	155	0.24
Assyrian/Chaldean/Syriac (11)	11	0.02
Australian (0)	23	0.04
Austrian (35)	94	0.15
Belgian (44)	101	0.16
Brazilian (86)	101	0.16
British (10)	47	0.07
Bulgarian (8)	8	0.01
Canadian (39)	353	0.55
Carpatho Rusyn (0)	10	0.02
Croatian (13)	115	0.18
Czech (79)	295	0.46
Czechoslovakian (103)	222	0.35
Danish (10)	168	0.26
Dutch (136)	923	1.45
Eastern European (10)	10	0.02
English (1,275)	5,231	8.19
European (494)	613	0.96
Finnish (35)	291	0.46
French, ex. Basque (762)	4,438	6.95
French Canadian (708)	1,822	2.85
German (2,786)	10,727	16.80
Greek (78)	350	0.55
Guyanese (10)	32	0.05
Hungarian (663)	2,139	3.35
Irish (2,185)	10,032	15.72
Italian (1,048)	3,179	4.98
Latvian (10)	42	0.07
Lithuanian (126)	381	0.60
Macedonian (7)	7	0.01
Maltese (163)	342	0.54
Norwegian (26)	275	0.43
Pennsylvania German (74)	118	0.18
Polish (2,805)	6,619	10.37
Portuguese (20)	154	0.24
Romanian (138)	162	0.25
Russian (88)	305	0.48
Scandinavian (44)	98	0.15
Scotch-Irish (560)	1,226	1.92
Scottish (380)	1,341	2.10
Serbian (0)	11	0.02
Slavic (0)	20	0.03
Slovak (25)	243	0.38
Slovene (0)	8	0.01
Swedish (135)	438	0.69
Swiss (0)	15	0.02
Ukrainian (75)	101	0.16
Welsh (38)	314	0.49
West Indian, ex. Hispanic (74)	74	0.12
Jamaican (18)	18	0.03
West Indian (56)	56	0.09
Yugoslavian (0)	16	0.03

Hispanic Origin	Population	%
Hispanic or Latino (of any race)	3,209	5.08
Central American, ex. Mexican	77	0.12
Costa Rican	4	0.01
Guatemalan	16	0.03
Honduran	15	0.02
Nicaraguan	17	0.03
Panamanian	11	0.02
Salvadoran	14	0.02
Cuban	55	0.09
Dominican Republic	7	0.01
Mexican	2,344	3.71
Puerto Rican	446	0.71
South American	56	0.09
Argentinean	23	0.04
Bolivian	2	<0.01
Chilean	6	0.01
Colombian	4	0.01
Ecuadorian	7	0.01
Peruvian	10	0.02
Uruguayan	2	<0.01
Venezuelan	2	<0.01
Other Hispanic or Latino	224	0.35

Race*	Population	%
African-American/Black (10,004)	10,865	17.21
Not Hispanic (9,896)	10,671	16.90
Hispanic (108)	194	0.31
American Indian/Alaska Native (336)	920	1.46
Not Hispanic (285)	808	1.28
Hispanic (51)	112	0.18
Apache (4)	10	0.02
Blackfeet (12)	39	0.06
Canadian/French Am. Ind. (10)	13	0.02
Central American Ind. (0)	3	<0.01
Cherokee (41)	217	0.34
Cheyenne (0)	2	<0.01
Chickasaw (1)	5	0.01
Chippewa (59)	114	0.18
Choctaw (1)	8	0.01
Comanche (3)	3	<0.01
Cree (1)	2	<0.01
Creek (3)	4	0.01
Crow (0)	2	<0.01
Delaware (6)	18	0.03
Hopi (0)	2	<0.01
Iroquois (13)	43	0.07
Lumbee (27)	43	0.07
Menominee (0)	1	<0.01
Mexican American Ind. (4)	7	0.01
Navajo (1)	5	0.01
Osage (2)	4	0.01
Ottawa (9)	16	0.03
Pima (0)	1	<0.01
Potawatomi (1)	3	<0.01
Pueblo (0)	1	<0.01
Seminole (0)	4	0.01
Sioux (0)	13	0.02
South American Ind. (0)	5	0.01
Spanish American Ind. (1)	1	<0.01
Tlingit-Haida *(Alaska Native)* (1)	4	0.01
Yaqui (4)	4	0.01
Yuman (0)	1	<0.01
Asian (1,121)	1,324	2.10
Not Hispanic (1,111)	1,294	2.05
Hispanic (10)	30	0.05
Cambodian (15)	17	0.03
Chinese, ex. Taiwanese (98)	123	0.19
Filipino (234)	308	0.49
Hmong (5)	8	0.01
Indian (289)	312	0.49
Indonesian (4)	5	0.01
Japanese (31)	81	0.13
Korean (49)	69	0.11
Laotian (1)	5	0.01
Malaysian (2)	2	<0.01
Pakistani (243)	252	0.40
Thai (14)	20	0.03
Vietnamese (86)	90	0.14
Hawaii Native/Pacific Islander (20)	63	0.10
Not Hispanic (16)	49	0.08
Hispanic (4)	14	0.02
Guamanian/Chamorro (3)	3	<0.01
Native Hawaiian (7)	19	0.03
Samoan (1)	2	<0.01
White (49,229)	50,686	80.29
Not Hispanic (47,177)	48,415	76.69
Hispanic (2,052)	2,271	3.60

Tecumseh

Place Type: City
County: Lenawee
Population: 8,521†

Ancestry‡	Population	%
American (553)	553	6.39
Armenian (5)	15	0.17
Austrian (9)	9	0.10
Belgian (0)	16	0.18
British (9)	9	0.10
Cajun (0)	52	0.60
Canadian (43)	98	1.13
Croatian (0)	12	0.14
Czechoslovakian (28)	28	0.32
Danish (0)	68	0.79
Dutch (78)	388	4.48
English (525)	1,632	18.86
European (20)	56	0.65
Finnish (21)	32	0.37
French, ex. Basque (91)	551	6.37
French Canadian (22)	126	1.46
German (918)	3,422	39.55
Hungarian (22)	111	1.28
Irish (347)	1,413	16.33
Italian (148)	464	5.36
Lithuanian (18)	27	0.31
Maltese (0)	19	0.22
Norwegian (17)	153	1.77
Polish (191)	642	7.42
Portuguese (0)	10	0.12
Russian (24)	45	0.52
Scandinavian (9)	55	0.64
Scotch-Irish (58)	213	2.46
Scottish (128)	196	2.27
Swedish (0)	90	1.04
Swiss (0)	133	1.54
Ukrainian (0)	18	0.21
Welsh (0)	81	0.94

Hispanic Origin	Population	%
Hispanic or Latino (of any race)	379	4.45
Central American, ex. Mexican	9	0.11
Costa Rican	2	0.02
Guatemalan	5	0.06
Panamanian	1	0.01
Salvadoran	1	0.01
Cuban	2	0.02
Dominican Republic	4	0.05
Mexican	288	3.38
Puerto Rican	30	0.35
South American	7	0.08
Chilean	1	0.01
Colombian	6	0.07
Other Hispanic or Latino	39	0.46

Race*	Population	%
African-American/Black (34)	86	1.01
Not Hispanic (32)	68	0.80
Hispanic (2)	18	0.21
American Indian/Alaska Native (37)	78	0.92
Not Hispanic (30)	65	0.76
Hispanic (7)	13	0.15
Apache (0)	2	0.02
Canadian/French Am. Ind. (1)	1	0.01
Cherokee (10)	18	0.21
Cheyenne (0)	1	0.01
Chippewa (13)	17	0.20
Choctaw (1)	3	0.04
Comanche (1)	1	0.01
Delaware (0)	1	0.01
South American Ind. (0)	1	0.01
Asian (62)	83	0.97
Not Hispanic (62)	82	0.96
Hispanic (0)	1	0.01
Chinese, ex. Taiwanese (12)	15	0.18
Filipino (7)	12	0.14
Indian (7)	7	0.08
Japanese (9)	17	0.20
Korean (12)	17	0.20
Pakistani (5)	5	0.06
Vietnamese (9)	9	0.11
Hawaii Native/Pacific Islander (1)	3	0.04
Not Hispanic (1)	1	0.01
Hispanic (0)	2	0.02

*Notes: † The Census 2010 population figure is used to calculate the percentages in the Hispanic Origin and Race categories. Ancestry percentages are based on the 2006-2010 American Community Survey population (not shown); ‡ Numbers in parentheses indicate the number of people reporting a single ancestry; * Numbers in parentheses indicate the number of persons reporting this race alone, not in combination with any other race; Please refer to the Explanation of Data for more information.*

Native Hawaiian (1)	1	0.01
White (8,182)	8,310	97.52
Not Hispanic (7,926)	8,012	94.03
Hispanic (256)	298	3.50

Temperance

Place Type: CDP
County: Monroe
Population: 8,517†

Ancestry‡	Population	%
American (290)	290	3.44
Arab (56)	93	1.10
Arab (0)	11	0.13
Iraqi (10)	10	0.12
Jordanian (13)	13	0.15
Lebanese (33)	59	0.70
Belgian (21)	42	0.50
British (28)	110	1.30
Bulgarian (8)	29	0.34
Canadian (0)	12	0.14
Czech (16)	16	0.19
Dutch (76)	230	2.73
English (250)	1,037	12.29
European (71)	80	0.95
Finnish (12)	35	0.41
French, ex. Basque (120)	608	7.20
French Canadian (25)	167	1.98
German (1,171)	3,391	40.18
Greek (9)	30	0.36
Hungarian (77)	178	2.11
Irish (211)	1,368	16.21
Italian (114)	625	7.41
Norwegian (11)	45	0.53
Polish (538)	1,338	15.85
Romanian (20)	20	0.24
Russian (10)	74	0.88
Scandinavian (20)	40	0.47
Scotch-Irish (71)	140	1.66
Scottish (38)	142	1.68
Slovak (0)	63	0.75
Slovene (0)	13	0.15
Swedish (10)	62	0.73
Swiss (0)	8	0.09
Ukrainian (10)	19	0.23
Welsh (34)	52	0.62

Hispanic Origin	Population	%
Hispanic or Latino (of any race)	190	2.23
Central American, ex. Mexican	11	0.13
Costa Rican	5	0.06
Guatemalan	6	0.07
Cuban	6	0.07
Mexican	142	1.67
Puerto Rican	11	0.13
South American	7	0.08
Argentinean	2	0.02
Colombian	1	0.01
Peruvian	3	0.04
Venezuelan	1	0.01
Other Hispanic or Latino	13	0.15

Race*	Population	%
African-American/Black (35)	53	0.62
Not Hispanic (33)	49	0.58
Hispanic (2)	4	0.05
American Indian/Alaska Native (17)	59	0.69
Not Hispanic (14)	52	0.61
Hispanic (3)	7	0.08
Cherokee (5)	20	0.23
Chippewa (1)	2	0.02
Comanche (0)	2	0.02
Iroquois (0)	1	0.01
Kiowa (1)	3	0.04
Mexican American Ind. (2)	2	0.02
Navajo (0)	2	0.02
Ottawa (3)	3	0.04
Sioux (0)	1	0.01
Asian (70)	84	0.99
Not Hispanic (69)	82	0.96
Hispanic (1)	2	0.02
Chinese, ex. Taiwanese (20)	25	0.29
Filipino (13)	15	0.18
Indian (5)	8	0.09
Indonesian (1)	1	0.01
Japanese (5)	6	0.07
Korean (5)	9	0.11
Thai (1)	1	0.01
Vietnamese (13)	13	0.15
Hawaii Native/Pacific Islander (2)	2	0.02
Not Hispanic (2)	2	0.02
White (8,260)	8,341	97.93
Not Hispanic (8,127)	8,191	96.17
Hispanic (133)	150	1.76

Texas

Place Type: Charter Township
County: Kalamazoo
Population: 14,697†

Ancestry‡	Population	%
African, Sub-Saharan (63)	63	0.45
African (26)	26	0.19
Nigerian (32)	32	0.23
South African (5)	5	0.04
American (409)	409	2.92
Arab (46)	142	1.02
Arab (0)	48	0.34
Egyptian (46)	46	0.33
Palestinian (0)	48	0.34
Austrian (0)	9	0.06
Belgian (0)	50	0.36
British (44)	102	0.73
Canadian (119)	133	0.95
Croatian (0)	41	0.29
Czech (22)	123	0.88
Czechoslovakian (0)	11	0.08
Danish (35)	127	0.91
Dutch (957)	1,885	13.48
Eastern European (12)	12	0.09
English (503)	2,044	14.62
European (153)	185	1.32
Finnish (28)	119	0.85
French, ex. Basque (73)	655	4.68
French Canadian (41)	145	1.04
German (1,241)	4,420	31.61
Greek (0)	88	0.63
Hungarian (79)	286	2.05
Irish (417)	2,073	14.83
Italian (145)	830	5.94
Lithuanian (0)	89	0.64
Luxemburger (13)	13	0.09
Northern European (73)	73	0.52
Norwegian (11)	106	0.76
Polish (362)	1,059	7.57
Romanian (0)	33	0.24
Russian (16)	48	0.34
Scandinavian (0)	11	0.08
Scotch-Irish (32)	187	1.34
Scottish (145)	601	4.30
Serbian (15)	15	0.11
Slovak (0)	10	0.07
Slovene (0)	22	0.16
Swedish (51)	242	1.73
Swiss (0)	49	0.35
Ukrainian (8)	29	0.21
Yugoslavian (0)	10	0.07

Hispanic Origin	Population	%
Hispanic or Latino (of any race)	305	2.08
Central American, ex. Mexican	18	0.12
Costa Rican	3	0.02
Guatemalan	10	0.07
Panamanian	2	0.01
Salvadoran	3	0.02
Cuban	15	0.10
Dominican Republic	5	0.03
Mexican	178	1.21
Puerto Rican	39	0.27
South American	32	0.22
Argentinean	3	0.02
Chilean	5	0.03
Colombian	16	0.11
Peruvian	1	0.01
Venezuelan	7	0.05
Other Hispanic or Latino	18	0.12

Race*	Population	%
African-American/Black (367)	485	3.30
Not Hispanic (363)	476	3.24
Hispanic (4)	9	0.06
American Indian/Alaska Native (39)	115	0.78
Not Hispanic (33)	98	0.67
Hispanic (6)	17	0.12
Blackfeet (0)	2	0.01
Central American Ind. (0)	1	0.01
Cherokee (4)	22	0.15
Chippewa (6)	12	0.08
Choctaw (3)	4	0.03
Cree (1)	1	0.01
Creek (1)	1	0.01
Iroquois (0)	1	0.01
Mexican American Ind. (4)	5	0.03
Ottawa (1)	2	0.01
Potawatomi (5)	6	0.04
Sioux (0)	1	0.01
Yaqui (0)	1	0.01
Asian (609)	732	4.98
Not Hispanic (607)	720	4.90
Hispanic (2)	12	0.08
Bangladeshi (7)	7	0.05
Burmese (1)	1	0.01
Cambodian (1)	1	0.01
Chinese, ex. Taiwanese (120)	152	1.03
Filipino (29)	54	0.37
Indian (276)	292	1.99
Japanese (9)	16	0.11
Korean (52)	76	0.52
Laotian (8)	8	0.05
Malaysian (4)	5	0.03
Nepalese (1)	2	0.01
Pakistani (53)	55	0.37
Sri Lankan (1)	2	0.01
Taiwanese (18)	23	0.16
Thai (6)	6	0.04
Vietnamese (9)	9	0.06
Hawaii Native/Pacific Islander (5)	17	0.12
Not Hispanic (5)	14	0.10
Hispanic (0)	3	0.02
Guamanian/Chamorro (2)	2	0.01
Native Hawaiian (3)	10	0.07
White (13,317)	13,577	92.38
Not Hispanic (13,112)	13,343	90.79
Hispanic (205)	234	1.59

Thomas

Place Type: Township
County: Saginaw
Population: 11,985†

Ancestry‡	Population	%
American (447)	447	3.73
Arab (7)	20	0.17
Jordanian (7)	7	0.06
Lebanese (0)	13	0.11
Austrian (0)	55	0.46
Belgian (0)	14	0.12
British (15)	15	0.13
Canadian (13)	13	0.11
Czech (29)	86	0.72
Czechoslovakian (0)	19	0.16
Danish (39)	88	0.73
Dutch (15)	291	2.43
English (393)	1,357	11.32
Estonian (12)	12	0.10
European (57)	90	0.75
Finnish (27)	27	0.23

*Notes: † The Census 2010 population figure is used to calculate the percentages in the Hispanic Origin and Race categories. Ancestry percentages are based on the 2006-2010 American Community Survey population (not shown); ‡ Numbers in parentheses indicate the number of people reporting a single ancestry; * Numbers in parentheses indicate the number of persons reporting this race alone, not in combination with any other race; Please refer to the Explanation of Data for more information.*

French, ex. Basque (101)	856	7.14
French Canadian (95)	243	2.03
German (1,801)	5,041	42.07
Greek (83)	130	1.08
Hungarian (47)	97	0.81
Irish (298)	2,254	18.81
Italian (73)	345	2.88
Lithuanian (27)	56	0.47
Norwegian (49)	57	0.48
Pennsylvania German (0)	9	0.08
Polish (659)	1,719	14.35
Russian (46)	109	0.91
Scandinavian (15)	15	0.13
Scotch-Irish (50)	197	1.64
Scottish (45)	456	3.81
Slavic (0)	15	0.13
Slovak (19)	80	0.67
Swedish (18)	99	0.83
Swiss (26)	56	0.47
Ukrainian (7)	31	0.26
Welsh (0)	34	0.28
West Indian, ex. Hispanic (0)	9	0.08
Jamaican (0)	9	0.08
Yugoslavian (17)	33	0.28

Hispanic Origin	Population	%
Hispanic or Latino (of any race)	424	3.54
Central American, ex. Mexican	8	0.07
Guatemalan	1	0.01
Honduran	1	0.01
Salvadoran	6	0.05
Cuban	2	0.02
Mexican	380	3.17
Puerto Rican	7	0.06
South American	3	0.03
Paraguayan	1	0.01
Peruvian	1	0.01
Venezuelan	1	0.01
Other Hispanic or Latino	24	0.20

Race*	Population	%
African-American/Black (129)	157	1.31
Not Hispanic (124)	149	1.24
Hispanic (5)	8	0.07
American Indian/Alaska Native (28)	65	0.54
Not Hispanic (26)	54	0.45
Hispanic (2)	11	0.09
Apache (0)	1	0.01
Cherokee (0)	4	0.03
Chippewa (13)	18	0.15
Choctaw (1)	4	0.03
Creek (0)	2	0.02
Potawatomi (2)	2	0.02
Sioux (1)	4	0.03
Asian (136)	180	1.50
Not Hispanic (136)	178	1.49
Hispanic (0)	2	0.02
Bangladeshi (2)	2	0.02
Chinese, ex. Taiwanese (7)	11	0.09
Filipino (22)	26	0.22
Indian (57)	62	0.52
Japanese (7)	15	0.13
Korean (13)	28	0.23
Pakistani (18)	18	0.15
Taiwanese (1)	4	0.03
Thai (0)	1	0.01
Vietnamese (3)	4	0.03
Hawaii Native/Pacific Islander (3)	5	0.04
Not Hispanic (3)	5	0.04
Guamanian/Chamorro (1)	1	0.01
Native Hawaiian (2)	2	0.02
White (11,479)	11,610	96.87
Not Hispanic (11,176)	11,271	94.04
Hispanic (303)	339	2.83

Thornapple

Place Type: Township
County: Barry
Population: 7,884†

Ancestry‡	Population	%
American (987)	987	12.67
Belgian (0)	7	0.09
British (0)	69	0.89
Croatian (14)	33	0.42
Czechoslovakian (0)	15	0.19
Danish (34)	159	2.04
Dutch (1,201)	2,027	26.03
English (132)	986	12.66
European (97)	97	1.25
Finnish (5)	38	0.49
French, ex. Basque (25)	497	6.38
French Canadian (35)	87	1.12
German (537)	1,878	24.12
Hungarian (0)	16	0.21
Irish (127)	782	10.04
Italian (42)	53	0.68
Lithuanian (6)	22	0.28
Northern European (15)	15	0.19
Norwegian (0)	26	0.33
Polish (44)	367	4.71
Scandinavian (0)	7	0.09
Scotch-Irish (19)	162	2.08
Scottish (0)	153	1.96
Swedish (53)	257	3.30
Swiss (0)	10	0.13
Welsh (0)	12	0.15

Hispanic Origin	Population	%
Hispanic or Latino (of any race)	221	2.80
Central American, ex. Mexican	11	0.14
Costa Rican	1	0.01
Guatemalan	5	0.06
Salvadoran	5	0.06
Cuban	2	0.03
Mexican	163	2.07
Puerto Rican	23	0.29
South American	3	0.04
Colombian	3	0.04
Other Hispanic or Latino	19	0.24

Race*	Population	%
African-American/Black (30)	74	0.94
Not Hispanic (30)	72	0.91
Hispanic (0)	2	0.03
American Indian/Alaska Native (36)	82	1.04
Not Hispanic (33)	71	0.90
Hispanic (3)	11	0.14
Blackfeet (0)	1	0.01
Cherokee (2)	7	0.09
Chippewa (12)	22	0.28
Iroquois (0)	3	0.04
Lumbee (1)	1	0.01
Ottawa (1)	9	0.11
Potawatomi (13)	21	0.27
Seminole (0)	1	0.01
Sioux (1)	1	0.01
Asian (35)	59	0.75
Not Hispanic (32)	52	0.66
Hispanic (3)	7	0.09
Chinese, ex. Taiwanese (11)	14	0.18
Filipino (6)	16	0.20
Indian (3)	5	0.06
Indonesian (1)	1	0.01
Japanese (1)	2	0.03
Korean (12)	17	0.22
Vietnamese (1)	2	0.03
Hawaii Native/Pacific Islander (2)	3	0.04
Not Hispanic (1)	2	0.03
Hispanic (1)	1	0.01
Guamanian/Chamorro (2)	2	0.03
Native Hawaiian (0)	1	0.01
White (7,605)	7,715	97.86
Not Hispanic (7,458)	7,557	95.85
Hispanic (147)	158	2.00

Three Rivers

Place Type: City
County: St. Joseph
Population: 7,811†

Ancestry‡	Population	%
African, Sub-Saharan (18)	18	0.23
African (18)	18	0.23
American (1,349)	1,349	17.29
Arab (16)	16	0.21
Lebanese (16)	16	0.21
Canadian (0)	14	0.18
Croatian (7)	7	0.09
Czech (0)	5	0.06
Danish (8)	27	0.35
Dutch (69)	342	4.38
English (332)	811	10.39
European (14)	32	0.41
Finnish (0)	54	0.69
French, ex. Basque (7)	200	2.56
French Canadian (9)	40	0.51
German (1,059)	2,125	27.24
Greek (7)	7	0.09
Hungarian (0)	11	0.14
Irish (252)	755	9.68
Italian (66)	122	1.56
Lithuanian (0)	15	0.19
Norwegian (0)	40	0.51
Polish (81)	313	4.01
Portuguese (7)	7	0.09
Russian (7)	7	0.09
Scotch-Irish (13)	98	1.26
Scottish (0)	112	1.44
Swedish (15)	26	0.33
Swiss (0)	20	0.26
Ukrainian (10)	81	1.04

Hispanic Origin	Population	%
Hispanic or Latino (of any race)	408	5.22
Central American, ex. Mexican	18	0.23
Costa Rican	1	0.01
Guatemalan	3	0.04
Honduran	1	0.01
Panamanian	1	0.01
Salvadoran	12	0.15
Cuban	7	0.09
Dominican Republic	1	0.01
Mexican	280	3.58
Puerto Rican	71	0.91
South American	8	0.10
Argentinean	1	0.01
Venezuelan	7	0.09
Other Hispanic or Latino	23	0.29

Race*	Population	%
African-American/Black (791)	982	12.57
Not Hispanic (771)	951	12.18
Hispanic (20)	31	0.40
American Indian/Alaska Native (44)	102	1.31
Not Hispanic (33)	86	1.10
Hispanic (11)	16	0.20
Apache (1)	5	0.06
Blackfeet (0)	4	0.05
Canadian/French Am. Ind. (1)	1	0.01
Cherokee (4)	18	0.23
Chippewa (3)	4	0.05
Choctaw (2)	4	0.05
Navajo (3)	3	0.04
Ottawa (4)	5	0.06
Potawatomi (2)	5	0.06
Seminole (0)	1	0.01
South American Ind. (1)	1	0.01
Asian (70)	108	1.38
Not Hispanic (69)	103	1.32
Hispanic (1)	5	0.06
Bangladeshi (5)	5	0.06
Cambodian (1)	5	0.06
Chinese, ex. Taiwanese (6)	6	0.08
Filipino (14)	23	0.29

SECTION TWO

*Notes: † The Census 2010 population figure is used to calculate the percentages in the Hispanic Origin and Race categories. Ancestry percentages are based on the 2006-2010 American Community Survey population (not shown); ‡ Numbers in parentheses indicate the number of people reporting a single ancestry; * Numbers in parentheses indicate the number of persons reporting this race alone, not in combination with any other race; Please refer to the Explanation of Data for more information.*

Indian (19)	20	0.26
Indonesian (1)	1	0.01
Japanese (3)	7	0.09
Korean (12)	28	0.36
Laotian (0)	1	0.01
Pakistani (2)	2	0.03
Vietnamese (7)	8	0.10
Hawaii Native/Pacific Islander (0)	3	0.04
Not Hispanic (0)	3	0.04
Native Hawaiian (0)	1	0.01
White (6,453)	6,748	86.39
Not Hispanic (6,260)	6,510	83.34
Hispanic (193)	238	3.05

Tittabawassee

Place Type: Township
County: Saginaw
Population: 9,726†

Ancestry‡	Population	%
African, Sub-Saharan (18)	18	0.19
African (18)	18	0.19
American (351)	351	3.73
Arab (39)	39	0.41
Lebanese (8)	8	0.09
Moroccan (31)	31	0.33
Austrian (13)	13	0.14
Belgian (0)	11	0.12
British (12)	38	0.40
Canadian (31)	41	0.44
Czech (18)	26	0.28
Dutch (41)	291	3.10
English (160)	884	9.40
European (84)	84	0.89
Finnish (0)	144	1.53
French, ex. Basque (154)	974	10.36
French Canadian (39)	155	1.65
German (1,428)	3,717	39.54
Greek (9)	45	0.48
Hungarian (21)	49	0.52
Irish (352)	1,129	12.01
Italian (93)	502	5.34
Maltese (9)	27	0.29
Norwegian (14)	45	0.48
Pennsylvania German (35)	47	0.50
Polish (314)	1,188	12.64
Romanian (0)	11	0.12
Russian (20)	105	1.12
Scandinavian (20)	31	0.33
Scotch-Irish (86)	217	2.31
Scottish (17)	284	3.02
Slavic (0)	9	0.10
Slovak (17)	17	0.18
Swedish (111)	209	2.22
Swiss (0)	10	0.11
Ukrainian (9)	9	0.10
Welsh (0)	12	0.13
Yugoslavian (0)	13	0.14

Hispanic Origin	Population	%
Hispanic or Latino (of any race)	288	2.96
Central American, ex. Mexican	1	0.01
Costa Rican	1	0.01
Cuban	2	0.02
Mexican	246	2.53
Puerto Rican	9	0.09
South American	3	0.03
Argentinean	1	0.01
Colombian	1	0.01
Peruvian	1	0.01
Other Hispanic or Latino	27	0.28

Race*	Population	%
African-American/Black (888)	924	9.50
Not Hispanic (888)	920	9.46
Hispanic (0)	4	0.04
American Indian/Alaska Native (51)	94	0.97
Not Hispanic (46)	81	0.83
Hispanic (5)	13	0.13
Blackfeet (0)	3	0.03
Canadian/French Am. Ind. (0)	1	0.01
Cherokee (8)	13	0.13
Cheyenne (1)	1	0.01
Chippewa (19)	32	0.33
Inupiat *(Alaska Native)* (0)	1	0.01
Iroquois (0)	1	0.01
Shoshone (0)	1	0.01
Sioux (0)	1	0.01
Spanish American Ind. (1)	1	0.01
Tlingit-Haida *(Alaska Native)* (1)	1	0.01
Asian (44)	60	0.62
Not Hispanic (44)	59	0.61
Hispanic (0)	1	0.01
Chinese, ex. Taiwanese (18)	24	0.25
Filipino (9)	14	0.14
Indian (1)	2	0.02
Japanese (0)	2	0.02
Korean (5)	7	0.07
Pakistani (4)	4	0.04
Vietnamese (2)	2	0.02
Hawaii Native/Pacific Islander (3)	4	0.04
Not Hispanic (3)	4	0.04
Guamanian/Chamorro (1)	1	0.01
Native Hawaiian (1)	2	0.02
Tongan (1)	1	0.01
White (8,579)	8,688	89.33
Not Hispanic (8,372)	8,453	86.91
Hispanic (207)	235	2.42

Traverse City

Place Type: City
County: Grand Traverse
Population: 14,482†

Ancestry‡	Population	%
African, Sub-Saharan (18)	40	0.27
African (10)	32	0.22
Other Sub-Saharan African (8)	8	0.05
American (883)	883	6.04
Austrian (8)	103	0.71
Basque (0)	74	0.51
Belgian (29)	29	0.20
British (21)	67	0.46
Canadian (30)	42	0.29
Croatian (28)	36	0.25
Czech (20)	182	1.25
Czechoslovakian (55)	77	0.53
Danish (8)	143	0.98
Dutch (118)	579	3.96
Eastern European (19)	45	0.31
English (417)	2,381	16.30
European (476)	487	3.33
Finnish (153)	290	1.99
French, ex. Basque (76)	1,221	8.36
French Canadian (62)	271	1.86
German (1,091)	4,353	29.80
Greek (39)	122	0.84
Hungarian (7)	33	0.23
Irish (536)	2,720	18.62
Italian (131)	419	2.87
Lithuanian (9)	61	0.42
Maltese (24)	24	0.16
New Zealander (8)	8	0.05
Northern European (128)	128	0.88
Norwegian (41)	300	2.05
Pennsylvania German (10)	10	0.07
Polish (392)	1,443	9.88
Romanian (65)	95	0.65
Russian (0)	21	0.14
Scandinavian (39)	110	0.75
Scotch-Irish (90)	609	4.17
Scottish (159)	631	4.32
Serbian (0)	8	0.05
Slavic (0)	23	0.16
Slovak (0)	26	0.18
Swedish (119)	495	3.39
Swiss (0)	24	0.16
Ukrainian (0)	69	0.47
Welsh (0)	100	0.68
West Indian, ex. Hispanic (0)	5	0.03
Jamaican (0)	5	0.03
Yugoslavian (0)	13	0.09

Hispanic Origin	Population	%
Hispanic or Latino (of any race)	273	1.89
Central American, ex. Mexican	12	0.08
Costa Rican	2	0.01
Guatemalan	6	0.04
Nicaraguan	1	0.01
Panamanian	2	0.01
Salvadoran	1	0.01
Cuban	12	0.08
Dominican Republic	1	0.01
Mexican	156	1.08
Puerto Rican	31	0.21
South American	15	0.10
Argentinean	2	0.01
Colombian	8	0.06
Ecuadorian	1	0.01
Peruvian	3	0.02
Venezuelan	1	0.01
Other Hispanic or Latino	46	0.32

Race*	Population	%
African-American/Black (103)	204	1.41
Not Hispanic (103)	198	1.37
Hispanic (0)	6	0.04
American Indian/Alaska Native (255)	372	2.57
Not Hispanic (233)	339	2.34
Hispanic (22)	33	0.23
Alaska Athabascan *(Ala. Nat.)* (2)	2	0.01
Apache (1)	4	0.03
Blackfeet (0)	3	0.02
Canadian/French Am. Ind. (5)	8	0.06
Cherokee (7)	20	0.14
Chippewa (129)	162	1.12
Choctaw (1)	2	0.01
Iroquois (2)	6	0.04
Lumbee (0)	1	0.01
Menominee (0)	2	0.01
Mexican American Ind. (5)	11	0.08
Navajo (2)	4	0.03
Ottawa (16)	44	0.30
Potawatomi (1)	1	0.01
Shoshone (0)	1	0.01
Sioux (3)	5	0.03
Asian (99)	161	1.11
Not Hispanic (99)	153	1.06
Hispanic (0)	8	0.06
Bangladeshi (3)	3	0.02
Chinese, ex. Taiwanese (12)	28	0.19
Filipino (9)	18	0.12
Hmong (1)	1	0.01
Indian (10)	19	0.13
Indonesian (1)	3	0.02
Japanese (4)	11	0.08
Korean (16)	27	0.19
Laotian (9)	13	0.09
Malaysian (1)	1	0.01
Pakistani (1)	1	0.01
Sri Lankan (1)	1	0.01
Thai (8)	12	0.08
Vietnamese (10)	13	0.09
Hawaii Native/Pacific Islander (5)	21	0.15
Not Hispanic (5)	15	0.10
Hispanic (0)	6	0.04
Guamanian/Chamorro (0)	3	0.02
Native Hawaiian (1)	6	0.04
White (13,670)	13,925	96.15
Not Hispanic (13,523)	13,742	94.89
Hispanic (147)	183	1.26

Traverse City

Place Type: City
County: Grand Traverse
Population: 14,674†

*Notes: † The Census 2010 population figure is used to calculate the percentages in the Hispanic Origin and Race categories. Ancestry percentages are based on the 2006-2010 American Community Survey population (not shown); ‡ Numbers in parentheses indicate the number of people reporting a single ancestry; * Numbers in parentheses indicate the number of persons reporting this race alone, not in combination with any other race; Please refer to the Explanation of Data for more information.*

Ancestry‡	Population	%
African, Sub-Saharan (18)	40	0.27
African (10)	32	0.22
Other Sub-Saharan African (8)	8	0.05
American (925)	925	6.26
Austrian (8)	103	0.70
Basque (0)	74	0.50
Belgian (29)	29	0.20
British (21)	67	0.45
Canadian (30)	42	0.28
Croatian (28)	36	0.24
Czech (20)	182	1.23
Czechoslovakian (55)	77	0.52
Danish (8)	143	0.97
Dutch (118)	579	3.92
Eastern European (19)	45	0.30
English (417)	2,395	16.21
European (476)	487	3.30
Finnish (153)	290	1.96
French, ex. Basque (76)	1,221	8.27
French Canadian (62)	271	1.83
German (1,091)	4,399	29.78
Greek (39)	122	0.83
Hungarian (7)	41	0.28
Irish (543)	2,727	18.46
Italian (131)	419	2.84
Lithuanian (9)	61	0.41
Maltese (24)	24	0.16
New Zealander (8)	8	0.05
Northern European (128)	128	0.87
Norwegian (41)	300	2.03
Pennsylvania German (10)	10	0.07
Polish (392)	1,451	9.82
Romanian (65)	95	0.64
Russian (0)	21	0.14
Scandinavian (39)	110	0.74
Scotch-Irish (90)	609	4.12
Scottish (159)	647	4.38
Serbian (0)	8	0.05
Slavic (0)	23	0.16
Slovak (0)	26	0.18
Swedish (119)	495	3.35
Swiss (0)	24	0.16
Ukrainian (0)	69	0.47
Welsh (5)	105	0.71
West Indian, ex. Hispanic (0)	5	0.03
Jamaican (0)	5	0.03
Yugoslavian (0)	13	0.09

Hispanic Origin	Population	%
Hispanic or Latino (of any race)	280	1.91
Central American, ex. Mexican	12	0.08
Costa Rican	2	0.01
Guatemalan	6	0.04
Nicaraguan	1	0.01
Panamanian	2	0.01
Salvadoran	1	0.01
Cuban	12	0.08
Dominican Republic	1	0.01
Mexican	163	1.11
Puerto Rican	31	0.21
South American	15	0.10
Argentinean	2	0.01
Colombian	8	0.05
Ecuadorian	1	0.01
Peruvian	3	0.02
Venezuelan	1	0.01
Other Hispanic or Latino	46	0.31

Race*	Population	%
African-American/Black (103)	210	1.43
Not Hispanic (103)	204	1.39
Hispanic (0)	6	0.04
American Indian/Alaska Native (260)	378	2.58
Not Hispanic (238)	345	2.35
Hispanic (22)	33	0.22
Alaska Athabascan *(Ala. Nat.)* (2)	2	0.01
Apache (1)	4	0.03
Blackfeet (0)	3	0.02
Canadian/French Am. Ind. (5)	8	0.05
Cherokee (7)	20	0.14
Chippewa (132)	166	1.13
Choctaw (1)	2	0.01
Iroquois (2)	6	0.04
Lumbee (0)	1	0.01
Menominee (0)	2	0.01
Mexican American Ind. (5)	11	0.07
Navajo (2)	4	0.03
Ottawa (16)	45	0.31
Potawatomi (1)	1	0.01
Shoshone (0)	1	0.01
Sioux (3)	5	0.03
Asian (99)	165	1.12
Not Hispanic (99)	157	1.07
Hispanic (0)	8	0.05
Bangladeshi (3)	3	0.02
Chinese, ex. Taiwanese (12)	28	0.19
Filipino (9)	21	0.14
Hmong (1)	1	0.01
Indian (10)	19	0.13
Indonesian (1)	3	0.02
Japanese (4)	11	0.07
Korean (16)	28	0.19
Laotian (9)	13	0.09
Malaysian (1)	1	0.01
Pakistani (1)	1	0.01
Sri Lankan (1)	1	0.01
Thai (8)	12	0.08
Vietnamese (10)	13	0.09
Hawaii Native/Pacific Islander (5)	21	0.14
Not Hispanic (5)	15	0.10
Hispanic (0)	6	0.04
Guamanian/Chamorro (0)	3	0.02
Native Hawaiian (1)	6	0.04
White (13,846)	14,112	96.17
Not Hispanic (13,692)	13,922	94.88
Hispanic (154)	190	1.29

Trenton

Place Type: City
County: Wayne
Population: 18,853†

Ancestry‡	Population	%
African, Sub-Saharan (107)	111	0.58
African (98)	102	0.54
Cape Verdean (9)	9	0.05
Albanian (28)	39	0.20
American (613)	613	3.22
Arab (17)	37	0.19
Egyptian (17)	17	0.09
Lebanese (0)	20	0.10
Armenian (94)	146	0.77
Austrian (41)	115	0.60
Belgian (16)	48	0.25
British (23)	33	0.17
Canadian (28)	110	0.58
Croatian (0)	56	0.29
Czech (28)	98	0.51
Czechoslovakian (5)	5	0.03
Danish (9)	43	0.23
Dutch (50)	324	1.70
English (686)	2,635	13.83
European (88)	88	0.46
Finnish (35)	127	0.67
French, ex. Basque (406)	2,120	11.13
French Canadian (237)	651	3.42
German (967)	4,784	25.11
Greek (106)	312	1.64
Hungarian (214)	1,187	6.23
Irish (554)	3,142	16.49
Italian (809)	1,875	9.84
Latvian (0)	30	0.16
Lithuanian (34)	69	0.36
Macedonian (7)	21	0.11
Maltese (21)	62	0.33
Northern European (0)	8	0.04
Norwegian (9)	20	0.10
Polish (983)	2,619	13.75
Portuguese (0)	26	0.14
Romanian (0)	38	0.20
Russian (15)	141	0.74
Scandinavian (0)	8	0.04
Scotch-Irish (126)	406	2.13
Scottish (163)	821	4.31
Serbian (15)	25	0.13
Slavic (0)	9	0.05
Slovak (16)	23	0.12
Slovene (17)	17	0.09
Swedish (9)	107	0.56
Swiss (0)	18	0.09
Ukrainian (45)	82	0.43
Welsh (0)	88	0.46
Yugoslavian (59)	59	0.31

Hispanic Origin	Population	%
Hispanic or Latino (of any race)	598	3.17
Central American, ex. Mexican	11	0.06
Guatemalan	4	0.02
Honduran	2	0.01
Nicaraguan	1	0.01
Panamanian	4	0.02
Cuban	14	0.07
Mexican	438	2.32
Puerto Rican	56	0.30
South American	27	0.14
Argentinean	12	0.06
Chilean	2	0.01
Colombian	9	0.05
Peruvian	2	0.01
Venezuelan	1	0.01
Other South American	1	0.01
Other Hispanic or Latino	52	0.28

Race*	Population	%
African-American/Black (254)	329	1.75
Not Hispanic (251)	323	1.71
Hispanic (3)	6	0.03
American Indian/Alaska Native (95)	198	1.05
Not Hispanic (89)	188	1.00
Hispanic (6)	10	0.05
Blackfeet (1)	5	0.03
Canadian/French Am. Ind. (0)	8	0.04
Central American Ind. (1)	6	0.03
Cherokee (8)	36	0.19
Chippewa (25)	46	0.24
Choctaw (1)	1	0.01
Delaware (1)	1	0.01
Iroquois (5)	16	0.08
Lumbee (6)	7	0.04
Menominee (8)	9	0.05
Mexican American Ind. (2)	3	0.02
Navajo (1)	5	0.03
Osage (4)	4	0.02
Ottawa (5)	5	0.03
Potawatomi (1)	1	0.01
Sioux (2)	3	0.02
Spanish American Ind. (1)	1	0.01
Asian (133)	202	1.07
Not Hispanic (133)	190	1.01
Hispanic (0)	12	0.06
Chinese, ex. Taiwanese (24)	30	0.16
Filipino (42)	63	0.33
Indian (16)	23	0.12
Indonesian (2)	2	0.01
Japanese (14)	27	0.14
Korean (20)	30	0.16
Pakistani (5)	7	0.04
Thai (2)	3	0.02
Vietnamese (5)	16	0.08
Hawaii Native/Pacific Islander (3)	12	0.06
Not Hispanic (2)	11	0.06
Hispanic (1)	1	0.01
Guamanian/Chamorro (2)	2	0.01
Native Hawaiian (0)	9	0.05
Samoan (0)	1	0.01
White (18,009)	18,260	96.85
Not Hispanic (17,549)	17,762	94.21
Hispanic (460)	498	2.64

*Notes: † The Census 2010 population figure is used to calculate the percentages in the Hispanic Origin and Race categories. Ancestry percentages are based on the 2006-2010 American Community Survey population (not shown); ‡ Numbers in parentheses indicate the number of people reporting a single ancestry; * Numbers in parentheses indicate the number of persons reporting this race alone, not in combination with any other race; Please refer to the Explanation of Data for more information.*

Troy

Place Type: City
County: Oakland
Population: 80,980†

Ancestry‡	Population	%
African, Sub-Saharan (191)	191	0.24
African (69)	69	0.09
Ghanaian (37)	37	0.05
Nigerian (63)	63	0.08
Other Sub-Saharan African (22)	22	0.03
Albanian (612)	612	0.76
American (2,507)	2,507	3.10
Arab (2,511)	3,081	3.80
Arab (750)	929	1.15
Egyptian (286)	286	0.35
Iraqi (594)	722	0.89
Jordanian (60)	66	0.08
Lebanese (621)	752	0.93
Palestinian (29)	29	0.04
Syrian (87)	145	0.18
Other Arab (84)	152	0.19
Armenian (133)	338	0.42
Assyrian/Chaldean/Syriac (1,350)	1,643	2.03
Australian (54)	54	0.07
Austrian (62)	269	0.33
Belgian (162)	722	0.89
Brazilian (38)	38	0.05
British (109)	275	0.34
Bulgarian (44)	44	0.05
Canadian (124)	446	0.55
Celtic (0)	60	0.07
Croatian (89)	274	0.34
Czech (23)	280	0.35
Czechoslovakian (111)	258	0.32
Danish (113)	376	0.46
Dutch (266)	1,546	1.91
Eastern European (137)	163	0.20
English (1,902)	8,083	9.98
Estonian (13)	13	0.02
European (760)	913	1.13
Finnish (235)	674	0.83
French, ex. Basque (350)	3,424	4.23
French Canadian (474)	1,265	1.56
German (3,915)	15,482	19.12
German Russian (22)	22	0.03
Greek (608)	1,057	1.31
Hungarian (190)	685	0.85
Iranian (202)	218	0.27
Irish (2,069)	9,427	11.64
Italian (2,327)	6,643	8.20
Latvian (32)	32	0.04
Lithuanian (62)	444	0.55
Luxemburger (0)	9	0.01
Macedonian (186)	223	0.28
Maltese (28)	90	0.11
Northern European (91)	91	0.11
Norwegian (144)	594	0.73
Pennsylvania German (8)	20	0.02
Polish (3,348)	9,135	11.28
Portuguese (45)	98	0.12
Romanian (915)	1,184	1.46
Russian (419)	931	1.15
Scandinavian (66)	86	0.11
Scotch-Irish (426)	1,480	1.83
Scottish (615)	2,454	3.03
Serbian (148)	333	0.41
Slavic (24)	139	0.17
Slovak (140)	277	0.34
Slovene (0)	44	0.05
Swedish (433)	1,278	1.58
Swiss (19)	246	0.30
Turkish (61)	70	0.09
Ukrainian (423)	845	1.04
Welsh (40)	609	0.75
West Indian, ex. Hispanic (119)	198	0.24
Haitian (10)	28	0.03
Jamaican (109)	156	0.19
West Indian (0)	14	0.02
Yugoslavian (279)	338	0.42

Hispanic Origin	Population	%
Hispanic or Latino (of any race)	1,710	2.11
Central American, ex. Mexican	210	0.26
Costa Rican	7	0.01
Guatemalan	25	0.03
Honduran	15	0.02
Nicaraguan	5	0.01
Panamanian	2	<0.01
Salvadoran	156	0.19
Cuban	47	0.06
Dominican Republic	8	0.01
Mexican	825	1.02
Puerto Rican	130	0.16
South American	262	0.32
Argentinean	42	0.05
Bolivian	5	0.01
Chilean	13	0.02
Colombian	77	0.10
Ecuadorian	26	0.03
Paraguayan	4	<0.01
Peruvian	62	0.08
Uruguayan	1	<0.01
Venezuelan	27	0.03
Other South American	5	0.01
Other Hispanic or Latino	228	0.28

Race*	Population	%
African-American/Black (3,240)	3,655	4.51
Not Hispanic (3,210)	3,595	4.44
Hispanic (30)	60	0.07
American Indian/Alaska Native (151)	445	0.55
Not Hispanic (124)	384	0.47
Hispanic (27)	61	0.08
Apache (1)	7	0.01
Blackfeet (0)	4	<0.01
Canadian/French Am. Ind. (3)	5	0.01
Central American Ind. (1)	3	<0.01
Cherokee (4)	80	0.10
Chickasaw (0)	4	<0.01
Chippewa (17)	52	0.06
Choctaw (2)	8	0.01
Creek (0)	1	<0.01
Hopi (0)	3	<0.01
Iroquois (13)	22	0.03
Lumbee (1)	5	0.01
Menominee (0)	1	<0.01
Mexican American Ind. (5)	9	0.01
Navajo (1)	1	<0.01
Osage (0)	1	<0.01
Ottawa (7)	14	0.02
Potawatomi (3)	9	0.01
Seminole (0)	4	<0.01
Sioux (2)	4	<0.01
South American Ind. (2)	3	<0.01
Spanish American Ind. (1)	1	<0.01
Yaqui (0)	4	<0.01
Asian (15,462)	16,417	20.27
Not Hispanic (15,439)	16,356	20.20
Hispanic (23)	61	0.08
Bangladeshi (213)	232	0.29
Burmese (1)	4	<0.01
Cambodian (8)	14	0.02
Chinese, ex. Taiwanese (3,653)	3,809	4.70
Filipino (953)	1,121	1.38
Hmong (36)	36	0.04
Indian (7,331)	7,564	9.34
Indonesian (6)	10	0.01
Japanese (301)	386	0.48
Korean (1,373)	1,465	1.81
Laotian (20)	20	0.02
Malaysian (10)	11	0.01
Nepalese (31)	36	0.04
Pakistani (607)	663	0.82
Sri Lankan (34)	36	0.04
Taiwanese (393)	415	0.51
Thai (42)	50	0.06
Vietnamese (241)	257	0.32
Hawaii Native/Pacific Islander (1)	90	0.11
Not Hispanic (1)	84	0.10
Hispanic (0)	6	0.01
Guamanian/Chamorro (0)	4	<0.01
Native Hawaiian (0)	12	0.01
Samoan (0)	2	<0.01
White (59,998)	61,356	75.77
Not Hispanic (58,869)	60,096	74.21
Hispanic (1,129)	1,260	1.56

Tyrone

Place Type: Township
County: Livingston
Population: 10,020†

Ancestry‡	Population	%
African, Sub-Saharan (0)	9	0.09
African (0)	9	0.09
Albanian (9)	9	0.09
American (663)	663	6.63
Arab (140)	218	2.18
Arab (36)	36	0.36
Jordanian (18)	18	0.18
Lebanese (0)	78	0.78
Palestinian (71)	71	0.71
Syrian (15)	15	0.15
Armenian (9)	9	0.09
Austrian (29)	62	0.62
Belgian (11)	45	0.45
British (71)	71	0.71
Canadian (27)	40	0.40
Czech (29)	87	0.87
Czechoslovakian (0)	24	0.24
Danish (36)	66	0.66
Dutch (99)	328	3.28
Eastern European (39)	39	0.39
English (323)	1,255	12.55
European (104)	104	1.04
Finnish (48)	107	1.07
French, ex. Basque (123)	604	6.04
French Canadian (62)	334	3.34
German (911)	2,676	26.76
Greek (12)	58	0.58
Hungarian (82)	221	2.21
Irish (374)	1,451	14.51
Israeli (0)	9	0.09
Italian (199)	439	4.39
Lithuanian (26)	54	0.54
Macedonian (57)	147	1.47
Norwegian (43)	77	0.77
Pennsylvania German (8)	8	0.08
Polish (555)	1,445	14.45
Portuguese (9)	18	0.18
Romanian (13)	13	0.13
Russian (16)	44	0.44
Scandinavian (9)	27	0.27
Scotch-Irish (10)	99	0.99
Scottish (56)	363	3.63
Slavic (0)	9	0.09
Slovak (10)	10	0.10
Swedish (35)	338	3.38
Swiss (0)	35	0.35
Ukrainian (29)	38	0.38
Welsh (29)	80	0.80
Yugoslavian (10)	19	0.19

Hispanic Origin	Population	%
Hispanic or Latino (of any race)	219	2.19
Central American, ex. Mexican	10	0.10
Guatemalan	7	0.07
Nicaraguan	2	0.02
Panamanian	1	0.01
Cuban	1	0.01
Dominican Republic	4	0.04
Mexican	148	1.48
Puerto Rican	9	0.09
South American	11	0.11
Colombian	5	0.05
Ecuadorian	1	0.01

*Notes: † The Census 2010 population figure is used to calculate the percentages in the Hispanic Origin and Race categories. Ancestry percentages are based on the 2006-2010 American Community Survey population (not shown); ‡ Numbers in parentheses indicate the number of people reporting a single ancestry; * Numbers in parentheses indicate the number of persons reporting this race alone, not in combination with any other race; Please refer to the Explanation of Data for more information.*

Peruvian	5	0.05
Other Hispanic or Latino	36	0.36

Race*	Population	%
African-American/Black (50)	82	0.82
Not Hispanic (42)	70	0.70
Hispanic (8)	12	0.12
American Indian/Alaska Native (36)	134	1.34
Not Hispanic (34)	123	1.23
Hispanic (2)	11	0.11
Blackfeet (0)	7	0.07
Cherokee (1)	19	0.19
Chippewa (11)	36	0.36
Choctaw (1)	1	0.01
Crow (0)	4	0.04
Iroquois (5)	11	0.11
Lumbee (0)	3	0.03
Navajo (2)	2	0.02
Ottawa (1)	4	0.04
Asian (70)	104	1.04
Not Hispanic (70)	98	0.98
Hispanic (0)	6	0.06
Cambodian (2)	2	0.02
Chinese, ex. Taiwanese (5)	6	0.06
Filipino (5)	9	0.09
Hmong (6)	6	0.06
Indian (21)	27	0.27
Japanese (0)	3	0.03
Korean (13)	25	0.25
Laotian (0)	3	0.03
Malaysian (1)	1	0.01
Taiwanese (4)	4	0.04
Vietnamese (11)	15	0.15
Hawaii Native/Pacific Islander (2)	5	0.05
Not Hispanic (2)	4	0.04
Hispanic (0)	1	0.01
Native Hawaiian (1)	3	0.03
Samoan (1)	1	0.01
White (9,656)	9,804	97.84
Not Hispanic (9,514)	9,639	96.20
Hispanic (142)	165	1.65

Union

Place Type: Charter Township
County: Isabella
Population: 12,927†

Ancestry‡	Population	%
Albanian (0)	9	0.07
American (535)	535	4.43
Arab (12)	125	1.03
Arab (0)	3	0.02
Egyptian (0)	49	0.41
Lebanese (0)	61	0.50
Syrian (12)	12	0.10
Armenian (3)	13	0.11
Austrian (0)	7	0.06
Belgian (21)	46	0.38
British (54)	172	1.42
Bulgarian (13)	22	0.18
Cajun (3)	8	0.07
Canadian (14)	79	0.65
Croatian (3)	3	0.02
Czech (28)	95	0.79
Czechoslovakian (0)	3	0.02
Danish (35)	176	1.46
Dutch (142)	457	3.78
Eastern European (20)	20	0.17
English (593)	1,683	13.92
European (153)	153	1.27
Finnish (21)	192	1.59
French, ex. Basque (121)	732	6.06
French Canadian (251)	462	3.82
German (973)	3,697	30.58
Greek (4)	75	0.62
Hungarian (14)	138	1.14
Icelander (0)	43	0.36
Irish (275)	2,037	16.85
Italian (310)	807	6.68
Latvian (0)	17	0.14
Lithuanian (0)	15	0.12
Norwegian (11)	166	1.37
Polish (282)	1,015	8.40
Portuguese (0)	30	0.25
Romanian (0)	19	0.16
Russian (40)	78	0.65
Scotch-Irish (46)	130	1.08
Scottish (136)	426	3.52
Serbian (0)	3	0.02
Slavic (0)	39	0.32
Slovak (2)	24	0.20
Swedish (39)	313	2.59
Swiss (7)	54	0.45
Turkish (3)	3	0.02
Ukrainian (19)	65	0.54
Welsh (12)	158	1.31
Yugoslavian (46)	46	0.38

Hispanic Origin	Population	%
Hispanic or Latino (of any race)	416	3.22
Central American, ex. Mexican	9	0.07
Costa Rican	1	0.01
Guatemalan	1	0.01
Honduran	1	0.01
Panamanian	4	0.03
Salvadoran	2	0.02
Cuban	7	0.05
Dominican Republic	5	0.04
Mexican	320	2.48
Puerto Rican	25	0.19
South American	10	0.08
Colombian	7	0.05
Ecuadorian	1	0.01
Other South American	2	0.02
Other Hispanic or Latino	40	0.31

Race*	Population	%
African-American/Black (485)	622	4.81
Not Hispanic (476)	603	4.66
Hispanic (9)	19	0.15
American Indian/Alaska Native (419)	607	4.70
Not Hispanic (363)	512	3.96
Hispanic (56)	95	0.73
Alaska Athabascan *(Ala. Nat.)* (0)	1	0.01
Canadian/French Am. Ind. (11)	13	0.10
Cherokee (6)	15	0.12
Chippewa (253)	337	2.61
Choctaw (0)	4	0.03
Creek (0)	1	0.01
Iroquois (11)	14	0.11
Lumbee (1)	1	0.01
Menominee (0)	1	0.01
Mexican American Ind. (0)	1	0.01
Navajo (2)	3	0.02
Ottawa (9)	14	0.11
Potawatomi (13)	16	0.12
Pueblo (0)	4	0.03
Sioux (4)	4	0.03
Spanish American Ind. (5)	5	0.04
Asian (243)	309	2.39
Not Hispanic (242)	303	2.34
Hispanic (1)	6	0.05
Chinese, ex. Taiwanese (70)	82	0.63
Filipino (20)	41	0.32
Hmong (5)	5	0.04
Indian (55)	66	0.51
Japanese (12)	23	0.18
Korean (46)	61	0.47
Malaysian (1)	1	0.01
Pakistani (1)	1	0.01
Taiwanese (3)	5	0.04
Thai (0)	1	0.01
Vietnamese (19)	27	0.21
Hawaii Native/Pacific Islander (1)	14	0.11
Not Hispanic (1)	10	0.08
Hispanic (0)	4	0.03
Native Hawaiian (0)	8	0.06
Samoan (1)	5	0.04
White (11,325)	11,666	90.25
Not Hispanic (11,112)	11,396	88.16
Hispanic (213)	270	2.09

Van Buren

Place Type: Charter Township
County: Wayne
Population: 28,821†

Ancestry‡	Population	%
African, Sub-Saharan (334)	354	1.27
African (315)	335	1.20
Nigerian (19)	19	0.07
Albanian (39)	39	0.14
American (1,294)	1,294	4.63
Arab (254)	297	1.06
Arab (201)	201	0.72
Lebanese (19)	55	0.20
Moroccan (20)	20	0.07
Syrian (0)	7	0.03
Other Arab (14)	14	0.05
Armenian (27)	95	0.34
Assyrian/Chaldean/Syriac (0)	14	0.05
Austrian (8)	46	0.16
Belgian (0)	24	0.09
British (18)	73	0.26
Canadian (7)	54	0.19
Croatian (0)	21	0.08
Czech (64)	113	0.40
Czechoslovakian (0)	44	0.16
Danish (0)	56	0.20
Dutch (84)	503	1.80
English (415)	2,040	7.29
European (83)	132	0.47
Finnish (111)	212	0.76
French, ex. Basque (178)	1,249	4.47
French Canadian (153)	611	2.18
German (1,706)	6,185	22.11
Greek (33)	69	0.25
Hungarian (112)	445	1.59
Irish (587)	3,146	11.25
Italian (376)	1,237	4.42
Lithuanian (40)	102	0.36
Maltese (42)	57	0.20
Norwegian (32)	300	1.07
Polish (829)	2,288	8.18
Portuguese (0)	20	0.07
Romanian (29)	29	0.10
Russian (24)	104	0.37
Scotch-Irish (128)	501	1.79
Scottish (154)	739	2.64
Serbian (5)	5	0.02
Slavic (0)	21	0.08
Slovak (0)	59	0.21
Slovene (0)	39	0.14
Swedish (44)	203	0.73
Swiss (0)	29	0.10
Ukrainian (22)	87	0.31
Welsh (22)	158	0.56
West Indian, ex. Hispanic (89)	146	0.52
Haitian (9)	9	0.03
Jamaican (80)	137	0.49

Hispanic Origin	Population	%
Hispanic or Latino (of any race)	786	2.73
Central American, ex. Mexican	47	0.16
Costa Rican	2	0.01
Guatemalan	11	0.04
Honduran	9	0.03
Nicaraguan	9	0.03
Panamanian	8	0.03
Salvadoran	8	0.03
Cuban	17	0.06
Dominican Republic	12	0.04
Mexican	497	1.72
Puerto Rican	110	0.38
South American	35	0.12
Bolivian	3	0.01
Chilean	3	0.01
Colombian	11	0.04

*Notes: † The Census 2010 population figure is used to calculate the percentages in the Hispanic Origin and Race categories. Ancestry percentages are based on the 2006-2010 American Community Survey population (not shown); ‡ Numbers in parentheses indicate the number of people reporting a single ancestry; * Numbers in parentheses indicate the number of persons reporting this race alone, not in combination with any other race; Please refer to the Explanation of Data for more information.*

Ecuadorian	7	0.02
Peruvian	7	0.02
Venezuelan	3	0.01
Other South American	1	<0.01
Other Hispanic or Latino	68	0.24

Race*	Population	%
African-American/Black (8,261)	8,794	30.51
Not Hispanic (8,217)	8,720	30.26
Hispanic (44)	74	0.26
American Indian/Alaska Native (146)	411	1.43
Not Hispanic (132)	381	1.32
Hispanic (14)	30	0.10
Apache (0)	1	<0.01
Blackfeet (4)	30	0.10
Canadian/French Am. Ind. (7)	7	0.02
Cherokee (14)	80	0.28
Chickasaw (0)	2	0.01
Chippewa (19)	35	0.12
Choctaw (2)	8	0.03
Creek (6)	7	0.02
Delaware (3)	4	0.01
Hopi (2)	2	0.01
Inupiat *(Alaska Native)* (0)	1	<0.01
Iroquois (5)	5	0.02
Lumbee (1)	3	0.01
Navajo (1)	2	0.01
Ottawa (4)	4	0.01
Potawatomi (8)	11	0.04
Seminole (0)	1	<0.01
Sioux (2)	6	0.02
Tlingit-Haida *(Alaska Native)* (0)	1	<0.01
Yakama (0)	4	0.01
Asian (718)	884	3.07
Not Hispanic (716)	873	3.03
Hispanic (2)	11	0.04
Bangladeshi (24)	24	0.08
Cambodian (3)	3	0.01
Chinese, ex. Taiwanese (88)	102	0.35
Filipino (169)	229	0.79
Indian (258)	291	1.01
Indonesian (4)	4	0.01
Japanese (19)	37	0.13
Korean (38)	53	0.18
Laotian (3)	3	0.01
Malaysian (2)	2	0.01
Pakistani (24)	24	0.08
Sri Lankan (6)	6	0.02
Thai (6)	10	0.03
Vietnamese (50)	65	0.23
Hawaii Native/Pacific Islander (14)	23	0.08
Not Hispanic (13)	21	0.07
Hispanic (1)	2	0.01
Fijian (1)	1	<0.01
Guamanian/Chamorro (1)	2	0.01
Native Hawaiian (9)	12	0.04
White (18,612)	19,308	66.99
Not Hispanic (18,153)	18,783	65.17
Hispanic (459)	525	1.82

Vienna

Place Type: Charter Township
County: Genesee
Population: 13,255†

Ancestry‡	Population	%
American (926)	926	6.91
Arab (9)	22	0.16
Arab (9)	9	0.07
Syrian (0)	13	0.10
Armenian (12)	23	0.17
Assyrian/Chaldean/Syriac (13)	30	0.22
Austrian (0)	39	0.29
Belgian (21)	29	0.22
British (26)	44	0.33
Canadian (7)	48	0.36
Croatian (10)	10	0.07
Czech (14)	118	0.88
Czechoslovakian (0)	28	0.21
Danish (0)	110	0.82
Dutch (154)	346	2.58
English (493)	1,585	11.82
European (173)	177	1.32
Finnish (25)	152	1.13
French, ex. Basque (225)	1,001	7.46
French Canadian (106)	424	3.16
German (1,085)	3,380	25.21
Greek (0)	20	0.15
Hungarian (69)	388	2.89
Icelander (0)	7	0.05
Irish (556)	2,117	15.79
Italian (108)	287	2.14
Lithuanian (0)	14	0.10
Norwegian (19)	59	0.44
Pennsylvania German (74)	74	0.55
Polish (280)	1,141	8.51
Portuguese (0)	28	0.21
Russian (16)	106	0.79
Scotch-Irish (153)	244	1.82
Scottish (150)	452	3.37
Serbian (8)	8	0.06
Slavic (0)	47	0.35
Slovak (13)	50	0.37
Swedish (24)	161	1.20
Swiss (0)	15	0.11
Ukrainian (11)	20	0.15
Welsh (0)	102	0.76

Hispanic Origin	Population	%
Hispanic or Latino (of any race)	351	2.65
Central American, ex. Mexican	4	0.03
Costa Rican	1	0.01
Honduran	2	0.02
Panamanian	1	0.01
Cuban	4	0.03
Mexican	295	2.23
Puerto Rican	13	0.10
South American	5	0.04
Colombian	4	0.03
Peruvian	1	0.01
Other Hispanic or Latino	30	0.23

Race*	Population	%
African-American/Black (237)	320	2.41
Not Hispanic (235)	311	2.35
Hispanic (2)	9	0.07
American Indian/Alaska Native (81)	212	1.60
Not Hispanic (69)	198	1.49
Hispanic (12)	14	0.11
Blackfeet (0)	9	0.07
Canadian/French Am. Ind. (1)	1	0.01
Cherokee (6)	38	0.29
Chickasaw (2)	2	0.02
Chippewa (26)	56	0.42
Choctaw (6)	13	0.10
Crow (0)	1	0.01
Iroquois (4)	8	0.06
Mexican American Ind. (2)	2	0.02
Navajo (4)	4	0.03
Potawatomi (1)	2	0.02
Asian (47)	81	0.61
Not Hispanic (47)	77	0.58
Hispanic (0)	4	0.03
Chinese, ex. Taiwanese (5)	10	0.08
Filipino (6)	8	0.06
Hmong (7)	7	0.05
Indian (9)	13	0.10
Indonesian (0)	3	0.02
Japanese (3)	8	0.06
Korean (14)	23	0.17
Taiwanese (1)	1	0.01
Thai (0)	5	0.04
Hawaii Native/Pacific Islander (3)	12	0.09
Not Hispanic (3)	10	0.08
Hispanic (0)	2	0.02
Guamanian/Chamorro (0)	1	0.01
Native Hawaiian (1)	1	0.01
White (12,555)	12,799	96.56
Not Hispanic (12,315)	12,528	94.52
Hispanic (240)	271	2.04

Walker

Place Type: City
County: Kent
Population: 23,537†

Ancestry‡	Population	%
African, Sub-Saharan (117)	163	0.70
African (117)	163	0.70
American (599)	599	2.57
Arab (157)	182	0.78
Arab (52)	77	0.33
Egyptian (18)	18	0.08
Other Arab (87)	87	0.37
Austrian (0)	63	0.27
Belgian (12)	86	0.37
British (47)	148	0.64
Canadian (0)	11	0.05
Croatian (0)	17	0.07
Czech (49)	202	0.87
Czechoslovakian (15)	54	0.23
Danish (49)	100	0.43
Dutch (2,839)	5,992	25.73
English (512)	2,372	10.18
European (74)	84	0.36
Finnish (9)	63	0.27
French, ex. Basque (109)	829	3.56
French Canadian (22)	111	0.48
German (1,667)	6,044	25.95
Greek (45)	182	0.78
Hungarian (305)	531	2.28
Irish (661)	3,848	16.52
Italian (234)	763	3.28
Latvian (9)	68	0.29
Lithuanian (139)	395	1.70
Northern European (14)	14	0.06
Norwegian (56)	210	0.90
Pennsylvania German (29)	48	0.21
Polish (1,339)	3,622	15.55
Portuguese (0)	24	0.10
Russian (16)	182	0.78
Scandinavian (41)	187	0.80
Scotch-Irish (73)	314	1.35
Scottish (69)	325	1.40
Slovak (48)	88	0.38
Swedish (85)	382	1.64
Ukrainian (0)	33	0.14
Welsh (40)	187	0.80
Yugoslavian (0)	12	0.05

Hispanic Origin	Population	%
Hispanic or Latino (of any race)	973	4.13
Central American, ex. Mexican	52	0.22
Guatemalan	32	0.14
Honduran	10	0.04
Nicaraguan	2	0.01
Panamanian	5	0.02
Salvadoran	3	0.01
Cuban	26	0.11
Dominican Republic	28	0.12
Mexican	656	2.79
Puerto Rican	85	0.36
South American	40	0.17
Argentinean	7	0.03
Bolivian	2	0.01
Colombian	18	0.08
Peruvian	4	0.02
Uruguayan	2	0.01
Venezuelan	7	0.03
Other Hispanic or Latino	86	0.37

Race*	Population	%
African-American/Black (665)	877	3.73
Not Hispanic (640)	827	3.51
Hispanic (25)	50	0.21
American Indian/Alaska Native (107)	248	1.05
Not Hispanic (96)	219	0.93
Hispanic (11)	29	0.12

*Notes: † The Census 2010 population figure is used to calculate the percentages in the Hispanic Origin and Race categories. Ancestry percentages are based on the 2006-2010 American Community Survey population (not shown); ‡ Numbers in parentheses indicate the number of people reporting a single ancestry; * Numbers in parentheses indicate the number of persons reporting this race alone, not in combination with any other race; Please refer to the Explanation of Data for more information.*

Apache (1)	4	0.02
Blackfeet (1)	2	0.01
Canadian/French Am. Ind. (2)	3	0.01
Cherokee (4)	19	0.08
Chippewa (24)	51	0.22
Delaware (1)	1	<0.01
Inupiat *(Alaska Native)* (1)	1	<0.01
Iroquois (0)	1	<0.01
Mexican American Ind. (0)	1	<0.01
Navajo (2)	2	0.01
Ottawa (25)	31	0.13
Potawatomi (2)	11	0.05
Sioux (1)	5	0.02
Tlingit-Haida *(Alaska Native)* (0)	4	0.02
Yaqui (0)	1	<0.01
Asian (455)	563	2.39
Not Hispanic (454)	552	2.35
Hispanic (1)	11	0.05
Cambodian (2)	6	0.03
Chinese, ex. Taiwanese (34)	52	0.22
Filipino (48)	79	0.34
Hmong (4)	4	0.02
Indian (217)	224	0.95
Indonesian (1)	4	0.02
Japanese (14)	37	0.16
Korean (56)	70	0.30
Laotian (4)	5	0.02
Nepalese (11)	11	0.05
Pakistani (4)	4	0.02
Taiwanese (0)	1	<0.01
Thai (4)	7	0.03
Vietnamese (47)	55	0.23
Hawaii Native/Pacific Islander (6)	15	0.06
Not Hispanic (3)	12	0.05
Hispanic (3)	3	0.01
Guamanian/Chamorro (4)	4	0.02
Native Hawaiian (1)	6	0.03
White (21,478)	21,922	93.14
Not Hispanic (20,964)	21,318	90.57
Hispanic (514)	604	2.57

Warren

Place Type: City
County: Macomb
Population: 134,056†

Ancestry‡	Population	%
African, Sub-Saharan (539)	591	0.44
African (438)	490	0.36
Kenyan (40)	40	0.03
Senegalese (20)	20	0.01
Other Sub-Saharan African (41)	41	0.03
Albanian (524)	534	0.39
American (4,766)	4,766	3.51
Arab (1,921)	2,804	2.06
Arab (190)	309	0.23
Egyptian (8)	62	0.05
Iraqi (707)	932	0.69
Jordanian (164)	174	0.13
Lebanese (528)	891	0.66
Palestinian (13)	19	0.01
Syrian (92)	160	0.12
Other Arab (219)	257	0.19
Armenian (460)	528	0.39
Assyrian/Chaldean/Syriac (2,077)	2,627	1.93
Australian (0)	26	0.02
Austrian (115)	351	0.26
Belgian (465)	1,678	1.24
British (207)	441	0.32
Bulgarian (7)	44	0.03
Canadian (219)	635	0.47
Celtic (0)	23	0.02
Croatian (99)	406	0.30
Czech (69)	386	0.28
Czechoslovakian (87)	276	0.20
Danish (70)	225	0.17
Dutch (328)	1,603	1.18
Eastern European (8)	8	0.01
English (2,046)	9,746	7.18
European (549)	600	0.44
Finnish (281)	969	0.71
French, ex. Basque (1,042)	7,214	5.31
French Canadian (1,135)	2,892	2.13
German (7,035)	26,458	19.48
Greek (331)	894	0.66
Hungarian (235)	1,275	0.94
Iranian (213)	226	0.17
Irish (3,645)	16,937	12.47
Italian (5,164)	13,557	9.98
Latvian (8)	29	0.02
Lithuanian (157)	597	0.44
Macedonian (104)	114	0.08
Maltese (133)	320	0.24
Northern European (27)	27	0.02
Norwegian (182)	765	0.56
Pennsylvania German (10)	30	0.02
Polish (12,605)	26,655	19.63
Portuguese (17)	82	0.06
Romanian (599)	955	0.70
Russian (331)	1,211	0.89
Scandinavian (5)	34	0.03
Scotch-Irish (626)	1,965	1.45
Scottish (704)	2,448	1.80
Serbian (161)	237	0.17
Slavic (9)	102	0.08
Slovak (429)	821	0.60
Slovene (57)	108	0.08
Swedish (174)	1,004	0.74
Swiss (23)	130	0.10
Turkish (9)	18	0.01
Ukrainian (1,353)	1,999	1.47
Welsh (61)	557	0.41
West Indian, ex. Hispanic (96)	109	0.08
Belizean (14)	14	0.01
Haitian (60)	73	0.05
Jamaican (22)	22	0.02
Yugoslavian (710)	990	0.73

Hispanic Origin	Population	%
Hispanic or Latino (of any race)	2,758	2.06
Central American, ex. Mexican	87	0.06
Costa Rican	1	<0.01
Guatemalan	35	0.03
Honduran	11	0.01
Nicaraguan	6	<0.01
Panamanian	8	0.01
Salvadoran	23	0.02
Other Central American	3	<0.01
Cuban	76	0.06
Dominican Republic	42	0.03
Mexican	1,650	1.23
Puerto Rican	405	0.30
South American	135	0.10
Argentinean	35	0.03
Bolivian	2	<0.01
Chilean	25	0.02
Colombian	20	0.01
Ecuadorian	19	0.01
Paraguayan	1	<0.01
Peruvian	13	0.01
Uruguayan	1	<0.01
Venezuelan	18	0.01
Other South American	1	<0.01
Other Hispanic or Latino	363	0.27

Race*	Population	%
African-American/Black (18,123)	19,712	14.70
Not Hispanic (17,978)	19,443	14.50
Hispanic (145)	269	0.20
American Indian/Alaska Native (562)	1,588	1.18
Not Hispanic (524)	1,461	1.09
Hispanic (38)	127	0.09
Alaska Athabascan *(Ala. Nat.)* (2)	3	<0.01
Aleut *(Alaska Native)* (0)	2	<0.01
Apache (5)	22	0.02
Blackfeet (2)	45	0.03
Canadian/French Am. Ind. (16)	38	0.03
Cherokee (72)	320	0.24
Cheyenne (1)	2	<0.01
Chickasaw (0)	2	<0.01
Chippewa (87)	171	0.13
Choctaw (3)	17	0.01
Comanche (0)	2	<0.01
Cree (1)	5	<0.01
Creek (0)	3	<0.01
Crow (0)	1	<0.01
Delaware (2)	2	<0.01
Hopi (0)	6	<0.01
Iroquois (21)	55	0.04
Lumbee (55)	77	0.06
Menominee (1)	1	<0.01
Mexican American Ind. (4)	8	0.01
Navajo (2)	8	0.01
Ottawa (23)	34	0.03
Pima (1)	1	<0.01
Potawatomi (4)	14	0.01
Puget Sound Salish (3)	3	<0.01
Seminole (0)	2	<0.01
Shoshone (1)	2	<0.01
Sioux (8)	29	0.02
South American Ind. (0)	1	<0.01
Spanish American Ind. (0)	1	<0.01
Tlingit-Haida *(Alaska Native)* (1)	1	<0.01
Yaqui (2)	2	<0.01
Asian (6,212)	7,263	5.42
Not Hispanic (6,170)	7,175	5.35
Hispanic (42)	88	0.07
Bangladeshi (956)	1,061	0.79
Burmese (0)	2	<0.01
Cambodian (30)	55	0.04
Chinese, ex. Taiwanese (297)	381	0.28
Filipino (1,183)	1,432	1.07
Hmong (1,170)	1,218	0.91
Indian (1,051)	1,254	0.94
Indonesian (5)	9	0.01
Japanese (65)	137	0.10
Korean (140)	202	0.15
Laotian (141)	178	0.13
Nepalese (3)	5	<0.01
Pakistani (192)	203	0.15
Sri Lankan (7)	7	0.01
Taiwanese (9)	11	0.01
Thai (33)	58	0.04
Vietnamese (544)	608	0.45
Hawaii Native/Pacific Islander (20)	153	0.11
Not Hispanic (18)	136	0.10
Hispanic (2)	17	0.01
Guamanian/Chamorro (2)	3	<0.01
Native Hawaiian (5)	36	0.03
Samoan (3)	7	0.01
White (105,088)	108,186	80.70
Not Hispanic (103,308)	106,146	79.18
Hispanic (1,780)	2,040	1.52

Washington

Place Type: Township
County: Macomb
Population: 25,139†

Ancestry‡	Population	%
African, Sub-Saharan (9)	9	0.04
African (9)	9	0.04
Albanian (372)	386	1.59
Alsatian (0)	10	0.04
American (1,253)	1,253	5.17
Arab (297)	466	1.92
Arab (0)	59	0.24
Egyptian (39)	39	0.16
Iraqi (111)	111	0.46
Jordanian (0)	6	0.02
Lebanese (29)	127	0.52
Palestinian (106)	106	0.44
Syrian (12)	18	0.07
Armenian (7)	28	0.12
Austrian (12)	30	0.12
Belgian (83)	457	1.89
British (8)	124	0.51
Bulgarian (0)	18	0.07

*Notes: † The Census 2010 population figure is used to calculate the percentages in the Hispanic Origin and Race categories. Ancestry percentages are based on the 2006-2010 American Community Survey population (not shown); ‡ Numbers in parentheses indicate the number of people reporting a single ancestry; * Numbers in parentheses indicate the number of persons reporting this race alone, not in combination with any other race; Please refer to the Explanation of Data for more information.*

Canadian (201)	351	1.45
Croatian (31)	93	0.38
Czech (22)	191	0.79
Czechoslovakian (123)	236	0.97
Danish (9)	64	0.26
Dutch (32)	495	2.04
English (632)	2,291	9.46
European (72)	107	0.44
Finnish (70)	214	0.88
French, ex. Basque (108)	1,350	5.57
French Canadian (220)	548	2.26
German (1,620)	6,676	27.56
Greek (101)	208	0.86
Hungarian (27)	401	1.66
Iranian (17)	17	0.07
Irish (440)	3,012	12.43
Italian (2,046)	4,163	17.19
Lithuanian (20)	129	0.53
Macedonian (277)	342	1.41
Maltese (23)	40	0.17
Northern European (8)	8	0.03
Norwegian (61)	181	0.75
Polish (1,374)	4,410	18.21
Romanian (149)	191	0.79
Russian (36)	249	1.03
Scandinavian (10)	19	0.08
Scotch-Irish (75)	356	1.47
Scottish (177)	602	2.49
Serbian (117)	137	0.57
Slavic (34)	51	0.21
Slovak (86)	188	0.78
Slovene (0)	24	0.10
Swedish (22)	222	0.92
Swiss (14)	49	0.20
Ukrainian (31)	208	0.86
Welsh (9)	69	0.28
Yugoslavian (27)	27	0.11

Hispanic Origin	Population	%
Hispanic or Latino (of any race)	971	3.86
Central American, ex. Mexican	12	0.05
Costa Rican	2	0.01
Guatemalan	7	0.03
Honduran	2	0.01
Panamanian	1	<0.01
Cuban	20	0.08
Mexican	755	3.00
Puerto Rican	62	0.25
South American	36	0.14
Argentinean	5	0.02
Chilean	1	<0.01
Colombian	7	0.03
Ecuadorian	1	<0.01
Peruvian	16	0.06
Venezuelan	6	0.02
Other Hispanic or Latino	86	0.34

Race*	Population	%
African-American/Black (395)	488	1.94
Not Hispanic (378)	467	1.86
Hispanic (17)	21	0.08
American Indian/Alaska Native (51)	165	0.66
Not Hispanic (33)	140	0.56
Hispanic (18)	25	0.10
Apache (0)	3	0.01
Blackfeet (1)	12	0.05
Canadian/French Am. Ind. (2)	4	0.02
Cherokee (2)	35	0.14
Chippewa (6)	27	0.11
Choctaw (1)	6	0.02
Comanche (0)	1	<0.01
Cree (0)	3	0.01
Hopi (1)	1	<0.01
Iroquois (1)	1	<0.01
Kiowa (1)	2	0.01
Lumbee (8)	15	0.06
Menominee (0)	1	<0.01
Mexican American Ind. (6)	7	0.03
Sioux (0)	2	0.01
Asian (263)	372	1.48
Not Hispanic (259)	357	1.42
Hispanic (4)	15	0.06
Cambodian (4)	4	0.02
Chinese, ex. Taiwanese (34)	47	0.19
Filipino (54)	92	0.37
Hmong (19)	19	0.08
Indian (51)	56	0.22
Japanese (15)	28	0.11
Korean (49)	58	0.23
Malaysian (1)	1	<0.01
Pakistani (7)	12	0.05
Taiwanese (4)	4	0.02
Thai (1)	1	<0.01
Vietnamese (22)	32	0.13
Hawaii Native/Pacific Islander (10)	20	0.08
Not Hispanic (10)	19	0.08
Hispanic (0)	1	<0.01
Guamanian/Chamorro (0)	3	0.01
Native Hawaiian (0)	4	0.02
White (23,824)	24,147	96.05
Not Hispanic (23,192)	23,477	93.39
Hispanic (632)	670	2.67

Waterford

Place Type: Charter Township
County: Oakland
Population: 71,707†

Ancestry‡	Population	%
African, Sub-Saharan (111)	133	0.19
African (63)	85	0.12
Ghanaian (34)	34	0.05
Nigerian (14)	14	0.02
Albanian (82)	153	0.21
American (3,571)	3,571	4.97
Arab (361)	666	0.93
Arab (72)	110	0.15
Egyptian (19)	47	0.07
Iraqi (123)	135	0.19
Lebanese (95)	253	0.35
Moroccan (0)	29	0.04
Other Arab (52)	92	0.13
Armenian (213)	435	0.61
Assyrian/Chaldean/Syriac (463)	527	0.73
Australian (0)	38	0.05
Austrian (46)	163	0.23
Belgian (21)	120	0.17
British (108)	271	0.38
Bulgarian (108)	108	0.15
Canadian (219)	625	0.87
Celtic (11)	56	0.08
Croatian (81)	174	0.24
Czech (157)	364	0.51
Czechoslovakian (25)	168	0.23
Danish (81)	326	0.45
Dutch (310)	1,900	2.65
Eastern European (42)	42	0.06
English (2,859)	10,085	14.05
European (511)	647	0.90
Finnish (228)	690	0.96
French, ex. Basque (477)	4,372	6.09
French Canadian (555)	1,465	2.04
German (5,185)	18,164	25.30
Greek (209)	571	0.80
Hungarian (294)	813	1.13
Irish (3,416)	12,416	17.29
Israeli (13)	26	0.04
Italian (1,316)	4,000	5.57
Latvian (0)	7	0.01
Lithuanian (35)	142	0.20
Macedonian (17)	28	0.04
Maltese (30)	125	0.17
Northern European (11)	11	0.02
Norwegian (263)	786	1.09
Pennsylvania German (17)	56	0.08
Polish (2,070)	6,336	8.82
Portuguese (27)	34	0.05
Romanian (213)	352	0.49
Russian (309)	825	1.15
Scandinavian (61)	103	0.14
Scotch-Irish (739)	1,716	2.39
Scottish (789)	2,800	3.90
Serbian (0)	62	0.09
Slavic (39)	69	0.10
Slovak (95)	186	0.26
Slovene (24)	83	0.12
Swedish (303)	1,259	1.75
Swiss (44)	84	0.12
Ukrainian (150)	324	0.45
Welsh (41)	725	1.01
West Indian, ex. Hispanic (33)	46	0.06
Haitian (12)	12	0.02
Jamaican (21)	34	0.05
Yugoslavian (41)	136	0.19

Hispanic Origin	Population	%
Hispanic or Latino (of any race)	4,557	6.36
Central American, ex. Mexican	124	0.17
Costa Rican	16	0.02
Guatemalan	30	0.04
Honduran	26	0.04
Nicaraguan	10	0.01
Panamanian	3	<0.01
Salvadoran	38	0.05
Other Central American	1	<0.01
Cuban	39	0.05
Dominican Republic	14	0.02
Mexican	3,316	4.62
Puerto Rican	639	0.89
South American	103	0.14
Argentinean	11	0.02
Chilean	18	0.03
Colombian	29	0.04
Ecuadorian	11	0.02
Paraguayan	3	<0.01
Peruvian	22	0.03
Venezuelan	9	0.01
Other Hispanic or Latino	322	0.45

Race*	Population	%
African-American/Black (3,374)	4,071	5.68
Not Hispanic (3,266)	3,871	5.40
Hispanic (108)	200	0.28
American Indian/Alaska Native (306)	807	1.13
Not Hispanic (254)	694	0.97
Hispanic (52)	113	0.16
Apache (2)	11	0.02
Blackfeet (2)	28	0.04
Canadian/French Am. Ind. (2)	5	0.01
Central American Ind. (3)	4	0.01
Cherokee (21)	157	0.22
Cheyenne (2)	2	<0.01
Chippewa (103)	167	0.23
Choctaw (2)	2	<0.01
Comanche (1)	2	<0.01
Cree (0)	1	<0.01
Creek (1)	1	<0.01
Delaware (4)	4	0.01
Hopi (1)	1	<0.01
Inupiat *(Alaska Native)* (1)	1	<0.01
Iroquois (8)	30	0.04
Kiowa (0)	1	<0.01
Lumbee (3)	9	0.01
Mexican American Ind. (8)	17	0.02
Navajo (2)	8	0.01
Ottawa (6)	22	0.03
Paiute (0)	1	<0.01
Potawatomi (10)	14	0.02
Seminole (0)	1	<0.01
Sioux (6)	12	0.02
South American Ind. (1)	1	<0.01
Spanish American Ind. (1)	1	<0.01
Tlingit-Haida *(Alaska Native)* (1)	3	<0.01
Asian (1,143)	1,527	2.13
Not Hispanic (1,131)	1,488	2.08
Hispanic (12)	39	0.05
Bangladeshi (11)	11	0.02
Cambodian (4)	6	0.01
Chinese, ex. Taiwanese (137)	186	0.26

*Notes: † The Census 2010 population figure is used to calculate the percentages in the Hispanic Origin and Race categories. Ancestry percentages are based on the 2006-2010 American Community Survey population (not shown); ‡ Numbers in parentheses indicate the number of people reporting a single ancestry; * Numbers in parentheses indicate the number of persons reporting this race alone, not in combination with any other race; Please refer to the Explanation of Data for more information.*

Filipino (236)	361	0.50
Hmong (213)	217	0.30
Indian (145)	178	0.25
Indonesian (2)	7	0.01
Japanese (51)	113	0.16
Korean (109)	166	0.23
Laotian (13)	15	0.02
Malaysian (0)	1	<0.01
Nepalese (57)	62	0.09
Pakistani (18)	22	0.03
Sri Lankan (0)	1	<0.01
Taiwanese (9)	11	0.02
Thai (18)	26	0.04
Vietnamese (75)	95	0.13
Hawaii Native/Pacific Islander (12)	58	0.08
Not Hispanic (10)	49	0.07
Hispanic (2)	9	0.01
Fijian (1)	1	<0.01
Guamanian/Chamorro (4)	5	0.01
Native Hawaiian (3)	16	0.02
Samoan (0)	1	<0.01
White (63,937)	65,528	91.38
Not Hispanic (61,103)	62,353	86.96
Hispanic (2,834)	3,175	4.43

Waverly

Place Type: CDP
County: Eaton
Population: 23,925†

Ancestry‡	Population	%
African, Sub-Saharan (122)	122	0.49
African (63)	63	0.25
Ethiopian (59)	59	0.24
Albanian (179)	179	0.72
American (761)	761	3.08
Arab (197)	361	1.46
Lebanese (189)	336	1.36
Palestinian (8)	8	0.03
Other Arab (0)	17	0.07
Armenian (0)	39	0.16
Austrian (0)	16	0.06
Belgian (0)	50	0.20
British (70)	96	0.39
Canadian (10)	28	0.11
Celtic (0)	17	0.07
Croatian (22)	29	0.12
Czech (43)	307	1.24
Czechoslovakian (46)	66	0.27
Danish (35)	195	0.79
Dutch (185)	1,148	4.64
Eastern European (12)	51	0.21
English (795)	3,160	12.77
European (362)	394	1.59
Finnish (48)	126	0.51
French, ex. Basque (67)	1,130	4.57
French Canadian (89)	378	1.53
German (1,879)	6,418	25.94
Greek (83)	130	0.53
Guyanese (0)	8	0.03
Hungarian (26)	120	0.49
Irish (570)	3,820	15.44
Italian (481)	1,245	5.03
Lithuanian (0)	47	0.19
Macedonian (16)	16	0.06
Northern European (58)	58	0.23
Norwegian (44)	192	0.78
Pennsylvania German (0)	10	0.04
Polish (445)	1,473	5.95
Portuguese (49)	49	0.20
Romanian (0)	33	0.13
Russian (14)	110	0.44
Scandinavian (0)	18	0.07
Scotch-Irish (185)	374	1.51
Scottish (172)	679	2.74
Serbian (0)	13	0.05
Slavic (0)	128	0.52
Slovak (15)	128	0.52
Slovene (0)	13	0.05
Swedish (80)	802	3.24
Swiss (0)	97	0.39
Turkish (7)	7	0.03
Ukrainian (22)	33	0.13
Welsh (14)	138	0.56
West Indian, ex. Hispanic (28)	28	0.11
Jamaican (28)	28	0.11
Yugoslavian (96)	96	0.39

Hispanic Origin	Population	%
Hispanic or Latino (of any race)	1,652	6.90
Central American, ex. Mexican	45	0.19
Costa Rican	5	0.02
Guatemalan	19	0.08
Honduran	2	0.01
Nicaraguan	7	0.03
Panamanian	7	0.03
Salvadoran	5	0.02
Cuban	143	0.60
Dominican Republic	7	0.03
Mexican	1,195	4.99
Puerto Rican	90	0.38
South American	47	0.20
Argentinean	6	0.03
Bolivian	5	0.02
Chilean	2	0.01
Colombian	10	0.04
Ecuadorian	15	0.06
Peruvian	2	0.01
Uruguayan	1	<0.01
Venezuelan	3	0.01
Other South American	3	0.01
Other Hispanic or Latino	125	0.52

Race*	Population	%
African-American/Black (3,313)	3,856	16.12
Not Hispanic (3,241)	3,712	15.52
Hispanic (72)	144	0.60
American Indian/Alaska Native (129)	361	1.51
Not Hispanic (111)	317	1.32
Hispanic (18)	44	0.18
Apache (1)	2	0.01
Blackfeet (1)	14	0.06
Canadian/French Am. Ind. (4)	6	0.03
Central American Ind. (2)	2	0.01
Cherokee (4)	51	0.21
Chippewa (33)	64	0.27
Choctaw (2)	6	0.03
Creek (1)	6	0.03
Crow (0)	1	<0.01
Iroquois (3)	13	0.05
Mexican American Ind. (3)	4	0.02
Navajo (1)	2	0.01
Osage (0)	1	<0.01
Ottawa (15)	28	0.12
Potawatomi (1)	4	0.02
Sioux (2)	3	0.01
Tohono O'Odham (0)	1	<0.01
Asian (1,014)	1,193	4.99
Not Hispanic (1,006)	1,180	4.93
Hispanic (8)	13	0.05
Burmese (4)	4	0.02
Cambodian (2)	4	0.02
Chinese, ex. Taiwanese (97)	117	0.49
Filipino (37)	54	0.23
Hmong (27)	40	0.17
Indian (438)	478	2.00
Indonesian (4)	7	0.03
Japanese (10)	29	0.12
Korean (55)	81	0.34
Laotian (11)	14	0.06
Nepalese (0)	1	<0.01
Pakistani (49)	56	0.23
Sri Lankan (5)	7	0.03
Taiwanese (1)	3	0.01
Thai (3)	7	0.03
Vietnamese (233)	247	1.03
Hawaii Native/Pacific Islander (1)	24	0.10
Not Hispanic (1)	16	0.07
Hispanic (0)	8	0.03
Guamanian/Chamorro (0)	1	<0.01
Native Hawaiian (0)	2	0.01
Samoan (1)	2	0.01
White (17,988)	18,811	78.62
Not Hispanic (17,117)	17,773	74.29
Hispanic (871)	1,038	4.34

Wayne

Place Type: City
County: Wayne
Population: 17,593†

Ancestry‡	Population	%
African, Sub-Saharan (51)	75	0.42
African (14)	14	0.08
Liberian (37)	37	0.21
Nigerian (0)	24	0.13
Albanian (210)	210	1.17
American (1,007)	1,007	5.62
Arab (29)	51	0.28
Arab (0)	12	0.07
Lebanese (21)	31	0.17
Moroccan (8)	8	0.04
Armenian (0)	8	0.04
Australian (0)	46	0.26
Austrian (0)	80	0.45
British (8)	37	0.21
Canadian (41)	97	0.54
Croatian (9)	32	0.18
Cypriot (9)	18	0.10
Czech (45)	61	0.34
Danish (21)	61	0.34
Dutch (137)	512	2.86
English (388)	1,722	9.61
European (71)	91	0.51
Finnish (96)	237	1.32
French, ex. Basque (66)	786	4.39
French Canadian (100)	368	2.05
German (840)	3,920	21.87
Greek (0)	69	0.38
Guyanese (18)	18	0.10
Hungarian (40)	224	1.25
Irish (459)	2,272	12.68
Italian (206)	661	3.69
Lithuanian (0)	13	0.07
Macedonian (20)	39	0.22
Norwegian (29)	167	0.93
Pennsylvania German (18)	34	0.19
Polish (445)	1,585	8.84
Portuguese (10)	24	0.13
Romanian (24)	34	0.19
Russian (0)	41	0.23
Scotch-Irish (75)	321	1.79
Scottish (68)	542	3.02
Slavic (0)	14	0.08
Slovak (25)	99	0.55
Slovene (0)	10	0.06
Swedish (50)	166	0.93
Swiss (0)	15	0.08
Ukrainian (11)	70	0.39
Welsh (13)	63	0.35
Yugoslavian (35)	35	0.20

Hispanic Origin	Population	%
Hispanic or Latino (of any race)	602	3.42
Central American, ex. Mexican	15	0.09
Costa Rican	1	0.01
Guatemalan	2	0.01
Honduran	6	0.03
Nicaraguan	4	0.02
Salvadoran	2	0.01
Cuban	18	0.10
Dominican Republic	6	0.03
Mexican	430	2.44
Puerto Rican	69	0.39
South American	20	0.11
Argentinean	2	0.01
Chilean	1	0.01
Colombian	13	0.07

*Notes: † The Census 2010 population figure is used to calculate the percentages in the Hispanic Origin and Race categories. Ancestry percentages are based on the 2006-2010 American Community Survey population (not shown); ‡ Numbers in parentheses indicate the number of people reporting a single ancestry; * Numbers in parentheses indicate the number of persons reporting this race alone, not in combination with any other race; Please refer to the Explanation of Data for more information.*

SECTION TWO

Ecuadorian	3	0.02
Venezuelan	1	0.01
Other Hispanic or Latino	44	0.25

Race*	Population	%
African-American/Black (3,000)	3,299	18.75
Not Hispanic (2,964)	3,238	18.41
Hispanic (36)	61	0.35
American Indian/Alaska Native (92)	268	1.52
Not Hispanic (75)	237	1.35
Hispanic (17)	31	0.18
Apache (2)	4	0.02
Blackfeet (0)	5	0.03
Canadian/French Am. Ind. (1)	3	0.02
Cherokee (4)	43	0.24
Chippewa (22)	47	0.27
Creek (1)	3	0.02
Delaware (1)	2	0.01
Iroquois (2)	11	0.06
Lumbee (1)	1	0.01
Mexican American Ind. (1)	4	0.02
Navajo (3)	8	0.05
Ottawa (6)	9	0.05
Potawatomi (2)	2	0.01
Shoshone (1)	3	0.02
Sioux (0)	1	0.01
Ute (0)	1	0.01
Asian (361)	436	2.48
Not Hispanic (360)	429	2.44
Hispanic (1)	7	0.04
Bangladeshi (3)	3	0.02
Chinese, ex. Taiwanese (28)	32	0.18
Filipino (36)	64	0.36
Indian (158)	165	0.94
Japanese (2)	16	0.09
Korean (89)	98	0.56
Nepalese (3)	3	0.02
Pakistani (23)	23	0.13
Thai (4)	4	0.02
Vietnamese (15)	17	0.10
Hawaii Native/Pacific Islander (6)	20	0.11
Not Hispanic (6)	19	0.11
Hispanic (0)	1	0.01
Guamanian/Chamorro (1)	1	0.01
Native Hawaiian (3)	8	0.05
Samoan (0)	2	0.01
White (13,420)	13,904	79.03
Not Hispanic (13,080)	13,494	76.70
Hispanic (340)	410	2.33

West Bloomfield

Place Type: Charter Township
County: Oakland
Population: 64,690†

Ancestry‡	Population	%
African, Sub-Saharan (238)	395	0.61
African (96)	96	0.15
Ethiopian (25)	25	0.04
Nigerian (93)	250	0.39
Senegalese (7)	7	0.01
Zimbabwean (17)	17	0.03
Albanian (281)	315	0.49
American (2,747)	2,747	4.25
Arab (3,524)	4,594	7.10
Arab (1,263)	1,506	2.33
Egyptian (74)	83	0.13
Iraqi (1,385)	1,775	2.74
Jordanian (32)	32	0.05
Lebanese (257)	453	0.70
Palestinian (53)	53	0.08
Syrian (93)	125	0.19
Other Arab (367)	567	0.88
Armenian (691)	814	1.26
Assyrian/Chaldean/Syriac (4,689)	5,475	8.46
Austrian (92)	398	0.62
Belgian (33)	276	0.43
Brazilian (18)	78	0.12
British (121)	157	0.24
Canadian (468)	611	0.94
Celtic (8)	8	0.01
Croatian (28)	61	0.09
Czech (40)	253	0.39
Czechoslovakian (19)	101	0.16
Danish (12)	152	0.23
Dutch (89)	541	0.84
Eastern European (831)	842	1.30
English (1,105)	3,993	6.17
European (1,037)	1,081	1.67
Finnish (234)	429	0.66
French, ex. Basque (371)	1,658	2.56
French Canadian (170)	823	1.27
German (1,845)	7,192	11.11
Greek (227)	347	0.54
Hungarian (506)	1,200	1.85
Iranian (583)	640	0.99
Irish (1,144)	4,166	6.44
Israeli (208)	268	0.41
Italian (896)	2,337	3.61
Latvian (41)	76	0.12
Lithuanian (129)	293	0.45
Luxemburger (10)	10	0.02
Macedonian (14)	36	0.06
Maltese (19)	44	0.07
Northern European (12)	12	0.02
Norwegian (82)	281	0.43
Polish (2,677)	6,341	9.80
Portuguese (8)	8	0.01
Romanian (222)	469	0.72
Russian (2,578)	4,873	7.53
Scandinavian (71)	101	0.16
Scotch-Irish (207)	594	0.92
Scottish (278)	924	1.43
Serbian (21)	84	0.13
Slavic (0)	35	0.05
Slovak (142)	224	0.35
Slovene (0)	31	0.05
Swedish (239)	647	1.00
Swiss (29)	81	0.13
Turkish (85)	85	0.13
Ukrainian (335)	433	0.67
Welsh (58)	221	0.34
West Indian, ex. Hispanic (9)	20	0.03
Jamaican (9)	20	0.03
Yugoslavian (61)	118	0.18

Hispanic Origin	Population	%
Hispanic or Latino (of any race)	1,042	1.61
Central American, ex. Mexican	64	0.10
Costa Rican	5	0.01
Guatemalan	22	0.03
Honduran	9	0.01
Nicaraguan	6	0.01
Panamanian	12	0.02
Salvadoran	10	0.02
Cuban	42	0.06
Dominican Republic	12	0.02
Mexican	514	0.79
Puerto Rican	93	0.14
South American	162	0.25
Argentinean	34	0.05
Bolivian	3	<0.01
Chilean	23	0.04
Colombian	51	0.08
Ecuadorian	8	0.01
Paraguayan	9	0.01
Peruvian	21	0.03
Uruguayan	4	0.01
Venezuelan	7	0.01
Other South American	2	<0.01
Other Hispanic or Latino	155	0.24

Race*	Population	%
African-American/Black (7,396)	7,750	11.98
Not Hispanic (7,338)	7,662	11.84
Hispanic (58)	88	0.14
American Indian/Alaska Native (72)	285	0.44
Not Hispanic (61)	261	0.40
Hispanic (11)	24	0.04
Apache (1)	3	<0.01
Blackfeet (1)	6	0.01
Central American Ind. (1)	2	<0.01
Cherokee (6)	44	0.07
Chippewa (9)	16	0.02
Choctaw (0)	2	<0.01
Cree (2)	2	<0.01
Creek (0)	1	<0.01
Iroquois (3)	10	0.02
Lumbee (1)	6	0.01
Mexican American Ind. (3)	3	<0.01
Navajo (2)	4	0.01
Ottawa (2)	3	<0.01
Potawatomi (3)	9	0.01
Seminole (0)	4	0.01
Sioux (1)	6	0.01
South American Ind. (0)	5	0.01
Tlingit-Haida *(Alaska Native)* (2)	2	<0.01
Asian (5,421)	6,156	9.52
Not Hispanic (5,412)	6,123	9.47
Hispanic (9)	33	0.05
Bangladeshi (33)	36	0.06
Burmese (4)	4	0.01
Chinese, ex. Taiwanese (730)	800	1.24
Filipino (256)	327	0.51
Indian (2,225)	2,336	3.61
Indonesian (8)	8	0.01
Japanese (872)	946	1.46
Korean (464)	518	0.80
Laotian (1)	3	<0.01
Malaysian (4)	5	0.01
Nepalese (7)	7	0.01
Pakistani (565)	600	0.93
Sri Lankan (8)	10	0.02
Taiwanese (72)	78	0.12
Thai (14)	23	0.04
Vietnamese (63)	72	0.11
Hawaii Native/Pacific Islander (6)	129	0.20
Not Hispanic (6)	127	0.20
Hispanic (0)	2	<0.01
Guamanian/Chamorro (0)	4	0.01
Native Hawaiian (2)	11	0.02
Samoan (1)	3	<0.01
White (50,227)	51,374	79.42
Not Hispanic (49,474)	50,541	78.13
Hispanic (753)	833	1.29

Westland

Place Type: City
County: Wayne
Population: 84,094†

Ancestry‡	Population	%
African, Sub-Saharan (339)	529	0.62
African (219)	321	0.38
Ethiopian (0)	19	0.02
Nigerian (106)	115	0.14
Senegalese (14)	74	0.09
Albanian (829)	829	0.98
American (4,473)	4,473	5.27
Arab (833)	1,262	1.49
Arab (357)	536	0.63
Egyptian (11)	21	0.02
Jordanian (180)	180	0.21
Lebanese (100)	245	0.29
Palestinian (119)	119	0.14
Syrian (27)	109	0.13
Other Arab (39)	52	0.06
Armenian (59)	94	0.11
Australian (0)	24	0.03
Austrian (82)	200	0.24
Belgian (60)	187	0.22
Brazilian (7)	7	0.01
British (115)	254	0.30
Bulgarian (20)	93	0.11
Canadian (298)	768	0.91
Croatian (91)	227	0.27
Czech (46)	469	0.55
Czechoslovakian (40)	55	0.06

*Notes: † The Census 2010 population figure is used to calculate the percentages in the Hispanic Origin and Race categories. Ancestry percentages are based on the 2006-2010 American Community Survey population (not shown); ‡ Numbers in parentheses indicate the number of people reporting a single ancestry; * Numbers in parentheses indicate the number of persons reporting this race alone, not in combination with any other race; Please refer to the Explanation of Data for more information.*

Danish (25)	285	0.34
Dutch (288)	1,255	1.48
Eastern European (24)	24	0.03
English (1,934)	6,916	8.15
European (669)	760	0.90
Finnish (228)	835	0.98
French, ex. Basque (571)	3,679	4.34
French Canadian (687)	1,562	1.84
German (3,675)	15,599	18.39
Greek (206)	554	0.65
Hungarian (284)	989	1.17
Irish (2,566)	11,189	13.19
Israeli (24)	24	0.03
Italian (1,938)	4,529	5.34
Latvian (11)	11	0.01
Lithuanian (81)	323	0.38
Macedonian (61)	61	0.07
Maltese (120)	287	0.34
Northern European (34)	34	0.04
Norwegian (202)	497	0.59
Pennsylvania German (8)	52	0.06
Polish (4,073)	9,616	11.34
Portuguese (5)	39	0.05
Romanian (446)	623	0.73
Russian (110)	564	0.66
Scandinavian (0)	17	0.02
Scotch-Irish (620)	1,528	1.80
Scottish (416)	2,029	2.39
Serbian (20)	171	0.20
Slavic (11)	77	0.09
Slovak (162)	248	0.29
Slovene (31)	31	0.04
Swedish (69)	863	1.02
Swiss (19)	72	0.08
Turkish (10)	30	0.04
Ukrainian (105)	515	0.61
Welsh (51)	376	0.44
West Indian, ex. Hispanic (153)	211	0.25
Jamaican (131)	131	0.15
West Indian (22)	80	0.09
Yugoslavian (265)	292	0.34

Hispanic Origin	Population	%
Hispanic or Latino (of any race)	3,165	3.76
Central American, ex. Mexican	59	0.07
Costa Rican	4	<0.01
Guatemalan	14	0.02
Honduran	9	0.01
Nicaraguan	14	0.02
Panamanian	7	0.01
Salvadoran	11	0.01
Cuban	94	0.11
Dominican Republic	16	0.02
Mexican	2,287	2.72
Puerto Rican	273	0.32
South American	118	0.14
Argentinean	15	0.02
Bolivian	8	0.01
Chilean	4	<0.01
Colombian	30	0.04
Ecuadorian	15	0.02
Peruvian	34	0.04
Uruguayan	4	<0.01
Venezuelan	8	0.01
Other Hispanic or Latino	318	0.38

Race*	Population	%
African-American/Black (14,489)	15,552	18.49
Not Hispanic (14,347)	15,336	18.24
Hispanic (142)	216	0.26
American Indian/Alaska Native (391)	1,034	1.23
Not Hispanic (353)	896	1.07
Hispanic (38)	138	0.16
Aleut *(Alaska Native)* (1)	1	<0.01
Apache (0)	1	<0.01
Blackfeet (2)	28	0.03
Canadian/French Am. Ind. (8)	11	0.01
Cherokee (21)	160	0.19
Cheyenne (0)	2	<0.01
Chickasaw (1)	3	<0.01
Chippewa (118)	179	0.21
Choctaw (0)	4	<0.01
Comanche (1)	4	<0.01
Cree (0)	3	<0.01
Creek (15)	25	0.03
Delaware (9)	15	0.02
Houma (0)	1	<0.01
Iroquois (18)	40	0.05
Lumbee (11)	20	0.02
Menominee (0)	1	<0.01
Mexican American Ind. (8)	16	0.02
Navajo (3)	3	<0.01
Osage (1)	1	<0.01
Ottawa (9)	14	0.02
Potawatomi (2)	4	<0.01
Seminole (0)	1	<0.01
Sioux (4)	8	0.01
Spanish American Ind. (1)	2	<0.01
Tsimshian *(Alaska Native)* (0)	1	<0.01
Yup'ik *(Alaska Native)* (0)	1	<0.01
Asian (2,548)	2,986	3.55
Not Hispanic (2,526)	2,934	3.49
Hispanic (22)	52	0.06
Bangladeshi (25)	25	0.03
Burmese (2)	2	<0.01
Cambodian (5)	16	0.02
Chinese, ex. Taiwanese (329)	367	0.44
Filipino (485)	602	0.72
Hmong (4)	4	<0.01
Indian (1,130)	1,188	1.41
Indonesian (0)	8	0.01
Japanese (51)	135	0.16
Korean (95)	132	0.16
Laotian (7)	10	0.01
Malaysian (11)	13	0.02
Pakistani (113)	126	0.15
Sri Lankan (7)	7	0.01
Taiwanese (4)	8	0.01
Thai (11)	22	0.03
Vietnamese (211)	241	0.29
Hawaii Native/Pacific Islander (13)	70	0.08
Not Hispanic (13)	63	0.07
Hispanic (0)	7	0.01
Guamanian/Chamorro (6)	12	0.01
Native Hawaiian (1)	15	0.02
Samoan (5)	13	0.02
White (63,737)	65,538	77.93
Not Hispanic (61,826)	63,362	75.35
Hispanic (1,911)	2,176	2.59

Westwood

Place Type: CDP
County: Kalamazoo
Population: 8,653†

Ancestry‡	Population	%
African, Sub-Saharan (47)	63	0.70
African (16)	16	0.18
Ghanaian (7)	15	0.17
Nigerian (8)	16	0.18
South African (16)	16	0.18
American (311)	311	3.43
Arab (22)	22	0.24
Egyptian (11)	11	0.12
Lebanese (11)	11	0.12
Armenian (0)	12	0.13
Austrian (12)	12	0.13
Belgian (0)	44	0.49
British (40)	74	0.82
Canadian (15)	39	0.43
Celtic (0)	16	0.18
Croatian (39)	39	0.43
Czech (0)	46	0.51
Czechoslovakian (14)	27	0.30
Danish (19)	48	0.53
Dutch (761)	1,365	15.07
English (627)	1,691	18.67
European (96)	113	1.25
Finnish (31)	163	1.80
French, ex. Basque (7)	291	3.21
French Canadian (18)	50	0.55
German (458)	2,090	23.08
Greek (11)	31	0.34
Hungarian (0)	46	0.51
Irish (208)	1,004	11.09
Italian (84)	331	3.65
Latvian (33)	73	0.81
Lithuanian (0)	53	0.59
Northern European (11)	11	0.12
Norwegian (0)	34	0.38
Polish (145)	499	5.51
Russian (12)	46	0.51
Scandinavian (0)	14	0.15
Scotch-Irish (48)	203	2.24
Scottish (14)	226	2.50
Slovak (0)	11	0.12
Slovene (12)	12	0.13
Swedish (85)	335	3.70
Swiss (0)	12	0.13
Ukrainian (13)	13	0.14
Welsh (66)	128	1.41
West Indian, ex. Hispanic (14)	24	0.26
British West Indian (0)	10	0.11
Trinidadian/Tobagonian (14)	14	0.15

Hispanic Origin	Population	%
Hispanic or Latino (of any race)	236	2.73
Central American, ex. Mexican	12	0.14
Costa Rican	1	0.01
Guatemalan	6	0.07
Honduran	4	0.05
Salvadoran	1	0.01
Cuban	8	0.09
Dominican Republic	2	0.02
Mexican	146	1.69
Puerto Rican	29	0.34
South American	9	0.10
Argentinean	2	0.02
Colombian	3	0.03
Ecuadorian	2	0.02
Venezuelan	2	0.02
Other Hispanic or Latino	30	0.35

Race*	Population	%
African-American/Black (995)	1,154	13.34
Not Hispanic (985)	1,120	12.94
Hispanic (10)	34	0.39
American Indian/Alaska Native (29)	86	0.99
Not Hispanic (27)	73	0.84
Hispanic (2)	13	0.15
Apache (0)	1	0.01
Arapaho (3)	3	0.03
Blackfeet (0)	2	0.02
Central American Ind. (0)	1	0.01
Cherokee (4)	9	0.10
Chippewa (7)	16	0.18
Choctaw (0)	4	0.05
Inupiat *(Alaska Native)* (1)	1	0.01
Iroquois (1)	3	0.03
Mexican American Ind. (2)	3	0.03
Ottawa (2)	3	0.03
Potawatomi (4)	10	0.12
Shoshone (0)	1	0.01
Asian (159)	231	2.67
Not Hispanic (158)	220	2.54
Hispanic (1)	11	0.13
Bangladeshi (1)	1	0.01
Burmese (0)	2	0.02
Chinese, ex. Taiwanese (31)	36	0.42
Filipino (25)	40	0.46
Indian (36)	42	0.49
Indonesian (1)	1	0.01
Japanese (7)	30	0.35
Korean (23)	28	0.32
Laotian (1)	1	0.01
Malaysian (5)	6	0.07
Taiwanese (0)	1	0.01
Thai (10)	13	0.15
Vietnamese (8)	8	0.09

*Notes: † The Census 2010 population figure is used to calculate the percentages in the Hispanic Origin and Race categories. Ancestry percentages are based on the 2006-2010 American Community Survey population (not shown); ‡ Numbers in parentheses indicate the number of people reporting a single ancestry; * Numbers in parentheses indicate the number of persons reporting this race alone, not in combination with any other race; Please refer to the Explanation of Data for more information.*

Hawaii Native/Pacific Islander (2)	10	0.12
Not Hispanic (2)	8	0.09
Hispanic (0)	2	0.02
Guamanian/Chamorro (2)	2	0.02
White (7,100)	7,343	84.86
Not Hispanic (6,989)	7,197	83.17
Hispanic (111)	146	1.69

White Lake

Place Type: Charter Township
County: Oakland
Population: 30,019†

Ancestry‡	Population	%
American (1,707)	1,707	5.75
Arab (68)	206	0.69
Iraqi (0)	25	0.08
Lebanese (28)	131	0.44
Syrian (40)	50	0.17
Armenian (35)	74	0.25
Assyrian/Chaldean/Syriac (48)	113	0.38
Austrian (0)	79	0.27
Belgian (11)	175	0.59
British (40)	59	0.20
Bulgarian (0)	18	0.06
Canadian (76)	296	1.00
Croatian (14)	63	0.21
Czech (89)	301	1.01
Czechoslovakian (14)	44	0.15
Danish (42)	220	0.74
Dutch (155)	742	2.50
Eastern European (8)	8	0.03
English (1,209)	4,143	13.96
European (480)	508	1.71
Finnish (84)	331	1.12
French, ex. Basque (326)	1,844	6.21
French Canadian (299)	766	2.58
German (1,759)	7,715	25.99
Greek (11)	209	0.70
Hungarian (149)	425	1.43
Iranian (9)	9	0.03
Irish (1,043)	5,282	17.79
Italian (778)	2,270	7.65
Latvian (10)	32	0.11
Lithuanian (16)	64	0.22
Luxemburger (0)	8	0.03
Macedonian (12)	12	0.04
Maltese (20)	71	0.24
Norwegian (114)	355	1.20
Polish (1,305)	3,437	11.58
Portuguese (0)	11	0.04
Romanian (36)	100	0.34
Russian (141)	421	1.42
Scotch-Irish (350)	729	2.46
Scottish (293)	1,111	3.74
Serbian (0)	7	0.02
Slavic (5)	24	0.08
Slovak (87)	186	0.63
Slovene (0)	7	0.02
Swedish (209)	611	2.06
Swiss (31)	125	0.42
Turkish (72)	72	0.24
Ukrainian (38)	131	0.44
Welsh (13)	202	0.68
Yugoslavian (11)	23	0.08

Hispanic Origin	Population	%
Hispanic or Latino (of any race)	899	2.99
Central American, ex. Mexican	25	0.08
Costa Rican	8	0.03
Guatemalan	12	0.04
Honduran	2	0.01
Panamanian	2	0.01
Salvadoran	1	<0.01
Cuban	33	0.11
Mexican	628	2.09
Puerto Rican	85	0.28
South American	38	0.13
Argentinean	8	0.03
Bolivian	1	<0.01
Chilean	4	0.01
Colombian	15	0.05
Paraguayan	5	0.02
Peruvian	5	0.02
Other Hispanic or Latino	90	0.30

Race*	Population	%
African-American/Black (335)	483	1.61
Not Hispanic (321)	455	1.52
Hispanic (14)	28	0.09
American Indian/Alaska Native (125)	335	1.12
Not Hispanic (110)	298	0.99
Hispanic (15)	37	0.12
Aleut *(Alaska Native)* (4)	4	0.01
Apache (1)	1	<0.01
Blackfeet (3)	15	0.05
Canadian/French Am. Ind. (2)	3	0.01
Cherokee (12)	69	0.23
Chippewa (43)	87	0.29
Choctaw (1)	1	<0.01
Colville (0)	1	<0.01
Comanche (1)	1	<0.01
Cree (0)	1	<0.01
Iroquois (5)	14	0.05
Lumbee (0)	1	<0.01
Mexican American Ind. (2)	2	0.01
Navajo (1)	3	0.01
Ottawa (5)	5	0.02
Potawatomi (1)	1	<0.01
Sioux (2)	4	0.01
South American Ind. (1)	1	<0.01
Asian (283)	377	1.26
Not Hispanic (271)	363	1.21
Hispanic (12)	14	0.05
Chinese, ex. Taiwanese (39)	49	0.16
Filipino (56)	79	0.26
Hmong (13)	13	0.04
Indian (47)	60	0.20
Japanese (18)	32	0.11
Korean (38)	60	0.20
Malaysian (1)	2	0.01
Pakistani (8)	10	0.03
Sri Lankan (1)	1	<0.01
Thai (6)	8	0.03
Vietnamese (43)	51	0.17
Hawaii Native/Pacific Islander (6)	20	0.07
Not Hispanic (3)	16	0.05
Hispanic (3)	4	0.01
Guamanian/Chamorro (3)	8	0.03
Native Hawaiian (2)	4	0.01
Samoan (1)	1	<0.01
White (28,613)	29,065	96.82
Not Hispanic (28,000)	28,384	94.55
Hispanic (613)	681	2.27

Wixom

Place Type: City
County: Oakland
Population: 13,498†

Ancestry‡	Population	%
African, Sub-Saharan (46)	59	0.44
African (34)	47	0.35
Nigerian (12)	12	0.09
Albanian (235)	235	1.75
American (358)	358	2.66
Arab (144)	199	1.48
Arab (71)	97	0.72
Iraqi (38)	45	0.33
Lebanese (0)	22	0.16
Other Arab (35)	35	0.26
Armenian (67)	109	0.81
Assyrian/Chaldean/Syriac (75)	82	0.61
Austrian (0)	37	0.27
Belgian (44)	114	0.85
British (18)	31	0.23
Bulgarian (162)	162	1.20
Canadian (10)	14	0.10
Croatian (6)	83	0.62
Czech (34)	80	0.59
Danish (38)	92	0.68
Dutch (22)	114	0.85
Eastern European (8)	8	0.06
English (422)	1,514	11.25
Estonian (0)	12	0.09
European (105)	105	0.78
Finnish (103)	326	2.42
French, ex. Basque (86)	800	5.95
French Canadian (132)	334	2.48
German (895)	3,256	24.20
Greek (27)	69	0.51
Hungarian (69)	202	1.50
Irish (331)	1,579	11.73
Italian (277)	786	5.84
Latvian (0)	24	0.18
Lithuanian (0)	84	0.62
Macedonian (38)	119	0.88
Maltese (14)	65	0.48
Norwegian (58)	135	1.00
Polish (346)	1,807	13.43
Romanian (81)	120	0.89
Russian (31)	155	1.15
Scandinavian (0)	103	0.77
Scotch-Irish (84)	166	1.23
Scottish (47)	362	2.69
Slovak (0)	76	0.56
Slovene (0)	41	0.30
Swedish (74)	143	1.06
Swiss (4)	40	0.30
Ukrainian (83)	188	1.40
Welsh (0)	77	0.57
Yugoslavian (48)	57	0.42

Hispanic Origin	Population	%
Hispanic or Latino (of any race)	684	5.07
Central American, ex. Mexican	87	0.64
Guatemalan	24	0.18
Honduran	7	0.05
Nicaraguan	2	0.01
Salvadoran	54	0.40
Cuban	12	0.09
Dominican Republic	4	0.03
Mexican	447	3.31
Puerto Rican	40	0.30
South American	28	0.21
Argentinean	9	0.07
Bolivian	1	0.01
Colombian	9	0.07
Ecuadorian	1	0.01
Paraguayan	4	0.03
Peruvian	2	0.01
Uruguayan	1	0.01
Venezuelan	1	0.01
Other Hispanic or Latino	66	0.49

Race*	Population	%
African-American/Black (1,501)	1,609	11.92
Not Hispanic (1,487)	1,577	11.68
Hispanic (14)	32	0.24
American Indian/Alaska Native (32)	114	0.84
Not Hispanic (31)	104	0.77
Hispanic (1)	10	0.07
Blackfeet (0)	4	0.03
Cherokee (5)	24	0.18
Chippewa (7)	24	0.18
Choctaw (1)	1	0.01
Cree (1)	1	0.01
Iroquois (3)	9	0.07
Ottawa (5)	5	0.04
Potawatomi (1)	1	0.01
Asian (657)	750	5.56
Not Hispanic (653)	743	5.50
Hispanic (4)	7	0.05
Bangladeshi (3)	3	0.02
Chinese, ex. Taiwanese (67)	78	0.58
Filipino (37)	53	0.39
Hmong (4)	4	0.03
Indian (268)	279	2.07

*Notes: † The Census 2010 population figure is used to calculate the percentages in the Hispanic Origin and Race categories. Ancestry percentages are based on the 2006-2010 American Community Survey population (not shown); ‡ Numbers in parentheses indicate the number of people reporting a single ancestry; * Numbers in parentheses indicate the number of persons reporting this race alone, not in combination with any other race; Please refer to the Explanation of Data for more information.*

Indonesian (1)	1	0.01
Japanese (74)	97	0.72
Korean (64)	74	0.55
Nepalese (53)	54	0.40
Pakistani (3)	4	0.03
Sri Lankan (3)	4	0.03
Taiwanese (2)	2	0.01
Thai (1)	2	0.01
Vietnamese (57)	58	0.43
Hawaii Native/Pacific Islander (1)	11	0.08
Not Hispanic (1)	11	0.08
Guamanian/Chamorro (1)	2	0.01
Native Hawaiian (0)	2	0.01
White (10,770)	11,012	81.58
Not Hispanic (10,387)	10,595	78.49
Hispanic (383)	417	3.09

Woodhaven

Place Type: City
County: Wayne
Population: 12,875†

Ancestry‡	Population	%
African, Sub-Saharan (37)	37	0.29
African (26)	26	0.20
Ugandan (11)	11	0.09
Albanian (75)	75	0.58
American (381)	381	2.96
Arab (74)	121	0.94
Arab (22)	28	0.22
Lebanese (0)	41	0.32
Other Arab (52)	52	0.40
Armenian (0)	6	0.05
Austrian (10)	10	0.08
Belgian (25)	35	0.27
Brazilian (0)	11	0.09
British (9)	15	0.12
Canadian (10)	10	0.08
Croatian (0)	12	0.09
Czech (0)	16	0.12
Czechoslovakian (22)	48	0.37
Danish (0)	10	0.08
Dutch (103)	366	2.85
English (230)	1,282	9.97
European (189)	195	1.52
Finnish (10)	130	1.01
French, ex. Basque (65)	756	5.88
French Canadian (118)	279	2.17
German (641)	3,219	25.03
Greek (2)	66	0.51
Hungarian (176)	726	5.64
Irish (345)	2,164	16.82
Israeli (26)	26	0.20
Italian (320)	908	7.06
Lithuanian (5)	62	0.48
Maltese (26)	52	0.40
Norwegian (10)	75	0.58
Pennsylvania German (0)	8	0.06
Polish (899)	2,249	17.49
Romanian (0)	56	0.44
Russian (44)	60	0.47
Scandinavian (10)	19	0.15
Scotch-Irish (129)	442	3.44
Scottish (69)	357	2.78
Serbian (6)	6	0.05
Slovak (66)	190	1.48
Slovene (0)	25	0.19
Swedish (21)	335	2.60
Swiss (11)	44	0.34
Ukrainian (26)	62	0.48
Welsh (15)	49	0.38
Yugoslavian (0)	52	0.40

Hispanic Origin	Population	%
Hispanic or Latino (of any race)	706	5.48
Central American, ex. Mexican	8	0.06
Costa Rican	1	0.01
Guatemalan	7	0.05
Cuban	10	0.08
Dominican Republic	3	0.02
Mexican	571	4.43
Puerto Rican	69	0.54
South American	14	0.11
Argentinean	1	0.01
Ecuadorian	6	0.05
Peruvian	3	0.02
Other South American	4	0.03
Other Hispanic or Latino	31	0.24

Race*	Population	%
African-American/Black (684)	794	6.17
Not Hispanic (673)	779	6.05
Hispanic (11)	15	0.12
American Indian/Alaska Native (40)	129	1.00
Not Hispanic (31)	106	0.82
Hispanic (9)	23	0.18
Apache (0)	1	0.01
Blackfeet (1)	5	0.04
Central American Ind. (0)	1	0.01
Cherokee (2)	26	0.20
Chippewa (8)	17	0.13
Inupiat *(Alaska Native)* (1)	1	0.01
Iroquois (5)	9	0.07
Lumbee (3)	3	0.02
Mexican American Ind. (2)	2	0.02
Ottawa (5)	6	0.05
Sioux (0)	1	0.01
Asian (298)	331	2.57
Not Hispanic (297)	330	2.56
Hispanic (1)	1	0.01
Bangladeshi (0)	2	0.02
Chinese, ex. Taiwanese (23)	28	0.22
Filipino (87)	99	0.77
Indian (72)	88	0.68
Japanese (5)	8	0.06
Korean (17)	22	0.17
Pakistani (37)	39	0.30
Thai (6)	6	0.05
Vietnamese (40)	40	0.31
Hawaii Native/Pacific Islander (0)	5	0.04
Not Hispanic (0)	3	0.02
Hispanic (0)	2	0.02
Native Hawaiian (0)	5	0.04
White (11,447)	11,668	90.63
Not Hispanic (10,967)	11,144	86.56
Hispanic (480)	524	4.07

Wyandotte

Place Type: City
County: Wayne
Population: 25,883†

Ancestry‡	Population	%
African, Sub-Saharan (0)	46	0.17
African (0)	46	0.17
American (840)	840	3.19
Arab (66)	76	0.29
Lebanese (41)	51	0.19
Syrian (17)	17	0.06
Other Arab (8)	8	0.03
Armenian (28)	53	0.20
Austrian (23)	93	0.35
Belgian (20)	64	0.24
British (7)	39	0.15
Canadian (58)	132	0.50
Croatian (10)	39	0.15
Czech (114)	187	0.71
Danish (0)	15	0.06
Dutch (57)	283	1.07
English (379)	2,243	8.51
European (142)	179	0.68
Finnish (57)	146	0.55
French, ex. Basque (174)	1,815	6.88
French Canadian (200)	725	2.75
German (1,123)	5,517	20.92
Greek (73)	300	1.14
Hungarian (378)	1,107	4.20
Icelander (0)	20	0.08
Iranian (0)	14	0.05
Irish (1,120)	4,227	16.03
Italian (924)	1,946	7.38
Latvian (0)	10	0.04
Lithuanian (9)	84	0.32
Macedonian (9)	19	0.07
Maltese (12)	69	0.26
Norwegian (43)	318	1.21
Polish (2,702)	5,299	20.10
Portuguese (0)	7	0.03
Romanian (23)	74	0.28
Russian (23)	144	0.55
Scandinavian (9)	9	0.03
Scotch-Irish (282)	601	2.28
Scottish (229)	957	3.63
Serbian (62)	72	0.27
Slovak (58)	172	0.65
Slovene (0)	9	0.03
Swedish (152)	372	1.41
Swiss (0)	43	0.16
Ukrainian (44)	243	0.92
Welsh (18)	119	0.45
Yugoslavian (0)	111	0.42

Hispanic Origin	Population	%
Hispanic or Latino (of any race)	1,312	5.07
Central American, ex. Mexican	12	0.05
Guatemalan	5	0.02
Honduran	2	0.01
Nicaraguan	1	<0.01
Panamanian	1	<0.01
Salvadoran	3	0.01
Cuban	22	0.08
Dominican Republic	4	0.02
Mexican	1,034	3.99
Puerto Rican	128	0.49
South American	29	0.11
Argentinean	2	0.01
Bolivian	2	0.01
Chilean	2	0.01
Colombian	9	0.03
Ecuadorian	6	0.02
Peruvian	2	0.01
Venezuelan	6	0.02
Other Hispanic or Latino	83	0.32

Race*	Population	%
African-American/Black (339)	499	1.93
Not Hispanic (327)	476	1.84
Hispanic (12)	23	0.09
American Indian/Alaska Native (182)	387	1.50
Not Hispanic (146)	334	1.29
Hispanic (36)	53	0.20
Apache (2)	4	0.02
Arapaho (0)	1	<0.01
Blackfeet (3)	10	0.04
Canadian/French Am. Ind. (7)	11	0.04
Cherokee (25)	84	0.32
Cheyenne (0)	1	<0.01
Chickasaw (1)	1	<0.01
Chippewa (39)	65	0.25
Choctaw (0)	1	<0.01
Comanche (1)	1	<0.01
Cree (0)	1	<0.01
Creek (1)	1	<0.01
Crow (0)	1	<0.01
Delaware (1)	3	0.01
Inupiat *(Alaska Native)* (1)	4	0.02
Iroquois (8)	18	0.07
Lumbee (12)	14	0.05
Mexican American Ind. (17)	19	0.07
Navajo (3)	3	0.01
Ottawa (1)	4	0.02
Potawatomi (4)	5	0.02
Pueblo (1)	6	0.02
Seminole (0)	4	0.02
Sioux (4)	11	0.04
South American Ind. (1)	1	<0.01
Spanish American Ind. (1)	1	<0.01
Tlingit-Haida *(Alaska Native)* (0)	3	0.01

*Notes: † The Census 2010 population figure is used to calculate the percentages in the Hispanic Origin and Race categories. Ancestry percentages are based on the 2006-2010 American Community Survey population (not shown); ‡ Numbers in parentheses indicate the number of people reporting a single ancestry; * Numbers in parentheses indicate the number of persons reporting this race alone, not in combination with any other race; Please refer to the Explanation of Data for more information.*

SECTION TWO

Asian (131)	191	0.74
Not Hispanic (129)	184	0.71
Hispanic (2)	7	0.03
Bangladeshi (0)	1	<0.01
Cambodian (6)	6	0.02
Chinese, ex. Taiwanese (32)	36	0.14
Filipino (34)	56	0.22
Hmong (0)	2	0.01
Indian (16)	22	0.08
Indonesian (0)	2	0.01
Japanese (14)	20	0.08
Korean (12)	21	0.08
Laotian (4)	4	0.02
Pakistani (0)	2	0.01
Thai (2)	3	0.01
Vietnamese (6)	9	0.03
Hawaii Native/Pacific Islander (6)	20	0.08
Not Hispanic (6)	19	0.07
Hispanic (0)	1	<0.01
Fijian (1)	1	<0.01
Native Hawaiian (2)	11	0.04
Samoan (0)	3	0.01
White (24,511)	24,960	96.43
Not Hispanic (23,562)	23,920	92.42
Hispanic (949)	1,040	4.02

Wyoming

Place Type: City
County: Kent
Population: 72,125†

Ancestry‡	Population	%
African, Sub-Saharan (157)	186	0.26
African (106)	135	0.19
Kenyan (14)	14	0.02
Liberian (4)	4	0.01
Sudanese (33)	33	0.05
American (2,297)	2,297	3.20
Arab (26)	257	0.36
Arab (11)	59	0.08
Lebanese (0)	48	0.07
Palestinian (0)	10	0.01
Syrian (15)	140	0.19
Armenian (59)	98	0.14
Australian (7)	7	0.01
Austrian (0)	22	0.03
Belgian (39)	70	0.10
Brazilian (12)	12	0.02
British (24)	169	0.24
Bulgarian (13)	25	0.03
Canadian (82)	134	0.19
Celtic (0)	29	0.04
Croatian (23)	38	0.05
Czech (54)	182	0.25
Czechoslovakian (22)	82	0.11
Danish (95)	259	0.36
Dutch (7,514)	16,185	22.54
Eastern European (12)	12	0.02
English (1,370)	6,612	9.21
European (497)	566	0.79
Finnish (147)	458	0.64
French, ex. Basque (334)	2,725	3.79
French Canadian (88)	478	0.67
German (3,215)	13,797	19.21
Greek (32)	52	0.07
Hungarian (86)	305	0.42
Iranian (13)	13	0.02
Irish (1,516)	8,298	11.55
Italian (608)	2,131	2.97
Latvian (19)	31	0.04
Lithuanian (38)	155	0.22
Macedonian (22)	182	0.25
Northern European (8)	19	0.03
Norwegian (88)	402	0.56
Pennsylvania German (15)	35	0.05
Polish (1,276)	4,679	6.52
Portuguese (14)	70	0.10
Russian (63)	342	0.48
Scandinavian (74)	175	0.24
Scotch-Irish (233)	849	1.18
Scottish (216)	1,319	1.84
Slovak (29)	57	0.08
Slovene (0)	29	0.04
Swedish (234)	1,403	1.95
Swiss (43)	217	0.30
Ukrainian (53)	112	0.16
Welsh (23)	300	0.42
West Indian, ex. Hispanic (33)	125	0.17
British West Indian (13)	13	0.02
Haitian (11)	21	0.03
Jamaican (9)	91	0.13
Yugoslavian (299)	299	0.42

Hispanic Origin	Population	%
Hispanic or Latino (of any race)	14,010	19.42
Central American, ex. Mexican	1,109	1.54
Costa Rican	6	0.01
Guatemalan	698	0.97
Honduran	138	0.19
Nicaraguan	26	0.04
Panamanian	6	0.01
Salvadoran	235	0.33
Cuban	747	1.04
Dominican Republic	543	0.75
Mexican	9,419	13.06
Puerto Rican	1,460	2.02
South American	148	0.21
Argentinean	15	0.02
Bolivian	3	<0.01
Chilean	6	0.01
Colombian	42	0.06
Ecuadorian	15	0.02
Paraguayan	2	<0.01
Peruvian	37	0.05
Uruguayan	4	0.01
Venezuelan	24	0.03
Other Hispanic or Latino	584	0.81

Race*	Population	%
African-American/Black (5,215)	6,610	9.16
Not Hispanic (4,756)	5,843	8.10
Hispanic (459)	767	1.06
American Indian/Alaska Native (450)	1,109	1.54
Not Hispanic (292)	814	1.13
Hispanic (158)	295	0.41
Alaska Athabascan *(Ala. Nat.)* (2)	2	<0.01
Apache (4)	7	0.01
Blackfeet (2)	27	0.04
Canadian/French Am. Ind. (0)	1	<0.01
Central American Ind. (1)	1	<0.01
Cherokee (17)	75	0.10
Chippewa (78)	152	0.21
Choctaw (5)	9	0.01
Comanche (0)	2	<0.01
Creek (0)	7	0.01
Iroquois (5)	24	0.03
Lumbee (1)	1	<0.01
Menominee (0)	1	<0.01
Mexican American Ind. (15)	19	0.03
Navajo (4)	6	0.01
Osage (0)	2	<0.01
Ottawa (57)	122	0.17
Pima (1)	1	<0.01
Potawatomi (48)	86	0.12
Puget Sound Salish (0)	1	<0.01
Sioux (3)	9	0.01
South American Ind. (3)	4	0.01
Spanish American Ind. (7)	9	0.01
Yuman (0)	2	<0.01
Asian (2,022)	2,386	3.31
Not Hispanic (1,992)	2,306	3.20
Hispanic (30)	80	0.11
Bangladeshi (5)	5	0.01
Burmese (13)	17	0.02
Cambodian (2)	9	0.01
Chinese, ex. Taiwanese (176)	244	0.34
Filipino (91)	168	0.23
Indian (150)	185	0.26
Indonesian (5)	10	0.01
Japanese (21)	60	0.08
Korean (161)	234	0.32
Laotian (11)	17	0.02
Malaysian (1)	1	<0.01
Pakistani (8)	10	0.01
Taiwanese (4)	4	0.01
Thai (13)	34	0.05
Vietnamese (1,309)	1,389	1.93
Hawaii Native/Pacific Islander (35)	111	0.15
Not Hispanic (26)	65	0.09
Hispanic (9)	46	0.06
Guamanian/Chamorro (3)	10	0.01
Native Hawaiian (14)	28	0.04
Samoan (3)	4	0.01
White (54,696)	57,143	79.23
Not Hispanic (49,208)	50,833	70.48
Hispanic (5,488)	6,310	8.75

York

Place Type: Charter Township
County: Washtenaw
Population: 8,708†

Ancestry‡	Population	%
African, Sub-Saharan (80)	80	0.93
African (57)	57	0.67
Cape Verdean (12)	12	0.14
Nigerian (11)	11	0.13
American (357)	357	4.17
Arab (12)	61	0.71
Arab (12)	23	0.27
Iraqi (0)	11	0.13
Lebanese (0)	19	0.22
Syrian (0)	8	0.09
Armenian (10)	41	0.48
Assyrian/Chaldean/Syriac (0)	11	0.13
Austrian (12)	30	0.35
Belgian (17)	17	0.20
British (0)	18	0.21
Canadian (33)	128	1.49
Czech (16)	54	0.63
Czechoslovakian (24)	45	0.53
Danish (12)	20	0.23
Dutch (0)	114	1.33
Eastern European (11)	11	0.13
English (530)	1,230	14.35
European (125)	134	1.56
Finnish (33)	135	1.58
French, ex. Basque (15)	244	2.85
French Canadian (13)	104	1.21
German (522)	2,027	23.66
Greek (0)	17	0.20
Hungarian (97)	238	2.78
Irish (200)	1,040	12.14
Italian (110)	404	4.71
Latvian (0)	29	0.34
Lithuanian (0)	52	0.61
Maltese (34)	34	0.40
Norwegian (11)	61	0.71
Pennsylvania German (14)	26	0.30
Polish (188)	1,168	13.63
Romanian (283)	311	3.63
Russian (27)	60	0.70
Scotch-Irish (24)	105	1.23
Scottish (70)	193	2.25
Serbian (3)	3	0.04
Swedish (10)	93	1.09
Ukrainian (0)	47	0.55
Welsh (19)	330	3.85
West Indian, ex. Hispanic (11)	11	0.13
Haitian (11)	11	0.13
Yugoslavian (0)	14	0.16

Hispanic Origin	Population	%
Hispanic or Latino (of any race)	428	4.92
Central American, ex. Mexican	17	0.20
Guatemalan	6	0.07
Honduran	3	0.03
Nicaraguan	3	0.03

*Notes: † The Census 2010 population figure is used to calculate the percentages in the Hispanic Origin and Race categories. Ancestry percentages are based on the 2006-2010 American Community Survey population (not shown); ‡ Numbers in parentheses indicate the number of people reporting a single ancestry; * Numbers in parentheses indicate the number of persons reporting this race alone, not in combination with any other race; Please refer to the Explanation of Data for more information.*

	Population	%
Panamanian	4	0.05
Salvadoran	1	0.01
Cuban	16	0.18
Dominican Republic	8	0.09
Mexican	283	3.25
Puerto Rican	54	0.62
South American	26	0.30
Argentinean	3	0.03
Colombian	12	0.14
Peruvian	3	0.03
Uruguayan	2	0.02
Venezuelan	6	0.07
Other Hispanic or Latino	24	0.28

Race*	Population	%
African-American/Black (883)	966	11.09
Not Hispanic (861)	939	10.78
Hispanic (22)	27	0.31
American Indian/Alaska Native (56)	122	1.40
Not Hispanic (53)	109	1.25
Hispanic (3)	13	0.15
Apache (0)	4	0.05
Blackfeet (2)	5	0.06
Cherokee (8)	27	0.31
Chippewa (13)	19	0.22
Colville (1)	1	0.01
Iroquois (0)	1	0.01
Lumbee (2)	6	0.07
Mexican American Ind. (0)	1	0.01
Ottawa (0)	1	0.01
Potawatomi (0)	1	0.01
Sioux (7)	9	0.10
Tohono O'Odham (2)	2	0.02
Ute (1)	1	0.01
Yakama (1)	1	0.01
Asian (149)	194	2.23
Not Hispanic (146)	186	2.14
Hispanic (3)	8	0.09
Cambodian (0)	1	0.01
Chinese, ex. Taiwanese (26)	32	0.37
Filipino (6)	16	0.18
Indian (49)	58	0.67
Japanese (15)	20	0.23
Korean (17)	22	0.25
Laotian (1)	1	0.01
Nepalese (1)	1	0.01
Pakistani (7)	9	0.10
Taiwanese (4)	4	0.05
Thai (2)	2	0.02
Vietnamese (7)	12	0.14
Hawaii Native/Pacific Islander (3)	9	0.10
Not Hispanic (3)	7	0.08
Hispanic (0)	2	0.02
Guamanian/Chamorro (1)	1	0.01
Native Hawaiian (0)	2	0.02
Tongan (2)	2	0.02
White (7,311)	7,459	85.66
Not Hispanic (7,054)	7,176	82.41
Hispanic (257)	283	3.25

Ypsilanti

Place Type: Charter Township
County: Washtenaw
Population: 53,362†

Ancestry‡	Population	%
African, Sub-Saharan (1,121)	1,227	2.31
African (594)	634	1.20
Ethiopian (19)	34	0.06
Ghanaian (71)	71	0.13
Nigerian (201)	216	0.41
Senegalese (22)	22	0.04
Somalian (114)	127	0.24
Other Sub-Saharan African (100)	123	0.23
American (3,184)	3,184	6.01
Arab (388)	551	1.04
Arab (117)	142	0.27
Egyptian (26)	26	0.05
Lebanese (13)	113	0.21
Moroccan (8)	46	0.09
Palestinian (17)	17	0.03
Other Arab (207)	207	0.39
Armenian (10)	30	0.06
Austrian (30)	72	0.14
Belgian (10)	53	0.10
British (92)	208	0.39
Canadian (82)	319	0.60
Celtic (10)	10	0.02
Croatian (0)	5	0.01
Czech (33)	200	0.38
Czechoslovakian (0)	16	0.03
Danish (46)	157	0.30
Dutch (192)	1,162	2.19
English (1,035)	4,649	8.77
European (597)	693	1.31
Finnish (147)	503	0.95
French, ex. Basque (262)	1,539	2.90
French Canadian (409)	714	1.35
German (2,548)	8,668	16.35
Greek (37)	311	0.59
Guyanese (0)	32	0.06
Hungarian (178)	275	0.52
Irish (1,007)	5,123	9.66
Italian (346)	1,553	2.93
Latvian (0)	19	0.04
Lithuanian (0)	53	0.10
Macedonian (8)	8	0.02
Maltese (12)	63	0.12
Norwegian (50)	192	0.36
Pennsylvania German (0)	20	0.04
Polish (624)	2,371	4.47
Portuguese (26)	80	0.15
Romanian (102)	260	0.49
Russian (19)	327	0.62
Scandinavian (0)	12	0.02
Scotch-Irish (235)	831	1.57
Scottish (304)	1,497	2.82
Serbian (8)	24	0.05
Slavic (0)	33	0.06
Slovak (0)	139	0.26
Slovene (0)	19	0.04
Swedish (121)	453	0.85
Swiss (0)	140	0.26
Turkish (6)	30	0.06
Ukrainian (101)	226	0.43
Welsh (54)	415	0.78
West Indian, ex. Hispanic (134)	269	0.51
Haitian (58)	107	0.20
Jamaican (41)	97	0.18
Trinidadian/Tobagonian (6)	14	0.03
West Indian (29)	51	0.10
Yugoslavian (0)	57	0.11

Hispanic Origin	Population	%
Hispanic or Latino (of any race)	2,476	4.64
Central American, ex. Mexican	473	0.89
Costa Rican	65	0.12
Guatemalan	104	0.19
Honduran	110	0.21
Nicaraguan	15	0.03
Panamanian	33	0.06
Salvadoran	139	0.26
Other Central American	7	0.01
Cuban	65	0.12
Dominican Republic	16	0.03
Mexican	1,329	2.49
Puerto Rican	247	0.46
South American	105	0.20
Argentinean	5	0.01
Bolivian	1	<0.01
Chilean	7	0.01
Colombian	27	0.05
Ecuadorian	18	0.03
Peruvian	24	0.04
Uruguayan	6	0.01
Venezuelan	17	0.03
Other Hispanic or Latino	241	0.45

Race*	Population	%
African-American/Black (17,528)	19,204	35.99
Not Hispanic (17,321)	18,884	35.39
Hispanic (207)	320	0.60
American Indian/Alaska Native (227)	842	1.58
Not Hispanic (200)	743	1.39
Hispanic (27)	99	0.19
Aleut *(Alaska Native)* (1)	2	<0.01
Apache (0)	2	<0.01
Arapaho (0)	1	<0.01
Blackfeet (8)	48	0.09
Canadian/French Am. Ind. (1)	3	0.01
Cherokee (22)	166	0.31
Chickasaw (1)	1	<0.01
Chippewa (39)	79	0.15
Choctaw (4)	27	0.05
Comanche (1)	1	<0.01
Cree (0)	2	<0.01
Creek (6)	11	0.02
Delaware (2)	5	0.01
Iroquois (9)	20	0.04
Lumbee (4)	5	0.01
Mexican American Ind. (3)	6	0.01
Navajo (3)	7	0.01
Ottawa (5)	7	0.01
Paiute (0)	1	<0.01
Potawatomi (0)	12	0.02
Pueblo (0)	2	<0.01
Seminole (1)	2	<0.01
Sioux (13)	24	0.04
South American Ind. (2)	7	0.01
Tlingit-Haida *(Alaska Native)* (6)	9	0.02
Ute (0)	1	<0.01
Yakama (1)	1	<0.01
Yuman (0)	1	<0.01
Asian (1,101)	1,552	2.91
Not Hispanic (1,092)	1,502	2.81
Hispanic (9)	50	0.09
Bangladeshi (0)	1	<0.01
Burmese (1)	1	<0.01
Cambodian (3)	5	0.01
Chinese, ex. Taiwanese (175)	246	0.46
Filipino (176)	272	0.51
Hmong (2)	2	<0.01
Indian (247)	306	0.57
Indonesian (9)	17	0.03
Japanese (41)	94	0.18
Korean (120)	204	0.38
Laotian (31)	40	0.07
Malaysian (6)	14	0.03
Nepalese (1)	1	<0.01
Pakistani (70)	77	0.14
Sri Lankan (10)	17	0.03
Taiwanese (11)	14	0.03
Thai (30)	47	0.09
Vietnamese (107)	154	0.29
Hawaii Native/Pacific Islander (28)	89	0.17
Not Hispanic (26)	84	0.16
Hispanic (2)	5	0.01
Fijian (1)	1	<0.01
Guamanian/Chamorro (1)	9	0.02
Native Hawaiian (4)	21	0.04
Samoan (15)	30	0.06
Tongan (1)	3	0.01
White (31,171)	33,245	62.30
Not Hispanic (29,956)	31,781	59.56
Hispanic (1,215)	1,464	2.74

Ypsilanti

Place Type: City
County: Washtenaw
Population: 19,435†

Ancestry‡	Population	%
African, Sub-Saharan (155)	164	0.81
African (54)	63	0.31
Nigerian (7)	7	0.03
Somalian (72)	72	0.36

*Notes: † The Census 2010 population figure is used to calculate the percentages in the Hispanic Origin and Race categories. Ancestry percentages are based on the 2006-2010 American Community Survey population (not shown); ‡ Numbers in parentheses indicate the number of people reporting a single ancestry; * Numbers in parentheses indicate the number of persons reporting this race alone, not in combination with any other race; Please refer to the Explanation of Data for more information.*

Ancestry (continued)	Population	%
Other Sub-Saharan African (22)	22	0.11
American (750)	750	3.71
Arab (143)	188	0.93
Arab (98)	98	0.49
Egyptian (13)	13	0.06
Jordanian (17)	17	0.08
Lebanese (0)	45	0.22
Palestinian (15)	15	0.07
Assyrian/Chaldean/Syriac (25)	25	0.12
Austrian (0)	124	0.61
Belgian (15)	58	0.29
Brazilian (31)	77	0.38
British (62)	113	0.56
Bulgarian (15)	15	0.07
Canadian (92)	130	0.64
Croatian (0)	29	0.14
Czech (0)	28	0.14
Czechoslovakian (0)	12	0.06
Danish (12)	97	0.48
Dutch (144)	451	2.23
Eastern European (18)	18	0.09
English (485)	1,652	8.18
European (263)	276	1.37
Finnish (191)	296	1.47
French, ex. Basque (59)	435	2.15
French Canadian (90)	309	1.53
German (993)	3,850	19.07
Greek (11)	23	0.11
Hungarian (24)	147	0.73
Icelander (0)	38	0.19
Irish (805)	2,679	13.27
Israeli (14)	14	0.07
Italian (368)	1,226	6.07
Latvian (16)	16	0.08
Lithuanian (40)	96	0.48
Macedonian (0)	9	0.04
Maltese (0)	11	0.05
Northern European (19)	19	0.09
Norwegian (27)	147	0.73
Polish (299)	1,180	5.84
Romanian (58)	70	0.35
Russian (43)	145	0.72
Scandinavian (16)	16	0.08
Scotch-Irish (42)	241	1.19
Scottish (131)	475	2.35
Serbian (26)	26	0.13
Slavic (0)	22	0.11
Slovak (14)	45	0.22
Slovene (0)	9	0.04
Swedish (56)	255	1.26
Swiss (0)	24	0.12
Ukrainian (0)	49	0.24
Welsh (28)	179	0.89
West Indian, ex. Hispanic (20)	71	0.35
Barbadian (0)	10	0.05
Haitian (10)	32	0.16
Jamaican (10)	10	0.05
Trinidadian/Tobagonian (0)	19	0.09

Hispanic Origin	Population	%
Hispanic or Latino (of any race)	758	3.90
Central American, ex. Mexican	71	0.37
Costa Rican	5	0.03
Guatemalan	17	0.09
Honduran	20	0.10
Nicaraguan	7	0.04
Panamanian	2	0.01
Salvadoran	20	0.10
Cuban	31	0.16
Dominican Republic	18	0.09
Mexican	414	2.13
Puerto Rican	76	0.39
South American	49	0.25
Bolivian	4	0.02
Chilean	2	0.01
Colombian	10	0.05
Ecuadorian	18	0.09
Peruvian	3	0.02
Uruguayan	3	0.02
Venezuelan	9	0.05
Other Hispanic or Latino	99	0.51

Race*	Population	%
African-American/Black (5,669)	6,207	31.94
Not Hispanic (5,596)	6,090	31.34
Hispanic (73)	117	0.60
American Indian/Alaska Native (113)	348	1.79
Not Hispanic (96)	311	1.60
Hispanic (17)	37	0.19
Apache (1)	5	0.03
Blackfeet (0)	24	0.12
Canadian/French Am. Ind. (3)	4	0.02
Cherokee (12)	49	0.25
Cheyenne (0)	1	0.01
Chickasaw (1)	1	0.01
Chippewa (12)	26	0.13
Choctaw (0)	2	0.01
Comanche (0)	2	0.01
Cree (0)	1	0.01
Creek (1)	7	0.04
Crow (0)	1	0.01
Iroquois (2)	11	0.06
Lumbee (0)	1	0.01
Menominee (1)	1	0.01
Mexican American Ind. (2)	2	0.01
Navajo (0)	1	0.01
Osage (0)	1	0.01
Ottawa (1)	5	0.03
Potawatomi (3)	6	0.03
Pueblo (1)	1	0.01
Seminole (0)	1	0.01
Sioux (2)	9	0.05
South American Ind. (0)	3	0.02
Tlingit-Haida *(Alaska Native)* (3)	4	0.02
Yup'ik *(Alaska Native)* (0)	1	0.01
Asian (657)	831	4.28
Not Hispanic (653)	818	4.21
Hispanic (4)	13	0.07
Chinese, ex. Taiwanese (129)	172	0.89
Filipino (48)	82	0.42
Hmong (5)	5	0.03
Indian (234)	259	1.33
Indonesian (5)	5	0.03
Japanese (45)	86	0.44
Korean (76)	96	0.49
Laotian (12)	22	0.11
Nepalese (4)	5	0.03
Pakistani (11)	11	0.06
Sri Lankan (3)	3	0.02
Taiwanese (15)	17	0.09
Thai (8)	25	0.13
Vietnamese (26)	33	0.17
Hawaii Native/Pacific Islander (7)	51	0.26
Not Hispanic (7)	49	0.25
Hispanic (0)	2	0.01
Marshallese (0)	2	0.01
Native Hawaiian (1)	7	0.04
Samoan (4)	10	0.05
White (11,952)	12,636	65.02
Not Hispanic (11,543)	12,160	62.57
Hispanic (409)	476	2.45

Zeeland

Place Type: Charter Township
County: Ottawa
Population: 9,971†

Ancestry‡	Population	%
American (662)	662	6.87
British (36)	75	0.78
Canadian (30)	58	0.60
Czech (0)	13	0.13
Czechoslovakian (8)	8	0.08
Danish (0)	64	0.66
Dutch (3,902)	5,488	56.97
English (128)	392	4.07
European (122)	191	1.98
Finnish (0)	49	0.51
French, ex. Basque (48)	160	1.66
German (170)	1,521	15.79
Irish (134)	509	5.28
Italian (80)	162	1.68
Latvian (0)	57	0.59
Norwegian (30)	223	2.31
Polish (69)	380	3.94
Portuguese (16)	16	0.17
Romanian (0)	20	0.21
Scandinavian (10)	20	0.21
Scotch-Irish (14)	59	0.61
Scottish (12)	61	0.63
Swedish (28)	108	1.12
Ukrainian (0)	15	0.16
Welsh (0)	123	1.28
West Indian, ex. Hispanic (14)	43	0.45
Belizean (14)	43	0.45

Hispanic Origin	Population	%
Hispanic or Latino (of any race)	697	6.99
Central American, ex. Mexican	10	0.10
Costa Rican	2	0.02
Guatemalan	4	0.04
Honduran	2	0.02
Nicaraguan	2	0.02
Cuban	7	0.07
Dominican Republic	9	0.09
Mexican	579	5.81
Puerto Rican	36	0.36
South American	12	0.12
Chilean	3	0.03
Colombian	6	0.06
Paraguayan	1	0.01
Peruvian	2	0.02
Other Hispanic or Latino	44	0.44

Race*	Population	%
African-American/Black (72)	120	1.20
Not Hispanic (66)	110	1.10
Hispanic (6)	10	0.10
American Indian/Alaska Native (37)	93	0.93
Not Hispanic (17)	51	0.51
Hispanic (20)	42	0.42
Apache (0)	1	0.01
Arapaho (0)	1	0.01
Cherokee (2)	13	0.13
Chippewa (4)	8	0.08
Creek (0)	1	0.01
Crow (1)	1	0.01
Mexican American Ind. (1)	1	0.01
Navajo (3)	8	0.08
Ottawa (2)	8	0.08
Potawatomi (0)	1	0.01
Shoshone (0)	1	0.01
Sioux (0)	6	0.06
Spanish American Ind. (1)	5	0.05
Asian (322)	382	3.83
Not Hispanic (314)	365	3.66
Hispanic (8)	17	0.17
Bangladeshi (2)	2	0.02
Cambodian (60)	74	0.74
Chinese, ex. Taiwanese (23)	34	0.34
Filipino (10)	21	0.21
Indian (13)	19	0.19
Indonesian (0)	5	0.05
Korean (14)	29	0.29
Laotian (131)	153	1.53
Pakistani (1)	1	0.01
Taiwanese (1)	2	0.02
Thai (7)	11	0.11
Vietnamese (23)	34	0.34
Hawaii Native/Pacific Islander (2)	8	0.08
Not Hispanic (1)	6	0.06
Hispanic (1)	2	0.02
Guamanian/Chamorro (1)	1	0.01
Native Hawaiian (1)	4	0.04
White (9,123)	9,291	93.18
Not Hispanic (8,742)	8,859	88.85
Hispanic (381)	432	4.33

*Notes: † The Census 2010 population figure is used to calculate the percentages in the Hispanic Origin and Race categories. Ancestry percentages are based on the 2006-2010 American Community Survey population (not shown); ‡ Numbers in parentheses indicate the number of people reporting a single ancestry; * Numbers in parentheses indicate the number of persons reporting this race alone, not in combination with any other race; Please refer to the Explanation of Data for more information.*

MINNESOTA

Place Type: State
Population: 5,303,925†

Ancestry‡	Population	%
Afghan (452)	452	0.01
African, Sub-Saharan (90,503)	99,186	1.89
African (23,168)	27,740	0.53
Cape Verdean (10)	10	<0.01
Ethiopian (13,425)	14,183	0.27
Ghanaian (964)	995	0.02
Kenyan (3,211)	3,671	0.07
Liberian (7,046)	7,611	0.15
Nigerian (5,062)	6,014	0.11
Senegalese (0)	37	<0.01
Sierra Leonean (320)	415	0.01
Somalian (31,931)	32,449	0.62
South African (393)	536	0.01
Sudanese (1,709)	1,787	0.03
Ugandan (386)	424	0.01
Zimbabwean (92)	124	<0.01
Other Sub-Saharan African (2,786)	3,190	0.06
Albanian (184)	239	<0.01
Alsatian (42)	145	<0.01
American (142,698)	142,698	2.72
Arab (10,709)	18,803	0.36
Arab (1,508)	2,047	0.04
Egyptian (2,266)	2,752	0.05
Iraqi (515)	620	0.01
Jordanian (353)	442	0.01
Lebanese (2,207)	6,905	0.13
Moroccan (920)	1,165	0.02
Palestinian (903)	1,135	0.02
Syrian (246)	921	0.02
Other Arab (1,791)	2,816	0.05
Armenian (517)	1,299	0.02
Assyrian/Chaldean/Syriac (24)	77	<0.01
Australian (393)	1,136	0.02
Austrian (3,288)	18,518	0.35
Basque (70)	120	<0.01
Belgian (4,154)	16,141	0.31
Brazilian (794)	1,383	0.03
British (5,806)	14,024	0.27
Bulgarian (405)	868	0.02
Cajun (69)	121	<0.01
Canadian (3,182)	7,405	0.14
Carpatho Rusyn (37)	250	<0.01
Celtic (266)	582	0.01
Croatian (2,233)	8,558	0.16
Cypriot (13)	15	<0.01
Czech (24,643)	100,809	1.92
Czechoslovakian (4,563)	10,843	0.21
Danish (16,438)	86,508	1.65
Dutch (25,614)	106,516	2.03
Eastern European (4,709)	5,504	0.10
English (61,594)	328,807	6.27
Estonian (262)	594	0.01
European (54,946)	60,621	1.16
Finnish (36,566)	103,159	1.97
French, ex. Basque (22,652)	214,073	4.08
French Canadian (15,014)	54,739	1.04
German (692,437)	1,959,455	37.38
German Russian (209)	470	0.01
Greek (4,013)	12,277	0.23
Guyanese (959)	1,294	0.02
Hungarian (3,121)	13,958	0.27
Icelander (842)	3,875	0.07
Iranian (1,801)	2,467	0.05
Irish (100,877)	599,902	11.44
Israeli (640)	894	0.02
Italian (30,819)	128,278	2.45
Latvian (1,367)	3,010	0.06
Lithuanian (1,964)	6,775	0.13
Luxemburger (1,392)	5,789	0.11
Macedonian (73)	243	<0.01
Maltese (37)	104	<0.01
New Zealander (68)	134	<0.01
Northern European (10,544)	11,416	0.22
Norwegian (273,696)	866,785	16.54
Pennsylvania German (1,192)	2,396	0.05
Polish (60,122)	257,292	4.91
Portuguese (1,201)	3,749	0.07
Romanian (2,762)	6,304	0.12
Russian (16,334)	44,525	0.85
Scandinavian (47,371)	77,745	1.48
Scotch-Irish (12,502)	52,686	1.01
Scottish (11,726)	68,934	1.32
Serbian (1,328)	4,348	0.08
Slavic (1,523)	4,296	0.08
Slovak (2,269)	8,206	0.16
Slovene (3,582)	9,800	0.19
Soviet Union (16)	18	<0.01
Swedish (103,796)	496,174	9.47
Swiss (3,548)	23,180	0.44
Turkish (506)	1,123	0.02
Ukrainian (7,073)	15,132	0.29
Welsh (3,544)	25,064	0.48
West Indian, ex. Hispanic (3,023)	4,756	0.09
Bahamian (78)	169	<0.01
Barbadian (84)	84	<0.01
Belizean (81)	107	<0.01
Bermudan (12)	20	<0.01
British West Indian (52)	79	<0.01
Dutch West Indian (70)	161	<0.01
Haitian (452)	710	0.01
Jamaican (1,366)	2,177	0.04
Trinidadian/Tobagonian (116)	260	<0.01
U.S. Virgin Islander (0)	43	<0.01
West Indian (678)	878	0.02
Other West Indian (34)	68	<0.01
Yugoslavian (4,620)	8,826	0.17

Hispanic Origin	Population	%
Hispanic or Latino (of any race)	250,258	4.72
Central American, ex. Mexican	19,908	0.38
Costa Rican	785	0.01
Guatemalan	6,754	0.13
Honduran	3,186	0.06
Nicaraguan	970	0.02
Panamanian	906	0.02
Salvadoran	7,175	0.14
Other Central American	132	<0.01
Cuban	3,661	0.07
Dominican Republic	1,294	0.02
Mexican	176,007	3.32
Puerto Rican	10,807	0.20
South American	18,075	0.34
Argentinean	1,008	0.02
Bolivian	430	0.01
Chilean	1,057	0.02
Colombian	4,484	0.08
Ecuadorian	7,290	0.14
Paraguayan	287	0.01
Peruvian	2,028	0.04
Uruguayan	223	<0.01
Venezuelan	1,017	0.02
Other South American	251	<0.01
Other Hispanic or Latino	20,506	0.39

Race*	Population	%
African-American/Black (274,412)	327,548	6.18
Not Hispanic (269,141)	316,870	5.97
Hispanic (5,271)	10,678	0.20
American Indian/Alaska Native (60,916)	101,900	1.92
Not Hispanic (55,421)	90,505	1.71
Hispanic (5,495)	11,395	0.21
Alaska Athabascan *(Ala. Nat.)* (46)	80	<0.01
Aleut *(Alaska Native)* (61)	99	<0.01
Apache (133)	337	0.01
Arapaho (18)	36	<0.01
Blackfeet (123)	742	0.01
Canadian/French Am. Ind. (220)	470	0.01
Central American Ind. (79)	131	<0.01
Cherokee (528)	3,147	0.06
Cheyenne (62)	131	<0.01
Chickasaw (32)	109	<0.01
Chippewa (33,165)	44,213	0.83
Choctaw (167)	587	0.01
Colville (13)	16	<0.01
Comanche (45)	116	<0.01
Cree (68)	245	<0.01
Creek (58)	202	<0.01
Crow (59)	98	<0.01
Delaware (35)	82	<0.01
Hopi (15)	32	<0.01
Houma (8)	14	<0.01
Inupiat *(Alaska Native)* (65)	137	<0.01
Iroquois (238)	625	0.01
Kiowa (28)	51	<0.01
Lumbee (33)	54	<0.01
Menominee (111)	176	<0.01
Mexican American Ind. (936)	1,481	0.03
Navajo (225)	388	0.01
Osage (23)	62	<0.01
Ottawa (48)	93	<0.01
Paiute (18)	26	<0.01
Pima (17)	28	<0.01
Potawatomi (163)	263	<0.01
Pueblo (47)	95	<0.01
Puget Sound Salish (17)	35	<0.01
Seminole (24)	153	<0.01
Shoshone (25)	52	<0.01
Sioux (5,418)	8,691	0.16
South American Ind. (179)	390	0.01
Spanish American Ind. (120)	177	<0.01
Tlingit-Haida *(Alaska Native)* (29)	86	<0.01
Tohono O'Odham (19)	29	<0.01
Tsimshian *(Alaska Native)* (6)	9	<0.01
Ute (23)	45	<0.01
Yakama (16)	31	<0.01
Yaqui (21)	55	<0.01
Yuman (27)	37	<0.01
Yup'ik *(Alaska Native)* (39)	82	<0.01
Asian (214,234)	247,132	4.66
Not Hispanic (212,996)	243,897	4.60
Hispanic (1,238)	3,235	0.06
Bangladeshi (746)	858	0.02
Bhutanese (246)	284	0.01
Burmese (3,633)	3,763	0.07
Cambodian (7,850)	9,543	0.18
Chinese, ex. Taiwanese (23,482)	28,776	0.54
Filipino (9,464)	15,660	0.30
Hmong (63,619)	66,181	1.25
Indian (33,031)	38,097	0.72
Indonesian (427)	665	0.01
Japanese (3,611)	7,995	0.15
Korean (14,982)	20,995	0.40
Laotian (10,065)	12,009	0.23
Malaysian (292)	431	0.01
Nepalese (1,296)	1,438	0.03
Pakistani (2,402)	2,840	0.05
Sri Lankan (771)	944	0.02
Taiwanese (1,078)	1,365	0.03
Thai (1,596)	2,734	0.05
Vietnamese (23,544)	27,086	0.51
Hawaii Native/Pacific Islander (2,156)	6,206	0.12
Not Hispanic (1,860)	5,232	0.10
Hispanic (296)	974	0.02
Fijian (40)	61	<0.01
Guamanian/Chamorro (378)	727	0.01
Marshallese (34)	50	<0.01
Native Hawaiian (573)	1,847	0.03
Samoan (299)	640	0.01
Tongan (60)	100	<0.01
White (4,524,062)	4,634,915	87.39
Not Hispanic (4,405,142)	4,497,934	84.80
Hispanic (118,920)	136,981	2.58

*Notes: † The Census 2010 population figure is used to calculate the percentages in the Hispanic Origin and Race categories. Ancestry percentages are based on the 2006-2010 American Community Survey population (not shown); ‡ Numbers in parentheses indicate the number of people reporting a single ancestry; * Numbers in parentheses indicate the number of persons reporting this race alone, not in combination with any other race; Please refer to the Explanation of Data for more information.*

Albert Lea

Place Type: City
County: Freeborn
Population: 18,016†

Ancestry‡	Population	%
African, Sub-Saharan (59)	77	0.43
African (24)	24	0.13
Kenyan (8)	8	0.04
Liberian (9)	18	0.10
Nigerian (18)	27	0.15
American (584)	584	3.23
Arab (8)	8	0.04
Egyptian (8)	8	0.04
Austrian (0)	10	0.06
Belgian (0)	19	0.11
British (17)	17	0.09
Czech (148)	308	1.70
Czechoslovakian (7)	40	0.22
Danish (396)	1,249	6.91
Dutch (111)	423	2.34
Eastern European (20)	20	0.11
English (240)	810	4.48
European (20)	20	0.11
French, ex. Basque (28)	306	1.69
French Canadian (105)	147	0.81
German (2,482)	6,492	35.89
Greek (0)	10	0.06
Icelander (0)	8	0.04
Irish (244)	1,388	7.67
Israeli (0)	11	0.06
Italian (24)	121	0.67
Luxemburger (0)	18	0.10
Northern European (52)	52	0.29
Norwegian (2,795)	6,275	34.69
Pennsylvania German (10)	10	0.06
Polish (65)	397	2.19
Romanian (0)	9	0.05
Russian (0)	40	0.22
Scandinavian (170)	247	1.37
Scotch-Irish (76)	158	0.87
Scottish (21)	312	1.72
Swedish (113)	635	3.51
Swiss (9)	30	0.17
Ukrainian (0)	14	0.08
Welsh (21)	32	0.18

Hispanic Origin	Population	%
Hispanic or Latino (of any race)	2,380	13.21
Central American, ex. Mexican	43	0.24
Costa Rican	1	0.01
Guatemalan	21	0.12
Honduran	4	0.02
Nicaraguan	7	0.04
Salvadoran	10	0.06
Cuban	63	0.35
Dominican Republic	3	0.02
Mexican	2,051	11.38
Puerto Rican	97	0.54
South American	15	0.08
Bolivian	1	0.01
Colombian	8	0.04
Peruvian	1	0.01
Venezuelan	5	0.03
Other Hispanic or Latino	108	0.60

Race*	Population	%
African-American/Black (204)	290	1.61
Not Hispanic (177)	246	1.37
Hispanic (27)	44	0.24
American Indian/Alaska Native (49)	142	0.79
Not Hispanic (40)	122	0.68
Hispanic (9)	20	0.11
Blackfeet (0)	1	0.01
Canadian/French Am. Ind. (1)	2	0.01
Cherokee (1)	8	0.04
Chickasaw (0)	1	0.01
Chippewa (13)	19	0.11
Crow (0)	1	0.01
Mexican American Ind. (0)	6	0.03
Navajo (1)	2	0.01
Potawatomi (1)	2	0.01
Sioux (5)	12	0.07
Asian (204)	270	1.50
Not Hispanic (198)	253	1.40
Hispanic (6)	17	0.09
Burmese (48)	52	0.29
Cambodian (5)	6	0.03
Chinese, ex. Taiwanese (14)	17	0.09
Filipino (9)	33	0.18
Hmong (12)	12	0.07
Indian (14)	15	0.08
Japanese (5)	17	0.09
Korean (13)	27	0.15
Laotian (29)	31	0.17
Nepalese (3)	3	0.02
Thai (10)	17	0.09
Vietnamese (21)	34	0.19
Hawaii Native/Pacific Islander (15)	21	0.12
Not Hispanic (7)	10	0.06
Hispanic (8)	11	0.06
Guamanian/Chamorro (3)	4	0.02
Native Hawaiian (8)	8	0.04
Samoan (0)	1	0.01
White (16,213)	16,567	91.96
Not Hispanic (15,002)	15,187	84.30
Hispanic (1,211)	1,380	7.66

Alexandria

Place Type: City
County: Douglas
Population: 11,070†

Ancestry‡	Population	%
African, Sub-Saharan (112)	112	1.01
Ethiopian (112)	112	1.01
American (357)	357	3.22
Austrian (8)	13	0.12
Belgian (14)	23	0.21
British (11)	19	0.17
Croatian (0)	16	0.14
Czech (86)	201	1.81
Czechoslovakian (10)	78	0.70
Danish (0)	184	1.66
Dutch (61)	231	2.08
English (13)	284	2.56
European (107)	120	1.08
Finnish (32)	150	1.35
French, ex. Basque (16)	265	2.39
French Canadian (26)	61	0.55
German (2,176)	4,614	41.59
Irish (167)	1,251	11.28
Italian (30)	146	1.32
Lithuanian (0)	14	0.13
Northern European (46)	46	0.41
Norwegian (933)	2,772	24.99
Polish (93)	422	3.80
Russian (0)	25	0.23
Scandinavian (133)	142	1.28
Scotch-Irish (50)	156	1.41
Scottish (82)	176	1.59
Swedish (447)	1,551	13.98
Swiss (8)	37	0.33
Ukrainian (16)	41	0.37
Welsh (0)	56	0.50

Hispanic Origin	Population	%
Hispanic or Latino (of any race)	165	1.49
Central American, ex. Mexican	5	0.05
Guatemalan	5	0.05
Cuban	1	0.01
Mexican	103	0.93
Puerto Rican	19	0.17
South American	11	0.10
Argentinean	1	0.01
Colombian	8	0.07
Peruvian	2	0.02
Other Hispanic or Latino	26	0.23

Race*	Population	%
African-American/Black (94)	158	1.43
Not Hispanic (92)	154	1.39
Hispanic (2)	4	0.04
American Indian/Alaska Native (44)	93	0.84
Not Hispanic (41)	84	0.76
Hispanic (3)	9	0.08
Apache (1)	1	0.01
Canadian/French Am. Ind. (0)	1	0.01
Cherokee (1)	1	0.01
Chickasaw (0)	1	0.01
Chippewa (12)	34	0.31
Sioux (5)	8	0.07
Asian (77)	98	0.89
Not Hispanic (76)	95	0.86
Hispanic (1)	3	0.03
Chinese, ex. Taiwanese (25)	25	0.23
Filipino (14)	16	0.14
Hmong (1)	1	0.01
Indian (7)	11	0.10
Japanese (0)	6	0.05
Korean (14)	19	0.17
Laotian (1)	1	0.01
Nepalese (1)	1	0.01
Thai (0)	3	0.03
Vietnamese (9)	9	0.08
Hawaii Native/Pacific Islander (2)	5	0.05
Not Hispanic (2)	5	0.05
Native Hawaiian (1)	2	0.02
White (10,664)	10,810	97.65
Not Hispanic (10,564)	10,691	96.58
Hispanic (100)	119	1.07

Andover

Place Type: City
County: Anoka
Population: 30,598†

Ancestry‡	Population	%
African, Sub-Saharan (332)	332	1.10
Ethiopian (9)	9	0.03
Kenyan (43)	43	0.14
Liberian (124)	124	0.41
Nigerian (43)	43	0.14
South African (13)	13	0.04
Other Sub-Saharan African (100)	100	0.33
American (970)	970	3.22
Arab (0)	82	0.27
Lebanese (0)	74	0.25
Other Arab (0)	8	0.03
Austrian (3)	36	0.12
Belgian (0)	37	0.12
Brazilian (24)	24	0.08
British (20)	87	0.29
Canadian (44)	74	0.25
Croatian (0)	46	0.15
Czech (109)	588	1.95
Czechoslovakian (23)	131	0.44
Danish (63)	561	1.86
Dutch (225)	621	2.06
Eastern European (9)	9	0.03
English (270)	1,830	6.08
European (635)	645	2.14
Finnish (231)	586	1.95
French, ex. Basque (135)	1,669	5.55
French Canadian (84)	379	1.26
German (4,066)	12,587	41.82
Greek (0)	41	0.14
Hungarian (0)	46	0.15
Icelander (0)	9	0.03
Irish (391)	3,395	11.28
Italian (209)	791	2.63
Latvian (0)	58	0.19
Luxemburger (0)	9	0.03
Northern European (10)	62	0.21
Norwegian (1,607)	5,614	18.65
Polish (619)	2,488	8.27
Portuguese (16)	107	0.36

*Notes: † The Census 2010 population figure is used to calculate the percentages in the Hispanic Origin and Race categories. Ancestry percentages are based on the 2006-2010 American Community Survey population (not shown); ‡ Numbers in parentheses indicate the number of people reporting a single ancestry; * Numbers in parentheses indicate the number of persons reporting this race alone, not in combination with any other race; Please refer to the Explanation of Data for more information.*

Russian (43)	205	0.68
Scandinavian (386)	707	2.35
Scotch-Irish (35)	210	0.70
Scottish (39)	289	0.96
Serbian (28)	46	0.15
Slavic (9)	65	0.22
Slovak (0)	9	0.03
Slovene (0)	41	0.14
Swedish (761)	3,749	12.46
Swiss (21)	126	0.42
Turkish (0)	11	0.04
Ukrainian (74)	146	0.49
Welsh (30)	40	0.13
West Indian, ex. Hispanic (8)	28	0.09
Jamaican (8)	28	0.09
Yugoslavian (67)	79	0.26

Hispanic Origin	Population	%
Hispanic or Latino (of any race)	622	2.03
Central American, ex. Mexican	55	0.18
Costa Rican	8	0.03
Guatemalan	26	0.08
Honduran	14	0.05
Nicaraguan	1	<0.01
Panamanian	1	<0.01
Salvadoran	5	0.02
Cuban	3	0.01
Dominican Republic	2	0.01
Mexican	378	1.24
Puerto Rican	62	0.20
South American	48	0.16
Argentinean	3	0.01
Chilean	3	0.01
Colombian	13	0.04
Ecuadorian	7	0.02
Paraguayan	5	0.02
Peruvian	12	0.04
Venezuelan	3	0.01
Other South American	2	0.01
Other Hispanic or Latino	74	0.24

Race*	Population	%
African-American/Black (518)	699	2.28
Not Hispanic (504)	668	2.18
Hispanic (14)	31	0.10
American Indian/Alaska Native (104)	272	0.89
Not Hispanic (94)	253	0.83
Hispanic (10)	19	0.06
Canadian/French Am. Ind. (2)	2	0.01
Cherokee (4)	8	0.03
Chippewa (59)	119	0.39
Delaware (0)	1	<0.01
Iroquois (0)	4	0.01
Mexican American Ind. (2)	3	0.01
Sioux (6)	23	0.08
Asian (683)	899	2.94
Not Hispanic (681)	874	2.86
Hispanic (2)	25	0.08
Bangladeshi (1)	1	<0.01
Cambodian (8)	21	0.07
Chinese, ex. Taiwanese (80)	96	0.31
Filipino (31)	74	0.24
Hmong (203)	207	0.68
Indian (86)	112	0.37
Indonesian (5)	5	0.02
Japanese (14)	48	0.16
Korean (81)	105	0.34
Laotian (24)	37	0.12
Pakistani (5)	7	0.02
Taiwanese (0)	1	<0.01
Thai (4)	4	0.01
Vietnamese (53)	105	0.34
Hawaii Native/Pacific Islander (3)	27	0.09
Not Hispanic (3)	19	0.06
Hispanic (0)	8	0.03
Native Hawaiian (0)	5	0.02
White (28,525)	29,079	95.04
Not Hispanic (28,170)	28,651	93.64
Hispanic (355)	428	1.40

Anoka

Place Type: City
County: Anoka
Population: 17,142†

Ancestry‡	Population	%
African, Sub-Saharan (216)	224	1.28
African (33)	33	0.19
Ethiopian (103)	103	0.59
Liberian (45)	45	0.26
Nigerian (10)	18	0.10
Somalian (10)	10	0.06
Other Sub-Saharan African (15)	15	0.09
American (612)	612	3.51
Arab (45)	56	0.32
Lebanese (45)	56	0.32
Austrian (13)	31	0.18
Belgian (0)	77	0.44
British (14)	14	0.08
Bulgarian (34)	50	0.29
Celtic (0)	15	0.09
Czech (21)	191	1.09
Czechoslovakian (9)	26	0.15
Danish (39)	251	1.44
Dutch (67)	403	2.31
Eastern European (20)	20	0.11
English (258)	1,176	6.74
European (569)	569	3.26
Finnish (98)	298	1.71
French, ex. Basque (35)	771	4.42
French Canadian (23)	295	1.69
German (1,625)	5,621	32.21
Greek (9)	183	1.05
Hungarian (19)	87	0.50
Icelander (8)	19	0.11
Irish (210)	1,915	10.97
Italian (55)	586	3.36
Lithuanian (11)	11	0.06
Northern European (67)	67	0.38
Norwegian (972)	2,901	16.63
Polish (283)	1,036	5.94
Portuguese (102)	137	0.79
Romanian (40)	40	0.23
Russian (39)	276	1.58
Scandinavian (248)	361	2.07
Scotch-Irish (21)	194	1.11
Scottish (13)	121	0.69
Slavic (0)	5	0.03
Slovak (0)	17	0.10
Slovene (11)	11	0.06
Swedish (445)	1,772	10.16
Swiss (69)	168	0.96
Ukrainian (0)	43	0.25
Welsh (0)	49	0.28
Yugoslavian (11)	11	0.06

Hispanic Origin	Population	%
Hispanic or Latino (of any race)	713	4.16
Central American, ex. Mexican	74	0.43
Costa Rican	4	0.02
Guatemalan	38	0.22
Honduran	13	0.08
Panamanian	1	0.01
Salvadoran	18	0.11
Cuban	8	0.05
Dominican Republic	1	0.01
Mexican	471	2.75
Puerto Rican	52	0.30
South American	44	0.26
Argentinean	6	0.04
Bolivian	1	0.01
Colombian	14	0.08
Ecuadorian	13	0.08
Peruvian	3	0.02
Venezuelan	3	0.02
Other South American	4	0.02
Other Hispanic or Latino	63	0.37

Race*	Population	%
African-American/Black (805)	1,033	6.03
Not Hispanic (781)	988	5.76
Hispanic (24)	45	0.26
American Indian/Alaska Native (168)	357	2.08
Not Hispanic (160)	326	1.90
Hispanic (8)	31	0.18
Apache (1)	2	0.01
Blackfeet (2)	5	0.03
Canadian/French Am. Ind. (6)	6	0.04
Cherokee (4)	21	0.12
Chippewa (62)	100	0.58
Creek (0)	1	0.01
Delaware (0)	1	0.01
Lumbee (3)	3	0.02
Navajo (2)	4	0.02
Potawatomi (1)	1	0.01
Pueblo (0)	1	0.01
Seminole (0)	2	0.01
Shoshone (0)	3	0.02
Sioux (11)	19	0.11
South American Ind. (2)	2	0.01
Tlingit-Haida *(Alaska Native)* (0)	1	0.01
Asian (301)	394	2.30
Not Hispanic (298)	387	2.26
Hispanic (3)	7	0.04
Burmese (1)	1	0.01
Cambodian (7)	23	0.13
Chinese, ex. Taiwanese (19)	27	0.16
Filipino (34)	56	0.33
Hmong (78)	94	0.55
Indian (28)	42	0.25
Indonesian (3)	3	0.02
Japanese (6)	23	0.13
Korean (33)	51	0.30
Laotian (6)	10	0.06
Pakistani (0)	1	0.01
Sri Lankan (4)	4	0.02
Taiwanese (1)	1	0.01
Thai (5)	6	0.04
Vietnamese (41)	58	0.34
Hawaii Native/Pacific Islander (2)	13	0.08
Not Hispanic (2)	12	0.07
Hispanic (0)	1	0.01
Native Hawaiian (0)	10	0.06
White (15,082)	15,543	90.67
Not Hispanic (14,751)	15,154	88.40
Hispanic (331)	389	2.27

Apple Valley

Place Type: City
County: Dakota
Population: 49,084†

Ancestry‡	Population	%
African, Sub-Saharan (1,176)	1,205	2.47
African (342)	342	0.70
Ethiopian (422)	422	0.87
Kenyan (34)	34	0.07
Liberian (73)	102	0.21
Nigerian (93)	93	0.19
Somalian (102)	102	0.21
South African (44)	44	0.09
Other Sub-Saharan African (66)	66	0.14
American (1,066)	1,066	2.19
Arab (153)	191	0.39
Arab (14)	14	0.03
Lebanese (21)	59	0.12
Other Arab (118)	118	0.24
Armenian (16)	16	0.03
Assyrian/Chaldean/Syriac (0)	13	0.03
Austrian (38)	295	0.61
Belgian (37)	166	0.34
British (137)	257	0.53
Bulgarian (36)	43	0.09
Canadian (67)	117	0.24
Croatian (37)	106	0.22
Czech (178)	735	1.51

SECTION TWO

*Notes: † The Census 2010 population figure is used to calculate the percentages in the Hispanic Origin and Race categories. Ancestry percentages are based on the 2006-2010 American Community Survey population (not shown); ‡ Numbers in parentheses indicate the number of people reporting a single ancestry; * Numbers in parentheses indicate the number of persons reporting this race alone, not in combination with any other race; Please refer to the Explanation of Data for more information.*

Czechoslovakian (119)	277	0.57
Danish (78)	447	0.92
Dutch (145)	860	1.76
Eastern European (42)	42	0.09
English (605)	3,935	8.07
European (800)	825	1.69
Finnish (183)	537	1.10
French, ex. Basque (259)	2,008	4.12
French Canadian (163)	392	0.80
German (5,345)	17,799	36.51
Greek (16)	150	0.31
Guyanese (9)	9	0.02
Hungarian (11)	111	0.23
Icelander (13)	13	0.03
Iranian (4)	4	0.01
Irish (1,264)	6,781	13.91
Italian (427)	1,529	3.14
Latvian (0)	8	0.02
Lithuanian (0)	70	0.14
Luxemburger (9)	49	0.10
Northern European (318)	318	0.65
Norwegian (2,459)	8,144	16.71
Pennsylvania German (15)	15	0.03
Polish (523)	1,969	4.04
Portuguese (0)	19	0.04
Romanian (26)	52	0.11
Russian (288)	502	1.03
Scandinavian (316)	583	1.20
Scotch-Irish (120)	440	0.90
Scottish (142)	1,041	2.14
Serbian (8)	15	0.03
Slavic (0)	48	0.10
Slovak (12)	50	0.10
Slovene (0)	27	0.06
Swedish (752)	4,120	8.45
Swiss (70)	227	0.47
Ukrainian (78)	129	0.26
Welsh (55)	541	1.11
West Indian, ex. Hispanic (11)	11	0.02
Trinidadian/Tobagonian (11)	11	0.02
Yugoslavian (21)	34	0.07

Hispanic Origin	Population	%
Hispanic or Latino (of any race)	2,427	4.94
Central American, ex. Mexican	137	0.28
Costa Rican	10	0.02
Guatemalan	36	0.07
Honduran	16	0.03
Nicaraguan	10	0.02
Panamanian	12	0.02
Salvadoran	53	0.11
Cuban	41	0.08
Dominican Republic	23	0.05
Mexican	1,586	3.23
Puerto Rican	127	0.26
South American	312	0.64
Argentinean	25	0.05
Bolivian	4	0.01
Chilean	9	0.02
Colombian	84	0.17
Ecuadorian	124	0.25
Paraguayan	4	0.01
Peruvian	19	0.04
Uruguayan	3	0.01
Venezuelan	33	0.07
Other South American	7	0.01
Other Hispanic or Latino	201	0.41

Race*	Population	%
African-American/Black (2,689)	3,370	6.87
Not Hispanic (2,649)	3,265	6.65
Hispanic (40)	105	0.21
American Indian/Alaska Native (191)	467	0.95
Not Hispanic (153)	363	0.74
Hispanic (38)	104	0.21
Apache (0)	4	0.01
Blackfeet (2)	8	0.02
Canadian/French Am. Ind. (0)	1	<0.01
Cherokee (4)	32	0.07
Chippewa (54)	94	0.19
Choctaw (1)	3	0.01
Colville (0)	1	<0.01
Cree (2)	3	0.01
Crow (0)	1	<0.01
Delaware (0)	3	0.01
Iroquois (2)	3	0.01
Menominee (1)	1	<0.01
Mexican American Ind. (4)	7	0.01
Navajo (0)	5	0.01
Osage (0)	6	0.01
Ottawa (1)	2	<0.01
Potawatomi (1)	3	0.01
Sioux (25)	47	0.10
South American Ind. (0)	5	0.01
Tlingit-Haida *(Alaska Native)* (0)	2	<0.01
Asian (2,611)	3,081	6.28
Not Hispanic (2,601)	3,041	6.20
Hispanic (10)	40	0.08
Bangladeshi (15)	18	0.04
Burmese (16)	16	0.03
Cambodian (88)	122	0.25
Chinese, ex. Taiwanese (459)	532	1.08
Filipino (150)	226	0.46
Hmong (72)	76	0.15
Indian (597)	658	1.34
Indonesian (26)	31	0.06
Japanese (77)	159	0.32
Korean (260)	346	0.70
Laotian (135)	170	0.35
Malaysian (8)	12	0.02
Nepalese (23)	24	0.05
Pakistani (61)	63	0.13
Sri Lankan (5)	8	0.02
Taiwanese (20)	27	0.06
Thai (33)	47	0.10
Vietnamese (416)	498	1.01
Hawaii Native/Pacific Islander (34)	79	0.16
Not Hispanic (34)	78	0.16
Hispanic (0)	1	<0.01
Guamanian/Chamorro (3)	7	0.01
Marshallese (2)	2	<0.01
Native Hawaiian (6)	29	0.06
Samoan (3)	5	0.01
Tongan (6)	6	0.01
White (41,121)	42,418	86.42
Not Hispanic (39,962)	41,035	83.60
Hispanic (1,159)	1,383	2.82

Arden Hills

Place Type: City
County: Ramsey
Population: 9,552†

Ancestry‡	Population	%
American (307)	307	3.23
Arab (20)	28	0.29
Lebanese (20)	28	0.29
British (0)	89	0.94
Czech (85)	238	2.51
Czechoslovakian (0)	3	0.03
Danish (59)	225	2.37
Dutch (110)	263	2.77
English (135)	774	8.15
European (126)	126	1.33
Finnish (35)	110	1.16
French, ex. Basque (77)	440	4.63
French Canadian (0)	15	0.16
German (867)	2,952	31.08
Greek (28)	40	0.42
Hungarian (0)	13	0.14
Irish (283)	1,382	14.55
Italian (47)	234	2.46
Luxemburger (0)	36	0.38
Northern European (24)	24	0.25
Norwegian (451)	1,410	14.85
Polish (85)	417	4.39
Russian (23)	99	1.04
Scandinavian (155)	312	3.28
Scotch-Irish (29)	54	0.57
Scottish (0)	158	1.66
Slovak (10)	23	0.24
Slovene (9)	21	0.22
Swedish (445)	1,410	14.85
Swiss (17)	53	0.56
Ukrainian (26)	71	0.75
Welsh (28)	152	1.60
West Indian, ex. Hispanic (11)	28	0.29
Haitian (11)	11	0.12
Jamaican (0)	17	0.18

Hispanic Origin	Population	%
Hispanic or Latino (of any race)	263	2.75
Central American, ex. Mexican	25	0.26
Guatemalan	11	0.12
Honduran	6	0.06
Panamanian	1	0.01
Salvadoran	7	0.07
Cuban	10	0.10
Mexican	157	1.64
Puerto Rican	10	0.10
South American	40	0.42
Argentinean	1	0.01
Bolivian	1	0.01
Chilean	4	0.04
Colombian	7	0.07
Ecuadorian	4	0.04
Paraguayan	6	0.06
Peruvian	7	0.07
Venezuelan	10	0.10
Other Hispanic or Latino	21	0.22

Race*	Population	%
African-American/Black (159)	211	2.21
Not Hispanic (154)	198	2.07
Hispanic (5)	13	0.14
American Indian/Alaska Native (23)	69	0.72
Not Hispanic (21)	58	0.61
Hispanic (2)	11	0.12
Blackfeet (1)	1	0.01
Canadian/French Am. Ind. (0)	1	0.01
Cherokee (0)	3	0.03
Chippewa (12)	24	0.25
Choctaw (0)	1	0.01
Iroquois (1)	1	0.01
Mexican American Ind. (1)	1	0.01
Sioux (1)	6	0.06
South American Ind. (0)	1	0.01
Spanish American Ind. (0)	1	0.01
Yuman (1)	1	0.01
Asian (468)	563	5.89
Not Hispanic (464)	554	5.80
Hispanic (4)	9	0.09
Bangladeshi (2)	3	0.03
Cambodian (8)	8	0.08
Chinese, ex. Taiwanese (115)	134	1.40
Filipino (22)	41	0.43
Hmong (100)	103	1.08
Indian (58)	74	0.77
Japanese (15)	32	0.34
Korean (43)	51	0.53
Laotian (21)	25	0.26
Malaysian (0)	1	0.01
Pakistani (3)	6	0.06
Sri Lankan (1)	2	0.02
Taiwanese (22)	23	0.24
Thai (6)	6	0.06
Vietnamese (38)	53	0.55
Hawaii Native/Pacific Islander (0)	5	0.05
Not Hispanic (0)	5	0.05
Native Hawaiian (0)	4	0.04
White (8,630)	8,789	92.01
Not Hispanic (8,475)	8,623	90.27
Hispanic (155)	166	1.74

Austin

Place Type: City
County: Mower
Population: 24,718†

*Notes: † The Census 2010 population figure is used to calculate the percentages in the Hispanic Origin and Race categories. Ancestry percentages are based on the 2006-2010 American Community Survey population (not shown); ‡ Numbers in parentheses indicate the number of people reporting a single ancestry; * Numbers in parentheses indicate the number of persons reporting this race alone, not in combination with any other race; Please refer to the Explanation of Data for more information.*

Ancestry‡	Population	%
African, Sub-Saharan (228)	234	0.96
African (39)	42	0.17
Ethiopian (61)	61	0.25
Sudanese (103)	106	0.43
Other Sub-Saharan African (25)	25	0.10
American (851)	851	3.48
Arab (45)	49	0.20
Lebanese (14)	18	0.07
Palestinian (31)	31	0.13
Austrian (0)	15	0.06
Belgian (8)	41	0.17
British (0)	10	0.04
Canadian (19)	93	0.38
Croatian (40)	123	0.50
Czech (147)	575	2.35
Czechoslovakian (19)	80	0.33
Danish (119)	594	2.43
Dutch (142)	572	2.34
English (643)	1,496	6.12
European (67)	117	0.48
Finnish (56)	190	0.78
French, ex. Basque (96)	661	2.70
French Canadian (27)	96	0.39
German (3,342)	8,566	35.05
Hungarian (10)	26	0.11
Irish (578)	2,804	11.47
Italian (49)	246	1.01
Norwegian (2,476)	5,562	22.76
Pennsylvania German (11)	25	0.10
Polish (151)	466	1.91
Portuguese (28)	28	0.11
Russian (18)	56	0.23
Scandinavian (5)	54	0.22
Scotch-Irish (25)	200	0.82
Scottish (85)	262	1.07
Slavic (24)	24	0.10
Swedish (124)	812	3.32
Swiss (10)	93	0.38
Turkish (0)	19	0.08
Welsh (0)	108	0.44
West Indian, ex. Hispanic (74)	101	0.41
Dutch West Indian (50)	50	0.20
West Indian (24)	51	0.21
Yugoslavian (58)	58	0.24

Hispanic Origin	Population	%
Hispanic or Latino (of any race)	3,796	15.36
Central American, ex. Mexican	187	0.76
Costa Rican	2	0.01
Guatemalan	136	0.55
Honduran	9	0.04
Nicaraguan	1	<0.01
Salvadoran	39	0.16
Cuban	62	0.25
Dominican Republic	1	<0.01
Mexican	3,266	13.21
Puerto Rican	28	0.11
South American	23	0.09
Argentinean	1	<0.01
Bolivian	4	0.02
Chilean	3	0.01
Colombian	9	0.04
Ecuadorian	2	0.01
Peruvian	1	<0.01
Venezuelan	2	0.01
Other South American	1	<0.01
Other Hispanic or Latino	229	0.93

Race*	Population	%
African-American/Black (749)	990	4.01
Not Hispanic (725)	948	3.84
Hispanic (24)	42	0.17
American Indian/Alaska Native (79)	181	0.73
Not Hispanic (44)	125	0.51
Hispanic (35)	56	0.23
Apache (0)	2	0.01
Blackfeet (2)	5	0.02
Cherokee (2)	10	0.04
Chippewa (16)	32	0.13
Creek (0)	1	<0.01
Inupiat *(Alaska Native)* (0)	2	0.01
Iroquois (1)	1	<0.01
Mexican American Ind. (1)	1	<0.01
Navajo (1)	1	<0.01
Sioux (10)	17	0.07
South American Ind. (0)	1	<0.01
Tlingit-Haida *(Alaska Native)* (0)	1	<0.01
Asian (599)	733	2.97
Not Hispanic (586)	697	2.82
Hispanic (13)	36	0.15
Burmese (2)	2	0.01
Cambodian (11)	22	0.09
Chinese, ex. Taiwanese (80)	87	0.35
Filipino (43)	64	0.26
Hmong (8)	14	0.06
Indian (65)	86	0.35
Japanese (13)	23	0.09
Korean (34)	48	0.19
Laotian (138)	169	0.68
Nepalese (1)	1	<0.01
Sri Lankan (4)	4	0.02
Thai (4)	17	0.07
Vietnamese (160)	181	0.73
Hawaii Native/Pacific Islander (39)	54	0.22
Not Hispanic (35)	43	0.17
Hispanic (4)	11	0.04
Fijian (0)	1	<0.01
Guamanian/Chamorro (4)	7	0.03
Native Hawaiian (3)	7	0.03
Samoan (2)	2	0.01
White (21,466)	21,976	88.91
Not Hispanic (19,122)	19,454	78.70
Hispanic (2,344)	2,522	10.20

Baxter

Place Type: City
County: Crow Wing
Population: 7,610†

Ancestry‡	Population	%
American (114)	114	1.55
Canadian (19)	19	0.26
Croatian (0)	14	0.19
Czech (0)	66	0.90
Czechoslovakian (0)	15	0.20
Danish (38)	117	1.59
Dutch (79)	246	3.35
English (142)	417	5.68
Estonian (14)	14	0.19
European (83)	83	1.13
Finnish (45)	100	1.36
French, ex. Basque (31)	339	4.62
French Canadian (0)	146	1.99
German (769)	3,184	43.37
German Russian (0)	50	0.68
Greek (121)	132	1.80
Hungarian (0)	14	0.19
Irish (299)	852	11.60
Italian (16)	204	2.78
Northern European (103)	103	1.40
Norwegian (489)	1,335	18.18
Polish (32)	286	3.90
Portuguese (0)	12	0.16
Russian (63)	192	2.62
Scandinavian (81)	448	6.10
Scotch-Irish (114)	125	1.70
Scottish (28)	79	1.08
Serbian (0)	10	0.14
Swedish (143)	1,033	14.07
Swiss (0)	57	0.78
Yugoslavian (10)	10	0.14

Hispanic Origin	Population	%
Hispanic or Latino (of any race)	82	1.08
Central American, ex. Mexican	7	0.09
Costa Rican	1	0.01
Guatemalan	2	0.03
Honduran	4	0.05
Mexican	59	0.78
Puerto Rican	4	0.05
South American	7	0.09
Colombian	5	0.07
Peruvian	2	0.03
Other Hispanic or Latino	5	0.07

Race*	Population	%
African-American/Black (37)	67	0.88
Not Hispanic (30)	59	0.78
Hispanic (7)	8	0.11
American Indian/Alaska Native (35)	74	0.97
Not Hispanic (31)	70	0.92
Hispanic (4)	4	0.05
Apache (1)	4	0.05
Blackfeet (0)	3	0.04
Cherokee (1)	4	0.05
Chippewa (7)	21	0.28
Cree (0)	1	0.01
Crow (0)	1	0.01
Iroquois (7)	7	0.09
Mexican American Ind. (1)	1	0.01
Sioux (4)	5	0.07
Asian (66)	96	1.26
Not Hispanic (66)	96	1.26
Chinese, ex. Taiwanese (16)	20	0.26
Filipino (7)	11	0.14
Indian (8)	14	0.18
Japanese (3)	10	0.13
Korean (12)	17	0.22
Laotian (2)	4	0.05
Pakistani (1)	1	0.01
Vietnamese (17)	19	0.25
Hawaii Native/Pacific Islander (5)	11	0.14
Not Hispanic (4)	10	0.13
Hispanic (1)	1	0.01
Guamanian/Chamorro (2)	5	0.07
Native Hawaiian (0)	1	0.01
White (7,344)	7,446	97.84
Not Hispanic (7,294)	7,388	97.08
Hispanic (50)	58	0.76

Bemidji

Place Type: City
County: Beltrami
Population: 13,431†

Ancestry‡	Population	%
African, Sub-Saharan (41)	54	0.41
African (41)	54	0.41
American (763)	763	5.78
Arab (24)	33	0.25
Moroccan (23)	23	0.17
Palestinian (1)	1	0.01
Syrian (0)	9	0.07
Austrian (0)	19	0.14
Belgian (17)	29	0.22
British (26)	26	0.20
Canadian (0)	164	1.24
Carpatho Rusyn (0)	8	0.06
Croatian (0)	51	0.39
Czech (151)	350	2.65
Czechoslovakian (73)	73	0.55
Danish (51)	248	1.88
Dutch (0)	109	0.83
English (196)	786	5.95
European (84)	96	0.73
Finnish (72)	395	2.99
French, ex. Basque (92)	609	4.61
French Canadian (44)	183	1.39
German (1,151)	4,065	30.77
Greek (14)	50	0.38
Hungarian (47)	93	0.70
Irish (144)	1,171	8.87
Italian (75)	548	4.15
Luxemburger (0)	9	0.07
Norwegian (1,075)	2,522	19.09
Polish (134)	501	3.79
Russian (17)	26	0.20

*Notes: † The Census 2010 population figure is used to calculate the percentages in the Hispanic Origin and Race categories. Ancestry percentages are based on the 2006-2010 American Community Survey population (not shown); ‡ Numbers in parentheses indicate the number of people reporting a single ancestry; * Numbers in parentheses indicate the number of persons reporting this race alone, not in combination with any other race; Please refer to the Explanation of Data for more information.*

Scandinavian (168)	264	2.00
Scotch-Irish (17)	139	1.05
Scottish (60)	159	1.20
Serbian (7)	7	0.05
Slovak (0)	37	0.28
Slovene (0)	5	0.04
Swedish (114)	940	7.12
Ukrainian (9)	17	0.13
Yugoslavian (0)	79	0.60

Hispanic Origin	Population	%
Hispanic or Latino (of any race)	250	1.86
Central American, ex. Mexican	11	0.08
Guatemalan	2	0.01
Honduran	4	0.03
Nicaraguan	1	0.01
Panamanian	4	0.03
Cuban	4	0.03
Dominican Republic	2	0.01
Mexican	167	1.24
Puerto Rican	22	0.16
South American	13	0.10
Argentinean	1	0.01
Chilean	1	0.01
Colombian	4	0.03
Ecuadorian	1	0.01
Peruvian	4	0.03
Venezuelan	2	0.01
Other Hispanic or Latino	31	0.23

Race*	Population	%
African-American/Black (155)	310	2.31
Not Hispanic (148)	298	2.22
Hispanic (7)	12	0.09
American Indian/Alaska Native (1,523)	1,983	14.76
Not Hispanic (1,462)	1,895	14.11
Hispanic (61)	88	0.66
Alaska Athabascan *(Ala. Nat.)* (1)	1	0.01
Aleut *(Alaska Native)* (1)	1	0.01
Apache (1)	3	0.02
Blackfeet (0)	1	0.01
Canadian/French Am. Ind. (5)	5	0.04
Cherokee (3)	4	0.03
Chippewa (967)	1,166	8.68
Comanche (3)	3	0.02
Cree (0)	1	0.01
Crow (3)	3	0.02
Hopi (1)	1	0.01
Inupiat *(Alaska Native)* (5)	8	0.06
Iroquois (3)	7	0.05
Mexican American Ind. (7)	7	0.05
Navajo (3)	5	0.04
Ottawa (0)	1	0.01
Paiute (1)	1	0.01
Potawatomi (1)	1	0.01
Seminole (0)	1	0.01
Sioux (50)	62	0.46
South American Ind. (1)	1	0.01
Tlingit-Haida *(Alaska Native)* (0)	1	0.01
Ute (1)	1	0.01
Asian (187)	235	1.75
Not Hispanic (186)	225	1.68
Hispanic (1)	10	0.07
Chinese, ex. Taiwanese (45)	62	0.46
Filipino (16)	30	0.22
Hmong (1)	1	0.01
Indian (43)	48	0.36
Japanese (11)	16	0.12
Korean (44)	54	0.40
Laotian (1)	1	0.01
Malaysian (3)	10	0.07
Nepalese (5)	5	0.04
Pakistani (2)	2	0.01
Thai (2)	2	0.01
Vietnamese (2)	4	0.03
Hawaii Native/Pacific Islander (8)	14	0.10
Not Hispanic (8)	13	0.10
Hispanic (0)	1	0.01
Guamanian/Chamorro (0)	3	0.02
Native Hawaiian (5)	7	0.05
Samoan (3)	4	0.03
White (10,923)	11,452	85.27
Not Hispanic (10,817)	11,314	84.24
Hispanic (106)	138	1.03

Big Lake

Place Type: City
County: Sherburne
Population: 10,060†

Ancestry‡	Population	%
American (581)	581	6.02
Arab (12)	12	0.12
Lebanese (12)	12	0.12
Austrian (0)	20	0.21
Czech (53)	283	2.93
Czechoslovakian (0)	23	0.24
Danish (16)	74	0.77
Dutch (10)	176	1.82
English (32)	598	6.19
European (67)	67	0.69
Finnish (109)	242	2.51
French, ex. Basque (23)	479	4.96
French Canadian (38)	115	1.19
German (807)	3,577	37.03
Greek (0)	16	0.17
Irish (119)	1,072	11.10
Italian (55)	239	2.47
Lithuanian (13)	13	0.13
Norwegian (562)	1,842	19.07
Polish (149)	620	6.42
Portuguese (21)	42	0.43
Russian (16)	27	0.28
Scandinavian (112)	343	3.55
Scotch-Irish (43)	175	1.81
Scottish (34)	151	1.56
Slovak (11)	11	0.11
Swedish (146)	1,077	11.15
Ukrainian (13)	13	0.13

Hispanic Origin	Population	%
Hispanic or Latino (of any race)	371	3.69
Central American, ex. Mexican	50	0.50
Costa Rican	11	0.11
Guatemalan	26	0.26
Honduran	1	0.01
Salvadoran	12	0.12
Cuban	9	0.09
Mexican	208	2.07
Puerto Rican	23	0.23
South American	32	0.32
Argentinean	7	0.07
Chilean	13	0.13
Colombian	6	0.06
Ecuadorian	1	0.01
Peruvian	4	0.04
Other South American	1	0.01
Other Hispanic or Latino	49	0.49

Race*	Population	%
African-American/Black (176)	283	2.81
Not Hispanic (174)	273	2.71
Hispanic (2)	10	0.10
American Indian/Alaska Native (43)	108	1.07
Not Hispanic (39)	98	0.97
Hispanic (4)	10	0.10
Blackfeet (0)	3	0.03
Cherokee (0)	2	0.02
Chippewa (15)	32	0.32
Iroquois (0)	1	0.01
Mexican American Ind. (1)	1	0.01
Navajo (4)	4	0.04
Sioux (6)	12	0.12
Asian (121)	193	1.92
Not Hispanic (120)	191	1.90
Hispanic (1)	2	0.02
Cambodian (2)	8	0.08
Chinese, ex. Taiwanese (8)	14	0.14
Filipino (11)	26	0.26
Hmong (29)	32	0.32
Indian (7)	10	0.10
Indonesian (0)	1	0.01
Japanese (7)	20	0.20
Korean (15)	31	0.31
Laotian (17)	19	0.19
Nepalese (1)	3	0.03
Pakistani (8)	8	0.08
Thai (4)	8	0.08
Vietnamese (5)	16	0.16
Hawaii Native/Pacific Islander (1)	10	0.10
Not Hispanic (1)	9	0.09
Hispanic (0)	1	0.01
Native Hawaiian (1)	8	0.08
White (9,300)	9,557	95.00
Not Hispanic (9,116)	9,338	92.82
Hispanic (184)	219	2.18

Blaine

Place Type: City
County: Anoka
Population: 57,186†

Ancestry‡	Population	%
African, Sub-Saharan (716)	864	1.56
African (403)	475	0.86
Ethiopian (79)	79	0.14
Ghanaian (11)	11	0.02
Kenyan (29)	29	0.05
Liberian (20)	47	0.08
Nigerian (137)	186	0.34
Somalian (26)	26	0.05
Other Sub-Saharan African (11)	11	0.02
Albanian (15)	15	0.03
American (1,505)	1,505	2.72
Arab (240)	324	0.58
Arab (25)	25	0.05
Egyptian (59)	59	0.11
Jordanian (28)	28	0.05
Lebanese (0)	75	0.14
Palestinian (128)	128	0.23
Syrian (0)	9	0.02
Armenian (12)	12	0.02
Australian (0)	41	0.07
Austrian (34)	163	0.29
Belgian (15)	37	0.07
Brazilian (9)	9	0.02
British (25)	78	0.14
Bulgarian (0)	9	0.02
Canadian (18)	107	0.19
Celtic (20)	20	0.04
Croatian (23)	86	0.16
Czech (273)	1,180	2.13
Czechoslovakian (84)	99	0.18
Danish (126)	865	1.56
Dutch (162)	881	1.59
English (539)	3,016	5.44
European (422)	509	0.92
Finnish (266)	951	1.72
French, ex. Basque (226)	2,547	4.60
French Canadian (133)	601	1.08
German (5,568)	20,028	36.14
Greek (0)	42	0.08
Hungarian (15)	363	0.66
Iranian (12)	33	0.06
Irish (1,046)	6,365	11.49
Italian (431)	1,694	3.06
Latvian (8)	8	0.01
Lithuanian (5)	54	0.10
Luxemburger (0)	42	0.08
Northern European (287)	308	0.56
Norwegian (2,348)	8,556	15.44
Polish (990)	3,654	6.59
Portuguese (16)	79	0.14
Romanian (51)	76	0.14
Russian (151)	571	1.03
Scandinavian (626)	1,099	1.98
Scotch-Irish (39)	313	0.56
Scottish (114)	648	1.17

*Notes: † The Census 2010 population figure is used to calculate the percentages in the Hispanic Origin and Race categories. Ancestry percentages are based on the 2006-2010 American Community Survey population (not shown); ‡ Numbers in parentheses indicate the number of people reporting a single ancestry; * Numbers in parentheses indicate the number of persons reporting this race alone, not in combination with any other race; Please refer to the Explanation of Data for more information.*

Serbian (0)	35	0.06
Slavic (8)	98	0.18
Slovak (30)	100	0.18
Slovene (54)	154	0.28
Swedish (1,174)	6,373	11.50
Swiss (38)	152	0.27
Ukrainian (71)	172	0.31
Welsh (21)	312	0.56
West Indian, ex. Hispanic (165)	165	0.30
Haitian (22)	22	0.04
West Indian (143)	143	0.26
Yugoslavian (291)	323	0.58

Hispanic Origin	Population	%
Hispanic or Latino (of any race)	1,842	3.22
Central American, ex. Mexican	165	0.29
Costa Rican	12	0.02
Guatemalan	34	0.06
Honduran	29	0.05
Nicaraguan	13	0.02
Panamanian	9	0.02
Salvadoran	68	0.12
Cuban	17	0.03
Dominican Republic	27	0.05
Mexican	1,204	2.11
Puerto Rican	116	0.20
South American	145	0.25
Argentinean	11	0.02
Bolivian	1	<0.01
Chilean	6	0.01
Colombian	45	0.08
Ecuadorian	23	0.04
Peruvian	38	0.07
Uruguayan	7	0.01
Venezuelan	6	0.01
Other South American	8	0.01
Other Hispanic or Latino	168	0.29

Race*	Population	%
African-American/Black (2,132)	2,659	4.65
Not Hispanic (2,108)	2,600	4.55
Hispanic (24)	59	0.10
American Indian/Alaska Native (305)	758	1.33
Not Hispanic (276)	693	1.21
Hispanic (29)	65	0.11
Apache (0)	2	<0.01
Arapaho (0)	1	<0.01
Blackfeet (0)	5	0.01
Canadian/French Am. Ind. (0)	3	0.01
Central American Ind. (0)	4	0.01
Cherokee (9)	20	0.03
Chippewa (171)	316	0.55
Choctaw (0)	8	0.01
Cree (2)	7	0.01
Crow (0)	1	<0.01
Delaware (2)	2	<0.01
Iroquois (0)	2	<0.01
Lumbee (1)	1	<0.01
Mexican American Ind. (6)	9	0.02
Navajo (4)	6	0.01
Ottawa (3)	5	0.01
Potawatomi (1)	1	<0.01
Seminole (0)	1	<0.01
Sioux (16)	39	0.07
South American Ind. (1)	1	<0.01
Tlingit-Haida *(Alaska Native)* (1)	1	<0.01
Ute (3)	3	0.01
Yuman (1)	3	0.01
Yup'ik *(Alaska Native)* (1)	2	<0.01
Asian (4,468)	5,019	8.78
Not Hispanic (4,450)	4,987	8.72
Hispanic (18)	32	0.06
Bangladeshi (21)	21	0.04
Burmese (1)	3	0.01
Cambodian (51)	76	0.13
Chinese, ex. Taiwanese (411)	516	0.90
Filipino (172)	279	0.49
Hmong (905)	950	1.66
Indian (922)	1,015	1.77
Indonesian (15)	17	0.03
Japanese (43)	122	0.21
Korean (263)	364	0.64
Laotian (93)	122	0.21
Malaysian (1)	2	<0.01
Nepalese (11)	12	0.02
Pakistani (157)	171	0.30
Sri Lankan (5)	7	0.01
Taiwanese (6)	8	0.01
Thai (22)	50	0.09
Vietnamese (1,143)	1,233	2.16
Hawaii Native/Pacific Islander (14)	54	0.09
Not Hispanic (12)	48	0.08
Hispanic (2)	6	0.01
Guamanian/Chamorro (4)	5	0.01
Native Hawaiian (8)	27	0.05
Samoan (0)	3	0.01
White (48,045)	49,477	86.52
Not Hispanic (47,052)	48,319	84.49
Hispanic (993)	1,158	2.02

Bloomington

Place Type: City
County: Hennepin
Population: 82,893†

Ancestry‡	Population	%
African, Sub-Saharan (1,952)	2,137	2.59
African (514)	565	0.68
Ethiopian (182)	195	0.24
Kenyan (24)	24	0.03
Liberian (32)	32	0.04
Nigerian (186)	186	0.23
Somalian (800)	911	1.10
Sudanese (120)	120	0.15
Other Sub-Saharan African (94)	104	0.13
American (1,715)	1,715	2.08
Arab (74)	214	0.26
Egyptian (20)	26	0.03
Lebanese (17)	98	0.12
Moroccan (14)	14	0.02
Palestinian (8)	8	0.01
Other Arab (15)	68	0.08
Armenian (8)	53	0.06
Australian (0)	10	0.01
Austrian (42)	257	0.31
Belgian (37)	128	0.15
Brazilian (0)	18	0.02
British (95)	191	0.23
Bulgarian (0)	10	0.01
Cajun (8)	8	0.01
Canadian (91)	116	0.14
Carpatho Rusyn (0)	12	0.01
Celtic (0)	8	0.01
Croatian (12)	67	0.08
Czech (357)	1,412	1.71
Czechoslovakian (64)	193	0.23
Danish (238)	1,261	1.53
Dutch (321)	1,280	1.55
Eastern European (43)	66	0.08
English (1,281)	6,552	7.93
European (1,057)	1,213	1.47
Finnish (383)	1,324	1.60
French, ex. Basque (250)	2,717	3.29
French Canadian (136)	546	0.66
German (8,278)	25,491	30.85
Greek (80)	149	0.18
Guyanese (38)	38	0.05
Hungarian (34)	174	0.21
Icelander (26)	68	0.08
Iranian (92)	117	0.14
Irish (1,881)	9,711	11.75
Israeli (0)	14	0.02
Italian (554)	2,214	2.68
Latvian (45)	82	0.10
Lithuanian (71)	175	0.21
Luxemburger (53)	110	0.13
Maltese (0)	7	0.01
Northern European (152)	162	0.20
Norwegian (4,297)	13,151	15.92
Pennsylvania German (0)	16	0.02
Polish (692)	3,105	3.76
Portuguese (22)	22	0.03
Romanian (26)	66	0.08
Russian (172)	669	0.81
Scandinavian (834)	1,292	1.56
Scotch-Irish (240)	925	1.12
Scottish (245)	1,586	1.92
Serbian (0)	7	0.01
Slavic (0)	41	0.05
Slovak (130)	335	0.41
Slovene (71)	102	0.12
Swedish (2,596)	9,528	11.53
Swiss (69)	320	0.39
Ukrainian (154)	223	0.27
Welsh (75)	337	0.41
West Indian, ex. Hispanic (63)	63	0.08
Haitian (22)	22	0.03
Jamaican (10)	10	0.01
Trinidadian/Tobagonian (31)	31	0.04
Yugoslavian (48)	138	0.17

Hispanic Origin	Population	%
Hispanic or Latino (of any race)	5,623	6.78
Central American, ex. Mexican	604	0.73
Costa Rican	27	0.03
Guatemalan	124	0.15
Honduran	50	0.06
Nicaraguan	19	0.02
Panamanian	35	0.04
Salvadoran	349	0.42
Cuban	89	0.11
Dominican Republic	26	0.03
Mexican	3,861	4.66
Puerto Rican	255	0.31
South American	340	0.41
Argentinean	16	0.02
Bolivian	20	0.02
Chilean	28	0.03
Colombian	104	0.13
Ecuadorian	89	0.11
Paraguayan	7	0.01
Peruvian	46	0.06
Uruguayan	6	0.01
Venezuelan	8	0.01
Other South American	16	0.02
Other Hispanic or Latino	448	0.54

Race*	Population	%
African-American/Black (5,957)	7,322	8.83
Not Hispanic (5,839)	7,067	8.53
Hispanic (118)	255	0.31
American Indian/Alaska Native (329)	945	1.14
Not Hispanic (267)	803	0.97
Hispanic (62)	142	0.17
Alaska Athabascan *(Ala. Nat.)* (0)	3	<0.01
Aleut *(Alaska Native)* (1)	1	<0.01
Apache (0)	1	<0.01
Blackfeet (2)	23	0.03
Canadian/French Am. Ind. (2)	3	<0.01
Cherokee (8)	70	0.08
Cheyenne (0)	1	<0.01
Chippewa (122)	228	0.28
Choctaw (0)	9	0.01
Comanche (0)	5	0.01
Cree (2)	6	0.01
Creek (1)	2	<0.01
Delaware (3)	4	<0.01
Inupiat *(Alaska Native)* (1)	1	<0.01
Iroquois (2)	9	0.01
Mexican American Ind. (21)	33	0.04
Navajo (1)	1	<0.01
Ottawa (2)	2	<0.01
Potawatomi (4)	5	0.01
Seminole (0)	1	<0.01
Sioux (41)	86	0.10
South American Ind. (4)	9	0.01
Spanish American Ind. (4)	4	<0.01
Tlingit-Haida *(Alaska Native)* (1)	4	<0.01
Ute (1)	2	<0.01

*Notes: † The Census 2010 population figure is used to calculate the percentages in the Hispanic Origin and Race categories. Ancestry percentages are based on the 2006-2010 American Community Survey population (not shown); ‡ Numbers in parentheses indicate the number of people reporting a single ancestry; * Numbers in parentheses indicate the number of persons reporting this race alone, not in combination with any other race; Please refer to the Explanation of Data for more information.*

Yuman (0)	1	<0.01
Yup'ik *(Alaska Native)* (0)	1	<0.01
Asian (4,860)	5,563	6.71
Not Hispanic (4,835)	5,499	6.63
Hispanic (25)	64	0.08
Bangladeshi (11)	15	0.02
Burmese (17)	17	0.02
Cambodian (498)	585	0.71
Chinese, ex. Taiwanese (785)	907	1.09
Filipino (262)	392	0.47
Hmong (122)	128	0.15
Indian (727)	840	1.01
Indonesian (7)	14	0.02
Japanese (117)	212	0.26
Korean (337)	463	0.56
Laotian (285)	336	0.41
Malaysian (2)	5	0.01
Nepalese (31)	34	0.04
Pakistani (62)	71	0.09
Sri Lankan (58)	60	0.07
Taiwanese (15)	21	0.03
Thai (41)	65	0.08
Vietnamese (1,218)	1,334	1.61
Hawaii Native/Pacific Islander (44)	141	0.17
Not Hispanic (33)	115	0.14
Hispanic (11)	26	0.03
Guamanian/Chamorro (5)	10	0.01
Native Hawaiian (6)	30	0.04
Samoan (11)	18	0.02
Tongan (2)	7	0.01
White (66,087)	68,361	82.47
Not Hispanic (63,974)	65,908	79.51
Hispanic (2,113)	2,453	2.96

Brainerd

Place Type: City
County: Crow Wing
Population: 13,590†

Ancestry‡	Population	%
American (610)	610	4.44
Arab (81)	81	0.59
Moroccan (81)	81	0.59
Austrian (0)	40	0.29
British (21)	30	0.22
Cajun (0)	22	0.16
Canadian (22)	92	0.67
Croatian (0)	7	0.05
Czech (0)	189	1.38
Czechoslovakian (64)	118	0.86
Danish (31)	198	1.44
Dutch (109)	283	2.06
English (401)	1,196	8.70
European (197)	197	1.43
Finnish (48)	182	1.32
French, ex. Basque (53)	642	4.67
French Canadian (53)	248	1.80
German (1,723)	5,438	39.57
Hungarian (0)	43	0.31
Icelander (0)	25	0.18
Irish (294)	1,754	12.76
Italian (14)	209	1.52
Lithuanian (15)	50	0.36
Northern European (50)	50	0.36
Norwegian (653)	2,362	17.19
Pennsylvania German (0)	22	0.16
Polish (85)	453	3.30
Portuguese (0)	33	0.24
Russian (7)	22	0.16
Scandinavian (214)	334	2.43
Scotch-Irish (11)	155	1.13
Scottish (21)	182	1.32
Serbian (0)	47	0.34
Slovak (10)	44	0.32
Swedish (219)	935	6.80
Swiss (10)	34	0.25
Welsh (0)	40	0.29
West Indian, ex. Hispanic (15)	15	0.11
Jamaican (15)	15	0.11
Yugoslavian (12)	27	0.20

Hispanic Origin	Population	%
Hispanic or Latino (of any race)	249	1.83
Central American, ex. Mexican	6	0.04
Honduran	2	0.01
Nicaraguan	2	0.01
Salvadoran	2	0.01
Cuban	13	0.10
Mexican	166	1.22
Puerto Rican	24	0.18
South American	11	0.08
Argentinean	1	0.01
Chilean	2	0.01
Colombian	5	0.04
Ecuadorian	3	0.02
Other Hispanic or Latino	29	0.21

Race*	Population	%
African-American/Black (162)	310	2.28
Not Hispanic (158)	304	2.24
Hispanic (4)	6	0.04
American Indian/Alaska Native (223)	425	3.13
Not Hispanic (198)	381	2.80
Hispanic (25)	44	0.32
Apache (0)	2	0.01
Blackfeet (0)	1	0.01
Canadian/French Am. Ind. (0)	1	0.01
Cherokee (3)	8	0.06
Chippewa (120)	203	1.49
Cree (0)	2	0.01
Creek (0)	1	0.01
Iroquois (0)	6	0.04
Menominee (0)	1	0.01
Mexican American Ind. (2)	2	0.01
Navajo (2)	14	0.10
Pueblo (0)	1	0.01
Sioux (12)	16	0.12
South American Ind. (2)	3	0.02
Asian (46)	102	0.75
Not Hispanic (46)	100	0.74
Hispanic (0)	2	0.01
Chinese, ex. Taiwanese (2)	11	0.08
Filipino (14)	25	0.18
Indian (5)	11	0.08
Indonesian (1)	2	0.01
Japanese (3)	14	0.10
Korean (15)	30	0.22
Thai (2)	6	0.04
Vietnamese (1)	1	0.01
Hawaii Native/Pacific Islander (3)	8	0.06
Not Hispanic (3)	8	0.06
Guamanian/Chamorro (2)	3	0.02
Native Hawaiian (0)	2	0.01
White (12,704)	13,091	96.33
Not Hispanic (12,553)	12,910	95.00
Hispanic (151)	181	1.33

Brooklyn Center

Place Type: City
County: Hennepin
Population: 30,104†

Ancestry‡	Population	%
African, Sub-Saharan (2,539)	2,998	10.10
African (767)	970	3.27
Ethiopian (707)	742	2.50
Liberian (628)	796	2.68
Nigerian (26)	26	0.09
Sierra Leonean (20)	20	0.07
Somalian (312)	356	1.20
Other Sub-Saharan African (79)	88	0.30
American (498)	498	1.68
Arab (70)	132	0.44
Egyptian (36)	36	0.12
Lebanese (10)	22	0.07
Other Arab (24)	74	0.25
Austrian (6)	56	0.19
Belgian (0)	39	0.13
British (13)	25	0.08
Canadian (11)	27	0.09
Croatian (13)	13	0.04
Czech (34)	136	0.46
Czechoslovakian (16)	33	0.11
Danish (23)	163	0.55
Dutch (34)	189	0.64
English (283)	1,493	5.03
European (269)	269	0.91
Finnish (139)	605	2.04
French, ex. Basque (85)	801	2.70
French Canadian (107)	274	0.92
German (1,710)	5,332	17.97
Greek (11)	11	0.04
Guyanese (132)	142	0.48
Hungarian (0)	90	0.30
Irish (269)	1,617	5.45
Italian (27)	251	0.85
Latvian (0)	6	0.02
Lithuanian (8)	8	0.03
Luxemburger (11)	24	0.08
Northern European (74)	74	0.25
Norwegian (541)	2,248	7.58
Polish (245)	713	2.40
Portuguese (13)	13	0.04
Romanian (0)	37	0.12
Russian (55)	132	0.44
Scandinavian (149)	278	0.94
Scotch-Irish (55)	141	0.48
Scottish (23)	203	0.68
Serbian (10)	10	0.03
Slovak (23)	55	0.19
Slovene (10)	31	0.10
Swedish (628)	2,522	8.50
Swiss (56)	90	0.30
Ukrainian (19)	86	0.29
Welsh (0)	66	0.22
West Indian, ex. Hispanic (0)	14	0.05
Trinidadian/Tobagonian (0)	14	0.05
Yugoslavian (7)	7	0.02

Hispanic Origin	Population	%
Hispanic or Latino (of any race)	2,889	9.60
Central American, ex. Mexican	202	0.67
Costa Rican	12	0.04
Guatemalan	78	0.26
Honduran	25	0.08
Nicaraguan	7	0.02
Panamanian	1	<0.01
Salvadoran	79	0.26
Cuban	30	0.10
Dominican Republic	19	0.06
Mexican	2,204	7.32
Puerto Rican	104	0.35
South American	142	0.47
Argentinean	5	0.02
Bolivian	3	0.01
Chilean	6	0.02
Colombian	15	0.05
Ecuadorian	81	0.27
Paraguayan	5	0.02
Peruvian	11	0.04
Uruguayan	1	<0.01
Venezuelan	1	<0.01
Other South American	14	0.05
Other Hispanic or Latino	188	0.62

Race*	Population	%
African-American/Black (7,810)	8,692	28.87
Not Hispanic (7,744)	8,530	28.34
Hispanic (66)	162	0.54
American Indian/Alaska Native (232)	496	1.65
Not Hispanic (182)	412	1.37
Hispanic (50)	84	0.28
Apache (0)	5	0.02
Blackfeet (0)	6	0.02
Canadian/French Am. Ind. (1)	1	<0.01
Central American Ind. (3)	3	0.01
Cherokee (3)	41	0.14
Chippewa (82)	136	0.45

*Notes: † The Census 2010 population figure is used to calculate the percentages in the Hispanic Origin and Race categories. Ancestry percentages are based on the 2006-2010 American Community Survey population (not shown); ‡ Numbers in parentheses indicate the number of people reporting a single ancestry; * Numbers in parentheses indicate the number of persons reporting this race alone, not in combination with any other race; Please refer to the Explanation of Data for more information.*

Choctaw (2)	4	0.01
Cree (0)	1	<0.01
Crow (3)	3	0.01
Delaware (1)	1	<0.01
Iroquois (1)	6	0.02
Menominee (1)	2	0.01
Mexican American Ind. (10)	11	0.04
Navajo (0)	1	<0.01
Osage (1)	1	<0.01
Paiute (0)	1	<0.01
Seminole (0)	1	<0.01
Sioux (9)	23	0.08
South American Ind. (3)	4	0.01
Spanish American Ind. (1)	2	0.01
Tohono O'Odham (2)	2	0.01
Ute (1)	1	<0.01
Asian (4,309)	4,584	15.23
Not Hispanic (4,291)	4,544	15.09
Hispanic (18)	40	0.13
Bangladeshi (2)	2	0.01
Cambodian (54)	65	0.22
Chinese, ex. Taiwanese (73)	116	0.39
Filipino (63)	108	0.36
Hmong (3,105)	3,170	10.53
Indian (158)	215	0.71
Indonesian (0)	2	0.01
Japanese (16)	33	0.11
Korean (30)	55	0.18
Laotian (309)	355	1.18
Malaysian (2)	2	0.01
Nepalese (0)	1	<0.01
Pakistani (5)	9	0.03
Sri Lankan (1)	2	0.01
Taiwanese (2)	2	0.01
Thai (19)	33	0.11
Vietnamese (244)	265	0.88
Hawaii Native/Pacific Islander (20)	45	0.15
Not Hispanic (11)	34	0.11
Hispanic (9)	11	0.04
Fijian (4)	4	0.01
Guamanian/Chamorro (7)	7	0.02
Native Hawaiian (4)	13	0.04
Samoan (1)	1	<0.01
White (14,788)	15,911	52.85
Not Hispanic (13,815)	14,775	49.08
Hispanic (973)	1,136	3.77

Brooklyn Park

Place Type: City
County: Hennepin
Population: 75,781†

Ancestry‡	Population	%
Afghan (49)	49	0.07
African, Sub-Saharan (6,987)	7,751	10.53
African (1,269)	1,456	1.98
Ethiopian (305)	305	0.41
Ghanaian (128)	138	0.19
Kenyan (239)	404	0.55
Liberian (3,100)	3,237	4.40
Nigerian (1,377)	1,642	2.23
Sierra Leonean (76)	76	0.10
Somalian (214)	214	0.29
Ugandan (141)	141	0.19
Other Sub-Saharan African (138)	138	0.19
Albanian (17)	17	0.02
American (878)	878	1.19
Arab (759)	992	1.35
Arab (13)	13	0.02
Egyptian (42)	42	0.06
Jordanian (29)	118	0.16
Lebanese (0)	8	0.01
Palestinian (290)	290	0.39
Syrian (0)	8	0.01
Other Arab (385)	513	0.70
Austrian (61)	230	0.31
Belgian (10)	42	0.06
British (62)	129	0.18
Croatian (12)	50	0.07
Czech (204)	800	1.09
Czechoslovakian (49)	49	0.07
Danish (76)	707	0.96
Dutch (69)	558	0.76
English (627)	3,512	4.77
European (791)	981	1.33
Finnish (313)	1,008	1.37
French, ex. Basque (317)	2,863	3.89
French Canadian (104)	480	0.65
German (5,039)	17,479	23.74
German Russian (18)	18	0.02
Greek (11)	189	0.26
Guyanese (78)	78	0.11
Hungarian (64)	146	0.20
Icelander (13)	86	0.12
Iranian (17)	17	0.02
Irish (672)	4,896	6.65
Italian (197)	1,522	2.07
Latvian (8)	16	0.02
Lithuanian (9)	68	0.09
Luxemburger (0)	40	0.05
Northern European (13)	13	0.02
Norwegian (1,702)	7,255	9.85
Pennsylvania German (13)	35	0.05
Polish (560)	2,807	3.81
Romanian (135)	145	0.20
Russian (229)	630	0.86
Scandinavian (395)	607	0.82
Scotch-Irish (41)	410	0.56
Scottish (170)	751	1.02
Serbian (0)	19	0.03
Slavic (8)	24	0.03
Slovak (49)	91	0.12
Slovene (26)	75	0.10
Swedish (1,083)	5,012	6.81
Swiss (14)	223	0.30
Ukrainian (45)	170	0.23
Welsh (28)	228	0.31
West Indian, ex. Hispanic (58)	121	0.16
Jamaican (49)	112	0.15
Other West Indian (9)	9	0.01
Yugoslavian (14)	82	0.11

Hispanic Origin	Population	%
Hispanic or Latino (of any race)	4,841	6.39
Central American, ex. Mexican	429	0.57
Costa Rican	16	0.02
Guatemalan	126	0.17
Honduran	75	0.10
Nicaraguan	35	0.05
Panamanian	15	0.02
Salvadoran	161	0.21
Other Central American	1	<0.01
Cuban	56	0.07
Dominican Republic	34	0.04
Mexican	3,649	4.82
Puerto Rican	195	0.26
South American	196	0.26
Argentinean	14	0.02
Bolivian	5	0.01
Chilean	9	0.01
Colombian	36	0.05
Ecuadorian	71	0.09
Peruvian	34	0.04
Uruguayan	2	<0.01
Venezuelan	15	0.02
Other South American	10	0.01
Other Hispanic or Latino	282	0.37

Race*	Population	%
African-American/Black (18,480)	20,244	26.71
Not Hispanic (18,321)	19,939	26.31
Hispanic (159)	305	0.40
American Indian/Alaska Native (379)	999	1.32
Not Hispanic (313)	834	1.10
Hispanic (66)	165	0.22
Apache (1)	2	<0.01
Blackfeet (6)	23	0.03
Canadian/French Am. Ind. (2)	3	<0.01
Central American Ind. (2)	3	<0.01
Cherokee (5)	48	0.06
Cheyenne (2)	2	<0.01
Chickasaw (0)	2	<0.01
Chippewa (148)	275	0.36
Choctaw (0)	11	0.01
Comanche (0)	2	<0.01
Cree (0)	1	<0.01
Creek (1)	6	0.01
Inupiat *(Alaska Native)* (2)	2	<0.01
Iroquois (1)	11	0.01
Lumbee (0)	1	<0.01
Menominee (0)	4	0.01
Mexican American Ind. (25)	32	0.04
Navajo (1)	3	<0.01
Ottawa (1)	1	<0.01
Potawatomi (1)	2	<0.01
Pueblo (3)	3	<0.01
Seminole (0)	1	<0.01
Sioux (35)	71	0.09
South American Ind. (1)	10	0.01
Spanish American Ind. (6)	6	0.01
Tlingit-Haida *(Alaska Native)* (0)	2	<0.01
Tsimshian *(Alaska Native)* (0)	1	<0.01
Yup'ik *(Alaska Native)* (2)	2	<0.01
Asian (11,687)	12,465	16.45
Not Hispanic (11,658)	12,401	16.36
Hispanic (29)	64	0.08
Bangladeshi (18)	25	0.03
Burmese (4)	8	0.01
Cambodian (252)	294	0.39
Chinese, ex. Taiwanese (316)	481	0.63
Filipino (165)	262	0.35
Hmong (4,964)	5,151	6.80
Indian (888)	1,072	1.41
Indonesian (9)	13	0.02
Japanese (31)	77	0.10
Korean (245)	380	0.50
Laotian (1,453)	1,597	2.11
Malaysian (2)	6	0.01
Nepalese (10)	12	0.02
Pakistani (54)	63	0.08
Sri Lankan (13)	16	0.02
Taiwanese (0)	3	<0.01
Thai (34)	62	0.08
Vietnamese (2,593)	2,774	3.66
Hawaii Native/Pacific Islander (42)	148	0.20
Not Hispanic (26)	116	0.15
Hispanic (16)	32	0.04
Guamanian/Chamorro (6)	18	0.02
Native Hawaiian (7)	19	0.03
Samoan (2)	9	0.01
Tongan (5)	5	0.01
White (39,594)	41,877	55.26
Not Hispanic (37,948)	39,962	52.73
Hispanic (1,646)	1,915	2.53

Buffalo

Place Type: City
County: Wright
Population: 15,453†

Ancestry‡	Population	%
African, Sub-Saharan (89)	89	0.60
Somalian (89)	89	0.60
American (688)	688	4.66
Arab (12)	24	0.16
Lebanese (12)	24	0.16
Australian (16)	16	0.11
Austrian (13)	39	0.26
Belgian (0)	27	0.18
Canadian (17)	17	0.12
Croatian (17)	32	0.22
Czech (17)	256	1.73
Danish (41)	343	2.32
Dutch (127)	322	2.18
English (108)	968	6.55
Finnish (182)	507	3.43
French, ex. Basque (90)	480	3.25
French Canadian (69)	242	1.64

*Notes: † The Census 2010 population figure is used to calculate the percentages in the Hispanic Origin and Race categories. Ancestry percentages are based on the 2006-2010 American Community Survey population (not shown); ‡ Numbers in parentheses indicate the number of people reporting a single ancestry; * Numbers in parentheses indicate the number of persons reporting this race alone, not in combination with any other race; Please refer to the Explanation of Data for more information.*

German (2,380)	6,325	42.82
Greek (28)	28	0.19
Hungarian (13)	51	0.35
Icelander (0)	14	0.09
Irish (150)	1,368	9.26
Italian (86)	249	1.69
Latvian (10)	10	0.07
Northern European (79)	79	0.53
Norwegian (680)	2,440	16.52
Polish (252)	942	6.38
Portuguese (0)	14	0.09
Russian (10)	51	0.35
Scandinavian (180)	193	1.31
Scotch-Irish (12)	77	0.52
Scottish (46)	186	1.26
Swedish (289)	1,901	12.87
Swiss (0)	16	0.11
Ukrainian (0)	30	0.20
Welsh (0)	92	0.62

Hispanic Origin	Population	%
Hispanic or Latino (of any race)	428	2.77
Central American, ex. Mexican	22	0.14
Costa Rican	3	0.02
Guatemalan	6	0.04
Honduran	3	0.02
Nicaraguan	1	0.01
Panamanian	2	0.01
Salvadoran	7	0.05
Cuban	2	0.01
Dominican Republic	1	0.01
Mexican	316	2.04
Puerto Rican	34	0.22
South American	12	0.08
Colombian	11	0.07
Paraguayan	1	0.01
Other Hispanic or Latino	41	0.27

Race*	Population	%
African-American/Black (120)	258	1.67
Not Hispanic (117)	250	1.62
Hispanic (3)	8	0.05
American Indian/Alaska Native (80)	164	1.06
Not Hispanic (77)	142	0.92
Hispanic (3)	22	0.14
Apache (1)	2	0.01
Canadian/French Am. Ind. (1)	1	0.01
Cherokee (0)	7	0.05
Chippewa (41)	63	0.41
Choctaw (1)	1	0.01
Cree (1)	1	0.01
Creek (0)	1	0.01
Menominee (0)	1	0.01
Mexican American Ind. (0)	1	0.01
Potawatomi (4)	4	0.03
Sioux (5)	11	0.07
Asian (138)	198	1.28
Not Hispanic (137)	197	1.27
Hispanic (1)	1	0.01
Bangladeshi (0)	1	0.01
Chinese, ex. Taiwanese (38)	43	0.28
Filipino (20)	33	0.21
Indian (4)	8	0.05
Japanese (4)	15	0.10
Korean (24)	40	0.26
Laotian (14)	22	0.14
Pakistani (3)	7	0.05
Thai (5)	6	0.04
Vietnamese (11)	15	0.10
Hawaii Native/Pacific Islander (6)	9	0.06
Not Hispanic (6)	9	0.06
Guamanian/Chamorro (3)	3	0.02
White (14,694)	14,982	96.95
Not Hispanic (14,433)	14,671	94.94
Hispanic (261)	311	2.01

Burnsville

Place Type: City
County: Dakota
Population: 60,306†

Ancestry‡	Population	%
African, Sub-Saharan (2,420)	2,499	4.12
African (276)	331	0.55
Ethiopian (85)	109	0.18
Ghanaian (9)	9	0.01
Kenyan (274)	274	0.45
Liberian (55)	55	0.09
Nigerian (155)	155	0.26
Sierra Leonean (11)	11	0.02
Somalian (1,295)	1,295	2.13
Sudanese (162)	162	0.27
Other Sub-Saharan African (98)	98	0.16
American (1,222)	1,222	2.01
Arab (169)	243	0.40
Arab (0)	24	0.04
Egyptian (74)	74	0.12
Lebanese (35)	60	0.10
Moroccan (14)	28	0.05
Syrian (46)	57	0.09
Australian (0)	10	0.02
Austrian (143)	360	0.59
Belgian (0)	121	0.20
Brazilian (67)	67	0.11
British (95)	252	0.42
Canadian (53)	91	0.15
Croatian (10)	10	0.02
Czech (215)	1,084	1.79
Czechoslovakian (117)	265	0.44
Danish (154)	939	1.55
Dutch (277)	968	1.59
Eastern European (27)	39	0.06
English (608)	4,452	7.34
European (844)	882	1.45
Finnish (277)	666	1.10
French, ex. Basque (154)	2,169	3.57
French Canadian (150)	464	0.76
German (6,460)	19,594	32.28
Greek (84)	293	0.48
Hungarian (21)	124	0.20
Icelander (8)	45	0.07
Iranian (53)	53	0.09
Irish (1,227)	8,209	13.53
Israeli (7)	7	0.01
Italian (314)	1,579	2.60
Latvian (30)	53	0.09
Lithuanian (30)	146	0.24
Luxemburger (0)	41	0.07
Northern European (72)	77	0.13
Norwegian (2,757)	9,298	15.32
Pennsylvania German (0)	22	0.04
Polish (416)	2,117	3.49
Portuguese (32)	91	0.15
Romanian (0)	33	0.05
Russian (95)	407	0.67
Scandinavian (893)	1,202	1.98
Scotch-Irish (105)	837	1.38
Scottish (148)	663	1.09
Slavic (0)	50	0.08
Slovak (16)	130	0.21
Slovene (8)	19	0.03
Swedish (919)	5,316	8.76
Swiss (51)	157	0.26
Turkish (13)	13	0.02
Ukrainian (215)	304	0.50
Welsh (10)	386	0.64
West Indian, ex. Hispanic (30)	30	0.05
West Indian (30)	30	0.05
Yugoslavian (93)	127	0.21

Hispanic Origin	Population	%
Hispanic or Latino (of any race)	4,756	7.89
Central American, ex. Mexican	593	0.98
Costa Rican	26	0.04
Guatemalan	88	0.15
Honduran	65	0.11
Nicaraguan	17	0.03
Panamanian	18	0.03
Salvadoran	372	0.62
Other Central American	7	0.01
Cuban	47	0.08
Dominican Republic	28	0.05
Mexican	2,966	4.92
Puerto Rican	203	0.34
South American	466	0.77
Argentinean	14	0.02
Bolivian	9	0.01
Chilean	16	0.03
Colombian	101	0.17
Ecuadorian	222	0.37
Paraguayan	6	0.01
Peruvian	46	0.08
Uruguayan	5	0.01
Venezuelan	36	0.06
Other South American	11	0.02
Other Hispanic or Latino	453	0.75

Race*	Population	%
African-American/Black (6,046)	7,104	11.78
Not Hispanic (5,926)	6,879	11.41
Hispanic (120)	225	0.37
American Indian/Alaska Native (215)	676	1.12
Not Hispanic (175)	574	0.95
Hispanic (40)	102	0.17
Apache (3)	4	0.01
Blackfeet (3)	10	0.02
Central American Ind. (0)	4	0.01
Cherokee (8)	60	0.10
Chickasaw (0)	6	0.01
Chippewa (59)	148	0.25
Choctaw (4)	8	0.01
Colville (1)	1	<0.01
Comanche (0)	2	<0.01
Cree (0)	2	<0.01
Creek (0)	3	<0.01
Crow (0)	1	<0.01
Hopi (1)	1	<0.01
Iroquois (0)	4	0.01
Lumbee (1)	1	<0.01
Menominee (4)	8	0.01
Mexican American Ind. (10)	16	0.03
Navajo (5)	9	0.01
Potawatomi (4)	4	0.01
Seminole (2)	2	<0.01
Shoshone (0)	1	<0.01
Sioux (26)	72	0.12
South American Ind. (5)	9	0.01
Spanish American Ind. (0)	3	<0.01
Asian (3,043)	3,610	5.99
Not Hispanic (3,020)	3,546	5.88
Hispanic (23)	64	0.11
Bangladeshi (25)	32	0.05
Bhutanese (1)	1	<0.01
Burmese (11)	11	0.02
Cambodian (296)	367	0.61
Chinese, ex. Taiwanese (229)	336	0.56
Filipino (202)	302	0.50
Hmong (144)	162	0.27
Indian (456)	560	0.93
Indonesian (4)	8	0.01
Japanese (70)	128	0.21
Korean (239)	336	0.56
Laotian (289)	340	0.56
Malaysian (6)	9	0.01
Nepalese (16)	16	0.03
Pakistani (57)	68	0.11
Sri Lankan (23)	33	0.05
Taiwanese (2)	2	<0.01
Thai (40)	67	0.11
Vietnamese (731)	823	1.36
Hawaii Native/Pacific Islander (52)	144	0.24
Not Hispanic (46)	125	0.21
Hispanic (6)	19	0.03
Guamanian/Chamorro (5)	19	0.03
Native Hawaiian (12)	41	0.07

*Notes: † The Census 2010 population figure is used to calculate the percentages in the Hispanic Origin and Race categories. Ancestry percentages are based on the 2006-2010 American Community Survey population (not shown); ‡ Numbers in parentheses indicate the number of people reporting a single ancestry; * Numbers in parentheses indicate the number of persons reporting this race alone, not in combination with any other race; Please refer to the Explanation of Data for more information.*

Samoan (11)	16	0.03
White (46,731)	48,619	80.62
Not Hispanic (44,563)	46,067	76.39
Hispanic (2,168)	2,552	4.23

Cambridge

Place Type: City
County: Isanti
Population: 8,111†

Ancestry‡	Population	%
African, Sub-Saharan (62)	86	1.09
African (0)	24	0.31
Kenyan (48)	48	0.61
Somalian (14)	14	0.18
American (341)	341	4.33
Austrian (0)	9	0.11
Belgian (8)	8	0.10
British (0)	14	0.18
Czech (11)	90	1.14
Czechoslovakian (46)	46	0.58
Danish (23)	131	1.66
Dutch (37)	90	1.14
English (106)	486	6.18
European (59)	90	1.14
Finnish (23)	98	1.25
French, ex. Basque (34)	275	3.50
French Canadian (42)	89	1.13
German (1,066)	3,042	38.66
Hungarian (0)	21	0.27
Irish (73)	681	8.66
Italian (18)	209	2.66
Latvian (0)	12	0.15
Lithuanian (0)	12	0.15
Norwegian (502)	1,596	20.28
Pennsylvania German (29)	29	0.37
Polish (26)	239	3.04
Portuguese (14)	14	0.18
Russian (51)	116	1.47
Scandinavian (101)	117	1.49
Scotch-Irish (0)	39	0.50
Scottish (0)	41	0.52
Slovak (12)	12	0.15
Swedish (631)	1,497	19.03
Swiss (29)	82	1.04
Welsh (0)	39	0.50

Hispanic Origin	Population	%
Hispanic or Latino (of any race)	140	1.73
Central American, ex. Mexican	10	0.12
Guatemalan	2	0.02
Honduran	6	0.07
Panamanian	1	0.01
Salvadoran	1	0.01
Cuban	5	0.06
Mexican	75	0.92
Puerto Rican	11	0.14
South American	15	0.18
Argentinean	1	0.01
Bolivian	1	0.01
Colombian	3	0.04
Peruvian	10	0.12
Other Hispanic or Latino	24	0.30

Race*	Population	%
African-American/Black (81)	147	1.81
Not Hispanic (75)	134	1.65
Hispanic (6)	13	0.16
American Indian/Alaska Native (40)	123	1.52
Not Hispanic (38)	110	1.36
Hispanic (2)	13	0.16
Blackfeet (0)	1	0.01
Cherokee (3)	6	0.07
Chickasaw (0)	3	0.04
Chippewa (7)	31	0.38
Choctaw (1)	1	0.01
Menominee (1)	1	0.01
Sioux (2)	10	0.12
South American Ind. (0)	1	0.01
Asian (113)	152	1.87
Not Hispanic (113)	152	1.87
Cambodian (2)	10	0.12
Chinese, ex. Taiwanese (12)	20	0.25
Filipino (44)	54	0.67
Hmong (2)	5	0.06
Japanese (0)	1	0.01
Korean (19)	32	0.39
Laotian (4)	14	0.17
Sri Lankan (1)	1	0.01
Thai (1)	5	0.06
Vietnamese (15)	15	0.18
Hawaii Native/Pacific Islander (2)	2	0.02
Hispanic (2)	2	0.02
White (7,667)	7,836	96.61
Not Hispanic (7,582)	7,737	95.39
Hispanic (85)	99	1.22

Champlin

Place Type: City
County: Hennepin
Population: 23,089†

Ancestry‡	Population	%
African, Sub-Saharan (742)	742	3.26
African (94)	94	0.41
Kenyan (93)	93	0.41
Liberian (44)	44	0.19
Nigerian (293)	293	1.29
Somalian (75)	75	0.33
Other Sub-Saharan African (143)	143	0.63
Alsatian (0)	10	0.04
American (732)	732	3.22
Arab (13)	55	0.24
Lebanese (8)	8	0.04
Syrian (5)	47	0.21
Austrian (15)	15	0.07
Belgian (10)	20	0.09
British (17)	87	0.38
Canadian (11)	84	0.37
Croatian (0)	11	0.05
Czech (67)	426	1.87
Czechoslovakian (0)	12	0.05
Danish (118)	436	1.92
Dutch (209)	638	2.81
Eastern European (8)	22	0.10
English (170)	1,230	5.41
European (561)	601	2.64
Finnish (127)	528	2.32
French, ex. Basque (115)	1,082	4.76
French Canadian (0)	141	0.62
German (2,432)	8,393	36.91
Greek (32)	32	0.14
Guyanese (0)	11	0.05
Hungarian (7)	93	0.41
Iranian (134)	134	0.59
Irish (564)	2,828	12.44
Italian (183)	688	3.03
Lithuanian (103)	138	0.61
Luxemburger (0)	12	0.05
Northern European (58)	58	0.26
Norwegian (1,262)	4,306	18.93
Polish (198)	1,402	6.17
Portuguese (13)	50	0.22
Russian (10)	107	0.47
Scandinavian (303)	390	1.71
Scotch-Irish (55)	178	0.78
Scottish (65)	328	1.44
Serbian (0)	63	0.28
Slavic (15)	15	0.07
Slovak (0)	39	0.17
Soviet Union (16)	16	0.07
Swedish (616)	2,715	11.94
Swiss (12)	117	0.51
Ukrainian (42)	42	0.18
Welsh (0)	47	0.21
Yugoslavian (5)	5	0.02

Hispanic Origin	Population	%
Hispanic or Latino (of any race)	472	2.04
Central American, ex. Mexican	53	0.23
Costa Rican	2	0.01
Guatemalan	15	0.06
Honduran	1	<0.01
Nicaraguan	5	0.02
Panamanian	4	0.02
Salvadoran	26	0.11
Cuban	4	0.02
Dominican Republic	1	<0.01
Mexican	255	1.10
Puerto Rican	41	0.18
South American	69	0.30
Argentinean	2	0.01
Bolivian	6	0.03
Chilean	5	0.02
Colombian	26	0.11
Ecuadorian	11	0.05
Paraguayan	1	<0.01
Peruvian	15	0.06
Venezuelan	3	0.01
Other Hispanic or Latino	49	0.21

Race*	Population	%
African-American/Black (1,109)	1,343	5.82
Not Hispanic (1,106)	1,324	5.73
Hispanic (3)	19	0.08
American Indian/Alaska Native (90)	216	0.94
Not Hispanic (85)	195	0.84
Hispanic (5)	21	0.09
Blackfeet (2)	6	0.03
Canadian/French Am. Ind. (0)	1	<0.01
Cherokee (1)	9	0.04
Chippewa (55)	93	0.40
Choctaw (1)	1	<0.01
Creek (0)	2	0.01
Delaware (1)	1	<0.01
Inupiat *(Alaska Native)* (0)	1	<0.01
Mexican American Ind. (1)	3	0.01
Pueblo (2)	2	0.01
Puget Sound Salish (0)	4	0.02
Shoshone (2)	2	0.01
Sioux (7)	21	0.09
South American Ind. (0)	1	<0.01
Asian (714)	871	3.77
Not Hispanic (713)	866	3.75
Hispanic (1)	5	0.02
Bangladeshi (0)	3	0.01
Burmese (1)	1	<0.01
Cambodian (7)	12	0.05
Chinese, ex. Taiwanese (50)	80	0.35
Filipino (44)	70	0.30
Hmong (190)	201	0.87
Indian (77)	103	0.45
Indonesian (1)	1	<0.01
Japanese (13)	33	0.14
Korean (77)	103	0.45
Laotian (86)	100	0.43
Nepalese (1)	1	<0.01
Pakistani (3)	4	0.02
Sri Lankan (2)	2	0.01
Taiwanese (1)	5	0.02
Thai (11)	15	0.06
Vietnamese (102)	117	0.51
Hawaii Native/Pacific Islander (7)	26	0.11
Not Hispanic (4)	22	0.10
Hispanic (3)	4	0.02
Guamanian/Chamorro (3)	4	0.02
Native Hawaiian (4)	7	0.03
Samoan (0)	1	<0.01
White (20,551)	21,013	91.01
Not Hispanic (20,239)	20,652	89.45
Hispanic (312)	361	1.56

SECTION TWO

*Notes: † The Census 2010 population figure is used to calculate the percentages in the Hispanic Origin and Race categories. Ancestry percentages are based on the 2006-2010 American Community Survey population (not shown); ‡ Numbers in parentheses indicate the number of people reporting a single ancestry; * Numbers in parentheses indicate the number of persons reporting this race alone, not in combination with any other race; Please refer to the Explanation of Data for more information.*

Chanhassen

Place Type: City
County: Carver
Population: 22,952†

Ancestry‡	Population	%
Afghan (11)	11	0.05
African, Sub-Saharan (31)	99	0.43
African (31)	99	0.43
American (437)	437	1.91
Arab (73)	142	0.62
Arab (49)	49	0.21
Egyptian (0)	49	0.21
Lebanese (0)	20	0.09
Other Arab (24)	24	0.11
Australian (23)	23	0.10
Austrian (30)	127	0.56
Belgian (0)	33	0.14
British (60)	103	0.45
Canadian (8)	80	0.35
Croatian (0)	111	0.49
Czech (242)	703	3.08
Czechoslovakian (14)	49	0.21
Danish (98)	448	1.96
Dutch (230)	608	2.66
Eastern European (135)	135	0.59
English (333)	1,852	8.10
Estonian (19)	56	0.25
European (541)	571	2.50
Finnish (44)	287	1.26
French, ex. Basque (52)	852	3.73
French Canadian (53)	213	0.93
German (2,255)	9,227	40.38
Greek (0)	87	0.38
Hungarian (0)	61	0.27
Iranian (60)	127	0.56
Irish (459)	3,514	15.38
Israeli (30)	30	0.13
Italian (291)	764	3.34
Latvian (9)	9	0.04
Lithuanian (0)	31	0.14
Luxemburger (55)	69	0.30
Northern European (176)	176	0.77
Norwegian (1,131)	3,714	16.25
Pennsylvania German (0)	19	0.08
Polish (134)	1,121	4.91
Portuguese (0)	57	0.25
Romanian (12)	12	0.05
Russian (40)	203	0.89
Scandinavian (323)	540	2.36
Scotch-Irish (120)	430	1.88
Scottish (176)	437	1.91
Slovak (0)	31	0.14
Slovene (0)	58	0.25
Swedish (563)	2,897	12.68
Swiss (51)	133	0.58
Ukrainian (29)	34	0.15
Welsh (12)	157	0.69

Hispanic Origin	Population	%
Hispanic or Latino (of any race)	525	2.29
Central American, ex. Mexican	43	0.19
Costa Rican	1	<0.01
Guatemalan	20	0.09
Honduran	14	0.06
Nicaraguan	3	0.01
Panamanian	1	<0.01
Salvadoran	4	0.02
Cuban	6	0.03
Dominican Republic	10	0.04
Mexican	311	1.36
Puerto Rican	31	0.14
South American	67	0.29
Argentinean	1	<0.01
Bolivian	12	0.05
Chilean	4	0.02
Colombian	23	0.10
Ecuadorian	8	0.03
Peruvian	6	0.03
Venezuelan	13	0.06
Other Hispanic or Latino	57	0.25

Race*	Population	%
African-American/Black (254)	361	1.57
Not Hispanic (244)	346	1.51
Hispanic (10)	15	0.07
American Indian/Alaska Native (24)	87	0.38
Not Hispanic (16)	73	0.32
Hispanic (8)	14	0.06
Alaska Athabascan *(Ala. Nat.)* (0)	1	<0.01
Apache (3)	3	0.01
Blackfeet (0)	1	<0.01
Canadian/French Am. Ind. (1)	2	0.01
Central American Ind. (2)	2	0.01
Cherokee (0)	10	0.04
Chippewa (8)	18	0.08
Creek (0)	1	<0.01
Crow (0)	1	<0.01
Iroquois (1)	1	<0.01
Kiowa (0)	1	<0.01
Sioux (1)	7	0.03
South American Ind. (2)	2	0.01
Asian (887)	1,068	4.65
Not Hispanic (885)	1,057	4.61
Hispanic (2)	11	0.05
Bangladeshi (12)	13	0.06
Cambodian (63)	66	0.29
Chinese, ex. Taiwanese (148)	186	0.81
Filipino (67)	102	0.44
Hmong (16)	16	0.07
Indian (149)	161	0.70
Indonesian (0)	2	0.01
Japanese (15)	36	0.16
Korean (111)	148	0.64
Laotian (72)	80	0.35
Malaysian (0)	1	<0.01
Nepalese (6)	6	0.03
Pakistani (9)	10	0.04
Sri Lankan (1)	2	0.01
Taiwanese (2)	4	0.02
Thai (5)	13	0.06
Vietnamese (177)	198	0.86
Hawaii Native/Pacific Islander (2)	5	0.02
Not Hispanic (1)	4	0.02
Hispanic (1)	1	<0.01
Native Hawaiian (2)	4	0.02
White (21,235)	21,561	93.94
Not Hispanic (20,952)	21,241	92.55
Hispanic (283)	320	1.39

Chaska

Place Type: City
County: Carver
Population: 23,770†

Ancestry‡	Population	%
African, Sub-Saharan (86)	169	0.74
African (49)	108	0.47
Ethiopian (37)	61	0.27
American (438)	438	1.90
Arab (0)	143	0.62
Lebanese (0)	143	0.62
Australian (44)	44	0.19
Austrian (10)	147	0.64
Belgian (0)	63	0.27
British (17)	62	0.27
Bulgarian (0)	22	0.10
Canadian (0)	17	0.07
Croatian (13)	37	0.16
Czech (58)	544	2.37
Czechoslovakian (0)	38	0.17
Danish (33)	322	1.40
Dutch (109)	526	2.29
English (384)	1,813	7.89
European (312)	312	1.36
Finnish (67)	228	0.99
French, ex. Basque (151)	1,164	5.06
French Canadian (59)	250	1.09
German (2,983)	8,732	37.98
Hungarian (0)	61	0.27
Icelander (15)	15	0.07
Irish (456)	3,161	13.75
Italian (108)	824	3.58
Latvian (63)	92	0.40
Lithuanian (0)	20	0.09
Luxemburger (0)	26	0.11
Northern European (27)	27	0.12
Norwegian (1,083)	3,348	14.56
Pennsylvania German (0)	21	0.09
Polish (159)	737	3.21
Portuguese (0)	56	0.24
Romanian (424)	444	1.93
Russian (97)	188	0.82
Scandinavian (101)	278	1.21
Scotch-Irish (59)	313	1.36
Scottish (96)	480	2.09
Slovak (15)	15	0.07
Slovene (30)	30	0.13
Swedish (447)	1,841	8.01
Swiss (26)	54	0.23
Ukrainian (85)	166	0.72
Welsh (8)	54	0.23
Yugoslavian (13)	31	0.13

Hispanic Origin	Population	%
Hispanic or Latino (of any race)	2,030	8.54
Central American, ex. Mexican	228	0.96
Costa Rican	7	0.03
Guatemalan	115	0.48
Honduran	51	0.21
Nicaraguan	6	0.03
Panamanian	7	0.03
Salvadoran	42	0.18
Cuban	11	0.05
Dominican Republic	14	0.06
Mexican	1,434	6.03
Puerto Rican	41	0.17
South American	87	0.37
Argentinean	4	0.02
Chilean	4	0.02
Colombian	13	0.05
Ecuadorian	10	0.04
Paraguayan	4	0.02
Peruvian	47	0.20
Uruguayan	1	<0.01
Venezuelan	3	0.01
Other South American	1	<0.01
Other Hispanic or Latino	215	0.90

Race*	Population	%
African-American/Black (590)	772	3.25
Not Hispanic (553)	723	3.04
Hispanic (37)	49	0.21
American Indian/Alaska Native (97)	194	0.82
Not Hispanic (93)	175	0.74
Hispanic (4)	19	0.08
Blackfeet (1)	3	0.01
Canadian/French Am. Ind. (0)	1	<0.01
Cherokee (1)	12	0.05
Chippewa (33)	58	0.24
Iroquois (0)	2	0.01
Lumbee (2)	2	0.01
Puget Sound Salish (0)	4	0.02
Sioux (13)	20	0.08
South American Ind. (0)	2	0.01
Asian (871)	1,026	4.32
Not Hispanic (857)	1,006	4.23
Hispanic (14)	20	0.08
Bangladeshi (16)	18	0.08
Burmese (1)	1	<0.01
Cambodian (53)	65	0.27
Chinese, ex. Taiwanese (124)	159	0.67
Filipino (99)	115	0.48
Hmong (22)	32	0.13
Indian (124)	147	0.62
Indonesian (9)	9	0.04
Japanese (14)	34	0.14
Korean (77)	117	0.49

*Notes: † The Census 2010 population figure is used to calculate the percentages in the Hispanic Origin and Race categories. Ancestry percentages are based on the 2006-2010 American Community Survey population (not shown); ‡ Numbers in parentheses indicate the number of people reporting a single ancestry; * Numbers in parentheses indicate the number of persons reporting this race alone, not in combination with any other race; Please refer to the Explanation of Data for more information.*

Laotian (105)	124	0.52
Nepalese (9)	10	0.04
Pakistani (10)	10	0.04
Sri Lankan (11)	15	0.06
Taiwanese (1)	5	0.02
Thai (10)	16	0.07
Vietnamese (141)	163	0.69
Hawaii Native/Pacific Islander (7)	17	0.07
Not Hispanic (4)	14	0.06
Hispanic (3)	3	0.01
Guamanian/Chamorro (1)	1	<0.01
Native Hawaiian (1)	2	0.01
Samoan (0)	1	<0.01
White (20,931)	21,363	89.87
Not Hispanic (19,814)	20,166	84.84
Hispanic (1,117)	1,197	5.04

Cloquet

Place Type: City
County: Carlton
Population: 12,124†

Ancestry‡	Population	%
African, Sub-Saharan (0)	110	0.92
Nigerian (0)	92	0.77
Other Sub-Saharan African (0)	18	0.15
American (243)	243	2.02
Arab (0)	130	1.08
Syrian (0)	130	1.08
Austrian (0)	22	0.18
Belgian (0)	51	0.42
British (14)	26	0.22
Canadian (10)	12	0.10
Croatian (10)	10	0.08
Czech (35)	151	1.26
Czechoslovakian (0)	13	0.11
Danish (16)	218	1.81
Dutch (13)	208	1.73
English (148)	614	5.11
European (50)	50	0.42
Finnish (1,152)	1,993	16.58
French, ex. Basque (92)	558	4.64
French Canadian (70)	350	2.91
German (628)	2,514	20.92
Greek (0)	123	1.02
Icelander (51)	51	0.42
Irish (108)	912	7.59
Italian (72)	363	3.02
Luxemburger (0)	14	0.12
Northern European (2)	2	0.02
Norwegian (570)	1,781	14.82
Polish (290)	1,035	8.61
Romanian (0)	8	0.07
Russian (30)	30	0.25
Scandinavian (139)	212	1.76
Scotch-Irish (0)	52	0.43
Scottish (15)	199	1.66
Slavic (29)	29	0.24
Slovene (0)	16	0.13
Swedish (302)	1,316	10.95
Swiss (0)	56	0.47
Welsh (0)	60	0.50
Yugoslavian (10)	22	0.18

Hispanic Origin	Population	%
Hispanic or Latino (of any race)	162	1.34
Central American, ex. Mexican	6	0.05
Guatemalan	4	0.03
Honduran	2	0.02
Cuban	9	0.07
Mexican	104	0.86
Puerto Rican	17	0.14
South American	3	0.02
Chilean	2	0.02
Colombian	1	0.01
Other Hispanic or Latino	23	0.19

Race*	Population	%
African-American/Black (53)	135	1.11
Not Hispanic (52)	132	1.09
Hispanic (1)	3	0.02
American Indian/Alaska Native (1,304)	1,649	13.60
Not Hispanic (1,271)	1,592	13.13
Hispanic (33)	57	0.47
Aleut *(Alaska Native)* (4)	4	0.03
Apache (1)	2	0.02
Canadian/French Am. Ind. (7)	18	0.15
Cherokee (5)	10	0.08
Cheyenne (1)	1	0.01
Chippewa (1,061)	1,289	10.63
Cree (1)	2	0.02
Inupiat *(Alaska Native)* (6)	6	0.05
Iroquois (0)	1	0.01
Menominee (1)	1	0.01
Mexican American Ind. (1)	2	0.02
Ottawa (1)	2	0.02
Sioux (8)	8	0.07
Asian (66)	109	0.90
Not Hispanic (66)	107	0.88
Hispanic (0)	2	0.02
Cambodian (1)	1	0.01
Chinese, ex. Taiwanese (20)	21	0.17
Filipino (20)	37	0.31
Indian (0)	1	0.01
Indonesian (1)	1	0.01
Japanese (3)	13	0.11
Korean (15)	18	0.15
Laotian (1)	2	0.02
Malaysian (0)	1	0.01
Thai (2)	3	0.02
Vietnamese (2)	8	0.07
Hawaii Native/Pacific Islander (2)	15	0.12
Not Hispanic (1)	5	0.04
Hispanic (1)	10	0.08
Native Hawaiian (0)	5	0.04
Samoan (1)	9	0.07
White (10,233)	10,641	87.77
Not Hispanic (10,160)	10,537	86.91
Hispanic (73)	104	0.86

Columbia Heights

Place Type: City
County: Anoka
Population: 19,496†

Ancestry‡	Population	%
African, Sub-Saharan (1,682)	1,720	8.82
African (638)	676	3.47
Ethiopian (55)	55	0.28
Nigerian (30)	30	0.15
Somalian (959)	959	4.92
American (246)	246	1.26
Arab (312)	457	2.34
Egyptian (149)	149	0.76
Lebanese (20)	41	0.21
Moroccan (113)	175	0.90
Other Arab (30)	92	0.47
Austrian (8)	40	0.21
Belgian (11)	59	0.30
Brazilian (0)	20	0.10
British (10)	34	0.17
Canadian (0)	23	0.12
Carpatho Rusyn (0)	11	0.06
Croatian (8)	32	0.16
Czech (131)	280	1.44
Czechoslovakian (32)	59	0.30
Danish (38)	183	0.94
Dutch (48)	194	0.99
Eastern European (15)	40	0.21
English (130)	871	4.47
European (146)	174	0.89
Finnish (60)	153	0.78
French, ex. Basque (56)	765	3.92
French Canadian (206)	348	1.78
German (1,212)	4,953	25.40
German Russian (0)	9	0.05
Greek (0)	9	0.05
Hungarian (0)	48	0.25
Icelander (0)	42	0.22
Irish (418)	2,290	11.74
Italian (130)	232	1.19
Lithuanian (12)	12	0.06
Luxemburger (0)	8	0.04
Northern European (31)	31	0.16
Norwegian (562)	2,062	10.57
Polish (491)	1,591	8.16
Russian (0)	122	0.63
Scandinavian (69)	130	0.67
Scotch-Irish (42)	144	0.74
Scottish (16)	66	0.34
Slavic (0)	12	0.06
Slovak (60)	138	0.71
Slovene (0)	36	0.18
Swedish (303)	1,665	8.54
Swiss (9)	36	0.18
Ukrainian (196)	237	1.22
Welsh (10)	25	0.13
West Indian, ex. Hispanic (0)	10	0.05
Bahamian (0)	10	0.05
Yugoslavian (54)	65	0.33

Hispanic Origin	Population	%
Hispanic or Latino (of any race)	2,319	11.89
Central American, ex. Mexican	131	0.67
Costa Rican	6	0.03
Guatemalan	31	0.16
Honduran	9	0.05
Nicaraguan	18	0.09
Panamanian	5	0.03
Salvadoran	60	0.31
Other Central American	2	0.01
Cuban	11	0.06
Dominican Republic	16	0.08
Mexican	1,469	7.53
Puerto Rican	56	0.29
South American	462	2.37
Argentinean	3	0.02
Chilean	5	0.03
Colombian	23	0.12
Ecuadorian	404	2.07
Paraguayan	2	0.01
Peruvian	21	0.11
Venezuelan	1	0.01
Other South American	3	0.02
Other Hispanic or Latino	174	0.89

Race*	Population	%
African-American/Black (2,629)	3,072	15.76
Not Hispanic (2,596)	3,011	15.44
Hispanic (33)	61	0.31
American Indian/Alaska Native (298)	579	2.97
Not Hispanic (249)	483	2.48
Hispanic (49)	96	0.49
Aleut *(Alaska Native)* (1)	1	0.01
Apache (0)	3	0.02
Blackfeet (0)	6	0.03
Canadian/French Am. Ind. (0)	1	0.01
Cherokee (3)	29	0.15
Cheyenne (1)	1	0.01
Chippewa (136)	202	1.04
Choctaw (1)	6	0.03
Cree (1)	2	0.01
Creek (0)	2	0.01
Inupiat *(Alaska Native)* (1)	1	0.01
Iroquois (1)	2	0.01
Mexican American Ind. (16)	18	0.09
Navajo (1)	1	0.01
Potawatomi (2)	2	0.01
Seminole (0)	1	0.01
Sioux (17)	25	0.13
South American Ind. (6)	16	0.08
Spanish American Ind. (2)	2	0.01
Asian (930)	1,083	5.55
Not Hispanic (927)	1,068	5.48
Hispanic (3)	15	0.08
Cambodian (16)	27	0.14
Chinese, ex. Taiwanese (239)	258	1.32
Filipino (88)	102	0.52

*Notes: † The Census 2010 population figure is used to calculate the percentages in the Hispanic Origin and Race categories. Ancestry percentages are based on the 2006-2010 American Community Survey population (not shown); ‡ Numbers in parentheses indicate the number of people reporting a single ancestry; * Numbers in parentheses indicate the number of persons reporting this race alone, not in combination with any other race; Please refer to the Explanation of Data for more information.*

Hmong (166)	168	0.86
Indian (126)	173	0.89
Indonesian (2)	5	0.03
Japanese (26)	53	0.27
Korean (47)	79	0.41
Laotian (15)	18	0.09
Nepalese (2)	2	0.01
Pakistani (24)	33	0.17
Sri Lankan (1)	1	0.01
Taiwanese (2)	3	0.02
Thai (2)	7	0.04
Vietnamese (119)	141	0.72
Hawaii Native/Pacific Islander (14)	39	0.20
Not Hispanic (13)	30	0.15
Hispanic (1)	9	0.05
Guamanian/Chamorro (2)	2	0.01
Native Hawaiian (10)	12	0.06
Samoan (1)	2	0.01
Tongan (0)	1	0.01
White (13,588)	14,305	73.37
Not Hispanic (12,657)	13,258	68.00
Hispanic (931)	1,047	5.37

Coon Rapids

Place Type: City
County: Anoka
Population: 61,476†

Ancestry‡	Population	%
African, Sub-Saharan (1,035)	1,187	1.91
African (422)	504	0.81
Ethiopian (129)	159	0.26
Kenyan (77)	77	0.12
Liberian (121)	161	0.26
Nigerian (66)	66	0.11
Somalian (168)	168	0.27
Sudanese (39)	39	0.06
Other Sub-Saharan African (13)	13	0.02
American (2,190)	2,190	3.53
Arab (382)	579	0.93
Egyptian (89)	89	0.14
Iraqi (83)	83	0.13
Lebanese (35)	152	0.25
Syrian (7)	14	0.02
Other Arab (168)	241	0.39
Austrian (73)	271	0.44
Belgian (0)	77	0.12
British (62)	141	0.23
Bulgarian (52)	52	0.08
Canadian (12)	22	0.04
Croatian (10)	102	0.16
Czech (151)	762	1.23
Czechoslovakian (0)	38	0.06
Danish (108)	717	1.16
Dutch (288)	1,088	1.76
Eastern European (13)	13	0.02
English (648)	3,603	5.81
European (1,099)	1,158	1.87
Finnish (320)	1,264	2.04
French, ex. Basque (521)	3,229	5.21
French Canadian (243)	846	1.36
German (6,163)	21,612	34.86
Greek (24)	111	0.18
Hungarian (31)	67	0.11
Icelander (10)	50	0.08
Iranian (33)	101	0.16
Irish (981)	7,539	12.16
Italian (363)	1,491	2.41
Latvian (10)	10	0.02
Lithuanian (87)	96	0.15
Luxemburger (0)	28	0.05
Northern European (273)	352	0.57
Norwegian (2,760)	10,318	16.64
Pennsylvania German (9)	39	0.06
Polish (909)	4,024	6.49
Portuguese (0)	16	0.03
Romanian (60)	60	0.10
Russian (399)	759	1.22
Scandinavian (478)	758	1.22
Scotch-Irish (130)	637	1.03
Scottish (113)	725	1.17
Serbian (0)	9	0.01
Slavic (0)	31	0.05
Slovak (49)	88	0.14
Slovene (27)	98	0.16
Swedish (1,565)	7,001	11.29
Swiss (0)	100	0.16
Turkish (0)	13	0.02
Ukrainian (429)	714	1.15
Welsh (15)	188	0.30
West Indian, ex. Hispanic (12)	34	0.05
Jamaican (12)	34	0.05
Yugoslavian (118)	139	0.22

Hispanic Origin	Population	%
Hispanic or Latino (of any race)	1,989	3.24
Central American, ex. Mexican	189	0.31
Costa Rican	16	0.03
Guatemalan	53	0.09
Honduran	29	0.05
Nicaraguan	15	0.02
Panamanian	14	0.02
Salvadoran	62	0.10
Cuban	49	0.08
Dominican Republic	14	0.02
Mexican	1,326	2.16
Puerto Rican	153	0.25
South American	115	0.19
Argentinean	8	0.01
Bolivian	4	0.01
Chilean	9	0.01
Colombian	35	0.06
Ecuadorian	20	0.03
Peruvian	28	0.05
Uruguayan	1	<0.01
Venezuelan	10	0.02
Other Hispanic or Latino	143	0.23

Race*	Population	%
African-American/Black (3,384)	4,281	6.96
Not Hispanic (3,333)	4,148	6.75
Hispanic (51)	133	0.22
American Indian/Alaska Native (438)	1,012	1.65
Not Hispanic (391)	912	1.48
Hispanic (47)	100	0.16
Apache (2)	2	<0.01
Blackfeet (3)	15	0.02
Canadian/French Am. Ind. (1)	3	<0.01
Cherokee (10)	51	0.08
Chickasaw (3)	4	0.01
Chippewa (217)	383	0.62
Choctaw (4)	10	0.02
Cree (3)	4	0.01
Creek (0)	4	0.01
Delaware (3)	3	<0.01
Hopi (1)	2	<0.01
Inupiat *(Alaska Native)* (1)	2	<0.01
Iroquois (5)	19	0.03
Kiowa (3)	4	0.01
Lumbee (2)	2	<0.01
Menominee (0)	4	0.01
Mexican American Ind. (12)	17	0.03
Navajo (0)	2	<0.01
Osage (0)	1	<0.01
Ottawa (1)	7	0.01
Potawatomi (3)	3	<0.01
Seminole (0)	4	0.01
Shoshone (0)	1	<0.01
Sioux (39)	67	0.11
South American Ind. (0)	2	<0.01
Tlingit-Haida *(Alaska Native)* (1)	2	<0.01
Yup'ik *(Alaska Native)* (3)	3	<0.01
Asian (2,157)	2,641	4.30
Not Hispanic (2,150)	2,598	4.23
Hispanic (7)	43	0.07
Bangladeshi (2)	2	<0.01
Burmese (2)	5	0.01
Cambodian (32)	47	0.08
Chinese, ex. Taiwanese (158)	217	0.35
Filipino (87)	175	0.28
Hmong (745)	765	1.24
Indian (266)	329	0.54
Indonesian (7)	7	0.01
Japanese (24)	71	0.12
Korean (134)	228	0.37
Laotian (69)	86	0.14
Malaysian (3)	10	0.02
Nepalese (2)	4	0.01
Pakistani (48)	56	0.09
Sri Lankan (8)	8	0.01
Taiwanese (4)	4	0.01
Thai (29)	53	0.09
Vietnamese (404)	480	0.78
Hawaii Native/Pacific Islander (16)	64	0.10
Not Hispanic (14)	57	0.09
Hispanic (2)	7	0.01
Guamanian/Chamorro (4)	7	0.01
Native Hawaiian (3)	15	0.02
Samoan (0)	4	0.01
White (52,847)	54,585	88.79
Not Hispanic (51,859)	53,402	86.87
Hispanic (988)	1,183	1.92

Cottage Grove

Place Type: City
County: Washington
Population: 34,589†

Ancestry‡	Population	%
African, Sub-Saharan (643)	822	2.42
African (217)	232	0.68
Ethiopian (134)	149	0.44
Kenyan (72)	104	0.31
Liberian (28)	28	0.08
Nigerian (148)	241	0.71
Other Sub-Saharan African (44)	68	0.20
American (1,398)	1,398	4.11
Arab (0)	47	0.14
Lebanese (0)	38	0.11
Syrian (0)	9	0.03
Austrian (55)	167	0.49
Belgian (35)	57	0.17
British (47)	98	0.29
Canadian (0)	17	0.05
Carpatho Rusyn (0)	7	0.02
Croatian (22)	89	0.26
Czech (93)	538	1.58
Czechoslovakian (12)	84	0.25
Danish (116)	604	1.78
Dutch (134)	521	1.53
English (385)	2,137	6.28
European (465)	480	1.41
Finnish (50)	434	1.28
French, ex. Basque (100)	1,471	4.32
French Canadian (151)	452	1.33
German (3,912)	13,665	40.16
Greek (0)	93	0.27
Hungarian (69)	135	0.40
Irish (660)	4,597	13.51
Italian (429)	1,572	4.62
Latvian (0)	10	0.03
Lithuanian (0)	53	0.16
Luxemburger (0)	24	0.07
Norwegian (991)	4,472	13.14
Polish (383)	2,264	6.65
Portuguese (26)	42	0.12
Romanian (10)	10	0.03
Russian (37)	280	0.82
Scandinavian (232)	437	1.28
Scotch-Irish (26)	263	0.77
Scottish (108)	303	0.89
Slavic (10)	10	0.03
Slovak (10)	61	0.18
Slovene (9)	61	0.18
Swedish (512)	2,939	8.64
Swiss (18)	204	0.60
Ukrainian (64)	135	0.40
Welsh (12)	79	0.23

*Notes: † The Census 2010 population figure is used to calculate the percentages in the Hispanic Origin and Race categories. Ancestry percentages are based on the 2006-2010 American Community Survey population (not shown); ‡ Numbers in parentheses indicate the number of people reporting a single ancestry; * Numbers in parentheses indicate the number of persons reporting this race alone, not in combination with any other race; Please refer to the Explanation of Data for more information.*

Yugoslavian (15)	51	0.15

Hispanic Origin	Population	%
Hispanic or Latino (of any race)	1,658	4.79
Central American, ex. Mexican	135	0.39
Costa Rican	3	0.01
Guatemalan	44	0.13
Honduran	16	0.05
Nicaraguan	6	0.02
Panamanian	14	0.04
Salvadoran	51	0.15
Other Central American	1	<0.01
Cuban	19	0.05
Dominican Republic	10	0.03
Mexican	1,181	3.41
Puerto Rican	136	0.39
South American	89	0.26
Argentinean	8	0.02
Bolivian	1	<0.01
Colombian	33	0.10
Ecuadorian	10	0.03
Paraguayan	2	0.01
Peruvian	21	0.06
Uruguayan	1	<0.01
Venezuelan	12	0.03
Other South American	1	<0.01
Other Hispanic or Latino	88	0.25

Race*	Population	%
African-American/Black (1,348)	1,704	4.93
Not Hispanic (1,315)	1,631	4.72
Hispanic (33)	73	0.21
American Indian/Alaska Native (175)	394	1.14
Not Hispanic (155)	344	0.99
Hispanic (20)	50	0.14
Apache (1)	3	0.01
Canadian/French Am. Ind. (0)	5	0.01
Central American Ind. (2)	2	0.01
Cherokee (5)	18	0.05
Chippewa (62)	102	0.29
Choctaw (6)	9	0.03
Cree (0)	6	0.02
Creek (0)	2	0.01
Iroquois (1)	2	0.01
Menominee (1)	2	0.01
Mexican American Ind. (2)	6	0.02
Navajo (1)	4	0.01
Sioux (34)	65	0.19
South American Ind. (1)	9	0.03
Spanish American Ind. (0)	1	<0.01
Ute (2)	6	0.02
Asian (1,820)	2,042	5.90
Not Hispanic (1,814)	2,028	5.86
Hispanic (6)	14	0.04
Bangladeshi (7)	7	0.02
Cambodian (109)	126	0.36
Chinese, ex. Taiwanese (100)	130	0.38
Filipino (135)	207	0.60
Hmong (863)	890	2.57
Indian (145)	162	0.47
Indonesian (0)	1	<0.01
Japanese (17)	58	0.17
Korean (91)	123	0.36
Laotian (54)	57	0.16
Malaysian (2)	3	0.01
Pakistani (32)	38	0.11
Sri Lankan (5)	5	0.01
Taiwanese (1)	2	0.01
Thai (6)	15	0.04
Vietnamese (154)	189	0.55
Hawaii Native/Pacific Islander (20)	55	0.16
Not Hispanic (15)	45	0.13
Hispanic (5)	10	0.03
Guamanian/Chamorro (8)	17	0.05
Native Hawaiian (4)	12	0.03
Samoan (1)	7	0.02
Tongan (1)	2	0.01
White (29,921)	30,672	88.68
Not Hispanic (28,911)	29,547	85.42
Hispanic (1,010)	1,125	3.25

Crookston

Place Type: City
County: Polk
Population: 7,891†

Ancestry‡	Population	%
African, Sub-Saharan (15)	15	0.19
Other Sub-Saharan African (15)	15	0.19
American (200)	200	2.53
Arab (10)	10	0.13
Lebanese (10)	10	0.13
Austrian (0)	10	0.13
Belgian (0)	12	0.15
British (0)	17	0.22
Czech (19)	88	1.11
Danish (34)	69	0.87
Dutch (27)	137	1.73
English (31)	351	4.44
European (16)	16	0.20
Finnish (9)	76	0.96
French, ex. Basque (92)	665	8.42
French Canadian (60)	92	1.16
German (719)	2,855	36.14
German Russian (0)	15	0.19
Greek (0)	6	0.08
Hungarian (0)	1	0.01
Icelander (0)	16	0.20
Irish (64)	619	7.84
Italian (14)	148	1.87
Luxemburger (0)	22	0.28
Norwegian (850)	2,767	35.03
Pennsylvania German (0)	33	0.42
Polish (113)	355	4.49
Portuguese (0)	34	0.43
Russian (19)	50	0.63
Scandinavian (14)	57	0.72
Scotch-Irish (0)	41	0.52
Scottish (22)	104	1.32
Slavic (0)	18	0.23
Slovak (20)	24	0.30
Swedish (82)	450	5.70
Welsh (0)	34	0.43
West Indian, ex. Hispanic (0)	11	0.14
Haitian (0)	11	0.14

Hispanic Origin	Population	%
Hispanic or Latino (of any race)	871	11.04
Central American, ex. Mexican	38	0.48
Guatemalan	8	0.10
Honduran	10	0.13
Nicaraguan	3	0.04
Panamanian	1	0.01
Salvadoran	16	0.20
Cuban	8	0.10
Dominican Republic	5	0.06
Mexican	686	8.69
Puerto Rican	29	0.37
South American	4	0.05
Chilean	1	0.01
Colombian	2	0.03
Peruvian	1	0.01
Other Hispanic or Latino	101	1.28

Race*	Population	%
African-American/Black (112)	151	1.91
Not Hispanic (99)	126	1.60
Hispanic (13)	25	0.32
American Indian/Alaska Native (131)	227	2.88
Not Hispanic (109)	179	2.27
Hispanic (22)	48	0.61
Apache (1)	1	0.01
Blackfeet (0)	1	0.01
Canadian/French Am. Ind. (1)	3	0.04
Cherokee (8)	14	0.18
Cheyenne (8)	8	0.10
Chippewa (47)	68	0.86
Delaware (1)	4	0.05
Kiowa (5)	6	0.08
Mexican American Ind. (0)	1	0.01
Navajo (0)	6	0.08
Sioux (17)	20	0.25
Asian (125)	152	1.93
Not Hispanic (124)	144	1.82
Hispanic (1)	8	0.10
Cambodian (0)	3	0.04
Chinese, ex. Taiwanese (24)	28	0.35
Filipino (5)	14	0.18
Indian (8)	8	0.10
Japanese (4)	10	0.13
Korean (77)	85	1.08
Laotian (1)	1	0.01
Nepalese (2)	2	0.03
Pakistani (0)	3	0.04
Thai (1)	2	0.03
Hawaii Native/Pacific Islander (0)	3	0.04
Not Hispanic (0)	2	0.03
Hispanic (0)	1	0.01
Native Hawaiian (0)	1	0.01
White (7,121)	7,286	92.33
Not Hispanic (6,576)	6,677	84.62
Hispanic (545)	609	7.72

Crystal

Place Type: City
County: Hennepin
Population: 22,151†

Ancestry‡	Population	%
African, Sub-Saharan (399)	440	1.99
African (104)	123	0.56
Ethiopian (5)	14	0.06
Kenyan (72)	72	0.33
Liberian (206)	219	0.99
Nigerian (12)	12	0.05
American (632)	632	2.87
Arab (83)	99	0.45
Arab (0)	7	0.03
Egyptian (42)	42	0.19
Moroccan (37)	37	0.17
Other Arab (4)	13	0.06
Austrian (0)	33	0.15
Belgian (0)	10	0.05
British (19)	28	0.13
Croatian (9)	17	0.08
Czech (82)	424	1.92
Czechoslovakian (10)	48	0.22
Danish (89)	274	1.24
Dutch (95)	607	2.75
Eastern European (5)	5	0.02
English (260)	1,469	6.66
European (290)	317	1.44
Finnish (162)	349	1.58
French, ex. Basque (76)	871	3.95
French Canadian (57)	382	1.73
German (2,246)	7,430	33.68
Greek (0)	41	0.19
Hungarian (51)	61	0.28
Icelander (0)	26	0.12
Iranian (9)	9	0.04
Irish (291)	2,325	10.54
Israeli (18)	18	0.08
Italian (228)	676	3.06
Latvian (10)	10	0.05
Lithuanian (0)	70	0.32
Luxemburger (0)	31	0.14
Northern European (0)	15	0.07
Norwegian (941)	3,082	13.97
Polish (326)	1,317	5.97
Portuguese (0)	9	0.04
Russian (86)	263	1.19
Scandinavian (249)	442	2.00
Scotch-Irish (55)	301	1.36
Scottish (0)	257	1.17
Serbian (0)	10	0.05
Slavic (3)	14	0.06
Slovak (17)	27	0.12
Slovene (0)	15	0.07
Swedish (376)	1,931	8.75

*Notes: † The Census 2010 population figure is used to calculate the percentages in the Hispanic Origin and Race categories. Ancestry percentages are based on the 2006-2010 American Community Survey population (not shown); ‡ Numbers in parentheses indicate the number of people reporting a single ancestry; * Numbers in parentheses indicate the number of persons reporting this race alone, not in combination with any other race; Please refer to the Explanation of Data for more information.*

Swiss (10)	82	0.37
Ukrainian (9)	77	0.35
Welsh (13)	69	0.31
Yugoslavian (33)	94	0.43

Hispanic Origin	Population	%
Hispanic or Latino (of any race)	1,436	6.48
Central American, ex. Mexican	116	0.52
Costa Rican	9	0.04
Guatemalan	32	0.14
Honduran	25	0.11
Nicaraguan	2	0.01
Panamanian	8	0.04
Salvadoran	40	0.18
Cuban	11	0.05
Dominican Republic	23	0.10
Mexican	1,038	4.69
Puerto Rican	73	0.33
South American	84	0.38
Argentinean	6	0.03
Chilean	4	0.02
Colombian	22	0.10
Ecuadorian	21	0.09
Peruvian	14	0.06
Uruguayan	2	0.01
Venezuelan	11	0.05
Other South American	4	0.02
Other Hispanic or Latino	91	0.41

Race*	Population	%
African-American/Black (2,333)	2,769	12.50
Not Hispanic (2,267)	2,662	12.02
Hispanic (66)	107	0.48
American Indian/Alaska Native (152)	375	1.69
Not Hispanic (123)	308	1.39
Hispanic (29)	67	0.30
Apache (1)	1	<0.01
Blackfeet (0)	3	0.01
Canadian/French Am. Ind. (1)	1	<0.01
Cherokee (2)	12	0.05
Cheyenne (1)	1	<0.01
Chippewa (59)	107	0.48
Colville (1)	1	<0.01
Cree (0)	2	0.01
Creek (1)	1	<0.01
Iroquois (1)	3	0.01
Mexican American Ind. (10)	16	0.07
Navajo (1)	4	0.02
Osage (1)	3	0.01
Pueblo (0)	1	<0.01
Seminole (0)	1	<0.01
Sioux (10)	17	0.08
South American Ind. (0)	1	<0.01
Spanish American Ind. (5)	5	0.02
Asian (862)	1,076	4.86
Not Hispanic (856)	1,056	4.77
Hispanic (6)	20	0.09
Bangladeshi (8)	9	0.04
Burmese (5)	5	0.02
Cambodian (25)	26	0.12
Chinese, ex. Taiwanese (74)	101	0.46
Filipino (78)	135	0.61
Hmong (165)	180	0.81
Indian (101)	123	0.56
Indonesian (5)	8	0.04
Japanese (10)	34	0.15
Korean (74)	123	0.56
Laotian (108)	118	0.53
Malaysian (1)	3	0.01
Nepalese (2)	2	0.01
Pakistani (7)	8	0.04
Sri Lankan (5)	6	0.03
Thai (12)	22	0.10
Vietnamese (135)	165	0.74
Hawaii Native/Pacific Islander (7)	54	0.24
Not Hispanic (6)	48	0.22
Hispanic (1)	6	0.03
Guamanian/Chamorro (1)	3	0.01
Native Hawaiian (0)	13	0.06
Samoan (3)	4	0.02
Tongan (1)	4	0.02
White (17,289)	18,033	81.41
Not Hispanic (16,712)	17,349	78.32
Hispanic (577)	684	3.09

Detroit Lakes

Place Type: City
County: Becker
Population: 8,569†

Ancestry‡	Population	%
American (209)	209	2.47
Austrian (0)	17	0.20
Belgian (0)	119	1.40
Czech (65)	157	1.85
Danish (21)	85	1.00
Dutch (34)	150	1.77
English (107)	585	6.91
European (32)	32	0.38
Finnish (22)	234	2.76
French, ex. Basque (21)	471	5.56
French Canadian (39)	148	1.75
German (1,268)	3,846	45.40
Hungarian (0)	17	0.20
Icelander (0)	26	0.31
Irish (48)	632	7.46
Italian (10)	66	0.78
Northern European (16)	16	0.19
Norwegian (861)	2,517	29.71
Polish (74)	308	3.64
Russian (22)	40	0.47
Scandinavian (65)	102	1.20
Scotch-Irish (48)	120	1.42
Scottish (0)	111	1.31
Serbian (0)	29	0.34
Swedish (126)	1,003	11.84
Swiss (0)	32	0.38
Ukrainian (13)	23	0.27
Welsh (0)	38	0.45
West Indian, ex. Hispanic (11)	11	0.13
Trinidadian/Tobagonian (11)	11	0.13

Hispanic Origin	Population	%
Hispanic or Latino (of any race)	140	1.63
Central American, ex. Mexican	6	0.07
Guatemalan	4	0.05
Honduran	1	0.01
Panamanian	1	0.01
Cuban	2	0.02
Dominican Republic	3	0.04
Mexican	104	1.21
Puerto Rican	7	0.08
South American	1	0.01
Chilean	1	0.01
Other Hispanic or Latino	17	0.20

Race*	Population	%
African-American/Black (62)	95	1.11
Not Hispanic (57)	87	1.02
Hispanic (5)	8	0.09
American Indian/Alaska Native (375)	562	6.56
Not Hispanic (359)	536	6.26
Hispanic (16)	26	0.30
Blackfeet (1)	1	0.01
Canadian/French Am. Ind. (0)	4	0.05
Cherokee (0)	7	0.08
Chippewa (237)	330	3.85
Choctaw (0)	1	0.01
Iroquois (3)	5	0.06
Mexican American Ind. (0)	1	0.01
Navajo (2)	3	0.04
Potawatomi (1)	1	0.01
Seminole (1)	1	0.01
Sioux (13)	19	0.22
Asian (67)	103	1.20
Not Hispanic (67)	102	1.19
Hispanic (0)	1	0.01
Chinese, ex. Taiwanese (17)	17	0.20
Filipino (8)	22	0.26
Indian (8)	11	0.13
Japanese (1)	4	0.05
Korean (12)	20	0.23
Laotian (2)	3	0.04
Thai (0)	1	0.01
Vietnamese (17)	20	0.23
Hawaii Native/Pacific Islander (5)	14	0.16
Not Hispanic (5)	11	0.13
Hispanic (0)	3	0.04
Native Hawaiian (5)	6	0.07
Samoan (0)	1	0.01
White (7,761)	7,993	93.28
Not Hispanic (7,701)	7,917	92.39
Hispanic (60)	76	0.89

Duluth

Place Type: City
County: St. Louis
Population: 86,265†

Ancestry‡	Population	%
African, Sub-Saharan (217)	217	0.25
African (66)	66	0.08
Ethiopian (13)	13	0.02
Nigerian (31)	31	0.04
Somalian (25)	25	0.03
Other Sub-Saharan African (82)	82	0.10
American (2,075)	2,075	2.41
Arab (101)	283	0.33
Arab (0)	11	0.01
Iraqi (0)	12	0.01
Lebanese (50)	173	0.20
Moroccan (21)	39	0.05
Palestinian (10)	28	0.03
Syrian (20)	20	0.02
Australian (0)	20	0.02
Austrian (88)	326	0.38
Belgian (39)	300	0.35
Brazilian (0)	23	0.03
British (150)	328	0.38
Bulgarian (0)	12	0.01
Cajun (17)	17	0.02
Canadian (86)	200	0.23
Carpatho Rusyn (0)	14	0.02
Celtic (56)	56	0.07
Croatian (205)	423	0.49
Czech (149)	983	1.14
Czechoslovakian (116)	216	0.25
Danish (105)	834	0.97
Dutch (237)	1,030	1.20
Eastern European (29)	73	0.08
English (1,165)	6,024	7.00
Estonian (13)	13	0.02
European (727)	782	0.91
Finnish (2,012)	5,228	6.07
French, ex. Basque (514)	4,995	5.80
French Canadian (557)	1,579	1.83
German (5,768)	22,193	25.79
Greek (197)	483	0.56
Hungarian (64)	230	0.27
Icelander (11)	127	0.15
Iranian (14)	14	0.02
Irish (1,865)	9,777	11.36
Italian (1,428)	4,997	5.81
Latvian (0)	12	0.01
Lithuanian (52)	130	0.15
Luxemburger (0)	11	0.01
Macedonian (0)	9	0.01
Northern European (209)	217	0.25
Norwegian (3,761)	14,060	16.34
Polish (1,470)	5,804	6.74
Portuguese (53)	139	0.16
Romanian (14)	69	0.08
Russian (118)	473	0.55
Scandinavian (1,260)	2,182	2.54
Scotch-Irish (176)	1,318	1.53
Scottish (319)	1,892	2.20
Serbian (128)	282	0.33
Slavic (118)	256	0.30

*Notes: † The Census 2010 population figure is used to calculate the percentages in the Hispanic Origin and Race categories. Ancestry percentages are based on the 2006-2010 American Community Survey population (not shown); ‡ Numbers in parentheses indicate the number of people reporting a single ancestry; * Numbers in parentheses indicate the number of persons reporting this race alone, not in combination with any other race; Please refer to the Explanation of Data for more information.*

Ancestry (continued)	Population	%
Slovak (56)	112	0.13
Slovene (130)	371	0.43
Swedish (2,622)	12,102	14.06
Swiss (30)	186	0.22
Turkish (4)	30	0.03
Ukrainian (70)	194	0.23
Welsh (41)	377	0.44
West Indian, ex. Hispanic (19)	19	0.02
Jamaican (12)	12	0.01
Trinidadian/Tobagonian (7)	7	0.01
Yugoslavian (81)	266	0.31

Hispanic Origin	Population	%
Hispanic or Latino (of any race)	1,305	1.51
Central American, ex. Mexican	73	0.08
Costa Rican	6	0.01
Guatemalan	39	0.05
Honduran	10	0.01
Nicaraguan	1	<0.01
Panamanian	5	0.01
Salvadoran	10	0.01
Other Central American	2	<0.01
Cuban	57	0.07
Dominican Republic	2	<0.01
Mexican	717	0.83
Puerto Rican	144	0.17
South American	109	0.13
Argentinean	12	0.01
Bolivian	5	0.01
Chilean	2	<0.01
Colombian	57	0.07
Ecuadorian	2	<0.01
Paraguayan	3	<0.01
Peruvian	21	0.02
Venezuelan	7	0.01
Other Hispanic or Latino	203	0.24

Race*	Population	%
African-American/Black (1,988)	3,019	3.50
Not Hispanic (1,955)	2,922	3.39
Hispanic (33)	97	0.11
American Indian/Alaska Native (2,134)	3,512	4.07
Not Hispanic (2,011)	3,301	3.83
Hispanic (123)	211	0.24
Alaska Athabascan *(Ala. Nat.)* (1)	1	<0.01
Apache (3)	4	<0.01
Blackfeet (5)	22	0.03
Canadian/French Am. Ind. (14)	28	0.03
Central American Ind. (2)	2	<0.01
Cherokee (16)	57	0.07
Cheyenne (3)	3	<0.01
Chippewa (1,100)	1,661	1.93
Choctaw (4)	13	0.02
Cree (1)	7	0.01
Creek (1)	4	<0.01
Delaware (0)	1	<0.01
Hopi (0)	1	<0.01
Inupiat *(Alaska Native)* (1)	2	<0.01
Iroquois (6)	14	0.02
Kiowa (0)	1	<0.01
Menominee (13)	14	0.02
Mexican American Ind. (18)	30	0.03
Navajo (6)	7	0.01
Osage (0)	2	<0.01
Ottawa (3)	3	<0.01
Paiute (0)	2	<0.01
Potawatomi (8)	9	0.01
Pueblo (1)	1	<0.01
Puget Sound Salish (4)	5	0.01
Shoshone (1)	2	<0.01
Sioux (71)	111	0.13
South American Ind. (0)	1	<0.01
Ute (0)	2	<0.01
Yakama (1)	1	<0.01
Yaqui (4)	8	0.01
Yuman (0)	1	<0.01
Asian (1,293)	1,725	2.00
Not Hispanic (1,287)	1,701	1.97
Hispanic (6)	24	0.03
Bhutanese (1)	1	<0.01
Burmese (1)	3	<0.01
Cambodian (21)	25	0.03
Chinese, ex. Taiwanese (329)	392	0.45
Filipino (91)	174	0.20
Hmong (143)	159	0.18
Indian (155)	195	0.23
Indonesian (6)	11	0.01
Japanese (59)	135	0.16
Korean (196)	288	0.33
Laotian (15)	26	0.03
Malaysian (8)	8	0.01
Nepalese (20)	21	0.02
Pakistani (31)	32	0.04
Sri Lankan (13)	20	0.02
Taiwanese (15)	16	0.02
Thai (12)	22	0.03
Vietnamese (133)	186	0.22
Hawaii Native/Pacific Islander (29)	80	0.09
Not Hispanic (28)	75	0.09
Hispanic (1)	5	0.01
Guamanian/Chamorro (4)	6	0.01
Marshallese (2)	2	<0.01
Native Hawaiian (11)	34	0.04
Samoan (3)	7	0.01
White (77,968)	80,430	93.24
Not Hispanic (77,184)	79,482	92.14
Hispanic (784)	948	1.10

Eagan

Place Type: City
County: Dakota
Population: 64,206†

Ancestry‡	Population	%
Afghan (26)	26	0.04
African, Sub-Saharan (1,532)	1,632	2.53
African (163)	234	0.36
Ethiopian (704)	713	1.11
Kenyan (169)	169	0.26
Liberian (0)	11	0.02
Somalian (450)	459	0.71
Other Sub-Saharan African (46)	46	0.07
American (1,362)	1,362	2.11
Arab (272)	316	0.49
Arab (56)	56	0.09
Egyptian (92)	108	0.17
Lebanese (92)	120	0.19
Moroccan (7)	7	0.01
Palestinian (10)	10	0.02
Other Arab (15)	15	0.02
Assyrian/Chaldean/Syriac (10)	10	0.02
Austrian (23)	121	0.19
Belgian (15)	219	0.34
Brazilian (0)	10	0.02
British (127)	198	0.31
Bulgarian (18)	18	0.03
Canadian (135)	206	0.32
Carpatho Rusyn (0)	28	0.04
Croatian (37)	187	0.29
Czech (156)	1,438	2.23
Czechoslovakian (94)	120	0.19
Danish (159)	1,017	1.58
Dutch (213)	1,237	1.92
Eastern European (132)	169	0.26
English (780)	4,932	7.65
European (1,117)	1,240	1.92
Finnish (108)	748	1.16
French, ex. Basque (189)	2,492	3.86
French Canadian (163)	577	0.89
German (5,801)	23,461	36.38
Greek (11)	76	0.12
Hungarian (22)	172	0.27
Icelander (8)	135	0.21
Iranian (17)	23	0.04
Irish (1,280)	9,254	14.35
Israeli (0)	4	0.01
Italian (221)	1,707	2.65
Latvian (0)	60	0.09
Lithuanian (32)	117	0.18
Luxemburger (0)	80	0.12
Northern European (217)	217	0.34
Norwegian (2,582)	10,229	15.86
Pennsylvania German (0)	19	0.03
Polish (636)	2,849	4.42
Portuguese (21)	118	0.18
Romanian (26)	75	0.12
Russian (443)	1,071	1.66
Scandinavian (728)	1,335	2.07
Scotch-Irish (111)	583	0.90
Scottish (144)	1,275	1.98
Serbian (75)	146	0.23
Slavic (23)	78	0.12
Slovak (62)	281	0.44
Slovene (8)	39	0.06
Swedish (877)	5,297	8.21
Swiss (52)	225	0.35
Turkish (20)	80	0.12
Ukrainian (255)	399	0.62
Welsh (70)	430	0.67
West Indian, ex. Hispanic (88)	99	0.15
Jamaican (88)	99	0.15
Yugoslavian (49)	121	0.19

Hispanic Origin	Population	%
Hispanic or Latino (of any race)	2,892	4.50
Central American, ex. Mexican	237	0.37
Costa Rican	10	0.02
Guatemalan	63	0.10
Honduran	45	0.07
Nicaraguan	21	0.03
Panamanian	14	0.02
Salvadoran	83	0.13
Other Central American	1	<0.01
Cuban	46	0.07
Dominican Republic	23	0.04
Mexican	1,948	3.03
Puerto Rican	188	0.29
South American	260	0.40
Argentinean	7	0.01
Bolivian	16	0.02
Chilean	40	0.06
Colombian	90	0.14
Ecuadorian	35	0.05
Paraguayan	5	0.01
Peruvian	42	0.07
Venezuelan	25	0.04
Other Hispanic or Latino	190	0.30

Race*	Population	%
African-American/Black (3,609)	4,441	6.92
Not Hispanic (3,518)	4,267	6.65
Hispanic (91)	174	0.27
American Indian/Alaska Native (208)	623	0.97
Not Hispanic (182)	502	0.78
Hispanic (26)	121	0.19
Apache (0)	1	<0.01
Blackfeet (0)	8	0.01
Canadian/French Am. Ind. (1)	1	<0.01
Central American Ind. (0)	2	<0.01
Cherokee (4)	30	0.05
Chickasaw (0)	2	<0.01
Chippewa (62)	144	0.22
Choctaw (4)	7	0.01
Cree (1)	1	<0.01
Crow (3)	4	0.01
Delaware (0)	4	0.01
Hopi (1)	3	<0.01
Iroquois (1)	4	0.01
Lumbee (0)	2	<0.01
Menominee (2)	2	<0.01
Mexican American Ind. (4)	14	0.02
Navajo (3)	10	0.02
Potawatomi (0)	2	<0.01
Pueblo (0)	1	<0.01
Sioux (28)	56	0.09
South American Ind. (3)	3	<0.01
Spanish American Ind. (2)	2	<0.01
Tlingit-Haida *(Alaska Native)* (4)	4	0.01
Tohono O'Odham (0)	3	<0.01

*Notes: † The Census 2010 population figure is used to calculate the percentages in the Hispanic Origin and Race categories. Ancestry percentages are based on the 2006-2010 American Community Survey population (not shown); ‡ Numbers in parentheses indicate the number of people reporting a single ancestry; * Numbers in parentheses indicate the number of persons reporting this race alone, not in combination with any other race; Please refer to the Explanation of Data for more information.*

Yaqui (1)	2	<0.01
Yuman (0)	1	<0.01
Yup'ik *(Alaska Native)* (1)	2	<0.01
Asian (5,065)	5,703	8.88
Not Hispanic (5,043)	5,660	8.82
Hispanic (22)	43	0.07
Bangladeshi (52)	63	0.10
Burmese (15)	18	0.03
Cambodian (350)	404	0.63
Chinese, ex. Taiwanese (516)	629	0.98
Filipino (333)	444	0.69
Hmong (241)	255	0.40
Indian (1,662)	1,778	2.77
Indonesian (11)	14	0.02
Japanese (69)	164	0.26
Korean (327)	443	0.69
Laotian (331)	375	0.58
Malaysian (1)	5	0.01
Nepalese (45)	49	0.08
Pakistani (126)	134	0.21
Sri Lankan (23)	30	0.05
Taiwanese (23)	39	0.06
Thai (33)	50	0.08
Vietnamese (691)	783	1.22
Hawaii Native/Pacific Islander (27)	83	0.13
Not Hispanic (26)	76	0.12
Hispanic (1)	7	0.01
Guamanian/Chamorro (2)	3	<0.01
Native Hawaiian (8)	25	0.04
Samoan (4)	7	0.01
White (52,338)	54,004	84.11
Not Hispanic (50,866)	52,253	81.38
Hispanic (1,472)	1,751	2.73

East Bethel

Place Type: City
County: Anoka
Population: 11,626†

Ancestry‡	Population	%
American (816)	816	7.03
Arab (0)	13	0.11
Lebanese (0)	13	0.11
Austrian (0)	40	0.34
Belgian (36)	88	0.76
Czech (10)	317	2.73
Czechoslovakian (55)	64	0.55
Danish (21)	117	1.01
Dutch (0)	60	0.52
English (114)	486	4.19
European (335)	335	2.89
Finnish (52)	225	1.94
French, ex. Basque (22)	494	4.26
French Canadian (41)	239	2.06
German (1,173)	4,097	35.32
Greek (0)	10	0.09
Icelander (0)	11	0.09
Irish (167)	1,349	11.63
Italian (57)	178	1.53
Latvian (0)	6	0.05
Lithuanian (0)	8	0.07
Norwegian (662)	2,177	18.77
Polish (150)	1,197	10.32
Portuguese (11)	11	0.09
Romanian (0)	11	0.09
Russian (0)	85	0.73
Scandinavian (45)	100	0.86
Scotch-Irish (9)	70	0.60
Scottish (26)	158	1.36
Slavic (28)	28	0.24
Slovak (13)	37	0.32
Swedish (366)	1,430	12.33
Swiss (0)	33	0.28
Ukrainian (50)	78	0.67
Welsh (37)	66	0.57
West Indian, ex. Hispanic (0)	24	0.21
Jamaican (0)	24	0.21
Yugoslavian (0)	13	0.11

Hispanic Origin	Population	%
Hispanic or Latino (of any race)	121	1.04
Central American, ex. Mexican	14	0.12
Guatemalan	3	0.03
Honduran	3	0.03
Panamanian	8	0.07
Cuban	6	0.05
Mexican	76	0.65
Puerto Rican	8	0.07
South American	1	0.01
Peruvian	1	0.01
Other Hispanic or Latino	16	0.14

Race*	Population	%
African-American/Black (50)	94	0.81
Not Hispanic (49)	92	0.79
Hispanic (1)	2	0.02
American Indian/Alaska Native (60)	102	0.88
Not Hispanic (56)	96	0.83
Hispanic (4)	6	0.05
Apache (0)	1	0.01
Canadian/French Am. Ind. (1)	1	0.01
Cherokee (0)	1	0.01
Chippewa (37)	47	0.40
Choctaw (1)	2	0.02
Cree (0)	1	0.01
Pima (1)	1	0.01
Sioux (1)	2	0.02
Asian (183)	246	2.12
Not Hispanic (180)	241	2.07
Hispanic (3)	5	0.04
Cambodian (3)	11	0.09
Chinese, ex. Taiwanese (4)	15	0.13
Filipino (9)	15	0.13
Hmong (103)	110	0.95
Indian (9)	15	0.13
Indonesian (0)	4	0.03
Japanese (1)	12	0.10
Korean (27)	37	0.32
Laotian (2)	8	0.07
Pakistani (1)	1	0.01
Thai (3)	5	0.04
Vietnamese (9)	13	0.11
Hawaii Native/Pacific Islander (2)	15	0.13
Not Hispanic (2)	14	0.12
Hispanic (0)	1	0.01
Native Hawaiian (1)	1	0.01
Samoan (0)	1	0.01
White (11,147)	11,286	97.08
Not Hispanic (11,076)	11,200	96.34
Hispanic (71)	86	0.74

East Grand Forks

Place Type: City
County: Polk
Population: 8,601†

Ancestry‡	Population	%
American (140)	140	1.67
Belgian (21)	74	0.88
British (29)	29	0.35
Czech (64)	248	2.96
Czechoslovakian (86)	113	1.35
Danish (30)	153	1.82
Dutch (14)	191	2.28
English (94)	530	6.32
Estonian (14)	14	0.17
Finnish (15)	32	0.38
French, ex. Basque (83)	473	5.64
French Canadian (27)	109	1.30
German (878)	2,823	33.66
Greek (14)	14	0.17
Icelander (0)	20	0.24
Irish (215)	940	11.21
Italian (12)	94	1.12
Lithuanian (0)	16	0.19
Norwegian (812)	2,937	35.02
Pennsylvania German (11)	11	0.13
Polish (145)	408	4.87
Romanian (9)	9	0.11
Russian (0)	37	0.44
Scandinavian (89)	146	1.74
Scotch-Irish (72)	125	1.49
Scottish (10)	41	0.49
Slovak (17)	48	0.57
Swedish (129)	904	10.78
Welsh (0)	17	0.20

Hispanic Origin	Population	%
Hispanic or Latino (of any race)	563	6.55
Central American, ex. Mexican	11	0.13
Costa Rican	2	0.02
Guatemalan	3	0.03
Honduran	1	0.01
Nicaraguan	2	0.02
Panamanian	1	0.01
Salvadoran	2	0.02
Cuban	1	0.01
Dominican Republic	1	0.01
Mexican	416	4.84
Puerto Rican	10	0.12
South American	19	0.22
Argentinean	1	0.01
Bolivian	5	0.06
Chilean	1	0.01
Colombian	5	0.06
Ecuadorian	7	0.08
Other Hispanic or Latino	105	1.22

Race*	Population	%
African-American/Black (109)	150	1.74
Not Hispanic (103)	139	1.62
Hispanic (6)	11	0.13
American Indian/Alaska Native (154)	295	3.43
Not Hispanic (141)	259	3.01
Hispanic (13)	36	0.42
Blackfeet (1)	1	0.01
Canadian/French Am. Ind. (0)	1	0.01
Cherokee (0)	3	0.03
Chickasaw (0)	2	0.02
Chippewa (60)	109	1.27
Choctaw (3)	4	0.05
Iroquois (0)	1	0.01
Menominee (1)	1	0.01
Seminole (0)	1	0.01
Sioux (18)	29	0.34
Asian (48)	78	0.91
Not Hispanic (44)	73	0.85
Hispanic (4)	5	0.06
Chinese, ex. Taiwanese (6)	10	0.12
Filipino (8)	20	0.23
Hmong (9)	9	0.10
Indian (2)	3	0.03
Japanese (1)	8	0.09
Korean (7)	11	0.13
Laotian (5)	6	0.07
Pakistani (1)	1	0.01
Taiwanese (1)	4	0.05
Thai (2)	2	0.02
Vietnamese (1)	1	0.01
Hawaii Native/Pacific Islander (1)	8	0.09
Not Hispanic (1)	4	0.05
Hispanic (0)	4	0.05
Guamanian/Chamorro (0)	1	0.01
Samoan (1)	6	0.07
White (7,836)	8,056	93.66
Not Hispanic (7,571)	7,728	89.85
Hispanic (265)	328	3.81

Eden Prairie

Place Type: City
County: Hennepin
Population: 60,797†

Ancestry‡	Population	%
Afghan (30)	30	0.05
African, Sub-Saharan (1,772)	2,093	3.53
African (51)	75	0.13

*Notes: † The Census 2010 population figure is used to calculate the percentages in the Hispanic Origin and Race categories. Ancestry percentages are based on the 2006-2010 American Community Survey population (not shown); ‡ Numbers in parentheses indicate the number of people reporting a single ancestry; * Numbers in parentheses indicate the number of persons reporting this race alone, not in combination with any other race; Please refer to the Explanation of Data for more information.*

Ethiopian (77)	222	0.37
Kenyan (36)	47	0.08
Liberian (34)	34	0.06
Somalian (1,509)	1,636	2.76
South African (53)	67	0.11
Other Sub-Saharan African (12)	12	0.02
American (1,357)	1,357	2.29
Arab (438)	458	0.77
Arab (86)	86	0.15
Egyptian (214)	214	0.36
Lebanese (138)	158	0.27
Austrian (21)	465	0.79
Belgian (27)	204	0.34
Brazilian (12)	60	0.10
British (123)	259	0.44
Canadian (35)	72	0.12
Croatian (0)	27	0.05
Czech (211)	996	1.68
Czechoslovakian (0)	53	0.09
Danish (118)	908	1.53
Dutch (241)	964	1.63
Eastern European (83)	83	0.14
English (1,012)	4,638	7.83
Estonian (0)	32	0.05
European (633)	748	1.26
Finnish (180)	489	0.83
French, ex. Basque (193)	2,224	3.76
French Canadian (54)	393	0.66
German (5,974)	20,081	33.91
German Russian (0)	10	0.02
Greek (347)	724	1.22
Guyanese (0)	12	0.02
Hungarian (9)	84	0.14
Icelander (35)	137	0.23
Iranian (72)	87	0.15
Irish (1,366)	7,513	12.69
Italian (549)	2,091	3.53
Latvian (76)	128	0.22
Lithuanian (78)	171	0.29
Luxemburger (20)	61	0.10
Northern European (244)	244	0.41
Norwegian (2,404)	8,151	13.76
Pennsylvania German (0)	25	0.04
Polish (367)	2,160	3.65
Portuguese (9)	66	0.11
Romanian (0)	56	0.09
Russian (401)	943	1.59
Scandinavian (509)	943	1.59
Scotch-Irish (250)	820	1.38
Scottish (288)	1,119	1.89
Serbian (13)	23	0.04
Slavic (9)	139	0.23
Slovak (15)	95	0.16
Slovene (9)	36	0.06
Swedish (974)	5,463	9.23
Swiss (113)	272	0.46
Turkish (9)	33	0.06
Ukrainian (136)	233	0.39
Welsh (62)	333	0.56
West Indian, ex. Hispanic (18)	49	0.08
Bahamian (0)	12	0.02
Belizean (0)	19	0.03
Haitian (8)	8	0.01
Trinidadian/Tobagonian (10)	10	0.02
Yugoslavian (40)	56	0.09

Hispanic Origin	Population	%
Hispanic or Latino (of any race)	1,840	3.03
Central American, ex. Mexican	148	0.24
Costa Rican	18	0.03
Guatemalan	57	0.09
Honduran	22	0.04
Nicaraguan	7	0.01
Panamanian	25	0.04
Salvadoran	19	0.03
Cuban	50	0.08
Dominican Republic	18	0.03
Mexican	993	1.63
Puerto Rican	147	0.24
South American	309	0.51
Argentinean	37	0.06
Bolivian	12	0.02
Chilean	19	0.03
Colombian	92	0.15
Ecuadorian	42	0.07
Paraguayan	9	0.01
Peruvian	49	0.08
Uruguayan	3	<0.01
Venezuelan	46	0.08
Other Hispanic or Latino	175	0.29

Race*	Population	%
African-American/Black (3,398)	3,932	6.47
Not Hispanic (3,360)	3,853	6.34
Hispanic (38)	79	0.13
American Indian/Alaska Native (114)	384	0.63
Not Hispanic (94)	332	0.55
Hispanic (20)	52	0.09
Blackfeet (1)	2	<0.01
Canadian/French Am. Ind. (0)	1	<0.01
Central American Ind. (2)	2	<0.01
Cherokee (5)	32	0.05
Chickasaw (2)	2	<0.01
Chippewa (37)	96	0.16
Choctaw (0)	2	<0.01
Cree (0)	1	<0.01
Delaware (0)	1	<0.01
Hopi (0)	3	<0.01
Iroquois (2)	3	<0.01
Mexican American Ind. (7)	8	0.01
Osage (0)	3	<0.01
Sioux (7)	32	0.05
South American Ind. (4)	12	0.02
Asian (5,566)	6,167	10.14
Not Hispanic (5,551)	6,121	10.07
Hispanic (15)	46	0.08
Bangladeshi (22)	24	0.04
Burmese (3)	3	<0.01
Cambodian (194)	226	0.37
Chinese, ex. Taiwanese (1,031)	1,167	1.92
Filipino (191)	286	0.47
Hmong (45)	47	0.08
Indian (2,561)	2,688	4.42
Indonesian (23)	29	0.05
Japanese (92)	164	0.27
Korean (369)	443	0.73
Laotian (60)	91	0.15
Malaysian (10)	15	0.02
Nepalese (24)	24	0.04
Pakistani (137)	167	0.27
Sri Lankan (40)	43	0.07
Taiwanese (29)	38	0.06
Thai (14)	38	0.06
Vietnamese (516)	597	0.98
Hawaii Native/Pacific Islander (22)	63	0.10
Not Hispanic (21)	56	0.09
Hispanic (1)	7	0.01
Guamanian/Chamorro (8)	15	0.02
Native Hawaiian (4)	19	0.03
Samoan (6)	10	0.02
White (49,695)	50,893	83.71
Not Hispanic (48,654)	49,686	81.72
Hispanic (1,041)	1,207	1.99

Edina

Place Type: City
County: Hennepin
Population: 47,941†

Ancestry‡	Population	%
African, Sub-Saharan (701)	761	1.60
African (58)	107	0.23
Ethiopian (60)	60	0.13
Ghanaian (70)	70	0.15
Nigerian (19)	19	0.04
Somalian (379)	390	0.82
Sudanese (115)	115	0.24
Albanian (0)	8	0.02
American (1,108)	1,108	2.34
Arab (67)	141	0.30
Arab (0)	9	0.02
Egyptian (13)	13	0.03
Lebanese (26)	91	0.19
Syrian (7)	7	0.01
Other Arab (21)	21	0.04
Austrian (39)	194	0.41
Belgian (20)	226	0.48
Brazilian (10)	10	0.02
British (244)	410	0.86
Canadian (22)	106	0.22
Croatian (11)	116	0.24
Czech (100)	544	1.15
Czechoslovakian (29)	78	0.16
Danish (182)	1,176	2.48
Dutch (305)	834	1.76
Eastern European (212)	227	0.48
English (903)	5,164	10.88
European (657)	744	1.57
Finnish (167)	642	1.35
French, ex. Basque (229)	1,669	3.52
French Canadian (84)	268	0.56
German (3,831)	13,838	29.17
Greek (311)	521	1.10
Hungarian (58)	124	0.26
Icelander (0)	50	0.11
Iranian (54)	63	0.13
Irish (1,479)	7,387	15.57
Israeli (0)	15	0.03
Italian (405)	1,542	3.25
Latvian (46)	317	0.67
Lithuanian (46)	160	0.34
Luxemburger (17)	25	0.05
Macedonian (15)	58	0.12
Maltese (0)	9	0.02
Northern European (142)	178	0.38
Norwegian (2,215)	7,074	14.91
Pennsylvania German (0)	16	0.03
Polish (420)	1,783	3.76
Portuguese (12)	35	0.07
Romanian (55)	203	0.43
Russian (336)	896	1.89
Scandinavian (643)	1,110	2.34
Scotch-Irish (204)	895	1.89
Scottish (208)	1,697	3.58
Serbian (0)	62	0.13
Slavic (0)	44	0.09
Slovak (40)	200	0.42
Slovene (16)	95	0.20
Swedish (1,409)	5,740	12.10
Swiss (16)	381	0.80
Ukrainian (90)	213	0.45
Welsh (87)	554	1.17
West Indian, ex. Hispanic (9)	9	0.02
Trinidadian/Tobagonian (9)	9	0.02
Yugoslavian (299)	485	1.02

Hispanic Origin	Population	%
Hispanic or Latino (of any race)	1,101	2.30
Central American, ex. Mexican	89	0.19
Costa Rican	7	0.01
Guatemalan	48	0.10
Honduran	1	<0.01
Nicaraguan	6	0.01
Panamanian	12	0.03
Salvadoran	14	0.03
Other Central American	1	<0.01
Cuban	52	0.11
Dominican Republic	4	0.01
Mexican	505	1.05
Puerto Rican	79	0.16
South American	219	0.46
Argentinean	28	0.06
Bolivian	7	0.01
Chilean	14	0.03
Colombian	91	0.19
Ecuadorian	36	0.08
Paraguayan	4	0.01
Peruvian	19	0.04
Uruguayan	5	0.01

*Notes: † The Census 2010 population figure is used to calculate the percentages in the Hispanic Origin and Race categories. Ancestry percentages are based on the 2006-2010 American Community Survey population (not shown); ‡ Numbers in parentheses indicate the number of people reporting a single ancestry; * Numbers in parentheses indicate the number of persons reporting this race alone, not in combination with any other race; Please refer to the Explanation of Data for more information.*

Venezuelan	11	0.02
Other South American	4	0.01
Other Hispanic or Latino	153	0.32

Race*	Population	%
African-American/Black (1,446)	1,737	3.62
Not Hispanic (1,424)	1,688	3.52
Hispanic (22)	49	0.10
American Indian/Alaska Native (94)	267	0.56
Not Hispanic (78)	222	0.46
Hispanic (16)	45	0.09
Apache (2)	2	<0.01
Blackfeet (2)	5	0.01
Canadian/French Am. Ind. (0)	1	<0.01
Central American Ind. (1)	1	<0.01
Cherokee (4)	14	0.03
Cheyenne (0)	1	<0.01
Chippewa (24)	59	0.12
Choctaw (1)	2	<0.01
Comanche (0)	1	<0.01
Creek (0)	4	0.01
Iroquois (2)	4	0.01
Mexican American Ind. (3)	3	0.01
Navajo (2)	3	0.01
Potawatomi (0)	2	<0.01
Seminole (0)	1	<0.01
Sioux (11)	25	0.05
South American Ind. (1)	3	0.01
Spanish American Ind. (0)	4	0.01
Asian (2,936)	3,391	7.07
Not Hispanic (2,914)	3,350	6.99
Hispanic (22)	41	0.09
Bangladeshi (12)	18	0.04
Bhutanese (8)	8	0.02
Burmese (1)	1	<0.01
Cambodian (19)	25	0.05
Chinese, ex. Taiwanese (625)	732	1.53
Filipino (86)	136	0.28
Hmong (16)	16	0.03
Indian (1,533)	1,615	3.37
Indonesian (7)	12	0.03
Japanese (84)	134	0.28
Korean (283)	370	0.77
Laotian (9)	13	0.03
Malaysian (3)	3	0.01
Nepalese (20)	20	0.04
Pakistani (43)	47	0.10
Sri Lankan (14)	16	0.03
Taiwanese (20)	31	0.06
Thai (27)	28	0.06
Vietnamese (84)	102	0.21
Hawaii Native/Pacific Islander (16)	36	0.08
Not Hispanic (16)	34	0.07
Hispanic (0)	2	<0.01
Native Hawaiian (10)	11	0.02
Tongan (0)	4	0.01
White (42,237)	43,013	89.72
Not Hispanic (41,535)	42,240	88.11
Hispanic (702)	773	1.61

Elk River

Place Type: City
County: Sherburne
Population: 22,974†

Ancestry‡	Population	%
African, Sub-Saharan (0)	28	0.12
South African (0)	28	0.12
American (501)	501	2.23
Austrian (70)	175	0.78
Belgian (0)	11	0.05
Brazilian (0)	5	0.02
British (12)	82	0.36
Canadian (9)	9	0.04
Croatian (13)	13	0.06
Czech (95)	350	1.55
Czechoslovakian (0)	49	0.22
Danish (46)	328	1.46
Dutch (102)	502	2.23
English (642)	1,792	7.96
European (221)	259	1.15
Finnish (169)	382	1.70
French, ex. Basque (169)	1,070	4.75
French Canadian (60)	319	1.42
German (2,996)	9,351	41.53
Greek (0)	9	0.04
Hungarian (26)	83	0.37
Irish (369)	2,657	11.80
Italian (151)	614	2.73
Lithuanian (0)	42	0.19
Norwegian (1,312)	3,721	16.53
Polish (264)	1,421	6.31
Romanian (0)	10	0.04
Russian (211)	308	1.37
Scandinavian (429)	679	3.02
Scotch-Irish (39)	129	0.57
Scottish (44)	311	1.38
Serbian (13)	13	0.06
Slovak (9)	32	0.14
Slovene (21)	59	0.26
Swedish (473)	2,741	12.17
Swiss (0)	203	0.90
Turkish (0)	19	0.08
Ukrainian (183)	202	0.90
Welsh (12)	87	0.39
Yugoslavian (13)	44	0.20

Hispanic Origin	Population	%
Hispanic or Latino (of any race)	718	3.13
Central American, ex. Mexican	45	0.20
Guatemalan	26	0.11
Honduran	12	0.05
Nicaraguan	4	0.02
Panamanian	2	0.01
Salvadoran	1	<0.01
Cuban	7	0.03
Dominican Republic	12	0.05
Mexican	502	2.19
Puerto Rican	51	0.22
South American	45	0.20
Argentinean	1	<0.01
Chilean	1	<0.01
Colombian	14	0.06
Paraguayan	10	0.04
Peruvian	13	0.06
Venezuelan	6	0.03
Other Hispanic or Latino	56	0.24

Race*	Population	%
African-American/Black (444)	612	2.66
Not Hispanic (417)	576	2.51
Hispanic (27)	36	0.16
American Indian/Alaska Native (94)	245	1.07
Not Hispanic (90)	240	1.04
Hispanic (4)	5	0.02
Aleut *(Alaska Native)* (1)	1	<0.01
Apache (1)	1	<0.01
Blackfeet (0)	6	0.03
Canadian/French Am. Ind. (0)	1	<0.01
Cherokee (4)	10	0.04
Chippewa (31)	78	0.34
Choctaw (1)	8	0.03
Creek (0)	1	<0.01
Iroquois (0)	4	0.02
Mexican American Ind. (2)	2	0.01
Potawatomi (4)	9	0.04
Seminole (0)	1	<0.01
Sioux (1)	8	0.03
Yup'ik *(Alaska Native)* (3)	3	0.01
Asian (383)	503	2.19
Not Hispanic (382)	493	2.15
Hispanic (1)	10	0.04
Bangladeshi (4)	4	0.02
Cambodian (2)	7	0.03
Chinese, ex. Taiwanese (31)	38	0.17
Filipino (39)	81	0.35
Hmong (45)	45	0.20
Indian (53)	62	0.27
Indonesian (1)	1	<0.01
Japanese (11)	22	0.10
Korean (45)	78	0.34
Laotian (45)	61	0.27
Nepalese (1)	2	0.01
Pakistani (22)	23	0.10
Thai (15)	24	0.10
Vietnamese (6)	16	0.07
Hawaii Native/Pacific Islander (7)	21	0.09
Not Hispanic (7)	18	0.08
Hispanic (0)	3	0.01
Guamanian/Chamorro (0)	3	0.01
Native Hawaiian (0)	3	0.01
Samoan (1)	1	<0.01
White (21,451)	21,867	95.18
Not Hispanic (20,950)	21,315	92.78
Hispanic (501)	552	2.40

Fairmont

Place Type: City
County: Martin
Population: 10,666†

Ancestry‡	Population	%
American (328)	328	3.09
Austrian (0)	16	0.15
Belgian (0)	12	0.11
Canadian (0)	29	0.27
Czech (0)	29	0.27
Czechoslovakian (0)	9	0.08
Danish (174)	421	3.96
Dutch (91)	256	2.41
English (173)	552	5.19
European (139)	139	1.31
Finnish (12)	87	0.82
French, ex. Basque (11)	294	2.77
French Canadian (69)	79	0.74
German (2,704)	5,847	55.01
Iranian (0)	96	0.90
Irish (111)	1,095	10.30
Italian (27)	197	1.85
Northern European (12)	12	0.11
Norwegian (654)	1,715	16.14
Polish (106)	613	5.77
Portuguese (15)	15	0.14
Russian (22)	49	0.46
Scotch-Irish (11)	53	0.50
Scottish (0)	19	0.18
Slavic (0)	14	0.13
Swedish (68)	665	6.26
Swiss (0)	13	0.12
Ukrainian (0)	41	0.39
Welsh (14)	83	0.78
West Indian, ex. Hispanic (0)	11	0.10
Bahamian (0)	11	0.10
Yugoslavian (0)	37	0.35

Hispanic Origin	Population	%
Hispanic or Latino (of any race)	564	5.29
Central American, ex. Mexican	63	0.59
Costa Rican	1	0.01
Guatemalan	54	0.51
Honduran	4	0.04
Nicaraguan	1	0.01
Salvadoran	3	0.03
Cuban	11	0.10
Dominican Republic	2	0.02
Mexican	411	3.85
Puerto Rican	18	0.17
South American	6	0.06
Argentinean	1	0.01
Chilean	4	0.04
Peruvian	1	0.01
Other Hispanic or Latino	53	0.50

Race*	Population	%
African-American/Black (49)	78	0.73
Not Hispanic (47)	68	0.64
Hispanic (2)	10	0.09
American Indian/Alaska Native (27)	43	0.40

*Notes: † The Census 2010 population figure is used to calculate the percentages in the Hispanic Origin and Race categories. Ancestry percentages are based on the 2006-2010 American Community Survey population (not shown); ‡ Numbers in parentheses indicate the number of people reporting a single ancestry; * Numbers in parentheses indicate the number of persons reporting this race alone, not in combination with any other race; Please refer to the Explanation of Data for more information.*

Not Hispanic (23)	35	0.33
Hispanic (4)	8	0.08
Cherokee (0)	4	0.04
Chippewa (3)	8	0.08
Navajo (3)	3	0.03
Sioux (3)	3	0.03
Asian (71)	95	0.89
Not Hispanic (71)	88	0.83
Hispanic (0)	7	0.07
Bangladeshi (3)	3	0.03
Cambodian (0)	2	0.02
Chinese, ex. Taiwanese (13)	14	0.13
Filipino (7)	7	0.07
Hmong (12)	12	0.11
Indian (11)	12	0.11
Indonesian (1)	1	0.01
Japanese (2)	12	0.11
Korean (4)	11	0.10
Laotian (4)	6	0.06
Vietnamese (12)	16	0.15
Hawaii Native/Pacific Islander (5)	7	0.07
Not Hispanic (4)	5	0.05
Hispanic (1)	2	0.02
Guamanian/Chamorro (1)	2	0.02
Native Hawaiian (3)	3	0.03
White (10,200)	10,307	96.63
Not Hispanic (9,908)	9,957	93.35
Hispanic (292)	350	3.28

Faribault

Place Type: City
County: Rice
Population: 23,352†

Ancestry‡	Population	%
African, Sub-Saharan (456)	482	2.09
African (17)	43	0.19
Kenyan (39)	39	0.17
Somalian (400)	400	1.74
American (838)	838	3.64
Arab (9)	9	0.04
Moroccan (9)	9	0.04
Austrian (0)	20	0.09
Belgian (0)	100	0.43
British (14)	14	0.06
Croatian (0)	31	0.13
Czech (304)	765	3.32
Czechoslovakian (7)	60	0.26
Danish (69)	443	1.92
Dutch (110)	505	2.19
English (337)	1,069	4.64
European (104)	114	0.49
Finnish (39)	421	1.83
French, ex. Basque (130)	1,207	5.24
French Canadian (101)	195	0.85
German (2,756)	7,972	34.61
Greek (10)	26	0.11
Hungarian (0)	26	0.11
Iranian (9)	9	0.04
Irish (292)	2,786	12.10
Italian (136)	223	0.97
Northern European (14)	14	0.06
Norwegian (760)	3,257	14.14
Polish (70)	551	2.39
Russian (21)	198	0.86
Scandinavian (70)	144	0.63
Scotch-Irish (45)	94	0.41
Scottish (46)	219	0.95
Slovak (0)	24	0.10
Swedish (182)	908	3.94
Swiss (7)	106	0.46
Welsh (0)	65	0.28
West Indian, ex. Hispanic (12)	12	0.05
West Indian (12)	12	0.05

Hispanic Origin	Population	%
Hispanic or Latino (of any race)	3,026	12.96
Central American, ex. Mexican	219	0.94
Costa Rican	1	<0.01
Guatemalan	118	0.51
Honduran	14	0.06
Nicaraguan	10	0.04
Salvadoran	70	0.30
Other Central American	6	0.03
Cuban	13	0.06
Dominican Republic	1	<0.01
Mexican	2,599	11.13
Puerto Rican	50	0.21
South American	31	0.13
Argentinean	1	<0.01
Bolivian	1	<0.01
Chilean	9	0.04
Colombian	12	0.05
Paraguayan	1	<0.01
Peruvian	6	0.03
Venezuelan	1	<0.01
Other Hispanic or Latino	113	0.48

Race*	Population	%
African-American/Black (1,764)	1,935	8.29
Not Hispanic (1,723)	1,861	7.97
Hispanic (41)	74	0.32
American Indian/Alaska Native (216)	319	1.37
Not Hispanic (188)	279	1.19
Hispanic (28)	40	0.17
Alaska Athabascan *(Ala. Nat.)* (0)	1	<0.01
Aleut *(Alaska Native)* (1)	2	0.01
Apache (0)	1	<0.01
Blackfeet (1)	2	0.01
Cherokee (0)	10	0.04
Chippewa (22)	40	0.17
Choctaw (2)	2	0.01
Colville (3)	3	0.01
Iroquois (3)	3	0.01
Mexican American Ind. (2)	2	0.01
Sioux (13)	32	0.14
South American Ind. (0)	1	<0.01
Ute (0)	3	0.01
Asian (494)	595	2.55
Not Hispanic (484)	574	2.46
Hispanic (10)	21	0.09
Burmese (4)	4	0.02
Cambodian (138)	172	0.74
Chinese, ex. Taiwanese (72)	101	0.43
Filipino (16)	35	0.15
Hmong (11)	15	0.06
Indian (16)	25	0.11
Japanese (6)	17	0.07
Korean (61)	77	0.33
Laotian (3)	12	0.05
Nepalese (0)	1	<0.01
Pakistani (1)	1	<0.01
Taiwanese (0)	16	0.07
Thai (3)	9	0.04
Vietnamese (54)	57	0.24
Hawaii Native/Pacific Islander (14)	32	0.14
Not Hispanic (14)	28	0.12
Hispanic (0)	4	0.02
Guamanian/Chamorro (6)	6	0.03
Native Hawaiian (3)	11	0.05
Samoan (4)	6	0.03
White (19,296)	19,806	84.82
Not Hispanic (17,590)	17,874	76.54
Hispanic (1,706)	1,932	8.27

Farmington

Place Type: City
County: Dakota
Population: 21,086†

Ancestry‡	Population	%
African, Sub-Saharan (11)	18	0.09
African (11)	18	0.09
American (548)	548	2.79
Arab (0)	37	0.19
Lebanese (0)	11	0.06
Palestinian (0)	13	0.07
Other Arab (0)	13	0.07
Armenian (0)	8	0.04
Austrian (13)	93	0.47
Belgian (0)	12	0.06
British (0)	32	0.16
Canadian (12)	12	0.06
Carpatho Rusyn (0)	13	0.07
Croatian (14)	62	0.32
Czech (48)	316	1.61
Czechoslovakian (30)	40	0.20
Danish (76)	440	2.24
Dutch (73)	379	1.93
Eastern European (0)	7	0.04
English (263)	1,357	6.90
European (206)	252	1.28
Finnish (40)	248	1.26
French, ex. Basque (55)	690	3.51
French Canadian (54)	177	0.90
German (1,955)	7,948	40.43
Greek (34)	104	0.53
Hungarian (33)	43	0.22
Irish (402)	3,204	16.30
Italian (229)	612	3.11
Lithuanian (0)	34	0.17
Luxemburger (0)	13	0.07
Northern European (8)	20	0.10
Norwegian (702)	3,246	16.51
Pennsylvania German (12)	12	0.06
Polish (49)	696	3.54
Portuguese (0)	19	0.10
Russian (102)	195	0.99
Scandinavian (217)	253	1.29
Scotch-Irish (57)	190	0.97
Scottish (24)	310	1.58
Slovak (0)	48	0.24
Slovene (0)	34	0.17
Swedish (294)	1,838	9.35
Swiss (23)	23	0.12
Ukrainian (10)	10	0.05
Welsh (14)	177	0.90
West Indian, ex. Hispanic (16)	33	0.17
West Indian (16)	33	0.17

Hispanic Origin	Population	%
Hispanic or Latino (of any race)	767	3.64
Central American, ex. Mexican	70	0.33
Costa Rican	1	<0.01
Guatemalan	19	0.09
Honduran	17	0.08
Nicaraguan	3	0.01
Salvadoran	30	0.14
Cuban	12	0.06
Dominican Republic	16	0.08
Mexican	467	2.21
Puerto Rican	83	0.39
South American	61	0.29
Argentinean	8	0.04
Bolivian	3	0.01
Chilean	3	0.01
Colombian	23	0.11
Ecuadorian	5	0.02
Paraguayan	1	<0.01
Peruvian	9	0.04
Venezuelan	1	<0.01
Other South American	8	0.04
Other Hispanic or Latino	58	0.28

Race*	Population	%
African-American/Black (451)	661	3.13
Not Hispanic (420)	606	2.87
Hispanic (31)	55	0.26
American Indian/Alaska Native (108)	265	1.26
Not Hispanic (79)	195	0.92
Hispanic (29)	70	0.33
Alaska Athabascan *(Ala. Nat.)* (2)	2	0.01
Arapaho (0)	2	0.01
Central American Ind. (1)	1	<0.01
Cherokee (1)	19	0.09
Chippewa (25)	52	0.25
Comanche (1)	1	<0.01
Creek (1)	1	<0.01

*Notes: † The Census 2010 population figure is used to calculate the percentages in the Hispanic Origin and Race categories. Ancestry percentages are based on the 2006-2010 American Community Survey population (not shown); ‡ Numbers in parentheses indicate the number of people reporting a single ancestry; * Numbers in parentheses indicate the number of persons reporting this race alone, not in combination with any other race; Please refer to the Explanation of Data for more information.*

Iroquois (1)	2	0.01
Mexican American Ind. (0)	9	0.04
Navajo (0)	3	0.01
Potawatomi (3)	7	0.03
Sioux (18)	32	0.15
South American Ind. (1)	1	<0.01
Asian (749)	977	4.63
Not Hispanic (744)	956	4.53
Hispanic (5)	21	0.10
Bangladeshi (17)	21	0.10
Cambodian (82)	102	0.48
Chinese, ex. Taiwanese (62)	80	0.38
Filipino (103)	148	0.70
Hmong (57)	66	0.31
Indian (98)	131	0.62
Indonesian (1)	3	0.01
Japanese (5)	35	0.17
Korean (61)	107	0.51
Laotian (81)	89	0.42
Nepalese (5)	6	0.03
Pakistani (8)	8	0.04
Taiwanese (6)	11	0.05
Thai (11)	21	0.10
Vietnamese (110)	140	0.66
Hawaii Native/Pacific Islander (15)	33	0.16
Not Hispanic (14)	29	0.14
Hispanic (1)	4	0.02
Native Hawaiian (11)	15	0.07
Samoan (0)	2	0.01
White (18,935)	19,467	92.32
Not Hispanic (18,560)	18,990	90.06
Hispanic (375)	477	2.26

Fergus Falls

Place Type: City
County: Otter Tail
Population: 13,138†

Ancestry‡	Population	%
African, Sub-Saharan (8)	16	0.12
Nigerian (8)	16	0.12
American (589)	589	4.41
Belgian (8)	20	0.15
British (14)	14	0.10
Canadian (13)	13	0.10
Czech (15)	118	0.88
Danish (22)	302	2.26
Dutch (34)	70	0.52
English (342)	1,050	7.86
European (73)	73	0.55
Finnish (105)	224	1.68
French, ex. Basque (19)	369	2.76
French Canadian (12)	88	0.66
German (1,652)	5,864	43.92
Greek (11)	28	0.21
Icelander (0)	55	0.41
Irish (77)	872	6.53
Italian (0)	61	0.46
Luxemburger (0)	13	0.10
Norwegian (2,208)	5,327	39.89
Polish (59)	478	3.58
Portuguese (0)	24	0.18
Russian (14)	74	0.55
Scandinavian (176)	219	1.64
Scotch-Irish (28)	231	1.73
Scottish (7)	152	1.14
Slovak (8)	8	0.06
Swedish (361)	1,192	8.93
Swiss (0)	22	0.16
Ukrainian (22)	22	0.16
Welsh (14)	14	0.10
Yugoslavian (0)	5	0.04

Hispanic Origin	Population	%
Hispanic or Latino (of any race)	205	1.56
Central American, ex. Mexican	3	0.02
Guatemalan	3	0.02
Cuban	2	0.02
Mexican	141	1.07
Puerto Rican	24	0.18
South American	16	0.12
Colombian	11	0.08
Peruvian	2	0.02
Venezuelan	3	0.02
Other Hispanic or Latino	19	0.14

Race*	Population	%
African-American/Black (147)	197	1.50
Not Hispanic (145)	193	1.47
Hispanic (2)	4	0.03
American Indian/Alaska Native (106)	188	1.43
Not Hispanic (102)	181	1.38
Hispanic (4)	7	0.05
Alaska Athabascan *(Ala. Nat.)* (1)	1	0.01
Canadian/French Am. Ind. (1)	1	0.01
Cherokee (3)	6	0.05
Chippewa (45)	64	0.49
Choctaw (2)	2	0.02
Cree (0)	2	0.02
Inupiat *(Alaska Native)* (1)	3	0.02
Mexican American Ind. (1)	1	0.01
Sioux (11)	16	0.12
South American Ind. (0)	1	0.01
Yup'ik *(Alaska Native)* (1)	1	0.01
Asian (87)	146	1.11
Not Hispanic (87)	144	1.10
Hispanic (0)	2	0.02
Chinese, ex. Taiwanese (27)	33	0.25
Filipino (10)	23	0.18
Hmong (1)	1	0.01
Indian (8)	11	0.08
Japanese (6)	17	0.13
Korean (14)	25	0.19
Laotian (1)	9	0.07
Pakistani (1)	2	0.02
Taiwanese (3)	3	0.02
Thai (6)	6	0.05
Vietnamese (7)	9	0.07
Hawaii Native/Pacific Islander (2)	8	0.06
Not Hispanic (2)	8	0.06
Guamanian/Chamorro (0)	2	0.02
Native Hawaiian (1)	1	0.01
Samoan (1)	5	0.04
White (12,544)	12,742	96.99
Not Hispanic (12,407)	12,591	95.84
Hispanic (137)	151	1.15

Forest Lake

Place Type: City
County: Washington
Population: 18,375†

Ancestry‡	Population	%
African, Sub-Saharan (11)	11	0.06
African (11)	11	0.06
American (671)	671	3.78
Austrian (41)	204	1.15
Brazilian (41)	41	0.23
British (64)	64	0.36
Canadian (50)	50	0.28
Croatian (12)	30	0.17
Czech (79)	298	1.68
Czechoslovakian (0)	46	0.26
Danish (55)	356	2.01
Dutch (118)	464	2.61
English (263)	1,000	5.63
European (80)	111	0.63
Finnish (26)	227	1.28
French, ex. Basque (171)	1,201	6.77
French Canadian (154)	409	2.30
German (1,888)	7,376	41.56
Greek (22)	33	0.19
Hungarian (72)	110	0.62
Irish (349)	2,622	14.77
Italian (103)	438	2.47
Latvian (23)	23	0.13
Macedonian (0)	11	0.06
Norwegian (846)	2,647	14.92
Polish (227)	810	4.56
Russian (17)	94	0.53
Scandinavian (117)	218	1.23
Scotch-Irish (82)	175	0.99
Scottish (31)	143	0.81
Serbian (0)	35	0.20
Slavic (44)	55	0.31
Slovak (0)	20	0.11
Swedish (523)	2,479	13.97
Swiss (0)	159	0.90
Welsh (0)	69	0.39
West Indian, ex. Hispanic (29)	29	0.16
West Indian (29)	29	0.16
Yugoslavian (8)	8	0.05

Hispanic Origin	Population	%
Hispanic or Latino (of any race)	430	2.34
Central American, ex. Mexican	43	0.23
Costa Rican	2	0.01
Guatemalan	11	0.06
Honduran	6	0.03
Nicaraguan	5	0.03
Panamanian	2	0.01
Salvadoran	11	0.06
Other Central American	6	0.03
Cuban	8	0.04
Dominican Republic	6	0.03
Mexican	287	1.56
Puerto Rican	26	0.14
South American	22	0.12
Argentinean	1	0.01
Bolivian	2	0.01
Chilean	1	0.01
Colombian	5	0.03
Ecuadorian	1	0.01
Paraguayan	3	0.02
Peruvian	6	0.03
Venezuelan	3	0.02
Other Hispanic or Latino	38	0.21

Race*	Population	%
African-American/Black (195)	322	1.75
Not Hispanic (193)	304	1.65
Hispanic (2)	18	0.10
American Indian/Alaska Native (73)	184	1.00
Not Hispanic (66)	170	0.93
Hispanic (7)	14	0.08
Alaska Athabascan *(Ala. Nat.)* (1)	1	0.01
Apache (1)	2	0.01
Blackfeet (3)	4	0.02
Canadian/French Am. Ind. (1)	1	0.01
Cherokee (0)	7	0.04
Chickasaw (0)	1	0.01
Chippewa (19)	47	0.26
Choctaw (0)	1	0.01
Creek (0)	1	0.01
Iroquois (0)	1	0.01
Menominee (0)	1	0.01
Navajo (2)	2	0.01
Osage (1)	1	0.01
Pueblo (2)	2	0.01
Sioux (9)	22	0.12
Asian (269)	350	1.90
Not Hispanic (267)	348	1.89
Hispanic (2)	2	0.01
Cambodian (6)	12	0.07
Chinese, ex. Taiwanese (28)	40	0.22
Filipino (11)	22	0.12
Hmong (109)	116	0.63
Indian (21)	30	0.16
Japanese (4)	21	0.11
Korean (43)	59	0.32
Laotian (6)	11	0.06
Malaysian (2)	2	0.01
Pakistani (2)	2	0.01
Sri Lankan (0)	2	0.01
Thai (3)	8	0.04
Vietnamese (14)	22	0.12
Hawaii Native/Pacific Islander (10)	24	0.13
Not Hispanic (10)	22	0.12

*Notes: † The Census 2010 population figure is used to calculate the percentages in the Hispanic Origin and Race categories. Ancestry percentages are based on the 2006-2010 American Community Survey population (not shown); ‡ Numbers in parentheses indicate the number of people reporting a single ancestry; * Numbers in parentheses indicate the number of persons reporting this race alone, not in combination with any other race; Please refer to the Explanation of Data for more information.*

Hispanic (0)	2	0.01
Native Hawaiian (6)	12	0.07
Tongan (4)	4	0.02
White (17,394)	17,686	96.25
Not Hispanic (17,114)	17,388	94.63
Hispanic (280)	298	1.62

Fridley

Place Type: City
County: Anoka
Population: 27,208†

Ancestry‡	Population	%
African, Sub-Saharan (1,179)	1,210	4.41
African (531)	562	2.05
Ethiopian (102)	102	0.37
Kenyan (5)	5	0.02
Somalian (541)	541	1.97
American (751)	751	2.73
Arab (378)	439	1.60
Arab (326)	326	1.19
Egyptian (43)	52	0.19
Lebanese (9)	61	0.22
Austrian (10)	99	0.36
Belgian (0)	14	0.05
British (20)	76	0.28
Canadian (0)	33	0.12
Croatian (0)	24	0.09
Czech (193)	596	2.17
Czechoslovakian (23)	32	0.12
Danish (12)	326	1.19
Dutch (117)	431	1.57
Eastern European (7)	7	0.03
English (427)	1,662	6.05
European (256)	321	1.17
Finnish (90)	300	1.09
French, ex. Basque (123)	1,067	3.88
French Canadian (103)	519	1.89
German (2,519)	8,273	30.12
Greek (0)	26	0.09
Guyanese (110)	151	0.55
Hungarian (14)	208	0.76
Icelander (5)	5	0.02
Iranian (17)	17	0.06
Irish (481)	2,796	10.18
Italian (229)	619	2.25
Lithuanian (0)	7	0.03
Northern European (32)	32	0.12
Norwegian (913)	3,536	12.87
Pennsylvania German (0)	10	0.04
Polish (689)	2,419	8.81
Russian (24)	149	0.54
Scandinavian (398)	619	2.25
Scotch-Irish (41)	295	1.07
Scottish (51)	251	0.91
Serbian (0)	44	0.16
Slavic (0)	12	0.04
Slovak (14)	90	0.33
Slovene (31)	62	0.23
Swedish (530)	2,472	9.00
Swiss (0)	45	0.16
Ukrainian (259)	270	0.98
Welsh (0)	53	0.19
West Indian, ex. Hispanic (0)	35	0.13
Trinidadian/Tobagonian (0)	35	0.13
Yugoslavian (276)	289	1.05

Hispanic Origin	Population	%
Hispanic or Latino (of any race)	1,976	7.26
Central American, ex. Mexican	189	0.69
Costa Rican	7	0.03
Guatemalan	67	0.25
Honduran	35	0.13
Nicaraguan	7	0.03
Panamanian	3	0.01
Salvadoran	70	0.26
Cuban	18	0.07
Dominican Republic	21	0.08
Mexican	1,397	5.13
Puerto Rican	68	0.25
South American	139	0.51
Argentinean	8	0.03
Bolivian	5	0.02
Chilean	15	0.06
Colombian	20	0.07
Ecuadorian	73	0.27
Peruvian	14	0.05
Uruguayan	1	<0.01
Venezuelan	3	0.01
Other Hispanic or Latino	144	0.53

Race*	Population	%
African-American/Black (3,015)	3,663	13.46
Not Hispanic (2,968)	3,568	13.11
Hispanic (47)	95	0.35
American Indian/Alaska Native (321)	655	2.41
Not Hispanic (264)	558	2.05
Hispanic (57)	97	0.36
Alaska Athabascan *(Ala. Nat.)* (1)	1	<0.01
Apache (2)	2	0.01
Blackfeet (4)	14	0.05
Canadian/French Am. Ind. (1)	3	0.01
Cherokee (5)	30	0.11
Chippewa (157)	230	0.85
Choctaw (1)	4	0.01
Cree (0)	4	0.01
Delaware (3)	3	0.01
Iroquois (0)	2	0.01
Lumbee (0)	1	<0.01
Mexican American Ind. (8)	10	0.04
Navajo (2)	3	0.01
Osage (1)	1	<0.01
Seminole (0)	8	0.03
Sioux (16)	41	0.15
South American Ind. (0)	6	0.02
Tlingit-Haida *(Alaska Native)* (0)	1	<0.01
Asian (1,344)	1,577	5.80
Not Hispanic (1,324)	1,543	5.67
Hispanic (20)	34	0.12
Bangladeshi (1)	2	0.01
Cambodian (13)	15	0.06
Chinese, ex. Taiwanese (201)	262	0.96
Filipino (71)	115	0.42
Hmong (390)	419	1.54
Indian (257)	303	1.11
Indonesian (1)	3	0.01
Japanese (24)	44	0.16
Korean (82)	123	0.45
Laotian (28)	38	0.14
Malaysian (0)	1	<0.01
Pakistani (37)	41	0.15
Sri Lankan (0)	3	0.01
Taiwanese (2)	2	0.01
Thai (10)	14	0.05
Vietnamese (156)	178	0.65
Hawaii Native/Pacific Islander (14)	34	0.12
Not Hispanic (11)	29	0.11
Hispanic (3)	5	0.02
Guamanian/Chamorro (7)	7	0.03
Native Hawaiian (2)	7	0.03
Samoan (4)	4	0.01
Tongan (0)	1	<0.01
White (20,457)	21,449	78.83
Not Hispanic (19,620)	20,475	75.25
Hispanic (837)	974	3.58

Golden Valley

Place Type: City
County: Hennepin
Population: 20,371†

Ancestry‡	Population	%
African, Sub-Saharan (317)	342	1.69
African (175)	175	0.87
Liberian (90)	115	0.57
Sierra Leonean (24)	24	0.12
South African (20)	20	0.10
Other Sub-Saharan African (8)	8	0.04
American (327)	327	1.62
Arab (8)	61	0.30
Iraqi (0)	11	0.05
Lebanese (0)	25	0.12
Moroccan (8)	25	0.12
Austrian (0)	106	0.53
Belgian (0)	25	0.12
British (52)	106	0.53
Canadian (49)	112	0.55
Croatian (11)	30	0.15
Czech (145)	313	1.55
Czechoslovakian (0)	32	0.16
Danish (26)	308	1.53
Dutch (64)	230	1.14
Eastern European (155)	155	0.77
English (365)	1,573	7.79
European (371)	457	2.26
Finnish (90)	264	1.31
French, ex. Basque (176)	776	3.84
French Canadian (13)	100	0.50
German (2,203)	6,220	30.82
Greek (0)	57	0.28
Hungarian (96)	182	0.90
Icelander (0)	61	0.30
Iranian (22)	22	0.11
Irish (465)	2,218	10.99
Israeli (29)	41	0.20
Italian (101)	383	1.90
Latvian (24)	66	0.33
Lithuanian (10)	30	0.15
Luxemburger (0)	10	0.05
Northern European (156)	156	0.77
Norwegian (819)	2,949	14.61
Pennsylvania German (15)	23	0.11
Polish (287)	938	4.65
Portuguese (13)	13	0.06
Romanian (26)	191	0.95
Russian (254)	640	3.17
Scandinavian (224)	288	1.43
Scotch-Irish (32)	264	1.31
Scottish (34)	500	2.48
Serbian (0)	16	0.08
Slovak (24)	55	0.27
Slovene (0)	24	0.12
Swedish (682)	2,054	10.18
Swiss (33)	50	0.25
Ukrainian (74)	182	0.90
Welsh (8)	78	0.39
West Indian, ex. Hispanic (44)	60	0.30
Haitian (15)	15	0.07
Jamaican (29)	45	0.22
Yugoslavian (10)	10	0.05

Hispanic Origin	Population	%
Hispanic or Latino (of any race)	538	2.64
Central American, ex. Mexican	66	0.32
Costa Rican	3	0.01
Guatemalan	32	0.16
Honduran	6	0.03
Nicaraguan	7	0.03
Panamanian	2	0.01
Salvadoran	16	0.08
Cuban	15	0.07
Dominican Republic	6	0.03
Mexican	246	1.21
Puerto Rican	38	0.19
South American	105	0.52
Argentinean	13	0.06
Bolivian	4	0.02
Chilean	9	0.04
Colombian	37	0.18
Ecuadorian	13	0.06
Paraguayan	4	0.02
Peruvian	20	0.10
Uruguayan	1	<0.01
Venezuelan	3	0.01
Other South American	1	<0.01
Other Hispanic or Latino	62	0.30

*Notes: † The Census 2010 population figure is used to calculate the percentages in the Hispanic Origin and Race categories. Ancestry percentages are based on the 2006-2010 American Community Survey population (not shown); ‡ Numbers in parentheses indicate the number of people reporting a single ancestry; * Numbers in parentheses indicate the number of persons reporting this race alone, not in combination with any other race; Please refer to the Explanation of Data for more information.*

Race*	Population	%
African-American/Black (1,441)	1,724	8.46
Not Hispanic (1,412)	1,676	8.23
Hispanic (29)	48	0.24
American Indian/Alaska Native (85)	205	1.01
Not Hispanic (72)	179	0.88
Hispanic (13)	26	0.13
Central American Ind. (0)	1	<0.01
Cherokee (4)	15	0.07
Chippewa (42)	69	0.34
Choctaw (1)	2	0.01
Creek (0)	5	0.02
Crow (3)	3	0.01
Delaware (0)	1	<0.01
Iroquois (1)	6	0.03
Kiowa (1)	1	<0.01
Mexican American Ind. (3)	3	0.01
Ottawa (1)	1	<0.01
Potawatomi (0)	1	<0.01
Seminole (0)	1	<0.01
Sioux (3)	7	0.03
South American Ind. (3)	3	0.01
Asian (723)	929	4.56
Not Hispanic (708)	899	4.41
Hispanic (15)	30	0.15
Bangladeshi (5)	5	0.02
Cambodian (7)	7	0.03
Chinese, ex. Taiwanese (125)	171	0.84
Filipino (40)	76	0.37
Hmong (62)	67	0.33
Indian (153)	183	0.90
Indonesian (1)	1	<0.01
Japanese (28)	52	0.26
Korean (98)	141	0.69
Laotian (64)	68	0.33
Malaysian (1)	5	0.02
Nepalese (1)	1	<0.01
Pakistani (30)	31	0.15
Sri Lankan (5)	6	0.03
Taiwanese (4)	4	0.02
Thai (2)	7	0.03
Vietnamese (61)	74	0.36
Hawaii Native/Pacific Islander (4)	15	0.07
Not Hispanic (4)	13	0.06
Hispanic (0)	2	0.01
Fijian (1)	1	<0.01
Native Hawaiian (0)	3	0.01
White (17,390)	17,856	87.65
Not Hispanic (17,113)	17,523	86.02
Hispanic (277)	333	1.63

Grand Rapids

Place Type: City
County: Itasca
Population: 10,869†

Ancestry‡	Population	%
American (648)	648	6.02
Arab (29)	29	0.27
Lebanese (16)	16	0.15
Other Arab (13)	13	0.12
Austrian (0)	33	0.31
British (0)	8	0.07
Canadian (0)	14	0.13
Croatian (31)	47	0.44
Czech (159)	189	1.76
Czechoslovakian (15)	71	0.66
Danish (22)	186	1.73
Dutch (80)	189	1.76
Eastern European (13)	13	0.12
English (132)	794	7.38
European (62)	62	0.58
Finnish (250)	513	4.77
French, ex. Basque (85)	665	6.18
French Canadian (28)	194	1.80
German (951)	3,144	29.21
Hungarian (14)	14	0.13
Irish (404)	1,454	13.51
Italian (144)	531	4.93
Norwegian (617)	2,261	21.01
Pennsylvania German (0)	17	0.16
Polish (71)	228	2.12
Romanian (0)	9	0.08
Russian (0)	17	0.16
Scandinavian (118)	144	1.34
Scotch-Irish (29)	189	1.76
Scottish (77)	188	1.75
Serbian (22)	134	1.25
Slovak (0)	17	0.16
Slovene (11)	62	0.58
Swedish (225)	1,294	12.02
Swiss (0)	56	0.52
Welsh (23)	23	0.21
Yugoslavian (15)	44	0.41

Hispanic Origin	Population	%
Hispanic or Latino (of any race)	131	1.21
Central American, ex. Mexican	9	0.08
Guatemalan	2	0.02
Honduran	5	0.05
Nicaraguan	1	0.01
Panamanian	1	0.01
Cuban	5	0.05
Dominican Republic	1	0.01
Mexican	75	0.69
Puerto Rican	12	0.11
South American	10	0.09
Chilean	6	0.06
Ecuadorian	1	0.01
Peruvian	3	0.03
Other Hispanic or Latino	19	0.17

Race*	Population	%
African-American/Black (66)	117	1.08
Not Hispanic (66)	109	1.00
Hispanic (0)	8	0.07
American Indian/Alaska Native (206)	341	3.14
Not Hispanic (203)	335	3.08
Hispanic (3)	6	0.06
Aleut *(Alaska Native)* (0)	4	0.04
Blackfeet (0)	2	0.02
Cherokee (0)	10	0.09
Chippewa (104)	157	1.44
Comanche (0)	2	0.02
Iroquois (0)	1	0.01
Potawatomi (0)	8	0.07
Sioux (4)	6	0.06
Asian (64)	95	0.87
Not Hispanic (64)	95	0.87
Chinese, ex. Taiwanese (18)	21	0.19
Filipino (8)	17	0.16
Hmong (6)	6	0.06
Indian (11)	16	0.15
Indonesian (1)	2	0.02
Japanese (4)	9	0.08
Korean (9)	21	0.19
Laotian (0)	1	0.01
Thai (0)	1	0.01
Vietnamese (2)	4	0.04
Hawaii Native/Pacific Islander (0)	4	0.04
Not Hispanic (0)	3	0.03
Hispanic (0)	1	0.01
Native Hawaiian (0)	3	0.03
White (10,286)	10,493	96.54
Not Hispanic (10,207)	10,394	95.63
Hispanic (79)	99	0.91

Ham Lake

Place Type: City
County: Anoka
Population: 15,296†

Ancestry‡	Population	%
African, Sub-Saharan (0)	8	0.05
African (0)	8	0.05
American (642)	642	4.29
Arab (0)	30	0.20
Lebanese (0)	30	0.20
Armenian (28)	28	0.19
Australian (0)	25	0.17
Austrian (35)	92	0.62
Belgian (0)	8	0.05
British (10)	26	0.17
Canadian (7)	11	0.07
Carpatho Rusyn (0)	6	0.04
Czech (63)	254	1.70
Czechoslovakian (14)	25	0.17
Danish (22)	245	1.64
Dutch (21)	301	2.01
Eastern European (0)	8	0.05
English (150)	886	5.93
European (444)	611	4.09
Finnish (18)	163	1.09
French, ex. Basque (35)	775	5.18
French Canadian (71)	348	2.33
German (1,769)	5,819	38.92
Greek (23)	77	0.51
Guyanese (33)	33	0.22
Hungarian (17)	102	0.68
Icelander (0)	22	0.15
Irish (307)	2,084	13.94
Italian (43)	353	2.36
Lithuanian (19)	78	0.52
Luxemburger (0)	19	0.13
Northern European (22)	22	0.15
Norwegian (780)	2,805	18.76
Pennsylvania German (10)	10	0.07
Polish (220)	938	6.27
Portuguese (28)	28	0.19
Russian (61)	126	0.84
Scandinavian (85)	107	0.72
Scotch-Irish (7)	111	0.74
Scottish (28)	149	1.00
Serbian (15)	45	0.30
Slovak (0)	7	0.05
Swedish (374)	2,045	13.68
Swiss (0)	95	0.64
Ukrainian (59)	128	0.86
Welsh (11)	24	0.16
Yugoslavian (5)	21	0.14

Hispanic Origin	Population	%
Hispanic or Latino (of any race)	337	2.20
Central American, ex. Mexican	19	0.12
Costa Rican	1	0.01
Guatemalan	14	0.09
Nicaraguan	2	0.01
Salvadoran	2	0.01
Cuban	10	0.07
Mexican	215	1.41
Puerto Rican	27	0.18
South American	30	0.20
Argentinean	1	0.01
Chilean	2	0.01
Colombian	9	0.06
Ecuadorian	6	0.04
Paraguayan	1	0.01
Peruvian	8	0.05
Other South American	3	0.02
Other Hispanic or Latino	36	0.24

Race*	Population	%
African-American/Black (103)	149	0.97
Not Hispanic (100)	136	0.89
Hispanic (3)	13	0.08
American Indian/Alaska Native (56)	116	0.76
Not Hispanic (49)	96	0.63
Hispanic (7)	20	0.13
Blackfeet (0)	3	0.02
Cherokee (1)	5	0.03
Chippewa (25)	45	0.29
Choctaw (0)	1	0.01
Cree (1)	1	0.01
Crow (0)	1	0.01
Iroquois (0)	1	0.01
Navajo (1)	1	0.01
Potawatomi (3)	3	0.02

*Notes: † The Census 2010 population figure is used to calculate the percentages in the Hispanic Origin and Race categories. Ancestry percentages are based on the 2006-2010 American Community Survey population (not shown); ‡ Numbers in parentheses indicate the number of people reporting a single ancestry; * Numbers in parentheses indicate the number of persons reporting this race alone, not in combination with any other race; Please refer to the Explanation of Data for more information.*

Sioux (7)	12	0.08
Asian (375)	461	3.01
Not Hispanic (369)	450	2.94
Hispanic (6)	11	0.07
Cambodian (2)	3	0.02
Chinese, ex. Taiwanese (9)	15	0.10
Filipino (17)	35	0.23
Hmong (215)	218	1.43
Indian (32)	39	0.25
Japanese (5)	18	0.12
Korean (25)	49	0.32
Laotian (6)	10	0.07
Pakistani (8)	9	0.06
Taiwanese (1)	1	0.01
Thai (0)	1	0.01
Vietnamese (38)	43	0.28
Hawaii Native/Pacific Islander (5)	14	0.09
Not Hispanic (3)	7	0.05
Hispanic (2)	7	0.05
Guamanian/Chamorro (2)	2	0.01
Native Hawaiian (3)	11	0.07
White (14,433)	14,620	95.58
Not Hispanic (14,269)	14,418	94.26
Hispanic (164)	202	1.32

Hastings

Place Type: City
County: Dakota
Population: 22,172†

Ancestry‡	Population	%
African, Sub-Saharan (68)	68	0.31
Ethiopian (68)	68	0.31
American (1,090)	1,090	5.05
Arab (25)	35	0.16
Lebanese (25)	35	0.16
Australian (0)	14	0.06
Austrian (61)	113	0.52
Belgian (18)	83	0.38
British (0)	27	0.13
Canadian (11)	11	0.05
Czech (48)	268	1.24
Czechoslovakian (0)	24	0.11
Danish (55)	309	1.43
Dutch (15)	258	1.19
English (247)	1,243	5.76
European (332)	357	1.65
Finnish (102)	276	1.28
French, ex. Basque (72)	1,119	5.18
French Canadian (84)	113	0.52
German (3,721)	10,210	47.29
German Russian (26)	26	0.12
Greek (0)	23	0.11
Hungarian (10)	17	0.08
Irish (428)	3,632	16.82
Italian (59)	285	1.32
Latvian (14)	14	0.06
Lithuanian (5)	5	0.02
Luxemburger (25)	47	0.22
New Zealander (20)	41	0.19
Northern European (9)	9	0.04
Norwegian (1,087)	3,184	14.75
Polish (119)	687	3.18
Portuguese (25)	25	0.12
Romanian (9)	48	0.22
Russian (12)	130	0.60
Scandinavian (78)	169	0.78
Scotch-Irish (48)	302	1.40
Scottish (44)	274	1.27
Serbian (0)	3	0.01
Slovak (0)	13	0.06
Swedish (366)	1,706	7.90
Swiss (14)	157	0.73
Ukrainian (64)	64	0.30
Welsh (9)	63	0.29
West Indian, ex. Hispanic (0)	12	0.06
British West Indian (0)	12	0.06
Yugoslavian (8)	8	0.04

Hispanic Origin	Population	%
Hispanic or Latino (of any race)	580	2.62
Central American, ex. Mexican	37	0.17
Costa Rican	1	<0.01
Guatemalan	13	0.06
Honduran	4	0.02
Nicaraguan	2	0.01
Panamanian	12	0.05
Salvadoran	5	0.02
Cuban	16	0.07
Dominican Republic	7	0.03
Mexican	400	1.80
Puerto Rican	54	0.24
South American	27	0.12
Colombian	13	0.06
Ecuadorian	4	0.02
Peruvian	2	0.01
Venezuelan	8	0.04
Other Hispanic or Latino	39	0.18

Race*	Population	%
African-American/Black (361)	550	2.48
Not Hispanic (349)	509	2.30
Hispanic (12)	41	0.18
American Indian/Alaska Native (107)	247	1.11
Not Hispanic (101)	221	1.00
Hispanic (6)	26	0.12
Apache (1)	1	<0.01
Blackfeet (0)	4	0.02
Canadian/French Am. Ind. (1)	4	0.02
Cherokee (3)	23	0.10
Chickasaw (0)	2	0.01
Chippewa (30)	72	0.32
Choctaw (0)	3	0.01
Colville (2)	2	0.01
Comanche (0)	4	0.02
Iroquois (1)	2	0.01
Mexican American Ind. (5)	9	0.04
Navajo (1)	1	<0.01
Pueblo (0)	1	<0.01
Seminole (0)	1	<0.01
Sioux (14)	24	0.11
Yup'ik *(Alaska Native)* (1)	2	0.01
Asian (201)	307	1.38
Not Hispanic (198)	296	1.34
Hispanic (3)	11	0.05
Cambodian (1)	2	0.01
Chinese, ex. Taiwanese (29)	40	0.18
Filipino (38)	64	0.29
Hmong (17)	17	0.08
Indian (36)	50	0.23
Japanese (9)	24	0.11
Korean (32)	53	0.24
Pakistani (2)	6	0.03
Sri Lankan (4)	5	0.02
Taiwanese (3)	4	0.02
Thai (3)	7	0.03
Vietnamese (18)	26	0.12
Hawaii Native/Pacific Islander (6)	23	0.10
Not Hispanic (6)	18	0.08
Hispanic (0)	5	0.02
Guamanian/Chamorro (0)	4	0.02
Native Hawaiian (0)	5	0.02
Samoan (1)	1	<0.01
White (20,867)	21,292	96.03
Not Hispanic (20,555)	20,899	94.26
Hispanic (312)	393	1.77

Hermantown

Place Type: City
County: St. Louis
Population: 9,414†

Ancestry‡	Population	%
American (224)	224	2.45
Austrian (0)	34	0.37
Belgian (12)	83	0.91
British (13)	90	0.98
Bulgarian (0)	13	0.14
Croatian (24)	68	0.74
Czech (20)	82	0.90
Danish (8)	35	0.38
Dutch (42)	163	1.78
English (50)	467	5.10
Estonian (0)	12	0.13
European (136)	136	1.49
Finnish (256)	842	9.20
French, ex. Basque (72)	492	5.38
French Canadian (72)	147	1.61
German (698)	2,580	28.20
Greek (24)	70	0.77
Hungarian (31)	31	0.34
Icelander (8)	8	0.09
Irish (133)	801	8.76
Italian (161)	480	5.25
Lithuanian (11)	34	0.37
Norwegian (446)	1,441	15.75
Polish (198)	871	9.52
Russian (0)	14	0.15
Scandinavian (144)	307	3.36
Scotch-Irish (14)	60	0.66
Scottish (145)	286	3.13
Serbian (0)	12	0.13
Slavic (16)	16	0.17
Slovak (16)	41	0.45
Slovene (28)	43	0.47
Swedish (471)	1,687	18.44
Swiss (0)	46	0.50
Turkish (0)	32	0.35
Ukrainian (0)	9	0.10
Welsh (0)	24	0.26
Yugoslavian (0)	25	0.27

Hispanic Origin	Population	%
Hispanic or Latino (of any race)	204	2.17
Central American, ex. Mexican	5	0.05
Guatemalan	3	0.03
Honduran	1	0.01
Other Central American	1	0.01
Cuban	4	0.04
Dominican Republic	3	0.03
Mexican	146	1.55
Puerto Rican	24	0.25
South American	7	0.07
Colombian	3	0.03
Peruvian	4	0.04
Other Hispanic or Latino	15	0.16

Race*	Population	%
African-American/Black (225)	269	2.86
Not Hispanic (220)	258	2.74
Hispanic (5)	11	0.12
American Indian/Alaska Native (109)	163	1.73
Not Hispanic (106)	155	1.65
Hispanic (3)	8	0.08
Apache (1)	1	0.01
Blackfeet (3)	3	0.03
Canadian/French Am. Ind. (1)	1	0.01
Cherokee (2)	5	0.05
Chippewa (48)	77	0.82
Crow (1)	1	0.01
Iroquois (1)	1	0.01
Mexican American Ind. (1)	1	0.01
Pueblo (0)	2	0.02
Sioux (18)	18	0.19
Asian (116)	152	1.61
Not Hispanic (115)	148	1.57
Hispanic (1)	4	0.04
Chinese, ex. Taiwanese (4)	9	0.10
Filipino (5)	16	0.17
Hmong (11)	13	0.14
Indian (42)	48	0.51
Japanese (3)	10	0.11
Korean (17)	18	0.19
Laotian (5)	5	0.05
Pakistani (12)	12	0.13
Taiwanese (1)	1	0.01
Thai (5)	5	0.05
Vietnamese (8)	11	0.12

*Notes: † The Census 2010 population figure is used to calculate the percentages in the Hispanic Origin and Race categories. Ancestry percentages are based on the 2006-2010 American Community Survey population (not shown); ‡ Numbers in parentheses indicate the number of people reporting a single ancestry; * Numbers in parentheses indicate the number of persons reporting this race alone, not in combination with any other race; Please refer to the Explanation of Data for more information.*

Hawaii Native/Pacific Islander (4)	9	0.10
Not Hispanic (3)	8	0.08
Hispanic (1)	1	0.01
Guamanian/Chamorro (2)	2	0.02
Marshallese (1)	1	0.01
Native Hawaiian (1)	5	0.05
White (8,764)	8,900	94.54
Not Hispanic (8,645)	8,748	92.93
Hispanic (119)	152	1.61

Hibbing

Place Type: City
County: St. Louis
Population: 16,361†

Ancestry‡	Population	%
Albanian (15)	15	0.09
American (447)	447	2.73
Austrian (20)	58	0.35
Belgian (15)	89	0.54
British (11)	11	0.07
Canadian (30)	32	0.20
Croatian (180)	434	2.65
Czech (39)	130	0.79
Czechoslovakian (13)	58	0.35
Danish (45)	177	1.08
Dutch (14)	237	1.45
English (169)	1,438	8.77
European (62)	62	0.38
Finnish (814)	2,018	12.31
French, ex. Basque (28)	1,201	7.32
French Canadian (97)	338	2.06
German (972)	4,468	27.25
Greek (10)	25	0.15
Hungarian (0)	13	0.08
Irish (172)	1,661	10.13
Italian (674)	1,734	10.58
Lithuanian (6)	16	0.10
Northern European (11)	11	0.07
Norwegian (556)	2,278	13.89
Pennsylvania German (0)	13	0.08
Polish (141)	685	4.18
Portuguese (9)	9	0.05
Romanian (29)	39	0.24
Russian (0)	10	0.06
Scandinavian (127)	157	0.96
Scotch-Irish (54)	274	1.67
Scottish (22)	201	1.23
Serbian (88)	374	2.28
Slavic (71)	155	0.95
Slovak (20)	45	0.27
Slovene (335)	702	4.28
Swedish (289)	1,821	11.11
Swiss (0)	7	0.04
Ukrainian (22)	81	0.49
Welsh (21)	21	0.13
Yugoslavian (39)	159	0.97

Hispanic Origin	Population	%
Hispanic or Latino (of any race)	179	1.09
Central American, ex. Mexican	13	0.08
Costa Rican	3	0.02
Guatemalan	4	0.02
Salvadoran	6	0.04
Cuban	2	0.01
Dominican Republic	1	0.01
Mexican	111	0.68
Puerto Rican	24	0.15
South American	7	0.04
Chilean	4	0.02
Peruvian	3	0.02
Other Hispanic or Latino	21	0.13

Race*	Population	%
African-American/Black (90)	215	1.31
Not Hispanic (90)	207	1.27
Hispanic (0)	8	0.05
American Indian/Alaska Native (154)	300	1.83
Not Hispanic (149)	289	1.77
Hispanic (5)	11	0.07
Alaska Athabascan *(Ala. Nat.)* (0)	1	0.01
Aleut *(Alaska Native)* (0)	2	0.01
Blackfeet (0)	3	0.02
Canadian/French Am. Ind. (1)	4	0.02
Cherokee (1)	7	0.04
Chippewa (64)	115	0.70
Choctaw (11)	11	0.07
Cree (1)	1	0.01
Creek (1)	1	0.01
Navajo (1)	1	0.01
Osage (1)	1	0.01
Sioux (7)	14	0.09
Tlingit-Haida *(Alaska Native)* (2)	2	0.01
Asian (72)	111	0.68
Not Hispanic (70)	108	0.66
Hispanic (2)	3	0.02
Cambodian (0)	1	0.01
Chinese, ex. Taiwanese (8)	12	0.07
Filipino (17)	24	0.15
Indian (14)	15	0.09
Japanese (4)	19	0.12
Korean (12)	20	0.12
Laotian (1)	1	0.01
Malaysian (1)	1	0.01
Taiwanese (1)	1	0.01
Thai (0)	2	0.01
Vietnamese (6)	7	0.04
Hawaii Native/Pacific Islander (2)	2	0.01
Not Hispanic (1)	1	0.01
Hispanic (1)	1	0.01
Guamanian/Chamorro (1)	1	0.01
White (15,698)	15,990	97.73
Not Hispanic (15,588)	15,861	96.94
Hispanic (110)	129	0.79

Hopkins

Place Type: City
County: Hennepin
Population: 17,591†

Ancestry‡	Population	%
Afghan (29)	29	0.17
African, Sub-Saharan (1,168)	1,168	6.70
African (118)	118	0.68
Ethiopian (308)	308	1.77
Ghanaian (14)	14	0.08
Kenyan (60)	60	0.34
Nigerian (60)	60	0.34
Somalian (598)	598	3.43
Other Sub-Saharan African (10)	10	0.06
American (225)	225	1.29
Arab (15)	15	0.09
Moroccan (15)	15	0.09
Austrian (18)	48	0.28
British (0)	47	0.27
Canadian (0)	35	0.20
Czech (98)	345	1.98
Czechoslovakian (0)	98	0.56
Danish (72)	220	1.26
Dutch (47)	263	1.51
English (156)	1,147	6.58
European (177)	177	1.02
Finnish (60)	217	1.25
French, ex. Basque (24)	426	2.45
French Canadian (27)	80	0.46
German (1,275)	5,111	29.34
German Russian (11)	21	0.12
Greek (29)	29	0.17
Hungarian (29)	138	0.79
Icelander (14)	38	0.22
Iranian (7)	7	0.04
Irish (458)	1,917	11.00
Italian (80)	475	2.73
Latvian (25)	25	0.14
Lithuanian (17)	25	0.14
Northern European (0)	11	0.06
Norwegian (714)	2,623	15.06
Pennsylvania German (0)	16	0.09
Polish (117)	689	3.96
Portuguese (0)	41	0.24
Russian (78)	377	2.16
Scandinavian (198)	318	1.83
Scotch-Irish (27)	196	1.13
Scottish (15)	196	1.13
Slavic (8)	8	0.05
Slovak (52)	100	0.57
Slovene (0)	17	0.10
Swedish (268)	1,422	8.16
Swiss (0)	96	0.55
Ukrainian (9)	9	0.05
Welsh (28)	120	0.69
West Indian, ex. Hispanic (46)	46	0.26
Jamaican (46)	46	0.26
Yugoslavian (13)	39	0.22

Hispanic Origin	Population	%
Hispanic or Latino (of any race)	1,390	7.90
Central American, ex. Mexican	86	0.49
Costa Rican	5	0.03
Guatemalan	33	0.19
Honduran	6	0.03
Nicaraguan	4	0.02
Panamanian	5	0.03
Salvadoran	30	0.17
Other Central American	3	0.02
Cuban	12	0.07
Dominican Republic	24	0.14
Mexican	1,051	5.97
Puerto Rican	59	0.34
South American	93	0.53
Argentinean	1	0.01
Bolivian	9	0.05
Chilean	1	0.01
Colombian	11	0.06
Ecuadorian	38	0.22
Paraguayan	4	0.02
Peruvian	15	0.09
Uruguayan	5	0.03
Venezuelan	6	0.03
Other South American	3	0.02
Other Hispanic or Latino	65	0.37

Race*	Population	%
African-American/Black (2,371)	2,709	15.40
Not Hispanic (2,324)	2,629	14.95
Hispanic (47)	80	0.45
American Indian/Alaska Native (104)	283	1.61
Not Hispanic (92)	240	1.36
Hispanic (12)	43	0.24
Apache (0)	5	0.03
Blackfeet (1)	1	0.01
Canadian/French Am. Ind. (0)	3	0.02
Cherokee (3)	24	0.14
Chippewa (41)	73	0.41
Choctaw (1)	2	0.01
Iroquois (1)	4	0.02
Menominee (1)	1	0.01
Mexican American Ind. (4)	6	0.03
Navajo (1)	1	0.01
Seminole (0)	2	0.01
Sioux (1)	9	0.05
Asian (1,494)	1,660	9.44
Not Hispanic (1,483)	1,636	9.30
Hispanic (11)	24	0.14
Bangladeshi (14)	17	0.10
Burmese (1)	1	0.01
Cambodian (53)	60	0.34
Chinese, ex. Taiwanese (117)	144	0.82
Filipino (42)	67	0.38
Hmong (21)	22	0.13
Indian (972)	1,001	5.69
Indonesian (1)	2	0.01
Japanese (17)	41	0.23
Korean (63)	94	0.53
Laotian (42)	46	0.26
Malaysian (2)	3	0.02
Nepalese (7)	7	0.04
Pakistani (6)	12	0.07

*Notes: † The Census 2010 population figure is used to calculate the percentages in the Hispanic Origin and Race categories. Ancestry percentages are based on the 2006-2010 American Community Survey population (not shown); ‡ Numbers in parentheses indicate the number of people reporting a single ancestry; * Numbers in parentheses indicate the number of persons reporting this race alone, not in combination with any other race; Please refer to the Explanation of Data for more information.*

Sri Lankan (15)	15	0.09
Taiwanese (1)	1	0.01
Thai (4)	4	0.02
Vietnamese (83)	93	0.53
Hawaii Native/Pacific Islander (8)	32	0.18
Not Hispanic (6)	21	0.12
Hispanic (2)	11	0.06
Guamanian/Chamorro (1)	4	0.02
Native Hawaiian (4)	11	0.06
Samoan (3)	6	0.03
White (12,384)	12,956	73.65
Not Hispanic (11,721)	12,205	69.38
Hispanic (663)	751	4.27

Hugo

Place Type: City
County: Washington
Population: 13,332†

Ancestry‡	Population	%
American (370)	370	3.05
Arab (8)	8	0.07
Lebanese (8)	8	0.07
Armenian (30)	30	0.25
Austrian (0)	47	0.39
Belgian (0)	19	0.16
Croatian (0)	10	0.08
Czech (19)	229	1.89
Czechoslovakian (0)	9	0.07
Danish (70)	235	1.94
Dutch (26)	166	1.37
English (122)	847	6.98
European (173)	184	1.52
Finnish (62)	183	1.51
French, ex. Basque (150)	1,233	10.17
French Canadian (31)	270	2.23
German (1,322)	5,267	43.42
Hungarian (0)	19	0.16
Iranian (16)	16	0.13
Irish (233)	2,038	16.80
Italian (187)	1,022	8.43
Lithuanian (0)	19	0.16
Norwegian (343)	1,505	12.41
Polish (151)	686	5.66
Portuguese (0)	28	0.23
Russian (8)	76	0.63
Scandinavian (94)	365	3.01
Scotch-Irish (80)	159	1.31
Scottish (0)	111	0.92
Serbian (0)	46	0.38
Slovene (9)	22	0.18
Swedish (287)	1,261	10.40
Swiss (29)	183	1.51
Turkish (11)	34	0.28
Ukrainian (14)	30	0.25
Welsh (8)	50	0.41
Yugoslavian (17)	17	0.14

Hispanic Origin	Population	%
Hispanic or Latino (of any race)	319	2.39
Central American, ex. Mexican	23	0.17
Costa Rican	2	0.02
Guatemalan	8	0.06
Honduran	4	0.03
Panamanian	2	0.02
Salvadoran	7	0.05
Cuban	6	0.05
Dominican Republic	1	0.01
Mexican	202	1.52
Puerto Rican	17	0.13
South American	31	0.23
Chilean	5	0.04
Colombian	15	0.11
Ecuadorian	7	0.05
Peruvian	1	0.01
Venezuelan	3	0.02
Other Hispanic or Latino	39	0.29

Race*	Population	%
African-American/Black (105)	178	1.34
Not Hispanic (103)	169	1.27
Hispanic (2)	9	0.07
American Indian/Alaska Native (39)	100	0.75
Not Hispanic (36)	84	0.63
Hispanic (3)	16	0.12
Apache (1)	1	0.01
Blackfeet (0)	6	0.05
Canadian/French Am. Ind. (1)	2	0.02
Cherokee (0)	4	0.03
Chippewa (22)	38	0.29
Ottawa (1)	1	0.01
Sioux (9)	17	0.13
Asian (465)	564	4.23
Not Hispanic (461)	552	4.14
Hispanic (4)	12	0.09
Cambodian (12)	14	0.11
Chinese, ex. Taiwanese (15)	25	0.19
Filipino (36)	53	0.40
Hmong (252)	264	1.98
Indian (28)	48	0.36
Japanese (3)	36	0.27
Korean (23)	41	0.31
Laotian (4)	5	0.04
Sri Lankan (0)	1	0.01
Taiwanese (1)	2	0.02
Vietnamese (39)	46	0.35
Hawaii Native/Pacific Islander (4)	23	0.17
Not Hispanic (4)	23	0.17
Native Hawaiian (1)	11	0.08
White (12,381)	12,628	94.72
Not Hispanic (12,191)	12,391	92.94
Hispanic (190)	237	1.78

Hutchinson

Place Type: City
County: McLeod
Population: 14,178†

Ancestry‡	Population	%
African, Sub-Saharan (54)	88	0.62
Ethiopian (44)	44	0.31
Nigerian (10)	44	0.31
American (434)	434	3.06
Arab (0)	73	0.51
Arab (0)	73	0.51
Austrian (0)	29	0.20
Belgian (11)	11	0.08
British (0)	12	0.08
Croatian (28)	28	0.20
Czech (157)	474	3.34
Czechoslovakian (0)	26	0.18
Danish (172)	436	3.07
Dutch (11)	250	1.76
English (172)	694	4.89
European (128)	128	0.90
Finnish (146)	302	2.13
French, ex. Basque (79)	445	3.14
French Canadian (0)	39	0.27
German (3,465)	7,509	52.93
Hungarian (35)	47	0.33
Icelander (46)	75	0.53
Irish (114)	1,519	10.71
Italian (0)	4	0.03
Northern European (28)	28	0.20
Norwegian (730)	2,403	16.94
Polish (50)	357	2.52
Portuguese (51)	88	0.62
Romanian (0)	36	0.25
Russian (27)	40	0.28
Scandinavian (88)	240	1.69
Scotch-Irish (0)	70	0.49
Scottish (26)	180	1.27
Slavic (8)	8	0.06
Slovene (13)	66	0.47
Swedish (158)	1,084	7.64
Swiss (0)	80	0.56
Ukrainian (0)	16	0.11
Welsh (0)	31	0.22

Hispanic Origin	Population	%
Hispanic or Latino (of any race)	534	3.77
Central American, ex. Mexican	30	0.21
Guatemalan	10	0.07
Honduran	14	0.10
Panamanian	3	0.02
Salvadoran	3	0.02
Mexican	423	2.98
Puerto Rican	19	0.13
South American	7	0.05
Bolivian	1	0.01
Colombian	2	0.01
Ecuadorian	1	0.01
Peruvian	3	0.02
Other Hispanic or Latino	55	0.39

Race*	Population	%
African-American/Black (127)	196	1.38
Not Hispanic (118)	183	1.29
Hispanic (9)	13	0.09
American Indian/Alaska Native (41)	91	0.64
Not Hispanic (37)	86	0.61
Hispanic (4)	5	0.04
Aleut *(Alaska Native)* (0)	3	0.02
Cherokee (0)	5	0.04
Chippewa (12)	20	0.14
Inupiat *(Alaska Native)* (1)	1	0.01
Iroquois (1)	6	0.04
Mexican American Ind. (1)	1	0.01
Osage (2)	2	0.01
Sioux (2)	6	0.04
Asian (151)	207	1.46
Not Hispanic (149)	199	1.40
Hispanic (2)	8	0.06
Chinese, ex. Taiwanese (29)	31	0.22
Filipino (15)	28	0.20
Hmong (5)	6	0.04
Indian (46)	50	0.35
Japanese (7)	19	0.13
Korean (13)	28	0.20
Taiwanese (3)	8	0.06
Thai (6)	8	0.06
Vietnamese (20)	26	0.18
Hawaii Native/Pacific Islander (12)	13	0.09
Not Hispanic (11)	12	0.08
Hispanic (1)	1	0.01
Guamanian/Chamorro (1)	2	0.01
Native Hawaiian (4)	4	0.03
White (13,531)	13,704	96.66
Not Hispanic (13,167)	13,318	93.93
Hispanic (364)	386	2.72

Inver Grove Heights

Place Type: City
County: Dakota
Population: 33,880†

Ancestry‡	Population	%
African, Sub-Saharan (169)	189	0.57
African (9)	20	0.06
Ethiopian (85)	85	0.25
Ghanaian (8)	8	0.02
Nigerian (0)	9	0.03
Sierra Leonean (31)	31	0.09
Somalian (36)	36	0.11
American (959)	959	2.88
Arab (259)	288	0.86
Egyptian (112)	112	0.34
Lebanese (136)	165	0.49
Other Arab (11)	11	0.03
Austrian (18)	168	0.50
Basque (10)	10	0.03
Belgian (0)	10	0.03
Brazilian (87)	97	0.29
British (31)	81	0.24
Cajun (12)	12	0.04

*Notes: † The Census 2010 population figure is used to calculate the percentages in the Hispanic Origin and Race categories. Ancestry percentages are based on the 2006-2010 American Community Survey population (not shown); ‡ Numbers in parentheses indicate the number of people reporting a single ancestry; * Numbers in parentheses indicate the number of persons reporting this race alone, not in combination with any other race; Please refer to the Explanation of Data for more information.*

Canadian (59)	71	0.21
Croatian (9)	58	0.17
Czech (68)	721	2.16
Czechoslovakian (11)	36	0.11
Danish (82)	418	1.25
Dutch (68)	662	1.98
English (257)	2,173	6.52
European (289)	354	1.06
Finnish (74)	368	1.10
French, ex. Basque (141)	1,466	4.40
French Canadian (219)	648	1.94
German (3,810)	14,302	42.88
Greek (46)	115	0.34
Guyanese (0)	9	0.03
Hungarian (14)	97	0.29
Icelander (0)	9	0.03
Irish (607)	4,762	14.28
Israeli (0)	39	0.12
Italian (171)	933	2.80
Latvian (12)	12	0.04
Lithuanian (0)	71	0.21
Luxemburger (0)	31	0.09
Macedonian (8)	8	0.02
Northern European (35)	35	0.10
Norwegian (1,177)	4,761	14.27
Polish (430)	1,977	5.93
Portuguese (0)	20	0.06
Romanian (95)	125	0.37
Russian (87)	203	0.61
Scandinavian (196)	462	1.39
Scotch-Irish (64)	502	1.51
Scottish (48)	429	1.29
Serbian (55)	97	0.29
Slovak (0)	46	0.14
Slovene (18)	75	0.22
Swedish (310)	2,486	7.45
Swiss (0)	206	0.62
Turkish (10)	10	0.03
Ukrainian (175)	262	0.79
Welsh (0)	79	0.24
West Indian, ex. Hispanic (0)	21	0.06
Jamaican (0)	21	0.06
Yugoslavian (11)	19	0.06

Hispanic Origin	Population	%
Hispanic or Latino (of any race)	3,024	8.93
Central American, ex. Mexican	230	0.68
Costa Rican	4	0.01
Guatemalan	34	0.10
Honduran	48	0.14
Nicaraguan	33	0.10
Panamanian	8	0.02
Salvadoran	103	0.30
Cuban	26	0.08
Dominican Republic	28	0.08
Mexican	2,314	6.83
Puerto Rican	218	0.64
South American	90	0.27
Argentinean	5	0.01
Bolivian	2	0.01
Chilean	1	<0.01
Colombian	36	0.11
Ecuadorian	17	0.05
Paraguayan	3	0.01
Peruvian	20	0.06
Venezuelan	6	0.02
Other Hispanic or Latino	118	0.35

Race*	Population	%
African-American/Black (1,271)	1,715	5.06
Not Hispanic (1,234)	1,613	4.76
Hispanic (37)	102	0.30
American Indian/Alaska Native (148)	388	1.15
Not Hispanic (114)	309	0.91
Hispanic (34)	79	0.23
Apache (0)	4	0.01
Blackfeet (0)	4	0.01
Canadian/French Am. Ind. (3)	3	0.01
Cherokee (6)	19	0.06
Chippewa (55)	113	0.33
Cree (1)	2	0.01
Creek (0)	1	<0.01
Crow (0)	2	0.01
Delaware (2)	2	0.01
Iroquois (6)	10	0.03
Mexican American Ind. (11)	17	0.05
Navajo (0)	1	<0.01
Sioux (12)	35	0.10
South American Ind. (0)	1	<0.01
Spanish American Ind. (1)	1	<0.01
Yup'ik *(Alaska Native)* (3)	3	0.01
Asian (1,158)	1,404	4.14
Not Hispanic (1,150)	1,363	4.02
Hispanic (8)	41	0.12
Bangladeshi (17)	17	0.05
Cambodian (35)	53	0.16
Chinese, ex. Taiwanese (101)	138	0.41
Filipino (143)	221	0.65
Hmong (285)	303	0.89
Indian (192)	231	0.68
Indonesian (5)	5	0.01
Japanese (24)	56	0.17
Korean (109)	151	0.45
Laotian (15)	21	0.06
Malaysian (1)	1	<0.01
Nepalese (6)	6	0.02
Pakistani (20)	27	0.08
Sri Lankan (5)	8	0.02
Taiwanese (4)	9	0.03
Thai (2)	10	0.03
Vietnamese (124)	142	0.42
Hawaii Native/Pacific Islander (21)	60	0.18
Not Hispanic (17)	54	0.16
Hispanic (4)	6	0.02
Guamanian/Chamorro (2)	6	0.02
Native Hawaiian (13)	29	0.09
Samoan (0)	1	<0.01
Tongan (4)	9	0.03
White (29,019)	29,988	88.51
Not Hispanic (27,551)	28,244	83.36
Hispanic (1,468)	1,744	5.15

Lake Elmo

Place Type: City
County: Washington
Population: 8,069†

Ancestry‡	Population	%
American (218)	218	2.77
Arab (0)	12	0.15
Syrian (0)	12	0.15
Armenian (11)	11	0.14
Austrian (23)	45	0.57
Brazilian (0)	31	0.39
British (0)	21	0.27
Canadian (11)	11	0.14
Czech (12)	132	1.68
Czechoslovakian (12)	12	0.15
Danish (24)	106	1.35
Dutch (9)	142	1.80
English (79)	644	8.17
European (150)	161	2.04
Finnish (0)	42	0.53
French, ex. Basque (56)	334	4.24
French Canadian (75)	115	1.46
German (1,039)	3,147	39.95
Hungarian (32)	55	0.70
Irish (195)	1,453	18.44
Italian (32)	283	3.59
Luxemburger (0)	53	0.67
Northern European (47)	47	0.60
Norwegian (296)	1,126	14.29
Polish (156)	414	5.26
Romanian (0)	12	0.15
Russian (11)	27	0.34
Scandinavian (52)	52	0.66
Scotch-Irish (0)	55	0.70
Scottish (8)	119	1.51
Serbian (11)	22	0.28
Swedish (194)	974	12.36
Swiss (0)	46	0.58
Ukrainian (0)	6	0.08
Welsh (11)	33	0.42
Yugoslavian (10)	34	0.43

Hispanic Origin	Population	%
Hispanic or Latino (of any race)	279	3.46
Central American, ex. Mexican	9	0.11
Guatemalan	1	0.01
Panamanian	8	0.10
Cuban	5	0.06
Mexican	220	2.73
Puerto Rican	12	0.15
South American	20	0.25
Bolivian	1	0.01
Chilean	5	0.06
Colombian	12	0.15
Ecuadorian	2	0.02
Other Hispanic or Latino	13	0.16

Race*	Population	%
African-American/Black (65)	118	1.46
Not Hispanic (62)	114	1.41
Hispanic (3)	4	0.05
American Indian/Alaska Native (28)	75	0.93
Not Hispanic (27)	72	0.89
Hispanic (1)	3	0.04
Canadian/French Am. Ind. (1)	1	0.01
Cherokee (0)	5	0.06
Chippewa (6)	15	0.19
Choctaw (0)	3	0.04
Iroquois (1)	1	0.01
Menominee (2)	2	0.02
Potawatomi (0)	1	0.01
Sioux (5)	8	0.10
Yup'ik *(Alaska Native)* (1)	1	0.01
Asian (266)	318	3.94
Not Hispanic (263)	315	3.90
Hispanic (3)	3	0.04
Chinese, ex. Taiwanese (30)	35	0.43
Filipino (5)	26	0.32
Hmong (149)	149	1.85
Indian (15)	21	0.26
Japanese (6)	13	0.16
Korean (28)	40	0.50
Laotian (1)	1	0.01
Thai (1)	1	0.01
Vietnamese (13)	16	0.20
Hawaii Native/Pacific Islander (1)	3	0.04
Not Hispanic (1)	3	0.04
Native Hawaiian (0)	2	0.02
White (7,451)	7,596	94.14
Not Hispanic (7,288)	7,425	92.02
Hispanic (163)	171	2.12

Lakeville

Place Type: City
County: Dakota
Population: 55,954†

Ancestry‡	Population	%
African, Sub-Saharan (101)	171	0.32
African (49)	68	0.13
Kenyan (7)	33	0.06
South African (25)	50	0.09
Zimbabwean (11)	11	0.02
Other Sub-Saharan African (9)	9	0.02
American (1,989)	1,989	3.68
Arab (92)	128	0.24
Egyptian (83)	83	0.15
Lebanese (9)	25	0.05
Syrian (0)	20	0.04
Armenian (5)	11	0.02
Australian (14)	14	0.03
Austrian (12)	224	0.41
Belgian (76)	208	0.39
British (65)	172	0.32
Canadian (0)	10	0.02

*Notes: † The Census 2010 population figure is used to calculate the percentages in the Hispanic Origin and Race categories. Ancestry percentages are based on the 2006-2010 American Community Survey population (not shown); ‡ Numbers in parentheses indicate the number of people reporting a single ancestry; * Numbers in parentheses indicate the number of persons reporting this race alone, not in combination with any other race; Please refer to the Explanation of Data for more information.*

Celtic (0)	32	0.06
Croatian (14)	35	0.06
Czech (382)	1,054	1.95
Czechoslovakian (57)	101	0.19
Danish (118)	880	1.63
Dutch (253)	1,181	2.19
English (986)	3,772	6.99
Estonian (0)	14	0.03
European (640)	736	1.36
Finnish (69)	407	0.75
French, ex. Basque (195)	1,687	3.13
French Canadian (44)	397	0.74
German (7,617)	21,740	40.27
Greek (19)	257	0.48
Guyanese (23)	74	0.14
Hungarian (39)	194	0.36
Icelander (0)	13	0.02
Irish (1,210)	7,031	13.02
Italian (446)	1,698	3.15
Latvian (0)	9	0.02
Lithuanian (10)	41	0.08
Luxemburger (0)	53	0.10
Northern European (214)	241	0.45
Norwegian (2,606)	9,186	17.02
Pennsylvania German (21)	64	0.12
Polish (544)	2,305	4.27
Portuguese (22)	75	0.14
Romanian (58)	68	0.13
Russian (247)	600	1.11
Scandinavian (800)	1,202	2.23
Scotch-Irish (161)	370	0.69
Scottish (148)	879	1.63
Serbian (0)	8	0.01
Slavic (18)	46	0.09
Slovak (30)	102	0.19
Slovene (61)	112	0.21
Swedish (1,007)	5,268	9.76
Swiss (7)	204	0.38
Turkish (20)	20	0.04
Ukrainian (154)	311	0.58
Welsh (13)	159	0.29
West Indian, ex. Hispanic (60)	108	0.20
Bahamian (10)	10	0.02
Haitian (24)	24	0.04
Jamaican (26)	26	0.05
West Indian (0)	14	0.03
Other West Indian (0)	34	0.06
Yugoslavian (12)	26	0.05

Hispanic Origin	Population	%
Hispanic or Latino (of any race)	1,955	3.49
Central American, ex. Mexican	155	0.28
Costa Rican	12	0.02
Guatemalan	47	0.08
Honduran	14	0.03
Nicaraguan	14	0.03
Panamanian	15	0.03
Salvadoran	53	0.09
Cuban	38	0.07
Dominican Republic	9	0.02
Mexican	1,296	2.32
Puerto Rican	150	0.27
South American	123	0.22
Argentinean	2	<0.01
Bolivian	9	0.02
Chilean	6	0.01
Colombian	41	0.07
Ecuadorian	28	0.05
Paraguayan	1	<0.01
Peruvian	14	0.03
Uruguayan	5	0.01
Venezuelan	9	0.02
Other South American	8	0.01
Other Hispanic or Latino	184	0.33

Race*	Population	%
African-American/Black (1,407)	1,993	3.56
Not Hispanic (1,386)	1,925	3.44
Hispanic (21)	68	0.12
American Indian/Alaska Native (200)	455	0.81
Not Hispanic (178)	393	0.70
Hispanic (22)	62	0.11
Alaska Athabascan *(Ala. Nat.)* (2)	2	<0.01
Aleut *(Alaska Native)* (0)	1	<0.01
Blackfeet (0)	3	0.01
Canadian/French Am. Ind. (2)	2	<0.01
Cherokee (4)	24	0.04
Chickasaw (0)	2	<0.01
Chippewa (74)	106	0.19
Choctaw (1)	5	0.01
Comanche (0)	2	<0.01
Creek (10)	11	0.02
Crow (0)	1	<0.01
Hopi (1)	1	<0.01
Iroquois (0)	5	0.01
Kiowa (0)	2	<0.01
Lumbee (2)	3	0.01
Mexican American Ind. (6)	10	0.02
Osage (0)	1	<0.01
Ottawa (1)	4	0.01
Potawatomi (1)	2	<0.01
Seminole (0)	3	0.01
Shoshone (1)	4	0.01
Sioux (29)	46	0.08
Ute (2)	2	<0.01
Yup'ik *(Alaska Native)* (1)	5	0.01
Asian (2,276)	2,812	5.03
Not Hispanic (2,264)	2,764	4.94
Hispanic (12)	48	0.09
Bangladeshi (10)	12	0.02
Burmese (2)	2	<0.01
Cambodian (214)	244	0.44
Chinese, ex. Taiwanese (344)	417	0.75
Filipino (143)	239	0.43
Hmong (94)	101	0.18
Indian (404)	498	0.89
Indonesian (5)	17	0.03
Japanese (27)	104	0.19
Korean (215)	330	0.59
Laotian (125)	159	0.28
Malaysian (13)	13	0.02
Nepalese (20)	20	0.04
Pakistani (74)	85	0.15
Taiwanese (6)	8	0.01
Thai (14)	47	0.08
Vietnamese (439)	504	0.90
Hawaii Native/Pacific Islander (21)	61	0.11
Not Hispanic (21)	55	0.10
Hispanic (0)	6	0.01
Guamanian/Chamorro (1)	4	0.01
Native Hawaiian (12)	26	0.05
Samoan (1)	2	<0.01
White (49,970)	51,244	91.58
Not Hispanic (48,857)	49,920	89.22
Hispanic (1,113)	1,324	2.37

Lino Lakes

Place Type: City
County: Anoka
Population: 20,216†

Ancestry‡	Population	%
African, Sub-Saharan (48)	143	0.72
African (38)	41	0.21
Ethiopian (0)	82	0.41
Kenyan (0)	10	0.05
Somalian (10)	10	0.05
American (833)	833	4.21
Arab (0)	59	0.30
Arab (0)	8	0.04
Lebanese (0)	43	0.22
Other Arab (0)	8	0.04
Armenian (0)	59	0.30
Australian (9)	9	0.05
Austrian (7)	76	0.38
Belgian (0)	49	0.25
British (32)	43	0.22
Cajun (8)	8	0.04
Canadian (16)	43	0.22
Celtic (16)	16	0.08
Croatian (9)	21	0.11
Czech (59)	343	1.73
Czechoslovakian (8)	38	0.19
Danish (7)	291	1.47
Dutch (60)	388	1.96
English (143)	1,081	5.46
European (103)	112	0.57
Finnish (116)	455	2.30
French, ex. Basque (142)	1,229	6.21
French Canadian (219)	522	2.64
German (2,335)	7,925	40.06
Hungarian (87)	103	0.52
Icelander (0)	8	0.04
Irish (364)	2,367	11.96
Italian (194)	803	4.06
Lithuanian (0)	28	0.14
Northern European (39)	39	0.20
Norwegian (879)	3,444	17.41
Polish (251)	1,281	6.47
Romanian (10)	41	0.21
Russian (8)	115	0.58
Scandinavian (272)	522	2.64
Scotch-Irish (43)	190	0.96
Scottish (25)	169	0.85
Slavic (8)	8	0.04
Slovak (0)	60	0.30
Slovene (20)	54	0.27
Swedish (292)	2,169	10.96
Swiss (36)	139	0.70
Ukrainian (42)	58	0.29
Welsh (12)	67	0.34
West Indian, ex. Hispanic (9)	29	0.15
Haitian (9)	29	0.15
Yugoslavian (24)	52	0.26

Hispanic Origin	Population	%
Hispanic or Latino (of any race)	373	1.85
Central American, ex. Mexican	28	0.14
Costa Rican	5	0.02
Guatemalan	19	0.09
Panamanian	1	<0.01
Salvadoran	3	0.01
Cuban	4	0.02
Dominican Republic	6	0.03
Mexican	167	0.83
Puerto Rican	21	0.10
South American	40	0.20
Argentinean	7	0.03
Chilean	1	<0.01
Colombian	18	0.09
Ecuadorian	3	0.01
Peruvian	3	0.01
Venezuelan	8	0.04
Other Hispanic or Latino	107	0.53

Race*	Population	%
African-American/Black (550)	638	3.16
Not Hispanic (540)	627	3.10
Hispanic (10)	11	0.05
American Indian/Alaska Native (139)	208	1.03
Not Hispanic (134)	198	0.98
Hispanic (5)	10	0.05
Blackfeet (0)	2	0.01
Cherokee (0)	4	0.02
Cheyenne (1)	4	0.02
Chippewa (22)	44	0.22
Choctaw (0)	1	<0.01
Iroquois (0)	1	<0.01
Kiowa (1)	2	0.01
Menominee (1)	1	<0.01
Mexican American Ind. (2)	2	0.01
Ottawa (0)	2	0.01
Potawatomi (0)	1	<0.01
Seminole (0)	1	<0.01
Sioux (3)	9	0.04
South American Ind. (0)	3	0.01
Asian (754)	910	4.50
Not Hispanic (750)	899	4.45
Hispanic (4)	11	0.05

SECTION TWO

*Notes: † The Census 2010 population figure is used to calculate the percentages in the Hispanic Origin and Race categories. Ancestry percentages are based on the 2006-2010 American Community Survey population (not shown); ‡ Numbers in parentheses indicate the number of people reporting a single ancestry; * Numbers in parentheses indicate the number of persons reporting this race alone, not in combination with any other race; Please refer to the Explanation of Data for more information.*

Cambodian (9)	11	0.05
Chinese, ex. Taiwanese (58)	76	0.38
Filipino (13)	49	0.24
Hmong (334)	358	1.77
Indian (64)	78	0.39
Indonesian (1)	1	<0.01
Japanese (3)	19	0.09
Korean (71)	111	0.55
Laotian (6)	8	0.04
Malaysian (4)	6	0.03
Pakistani (4)	4	0.02
Taiwanese (6)	6	0.03
Thai (6)	11	0.05
Vietnamese (79)	97	0.48
Hawaii Native/Pacific Islander (16)	28	0.14
Not Hispanic (15)	27	0.13
Hispanic (1)	1	<0.01
Guamanian/Chamorro (1)	1	<0.01
Native Hawaiian (11)	17	0.08
White (18,369)	18,659	92.30
Not Hispanic (18,098)	18,368	90.86
Hispanic (271)	291	1.44

Little Canada

Place Type: City
County: Ramsey
Population: 9,773†

Ancestry‡	Population	%
African, Sub-Saharan (121)	137	1.42
African (0)	16	0.17
Ethiopian (75)	75	0.78
Kenyan (12)	12	0.12
Other Sub-Saharan African (34)	34	0.35
American (226)	226	2.34
Arab (50)	60	0.62
Arab (28)	28	0.29
Lebanese (22)	32	0.33
Austrian (12)	71	0.73
British (0)	10	0.10
Czech (28)	135	1.40
Czechoslovakian (0)	16	0.17
Danish (32)	155	1.60
Dutch (20)	137	1.42
English (62)	565	5.84
Estonian (0)	24	0.25
European (41)	41	0.42
Finnish (54)	76	0.79
French, ex. Basque (32)	573	5.93
French Canadian (53)	208	2.15
German (880)	3,239	33.50
Greek (0)	12	0.12
Hungarian (16)	56	0.58
Iranian (11)	11	0.11
Irish (230)	1,420	14.69
Italian (112)	495	5.12
Luxemburger (0)	33	0.34
Northern European (71)	71	0.73
Norwegian (340)	1,233	12.75
Pennsylvania German (0)	11	0.11
Polish (79)	408	4.22
Russian (0)	12	0.12
Scandinavian (38)	58	0.60
Scotch-Irish (13)	140	1.45
Scottish (27)	120	1.24
Slovene (0)	8	0.08
Swedish (186)	865	8.95
Swiss (8)	51	0.53
Welsh (0)	111	1.15
Yugoslavian (0)	19	0.20

Hispanic Origin	Population	%
Hispanic or Latino (of any race)	566	5.79
Central American, ex. Mexican	60	0.61
Costa Rican	5	0.05
Guatemalan	12	0.12
Honduran	18	0.18
Nicaraguan	7	0.07
Panamanian	3	0.03
Salvadoran	15	0.15
Cuban	7	0.07
Dominican Republic	1	0.01
Mexican	398	4.07
Puerto Rican	18	0.18
South American	27	0.28
Argentinean	3	0.03
Colombian	12	0.12
Ecuadorian	6	0.06
Uruguayan	4	0.04
Venezuelan	2	0.02
Other Hispanic or Latino	55	0.56

Race*	Population	%
African-American/Black (641)	766	7.84
Not Hispanic (631)	743	7.60
Hispanic (10)	23	0.24
American Indian/Alaska Native (51)	115	1.18
Not Hispanic (35)	82	0.84
Hispanic (16)	33	0.34
Apache (1)	2	0.02
Cherokee (0)	6	0.06
Chippewa (25)	47	0.48
Cree (2)	2	0.02
Hopi (1)	1	0.01
Seminole (1)	1	0.01
Sioux (5)	8	0.08
Yup'ik *(Alaska Native)* (1)	1	0.01
Asian (1,280)	1,343	13.74
Not Hispanic (1,275)	1,334	13.65
Hispanic (5)	9	0.09
Bangladeshi (7)	7	0.07
Burmese (1)	1	0.01
Cambodian (19)	33	0.34
Chinese, ex. Taiwanese (110)	146	1.49
Filipino (26)	36	0.37
Hmong (638)	650	6.65
Indian (127)	141	1.44
Japanese (2)	5	0.05
Korean (40)	45	0.46
Laotian (16)	19	0.19
Malaysian (2)	3	0.03
Nepalese (3)	3	0.03
Pakistani (6)	9	0.09
Taiwanese (9)	9	0.09
Thai (4)	6	0.06
Vietnamese (183)	207	2.12
Hawaii Native/Pacific Islander (3)	16	0.16
Not Hispanic (3)	14	0.14
Hispanic (0)	2	0.02
Guamanian/Chamorro (1)	1	0.01
Native Hawaiian (1)	4	0.04
Samoan (1)	2	0.02
White (7,287)	7,500	76.74
Not Hispanic (7,053)	7,238	74.06
Hispanic (234)	262	2.68

Little Falls

Place Type: City
County: Morrison
Population: 8,343†

Ancestry‡	Population	%
American (367)	367	4.40
Austrian (0)	8	0.10
Belgian (0)	12	0.14
Canadian (12)	12	0.14
Czech (23)	156	1.87
Czechoslovakian (0)	7	0.08
Danish (0)	155	1.86
Dutch (45)	161	1.93
English (206)	414	4.96
Finnish (8)	19	0.23
French, ex. Basque (84)	877	10.50
French Canadian (40)	96	1.15
German (1,078)	3,661	43.84
Icelander (11)	11	0.13
Irish (118)	725	8.68
Italian (66)	265	3.17
Luxemburger (0)	9	0.11
Northern European (10)	10	0.12
Norwegian (291)	1,109	13.28
Polish (562)	1,369	16.40
Russian (11)	14	0.17
Scandinavian (12)	42	0.50
Scotch-Irish (0)	21	0.25
Scottish (23)	95	1.14
Slovak (0)	55	0.66
Slovene (12)	12	0.14
Swedish (117)	904	10.83
Welsh (0)	29	0.35

Hispanic Origin	Population	%
Hispanic or Latino (of any race)	116	1.39
Central American, ex. Mexican	2	0.02
Costa Rican	1	0.01
Salvadoran	1	0.01
Mexican	79	0.95
Puerto Rican	8	0.10
South American	3	0.04
Colombian	3	0.04
Other Hispanic or Latino	24	0.29

Race*	Population	%
African-American/Black (66)	118	1.41
Not Hispanic (66)	117	1.40
Hispanic (0)	1	0.01
American Indian/Alaska Native (32)	115	1.38
Not Hispanic (31)	110	1.32
Hispanic (1)	5	0.06
Aleut *(Alaska Native)* (0)	1	0.01
Apache (0)	2	0.02
Cherokee (0)	14	0.17
Chickasaw (0)	1	0.01
Chippewa (15)	48	0.58
Choctaw (0)	2	0.02
Creek (0)	1	0.01
Sioux (1)	7	0.08
Asian (45)	77	0.92
Not Hispanic (45)	77	0.92
Chinese, ex. Taiwanese (5)	12	0.14
Filipino (1)	5	0.06
Indian (10)	14	0.17
Indonesian (0)	1	0.01
Japanese (1)	4	0.05
Korean (3)	7	0.08
Laotian (2)	4	0.05
Thai (1)	3	0.04
Vietnamese (21)	21	0.25
Hawaii Native/Pacific Islander (3)	16	0.19
Not Hispanic (1)	13	0.16
Hispanic (2)	3	0.04
Fijian (1)	2	0.02
Guamanian/Chamorro (0)	4	0.05
Native Hawaiian (0)	11	0.13
Samoan (2)	3	0.04
White (8,021)	8,175	97.99
Not Hispanic (7,939)	8,078	96.82
Hispanic (82)	97	1.16

Mahtomedi

Place Type: City
County: Washington
Population: 7,676†

Ancestry‡	Population	%
African, Sub-Saharan (61)	61	0.79
Somalian (43)	43	0.56
South African (18)	18	0.23
American (524)	524	6.81
Austrian (9)	67	0.87
British (9)	22	0.29
Canadian (0)	28	0.36
Czech (84)	123	1.60
Danish (11)	163	2.12
Dutch (41)	150	1.95
English (113)	644	8.36
European (102)	102	1.32

*Notes: † The Census 2010 population figure is used to calculate the percentages in the Hispanic Origin and Race categories. Ancestry percentages are based on the 2006-2010 American Community Survey population (not shown); ‡ Numbers in parentheses indicate the number of people reporting a single ancestry; * Numbers in parentheses indicate the number of persons reporting this race alone, not in combination with any other race; Please refer to the Explanation of Data for more information.*

Finnish (0)	75	0.97
French, ex. Basque (60)	579	7.52
French Canadian (74)	148	1.92
German (992)	3,144	40.84
Hungarian (0)	19	0.25
Icelander (0)	3	0.04
Irish (225)	1,199	15.57
Italian (50)	256	3.33
Northern European (87)	87	1.13
Norwegian (280)	826	10.73
Polish (49)	315	4.09
Scandinavian (77)	167	2.17
Scotch-Irish (8)	86	1.12
Scottish (25)	131	1.70
Slavic (0)	32	0.42
Slovak (0)	18	0.23
Slovene (10)	23	0.30
Swedish (293)	863	11.21
Swiss (27)	55	0.71
Welsh (0)	71	0.92

Hispanic Origin	Population	%
Hispanic or Latino (of any race)	96	1.25
Central American, ex. Mexican	2	0.03
Guatemalan	1	0.01
Nicaraguan	1	0.01
Cuban	3	0.04
Mexican	59	0.77
Puerto Rican	8	0.10
South American	13	0.17
Chilean	1	0.01
Colombian	4	0.05
Ecuadorian	2	0.03
Peruvian	2	0.03
Venezuelan	4	0.05
Other Hispanic or Latino	11	0.14

Race*	Population	%
African-American/Black (176)	236	3.07
Not Hispanic (176)	233	3.04
Hispanic (0)	3	0.04
American Indian/Alaska Native (18)	46	0.60
Not Hispanic (18)	41	0.53
Hispanic (0)	5	0.07
Alaska Athabascan *(Ala. Nat.)* (0)	1	0.01
Canadian/French Am. Ind. (1)	1	0.01
Cherokee (2)	3	0.04
Chippewa (5)	9	0.12
Choctaw (0)	2	0.03
Iroquois (0)	2	0.03
Sioux (5)	7	0.09
Asian (93)	138	1.80
Not Hispanic (93)	136	1.77
Hispanic (0)	2	0.03
Chinese, ex. Taiwanese (6)	10	0.13
Filipino (3)	13	0.17
Hmong (26)	30	0.39
Indian (16)	27	0.35
Japanese (4)	8	0.10
Korean (23)	29	0.38
Pakistani (1)	4	0.05
Sri Lankan (1)	4	0.05
Taiwanese (1)	4	0.05
Vietnamese (3)	8	0.10
Hawaii Native/Pacific Islander (4)	6	0.08
Not Hispanic (4)	6	0.08
Native Hawaiian (2)	4	0.05
White (7,229)	7,360	95.88
Not Hispanic (7,155)	7,277	94.80
Hispanic (74)	83	1.08

Mankato

Place Type: City
County: Blue Earth
Population: 39,305†

Ancestry‡	Population	%
African, Sub-Saharan (847)	907	2.38
African (181)	241	0.63
Ethiopian (15)	15	0.04
Nigerian (65)	65	0.17
Somalian (395)	395	1.03
Sudanese (191)	191	0.50
American (868)	868	2.27
Arab (175)	256	0.67
Arab (60)	60	0.16
Lebanese (67)	136	0.36
Moroccan (48)	48	0.13
Syrian (0)	12	0.03
Australian (0)	10	0.03
Austrian (12)	116	0.30
Belgian (130)	226	0.59
British (108)	185	0.48
Canadian (0)	29	0.08
Carpatho Rusyn (9)	19	0.05
Croatian (19)	40	0.10
Czech (163)	696	1.82
Czechoslovakian (17)	44	0.12
Danish (95)	754	1.97
Dutch (221)	856	2.24
English (348)	1,826	4.78
European (283)	299	0.78
Finnish (25)	133	0.35
French, ex. Basque (95)	1,100	2.88
French Canadian (70)	229	0.60
German (8,023)	19,218	50.33
Greek (26)	34	0.09
Hungarian (0)	25	0.07
Icelander (9)	37	0.10
Irish (894)	4,882	12.78
Italian (298)	618	1.62
Latvian (44)	44	0.12
Luxemburger (0)	41	0.11
Northern European (21)	30	0.08
Norwegian (2,078)	6,337	16.59
Pennsylvania German (0)	10	0.03
Polish (203)	1,072	2.81
Romanian (0)	19	0.05
Russian (0)	109	0.29
Scandinavian (269)	448	1.17
Scotch-Irish (175)	335	0.88
Scottish (118)	481	1.26
Serbian (0)	12	0.03
Slavic (29)	29	0.08
Slovak (0)	20	0.05
Slovene (0)	9	0.02
Swedish (399)	2,464	6.45
Swiss (45)	158	0.41
Ukrainian (59)	70	0.18
Welsh (39)	259	0.68

Hispanic Origin	Population	%
Hispanic or Latino (of any race)	1,151	2.93
Central American, ex. Mexican	55	0.14
Costa Rican	11	0.03
Guatemalan	17	0.04
Honduran	6	0.02
Nicaraguan	3	0.01
Panamanian	3	0.01
Salvadoran	15	0.04
Cuban	17	0.04
Dominican Republic	7	0.02
Mexican	843	2.14
Puerto Rican	48	0.12
South American	68	0.17
Argentinean	2	0.01
Bolivian	6	0.02
Chilean	9	0.02
Colombian	25	0.06
Ecuadorian	5	0.01
Paraguayan	3	0.01
Peruvian	10	0.03
Venezuelan	7	0.02
Other South American	1	<0.01
Other Hispanic or Latino	113	0.29

Race*	Population	%
African-American/Black (1,583)	1,964	5.00
Not Hispanic (1,560)	1,912	4.86
Hispanic (23)	52	0.13
American Indian/Alaska Native (132)	317	0.81
Not Hispanic (104)	266	0.68
Hispanic (28)	51	0.13
Alaska Athabascan *(Ala. Nat.)* (0)	1	<0.01
Apache (1)	3	0.01
Blackfeet (0)	2	0.01
Canadian/French Am. Ind. (0)	2	0.01
Cherokee (6)	18	0.05
Cheyenne (1)	1	<0.01
Chippewa (24)	40	0.10
Choctaw (0)	3	0.01
Creek (0)	4	0.01
Crow (0)	1	<0.01
Delaware (1)	1	<0.01
Inupiat *(Alaska Native)* (6)	6	0.02
Iroquois (0)	2	0.01
Menominee (0)	1	<0.01
Mexican American Ind. (4)	7	0.02
Potawatomi (4)	4	0.01
Pueblo (1)	2	0.01
Puget Sound Salish (5)	5	0.01
Seminole (0)	4	0.01
Sioux (17)	34	0.09
South American Ind. (2)	2	0.01
Spanish American Ind. (1)	1	<0.01
Tlingit-Haida *(Alaska Native)* (1)	1	<0.01
Yaqui (0)	4	0.01
Yup'ik *(Alaska Native)* (0)	4	0.01
Asian (1,094)	1,337	3.40
Not Hispanic (1,092)	1,325	3.37
Hispanic (2)	12	0.03
Bangladeshi (20)	21	0.05
Burmese (2)	2	0.01
Cambodian (39)	61	0.16
Chinese, ex. Taiwanese (113)	143	0.36
Filipino (47)	90	0.23
Hmong (71)	76	0.19
Indian (196)	222	0.56
Indonesian (1)	1	<0.01
Japanese (30)	59	0.15
Korean (142)	183	0.47
Laotian (32)	44	0.11
Malaysian (3)	3	0.01
Nepalese (61)	64	0.16
Pakistani (47)	51	0.13
Sri Lankan (14)	19	0.05
Taiwanese (17)	19	0.05
Thai (8)	23	0.06
Vietnamese (144)	163	0.41
Hawaii Native/Pacific Islander (16)	41	0.10
Not Hispanic (16)	40	0.10
Hispanic (0)	1	<0.01
Guamanian/Chamorro (6)	8	0.02
Marshallese (1)	1	<0.01
Native Hawaiian (1)	10	0.03
Samoan (6)	7	0.02
White (35,350)	36,074	91.78
Not Hispanic (34,654)	35,267	89.73
Hispanic (696)	807	2.05

Mankato

Place Type: City
County: Blue Earth
Population: 39,309†

Ancestry‡	Population	%
African, Sub-Saharan (847)	907	2.38
African (181)	241	0.63
Ethiopian (15)	15	0.04
Nigerian (65)	65	0.17
Somalian (395)	395	1.03
Sudanese (191)	191	0.50
American (868)	868	2.27
Arab (175)	256	0.67
Arab (60)	60	0.16
Lebanese (67)	136	0.36
Moroccan (48)	48	0.13
Syrian (0)	12	0.03

*Notes: † The Census 2010 population figure is used to calculate the percentages in the Hispanic Origin and Race categories. Ancestry percentages are based on the 2006-2010 American Community Survey population (not shown); ‡ Numbers in parentheses indicate the number of people reporting a single ancestry; * Numbers in parentheses indicate the number of persons reporting this race alone, not in combination with any other race; Please refer to the Explanation of Data for more information.*

Australian (0)	10	0.03
Austrian (12)	116	0.30
Belgian (130)	226	0.59
British (108)	185	0.48
Canadian (0)	29	0.08
Carpatho Rusyn (9)	19	0.05
Croatian (19)	40	0.10
Czech (163)	696	1.82
Czechoslovakian (17)	44	0.12
Danish (95)	754	1.97
Dutch (221)	856	2.24
English (348)	1,826	4.78
European (283)	299	0.78
Finnish (25)	133	0.35
French, ex. Basque (95)	1,100	2.88
French Canadian (70)	229	0.60
German (8,023)	19,218	50.33
Greek (26)	34	0.09
Hungarian (0)	25	0.07
Icelander (9)	37	0.10
Irish (894)	4,882	12.78
Italian (298)	618	1.62
Latvian (44)	44	0.12
Luxemburger (0)	41	0.11
Northern European (21)	30	0.08
Norwegian (2,078)	6,337	16.59
Pennsylvania German (0)	10	0.03
Polish (203)	1,072	2.81
Romanian (0)	19	0.05
Russian (0)	109	0.29
Scandinavian (269)	448	1.17
Scotch-Irish (175)	335	0.88
Scottish (118)	481	1.26
Serbian (0)	12	0.03
Slavic (29)	29	0.08
Slovak (0)	20	0.05
Slovene (0)	9	0.02
Swedish (399)	2,464	6.45
Swiss (45)	158	0.41
Ukrainian (59)	70	0.18
Welsh (39)	259	0.68

Hispanic Origin	Population	%
Hispanic or Latino (of any race)	1,153	2.93
Central American, ex. Mexican	55	0.14
Costa Rican	11	0.03
Guatemalan	17	0.04
Honduran	6	0.02
Nicaraguan	3	0.01
Panamanian	3	0.01
Salvadoran	15	0.04
Cuban	17	0.04
Dominican Republic	7	0.02
Mexican	845	2.15
Puerto Rican	48	0.12
South American	68	0.17
Argentinean	2	0.01
Bolivian	6	0.02
Chilean	9	0.02
Colombian	25	0.06
Ecuadorian	5	0.01
Paraguayan	3	0.01
Peruvian	10	0.03
Venezuelan	7	0.02
Other South American	1	<0.01
Other Hispanic or Latino	113	0.29

Race*	Population	%
African-American/Black (1,583)	1,964	5.00
Not Hispanic (1,560)	1,912	4.86
Hispanic (23)	52	0.13
American Indian/Alaska Native (132)	317	0.81
Not Hispanic (104)	266	0.68
Hispanic (28)	51	0.13
Alaska Athabascan *(Ala. Nat.)* (0)	1	<0.01
Apache (1)	3	0.01
Blackfeet (0)	2	0.01
Canadian/French Am. Ind. (0)	2	0.01
Cherokee (6)	18	0.05
Cheyenne (1)	1	<0.01
Chippewa (24)	40	0.10
Choctaw (0)	3	0.01
Creek (0)	4	0.01
Crow (0)	1	<0.01
Delaware (1)	1	<0.01
Inupiat *(Alaska Native)* (6)	6	0.02
Iroquois (0)	2	0.01
Menominee (0)	1	<0.01
Mexican American Ind. (4)	7	0.02
Potawatomi (4)	4	0.01
Pueblo (1)	2	0.01
Puget Sound Salish (5)	5	0.01
Seminole (0)	4	0.01
Sioux (17)	34	0.09
South American Ind. (2)	2	0.01
Spanish American Ind. (1)	1	<0.01
Tlingit-Haida *(Alaska Native)* (1)	1	<0.01
Yaqui (0)	4	0.01
Yup'ik *(Alaska Native)* (0)	4	0.01
Asian (1,094)	1,337	3.40
Not Hispanic (1,092)	1,325	3.37
Hispanic (2)	12	0.03
Bangladeshi (20)	21	0.05
Burmese (2)	2	0.01
Cambodian (39)	61	0.16
Chinese, ex. Taiwanese (113)	143	0.36
Filipino (47)	90	0.23
Hmong (71)	76	0.19
Indian (196)	222	0.56
Indonesian (1)	1	<0.01
Japanese (30)	59	0.15
Korean (142)	183	0.47
Laotian (32)	44	0.11
Malaysian (3)	3	0.01
Nepalese (61)	64	0.16
Pakistani (47)	51	0.13
Sri Lankan (14)	19	0.05
Taiwanese (17)	19	0.05
Thai (8)	23	0.06
Vietnamese (144)	163	0.41
Hawaii Native/Pacific Islander (16)	41	0.10
Not Hispanic (16)	40	0.10
Hispanic (0)	1	<0.01
Guamanian/Chamorro (6)	8	0.02
Marshallese (1)	1	<0.01
Native Hawaiian (1)	10	0.03
Samoan (6)	7	0.02
White (35,353)	36,077	91.78
Not Hispanic (34,656)	35,269	89.72
Hispanic (697)	808	2.06

Maple Grove

Place Type: City
County: Hennepin
Population: 61,567†

Ancestry‡	Population	%
African, Sub-Saharan (755)	772	1.31
African (420)	420	0.71
Ethiopian (47)	47	0.08
Kenyan (16)	16	0.03
Liberian (34)	42	0.07
Nigerian (221)	230	0.39
South African (17)	17	0.03
Albanian (0)	12	0.02
American (1,245)	1,245	2.11
Arab (309)	358	0.61
Egyptian (47)	47	0.08
Jordanian (117)	117	0.20
Lebanese (79)	110	0.19
Palestinian (29)	36	0.06
Syrian (0)	11	0.02
Other Arab (37)	37	0.06
Armenian (35)	45	0.08
Assyrian/Chaldean/Syriac (0)	16	0.03
Australian (30)	40	0.07
Austrian (0)	249	0.42
Belgian (35)	223	0.38
Brazilian (3)	3	0.01
British (50)	259	0.44
Canadian (41)	138	0.23
Carpatho Rusyn (0)	12	0.02
Celtic (14)	14	0.02
Croatian (42)	85	0.14
Czech (181)	1,056	1.79
Czechoslovakian (96)	233	0.39
Danish (239)	1,152	1.95
Dutch (158)	1,095	1.85
Eastern European (91)	100	0.17
English (753)	4,032	6.83
European (790)	838	1.42
Finnish (221)	997	1.69
French, ex. Basque (203)	2,770	4.69
French Canadian (227)	741	1.26
German (6,691)	22,394	37.93
Greek (79)	238	0.40
Guyanese (6)	6	0.01
Hungarian (80)	250	0.42
Icelander (25)	107	0.18
Iranian (69)	69	0.12
Irish (1,110)	6,811	11.54
Italian (289)	1,499	2.54
Latvian (67)	123	0.21
Lithuanian (36)	94	0.16
Luxemburger (0)	16	0.03
New Zealander (0)	10	0.02
Northern European (186)	186	0.32
Norwegian (2,656)	10,177	17.24
Pennsylvania German (0)	9	0.02
Polish (688)	3,118	5.28
Portuguese (0)	21	0.04
Romanian (8)	39	0.07
Russian (992)	1,642	2.78
Scandinavian (458)	917	1.55
Scotch-Irish (138)	494	0.84
Scottish (230)	970	1.64
Serbian (15)	40	0.07
Slavic (11)	59	0.10
Slovak (8)	31	0.05
Slovene (77)	121	0.20
Swedish (1,249)	6,556	11.10
Swiss (108)	463	0.78
Turkish (14)	14	0.02
Ukrainian (141)	390	0.66
Welsh (32)	505	0.86
West Indian, ex. Hispanic (13)	36	0.06
Haitian (3)	3	0.01
West Indian (10)	33	0.06
Yugoslavian (23)	65	0.11

Hispanic Origin	Population	%
Hispanic or Latino (of any race)	1,545	2.51
Central American, ex. Mexican	135	0.22
Costa Rican	14	0.02
Guatemalan	48	0.08
Honduran	42	0.07
Nicaraguan	10	0.02
Panamanian	2	<0.01
Salvadoran	19	0.03
Cuban	27	0.04
Dominican Republic	5	0.01
Mexican	788	1.28
Puerto Rican	120	0.19
South American	323	0.52
Argentinean	36	0.06
Bolivian	21	0.03
Chilean	26	0.04
Colombian	119	0.19
Ecuadorian	28	0.05
Paraguayan	2	<0.01
Peruvian	70	0.11
Uruguayan	3	<0.01
Venezuelan	17	0.03
Other South American	1	<0.01
Other Hispanic or Latino	147	0.24

Race*	Population	%
African-American/Black (2,568)	3,157	5.13
Not Hispanic (2,513)	3,062	4.97

*Notes: † The Census 2010 population figure is used to calculate the percentages in the Hispanic Origin and Race categories. Ancestry percentages are based on the 2006-2010 American Community Survey population (not shown); ‡ Numbers in parentheses indicate the number of people reporting a single ancestry; * Numbers in parentheses indicate the number of persons reporting this race alone, not in combination with any other race; Please refer to the Explanation of Data for more information.*

Hispanic (55)	95	0.15
American Indian/Alaska Native (170)	415	0.67
Not Hispanic (154)	377	0.61
Hispanic (16)	38	0.06
Alaska Athabascan *(Ala. Nat.)* (1)	1	<0.01
Blackfeet (0)	1	<0.01
Canadian/French Am. Ind. (2)	3	<0.01
Central American Ind. (3)	3	<0.01
Cherokee (3)	25	0.04
Cheyenne (0)	1	<0.01
Chippewa (62)	130	0.21
Choctaw (2)	10	0.02
Comanche (2)	4	0.01
Cree (0)	3	<0.01
Creek (1)	1	<0.01
Iroquois (2)	3	<0.01
Kiowa (1)	1	<0.01
Menominee (1)	3	<0.01
Mexican American Ind. (2)	5	0.01
Navajo (2)	2	<0.01
Sioux (9)	25	0.04
South American Ind. (1)	11	0.02
Spanish American Ind. (1)	1	<0.01
Yakama (3)	3	<0.01
Asian (3,807)	4,347	7.06
Not Hispanic (3,801)	4,329	7.03
Hispanic (6)	18	0.03
Bangladeshi (52)	58	0.09
Cambodian (66)	74	0.12
Chinese, ex. Taiwanese (759)	855	1.39
Filipino (181)	308	0.50
Hmong (124)	136	0.22
Indian (1,359)	1,440	2.34
Indonesian (9)	10	0.02
Japanese (45)	109	0.18
Korean (389)	509	0.83
Laotian (145)	169	0.27
Malaysian (1)	2	<0.01
Nepalese (10)	13	0.02
Pakistani (86)	99	0.16
Sri Lankan (25)	32	0.05
Taiwanese (20)	24	0.04
Thai (11)	19	0.03
Vietnamese (410)	450	0.73
Hawaii Native/Pacific Islander (26)	79	0.13
Not Hispanic (24)	74	0.12
Hispanic (2)	5	0.01
Fijian (4)	4	0.01
Guamanian/Chamorro (5)	6	0.01
Native Hawaiian (5)	30	0.05
Samoan (11)	22	0.04
White (53,164)	54,374	88.32
Not Hispanic (52,222)	53,322	86.61
Hispanic (942)	1,052	1.71

Maplewood

Place Type: City
County: Ramsey
Population: 38,018†

Ancestry‡	Population	%
African, Sub-Saharan (444)	577	1.56
African (101)	217	0.59
Kenyan (23)	40	0.11
Liberian (92)	92	0.25
Nigerian (228)	228	0.61
American (955)	955	2.58
Arab (74)	330	0.89
Arab (32)	32	0.09
Egyptian (0)	145	0.39
Lebanese (0)	87	0.23
Palestinian (42)	42	0.11
Syrian (0)	13	0.04
Other Arab (0)	11	0.03
Armenian (0)	10	0.03
Austrian (66)	237	0.64
Basque (0)	11	0.03
Belgian (27)	52	0.14
British (15)	23	0.06
Canadian (0)	15	0.04
Croatian (0)	10	0.03
Czech (166)	782	2.11
Czechoslovakian (10)	28	0.08
Danish (77)	498	1.34
Dutch (98)	368	0.99
Eastern European (0)	11	0.03
English (244)	2,093	5.64
European (328)	328	0.88
Finnish (65)	263	0.71
French, ex. Basque (80)	2,199	5.93
French Canadian (227)	598	1.61
German (3,192)	11,485	30.97
Greek (47)	47	0.13
Guyanese (31)	31	0.08
Hungarian (42)	180	0.49
Irish (711)	5,070	13.67
Italian (531)	1,756	4.74
Latvian (7)	21	0.06
Lithuanian (28)	28	0.08
Luxemburger (0)	23	0.06
Northern European (376)	429	1.16
Norwegian (1,261)	4,522	12.19
Polish (546)	2,356	6.35
Romanian (29)	29	0.08
Russian (57)	130	0.35
Scandinavian (72)	243	0.66
Scotch-Irish (60)	259	0.70
Scottish (71)	404	1.09
Serbian (11)	11	0.03
Slovak (9)	42	0.11
Slovene (13)	25	0.07
Swedish (701)	3,646	9.83
Swiss (0)	94	0.25
Turkish (41)	148	0.40
Ukrainian (22)	22	0.06
Welsh (0)	87	0.23
West Indian, ex. Hispanic (0)	8	0.02
Bermudan (0)	8	0.02
Yugoslavian (30)	77	0.21

Hispanic Origin	Population	%
Hispanic or Latino (of any race)	2,342	6.16
Central American, ex. Mexican	238	0.63
Costa Rican	3	0.01
Guatemalan	38	0.10
Honduran	19	0.05
Nicaraguan	7	0.02
Panamanian	9	0.02
Salvadoran	161	0.42
Other Central American	1	<0.01
Cuban	22	0.06
Dominican Republic	11	0.03
Mexican	1,668	4.39
Puerto Rican	108	0.28
South American	65	0.17
Argentinean	8	0.02
Chilean	5	0.01
Colombian	26	0.07
Ecuadorian	3	0.01
Peruvian	8	0.02
Uruguayan	1	<0.01
Venezuelan	9	0.02
Other South American	5	0.01
Other Hispanic or Latino	230	0.60

Race*	Population	%
African-American/Black (3,122)	3,701	9.73
Not Hispanic (3,029)	3,538	9.31
Hispanic (93)	163	0.43
American Indian/Alaska Native (197)	480	1.26
Not Hispanic (160)	388	1.02
Hispanic (37)	92	0.24
Alaska Athabascan *(Ala. Nat.)* (1)	1	<0.01
Blackfeet (0)	6	0.02
Canadian/French Am. Ind. (1)	1	<0.01
Central American Ind. (1)	1	<0.01
Cherokee (3)	17	0.04
Cheyenne (0)	1	<0.01
Chippewa (55)	99	0.26
Choctaw (0)	1	<0.01
Comanche (3)	3	0.01
Cree (1)	2	0.01
Delaware (0)	3	0.01
Iroquois (2)	8	0.02
Kiowa (1)	1	<0.01
Menominee (1)	2	0.01
Mexican American Ind. (8)	19	0.05
Navajo (1)	1	<0.01
Ottawa (0)	1	<0.01
Shoshone (0)	1	<0.01
Sioux (33)	64	0.17
Asian (3,963)	4,258	11.20
Not Hispanic (3,939)	4,209	11.07
Hispanic (24)	49	0.13
Bangladeshi (2)	4	0.01
Burmese (220)	224	0.59
Cambodian (95)	107	0.28
Chinese, ex. Taiwanese (200)	257	0.68
Filipino (109)	164	0.43
Hmong (2,428)	2,512	6.61
Indian (199)	265	0.70
Indonesian (3)	8	0.02
Japanese (18)	39	0.10
Korean (86)	145	0.38
Laotian (25)	34	0.09
Malaysian (5)	5	0.01
Pakistani (27)	28	0.07
Sri Lankan (6)	8	0.02
Taiwanese (6)	11	0.03
Thai (17)	25	0.07
Vietnamese (322)	358	0.94
Hawaii Native/Pacific Islander (21)	70	0.18
Not Hispanic (13)	51	0.13
Hispanic (8)	19	0.05
Guamanian/Chamorro (1)	1	<0.01
Native Hawaiian (7)	17	0.04
Samoan (9)	13	0.03
Tongan (2)	3	0.01
White (28,719)	29,684	78.08
Not Hispanic (27,598)	28,405	74.71
Hispanic (1,121)	1,279	3.36

Marshall

Place Type: City
County: Lyon
Population: 13,680†

Ancestry‡	Population	%
African, Sub-Saharan (158)	158	1.18
African (68)	68	0.51
Ethiopian (79)	79	0.59
Nigerian (11)	11	0.08
American (249)	249	1.85
Arab (74)	74	0.55
Egyptian (63)	63	0.47
Jordanian (11)	11	0.08
Austrian (0)	46	0.34
Belgian (287)	933	6.95
British (10)	69	0.51
Canadian (0)	10	0.07
Croatian (0)	14	0.10
Czech (62)	176	1.31
Danish (78)	471	3.51
Dutch (102)	641	4.77
English (88)	566	4.22
European (71)	71	0.53
Finnish (22)	92	0.69
French, ex. Basque (13)	478	3.56
French Canadian (25)	122	0.91
German (2,355)	6,189	46.09
Icelander (0)	19	0.14
Irish (215)	1,390	10.35
Italian (40)	135	1.01
Lithuanian (25)	100	0.74
Luxemburger (0)	45	0.34
Norwegian (562)	2,339	17.42
Polish (71)	408	3.04
Romanian (6)	6	0.04

*Notes: † The Census 2010 population figure is used to calculate the percentages in the Hispanic Origin and Race categories. Ancestry percentages are based on the 2006-2010 American Community Survey population (not shown); ‡ Numbers in parentheses indicate the number of people reporting a single ancestry; * Numbers in parentheses indicate the number of persons reporting this race alone, not in combination with any other race; Please refer to the Explanation of Data for more information.*

Ancestry (cont.)	Population	%
Russian (0)	54	0.40
Scandinavian (55)	80	0.60
Scotch-Irish (48)	152	1.13
Scottish (12)	36	0.27
Slovene (0)	39	0.29
Swedish (121)	768	5.72
Swiss (0)	54	0.40
Welsh (0)	13	0.10
West Indian, ex. Hispanic (0)	23	0.17
Bahamian (0)	23	0.17

Hispanic Origin	Population	%
Hispanic or Latino (of any race)	1,063	7.77
Central American, ex. Mexican	223	1.63
Guatemalan	131	0.96
Honduran	49	0.36
Nicaraguan	23	0.17
Panamanian	3	0.02
Salvadoran	17	0.12
Cuban	1	0.01
Dominican Republic	3	0.02
Mexican	677	4.95
Puerto Rican	17	0.12
South American	25	0.18
Colombian	11	0.08
Ecuadorian	1	0.01
Peruvian	7	0.05
Venezuelan	6	0.04
Other Hispanic or Latino	117	0.86

Race*	Population	%
African-American/Black (544)	667	4.88
Not Hispanic (534)	647	4.73
Hispanic (10)	20	0.15
American Indian/Alaska Native (84)	149	1.09
Not Hispanic (59)	114	0.83
Hispanic (25)	35	0.26
Blackfeet (0)	2	0.01
Cherokee (0)	3	0.02
Chickasaw (8)	8	0.06
Chippewa (11)	20	0.15
Iroquois (0)	1	0.01
Mexican American Ind. (12)	12	0.09
Sioux (4)	6	0.04
Asian (410)	472	3.45
Not Hispanic (408)	464	3.39
Hispanic (2)	8	0.06
Burmese (1)	1	0.01
Chinese, ex. Taiwanese (15)	20	0.15
Filipino (11)	24	0.18
Hmong (91)	98	0.72
Indian (108)	118	0.86
Indonesian (0)	2	0.01
Japanese (7)	13	0.10
Korean (28)	38	0.28
Laotian (11)	13	0.10
Nepalese (97)	99	0.72
Pakistani (3)	5	0.04
Sri Lankan (5)	5	0.04
Thai (10)	11	0.08
Vietnamese (15)	17	0.12
Hawaii Native/Pacific Islander (4)	14	0.10
Not Hispanic (3)	13	0.10
Hispanic (1)	1	0.01
Native Hawaiian (0)	2	0.01
Samoan (2)	6	0.04
White (11,874)	12,111	88.53
Not Hispanic (11,395)	11,575	84.61
Hispanic (479)	536	3.92

Mendota Heights

Place Type: City
County: Dakota
Population: 11,071†

Ancestry‡	Population	%
African, Sub-Saharan (105)	105	0.94
Kenyan (12)	12	0.11
Somalian (93)	93	0.83
American (199)	199	1.77
Arab (6)	65	0.58
Lebanese (6)	65	0.58
Austrian (29)	92	0.82
Belgian (9)	21	0.19
British (22)	77	0.69
Canadian (7)	29	0.26
Czech (59)	341	3.04
Czechoslovakian (6)	6	0.05
Danish (72)	196	1.75
Dutch (31)	147	1.31
Eastern European (85)	85	0.76
English (236)	898	8.00
European (143)	150	1.34
Finnish (27)	108	0.96
French, ex. Basque (76)	512	4.56
French Canadian (42)	209	1.86
German (1,168)	4,184	37.29
Greek (0)	43	0.38
Hungarian (0)	9	0.08
Iranian (15)	15	0.13
Irish (655)	3,119	27.80
Italian (116)	436	3.89
Latvian (0)	12	0.11
Lithuanian (31)	66	0.59
Luxemburger (22)	72	0.64
Norwegian (326)	1,215	10.83
Polish (60)	468	4.17
Romanian (16)	52	0.46
Russian (249)	347	3.09
Scandinavian (39)	39	0.35
Scotch-Irish (0)	51	0.45
Scottish (38)	263	2.34
Serbian (8)	8	0.07
Slovene (0)	8	0.07
Swedish (173)	887	7.91
Swiss (0)	81	0.72
Ukrainian (0)	4	0.04
Welsh (10)	274	2.44
Yugoslavian (9)	18	0.16

Hispanic Origin	Population	%
Hispanic or Latino (of any race)	323	2.92
Central American, ex. Mexican	22	0.20
Costa Rican	1	0.01
Guatemalan	17	0.15
Honduran	1	0.01
Nicaraguan	1	0.01
Salvadoran	2	0.02
Cuban	12	0.11
Dominican Republic	3	0.03
Mexican	208	1.88
Puerto Rican	14	0.13
South American	47	0.42
Argentinean	3	0.03
Bolivian	1	0.01
Chilean	7	0.06
Colombian	15	0.14
Ecuadorian	4	0.04
Paraguayan	2	0.02
Peruvian	15	0.14
Other Hispanic or Latino	17	0.15

Race*	Population	%
African-American/Black (164)	229	2.07
Not Hispanic (161)	222	2.01
Hispanic (3)	7	0.06
American Indian/Alaska Native (17)	50	0.45
Not Hispanic (8)	30	0.27
Hispanic (9)	20	0.18
Cherokee (0)	1	0.01
Chippewa (2)	7	0.06
Iroquois (0)	5	0.05
Menominee (1)	1	0.01
Mexican American Ind. (3)	3	0.03
Sioux (2)	9	0.08
South American Ind. (1)	1	0.01
Spanish American Ind. (1)	1	0.01
Asian (241)	329	2.97
Not Hispanic (240)	324	2.93
Hispanic (1)	5	0.05
Bangladeshi (3)	3	0.03
Cambodian (5)	5	0.05
Chinese, ex. Taiwanese (46)	61	0.55
Filipino (18)	39	0.35
Hmong (19)	20	0.18
Indian (59)	62	0.56
Indonesian (1)	4	0.04
Japanese (9)	24	0.22
Korean (45)	55	0.50
Laotian (0)	1	0.01
Nepalese (0)	1	0.01
Pakistani (0)	3	0.03
Sri Lankan (4)	4	0.04
Taiwanese (6)	10	0.09
Thai (6)	12	0.11
Vietnamese (14)	29	0.26
Hawaii Native/Pacific Islander (2)	8	0.07
Not Hispanic (2)	7	0.06
Hispanic (0)	1	0.01
Marshallese (1)	1	0.01
Native Hawaiian (0)	1	0.01
White (10,383)	10,567	95.45
Not Hispanic (10,173)	10,319	93.21
Hispanic (210)	248	2.24

Minneapolis

Place Type: City
County: Hennepin
Population: 382,578†

Ancestry‡	Population	%
African, Sub-Saharan (25,644)	27,138	7.15
African (7,819)	8,873	2.34
Ethiopian (3,611)	3,714	0.98
Ghanaian (122)	131	0.03
Kenyan (53)	93	0.02
Liberian (758)	791	0.21
Nigerian (453)	499	0.13
Senegalese (0)	37	0.01
Sierra Leonean (34)	44	0.01
Somalian (12,232)	12,303	3.24
South African (12)	12	<0.01
Sudanese (131)	131	0.03
Ugandan (28)	28	0.01
Other Sub-Saharan African (391)	482	0.13
Albanian (36)	53	0.01
Alsatian (0)	23	0.01
American (5,037)	5,037	1.33
Arab (1,271)	2,389	0.63
Arab (168)	229	0.06
Egyptian (345)	392	0.10
Iraqi (11)	11	<0.01
Lebanese (222)	918	0.24
Moroccan (157)	168	0.04
Palestinian (16)	61	0.02
Syrian (8)	105	0.03
Other Arab (344)	505	0.13
Armenian (72)	214	0.06
Australian (52)	159	0.04
Austrian (232)	1,469	0.39
Belgian (210)	962	0.25
Brazilian (52)	149	0.04
British (711)	1,812	0.48
Bulgarian (52)	120	0.03
Cajun (16)	16	<0.01
Canadian (377)	784	0.21
Carpatho Rusyn (11)	21	0.01
Celtic (38)	160	0.04
Croatian (109)	558	0.15
Cypriot (13)	13	<0.01
Czech (1,027)	5,254	1.38
Czechoslovakian (229)	586	0.15
Danish (942)	5,219	1.37
Dutch (959)	5,978	1.57
Eastern European (743)	1,072	0.28
English (4,112)	24,174	6.37
Estonian (38)	72	0.02
European (6,073)	6,854	1.81

*Notes: † The Census 2010 population figure is used to calculate the percentages in the Hispanic Origin and Race categories. Ancestry percentages are based on the 2006-2010 American Community Survey population (not shown); ‡ Numbers in parentheses indicate the number of people reporting a single ancestry; * Numbers in parentheses indicate the number of persons reporting this race alone, not in combination with any other race; Please refer to the Explanation of Data for more information.*

Finnish (1,192)	3,786	1.00
French, ex. Basque (1,570)	12,885	3.39
French Canadian (570)	2,697	0.71
German (23,915)	88,406	23.29
German Russian (82)	128	0.03
Greek (469)	1,326	0.35
Guyanese (144)	189	0.05
Hungarian (200)	1,261	0.33
Icelander (34)	174	0.05
Iranian (158)	280	0.07
Irish (8,375)	42,359	11.16
Israeli (26)	72	0.02
Italian (2,261)	9,248	2.44
Latvian (207)	453	0.12
Lithuanian (291)	913	0.24
Luxemburger (67)	194	0.05
Macedonian (0)	17	<0.01
New Zealander (11)	11	<0.01
Northern European (803)	881	0.23
Norwegian (11,380)	41,603	10.96
Pennsylvania German (8)	115	0.03
Polish (3,751)	14,605	3.85
Portuguese (64)	301	0.08
Romanian (109)	557	0.15
Russian (1,426)	4,282	1.13
Scandinavian (2,853)	4,614	1.22
Scotch-Irish (1,194)	4,463	1.18
Scottish (794)	6,097	1.61
Serbian (90)	318	0.08
Slavic (98)	308	0.08
Slovak (226)	857	0.23
Slovene (162)	437	0.12
Swedish (6,541)	30,230	7.96
Swiss (164)	1,707	0.45
Turkish (90)	143	0.04
Ukrainian (760)	1,628	0.43
Welsh (363)	2,689	0.71
West Indian, ex. Hispanic (763)	1,185	0.31
Bahamian (19)	32	0.01
Barbadian (16)	16	<0.01
Belizean (10)	17	<0.01
British West Indian (10)	10	<0.01
Haitian (81)	222	0.06
Jamaican (370)	510	0.13
Trinidadian/Tobagonian (33)	113	0.03
West Indian (224)	265	0.07
Yugoslavian (88)	340	0.09

Hispanic Origin	Population	%
Hispanic or Latino (of any race)	40,073	10.47
Central American, ex. Mexican	2,258	0.59
Costa Rican	113	0.03
Guatemalan	980	0.26
Honduran	286	0.07
Nicaraguan	152	0.04
Panamanian	126	0.03
Salvadoran	586	0.15
Other Central American	15	<0.01
Cuban	553	0.14
Dominican Republic	177	0.05
Mexican	26,643	6.96
Puerto Rican	1,364	0.36
South American	6,270	1.64
Argentinean	174	0.05
Bolivian	50	0.01
Chilean	155	0.04
Colombian	568	0.15
Ecuadorian	4,792	1.25
Paraguayan	33	0.01
Peruvian	263	0.07
Uruguayan	40	0.01
Venezuelan	142	0.04
Other South American	53	0.01
Other Hispanic or Latino	2,808	0.73

Race*	Population	%
African-American/Black (71,098)	79,967	20.90
Not Hispanic (69,971)	77,889	20.36
Hispanic (1,127)	2,078	0.54
American Indian/Alaska Native (7,601)	13,381	3.50
Not Hispanic (6,351)	10,662	2.79
Hispanic (1,250)	2,719	0.71
Alaska Athabascan *(Ala. Nat.)* (5)	11	<0.01
Aleut *(Alaska Native)* (2)	8	<0.01
Apache (11)	41	0.01
Arapaho (4)	5	<0.01
Blackfeet (12)	141	0.04
Canadian/French Am. Ind. (24)	42	0.01
Central American Ind. (12)	35	0.01
Cherokee (59)	499	0.13
Cheyenne (7)	24	0.01
Chickasaw (5)	15	<0.01
Chippewa (3,283)	4,363	1.14
Choctaw (8)	84	0.02
Colville (2)	3	<0.01
Comanche (15)	22	0.01
Cree (8)	36	0.01
Creek (6)	38	0.01
Crow (14)	19	<0.01
Delaware (3)	9	<0.01
Hopi (2)	5	<0.01
Houma (0)	2	<0.01
Inupiat *(Alaska Native)* (4)	14	<0.01
Iroquois (50)	106	0.03
Kiowa (3)	6	<0.01
Lumbee (5)	8	<0.01
Menominee (41)	46	0.01
Mexican American Ind. (229)	365	0.10
Navajo (37)	46	0.01
Osage (1)	1	<0.01
Ottawa (6)	10	<0.01
Paiute (2)	2	<0.01
Pima (2)	2	<0.01
Potawatomi (44)	62	0.02
Pueblo (6)	12	<0.01
Puget Sound Salish (1)	3	<0.01
Seminole (3)	28	0.01
Shoshone (5)	6	<0.01
Sioux (921)	1,306	0.34
South American Ind. (58)	92	0.02
Spanish American Ind. (41)	73	0.02
Tlingit-Haida *(Alaska Native)* (3)	11	<0.01
Tohono O'Odham (7)	7	<0.01
Tsimshian *(Alaska Native)* (2)	2	<0.01
Ute (1)	6	<0.01
Yakama (3)	10	<0.01
Yaqui (4)	7	<0.01
Yuman (6)	6	<0.01
Yup'ik *(Alaska Native)* (2)	4	<0.01
Asian (21,553)	25,227	6.59
Not Hispanic (21,399)	24,848	6.49
Hispanic (154)	379	0.10
Bangladeshi (52)	59	0.02
Bhutanese (8)	32	0.01
Burmese (10)	18	<0.01
Cambodian (305)	389	0.10
Chinese, ex. Taiwanese (3,131)	3,819	1.00
Filipino (682)	1,246	0.33
Hmong (7,253)	7,512	1.96
Indian (2,860)	3,539	0.93
Indonesian (68)	96	0.03
Japanese (558)	1,158	0.30
Korean (2,162)	2,700	0.71
Laotian (966)	1,166	0.30
Malaysian (101)	123	0.03
Nepalese (98)	133	0.03
Pakistani (146)	199	0.05
Sri Lankan (69)	90	0.02
Taiwanese (240)	258	0.07
Thai (174)	311	0.08
Vietnamese (1,493)	1,760	0.46
Hawaii Native/Pacific Islander (179)	719	0.19
Not Hispanic (168)	601	0.16
Hispanic (11)	118	0.03
Fijian (1)	5	<0.01
Guamanian/Chamorro (28)	64	0.02
Marshallese (5)	12	<0.01
Native Hawaiian (49)	191	0.05
Samoan (27)	72	0.02
Tongan (4)	11	<0.01
White (244,086)	257,575	67.33
Not Hispanic (230,650)	241,570	63.14
Hispanic (13,436)	16,005	4.18

Minnetonka

Place Type: City
County: Hennepin
Population: 49,734[†]

Ancestry[‡]	Population	%
African, Sub-Saharan (568)	581	1.17
African (85)	98	0.20
Ethiopian (47)	47	0.09
Kenyan (222)	222	0.45
Liberian (13)	13	0.03
Somalian (193)	193	0.39
Other Sub-Saharan African (8)	8	0.02
American (1,803)	1,803	3.64
Arab (10)	151	0.30
Iraqi (10)	38	0.08
Lebanese (0)	73	0.15
Moroccan (0)	40	0.08
Armenian (8)	24	0.05
Australian (10)	40	0.08
Austrian (68)	295	0.60
Belgian (66)	106	0.21
Brazilian (7)	15	0.03
British (170)	307	0.62
Bulgarian (0)	11	0.02
Canadian (33)	45	0.09
Celtic (7)	7	0.01
Croatian (20)	65	0.13
Czech (286)	1,271	2.56
Czechoslovakian (27)	52	0.10
Danish (218)	1,143	2.31
Dutch (169)	821	1.66
Eastern European (634)	657	1.33
English (841)	5,149	10.39
Estonian (22)	22	0.04
European (836)	855	1.72
Finnish (256)	634	1.28
French, ex. Basque (104)	1,578	3.18
French Canadian (102)	237	0.48
German (4,381)	15,746	31.77
German Russian (10)	10	0.02
Greek (135)	253	0.51
Hungarian (83)	300	0.61
Icelander (8)	54	0.11
Iranian (10)	10	0.02
Irish (1,238)	6,985	14.09
Israeli (71)	71	0.14
Italian (308)	1,262	2.55
Latvian (24)	93	0.19
Lithuanian (72)	367	0.74
Luxemburger (27)	135	0.27
Northern European (124)	124	0.25
Norwegian (2,063)	7,112	14.35
Pennsylvania German (22)	63	0.13
Polish (497)	2,657	5.36
Portuguese (33)	71	0.14
Romanian (199)	285	0.57
Russian (903)	1,813	3.66
Scandinavian (688)	1,012	2.04
Scotch-Irish (272)	764	1.54
Scottish (175)	1,145	2.31
Serbian (7)	37	0.07
Slavic (11)	29	0.06
Slovak (32)	144	0.29
Slovene (63)	163	0.33
Swedish (1,523)	6,106	12.32
Swiss (82)	440	0.89
Turkish (40)	50	0.10
Ukrainian (127)	248	0.50
Welsh (64)	612	1.23
West Indian, ex. Hispanic (41)	88	0.18
British West Indian (16)	16	0.03
Jamaican (25)	72	0.15
Yugoslavian (162)	172	0.35

SECTION TWO

*Notes: † The Census 2010 population figure is used to calculate the percentages in the Hispanic Origin and Race categories. Ancestry percentages are based on the 2006-2010 American Community Survey population (not shown); ‡ Numbers in parentheses indicate the number of people reporting a single ancestry; * Numbers in parentheses indicate the number of persons reporting this race alone, not in combination with any other race; Please refer to the Explanation of Data for more information.*

Hispanic Origin	Population	%
Hispanic or Latino (of any race)	1,169	2.35
Central American, ex. Mexican	102	0.21
Costa Rican	17	0.03
Guatemalan	42	0.08
Honduran	16	0.03
Nicaraguan	6	0.01
Panamanian	5	0.01
Salvadoran	16	0.03
Cuban	30	0.06
Dominican Republic	11	0.02
Mexican	616	1.24
Puerto Rican	59	0.12
South American	235	0.47
Argentinean	32	0.06
Bolivian	15	0.03
Chilean	21	0.04
Colombian	80	0.16
Ecuadorian	27	0.05
Paraguayan	6	0.01
Peruvian	31	0.06
Uruguayan	2	<0.01
Venezuelan	20	0.04
Other South American	1	<0.01
Other Hispanic or Latino	116	0.23

Race*	Population	%
African-American/Black (1,855)	2,297	4.62
Not Hispanic (1,837)	2,250	4.52
Hispanic (18)	47	0.09
American Indian/Alaska Native (132)	337	0.68
Not Hispanic (103)	276	0.55
Hispanic (29)	61	0.12
Alaska Athabascan *(Ala. Nat.)* (0)	1	<0.01
Aleut *(Alaska Native)* (2)	2	<0.01
Apache (1)	3	0.01
Blackfeet (2)	7	0.01
Canadian/French Am. Ind. (1)	4	0.01
Cherokee (4)	14	0.03
Chickasaw (0)	1	<0.01
Chippewa (32)	62	0.12
Choctaw (0)	3	0.01
Colville (2)	2	<0.01
Cree (1)	1	<0.01
Creek (1)	1	<0.01
Iroquois (1)	6	0.01
Menominee (0)	1	<0.01
Mexican American Ind. (7)	7	0.01
Navajo (0)	1	<0.01
Pima (1)	1	<0.01
Potawatomi (4)	4	0.01
Seminole (0)	1	<0.01
Shoshone (4)	4	0.01
Sioux (14)	32	0.06
South American Ind. (2)	4	0.01
Spanish American Ind. (6)	6	0.01
Tlingit-Haida *(Alaska Native)* (0)	3	0.01
Yuman (1)	1	<0.01
Yup'ik *(Alaska Native)* (0)	1	<0.01
Asian (1,565)	1,996	4.01
Not Hispanic (1,558)	1,979	3.98
Hispanic (7)	17	0.03
Bangladeshi (11)	12	0.02
Burmese (1)	1	<0.01
Cambodian (43)	54	0.11
Chinese, ex. Taiwanese (279)	369	0.74
Filipino (80)	143	0.29
Hmong (22)	23	0.05
Indian (563)	608	1.22
Indonesian (2)	6	0.01
Japanese (52)	95	0.19
Korean (218)	325	0.65
Laotian (19)	24	0.05
Malaysian (1)	3	0.01
Nepalese (13)	13	0.03
Pakistani (42)	49	0.10
Sri Lankan (13)	15	0.03
Taiwanese (18)	24	0.05
Thai (25)	38	0.08
Vietnamese (102)	132	0.27
Hawaii Native/Pacific Islander (9)	29	0.06
Not Hispanic (8)	27	0.05
Hispanic (1)	2	<0.01
Native Hawaiian (4)	8	0.02
Samoan (1)	1	<0.01
White (44,780)	45,695	91.88
Not Hispanic (44,081)	44,903	90.29
Hispanic (699)	792	1.59

Monticello

Place Type: City
County: Wright
Population: 12,759†

Ancestry‡	Population	%
American (362)	362	2.96
Arab (0)	15	0.12
Lebanese (0)	15	0.12
Austrian (9)	40	0.33
Canadian (14)	23	0.19
Croatian (0)	31	0.25
Czech (48)	177	1.45
Czechoslovakian (0)	11	0.09
Danish (12)	94	0.77
Dutch (45)	308	2.52
English (104)	779	6.37
European (73)	73	0.60
Finnish (70)	168	1.37
French, ex. Basque (208)	1,109	9.07
French Canadian (41)	234	1.91
German (1,887)	5,188	42.42
Greek (0)	51	0.42
Hungarian (13)	13	0.11
Irish (229)	1,594	13.03
Italian (19)	91	0.74
Norwegian (624)	2,167	17.72
Polish (305)	886	7.24
Russian (0)	62	0.51
Scandinavian (90)	136	1.11
Scotch-Irish (8)	62	0.51
Scottish (25)	234	1.91
Slavic (0)	18	0.15
Slovak (0)	14	0.11
Swedish (311)	984	8.05
Swiss (0)	16	0.13
Ukrainian (0)	11	0.09
Welsh (50)	123	1.01
Yugoslavian (64)	64	0.52

Hispanic Origin	Population	%
Hispanic or Latino (of any race)	686	5.38
Central American, ex. Mexican	105	0.82
Costa Rican	5	0.04
Guatemalan	35	0.27
Honduran	20	0.16
Nicaraguan	2	0.02
Panamanian	2	0.02
Salvadoran	41	0.32
Cuban	23	0.18
Dominican Republic	4	0.03
Mexican	420	3.29
Puerto Rican	29	0.23
South American	42	0.33
Chilean	9	0.07
Colombian	5	0.04
Ecuadorian	3	0.02
Peruvian	21	0.16
Venezuelan	1	0.01
Other South American	3	0.02
Other Hispanic or Latino	63	0.49

Race*	Population	%
African-American/Black (195)	309	2.42
Not Hispanic (192)	302	2.37
Hispanic (3)	7	0.05
American Indian/Alaska Native (64)	124	0.97
Not Hispanic (61)	117	0.92
Hispanic (3)	7	0.05
Aleut *(Alaska Native)* (3)	3	0.02
Apache (5)	5	0.04
Blackfeet (0)	1	0.01
Canadian/French Am. Ind. (0)	1	0.01
Cherokee (1)	2	0.02
Chippewa (25)	41	0.32
Delaware (0)	2	0.02
Iroquois (2)	3	0.02
Mexican American Ind. (0)	1	0.01
Ottawa (4)	4	0.03
Sioux (6)	10	0.08
South American Ind. (0)	1	0.01
Asian (130)	197	1.54
Not Hispanic (130)	196	1.54
Hispanic (0)	1	0.01
Chinese, ex. Taiwanese (16)	26	0.20
Filipino (12)	25	0.20
Hmong (4)	4	0.03
Indian (32)	43	0.34
Indonesian (0)	3	0.02
Japanese (2)	10	0.08
Korean (31)	43	0.34
Laotian (18)	25	0.20
Thai (1)	6	0.05
Vietnamese (7)	16	0.13
Hawaii Native/Pacific Islander (4)	14	0.11
Not Hispanic (4)	14	0.11
Guamanian/Chamorro (3)	3	0.02
Native Hawaiian (0)	7	0.05
White (11,812)	12,065	94.56
Not Hispanic (11,452)	11,669	91.46
Hispanic (360)	396	3.10

Moorhead

Place Type: City
County: Clay
Population: 38,065†

Ancestry‡	Population	%
African, Sub-Saharan (445)	455	1.24
African (146)	146	0.40
Ethiopian (48)	48	0.13
Somalian (156)	166	0.45
Sudanese (86)	86	0.23
Other Sub-Saharan African (9)	9	0.02
Albanian (7)	7	0.02
American (645)	645	1.76
Arab (334)	375	1.02
Arab (5)	5	0.01
Iraqi (175)	175	0.48
Lebanese (0)	23	0.06
Syrian (0)	18	0.05
Other Arab (154)	154	0.42
Armenian (0)	10	0.03
Austrian (14)	46	0.13
Belgian (53)	88	0.24
British (172)	209	0.57
Bulgarian (18)	18	0.05
Canadian (9)	9	0.02
Celtic (12)	12	0.03
Czech (166)	508	1.38
Czechoslovakian (13)	77	0.21
Danish (86)	518	1.41
Dutch (72)	433	1.18
English (303)	1,805	4.92
Estonian (0)	12	0.03
European (215)	215	0.59
Finnish (152)	484	1.32
French, ex. Basque (241)	1,355	3.69
French Canadian (75)	352	0.96
German (4,420)	13,204	35.96
German Russian (15)	15	0.04
Greek (8)	157	0.43
Hungarian (14)	14	0.04
Icelander (14)	61	0.17
Irish (625)	2,931	7.98
Italian (180)	507	1.38
Luxemburger (0)	13	0.04
Maltese (0)	10	0.03
Northern European (105)	105	0.29

*Notes: † The Census 2010 population figure is used to calculate the percentages in the Hispanic Origin and Race categories. Ancestry percentages are based on the 2006-2010 American Community Survey population (not shown); ‡ Numbers in parentheses indicate the number of people reporting a single ancestry; * Numbers in parentheses indicate the number of persons reporting this race alone, not in combination with any other race; Please refer to the Explanation of Data for more information.*

Ancestry (continued)	Population	%
Norwegian (6,281)	13,231	36.03
Polish (322)	1,443	3.93
Portuguese (0)	56	0.15
Romanian (12)	25	0.07
Russian (53)	492	1.34
Scandinavian (438)	564	1.54
Scotch-Irish (55)	330	0.90
Scottish (80)	339	0.92
Slavic (0)	16	0.04
Slovak (12)	33	0.09
Slovene (0)	22	0.06
Swedish (358)	3,044	8.29
Swiss (13)	98	0.27
Ukrainian (10)	54	0.15
Welsh (16)	85	0.23
West Indian, ex. Hispanic (21)	21	0.06
Bermudan (12)	12	0.03
Jamaican (9)	9	0.02
Yugoslavian (65)	85	0.23

Hispanic Origin	Population	%
Hispanic or Latino (of any race)	1,576	4.14
Central American, ex. Mexican	36	0.09
Costa Rican	8	0.02
Guatemalan	8	0.02
Honduran	7	0.02
Nicaraguan	2	0.01
Panamanian	4	0.01
Salvadoran	7	0.02
Cuban	7	0.02
Dominican Republic	2	0.01
Mexican	1,181	3.10
Puerto Rican	46	0.12
South American	41	0.11
Argentinean	2	0.01
Chilean	5	0.01
Colombian	18	0.05
Ecuadorian	7	0.02
Paraguayan	3	0.01
Peruvian	4	0.01
Venezuelan	2	0.01
Other Hispanic or Latino	263	0.69

Race*	Population	%
African-American/Black (775)	1,091	2.87
Not Hispanic (761)	1,044	2.74
Hispanic (14)	47	0.12
American Indian/Alaska Native (580)	958	2.52
Not Hispanic (544)	884	2.32
Hispanic (36)	74	0.19
Apache (1)	2	0.01
Blackfeet (1)	5	0.01
Canadian/French Am. Ind. (0)	1	<0.01
Cherokee (2)	21	0.06
Cheyenne (1)	1	<0.01
Chippewa (215)	345	0.91
Choctaw (2)	7	0.02
Comanche (1)	1	<0.01
Cree (10)	11	0.03
Creek (1)	1	<0.01
Crow (1)	1	<0.01
Iroquois (0)	8	0.02
Lumbee (1)	3	0.01
Mexican American Ind. (1)	2	0.01
Navajo (5)	17	0.04
Ottawa (0)	1	<0.01
Pima (1)	1	<0.01
Potawatomi (1)	1	<0.01
Sioux (95)	124	0.33
Yakama (0)	1	<0.01
Asian (758)	1,005	2.64
Not Hispanic (749)	977	2.57
Hispanic (9)	28	0.07
Bangladeshi (4)	4	0.01
Burmese (2)	2	0.01
Cambodian (7)	13	0.03
Chinese, ex. Taiwanese (68)	90	0.24
Filipino (36)	90	0.24
Hmong (18)	20	0.05
Indian (61)	91	0.24
Indonesian (2)	2	0.01
Japanese (41)	74	0.19
Korean (99)	144	0.38
Laotian (21)	32	0.08
Malaysian (3)	3	0.01
Nepalese (165)	180	0.47
Pakistani (5)	10	0.03
Sri Lankan (34)	34	0.09
Taiwanese (4)	4	0.01
Thai (10)	27	0.07
Vietnamese (120)	138	0.36
Hawaii Native/Pacific Islander (17)	50	0.13
Not Hispanic (14)	36	0.09
Hispanic (3)	14	0.04
Guamanian/Chamorro (4)	12	0.03
Marshallese (1)	1	<0.01
Native Hawaiian (7)	16	0.04
Samoan (0)	1	<0.01
White (34,530)	35,440	93.10
Not Hispanic (33,572)	34,336	90.20
Hispanic (958)	1,104	2.90

Mound

Place Type: City
County: Hennepin
Population: 9,052†

Ancestry‡	Population	%
African, Sub-Saharan (14)	14	0.15
Ethiopian (14)	14	0.15
American (105)	105	1.16
Austrian (0)	12	0.13
Belgian (0)	59	0.65
British (0)	20	0.22
Bulgarian (0)	13	0.14
Czech (23)	192	2.12
Danish (35)	192	2.12
Dutch (67)	189	2.09
English (120)	815	9.02
Estonian (63)	63	0.70
European (107)	107	1.18
Finnish (10)	152	1.68
French, ex. Basque (20)	321	3.55
French Canadian (0)	108	1.20
German (1,361)	3,591	39.74
Greek (14)	38	0.42
Icelander (9)	9	0.10
Irish (160)	1,143	12.65
Italian (135)	404	4.47
Lithuanian (0)	15	0.17
Luxemburger (10)	10	0.11
Northern European (7)	7	0.08
Norwegian (404)	1,479	16.37
Polish (90)	473	5.23
Portuguese (21)	21	0.23
Romanian (0)	10	0.11
Russian (62)	143	1.58
Scandinavian (70)	98	1.08
Scotch-Irish (12)	153	1.69
Scottish (58)	325	3.60
Serbian (0)	8	0.09
Slovak (10)	18	0.20
Swedish (325)	1,136	12.57
Swiss (0)	10	0.11
Welsh (0)	38	0.42
Yugoslavian (0)	23	0.25

Hispanic Origin	Population	%
Hispanic or Latino (of any race)	164	1.81
Central American, ex. Mexican	9	0.10
Guatemalan	5	0.06
Honduran	2	0.02
Nicaraguan	1	0.01
Salvadoran	1	0.01
Cuban	3	0.03
Mexican	114	1.26
Puerto Rican	11	0.12
South American	16	0.18
Argentinean	5	0.06
Bolivian	1	0.01
Colombian	4	0.04
Peruvian	6	0.07
Other Hispanic or Latino	11	0.12

Race*	Population	%
African-American/Black (80)	132	1.46
Not Hispanic (77)	120	1.33
Hispanic (3)	12	0.13
American Indian/Alaska Native (23)	50	0.55
Not Hispanic (22)	47	0.52
Hispanic (1)	3	0.03
Blackfeet (0)	3	0.03
Cherokee (1)	1	0.01
Chippewa (9)	16	0.18
Delaware (0)	1	0.01
Mexican American Ind. (1)	3	0.03
Sioux (3)	5	0.06
Asian (115)	162	1.79
Not Hispanic (114)	160	1.77
Hispanic (1)	2	0.02
Cambodian (6)	7	0.08
Chinese, ex. Taiwanese (27)	39	0.43
Filipino (9)	16	0.18
Hmong (8)	8	0.09
Indian (8)	18	0.20
Japanese (7)	15	0.17
Korean (21)	29	0.32
Laotian (10)	12	0.13
Pakistani (1)	1	0.01
Thai (5)	7	0.08
Vietnamese (6)	7	0.08
Hawaii Native/Pacific Islander (3)	10	0.11
Not Hispanic (3)	10	0.11
Guamanian/Chamorro (1)	2	0.02
Native Hawaiian (2)	5	0.06
Samoan (0)	3	0.03
White (8,668)	8,781	97.01
Not Hispanic (8,553)	8,661	95.68
Hispanic (115)	120	1.33

Mounds View

Place Type: City
County: Ramsey
Population: 12,155†

Ancestry‡	Population	%
African, Sub-Saharan (168)	178	1.47
African (31)	36	0.30
Ethiopian (8)	8	0.07
Nigerian (101)	101	0.83
Somalian (0)	5	0.04
Other Sub-Saharan African (28)	28	0.23
Albanian (0)	11	0.09
American (262)	262	2.16
Arab (47)	86	0.71
Arab (0)	19	0.16
Lebanese (36)	56	0.46
Syrian (11)	11	0.09
Assyrian/Chaldean/Syriac (10)	10	0.08
Austrian (9)	27	0.22
Belgian (0)	8	0.07
British (10)	40	0.33
Czech (11)	104	0.86
Czechoslovakian (0)	93	0.77
Danish (18)	65	0.54
Dutch (75)	160	1.32
English (109)	736	6.08
European (102)	113	0.93
Finnish (59)	144	1.19
French, ex. Basque (42)	559	4.62
French Canadian (20)	174	1.44
German (1,323)	3,977	32.85
Greek (0)	9	0.07
Hungarian (11)	48	0.40
Iranian (31)	31	0.26
Irish (359)	1,504	12.42
Italian (119)	639	5.28
Northern European (99)	99	0.82

*Notes: † The Census 2010 population figure is used to calculate the percentages in the Hispanic Origin and Race categories. Ancestry percentages are based on the 2006-2010 American Community Survey population (not shown); ‡ Numbers in parentheses indicate the number of people reporting a single ancestry; * Numbers in parentheses indicate the number of persons reporting this race alone, not in combination with any other race; Please refer to the Explanation of Data for more information.*

Norwegian (434)	2,100	17.35
Polish (171)	686	5.67
Romanian (0)	22	0.18
Russian (5)	109	0.90
Scandinavian (163)	197	1.63
Scotch-Irish (0)	59	0.49
Scottish (44)	200	1.65
Slavic (0)	18	0.15
Slovak (9)	27	0.22
Slovene (0)	12	0.10
Swedish (346)	1,717	14.18
Swiss (7)	48	0.40
Ukrainian (11)	11	0.09
Yugoslavian (106)	106	0.88

Hispanic Origin	Population	%
Hispanic or Latino (of any race)	611	5.03
Central American, ex. Mexican	58	0.48
Guatemalan	19	0.16
Honduran	9	0.07
Nicaraguan	10	0.08
Panamanian	1	0.01
Salvadoran	19	0.16
Cuban	4	0.03
Dominican Republic	2	0.02
Mexican	440	3.62
Puerto Rican	31	0.26
South American	43	0.35
Argentinean	2	0.02
Bolivian	1	0.01
Chilean	5	0.04
Colombian	20	0.16
Ecuadorian	5	0.04
Paraguayan	1	0.01
Peruvian	5	0.04
Venezuelan	3	0.02
Other South American	1	0.01
Other Hispanic or Latino	33	0.27

Race*	Population	%
African-American/Black (664)	848	6.98
Not Hispanic (648)	806	6.63
Hispanic (16)	42	0.35
American Indian/Alaska Native (92)	182	1.50
Not Hispanic (85)	156	1.28
Hispanic (7)	26	0.21
Blackfeet (1)	2	0.02
Cherokee (0)	7	0.06
Chippewa (47)	69	0.57
Choctaw (0)	1	0.01
Comanche (0)	4	0.03
Menominee (0)	1	0.01
Pueblo (0)	1	0.01
Sioux (5)	6	0.05
South American Ind. (1)	2	0.02
Tlingit-Haida *(Alaska Native)* (1)	1	0.01
Asian (850)	938	7.72
Not Hispanic (840)	921	7.58
Hispanic (10)	17	0.14
Bangladeshi (2)	2	0.02
Cambodian (17)	22	0.18
Chinese, ex. Taiwanese (99)	106	0.87
Filipino (53)	76	0.63
Hmong (312)	321	2.64
Indian (175)	182	1.50
Japanese (7)	26	0.21
Korean (26)	37	0.30
Laotian (40)	48	0.39
Nepalese (2)	2	0.02
Pakistani (5)	6	0.05
Taiwanese (2)	2	0.02
Thai (4)	10	0.08
Vietnamese (84)	93	0.77
Hawaii Native/Pacific Islander (9)	19	0.16
Not Hispanic (9)	15	0.12
Hispanic (0)	4	0.03
Native Hawaiian (3)	7	0.06
Samoan (2)	5	0.04
Tongan (0)	4	0.03
White (9,888)	10,223	84.11
Not Hispanic (9,634)	9,913	81.55
Hispanic (254)	310	2.55

New Brighton

Place Type: City
County: Ramsey
Population: 21,456†

Ancestry‡	Population	%
African, Sub-Saharan (310)	382	1.79
African (45)	83	0.39
Ethiopian (134)	134	0.63
Kenyan (104)	120	0.56
Liberian (27)	27	0.13
Nigerian (0)	18	0.08
Albanian (44)	44	0.21
Alsatian (15)	15	0.07
American (503)	503	2.36
Arab (98)	203	0.95
Arab (16)	30	0.14
Iraqi (45)	45	0.21
Lebanese (37)	128	0.60
Austrian (18)	28	0.13
Belgian (0)	32	0.15
British (40)	62	0.29
Bulgarian (48)	48	0.23
Canadian (0)	10	0.05
Croatian (0)	18	0.08
Czech (80)	389	1.82
Czechoslovakian (0)	70	0.33
Danish (29)	336	1.58
Dutch (168)	532	2.49
English (161)	1,490	6.99
European (195)	229	1.07
Finnish (168)	381	1.79
French, ex. Basque (69)	750	3.52
French Canadian (54)	196	0.92
German (2,030)	6,306	29.57
Greek (0)	28	0.13
Hungarian (26)	86	0.40
Icelander (0)	43	0.20
Iranian (0)	9	0.04
Irish (307)	2,845	13.34
Italian (161)	510	2.39
Lithuanian (0)	25	0.12
Luxemburger (0)	61	0.29
Northern European (60)	60	0.28
Norwegian (1,003)	2,996	14.05
Polish (351)	1,392	6.53
Russian (22)	154	0.72
Scandinavian (196)	334	1.57
Scotch-Irish (36)	266	1.25
Scottish (61)	311	1.46
Slavic (0)	14	0.07
Slovak (17)	36	0.17
Slovene (29)	37	0.17
Swedish (835)	2,664	12.49
Swiss (34)	185	0.87
Ukrainian (19)	42	0.20
Welsh (0)	84	0.39
Yugoslavian (72)	97	0.45

Hispanic Origin	Population	%
Hispanic or Latino (of any race)	934	4.35
Central American, ex. Mexican	61	0.28
Guatemalan	18	0.08
Honduran	17	0.08
Nicaraguan	8	0.04
Panamanian	2	0.01
Salvadoran	15	0.07
Other Central American	1	<0.01
Cuban	17	0.08
Dominican Republic	7	0.03
Mexican	644	3.00
Puerto Rican	38	0.18
South American	93	0.43
Argentinean	2	0.01
Chilean	12	0.06
Colombian	31	0.14
Ecuadorian	30	0.14
Paraguayan	6	0.03
Peruvian	9	0.04
Venezuelan	3	0.01
Other Hispanic or Latino	74	0.34

Race*	Population	%
African-American/Black (1,425)	1,719	8.01
Not Hispanic (1,406)	1,679	7.83
Hispanic (19)	40	0.19
American Indian/Alaska Native (85)	235	1.10
Not Hispanic (72)	201	0.94
Hispanic (13)	34	0.16
Blackfeet (0)	4	0.02
Canadian/French Am. Ind. (0)	5	0.02
Cherokee (0)	8	0.04
Chippewa (41)	83	0.39
Choctaw (0)	1	<0.01
Iroquois (3)	3	0.01
Mexican American Ind. (4)	8	0.04
Navajo (1)	1	<0.01
Seminole (0)	1	<0.01
Shoshone (0)	2	0.01
Sioux (7)	14	0.07
South American Ind. (0)	1	<0.01
Tohono O'Odham (0)	1	<0.01
Asian (1,303)	1,453	6.77
Not Hispanic (1,299)	1,442	6.72
Hispanic (4)	11	0.05
Cambodian (29)	36	0.17
Chinese, ex. Taiwanese (356)	387	1.80
Filipino (113)	142	0.66
Hmong (77)	81	0.38
Indian (266)	275	1.28
Indonesian (1)	2	0.01
Japanese (17)	41	0.19
Korean (109)	126	0.59
Laotian (5)	6	0.03
Malaysian (4)	4	0.02
Nepalese (24)	27	0.13
Pakistani (11)	15	0.07
Sri Lankan (1)	1	<0.01
Taiwanese (14)	18	0.08
Thai (6)	8	0.04
Vietnamese (219)	245	1.14
Hawaii Native/Pacific Islander (6)	23	0.11
Not Hispanic (6)	22	0.10
Hispanic (0)	1	<0.01
Guamanian/Chamorro (0)	4	0.02
Native Hawaiian (2)	7	0.03
Samoan (0)	3	0.01
Tongan (0)	1	<0.01
White (17,581)	18,100	84.36
Not Hispanic (17,192)	17,647	82.25
Hispanic (389)	453	2.11

New Hope

Place Type: City
County: Hennepin
Population: 20,339†

Ancestry‡	Population	%
African, Sub-Saharan (783)	812	4.00
African (363)	381	1.88
Ghanaian (29)	29	0.14
Liberian (139)	150	0.74
Somalian (177)	177	0.87
Other Sub-Saharan African (75)	75	0.37
American (522)	522	2.57
Arab (243)	309	1.52
Arab (156)	156	0.77
Egyptian (29)	29	0.14
Lebanese (0)	22	0.11
Moroccan (21)	21	0.10
Palestinian (37)	65	0.32
Syrian (0)	16	0.08
Armenian (0)	13	0.06
Austrian (0)	22	0.11
Belgian (12)	24	0.12

*Notes: † The Census 2010 population figure is used to calculate the percentages in the Hispanic Origin and Race categories. Ancestry percentages are based on the 2006-2010 American Community Survey population (not shown); ‡ Numbers in parentheses indicate the number of people reporting a single ancestry; * Numbers in parentheses indicate the number of persons reporting this race alone, not in combination with any other race; Please refer to the Explanation of Data for more information.*

British (29)	44	0.22
Canadian (19)	19	0.09
Celtic (0)	30	0.15
Croatian (40)	67	0.33
Czech (130)	294	1.45
Czechoslovakian (34)	34	0.17
Danish (91)	297	1.46
Dutch (88)	299	1.47
Eastern European (12)	36	0.18
English (247)	1,371	6.76
European (238)	258	1.27
Finnish (71)	250	1.23
French, ex. Basque (118)	927	4.57
French Canadian (77)	145	0.71
German (2,048)	5,774	28.47
Greek (62)	94	0.46
Guyanese (0)	37	0.18
Hungarian (0)	43	0.21
Iranian (10)	19	0.09
Irish (367)	1,868	9.21
Israeli (55)	55	0.27
Italian (56)	506	2.49
Lithuanian (12)	46	0.23
Luxemburger (0)	12	0.06
Northern European (42)	42	0.21
Norwegian (759)	2,962	14.60
Pennsylvania German (0)	20	0.10
Polish (250)	768	3.79
Portuguese (0)	12	0.06
Romanian (82)	102	0.50
Russian (154)	251	1.24
Scandinavian (246)	336	1.66
Scotch-Irish (34)	210	1.04
Scottish (93)	271	1.34
Serbian (0)	4	0.02
Slovak (32)	64	0.32
Slovene (15)	26	0.13
Swedish (439)	2,021	9.96
Swiss (0)	81	0.40
Welsh (8)	69	0.34
West Indian, ex. Hispanic (40)	88	0.43
Haitian (25)	25	0.12
Jamaican (15)	39	0.19
West Indian (0)	24	0.12
Yugoslavian (53)	63	0.31

Hispanic Origin	Population	%
Hispanic or Latino (of any race)	1,330	6.54
Central American, ex. Mexican	60	0.29
Guatemalan	23	0.11
Honduran	15	0.07
Nicaraguan	1	<0.01
Panamanian	2	0.01
Salvadoran	19	0.09
Cuban	22	0.11
Dominican Republic	6	0.03
Mexican	1,066	5.24
Puerto Rican	33	0.16
South American	93	0.46
Argentinean	3	0.01
Bolivian	1	<0.01
Chilean	4	0.02
Colombian	25	0.12
Ecuadorian	32	0.16
Peruvian	19	0.09
Uruguayan	6	0.03
Venezuelan	1	<0.01
Other South American	2	0.01
Other Hispanic or Latino	50	0.25

Race*	Population	%
African-American/Black (2,993)	3,463	17.03
Not Hispanic (2,965)	3,406	16.75
Hispanic (28)	57	0.28
American Indian/Alaska Native (90)	318	1.56
Not Hispanic (80)	282	1.39
Hispanic (10)	36	0.18
Alaska Athabascan *(Ala. Nat.)* (1)	1	<0.01
Apache (1)	3	0.01
Blackfeet (0)	3	0.01
Cherokee (2)	16	0.08
Chippewa (44)	97	0.48
Choctaw (1)	1	<0.01
Cree (0)	2	0.01
Hopi (0)	1	<0.01
Inupiat *(Alaska Native)* (0)	1	<0.01
Iroquois (0)	2	0.01
Mexican American Ind. (6)	12	0.06
Navajo (0)	1	<0.01
Osage (1)	1	<0.01
Potawatomi (1)	1	<0.01
Pueblo (0)	1	<0.01
Seminole (3)	4	0.02
Sioux (8)	28	0.14
South American Ind. (1)	2	0.01
Asian (779)	904	4.44
Not Hispanic (772)	887	4.36
Hispanic (7)	17	0.08
Bangladeshi (4)	4	0.02
Burmese (3)	3	0.01
Cambodian (22)	27	0.13
Chinese, ex. Taiwanese (96)	117	0.58
Filipino (59)	76	0.37
Hmong (126)	135	0.66
Indian (120)	129	0.63
Indonesian (8)	12	0.06
Japanese (3)	27	0.13
Korean (41)	57	0.28
Laotian (106)	122	0.60
Nepalese (5)	5	0.02
Pakistani (6)	6	0.03
Sri Lankan (4)	4	0.02
Taiwanese (9)	10	0.05
Thai (3)	3	0.01
Vietnamese (137)	150	0.74
Hawaii Native/Pacific Islander (4)	25	0.12
Not Hispanic (4)	18	0.09
Hispanic (0)	7	0.03
Guamanian/Chamorro (0)	1	<0.01
Native Hawaiian (2)	11	0.05
Samoan (0)	2	0.01
White (15,157)	15,790	77.63
Not Hispanic (14,522)	15,074	74.11
Hispanic (635)	716	3.52

New Ulm

Place Type: City
County: Brown
Population: 13,522†

Ancestry‡	Population	%
American (559)	559	4.14
Arab (12)	12	0.09
Arab (12)	12	0.09
Austrian (11)	41	0.30
Belgian (22)	72	0.53
British (8)	31	0.23
Canadian (0)	41	0.30
Croatian (0)	8	0.06
Czech (41)	310	2.29
Czechoslovakian (0)	12	0.09
Danish (61)	229	1.70
Dutch (52)	185	1.37
Eastern European (18)	18	0.13
English (118)	410	3.04
European (105)	105	0.78
Finnish (25)	57	0.42
French, ex. Basque (25)	244	1.81
French Canadian (0)	55	0.41
German (5,828)	8,740	64.70
Hungarian (0)	17	0.13
Irish (74)	717	5.31
Italian (43)	211	1.56
Luxemburger (0)	11	0.08
Northern European (21)	21	0.16
Norwegian (661)	1,670	12.36
Polish (82)	263	1.95
Russian (19)	53	0.39
Scandinavian (55)	88	0.65
Scotch-Irish (32)	252	1.87
Scottish (10)	51	0.38
Slovak (0)	9	0.07
Swedish (175)	729	5.40
Swiss (10)	61	0.45
Welsh (14)	158	1.17
Yugoslavian (9)	9	0.07

Hispanic Origin	Population	%
Hispanic or Latino (of any race)	241	1.78
Central American, ex. Mexican	11	0.08
Costa Rican	3	0.02
Guatemalan	4	0.03
Honduran	1	0.01
Panamanian	2	0.01
Salvadoran	1	0.01
Dominican Republic	1	0.01
Mexican	181	1.34
Puerto Rican	12	0.09
South American	14	0.10
Bolivian	1	0.01
Chilean	7	0.05
Colombian	2	0.01
Venezuelan	4	0.03
Other Hispanic or Latino	22	0.16

Race*	Population	%
African-American/Black (42)	79	0.58
Not Hispanic (41)	77	0.57
Hispanic (1)	2	0.01
American Indian/Alaska Native (11)	34	0.25
Not Hispanic (11)	31	0.23
Hispanic (0)	3	0.02
Cherokee (0)	4	0.03
Chickasaw (1)	1	0.01
Chippewa (3)	8	0.06
Navajo (0)	1	0.01
Potawatomi (0)	1	0.01
Sioux (4)	5	0.04
Asian (88)	121	0.89
Not Hispanic (88)	119	0.88
Hispanic (0)	2	0.01
Cambodian (3)	3	0.02
Chinese, ex. Taiwanese (16)	17	0.13
Filipino (14)	22	0.16
Indian (16)	24	0.18
Japanese (3)	8	0.06
Korean (22)	31	0.23
Vietnamese (14)	14	0.10
Hawaii Native/Pacific Islander (2)	4	0.03
Not Hispanic (2)	2	0.01
Hispanic (0)	2	0.01
Guamanian/Chamorro (1)	1	0.01
Native Hawaiian (1)	1	0.01
White (13,220)	13,318	98.49
Not Hispanic (13,055)	13,138	97.16
Hispanic (165)	180	1.33

North Branch

Place Type: City
County: Chisago
Population: 10,125†

Ancestry‡	Population	%
African, Sub-Saharan (43)	43	0.43
Ethiopian (22)	22	0.22
Kenyan (10)	10	0.10
Somalian (11)	11	0.11
American (309)	309	3.10
Arab (0)	11	0.11
Lebanese (0)	11	0.11
Austrian (0)	39	0.39
Belgian (0)	21	0.21
British (0)	11	0.11
Czech (59)	140	1.40
Czechoslovakian (16)	16	0.16
Danish (44)	170	1.70
Dutch (0)	133	1.33
English (75)	359	3.60

*Notes: † The Census 2010 population figure is used to calculate the percentages in the Hispanic Origin and Race categories. Ancestry percentages are based on the 2006-2010 American Community Survey population (not shown); ‡ Numbers in parentheses indicate the number of people reporting a single ancestry; * Numbers in parentheses indicate the number of persons reporting this race alone, not in combination with any other race; Please refer to the Explanation of Data for more information.*

Ancestry	Population	%
European (49)	49	0.49
Finnish (9)	65	0.65
French, ex. Basque (7)	779	7.81
French Canadian (155)	277	2.78
German (1,334)	4,431	44.41
Greek (0)	23	0.23
Irish (177)	1,223	12.26
Italian (9)	205	2.05
Norwegian (450)	1,494	14.97
Polish (131)	869	8.71
Portuguese (0)	14	0.14
Russian (13)	129	1.29
Scandinavian (80)	115	1.15
Scotch-Irish (0)	79	0.79
Scottish (43)	69	0.69
Slovene (0)	35	0.35
Swedish (521)	1,739	17.43
Swiss (0)	31	0.31
Ukrainian (18)	27	0.27
Welsh (30)	55	0.55

Hispanic Origin	Population	%
Hispanic or Latino (of any race)	189	1.87
Central American, ex. Mexican	8	0.08
Guatemalan	2	0.02
Nicaraguan	1	0.01
Salvadoran	5	0.05
Cuban	2	0.02
Mexican	157	1.55
Puerto Rican	6	0.06
South American	7	0.07
Argentinean	1	0.01
Bolivian	1	0.01
Colombian	1	0.01
Paraguayan	1	0.01
Peruvian	3	0.03
Other Hispanic or Latino	9	0.09

Race*	Population	%
African-American/Black (52)	88	0.87
Not Hispanic (50)	84	0.83
Hispanic (2)	4	0.04
American Indian/Alaska Native (42)	91	0.90
Not Hispanic (38)	85	0.84
Hispanic (4)	6	0.06
Cherokee (0)	4	0.04
Chickasaw (1)	1	0.01
Chippewa (16)	23	0.23
Choctaw (0)	3	0.03
Comanche (1)	1	0.01
Iroquois (1)	1	0.01
Pueblo (1)	1	0.01
Puget Sound Salish (1)	1	0.01
Sioux (5)	9	0.09
South American Ind. (0)	2	0.02
Asian (84)	125	1.23
Not Hispanic (82)	123	1.21
Hispanic (2)	2	0.02
Chinese, ex. Taiwanese (3)	13	0.13
Filipino (7)	14	0.14
Hmong (42)	46	0.45
Indian (4)	7	0.07
Indonesian (0)	3	0.03
Japanese (3)	8	0.08
Korean (10)	26	0.26
Laotian (4)	6	0.06
Nepalese (1)	1	0.01
Thai (1)	1	0.01
Vietnamese (1)	6	0.06
Hawaii Native/Pacific Islander (1)	14	0.14
Not Hispanic (1)	14	0.14
Guamanian/Chamorro (1)	6	0.06
Native Hawaiian (0)	3	0.03
White (9,785)	9,909	97.87
Not Hispanic (9,635)	9,749	96.29
Hispanic (150)	160	1.58

North Mankato

Place Type: City
County: Nicollet
Population: 13,394†

Ancestry‡	Population	%
African, Sub-Saharan (19)	32	0.24
African (0)	13	0.10
Kenyan (19)	19	0.14
American (339)	339	2.58
Arab (18)	28	0.21
Lebanese (18)	28	0.21
Austrian (0)	79	0.60
Belgian (4)	4	0.03
British (8)	46	0.35
Canadian (14)	14	0.11
Czech (99)	235	1.79
Czechoslovakian (28)	37	0.28
Danish (33)	456	3.47
Dutch (99)	503	3.83
Eastern European (15)	15	0.11
English (48)	583	4.43
European (96)	139	1.06
Finnish (23)	63	0.48
French, ex. Basque (12)	297	2.26
French Canadian (23)	113	0.86
German (2,856)	7,044	53.58
Irish (339)	1,852	14.09
Italian (26)	403	3.07
Luxemburger (0)	46	0.35
Northern European (43)	43	0.33
Norwegian (568)	1,959	14.90
Pennsylvania German (0)	8	0.06
Polish (85)	291	2.21
Russian (9)	65	0.49
Scandinavian (40)	201	1.53
Scotch-Irish (26)	110	0.84
Scottish (0)	98	0.75
Slovene (13)	61	0.46
Swedish (278)	898	6.83
Swiss (43)	85	0.65
Ukrainian (22)	22	0.17
Welsh (38)	212	1.61
Yugoslavian (8)	27	0.21

Hispanic Origin	Population	%
Hispanic or Latino (of any race)	400	2.99
Central American, ex. Mexican	17	0.13
Guatemalan	6	0.04
Nicaraguan	2	0.01
Salvadoran	9	0.07
Cuban	1	0.01
Mexican	323	2.41
Puerto Rican	6	0.04
South American	16	0.12
Argentinean	1	0.01
Bolivian	1	0.01
Colombian	4	0.03
Ecuadorian	1	0.01
Peruvian	3	0.02
Uruguayan	4	0.03
Venezuelan	2	0.01
Other Hispanic or Latino	37	0.28

Race*	Population	%
African-American/Black (277)	337	2.52
Not Hispanic (270)	330	2.46
Hispanic (7)	7	0.05
American Indian/Alaska Native (30)	81	0.60
Not Hispanic (22)	69	0.52
Hispanic (8)	12	0.09
Alaska Athabascan *(Ala. Nat.)* (1)	1	0.01
Canadian/French Am. Ind. (1)	6	0.04
Cherokee (1)	10	0.07
Chippewa (12)	16	0.12
Iroquois (1)	1	0.01
Mexican American Ind. (1)	1	0.01
Sioux (1)	6	0.04
Asian (228)	281	2.10
Not Hispanic (227)	279	2.08
Hispanic (1)	2	0.01
Bangladeshi (3)	3	0.02
Burmese (1)	1	0.01
Cambodian (6)	8	0.06
Chinese, ex. Taiwanese (29)	40	0.30
Filipino (20)	39	0.29
Indian (20)	25	0.19
Indonesian (1)	1	0.01
Japanese (8)	12	0.09
Korean (42)	52	0.39
Laotian (8)	10	0.07
Nepalese (1)	2	0.01
Pakistani (13)	13	0.10
Sri Lankan (5)	6	0.04
Thai (3)	8	0.06
Vietnamese (58)	66	0.49
Hawaii Native/Pacific Islander (1)	3	0.02
Not Hispanic (1)	3	0.02
Guamanian/Chamorro (1)	1	0.01
Native Hawaiian (0)	2	0.01
White (12,575)	12,742	95.13
Not Hispanic (12,320)	12,458	93.01
Hispanic (255)	284	2.12

North St. Paul

Place Type: City
County: Ramsey
Population: 11,460†

Ancestry‡	Population	%
African, Sub-Saharan (266)	266	2.34
African (179)	179	1.57
Kenyan (32)	32	0.28
Nigerian (55)	55	0.48
American (133)	133	1.17
Austrian (28)	75	0.66
British (29)	88	0.77
Canadian (0)	10	0.09
Czech (10)	185	1.62
Czechoslovakian (9)	45	0.40
Danish (22)	72	0.63
Dutch (42)	184	1.62
English (137)	557	4.89
European (149)	149	1.31
Finnish (13)	49	0.43
French, ex. Basque (60)	418	3.67
French Canadian (46)	184	1.62
German (1,252)	4,158	36.52
Greek (0)	12	0.11
Hungarian (92)	136	1.19
Icelander (0)	23	0.20
Irish (393)	1,624	14.26
Italian (134)	550	4.83
Luxemburger (10)	36	0.32
Macedonian (0)	12	0.11
Northern European (10)	21	0.18
Norwegian (530)	1,690	14.84
Polish (224)	446	3.92
Portuguese (0)	10	0.09
Romanian (0)	11	0.10
Russian (9)	43	0.38
Scandinavian (53)	91	0.80
Scotch-Irish (24)	89	0.78
Scottish (20)	74	0.65
Serbian (0)	10	0.09
Swedish (264)	1,305	11.46
Swiss (9)	52	0.46
Ukrainian (0)	9	0.08
Welsh (73)	81	0.71

Hispanic Origin	Population	%
Hispanic or Latino (of any race)	557	4.86
Central American, ex. Mexican	20	0.17
Costa Rican	1	0.01
Guatemalan	6	0.05
Honduran	9	0.08
Salvadoran	4	0.03
Cuban	7	0.06

*Notes: † The Census 2010 population figure is used to calculate the percentages in the Hispanic Origin and Race categories. Ancestry percentages are based on the 2006-2010 American Community Survey population (not shown); ‡ Numbers in parentheses indicate the number of people reporting a single ancestry; * Numbers in parentheses indicate the number of persons reporting this race alone, not in combination with any other race; Please refer to the Explanation of Data for more information.*

Mexican	466	4.07
Puerto Rican	14	0.12
South American	16	0.14
Colombian	9	0.08
Ecuadorian	2	0.02
Venezuelan	5	0.04
Other Hispanic or Latino	34	0.30

Race*	Population	%
African-American/Black (801)	972	8.48
Not Hispanic (789)	950	8.29
Hispanic (12)	22	0.19
American Indian/Alaska Native (72)	155	1.35
Not Hispanic (50)	122	1.06
Hispanic (22)	33	0.29
Apache (6)	6	0.05
Cherokee (0)	7	0.06
Chippewa (32)	61	0.53
Choctaw (1)	1	0.01
Houma (0)	1	0.01
Iroquois (0)	1	0.01
Menominee (0)	1	0.01
Mexican American Ind. (2)	5	0.04
Navajo (0)	1	0.01
Potawatomi (1)	1	0.01
Sioux (9)	18	0.16
Yaqui (1)	3	0.03
Yup'ik *(Alaska Native)* (1)	1	0.01
Asian (762)	820	7.16
Not Hispanic (762)	817	7.13
Hispanic (0)	3	0.03
Burmese (10)	10	0.09
Cambodian (10)	11	0.10
Chinese, ex. Taiwanese (40)	48	0.42
Filipino (29)	47	0.41
Hmong (521)	546	4.76
Indian (30)	38	0.33
Japanese (4)	8	0.07
Korean (22)	32	0.28
Laotian (2)	2	0.02
Thai (5)	9	0.08
Vietnamese (36)	42	0.37
Hawaii Native/Pacific Islander (11)	22	0.19
Not Hispanic (7)	15	0.13
Hispanic (4)	7	0.06
Guamanian/Chamorro (4)	6	0.05
Native Hawaiian (2)	7	0.06
Samoan (1)	2	0.02
White (9,300)	9,601	83.78
Not Hispanic (9,018)	9,264	80.84
Hispanic (282)	337	2.94

Northfield

Place Type: City
County: Rice
Population: 18,860†

Ancestry‡	Population	%
African, Sub-Saharan (246)	270	1.47
African (136)	136	0.74
Ghanaian (0)	12	0.07
Nigerian (11)	23	0.12
Sudanese (65)	65	0.35
Zimbabwean (11)	11	0.06
Other Sub-Saharan African (23)	23	0.12
American (572)	572	3.10
Arab (24)	35	0.19
Lebanese (0)	11	0.06
Palestinian (12)	12	0.07
Other Arab (12)	12	0.07
Armenian (51)	118	0.64
Assyrian/Chaldean/Syriac (0)	12	0.07
Austrian (13)	58	0.31
Belgian (0)	11	0.06
British (16)	130	0.71
Cajun (0)	10	0.05
Canadian (0)	41	0.22
Czech (152)	479	2.60
Czechoslovakian (58)	82	0.45
Danish (59)	454	2.46
Dutch (74)	363	1.97
English (328)	1,958	10.63
European (315)	364	1.98
Finnish (9)	161	0.87
French, ex. Basque (0)	671	3.64
French Canadian (32)	130	0.71
German (1,633)	6,846	37.16
Greek (47)	71	0.39
Hungarian (23)	169	0.92
Iranian (12)	12	0.07
Irish (205)	2,236	12.14
Italian (97)	481	2.61
Latvian (0)	21	0.11
Lithuanian (0)	52	0.28
Northern European (34)	50	0.27
Norwegian (1,301)	3,634	19.73
Pennsylvania German (0)	8	0.04
Polish (233)	842	4.57
Russian (45)	244	1.32
Scandinavian (125)	321	1.74
Scotch-Irish (96)	382	2.07
Scottish (37)	403	2.19
Slovak (0)	15	0.08
Slovene (0)	21	0.11
Swedish (500)	1,879	10.20
Swiss (15)	49	0.27
Ukrainian (0)	57	0.31
Welsh (19)	119	0.65

Hispanic Origin	Population	%
Hispanic or Latino (of any race)	1,666	8.83
Central American, ex. Mexican	49	0.26
Costa Rican	4	0.02
Guatemalan	27	0.14
Honduran	4	0.02
Nicaraguan	1	0.01
Panamanian	4	0.02
Salvadoran	9	0.05
Cuban	33	0.17
Dominican Republic	1	0.01
Mexican	1,388	7.36
Puerto Rican	43	0.23
South American	68	0.36
Argentinean	9	0.05
Bolivian	5	0.03
Chilean	4	0.02
Colombian	24	0.13
Ecuadorian	11	0.06
Paraguayan	1	0.01
Peruvian	10	0.05
Venezuelan	4	0.02
Other Hispanic or Latino	84	0.45

Race*	Population	%
African-American/Black (247)	394	2.09
Not Hispanic (238)	372	1.97
Hispanic (9)	22	0.12
American Indian/Alaska Native (47)	129	0.68
Not Hispanic (29)	94	0.50
Hispanic (18)	35	0.19
Alaska Athabascan *(Ala. Nat.)* (0)	1	0.01
Blackfeet (0)	1	0.01
Cherokee (1)	18	0.10
Chippewa (12)	28	0.15
Choctaw (0)	2	0.01
Comanche (0)	1	0.01
Houma (0)	1	0.01
Inupiat *(Alaska Native)* (0)	1	0.01
Iroquois (0)	2	0.01
Mexican American Ind. (7)	9	0.05
Pueblo (0)	1	0.01
Sioux (2)	6	0.03
South American Ind. (0)	1	0.01
Spanish American Ind. (2)	3	0.02
Asian (671)	865	4.59
Not Hispanic (663)	841	4.46
Hispanic (8)	24	0.13
Bangladeshi (5)	7	0.04
Burmese (4)	7	0.04
Cambodian (5)	9	0.05
Chinese, ex. Taiwanese (178)	234	1.24
Filipino (33)	61	0.32
Hmong (80)	85	0.45
Indian (77)	101	0.54
Indonesian (2)	2	0.01
Japanese (53)	111	0.59
Korean (89)	120	0.64
Laotian (2)	5	0.03
Nepalese (0)	1	0.01
Pakistani (2)	5	0.03
Sri Lankan (2)	3	0.02
Taiwanese (0)	6	0.03
Thai (8)	14	0.07
Vietnamese (98)	116	0.62
Hawaii Native/Pacific Islander (8)	23	0.12
Not Hispanic (8)	15	0.08
Hispanic (0)	8	0.04
Native Hawaiian (4)	8	0.04
Samoan (0)	3	0.02
White (16,669)	17,063	90.47
Not Hispanic (15,891)	16,217	85.99
Hispanic (778)	846	4.49

Northfield

Place Type: City
County: Rice
Population: 20,007†

Ancestry‡	Population	%
African, Sub-Saharan (246)	270	1.39
African (136)	136	0.70
Ghanaian (0)	12	0.06
Nigerian (11)	23	0.12
Sudanese (65)	65	0.33
Zimbabwean (11)	11	0.06
Other Sub-Saharan African (23)	23	0.12
American (594)	594	3.06
Arab (24)	35	0.18
Lebanese (0)	11	0.06
Palestinian (12)	12	0.06
Other Arab (12)	12	0.06
Armenian (51)	118	0.61
Assyrian/Chaldean/Syriac (0)	12	0.06
Austrian (13)	58	0.30
Belgian (0)	11	0.06
British (16)	130	0.67
Cajun (0)	21	0.11
Canadian (0)	41	0.21
Czech (152)	529	2.72
Czechoslovakian (58)	91	0.47
Danish (89)	526	2.71
Dutch (74)	413	2.13
English (328)	2,060	10.61
European (337)	386	1.99
Finnish (9)	161	0.83
French, ex. Basque (0)	738	3.80
French Canadian (32)	148	0.76
German (1,692)	7,245	37.32
Greek (47)	71	0.37
Hungarian (23)	169	0.87
Iranian (12)	12	0.06
Irish (216)	2,343	12.07
Italian (97)	534	2.75
Latvian (0)	21	0.11
Lithuanian (0)	52	0.27
Northern European (34)	50	0.26
Norwegian (1,362)	3,994	20.57
Pennsylvania German (0)	8	0.04
Polish (244)	881	4.54
Russian (45)	244	1.26
Scandinavian (136)	332	1.71
Scotch-Irish (96)	382	1.97
Scottish (37)	429	2.21
Slovak (0)	15	0.08
Slovene (0)	21	0.11
Swedish (511)	2,025	10.43
Swiss (15)	59	0.30
Ukrainian (0)	98	0.50

*Notes: † The Census 2010 population figure is used to calculate the percentages in the Hispanic Origin and Race categories. Ancestry percentages are based on the 2006-2010 American Community Survey population (not shown); ‡ Numbers in parentheses indicate the number of people reporting a single ancestry; * Numbers in parentheses indicate the number of persons reporting this race alone, not in combination with any other race; Please refer to the Explanation of Data for more information.*

Welsh (19)	168	0.87

Hispanic Origin	Population	%
Hispanic or Latino (of any race)	1,685	8.42
Central American, ex. Mexican	52	0.26
Costa Rican	7	0.03
Guatemalan	27	0.13
Honduran	4	0.02
Nicaraguan	1	<0.01
Panamanian	4	0.02
Salvadoran	9	0.04
Cuban	33	0.16
Dominican Republic	1	<0.01
Mexican	1,403	7.01
Puerto Rican	43	0.21
South American	68	0.34
Argentinean	9	0.04
Bolivian	5	0.02
Chilean	4	0.02
Colombian	24	0.12
Ecuadorian	11	0.05
Paraguayan	1	<0.01
Peruvian	10	0.05
Venezuelan	4	0.02
Other Hispanic or Latino	85	0.42

Race*	Population	%
African-American/Black (257)	405	2.02
Not Hispanic (248)	383	1.91
Hispanic (9)	22	0.11
American Indian/Alaska Native (49)	133	0.66
Not Hispanic (30)	97	0.48
Hispanic (19)	36	0.18
Alaska Athabascan *(Ala. Nat.)* (0)	1	<0.01
Blackfeet (0)	1	<0.01
Cherokee (1)	18	0.09
Chippewa (12)	29	0.14
Choctaw (0)	2	0.01
Comanche (0)	1	<0.01
Houma (0)	1	<0.01
Inupiat *(Alaska Native)* (0)	1	<0.01
Iroquois (0)	2	0.01
Mexican American Ind. (7)	9	0.04
Pueblo (0)	1	<0.01
Sioux (2)	6	0.03
South American Ind. (0)	1	<0.01
Spanish American Ind. (2)	3	0.01
Asian (691)	889	4.44
Not Hispanic (683)	865	4.32
Hispanic (8)	24	0.12
Bangladeshi (5)	7	0.03
Burmese (4)	7	0.03
Cambodian (5)	9	0.04
Chinese, ex. Taiwanese (188)	246	1.23
Filipino (34)	62	0.31
Hmong (80)	85	0.42
Indian (77)	102	0.51
Indonesian (2)	2	0.01
Japanese (53)	112	0.56
Korean (95)	127	0.63
Laotian (2)	5	0.02
Nepalese (0)	1	<0.01
Pakistani (2)	5	0.02
Sri Lankan (2)	3	0.01
Taiwanese (0)	6	0.03
Thai (8)	15	0.07
Vietnamese (100)	118	0.59
Hawaii Native/Pacific Islander (8)	23	0.11
Not Hispanic (8)	15	0.07
Hispanic (0)	8	0.04
Native Hawaiian (4)	8	0.04
Samoan (0)	3	0.01
White (17,763)	18,164	90.79
Not Hispanic (16,978)	17,311	86.52
Hispanic (785)	853	4.26

Oak Grove

Place Type: City
County: Anoka
Population: 8,031†

Ancestry‡	Population	%
American (176)	176	2.23
Arab (9)	9	0.11
Other Arab (9)	9	0.11
Brazilian (9)	9	0.11
Czech (19)	195	2.47
Danish (33)	146	1.85
Dutch (28)	57	0.72
English (107)	617	7.83
European (168)	318	4.04
Finnish (32)	101	1.28
French, ex. Basque (32)	474	6.01
French Canadian (33)	145	1.84
German (826)	3,196	40.55
Greek (0)	11	0.14
Hungarian (0)	11	0.14
Irish (149)	1,018	12.92
Italian (52)	316	4.01
Norwegian (296)	1,427	18.11
Polish (87)	668	8.48
Portuguese (11)	22	0.28
Russian (0)	63	0.80
Scandinavian (53)	239	3.03
Scotch-Irish (11)	72	0.91
Scottish (0)	42	0.53
Swedish (185)	1,200	15.23
Swiss (8)	19	0.24
Welsh (0)	7	0.09
Yugoslavian (9)	9	0.11

Hispanic Origin	Population	%
Hispanic or Latino (of any race)	94	1.17
Central American, ex. Mexican	9	0.11
Costa Rican	2	0.02
Guatemalan	3	0.04
Nicaraguan	1	0.01
Panamanian	2	0.02
Salvadoran	1	0.01
Cuban	1	0.01
Mexican	66	0.82
Puerto Rican	7	0.09
South American	3	0.04
Chilean	1	0.01
Colombian	2	0.02
Other Hispanic or Latino	8	0.10

Race*	Population	%
African-American/Black (40)	68	0.85
Not Hispanic (40)	67	0.83
Hispanic (0)	1	0.01
American Indian/Alaska Native (21)	65	0.81
Not Hispanic (13)	57	0.71
Hispanic (8)	8	0.10
Alaska Athabascan *(Ala. Nat.)* (1)	1	0.01
Canadian/French Am. Ind. (0)	1	0.01
Cherokee (4)	9	0.11
Chippewa (5)	17	0.21
Choctaw (0)	1	0.01
Sioux (4)	7	0.09
Asian (150)	186	2.32
Not Hispanic (150)	185	2.30
Hispanic (0)	1	0.01
Cambodian (1)	1	0.01
Chinese, ex. Taiwanese (8)	8	0.10
Filipino (17)	30	0.37
Hmong (102)	103	1.28
Indian (3)	3	0.04
Japanese (0)	8	0.10
Korean (6)	15	0.19
Nepalese (0)	1	0.01
Pakistani (0)	1	0.01
Thai (2)	4	0.05
Vietnamese (0)	1	0.01
White (7,690)	7,792	97.02
Not Hispanic (7,633)	7,728	96.23
Hispanic (57)	64	0.80

Oakdale

Place Type: City
County: Washington
Population: 27,378†

Ancestry‡	Population	%
Afghan (53)	53	0.19
African, Sub-Saharan (917)	1,013	3.70
African (395)	491	1.79
Ethiopian (49)	49	0.18
Ghanaian (88)	88	0.32
Kenyan (126)	126	0.46
Nigerian (259)	259	0.95
American (1,058)	1,058	3.86
Arab (95)	195	0.71
Arab (7)	17	0.06
Egyptian (28)	98	0.36
Lebanese (28)	48	0.18
Palestinian (12)	12	0.04
Other Arab (20)	20	0.07
Armenian (0)	15	0.05
Austrian (12)	102	0.37
Brazilian (71)	71	0.26
British (14)	97	0.35
Bulgarian (12)	47	0.17
Canadian (24)	74	0.27
Croatian (0)	36	0.13
Czech (109)	603	2.20
Czechoslovakian (39)	39	0.14
Danish (86)	475	1.73
Dutch (57)	386	1.41
Eastern European (24)	24	0.09
English (178)	1,605	5.86
European (290)	320	1.17
Finnish (13)	271	0.99
French, ex. Basque (68)	1,789	6.53
French Canadian (109)	377	1.38
German (3,143)	10,611	38.76
Greek (15)	51	0.19
Hungarian (26)	92	0.34
Irish (551)	3,316	12.11
Italian (299)	1,513	5.53
Latvian (15)	15	0.05
Luxemburger (0)	12	0.04
Maltese (0)	10	0.04
Northern European (20)	20	0.07
Norwegian (940)	3,610	13.19
Polish (512)	1,936	7.07
Portuguese (9)	9	0.03
Romanian (18)	44	0.16
Russian (12)	175	0.64
Scandinavian (113)	294	1.07
Scotch-Irish (97)	243	0.89
Scottish (52)	328	1.20
Serbian (39)	59	0.22
Slovene (13)	13	0.05
Swedish (524)	2,389	8.73
Swiss (42)	197	0.72
Ukrainian (31)	99	0.36
Welsh (22)	106	0.39
West Indian, ex. Hispanic (56)	56	0.20
Belizean (56)	56	0.20

Hispanic Origin	Population	%
Hispanic or Latino (of any race)	1,172	4.28
Central American, ex. Mexican	83	0.30
Costa Rican	5	0.02
Guatemalan	24	0.09
Honduran	10	0.04
Nicaraguan	8	0.03
Panamanian	8	0.03
Salvadoran	27	0.10
Other Central American	1	<0.01
Cuban	20	0.07
Dominican Republic	5	0.02
Mexican	845	3.09

*Notes: † The Census 2010 population figure is used to calculate the percentages in the Hispanic Origin and Race categories. Ancestry percentages are based on the 2006-2010 American Community Survey population (not shown); ‡ Numbers in parentheses indicate the number of people reporting a single ancestry; * Numbers in parentheses indicate the number of persons reporting this race alone, not in combination with any other race; Please refer to the Explanation of Data for more information.*

Puerto Rican	86	0.31
South American	57	0.21
Argentinean	1	<0.01
Bolivian	2	0.01
Chilean	4	0.01
Colombian	23	0.08
Ecuadorian	11	0.04
Paraguayan	3	0.01
Peruvian	6	0.02
Uruguayan	5	0.02
Venezuelan	2	0.01
Other Hispanic or Latino	76	0.28

Race*	Population	%
African-American/Black (1,649)	2,032	7.42
Not Hispanic (1,609)	1,931	7.05
Hispanic (40)	101	0.37
American Indian/Alaska Native (112)	306	1.12
Not Hispanic (94)	250	0.91
Hispanic (18)	56	0.20
Alaska Athabascan *(Ala. Nat.)* (5)	5	0.02
Apache (0)	1	<0.01
Cherokee (0)	11	0.04
Cheyenne (0)	1	<0.01
Chippewa (37)	72	0.26
Choctaw (0)	1	<0.01
Cree (0)	1	<0.01
Iroquois (3)	6	0.02
Mexican American Ind. (4)	5	0.02
Pima (1)	1	<0.01
Sioux (14)	24	0.09
Spanish American Ind. (1)	1	<0.01
Asian (2,232)	2,424	8.85
Not Hispanic (2,218)	2,397	8.76
Hispanic (14)	27	0.10
Bangladeshi (3)	3	0.01
Cambodian (84)	90	0.33
Chinese, ex. Taiwanese (69)	93	0.34
Filipino (61)	81	0.30
Hmong (1,473)	1,524	5.57
Indian (100)	114	0.42
Indonesian (2)	6	0.02
Japanese (18)	51	0.19
Korean (77)	114	0.42
Laotian (26)	32	0.12
Malaysian (0)	1	<0.01
Nepalese (2)	4	0.01
Pakistani (17)	18	0.07
Sri Lankan (3)	3	0.01
Taiwanese (4)	6	0.02
Thai (3)	6	0.02
Vietnamese (165)	178	0.65
Hawaii Native/Pacific Islander (8)	44	0.16
Not Hispanic (8)	33	0.12
Hispanic (0)	11	0.04
Fijian (1)	1	<0.01
Guamanian/Chamorro (2)	4	0.01
Native Hawaiian (2)	7	0.03
Samoan (1)	3	0.01
White (22,293)	22,946	83.81
Not Hispanic (21,658)	22,178	81.01
Hispanic (635)	768	2.81

Otsego

Place Type: City
County: Wright
Population: 13,571†

Ancestry‡	Population	%
African, Sub-Saharan (97)	107	0.85
Ethiopian (21)	31	0.25
Kenyan (20)	20	0.16
Liberian (56)	56	0.45
American (409)	409	3.27
Austrian (0)	60	0.48
Belgian (15)	15	0.12
British (0)	43	0.34
Canadian (0)	10	0.08
Croatian (0)	71	0.57
Czech (76)	376	3.00
Danish (15)	125	1.00
Dutch (38)	197	1.57
Eastern European (41)	41	0.33
English (51)	641	5.12
European (78)	92	0.73
Finnish (36)	264	2.11
French, ex. Basque (68)	943	7.53
French Canadian (77)	146	1.17
German (1,817)	5,363	42.83
Greek (0)	25	0.20
Hungarian (10)	46	0.37
Iranian (0)	25	0.20
Irish (258)	1,529	12.21
Italian (72)	431	3.44
Norwegian (607)	2,287	18.27
Polish (221)	800	6.39
Portuguese (0)	29	0.23
Russian (135)	176	1.41
Scandinavian (63)	180	1.44
Scotch-Irish (35)	104	0.83
Scottish (15)	172	1.37
Slovak (44)	111	0.89
Swedish (358)	1,363	10.89
Swiss (0)	26	0.21
Ukrainian (15)	15	0.12
Welsh (14)	24	0.19

Hispanic Origin	Population	%
Hispanic or Latino (of any race)	329	2.42
Central American, ex. Mexican	32	0.24
Costa Rican	2	0.01
Guatemalan	7	0.05
Honduran	1	0.01
Nicaraguan	7	0.05
Panamanian	2	0.01
Salvadoran	13	0.10
Cuban	3	0.02
Dominican Republic	4	0.03
Mexican	208	1.53
Puerto Rican	28	0.21
South American	31	0.23
Bolivian	1	0.01
Chilean	9	0.07
Colombian	3	0.02
Ecuadorian	2	0.01
Paraguayan	2	0.01
Peruvian	9	0.07
Venezuelan	5	0.04
Other Hispanic or Latino	23	0.17

Race*	Population	%
African-American/Black (242)	347	2.56
Not Hispanic (239)	336	2.48
Hispanic (3)	11	0.08
American Indian/Alaska Native (56)	135	0.99
Not Hispanic (52)	117	0.86
Hispanic (4)	18	0.13
Cherokee (4)	5	0.04
Chickasaw (1)	1	0.01
Chippewa (23)	48	0.35
Iroquois (1)	7	0.05
Mexican American Ind. (1)	1	0.01
Navajo (1)	1	0.01
Seminole (0)	1	0.01
Sioux (5)	5	0.04
Asian (239)	332	2.45
Not Hispanic (236)	326	2.40
Hispanic (3)	6	0.04
Burmese (2)	2	0.01
Cambodian (4)	7	0.05
Chinese, ex. Taiwanese (11)	35	0.26
Filipino (20)	40	0.29
Hmong (45)	47	0.35
Indian (10)	19	0.14
Indonesian (1)	3	0.02
Japanese (5)	6	0.04
Korean (31)	62	0.46
Laotian (47)	61	0.45
Taiwanese (1)	5	0.04
Thai (3)	5	0.04
Vietnamese (44)	52	0.38
Hawaii Native/Pacific Islander (18)	28	0.21
Not Hispanic (18)	27	0.20
Hispanic (0)	1	0.01
Fijian (8)	8	0.06
Guamanian/Chamorro (6)	7	0.05
Native Hawaiian (0)	5	0.04
White (12,652)	12,890	94.98
Not Hispanic (12,464)	12,670	93.36
Hispanic (188)	220	1.62

Owatonna

Place Type: City
County: Steele
Population: 25,599†

Ancestry‡	Population	%
African, Sub-Saharan (372)	401	1.58
African (51)	80	0.32
Somalian (321)	321	1.27
American (878)	878	3.47
Arab (14)	14	0.06
Lebanese (14)	14	0.06
Austrian (0)	11	0.04
Belgian (7)	58	0.23
British (12)	35	0.14
Canadian (17)	44	0.17
Croatian (0)	45	0.18
Czech (446)	1,381	5.45
Czechoslovakian (98)	128	0.51
Danish (238)	851	3.36
Dutch (97)	367	1.45
English (305)	1,466	5.79
European (95)	129	0.51
Finnish (15)	121	0.48
French, ex. Basque (31)	636	2.51
French Canadian (178)	456	1.80
German (3,656)	9,879	39.02
German Russian (0)	48	0.19
Greek (44)	56	0.22
Hungarian (0)	54	0.21
Irish (406)	2,240	8.85
Italian (48)	220	0.87
Lithuanian (25)	56	0.22
Luxemburger (22)	38	0.15
Northern European (34)	80	0.32
Norwegian (1,415)	4,433	17.51
Pennsylvania German (0)	17	0.07
Polish (177)	611	2.41
Portuguese (0)	12	0.05
Russian (0)	28	0.11
Scandinavian (117)	200	0.79
Scotch-Irish (52)	176	0.70
Scottish (17)	95	0.38
Swedish (261)	1,154	4.56
Swiss (3)	27	0.11
Ukrainian (15)	15	0.06
Welsh (0)	62	0.24
Yugoslavian (13)	37	0.15

Hispanic Origin	Population	%
Hispanic or Latino (of any race)	1,868	7.30
Central American, ex. Mexican	79	0.31
Costa Rican	6	0.02
Guatemalan	29	0.11
Honduran	8	0.03
Nicaraguan	1	<0.01
Panamanian	4	0.02
Salvadoran	31	0.12
Cuban	13	0.05
Mexican	1,573	6.14
Puerto Rican	43	0.17
South American	12	0.05
Colombian	8	0.03
Ecuadorian	2	0.01
Peruvian	2	0.01
Other Hispanic or Latino	148	0.58

*Notes: † The Census 2010 population figure is used to calculate the percentages in the Hispanic Origin and Race categories. Ancestry percentages are based on the 2006-2010 American Community Survey population (not shown); ‡ Numbers in parentheses indicate the number of people reporting a single ancestry; * Numbers in parentheses indicate the number of persons reporting this race alone, not in combination with any other race; Please refer to the Explanation of Data for more information.*

Race*	Population	%
African-American/Black (984)	1,141	4.46
Not Hispanic (974)	1,121	4.38
Hispanic (10)	20	0.08
American Indian/Alaska Native (66)	146	0.57
Not Hispanic (53)	115	0.45
Hispanic (13)	31	0.12
Aleut *(Alaska Native)* (1)	2	0.01
Apache (2)	5	0.02
Blackfeet (0)	5	0.02
Cherokee (5)	9	0.04
Chippewa (20)	33	0.13
Choctaw (0)	1	<0.01
Colville (1)	1	<0.01
Comanche (0)	7	0.03
Creek (0)	1	<0.01
Hopi (0)	1	<0.01
Inupiat *(Alaska Native)* (1)	1	<0.01
Lumbee (1)	1	<0.01
Mexican American Ind. (1)	2	0.01
Potawatomi (0)	4	0.02
Seminole (2)	2	0.01
Sioux (4)	10	0.04
Spanish American Ind. (2)	2	0.01
Asian (237)	319	1.25
Not Hispanic (234)	309	1.21
Hispanic (3)	10	0.04
Cambodian (7)	8	0.03
Chinese, ex. Taiwanese (39)	50	0.20
Filipino (19)	41	0.16
Hmong (20)	21	0.08
Indian (50)	62	0.24
Japanese (14)	30	0.12
Korean (41)	58	0.23
Laotian (0)	2	0.01
Nepalese (3)	3	0.01
Pakistani (3)	3	0.01
Thai (4)	5	0.02
Vietnamese (27)	38	0.15
Hawaii Native/Pacific Islander (3)	9	0.04
Not Hispanic (3)	7	0.03
Hispanic (0)	2	0.01
Native Hawaiian (1)	5	0.02
Samoan (0)	1	<0.01
White (23,350)	23,717	92.65
Not Hispanic (22,172)	22,439	87.66
Hispanic (1,178)	1,278	4.99

Plymouth

Place Type: City
County: Hennepin
Population: 70,576†

Ancestry‡	Population	%
African, Sub-Saharan (935)	969	1.40
African (463)	481	0.70
Ethiopian (92)	108	0.16
Kenyan (175)	175	0.25
Liberian (63)	63	0.09
Nigerian (73)	73	0.11
Somalian (69)	69	0.10
Albanian (5)	5	0.01
American (1,831)	1,831	2.65
Arab (297)	425	0.61
Arab (41)	41	0.06
Egyptian (86)	86	0.12
Jordanian (26)	26	0.04
Lebanese (32)	142	0.21
Moroccan (87)	87	0.13
Syrian (25)	43	0.06
Armenian (41)	68	0.10
Australian (0)	19	0.03
Austrian (47)	325	0.47
Belgian (63)	215	0.31
Brazilian (38)	55	0.08
British (101)	258	0.37
Canadian (76)	185	0.27
Celtic (14)	32	0.05
Croatian (62)	179	0.26
Czech (203)	985	1.42
Czechoslovakian (10)	27	0.04
Danish (411)	1,215	1.76
Dutch (287)	1,420	2.05
Eastern European (295)	305	0.44
English (955)	4,659	6.74
European (978)	1,064	1.54
Finnish (507)	1,357	1.96
French, ex. Basque (258)	2,969	4.29
French Canadian (132)	584	0.84
German (6,991)	22,574	32.64
Greek (67)	171	0.25
Guyanese (10)	10	0.01
Hungarian (27)	287	0.41
Icelander (0)	52	0.08
Iranian (142)	160	0.23
Irish (1,605)	8,110	11.72
Israeli (78)	78	0.11
Italian (444)	2,047	2.96
Latvian (15)	21	0.03
Lithuanian (37)	153	0.22
Luxemburger (11)	77	0.11
Macedonian (23)	23	0.03
New Zealander (0)	9	0.01
Northern European (340)	340	0.49
Norwegian (3,644)	11,572	16.73
Pennsylvania German (0)	12	0.02
Polish (699)	3,321	4.80
Portuguese (0)	102	0.15
Romanian (49)	183	0.26
Russian (1,010)	1,782	2.58
Scandinavian (870)	1,235	1.79
Scotch-Irish (241)	667	0.96
Scottish (122)	755	1.09
Serbian (12)	26	0.04
Slavic (54)	89	0.13
Slovak (32)	100	0.14
Slovene (22)	56	0.08
Swedish (1,695)	7,210	10.42
Swiss (121)	259	0.37
Turkish (13)	13	0.02
Ukrainian (173)	399	0.58
Welsh (76)	542	0.78
West Indian, ex. Hispanic (14)	25	0.04
Barbadian (14)	14	0.02
Jamaican (0)	11	0.02
Yugoslavian (32)	93	0.13

Hispanic Origin	Population	%
Hispanic or Latino (of any race)	2,117	3.00
Central American, ex. Mexican	161	0.23
Costa Rican	17	0.02
Guatemalan	72	0.10
Honduran	14	0.02
Nicaraguan	12	0.02
Panamanian	15	0.02
Salvadoran	30	0.04
Other Central American	1	<0.01
Cuban	51	0.07
Dominican Republic	18	0.03
Mexican	1,145	1.62
Puerto Rican	126	0.18
South American	385	0.55
Argentinean	28	0.04
Bolivian	6	0.01
Chilean	55	0.08
Colombian	135	0.19
Ecuadorian	53	0.08
Paraguayan	7	0.01
Peruvian	57	0.08
Uruguayan	5	0.01
Venezuelan	37	0.05
Other South American	2	<0.01
Other Hispanic or Latino	231	0.33

Race*	Population	%
African-American/Black (3,704)	4,381	6.21
Not Hispanic (3,661)	4,286	6.07
Hispanic (43)	95	0.13
American Indian/Alaska Native (188)	543	0.77
Not Hispanic (170)	471	0.67
Hispanic (18)	72	0.10
Aleut *(Alaska Native)* (0)	6	0.01
Apache (0)	2	<0.01
Blackfeet (0)	3	<0.01
Canadian/French Am. Ind. (2)	3	<0.01
Cherokee (4)	35	0.05
Chippewa (65)	130	0.18
Choctaw (0)	10	0.01
Cree (0)	1	<0.01
Creek (0)	1	<0.01
Crow (2)	2	<0.01
Houma (0)	1	<0.01
Inupiat *(Alaska Native)* (1)	1	<0.01
Iroquois (0)	2	<0.01
Menominee (0)	3	<0.01
Mexican American Ind. (2)	16	0.02
Navajo (3)	5	0.01
Osage (1)	1	<0.01
Ottawa (0)	2	<0.01
Pima (0)	2	<0.01
Pueblo (0)	2	<0.01
Seminole (0)	2	<0.01
Sioux (32)	68	0.10
South American Ind. (2)	6	0.01
Yuman (1)	1	<0.01
Asian (4,888)	5,506	7.80
Not Hispanic (4,867)	5,454	7.73
Hispanic (21)	52	0.07
Bangladeshi (22)	22	0.03
Burmese (4)	4	0.01
Cambodian (25)	43	0.06
Chinese, ex. Taiwanese (929)	1,072	1.52
Filipino (155)	226	0.32
Hmong (116)	123	0.17
Indian (2,335)	2,439	3.46
Indonesian (0)	4	0.01
Japanese (123)	212	0.30
Korean (484)	604	0.86
Laotian (43)	62	0.09
Malaysian (11)	14	0.02
Nepalese (14)	15	0.02
Pakistani (69)	89	0.13
Sri Lankan (15)	18	0.03
Taiwanese (67)	71	0.10
Thai (22)	33	0.05
Vietnamese (331)	383	0.54
Hawaii Native/Pacific Islander (22)	68	0.10
Not Hispanic (20)	56	0.08
Hispanic (2)	12	0.02
Guamanian/Chamorro (8)	13	0.02
Marshallese (1)	1	<0.01
Native Hawaiian (5)	30	0.04
Samoan (6)	8	0.01
White (59,460)	60,899	86.29
Not Hispanic (58,240)	59,494	84.30
Hispanic (1,220)	1,405	1.99

Prior Lake

Place Type: City
County: Scott
Population: 22,796†

Ancestry‡	Population	%
African, Sub-Saharan (14)	30	0.14
African (0)	15	0.07
Ethiopian (14)	14	0.06
Other Sub-Saharan African (0)	1	<0.01
American (633)	633	2.85
Arab (6)	30	0.14
Lebanese (6)	30	0.14
Armenian (0)	60	0.27
Australian (0)	9	0.04
Austrian (12)	48	0.22
Belgian (26)	71	0.32
British (0)	52	0.23
Canadian (0)	10	0.05
Croatian (21)	73	0.33

*Notes: † The Census 2010 population figure is used to calculate the percentages in the Hispanic Origin and Race categories. Ancestry percentages are based on the 2006-2010 American Community Survey population (not shown); ‡ Numbers in parentheses indicate the number of people reporting a single ancestry; * Numbers in parentheses indicate the number of persons reporting this race alone, not in combination with any other race; Please refer to the Explanation of Data for more information.*

Ancestry	Population	%
Czech (61)	599	2.70
Czechoslovakian (57)	98	0.44
Danish (12)	118	0.53
Dutch (150)	765	3.45
Eastern European (27)	27	0.12
English (426)	1,960	8.83
European (432)	454	2.05
Finnish (40)	258	1.16
French, ex. Basque (52)	719	3.24
French Canadian (56)	166	0.75
German (2,966)	8,838	39.82
Greek (28)	28	0.13
Hungarian (11)	98	0.44
Icelander (34)	34	0.15
Irish (681)	3,076	13.86
Italian (191)	741	3.34
Latvian (32)	42	0.19
Lithuanian (0)	36	0.16
Luxemburger (29)	29	0.13
Northern European (41)	41	0.18
Norwegian (949)	3,596	16.20
Pennsylvania German (36)	36	0.16
Polish (188)	1,187	5.35
Portuguese (38)	68	0.31
Russian (211)	326	1.47
Scandinavian (167)	342	1.54
Scotch-Irish (63)	250	1.13
Scottish (49)	277	1.25
Serbian (9)	16	0.07
Slavic (0)	11	0.05
Slovak (44)	81	0.36
Slovene (0)	8	0.04
Swedish (521)	2,511	11.31
Swiss (0)	72	0.32
Turkish (0)	28	0.13
Ukrainian (40)	189	0.85
Welsh (14)	89	0.40
West Indian, ex. Hispanic (0)	22	0.10
Bahamian (0)	22	0.10
Yugoslavian (52)	99	0.45

Hispanic Origin	Population	%
Hispanic or Latino (of any race)	482	2.11
Central American, ex. Mexican	30	0.13
Guatemalan	14	0.06
Honduran	5	0.02
Nicaraguan	1	<0.01
Panamanian	7	0.03
Salvadoran	3	0.01
Cuban	10	0.04
Mexican	322	1.41
Puerto Rican	53	0.23
South American	39	0.17
Argentinean	12	0.05
Chilean	4	0.02
Colombian	10	0.04
Ecuadorian	3	0.01
Paraguayan	1	<0.01
Peruvian	6	0.03
Uruguayan	2	0.01
Venezuelan	1	<0.01
Other Hispanic or Latino	28	0.12

Race*	Population	%
African-American/Black (341)	484	2.12
Not Hispanic (334)	462	2.03
Hispanic (7)	22	0.10
American Indian/Alaska Native (357)	620	2.72
Not Hispanic (338)	565	2.48
Hispanic (19)	55	0.24
Canadian/French Am. Ind. (1)	3	0.01
Central American Ind. (1)	1	<0.01
Cherokee (2)	10	0.04
Chickasaw (0)	3	0.01
Chippewa (68)	90	0.39
Cree (0)	1	<0.01
Iroquois (4)	6	0.03
Mexican American Ind. (5)	6	0.03
Navajo (0)	4	0.02
Osage (0)	1	<0.01
Pima (1)	2	0.01
Puget Sound Salish (0)	1	<0.01
Seminole (1)	1	<0.01
Sioux (191)	350	1.54
South American Ind. (1)	1	<0.01
Spanish American Ind. (0)	1	<0.01
Asian (690)	842	3.69
Not Hispanic (688)	838	3.68
Hispanic (2)	4	0.02
Bangladeshi (4)	5	0.02
Burmese (5)	5	0.02
Cambodian (50)	66	0.29
Chinese, ex. Taiwanese (116)	148	0.65
Filipino (34)	54	0.24
Hmong (17)	17	0.07
Indian (133)	155	0.68
Indonesian (2)	4	0.02
Japanese (7)	22	0.10
Korean (56)	79	0.35
Laotian (24)	38	0.17
Malaysian (1)	1	<0.01
Nepalese (3)	3	0.01
Pakistani (10)	10	0.04
Sri Lankan (1)	1	<0.01
Taiwanese (3)	7	0.03
Thai (2)	13	0.06
Vietnamese (166)	198	0.87
Hawaii Native/Pacific Islander (8)	25	0.11
Not Hispanic (8)	25	0.11
Guamanian/Chamorro (4)	6	0.03
Native Hawaiian (2)	8	0.04
White (20,735)	21,247	93.20
Not Hispanic (20,431)	20,883	91.61
Hispanic (304)	364	1.60

Ramsey

Place Type: City
County: Anoka
Population: 23,668[†]

Ancestry[‡]	Population	%
African, Sub-Saharan (291)	291	1.27
African (71)	71	0.31
Ethiopian (26)	26	0.11
Nigerian (20)	20	0.09
Sierra Leonean (112)	112	0.49
Other Sub-Saharan African (62)	62	0.27
American (605)	605	2.64
Arab (10)	47	0.21
Lebanese (10)	47	0.21
Australian (6)	6	0.03
Austrian (0)	48	0.21
Belgian (9)	81	0.35
British (31)	51	0.22
Canadian (0)	18	0.08
Czech (69)	290	1.26
Czechoslovakian (16)	54	0.24
Danish (28)	586	2.56
Dutch (83)	474	2.07
English (217)	1,404	6.12
European (390)	430	1.88
Finnish (149)	497	2.17
French, ex. Basque (101)	1,307	5.70
French Canadian (225)	423	1.85
German (2,410)	8,565	37.36
Greek (12)	39	0.17
Hungarian (0)	85	0.37
Icelander (0)	11	0.05
Irish (502)	2,819	12.30
Israeli (62)	62	0.27
Italian (257)	997	4.35
Latvian (0)	17	0.07
Lithuanian (0)	22	0.10
Macedonian (9)	9	0.04
Northern European (18)	18	0.08
Norwegian (1,052)	3,996	17.43
Pennsylvania German (10)	10	0.04
Polish (442)	1,771	7.73
Portuguese (0)	45	0.20
Romanian (7)	52	0.23
Russian (252)	371	1.62
Scandinavian (167)	423	1.85
Scotch-Irish (12)	240	1.05
Scottish (24)	160	0.70
Serbian (12)	12	0.05
Slavic (7)	16	0.07
Slovak (0)	38	0.17
Swedish (398)	2,508	10.94
Swiss (0)	43	0.19
Ukrainian (111)	184	0.80
Welsh (21)	131	0.57
Yugoslavian (0)	9	0.04

Hispanic Origin	Population	%
Hispanic or Latino (of any race)	566	2.39
Central American, ex. Mexican	37	0.16
Costa Rican	1	<0.01
Guatemalan	16	0.07
Nicaraguan	2	0.01
Panamanian	6	0.03
Salvadoran	12	0.05
Cuban	16	0.07
Mexican	387	1.64
Puerto Rican	31	0.13
South American	56	0.24
Argentinean	7	0.03
Bolivian	3	0.01
Chilean	5	0.02
Colombian	26	0.11
Ecuadorian	1	<0.01
Paraguayan	1	<0.01
Peruvian	6	0.03
Venezuelan	7	0.03
Other Hispanic or Latino	39	0.16

Race*	Population	%
African-American/Black (662)	783	3.31
Not Hispanic (658)	767	3.24
Hispanic (4)	16	0.07
American Indian/Alaska Native (106)	235	0.99
Not Hispanic (91)	205	0.87
Hispanic (15)	30	0.13
Apache (1)	1	<0.01
Blackfeet (1)	1	<0.01
Canadian/French Am. Ind. (1)	1	<0.01
Cherokee (0)	1	<0.01
Chippewa (69)	103	0.44
Creek (1)	3	0.01
Iroquois (0)	4	0.02
Mexican American Ind. (3)	3	0.01
Navajo (0)	5	0.02
Seminole (0)	1	<0.01
Sioux (6)	21	0.09
South American Ind. (0)	4	0.02
Asian (573)	731	3.09
Not Hispanic (569)	721	3.05
Hispanic (4)	10	0.04
Bangladeshi (1)	4	0.02
Cambodian (5)	6	0.03
Chinese, ex. Taiwanese (50)	65	0.27
Filipino (36)	60	0.25
Hmong (206)	216	0.91
Indian (55)	83	0.35
Japanese (6)	26	0.11
Korean (56)	91	0.38
Laotian (29)	35	0.15
Pakistani (5)	9	0.04
Thai (12)	20	0.08
Vietnamese (66)	88	0.37
Hawaii Native/Pacific Islander (5)	10	0.04
Not Hispanic (5)	9	0.04
Hispanic (0)	1	<0.01
Native Hawaiian (4)	4	0.02
Samoan (0)	1	<0.01
White (21,732)	22,115	93.44
Not Hispanic (21,415)	21,747	91.88
Hispanic (317)	368	1.55

*Notes: † The Census 2010 population figure is used to calculate the percentages in the Hispanic Origin and Race categories. Ancestry percentages are based on the 2006-2010 American Community Survey population (not shown); ‡ Numbers in parentheses indicate the number of people reporting a single ancestry; * Numbers in parentheses indicate the number of persons reporting this race alone, not in combination with any other race; Please refer to the Explanation of Data for more information.*

Red Wing

Place Type: City
County: Goodhue
Population: 16,459†

Ancestry‡	Population	%
American (517)	517	3.14
Armenian (20)	20	0.12
Australian (0)	20	0.12
Austrian (0)	13	0.08
Belgian (0)	11	0.07
British (26)	77	0.47
Canadian (0)	18	0.11
Czech (120)	310	1.88
Czechoslovakian (0)	20	0.12
Danish (13)	283	1.72
Dutch (70)	355	2.16
Eastern European (18)	29	0.18
English (185)	1,107	6.73
European (197)	197	1.20
Finnish (18)	52	0.32
French, ex. Basque (90)	379	2.30
French Canadian (96)	304	1.85
German (2,694)	7,497	45.58
Greek (0)	14	0.09
Hungarian (16)	36	0.22
Irish (362)	1,780	10.82
Italian (129)	361	2.19
Latvian (11)	11	0.07
Lithuanian (19)	54	0.33
Luxemburger (12)	12	0.07
Norwegian (980)	3,114	18.93
Polish (99)	357	2.17
Romanian (0)	14	0.09
Russian (6)	24	0.15
Scandinavian (212)	355	2.16
Scotch-Irish (13)	178	1.08
Scottish (11)	337	2.05
Serbian (0)	13	0.08
Slovak (0)	46	0.28
Swedish (564)	2,237	13.60
Swiss (25)	109	0.66
Ukrainian (7)	39	0.24
Welsh (21)	85	0.52

Hispanic Origin	Population	%
Hispanic or Latino (of any race)	607	3.69
Central American, ex. Mexican	54	0.33
Guatemalan	36	0.22
Honduran	1	0.01
Salvadoran	17	0.10
Cuban	11	0.07
Dominican Republic	4	0.02
Mexican	426	2.59
Puerto Rican	34	0.21
South American	15	0.09
Argentinean	1	0.01
Chilean	2	0.01
Colombian	5	0.03
Ecuadorian	2	0.01
Peruvian	3	0.02
Venezuelan	2	0.01
Other Hispanic or Latino	63	0.38

Race*	Population	%
African-American/Black (312)	473	2.87
Not Hispanic (303)	459	2.79
Hispanic (9)	14	0.09
American Indian/Alaska Native (366)	522	3.17
Not Hispanic (330)	470	2.86
Hispanic (36)	52	0.32
Aleut *(Alaska Native)* (13)	13	0.08
Apache (1)	1	0.01
Arapaho (0)	1	0.01
Blackfeet (0)	7	0.04
Canadian/French Am. Ind. (6)	7	0.04
Cherokee (4)	10	0.06
Cheyenne (0)	2	0.01
Chippewa (37)	55	0.33
Comanche (3)	3	0.02
Cree (7)	7	0.04
Crow (6)	6	0.04
Menominee (0)	1	0.01
Mexican American Ind. (7)	8	0.05
Potawatomi (0)	1	0.01
Sioux (201)	270	1.64
Asian (129)	179	1.09
Not Hispanic (127)	177	1.08
Hispanic (2)	2	0.01
Cambodian (1)	1	0.01
Chinese, ex. Taiwanese (25)	36	0.22
Filipino (16)	29	0.18
Hmong (14)	15	0.09
Indian (19)	25	0.15
Japanese (5)	9	0.05
Korean (21)	35	0.21
Laotian (3)	3	0.02
Thai (1)	1	0.01
Vietnamese (22)	23	0.14
Hawaii Native/Pacific Islander (5)	18	0.11
Not Hispanic (5)	18	0.11
Guamanian/Chamorro (1)	6	0.04
Native Hawaiian (1)	7	0.04
White (15,064)	15,422	93.70
Not Hispanic (14,771)	15,062	91.51
Hispanic (293)	360	2.19

Richfield

Place Type: City
County: Hennepin
Population: 35,228†

Ancestry‡	Population	%
African, Sub-Saharan (1,080)	1,269	3.65
African (291)	388	1.12
Ethiopian (55)	55	0.16
Ghanaian (119)	119	0.34
Kenyan (101)	110	0.32
Liberian (127)	127	0.37
Nigerian (51)	51	0.15
Somalian (300)	300	0.86
Other Sub-Saharan African (36)	119	0.34
American (607)	607	1.75
Arab (114)	199	0.57
Egyptian (35)	35	0.10
Jordanian (27)	27	0.08
Lebanese (34)	119	0.34
Other Arab (18)	18	0.05
Australian (0)	8	0.02
Austrian (12)	26	0.07
Belgian (0)	18	0.05
British (55)	102	0.29
Canadian (26)	26	0.07
Croatian (10)	39	0.11
Czech (107)	472	1.36
Czechoslovakian (20)	20	0.06
Danish (48)	464	1.33
Dutch (99)	592	1.70
Eastern European (61)	71	0.20
English (240)	1,957	5.63
European (223)	349	1.00
Finnish (105)	260	0.75
French, ex. Basque (76)	1,058	3.04
French Canadian (42)	282	0.81
German (2,691)	8,646	24.86
Greek (13)	78	0.22
Guyanese (186)	236	0.68
Hungarian (61)	121	0.35
Icelander (7)	13	0.04
Iranian (10)	10	0.03
Irish (677)	3,440	9.89
Italian (120)	807	2.32
Latvian (10)	19	0.05
Lithuanian (18)	43	0.12
Northern European (63)	80	0.23
Norwegian (1,395)	4,548	13.08
Pennsylvania German (10)	24	0.07
Polish (284)	1,055	3.03
Romanian (20)	40	0.12
Russian (57)	263	0.76
Scandinavian (240)	419	1.20
Scotch-Irish (66)	417	1.20
Scottish (57)	468	1.35
Serbian (9)	9	0.03
Slovak (22)	108	0.31
Slovene (0)	25	0.07
Swedish (677)	3,383	9.73
Swiss (12)	187	0.54
Ukrainian (17)	17	0.05
Welsh (28)	118	0.34
West Indian, ex. Hispanic (9)	9	0.03
Bahamian (9)	9	0.03
Yugoslavian (66)	79	0.23

Hispanic Origin	Population	%
Hispanic or Latino (of any race)	6,436	18.27
Central American, ex. Mexican	455	1.29
Costa Rican	15	0.04
Guatemalan	73	0.21
Honduran	34	0.10
Nicaraguan	16	0.05
Panamanian	19	0.05
Salvadoran	298	0.85
Cuban	58	0.16
Dominican Republic	50	0.14
Mexican	5,191	14.74
Puerto Rican	98	0.28
South American	243	0.69
Argentinean	8	0.02
Bolivian	4	0.01
Chilean	15	0.04
Colombian	42	0.12
Ecuadorian	136	0.39
Peruvian	15	0.04
Uruguayan	3	0.01
Venezuelan	17	0.05
Other South American	3	0.01
Other Hispanic or Latino	341	0.97

Race*	Population	%
African-American/Black (3,242)	3,839	10.90
Not Hispanic (3,152)	3,660	10.39
Hispanic (90)	179	0.51
American Indian/Alaska Native (295)	617	1.75
Not Hispanic (225)	448	1.27
Hispanic (70)	169	0.48
Alaska Athabascan *(Ala. Nat.)* (0)	1	<0.01
Apache (1)	3	0.01
Blackfeet (0)	1	<0.01
Central American Ind. (3)	4	0.01
Cherokee (2)	23	0.07
Cheyenne (1)	1	<0.01
Chickasaw (0)	2	0.01
Chippewa (90)	158	0.45
Choctaw (0)	2	0.01
Comanche (0)	1	<0.01
Cree (0)	1	<0.01
Creek (1)	6	0.02
Iroquois (2)	7	0.02
Kiowa (0)	1	<0.01
Mexican American Ind. (21)	28	0.08
Navajo (5)	6	0.02
Potawatomi (2)	3	0.01
Pueblo (0)	2	0.01
Sioux (31)	39	0.11
South American Ind. (3)	3	0.01
Yaqui (2)	5	0.01
Asian (2,163)	2,448	6.95
Not Hispanic (2,150)	2,411	6.84
Hispanic (13)	37	0.11
Bangladeshi (4)	4	0.01
Bhutanese (1)	1	<0.01
Burmese (16)	16	0.05
Cambodian (117)	143	0.41
Chinese, ex. Taiwanese (370)	431	1.22
Filipino (170)	219	0.62
Hmong (44)	50	0.14
Indian (544)	618	1.75

*Notes: † The Census 2010 population figure is used to calculate the percentages in the Hispanic Origin and Race categories. Ancestry percentages are based on the 2006-2010 American Community Survey population (not shown); ‡ Numbers in parentheses indicate the number of people reporting a single ancestry; * Numbers in parentheses indicate the number of persons reporting this race alone, not in combination with any other race; Please refer to the Explanation of Data for more information.*

Indonesian (1)	3	0.01
Japanese (23)	60	0.17
Korean (89)	134	0.38
Laotian (185)	203	0.58
Malaysian (3)	4	0.01
Nepalese (22)	24	0.07
Pakistani (25)	27	0.08
Sri Lankan (26)	27	0.08
Taiwanese (9)	15	0.04
Thai (14)	23	0.07
Vietnamese (397)	438	1.24
Hawaii Native/Pacific Islander (21)	55	0.16
Not Hispanic (17)	37	0.11
Hispanic (4)	18	0.05
Fijian (1)	1	<0.01
Guamanian/Chamorro (2)	5	0.01
Native Hawaiian (9)	15	0.04
Samoan (2)	6	0.02
White (24,606)	25,620	72.73
Not Hispanic (22,260)	22,985	65.25
Hispanic (2,346)	2,635	7.48

Robbinsdale

Place Type: City
County: Hennepin
Population: 13,953†

Ancestry‡	Population	%
Afghan (5)	5	0.04
African, Sub-Saharan (265)	343	2.47
African (153)	167	1.20
Nigerian (33)	65	0.47
Somalian (43)	43	0.31
Zimbabwean (36)	68	0.49
American (333)	333	2.40
Arab (0)	35	0.25
Arab (0)	16	0.12
Egyptian (0)	8	0.06
Moroccan (0)	11	0.08
Australian (12)	37	0.27
Austrian (22)	73	0.53
Belgian (0)	34	0.24
British (29)	29	0.21
Canadian (11)	11	0.08
Czech (65)	223	1.61
Danish (45)	128	0.92
Dutch (107)	326	2.35
Eastern European (9)	9	0.06
English (144)	860	6.20
European (164)	188	1.35
Finnish (82)	263	1.90
French, ex. Basque (107)	488	3.52
French Canadian (62)	143	1.03
German (1,018)	4,487	32.33
Greek (0)	135	0.97
Hungarian (11)	33	0.24
Irish (266)	1,865	13.44
Italian (52)	310	2.23
Lithuanian (15)	36	0.26
Luxemburger (12)	53	0.38
Northern European (11)	11	0.08
Norwegian (739)	1,977	14.25
Polish (267)	1,144	8.24
Portuguese (0)	12	0.09
Romanian (38)	75	0.54
Russian (16)	115	0.83
Scandinavian (70)	116	0.84
Scotch-Irish (48)	141	1.02
Scottish (12)	143	1.03
Slavic (0)	10	0.07
Slovak (10)	18	0.13
Slovene (9)	30	0.22
Swedish (306)	1,510	10.88
Swiss (0)	20	0.14
Ukrainian (0)	34	0.24
Welsh (10)	203	1.46

Hispanic Origin	Population	%
Hispanic or Latino (of any race)	647	4.64
Central American, ex. Mexican	72	0.52
Costa Rican	4	0.03
Guatemalan	11	0.08
Honduran	2	0.01
Nicaraguan	19	0.14
Panamanian	4	0.03
Salvadoran	31	0.22
Other Central American	1	0.01
Cuban	19	0.14
Dominican Republic	13	0.09
Mexican	396	2.84
Puerto Rican	49	0.35
South American	38	0.27
Argentinean	5	0.04
Chilean	1	0.01
Colombian	15	0.11
Ecuadorian	10	0.07
Paraguayan	1	0.01
Peruvian	6	0.04
Other Hispanic or Latino	60	0.43

Race*	Population	%
African-American/Black (1,931)	2,274	16.30
Not Hispanic (1,895)	2,212	15.85
Hispanic (36)	62	0.44
American Indian/Alaska Native (68)	198	1.42
Not Hispanic (59)	173	1.24
Hispanic (9)	25	0.18
Aleut *(Alaska Native)* (1)	1	0.01
Apache (0)	1	0.01
Blackfeet (0)	2	0.01
Cherokee (0)	11	0.08
Chippewa (27)	57	0.41
Choctaw (0)	1	0.01
Comanche (0)	1	0.01
Inupiat *(Alaska Native)* (0)	1	0.01
Menominee (1)	1	0.01
Navajo (0)	5	0.04
Potawatomi (1)	1	0.01
Seminole (0)	1	0.01
Sioux (12)	19	0.14
Spanish American Ind. (0)	1	0.01
Yaqui (1)	2	0.01
Asian (455)	571	4.09
Not Hispanic (454)	559	4.01
Hispanic (1)	12	0.09
Cambodian (6)	8	0.06
Chinese, ex. Taiwanese (41)	56	0.40
Filipino (14)	28	0.20
Hmong (168)	175	1.25
Indian (50)	68	0.49
Japanese (7)	24	0.17
Korean (37)	56	0.40
Laotian (33)	39	0.28
Nepalese (1)	3	0.02
Pakistani (11)	12	0.09
Thai (3)	9	0.06
Vietnamese (71)	83	0.59
Hawaii Native/Pacific Islander (8)	16	0.11
Not Hispanic (8)	16	0.11
Guamanian/Chamorro (0)	1	0.01
Native Hawaiian (3)	8	0.06
White (10,671)	11,183	80.15
Not Hispanic (10,395)	10,843	77.71
Hispanic (276)	340	2.44

Rochester

Place Type: City
County: Olmsted
Population: 106,769†

Ancestry‡	Population	%
African, Sub-Saharan (3,474)	3,552	3.41
African (390)	455	0.44
Ethiopian (239)	239	0.23
Ghanaian (45)	45	0.04
Kenyan (15)	15	0.01
Liberian (14)	14	0.01
Nigerian (33)	46	0.04
Somalian (2,488)	2,488	2.39
South African (25)	25	0.02
Sudanese (189)	189	0.18
Zimbabwean (28)	28	0.03
Other Sub-Saharan African (8)	8	0.01
American (3,004)	3,004	2.88
Arab (340)	472	0.45
Arab (63)	107	0.10
Egyptian (90)	113	0.11
Jordanian (7)	7	0.01
Lebanese (44)	62	0.06
Moroccan (44)	56	0.05
Palestinian (37)	37	0.04
Other Arab (55)	90	0.09
Armenian (20)	20	0.02
Australian (0)	11	0.01
Austrian (36)	335	0.32
Belgian (53)	235	0.23
Brazilian (63)	63	0.06
British (178)	396	0.38
Bulgarian (0)	36	0.03
Canadian (118)	201	0.19
Celtic (40)	60	0.06
Croatian (38)	208	0.20
Czech (446)	1,637	1.57
Czechoslovakian (22)	90	0.09
Danish (154)	1,374	1.32
Dutch (446)	2,422	2.32
Eastern European (64)	64	0.06
English (1,648)	7,313	7.02
European (1,101)	1,275	1.22
Finnish (248)	827	0.79
French, ex. Basque (360)	2,830	2.72
French Canadian (147)	611	0.59
German (12,216)	35,337	33.91
Greek (99)	355	0.34
Guyanese (0)	10	0.01
Hungarian (59)	328	0.31
Icelander (0)	14	0.01
Iranian (16)	31	0.03
Irish (2,402)	11,229	10.78
Italian (466)	1,875	1.80
Latvian (0)	44	0.04
Lithuanian (30)	115	0.11
Luxemburger (86)	299	0.29
Macedonian (0)	11	0.01
Maltese (26)	26	0.02
Northern European (179)	226	0.22
Norwegian (5,343)	15,760	15.12
Pennsylvania German (8)	39	0.04
Polish (814)	3,212	3.08
Portuguese (26)	111	0.11
Romanian (178)	226	0.22
Russian (152)	622	0.60
Scandinavian (548)	840	0.81
Scotch-Irish (249)	1,048	1.01
Scottish (306)	1,306	1.25
Serbian (36)	45	0.04
Slavic (11)	72	0.07
Slovak (34)	169	0.16
Slovene (0)	89	0.09
Swedish (900)	5,106	4.90
Swiss (166)	643	0.62
Turkish (69)	104	0.10
Ukrainian (69)	158	0.15
Welsh (121)	552	0.53
West Indian, ex. Hispanic (75)	75	0.07
Bahamian (10)	10	0.01
Haitian (25)	25	0.02
Jamaican (40)	40	0.04
Yugoslavian (467)	490	0.47

Hispanic Origin	Population	%
Hispanic or Latino (of any race)	5,508	5.16
Central American, ex. Mexican	259	0.24
Costa Rican	14	0.01
Guatemalan	119	0.11
Honduran	30	0.03
Nicaraguan	27	0.03
Panamanian	14	0.01

*Notes: † The Census 2010 population figure is used to calculate the percentages in the Hispanic Origin and Race categories. Ancestry percentages are based on the 2006-2010 American Community Survey population (not shown); ‡ Numbers in parentheses indicate the number of people reporting a single ancestry; * Numbers in parentheses indicate the number of persons reporting this race alone, not in combination with any other race; Please refer to the Explanation of Data for more information.*

	Population	%
Salvadoran	51	0.05
Other Central American	4	<0.01
Cuban	98	0.09
Dominican Republic	56	0.05
Mexican	3,922	3.67
Puerto Rican	362	0.34
South American	396	0.37
Argentinean	46	0.04
Bolivian	6	0.01
Chilean	46	0.04
Colombian	138	0.13
Ecuadorian	26	0.02
Paraguayan	8	0.01
Peruvian	67	0.06
Uruguayan	11	0.01
Venezuelan	47	0.04
Other South American	1	<0.01
Other Hispanic or Latino	415	0.39

Race*	Population	%
African-American/Black (6,703)	7,914	7.41
Not Hispanic (6,586)	7,698	7.21
Hispanic (117)	216	0.20
American Indian/Alaska Native (303)	781	0.73
Not Hispanic (251)	659	0.62
Hispanic (52)	122	0.11
Alaska Athabascan *(Ala. Nat.)* (1)	1	<0.01
Aleut *(Alaska Native)* (1)	1	<0.01
Apache (0)	10	0.01
Blackfeet (2)	4	<0.01
Canadian/French Am. Ind. (0)	6	0.01
Cherokee (7)	81	0.08
Cheyenne (2)	2	<0.01
Chickasaw (1)	3	<0.01
Chippewa (71)	128	0.12
Choctaw (3)	13	0.01
Comanche (1)	2	<0.01
Cree (0)	1	<0.01
Creek (1)	5	<0.01
Crow (0)	1	<0.01
Delaware (5)	9	0.01
Hopi (1)	1	<0.01
Inupiat *(Alaska Native)* (1)	5	<0.01
Iroquois (0)	3	<0.01
Kiowa (0)	1	<0.01
Menominee (2)	6	0.01
Mexican American Ind. (15)	23	0.02
Navajo (4)	5	<0.01
Osage (0)	1	<0.01
Pima (1)	1	<0.01
Potawatomi (2)	6	0.01
Seminole (0)	6	0.01
Sioux (30)	65	0.06
South American Ind. (0)	3	<0.01
Spanish American Ind. (0)	1	<0.01
Tlingit-Haida *(Alaska Native)* (2)	4	<0.01
Yakama (1)	1	<0.01
Yuman (1)	1	<0.01
Yup'ik *(Alaska Native)* (0)	3	<0.01
Asian (7,246)	8,325	7.80
Not Hispanic (7,212)	8,223	7.70
Hispanic (34)	102	0.10
Bangladeshi (57)	60	0.06
Burmese (13)	15	0.01
Cambodian (1,277)	1,512	1.42
Chinese, ex. Taiwanese (1,068)	1,260	1.18
Filipino (358)	520	0.49
Hmong (240)	256	0.24
Indian (1,320)	1,479	1.39
Indonesian (10)	15	0.01
Japanese (158)	262	0.25
Korean (433)	574	0.54
Laotian (598)	735	0.69
Malaysian (7)	14	0.01
Nepalese (25)	29	0.03
Pakistani (137)	150	0.14
Sri Lankan (11)	19	0.02
Taiwanese (46)	51	0.05
Thai (100)	156	0.15
Vietnamese (969)	1,107	1.04
Hawaii Native/Pacific Islander (39)	117	0.11
Not Hispanic (38)	106	0.10
Hispanic (1)	11	0.01
Guamanian/Chamorro (3)	12	0.01
Native Hawaiian (18)	34	0.03
Samoan (12)	24	0.02
Tongan (1)	1	<0.01
White (87,500)	89,881	84.18
Not Hispanic (84,608)	86,629	81.14
Hispanic (2,892)	3,252	3.05

Rogers

Place Type: City
County: Hennepin
Population: 8,597†

Ancestry‡	Population	%
African, Sub-Saharan (86)	86	1.12
African (86)	86	1.12
American (225)	225	2.94
Austrian (19)	19	0.25
British (26)	26	0.34
Canadian (0)	14	0.18
Croatian (13)	13	0.17
Czech (26)	79	1.03
Czechoslovakian (14)	14	0.18
Danish (25)	94	1.23
Dutch (13)	53	0.69
English (50)	508	6.63
European (40)	40	0.52
Finnish (53)	274	3.58
French, ex. Basque (12)	369	4.82
French Canadian (15)	88	1.15
German (1,302)	3,149	41.10
Greek (0)	44	0.57
Hungarian (0)	27	0.35
Irish (127)	948	12.37
Italian (26)	134	1.75
Northern European (27)	27	0.35
Norwegian (563)	1,538	20.08
Polish (131)	357	4.66
Romanian (0)	29	0.38
Russian (137)	166	2.17
Scandinavian (89)	233	3.04
Scotch-Irish (45)	91	1.19
Scottish (0)	140	1.83
Slavic (0)	26	0.34
Slovak (0)	13	0.17
Swedish (102)	730	9.53
Swiss (0)	14	0.18
Ukrainian (0)	14	0.18
Welsh (0)	13	0.17
Yugoslavian (0)	6	0.08

Hispanic Origin	Population	%
Hispanic or Latino (of any race)	160	1.86
Central American, ex. Mexican	23	0.27
Guatemalan	8	0.09
Salvadoran	15	0.17
Mexican	96	1.12
Puerto Rican	5	0.06
South American	25	0.29
Argentinean	4	0.05
Chilean	1	0.01
Colombian	2	0.02
Ecuadorian	5	0.06
Paraguayan	1	0.01
Peruvian	9	0.10
Uruguayan	2	0.02
Venezuelan	1	0.01
Other Hispanic or Latino	11	0.13

Race*	Population	%
African-American/Black (205)	266	3.09
Not Hispanic (204)	264	3.07
Hispanic (1)	2	0.02
American Indian/Alaska Native (11)	48	0.56
Not Hispanic (11)	47	0.55
Hispanic (0)	1	0.01
Cherokee (2)	5	0.06
Chippewa (5)	19	0.22
Ottawa (0)	1	0.01
Sioux (0)	4	0.05
Asian (302)	382	4.44
Not Hispanic (299)	376	4.37
Hispanic (3)	6	0.07
Cambodian (7)	12	0.14
Chinese, ex. Taiwanese (16)	32	0.37
Filipino (13)	34	0.40
Hmong (48)	53	0.62
Indian (55)	62	0.72
Japanese (6)	20	0.23
Korean (34)	42	0.49
Laotian (64)	64	0.74
Malaysian (0)	4	0.05
Pakistani (13)	13	0.15
Thai (7)	10	0.12
Vietnamese (27)	40	0.47
Hawaii Native/Pacific Islander (0)	3	0.03
Not Hispanic (0)	3	0.03
Native Hawaiian (0)	1	0.01
White (7,853)	8,023	93.32
Not Hispanic (7,765)	7,916	92.08
Hispanic (88)	107	1.24

Rosemount

Place Type: City
County: Dakota
Population: 21,874†

Ancestry‡	Population	%
Afghan (11)	11	0.05
African, Sub-Saharan (468)	613	2.96
African (83)	120	0.58
Ethiopian (53)	53	0.26
Kenyan (66)	66	0.32
Liberian (56)	56	0.27
Nigerian (26)	80	0.39
Somalian (34)	34	0.16
Sudanese (115)	115	0.56
Ugandan (10)	10	0.05
Other Sub-Saharan African (25)	79	0.38
American (535)	535	2.58
Arab (205)	264	1.27
Jordanian (45)	45	0.22
Moroccan (50)	50	0.24
Palestinian (110)	169	0.82
Austrian (12)	40	0.19
Belgian (11)	31	0.15
British (45)	78	0.38
Canadian (49)	88	0.42
Carpatho Rusyn (0)	7	0.03
Croatian (0)	58	0.28
Czech (34)	279	1.35
Czechoslovakian (0)	19	0.09
Danish (85)	567	2.74
Dutch (100)	391	1.89
English (139)	1,236	5.97
European (133)	206	0.99
Finnish (106)	261	1.26
French, ex. Basque (38)	841	4.06
French Canadian (165)	382	1.84
German (2,565)	8,748	42.24
Greek (25)	41	0.20
Guyanese (0)	30	0.14
Hungarian (0)	24	0.12
Icelander (0)	9	0.04
Iranian (0)	34	0.16
Irish (426)	3,200	15.45
Israeli (0)	59	0.28
Italian (165)	975	4.71
Lithuanian (12)	52	0.25
Luxemburger (0)	30	0.14
Northern European (54)	54	0.26
Norwegian (750)	3,248	15.68
Polish (120)	807	3.90
Russian (56)	135	0.65
Scandinavian (241)	408	1.97

*Notes: † The Census 2010 population figure is used to calculate the percentages in the Hispanic Origin and Race categories. Ancestry percentages are based on the 2006-2010 American Community Survey population (not shown); ‡ Numbers in parentheses indicate the number of people reporting a single ancestry; * Numbers in parentheses indicate the number of persons reporting this race alone, not in combination with any other race; Please refer to the Explanation of Data for more information.*

Scotch-Irish (118)	344	1.66
Scottish (59)	200	0.97
Serbian (0)	30	0.14
Slavic (18)	18	0.09
Slovak (0)	86	0.42
Slovene (0)	16	0.08
Swedish (324)	2,317	11.19
Swiss (11)	47	0.23
Ukrainian (26)	94	0.45
Welsh (0)	190	0.92
Yugoslavian (21)	46	0.22

Hispanic Origin	Population	%
Hispanic or Latino (of any race)	687	3.14
Central American, ex. Mexican	52	0.24
Costa Rican	4	0.02
Guatemalan	16	0.07
Honduran	13	0.06
Nicaraguan	2	0.01
Panamanian	6	0.03
Salvadoran	11	0.05
Cuban	10	0.05
Mexican	427	1.95
Puerto Rican	70	0.32
South American	66	0.30
Argentinean	1	<0.01
Bolivian	1	<0.01
Chilean	6	0.03
Colombian	30	0.14
Ecuadorian	6	0.03
Paraguayan	4	0.02
Peruvian	6	0.03
Uruguayan	3	0.01
Venezuelan	8	0.04
Other South American	1	<0.01
Other Hispanic or Latino	62	0.28

Race*	Population	%
African-American/Black (667)	901	4.12
Not Hispanic (663)	874	4.00
Hispanic (4)	27	0.12
American Indian/Alaska Native (83)	214	0.98
Not Hispanic (58)	173	0.79
Hispanic (25)	41	0.19
Blackfeet (0)	1	<0.01
Cherokee (2)	11	0.05
Cheyenne (1)	1	<0.01
Chickasaw (0)	1	<0.01
Chippewa (18)	52	0.24
Choctaw (1)	4	0.02
Comanche (1)	1	<0.01
Cree (0)	1	<0.01
Iroquois (1)	1	<0.01
Kiowa (0)	1	<0.01
Lumbee (0)	3	0.01
Menominee (0)	2	0.01
Mexican American Ind. (0)	1	<0.01
Navajo (0)	3	0.01
Shoshone (1)	1	<0.01
Sioux (12)	29	0.13
South American Ind. (6)	7	0.03
Asian (1,218)	1,426	6.52
Not Hispanic (1,213)	1,410	6.45
Hispanic (5)	16	0.07
Bangladeshi (8)	8	0.04
Burmese (2)	2	0.01
Cambodian (44)	60	0.27
Chinese, ex. Taiwanese (96)	122	0.56
Filipino (140)	182	0.83
Hmong (53)	56	0.26
Indian (346)	376	1.72
Japanese (16)	32	0.15
Korean (95)	154	0.70
Laotian (65)	75	0.34
Nepalese (7)	8	0.04
Pakistani (109)	112	0.51
Sri Lankan (12)	16	0.07
Taiwanese (1)	5	0.02
Thai (8)	13	0.06
Vietnamese (165)	184	0.84
Hawaii Native/Pacific Islander (6)	29	0.13
Not Hispanic (6)	29	0.13
Guamanian/Chamorro (2)	6	0.03
Native Hawaiian (4)	8	0.04
Samoan (0)	12	0.05
White (19,106)	19,597	89.59
Not Hispanic (18,713)	19,140	87.50
Hispanic (393)	457	2.09

Roseville

Place Type: City
County: Ramsey
Population: 33,660†

Ancestry‡	Population	%
African, Sub-Saharan (608)	669	2.01
African (134)	195	0.59
Ethiopian (101)	101	0.30
Kenyan (24)	24	0.07
Somalian (120)	120	0.36
Sudanese (35)	35	0.11
Ugandan (132)	132	0.40
Other Sub-Saharan African (62)	62	0.19
American (568)	568	1.71
Arab (117)	162	0.49
Arab (92)	101	0.30
Lebanese (9)	15	0.05
Other Arab (16)	46	0.14
Australian (0)	10	0.03
Austrian (103)	393	1.18
Belgian (0)	35	0.11
Brazilian (12)	23	0.07
British (75)	138	0.41
Canadian (13)	110	0.33
Croatian (8)	26	0.08
Czech (90)	805	2.42
Czechoslovakian (19)	63	0.19
Danish (112)	523	1.57
Dutch (101)	526	1.58
Eastern European (0)	13	0.04
English (346)	2,850	8.57
European (381)	440	1.32
Finnish (148)	445	1.34
French, ex. Basque (120)	1,555	4.68
French Canadian (192)	527	1.58
German (3,352)	12,189	36.65
Greek (45)	119	0.36
Hungarian (0)	137	0.41
Iranian (40)	40	0.12
Irish (962)	5,041	15.16
Israeli (25)	25	0.08
Italian (158)	739	2.22
Latvian (24)	24	0.07
Lithuanian (14)	65	0.20
Luxemburger (11)	46	0.14
Northern European (138)	171	0.51
Norwegian (1,473)	5,311	15.97
Polish (421)	1,942	5.84
Portuguese (25)	55	0.17
Romanian (37)	60	0.18
Russian (58)	197	0.59
Scandinavian (172)	357	1.07
Scotch-Irish (158)	710	2.13
Scottish (121)	639	1.92
Serbian (0)	52	0.16
Slavic (11)	32	0.10
Slovak (11)	49	0.15
Slovene (8)	77	0.23
Swedish (904)	3,809	11.45
Swiss (23)	233	0.70
Turkish (12)	22	0.07
Ukrainian (9)	49	0.15
Welsh (0)	73	0.22
West Indian, ex. Hispanic (27)	58	0.17
British West Indian (18)	18	0.05
Jamaican (9)	29	0.09
West Indian (0)	11	0.03
Yugoslavian (8)	79	0.24

Hispanic Origin	Population	%
Hispanic or Latino (of any race)	1,551	4.61
Central American, ex. Mexican	171	0.51
Costa Rican	12	0.04
Guatemalan	55	0.16
Honduran	36	0.11
Nicaraguan	4	0.01
Panamanian	13	0.04
Salvadoran	51	0.15
Cuban	27	0.08
Dominican Republic	13	0.04
Mexican	1,001	2.97
Puerto Rican	58	0.17
South American	168	0.50
Argentinean	22	0.07
Bolivian	5	0.01
Chilean	18	0.05
Colombian	62	0.18
Ecuadorian	19	0.06
Paraguayan	7	0.02
Peruvian	18	0.05
Uruguayan	1	<0.01
Venezuelan	14	0.04
Other South American	2	0.01
Other Hispanic or Latino	113	0.34

Race*	Population	%
African-American/Black (2,083)	2,474	7.35
Not Hispanic (2,038)	2,389	7.10
Hispanic (45)	85	0.25
American Indian/Alaska Native (168)	421	1.25
Not Hispanic (132)	342	1.02
Hispanic (36)	79	0.23
Apache (5)	12	0.04
Blackfeet (0)	4	0.01
Central American Ind. (1)	1	<0.01
Cherokee (2)	14	0.04
Cheyenne (0)	2	0.01
Chippewa (66)	134	0.40
Choctaw (1)	7	0.02
Iroquois (0)	2	0.01
Mexican American Ind. (3)	8	0.02
Navajo (0)	6	0.02
Ottawa (1)	1	<0.01
Pueblo (0)	2	0.01
Sioux (27)	65	0.19
South American Ind. (1)	3	0.01
Asian (2,442)	2,745	8.16
Not Hispanic (2,436)	2,729	8.11
Hispanic (6)	16	0.05
Bangladeshi (8)	8	0.02
Bhutanese (18)	18	0.05
Burmese (271)	275	0.82
Cambodian (33)	50	0.15
Chinese, ex. Taiwanese (453)	504	1.50
Filipino (90)	129	0.38
Hmong (401)	413	1.23
Indian (299)	349	1.04
Indonesian (6)	9	0.03
Japanese (95)	148	0.44
Korean (263)	321	0.95
Laotian (23)	29	0.09
Malaysian (5)	5	0.01
Nepalese (35)	41	0.12
Pakistani (36)	45	0.13
Sri Lankan (14)	22	0.07
Taiwanese (32)	37	0.11
Thai (16)	20	0.06
Vietnamese (258)	282	0.84
Hawaii Native/Pacific Islander (11)	45	0.13
Not Hispanic (11)	43	0.13
Hispanic (0)	2	0.01
Native Hawaiian (3)	20	0.06
Samoan (5)	8	0.02
Tongan (1)	2	0.01
White (27,369)	28,173	83.70
Not Hispanic (26,700)	27,376	81.33
Hispanic (669)	797	2.37

*Notes: † The Census 2010 population figure is used to calculate the percentages in the Hispanic Origin and Race categories. Ancestry percentages are based on the 2006-2010 American Community Survey population (not shown); ‡ Numbers in parentheses indicate the number of people reporting a single ancestry; * Numbers in parentheses indicate the number of persons reporting this race alone, not in combination with any other race; Please refer to the Explanation of Data for more information.*

Sartell

Place Type: City
County: Stearns
Population: 13,630†

Ancestry‡	Population	%
American (285)	285	2.26
Arab (56)	79	0.63
Egyptian (56)	56	0.44
Iraqi (0)	23	0.18
Armenian (0)	27	0.21
Austrian (0)	56	0.44
Belgian (14)	57	0.45
British (15)	15	0.12
Canadian (0)	17	0.13
Czech (47)	342	2.71
Czechoslovakian (26)	40	0.32
Danish (27)	196	1.55
Dutch (25)	283	2.24
English (95)	733	5.81
European (48)	48	0.38
Finnish (31)	80	0.63
French, ex. Basque (193)	821	6.50
French Canadian (11)	207	1.64
German (2,766)	6,966	55.19
German Russian (0)	13	0.10
Hungarian (0)	41	0.32
Icelander (0)	47	0.37
Irish (135)	1,208	9.57
Italian (45)	165	1.31
Luxemburger (0)	3	0.02
Northern European (34)	34	0.27
Norwegian (603)	2,087	16.53
Polish (352)	1,188	9.41
Portuguese (0)	31	0.25
Romanian (56)	69	0.55
Russian (104)	132	1.05
Scandinavian (87)	149	1.18
Scotch-Irish (0)	36	0.29
Scottish (30)	192	1.52
Slovak (0)	24	0.19
Slovene (10)	36	0.29
Swedish (124)	662	5.24
Swiss (0)	26	0.21
Ukrainian (0)	53	0.42
Welsh (15)	15	0.12
West Indian, ex. Hispanic (9)	9	0.07
Haitian (9)	9	0.07

Hispanic Origin	Population	%
Hispanic or Latino (of any race)	189	1.39
Central American, ex. Mexican	13	0.10
Costa Rican	3	0.02
Guatemalan	4	0.03
Honduran	2	0.01
Nicaraguan	4	0.03
Cuban	10	0.07
Dominican Republic	3	0.02
Mexican	108	0.79
Puerto Rican	11	0.08
South American	13	0.10
Bolivian	1	0.01
Colombian	12	0.09
Other Hispanic or Latino	31	0.23

Race*	Population	%
African-American/Black (127)	198	1.45
Not Hispanic (126)	197	1.45
Hispanic (1)	1	0.01
American Indian/Alaska Native (33)	61	0.45
Not Hispanic (18)	41	0.30
Hispanic (15)	20	0.15
Cherokee (2)	3	0.02
Chippewa (13)	21	0.15
Cree (0)	1	0.01
Mexican American Ind. (1)	2	0.01
Sioux (1)	3	0.02
Asian (218)	296	2.17
Not Hispanic (217)	293	2.15
Hispanic (1)	3	0.02
Bangladeshi (0)	3	0.02
Cambodian (3)	9	0.07
Chinese, ex. Taiwanese (31)	41	0.30
Filipino (20)	33	0.24
Indian (32)	35	0.26
Indonesian (1)	2	0.01
Japanese (4)	15	0.11
Korean (28)	51	0.37
Laotian (20)	22	0.16
Nepalese (2)	3	0.02
Pakistani (11)	11	0.08
Sri Lankan (4)	4	0.03
Taiwanese (3)	3	0.02
Thai (3)	5	0.04
Vietnamese (39)	51	0.37
Hawaii Native/Pacific Islander (5)	10	0.07
Not Hispanic (3)	8	0.06
Hispanic (2)	2	0.01
Guamanian/Chamorro (2)	2	0.01
Native Hawaiian (3)	6	0.04
Samoan (0)	1	0.01
White (12,995)	13,178	96.68
Not Hispanic (12,892)	13,058	95.80
Hispanic (103)	120	0.88

Sartell

Place Type: City
County: Stearns
Population: 15,876†

Ancestry‡	Population	%
American (323)	323	2.19
Arab (56)	79	0.54
Egyptian (56)	56	0.38
Iraqi (0)	23	0.16
Armenian (0)	27	0.18
Austrian (0)	66	0.45
Belgian (14)	57	0.39
British (15)	15	0.10
Canadian (0)	17	0.12
Croatian (0)	10	0.07
Czech (47)	342	2.32
Czechoslovakian (41)	55	0.37
Danish (27)	231	1.57
Dutch (25)	283	1.92
English (95)	841	5.70
European (48)	48	0.33
Finnish (58)	107	0.73
French, ex. Basque (193)	926	6.28
French Canadian (21)	228	1.55
German (3,443)	8,210	55.64
German Russian (0)	13	0.09
Hungarian (0)	41	0.28
Icelander (0)	47	0.32
Irish (135)	1,254	8.50
Italian (54)	271	1.84
Luxemburger (0)	3	0.02
Northern European (34)	34	0.23
Norwegian (721)	2,328	15.78
Polish (398)	1,360	9.22
Portuguese (0)	31	0.21
Romanian (56)	69	0.47
Russian (104)	192	1.30
Scandinavian (87)	149	1.01
Scotch-Irish (17)	77	0.52
Scottish (30)	259	1.76
Slovak (0)	24	0.16
Slovene (10)	57	0.39
Swedish (145)	766	5.19
Swiss (0)	26	0.18
Ukrainian (0)	53	0.36
Welsh (15)	15	0.10
West Indian, ex. Hispanic (20)	37	0.25
Haitian (9)	9	0.06
West Indian (11)	28	0.19

Hispanic Origin	Population	%
Hispanic or Latino (of any race)	228	1.44
Central American, ex. Mexican	14	0.09
Costa Rican	3	0.02
Guatemalan	4	0.03
Honduran	2	0.01
Nicaraguan	5	0.03
Cuban	15	0.09
Dominican Republic	4	0.03
Mexican	135	0.85
Puerto Rican	13	0.08
South American	14	0.09
Bolivian	1	0.01
Colombian	13	0.08
Other Hispanic or Latino	33	0.21

Race*	Population	%
African-American/Black (138)	226	1.42
Not Hispanic (135)	223	1.40
Hispanic (3)	3	0.02
American Indian/Alaska Native (37)	71	0.45
Not Hispanic (22)	51	0.32
Hispanic (15)	20	0.13
Cherokee (2)	3	0.02
Chippewa (15)	23	0.14
Cree (0)	1	0.01
Mexican American Ind. (1)	2	0.01
Sioux (1)	3	0.02
Asian (244)	327	2.06
Not Hispanic (243)	324	2.04
Hispanic (1)	3	0.02
Bangladeshi (0)	3	0.02
Cambodian (3)	9	0.06
Chinese, ex. Taiwanese (31)	42	0.26
Filipino (21)	35	0.22
Indian (35)	38	0.24
Indonesian (1)	1	0.01
Japanese (4)	15	0.09
Korean (28)	51	0.32
Laotian (30)	33	0.21
Nepalese (2)	3	0.02
Pakistani (11)	11	0.07
Sri Lankan (4)	4	0.03
Taiwanese (3)	3	0.02
Thai (3)	5	0.03
Vietnamese (50)	66	0.42
Hawaii Native/Pacific Islander (5)	10	0.06
Not Hispanic (3)	8	0.05
Hispanic (2)	2	0.01
Guamanian/Chamorro (2)	2	0.01
Native Hawaiian (3)	6	0.04
Samoan (0)	1	0.01
White (15,160)	15,370	96.81
Not Hispanic (15,033)	15,226	95.91
Hispanic (127)	144	0.91

Sauk Rapids

Place Type: City
County: Benton
Population: 12,773†

Ancestry‡	Population	%
American (519)	519	4.16
Australian (0)	12	0.10
Austrian (13)	25	0.20
Belgian (10)	31	0.25
Czech (60)	165	1.32
Czechoslovakian (0)	19	0.15
Danish (0)	182	1.46
Dutch (79)	130	1.04
English (110)	574	4.60
European (66)	81	0.65
Finnish (97)	318	2.55
French, ex. Basque (72)	493	3.95
French Canadian (0)	26	0.21
German (2,838)	6,858	54.94
Greek (0)	17	0.14
Hungarian (7)	43	0.34
Icelander (0)	43	0.34
Irish (193)	810	6.49
Italian (19)	175	1.40

*Notes: † The Census 2010 population figure is used to calculate the percentages in the Hispanic Origin and Race categories. Ancestry percentages are based on the 2006-2010 American Community Survey population (not shown); ‡ Numbers in parentheses indicate the number of people reporting a single ancestry; * Numbers in parentheses indicate the number of persons reporting this race alone, not in combination with any other race; Please refer to the Explanation of Data for more information.*

Luxemburger (0)	25	0.20
Norwegian (362)	1,553	12.44
Polish (212)	1,661	13.31
Russian (18)	194	1.55
Scandinavian (86)	112	0.90
Scotch-Irish (30)	69	0.55
Scottish (0)	112	0.90
Serbian (0)	11	0.09
Slovene (8)	54	0.43
Swedish (207)	942	7.55
Swiss (0)	14	0.11

Hispanic Origin	Population	%
Hispanic or Latino (of any race)	229	1.79
Central American, ex. Mexican	5	0.04
Costa Rican	1	0.01
Guatemalan	2	0.02
Panamanian	1	0.01
Salvadoran	1	0.01
Cuban	29	0.23
Mexican	151	1.18
Puerto Rican	15	0.12
South American	15	0.12
Chilean	3	0.02
Colombian	5	0.04
Paraguayan	5	0.04
Peruvian	1	0.01
Venezuelan	1	0.01
Other Hispanic or Latino	14	0.11

Race*	Population	%
African-American/Black (150)	261	2.04
Not Hispanic (147)	255	2.00
Hispanic (3)	6	0.05
American Indian/Alaska Native (65)	122	0.96
Not Hispanic (58)	109	0.85
Hispanic (7)	13	0.10
Canadian/French Am. Ind. (1)	1	0.01
Cherokee (8)	13	0.10
Chippewa (20)	34	0.27
Mexican American Ind. (1)	2	0.02
Sioux (7)	8	0.06
Asian (149)	211	1.65
Not Hispanic (147)	205	1.60
Hispanic (2)	6	0.05
Bangladeshi (0)	1	0.01
Cambodian (5)	5	0.04
Chinese, ex. Taiwanese (5)	9	0.07
Filipino (13)	27	0.21
Hmong (4)	4	0.03
Indian (13)	26	0.20
Japanese (3)	4	0.03
Korean (26)	40	0.31
Laotian (21)	31	0.24
Malaysian (0)	3	0.02
Nepalese (1)	1	0.01
Pakistani (5)	5	0.04
Thai (3)	4	0.03
Vietnamese (40)	45	0.35
Hawaii Native/Pacific Islander (2)	6	0.05
Not Hispanic (2)	6	0.05
Guamanian/Chamorro (1)	1	0.01
Native Hawaiian (1)	2	0.02
White (12,125)	12,346	96.66
Not Hispanic (11,978)	12,174	95.31
Hispanic (147)	172	1.35

Savage

Place Type: City
County: Scott
Population: 26,911†

Ancestry‡	Population	%
Afghan (22)	22	0.08
African, Sub-Saharan (743)	743	2.79
African (212)	212	0.80
Ethiopian (109)	109	0.41
Ghanaian (39)	39	0.15
Kenyan (57)	57	0.21
Somalian (267)	267	1.00
Other Sub-Saharan African (59)	59	0.22
American (1,159)	1,159	4.36
Arab (9)	80	0.30
Iraqi (0)	24	0.09
Lebanese (0)	12	0.05
Palestinian (9)	32	0.12
Other Arab (0)	12	0.05
Austrian (17)	102	0.38
Basque (8)	8	0.03
Belgian (0)	71	0.27
British (11)	11	0.04
Bulgarian (9)	22	0.08
Canadian (15)	15	0.06
Croatian (16)	54	0.20
Czech (152)	764	2.87
Czechoslovakian (23)	44	0.17
Danish (75)	577	2.17
Dutch (103)	276	1.04
Eastern European (14)	14	0.05
English (408)	1,633	6.14
European (265)	304	1.14
Finnish (26)	135	0.51
French, ex. Basque (97)	1,295	4.87
French Canadian (18)	197	0.74
German (3,031)	9,944	37.37
Greek (15)	66	0.25
Hungarian (0)	41	0.15
Iranian (115)	115	0.43
Irish (680)	3,617	13.59
Italian (248)	850	3.19
Lithuanian (17)	97	0.36
Luxemburger (0)	33	0.12
Northern European (15)	15	0.06
Norwegian (1,071)	4,644	17.45
Polish (93)	841	3.16
Portuguese (8)	21	0.08
Romanian (0)	10	0.04
Russian (141)	331	1.24
Scandinavian (242)	402	1.51
Scotch-Irish (58)	109	0.41
Scottish (111)	493	1.85
Slavic (0)	14	0.05
Slovak (10)	22	0.08
Slovene (0)	22	0.08
Swedish (318)	2,091	7.86
Swiss (6)	91	0.34
Turkish (22)	22	0.08
Ukrainian (111)	162	0.61
Welsh (0)	89	0.33
West Indian, ex. Hispanic (9)	9	0.03
Belizean (9)	9	0.03
Yugoslavian (0)	9	0.03

Hispanic Origin	Population	%
Hispanic or Latino (of any race)	918	3.41
Central American, ex. Mexican	90	0.33
Costa Rican	6	0.02
Guatemalan	17	0.06
Honduran	15	0.06
Panamanian	1	<0.01
Salvadoran	51	0.19
Cuban	10	0.04
Dominican Republic	4	0.01
Mexican	595	2.21
Puerto Rican	50	0.19
South American	87	0.32
Argentinean	2	0.01
Bolivian	7	0.03
Chilean	1	<0.01
Colombian	45	0.17
Ecuadorian	16	0.06
Peruvian	9	0.03
Uruguayan	1	<0.01
Venezuelan	5	0.02
Other South American	1	<0.01
Other Hispanic or Latino	82	0.30

Race*	Population	%
African-American/Black (1,161)	1,440	5.35
Not Hispanic (1,149)	1,401	5.21
Hispanic (12)	39	0.14
American Indian/Alaska Native (119)	285	1.06
Not Hispanic (105)	245	0.91
Hispanic (14)	40	0.15
Alaska Athabascan *(Ala. Nat.)* (0)	1	<0.01
Apache (2)	3	0.01
Blackfeet (0)	5	0.02
Central American Ind. (1)	1	<0.01
Cherokee (2)	19	0.07
Cheyenne (0)	4	0.01
Chippewa (39)	82	0.30
Choctaw (0)	2	0.01
Iroquois (1)	5	0.02
Menominee (1)	1	<0.01
Mexican American Ind. (1)	7	0.03
Navajo (1)	2	0.01
Potawatomi (1)	1	<0.01
Seminole (1)	1	<0.01
Sioux (16)	27	0.10
South American Ind. (1)	4	0.01
Spanish American Ind. (2)	2	0.01
Yuman (1)	1	<0.01
Asian (2,269)	2,508	9.32
Not Hispanic (2,258)	2,487	9.24
Hispanic (11)	21	0.08
Bangladeshi (16)	17	0.06
Burmese (1)	1	<0.01
Cambodian (401)	447	1.66
Chinese, ex. Taiwanese (262)	317	1.18
Filipino (65)	126	0.47
Hmong (54)	68	0.25
Indian (264)	293	1.09
Indonesian (2)	2	0.01
Japanese (21)	47	0.17
Korean (109)	149	0.55
Laotian (197)	213	0.79
Malaysian (0)	1	<0.01
Nepalese (6)	6	0.02
Pakistani (13)	19	0.07
Sri Lankan (26)	27	0.10
Taiwanese (4)	5	0.02
Thai (21)	32	0.12
Vietnamese (648)	685	2.55
Hawaii Native/Pacific Islander (68)	98	0.36
Not Hispanic (67)	96	0.36
Hispanic (1)	2	0.01
Fijian (1)	1	<0.01
Guamanian/Chamorro (2)	5	0.02
Native Hawaiian (3)	10	0.04
Samoan (12)	12	0.04
White (22,240)	22,832	84.84
Not Hispanic (21,790)	22,286	82.81
Hispanic (450)	546	2.03

Shakopee

Place Type: City
County: Scott
Population: 37,076†

Ancestry‡	Population	%
Afghan (175)	175	0.50
African, Sub-Saharan (612)	689	1.96
African (122)	153	0.44
Ethiopian (164)	164	0.47
Kenyan (9)	9	0.03
Liberian (75)	80	0.23
Nigerian (25)	25	0.07
Somalian (186)	186	0.53
Sudanese (8)	49	0.14
Other Sub-Saharan African (23)	23	0.07
American (925)	925	2.64
Arab (36)	61	0.17
Arab (24)	24	0.07
Jordanian (12)	12	0.03
Lebanese (0)	25	0.07
Austrian (8)	59	0.17
Belgian (9)	44	0.13
Brazilian (7)	7	0.02

*Notes: † The Census 2010 population figure is used to calculate the percentages in the Hispanic Origin and Race categories. Ancestry percentages are based on the 2006-2010 American Community Survey population (not shown); ‡ Numbers in parentheses indicate the number of people reporting a single ancestry; * Numbers in parentheses indicate the number of persons reporting this race alone, not in combination with any other race; Please refer to the Explanation of Data for more information.*

British (17)	76	0.22
Canadian (17)	17	0.05
Croatian (14)	28	0.08
Czech (149)	715	2.04
Czechoslovakian (85)	176	0.50
Danish (34)	475	1.35
Dutch (139)	1,060	3.02
English (367)	1,885	5.37
European (219)	247	0.70
Finnish (112)	478	1.36
French, ex. Basque (167)	1,007	2.87
French Canadian (54)	263	0.75
German (4,835)	13,371	38.12
Greek (26)	137	0.39
Guyanese (0)	16	0.05
Hungarian (0)	79	0.23
Icelander (7)	31	0.09
Iranian (41)	41	0.12
Irish (567)	3,726	10.62
Italian (167)	678	1.93
Latvian (0)	15	0.04
Lithuanian (0)	10	0.03
Luxemburger (10)	53	0.15
Northern European (24)	24	0.07
Norwegian (1,180)	4,065	11.59
Pennsylvania German (41)	53	0.15
Polish (339)	1,654	4.72
Romanian (6)	60	0.17
Russian (520)	764	2.18
Scandinavian (268)	510	1.45
Scotch-Irish (41)	276	0.79
Scottish (51)	245	0.70
Serbian (0)	9	0.03
Slavic (0)	43	0.12
Slovak (0)	11	0.03
Slovene (10)	18	0.05
Swedish (265)	2,176	6.20
Swiss (25)	95	0.27
Ukrainian (160)	221	0.63
Welsh (17)	85	0.24
Yugoslavian (0)	20	0.06

Hispanic Origin	Population	%
Hispanic or Latino (of any race)	2,890	7.79
Central American, ex. Mexican	244	0.66
Costa Rican	12	0.03
Guatemalan	50	0.13
Honduran	80	0.22
Nicaraguan	1	<0.01
Panamanian	13	0.04
Salvadoran	88	0.24
Cuban	14	0.04
Dominican Republic	6	0.02
Mexican	2,195	5.92
Puerto Rican	108	0.29
South American	94	0.25
Argentinean	8	0.02
Bolivian	1	<0.01
Chilean	12	0.03
Colombian	42	0.11
Ecuadorian	8	0.02
Peruvian	12	0.03
Venezuelan	5	0.01
Other South American	6	0.02
Other Hispanic or Latino	229	0.62

Race*	Population	%
African-American/Black (1,601)	1,951	5.26
Not Hispanic (1,550)	1,881	5.07
Hispanic (51)	70	0.19
American Indian/Alaska Native (433)	664	1.79
Not Hispanic (383)	589	1.59
Hispanic (50)	75	0.20
Aleut *(Alaska Native)* (0)	1	<0.01
Apache (4)	4	0.01
Arapaho (0)	1	<0.01
Blackfeet (2)	3	0.01
Canadian/French Am. Ind. (3)	3	0.01
Central American Ind. (0)	1	<0.01
Cherokee (4)	10	0.03
Chickasaw (1)	1	<0.01
Chippewa (67)	106	0.29
Choctaw (0)	1	<0.01
Creek (2)	2	0.01
Iroquois (1)	1	<0.01
Mexican American Ind. (11)	11	0.03
Navajo (2)	4	0.01
Osage (1)	1	<0.01
Paiute (0)	2	0.01
Potawatomi (3)	3	0.01
Pueblo (1)	1	<0.01
Sioux (90)	182	0.49
South American Ind. (5)	10	0.03
Tohono O'Odham (2)	2	0.01
Yaqui (3)	3	0.01
Asian (3,822)	4,195	11.31
Not Hispanic (3,796)	4,138	11.16
Hispanic (26)	57	0.15
Bangladeshi (12)	14	0.04
Burmese (6)	6	0.02
Cambodian (517)	580	1.56
Chinese, ex. Taiwanese (302)	355	0.96
Filipino (98)	155	0.42
Hmong (58)	63	0.17
Indian (981)	1,043	2.81
Indonesian (19)	24	0.06
Japanese (10)	49	0.13
Korean (124)	207	0.56
Laotian (368)	420	1.13
Malaysian (10)	13	0.04
Nepalese (24)	26	0.07
Pakistani (60)	63	0.17
Sri Lankan (6)	6	0.02
Taiwanese (13)	15	0.04
Thai (35)	69	0.19
Vietnamese (799)	902	2.43
Hawaii Native/Pacific Islander (6)	53	0.14
Not Hispanic (4)	23	0.06
Hispanic (2)	30	0.08
Fijian (1)	1	<0.01
Guamanian/Chamorro (4)	4	0.01
Native Hawaiian (0)	20	0.05
Samoan (0)	3	0.01
White (28,537)	29,391	79.27
Not Hispanic (27,544)	28,246	76.18
Hispanic (993)	1,145	3.09

Shoreview

Place Type: City
County: Ramsey
Population: 25,043[†]

Ancestry[‡]	Population	%
African, Sub-Saharan (35)	45	0.18
African (31)	41	0.16
Kenyan (1)	1	<0.01
Other Sub-Saharan African (3)	3	0.01
American (722)	722	2.90
Arab (197)	355	1.43
Arab (0)	10	0.04
Egyptian (89)	89	0.36
Lebanese (60)	208	0.84
Moroccan (27)	27	0.11
Other Arab (21)	21	0.08
Armenian (8)	8	0.03
Austrian (25)	142	0.57
Belgian (9)	59	0.24
British (0)	43	0.17
Bulgarian (0)	13	0.05
Canadian (9)	21	0.08
Croatian (40)	65	0.26
Czech (196)	645	2.59
Czechoslovakian (12)	55	0.22
Danish (93)	496	1.99
Dutch (31)	370	1.49
Eastern European (11)	11	0.04
English (186)	1,988	7.98
European (375)	387	1.55
Finnish (70)	218	0.88
French, ex. Basque (61)	1,084	4.35
French Canadian (44)	279	1.12
German (2,527)	9,525	38.25
Greek (64)	156	0.63
Guyanese (60)	60	0.24
Hungarian (71)	163	0.65
Iranian (27)	27	0.11
Irish (688)	4,256	17.09
Italian (342)	885	3.55
Latvian (15)	15	0.06
Lithuanian (0)	45	0.18
Luxemburger (14)	61	0.24
Northern European (286)	286	1.15
Norwegian (1,106)	4,048	16.26
Pennsylvania German (0)	7	0.03
Polish (420)	1,606	6.45
Portuguese (0)	11	0.04
Romanian (25)	64	0.26
Russian (43)	137	0.55
Scandinavian (241)	508	2.04
Scotch-Irish (114)	342	1.37
Scottish (54)	403	1.62
Slavic (0)	32	0.13
Slovak (19)	31	0.12
Slovene (0)	25	0.10
Swedish (803)	2,915	11.71
Swiss (12)	175	0.70
Ukrainian (50)	120	0.48
Welsh (26)	56	0.22
West Indian, ex. Hispanic (12)	12	0.05
Haitian (12)	12	0.05
Yugoslavian (0)	23	0.09

Hispanic Origin	Population	%
Hispanic or Latino (of any race)	541	2.16
Central American, ex. Mexican	39	0.16
Costa Rican	1	<0.01
Guatemalan	15	0.06
Honduran	6	0.02
Nicaraguan	1	<0.01
Panamanian	2	0.01
Salvadoran	14	0.06
Cuban	18	0.07
Dominican Republic	4	0.02
Mexican	296	1.18
Puerto Rican	35	0.14
South American	99	0.40
Argentinean	12	0.05
Bolivian	4	0.02
Chilean	5	0.02
Colombian	44	0.18
Ecuadorian	3	0.01
Paraguayan	1	<0.01
Peruvian	14	0.06
Uruguayan	6	0.02
Venezuelan	10	0.04
Other Hispanic or Latino	50	0.20

Race*	Population	%
African-American/Black (560)	749	2.99
Not Hispanic (555)	732	2.92
Hispanic (5)	17	0.07
American Indian/Alaska Native (90)	206	0.82
Not Hispanic (77)	177	0.71
Hispanic (13)	29	0.12
Apache (0)	2	0.01
Canadian/French Am. Ind. (0)	3	0.01
Cherokee (0)	5	0.02
Chippewa (36)	66	0.26
Iroquois (0)	1	<0.01
Menominee (0)	1	<0.01
Mexican American Ind. (2)	3	0.01
Ottawa (0)	2	0.01
Seminole (0)	4	0.02
Sioux (10)	18	0.07
South American Ind. (1)	2	0.01
Spanish American Ind. (2)	2	0.01
Asian (1,792)	2,030	8.11
Not Hispanic (1,791)	2,021	8.07
Hispanic (1)	9	0.04

*Notes: † The Census 2010 population figure is used to calculate the percentages in the Hispanic Origin and Race categories. Ancestry percentages are based on the 2006-2010 American Community Survey population (not shown); ‡ Numbers in parentheses indicate the number of people reporting a single ancestry; * Numbers in parentheses indicate the number of persons reporting this race alone, not in combination with any other race; Please refer to the Explanation of Data for more information.*

Burmese (1)	1	<0.01
Cambodian (12)	15	0.06
Chinese, ex. Taiwanese (646)	700	2.80
Filipino (52)	80	0.32
Hmong (134)	150	0.60
Indian (476)	506	2.02
Indonesian (0)	1	<0.01
Japanese (47)	98	0.39
Korean (165)	211	0.84
Laotian (7)	8	0.03
Nepalese (0)	1	<0.01
Pakistani (19)	35	0.14
Sri Lankan (0)	3	0.01
Taiwanese (38)	48	0.19
Thai (14)	23	0.09
Vietnamese (128)	146	0.58
Hawaii Native/Pacific Islander (8)	20	0.08
Not Hispanic (6)	17	0.07
Hispanic (2)	3	0.01
Guamanian/Chamorro (2)	6	0.02
Native Hawaiian (1)	7	0.03
Samoan (2)	2	0.01
White (21,897)	22,399	89.44
Not Hispanic (21,556)	22,007	87.88
Hispanic (341)	392	1.57

South St. Paul

Place Type: City
County: Dakota
Population: 20,160†

Ancestry‡	Population	%
African, Sub-Saharan (127)	127	0.63
African (102)	102	0.50
Ethiopian (10)	10	0.05
Kenyan (15)	15	0.07
American (465)	465	2.29
Arab (42)	148	0.73
Lebanese (42)	148	0.73
Australian (0)	11	0.05
Austrian (53)	123	0.61
Belgian (0)	20	0.10
Brazilian (0)	26	0.13
British (0)	50	0.25
Croatian (56)	149	0.73
Czech (90)	418	2.06
Czechoslovakian (48)	86	0.42
Danish (145)	297	1.46
Dutch (87)	414	2.04
Eastern European (17)	17	0.08
English (209)	1,197	5.90
European (407)	441	2.17
Finnish (76)	162	0.80
French, ex. Basque (62)	714	3.52
French Canadian (74)	401	1.98
German (2,383)	7,506	37.00
Greek (10)	50	0.25
Hungarian (0)	24	0.12
Irish (531)	2,971	14.65
Italian (143)	516	2.54
Latvian (0)	9	0.04
Lithuanian (0)	34	0.17
Luxemburger (25)	50	0.25
Northern European (0)	8	0.04
Norwegian (361)	1,908	9.41
Pennsylvania German (0)	13	0.06
Polish (353)	1,283	6.32
Romanian (14)	96	0.47
Russian (49)	134	0.66
Scandinavian (81)	230	1.13
Scotch-Irish (40)	344	1.70
Scottish (22)	238	1.17
Serbian (71)	82	0.40
Slovak (0)	8	0.04
Slovene (0)	10	0.05
Swedish (150)	1,222	6.02
Swiss (13)	41	0.20
Ukrainian (0)	65	0.32
Welsh (19)	142	0.70
West Indian, ex. Hispanic (12)	28	0.14
Haitian (12)	28	0.14
Yugoslavian (11)	36	0.18

Hispanic Origin	Population	%
Hispanic or Latino (of any race)	2,457	12.19
Central American, ex. Mexican	141	0.70
Costa Rican	1	<0.01
Guatemalan	12	0.06
Honduran	16	0.08
Nicaraguan	10	0.05
Salvadoran	102	0.51
Cuban	26	0.13
Dominican Republic	10	0.05
Mexican	1,905	9.45
Puerto Rican	153	0.76
South American	31	0.15
Argentinean	2	0.01
Chilean	2	0.01
Colombian	9	0.04
Ecuadorian	6	0.03
Peruvian	6	0.03
Venezuelan	6	0.03
Other Hispanic or Latino	191	0.95

Race*	Population	%
African-American/Black (788)	1,113	5.52
Not Hispanic (739)	1,000	4.96
Hispanic (49)	113	0.56
American Indian/Alaska Native (152)	332	1.65
Not Hispanic (121)	256	1.27
Hispanic (31)	76	0.38
Alaska Athabascan *(Ala. Nat.)* (1)	1	<0.01
Apache (0)	3	0.01
Canadian/French Am. Ind. (1)	5	0.02
Central American Ind. (1)	1	<0.01
Cherokee (2)	14	0.07
Chippewa (54)	82	0.41
Choctaw (0)	1	<0.01
Cree (0)	4	0.02
Crow (3)	3	0.01
Iroquois (1)	2	0.01
Mexican American Ind. (3)	4	0.02
Navajo (2)	3	0.01
Osage (1)	1	<0.01
Ottawa (1)	1	<0.01
Puget Sound Salish (0)	1	<0.01
Sioux (14)	23	0.11
Asian (248)	373	1.85
Not Hispanic (242)	352	1.75
Hispanic (6)	21	0.10
Bangladeshi (3)	3	0.01
Cambodian (17)	30	0.15
Chinese, ex. Taiwanese (29)	49	0.24
Filipino (27)	63	0.31
Hmong (70)	72	0.36
Indian (26)	30	0.15
Japanese (6)	20	0.10
Korean (19)	41	0.20
Laotian (9)	10	0.05
Sri Lankan (4)	8	0.04
Taiwanese (2)	2	0.01
Thai (2)	2	0.01
Vietnamese (20)	27	0.13
Hawaii Native/Pacific Islander (17)	37	0.18
Not Hispanic (16)	33	0.16
Hispanic (1)	4	0.02
Guamanian/Chamorro (6)	12	0.06
Native Hawaiian (0)	6	0.03
Samoan (1)	1	<0.01
Tongan (0)	1	<0.01
White (17,191)	17,827	88.43
Not Hispanic (16,101)	16,546	82.07
Hispanic (1,090)	1,281	6.35

St. Anthony

Place Type: City
County: Hennepin and Ramsey
Population: 8,226†

Ancestry‡	Population	%
African, Sub-Saharan (109)	147	1.81
African (59)	59	0.73
Ethiopian (17)	17	0.21
Kenyan (10)	10	0.12
Other Sub-Saharan African (23)	61	0.75
American (99)	99	1.22
Arab (144)	144	1.78
Lebanese (8)	8	0.10
Palestinian (56)	56	0.69
Other Arab (80)	80	0.99
Armenian (7)	7	0.09
Austrian (10)	21	0.26
Belgian (13)	13	0.16
Bulgarian (28)	28	0.35
Canadian (10)	10	0.12
Czech (29)	183	2.26
Czechoslovakian (0)	23	0.28
Danish (35)	201	2.48
Dutch (20)	124	1.53
Eastern European (15)	23	0.28
English (71)	489	6.03
European (170)	185	2.28
Finnish (41)	111	1.37
French, ex. Basque (52)	321	3.96
French Canadian (37)	122	1.51
German (701)	2,419	29.84
Greek (30)	30	0.37
Hungarian (0)	14	0.17
Iranian (19)	28	0.35
Irish (241)	998	12.31
Italian (84)	301	3.71
Norwegian (312)	1,384	17.07
Pennsylvania German (0)	11	0.14
Polish (277)	904	11.15
Romanian (6)	18	0.22
Russian (17)	84	1.04
Scandinavian (20)	42	0.52
Scotch-Irish (9)	109	1.34
Scottish (22)	105	1.30
Slavic (0)	24	0.30
Slovak (0)	43	0.53
Slovene (11)	11	0.14
Swedish (318)	1,058	13.05
Swiss (0)	70	0.86
Ukrainian (19)	80	0.99
Welsh (19)	33	0.41
Yugoslavian (34)	34	0.42

Hispanic Origin	Population	%
Hispanic or Latino (of any race)	237	2.88
Central American, ex. Mexican	18	0.22
Costa Rican	2	0.02
Guatemalan	6	0.07
Honduran	2	0.02
Nicaraguan	1	0.01
Salvadoran	7	0.09
Cuban	11	0.13
Dominican Republic	4	0.05
Mexican	131	1.59
Puerto Rican	9	0.11
South American	52	0.63
Argentinean	4	0.05
Chilean	5	0.06
Colombian	10	0.12
Ecuadorian	22	0.27
Peruvian	8	0.10
Venezuelan	3	0.04
Other Hispanic or Latino	12	0.15

Race*	Population	%
African-American/Black (414)	483	5.87
Not Hispanic (410)	472	5.74
Hispanic (4)	11	0.13
American Indian/Alaska Native (46)	87	1.06
Not Hispanic (29)	60	0.73
Hispanic (17)	27	0.33
Chippewa (20)	39	0.47
Iroquois (2)	2	0.02
Mexican American Ind. (5)	5	0.06

*Notes: † The Census 2010 population figure is used to calculate the percentages in the Hispanic Origin and Race categories. Ancestry percentages are based on the 2006-2010 American Community Survey population (not shown); ‡ Numbers in parentheses indicate the number of people reporting a single ancestry; * Numbers in parentheses indicate the number of persons reporting this race alone, not in combination with any other race; Please refer to the Explanation of Data for more information.*

Sioux (2)	4	0.05
South American Ind. (1)	1	0.01
Spanish American Ind. (8)	8	0.10
Asian (483)	559	6.80
Not Hispanic (481)	555	6.75
Hispanic (2)	4	0.05
Burmese (0)	2	0.02
Cambodian (4)	6	0.07
Chinese, ex. Taiwanese (116)	141	1.71
Filipino (24)	44	0.53
Hmong (21)	21	0.26
Indian (103)	123	1.50
Indonesian (10)	11	0.13
Japanese (31)	42	0.51
Korean (48)	66	0.80
Laotian (5)	6	0.07
Malaysian (1)	1	0.01
Nepalese (7)	7	0.09
Pakistani (6)	6	0.07
Sri Lankan (2)	2	0.02
Taiwanese (6)	10	0.12
Thai (1)	2	0.02
Vietnamese (59)	73	0.89
Hawaii Native/Pacific Islander (7)	20	0.24
Not Hispanic (7)	19	0.23
Hispanic (0)	1	0.01
Native Hawaiian (5)	9	0.11
White (6,999)	7,164	87.09
Not Hispanic (6,900)	7,038	85.56
Hispanic (99)	126	1.53

St. Cloud

Place Type: City
County: Stearns
Population: 52,661†

Ancestry‡	Population	%
African, Sub-Saharan (1,333)	1,623	3.13
African (347)	554	1.07
Ethiopian (62)	62	0.12
Kenyan (93)	128	0.25
Liberian (170)	170	0.33
Nigerian (17)	17	0.03
Somalian (644)	657	1.27
Ugandan (0)	35	0.07
American (1,315)	1,315	2.54
Arab (34)	107	0.21
Lebanese (34)	70	0.14
Palestinian (0)	10	0.02
Syrian (0)	27	0.05
Armenian (0)	31	0.06
Austrian (30)	267	0.52
Belgian (58)	254	0.49
Brazilian (0)	120	0.23
British (0)	52	0.10
Canadian (47)	60	0.12
Croatian (10)	59	0.11
Czech (149)	845	1.63
Czechoslovakian (35)	54	0.10
Danish (77)	501	0.97
Dutch (67)	692	1.34
English (348)	2,323	4.48
European (696)	747	1.44
Finnish (137)	626	1.21
French, ex. Basque (185)	1,750	3.38
French Canadian (80)	495	0.96
German (10,033)	23,555	45.46
Greek (0)	22	0.04
Hungarian (0)	177	0.34
Icelander (9)	17	0.03
Irish (908)	5,382	10.39
Italian (388)	1,338	2.58
Lithuanian (0)	82	0.16
Luxemburger (10)	83	0.16
Northern European (52)	67	0.13
Norwegian (1,429)	5,997	11.57
Pennsylvania German (27)	47	0.09
Polish (630)	3,674	7.09
Portuguese (0)	42	0.08
Romanian (53)	115	0.22
Russian (45)	240	0.46
Scandinavian (423)	768	1.48
Scotch-Irish (65)	388	0.75
Scottish (20)	432	0.83
Serbian (0)	19	0.04
Slavic (40)	85	0.16
Slovak (12)	80	0.15
Slovene (28)	100	0.19
Swedish (555)	3,563	6.88
Swiss (0)	107	0.21
Ukrainian (12)	125	0.24
Welsh (22)	196	0.38
West Indian, ex. Hispanic (30)	30	0.06
Haitian (20)	20	0.04
Jamaican (10)	10	0.02
Yugoslavian (7)	62	0.12

Hispanic Origin	Population	%
Hispanic or Latino (of any race)	1,173	2.23
Central American, ex. Mexican	80	0.15
Costa Rican	10	0.02
Guatemalan	19	0.04
Honduran	10	0.02
Nicaraguan	9	0.02
Panamanian	6	0.01
Salvadoran	25	0.05
Other Central American	1	<0.01
Cuban	28	0.05
Dominican Republic	12	0.02
Mexican	731	1.39
Puerto Rican	119	0.23
South American	95	0.18
Argentinean	7	0.01
Bolivian	2	<0.01
Chilean	13	0.02
Colombian	36	0.07
Ecuadorian	7	0.01
Paraguayan	5	0.01
Peruvian	11	0.02
Venezuelan	12	0.02
Other South American	2	<0.01
Other Hispanic or Latino	108	0.21

Race*	Population	%
African-American/Black (3,744)	4,356	8.27
Not Hispanic (3,705)	4,272	8.11
Hispanic (39)	84	0.16
American Indian/Alaska Native (261)	564	1.07
Not Hispanic (229)	502	0.95
Hispanic (32)	62	0.12
Apache (0)	4	0.01
Blackfeet (6)	9	0.02
Canadian/French Am. Ind. (3)	9	0.02
Cherokee (3)	24	0.05
Chickasaw (0)	4	0.01
Chippewa (89)	153	0.29
Choctaw (5)	13	0.02
Comanche (0)	1	<0.01
Cree (1)	1	<0.01
Creek (1)	4	0.01
Crow (0)	1	<0.01
Inupiat *(Alaska Native)* (1)	2	<0.01
Iroquois (1)	1	<0.01
Menominee (0)	2	<0.01
Mexican American Ind. (6)	7	0.01
Navajo (1)	1	<0.01
Osage (1)	1	<0.01
Ottawa (2)	2	<0.01
Potawatomi (1)	3	0.01
Pueblo (0)	1	<0.01
Sioux (27)	54	0.10
South American Ind. (1)	1	<0.01
Yaqui (1)	1	<0.01
Yuman (1)	1	<0.01
Asian (1,882)	2,199	4.18
Not Hispanic (1,858)	2,163	4.11
Hispanic (24)	36	0.07
Bangladeshi (19)	21	0.04
Burmese (3)	3	0.01
Cambodian (37)	49	0.09
Chinese, ex. Taiwanese (272)	329	0.62
Filipino (92)	142	0.27
Hmong (106)	110	0.21
Indian (273)	318	0.60
Indonesian (5)	7	0.01
Japanese (55)	102	0.19
Korean (150)	189	0.36
Laotian (234)	284	0.54
Malaysian (11)	17	0.03
Nepalese (72)	75	0.14
Pakistani (24)	24	0.05
Sri Lankan (19)	19	0.04
Taiwanese (7)	8	0.02
Thai (23)	35	0.07
Vietnamese (362)	402	0.76
Hawaii Native/Pacific Islander (13)	61	0.12
Not Hispanic (13)	53	0.10
Hispanic (0)	8	0.02
Guamanian/Chamorro (2)	12	0.02
Marshallese (1)	1	<0.01
Native Hawaiian (8)	20	0.04
Samoan (1)	3	0.01
White (45,149)	46,243	87.81
Not Hispanic (44,599)	45,562	86.52
Hispanic (550)	681	1.29

St. Cloud

Place Type: City
County: Stearns
Population: 65,842†

Ancestry‡	Population	%
African, Sub-Saharan (1,500)	2,082	3.20
African (499)	976	1.50
Ethiopian (62)	62	0.10
Kenyan (93)	128	0.20
Liberian (185)	207	0.32
Nigerian (17)	17	0.03
Somalian (644)	657	1.01
Ugandan (0)	35	0.05
Alsatian (8)	8	0.01
American (1,732)	1,732	2.66
Arab (44)	117	0.18
Egyptian (10)	10	0.02
Lebanese (34)	70	0.11
Palestinian (0)	10	0.02
Syrian (0)	27	0.04
Armenian (0)	31	0.05
Austrian (48)	323	0.50
Basque (18)	38	0.06
Belgian (58)	254	0.39
Brazilian (0)	120	0.18
British (10)	75	0.12
Canadian (47)	60	0.09
Croatian (10)	59	0.09
Czech (179)	1,053	1.62
Czechoslovakian (43)	62	0.10
Danish (99)	542	0.83
Dutch (76)	906	1.39
English (440)	2,721	4.18
European (1,077)	1,128	1.73
Finnish (154)	680	1.04
French, ex. Basque (246)	2,272	3.49
French Canadian (88)	610	0.94
German (12,443)	29,609	45.44
Greek (7)	29	0.04
Hungarian (10)	228	0.35
Icelander (9)	17	0.03
Irish (1,102)	7,003	10.75
Italian (419)	1,510	2.32
Lithuanian (0)	82	0.13
Luxemburger (24)	121	0.19
Northern European (68)	83	0.13
Norwegian (1,768)	7,126	10.94
Pennsylvania German (27)	47	0.07
Polish (851)	4,533	6.96
Portuguese (0)	42	0.06
Romanian (53)	115	0.18

*Notes: † The Census 2010 population figure is used to calculate the percentages in the Hispanic Origin and Race categories. Ancestry percentages are based on the 2006-2010 American Community Survey population (not shown); ‡ Numbers in parentheses indicate the number of people reporting a single ancestry; * Numbers in parentheses indicate the number of persons reporting this race alone, not in combination with any other race; Please refer to the Explanation of Data for more information.*

Russian (54)	249	0.38
Scandinavian (515)	906	1.39
Scotch-Irish (119)	475	0.73
Scottish (20)	549	0.84
Serbian (0)	19	0.03
Slavic (40)	105	0.16
Slovak (12)	80	0.12
Slovene (28)	100	0.15
Swedish (725)	4,319	6.63
Swiss (0)	140	0.21
Ukrainian (12)	138	0.21
Welsh (22)	220	0.34
West Indian, ex. Hispanic (40)	155	0.24
Haitian (20)	29	0.04
Jamaican (20)	126	0.19
Yugoslavian (7)	76	0.12

Hispanic Origin	Population	%
Hispanic or Latino (of any race)	1,597	2.43
Central American, ex. Mexican	94	0.14
Costa Rican	10	0.02
Guatemalan	20	0.03
Honduran	12	0.02
Nicaraguan	13	0.02
Panamanian	9	0.01
Salvadoran	29	0.04
Other Central American	1	<0.01
Cuban	51	0.08
Dominican Republic	13	0.02
Mexican	995	1.51
Puerto Rican	148	0.22
South American	123	0.19
Argentinean	8	0.01
Bolivian	3	<0.01
Chilean	19	0.03
Colombian	47	0.07
Ecuadorian	8	0.01
Paraguayan	5	0.01
Peruvian	16	0.02
Venezuelan	15	0.02
Other South American	2	<0.01
Other Hispanic or Latino	173	0.26

Race*	Population	%
African-American/Black (5,152)	5,993	9.10
Not Hispanic (5,101)	5,891	8.95
Hispanic (51)	102	0.15
American Indian/Alaska Native (443)	852	1.29
Not Hispanic (398)	768	1.17
Hispanic (45)	84	0.13
Apache (0)	4	0.01
Blackfeet (7)	14	0.02
Canadian/French Am. Ind. (4)	10	0.02
Cherokee (3)	43	0.07
Chickasaw (0)	4	0.01
Chippewa (135)	215	0.33
Choctaw (5)	13	0.02
Comanche (0)	1	<0.01
Cree (1)	1	<0.01
Creek (1)	5	0.01
Crow (0)	1	<0.01
Inupiat *(Alaska Native)* (1)	2	<0.01
Iroquois (2)	4	0.01
Menominee (0)	2	<0.01
Mexican American Ind. (7)	13	0.02
Navajo (1)	1	<0.01
Osage (1)	1	<0.01
Ottawa (2)	2	<0.01
Paiute (4)	4	0.01
Potawatomi (2)	4	0.01
Pueblo (1)	2	<0.01
Sioux (35)	71	0.11
South American Ind. (2)	2	<0.01
Yaqui (1)	1	<0.01
Yuman (1)	1	<0.01
Asian (2,419)	2,834	4.30
Not Hispanic (2,393)	2,790	4.24
Hispanic (26)	44	0.07
Bangladeshi (25)	29	0.04
Burmese (3)	3	<0.01
Cambodian (37)	50	0.08
Chinese, ex. Taiwanese (319)	385	0.58
Filipino (112)	178	0.27
Hmong (133)	137	0.21
Indian (352)	413	0.63
Indonesian (6)	8	0.01
Japanese (64)	124	0.19
Korean (166)	217	0.33
Laotian (330)	405	0.62
Malaysian (19)	34	0.05
Nepalese (202)	207	0.31
Pakistani (25)	26	0.04
Sri Lankan (29)	31	0.05
Taiwanese (8)	9	0.01
Thai (23)	37	0.06
Vietnamese (379)	422	0.64
Hawaii Native/Pacific Islander (16)	73	0.11
Not Hispanic (16)	64	0.10
Hispanic (0)	9	0.01
Guamanian/Chamorro (3)	14	0.02
Marshallese (1)	1	<0.01
Native Hawaiian (9)	23	0.03
Samoan (2)	4	0.01
White (55,693)	57,170	86.83
Not Hispanic (54,854)	56,170	85.31
Hispanic (839)	1,000	1.52

St. Louis Park

Place Type: City
County: Hennepin
Population: 45,250†

Ancestry‡	Population	%
African, Sub-Saharan (1,292)	1,380	3.09
African (252)	292	0.65
Ethiopian (115)	118	0.26
Kenyan (174)	202	0.45
Liberian (8)	8	0.02
Somalian (561)	561	1.26
South African (7)	7	0.02
Other Sub-Saharan African (175)	192	0.43
Alsatian (10)	10	0.02
American (1,050)	1,050	2.35
Arab (117)	173	0.39
Arab (0)	6	0.01
Lebanese (73)	101	0.23
Moroccan (32)	54	0.12
Other Arab (12)	12	0.03
Armenian (24)	36	0.08
Australian (11)	27	0.06
Austrian (61)	230	0.51
Belgian (0)	143	0.32
Brazilian (18)	18	0.04
British (132)	278	0.62
Canadian (19)	64	0.14
Croatian (12)	80	0.18
Czech (33)	726	1.63
Czechoslovakian (78)	180	0.40
Danish (211)	712	1.59
Dutch (160)	715	1.60
Eastern European (451)	463	1.04
English (431)	3,375	7.56
Estonian (22)	60	0.13
European (539)	582	1.30
Finnish (243)	710	1.59
French, ex. Basque (72)	1,640	3.67
French Canadian (124)	351	0.79
German (3,940)	14,260	31.93
Greek (65)	162	0.36
Guyanese (36)	36	0.08
Hungarian (24)	133	0.30
Icelander (10)	29	0.06
Iranian (36)	36	0.08
Irish (864)	5,712	12.79
Israeli (134)	134	0.30
Italian (264)	1,366	3.06
Latvian (69)	120	0.27
Lithuanian (94)	276	0.62
Luxemburger (7)	68	0.15
Northern European (91)	91	0.20
Norwegian (1,666)	6,374	14.27
Pennsylvania German (9)	9	0.02
Polish (520)	2,635	5.90
Portuguese (12)	49	0.11
Romanian (135)	248	0.56
Russian (661)	1,348	3.02
Scandinavian (521)	949	2.12
Scotch-Irish (175)	608	1.36
Scottish (171)	1,013	2.27
Serbian (36)	83	0.19
Slavic (7)	46	0.10
Slovak (14)	107	0.24
Slovene (45)	111	0.25
Swedish (971)	4,663	10.44
Swiss (39)	339	0.76
Ukrainian (78)	194	0.43
Welsh (23)	288	0.64
West Indian, ex. Hispanic (63)	63	0.14
West Indian (49)	49	0.11
Other West Indian (14)	14	0.03
Yugoslavian (76)	122	0.27

Hispanic Origin	Population	%
Hispanic or Latino (of any race)	1,941	4.29
Central American, ex. Mexican	167	0.37
Costa Rican	25	0.06
Guatemalan	49	0.11
Honduran	26	0.06
Nicaraguan	11	0.02
Panamanian	17	0.04
Salvadoran	36	0.08
Other Central American	3	0.01
Cuban	38	0.08
Dominican Republic	12	0.03
Mexican	1,150	2.54
Puerto Rican	124	0.27
South American	306	0.68
Argentinean	28	0.06
Bolivian	12	0.03
Chilean	20	0.04
Colombian	70	0.15
Ecuadorian	91	0.20
Paraguayan	4	0.01
Peruvian	55	0.12
Uruguayan	10	0.02
Venezuelan	8	0.02
Other South American	8	0.02
Other Hispanic or Latino	144	0.32

Race*	Population	%
African-American/Black (3,372)	4,060	8.97
Not Hispanic (3,319)	3,954	8.74
Hispanic (53)	106	0.23
American Indian/Alaska Native (205)	532	1.18
Not Hispanic (175)	447	0.99
Hispanic (30)	85	0.19
Blackfeet (0)	7	0.02
Canadian/French Am. Ind. (1)	2	<0.01
Cherokee (3)	34	0.08
Cheyenne (0)	2	<0.01
Chippewa (71)	134	0.30
Comanche (0)	1	<0.01
Cree (0)	3	0.01
Creek (1)	2	<0.01
Crow (0)	1	<0.01
Iroquois (0)	6	0.01
Mexican American Ind. (11)	19	0.04
Pima (0)	1	<0.01
Pueblo (1)	4	0.01
Seminole (0)	1	<0.01
Sioux (47)	68	0.15
South American Ind. (6)	12	0.03
Spanish American Ind. (0)	1	<0.01
Tlingit-Haida *(Alaska Native)* (1)	4	0.01
Yuman (0)	1	<0.01
Asian (1,737)	2,164	4.78
Not Hispanic (1,734)	2,141	4.73
Hispanic (3)	23	0.05
Bangladeshi (18)	23	0.05

*Notes: † The Census 2010 population figure is used to calculate the percentages in the Hispanic Origin and Race categories. Ancestry percentages are based on the 2006-2010 American Community Survey population (not shown); ‡ Numbers in parentheses indicate the number of people reporting a single ancestry; * Numbers in parentheses indicate the number of persons reporting this race alone, not in combination with any other race; Please refer to the Explanation of Data for more information.*

Burmese (1)	1	<0.01
Cambodian (46)	60	0.13
Chinese, ex. Taiwanese (256)	344	0.76
Filipino (97)	176	0.39
Hmong (43)	52	0.11
Indian (557)	625	1.38
Indonesian (14)	16	0.04
Japanese (96)	175	0.39
Korean (212)	293	0.65
Laotian (42)	53	0.12
Malaysian (3)	3	0.01
Nepalese (12)	13	0.03
Pakistani (10)	14	0.03
Sri Lankan (30)	32	0.07
Taiwanese (13)	14	0.03
Thai (20)	28	0.06
Vietnamese (179)	212	0.47
Hawaii Native/Pacific Islander (41)	81	0.18
Not Hispanic (36)	69	0.15
Hispanic (5)	12	0.03
Fijian (11)	13	0.03
Guamanian/Chamorro (0)	2	<0.01
Native Hawaiian (13)	27	0.06
Samoan (13)	17	0.04
White (37,686)	38,917	86.00
Not Hispanic (36,745)	37,794	83.52
Hispanic (941)	1,123	2.48

St. Michael

Place Type: City
County: Wright
Population: 16,399†

Ancestry‡	Population	%
African, Sub-Saharan (232)	232	1.51
African (13)	13	0.08
Liberian (192)	192	1.25
Nigerian (9)	9	0.06
Other Sub-Saharan African (18)	18	0.12
American (211)	211	1.37
Austrian (0)	68	0.44
Belgian (0)	31	0.20
British (44)	70	0.46
Canadian (34)	34	0.22
Croatian (0)	9	0.06
Czech (170)	311	2.02
Danish (15)	215	1.40
Dutch (139)	386	2.51
English (108)	863	5.61
European (220)	255	1.66
Finnish (20)	237	1.54
French, ex. Basque (30)	662	4.30
French Canadian (16)	74	0.48
German (2,618)	7,166	46.58
Greek (15)	15	0.10
Irish (200)	2,202	14.31
Italian (227)	565	3.67
Norwegian (778)	2,766	17.98
Polish (255)	1,356	8.81
Portuguese (7)	39	0.25
Russian (25)	54	0.35
Scandinavian (178)	238	1.55
Scotch-Irish (49)	154	1.00
Scottish (0)	227	1.48
Slovak (9)	78	0.51
Swedish (227)	1,530	9.95
Ukrainian (37)	49	0.32
Welsh (27)	149	0.97
Yugoslavian (54)	86	0.56

Hispanic Origin	Population	%
Hispanic or Latino (of any race)	311	1.90
Central American, ex. Mexican	31	0.19
Guatemalan	16	0.10
Honduran	5	0.03
Nicaraguan	1	0.01
Salvadoran	9	0.05
Cuban	13	0.08
Dominican Republic	1	0.01
Mexican	169	1.03
Puerto Rican	19	0.12
South American	31	0.19
Argentinean	3	0.02
Chilean	1	0.01
Colombian	18	0.11
Ecuadorian	1	0.01
Paraguayan	1	0.01
Peruvian	1	0.01
Venezuelan	3	0.02
Other South American	3	0.02
Other Hispanic or Latino	47	0.29

Race*	Population	%
African-American/Black (308)	400	2.44
Not Hispanic (300)	375	2.29
Hispanic (8)	25	0.15
American Indian/Alaska Native (35)	106	0.65
Not Hispanic (31)	97	0.59
Hispanic (4)	9	0.05
Apache (0)	2	0.01
Blackfeet (0)	3	0.02
Cherokee (1)	2	0.01
Chippewa (16)	42	0.26
Choctaw (0)	1	0.01
Comanche (1)	1	0.01
Creek (2)	2	0.01
Iroquois (3)	3	0.02
Mexican American Ind. (1)	1	0.01
Navajo (1)	4	0.02
Sioux (2)	9	0.05
South American Ind. (0)	3	0.02
Asian (395)	487	2.97
Not Hispanic (395)	483	2.95
Hispanic (0)	4	0.02
Burmese (2)	2	0.01
Cambodian (10)	11	0.07
Chinese, ex. Taiwanese (31)	40	0.24
Filipino (30)	52	0.32
Hmong (82)	83	0.51
Indian (36)	48	0.29
Japanese (3)	9	0.05
Korean (32)	60	0.37
Laotian (103)	114	0.70
Malaysian (1)	1	0.01
Pakistani (2)	2	0.01
Thai (1)	1	0.01
Vietnamese (39)	47	0.29
Hawaii Native/Pacific Islander (6)	15	0.09
Not Hispanic (5)	13	0.08
Hispanic (1)	2	0.01
Fijian (2)	2	0.01
Guamanian/Chamorro (0)	1	0.01
Native Hawaiian (4)	9	0.05
Samoan (0)	1	0.01
White (15,293)	15,552	94.84
Not Hispanic (15,116)	15,342	93.55
Hispanic (177)	210	1.28

St. Paul

Place Type: City
County: Ramsey
Population: 285,068†

Ancestry‡	Population	%
African, Sub-Saharan (12,710)	13,900	4.93
African (2,546)	3,110	1.10
Ethiopian (3,607)	3,839	1.36
Ghanaian (263)	263	0.09
Kenyan (235)	262	0.09
Liberian (221)	248	0.09
Nigerian (374)	450	0.16
Sierra Leonean (10)	95	0.03
Somalian (4,589)	4,697	1.67
South African (42)	67	0.02
Sudanese (160)	188	0.07
Ugandan (73)	73	0.03
Other Sub-Saharan African (590)	608	0.22
Albanian (7)	7	<0.01
Alsatian (0)	25	0.01
American (4,609)	4,609	1.63
Arab (463)	991	0.35
Arab (40)	108	0.04
Egyptian (31)	44	0.02
Iraqi (38)	45	0.02
Jordanian (26)	26	0.01
Lebanese (178)	509	0.18
Moroccan (73)	81	0.03
Palestinian (27)	27	0.01
Syrian (18)	45	0.02
Other Arab (32)	106	0.04
Australian (12)	72	0.03
Austrian (85)	1,232	0.44
Basque (15)	27	0.01
Belgian (86)	582	0.21
Brazilian (40)	60	0.02
British (368)	996	0.35
Bulgarian (30)	70	0.02
Canadian (107)	420	0.15
Carpatho Rusyn (10)	42	0.01
Celtic (8)	8	<0.01
Croatian (34)	338	0.12
Czech (693)	3,697	1.31
Czechoslovakian (145)	326	0.12
Danish (389)	3,307	1.17
Dutch (545)	3,582	1.27
Eastern European (497)	520	0.18
English (2,224)	15,435	5.47
Estonian (14)	80	0.03
European (2,926)	3,305	1.17
Finnish (486)	2,347	0.83
French, ex. Basque (1,289)	10,020	3.55
French Canadian (709)	2,602	0.92
German (17,205)	67,025	23.76
German Russian (0)	37	0.01
Greek (174)	622	0.22
Guyanese (0)	13	<0.01
Hungarian (371)	1,133	0.40
Icelander (42)	141	0.05
Iranian (191)	204	0.07
Irish (6,682)	34,326	12.17
Israeli (13)	43	0.02
Italian (2,328)	8,559	3.03
Latvian (167)	262	0.09
Lithuanian (162)	479	0.17
Luxemburger (43)	218	0.08
Maltese (0)	14	<0.01
New Zealander (11)	11	<0.01
Northern European (743)	785	0.28
Norwegian (5,599)	24,039	8.52
Pennsylvania German (22)	65	0.02
Polish (2,297)	9,921	3.52
Portuguese (90)	204	0.07
Romanian (273)	587	0.21
Russian (894)	2,579	0.91
Scandinavian (1,450)	2,612	0.93
Scotch-Irish (734)	2,890	1.02
Scottish (419)	3,738	1.33
Serbian (37)	133	0.05
Slavic (45)	152	0.05
Slovak (87)	308	0.11
Slovene (53)	277	0.10
Swedish (3,071)	18,089	6.41
Swiss (111)	945	0.34
Turkish (29)	79	0.03
Ukrainian (256)	653	0.23
Welsh (188)	1,272	0.45
West Indian, ex. Hispanic (419)	638	0.23
Bahamian (11)	11	<0.01
British West Indian (8)	8	<0.01
Dutch West Indian (0)	35	0.01
Haitian (77)	94	0.03
Jamaican (206)	325	0.12
U.S. Virgin Islander (0)	33	0.01
West Indian (117)	132	0.05
Yugoslavian (62)	225	0.08

Hispanic Origin	Population	%
Hispanic or Latino (of any race)	27,311	9.58

*Notes: † The Census 2010 population figure is used to calculate the percentages in the Hispanic Origin and Race categories. Ancestry percentages are based on the 2006-2010 American Community Survey population (not shown); ‡ Numbers in parentheses indicate the number of people reporting a single ancestry; * Numbers in parentheses indicate the number of persons reporting this race alone, not in combination with any other race; Please refer to the Explanation of Data for more information.*

Central American, ex. Mexican	2,933	1.03
Costa Rican	52	0.02
Guatemalan	583	0.20
Honduran	377	0.13
Nicaraguan	88	0.03
Panamanian	74	0.03
Salvadoran	1,731	0.61
Other Central American	28	0.01
Cuban	445	0.16
Dominican Republic	209	0.07
Mexican	19,490	6.84
Puerto Rican	1,310	0.46
South American	1,032	0.36
Argentinean	85	0.03
Bolivian	43	0.02
Chilean	74	0.03
Colombian	351	0.12
Ecuadorian	148	0.05
Paraguayan	31	0.01
Peruvian	154	0.05
Uruguayan	36	0.01
Venezuelan	86	0.03
Other South American	24	0.01
Other Hispanic or Latino	1,892	0.66

Race*	Population	%
African-American/Black (44,728)	51,296	17.99
Not Hispanic (43,620)	49,191	17.26
Hispanic (1,108)	2,105	0.74
American Indian/Alaska Native (3,016)	6,725	2.36
Not Hispanic (2,316)	5,276	1.85
Hispanic (700)	1,449	0.51
Alaska Athabascan *(Ala. Nat.)* (2)	6	<0.01
Aleut *(Alaska Native)* (5)	9	<0.01
Apache (13)	36	0.01
Arapaho (5)	7	<0.01
Blackfeet (16)	86	0.03
Canadian/French Am. Ind. (13)	36	0.01
Central American Ind. (15)	21	0.01
Cherokee (33)	274	0.10
Cheyenne (5)	12	<0.01
Chickasaw (1)	9	<0.01
Chippewa (940)	1,584	0.56
Choctaw (16)	81	0.03
Comanche (2)	6	<0.01
Cree (4)	17	0.01
Creek (2)	14	<0.01
Crow (3)	6	<0.01
Delaware (0)	4	<0.01
Hopi (1)	1	<0.01
Inupiat *(Alaska Native)* (0)	4	<0.01
Iroquois (16)	43	0.02
Kiowa (1)	1	<0.01
Lumbee (2)	3	<0.01
Menominee (6)	11	<0.01
Mexican American Ind. (103)	198	0.07
Navajo (27)	35	0.01
Ottawa (1)	1	<0.01
Paiute (1)	1	<0.01
Potawatomi (5)	11	<0.01
Pueblo (5)	8	<0.01
Puget Sound Salish (1)	3	<0.01
Seminole (5)	21	0.01
Shoshone (2)	4	<0.01
Sioux (440)	807	0.28
South American Ind. (14)	33	0.01
Spanish American Ind. (11)	13	<0.01
Tlingit-Haida *(Alaska Native)* (5)	8	<0.01
Tohono O'Odham (1)	1	<0.01
Ute (0)	5	<0.01
Yakama (2)	6	<0.01
Yaqui (1)	2	<0.01
Yuman (2)	2	<0.01
Yup'ik *(Alaska Native)* (2)	7	<0.01
Asian (42,695)	45,480	15.95
Not Hispanic (42,494)	45,032	15.80
Hispanic (201)	448	0.16
Bangladeshi (47)	47	0.02
Bhutanese (155)	167	0.06
Burmese (2,523)	2,587	0.91
Cambodian (989)	1,177	0.41
Chinese, ex. Taiwanese (1,370)	1,759	0.62
Filipino (692)	1,099	0.39
Hmong (28,591)	29,662	10.41
Indian (1,467)	2,218	0.78
Indonesian (41)	70	0.02
Japanese (233)	542	0.19
Korean (974)	1,360	0.48
Laotian (253)	379	0.13
Malaysian (14)	24	0.01
Nepalese (97)	117	0.04
Pakistani (52)	73	0.03
Sri Lankan (64)	80	0.03
Taiwanese (63)	82	0.03
Thai (139)	228	0.08
Vietnamese (2,145)	2,357	0.83
Hawaii Native/Pacific Islander (154)	601	0.21
Not Hispanic (120)	500	0.18
Hispanic (34)	101	0.04
Fijian (4)	12	<0.01
Guamanian/Chamorro (28)	45	0.02
Marshallese (4)	5	<0.01
Native Hawaiian (33)	114	0.04
Samoan (30)	60	0.02
Tongan (8)	8	<0.01
White (171,365)	181,147	63.55
Not Hispanic (159,437)	167,111	58.62
Hispanic (11,928)	14,036	4.92

St. Peter

Place Type: City
County: Nicollet
Population: 11,196†

Ancestry‡	Population	%
African, Sub-Saharan (79)	90	0.82
African (28)	39	0.35
Ethiopian (13)	13	0.12
Somalian (38)	38	0.34
American (124)	124	1.13
Arab (0)	67	0.61
Arab (0)	12	0.11
Lebanese (0)	42	0.38
Syrian (0)	13	0.12
Austrian (0)	83	0.75
Belgian (46)	167	1.52
British (0)	17	0.15
Canadian (8)	48	0.44
Czech (10)	238	2.16
Danish (27)	159	1.44
Dutch (30)	177	1.61
Eastern European (0)	7	0.06
English (113)	633	5.75
European (67)	82	0.74
Finnish (19)	168	1.52
French, ex. Basque (39)	251	2.28
French Canadian (13)	126	1.14
German (1,908)	4,765	43.25
Greek (9)	9	0.08
Hungarian (21)	36	0.33
Irish (203)	1,233	11.19
Italian (106)	281	2.55
Luxemburger (10)	28	0.25
Northern European (38)	38	0.34
Norwegian (555)	2,084	18.92
Polish (4)	262	2.38
Portuguese (8)	38	0.34
Romanian (21)	34	0.31
Russian (11)	56	0.51
Scandinavian (139)	190	1.72
Scotch-Irish (50)	143	1.30
Scottish (17)	145	1.32
Serbian (0)	11	0.10
Slovak (0)	25	0.23
Slovene (0)	26	0.24
Swedish (274)	1,320	11.98
Swiss (25)	63	0.57
Ukrainian (0)	18	0.16
Welsh (49)	92	0.84
Yugoslavian (0)	8	0.07

Hispanic Origin	Population	%
Hispanic or Latino (of any race)	718	6.41
Central American, ex. Mexican	39	0.35
Guatemalan	19	0.17
Honduran	7	0.06
Nicaraguan	2	0.02
Panamanian	1	0.01
Salvadoran	10	0.09
Cuban	4	0.04
Mexican	582	5.20
Puerto Rican	12	0.11
South American	21	0.19
Argentinean	9	0.08
Bolivian	1	0.01
Colombian	6	0.05
Ecuadorian	3	0.03
Peruvian	2	0.02
Other Hispanic or Latino	60	0.54

Race*	Population	%
African-American/Black (369)	443	3.96
Not Hispanic (367)	437	3.90
Hispanic (2)	6	0.05
American Indian/Alaska Native (64)	138	1.23
Not Hispanic (47)	107	0.96
Hispanic (17)	31	0.28
Apache (0)	2	0.02
Blackfeet (0)	1	0.01
Canadian/French Am. Ind. (0)	1	0.01
Cherokee (0)	4	0.04
Chippewa (8)	30	0.27
Comanche (0)	1	0.01
Iroquois (1)	6	0.05
Mexican American Ind. (4)	4	0.04
Sioux (5)	12	0.11
Spanish American Ind. (1)	1	0.01
Asian (180)	248	2.22
Not Hispanic (179)	244	2.18
Hispanic (1)	4	0.04
Bangladeshi (4)	4	0.04
Burmese (1)	1	0.01
Cambodian (4)	8	0.07
Chinese, ex. Taiwanese (39)	46	0.41
Filipino (11)	31	0.28
Hmong (49)	51	0.46
Indian (16)	26	0.23
Japanese (6)	21	0.19
Korean (26)	37	0.33
Laotian (3)	3	0.03
Malaysian (1)	1	0.01
Sri Lankan (1)	1	0.01
Thai (3)	6	0.05
Vietnamese (3)	5	0.04
Hawaii Native/Pacific Islander (0)	9	0.08
Not Hispanic (0)	9	0.08
Native Hawaiian (0)	1	0.01
White (10,091)	10,300	92.00
Not Hispanic (9,698)	9,865	88.11
Hispanic (393)	435	3.89

Stillwater

Place Type: City
County: Washington
Population: 18,225†

Ancestry‡	Population	%
African, Sub-Saharan (65)	69	0.39
African (65)	65	0.37
Ethiopian (0)	4	0.02
American (602)	602	3.38
Arab (63)	70	0.39
Egyptian (30)	30	0.17
Lebanese (33)	40	0.22
Austrian (37)	125	0.70
Belgian (0)	26	0.15
British (26)	62	0.35
Canadian (0)	9	0.05

*Notes: † The Census 2010 population figure is used to calculate the percentages in the Hispanic Origin and Race categories. Ancestry percentages are based on the 2006-2010 American Community Survey population (not shown); ‡ Numbers in parentheses indicate the number of people reporting a single ancestry; * Numbers in parentheses indicate the number of persons reporting this race alone, not in combination with any other race; Please refer to the Explanation of Data for more information.*

Ancestry	Population	%
Croatian (0)	18	0.10
Czech (57)	293	1.65
Czechoslovakian (13)	41	0.23
Danish (76)	341	1.92
Dutch (75)	485	2.72
English (326)	1,450	8.14
Estonian (8)	16	0.09
European (314)	345	1.94
Finnish (74)	189	1.06
French, ex. Basque (199)	955	5.36
French Canadian (61)	261	1.47
German (2,289)	6,611	37.13
Greek (15)	50	0.28
Hungarian (0)	29	0.16
Icelander (0)	19	0.11
Irish (562)	2,982	16.75
Italian (152)	676	3.80
Luxemburger (0)	29	0.16
Northern European (82)	82	0.46
Norwegian (763)	2,652	14.90
Pennsylvania German (0)	16	0.09
Polish (143)	698	3.92
Russian (0)	129	0.72
Scandinavian (271)	441	2.48
Scotch-Irish (66)	370	2.08
Scottish (94)	336	1.89
Serbian (24)	24	0.13
Slovak (0)	45	0.25
Slovene (0)	9	0.05
Swedish (368)	2,046	11.49
Swiss (59)	215	1.21
Ukrainian (2)	37	0.21
Welsh (0)	109	0.61
Yugoslavian (14)	28	0.16

Hispanic Origin	Population	%
Hispanic or Latino (of any race)	349	1.91
Central American, ex. Mexican	48	0.26
Costa Rican	4	0.02
Guatemalan	30	0.16
Honduran	3	0.02
Panamanian	4	0.02
Salvadoran	5	0.03
Other Central American	2	0.01
Cuban	16	0.09
Dominican Republic	2	0.01
Mexican	188	1.03
Puerto Rican	33	0.18
South American	32	0.18
Argentinean	2	0.01
Chilean	5	0.03
Colombian	20	0.11
Peruvian	2	0.01
Uruguayan	3	0.02
Other Hispanic or Latino	30	0.16

Race*	Population	%
African-American/Black (178)	301	1.65
Not Hispanic (168)	282	1.55
Hispanic (10)	19	0.10
American Indian/Alaska Native (66)	151	0.83
Not Hispanic (66)	144	0.79
Hispanic (0)	7	0.04
Aleut *(Alaska Native)* (1)	1	0.01
Apache (0)	1	0.01
Blackfeet (1)	2	0.01
Canadian/French Am. Ind. (0)	1	0.01
Cherokee (1)	2	0.01
Cheyenne (0)	2	0.01
Chickasaw (0)	1	0.01
Chippewa (18)	48	0.26
Choctaw (0)	2	0.01
Inupiat *(Alaska Native)* (4)	4	0.02
Mexican American Ind. (0)	2	0.01
Pima (2)	2	0.01
Sioux (9)	13	0.07
South American Ind. (0)	1	0.01
Tlingit-Haida *(Alaska Native)* (0)	1	0.01
Asian (205)	323	1.77
Not Hispanic (204)	315	1.73
Hispanic (1)	8	0.04
Burmese (3)	3	0.02
Cambodian (1)	9	0.05
Chinese, ex. Taiwanese (27)	38	0.21
Filipino (19)	53	0.29
Hmong (19)	20	0.11
Indian (35)	49	0.27
Japanese (5)	23	0.13
Korean (49)	76	0.42
Pakistani (5)	6	0.03
Sri Lankan (1)	1	0.01
Taiwanese (0)	1	0.01
Thai (3)	6	0.03
Vietnamese (26)	34	0.19
Hawaii Native/Pacific Islander (4)	9	0.05
Not Hispanic (4)	9	0.05
Native Hawaiian (2)	4	0.02
White (17,339)	17,640	96.79
Not Hispanic (17,124)	17,396	95.45
Hispanic (215)	244	1.34

Thief River Falls

Place Type: City
County: Pennington
Population: 8,573†

Ancestry‡	Population	%
African, Sub-Saharan (6)	32	0.37
African (6)	19	0.22
Nigerian (0)	13	0.15
American (114)	114	1.33
Austrian (0)	5	0.06
Belgian (0)	7	0.08
British (0)	8	0.09
Canadian (0)	21	0.25
Croatian (0)	7	0.08
Czech (11)	283	3.31
Danish (57)	125	1.46
Dutch (16)	67	0.78
English (97)	437	5.11
European (10)	10	0.12
Finnish (48)	200	2.34
French, ex. Basque (122)	393	4.59
French Canadian (7)	81	0.95
German (770)	2,351	27.48
Icelander (11)	16	0.19
Irish (194)	783	9.15
Italian (0)	28	0.33
Luxemburger (0)	15	0.18
Norwegian (1,738)	3,930	45.94
Polish (51)	169	1.98
Russian (12)	80	0.94
Scandinavian (56)	85	0.99
Scotch-Irish (0)	60	0.70
Scottish (0)	25	0.29
Slovene (5)	11	0.13
Swedish (213)	1,304	15.24
Swiss (57)	57	0.67
Ukrainian (0)	11	0.13
Yugoslavian (14)	57	0.67

Hispanic Origin	Population	%
Hispanic or Latino (of any race)	273	3.18
Central American, ex. Mexican	12	0.14
Costa Rican	1	0.01
Guatemalan	2	0.02
Panamanian	9	0.10
Mexican	200	2.33
Puerto Rican	9	0.10
South American	7	0.08
Colombian	6	0.07
Venezuelan	1	0.01
Other Hispanic or Latino	45	0.52

Race*	Population	%
African-American/Black (179)	233	2.72
Not Hispanic (170)	221	2.58
Hispanic (9)	12	0.14
American Indian/Alaska Native (165)	265	3.09
Not Hispanic (149)	237	2.76
Hispanic (16)	28	0.33
Blackfeet (4)	4	0.05
Canadian/French Am. Ind. (1)	2	0.02
Cherokee (0)	2	0.02
Cheyenne (2)	3	0.03
Chippewa (72)	97	1.13
Choctaw (0)	1	0.01
Navajo (1)	1	0.01
Potawatomi (0)	2	0.02
Shoshone (1)	1	0.01
Sioux (13)	14	0.16
Asian (59)	94	1.10
Not Hispanic (59)	94	1.10
Bangladeshi (0)	1	0.01
Chinese, ex. Taiwanese (13)	19	0.22
Filipino (14)	24	0.28
Indian (18)	19	0.22
Japanese (1)	1	0.01
Korean (7)	19	0.22
Laotian (2)	2	0.02
Pakistani (1)	1	0.01
Vietnamese (0)	4	0.05
Hawaii Native/Pacific Islander (0)	1	0.01
Not Hispanic (0)	1	0.01
White (7,888)	8,077	94.21
Not Hispanic (7,752)	7,911	92.28
Hispanic (136)	166	1.94

Vadnais Heights

Place Type: City
County: Ramsey
Population: 12,302†

Ancestry‡	Population	%
African, Sub-Saharan (66)	93	0.76
African (51)	51	0.42
Other Sub-Saharan African (15)	42	0.34
American (234)	234	1.91
Arab (0)	39	0.32
Lebanese (0)	39	0.32
Austrian (16)	31	0.25
Belgian (0)	7	0.06
British (16)	16	0.13
Canadian (17)	33	0.27
Czech (104)	140	1.14
Czechoslovakian (0)	26	0.21
Danish (114)	285	2.32
Dutch (25)	240	1.95
English (103)	677	5.51
European (124)	151	1.23
Finnish (64)	126	1.03
French, ex. Basque (54)	621	5.06
French Canadian (62)	193	1.57
German (1,530)	4,610	37.54
Greek (0)	10	0.08
Hungarian (26)	39	0.32
Irish (190)	1,411	11.49
Italian (136)	387	3.15
Latvian (12)	12	0.10
Lithuanian (0)	9	0.07
Northern European (74)	74	0.60
Norwegian (546)	1,728	14.07
Polish (138)	663	5.40
Portuguese (0)	15	0.12
Russian (14)	70	0.57
Scandinavian (123)	137	1.12
Scotch-Irish (18)	54	0.44
Scottish (20)	76	0.62
Serbian (15)	31	0.25
Slavic (0)	21	0.17
Slovak (0)	21	0.17
Slovene (0)	13	0.11
Swedish (473)	1,786	14.54
Swiss (16)	161	1.31
Ukrainian (28)	28	0.23
Welsh (50)	108	0.88
West Indian, ex. Hispanic (142)	142	1.16
Jamaican (142)	142	1.16

*Notes: † The Census 2010 population figure is used to calculate the percentages in the Hispanic Origin and Race categories. Ancestry percentages are based on the 2006-2010 American Community Survey population (not shown); ‡ Numbers in parentheses indicate the number of people reporting a single ancestry; * Numbers in parentheses indicate the number of persons reporting this race alone, not in combination with any other race; Please refer to the Explanation of Data for more information.*

Hispanic Origin	Population	%
Hispanic or Latino (of any race)	346	2.81
Central American, ex. Mexican	5	0.04
Guatemalan	4	0.03
Honduran	1	0.01
Cuban	6	0.05
Dominican Republic	9	0.07
Mexican	244	1.98
Puerto Rican	16	0.13
South American	30	0.24
Argentinean	4	0.03
Bolivian	1	0.01
Chilean	1	0.01
Colombian	19	0.15
Ecuadorian	3	0.02
Paraguayan	1	0.01
Venezuelan	1	0.01
Other Hispanic or Latino	36	0.29

Race*	Population	%
African-American/Black (445)	574	4.67
Not Hispanic (442)	551	4.48
Hispanic (3)	23	0.19
American Indian/Alaska Native (56)	149	1.21
Not Hispanic (36)	117	0.95
Hispanic (20)	32	0.26
Blackfeet (0)	1	0.01
Cherokee (0)	8	0.07
Chippewa (18)	53	0.43
Choctaw (0)	4	0.03
Hopi (0)	2	0.02
Iroquois (2)	4	0.03
Kiowa (1)	1	0.01
Mexican American Ind. (2)	3	0.02
Osage (0)	1	0.01
Seminole (0)	2	0.02
Sioux (13)	27	0.22
Asian (930)	1,012	8.23
Not Hispanic (930)	1,008	8.19
Hispanic (0)	4	0.03
Bangladeshi (0)	2	0.02
Cambodian (6)	6	0.05
Chinese, ex. Taiwanese (78)	98	0.80
Filipino (28)	47	0.38
Hmong (564)	578	4.70
Indian (56)	67	0.54
Japanese (5)	20	0.16
Korean (33)	48	0.39
Laotian (5)	5	0.04
Pakistani (10)	15	0.12
Sri Lankan (0)	2	0.02
Taiwanese (8)	9	0.07
Thai (5)	11	0.09
Vietnamese (68)	75	0.61
Hawaii Native/Pacific Islander (5)	20	0.16
Not Hispanic (2)	9	0.07
Hispanic (3)	11	0.09
Guamanian/Chamorro (5)	6	0.05
Native Hawaiian (0)	4	0.03
Samoan (0)	1	0.01
White (10,443)	10,683	86.84
Not Hispanic (10,293)	10,490	85.27
Hispanic (150)	193	1.57

Virginia

Place Type: City
County: St. Louis
Population: 8,712†

Ancestry‡	Population	%
American (258)	258	2.94
Australian (8)	8	0.09
Austrian (8)	23	0.26
Belgian (13)	13	0.15
British (12)	28	0.32
Croatian (41)	251	2.86
Czech (0)	18	0.21
Czechoslovakian (0)	9	0.10
Danish (11)	77	0.88
Dutch (19)	65	0.74
English (132)	571	6.51
European (31)	31	0.35
Finnish (719)	1,733	19.77
French, ex. Basque (63)	408	4.65
French Canadian (12)	147	1.68
German (627)	1,765	20.13
Greek (10)	30	0.34
Hungarian (0)	12	0.14
Irish (126)	651	7.43
Italian (234)	869	9.91
Lithuanian (8)	18	0.21
Northern European (8)	8	0.09
Norwegian (266)	1,072	12.23
Polish (91)	391	4.46
Romanian (14)	44	0.50
Russian (0)	8	0.09
Scandinavian (49)	64	0.73
Scotch-Irish (8)	40	0.46
Scottish (7)	105	1.20
Serbian (0)	36	0.41
Slavic (14)	48	0.55
Slovak (0)	24	0.27
Slovene (118)	347	3.96
Swedish (188)	1,146	13.07
Swiss (0)	26	0.30
Ukrainian (19)	32	0.37
Welsh (0)	41	0.47
Yugoslavian (25)	59	0.67

Hispanic Origin	Population	%
Hispanic or Latino (of any race)	128	1.47
Central American, ex. Mexican	10	0.11
Guatemalan	4	0.05
Honduran	1	0.01
Panamanian	4	0.05
Salvadoran	1	0.01
Cuban	2	0.02
Mexican	79	0.91
Puerto Rican	9	0.10
South American	19	0.22
Bolivian	5	0.06
Chilean	1	0.01
Colombian	4	0.05
Ecuadorian	1	0.01
Peruvian	8	0.09
Other Hispanic or Latino	9	0.10

Race*	Population	%
African-American/Black (136)	231	2.65
Not Hispanic (136)	222	2.55
Hispanic (0)	9	0.10
American Indian/Alaska Native (264)	404	4.64
Not Hispanic (258)	389	4.47
Hispanic (6)	15	0.17
Alaska Athabascan *(Ala. Nat.)* (1)	1	0.01
Blackfeet (0)	1	0.01
Canadian/French Am. Ind. (4)	7	0.08
Cherokee (1)	9	0.10
Chippewa (181)	235	2.70
Cree (0)	4	0.05
Crow (1)	1	0.01
Menominee (1)	3	0.03
Mexican American Ind. (2)	6	0.07
Sioux (9)	13	0.15
Asian (46)	66	0.76
Not Hispanic (46)	64	0.73
Hispanic (0)	2	0.02
Chinese, ex. Taiwanese (15)	20	0.23
Filipino (5)	9	0.10
Indian (1)	1	0.01
Japanese (3)	3	0.03
Korean (11)	19	0.22
Vietnamese (5)	14	0.16
Hawaii Native/Pacific Islander (2)	3	0.03
Not Hispanic (2)	3	0.03
Native Hawaiian (2)	3	0.03
White (7,987)	8,229	94.46
Not Hispanic (7,923)	8,132	93.34
Hispanic (64)	97	1.11

Waconia

Place Type: City
County: Carver
Population: 10,697†

Ancestry‡	Population	%
American (405)	405	3.99
Austrian (0)	9	0.09
British (0)	4	0.04
Canadian (41)	41	0.40
Croatian (0)	53	0.52
Czech (134)	470	4.63
Czechoslovakian (0)	11	0.11
Danish (22)	87	0.86
Dutch (56)	342	3.37
English (121)	698	6.87
European (23)	36	0.35
Finnish (35)	93	0.92
French, ex. Basque (35)	376	3.70
French Canadian (16)	45	0.44
German (2,388)	5,055	49.76
Greek (49)	75	0.74
Hungarian (0)	16	0.16
Irish (185)	838	8.25
Italian (0)	296	2.91
Lithuanian (0)	26	0.26
Macedonian (0)	14	0.14
Norwegian (546)	1,976	19.45
Polish (73)	403	3.97
Russian (0)	82	0.81
Scandinavian (111)	145	1.43
Scotch-Irish (0)	24	0.24
Scottish (37)	323	3.18
Serbian (0)	30	0.30
Slovak (0)	14	0.14
Slovene (14)	27	0.27
Swedish (220)	937	9.22
Swiss (21)	33	0.32
Ukrainian (11)	30	0.30
Welsh (9)	9	0.09
West Indian, ex. Hispanic (28)	28	0.28
Barbadian (28)	28	0.28

Hispanic Origin	Population	%
Hispanic or Latino (of any race)	266	2.49
Central American, ex. Mexican	17	0.16
Guatemalan	7	0.07
Honduran	7	0.07
Panamanian	1	0.01
Salvadoran	2	0.02
Cuban	11	0.10
Mexican	147	1.37
Puerto Rican	16	0.15
South American	41	0.38
Argentinean	1	0.01
Chilean	10	0.09
Colombian	10	0.09
Ecuadorian	9	0.08
Paraguayan	1	0.01
Peruvian	9	0.08
Uruguayan	1	0.01
Other Hispanic or Latino	34	0.32

Race*	Population	%
African-American/Black (113)	153	1.43
Not Hispanic (106)	143	1.34
Hispanic (7)	10	0.09
American Indian/Alaska Native (29)	59	0.55
Not Hispanic (27)	55	0.51
Hispanic (2)	4	0.04
Blackfeet (0)	2	0.02
Cherokee (0)	8	0.07
Chippewa (13)	21	0.20
Creek (1)	1	0.01
Mexican American Ind. (1)	1	0.01
Osage (0)	3	0.03
Sioux (2)	3	0.03
Asian (119)	171	1.60
Not Hispanic (118)	163	1.52

*Notes: † The Census 2010 population figure is used to calculate the percentages in the Hispanic Origin and Race categories. Ancestry percentages are based on the 2006-2010 American Community Survey population (not shown); ‡ Numbers in parentheses indicate the number of people reporting a single ancestry; * Numbers in parentheses indicate the number of persons reporting this race alone, not in combination with any other race; Please refer to the Explanation of Data for more information.*

Hispanic (1)	8	0.07
Cambodian (16)	16	0.15
Chinese, ex. Taiwanese (15)	15	0.14
Filipino (17)	38	0.36
Indian (11)	20	0.19
Japanese (10)	17	0.16
Korean (23)	31	0.29
Laotian (10)	10	0.09
Nepalese (1)	3	0.03
Thai (2)	2	0.02
Vietnamese (3)	5	0.05
Hawaii Native/Pacific Islander (2)	10	0.09
Not Hispanic (1)	6	0.06
Hispanic (1)	4	0.04
Guamanian/Chamorro (1)	1	0.01
Samoan (0)	1	0.01
White (10,236)	10,342	96.68
Not Hispanic (10,075)	10,165	95.03
Hispanic (161)	177	1.65

Waseca

Place Type: City
County: Waseca
Population: 9,410†

Ancestry‡	Population	%
American (222)	222	2.36
Australian (18)	18	0.19
Austrian (0)	16	0.17
Belgian (0)	12	0.13
British (20)	20	0.21
Canadian (12)	12	0.13
Croatian (0)	16	0.17
Czech (0)	77	0.82
Czechoslovakian (0)	43	0.46
Danish (0)	122	1.29
Dutch (27)	266	2.82
English (145)	600	6.37
European (0)	8	0.08
Finnish (0)	48	0.51
French, ex. Basque (46)	308	3.27
French Canadian (16)	16	0.17
German (1,662)	4,977	52.80
Hungarian (0)	104	1.10
Icelander (0)	137	1.45
Irish (223)	1,613	17.11
Italian (13)	184	1.95
Latvian (0)	10	0.11
Norwegian (472)	2,028	21.51
Polish (37)	361	3.83
Russian (0)	4	0.04
Scandinavian (18)	28	0.30
Scotch-Irish (0)	83	0.88
Scottish (0)	60	0.64
Slovak (19)	19	0.20
Swedish (78)	658	6.98
Swiss (16)	49	0.52
Welsh (0)	40	0.42

Hispanic Origin	Population	%
Hispanic or Latino (of any race)	845	8.98
Central American, ex. Mexican	14	0.15
Guatemalan	2	0.02
Honduran	6	0.06
Panamanian	1	0.01
Salvadoran	5	0.05
Cuban	7	0.07
Dominican Republic	5	0.05
Mexican	721	7.66
Puerto Rican	31	0.33
South American	14	0.15
Chilean	1	0.01
Colombian	11	0.12
Peruvian	1	0.01
Venezuelan	1	0.01
Other Hispanic or Latino	53	0.56

Race*	Population	%
African-American/Black (350)	445	4.73
Not Hispanic (342)	425	4.52
Hispanic (8)	20	0.21
American Indian/Alaska Native (137)	192	2.04
Not Hispanic (118)	168	1.79
Hispanic (19)	24	0.26
Apache (1)	1	0.01
Arapaho (3)	3	0.03
Blackfeet (0)	6	0.06
Cherokee (4)	11	0.12
Cheyenne (0)	1	0.01
Chippewa (19)	32	0.34
Menominee (3)	3	0.03
Mexican American Ind. (8)	8	0.09
Navajo (3)	3	0.03
Potawatomi (0)	1	0.01
Pueblo (2)	2	0.02
Sioux (23)	24	0.26
Tohono O'Odham (5)	6	0.06
Ute (2)	2	0.02
Yaqui (0)	1	0.01
Asian (93)	123	1.31
Not Hispanic (92)	117	1.24
Hispanic (1)	6	0.06
Bangladeshi (2)	3	0.03
Chinese, ex. Taiwanese (19)	23	0.24
Filipino (12)	19	0.20
Hmong (9)	9	0.10
Indian (15)	16	0.17
Japanese (2)	6	0.06
Korean (11)	17	0.18
Laotian (1)	2	0.02
Nepalese (2)	2	0.02
Pakistani (6)	8	0.09
Thai (3)	7	0.07
Vietnamese (3)	4	0.04
Hawaii Native/Pacific Islander (2)	10	0.11
Not Hispanic (1)	7	0.07
Hispanic (1)	3	0.03
Guamanian/Chamorro (1)	2	0.02
Native Hawaiian (1)	4	0.04
Tongan (0)	1	0.01
White (8,377)	8,587	91.25
Not Hispanic (7,860)	7,994	84.95
Hispanic (517)	593	6.30

West St. Paul

Place Type: City
County: Dakota
Population: 19,540†

Ancestry‡	Population	%
African, Sub-Saharan (146)	157	0.80
Ethiopian (111)	111	0.57
Nigerian (0)	11	0.06
Somalian (35)	35	0.18
American (290)	290	1.48
Arab (140)	285	1.45
Egyptian (108)	182	0.93
Lebanese (32)	103	0.52
Austrian (29)	139	0.71
Belgian (0)	15	0.08
Brazilian (11)	11	0.06
British (8)	40	0.20
Canadian (14)	23	0.12
Croatian (15)	56	0.29
Czech (29)	380	1.93
Czechoslovakian (0)	21	0.11
Danish (51)	310	1.58
Dutch (71)	293	1.49
Eastern European (182)	182	0.93
English (196)	1,119	5.70
European (194)	194	0.99
Finnish (33)	278	1.42
French, ex. Basque (111)	932	4.75
French Canadian (43)	249	1.27
German (1,917)	6,559	33.40
German Russian (14)	14	0.07
Greek (18)	106	0.54
Hungarian (0)	22	0.11
Icelander (18)	18	0.09
Irish (626)	3,425	17.44
Italian (199)	495	2.52
Lithuanian (10)	10	0.05
Luxemburger (8)	17	0.09
Northern European (22)	22	0.11
Norwegian (613)	1,807	9.20
Pennsylvania German (31)	76	0.39
Polish (201)	884	4.50
Portuguese (9)	9	0.05
Russian (59)	107	0.54
Scandinavian (87)	133	0.68
Scotch-Irish (78)	281	1.43
Scottish (24)	215	1.09
Serbian (0)	19	0.10
Slovene (0)	64	0.33
Swedish (264)	1,542	7.85
Swiss (0)	83	0.42
Ukrainian (52)	110	0.56
Welsh (0)	47	0.24
West Indian, ex. Hispanic (0)	10	0.05
U.S. Virgin Islander (0)	10	0.05
Yugoslavian (0)	14	0.07

Hispanic Origin	Population	%
Hispanic or Latino (of any race)	3,803	19.46
Central American, ex. Mexican	294	1.50
Costa Rican	4	0.02
Guatemalan	29	0.15
Honduran	72	0.37
Nicaraguan	11	0.06
Panamanian	18	0.09
Salvadoran	150	0.77
Other Central American	10	0.05
Cuban	33	0.17
Dominican Republic	16	0.08
Mexican	3,023	15.47
Puerto Rican	158	0.81
South American	79	0.40
Argentinean	9	0.05
Chilean	9	0.05
Colombian	31	0.16
Ecuadorian	5	0.03
Peruvian	11	0.06
Uruguayan	1	0.01
Venezuelan	13	0.07
Other Hispanic or Latino	200	1.02

Race*	Population	%
African-American/Black (1,164)	1,477	7.56
Not Hispanic (1,098)	1,341	6.86
Hispanic (66)	136	0.70
American Indian/Alaska Native (167)	385	1.97
Not Hispanic (127)	271	1.39
Hispanic (40)	114	0.58
Apache (2)	2	0.01
Blackfeet (0)	5	0.03
Canadian/French Am. Ind. (0)	1	0.01
Cherokee (3)	12	0.06
Chippewa (47)	68	0.35
Choctaw (1)	2	0.01
Cree (0)	1	0.01
Crow (1)	1	0.01
Inupiat *(Alaska Native)* (1)	3	0.02
Iroquois (2)	2	0.01
Kiowa (1)	1	0.01
Menominee (1)	3	0.02
Mexican American Ind. (15)	30	0.15
Navajo (1)	1	0.01
Osage (0)	5	0.03
Seminole (0)	3	0.02
Sioux (44)	64	0.33
South American Ind. (0)	2	0.01
Tlingit-Haida *(Alaska Native)* (0)	1	0.01
Asian (424)	517	2.65
Not Hispanic (419)	492	2.52
Hispanic (5)	25	0.13
Cambodian (33)	37	0.19
Chinese, ex. Taiwanese (67)	90	0.46
Filipino (106)	138	0.71

*Notes: † The Census 2010 population figure is used to calculate the percentages in the Hispanic Origin and Race categories. Ancestry percentages are based on the 2006-2010 American Community Survey population (not shown); ‡ Numbers in parentheses indicate the number of people reporting a single ancestry; * Numbers in parentheses indicate the number of persons reporting this race alone, not in combination with any other race; Please refer to the Explanation of Data for more information.*

Hmong (85)	87	0.45
Indian (18)	24	0.12
Indonesian (1)	1	0.01
Japanese (10)	16	0.08
Korean (29)	41	0.21
Laotian (5)	6	0.03
Nepalese (2)	4	0.02
Pakistani (2)	6	0.03
Sri Lankan (2)	2	0.01
Taiwanese (6)	6	0.03
Thai (1)	5	0.03
Vietnamese (35)	40	0.20
Hawaii Native/Pacific Islander (11)	32	0.16
Not Hispanic (8)	27	0.14
Hispanic (3)	5	0.03
Guamanian/Chamorro (0)	1	0.01
Native Hawaiian (1)	12	0.06
Samoan (4)	4	0.02
White (15,247)	16,008	81.92
Not Hispanic (13,658)	14,033	71.82
Hispanic (1,589)	1,975	10.11

Hispanic Origin	Population	%
Hispanic or Latino (of any race)	788	3.37
Central American, ex. Mexican	35	0.15
Costa Rican	4	0.02
Guatemalan	13	0.06
Honduran	6	0.03
Panamanian	5	0.02
Salvadoran	7	0.03
Cuban	19	0.08
Dominican Republic	2	0.01
Mexican	607	2.59
Puerto Rican	45	0.19
South American	34	0.15
Argentinean	6	0.03
Chilean	4	0.02
Colombian	11	0.05
Ecuadorian	1	<0.01
Paraguayan	1	<0.01
Peruvian	5	0.02
Venezuelan	6	0.03
Other Hispanic or Latino	46	0.20

White Bear Lake

Place Type: City
County: Ramsey
Population: 23,394†

Ancestry‡	Population	%
African, Sub-Saharan (93)	93	0.40
African (93)	93	0.40
Alsatian (9)	9	0.04
American (569)	569	2.45
Arab (100)	192	0.83
Iraqi (79)	79	0.34
Lebanese (12)	83	0.36
Moroccan (9)	9	0.04
Syrian (0)	21	0.09
Australian (0)	8	0.03
Austrian (77)	171	0.74
Belgian (17)	40	0.17
British (16)	67	0.29
Canadian (30)	62	0.27
Croatian (23)	46	0.20
Czech (102)	552	2.38
Czechoslovakian (0)	31	0.13
Danish (66)	613	2.64
Dutch (42)	249	1.07
Eastern European (28)	28	0.12
English (233)	2,034	8.76
European (270)	392	1.69
Finnish (134)	455	1.96
French, ex. Basque (137)	1,271	5.47
French Canadian (125)	463	1.99
German (3,179)	10,105	43.50
Greek (11)	72	0.31
Hungarian (13)	69	0.30
Icelander (0)	10	0.04
Iranian (10)	29	0.12
Irish (674)	3,647	15.70
Italian (200)	958	4.12
Latvian (13)	13	0.06
Lithuanian (0)	14	0.06
Luxemburger (0)	14	0.06
Northern European (300)	300	1.29
Norwegian (1,012)	3,420	14.72
Polish (383)	1,208	5.20
Portuguese (10)	17	0.07
Russian (11)	138	0.59
Scandinavian (203)	346	1.49
Scotch-Irish (69)	269	1.16
Scottish (63)	330	1.42
Serbian (0)	10	0.04
Slavic (12)	12	0.05
Slovak (34)	34	0.15
Slovene (22)	33	0.14
Swedish (446)	2,669	11.49
Swiss (0)	96	0.41
Ukrainian (0)	23	0.10
Welsh (0)	76	0.33

Race*	Population	%
African-American/Black (577)	851	3.64
Not Hispanic (570)	810	3.46
Hispanic (7)	41	0.18
American Indian/Alaska Native (97)	291	1.24
Not Hispanic (82)	237	1.01
Hispanic (15)	54	0.23
Blackfeet (0)	4	0.02
Canadian/French Am. Ind. (1)	3	0.01
Central American Ind. (1)	1	<0.01
Cherokee (3)	10	0.04
Chippewa (29)	71	0.30
Comanche (0)	1	<0.01
Iroquois (1)	1	<0.01
Mexican American Ind. (3)	8	0.03
Ottawa (0)	1	<0.01
Sioux (5)	29	0.12
Asian (840)	1,038	4.44
Not Hispanic (837)	1,021	4.36
Hispanic (3)	17	0.07
Cambodian (7)	10	0.04
Chinese, ex. Taiwanese (57)	103	0.44
Filipino (34)	61	0.26
Hmong (437)	454	1.94
Indian (116)	137	0.59
Indonesian (3)	8	0.03
Japanese (16)	38	0.16
Korean (49)	81	0.35
Laotian (1)	1	<0.01
Malaysian (1)	1	<0.01
Nepalese (1)	1	<0.01
Pakistani (3)	4	0.02
Taiwanese (3)	5	0.02
Thai (6)	7	0.03
Vietnamese (66)	96	0.41
Hawaii Native/Pacific Islander (5)	31	0.13
Not Hispanic (5)	23	0.10
Hispanic (0)	8	0.03
Fijian (0)	2	0.01
Native Hawaiian (0)	14	0.06
Samoan (0)	2	0.01
Tongan (5)	5	0.02
White (21,045)	21,576	92.23
Not Hispanic (20,591)	21,041	89.94
Hispanic (454)	535	2.29

White Bear Lake

Place Type: City
County: Ramsey
Population: 23,797†

Ancestry‡	Population	%
African, Sub-Saharan (93)	93	0.40
African (93)	93	0.40
Alsatian (9)	9	0.04
American (578)	578	2.46
Arab (100)	192	0.82
Iraqi (79)	79	0.34
Lebanese (12)	83	0.35
Moroccan (9)	9	0.04
Syrian (0)	21	0.09
Australian (0)	8	0.03
Austrian (77)	171	0.73
Belgian (17)	40	0.17
British (16)	67	0.29
Canadian (30)	62	0.26
Croatian (23)	46	0.20
Czech (102)	552	2.35
Czechoslovakian (0)	43	0.18
Danish (66)	613	2.61
Dutch (42)	249	1.06
Eastern European (28)	28	0.12
English (233)	2,037	8.68
European (270)	392	1.67
Finnish (134)	455	1.94
French, ex. Basque (137)	1,295	5.52
French Canadian (125)	463	1.97
German (3,264)	10,281	43.82
Greek (11)	72	0.31
Hungarian (13)	69	0.29
Icelander (0)	10	0.04
Iranian (10)	29	0.12
Irish (674)	3,650	15.56
Italian (213)	971	4.14
Latvian (13)	13	0.06
Lithuanian (0)	14	0.06
Luxemburger (0)	14	0.06
Northern European (300)	300	1.28
Norwegian (1,012)	3,420	14.58
Polish (393)	1,230	5.24
Portuguese (10)	17	0.07
Russian (11)	138	0.59
Scandinavian (203)	346	1.47
Scotch-Irish (69)	269	1.15
Scottish (63)	330	1.41
Serbian (0)	10	0.04
Slavic (12)	12	0.05
Slovak (34)	34	0.14
Slovene (22)	33	0.14
Swedish (446)	2,726	11.62
Swiss (10)	116	0.49
Ukrainian (0)	23	0.10
Welsh (0)	76	0.32

Hispanic Origin	Population	%
Hispanic or Latino (of any race)	791	3.32
Central American, ex. Mexican	36	0.15
Costa Rican	5	0.02
Guatemalan	13	0.05
Honduran	6	0.03
Panamanian	5	0.02
Salvadoran	7	0.03
Cuban	19	0.08
Dominican Republic	2	0.01
Mexican	609	2.56
Puerto Rican	45	0.19
South American	34	0.14
Argentinean	6	0.03
Chilean	4	0.02
Colombian	11	0.05
Ecuadorian	1	<0.01
Paraguayan	1	<0.01
Peruvian	5	0.02
Venezuelan	6	0.03
Other Hispanic or Latino	46	0.19

Race*	Population	%
African-American/Black (589)	863	3.63
Not Hispanic (582)	822	3.45
Hispanic (7)	41	0.17
American Indian/Alaska Native (97)	291	1.22
Not Hispanic (82)	237	1.00
Hispanic (15)	54	0.23
Blackfeet (0)	4	0.02
Canadian/French Am. Ind. (1)	3	0.01
Central American Ind. (1)	1	<0.01
Cherokee (3)	10	0.04

*Notes: † The Census 2010 population figure is used to calculate the percentages in the Hispanic Origin and Race categories. Ancestry percentages are based on the 2006-2010 American Community Survey population (not shown); ‡ Numbers in parentheses indicate the number of people reporting a single ancestry; * Numbers in parentheses indicate the number of persons reporting this race alone, not in combination with any other race; Please refer to the Explanation of Data for more information.*

Chippewa (29)	71	0.30
Comanche (0)	1	<0.01
Iroquois (1)	1	<0.01
Mexican American Ind. (3)	8	0.03
Ottawa (0)	1	<0.01
Sioux (5)	29	0.12
Asian (842)	1,041	4.37
Not Hispanic (839)	1,024	4.30
Hispanic (3)	17	0.07
Cambodian (7)	10	0.04
Chinese, ex. Taiwanese (58)	104	0.44
Filipino (34)	61	0.26
Hmong (437)	454	1.91
Indian (116)	137	0.58
Indonesian (3)	8	0.03
Japanese (16)	38	0.16
Korean (50)	83	0.35
Laotian (1)	1	<0.01
Malaysian (1)	1	<0.01
Nepalese (1)	1	<0.01
Pakistani (3)	4	0.02
Taiwanese (3)	5	0.02
Thai (6)	7	0.03
Vietnamese (66)	96	0.40
Hawaii Native/Pacific Islander (5)	31	0.13
Not Hispanic (5)	23	0.10
Hispanic (0)	8	0.03
Fijian (0)	2	0.01
Native Hawaiian (0)	14	0.06
Samoan (0)	2	0.01
Tongan (5)	5	0.02
White (21,433)	21,965	92.30
Not Hispanic (20,976)	21,427	90.04
Hispanic (457)	538	2.26

White Bear

Place Type: Township
County: Ramsey
Population: 10,949†

Ancestry‡	Population	%
American (466)	466	4.30
Arab (25)	65	0.60
Lebanese (12)	52	0.48
Palestinian (13)	13	0.12
Austrian (0)	80	0.74
Belgian (0)	46	0.42
British (19)	28	0.26
Canadian (14)	23	0.21
Czech (0)	150	1.38
Danish (36)	177	1.63
Dutch (23)	171	1.58
Eastern European (0)	14	0.13
English (178)	903	8.32
European (46)	46	0.42
Finnish (20)	175	1.61
French, ex. Basque (82)	759	7.00
French Canadian (52)	258	2.38
German (1,157)	4,505	41.52
Hungarian (14)	35	0.32
Irish (196)	1,880	17.33
Italian (98)	460	4.24
Lithuanian (0)	24	0.22
Northern European (26)	40	0.37
Norwegian (550)	1,946	17.94
Polish (197)	794	7.32
Russian (20)	114	1.05
Scandinavian (51)	183	1.69
Scotch-Irish (14)	105	0.97
Scottish (8)	98	0.90
Serbian (0)	60	0.55
Slavic (0)	11	0.10
Slovene (0)	27	0.25
Swedish (274)	1,491	13.74
Swiss (0)	146	1.35
Turkish (0)	16	0.15
Ukrainian (0)	22	0.20
Welsh (14)	40	0.37
Yugoslavian (15)	25	0.23

Hispanic Origin	Population	%
Hispanic or Latino (of any race)	266	2.43
Central American, ex. Mexican	38	0.35
Costa Rican	6	0.05
Guatemalan	10	0.09
Honduran	11	0.10
Nicaraguan	1	0.01
Panamanian	8	0.07
Salvadoran	2	0.02
Cuban	15	0.14
Dominican Republic	2	0.02
Mexican	133	1.21
Puerto Rican	24	0.22
South American	31	0.28
Colombian	17	0.16
Ecuadorian	9	0.08
Peruvian	4	0.04
Venezuelan	1	0.01
Other Hispanic or Latino	23	0.21

Race*	Population	%
African-American/Black (80)	127	1.16
Not Hispanic (74)	107	0.98
Hispanic (6)	20	0.18
American Indian/Alaska Native (41)	104	0.95
Not Hispanic (36)	77	0.70
Hispanic (5)	27	0.25
Aleut *(Alaska Native)* (1)	1	0.01
Blackfeet (0)	2	0.02
Cherokee (1)	4	0.04
Chickasaw (0)	1	0.01
Chippewa (9)	12	0.11
Cree (0)	2	0.02
Kiowa (0)	1	0.01
Mexican American Ind. (4)	14	0.13
Sioux (8)	20	0.18
Asian (239)	301	2.75
Not Hispanic (235)	290	2.65
Hispanic (4)	11	0.10
Chinese, ex. Taiwanese (30)	31	0.28
Filipino (8)	15	0.14
Hmong (99)	102	0.93
Indian (23)	26	0.24
Indonesian (0)	1	0.01
Japanese (14)	33	0.30
Korean (27)	51	0.47
Laotian (4)	5	0.05
Pakistani (1)	1	0.01
Thai (2)	8	0.07
Vietnamese (18)	18	0.16
Hawaii Native/Pacific Islander (6)	11	0.10
Not Hispanic (6)	10	0.09
Hispanic (0)	1	0.01
Native Hawaiian (1)	4	0.04
Samoan (0)	1	0.01
Tongan (2)	2	0.02
White (10,352)	10,506	95.95
Not Hispanic (10,210)	10,327	94.32
Hispanic (142)	179	1.63

Willmar

Place Type: City
County: Kandiyohi
Population: 19,610†

Ancestry‡	Population	%
African, Sub-Saharan (464)	464	2.40
Ethiopian (13)	13	0.07
Somalian (451)	451	2.33
American (386)	386	2.00
Austrian (10)	10	0.05
Belgian (32)	41	0.21
British (29)	41	0.21
Canadian (11)	11	0.06
Czech (73)	210	1.09
Czechoslovakian (13)	21	0.11
Danish (114)	356	1.84
Dutch (482)	868	4.49
English (102)	689	3.56
European (87)	92	0.48
Finnish (23)	140	0.72
French, ex. Basque (31)	353	1.83
French Canadian (0)	130	0.67
German (2,232)	5,888	30.45
Greek (11)	11	0.06
Hungarian (0)	10	0.05
Iranian (6)	6	0.03
Irish (224)	1,245	6.44
Italian (33)	173	0.89
Luxemburger (0)	39	0.20
Northern European (13)	13	0.07
Norwegian (1,652)	4,617	23.88
Pennsylvania German (13)	13	0.07
Polish (77)	340	1.76
Portuguese (0)	14	0.07
Russian (0)	88	0.46
Scandinavian (220)	233	1.21
Scotch-Irish (10)	92	0.48
Scottish (24)	154	0.80
Slavic (0)	8	0.04
Swedish (421)	2,195	11.35
Swiss (19)	88	0.46
Ukrainian (10)	39	0.20
Welsh (0)	10	0.05
West Indian, ex. Hispanic (9)	9	0.05
Other West Indian (9)	9	0.05
Yugoslavian (0)	21	0.11

Hispanic Origin	Population	%
Hispanic or Latino (of any race)	4,099	20.90
Central American, ex. Mexican	566	2.89
Costa Rican	5	0.03
Guatemalan	135	0.69
Honduran	337	1.72
Nicaraguan	14	0.07
Panamanian	6	0.03
Salvadoran	66	0.34
Other Central American	3	0.02
Cuban	21	0.11
Dominican Republic	4	0.02
Mexican	2,934	14.96
Puerto Rican	35	0.18
South American	60	0.31
Bolivian	8	0.04
Chilean	12	0.06
Colombian	9	0.05
Ecuadorian	14	0.07
Paraguayan	2	0.01
Peruvian	14	0.07
Venezuelan	1	0.01
Other Hispanic or Latino	479	2.44

Race*	Population	%
African-American/Black (933)	1,042	5.31
Not Hispanic (908)	988	5.04
Hispanic (25)	54	0.28
American Indian/Alaska Native (93)	202	1.03
Not Hispanic (80)	143	0.73
Hispanic (13)	59	0.30
Apache (1)	1	0.01
Blackfeet (0)	1	0.01
Cherokee (2)	7	0.04
Chickasaw (0)	2	0.01
Chippewa (12)	21	0.11
Choctaw (0)	1	0.01
Comanche (0)	5	0.03
Mexican American Ind. (0)	4	0.02
Paiute (1)	1	0.01
Pima (2)	5	0.03
Sioux (25)	31	0.16
South American Ind. (3)	3	0.02
Spanish American Ind. (0)	1	0.01
Yuman (0)	3	0.02
Asian (111)	180	0.92
Not Hispanic (106)	164	0.84
Hispanic (5)	16	0.08
Cambodian (2)	4	0.02
Chinese, ex. Taiwanese (27)	31	0.16
Filipino (28)	59	0.30

*Notes: † The Census 2010 population figure is used to calculate the percentages in the Hispanic Origin and Race categories. Ancestry percentages are based on the 2006-2010 American Community Survey population (not shown); ‡ Numbers in parentheses indicate the number of people reporting a single ancestry; * Numbers in parentheses indicate the number of persons reporting this race alone, not in combination with any other race; Please refer to the Explanation of Data for more information.*

Indian (12)	14	0.07
Indonesian (1)	3	0.02
Japanese (0)	4	0.02
Korean (17)	24	0.12
Laotian (1)	1	0.01
Pakistani (10)	15	0.08
Thai (0)	4	0.02
Vietnamese (11)	14	0.07
Hawaii Native/Pacific Islander (15)	22	0.11
Not Hispanic (14)	20	0.10
Hispanic (1)	2	0.01
Guamanian/Chamorro (1)	1	0.01
Native Hawaiian (4)	5	0.03
Samoan (10)	12	0.06
White (17,037)	17,371	88.58
Not Hispanic (14,192)	14,376	73.31
Hispanic (2,845)	2,995	15.27

Winona

Place Type: City
County: Winona
Population: 27,592†

Ancestry‡	Population	%
African, Sub-Saharan (68)	98	0.35
African (29)	59	0.21
South African (39)	39	0.14
American (740)	740	2.68
Arab (38)	101	0.37
Arab (4)	4	0.01
Lebanese (0)	15	0.05
Other Arab (34)	82	0.30
Australian (0)	10	0.04
Austrian (0)	103	0.37
Belgian (21)	70	0.25
Brazilian (0)	29	0.10
British (17)	39	0.14
Bulgarian (33)	33	0.12
Canadian (4)	23	0.08
Croatian (0)	23	0.08
Czech (94)	387	1.40
Czechoslovakian (0)	36	0.13
Danish (35)	275	0.99
Dutch (26)	297	1.07
Eastern European (13)	13	0.05
English (446)	1,729	6.25
European (116)	116	0.42
Finnish (66)	133	0.48
French, ex. Basque (60)	977	3.53
French Canadian (71)	126	0.46
German (4,312)	11,598	41.93
Greek (28)	90	0.33
Hungarian (74)	151	0.55
Irish (749)	3,471	12.55
Italian (89)	652	2.36
Lithuanian (10)	79	0.29
Luxemburger (32)	136	0.49
Northern European (13)	52	0.19
Norwegian (1,169)	4,421	15.98
Polish (1,197)	3,245	11.73
Portuguese (8)	8	0.03
Russian (12)	54	0.20
Scandinavian (98)	171	0.62
Scotch-Irish (74)	385	1.39
Scottish (81)	270	0.98
Serbian (0)	24	0.09
Slavic (0)	26	0.09
Slovak (0)	16	0.06
Slovene (0)	17	0.06
Swedish (149)	1,332	4.82
Swiss (28)	146	0.53
Ukrainian (0)	11	0.04
Welsh (0)	184	0.67
West Indian, ex. Hispanic (13)	13	0.05
West Indian (13)	13	0.05
Yugoslavian (14)	42	0.15

Hispanic Origin	Population	%
Hispanic or Latino (of any race)	460	1.67
Central American, ex. Mexican	17	0.06
Costa Rican	2	0.01
Guatemalan	4	0.01
Honduran	5	0.02
Nicaraguan	2	0.01
Panamanian	2	0.01
Salvadoran	2	0.01
Cuban	26	0.09
Mexican	311	1.13
Puerto Rican	38	0.14
South American	34	0.12
Bolivian	1	<0.01
Chilean	2	0.01
Colombian	13	0.05
Ecuadorian	7	0.03
Paraguayan	3	0.01
Peruvian	1	<0.01
Venezuelan	7	0.03
Other Hispanic or Latino	34	0.12

Race*	Population	%
African-American/Black (528)	685	2.48
Not Hispanic (527)	676	2.45
Hispanic (1)	9	0.03
American Indian/Alaska Native (73)	165	0.60
Not Hispanic (63)	144	0.52
Hispanic (10)	21	0.08
Aleut *(Alaska Native)* (1)	2	0.01
Apache (1)	2	0.01
Blackfeet (1)	1	<0.01
Cherokee (2)	19	0.07
Chippewa (14)	18	0.07
Choctaw (1)	1	<0.01
Comanche (0)	1	<0.01
Cree (0)	2	0.01
Iroquois (1)	6	0.02
Menominee (1)	1	<0.01
Navajo (0)	1	<0.01
Paiute (1)	1	<0.01
Puget Sound Salish (0)	1	<0.01
Seminole (0)	1	<0.01
Sioux (11)	12	0.04
South American Ind. (0)	1	<0.01
Ute (0)	1	<0.01
Asian (808)	897	3.25
Not Hispanic (805)	890	3.23
Hispanic (3)	7	0.03
Bangladeshi (6)	7	0.03
Cambodian (6)	12	0.04
Chinese, ex. Taiwanese (168)	177	0.64
Filipino (23)	42	0.15
Hmong (218)	218	0.79
Indian (67)	76	0.28
Japanese (20)	34	0.12
Korean (111)	126	0.46
Laotian (3)	4	0.01
Malaysian (2)	4	0.01
Nepalese (20)	21	0.08
Pakistani (5)	6	0.02
Sri Lankan (7)	8	0.03
Taiwanese (26)	27	0.10
Thai (7)	8	0.03
Vietnamese (28)	35	0.13
Hawaii Native/Pacific Islander (2)	18	0.07
Not Hispanic (2)	18	0.07
Guamanian/Chamorro (2)	4	0.01
Native Hawaiian (0)	3	0.01
Samoan (0)	4	0.01
White (25,664)	26,018	94.30
Not Hispanic (25,388)	25,699	93.14
Hispanic (276)	319	1.16

Woodbury

Place Type: City
County: Washington
Population: 61,961†

Ancestry‡	Population	%
African, Sub-Saharan (754)	899	1.51
African (115)	260	0.44
Ethiopian (229)	229	0.39
Kenyan (69)	69	0.12
Liberian (42)	42	0.07
Nigerian (137)	137	0.23
Sudanese (143)	143	0.24
Other Sub-Saharan African (19)	19	0.03
American (1,484)	1,484	2.50
Arab (137)	367	0.62
Egyptian (44)	54	0.09
Lebanese (22)	100	0.17
Palestinian (0)	25	0.04
Syrian (71)	83	0.14
Other Arab (0)	105	0.18
Austrian (30)	246	0.41
Belgian (30)	215	0.36
Brazilian (26)	37	0.06
British (48)	113	0.19
Canadian (48)	158	0.27
Celtic (8)	8	0.01
Croatian (13)	86	0.14
Czech (199)	809	1.36
Czechoslovakian (37)	151	0.25
Danish (162)	1,068	1.80
Dutch (143)	746	1.25
Eastern European (21)	21	0.04
English (1,018)	4,873	8.20
European (900)	1,021	1.72
Finnish (230)	612	1.03
French, ex. Basque (261)	2,354	3.96
French Canadian (206)	684	1.15
German (6,458)	21,774	36.63
Greek (41)	228	0.38
Hungarian (39)	178	0.30
Icelander (12)	95	0.16
Iranian (74)	97	0.16
Irish (1,599)	9,331	15.70
Israeli (14)	14	0.02
Italian (518)	2,605	4.38
Latvian (19)	39	0.07
Lithuanian (9)	68	0.11
Luxemburger (9)	74	0.12
Macedonian (18)	18	0.03
New Zealander (9)	18	0.03
Northern European (277)	306	0.51
Norwegian (2,046)	7,461	12.55
Pennsylvania German (0)	16	0.03
Polish (690)	3,475	5.85
Portuguese (63)	97	0.16
Russian (208)	611	1.03
Scandinavian (479)	832	1.40
Scotch-Irish (151)	669	1.13
Scottish (119)	645	1.09
Serbian (19)	41	0.07
Slavic (74)	113	0.19
Slovak (17)	89	0.15
Slovene (28)	39	0.07
Swedish (1,179)	5,100	8.58
Swiss (61)	338	0.57
Turkish (22)	29	0.05
Ukrainian (71)	172	0.29
Welsh (77)	331	0.56
West Indian, ex. Hispanic (36)	63	0.11
Haitian (12)	12	0.02
Jamaican (24)	51	0.09
Yugoslavian (11)	80	0.13

Hispanic Origin	Population	%
Hispanic or Latino (of any race)	2,329	3.76
Central American, ex. Mexican	182	0.29
Costa Rican	20	0.03
Guatemalan	43	0.07
Honduran	23	0.04
Nicaraguan	10	0.02
Panamanian	28	0.05
Salvadoran	58	0.09
Cuban	80	0.13
Dominican Republic	21	0.03
Mexican	1,284	2.07
Puerto Rican	227	0.37

SECTION TWO

*Notes: † The Census 2010 population figure is used to calculate the percentages in the Hispanic Origin and Race categories. Ancestry percentages are based on the 2006-2010 American Community Survey population (not shown); ‡ Numbers in parentheses indicate the number of people reporting a single ancestry; * Numbers in parentheses indicate the number of persons reporting this race alone, not in combination with any other race; Please refer to the Explanation of Data for more information.*

South American	373	0.60
Argentinean	16	0.03
Bolivian	9	0.01
Chilean	24	0.04
Colombian	169	0.27
Ecuadorian	23	0.04
Paraguayan	4	0.01
Peruvian	66	0.11
Uruguayan	8	0.01
Venezuelan	47	0.08
Other South American	7	0.01
Other Hispanic or Latino	162	0.26

Race*	Population	%
African-American/Black (3,487)	4,148	6.69
Not Hispanic (3,392)	3,994	6.45
Hispanic (95)	154	0.25
American Indian/Alaska Native (171)	471	0.76
Not Hispanic (147)	388	0.63
Hispanic (24)	83	0.13
Aleut *(Alaska Native)* (1)	1	<0.01
Apache (1)	2	<0.01
Blackfeet (0)	6	0.01
Canadian/French Am. Ind. (1)	1	<0.01
Central American Ind. (1)	1	<0.01
Cherokee (1)	34	0.05
Chickasaw (1)	1	<0.01
Chippewa (46)	94	0.15
Choctaw (0)	6	0.01
Comanche (0)	2	<0.01
Cree (0)	3	<0.01
Creek (2)	4	0.01
Houma (0)	1	<0.01
Iroquois (4)	6	0.01
Menominee (1)	2	<0.01
Mexican American Ind. (2)	4	0.01
Navajo (1)	2	<0.01
Osage (0)	2	<0.01
Pima (1)	1	<0.01
Potawatomi (3)	3	<0.01
Pueblo (0)	4	0.01
Seminole (1)	6	0.01
Sioux (33)	61	0.10
South American Ind. (0)	7	0.01
Tohono O'Odham (0)	2	<0.01
Ute (1)	1	<0.01
Yup'ik *(Alaska Native)* (0)	3	<0.01
Asian (5,660)	6,301	10.17
Not Hispanic (5,645)	6,264	10.11
Hispanic (15)	37	0.06
Bangladeshi (25)	25	0.04
Burmese (9)	9	0.01
Cambodian (133)	155	0.25
Chinese, ex. Taiwanese (976)	1,122	1.81
Filipino (358)	479	0.77
Hmong (1,054)	1,103	1.78
Indian (1,557)	1,647	2.66
Indonesian (8)	11	0.02
Japanese (116)	223	0.36
Korean (431)	546	0.88
Laotian (25)	35	0.06
Malaysian (4)	10	0.02
Nepalese (6)	6	0.01
Pakistani (94)	114	0.18
Sri Lankan (23)	28	0.05
Taiwanese (88)	97	0.16
Thai (17)	34	0.05
Vietnamese (520)	581	0.94
Hawaii Native/Pacific Islander (15)	70	0.11
Not Hispanic (15)	69	0.11
Hispanic (0)	1	<0.01
Guamanian/Chamorro (4)	5	0.01
Native Hawaiian (2)	21	0.03
Tongan (2)	2	<0.01
White (50,462)	51,876	83.72
Not Hispanic (49,016)	50,229	81.07
Hispanic (1,446)	1,647	2.66

Worthington

Place Type: City
County: Nobles
Population: 12,764†

Ancestry‡	Population	%
African, Sub-Saharan (351)	351	2.84
Ethiopian (112)	112	0.91
Liberian (239)	239	1.93
American (172)	172	1.39
Australian (12)	12	0.10
Austrian (0)	7	0.06
Belgian (0)	28	0.23
British (0)	10	0.08
Canadian (10)	10	0.08
Czech (29)	92	0.74
Czechoslovakian (7)	7	0.06
Danish (30)	117	0.95
Dutch (336)	536	4.34
English (145)	508	4.11
European (9)	9	0.07
French, ex. Basque (38)	264	2.14
French Canadian (0)	26	0.21
German (2,194)	3,942	31.90
Greek (12)	12	0.10
Icelander (0)	12	0.10
Irish (72)	643	5.20
Italian (59)	106	0.86
Luxemburger (18)	38	0.31
Norwegian (294)	895	7.24
Polish (0)	47	0.38
Romanian (9)	20	0.16
Russian (0)	10	0.08
Scandinavian (67)	131	1.06
Scotch-Irish (17)	43	0.35
Scottish (0)	141	1.14
Slovak (0)	9	0.07
Swedish (355)	671	5.43
Swiss (10)	32	0.26
Welsh (0)	15	0.12

Hispanic Origin	Population	%
Hispanic or Latino (of any race)	4,521	35.42
Central American, ex. Mexican	1,619	12.68
Guatemalan	906	7.10
Honduran	139	1.09
Nicaraguan	61	0.48
Panamanian	1	0.01
Salvadoran	500	3.92
Other Central American	12	0.09
Cuban	3	0.02
Dominican Republic	1	0.01
Mexican	2,367	18.54
Puerto Rican	29	0.23
South American	15	0.12
Bolivian	1	0.01
Colombian	8	0.06
Ecuadorian	4	0.03
Venezuelan	2	0.02
Other Hispanic or Latino	487	3.82

Race*	Population	%
African-American/Black (698)	770	6.03
Not Hispanic (682)	744	5.83
Hispanic (16)	26	0.20
American Indian/Alaska Native (91)	149	1.17
Not Hispanic (51)	87	0.68
Hispanic (40)	62	0.49
Central American Ind. (6)	6	0.05
Cherokee (0)	2	0.02
Chippewa (13)	25	0.20
Choctaw (3)	3	0.02
Cree (1)	3	0.02
Mexican American Ind. (6)	6	0.05
Potawatomi (0)	1	0.01
Sioux (12)	17	0.13
South American Ind. (1)	3	0.02
Yup'ik *(Alaska Native)* (0)	4	0.03
Asian (1,104)	1,211	9.49
Not Hispanic (1,081)	1,175	9.21
Hispanic (23)	36	0.28
Burmese (282)	296	2.32
Cambodian (2)	2	0.02
Chinese, ex. Taiwanese (33)	36	0.28
Filipino (4)	15	0.12
Hmong (0)	1	0.01
Indian (37)	50	0.39
Korean (11)	16	0.13
Laotian (484)	529	4.14
Malaysian (1)	1	0.01
Thai (58)	61	0.48
Vietnamese (128)	147	1.15
Hawaii Native/Pacific Islander (9)	18	0.14
Not Hispanic (7)	10	0.08
Hispanic (2)	8	0.06
Guamanian/Chamorro (6)	12	0.09
Native Hawaiian (3)	4	0.03
White (7,936)	8,186	64.13
Not Hispanic (6,238)	6,360	49.83
Hispanic (1,698)	1,826	14.31

Wyoming

Place Type: City
County: Chisago
Population: 7,791†

Ancestry‡	Population	%
American (42)	42	0.55
Arab (0)	14	0.18
Lebanese (0)	14	0.18
Austrian (0)	12	0.16
Belgian (0)	10	0.13
Czech (0)	85	1.11
Czechoslovakian (0)	12	0.16
Danish (21)	105	1.37
Dutch (0)	66	0.86
English (83)	799	10.40
European (115)	115	1.50
Finnish (16)	114	1.48
French, ex. Basque (27)	624	8.13
French Canadian (58)	217	2.83
German (1,147)	3,678	47.89
German Russian (15)	30	0.39
Icelander (17)	17	0.22
Irish (180)	1,041	13.55
Italian (11)	274	3.57
Luxemburger (0)	10	0.13
Norwegian (268)	1,095	14.26
Polish (87)	766	9.97
Portuguese (0)	14	0.18
Russian (0)	138	1.80
Scandinavian (170)	261	3.40
Scotch-Irish (14)	49	0.64
Scottish (0)	72	0.94
Slavic (0)	22	0.29
Swedish (157)	1,276	16.61
Swiss (0)	20	0.26
Welsh (0)	12	0.16
Yugoslavian (0)	151	1.97

Hispanic Origin	Population	%
Hispanic or Latino (of any race)	130	1.67
Central American, ex. Mexican	12	0.15
Costa Rican	1	0.01
Guatemalan	2	0.03
Honduran	1	0.01
Panamanian	1	0.01
Salvadoran	7	0.09
Cuban	5	0.06
Dominican Republic	1	0.01
Mexican	85	1.09
Puerto Rican	7	0.09
South American	12	0.15
Colombian	10	0.13
Ecuadorian	1	0.01
Venezuelan	1	0.01
Other Hispanic or Latino	8	0.10

*Notes: † The Census 2010 population figure is used to calculate the percentages in the Hispanic Origin and Race categories. Ancestry percentages are based on the 2006-2010 American Community Survey population (not shown); ‡ Numbers in parentheses indicate the number of people reporting a single ancestry; * Numbers in parentheses indicate the number of persons reporting this race alone, not in combination with any other race; Please refer to the Explanation of Data for more information.*

Race*	Population	%
African-American/Black (28)	62	0.80
Not Hispanic (28)	58	0.74
Hispanic (0)	4	0.05
American Indian/Alaska Native (29)	72	0.92
Not Hispanic (29)	70	0.90
Hispanic (0)	2	0.03
Blackfeet (0)	5	0.06
Cherokee (4)	4	0.05
Chippewa (17)	29	0.37
Comanche (0)	1	0.01
Cree (0)	1	0.01
Ottawa (0)	2	0.03
Sioux (1)	1	0.01
Asian (72)	99	1.27
Not Hispanic (68)	95	1.22
Hispanic (4)	4	0.05
Cambodian (4)	4	0.05
Chinese, ex. Taiwanese (6)	10	0.13
Filipino (8)	10	0.13
Hmong (31)	31	0.40
Indian (6)	7	0.09
Japanese (1)	4	0.05
Korean (6)	19	0.24
Vietnamese (10)	14	0.18
Hawaii Native/Pacific Islander (0)	6	0.08
Not Hispanic (0)	6	0.08
Samoan (0)	6	0.08
White (7,526)	7,627	97.90
Not Hispanic (7,438)	7,530	96.65
Hispanic (88)	97	1.25

SECTION TWO

*Notes: † The Census 2010 population figure is used to calculate the percentages in the Hispanic Origin and Race categories. Ancestry percentages are based on the 2006-2010 American Community Survey population (not shown); ‡ Numbers in parentheses indicate the number of people reporting a single ancestry; * Numbers in parentheses indicate the number of persons reporting this race alone, not in combination with any other race; Please refer to the Explanation of Data for more information.*

MISSISSIPPI

Place Type: State
Population: 2,967,297†

Ancestry‡	Population	%
African, Sub-Saharan (22,056)	24,715	0.84
African (20,944)	23,459	0.80
Cape Verdean (9)	17	<0.01
Ethiopian (47)	58	<0.01
Ghanaian (237)	251	0.01
Kenyan (60)	60	<0.01
Liberian (13)	13	<0.01
Nigerian (364)	397	0.01
South African (65)	84	<0.01
Sudanese (157)	172	0.01
Other Sub-Saharan African (160)	204	0.01
Albanian (15)	15	<0.01
Alsatian (0)	32	<0.01
American (349,153)	349,153	11.87
Arab (4,427)	6,984	0.24
Arab (522)	748	0.03
Egyptian (256)	277	0.01
Iraqi (74)	74	<0.01
Jordanian (199)	223	0.01
Lebanese (2,567)	4,229	0.14
Moroccan (46)	118	<0.01
Palestinian (253)	258	0.01
Syrian (201)	721	0.02
Other Arab (309)	336	0.01
Armenian (130)	179	0.01
Assyrian/Chaldean/Syriac (54)	92	<0.01
Australian (129)	221	0.01
Austrian (432)	1,445	0.05
Basque (47)	47	<0.01
Belgian (258)	656	0.02
Brazilian (193)	300	0.01
British (4,343)	7,308	0.25
Bulgarian (58)	94	<0.01
Cajun (890)	2,097	0.07
Canadian (872)	1,725	0.06
Celtic (300)	488	0.02
Croatian (592)	1,054	0.04
Czech (799)	1,975	0.07
Czechoslovakian (391)	688	0.02
Danish (732)	2,760	0.09
Dutch (4,570)	23,177	0.79
Eastern European (123)	129	<0.01
English (148,060)	251,326	8.54
Estonian (28)	28	<0.01
European (17,041)	19,577	0.67
Finnish (435)	1,061	0.04
French, ex. Basque (30,259)	85,806	2.92
French Canadian (4,195)	6,902	0.23
German (59,483)	179,323	6.10
German Russian (8)	41	<0.01
Greek (1,431)	3,217	0.11
Guyanese (157)	197	0.01
Hungarian (703)	2,297	0.08
Icelander (52)	162	0.01
Iranian (507)	661	0.02
Irish (125,517)	285,021	9.69
Israeli (19)	66	<0.01
Italian (22,820)	52,821	1.80
Latvian (104)	196	0.01
Lithuanian (391)	769	0.03
Luxemburger (14)	35	<0.01
Macedonian (46)	55	<0.01
Maltese (34)	85	<0.01
New Zealander (21)	37	<0.01
Northern European (881)	881	0.03
Norwegian (2,671)	6,939	0.24
Pennsylvania German (129)	214	0.01
Polish (5,569)	15,189	0.52
Portuguese (783)	1,505	0.05
Romanian (172)	314	0.01
Russian (1,622)	3,469	0.12
Scandinavian (506)	1,349	0.05
Scotch-Irish (41,898)	66,784	2.27
Scottish (23,163)	47,248	1.61
Serbian (47)	166	0.01
Slavic (223)	913	0.03
Slovak (420)	796	0.03
Slovene (43)	218	0.01
Swedish (2,650)	8,572	0.29
Swiss (641)	2,359	0.08
Turkish (177)	245	0.01
Ukrainian (314)	709	0.02
Welsh (3,431)	9,225	0.31
West Indian, ex. Hispanic (1,405)	2,403	0.08
Bahamian (111)	120	<0.01
Barbadian (12)	12	<0.01
Belizean (60)	83	<0.01
Bermudan (60)	109	<0.01
British West Indian (107)	115	<0.01
Dutch West Indian (82)	327	0.01
Haitian (216)	453	0.02
Jamaican (610)	962	0.03
Trinidadian/Tobagonian (41)	69	<0.01
U.S. Virgin Islander (0)	12	<0.01
West Indian (76)	101	<0.01
Other West Indian (30)	40	<0.01
Yugoslavian (732)	1,687	0.06

Hispanic Origin	Population	%
Hispanic or Latino (of any race)	81,481	2.75
Central American, ex. Mexican	8,343	0.28
Costa Rican	317	0.01
Guatemalan	2,978	0.10
Honduran	2,448	0.08
Nicaraguan	700	0.02
Panamanian	670	0.02
Salvadoran	1,174	0.04
Other Central American	56	<0.01
Cuban	2,063	0.07
Dominican Republic	733	0.02
Mexican	52,459	1.77
Puerto Rican	5,888	0.20
South American	2,833	0.10
Argentinean	276	0.01
Bolivian	87	<0.01
Chilean	146	<0.01
Colombian	1,025	0.03
Ecuadorian	298	0.01
Paraguayan	37	<0.01
Peruvian	473	0.02
Uruguayan	49	<0.01
Venezuelan	412	0.01
Other South American	30	<0.01
Other Hispanic or Latino	9,162	0.31

Race*	Population	%
African-American/Black (1,098,385)	1,115,801	37.60
Not Hispanic (1,093,512)	1,109,300	37.38
Hispanic (4,873)	6,501	0.22
American Indian/Alaska Native (15,030)	25,910	0.87
Not Hispanic (13,845)	23,657	0.80
Hispanic (1,185)	2,253	0.08
Alaska Athabascan *(Ala. Nat.)* (22)	32	<0.01
Aleut *(Alaska Native)* (17)	26	<0.01
Apache (107)	266	0.01
Arapaho (1)	5	<0.01
Blackfeet (53)	305	0.01
Canadian/French Am. Ind. (26)	60	<0.01
Central American Ind. (38)	83	<0.01
Cherokee (947)	3,431	0.12
Cheyenne (13)	37	<0.01
Chickasaw (100)	272	0.01
Chippewa (87)	171	0.01
Choctaw (7,539)	9,260	0.31
Colville (5)	6	<0.01
Comanche (20)	50	<0.01
Cree (6)	18	<0.01
Creek (171)	359	0.01
Crow (9)	20	<0.01
Delaware (11)	21	<0.01
Hopi (1)	3	<0.01
Houma (270)	393	0.01
Inupiat *(Alaska Native)* (11)	23	<0.01
Iroquois (41)	119	<0.01
Kiowa (5)	14	<0.01
Lumbee (37)	54	<0.01
Menominee (2)	10	<0.01
Mexican American Ind. (308)	448	0.02
Navajo (87)	163	0.01
Osage (18)	38	<0.01
Ottawa (11)	26	<0.01
Paiute (7)	7	<0.01
Pima (6)	9	<0.01
Potawatomi (49)	76	<0.01
Pueblo (15)	32	<0.01
Puget Sound Salish (25)	35	<0.01
Seminole (57)	123	<0.01
Shoshone (6)	9	<0.01
Sioux (131)	287	0.01
South American Ind. (16)	47	<0.01
Spanish American Ind. (18)	48	<0.01
Tlingit-Haida *(Alaska Native)* (8)	19	<0.01
Tohono O'Odham (3)	6	<0.01
Tsimshian *(Alaska Native)* (0)	2	<0.01
Ute (2)	2	<0.01
Yakama (3)	6	<0.01
Yaqui (15)	24	<0.01
Yuman (6)	7	<0.01
Yup'ik *(Alaska Native)* (5)	5	<0.01
Asian (25,742)	32,560	1.10
Not Hispanic (25,477)	31,595	1.06
Hispanic (265)	965	0.03
Bangladeshi (116)	126	<0.01
Burmese (35)	37	<0.01
Cambodian (237)	302	0.01
Chinese, ex. Taiwanese (4,317)	5,168	0.17
Filipino (3,562)	5,638	0.19
Hmong (29)	50	<0.01
Indian (5,494)	6,458	0.22
Indonesian (80)	129	<0.01
Japanese (807)	1,752	0.06
Korean (1,537)	2,301	0.08
Laotian (228)	285	0.01
Malaysian (40)	65	<0.01
Nepalese (77)	88	<0.01
Pakistani (449)	546	0.02
Sri Lankan (96)	109	<0.01
Taiwanese (150)	172	0.01
Thai (465)	703	0.02
Vietnamese (7,025)	7,721	0.26
Hawaii Native/Pacific Islander (1,187)	2,776	0.09
Not Hispanic (948)	2,155	0.07
Hispanic (239)	621	0.02
Fijian (5)	12	<0.01
Guamanian/Chamorro (560)	817	0.03
Marshallese (12)	18	<0.01
Native Hawaiian (252)	699	0.02
Samoan (135)	329	0.01
Tongan (5)	16	<0.01
White (1,754,684)	1,782,807	60.08
Not Hispanic (1,722,287)	1,745,642	58.83
Hispanic (32,397)	37,165	1.25

*Notes: † The Census 2010 population figure is used to calculate the percentages in the Hispanic Origin and Race categories. Ancestry percentages are based on the 2006-2010 American Community Survey population (not shown); ‡ Numbers in parentheses indicate the number of people reporting a single ancestry; * Numbers in parentheses indicate the number of persons reporting this race alone, not in combination with any other race; Please refer to the Explanation of Data for more information.*

Bay St. Louis

Place Type: City
County: Hancock
Population: 9,260†

Ancestry‡	Population	%
African, Sub-Saharan (18)	18	0.19
African (18)	18	0.19
American (396)	396	4.24
Austrian (0)	31	0.33
British (0)	103	1.10
Danish (11)	197	2.11
Dutch (0)	44	0.47
English (751)	1,305	13.96
European (69)	69	0.74
French, ex. Basque (794)	1,637	17.51
French Canadian (10)	22	0.24
German (565)	1,288	13.78
Greek (17)	35	0.37
Irish (663)	1,286	13.76
Italian (216)	470	5.03
Norwegian (35)	48	0.51
Scotch-Irish (126)	203	2.17
Scottish (0)	47	0.50
Swedish (0)	147	1.57
Swiss (17)	43	0.46
Welsh (16)	16	0.17

Hispanic Origin	Population	%
Hispanic or Latino (of any race)	332	3.59
Central American, ex. Mexican	58	0.63
Costa Rican	1	0.01
Guatemalan	4	0.04
Honduran	34	0.37
Nicaraguan	14	0.15
Panamanian	2	0.02
Salvadoran	2	0.02
Other Central American	1	0.01
Cuban	18	0.19
Dominican Republic	9	0.10
Mexican	118	1.27
Puerto Rican	94	1.02
South American	4	0.04
Ecuadorian	1	0.01
Peruvian	3	0.03
Other Hispanic or Latino	31	0.33

Race*	Population	%
African-American/Black (1,175)	1,294	13.97
Not Hispanic (1,151)	1,261	13.62
Hispanic (24)	33	0.36
American Indian/Alaska Native (30)	91	0.98
Not Hispanic (28)	85	0.92
Hispanic (2)	6	0.06
Aleut *(Alaska Native)* (1)	1	0.01
Arapaho (0)	2	0.02
Cherokee (5)	13	0.14
Chickasaw (0)	1	0.01
Chippewa (1)	1	0.01
Choctaw (3)	16	0.17
Creek (1)	1	0.01
Houma (5)	5	0.05
Mexican American Ind. (0)	1	0.01
Navajo (1)	1	0.01
Paiute (1)	1	0.01
Seminole (1)	2	0.02
Sioux (1)	1	0.01
Yaqui (0)	1	0.01
Asian (108)	141	1.52
Not Hispanic (108)	140	1.51
Hispanic (0)	1	0.01
Chinese, ex. Taiwanese (8)	12	0.13
Filipino (19)	29	0.31
Indian (24)	27	0.29
Indonesian (1)	1	0.01
Japanese (6)	15	0.16
Korean (8)	10	0.11
Pakistani (1)	1	0.01
Taiwanese (1)	2	0.02
Thai (1)	6	0.06
Vietnamese (27)	31	0.33
Hawaii Native/Pacific Islander (5)	11	0.12
Not Hispanic (5)	11	0.12
Guamanian/Chamorro (0)	1	0.01
Samoan (2)	6	0.06
Tongan (1)	1	0.01
White (7,656)	7,836	84.62
Not Hispanic (7,437)	7,607	82.15
Hispanic (219)	229	2.47

Biloxi

Place Type: City
County: Harrison
Population: 44,054†

Ancestry‡	Population	%
African, Sub-Saharan (175)	209	0.48
African (175)	209	0.48
Albanian (10)	10	0.02
American (3,184)	3,184	7.25
Arab (93)	131	0.30
Egyptian (11)	11	0.03
Lebanese (82)	102	0.23
Moroccan (0)	18	0.04
Austrian (12)	217	0.49
Belgian (15)	28	0.06
Brazilian (38)	38	0.09
British (181)	260	0.59
Cajun (22)	95	0.22
Canadian (34)	112	0.26
Croatian (159)	320	0.73
Czech (40)	80	0.18
Czechoslovakian (9)	9	0.02
Danish (0)	69	0.16
Dutch (89)	389	0.89
English (1,949)	4,029	9.17
European (474)	534	1.22
Finnish (18)	38	0.09
French, ex. Basque (1,180)	3,788	8.62
French Canadian (330)	623	1.42
German (1,763)	4,646	10.58
Greek (79)	157	0.36
Hungarian (88)	135	0.31
Icelander (27)	27	0.06
Irish (1,875)	5,475	12.47
Italian (835)	2,863	6.52
Lithuanian (13)	28	0.06
Northern European (17)	17	0.04
Norwegian (89)	162	0.37
Polish (136)	673	1.53
Portuguese (0)	26	0.06
Russian (63)	215	0.49
Scandinavian (48)	86	0.20
Scotch-Irish (435)	1,029	2.34
Scottish (315)	773	1.76
Slavic (50)	216	0.49
Slovak (31)	62	0.14
Slovene (12)	12	0.03
Swedish (53)	240	0.55
Swiss (0)	58	0.13
Ukrainian (16)	104	0.24
Welsh (245)	348	0.79
West Indian, ex. Hispanic (159)	211	0.48
Jamaican (159)	197	0.45
West Indian (0)	14	0.03
Yugoslavian (94)	650	1.48

Hispanic Origin	Population	%
Hispanic or Latino (of any race)	3,847	8.73
Central American, ex. Mexican	655	1.49
Costa Rican	15	0.03
Guatemalan	244	0.55
Honduran	195	0.44
Nicaraguan	71	0.16
Panamanian	48	0.11
Salvadoran	72	0.16
Other Central American	10	0.02
Cuban	99	0.22
Dominican Republic	43	0.10
Mexican	2,107	4.78
Puerto Rican	382	0.87
South American	256	0.58
Argentinean	10	0.02
Bolivian	5	0.01
Chilean	12	0.03
Colombian	81	0.18
Ecuadorian	41	0.09
Peruvian	78	0.18
Uruguayan	6	0.01
Venezuelan	23	0.05
Other Hispanic or Latino	305	0.69

Race*	Population	%
African-American/Black (8,632)	9,209	20.90
Not Hispanic (8,491)	9,005	20.44
Hispanic (141)	204	0.46
American Indian/Alaska Native (221)	534	1.21
Not Hispanic (160)	426	0.97
Hispanic (61)	108	0.25
Alaska Athabascan *(Ala. Nat.)* (2)	3	0.01
Apache (6)	10	0.02
Blackfeet (5)	11	0.02
Canadian/French Am. Ind. (0)	1	<0.01
Cherokee (22)	89	0.20
Chippewa (2)	2	<0.01
Choctaw (8)	45	0.10
Comanche (6)	8	0.02
Cree (0)	1	<0.01
Creek (6)	17	0.04
Houma (5)	10	0.02
Inupiat *(Alaska Native)* (0)	1	<0.01
Iroquois (4)	13	0.03
Lumbee (5)	5	0.01
Menominee (0)	3	0.01
Mexican American Ind. (19)	24	0.05
Navajo (3)	3	0.01
Osage (1)	1	<0.01
Potawatomi (7)	9	0.02
Sioux (12)	15	0.03
South American Ind. (0)	2	<0.01
Yakama (1)	1	<0.01
Asian (1,951)	2,408	5.47
Not Hispanic (1,923)	2,339	5.31
Hispanic (28)	69	0.16
Bangladeshi (4)	7	0.02
Burmese (2)	3	0.01
Cambodian (14)	19	0.04
Chinese, ex. Taiwanese (123)	193	0.44
Filipino (324)	489	1.11
Hmong (2)	2	<0.01
Indian (84)	111	0.25
Indonesian (10)	12	0.03
Japanese (81)	147	0.33
Korean (119)	198	0.45
Laotian (22)	27	0.06
Pakistani (10)	11	0.02
Taiwanese (2)	5	0.01
Thai (36)	64	0.15
Vietnamese (1,034)	1,096	2.49
Hawaii Native/Pacific Islander (108)	206	0.47
Not Hispanic (84)	171	0.39
Hispanic (24)	35	0.08
Fijian (1)	1	<0.01
Guamanian/Chamorro (67)	85	0.19
Marshallese (3)	3	0.01
Native Hawaiian (22)	43	0.10
Samoan (5)	27	0.06
Tongan (0)	1	<0.01
White (30,129)	31,277	71.00
Not Hispanic (28,402)	29,328	66.57
Hispanic (1,727)	1,949	4.42

Booneville

Place Type: City
County: Prentiss
Population: 8,743†

*Notes: † The Census 2010 population figure is used to calculate the percentages in the Hispanic Origin and Race categories. Ancestry percentages are based on the 2006-2010 American Community Survey population (not shown); ‡ Numbers in parentheses indicate the number of people reporting a single ancestry; * Numbers in parentheses indicate the number of persons reporting this race alone, not in combination with any other race; Please refer to the Explanation of Data for more information.*

Ancestry‡	Population	%
American (1,027)	1,027	11.73
Arab (8)	8	0.09
Egyptian (8)	8	0.09
Danish (0)	17	0.19
Dutch (39)	80	0.91
English (463)	1,132	12.93
European (55)	55	0.63
French, ex. Basque (16)	80	0.91
German (80)	683	7.80
Irish (923)	1,643	18.77
Italian (16)	73	0.83
Polish (10)	106	1.21
Portuguese (13)	13	0.15
Scotch-Irish (184)	207	2.36
Scottish (20)	159	1.82
Swedish (0)	38	0.43
Welsh (0)	13	0.15

Hispanic Origin	Population	%
Hispanic or Latino (of any race)	165	1.89
Central American, ex. Mexican	43	0.49
Guatemalan	26	0.30
Honduran	2	0.02
Nicaraguan	2	0.02
Panamanian	3	0.03
Salvadoran	10	0.11
Dominican Republic	5	0.06
Mexican	89	1.02
Puerto Rican	9	0.10
South American	3	0.03
Colombian	2	0.02
Peruvian	1	0.01
Other Hispanic or Latino	16	0.18

Race*	Population	%
African-American/Black (1,771)	1,845	21.10
Not Hispanic (1,767)	1,833	20.97
Hispanic (4)	12	0.14
American Indian/Alaska Native (25)	47	0.54
Not Hispanic (10)	31	0.35
Hispanic (15)	16	0.18
Central American Ind. (6)	6	0.07
Cherokee (4)	18	0.21
Chickasaw (0)	1	0.01
Choctaw (1)	5	0.06
Mexican American Ind. (7)	7	0.08
Pima (0)	1	0.01
South American Ind. (1)	2	0.02
Asian (14)	26	0.30
Not Hispanic (14)	23	0.26
Hispanic (0)	3	0.03
Chinese, ex. Taiwanese (5)	6	0.07
Filipino (4)	5	0.06
Indian (1)	7	0.08
Japanese (3)	3	0.03
Korean (1)	3	0.03
Pakistani (0)	1	0.01
Taiwanese (0)	1	0.01
Hawaii Native/Pacific Islander (3)	5	0.06
Not Hispanic (2)	3	0.03
Hispanic (1)	2	0.02
Guamanian/Chamorro (3)	3	0.03
Native Hawaiian (0)	1	0.01
White (6,736)	6,832	78.14
Not Hispanic (6,678)	6,770	77.43
Hispanic (58)	62	0.71

Brandon

Place Type: City
County: Rankin
Population: 21,705†

Ancestry‡	Population	%
African, Sub-Saharan (48)	48	0.23
African (48)	48	0.23
American (2,764)	2,764	13.12
Arab (0)	41	0.19
Lebanese (0)	19	0.09
Moroccan (0)	11	0.05
Other Arab (0)	11	0.05
Bulgarian (0)	36	0.17
Canadian (0)	9	0.04
Czechoslovakian (16)	44	0.21
Danish (13)	13	0.06
Dutch (4)	198	0.94
English (1,266)	2,869	13.62
European (243)	243	1.15
Finnish (0)	6	0.03
French, ex. Basque (148)	648	3.08
French Canadian (13)	48	0.23
German (402)	1,784	8.47
Greek (0)	20	0.09
Hungarian (11)	36	0.17
Irish (1,348)	2,957	14.03
Italian (170)	752	3.57
Lithuanian (12)	12	0.06
Maltese (0)	32	0.15
Norwegian (47)	138	0.65
Polish (27)	118	0.56
Romanian (27)	27	0.13
Russian (24)	24	0.11
Scotch-Irish (549)	816	3.87
Scottish (382)	580	2.75
Swedish (0)	135	0.64
Welsh (43)	188	0.89
West Indian, ex. Hispanic (22)	22	0.10
Haitian (22)	22	0.10

Hispanic Origin	Population	%
Hispanic or Latino (of any race)	358	1.65
Central American, ex. Mexican	64	0.29
Costa Rican	4	0.02
Guatemalan	18	0.08
Honduran	20	0.09
Nicaraguan	11	0.05
Panamanian	1	<0.01
Salvadoran	10	0.05
Cuban	6	0.03
Mexican	185	0.85
Puerto Rican	38	0.18
South American	26	0.12
Argentinean	2	0.01
Bolivian	2	0.01
Chilean	2	0.01
Colombian	4	0.02
Ecuadorian	1	<0.01
Peruvian	11	0.05
Uruguayan	1	<0.01
Venezuelan	3	0.01
Other Hispanic or Latino	39	0.18

Race*	Population	%
African-American/Black (3,659)	3,757	17.31
Not Hispanic (3,638)	3,729	17.18
Hispanic (21)	28	0.13
American Indian/Alaska Native (39)	88	0.41
Not Hispanic (36)	82	0.38
Hispanic (3)	6	0.03
Apache (1)	2	0.01
Cherokee (6)	11	0.05
Chickasaw (3)	3	0.01
Chippewa (1)	3	0.01
Choctaw (6)	7	0.03
Navajo (0)	1	<0.01
Puget Sound Salish (4)	4	0.02
Sioux (1)	4	0.02
Tohono O'Odham (3)	3	0.01
Asian (213)	262	1.21
Not Hispanic (210)	257	1.18
Hispanic (3)	5	0.02
Chinese, ex. Taiwanese (31)	40	0.18
Filipino (20)	27	0.12
Indian (65)	73	0.34
Indonesian (3)	3	0.01
Japanese (9)	19	0.09
Korean (9)	13	0.06
Pakistani (1)	4	0.02
Thai (0)	1	<0.01
Vietnamese (65)	75	0.35
Hawaii Native/Pacific Islander (13)	15	0.07
Not Hispanic (13)	15	0.07
Guamanian/Chamorro (9)	9	0.04
Native Hawaiian (1)	4	0.02
Samoan (0)	1	<0.01
White (17,495)	17,641	81.28
Not Hispanic (17,282)	17,419	80.25
Hispanic (213)	222	1.02

Brookhaven

Place Type: City
County: Lincoln
Population: 12,513†

Ancestry‡	Population	%
African, Sub-Saharan (149)	149	1.18
African (149)	149	1.18
American (1,435)	1,435	11.37
Arab (15)	41	0.32
Syrian (15)	41	0.32
Dutch (13)	51	0.40
English (563)	1,048	8.31
European (103)	103	0.82
French, ex. Basque (124)	216	1.71
German (74)	283	2.24
Irish (297)	610	4.83
Italian (25)	143	1.13
Norwegian (0)	10	0.08
Scotch-Irish (61)	188	1.49
Scottish (19)	122	0.97
Swedish (0)	12	0.10
West Indian, ex. Hispanic (12)	12	0.10
Barbadian (12)	12	0.10

Hispanic Origin	Population	%
Hispanic or Latino (of any race)	118	0.94
Central American, ex. Mexican	9	0.07
Guatemalan	1	0.01
Honduran	3	0.02
Salvadoran	5	0.04
Cuban	4	0.03
Mexican	60	0.48
Puerto Rican	8	0.06
South American	3	0.02
Ecuadorian	1	0.01
Venezuelan	2	0.02
Other Hispanic or Latino	34	0.27

Race*	Population	%
African-American/Black (6,772)	6,876	54.95
Not Hispanic (6,747)	6,845	54.70
Hispanic (25)	31	0.25
American Indian/Alaska Native (10)	51	0.41
Not Hispanic (10)	48	0.38
Hispanic (0)	3	0.02
Blackfeet (0)	3	0.02
Cherokee (1)	14	0.11
Chippewa (0)	1	0.01
Choctaw (0)	2	0.02
Creek (4)	5	0.04
Asian (93)	120	0.96
Not Hispanic (93)	118	0.94
Hispanic (0)	2	0.02
Cambodian (0)	5	0.04
Chinese, ex. Taiwanese (28)	32	0.26
Filipino (8)	10	0.08
Indian (48)	50	0.40
Japanese (0)	15	0.12
Korean (3)	4	0.03
Vietnamese (0)	3	0.02
Hawaii Native/Pacific Islander (1)	3	0.02
Not Hispanic (1)	1	0.01
Hispanic (0)	2	0.02
Guamanian/Chamorro (0)	2	0.02
White (5,482)	5,566	44.48
Not Hispanic (5,421)	5,497	43.93
Hispanic (61)	69	0.55

*Notes: † The Census 2010 population figure is used to calculate the percentages in the Hispanic Origin and Race categories. Ancestry percentages are based on the 2006-2010 American Community Survey population (not shown); ‡ Numbers in parentheses indicate the number of people reporting a single ancestry; * Numbers in parentheses indicate the number of persons reporting this race alone, not in combination with any other race; Please refer to the Explanation of Data for more information.*

Byram

Place Type: City
County: Hinds
Population: 11,489†

Ancestry‡	Population	%
African, Sub-Saharan (28)	28	0.27
African (28)	28	0.27
American (858)	858	8.16
Arab (61)	61	0.58
Jordanian (12)	12	0.11
Other Arab (49)	49	0.47
Austrian (0)	14	0.13
British (0)	20	0.19
Dutch (16)	34	0.32
English (463)	696	6.62
Estonian (17)	17	0.16
European (72)	72	0.68
French, ex. Basque (39)	406	3.86
German (248)	588	5.59
Greek (12)	24	0.23
Hungarian (13)	13	0.12
Irish (447)	875	8.32
Italian (23)	172	1.64
Norwegian (26)	26	0.25
Polish (14)	28	0.27
Russian (8)	26	0.25
Scotch-Irish (236)	384	3.65
Scottish (24)	126	1.20
Swedish (0)	14	0.13
Welsh (21)	33	0.31

Hispanic Origin	Population	%
Hispanic or Latino (of any race)	122	1.06
Central American, ex. Mexican	8	0.07
Costa Rican	1	0.01
Guatemalan	2	0.02
Honduran	4	0.03
Panamanian	1	0.01
Cuban	8	0.07
Mexican	62	0.54
Puerto Rican	15	0.13
South American	10	0.09
Argentinean	2	0.02
Chilean	1	0.01
Colombian	4	0.03
Peruvian	1	0.01
Uruguayan	1	0.01
Venezuelan	1	0.01
Other Hispanic or Latino	19	0.17

Race*	Population	%
African-American/Black (5,990)	6,051	52.67
Not Hispanic (5,973)	6,030	52.48
Hispanic (17)	21	0.18
American Indian/Alaska Native (25)	57	0.50
Not Hispanic (22)	53	0.46
Hispanic (3)	4	0.03
Blackfeet (1)	2	0.02
Cherokee (4)	6	0.05
Choctaw (3)	6	0.05
Iroquois (0)	1	0.01
Seminole (0)	1	0.01
Asian (96)	112	0.97
Not Hispanic (93)	109	0.95
Hispanic (3)	3	0.03
Chinese, ex. Taiwanese (14)	20	0.17
Filipino (22)	25	0.22
Indian (28)	31	0.27
Japanese (1)	3	0.03
Korean (6)	7	0.06
Thai (3)	3	0.03
Vietnamese (18)	22	0.19
Hawaii Native/Pacific Islander (1)	1	0.01
Not Hispanic (1)	1	0.01
Guamanian/Chamorro (1)	1	0.01
White (5,247)	5,326	46.36
Not Hispanic (5,178)	5,250	45.70
Hispanic (69)	76	0.66

Canton

Place Type: City
County: Madison
Population: 13,189†

Ancestry‡	Population	%
African, Sub-Saharan (12)	12	0.09
African (12)	12	0.09
American (1,234)	1,234	9.44
British (15)	23	0.18
Dutch (0)	21	0.16
English (304)	430	3.29
European (75)	75	0.57
French, ex. Basque (0)	112	0.86
German (68)	243	1.86
Irish (172)	358	2.74
Italian (10)	86	0.66
Polish (10)	10	0.08
Portuguese (10)	10	0.08
Scotch-Irish (136)	176	1.35
Scottish (0)	46	0.35
Welsh (0)	19	0.15

Hispanic Origin	Population	%
Hispanic or Latino (of any race)	726	5.50
Central American, ex. Mexican	167	1.27
Costa Rican	1	0.01
Guatemalan	132	1.00
Honduran	21	0.16
Nicaraguan	5	0.04
Panamanian	3	0.02
Salvadoran	5	0.04
Cuban	6	0.05
Dominican Republic	2	0.02
Mexican	437	3.31
Puerto Rican	10	0.08
South American	4	0.03
Chilean	1	0.01
Peruvian	3	0.02
Other Hispanic or Latino	100	0.76

Race*	Population	%
African-American/Black (9,850)	9,895	75.02
Not Hispanic (9,818)	9,858	74.74
Hispanic (32)	37	0.28
American Indian/Alaska Native (26)	52	0.39
Not Hispanic (25)	41	0.31
Hispanic (1)	11	0.08
Choctaw (5)	5	0.04
Houma (3)	3	0.02
Mexican American Ind. (0)	1	0.01
Navajo (0)	1	0.01
Seminole (1)	1	0.01
Asian (81)	92	0.70
Not Hispanic (79)	84	0.64
Hispanic (2)	8	0.06
Chinese, ex. Taiwanese (20)	20	0.15
Filipino (13)	14	0.11
Indian (28)	28	0.21
Japanese (0)	3	0.02
Korean (10)	10	0.08
Laotian (2)	2	0.02
Nepalese (1)	1	0.01
Vietnamese (4)	4	0.03
Hawaii Native/Pacific Islander (8)	23	0.17
Not Hispanic (0)	2	0.02
Hispanic (8)	21	0.16
Guamanian/Chamorro (8)	19	0.14
Native Hawaiian (0)	2	0.02
Samoan (0)	1	0.01
White (2,573)	2,631	19.95
Not Hispanic (2,477)	2,513	19.05
Hispanic (96)	118	0.89

Clarksdale

Place Type: City
County: Coahoma
Population: 17,962†

Ancestry‡	Population	%
African, Sub-Saharan (131)	164	0.90
African (112)	112	0.61
Nigerian (19)	52	0.28
American (552)	552	3.02
Arab (35)	52	0.28
Lebanese (23)	40	0.22
Syrian (12)	12	0.07
British (0)	10	0.05
Dutch (30)	46	0.25
English (430)	604	3.30
European (7)	15	0.08
French, ex. Basque (17)	54	0.30
German (100)	296	1.62
Greek (17)	17	0.09
Irish (248)	560	3.06
Italian (231)	307	1.68
Norwegian (0)	16	0.09
Polish (70)	70	0.38
Scotch-Irish (239)	394	2.16
Scottish (131)	160	0.88
Swedish (9)	25	0.14
Swiss (0)	7	0.04
Welsh (0)	28	0.15
West Indian, ex. Hispanic (16)	16	0.09
Jamaican (16)	16	0.09

Hispanic Origin	Population	%
Hispanic or Latino (of any race)	168	0.94
Central American, ex. Mexican	21	0.12
Costa Rican	1	0.01
Guatemalan	20	0.11
Cuban	6	0.03
Mexican	73	0.41
Puerto Rican	34	0.19
South American	1	0.01
Venezuelan	1	0.01
Other Hispanic or Latino	33	0.18

Race*	Population	%
African-American/Black (14,184)	14,256	79.37
Not Hispanic (14,140)	14,198	79.04
Hispanic (44)	58	0.32
American Indian/Alaska Native (21)	42	0.23
Not Hispanic (18)	39	0.22
Hispanic (3)	3	0.02
Blackfeet (0)	1	0.01
Cherokee (0)	5	0.03
Chickasaw (0)	1	0.01
Choctaw (0)	2	0.01
Asian (102)	133	0.74
Not Hispanic (98)	118	0.66
Hispanic (4)	15	0.08
Bangladeshi (4)	4	0.02
Chinese, ex. Taiwanese (55)	62	0.35
Filipino (14)	17	0.09
Indian (15)	27	0.15
Japanese (0)	2	0.01
Korean (2)	8	0.04
Laotian (2)	2	0.01
Pakistani (2)	2	0.01
Vietnamese (7)	9	0.05
Hawaii Native/Pacific Islander (0)	7	0.04
Hispanic (0)	7	0.04
Guamanian/Chamorro (0)	4	0.02
Native Hawaiian (0)	1	0.01
White (3,496)	3,547	19.75
Not Hispanic (3,460)	3,506	19.52
Hispanic (36)	41	0.23

Cleveland

Place Type: City
County: Bolivar
Population: 12,334†

Ancestry‡	Population	%
African, Sub-Saharan (23)	23	0.18
Nigerian (15)	15	0.12
South African (8)	8	0.06

*Notes: † The Census 2010 population figure is used to calculate the percentages in the Hispanic Origin and Race categories. Ancestry percentages are based on the 2006-2010 American Community Survey population (not shown); ‡ Numbers in parentheses indicate the number of people reporting a single ancestry; * Numbers in parentheses indicate the number of persons reporting this race alone, not in combination with any other race; Please refer to the Explanation of Data for more information.*

American (1,755)	1,755	14.00
Australian (10)	10	0.08
British (34)	34	0.27
Dutch (0)	60	0.48
English (461)	753	6.01
European (10)	160	1.28
French, ex. Basque (0)	72	0.57
German (105)	461	3.68
Irish (551)	838	6.68
Italian (365)	418	3.33
Norwegian (0)	21	0.17
Polish (69)	69	0.55
Scotch-Irish (180)	247	1.97
Scottish (59)	139	1.11
Swedish (0)	55	0.44
Welsh (13)	13	0.10

Hispanic Origin	Population	%
Hispanic or Latino (of any race)	187	1.52
Central American, ex. Mexican	3	0.02
Honduran	3	0.02
Cuban	3	0.02
Mexican	136	1.10
Puerto Rican	9	0.07
South American	6	0.05
Colombian	4	0.03
Peruvian	2	0.02
Other Hispanic or Latino	30	0.24

Race*	Population	%
African-American/Black (6,189)	6,226	50.48
Not Hispanic (6,159)	6,195	50.23
Hispanic (30)	31	0.25
American Indian/Alaska Native (6)	38	0.31
Not Hispanic (5)	31	0.25
Hispanic (1)	7	0.06
Cherokee (0)	10	0.08
Choctaw (1)	11	0.09
Asian (118)	152	1.23
Not Hispanic (117)	149	1.21
Hispanic (1)	3	0.02
Bangladeshi (7)	7	0.06
Chinese, ex. Taiwanese (36)	43	0.35
Filipino (22)	27	0.22
Indian (32)	37	0.30
Japanese (1)	2	0.02
Korean (6)	7	0.06
Sri Lankan (2)	2	0.02
Thai (4)	6	0.05
Vietnamese (7)	11	0.09
Hawaii Native/Pacific Islander (10)	14	0.11
Not Hispanic (10)	14	0.11
Native Hawaiian (1)	3	0.02
Samoan (9)	9	0.07
White (5,859)	5,925	48.04
Not Hispanic (5,768)	5,825	47.23
Hispanic (91)	100	0.81

Clinton

Place Type: City
County: Hinds
Population: 25,216†

Ancestry‡	Population	%
African, Sub-Saharan (93)	93	0.37
African (93)	93	0.37
Alsatian (0)	15	0.06
American (1,820)	1,820	7.24
Arab (21)	44	0.18
Lebanese (21)	36	0.14
Syrian (0)	8	0.03
Australian (11)	35	0.14
Austrian (11)	11	0.04
Belgian (18)	18	0.07
British (73)	160	0.64
Bulgarian (40)	40	0.16
Cajun (15)	23	0.09
Canadian (22)	84	0.33
Celtic (28)	28	0.11
Czech (10)	37	0.15
Danish (0)	12	0.05
Dutch (66)	204	0.81
English (1,574)	2,821	11.22
European (85)	146	0.58
Finnish (14)	55	0.22
French, ex. Basque (276)	652	2.59
French Canadian (30)	63	0.25
German (481)	1,647	6.55
Greek (0)	14	0.06
Hungarian (0)	29	0.12
Iranian (17)	17	0.07
Irish (1,066)	2,478	9.86
Italian (240)	480	1.91
Latvian (0)	13	0.05
Norwegian (22)	78	0.31
Polish (42)	280	1.11
Portuguese (0)	60	0.24
Scandinavian (3)	3	0.01
Scotch-Irish (612)	1,046	4.16
Scottish (318)	742	2.95
Serbian (0)	5	0.02
Swedish (8)	59	0.23
Swiss (32)	32	0.13
Ukrainian (21)	110	0.44
Welsh (62)	156	0.62
West Indian, ex. Hispanic (13)	27	0.11
Jamaican (13)	27	0.11
Yugoslavian (36)	43	0.17

Hispanic Origin	Population	%
Hispanic or Latino (of any race)	373	1.48
Central American, ex. Mexican	37	0.15
Guatemalan	18	0.07
Honduran	13	0.05
Panamanian	1	<0.01
Salvadoran	5	0.02
Cuban	6	0.02
Dominican Republic	3	0.01
Mexican	244	0.97
Puerto Rican	22	0.09
South American	19	0.08
Argentinean	2	0.01
Colombian	2	0.01
Ecuadorian	5	0.02
Paraguayan	1	<0.01
Peruvian	1	<0.01
Uruguayan	1	<0.01
Venezuelan	7	0.03
Other Hispanic or Latino	42	0.17

Race*	Population	%
African-American/Black (8,542)	8,684	34.44
Not Hispanic (8,527)	8,666	34.37
Hispanic (15)	18	0.07
American Indian/Alaska Native (56)	146	0.58
Not Hispanic (47)	131	0.52
Hispanic (9)	15	0.06
Apache (0)	1	<0.01
Cherokee (4)	22	0.09
Chippewa (2)	3	0.01
Choctaw (8)	22	0.09
Creek (1)	2	0.01
Iroquois (0)	1	<0.01
Lumbee (0)	2	0.01
Mexican American Ind. (3)	3	0.01
Sioux (2)	2	0.01
Tlingit-Haida *(Alaska Native)* (1)	1	<0.01
Asian (1,029)	1,095	4.34
Not Hispanic (1,027)	1,093	4.33
Hispanic (2)	2	0.01
Bangladeshi (4)	4	0.02
Chinese, ex. Taiwanese (160)	167	0.66
Filipino (36)	46	0.18
Hmong (3)	3	0.01
Indian (622)	635	2.52
Indonesian (2)	2	0.01
Japanese (5)	10	0.04
Korean (39)	46	0.18
Laotian (0)	1	<0.01
Nepalese (14)	14	0.06
Pakistani (9)	14	0.06
Taiwanese (1)	1	<0.01
Thai (2)	7	0.03
Vietnamese (121)	124	0.49
Hawaii Native/Pacific Islander (6)	27	0.11
Not Hispanic (6)	23	0.09
Hispanic (0)	4	0.02
Guamanian/Chamorro (1)	2	0.01
Native Hawaiian (1)	7	0.03
Tongan (0)	1	<0.01
White (15,163)	15,351	60.88
Not Hispanic (14,982)	15,154	60.10
Hispanic (181)	197	0.78

Columbus

Place Type: City
County: Lowndes
Population: 23,640†

Ancestry‡	Population	%
African, Sub-Saharan (93)	111	0.47
African (84)	102	0.43
Nigerian (9)	9	0.04
American (1,683)	1,683	7.08
Arab (49)	89	0.37
Lebanese (49)	89	0.37
Austrian (0)	11	0.05
British (47)	62	0.26
Czech (16)	39	0.16
Danish (0)	42	0.18
Dutch (9)	101	0.42
English (1,132)	1,859	7.82
European (63)	70	0.29
French, ex. Basque (114)	260	1.09
French Canadian (54)	64	0.27
German (224)	741	3.12
Greek (0)	28	0.12
Hungarian (17)	40	0.17
Irish (739)	1,516	6.38
Italian (66)	149	0.63
Lithuanian (22)	36	0.15
Northern European (15)	15	0.06
Norwegian (25)	59	0.25
Polish (27)	86	0.36
Russian (0)	52	0.22
Scotch-Irish (353)	623	2.62
Scottish (381)	582	2.45
Swedish (60)	60	0.25
Swiss (22)	22	0.09
Ukrainian (0)	20	0.08
Welsh (0)	70	0.29
West Indian, ex. Hispanic (7)	7	0.03
Jamaican (7)	7	0.03

Hispanic Origin	Population	%
Hispanic or Latino (of any race)	337	1.43
Central American, ex. Mexican	28	0.12
Costa Rican	2	0.01
Guatemalan	9	0.04
Honduran	4	0.02
Nicaraguan	5	0.02
Panamanian	4	0.02
Salvadoran	4	0.02
Cuban	9	0.04
Mexican	193	0.82
Puerto Rican	28	0.12
South American	19	0.08
Argentinean	2	0.01
Bolivian	1	<0.01
Chilean	2	0.01
Colombian	6	0.03
Ecuadorian	2	0.01
Peruvian	4	0.02
Venezuelan	1	<0.01
Other South American	1	<0.01
Other Hispanic or Latino	60	0.25

*Notes: † The Census 2010 population figure is used to calculate the percentages in the Hispanic Origin and Race categories. Ancestry percentages are based on the 2006-2010 American Community Survey population (not shown); ‡ Numbers in parentheses indicate the number of people reporting a single ancestry; * Numbers in parentheses indicate the number of persons reporting this race alone, not in combination with any other race; Please refer to the Explanation of Data for more information.*

Race*	Population	%
African-American/Black (14,187)	14,350	60.70
Not Hispanic (14,136)	14,290	60.45
Hispanic (51)	60	0.25
American Indian/Alaska Native (42)	116	0.49
Not Hispanic (41)	111	0.47
Hispanic (1)	5	0.02
Aleut *(Alaska Native)* (2)	7	0.03
Apache (0)	1	<0.01
Blackfeet (0)	1	<0.01
Cherokee (1)	11	0.05
Chippewa (0)	1	<0.01
Choctaw (1)	7	0.03
Cree (0)	1	<0.01
Houma (1)	1	<0.01
Lumbee (0)	1	<0.01
Seminole (0)	1	<0.01
Shoshone (1)	1	<0.01
Sioux (0)	1	<0.01
South American Ind. (1)	1	<0.01
Yaqui (0)	2	0.01
Asian (164)	229	0.97
Not Hispanic (161)	218	0.92
Hispanic (3)	11	0.05
Bangladeshi (3)	3	0.01
Chinese, ex. Taiwanese (40)	47	0.20
Filipino (30)	39	0.16
Hmong (1)	1	<0.01
Indian (15)	22	0.09
Japanese (4)	15	0.06
Korean (21)	26	0.11
Malaysian (0)	1	<0.01
Nepalese (3)	3	0.01
Pakistani (16)	17	0.07
Taiwanese (1)	1	<0.01
Thai (7)	14	0.06
Vietnamese (20)	21	0.09
Hawaii Native/Pacific Islander (3)	13	0.05
Not Hispanic (3)	13	0.05
Guamanian/Chamorro (3)	3	0.01
Native Hawaiian (0)	1	<0.01
White (8,842)	9,036	38.22
Not Hispanic (8,718)	8,893	37.62
Hispanic (124)	143	0.60

Corinth

Place Type: City
County: Alcorn
Population: 14,573†

Ancestry‡	Population	%
American (2,079)	2,079	14.29
British (17)	32	0.22
Danish (0)	23	0.16
Dutch (0)	217	1.49
English (832)	1,778	12.22
European (181)	181	1.24
Finnish (8)	8	0.05
French, ex. Basque (70)	203	1.40
French Canadian (23)	23	0.16
German (241)	857	5.89
Irish (1,307)	2,420	16.63
Italian (308)	341	2.34
Norwegian (0)	36	0.25
Polish (22)	58	0.40
Russian (0)	14	0.10
Scotch-Irish (240)	335	2.30
Scottish (183)	365	2.51
Swedish (0)	38	0.26
Welsh (50)	204	1.40

Hispanic Origin	Population	%
Hispanic or Latino (of any race)	769	5.28
Central American, ex. Mexican	44	0.30
Costa Rican	1	0.01
Guatemalan	31	0.21
Honduran	4	0.03
Nicaraguan	1	0.01
Panamanian	3	0.02
Salvadoran	4	0.03
Cuban	6	0.04
Mexican	624	4.28
Puerto Rican	31	0.21
South American	8	0.05
Argentinean	5	0.03
Colombian	2	0.01
Ecuadorian	1	0.01
Other Hispanic or Latino	56	0.38

Race*	Population	%
African-American/Black (3,386)	3,488	23.93
Not Hispanic (3,374)	3,472	23.82
Hispanic (12)	16	0.11
American Indian/Alaska Native (30)	94	0.65
Not Hispanic (18)	79	0.54
Hispanic (12)	15	0.10
Blackfeet (0)	1	0.01
Cherokee (0)	21	0.14
Chickasaw (2)	2	0.01
Choctaw (2)	5	0.03
Comanche (2)	2	0.01
Creek (3)	3	0.02
Iroquois (0)	1	0.01
Mexican American Ind. (11)	13	0.09
Navajo (0)	1	0.01
Sioux (0)	1	0.01
Yaqui (1)	1	0.01
Asian (74)	92	0.63
Not Hispanic (74)	91	0.62
Hispanic (0)	1	0.01
Chinese, ex. Taiwanese (11)	11	0.08
Filipino (13)	22	0.15
Indian (23)	24	0.16
Indonesian (1)	1	0.01
Japanese (3)	7	0.05
Korean (4)	7	0.05
Thai (1)	1	0.01
Vietnamese (15)	15	0.10
Hawaii Native/Pacific Islander (6)	7	0.05
Not Hispanic (3)	4	0.03
Hispanic (3)	3	0.02
Guamanian/Chamorro (6)	6	0.04
Native Hawaiian (0)	1	0.01
White (10,408)	10,599	72.73
Not Hispanic (10,163)	10,313	70.77
Hispanic (245)	286	1.96

D'Iberville

Place Type: City
County: Harrison
Population: 9,486†

Ancestry‡	Population	%
African, Sub-Saharan (16)	16	0.18
African (16)	16	0.18
American (682)	682	7.66
Arab (0)	16	0.18
Lebanese (0)	16	0.18
Czech (0)	13	0.15
Czechoslovakian (72)	72	0.81
Danish (0)	16	0.18
Dutch (38)	90	1.01
English (448)	804	9.03
European (124)	124	1.39
French, ex. Basque (445)	1,267	14.23
French Canadian (13)	66	0.74
German (163)	709	7.96
Greek (13)	13	0.15
Hungarian (0)	12	0.13
Irish (195)	987	11.08
Italian (119)	409	4.59
Norwegian (0)	16	0.18
Polish (127)	295	3.31
Portuguese (0)	27	0.30
Russian (45)	53	0.60
Scotch-Irish (214)	494	5.55
Scottish (0)	78	0.88
Slavic (50)	392	4.40
Swedish (0)	13	0.15
Welsh (21)	44	0.49
West Indian, ex. Hispanic (0)	28	0.31
Trinidadian/Tobagonian (0)	28	0.31

Hispanic Origin	Population	%
Hispanic or Latino (of any race)	458	4.83
Central American, ex. Mexican	24	0.25
Costa Rican	2	0.02
Guatemalan	1	0.01
Honduran	3	0.03
Nicaraguan	8	0.08
Panamanian	7	0.07
Salvadoran	3	0.03
Cuban	48	0.51
Dominican Republic	4	0.04
Mexican	233	2.46
Puerto Rican	82	0.86
South American	16	0.17
Argentinean	1	0.01
Bolivian	2	0.02
Colombian	2	0.02
Ecuadorian	4	0.04
Peruvian	4	0.04
Venezuelan	3	0.03
Other Hispanic or Latino	51	0.54

Race*	Population	%
African-American/Black (1,490)	1,642	17.31
Not Hispanic (1,473)	1,612	16.99
Hispanic (17)	30	0.32
American Indian/Alaska Native (50)	122	1.29
Not Hispanic (41)	105	1.11
Hispanic (9)	17	0.18
Apache (4)	4	0.04
Blackfeet (1)	3	0.03
Canadian/French Am. Ind. (0)	1	0.01
Cherokee (12)	42	0.44
Chickasaw (3)	3	0.03
Chippewa (0)	4	0.04
Choctaw (3)	10	0.11
Comanche (1)	1	0.01
Iroquois (2)	2	0.02
Mexican American Ind. (0)	3	0.03
Asian (788)	879	9.27
Not Hispanic (780)	869	9.16
Hispanic (8)	10	0.11
Bangladeshi (2)	2	0.02
Chinese, ex. Taiwanese (36)	45	0.47
Filipino (63)	85	0.90
Indian (16)	21	0.22
Indonesian (0)	1	0.01
Japanese (6)	21	0.22
Korean (24)	31	0.33
Thai (11)	20	0.21
Vietnamese (609)	639	6.74
Hawaii Native/Pacific Islander (10)	22	0.23
Not Hispanic (10)	18	0.19
Hispanic (0)	4	0.04
Guamanian/Chamorro (7)	8	0.08
Native Hawaiian (0)	1	0.01
Samoan (0)	4	0.04
White (6,724)	6,989	73.68
Not Hispanic (6,451)	6,671	70.32
Hispanic (273)	318	3.35

Diamondhead

Place Type: CDP
County: Hancock
Population: 8,425†

Ancestry‡	Population	%
American (526)	526	6.63
British (33)	33	0.42
Cajun (8)	20	0.25
Canadian (12)	38	0.48
Czech (0)	13	0.16
Danish (12)	25	0.32
Dutch (22)	140	1.76

*Notes: † The Census 2010 population figure is used to calculate the percentages in the Hispanic Origin and Race categories. Ancestry percentages are based on the 2006-2010 American Community Survey population (not shown); ‡ Numbers in parentheses indicate the number of people reporting a single ancestry; * Numbers in parentheses indicate the number of persons reporting this race alone, not in combination with any other race; Please refer to the Explanation of Data for more information.*

English (365)	947	11.93
European (42)	75	0.95
French, ex. Basque (370)	943	11.88
French Canadian (40)	40	0.50
German (585)	1,493	18.81
Greek (0)	13	0.16
Hungarian (12)	12	0.15
Icelander (0)	16	0.20
Irish (650)	1,360	17.14
Italian (329)	537	6.77
Lithuanian (0)	12	0.15
Northern European (24)	24	0.30
Norwegian (75)	89	1.12
Polish (23)	157	1.98
Portuguese (0)	11	0.14
Romanian (0)	14	0.18
Russian (51)	59	0.74
Scotch-Irish (165)	217	2.73
Scottish (73)	156	1.97
Slavic (0)	10	0.13
Slovene (11)	11	0.14
Swedish (24)	49	0.62
Welsh (11)	55	0.69
West Indian, ex. Hispanic (10)	10	0.13
Bermudan (10)	10	0.13
Yugoslavian (241)	241	3.04

Hispanic Origin	**Population**	**%**
Hispanic or Latino (of any race)	278	3.30
Central American, ex. Mexican	74	0.88
Costa Rican	9	0.11
Guatemalan	8	0.09
Honduran	37	0.44
Nicaraguan	7	0.08
Panamanian	9	0.11
Salvadoran	4	0.05
Cuban	15	0.18
Dominican Republic	3	0.04
Mexican	72	0.85
Puerto Rican	27	0.32
South American	17	0.20
Chilean	2	0.02
Colombian	8	0.09
Ecuadorian	6	0.07
Peruvian	1	0.01
Other Hispanic or Latino	70	0.83

Race*	**Population**	**%**
African-American/Black (243)	274	3.25
Not Hispanic (237)	267	3.17
Hispanic (6)	7	0.08
American Indian/Alaska Native (34)	71	0.84
Not Hispanic (30)	60	0.71
Hispanic (4)	11	0.13
Blackfeet (0)	1	0.01
Cherokee (5)	18	0.21
Chickasaw (1)	1	0.01
Chippewa (0)	2	0.02
Choctaw (7)	9	0.11
Comanche (0)	1	0.01
Delaware (0)	1	0.01
Houma (4)	5	0.06
Iroquois (1)	2	0.02
Seminole (1)	3	0.04
Sioux (2)	4	0.05
South American Ind. (0)	2	0.02
Asian (92)	132	1.57
Not Hispanic (89)	124	1.47
Hispanic (3)	8	0.09
Chinese, ex. Taiwanese (15)	18	0.21
Filipino (22)	32	0.38
Indian (27)	31	0.37
Indonesian (2)	4	0.05
Japanese (9)	15	0.18
Korean (8)	14	0.17
Thai (2)	3	0.04
Vietnamese (5)	12	0.14
Hawaii Native/Pacific Islander (9)	14	0.17
Not Hispanic (8)	13	0.15
Hispanic (1)	1	0.01
Guamanian/Chamorro (1)	1	0.01
Native Hawaiian (5)	6	0.07
White (7,915)	8,013	95.11
Not Hispanic (7,692)	7,774	92.27
Hispanic (223)	239	2.84

Flowood

Place Type: City
County: Rankin
Population: 7,823†

Ancestry‡	**Population**	**%**
American (939)	939	12.38
Arab (93)	93	1.23
Lebanese (93)	93	1.23
Armenian (0)	11	0.15
Australian (13)	13	0.17
Austrian (0)	16	0.21
British (12)	12	0.16
Canadian (28)	28	0.37
Danish (0)	29	0.38
Dutch (14)	14	0.18
English (402)	698	9.20
European (67)	78	1.03
Finnish (0)	17	0.22
French, ex. Basque (117)	354	4.67
French Canadian (14)	14	0.18
German (364)	882	11.63
Greek (15)	47	0.62
Irish (275)	525	6.92
Italian (133)	205	2.70
Lithuanian (0)	12	0.16
Norwegian (25)	85	1.12
Polish (31)	61	0.80
Portuguese (27)	27	0.36
Russian (0)	25	0.33
Scotch-Irish (236)	398	5.25
Scottish (94)	163	2.15
Swedish (149)	149	1.96

Hispanic Origin	**Population**	**%**
Hispanic or Latino (of any race)	185	2.36
Central American, ex. Mexican	16	0.20
Costa Rican	1	0.01
Guatemalan	4	0.05
Honduran	7	0.09
Nicaraguan	4	0.05
Cuban	10	0.13
Dominican Republic	3	0.04
Mexican	86	1.10
Puerto Rican	22	0.28
South American	28	0.36
Argentinean	3	0.04
Chilean	1	0.01
Colombian	10	0.13
Peruvian	3	0.04
Uruguayan	1	0.01
Venezuelan	10	0.13
Other Hispanic or Latino	20	0.26

Race*	**Population**	**%**
African-American/Black (1,455)	1,505	19.24
Not Hispanic (1,444)	1,491	19.06
Hispanic (11)	14	0.18
American Indian/Alaska Native (15)	44	0.56
Not Hispanic (13)	37	0.47
Hispanic (2)	7	0.09
Blackfeet (0)	1	0.01
Cherokee (4)	9	0.12
Cheyenne (0)	1	0.01
Choctaw (2)	10	0.13
Kiowa (1)	4	0.05
Spanish American Ind. (1)	1	0.01
Asian (295)	323	4.13
Not Hispanic (295)	321	4.10
Hispanic (0)	2	0.03
Burmese (4)	4	0.05
Cambodian (0)	2	0.03
Chinese, ex. Taiwanese (90)	90	1.15
Filipino (30)	33	0.42
Indian (75)	85	1.09
Indonesian (1)	1	0.01
Japanese (2)	4	0.05
Korean (14)	19	0.24
Malaysian (1)	1	0.01
Pakistani (7)	7	0.09
Taiwanese (5)	6	0.08
Thai (2)	2	0.03
Vietnamese (54)	55	0.70
Hawaii Native/Pacific Islander (0)	2	0.03
Not Hispanic (0)	2	0.03
Native Hawaiian (0)	1	0.01
White (5,886)	5,966	76.26
Not Hispanic (5,787)	5,858	74.88
Hispanic (99)	108	1.38

Gautier

Place Type: City
County: Jackson
Population: 18,572†

Ancestry‡	**Population**	**%**
African, Sub-Saharan (1,087)	1,087	6.01
African (1,074)	1,074	5.94
Liberian (13)	13	0.07
American (1,724)	1,724	9.53
Arab (0)	15	0.08
Syrian (0)	15	0.08
Belgian (0)	10	0.06
British (53)	110	0.61
Canadian (16)	16	0.09
Croatian (22)	30	0.17
Danish (13)	63	0.35
Dutch (9)	70	0.39
English (663)	1,334	7.38
European (139)	139	0.77
Finnish (0)	56	0.31
French, ex. Basque (789)	1,249	6.91
French Canadian (12)	111	0.61
German (579)	1,432	7.92
Greek (0)	10	0.06
Hungarian (14)	14	0.08
Irish (624)	1,810	10.01
Italian (231)	438	2.42
New Zealander (13)	13	0.07
Norwegian (20)	30	0.17
Polish (24)	120	0.66
Portuguese (23)	41	0.23
Russian (0)	9	0.05
Scotch-Irish (298)	412	2.28
Scottish (32)	180	1.00
Slavic (0)	8	0.04
Slovak (0)	17	0.09
Swedish (52)	88	0.49
Turkish (16)	16	0.09
Ukrainian (8)	8	0.04
Welsh (49)	121	0.67
Yugoslavian (11)	11	0.06

Hispanic Origin	**Population**	**%**
Hispanic or Latino (of any race)	990	5.33
Central American, ex. Mexican	65	0.35
Costa Rican	3	0.02
Guatemalan	8	0.04
Honduran	25	0.13
Nicaraguan	7	0.04
Panamanian	11	0.06
Salvadoran	8	0.04
Other Central American	3	0.02
Cuban	24	0.13
Dominican Republic	35	0.19
Mexican	545	2.93
Puerto Rican	221	1.19
South American	35	0.19
Argentinean	2	0.01
Chilean	1	0.01
Colombian	6	0.03
Ecuadorian	8	0.04

*Notes: † The Census 2010 population figure is used to calculate the percentages in the Hispanic Origin and Race categories. Ancestry percentages are based on the 2006-2010 American Community Survey population (not shown); ‡ Numbers in parentheses indicate the number of people reporting a single ancestry; * Numbers in parentheses indicate the number of persons reporting this race alone, not in combination with any other race; Please refer to the Explanation of Data for more information.*

Peruvian	15	0.08
Venezuelan	3	0.02
Other Hispanic or Latino	65	0.35

Race*	Population	%
African-American/Black (6,012)	6,262	33.72
Not Hispanic (5,976)	6,191	33.34
Hispanic (36)	71	0.38
American Indian/Alaska Native (102)	221	1.19
Not Hispanic (98)	203	1.09
Hispanic (4)	18	0.10
Aleut *(Alaska Native)* (4)	4	0.02
Blackfeet (1)	7	0.04
Cherokee (11)	41	0.22
Chippewa (1)	1	0.01
Choctaw (35)	56	0.30
Cree (0)	1	0.01
Creek (9)	13	0.07
Iroquois (2)	2	0.01
Lumbee (2)	2	0.01
Navajo (0)	2	0.01
Ottawa (1)	1	0.01
Paiute (1)	1	0.01
Pueblo (1)	1	0.01
Sioux (0)	1	0.01
Spanish American Ind. (1)	1	0.01
Asian (274)	355	1.91
Not Hispanic (272)	346	1.86
Hispanic (2)	9	0.05
Cambodian (7)	8	0.04
Chinese, ex. Taiwanese (16)	23	0.12
Filipino (49)	86	0.46
Indian (43)	47	0.25
Indonesian (1)	1	0.01
Japanese (11)	19	0.10
Korean (8)	13	0.07
Laotian (2)	3	0.02
Malaysian (0)	1	0.01
Sri Lankan (0)	1	0.01
Taiwanese (2)	2	0.01
Thai (3)	9	0.05
Vietnamese (121)	141	0.76
Hawaii Native/Pacific Islander (8)	22	0.12
Not Hispanic (8)	20	0.11
Hispanic (0)	2	0.01
Guamanian/Chamorro (1)	3	0.02
Native Hawaiian (5)	10	0.05
Samoan (0)	1	0.01
White (11,355)	11,673	62.85
Not Hispanic (10,866)	11,138	59.97
Hispanic (489)	535	2.88

Greenville

Place Type: City
County: Washington
Population: 34,400†

Ancestry‡	Population	%
African, Sub-Saharan (363)	459	1.31
African (363)	459	1.31
American (995)	995	2.83
Arab (76)	96	0.27
Lebanese (50)	70	0.20
Syrian (26)	26	0.07
Assyrian/Chaldean/Syriac (3)	3	0.01
British (32)	32	0.09
Celtic (0)	6	0.02
Czech (0)	16	0.05
Danish (0)	11	0.03
Dutch (10)	86	0.24
English (932)	1,378	3.92
European (104)	104	0.30
French, ex. Basque (20)	326	0.93
French Canadian (18)	32	0.09
German (199)	846	2.41
Iranian (209)	209	0.59
Irish (377)	1,422	4.05
Italian (308)	626	1.78
Latvian (14)	14	0.04
Polish (14)	14	0.04
Portuguese (16)	16	0.05
Russian (47)	47	0.13
Scandinavian (0)	3	0.01
Scotch-Irish (202)	344	0.98
Scottish (129)	291	0.83
Swedish (5)	16	0.05
Ukrainian (17)	17	0.05
Welsh (0)	7	0.02
West Indian, ex. Hispanic (29)	29	0.08
Dutch West Indian (29)	29	0.08

Hispanic Origin	Population	%
Hispanic or Latino (of any race)	293	0.85
Central American, ex. Mexican	16	0.05
Guatemalan	6	0.02
Honduran	6	0.02
Nicaraguan	1	<0.01
Panamanian	2	0.01
Salvadoran	1	<0.01
Cuban	10	0.03
Dominican Republic	5	0.01
Mexican	162	0.47
Puerto Rican	29	0.08
South American	8	0.02
Argentinean	1	<0.01
Colombian	3	0.01
Ecuadorian	4	0.01
Other Hispanic or Latino	63	0.18

Race*	Population	%
African-American/Black (26,849)	26,986	78.45
Not Hispanic (26,750)	26,875	78.13
Hispanic (99)	111	0.32
American Indian/Alaska Native (52)	103	0.30
Not Hispanic (45)	91	0.26
Hispanic (7)	12	0.03
Canadian/French Am. Ind. (1)	1	<0.01
Cherokee (2)	7	0.02
Chippewa (0)	1	<0.01
Choctaw (1)	4	0.01
Cree (1)	1	<0.01
Iroquois (1)	1	<0.01
Mexican American Ind. (5)	5	0.01
Sioux (1)	1	<0.01
Asian (251)	286	0.83
Not Hispanic (251)	282	0.82
Hispanic (0)	4	0.01
Bangladeshi (4)	4	0.01
Chinese, ex. Taiwanese (87)	98	0.28
Filipino (20)	27	0.08
Indian (76)	79	0.23
Indonesian (1)	1	<0.01
Japanese (4)	5	0.01
Korean (14)	17	0.05
Malaysian (0)	1	<0.01
Pakistani (6)	6	0.02
Taiwanese (4)	4	0.01
Thai (5)	5	0.01
Vietnamese (21)	25	0.07
Hawaii Native/Pacific Islander (8)	17	0.05
Not Hispanic (5)	14	0.04
Hispanic (3)	3	0.01
Guamanian/Chamorro (5)	6	0.02
Native Hawaiian (3)	6	0.02
Samoan (0)	2	0.01
White (6,963)	7,088	20.60
Not Hispanic (6,894)	6,998	20.34
Hispanic (69)	90	0.26

Greenwood

Place Type: City
County: Leflore
Population: 15,205†

Ancestry‡	Population	%
African, Sub-Saharan (65)	65	0.41
African (65)	65	0.41
American (1,127)	1,127	7.10
Arab (106)	450	2.84
Lebanese (106)	278	1.75
Syrian (0)	172	1.08
British (31)	31	0.20
Canadian (20)	20	0.13
Celtic (10)	10	0.06
Dutch (9)	90	0.57
English (291)	601	3.79
European (4)	4	0.03
French, ex. Basque (17)	73	0.46
German (108)	303	1.91
Irish (349)	527	3.32
Italian (53)	162	1.02
Scotch-Irish (224)	309	1.95
Scottish (85)	249	1.57
Swedish (15)	15	0.09
Swiss (0)	11	0.07
West Indian, ex. Hispanic (6)	27	0.17
Jamaican (6)	27	0.17

Hispanic Origin	Population	%
Hispanic or Latino (of any race)	163	1.07
Central American, ex. Mexican	19	0.12
Costa Rican	1	0.01
Guatemalan	10	0.07
Honduran	1	0.01
Panamanian	1	0.01
Salvadoran	6	0.04
Cuban	4	0.03
Dominican Republic	1	0.01
Mexican	103	0.68
Puerto Rican	15	0.10
South American	1	0.01
Venezuelan	1	0.01
Other Hispanic or Latino	20	0.13

Race*	Population	%
African-American/Black (10,221)	10,304	67.77
Not Hispanic (10,182)	10,244	67.37
Hispanic (39)	60	0.39
American Indian/Alaska Native (22)	42	0.28
Not Hispanic (21)	40	0.26
Hispanic (1)	2	0.01
Blackfeet (0)	2	0.01
Central American Ind. (1)	1	0.01
Cherokee (0)	1	0.01
Chickasaw (0)	1	0.01
Choctaw (0)	1	0.01
Asian (135)	150	0.99
Not Hispanic (135)	150	0.99
Chinese, ex. Taiwanese (56)	58	0.38
Filipino (17)	24	0.16
Indian (46)	50	0.33
Korean (11)	12	0.08
Vietnamese (4)	5	0.03
Hawaii Native/Pacific Islander (2)	15	0.10
Not Hispanic (2)	9	0.06
Hispanic (0)	6	0.04
Native Hawaiian (0)	3	0.02
Samoan (1)	1	0.01
White (4,669)	4,724	31.07
Not Hispanic (4,623)	4,663	30.67
Hispanic (46)	61	0.40

Grenada

Place Type: City
County: Grenada
Population: 13,092†

Ancestry‡	Population	%
African, Sub-Saharan (66)	66	0.49
African (66)	66	0.49
American (1,148)	1,148	8.56
Arab (8)	8	0.06
Arab (8)	8	0.06
Austrian (31)	31	0.23
British (12)	12	0.09
Dutch (13)	162	1.21
English (337)	907	6.76

*Notes: † The Census 2010 population figure is used to calculate the percentages in the Hispanic Origin and Race categories. Ancestry percentages are based on the 2006-2010 American Community Survey population (not shown); ‡ Numbers in parentheses indicate the number of people reporting a single ancestry; * Numbers in parentheses indicate the number of persons reporting this race alone, not in combination with any other race; Please refer to the Explanation of Data for more information.*

European (68)	70	0.52
French, ex. Basque (79)	153	1.14
French Canadian (0)	18	0.13
German (168)	715	5.33
Guyanese (20)	20	0.15
Irish (518)	1,055	7.86
Italian (31)	87	0.65
Norwegian (14)	14	0.10
Pennsylvania German (7)	7	0.05
Polish (0)	30	0.22
Scotch-Irish (219)	286	2.13
Scottish (45)	84	0.63
Swedish (22)	22	0.16
Swiss (0)	24	0.18
West Indian, ex. Hispanic (13)	13	0.10
British West Indian (13)	13	0.10

Hispanic Origin	Population	%
Hispanic or Latino (of any race)	122	0.93
Central American, ex. Mexican	9	0.07
Costa Rican	1	0.01
Guatemalan	6	0.05
Nicaraguan	1	0.01
Salvadoran	1	0.01
Mexican	75	0.57
Puerto Rican	17	0.13
Other Hispanic or Latino	21	0.16

Race*	Population	%
African-American/Black (7,027)	7,094	54.19
Not Hispanic (6,998)	7,061	53.93
Hispanic (29)	33	0.25
American Indian/Alaska Native (24)	78	0.60
Not Hispanic (22)	74	0.57
Hispanic (2)	4	0.03
Blackfeet (0)	3	0.02
Cherokee (6)	26	0.20
Cheyenne (0)	1	0.01
Chickasaw (0)	2	0.02
Choctaw (6)	21	0.16
Creek (0)	2	0.02
Delaware (0)	1	0.01
Iroquois (0)	3	0.02
Osage (1)	1	0.01
Ute (1)	1	0.01
Asian (39)	59	0.45
Not Hispanic (39)	59	0.45
Chinese, ex. Taiwanese (16)	23	0.18
Filipino (6)	9	0.07
Indian (11)	12	0.09
Japanese (3)	5	0.04
Korean (3)	4	0.03
Vietnamese (0)	2	0.02
Hawaii Native/Pacific Islander (2)	6	0.05
Not Hispanic (0)	4	0.03
Hispanic (2)	2	0.02
Guamanian/Chamorro (2)	3	0.02
White (5,861)	5,946	45.42
Not Hispanic (5,799)	5,878	44.90
Hispanic (62)	68	0.52

Gulfport

Place Type: City
County: Harrison
Population: 67,793†

Ancestry‡	Population	%
African, Sub-Saharan (4,615)	5,081	7.67
African (4,577)	5,043	7.61
Other Sub-Saharan African (38)	38	0.06
American (4,429)	4,429	6.68
Arab (453)	589	0.89
Arab (0)	96	0.14
Egyptian (125)	125	0.19
Lebanese (299)	313	0.47
Syrian (0)	26	0.04
Other Arab (29)	29	0.04
Austrian (16)	54	0.08
Belgian (0)	35	0.05
British (141)	199	0.30
Cajun (100)	100	0.15
Canadian (50)	78	0.12
Celtic (0)	51	0.08
Croatian (24)	24	0.04
Czech (0)	15	0.02
Danish (0)	138	0.21
Dutch (139)	925	1.40
English (2,123)	5,362	8.09
European (156)	267	0.40
Finnish (9)	9	0.01
French, ex. Basque (1,292)	4,010	6.05
French Canadian (213)	325	0.49
German (1,649)	6,147	9.27
Greek (26)	166	0.25
Guyanese (33)	73	0.11
Hungarian (15)	176	0.27
Icelander (0)	7	0.01
Iranian (27)	27	0.04
Irish (2,181)	7,434	11.22
Italian (1,088)	2,439	3.68
Lithuanian (65)	106	0.16
Northern European (18)	18	0.03
Norwegian (120)	396	0.60
Pennsylvania German (10)	69	0.10
Polish (266)	968	1.46
Portuguese (89)	144	0.22
Russian (186)	231	0.35
Scandinavian (0)	47	0.07
Scotch-Irish (670)	1,413	2.13
Scottish (479)	953	1.44
Slavic (0)	25	0.04
Slovak (9)	87	0.13
Swedish (21)	206	0.31
Swiss (6)	20	0.03
Ukrainian (0)	14	0.02
Welsh (19)	271	0.41
West Indian, ex. Hispanic (126)	200	0.30
British West Indian (0)	8	0.01
Dutch West Indian (9)	9	0.01
Jamaican (89)	143	0.22
U.S. Virgin Islander (0)	12	0.02
West Indian (28)	28	0.04
Yugoslavian (50)	87	0.13

Hispanic Origin	Population	%
Hispanic or Latino (of any race)	3,519	5.19
Central American, ex. Mexican	640	0.94
Costa Rican	20	0.03
Guatemalan	101	0.15
Honduran	365	0.54
Nicaraguan	42	0.06
Panamanian	34	0.05
Salvadoran	71	0.10
Other Central American	7	0.01
Cuban	121	0.18
Dominican Republic	53	0.08
Mexican	1,819	2.68
Puerto Rican	396	0.58
South American	149	0.22
Argentinean	12	0.02
Bolivian	1	<0.01
Chilean	4	0.01
Colombian	65	0.10
Ecuadorian	30	0.04
Peruvian	25	0.04
Venezuelan	11	0.02
Other South American	1	<0.01
Other Hispanic or Latino	341	0.50

Race*	Population	%
African-American/Black (24,453)	25,395	37.46
Not Hispanic (24,266)	25,079	36.99
Hispanic (187)	316	0.47
American Indian/Alaska Native (263)	714	1.05
Not Hispanic (223)	632	0.93
Hispanic (40)	82	0.12
Alaska Athabascan *(Ala. Nat.)* (0)	1	<0.01
Apache (11)	16	0.02
Blackfeet (3)	26	0.04
Canadian/French Am. Ind. (2)	2	<0.01
Central American Ind. (3)	4	0.01
Cherokee (35)	156	0.23
Cheyenne (0)	3	<0.01
Chickasaw (1)	11	0.02
Chippewa (7)	22	0.03
Choctaw (21)	77	0.11
Colville (1)	1	<0.01
Comanche (0)	8	0.01
Creek (5)	7	0.01
Crow (1)	3	<0.01
Delaware (1)	1	<0.01
Houma (5)	5	0.01
Inupiat *(Alaska Native)* (0)	1	<0.01
Iroquois (6)	12	0.02
Lumbee (5)	6	0.01
Mexican American Ind. (7)	11	0.02
Navajo (6)	7	0.01
Ottawa (3)	10	0.01
Pima (3)	3	<0.01
Potawatomi (3)	3	<0.01
Seminole (1)	2	<0.01
Shoshone (0)	1	<0.01
Sioux (8)	15	0.02
South American Ind. (0)	2	<0.01
Spanish American Ind. (2)	7	0.01
Tlingit-Haida *(Alaska Native)* (2)	3	<0.01
Yuman (1)	1	<0.01
Asian (1,149)	1,613	2.38
Not Hispanic (1,134)	1,551	2.29
Hispanic (15)	62	0.09
Burmese (5)	5	0.01
Cambodian (14)	15	0.02
Chinese, ex. Taiwanese (90)	132	0.19
Filipino (438)	654	0.96
Hmong (0)	1	<0.01
Indian (72)	121	0.18
Indonesian (1)	6	0.01
Japanese (38)	101	0.15
Korean (50)	93	0.14
Laotian (2)	5	0.01
Malaysian (1)	3	<0.01
Pakistani (10)	17	0.03
Sri Lankan (1)	2	<0.01
Taiwanese (1)	1	<0.01
Thai (89)	105	0.15
Vietnamese (297)	345	0.51
Hawaii Native/Pacific Islander (94)	187	0.28
Not Hispanic (87)	156	0.23
Hispanic (7)	31	0.05
Guamanian/Chamorro (59)	82	0.12
Native Hawaiian (17)	51	0.08
Samoan (3)	11	0.02
White (38,544)	40,115	59.17
Not Hispanic (37,038)	38,301	56.50
Hispanic (1,506)	1,814	2.68

Hattiesburg

Place Type: City
County: Forrest
Population: 45,989†

Ancestry‡	Population	%
African, Sub-Saharan (295)	571	1.25
African (285)	561	1.23
Nigerian (10)	10	0.02
American (2,014)	2,014	4.41
Arab (38)	91	0.20
Jordanian (10)	10	0.02
Lebanese (28)	81	0.18
Australian (12)	12	0.03
Austrian (7)	7	0.02
Belgian (12)	12	0.03
British (149)	239	0.52
Cajun (10)	23	0.05
Canadian (0)	9	0.02
Celtic (0)	23	0.05
Croatian (0)	12	0.03
Czech (0)	45	0.10

*Notes: † The Census 2010 population figure is used to calculate the percentages in the Hispanic Origin and Race categories. Ancestry percentages are based on the 2006-2010 American Community Survey population (not shown); ‡ Numbers in parentheses indicate the number of people reporting a single ancestry; * Numbers in parentheses indicate the number of persons reporting this race alone, not in combination with any other race; Please refer to the Explanation of Data for more information.*

Czechoslovakian (4)	48	0.11
Danish (0)	81	0.18
Dutch (68)	164	0.36
English (1,802)	3,471	7.59
European (174)	248	0.54
French, ex. Basque (270)	1,270	2.78
French Canadian (17)	45	0.10
German (990)	2,988	6.54
Greek (17)	67	0.15
Hungarian (9)	66	0.14
Irish (1,092)	3,096	6.77
Italian (388)	918	2.01
Lithuanian (7)	39	0.09
Northern European (7)	7	0.02
Norwegian (41)	73	0.16
Polish (61)	219	0.48
Portuguese (13)	41	0.09
Romanian (0)	10	0.02
Russian (39)	87	0.19
Scandinavian (13)	71	0.16
Scotch-Irish (844)	1,198	2.62
Scottish (531)	1,263	2.76
Slavic (12)	20	0.04
Swedish (24)	212	0.46
Swiss (0)	19	0.04
Turkish (14)	50	0.11
Ukrainian (13)	13	0.03
Welsh (29)	111	0.24
West Indian, ex. Hispanic (10)	45	0.10
Dutch West Indian (0)	12	0.03
Jamaican (10)	33	0.07
Yugoslavian (0)	9	0.02

Hispanic Origin	Population	%
Hispanic or Latino (of any race)	1,996	4.34
Central American, ex. Mexican	149	0.32
Costa Rican	8	0.02
Guatemalan	40	0.09
Honduran	59	0.13
Nicaraguan	9	0.02
Panamanian	14	0.03
Salvadoran	14	0.03
Other Central American	5	0.01
Cuban	47	0.10
Dominican Republic	8	0.02
Mexican	1,457	3.17
Puerto Rican	78	0.17
South American	85	0.18
Argentinean	3	0.01
Bolivian	4	0.01
Chilean	3	0.01
Colombian	29	0.06
Ecuadorian	9	0.02
Peruvian	11	0.02
Venezuelan	26	0.06
Other Hispanic or Latino	172	0.37

Race*	Population	%
African-American/Black (24,391)	24,797	53.92
Not Hispanic (24,282)	24,641	53.58
Hispanic (109)	156	0.34
American Indian/Alaska Native (112)	314	0.68
Not Hispanic (85)	251	0.55
Hispanic (27)	63	0.14
Aleut *(Alaska Native)* (0)	1	<0.01
Apache (1)	1	<0.01
Blackfeet (1)	1	<0.01
Canadian/French Am. Ind. (1)	1	<0.01
Central American Ind. (1)	1	<0.01
Cherokee (3)	48	0.10
Cheyenne (0)	1	<0.01
Chickasaw (0)	3	0.01
Choctaw (15)	35	0.08
Comanche (1)	1	<0.01
Creek (6)	11	0.02
Crow (0)	1	<0.01
Hopi (1)	1	<0.01
Houma (3)	3	0.01
Inupiat *(Alaska Native)* (0)	2	<0.01
Mexican American Ind. (12)	13	0.03
Osage (0)	1	<0.01
Seminole (1)	1	<0.01
Shoshone (0)	1	<0.01
Sioux (2)	2	<0.01
South American Ind. (0)	1	<0.01
Spanish American Ind. (0)	12	0.03
Tlingit-Haida *(Alaska Native)* (0)	1	<0.01
Asian (435)	547	1.19
Not Hispanic (431)	527	1.15
Hispanic (4)	20	0.04
Burmese (3)	3	0.01
Cambodian (1)	1	<0.01
Chinese, ex. Taiwanese (111)	135	0.29
Filipino (34)	65	0.14
Indian (119)	136	0.30
Indonesian (1)	2	<0.01
Japanese (8)	22	0.05
Korean (37)	48	0.10
Laotian (1)	1	<0.01
Nepalese (15)	17	0.04
Pakistani (7)	8	0.02
Taiwanese (4)	4	0.01
Thai (4)	13	0.03
Vietnamese (59)	65	0.14
Hawaii Native/Pacific Islander (28)	53	0.12
Not Hispanic (18)	40	0.09
Hispanic (10)	13	0.03
Guamanian/Chamorro (10)	12	0.03
Native Hawaiian (7)	16	0.03
Samoan (6)	12	0.03
White (19,266)	19,745	42.93
Not Hispanic (18,615)	19,016	41.35
Hispanic (651)	729	1.59

Hernando

Place Type: City
County: DeSoto
Population: 14,090†

Ancestry‡	Population	%
African, Sub-Saharan (13)	13	0.10
African (13)	13	0.10
American (1,395)	1,395	10.53
Arab (9)	209	1.58
Lebanese (0)	100	0.75
Syrian (9)	109	0.82
Austrian (0)	29	0.22
Brazilian (92)	92	0.69
British (12)	51	0.38
Canadian (0)	7	0.05
Croatian (26)	50	0.38
Czechoslovakian (0)	18	0.14
Dutch (170)	342	2.58
English (721)	1,490	11.24
European (170)	193	1.46
French, ex. Basque (55)	192	1.45
French Canadian (39)	64	0.48
German (356)	1,113	8.40
Irish (736)	2,047	15.45
Italian (245)	501	3.78
Norwegian (13)	19	0.14
Polish (162)	273	2.06
Portuguese (0)	12	0.09
Scandinavian (0)	25	0.19
Scotch-Irish (156)	482	3.64
Scottish (193)	421	3.18
Welsh (16)	52	0.39
Yugoslavian (0)	22	0.17

Hispanic Origin	Population	%
Hispanic or Latino (of any race)	774	5.49
Central American, ex. Mexican	15	0.11
Guatemalan	4	0.03
Honduran	4	0.03
Nicaraguan	1	0.01
Panamanian	4	0.03
Salvadoran	2	0.01
Cuban	12	0.09
Dominican Republic	4	0.03
Mexican	682	4.84
Puerto Rican	11	0.08
South American	9	0.06
Argentinean	2	0.01
Colombian	6	0.04
Peruvian	1	0.01
Other Hispanic or Latino	41	0.29

Race*	Population	%
African-American/Black (1,842)	1,900	13.48
Not Hispanic (1,835)	1,887	13.39
Hispanic (7)	13	0.09
American Indian/Alaska Native (29)	66	0.47
Not Hispanic (28)	61	0.43
Hispanic (1)	5	0.04
Apache (4)	4	0.03
Cherokee (7)	20	0.14
Chickasaw (0)	2	0.01
Chippewa (3)	3	0.02
Choctaw (3)	5	0.04
Inupiat *(Alaska Native)* (1)	1	0.01
Sioux (3)	4	0.03
Asian (145)	193	1.37
Not Hispanic (144)	192	1.36
Hispanic (1)	1	0.01
Chinese, ex. Taiwanese (32)	45	0.32
Filipino (12)	27	0.19
Indian (69)	74	0.53
Japanese (9)	14	0.10
Korean (6)	17	0.12
Laotian (2)	3	0.02
Pakistani (1)	3	0.02
Thai (1)	4	0.03
Vietnamese (8)	12	0.09
Hawaii Native/Pacific Islander (3)	4	0.03
Not Hispanic (3)	3	0.02
Hispanic (0)	1	0.01
Native Hawaiian (3)	3	0.02
White (11,491)	11,633	82.56
Not Hispanic (11,171)	11,279	80.05
Hispanic (320)	354	2.51

Holly Springs

Place Type: City
County: Marshall
Population: 7,699†

Ancestry‡	Population	%
African, Sub-Saharan (15)	15	0.19
African (15)	15	0.19
American (667)	667	8.52
British (62)	62	0.79
English (191)	325	4.15
European (25)	25	0.32
French, ex. Basque (0)	117	1.49
German (191)	275	3.51
Irish (78)	212	2.71
Scotch-Irish (73)	125	1.60
Scottish (59)	59	0.75
Welsh (15)	15	0.19

Hispanic Origin	Population	%
Hispanic or Latino (of any race)	96	1.25
Central American, ex. Mexican	2	0.03
Panamanian	2	0.03
Cuban	2	0.03
Mexican	58	0.75
Puerto Rican	5	0.06
Other Hispanic or Latino	29	0.38

Race*	Population	%
African-American/Black (6,100)	6,133	79.66
Not Hispanic (6,069)	6,097	79.19
Hispanic (31)	36	0.47
American Indian/Alaska Native (13)	24	0.31
Not Hispanic (12)	21	0.27
Hispanic (1)	3	0.04
Blackfeet (0)	1	0.01
Central American Ind. (0)	1	0.01

*Notes: † The Census 2010 population figure is used to calculate the percentages in the Hispanic Origin and Race categories. Ancestry percentages are based on the 2006-2010 American Community Survey population (not shown); ‡ Numbers in parentheses indicate the number of people reporting a single ancestry; * Numbers in parentheses indicate the number of persons reporting this race alone, not in combination with any other race; Please refer to the Explanation of Data for more information.*

Cherokee (0)	4	0.05
Chickasaw (1)	1	0.01
Choctaw (0)	1	0.01
Mexican American Ind. (1)	1	0.01
Asian (14)	19	0.25
Not Hispanic (14)	17	0.22
Hispanic (0)	2	0.03
Chinese, ex. Taiwanese (1)	1	0.01
Indian (11)	12	0.16
Korean (2)	5	0.06
Hawaii Native/Pacific Islander (0)	3	0.04
Not Hispanic (0)	1	0.01
Hispanic (0)	2	0.03
Native Hawaiian (0)	2	0.03
White (1,488)	1,515	19.68
Not Hispanic (1,471)	1,493	19.39
Hispanic (17)	22	0.29

Horn Lake

Place Type: City
County: DeSoto
Population: 26,066†

Ancestry‡	Population	%
African, Sub-Saharan (31)	31	0.12
African (31)	31	0.12
American (2,244)	2,244	8.80
Arab (80)	91	0.36
Lebanese (0)	11	0.04
Other Arab (80)	80	0.31
Austrian (22)	22	0.09
British (0)	41	0.16
Cajun (0)	5	0.02
Czech (16)	16	0.06
Danish (0)	24	0.09
Dutch (0)	337	1.32
English (664)	1,419	5.57
European (164)	177	0.69
French, ex. Basque (295)	628	2.46
German (708)	2,354	9.23
Iranian (36)	36	0.14
Irish (1,209)	3,644	14.29
Italian (327)	778	3.05
Norwegian (61)	107	0.42
Polish (167)	309	1.21
Scotch-Irish (211)	485	1.90
Scottish (186)	479	1.88
Slovak (20)	20	0.08
Swedish (86)	111	0.44
Welsh (48)	58	0.23
West Indian, ex. Hispanic (12)	12	0.05
Dutch West Indian (12)	12	0.05

Hispanic Origin	Population	%
Hispanic or Latino (of any race)	2,093	8.03
Central American, ex. Mexican	103	0.40
Costa Rican	10	0.04
Guatemalan	15	0.06
Honduran	21	0.08
Nicaraguan	11	0.04
Panamanian	21	0.08
Salvadoran	25	0.10
Cuban	25	0.10
Dominican Republic	3	0.01
Mexican	1,701	6.53
Puerto Rican	62	0.24
South American	52	0.20
Argentinean	5	0.02
Bolivian	1	<0.01
Chilean	5	0.02
Colombian	16	0.06
Ecuadorian	13	0.05
Peruvian	6	0.02
Venezuelan	3	0.01
Other South American	3	0.01
Other Hispanic or Latino	147	0.56

Race*	Population	%
African-American/Black (8,565)	8,851	33.96
Not Hispanic (8,537)	8,791	33.73
Hispanic (28)	60	0.23
American Indian/Alaska Native (94)	238	0.91
Not Hispanic (66)	188	0.72
Hispanic (28)	50	0.19
Apache (0)	7	0.03
Blackfeet (0)	6	0.02
Canadian/French Am. Ind. (0)	1	<0.01
Cherokee (6)	49	0.19
Chickasaw (1)	2	0.01
Chippewa (1)	4	0.02
Choctaw (9)	23	0.09
Comanche (0)	2	0.01
Cree (1)	2	0.01
Creek (0)	1	<0.01
Delaware (0)	3	0.01
Iroquois (0)	3	0.01
Mexican American Ind. (7)	7	0.03
Potawatomi (1)	1	<0.01
Seminole (0)	2	0.01
Sioux (1)	1	<0.01
Spanish American Ind. (6)	9	0.03
Yaqui (1)	1	<0.01
Asian (263)	350	1.34
Not Hispanic (251)	329	1.26
Hispanic (12)	21	0.08
Burmese (4)	4	0.02
Cambodian (28)	31	0.12
Chinese, ex. Taiwanese (78)	84	0.32
Filipino (56)	93	0.36
Indian (30)	36	0.14
Japanese (4)	13	0.05
Korean (10)	24	0.09
Laotian (12)	13	0.05
Pakistani (11)	11	0.04
Sri Lankan (4)	5	0.02
Taiwanese (2)	2	0.01
Thai (8)	8	0.03
Vietnamese (8)	13	0.05
Hawaii Native/Pacific Islander (13)	28	0.11
Not Hispanic (11)	21	0.08
Hispanic (2)	7	0.03
Guamanian/Chamorro (3)	5	0.02
Native Hawaiian (4)	6	0.02
Samoan (1)	6	0.02
White (15,367)	15,884	60.94
Not Hispanic (14,664)	15,038	57.69
Hispanic (703)	846	3.25

Indianola

Place Type: City
County: Sunflower
Population: 10,683†

Ancestry‡	Population	%
African, Sub-Saharan (213)	213	1.96
African (213)	213	1.96
American (438)	438	4.02
British (0)	6	0.06
Dutch (0)	37	0.34
English (154)	262	2.41
European (9)	9	0.08
French, ex. Basque (0)	46	0.42
German (15)	120	1.10
Irish (177)	442	4.06
Italian (63)	96	0.88
Scotch-Irish (81)	127	1.17
Scottish (15)	21	0.19

Hispanic Origin	Population	%
Hispanic or Latino (of any race)	175	1.64
Central American, ex. Mexican	5	0.05
Nicaraguan	3	0.03
Panamanian	1	0.01
Salvadoran	1	0.01
Cuban	3	0.03
Mexican	110	1.03
Puerto Rican	10	0.09
Other Hispanic or Latino	47	0.44

Race*	Population	%
African-American/Black (8,480)	8,512	79.68
Not Hispanic (8,416)	8,446	79.06
Hispanic (64)	66	0.62
American Indian/Alaska Native (21)	38	0.36
Not Hispanic (21)	38	0.36
Cherokee (0)	1	0.01
Choctaw (2)	7	0.07
Asian (50)	55	0.51
Not Hispanic (50)	55	0.51
Chinese, ex. Taiwanese (28)	30	0.28
Indian (11)	12	0.11
Korean (5)	5	0.05
Vietnamese (5)	5	0.05
Hawaii Native/Pacific Islander (0)	4	0.04
Not Hispanic (0)	4	0.04
White (2,003)	2,037	19.07
Not Hispanic (1,972)	2,002	18.74
Hispanic (31)	35	0.33

Jackson

Place Type: City
County: Hinds
Population: 173,514†

Ancestry‡	Population	%
African, Sub-Saharan (1,798)	1,884	1.07
African (1,546)	1,624	0.93
Cape Verdean (9)	17	0.01
Ghanaian (137)	137	0.08
Nigerian (88)	88	0.05
Sudanese (18)	18	0.01
American (5,360)	5,360	3.05
Arab (273)	398	0.23
Arab (17)	17	0.01
Lebanese (256)	376	0.21
Palestinian (0)	5	<0.01
Australian (0)	11	0.01
Austrian (0)	26	0.01
Belgian (7)	30	0.02
British (231)	433	0.25
Cajun (0)	8	<0.01
Canadian (7)	17	0.01
Croatian (0)	15	0.01
Czech (10)	49	0.03
Danish (24)	67	0.04
Dutch (129)	413	0.24
Eastern European (7)	7	<0.01
English (3,003)	5,716	3.26
European (904)	1,060	0.60
Finnish (0)	69	0.04
French, ex. Basque (445)	1,353	0.77
French Canadian (35)	63	0.04
German (1,070)	3,795	2.16
Greek (18)	27	0.02
Hungarian (7)	49	0.03
Irish (2,358)	5,401	3.08
Israeli (9)	9	0.01
Italian (429)	965	0.55
Lithuanian (25)	25	0.01
Northern European (99)	99	0.06
Norwegian (56)	121	0.07
Polish (127)	343	0.20
Portuguese (43)	51	0.03
Romanian (0)	11	0.01
Russian (62)	129	0.07
Scandinavian (33)	143	0.08
Scotch-Irish (1,660)	2,496	1.42
Scottish (630)	1,416	0.81
Slovak (0)	40	0.02
Swedish (123)	224	0.13
Swiss (0)	62	0.04
Ukrainian (0)	7	<0.01
Welsh (144)	354	0.20
West Indian, ex. Hispanic (112)	361	0.21
Haitian (49)	269	0.15
Jamaican (50)	79	0.05
West Indian (13)	13	0.01

*Notes: † The Census 2010 population figure is used to calculate the percentages in the Hispanic Origin and Race categories. Ancestry percentages are based on the 2006-2010 American Community Survey population (not shown); ‡ Numbers in parentheses indicate the number of people reporting a single ancestry; * Numbers in parentheses indicate the number of persons reporting this race alone, not in combination with any other race; Please refer to the Explanation of Data for more information.*

Hispanic Origin	Population	%
Hispanic or Latino (of any race)	2,723	1.57
Central American, ex. Mexican	296	0.17
Costa Rican	7	<0.01
Guatemalan	54	0.03
Honduran	155	0.09
Nicaraguan	24	0.01
Panamanian	22	0.01
Salvadoran	34	0.02
Cuban	76	0.04
Dominican Republic	25	0.01
Mexican	1,694	0.98
Puerto Rican	169	0.10
South American	87	0.05
Argentinean	18	0.01
Bolivian	5	<0.01
Chilean	4	<0.01
Colombian	29	0.02
Ecuadorian	12	0.01
Paraguayan	2	<0.01
Peruvian	8	<0.01
Uruguayan	1	<0.01
Venezuelan	7	<0.01
Other South American	1	<0.01
Other Hispanic or Latino	376	0.22

Race*	Population	%
African-American/Black (137,716)	138,940	80.07
Not Hispanic (137,265)	138,363	79.74
Hispanic (451)	577	0.33
American Indian/Alaska Native (248)	732	0.42
Not Hispanic (232)	674	0.39
Hispanic (16)	58	0.03
Alaska Athabascan *(Ala. Nat.)* (1)	2	<0.01
Aleut *(Alaska Native)* (1)	1	<0.01
Apache (1)	18	0.01
Blackfeet (2)	20	0.01
Canadian/French Am. Ind. (1)	3	<0.01
Cherokee (26)	94	0.05
Cheyenne (0)	2	<0.01
Chickasaw (0)	2	<0.01
Chippewa (1)	2	<0.01
Choctaw (16)	71	0.04
Comanche (1)	1	<0.01
Creek (1)	10	0.01
Crow (0)	1	<0.01
Houma (3)	4	<0.01
Iroquois (0)	1	<0.01
Lumbee (1)	1	<0.01
Mexican American Ind. (1)	3	<0.01
Navajo (0)	5	<0.01
Pueblo (1)	3	<0.01
Seminole (1)	2	<0.01
Sioux (4)	14	0.01
Asian (676)	939	0.54
Not Hispanic (660)	880	0.51
Hispanic (16)	59	0.03
Bangladeshi (12)	12	0.01
Cambodian (1)	3	<0.01
Chinese, ex. Taiwanese (153)	200	0.12
Filipino (46)	83	0.05
Indian (261)	327	0.19
Indonesian (1)	1	<0.01
Japanese (16)	52	0.03
Korean (45)	68	0.04
Laotian (10)	10	0.01
Malaysian (0)	3	<0.01
Nepalese (3)	3	<0.01
Pakistani (21)	23	0.01
Taiwanese (7)	8	<0.01
Thai (3)	12	0.01
Vietnamese (60)	74	0.04
Hawaii Native/Pacific Islander (39)	130	0.07
Not Hispanic (18)	88	0.05
Hispanic (21)	42	0.02
Fijian (0)	1	<0.01
Guamanian/Chamorro (22)	35	0.02
Marshallese (0)	3	<0.01
Native Hawaiian (7)	34	0.02
Samoan (3)	12	0.01
White (31,961)	33,021	19.03
Not Hispanic (31,194)	32,094	18.50
Hispanic (767)	927	0.53

Laurel

Place Type: City
County: Jones
Population: 18,540†

Ancestry‡	Population	%
African, Sub-Saharan (192)	192	1.04
African (192)	192	1.04
American (1,362)	1,362	7.36
Arab (40)	40	0.22
Lebanese (40)	40	0.22
British (0)	10	0.05
Dutch (37)	65	0.35
English (433)	972	5.25
European (108)	108	0.58
French, ex. Basque (23)	123	0.66
French Canadian (47)	47	0.25
German (380)	763	4.12
Hungarian (13)	20	0.11
Icelander (0)	16	0.09
Irish (476)	925	5.00
Italian (32)	143	0.77
Norwegian (0)	13	0.07
Polish (0)	42	0.23
Russian (24)	24	0.13
Scotch-Irish (458)	590	3.19
Scottish (174)	345	1.86
Swedish (0)	16	0.09
Swiss (0)	37	0.20

Hispanic Origin	Population	%
Hispanic or Latino (of any race)	1,424	7.68
Central American, ex. Mexican	118	0.64
Costa Rican	1	0.01
Guatemalan	35	0.19
Honduran	9	0.05
Nicaraguan	9	0.05
Panamanian	61	0.33
Salvadoran	3	0.02
Cuban	28	0.15
Dominican Republic	1	0.01
Mexican	1,148	6.19
Puerto Rican	19	0.10
South American	9	0.05
Argentinean	4	0.02
Chilean	1	0.01
Colombian	1	0.01
Ecuadorian	1	0.01
Peruvian	1	0.01
Other South American	1	0.01
Other Hispanic or Latino	101	0.54

Race*	Population	%
African-American/Black (11,372)	11,507	62.07
Not Hispanic (11,330)	11,433	61.67
Hispanic (42)	74	0.40
American Indian/Alaska Native (20)	75	0.40
Not Hispanic (9)	41	0.22
Hispanic (11)	34	0.18
Blackfeet (0)	3	0.02
Cherokee (0)	17	0.09
Choctaw (4)	7	0.04
Creek (1)	1	0.01
Mexican American Ind. (2)	7	0.04
Navajo (0)	3	0.02
Sioux (2)	3	0.02
Spanish American Ind. (2)	2	0.01
Asian (128)	152	0.82
Not Hispanic (128)	140	0.76
Hispanic (0)	12	0.06
Chinese, ex. Taiwanese (37)	39	0.21
Filipino (12)	15	0.08
Indian (45)	49	0.26
Japanese (1)	3	0.02
Thai (3)	4	0.02
Vietnamese (27)	30	0.16
Hawaii Native/Pacific Islander (8)	24	0.13
Not Hispanic (3)	6	0.03
Hispanic (5)	18	0.10
Guamanian/Chamorro (1)	2	0.01
Native Hawaiian (1)	1	0.01
Samoan (6)	7	0.04
White (6,011)	6,151	33.18
Not Hispanic (5,517)	5,608	30.25
Hispanic (494)	543	2.93

Long Beach

Place Type: City
County: Harrison
Population: 14,792†

Ancestry‡	Population	%
African, Sub-Saharan (229)	229	1.55
African (229)	229	1.55
American (1,191)	1,191	8.06
Arab (0)	75	0.51
Lebanese (0)	75	0.51
Austrian (0)	12	0.08
Belgian (0)	21	0.14
British (97)	147	1.00
Cajun (0)	40	0.27
Canadian (15)	15	0.10
Croatian (12)	12	0.08
Czech (73)	73	0.49
Czechoslovakian (0)	13	0.09
Danish (28)	118	0.80
Dutch (39)	211	1.43
English (496)	1,659	11.23
European (355)	355	2.40
Finnish (11)	11	0.07
French, ex. Basque (206)	1,140	7.72
French Canadian (28)	102	0.69
German (711)	2,643	17.90
Greek (8)	8	0.05
Hungarian (14)	80	0.54
Iranian (13)	43	0.29
Irish (559)	2,263	15.32
Italian (474)	1,179	7.98
Lithuanian (0)	13	0.09
Northern European (33)	33	0.22
Norwegian (63)	121	0.82
Polish (92)	176	1.19
Portuguese (12)	12	0.08
Russian (39)	141	0.95
Scandinavian (0)	13	0.09
Scotch-Irish (184)	345	2.34
Scottish (81)	258	1.75
Slovak (0)	9	0.06
Swedish (60)	176	1.19
Swiss (0)	14	0.09
Welsh (15)	40	0.27
Yugoslavian (0)	51	0.35

Hispanic Origin	Population	%
Hispanic or Latino (of any race)	541	3.66
Central American, ex. Mexican	86	0.58
Costa Rican	3	0.02
Guatemalan	9	0.06
Honduran	44	0.30
Nicaraguan	12	0.08
Panamanian	12	0.08
Salvadoran	6	0.04
Cuban	13	0.09
Dominican Republic	14	0.09
Mexican	243	1.64
Puerto Rican	89	0.60
South American	14	0.09
Argentinean	2	0.01
Colombian	6	0.04
Ecuadorian	1	0.01
Peruvian	1	0.01
Venezuelan	4	0.03
Other Hispanic or Latino	82	0.55

*Notes: † The Census 2010 population figure is used to calculate the percentages in the Hispanic Origin and Race categories. Ancestry percentages are based on the 2006-2010 American Community Survey population (not shown); ‡ Numbers in parentheses indicate the number of people reporting a single ancestry; * Numbers in parentheses indicate the number of persons reporting this race alone, not in combination with any other race; Please refer to the Explanation of Data for more information.*

Race*	Population	%
African-American/Black (1,224)	1,328	8.98
Not Hispanic (1,207)	1,293	8.74
Hispanic (17)	35	0.24
American Indian/Alaska Native (71)	158	1.07
Not Hispanic (62)	138	0.93
Hispanic (9)	20	0.14
Apache (0)	3	0.02
Blackfeet (2)	2	0.01
Canadian/French Am. Ind. (0)	4	0.03
Cherokee (6)	27	0.18
Cheyenne (4)	4	0.03
Chickasaw (0)	1	0.01
Chippewa (3)	5	0.03
Choctaw (13)	32	0.22
Creek (2)	2	0.01
Houma (4)	7	0.05
Lumbee (2)	4	0.03
Menominee (0)	1	0.01
Mexican American Ind. (5)	5	0.03
Navajo (0)	4	0.03
Pueblo (0)	1	0.01
Sioux (1)	2	0.01
South American Ind. (0)	4	0.03
Asian (382)	486	3.29
Not Hispanic (377)	462	3.12
Hispanic (5)	24	0.16
Chinese, ex. Taiwanese (33)	38	0.26
Filipino (112)	163	1.10
Indian (16)	18	0.12
Indonesian (0)	2	0.01
Japanese (21)	39	0.26
Korean (12)	24	0.16
Pakistani (5)	5	0.03
Taiwanese (1)	1	0.01
Thai (2)	6	0.04
Vietnamese (172)	185	1.25
Hawaii Native/Pacific Islander (14)	23	0.16
Not Hispanic (11)	20	0.14
Hispanic (3)	3	0.02
Guamanian/Chamorro (6)	9	0.06
Native Hawaiian (6)	9	0.06
White (12,642)	12,901	87.22
Not Hispanic (12,358)	12,567	84.96
Hispanic (284)	334	2.26

Madison

Place Type: City
County: Madison
Population: 24,149†

Ancestry‡	Population	%
African, Sub-Saharan (14)	14	0.06
Nigerian (14)	14	0.06
American (3,373)	3,373	14.48
Arab (113)	209	0.90
Arab (31)	31	0.13
Lebanese (82)	135	0.58
Moroccan (0)	43	0.18
Armenian (0)	10	0.04
British (70)	143	0.61
Bulgarian (5)	5	0.02
Cajun (0)	22	0.09
Canadian (9)	37	0.16
Czech (0)	20	0.09
Danish (24)	24	0.10
Dutch (66)	155	0.67
Eastern European (11)	11	0.05
English (2,442)	4,373	18.77
European (424)	439	1.88
Finnish (0)	86	0.37
French, ex. Basque (248)	1,058	4.54
French Canadian (125)	233	1.00
German (397)	2,175	9.34
Greek (48)	199	0.85
Hungarian (0)	9	0.04
Iranian (13)	26	0.11
Irish (1,351)	3,152	13.53
Italian (234)	783	3.36
Northern European (12)	12	0.05
Norwegian (61)	143	0.61
Polish (0)	171	0.73
Romanian (0)	19	0.08
Russian (120)	134	0.58
Scotch-Irish (804)	1,102	4.73
Scottish (575)	1,367	5.87
Swedish (54)	109	0.47
Swiss (11)	82	0.35
Turkish (10)	10	0.04
Welsh (129)	188	0.81

Hispanic Origin	Population	%
Hispanic or Latino (of any race)	279	1.16
Central American, ex. Mexican	30	0.12
Costa Rican	1	<0.01
Guatemalan	4	0.02
Honduran	7	0.03
Nicaraguan	4	0.02
Panamanian	5	0.02
Salvadoran	9	0.04
Cuban	11	0.05
Dominican Republic	3	0.01
Mexican	128	0.53
Puerto Rican	16	0.07
South American	44	0.18
Argentinean	6	0.02
Bolivian	3	0.01
Colombian	14	0.06
Ecuadorian	4	0.02
Peruvian	6	0.02
Venezuelan	11	0.05
Other Hispanic or Latino	47	0.19

Race*	Population	%
African-American/Black (2,471)	2,538	10.51
Not Hispanic (2,467)	2,527	10.46
Hispanic (4)	11	0.05
American Indian/Alaska Native (25)	66	0.27
Not Hispanic (19)	60	0.25
Hispanic (6)	6	0.02
Alaska Athabascan *(Ala. Nat.)* (6)	6	0.02
Apache (2)	2	0.01
Cherokee (0)	9	0.04
Chickasaw (3)	7	0.03
Chippewa (1)	1	<0.01
Choctaw (2)	16	0.07
Creek (0)	2	0.01
Houma (1)	1	<0.01
Iroquois (2)	2	0.01
Potawatomi (1)	1	<0.01
Asian (771)	859	3.56
Not Hispanic (769)	856	3.54
Hispanic (2)	3	0.01
Bangladeshi (11)	11	0.05
Burmese (7)	7	0.03
Cambodian (6)	6	0.02
Chinese, ex. Taiwanese (186)	203	0.84
Filipino (18)	36	0.15
Indian (295)	315	1.30
Japanese (27)	34	0.14
Korean (49)	60	0.25
Malaysian (2)	2	0.01
Nepalese (1)	1	<0.01
Pakistani (60)	60	0.25
Taiwanese (9)	9	0.04
Thai (8)	15	0.06
Vietnamese (76)	78	0.32
Hawaii Native/Pacific Islander (3)	8	0.03
Not Hispanic (3)	8	0.03
Native Hawaiian (2)	3	0.01
White (20,645)	20,784	86.07
Not Hispanic (20,427)	20,551	85.10
Hispanic (218)	233	0.96

McComb

Place Type: City
County: Pike
Population: 12,790†

Ancestry‡	Population	%
American (2,637)	2,637	20.39
Arab (8)	8	0.06
Lebanese (8)	8	0.06
British (64)	76	0.59
Cajun (0)	9	0.07
Dutch (0)	54	0.42
English (653)	891	6.89
European (51)	51	0.39
French, ex. Basque (87)	141	1.09
German (157)	355	2.75
Irish (217)	537	4.15
Italian (9)	88	0.68
Latvian (9)	9	0.07
Polish (0)	38	0.29
Scotch-Irish (202)	292	2.26
Scottish (31)	48	0.37
Swedish (0)	10	0.08
Welsh (0)	13	0.10
West Indian, ex. Hispanic (19)	19	0.15
Other West Indian (19)	19	0.15

Hispanic Origin	Population	%
Hispanic or Latino (of any race)	180	1.41
Central American, ex. Mexican	30	0.23
Guatemalan	11	0.09
Honduran	11	0.09
Panamanian	2	0.02
Salvadoran	6	0.05
Cuban	4	0.03
Dominican Republic	3	0.02
Mexican	73	0.57
Puerto Rican	11	0.09
South American	8	0.06
Colombian	5	0.04
Peruvian	1	0.01
Venezuelan	2	0.02
Other Hispanic or Latino	51	0.40

Race*	Population	%
African-American/Black (8,479)	8,541	66.78
Not Hispanic (8,437)	8,491	66.39
Hispanic (42)	50	0.39
American Indian/Alaska Native (22)	64	0.50
Not Hispanic (22)	59	0.46
Hispanic (0)	5	0.04
Apache (2)	2	0.02
Blackfeet (0)	1	0.01
Canadian/French Am. Ind. (1)	1	0.01
Cherokee (2)	9	0.07
Choctaw (1)	4	0.03
Creek (0)	1	0.01
Houma (2)	4	0.03
Sioux (1)	1	0.01
Asian (116)	135	1.06
Not Hispanic (116)	132	1.03
Hispanic (0)	3	0.02
Cambodian (2)	2	0.02
Chinese, ex. Taiwanese (18)	20	0.16
Filipino (9)	10	0.08
Indian (53)	60	0.47
Japanese (5)	9	0.07
Korean (4)	4	0.03
Vietnamese (24)	24	0.19
Hawaii Native/Pacific Islander (7)	13	0.10
Not Hispanic (0)	6	0.05
Hispanic (7)	7	0.05
Guamanian/Chamorro (7)	7	0.05
Native Hawaiian (0)	3	0.02
White (3,993)	4,063	31.77
Not Hispanic (3,941)	4,005	31.31
Hispanic (52)	58	0.45

*Notes: † The Census 2010 population figure is used to calculate the percentages in the Hispanic Origin and Race categories. Ancestry percentages are based on the 2006-2010 American Community Survey population (not shown); ‡ Numbers in parentheses indicate the number of people reporting a single ancestry; * Numbers in parentheses indicate the number of persons reporting this race alone, not in combination with any other race; Please refer to the Explanation of Data for more information.*

Meridian

Place Type: City
County: Lauderdale
Population: 41,148†

Ancestry‡	Population	%
African, Sub-Saharan (381)	404	0.99
African (381)	404	0.99
American (3,488)	3,488	8.52
Arab (74)	153	0.37
Egyptian (0)	5	0.01
Lebanese (74)	95	0.23
Syrian (0)	53	0.13
Austrian (9)	9	0.02
Belgian (0)	15	0.04
British (14)	100	0.24
Canadian (39)	39	0.10
Czech (0)	15	0.04
Danish (38)	38	0.09
Dutch (23)	47	0.11
English (3,233)	4,196	10.25
European (267)	267	0.65
French, ex. Basque (302)	764	1.87
French Canadian (15)	42	0.10
German (490)	1,387	3.39
Hungarian (11)	50	0.12
Irish (823)	2,337	5.71
Italian (78)	448	1.09
Latvian (24)	24	0.06
Northern European (43)	43	0.11
Norwegian (54)	181	0.44
Pennsylvania German (9)	20	0.05
Polish (11)	174	0.43
Russian (0)	75	0.18
Scandinavian (83)	96	0.23
Scotch-Irish (567)	896	2.19
Scottish (561)	775	1.89
Slovak (17)	17	0.04
Swedish (28)	61	0.15
Swiss (32)	41	0.10
Welsh (12)	150	0.37
West Indian, ex. Hispanic (50)	50	0.12
Bahamian (31)	31	0.08
Haitian (19)	19	0.05

Hispanic Origin	Population	%
Hispanic or Latino (of any race)	719	1.75
Central American, ex. Mexican	63	0.15
Costa Rican	10	0.02
Guatemalan	21	0.05
Honduran	10	0.02
Nicaraguan	2	<0.01
Panamanian	18	0.04
Salvadoran	1	<0.01
Other Central American	1	<0.01
Cuban	12	0.03
Dominican Republic	13	0.03
Mexican	406	0.99
Puerto Rican	72	0.17
South American	32	0.08
Bolivian	1	<0.01
Chilean	1	<0.01
Colombian	10	0.02
Ecuadorian	1	<0.01
Paraguayan	1	<0.01
Peruvian	2	<0.01
Venezuelan	13	0.03
Other South American	3	0.01
Other Hispanic or Latino	121	0.29

Race*	Population	%
African-American/Black (25,327)	25,576	62.16
Not Hispanic (25,208)	25,425	61.79
Hispanic (119)	151	0.37
American Indian/Alaska Native (115)	205	0.50
Not Hispanic (88)	165	0.40
Hispanic (27)	40	0.10
Apache (0)	1	<0.01
Cherokee (8)	27	0.07
Choctaw (14)	21	0.05
Creek (3)	3	0.01
Houma (0)	2	<0.01
Mexican American Ind. (11)	11	0.03
Navajo (1)	1	<0.01
Pueblo (2)	7	0.02
Sioux (0)	1	<0.01
Spanish American Ind. (0)	3	0.01
Asian (390)	469	1.14
Not Hispanic (386)	460	1.12
Hispanic (4)	9	0.02
Cambodian (2)	2	<0.01
Chinese, ex. Taiwanese (52)	60	0.15
Filipino (134)	157	0.38
Indian (101)	125	0.30
Indonesian (1)	1	<0.01
Japanese (8)	17	0.04
Korean (16)	23	0.06
Laotian (0)	1	<0.01
Pakistani (22)	27	0.07
Thai (17)	18	0.04
Vietnamese (22)	24	0.06
Hawaii Native/Pacific Islander (10)	43	0.10
Not Hispanic (5)	33	0.08
Hispanic (5)	10	0.02
Guamanian/Chamorro (7)	25	0.06
Native Hawaiian (0)	6	0.01
Samoan (2)	8	0.02
White (14,696)	14,942	36.31
Not Hispanic (14,415)	14,627	35.55
Hispanic (281)	315	0.77

Moss Point

Place Type: City
County: Jackson
Population: 13,704†

Ancestry‡	Population	%
African, Sub-Saharan (1,483)	1,483	10.62
African (1,483)	1,483	10.62
American (797)	797	5.71
British (26)	106	0.76
Danish (0)	6	0.04
Dutch (16)	38	0.27
English (176)	374	2.68
European (132)	132	0.95
Finnish (20)	27	0.19
French, ex. Basque (87)	247	1.77
French Canadian (16)	16	0.11
German (132)	674	4.83
Irish (194)	406	2.91
Italian (45)	117	0.84
Northern European (10)	10	0.07
Polish (10)	40	0.29
Portuguese (20)	34	0.24
Russian (18)	26	0.19
Scotch-Irish (60)	103	0.74
Scottish (21)	53	0.38
Slovak (13)	13	0.09
Swedish (25)	34	0.24
Welsh (0)	11	0.08

Hispanic Origin	Population	%
Hispanic or Latino (of any race)	254	1.85
Central American, ex. Mexican	23	0.17
Guatemalan	7	0.05
Honduran	5	0.04
Nicaraguan	5	0.04
Salvadoran	6	0.04
Cuban	4	0.03
Dominican Republic	10	0.07
Mexican	128	0.93
Puerto Rican	36	0.26
South American	3	0.02
Venezuelan	3	0.02
Other Hispanic or Latino	50	0.36

Race*	Population	%
African-American/Black (10,080)	10,196	74.40
Not Hispanic (10,048)	10,152	74.08
Hispanic (32)	44	0.32
American Indian/Alaska Native (28)	90	0.66
Not Hispanic (28)	85	0.62
Hispanic (0)	5	0.04
Central American Ind. (0)	5	0.04
Cherokee (0)	16	0.12
Choctaw (6)	11	0.08
Creek (1)	2	0.01
Asian (60)	83	0.61
Not Hispanic (60)	77	0.56
Hispanic (0)	6	0.04
Cambodian (1)	4	0.03
Chinese, ex. Taiwanese (6)	7	0.05
Filipino (15)	22	0.16
Indian (1)	4	0.03
Japanese (4)	5	0.04
Thai (2)	4	0.03
Vietnamese (28)	34	0.25
Hawaii Native/Pacific Islander (4)	15	0.11
Not Hispanic (4)	13	0.09
Hispanic (0)	2	0.01
Guamanian/Chamorro (3)	5	0.04
Native Hawaiian (0)	2	0.01
Samoan (1)	4	0.03
White (3,280)	3,363	24.54
Not Hispanic (3,172)	3,238	23.63
Hispanic (108)	125	0.91

Natchez

Place Type: City
County: Adams
Population: 15,792†

Ancestry‡	Population	%
African, Sub-Saharan (129)	173	1.06
African (118)	162	1.00
Ghanaian (11)	11	0.07
American (971)	971	5.96
Arab (58)	58	0.36
Arab (49)	49	0.30
Lebanese (9)	9	0.06
Belgian (10)	21	0.13
British (32)	32	0.20
Cajun (10)	21	0.13
Danish (0)	11	0.07
Dutch (0)	65	0.40
English (549)	1,394	8.56
European (69)	161	0.99
Finnish (10)	10	0.06
French, ex. Basque (95)	440	2.70
French Canadian (9)	9	0.06
German (294)	708	4.35
Hungarian (8)	8	0.05
Irish (368)	1,212	7.45
Italian (116)	210	1.29
Norwegian (23)	70	0.43
Polish (28)	66	0.41
Romanian (0)	8	0.05
Russian (0)	8	0.05
Scotch-Irish (228)	321	1.97
Scottish (135)	577	3.54
Swedish (22)	31	0.19
Ukrainian (0)	8	0.05
Welsh (33)	71	0.44

Hispanic Origin	Population	%
Hispanic or Latino (of any race)	179	1.13
Central American, ex. Mexican	8	0.05
Guatemalan	3	0.02
Honduran	3	0.02
Nicaraguan	1	0.01
Salvadoran	1	0.01
Cuban	8	0.05
Mexican	108	0.68
Puerto Rican	20	0.13
South American	8	0.05
Argentinean	1	0.01
Ecuadorian	5	0.03

*Notes: † The Census 2010 population figure is used to calculate the percentages in the Hispanic Origin and Race categories. Ancestry percentages are based on the 2006-2010 American Community Survey population (not shown); ‡ Numbers in parentheses indicate the number of people reporting a single ancestry; * Numbers in parentheses indicate the number of persons reporting this race alone, not in combination with any other race; Please refer to the Explanation of Data for more information.*

Peruvian	2	0.01
Other Hispanic or Latino	27	0.17

Race*	Population	%
African-American/Black (9,213)	9,340	59.14
Not Hispanic (9,176)	9,292	58.84
Hispanic (37)	48	0.30
American Indian/Alaska Native (35)	91	0.58
Not Hispanic (31)	82	0.52
Hispanic (4)	9	0.06
Cherokee (4)	24	0.15
Chickasaw (0)	1	0.01
Chippewa (3)	3	0.02
Choctaw (0)	8	0.05
Creek (1)	4	0.03
Delaware (1)	1	0.01
Iroquois (0)	1	0.01
Menominee (0)	2	0.01
South American Ind. (0)	3	0.02
Asian (59)	82	0.52
Not Hispanic (59)	82	0.52
Cambodian (1)	1	0.01
Chinese, ex. Taiwanese (15)	15	0.09
Filipino (2)	7	0.04
Indian (12)	18	0.11
Japanese (1)	3	0.02
Korean (6)	6	0.04
Pakistani (2)	2	0.01
Thai (3)	3	0.02
Vietnamese (17)	17	0.11
Hawaii Native/Pacific Islander (0)	11	0.07
Not Hispanic (0)	10	0.06
Hispanic (0)	1	0.01
Native Hawaiian (0)	1	0.01
Samoan (0)	3	0.02
White (6,248)	6,359	40.27
Not Hispanic (6,185)	6,291	39.84
Hispanic (63)	68	0.43

New Albany

Place Type: City
County: Union
Population: 8,034†

Ancestry‡	Population	%
African, Sub-Saharan (262)	262	3.28
African (262)	262	3.28
American (1,607)	1,607	20.09
British (27)	27	0.34
Dutch (22)	66	0.83
English (359)	480	6.00
European (34)	34	0.43
French, ex. Basque (100)	134	1.68
German (272)	568	7.10
Irish (196)	501	6.26
Italian (13)	57	0.71
Polish (41)	102	1.28
Russian (0)	17	0.21
Scotch-Irish (126)	176	2.20
Scottish (145)	177	2.21
Swedish (73)	73	0.91

Hispanic Origin	Population	%
Hispanic or Latino (of any race)	667	8.30
Central American, ex. Mexican	42	0.52
Guatemalan	5	0.06
Honduran	23	0.29
Nicaraguan	1	0.01
Salvadoran	13	0.16
Cuban	2	0.02
Mexican	588	7.32
Puerto Rican	2	0.02
Other Hispanic or Latino	33	0.41

Race*	Population	%
African-American/Black (2,507)	2,610	32.49
Not Hispanic (2,492)	2,588	32.21
Hispanic (15)	22	0.27
American Indian/Alaska Native (17)	39	0.49
Not Hispanic (6)	28	0.35
Hispanic (11)	11	0.14
Blackfeet (0)	5	0.06
Cherokee (1)	15	0.19
Iroquois (0)	1	0.01
Mexican American Ind. (2)	2	0.02
Asian (27)	48	0.60
Not Hispanic (27)	48	0.60
Chinese, ex. Taiwanese (8)	8	0.10
Filipino (3)	8	0.10
Japanese (3)	12	0.15
Korean (1)	2	0.02
Sri Lankan (1)	1	0.01
Vietnamese (5)	7	0.09
Hawaii Native/Pacific Islander (0)	3	0.04
Not Hispanic (0)	3	0.04
Native Hawaiian (0)	3	0.04
White (4,884)	5,023	62.52
Not Hispanic (4,705)	4,826	60.07
Hispanic (179)	197	2.45

Ocean Springs

Place Type: City
County: Jackson
Population: 17,442†

Ancestry‡	Population	%
African, Sub-Saharan (206)	206	1.19
African (206)	206	1.19
American (1,635)	1,635	9.47
Arab (0)	62	0.36
Lebanese (0)	15	0.09
Syrian (0)	31	0.18
Other Arab (0)	16	0.09
Assyrian/Chaldean/Syriac (12)	50	0.29
Australian (0)	13	0.08
Austrian (38)	38	0.22
Belgian (0)	17	0.10
British (0)	73	0.42
Cajun (56)	56	0.32
Canadian (17)	17	0.10
Croatian (35)	57	0.33
Czech (0)	14	0.08
Danish (12)	37	0.21
Dutch (136)	377	2.18
English (1,193)	2,446	14.17
European (179)	179	1.04
Finnish (40)	71	0.41
French, ex. Basque (514)	1,449	8.40
French Canadian (13)	65	0.38
German (1,096)	2,562	14.85
Greek (16)	86	0.50
Hungarian (25)	191	1.11
Irish (827)	2,288	13.26
Italian (372)	773	4.48
Lithuanian (46)	68	0.39
Norwegian (47)	128	0.74
Pennsylvania German (15)	15	0.09
Polish (35)	107	0.62
Portuguese (19)	57	0.33
Russian (47)	119	0.69
Scotch-Irish (594)	930	5.39
Scottish (35)	338	1.96
Slavic (0)	16	0.09
Slovak (12)	12	0.07
Swedish (53)	204	1.18
Swiss (52)	68	0.39
Welsh (0)	63	0.37
Yugoslavian (0)	13	0.08

Hispanic Origin	Population	%
Hispanic or Latino (of any race)	728	4.17
Central American, ex. Mexican	85	0.49
Costa Rican	9	0.05
Guatemalan	16	0.09
Honduran	12	0.07
Nicaraguan	22	0.13
Panamanian	20	0.11
Salvadoran	6	0.03
Cuban	31	0.18
Dominican Republic	5	0.03
Mexican	326	1.87
Puerto Rican	93	0.53
South American	78	0.45
Argentinean	5	0.03
Bolivian	3	0.02
Chilean	21	0.12
Colombian	27	0.15
Ecuadorian	4	0.02
Peruvian	10	0.06
Uruguayan	1	0.01
Venezuelan	6	0.03
Other South American	1	0.01
Other Hispanic or Latino	110	0.63

Race*	Population	%
African-American/Black (1,298)	1,422	8.15
Not Hispanic (1,281)	1,392	7.98
Hispanic (17)	30	0.17
American Indian/Alaska Native (67)	180	1.03
Not Hispanic (57)	156	0.89
Hispanic (10)	24	0.14
Aleut *(Alaska Native)* (1)	1	0.01
Apache (3)	7	0.04
Canadian/French Am. Ind. (1)	2	0.01
Cherokee (15)	41	0.24
Chippewa (3)	6	0.03
Choctaw (8)	11	0.06
Cree (0)	1	0.01
Creek (2)	8	0.05
Houma (0)	1	0.01
Iroquois (0)	1	0.01
Mexican American Ind. (1)	1	0.01
Osage (0)	2	0.01
Ottawa (0)	1	0.01
Potawatomi (2)	2	0.01
Seminole (1)	1	0.01
Sioux (4)	6	0.03
South American Ind. (0)	2	0.01
Spanish American Ind. (1)	1	0.01
Asian (544)	696	3.99
Not Hispanic (542)	677	3.88
Hispanic (2)	19	0.11
Burmese (1)	1	0.01
Cambodian (2)	2	0.01
Chinese, ex. Taiwanese (57)	75	0.43
Filipino (76)	133	0.76
Hmong (10)	14	0.08
Indian (24)	32	0.18
Indonesian (2)	2	0.01
Japanese (19)	42	0.24
Korean (17)	37	0.21
Laotian (12)	13	0.07
Pakistani (40)	47	0.27
Sri Lankan (2)	2	0.01
Taiwanese (4)	6	0.03
Thai (12)	17	0.10
Vietnamese (255)	276	1.58
Hawaii Native/Pacific Islander (12)	22	0.13
Not Hispanic (11)	19	0.11
Hispanic (1)	3	0.02
Guamanian/Chamorro (1)	2	0.01
Native Hawaiian (10)	16	0.09
White (14,901)	15,260	87.49
Not Hispanic (14,479)	14,766	84.66
Hispanic (422)	494	2.83

Olive Branch

Place Type: City
County: DeSoto
Population: 33,484†

Ancestry‡	Population	%
African, Sub-Saharan (211)	211	0.66
African (211)	211	0.66
American (4,658)	4,658	14.60
Arab (312)	349	1.09
Arab (44)	44	0.14

SECTION TWO

*Notes: † The Census 2010 population figure is used to calculate the percentages in the Hispanic Origin and Race categories. Ancestry percentages are based on the 2006-2010 American Community Survey population (not shown); ‡ Numbers in parentheses indicate the number of people reporting a single ancestry; * Numbers in parentheses indicate the number of persons reporting this race alone, not in combination with any other race; Please refer to the Explanation of Data for more information.*

Jordanian (25)	25	0.08
Lebanese (6)	43	0.13
Palestinian (237)	237	0.74
Australian (5)	18	0.06
Austrian (0)	9	0.03
British (17)	37	0.12
Canadian (8)	8	0.03
Croatian (0)	10	0.03
Czech (54)	54	0.17
Czechoslovakian (0)	34	0.11
Danish (15)	51	0.16
Dutch (76)	344	1.08
English (1,700)	3,179	9.96
European (413)	523	1.64
French, ex. Basque (326)	833	2.61
French Canadian (8)	45	0.14
German (971)	2,771	8.68
Greek (17)	34	0.11
Iranian (35)	35	0.11
Irish (1,327)	3,471	10.88
Italian (345)	965	3.02
Lithuanian (0)	34	0.11
Norwegian (12)	26	0.08
Polish (28)	171	0.54
Portuguese (6)	6	0.02
Scandinavian (13)	51	0.16
Scotch-Irish (691)	1,164	3.65
Scottish (612)	990	3.10
Serbian (0)	18	0.06
Slovak (31)	31	0.10
Swedish (34)	52	0.16
Swiss (0)	19	0.06
Welsh (122)	201	0.63
West Indian, ex. Hispanic (85)	85	0.27
Haitian (85)	85	0.27
Yugoslavian (0)	45	0.14

Hispanic Origin	Population	%
Hispanic or Latino (of any race)	1,397	4.17
Central American, ex. Mexican	136	0.41
Costa Rican	4	0.01
Guatemalan	46	0.14
Honduran	30	0.09
Nicaraguan	3	0.01
Panamanian	10	0.03
Salvadoran	43	0.13
Cuban	15	0.04
Dominican Republic	13	0.04
Mexican	1,021	3.05
Puerto Rican	67	0.20
South American	75	0.22
Argentinean	2	0.01
Bolivian	2	0.01
Chilean	5	0.01
Colombian	34	0.10
Ecuadorian	5	0.01
Paraguayan	3	0.01
Peruvian	12	0.04
Uruguayan	1	<0.01
Venezuelan	11	0.03
Other Hispanic or Latino	70	0.21

Race*	Population	%
African-American/Black (7,743)	7,980	23.83
Not Hispanic (7,696)	7,901	23.60
Hispanic (47)	79	0.24
American Indian/Alaska Native (61)	170	0.51
Not Hispanic (47)	140	0.42
Hispanic (14)	30	0.09
Apache (0)	1	<0.01
Blackfeet (0)	2	0.01
Canadian/French Am. Ind. (3)	3	0.01
Cherokee (15)	40	0.12
Chippewa (0)	3	0.01
Choctaw (4)	8	0.02
Comanche (0)	1	<0.01
Creek (1)	1	<0.01
Crow (0)	1	<0.01
Houma (2)	2	0.01
Lumbee (0)	1	<0.01
Mexican American Ind. (7)	7	0.02
Navajo (4)	5	0.01
Potawatomi (1)	1	<0.01
Seminole (0)	2	0.01
Sioux (0)	2	0.01
Asian (435)	538	1.61
Not Hispanic (434)	532	1.59
Hispanic (1)	6	0.02
Cambodian (2)	3	0.01
Chinese, ex. Taiwanese (67)	72	0.22
Filipino (95)	139	0.42
Indian (74)	84	0.25
Indonesian (2)	4	0.01
Japanese (16)	26	0.08
Korean (38)	54	0.16
Laotian (11)	11	0.03
Malaysian (3)	3	0.01
Pakistani (2)	2	0.01
Taiwanese (2)	2	0.01
Thai (17)	21	0.06
Vietnamese (89)	90	0.27
Hawaii Native/Pacific Islander (23)	40	0.12
Not Hispanic (23)	30	0.09
Hispanic (0)	10	0.03
Fijian (0)	1	<0.01
Guamanian/Chamorro (14)	14	0.04
Marshallese (1)	1	<0.01
Native Hawaiian (7)	9	0.03
White (23,940)	24,357	72.74
Not Hispanic (23,493)	23,804	71.09
Hispanic (447)	553	1.65

Oxford

Place Type: City
County: Lafayette
Population: 18,916†

Ancestry‡	Population	%
African, Sub-Saharan (36)	36	0.20
African (9)	9	0.05
Nigerian (27)	27	0.15
American (861)	861	4.79
Arab (106)	136	0.76
Egyptian (53)	53	0.29
Iraqi (33)	33	0.18
Lebanese (20)	50	0.28
Austrian (0)	18	0.10
Basque (13)	13	0.07
British (173)	224	1.25
Canadian (0)	7	0.04
Danish (28)	59	0.33
Dutch (36)	159	0.88
English (846)	2,238	12.44
European (195)	213	1.18
Finnish (10)	10	0.06
French, ex. Basque (86)	324	1.80
French Canadian (0)	30	0.17
German (379)	1,409	7.83
Greek (26)	26	0.14
Hungarian (9)	31	0.17
Iranian (22)	67	0.37
Irish (610)	1,787	9.93
Italian (203)	504	2.80
Lithuanian (14)	14	0.08
Norwegian (0)	42	0.23
Pennsylvania German (14)	14	0.08
Polish (34)	100	0.56
Portuguese (10)	10	0.06
Russian (0)	16	0.09
Scandinavian (20)	20	0.11
Scotch-Irish (722)	1,279	7.11
Scottish (184)	362	2.01
Swedish (39)	216	1.20
Swiss (12)	65	0.36
Welsh (73)	168	0.93
Yugoslavian (6)	6	0.03

Hispanic Origin	Population	%
Hispanic or Latino (of any race)	465	2.46
Central American, ex. Mexican	67	0.35
Costa Rican	6	0.03
Guatemalan	22	0.12
Honduran	23	0.12
Nicaraguan	7	0.04
Panamanian	2	0.01
Salvadoran	7	0.04
Cuban	10	0.05
Mexican	279	1.47
Puerto Rican	24	0.13
South American	28	0.15
Argentinean	3	0.02
Bolivian	6	0.03
Chilean	4	0.02
Colombian	7	0.04
Ecuadorian	2	0.01
Peruvian	2	0.01
Uruguayan	4	0.02
Other Hispanic or Latino	57	0.30

Race*	Population	%
African-American/Black (4,130)	4,195	22.18
Not Hispanic (4,122)	4,181	22.10
Hispanic (8)	14	0.07
American Indian/Alaska Native (61)	116	0.61
Not Hispanic (29)	82	0.43
Hispanic (32)	34	0.18
Apache (1)	1	0.01
Cherokee (6)	17	0.09
Chickasaw (2)	4	0.02
Choctaw (1)	4	0.02
Comanche (0)	1	0.01
Mexican American Ind. (26)	27	0.14
Navajo (0)	1	0.01
Osage (2)	3	0.02
Potawatomi (1)	1	0.01
Seminole (0)	1	0.01
Sioux (1)	1	0.01
Asian (621)	714	3.77
Not Hispanic (620)	709	3.75
Hispanic (1)	5	0.03
Bangladeshi (9)	9	0.05
Chinese, ex. Taiwanese (176)	194	1.03
Filipino (11)	30	0.16
Indian (212)	220	1.16
Indonesian (3)	5	0.03
Japanese (18)	32	0.17
Korean (59)	67	0.35
Malaysian (2)	3	0.02
Nepalese (17)	18	0.10
Pakistani (9)	11	0.06
Sri Lankan (27)	27	0.14
Taiwanese (6)	6	0.03
Thai (10)	12	0.06
Vietnamese (54)	58	0.31
Hawaii Native/Pacific Islander (13)	21	0.11
Not Hispanic (9)	15	0.08
Hispanic (4)	6	0.03
Fijian (1)	1	0.01
Guamanian/Chamorro (4)	4	0.02
Native Hawaiian (7)	10	0.05
Samoan (1)	1	0.01
White (13,674)	13,848	73.21
Not Hispanic (13,465)	13,622	72.01
Hispanic (209)	226	1.19

Pascagoula

Place Type: City
County: Jackson
Population: 22,392†

Ancestry‡	Population	%
African, Sub-Saharan (741)	741	3.23
African (741)	741	3.23
American (2,377)	2,377	10.36
Arab (8)	8	0.03
Lebanese (8)	8	0.03
Armenian (9)	9	0.04
British (71)	154	0.67

*Notes: † The Census 2010 population figure is used to calculate the percentages in the Hispanic Origin and Race categories. Ancestry percentages are based on the 2006-2010 American Community Survey population (not shown); ‡ Numbers in parentheses indicate the number of people reporting a single ancestry; * Numbers in parentheses indicate the number of persons reporting this race alone, not in combination with any other race; Please refer to the Explanation of Data for more information.*

Cajun (9)	9	0.04
Canadian (37)	37	0.16
Croatian (30)	30	0.13
Danish (35)	46	0.20
Dutch (8)	69	0.30
English (1,540)	2,347	10.23
European (375)	375	1.63
Finnish (10)	31	0.14
French, ex. Basque (476)	1,267	5.52
French Canadian (92)	187	0.81
German (489)	1,392	6.07
Greek (25)	39	0.17
Hungarian (0)	2	0.01
Irish (744)	2,202	9.60
Italian (192)	364	1.59
Macedonian (0)	9	0.04
Norwegian (21)	104	0.45
Polish (46)	129	0.56
Portuguese (7)	56	0.24
Russian (0)	11	0.05
Scotch-Irish (172)	423	1.84
Scottish (187)	328	1.43
Serbian (7)	7	0.03
Swedish (15)	163	0.71
Welsh (0)	88	0.38
West Indian, ex. Hispanic (37)	57	0.25
Bermudan (37)	37	0.16
Jamaican (0)	10	0.04
Other West Indian (0)	10	0.04
Yugoslavian (10)	10	0.04

Hispanic Origin	Population	%
Hispanic or Latino (of any race)	2,472	11.04
Central American, ex. Mexican	121	0.54
Costa Rican	3	0.01
Guatemalan	35	0.16
Honduran	48	0.21
Nicaraguan	7	0.03
Panamanian	8	0.04
Salvadoran	20	0.09
Cuban	52	0.23
Dominican Republic	177	0.79
Mexican	909	4.06
Puerto Rican	1,014	4.53
South American	47	0.21
Argentinean	4	0.02
Chilean	6	0.03
Colombian	15	0.07
Ecuadorian	6	0.03
Peruvian	8	0.04
Venezuelan	8	0.04
Other Hispanic or Latino	152	0.68

Race*	Population	%
African-American/Black (7,317)	7,522	33.59
Not Hispanic (7,184)	7,347	32.81
Hispanic (133)	175	0.78
American Indian/Alaska Native (69)	164	0.73
Not Hispanic (59)	138	0.62
Hispanic (10)	26	0.12
Apache (0)	2	0.01
Blackfeet (1)	3	0.01
Canadian/French Am. Ind. (0)	1	<0.01
Central American Ind. (0)	1	<0.01
Cherokee (3)	28	0.13
Chippewa (0)	2	0.01
Choctaw (11)	21	0.09
Creek (3)	10	0.04
Inupiat *(Alaska Native)* (0)	1	<0.01
Iroquois (0)	1	<0.01
Lumbee (1)	1	<0.01
Navajo (6)	9	0.04
Osage (0)	1	<0.01
Ottawa (0)	2	0.01
Pueblo (1)	1	<0.01
Sioux (4)	7	0.03
South American Ind. (3)	3	0.01
Spanish American Ind. (0)	1	<0.01
Tlingit-Haida *(Alaska Native)* (1)	1	<0.01
Asian (224)	289	1.29
Not Hispanic (210)	264	1.18
Hispanic (14)	25	0.11
Cambodian (9)	9	0.04
Chinese, ex. Taiwanese (27)	38	0.17
Filipino (30)	53	0.24
Indian (42)	54	0.24
Indonesian (1)	1	<0.01
Japanese (3)	12	0.05
Korean (5)	11	0.05
Laotian (0)	4	0.02
Thai (1)	1	<0.01
Vietnamese (87)	97	0.43
Hawaii Native/Pacific Islander (14)	38	0.17
Not Hispanic (9)	26	0.12
Hispanic (5)	12	0.05
Guamanian/Chamorro (7)	17	0.08
Native Hawaiian (2)	6	0.03
Samoan (2)	3	0.01
White (13,169)	13,477	60.19
Not Hispanic (12,200)	12,403	55.39
Hispanic (969)	1,074	4.80

Pearl

Place Type: City
County: Rankin
Population: 25,092†

Ancestry‡	Population	%
African, Sub-Saharan (399)	449	1.79
African (399)	449	1.79
American (3,013)	3,013	12.02
Austrian (25)	25	0.10
British (19)	33	0.13
Cajun (27)	27	0.11
Czech (37)	37	0.15
Danish (32)	32	0.13
Dutch (28)	255	1.02
English (915)	1,628	6.50
European (265)	341	1.36
French, ex. Basque (317)	856	3.42
French Canadian (86)	86	0.34
German (852)	2,228	8.89
Greek (0)	51	0.20
Hungarian (17)	17	0.07
Irish (1,316)	3,340	13.33
Italian (385)	558	2.23
Luxemburger (14)	14	0.06
Norwegian (0)	41	0.16
Polish (141)	192	0.77
Portuguese (0)	13	0.05
Scotch-Irish (537)	752	3.00
Scottish (185)	321	1.28
Slovak (0)	63	0.25
Slovene (0)	117	0.47
Swedish (7)	24	0.10
Swiss (11)	11	0.04
Ukrainian (6)	6	0.02
Welsh (51)	72	0.29
West Indian, ex. Hispanic (0)	13	0.05
Belizean (0)	13	0.05

Hispanic Origin	Population	%
Hispanic or Latino (of any race)	1,598	6.37
Central American, ex. Mexican	349	1.39
Costa Rican	12	0.05
Guatemalan	107	0.43
Honduran	124	0.49
Nicaraguan	51	0.20
Panamanian	8	0.03
Salvadoran	47	0.19
Cuban	28	0.11
Dominican Republic	1	<0.01
Mexican	973	3.88
Puerto Rican	46	0.18
South American	30	0.12
Argentinean	5	0.02
Bolivian	3	0.01
Chilean	1	<0.01
Colombian	15	0.06
Ecuadorian	1	<0.01
Peruvian	3	0.01
Venezuelan	2	0.01
Other Hispanic or Latino	171	0.68

Race*	Population	%
African-American/Black (5,768)	5,978	23.82
Not Hispanic (5,732)	5,918	23.59
Hispanic (36)	60	0.24
American Indian/Alaska Native (57)	172	0.69
Not Hispanic (44)	147	0.59
Hispanic (13)	25	0.10
Apache (4)	6	0.02
Blackfeet (0)	2	0.01
Canadian/French Am. Ind. (0)	4	0.02
Cherokee (4)	19	0.08
Chickasaw (1)	10	0.04
Chippewa (1)	3	0.01
Choctaw (3)	13	0.05
Creek (2)	2	0.01
Crow (0)	2	0.01
Houma (3)	3	0.01
Iroquois (0)	2	0.01
Mexican American Ind. (4)	5	0.02
Puget Sound Salish (1)	3	0.01
Sioux (1)	1	<0.01
Ute (1)	1	<0.01
Yakama (1)	1	<0.01
Asian (217)	274	1.09
Not Hispanic (215)	271	1.08
Hispanic (2)	3	0.01
Cambodian (1)	5	0.02
Chinese, ex. Taiwanese (22)	29	0.12
Filipino (44)	65	0.26
Indian (76)	86	0.34
Indonesian (1)	2	0.01
Japanese (15)	23	0.09
Korean (8)	13	0.05
Malaysian (0)	1	<0.01
Pakistani (2)	2	0.01
Thai (9)	10	0.04
Vietnamese (27)	29	0.12
Hawaii Native/Pacific Islander (53)	81	0.32
Not Hispanic (53)	63	0.25
Hispanic (0)	18	0.07
Guamanian/Chamorro (26)	35	0.14
Native Hawaiian (3)	4	0.02
Tongan (1)	2	0.01
White (17,525)	17,889	71.29
Not Hispanic (17,103)	17,398	69.34
Hispanic (422)	491	1.96

Petal

Place Type: City
County: Forrest
Population: 10,454†

Ancestry‡	Population	%
American (1,955)	1,955	18.98
Arab (21)	60	0.58
Lebanese (21)	60	0.58
Australian (0)	14	0.14
Austrian (0)	4	0.04
British (18)	18	0.17
Cajun (9)	9	0.09
Czechoslovakian (15)	44	0.43
Dutch (0)	189	1.83
English (973)	1,471	14.28
European (95)	95	0.92
French, ex. Basque (176)	424	4.12
French Canadian (0)	35	0.34
German (481)	1,142	11.09
Irish (545)	1,100	10.68
Italian (110)	218	2.12
Norwegian (0)	84	0.82
Polish (46)	110	1.07
Portuguese (13)	13	0.13
Scotch-Irish (179)	319	3.10
Scottish (114)	184	1.79

*Notes: † The Census 2010 population figure is used to calculate the percentages in the Hispanic Origin and Race categories. Ancestry percentages are based on the 2006-2010 American Community Survey population (not shown); ‡ Numbers in parentheses indicate the number of people reporting a single ancestry; * Numbers in parentheses indicate the number of persons reporting this race alone, not in combination with any other race; Please refer to the Explanation of Data for more information.*

Swedish (0)	40	0.39
Swiss (9)	9	0.09
Welsh (0)	41	0.40

Hispanic Origin	Population	%
Hispanic or Latino (of any race)	361	3.45
Central American, ex. Mexican	48	0.46
Guatemalan	2	0.02
Honduran	13	0.12
Nicaraguan	6	0.06
Panamanian	5	0.05
Salvadoran	22	0.21
Cuban	9	0.09
Dominican Republic	1	0.01
Mexican	213	2.04
Puerto Rican	20	0.19
South American	34	0.33
Argentinean	1	0.01
Chilean	1	0.01
Colombian	15	0.14
Ecuadorian	5	0.05
Peruvian	2	0.02
Venezuelan	10	0.10
Other Hispanic or Latino	36	0.34

Race*	Population	%
African-American/Black (1,039)	1,116	10.68
Not Hispanic (1,037)	1,100	10.52
Hispanic (2)	16	0.15
American Indian/Alaska Native (25)	79	0.76
Not Hispanic (23)	77	0.74
Hispanic (2)	2	0.02
Apache (0)	2	0.02
Cherokee (7)	20	0.19
Cheyenne (1)	1	0.01
Choctaw (5)	22	0.21
Creek (2)	3	0.03
Iroquois (2)	7	0.07
Mexican American Ind. (2)	2	0.02
Sioux (1)	2	0.02
Asian (78)	113	1.08
Not Hispanic (78)	111	1.06
Hispanic (0)	2	0.02
Chinese, ex. Taiwanese (12)	15	0.14
Filipino (4)	15	0.14
Hmong (1)	3	0.03
Indian (4)	6	0.06
Japanese (3)	16	0.15
Korean (6)	11	0.11
Laotian (4)	4	0.04
Pakistani (1)	3	0.03
Thai (2)	3	0.03
Vietnamese (34)	37	0.35
Hawaii Native/Pacific Islander (0)	8	0.08
Not Hispanic (0)	8	0.08
Guamanian/Chamorro (0)	4	0.04
Native Hawaiian (0)	3	0.03
Samoan (0)	1	0.01
White (8,997)	9,161	87.63
Not Hispanic (8,811)	8,946	85.57
Hispanic (186)	215	2.06

Picayune

Place Type: City
County: Pearl River
Population: 10,878†

Ancestry‡	Population	%
African, Sub-Saharan (22)	22	0.20
African (22)	22	0.20
American (837)	837	7.55
Arab (33)	51	0.46
Lebanese (33)	51	0.46
Austrian (7)	7	0.06
British (19)	93	0.84
Celtic (17)	17	0.15
Czechoslovakian (7)	7	0.06
Dutch (0)	21	0.19
English (700)	1,039	9.37
European (12)	12	0.11
French, ex. Basque (142)	698	6.30
French Canadian (49)	70	0.63
German (148)	746	6.73
Iranian (6)	6	0.05
Irish (457)	815	7.35
Italian (278)	494	4.46
Latvian (0)	12	0.11
Norwegian (0)	15	0.14
Polish (27)	179	1.61
Portuguese (9)	9	0.08
Russian (0)	133	1.20
Scotch-Irish (204)	327	2.95
Scottish (47)	167	1.51
Swedish (21)	21	0.19
Welsh (9)	45	0.41
West Indian, ex. Hispanic (0)	12	0.11
Dutch West Indian (0)	12	0.11

Hispanic Origin	Population	%
Hispanic or Latino (of any race)	333	3.06
Central American, ex. Mexican	57	0.52
Guatemalan	5	0.05
Honduran	28	0.26
Nicaraguan	10	0.09
Panamanian	8	0.07
Salvadoran	4	0.04
Other Central American	2	0.02
Cuban	10	0.09
Mexican	152	1.40
Puerto Rican	45	0.41
South American	11	0.10
Argentinean	1	0.01
Bolivian	3	0.03
Colombian	5	0.05
Peruvian	1	0.01
Venezuelan	1	0.01
Other Hispanic or Latino	58	0.53

Race*	Population	%
African-American/Black (3,996)	4,118	37.86
Not Hispanic (3,986)	4,101	37.70
Hispanic (10)	17	0.16
American Indian/Alaska Native (32)	105	0.97
Not Hispanic (32)	93	0.85
Hispanic (0)	12	0.11
Aleut *(Alaska Native)* (1)	3	0.03
Apache (0)	1	0.01
Blackfeet (2)	3	0.03
Cherokee (3)	15	0.14
Chickasaw (1)	1	0.01
Chippewa (0)	1	0.01
Choctaw (4)	11	0.10
Creek (3)	3	0.03
Houma (6)	19	0.17
Navajo (0)	2	0.02
Seminole (0)	1	0.01
Asian (66)	99	0.91
Not Hispanic (64)	88	0.81
Hispanic (2)	11	0.10
Chinese, ex. Taiwanese (21)	24	0.22
Filipino (10)	22	0.20
Indian (7)	12	0.11
Japanese (4)	9	0.08
Korean (2)	2	0.02
Thai (1)	1	0.01
Vietnamese (18)	21	0.19
Hawaii Native/Pacific Islander (4)	11	0.10
Not Hispanic (4)	11	0.10
Native Hawaiian (4)	4	0.04
White (6,449)	6,635	60.99
Not Hispanic (6,269)	6,431	59.12
Hispanic (180)	204	1.88

Ridgeland

Place Type: City
County: Madison
Population: 24,047†

Ancestry‡	Population	%
African, Sub-Saharan (166)	196	0.83
African (7)	22	0.09
Nigerian (80)	80	0.34
Sudanese (79)	94	0.40
American (2,334)	2,334	9.93
Arab (105)	162	0.69
Lebanese (91)	148	0.63
Other Arab (14)	14	0.06
Armenian (26)	26	0.11
British (17)	175	0.74
Cajun (0)	9	0.04
Canadian (17)	17	0.07
Czech (16)	30	0.13
Czechoslovakian (14)	21	0.09
Danish (27)	27	0.11
Dutch (46)	106	0.45
Eastern European (15)	15	0.06
English (2,020)	3,323	14.14
European (142)	168	0.71
French, ex. Basque (145)	505	2.15
French Canadian (10)	47	0.20
German (904)	2,373	10.10
Greek (93)	126	0.54
Hungarian (0)	23	0.10
Irish (1,174)	2,674	11.38
Italian (229)	354	1.51
Lithuanian (7)	7	0.03
Northern European (20)	20	0.09
Norwegian (140)	166	0.71
Polish (28)	169	0.72
Romanian (0)	25	0.11
Russian (21)	38	0.16
Scotch-Irish (202)	480	2.04
Scottish (265)	651	2.77
Serbian (7)	40	0.17
Swedish (30)	78	0.33
Turkish (36)	36	0.15
Ukrainian (32)	32	0.14
Welsh (28)	128	0.54
West Indian, ex. Hispanic (58)	58	0.25
Jamaican (58)	58	0.25

Hispanic Origin	Population	%
Hispanic or Latino (of any race)	1,133	4.71
Central American, ex. Mexican	103	0.43
Costa Rican	7	0.03
Guatemalan	32	0.13
Honduran	47	0.20
Nicaraguan	3	0.01
Panamanian	4	0.02
Salvadoran	10	0.04
Cuban	32	0.13
Dominican Republic	7	0.03
Mexican	661	2.75
Puerto Rican	35	0.15
South American	127	0.53
Argentinean	17	0.07
Bolivian	1	<0.01
Chilean	14	0.06
Colombian	36	0.15
Ecuadorian	6	0.02
Peruvian	26	0.11
Uruguayan	4	0.02
Venezuelan	20	0.08
Other South American	3	0.01
Other Hispanic or Latino	168	0.70

Race*	Population	%
African-American/Black (7,864)	7,995	33.25
Not Hispanic (7,823)	7,946	33.04
Hispanic (41)	49	0.20
American Indian/Alaska Native (44)	120	0.50
Not Hispanic (37)	98	0.41
Hispanic (7)	22	0.09
Aleut *(Alaska Native)* (1)	1	<0.01
Apache (3)	3	0.01
Blackfeet (0)	3	0.01
Cherokee (3)	20	0.08
Choctaw (10)	19	0.08

*Notes: † The Census 2010 population figure is used to calculate the percentages in the Hispanic Origin and Race categories. Ancestry percentages are based on the 2006-2010 American Community Survey population (not shown); ‡ Numbers in parentheses indicate the number of people reporting a single ancestry; * Numbers in parentheses indicate the number of persons reporting this race alone, not in combination with any other race; Please refer to the Explanation of Data for more information.*

Cree (0)	1	<0.01
Creek (1)	2	0.01
Houma (1)	1	<0.01
Mexican American Ind. (1)	6	0.02
Navajo (1)	1	<0.01
Osage (1)	1	<0.01
Tlingit-Haida *(Alaska Native)* (0)	1	<0.01
Asian (960)	1,067	4.44
Not Hispanic (953)	1,047	4.35
Hispanic (7)	20	0.08
Bangladeshi (6)	11	0.05
Cambodian (12)	12	0.05
Chinese, ex. Taiwanese (148)	163	0.68
Filipino (56)	71	0.30
Indian (438)	474	1.97
Indonesian (1)	2	0.01
Japanese (62)	86	0.36
Korean (43)	56	0.23
Laotian (1)	1	<0.01
Malaysian (1)	1	<0.01
Pakistani (27)	30	0.12
Taiwanese (12)	12	0.05
Thai (11)	14	0.06
Vietnamese (117)	118	0.49
Hawaii Native/Pacific Islander (9)	24	0.10
Not Hispanic (9)	23	0.10
Hispanic (0)	1	<0.01
Guamanian/Chamorro (2)	2	0.01
Native Hawaiian (1)	4	0.02
Samoan (1)	2	0.01
White (14,302)	14,529	60.42
Not Hispanic (13,823)	14,013	58.27
Hispanic (479)	516	2.15

Senatobia

Place Type: City
County: Tate
Population: 8,165†

Ancestry‡	Population	%
African, Sub-Saharan (20)	20	0.25
African (20)	20	0.25
American (1,517)	1,517	19.06
Bulgarian (13)	13	0.16
Canadian (32)	32	0.40
Czech (0)	15	0.19
Dutch (0)	20	0.25
English (775)	1,038	13.04
French, ex. Basque (115)	251	3.15
French Canadian (12)	12	0.15
German (76)	496	6.23
Irish (473)	618	7.77
Italian (44)	83	1.04
Norwegian (22)	22	0.28
Scotch-Irish (184)	229	2.88
Scottish (79)	139	1.75
Welsh (17)	17	0.21

Hispanic Origin	Population	%
Hispanic or Latino (of any race)	192	2.35
Central American, ex. Mexican	10	0.12
Honduran	5	0.06
Panamanian	1	0.01
Salvadoran	4	0.05
Cuban	3	0.04
Mexican	138	1.69
Puerto Rican	11	0.13
South American	8	0.10
Bolivian	2	0.02
Peruvian	2	0.02
Venezuelan	4	0.05
Other Hispanic or Latino	22	0.27

Race*	Population	%
African-American/Black (2,861)	2,915	35.70
Not Hispanic (2,855)	2,905	35.58
Hispanic (6)	10	0.12
American Indian/Alaska Native (16)	39	0.48
Not Hispanic (16)	36	0.44
Hispanic (0)	3	0.04
Blackfeet (1)	1	0.01
Cherokee (2)	5	0.06
Choctaw (0)	1	0.01
Houma (0)	1	0.01
Navajo (1)	1	0.01
Osage (0)	1	0.01
Potawatomi (3)	3	0.04
Tlingit-Haida *(Alaska Native)* (0)	1	0.01
Asian (24)	42	0.51
Not Hispanic (24)	41	0.50
Hispanic (0)	1	0.01
Chinese, ex. Taiwanese (6)	9	0.11
Filipino (5)	12	0.15
Indian (7)	10	0.12
Indonesian (0)	2	0.02
Korean (1)	1	0.01
Laotian (0)	1	0.01
Pakistani (1)	1	0.01
Vietnamese (4)	4	0.05
Hawaii Native/Pacific Islander (2)	8	0.10
Not Hispanic (1)	7	0.09
Hispanic (1)	1	0.01
Guamanian/Chamorro (2)	2	0.02
Native Hawaiian (0)	1	0.01
Samoan (0)	2	0.02
White (5,057)	5,152	63.10
Not Hispanic (4,989)	5,060	61.97
Hispanic (68)	92	1.13

Southaven

Place Type: City
County: DeSoto
Population: 48,982†

Ancestry‡	Population	%
African, Sub-Saharan (134)	152	0.33
African (75)	93	0.20
Kenyan (59)	59	0.13
American (5,184)	5,184	11.09
Arab (51)	79	0.17
Arab (0)	28	0.06
Moroccan (31)	31	0.07
Syrian (20)	20	0.04
Belgian (8)	21	0.04
Brazilian (11)	11	0.02
British (78)	187	0.40
Cajun (19)	86	0.18
Canadian (0)	28	0.06
Croatian (34)	34	0.07
Czech (0)	12	0.03
Danish (21)	55	0.12
Dutch (75)	480	1.03
English (2,290)	4,576	9.79
European (518)	596	1.28
Finnish (24)	42	0.09
French, ex. Basque (240)	858	1.84
French Canadian (47)	68	0.15
German (1,636)	4,626	9.90
Greek (47)	75	0.16
Hungarian (22)	44	0.09
Icelander (9)	9	0.02
Irish (2,762)	6,635	14.19
Italian (698)	1,254	2.68
Lithuanian (0)	12	0.03
Norwegian (9)	109	0.23
Polish (179)	328	0.70
Portuguese (9)	35	0.07
Russian (0)	32	0.07
Scandinavian (17)	33	0.07
Scotch-Irish (600)	915	1.96
Scottish (575)	1,227	2.62
Slovak (0)	10	0.02
Swedish (116)	321	0.69
Swiss (14)	27	0.06
Ukrainian (8)	8	0.02
Welsh (130)	181	0.39
West Indian, ex. Hispanic (62)	62	0.13
Belizean (37)	37	0.08
Haitian (10)	10	0.02
Jamaican (15)	15	0.03

Hispanic Origin	Population	%
Hispanic or Latino (of any race)	2,472	5.05
Central American, ex. Mexican	151	0.31
Costa Rican	10	0.02
Guatemalan	28	0.06
Honduran	38	0.08
Nicaraguan	9	0.02
Panamanian	16	0.03
Salvadoran	48	0.10
Other Central American	2	<0.01
Cuban	28	0.06
Dominican Republic	9	0.02
Mexican	1,991	4.06
Puerto Rican	92	0.19
South American	92	0.19
Argentinean	10	0.02
Bolivian	12	0.02
Chilean	3	0.01
Colombian	20	0.04
Ecuadorian	14	0.03
Peruvian	14	0.03
Uruguayan	5	0.01
Venezuelan	14	0.03
Other Hispanic or Latino	109	0.22

Race*	Population	%
African-American/Black (10,852)	11,210	22.89
Not Hispanic (10,827)	11,164	22.79
Hispanic (25)	46	0.09
American Indian/Alaska Native (153)	369	0.75
Not Hispanic (120)	314	0.64
Hispanic (33)	55	0.11
Apache (4)	8	0.02
Blackfeet (1)	10	0.02
Cherokee (38)	114	0.23
Cheyenne (0)	1	<0.01
Chickasaw (2)	5	0.01
Chippewa (4)	6	0.01
Choctaw (10)	22	0.04
Comanche (0)	1	<0.01
Cree (1)	1	<0.01
Creek (1)	1	<0.01
Delaware (2)	2	<0.01
Inupiat *(Alaska Native)* (1)	1	<0.01
Iroquois (1)	1	<0.01
Mexican American Ind. (13)	16	0.03
Navajo (0)	2	<0.01
Potawatomi (1)	1	<0.01
Seminole (0)	2	<0.01
Shoshone (4)	4	0.01
Sioux (4)	10	0.02
South American Ind. (4)	4	0.01
Asian (841)	1,055	2.15
Not Hispanic (833)	1,031	2.10
Hispanic (8)	24	0.05
Bangladeshi (8)	8	0.02
Burmese (1)	1	<0.01
Cambodian (42)	54	0.11
Chinese, ex. Taiwanese (145)	178	0.36
Filipino (148)	220	0.45
Indian (208)	235	0.48
Indonesian (2)	2	<0.01
Japanese (15)	46	0.09
Korean (49)	85	0.17
Laotian (27)	29	0.06
Malaysian (1)	1	<0.01
Pakistani (0)	1	<0.01
Sri Lankan (3)	5	0.01
Taiwanese (2)	2	<0.01
Thai (7)	7	0.01
Vietnamese (159)	176	0.36
Hawaii Native/Pacific Islander (28)	64	0.13
Not Hispanic (25)	49	0.10
Hispanic (3)	15	0.03
Fijian (0)	2	<0.01
Guamanian/Chamorro (10)	15	0.03
Native Hawaiian (6)	16	0.03

*Notes: † The Census 2010 population figure is used to calculate the percentages in the Hispanic Origin and Race categories. Ancestry percentages are based on the 2006-2010 American Community Survey population (not shown); ‡ Numbers in parentheses indicate the number of people reporting a single ancestry; * Numbers in parentheses indicate the number of persons reporting this race alone, not in combination with any other race; Please refer to the Explanation of Data for more information.*

Samoan (8)	14	0.03
White (34,787)	35,533	72.54
Not Hispanic (33,992)	34,591	70.62
Hispanic (795)	942	1.92

St. Martin

Place Type: CDP
County: Jackson
Population: 7,730†

Ancestry‡	Population	%
African, Sub-Saharan (137)	137	2.05
African (137)	137	2.05
American (929)	929	13.92
Austrian (0)	20	0.30
Dutch (0)	39	0.58
English (332)	412	6.17
French, ex. Basque (213)	657	9.84
French Canadian (60)	60	0.90
German (244)	733	10.98
Hungarian (0)	112	1.68
Irish (265)	528	7.91
Italian (117)	327	4.90
Polish (32)	138	2.07
Portuguese (0)	14	0.21
Russian (20)	20	0.30
Scotch-Irish (76)	144	2.16
Scottish (7)	44	0.66
Turkish (8)	8	0.12
Yugoslavian (14)	14	0.21

Hispanic Origin	Population	%
Hispanic or Latino (of any race)	316	4.09
Central American, ex. Mexican	40	0.52
Costa Rican	7	0.09
Guatemalan	2	0.03
Honduran	6	0.08
Nicaraguan	3	0.04
Panamanian	11	0.14
Salvadoran	11	0.14
Cuban	19	0.25
Dominican Republic	1	0.01
Mexican	127	1.64
Puerto Rican	37	0.48
South American	26	0.34
Argentinean	1	0.01
Bolivian	1	0.01
Colombian	8	0.10
Paraguayan	1	0.01
Peruvian	4	0.05
Venezuelan	11	0.14
Other Hispanic or Latino	66	0.85

Race*	Population	%
African-American/Black (1,039)	1,147	14.84
Not Hispanic (1,025)	1,124	14.54
Hispanic (14)	23	0.30
American Indian/Alaska Native (28)	58	0.75
Not Hispanic (24)	51	0.66
Hispanic (4)	7	0.09
Cherokee (1)	9	0.12
Chippewa (2)	2	0.03
Choctaw (9)	11	0.14
Iroquois (1)	1	0.01
Menominee (0)	1	0.01
Mexican American Ind. (2)	2	0.03
Potawatomi (1)	4	0.05
Seminole (0)	2	0.03
Spanish American Ind. (1)	1	0.01
Asian (746)	834	10.79
Not Hispanic (743)	822	10.63
Hispanic (3)	12	0.16
Bangladeshi (1)	1	0.01
Chinese, ex. Taiwanese (21)	35	0.45
Filipino (34)	64	0.83
Indian (24)	31	0.40
Japanese (22)	35	0.45
Korean (8)	21	0.27
Thai (9)	12	0.16
Vietnamese (607)	628	8.12
Hawaii Native/Pacific Islander (9)	16	0.21
Not Hispanic (9)	15	0.19
Hispanic (0)	1	0.01
Guamanian/Chamorro (5)	5	0.06
Native Hawaiian (1)	4	0.05
Samoan (1)	1	0.01
White (5,577)	5,788	74.88
Not Hispanic (5,413)	5,588	72.29
Hispanic (164)	200	2.59

Starkville

Place Type: City
County: Oktibbeha
Population: 23,888†

Ancestry‡	Population	%
African, Sub-Saharan (184)	248	1.06
African (184)	248	1.06
American (1,837)	1,837	7.84
Arab (74)	119	0.51
Arab (20)	20	0.09
Egyptian (31)	31	0.13
Lebanese (23)	68	0.29
Austrian (0)	40	0.17
British (60)	91	0.39
Canadian (9)	9	0.04
Czech (0)	31	0.13
Danish (0)	49	0.21
Dutch (151)	282	1.20
English (1,450)	3,127	13.34
European (365)	414	1.77
French, ex. Basque (228)	777	3.32
French Canadian (29)	54	0.23
German (775)	2,119	9.04
Greek (42)	138	0.59
Hungarian (11)	11	0.05
Irish (749)	2,381	10.16
Israeli (10)	51	0.22
Italian (47)	264	1.13
Lithuanian (10)	10	0.04
Norwegian (12)	39	0.17
Polish (51)	67	0.29
Portuguese (0)	16	0.07
Russian (41)	49	0.21
Scotch-Irish (587)	833	3.55
Scottish (283)	783	3.34
Serbian (26)	34	0.15
Slavic (48)	48	0.20
Slovene (7)	7	0.03
Swedish (33)	84	0.36
Swiss (20)	76	0.32
Turkish (35)	35	0.15
Ukrainian (13)	13	0.06
Welsh (33)	150	0.64

Hispanic Origin	Population	%
Hispanic or Latino (of any race)	429	1.80
Central American, ex. Mexican	31	0.13
Guatemalan	5	0.02
Honduran	11	0.05
Nicaraguan	9	0.04
Panamanian	4	0.02
Salvadoran	2	0.01
Cuban	17	0.07
Dominican Republic	3	0.01
Mexican	190	0.80
Puerto Rican	50	0.21
South American	87	0.36
Argentinean	4	0.02
Bolivian	1	<0.01
Chilean	1	<0.01
Colombian	31	0.13
Paraguayan	3	0.01
Peruvian	14	0.06
Venezuelan	33	0.14
Other Hispanic or Latino	51	0.21

Race*	Population	%
African-American/Black (8,274)	8,434	35.31
Not Hispanic (8,239)	8,387	35.11
Hispanic (35)	47	0.20
American Indian/Alaska Native (48)	120	0.50
Not Hispanic (44)	112	0.47
Hispanic (4)	8	0.03
Apache (4)	5	0.02
Blackfeet (1)	1	<0.01
Cherokee (5)	20	0.08
Chickasaw (2)	3	0.01
Choctaw (20)	29	0.12
Creek (1)	1	<0.01
Houma (1)	2	0.01
Inupiat *(Alaska Native)* (1)	1	<0.01
Iroquois (1)	1	<0.01
Menominee (1)	1	<0.01
Sioux (0)	1	<0.01
South American Ind. (1)	1	<0.01
Asian (894)	1,015	4.25
Not Hispanic (889)	1,002	4.19
Hispanic (5)	13	0.05
Bangladeshi (11)	11	0.05
Burmese (2)	2	0.01
Cambodian (1)	2	0.01
Chinese, ex. Taiwanese (327)	348	1.46
Filipino (29)	55	0.23
Indian (248)	268	1.12
Indonesian (9)	17	0.07
Japanese (10)	36	0.15
Korean (96)	112	0.47
Malaysian (1)	2	0.01
Nepalese (21)	23	0.10
Pakistani (15)	15	0.06
Sri Lankan (40)	40	0.17
Taiwanese (13)	14	0.06
Thai (9)	9	0.04
Vietnamese (34)	40	0.17
Hawaii Native/Pacific Islander (13)	34	0.14
Not Hispanic (10)	27	0.11
Hispanic (3)	7	0.03
Guamanian/Chamorro (5)	7	0.03
Native Hawaiian (7)	25	0.10
Samoan (0)	4	0.02
White (14,246)	14,495	60.68
Not Hispanic (13,979)	14,206	59.47
Hispanic (267)	289	1.21

Tupelo

Place Type: City
County: Lee
Population: 34,546†

Ancestry‡	Population	%
African, Sub-Saharan (35)	75	0.22
African (35)	75	0.22
American (3,310)	3,310	9.63
Arab (17)	75	0.22
Lebanese (17)	75	0.22
Austrian (0)	34	0.10
British (41)	41	0.12
Cajun (0)	10	0.03
Canadian (5)	54	0.16
Croatian (8)	19	0.06
Czech (13)	31	0.09
Czechoslovakian (34)	34	0.10
Dutch (313)	479	1.39
English (1,904)	3,692	10.74
European (278)	318	0.93
French, ex. Basque (260)	602	1.75
French Canadian (0)	10	0.03
German (696)	1,764	5.13
Greek (41)	50	0.15
Hungarian (16)	26	0.08
Icelander (0)	12	0.03
Irish (1,279)	2,943	8.56
Italian (340)	996	2.90
Lithuanian (0)	11	0.03

*Notes: † The Census 2010 population figure is used to calculate the percentages in the Hispanic Origin and Race categories. Ancestry percentages are based on the 2006-2010 American Community Survey population (not shown); ‡ Numbers in parentheses indicate the number of people reporting a single ancestry; * Numbers in parentheses indicate the number of persons reporting this race alone, not in combination with any other race; Please refer to the Explanation of Data for more information.*

Ancestry	Population	%
Norwegian (22)	93	0.27
Polish (44)	148	0.43
Portuguese (15)	25	0.07
Romanian (19)	29	0.08
Russian (36)	36	0.10
Scandinavian (0)	24	0.07
Scotch-Irish (582)	872	2.54
Scottish (269)	575	1.67
Slavic (0)	6	0.02
Slovak (0)	9	0.03
Slovene (0)	9	0.03
Swedish (10)	54	0.16
Swiss (0)	25	0.07
Ukrainian (11)	11	0.03
Welsh (30)	90	0.26

Hispanic Origin	Population	%
Hispanic or Latino (of any race)	1,205	3.49
Central American, ex. Mexican	80	0.23
Costa Rican	2	0.01
Guatemalan	45	0.13
Honduran	8	0.02
Nicaraguan	4	0.01
Panamanian	5	0.01
Salvadoran	15	0.04
Other Central American	1	<0.01
Cuban	33	0.10
Mexican	929	2.69
Puerto Rican	39	0.11
South American	21	0.06
Bolivian	4	0.01
Chilean	1	<0.01
Colombian	6	0.02
Ecuadorian	1	<0.01
Peruvian	3	0.01
Venezuelan	6	0.02
Other Hispanic or Latino	103	0.30

Race*	Population	%
African-American/Black (12,709)	13,020	37.69
Not Hispanic (12,634)	12,918	37.39
Hispanic (75)	102	0.30
American Indian/Alaska Native (45)	138	0.40
Not Hispanic (37)	109	0.32
Hispanic (8)	29	0.08
Blackfeet (0)	2	0.01
Central American Ind. (0)	2	0.01
Cherokee (6)	20	0.06
Chickasaw (0)	6	0.02
Choctaw (8)	18	0.05
Iroquois (2)	2	0.01
Mexican American Ind. (1)	3	0.01
Navajo (1)	5	0.01
Potawatomi (3)	3	0.01
Pueblo (0)	1	<0.01
Sioux (0)	1	<0.01
South American Ind. (0)	1	<0.01
Spanish American Ind. (0)	1	<0.01
Asian (339)	418	1.21
Not Hispanic (335)	409	1.18
Hispanic (4)	9	0.03
Cambodian (1)	3	0.01
Chinese, ex. Taiwanese (54)	64	0.19
Filipino (16)	26	0.08
Indian (106)	115	0.33
Indonesian (3)	3	0.01
Japanese (12)	18	0.05
Korean (22)	39	0.11
Laotian (31)	36	0.10
Malaysian (0)	1	<0.01
Pakistani (9)	10	0.03
Sri Lankan (2)	2	0.01
Taiwanese (6)	6	0.02
Thai (3)	6	0.02
Vietnamese (62)	68	0.20
Hawaii Native/Pacific Islander (4)	25	0.07
Not Hispanic (3)	15	0.04
Hispanic (1)	10	0.03
Guamanian/Chamorro (1)	1	<0.01
Native Hawaiian (2)	9	0.03
Samoan (1)	5	0.01
White (20,283)	20,688	59.89
Not Hispanic (19,929)	20,267	58.67
Hispanic (354)	421	1.22

Vicksburg

Place Type: City
County: Warren
Population: 23,856†

Ancestry‡	Population	%
African, Sub-Saharan (237)	300	1.24
African (144)	193	0.80
Ghanaian (42)	56	0.23
Other Sub-Saharan African (51)	51	0.21
American (1,616)	1,616	6.68
Arab (66)	174	0.72
Lebanese (66)	174	0.72
Austrian (7)	21	0.09
Belgian (0)	9	0.04
British (44)	57	0.24
Canadian (0)	8	0.03
Celtic (8)	8	0.03
Danish (13)	45	0.19
Dutch (0)	52	0.21
English (645)	1,129	4.67
European (47)	55	0.23
French, ex. Basque (120)	381	1.58
French Canadian (25)	61	0.25
German (436)	877	3.63
Greek (0)	9	0.04
Irish (568)	1,185	4.90
Italian (236)	529	2.19
Norwegian (10)	50	0.21
Polish (0)	36	0.15
Russian (15)	15	0.06
Scotch-Irish (152)	349	1.44
Scottish (146)	347	1.43
Swedish (64)	140	0.58
Swiss (15)	48	0.20
Welsh (48)	71	0.29
West Indian, ex. Hispanic (0)	33	0.14
Dutch West Indian (0)	10	0.04
Jamaican (0)	23	0.10

Hispanic Origin	Population	%
Hispanic or Latino (of any race)	409	1.71
Central American, ex. Mexican	24	0.10
Costa Rican	1	<0.01
Guatemalan	8	0.03
Honduran	8	0.03
Nicaraguan	4	0.02
Panamanian	2	0.01
Salvadoran	1	<0.01
Cuban	9	0.04
Dominican Republic	4	0.02
Mexican	272	1.14
Puerto Rican	34	0.14
South American	10	0.04
Argentinean	1	<0.01
Chilean	2	0.01
Colombian	4	0.02
Ecuadorian	1	<0.01
Peruvian	1	<0.01
Venezuelan	1	<0.01
Other Hispanic or Latino	56	0.23

Race*	Population	%
African-American/Black (15,763)	15,876	66.55
Not Hispanic (15,715)	15,812	66.28
Hispanic (48)	64	0.27
American Indian/Alaska Native (58)	116	0.49
Not Hispanic (41)	95	0.40
Hispanic (17)	21	0.09
Aleut *(Alaska Native)* (1)	2	0.01
Blackfeet (1)	2	0.01
Cherokee (2)	24	0.10
Choctaw (5)	13	0.05
Comanche (0)	1	<0.01
Creek (1)	3	0.01
Iroquois (1)	1	<0.01
Mexican American Ind. (1)	1	<0.01
Navajo (3)	3	0.01
Pueblo (1)	1	<0.01
Seminole (0)	1	<0.01
Sioux (8)	8	0.03
Spanish American Ind. (2)	2	0.01
Asian (211)	247	1.04
Not Hispanic (210)	241	1.01
Hispanic (1)	6	0.03
Cambodian (1)	1	<0.01
Chinese, ex. Taiwanese (27)	32	0.13
Filipino (42)	47	0.20
Indian (106)	118	0.49
Japanese (6)	11	0.05
Korean (7)	9	0.04
Malaysian (1)	1	<0.01
Pakistani (8)	8	0.03
Vietnamese (9)	10	0.04
Hawaii Native/Pacific Islander (8)	15	0.06
Not Hispanic (8)	14	0.06
Hispanic (0)	1	<0.01
Guamanian/Chamorro (8)	10	0.04
Tongan (0)	1	<0.01
White (7,469)	7,610	31.90
Not Hispanic (7,301)	7,419	31.10
Hispanic (168)	191	0.80

West Point

Place Type: City
County: Clay
Population: 11,307†

Ancestry‡	Population	%
African, Sub-Saharan (68)	68	0.59
African (68)	68	0.59
American (520)	520	4.53
Australian (0)	7	0.06
Czech (16)	16	0.14
Dutch (9)	78	0.68
English (715)	1,482	12.92
European (51)	51	0.44
French, ex. Basque (34)	153	1.33
French Canadian (0)	6	0.05
German (87)	433	3.78
Irish (367)	855	7.46
Italian (42)	100	0.87
Polish (0)	50	0.44
Scotch-Irish (144)	249	2.17
Scottish (142)	161	1.40
Swedish (12)	45	0.39
Swiss (7)	14	0.12
Welsh (0)	41	0.36

Hispanic Origin	Population	%
Hispanic or Latino (of any race)	99	0.88
Central American, ex. Mexican	3	0.03
Guatemalan	1	0.01
Salvadoran	2	0.02
Mexican	61	0.54
Puerto Rican	1	0.01
South American	1	0.01
Venezuelan	1	0.01
Other Hispanic or Latino	33	0.29

Race*	Population	%
African-American/Black (6,943)	6,973	61.67
Not Hispanic (6,917)	6,946	61.43
Hispanic (26)	27	0.24
American Indian/Alaska Native (10)	37	0.33
Not Hispanic (10)	33	0.29
Hispanic (0)	4	0.04
Apache (1)	2	0.02
Cherokee (6)	10	0.09
Choctaw (1)	2	0.02
Sioux (0)	5	0.04
Asian (20)	28	0.25
Not Hispanic (19)	26	0.23

*Notes: † The Census 2010 population figure is used to calculate the percentages in the Hispanic Origin and Race categories. Ancestry percentages are based on the 2006-2010 American Community Survey population (not shown); ‡ Numbers in parentheses indicate the number of people reporting a single ancestry; * Numbers in parentheses indicate the number of persons reporting this race alone, not in combination with any other race; Please refer to the Explanation of Data for more information.*

Hispanic (1)	2	0.02
Chinese, ex. Taiwanese (0)	1	0.01
Filipino (5)	7	0.06
Indian (6)	7	0.06
Japanese (1)	2	0.02
Korean (4)	4	0.04
Pakistani (2)	2	0.02
Sri Lankan (1)	1	0.01
Hawaii Native/Pacific Islander (2)	4	0.04
Not Hispanic (2)	3	0.03
Hispanic (0)	1	0.01
Guamanian/Chamorro (1)	1	0.01
White (4,248)	4,286	37.91
Not Hispanic (4,212)	4,243	37.53
Hispanic (36)	43	0.38

Yazoo City

Place Type: City
County: Yazoo
Population: 11,403†

Ancestry‡	Population	%
African, Sub-Saharan (89)	89	0.76
African (89)	89	0.76
American (479)	479	4.11
Arab (9)	26	0.22
Lebanese (9)	26	0.22
Armenian (10)	10	0.09
British (9)	9	0.08
English (326)	351	3.01
French, ex. Basque (0)	75	0.64
German (31)	103	0.88
Irish (195)	271	2.33
Italian (15)	22	0.19
Scotch-Irish (36)	67	0.58
Scottish (13)	76	0.65
Swedish (0)	10	0.09
Swiss (0)	9	0.08

Hispanic Origin	Population	%
Hispanic or Latino (of any race)	79	0.69
Central American, ex. Mexican	2	0.02
Guatemalan	1	0.01
Panamanian	1	0.01
Mexican	44	0.39
Puerto Rican	9	0.08
South American	1	0.01
Paraguayan	1	0.01
Other Hispanic or Latino	23	0.20

Race*	Population	%
African-American/Black (9,405)	9,456	82.93
Not Hispanic (9,355)	9,402	82.45
Hispanic (50)	54	0.47
American Indian/Alaska Native (18)	41	0.36
Not Hispanic (17)	38	0.33
Hispanic (1)	3	0.03
Canadian/French Am. Ind. (1)	1	0.01
Cherokee (1)	1	0.01
Choctaw (0)	1	0.01
Navajo (0)	1	0.01
Asian (60)	70	0.61
Not Hispanic (60)	70	0.61
Chinese, ex. Taiwanese (7)	7	0.06
Filipino (14)	14	0.12
Indian (30)	36	0.32
Korean (5)	5	0.04
Laotian (4)	4	0.04
Hawaii Native/Pacific Islander (0)	6	0.05
Not Hispanic (0)	4	0.04
Hispanic (0)	2	0.02
Native Hawaiian (0)	1	0.01
White (1,846)	1,880	16.49
Not Hispanic (1,834)	1,867	16.37
Hispanic (12)	13	0.11

*Notes: † The Census 2010 population figure is used to calculate the percentages in the Hispanic Origin and Race categories. Ancestry percentages are based on the 2006-2010 American Community Survey population (not shown); ‡ Numbers in parentheses indicate the number of people reporting a single ancestry; * Numbers in parentheses indicate the number of persons reporting this race alone, not in combination with any other race; Please refer to the Explanation of Data for more information.*

MISSOURI

Place Type: State
Population: 5,988,927†

Ancestry‡	Population	%
Afghan (1,433)	1,433	0.02
African, Sub-Saharan (31,460)	37,706	0.64
African (21,744)	26,968	0.46
Cape Verdean (15)	90	<0.01
Ethiopian (1,377)	1,441	0.02
Ghanaian (416)	433	0.01
Kenyan (916)	994	0.02
Liberian (796)	873	0.01
Nigerian (2,328)	2,523	0.04
Senegalese (69)	69	<0.01
Sierra Leonean (149)	149	<0.01
Somalian (1,366)	1,366	0.02
South African (365)	535	0.01
Sudanese (523)	707	0.01
Ugandan (87)	87	<0.01
Zimbabwean (99)	108	<0.01
Other Sub-Saharan African (1,210)	1,363	0.02
Albanian (2,164)	2,687	0.05
Alsatian (110)	268	<0.01
American (552,994)	552,994	9.34
Arab (10,060)	16,327	0.28
Arab (2,832)	3,669	0.06
Egyptian (921)	1,273	0.02
Iraqi (1,020)	1,159	0.02
Jordanian (317)	475	0.01
Lebanese (1,975)	5,118	0.09
Moroccan (662)	956	0.02
Palestinian (517)	744	0.01
Syrian (499)	1,200	0.02
Other Arab (1,317)	1,733	0.03
Armenian (1,041)	2,260	0.04
Assyrian/Chaldean/Syriac (25)	70	<0.01
Australian (610)	1,495	0.03
Austrian (2,682)	12,116	0.20
Basque (160)	258	<0.01
Belgian (1,805)	5,561	0.09
Brazilian (1,043)	1,530	0.03
British (9,371)	19,268	0.33
Bulgarian (1,241)	1,611	0.03
Cajun (582)	1,267	0.02
Canadian (3,200)	6,463	0.11
Carpatho Rusyn (0)	9	<0.01
Celtic (391)	734	0.01
Croatian (3,331)	9,856	0.17
Cypriot (87)	87	<0.01
Czech (8,608)	30,187	0.51
Czechoslovakian (2,653)	5,759	0.10
Danish (5,811)	20,826	0.35
Dutch (21,353)	115,789	1.96
Eastern European (3,080)	3,436	0.06
English (217,479)	613,509	10.36
Estonian (87)	423	0.01
European (57,038)	64,904	1.10
Finnish (1,051)	4,359	0.07
French, ex. Basque (37,138)	225,631	3.81
French Canadian (5,842)	15,717	0.27
German (640,703)	1,605,541	27.11
German Russian (172)	369	0.01
Greek (6,109)	15,635	0.26
Guyanese (128)	180	<0.01
Hungarian (4,712)	14,513	0.25
Icelander (177)	515	0.01
Iranian (2,278)	3,078	0.05
Irish (218,780)	876,760	14.80
Israeli (506)	726	0.01
Italian (73,144)	215,204	3.63
Latvian (352)	792	0.01
Lithuanian (2,144)	6,141	0.10
Luxemburger (217)	505	0.01
Macedonian (437)	615	0.01
Maltese (25)	126	<0.01
New Zealander (252)	439	0.01
Northern European (3,078)	3,384	0.06
Norwegian (14,245)	45,415	0.77
Pennsylvania German (2,734)	4,172	0.07
Polish (32,688)	108,835	1.84
Portuguese (1,880)	5,981	0.10
Romanian (2,797)	5,220	0.09
Russian (14,106)	31,898	0.54
Scandinavian (2,541)	7,357	0.12
Scotch-Irish (43,380)	115,144	1.94
Scottish (32,362)	111,202	1.88
Serbian (1,167)	2,448	0.04
Slavic (496)	1,643	0.03
Slovak (1,655)	5,031	0.08
Slovene (420)	1,336	0.02
Soviet Union (18)	18	<0.01
Swedish (16,387)	64,889	1.10
Swiss (5,600)	24,908	0.42
Turkish (1,127)	1,633	0.03
Ukrainian (3,937)	7,893	0.13
Welsh (8,767)	40,759	0.69
West Indian, ex. Hispanic (3,899)	6,838	0.12
Bahamian (237)	314	0.01
Barbadian (12)	58	<0.01
Belizean (200)	241	<0.01
Bermudan (18)	18	<0.01
British West Indian (238)	262	<0.01
Dutch West Indian (285)	984	0.02
Haitian (998)	1,278	0.02
Jamaican (1,336)	2,537	0.04
Trinidadian/Tobagonian (109)	229	<0.01
U.S. Virgin Islander (0)	3	<0.01
West Indian (452)	860	0.01
Other West Indian (14)	54	<0.01
Yugoslavian (11,757)	13,707	0.23

Hispanic Origin	Population	%
Hispanic or Latino (of any race)	212,470	3.55
Central American, ex. Mexican	17,763	0.30
Costa Rican	587	0.01
Guatemalan	6,610	0.11
Honduran	3,657	0.06
Nicaraguan	843	0.01
Panamanian	1,349	0.02
Salvadoran	4,628	0.08
Other Central American	89	<0.01
Cuban	4,979	0.08
Dominican Republic	1,503	0.03
Mexican	147,254	2.46
Puerto Rican	12,236	0.20
South American	8,731	0.15
Argentinean	991	0.02
Bolivian	471	0.01
Chilean	665	0.01
Colombian	2,659	0.04
Ecuadorian	937	0.02
Paraguayan	128	<0.01
Peruvian	1,687	0.03
Uruguayan	179	<0.01
Venezuelan	901	0.02
Other South American	113	<0.01
Other Hispanic or Latino	20,004	0.33

Race*	Population	%
African-American/Black (693,391)	747,474	12.48
Not Hispanic (687,149)	736,574	12.30
Hispanic (6,242)	10,900	0.18
American Indian/Alaska Native (27,376)	72,376	1.21
Not Hispanic (24,062)	65,131	1.09
Hispanic (3,314)	7,245	0.12
Alaska Athabascan *(Ala. Nat.)* (56)	98	<0.01
Aleut *(Alaska Native)* (57)	92	<0.01
Apache (392)	1,183	0.02
Arapaho (47)	120	<0.01
Blackfeet (375)	2,473	0.04
Canadian/French Am. Ind. (37)	127	<0.01
Central American Ind. (48)	91	<0.01
Cherokee (8,081)	25,373	0.42
Cheyenne (84)	212	<0.01
Chickasaw (345)	789	0.01
Chippewa (493)	945	0.02
Choctaw (1,141)	2,793	0.05
Colville (15)	20	<0.01
Comanche (120)	304	0.01
Cree (33)	106	<0.01
Creek (463)	998	0.02
Crow (43)	154	<0.01
Delaware (191)	394	0.01
Hopi (33)	92	<0.01
Houma (12)	31	<0.01
Inupiat *(Alaska Native)* (50)	113	<0.01
Iroquois (700)	1,261	0.02
Kiowa (66)	143	<0.01
Lumbee (105)	171	<0.01
Menominee (25)	43	<0.01
Mexican American Ind. (731)	1,147	0.02
Navajo (344)	798	0.01
Osage (246)	799	0.01
Ottawa (154)	240	<0.01
Paiute (18)	41	<0.01
Pima (26)	33	<0.01
Potawatomi (401)	723	0.01
Pueblo (101)	187	<0.01
Puget Sound Salish (23)	35	<0.01
Seminole (116)	400	0.01
Shoshone (53)	107	<0.01
Sioux (825)	2,159	0.04
South American Ind. (97)	226	<0.01
Spanish American Ind. (68)	104	<0.01
Tlingit-Haida *(Alaska Native)* (69)	125	<0.01
Tohono O'Odham (18)	29	<0.01
Tsimshian *(Alaska Native)* (2)	7	<0.01
Ute (40)	81	<0.01
Yakama (8)	17	<0.01
Yaqui (29)	95	<0.01
Yuman (22)	30	<0.01
Yup'ik *(Alaska Native)* (25)	45	<0.01
Asian (98,083)	123,571	2.06
Not Hispanic (97,221)	121,013	2.02
Hispanic (862)	2,558	0.04
Bangladeshi (449)	530	0.01
Bhutanese (231)	309	0.01
Burmese (794)	842	0.01
Cambodian (1,002)	1,328	0.02
Chinese, ex. Taiwanese (20,693)	24,457	0.41
Filipino (10,914)	17,706	0.30
Hmong (1,248)	1,329	0.02
Indian (23,223)	26,263	0.44
Indonesian (290)	475	0.01
Japanese (3,186)	7,084	0.12
Korean (9,249)	12,689	0.21
Laotian (894)	1,180	0.02
Malaysian (213)	344	0.01
Nepalese (465)	566	0.01
Pakistani (3,250)	3,710	0.06
Sri Lankan (297)	341	0.01
Taiwanese (1,343)	1,632	0.03
Thai (1,593)	2,471	0.04
Vietnamese (14,523)	16,530	0.28
Hawaii Native/Pacific Islander (6,261)	11,296	0.19
Not Hispanic (5,763)	10,075	0.17
Hispanic (498)	1,221	0.02
Fijian (50)	93	<0.01
Guamanian/Chamorro (969)	1,551	0.03
Marshallese (134)	174	<0.01
Native Hawaiian (958)	2,673	0.04
Samoan (1,557)	2,740	0.05
Tongan (74)	156	<0.01
White (4,958,770)	5,070,826	84.67
Not Hispanic (4,850,748)	4,947,306	82.61
Hispanic (108,022)	123,520	2.06

*Notes: † The Census 2010 population figure is used to calculate the percentages in the Hispanic Origin and Race categories. Ancestry percentages are based on the 2006-2010 American Community Survey population (not shown); ‡ Numbers in parentheses indicate the number of people reporting a single ancestry; * Numbers in parentheses indicate the number of persons reporting this race alone, not in combination with any other race; Please refer to the Explanation of Data for more information.*

Affton

Place Type: CDP
County: St. Louis
Population: 20,307†

Ancestry‡	Population	%
Albanian (215)	242	1.20
American (1,325)	1,325	6.59
Arab (109)	189	0.94
Arab (35)	106	0.53
Iraqi (19)	19	0.09
Lebanese (55)	64	0.32
Austrian (30)	75	0.37
Belgian (39)	122	0.61
Brazilian (9)	9	0.04
British (16)	67	0.33
Croatian (114)	247	1.23
Czech (139)	316	1.57
Czechoslovakian (12)	124	0.62
Danish (0)	10	0.05
Dutch (74)	312	1.55
English (444)	1,795	8.92
European (208)	208	1.03
French, ex. Basque (56)	1,377	6.85
German (3,315)	8,301	41.27
Greek (45)	130	0.65
Hungarian (27)	85	0.42
Iranian (10)	10	0.05
Irish (728)	3,587	17.83
Italian (694)	1,713	8.52
Lithuanian (13)	13	0.06
Macedonian (194)	194	0.96
Norwegian (16)	127	0.63
Polish (239)	882	4.38
Romanian (0)	27	0.13
Russian (10)	49	0.24
Scotch-Irish (38)	202	1.00
Scottish (120)	357	1.77
Serbian (31)	43	0.21
Slavic (0)	16	0.08
Slovak (13)	93	0.46
Slovene (12)	55	0.27
Swedish (37)	193	0.96
Swiss (14)	32	0.16
Ukrainian (15)	43	0.21
Welsh (0)	97	0.48
Yugoslavian (1,150)	1,150	5.72

Hispanic Origin	Population	%
Hispanic or Latino (of any race)	419	2.06
Central American, ex. Mexican	29	0.14
Costa Rican	2	0.01
Guatemalan	18	0.09
Honduran	4	0.02
Nicaraguan	2	0.01
Panamanian	2	0.01
Other Central American	1	<0.01
Cuban	12	0.06
Dominican Republic	1	<0.01
Mexican	251	1.24
Puerto Rican	20	0.10
South American	38	0.19
Argentinean	8	0.04
Bolivian	4	0.02
Chilean	2	0.01
Colombian	4	0.02
Ecuadorian	8	0.04
Paraguayan	2	0.01
Peruvian	3	0.01
Uruguayan	3	0.01
Venezuelan	3	0.01
Other South American	1	<0.01
Other Hispanic or Latino	68	0.33

Race*	Population	%
African-American/Black (343)	437	2.15
Not Hispanic (337)	424	2.09
Hispanic (6)	13	0.06
American Indian/Alaska Native (32)	108	0.53
Not Hispanic (26)	94	0.46
Hispanic (6)	14	0.07
Alaska Athabascan *(Ala. Nat.)* (1)	1	<0.01
Aleut *(Alaska Native)* (1)	1	<0.01
Apache (1)	8	0.04
Arapaho (0)	2	0.01
Blackfeet (0)	1	<0.01
Cherokee (8)	29	0.14
Chippewa (3)	10	0.05
Choctaw (1)	2	0.01
Mexican American Ind. (3)	9	0.04
Osage (1)	2	0.01
Sioux (0)	6	0.03
South American Ind. (1)	1	<0.01
Asian (417)	517	2.55
Not Hispanic (409)	506	2.49
Hispanic (8)	11	0.05
Bangladeshi (4)	4	0.02
Cambodian (1)	1	<0.01
Chinese, ex. Taiwanese (28)	49	0.24
Filipino (46)	69	0.34
Indian (70)	78	0.38
Indonesian (0)	1	<0.01
Japanese (8)	14	0.07
Korean (13)	26	0.13
Laotian (2)	6	0.03
Pakistani (0)	1	<0.01
Sri Lankan (0)	1	<0.01
Taiwanese (1)	1	<0.01
Thai (3)	12	0.06
Vietnamese (201)	228	1.12
Hawaii Native/Pacific Islander (3)	16	0.08
Not Hispanic (3)	16	0.08
Guamanian/Chamorro (0)	2	0.01
Native Hawaiian (0)	3	0.01
Samoan (1)	5	0.02
White (19,163)	19,420	95.63
Not Hispanic (18,845)	19,080	93.96
Hispanic (318)	340	1.67

Arnold

Place Type: City
County: Jefferson
Population: 20,808†

Ancestry‡	Population	%
African, Sub-Saharan (12)	33	0.16
African (12)	33	0.16
American (1,563)	1,563	7.53
Arab (52)	52	0.25
Lebanese (52)	52	0.25
Austrian (0)	55	0.27
British (25)	46	0.22
Canadian (0)	15	0.07
Croatian (0)	45	0.22
Czech (10)	159	0.77
Czechoslovakian (71)	71	0.34
Danish (32)	96	0.46
Dutch (34)	228	1.10
English (483)	2,057	9.91
European (68)	121	0.58
Finnish (0)	51	0.25
French, ex. Basque (110)	1,059	5.10
French Canadian (28)	63	0.30
German (3,179)	8,813	42.47
Greek (71)	97	0.47
Hungarian (12)	104	0.50
Irish (928)	4,394	21.17
Italian (311)	950	4.58
Latvian (16)	16	0.08
Norwegian (48)	106	0.51
Polish (341)	558	2.69
Romanian (27)	95	0.46
Russian (42)	320	1.54
Scandinavian (0)	33	0.16
Scotch-Irish (102)	200	0.96
Scottish (86)	253	1.22
Slavic (17)	17	0.08
Slovak (0)	15	0.07
Swedish (0)	15	0.07
Swiss (0)	17	0.08
Ukrainian (9)	71	0.34
Welsh (45)	135	0.65
West Indian, ex. Hispanic (0)	16	0.08
Dutch West Indian (0)	16	0.08
Yugoslavian (171)	209	1.01

Hispanic Origin	Population	%
Hispanic or Latino (of any race)	455	2.19
Central American, ex. Mexican	20	0.10
Costa Rican	2	0.01
Guatemalan	11	0.05
Honduran	7	0.03
Cuban	6	0.03
Dominican Republic	2	0.01
Mexican	308	1.48
Puerto Rican	24	0.12
South American	30	0.14
Argentinean	1	<0.01
Bolivian	2	0.01
Chilean	2	0.01
Colombian	17	0.08
Ecuadorian	1	<0.01
Peruvian	4	0.02
Venezuelan	2	0.01
Other South American	1	<0.01
Other Hispanic or Latino	65	0.31

Race*	Population	%
African-American/Black (116)	203	0.98
Not Hispanic (112)	196	0.94
Hispanic (4)	7	0.03
American Indian/Alaska Native (47)	160	0.77
Not Hispanic (43)	141	0.68
Hispanic (4)	19	0.09
Apache (1)	1	<0.01
Blackfeet (2)	9	0.04
Cherokee (13)	71	0.34
Chippewa (1)	4	0.02
Choctaw (4)	12	0.06
Comanche (1)	4	0.02
Creek (0)	2	0.01
Crow (0)	1	<0.01
Iroquois (1)	2	0.01
Mexican American Ind. (0)	1	<0.01
Navajo (1)	2	0.01
Sioux (1)	5	0.02
Yuman (1)	1	<0.01
Yup'ik *(Alaska Native)* (1)	1	<0.01
Asian (185)	258	1.24
Not Hispanic (182)	246	1.18
Hispanic (3)	12	0.06
Cambodian (0)	1	<0.01
Chinese, ex. Taiwanese (31)	34	0.16
Filipino (45)	66	0.32
Indian (20)	23	0.11
Japanese (8)	29	0.14
Korean (16)	28	0.13
Laotian (8)	12	0.06
Nepalese (2)	2	0.01
Pakistani (0)	1	<0.01
Thai (9)	12	0.06
Vietnamese (33)	35	0.17
Hawaii Native/Pacific Islander (5)	14	0.07
Not Hispanic (5)	14	0.07
Native Hawaiian (4)	11	0.05
Samoan (1)	3	0.01
White (20,046)	20,320	97.65
Not Hispanic (19,754)	19,992	96.08
Hispanic (292)	328	1.58

Aurora

Place Type: City
County: Lawrence
Population: 7,508†

Ancestry‡	Population	%
American (897)	897	11.95

*Notes: † The Census 2010 population figure is used to calculate the percentages in the Hispanic Origin and Race categories. Ancestry percentages are based on the 2006-2010 American Community Survey population (not shown); ‡ Numbers in parentheses indicate the number of people reporting a single ancestry; * Numbers in parentheses indicate the number of persons reporting this race alone, not in combination with any other race; Please refer to the Explanation of Data for more information.*

Arab (0)	17	0.23
Lebanese (0)	17	0.23
Austrian (0)	13	0.17
British (0)	51	0.68
Czech (10)	10	0.13
Danish (0)	13	0.17
Dutch (61)	287	3.82
English (464)	872	11.62
European (0)	19	0.25
French, ex. Basque (46)	282	3.76
German (421)	1,390	18.52
Irish (560)	1,542	20.55
Italian (23)	138	1.84
Norwegian (13)	80	1.07
Polish (14)	41	0.55
Portuguese (0)	4	0.05
Russian (0)	9	0.12
Scotch-Irish (39)	140	1.87
Scottish (88)	227	3.02
Swedish (44)	130	1.73
Welsh (0)	46	0.61
West Indian, ex. Hispanic (55)	55	0.73
Dutch West Indian (55)	55	0.73

Hispanic Origin	Population	%
Hispanic or Latino (of any race)	563	7.50
Central American, ex. Mexican	19	0.25
Guatemalan	9	0.12
Honduran	1	0.01
Nicaraguan	2	0.03
Salvadoran	7	0.09
Mexican	494	6.58
Puerto Rican	8	0.11
South American	6	0.08
Argentinean	3	0.04
Colombian	1	0.01
Ecuadorian	1	0.01
Paraguayan	1	0.01
Other Hispanic or Latino	36	0.48

Race*	Population	%
African-American/Black (25)	47	0.63
Not Hispanic (19)	40	0.53
Hispanic (6)	7	0.09
American Indian/Alaska Native (65)	146	1.94
Not Hispanic (59)	130	1.73
Hispanic (6)	16	0.21
Alaska Athabascan *(Ala. Nat.)* (1)	1	0.01
Apache (3)	4	0.05
Arapaho (1)	4	0.05
Blackfeet (0)	2	0.03
Canadian/French Am. Ind. (0)	1	0.01
Cherokee (21)	52	0.69
Cheyenne (0)	1	0.01
Chickasaw (1)	4	0.05
Choctaw (1)	5	0.07
Comanche (0)	4	0.05
Creek (6)	12	0.16
Iroquois (5)	6	0.08
Mexican American Ind. (2)	2	0.03
Navajo (4)	4	0.05
Potawatomi (1)	3	0.04
Sioux (2)	4	0.05
Tlingit-Haida *(Alaska Native)* (0)	4	0.05
Asian (13)	23	0.31
Not Hispanic (13)	22	0.29
Hispanic (0)	1	0.01
Chinese, ex. Taiwanese (3)	3	0.04
Filipino (7)	12	0.16
Indian (2)	5	0.07
Japanese (0)	1	0.01
Korean (1)	2	0.03
Hawaii Native/Pacific Islander (8)	9	0.12
Not Hispanic (3)	4	0.05
Hispanic (5)	5	0.07
Guamanian/Chamorro (5)	5	0.07
Native Hawaiian (1)	2	0.03
Samoan (2)	2	0.03
White (6,933)	7,064	94.09
Not Hispanic (6,744)	6,843	91.14
Hispanic (189)	221	2.94

Ballwin

Place Type: City
County: St. Louis
Population: 30,404†

Ancestry‡	Population	%
African, Sub-Saharan (0)	48	0.16
South African (0)	48	0.16
Albanian (321)	321	1.05
American (1,867)	1,867	6.12
Arab (137)	238	0.78
Arab (57)	57	0.19
Egyptian (26)	48	0.16
Lebanese (23)	66	0.22
Syrian (0)	15	0.05
Other Arab (31)	52	0.17
Armenian (15)	30	0.10
Australian (28)	28	0.09
Austrian (38)	230	0.75
Basque (14)	14	0.05
Belgian (14)	25	0.08
Brazilian (52)	52	0.17
British (63)	171	0.56
Bulgarian (241)	258	0.85
Canadian (14)	119	0.39
Croatian (22)	36	0.12
Czech (94)	213	0.70
Czechoslovakian (32)	60	0.20
Danish (12)	242	0.79
Dutch (121)	644	2.11
Eastern European (17)	17	0.06
English (917)	4,355	14.28
European (232)	246	0.81
French, ex. Basque (253)	1,608	5.27
French Canadian (13)	152	0.50
German (3,846)	11,211	36.76
Greek (105)	257	0.84
Hungarian (38)	125	0.41
Irish (1,488)	6,189	20.29
Italian (652)	2,433	7.98
Latvian (0)	14	0.05
Lithuanian (77)	126	0.41
Macedonian (10)	10	0.03
Northern European (35)	35	0.11
Norwegian (200)	391	1.28
Polish (368)	1,024	3.36
Portuguese (26)	66	0.22
Romanian (12)	24	0.08
Russian (166)	316	1.04
Scandinavian (40)	86	0.28
Scotch-Irish (280)	664	2.18
Scottish (195)	948	3.11
Slavic (0)	13	0.04
Slovak (0)	41	0.13
Slovene (0)	12	0.04
Swedish (152)	409	1.34
Swiss (0)	62	0.20
Ukrainian (40)	60	0.20
Welsh (29)	176	0.58
West Indian, ex. Hispanic (15)	15	0.05
Jamaican (15)	15	0.05
Yugoslavian (0)	10	0.03

Hispanic Origin	Population	%
Hispanic or Latino (of any race)	733	2.41
Central American, ex. Mexican	43	0.14
Costa Rican	4	0.01
Guatemalan	23	0.08
Honduran	5	0.02
Nicaraguan	1	<0.01
Panamanian	5	0.02
Salvadoran	3	0.01
Other Central American	2	0.01
Cuban	35	0.12
Dominican Republic	7	0.02
Mexican	360	1.18
Puerto Rican	84	0.28
South American	105	0.35
Argentinean	17	0.06
Bolivian	8	0.03
Chilean	15	0.05
Colombian	19	0.06
Ecuadorian	7	0.02
Peruvian	33	0.11
Uruguayan	1	<0.01
Venezuelan	5	0.02
Other Hispanic or Latino	99	0.33

Race*	Population	%
African-American/Black (748)	916	3.01
Not Hispanic (736)	898	2.95
Hispanic (12)	18	0.06
American Indian/Alaska Native (68)	184	0.61
Not Hispanic (61)	166	0.55
Hispanic (7)	18	0.06
Apache (1)	1	<0.01
Blackfeet (0)	5	0.02
Canadian/French Am. Ind. (0)	1	<0.01
Cherokee (28)	60	0.20
Chippewa (2)	2	0.01
Choctaw (3)	3	0.01
Colville (0)	1	<0.01
Creek (0)	2	0.01
Crow (0)	6	0.02
Delaware (1)	1	<0.01
Iroquois (0)	1	<0.01
Mexican American Ind. (2)	2	0.01
Ottawa (1)	1	<0.01
Pueblo (0)	4	0.01
Sioux (1)	4	0.01
South American Ind. (0)	2	0.01
Tohono O'Odham (2)	2	0.01
Asian (1,704)	1,935	6.36
Not Hispanic (1,703)	1,923	6.32
Hispanic (1)	12	0.04
Bangladeshi (15)	18	0.06
Burmese (6)	6	0.02
Cambodian (2)	2	0.01
Chinese, ex. Taiwanese (408)	445	1.46
Filipino (138)	191	0.63
Indian (601)	628	2.07
Indonesian (5)	5	0.02
Japanese (18)	57	0.19
Korean (171)	197	0.65
Laotian (1)	4	0.01
Malaysian (1)	1	<0.01
Nepalese (8)	8	0.03
Pakistani (169)	186	0.61
Sri Lankan (1)	4	0.01
Taiwanese (20)	20	0.07
Thai (9)	13	0.04
Vietnamese (65)	80	0.26
Hawaii Native/Pacific Islander (8)	16	0.05
Not Hispanic (8)	15	0.05
Hispanic (0)	1	<0.01
Marshallese (1)	1	<0.01
Native Hawaiian (2)	6	0.02
White (27,162)	27,644	90.92
Not Hispanic (26,670)	27,096	89.12
Hispanic (492)	548	1.80

Bellefontaine Neighbors

Place Type: City
County: St. Louis
Population: 10,860†

Ancestry‡	Population	%
African, Sub-Saharan (76)	183	1.68
African (76)	183	1.68
American (1,256)	1,256	11.50
Arab (0)	9	0.08
Lebanese (0)	9	0.08
Austrian (17)	58	0.53
Belgian (0)	20	0.18
Canadian (25)	25	0.23
Czech (0)	33	0.30

*Notes: † The Census 2010 population figure is used to calculate the percentages in the Hispanic Origin and Race categories. Ancestry percentages are based on the 2006-2010 American Community Survey population (not shown); ‡ Numbers in parentheses indicate the number of people reporting a single ancestry; * Numbers in parentheses indicate the number of persons reporting this race alone, not in combination with any other race; Please refer to the Explanation of Data for more information.*

Czechoslovakian (0)	8	0.07
Dutch (0)	20	0.18
English (176)	282	2.58
French, ex. Basque (12)	39	0.36
French Canadian (0)	8	0.07
German (283)	918	8.41
Greek (0)	84	0.77
Hungarian (55)	55	0.50
Irish (180)	557	5.10
Italian (268)	540	4.95
Lithuanian (0)	8	0.07
Pennsylvania German (0)	8	0.07
Polish (39)	121	1.11
Scandinavian (0)	5	0.05
Scotch-Irish (6)	85	0.78
Scottish (0)	27	0.25
Slovak (0)	26	0.24
Swedish (0)	57	0.52
Welsh (0)	23	0.21

Hispanic Origin	Population	%
Hispanic or Latino (of any race)	54	0.50
Central American, ex. Mexican	4	0.04
Guatemalan	1	0.01
Honduran	1	0.01
Panamanian	2	0.02
Cuban	8	0.07
Dominican Republic	2	0.02
Mexican	20	0.18
Puerto Rican	3	0.03
South American	5	0.05
Colombian	1	0.01
Venezuelan	4	0.04
Other Hispanic or Latino	12	0.11

Race*	Population	%
African-American/Black (7,892)	8,001	73.67
Not Hispanic (7,874)	7,977	73.45
Hispanic (18)	24	0.22
American Indian/Alaska Native (12)	40	0.37
Not Hispanic (12)	37	0.34
Hispanic (0)	3	0.03
Blackfeet (0)	3	0.03
Cherokee (4)	14	0.13
Chippewa (1)	1	0.01
Choctaw (2)	3	0.03
Inupiat *(Alaska Native)* (1)	1	0.01
Menominee (2)	2	0.02
South American Ind. (0)	2	0.02
Asian (18)	34	0.31
Not Hispanic (18)	34	0.31
Chinese, ex. Taiwanese (4)	4	0.04
Filipino (2)	6	0.06
Indian (6)	7	0.06
Japanese (2)	3	0.03
Korean (3)	8	0.07
Thai (0)	1	0.01
Vietnamese (1)	1	0.01
Hawaii Native/Pacific Islander (1)	6	0.06
Not Hispanic (1)	6	0.06
Fijian (1)	1	0.01
White (2,792)	2,881	26.53
Not Hispanic (2,770)	2,857	26.31
Hispanic (22)	24	0.22

Belton

Place Type: City
County: Cass
Population: 23,116†

Ancestry‡	Population	%
African, Sub-Saharan (125)	125	0.54
African (116)	116	0.50
Nigerian (9)	9	0.04
Alsatian (10)	10	0.04
American (2,010)	2,010	8.70
Arab (0)	18	0.08
Syrian (0)	18	0.08
Australian (43)	43	0.19
Austrian (0)	15	0.06
British (53)	72	0.31
Cajun (62)	62	0.27
Canadian (41)	192	0.83
Croatian (0)	42	0.18
Czech (8)	79	0.34
Czechoslovakian (13)	30	0.13
Danish (56)	246	1.07
Dutch (38)	453	1.96
Eastern European (43)	43	0.19
English (796)	2,115	9.16
European (303)	387	1.68
Finnish (0)	12	0.05
French, ex. Basque (133)	742	3.21
French Canadian (103)	224	0.97
German (2,149)	6,015	26.05
Greek (0)	53	0.23
Hungarian (0)	24	0.10
Irish (769)	3,192	13.82
Italian (173)	836	3.62
Luxemburger (0)	13	0.06
Norwegian (76)	254	1.10
Polish (148)	435	1.88
Portuguese (24)	24	0.10
Russian (0)	65	0.28
Scandinavian (11)	11	0.05
Scotch-Irish (186)	635	2.75
Scottish (111)	677	2.93
Slovak (14)	14	0.06
Swedish (59)	265	1.15
Swiss (0)	52	0.23
Ukrainian (50)	104	0.45
Welsh (17)	249	1.08
West Indian, ex. Hispanic (57)	74	0.32
Jamaican (57)	74	0.32

Hispanic Origin	Population	%
Hispanic or Latino (of any race)	1,874	8.11
Central American, ex. Mexican	88	0.38
Costa Rican	5	0.02
Guatemalan	10	0.04
Honduran	44	0.19
Panamanian	7	0.03
Salvadoran	22	0.10
Cuban	23	0.10
Dominican Republic	2	0.01
Mexican	1,503	6.50
Puerto Rican	80	0.35
South American	46	0.20
Argentinean	4	0.02
Bolivian	3	0.01
Chilean	4	0.02
Colombian	9	0.04
Ecuadorian	12	0.05
Peruvian	6	0.03
Uruguayan	2	0.01
Venezuelan	6	0.03
Other Hispanic or Latino	132	0.57

Race*	Population	%
African-American/Black (1,383)	1,650	7.14
Not Hispanic (1,342)	1,588	6.87
Hispanic (41)	62	0.27
American Indian/Alaska Native (146)	353	1.53
Not Hispanic (128)	312	1.35
Hispanic (18)	41	0.18
Apache (1)	1	<0.01
Blackfeet (2)	9	0.04
Central American Ind. (0)	1	<0.01
Cherokee (35)	103	0.45
Cheyenne (3)	4	0.02
Chickasaw (2)	9	0.04
Chippewa (1)	2	0.01
Choctaw (8)	13	0.06
Colville (1)	1	<0.01
Creek (4)	7	0.03
Delaware (1)	1	<0.01
Iroquois (1)	8	0.03
Kiowa (0)	1	<0.01
Lumbee (1)	3	0.01
Mexican American Ind. (2)	5	0.02
Navajo (6)	6	0.03
Osage (3)	3	0.01
Potawatomi (1)	4	0.02
Pueblo (3)	3	0.01
Seminole (0)	1	<0.01
Shoshone (3)	3	0.01
Sioux (3)	10	0.04
South American Ind. (0)	1	<0.01
Spanish American Ind. (0)	1	<0.01
Asian (197)	336	1.45
Not Hispanic (196)	318	1.38
Hispanic (1)	18	0.08
Cambodian (1)	1	<0.01
Chinese, ex. Taiwanese (37)	55	0.24
Filipino (52)	105	0.45
Indian (32)	40	0.17
Indonesian (3)	5	0.02
Japanese (19)	45	0.19
Korean (20)	41	0.18
Laotian (4)	5	0.02
Taiwanese (0)	2	0.01
Thai (4)	11	0.05
Vietnamese (19)	29	0.13
Hawaii Native/Pacific Islander (28)	72	0.31
Not Hispanic (27)	61	0.26
Hispanic (1)	11	0.05
Guamanian/Chamorro (1)	2	0.01
Native Hawaiian (9)	38	0.16
Samoan (18)	24	0.10
White (19,800)	20,463	88.52
Not Hispanic (18,957)	19,479	84.27
Hispanic (843)	984	4.26

Berkeley

Place Type: City
County: St. Louis
Population: 8,978†

Ancestry‡	Population	%
African, Sub-Saharan (354)	444	4.86
African (336)	426	4.66
South African (18)	18	0.20
American (203)	203	2.22
Croatian (12)	12	0.13
Czech (0)	15	0.16
Czechoslovakian (13)	13	0.14
Dutch (0)	9	0.10
English (45)	239	2.61
French, ex. Basque (114)	164	1.79
French Canadian (22)	22	0.24
German (154)	339	3.71
Greek (13)	13	0.14
Iranian (12)	12	0.13
Irish (52)	206	2.25
Italian (14)	144	1.58
Norwegian (0)	6	0.07
Polish (9)	53	0.58
Russian (14)	29	0.32
Swedish (0)	36	0.39
Yugoslavian (12)	12	0.13

Hispanic Origin	Population	%
Hispanic or Latino (of any race)	312	3.48
Central American, ex. Mexican	32	0.36
Guatemalan	1	0.01
Honduran	18	0.20
Nicaraguan	2	0.02
Panamanian	3	0.03
Salvadoran	8	0.09
Cuban	4	0.04
Dominican Republic	14	0.16
Mexican	223	2.48
Puerto Rican	20	0.22
South American	3	0.03
Colombian	1	0.01
Ecuadorian	1	0.01
Venezuelan	1	0.01
Other Hispanic or Latino	16	0.18

*Notes: † The Census 2010 population figure is used to calculate the percentages in the Hispanic Origin and Race categories. Ancestry percentages are based on the 2006-2010 American Community Survey population (not shown); ‡ Numbers in parentheses indicate the number of people reporting a single ancestry; * Numbers in parentheses indicate the number of persons reporting this race alone, not in combination with any other race; Please refer to the Explanation of Data for more information.*

Race*	Population	%
African-American/Black (7,346)	7,471	83.21
Not Hispanic (7,312)	7,423	82.68
Hispanic (34)	48	0.53
American Indian/Alaska Native (21)	63	0.70
Not Hispanic (19)	60	0.67
Hispanic (2)	3	0.03
Alaska Athabascan *(Ala. Nat.)* (0)	2	0.02
Apache (1)	1	0.01
Blackfeet (0)	1	0.01
Cherokee (4)	16	0.18
Choctaw (1)	3	0.03
Creek (1)	1	0.01
Inupiat *(Alaska Native)* (0)	1	0.01
Navajo (1)	1	0.01
Asian (33)	52	0.58
Not Hispanic (33)	47	0.52
Hispanic (0)	5	0.06
Filipino (22)	25	0.28
Indian (3)	5	0.06
Japanese (2)	6	0.07
Korean (2)	7	0.08
Sri Lankan (1)	1	0.01
Thai (1)	2	0.02
Vietnamese (1)	1	0.01
Hawaii Native/Pacific Islander (5)	8	0.09
Not Hispanic (4)	5	0.06
Hispanic (1)	3	0.03
Native Hawaiian (1)	2	0.02
Samoan (4)	4	0.04
White (1,281)	1,386	15.44
Not Hispanic (1,154)	1,247	13.89
Hispanic (127)	139	1.55

Blue Springs

Place Type: City
County: Jackson
Population: 52,575†

Ancestry‡	Population	%
African, Sub-Saharan (47)	92	0.18
African (31)	76	0.15
Ghanaian (16)	16	0.03
Albanian (57)	57	0.11
American (4,189)	4,189	8.13
Arab (118)	145	0.28
Arab (0)	8	0.02
Lebanese (118)	137	0.27
Austrian (42)	141	0.27
Belgian (12)	12	0.02
Brazilian (22)	22	0.04
British (69)	109	0.21
Canadian (67)	67	0.13
Celtic (10)	10	0.02
Croatian (53)	88	0.17
Czech (101)	546	1.06
Czechoslovakian (19)	30	0.06
Danish (66)	238	0.46
Dutch (180)	1,144	2.22
Eastern European (13)	13	0.03
English (2,446)	6,295	12.22
European (711)	807	1.57
Finnish (28)	69	0.13
French, ex. Basque (279)	1,686	3.27
French Canadian (27)	98	0.19
German (5,055)	13,516	26.24
German Russian (0)	18	0.03
Greek (14)	67	0.13
Hungarian (27)	60	0.12
Iranian (0)	15	0.03
Irish (1,677)	7,349	14.27
Italian (926)	2,684	5.21
Lithuanian (38)	38	0.07
Macedonian (7)	7	0.01
Northern European (25)	44	0.09
Norwegian (112)	714	1.39
Polish (344)	1,040	2.02
Portuguese (19)	41	0.08
Russian (13)	173	0.34
Scotch-Irish (480)	1,162	2.26
Scottish (348)	1,077	2.09
Serbian (24)	51	0.10
Slavic (0)	4	0.01
Slovak (22)	65	0.13
Slovene (0)	15	0.03
Swedish (176)	597	1.16
Swiss (24)	116	0.23
Welsh (62)	402	0.78
Yugoslavian (5)	5	0.01

Hispanic Origin	Population	%
Hispanic or Latino (of any race)	2,618	4.98
Central American, ex. Mexican	125	0.24
Costa Rican	8	0.02
Guatemalan	21	0.04
Honduran	51	0.10
Nicaraguan	8	0.02
Panamanian	11	0.02
Salvadoran	26	0.05
Cuban	49	0.09
Dominican Republic	25	0.05
Mexican	1,944	3.70
Puerto Rican	146	0.28
South American	83	0.16
Argentinean	1	<0.01
Chilean	8	0.02
Colombian	27	0.05
Ecuadorian	8	0.02
Paraguayan	1	<0.01
Peruvian	23	0.04
Venezuelan	13	0.02
Other South American	2	<0.01
Other Hispanic or Latino	246	0.47

Race*	Population	%
African-American/Black (3,257)	4,016	7.64
Not Hispanic (3,185)	3,865	7.35
Hispanic (72)	151	0.29
American Indian/Alaska Native (241)	663	1.26
Not Hispanic (205)	563	1.07
Hispanic (36)	100	0.19
Alaska Athabascan *(Ala. Nat.)* (0)	1	<0.01
Aleut *(Alaska Native)* (2)	2	<0.01
Apache (3)	19	0.04
Arapaho (3)	3	0.01
Blackfeet (2)	27	0.05
Canadian/French Am. Ind. (0)	1	<0.01
Cherokee (70)	239	0.45
Cheyenne (1)	2	<0.01
Chickasaw (6)	8	0.02
Chippewa (4)	9	0.02
Choctaw (19)	34	0.06
Colville (1)	1	<0.01
Comanche (1)	1	<0.01
Cree (0)	5	0.01
Creek (2)	8	0.02
Delaware (1)	3	0.01
Hopi (2)	2	<0.01
Inupiat *(Alaska Native)* (3)	4	0.01
Iroquois (5)	7	0.01
Mexican American Ind. (6)	8	0.02
Navajo (6)	11	0.02
Osage (1)	4	0.01
Ottawa (3)	5	0.01
Potawatomi (8)	18	0.03
Pueblo (3)	8	0.02
Seminole (3)	10	0.02
Shoshone (0)	3	0.01
Sioux (12)	30	0.06
South American Ind. (0)	4	0.01
Spanish American Ind. (0)	5	0.01
Tlingit-Haida *(Alaska Native)* (0)	6	0.01
Yaqui (1)	3	0.01
Asian (654)	996	1.89
Not Hispanic (652)	966	1.84
Hispanic (2)	30	0.06
Burmese (0)	3	0.01
Cambodian (2)	4	0.01
Chinese, ex. Taiwanese (92)	129	0.25
Filipino (145)	266	0.51
Hmong (16)	16	0.03
Indian (137)	164	0.31
Indonesian (4)	4	0.01
Japanese (19)	64	0.12
Korean (73)	135	0.26
Laotian (10)	15	0.03
Malaysian (0)	5	0.01
Pakistani (23)	26	0.05
Sri Lankan (1)	1	<0.01
Taiwanese (14)	17	0.03
Thai (10)	37	0.07
Vietnamese (90)	106	0.20
Hawaii Native/Pacific Islander (82)	175	0.33
Not Hispanic (82)	167	0.32
Hispanic (0)	8	0.02
Guamanian/Chamorro (5)	20	0.04
Native Hawaiian (19)	52	0.10
Samoan (47)	82	0.16
Tongan (6)	18	0.03
White (46,051)	47,566	90.47
Not Hispanic (44,463)	45,710	86.94
Hispanic (1,588)	1,856	3.53

Bolivar

Place Type: City
County: Polk
Population: 10,325†

Ancestry‡	Population	%
Albanian (18)	18	0.18
American (640)	640	6.26
Austrian (10)	10	0.10
British (15)	25	0.24
Czech (14)	14	0.14
Danish (15)	100	0.98
Dutch (60)	315	3.08
English (798)	1,581	15.47
European (52)	52	0.51
French, ex. Basque (71)	527	5.16
French Canadian (14)	42	0.41
German (547)	1,780	17.41
Irish (440)	1,527	14.94
Italian (300)	538	5.26
Norwegian (80)	139	1.36
Pennsylvania German (12)	12	0.12
Polish (31)	125	1.22
Romanian (125)	125	1.22
Russian (32)	32	0.31
Scotch-Irish (165)	488	4.77
Scottish (0)	263	2.57
Swedish (15)	39	0.38
Swiss (0)	25	0.24
Turkish (0)	42	0.41
Ukrainian (0)	13	0.13
Welsh (43)	59	0.58

Hispanic Origin	Population	%
Hispanic or Latino (of any race)	259	2.51
Central American, ex. Mexican	9	0.09
Guatemalan	4	0.04
Honduran	2	0.02
Panamanian	3	0.03
Cuban	6	0.06
Mexican	179	1.73
Puerto Rican	18	0.17
South American	18	0.17
Argentinean	2	0.02
Chilean	1	0.01
Colombian	1	0.01
Ecuadorian	2	0.02
Peruvian	2	0.02
Uruguayan	4	0.04
Venezuelan	6	0.06
Other Hispanic or Latino	29	0.28

Race*	Population	%
African-American/Black (155)	219	2.12

*Notes: † The Census 2010 population figure is used to calculate the percentages in the Hispanic Origin and Race categories. Ancestry percentages are based on the 2006-2010 American Community Survey population (not shown); ‡ Numbers in parentheses indicate the number of people reporting a single ancestry; * Numbers in parentheses indicate the number of persons reporting this race alone, not in combination with any other race; Please refer to the Explanation of Data for more information.*

Not Hispanic (147)	208	2.01
Hispanic (8)	11	0.11
American Indian/Alaska Native (54)	137	1.33
Not Hispanic (50)	132	1.28
Hispanic (4)	5	0.05
Apache (0)	3	0.03
Blackfeet (1)	11	0.11
Cherokee (20)	54	0.52
Cheyenne (1)	1	0.01
Chickasaw (1)	1	0.01
Chippewa (0)	1	0.01
Choctaw (1)	4	0.04
Creek (2)	2	0.02
Delaware (2)	5	0.05
Iroquois (0)	2	0.02
Mexican American Ind. (1)	1	0.01
Navajo (1)	1	0.01
Seminole (1)	2	0.02
Sioux (2)	5	0.05
Asian (64)	95	0.92
Not Hispanic (64)	91	0.88
Hispanic (0)	4	0.04
Chinese, ex. Taiwanese (15)	18	0.17
Filipino (7)	15	0.15
Hmong (3)	3	0.03
Indian (17)	22	0.21
Japanese (0)	7	0.07
Korean (9)	13	0.13
Thai (2)	3	0.03
Vietnamese (5)	10	0.10
Hawaii Native/Pacific Islander (4)	12	0.12
Not Hispanic (4)	12	0.12
Guamanian/Chamorro (2)	4	0.04
Native Hawaiian (0)	2	0.02
Samoan (2)	4	0.04
White (9,790)	9,968	96.54
Not Hispanic (9,633)	9,795	94.87
Hispanic (157)	173	1.68

Boonville

Place Type: City
County: Cooper
Population: 8,319†

Ancestry‡	Population	%
African, Sub-Saharan (22)	22	0.26
African (9)	9	0.11
South African (13)	13	0.15
American (546)	546	6.51
Arab (5)	5	0.06
Moroccan (5)	5	0.06
British (45)	45	0.54
Czech (0)	45	0.54
Dutch (23)	148	1.76
English (235)	737	8.78
European (93)	93	1.11
French, ex. Basque (10)	185	2.20
French Canadian (0)	8	0.10
German (1,607)	2,814	33.54
Greek (73)	73	0.87
Irish (494)	1,403	16.72
Italian (142)	237	2.82
Latvian (8)	8	0.10
Norwegian (0)	58	0.69
Polish (9)	71	0.85
Russian (0)	17	0.20
Scotch-Irish (41)	228	2.72
Scottish (8)	71	0.85
Slovak (0)	12	0.14
Swedish (25)	37	0.44
Swiss (27)	99	1.18
Turkish (0)	12	0.14
Ukrainian (33)	33	0.39
Welsh (0)	123	1.47
West Indian, ex. Hispanic (0)	9	0.11
Dutch West Indian (0)	9	0.11

Hispanic Origin	Population	%
Hispanic or Latino (of any race)	158	1.90
Central American, ex. Mexican	9	0.11
Guatemalan	1	0.01
Honduran	2	0.02
Panamanian	4	0.05
Salvadoran	2	0.02
Cuban	1	0.01
Mexican	120	1.44
Puerto Rican	13	0.16
South American	4	0.05
Colombian	1	0.01
Ecuadorian	1	0.01
Venezuelan	2	0.02
Other Hispanic or Latino	11	0.13

Race*	Population	%
African-American/Black (1,109)	1,233	14.82
Not Hispanic (1,104)	1,223	14.70
Hispanic (5)	10	0.12
American Indian/Alaska Native (33)	83	1.00
Not Hispanic (25)	71	0.85
Hispanic (8)	12	0.14
Apache (3)	3	0.04
Cherokee (12)	25	0.30
Chippewa (0)	2	0.02
Choctaw (1)	1	0.01
Creek (1)	1	0.01
Mexican American Ind. (3)	4	0.05
Navajo (0)	1	0.01
Potawatomi (1)	1	0.01
Sioux (1)	1	0.01
Asian (47)	66	0.79
Not Hispanic (47)	65	0.78
Hispanic (0)	1	0.01
Cambodian (2)	5	0.06
Chinese, ex. Taiwanese (15)	18	0.22
Filipino (4)	11	0.13
Indian (18)	23	0.28
Japanese (0)	3	0.04
Korean (2)	6	0.07
Thai (0)	1	0.01
Hawaii Native/Pacific Islander (3)	7	0.08
Not Hispanic (3)	6	0.07
Hispanic (0)	1	0.01
Native Hawaiian (2)	5	0.06
Samoan (1)	1	0.01
White (6,915)	7,092	85.25
Not Hispanic (6,801)	6,969	83.77
Hispanic (114)	123	1.48

Branson

Place Type: City
County: Taney
Population: 10,520†

Ancestry‡	Population	%
American (805)	805	8.17
Arab (43)	43	0.44
Iraqi (43)	43	0.44
British (188)	188	1.91
Bulgarian (25)	25	0.25
Cajun (78)	78	0.79
Canadian (16)	33	0.33
Czech (0)	67	0.68
Danish (12)	12	0.12
Dutch (29)	341	3.46
English (728)	1,548	15.71
European (20)	20	0.20
Finnish (0)	72	0.73
French, ex. Basque (14)	296	3.00
French Canadian (76)	76	0.77
German (590)	2,084	21.15
Greek (40)	40	0.41
Irish (784)	1,601	16.25
Italian (184)	347	3.52
Macedonian (19)	19	0.19
Norwegian (47)	208	2.11
Pennsylvania German (0)	16	0.16
Polish (26)	190	1.93
Romanian (30)	39	0.40
Scotch-Irish (177)	359	3.64
Scottish (80)	298	3.02
Swedish (44)	123	1.25
Swiss (0)	128	1.30
Welsh (29)	105	1.07
Yugoslavian (19)	19	0.19

Hispanic Origin	Population	%
Hispanic or Latino (of any race)	928	8.82
Central American, ex. Mexican	76	0.72
Costa Rican	2	0.02
Guatemalan	23	0.22
Honduran	10	0.10
Nicaraguan	9	0.09
Panamanian	4	0.04
Salvadoran	25	0.24
Other Central American	3	0.03
Cuban	6	0.06
Mexican	729	6.93
Puerto Rican	25	0.24
South American	23	0.22
Bolivian	1	0.01
Colombian	17	0.16
Ecuadorian	1	0.01
Peruvian	4	0.04
Other Hispanic or Latino	69	0.66

Race*	Population	%
African-American/Black (207)	260	2.47
Not Hispanic (184)	223	2.12
Hispanic (23)	37	0.35
American Indian/Alaska Native (92)	207	1.97
Not Hispanic (80)	180	1.71
Hispanic (12)	27	0.26
Apache (1)	2	0.02
Blackfeet (0)	3	0.03
Cherokee (31)	72	0.68
Chickasaw (3)	4	0.04
Chippewa (2)	5	0.05
Choctaw (6)	11	0.10
Comanche (1)	2	0.02
Cree (0)	1	0.01
Creek (0)	2	0.02
Inupiat *(Alaska Native)* (1)	3	0.03
Iroquois (1)	1	0.01
Kiowa (0)	1	0.01
Menominee (1)	1	0.01
Mexican American Ind. (7)	7	0.07
Navajo (5)	5	0.05
Osage (1)	2	0.02
Ottawa (0)	1	0.01
Seminole (1)	1	0.01
Sioux (6)	10	0.10
Asian (159)	216	2.05
Not Hispanic (154)	205	1.95
Hispanic (5)	11	0.10
Chinese, ex. Taiwanese (14)	18	0.17
Filipino (27)	41	0.39
Hmong (12)	12	0.11
Indian (32)	42	0.40
Indonesian (1)	1	0.01
Japanese (6)	26	0.25
Korean (19)	21	0.20
Laotian (1)	1	0.01
Nepalese (1)	1	0.01
Pakistani (2)	2	0.02
Thai (15)	18	0.17
Vietnamese (24)	30	0.29
Hawaii Native/Pacific Islander (13)	29	0.28
Not Hispanic (13)	27	0.26
Hispanic (0)	2	0.02
Guamanian/Chamorro (3)	7	0.07
Native Hawaiian (0)	7	0.07
Samoan (7)	15	0.14
White (9,358)	9,608	91.33
Not Hispanic (8,956)	9,132	86.81
Hispanic (402)	476	4.52

*Notes: † The Census 2010 population figure is used to calculate the percentages in the Hispanic Origin and Race categories. Ancestry percentages are based on the 2006-2010 American Community Survey population (not shown); ‡ Numbers in parentheses indicate the number of people reporting a single ancestry; * Numbers in parentheses indicate the number of persons reporting this race alone, not in combination with any other race; Please refer to the Explanation of Data for more information.*

Brentwood

Place Type: City
County: St. Louis
Population: 8,055†

Ancestry‡	Population	%
African, Sub-Saharan (26)	26	0.33
Nigerian (26)	26	0.33
Albanian (9)	9	0.11
American (451)	451	5.66
Arab (14)	55	0.69
Lebanese (14)	55	0.69
Brazilian (12)	12	0.15
British (9)	47	0.59
Canadian (12)	12	0.15
Croatian (0)	46	0.58
Czech (3)	57	0.71
Danish (40)	49	0.61
Dutch (0)	46	0.58
Eastern European (9)	9	0.11
English (382)	1,360	17.06
European (231)	241	3.02
Finnish (0)	33	0.41
French, ex. Basque (23)	469	5.88
French Canadian (15)	15	0.19
German (1,207)	2,850	35.75
Greek (9)	21	0.26
Guyanese (20)	20	0.25
Hungarian (0)	13	0.16
Irish (400)	1,603	20.11
Italian (136)	539	6.76
Lithuanian (0)	15	0.19
Norwegian (12)	54	0.68
Polish (44)	216	2.71
Romanian (0)	37	0.46
Russian (34)	191	2.40
Scandinavian (29)	29	0.36
Scotch-Irish (68)	194	2.43
Scottish (48)	148	1.86
Serbian (0)	17	0.21
Slavic (0)	10	0.13
Slovak (22)	22	0.28
Swedish (0)	10	0.13
Swiss (0)	25	0.31
Turkish (17)	17	0.21
Ukrainian (0)	14	0.18
Welsh (0)	52	0.65
Yugoslavian (14)	25	0.31

Hispanic Origin	Population	%
Hispanic or Latino (of any race)	223	2.77
Central American, ex. Mexican	16	0.20
Costa Rican	2	0.02
Guatemalan	2	0.02
Honduran	4	0.05
Nicaraguan	4	0.05
Panamanian	4	0.05
Cuban	9	0.11
Dominican Republic	1	0.01
Mexican	84	1.04
Puerto Rican	24	0.30
South American	63	0.78
Argentinean	9	0.11
Bolivian	4	0.05
Chilean	4	0.05
Colombian	15	0.19
Ecuadorian	2	0.02
Peruvian	18	0.22
Venezuelan	5	0.06
Other South American	6	0.07
Other Hispanic or Latino	26	0.32

Race*	Population	%
African-American/Black (250)	306	3.80
Not Hispanic (241)	291	3.61
Hispanic (9)	15	0.19
American Indian/Alaska Native (8)	46	0.57
Not Hispanic (5)	41	0.51
Hispanic (3)	5	0.06
Blackfeet (0)	6	0.07
Cherokee (3)	15	0.19
Cheyenne (0)	1	0.01
Chippewa (1)	4	0.05
Crow (0)	2	0.02
Kiowa (0)	1	0.01
Potawatomi (0)	1	0.01
Sioux (0)	1	0.01
South American Ind. (0)	2	0.02
Asian (547)	610	7.57
Not Hispanic (545)	606	7.52
Hispanic (2)	4	0.05
Bangladeshi (1)	1	0.01
Burmese (1)	1	0.01
Chinese, ex. Taiwanese (89)	95	1.18
Filipino (29)	53	0.66
Indian (167)	186	2.31
Indonesian (1)	5	0.06
Japanese (65)	72	0.89
Korean (106)	111	1.38
Pakistani (20)	21	0.26
Taiwanese (16)	16	0.20
Thai (8)	11	0.14
Vietnamese (22)	25	0.31
Hawaii Native/Pacific Islander (1)	6	0.07
Not Hispanic (1)	5	0.06
Hispanic (0)	1	0.01
Guamanian/Chamorro (0)	2	0.02
Native Hawaiian (1)	1	0.01
White (7,047)	7,185	89.20
Not Hispanic (6,891)	7,013	87.06
Hispanic (156)	172	2.14

Bridgeton

Place Type: City
County: St. Louis
Population: 11,550†

Ancestry‡	Population	%
African, Sub-Saharan (60)	60	0.49
African (60)	60	0.49
American (597)	597	4.88
Arab (155)	155	1.27
Arab (155)	155	1.27
Austrian (17)	35	0.29
British (31)	31	0.25
Canadian (18)	29	0.24
Croatian (13)	23	0.19
Czech (54)	130	1.06
Danish (43)	72	0.59
Dutch (42)	116	0.95
Eastern European (0)	14	0.11
English (407)	1,248	10.20
European (39)	60	0.49
French, ex. Basque (70)	580	4.74
German (1,050)	2,852	23.31
Greek (14)	97	0.79
Hungarian (21)	50	0.41
Irish (402)	1,821	14.88
Italian (242)	747	6.11
Norwegian (12)	43	0.35
Polish (146)	267	2.18
Russian (0)	13	0.11
Scotch-Irish (75)	380	3.11
Scottish (73)	155	1.27
Swedish (0)	27	0.22
Swiss (13)	113	0.92
Welsh (10)	18	0.15
West Indian, ex. Hispanic (28)	28	0.23
Belizean (28)	28	0.23

Hispanic Origin	Population	%
Hispanic or Latino (of any race)	743	6.43
Central American, ex. Mexican	50	0.43
Guatemalan	33	0.29
Honduran	4	0.03
Nicaraguan	2	0.02
Panamanian	2	0.02
Salvadoran	9	0.08
Cuban	6	0.05
Mexican	579	5.01
Puerto Rican	38	0.33
South American	22	0.19
Bolivian	1	0.01
Chilean	1	0.01
Colombian	8	0.07
Ecuadorian	1	0.01
Peruvian	8	0.07
Venezuelan	3	0.03
Other Hispanic or Latino	48	0.42

Race*	Population	%
African-American/Black (2,162)	2,313	20.03
Not Hispanic (2,141)	2,285	19.78
Hispanic (21)	28	0.24
American Indian/Alaska Native (25)	71	0.61
Not Hispanic (20)	64	0.55
Hispanic (5)	7	0.06
Blackfeet (0)	7	0.06
Cherokee (5)	20	0.17
Chickasaw (0)	1	0.01
Creek (0)	3	0.03
Mexican American Ind. (4)	5	0.04
Seminole (0)	1	0.01
Sioux (1)	3	0.03
Asian (288)	339	2.94
Not Hispanic (288)	337	2.92
Hispanic (0)	2	0.02
Bangladeshi (7)	7	0.06
Chinese, ex. Taiwanese (65)	71	0.61
Filipino (38)	50	0.43
Indian (74)	86	0.74
Indonesian (9)	16	0.14
Japanese (5)	10	0.09
Korean (7)	18	0.16
Laotian (11)	14	0.12
Malaysian (2)	2	0.02
Nepalese (1)	1	0.01
Pakistani (6)	12	0.10
Taiwanese (2)	3	0.03
Thai (3)	4	0.03
Vietnamese (41)	45	0.39
Hawaii Native/Pacific Islander (2)	17	0.15
Not Hispanic (2)	15	0.13
Hispanic (0)	2	0.02
Guamanian/Chamorro (1)	1	0.01
Native Hawaiian (0)	3	0.03
White (8,362)	8,569	74.19
Not Hispanic (8,130)	8,311	71.96
Hispanic (232)	258	2.23

Cameron

Place Type: City
County: Clinton
Population: 9,933†

Ancestry‡	Population	%
African, Sub-Saharan (18)	41	0.42
African (0)	14	0.14
Liberian (0)	9	0.09
Other Sub-Saharan African (18)	18	0.18
American (1,013)	1,013	10.41
Arab (10)	30	0.31
Jordanian (10)	20	0.21
Moroccan (0)	10	0.10
Austrian (22)	36	0.37
Belgian (31)	31	0.32
Canadian (7)	48	0.49
Celtic (0)	14	0.14
Czech (0)	24	0.25
Danish (10)	71	0.73
Dutch (25)	324	3.33
English (415)	866	8.90
European (134)	134	1.38
French, ex. Basque (76)	301	3.09
French Canadian (21)	53	0.54
German (1,027)	2,496	25.65
Greek (0)	7	0.07

SECTION TWO

*Notes: † The Census 2010 population figure is used to calculate the percentages in the Hispanic Origin and Race categories. Ancestry percentages are based on the 2006-2010 American Community Survey population (not shown); ‡ Numbers in parentheses indicate the number of people reporting a single ancestry; * Numbers in parentheses indicate the number of persons reporting this race alone, not in combination with any other race; Please refer to the Explanation of Data for more information.*

Hungarian (0)	24	0.25
Irish (493)	1,667	17.13
Italian (78)	165	1.70
Norwegian (23)	56	0.58
Polish (14)	54	0.55
Russian (0)	69	0.71
Scotch-Irish (291)	411	4.22
Scottish (41)	102	1.05
Swedish (0)	90	0.92
Swiss (0)	54	0.55
Welsh (17)	50	0.51
West Indian, ex. Hispanic (13)	13	0.13
Haitian (13)	13	0.13

Hispanic Origin	Population	%
Hispanic or Latino (of any race)	197	1.98
Central American, ex. Mexican	4	0.04
Guatemalan	4	0.04
Cuban	4	0.04
Mexican	137	1.38
Puerto Rican	1	0.01
South American	2	0.02
Chilean	1	0.01
Peruvian	1	0.01
Other Hispanic or Latino	49	0.49

Race*	Population	%
African-American/Black (1,469)	1,514	15.24
Not Hispanic (1,463)	1,508	15.18
Hispanic (6)	6	0.06
American Indian/Alaska Native (51)	92	0.93
Not Hispanic (50)	89	0.90
Hispanic (1)	3	0.03
Cherokee (13)	19	0.19
Chippewa (5)	5	0.05
Creek (1)	1	0.01
Delaware (0)	1	0.01
Navajo (2)	2	0.02
Osage (2)	2	0.02
Sioux (0)	1	0.01
Yup'ik *(Alaska Native)* (1)	1	0.01
Asian (47)	70	0.70
Not Hispanic (47)	69	0.69
Hispanic (0)	1	0.01
Chinese, ex. Taiwanese (5)	6	0.06
Filipino (8)	15	0.15
Indian (16)	18	0.18
Japanese (1)	1	0.01
Korean (6)	6	0.06
Thai (1)	1	0.01
Vietnamese (6)	6	0.06
Hawaii Native/Pacific Islander (4)	20	0.20
Not Hispanic (4)	18	0.18
Hispanic (0)	2	0.02
Native Hawaiian (0)	2	0.02
Samoan (0)	1	0.01
White (8,235)	8,324	83.80
Not Hispanic (8,077)	8,158	82.13
Hispanic (158)	166	1.67

Cape Girardeau

Place Type: City
County: Cape Girardeau
Population: 37,941†

Ancestry‡	Population	%
African, Sub-Saharan (97)	106	0.28
African (74)	83	0.22
Nigerian (23)	23	0.06
Albanian (0)	12	0.03
American (3,328)	3,328	8.90
Arab (24)	68	0.18
Lebanese (11)	55	0.15
Other Arab (13)	13	0.03
Assyrian/Chaldean/Syriac (9)	9	0.02
Austrian (14)	19	0.05
Belgian (0)	11	0.03
British (138)	232	0.62
Canadian (0)	14	0.04
Celtic (9)	9	0.02
Croatian (29)	58	0.16
Czech (0)	61	0.16
Czechoslovakian (0)	100	0.27
Danish (78)	94	0.25
Dutch (158)	894	2.39
Eastern European (14)	14	0.04
English (1,172)	3,447	9.21
European (226)	323	0.86
Finnish (15)	60	0.16
French, ex. Basque (175)	1,483	3.96
French Canadian (11)	21	0.06
German (5,411)	11,461	30.64
Greek (19)	19	0.05
Hungarian (90)	150	0.40
Irish (1,163)	4,753	12.71
Italian (374)	899	2.40
Latvian (21)	21	0.06
Norwegian (13)	211	0.56
Polish (268)	611	1.63
Portuguese (17)	28	0.07
Romanian (10)	10	0.03
Russian (7)	29	0.08
Scandinavian (0)	15	0.04
Scotch-Irish (301)	789	2.11
Scottish (190)	705	1.88
Swedish (126)	283	0.76
Swiss (8)	156	0.42
Ukrainian (16)	67	0.18
Welsh (64)	284	0.76
West Indian, ex. Hispanic (23)	51	0.14
Dutch West Indian (23)	44	0.12
Haitian (0)	7	0.02

Hispanic Origin	Population	%
Hispanic or Latino (of any race)	1,046	2.76
Central American, ex. Mexican	111	0.29
Costa Rican	5	0.01
Guatemalan	16	0.04
Honduran	69	0.18
Nicaraguan	2	0.01
Panamanian	11	0.03
Salvadoran	8	0.02
Cuban	16	0.04
Dominican Republic	2	0.01
Mexican	709	1.87
Puerto Rican	70	0.18
South American	43	0.11
Argentinean	3	0.01
Bolivian	2	0.01
Colombian	22	0.06
Ecuadorian	1	<0.01
Peruvian	11	0.03
Venezuelan	4	0.01
Other Hispanic or Latino	95	0.25

Race*	Population	%
African-American/Black (4,839)	5,420	14.29
Not Hispanic (4,807)	5,345	14.09
Hispanic (32)	75	0.20
American Indian/Alaska Native (87)	312	0.82
Not Hispanic (81)	277	0.73
Hispanic (6)	35	0.09
Apache (1)	6	0.02
Blackfeet (1)	13	0.03
Canadian/French Am. Ind. (0)	1	<0.01
Cherokee (31)	108	0.28
Chickasaw (0)	1	<0.01
Chippewa (0)	2	0.01
Choctaw (2)	10	0.03
Comanche (0)	1	<0.01
Creek (0)	3	0.01
Crow (1)	4	0.01
Iroquois (1)	2	0.01
Mexican American Ind. (3)	6	0.02
Navajo (0)	1	<0.01
Osage (1)	2	0.01
Sioux (3)	13	0.03
South American Ind. (1)	1	<0.01
Asian (718)	859	2.26
Not Hispanic (716)	840	2.21
Hispanic (2)	19	0.05
Bangladeshi (8)	10	0.03
Burmese (1)	1	<0.01
Cambodian (2)	3	0.01
Chinese, ex. Taiwanese (227)	257	0.68
Filipino (34)	61	0.16
Indian (168)	203	0.54
Indonesian (0)	3	0.01
Japanese (73)	87	0.23
Korean (36)	53	0.14
Laotian (2)	2	0.01
Malaysian (0)	1	<0.01
Nepalese (26)	27	0.07
Pakistani (32)	48	0.13
Sri Lankan (9)	9	0.02
Taiwanese (8)	12	0.03
Thai (15)	21	0.06
Vietnamese (40)	46	0.12
Hawaii Native/Pacific Islander (17)	37	0.10
Not Hispanic (13)	29	0.08
Hispanic (4)	8	0.02
Guamanian/Chamorro (1)	1	<0.01
Marshallese (1)	1	<0.01
Native Hawaiian (3)	15	0.04
Samoan (7)	13	0.03
White (30,783)	31,619	83.34
Not Hispanic (30,432)	31,185	82.19
Hispanic (351)	434	1.14

Carthage

Place Type: City
County: Jasper
Population: 14,378†

Ancestry‡	Population	%
American (1,158)	1,158	8.20
British (10)	10	0.07
Czechoslovakian (28)	39	0.28
Danish (11)	30	0.21
Dutch (11)	250	1.77
English (528)	1,108	7.85
European (26)	26	0.18
French, ex. Basque (142)	497	3.52
French Canadian (0)	16	0.11
German (581)	2,407	17.05
Iranian (23)	23	0.16
Irish (288)	1,333	9.44
Italian (52)	118	0.84
Norwegian (23)	48	0.34
Polish (38)	93	0.66
Russian (0)	17	0.12
Scandinavian (0)	12	0.09
Scotch-Irish (110)	404	2.86
Scottish (40)	168	1.19
Swedish (11)	39	0.28
Swiss (13)	32	0.23
Welsh (0)	103	0.73
West Indian, ex. Hispanic (0)	31	0.22
Dutch West Indian (0)	31	0.22

Hispanic Origin	Population	%
Hispanic or Latino (of any race)	3,685	25.63
Central American, ex. Mexican	2,060	14.33
Costa Rican	3	0.02
Guatemalan	1,840	12.80
Honduran	41	0.29
Nicaraguan	1	0.01
Salvadoran	175	1.22
Cuban	1	0.01
Dominican Republic	3	0.02
Mexican	1,286	8.94
Puerto Rican	27	0.19
South American	12	0.08
Bolivian	2	0.01
Chilean	1	0.01
Colombian	3	0.02
Ecuadorian	1	0.01
Peruvian	5	0.03

*Notes: † The Census 2010 population figure is used to calculate the percentages in the Hispanic Origin and Race categories. Ancestry percentages are based on the 2006-2010 American Community Survey population (not shown); ‡ Numbers in parentheses indicate the number of people reporting a single ancestry; * Numbers in parentheses indicate the number of persons reporting this race alone, not in combination with any other race; Please refer to the Explanation of Data for more information.*

Other Hispanic or Latino	296	2.06

Race*	Population	%
African-American/Black (222)	357	2.48
Not Hispanic (187)	292	2.03
Hispanic (35)	65	0.45
American Indian/Alaska Native (142)	332	2.31
Not Hispanic (117)	268	1.86
Hispanic (25)	64	0.45
Alaska Athabascan *(Ala. Nat.)* (1)	2	0.01
Apache (2)	2	0.01
Blackfeet (1)	4	0.03
Cherokee (41)	133	0.93
Cheyenne (0)	1	0.01
Chickasaw (0)	1	0.01
Chippewa (0)	2	0.01
Choctaw (5)	20	0.14
Comanche (1)	1	0.01
Creek (3)	3	0.02
Delaware (2)	4	0.03
Iroquois (7)	10	0.07
Mexican American Ind. (4)	11	0.08
Navajo (7)	21	0.15
Osage (0)	1	0.01
Ottawa (4)	5	0.03
Sioux (0)	7	0.05
Tlingit-Haida *(Alaska Native)* (6)	6	0.04
Tohono O'Odham (0)	1	0.01
Asian (146)	179	1.24
Not Hispanic (146)	176	1.22
Hispanic (0)	3	0.02
Chinese, ex. Taiwanese (4)	7	0.05
Filipino (16)	32	0.22
Indian (6)	12	0.08
Indonesian (1)	1	0.01
Japanese (2)	3	0.02
Korean (16)	26	0.18
Malaysian (1)	1	0.01
Thai (1)	1	0.01
Vietnamese (97)	97	0.67
Hawaii Native/Pacific Islander (92)	104	0.72
Not Hispanic (43)	51	0.35
Hispanic (49)	53	0.37
Guamanian/Chamorro (66)	69	0.48
Native Hawaiian (4)	8	0.06
White (10,581)	11,018	76.63
Not Hispanic (9,912)	10,178	70.79
Hispanic (669)	840	5.84

Chesterfield

Place Type: City
County: St. Louis
Population: 47,484†

Ancestry‡	Population	%
African, Sub-Saharan (121)	327	0.69
African (0)	206	0.44
Ethiopian (57)	57	0.12
Somalian (64)	64	0.14
Albanian (0)	24	0.05
American (3,055)	3,055	6.47
Arab (25)	129	0.27
Lebanese (25)	38	0.08
Moroccan (0)	37	0.08
Syrian (0)	54	0.11
Armenian (25)	34	0.07
Australian (30)	44	0.09
Austrian (0)	225	0.48
Basque (0)	28	0.06
Belgian (23)	149	0.32
Brazilian (0)	15	0.03
British (73)	247	0.52
Bulgarian (106)	106	0.22
Canadian (82)	109	0.23
Croatian (63)	317	0.67
Czech (142)	358	0.76
Czechoslovakian (17)	17	0.04
Danish (26)	208	0.44
Dutch (95)	474	1.00
Eastern European (398)	409	0.87
English (1,583)	5,613	11.88
European (957)	1,032	2.18
Finnish (0)	44	0.09
French, ex. Basque (216)	2,235	4.73
French Canadian (48)	82	0.17
German (5,855)	14,942	31.62
Greek (418)	559	1.18
Hungarian (164)	285	0.60
Iranian (12)	12	0.03
Irish (2,061)	8,053	17.04
Israeli (45)	56	0.12
Italian (986)	2,663	5.64
Latvian (17)	17	0.04
Lithuanian (32)	141	0.30
Northern European (106)	106	0.22
Norwegian (81)	487	1.03
Polish (623)	1,866	3.95
Portuguese (0)	47	0.10
Romanian (39)	91	0.19
Russian (1,300)	2,335	4.94
Scandinavian (0)	50	0.11
Scotch-Irish (393)	1,042	2.21
Scottish (221)	1,164	2.46
Serbian (0)	40	0.08
Slavic (0)	12	0.03
Slovak (47)	96	0.20
Slovene (13)	13	0.03
Swedish (64)	554	1.17
Swiss (77)	336	0.71
Ukrainian (131)	204	0.43
Welsh (32)	376	0.80
West Indian, ex. Hispanic (24)	50	0.11
Jamaican (24)	50	0.11
Yugoslavian (45)	45	0.10

Hispanic Origin	Population	%
Hispanic or Latino (of any race)	1,323	2.79
Central American, ex. Mexican	65	0.14
Costa Rican	1	<0.01
Guatemalan	20	0.04
Honduran	16	0.03
Nicaraguan	3	0.01
Panamanian	9	0.02
Salvadoran	15	0.03
Other Central American	1	<0.01
Cuban	57	0.12
Dominican Republic	4	0.01
Mexican	721	1.52
Puerto Rican	106	0.22
South American	209	0.44
Argentinean	55	0.12
Bolivian	16	0.03
Chilean	16	0.03
Colombian	37	0.08
Ecuadorian	7	0.01
Paraguayan	4	0.01
Peruvian	49	0.10
Uruguayan	2	<0.01
Venezuelan	23	0.05
Other Hispanic or Latino	161	0.34

Race*	Population	%
African-American/Black (1,257)	1,408	2.97
Not Hispanic (1,235)	1,370	2.89
Hispanic (22)	38	0.08
American Indian/Alaska Native (74)	211	0.44
Not Hispanic (63)	192	0.40
Hispanic (11)	19	0.04
Apache (2)	2	<0.01
Blackfeet (0)	3	0.01
Cherokee (19)	60	0.13
Chickasaw (4)	8	0.02
Chippewa (0)	3	0.01
Choctaw (1)	6	0.01
Creek (3)	11	0.02
Inupiat *(Alaska Native)* (0)	1	<0.01
Iroquois (2)	2	<0.01
Lumbee (0)	2	<0.01
Menominee (1)	1	<0.01
Mexican American Ind. (3)	6	0.01
Navajo (0)	2	<0.01
Osage (2)	3	0.01
Pueblo (3)	3	0.01
Sioux (0)	10	0.02
South American Ind. (4)	4	0.01
Asian (4,091)	4,429	9.33
Not Hispanic (4,076)	4,399	9.26
Hispanic (15)	30	0.06
Bangladeshi (12)	17	0.04
Burmese (11)	11	0.02
Cambodian (3)	3	0.01
Chinese, ex. Taiwanese (1,394)	1,469	3.09
Filipino (173)	223	0.47
Indian (1,323)	1,394	2.94
Indonesian (2)	4	0.01
Japanese (88)	143	0.30
Korean (474)	509	1.07
Nepalese (12)	12	0.03
Pakistani (271)	281	0.59
Sri Lankan (20)	20	0.04
Taiwanese (121)	136	0.29
Thai (33)	45	0.09
Vietnamese (53)	70	0.15
Hawaii Native/Pacific Islander (15)	32	0.07
Not Hispanic (14)	28	0.06
Hispanic (1)	4	0.01
Guamanian/Chamorro (1)	2	<0.01
Native Hawaiian (5)	9	0.02
Samoan (8)	10	0.02
White (41,078)	41,635	87.68
Not Hispanic (40,163)	40,654	85.62
Hispanic (915)	981	2.07

Chillicothe

Place Type: City
County: Livingston
Population: 9,515†

Ancestry‡	Population	%
African, Sub-Saharan (0)	47	0.53
Sudanese (0)	47	0.53
Alsatian (12)	12	0.14
American (727)	727	8.20
British (0)	17	0.19
Czech (11)	24	0.27
Dutch (17)	81	0.91
English (595)	1,245	14.04
French, ex. Basque (29)	170	1.92
French Canadian (0)	23	0.26
German (667)	2,035	22.95
Guyanese (16)	16	0.18
Hungarian (0)	14	0.16
Irish (369)	1,197	13.50
Italian (103)	179	2.02
Norwegian (68)	68	0.77
Polish (0)	24	0.27
Portuguese (0)	31	0.35
Scandinavian (0)	36	0.41
Scotch-Irish (64)	120	1.35
Scottish (49)	317	3.58
Swedish (44)	84	0.95
Swiss (6)	32	0.36
Welsh (17)	87	0.98

Hispanic Origin	Population	%
Hispanic or Latino (of any race)	143	1.50
Central American, ex. Mexican	4	0.04
Guatemalan	1	0.01
Panamanian	1	0.01
Salvadoran	2	0.02
Cuban	3	0.03
Dominican Republic	3	0.03
Mexican	115	1.21
Puerto Rican	3	0.03
South American	4	0.04
Bolivian	3	0.03
Venezuelan	1	0.01
Other Hispanic or Latino	11	0.12

*Notes: † The Census 2010 population figure is used to calculate the percentages in the Hispanic Origin and Race categories. Ancestry percentages are based on the 2006-2010 American Community Survey population (not shown); ‡ Numbers in parentheses indicate the number of people reporting a single ancestry; * Numbers in parentheses indicate the number of persons reporting this race alone, not in combination with any other race; Please refer to the Explanation of Data for more information.*

Race*	Population	%
African-American/Black (353)	431	4.53
Not Hispanic (352)	429	4.51
Hispanic (1)	2	0.02
American Indian/Alaska Native (41)	77	0.81
Not Hispanic (39)	72	0.76
Hispanic (2)	5	0.05
Apache (3)	5	0.05
Blackfeet (1)	1	0.01
Cherokee (5)	21	0.22
Chippewa (3)	3	0.03
Choctaw (1)	2	0.02
Comanche (0)	1	0.01
Creek (0)	1	0.01
Potawatomi (1)	1	0.01
Sioux (2)	5	0.05
Asian (33)	62	0.65
Not Hispanic (33)	62	0.65
Chinese, ex. Taiwanese (7)	15	0.16
Filipino (9)	17	0.18
Indian (7)	8	0.08
Japanese (1)	5	0.05
Korean (1)	3	0.03
Pakistani (3)	3	0.03
Thai (0)	1	0.01
Vietnamese (2)	2	0.02
Hawaii Native/Pacific Islander (1)	3	0.03
Not Hispanic (1)	3	0.03
Guamanian/Chamorro (1)	1	0.01
Native Hawaiian (0)	1	0.01
White (8,896)	9,035	94.96
Not Hispanic (8,808)	8,940	93.96
Hispanic (88)	95	1.00

Clayton

Place Type: City
County: St. Louis
Population: 15,939†

Ancestry‡	Population	%
African, Sub-Saharan (12)	55	0.36
African (12)	12	0.08
South African (0)	43	0.28
American (1,834)	1,834	11.96
Arab (185)	185	1.21
Egyptian (65)	65	0.42
Lebanese (104)	104	0.68
Other Arab (16)	16	0.10
Austrian (16)	153	1.00
Brazilian (0)	14	0.09
British (78)	129	0.84
Bulgarian (15)	15	0.10
Canadian (14)	14	0.09
Czech (12)	99	0.65
Czechoslovakian (13)	13	0.08
Danish (11)	24	0.16
Dutch (11)	144	0.94
Eastern European (184)	184	1.20
English (237)	1,538	10.03
European (419)	540	3.52
Finnish (0)	11	0.07
French, ex. Basque (43)	556	3.63
French Canadian (16)	66	0.43
German (1,143)	3,519	22.94
Greek (43)	79	0.52
Hungarian (0)	115	0.75
Iranian (114)	114	0.74
Irish (585)	2,057	13.41
Israeli (19)	19	0.12
Italian (210)	753	4.91
Latvian (79)	79	0.52
Lithuanian (0)	7	0.05
Norwegian (26)	225	1.47
Pennsylvania German (12)	12	0.08
Polish (100)	585	3.81
Portuguese (0)	12	0.08
Romanian (14)	54	0.35
Russian (397)	732	4.77
Scandinavian (0)	31	0.20
Scotch-Irish (125)	308	2.01
Scottish (51)	463	3.02
Slavic (0)	12	0.08
Slovak (17)	17	0.11
Slovene (18)	34	0.22
Swedish (52)	272	1.77
Swiss (11)	81	0.53
Ukrainian (40)	52	0.34
Welsh (11)	112	0.73

Hispanic Origin	Population	%
Hispanic or Latino (of any race)	488	3.06
Central American, ex. Mexican	32	0.20
Costa Rican	6	0.04
Guatemalan	6	0.04
Honduran	5	0.03
Nicaraguan	3	0.02
Panamanian	7	0.04
Salvadoran	5	0.03
Cuban	44	0.28
Dominican Republic	8	0.05
Mexican	155	0.97
Puerto Rican	39	0.24
South American	150	0.94
Argentinean	32	0.20
Bolivian	3	0.02
Chilean	12	0.08
Colombian	45	0.28
Ecuadorian	18	0.11
Paraguayan	3	0.02
Peruvian	14	0.09
Uruguayan	9	0.06
Venezuelan	14	0.09
Other Hispanic or Latino	60	0.38

Race*	Population	%
African-American/Black (1,305)	1,396	8.76
Not Hispanic (1,292)	1,375	8.63
Hispanic (13)	21	0.13
American Indian/Alaska Native (26)	80	0.50
Not Hispanic (21)	68	0.43
Hispanic (5)	12	0.08
Apache (1)	2	0.01
Blackfeet (0)	2	0.01
Cherokee (5)	21	0.13
Chickasaw (0)	1	0.01
Chippewa (1)	1	0.01
Choctaw (0)	4	0.03
Iroquois (2)	3	0.02
Lumbee (0)	1	0.01
Mexican American Ind. (1)	1	0.01
Navajo (1)	3	0.02
Potawatomi (0)	1	0.01
Seminole (0)	1	0.01
Sioux (2)	2	0.01
South American Ind. (1)	2	0.01
Tlingit-Haida *(Alaska Native)* (0)	1	0.01
Asian (1,722)	1,969	12.35
Not Hispanic (1,711)	1,949	12.23
Hispanic (11)	20	0.13
Bangladeshi (1)	1	0.01
Burmese (3)	4	0.03
Chinese, ex. Taiwanese (784)	878	5.51
Filipino (25)	56	0.35
Indian (328)	382	2.40
Indonesian (1)	2	0.01
Japanese (74)	122	0.77
Korean (294)	328	2.06
Malaysian (0)	2	0.01
Nepalese (7)	8	0.05
Pakistani (18)	23	0.14
Sri Lankan (7)	10	0.06
Taiwanese (67)	85	0.53
Thai (25)	32	0.20
Vietnamese (27)	39	0.24
Hawaii Native/Pacific Islander (5)	28	0.18
Not Hispanic (3)	24	0.15
Hispanic (2)	4	0.03
Fijian (0)	3	0.02
Native Hawaiian (1)	3	0.02
Samoan (0)	1	0.01
White (12,431)	12,759	80.05
Not Hispanic (12,060)	12,362	77.56
Hispanic (371)	397	2.49

Clinton

Place Type: City
County: Henry
Population: 9,008†

Ancestry‡	Population	%
African, Sub-Saharan (0)	42	0.45
African (0)	42	0.45
American (1,236)	1,236	13.37
Austrian (0)	23	0.25
Czech (27)	71	0.77
Danish (0)	21	0.23
Dutch (11)	257	2.78
Eastern European (9)	9	0.10
English (486)	1,163	12.58
French, ex. Basque (20)	226	2.44
French Canadian (19)	29	0.31
German (934)	2,929	31.67
Greek (0)	14	0.15
Irish (295)	1,762	19.05
Italian (51)	312	3.37
Norwegian (0)	22	0.24
Polish (58)	183	1.98
Portuguese (0)	5	0.05
Romanian (0)	31	0.34
Russian (0)	22	0.24
Scotch-Irish (57)	391	4.23
Scottish (92)	165	1.78
Swedish (9)	82	0.89
Swiss (8)	55	0.59
Welsh (0)	15	0.16

Hispanic Origin	Population	%
Hispanic or Latino (of any race)	177	1.96
Central American, ex. Mexican	9	0.10
Guatemalan	1	0.01
Honduran	2	0.02
Salvadoran	6	0.07
Cuban	1	0.01
Mexican	142	1.58
Puerto Rican	9	0.10
South American	2	0.02
Chilean	1	0.01
Colombian	1	0.01
Other Hispanic or Latino	14	0.16

Race*	Population	%
African-American/Black (171)	230	2.55
Not Hispanic (164)	221	2.45
Hispanic (7)	9	0.10
American Indian/Alaska Native (40)	112	1.24
Not Hispanic (36)	103	1.14
Hispanic (4)	9	0.10
Apache (1)	1	0.01
Blackfeet (1)	2	0.02
Cherokee (13)	36	0.40
Chickasaw (0)	4	0.04
Choctaw (4)	10	0.11
Crow (0)	1	0.01
Delaware (1)	2	0.02
Iroquois (2)	3	0.03
Lumbee (1)	1	0.01
Mexican American Ind. (1)	2	0.02
Sioux (1)	4	0.04
Ute (1)	1	0.01
Asian (25)	43	0.48
Not Hispanic (25)	43	0.48
Chinese, ex. Taiwanese (9)	9	0.10
Filipino (11)	21	0.23
Indian (3)	3	0.03
Japanese (0)	3	0.03
Korean (0)	4	0.04
Pakistani (1)	1	0.01

*Notes: † The Census 2010 population figure is used to calculate the percentages in the Hispanic Origin and Race categories. Ancestry percentages are based on the 2006-2010 American Community Survey population (not shown); ‡ Numbers in parentheses indicate the number of people reporting a single ancestry; * Numbers in parentheses indicate the number of persons reporting this race alone, not in combination with any other race; Please refer to the Explanation of Data for more information.*

Thai (1)	1	0.01
Hawaii Native/Pacific Islander (1)	1	0.01
Not Hispanic (1)	1	0.01
Native Hawaiian (1)	1	0.01
White (8,566)	8,727	96.88
Not Hispanic (8,462)	8,602	95.49
Hispanic (104)	125	1.39

Columbia

Place Type: City
County: Boone
Population: 108,500†

Ancestry‡	Population	%
African, Sub-Saharan (791)	1,126	1.08
African (484)	819	0.78
Ghanaian (61)	61	0.06
Kenyan (115)	115	0.11
Nigerian (28)	28	0.03
South African (26)	26	0.02
Zimbabwean (26)	26	0.02
Other Sub-Saharan African (51)	51	0.05
Albanian (14)	14	0.01
Alsatian (0)	17	0.02
American (4,116)	4,116	3.93
Arab (877)	1,125	1.08
Arab (500)	578	0.55
Egyptian (39)	39	0.04
Iraqi (37)	85	0.08
Jordanian (37)	37	0.04
Lebanese (58)	84	0.08
Palestinian (48)	73	0.07
Syrian (25)	38	0.04
Other Arab (133)	191	0.18
Armenian (0)	56	0.05
Australian (14)	14	0.01
Austrian (13)	220	0.21
Belgian (31)	68	0.06
Brazilian (116)	152	0.15
British (265)	684	0.65
Bulgarian (47)	47	0.04
Cajun (12)	12	0.01
Canadian (74)	126	0.12
Croatian (31)	128	0.12
Czech (246)	664	0.63
Czechoslovakian (45)	136	0.13
Danish (109)	490	0.47
Dutch (549)	1,854	1.77
Eastern European (89)	99	0.09
English (4,313)	12,917	12.35
Estonian (0)	34	0.03
European (1,815)	2,082	1.99
Finnish (79)	119	0.11
French, ex. Basque (393)	3,539	3.38
French Canadian (117)	352	0.34
German (11,041)	30,374	29.03
Greek (348)	680	0.65
Hungarian (354)	676	0.65
Iranian (232)	316	0.30
Irish (3,395)	14,988	14.33
Italian (977)	3,742	3.58
Latvian (0)	95	0.09
Lithuanian (40)	319	0.30
Macedonian (71)	71	0.07
Maltese (10)	10	0.01
Northern European (223)	238	0.23
Norwegian (364)	1,235	1.18
Pennsylvania German (99)	122	0.12
Polish (487)	2,107	2.01
Portuguese (146)	194	0.19
Romanian (34)	116	0.11
Russian (543)	1,054	1.01
Scandinavian (58)	130	0.12
Scotch-Irish (988)	3,044	2.91
Scottish (627)	2,736	2.62
Serbian (12)	91	0.09
Slavic (9)	111	0.11
Slovak (32)	101	0.10
Soviet Union (10)	10	0.01
Swedish (334)	1,423	1.36
Swiss (122)	683	0.65
Turkish (50)	60	0.06
Ukrainian (83)	187	0.18
Welsh (86)	1,194	1.14
West Indian, ex. Hispanic (64)	135	0.13
Bahamian (0)	9	0.01
Dutch West Indian (0)	13	0.01
Haitian (64)	71	0.07
Jamaican (0)	42	0.04
Yugoslavian (306)	361	0.35

Hispanic Origin	Population	%
Hispanic or Latino (of any race)	3,729	3.44
Central American, ex. Mexican	220	0.20
Costa Rican	9	0.01
Guatemalan	56	0.05
Honduran	60	0.06
Nicaraguan	26	0.02
Panamanian	32	0.03
Salvadoran	36	0.03
Other Central American	1	<0.01
Cuban	174	0.16
Dominican Republic	27	0.02
Mexican	2,320	2.14
Puerto Rican	311	0.29
South American	334	0.31
Argentinean	24	0.02
Bolivian	32	0.03
Chilean	15	0.01
Colombian	96	0.09
Ecuadorian	32	0.03
Paraguayan	8	0.01
Peruvian	98	0.09
Uruguayan	7	0.01
Venezuelan	17	0.02
Other South American	5	<0.01
Other Hispanic or Latino	343	0.32

Race*	Population	%
African-American/Black (12,217)	13,972	12.88
Not Hispanic (12,083)	13,723	12.65
Hispanic (134)	249	0.23
American Indian/Alaska Native (362)	1,186	1.09
Not Hispanic (296)	1,022	0.94
Hispanic (66)	164	0.15
Alaska Athabascan *(Ala. Nat.)* (6)	6	0.01
Aleut *(Alaska Native)* (1)	3	<0.01
Apache (10)	24	0.02
Blackfeet (8)	45	0.04
Canadian/French Am. Ind. (0)	1	<0.01
Central American Ind. (1)	2	<0.01
Cherokee (109)	400	0.37
Cheyenne (0)	1	<0.01
Chickasaw (3)	9	0.01
Chippewa (10)	11	0.01
Choctaw (5)	32	0.03
Colville (1)	1	<0.01
Comanche (0)	3	<0.01
Creek (6)	10	0.01
Crow (0)	1	<0.01
Delaware (1)	2	<0.01
Hopi (0)	2	<0.01
Houma (1)	3	<0.01
Inupiat *(Alaska Native)* (1)	2	<0.01
Iroquois (11)	28	0.03
Kiowa (1)	6	0.01
Lumbee (2)	2	<0.01
Menominee (0)	1	<0.01
Mexican American Ind. (12)	25	0.02
Navajo (3)	8	0.01
Osage (6)	12	0.01
Ottawa (1)	2	<0.01
Paiute (0)	3	<0.01
Potawatomi (5)	11	0.01
Pueblo (5)	5	<0.01
Puget Sound Salish (1)	1	<0.01
Seminole (1)	5	<0.01
Shoshone (1)	2	<0.01
Sioux (7)	26	0.02
South American Ind. (3)	14	0.01
Tlingit-Haida *(Alaska Native)* (0)	1	<0.01
Yaqui (0)	1	<0.01
Yup'ik *(Alaska Native)* (1)	1	<0.01
Asian (5,628)	6,552	6.04
Not Hispanic (5,604)	6,488	5.98
Hispanic (24)	64	0.06
Bangladeshi (67)	82	0.08
Burmese (97)	97	0.09
Cambodian (288)	329	0.30
Chinese, ex. Taiwanese (1,701)	1,873	1.73
Filipino (301)	481	0.44
Hmong (1)	2	<0.01
Indian (1,282)	1,413	1.30
Indonesian (13)	17	0.02
Japanese (114)	266	0.25
Korean (839)	975	0.90
Laotian (12)	19	0.02
Malaysian (18)	28	0.03
Nepalese (30)	36	0.03
Pakistani (136)	144	0.13
Sri Lankan (34)	36	0.03
Taiwanese (136)	146	0.13
Thai (82)	121	0.11
Vietnamese (304)	352	0.32
Hawaii Native/Pacific Islander (69)	167	0.15
Not Hispanic (59)	150	0.14
Hispanic (10)	17	0.02
Guamanian/Chamorro (21)	33	0.03
Native Hawaiian (24)	67	0.06
Samoan (5)	22	0.02
Tongan (3)	3	<0.01
White (85,742)	88,766	81.81
Not Hispanic (83,542)	86,238	79.48
Hispanic (2,200)	2,528	2.33

Concord

Place Type: CDP
County: St. Louis
Population: 16,421†

Ancestry‡	Population	%
African, Sub-Saharan (14)	14	0.09
Nigerian (14)	14	0.09
Albanian (153)	153	0.97
American (735)	735	4.64
Arab (40)	133	0.84
Jordanian (16)	16	0.10
Lebanese (7)	88	0.56
Other Arab (17)	29	0.18
Austrian (38)	122	0.77
British (15)	32	0.20
Bulgarian (15)	15	0.09
Cajun (11)	11	0.07
Canadian (0)	18	0.11
Croatian (77)	108	0.68
Czech (114)	440	2.78
Czechoslovakian (0)	24	0.15
Danish (65)	114	0.72
Dutch (134)	337	2.13
Eastern European (35)	35	0.22
English (281)	1,354	8.55
European (284)	296	1.87
Finnish (0)	9	0.06
French, ex. Basque (148)	1,071	6.76
French Canadian (23)	65	0.41
German (3,413)	7,910	49.94
Greek (27)	59	0.37
Hungarian (21)	93	0.59
Irish (646)	3,429	21.65
Italian (405)	1,602	10.11
Lithuanian (11)	49	0.31
Macedonian (0)	15	0.09
Norwegian (19)	67	0.42
Polish (43)	407	2.57
Romanian (43)	70	0.44
Russian (34)	34	0.21
Scandinavian (0)	15	0.09
Scotch-Irish (91)	304	1.92

*Notes: † The Census 2010 population figure is used to calculate the percentages in the Hispanic Origin and Race categories. Ancestry percentages are based on the 2006-2010 American Community Survey population (not shown); ‡ Numbers in parentheses indicate the number of people reporting a single ancestry; * Numbers in parentheses indicate the number of persons reporting this race alone, not in combination with any other race; Please refer to the Explanation of Data for more information.*

Scottish (24)	101	0.64
Slavic (6)	6	0.04
Slovak (10)	10	0.06
Slovene (11)	11	0.07
Swedish (80)	173	1.09
Swiss (22)	251	1.58
Ukrainian (17)	26	0.16
Welsh (14)	117	0.74
Yugoslavian (219)	233	1.47

Hispanic Origin	Population	%
Hispanic or Latino (of any race)	231	1.41
Central American, ex. Mexican	21	0.13
Costa Rican	3	0.02
Guatemalan	13	0.08
Honduran	4	0.02
Panamanian	1	0.01
Cuban	7	0.04
Mexican	107	0.65
Puerto Rican	22	0.13
South American	23	0.14
Bolivian	3	0.02
Chilean	2	0.01
Colombian	9	0.05
Ecuadorian	4	0.02
Paraguayan	1	0.01
Peruvian	4	0.02
Other Hispanic or Latino	51	0.31

Race*	Population	%
African-American/Black (106)	157	0.96
Not Hispanic (103)	151	0.92
Hispanic (3)	6	0.04
American Indian/Alaska Native (23)	78	0.48
Not Hispanic (18)	67	0.41
Hispanic (5)	11	0.07
Aleut *(Alaska Native)* (1)	2	0.01
Apache (0)	1	0.01
Blackfeet (0)	1	0.01
Central American Ind. (0)	1	0.01
Cherokee (0)	23	0.14
Chickasaw (4)	4	0.02
Chippewa (4)	4	0.02
Choctaw (2)	5	0.03
Creek (0)	2	0.01
Crow (0)	1	0.01
Mexican American Ind. (3)	5	0.03
Osage (0)	6	0.04
Sioux (0)	1	0.01
Asian (275)	351	2.14
Not Hispanic (270)	342	2.08
Hispanic (5)	9	0.05
Bangladeshi (1)	1	0.01
Cambodian (4)	4	0.02
Chinese, ex. Taiwanese (54)	67	0.41
Filipino (62)	83	0.51
Indian (32)	36	0.22
Indonesian (1)	4	0.02
Japanese (8)	17	0.10
Korean (16)	19	0.12
Laotian (1)	1	0.01
Taiwanese (1)	1	0.01
Thai (4)	5	0.03
Vietnamese (84)	86	0.52
Hawaii Native/Pacific Islander (4)	10	0.06
Not Hispanic (4)	9	0.05
Hispanic (0)	1	0.01
Guamanian/Chamorro (1)	1	0.01
Native Hawaiian (0)	3	0.02
Samoan (0)	1	0.01
White (15,771)	15,950	97.13
Not Hispanic (15,622)	15,782	96.11
Hispanic (149)	168	1.02

Crestwood

Place Type: City
County: St. Louis
Population: 11,912†

Ancestry‡	Population	%
African, Sub-Saharan (0)	24	0.20
Other Sub-Saharan African (0)	24	0.20
American (620)	620	5.21
Arab (7)	46	0.39
Lebanese (7)	27	0.23
Syrian (0)	19	0.16
Armenian (64)	64	0.54
Austrian (23)	101	0.85
Belgian (0)	19	0.16
British (42)	42	0.35
Canadian (8)	66	0.55
Croatian (66)	122	1.03
Czech (19)	171	1.44
Czechoslovakian (0)	10	0.08
Danish (9)	9	0.08
Dutch (24)	315	2.65
Eastern European (19)	19	0.16
English (302)	1,409	11.85
European (31)	31	0.26
Finnish (0)	14	0.12
French, ex. Basque (65)	479	4.03
French Canadian (11)	24	0.20
German (2,352)	5,819	48.93
Greek (28)	28	0.24
Hungarian (15)	56	0.47
Irish (437)	2,517	21.17
Israeli (14)	14	0.12
Italian (324)	839	7.06
Latvian (0)	7	0.06
Lithuanian (32)	41	0.34
Luxemburger (0)	10	0.08
Northern European (108)	108	0.91
Norwegian (11)	128	1.08
Polish (104)	323	2.72
Portuguese (0)	3	0.03
Romanian (46)	46	0.39
Russian (19)	110	0.92
Scotch-Irish (44)	216	1.82
Scottish (83)	287	2.41
Serbian (26)	50	0.42
Slavic (0)	25	0.21
Slovak (0)	14	0.12
Swedish (34)	133	1.12
Swiss (41)	122	1.03
Ukrainian (44)	60	0.50
Welsh (22)	115	0.97
Yugoslavian (29)	69	0.58

Hispanic Origin	Population	%
Hispanic or Latino (of any race)	229	1.92
Central American, ex. Mexican	37	0.31
Guatemalan	29	0.24
Honduran	1	0.01
Nicaraguan	1	0.01
Salvadoran	3	0.03
Other Central American	3	0.03
Cuban	5	0.04
Dominican Republic	3	0.03
Mexican	108	0.91
Puerto Rican	10	0.08
South American	29	0.24
Argentinean	13	0.11
Bolivian	1	0.01
Chilean	2	0.02
Colombian	6	0.05
Ecuadorian	1	0.01
Peruvian	6	0.05
Other Hispanic or Latino	37	0.31

Race*	Population	%
African-American/Black (191)	258	2.17
Not Hispanic (189)	250	2.10
Hispanic (2)	8	0.07
American Indian/Alaska Native (18)	66	0.55
Not Hispanic (12)	58	0.49
Hispanic (6)	8	0.07
Apache (1)	5	0.04
Blackfeet (1)	1	0.01
Central American Ind. (2)	2	0.02
Cherokee (2)	19	0.16
Chippewa (0)	1	0.01
Choctaw (0)	3	0.03
Delaware (1)	1	0.01
Mexican American Ind. (1)	2	0.02
Sioux (3)	4	0.03
Yaqui (1)	1	0.01
Asian (280)	369	3.10
Not Hispanic (280)	361	3.03
Hispanic (0)	8	0.07
Cambodian (4)	6	0.05
Chinese, ex. Taiwanese (64)	92	0.77
Filipino (12)	37	0.31
Indian (54)	64	0.54
Indonesian (1)	4	0.03
Japanese (12)	25	0.21
Korean (17)	24	0.20
Laotian (2)	6	0.05
Malaysian (1)	2	0.02
Nepalese (1)	3	0.03
Pakistani (9)	9	0.08
Sri Lankan (0)	3	0.03
Taiwanese (2)	3	0.03
Thai (3)	6	0.05
Vietnamese (64)	83	0.70
Hawaii Native/Pacific Islander (7)	23	0.19
Not Hispanic (6)	16	0.13
Hispanic (1)	7	0.06
Guamanian/Chamorro (1)	8	0.07
Native Hawaiian (6)	12	0.10
Samoan (0)	2	0.02
Tongan (0)	1	0.01
White (11,168)	11,350	95.28
Not Hispanic (11,014)	11,182	93.87
Hispanic (154)	168	1.41

Creve Coeur

Place Type: City
County: St. Louis
Population: 17,833†

Ancestry‡	Population	%
African, Sub-Saharan (63)	163	0.93
African (45)	145	0.82
Nigerian (9)	9	0.05
Ugandan (9)	9	0.05
American (1,807)	1,807	10.28
Arab (36)	47	0.27
Lebanese (24)	24	0.14
Syrian (12)	23	0.13
Armenian (12)	12	0.07
Austrian (52)	125	0.71
Belgian (13)	49	0.28
Brazilian (14)	14	0.08
British (39)	48	0.27
Canadian (20)	54	0.31
Celtic (14)	14	0.08
Croatian (32)	61	0.35
Cypriot (47)	47	0.27
Czech (52)	154	0.88
Danish (0)	30	0.17
Dutch (53)	149	0.85
Eastern European (227)	227	1.29
English (372)	1,377	7.83
European (347)	347	1.97
Finnish (0)	13	0.07
French, ex. Basque (107)	546	3.11
French Canadian (0)	9	0.05
German (1,732)	4,745	26.99
Greek (163)	242	1.38
Guyanese (0)	20	0.11
Hungarian (23)	82	0.47
Iranian (24)	24	0.14
Irish (436)	2,200	12.51
Israeli (28)	28	0.16
Italian (307)	786	4.47
Latvian (7)	7	0.04
Lithuanian (49)	54	0.31
Northern European (51)	51	0.29

*Notes: † The Census 2010 population figure is used to calculate the percentages in the Hispanic Origin and Race categories. Ancestry percentages are based on the 2006-2010 American Community Survey population (not shown); ‡ Numbers in parentheses indicate the number of people reporting a single ancestry; * Numbers in parentheses indicate the number of persons reporting this race alone, not in combination with any other race; Please refer to the Explanation of Data for more information.*

Norwegian (54)	143	0.81
Polish (335)	1,060	6.03
Romanian (23)	65	0.37
Russian (856)	1,375	7.82
Scandinavian (14)	55	0.31
Scotch-Irish (118)	212	1.21
Scottish (77)	238	1.35
Slovak (13)	36	0.20
Slovene (0)	39	0.22
Swedish (12)	153	0.87
Swiss (47)	115	0.65
Turkish (19)	19	0.11
Ukrainian (67)	138	0.78
Welsh (0)	133	0.76
West Indian, ex. Hispanic (20)	20	0.11
Jamaican (9)	9	0.05
Other West Indian (11)	11	0.06
Yugoslavian (34)	34	0.19

Hispanic Origin	Population	%
Hispanic or Latino (of any race)	461	2.59
Central American, ex. Mexican	29	0.16
Guatemalan	12	0.07
Honduran	2	0.01
Nicaraguan	1	0.01
Panamanian	4	0.02
Salvadoran	10	0.06
Cuban	24	0.13
Dominican Republic	5	0.03
Mexican	203	1.14
Puerto Rican	48	0.27
South American	120	0.67
Argentinean	33	0.19
Bolivian	6	0.03
Chilean	4	0.02
Colombian	45	0.25
Ecuadorian	2	0.01
Peruvian	8	0.04
Uruguayan	2	0.01
Venezuelan	16	0.09
Other South American	4	0.02
Other Hispanic or Latino	32	0.18

Race*	Population	%
African-American/Black (1,278)	1,391	7.80
Not Hispanic (1,264)	1,366	7.66
Hispanic (14)	25	0.14
American Indian/Alaska Native (34)	108	0.61
Not Hispanic (31)	101	0.57
Hispanic (3)	7	0.04
Blackfeet (0)	2	0.01
Cherokee (7)	27	0.15
Chickasaw (0)	2	0.01
Chippewa (0)	5	0.03
Crow (0)	1	0.01
Iroquois (1)	1	0.01
Seminole (3)	3	0.02
Sioux (1)	8	0.04
South American Ind. (1)	1	0.01
Ute (2)	2	0.01
Asian (1,800)	1,982	11.11
Not Hispanic (1,798)	1,971	11.05
Hispanic (2)	11	0.06
Bangladeshi (1)	1	0.01
Burmese (4)	4	0.02
Cambodian (2)	2	0.01
Chinese, ex. Taiwanese (445)	500	2.80
Filipino (76)	92	0.52
Indian (814)	866	4.86
Indonesian (2)	3	0.02
Japanese (27)	44	0.25
Korean (174)	198	1.11
Laotian (3)	5	0.03
Malaysian (2)	2	0.01
Pakistani (83)	100	0.56
Sri Lankan (22)	25	0.14
Taiwanese (38)	41	0.23
Thai (21)	26	0.15
Vietnamese (24)	27	0.15
Hawaii Native/Pacific Islander (3)	15	0.08
Not Hispanic (3)	13	0.07
Hispanic (0)	2	0.01
Guamanian/Chamorro (2)	2	0.01
Native Hawaiian (0)	4	0.02
White (14,251)	14,539	81.53
Not Hispanic (13,936)	14,195	79.60
Hispanic (315)	344	1.93

Dardenne Prairie

Place Type: City
County: St. Charles
Population: 11,494†

Ancestry‡	Population	%
African, Sub-Saharan (27)	27	0.26
African (27)	27	0.26
American (512)	512	4.98
Arab (0)	32	0.31
Lebanese (0)	32	0.31
Austrian (7)	33	0.32
British (29)	44	0.43
Croatian (0)	31	0.30
Czech (0)	93	0.90
Danish (15)	96	0.93
Dutch (72)	143	1.39
English (443)	1,215	11.81
European (236)	263	2.56
French, ex. Basque (19)	512	4.98
German (1,261)	3,394	32.98
Greek (27)	39	0.38
Hungarian (18)	113	1.10
Irish (582)	1,873	18.20
Italian (268)	1,020	9.91
Lithuanian (0)	29	0.28
New Zealander (0)	13	0.13
Northern European (13)	13	0.13
Norwegian (17)	109	1.06
Polish (117)	419	4.07
Russian (30)	79	0.77
Scandinavian (0)	10	0.10
Scotch-Irish (111)	240	2.33
Scottish (56)	229	2.23
Swedish (87)	167	1.62
Swiss (0)	30	0.29
Turkish (23)	23	0.22
Ukrainian (0)	11	0.11
Welsh (24)	98	0.95

Hispanic Origin	Population	%
Hispanic or Latino (of any race)	234	2.04
Central American, ex. Mexican	23	0.20
Guatemalan	10	0.09
Panamanian	10	0.09
Salvadoran	3	0.03
Cuban	11	0.10
Mexican	149	1.30
Puerto Rican	14	0.12
South American	26	0.23
Argentinean	1	0.01
Chilean	2	0.02
Colombian	11	0.10
Ecuadorian	1	0.01
Peruvian	7	0.06
Venezuelan	1	0.01
Other South American	3	0.03
Other Hispanic or Latino	11	0.10

Race*	Population	%
African-American/Black (404)	481	4.18
Not Hispanic (403)	476	4.14
Hispanic (1)	5	0.04
American Indian/Alaska Native (17)	52	0.45
Not Hispanic (16)	45	0.39
Hispanic (1)	7	0.06
Apache (0)	2	0.02
Blackfeet (1)	3	0.03
Cherokee (3)	21	0.18
Cheyenne (1)	1	0.01
Choctaw (0)	1	0.01
Mexican American Ind. (0)	3	0.03
Potawatomi (1)	1	0.01
Seminole (0)	1	0.01
South American Ind. (0)	1	0.01
Ute (1)	1	0.01
Asian (404)	466	4.05
Not Hispanic (404)	464	4.04
Hispanic (0)	2	0.02
Chinese, ex. Taiwanese (82)	96	0.84
Filipino (43)	55	0.48
Indian (170)	175	1.52
Japanese (10)	20	0.17
Korean (13)	23	0.20
Laotian (8)	8	0.07
Nepalese (1)	2	0.02
Pakistani (15)	17	0.15
Sri Lankan (1)	2	0.02
Taiwanese (5)	6	0.05
Thai (5)	6	0.05
Vietnamese (45)	59	0.51
Hawaii Native/Pacific Islander (5)	16	0.14
Not Hispanic (5)	14	0.12
Hispanic (0)	2	0.02
Guamanian/Chamorro (0)	2	0.02
Marshallese (1)	1	0.01
Native Hawaiian (2)	9	0.08
Samoan (1)	3	0.03
White (10,423)	10,589	92.13
Not Hispanic (10,262)	10,405	90.53
Hispanic (161)	184	1.60

Des Peres

Place Type: City
County: St. Louis
Population: 8,373†

Ancestry‡	Population	%
Alsatian (0)	17	0.20
American (260)	260	3.10
Arab (0)	16	0.19
Lebanese (0)	16	0.19
Australian (0)	13	0.15
Austrian (0)	22	0.26
British (41)	55	0.65
Canadian (32)	32	0.38
Croatian (0)	30	0.36
Czech (41)	62	0.74
Czechoslovakian (0)	10	0.12
Danish (15)	39	0.46
Dutch (48)	123	1.46
Eastern European (12)	12	0.14
English (398)	1,358	16.17
European (64)	64	0.76
French, ex. Basque (27)	514	6.12
French Canadian (22)	22	0.26
German (1,160)	3,671	43.72
Greek (0)	26	0.31
Hungarian (7)	7	0.08
Irish (557)	2,615	31.14
Italian (188)	582	6.93
Lithuanian (8)	8	0.10
Macedonian (0)	7	0.08
Norwegian (26)	118	1.41
Polish (32)	308	3.67
Portuguese (0)	12	0.14
Romanian (17)	32	0.38
Russian (23)	136	1.62
Scotch-Irish (67)	235	2.80
Scottish (56)	340	4.05
Slovak (0)	30	0.36
Slovene (0)	84	1.00
Swedish (0)	190	2.26
Swiss (0)	70	0.83
Ukrainian (28)	42	0.50
Welsh (21)	77	0.92

Hispanic Origin	Population	%
Hispanic or Latino (of any race)	112	1.34
Central American, ex. Mexican	18	0.21

*Notes: † The Census 2010 population figure is used to calculate the percentages in the Hispanic Origin and Race categories. Ancestry percentages are based on the 2006-2010 American Community Survey population (not shown); ‡ Numbers in parentheses indicate the number of people reporting a single ancestry; * Numbers in parentheses indicate the number of persons reporting this race alone, not in combination with any other race; Please refer to the Explanation of Data for more information.*

Costa Rican	1	0.01
Guatemalan	17	0.20
Cuban	1	0.01
Dominican Republic	1	0.01
Mexican	52	0.62
Puerto Rican	3	0.04
South American	24	0.29
Argentinean	2	0.02
Bolivian	5	0.06
Chilean	5	0.06
Colombian	5	0.06
Peruvian	4	0.05
Venezuelan	3	0.04
Other Hispanic or Latino	13	0.16

Race*	Population	%
African-American/Black (79)	95	1.13
Not Hispanic (76)	92	1.10
Hispanic (3)	3	0.04
American Indian/Alaska Native (14)	24	0.29
Not Hispanic (12)	20	0.24
Hispanic (2)	4	0.05
Cherokee (0)	3	0.04
Iroquois (0)	1	0.01
Mexican American Ind. (6)	6	0.07
Asian (262)	332	3.97
Not Hispanic (261)	329	3.93
Hispanic (1)	3	0.04
Burmese (0)	3	0.04
Cambodian (3)	3	0.04
Chinese, ex. Taiwanese (32)	55	0.66
Filipino (35)	59	0.70
Indian (91)	96	1.15
Indonesian (1)	1	0.01
Japanese (8)	15	0.18
Korean (18)	25	0.30
Malaysian (1)	7	0.08
Pakistani (23)	29	0.35
Sri Lankan (1)	1	0.01
Taiwanese (3)	3	0.04
Thai (5)	8	0.10
Vietnamese (19)	27	0.32
Hawaii Native/Pacific Islander (2)	8	0.10
Not Hispanic (2)	8	0.10
Tongan (1)	1	0.01
White (7,894)	7,990	95.43
Not Hispanic (7,809)	7,900	94.35
Hispanic (85)	90	1.07

Dexter

Place Type: City
County: Stoddard
Population: 7,864†

Ancestry‡	Population	%
American (1,544)	1,544	19.66
British (11)	11	0.14
Czech (0)	52	0.66
Dutch (16)	296	3.77
English (313)	586	7.46
European (67)	67	0.85
French, ex. Basque (8)	52	0.66
French Canadian (8)	8	0.10
German (462)	1,318	16.78
Irish (412)	1,154	14.69
Italian (93)	169	2.15
Norwegian (10)	63	0.80
Polish (0)	80	1.02
Portuguese (8)	8	0.10
Scotch-Irish (0)	31	0.39
Scottish (27)	128	1.63
Swedish (0)	25	0.32
Swiss (9)	9	0.11

Hispanic Origin	Population	%
Hispanic or Latino (of any race)	148	1.88
Cuban	6	0.08
Dominican Republic	1	0.01
Mexican	105	1.34
Puerto Rican	14	0.18
South American	4	0.05
Colombian	2	0.03
Peruvian	2	0.03
Other Hispanic or Latino	18	0.23

Race*	Population	%
African-American/Black (38)	59	0.75
Not Hispanic (37)	56	0.71
Hispanic (1)	3	0.04
American Indian/Alaska Native (39)	94	1.20
Not Hispanic (32)	77	0.98
Hispanic (7)	17	0.22
Apache (0)	2	0.03
Cherokee (16)	43	0.55
Chippewa (1)	1	0.01
Choctaw (1)	1	0.01
Iroquois (0)	1	0.01
Mexican American Ind. (1)	2	0.03
Navajo (2)	5	0.06
Potawatomi (0)	1	0.01
Sioux (0)	1	0.01
Asian (19)	35	0.45
Not Hispanic (19)	35	0.45
Chinese, ex. Taiwanese (0)	3	0.04
Filipino (4)	8	0.10
Indian (5)	12	0.15
Japanese (1)	5	0.06
Korean (0)	5	0.06
Thai (1)	3	0.04
Vietnamese (3)	3	0.04
Hawaii Native/Pacific Islander (2)	5	0.06
Not Hispanic (0)	3	0.04
Hispanic (2)	2	0.03
Native Hawaiian (2)	2	0.03
White (7,639)	7,746	98.50
Not Hispanic (7,537)	7,626	96.97
Hispanic (102)	120	1.53

Ellisville

Place Type: City
County: St. Louis
Population: 9,133†

Ancestry‡	Population	%
African, Sub-Saharan (0)	17	0.19
African (0)	17	0.19
Albanian (0)	25	0.27
American (640)	640	7.03
Arab (11)	45	0.49
Arab (11)	11	0.12
Moroccan (0)	34	0.37
Austrian (0)	12	0.13
British (0)	57	0.63
Czech (77)	195	2.14
Danish (0)	63	0.69
Dutch (14)	87	0.96
English (377)	1,220	13.40
European (157)	157	1.72
French, ex. Basque (55)	460	5.05
German (1,650)	3,485	38.29
Greek (11)	11	0.12
Hungarian (0)	14	0.15
Irish (372)	1,402	15.40
Italian (202)	665	7.31
Lithuanian (0)	13	0.14
Northern European (45)	45	0.49
Norwegian (34)	152	1.67
Polish (127)	420	4.61
Romanian (43)	61	0.67
Russian (11)	23	0.25
Scotch-Irish (14)	29	0.32
Scottish (77)	147	1.62
Slovak (0)	25	0.27
Swedish (8)	174	1.91
Swiss (36)	90	0.99
Welsh (0)	24	0.26
West Indian, ex. Hispanic (58)	58	0.64
West Indian (58)	58	0.64

Hispanic Origin	Population	%
Hispanic or Latino (of any race)	223	2.44
Central American, ex. Mexican	9	0.10
Guatemalan	5	0.05
Honduran	2	0.02
Panamanian	2	0.02
Cuban	11	0.12
Dominican Republic	2	0.02
Mexican	136	1.49
Puerto Rican	9	0.10
South American	23	0.25
Argentinean	8	0.09
Bolivian	2	0.02
Colombian	2	0.02
Ecuadorian	1	0.01
Peruvian	9	0.10
Venezuelan	1	0.01
Other Hispanic or Latino	33	0.36

Race*	Population	%
African-American/Black (173)	210	2.30
Not Hispanic (170)	205	2.24
Hispanic (3)	5	0.05
American Indian/Alaska Native (12)	42	0.46
Not Hispanic (11)	37	0.41
Hispanic (1)	5	0.05
Canadian/French Am. Ind. (0)	2	0.02
Cherokee (4)	18	0.20
Choctaw (1)	3	0.03
Mexican American Ind. (1)	3	0.03
Osage (0)	1	0.01
Potawatomi (0)	1	0.01
Sioux (0)	1	0.01
South American Ind. (1)	1	0.01
Asian (392)	444	4.86
Not Hispanic (392)	440	4.82
Hispanic (0)	4	0.04
Bangladeshi (13)	13	0.14
Burmese (1)	3	0.03
Cambodian (0)	1	0.01
Chinese, ex. Taiwanese (91)	100	1.09
Filipino (37)	49	0.54
Indian (157)	168	1.84
Japanese (6)	15	0.16
Korean (27)	27	0.30
Laotian (3)	3	0.03
Pakistani (34)	37	0.41
Taiwanese (1)	1	0.01
Thai (2)	2	0.02
Vietnamese (16)	20	0.22
White (8,371)	8,490	92.96
Not Hispanic (8,216)	8,319	91.09
Hispanic (155)	171	1.87

Eureka

Place Type: City
County: St. Louis
Population: 10,189†

Ancestry‡	Population	%
African, Sub-Saharan (31)	31	0.32
African (31)	31	0.32
American (567)	567	5.84
Arab (0)	9	0.09
Arab (0)	9	0.09
Austrian (0)	10	0.10
British (65)	65	0.67
Canadian (15)	15	0.15
Croatian (10)	30	0.31
Czech (38)	190	1.96
Czechoslovakian (0)	9	0.09
Danish (20)	41	0.42
Dutch (47)	204	2.10
Eastern European (41)	49	0.50
English (307)	1,061	10.93
European (123)	130	1.34
Finnish (0)	18	0.19
French, ex. Basque (202)	584	6.02
German (991)	2,637	27.17

*Notes: † The Census 2010 population figure is used to calculate the percentages in the Hispanic Origin and Race categories. Ancestry percentages are based on the 2006-2010 American Community Survey population (not shown); ‡ Numbers in parentheses indicate the number of people reporting a single ancestry; * Numbers in parentheses indicate the number of persons reporting this race alone, not in combination with any other race; Please refer to the Explanation of Data for more information.*

Greek (9)	62	0.64
Hungarian (9)	76	0.78
Irish (544)	2,072	21.35
Italian (103)	653	6.73
Northern European (40)	83	0.86
Norwegian (79)	97	1.00
Polish (81)	348	3.59
Portuguese (8)	8	0.08
Romanian (76)	85	0.88
Russian (61)	170	1.75
Scotch-Irish (85)	163	1.68
Scottish (22)	266	2.74
Slavic (0)	14	0.14
Swedish (22)	69	0.71
Ukrainian (10)	10	0.10
Welsh (18)	54	0.56

Hispanic Origin	Population	%
Hispanic or Latino (of any race)	204	2.00
Central American, ex. Mexican	14	0.14
Costa Rican	1	0.01
Guatemalan	13	0.13
Cuban	2	0.02
Dominican Republic	3	0.03
Mexican	125	1.23
Puerto Rican	14	0.14
South American	32	0.31
Argentinean	7	0.07
Bolivian	4	0.04
Chilean	3	0.03
Colombian	4	0.04
Ecuadorian	5	0.05
Peruvian	5	0.05
Venezuelan	4	0.04
Other Hispanic or Latino	14	0.14

Race*	Population	%
African-American/Black (83)	130	1.28
Not Hispanic (82)	121	1.19
Hispanic (1)	9	0.09
American Indian/Alaska Native (25)	85	0.83
Not Hispanic (23)	79	0.78
Hispanic (2)	6	0.06
Apache (0)	9	0.09
Blackfeet (0)	4	0.04
Cherokee (10)	22	0.22
Chippewa (0)	1	0.01
Navajo (1)	2	0.02
Paiute (1)	1	0.01
Potawatomi (0)	5	0.05
Sioux (0)	5	0.05
South American Ind. (2)	6	0.06
Asian (194)	264	2.59
Not Hispanic (192)	260	2.55
Hispanic (2)	4	0.04
Cambodian (3)	3	0.03
Chinese, ex. Taiwanese (24)	38	0.37
Filipino (19)	37	0.36
Indian (105)	108	1.06
Japanese (3)	16	0.16
Korean (12)	25	0.25
Laotian (3)	3	0.03
Pakistani (6)	7	0.07
Sri Lankan (1)	1	0.01
Thai (1)	7	0.07
Vietnamese (11)	13	0.13
Hawaii Native/Pacific Islander (6)	8	0.08
Not Hispanic (6)	8	0.08
Native Hawaiian (5)	7	0.07
Samoan (1)	1	0.01
White (9,671)	9,845	96.62
Not Hispanic (9,532)	9,674	94.95
Hispanic (139)	171	1.68

Excelsior Springs

Place Type: City
County: Clay
Population: 11,084†

Ancestry‡	Population	%
African, Sub-Saharan (9)	9	0.08
South African (9)	9	0.08
American (1,464)	1,464	13.17
Belgian (13)	13	0.12
British (12)	23	0.21
Czech (50)	50	0.45
Czechoslovakian (32)	32	0.29
Danish (0)	119	1.07
Dutch (104)	357	3.21
English (542)	1,417	12.75
European (40)	40	0.36
French, ex. Basque (25)	351	3.16
French Canadian (22)	60	0.54
German (1,014)	2,876	25.87
Greek (0)	27	0.24
Irish (415)	1,917	17.24
Italian (108)	274	2.46
Norwegian (14)	54	0.49
Polish (131)	272	2.45
Romanian (0)	18	0.16
Russian (10)	10	0.09
Scotch-Irish (46)	94	0.85
Scottish (61)	110	0.99
Swedish (0)	83	0.75
Swiss (29)	51	0.46
Ukrainian (10)	21	0.19
Welsh (67)	241	2.17

Hispanic Origin	Population	%
Hispanic or Latino (of any race)	369	3.33
Central American, ex. Mexican	25	0.23
Costa Rican	1	0.01
Guatemalan	6	0.05
Honduran	9	0.08
Panamanian	4	0.04
Salvadoran	5	0.05
Cuban	10	0.09
Dominican Republic	2	0.02
Mexican	250	2.26
Puerto Rican	33	0.30
South American	3	0.03
Colombian	2	0.02
Peruvian	1	0.01
Other Hispanic or Latino	46	0.42

Race*	Population	%
African-American/Black (313)	444	4.01
Not Hispanic (299)	415	3.74
Hispanic (14)	29	0.26
American Indian/Alaska Native (83)	186	1.68
Not Hispanic (72)	160	1.44
Hispanic (11)	26	0.23
Blackfeet (0)	13	0.12
Cherokee (37)	81	0.73
Cheyenne (1)	1	0.01
Chickasaw (0)	3	0.03
Chippewa (1)	3	0.03
Choctaw (3)	6	0.05
Cree (0)	1	0.01
Creek (1)	1	0.01
Kiowa (4)	4	0.04
Mexican American Ind. (2)	3	0.03
Navajo (1)	2	0.02
Osage (1)	1	0.01
Potawatomi (2)	4	0.04
Sioux (7)	14	0.13
Yaqui (1)	1	0.01
Asian (53)	78	0.70
Not Hispanic (53)	74	0.67
Hispanic (0)	4	0.04
Bangladeshi (4)	4	0.04
Chinese, ex. Taiwanese (23)	26	0.23
Filipino (6)	16	0.14
Indian (7)	8	0.07
Japanese (2)	6	0.05
Korean (2)	3	0.03
Taiwanese (0)	1	0.01
Thai (3)	3	0.03
Vietnamese (3)	5	0.05
Hawaii Native/Pacific Islander (13)	19	0.17
Not Hispanic (7)	13	0.12
Hispanic (6)	6	0.05
Native Hawaiian (1)	5	0.05
White (10,267)	10,510	94.82
Not Hispanic (10,046)	10,247	92.45
Hispanic (221)	263	2.37

Farmington

Place Type: City
County: St. Francois
Population: 16,240†

Ancestry‡	Population	%
Alsatian (13)	13	0.08
American (1,475)	1,475	9.14
Arab (40)	40	0.25
Moroccan (40)	40	0.25
Austrian (0)	18	0.11
Belgian (0)	13	0.08
British (0)	27	0.17
Czech (15)	56	0.35
Czechoslovakian (17)	17	0.11
Danish (23)	48	0.30
Dutch (42)	395	2.45
English (438)	1,289	7.98
European (170)	170	1.05
Finnish (0)	15	0.09
French, ex. Basque (315)	1,272	7.88
French Canadian (18)	47	0.29
German (1,702)	4,153	25.73
Greek (10)	33	0.20
Hungarian (13)	13	0.08
Irish (490)	2,445	15.15
Italian (226)	550	3.41
Lithuanian (26)	35	0.22
Norwegian (10)	92	0.57
Pennsylvania German (29)	29	0.18
Polish (71)	218	1.35
Russian (0)	11	0.07
Scandinavian (7)	7	0.04
Scotch-Irish (114)	196	1.21
Scottish (126)	512	3.17
Swedish (37)	132	0.82
Welsh (17)	81	0.50
West Indian, ex. Hispanic (10)	19	0.12
British West Indian (10)	10	0.06
Dutch West Indian (0)	9	0.06
Yugoslavian (17)	32	0.20

Hispanic Origin	Population	%
Hispanic or Latino (of any race)	247	1.52
Central American, ex. Mexican	15	0.09
Guatemalan	2	0.01
Honduran	6	0.04
Panamanian	3	0.02
Salvadoran	4	0.02
Cuban	3	0.02
Dominican Republic	7	0.04
Mexican	164	1.01
Puerto Rican	12	0.07
South American	6	0.04
Colombian	1	0.01
Ecuadorian	2	0.01
Peruvian	2	0.01
Venezuelan	1	0.01
Other Hispanic or Latino	40	0.25

Race*	Population	%
African-American/Black (1,160)	1,223	7.53
Not Hispanic (1,152)	1,215	7.48
Hispanic (8)	8	0.05
American Indian/Alaska Native (52)	128	0.79
Not Hispanic (50)	124	0.76
Hispanic (2)	4	0.02
Aleut *(Alaska Native)* (1)	1	0.01
Apache (3)	6	0.04
Blackfeet (0)	2	0.01
Cherokee (10)	40	0.25

SECTION TWO

*Notes: † The Census 2010 population figure is used to calculate the percentages in the Hispanic Origin and Race categories. Ancestry percentages are based on the 2006-2010 American Community Survey population (not shown); ‡ Numbers in parentheses indicate the number of people reporting a single ancestry; * Numbers in parentheses indicate the number of persons reporting this race alone, not in combination with any other race; Please refer to the Explanation of Data for more information.*

	Population	%
Chickasaw (3)	3	0.02
Chippewa (1)	1	0.01
Choctaw (1)	4	0.02
Creek (4)	4	0.02
Crow (1)	1	0.01
Navajo (1)	1	0.01
Potawatomi (1)	1	0.01
Sioux (1)	6	0.04
South American Ind. (1)	1	0.01
Asian (130)	161	0.99
Not Hispanic (129)	158	0.97
Hispanic (1)	3	0.02
Chinese, ex. Taiwanese (26)	31	0.19
Filipino (31)	44	0.27
Indian (28)	29	0.18
Japanese (3)	16	0.10
Korean (8)	9	0.06
Laotian (1)	1	0.01
Sri Lankan (8)	8	0.05
Thai (15)	15	0.09
Vietnamese (4)	6	0.04
Hawaii Native/Pacific Islander (7)	12	0.07
Not Hispanic (7)	10	0.06
Hispanic (0)	2	0.01
Native Hawaiian (1)	4	0.02
Tongan (0)	1	0.01
White (14,658)	14,837	91.36
Not Hispanic (14,483)	14,648	90.20
Hispanic (175)	189	1.16

Ferguson

Place Type: City
County: St. Louis
Population: 21,203†

Ancestry‡	Population	%
African, Sub-Saharan (706)	797	3.73
African (695)	749	3.51
Cape Verdean (0)	37	0.17
Ethiopian (11)	11	0.05
American (319)	319	1.49
Arab (0)	26	0.12
Moroccan (0)	26	0.12
Austrian (0)	17	0.08
British (8)	28	0.13
Croatian (0)	16	0.07
Czech (24)	43	0.20
Danish (10)	25	0.12
Dutch (24)	109	0.51
English (270)	1,123	5.26
European (145)	145	0.68
French, ex. Basque (188)	575	2.69
German (909)	3,151	14.77
German Russian (0)	29	0.14
Hungarian (0)	34	0.16
Iranian (5)	17	0.08
Irish (412)	2,061	9.66
Italian (192)	488	2.29
Lithuanian (13)	27	0.13
Norwegian (13)	28	0.13
Polish (154)	317	1.49
Romanian (0)	17	0.08
Russian (21)	82	0.38
Scotch-Irish (52)	182	0.85
Scottish (180)	276	1.29
Slovak (0)	10	0.05
Swedish (14)	93	0.44
Swiss (0)	35	0.16
Welsh (14)	70	0.33
West Indian, ex. Hispanic (0)	45	0.21
Jamaican (0)	45	0.21

Hispanic Origin	Population	%
Hispanic or Latino (of any race)	260	1.23
Central American, ex. Mexican	15	0.07
Costa Rican	1	<0.01
Guatemalan	4	0.02
Nicaraguan	1	<0.01
Panamanian	2	0.01
Salvadoran	7	0.03
Cuban	18	0.08
Mexican	138	0.65
Puerto Rican	42	0.20
South American	23	0.11
Bolivian	4	0.02
Chilean	2	0.01
Colombian	7	0.03
Ecuadorian	1	<0.01
Venezuelan	9	0.04
Other Hispanic or Latino	24	0.11

Race*	Population	%
African-American/Black (14,297)	14,631	69.00
Not Hispanic (14,252)	14,567	68.70
Hispanic (45)	64	0.30
American Indian/Alaska Native (80)	193	0.91
Not Hispanic (78)	187	0.88
Hispanic (2)	6	0.03
Apache (0)	3	0.01
Blackfeet (0)	5	0.02
Cherokee (10)	50	0.24
Chickasaw (1)	3	0.01
Choctaw (3)	8	0.04
Comanche (0)	1	<0.01
Creek (0)	2	0.01
Iroquois (0)	1	<0.01
Navajo (0)	1	<0.01
Shoshone (2)	2	0.01
Sioux (1)	4	0.02
Ute (1)	1	<0.01
Asian (103)	170	0.80
Not Hispanic (102)	167	0.79
Hispanic (1)	3	0.01
Chinese, ex. Taiwanese (13)	20	0.09
Filipino (14)	39	0.18
Indian (11)	15	0.07
Indonesian (0)	2	0.01
Japanese (8)	19	0.09
Korean (4)	10	0.05
Laotian (1)	2	0.01
Taiwanese (2)	2	0.01
Thai (6)	6	0.03
Vietnamese (44)	51	0.24
Hawaii Native/Pacific Islander (4)	27	0.13
Not Hispanic (4)	23	0.11
Hispanic (0)	4	0.02
Guamanian/Chamorro (0)	3	0.01
Native Hawaiian (0)	3	0.01
Samoan (1)	6	0.03
White (6,206)	6,541	30.85
Not Hispanic (6,093)	6,411	30.24
Hispanic (113)	130	0.61

Festus

Place Type: City
County: Jefferson
Population: 11,602†

Ancestry‡	Population	%
American (857)	857	7.58
Armenian (0)	71	0.63
Austrian (0)	17	0.15
British (0)	10	0.09
Bulgarian (17)	17	0.15
Canadian (29)	29	0.26
Croatian (0)	20	0.18
Czech (0)	17	0.15
Czechoslovakian (0)	24	0.21
Danish (0)	8	0.07
Dutch (38)	401	3.55
English (501)	1,316	11.64
European (66)	66	0.58
French, ex. Basque (193)	1,166	10.31
French Canadian (30)	160	1.41
German (1,507)	4,049	35.80
Greek (30)	45	0.40
Hungarian (10)	43	0.38
Irish (309)	1,467	12.97
Italian (127)	436	3.86
Norwegian (3)	25	0.22
Polish (18)	152	1.34
Russian (116)	189	1.67
Scotch-Irish (86)	162	1.43
Scottish (113)	201	1.78
Slovak (0)	18	0.16
Swedish (0)	27	0.24
Swiss (0)	25	0.22
Turkish (26)	26	0.23
Welsh (18)	55	0.49

Hispanic Origin	Population	%
Hispanic or Latino (of any race)	141	1.22
Central American, ex. Mexican	7	0.06
Guatemalan	2	0.02
Honduran	2	0.02
Salvadoran	3	0.03
Dominican Republic	1	0.01
Mexican	96	0.83
Puerto Rican	14	0.12
South American	2	0.02
Chilean	1	0.01
Ecuadorian	1	0.01
Other Hispanic or Latino	21	0.18

Race*	Population	%
African-American/Black (389)	527	4.54
Not Hispanic (386)	520	4.48
Hispanic (3)	7	0.06
American Indian/Alaska Native (25)	90	0.78
Not Hispanic (23)	84	0.72
Hispanic (2)	6	0.05
Apache (0)	1	0.01
Arapaho (0)	3	0.03
Blackfeet (0)	5	0.04
Cherokee (8)	27	0.23
Chickasaw (1)	1	0.01
Choctaw (1)	2	0.02
Cree (0)	4	0.03
Mexican American Ind. (2)	2	0.02
Sioux (4)	11	0.09
Asian (93)	119	1.03
Not Hispanic (93)	118	1.02
Hispanic (0)	1	0.01
Bangladeshi (0)	3	0.03
Chinese, ex. Taiwanese (18)	22	0.19
Filipino (29)	42	0.36
Indian (11)	13	0.11
Japanese (2)	4	0.03
Korean (7)	12	0.10
Laotian (4)	4	0.03
Taiwanese (2)	3	0.03
Thai (3)	8	0.07
Vietnamese (12)	12	0.10
Hawaii Native/Pacific Islander (5)	10	0.09
Not Hispanic (5)	10	0.09
Guamanian/Chamorro (1)	2	0.02
Native Hawaiian (1)	3	0.03
Samoan (1)	2	0.02
White (10,843)	11,061	95.34
Not Hispanic (10,736)	10,939	94.29
Hispanic (107)	122	1.05

Florissant

Place Type: City
County: St. Louis
Population: 52,158†

Ancestry‡	Population	%
African, Sub-Saharan (1,193)	1,387	2.64
African (1,005)	1,199	2.29
Kenyan (96)	96	0.18
Nigerian (74)	74	0.14
Ugandan (18)	18	0.03
American (2,337)	2,337	4.45
Arab (173)	173	0.33
Arab (55)	55	0.10
Palestinian (22)	22	0.04

*Notes: † The Census 2010 population figure is used to calculate the percentages in the Hispanic Origin and Race categories. Ancestry percentages are based on the 2006-2010 American Community Survey population (not shown); ‡ Numbers in parentheses indicate the number of people reporting a single ancestry; * Numbers in parentheses indicate the number of persons reporting this race alone, not in combination with any other race; Please refer to the Explanation of Data for more information.*

Syrian (16)	16	0.03
Other Arab (80)	80	0.15
Austrian (118)	304	0.58
Belgian (0)	162	0.31
British (26)	54	0.10
Bulgarian (12)	12	0.02
Cajun (28)	44	0.08
Canadian (36)	64	0.12
Croatian (69)	153	0.29
Czech (31)	247	0.47
Czechoslovakian (15)	60	0.11
Danish (0)	262	0.50
Dutch (85)	878	1.67
English (1,142)	4,721	9.00
European (328)	389	0.74
French, ex. Basque (325)	2,966	5.65
French Canadian (65)	142	0.27
German (5,334)	15,355	29.27
Greek (16)	132	0.25
Guyanese (35)	35	0.07
Hungarian (27)	54	0.10
Iranian (11)	66	0.13
Irish (2,282)	8,964	17.09
Italian (921)	3,374	6.43
Lithuanian (12)	112	0.21
Luxemburger (0)	12	0.02
Macedonian (0)	9	0.02
Norwegian (137)	455	0.87
Polish (441)	1,784	3.40
Portuguese (17)	36	0.07
Russian (0)	155	0.30
Scotch-Irish (328)	854	1.63
Scottish (194)	711	1.36
Slavic (19)	81	0.15
Slovak (27)	99	0.19
Swedish (144)	430	0.82
Swiss (40)	586	1.12
Ukrainian (14)	111	0.21
Welsh (68)	253	0.48
West Indian, ex. Hispanic (12)	53	0.10
Haitian (12)	34	0.06
Jamaican (0)	19	0.04
Yugoslavian (16)	16	0.03

Hispanic Origin	Population	%
Hispanic or Latino (of any race)	1,029	1.97
Central American, ex. Mexican	62	0.12
Costa Rican	6	0.01
Guatemalan	9	0.02
Honduran	11	0.02
Nicaraguan	9	0.02
Panamanian	12	0.02
Salvadoran	15	0.03
Cuban	34	0.07
Dominican Republic	32	0.06
Mexican	578	1.11
Puerto Rican	135	0.26
South American	81	0.16
Argentinean	6	0.01
Bolivian	2	<0.01
Chilean	4	0.01
Colombian	33	0.06
Ecuadorian	16	0.03
Paraguayan	1	<0.01
Peruvian	11	0.02
Venezuelan	8	0.02
Other Hispanic or Latino	107	0.21

Race*	Population	%
African-American/Black (13,957)	14,741	28.26
Not Hispanic (13,889)	14,617	28.02
Hispanic (68)	124	0.24
American Indian/Alaska Native (117)	389	0.75
Not Hispanic (109)	353	0.68
Hispanic (8)	36	0.07
Alaska Athabascan *(Ala. Nat.)* (0)	1	<0.01
Aleut *(Alaska Native)* (3)	3	0.01
Apache (0)	5	0.01
Blackfeet (1)	14	0.03
Cherokee (27)	106	0.20
Chickasaw (5)	17	0.03
Chippewa (2)	4	0.01
Choctaw (1)	12	0.02
Comanche (1)	3	0.01
Cree (0)	2	<0.01
Creek (2)	8	0.02
Crow (1)	1	<0.01
Delaware (0)	2	<0.01
Hopi (1)	1	<0.01
Iroquois (3)	4	0.01
Kiowa (0)	1	<0.01
Mexican American Ind. (1)	1	<0.01
Navajo (2)	4	0.01
Osage (0)	3	0.01
Ottawa (1)	4	0.01
Potawatomi (0)	2	<0.01
Seminole (0)	1	<0.01
Shoshone (0)	2	<0.01
Sioux (2)	11	0.02
Spanish American Ind. (0)	2	<0.01
Tlingit-Haida *(Alaska Native)* (1)	1	<0.01
Ute (0)	3	0.01
Asian (398)	664	1.27
Not Hispanic (394)	643	1.23
Hispanic (4)	21	0.04
Cambodian (0)	3	0.01
Chinese, ex. Taiwanese (52)	77	0.15
Filipino (63)	140	0.27
Indian (27)	50	0.10
Indonesian (0)	2	<0.01
Japanese (15)	54	0.10
Korean (23)	57	0.11
Laotian (0)	2	<0.01
Malaysian (3)	10	0.02
Nepalese (0)	1	<0.01
Pakistani (18)	21	0.04
Taiwanese (1)	1	<0.01
Thai (19)	28	0.05
Vietnamese (158)	191	0.37
Hawaii Native/Pacific Islander (20)	56	0.11
Not Hispanic (19)	53	0.10
Hispanic (1)	3	0.01
Fijian (1)	6	0.01
Guamanian/Chamorro (11)	12	0.02
Native Hawaiian (2)	15	0.03
Samoan (2)	7	0.01
White (36,148)	37,198	71.32
Not Hispanic (35,559)	36,506	69.99
Hispanic (589)	692	1.33

Fort Leonard Wood

Place Type: CDP
County: Pulaski
Population: 15,061†

Ancestry‡	Population	%
African, Sub-Saharan (17)	17	0.11
African (3)	3	0.02
Other Sub-Saharan African (14)	14	0.09
American (424)	424	2.78
Arab (52)	86	0.56
Egyptian (36)	51	0.33
Lebanese (16)	35	0.23
Armenian (15)	15	0.10
Assyrian/Chaldean/Syriac (16)	16	0.11
Austrian (19)	61	0.40
Brazilian (8)	23	0.15
British (29)	62	0.41
Bulgarian (6)	6	0.04
Cajun (0)	69	0.45
Canadian (0)	9	0.06
Croatian (0)	41	0.27
Czech (0)	13	0.09
Czechoslovakian (32)	133	0.87
Danish (10)	10	0.07
Dutch (0)	105	0.69
English (321)	887	5.82
European (122)	122	0.80
Finnish (16)	165	1.08
French, ex. Basque (54)	582	3.82
French Canadian (19)	112	0.74
German (955)	3,466	22.75
Greek (14)	35	0.23
Hungarian (0)	46	0.30
Irish (811)	2,505	16.44
Italian (314)	1,139	7.48
Lithuanian (1)	1	0.01
Norwegian (8)	100	0.66
Polish (36)	317	2.08
Russian (77)	126	0.83
Scandinavian (9)	50	0.33
Scotch-Irish (72)	225	1.48
Scottish (138)	301	1.98
Swedish (43)	347	2.28
Swiss (0)	29	0.19
Ukrainian (48)	103	0.68
Welsh (69)	214	1.40
West Indian, ex. Hispanic (120)	241	1.58
Haitian (68)	94	0.62
Jamaican (52)	134	0.88
Trinidadian/Tobagonian (0)	13	0.09

Hispanic Origin	Population	%
Hispanic or Latino (of any race)	2,200	14.61
Central American, ex. Mexican	122	0.81
Costa Rican	12	0.08
Guatemalan	7	0.05
Honduran	24	0.16
Nicaraguan	17	0.11
Panamanian	18	0.12
Salvadoran	44	0.29
Cuban	65	0.43
Dominican Republic	73	0.48
Mexican	1,068	7.09
Puerto Rican	600	3.98
South American	123	0.82
Argentinean	6	0.04
Bolivian	2	0.01
Chilean	3	0.02
Colombian	64	0.42
Ecuadorian	24	0.16
Peruvian	17	0.11
Uruguayan	1	0.01
Venezuelan	6	0.04
Other Hispanic or Latino	149	0.99

Race*	Population	%
African-American/Black (2,487)	2,828	18.78
Not Hispanic (2,323)	2,586	17.17
Hispanic (164)	242	1.61
American Indian/Alaska Native (157)	327	2.17
Not Hispanic (127)	272	1.81
Hispanic (30)	55	0.37
Alaska Athabascan *(Ala. Nat.)* (1)	1	0.01
Aleut *(Alaska Native)* (1)	1	0.01
Apache (3)	6	0.04
Blackfeet (4)	13	0.09
Cherokee (22)	71	0.47
Chickasaw (5)	6	0.04
Chippewa (4)	10	0.07
Choctaw (4)	22	0.15
Creek (5)	5	0.03
Crow (1)	1	0.01
Delaware (2)	2	0.01
Hopi (0)	1	0.01
Houma (1)	1	0.01
Inupiat *(Alaska Native)* (1)	2	0.01
Iroquois (1)	2	0.01
Kiowa (1)	2	0.01
Lumbee (6)	8	0.05
Mexican American Ind. (4)	7	0.05
Navajo (14)	19	0.13
Osage (0)	1	0.01
Paiute (1)	1	0.01
Pueblo (4)	4	0.03
Seminole (0)	6	0.04
Sioux (9)	12	0.08
South American Ind. (1)	1	0.01
Tlingit-Haida *(Alaska Native)* (2)	2	0.01

*Notes: † The Census 2010 population figure is used to calculate the percentages in the Hispanic Origin and Race categories. Ancestry percentages are based on the 2006-2010 American Community Survey population (not shown); ‡ Numbers in parentheses indicate the number of people reporting a single ancestry; * Numbers in parentheses indicate the number of persons reporting this race alone, not in combination with any other race; Please refer to the Explanation of Data for more information.*

Yakama (1)	1	0.01
Yaqui (4)	5	0.03
Yup'ik *(Alaska Native)* (1)	1	0.01
Asian (385)	611	4.06
Not Hispanic (359)	545	3.62
Hispanic (26)	66	0.44
Bangladeshi (2)	2	0.01
Burmese (3)	6	0.04
Cambodian (9)	12	0.08
Chinese, ex. Taiwanese (37)	88	0.58
Filipino (110)	205	1.36
Hmong (5)	5	0.03
Indian (23)	38	0.25
Indonesian (4)	8	0.05
Japanese (7)	43	0.29
Korean (84)	130	0.86
Laotian (8)	10	0.07
Malaysian (1)	4	0.03
Nepalese (10)	11	0.07
Pakistani (7)	8	0.05
Sri Lankan (2)	2	0.01
Taiwanese (3)	4	0.03
Thai (5)	17	0.11
Vietnamese (29)	42	0.28
Hawaii Native/Pacific Islander (111)	197	1.31
Not Hispanic (107)	172	1.14
Hispanic (4)	25	0.17
Fijian (1)	1	0.01
Guamanian/Chamorro (37)	42	0.28
Marshallese (2)	4	0.03
Native Hawaiian (10)	55	0.37
Samoan (29)	56	0.37
White (10,627)	11,214	74.46
Not Hispanic (9,402)	9,853	65.42
Hispanic (1,225)	1,361	9.04

Fulton

Place Type: City
County: Callaway
Population: 12,790†

Ancestry‡	Population	%
African, Sub-Saharan (165)	165	1.31
African (116)	116	0.92
Somalian (13)	13	0.10
Other Sub-Saharan African (36)	36	0.29
American (1,674)	1,674	13.27
Arab (21)	30	0.24
Arab (0)	9	0.07
Iraqi (8)	8	0.06
Moroccan (13)	13	0.10
Austrian (0)	24	0.19
British (0)	49	0.39
Bulgarian (9)	9	0.07
Croatian (11)	30	0.24
Czech (48)	110	0.87
Danish (16)	51	0.40
Dutch (53)	229	1.81
English (379)	1,243	9.85
European (76)	76	0.60
Finnish (0)	12	0.10
French, ex. Basque (151)	538	4.26
French Canadian (13)	13	0.10
German (1,371)	3,483	27.60
Greek (23)	44	0.35
Iranian (14)	39	0.31
Irish (425)	1,570	12.44
Italian (64)	212	1.68
Northern European (56)	73	0.58
Norwegian (71)	99	0.78
Polish (7)	74	0.59
Russian (13)	33	0.26
Scandinavian (5)	24	0.19
Scotch-Irish (162)	267	2.12
Scottish (145)	345	2.73
Slovak (17)	17	0.13
Swedish (39)	131	1.04
Swiss (0)	63	0.50
Welsh (11)	117	0.93
West Indian, ex. Hispanic (38)	38	0.30
Haitian (10)	10	0.08
Jamaican (28)	28	0.22

Hispanic Origin	Population	%
Hispanic or Latino (of any race)	270	2.11
Central American, ex. Mexican	13	0.10
Costa Rican	7	0.05
Panamanian	3	0.02
Salvadoran	3	0.02
Cuban	8	0.06
Dominican Republic	2	0.02
Mexican	161	1.26
Puerto Rican	17	0.13
South American	16	0.13
Argentinean	7	0.05
Bolivian	1	0.01
Colombian	4	0.03
Ecuadorian	1	0.01
Peruvian	2	0.02
Uruguayan	1	0.01
Other Hispanic or Latino	53	0.41

Race*	Population	%
African-American/Black (1,531)	1,702	13.31
Not Hispanic (1,515)	1,666	13.03
Hispanic (16)	36	0.28
American Indian/Alaska Native (62)	144	1.13
Not Hispanic (59)	132	1.03
Hispanic (3)	12	0.09
Apache (0)	1	0.01
Blackfeet (2)	5	0.04
Cherokee (20)	50	0.39
Cheyenne (0)	3	0.02
Chippewa (1)	1	0.01
Choctaw (6)	7	0.05
Comanche (1)	1	0.01
Creek (2)	2	0.02
Iroquois (0)	3	0.02
Menominee (0)	1	0.01
Mexican American Ind. (1)	3	0.02
Navajo (3)	4	0.03
Potawatomi (1)	4	0.03
Pueblo (0)	1	0.01
Sioux (5)	7	0.05
Asian (148)	181	1.42
Not Hispanic (148)	180	1.41
Hispanic (0)	1	0.01
Bhutanese (0)	1	0.01
Chinese, ex. Taiwanese (41)	44	0.34
Filipino (21)	29	0.23
Indian (26)	29	0.23
Indonesian (3)	3	0.02
Japanese (3)	8	0.06
Korean (26)	26	0.20
Malaysian (0)	1	0.01
Nepalese (8)	9	0.07
Pakistani (0)	1	0.01
Taiwanese (1)	1	0.01
Thai (6)	6	0.05
Vietnamese (5)	6	0.05
Hawaii Native/Pacific Islander (6)	15	0.12
Not Hispanic (4)	13	0.10
Hispanic (2)	2	0.02
Fijian (0)	1	0.01
Guamanian/Chamorro (0)	2	0.02
Native Hawaiian (4)	6	0.05
Samoan (0)	2	0.02
White (10,668)	10,937	85.51
Not Hispanic (10,521)	10,766	84.18
Hispanic (147)	171	1.34

Gladstone

Place Type: City
County: Clay
Population: 25,410†

Ancestry‡	Population	%
African, Sub-Saharan (99)	99	0.39
African (35)	35	0.14
Nigerian (22)	22	0.09
Other Sub-Saharan African (42)	42	0.16
Albanian (0)	19	0.07
American (2,274)	2,274	8.92
Arab (18)	20	0.08
Egyptian (18)	18	0.07
Syrian (0)	2	0.01
Australian (0)	15	0.06
Austrian (29)	98	0.38
Belgian (54)	62	0.24
Brazilian (13)	13	0.05
British (26)	121	0.47
Cajun (12)	12	0.05
Canadian (13)	27	0.11
Croatian (17)	17	0.07
Czech (35)	207	0.81
Czechoslovakian (26)	26	0.10
Danish (33)	149	0.58
Dutch (37)	389	1.53
English (1,151)	3,475	13.63
European (443)	513	2.01
French, ex. Basque (210)	704	2.76
French Canadian (33)	129	0.51
German (2,441)	7,119	27.92
Greek (12)	51	0.20
Hungarian (0)	12	0.05
Irish (1,473)	5,067	19.87
Italian (745)	1,498	5.87
Lithuanian (0)	12	0.05
Luxemburger (16)	16	0.06
Northern European (18)	18	0.07
Norwegian (26)	258	1.01
Pennsylvania German (9)	9	0.04
Polish (320)	763	2.99
Portuguese (70)	99	0.39
Romanian (0)	46	0.18
Russian (41)	58	0.23
Scandinavian (11)	18	0.07
Scotch-Irish (130)	414	1.62
Scottish (242)	568	2.23
Serbian (10)	10	0.04
Swedish (107)	511	2.00
Swiss (0)	73	0.29
Turkish (8)	8	0.03
Ukrainian (0)	19	0.07
Welsh (148)	293	1.15
West Indian, ex. Hispanic (0)	9	0.04
Barbadian (0)	9	0.04
Yugoslavian (79)	79	0.31

Hispanic Origin	Population	%
Hispanic or Latino (of any race)	1,848	7.27
Central American, ex. Mexican	74	0.29
Costa Rican	3	0.01
Guatemalan	30	0.12
Honduran	15	0.06
Nicaraguan	10	0.04
Panamanian	4	0.02
Salvadoran	12	0.05
Cuban	69	0.27
Dominican Republic	9	0.04
Mexican	1,469	5.78
Puerto Rican	68	0.27
South American	54	0.21
Argentinean	3	0.01
Bolivian	2	0.01
Chilean	1	<0.01
Colombian	13	0.05
Ecuadorian	7	0.03
Paraguayan	12	0.05
Peruvian	9	0.04
Venezuelan	4	0.02
Other South American	3	0.01
Other Hispanic or Latino	105	0.41

Race*	Population	%
African-American/Black (1,316)	1,682	6.62
Not Hispanic (1,287)	1,604	6.31
Hispanic (29)	78	0.31

*Notes: † The Census 2010 population figure is used to calculate the percentages in the Hispanic Origin and Race categories. Ancestry percentages are based on the 2006-2010 American Community Survey population (not shown); ‡ Numbers in parentheses indicate the number of people reporting a single ancestry; * Numbers in parentheses indicate the number of persons reporting this race alone, not in combination with any other race; Please refer to the Explanation of Data for more information.*

American Indian/Alaska Native (156)	410	1.61
Not Hispanic (129)	354	1.39
Hispanic (27)	56	0.22
Apache (2)	3	0.01
Blackfeet (4)	15	0.06
Cherokee (41)	143	0.56
Chickasaw (2)	4	0.02
Chippewa (2)	3	0.01
Choctaw (9)	20	0.08
Creek (1)	9	0.04
Delaware (1)	2	0.01
Houma (1)	1	<0.01
Iroquois (5)	8	0.03
Kiowa (1)	3	0.01
Mexican American Ind. (0)	6	0.02
Navajo (1)	3	0.01
Osage (2)	3	0.01
Potawatomi (15)	16	0.06
Seminole (1)	2	0.01
Sioux (4)	10	0.04
Asian (440)	617	2.43
Not Hispanic (433)	599	2.36
Hispanic (7)	18	0.07
Cambodian (7)	7	0.03
Chinese, ex. Taiwanese (45)	71	0.28
Filipino (97)	156	0.61
Hmong (2)	3	0.01
Indian (30)	46	0.18
Indonesian (0)	1	<0.01
Japanese (17)	29	0.11
Korean (36)	67	0.26
Laotian (4)	4	0.02
Malaysian (4)	4	0.02
Pakistani (8)	9	0.04
Taiwanese (3)	3	0.01
Thai (7)	20	0.08
Vietnamese (160)	173	0.68
Hawaii Native/Pacific Islander (148)	194	0.76
Not Hispanic (143)	186	0.73
Hispanic (5)	8	0.03
Fijian (0)	3	0.01
Guamanian/Chamorro (1)	11	0.04
Native Hawaiian (10)	33	0.13
Samoan (2)	17	0.07
White (21,805)	22,617	89.01
Not Hispanic (20,847)	21,469	84.49
Hispanic (958)	1,148	4.52

Grain Valley

Place Type: City
County: Jackson
Population: 12,854†

Ancestry‡	Population	%
American (470)	470	4.11
Arab (0)	14	0.12
Lebanese (0)	14	0.12
Austrian (12)	25	0.22
Belgian (0)	24	0.21
British (0)	30	0.26
Canadian (19)	19	0.17
Czech (21)	45	0.39
Czechoslovakian (17)	51	0.45
Danish (0)	8	0.07
Dutch (24)	275	2.41
Eastern European (10)	10	0.09
English (403)	1,445	12.64
European (137)	239	2.09
Finnish (0)	13	0.11
French, ex. Basque (22)	289	2.53
French Canadian (13)	74	0.65
German (1,269)	2,790	24.41
Greek (27)	55	0.48
Hungarian (0)	9	0.08
Irish (308)	1,508	13.20
Italian (219)	686	6.00
Lithuanian (0)	13	0.11
Northern European (54)	68	0.60
Norwegian (36)	249	2.18
Polish (122)	202	1.77
Russian (0)	17	0.15
Scotch-Irish (151)	205	1.79
Scottish (45)	212	1.86
Slovene (15)	31	0.27
Swedish (81)	385	3.37
Welsh (34)	140	1.23

Hispanic Origin	Population	%
Hispanic or Latino (of any race)	632	4.92
Central American, ex. Mexican	36	0.28
Costa Rican	3	0.02
Guatemalan	6	0.05
Honduran	6	0.05
Nicaraguan	1	0.01
Panamanian	8	0.06
Salvadoran	12	0.09
Cuban	7	0.05
Mexican	483	3.76
Puerto Rican	52	0.40
South American	9	0.07
Bolivian	1	0.01
Colombian	2	0.02
Peruvian	2	0.02
Venezuelan	4	0.03
Other Hispanic or Latino	45	0.35

Race*	Population	%
African-American/Black (327)	428	3.33
Not Hispanic (315)	405	3.15
Hispanic (12)	23	0.18
American Indian/Alaska Native (73)	181	1.41
Not Hispanic (51)	140	1.09
Hispanic (22)	41	0.32
Aleut *(Alaska Native)* (3)	3	0.02
Apache (1)	2	0.02
Blackfeet (1)	7	0.05
Cherokee (10)	38	0.30
Chickasaw (1)	1	0.01
Chippewa (2)	3	0.02
Choctaw (9)	14	0.11
Creek (3)	5	0.04
Inupiat *(Alaska Native)* (0)	1	0.01
Iroquois (1)	1	0.01
Lumbee (0)	2	0.02
Mexican American Ind. (5)	9	0.07
Navajo (1)	1	0.01
Paiute (2)	2	0.02
Potawatomi (0)	2	0.02
Sioux (10)	18	0.14
South American Ind. (1)	7	0.05
Asian (80)	149	1.16
Not Hispanic (78)	139	1.08
Hispanic (2)	10	0.08
Cambodian (0)	1	0.01
Chinese, ex. Taiwanese (18)	22	0.17
Filipino (20)	39	0.30
Hmong (7)	7	0.05
Indian (12)	22	0.17
Japanese (1)	9	0.07
Korean (8)	22	0.17
Taiwanese (0)	1	0.01
Thai (2)	3	0.02
Vietnamese (12)	13	0.10
Hawaii Native/Pacific Islander (17)	45	0.35
Not Hispanic (15)	39	0.30
Hispanic (2)	6	0.05
Fijian (0)	3	0.02
Guamanian/Chamorro (0)	1	0.01
Marshallese (1)	1	0.01
Native Hawaiian (5)	17	0.13
Samoan (7)	11	0.09
Tongan (1)	5	0.04
White (11,904)	12,173	94.70
Not Hispanic (11,528)	11,735	91.29
Hispanic (376)	438	3.41

Grandview

Place Type: City
County: Jackson
Population: 24,475†

Ancestry‡	Population	%
African, Sub-Saharan (187)	187	0.77
African (146)	146	0.60
Nigerian (41)	41	0.17
American (1,245)	1,245	5.10
Arab (114)	128	0.52
Arab (10)	10	0.04
Egyptian (58)	58	0.24
Lebanese (7)	21	0.09
Moroccan (28)	28	0.11
Palestinian (11)	11	0.05
Austrian (13)	31	0.13
Belgian (0)	41	0.17
British (34)	81	0.33
Croatian (17)	17	0.07
Czech (0)	21	0.09
Danish (70)	172	0.70
Dutch (95)	445	1.82
English (445)	1,450	5.94
European (160)	160	0.66
Finnish (15)	34	0.14
French, ex. Basque (40)	638	2.61
French Canadian (8)	34	0.14
German (1,245)	3,277	13.42
Greek (0)	13	0.05
Icelander (0)	40	0.16
Irish (714)	2,099	8.60
Italian (80)	450	1.84
Lithuanian (8)	30	0.12
Norwegian (19)	89	0.36
Pennsylvania German (0)	16	0.07
Polish (61)	197	0.81
Portuguese (12)	12	0.05
Russian (0)	33	0.14
Scotch-Irish (233)	409	1.67
Scottish (45)	116	0.48
Slavic (13)	13	0.05
Swedish (36)	138	0.57
Swiss (0)	11	0.05
Ukrainian (0)	39	0.16
Welsh (75)	286	1.17
West Indian, ex. Hispanic (64)	64	0.26
Haitian (14)	14	0.06
West Indian (50)	50	0.20
Yugoslavian (0)	5	0.02

Hispanic Origin	Population	%
Hispanic or Latino (of any race)	2,379	9.72
Central American, ex. Mexican	404	1.65
Costa Rican	1	<0.01
Guatemalan	24	0.10
Honduran	34	0.14
Nicaraguan	1	<0.01
Panamanian	10	0.04
Salvadoran	331	1.35
Other Central American	3	0.01
Cuban	21	0.09
Dominican Republic	22	0.09
Mexican	1,633	6.67
Puerto Rican	77	0.31
South American	31	0.13
Argentinean	1	<0.01
Chilean	1	<0.01
Colombian	4	0.02
Ecuadorian	4	0.02
Paraguayan	8	0.03
Peruvian	4	0.02
Venezuelan	9	0.04
Other Hispanic or Latino	191	0.78

Race*	Population	%
African-American/Black (9,997)	10,657	43.54
Not Hispanic (9,908)	10,478	42.81
Hispanic (89)	179	0.73

*Notes: † The Census 2010 population figure is used to calculate the percentages in the Hispanic Origin and Race categories. Ancestry percentages are based on the 2006-2010 American Community Survey population (not shown); ‡ Numbers in parentheses indicate the number of people reporting a single ancestry; * Numbers in parentheses indicate the number of persons reporting this race alone, not in combination with any other race; Please refer to the Explanation of Data for more information.*

American Indian/Alaska Native (131)	434	1.77
Not Hispanic (92)	358	1.46
Hispanic (39)	76	0.31
Apache (3)	7	0.03
Blackfeet (9)	35	0.14
Central American Ind. (0)	3	0.01
Cherokee (22)	108	0.44
Chickasaw (2)	10	0.04
Chippewa (1)	1	<0.01
Choctaw (4)	22	0.09
Comanche (4)	4	0.02
Creek (3)	6	0.02
Crow (0)	1	<0.01
Delaware (1)	1	<0.01
Iroquois (6)	9	0.04
Lumbee (1)	1	<0.01
Mexican American Ind. (3)	6	0.02
Navajo (2)	9	0.04
Osage (0)	1	<0.01
Potawatomi (4)	4	0.02
Seminole (3)	6	0.02
Sioux (4)	11	0.04
South American Ind. (0)	4	0.02
Asian (263)	396	1.62
Not Hispanic (258)	376	1.54
Hispanic (5)	20	0.08
Burmese (1)	1	<0.01
Cambodian (4)	5	0.02
Chinese, ex. Taiwanese (43)	59	0.24
Filipino (38)	80	0.33
Hmong (7)	7	0.03
Indian (11)	25	0.10
Indonesian (3)	4	0.02
Japanese (13)	35	0.14
Korean (59)	85	0.35
Laotian (1)	4	0.02
Malaysian (4)	4	0.02
Nepalese (1)	1	<0.01
Pakistani (7)	8	0.03
Sri Lankan (1)	2	0.01
Taiwanese (5)	6	0.02
Thai (3)	13	0.05
Vietnamese (49)	61	0.25
Hawaii Native/Pacific Islander (18)	49	0.20
Not Hispanic (16)	41	0.17
Hispanic (2)	8	0.03
Guamanian/Chamorro (1)	14	0.06
Native Hawaiian (9)	18	0.07
Samoan (3)	4	0.02
White (11,834)	12,599	51.48
Not Hispanic (11,014)	11,642	47.57
Hispanic (820)	957	3.91

Hannibal

Place Type: City
County: Marion
Population: 17,916[†]

Ancestry[‡]	Population	%
African, Sub-Saharan (16)	16	0.09
African (16)	16	0.09
American (2,389)	2,389	13.41
Arab (7)	16	0.09
Lebanese (7)	16	0.09
Croatian (0)	8	0.04
Czech (20)	48	0.27
Czechoslovakian (44)	65	0.36
Danish (0)	23	0.13
Dutch (119)	374	2.10
English (777)	1,694	9.51
European (157)	157	0.88
French, ex. Basque (177)	517	2.90
German (2,008)	3,807	21.36
Greek (0)	10	0.06
Hungarian (0)	8	0.04
Iranian (35)	35	0.20
Irish (615)	1,683	9.44
Italian (182)	382	2.14
Lithuanian (14)	14	0.08
Norwegian (84)	125	0.70
Polish (114)	296	1.66
Romanian (36)	36	0.20
Russian (11)	11	0.06
Scandinavian (65)	65	0.36
Scotch-Irish (196)	446	2.50
Scottish (78)	370	2.08
Slovak (20)	20	0.11
Swedish (67)	143	0.80
Swiss (8)	90	0.51
Ukrainian (22)	22	0.12
Welsh (18)	112	0.63

Hispanic Origin	Population	%
Hispanic or Latino (of any race)	324	1.81
Central American, ex. Mexican	9	0.05
Costa Rican	2	0.01
Guatemalan	1	0.01
Honduran	6	0.03
Cuban	6	0.03
Dominican Republic	6	0.03
Mexican	204	1.14
Puerto Rican	19	0.11
South American	20	0.11
Argentinean	3	0.02
Chilean	5	0.03
Colombian	4	0.02
Ecuadorian	1	0.01
Peruvian	3	0.02
Venezuelan	4	0.02
Other Hispanic or Latino	60	0.33

Race*	Population	%
African-American/Black (1,264)	1,568	8.75
Not Hispanic (1,249)	1,544	8.62
Hispanic (15)	24	0.13
American Indian/Alaska Native (39)	168	0.94
Not Hispanic (34)	145	0.81
Hispanic (5)	23	0.13
Apache (0)	5	0.03
Arapaho (0)	1	0.01
Blackfeet (1)	6	0.03
Cherokee (10)	64	0.36
Chippewa (1)	2	0.01
Choctaw (6)	8	0.04
Mexican American Ind. (0)	3	0.02
Pueblo (0)	1	0.01
Sioux (2)	6	0.03
Spanish American Ind. (1)	1	0.01
Asian (115)	155	0.87
Not Hispanic (115)	148	0.83
Hispanic (0)	7	0.04
Chinese, ex. Taiwanese (14)	17	0.09
Filipino (19)	34	0.19
Indian (27)	32	0.18
Japanese (12)	17	0.09
Korean (6)	9	0.05
Pakistani (5)	5	0.03
Taiwanese (1)	3	0.02
Thai (3)	3	0.02
Vietnamese (19)	21	0.12
Hawaii Native/Pacific Islander (16)	24	0.13
Not Hispanic (16)	24	0.13
Fijian (8)	9	0.05
Guamanian/Chamorro (2)	3	0.02
Native Hawaiian (1)	1	0.01
Samoan (0)	1	0.01
White (15,917)	16,368	91.36
Not Hispanic (15,743)	16,138	90.08
Hispanic (174)	230	1.28

Harrisonville

Place Type: City
County: Cass
Population: 10,019[†]

Ancestry[‡]	Population	%
American (831)	831	8.33
Australian (0)	21	0.21
Belgian (0)	8	0.08
British (0)	8	0.08
Croatian (0)	13	0.13
Czech (0)	16	0.16
Dutch (27)	238	2.39
English (321)	1,144	11.47
European (13)	13	0.13
French, ex. Basque (0)	155	1.55
French Canadian (20)	59	0.59
German (917)	2,766	27.73
Greek (22)	65	0.65
Irish (711)	1,953	19.58
Italian (203)	372	3.73
Norwegian (28)	70	0.70
Polish (44)	81	0.81
Russian (12)	29	0.29
Scandinavian (0)	63	0.63
Scotch-Irish (69)	201	2.02
Scottish (17)	66	0.66
Swedish (56)	130	1.30
Swiss (0)	16	0.16
Welsh (52)	76	0.76

Hispanic Origin	Population	%
Hispanic or Latino (of any race)	265	2.64
Central American, ex. Mexican	13	0.13
Guatemalan	3	0.03
Honduran	3	0.03
Nicaraguan	4	0.04
Salvadoran	3	0.03
Cuban	4	0.04
Mexican	187	1.87
Puerto Rican	20	0.20
South American	8	0.08
Chilean	6	0.06
Peruvian	1	0.01
Venezuelan	1	0.01
Other Hispanic or Latino	33	0.33

Race*	Population	%
African-American/Black (115)	164	1.64
Not Hispanic (114)	162	1.62
Hispanic (1)	2	0.02
American Indian/Alaska Native (69)	157	1.57
Not Hispanic (68)	151	1.51
Hispanic (1)	6	0.06
Alaska Athabascan *(Ala. Nat.)* (2)	2	0.02
Aleut *(Alaska Native)* (2)	2	0.02
Blackfeet (0)	2	0.02
Canadian/French Am. Ind. (0)	1	0.01
Cherokee (26)	60	0.60
Chickasaw (1)	2	0.02
Chippewa (0)	4	0.04
Choctaw (3)	4	0.04
Creek (1)	9	0.09
Mexican American Ind. (0)	1	0.01
Navajo (4)	5	0.05
Osage (1)	5	0.05
Potawatomi (5)	9	0.09
Seminole (0)	5	0.05
Sioux (2)	10	0.10
Spanish American Ind. (1)	1	0.01
Asian (64)	80	0.80
Not Hispanic (57)	73	0.73
Hispanic (7)	7	0.07
Cambodian (5)	7	0.07
Chinese, ex. Taiwanese (9)	15	0.15
Filipino (8)	12	0.12
Indian (20)	22	0.22
Japanese (2)	2	0.02
Korean (2)	2	0.02
Laotian (6)	6	0.06
Pakistani (1)	1	0.01
Thai (1)	2	0.02
Vietnamese (9)	11	0.11
Hawaii Native/Pacific Islander (4)	16	0.16
Not Hispanic (4)	13	0.13
Hispanic (0)	3	0.03
Guamanian/Chamorro (4)	6	0.06
Native Hawaiian (0)	4	0.04

*Notes: † The Census 2010 population figure is used to calculate the percentages in the Hispanic Origin and Race categories. Ancestry percentages are based on the 2006-2010 American Community Survey population (not shown); ‡ Numbers in parentheses indicate the number of people reporting a single ancestry; * Numbers in parentheses indicate the number of persons reporting this race alone, not in combination with any other race; Please refer to the Explanation of Data for more information.*

Samoan (0)	2	0.02
White (9,518)	9,679	96.61
Not Hispanic (9,360)	9,506	94.88
Hispanic (158)	173	1.73

Hazelwood

Place Type: City
County: St. Louis
Population: 25,703†

Ancestry‡	Population	%
African, Sub-Saharan (532)	609	2.37
African (381)	422	1.64
Kenyan (52)	70	0.27
Nigerian (83)	83	0.32
Other Sub-Saharan African (16)	34	0.13
Albanian (0)	35	0.14
American (1,294)	1,294	5.03
Arab (86)	135	0.52
Arab (86)	86	0.33
Lebanese (0)	49	0.19
Austrian (0)	28	0.11
Basque (17)	17	0.07
Belgian (15)	15	0.06
British (37)	80	0.31
Croatian (0)	9	0.03
Czech (31)	31	0.12
Czechoslovakian (14)	14	0.05
Danish (24)	81	0.31
Dutch (88)	321	1.25
English (566)	1,795	6.98
European (145)	185	0.72
Finnish (0)	11	0.04
French, ex. Basque (24)	912	3.55
French Canadian (10)	57	0.22
German (2,445)	6,653	25.87
Greek (15)	52	0.20
Hungarian (20)	82	0.32
Iranian (40)	40	0.16
Irish (1,023)	3,922	15.25
Italian (562)	1,386	5.39
Lithuanian (17)	27	0.10
Northern European (7)	7	0.03
Norwegian (32)	95	0.37
Polish (210)	678	2.64
Portuguese (0)	33	0.13
Romanian (0)	13	0.05
Russian (133)	174	0.68
Scandinavian (68)	68	0.26
Scotch-Irish (169)	427	1.66
Scottish (172)	410	1.59
Slavic (0)	11	0.04
Slovak (0)	27	0.10
Swedish (12)	144	0.56
Swiss (0)	87	0.34
Ukrainian (0)	26	0.10
Welsh (0)	157	0.61
West Indian, ex. Hispanic (43)	43	0.17
West Indian (43)	43	0.17

Hispanic Origin	Population	%
Hispanic or Latino (of any race)	776	3.02
Central American, ex. Mexican	71	0.28
Costa Rican	7	0.03
Guatemalan	28	0.11
Honduran	5	0.02
Nicaraguan	7	0.03
Panamanian	8	0.03
Salvadoran	13	0.05
Other Central American	3	0.01
Cuban	15	0.06
Dominican Republic	13	0.05
Mexican	508	1.98
Puerto Rican	52	0.20
South American	38	0.15
Bolivian	1	<0.01
Colombian	12	0.05
Ecuadorian	9	0.04
Peruvian	1	<0.01
Uruguayan	2	0.01
Venezuelan	13	0.05
Other Hispanic or Latino	79	0.31

Race*	Population	%
African-American/Black (7,835)	8,217	31.97
Not Hispanic (7,812)	8,174	31.80
Hispanic (23)	43	0.17
American Indian/Alaska Native (69)	224	0.87
Not Hispanic (57)	201	0.78
Hispanic (12)	23	0.09
Apache (4)	7	0.03
Blackfeet (2)	9	0.04
Cherokee (13)	71	0.28
Chickasaw (0)	1	<0.01
Choctaw (5)	7	0.03
Comanche (1)	1	<0.01
Cree (0)	4	0.02
Creek (1)	1	<0.01
Crow (0)	2	0.01
Iroquois (0)	1	<0.01
Mexican American Ind. (1)	5	0.02
Navajo (0)	1	<0.01
Osage (1)	5	0.02
Sioux (3)	9	0.04
Asian (353)	477	1.86
Not Hispanic (353)	469	1.82
Hispanic (0)	8	0.03
Cambodian (3)	3	0.01
Chinese, ex. Taiwanese (62)	88	0.34
Filipino (83)	127	0.49
Indian (84)	94	0.37
Indonesian (2)	2	0.01
Japanese (10)	19	0.07
Korean (10)	18	0.07
Laotian (1)	1	<0.01
Malaysian (1)	1	<0.01
Nepalese (4)	4	0.02
Pakistani (12)	14	0.05
Sri Lankan (1)	1	<0.01
Taiwanese (13)	13	0.05
Thai (5)	9	0.04
Vietnamese (44)	55	0.21
Hawaii Native/Pacific Islander (10)	26	0.10
Not Hispanic (10)	26	0.10
Fijian (2)	3	0.01
Native Hawaiian (2)	9	0.04
Samoan (3)	7	0.03
Tongan (1)	4	0.02
White (16,484)	17,043	66.31
Not Hispanic (16,090)	16,578	64.50
Hispanic (394)	465	1.81

Independence

Place Type: City
County: Jackson
Population: 116,830†

Ancestry‡	Population	%
African, Sub-Saharan (83)	178	0.15
African (83)	178	0.15
Albanian (25)	48	0.04
American (9,002)	9,002	7.79
Arab (13)	61	0.05
Arab (0)	32	0.03
Lebanese (0)	16	0.01
Syrian (13)	13	0.01
Armenian (134)	147	0.13
Australian (0)	43	0.04
Austrian (52)	148	0.13
Belgian (35)	65	0.06
British (195)	481	0.42
Canadian (104)	175	0.15
Celtic (0)	9	0.01
Croatian (101)	398	0.34
Czech (64)	324	0.28
Czechoslovakian (74)	86	0.07
Danish (270)	781	0.68
Dutch (667)	2,728	2.36
English (5,454)	14,387	12.45
European (896)	1,120	0.97
Finnish (0)	90	0.08
French, ex. Basque (368)	2,998	2.59
French Canadian (202)	642	0.56
German (7,987)	25,265	21.86
Greek (123)	355	0.31
Hungarian (71)	230	0.20
Irish (4,690)	17,194	14.88
Italian (1,779)	4,491	3.89
Lithuanian (50)	69	0.06
Luxemburger (0)	16	0.01
Maltese (0)	45	0.04
Northern European (12)	12	0.01
Norwegian (474)	1,052	0.91
Pennsylvania German (115)	138	0.12
Polish (348)	1,210	1.05
Portuguese (0)	43	0.04
Romanian (10)	10	0.01
Russian (117)	258	0.22
Scandinavian (15)	84	0.07
Scotch-Irish (1,170)	3,196	2.77
Scottish (689)	2,648	2.29
Serbian (19)	197	0.17
Slavic (20)	87	0.08
Slovak (39)	101	0.09
Slovene (11)	11	0.01
Swedish (759)	1,939	1.68
Swiss (51)	200	0.17
Turkish (0)	12	0.01
Ukrainian (0)	99	0.09
Welsh (195)	1,031	0.89
West Indian, ex. Hispanic (0)	57	0.05
Dutch West Indian (0)	45	0.04
West Indian (0)	12	0.01
Yugoslavian (50)	72	0.06

Hispanic Origin	Population	%
Hispanic or Latino (of any race)	8,999	7.70
Central American, ex. Mexican	993	0.85
Costa Rican	10	0.01
Guatemalan	265	0.23
Honduran	379	0.32
Nicaraguan	20	0.02
Panamanian	38	0.03
Salvadoran	276	0.24
Other Central American	5	<0.01
Cuban	152	0.13
Dominican Republic	208	0.18
Mexican	6,468	5.54
Puerto Rican	301	0.26
South American	215	0.18
Argentinean	25	0.02
Bolivian	9	0.01
Chilean	10	0.01
Colombian	98	0.08
Ecuadorian	25	0.02
Peruvian	18	0.02
Uruguayan	7	0.01
Venezuelan	18	0.02
Other South American	5	<0.01
Other Hispanic or Latino	662	0.57

Race*	Population	%
African-American/Black (6,498)	8,092	6.93
Not Hispanic (6,265)	7,659	6.56
Hispanic (233)	433	0.37
American Indian/Alaska Native (736)	1,960	1.68
Not Hispanic (601)	1,666	1.43
Hispanic (135)	294	0.25
Alaska Athabascan *(Ala. Nat.)* (0)	2	<0.01
Aleut *(Alaska Native)* (1)	1	<0.01
Apache (14)	43	0.04
Arapaho (0)	2	<0.01
Blackfeet (11)	85	0.07
Canadian/French Am. Ind. (1)	1	<0.01
Cherokee (188)	674	0.58
Cheyenne (0)	7	0.01
Chickasaw (7)	10	0.01
Chippewa (11)	24	0.02

*Notes: † The Census 2010 population figure is used to calculate the percentages in the Hispanic Origin and Race categories. Ancestry percentages are based on the 2006-2010 American Community Survey population (not shown); ‡ Numbers in parentheses indicate the number of people reporting a single ancestry; * Numbers in parentheses indicate the number of persons reporting this race alone, not in combination with any other race; Please refer to the Explanation of Data for more information.*

Choctaw (25)	69	0.06
Colville (2)	2	<0.01
Comanche (0)	8	0.01
Cree (0)	2	<0.01
Creek (27)	42	0.04
Crow (2)	4	<0.01
Delaware (9)	26	0.02
Hopi (2)	3	<0.01
Houma (2)	3	<0.01
Iroquois (10)	17	0.01
Kiowa (2)	7	0.01
Lumbee (3)	4	<0.01
Menominee (2)	2	<0.01
Mexican American Ind. (15)	31	0.03
Navajo (6)	24	0.02
Osage (8)	32	0.03
Ottawa (1)	2	<0.01
Potawatomi (15)	17	0.01
Pueblo (6)	11	0.01
Seminole (3)	12	0.01
Shoshone (3)	3	<0.01
Sioux (53)	88	0.08
South American Ind. (0)	5	<0.01
Spanish American Ind. (4)	9	0.01
Ute (7)	8	0.01
Yakama (1)	5	<0.01
Yaqui (1)	1	<0.01
Asian (1,143)	1,657	1.42
Not Hispanic (1,114)	1,567	1.34
Hispanic (29)	90	0.08
Bangladeshi (1)	1	<0.01
Cambodian (13)	17	0.01
Chinese, ex. Taiwanese (208)	288	0.25
Filipino (282)	471	0.40
Hmong (26)	30	0.03
Indian (110)	151	0.13
Indonesian (3)	3	<0.01
Japanese (42)	135	0.12
Korean (76)	144	0.12
Laotian (49)	63	0.05
Malaysian (0)	6	0.01
Pakistani (23)	29	0.02
Taiwanese (6)	9	0.01
Thai (26)	35	0.03
Vietnamese (217)	246	0.21
Hawaii Native/Pacific Islander (815)	1,184	1.01
Not Hispanic (771)	1,085	0.93
Hispanic (44)	99	0.08
Fijian (1)	1	<0.01
Guamanian/Chamorro (12)	38	0.03
Marshallese (1)	1	<0.01
Native Hawaiian (39)	121	0.10
Samoan (647)	940	0.80
Tongan (25)	51	0.04
White (100,112)	103,552	88.63
Not Hispanic (96,086)	98,789	84.56
Hispanic (4,026)	4,763	4.08

Jackson

Place Type: City
County: Cape Girardeau
Population: 13,758†

Ancestry‡	Population	%
American (1,302)	1,302	9.70
Austrian (12)	26	0.19
Belgian (13)	27	0.20
British (53)	123	0.92
Canadian (0)	15	0.11
Czech (0)	18	0.13
Dutch (87)	305	2.27
English (337)	1,104	8.23
European (96)	172	1.28
French, ex. Basque (138)	570	4.25
German (2,743)	5,001	37.27
Greek (63)	81	0.60
Iranian (13)	13	0.10
Irish (754)	2,251	16.77
Italian (77)	151	1.13
Norwegian (15)	29	0.22
Polish (0)	120	0.89
Scandinavian (15)	15	0.11
Scotch-Irish (93)	244	1.82
Scottish (109)	263	1.96
Serbian (0)	12	0.09
Swedish (10)	141	1.05
Welsh (16)	88	0.66

Hispanic Origin	Population	%
Hispanic or Latino (of any race)	170	1.24
Central American, ex. Mexican	9	0.07
Guatemalan	5	0.04
Nicaraguan	4	0.03
Cuban	4	0.03
Dominican Republic	4	0.03
Mexican	112	0.81
Puerto Rican	10	0.07
South American	7	0.05
Chilean	1	0.01
Colombian	6	0.04
Other Hispanic or Latino	24	0.17

Race*	Population	%
African-American/Black (227)	313	2.28
Not Hispanic (225)	311	2.26
Hispanic (2)	2	0.01
American Indian/Alaska Native (37)	81	0.59
Not Hispanic (36)	78	0.57
Hispanic (1)	3	0.02
Cherokee (17)	42	0.31
Chickasaw (1)	1	0.01
Chippewa (1)	2	0.01
Choctaw (0)	1	0.01
Creek (4)	4	0.03
Mexican American Ind. (0)	2	0.01
Navajo (0)	1	0.01
Sioux (3)	5	0.04
Yup'ik *(Alaska Native)* (1)	1	0.01
Asian (79)	130	0.94
Not Hispanic (71)	122	0.89
Hispanic (8)	8	0.06
Chinese, ex. Taiwanese (7)	16	0.12
Filipino (25)	42	0.31
Indian (10)	13	0.09
Indonesian (4)	4	0.03
Japanese (6)	13	0.09
Korean (2)	9	0.07
Pakistani (4)	4	0.03
Taiwanese (1)	1	0.01
Thai (4)	7	0.05
Vietnamese (7)	9	0.07
Hawaii Native/Pacific Islander (1)	5	0.04
Not Hispanic (1)	5	0.04
Guamanian/Chamorro (0)	1	0.01
Samoan (1)	2	0.01
White (13,182)	13,360	97.11
Not Hispanic (13,075)	13,240	96.23
Hispanic (107)	120	0.87

Jefferson City

Place Type: City
County: Cole
Population: 43,079†

Ancestry‡	Population	%
African, Sub-Saharan (569)	677	1.60
African (346)	384	0.91
Ghanaian (85)	85	0.20
Kenyan (19)	29	0.07
Nigerian (19)	79	0.19
Other Sub-Saharan African (100)	100	0.24
American (2,434)	2,434	5.74
Arab (76)	144	0.34
Egyptian (0)	34	0.08
Lebanese (59)	74	0.17
Moroccan (17)	36	0.08
Austrian (44)	58	0.14
Belgian (0)	10	0.02
British (54)	131	0.31
Celtic (13)	13	0.03
Czech (0)	76	0.18
Czechoslovakian (10)	39	0.09
Danish (26)	106	0.25
Dutch (147)	843	1.99
English (1,343)	4,717	11.13
European (379)	550	1.30
French, ex. Basque (245)	1,826	4.31
German (8,092)	15,606	36.83
Greek (0)	24	0.06
Hungarian (0)	41	0.10
Iranian (0)	11	0.03
Irish (1,272)	4,767	11.25
Italian (232)	1,146	2.70
Latvian (8)	8	0.02
Lithuanian (0)	9	0.02
Northern European (60)	60	0.14
Norwegian (102)	337	0.80
Pennsylvania German (12)	21	0.05
Polish (116)	434	1.02
Portuguese (41)	76	0.18
Russian (73)	225	0.53
Scandinavian (19)	94	0.22
Scotch-Irish (281)	795	1.88
Scottish (164)	726	1.71
Slovak (36)	67	0.16
Slovene (0)	15	0.04
Swedish (94)	409	0.97
Swiss (24)	175	0.41
Turkish (0)	47	0.11
Welsh (53)	321	0.76
West Indian, ex. Hispanic (161)	370	0.87
Bahamian (98)	98	0.23
Jamaican (63)	272	0.64
Yugoslavian (13)	13	0.03

Hispanic Origin	Population	%
Hispanic or Latino (of any race)	1,103	2.56
Central American, ex. Mexican	130	0.30
Costa Rican	1	<0.01
Guatemalan	17	0.04
Honduran	20	0.05
Nicaraguan	56	0.13
Panamanian	19	0.04
Salvadoran	17	0.04
Cuban	32	0.07
Dominican Republic	6	0.01
Mexican	722	1.68
Puerto Rican	72	0.17
South American	40	0.09
Argentinean	4	0.01
Bolivian	10	0.02
Chilean	11	0.03
Colombian	8	0.02
Ecuadorian	4	0.01
Venezuelan	2	<0.01
Other South American	1	<0.01
Other Hispanic or Latino	101	0.23

Race*	Population	%
African-American/Black (7,263)	7,837	18.19
Not Hispanic (7,188)	7,715	17.91
Hispanic (75)	122	0.28
American Indian/Alaska Native (142)	397	0.92
Not Hispanic (124)	357	0.83
Hispanic (18)	40	0.09
Apache (1)	1	<0.01
Arapaho (2)	2	<0.01
Blackfeet (1)	11	0.03
Canadian/French Am. Ind. (1)	2	<0.01
Central American Ind. (0)	1	<0.01
Cherokee (38)	125	0.29
Cheyenne (3)	3	0.01
Chickasaw (4)	4	0.01
Chippewa (2)	7	0.02
Choctaw (2)	16	0.04
Comanche (1)	1	<0.01
Creek (6)	9	0.02
Iroquois (2)	4	0.01

*Notes: † The Census 2010 population figure is used to calculate the percentages in the Hispanic Origin and Race categories. Ancestry percentages are based on the 2006-2010 American Community Survey population (not shown); ‡ Numbers in parentheses indicate the number of people reporting a single ancestry; * Numbers in parentheses indicate the number of persons reporting this race alone, not in combination with any other race; Please refer to the Explanation of Data for more information.*

Lumbee (1)	2	<0.01
Mexican American Ind. (4)	6	0.01
Navajo (0)	1	<0.01
Osage (0)	5	0.01
Pueblo (2)	2	<0.01
Seminole (0)	2	<0.01
Shoshone (0)	1	<0.01
Sioux (1)	2	<0.01
Tlingit-Haida *(Alaska Native)* (1)	1	<0.01
Ute (1)	6	0.01
Asian (755)	951	2.21
Not Hispanic (749)	933	2.17
Hispanic (6)	18	0.04
Bangladeshi (2)	3	0.01
Burmese (3)	3	0.01
Cambodian (7)	13	0.03
Chinese, ex. Taiwanese (96)	131	0.30
Filipino (72)	133	0.31
Hmong (5)	5	0.01
Indian (428)	449	1.04
Japanese (19)	45	0.10
Korean (26)	53	0.12
Laotian (6)	6	0.01
Nepalese (2)	2	<0.01
Pakistani (20)	22	0.05
Sri Lankan (7)	8	0.02
Taiwanese (3)	5	0.01
Thai (2)	6	0.01
Vietnamese (32)	41	0.10
Hawaii Native/Pacific Islander (25)	49	0.11
Not Hispanic (23)	45	0.10
Hispanic (2)	4	0.01
Guamanian/Chamorro (7)	8	0.02
Native Hawaiian (2)	11	0.03
Samoan (7)	10	0.02
Tongan (2)	2	<0.01
White (33,599)	34,445	79.96
Not Hispanic (33,021)	33,767	78.38
Hispanic (578)	678	1.57

Jennings

Place Type: City
County: St. Louis
Population: 14,712†

Ancestry‡	Population	%
African, Sub-Saharan (55)	218	1.47
African (15)	178	1.20
Nigerian (40)	40	0.27
American (287)	287	1.94
Austrian (0)	29	0.20
Czech (0)	16	0.11
English (71)	225	1.52
French, ex. Basque (39)	182	1.23
German (216)	669	4.51
Irish (44)	369	2.49
Italian (18)	18	0.12
Polish (13)	29	0.20
Portuguese (0)	17	0.11
Scotch-Irish (0)	28	0.19
Scottish (10)	27	0.18
West Indian, ex. Hispanic (39)	39	0.26
Haitian (23)	23	0.16
Jamaican (16)	16	0.11

Hispanic Origin	Population	%
Hispanic or Latino (of any race)	90	0.61
Central American, ex. Mexican	4	0.03
Guatemalan	1	0.01
Panamanian	2	0.01
Salvadoran	1	0.01
Cuban	9	0.06
Dominican Republic	2	0.01
Mexican	33	0.22
Puerto Rican	19	0.13
Other Hispanic or Latino	23	0.16

Race*	Population	%
African-American/Black (13,210)	13,363	90.83
Not Hispanic (13,173)	13,310	90.47
Hispanic (37)	53	0.36
American Indian/Alaska Native (21)	68	0.46
Not Hispanic (21)	63	0.43
Hispanic (0)	5	0.03
Blackfeet (0)	4	0.03
Cherokee (4)	22	0.15
Choctaw (0)	5	0.03
Mexican American Ind. (0)	1	0.01
Navajo (0)	2	0.01
Asian (24)	43	0.29
Not Hispanic (24)	40	0.27
Hispanic (0)	3	0.02
Burmese (0)	1	0.01
Cambodian (1)	1	0.01
Chinese, ex. Taiwanese (7)	12	0.08
Filipino (8)	14	0.10
Indian (4)	7	0.05
Japanese (1)	4	0.03
Korean (0)	1	0.01
Vietnamese (1)	3	0.02
Hawaii Native/Pacific Islander (0)	13	0.09
Not Hispanic (0)	9	0.06
Hispanic (0)	4	0.03
Guamanian/Chamorro (0)	1	0.01
Native Hawaiian (0)	1	0.01
Samoan (0)	2	0.01
White (1,256)	1,360	9.24
Not Hispanic (1,237)	1,332	9.05
Hispanic (19)	28	0.19

Joplin

Place Type: City
County: Jasper
Population: 50,150†

Ancestry‡	Population	%
African, Sub-Saharan (62)	96	0.19
African (62)	96	0.19
Albanian (22)	22	0.04
American (4,318)	4,318	8.73
Arab (16)	79	0.16
Arab (0)	35	0.07
Iraqi (8)	8	0.02
Lebanese (8)	25	0.05
Syrian (0)	11	0.02
Armenian (0)	26	0.05
Australian (16)	16	0.03
Austrian (0)	70	0.14
Belgian (97)	108	0.22
Brazilian (12)	21	0.04
British (100)	183	0.37
Bulgarian (0)	17	0.03
Canadian (0)	8	0.02
Croatian (38)	94	0.19
Czech (15)	55	0.11
Danish (23)	107	0.22
Dutch (129)	1,183	2.39
Eastern European (20)	20	0.04
English (2,776)	6,501	13.15
European (502)	598	1.21
French, ex. Basque (535)	1,958	3.96
French Canadian (63)	191	0.39
German (3,456)	10,241	20.71
Greek (65)	120	0.24
Hungarian (0)	45	0.09
Iranian (0)	17	0.03
Irish (1,718)	7,250	14.66
Israeli (10)	10	0.02
Italian (369)	1,509	3.05
Lithuanian (0)	39	0.08
Northern European (143)	143	0.29
Norwegian (108)	258	0.52
Pennsylvania German (11)	11	0.02
Polish (123)	414	0.84
Portuguese (14)	80	0.16
Russian (170)	239	0.48
Scandinavian (0)	29	0.06
Scotch-Irish (478)	1,128	2.28
Scottish (165)	753	1.52
Slavic (25)	60	0.12
Slovak (0)	27	0.05
Swedish (134)	585	1.18
Swiss (0)	95	0.19
Ukrainian (27)	27	0.05
Welsh (106)	378	0.76
West Indian, ex. Hispanic (8)	8	0.02
British West Indian (8)	8	0.02

Hispanic Origin	Population	%
Hispanic or Latino (of any race)	2,241	4.47
Central American, ex. Mexican	166	0.33
Guatemalan	76	0.15
Honduran	44	0.09
Nicaraguan	5	0.01
Panamanian	8	0.02
Salvadoran	33	0.07
Cuban	25	0.05
Dominican Republic	5	0.01
Mexican	1,568	3.13
Puerto Rican	207	0.41
South American	52	0.10
Argentinean	2	<0.01
Bolivian	2	<0.01
Chilean	6	0.01
Colombian	15	0.03
Ecuadorian	12	0.02
Peruvian	8	0.02
Uruguayan	1	<0.01
Venezuelan	6	0.01
Other Hispanic or Latino	218	0.43

Race*	Population	%
African-American/Black (1,657)	2,373	4.73
Not Hispanic (1,622)	2,285	4.56
Hispanic (35)	88	0.18
American Indian/Alaska Native (911)	1,715	3.42
Not Hispanic (832)	1,583	3.16
Hispanic (79)	132	0.26
Alaska Athabascan *(Ala. Nat.)* (1)	1	<0.01
Apache (10)	20	0.04
Arapaho (4)	6	0.01
Blackfeet (7)	34	0.07
Canadian/French Am. Ind. (0)	1	<0.01
Central American Ind. (3)	3	0.01
Cherokee (326)	689	1.37
Cheyenne (0)	3	0.01
Chickasaw (16)	30	0.06
Chippewa (20)	26	0.05
Choctaw (31)	67	0.13
Comanche (5)	7	0.01
Cree (3)	5	0.01
Creek (32)	48	0.10
Crow (2)	2	<0.01
Delaware (13)	29	0.06
Inupiat *(Alaska Native)* (2)	2	<0.01
Iroquois (32)	51	0.10
Kiowa (4)	4	0.01
Lumbee (1)	1	<0.01
Menominee (1)	1	<0.01
Mexican American Ind. (14)	19	0.04
Navajo (5)	8	0.02
Osage (13)	27	0.05
Ottawa (12)	22	0.04
Paiute (4)	4	0.01
Potawatomi (6)	16	0.03
Pueblo (1)	2	<0.01
Seminole (2)	9	0.02
Shoshone (2)	2	<0.01
Sioux (14)	35	0.07
Spanish American Ind. (3)	3	0.01
Tlingit-Haida *(Alaska Native)* (2)	3	0.01
Yaqui (1)	1	<0.01
Yup'ik *(Alaska Native)* (0)	1	<0.01
Asian (801)	1,011	2.02
Not Hispanic (795)	986	1.97
Hispanic (6)	25	0.05
Bangladeshi (1)	2	<0.01
Cambodian (2)	2	<0.01

*Notes: † The Census 2010 population figure is used to calculate the percentages in the Hispanic Origin and Race categories. Ancestry percentages are based on the 2006-2010 American Community Survey population (not shown); ‡ Numbers in parentheses indicate the number of people reporting a single ancestry; * Numbers in parentheses indicate the number of persons reporting this race alone, not in combination with any other race; Please refer to the Explanation of Data for more information.*

Chinese, ex. Taiwanese (118)	146	0.29
Filipino (120)	185	0.37
Hmong (26)	27	0.05
Indian (169)	194	0.39
Indonesian (16)	18	0.04
Japanese (36)	69	0.14
Korean (48)	78	0.16
Malaysian (0)	1	<0.01
Nepalese (2)	4	0.01
Pakistani (63)	67	0.13
Sri Lankan (2)	4	0.01
Taiwanese (15)	15	0.03
Thai (24)	30	0.06
Vietnamese (134)	142	0.28
Hawaii Native/Pacific Islander (154)	238	0.47
Not Hispanic (148)	222	0.44
Hispanic (6)	16	0.03
Guamanian/Chamorro (6)	19	0.04
Native Hawaiian (26)	52	0.10
Samoan (12)	27	0.05
Tongan (2)	2	<0.01
White (43,954)	45,640	91.01
Not Hispanic (42,904)	44,377	88.49
Hispanic (1,050)	1,263	2.52

Kansas City

Place Type: City
County: Jackson
Population: 459,787†

Ancestry‡	Population	%
Afghan (145)	145	0.03
African, Sub-Saharan (6,077)	7,251	1.59
African (3,192)	4,120	0.91
Cape Verdean (8)	46	0.01
Ethiopian (302)	302	0.07
Ghanaian (87)	87	0.02
Kenyan (142)	142	0.03
Liberian (332)	356	0.08
Nigerian (694)	727	0.16
Senegalese (29)	29	0.01
Somalian (555)	555	0.12
South African (141)	164	0.04
Sudanese (435)	544	0.12
Ugandan (4)	4	<0.01
Other Sub-Saharan African (156)	175	0.04
Albanian (120)	120	0.03
Alsatian (22)	33	0.01
American (48,909)	48,909	10.75
Arab (1,425)	2,176	0.48
Arab (419)	528	0.12
Egyptian (75)	151	0.03
Iraqi (164)	164	0.04
Jordanian (0)	109	0.02
Lebanese (170)	344	0.08
Moroccan (166)	166	0.04
Palestinian (108)	217	0.05
Syrian (91)	177	0.04
Other Arab (232)	320	0.07
Armenian (184)	321	0.07
Australian (73)	89	0.02
Austrian (208)	766	0.17
Belgian (280)	753	0.17
Brazilian (203)	224	0.05
British (672)	1,211	0.27
Bulgarian (48)	112	0.02
Cajun (8)	17	<0.01
Canadian (253)	514	0.11
Celtic (42)	71	0.02
Croatian (342)	1,349	0.30
Czech (534)	1,638	0.36
Czechoslovakian (140)	344	0.08
Danish (502)	2,006	0.44
Dutch (1,012)	6,489	1.43
Eastern European (125)	149	0.03
English (11,829)	38,104	8.38
European (3,801)	4,255	0.94
Finnish (66)	239	0.05
French, ex. Basque (1,579)	10,371	2.28
French Canadian (331)	1,136	0.25
German (27,417)	82,136	18.06
German Russian (6)	41	0.01
Greek (583)	1,124	0.25
Hungarian (277)	794	0.17
Icelander (0)	35	0.01
Iranian (217)	325	0.07
Irish (13,497)	53,239	11.70
Israeli (8)	14	<0.01
Italian (6,070)	16,306	3.58
Latvian (30)	52	0.01
Lithuanian (254)	542	0.12
Luxemburger (36)	51	0.01
Macedonian (15)	15	<0.01
Northern European (379)	472	0.10
Norwegian (1,266)	4,020	0.88
Pennsylvania German (31)	103	0.02
Polish (1,912)	6,093	1.34
Portuguese (217)	497	0.11
Romanian (183)	243	0.05
Russian (863)	2,405	0.53
Scandinavian (278)	775	0.17
Scotch-Irish (2,983)	8,013	1.76
Scottish (2,346)	8,260	1.82
Serbian (162)	246	0.05
Slavic (90)	109	0.02
Slovak (122)	347	0.08
Slovene (29)	152	0.03
Swedish (1,846)	6,140	1.35
Swiss (261)	1,546	0.34
Turkish (112)	156	0.03
Ukrainian (151)	473	0.10
Welsh (712)	3,415	0.75
West Indian, ex. Hispanic (917)	1,348	0.30
British West Indian (139)	148	0.03
Dutch West Indian (4)	24	0.01
Haitian (266)	289	0.06
Jamaican (363)	532	0.12
Trinidadian/Tobagonian (57)	57	0.01
West Indian (88)	298	0.07
Yugoslavian (280)	445	0.10

Hispanic Origin	Population	%
Hispanic or Latino (of any race)	45,953	9.99
Central American, ex. Mexican	2,758	0.60
Costa Rican	92	0.02
Guatemalan	671	0.15
Honduran	884	0.19
Nicaraguan	75	0.02
Panamanian	127	0.03
Salvadoran	893	0.19
Other Central American	16	<0.01
Cuban	1,327	0.29
Dominican Republic	301	0.07
Mexican	35,930	7.81
Puerto Rican	1,474	0.32
South American	1,108	0.24
Argentinean	103	0.02
Bolivian	59	0.01
Chilean	93	0.02
Colombian	364	0.08
Ecuadorian	132	0.03
Paraguayan	24	0.01
Peruvian	176	0.04
Uruguayan	22	<0.01
Venezuelan	111	0.02
Other South American	24	0.01
Other Hispanic or Latino	3,055	0.66

Race*	Population	%
African-American/Black (137,540)	145,396	31.62
Not Hispanic (135,916)	142,748	31.05
Hispanic (1,624)	2,648	0.58
American Indian/Alaska Native (2,331)	6,745	1.47
Not Hispanic (1,823)	5,584	1.21
Hispanic (508)	1,161	0.25
Alaska Athabascan *(Ala. Nat.)* (1)	4	<0.01
Aleut *(Alaska Native)* (3)	4	<0.01
Apache (32)	89	0.02
Arapaho (2)	7	<0.01
Blackfeet (22)	284	0.06
Canadian/French Am. Ind. (3)	10	<0.01
Central American Ind. (2)	8	<0.01
Cherokee (411)	1,693	0.37
Cheyenne (9)	22	<0.01
Chickasaw (27)	97	0.02
Chippewa (46)	84	0.02
Choctaw (119)	325	0.07
Colville (2)	5	<0.01
Comanche (6)	15	<0.01
Cree (4)	16	<0.01
Creek (56)	150	0.03
Crow (8)	27	0.01
Delaware (22)	37	0.01
Hopi (2)	8	<0.01
Inupiat *(Alaska Native)* (3)	9	<0.01
Iroquois (33)	72	0.02
Kiowa (14)	28	0.01
Lumbee (3)	14	<0.01
Menominee (1)	5	<0.01
Mexican American Ind. (122)	173	0.04
Navajo (19)	60	0.01
Osage (14)	51	0.01
Ottawa (6)	13	<0.01
Paiute (1)	5	<0.01
Potawatomi (61)	135	0.03
Pueblo (11)	29	0.01
Puget Sound Salish (2)	2	<0.01
Seminole (22)	69	0.02
Shoshone (3)	4	<0.01
Sioux (70)	218	0.05
South American Ind. (11)	28	0.01
Spanish American Ind. (8)	15	<0.01
Tlingit-Haida *(Alaska Native)* (6)	8	<0.01
Tohono O'Odham (1)	1	<0.01
Tsimshian *(Alaska Native)* (0)	3	<0.01
Ute (2)	4	<0.01
Yakama (0)	1	<0.01
Yaqui (4)	6	<0.01
Yuman (0)	1	<0.01
Yup'ik *(Alaska Native)* (3)	10	<0.01
Asian (11,399)	14,160	3.08
Not Hispanic (11,275)	13,781	3.00
Hispanic (124)	379	0.08
Bangladeshi (64)	75	0.02
Burmese (257)	262	0.06
Cambodian (272)	350	0.08
Chinese, ex. Taiwanese (1,374)	1,759	0.38
Filipino (1,219)	1,887	0.41
Hmong (61)	70	0.02
Indian (1,640)	1,958	0.43
Indonesian (42)	73	0.02
Japanese (292)	708	0.15
Korean (816)	1,120	0.24
Laotian (128)	170	0.04
Malaysian (57)	71	0.02
Nepalese (20)	22	<0.01
Pakistani (475)	553	0.12
Sri Lankan (23)	24	0.01
Taiwanese (108)	138	0.03
Thai (167)	262	0.06
Vietnamese (3,793)	4,128	0.90
Hawaii Native/Pacific Islander (861)	1,467	0.32
Not Hispanic (787)	1,258	0.27
Hispanic (74)	209	0.05
Fijian (5)	19	<0.01
Guamanian/Chamorro (107)	157	0.03
Marshallese (30)	38	0.01
Native Hawaiian (113)	266	0.06
Samoan (173)	333	0.07
Tongan (1)	5	<0.01
White (272,305)	284,126	61.80
Not Hispanic (252,257)	261,254	56.82
Hispanic (20,048)	22,872	4.97

*Notes: † The Census 2010 population figure is used to calculate the percentages in the Hispanic Origin and Race categories. Ancestry percentages are based on the 2006-2010 American Community Survey population (not shown); ‡ Numbers in parentheses indicate the number of people reporting a single ancestry; * Numbers in parentheses indicate the number of persons reporting this race alone, not in combination with any other race; Please refer to the Explanation of Data for more information.*

Kearney

Place Type: City
County: Clay
Population: 8,381†

Ancestry‡	Population	%
American (665)	665	8.46
Arab (0)	46	0.58
Syrian (0)	46	0.58
Austrian (49)	49	0.62
Belgian (0)	16	0.20
Czech (13)	61	0.78
Danish (24)	47	0.60
Dutch (96)	177	2.25
English (338)	838	10.66
European (188)	188	2.39
French, ex. Basque (16)	215	2.73
French Canadian (0)	27	0.34
German (649)	2,625	33.38
Irish (321)	1,713	21.78
Italian (44)	322	4.09
Norwegian (26)	57	0.72
Polish (47)	242	3.08
Portuguese (16)	27	0.34
Russian (0)	27	0.34
Scotch-Irish (64)	221	2.81
Scottish (29)	167	2.12
Swedish (31)	266	3.38
Swiss (0)	16	0.20
Ukrainian (0)	38	0.48
Welsh (18)	116	1.48
Yugoslavian (0)	13	0.17

Hispanic Origin	Population	%
Hispanic or Latino (of any race)	274	3.27
Central American, ex. Mexican	13	0.16
Guatemalan	3	0.04
Honduran	8	0.10
Panamanian	2	0.02
Cuban	5	0.06
Mexican	203	2.42
Puerto Rican	23	0.27
South American	9	0.11
Chilean	4	0.05
Peruvian	1	0.01
Venezuelan	4	0.05
Other Hispanic or Latino	21	0.25

Race*	Population	%
African-American/Black (32)	82	0.98
Not Hispanic (31)	77	0.92
Hispanic (1)	5	0.06
American Indian/Alaska Native (34)	84	1.00
Not Hispanic (30)	69	0.82
Hispanic (4)	15	0.18
Apache (0)	5	0.06
Canadian/French Am. Ind. (2)	3	0.04
Cherokee (7)	23	0.27
Chickasaw (0)	1	0.01
Choctaw (6)	6	0.07
Comanche (1)	1	0.01
Creek (1)	1	0.01
Iroquois (1)	1	0.01
Menominee (3)	3	0.04
Mexican American Ind. (0)	5	0.06
Potawatomi (1)	2	0.02
Sioux (2)	4	0.05
South American Ind. (1)	1	0.01
Ute (1)	1	0.01
Asian (33)	63	0.75
Not Hispanic (33)	57	0.68
Hispanic (0)	6	0.07
Chinese, ex. Taiwanese (19)	22	0.26
Filipino (3)	18	0.21
Indian (7)	8	0.10
Japanese (1)	6	0.07
Korean (2)	6	0.07
Thai (0)	4	0.05
Hawaii Native/Pacific Islander (8)	17	0.20
Not Hispanic (8)	17	0.20
Samoan (7)	14	0.17
White (8,061)	8,207	97.92
Not Hispanic (7,889)	7,998	95.43
Hispanic (172)	209	2.49

Kennett

Place Type: City
County: Dunklin
Population: 10,932†

Ancestry‡	Population	%
African, Sub-Saharan (8)	8	0.07
African (8)	8	0.07
American (1,305)	1,305	11.58
Belgian (17)	17	0.15
British (0)	10	0.09
Bulgarian (0)	9	0.08
Czech (8)	8	0.07
Dutch (12)	121	1.07
English (340)	776	6.89
European (32)	46	0.41
French, ex. Basque (41)	323	2.87
German (297)	874	7.76
Irish (738)	1,731	15.36
Italian (0)	49	0.43
Lithuanian (0)	11	0.10
Norwegian (31)	46	0.41
Pennsylvania German (0)	9	0.08
Polish (0)	32	0.28
Scotch-Irish (150)	232	2.06
Scottish (62)	88	0.78
Swedish (8)	54	0.48
Swiss (0)	13	0.12
Ukrainian (0)	35	0.31
Welsh (0)	17	0.15

Hispanic Origin	Population	%
Hispanic or Latino (of any race)	388	3.55
Central American, ex. Mexican	3	0.03
Honduran	3	0.03
Cuban	2	0.02
Mexican	319	2.92
Puerto Rican	8	0.07
South American	12	0.11
Argentinean	2	0.02
Colombian	5	0.05
Paraguayan	3	0.03
Peruvian	2	0.02
Other Hispanic or Latino	44	0.40

Race*	Population	%
African-American/Black (1,766)	1,880	17.20
Not Hispanic (1,749)	1,863	17.04
Hispanic (17)	17	0.16
American Indian/Alaska Native (24)	68	0.62
Not Hispanic (24)	66	0.60
Hispanic (0)	2	0.02
Blackfeet (3)	3	0.03
Cherokee (8)	28	0.26
Chippewa (1)	1	0.01
Choctaw (2)	3	0.03
Creek (0)	1	0.01
Paiute (1)	1	0.01
Asian (63)	83	0.76
Not Hispanic (63)	83	0.76
Chinese, ex. Taiwanese (12)	12	0.11
Filipino (25)	27	0.25
Indian (9)	13	0.12
Japanese (0)	9	0.08
Korean (1)	1	0.01
Taiwanese (3)	3	0.03
Thai (7)	7	0.06
Vietnamese (4)	7	0.06
Hawaii Native/Pacific Islander (7)	13	0.12
Not Hispanic (7)	13	0.12
Guamanian/Chamorro (6)	10	0.09
Native Hawaiian (1)	1	0.01
White (8,752)	8,924	81.63
Not Hispanic (8,516)	8,680	79.40
Hispanic (236)	244	2.23

Kirksville

Place Type: City
County: Adair
Population: 17,505†

Ancestry‡	Population	%
African, Sub-Saharan (58)	59	0.34
African (32)	33	0.19
Nigerian (13)	13	0.07
Sudanese (13)	13	0.07
American (1,553)	1,553	8.92
Arab (13)	23	0.13
Lebanese (13)	23	0.13
Armenian (0)	7	0.04
Belgian (39)	56	0.32
British (47)	47	0.27
Bulgarian (67)	67	0.38
Canadian (0)	8	0.05
Croatian (16)	16	0.09
Czech (40)	123	0.71
Czechoslovakian (12)	59	0.34
Danish (67)	129	0.74
Dutch (84)	408	2.34
English (898)	2,328	13.37
European (163)	173	0.99
French, ex. Basque (56)	469	2.69
French Canadian (61)	103	0.59
German (1,769)	5,097	29.27
Greek (1)	46	0.26
Hungarian (0)	53	0.30
Iranian (25)	25	0.14
Irish (935)	3,068	17.62
Italian (307)	692	3.97
Lithuanian (0)	45	0.26
Northern European (37)	37	0.21
Norwegian (62)	237	1.36
Polish (85)	255	1.46
Portuguese (0)	18	0.10
Romanian (10)	21	0.12
Russian (37)	49	0.28
Scandinavian (11)	69	0.40
Scotch-Irish (180)	425	2.44
Scottish (76)	458	2.63
Slovak (13)	13	0.07
Slovene (0)	16	0.09
Swedish (60)	207	1.19
Swiss (0)	34	0.20
Turkish (0)	11	0.06
Ukrainian (13)	13	0.07
Welsh (113)	288	1.65
West Indian, ex. Hispanic (21)	21	0.12
Dutch West Indian (12)	12	0.07
Jamaican (9)	9	0.05
Yugoslavian (0)	15	0.09

Hispanic Origin	Population	%
Hispanic or Latino (of any race)	473	2.70
Central American, ex. Mexican	43	0.25
Costa Rican	9	0.05
Guatemalan	9	0.05
Honduran	5	0.03
Nicaraguan	2	0.01
Panamanian	6	0.03
Salvadoran	12	0.07
Cuban	6	0.03
Dominican Republic	2	0.01
Mexican	290	1.66
Puerto Rican	34	0.19
South American	41	0.23
Argentinean	5	0.03
Bolivian	3	0.02
Chilean	2	0.01
Colombian	15	0.09
Ecuadorian	4	0.02
Peruvian	7	0.04
Venezuelan	5	0.03

*Notes: † The Census 2010 population figure is used to calculate the percentages in the Hispanic Origin and Race categories. Ancestry percentages are based on the 2006-2010 American Community Survey population (not shown); ‡ Numbers in parentheses indicate the number of people reporting a single ancestry; * Numbers in parentheses indicate the number of persons reporting this race alone, not in combination with any other race; Please refer to the Explanation of Data for more information.*

SECTION TWO

Other Hispanic or Latino	57	0.33

Race*	Population	%
African-American/Black (389)	523	2.99
Not Hispanic (374)	501	2.86
Hispanic (15)	22	0.13
American Indian/Alaska Native (38)	144	0.82
Not Hispanic (32)	122	0.70
Hispanic (6)	22	0.13
Apache (1)	1	0.01
Blackfeet (0)	5	0.03
Cherokee (11)	45	0.26
Cheyenne (0)	4	0.02
Chickasaw (0)	1	0.01
Chippewa (2)	5	0.03
Choctaw (0)	2	0.01
Cree (0)	1	0.01
Delaware (0)	1	0.01
Iroquois (0)	1	0.01
Kiowa (0)	1	0.01
Lumbee (0)	1	0.01
Mexican American Ind. (1)	2	0.01
Navajo (2)	2	0.01
Osage (0)	1	0.01
Seminole (0)	1	0.01
Sioux (1)	10	0.06
Spanish American Ind. (0)	4	0.02
Asian (413)	517	2.95
Not Hispanic (413)	512	2.92
Hispanic (0)	5	0.03
Bangladeshi (3)	3	0.02
Chinese, ex. Taiwanese (112)	124	0.71
Filipino (26)	51	0.29
Indian (72)	82	0.47
Indonesian (1)	1	0.01
Japanese (17)	37	0.21
Korean (27)	45	0.26
Laotian (3)	3	0.02
Nepalese (31)	32	0.18
Pakistani (9)	11	0.06
Sri Lankan (16)	17	0.10
Taiwanese (7)	8	0.05
Thai (4)	9	0.05
Vietnamese (56)	66	0.38
Hawaii Native/Pacific Islander (13)	25	0.14
Not Hispanic (12)	23	0.13
Hispanic (1)	2	0.01
Guamanian/Chamorro (1)	6	0.03
Native Hawaiian (2)	4	0.02
Samoan (6)	11	0.06
White (16,160)	16,499	94.25
Not Hispanic (15,878)	16,175	92.40
Hispanic (282)	324	1.85

Kirkwood

Place Type: City
County: St. Louis
Population: 27,540†

Ancestry‡	Population	%
African, Sub-Saharan (57)	57	0.21
African (57)	57	0.21
Albanian (77)	90	0.33
Alsatian (0)	27	0.10
American (1,051)	1,051	3.83
Arab (140)	173	0.63
Lebanese (0)	33	0.12
Palestinian (48)	48	0.18
Syrian (92)	92	0.34
Austrian (30)	96	0.35
British (162)	252	0.92
Cajun (0)	10	0.04
Canadian (75)	99	0.36
Celtic (37)	37	0.13
Croatian (0)	28	0.10
Czech (60)	285	1.04
Czechoslovakian (15)	59	0.22
Danish (15)	154	0.56
Dutch (149)	573	2.09
Eastern European (67)	88	0.32
English (851)	3,886	14.18
European (449)	466	1.70
Finnish (0)	27	0.10
French, ex. Basque (220)	1,566	5.71
French Canadian (9)	141	0.51
German (4,283)	11,542	42.11
Greek (0)	65	0.24
Hungarian (58)	161	0.59
Irish (1,379)	6,028	21.99
Italian (490)	1,930	7.04
Latvian (9)	9	0.03
Lithuanian (14)	58	0.21
Macedonian (17)	63	0.23
Northern European (11)	11	0.04
Norwegian (54)	222	0.81
Polish (170)	799	2.91
Portuguese (37)	45	0.16
Romanian (30)	30	0.11
Russian (81)	218	0.80
Scandinavian (0)	66	0.24
Scotch-Irish (137)	652	2.38
Scottish (223)	795	2.90
Serbian (0)	11	0.04
Slavic (0)	18	0.07
Slovak (0)	82	0.30
Slovene (15)	15	0.05
Swedish (55)	446	1.63
Swiss (24)	225	0.82
Ukrainian (31)	65	0.24
Welsh (235)	521	1.90
West Indian, ex. Hispanic (0)	18	0.07
Jamaican (0)	18	0.07
Yugoslavian (11)	43	0.16

Hispanic Origin	Population	%
Hispanic or Latino (of any race)	507	1.84
Central American, ex. Mexican	72	0.26
Costa Rican	5	0.02
Guatemalan	27	0.10
Honduran	13	0.05
Nicaraguan	16	0.06
Panamanian	5	0.02
Salvadoran	4	0.01
Other Central American	2	0.01
Cuban	18	0.07
Dominican Republic	11	0.04
Mexican	223	0.81
Puerto Rican	53	0.19
South American	74	0.27
Argentinean	12	0.04
Bolivian	1	<0.01
Chilean	4	0.01
Colombian	23	0.08
Ecuadorian	4	0.01
Peruvian	16	0.06
Uruguayan	2	0.01
Venezuelan	12	0.04
Other Hispanic or Latino	56	0.20

Race*	Population	%
African-American/Black (1,927)	2,139	7.77
Not Hispanic (1,911)	2,106	7.65
Hispanic (16)	33	0.12
American Indian/Alaska Native (36)	159	0.58
Not Hispanic (21)	131	0.48
Hispanic (15)	28	0.10
Apache (0)	3	0.01
Central American Ind. (2)	2	0.01
Cherokee (3)	35	0.13
Cheyenne (0)	6	0.02
Chippewa (1)	3	0.01
Choctaw (2)	10	0.04
Cree (1)	1	<0.01
Creek (1)	1	<0.01
Lumbee (1)	1	<0.01
Mexican American Ind. (5)	7	0.03
Osage (0)	1	<0.01
Potawatomi (0)	1	<0.01
Pueblo (2)	2	0.01
Shoshone (0)	1	<0.01
Sioux (0)	5	0.02
South American Ind. (1)	1	<0.01
Asian (394)	530	1.92
Not Hispanic (393)	524	1.90
Hispanic (1)	6	0.02
Chinese, ex. Taiwanese (104)	128	0.46
Filipino (51)	94	0.34
Hmong (0)	1	<0.01
Indian (98)	111	0.40
Indonesian (0)	5	0.02
Japanese (24)	48	0.17
Korean (42)	54	0.20
Laotian (2)	4	0.01
Pakistani (9)	12	0.04
Taiwanese (2)	4	0.01
Thai (11)	13	0.05
Vietnamese (38)	47	0.17
Hawaii Native/Pacific Islander (5)	25	0.09
Not Hispanic (5)	23	0.08
Hispanic (0)	2	0.01
Fijian (1)	1	<0.01
Guamanian/Chamorro (1)	2	0.01
Marshallese (0)	5	0.02
Native Hawaiian (1)	3	0.01
Samoan (2)	3	0.01
White (24,634)	25,015	90.83
Not Hispanic (24,280)	24,633	89.44
Hispanic (354)	382	1.39

Ladue

Place Type: City
County: St. Louis
Population: 8,521†

Ancestry‡	Population	%
Alsatian (11)	11	0.13
American (970)	970	11.46
Arab (7)	66	0.78
Egyptian (7)	13	0.15
Syrian (0)	12	0.14
Other Arab (0)	41	0.48
Armenian (10)	10	0.12
Australian (0)	18	0.21
Austrian (15)	27	0.32
Belgian (0)	34	0.40
Brazilian (13)	13	0.15
British (70)	97	1.15
Canadian (0)	11	0.13
Croatian (11)	20	0.24
Czech (12)	12	0.14
Danish (50)	79	0.93
Dutch (19)	98	1.16
Eastern European (49)	49	0.58
English (405)	1,457	17.21
European (367)	367	4.33
French, ex. Basque (49)	316	3.73
French Canadian (2)	2	0.02
German (816)	2,338	27.61
Greek (46)	83	0.98
Hungarian (0)	63	0.74
Irish (462)	1,657	19.57
Italian (69)	248	2.93
Lithuanian (23)	62	0.73
Northern European (8)	8	0.09
Norwegian (22)	90	1.06
Polish (141)	325	3.84
Romanian (0)	8	0.09
Russian (165)	370	4.37
Scandinavian (9)	9	0.11
Scotch-Irish (118)	170	2.01
Scottish (101)	239	2.82
Slovak (0)	16	0.19
Swedish (8)	65	0.77
Swiss (0)	75	0.89
Ukrainian (24)	40	0.47
Welsh (31)	93	1.10

*Notes: † The Census 2010 population figure is used to calculate the percentages in the Hispanic Origin and Race categories. Ancestry percentages are based on the 2006-2010 American Community Survey population (not shown); ‡ Numbers in parentheses indicate the number of people reporting a single ancestry; * Numbers in parentheses indicate the number of persons reporting this race alone, not in combination with any other race; Please refer to the Explanation of Data for more information.*

Hispanic Origin	Population	%
Hispanic or Latino (of any race)	120	1.41
Central American, ex. Mexican	9	0.11
Guatemalan	8	0.09
Salvadoran	1	0.01
Cuban	7	0.08
Dominican Republic	1	0.01
Mexican	53	0.62
Puerto Rican	3	0.04
South American	29	0.34
Argentinean	8	0.09
Bolivian	1	0.01
Colombian	10	0.12
Ecuadorian	4	0.05
Peruvian	6	0.07
Other Hispanic or Latino	18	0.21

Race*	Population	%
African-American/Black (84)	99	1.16
Not Hispanic (83)	98	1.15
Hispanic (1)	1	0.01
American Indian/Alaska Native (7)	26	0.31
Not Hispanic (7)	25	0.29
Hispanic (0)	1	0.01
Blackfeet (1)	1	0.01
Cherokee (2)	9	0.11
Chickasaw (0)	3	0.04
Mexican American Ind. (0)	1	0.01
Seminole (0)	1	0.01
Spanish American Ind. (1)	1	0.01
Asian (263)	338	3.97
Not Hispanic (261)	331	3.88
Hispanic (2)	7	0.08
Burmese (4)	7	0.08
Chinese, ex. Taiwanese (84)	104	1.22
Filipino (9)	16	0.19
Indian (86)	96	1.13
Japanese (11)	30	0.35
Korean (37)	42	0.49
Nepalese (1)	1	0.01
Pakistani (10)	17	0.20
Sri Lankan (1)	5	0.06
Taiwanese (2)	2	0.02
Thai (2)	4	0.05
Vietnamese (9)	17	0.20
Hawaii Native/Pacific Islander (8)	13	0.15
Not Hispanic (8)	13	0.15
Guamanian/Chamorro (2)	2	0.02
Native Hawaiian (4)	8	0.09
White (8,020)	8,134	95.46
Not Hispanic (7,925)	8,030	94.24
Hispanic (95)	104	1.22

Lake St. Louis

Place Type: City
County: St. Charles
Population: 14,545†

Ancestry‡	Population	%
Alsatian (0)	9	0.06
American (905)	905	6.51
Arab (13)	46	0.33
Egyptian (13)	13	0.09
Lebanese (0)	33	0.24
Austrian (0)	20	0.14
Belgian (12)	26	0.19
Brazilian (15)	15	0.11
British (31)	54	0.39
Canadian (0)	13	0.09
Czech (0)	101	0.73
Czechoslovakian (86)	99	0.71
Danish (63)	105	0.76
Dutch (120)	292	2.10
Eastern European (10)	10	0.07
English (656)	2,063	14.84
European (267)	319	2.29
Finnish (82)	82	0.59
French, ex. Basque (73)	473	3.40
French Canadian (10)	35	0.25
German (1,937)	4,703	33.83
Greek (19)	30	0.22
Hungarian (19)	61	0.44
Iranian (13)	50	0.36
Irish (668)	2,811	20.22
Italian (290)	1,077	7.75
Lithuanian (0)	51	0.37
Norwegian (129)	230	1.65
Polish (107)	538	3.87
Portuguese (0)	31	0.22
Russian (83)	111	0.80
Scandinavian (0)	36	0.26
Scotch-Irish (102)	276	1.99
Scottish (103)	356	2.56
Slovak (15)	45	0.32
Slovene (15)	15	0.11
Swedish (38)	262	1.88
Swiss (0)	96	0.69
Welsh (0)	43	0.31
West Indian, ex. Hispanic (0)	10	0.07
West Indian (0)	10	0.07
Yugoslavian (0)	76	0.55

Hispanic Origin	Population	%
Hispanic or Latino (of any race)	305	2.10
Central American, ex. Mexican	32	0.22
Guatemalan	11	0.08
Honduran	7	0.05
Nicaraguan	6	0.04
Panamanian	7	0.05
Salvadoran	1	0.01
Cuban	17	0.12
Dominican Republic	6	0.04
Mexican	141	0.97
Puerto Rican	42	0.29
South American	33	0.23
Argentinean	2	0.01
Bolivian	2	0.01
Chilean	1	0.01
Colombian	10	0.07
Ecuadorian	11	0.08
Paraguayan	1	0.01
Peruvian	1	0.01
Venezuelan	5	0.03
Other Hispanic or Latino	34	0.23

Race*	Population	%
African-American/Black (555)	618	4.25
Not Hispanic (553)	610	4.19
Hispanic (2)	8	0.06
American Indian/Alaska Native (37)	89	0.61
Not Hispanic (36)	79	0.54
Hispanic (1)	10	0.07
Alaska Athabascan *(Ala. Nat.)* (1)	1	0.01
Aleut *(Alaska Native)* (3)	3	0.02
Blackfeet (0)	5	0.03
Central American Ind. (0)	5	0.03
Cherokee (8)	21	0.14
Chippewa (1)	3	0.02
Creek (0)	1	0.01
Delaware (0)	1	0.01
Iroquois (2)	2	0.01
Lumbee (1)	2	0.01
Mexican American Ind. (0)	1	0.01
Osage (0)	2	0.01
Ottawa (6)	6	0.04
Sioux (3)	5	0.03
Asian (310)	364	2.50
Not Hispanic (309)	361	2.48
Hispanic (1)	3	0.02
Chinese, ex. Taiwanese (37)	41	0.28
Filipino (34)	49	0.34
Indian (155)	164	1.13
Japanese (8)	19	0.13
Korean (22)	28	0.19
Laotian (2)	2	0.01
Pakistani (21)	25	0.17
Sri Lankan (4)	4	0.03
Taiwanese (1)	1	0.01
Thai (4)	6	0.04
Vietnamese (16)	22	0.15
Hawaii Native/Pacific Islander (14)	26	0.18
Not Hispanic (12)	23	0.16
Hispanic (2)	3	0.02
Guamanian/Chamorro (6)	6	0.04
Native Hawaiian (1)	7	0.05
Samoan (0)	2	0.01
White (13,415)	13,562	93.24
Not Hispanic (13,178)	13,303	91.46
Hispanic (237)	259	1.78

Lebanon

Place Type: City
County: Laclede
Population: 14,474†

Ancestry‡	Population	%
African, Sub-Saharan (31)	62	0.44
Kenyan (0)	31	0.22
Sudanese (31)	31	0.22
American (1,684)	1,684	11.85
Arab (32)	32	0.23
Arab (21)	21	0.15
Egyptian (11)	11	0.08
Australian (18)	31	0.22
British (20)	85	0.60
Cajun (11)	11	0.08
Croatian (0)	13	0.09
Czech (0)	24	0.17
Czechoslovakian (0)	16	0.11
Danish (0)	9	0.06
Dutch (19)	317	2.23
Eastern European (14)	14	0.10
English (588)	1,281	9.01
European (163)	183	1.29
French, ex. Basque (68)	405	2.85
German (743)	2,165	15.23
Greek (0)	40	0.28
Hungarian (8)	8	0.06
Iranian (50)	50	0.35
Irish (513)	1,743	12.27
Italian (55)	149	1.05
Lithuanian (0)	10	0.07
Norwegian (44)	140	0.99
Pennsylvania German (0)	35	0.25
Polish (52)	157	1.10
Russian (0)	9	0.06
Scandinavian (16)	16	0.11
Scotch-Irish (123)	280	1.97
Scottish (55)	145	1.02
Swedish (36)	83	0.58
Swiss (0)	28	0.20
Welsh (31)	68	0.48
West Indian, ex. Hispanic (0)	6	0.04
Dutch West Indian (0)	6	0.04

Hispanic Origin	Population	%
Hispanic or Latino (of any race)	380	2.63
Central American, ex. Mexican	14	0.10
Costa Rican	3	0.02
Guatemalan	1	0.01
Nicaraguan	4	0.03
Panamanian	1	0.01
Salvadoran	5	0.03
Cuban	14	0.10
Dominican Republic	1	0.01
Mexican	273	1.89
Puerto Rican	38	0.26
South American	3	0.02
Argentinean	1	0.01
Colombian	2	0.01
Other Hispanic or Latino	37	0.26

Race*	Population	%
African-American/Black (188)	291	2.01
Not Hispanic (185)	284	1.96
Hispanic (3)	7	0.05
American Indian/Alaska Native (89)	244	1.69
Not Hispanic (83)	231	1.60

*Notes: † The Census 2010 population figure is used to calculate the percentages in the Hispanic Origin and Race categories. Ancestry percentages are based on the 2006-2010 American Community Survey population (not shown); ‡ Numbers in parentheses indicate the number of people reporting a single ancestry; * Numbers in parentheses indicate the number of persons reporting this race alone, not in combination with any other race; Please refer to the Explanation of Data for more information.*

Hispanic (6)	13	0.09
Apache (0)	1	0.01
Arapaho (2)	2	0.01
Blackfeet (1)	15	0.10
Central American Ind. (1)	1	0.01
Cherokee (17)	73	0.50
Chippewa (1)	1	0.01
Choctaw (2)	11	0.08
Comanche (0)	2	0.01
Creek (2)	3	0.02
Crow (0)	1	0.01
Iroquois (1)	4	0.03
Lumbee (7)	7	0.05
Mexican American Ind. (1)	2	0.01
Navajo (1)	1	0.01
Osage (1)	2	0.01
Potawatomi (6)	9	0.06
Seminole (0)	1	0.01
Shoshone (0)	1	0.01
Sioux (1)	4	0.03
Ute (1)	1	0.01
Yuman (1)	1	0.01
Asian (102)	176	1.22
Not Hispanic (97)	168	1.16
Hispanic (5)	8	0.06
Burmese (0)	4	0.03
Cambodian (3)	3	0.02
Chinese, ex. Taiwanese (9)	20	0.14
Filipino (42)	63	0.44
Indian (11)	12	0.08
Japanese (6)	21	0.15
Korean (10)	25	0.17
Pakistani (10)	10	0.07
Taiwanese (2)	5	0.03
Thai (1)	4	0.03
Vietnamese (3)	8	0.06
Hawaii Native/Pacific Islander (10)	22	0.15
Not Hispanic (8)	18	0.12
Hispanic (2)	4	0.03
Guamanian/Chamorro (3)	5	0.03
Native Hawaiian (5)	8	0.06
Samoan (2)	6	0.04
Tongan (0)	2	0.01
White (13,625)	13,963	96.47
Not Hispanic (13,399)	13,698	94.64
Hispanic (226)	265	1.83

Lee's Summit

Place Type: City
County: Jackson
Population: 91,364†

Ancestry‡	Population	%
African, Sub-Saharan (51)	51	0.06
African (32)	32	0.04
Kenyan (19)	19	0.02
Albanian (0)	10	0.01
American (6,116)	6,116	7.03
Arab (138)	259	0.30
Arab (12)	12	0.01
Egyptian (55)	66	0.08
Jordanian (44)	44	0.05
Lebanese (0)	110	0.13
Palestinian (27)	27	0.03
Armenian (0)	30	0.03
Australian (11)	11	0.01
Austrian (86)	268	0.31
Basque (0)	6	0.01
Belgian (54)	154	0.18
Brazilian (17)	17	0.02
British (122)	424	0.49
Canadian (102)	230	0.26
Carpatho Rusyn (0)	9	0.01
Croatian (136)	204	0.23
Czech (123)	320	0.37
Czechoslovakian (26)	87	0.10
Danish (174)	568	0.65
Dutch (388)	1,662	1.91
Eastern European (51)	51	0.06
English (4,000)	12,197	14.02
Estonian (55)	270	0.31
European (1,266)	1,321	1.52
Finnish (16)	103	0.12
French, ex. Basque (292)	2,130	2.45
French Canadian (136)	217	0.25
German (8,392)	24,716	28.40
Greek (51)	155	0.18
Hungarian (58)	151	0.17
Icelander (0)	24	0.03
Iranian (232)	257	0.30
Irish (3,328)	14,211	16.33
Italian (1,414)	3,354	3.85
Lithuanian (40)	83	0.10
Luxemburger (7)	18	0.02
Northern European (110)	110	0.13
Norwegian (384)	1,464	1.68
Pennsylvania German (13)	37	0.04
Polish (379)	1,809	2.08
Portuguese (32)	45	0.05
Romanian (8)	38	0.04
Russian (139)	421	0.48
Scandinavian (80)	165	0.19
Scotch-Irish (678)	2,089	2.40
Scottish (464)	2,000	2.30
Serbian (25)	25	0.03
Slavic (29)	58	0.07
Slovak (19)	138	0.16
Slovene (0)	13	0.01
Swedish (565)	1,887	2.17
Swiss (98)	443	0.51
Turkish (12)	12	0.01
Ukrainian (15)	34	0.04
Welsh (185)	915	1.05
West Indian, ex. Hispanic (54)	54	0.06
British West Indian (10)	10	0.01
Haitian (16)	16	0.02
Jamaican (28)	28	0.03
Yugoslavian (4)	56	0.06

Hispanic Origin	Population	%
Hispanic or Latino (of any race)	3,529	3.86
Central American, ex. Mexican	257	0.28
Costa Rican	17	0.02
Guatemalan	63	0.07
Honduran	70	0.08
Nicaraguan	10	0.01
Panamanian	39	0.04
Salvadoran	53	0.06
Other Central American	5	0.01
Cuban	56	0.06
Dominican Republic	28	0.03
Mexican	2,467	2.70
Puerto Rican	218	0.24
South American	245	0.27
Argentinean	21	0.02
Bolivian	8	0.01
Chilean	6	0.01
Colombian	75	0.08
Ecuadorian	33	0.04
Paraguayan	4	<0.01
Peruvian	64	0.07
Uruguayan	5	0.01
Venezuelan	28	0.03
Other South American	1	<0.01
Other Hispanic or Latino	258	0.28

Race*	Population	%
African-American/Black (7,632)	8,624	9.44
Not Hispanic (7,508)	8,400	9.19
Hispanic (124)	224	0.25
American Indian/Alaska Native (289)	841	0.92
Not Hispanic (248)	703	0.77
Hispanic (41)	138	0.15
Alaska Athabascan *(Ala. Nat.)* (0)	3	<0.01
Apache (1)	9	0.01
Blackfeet (3)	34	0.04
Canadian/French Am. Ind. (0)	3	<0.01
Central American Ind. (2)	2	<0.01
Cherokee (84)	257	0.28
Cheyenne (0)	1	<0.01
Chickasaw (3)	8	0.01
Chippewa (8)	15	0.02
Choctaw (27)	47	0.05
Comanche (2)	2	<0.01
Cree (0)	1	<0.01
Creek (4)	11	0.01
Crow (1)	1	<0.01
Delaware (1)	5	0.01
Iroquois (2)	6	0.01
Kiowa (0)	3	<0.01
Mexican American Ind. (15)	25	0.03
Navajo (3)	7	0.01
Osage (3)	11	0.01
Ottawa (1)	1	<0.01
Potawatomi (6)	13	0.01
Pueblo (3)	4	<0.01
Seminole (3)	5	0.01
Shoshone (0)	1	<0.01
Sioux (13)	29	0.03
South American Ind. (0)	5	0.01
Tlingit-Haida *(Alaska Native)* (1)	3	<0.01
Tohono O'Odham (1)	1	<0.01
Ute (2)	2	<0.01
Yaqui (0)	1	<0.01
Asian (1,535)	2,122	2.32
Not Hispanic (1,521)	2,082	2.28
Hispanic (14)	40	0.04
Bangladeshi (18)	20	0.02
Cambodian (45)	57	0.06
Chinese, ex. Taiwanese (321)	411	0.45
Filipino (171)	331	0.36
Hmong (11)	12	0.01
Indian (257)	303	0.33
Indonesian (4)	7	0.01
Japanese (46)	148	0.16
Korean (172)	244	0.27
Laotian (21)	37	0.04
Malaysian (4)	5	0.01
Nepalese (6)	6	0.01
Pakistani (88)	100	0.11
Sri Lankan (2)	7	0.01
Taiwanese (9)	22	0.02
Thai (16)	31	0.03
Vietnamese (284)	320	0.35
Hawaii Native/Pacific Islander (114)	222	0.24
Not Hispanic (109)	203	0.22
Hispanic (5)	19	0.02
Fijian (1)	1	<0.01
Guamanian/Chamorro (17)	28	0.03
Marshallese (2)	2	<0.01
Native Hawaiian (13)	65	0.07
Samoan (40)	65	0.07
Tongan (6)	8	0.01
White (78,634)	80,625	88.25
Not Hispanic (76,502)	78,166	85.55
Hispanic (2,132)	2,459	2.69

Lemay

Place Type: CDP
County: St. Louis
Population: 16,645†

Ancestry‡	Population	%
American (1,141)	1,141	7.17
Arab (106)	185	1.16
Arab (0)	50	0.31
Lebanese (13)	42	0.26
Other Arab (93)	93	0.58
Austrian (13)	47	0.30
British (14)	27	0.17
Canadian (72)	72	0.45
Croatian (25)	60	0.38
Czech (62)	182	1.14
Czechoslovakian (13)	13	0.08
Dutch (31)	233	1.46
English (389)	997	6.26
European (23)	36	0.23
French, ex. Basque (159)	1,289	8.09

*Notes: † The Census 2010 population figure is used to calculate the percentages in the Hispanic Origin and Race categories. Ancestry percentages are based on the 2006-2010 American Community Survey population (not shown); ‡ Numbers in parentheses indicate the number of people reporting a single ancestry; * Numbers in parentheses indicate the number of persons reporting this race alone, not in combination with any other race; Please refer to the Explanation of Data for more information.*

German (2,749)	6,314	39.65
Hungarian (10)	68	0.43
Irish (568)	2,449	15.38
Italian (505)	1,204	7.56
Lithuanian (13)	13	0.08
Norwegian (22)	77	0.48
Polish (195)	391	2.46
Russian (36)	59	0.37
Scandinavian (37)	189	1.19
Scotch-Irish (37)	118	0.74
Scottish (61)	214	1.34
Serbian (4)	16	0.10
Slovak (0)	10	0.06
Swedish (0)	75	0.47
Swiss (54)	70	0.44
Welsh (20)	91	0.57
Yugoslavian (1,559)	1,654	10.39

Hispanic Origin	Population	%
Hispanic or Latino (of any race)	517	3.11
Central American, ex. Mexican	15	0.09
Honduran	3	0.02
Nicaraguan	7	0.04
Panamanian	4	0.02
Salvadoran	1	0.01
Cuban	17	0.10
Dominican Republic	3	0.02
Mexican	378	2.27
Puerto Rican	27	0.16
South American	7	0.04
Bolivian	3	0.02
Colombian	2	0.01
Ecuadorian	2	0.01
Other Hispanic or Latino	70	0.42

Race*	Population	%
African-American/Black (288)	413	2.48
Not Hispanic (284)	396	2.38
Hispanic (4)	17	0.10
American Indian/Alaska Native (49)	129	0.78
Not Hispanic (43)	116	0.70
Hispanic (6)	13	0.08
Apache (0)	2	0.01
Blackfeet (3)	3	0.02
Central American Ind. (1)	1	0.01
Cherokee (23)	57	0.34
Cheyenne (0)	1	0.01
Chippewa (0)	1	0.01
Choctaw (1)	3	0.02
Creek (0)	3	0.02
Delaware (1)	1	0.01
Iroquois (4)	5	0.03
Mexican American Ind. (1)	1	0.01
Navajo (1)	5	0.03
Shoshone (1)	3	0.02
Sioux (0)	2	0.01
Tlingit-Haida *(Alaska Native)* (0)	3	0.02
Asian (278)	349	2.10
Not Hispanic (278)	348	2.09
Hispanic (0)	1	0.01
Cambodian (0)	1	0.01
Chinese, ex. Taiwanese (28)	34	0.20
Filipino (23)	45	0.27
Indian (10)	12	0.07
Japanese (6)	14	0.08
Korean (10)	22	0.13
Laotian (5)	5	0.03
Pakistani (1)	1	0.01
Thai (4)	4	0.02
Vietnamese (184)	189	1.14
Hawaii Native/Pacific Islander (6)	24	0.14
Not Hispanic (6)	24	0.14
Native Hawaiian (1)	2	0.01
Samoan (2)	2	0.01
White (15,581)	15,850	95.22
Not Hispanic (15,255)	15,497	93.10
Hispanic (326)	353	2.12

Liberty

Place Type: City
County: Clay
Population: 29,149†

Ancestry‡	Population	%
African, Sub-Saharan (84)	115	0.40
African (14)	45	0.16
Kenyan (15)	15	0.05
Other Sub-Saharan African (55)	55	0.19
American (3,229)	3,229	11.27
Arab (9)	9	0.03
Moroccan (9)	9	0.03
Austrian (0)	26	0.09
Basque (7)	7	0.02
Belgian (15)	71	0.25
British (129)	176	0.61
Canadian (26)	39	0.14
Czech (39)	269	0.94
Czechoslovakian (44)	60	0.21
Danish (64)	174	0.61
Dutch (222)	649	2.27
Eastern European (17)	42	0.15
English (1,248)	4,173	14.57
European (243)	271	0.95
French, ex. Basque (143)	608	2.12
French Canadian (41)	57	0.20
German (2,969)	8,353	29.16
Greek (13)	50	0.17
Hungarian (14)	57	0.20
Iranian (47)	47	0.16
Irish (1,396)	5,094	17.78
Italian (628)	1,385	4.84
Luxemburger (11)	11	0.04
Northern European (26)	26	0.09
Norwegian (69)	353	1.23
Polish (142)	578	2.02
Portuguese (18)	18	0.06
Russian (42)	83	0.29
Scandinavian (31)	31	0.11
Scotch-Irish (271)	887	3.10
Scottish (261)	850	2.97
Serbian (0)	18	0.06
Slovak (68)	79	0.28
Swedish (189)	823	2.87
Swiss (23)	103	0.36
Ukrainian (0)	16	0.06
Welsh (108)	255	0.89
West Indian, ex. Hispanic (0)	11	0.04
Haitian (0)	11	0.04
Yugoslavian (0)	10	0.03

Hispanic Origin	Population	%
Hispanic or Latino (of any race)	1,188	4.08
Central American, ex. Mexican	30	0.10
Costa Rican	3	0.01
Guatemalan	8	0.03
Honduran	8	0.03
Nicaraguan	2	0.01
Panamanian	7	0.02
Salvadoran	2	0.01
Cuban	18	0.06
Dominican Republic	11	0.04
Mexican	881	3.02
Puerto Rican	87	0.30
South American	43	0.15
Argentinean	3	0.01
Bolivian	3	0.01
Chilean	3	0.01
Colombian	3	0.01
Ecuadorian	6	0.02
Peruvian	24	0.08
Other South American	1	<0.01
Other Hispanic or Latino	118	0.40

Race*	Population	%
African-American/Black (1,038)	1,375	4.72
Not Hispanic (1,021)	1,313	4.50
Hispanic (17)	62	0.21
American Indian/Alaska Native (135)	381	1.31
Not Hispanic (124)	356	1.22
Hispanic (11)	25	0.09
Apache (0)	8	0.03
Blackfeet (3)	16	0.05
Cherokee (37)	121	0.42
Chickasaw (3)	3	0.01
Chippewa (2)	4	0.01
Choctaw (9)	19	0.07
Comanche (0)	4	0.01
Creek (1)	11	0.04
Crow (0)	2	0.01
Delaware (1)	4	0.01
Iroquois (4)	13	0.04
Kiowa (1)	1	<0.01
Menominee (1)	1	<0.01
Mexican American Ind. (3)	3	0.01
Navajo (4)	10	0.03
Osage (2)	6	0.02
Ottawa (0)	1	<0.01
Potawatomi (8)	15	0.05
Pueblo (0)	1	<0.01
Seminole (0)	9	0.03
Shoshone (3)	3	0.01
Sioux (2)	9	0.03
South American Ind. (1)	1	<0.01
Asian (285)	443	1.52
Not Hispanic (282)	430	1.48
Hispanic (3)	13	0.04
Cambodian (0)	2	0.01
Chinese, ex. Taiwanese (78)	103	0.35
Filipino (42)	91	0.31
Indian (35)	46	0.16
Japanese (17)	55	0.19
Korean (25)	49	0.17
Laotian (3)	6	0.02
Malaysian (0)	2	0.01
Nepalese (3)	3	0.01
Pakistani (9)	9	0.03
Sri Lankan (8)	8	0.03
Thai (16)	23	0.08
Vietnamese (36)	38	0.13
Hawaii Native/Pacific Islander (30)	61	0.21
Not Hispanic (27)	54	0.19
Hispanic (3)	7	0.02
Guamanian/Chamorro (13)	21	0.07
Native Hawaiian (8)	24	0.08
Samoan (2)	8	0.03
White (26,649)	27,353	93.84
Not Hispanic (25,836)	26,442	90.71
Hispanic (813)	911	3.13

Manchester

Place Type: City
County: St. Louis
Population: 18,094†

Ancestry‡	Population	%
African, Sub-Saharan (253)	253	1.39
Nigerian (239)	239	1.31
South African (14)	14	0.08
American (921)	921	5.06
Arab (130)	167	0.92
Arab (0)	12	0.07
Jordanian (93)	93	0.51
Lebanese (37)	53	0.29
Syrian (0)	9	0.05
Armenian (9)	24	0.13
Austrian (0)	104	0.57
Belgian (15)	48	0.26
Brazilian (0)	33	0.18
British (74)	86	0.47
Bulgarian (0)	22	0.12
Canadian (13)	13	0.07
Croatian (14)	55	0.30
Czech (58)	150	0.82
Danish (43)	75	0.41
Dutch (112)	461	2.53
English (575)	2,221	12.19

*Notes: † The Census 2010 population figure is used to calculate the percentages in the Hispanic Origin and Race categories. Ancestry percentages are based on the 2006-2010 American Community Survey population (not shown); ‡ Numbers in parentheses indicate the number of people reporting a single ancestry; * Numbers in parentheses indicate the number of persons reporting this race alone, not in combination with any other race; Please refer to the Explanation of Data for more information.*

European (141)	141	0.77
Finnish (0)	14	0.08
French, ex. Basque (68)	756	4.15
French Canadian (13)	13	0.07
German (2,375)	7,079	38.86
Greek (0)	63	0.35
Hungarian (20)	55	0.30
Irish (904)	3,627	19.91
Israeli (0)	12	0.07
Italian (315)	1,189	6.53
Lithuanian (15)	15	0.08
Norwegian (51)	249	1.37
Polish (282)	582	3.20
Romanian (15)	15	0.08
Russian (64)	174	0.96
Scandinavian (15)	97	0.53
Scotch-Irish (95)	327	1.80
Scottish (136)	459	2.52
Slovak (43)	102	0.56
Swedish (0)	402	2.21
Swiss (34)	65	0.36
Ukrainian (63)	90	0.49
Welsh (39)	186	1.02
Yugoslavian (97)	133	0.73

Hispanic Origin	Population	%
Hispanic or Latino (of any race)	525	2.90
Central American, ex. Mexican	31	0.17
Costa Rican	4	0.02
Guatemalan	7	0.04
Honduran	4	0.02
Nicaraguan	5	0.03
Panamanian	3	0.02
Salvadoran	8	0.04
Cuban	12	0.07
Dominican Republic	8	0.04
Mexican	329	1.82
Puerto Rican	27	0.15
South American	70	0.39
Argentinean	9	0.05
Bolivian	3	0.02
Chilean	8	0.04
Colombian	13	0.07
Ecuadorian	3	0.02
Peruvian	24	0.13
Uruguayan	2	0.01
Venezuelan	7	0.04
Other South American	1	0.01
Other Hispanic or Latino	48	0.27

Race*	Population	%
African-American/Black (565)	661	3.65
Not Hispanic (555)	645	3.56
Hispanic (10)	16	0.09
American Indian/Alaska Native (29)	119	0.66
Not Hispanic (22)	105	0.58
Hispanic (7)	14	0.08
Arapaho (1)	7	0.04
Blackfeet (0)	3	0.02
Canadian/French Am. Ind. (0)	1	0.01
Central American Ind. (1)	1	0.01
Cherokee (8)	27	0.15
Cheyenne (0)	1	0.01
Choctaw (2)	4	0.02
Comanche (1)	3	0.02
Creek (1)	2	0.01
Iroquois (0)	3	0.02
Mexican American Ind. (2)	5	0.03
Navajo (0)	1	0.01
Sioux (0)	2	0.01
South American Ind. (3)	3	0.02
Tlingit-Haida *(Alaska Native)* (1)	1	0.01
Asian (1,079)	1,283	7.09
Not Hispanic (1,078)	1,282	7.09
Hispanic (1)	1	0.01
Bangladeshi (24)	24	0.13
Burmese (5)	5	0.03
Cambodian (0)	1	0.01
Chinese, ex. Taiwanese (220)	246	1.36
Filipino (65)	100	0.55
Hmong (1)	1	0.01
Indian (427)	463	2.56
Japanese (13)	35	0.19
Korean (68)	102	0.56
Malaysian (11)	13	0.07
Nepalese (4)	4	0.02
Pakistani (155)	161	0.89
Sri Lankan (3)	3	0.02
Taiwanese (11)	11	0.06
Thai (6)	7	0.04
Vietnamese (32)	37	0.20
Hawaii Native/Pacific Islander (3)	9	0.05
Not Hispanic (3)	9	0.05
Native Hawaiian (2)	4	0.02
Samoan (1)	4	0.02
White (15,842)	16,205	89.56
Not Hispanic (15,543)	15,880	87.76
Hispanic (299)	325	1.80

Maplewood

Place Type: City
County: St. Louis
Population: 8,046†

Ancestry‡	Population	%
African, Sub-Saharan (32)	119	1.45
African (32)	73	0.89
Ethiopian (0)	46	0.56
American (258)	258	3.14
Arab (108)	119	1.45
Lebanese (0)	11	0.13
Moroccan (94)	94	1.14
Other Arab (14)	14	0.17
Austrian (24)	45	0.55
British (16)	66	0.80
Celtic (0)	11	0.13
Croatian (0)	12	0.15
Czech (34)	99	1.20
Danish (0)	7	0.09
Dutch (24)	98	1.19
Eastern European (14)	14	0.17
English (231)	901	10.95
European (51)	51	0.62
French, ex. Basque (49)	319	3.88
German (1,009)	2,645	32.15
Greek (37)	78	0.95
Hungarian (11)	44	0.53
Iranian (0)	26	0.32
Irish (235)	1,381	16.79
Italian (86)	400	4.86
Lithuanian (8)	19	0.23
Northern European (23)	23	0.28
Norwegian (18)	25	0.30
Polish (32)	173	2.10
Portuguese (0)	20	0.24
Romanian (18)	18	0.22
Russian (0)	51	0.62
Scandinavian (12)	26	0.32
Scotch-Irish (55)	207	2.52
Scottish (69)	120	1.46
Serbian (0)	63	0.77
Swedish (51)	92	1.12
Swiss (0)	59	0.72
Ukrainian (0)	15	0.18
Welsh (16)	71	0.86
West Indian, ex. Hispanic (9)	9	0.11
Jamaican (9)	9	0.11

Hispanic Origin	Population	%
Hispanic or Latino (of any race)	307	3.82
Central American, ex. Mexican	60	0.75
Guatemalan	11	0.14
Honduran	35	0.43
Nicaraguan	1	0.01
Panamanian	4	0.05
Salvadoran	9	0.11
Cuban	8	0.10
Dominican Republic	5	0.06
Mexican	163	2.03
Puerto Rican	20	0.25
South American	27	0.34
Argentinean	4	0.05
Bolivian	1	0.01
Colombian	8	0.10
Ecuadorian	4	0.05
Peruvian	10	0.12
Other Hispanic or Latino	24	0.30

Race*	Population	%
African-American/Black (1,384)	1,543	19.18
Not Hispanic (1,381)	1,532	19.04
Hispanic (3)	11	0.14
American Indian/Alaska Native (20)	99	1.23
Not Hispanic (16)	90	1.12
Hispanic (4)	9	0.11
Apache (1)	3	0.04
Blackfeet (0)	2	0.02
Cherokee (7)	38	0.47
Chickasaw (0)	2	0.02
Choctaw (1)	1	0.01
Comanche (0)	1	0.01
Creek (0)	1	0.01
Lumbee (1)	1	0.01
Sioux (0)	5	0.06
Yaqui (1)	1	0.01
Asian (279)	346	4.30
Not Hispanic (279)	342	4.25
Hispanic (0)	4	0.05
Burmese (2)	2	0.02
Chinese, ex. Taiwanese (142)	154	1.91
Filipino (11)	32	0.40
Hmong (0)	1	0.01
Indian (22)	32	0.40
Japanese (15)	26	0.32
Korean (23)	30	0.37
Laotian (5)	8	0.10
Malaysian (3)	4	0.05
Nepalese (2)	2	0.02
Pakistani (1)	1	0.01
Taiwanese (11)	13	0.16
Thai (5)	5	0.06
Vietnamese (23)	25	0.31
Hawaii Native/Pacific Islander (11)	20	0.25
Not Hispanic (11)	20	0.25
Fijian (1)	1	0.01
Guamanian/Chamorro (1)	1	0.01
Native Hawaiian (9)	9	0.11
Samoan (0)	2	0.02
White (5,966)	6,208	77.16
Not Hispanic (5,783)	6,005	74.63
Hispanic (183)	203	2.52

Marshall

Place Type: City
County: Saline
Population: 13,065†

Ancestry‡	Population	%
African, Sub-Saharan (70)	70	0.55
African (33)	33	0.26
Ghanaian (37)	37	0.29
American (904)	904	7.05
Arab (21)	39	0.30
Lebanese (0)	9	0.07
Syrian (21)	30	0.23
British (0)	9	0.07
Canadian (6)	6	0.05
Czech (18)	34	0.27
Czechoslovakian (0)	8	0.06
Dutch (11)	163	1.27
English (619)	1,689	13.17
European (280)	358	2.79
French, ex. Basque (18)	182	1.42
French Canadian (24)	43	0.34
German (1,423)	3,588	27.98
Hungarian (0)	21	0.16
Irish (640)	1,715	13.37
Italian (26)	117	0.91

*Notes: † The Census 2010 population figure is used to calculate the percentages in the Hispanic Origin and Race categories. Ancestry percentages are based on the 2006-2010 American Community Survey population (not shown); ‡ Numbers in parentheses indicate the number of people reporting a single ancestry; * Numbers in parentheses indicate the number of persons reporting this race alone, not in combination with any other race; Please refer to the Explanation of Data for more information.*

Norwegian (10)	75	0.58
Pennsylvania German (10)	10	0.08
Polish (56)	110	0.86
Portuguese (0)	9	0.07
Russian (8)	8	0.06
Scandinavian (21)	21	0.16
Scotch-Irish (84)	232	1.81
Scottish (25)	181	1.41
Serbian (12)	12	0.09
Swedish (0)	15	0.12
Swiss (5)	5	0.04
Welsh (26)	125	0.97
West Indian, ex. Hispanic (55)	64	0.50
Bahamian (55)	55	0.43
Dutch West Indian (0)	9	0.07

Hispanic Origin	Population	%
Hispanic or Latino (of any race)	1,723	13.19
Central American, ex. Mexican	817	6.25
Guatemalan	21	0.16
Honduran	21	0.16
Nicaraguan	22	0.17
Salvadoran	753	5.76
Cuban	4	0.03
Dominican Republic	2	0.02
Mexican	681	5.21
Puerto Rican	27	0.21
South American	17	0.13
Argentinean	3	0.02
Chilean	1	0.01
Colombian	2	0.02
Ecuadorian	6	0.05
Peruvian	1	0.01
Venezuelan	4	0.03
Other Hispanic or Latino	175	1.34

Race*	Population	%
African-American/Black (1,024)	1,225	9.38
Not Hispanic (1,008)	1,194	9.14
Hispanic (16)	31	0.24
American Indian/Alaska Native (52)	147	1.13
Not Hispanic (29)	114	0.87
Hispanic (23)	33	0.25
Apache (0)	2	0.02
Blackfeet (0)	1	0.01
Cherokee (3)	28	0.21
Cheyenne (1)	1	0.01
Choctaw (6)	9	0.07
Mexican American Ind. (10)	11	0.08
Navajo (3)	7	0.05
Osage (1)	1	0.01
Sioux (0)	12	0.09
Asian (92)	134	1.03
Not Hispanic (91)	127	0.97
Hispanic (1)	7	0.05
Cambodian (0)	2	0.02
Chinese, ex. Taiwanese (14)	21	0.16
Filipino (31)	44	0.34
Indian (18)	21	0.16
Indonesian (2)	2	0.02
Japanese (16)	23	0.18
Korean (3)	6	0.05
Pakistani (0)	1	0.01
Thai (2)	4	0.03
Vietnamese (5)	8	0.06
Hawaii Native/Pacific Islander (157)	177	1.35
Not Hispanic (151)	168	1.29
Hispanic (6)	9	0.07
Guamanian/Chamorro (13)	15	0.11
Native Hawaiian (13)	21	0.16
Samoan (5)	7	0.05
Tongan (3)	3	0.02
White (10,347)	10,702	81.91
Not Hispanic (9,740)	10,032	76.79
Hispanic (607)	670	5.13

Maryland Heights

Place Type: City
County: St. Louis
Population: 27,472†

Ancestry‡	Population	%
African, Sub-Saharan (81)	100	0.37
African (71)	71	0.26
Kenyan (10)	29	0.11
Albanian (93)	93	0.34
Alsatian (15)	15	0.05
American (1,171)	1,171	4.28
Arab (15)	15	0.05
Lebanese (15)	15	0.05
Australian (31)	31	0.11
Austrian (42)	95	0.35
Belgian (14)	28	0.10
Brazilian (0)	15	0.05
British (75)	183	0.67
Canadian (13)	33	0.12
Croatian (28)	109	0.40
Czech (25)	123	0.45
Czechoslovakian (0)	29	0.11
Danish (22)	34	0.12
Dutch (61)	263	0.96
Eastern European (12)	12	0.04
English (686)	3,137	11.46
European (224)	300	1.10
Finnish (0)	9	0.03
French, ex. Basque (53)	956	3.49
French Canadian (30)	75	0.27
German (3,168)	8,943	32.67
Greek (26)	98	0.36
Hungarian (47)	66	0.24
Irish (968)	4,395	16.05
Italian (400)	1,346	4.92
Lithuanian (0)	32	0.12
Maltese (0)	11	0.04
Norwegian (33)	139	0.51
Polish (83)	554	2.02
Portuguese (0)	45	0.16
Romanian (22)	22	0.08
Russian (186)	332	1.21
Scandinavian (0)	30	0.11
Scotch-Irish (177)	552	2.02
Scottish (75)	372	1.36
Serbian (14)	115	0.42
Slavic (14)	14	0.05
Slovak (0)	10	0.04
Slovene (0)	100	0.37
Swedish (61)	233	0.85
Swiss (0)	10	0.04
Turkish (16)	25	0.09
Ukrainian (71)	97	0.35
Welsh (23)	220	0.80
West Indian, ex. Hispanic (45)	152	0.56
Dutch West Indian (27)	27	0.10
Trinidadian/Tobagonian (18)	125	0.46
Yugoslavian (133)	147	0.54

Hispanic Origin	Population	%
Hispanic or Latino (of any race)	1,233	4.49
Central American, ex. Mexican	110	0.40
Costa Rican	6	0.02
Guatemalan	37	0.13
Honduran	28	0.10
Nicaraguan	9	0.03
Panamanian	15	0.05
Salvadoran	15	0.05
Cuban	18	0.07
Dominican Republic	12	0.04
Mexican	775	2.82
Puerto Rican	104	0.38
South American	106	0.39
Argentinean	11	0.04
Bolivian	5	0.02
Chilean	14	0.05
Colombian	26	0.09
Ecuadorian	13	0.05
Paraguayan	1	<0.01
Peruvian	17	0.06
Uruguayan	2	0.01
Venezuelan	17	0.06
Other Hispanic or Latino	108	0.39

Race*	Population	%
African-American/Black (3,262)	3,567	12.98
Not Hispanic (3,244)	3,505	12.76
Hispanic (18)	62	0.23
American Indian/Alaska Native (64)	192	0.70
Not Hispanic (55)	172	0.63
Hispanic (9)	20	0.07
Apache (0)	1	<0.01
Blackfeet (1)	12	0.04
Central American Ind. (0)	2	0.01
Cherokee (12)	57	0.21
Cheyenne (0)	1	<0.01
Chippewa (2)	3	0.01
Choctaw (7)	8	0.03
Comanche (0)	1	<0.01
Creek (1)	1	<0.01
Delaware (1)	1	<0.01
Iroquois (1)	1	<0.01
Kiowa (0)	2	0.01
Lumbee (3)	4	0.01
Mexican American Ind. (2)	3	0.01
Navajo (1)	1	<0.01
Osage (0)	2	0.01
Potawatomi (1)	1	<0.01
Seminole (0)	1	<0.01
Sioux (3)	8	0.03
Asian (2,696)	2,957	10.76
Not Hispanic (2,689)	2,941	10.71
Hispanic (7)	16	0.06
Bangladeshi (10)	11	0.04
Burmese (3)	6	0.02
Chinese, ex. Taiwanese (401)	453	1.65
Filipino (163)	214	0.78
Indian (1,540)	1,591	5.79
Indonesian (5)	6	0.02
Japanese (33)	63	0.23
Korean (208)	247	0.90
Laotian (5)	9	0.03
Malaysian (3)	4	0.01
Nepalese (11)	11	0.04
Pakistani (65)	70	0.25
Sri Lankan (5)	6	0.02
Taiwanese (37)	41	0.15
Thai (25)	34	0.12
Vietnamese (99)	119	0.43
Hawaii Native/Pacific Islander (13)	43	0.16
Not Hispanic (13)	39	0.14
Hispanic (0)	4	0.01
Fijian (1)	1	<0.01
Guamanian/Chamorro (0)	2	0.01
Native Hawaiian (1)	7	0.03
Samoan (8)	14	0.05
White (20,122)	20,671	75.24
Not Hispanic (19,613)	20,083	73.10
Hispanic (509)	588	2.14

Maryville

Place Type: City
County: Nodaway
Population: 11,972†

Ancestry‡	Population	%
African, Sub-Saharan (56)	65	0.56
African (29)	32	0.27
Nigerian (12)	12	0.10
Other Sub-Saharan African (15)	21	0.18
American (1,514)	1,514	12.95
Arab (0)	11	0.09
Other Arab (0)	11	0.09
Belgian (0)	13	0.11
Brazilian (11)	11	0.09
Canadian (13)	39	0.33
Croatian (0)	11	0.09

*Notes: † The Census 2010 population figure is used to calculate the percentages in the Hispanic Origin and Race categories. Ancestry percentages are based on the 2006-2010 American Community Survey population (not shown); ‡ Numbers in parentheses indicate the number of people reporting a single ancestry; * Numbers in parentheses indicate the number of persons reporting this race alone, not in combination with any other race; Please refer to the Explanation of Data for more information.*

SECTION TWO

Czech (0)	56	0.48
Czechoslovakian (8)	8	0.07
Danish (24)	72	0.62
Dutch (7)	131	1.12
English (313)	941	8.05
European (38)	38	0.32
French, ex. Basque (87)	275	2.35
French Canadian (0)	15	0.13
German (1,280)	3,992	34.13
Greek (0)	65	0.56
Hungarian (0)	24	0.21
Irish (381)	2,228	19.05
Italian (71)	396	3.39
Northern European (8)	8	0.07
Norwegian (41)	132	1.13
Polish (68)	286	2.45
Portuguese (9)	9	0.08
Russian (0)	15	0.13
Scandinavian (21)	59	0.50
Scotch-Irish (92)	141	1.21
Scottish (112)	384	3.28
Swedish (89)	239	2.04
Swiss (35)	124	1.06
Welsh (13)	87	0.74

Hispanic Origin	Population	%
Hispanic or Latino (of any race)	193	1.61
Central American, ex. Mexican	11	0.09
Guatemalan	2	0.02
Honduran	1	0.01
Nicaraguan	1	0.01
Panamanian	6	0.05
Salvadoran	1	0.01
Cuban	8	0.07
Dominican Republic	3	0.03
Mexican	140	1.17
Puerto Rican	8	0.07
South American	5	0.04
Bolivian	2	0.02
Colombian	1	0.01
Venezuelan	2	0.02
Other Hispanic or Latino	18	0.15

Race*	Population	%
African-American/Black (369)	428	3.58
Not Hispanic (366)	417	3.48
Hispanic (3)	11	0.09
American Indian/Alaska Native (29)	71	0.59
Not Hispanic (27)	67	0.56
Hispanic (2)	4	0.03
Apache (1)	1	0.01
Arapaho (1)	1	0.01
Blackfeet (1)	3	0.03
Cherokee (8)	19	0.16
Chickasaw (0)	1	0.01
Chippewa (1)	2	0.02
Choctaw (1)	1	0.01
Comanche (1)	1	0.01
Creek (0)	1	0.01
Iroquois (2)	2	0.02
Lumbee (0)	1	0.01
Mexican American Ind. (2)	2	0.02
Osage (0)	1	0.01
Potawatomi (0)	1	0.01
Sioux (0)	4	0.03
Asian (324)	368	3.07
Not Hispanic (323)	366	3.06
Hispanic (1)	2	0.02
Bangladeshi (7)	7	0.06
Cambodian (1)	1	0.01
Chinese, ex. Taiwanese (80)	91	0.76
Filipino (14)	30	0.25
Indian (111)	116	0.97
Indonesian (1)	2	0.02
Japanese (28)	35	0.29
Korean (58)	64	0.53
Laotian (0)	1	0.01
Nepalese (6)	6	0.05
Taiwanese (4)	4	0.03
Thai (0)	3	0.03
Vietnamese (7)	7	0.06
Hawaii Native/Pacific Islander (3)	10	0.08
Not Hispanic (3)	9	0.08
Hispanic (0)	1	0.01
Native Hawaiian (2)	5	0.04
Samoan (1)	4	0.03
White (11,052)	11,181	93.39
Not Hispanic (10,928)	11,041	92.22
Hispanic (124)	140	1.17

Mehlville

Place Type: CDP
County: St. Louis
Population: 28,380†

Ancestry‡	Population	%
Afghan (18)	18	0.07
Albanian (71)	84	0.31
American (992)	992	3.63
Arab (154)	294	1.07
Arab (85)	127	0.46
Jordanian (69)	69	0.25
Lebanese (0)	98	0.36
Austrian (50)	166	0.61
Belgian (0)	27	0.10
British (12)	59	0.22
Canadian (0)	12	0.04
Croatian (61)	109	0.40
Czech (105)	529	1.93
Czechoslovakian (21)	71	0.26
Danish (23)	63	0.23
Dutch (32)	386	1.41
English (713)	2,627	9.60
European (300)	346	1.26
Finnish (0)	32	0.12
French, ex. Basque (277)	1,434	5.24
French Canadian (12)	12	0.04
German (4,814)	11,617	42.45
Greek (27)	231	0.84
Hungarian (40)	121	0.44
Irish (1,267)	5,616	20.52
Italian (790)	1,871	6.84
Lithuanian (84)	95	0.35
Northern European (14)	14	0.05
Norwegian (45)	68	0.25
Polish (428)	1,022	3.73
Russian (21)	239	0.87
Scotch-Irish (103)	427	1.56
Scottish (141)	344	1.26
Serbian (78)	94	0.34
Slavic (16)	49	0.18
Slovak (11)	32	0.12
Slovene (0)	13	0.05
Swedish (108)	329	1.20
Swiss (22)	161	0.59
Turkish (162)	177	0.65
Welsh (11)	229	0.84
Yugoslavian (1,086)	1,206	4.41

Hispanic Origin	Population	%
Hispanic or Latino (of any race)	825	2.91
Central American, ex. Mexican	36	0.13
Guatemalan	16	0.06
Honduran	10	0.04
Nicaraguan	3	0.01
Panamanian	5	0.02
Salvadoran	2	0.01
Cuban	23	0.08
Dominican Republic	2	0.01
Mexican	586	2.06
Puerto Rican	42	0.15
South American	35	0.12
Argentinean	1	<0.01
Bolivian	6	0.02
Chilean	1	<0.01
Colombian	13	0.05
Ecuadorian	6	0.02
Peruvian	4	0.01
Uruguayan	2	0.01
Venezuelan	1	<0.01
Other South American	1	<0.01
Other Hispanic or Latino	101	0.36

Race*	Population	%
African-American/Black (856)	1,039	3.66
Not Hispanic (845)	1,007	3.55
Hispanic (11)	32	0.11
American Indian/Alaska Native (45)	132	0.47
Not Hispanic (34)	119	0.42
Hispanic (11)	13	0.05
Apache (1)	1	<0.01
Blackfeet (0)	10	0.04
Canadian/French Am. Ind. (0)	1	<0.01
Cherokee (12)	50	0.18
Chickasaw (2)	3	0.01
Chippewa (1)	2	0.01
Choctaw (5)	11	0.04
Inupiat *(Alaska Native)* (1)	1	<0.01
Kiowa (1)	1	<0.01
Lumbee (2)	2	0.01
Mexican American Ind. (5)	6	0.02
Navajo (1)	2	0.01
Osage (0)	1	<0.01
Potawatomi (1)	2	0.01
Sioux (3)	5	0.02
Asian (587)	725	2.55
Not Hispanic (581)	713	2.51
Hispanic (6)	12	0.04
Bangladeshi (2)	2	0.01
Cambodian (1)	3	0.01
Chinese, ex. Taiwanese (97)	113	0.40
Filipino (105)	135	0.48
Indian (63)	73	0.26
Japanese (4)	12	0.04
Korean (25)	41	0.14
Laotian (22)	26	0.09
Malaysian (2)	2	0.01
Nepalese (1)	1	<0.01
Pakistani (11)	15	0.05
Taiwanese (4)	6	0.02
Thai (12)	14	0.05
Vietnamese (221)	239	0.84
Hawaii Native/Pacific Islander (12)	30	0.11
Not Hispanic (11)	29	0.10
Hispanic (1)	1	<0.01
Guamanian/Chamorro (1)	1	<0.01
Native Hawaiian (2)	6	0.02
Samoan (4)	8	0.03
White (26,227)	26,652	93.91
Not Hispanic (25,674)	26,054	91.80
Hispanic (553)	598	2.11

Mexico

Place Type: City
County: Audrain
Population: 11,543†

Ancestry‡	Population	%
African, Sub-Saharan (28)	28	0.24
African (28)	28	0.24
American (2,032)	2,032	17.58
Arab (10)	40	0.35
Lebanese (10)	40	0.35
Belgian (0)	15	0.13
British (17)	36	0.31
Czech (8)	34	0.29
Danish (4)	4	0.03
Dutch (9)	135	1.17
English (404)	1,034	8.95
European (81)	81	0.70
French, ex. Basque (62)	267	2.31
French Canadian (0)	13	0.11
German (1,255)	2,632	22.77
Irish (429)	1,490	12.89
Italian (48)	125	1.08
Lithuanian (9)	21	0.18
Norwegian (9)	83	0.72
Polish (9)	46	0.40

*Notes: † The Census 2010 population figure is used to calculate the percentages in the Hispanic Origin and Race categories. Ancestry percentages are based on the 2006-2010 American Community Survey population (not shown); ‡ Numbers in parentheses indicate the number of people reporting a single ancestry; * Numbers in parentheses indicate the number of persons reporting this race alone, not in combination with any other race; Please refer to the Explanation of Data for more information.*

Russian (0)	30	0.26
Scotch-Irish (159)	308	2.66
Scottish (49)	300	2.60
Slavic (5)	5	0.04
Slovak (13)	18	0.16
Swedish (20)	30	0.26
Swiss (16)	38	0.33
Ukrainian (0)	8	0.07
Welsh (92)	156	1.35

Hispanic Origin	Population	%
Hispanic or Latino (of any race)	474	4.11
Central American, ex. Mexican	17	0.15
Guatemalan	1	0.01
Honduran	4	0.03
Nicaraguan	1	0.01
Panamanian	3	0.03
Salvadoran	8	0.07
Cuban	4	0.03
Mexican	391	3.39
Puerto Rican	18	0.16
South American	6	0.05
Argentinean	5	0.04
Venezuelan	1	0.01
Other Hispanic or Latino	38	0.33

Race*	Population	%
African-American/Black (960)	1,142	9.89
Not Hispanic (958)	1,136	9.84
Hispanic (2)	6	0.05
American Indian/Alaska Native (45)	98	0.85
Not Hispanic (43)	94	0.81
Hispanic (2)	4	0.03
Aleut *(Alaska Native)* (0)	2	0.02
Apache (1)	4	0.03
Blackfeet (1)	5	0.04
Cherokee (18)	32	0.28
Cheyenne (2)	2	0.02
Chickasaw (2)	2	0.02
Choctaw (0)	1	0.01
Creek (1)	1	0.01
Lumbee (0)	1	0.01
Osage (0)	1	0.01
Seminole (0)	1	0.01
Sioux (1)	4	0.03
South American Ind. (1)	1	0.01
Tlingit-Haida *(Alaska Native)* (0)	1	0.01
Yup'ik *(Alaska Native)* (0)	2	0.02
Asian (88)	124	1.07
Not Hispanic (88)	123	1.07
Hispanic (0)	1	0.01
Chinese, ex. Taiwanese (35)	35	0.30
Filipino (12)	21	0.18
Indian (16)	17	0.15
Japanese (1)	8	0.07
Korean (13)	25	0.22
Nepalese (4)	4	0.03
Pakistani (4)	4	0.03
Taiwanese (0)	1	0.01
Thai (2)	6	0.05
Hawaii Native/Pacific Islander (6)	11	0.10
Not Hispanic (2)	7	0.06
Hispanic (4)	4	0.03
Native Hawaiian (6)	7	0.06
White (9,933)	10,201	88.37
Not Hispanic (9,715)	9,963	86.31
Hispanic (218)	238	2.06

Moberly

Place Type: City
County: Randolph
Population: 13,974†

Ancestry‡	Population	%
African, Sub-Saharan (44)	44	0.31
African (44)	44	0.31
American (974)	974	6.93
Arab (109)	119	0.85
Arab (70)	70	0.50
Moroccan (18)	28	0.20
Palestinian (21)	21	0.15
Austrian (9)	21	0.15
Belgian (0)	7	0.05
British (42)	42	0.30
Cajun (0)	9	0.06
Czech (0)	54	0.38
Danish (6)	6	0.04
Dutch (117)	319	2.27
English (475)	1,037	7.38
European (9)	9	0.06
French, ex. Basque (52)	228	1.62
French Canadian (30)	56	0.40
German (1,975)	3,722	26.48
Greek (10)	10	0.07
Hungarian (0)	12	0.09
Irish (685)	2,082	14.81
Italian (53)	266	1.89
Northern European (15)	15	0.11
Norwegian (0)	49	0.35
Polish (7)	75	0.53
Portuguese (0)	17	0.12
Russian (0)	10	0.07
Scandinavian (0)	23	0.16
Scotch-Irish (86)	231	1.64
Scottish (70)	255	1.81
Swedish (17)	85	0.60
Swiss (0)	9	0.06
Welsh (22)	108	0.77

Hispanic Origin	Population	%
Hispanic or Latino (of any race)	299	2.14
Central American, ex. Mexican	12	0.09
Honduran	2	0.01
Panamanian	7	0.05
Salvadoran	3	0.02
Cuban	12	0.09
Mexican	217	1.55
Puerto Rican	18	0.13
South American	7	0.05
Chilean	1	0.01
Colombian	1	0.01
Paraguayan	4	0.03
Venezuelan	1	0.01
Other Hispanic or Latino	33	0.24

Race*	Population	%
African-American/Black (1,357)	1,574	11.26
Not Hispanic (1,347)	1,548	11.08
Hispanic (10)	26	0.19
American Indian/Alaska Native (49)	149	1.07
Not Hispanic (44)	125	0.89
Hispanic (5)	24	0.17
Apache (0)	3	0.02
Blackfeet (1)	9	0.06
Cherokee (15)	59	0.42
Chippewa (1)	4	0.03
Choctaw (3)	5	0.04
Inupiat *(Alaska Native)* (1)	1	0.01
Iroquois (0)	1	0.01
Menominee (0)	1	0.01
Mexican American Ind. (1)	4	0.03
Navajo (1)	6	0.04
Osage (2)	3	0.02
Potawatomi (2)	5	0.04
Seminole (1)	1	0.01
Sioux (1)	2	0.01
Tlingit-Haida *(Alaska Native)* (1)	1	0.01
Tohono O'Odham (1)	1	0.01
Asian (81)	127	0.91
Not Hispanic (81)	118	0.84
Hispanic (0)	9	0.06
Chinese, ex. Taiwanese (12)	17	0.12
Filipino (14)	32	0.23
Indian (17)	28	0.20
Indonesian (2)	2	0.01
Japanese (6)	18	0.13
Korean (4)	9	0.06
Pakistani (1)	1	0.01
Sri Lankan (1)	1	0.01
Taiwanese (3)	3	0.02
Thai (1)	5	0.04
Vietnamese (10)	11	0.08
Hawaii Native/Pacific Islander (2)	11	0.08
Not Hispanic (2)	10	0.07
Hispanic (0)	1	0.01
Native Hawaiian (0)	6	0.04
Samoan (0)	2	0.01
White (12,076)	12,416	88.85
Not Hispanic (11,876)	12,181	87.17
Hispanic (200)	235	1.68

Monett

Place Type: City
County: Barry
Population: 8,873†

Ancestry‡	Population	%
Albanian (54)	54	0.61
American (780)	780	8.86
Arab (0)	57	0.65
Lebanese (0)	57	0.65
Austrian (16)	16	0.18
British (8)	22	0.25
Czech (13)	55	0.63
Czechoslovakian (0)	19	0.22
Danish (7)	7	0.08
Dutch (7)	202	2.30
Eastern European (12)	12	0.14
English (294)	827	9.40
European (0)	8	0.09
French, ex. Basque (76)	377	4.28
German (486)	2,044	23.23
Hungarian (0)	11	0.13
Irish (311)	1,551	17.63
Italian (63)	390	4.43
Lithuanian (0)	19	0.22
Norwegian (3)	54	0.61
Polish (33)	68	0.77
Portuguese (0)	73	0.83
Russian (0)	20	0.23
Scotch-Irish (95)	181	2.06
Scottish (135)	303	3.44
Slovak (0)	31	0.35
Swedish (52)	88	1.00
Swiss (0)	76	0.86
Ukrainian (31)	31	0.35
Welsh (11)	66	0.75

Hispanic Origin	Population	%
Hispanic or Latino (of any race)	1,686	19.00
Central American, ex. Mexican	129	1.45
Guatemalan	107	1.21
Honduran	10	0.11
Panamanian	1	0.01
Salvadoran	11	0.12
Cuban	4	0.05
Mexican	1,450	16.34
Puerto Rican	22	0.25
South American	9	0.10
Bolivian	2	0.02
Colombian	4	0.05
Ecuadorian	1	0.01
Uruguayan	2	0.02
Other Hispanic or Latino	72	0.81

Race*	Population	%
African-American/Black (68)	102	1.15
Not Hispanic (42)	74	0.83
Hispanic (26)	28	0.32
American Indian/Alaska Native (77)	147	1.66
Not Hispanic (71)	133	1.50
Hispanic (6)	14	0.16
Aleut *(Alaska Native)* (1)	1	0.01
Blackfeet (0)	4	0.05
Central American Ind. (0)	1	0.01
Cherokee (28)	72	0.81
Chickasaw (0)	3	0.03
Choctaw (3)	5	0.06

SECTION TWO

*Notes: † The Census 2010 population figure is used to calculate the percentages in the Hispanic Origin and Race categories. Ancestry percentages are based on the 2006-2010 American Community Survey population (not shown); ‡ Numbers in parentheses indicate the number of people reporting a single ancestry; * Numbers in parentheses indicate the number of persons reporting this race alone, not in combination with any other race; Please refer to the Explanation of Data for more information.*

Comanche (1)	1	0.01
Creek (4)	4	0.05
Iroquois (1)	1	0.01
Mexican American Ind. (2)	3	0.03
Ottawa (1)	1	0.01
Sioux (2)	3	0.03
Ute (1)	1	0.01
Yaqui (1)	2	0.02
Asian (87)	115	1.30
Not Hispanic (82)	102	1.15
Hispanic (5)	13	0.15
Chinese, ex. Taiwanese (9)	13	0.15
Filipino (16)	31	0.35
Hmong (10)	10	0.11
Indian (19)	20	0.23
Japanese (7)	14	0.16
Korean (5)	7	0.08
Nepalese (3)	3	0.03
Taiwanese (2)	2	0.02
Thai (3)	4	0.05
Vietnamese (12)	14	0.16
Hawaii Native/Pacific Islander (9)	23	0.26
Not Hispanic (3)	11	0.12
Hispanic (6)	12	0.14
Guamanian/Chamorro (6)	6	0.07
Samoan (1)	10	0.11
White (7,705)	7,869	88.68
Not Hispanic (6,865)	6,980	78.67
Hispanic (840)	889	10.02

Murphy

Place Type: CDP
County: Jefferson
Population: 8,690†

Ancestry‡	Population	%
American (462)	462	5.18
Austrian (24)	24	0.27
Belgian (20)	20	0.22
Canadian (19)	19	0.21
Croatian (10)	25	0.28
Czech (27)	364	4.08
Czechoslovakian (0)	11	0.12
Danish (13)	13	0.15
Dutch (56)	174	1.95
English (362)	1,230	13.80
European (75)	75	0.84
French, ex. Basque (38)	416	4.67
French Canadian (32)	32	0.36
German (1,170)	3,391	38.05
Greek (6)	6	0.07
Hungarian (23)	23	0.26
Irish (140)	1,226	13.76
Italian (135)	424	4.76
Lithuanian (9)	9	0.10
Norwegian (27)	110	1.23
Polish (83)	197	2.21
Russian (0)	10	0.11
Scandinavian (0)	25	0.28
Scotch-Irish (48)	152	1.71
Scottish (84)	306	3.43
Swedish (0)	34	0.38
Swiss (0)	10	0.11

Hispanic Origin	Population	%
Hispanic or Latino (of any race)	208	2.39
Central American, ex. Mexican	8	0.09
Costa Rican	1	0.01
Honduran	6	0.07
Panamanian	1	0.01
Cuban	4	0.05
Mexican	148	1.70
Puerto Rican	19	0.22
South American	6	0.07
Bolivian	2	0.02
Colombian	1	0.01
Peruvian	3	0.03
Other Hispanic or Latino	23	0.26

Race*	Population	%
African-American/Black (81)	115	1.32
Not Hispanic (80)	114	1.31
Hispanic (1)	1	0.01
American Indian/Alaska Native (42)	121	1.39
Not Hispanic (34)	106	1.22
Hispanic (8)	15	0.17
Apache (4)	10	0.12
Blackfeet (0)	4	0.05
Cherokee (14)	26	0.30
Chickasaw (1)	1	0.01
Chippewa (1)	1	0.01
Choctaw (2)	4	0.05
Iroquois (2)	4	0.05
Kiowa (1)	1	0.01
Lumbee (1)	1	0.01
Navajo (1)	1	0.01
Potawatomi (1)	1	0.01
Seminole (0)	1	0.01
Sioux (1)	6	0.07
Asian (56)	93	1.07
Not Hispanic (56)	88	1.01
Hispanic (0)	5	0.06
Chinese, ex. Taiwanese (19)	27	0.31
Filipino (13)	33	0.38
Indian (5)	9	0.10
Japanese (0)	1	0.01
Korean (3)	4	0.05
Laotian (1)	1	0.01
Vietnamese (14)	14	0.16
Hawaii Native/Pacific Islander (4)	16	0.18
Not Hispanic (4)	14	0.16
Hispanic (0)	2	0.02
Guamanian/Chamorro (1)	10	0.12
Native Hawaiian (2)	2	0.02
White (8,279)	8,438	97.10
Not Hispanic (8,166)	8,299	95.50
Hispanic (113)	139	1.60

Neosho

Place Type: City
County: Newton
Population: 11,835†

Ancestry‡	Population	%
American (1,039)	1,039	8.87
Cajun (0)	14	0.12
Canadian (60)	77	0.66
Czech (0)	12	0.10
Danish (0)	23	0.20
Dutch (33)	207	1.77
English (436)	1,269	10.83
European (45)	62	0.53
French, ex. Basque (34)	597	5.09
French Canadian (55)	55	0.47
German (711)	2,090	17.83
Greek (19)	27	0.23
Hungarian (0)	28	0.24
Irish (444)	1,403	11.97
Italian (150)	325	2.77
Northern European (31)	40	0.34
Norwegian (73)	158	1.35
Pennsylvania German (9)	9	0.08
Polish (26)	169	1.44
Russian (43)	78	0.67
Scotch-Irish (82)	189	1.61
Scottish (7)	244	2.08
Slavic (0)	8	0.07
Swedish (40)	229	1.95
Welsh (12)	112	0.96

Hispanic Origin	Population	%
Hispanic or Latino (of any race)	1,337	11.30
Central American, ex. Mexican	327	2.76
Guatemalan	298	2.52
Honduran	6	0.05
Panamanian	2	0.02
Salvadoran	21	0.18
Cuban	5	0.04
Mexican	902	7.62
Puerto Rican	7	0.06
South American	4	0.03
Colombian	1	0.01
Ecuadorian	1	0.01
Venezuelan	2	0.02
Other Hispanic or Latino	92	0.78

Race*	Population	%
African-American/Black (118)	195	1.65
Not Hispanic (113)	185	1.56
Hispanic (5)	10	0.08
American Indian/Alaska Native (186)	363	3.07
Not Hispanic (182)	349	2.95
Hispanic (4)	14	0.12
Apache (2)	3	0.03
Blackfeet (0)	4	0.03
Cherokee (70)	144	1.22
Chickasaw (1)	3	0.03
Chippewa (0)	1	0.01
Choctaw (5)	6	0.05
Creek (1)	8	0.07
Delaware (2)	3	0.03
Iroquois (19)	27	0.23
Kiowa (0)	1	0.01
Mexican American Ind. (6)	8	0.07
Osage (0)	1	0.01
Ottawa (5)	5	0.04
Pima (1)	1	0.01
Potawatomi (1)	4	0.03
Pueblo (2)	2	0.02
Sioux (3)	6	0.05
South American Ind. (1)	1	0.01
Ute (0)	1	0.01
Yaqui (0)	1	0.01
Asian (103)	128	1.08
Not Hispanic (96)	118	1.00
Hispanic (7)	10	0.08
Cambodian (6)	6	0.05
Chinese, ex. Taiwanese (21)	24	0.20
Filipino (11)	21	0.18
Hmong (17)	18	0.15
Indian (6)	8	0.07
Japanese (5)	12	0.10
Korean (7)	9	0.08
Laotian (6)	6	0.05
Pakistani (1)	1	0.01
Taiwanese (3)	3	0.03
Thai (8)	9	0.08
Vietnamese (4)	11	0.09
Hawaii Native/Pacific Islander (284)	318	2.69
Not Hispanic (272)	303	2.56
Hispanic (12)	15	0.13
Guamanian/Chamorro (17)	18	0.15
Marshallese (1)	3	0.03
Native Hawaiian (13)	19	0.16
Samoan (1)	3	0.03
White (9,970)	10,273	86.80
Not Hispanic (9,554)	9,812	82.91
Hispanic (416)	461	3.90

Nevada

Place Type: City
County: Vernon
Population: 8,386†

Ancestry‡	Population	%
American (1,059)	1,059	12.97
Austrian (10)	10	0.12
British (0)	8	0.10
Danish (16)	16	0.20
Dutch (44)	243	2.98
English (453)	1,152	14.11
European (59)	72	0.88
French, ex. Basque (139)	471	5.77
French Canadian (82)	82	1.00
German (699)	2,347	28.75
Irish (191)	1,288	15.78
Italian (37)	129	1.58

*Notes: † The Census 2010 population figure is used to calculate the percentages in the Hispanic Origin and Race categories. Ancestry percentages are based on the 2006-2010 American Community Survey population (not shown); ‡ Numbers in parentheses indicate the number of people reporting a single ancestry; * Numbers in parentheses indicate the number of persons reporting this race alone, not in combination with any other race; Please refer to the Explanation of Data for more information.*

Ancestry	Population	%
Norwegian (0)	52	0.64
Pennsylvania German (40)	40	0.49
Polish (0)	65	0.80
Portuguese (21)	32	0.39
Russian (0)	85	1.04
Scotch-Irish (80)	249	3.05
Scottish (22)	156	1.91
Slovene (0)	19	0.23
Swedish (0)	28	0.34
Swiss (8)	29	0.36
Turkish (34)	34	0.42
Welsh (41)	59	0.72

Hispanic Origin	Population	%
Hispanic or Latino (of any race)	167	1.99
Central American, ex. Mexican	2	0.02
Honduran	2	0.02
Cuban	3	0.04
Dominican Republic	1	0.01
Mexican	127	1.51
Puerto Rican	7	0.08
South American	1	0.01
Ecuadorian	1	0.01
Other Hispanic or Latino	26	0.31

Race*	Population	%
African-American/Black (91)	121	1.44
Not Hispanic (89)	115	1.37
Hispanic (2)	6	0.07
American Indian/Alaska Native (67)	143	1.71
Not Hispanic (60)	130	1.55
Hispanic (7)	13	0.16
Aleut *(Alaska Native)* (1)	1	0.01
Apache (4)	7	0.08
Blackfeet (2)	3	0.04
Cherokee (15)	49	0.58
Chippewa (0)	1	0.01
Choctaw (1)	4	0.05
Creek (0)	1	0.01
Delaware (2)	2	0.02
Iroquois (1)	1	0.01
Navajo (0)	1	0.01
Osage (1)	4	0.05
Potawatomi (4)	4	0.05
Pueblo (0)	1	0.01
Shoshone (1)	1	0.01
Sioux (2)	5	0.06
Tohono O'Odham (1)	1	0.01
Asian (66)	85	1.01
Not Hispanic (66)	82	0.98
Hispanic (0)	3	0.04
Bangladeshi (4)	4	0.05
Bhutanese (1)	1	0.01
Chinese, ex. Taiwanese (14)	16	0.19
Filipino (6)	8	0.10
Indian (10)	14	0.17
Japanese (9)	11	0.13
Korean (3)	3	0.04
Sri Lankan (1)	2	0.02
Thai (3)	4	0.05
Vietnamese (14)	15	0.18
Hawaii Native/Pacific Islander (3)	5	0.06
Not Hispanic (3)	5	0.06
Samoan (2)	2	0.02
White (7,976)	8,098	96.57
Not Hispanic (7,884)	7,991	95.29
Hispanic (92)	107	1.28

Nixa

Place Type: City
County: Christian
Population: 19,022†

Ancestry‡	Population	%
American (4,111)	4,111	22.81
Arab (50)	50	0.28
Other Arab (50)	50	0.28
Austrian (6)	6	0.03
Belgian (0)	78	0.43
Brazilian (0)	44	0.24
British (49)	75	0.42
Cajun (27)	27	0.15
Canadian (7)	7	0.04
Czech (0)	90	0.50
Danish (18)	32	0.18
Dutch (41)	435	2.41
Eastern European (0)	12	0.07
English (869)	1,919	10.65
European (440)	440	2.44
Finnish (20)	55	0.31
French, ex. Basque (70)	563	3.12
French Canadian (64)	84	0.47
German (1,623)	4,369	24.24
Greek (26)	115	0.64
Hungarian (6)	27	0.15
Irish (719)	2,543	14.11
Italian (162)	600	3.33
Norwegian (86)	156	0.87
Pennsylvania German (9)	9	0.05
Polish (74)	302	1.68
Portuguese (18)	130	0.72
Russian (20)	86	0.48
Scandinavian (0)	10	0.06
Scotch-Irish (105)	239	1.33
Scottish (146)	452	2.51
Slavic (0)	9	0.05
Slovene (0)	12	0.07
Swedish (38)	225	1.25
Swiss (28)	38	0.21
Ukrainian (35)	64	0.36
Welsh (22)	122	0.68
West Indian, ex. Hispanic (93)	93	0.52
Haitian (93)	93	0.52
Yugoslavian (0)	9	0.05

Hispanic Origin	Population	%
Hispanic or Latino (of any race)	595	3.13
Central American, ex. Mexican	67	0.35
Costa Rican	2	0.01
Guatemalan	12	0.06
Honduran	6	0.03
Nicaraguan	5	0.03
Panamanian	2	0.01
Salvadoran	39	0.21
Other Central American	1	0.01
Cuban	24	0.13
Dominican Republic	3	0.02
Mexican	368	1.93
Puerto Rican	50	0.26
South American	25	0.13
Bolivian	1	0.01
Colombian	7	0.04
Peruvian	16	0.08
Venezuelan	1	0.01
Other Hispanic or Latino	58	0.30

Race*	Population	%
African-American/Black (175)	294	1.55
Not Hispanic (167)	278	1.46
Hispanic (8)	16	0.08
American Indian/Alaska Native (131)	322	1.69
Not Hispanic (114)	291	1.53
Hispanic (17)	31	0.16
Alaska Athabascan *(Ala. Nat.)* (0)	1	0.01
Apache (4)	4	0.02
Blackfeet (2)	7	0.04
Cherokee (37)	128	0.67
Chickasaw (0)	8	0.04
Chippewa (5)	7	0.04
Choctaw (10)	23	0.12
Comanche (0)	1	0.01
Creek (1)	3	0.02
Crow (0)	1	0.01
Delaware (1)	1	0.01
Iroquois (8)	10	0.05
Kiowa (1)	1	0.01
Mexican American Ind. (10)	12	0.06
Navajo (4)	5	0.03
Osage (3)	12	0.06
Pima (0)	1	0.01
Potawatomi (0)	2	0.01
Seminole (2)	2	0.01
Sioux (1)	10	0.05
Spanish American Ind. (2)	2	0.01
Asian (156)	248	1.30
Not Hispanic (152)	238	1.25
Hispanic (4)	10	0.05
Cambodian (7)	13	0.07
Chinese, ex. Taiwanese (7)	21	0.11
Filipino (44)	73	0.38
Hmong (6)	6	0.03
Indian (22)	32	0.17
Indonesian (2)	4	0.02
Japanese (4)	16	0.08
Korean (39)	56	0.29
Pakistani (1)	4	0.02
Sri Lankan (1)	1	0.01
Taiwanese (0)	1	0.01
Thai (2)	3	0.02
Vietnamese (14)	17	0.09
Hawaii Native/Pacific Islander (14)	33	0.17
Not Hispanic (11)	25	0.13
Hispanic (3)	8	0.04
Guamanian/Chamorro (4)	10	0.05
Native Hawaiian (1)	8	0.04
Samoan (4)	11	0.06
Tongan (1)	4	0.02
White (17,955)	18,353	96.48
Not Hispanic (17,625)	17,970	94.47
Hispanic (330)	383	2.01

O'Fallon

Place Type: City
County: St. Charles
Population: 79,329†

Ancestry‡	Population	%
African, Sub-Saharan (276)	332	0.44
African (276)	323	0.43
Zimbabwean (0)	9	0.01
Albanian (32)	51	0.07
American (5,359)	5,359	7.17
Arab (269)	403	0.54
Arab (138)	138	0.18
Lebanese (22)	121	0.16
Palestinian (104)	104	0.14
Syrian (5)	5	0.01
Other Arab (0)	35	0.05
Armenian (15)	111	0.15
Australian (16)	16	0.02
Austrian (0)	206	0.28
Basque (0)	26	0.03
Belgian (3)	52	0.07
Brazilian (38)	124	0.17
British (92)	349	0.47
Cajun (11)	11	0.01
Canadian (18)	58	0.08
Croatian (47)	138	0.18
Czech (107)	427	0.57
Czechoslovakian (75)	170	0.23
Danish (96)	328	0.44
Dutch (216)	1,344	1.80
English (2,293)	8,303	11.10
European (860)	1,068	1.43
Finnish (14)	100	0.13
French, ex. Basque (569)	3,535	4.73
French Canadian (145)	431	0.58
German (11,859)	29,723	39.75
Greek (68)	323	0.43
Hungarian (71)	160	0.21
Icelander (0)	42	0.06
Irish (3,073)	14,694	19.65
Italian (1,817)	5,841	7.81
Latvian (16)	16	0.02
Lithuanian (13)	42	0.06
Macedonian (6)	18	0.02
New Zealander (14)	53	0.07
Northern European (45)	45	0.06

SECTION TWO

*Notes: † The Census 2010 population figure is used to calculate the percentages in the Hispanic Origin and Race categories. Ancestry percentages are based on the 2006-2010 American Community Survey population (not shown); ‡ Numbers in parentheses indicate the number of people reporting a single ancestry; * Numbers in parentheses indicate the number of persons reporting this race alone, not in combination with any other race; Please refer to the Explanation of Data for more information.*

Norwegian (158)	720	0.96
Polish (644)	2,540	3.40
Portuguese (0)	40	0.05
Romanian (81)	117	0.16
Russian (145)	286	0.38
Scandinavian (46)	131	0.18
Scotch-Irish (422)	1,487	1.99
Scottish (410)	1,320	1.77
Slavic (8)	40	0.05
Slovak (32)	109	0.15
Swedish (167)	958	1.28
Swiss (117)	409	0.55
Turkish (45)	45	0.06
Ukrainian (26)	104	0.14
Welsh (161)	578	0.77
Yugoslavian (25)	68	0.09

Hispanic Origin	Population	%
Hispanic or Latino (of any race)	2,159	2.72
Central American, ex. Mexican	128	0.16
Costa Rican	1	<0.01
Guatemalan	46	0.06
Honduran	22	0.03
Nicaraguan	8	0.01
Panamanian	16	0.02
Salvadoran	35	0.04
Cuban	66	0.08
Dominican Republic	6	0.01
Mexican	1,347	1.70
Puerto Rican	189	0.24
South American	215	0.27
Argentinean	19	0.02
Bolivian	3	<0.01
Chilean	21	0.03
Colombian	62	0.08
Ecuadorian	37	0.05
Peruvian	37	0.05
Uruguayan	4	0.01
Venezuelan	32	0.04
Other Hispanic or Latino	208	0.26

Race*	Population	%
African-American/Black (3,164)	3,751	4.73
Not Hispanic (3,135)	3,684	4.64
Hispanic (29)	67	0.08
American Indian/Alaska Native (197)	547	0.69
Not Hispanic (162)	483	0.61
Hispanic (35)	64	0.08
Apache (7)	16	0.02
Arapaho (0)	1	<0.01
Blackfeet (5)	20	0.03
Cherokee (39)	163	0.21
Chickasaw (4)	4	0.01
Chippewa (2)	6	0.01
Choctaw (4)	22	0.03
Creek (4)	6	0.01
Crow (9)	10	0.01
Delaware (0)	5	0.01
Houma (3)	4	0.01
Iroquois (5)	7	0.01
Lumbee (2)	3	<0.01
Mexican American Ind. (10)	14	0.02
Navajo (3)	6	0.01
Osage (2)	5	0.01
Potawatomi (1)	4	0.01
Pueblo (1)	1	<0.01
Seminole (0)	3	<0.01
Shoshone (1)	1	<0.01
Sioux (3)	8	0.01
South American Ind. (4)	7	0.01
Spanish American Ind. (4)	5	0.01
Yaqui (0)	2	<0.01
Asian (2,499)	2,971	3.75
Not Hispanic (2,485)	2,943	3.71
Hispanic (14)	28	0.04
Bangladeshi (5)	6	0.01
Cambodian (5)	7	0.01
Chinese, ex. Taiwanese (323)	390	0.49
Filipino (201)	366	0.46
Indian (1,210)	1,257	1.58
Indonesian (7)	7	0.01
Japanese (29)	96	0.12
Korean (206)	290	0.37
Laotian (11)	12	0.02
Malaysian (8)	11	0.01
Nepalese (4)	4	0.01
Pakistani (84)	91	0.11
Sri Lankan (4)	4	0.01
Taiwanese (17)	21	0.03
Thai (20)	31	0.04
Vietnamese (274)	313	0.39
Hawaii Native/Pacific Islander (44)	77	0.10
Not Hispanic (40)	71	0.09
Hispanic (4)	6	0.01
Guamanian/Chamorro (14)	16	0.02
Native Hawaiian (12)	27	0.03
Samoan (8)	12	0.02
White (71,315)	72,663	91.60
Not Hispanic (69,979)	71,166	89.71
Hispanic (1,336)	1,497	1.89

Oak Grove

Place Type: City
County: Jackson
Population: 7,795†

Ancestry‡	Population	%
American (504)	504	6.81
Czech (0)	36	0.49
Danish (0)	22	0.30
Dutch (79)	182	2.46
English (420)	1,253	16.93
European (40)	112	1.51
French, ex. Basque (12)	236	3.19
French Canadian (21)	21	0.28
German (710)	2,305	31.15
Irish (383)	1,471	19.88
Italian (201)	445	6.01
Norwegian (0)	50	0.68
Polish (32)	231	3.12
Scotch-Irish (19)	175	2.36
Scottish (71)	146	1.97
Serbian (0)	10	0.14
Swedish (13)	84	1.14
Swiss (11)	41	0.55
Ukrainian (0)	19	0.26
Welsh (12)	22	0.30

Hispanic Origin	Population	%
Hispanic or Latino (of any race)	286	3.67
Central American, ex. Mexican	4	0.05
Guatemalan	1	0.01
Panamanian	2	0.03
Salvadoran	1	0.01
Cuban	3	0.04
Mexican	228	2.92
Puerto Rican	15	0.19
South American	9	0.12
Argentinean	1	0.01
Colombian	4	0.05
Peruvian	4	0.05
Other Hispanic or Latino	27	0.35

Race*	Population	%
African-American/Black (87)	132	1.69
Not Hispanic (82)	120	1.54
Hispanic (5)	12	0.15
American Indian/Alaska Native (63)	115	1.48
Not Hispanic (55)	103	1.32
Hispanic (8)	12	0.15
Alaska Athabascan *(Ala. Nat.)* (1)	1	0.01
Apache (0)	2	0.03
Blackfeet (0)	5	0.06
Canadian/French Am. Ind. (0)	1	0.01
Cherokee (22)	51	0.65
Chickasaw (3)	3	0.04
Chippewa (4)	5	0.06
Choctaw (3)	6	0.08
Creek (2)	2	0.03
Mexican American Ind. (0)	1	0.01
Potawatomi (1)	3	0.04
Seminole (3)	3	0.04
Sioux (3)	4	0.05
Asian (56)	83	1.06
Not Hispanic (54)	75	0.96
Hispanic (2)	8	0.10
Chinese, ex. Taiwanese (19)	20	0.26
Filipino (17)	26	0.33
Indian (13)	14	0.18
Japanese (3)	6	0.08
Korean (1)	9	0.12
Taiwanese (1)	2	0.03
Vietnamese (2)	6	0.08
Hawaii Native/Pacific Islander (9)	19	0.24
Not Hispanic (9)	19	0.24
Native Hawaiian (1)	1	0.01
Samoan (7)	17	0.22
White (7,379)	7,513	96.38
Not Hispanic (7,195)	7,307	93.74
Hispanic (184)	206	2.64

Oakville

Place Type: CDP
County: St. Louis
Population: 36,143†

Ancestry‡	Population	%
Afghan (16)	16	0.05
Albanian (0)	45	0.13
American (1,946)	1,946	5.52
Arab (50)	126	0.36
Arab (28)	28	0.08
Lebanese (22)	98	0.28
Armenian (0)	14	0.04
Austrian (36)	282	0.80
Belgian (23)	31	0.09
British (39)	138	0.39
Canadian (27)	69	0.20
Croatian (66)	349	0.99
Czech (126)	540	1.53
Czechoslovakian (20)	50	0.14
Danish (31)	46	0.13
Dutch (97)	698	1.98
English (857)	3,471	9.85
European (306)	330	0.94
French, ex. Basque (287)	2,829	8.02
French Canadian (0)	93	0.26
German (7,942)	18,478	52.42
Greek (47)	273	0.77
Hungarian (87)	328	0.93
Irish (1,012)	6,528	18.52
Italian (715)	2,836	8.04
Lithuanian (31)	62	0.18
Northern European (32)	32	0.09
Norwegian (39)	183	0.52
Polish (585)	1,633	4.63
Portuguese (10)	31	0.09
Romanian (57)	131	0.37
Russian (84)	238	0.68
Scotch-Irish (186)	628	1.78
Scottish (238)	630	1.79
Serbian (56)	56	0.16
Slavic (0)	28	0.08
Slovak (0)	140	0.40
Swedish (70)	398	1.13
Swiss (0)	226	0.64
Ukrainian (36)	77	0.22
Welsh (10)	111	0.31
Yugoslavian (177)	196	0.56

Hispanic Origin	Population	%
Hispanic or Latino (of any race)	518	1.43
Central American, ex. Mexican	36	0.10
Costa Rican	1	<0.01
Guatemalan	21	0.06
Honduran	8	0.02
Nicaraguan	1	<0.01
Panamanian	2	0.01

*Notes: † The Census 2010 population figure is used to calculate the percentages in the Hispanic Origin and Race categories. Ancestry percentages are based on the 2006-2010 American Community Survey population (not shown); ‡ Numbers in parentheses indicate the number of people reporting a single ancestry; * Numbers in parentheses indicate the number of persons reporting this race alone, not in combination with any other race; Please refer to the Explanation of Data for more information.*

Salvadoran	3	0.01
Cuban	25	0.07
Dominican Republic	9	0.02
Mexican	265	0.73
Puerto Rican	38	0.11
South American	37	0.10
Argentinean	2	0.01
Bolivian	1	<0.01
Colombian	15	0.04
Ecuadorian	6	0.02
Peruvian	11	0.03
Venezuelan	2	0.01
Other Hispanic or Latino	108	0.30

Race*	Population	%
African-American/Black (296)	421	1.16
Not Hispanic (294)	411	1.14
Hispanic (2)	10	0.03
American Indian/Alaska Native (35)	124	0.34
Not Hispanic (33)	120	0.33
Hispanic (2)	4	0.01
Blackfeet (0)	2	0.01
Cherokee (14)	51	0.14
Chickasaw (2)	3	0.01
Choctaw (0)	5	0.01
Delaware (2)	2	0.01
Inupiat *(Alaska Native)* (0)	1	<0.01
Iroquois (4)	4	0.01
Lumbee (2)	2	0.01
Menominee (0)	1	<0.01
Mexican American Ind. (1)	1	<0.01
Potawatomi (0)	1	<0.01
Sioux (0)	4	0.01
Ute (4)	4	0.01
Asian (633)	800	2.21
Not Hispanic (623)	786	2.17
Hispanic (10)	14	0.04
Bangladeshi (1)	3	0.01
Cambodian (5)	5	0.01
Chinese, ex. Taiwanese (98)	123	0.34
Filipino (100)	140	0.39
Indian (66)	76	0.21
Indonesian (3)	5	0.01
Japanese (9)	31	0.09
Korean (34)	58	0.16
Laotian (21)	22	0.06
Pakistani (18)	21	0.06
Sri Lankan (3)	3	0.01
Taiwanese (11)	11	0.03
Thai (10)	15	0.04
Vietnamese (205)	229	0.63
Hawaii Native/Pacific Islander (5)	17	0.05
Not Hispanic (5)	16	0.04
Hispanic (0)	1	<0.01
Fijian (0)	1	<0.01
Native Hawaiian (0)	3	0.01
Samoan (1)	1	<0.01
White (34,680)	35,030	96.92
Not Hispanic (34,297)	34,623	95.79
Hispanic (383)	407	1.13

Old Jamestown

Place Type: CDP
County: St. Louis
Population: 19,184†

Ancestry‡	Population	%
African, Sub-Saharan (1,148)	1,189	5.80
African (943)	967	4.72
Ghanaian (18)	35	0.17
Kenyan (63)	63	0.31
Nigerian (88)	88	0.43
Ugandan (36)	36	0.18
American (668)	668	3.26
Arab (30)	30	0.15
Arab (30)	30	0.15
Austrian (0)	52	0.25
British (8)	23	0.11
Canadian (0)	20	0.10
Croatian (10)	38	0.19
Czech (11)	152	0.74
Dutch (15)	181	0.88
English (343)	1,449	7.07
European (149)	149	0.73
Finnish (0)	18	0.09
French, ex. Basque (83)	569	2.77
German (1,548)	3,806	18.56
German Russian (0)	18	0.09
Greek (0)	11	0.05
Hungarian (0)	35	0.17
Irish (408)	1,797	8.76
Italian (487)	899	4.38
Northern European (78)	78	0.38
Norwegian (47)	74	0.36
Polish (169)	472	2.30
Portuguese (0)	15	0.07
Russian (14)	54	0.26
Scandinavian (0)	21	0.10
Scotch-Irish (75)	244	1.19
Scottish (134)	172	0.84
Slavic (0)	7	0.03
Slovak (24)	24	0.12
Swedish (12)	76	0.37
Swiss (0)	87	0.42
Welsh (16)	87	0.42
West Indian, ex. Hispanic (125)	125	0.61
Haitian (49)	49	0.24
Jamaican (58)	58	0.28
West Indian (18)	18	0.09

Hispanic Origin	Population	%
Hispanic or Latino (of any race)	275	1.43
Central American, ex. Mexican	24	0.13
Guatemalan	8	0.04
Panamanian	15	0.08
Salvadoran	1	0.01
Cuban	8	0.04
Dominican Republic	7	0.04
Mexican	149	0.78
Puerto Rican	33	0.17
South American	30	0.16
Chilean	4	0.02
Colombian	8	0.04
Ecuadorian	7	0.04
Peruvian	4	0.02
Venezuelan	5	0.03
Other South American	2	0.01
Other Hispanic or Latino	24	0.13

Race*	Population	%
African-American/Black (10,302)	10,576	55.13
Not Hispanic (10,253)	10,510	54.79
Hispanic (49)	66	0.34
American Indian/Alaska Native (27)	132	0.69
Not Hispanic (23)	116	0.60
Hispanic (4)	16	0.08
Apache (0)	4	0.02
Blackfeet (0)	12	0.06
Canadian/French Am. Ind. (0)	1	0.01
Cherokee (2)	26	0.14
Choctaw (0)	5	0.03
Cree (0)	1	0.01
Creek (0)	5	0.03
Iroquois (1)	1	0.01
Mexican American Ind. (0)	3	0.02
Navajo (2)	2	0.01
Seminole (0)	1	0.01
South American Ind. (1)	1	0.01
Asian (338)	399	2.08
Not Hispanic (336)	395	2.06
Hispanic (2)	4	0.02
Chinese, ex. Taiwanese (87)	121	0.63
Filipino (40)	48	0.25
Indian (60)	74	0.39
Japanese (4)	13	0.07
Korean (8)	20	0.10
Pakistani (11)	11	0.06
Thai (4)	5	0.03
Vietnamese (91)	104	0.54
Hawaii Native/Pacific Islander (11)	22	0.11
Not Hispanic (11)	22	0.11
Fijian (1)	2	0.01
Guamanian/Chamorro (1)	4	0.02
Native Hawaiian (4)	9	0.05
White (8,045)	8,286	43.19
Not Hispanic (7,928)	8,154	42.50
Hispanic (117)	132	0.69

Olivette

Place Type: City
County: St. Louis
Population: 7,737†

Ancestry‡	Population	%
African, Sub-Saharan (188)	188	2.45
African (162)	162	2.11
Ethiopian (26)	26	0.34
American (282)	282	3.68
Arab (0)	9	0.12
Moroccan (0)	9	0.12
Austrian (0)	68	0.89
British (10)	34	0.44
Bulgarian (57)	57	0.74
Canadian (9)	9	0.12
Czech (0)	11	0.14
Czechoslovakian (24)	67	0.87
Dutch (26)	62	0.81
Eastern European (49)	49	0.64
English (154)	635	8.29
European (155)	155	2.02
French, ex. Basque (20)	221	2.89
French Canadian (12)	12	0.16
German (491)	1,491	19.46
Greek (11)	31	0.40
Hungarian (17)	38	0.50
Iranian (22)	22	0.29
Irish (65)	545	7.11
Israeli (0)	10	0.13
Italian (24)	59	0.77
Latvian (0)	30	0.39
Lithuanian (10)	60	0.78
Northern European (33)	33	0.43
Norwegian (18)	73	0.95
Polish (188)	349	4.56
Portuguese (10)	10	0.13
Romanian (9)	37	0.48
Russian (363)	608	7.94
Scandinavian (0)	10	0.13
Scotch-Irish (45)	221	2.89
Scottish (20)	138	1.80
Serbian (25)	25	0.33
Slovak (0)	9	0.12
Swedish (7)	58	0.76
Swiss (19)	39	0.51
Ukrainian (45)	64	0.84
Welsh (0)	114	1.49
West Indian, ex. Hispanic (15)	15	0.20
Jamaican (15)	15	0.20

Hispanic Origin	Population	%
Hispanic or Latino (of any race)	258	3.33
Central American, ex. Mexican	34	0.44
Costa Rican	1	0.01
Guatemalan	23	0.30
Honduran	8	0.10
Panamanian	1	0.01
Salvadoran	1	0.01
Cuban	9	0.12
Mexican	122	1.58
Puerto Rican	20	0.26
South American	44	0.57
Argentinean	12	0.16
Chilean	3	0.04
Colombian	16	0.21
Ecuadorian	2	0.03
Peruvian	9	0.12
Venezuelan	2	0.03
Other Hispanic or Latino	29	0.37

*Notes: † The Census 2010 population figure is used to calculate the percentages in the Hispanic Origin and Race categories. Ancestry percentages are based on the 2006-2010 American Community Survey population (not shown); ‡ Numbers in parentheses indicate the number of people reporting a single ancestry; * Numbers in parentheses indicate the number of persons reporting this race alone, not in combination with any other race; Please refer to the Explanation of Data for more information.*

Race*	Population	%
African-American/Black (1,848)	1,964	25.38
Not Hispanic (1,839)	1,944	25.13
Hispanic (9)	20	0.26
American Indian/Alaska Native (18)	65	0.84
Not Hispanic (13)	57	0.74
Hispanic (5)	8	0.10
Blackfeet (0)	1	0.01
Central American Ind. (2)	2	0.03
Cherokee (2)	21	0.27
Chickasaw (5)	6	0.08
Choctaw (1)	4	0.05
Creek (0)	4	0.05
Iroquois (0)	1	0.01
Mexican American Ind. (2)	2	0.03
Paiute (1)	1	0.01
Asian (826)	898	11.61
Not Hispanic (824)	893	11.54
Hispanic (2)	5	0.06
Cambodian (1)	1	0.01
Chinese, ex. Taiwanese (389)	411	5.31
Filipino (27)	45	0.58
Indian (237)	254	3.28
Indonesian (1)	1	0.01
Japanese (24)	31	0.40
Korean (68)	76	0.98
Malaysian (1)	1	0.01
Nepalese (4)	4	0.05
Pakistani (5)	6	0.08
Taiwanese (15)	21	0.27
Thai (3)	3	0.04
Vietnamese (36)	38	0.49
Hawaii Native/Pacific Islander (3)	5	0.06
Not Hispanic (3)	5	0.06
Native Hawaiian (3)	4	0.05
White (4,715)	4,880	63.07
Not Hispanic (4,606)	4,759	61.51
Hispanic (109)	121	1.56

Overland

Place Type: City
County: St. Louis
Population: 16,062†

Ancestry‡	Population	%
African, Sub-Saharan (183)	390	2.41
African (152)	341	2.11
Ethiopian (31)	49	0.30
Alsatian (0)	11	0.07
American (1,497)	1,497	9.26
Arab (0)	46	0.28
Arab (0)	18	0.11
Lebanese (0)	28	0.17
Austrian (0)	15	0.09
Brazilian (11)	11	0.07
British (33)	79	0.49
Canadian (19)	19	0.12
Celtic (18)	52	0.32
Croatian (29)	100	0.62
Czech (0)	31	0.19
Danish (0)	48	0.30
Dutch (23)	305	1.89
English (284)	1,219	7.54
European (130)	130	0.80
Finnish (0)	27	0.17
French, ex. Basque (73)	834	5.16
French Canadian (0)	11	0.07
German (1,492)	5,434	33.62
Greek (10)	10	0.06
Hungarian (24)	65	0.40
Iranian (37)	37	0.23
Irish (607)	3,392	20.99
Israeli (22)	58	0.36
Italian (374)	907	5.61
Lithuanian (10)	19	0.12
Norwegian (39)	70	0.43
Pennsylvania German (14)	14	0.09
Polish (87)	382	2.36
Portuguese (0)	13	0.08
Romanian (52)	52	0.32
Russian (93)	199	1.23
Scotch-Irish (63)	265	1.64
Scottish (136)	288	1.78
Slovak (66)	95	0.59
Swedish (39)	271	1.68
Swiss (42)	147	0.91
Turkish (0)	10	0.06
Ukrainian (24)	24	0.15
Welsh (0)	68	0.42
West Indian, ex. Hispanic (0)	12	0.07
Jamaican (0)	12	0.07
Yugoslavian (0)	11	0.07

Hispanic Origin	Population	%
Hispanic or Latino (of any race)	1,027	6.39
Central American, ex. Mexican	89	0.55
Guatemalan	19	0.12
Honduran	17	0.11
Nicaraguan	11	0.07
Panamanian	8	0.05
Salvadoran	34	0.21
Cuban	26	0.16
Dominican Republic	7	0.04
Mexican	760	4.73
Puerto Rican	28	0.17
South American	28	0.17
Argentinean	1	0.01
Bolivian	13	0.08
Chilean	1	0.01
Colombian	7	0.04
Ecuadorian	1	0.01
Peruvian	2	0.01
Uruguayan	1	0.01
Venezuelan	2	0.01
Other Hispanic or Latino	89	0.55

Race*	Population	%
African-American/Black (2,628)	2,927	18.22
Not Hispanic (2,590)	2,867	17.85
Hispanic (38)	60	0.37
American Indian/Alaska Native (49)	164	1.02
Not Hispanic (39)	139	0.87
Hispanic (10)	25	0.16
Apache (1)	1	0.01
Arapaho (0)	4	0.02
Blackfeet (0)	5	0.03
Cherokee (7)	47	0.29
Cheyenne (1)	1	0.01
Chickasaw (1)	3	0.02
Chippewa (0)	2	0.01
Choctaw (1)	10	0.06
Delaware (0)	1	0.01
Hopi (0)	3	0.02
Iroquois (4)	4	0.02
Mexican American Ind. (0)	3	0.02
Navajo (0)	1	0.01
Sioux (4)	4	0.02
Asian (518)	600	3.74
Not Hispanic (510)	586	3.65
Hispanic (8)	14	0.09
Bangladeshi (0)	2	0.01
Cambodian (1)	1	0.01
Chinese, ex. Taiwanese (101)	119	0.74
Filipino (100)	125	0.78
Indian (57)	64	0.40
Indonesian (0)	3	0.02
Japanese (4)	15	0.09
Korean (21)	36	0.22
Laotian (0)	4	0.02
Nepalese (1)	1	0.01
Pakistani (7)	7	0.04
Taiwanese (1)	1	0.01
Thai (7)	7	0.04
Vietnamese (197)	213	1.33
Hawaii Native/Pacific Islander (2)	14	0.09
Not Hispanic (2)	14	0.09
Native Hawaiian (2)	9	0.06
White (11,770)	12,207	76.00
Not Hispanic (11,448)	11,823	73.61
Hispanic (322)	384	2.39

Ozark

Place Type: City
County: Christian
Population: 17,820†

Ancestry‡	Population	%
American (4,054)	4,054	24.39
Armenian (10)	22	0.13
Austrian (0)	9	0.05
Belgian (19)	19	0.11
Brazilian (13)	13	0.08
British (26)	57	0.34
Canadian (7)	7	0.04
Czech (10)	85	0.51
Danish (13)	118	0.71
Dutch (81)	290	1.74
English (564)	1,713	10.31
European (183)	236	1.42
French, ex. Basque (45)	592	3.56
French Canadian (17)	67	0.40
German (1,431)	3,734	22.46
Greek (27)	46	0.28
Hungarian (12)	12	0.07
Iranian (21)	21	0.13
Irish (552)	1,924	11.58
Italian (105)	416	2.50
Norwegian (71)	328	1.97
Polish (34)	186	1.12
Portuguese (17)	83	0.50
Romanian (0)	17	0.10
Russian (13)	100	0.60
Scotch-Irish (131)	437	2.63
Scottish (109)	285	1.71
Swedish (55)	107	0.64
Swiss (11)	11	0.07
Welsh (0)	22	0.13

Hispanic Origin	Population	%
Hispanic or Latino (of any race)	572	3.21
Central American, ex. Mexican	28	0.16
Costa Rican	3	0.02
Guatemalan	7	0.04
Honduran	9	0.05
Panamanian	2	0.01
Salvadoran	7	0.04
Cuban	13	0.07
Mexican	419	2.35
Puerto Rican	42	0.24
South American	22	0.12
Argentinean	5	0.03
Chilean	2	0.01
Colombian	9	0.05
Ecuadorian	5	0.03
Venezuelan	1	0.01
Other Hispanic or Latino	48	0.27

Race*	Population	%
African-American/Black (150)	273	1.53
Not Hispanic (146)	260	1.46
Hispanic (4)	13	0.07
American Indian/Alaska Native (97)	234	1.31
Not Hispanic (80)	207	1.16
Hispanic (17)	27	0.15
Blackfeet (1)	12	0.07
Cherokee (31)	96	0.54
Chickasaw (1)	5	0.03
Chippewa (0)	1	0.01
Choctaw (10)	17	0.10
Comanche (1)	3	0.02
Creek (0)	1	0.01
Iroquois (5)	9	0.05
Kiowa (1)	1	0.01
Mexican American Ind. (2)	2	0.01
Osage (1)	2	0.01
Ottawa (1)	1	0.01
Potawatomi (3)	4	0.02

*Notes: † The Census 2010 population figure is used to calculate the percentages in the Hispanic Origin and Race categories. Ancestry percentages are based on the 2006-2010 American Community Survey population (not shown); ‡ Numbers in parentheses indicate the number of people reporting a single ancestry; * Numbers in parentheses indicate the number of persons reporting this race alone, not in combination with any other race; Please refer to the Explanation of Data for more information.*

Pueblo (2)	2	0.01
Sioux (6)	8	0.04
Tlingit-Haida *(Alaska Native)* (0)	3	0.02
Yaqui (0)	1	0.01
Asian (96)	168	0.94
Not Hispanic (94)	155	0.87
Hispanic (2)	13	0.07
Cambodian (2)	2	0.01
Chinese, ex. Taiwanese (14)	25	0.14
Filipino (18)	48	0.27
Indian (10)	18	0.10
Japanese (1)	10	0.06
Korean (19)	29	0.16
Pakistani (10)	11	0.06
Taiwanese (3)	3	0.02
Thai (0)	2	0.01
Vietnamese (12)	15	0.08
Hawaii Native/Pacific Islander (18)	47	0.26
Not Hispanic (18)	45	0.25
Hispanic (0)	2	0.01
Fijian (0)	4	0.02
Guamanian/Chamorro (2)	2	0.01
Marshallese (0)	1	0.01
Native Hawaiian (2)	15	0.08
Samoan (8)	11	0.06
Tongan (1)	1	0.01
White (16,957)	17,311	97.14
Not Hispanic (16,580)	16,895	94.81
Hispanic (377)	416	2.33

Park Hills

Place Type: City
County: St. Francois
Population: 8,759†

Ancestry‡	Population	%
American (1,567)	1,567	18.17
Dutch (30)	206	2.39
English (479)	997	11.56
European (0)	12	0.14
French, ex. Basque (221)	693	8.03
German (508)	1,888	21.89
Greek (9)	9	0.10
Irish (823)	1,728	20.03
Italian (0)	266	3.08
Norwegian (0)	34	0.39
Polish (58)	142	1.65
Portuguese (0)	11	0.13
Russian (0)	15	0.17
Scotch-Irish (67)	120	1.39
Scottish (25)	95	1.10
Welsh (65)	76	0.88

Hispanic Origin	Population	%
Hispanic or Latino (of any race)	111	1.27
Central American, ex. Mexican	5	0.06
Honduran	2	0.02
Nicaraguan	1	0.01
Panamanian	2	0.02
Cuban	1	0.01
Mexican	73	0.83
Puerto Rican	5	0.06
South American	6	0.07
Venezuelan	1	0.01
Other South American	5	0.06
Other Hispanic or Latino	21	0.24

Race*	Population	%
African-American/Black (172)	217	2.48
Not Hispanic (172)	212	2.42
Hispanic (0)	5	0.06
American Indian/Alaska Native (41)	95	1.08
Not Hispanic (40)	87	0.99
Hispanic (1)	8	0.09
Alaska Athabascan *(Ala. Nat.)* (1)	1	0.01
Aleut *(Alaska Native)* (0)	1	0.01
Blackfeet (6)	12	0.14
Cherokee (7)	25	0.29
Cheyenne (0)	3	0.03
Chickasaw (1)	1	0.01
Chippewa (0)	1	0.01
Iroquois (0)	2	0.02
Mexican American Ind. (0)	2	0.02
Navajo (1)	2	0.02
Shoshone (0)	1	0.01
Sioux (1)	1	0.01
Asian (36)	57	0.65
Not Hispanic (35)	53	0.61
Hispanic (1)	4	0.05
Chinese, ex. Taiwanese (20)	24	0.27
Filipino (1)	5	0.06
Indian (1)	2	0.02
Japanese (2)	12	0.14
Korean (1)	5	0.06
Vietnamese (7)	11	0.13
Hawaii Native/Pacific Islander (11)	15	0.17
Not Hispanic (11)	12	0.14
Hispanic (0)	3	0.03
Native Hawaiian (3)	3	0.03
Samoan (5)	5	0.06
White (8,351)	8,474	96.75
Not Hispanic (8,284)	8,387	95.75
Hispanic (67)	87	0.99

Perryville

Place Type: City
County: Perry
Population: 8,225†

Ancestry‡	Population	%
American (1,032)	1,032	12.62
Armenian (16)	16	0.20
Belgian (0)	27	0.33
British (0)	8	0.10
Canadian (6)	17	0.21
Czech (0)	45	0.55
Danish (0)	10	0.12
Dutch (19)	92	1.13
English (163)	457	5.59
European (49)	59	0.72
French, ex. Basque (160)	956	11.69
German (2,050)	3,805	46.54
Hungarian (0)	10	0.12
Irish (104)	694	8.49
Italian (96)	222	2.72
Polish (16)	68	0.83
Scotch-Irish (38)	83	1.02
Scottish (8)	50	0.61
Swedish (12)	38	0.46
Swiss (0)	9	0.11

Hispanic Origin	Population	%
Hispanic or Latino (of any race)	221	2.69
Central American, ex. Mexican	19	0.23
Guatemalan	14	0.17
Honduran	4	0.05
Salvadoran	1	0.01
Dominican Republic	1	0.01
Mexican	170	2.07
Puerto Rican	10	0.12
South American	3	0.04
Colombian	2	0.02
Peruvian	1	0.01
Other Hispanic or Latino	18	0.22

Race*	Population	%
African-American/Black (62)	85	1.03
Not Hispanic (57)	80	0.97
Hispanic (5)	5	0.06
American Indian/Alaska Native (32)	80	0.97
Not Hispanic (21)	69	0.84
Hispanic (11)	11	0.13
Arapaho (1)	1	0.01
Blackfeet (0)	2	0.02
Cherokee (5)	29	0.35
Chickasaw (1)	1	0.01
Creek (1)	2	0.02
Kiowa (1)	1	0.01
Mexican American Ind. (8)	8	0.10
Potawatomi (5)	5	0.06
Shoshone (3)	3	0.04
Sioux (0)	3	0.04
Asian (74)	102	1.24
Not Hispanic (74)	101	1.23
Hispanic (0)	1	0.01
Chinese, ex. Taiwanese (10)	13	0.16
Filipino (11)	13	0.16
Indian (6)	6	0.07
Japanese (24)	27	0.33
Korean (0)	1	0.01
Laotian (10)	13	0.16
Thai (3)	8	0.10
Vietnamese (6)	7	0.09
Hawaii Native/Pacific Islander (6)	21	0.26
Not Hispanic (1)	15	0.18
Hispanic (5)	6	0.07
Guamanian/Chamorro (6)	9	0.11
Native Hawaiian (0)	6	0.07
Samoan (0)	1	0.01
White (7,841)	7,943	96.57
Not Hispanic (7,754)	7,849	95.43
Hispanic (87)	94	1.14

Pleasant Hill

Place Type: City
County: Cass
Population: 8,113†

Ancestry‡	Population	%
African, Sub-Saharan (0)	18	0.23
African (0)	18	0.23
American (1,023)	1,023	13.17
Arab (31)	64	0.82
Syrian (31)	64	0.82
Belgian (0)	8	0.10
British (11)	20	0.26
Cajun (0)	46	0.59
Croatian (16)	31	0.40
Czech (12)	37	0.48
Dutch (50)	151	1.94
English (342)	973	12.52
European (95)	112	1.44
Finnish (12)	35	0.45
French, ex. Basque (49)	240	3.09
French Canadian (11)	34	0.44
German (658)	1,803	23.21
Greek (0)	48	0.62
Hungarian (0)	14	0.18
Irish (335)	1,259	16.21
Italian (37)	115	1.48
Norwegian (106)	195	2.51
Polish (34)	51	0.66
Portuguese (0)	13	0.17
Scandinavian (6)	6	0.08
Scotch-Irish (7)	155	2.00
Scottish (87)	227	2.92
Swedish (0)	170	2.19
Welsh (13)	53	0.68

Hispanic Origin	Population	%
Hispanic or Latino (of any race)	298	3.67
Central American, ex. Mexican	18	0.22
Guatemalan	3	0.04
Honduran	6	0.07
Panamanian	5	0.06
Salvadoran	4	0.05
Cuban	3	0.04
Mexican	220	2.71
Puerto Rican	20	0.25
South American	8	0.10
Chilean	3	0.04
Colombian	5	0.06
Other Hispanic or Latino	29	0.36

Race*	Population	%
African-American/Black (57)	95	1.17
Not Hispanic (52)	89	1.10

*Notes: † The Census 2010 population figure is used to calculate the percentages in the Hispanic Origin and Race categories. Ancestry percentages are based on the 2006-2010 American Community Survey population (not shown); ‡ Numbers in parentheses indicate the number of people reporting a single ancestry; * Numbers in parentheses indicate the number of persons reporting this race alone, not in combination with any other race; Please refer to the Explanation of Data for more information.*

Hispanic (5)	6	0.07
American Indian/Alaska Native (40)	86	1.06
Not Hispanic (37)	81	1.00
Hispanic (3)	5	0.06
Blackfeet (0)	2	0.02
Canadian/French Am. Ind. (0)	1	0.01
Cherokee (10)	31	0.38
Chickasaw (2)	2	0.02
Comanche (2)	3	0.04
Creek (1)	2	0.02
Houma (1)	1	0.01
Iroquois (3)	5	0.06
Mexican American Ind. (1)	1	0.01
Navajo (2)	2	0.02
Osage (0)	2	0.02
South American Ind. (2)	3	0.04
Asian (43)	81	1.00
Not Hispanic (43)	72	0.89
Hispanic (0)	9	0.11
Burmese (7)	7	0.09
Cambodian (4)	4	0.05
Chinese, ex. Taiwanese (14)	15	0.18
Filipino (6)	20	0.25
Indian (0)	2	0.02
Japanese (1)	6	0.07
Korean (2)	6	0.07
Laotian (2)	2	0.02
Pakistani (1)	1	0.01
Thai (0)	9	0.11
Vietnamese (2)	4	0.05
Hawaii Native/Pacific Islander (6)	7	0.09
Not Hispanic (4)	5	0.06
Hispanic (2)	2	0.02
Guamanian/Chamorro (3)	3	0.04
Samoan (2)	2	0.02
Tongan (1)	1	0.01
White (7,734)	7,872	97.03
Not Hispanic (7,566)	7,678	94.64
Hispanic (168)	194	2.39

Poplar Bluff

Place Type: City
County: Butler
Population: 17,023†

Ancestry‡	Population	%
American (2,293)	2,293	13.39
Arab (0)	32	0.19
Syrian (0)	32	0.19
Armenian (9)	9	0.05
Austrian (6)	6	0.04
British (39)	63	0.37
Canadian (8)	8	0.05
Czech (0)	31	0.18
Czechoslovakian (10)	20	0.12
Danish (0)	9	0.05
Dutch (24)	358	2.09
English (750)	1,489	8.70
European (203)	203	1.19
French, ex. Basque (46)	334	1.95
French Canadian (0)	69	0.40
German (808)	2,660	15.53
Greek (12)	12	0.07
Irish (1,096)	2,970	17.35
Italian (67)	272	1.59
Lithuanian (2)	5	0.03
Norwegian (33)	54	0.32
Pennsylvania German (41)	41	0.24
Polish (23)	141	0.82
Scotch-Irish (71)	217	1.27
Scottish (178)	280	1.64
Slovak (11)	11	0.06
Swedish (37)	66	0.39
Swiss (0)	43	0.25
Welsh (24)	82	0.48
West Indian, ex. Hispanic (0)	18	0.11
West Indian (0)	18	0.11
Yugoslavian (16)	16	0.09

Hispanic Origin	Population	%
Hispanic or Latino (of any race)	376	2.21
Central American, ex. Mexican	18	0.11
Guatemalan	2	0.01
Honduran	8	0.05
Nicaraguan	6	0.04
Panamanian	2	0.01
Cuban	4	0.02
Dominican Republic	10	0.06
Mexican	269	1.58
Puerto Rican	30	0.18
South American	3	0.02
Colombian	2	0.01
Peruvian	1	0.01
Other Hispanic or Latino	42	0.25

Race*	Population	%
African-American/Black (1,698)	1,961	11.52
Not Hispanic (1,683)	1,929	11.33
Hispanic (15)	32	0.19
American Indian/Alaska Native (90)	254	1.49
Not Hispanic (88)	248	1.46
Hispanic (2)	6	0.04
Aleut *(Alaska Native)* (1)	2	0.01
Apache (6)	13	0.08
Blackfeet (6)	12	0.07
Canadian/French Am. Ind. (0)	2	0.01
Cherokee (29)	81	0.48
Chickasaw (1)	3	0.02
Chippewa (1)	3	0.02
Choctaw (2)	5	0.03
Creek (1)	6	0.04
Crow (0)	1	0.01
Iroquois (2)	4	0.02
Menominee (1)	1	0.01
Mexican American Ind. (0)	1	0.01
Navajo (0)	3	0.02
Osage (1)	3	0.02
Potawatomi (2)	2	0.01
Seminole (0)	4	0.02
Sioux (3)	8	0.05
Asian (152)	202	1.19
Not Hispanic (152)	201	1.18
Hispanic (0)	1	0.01
Cambodian (1)	7	0.04
Chinese, ex. Taiwanese (19)	28	0.16
Filipino (17)	25	0.15
Indian (47)	50	0.29
Japanese (9)	24	0.14
Korean (9)	12	0.07
Pakistani (31)	31	0.18
Thai (11)	11	0.06
Vietnamese (2)	8	0.05
Hawaii Native/Pacific Islander (11)	25	0.15
Not Hispanic (11)	24	0.14
Hispanic (0)	1	0.01
Native Hawaiian (7)	13	0.08
White (14,434)	14,879	87.41
Not Hispanic (14,263)	14,671	86.18
Hispanic (171)	208	1.22

Raymore

Place Type: City
County: Cass
Population: 19,206†

Ancestry‡	Population	%
African, Sub-Saharan (9)	9	0.05
African (9)	9	0.05
American (2,098)	2,098	11.65
Armenian (0)	16	0.09
Australian (16)	16	0.09
Austrian (15)	15	0.08
Belgian (12)	36	0.20
British (0)	44	0.24
Cajun (19)	19	0.11
Canadian (8)	8	0.04
Croatian (16)	16	0.09
Czech (0)	112	0.62
Czechoslovakian (12)	12	0.07
Danish (17)	101	0.56
Dutch (39)	243	1.35
Eastern European (10)	10	0.06
English (1,021)	2,630	14.60
European (426)	426	2.37
French, ex. Basque (70)	599	3.33
French Canadian (13)	109	0.61
German (1,584)	4,393	24.39
Greek (0)	23	0.13
Hungarian (0)	10	0.06
Irish (562)	2,507	13.92
Italian (268)	644	3.58
Lithuanian (14)	44	0.24
Macedonian (16)	34	0.19
Northern European (15)	15	0.08
Norwegian (65)	156	0.87
Polish (94)	352	1.95
Portuguese (0)	17	0.09
Russian (30)	99	0.55
Scotch-Irish (175)	422	2.34
Scottish (217)	479	2.66
Swedish (45)	343	1.90
Swiss (12)	28	0.16
Ukrainian (10)	10	0.06
Welsh (39)	149	0.83

Hispanic Origin	Population	%
Hispanic or Latino (of any race)	624	3.25
Central American, ex. Mexican	71	0.37
Costa Rican	5	0.03
Guatemalan	20	0.10
Honduran	16	0.08
Panamanian	17	0.09
Salvadoran	13	0.07
Cuban	16	0.08
Dominican Republic	2	0.01
Mexican	385	2.00
Puerto Rican	54	0.28
South American	34	0.18
Argentinean	3	0.02
Bolivian	1	0.01
Chilean	6	0.03
Colombian	8	0.04
Ecuadorian	8	0.04
Paraguayan	1	0.01
Peruvian	7	0.04
Other Hispanic or Latino	62	0.32

Race*	Population	%
African-American/Black (1,506)	1,712	8.91
Not Hispanic (1,492)	1,690	8.80
Hispanic (14)	22	0.11
American Indian/Alaska Native (81)	228	1.19
Not Hispanic (74)	214	1.11
Hispanic (7)	14	0.07
Apache (2)	2	0.01
Blackfeet (0)	9	0.05
Cherokee (20)	88	0.46
Chickasaw (3)	4	0.02
Chippewa (1)	1	0.01
Choctaw (4)	12	0.06
Comanche (2)	2	0.01
Creek (3)	7	0.04
Delaware (1)	1	0.01
Hopi (0)	5	0.03
Iroquois (3)	7	0.04
Mexican American Ind. (1)	2	0.01
Osage (2)	7	0.04
Ottawa (4)	4	0.02
Potawatomi (1)	10	0.05
Sioux (1)	8	0.04
Asian (160)	277	1.44
Not Hispanic (160)	275	1.43
Hispanic (0)	2	0.01
Cambodian (5)	8	0.04
Chinese, ex. Taiwanese (21)	46	0.24
Filipino (24)	64	0.33
Indian (47)	54	0.28
Indonesian (0)	1	0.01

*Notes: † The Census 2010 population figure is used to calculate the percentages in the Hispanic Origin and Race categories. Ancestry percentages are based on the 2006-2010 American Community Survey population (not shown); ‡ Numbers in parentheses indicate the number of people reporting a single ancestry; * Numbers in parentheses indicate the number of persons reporting this race alone, not in combination with any other race; Please refer to the Explanation of Data for more information.*

Japanese (8)	23	0.12
Korean (21)	38	0.20
Laotian (1)	2	0.01
Malaysian (1)	4	0.02
Pakistani (15)	17	0.09
Taiwanese (1)	1	0.01
Thai (6)	15	0.08
Vietnamese (5)	8	0.04
Hawaii Native/Pacific Islander (10)	17	0.09
Not Hispanic (10)	16	0.08
Hispanic (0)	1	0.01
Guamanian/Chamorro (7)	8	0.04
Native Hawaiian (1)	1	0.01
Samoan (1)	3	0.02
Tongan (1)	1	0.01
White (16,870)	17,298	90.07
Not Hispanic (16,426)	16,799	87.47
Hispanic (444)	499	2.60

Raytown

Place Type: City
County: Jackson
Population: 29,526†

Ancestry‡	Population	%
African, Sub-Saharan (112)	124	0.42
African (112)	124	0.42
American (3,762)	3,762	12.76
Arab (146)	146	0.50
Arab (72)	72	0.24
Egyptian (27)	27	0.09
Lebanese (16)	16	0.05
Other Arab (31)	31	0.11
Austrian (14)	25	0.08
Belgian (35)	35	0.12
British (102)	158	0.54
Croatian (0)	49	0.17
Czech (22)	223	0.76
Czechoslovakian (12)	25	0.08
Danish (11)	56	0.19
Dutch (153)	496	1.68
Eastern European (33)	45	0.15
English (1,180)	3,253	11.03
European (192)	232	0.79
Finnish (11)	11	0.04
French, ex. Basque (153)	1,037	3.52
French Canadian (48)	110	0.37
German (1,896)	6,114	20.73
Greek (17)	17	0.06
Hungarian (12)	20	0.07
Irish (834)	3,291	11.16
Italian (332)	853	2.89
Lithuanian (13)	21	0.07
Northern European (23)	23	0.08
Norwegian (50)	177	0.60
Pennsylvania German (0)	50	0.17
Polish (83)	410	1.39
Portuguese (0)	57	0.19
Russian (7)	50	0.17
Scandinavian (0)	50	0.17
Scotch-Irish (243)	501	1.70
Scottish (163)	512	1.74
Slavic (0)	8	0.03
Slovak (0)	28	0.09
Slovene (0)	8	0.03
Swedish (66)	252	0.85
Swiss (14)	78	0.26
Ukrainian (0)	14	0.05
Welsh (0)	233	0.79
West Indian, ex. Hispanic (12)	52	0.18
Belizean (4)	4	0.01
Dutch West Indian (0)	40	0.14
Haitian (8)	8	0.03
Yugoslavian (0)	39	0.13

Hispanic Origin	Population	%
Hispanic or Latino (of any race)	1,513	5.12
Central American, ex. Mexican	160	0.54
Costa Rican	3	0.01
Guatemalan	15	0.05
Honduran	33	0.11
Nicaraguan	1	<0.01
Panamanian	4	0.01
Salvadoran	103	0.35
Other Central American	1	<0.01
Cuban	17	0.06
Dominican Republic	12	0.04
Mexican	1,084	3.67
Puerto Rican	61	0.21
South American	39	0.13
Argentinean	7	0.02
Bolivian	2	0.01
Chilean	6	0.02
Colombian	14	0.05
Ecuadorian	4	0.01
Peruvian	5	0.02
Venezuelan	1	<0.01
Other Hispanic or Latino	140	0.47

Race*	Population	%
African-American/Black (7,421)	8,049	27.26
Not Hispanic (7,362)	7,910	26.79
Hispanic (59)	139	0.47
American Indian/Alaska Native (135)	459	1.55
Not Hispanic (115)	409	1.39
Hispanic (20)	50	0.17
Alaska Athabascan *(Ala. Nat.)* (2)	2	0.01
Apache (4)	13	0.04
Blackfeet (5)	20	0.07
Canadian/French Am. Ind. (0)	1	<0.01
Central American Ind. (4)	5	0.02
Cherokee (29)	124	0.42
Cheyenne (0)	4	0.01
Chickasaw (2)	3	0.01
Chippewa (8)	16	0.05
Choctaw (4)	12	0.04
Comanche (1)	4	0.01
Creek (1)	9	0.03
Crow (0)	4	0.01
Delaware (1)	6	0.02
Iroquois (3)	6	0.02
Lumbee (1)	2	0.01
Mexican American Ind. (6)	11	0.04
Navajo (0)	5	0.02
Osage (0)	2	0.01
Ottawa (2)	2	0.01
Potawatomi (9)	13	0.04
Seminole (2)	2	0.01
Shoshone (0)	1	<0.01
Sioux (8)	20	0.07
Yaqui (0)	4	0.01
Asian (301)	475	1.61
Not Hispanic (297)	456	1.54
Hispanic (4)	19	0.06
Cambodian (28)	34	0.12
Chinese, ex. Taiwanese (19)	36	0.12
Filipino (70)	119	0.40
Hmong (1)	1	<0.01
Indian (19)	37	0.13
Indonesian (0)	4	0.01
Japanese (13)	30	0.10
Korean (32)	56	0.19
Laotian (11)	15	0.05
Nepalese (4)	4	0.01
Pakistani (19)	19	0.06
Taiwanese (3)	5	0.02
Thai (2)	6	0.02
Vietnamese (63)	84	0.28
Hawaii Native/Pacific Islander (61)	125	0.42
Not Hispanic (52)	107	0.36
Hispanic (9)	18	0.06
Guamanian/Chamorro (14)	17	0.06
Native Hawaiian (11)	25	0.08
Samoan (10)	27	0.09
White (20,000)	20,877	70.71
Not Hispanic (19,274)	20,041	67.88
Hispanic (726)	836	2.83

Republic

Place Type: City
County: Greene
Population: 14,751†

Ancestry‡	Population	%
African, Sub-Saharan (14)	14	0.10
South African (14)	14	0.10
American (1,594)	1,594	11.57
Arab (0)	12	0.09
Arab (0)	12	0.09
Austrian (0)	12	0.09
British (15)	15	0.11
Canadian (15)	43	0.31
Czech (64)	75	0.54
Danish (0)	116	0.84
Dutch (106)	544	3.95
English (1,115)	2,111	15.33
European (101)	126	0.91
French, ex. Basque (30)	432	3.14
French Canadian (31)	99	0.72
German (1,173)	3,293	23.91
Greek (9)	9	0.07
Hungarian (0)	14	0.10
Irish (582)	2,436	17.69
Italian (192)	402	2.92
Norwegian (26)	61	0.44
Polish (34)	194	1.41
Romanian (0)	61	0.44
Russian (0)	30	0.22
Scandinavian (0)	20	0.15
Scotch-Irish (55)	215	1.56
Scottish (38)	254	1.84
Swedish (85)	170	1.23
Swiss (0)	15	0.11
Welsh (41)	156	1.13

Hispanic Origin	Population	%
Hispanic or Latino (of any race)	320	2.17
Central American, ex. Mexican	31	0.21
Costa Rican	2	0.01
Guatemalan	16	0.11
Nicaraguan	1	0.01
Panamanian	6	0.04
Salvadoran	6	0.04
Cuban	6	0.04
Dominican Republic	2	0.01
Mexican	207	1.40
Puerto Rican	21	0.14
South American	8	0.05
Chilean	1	0.01
Ecuadorian	4	0.03
Venezuelan	1	0.01
Other South American	2	0.01
Other Hispanic or Latino	45	0.31

Race*	Population	%
African-American/Black (97)	184	1.25
Not Hispanic (90)	169	1.15
Hispanic (7)	15	0.10
American Indian/Alaska Native (85)	208	1.41
Not Hispanic (81)	195	1.32
Hispanic (4)	13	0.09
Apache (0)	1	0.01
Blackfeet (0)	5	0.03
Canadian/French Am. Ind. (1)	1	0.01
Cherokee (37)	89	0.60
Chickasaw (0)	4	0.03
Chippewa (0)	3	0.02
Choctaw (3)	5	0.03
Creek (0)	1	0.01
Iroquois (2)	4	0.03
Mexican American Ind. (4)	6	0.04
Osage (3)	5	0.03
Ottawa (0)	1	0.01
Potawatomi (1)	1	0.01
Seminole (1)	1	0.01
Shoshone (0)	1	0.01
Sioux (2)	3	0.02

SECTION TWO

*Notes: † The Census 2010 population figure is used to calculate the percentages in the Hispanic Origin and Race categories. Ancestry percentages are based on the 2006-2010 American Community Survey population (not shown); ‡ Numbers in parentheses indicate the number of people reporting a single ancestry; * Numbers in parentheses indicate the number of persons reporting this race alone, not in combination with any other race; Please refer to the Explanation of Data for more information.*

Spanish American Ind. (1)	1	0.01
Asian (81)	138	0.94
Not Hispanic (79)	134	0.91
Hispanic (2)	4	0.03
Chinese, ex. Taiwanese (20)	22	0.15
Filipino (14)	31	0.21
Indian (5)	6	0.04
Indonesian (0)	2	0.01
Japanese (11)	16	0.11
Korean (8)	27	0.18
Laotian (2)	6	0.04
Pakistani (0)	4	0.03
Taiwanese (0)	3	0.02
Thai (3)	4	0.03
Vietnamese (13)	19	0.13
Hawaii Native/Pacific Islander (1)	14	0.09
Not Hispanic (1)	14	0.09
Native Hawaiian (0)	8	0.05
Samoan (1)	5	0.03
White (14,103)	14,376	97.46
Not Hispanic (13,925)	14,157	95.97
Hispanic (178)	219	1.48

Richmond Heights

Place Type: City
County: St. Louis
Population: 8,603†

Ancestry‡	Population	%
African, Sub-Saharan (42)	42	0.48
African (42)	42	0.48
American (844)	844	9.63
Arab (0)	36	0.41
Egyptian (0)	11	0.13
Lebanese (0)	25	0.29
Armenian (0)	7	0.08
Austrian (0)	16	0.18
Belgian (0)	13	0.15
British (0)	38	0.43
Cajun (0)	7	0.08
Canadian (0)	8	0.09
Croatian (0)	5	0.06
Czech (8)	40	0.46
Czechoslovakian (0)	9	0.10
Danish (0)	77	0.88
Dutch (136)	256	2.92
English (226)	1,110	12.66
European (135)	135	1.54
Finnish (0)	22	0.25
French, ex. Basque (107)	363	4.14
French Canadian (0)	7	0.08
German (895)	2,776	31.66
Greek (32)	54	0.62
Hungarian (0)	60	0.68
Iranian (14)	14	0.16
Irish (338)	1,674	19.09
Italian (156)	515	5.87
Lithuanian (11)	37	0.42
Norwegian (15)	88	1.00
Pennsylvania German (38)	38	0.43
Polish (84)	382	4.36
Portuguese (0)	20	0.23
Romanian (0)	19	0.22
Russian (59)	82	0.94
Scotch-Irish (78)	215	2.45
Scottish (21)	324	3.70
Serbian (15)	15	0.17
Slovak (0)	23	0.26
Swedish (14)	139	1.59
Swiss (6)	72	0.82
Turkish (12)	28	0.32
Ukrainian (8)	15	0.17
Welsh (0)	11	0.13
Yugoslavian (0)	8	0.09

Hispanic Origin	Population	%
Hispanic or Latino (of any race)	197	2.29
Central American, ex. Mexican	15	0.17
Costa Rican	2	0.02
Guatemalan	5	0.06
Honduran	3	0.03
Nicaraguan	2	0.02
Panamanian	2	0.02
Salvadoran	1	0.01
Cuban	10	0.12
Dominican Republic	2	0.02
Mexican	91	1.06
Puerto Rican	23	0.27
South American	33	0.38
Argentinean	9	0.10
Bolivian	2	0.02
Chilean	2	0.02
Colombian	6	0.07
Ecuadorian	3	0.03
Peruvian	7	0.08
Uruguayan	1	0.01
Venezuelan	2	0.02
Other South American	1	0.01
Other Hispanic or Latino	23	0.27

Race*	Population	%
African-American/Black (1,002)	1,085	12.61
Not Hispanic (988)	1,066	12.39
Hispanic (14)	19	0.22
American Indian/Alaska Native (17)	51	0.59
Not Hispanic (15)	47	0.55
Hispanic (2)	4	0.05
Aleut *(Alaska Native)* (2)	2	0.02
Apache (1)	1	0.01
Blackfeet (1)	1	0.01
Canadian/French Am. Ind. (1)	1	0.01
Cherokee (2)	11	0.13
Choctaw (0)	2	0.02
Creek (1)	2	0.02
Delaware (1)	1	0.01
Iroquois (0)	1	0.01
Osage (0)	1	0.01
Pueblo (0)	2	0.02
Sioux (1)	2	0.02
Asian (359)	413	4.80
Not Hispanic (358)	412	4.79
Hispanic (1)	1	0.01
Chinese, ex. Taiwanese (143)	153	1.78
Filipino (26)	31	0.36
Indian (69)	78	0.91
Japanese (20)	27	0.31
Korean (59)	67	0.78
Nepalese (2)	2	0.02
Pakistani (2)	3	0.03
Sri Lankan (1)	2	0.02
Taiwanese (11)	12	0.14
Thai (3)	6	0.07
Vietnamese (8)	14	0.16
Hawaii Native/Pacific Islander (2)	4	0.05
Not Hispanic (2)	4	0.05
Guamanian/Chamorro (1)	1	0.01
Native Hawaiian (0)	2	0.02
Tongan (1)	1	0.01
White (7,030)	7,156	83.18
Not Hispanic (6,889)	7,011	81.49
Hispanic (141)	145	1.69

Rolla

Place Type: City
County: Phelps
Population: 19,559†

Ancestry‡	Population	%
African, Sub-Saharan (29)	29	0.15
Other Sub-Saharan African (29)	29	0.15
American (1,266)	1,266	6.61
Arab (16)	34	0.18
Lebanese (0)	5	0.03
Syrian (0)	5	0.03
Other Arab (16)	24	0.13
Armenian (0)	39	0.20
Australian (9)	9	0.05
Austrian (20)	39	0.20
Brazilian (51)	51	0.27
British (61)	81	0.42
Cajun (27)	27	0.14
Croatian (0)	11	0.06
Czech (0)	51	0.27
Czechoslovakian (48)	148	0.77
Danish (33)	39	0.20
Dutch (128)	340	1.78
English (908)	2,383	12.45
European (203)	203	1.06
Finnish (0)	10	0.05
French, ex. Basque (52)	668	3.49
French Canadian (0)	22	0.11
German (1,958)	5,477	28.61
Greek (12)	125	0.65
Hungarian (0)	19	0.10
Icelander (0)	33	0.17
Irish (559)	2,227	11.63
Italian (157)	672	3.51
Norwegian (37)	159	0.83
Pennsylvania German (7)	7	0.04
Polish (76)	452	2.36
Portuguese (16)	38	0.20
Romanian (0)	12	0.06
Russian (0)	79	0.41
Scandinavian (69)	101	0.53
Scotch-Irish (157)	430	2.25
Scottish (153)	585	3.06
Slavic (6)	22	0.11
Slovak (0)	17	0.09
Swedish (0)	195	1.02
Swiss (0)	38	0.20
Turkish (42)	42	0.22
Welsh (29)	64	0.33
West Indian, ex. Hispanic (6)	6	0.03
Jamaican (6)	6	0.03

Hispanic Origin	Population	%
Hispanic or Latino (of any race)	512	2.62
Central American, ex. Mexican	24	0.12
Costa Rican	2	0.01
Guatemalan	5	0.03
Honduran	5	0.03
Panamanian	7	0.04
Salvadoran	5	0.03
Cuban	16	0.08
Dominican Republic	3	0.02
Mexican	305	1.56
Puerto Rican	66	0.34
South American	31	0.16
Argentinean	4	0.02
Bolivian	1	0.01
Chilean	2	0.01
Colombian	10	0.05
Peruvian	7	0.04
Uruguayan	1	0.01
Venezuelan	6	0.03
Other Hispanic or Latino	67	0.34

Race*	Population	%
African-American/Black (803)	993	5.08
Not Hispanic (782)	959	4.90
Hispanic (21)	34	0.17
American Indian/Alaska Native (84)	218	1.11
Not Hispanic (71)	195	1.00
Hispanic (13)	23	0.12
Apache (6)	8	0.04
Blackfeet (0)	6	0.03
Cherokee (29)	70	0.36
Chickasaw (1)	3	0.02
Chippewa (1)	1	0.01
Choctaw (8)	15	0.08
Comanche (1)	2	0.01
Creek (1)	1	0.01
Crow (3)	4	0.02
Delaware (0)	2	0.01
Iroquois (1)	2	0.01
Mexican American Ind. (1)	1	0.01
Navajo (2)	5	0.03
Osage (0)	3	0.02

*Notes: † The Census 2010 population figure is used to calculate the percentages in the Hispanic Origin and Race categories. Ancestry percentages are based on the 2006-2010 American Community Survey population (not shown); ‡ Numbers in parentheses indicate the number of people reporting a single ancestry; * Numbers in parentheses indicate the number of persons reporting this race alone, not in combination with any other race; Please refer to the Explanation of Data for more information.*

Potawatomi (1)	1	0.01
Shoshone (1)	2	0.01
Sioux (5)	6	0.03
South American Ind. (0)	1	0.01
Ute (0)	1	0.01
Asian (1,115)	1,279	6.54
Not Hispanic (1,112)	1,270	6.49
Hispanic (3)	9	0.05
Bangladeshi (6)	6	0.03
Cambodian (3)	3	0.02
Chinese, ex. Taiwanese (349)	365	1.87
Filipino (60)	92	0.47
Hmong (2)	2	0.01
Indian (449)	471	2.41
Indonesian (1)	1	0.01
Japanese (27)	44	0.22
Korean (71)	83	0.42
Laotian (0)	1	0.01
Malaysian (15)	15	0.08
Nepalese (9)	9	0.05
Pakistani (17)	17	0.09
Sri Lankan (19)	19	0.10
Taiwanese (16)	17	0.09
Thai (9)	12	0.06
Vietnamese (36)	40	0.20
Hawaii Native/Pacific Islander (17)	51	0.26
Not Hispanic (13)	46	0.24
Hispanic (4)	5	0.03
Guamanian/Chamorro (1)	6	0.03
Native Hawaiian (2)	16	0.08
Samoan (3)	5	0.03
White (16,960)	17,430	89.11
Not Hispanic (16,590)	17,026	87.05
Hispanic (370)	404	2.07

Sappington

Place Type: CDP
County: St. Louis
Population: 7,580†

Ancestry‡	Population	%
Afghan (45)	45	0.56
Albanian (196)	196	2.46
American (393)	393	4.92
Armenian (17)	17	0.21
Austrian (0)	8	0.10
Belgian (0)	26	0.33
British (34)	67	0.84
Cajun (0)	10	0.13
Croatian (27)	120	1.50
Czech (24)	70	0.88
Czechoslovakian (25)	25	0.31
Danish (0)	28	0.35
Dutch (0)	162	2.03
English (163)	786	9.85
European (17)	17	0.21
Finnish (0)	12	0.15
French, ex. Basque (0)	335	4.20
German (1,755)	4,065	50.93
Greek (0)	34	0.43
Hungarian (16)	40	0.50
Irish (305)	2,000	25.06
Italian (186)	618	7.74
Lithuanian (0)	9	0.11
Luxemburger (8)	8	0.10
Norwegian (21)	31	0.39
Polish (83)	378	4.74
Portuguese (0)	15	0.19
Russian (23)	23	0.29
Scotch-Irish (10)	48	0.60
Scottish (13)	121	1.52
Serbian (0)	31	0.39
Slovak (15)	29	0.36
Swedish (13)	122	1.53
Swiss (17)	109	1.37
Welsh (9)	82	1.03
Yugoslavian (61)	79	0.99

Hispanic Origin	Population	%
Hispanic or Latino (of any race)	146	1.93
Central American, ex. Mexican	15	0.20
Costa Rican	4	0.05
Guatemalan	4	0.05
Honduran	6	0.08
Nicaraguan	1	0.01
Cuban	1	0.01
Mexican	81	1.07
Puerto Rican	12	0.16
South American	19	0.25
Argentinean	3	0.04
Bolivian	4	0.05
Colombian	6	0.08
Peruvian	4	0.05
Venezuelan	2	0.03
Other Hispanic or Latino	18	0.24

Race*	Population	%
African-American/Black (112)	149	1.97
Not Hispanic (112)	147	1.94
Hispanic (0)	2	0.03
American Indian/Alaska Native (8)	33	0.44
Not Hispanic (5)	22	0.29
Hispanic (3)	11	0.15
Apache (1)	1	0.01
Cherokee (4)	10	0.13
Chippewa (0)	4	0.05
Creek (1)	2	0.03
Mexican American Ind. (1)	3	0.04
Sioux (0)	1	0.01
South American Ind. (1)	1	0.01
Asian (206)	260	3.43
Not Hispanic (205)	258	3.40
Hispanic (1)	2	0.03
Chinese, ex. Taiwanese (28)	28	0.37
Filipino (21)	34	0.45
Indian (64)	67	0.88
Indonesian (2)	2	0.03
Japanese (7)	13	0.17
Korean (18)	23	0.30
Laotian (3)	3	0.04
Pakistani (1)	1	0.01
Sri Lankan (1)	1	0.01
Taiwanese (4)	4	0.05
Thai (1)	1	0.01
Vietnamese (45)	45	0.59
Hawaii Native/Pacific Islander (3)	7	0.09
Not Hispanic (3)	6	0.08
Hispanic (0)	1	0.01
Guamanian/Chamorro (2)	6	0.08
Native Hawaiian (1)	1	0.01
White (7,097)	7,218	95.22
Not Hispanic (6,999)	7,102	93.69
Hispanic (98)	116	1.53

Sedalia

Place Type: City
County: Pettis
Population: 21,387†

Ancestry‡	Population	%
African, Sub-Saharan (48)	48	0.23
African (48)	48	0.23
American (2,390)	2,390	11.30
Arab (12)	12	0.06
Palestinian (12)	12	0.06
Belgian (6)	86	0.41
British (9)	82	0.39
Cajun (0)	15	0.07
Celtic (0)	8	0.04
Czech (25)	126	0.60
Czechoslovakian (0)	10	0.05
Danish (0)	10	0.05
Dutch (120)	480	2.27
English (779)	2,148	10.16
European (235)	260	1.23
French, ex. Basque (106)	578	2.73
French Canadian (22)	89	0.42
German (2,368)	5,902	27.92
Greek (0)	8	0.04
Hungarian (18)	23	0.11
Irish (749)	3,096	14.64
Italian (83)	237	1.12
New Zealander (0)	82	0.39
Norwegian (52)	127	0.60
Pennsylvania German (64)	64	0.30
Polish (38)	215	1.02
Portuguese (0)	12	0.06
Romanian (0)	7	0.03
Russian (6)	6	0.03
Scotch-Irish (152)	594	2.81
Scottish (51)	349	1.65
Serbian (11)	11	0.05
Slovak (20)	29	0.14
Swedish (30)	179	0.85
Swiss (0)	27	0.13
Ukrainian (96)	102	0.48
Welsh (13)	46	0.22

Hispanic Origin	Population	%
Hispanic or Latino (of any race)	1,931	9.03
Central American, ex. Mexican	180	0.84
Guatemalan	43	0.20
Honduran	24	0.11
Nicaraguan	1	<0.01
Panamanian	8	0.04
Salvadoran	104	0.49
Cuban	21	0.10
Dominican Republic	1	<0.01
Mexican	1,495	6.99
Puerto Rican	64	0.30
South American	37	0.17
Argentinean	2	0.01
Bolivian	1	<0.01
Colombian	8	0.04
Ecuadorian	9	0.04
Uruguayan	1	<0.01
Venezuelan	16	0.07
Other Hispanic or Latino	133	0.62

Race*	Population	%
African-American/Black (1,103)	1,455	6.80
Not Hispanic (1,090)	1,415	6.62
Hispanic (13)	40	0.19
American Indian/Alaska Native (115)	286	1.34
Not Hispanic (87)	236	1.10
Hispanic (28)	50	0.23
Apache (9)	17	0.08
Arapaho (0)	2	0.01
Blackfeet (0)	9	0.04
Cherokee (35)	103	0.48
Chickasaw (5)	10	0.05
Chippewa (2)	2	0.01
Choctaw (1)	7	0.03
Crow (1)	1	<0.01
Iroquois (1)	2	0.01
Kiowa (0)	3	0.01
Mexican American Ind. (7)	10	0.05
Navajo (2)	4	0.02
Osage (1)	4	0.02
Pueblo (0)	1	<0.01
Puget Sound Salish (1)	1	<0.01
Seminole (2)	3	0.01
Sioux (2)	16	0.07
Yaqui (0)	1	<0.01
Asian (146)	214	1.00
Not Hispanic (146)	212	0.99
Hispanic (0)	2	0.01
Bangladeshi (1)	1	<0.01
Chinese, ex. Taiwanese (16)	19	0.09
Filipino (73)	109	0.51
Hmong (1)	1	<0.01
Indian (22)	26	0.12
Indonesian (0)	1	<0.01
Japanese (6)	17	0.08
Korean (6)	16	0.07
Nepalese (1)	1	<0.01
Taiwanese (2)	6	0.03

*Notes: † The Census 2010 population figure is used to calculate the percentages in the Hispanic Origin and Race categories. Ancestry percentages are based on the 2006-2010 American Community Survey population (not shown); ‡ Numbers in parentheses indicate the number of people reporting a single ancestry; * Numbers in parentheses indicate the number of persons reporting this race alone, not in combination with any other race; Please refer to the Explanation of Data for more information.*

Thai (4)	6	0.03
Vietnamese (12)	13	0.06
Hawaii Native/Pacific Islander (22)	41	0.19
Not Hispanic (21)	35	0.16
Hispanic (1)	6	0.03
Guamanian/Chamorro (1)	3	0.01
Native Hawaiian (13)	16	0.07
Samoan (1)	6	0.03
Tongan (0)	1	<0.01
White (18,246)	18,841	88.10
Not Hispanic (17,570)	18,059	84.44
Hispanic (676)	782	3.66

Sikeston

Place Type: City
County: Scott
Population: 16,318†

Ancestry‡	Population	%
African, Sub-Saharan (25)	25	0.15
African (10)	10	0.06
Nigerian (15)	15	0.09
American (2,156)	2,156	13.17
Brazilian (0)	8	0.05
British (10)	41	0.25
Cajun (8)	8	0.05
Czech (14)	14	0.09
Czechoslovakian (16)	16	0.10
Danish (40)	56	0.34
Dutch (68)	138	0.84
English (594)	1,359	8.30
European (73)	85	0.52
French, ex. Basque (104)	417	2.55
French Canadian (10)	10	0.06
German (965)	2,074	12.67
Greek (8)	24	0.15
Irish (366)	1,808	11.05
Italian (74)	88	0.54
New Zealander (0)	6	0.04
Norwegian (28)	74	0.45
Pennsylvania German (8)	8	0.05
Polish (50)	50	0.31
Scotch-Irish (163)	290	1.77
Scottish (123)	293	1.79
Swedish (16)	34	0.21
Welsh (25)	71	0.43
West Indian, ex. Hispanic (23)	23	0.14
Jamaican (23)	23	0.14

Hispanic Origin	Population	%
Hispanic or Latino (of any race)	378	2.32
Central American, ex. Mexican	15	0.09
Costa Rican	3	0.02
Guatemalan	1	0.01
Honduran	6	0.04
Salvadoran	5	0.03
Cuban	1	0.01
Mexican	323	1.98
Puerto Rican	15	0.09
South American	1	0.01
Chilean	1	0.01
Other Hispanic or Latino	23	0.14

Race*	Population	%
African-American/Black (4,275)	4,502	27.59
Not Hispanic (4,246)	4,468	27.38
Hispanic (29)	34	0.21
American Indian/Alaska Native (24)	102	0.63
Not Hispanic (20)	97	0.59
Hispanic (4)	5	0.03
Apache (1)	1	0.01
Cherokee (4)	30	0.18
Cheyenne (0)	1	0.01
Chickasaw (1)	3	0.02
Choctaw (3)	9	0.06
Mexican American Ind. (2)	2	0.01
Potawatomi (2)	3	0.02
Seminole (0)	2	0.01
Sioux (1)	1	0.01
Tlingit-Haida *(Alaska Native)* (0)	2	0.01
Asian (138)	161	0.99
Not Hispanic (133)	154	0.94
Hispanic (5)	7	0.04
Cambodian (3)	3	0.02
Chinese, ex. Taiwanese (23)	29	0.18
Filipino (34)	42	0.26
Indian (22)	25	0.15
Japanese (3)	9	0.06
Korean (2)	6	0.04
Pakistani (22)	22	0.13
Thai (2)	3	0.02
Vietnamese (24)	24	0.15
Hawaii Native/Pacific Islander (7)	14	0.09
Not Hispanic (7)	13	0.08
Hispanic (0)	1	0.01
Native Hawaiian (1)	8	0.05
Samoan (2)	2	0.01
White (11,415)	11,725	71.85
Not Hispanic (11,231)	11,514	70.56
Hispanic (184)	211	1.29

Smithville

Place Type: City
County: Clay
Population: 8,425†

Ancestry‡	Population	%
American (594)	594	7.52
Arab (0)	12	0.15
Syrian (0)	12	0.15
Armenian (9)	9	0.11
Austrian (0)	15	0.19
Belgian (9)	9	0.11
British (12)	46	0.58
Czech (0)	47	0.60
Danish (0)	32	0.41
Dutch (61)	246	3.12
English (373)	1,306	16.54
European (81)	113	1.43
Finnish (0)	8	0.10
French, ex. Basque (12)	120	1.52
French Canadian (0)	25	0.32
German (977)	2,681	33.95
Irish (378)	1,496	18.95
Italian (349)	605	7.66
Lithuanian (0)	112	1.42
Norwegian (62)	88	1.11
Polish (49)	241	3.05
Russian (29)	29	0.37
Scotch-Irish (102)	181	2.29
Scottish (29)	148	1.87
Swedish (70)	193	2.44
Welsh (56)	112	1.42

Hispanic Origin	Population	%
Hispanic or Latino (of any race)	220	2.61
Central American, ex. Mexican	10	0.12
Guatemalan	6	0.07
Honduran	2	0.02
Nicaraguan	1	0.01
Panamanian	1	0.01
Cuban	8	0.09
Dominican Republic	16	0.19
Mexican	166	1.97
Puerto Rican	4	0.05
South American	1	0.01
Colombian	1	0.01
Other Hispanic or Latino	15	0.18

Race*	Population	%
African-American/Black (57)	86	1.02
Not Hispanic (51)	80	0.95
Hispanic (6)	6	0.07
American Indian/Alaska Native (41)	104	1.23
Not Hispanic (40)	98	1.16
Hispanic (1)	6	0.07
Cherokee (13)	35	0.42
Chippewa (3)	5	0.06
Choctaw (4)	10	0.12
Creek (4)	4	0.05
Mexican American Ind. (1)	2	0.02
Navajo (1)	1	0.01
Osage (0)	2	0.02
Potawatomi (5)	6	0.07
Sioux (0)	1	0.01
Asian (56)	104	1.23
Not Hispanic (55)	101	1.20
Hispanic (1)	3	0.04
Chinese, ex. Taiwanese (20)	24	0.28
Filipino (8)	25	0.30
Indian (8)	12	0.14
Indonesian (3)	3	0.04
Japanese (2)	14	0.17
Korean (4)	7	0.08
Laotian (0)	1	0.01
Thai (1)	1	0.01
Vietnamese (9)	15	0.18
Hawaii Native/Pacific Islander (3)	12	0.14
Not Hispanic (3)	12	0.14
Fijian (2)	2	0.02
Guamanian/Chamorro (1)	1	0.01
Native Hawaiian (0)	6	0.07
Samoan (0)	2	0.02
White (8,084)	8,228	97.66
Not Hispanic (7,924)	8,051	95.56
Hispanic (160)	177	2.10

Spanish Lake

Place Type: CDP
County: St. Louis
Population: 19,650†

Ancestry‡	Population	%
African, Sub-Saharan (1,479)	1,547	7.10
African (1,444)	1,512	6.93
Nigerian (35)	35	0.16
American (332)	332	1.52
Austrian (30)	44	0.20
Croatian (0)	11	0.05
Danish (16)	16	0.07
Dutch (0)	43	0.20
Eastern European (12)	12	0.06
English (168)	748	3.43
European (90)	139	0.64
French, ex. Basque (0)	308	1.41
French Canadian (0)	25	0.11
German (930)	1,880	8.62
Greek (21)	21	0.10
Hungarian (78)	116	0.53
Irish (184)	1,095	5.02
Italian (147)	409	1.88
Lithuanian (0)	42	0.19
Norwegian (9)	9	0.04
Polish (71)	214	0.98
Russian (0)	34	0.16
Scotch-Irish (0)	65	0.30
Scottish (50)	76	0.35
Swedish (0)	25	0.11
Welsh (0)	16	0.07
West Indian, ex. Hispanic (38)	38	0.17
Haitian (19)	19	0.09
Jamaican (19)	19	0.09
Yugoslavian (14)	14	0.06

Hispanic Origin	Population	%
Hispanic or Latino (of any race)	244	1.24
Central American, ex. Mexican	14	0.07
Guatemalan	4	0.02
Nicaraguan	2	0.01
Panamanian	7	0.04
Salvadoran	1	0.01
Cuban	5	0.03
Dominican Republic	10	0.05
Mexican	130	0.66
Puerto Rican	36	0.18
South American	3	0.02
Argentinean	1	0.01

*Notes: † The Census 2010 population figure is used to calculate the percentages in the Hispanic Origin and Race categories. Ancestry percentages are based on the 2006-2010 American Community Survey population (not shown); ‡ Numbers in parentheses indicate the number of people reporting a single ancestry; * Numbers in parentheses indicate the number of persons reporting this race alone, not in combination with any other race; Please refer to the Explanation of Data for more information.*

Colombian	1	0.01
Peruvian	1	0.01
Other Hispanic or Latino	46	0.23

Race*	Population	%
African-American/Black (15,116)	15,524	79.00
Not Hispanic (15,045)	15,412	78.43
Hispanic (71)	112	0.57
American Indian/Alaska Native (46)	198	1.01
Not Hispanic (38)	181	0.92
Hispanic (8)	17	0.09
Blackfeet (1)	18	0.09
Cherokee (8)	47	0.24
Chippewa (1)	2	0.01
Choctaw (1)	14	0.07
Hopi (0)	2	0.01
Houma (0)	1	0.01
Kiowa (0)	1	0.01
Navajo (0)	3	0.02
Osage (5)	5	0.03
Seminole (1)	1	0.01
Sioux (1)	1	0.01
Yuman (0)	1	0.01
Asian (75)	125	0.64
Not Hispanic (75)	125	0.64
Chinese, ex. Taiwanese (11)	22	0.11
Filipino (16)	24	0.12
Indian (14)	27	0.14
Japanese (5)	11	0.06
Korean (12)	12	0.06
Thai (3)	5	0.03
Vietnamese (5)	10	0.05
Hawaii Native/Pacific Islander (6)	24	0.12
Not Hispanic (4)	14	0.07
Hispanic (2)	10	0.05
Guamanian/Chamorro (2)	3	0.02
Native Hawaiian (2)	6	0.03
Samoan (2)	11	0.06
White (3,882)	4,195	21.35
Not Hispanic (3,808)	4,098	20.85
Hispanic (74)	97	0.49

Springfield

Place Type: City
County: Christian
Population: 159,498†

Ancestry‡	Population	%
African, Sub-Saharan (251)	387	0.24
African (192)	328	0.21
Cape Verdean (7)	7	<0.01
Ethiopian (28)	28	0.02
South African (7)	7	<0.01
Other Sub-Saharan African (17)	17	0.01
Alsatian (0)	15	0.01
American (25,097)	25,097	15.79
Arab (151)	279	0.18
Arab (79)	116	0.07
Egyptian (16)	35	0.02
Lebanese (29)	63	0.04
Moroccan (9)	26	0.02
Syrian (9)	20	0.01
Other Arab (9)	19	0.01
Armenian (11)	39	0.02
Australian (13)	13	0.01
Austrian (28)	218	0.14
Basque (9)	9	0.01
Belgian (12)	136	0.09
Brazilian (17)	38	0.02
British (437)	756	0.48
Bulgarian (0)	40	0.03
Cajun (18)	59	0.04
Canadian (169)	236	0.15
Celtic (0)	14	0.01
Croatian (12)	27	0.02
Czech (346)	795	0.50
Czechoslovakian (34)	67	0.04
Danish (216)	889	0.56
Dutch (662)	3,470	2.18
Eastern European (7)	7	<0.01
English (6,288)	17,952	11.29
Estonian (16)	30	0.02
European (1,570)	2,217	1.39
Finnish (61)	167	0.11
French, ex. Basque (1,079)	5,365	3.38
French Canadian (263)	847	0.53
German (12,880)	35,757	22.50
Greek (165)	444	0.28
Guyanese (0)	30	0.02
Hungarian (54)	335	0.21
Icelander (0)	10	0.01
Iranian (50)	86	0.05
Irish (5,907)	22,991	14.46
Israeli (7)	31	0.02
Italian (1,517)	4,295	2.70
Latvian (0)	12	0.01
Lithuanian (19)	205	0.13
Maltese (0)	11	0.01
Northern European (74)	74	0.05
Norwegian (839)	1,851	1.16
Pennsylvania German (0)	25	0.02
Polish (659)	2,555	1.61
Portuguese (74)	163	0.10
Romanian (46)	162	0.10
Russian (245)	707	0.44
Scandinavian (141)	283	0.18
Scotch-Irish (1,597)	4,020	2.53
Scottish (1,242)	4,372	2.75
Serbian (14)	33	0.02
Slavic (0)	27	0.02
Slovak (9)	29	0.02
Slovene (18)	34	0.02
Swedish (723)	2,320	1.46
Swiss (117)	574	0.36
Turkish (17)	28	0.02
Ukrainian (27)	95	0.06
Welsh (280)	1,243	0.78
West Indian, ex. Hispanic (62)	107	0.07
Bahamian (12)	12	0.01
Belizean (9)	9	0.01
Dutch West Indian (14)	14	0.01
Haitian (19)	19	0.01
Jamaican (8)	20	0.01
West Indian (0)	33	0.02
Yugoslavian (61)	156	0.10

Hispanic Origin	Population	%
Hispanic or Latino (of any race)	5,851	3.67
Central American, ex. Mexican	427	0.27
Costa Rican	28	0.02
Guatemalan	53	0.03
Honduran	120	0.08
Nicaraguan	40	0.03
Panamanian	29	0.02
Salvadoran	154	0.10
Other Central American	3	<0.01
Cuban	107	0.07
Dominican Republic	33	0.02
Mexican	3,879	2.43
Puerto Rican	470	0.29
South American	256	0.16
Argentinean	29	0.02
Bolivian	7	<0.01
Chilean	23	0.01
Colombian	92	0.06
Ecuadorian	25	0.02
Paraguayan	4	<0.01
Peruvian	35	0.02
Uruguayan	5	<0.01
Venezuelan	31	0.02
Other South American	5	<0.01
Other Hispanic or Latino	679	0.43

Race*	Population	%
African-American/Black (6,524)	8,740	5.48
Not Hispanic (6,397)	8,435	5.29
Hispanic (127)	305	0.19
American Indian/Alaska Native (1,233)	3,138	1.97
Not Hispanic (1,076)	2,817	1.77
Hispanic (157)	321	0.20
Alaska Athabascan *(Ala. Nat.)* (3)	5	<0.01
Aleut *(Alaska Native)* (0)	3	<0.01
Apache (21)	70	0.04
Arapaho (2)	4	<0.01
Blackfeet (8)	90	0.06
Canadian/French Am. Ind. (2)	4	<0.01
Central American Ind. (2)	2	<0.01
Cherokee (340)	1,076	0.67
Cheyenne (1)	4	<0.01
Chickasaw (9)	30	0.02
Chippewa (25)	45	0.03
Choctaw (42)	109	0.07
Colville (3)	3	<0.01
Comanche (18)	43	0.03
Cree (2)	4	<0.01
Creek (12)	28	0.02
Crow (2)	5	<0.01
Delaware (8)	17	0.01
Hopi (3)	7	<0.01
Houma (1)	2	<0.01
Inupiat *(Alaska Native)* (5)	13	0.01
Iroquois (30)	53	0.03
Kiowa (5)	7	<0.01
Lumbee (2)	5	<0.01
Menominee (1)	1	<0.01
Mexican American Ind. (51)	78	0.05
Navajo (22)	49	0.03
Osage (4)	17	0.01
Ottawa (10)	15	0.01
Paiute (1)	1	<0.01
Pima (1)	1	<0.01
Potawatomi (22)	34	0.02
Pueblo (5)	10	0.01
Puget Sound Salish (2)	2	<0.01
Seminole (14)	25	0.02
Shoshone (0)	2	<0.01
Sioux (46)	86	0.05
South American Ind. (0)	1	<0.01
Spanish American Ind. (4)	4	<0.01
Tlingit-Haida *(Alaska Native)* (5)	8	0.01
Tohono O'Odham (1)	5	<0.01
Ute (2)	2	<0.01
Yakama (2)	3	<0.01
Yaqui (6)	9	0.01
Yup'ik *(Alaska Native)* (1)	1	<0.01
Asian (3,015)	3,845	2.41
Not Hispanic (2,980)	3,753	2.35
Hispanic (35)	92	0.06
Bangladeshi (16)	16	0.01
Burmese (57)	57	0.04
Cambodian (32)	52	0.03
Chinese, ex. Taiwanese (832)	943	0.59
Filipino (341)	553	0.35
Hmong (42)	44	0.03
Indian (402)	472	0.30
Indonesian (12)	25	0.02
Japanese (111)	254	0.16
Korean (376)	542	0.34
Laotian (12)	17	0.01
Malaysian (4)	10	0.01
Nepalese (9)	9	0.01
Pakistani (22)	32	0.02
Sri Lankan (9)	10	0.01
Taiwanese (42)	47	0.03
Thai (51)	81	0.05
Vietnamese (512)	598	0.37
Hawaii Native/Pacific Islander (267)	437	0.27
Not Hispanic (254)	407	0.26
Hispanic (13)	30	0.02
Fijian (2)	2	<0.01
Guamanian/Chamorro (52)	71	0.04
Marshallese (35)	45	0.03
Native Hawaiian (40)	118	0.07
Samoan (63)	89	0.06
Tongan (3)	6	<0.01
White (141,526)	146,257	91.70
Not Hispanic (138,495)	142,587	89.40
Hispanic (3,031)	3,670	2.30

*Notes: † The Census 2010 population figure is used to calculate the percentages in the Hispanic Origin and Race categories. Ancestry percentages are based on the 2006-2010 American Community Survey population (not shown); ‡ Numbers in parentheses indicate the number of people reporting a single ancestry; * Numbers in parentheses indicate the number of persons reporting this race alone, not in combination with any other race; Please refer to the Explanation of Data for more information.*

St. Ann

Place Type: City
County: St. Louis
Population: 13,020†

Ancestry‡	Population	%
African, Sub-Saharan (362)	395	3.02
African (219)	252	1.93
Ethiopian (128)	128	0.98
Kenyan (15)	15	0.11
Alsatian (0)	13	0.10
American (1,017)	1,017	7.78
Arab (0)	21	0.16
Lebanese (0)	21	0.16
Austrian (0)	12	0.09
Brazilian (26)	26	0.20
British (43)	57	0.44
Croatian (0)	36	0.28
Czech (8)	93	0.71
Czechoslovakian (16)	27	0.21
Danish (11)	63	0.48
Dutch (0)	175	1.34
English (215)	1,051	8.04
European (72)	72	0.55
Finnish (42)	42	0.32
French, ex. Basque (74)	668	5.11
French Canadian (11)	65	0.50
German (1,229)	3,701	28.31
Greek (33)	71	0.54
Hungarian (15)	65	0.50
Irish (567)	2,490	19.05
Italian (180)	382	2.92
Lithuanian (91)	166	1.27
Norwegian (22)	77	0.59
Polish (56)	450	3.44
Portuguese (0)	13	0.10
Russian (14)	71	0.54
Scandinavian (13)	27	0.21
Scotch-Irish (0)	203	1.55
Scottish (28)	298	2.28
Slovak (0)	16	0.12
Swedish (0)	29	0.22
Swiss (0)	31	0.24
Welsh (16)	90	0.69

Hispanic Origin	Population	%
Hispanic or Latino (of any race)	745	5.72
Central American, ex. Mexican	95	0.73
Costa Rican	3	0.02
Guatemalan	22	0.17
Honduran	24	0.18
Nicaraguan	4	0.03
Panamanian	8	0.06
Salvadoran	32	0.25
Other Central American	2	0.02
Cuban	7	0.05
Dominican Republic	7	0.05
Mexican	498	3.82
Puerto Rican	54	0.41
South American	32	0.25
Bolivian	2	0.02
Chilean	1	0.01
Colombian	20	0.15
Peruvian	6	0.05
Venezuelan	2	0.02
Other South American	1	0.01
Other Hispanic or Latino	52	0.40

Race*	Population	%
African-American/Black (2,879)	3,123	23.99
Not Hispanic (2,846)	3,069	23.57
Hispanic (33)	54	0.41
American Indian/Alaska Native (45)	135	1.04
Not Hispanic (34)	117	0.90
Hispanic (11)	18	0.14
Apache (0)	7	0.05
Blackfeet (0)	7	0.05
Cherokee (5)	34	0.26
Chickasaw (0)	1	0.01
Choctaw (0)	7	0.05
Creek (0)	1	0.01
Crow (0)	2	0.02
Mexican American Ind. (2)	3	0.02
Navajo (0)	2	0.02
Pueblo (0)	3	0.02
Seminole (0)	1	0.01
Sioux (0)	4	0.03
Asian (287)	334	2.57
Not Hispanic (286)	329	2.53
Hispanic (1)	5	0.04
Bangladeshi (4)	5	0.04
Cambodian (0)	1	0.01
Chinese, ex. Taiwanese (75)	87	0.67
Filipino (34)	48	0.37
Indian (37)	52	0.40
Indonesian (0)	2	0.02
Japanese (4)	10	0.08
Korean (16)	21	0.16
Laotian (2)	4	0.03
Pakistani (3)	8	0.06
Taiwanese (3)	4	0.03
Thai (4)	7	0.05
Vietnamese (84)	95	0.73
Hawaii Native/Pacific Islander (1)	14	0.11
Not Hispanic (1)	13	0.10
Hispanic (0)	1	0.01
Samoan (0)	1	0.01
Tongan (1)	1	0.01
White (9,052)	9,347	71.79
Not Hispanic (8,768)	9,024	69.31
Hispanic (284)	323	2.48

St. Charles

Place Type: City
County: St. Charles
Population: 65,794†

Ancestry‡	Population	%
African, Sub-Saharan (78)	139	0.21
African (37)	50	0.08
South African (12)	12	0.02
Ugandan (8)	8	0.01
Other Sub-Saharan African (21)	69	0.11
American (3,574)	3,574	5.47
Arab (14)	60	0.09
Arab (0)	11	0.02
Lebanese (14)	32	0.05
Other Arab (0)	17	0.03
Armenian (10)	10	0.02
Australian (0)	11	0.02
Austrian (28)	199	0.30
Basque (28)	28	0.04
Belgian (26)	53	0.08
Brazilian (51)	107	0.16
British (33)	174	0.27
Bulgarian (0)	25	0.04
Cajun (12)	12	0.02
Canadian (114)	179	0.27
Celtic (0)	12	0.02
Croatian (38)	89	0.14
Czech (47)	359	0.55
Czechoslovakian (68)	109	0.17
Danish (44)	391	0.60
Dutch (238)	1,128	1.73
Eastern European (92)	92	0.14
English (2,131)	7,643	11.69
European (1,080)	1,127	1.72
Finnish (0)	59	0.09
French, ex. Basque (403)	3,748	5.73
French Canadian (41)	101	0.15
German (11,696)	26,831	41.04
Greek (172)	517	0.79
Guyanese (11)	11	0.02
Hungarian (136)	292	0.45
Irish (2,558)	11,313	17.31
Italian (1,378)	3,813	5.83
Lithuanian (52)	277	0.42
Macedonian (0)	12	0.02
Norwegian (130)	487	0.74
Pennsylvania German (0)	11	0.02
Polish (398)	1,507	2.31
Portuguese (8)	63	0.10
Romanian (81)	134	0.20
Russian (146)	370	0.57
Scandinavian (23)	225	0.34
Scotch-Irish (421)	1,240	1.90
Scottish (383)	1,280	1.96
Serbian (31)	49	0.07
Slavic (0)	12	0.02
Slovak (35)	55	0.08
Slovene (0)	21	0.03
Swedish (217)	629	0.96
Swiss (12)	308	0.47
Ukrainian (36)	90	0.14
Welsh (41)	617	0.94
West Indian, ex. Hispanic (208)	232	0.35
Belizean (111)	111	0.17
British West Indian (2)	2	<0.01
Jamaican (13)	37	0.06
West Indian (82)	82	0.13
Yugoslavian (47)	61	0.09

Hispanic Origin	Population	%
Hispanic or Latino (of any race)	2,759	4.19
Central American, ex. Mexican	203	0.31
Costa Rican	3	<0.01
Guatemalan	52	0.08
Honduran	42	0.06
Nicaraguan	26	0.04
Panamanian	60	0.09
Salvadoran	16	0.02
Other Central American	4	0.01
Cuban	39	0.06
Dominican Republic	11	0.02
Mexican	1,892	2.88
Puerto Rican	173	0.26
South American	177	0.27
Argentinean	18	0.03
Bolivian	4	0.01
Chilean	17	0.03
Colombian	41	0.06
Ecuadorian	43	0.07
Paraguayan	5	0.01
Peruvian	25	0.04
Uruguayan	15	0.02
Venezuelan	8	0.01
Other South American	1	<0.01
Other Hispanic or Latino	264	0.40

Race*	Population	%
African-American/Black (3,889)	4,548	6.91
Not Hispanic (3,838)	4,445	6.76
Hispanic (51)	103	0.16
American Indian/Alaska Native (182)	536	0.81
Not Hispanic (134)	445	0.68
Hispanic (48)	91	0.14
Apache (1)	9	0.01
Blackfeet (2)	17	0.03
Central American Ind. (3)	3	<0.01
Cherokee (29)	139	0.21
Chickasaw (0)	4	0.01
Chippewa (7)	17	0.03
Choctaw (9)	17	0.03
Comanche (1)	1	<0.01
Cree (3)	3	<0.01
Creek (6)	11	0.02
Crow (0)	1	<0.01
Iroquois (4)	9	0.01
Kiowa (0)	1	<0.01
Lumbee (1)	1	<0.01
Mexican American Ind. (14)	22	0.03
Navajo (3)	7	0.01
Osage (0)	1	<0.01
Ottawa (1)	1	<0.01
Potawatomi (1)	1	<0.01
Pueblo (1)	1	<0.01
Sioux (9)	27	0.04
South American Ind. (0)	5	0.01

*Notes: † The Census 2010 population figure is used to calculate the percentages in the Hispanic Origin and Race categories. Ancestry percentages are based on the 2006-2010 American Community Survey population (not shown); ‡ Numbers in parentheses indicate the number of people reporting a single ancestry; * Numbers in parentheses indicate the number of persons reporting this race alone, not in combination with any other race; Please refer to the Explanation of Data for more information.*

Ute (0)	5	0.01
Yaqui (0)	1	<0.01
Yuman (0)	1	<0.01
Asian (1,673)	1,964	2.99
Not Hispanic (1,664)	1,947	2.96
Hispanic (9)	17	0.03
Chinese, ex. Taiwanese (300)	338	0.51
Filipino (131)	213	0.32
Indian (693)	719	1.09
Indonesian (3)	3	<0.01
Japanese (78)	132	0.20
Korean (152)	182	0.28
Laotian (13)	17	0.03
Malaysian (4)	4	0.01
Nepalese (25)	27	0.04
Pakistani (37)	38	0.06
Sri Lankan (4)	6	0.01
Taiwanese (13)	13	0.02
Thai (30)	42	0.06
Vietnamese (122)	140	0.21
Hawaii Native/Pacific Islander (47)	87	0.13
Not Hispanic (40)	75	0.11
Hispanic (7)	12	0.02
Fijian (4)	4	0.01
Guamanian/Chamorro (10)	16	0.02
Marshallese (2)	2	<0.01
Native Hawaiian (14)	30	0.05
Samoan (1)	2	<0.01
White (57,557)	58,714	89.24
Not Hispanic (56,117)	57,149	86.86
Hispanic (1,440)	1,565	2.38

St. Joseph

Place Type: City
County: Buchanan
Population: 76,780†

Ancestry‡	Population	%
African, Sub-Saharan (257)	296	0.39
African (53)	92	0.12
Ghanaian (57)	57	0.08
Liberian (52)	52	0.07
Nigerian (40)	40	0.05
Senegalese (34)	34	0.04
Sierra Leonean (13)	13	0.02
Sudanese (8)	8	0.01
American (6,487)	6,487	8.55
Arab (159)	170	0.22
Arab (39)	39	0.05
Lebanese (23)	34	0.04
Moroccan (97)	97	0.13
Armenian (38)	54	0.07
Austrian (9)	64	0.08
Belgian (55)	145	0.19
British (49)	124	0.16
Bulgarian (26)	26	0.03
Cajun (0)	11	0.01
Canadian (21)	94	0.12
Croatian (18)	37	0.05
Czech (25)	62	0.08
Czechoslovakian (14)	14	0.02
Danish (103)	361	0.48
Dutch (299)	1,671	2.20
Eastern European (51)	66	0.09
English (3,216)	7,611	10.03
European (476)	581	0.77
French, ex. Basque (456)	2,772	3.65
French Canadian (90)	196	0.26
German (7,830)	20,237	26.66
Greek (30)	84	0.11
Hungarian (19)	66	0.09
Icelander (0)	8	0.01
Iranian (28)	42	0.06
Irish (4,099)	13,398	17.65
Italian (914)	2,031	2.68
Lithuanian (10)	10	0.01
Luxemburger (15)	45	0.06
Northern European (64)	72	0.09
Norwegian (92)	461	0.61
Pennsylvania German (12)	19	0.03
Polish (488)	1,667	2.20
Portuguese (28)	156	0.21
Romanian (46)	83	0.11
Russian (23)	162	0.21
Scandinavian (16)	25	0.03
Scotch-Irish (575)	1,409	1.86
Scottish (379)	1,311	1.73
Slavic (0)	14	0.02
Swedish (217)	668	0.88
Swiss (143)	660	0.87
Turkish (18)	18	0.02
Ukrainian (70)	150	0.20
Welsh (141)	420	0.55
West Indian, ex. Hispanic (32)	69	0.09
Dutch West Indian (0)	9	0.01
Jamaican (0)	28	0.04
West Indian (32)	32	0.04
Yugoslavian (27)	52	0.07

Hispanic Origin	Population	%
Hispanic or Latino (of any race)	4,414	5.75
Central American, ex. Mexican	400	0.52
Costa Rican	5	0.01
Guatemalan	249	0.32
Honduran	38	0.05
Nicaraguan	25	0.03
Panamanian	13	0.02
Salvadoran	69	0.09
Other Central American	1	<0.01
Cuban	114	0.15
Dominican Republic	6	0.01
Mexican	3,263	4.25
Puerto Rican	147	0.19
South American	77	0.10
Argentinean	11	0.01
Bolivian	3	<0.01
Chilean	1	<0.01
Colombian	24	0.03
Peruvian	3	<0.01
Uruguayan	3	<0.01
Venezuelan	32	0.04
Other Hispanic or Latino	407	0.53

Race*	Population	%
African-American/Black (4,585)	5,719	7.45
Not Hispanic (4,501)	5,551	7.23
Hispanic (84)	168	0.22
American Indian/Alaska Native (347)	872	1.14
Not Hispanic (290)	742	0.97
Hispanic (57)	130	0.17
Apache (5)	12	0.02
Blackfeet (7)	13	0.02
Canadian/French Am. Ind. (0)	3	<0.01
Central American Ind. (1)	1	<0.01
Cherokee (47)	214	0.28
Cheyenne (0)	2	<0.01
Chickasaw (0)	2	<0.01
Chippewa (2)	8	0.01
Choctaw (7)	16	0.02
Comanche (2)	2	<0.01
Cree (1)	4	0.01
Creek (1)	6	0.01
Crow (5)	8	0.01
Delaware (0)	5	0.01
Inupiat *(Alaska Native)* (1)	5	0.01
Iroquois (6)	15	0.02
Kiowa (5)	6	0.01
Menominee (2)	2	<0.01
Mexican American Ind. (8)	13	0.02
Navajo (2)	5	0.01
Osage (0)	3	<0.01
Potawatomi (12)	22	0.03
Pueblo (0)	2	<0.01
Puget Sound Salish (6)	8	0.01
Seminole (0)	1	<0.01
Shoshone (1)	2	<0.01
Sioux (18)	48	0.06
Spanish American Ind. (3)	3	<0.01
Tlingit-Haida *(Alaska Native)* (1)	4	0.01
Asian (674)	912	1.19
Not Hispanic (656)	883	1.15
Hispanic (18)	29	0.04
Bangladeshi (6)	6	0.01
Burmese (40)	40	0.05
Cambodian (1)	2	<0.01
Chinese, ex. Taiwanese (119)	139	0.18
Filipino (95)	161	0.21
Indian (169)	193	0.25
Indonesian (1)	2	<0.01
Japanese (21)	57	0.07
Korean (63)	95	0.12
Laotian (0)	2	<0.01
Malaysian (2)	5	0.01
Pakistani (32)	35	0.05
Taiwanese (4)	9	0.01
Thai (8)	10	0.01
Vietnamese (87)	96	0.13
Hawaii Native/Pacific Islander (183)	257	0.33
Not Hispanic (147)	210	0.27
Hispanic (36)	47	0.06
Guamanian/Chamorro (58)	66	0.09
Marshallese (1)	1	<0.01
Native Hawaiian (50)	77	0.10
Samoan (12)	31	0.04
White (67,384)	69,307	90.27
Not Hispanic (65,053)	66,612	86.76
Hispanic (2,331)	2,695	3.51

St. Louis

Place Type: City
County: St. Louis city
Population: 319,294†

Ancestry‡	Population	%
Afghan (926)	926	0.29
African, Sub-Saharan (6,117)	6,762	2.12
African (3,976)	4,621	1.45
Ethiopian (246)	246	0.08
Ghanaian (18)	18	0.01
Kenyan (266)	266	0.08
Liberian (273)	273	0.09
Nigerian (327)	327	0.10
Sierra Leonean (125)	125	0.04
Somalian (533)	533	0.17
South African (12)	12	<0.01
Sudanese (36)	36	0.01
Ugandan (12)	12	<0.01
Zimbabwean (24)	24	0.01
Other Sub-Saharan African (269)	269	0.08
Albanian (442)	587	0.18
Alsatian (0)	8	<0.01
American (11,071)	11,071	3.47
Arab (1,492)	2,332	0.73
Arab (176)	244	0.08
Egyptian (82)	109	0.03
Iraqi (679)	723	0.23
Jordanian (9)	9	<0.01
Lebanese (412)	1,013	0.32
Moroccan (34)	34	0.01
Palestinian (12)	20	0.01
Syrian (18)	88	0.03
Other Arab (70)	92	0.03
Armenian (36)	160	0.05
Australian (23)	48	0.02
Austrian (175)	765	0.24
Belgian (68)	302	0.09
Brazilian (143)	143	0.04
British (288)	690	0.22
Bulgarian (86)	143	0.04
Cajun (10)	10	<0.01
Canadian (107)	210	0.07
Celtic (22)	40	0.01
Croatian (308)	875	0.27
Cypriot (24)	24	0.01
Czech (328)	1,655	0.52
Czechoslovakian (114)	307	0.10
Danish (123)	586	0.18
Dutch (337)	2,071	0.65

*Notes: † The Census 2010 population figure is used to calculate the percentages in the Hispanic Origin and Race categories. Ancestry percentages are based on the 2006-2010 American Community Survey population (not shown); ‡ Numbers in parentheses indicate the number of people reporting a single ancestry; * Numbers in parentheses indicate the number of persons reporting this race alone, not in combination with any other race; Please refer to the Explanation of Data for more information.*

Eastern European (314)	356	0.11
English (3,381)	14,777	4.64
Estonian (0)	9	<0.01
European (5,238)	6,123	1.92
Finnish (0)	76	0.02
French, ex. Basque (950)	8,663	2.72
French Canadian (140)	503	0.16
German (17,780)	51,664	16.21
Greek (261)	528	0.17
Guyanese (18)	18	0.01
Hungarian (291)	1,122	0.35
Icelander (0)	30	0.01
Iranian (179)	307	0.10
Irish (7,168)	31,486	9.88
Israeli (34)	58	0.02
Italian (4,730)	11,751	3.69
Latvian (7)	14	<0.01
Lithuanian (167)	416	0.13
Macedonian (34)	53	0.02
Maltese (0)	12	<0.01
Northern European (56)	56	0.02
Norwegian (294)	1,089	0.34
Polish (1,935)	6,363	2.00
Portuguese (28)	53	0.02
Romanian (165)	236	0.07
Russian (751)	1,765	0.55
Scandinavian (95)	286	0.09
Scotch-Irish (1,090)	3,000	0.94
Scottish (850)	2,792	0.88
Serbian (112)	241	0.08
Slavic (8)	61	0.02
Slovak (90)	328	0.10
Slovene (43)	65	0.02
Soviet Union (8)	8	<0.01
Swedish (360)	1,721	0.54
Swiss (180)	758	0.24
Turkish (240)	290	0.09
Ukrainian (123)	315	0.10
Welsh (288)	1,263	0.40
West Indian, ex. Hispanic (581)	785	0.25
Bermudan (14)	14	<0.01
British West Indian (11)	11	<0.01
Haitian (278)	324	0.10
Jamaican (246)	368	0.12
Trinidadian/Tobagonian (11)	11	<0.01
West Indian (21)	57	0.02
Yugoslavian (2,646)	2,707	0.85

Hispanic Origin	Population	%
Hispanic or Latino (of any race)	11,130	3.49
Central American, ex. Mexican	954	0.30
Costa Rican	32	0.01
Guatemalan	139	0.04
Honduran	449	0.14
Nicaraguan	106	0.03
Panamanian	81	0.03
Salvadoran	138	0.04
Other Central American	9	<0.01
Cuban	474	0.15
Dominican Republic	75	0.02
Mexican	7,163	2.24
Puerto Rican	700	0.22
South American	590	0.18
Argentinean	70	0.02
Bolivian	39	0.01
Chilean	52	0.02
Colombian	178	0.06
Ecuadorian	52	0.02
Paraguayan	4	<0.01
Peruvian	115	0.04
Uruguayan	13	<0.01
Venezuelan	59	0.02
Other South American	8	<0.01
Other Hispanic or Latino	1,174	0.37

Race*	Population	%
African-American/Black (157,160)	161,796	50.67
Not Hispanic (156,389)	160,631	50.31
Hispanic (771)	1,165	0.36
American Indian/Alaska Native (838)	3,081	0.96
Not Hispanic (684)	2,760	0.86
Hispanic (154)	321	0.10
Alaska Athabascan *(Ala. Nat.)* (2)	9	<0.01
Apache (17)	41	0.01
Arapaho (3)	7	<0.01
Blackfeet (18)	161	0.05
Canadian/French Am. Ind. (1)	6	<0.01
Central American Ind. (5)	9	<0.01
Cherokee (137)	826	0.26
Cheyenne (2)	4	<0.01
Chickasaw (3)	22	0.01
Chippewa (12)	23	0.01
Choctaw (24)	95	0.03
Comanche (3)	5	<0.01
Cree (4)	9	<0.01
Creek (10)	29	0.01
Crow (0)	8	<0.01
Delaware (2)	4	<0.01
Hopi (8)	17	0.01
Houma (1)	1	<0.01
Inupiat *(Alaska Native)* (0)	3	<0.01
Iroquois (15)	28	0.01
Kiowa (6)	8	<0.01
Lumbee (2)	6	<0.01
Mexican American Ind. (34)	58	0.02
Navajo (10)	34	0.01
Osage (1)	9	<0.01
Ottawa (1)	2	<0.01
Paiute (0)	1	<0.01
Pima (0)	2	<0.01
Potawatomi (2)	8	<0.01
Pueblo (2)	4	<0.01
Puget Sound Salish (1)	1	<0.01
Seminole (1)	10	<0.01
Shoshone (1)	5	<0.01
Sioux (11)	76	0.02
South American Ind. (3)	10	<0.01
Spanish American Ind. (3)	5	<0.01
Tlingit-Haida *(Alaska Native)* (2)	5	<0.01
Tohono O'Odham (1)	1	<0.01
Ute (2)	3	<0.01
Yaqui (0)	3	<0.01
Yuman (0)	1	<0.01
Yup'ik *(Alaska Native)* (1)	1	<0.01
Asian (9,291)	11,185	3.50
Not Hispanic (9,233)	11,013	3.45
Hispanic (58)	172	0.05
Bangladeshi (23)	26	0.01
Bhutanese (229)	306	0.10
Burmese (234)	241	0.08
Cambodian (53)	73	0.02
Chinese, ex. Taiwanese (1,787)	2,130	0.67
Filipino (562)	870	0.27
Hmong (3)	5	<0.01
Indian (1,613)	1,885	0.59
Indonesian (24)	36	0.01
Japanese (212)	408	0.13
Korean (515)	679	0.21
Laotian (251)	290	0.09
Malaysian (14)	26	0.01
Nepalese (87)	161	0.05
Pakistani (91)	107	0.03
Sri Lankan (9)	11	<0.01
Taiwanese (142)	173	0.05
Thai (87)	118	0.04
Vietnamese (2,835)	3,058	0.96
Hawaii Native/Pacific Islander (74)	362	0.11
Not Hispanic (62)	304	0.10
Hispanic (12)	58	0.02
Fijian (3)	5	<0.01
Guamanian/Chamorro (11)	45	0.01
Marshallese (0)	1	<0.01
Native Hawaiian (31)	120	0.04
Samoan (10)	55	0.02
Tongan (1)	1	<0.01
White (140,267)	146,158	45.78
Not Hispanic (134,702)	139,920	43.82
Hispanic (5,565)	6,238	1.95

St. Peters

Place Type: City
County: St. Charles
Population: 52,575†

Ancestry‡	Population	%
African, Sub-Saharan (236)	241	0.46
African (129)	134	0.25
Somalian (77)	77	0.15
Other Sub-Saharan African (30)	30	0.06
American (3,202)	3,202	6.06
Arab (65)	85	0.16
Arab (38)	38	0.07
Egyptian (20)	20	0.04
Jordanian (0)	11	0.02
Lebanese (7)	7	0.01
Syrian (0)	9	0.02
Australian (13)	41	0.08
Austrian (68)	267	0.51
Belgian (27)	52	0.10
Brazilian (29)	40	0.08
British (81)	106	0.20
Bulgarian (113)	113	0.21
Cajun (11)	19	0.04
Canadian (1)	56	0.11
Croatian (11)	23	0.04
Czech (84)	245	0.46
Czechoslovakian (8)	24	0.05
Danish (23)	75	0.14
Dutch (134)	1,047	1.98
Eastern European (11)	11	0.02
English (1,540)	5,910	11.18
European (821)	878	1.66
Finnish (0)	9	0.02
French, ex. Basque (259)	2,833	5.36
French Canadian (34)	152	0.29
German (8,279)	22,461	42.50
German Russian (10)	10	0.02
Greek (100)	293	0.55
Hungarian (38)	132	0.25
Icelander (16)	16	0.03
Iranian (82)	97	0.18
Irish (2,043)	10,466	19.80
Israeli (0)	9	0.02
Italian (989)	3,762	7.12
Latvian (0)	12	0.02
Lithuanian (18)	159	0.30
Norwegian (97)	582	1.10
Pennsylvania German (14)	104	0.20
Polish (392)	1,925	3.64
Portuguese (13)	39	0.07
Romanian (20)	44	0.08
Russian (126)	243	0.46
Scandinavian (13)	86	0.16
Scotch-Irish (525)	985	1.86
Scottish (361)	998	1.89
Serbian (0)	9	0.02
Slavic (33)	79	0.15
Slovak (0)	77	0.15
Swedish (43)	565	1.07
Swiss (36)	215	0.41
Turkish (5)	5	0.01
Ukrainian (31)	106	0.20
Welsh (107)	385	0.73
West Indian, ex. Hispanic (23)	71	0.13
Trinidadian/Tobagonian (23)	23	0.04
West Indian (0)	48	0.09
Yugoslavian (53)	74	0.14

Hispanic Origin	Population	%
Hispanic or Latino (of any race)	1,319	2.51
Central American, ex. Mexican	128	0.24
Costa Rican	15	0.03
Guatemalan	36	0.07
Honduran	49	0.09
Nicaraguan	1	<0.01
Panamanian	13	0.02
Salvadoran	14	0.03
Cuban	47	0.09

*Notes: † The Census 2010 population figure is used to calculate the percentages in the Hispanic Origin and Race categories. Ancestry percentages are based on the 2006-2010 American Community Survey population (not shown); ‡ Numbers in parentheses indicate the number of people reporting a single ancestry; * Numbers in parentheses indicate the number of persons reporting this race alone, not in combination with any other race; Please refer to the Explanation of Data for more information.*

	Population	%
Dominican Republic	16	0.03
Mexican	785	1.49
Puerto Rican	138	0.26
South American	90	0.17
Argentinean	4	0.01
Bolivian	3	0.01
Chilean	10	0.02
Colombian	21	0.04
Ecuadorian	15	0.03
Paraguayan	1	<0.01
Peruvian	17	0.03
Uruguayan	5	0.01
Venezuelan	14	0.03
Other Hispanic or Latino	115	0.22

Race*	Population	%
African-American/Black (1,939)	2,306	4.39
Not Hispanic (1,921)	2,268	4.31
Hispanic (18)	38	0.07
American Indian/Alaska Native (96)	361	0.69
Not Hispanic (71)	298	0.57
Hispanic (25)	63	0.12
Alaska Athabascan *(Ala. Nat.)* (1)	1	<0.01
Aleut *(Alaska Native)* (1)	1	<0.01
Apache (0)	7	0.01
Arapaho (1)	1	<0.01
Blackfeet (0)	12	0.02
Canadian/French Am. Ind. (3)	3	0.01
Cherokee (23)	120	0.23
Chickasaw (0)	2	<0.01
Chippewa (2)	3	0.01
Choctaw (1)	10	0.02
Comanche (1)	1	<0.01
Cree (3)	3	0.01
Creek (1)	9	0.02
Delaware (1)	2	<0.01
Iroquois (0)	6	0.01
Lumbee (1)	1	<0.01
Mexican American Ind. (3)	8	0.02
Osage (0)	4	0.01
Ottawa (2)	2	<0.01
Pueblo (2)	2	<0.01
Seminole (0)	1	<0.01
Sioux (5)	12	0.02
South American Ind. (3)	6	0.01
Spanish American Ind. (5)	6	0.01
Ute (1)	2	<0.01
Asian (971)	1,262	2.40
Not Hispanic (967)	1,253	2.38
Hispanic (4)	9	0.02
Bangladeshi (0)	1	<0.01
Cambodian (1)	3	0.01
Chinese, ex. Taiwanese (173)	207	0.39
Filipino (163)	258	0.49
Indian (290)	326	0.62
Indonesian (1)	3	0.01
Japanese (25)	60	0.11
Korean (94)	124	0.24
Laotian (1)	1	<0.01
Malaysian (2)	3	0.01
Nepalese (2)	3	0.01
Pakistani (15)	25	0.05
Taiwanese (10)	19	0.04
Thai (28)	32	0.06
Vietnamese (133)	160	0.30
Hawaii Native/Pacific Islander (33)	67	0.13
Not Hispanic (29)	58	0.11
Hispanic (4)	9	0.02
Guamanian/Chamorro (12)	16	0.03
Native Hawaiian (4)	20	0.04
Samoan (3)	10	0.02
White (48,196)	49,048	93.29
Not Hispanic (47,414)	48,164	91.61
Hispanic (782)	884	1.68

Sunset Hills

Place Type: City
County: St. Louis
Population: 8,496†

Ancestry‡	Population	%
African, Sub-Saharan (28)	28	0.33
African (28)	28	0.33
Albanian (24)	35	0.42
Alsatian (0)	11	0.13
American (446)	446	5.29
Arab (28)	102	1.21
Lebanese (0)	74	0.88
Other Arab (28)	28	0.33
Austrian (0)	34	0.40
Belgian (0)	49	0.58
British (9)	19	0.23
Croatian (287)	318	3.77
Czech (40)	77	0.91
Dutch (12)	104	1.23
English (230)	920	10.92
European (210)	222	2.64
French, ex. Basque (122)	473	5.61
German (1,657)	3,569	42.37
Greek (135)	174	2.07
Hungarian (57)	103	1.22
Irish (459)	1,630	19.35
Italian (233)	694	8.24
Latvian (0)	10	0.12
Lithuanian (9)	9	0.11
Norwegian (27)	36	0.43
Polish (19)	100	1.19
Portuguese (0)	9	0.11
Romanian (8)	8	0.09
Russian (39)	50	0.59
Scotch-Irish (52)	109	1.29
Scottish (20)	92	1.09
Serbian (0)	10	0.12
Swedish (20)	120	1.42
Swiss (13)	297	3.53
Ukrainian (28)	28	0.33
Welsh (0)	81	0.96
West Indian, ex. Hispanic (0)	16	0.19
Barbadian (0)	16	0.19
Yugoslavian (16)	16	0.19

Hispanic Origin	Population	%
Hispanic or Latino (of any race)	139	1.64
Central American, ex. Mexican	16	0.19
Guatemalan	12	0.14
Honduran	2	0.02
Panamanian	1	0.01
Salvadoran	1	0.01
Cuban	2	0.02
Mexican	69	0.81
Puerto Rican	8	0.09
South American	17	0.20
Argentinean	5	0.06
Colombian	5	0.06
Peruvian	3	0.04
Venezuelan	4	0.05
Other Hispanic or Latino	27	0.32

Race*	Population	%
African-American/Black (129)	174	2.05
Not Hispanic (129)	169	1.99
Hispanic (0)	5	0.06
American Indian/Alaska Native (17)	48	0.56
Not Hispanic (13)	38	0.45
Hispanic (4)	10	0.12
Apache (0)	4	0.05
Blackfeet (0)	3	0.04
Cherokee (9)	19	0.22
Cheyenne (0)	1	0.01
Chippewa (0)	2	0.02
Choctaw (1)	1	0.01
Iroquois (1)	1	0.01
Mexican American Ind. (1)	5	0.06
Osage (0)	4	0.05
South American Ind. (2)	2	0.02
Asian (199)	254	2.99
Not Hispanic (198)	249	2.93
Hispanic (1)	5	0.06
Chinese, ex. Taiwanese (48)	54	0.64
Filipino (34)	54	0.64
Indian (36)	50	0.59
Indonesian (0)	3	0.04
Japanese (5)	7	0.08
Korean (24)	27	0.32
Laotian (8)	10	0.12
Nepalese (1)	1	0.01
Pakistani (4)	5	0.06
Taiwanese (1)	3	0.04
Thai (4)	5	0.06
Vietnamese (25)	27	0.32
Hawaii Native/Pacific Islander (2)	5	0.06
Not Hispanic (0)	3	0.04
Hispanic (2)	2	0.02
Guamanian/Chamorro (2)	2	0.02
White (7,992)	8,107	95.42
Not Hispanic (7,909)	8,007	94.24
Hispanic (83)	100	1.18

Town and Country

Place Type: City
County: St. Louis
Population: 10,815†

Ancestry‡	Population	%
African, Sub-Saharan (8)	8	0.07
African (8)	8	0.07
American (932)	932	8.62
Armenian (62)	62	0.57
Austrian (22)	134	1.24
Belgian (0)	11	0.10
Brazilian (29)	29	0.27
British (0)	33	0.31
Czech (11)	90	0.83
Danish (9)	28	0.26
Dutch (35)	188	1.74
Eastern European (9)	9	0.08
English (424)	1,603	14.83
Estonian (0)	15	0.14
European (15)	15	0.14
Finnish (0)	16	0.15
French, ex. Basque (59)	404	3.74
French Canadian (0)	11	0.10
German (1,680)	3,591	33.21
Greek (18)	18	0.17
Hungarian (5)	22	0.20
Iranian (107)	107	0.99
Irish (622)	1,795	16.60
Italian (350)	931	8.61
Lithuanian (0)	11	0.10
Norwegian (20)	63	0.58
Polish (167)	440	4.07
Portuguese (15)	75	0.69
Russian (80)	203	1.88
Scandinavian (0)	23	0.21
Scotch-Irish (169)	341	3.15
Scottish (53)	206	1.91
Serbian (36)	36	0.33
Swedish (37)	199	1.84
Swiss (104)	161	1.49
Ukrainian (21)	52	0.48
Welsh (0)	34	0.31
West Indian, ex. Hispanic (10)	10	0.09
Belizean (10)	10	0.09
Yugoslavian (0)	2	0.02

Hispanic Origin	Population	%
Hispanic or Latino (of any race)	189	1.75
Central American, ex. Mexican	16	0.15
Costa Rican	6	0.06
Guatemalan	2	0.02
Honduran	4	0.04
Nicaraguan	1	0.01
Panamanian	3	0.03
Cuban	9	0.08
Dominican Republic	3	0.03
Mexican	66	0.61
Puerto Rican	21	0.19
South American	43	0.40
Argentinean	13	0.12

*Notes: † The Census 2010 population figure is used to calculate the percentages in the Hispanic Origin and Race categories. Ancestry percentages are based on the 2006-2010 American Community Survey population (not shown); ‡ Numbers in parentheses indicate the number of people reporting a single ancestry; * Numbers in parentheses indicate the number of persons reporting this race alone, not in combination with any other race; Please refer to the Explanation of Data for more information.*

	Population	%
Bolivian	9	0.08
Colombian	11	0.10
Peruvian	3	0.03
Venezuelan	7	0.06
Other Hispanic or Latino	31	0.29

Race*	Population	%
African-American/Black (280)	307	2.84
Not Hispanic (276)	300	2.77
Hispanic (4)	7	0.06
American Indian/Alaska Native (12)	39	0.36
Not Hispanic (12)	35	0.32
Hispanic (0)	4	0.04
Blackfeet (0)	1	0.01
Cherokee (1)	5	0.05
Chippewa (2)	2	0.02
Choctaw (1)	3	0.03
Comanche (1)	1	0.01
Iroquois (0)	1	0.01
Lumbee (0)	1	0.01
Potawatomi (0)	1	0.01
Asian (812)	929	8.59
Not Hispanic (809)	919	8.50
Hispanic (3)	10	0.09
Bangladeshi (9)	9	0.08
Burmese (1)	1	0.01
Chinese, ex. Taiwanese (117)	144	1.33
Filipino (64)	85	0.79
Indian (314)	334	3.09
Indonesian (3)	3	0.03
Japanese (9)	17	0.16
Korean (54)	68	0.63
Laotian (0)	1	0.01
Pakistani (132)	153	1.41
Sri Lankan (4)	4	0.04
Taiwanese (29)	29	0.27
Thai (19)	20	0.18
Vietnamese (25)	33	0.31
Hawaii Native/Pacific Islander (10)	18	0.17
Not Hispanic (10)	17	0.16
Hispanic (0)	1	0.01
Guamanian/Chamorro (2)	2	0.02
Marshallese (1)	1	0.01
Native Hawaiian (0)	2	0.02
Samoan (3)	4	0.04
White (9,494)	9,641	89.14
Not Hispanic (9,350)	9,483	87.68
Hispanic (144)	158	1.46

Troy

Place Type: City
County: Lincoln
Population: 10,540†

Ancestry‡	Population	%
African, Sub-Saharan (19)	19	0.19
African (19)	19	0.19
Alsatian (0)	8	0.08
American (651)	651	6.44
Armenian (0)	18	0.18
Austrian (0)	25	0.25
British (45)	71	0.70
Czech (15)	58	0.57
Danish (0)	30	0.30
Dutch (0)	223	2.21
English (177)	748	7.40
European (115)	127	1.26
French, ex. Basque (10)	466	4.61
French Canadian (10)	10	0.10
German (1,413)	3,856	38.17
Hungarian (0)	22	0.22
Irish (364)	2,134	21.12
Italian (71)	578	5.72
Lithuanian (0)	19	0.19
Northern European (10)	10	0.10
Norwegian (0)	20	0.20
Polish (188)	413	4.09
Portuguese (0)	8	0.08
Russian (40)	59	0.58
Scandinavian (0)	15	0.15
Scotch-Irish (160)	280	2.77
Scottish (45)	125	1.24
Swedish (0)	41	0.41
Ukrainian (0)	9	0.09

Hispanic Origin	Population	%
Hispanic or Latino (of any race)	313	2.97
Central American, ex. Mexican	8	0.08
Costa Rican	1	0.01
Guatemalan	1	0.01
Honduran	1	0.01
Panamanian	5	0.05
Cuban	11	0.10
Mexican	239	2.27
Puerto Rican	21	0.20
South American	9	0.09
Colombian	2	0.02
Ecuadorian	1	0.01
Peruvian	5	0.05
Venezuelan	1	0.01
Other Hispanic or Latino	25	0.24

Race*	Population	%
African-American/Black (324)	448	4.25
Not Hispanic (317)	438	4.16
Hispanic (7)	10	0.09
American Indian/Alaska Native (43)	119	1.13
Not Hispanic (37)	107	1.02
Hispanic (6)	12	0.11
Apache (1)	3	0.03
Blackfeet (1)	4	0.04
Cherokee (9)	30	0.28
Cheyenne (0)	1	0.01
Chippewa (0)	1	0.01
Choctaw (2)	2	0.02
Colville (1)	1	0.01
Comanche (3)	3	0.03
Inupiat *(Alaska Native)* (0)	1	0.01
Mexican American Ind. (0)	1	0.01
Osage (3)	3	0.03
Potawatomi (3)	3	0.03
Puget Sound Salish (0)	1	0.01
Sioux (0)	2	0.02
Yup'ik *(Alaska Native)* (5)	5	0.05
Asian (79)	128	1.21
Not Hispanic (77)	121	1.15
Hispanic (2)	7	0.07
Chinese, ex. Taiwanese (21)	25	0.24
Filipino (13)	32	0.30
Indian (14)	17	0.16
Japanese (3)	9	0.09
Korean (6)	14	0.13
Pakistani (12)	12	0.11
Thai (3)	8	0.08
Vietnamese (6)	8	0.08
Hawaii Native/Pacific Islander (4)	8	0.08
Not Hispanic (3)	7	0.07
Hispanic (1)	1	0.01
Guamanian/Chamorro (1)	2	0.02
Native Hawaiian (2)	3	0.03
White (9,751)	9,995	94.83
Not Hispanic (9,571)	9,786	92.85
Hispanic (180)	209	1.98

Union

Place Type: City
County: Franklin
Population: 10,204†

Ancestry‡	Population	%
American (1,008)	1,008	10.26
Austrian (0)	16	0.16
British (12)	12	0.12
Czech (0)	32	0.33
Danish (14)	22	0.22
Dutch (58)	235	2.39
English (383)	789	8.03
European (130)	130	1.32
French, ex. Basque (37)	283	2.88
German (1,739)	3,937	40.09
Greek (0)	39	0.40
Hungarian (15)	15	0.15
Irish (400)	1,823	18.56
Italian (161)	367	3.74
Norwegian (9)	92	0.94
Polish (83)	206	2.10
Romanian (14)	58	0.59
Russian (86)	147	1.50
Scotch-Irish (18)	125	1.27
Scottish (39)	179	1.82
Slovak (0)	19	0.19
Swedish (23)	69	0.70
Swiss (0)	12	0.12
Welsh (0)	13	0.13

Hispanic Origin	Population	%
Hispanic or Latino (of any race)	146	1.43
Central American, ex. Mexican	11	0.11
Guatemalan	6	0.06
Honduran	1	0.01
Nicaraguan	3	0.03
Salvadoran	1	0.01
Cuban	7	0.07
Mexican	95	0.93
Puerto Rican	8	0.08
South American	2	0.02
Argentinean	1	0.01
Colombian	1	0.01
Other Hispanic or Latino	23	0.23

Race*	Population	%
African-American/Black (110)	185	1.81
Not Hispanic (110)	182	1.78
Hispanic (0)	3	0.03
American Indian/Alaska Native (57)	113	1.11
Not Hispanic (51)	104	1.02
Hispanic (6)	9	0.09
Blackfeet (5)	7	0.07
Cherokee (25)	48	0.47
Chickasaw (4)	4	0.04
Chippewa (2)	2	0.02
Choctaw (1)	1	0.01
Kiowa (0)	3	0.03
Lumbee (1)	1	0.01
Sioux (1)	1	0.01
Asian (43)	84	0.82
Not Hispanic (43)	80	0.78
Hispanic (0)	4	0.04
Cambodian (1)	2	0.02
Chinese, ex. Taiwanese (6)	7	0.07
Filipino (13)	25	0.25
Indian (3)	8	0.08
Japanese (3)	10	0.10
Korean (3)	11	0.11
Malaysian (0)	3	0.03
Thai (3)	5	0.05
Vietnamese (11)	14	0.14
Hawaii Native/Pacific Islander (3)	6	0.06
Not Hispanic (3)	6	0.06
Guamanian/Chamorro (1)	1	0.01
Samoan (0)	2	0.02
White (9,767)	9,929	97.30
Not Hispanic (9,674)	9,829	96.32
Hispanic (93)	100	0.98

University City

Place Type: City
County: St. Louis
Population: 35,371†

Ancestry‡	Population	%
African, Sub-Saharan (664)	722	2.02
African (409)	467	1.31
Ethiopian (167)	167	0.47
Liberian (54)	54	0.15
South African (17)	17	0.05
Other Sub-Saharan African (17)	17	0.05

*Notes: † The Census 2010 population figure is used to calculate the percentages in the Hispanic Origin and Race categories. Ancestry percentages are based on the 2006-2010 American Community Survey population (not shown); ‡ Numbers in parentheses indicate the number of people reporting a single ancestry; * Numbers in parentheses indicate the number of persons reporting this race alone, not in combination with any other race; Please refer to the Explanation of Data for more information.*

American (1,814)	1,814	5.08
Arab (31)	88	0.25
Arab (0)	20	0.06
Iraqi (11)	11	0.03
Lebanese (20)	37	0.10
Other Arab (0)	20	0.06
Armenian (0)	13	0.04
Australian (16)	49	0.14
Austrian (28)	102	0.29
Belgian (0)	36	0.10
British (55)	138	0.39
Canadian (24)	24	0.07
Croatian (26)	26	0.07
Czech (48)	177	0.50
Danish (33)	120	0.34
Dutch (51)	218	0.61
Eastern European (278)	340	0.95
English (679)	2,390	6.69
European (663)	787	2.20
Finnish (0)	14	0.04
French, ex. Basque (122)	676	1.89
French Canadian (93)	108	0.30
German (1,463)	5,343	14.96
Greek (10)	24	0.07
Hungarian (38)	105	0.29
Irish (860)	3,356	9.40
Italian (294)	840	2.35
Latvian (16)	25	0.07
Lithuanian (27)	222	0.62
Northern European (13)	29	0.08
Norwegian (48)	242	0.68
Pennsylvania German (12)	23	0.06
Polish (434)	1,180	3.30
Portuguese (0)	10	0.03
Romanian (74)	74	0.21
Russian (585)	1,369	3.83
Scandinavian (0)	49	0.14
Scotch-Irish (174)	484	1.36
Scottish (132)	595	1.67
Slovak (0)	27	0.08
Slovene (0)	11	0.03
Swedish (27)	172	0.48
Swiss (23)	112	0.31
Turkish (14)	14	0.04
Ukrainian (178)	289	0.81
Welsh (45)	170	0.48
West Indian, ex. Hispanic (52)	83	0.23
Bahamian (0)	31	0.09
Dutch West Indian (11)	11	0.03
West Indian (41)	41	0.11
Yugoslavian (13)	13	0.04

Hispanic Origin	Population	%
Hispanic or Latino (of any race)	979	2.77
Central American, ex. Mexican	103	0.29
Costa Rican	7	0.02
Guatemalan	35	0.10
Honduran	30	0.08
Nicaraguan	10	0.03
Panamanian	14	0.04
Salvadoran	7	0.02
Cuban	39	0.11
Dominican Republic	22	0.06
Mexican	429	1.21
Puerto Rican	85	0.24
South American	193	0.55
Argentinean	30	0.08
Bolivian	10	0.03
Chilean	13	0.04
Colombian	56	0.16
Ecuadorian	16	0.05
Paraguayan	2	0.01
Peruvian	33	0.09
Uruguayan	20	0.06
Venezuelan	12	0.03
Other South American	1	<0.01
Other Hispanic or Latino	108	0.31

Race*	Population	%
African-American/Black (14,535)	15,129	42.77
Not Hispanic (14,450)	15,010	42.44
Hispanic (85)	119	0.34
American Indian/Alaska Native (89)	364	1.03
Not Hispanic (69)	318	0.90
Hispanic (20)	46	0.13
Apache (1)	4	0.01
Arapaho (1)	3	0.01
Blackfeet (3)	28	0.08
Cherokee (11)	81	0.23
Chickasaw (0)	1	<0.01
Choctaw (1)	14	0.04
Creek (2)	4	0.01
Delaware (0)	1	<0.01
Houma (0)	4	0.01
Iroquois (1)	3	0.01
Lumbee (2)	5	0.01
Mexican American Ind. (11)	13	0.04
Navajo (3)	3	0.01
Osage (3)	5	0.01
Pima (0)	1	<0.01
Potawatomi (1)	2	0.01
Pueblo (0)	1	<0.01
Seminole (1)	4	0.01
Sioux (1)	4	0.01
South American Ind. (1)	9	0.03
Yaqui (0)	1	<0.01
Asian (1,504)	1,803	5.10
Not Hispanic (1,498)	1,786	5.05
Hispanic (6)	17	0.05
Bangladeshi (1)	1	<0.01
Burmese (3)	3	0.01
Chinese, ex. Taiwanese (710)	789	2.23
Filipino (61)	103	0.29
Indian (276)	317	0.90
Indonesian (3)	3	0.01
Japanese (51)	116	0.33
Korean (157)	194	0.55
Laotian (9)	9	0.03
Malaysian (1)	4	0.01
Nepalese (30)	32	0.09
Pakistani (25)	32	0.09
Sri Lankan (12)	12	0.03
Taiwanese (62)	77	0.22
Thai (9)	17	0.05
Vietnamese (47)	67	0.19
Hawaii Native/Pacific Islander (10)	31	0.09
Not Hispanic (4)	20	0.06
Hispanic (6)	11	0.03
Guamanian/Chamorro (3)	5	0.01
Native Hawaiian (0)	9	0.03
Samoan (4)	6	0.02
Tongan (1)	1	<0.01
White (17,954)	18,694	52.85
Not Hispanic (17,417)	18,099	51.17
Hispanic (537)	595	1.68

Warrensburg

Place Type: City
County: Johnson
Population: 18,838†

Ancestry‡	Population	%
African, Sub-Saharan (261)	280	1.52
African (138)	157	0.85
Ethiopian (79)	79	0.43
Ghanaian (8)	8	0.04
Kenyan (36)	36	0.19
American (880)	880	4.77
Arab (98)	113	0.61
Arab (35)	35	0.19
Syrian (0)	15	0.08
Other Arab (63)	63	0.34
Australian (0)	23	0.12
Austrian (29)	87	0.47
Belgian (29)	36	0.19
British (83)	83	0.45
Canadian (11)	11	0.06
Croatian (0)	13	0.07
Czech (36)	49	0.27
Danish (32)	86	0.47
Dutch (65)	325	1.76
English (775)	2,091	11.32
European (191)	224	1.21
Finnish (0)	29	0.16
French, ex. Basque (128)	682	3.69
French Canadian (1)	85	0.46
German (2,284)	6,197	33.56
Greek (12)	12	0.06
Hungarian (19)	19	0.10
Irish (551)	2,817	15.26
Italian (241)	859	4.65
Latvian (0)	17	0.09
Northern European (61)	61	0.33
Norwegian (48)	315	1.71
Pennsylvania German (0)	31	0.17
Polish (86)	355	1.92
Portuguese (13)	13	0.07
Russian (6)	55	0.30
Scotch-Irish (285)	555	3.01
Scottish (272)	730	3.95
Slovak (14)	39	0.21
Swedish (60)	530	2.87
Turkish (53)	53	0.29
Ukrainian (0)	81	0.44
Welsh (22)	141	0.76
West Indian, ex. Hispanic (29)	48	0.26
Belizean (29)	29	0.16
Haitian (0)	11	0.06
Jamaican (0)	8	0.04
Yugoslavian (0)	13	0.07

Hispanic Origin	Population	%
Hispanic or Latino (of any race)	590	3.13
Central American, ex. Mexican	36	0.19
Costa Rican	4	0.02
Guatemalan	5	0.03
Honduran	7	0.04
Nicaraguan	2	0.01
Panamanian	9	0.05
Salvadoran	9	0.05
Cuban	22	0.12
Dominican Republic	3	0.02
Mexican	366	1.94
Puerto Rican	55	0.29
South American	26	0.14
Argentinean	1	0.01
Bolivian	4	0.02
Colombian	5	0.03
Ecuadorian	1	0.01
Peruvian	6	0.03
Venezuelan	8	0.04
Other South American	1	0.01
Other Hispanic or Latino	82	0.44

Race*	Population	%
African-American/Black (1,408)	1,693	8.99
Not Hispanic (1,370)	1,640	8.71
Hispanic (38)	53	0.28
American Indian/Alaska Native (93)	239	1.27
Not Hispanic (78)	211	1.12
Hispanic (15)	28	0.15
Apache (2)	9	0.05
Arapaho (1)	1	0.01
Blackfeet (0)	3	0.02
Cherokee (24)	76	0.40
Cheyenne (0)	1	0.01
Chickasaw (1)	1	0.01
Chippewa (6)	10	0.05
Choctaw (4)	16	0.08
Creek (0)	3	0.02
Delaware (1)	1	0.01
Iroquois (2)	2	0.01
Mexican American Ind. (1)	4	0.02
Navajo (3)	8	0.04
Osage (0)	4	0.02
Potawatomi (2)	4	0.02
Pueblo (1)	1	0.01
Seminole (0)	1	0.01
Shoshone (1)	1	0.01

*Notes: † The Census 2010 population figure is used to calculate the percentages in the Hispanic Origin and Race categories. Ancestry percentages are based on the 2006-2010 American Community Survey population (not shown); ‡ Numbers in parentheses indicate the number of people reporting a single ancestry; * Numbers in parentheses indicate the number of persons reporting this race alone, not in combination with any other race; Please refer to the Explanation of Data for more information.*

Sioux (0)	4	0.02
South American Ind. (3)	3	0.02
Spanish American Ind. (1)	1	0.01
Yaqui (0)	3	0.02
Asian (520)	692	3.67
Not Hispanic (513)	679	3.60
Hispanic (7)	13	0.07
Bangladeshi (2)	7	0.04
Cambodian (3)	4	0.02
Chinese, ex. Taiwanese (116)	135	0.72
Filipino (51)	96	0.51
Indian (110)	119	0.63
Indonesian (0)	1	0.01
Japanese (45)	72	0.38
Korean (77)	97	0.51
Malaysian (3)	3	0.02
Nepalese (14)	15	0.08
Pakistani (2)	2	0.01
Taiwanese (11)	12	0.06
Thai (16)	31	0.16
Vietnamese (39)	52	0.28
Hawaii Native/Pacific Islander (40)	59	0.31
Not Hispanic (38)	55	0.29
Hispanic (2)	4	0.02
Guamanian/Chamorro (4)	9	0.05
Native Hawaiian (7)	14	0.07
Samoan (10)	14	0.07
Tongan (1)	1	0.01
White (16,065)	16,608	88.16
Not Hispanic (15,702)	16,194	85.96
Hispanic (363)	414	2.20

Warrenton

Place Type: City
County: Warren
Population: 7,880†

Ancestry‡	Population	%
American (640)	640	8.44
Australian (0)	19	0.25
Austrian (0)	16	0.21
British (0)	10	0.13
Czech (28)	227	2.99
Czechoslovakian (70)	70	0.92
Danish (17)	24	0.32
Dutch (40)	226	2.98
English (83)	667	8.79
French, ex. Basque (84)	338	4.46
German (1,397)	2,889	38.08
Greek (51)	141	1.86
Hungarian (27)	27	0.36
Irish (338)	1,561	20.58
Italian (0)	453	5.97
Norwegian (18)	86	1.13
Polish (72)	232	3.06
Russian (29)	29	0.38
Scandinavian (0)	53	0.70
Scotch-Irish (40)	228	3.01
Scottish (13)	22	0.29
Swedish (20)	83	1.09
Swiss (0)	10	0.13
Welsh (0)	98	1.29

Hispanic Origin	Population	%
Hispanic or Latino (of any race)	288	3.65
Central American, ex. Mexican	4	0.05
Honduran	1	0.01
Nicaraguan	1	0.01
Panamanian	1	0.01
Salvadoran	1	0.01
Cuban	6	0.08
Mexican	205	2.60
Puerto Rican	24	0.30
South American	11	0.14
Argentinean	1	0.01
Chilean	1	0.01
Colombian	7	0.09
Peruvian	2	0.03
Other Hispanic or Latino	38	0.48

Race*	Population	%
African-American/Black (162)	248	3.15
Not Hispanic (144)	229	2.91
Hispanic (18)	19	0.24
American Indian/Alaska Native (47)	83	1.05
Not Hispanic (40)	73	0.93
Hispanic (7)	10	0.13
Apache (4)	4	0.05
Blackfeet (6)	7	0.09
Canadian/French Am. Ind. (0)	1	0.01
Cherokee (12)	25	0.32
Chickasaw (0)	1	0.01
Choctaw (5)	5	0.06
Iroquois (0)	1	0.01
Mexican American Ind. (6)	8	0.10
Potawatomi (0)	1	0.01
Asian (55)	74	0.94
Not Hispanic (53)	66	0.84
Hispanic (2)	8	0.10
Chinese, ex. Taiwanese (22)	25	0.32
Filipino (6)	13	0.16
Indian (3)	5	0.06
Japanese (4)	7	0.09
Korean (3)	5	0.06
Pakistani (1)	2	0.03
Taiwanese (1)	2	0.03
Thai (2)	2	0.03
Vietnamese (12)	13	0.16
Hawaii Native/Pacific Islander (5)	6	0.08
Not Hispanic (5)	6	0.08
Marshallese (1)	1	0.01
Native Hawaiian (2)	3	0.04
White (7,402)	7,543	95.72
Not Hispanic (7,221)	7,348	93.25
Hispanic (181)	195	2.47

Washington

Place Type: City
County: Franklin
Population: 13,982†

Ancestry‡	Population	%
American (1,176)	1,176	8.42
Armenian (12)	30	0.21
Austrian (12)	50	0.36
Belgian (0)	8	0.06
British (36)	78	0.56
Cajun (0)	17	0.12
Canadian (0)	10	0.07
Croatian (0)	20	0.14
Czech (27)	159	1.14
Czechoslovakian (0)	15	0.11
Danish (16)	77	0.55
Dutch (56)	287	2.05
English (361)	1,053	7.54
European (92)	114	0.82
Finnish (9)	9	0.06
French, ex. Basque (225)	1,031	7.38
French Canadian (35)	35	0.25
German (4,036)	7,008	50.17
Greek (0)	11	0.08
Hungarian (22)	44	0.32
Irish (487)	2,346	16.80
Italian (211)	768	5.50
Lithuanian (9)	38	0.27
Northern European (43)	43	0.31
Norwegian (23)	53	0.38
Polish (92)	438	3.14
Portuguese (0)	10	0.07
Russian (12)	24	0.17
Scotch-Irish (16)	98	0.70
Scottish (103)	344	2.46
Slovak (24)	38	0.27
Slovene (18)	70	0.50
Swedish (41)	62	0.44
Swiss (30)	92	0.66
Welsh (0)	29	0.21

Hispanic Origin	Population	%
Hispanic or Latino (of any race)	299	2.14
Central American, ex. Mexican	10	0.07
Costa Rican	1	0.01
Guatemalan	4	0.03
Salvadoran	5	0.04
Cuban	1	0.01
Mexican	204	1.46
Puerto Rican	20	0.14
South American	10	0.07
Argentinean	1	0.01
Colombian	2	0.01
Ecuadorian	4	0.03
Venezuelan	3	0.02
Other Hispanic or Latino	54	0.39

Race*	Population	%
African-American/Black (96)	156	1.12
Not Hispanic (93)	150	1.07
Hispanic (3)	6	0.04
American Indian/Alaska Native (20)	75	0.54
Not Hispanic (17)	68	0.49
Hispanic (3)	7	0.05
Apache (1)	2	0.01
Blackfeet (0)	5	0.04
Cherokee (2)	29	0.21
Chickasaw (4)	6	0.04
Choctaw (1)	6	0.04
Iroquois (0)	4	0.03
Mexican American Ind. (1)	1	0.01
Osage (1)	1	0.01
Sioux (1)	1	0.01
Tlingit-Haida *(Alaska Native)* (1)	1	0.01
Asian (76)	99	0.71
Not Hispanic (76)	95	0.68
Hispanic (0)	4	0.03
Chinese, ex. Taiwanese (31)	33	0.24
Filipino (17)	23	0.16
Indian (11)	12	0.09
Japanese (0)	1	0.01
Korean (11)	20	0.14
Vietnamese (6)	9	0.06
Hawaii Native/Pacific Islander (10)	15	0.11
Not Hispanic (10)	15	0.11
Guamanian/Chamorro (2)	2	0.01
Native Hawaiian (2)	5	0.04
Samoan (0)	1	0.01
White (13,521)	13,682	97.85
Not Hispanic (13,334)	13,465	96.30
Hispanic (187)	217	1.55

Webb City

Place Type: City
County: Jasper
Population: 10,996†

Ancestry‡	Population	%
American (938)	938	8.71
Austrian (18)	50	0.46
British (0)	13	0.12
Czech (0)	14	0.13
Czechoslovakian (0)	51	0.47
Danish (0)	19	0.18
Dutch (14)	146	1.36
English (847)	1,686	15.66
European (35)	35	0.33
French, ex. Basque (126)	453	4.21
French Canadian (17)	17	0.16
German (640)	1,792	16.65
Irish (298)	1,551	14.41
Italian (238)	548	5.09
Norwegian (80)	80	0.74
Pennsylvania German (12)	12	0.11
Polish (55)	94	0.87
Scotch-Irish (120)	307	2.85
Scottish (96)	121	1.12
Swedish (18)	153	1.42
Swiss (23)	23	0.21
Welsh (18)	42	0.39

*Notes: † The Census 2010 population figure is used to calculate the percentages in the Hispanic Origin and Race categories. Ancestry percentages are based on the 2006-2010 American Community Survey population (not shown); ‡ Numbers in parentheses indicate the number of people reporting a single ancestry; * Numbers in parentheses indicate the number of persons reporting this race alone, not in combination with any other race; Please refer to the Explanation of Data for more information.*

Hispanic Origin	Population	%
Hispanic or Latino (of any race)	543	4.94
Central American, ex. Mexican	39	0.35
Costa Rican	1	0.01
Guatemalan	21	0.19
Honduran	1	0.01
Panamanian	3	0.03
Salvadoran	13	0.12
Cuban	1	0.01
Dominican Republic	1	0.01
Mexican	400	3.64
Puerto Rican	32	0.29
South American	12	0.11
Colombian	1	0.01
Ecuadorian	4	0.04
Paraguayan	3	0.03
Venezuelan	4	0.04
Other Hispanic or Latino	58	0.53

Race*	Population	%
African-American/Black (178)	278	2.53
Not Hispanic (163)	255	2.32
Hispanic (15)	23	0.21
American Indian/Alaska Native (160)	338	3.07
Not Hispanic (129)	289	2.63
Hispanic (31)	49	0.45
Apache (1)	2	0.02
Arapaho (1)	2	0.02
Blackfeet (3)	6	0.05
Canadian/French Am. Ind. (4)	4	0.04
Cherokee (48)	139	1.26
Cheyenne (1)	1	0.01
Chickasaw (0)	8	0.07
Chippewa (3)	6	0.05
Choctaw (2)	8	0.07
Creek (3)	3	0.03
Delaware (1)	1	0.01
Iroquois (9)	10	0.09
Mexican American Ind. (4)	6	0.05
Navajo (1)	2	0.02
Osage (3)	7	0.06
Ottawa (0)	2	0.02
Potawatomi (1)	4	0.04
Shoshone (1)	1	0.01
Sioux (3)	4	0.04
Spanish American Ind. (4)	4	0.04
Yakama (0)	1	0.01
Asian (101)	137	1.25
Not Hispanic (100)	129	1.17
Hispanic (1)	8	0.07
Chinese, ex. Taiwanese (14)	15	0.14
Filipino (29)	44	0.40
Indian (18)	21	0.19
Japanese (4)	10	0.09
Korean (10)	18	0.16
Sri Lankan (3)	3	0.03
Thai (2)	2	0.02
Vietnamese (20)	21	0.19
Hawaii Native/Pacific Islander (9)	13	0.12
Not Hispanic (9)	13	0.12
Guamanian/Chamorro (0)	1	0.01
Native Hawaiian (8)	11	0.10
Samoan (1)	1	0.01
White (9,975)	10,297	93.64
Not Hispanic (9,758)	10,033	91.24
Hispanic (217)	264	2.40

Webster Groves

Place Type: City
County: St. Louis
Population: 22,995†

Ancestry‡	Population	%
African, Sub-Saharan (45)	113	0.49
African (0)	14	0.06
Liberian (0)	44	0.19
Nigerian (0)	10	0.04
Zimbabwean (23)	23	0.10
Other Sub-Saharan African (22)	22	0.10
Albanian (9)	9	0.04
American (779)	779	3.39
Arab (0)	42	0.18
Syrian (0)	14	0.06
Other Arab (0)	28	0.12
Armenian (12)	63	0.27
Austrian (0)	79	0.34
Belgian (0)	33	0.14
British (73)	100	0.44
Bulgarian (13)	13	0.06
Canadian (11)	50	0.22
Croatian (8)	47	0.20
Czech (74)	212	0.92
Czechoslovakian (63)	102	0.44
Danish (11)	178	0.77
Dutch (73)	444	1.93
Eastern European (63)	79	0.34
English (874)	3,473	15.11
European (903)	933	4.06
Finnish (27)	35	0.15
French, ex. Basque (85)	1,482	6.45
French Canadian (26)	172	0.75
German (2,592)	7,443	32.38
German Russian (0)	53	0.23
Greek (21)	52	0.23
Hungarian (85)	302	1.31
Iranian (31)	51	0.22
Irish (1,175)	5,028	21.88
Italian (456)	1,538	6.69
Latvian (0)	33	0.14
Lithuanian (13)	36	0.16
Luxemburger (29)	38	0.17
Northern European (35)	54	0.23
Norwegian (67)	248	1.08
Pennsylvania German (10)	10	0.04
Polish (188)	679	2.95
Portuguese (21)	63	0.27
Romanian (21)	53	0.23
Russian (35)	279	1.21
Scandinavian (17)	27	0.12
Scotch-Irish (111)	392	1.71
Scottish (69)	758	3.30
Serbian (0)	18	0.08
Slavic (0)	12	0.05
Slovak (11)	63	0.27
Swedish (47)	396	1.72
Swiss (14)	137	0.60
Turkish (7)	7	0.03
Ukrainian (74)	177	0.77
Welsh (31)	306	1.33
Yugoslavian (43)	43	0.19

Hispanic Origin	Population	%
Hispanic or Latino (of any race)	365	1.59
Central American, ex. Mexican	29	0.13
Costa Rican	4	0.02
Guatemalan	19	0.08
Honduran	3	0.01
Panamanian	3	0.01
Cuban	14	0.06
Dominican Republic	2	0.01
Mexican	157	0.68
Puerto Rican	23	0.10
South American	80	0.35
Argentinean	15	0.07
Bolivian	2	0.01
Colombian	29	0.13
Ecuadorian	11	0.05
Peruvian	12	0.05
Venezuelan	11	0.05
Other Hispanic or Latino	60	0.26

Race*	Population	%
African-American/Black (1,522)	1,677	7.29
Not Hispanic (1,514)	1,651	7.18
Hispanic (8)	26	0.11
American Indian/Alaska Native (42)	120	0.52
Not Hispanic (39)	112	0.49
Hispanic (3)	8	0.03
Blackfeet (0)	1	<0.01
Canadian/French Am. Ind. (0)	1	<0.01
Central American Ind. (1)	1	<0.01
Cherokee (10)	22	0.10
Cheyenne (0)	3	0.01
Chippewa (3)	4	0.02
Choctaw (0)	3	0.01
Cree (0)	1	<0.01
Iroquois (0)	1	<0.01
Mexican American Ind. (2)	5	0.02
Navajo (0)	5	0.02
Osage (1)	2	0.01
Potawatomi (1)	1	<0.01
Sioux (0)	5	0.02
South American Ind. (0)	1	<0.01
Yup'ik *(Alaska Native)* (5)	5	0.02
Asian (345)	485	2.11
Not Hispanic (343)	483	2.10
Hispanic (2)	2	0.01
Bangladeshi (0)	1	<0.01
Bhutanese (1)	1	<0.01
Burmese (1)	2	0.01
Chinese, ex. Taiwanese (105)	132	0.57
Filipino (54)	86	0.37
Indian (70)	91	0.40
Indonesian (3)	5	0.02
Japanese (29)	50	0.22
Korean (27)	46	0.20
Malaysian (1)	1	<0.01
Nepalese (3)	3	0.01
Pakistani (1)	1	<0.01
Taiwanese (2)	3	0.01
Thai (5)	8	0.03
Vietnamese (29)	36	0.16
Hawaii Native/Pacific Islander (3)	17	0.07
Not Hispanic (3)	17	0.07
Guamanian/Chamorro (0)	2	0.01
Native Hawaiian (2)	3	0.01
Samoan (0)	1	<0.01
Tongan (1)	4	0.02
White (20,664)	20,976	91.22
Not Hispanic (20,384)	20,681	89.94
Hispanic (280)	295	1.28

Wentzville

Place Type: City
County: St. Charles
Population: 29,070†

Ancestry‡	Population	%
African, Sub-Saharan (107)	107	0.42
African (93)	93	0.37
South African (14)	14	0.06
American (1,485)	1,485	5.85
Arab (29)	74	0.29
Lebanese (0)	31	0.12
Moroccan (0)	14	0.06
Palestinian (29)	29	0.11
Armenian (0)	26	0.10
Austrian (0)	56	0.22
Brazilian (0)	11	0.04
British (27)	27	0.11
Croatian (17)	73	0.29
Czech (31)	183	0.72
Czechoslovakian (0)	26	0.10
Danish (22)	179	0.71
Dutch (90)	543	2.14
English (775)	2,682	10.56
European (182)	196	0.77
Finnish (0)	9	0.04
French, ex. Basque (288)	1,799	7.09
French Canadian (12)	91	0.36
German (3,988)	10,276	40.48
Greek (34)	65	0.26
Hungarian (0)	26	0.10
Iranian (46)	46	0.18
Irish (1,001)	5,003	19.71
Italian (513)	2,085	8.21
Lithuanian (0)	8	0.03
Luxemburger (0)	9	0.04

*Notes: † The Census 2010 population figure is used to calculate the percentages in the Hispanic Origin and Race categories. Ancestry percentages are based on the 2006-2010 American Community Survey population (not shown); ‡ Numbers in parentheses indicate the number of people reporting a single ancestry; * Numbers in parentheses indicate the number of persons reporting this race alone, not in combination with any other race; Please refer to the Explanation of Data for more information.*

Norwegian (10)	42	0.17
Polish (198)	980	3.86
Portuguese (0)	26	0.10
Romanian (7)	7	0.03
Russian (61)	140	0.55
Scandinavian (11)	11	0.04
Scotch-Irish (228)	554	2.18
Scottish (164)	424	1.67
Slovak (0)	25	0.10
Slovene (0)	28	0.11
Swedish (31)	281	1.11
Swiss (8)	148	0.58
Ukrainian (28)	79	0.31
Welsh (14)	105	0.41
Yugoslavian (0)	23	0.09

Hispanic Origin	Population	%
Hispanic or Latino (of any race)	788	2.71
Central American, ex. Mexican	45	0.15
Guatemalan	34	0.12
Honduran	4	0.01
Nicaraguan	3	0.01
Panamanian	3	0.01
Salvadoran	1	<0.01
Cuban	27	0.09
Dominican Republic	7	0.02
Mexican	515	1.77
Puerto Rican	65	0.22
South American	54	0.19
Argentinean	10	0.03
Chilean	6	0.02
Colombian	18	0.06
Ecuadorian	10	0.03
Peruvian	10	0.03
Other Hispanic or Latino	75	0.26

Race*	Population	%
African-American/Black (1,738)	2,055	7.07
Not Hispanic (1,728)	2,040	7.02
Hispanic (10)	15	0.05
American Indian/Alaska Native (76)	170	0.58
Not Hispanic (68)	156	0.54
Hispanic (8)	14	0.05
Aleut *(Alaska Native)* (3)	4	0.01
Apache (5)	6	0.02
Blackfeet (1)	9	0.03
Cherokee (10)	48	0.17
Chickasaw (1)	1	<0.01
Chippewa (2)	2	0.01
Choctaw (3)	6	0.02
Inupiat *(Alaska Native)* (4)	4	0.01
Iroquois (2)	3	0.01
Mexican American Ind. (4)	5	0.02
Navajo (3)	3	0.01
Ottawa (1)	1	<0.01
Puget Sound Salish (1)	1	<0.01
Sioux (6)	9	0.03
Tlingit-Haida *(Alaska Native)* (2)	2	0.01
Asian (356)	455	1.57
Not Hispanic (349)	443	1.52
Hispanic (7)	12	0.04
Cambodian (0)	1	<0.01
Chinese, ex. Taiwanese (56)	62	0.21
Filipino (58)	90	0.31
Indian (72)	82	0.28
Indonesian (1)	1	<0.01
Japanese (6)	17	0.06
Korean (69)	86	0.30
Laotian (0)	4	0.01
Nepalese (2)	2	0.01
Pakistani (2)	2	0.01
Taiwanese (2)	6	0.02
Thai (12)	15	0.05
Vietnamese (68)	78	0.27
Hawaii Native/Pacific Islander (1)	18	0.06
Not Hispanic (1)	15	0.05
Hispanic (0)	3	0.01
Guamanian/Chamorro (0)	6	0.02
Native Hawaiian (1)	1	<0.01
White (26,122)	26,628	91.60
Not Hispanic (25,606)	26,068	89.67
Hispanic (516)	560	1.93

West Plains

Place Type: City
County: Howell
Population: 11,986†

Ancestry‡	Population	%
African, Sub-Saharan (0)	21	0.18
African (0)	21	0.18
American (1,243)	1,243	10.57
Austrian (0)	1	0.01
British (13)	46	0.39
Canadian (10)	10	0.09
Croatian (22)	22	0.19
Czech (8)	8	0.07
Danish (0)	13	0.11
Dutch (43)	258	2.19
English (649)	1,363	11.59
European (49)	49	0.42
French, ex. Basque (0)	593	5.04
German (485)	2,032	17.28
Hungarian (15)	29	0.25
Irish (406)	1,935	16.46
Italian (73)	132	1.12
Latvian (8)	8	0.07
Lithuanian (0)	5	0.04
Norwegian (15)	82	0.70
Pennsylvania German (0)	12	0.10
Polish (44)	82	0.70
Russian (48)	76	0.65
Scotch-Irish (132)	416	3.54
Scottish (71)	149	1.27
Slovene (0)	9	0.08
Swedish (14)	69	0.59
Welsh (10)	10	0.09

Hispanic Origin	Population	%
Hispanic or Latino (of any race)	265	2.21
Central American, ex. Mexican	8	0.07
Costa Rican	4	0.03
Guatemalan	1	0.01
Honduran	1	0.01
Panamanian	2	0.02
Cuban	5	0.04
Dominican Republic	1	0.01
Mexican	195	1.63
Puerto Rican	6	0.05
South American	5	0.04
Argentinean	2	0.02
Colombian	3	0.03
Other Hispanic or Latino	45	0.38

Race*	Population	%
African-American/Black (101)	138	1.15
Not Hispanic (100)	136	1.13
Hispanic (1)	2	0.02
American Indian/Alaska Native (76)	184	1.54
Not Hispanic (75)	178	1.49
Hispanic (1)	6	0.05
Apache (0)	3	0.03
Arapaho (2)	2	0.02
Blackfeet (1)	8	0.07
Canadian/French Am. Ind. (0)	1	0.01
Cherokee (20)	68	0.57
Choctaw (3)	7	0.06
Comanche (0)	1	0.01
Delaware (2)	2	0.02
Hopi (2)	2	0.02
Kiowa (2)	2	0.02
Mexican American Ind. (0)	1	0.01
Navajo (4)	4	0.03
Potawatomi (0)	5	0.04
Shoshone (0)	1	0.01
Sioux (4)	5	0.04
Yuman (7)	7	0.06
Asian (102)	159	1.33
Not Hispanic (101)	152	1.27
Hispanic (1)	7	0.06
Chinese, ex. Taiwanese (39)	42	0.35
Filipino (19)	33	0.28
Indian (8)	17	0.14
Japanese (12)	29	0.24
Korean (11)	25	0.21
Laotian (1)	1	0.01
Pakistani (1)	1	0.01
Vietnamese (4)	8	0.07
Hawaii Native/Pacific Islander (6)	10	0.08
Not Hispanic (6)	10	0.08
Guamanian/Chamorro (1)	2	0.02
Native Hawaiian (3)	4	0.03
Samoan (1)	4	0.03
Tongan (1)	1	0.01
White (11,391)	11,594	96.73
Not Hispanic (11,239)	11,423	95.30
Hispanic (152)	171	1.43

Wildwood

Place Type: City
County: St. Louis
Population: 35,517†

Ancestry‡	Population	%
African, Sub-Saharan (34)	49	0.14
African (34)	49	0.14
American (1,579)	1,579	4.52
Arab (98)	163	0.47
Arab (59)	59	0.17
Iraqi (13)	13	0.04
Jordanian (0)	8	0.02
Lebanese (0)	49	0.14
Other Arab (26)	34	0.10
Armenian (0)	42	0.12
Australian (24)	97	0.28
Austrian (15)	179	0.51
Belgian (12)	79	0.23
Brazilian (7)	27	0.08
British (94)	117	0.33
Canadian (50)	64	0.18
Croatian (50)	179	0.51
Czech (50)	296	0.85
Czechoslovakian (22)	45	0.13
Danish (0)	57	0.16
Dutch (79)	438	1.25
Eastern European (9)	9	0.03
English (1,372)	4,773	13.65
Estonian (13)	13	0.04
European (537)	548	1.57
Finnish (73)	170	0.49
French, ex. Basque (217)	2,108	6.03
French Canadian (44)	69	0.20
German (5,803)	14,515	41.51
Greek (142)	279	0.80
Hungarian (93)	262	0.75
Iranian (42)	77	0.22
Irish (1,293)	6,952	19.88
Italian (940)	2,935	8.39
Latvian (0)	10	0.03
Lithuanian (31)	139	0.40
Macedonian (9)	9	0.03
New Zealander (16)	16	0.05
Northern European (23)	23	0.07
Norwegian (114)	487	1.39
Polish (355)	1,494	4.27
Portuguese (90)	149	0.43
Romanian (15)	45	0.13
Russian (290)	637	1.82
Scandinavian (11)	23	0.07
Scotch-Irish (322)	1,023	2.93
Scottish (265)	874	2.50
Serbian (55)	55	0.16
Slavic (0)	10	0.03
Slovak (8)	34	0.10
Slovene (11)	11	0.03
Swedish (314)	1,002	2.87
Swiss (40)	156	0.45
Ukrainian (109)	151	0.43

*Notes: † The Census 2010 population figure is used to calculate the percentages in the Hispanic Origin and Race categories. Ancestry percentages are based on the 2006-2010 American Community Survey population (not shown); ‡ Numbers in parentheses indicate the number of people reporting a single ancestry; * Numbers in parentheses indicate the number of persons reporting this race alone, not in combination with any other race; Please refer to the Explanation of Data for more information.*

Welsh (60)	277	0.79
Yugoslavian (153)	170	0.49

Hispanic Origin	Population	%
Hispanic or Latino (of any race)	830	2.34
Central American, ex. Mexican	66	0.19
Costa Rican	1	<0.01
Guatemalan	33	0.09
Honduran	12	0.03
Nicaraguan	6	0.02
Panamanian	8	0.02
Salvadoran	6	0.02
Cuban	60	0.17
Dominican Republic	10	0.03
Mexican	379	1.07
Puerto Rican	63	0.18
South American	123	0.35
Argentinean	27	0.08
Bolivian	4	0.01
Chilean	15	0.04
Colombian	24	0.07
Ecuadorian	11	0.03
Peruvian	16	0.05
Uruguayan	1	<0.01
Venezuelan	24	0.07
Other South American	1	<0.01
Other Hispanic or Latino	129	0.36

Race*	Population	%
African-American/Black (588)	719	2.02
Not Hispanic (581)	694	1.95
Hispanic (7)	25	0.07
American Indian/Alaska Native (68)	198	0.56
Not Hispanic (47)	163	0.46
Hispanic (21)	35	0.10
Apache (1)	4	0.01
Central American Ind. (1)	3	0.01
Cherokee (21)	85	0.24
Chickasaw (0)	1	<0.01
Chippewa (2)	3	0.01
Choctaw (1)	8	0.02
Creek (6)	9	0.03
Inupiat *(Alaska Native)* (3)	3	0.01
Iroquois (1)	1	<0.01
Mexican American Ind. (2)	3	0.01
Navajo (0)	1	<0.01
Osage (0)	5	0.01
Sioux (1)	5	0.01
Spanish American Ind. (4)	4	0.01
Yuman (6)	6	0.02
Asian (1,434)	1,699	4.78
Not Hispanic (1,433)	1,689	4.76
Hispanic (1)	10	0.03
Bangladeshi (12)	15	0.04
Burmese (1)	5	0.01
Chinese, ex. Taiwanese (417)	463	1.30
Filipino (75)	129	0.36
Hmong (3)	3	0.01
Indian (618)	666	1.88
Indonesian (14)	15	0.04
Japanese (29)	84	0.24
Korean (119)	145	0.41
Laotian (2)	5	0.01
Malaysian (3)	7	0.02
Pakistani (49)	54	0.15
Sri Lankan (3)	3	0.01
Taiwanese (4)	8	0.02
Thai (10)	13	0.04
Vietnamese (30)	44	0.12
Hawaii Native/Pacific Islander (10)	30	0.08
Not Hispanic (9)	29	0.08
Hispanic (1)	1	<0.01
Fijian (3)	3	0.01
Guamanian/Chamorro (1)	4	0.01
Native Hawaiian (1)	14	0.04
Tongan (0)	1	<0.01
White (32,740)	33,230	93.56
Not Hispanic (32,116)	32,557	91.67
Hispanic (624)	673	1.89

*Notes: † The Census 2010 population figure is used to calculate the percentages in the Hispanic Origin and Race categories. Ancestry percentages are based on the 2006-2010 American Community Survey population (not shown); ‡ Numbers in parentheses indicate the number of people reporting a single ancestry; * Numbers in parentheses indicate the number of persons reporting this race alone, not in combination with any other race; Please refer to the Explanation of Data for more information.*

MONTANA

Place Type: State
Population: 989,415†

Ancestry‡	Population	%
African, Sub-Saharan (822)	1,477	0.15
African (602)	1,091	0.11
Ethiopian (70)	106	0.01
Ghanaian (7)	7	<0.01
Liberian (119)	151	0.02
Nigerian (0)	66	0.01
Somalian (0)	32	<0.01
South African (24)	24	<0.01
Albanian (14)	14	<0.01
Alsatian (0)	35	<0.01
American (59,349)	59,349	6.09
Arab (868)	1,880	0.19
Arab (103)	229	0.02
Egyptian (0)	12	<0.01
Iraqi (27)	27	<0.01
Jordanian (10)	18	<0.01
Lebanese (330)	1,016	0.10
Palestinian (20)	33	<0.01
Syrian (33)	160	0.02
Other Arab (345)	385	0.04
Armenian (61)	175	0.02
Australian (153)	290	0.03
Austrian (1,484)	5,779	0.59
Basque (309)	633	0.07
Belgian (783)	2,361	0.24
Brazilian (98)	272	0.03
British (1,515)	3,148	0.32
Bulgarian (59)	149	0.02
Cajun (169)	357	0.04
Canadian (1,313)	2,526	0.26
Carpatho Rusyn (18)	18	<0.01
Celtic (66)	169	0.02
Croatian (891)	2,213	0.23
Czech (2,507)	8,637	0.89
Czechoslovakian (1,044)	2,198	0.23
Danish (3,885)	14,452	1.48
Dutch (6,813)	26,514	2.72
Eastern European (261)	326	0.03
English (33,536)	126,682	13.01
Estonian (115)	192	0.02
European (11,162)	12,265	1.26
Finnish (2,461)	7,362	0.76
French, ex. Basque (5,924)	39,850	4.09
French Canadian (3,401)	9,681	0.99
German (102,271)	283,211	29.08
German Russian (107)	130	0.01
Greek (745)	3,090	0.32
Hungarian (889)	3,432	0.35
Icelander (57)	356	0.04
Iranian (50)	137	0.01
Irish (42,960)	157,032	16.13
Israeli (15)	15	<0.01
Italian (10,688)	35,206	3.62
Latvian (222)	337	0.03
Lithuanian (400)	1,276	0.13
Luxemburger (137)	275	0.03
Macedonian (8)	8	<0.01
Maltese (5)	49	0.01
Northern European (1,528)	1,730	0.18
Norwegian (36,653)	95,971	9.86
Pennsylvania German (387)	798	0.08
Polish (5,952)	20,558	2.11
Portuguese (709)	2,543	0.26
Romanian (336)	890	0.09
Russian (2,055)	9,911	1.02
Scandinavian (4,296)	7,736	0.79
Scotch-Irish (8,582)	25,373	2.61
Scottish (9,182)	32,395	3.33
Serbian (204)	745	0.08
Slavic (364)	1,123	0.12
Slovak (348)	1,203	0.12
Slovene (339)	809	0.08
Swedish (7,762)	33,389	3.43
Swiss (1,337)	6,302	0.65
Turkish (61)	126	0.01
Ukrainian (1,136)	2,630	0.27
Welsh (1,727)	10,263	1.05
West Indian, ex. Hispanic (130)	398	0.04
Belizean (0)	34	<0.01
Dutch West Indian (0)	43	<0.01
Haitian (45)	47	<0.01
Jamaican (72)	244	0.03
West Indian (13)	13	<0.01
Other West Indian (0)	17	<0.01
Yugoslavian (956)	2,428	0.25

Hispanic Origin	Population	%
Hispanic or Latino (of any race)	28,565	2.89
Central American, ex. Mexican	735	0.07
Costa Rican	71	0.01
Guatemalan	200	0.02
Honduran	98	0.01
Nicaraguan	91	0.01
Panamanian	131	0.01
Salvadoran	140	0.01
Other Central American	4	<0.01
Cuban	421	0.04
Dominican Republic	95	0.01
Mexican	20,048	2.03
Puerto Rican	1,491	0.15
South American	997	0.10
Argentinean	115	0.01
Bolivian	49	<0.01
Chilean	105	0.01
Colombian	288	0.03
Ecuadorian	97	0.01
Paraguayan	11	<0.01
Peruvian	237	0.02
Uruguayan	8	<0.01
Venezuelan	67	0.01
Other South American	20	<0.01
Other Hispanic or Latino	4,778	0.48

Race*	Population	%
African-American/Black (4,027)	7,917	0.80
Not Hispanic (3,743)	7,159	0.72
Hispanic (284)	758	0.08
American Indian/Alaska Native (62,555)	78,601	7.94
Not Hispanic (59,902)	74,452	7.52
Hispanic (2,653)	4,149	0.42
Alaska Athabascan *(Ala. Nat.)* (49)	87	0.01
Aleut *(Alaska Native)* (57)	88	0.01
Apache (162)	360	0.04
Arapaho (340)	381	0.04
Blackfeet (11,210)	12,831	1.30
Canadian/French Am. Ind. (108)	207	0.02
Central American Ind. (4)	10	<0.01
Cherokee (473)	1,860	0.19
Cheyenne (5,232)	5,912	0.60
Chickasaw (36)	99	0.01
Chippewa (2,528)	4,284	0.43
Choctaw (126)	303	0.03
Colville (79)	122	0.01
Comanche (26)	67	0.01
Cree (239)	661	0.07
Creek (30)	98	0.01
Crow (7,949)	8,680	0.88
Delaware (9)	28	<0.01
Hopi (11)	29	<0.01
Houma (0)	2	<0.01
Inupiat *(Alaska Native)* (76)	135	0.01
Iroquois (65)	187	0.02
Kiowa (18)	30	<0.01
Lumbee (18)	21	<0.01
Menominee (6)	15	<0.01
Mexican American Ind. (91)	155	0.02
Navajo (434)	621	0.06
Osage (29)	70	0.01
Ottawa (13)	21	<0.01
Paiute (43)	61	0.01
Pima (13)	23	<0.01
Potawatomi (113)	202	0.02
Pueblo (57)	77	0.01
Puget Sound Salish (80)	125	0.01
Seminole (25)	57	0.01
Shoshone (122)	176	0.02
Sioux (1,809)	2,698	0.27
South American Ind. (7)	28	<0.01
Spanish American Ind. (8)	18	<0.01
Tlingit-Haida *(Alaska Native)* (76)	135	0.01
Tohono O'Odham (22)	27	<0.01
Tsimshian *(Alaska Native)* (9)	17	<0.01
Ute (28)	54	0.01
Yakama (43)	74	0.01
Yaqui (7)	27	<0.01
Yuman (25)	48	<0.01
Yup'ik *(Alaska Native)* (35)	67	0.01
Asian (6,253)	10,482	1.06
Not Hispanic (6,138)	9,992	1.01
Hispanic (115)	490	0.05
Bangladeshi (11)	11	<0.01
Bhutanese (4)	4	<0.01
Burmese (11)	14	<0.01
Cambodian (23)	28	<0.01
Chinese, ex. Taiwanese (1,227)	1,845	0.19
Filipino (1,383)	2,829	0.29
Hmong (221)	253	0.03
Indian (618)	930	0.09
Indonesian (50)	86	0.01
Japanese (850)	1,854	0.19
Korean (837)	1,369	0.14
Laotian (31)	51	0.01
Malaysian (21)	31	<0.01
Nepalese (25)	29	<0.01
Pakistani (26)	37	<0.01
Sri Lankan (9)	11	<0.01
Taiwanese (51)	83	0.01
Thai (189)	324	0.03
Vietnamese (297)	481	0.05
Hawaii Native/Pacific Islander (668)	1,732	0.18
Not Hispanic (609)	1,528	0.15
Hispanic (59)	204	0.02
Fijian (13)	23	<0.01
Guamanian/Chamorro (107)	228	0.02
Marshallese (3)	6	<0.01
Native Hawaiian (295)	868	0.09
Samoan (123)	267	0.03
Tongan (17)	37	<0.01
White (884,961)	908,645	91.84
Not Hispanic (868,628)	889,028	89.85
Hispanic (16,333)	19,617	1.98

*Notes: † The Census 2010 population figure is used to calculate the percentages in the Hispanic Origin and Race categories. Ancestry percentages are based on the 2006-2010 American Community Survey population (not shown); ‡ Numbers in parentheses indicate the number of people reporting a single ancestry; * Numbers in parentheses indicate the number of persons reporting this race alone, not in combination with any other race; Please refer to the Explanation of Data for more information.*

Anaconda-Deer Lodge County

Place Type: Special City
County: Deer Lodge
Population: 9,298†

Ancestry‡	Population	%
American (241)	241	2.60
Arab (28)	49	0.53
Lebanese (25)	25	0.27
Syrian (3)	24	0.26
Austrian (68)	241	2.60
Basque (14)	14	0.15
Belgian (9)	9	0.10
British (0)	35	0.38
Canadian (8)	8	0.09
Croatian (45)	155	1.67
Czech (12)	12	0.13
Czechoslovakian (11)	11	0.12
Danish (42)	149	1.61
Dutch (83)	349	3.76
English (202)	854	9.21
European (22)	45	0.49
Finnish (40)	102	1.10
French, ex. Basque (193)	547	5.90
French Canadian (14)	86	0.93
German (1,246)	2,800	30.20
Greek (0)	18	0.19
Hungarian (0)	22	0.24
Irish (865)	2,429	26.20
Italian (178)	543	5.86
Lithuanian (0)	21	0.23
Northern European (12)	12	0.13
Norwegian (212)	791	8.53
Pennsylvania German (7)	7	0.08
Polish (0)	58	0.63
Portuguese (0)	12	0.13
Romanian (15)	15	0.16
Russian (46)	117	1.26
Scandinavian (7)	23	0.25
Scotch-Irish (173)	330	3.56
Scottish (73)	262	2.83
Serbian (34)	45	0.49
Slavic (0)	8	0.09
Slovak (0)	18	0.19
Slovene (16)	16	0.17
Swedish (96)	481	5.19
Swiss (0)	19	0.20
Welsh (17)	115	1.24
Yugoslavian (16)	42	0.45

Hispanic Origin	Population	%
Hispanic or Latino (of any race)	271	2.91
Central American, ex. Mexican	6	0.06
Nicaraguan	1	0.01
Panamanian	1	0.01
Salvadoran	4	0.04
Cuban	4	0.04
Dominican Republic	5	0.05
Mexican	192	2.06
Puerto Rican	11	0.12
South American	3	0.03
Argentinean	1	0.01
Colombian	2	0.02
Other Hispanic or Latino	50	0.54

Race*	Population	%
African-American/Black (38)	91	0.98
Not Hispanic (36)	83	0.89
Hispanic (2)	8	0.09
American Indian/Alaska Native (285)	445	4.79
Not Hispanic (242)	389	4.18
Hispanic (43)	56	0.60
Alaska Athabascan *(Ala. Nat.)* (2)	2	0.02
Aleut *(Alaska Native)* (1)	2	0.02
Apache (2)	5	0.05
Blackfeet (7)	13	0.14
Canadian/French Am. Ind. (1)	1	0.01
Cherokee (11)	29	0.31
Cheyenne (9)	17	0.18
Chickasaw (0)	1	0.01
Chippewa (20)	35	0.38
Choctaw (0)	1	0.01
Comanche (0)	3	0.03
Cree (3)	4	0.04
Crow (22)	24	0.26
Iroquois (3)	5	0.05
Mexican American Ind. (1)	1	0.01
Navajo (2)	4	0.04
Osage (1)	1	0.01
Ottawa (0)	1	0.01
Paiute (1)	1	0.01
Pima (3)	3	0.03
Puget Sound Salish (0)	1	0.01
Seminole (2)	2	0.02
Sioux (12)	16	0.17
Tlingit-Haida *(Alaska Native)* (0)	2	0.02
Tohono O'Odham (5)	5	0.05
Ute (1)	1	0.01
Asian (29)	53	0.57
Not Hispanic (28)	50	0.54
Hispanic (1)	3	0.03
Chinese, ex. Taiwanese (15)	20	0.22
Filipino (7)	11	0.12
Indian (0)	5	0.05
Japanese (4)	7	0.08
Korean (1)	7	0.08
Hawaii Native/Pacific Islander (4)	17	0.18
Not Hispanic (2)	15	0.16
Hispanic (2)	2	0.02
Guamanian/Chamorro (1)	1	0.01
Native Hawaiian (3)	10	0.11
Samoan (0)	2	0.02
White (8,660)	8,882	95.53
Not Hispanic (8,518)	8,706	93.63
Hispanic (142)	176	1.89

Billings

Place Type: City
County: Yellowstone
Population: 104,170†

Ancestry‡	Population	%
African, Sub-Saharan (184)	326	0.32
African (177)	308	0.30
Ghanaian (7)	7	0.01
Nigerian (0)	11	0.01
American (9,034)	9,034	8.90
Arab (72)	72	0.07
Lebanese (59)	59	0.06
Palestinian (13)	13	0.01
Armenian (2)	2	<0.01
Australian (0)	25	0.02
Austrian (107)	509	0.50
Basque (0)	26	0.03
Belgian (91)	332	0.33
Brazilian (28)	59	0.06
British (84)	252	0.25
Bulgarian (10)	19	0.02
Cajun (30)	47	0.05
Canadian (194)	343	0.34
Celtic (13)	41	0.04
Croatian (72)	154	0.15
Czech (159)	810	0.80
Czechoslovakian (95)	221	0.22
Danish (337)	1,486	1.46
Dutch (286)	1,784	1.76
Eastern European (33)	45	0.04
English (2,364)	11,208	11.04
Estonian (0)	12	0.01
European (1,000)	1,058	1.04
Finnish (86)	599	0.59
French, ex. Basque (384)	3,701	3.64
French Canadian (275)	794	0.78
German (13,329)	33,137	32.63
German Russian (63)	83	0.08
Greek (84)	275	0.27
Hungarian (89)	399	0.39
Icelander (7)	87	0.09
Iranian (0)	15	0.01
Irish (3,956)	14,253	14.04
Italian (1,058)	3,554	3.50
Latvian (9)	9	0.01
Lithuanian (8)	185	0.18
Luxemburger (14)	17	0.02
Northern European (94)	102	0.10
Norwegian (3,896)	10,157	10.00
Pennsylvania German (46)	148	0.15
Polish (558)	1,903	1.87
Portuguese (45)	84	0.08
Romanian (0)	209	0.21
Russian (192)	1,785	1.76
Scandinavian (618)	1,038	1.02
Scotch-Irish (700)	2,220	2.19
Scottish (1,019)	3,331	3.28
Serbian (0)	20	0.02
Slavic (27)	150	0.15
Slovak (14)	37	0.04
Slovene (0)	45	0.04
Swedish (626)	3,328	3.28
Swiss (58)	503	0.50
Turkish (4)	12	0.01
Ukrainian (145)	253	0.25
Welsh (98)	1,095	1.08
West Indian, ex. Hispanic (20)	35	0.03
Dutch West Indian (0)	15	0.01
Jamaican (20)	20	0.02
Yugoslavian (161)	397	0.39

Hispanic Origin	Population	%
Hispanic or Latino (of any race)	5,456	5.24
Central American, ex. Mexican	103	0.10
Costa Rican	7	0.01
Guatemalan	33	0.03
Honduran	20	0.02
Nicaraguan	11	0.01
Panamanian	15	0.01
Salvadoran	17	0.02
Cuban	47	0.05
Dominican Republic	9	0.01
Mexican	4,214	4.05
Puerto Rican	227	0.22
South American	80	0.08
Argentinean	18	0.02
Bolivian	2	<0.01
Chilean	7	0.01
Colombian	26	0.02
Ecuadorian	4	<0.01
Peruvian	17	0.02
Venezuelan	5	<0.01
Other South American	1	<0.01
Other Hispanic or Latino	776	0.74

Race*	Population	%
African-American/Black (828)	1,593	1.53
Not Hispanic (750)	1,397	1.34
Hispanic (78)	196	0.19
American Indian/Alaska Native (4,619)	6,222	5.97
Not Hispanic (4,204)	5,562	5.34
Hispanic (415)	660	0.63
Alaska Athabascan *(Ala. Nat.)* (3)	10	0.01
Aleut *(Alaska Native)* (1)	2	<0.01
Apache (10)	26	0.02
Arapaho (68)	72	0.07
Blackfeet (183)	249	0.24
Canadian/French Am. Ind. (7)	14	0.01
Cherokee (23)	130	0.12
Cheyenne (609)	782	0.75
Chickasaw (3)	7	0.01
Chippewa (256)	386	0.37
Choctaw (8)	23	0.02
Colville (3)	5	<0.01
Comanche (5)	7	0.01
Cree (10)	24	0.02
Creek (5)	25	0.02
Crow (1,143)	1,383	1.33
Delaware (1)	5	<0.01

*Notes: † The Census 2010 population figure is used to calculate the percentages in the Hispanic Origin and Race categories. Ancestry percentages are based on the 2006-2010 American Community Survey population (not shown); ‡ Numbers in parentheses indicate the number of people reporting a single ancestry; * Numbers in parentheses indicate the number of persons reporting this race alone, not in combination with any other race; Please refer to the Explanation of Data for more information.*

Hopi (4)	6	0.01
Inupiat *(Alaska Native)* (12)	19	0.02
Iroquois (8)	11	0.01
Kiowa (4)	4	<0.01
Lumbee (4)	4	<0.01
Menominee (0)	1	<0.01
Mexican American Ind. (16)	21	0.02
Navajo (35)	48	0.05
Osage (0)	7	0.01
Ottawa (2)	5	<0.01
Paiute (2)	3	<0.01
Pima (0)	1	<0.01
Potawatomi (8)	13	0.01
Pueblo (3)	3	<0.01
Puget Sound Salish (1)	2	<0.01
Seminole (3)	10	0.01
Shoshone (17)	20	0.02
Sioux (222)	340	0.33
South American Ind. (1)	6	0.01
Tlingit-Haida *(Alaska Native)* (3)	5	<0.01
Tsimshian *(Alaska Native)* (3)	3	<0.01
Ute (5)	13	0.01
Yakama (1)	7	0.01
Yaqui (0)	3	<0.01
Yuman (3)	8	0.01
Yup'ik *(Alaska Native)* (0)	1	<0.01
Asian (778)	1,277	1.23
Not Hispanic (755)	1,198	1.15
Hispanic (23)	79	0.08
Burmese (0)	1	<0.01
Chinese, ex. Taiwanese (163)	246	0.24
Filipino (159)	317	0.30
Hmong (4)	5	<0.01
Indian (89)	117	0.11
Indonesian (10)	14	0.01
Japanese (90)	230	0.22
Korean (118)	174	0.17
Laotian (5)	6	0.01
Malaysian (3)	6	0.01
Nepalese (1)	1	<0.01
Pakistani (1)	2	<0.01
Sri Lankan (1)	1	<0.01
Taiwanese (6)	10	0.01
Thai (21)	37	0.04
Vietnamese (57)	72	0.07
Hawaii Native/Pacific Islander (93)	244	0.23
Not Hispanic (84)	212	0.20
Hispanic (9)	32	0.03
Fijian (1)	1	<0.01
Guamanian/Chamorro (5)	11	0.01
Marshallese (1)	2	<0.01
Native Hawaiian (33)	107	0.10
Samoan (35)	74	0.07
Tongan (5)	15	0.01
White (93,313)	96,154	92.30
Not Hispanic (90,503)	92,745	89.03
Hispanic (2,810)	3,409	3.27

Bozeman

Place Type: City
County: Gallatin
Population: 37,280†

Ancestry‡	Population	%
African, Sub-Saharan (8)	28	0.08
African (8)	28	0.08
American (1,091)	1,091	2.99
Arab (186)	270	0.74
Arab (66)	66	0.18
Lebanese (39)	123	0.34
Other Arab (81)	81	0.22
Armenian (14)	14	0.04
Australian (0)	13	0.04
Austrian (65)	313	0.86
Basque (17)	30	0.08
Belgian (84)	118	0.32
Brazilian (23)	39	0.11
British (68)	175	0.48
Cajun (0)	15	0.04
Canadian (9)	36	0.10
Croatian (18)	81	0.22
Czech (130)	410	1.13
Czechoslovakian (16)	31	0.09
Danish (59)	606	1.66
Dutch (256)	860	2.36
English (1,035)	4,645	12.75
Estonian (52)	52	0.14
European (755)	808	2.22
Finnish (53)	178	0.49
French, ex. Basque (390)	1,696	4.65
French Canadian (118)	303	0.83
German (3,366)	11,695	32.09
Greek (102)	256	0.70
Hungarian (116)	200	0.55
Iranian (0)	11	0.03
Irish (1,700)	7,337	20.13
Italian (478)	1,883	5.17
Latvian (13)	70	0.19
Lithuanian (11)	48	0.13
Luxemburger (0)	26	0.07
Northern European (163)	163	0.45
Norwegian (1,211)	3,406	9.35
Polish (213)	953	2.62
Portuguese (17)	136	0.37
Romanian (34)	61	0.17
Russian (78)	287	0.79
Scandinavian (129)	274	0.75
Scotch-Irish (283)	774	2.12
Scottish (413)	1,370	3.76
Slavic (26)	58	0.16
Slovak (0)	7	0.02
Slovene (3)	3	0.01
Swedish (288)	1,281	3.52
Swiss (78)	308	0.85
Turkish (7)	16	0.04
Ukrainian (37)	100	0.27
Welsh (73)	533	1.46
West Indian, ex. Hispanic (25)	53	0.15
Haitian (8)	8	0.02
Jamaican (17)	45	0.12
Yugoslavian (42)	52	0.14

Hispanic Origin	Population	%
Hispanic or Latino (of any race)	1,096	2.94
Central American, ex. Mexican	44	0.12
Costa Rican	2	0.01
Guatemalan	18	0.05
Honduran	1	<0.01
Nicaraguan	4	0.01
Panamanian	10	0.03
Salvadoran	8	0.02
Other Central American	1	<0.01
Cuban	26	0.07
Dominican Republic	7	0.02
Mexican	665	1.78
Puerto Rican	64	0.17
South American	104	0.28
Argentinean	13	0.03
Bolivian	8	0.02
Chilean	14	0.04
Colombian	21	0.06
Ecuadorian	10	0.03
Peruvian	25	0.07
Uruguayan	1	<0.01
Venezuelan	12	0.03
Other Hispanic or Latino	186	0.50

Race*	Population	%
African-American/Black (174)	314	0.84
Not Hispanic (168)	288	0.77
Hispanic (6)	26	0.07
American Indian/Alaska Native (414)	725	1.94
Not Hispanic (384)	653	1.75
Hispanic (30)	72	0.19
Alaska Athabascan *(Ala. Nat.)* (0)	1	<0.01
Aleut *(Alaska Native)* (3)	4	0.01
Apache (1)	3	0.01
Arapaho (1)	1	<0.01
Blackfeet (68)	100	0.27
Canadian/French Am. Ind. (5)	10	0.03
Central American Ind. (1)	1	<0.01
Cherokee (10)	55	0.15
Cheyenne (33)	48	0.13
Chickasaw (1)	3	0.01
Chippewa (22)	59	0.16
Choctaw (3)	8	0.02
Colville (0)	1	<0.01
Cree (0)	2	0.01
Creek (0)	4	0.01
Crow (67)	84	0.23
Hopi (0)	2	0.01
Inupiat *(Alaska Native)* (3)	9	0.02
Iroquois (0)	4	0.01
Kiowa (0)	2	0.01
Mexican American Ind. (1)	9	0.02
Navajo (4)	4	0.01
Paiute (3)	4	0.01
Pima (0)	2	0.01
Potawatomi (0)	1	<0.01
Pueblo (3)	3	0.01
Shoshone (7)	8	0.02
Sioux (26)	61	0.16
South American Ind. (0)	1	<0.01
Tlingit-Haida *(Alaska Native)* (1)	2	0.01
Yakama (1)	1	<0.01
Yaqui (0)	1	<0.01
Yup'ik *(Alaska Native)* (1)	3	0.01
Asian (715)	1,006	2.70
Not Hispanic (706)	975	2.62
Hispanic (9)	31	0.08
Bangladeshi (6)	6	0.02
Bhutanese (1)	1	<0.01
Burmese (0)	1	<0.01
Cambodian (0)	1	<0.01
Chinese, ex. Taiwanese (260)	320	0.86
Filipino (67)	128	0.34
Hmong (0)	1	<0.01
Indian (85)	109	0.29
Indonesian (8)	16	0.04
Japanese (88)	145	0.39
Korean (107)	148	0.40
Laotian (0)	1	<0.01
Malaysian (7)	8	0.02
Nepalese (3)	5	0.01
Pakistani (2)	5	0.01
Sri Lankan (2)	2	0.01
Taiwanese (13)	14	0.04
Thai (6)	18	0.05
Vietnamese (18)	26	0.07
Hawaii Native/Pacific Islander (39)	83	0.22
Not Hispanic (32)	72	0.19
Hispanic (7)	11	0.03
Guamanian/Chamorro (5)	10	0.03
Native Hawaiian (23)	44	0.12
Samoan (8)	11	0.03
White (34,910)	35,641	95.60
Not Hispanic (34,214)	34,829	93.43
Hispanic (696)	812	2.18

Butte-Silver Bow

Place Type: Consolidated Government
County: Silver Bow
Population: 33,525†

Ancestry‡	Population	%
African, Sub-Saharan (5)	5	0.02
African (5)	5	0.02
American (1,051)	1,051	3.20
Arab (189)	329	1.00
Arab (8)	8	0.02
Lebanese (14)	154	0.47
Other Arab (167)	167	0.51
Australian (0)	41	0.12
Austrian (237)	835	2.54
Basque (10)	24	0.07
British (9)	54	0.16
Bulgarian (13)	13	0.04
Canadian (40)	60	0.18

*Notes: † The Census 2010 population figure is used to calculate the percentages in the Hispanic Origin and Race categories. Ancestry percentages are based on the 2006-2010 American Community Survey population (not shown); ‡ Numbers in parentheses indicate the number of people reporting a single ancestry; * Numbers in parentheses indicate the number of persons reporting this race alone, not in combination with any other race; Please refer to the Explanation of Data for more information.*

Croatian (156)	259	0.79
Czech (0)	102	0.31
Czechoslovakian (26)	179	0.54
Danish (143)	395	1.20
Dutch (39)	556	1.69
English (1,180)	5,279	16.06
Estonian (10)	10	0.03
European (245)	245	0.75
Finnish (259)	827	2.52
French, ex. Basque (174)	1,922	5.85
French Canadian (183)	576	1.75
German (1,639)	7,702	23.44
Greek (12)	92	0.28
Hungarian (25)	111	0.34
Irish (3,306)	10,583	32.21
Italian (942)	2,667	8.12
Lithuanian (16)	33	0.10
Luxemburger (12)	12	0.04
Northern European (36)	36	0.11
Norwegian (610)	2,298	6.99
Pennsylvania German (14)	14	0.04
Polish (241)	797	2.43
Portuguese (11)	41	0.12
Russian (19)	230	0.70
Scandinavian (49)	111	0.34
Scotch-Irish (224)	847	2.58
Scottish (220)	748	2.28
Serbian (12)	181	0.55
Slavic (14)	52	0.16
Slovak (21)	79	0.24
Slovene (10)	28	0.09
Swedish (268)	977	2.97
Swiss (0)	68	0.21
Turkish (17)	17	0.05
Ukrainian (18)	52	0.16
Welsh (18)	455	1.38
Yugoslavian (112)	332	1.01

Hispanic Origin	Population	%
Hispanic or Latino (of any race)	1,227	3.66
Central American, ex. Mexican	12	0.04
Costa Rican	1	<0.01
Guatemalan	6	0.02
Nicaraguan	4	0.01
Salvadoran	1	<0.01
Cuban	10	0.03
Dominican Republic	2	0.01
Mexican	923	2.75
Puerto Rican	32	0.10
South American	27	0.08
Argentinean	1	<0.01
Chilean	5	0.01
Colombian	8	0.02
Ecuadorian	5	0.01
Peruvian	7	0.02
Venezuelan	1	<0.01
Other Hispanic or Latino	221	0.66

Race*	Population	%
African-American/Black (110)	190	0.57
Not Hispanic (102)	176	0.52
Hispanic (8)	14	0.04
American Indian/Alaska Native (633)	1,096	3.27
Not Hispanic (569)	940	2.80
Hispanic (64)	156	0.47
Alaska Athabascan *(Ala. Nat.)* (1)	2	0.01
Aleut *(Alaska Native)* (2)	2	0.01
Apache (4)	17	0.05
Arapaho (2)	4	0.01
Blackfeet (58)	98	0.29
Canadian/French Am. Ind. (0)	1	<0.01
Cherokee (12)	65	0.19
Cheyenne (17)	31	0.09
Chickasaw (0)	1	<0.01
Chippewa (62)	113	0.34
Choctaw (5)	6	0.02
Cree (3)	14	0.04
Creek (1)	4	0.01
Crow (32)	40	0.12
Inupiat *(Alaska Native)* (1)	1	<0.01
Iroquois (1)	4	0.01
Lumbee (3)	3	0.01
Menominee (1)	1	<0.01
Mexican American Ind. (6)	10	0.03
Navajo (3)	8	0.02
Ottawa (0)	1	<0.01
Potawatomi (0)	2	0.01
Puget Sound Salish (0)	2	0.01
Seminole (0)	1	<0.01
Shoshone (1)	1	<0.01
Sioux (12)	25	0.07
Asian (161)	267	0.80
Not Hispanic (159)	243	0.72
Hispanic (2)	24	0.07
Chinese, ex. Taiwanese (41)	56	0.17
Filipino (33)	76	0.23
Indian (24)	28	0.08
Indonesian (1)	1	<0.01
Japanese (12)	40	0.12
Korean (14)	24	0.07
Laotian (2)	2	0.01
Nepalese (2)	2	0.01
Pakistani (2)	2	0.01
Taiwanese (2)	9	0.03
Thai (4)	5	0.01
Vietnamese (7)	9	0.03
Hawaii Native/Pacific Islander (21)	50	0.15
Not Hispanic (20)	40	0.12
Hispanic (1)	10	0.03
Guamanian/Chamorro (2)	5	0.01
Native Hawaiian (12)	31	0.09
Samoan (4)	7	0.02
White (31,663)	32,339	96.46
Not Hispanic (30,901)	31,421	93.72
Hispanic (762)	918	2.74

Evergreen

Place Type: CDP
County: Flathead
Population: 7,616†

Ancestry‡	Population	%
American (288)	288	3.87
Austrian (3)	10	0.13
Belgian (0)	4	0.05
British (20)	20	0.27
Canadian (72)	76	1.02
Czech (3)	70	0.94
Czechoslovakian (0)	5	0.07
Danish (0)	120	1.61
Dutch (6)	238	3.20
English (260)	785	10.54
Finnish (17)	34	0.46
French, ex. Basque (101)	229	3.08
French Canadian (40)	97	1.30
German (707)	2,011	27.01
Hungarian (0)	17	0.23
Irish (264)	1,066	14.32
Italian (176)	452	6.07
Latvian (31)	31	0.42
Norwegian (279)	922	12.38
Polish (36)	87	1.17
Portuguese (59)	59	0.79
Russian (0)	47	0.63
Scandinavian (116)	239	3.21
Scotch-Irish (79)	126	1.69
Scottish (120)	268	3.60
Slovak (0)	28	0.38
Swedish (132)	263	3.53
Swiss (103)	103	1.38
Ukrainian (16)	16	0.21
Welsh (128)	195	2.62

Hispanic Origin	Population	%
Hispanic or Latino (of any race)	215	2.82
Central American, ex. Mexican	2	0.03
Costa Rican	1	0.01
Guatemalan	1	0.01
Cuban	2	0.03
Mexican	166	2.18
Puerto Rican	13	0.17
South American	3	0.04
Bolivian	1	0.01
Ecuadorian	1	0.01
Peruvian	1	0.01
Other Hispanic or Latino	29	0.38

Race*	Population	%
African-American/Black (16)	39	0.51
Not Hispanic (15)	37	0.49
Hispanic (1)	2	0.03
American Indian/Alaska Native (117)	266	3.49
Not Hispanic (97)	229	3.01
Hispanic (20)	37	0.49
Apache (0)	1	0.01
Arapaho (0)	1	0.01
Blackfeet (16)	22	0.29
Cherokee (19)	38	0.50
Chippewa (12)	30	0.39
Cree (0)	2	0.03
Crow (1)	2	0.03
Delaware (0)	3	0.04
Kiowa (1)	1	0.01
Navajo (2)	5	0.07
Potawatomi (1)	1	0.01
Pueblo (0)	3	0.04
Puget Sound Salish (2)	7	0.09
Seminole (0)	1	0.01
Sioux (1)	6	0.08
Yup'ik *(Alaska Native)* (1)	1	0.01
Asian (33)	62	0.81
Not Hispanic (33)	62	0.81
Chinese, ex. Taiwanese (5)	8	0.11
Filipino (9)	24	0.32
Indian (2)	4	0.05
Indonesian (0)	1	0.01
Japanese (6)	11	0.14
Korean (4)	7	0.09
Pakistani (0)	2	0.03
Vietnamese (5)	7	0.09
Hawaii Native/Pacific Islander (4)	13	0.17
Not Hispanic (3)	7	0.09
Hispanic (1)	6	0.08
Guamanian/Chamorro (2)	3	0.04
Native Hawaiian (0)	2	0.03
Samoan (2)	2	0.03
White (7,199)	7,391	97.05
Not Hispanic (7,080)	7,243	95.10
Hispanic (119)	148	1.94

Great Falls

Place Type: City
County: Cascade
Population: 58,505†

Ancestry‡	Population	%
African, Sub-Saharan (158)	437	0.76
African (158)	373	0.64
Liberian (0)	32	0.06
Nigerian (0)	32	0.06
American (2,887)	2,887	4.99
Arab (47)	72	0.12
Lebanese (47)	61	0.11
Syrian (0)	11	0.02
Austrian (20)	213	0.37
Basque (38)	65	0.11
Belgian (50)	221	0.38
British (134)	267	0.46
Cajun (24)	24	0.04
Canadian (72)	165	0.29
Croatian (36)	154	0.27
Czech (155)	671	1.16
Czechoslovakian (245)	321	0.55
Danish (197)	658	1.14
Dutch (235)	1,427	2.47
Eastern European (23)	23	0.04
English (1,730)	6,774	11.70
Estonian (10)	10	0.02

*Notes: † The Census 2010 population figure is used to calculate the percentages in the Hispanic Origin and Race categories. Ancestry percentages are based on the 2006-2010 American Community Survey population (not shown); ‡ Numbers in parentheses indicate the number of people reporting a single ancestry; * Numbers in parentheses indicate the number of persons reporting this race alone, not in combination with any other race; Please refer to the Explanation of Data for more information.*

European (821)	1,011	1.75
Finnish (182)	619	1.07
French, ex. Basque (295)	2,163	3.74
French Canadian (204)	673	1.16
German (4,862)	15,913	27.50
Greek (77)	264	0.46
Hungarian (65)	220	0.38
Irish (2,052)	9,556	16.51
Italian (722)	2,274	3.93
Latvian (9)	9	0.02
Lithuanian (84)	111	0.19
Luxemburger (33)	54	0.09
Northern European (12)	12	0.02
Norwegian (2,362)	6,293	10.87
Pennsylvania German (36)	42	0.07
Polish (677)	1,685	2.91
Portuguese (27)	206	0.36
Russian (168)	748	1.29
Scandinavian (183)	403	0.70
Scotch-Irish (387)	1,363	2.36
Scottish (388)	1,747	3.02
Serbian (17)	33	0.06
Slavic (6)	99	0.17
Slovak (50)	58	0.10
Slovene (76)	117	0.20
Swedish (410)	2,096	3.62
Swiss (0)	246	0.43
Turkish (7)	7	0.01
Ukrainian (169)	300	0.52
Welsh (72)	441	0.76
West Indian, ex. Hispanic (12)	109	0.19
Jamaican (12)	109	0.19
Yugoslavian (68)	199	0.34

Hispanic Origin	Population	%
Hispanic or Latino (of any race)	1,978	3.38
Central American, ex. Mexican	61	0.10
Costa Rican	7	0.01
Guatemalan	8	0.01
Honduran	5	0.01
Nicaraguan	7	0.01
Panamanian	14	0.02
Salvadoran	20	0.03
Cuban	28	0.05
Dominican Republic	19	0.03
Mexican	1,319	2.25
Puerto Rican	176	0.30
South American	47	0.08
Argentinean	2	<0.01
Bolivian	1	<0.01
Chilean	2	<0.01
Colombian	17	0.03
Ecuadorian	7	0.01
Peruvian	10	0.02
Uruguayan	1	<0.01
Venezuelan	4	0.01
Other South American	3	0.01
Other Hispanic or Latino	328	0.56

Race*	Population	%
African-American/Black (617)	1,106	1.89
Not Hispanic (583)	1,000	1.71
Hispanic (34)	106	0.18
American Indian/Alaska Native (2,942)	4,326	7.39
Not Hispanic (2,753)	3,999	6.84
Hispanic (189)	327	0.56
Alaska Athabascan *(Ala. Nat.)* (4)	4	0.01
Aleut *(Alaska Native)* (2)	4	0.01
Apache (3)	10	0.02
Arapaho (11)	18	0.03
Blackfeet (642)	784	1.34
Canadian/French Am. Ind. (6)	12	0.02
Cherokee (22)	86	0.15
Cheyenne (32)	44	0.08
Chickasaw (0)	3	0.01
Chippewa (321)	557	0.95
Choctaw (6)	14	0.02
Colville (0)	5	0.01
Comanche (0)	1	<0.01
Cree (38)	85	0.15
Creek (0)	3	0.01
Crow (25)	33	0.06
Delaware (3)	7	0.01
Hopi (1)	1	<0.01
Inupiat *(Alaska Native)* (3)	5	0.01
Iroquois (4)	10	0.02
Menominee (0)	3	0.01
Mexican American Ind. (4)	16	0.03
Navajo (19)	28	0.05
Osage (0)	1	<0.01
Paiute (0)	1	<0.01
Potawatomi (4)	9	0.02
Pueblo (8)	8	0.01
Puget Sound Salish (2)	7	0.01
Seminole (0)	2	<0.01
Shoshone (5)	19	0.03
Sioux (50)	105	0.18
Spanish American Ind. (0)	2	<0.01
Tlingit-Haida *(Alaska Native)* (7)	10	0.02
Tsimshian *(Alaska Native)* (1)	3	0.01
Ute (0)	2	<0.01
Yakama (0)	4	0.01
Yaqui (0)	1	<0.01
Yuman (8)	9	0.02
Yup'ik *(Alaska Native)* (1)	2	<0.01
Asian (520)	921	1.57
Not Hispanic (505)	860	1.47
Hispanic (15)	61	0.10
Burmese (1)	1	<0.01
Chinese, ex. Taiwanese (44)	95	0.16
Filipino (201)	372	0.64
Hmong (5)	6	0.01
Indian (38)	66	0.11
Indonesian (0)	2	<0.01
Japanese (59)	141	0.24
Korean (79)	139	0.24
Laotian (13)	18	0.03
Malaysian (2)	5	0.01
Nepalese (3)	3	0.01
Pakistani (2)	2	<0.01
Sri Lankan (0)	1	<0.01
Taiwanese (1)	1	<0.01
Thai (27)	49	0.08
Vietnamese (19)	30	0.05
Hawaii Native/Pacific Islander (76)	158	0.27
Not Hispanic (66)	135	0.23
Hispanic (10)	23	0.04
Fijian (1)	1	<0.01
Guamanian/Chamorro (33)	48	0.08
Marshallese (1)	1	<0.01
Native Hawaiian (29)	76	0.13
Samoan (4)	6	0.01
Tongan (3)	3	0.01
White (51,765)	53,815	91.98
Not Hispanic (50,723)	52,466	89.68
Hispanic (1,042)	1,349	2.31

Havre

Place Type: City
County: Hill
Population: 9,310†

Ancestry‡	Population	%
African, Sub-Saharan (23)	23	0.25
African (23)	23	0.25
American (424)	424	4.58
Arab (7)	7	0.08
Syrian (7)	7	0.08
Austrian (0)	28	0.30
Belgian (13)	13	0.14
British (33)	33	0.36
Canadian (18)	18	0.19
Croatian (9)	40	0.43
Czech (48)	131	1.41
Czechoslovakian (11)	21	0.23
Danish (17)	55	0.59
Dutch (61)	265	2.86
English (199)	908	9.80
European (218)	218	2.35
French, ex. Basque (40)	258	2.79
French Canadian (24)	54	0.58
German (862)	2,647	28.58
Irish (302)	1,407	15.19
Italian (62)	302	3.26
Norwegian (710)	1,933	20.87
Polish (23)	173	1.87
Russian (19)	53	0.57
Scandinavian (48)	56	0.60
Scotch-Irish (36)	95	1.03
Scottish (95)	229	2.47
Slovak (0)	17	0.18
Swedish (50)	282	3.05
Swiss (0)	63	0.68
Ukrainian (0)	20	0.22
Welsh (0)	68	0.73
Yugoslavian (23)	36	0.39

Hispanic Origin	Population	%
Hispanic or Latino (of any race)	237	2.55
Central American, ex. Mexican	11	0.12
Guatemalan	1	0.01
Honduran	3	0.03
Nicaraguan	1	0.01
Panamanian	3	0.03
Salvadoran	2	0.02
Other Central American	1	0.01
Cuban	4	0.04
Mexican	170	1.83
Puerto Rican	11	0.12
South American	2	0.02
Paraguayan	1	0.01
Uruguayan	1	0.01
Other Hispanic or Latino	39	0.42

Race*	Population	%
African-American/Black (40)	80	0.86
Not Hispanic (37)	74	0.79
Hispanic (3)	6	0.06
American Indian/Alaska Native (1,210)	1,489	15.99
Not Hispanic (1,152)	1,401	15.05
Hispanic (58)	88	0.95
Aleut *(Alaska Native)* (1)	2	0.02
Apache (3)	4	0.04
Blackfeet (81)	98	1.05
Canadian/French Am. Ind. (3)	3	0.03
Cherokee (2)	5	0.05
Cheyenne (12)	17	0.18
Chickasaw (0)	1	0.01
Chippewa (94)	151	1.62
Choctaw (4)	4	0.04
Colville (0)	1	0.01
Cree (9)	17	0.18
Crow (8)	11	0.12
Delaware (0)	1	0.01
Inupiat *(Alaska Native)* (1)	1	0.01
Iroquois (2)	3	0.03
Lumbee (0)	2	0.02
Mexican American Ind. (1)	2	0.02
Navajo (10)	14	0.15
Pima (1)	1	0.01
Potawatomi (1)	2	0.02
Pueblo (9)	9	0.10
Puget Sound Salish (3)	3	0.03
Shoshone (1)	1	0.01
Sioux (15)	37	0.40
Tlingit-Haida *(Alaska Native)* (5)	5	0.05
Yup'ik *(Alaska Native)* (3)	5	0.05
Asian (53)	112	1.20
Not Hispanic (52)	105	1.13
Hispanic (1)	7	0.08
Chinese, ex. Taiwanese (9)	19	0.20
Filipino (24)	44	0.47
Indian (1)	5	0.05
Japanese (9)	38	0.41
Korean (1)	9	0.10
Taiwanese (0)	1	0.01
Thai (4)	7	0.08
Vietnamese (1)	1	0.01
Hawaii Native/Pacific Islander (7)	25	0.27

*Notes: † The Census 2010 population figure is used to calculate the percentages in the Hispanic Origin and Race categories. Ancestry percentages are based on the 2006-2010 American Community Survey population (not shown); ‡ Numbers in parentheses indicate the number of people reporting a single ancestry; * Numbers in parentheses indicate the number of persons reporting this race alone, not in combination with any other race; Please refer to the Explanation of Data for more information.*

Not Hispanic (6)	24	0.26
Hispanic (1)	1	0.01
Guamanian/Chamorro (0)	9	0.10
Native Hawaiian (4)	9	0.10
Samoan (2)	4	0.04
White (7,601)	7,945	85.34
Not Hispanic (7,501)	7,802	83.80
Hispanic (100)	143	1.54

Helena Valley Southeast

Place Type: CDP
County: Lewis and Clark
Population: 8,227†

Ancestry‡	Population	%
American (284)	284	3.58
Australian (0)	36	0.45
Austrian (0)	68	0.86
British (43)	72	0.91
Czech (0)	29	0.37
Czechoslovakian (46)	61	0.77
Danish (12)	28	0.35
Dutch (0)	286	3.61
English (442)	1,254	15.83
European (86)	86	1.09
Finnish (38)	59	0.74
French, ex. Basque (0)	418	5.28
French Canadian (19)	64	0.81
German (1,102)	2,537	32.02
Irish (219)	1,489	18.79
Italian (105)	461	5.82
Norwegian (149)	450	5.68
Pennsylvania German (0)	12	0.15
Polish (72)	164	2.07
Portuguese (0)	26	0.33
Romanian (0)	22	0.28
Russian (0)	29	0.37
Scotch-Irish (95)	318	4.01
Scottish (101)	434	5.48
Slovak (0)	10	0.13
Swedish (88)	327	4.13
Swiss (0)	15	0.19
Welsh (11)	62	0.78

Hispanic Origin	Population	%
Hispanic or Latino (of any race)	202	2.46
Central American, ex. Mexican	4	0.05
Honduran	1	0.01
Salvadoran	3	0.04
Cuban	2	0.02
Dominican Republic	4	0.05
Mexican	124	1.51
Puerto Rican	10	0.12
South American	10	0.12
Bolivian	1	0.01
Colombian	2	0.02
Ecuadorian	1	0.01
Peruvian	6	0.07
Other Hispanic or Latino	48	0.58

Race*	Population	%
African-American/Black (24)	64	0.78
Not Hispanic (24)	58	0.70
Hispanic (0)	6	0.07
American Indian/Alaska Native (233)	421	5.12
Not Hispanic (222)	393	4.78
Hispanic (11)	28	0.34
Apache (0)	1	0.01
Blackfeet (39)	51	0.62
Cherokee (4)	24	0.29
Cheyenne (6)	14	0.17
Chippewa (46)	86	1.05
Cree (2)	8	0.10
Creek (1)	4	0.05
Inupiat *(Alaska Native)* (0)	1	0.01
Iroquois (1)	1	0.01
Mexican American Ind. (1)	2	0.02
Navajo (1)	3	0.04
Potawatomi (0)	2	0.02
Puget Sound Salish (5)	9	0.11
Sioux (5)	9	0.11
Asian (33)	58	0.70
Not Hispanic (33)	56	0.68
Hispanic (0)	2	0.02
Chinese, ex. Taiwanese (2)	5	0.06
Filipino (19)	27	0.33
Indian (1)	4	0.05
Japanese (4)	5	0.06
Korean (6)	10	0.12
Vietnamese (1)	6	0.07
Hawaii Native/Pacific Islander (6)	17	0.21
Not Hispanic (6)	15	0.18
Hispanic (0)	2	0.02
Fijian (0)	3	0.04
Guamanian/Chamorro (1)	2	0.02
Native Hawaiian (3)	6	0.07
Tongan (1)	3	0.04
White (7,621)	7,873	95.70
Not Hispanic (7,505)	7,721	93.85
Hispanic (116)	152	1.85

Helena Valley West Central

Place Type: CDP
County: Lewis and Clark
Population: 7,883†

Ancestry‡	Population	%
African, Sub-Saharan (119)	119	1.45
Liberian (119)	119	1.45
American (610)	610	7.44
Arab (14)	16	0.20
Arab (14)	14	0.17
Syrian (0)	2	0.02
Austrian (15)	26	0.32
Belgian (13)	24	0.29
Cajun (0)	47	0.57
Canadian (13)	21	0.26
Croatian (46)	98	1.20
Czech (12)	71	0.87
Czechoslovakian (12)	30	0.37
Danish (0)	87	1.06
Dutch (27)	175	2.13
English (166)	1,084	13.22
European (216)	216	2.64
Finnish (45)	89	1.09
French, ex. Basque (26)	310	3.78
French Canadian (24)	90	1.10
German (959)	2,289	27.92
Greek (0)	31	0.38
Irish (559)	1,642	20.03
Italian (81)	169	2.06
Lithuanian (0)	15	0.18
Northern European (51)	51	0.62
Norwegian (131)	526	6.42
Polish (45)	226	2.76
Portuguese (57)	214	2.61
Russian (0)	29	0.35
Scandinavian (26)	121	1.48
Scotch-Irish (131)	208	2.54
Scottish (113)	221	2.70
Swedish (45)	292	3.56
Swiss (20)	37	0.45
Ukrainian (0)	23	0.28
Welsh (0)	29	0.35
Yugoslavian (0)	9	0.11

Hispanic Origin	Population	%
Hispanic or Latino (of any race)	161	2.04
Central American, ex. Mexican	1	0.01
Nicaraguan	1	0.01
Cuban	3	0.04
Dominican Republic	1	0.01
Mexican	127	1.61
Puerto Rican	6	0.08
South American	2	0.03
Peruvian	2	0.03
Other Hispanic or Latino	21	0.27

Race*	Population	%
African-American/Black (27)	54	0.69
Not Hispanic (25)	50	0.63
Hispanic (2)	4	0.05
American Indian/Alaska Native (98)	190	2.41
Not Hispanic (90)	174	2.21
Hispanic (8)	16	0.20
Blackfeet (18)	30	0.38
Canadian/French Am. Ind. (0)	5	0.06
Cherokee (4)	12	0.15
Cheyenne (2)	2	0.03
Chippewa (18)	25	0.32
Choctaw (0)	2	0.03
Cree (0)	2	0.03
Creek (1)	1	0.01
Crow (2)	3	0.04
Hopi (1)	1	0.01
Mexican American Ind. (1)	1	0.01
Sioux (4)	12	0.15
Tlingit-Haida *(Alaska Native)* (0)	2	0.03
Asian (43)	85	1.08
Not Hispanic (42)	78	0.99
Hispanic (1)	7	0.09
Burmese (1)	1	0.01
Chinese, ex. Taiwanese (3)	12	0.15
Filipino (7)	30	0.38
Indian (5)	6	0.08
Japanese (5)	12	0.15
Korean (5)	5	0.06
Laotian (1)	4	0.05
Malaysian (1)	1	0.01
Nepalese (1)	1	0.01
Thai (1)	1	0.01
Vietnamese (2)	2	0.03
Hawaii Native/Pacific Islander (6)	20	0.25
Not Hispanic (6)	13	0.16
Hispanic (0)	7	0.09
Guamanian/Chamorro (1)	6	0.08
Native Hawaiian (0)	3	0.04
Samoan (1)	4	0.05
White (7,523)	7,673	97.34
Not Hispanic (7,418)	7,552	95.80
Hispanic (105)	121	1.53

Helena

Place Type: City
County: Lewis and Clark
Population: 28,190†

Ancestry‡	Population	%
American (1,259)	1,259	4.55
Arab (18)	138	0.50
Lebanese (8)	128	0.46
Other Arab (10)	10	0.04
Australian (38)	38	0.14
Austrian (34)	168	0.61
Basque (0)	32	0.12
Belgian (0)	11	0.04
British (54)	137	0.50
Bulgarian (0)	21	0.08
Cajun (13)	13	0.05
Canadian (15)	55	0.20
Croatian (53)	133	0.48
Czech (127)	263	0.95
Czechoslovakian (19)	52	0.19
Danish (79)	415	1.50
Dutch (83)	505	1.82
Eastern European (7)	45	0.16
English (789)	3,835	13.86
European (450)	487	1.76
Finnish (56)	254	0.92
French, ex. Basque (278)	1,564	5.65
French Canadian (85)	371	1.34
German (2,393)	7,629	27.57
Greek (21)	136	0.49
Hungarian (24)	48	0.17
Iranian (0)	20	0.07
Irish (1,204)	5,172	18.69

*Notes: † The Census 2010 population figure is used to calculate the percentages in the Hispanic Origin and Race categories. Ancestry percentages are based on the 2006-2010 American Community Survey population (not shown); ‡ Numbers in parentheses indicate the number of people reporting a single ancestry; * Numbers in parentheses indicate the number of persons reporting this race alone, not in combination with any other race; Please refer to the Explanation of Data for more information.*

Italian (405)	1,683	6.08
Latvian (0)	9	0.03
Lithuanian (14)	58	0.21
Maltese (0)	28	0.10
Northern European (21)	21	0.08
Norwegian (1,065)	2,724	9.84
Polish (378)	1,042	3.77
Portuguese (18)	86	0.31
Romanian (51)	72	0.26
Russian (32)	187	0.68
Scandinavian (130)	189	0.68
Scotch-Irish (330)	1,067	3.86
Scottish (352)	1,270	4.59
Serbian (7)	50	0.18
Slavic (21)	86	0.31
Slovak (20)	36	0.13
Slovene (45)	126	0.46
Swedish (237)	1,015	3.67
Swiss (0)	126	0.46
Ukrainian (0)	228	0.82
Welsh (56)	390	1.41
West Indian, ex. Hispanic (7)	27	0.10
Belizean (0)	20	0.07
Jamaican (7)	7	0.03
Yugoslavian (36)	89	0.32

Hispanic Origin	Population	%
Hispanic or Latino (of any race)	779	2.76
Central American, ex. Mexican	28	0.10
Costa Rican	3	0.01
Guatemalan	9	0.03
Honduran	5	0.02
Nicaraguan	5	0.02
Salvadoran	6	0.02
Cuban	25	0.09
Dominican Republic	6	0.02
Mexican	497	1.76
Puerto Rican	31	0.11
South American	24	0.09
Argentinean	6	0.02
Bolivian	1	<0.01
Chilean	1	<0.01
Colombian	9	0.03
Ecuadorian	1	<0.01
Paraguayan	1	<0.01
Peruvian	2	0.01
Venezuelan	3	0.01
Other Hispanic or Latino	168	0.60

Race*	Population	%
African-American/Black (118)	214	0.76
Not Hispanic (110)	195	0.69
Hispanic (8)	19	0.07
American Indian/Alaska Native (648)	1,108	3.93
Not Hispanic (607)	1,027	3.64
Hispanic (41)	81	0.29
Aleut *(Alaska Native)* (1)	3	0.01
Apache (5)	21	0.07
Arapaho (0)	1	<0.01
Blackfeet (76)	121	0.43
Canadian/French Am. Ind. (1)	2	0.01
Cherokee (14)	60	0.21
Cheyenne (26)	34	0.12
Chickasaw (5)	6	0.02
Chippewa (77)	152	0.54
Choctaw (2)	6	0.02
Colville (0)	1	<0.01
Cree (2)	10	0.04
Crow (5)	13	0.05
Hopi (1)	4	0.01
Inupiat *(Alaska Native)* (3)	5	0.02
Iroquois (4)	10	0.04
Mexican American Ind. (5)	5	0.02
Navajo (14)	27	0.10
Osage (0)	1	<0.01
Paiute (2)	3	0.01
Pima (2)	3	0.01
Potawatomi (1)	4	0.01
Pueblo (1)	1	<0.01
Puget Sound Salish (2)	4	0.01
Seminole (0)	1	<0.01
Shoshone (1)	1	<0.01
Sioux (41)	82	0.29
South American Ind. (1)	2	0.01
Tlingit-Haida *(Alaska Native)* (1)	3	0.01
Asian (205)	333	1.18
Not Hispanic (203)	317	1.12
Hispanic (2)	16	0.06
Burmese (1)	1	<0.01
Chinese, ex. Taiwanese (47)	68	0.24
Filipino (39)	84	0.30
Hmong (1)	1	<0.01
Indian (35)	44	0.16
Indonesian (1)	1	<0.01
Japanese (20)	53	0.19
Korean (36)	54	0.19
Laotian (2)	4	0.01
Nepalese (2)	2	0.01
Pakistani (2)	2	0.01
Taiwanese (1)	1	<0.01
Thai (3)	4	0.01
Vietnamese (4)	19	0.07
Hawaii Native/Pacific Islander (20)	46	0.16
Not Hispanic (19)	38	0.13
Hispanic (1)	8	0.03
Guamanian/Chamorro (1)	4	0.01
Native Hawaiian (8)	24	0.09
Samoan (5)	8	0.03
White (26,313)	27,017	95.84
Not Hispanic (25,831)	26,432	93.76
Hispanic (482)	585	2.08

Kalispell

Place Type: City
County: Flathead
Population: 19,927†

Ancestry‡	Population	%
African, Sub-Saharan (24)	67	0.35
African (24)	44	0.23
Nigerian (0)	23	0.12
American (731)	731	3.79
Arab (9)	24	0.12
Lebanese (9)	24	0.12
Austrian (20)	71	0.37
British (13)	118	0.61
Bulgarian (0)	9	0.05
Canadian (90)	108	0.56
Celtic (0)	16	0.08
Croatian (43)	43	0.22
Czech (48)	134	0.69
Czechoslovakian (0)	17	0.09
Danish (71)	289	1.50
Dutch (79)	571	2.96
Eastern European (18)	18	0.09
English (1,053)	2,621	13.58
European (183)	239	1.24
Finnish (154)	237	1.23
French, ex. Basque (68)	898	4.65
French Canadian (106)	195	1.01
German (2,136)	5,498	28.49
Greek (0)	45	0.23
Hungarian (0)	24	0.12
Irish (869)	2,782	14.42
Italian (118)	723	3.75
Lithuanian (47)	47	0.24
Northern European (52)	52	0.27
Norwegian (765)	2,325	12.05
Pennsylvania German (0)	14	0.07
Polish (188)	585	3.03
Portuguese (7)	7	0.04
Russian (57)	130	0.67
Scandinavian (95)	131	0.68
Scotch-Irish (179)	751	3.89
Scottish (110)	496	2.57
Serbian (0)	27	0.14
Slovak (14)	14	0.07
Swedish (215)	885	4.59
Swiss (68)	241	1.25
Ukrainian (157)	219	1.13
Welsh (31)	159	0.82
West Indian, ex. Hispanic (0)	17	0.09
Dutch West Indian (0)	17	0.09
Yugoslavian (30)	79	0.41

Hispanic Origin	Population	%
Hispanic or Latino (of any race)	568	2.85
Central American, ex. Mexican	20	0.10
Costa Rican	4	0.02
Guatemalan	2	0.01
Honduran	2	0.01
Panamanian	7	0.04
Salvadoran	5	0.03
Cuban	15	0.08
Dominican Republic	2	0.01
Mexican	382	1.92
Puerto Rican	39	0.20
South American	24	0.12
Argentinean	1	0.01
Bolivian	3	0.02
Chilean	2	0.01
Colombian	9	0.05
Peruvian	7	0.04
Venezuelan	2	0.01
Other Hispanic or Latino	86	0.43

Race*	Population	%
African-American/Black (49)	115	0.58
Not Hispanic (38)	98	0.49
Hispanic (11)	17	0.09
American Indian/Alaska Native (257)	567	2.85
Not Hispanic (232)	508	2.55
Hispanic (25)	59	0.30
Alaska Athabascan *(Ala. Nat.)* (0)	2	0.01
Aleut *(Alaska Native)* (4)	4	0.02
Apache (0)	6	0.03
Arapaho (1)	1	0.01
Blackfeet (47)	94	0.47
Canadian/French Am. Ind. (0)	1	0.01
Cherokee (9)	26	0.13
Cheyenne (3)	7	0.04
Chickasaw (0)	1	0.01
Chippewa (27)	52	0.26
Choctaw (3)	3	0.02
Colville (0)	3	0.02
Comanche (1)	2	0.01
Cree (1)	10	0.05
Creek (0)	3	0.02
Crow (2)	6	0.03
Hopi (0)	4	0.02
Inupiat *(Alaska Native)* (4)	12	0.06
Iroquois (0)	3	0.02
Mexican American Ind. (1)	1	0.01
Navajo (4)	7	0.04
Potawatomi (3)	7	0.04
Puget Sound Salish (3)	6	0.03
Seminole (2)	3	0.02
Sioux (12)	33	0.17
Tlingit-Haida *(Alaska Native)* (0)	4	0.02
Tohono O'Odham (0)	2	0.01
Tsimshian *(Alaska Native)* (1)	2	0.01
Yakama (3)	5	0.03
Yuman (1)	8	0.04
Asian (191)	316	1.59
Not Hispanic (187)	302	1.52
Hispanic (4)	14	0.07
Chinese, ex. Taiwanese (32)	53	0.27
Filipino (48)	92	0.46
Indian (20)	25	0.13
Indonesian (4)	4	0.02
Japanese (30)	60	0.30
Korean (25)	44	0.22
Nepalese (1)	2	0.01
Pakistani (1)	1	0.01
Sri Lankan (2)	2	0.01
Taiwanese (0)	3	0.02
Thai (2)	6	0.03
Vietnamese (11)	21	0.11
Hawaii Native/Pacific Islander (13)	32	0.16

*Notes: † The Census 2010 population figure is used to calculate the percentages in the Hispanic Origin and Race categories. Ancestry percentages are based on the 2006-2010 American Community Survey population (not shown); ‡ Numbers in parentheses indicate the number of people reporting a single ancestry; * Numbers in parentheses indicate the number of persons reporting this race alone, not in combination with any other race; Please refer to the Explanation of Data for more information.*

Not Hispanic (11)	26	0.13
Hispanic (2)	6	0.03
Guamanian/Chamorro (1)	3	0.02
Native Hawaiian (12)	25	0.13
Samoan (0)	2	0.01
White (18,776)	19,273	96.72
Not Hispanic (18,428)	18,860	94.65
Hispanic (348)	413	2.07

Miles City

Place Type: City
County: Custer
Population: 8,410†

Ancestry‡	Population	%
African, Sub-Saharan (0)	64	0.77
Ethiopian (0)	32	0.39
Somalian (0)	32	0.39
American (1,120)	1,120	13.48
Arab (0)	12	0.14
Arab (0)	12	0.14
Austrian (0)	29	0.35
Belgian (0)	10	0.12
British (11)	11	0.13
Canadian (13)	19	0.23
Czech (19)	55	0.66
Czechoslovakian (0)	12	0.14
Danish (37)	86	1.04
Dutch (0)	177	2.13
Eastern European (0)	15	0.18
English (147)	840	10.11
European (52)	52	0.63
Finnish (0)	31	0.37
French, ex. Basque (38)	271	3.26
French Canadian (34)	106	1.28
German (904)	2,853	34.34
German Russian (13)	13	0.16
Greek (4)	4	0.05
Hungarian (0)	26	0.31
Irish (342)	1,629	19.61
Italian (34)	185	2.23
Luxemburger (0)	7	0.08
Northern European (13)	13	0.16
Norwegian (458)	1,160	13.96
Pennsylvania German (0)	23	0.28
Polish (35)	213	2.56
Portuguese (0)	10	0.12
Russian (18)	83	1.00
Scandinavian (19)	59	0.71
Scotch-Irish (72)	205	2.47
Scottish (85)	292	3.51
Slovak (0)	18	0.22
Swedish (58)	329	3.96
Swiss (17)	47	0.57
Ukrainian (11)	28	0.34
Welsh (37)	95	1.14
Yugoslavian (11)	21	0.25

Hispanic Origin	Population	%
Hispanic or Latino (of any race)	205	2.44
Cuban	2	0.02
Mexican	160	1.90
Puerto Rican	15	0.18
South American	3	0.04
Ecuadorian	2	0.02
Peruvian	1	0.01
Other Hispanic or Latino	25	0.30

Race*	Population	%
African-American/Black (28)	48	0.57
Not Hispanic (27)	45	0.54
Hispanic (1)	3	0.04
American Indian/Alaska Native (144)	228	2.71
Not Hispanic (141)	216	2.57
Hispanic (3)	12	0.14
Apache (1)	1	0.01
Arapaho (3)	3	0.04
Blackfeet (3)	6	0.07
Canadian/French Am. Ind. (1)	1	0.01
Cherokee (1)	8	0.10
Cheyenne (25)	37	0.44
Chippewa (19)	27	0.32
Choctaw (1)	1	0.01
Cree (1)	1	0.01
Delaware (0)	1	0.01
Potawatomi (0)	1	0.01
Sioux (15)	24	0.29
Ute (1)	1	0.01
Yakama (0)	2	0.02
Asian (33)	59	0.70
Not Hispanic (33)	59	0.70
Chinese, ex. Taiwanese (12)	17	0.20
Filipino (6)	10	0.12
Indian (5)	6	0.07
Japanese (5)	17	0.20
Korean (2)	5	0.06
Taiwanese (1)	2	0.02
Thai (1)	5	0.06
Vietnamese (0)	1	0.01
Hawaii Native/Pacific Islander (8)	18	0.21
Not Hispanic (2)	12	0.14
Hispanic (6)	6	0.07
Guamanian/Chamorro (1)	3	0.04
Native Hawaiian (7)	13	0.15
Tongan (0)	1	0.01
White (8,012)	8,144	96.84
Not Hispanic (7,876)	7,995	95.07
Hispanic (136)	149	1.77

Missoula

Place Type: City
County: Missoula
Population: 66,788†

Ancestry‡	Population	%
African, Sub-Saharan (37)	37	0.06
African (13)	13	0.02
Ethiopian (11)	11	0.02
South African (13)	13	0.02
Alsatian (0)	13	0.02
American (3,375)	3,375	5.16
Arab (83)	217	0.33
Arab (0)	44	0.07
Lebanese (18)	95	0.15
Palestinian (0)	13	0.02
Other Arab (65)	65	0.10
Armenian (0)	5	0.01
Austrian (55)	300	0.46
Basque (12)	33	0.05
Belgian (0)	54	0.08
Brazilian (0)	20	0.03
British (157)	408	0.62
Cajun (28)	80	0.12
Canadian (44)	164	0.25
Celtic (28)	51	0.08
Croatian (62)	162	0.25
Czech (127)	421	0.64
Czechoslovakian (66)	105	0.16
Danish (274)	1,143	1.75
Dutch (381)	1,716	2.62
Eastern European (17)	17	0.03
English (2,043)	7,701	11.78
European (955)	1,028	1.57
Finnish (79)	327	0.50
French, ex. Basque (670)	2,778	4.25
French Canadian (84)	491	0.75
German (5,831)	17,110	26.17
German Russian (20)	20	0.03
Greek (78)	366	0.56
Hungarian (10)	233	0.36
Icelander (0)	12	0.02
Irish (4,234)	11,268	17.23
Israeli (15)	15	0.02
Italian (1,074)	3,421	5.23
Lithuanian (53)	121	0.19
Luxemburger (30)	44	0.07
Northern European (116)	191	0.29
Norwegian (2,153)	5,083	7.77
Pennsylvania German (19)	75	0.11
Polish (597)	1,739	2.66
Portuguese (53)	94	0.14
Romanian (41)	108	0.17
Russian (145)	607	0.93
Scandinavian (271)	518	0.79
Scotch-Irish (590)	2,051	3.14
Scottish (752)	2,469	3.78
Serbian (43)	114	0.17
Slavic (23)	38	0.06
Slovak (6)	99	0.15
Swedish (590)	2,000	3.06
Swiss (136)	464	0.71
Turkish (8)	8	0.01
Ukrainian (77)	171	0.26
Welsh (12)	544	0.83
West Indian, ex. Hispanic (0)	59	0.09
Jamaican (0)	42	0.06
Other West Indian (0)	17	0.03
Yugoslavian (0)	46	0.07

Hispanic Origin	Population	%
Hispanic or Latino (of any race)	1,943	2.91
Central American, ex. Mexican	72	0.11
Costa Rican	11	0.02
Guatemalan	19	0.03
Honduran	5	0.01
Nicaraguan	8	0.01
Panamanian	9	0.01
Salvadoran	19	0.03
Other Central American	1	<0.01
Cuban	75	0.11
Dominican Republic	5	0.01
Mexican	1,173	1.76
Puerto Rican	139	0.21
South American	147	0.22
Argentinean	14	0.02
Bolivian	5	0.01
Chilean	22	0.03
Colombian	59	0.09
Ecuadorian	10	0.01
Paraguayan	3	<0.01
Peruvian	28	0.04
Uruguayan	2	<0.01
Venezuelan	4	0.01
Other Hispanic or Latino	332	0.50

Race*	Population	%
African-American/Black (352)	727	1.09
Not Hispanic (327)	650	0.97
Hispanic (25)	77	0.12
American Indian/Alaska Native (1,838)	2,812	4.21
Not Hispanic (1,680)	2,533	3.79
Hispanic (158)	279	0.42
Alaska Athabascan *(Ala. Nat.)* (3)	6	0.01
Aleut *(Alaska Native)* (2)	6	0.01
Apache (12)	25	0.04
Arapaho (10)	12	0.02
Blackfeet (441)	597	0.89
Canadian/French Am. Ind. (13)	26	0.04
Central American Ind. (1)	1	<0.01
Cherokee (19)	101	0.15
Cheyenne (53)	65	0.10
Chickasaw (1)	4	0.01
Chippewa (77)	158	0.24
Choctaw (7)	20	0.03
Colville (11)	19	0.03
Comanche (2)	4	0.01
Cree (6)	32	0.05
Creek (1)	14	0.02
Crow (78)	96	0.14
Hopi (2)	2	<0.01
Inupiat *(Alaska Native)* (6)	10	0.01
Iroquois (6)	9	0.01
Kiowa (2)	3	<0.01
Menominee (1)	1	<0.01
Mexican American Ind. (10)	16	0.02
Navajo (26)	31	0.05
Osage (2)	8	0.01
Ottawa (0)	3	<0.01

*Notes: † The Census 2010 population figure is used to calculate the percentages in the Hispanic Origin and Race categories. Ancestry percentages are based on the 2006-2010 American Community Survey population (not shown); ‡ Numbers in parentheses indicate the number of people reporting a single ancestry; * Numbers in parentheses indicate the number of persons reporting this race alone, not in combination with any other race; Please refer to the Explanation of Data for more information.*

Paiute (8)	17	0.03
Pima (1)	1	<0.01
Potawatomi (10)	14	0.02
Pueblo (3)	6	0.01
Puget Sound Salish (4)	5	0.01
Seminole (1)	3	<0.01
Shoshone (7)	10	0.01
Sioux (54)	120	0.18
South American Ind. (1)	8	0.01
Spanish American Ind. (0)	1	<0.01
Tlingit-Haida *(Alaska Native)* (10)	14	0.02
Tohono O'Odham (1)	2	<0.01
Ute (3)	5	0.01
Yakama (4)	5	0.01
Yaqui (0)	3	<0.01
Yuman (1)	2	<0.01
Yup'ik *(Alaska Native)* (0)	5	0.01
Asian (809)	1,300	1.95
Not Hispanic (798)	1,267	1.90
Hispanic (11)	33	0.05
Bangladeshi (2)	2	<0.01
Bhutanese (3)	3	<0.01
Burmese (6)	6	0.01
Cambodian (8)	8	0.01
Chinese, ex. Taiwanese (185)	270	0.40
Filipino (75)	163	0.24
Hmong (34)	56	0.08
Indian (84)	133	0.20
Indonesian (4)	11	0.02
Japanese (144)	265	0.40
Korean (110)	164	0.25
Malaysian (4)	6	0.01
Nepalese (8)	8	0.01
Pakistani (9)	10	0.01
Sri Lankan (1)	2	<0.01
Taiwanese (9)	12	0.02
Thai (23)	38	0.06
Vietnamese (53)	75	0.11
Hawaii Native/Pacific Islander (69)	157	0.24
Not Hispanic (68)	145	0.22
Hispanic (1)	12	0.02
Fijian (2)	7	0.01
Guamanian/Chamorro (6)	17	0.03
Marshallese (1)	1	<0.01
Native Hawaiian (28)	66	0.10
Samoan (18)	28	0.04
Tongan (1)	1	<0.01
White (61,534)	63,275	94.74
Not Hispanic (60,313)	61,826	92.57
Hispanic (1,221)	1,449	2.17

*Notes: † The Census 2010 population figure is used to calculate the percentages in the Hispanic Origin and Race categories. Ancestry percentages are based on the 2006-2010 American Community Survey population (not shown); ‡ Numbers in parentheses indicate the number of people reporting a single ancestry; * Numbers in parentheses indicate the number of persons reporting this race alone, not in combination with any other race; Please refer to the Explanation of Data for more information.*

NEBRASKA

Place Type: State
Population: 1,826,341†

Ancestry‡	Population	%
Afghan (276)	287	0.02
African, Sub-Saharan (10,813)	12,490	0.69
African (5,007)	6,278	0.35
Cape Verdean (8)	8	<0.01
Ethiopian (271)	277	0.02
Ghanaian (194)	242	0.01
Kenyan (35)	35	<0.01
Liberian (73)	83	<0.01
Nigerian (473)	506	0.03
Sierra Leonean (9)	9	<0.01
Somalian (1,207)	1,300	0.07
South African (57)	160	0.01
Sudanese (2,941)	3,016	0.17
Ugandan (41)	41	<0.01
Zimbabwean (9)	9	<0.01
Other Sub-Saharan African (488)	526	0.03
Albanian (108)	139	0.01
Alsatian (18)	72	<0.01
American (65,793)	65,793	3.66
Arab (3,763)	6,036	0.34
Arab (782)	985	0.05
Egyptian (128)	194	0.01
Iraqi (1,006)	1,083	0.06
Jordanian (246)	303	0.02
Lebanese (770)	2,057	0.11
Moroccan (9)	27	<0.01
Palestinian (117)	133	0.01
Syrian (150)	650	0.04
Other Arab (555)	604	0.03
Armenian (62)	140	0.01
Assyrian/Chaldean/Syriac (8)	15	<0.01
Australian (93)	412	0.02
Austrian (677)	3,603	0.20
Basque (100)	310	0.02
Belgian (491)	2,089	0.12
Brazilian (249)	384	0.02
British (2,000)	4,810	0.27
Bulgarian (22)	50	<0.01
Cajun (108)	229	0.01
Canadian (765)	1,785	0.10
Celtic (85)	213	0.01
Croatian (529)	2,051	0.11
Czech (35,064)	97,986	5.45
Czechoslovakian (3,568)	6,161	0.34
Danish (13,351)	50,896	2.83
Dutch (7,733)	38,931	2.16
Eastern European (463)	499	0.03
English (42,810)	171,698	9.54
Estonian (61)	181	0.01
European (15,924)	17,510	0.97
Finnish (423)	1,933	0.11
French, ex. Basque (6,142)	49,173	2.73
French Canadian (1,805)	5,985	0.33
German (328,647)	746,586	41.50
German Russian (165)	273	0.02
Greek (1,288)	3,713	0.21
Hungarian (892)	3,420	0.19
Icelander (93)	238	0.01
Iranian (240)	509	0.03
Irish (52,460)	264,065	14.68
Israeli (83)	119	0.01
Italian (13,944)	50,059	2.78
Latvian (253)	479	0.03
Lithuanian (802)	2,702	0.15
Luxemburger (299)	951	0.05
Macedonian (0)	40	<0.01
Maltese (26)	62	<0.01
New Zealander (34)	64	<0.01
Northern European (953)	1,074	0.06
Norwegian (11,574)	37,936	2.11
Pennsylvania German (948)	2,567	0.14
Polish (20,686)	67,899	3.77
Portuguese (533)	1,926	0.11
Romanian (510)	1,180	0.07
Russian (2,692)	12,966	0.72
Scandinavian (2,121)	4,494	0.25
Scotch-Irish (8,380)	28,504	1.58
Scottish (6,279)	27,303	1.52
Serbian (252)	838	0.05
Slavic (458)	807	0.04
Slovak (549)	1,125	0.06
Slovene (110)	346	0.02
Swedish (22,087)	89,083	4.95
Swiss (1,355)	7,954	0.44
Turkish (178)	316	0.02
Ukrainian (1,035)	1,959	0.11
Welsh (1,929)	11,660	0.65
West Indian, ex. Hispanic (653)	1,258	0.07
Bahamian (51)	71	<0.01
Belizean (3)	3	<0.01
British West Indian (59)	59	<0.01
Dutch West Indian (11)	41	<0.01
Haitian (217)	309	0.02
Jamaican (179)	546	0.03
Trinidadian/Tobagonian (74)	86	<0.01
U.S. Virgin Islander (0)	66	<0.01
West Indian (59)	76	<0.01
Other West Indian (0)	1	<0.01
Yugoslavian (669)	1,161	0.06

Hispanic Origin	Population	%
Hispanic or Latino (of any race)	167,405	9.17
Central American, ex. Mexican	17,242	0.94
Costa Rican	166	0.01
Guatemalan	8,616	0.47
Honduran	1,547	0.08
Nicaraguan	347	0.02
Panamanian	398	0.02
Salvadoran	6,016	0.33
Other Central American	152	0.01
Cuban	2,152	0.12
Dominican Republic	358	0.02
Mexican	128,060	7.01
Puerto Rican	3,242	0.18
South American	2,824	0.15
Argentinean	243	0.01
Bolivian	86	<0.01
Chilean	228	0.01
Colombian	974	0.05
Ecuadorian	233	0.01
Paraguayan	38	<0.01
Peruvian	628	0.03
Uruguayan	24	<0.01
Venezuelan	319	0.02
Other South American	51	<0.01
Other Hispanic or Latino	13,527	0.74

Race*	Population	%
African-American/Black (82,885)	98,959	5.42
Not Hispanic (80,959)	95,189	5.21
Hispanic (1,926)	3,770	0.21
American Indian/Alaska Native (18,427)	29,816	1.63
Not Hispanic (14,797)	23,945	1.31
Hispanic (3,630)	5,871	0.32
Alaska Athabascan *(Ala. Nat.)* (19)	41	<0.01
Aleut *(Alaska Native)* (9)	15	<0.01
Apache (91)	293	0.02
Arapaho (31)	52	<0.01
Blackfeet (57)	302	0.02
Canadian/French Am. Ind. (29)	64	<0.01
Central American Ind. (111)	154	0.01
Cherokee (448)	1,989	0.11
Cheyenne (44)	118	0.01
Chickasaw (40)	96	0.01
Chippewa (219)	412	0.02
Choctaw (130)	351	0.02
Colville (2)	6	<0.01
Comanche (16)	31	<0.01
Cree (8)	36	<0.01
Creek (65)	149	0.01
Crow (8)	40	<0.01
Delaware (15)	34	<0.01
Hopi (4)	6	<0.01
Houma (1)	1	<0.01
Inupiat *(Alaska Native)* (19)	37	<0.01
Iroquois (68)	146	0.01
Kiowa (12)	23	<0.01
Lumbee (13)	24	<0.01
Menominee (5)	28	<0.01
Mexican American Ind. (646)	913	0.05
Navajo (168)	314	0.02
Osage (4)	25	<0.01
Ottawa (14)	23	<0.01
Paiute (10)	17	<0.01
Pima (17)	25	<0.01
Potawatomi (88)	162	0.01
Pueblo (20)	49	<0.01
Puget Sound Salish (8)	11	<0.01
Seminole (9)	38	<0.01
Shoshone (22)	36	<0.01
Sioux (4,294)	6,259	0.34
South American Ind. (26)	80	<0.01
Spanish American Ind. (73)	90	<0.01
Tlingit-Haida *(Alaska Native)* (11)	20	<0.01
Tohono O'Odham (2)	5	<0.01
Tsimshian *(Alaska Native)* (1)	1	<0.01
Ute (4)	7	<0.01
Yakama (12)	13	<0.01
Yaqui (8)	37	<0.01
Yuman (3)	8	<0.01
Yup'ik *(Alaska Native)* (11)	15	<0.01
Asian (32,293)	40,561	2.22
Not Hispanic (31,919)	39,398	2.16
Hispanic (374)	1,163	0.06
Bangladeshi (65)	70	<0.01
Bhutanese (34)	38	<0.01
Burmese (2,164)	2,250	0.12
Cambodian (155)	243	0.01
Chinese, ex. Taiwanese (4,543)	5,527	0.30
Filipino (2,741)	4,900	0.27
Hmong (161)	188	0.01
Indian (5,903)	6,708	0.37
Indonesian (102)	153	0.01
Japanese (1,538)	3,106	0.17
Korean (2,678)	3,815	0.21
Laotian (880)	1,130	0.06
Malaysian (97)	132	0.01
Nepalese (650)	698	0.04
Pakistani (342)	413	0.02
Sri Lankan (112)	116	0.01
Taiwanese (161)	216	0.01
Thai (531)	921	0.05
Vietnamese (7,910)	8,677	0.48
Hawaii Native/Pacific Islander (1,279)	2,823	0.15
Not Hispanic (966)	2,128	0.12
Hispanic (313)	695	0.04
Fijian (15)	19	<0.01
Guamanian/Chamorro (501)	729	0.04
Marshallese (50)	64	<0.01
Native Hawaiian (227)	794	0.04
Samoan (164)	345	0.02
Tongan (12)	25	<0.01
White (1,572,838)	1,607,717	88.03
Not Hispanic (1,499,753)	1,525,184	83.51
Hispanic (73,085)	82,533	4.52

*Notes: † The Census 2010 population figure is used to calculate the percentages in the Hispanic Origin and Race categories. Ancestry percentages are based on the 2006-2010 American Community Survey population (not shown); ‡ Numbers in parentheses indicate the number of people reporting a single ancestry; * Numbers in parentheses indicate the number of persons reporting this race alone, not in combination with any other race; Please refer to the Explanation of Data for more information.*

Alliance

Place Type: City
County: Box Butte
Population: 8,491†

Ancestry‡	Population	%
American (187)	187	2.19
Austrian (0)	15	0.18
Czech (32)	169	1.98
Danish (22)	141	1.65
Dutch (18)	244	2.86
English (251)	882	10.35
European (25)	25	0.29
French, ex. Basque (25)	150	1.76
German (1,912)	3,904	45.80
Greek (9)	26	0.31
Hungarian (13)	43	0.50
Irish (263)	1,541	18.08
Italian (23)	23	0.27
Northern European (13)	13	0.15
Norwegian (63)	239	2.80
Pennsylvania German (7)	7	0.08
Polish (17)	152	1.78
Russian (0)	38	0.45
Scotch-Irish (23)	157	1.84
Scottish (21)	190	2.23
Swedish (99)	236	2.77
Swiss (15)	55	0.65
Welsh (8)	110	1.29

Hispanic Origin	Population	%
Hispanic or Latino (of any race)	1,048	12.34
Central American, ex. Mexican	2	0.02
Guatemalan	2	0.02
Cuban	8	0.09
Mexican	943	11.11
Puerto Rican	6	0.07
South American	9	0.11
Colombian	8	0.09
Peruvian	1	0.01
Other Hispanic or Latino	80	0.94

Race*	Population	%
African-American/Black (45)	86	1.01
Not Hispanic (42)	81	0.95
Hispanic (3)	5	0.06
American Indian/Alaska Native (390)	518	6.10
Not Hispanic (317)	414	4.88
Hispanic (73)	104	1.22
Aleut *(Alaska Native)* (1)	1	0.01
Apache (2)	3	0.04
Blackfeet (1)	2	0.02
Cherokee (1)	5	0.06
Cheyenne (0)	1	0.01
Chickasaw (2)	2	0.02
Chippewa (1)	1	0.01
Choctaw (1)	1	0.01
Comanche (0)	1	0.01
Iroquois (0)	2	0.02
Mexican American Ind. (12)	17	0.20
Navajo (5)	11	0.13
Sioux (249)	319	3.76
Spanish American Ind. (1)	1	0.01
Yaqui (1)	5	0.06
Asian (27)	56	0.66
Not Hispanic (27)	50	0.59
Hispanic (0)	6	0.07
Cambodian (2)	3	0.04
Chinese, ex. Taiwanese (8)	8	0.09
Filipino (6)	22	0.26
Japanese (7)	8	0.09
Korean (4)	13	0.15
Vietnamese (0)	2	0.02
Hawaii Native/Pacific Islander (2)	6	0.07
Not Hispanic (1)	5	0.06
Hispanic (1)	1	0.01
Guamanian/Chamorro (1)	3	0.04
Native Hawaiian (0)	3	0.04
White (7,429)	7,651	90.11
Not Hispanic (6,905)	7,040	82.91
Hispanic (524)	611	7.20

Beatrice

Place Type: City
County: Gage
Population: 12,459†

Ancestry‡	Population	%
American (557)	557	4.43
Austrian (8)	17	0.14
British (45)	45	0.36
Canadian (0)	32	0.25
Czech (179)	676	5.37
Czechoslovakian (22)	51	0.41
Danish (46)	172	1.37
Dutch (49)	228	1.81
English (190)	1,095	8.70
European (47)	47	0.37
French, ex. Basque (115)	465	3.70
French Canadian (52)	52	0.41
German (3,542)	6,232	49.52
Greek (11)	35	0.28
Hungarian (0)	36	0.29
Irish (338)	1,597	12.69
Italian (100)	328	2.61
Luxemburger (8)	8	0.06
Northern European (79)	79	0.63
Norwegian (72)	166	1.32
Pennsylvania German (11)	11	0.09
Polish (36)	202	1.61
Russian (13)	97	0.77
Scandinavian (0)	15	0.12
Scotch-Irish (10)	64	0.51
Scottish (59)	129	1.03
Slovak (0)	11	0.09
Swedish (117)	347	2.76
Swiss (14)	66	0.52
Welsh (21)	121	0.96

Hispanic Origin	Population	%
Hispanic or Latino (of any race)	274	2.20
Central American, ex. Mexican	10	0.08
Guatemalan	4	0.03
Honduran	2	0.02
Panamanian	1	0.01
Salvadoran	2	0.02
Other Central American	1	0.01
Cuban	1	0.01
Mexican	211	1.69
Puerto Rican	12	0.10
South American	3	0.02
Colombian	2	0.02
Paraguayan	1	0.01
Other Hispanic or Latino	37	0.30

Race*	Population	%
African-American/Black (62)	118	0.95
Not Hispanic (62)	109	0.87
Hispanic (0)	9	0.07
American Indian/Alaska Native (60)	148	1.19
Not Hispanic (57)	133	1.07
Hispanic (3)	15	0.12
Arapaho (1)	1	0.01
Cherokee (1)	12	0.10
Cheyenne (1)	3	0.02
Chippewa (3)	4	0.03
Cree (0)	1	0.01
Creek (1)	3	0.02
Crow (0)	4	0.03
Mexican American Ind. (1)	1	0.01
Potawatomi (2)	8	0.06
Puget Sound Salish (1)	1	0.01
Seminole (0)	1	0.01
Sioux (12)	32	0.26
South American Ind. (0)	1	0.01
Asian (73)	104	0.83
Not Hispanic (68)	98	0.79
Hispanic (5)	6	0.05
Chinese, ex. Taiwanese (15)	16	0.13
Filipino (6)	9	0.07
Indian (8)	17	0.14
Japanese (4)	7	0.06
Korean (6)	11	0.09
Laotian (21)	33	0.26
Taiwanese (1)	1	0.01
Thai (3)	5	0.04
Vietnamese (2)	2	0.02
Hawaii Native/Pacific Islander (2)	9	0.07
Not Hispanic (2)	9	0.07
Guamanian/Chamorro (1)	1	0.01
Marshallese (1)	1	0.01
Native Hawaiian (0)	5	0.04
White (11,972)	12,165	97.64
Not Hispanic (11,842)	11,990	96.24
Hispanic (130)	175	1.40

Bellevue

Place Type: City
County: Sarpy
Population: 50,137†

Ancestry‡	Population	%
African, Sub-Saharan (1,018)	1,068	2.13
African (425)	434	0.86
Sudanese (587)	628	1.25
Zimbabwean (6)	6	0.01
Albanian (11)	22	0.04
American (1,839)	1,839	3.66
Arab (0)	41	0.08
Lebanese (0)	31	0.06
Syrian (0)	10	0.02
Australian (0)	11	0.02
Austrian (0)	139	0.28
Belgian (9)	46	0.09
British (142)	219	0.44
Canadian (23)	40	0.08
Celtic (29)	38	0.08
Croatian (32)	132	0.26
Czech (802)	2,355	4.69
Czechoslovakian (43)	59	0.12
Danish (250)	1,369	2.72
Dutch (150)	899	1.79
English (1,317)	4,800	9.55
Estonian (31)	31	0.06
European (757)	836	1.66
Finnish (25)	101	0.20
French, ex. Basque (226)	1,337	2.66
French Canadian (66)	228	0.45
German (4,917)	15,696	31.24
Greek (9)	89	0.18
Hungarian (36)	102	0.20
Irish (2,234)	7,922	15.77
Italian (557)	2,183	4.35
Lithuanian (44)	156	0.31
Luxemburger (18)	54	0.11
Northern European (10)	10	0.02
Norwegian (379)	1,288	2.56
Pennsylvania German (11)	20	0.04
Polish (716)	2,670	5.31
Portuguese (56)	87	0.17
Romanian (0)	33	0.07
Russian (36)	210	0.42
Scandinavian (38)	48	0.10
Scotch-Irish (335)	972	1.93
Scottish (287)	1,469	2.92
Serbian (24)	35	0.07
Slavic (0)	9	0.02
Slovak (49)	98	0.20
Slovene (0)	11	0.02
Swedish (337)	1,865	3.71
Swiss (23)	363	0.72
Ukrainian (12)	12	0.02
Welsh (86)	485	0.97
West Indian, ex. Hispanic (60)	147	0.29
Haitian (11)	20	0.04
Jamaican (49)	66	0.13
U.S. Virgin Islander (0)	61	0.12

*Notes: † The Census 2010 population figure is used to calculate the percentages in the Hispanic Origin and Race categories. Ancestry percentages are based on the 2006-2010 American Community Survey population (not shown); ‡ Numbers in parentheses indicate the number of people reporting a single ancestry; * Numbers in parentheses indicate the number of persons reporting this race alone, not in combination with any other race; Please refer to the Explanation of Data for more information.*

Yugoslavian (11)	11	0.02

Hispanic Origin	Population	%
Hispanic or Latino (of any race)	5,962	11.89
Central American, ex. Mexican	529	1.06
Costa Rican	10	0.02
Guatemalan	80	0.16
Honduran	60	0.12
Nicaraguan	23	0.05
Panamanian	40	0.08
Salvadoran	311	0.62
Other Central American	5	0.01
Cuban	64	0.13
Dominican Republic	21	0.04
Mexican	4,573	9.12
Puerto Rican	296	0.59
South American	73	0.15
Argentinean	2	<0.01
Bolivian	6	0.01
Chilean	11	0.02
Colombian	19	0.04
Ecuadorian	14	0.03
Peruvian	13	0.03
Venezuelan	8	0.02
Other Hispanic or Latino	406	0.81

Race*	Population	%
African-American/Black (3,019)	3,884	7.75
Not Hispanic (2,936)	3,691	7.36
Hispanic (83)	193	0.38
American Indian/Alaska Native (348)	787	1.57
Not Hispanic (258)	610	1.22
Hispanic (90)	177	0.35
Apache (2)	21	0.04
Blackfeet (6)	25	0.05
Central American Ind. (1)	1	<0.01
Cherokee (23)	90	0.18
Cheyenne (4)	5	0.01
Chickasaw (1)	7	0.01
Chippewa (8)	12	0.02
Choctaw (4)	9	0.02
Comanche (1)	1	<0.01
Creek (2)	4	0.01
Crow (1)	2	<0.01
Inupiat *(Alaska Native)* (2)	2	<0.01
Iroquois (2)	5	0.01
Kiowa (1)	1	<0.01
Lumbee (1)	1	<0.01
Menominee (2)	4	0.01
Mexican American Ind. (24)	31	0.06
Navajo (2)	5	0.01
Ottawa (1)	4	0.01
Pima (3)	3	0.01
Potawatomi (1)	13	0.03
Pueblo (0)	3	0.01
Seminole (0)	4	0.01
Shoshone (1)	2	<0.01
Sioux (56)	96	0.19
South American Ind. (1)	3	0.01
Ute (1)	1	<0.01
Yakama (1)	1	<0.01
Yaqui (1)	2	<0.01
Asian (1,157)	1,696	3.38
Not Hispanic (1,151)	1,640	3.27
Hispanic (6)	56	0.11
Burmese (3)	3	0.01
Cambodian (7)	11	0.02
Chinese, ex. Taiwanese (108)	144	0.29
Filipino (387)	603	1.20
Hmong (1)	5	0.01
Indian (119)	155	0.31
Japanese (104)	207	0.41
Korean (139)	226	0.45
Laotian (18)	20	0.04
Malaysian (0)	1	<0.01
Nepalese (66)	73	0.15
Pakistani (2)	3	0.01
Sri Lankan (2)	2	<0.01
Taiwanese (2)	2	<0.01
Thai (63)	99	0.20
Vietnamese (92)	97	0.19
Hawaii Native/Pacific Islander (94)	180	0.36
Not Hispanic (91)	166	0.33
Hispanic (3)	14	0.03
Guamanian/Chamorro (52)	61	0.12
Native Hawaiian (22)	71	0.14
Samoan (14)	22	0.04
White (40,886)	42,581	84.93
Not Hispanic (38,264)	39,475	78.73
Hispanic (2,622)	3,106	6.20

Blair

Place Type: City
County: Washington
Population: 7,990†

Ancestry‡	Population	%
American (284)	284	3.56
Arab (0)	28	0.35
Lebanese (0)	14	0.18
Syrian (0)	14	0.18
Assyrian/Chaldean/Syriac (8)	8	0.10
Austrian (0)	12	0.15
British (0)	5	0.06
Czech (103)	193	2.42
Czechoslovakian (0)	15	0.19
Danish (359)	1,373	17.21
Dutch (66)	131	1.64
English (391)	909	11.39
European (156)	156	1.95
French, ex. Basque (29)	310	3.88
German (1,222)	3,493	43.77
Irish (284)	1,508	18.90
Italian (51)	271	3.40
Norwegian (81)	185	2.32
Polish (26)	77	0.96
Portuguese (0)	9	0.11
Russian (0)	10	0.13
Scandinavian (6)	6	0.08
Scotch-Irish (68)	166	2.08
Scottish (65)	131	1.64
Swedish (173)	587	7.36
Swiss (0)	11	0.14
Welsh (33)	73	0.91

Hispanic Origin	Population	%
Hispanic or Latino (of any race)	234	2.93
Central American, ex. Mexican	13	0.16
Guatemalan	9	0.11
Honduran	2	0.03
Salvadoran	2	0.03
Cuban	3	0.04
Mexican	162	2.03
Puerto Rican	11	0.14
South American	4	0.05
Chilean	1	0.01
Venezuelan	3	0.04
Other Hispanic or Latino	41	0.51

Race*	Population	%
African-American/Black (65)	107	1.34
Not Hispanic (65)	105	1.31
Hispanic (0)	2	0.03
American Indian/Alaska Native (20)	61	0.76
Not Hispanic (19)	59	0.74
Hispanic (1)	2	0.03
Alaska Athabascan *(Ala. Nat.)* (0)	4	0.05
Cherokee (0)	13	0.16
Choctaw (1)	1	0.01
Cree (0)	1	0.01
Navajo (2)	2	0.03
Sioux (9)	11	0.14
Asian (23)	27	0.34
Not Hispanic (23)	26	0.33
Hispanic (0)	1	0.01
Chinese, ex. Taiwanese (8)	9	0.11
Filipino (6)	7	0.09
Indian (1)	1	0.01
Indonesian (0)	1	0.01
Japanese (2)	4	0.05
Korean (5)	5	0.06
Hawaii Native/Pacific Islander (5)	16	0.20
Not Hispanic (4)	12	0.15
Hispanic (1)	4	0.05
Guamanian/Chamorro (0)	3	0.04
Native Hawaiian (2)	5	0.06
Samoan (2)	9	0.11
White (7,706)	7,794	97.55
Not Hispanic (7,545)	7,623	95.41
Hispanic (161)	171	2.14

Chalco

Place Type: CDP
County: Sarpy
Population: 10,994†

Ancestry‡	Population	%
African, Sub-Saharan (8)	8	0.07
Nigerian (8)	8	0.07
American (213)	213	1.98
Arab (0)	12	0.11
Syrian (0)	12	0.11
Austrian (0)	85	0.79
British (12)	217	2.02
Canadian (0)	13	0.12
Croatian (0)	49	0.46
Czech (180)	623	5.81
Czechoslovakian (96)	115	1.07
Danish (67)	562	5.24
Dutch (21)	452	4.21
English (108)	814	7.58
European (88)	104	0.97
French, ex. Basque (17)	417	3.89
French Canadian (28)	58	0.54
German (1,427)	4,890	45.56
Greek (0)	17	0.16
Hungarian (103)	128	1.19
Irish (293)	1,983	18.48
Italian (152)	653	6.08
Latvian (15)	15	0.14
Lithuanian (17)	26	0.24
Luxemburger (32)	61	0.57
Northern European (29)	58	0.54
Norwegian (82)	414	3.86
Polish (222)	775	7.22
Russian (0)	34	0.32
Scandinavian (10)	20	0.19
Scotch-Irish (51)	119	1.11
Scottish (52)	212	1.98
Serbian (0)	37	0.34
Swedish (229)	617	5.75
Swiss (0)	30	0.28
Ukrainian (12)	12	0.11
Welsh (11)	125	1.16
Yugoslavian (0)	27	0.25

Hispanic Origin	Population	%
Hispanic or Latino (of any race)	580	5.28
Central American, ex. Mexican	40	0.36
Guatemalan	9	0.08
Honduran	6	0.05
Nicaraguan	1	0.01
Salvadoran	24	0.22
Cuban	5	0.05
Dominican Republic	4	0.04
Mexican	431	3.92
Puerto Rican	34	0.31
South American	23	0.21
Argentinean	3	0.03
Chilean	4	0.04
Colombian	3	0.03
Ecuadorian	7	0.06
Peruvian	2	0.02
Venezuelan	4	0.04
Other Hispanic or Latino	43	0.39

Race*	Population	%
African-American/Black (209)	317	2.88

SECTION TWO

*Notes: † The Census 2010 population figure is used to calculate the percentages in the Hispanic Origin and Race categories. Ancestry percentages are based on the 2006-2010 American Community Survey population (not shown); ‡ Numbers in parentheses indicate the number of people reporting a single ancestry; * Numbers in parentheses indicate the number of persons reporting this race alone, not in combination with any other race; Please refer to the Explanation of Data for more information.*

	Population	%
Not Hispanic (209)	309	2.81
Hispanic (0)	8	0.07
American Indian/Alaska Native (39)	113	1.03
Not Hispanic (31)	98	0.89
Hispanic (8)	15	0.14
Apache (1)	2	0.02
Blackfeet (1)	1	0.01
Cherokee (2)	24	0.22
Chickasaw (0)	1	0.01
Chippewa (1)	2	0.02
Choctaw (1)	2	0.02
Creek (2)	9	0.08
Menominee (0)	5	0.05
Mexican American Ind. (1)	4	0.04
Sioux (8)	18	0.16
Yup'ik *(Alaska Native)* (1)	1	0.01
Asian (150)	229	2.08
Not Hispanic (145)	222	2.02
Hispanic (5)	7	0.06
Chinese, ex. Taiwanese (13)	17	0.15
Filipino (29)	51	0.46
Hmong (2)	4	0.04
Indian (13)	21	0.19
Indonesian (0)	4	0.04
Japanese (5)	17	0.15
Korean (18)	34	0.31
Laotian (1)	3	0.03
Nepalese (3)	3	0.03
Pakistani (0)	3	0.03
Sri Lankan (5)	5	0.05
Taiwanese (1)	1	0.01
Thai (6)	13	0.12
Vietnamese (35)	47	0.43
Hawaii Native/Pacific Islander (4)	17	0.15
Not Hispanic (4)	17	0.15
Guamanian/Chamorro (1)	5	0.05
Native Hawaiian (1)	4	0.04
White (10,094)	10,352	94.16
Not Hispanic (9,794)	10,001	90.97
Hispanic (300)	351	3.19

Columbus

Place Type: City
County: Platte
Population: 22,111†

Ancestry‡	Population	%
American (534)	534	2.47
Arab (102)	152	0.70
Arab (31)	81	0.37
Jordanian (39)	39	0.18
Other Arab (32)	32	0.15
Austrian (0)	43	0.20
Belgian (0)	26	0.12
British (10)	10	0.05
Canadian (47)	47	0.22
Czech (508)	1,679	7.76
Czechoslovakian (54)	54	0.25
Danish (89)	335	1.55
Dutch (68)	521	2.41
English (479)	1,878	8.68
Estonian (0)	11	0.05
European (50)	50	0.23
French, ex. Basque (10)	382	1.77
French Canadian (24)	37	0.17
German (4,774)	10,390	48.01
Greek (23)	23	0.11
Hungarian (0)	75	0.35
Irish (316)	2,416	11.16
Italian (19)	308	1.42
Latvian (12)	38	0.18
Lithuanian (7)	7	0.03
Norwegian (100)	388	1.79
Pennsylvania German (13)	13	0.06
Polish (1,064)	2,405	11.11
Portuguese (3)	3	0.01
Russian (0)	41	0.19
Scandinavian (0)	7	0.03
Scotch-Irish (22)	261	1.21
Scottish (0)	92	0.43
Slovak (0)	12	0.06
Swedish (152)	901	4.16
Swiss (95)	356	1.65
Ukrainian (0)	21	0.10
Welsh (0)	61	0.28

Hispanic Origin	Population	%
Hispanic or Latino (of any race)	3,606	16.31
Central American, ex. Mexican	497	2.25
Guatemalan	253	1.14
Honduran	49	0.22
Nicaraguan	9	0.04
Panamanian	2	0.01
Salvadoran	165	0.75
Other Central American	19	0.09
Cuban	119	0.54
Mexican	2,669	12.07
Puerto Rican	51	0.23
South American	82	0.37
Argentinean	4	0.02
Bolivian	2	0.01
Chilean	6	0.03
Colombian	8	0.04
Ecuadorian	7	0.03
Peruvian	51	0.23
Venezuelan	4	0.02
Other Hispanic or Latino	188	0.85

Race*	Population	%
African-American/Black (113)	199	0.90
Not Hispanic (102)	173	0.78
Hispanic (11)	26	0.12
American Indian/Alaska Native (197)	303	1.37
Not Hispanic (80)	144	0.65
Hispanic (117)	159	0.72
Apache (0)	5	0.02
Arapaho (1)	1	<0.01
Blackfeet (0)	3	0.01
Central American Ind. (2)	2	0.01
Cherokee (11)	19	0.09
Cheyenne (0)	3	0.01
Chippewa (1)	1	<0.01
Choctaw (2)	3	0.01
Comanche (1)	1	<0.01
Creek (1)	3	0.01
Mexican American Ind. (21)	22	0.10
Navajo (1)	2	0.01
Potawatomi (1)	1	<0.01
Pueblo (0)	3	0.01
Sioux (23)	32	0.14
Spanish American Ind. (6)	9	0.04
Asian (109)	161	0.73
Not Hispanic (107)	147	0.66
Hispanic (2)	14	0.06
Chinese, ex. Taiwanese (23)	25	0.11
Filipino (9)	21	0.09
Indian (17)	20	0.09
Indonesian (0)	1	<0.01
Japanese (3)	14	0.06
Korean (28)	37	0.17
Laotian (1)	1	<0.01
Malaysian (1)	1	<0.01
Pakistani (2)	3	0.01
Taiwanese (1)	1	<0.01
Thai (5)	5	0.02
Vietnamese (17)	24	0.11
Hawaii Native/Pacific Islander (11)	26	0.12
Not Hispanic (5)	10	0.05
Hispanic (6)	16	0.07
Guamanian/Chamorro (6)	17	0.08
Native Hawaiian (1)	1	<0.01
Samoan (1)	1	<0.01
White (19,477)	19,824	89.66
Not Hispanic (18,027)	18,175	82.20
Hispanic (1,450)	1,649	7.46

Fremont

Place Type: City
County: Dodge
Population: 26,397†

Ancestry‡	Population	%
American (885)	885	3.37
Austrian (0)	18	0.07
British (10)	42	0.16
Canadian (0)	8	0.03
Czech (575)	1,953	7.45
Czechoslovakian (75)	164	0.63
Danish (281)	1,156	4.41
Dutch (67)	442	1.69
English (385)	2,432	9.27
European (253)	253	0.96
French, ex. Basque (58)	533	2.03
French Canadian (5)	14	0.05
German (5,302)	12,838	48.96
Greek (39)	74	0.28
Hungarian (0)	12	0.05
Irish (684)	3,733	14.24
Italian (75)	556	2.12
Lithuanian (0)	38	0.14
Luxemburger (0)	12	0.05
Northern European (13)	13	0.05
Norwegian (195)	574	2.19
Pennsylvania German (12)	43	0.16
Polish (137)	805	3.07
Romanian (12)	12	0.05
Russian (11)	125	0.48
Scandinavian (19)	39	0.15
Scotch-Irish (86)	293	1.12
Scottish (107)	279	1.06
Serbian (25)	25	0.10
Slavic (9)	9	0.03
Swedish (398)	1,862	7.10
Swiss (17)	94	0.36
Welsh (10)	105	0.40
Yugoslavian (0)	12	0.05

Hispanic Origin	Population	%
Hispanic or Latino (of any race)	3,149	11.93
Central American, ex. Mexican	617	2.34
Costa Rican	4	0.02
Guatemalan	278	1.05
Honduran	45	0.17
Nicaraguan	3	0.01
Panamanian	4	0.02
Salvadoran	273	1.03
Other Central American	10	0.04
Cuban	8	0.03
Dominican Republic	3	0.01
Mexican	2,123	8.04
Puerto Rican	30	0.11
South American	14	0.05
Argentinean	1	<0.01
Colombian	1	<0.01
Ecuadorian	2	0.01
Peruvian	10	0.04
Other Hispanic or Latino	354	1.34

Race*	Population	%
African-American/Black (172)	300	1.14
Not Hispanic (154)	261	0.99
Hispanic (18)	39	0.15
American Indian/Alaska Native (153)	257	0.97
Not Hispanic (105)	190	0.72
Hispanic (48)	67	0.25
Apache (0)	6	0.02
Arapaho (1)	1	<0.01
Blackfeet (1)	2	0.01
Canadian/French Am. Ind. (2)	3	0.01
Cherokee (5)	22	0.08
Cheyenne (1)	1	<0.01
Chickasaw (0)	2	0.01
Chippewa (3)	6	0.02
Choctaw (2)	8	0.03
Iroquois (0)	3	0.01

*Notes: † The Census 2010 population figure is used to calculate the percentages in the Hispanic Origin and Race categories. Ancestry percentages are based on the 2006-2010 American Community Survey population (not shown); ‡ Numbers in parentheses indicate the number of people reporting a single ancestry; * Numbers in parentheses indicate the number of persons reporting this race alone, not in combination with any other race; Please refer to the Explanation of Data for more information.*

Mexican American Ind. (4)	5	0.02
Navajo (5)	6	0.02
Pueblo (1)	1	<0.01
Seminole (1)	1	<0.01
Shoshone (0)	3	0.01
Sioux (52)	61	0.23
South American Ind. (1)	4	0.02
Spanish American Ind. (1)	1	<0.01
Asian (163)	242	0.92
Not Hispanic (156)	217	0.82
Hispanic (7)	25	0.09
Chinese, ex. Taiwanese (18)	31	0.12
Filipino (29)	55	0.21
Indian (13)	21	0.08
Japanese (22)	33	0.13
Korean (22)	39	0.15
Laotian (13)	15	0.06
Taiwanese (0)	2	0.01
Thai (3)	5	0.02
Vietnamese (35)	44	0.17
Hawaii Native/Pacific Islander (74)	100	0.38
Not Hispanic (30)	47	0.18
Hispanic (44)	53	0.20
Guamanian/Chamorro (62)	74	0.28
Native Hawaiian (4)	8	0.03
Samoan (1)	4	0.02
White (23,538)	23,900	90.54
Not Hispanic (22,524)	22,762	86.23
Hispanic (1,014)	1,138	4.31

Gering

Place Type: City
County: Scotts Bluff
Population: 8,500†

Ancestry‡	Population	%
American (169)	169	2.04
Arab (0)	20	0.24
Lebanese (0)	20	0.24
British (0)	9	0.11
Canadian (14)	14	0.17
Czech (85)	209	2.53
Danish (36)	123	1.49
Dutch (26)	281	3.40
English (299)	1,037	12.54
European (55)	67	0.81
Finnish (0)	18	0.22
French, ex. Basque (60)	282	3.41
French Canadian (0)	42	0.51
German (1,728)	3,664	44.30
Greek (78)	78	0.94
Irish (458)	1,080	13.06
Italian (47)	139	1.68
Lithuanian (0)	16	0.19
Norwegian (53)	230	2.78
Pennsylvania German (0)	11	0.13
Polish (12)	176	2.13
Russian (0)	176	2.13
Scandinavian (21)	127	1.54
Scotch-Irish (67)	185	2.24
Scottish (26)	146	1.77
Slovak (73)	73	0.88
Swedish (45)	219	2.65
Welsh (0)	10	0.12
West Indian, ex. Hispanic (0)	23	0.28
Haitian (0)	23	0.28

Hispanic Origin	Population	%
Hispanic or Latino (of any race)	1,461	17.19
Central American, ex. Mexican	14	0.16
Costa Rican	2	0.02
Guatemalan	3	0.04
Honduran	4	0.05
Salvadoran	5	0.06
Cuban	5	0.06
Dominican Republic	6	0.07
Mexican	1,265	14.88
Puerto Rican	6	0.07
South American	5	0.06
Colombian	1	0.01
Peruvian	3	0.04
Venezuelan	1	0.01
Other Hispanic or Latino	160	1.88

Race*	Population	%
African-American/Black (50)	80	0.94
Not Hispanic (43)	63	0.74
Hispanic (7)	17	0.20
American Indian/Alaska Native (126)	201	2.36
Not Hispanic (80)	116	1.36
Hispanic (46)	85	1.00
Arapaho (4)	4	0.05
Blackfeet (1)	5	0.06
Cherokee (2)	5	0.06
Chippewa (0)	3	0.04
Pueblo (1)	1	0.01
Puget Sound Salish (1)	1	0.01
Shoshone (1)	1	0.01
Sioux (64)	96	1.13
South American Ind. (0)	1	0.01
Spanish American Ind. (8)	9	0.11
Asian (33)	70	0.82
Not Hispanic (33)	62	0.73
Hispanic (0)	8	0.09
Chinese, ex. Taiwanese (5)	11	0.13
Filipino (6)	24	0.28
Indian (4)	5	0.06
Japanese (8)	18	0.21
Korean (4)	6	0.07
Vietnamese (3)	4	0.05
Hawaii Native/Pacific Islander (8)	8	0.09
Not Hispanic (7)	7	0.08
Hispanic (1)	1	0.01
Native Hawaiian (1)	1	0.01
Samoan (2)	2	0.02
White (7,612)	7,800	91.76
Not Hispanic (6,780)	6,863	80.74
Hispanic (832)	937	11.02

Grand Island

Place Type: City
County: Hall
Population: 48,520†

Ancestry‡	Population	%
African, Sub-Saharan (593)	593	1.26
African (47)	47	0.10
Ethiopian (15)	15	0.03
Somalian (216)	216	0.46
Sudanese (315)	315	0.67
American (1,807)	1,807	3.85
Arab (67)	120	0.26
Arab (0)	9	0.02
Lebanese (24)	57	0.12
Syrian (0)	11	0.02
Other Arab (43)	43	0.09
Austrian (0)	20	0.04
Belgian (8)	8	0.02
British (8)	69	0.15
Canadian (0)	26	0.06
Czech (601)	1,865	3.97
Czechoslovakian (66)	153	0.33
Danish (410)	1,497	3.19
Dutch (161)	782	1.66
Eastern European (17)	17	0.04
English (861)	3,725	7.93
Estonian (8)	8	0.02
European (178)	238	0.51
French, ex. Basque (164)	1,303	2.77
French Canadian (31)	232	0.49
German (7,170)	16,469	35.06
Greek (25)	81	0.17
Hungarian (0)	27	0.06
Irish (965)	5,359	11.41
Italian (114)	707	1.51
Norwegian (225)	604	1.29
Pennsylvania German (34)	151	0.32
Polish (881)	3,035	6.46
Russian (47)	191	0.41
Scandinavian (0)	32	0.07
Scotch-Irish (75)	540	1.15
Scottish (112)	490	1.04
Slavic (11)	11	0.02
Slovak (6)	49	0.10
Swedish (338)	1,407	3.00
Swiss (18)	104	0.22
Turkish (0)	11	0.02
Ukrainian (9)	9	0.02
Welsh (90)	355	0.76
Yugoslavian (12)	104	0.22

Hispanic Origin	Population	%
Hispanic or Latino (of any race)	12,933	26.65
Central American, ex. Mexican	2,689	5.54
Costa Rican	1	<0.01
Guatemalan	1,665	3.43
Honduran	225	0.46
Nicaraguan	20	0.04
Panamanian	9	0.02
Salvadoran	757	1.56
Other Central American	12	0.02
Cuban	528	1.09
Dominican Republic	1	<0.01
Mexican	8,126	16.75
Puerto Rican	92	0.19
South American	109	0.22
Argentinean	4	0.01
Bolivian	1	<0.01
Chilean	16	0.03
Colombian	55	0.11
Ecuadorian	2	<0.01
Peruvian	8	0.02
Uruguayan	4	0.01
Venezuelan	17	0.04
Other South American	2	<0.01
Other Hispanic or Latino	1,388	2.86

Race*	Population	%
African-American/Black (1,002)	1,279	2.64
Not Hispanic (885)	1,103	2.27
Hispanic (117)	176	0.36
American Indian/Alaska Native (503)	764	1.57
Not Hispanic (213)	368	0.76
Hispanic (290)	396	0.82
Apache (3)	8	0.02
Blackfeet (4)	7	0.01
Central American Ind. (27)	36	0.07
Cherokee (16)	41	0.08
Cheyenne (2)	2	<0.01
Chickasaw (2)	3	0.01
Chippewa (0)	3	0.01
Choctaw (1)	5	0.01
Creek (1)	1	<0.01
Crow (3)	5	0.01
Inupiat *(Alaska Native)* (1)	3	0.01
Iroquois (1)	1	<0.01
Lumbee (1)	1	<0.01
Mexican American Ind. (53)	77	0.16
Navajo (8)	11	0.02
Potawatomi (0)	2	<0.01
Seminole (1)	1	<0.01
Sioux (90)	147	0.30
Spanish American Ind. (2)	2	<0.01
Yakama (1)	1	<0.01
Asian (584)	772	1.59
Not Hispanic (556)	712	1.47
Hispanic (28)	60	0.12
Bangladeshi (1)	1	<0.01
Cambodian (1)	1	<0.01
Chinese, ex. Taiwanese (42)	59	0.12
Filipino (44)	102	0.21
Hmong (1)	1	<0.01
Indian (44)	61	0.13
Indonesian (2)	3	0.01
Japanese (6)	28	0.06
Korean (28)	40	0.08
Laotian (185)	232	0.48
Pakistani (2)	2	<0.01

*Notes: † The Census 2010 population figure is used to calculate the percentages in the Hispanic Origin and Race categories. Ancestry percentages are based on the 2006-2010 American Community Survey population (not shown); ‡ Numbers in parentheses indicate the number of people reporting a single ancestry; * Numbers in parentheses indicate the number of persons reporting this race alone, not in combination with any other race; Please refer to the Explanation of Data for more information.*

Taiwanese (0)	1	<0.01
Thai (11)	20	0.04
Vietnamese (158)	178	0.37
Hawaii Native/Pacific Islander (110)	159	0.33
Not Hispanic (32)	64	0.13
Hispanic (78)	95	0.20
Guamanian/Chamorro (87)	95	0.20
Native Hawaiian (7)	21	0.04
Samoan (7)	13	0.03
White (38,839)	39,796	82.02
Not Hispanic (33,280)	33,718	69.49
Hispanic (5,559)	6,078	12.53

Hastings

Place Type: City
County: Adams
Population: 24,907†

Ancestry‡	Population	%
African, Sub-Saharan (0)	13	0.05
African (0)	13	0.05
American (1,153)	1,153	4.66
Arab (19)	32	0.13
Syrian (19)	32	0.13
Austrian (10)	10	0.04
Belgian (0)	16	0.06
Brazilian (9)	9	0.04
British (18)	54	0.22
Croatian (0)	8	0.03
Czech (309)	983	3.98
Czechoslovakian (59)	73	0.30
Danish (69)	529	2.14
Dutch (115)	525	2.12
English (639)	2,280	9.22
European (266)	266	1.08
French, ex. Basque (161)	896	3.63
French Canadian (29)	67	0.27
German (5,915)	11,745	47.52
Hungarian (0)	11	0.04
Iranian (0)	10	0.04
Irish (535)	3,121	12.63
Italian (71)	322	1.30
Lithuanian (0)	12	0.05
Luxemburger (10)	10	0.04
Northern European (51)	51	0.21
Norwegian (40)	284	1.15
Pennsylvania German (18)	35	0.14
Polish (125)	518	2.10
Portuguese (10)	10	0.04
Russian (69)	260	1.05
Scandinavian (21)	56	0.23
Scotch-Irish (170)	548	2.22
Scottish (189)	568	2.30
Swedish (460)	1,223	4.95
Swiss (0)	107	0.43
Turkish (0)	9	0.04
Welsh (20)	190	0.77
West Indian, ex. Hispanic (6)	17	0.07
Bahamian (0)	11	0.04
British West Indian (6)	6	0.02
Yugoslavian (12)	29	0.12

Hispanic Origin	Population	%
Hispanic or Latino (of any race)	2,430	9.76
Central American, ex. Mexican	203	0.82
Costa Rican	1	<0.01
Guatemalan	64	0.26
Honduran	46	0.18
Nicaraguan	4	0.02
Panamanian	9	0.04
Salvadoran	78	0.31
Other Central American	1	<0.01
Cuban	222	0.89
Mexican	1,796	7.21
Puerto Rican	33	0.13
South American	21	0.08
Argentinean	2	0.01
Bolivian	1	<0.01
Colombian	8	0.03
Ecuadorian	1	<0.01
Peruvian	7	0.03
Venezuelan	2	0.01
Other Hispanic or Latino	155	0.62

Race*	Population	%
African-American/Black (237)	365	1.47
Not Hispanic (208)	322	1.29
Hispanic (29)	43	0.17
American Indian/Alaska Native (115)	232	0.93
Not Hispanic (89)	180	0.72
Hispanic (26)	52	0.21
Apache (3)	4	0.02
Central American Ind. (0)	5	0.02
Cherokee (5)	22	0.09
Chickasaw (0)	1	<0.01
Chippewa (2)	9	0.04
Choctaw (2)	3	0.01
Comanche (0)	1	<0.01
Cree (1)	4	0.02
Creek (1)	1	<0.01
Iroquois (1)	4	0.02
Mexican American Ind. (5)	6	0.02
Navajo (5)	5	0.02
Osage (1)	1	<0.01
Pima (0)	1	<0.01
Seminole (1)	2	0.01
Sioux (29)	45	0.18
Spanish American Ind. (5)	5	0.02
Yaqui (0)	1	<0.01
Asian (412)	474	1.90
Not Hispanic (410)	464	1.86
Hispanic (2)	10	0.04
Chinese, ex. Taiwanese (22)	25	0.10
Filipino (29)	47	0.19
Indian (21)	34	0.14
Japanese (8)	25	0.10
Korean (20)	32	0.13
Laotian (9)	10	0.04
Pakistani (3)	3	0.01
Thai (7)	8	0.03
Vietnamese (275)	284	1.14
Hawaii Native/Pacific Islander (15)	29	0.12
Not Hispanic (9)	17	0.07
Hispanic (6)	12	0.05
Guamanian/Chamorro (6)	13	0.05
Native Hawaiian (3)	7	0.03
Samoan (5)	6	0.02
White (22,511)	22,863	91.79
Not Hispanic (21,485)	21,733	87.26
Hispanic (1,026)	1,130	4.54

Kearney

Place Type: City
County: Buffalo
Population: 30,787†

Ancestry‡	Population	%
African, Sub-Saharan (39)	75	0.25
African (30)	66	0.22
Ugandan (9)	9	0.03
American (816)	816	2.70
Arab (83)	148	0.49
Arab (47)	47	0.16
Lebanese (36)	101	0.33
Australian (0)	11	0.04
Austrian (30)	105	0.35
Belgian (0)	22	0.07
Brazilian (10)	10	0.03
British (69)	156	0.52
Czech (362)	1,385	4.58
Czechoslovakian (22)	59	0.20
Danish (277)	1,218	4.03
Dutch (84)	461	1.53
Eastern European (9)	9	0.03
English (743)	2,824	9.35
European (250)	333	1.10
Finnish (0)	25	0.08
French, ex. Basque (56)	640	2.12
French Canadian (12)	95	0.31
German (5,653)	13,064	43.24
German Russian (12)	12	0.04
Greek (31)	146	0.48
Hungarian (0)	81	0.27
Irish (949)	4,439	14.69
Italian (146)	441	1.46
Northern European (20)	20	0.07
Norwegian (204)	601	1.99
Pennsylvania German (27)	43	0.14
Polish (459)	1,329	4.40
Romanian (0)	5	0.02
Russian (10)	175	0.58
Scandinavian (60)	70	0.23
Scotch-Irish (91)	370	1.22
Scottish (82)	404	1.34
Slavic (13)	13	0.04
Swedish (504)	2,160	7.15
Swiss (13)	144	0.48
Welsh (9)	95	0.31
West Indian, ex. Hispanic (38)	38	0.13
Jamaican (38)	38	0.13

Hispanic Origin	Population	%
Hispanic or Latino (of any race)	2,243	7.29
Central American, ex. Mexican	166	0.54
Costa Rican	2	0.01
Guatemalan	62	0.20
Honduran	7	0.02
Nicaraguan	7	0.02
Panamanian	6	0.02
Salvadoran	80	0.26
Other Central American	2	0.01
Cuban	16	0.05
Dominican Republic	4	0.01
Mexican	1,644	5.34
Puerto Rican	32	0.10
South American	79	0.26
Argentinean	2	0.01
Bolivian	1	<0.01
Chilean	5	0.02
Colombian	44	0.14
Ecuadorian	21	0.07
Uruguayan	1	<0.01
Venezuelan	5	0.02
Other Hispanic or Latino	302	0.98

Race*	Population	%
African-American/Black (315)	470	1.53
Not Hispanic (295)	433	1.41
Hispanic (20)	37	0.12
American Indian/Alaska Native (93)	220	0.71
Not Hispanic (72)	167	0.54
Hispanic (21)	53	0.17
Alaska Athabascan *(Ala. Nat.)* (1)	1	<0.01
Blackfeet (0)	2	0.01
Canadian/French Am. Ind. (0)	3	0.01
Central American Ind. (1)	1	<0.01
Cherokee (4)	26	0.08
Chickasaw (0)	3	0.01
Chippewa (0)	1	<0.01
Choctaw (0)	4	0.01
Creek (1)	2	0.01
Crow (0)	2	0.01
Delaware (1)	1	<0.01
Inupiat *(Alaska Native)* (1)	1	<0.01
Iroquois (0)	4	0.01
Menominee (0)	3	0.01
Mexican American Ind. (1)	9	0.03
Navajo (2)	4	0.01
Paiute (1)	1	<0.01
Pima (2)	2	0.01
Potawatomi (1)	1	<0.01
Pueblo (3)	3	0.01
Sioux (30)	61	0.20
Spanish American Ind. (3)	3	0.01
Asian (548)	632	2.05
Not Hispanic (540)	615	2.00
Hispanic (8)	17	0.06
Bangladeshi (9)	9	0.03

*Notes: † The Census 2010 population figure is used to calculate the percentages in the Hispanic Origin and Race categories. Ancestry percentages are based on the 2006-2010 American Community Survey population (not shown); ‡ Numbers in parentheses indicate the number of people reporting a single ancestry; * Numbers in parentheses indicate the number of persons reporting this race alone, not in combination with any other race; Please refer to the Explanation of Data for more information.*

Bhutanese (2)	2	0.01
Chinese, ex. Taiwanese (157)	162	0.53
Filipino (35)	44	0.14
Indian (53)	61	0.20
Japanese (166)	180	0.58
Korean (61)	81	0.26
Laotian (1)	1	<0.01
Malaysian (1)	1	<0.01
Nepalese (6)	7	0.02
Pakistani (3)	4	0.01
Sri Lankan (2)	2	0.01
Taiwanese (4)	4	0.01
Thai (10)	19	0.06
Vietnamese (30)	35	0.11
Hawaii Native/Pacific Islander (7)	19	0.06
Not Hispanic (4)	10	0.03
Hispanic (3)	9	0.03
Guamanian/Chamorro (1)	1	<0.01
Native Hawaiian (0)	7	0.02
Tongan (1)	2	0.01
White (28,416)	28,843	93.69
Not Hispanic (27,276)	27,583	89.59
Hispanic (1,140)	1,260	4.09

La Vista

Place Type: City
County: Sarpy
Population: 15,758†

Ancestry‡	Population	%
African, Sub-Saharan (181)	276	1.83
African (38)	85	0.57
Ethiopian (38)	38	0.25
Ghanaian (0)	48	0.32
Sudanese (105)	105	0.70
American (448)	448	2.98
Arab (42)	49	0.33
Arab (42)	42	0.28
Lebanese (0)	7	0.05
Austrian (0)	47	0.31
Belgian (0)	37	0.25
British (27)	59	0.39
Canadian (0)	15	0.10
Croatian (0)	115	0.76
Czech (149)	986	6.55
Czechoslovakian (7)	14	0.09
Danish (54)	264	1.75
Dutch (62)	330	2.19
English (469)	1,632	10.85
European (258)	258	1.71
French, ex. Basque (50)	371	2.47
French Canadian (49)	59	0.39
German (1,982)	5,916	39.32
Greek (8)	25	0.17
Hungarian (0)	53	0.35
Iranian (0)	17	0.11
Irish (444)	3,072	20.42
Italian (298)	777	5.16
Lithuanian (6)	153	1.02
Norwegian (163)	410	2.73
Pennsylvania German (0)	31	0.21
Polish (198)	1,118	7.43
Portuguese (0)	65	0.43
Romanian (0)	25	0.17
Russian (0)	61	0.41
Scandinavian (14)	83	0.55
Scotch-Irish (25)	275	1.83
Scottish (28)	227	1.51
Serbian (0)	14	0.09
Slovak (0)	14	0.09
Swedish (85)	491	3.26
Swiss (0)	36	0.24
Turkish (5)	5	0.03
Ukrainian (24)	24	0.16
Welsh (9)	190	1.26
Yugoslavian (0)	32	0.21

Hispanic Origin	Population	%
Hispanic or Latino (of any race)	1,026	6.51
Central American, ex. Mexican	96	0.61
Guatemalan	32	0.20
Honduran	9	0.06
Nicaraguan	3	0.02
Panamanian	11	0.07
Salvadoran	41	0.26
Cuban	4	0.03
Dominican Republic	8	0.05
Mexican	790	5.01
Puerto Rican	45	0.29
South American	33	0.21
Argentinean	1	0.01
Chilean	1	0.01
Colombian	18	0.11
Paraguayan	2	0.01
Peruvian	9	0.06
Venezuelan	1	0.01
Other South American	1	0.01
Other Hispanic or Latino	50	0.32

Race*	Population	%
African-American/Black (617)	835	5.30
Not Hispanic (599)	795	5.05
Hispanic (18)	40	0.25
American Indian/Alaska Native (69)	155	0.98
Not Hispanic (54)	122	0.77
Hispanic (15)	33	0.21
Aleut *(Alaska Native)* (1)	3	0.02
Apache (1)	1	0.01
Blackfeet (0)	1	0.01
Canadian/French Am. Ind. (7)	7	0.04
Cherokee (4)	18	0.11
Chickasaw (0)	2	0.01
Chippewa (7)	9	0.06
Comanche (0)	1	0.01
Creek (2)	4	0.03
Lumbee (1)	1	0.01
Mexican American Ind. (1)	4	0.03
Navajo (0)	5	0.03
Ottawa (1)	1	0.01
Paiute (0)	1	0.01
Potawatomi (1)	2	0.01
Pueblo (1)	1	0.01
Sioux (6)	12	0.08
South American Ind. (1)	2	0.01
Tlingit-Haida *(Alaska Native)* (1)	1	0.01
Asian (512)	625	3.97
Not Hispanic (506)	606	3.85
Hispanic (6)	19	0.12
Bhutanese (1)	1	0.01
Cambodian (2)	2	0.01
Chinese, ex. Taiwanese (31)	55	0.35
Filipino (77)	127	0.81
Indian (58)	72	0.46
Japanese (22)	43	0.27
Korean (54)	74	0.47
Laotian (5)	5	0.03
Nepalese (34)	34	0.22
Thai (13)	16	0.10
Vietnamese (186)	197	1.25
Hawaii Native/Pacific Islander (10)	27	0.17
Not Hispanic (9)	20	0.13
Hispanic (1)	7	0.04
Guamanian/Chamorro (1)	7	0.04
Native Hawaiian (6)	8	0.05
White (13,699)	14,084	89.38
Not Hispanic (13,181)	13,495	85.64
Hispanic (518)	589	3.74

Lexington

Place Type: City
County: Dawson
Population: 10,230†

Ancestry‡	Population	%
African, Sub-Saharan (551)	551	5.45
African (49)	49	0.48
Somalian (464)	464	4.59
Sudanese (38)	38	0.38
American (234)	234	2.31
Arab (29)	29	0.29
Lebanese (29)	29	0.29
British (9)	9	0.09
Canadian (10)	10	0.10
Czech (47)	156	1.54
Danish (39)	101	1.00
Dutch (38)	167	1.65
English (141)	388	3.84
European (22)	22	0.22
French, ex. Basque (38)	115	1.14
German (843)	1,766	17.47
Irish (78)	359	3.55
Italian (0)	81	0.80
Norwegian (41)	97	0.96
Polish (0)	61	0.60
Scandinavian (10)	10	0.10
Scotch-Irish (7)	69	0.68
Scottish (0)	62	0.61
Swedish (53)	224	2.22
Swiss (0)	36	0.36
Welsh (0)	22	0.22

Hispanic Origin	Population	%
Hispanic or Latino (of any race)	6,183	60.44
Central American, ex. Mexican	1,243	12.15
Guatemalan	891	8.71
Honduran	42	0.41
Nicaraguan	23	0.22
Panamanian	3	0.03
Salvadoran	281	2.75
Other Central American	3	0.03
Cuban	26	0.25
Dominican Republic	8	0.08
Mexican	4,524	44.22
Puerto Rican	9	0.09
South American	24	0.23
Argentinean	2	0.02
Bolivian	4	0.04
Chilean	3	0.03
Colombian	10	0.10
Peruvian	2	0.02
Venezuelan	2	0.02
Other South American	1	0.01
Other Hispanic or Latino	349	3.41

Race*	Population	%
African-American/Black (678)	705	6.89
Not Hispanic (649)	659	6.44
Hispanic (29)	46	0.45
American Indian/Alaska Native (120)	182	1.78
Not Hispanic (34)	60	0.59
Hispanic (86)	122	1.19
Apache (0)	2	0.02
Blackfeet (0)	1	0.01
Canadian/French Am. Ind. (0)	1	0.01
Central American Ind. (3)	4	0.04
Cherokee (0)	5	0.05
Cheyenne (0)	2	0.02
Mexican American Ind. (35)	45	0.44
Navajo (2)	3	0.03
Paiute (0)	1	0.01
Pima (1)	5	0.05
Pueblo (3)	3	0.03
Sioux (12)	20	0.20
Spanish American Ind. (2)	3	0.03
Yakama (0)	1	0.01
Asian (102)	117	1.14
Not Hispanic (100)	109	1.07
Hispanic (2)	8	0.08
Chinese, ex. Taiwanese (18)	18	0.18
Filipino (5)	9	0.09
Hmong (1)	1	0.01
Indian (8)	11	0.11
Japanese (2)	4	0.04
Korean (2)	2	0.02
Laotian (21)	23	0.22
Vietnamese (44)	44	0.43
Hawaii Native/Pacific Islander (36)	48	0.47
Not Hispanic (30)	34	0.33

*Notes: † The Census 2010 population figure is used to calculate the percentages in the Hispanic Origin and Race categories. Ancestry percentages are based on the 2006-2010 American Community Survey population (not shown); ‡ Numbers in parentheses indicate the number of people reporting a single ancestry; * Numbers in parentheses indicate the number of persons reporting this race alone, not in combination with any other race; Please refer to the Explanation of Data for more information.*

Hispanic (6)	14	0.14
Guamanian/Chamorro (19)	19	0.19
Marshallese (1)	5	0.05
Native Hawaiian (0)	1	0.01
Samoan (16)	16	0.16
White (5,919)	6,219	60.79
Not Hispanic (3,174)	3,214	31.42
Hispanic (2,745)	3,005	29.37

Lincoln

Place Type: City
County: Lancaster
Population: 258,379†

Ancestry‡	Population	%
Afghan (31)	31	0.01
African, Sub-Saharan (3,002)	3,548	1.40
African (1,889)	2,325	0.92
Ethiopian (109)	109	0.04
Ghanaian (11)	11	<0.01
Kenyan (23)	23	0.01
Liberian (7)	7	<0.01
Nigerian (142)	154	0.06
Sierra Leonean (9)	9	<0.01
South African (10)	108	0.04
Sudanese (703)	703	0.28
Ugandan (32)	32	0.01
Other Sub-Saharan African (67)	67	0.03
Albanian (43)	50	0.02
American (8,631)	8,631	3.41
Arab (1,481)	1,863	0.74
Arab (131)	131	0.05
Egyptian (18)	18	0.01
Iraqi (915)	992	0.39
Jordanian (80)	80	0.03
Lebanese (144)	352	0.14
Moroccan (0)	11	<0.01
Palestinian (10)	10	<0.01
Syrian (31)	93	0.04
Other Arab (152)	176	0.07
Armenian (35)	57	0.02
Australian (0)	25	0.01
Austrian (29)	442	0.17
Basque (13)	13	0.01
Belgian (94)	297	0.12
Brazilian (104)	130	0.05
British (410)	967	0.38
Cajun (8)	33	0.01
Canadian (159)	347	0.14
Celtic (14)	28	0.01
Croatian (103)	266	0.11
Czech (5,646)	15,960	6.31
Czechoslovakian (475)	1,016	0.40
Danish (1,179)	5,511	2.18
Dutch (1,225)	6,306	2.49
Eastern European (41)	41	0.02
English (6,030)	25,732	10.17
Estonian (0)	62	0.02
European (2,726)	2,985	1.18
Finnish (59)	327	0.13
French, ex. Basque (699)	6,760	2.67
French Canadian (326)	863	0.34
German (47,295)	110,551	43.69
German Russian (87)	105	0.04
Greek (295)	701	0.28
Hungarian (88)	443	0.18
Iranian (140)	237	0.09
Irish (6,963)	35,533	14.04
Israeli (18)	18	0.01
Italian (1,616)	5,359	2.12
Latvian (73)	196	0.08
Lithuanian (47)	208	0.08
Luxemburger (17)	64	0.03
New Zealander (0)	19	0.01
Northern European (191)	191	0.08
Norwegian (1,476)	5,033	1.99
Pennsylvania German (108)	300	0.12
Polish (1,978)	7,459	2.95
Portuguese (125)	626	0.25
Romanian (233)	371	0.15
Russian (499)	2,914	1.15
Scandinavian (258)	598	0.24
Scotch-Irish (1,388)	4,199	1.66
Scottish (938)	4,525	1.79
Serbian (32)	93	0.04
Slavic (34)	64	0.03
Slovak (74)	160	0.06
Slovene (0)	15	0.01
Swedish (2,798)	13,266	5.24
Swiss (154)	989	0.39
Turkish (69)	69	0.03
Ukrainian (378)	557	0.22
Welsh (375)	1,968	0.78
West Indian, ex. Hispanic (190)	447	0.18
Bahamian (38)	38	0.02
Dutch West Indian (0)	21	0.01
Haitian (43)	43	0.02
Jamaican (45)	281	0.11
Trinidadian/Tobagonian (55)	55	0.02
West Indian (9)	9	<0.01
Yugoslavian (217)	260	0.10

Hispanic Origin	Population	%
Hispanic or Latino (of any race)	16,182	6.26
Central American, ex. Mexican	1,430	0.55
Costa Rican	41	0.02
Guatemalan	682	0.26
Honduran	149	0.06
Nicaraguan	35	0.01
Panamanian	55	0.02
Salvadoran	459	0.18
Other Central American	9	<0.01
Cuban	212	0.08
Dominican Republic	49	0.02
Mexican	12,073	4.67
Puerto Rican	475	0.18
South American	702	0.27
Argentinean	85	0.03
Bolivian	15	0.01
Chilean	34	0.01
Colombian	196	0.08
Ecuadorian	52	0.02
Paraguayan	16	0.01
Peruvian	211	0.08
Uruguayan	6	<0.01
Venezuelan	75	0.03
Other South American	12	<0.01
Other Hispanic or Latino	1,241	0.48

Race*	Population	%
African-American/Black (9,824)	13,653	5.28
Not Hispanic (9,541)	13,002	5.03
Hispanic (283)	651	0.25
American Indian/Alaska Native (2,073)	4,061	1.57
Not Hispanic (1,611)	3,215	1.24
Hispanic (462)	846	0.33
Alaska Athabascan *(Ala. Nat.)* (1)	5	<0.01
Aleut *(Alaska Native)* (3)	4	<0.01
Apache (14)	61	0.02
Arapaho (2)	5	<0.01
Blackfeet (7)	37	0.01
Canadian/French Am. Ind. (3)	6	<0.01
Central American Ind. (0)	7	<0.01
Cherokee (46)	289	0.11
Cheyenne (6)	17	0.01
Chickasaw (4)	13	0.01
Chippewa (36)	78	0.03
Choctaw (28)	57	0.02
Comanche (5)	8	<0.01
Cree (1)	6	<0.01
Creek (3)	13	0.01
Crow (2)	4	<0.01
Delaware (4)	5	<0.01
Hopi (0)	1	<0.01
Inupiat *(Alaska Native)* (3)	5	<0.01
Iroquois (18)	39	0.02
Kiowa (2)	4	<0.01
Lumbee (1)	4	<0.01
Mexican American Ind. (46)	86	0.03
Navajo (28)	55	0.02
Osage (1)	9	<0.01
Ottawa (0)	1	<0.01
Paiute (1)	4	<0.01
Pima (0)	2	<0.01
Potawatomi (5)	9	<0.01
Pueblo (1)	1	<0.01
Seminole (3)	9	<0.01
Shoshone (1)	4	<0.01
Sioux (459)	790	0.31
South American Ind. (5)	17	0.01
Spanish American Ind. (10)	13	0.01
Tlingit-Haida *(Alaska Native)* (3)	4	<0.01
Yakama (1)	1	<0.01
Yuman (1)	3	<0.01
Yup'ik *(Alaska Native)* (5)	6	<0.01
Asian (9,773)	11,483	4.44
Not Hispanic (9,711)	11,292	4.37
Hispanic (62)	191	0.07
Bangladeshi (8)	8	<0.01
Bhutanese (11)	11	<0.01
Burmese (387)	395	0.15
Cambodian (61)	101	0.04
Chinese, ex. Taiwanese (1,481)	1,680	0.65
Filipino (306)	579	0.22
Hmong (3)	3	<0.01
Indian (1,085)	1,239	0.48
Indonesian (30)	40	0.02
Japanese (265)	563	0.22
Korean (653)	855	0.33
Laotian (59)	90	0.03
Malaysian (78)	95	0.04
Nepalese (42)	46	0.02
Pakistani (65)	79	0.03
Sri Lankan (31)	33	0.01
Taiwanese (54)	62	0.02
Thai (70)	145	0.06
Vietnamese (4,749)	5,039	1.95
Hawaii Native/Pacific Islander (147)	386	0.15
Not Hispanic (128)	326	0.13
Hispanic (19)	60	0.02
Fijian (11)	11	<0.01
Guamanian/Chamorro (36)	51	0.02
Marshallese (3)	6	<0.01
Native Hawaiian (15)	96	0.04
Samoan (23)	47	0.02
Tongan (0)	2	<0.01
White (222,331)	229,200	88.71
Not Hispanic (214,739)	220,308	85.27
Hispanic (7,592)	8,892	3.44

McCook

Place Type: City
County: Red Willow
Population: 7,698†

Ancestry‡	Population	%
African, Sub-Saharan (10)	10	0.13
Nigerian (10)	10	0.13
American (499)	499	6.46
Austrian (0)	11	0.14
British (0)	7	0.09
Canadian (7)	7	0.09
Czech (46)	229	2.96
Czechoslovakian (26)	26	0.34
Danish (24)	96	1.24
Dutch (54)	248	3.21
English (373)	1,029	13.31
European (120)	120	1.55
French, ex. Basque (20)	289	3.74
French Canadian (13)	13	0.17
German (1,629)	3,501	45.30
Irish (224)	1,048	13.56
Italian (102)	309	4.00
Norwegian (71)	118	1.53
Polish (16)	38	0.49
Portuguese (0)	34	0.44
Russian (6)	92	1.19
Scotch-Irish (14)	146	1.89

*Notes: † The Census 2010 population figure is used to calculate the percentages in the Hispanic Origin and Race categories. Ancestry percentages are based on the 2006-2010 American Community Survey population (not shown); ‡ Numbers in parentheses indicate the number of people reporting a single ancestry; * Numbers in parentheses indicate the number of persons reporting this race alone, not in combination with any other race; Please refer to the Explanation of Data for more information.*

Scottish (38)	151	1.95
Slovak (0)	31	0.40
Swedish (59)	296	3.83
Welsh (6)	25	0.32

Hispanic Origin	Population	%
Hispanic or Latino (of any race)	377	4.90
Central American, ex. Mexican	6	0.08
Guatemalan	6	0.08
Mexican	341	4.43
Puerto Rican	11	0.14
South American	3	0.04
Chilean	3	0.04
Other Hispanic or Latino	16	0.21

Race*	Population	%
African-American/Black (38)	76	0.99
Not Hispanic (38)	69	0.90
Hispanic (0)	7	0.09
American Indian/Alaska Native (39)	75	0.97
Not Hispanic (33)	65	0.84
Hispanic (6)	10	0.13
Apache (2)	2	0.03
Cherokee (4)	14	0.18
Chippewa (0)	1	0.01
Creek (0)	1	0.01
Inupiat *(Alaska Native)* (1)	1	0.01
Navajo (2)	4	0.05
Osage (0)	1	0.01
Sioux (14)	22	0.29
Tlingit-Haida *(Alaska Native)* (0)	2	0.03
Asian (29)	44	0.57
Not Hispanic (25)	40	0.52
Hispanic (4)	4	0.05
Chinese, ex. Taiwanese (5)	5	0.06
Filipino (12)	18	0.23
Japanese (4)	8	0.10
Korean (5)	7	0.09
Vietnamese (1)	2	0.03
Hawaii Native/Pacific Islander (1)	2	0.03
Not Hispanic (1)	1	0.01
Hispanic (0)	1	0.01
Samoan (1)	1	0.01
White (7,372)	7,471	97.05
Not Hispanic (7,143)	7,217	93.75
Hispanic (229)	254	3.30

Norfolk

Place Type: City
County: Madison
Population: 24,210†

Ancestry‡	Population	%
African, Sub-Saharan (65)	96	0.40
African (65)	96	0.40
American (701)	701	2.93
Arab (45)	91	0.38
Arab (34)	34	0.14
Lebanese (0)	46	0.19
Syrian (11)	11	0.05
Basque (24)	140	0.58
Belgian (0)	63	0.26
Brazilian (28)	28	0.12
British (0)	10	0.04
Canadian (0)	67	0.28
Czech (335)	1,184	4.94
Czechoslovakian (74)	117	0.49
Danish (87)	401	1.67
Dutch (39)	452	1.89
English (467)	1,747	7.29
European (104)	104	0.43
Finnish (36)	81	0.34
French, ex. Basque (54)	687	2.87
French Canadian (15)	76	0.32
German (6,878)	12,691	52.97
Greek (94)	129	0.54
Hungarian (0)	24	0.10
Icelander (12)	12	0.05
Iranian (2)	2	0.01
Irish (363)	2,819	11.76
Italian (55)	334	1.39
Lithuanian (0)	11	0.05
Norwegian (220)	534	2.23
Polish (108)	363	1.51
Russian (12)	64	0.27
Scandinavian (0)	3	0.01
Scotch-Irish (51)	215	0.90
Scottish (18)	131	0.55
Swedish (254)	1,312	5.48
Swiss (39)	117	0.49
Ukrainian (9)	9	0.04
Welsh (55)	85	0.35

Hispanic Origin	Population	%
Hispanic or Latino (of any race)	2,939	12.14
Central American, ex. Mexican	199	0.82
Costa Rican	4	0.02
Guatemalan	80	0.33
Honduran	24	0.10
Nicaraguan	12	0.05
Panamanian	5	0.02
Salvadoran	72	0.30
Other Central American	2	0.01
Cuban	109	0.45
Dominican Republic	2	0.01
Mexican	2,345	9.69
Puerto Rican	45	0.19
South American	45	0.19
Argentinean	4	0.02
Colombian	22	0.09
Ecuadorian	5	0.02
Paraguayan	2	0.01
Peruvian	1	<0.01
Venezuelan	4	0.02
Other South American	7	0.03
Other Hispanic or Latino	194	0.80

Race*	Population	%
African-American/Black (397)	590	2.44
Not Hispanic (375)	545	2.25
Hispanic (22)	45	0.19
American Indian/Alaska Native (340)	490	2.02
Not Hispanic (289)	415	1.71
Hispanic (51)	75	0.31
Apache (0)	1	<0.01
Blackfeet (0)	1	<0.01
Cherokee (2)	6	0.02
Crow (0)	4	0.02
Inupiat *(Alaska Native)* (0)	2	0.01
Mexican American Ind. (14)	15	0.06
Navajo (1)	1	<0.01
Pima (1)	1	<0.01
Potawatomi (2)	3	0.01
Puget Sound Salish (0)	1	<0.01
Sioux (108)	143	0.59
South American Ind. (0)	3	0.01
Spanish American Ind. (0)	1	<0.01
Tohono O'Odham (0)	1	<0.01
Yaqui (1)	1	<0.01
Asian (135)	194	0.80
Not Hispanic (131)	178	0.74
Hispanic (4)	16	0.07
Chinese, ex. Taiwanese (23)	30	0.12
Filipino (30)	52	0.21
Hmong (1)	1	<0.01
Indian (30)	36	0.15
Indonesian (0)	1	<0.01
Japanese (4)	13	0.05
Korean (15)	22	0.09
Laotian (0)	2	0.01
Pakistani (7)	9	0.04
Thai (4)	7	0.03
Vietnamese (16)	19	0.08
Hawaii Native/Pacific Islander (12)	26	0.11
Not Hispanic (6)	15	0.06
Hispanic (6)	11	0.05
Guamanian/Chamorro (8)	10	0.04
Marshallese (1)	2	0.01
Native Hawaiian (2)	7	0.03
Samoan (1)	2	0.01
White (21,313)	21,750	89.84
Not Hispanic (20,148)	20,433	84.40
Hispanic (1,165)	1,317	5.44

North Platte

Place Type: City
County: Lincoln
Population: 24,733†

Ancestry‡	Population	%
American (1,254)	1,254	5.07
Arab (0)	17	0.07
Syrian (0)	17	0.07
Austrian (31)	82	0.33
British (0)	41	0.17
Czech (194)	654	2.65
Czechoslovakian (12)	12	0.05
Danish (201)	619	2.50
Dutch (59)	660	2.67
English (912)	3,130	12.66
European (77)	88	0.36
Finnish (0)	21	0.08
French, ex. Basque (56)	940	3.80
French Canadian (25)	77	0.31
German (3,802)	9,055	36.63
German Russian (6)	6	0.02
Greek (11)	62	0.25
Hungarian (0)	12	0.05
Irish (1,165)	4,260	17.23
Italian (103)	573	2.32
Lithuanian (0)	25	0.10
Norwegian (137)	326	1.32
Pennsylvania German (55)	118	0.48
Polish (341)	690	2.79
Russian (10)	180	0.73
Scandinavian (0)	30	0.12
Scotch-Irish (143)	492	1.99
Scottish (100)	492	1.99
Slovene (0)	60	0.24
Swedish (348)	1,302	5.27
Swiss (0)	33	0.13
Ukrainian (10)	20	0.08
Welsh (13)	181	0.73

Hispanic Origin	Population	%
Hispanic or Latino (of any race)	2,170	8.77
Central American, ex. Mexican	37	0.15
Costa Rican	3	0.01
Guatemalan	9	0.04
Panamanian	4	0.02
Salvadoran	21	0.08
Cuban	9	0.04
Mexican	1,876	7.59
Puerto Rican	17	0.07
South American	9	0.04
Argentinean	1	<0.01
Colombian	1	<0.01
Ecuadorian	7	0.03
Other Hispanic or Latino	222	0.90

Race*	Population	%
African-American/Black (250)	402	1.63
Not Hispanic (224)	335	1.35
Hispanic (26)	67	0.27
American Indian/Alaska Native (172)	289	1.17
Not Hispanic (127)	219	0.89
Hispanic (45)	70	0.28
Apache (6)	10	0.04
Blackfeet (2)	6	0.02
Cherokee (8)	27	0.11
Chickasaw (0)	1	<0.01
Chippewa (5)	7	0.03
Choctaw (1)	2	0.01
Mexican American Ind. (4)	10	0.04
Navajo (11)	14	0.06
Sioux (55)	69	0.28
Spanish American Ind. (0)	1	<0.01
Yuman (0)	1	<0.01

*Notes: † The Census 2010 population figure is used to calculate the percentages in the Hispanic Origin and Race categories. Ancestry percentages are based on the 2006-2010 American Community Survey population (not shown); ‡ Numbers in parentheses indicate the number of people reporting a single ancestry; * Numbers in parentheses indicate the number of persons reporting this race alone, not in combination with any other race; Please refer to the Explanation of Data for more information.*

Yup'ik *(Alaska Native)* (3)	3	0.01
Asian (167)	231	0.93
Not Hispanic (163)	216	0.87
Hispanic (4)	15	0.06
Chinese, ex. Taiwanese (29)	39	0.16
Filipino (39)	67	0.27
Indian (18)	20	0.08
Indonesian (1)	1	<0.01
Japanese (26)	38	0.15
Korean (21)	32	0.13
Nepalese (2)	2	0.01
Pakistani (4)	4	0.02
Taiwanese (1)	1	<0.01
Thai (1)	3	0.01
Vietnamese (14)	16	0.06
Hawaii Native/Pacific Islander (5)	27	0.11
Not Hispanic (4)	16	0.06
Hispanic (1)	11	0.04
Guamanian/Chamorro (3)	6	0.02
Native Hawaiian (0)	8	0.03
Samoan (0)	2	0.01
Tongan (2)	2	0.01
White (23,025)	23,414	94.67
Not Hispanic (21,771)	22,021	89.03
Hispanic (1,254)	1,393	5.63

Omaha

Place Type: City
County: Douglas
Population: 408,958†

Ancestry‡	Population	%
Afghan (230)	241	0.06
African, Sub-Saharan (4,173)	4,839	1.19
African (1,922)	2,433	0.60
Cape Verdean (8)	8	<0.01
Ethiopian (82)	82	0.02
Ghanaian (183)	183	0.04
Kenyan (12)	12	<0.01
Liberian (66)	76	0.02
Nigerian (305)	326	0.08
Somalian (241)	322	0.08
South African (8)	8	<0.01
Sudanese (1,055)	1,060	0.26
Other Sub-Saharan African (291)	329	0.08
Albanian (54)	54	0.01
Alsatian (0)	7	<0.01
American (12,470)	12,470	3.06
Arab (1,359)	2,069	0.51
Arab (443)	580	0.14
Egyptian (82)	100	0.02
Jordanian (112)	169	0.04
Lebanese (382)	723	0.18
Moroccan (0)	7	<0.01
Palestinian (81)	81	0.02
Syrian (44)	172	0.04
Other Arab (215)	237	0.06
Armenian (18)	48	0.01
Australian (44)	215	0.05
Austrian (173)	836	0.21
Basque (41)	49	0.01
Belgian (114)	497	0.12
Brazilian (53)	136	0.03
British (415)	1,065	0.26
Bulgarian (14)	24	0.01
Cajun (12)	29	0.01
Canadian (203)	397	0.10
Celtic (10)	61	0.01
Croatian (250)	961	0.24
Czech (5,012)	16,370	4.02
Czechoslovakian (635)	1,311	0.32
Danish (2,679)	10,484	2.57
Dutch (1,471)	6,723	1.65
Eastern European (261)	297	0.07
English (7,103)	34,668	8.51
Estonian (0)	9	<0.01
European (4,301)	4,808	1.18
Finnish (93)	492	0.12
French, ex. Basque (1,445)	11,071	2.72
French Canadian (359)	1,322	0.32
German (40,118)	122,060	29.97
German Russian (10)	45	0.01
Greek (265)	890	0.22
Hungarian (294)	1,124	0.28
Icelander (8)	62	0.02
Iranian (65)	210	0.05
Irish (13,929)	68,484	16.81
Israeli (56)	91	0.02
Italian (5,936)	19,346	4.75
Latvian (118)	163	0.04
Lithuanian (454)	1,226	0.30
Luxemburger (52)	239	0.06
Maltese (9)	41	0.01
New Zealander (0)	11	<0.01
Northern European (270)	341	0.08
Norwegian (2,204)	8,514	2.09
Pennsylvania German (79)	444	0.11
Polish (5,397)	18,043	4.43
Portuguese (128)	345	0.08
Romanian (126)	327	0.08
Russian (1,096)	3,148	0.77
Scandinavian (482)	1,062	0.26
Scotch-Irish (1,978)	6,825	1.68
Scottish (1,167)	5,728	1.41
Serbian (143)	437	0.11
Slavic (262)	408	0.10
Slovak (143)	291	0.07
Slovene (27)	107	0.03
Swedish (3,580)	15,444	3.79
Swiss (241)	1,276	0.31
Turkish (63)	105	0.03
Ukrainian (341)	560	0.14
Welsh (319)	2,490	0.61
West Indian, ex. Hispanic (199)	295	0.07
British West Indian (53)	53	0.01
Dutch West Indian (11)	14	<0.01
Haitian (81)	92	0.02
Jamaican (33)	100	0.02
U.S. Virgin Islander (0)	5	<0.01
West Indian (21)	31	0.01
Yugoslavian (72)	166	0.04

Hispanic Origin	Population	%
Hispanic or Latino (of any race)	53,553	13.09
Central American, ex. Mexican	4,943	1.21
Costa Rican	41	0.01
Guatemalan	1,853	0.45
Honduran	518	0.13
Nicaraguan	95	0.02
Panamanian	124	0.03
Salvadoran	2,276	0.56
Other Central American	36	0.01
Cuban	365	0.09
Dominican Republic	152	0.04
Mexican	42,701	10.44
Puerto Rican	930	0.23
South American	749	0.18
Argentinean	71	0.02
Bolivian	33	0.01
Chilean	87	0.02
Colombian	270	0.07
Ecuadorian	46	0.01
Paraguayan	11	<0.01
Peruvian	123	0.03
Uruguayan	4	<0.01
Venezuelan	83	0.02
Other South American	21	0.01
Other Hispanic or Latino	3,713	0.91

Race*	Population	%
African-American/Black (55,950)	62,321	15.24
Not Hispanic (55,128)	60,775	14.86
Hispanic (822)	1,546	0.38
American Indian/Alaska Native (3,391)	6,649	1.63
Not Hispanic (2,263)	4,830	1.18
Hispanic (1,128)	1,819	0.44
Alaska Athabascan *(Ala. Nat.)* (9)	9	<0.01
Aleut *(Alaska Native)* (2)	4	<0.01
Apache (17)	68	0.02
Arapaho (6)	16	<0.01
Blackfeet (14)	124	0.03
Canadian/French Am. Ind. (6)	18	<0.01
Central American Ind. (46)	56	0.01
Cherokee (106)	528	0.13
Cheyenne (3)	13	<0.01
Chickasaw (13)	21	0.01
Chippewa (52)	96	0.02
Choctaw (26)	107	0.03
Colville (0)	1	<0.01
Comanche (2)	7	<0.01
Cree (1)	12	<0.01
Creek (19)	42	0.01
Crow (0)	4	<0.01
Delaware (0)	11	<0.01
Hopi (2)	2	<0.01
Houma (1)	1	<0.01
Iroquois (7)	27	0.01
Kiowa (6)	9	<0.01
Lumbee (1)	1	<0.01
Menominee (1)	11	<0.01
Mexican American Ind. (255)	362	0.09
Navajo (46)	80	0.02
Osage (1)	7	<0.01
Ottawa (6)	9	<0.01
Pima (1)	1	<0.01
Potawatomi (28)	49	0.01
Pueblo (2)	5	<0.01
Puget Sound Salish (3)	3	<0.01
Seminole (2)	12	<0.01
Shoshone (7)	10	<0.01
Sioux (390)	793	0.19
South American Ind. (6)	18	<0.01
Spanish American Ind. (29)	35	0.01
Tlingit-Haida *(Alaska Native)* (1)	2	<0.01
Tohono O'Odham (0)	1	<0.01
Ute (1)	2	<0.01
Yakama (7)	7	<0.01
Yaqui (2)	5	<0.01
Yup'ik *(Alaska Native)* (2)	3	<0.01
Asian (10,014)	12,307	3.01
Not Hispanic (9,889)	11,946	2.92
Hispanic (125)	361	0.09
Bangladeshi (20)	23	0.01
Bhutanese (20)	24	0.01
Burmese (1,703)	1,779	0.44
Cambodian (43)	67	0.02
Chinese, ex. Taiwanese (1,360)	1,700	0.42
Filipino (689)	1,256	0.31
Hmong (93)	108	0.03
Indian (2,461)	2,755	0.67
Indonesian (35)	46	0.01
Japanese (475)	925	0.23
Korean (748)	1,044	0.26
Laotian (99)	132	0.03
Malaysian (9)	15	<0.01
Nepalese (293)	312	0.08
Pakistani (121)	148	0.04
Sri Lankan (30)	30	0.01
Taiwanese (66)	93	0.02
Thai (172)	265	0.06
Vietnamese (1,059)	1,205	0.29
Hawaii Native/Pacific Islander (326)	793	0.19
Not Hispanic (253)	614	0.15
Hispanic (73)	179	0.04
Fijian (1)	1	<0.01
Guamanian/Chamorro (98)	149	0.04
Marshallese (8)	14	<0.01
Native Hawaiian (54)	222	0.05
Samoan (44)	133	0.03
Tongan (5)	10	<0.01
White (298,815)	309,021	75.56
Not Hispanic (278,172)	285,554	69.82
Hispanic (20,643)	23,467	5.74

*Notes: † The Census 2010 population figure is used to calculate the percentages in the Hispanic Origin and Race categories. Ancestry percentages are based on the 2006-2010 American Community Survey population (not shown); ‡ Numbers in parentheses indicate the number of people reporting a single ancestry; * Numbers in parentheses indicate the number of persons reporting this race alone, not in combination with any other race; Please refer to the Explanation of Data for more information.*

Papillion

Place Type: City
County: Sarpy
Population: 18,894†

Ancestry‡	Population	%
American (790)	790	4.20
Arab (6)	96	0.51
Lebanese (6)	64	0.34
Syrian (0)	32	0.17
Austrian (26)	100	0.53
Belgian (0)	67	0.36
British (55)	103	0.55
Cajun (25)	25	0.13
Canadian (20)	39	0.21
Croatian (0)	30	0.16
Czech (257)	871	4.63
Czechoslovakian (110)	152	0.81
Danish (138)	472	2.51
Dutch (29)	384	2.04
English (641)	2,317	12.31
European (129)	129	0.69
Finnish (0)	55	0.29
French, ex. Basque (36)	677	3.60
French Canadian (7)	65	0.35
German (2,666)	7,585	40.28
Greek (6)	16	0.08
Hungarian (24)	39	0.21
Irish (571)	3,612	19.18
Italian (343)	1,365	7.25
Lithuanian (16)	51	0.27
Luxemburger (12)	12	0.06
Norwegian (308)	774	4.11
Pennsylvania German (12)	42	0.22
Polish (367)	907	4.82
Portuguese (14)	32	0.17
Romanian (8)	23	0.12
Russian (42)	147	0.78
Scotch-Irish (65)	266	1.41
Scottish (93)	326	1.73
Serbian (18)	63	0.33
Swedish (249)	1,169	6.21
Swiss (46)	98	0.52
Ukrainian (0)	35	0.19
Welsh (30)	132	0.70
West Indian, ex. Hispanic (11)	11	0.06
Haitian (11)	11	0.06
Yugoslavian (0)	13	0.07

Hispanic Origin	Population	%
Hispanic or Latino (of any race)	987	5.22
Central American, ex. Mexican	79	0.42
Costa Rican	1	0.01
Guatemalan	16	0.08
Honduran	12	0.06
Panamanian	2	0.01
Salvadoran	48	0.25
Cuban	13	0.07
Dominican Republic	3	0.02
Mexican	637	3.37
Puerto Rican	77	0.41
South American	35	0.19
Argentinean	8	0.04
Bolivian	4	0.02
Chilean	2	0.01
Colombian	6	0.03
Ecuadorian	2	0.01
Peruvian	11	0.06
Uruguayan	2	0.01
Other Hispanic or Latino	143	0.76

Race*	Population	%
African-American/Black (617)	804	4.26
Not Hispanic (608)	772	4.09
Hispanic (9)	32	0.17
American Indian/Alaska Native (79)	189	1.00
Not Hispanic (57)	143	0.76
Hispanic (22)	46	0.24
Apache (3)	3	0.02
Cherokee (3)	24	0.13
Cheyenne (0)	4	0.02
Chickasaw (0)	6	0.03
Chippewa (3)	5	0.03
Choctaw (3)	5	0.03
Creek (0)	3	0.02
Delaware (3)	3	0.02
Iroquois (0)	2	0.01
Mexican American Ind. (1)	3	0.02
Navajo (1)	4	0.02
Ottawa (1)	1	0.01
Potawatomi (0)	1	0.01
Pueblo (1)	2	0.01
Seminole (0)	2	0.01
Sioux (10)	19	0.10
Tlingit-Haida *(Alaska Native)* (3)	3	0.02
Yaqui (0)	9	0.05
Asian (281)	424	2.24
Not Hispanic (280)	413	2.19
Hispanic (1)	11	0.06
Chinese, ex. Taiwanese (40)	55	0.29
Filipino (40)	84	0.44
Hmong (6)	6	0.03
Indian (24)	28	0.15
Japanese (27)	62	0.33
Korean (53)	76	0.40
Laotian (0)	1	0.01
Nepalese (4)	5	0.03
Pakistani (9)	9	0.05
Taiwanese (0)	5	0.03
Thai (9)	14	0.07
Vietnamese (63)	80	0.42
Hawaii Native/Pacific Islander (4)	36	0.19
Not Hispanic (4)	30	0.16
Hispanic (0)	6	0.03
Guamanian/Chamorro (1)	8	0.04
Native Hawaiian (2)	15	0.08
Samoan (0)	3	0.02
White (17,132)	17,601	93.16
Not Hispanic (16,546)	16,903	89.46
Hispanic (586)	698	3.69

Scottsbluff

Place Type: City
County: Scotts Bluff
Population: 15,039†

Ancestry‡	Population	%
African, Sub-Saharan (0)	7	0.05
African (0)	7	0.05
American (458)	458	3.09
Arab (0)	8	0.05
Lebanese (0)	8	0.05
Belgian (16)	106	0.71
British (11)	22	0.15
Czech (21)	200	1.35
Czechoslovakian (38)	38	0.26
Danish (0)	78	0.53
Dutch (22)	75	0.51
English (466)	1,599	10.77
European (65)	65	0.44
Finnish (12)	12	0.08
French, ex. Basque (7)	461	3.11
French Canadian (21)	21	0.14
German (2,645)	5,410	36.45
German Russian (9)	9	0.06
Greek (10)	61	0.41
Hungarian (7)	7	0.05
Iranian (30)	30	0.20
Irish (194)	1,330	8.96
Italian (57)	358	2.41
Norwegian (87)	276	1.86
Pennsylvania German (8)	8	0.05
Polish (35)	64	0.43
Russian (70)	347	2.34
Scandinavian (16)	16	0.11
Scotch-Irish (44)	216	1.46
Scottish (71)	235	1.58
Slovak (0)	12	0.08
Swedish (120)	338	2.28
Swiss (0)	65	0.44
Turkish (0)	14	0.09
Welsh (40)	97	0.65

Hispanic Origin	Population	%
Hispanic or Latino (of any race)	4,371	29.06
Central American, ex. Mexican	25	0.17
Costa Rican	1	0.01
Guatemalan	13	0.09
Honduran	6	0.04
Nicaraguan	2	0.01
Panamanian	2	0.01
Salvadoran	1	0.01
Cuban	19	0.13
Dominican Republic	2	0.01
Mexican	3,957	26.31
Puerto Rican	27	0.18
South American	26	0.17
Argentinean	1	0.01
Colombian	9	0.06
Peruvian	13	0.09
Venezuelan	3	0.02
Other Hispanic or Latino	315	2.09

Race*	Population	%
African-American/Black (125)	185	1.23
Not Hispanic (85)	121	0.80
Hispanic (40)	64	0.43
American Indian/Alaska Native (512)	646	4.30
Not Hispanic (340)	419	2.79
Hispanic (172)	227	1.51
Apache (0)	1	0.01
Blackfeet (0)	1	0.01
Cherokee (5)	24	0.16
Cheyenne (2)	4	0.03
Chippewa (7)	14	0.09
Iroquois (1)	3	0.02
Mexican American Ind. (15)	17	0.11
Navajo (1)	5	0.03
Sioux (288)	340	2.26
South American Ind. (2)	2	0.01
Asian (113)	145	0.96
Not Hispanic (106)	125	0.83
Hispanic (7)	20	0.13
Chinese, ex. Taiwanese (41)	46	0.31
Filipino (6)	15	0.10
Hmong (8)	8	0.05
Indian (7)	9	0.06
Japanese (37)	39	0.26
Korean (3)	7	0.05
Thai (1)	2	0.01
Vietnamese (6)	13	0.09
Hawaii Native/Pacific Islander (7)	23	0.15
Not Hispanic (4)	12	0.08
Hispanic (3)	11	0.07
Guamanian/Chamorro (2)	3	0.02
Native Hawaiian (4)	11	0.07
Samoan (0)	1	0.01
White (12,487)	12,763	84.87
Not Hispanic (9,983)	10,111	67.23
Hispanic (2,504)	2,652	17.63

South Sioux City

Place Type: City
County: Dakota
Population: 13,353†

Ancestry‡	Population	%
African, Sub-Saharan (319)	319	2.46
African (102)	102	0.79
Somalian (217)	217	1.67
American (467)	467	3.60
Arab (0)	17	0.13
Syrian (0)	17	0.13
British (11)	20	0.15
Canadian (0)	12	0.09
Czech (0)	23	0.18
Czechoslovakian (24)	32	0.25

*Notes: † The Census 2010 population figure is used to calculate the percentages in the Hispanic Origin and Race categories. Ancestry percentages are based on the 2006-2010 American Community Survey population (not shown); ‡ Numbers in parentheses indicate the number of people reporting a single ancestry; * Numbers in parentheses indicate the number of persons reporting this race alone, not in combination with any other race; Please refer to the Explanation of Data for more information.*

Danish (122)	352	2.71
Dutch (34)	347	2.67
English (186)	704	5.42
Finnish (16)	16	0.12
French, ex. Basque (84)	367	2.83
French Canadian (16)	50	0.39
German (1,267)	2,777	21.40
Greek (0)	20	0.15
Irish (405)	1,500	11.56
Italian (8)	109	0.84
Lithuanian (0)	13	0.10
Norwegian (101)	210	1.62
Polish (75)	135	1.04
Portuguese (0)	9	0.07
Russian (0)	39	0.30
Scandinavian (0)	9	0.07
Scotch-Irish (39)	77	0.59
Scottish (0)	82	0.63
Swedish (54)	390	3.01
Swiss (0)	11	0.08
Welsh (8)	49	0.38

Hispanic Origin	Population	%
Hispanic or Latino (of any race)	6,047	45.29
Central American, ex. Mexican	499	3.74
Guatemalan	306	2.29
Honduran	9	0.07
Nicaraguan	24	0.18
Panamanian	4	0.03
Salvadoran	156	1.17
Cuban	10	0.07
Dominican Republic	2	0.01
Mexican	5,246	39.29
Puerto Rican	31	0.23
South American	15	0.11
Chilean	1	0.01
Colombian	2	0.01
Ecuadorian	5	0.04
Peruvian	5	0.04
Venezuelan	2	0.01
Other Hispanic or Latino	244	1.83

Race*	Population	%
African-American/Black (625)	687	5.14
Not Hispanic (610)	663	4.97
Hispanic (15)	24	0.18
American Indian/Alaska Native (407)	509	3.81
Not Hispanic (330)	386	2.89
Hispanic (77)	123	0.92
Apache (0)	10	0.07
Central American Ind. (1)	2	0.01
Cherokee (5)	10	0.07
Cheyenne (1)	1	0.01
Choctaw (1)	1	0.01
Comanche (1)	1	0.01
Kiowa (0)	1	0.01
Mexican American Ind. (18)	24	0.18
Sioux (85)	113	0.85
Asian (385)	427	3.20
Not Hispanic (375)	416	3.12
Hispanic (10)	11	0.08
Cambodian (8)	10	0.07
Chinese, ex. Taiwanese (14)	21	0.16
Filipino (12)	18	0.13
Hmong (11)	14	0.10
Indian (12)	15	0.11
Indonesian (1)	1	0.01
Japanese (1)	4	0.03
Korean (4)	10	0.07
Laotian (153)	175	1.31
Malaysian (0)	2	0.01
Pakistani (1)	1	0.01
Thai (6)	9	0.07
Vietnamese (133)	144	1.08
Hawaii Native/Pacific Islander (21)	35	0.26
Not Hispanic (20)	23	0.17
Hispanic (1)	12	0.09
Guamanian/Chamorro (3)	9	0.07
Native Hawaiian (0)	1	0.01
Samoan (6)	6	0.04
White (8,368)	8,687	65.06
Not Hispanic (5,816)	5,957	44.61
Hispanic (2,552)	2,730	20.44

York

Place Type: City
County: York
Population: 7,766†

Ancestry‡	Population	%
African, Sub-Saharan (19)	30	0.38
African (0)	11	0.14
South African (19)	19	0.24
American (416)	416	5.29
Arab (10)	56	0.71
Lebanese (10)	37	0.47
Syrian (0)	19	0.24
Belgian (0)	12	0.15
British (0)	12	0.15
Canadian (8)	22	0.28
Czech (61)	375	4.77
Czechoslovakian (27)	27	0.34
Danish (49)	234	2.97
Dutch (22)	196	2.49
English (252)	1,119	14.22
European (202)	209	2.66
French, ex. Basque (20)	144	1.83
French Canadian (9)	9	0.11
German (1,659)	3,893	49.47
Hungarian (0)	7	0.09
Irish (281)	1,380	17.54
Italian (25)	43	0.55
Norwegian (54)	303	3.85
Pennsylvania German (26)	41	0.52
Polish (23)	106	1.35
Portuguese (0)	60	0.76
Russian (34)	71	0.90
Scotch-Irish (25)	100	1.27
Scottish (10)	140	1.78
Slovak (14)	14	0.18
Swedish (150)	464	5.90
Swiss (0)	16	0.20
Welsh (0)	69	0.88

Hispanic Origin	Population	%
Hispanic or Latino (of any race)	340	4.38
Central American, ex. Mexican	25	0.32
Guatemalan	7	0.09
Honduran	4	0.05
Salvadoran	14	0.18
Cuban	2	0.03
Mexican	254	3.27
Puerto Rican	19	0.24
South American	7	0.09
Ecuadorian	3	0.04
Peruvian	4	0.05
Other Hispanic or Latino	33	0.42

Race*	Population	%
African-American/Black (77)	110	1.42
Not Hispanic (70)	102	1.31
Hispanic (7)	8	0.10
American Indian/Alaska Native (27)	42	0.54
Not Hispanic (20)	34	0.44
Hispanic (7)	8	0.10
Cherokee (0)	1	0.01
Choctaw (1)	1	0.01
Mexican American Ind. (1)	1	0.01
Sioux (8)	10	0.13
Asian (52)	87	1.12
Not Hispanic (51)	78	1.00
Hispanic (1)	9	0.12
Chinese, ex. Taiwanese (11)	19	0.24
Filipino (17)	27	0.35
Indian (6)	9	0.12
Japanese (7)	20	0.26
Korean (6)	7	0.09
Thai (2)	2	0.03
Vietnamese (3)	12	0.15
Hawaii Native/Pacific Islander (4)	17	0.22
Not Hispanic (4)	10	0.13
Hispanic (0)	7	0.09
Native Hawaiian (4)	16	0.21
White (7,367)	7,450	95.93
Not Hispanic (7,192)	7,255	93.42
Hispanic (175)	195	2.51

*Notes: † The Census 2010 population figure is used to calculate the percentages in the Hispanic Origin and Race categories. Ancestry percentages are based on the 2006-2010 American Community Survey population (not shown); ‡ Numbers in parentheses indicate the number of people reporting a single ancestry; * Numbers in parentheses indicate the number of persons reporting this race alone, not in combination with any other race; Please refer to the Explanation of Data for more information.*

NEVADA

Place Type: State
Population: 2,700,551[†]

Ancestry[‡]	Population	%
Afghan (1,062)	1,101	0.04
African, Sub-Saharan (22,530)	26,691	1.01
African (14,144)	17,448	0.66
Cape Verdean (353)	401	0.02
Ethiopian (4,880)	5,088	0.19
Ghanaian (248)	262	0.01
Kenyan (264)	285	0.01
Liberian (221)	221	0.01
Nigerian (626)	716	0.03
Sierra Leonean (8)	8	<0.01
Somalian (252)	368	0.01
South African (587)	762	0.03
Sudanese (171)	177	0.01
Ugandan (28)	72	<0.01
Zimbabwean (26)	26	<0.01
Other Sub-Saharan African (722)	857	0.03
Albanian (923)	1,077	0.04
Alsatian (0)	148	0.01
American (99,327)	99,327	3.77
Arab (7,910)	12,140	0.46
Arab (1,100)	1,443	0.05
Egyptian (1,115)	1,310	0.05
Iraqi (771)	808	0.03
Jordanian (157)	240	0.01
Lebanese (2,913)	5,119	0.19
Moroccan (446)	825	0.03
Palestinian (258)	301	0.01
Syrian (495)	1,195	0.05
Other Arab (655)	899	0.03
Armenian (4,164)	5,479	0.21
Assyrian/Chaldean/Syriac (439)	555	0.02
Australian (594)	1,087	0.04
Austrian (2,113)	7,045	0.27
Basque (2,974)	5,390	0.20
Belgian (807)	2,236	0.08
Brazilian (1,546)	2,295	0.09
British (5,349)	9,693	0.37
Bulgarian (2,148)	2,352	0.09
Cajun (213)	416	0.02
Canadian (4,719)	8,634	0.33
Carpatho Rusyn (5)	5	<0.01
Celtic (311)	600	0.02
Croatian (1,552)	3,875	0.15
Czech (2,944)	10,271	0.39
Czechoslovakian (1,073)	2,396	0.09
Danish (5,342)	20,157	0.77
Dutch (7,689)	34,972	1.33
Eastern European (1,603)	2,003	0.08
English (77,698)	244,546	9.29
Estonian (69)	94	<0.01
European (22,617)	27,065	1.03
Finnish (1,561)	4,856	0.18
French, ex. Basque (11,923)	69,177	2.63
French Canadian (5,983)	12,651	0.48
German (104,445)	353,500	13.42
German Russian (72)	175	0.01
Greek (5,323)	11,346	0.43
Guyanese (216)	254	0.01
Hungarian (6,036)	14,122	0.54
Icelander (196)	551	0.02
Iranian (4,153)	4,677	0.18
Irish (76,437)	271,932	10.33
Israeli (1,137)	1,367	0.05
Italian (71,978)	169,273	6.43
Latvian (393)	820	0.03
Lithuanian (1,703)	4,432	0.17
Luxemburger (123)	338	0.01
Macedonian (343)	567	0.02
Maltese (495)	712	0.03
New Zealander (247)	339	0.01
Northern European (1,604)	1,929	0.07
Norwegian (14,141)	41,941	1.59
Pennsylvania German (457)	770	0.03
Polish (21,355)	60,741	2.31
Portuguese (6,450)	16,905	0.64
Romanian (2,322)	4,127	0.16
Russian (11,813)	27,290	1.04
Scandinavian (2,633)	6,213	0.24
Scotch-Irish (13,091)	36,943	1.40
Scottish (14,937)	50,899	1.93
Serbian (2,074)	3,114	0.12
Slavic (333)	1,230	0.05
Slovak (1,212)	3,617	0.14
Slovene (301)	743	0.03
Soviet Union (19)	38	<0.01
Swedish (10,146)	39,042	1.48
Swiss (2,254)	9,396	0.36
Turkish (1,284)	1,696	0.06
Ukrainian (2,188)	5,306	0.20
Welsh (3,263)	18,227	0.69
West Indian, ex. Hispanic (3,971)	6,573	0.25
Bahamian (73)	86	<0.01
Barbadian (47)	90	<0.01
Belizean (696)	830	0.03
British West Indian (64)	130	<0.01
Dutch West Indian (24)	107	<0.01
Haitian (774)	983	0.04
Jamaican (1,504)	2,950	0.11
Trinidadian/Tobagonian (190)	343	0.01
U.S. Virgin Islander (32)	32	<0.01
West Indian (567)	1,022	0.04
Yugoslavian (2,940)	4,514	0.17

Hispanic Origin	Population	%
Hispanic or Latino (of any race)	716,501	26.53
Central American, ex. Mexican	55,937	2.07
Costa Rican	1,433	0.05
Guatemalan	13,407	0.50
Honduran	4,481	0.17
Nicaraguan	4,475	0.17
Panamanian	1,615	0.06
Salvadoran	30,043	1.11
Other Central American	483	0.02
Cuban	21,459	0.79
Dominican Republic	2,446	0.09
Mexican	540,978	20.03
Puerto Rican	20,664	0.77
South American	19,056	0.71
Argentinean	3,419	0.13
Bolivian	481	0.02
Chilean	1,683	0.06
Colombian	5,230	0.19
Ecuadorian	2,045	0.08
Paraguayan	116	<0.01
Peruvian	4,581	0.17
Uruguayan	407	0.02
Venezuelan	878	0.03
Other South American	216	0.01
Other Hispanic or Latino	55,961	2.07

Race*	Population	%
African-American/Black (218,626)	254,452	9.42
Not Hispanic (208,058)	236,042	8.74
Hispanic (10,568)	18,410	0.68
American Indian/Alaska Native (32,062)	55,945	2.07
Not Hispanic (23,536)	40,994	1.52
Hispanic (8,526)	14,951	0.55
Alaska Athabascan *(Ala. Nat.)* (65)	119	<0.01
Aleut *(Alaska Native)* (75)	127	<0.01
Apache (642)	1,409	0.05
Arapaho (54)	84	<0.01
Blackfeet (236)	1,161	0.04
Canadian/French Am. Ind. (64)	143	0.01
Central American Ind. (83)	160	0.01
Cherokee (1,682)	6,200	0.23
Cheyenne (55)	148	0.01
Chickasaw (179)	387	0.01
Chippewa (476)	832	0.03
Choctaw (548)	1,469	0.05
Colville (26)	36	<0.01
Comanche (72)	197	0.01
Cree (48)	123	<0.01
Creek (155)	395	0.01
Crow (39)	79	<0.01
Delaware (29)	78	<0.01
Hopi (142)	239	0.01
Houma (3)	9	<0.01
Inupiat *(Alaska Native)* (81)	144	0.01
Iroquois (216)	511	0.02
Kiowa (40)	67	<0.01
Lumbee (53)	80	<0.01
Menominee (25)	33	<0.01
Mexican American Ind. (1,197)	1,930	0.07
Navajo (1,821)	2,597	0.10
Osage (58)	131	<0.01
Ottawa (53)	82	<0.01
Paiute (4,027)	4,859	0.18
Pima (70)	125	<0.01
Potawatomi (171)	290	0.01
Pueblo (301)	481	0.02
Puget Sound Salish (55)	85	<0.01
Seminole (54)	228	0.01
Shoshone (1,317)	1,788	0.07
Sioux (640)	1,328	0.05
South American Ind. (114)	233	0.01
Spanish American Ind. (146)	217	0.01
Tlingit-Haida *(Alaska Native)* (110)	201	0.01
Tohono O'Odham (66)	120	<0.01
Tsimshian *(Alaska Native)* (9)	18	<0.01
Ute (79)	166	0.01
Yakama (20)	33	<0.01
Yaqui (130)	266	0.01
Yuman (129)	190	0.01
Yup'ik *(Alaska Native)* (33)	57	<0.01
Asian (195,436)	242,916	9.00
Not Hispanic (191,047)	230,685	8.54
Hispanic (4,389)	12,231	0.45
Bangladeshi (425)	482	0.02
Bhutanese (158)	165	0.01
Burmese (301)	349	0.01
Cambodian (1,199)	1,630	0.06
Chinese, ex. Taiwanese (27,673)	38,108	1.41
Filipino (98,351)	123,891	4.59
Hmong (203)	254	0.01
Indian (11,671)	14,290	0.53
Indonesian (671)	1,165	0.04
Japanese (10,873)	21,364	0.79
Korean (13,896)	18,518	0.69
Laotian (1,952)	2,581	0.10
Malaysian (117)	237	0.01
Nepalese (205)	238	0.01
Pakistani (1,484)	1,793	0.07
Sri Lankan (517)	610	0.02
Taiwanese (1,138)	1,476	0.05
Thai (5,515)	7,783	0.29
Vietnamese (9,892)	12,366	0.46
Hawaii Native/Pacific Islander (16,871)	32,848	1.22
Not Hispanic (15,456)	28,415	1.05
Hispanic (1,415)	4,433	0.16
Fijian (251)	369	0.01
Guamanian/Chamorro (3,513)	5,512	0.20
Marshallese (90)	108	<0.01
Native Hawaiian (6,459)	16,339	0.61
Samoan (3,202)	5,257	0.19
Tongan (1,100)	1,590	0.06
White (1,786,688)	1,890,043	69.99
Not Hispanic (1,462,081)	1,527,298	56.56
Hispanic (324,607)	362,745	13.43

*Notes: † The Census 2010 population figure is used to calculate the percentages in the Hispanic Origin and Race categories. Ancestry percentages are based on the 2006-2010 American Community Survey population (not shown); ‡ Numbers in parentheses indicate the number of people reporting a single ancestry; * Numbers in parentheses indicate the number of persons reporting this race alone, not in combination with any other race; Please refer to the Explanation of Data for more information.*

Boulder City

Place Type: City
County: Clark
Population: 15,023†

Ancestry‡	Population	%
African, Sub-Saharan (8)	8	0.05
Ethiopian (8)	8	0.05
Alsatian (0)	10	0.06
American (830)	830	5.39
Arab (0)	10	0.06
Syrian (0)	10	0.06
Armenian (18)	18	0.12
Austrian (9)	51	0.33
Basque (15)	15	0.10
Belgian (11)	22	0.14
British (73)	109	0.71
Canadian (13)	49	0.32
Croatian (0)	24	0.16
Czech (27)	67	0.44
Czechoslovakian (18)	141	0.92
Danish (74)	140	0.91
Dutch (153)	357	2.32
English (722)	2,903	18.85
European (127)	147	0.95
Finnish (27)	27	0.18
French, ex. Basque (17)	557	3.62
French Canadian (59)	73	0.47
German (1,284)	3,876	25.17
Greek (12)	23	0.15
Hungarian (71)	121	0.79
Iranian (23)	23	0.15
Irish (464)	2,342	15.21
Italian (753)	1,389	9.02
Lithuanian (19)	28	0.18
Northern European (13)	25	0.16
Norwegian (345)	672	4.36
Polish (161)	462	3.00
Portuguese (23)	77	0.50
Russian (10)	157	1.02
Scandinavian (85)	135	0.88
Scotch-Irish (56)	306	1.99
Scottish (90)	426	2.77
Serbian (0)	17	0.11
Slovak (16)	16	0.10
Swedish (166)	499	3.24
Swiss (40)	77	0.50
Ukrainian (10)	21	0.14
Welsh (81)	185	1.20

Hispanic Origin	Population	%
Hispanic or Latino (of any race)	1,061	7.06
Central American, ex. Mexican	44	0.29
Costa Rican	11	0.07
Guatemalan	16	0.11
Honduran	10	0.07
Nicaraguan	1	0.01
Panamanian	2	0.01
Salvadoran	3	0.02
Other Central American	1	0.01
Cuban	23	0.15
Dominican Republic	7	0.05
Mexican	676	4.50
Puerto Rican	61	0.41
South American	45	0.30
Argentinean	5	0.03
Bolivian	7	0.05
Chilean	3	0.02
Colombian	12	0.08
Ecuadorian	1	0.01
Peruvian	11	0.07
Venezuelan	4	0.03
Other South American	2	0.01
Other Hispanic or Latino	205	1.36

Race*	Population	%
African-American/Black (130)	236	1.57
Not Hispanic (114)	199	1.32
Hispanic (16)	37	0.25
American Indian/Alaska Native (125)	281	1.87
Not Hispanic (111)	234	1.56
Hispanic (14)	47	0.31
Alaska Athabascan *(Ala. Nat.)* (1)	1	0.01
Aleut *(Alaska Native)* (2)	2	0.01
Apache (3)	8	0.05
Arapaho (1)	3	0.02
Blackfeet (1)	4	0.03
Canadian/French Am. Ind. (0)	1	0.01
Cherokee (14)	48	0.32
Chickasaw (1)	1	0.01
Chippewa (7)	9	0.06
Choctaw (3)	3	0.02
Creek (2)	7	0.05
Delaware (1)	2	0.01
Hopi (3)	4	0.03
Iroquois (2)	3	0.02
Menominee (1)	1	0.01
Mexican American Ind. (1)	1	0.01
Navajo (14)	22	0.15
Osage (0)	1	0.01
Pima (0)	1	0.01
Potawatomi (3)	5	0.03
Pueblo (4)	6	0.04
Shoshone (1)	1	0.01
Sioux (5)	17	0.11
Tlingit-Haida *(Alaska Native)* (1)	7	0.05
Yaqui (0)	1	0.01
Yuman (0)	2	0.01
Asian (169)	283	1.88
Not Hispanic (161)	257	1.71
Hispanic (8)	26	0.17
Burmese (2)	2	0.01
Chinese, ex. Taiwanese (20)	39	0.26
Filipino (38)	92	0.61
Indian (15)	17	0.11
Japanese (39)	71	0.47
Korean (24)	32	0.21
Malaysian (0)	3	0.02
Pakistani (5)	5	0.03
Thai (5)	7	0.05
Vietnamese (5)	9	0.06
Hawaii Native/Pacific Islander (40)	93	0.62
Not Hispanic (31)	71	0.47
Hispanic (9)	22	0.15
Guamanian/Chamorro (7)	10	0.07
Marshallese (1)	1	0.01
Native Hawaiian (12)	42	0.28
Samoan (6)	8	0.05
Tongan (0)	1	0.01
White (13,866)	14,278	95.04
Not Hispanic (13,215)	13,502	89.88
Hispanic (651)	776	5.17

Carson City

Place Type: Independent City
County: Carson City
Population: 55,274†

Ancestry‡	Population	%
African, Sub-Saharan (17)	97	0.18
African (17)	97	0.18
American (2,320)	2,320	4.19
Arab (184)	206	0.37
Arab (169)	169	0.31
Lebanese (0)	8	0.01
Syrian (15)	29	0.05
Armenian (35)	113	0.20
Australian (0)	25	0.05
Austrian (65)	140	0.25
Basque (125)	138	0.25
Belgian (131)	153	0.28
British (0)	21	0.04
Cajun (41)	75	0.14
Canadian (80)	92	0.17
Celtic (13)	24	0.04
Croatian (16)	90	0.16
Czech (27)	128	0.23
Czechoslovakian (5)	28	0.05
Danish (317)	826	1.49
Dutch (291)	1,063	1.92
English (1,770)	8,152	14.72
Estonian (0)	9	0.02
European (571)	728	1.31
Finnish (22)	147	0.27
French, ex. Basque (342)	1,880	3.40
French Canadian (121)	312	0.56
German (3,245)	11,801	21.31
Greek (47)	213	0.38
Hungarian (97)	581	1.05
Iranian (13)	13	0.02
Irish (1,655)	7,922	14.31
Israeli (39)	39	0.07
Italian (1,427)	4,260	7.69
Lithuanian (49)	98	0.18
Luxemburger (0)	15	0.03
Northern European (222)	222	0.40
Norwegian (352)	1,129	2.04
Pennsylvania German (16)	33	0.06
Polish (271)	854	1.54
Portuguese (318)	849	1.53
Romanian (19)	36	0.07
Russian (198)	549	0.99
Scandinavian (104)	334	0.60
Scotch-Irish (459)	1,297	2.34
Scottish (426)	1,831	3.31
Serbian (27)	35	0.06
Slavic (15)	53	0.10
Slovak (0)	26	0.05
Slovene (40)	56	0.10
Swedish (312)	1,311	2.37
Swiss (146)	366	0.66
Ukrainian (36)	108	0.20
Welsh (175)	914	1.65
West Indian, ex. Hispanic (0)	30	0.05
West Indian (0)	30	0.05
Yugoslavian (50)	79	0.14

Hispanic Origin	Population	%
Hispanic or Latino (of any race)	11,777	21.31
Central American, ex. Mexican	838	1.52
Costa Rican	17	0.03
Guatemalan	85	0.15
Honduran	73	0.13
Nicaraguan	320	0.58
Panamanian	7	0.01
Salvadoran	330	0.60
Other Central American	6	0.01
Cuban	65	0.12
Dominican Republic	2	<0.01
Mexican	9,215	16.67
Puerto Rican	167	0.30
South American	138	0.25
Argentinean	10	0.02
Bolivian	2	<0.01
Chilean	13	0.02
Colombian	51	0.09
Ecuadorian	17	0.03
Peruvian	39	0.07
Venezuelan	5	0.01
Other South American	1	<0.01
Other Hispanic or Latino	1,352	2.45

Race*	Population	%
African-American/Black (1,054)	1,297	2.35
Not Hispanic (1,003)	1,195	2.16
Hispanic (51)	102	0.18
American Indian/Alaska Native (1,306)	1,894	3.43
Not Hispanic (1,096)	1,563	2.83
Hispanic (210)	331	0.60
Alaska Athabascan *(Ala. Nat.)* (3)	3	0.01
Aleut *(Alaska Native)* (2)	3	0.01
Apache (12)	36	0.07
Blackfeet (10)	24	0.04
Canadian/French Am. Ind. (1)	4	0.01
Cherokee (46)	163	0.29
Cheyenne (1)	6	0.01
Chickasaw (1)	4	0.01
Chippewa (15)	25	0.05

*Notes: † The Census 2010 population figure is used to calculate the percentages in the Hispanic Origin and Race categories. Ancestry percentages are based on the 2006-2010 American Community Survey population (not shown); ‡ Numbers in parentheses indicate the number of people reporting a single ancestry; * Numbers in parentheses indicate the number of persons reporting this race alone, not in combination with any other race; Please refer to the Explanation of Data for more information.*

	Population	%
Choctaw (9)	34	0.06
Colville (0)	1	<0.01
Comanche (1)	4	0.01
Cree (5)	10	0.02
Creek (9)	15	0.03
Crow (5)	5	0.01
Delaware (1)	1	<0.01
Hopi (20)	29	0.05
Inupiat *(Alaska Native)* (2)	3	0.01
Iroquois (3)	18	0.03
Kiowa (3)	3	0.01
Mexican American Ind. (12)	32	0.06
Navajo (21)	39	0.07
Osage (2)	4	0.01
Paiute (154)	234	0.42
Pima (2)	2	<0.01
Potawatomi (5)	6	0.01
Pueblo (11)	16	0.03
Seminole (2)	6	0.01
Shoshone (44)	70	0.13
Sioux (19)	44	0.08
South American Ind. (1)	1	<0.01
Tlingit-Haida *(Alaska Native)* (7)	14	0.03
Tohono O'Odham (2)	4	0.01
Tsimshian *(Alaska Native)* (1)	3	0.01
Ute (2)	6	0.01
Yaqui (4)	6	0.01
Yuman (6)	7	0.01
Yup'ik *(Alaska Native)* (2)	2	<0.01
Asian (1,181)	1,641	2.97
Not Hispanic (1,139)	1,499	2.71
Hispanic (42)	142	0.26
Cambodian (2)	3	0.01
Chinese, ex. Taiwanese (182)	269	0.49
Filipino (382)	576	1.04
Hmong (7)	8	0.01
Indian (194)	210	0.38
Indonesian (13)	20	0.04
Japanese (121)	211	0.38
Korean (57)	93	0.17
Laotian (2)	3	0.01
Nepalese (2)	2	<0.01
Pakistani (4)	5	0.01
Sri Lankan (6)	6	0.01
Taiwanese (3)	6	0.01
Thai (25)	38	0.07
Vietnamese (83)	102	0.18
Hawaii Native/Pacific Islander (101)	241	0.44
Not Hispanic (91)	211	0.38
Hispanic (10)	30	0.05
Fijian (0)	1	<0.01
Guamanian/Chamorro (29)	42	0.08
Native Hawaiian (43)	134	0.24
Samoan (16)	21	0.04
Tongan (5)	9	0.02
White (44,807)	46,290	83.75
Not Hispanic (39,083)	40,034	72.43
Hispanic (5,724)	6,256	11.32

Cold Springs

Place Type: CDP
County: Washoe
Population: 8,544†

Ancestry‡	Population	%
American (837)	837	9.09
Armenian (0)	26	0.28
Basque (0)	25	0.27
Belgian (14)	14	0.15
British (83)	83	0.90
Canadian (18)	18	0.20
Danish (0)	82	0.89
Dutch (26)	168	1.83
English (240)	1,317	14.31
European (127)	139	1.51
French, ex. Basque (142)	483	5.25
French Canadian (0)	79	0.86
German (488)	2,044	22.21
Irish (65)	1,442	15.67
Italian (363)	682	7.41
New Zealander (0)	11	0.12
Norwegian (80)	270	2.93
Polish (20)	59	0.64
Portuguese (15)	72	0.78
Russian (0)	63	0.68
Scotch-Irish (58)	97	1.05
Scottish (24)	294	3.19
Serbian (36)	36	0.39
Swedish (54)	264	2.87
Swiss (7)	19	0.21
Turkish (23)	23	0.25
Welsh (0)	33	0.36
West Indian, ex. Hispanic (0)	100	1.09
Jamaican (0)	100	1.09

Hispanic Origin	Population	%
Hispanic or Latino (of any race)	1,211	14.17
Central American, ex. Mexican	114	1.33
Costa Rican	18	0.21
Guatemalan	40	0.47
Honduran	4	0.05
Nicaraguan	7	0.08
Panamanian	3	0.04
Salvadoran	41	0.48
Other Central American	1	0.01
Cuban	21	0.25
Mexican	912	10.67
Puerto Rican	36	0.42
South American	21	0.25
Argentinean	5	0.06
Bolivian	2	0.02
Chilean	4	0.05
Colombian	7	0.08
Ecuadorian	1	0.01
Peruvian	2	0.02
Other Hispanic or Latino	107	1.25

Race*	Population	%
African-American/Black (151)	207	2.42
Not Hispanic (147)	196	2.29
Hispanic (4)	11	0.13
American Indian/Alaska Native (98)	203	2.38
Not Hispanic (68)	153	1.79
Hispanic (30)	50	0.59
Apache (1)	6	0.07
Arapaho (4)	4	0.05
Blackfeet (0)	1	0.01
Cherokee (8)	25	0.29
Cheyenne (0)	1	0.01
Chickasaw (3)	6	0.07
Chippewa (0)	2	0.02
Choctaw (8)	14	0.16
Creek (0)	1	0.01
Crow (0)	1	0.01
Delaware (0)	1	0.01
Mexican American Ind. (4)	4	0.05
Navajo (4)	5	0.06
Osage (0)	3	0.04
Paiute (3)	7	0.08
Potawatomi (2)	2	0.02
Pueblo (1)	3	0.04
Shoshone (3)	6	0.07
Sioux (0)	5	0.06
South American Ind. (0)	2	0.02
Tlingit-Haida *(Alaska Native)* (2)	4	0.05
Yaqui (0)	1	0.01
Asian (170)	332	3.89
Not Hispanic (162)	303	3.55
Hispanic (8)	29	0.34
Chinese, ex. Taiwanese (14)	37	0.43
Filipino (93)	175	2.05
Hmong (2)	2	0.02
Indian (14)	16	0.19
Indonesian (0)	2	0.02
Japanese (12)	49	0.57
Korean (18)	36	0.42
Taiwanese (3)	3	0.04
Thai (3)	8	0.09
Vietnamese (4)	18	0.21
Hawaii Native/Pacific Islander (28)	67	0.78
Not Hispanic (28)	57	0.67
Hispanic (0)	10	0.12
Guamanian/Chamorro (11)	12	0.14
Native Hawaiian (13)	37	0.43
Samoan (1)	4	0.05
Tongan (1)	3	0.04
White (7,265)	7,602	88.97
Not Hispanic (6,632)	6,888	80.62
Hispanic (633)	714	8.36

Dayton

Place Type: CDP
County: Lyon
Population: 8,964†

Ancestry‡	Population	%
American (379)	379	3.86
Arab (19)	27	0.27
Lebanese (0)	8	0.08
Syrian (19)	19	0.19
Australian (0)	16	0.16
Austrian (34)	97	0.99
Canadian (0)	66	0.67
Croatian (0)	5	0.05
Danish (63)	63	0.64
Dutch (0)	44	0.45
English (371)	1,777	18.08
European (37)	92	0.94
Finnish (0)	93	0.95
French, ex. Basque (94)	506	5.15
French Canadian (0)	18	0.18
German (744)	2,247	22.86
Greek (0)	61	0.62
Hungarian (28)	28	0.28
Iranian (22)	22	0.22
Irish (255)	1,684	17.13
Italian (52)	775	7.89
Latvian (7)	7	0.07
Norwegian (48)	182	1.85
Polish (21)	68	0.69
Portuguese (282)	526	5.35
Russian (33)	62	0.63
Scandinavian (0)	15	0.15
Scotch-Irish (37)	181	1.84
Scottish (112)	689	7.01
Swedish (18)	291	2.96
Swiss (13)	13	0.13
Ukrainian (27)	27	0.27
Welsh (9)	60	0.61
Yugoslavian (0)	15	0.15

Hispanic Origin	Population	%
Hispanic or Latino (of any race)	1,444	16.11
Central American, ex. Mexican	154	1.72
Costa Rican	3	0.03
Guatemalan	8	0.09
Honduran	13	0.15
Nicaraguan	57	0.64
Panamanian	4	0.04
Salvadoran	69	0.77
Cuban	7	0.08
Dominican Republic	5	0.06
Mexican	1,089	12.15
Puerto Rican	44	0.49
South American	25	0.28
Bolivian	2	0.02
Chilean	3	0.03
Colombian	6	0.07
Ecuadorian	1	0.01
Peruvian	13	0.15
Other Hispanic or Latino	120	1.34

Race*	Population	%
African-American/Black (52)	117	1.31
Not Hispanic (45)	98	1.09
Hispanic (7)	19	0.21
American Indian/Alaska Native (124)	212	2.37
Not Hispanic (96)	165	1.84

*Notes: † The Census 2010 population figure is used to calculate the percentages in the Hispanic Origin and Race categories. Ancestry percentages are based on the 2006-2010 American Community Survey population (not shown); ‡ Numbers in parentheses indicate the number of people reporting a single ancestry; * Numbers in parentheses indicate the number of persons reporting this race alone, not in combination with any other race; Please refer to the Explanation of Data for more information.*

Hispanic (28)	47	0.52
Aleut *(Alaska Native)* (1)	1	0.01
Apache (3)	7	0.08
Blackfeet (0)	2	0.02
Cherokee (6)	15	0.17
Cheyenne (1)	1	0.01
Chickasaw (1)	3	0.03
Chippewa (2)	2	0.02
Choctaw (4)	10	0.11
Creek (0)	2	0.02
Hopi (2)	2	0.02
Inupiat *(Alaska Native)* (3)	3	0.03
Iroquois (4)	4	0.04
Mexican American Ind. (12)	12	0.13
Navajo (3)	3	0.03
Paiute (16)	25	0.28
Potawatomi (0)	1	0.01
Pueblo (1)	1	0.01
Seminole (0)	1	0.01
Shoshone (6)	9	0.10
Sioux (1)	1	0.01
Tlingit-Haida *(Alaska Native)* (4)	4	0.04
Ute (1)	2	0.02
Yaqui (0)	3	0.03
Yup'ik *(Alaska Native)* (1)	1	0.01
Asian (123)	220	2.45
Not Hispanic (111)	199	2.22
Hispanic (12)	21	0.23
Chinese, ex. Taiwanese (13)	26	0.29
Filipino (57)	110	1.23
Indian (19)	27	0.30
Indonesian (1)	1	0.01
Japanese (7)	19	0.21
Korean (10)	16	0.18
Taiwanese (3)	5	0.06
Thai (1)	2	0.02
Vietnamese (5)	6	0.07
Hawaii Native/Pacific Islander (12)	45	0.50
Not Hispanic (11)	42	0.47
Hispanic (1)	3	0.03
Guamanian/Chamorro (5)	7	0.08
Native Hawaiian (4)	22	0.25
Samoan (3)	12	0.13
White (7,776)	8,060	89.92
Not Hispanic (7,031)	7,233	80.69
Hispanic (745)	827	9.23

Elko

Place Type: City
County: Elko
Population: 18,297†

Ancestry‡	Population	%
African, Sub-Saharan (46)	46	0.26
Ghanaian (46)	46	0.26
American (3,011)	3,011	16.93
Australian (14)	14	0.08
Austrian (0)	8	0.04
Basque (200)	292	1.64
Belgian (0)	33	0.19
Brazilian (0)	13	0.07
British (23)	65	0.37
Canadian (40)	153	0.86
Croatian (0)	49	0.28
Czech (18)	25	0.14
Danish (42)	300	1.69
Dutch (15)	337	1.89
Eastern European (23)	23	0.13
English (575)	2,184	12.28
European (95)	113	0.64
Finnish (0)	57	0.32
French, ex. Basque (63)	387	2.18
French Canadian (0)	18	0.10
German (666)	2,637	14.83
Greek (162)	219	1.23
Hungarian (0)	29	0.16
Irish (496)	1,437	8.08
Italian (515)	1,002	5.63
Northern European (33)	33	0.19
Norwegian (131)	448	2.52
Polish (25)	191	1.07
Portuguese (18)	54	0.30
Russian (0)	38	0.21
Scandinavian (63)	123	0.69
Scotch-Irish (57)	238	1.34
Scottish (71)	364	2.05
Serbian (0)	9	0.05
Swedish (75)	346	1.95
Swiss (10)	83	0.47
Ukrainian (0)	13	0.07
Welsh (34)	325	1.83
Yugoslavian (0)	8	0.04

Hispanic Origin	Population	%
Hispanic or Latino (of any race)	4,824	26.36
Central American, ex. Mexican	25	0.14
Costa Rican	3	0.02
Guatemalan	6	0.03
Nicaraguan	5	0.03
Panamanian	1	0.01
Salvadoran	10	0.05
Cuban	3	0.02
Dominican Republic	4	0.02
Mexican	4,269	23.33
Puerto Rican	46	0.25
South American	68	0.37
Argentinean	1	0.01
Bolivian	2	0.01
Chilean	9	0.05
Colombian	7	0.04
Ecuadorian	2	0.01
Peruvian	41	0.22
Venezuelan	5	0.03
Other South American	1	0.01
Other Hispanic or Latino	409	2.24

Race*	Population	%
African-American/Black (183)	260	1.42
Not Hispanic (163)	218	1.19
Hispanic (20)	42	0.23
American Indian/Alaska Native (608)	841	4.60
Not Hispanic (497)	643	3.51
Hispanic (111)	198	1.08
Alaska Athabascan *(Ala. Nat.)* (2)	2	0.01
Apache (7)	9	0.05
Blackfeet (2)	5	0.03
Canadian/French Am. Ind. (1)	1	0.01
Central American Ind. (0)	3	0.02
Cherokee (17)	52	0.28
Cheyenne (0)	2	0.01
Chickasaw (3)	3	0.02
Chippewa (5)	8	0.04
Choctaw (5)	8	0.04
Comanche (1)	4	0.02
Hopi (1)	1	0.01
Inupiat *(Alaska Native)* (2)	2	0.01
Iroquois (4)	5	0.03
Kiowa (0)	1	0.01
Lumbee (1)	1	0.01
Mexican American Ind. (18)	20	0.11
Navajo (32)	41	0.22
Ottawa (2)	2	0.01
Paiute (29)	41	0.22
Pima (3)	3	0.02
Pueblo (2)	3	0.02
Puget Sound Salish (2)	2	0.01
Seminole (1)	2	0.01
Shoshone (85)	118	0.64
Sioux (5)	19	0.10
South American Ind. (2)	2	0.01
Tlingit-Haida *(Alaska Native)* (2)	6	0.03
Tohono O'Odham (0)	1	0.01
Tsimshian *(Alaska Native)* (1)	1	0.01
Ute (0)	1	0.01
Yuman (2)	5	0.03
Asian (249)	363	1.98
Not Hispanic (245)	337	1.84
Hispanic (4)	26	0.14
Chinese, ex. Taiwanese (73)	78	0.43
Filipino (61)	117	0.64
Indian (67)	83	0.45
Indonesian (3)	10	0.05
Japanese (13)	38	0.21
Korean (9)	19	0.10
Malaysian (1)	3	0.02
Thai (2)	2	0.01
Vietnamese (12)	15	0.08
Hawaii Native/Pacific Islander (18)	43	0.24
Not Hispanic (13)	29	0.16
Hispanic (5)	14	0.08
Guamanian/Chamorro (3)	4	0.02
Native Hawaiian (5)	9	0.05
Samoan (4)	13	0.07
Tongan (0)	8	0.04
White (14,430)	15,006	82.01
Not Hispanic (12,241)	12,513	68.39
Hispanic (2,189)	2,493	13.63

Enterprise

Place Type: CDP
County: Clark
Population: 108,481†

Ancestry‡	Population	%
Afghan (55)	55	0.06
African, Sub-Saharan (959)	1,148	1.15
African (279)	358	0.36
Cape Verdean (18)	42	0.04
Ethiopian (596)	596	0.60
Nigerian (43)	43	0.04
Somalian (0)	26	0.03
South African (0)	26	0.03
Other Sub-Saharan African (23)	57	0.06
Albanian (196)	218	0.22
Alsatian (0)	27	0.03
American (1,890)	1,890	1.90
Arab (763)	1,059	1.06
Arab (125)	143	0.14
Egyptian (22)	22	0.02
Jordanian (19)	57	0.06
Lebanese (517)	757	0.76
Moroccan (40)	40	0.04
Syrian (15)	15	0.02
Other Arab (25)	25	0.03
Armenian (149)	241	0.24
Assyrian/Chaldean/Syriac (16)	16	0.02
Australian (32)	32	0.03
Austrian (35)	206	0.21
Basque (36)	45	0.05
Belgian (0)	67	0.07
Brazilian (64)	98	0.10
British (218)	316	0.32
Bulgarian (244)	255	0.26
Canadian (226)	304	0.31
Celtic (0)	11	0.01
Croatian (9)	207	0.21
Czech (237)	477	0.48
Czechoslovakian (30)	139	0.14
Danish (48)	274	0.28
Dutch (126)	1,029	1.03
Eastern European (69)	113	0.11
English (1,645)	6,039	6.07
European (1,009)	1,201	1.21
Finnish (125)	315	0.32
French, ex. Basque (468)	2,246	2.26
French Canadian (508)	790	0.79
German (3,121)	11,862	11.92
Greek (92)	249	0.25
Hungarian (340)	536	0.54
Icelander (16)	16	0.02
Iranian (236)	236	0.24
Irish (2,456)	10,311	10.36
Israeli (63)	63	0.06
Italian (2,626)	6,957	6.99
Latvian (15)	15	0.02
Lithuanian (0)	25	0.03
Macedonian (107)	107	0.11
Maltese (67)	67	0.07

*Notes: † The Census 2010 population figure is used to calculate the percentages in the Hispanic Origin and Race categories. Ancestry percentages are based on the 2006-2010 American Community Survey population (not shown); ‡ Numbers in parentheses indicate the number of people reporting a single ancestry; * Numbers in parentheses indicate the number of persons reporting this race alone, not in combination with any other race; Please refer to the Explanation of Data for more information.*

New Zealander (9)	9	0.01
Norwegian (289)	995	1.00
Polish (1,002)	2,841	2.85
Portuguese (50)	282	0.28
Romanian (184)	251	0.25
Russian (265)	924	0.93
Scandinavian (57)	109	0.11
Scotch-Irish (285)	932	0.94
Scottish (380)	1,357	1.36
Serbian (236)	276	0.28
Slavic (31)	58	0.06
Slovak (44)	126	0.13
Slovene (46)	102	0.10
Swedish (507)	1,544	1.55
Swiss (44)	247	0.25
Turkish (317)	375	0.38
Ukrainian (16)	117	0.12
Welsh (20)	377	0.38
West Indian, ex. Hispanic (298)	372	0.37
Bahamian (0)	13	0.01
Belizean (6)	17	0.02
Haitian (110)	110	0.11
Jamaican (74)	91	0.09
Trinidadian/Tobagonian (44)	55	0.06
West Indian (64)	86	0.09
Yugoslavian (483)	498	0.50

Hispanic Origin	Population	%
Hispanic or Latino (of any race)	18,755	17.29
Central American, ex. Mexican	1,513	1.39
Costa Rican	58	0.05
Guatemalan	335	0.31
Honduran	109	0.10
Nicaraguan	160	0.15
Panamanian	98	0.09
Salvadoran	745	0.69
Other Central American	8	0.01
Cuban	921	0.85
Dominican Republic	170	0.16
Mexican	11,974	11.04
Puerto Rican	1,227	1.13
South American	1,091	1.01
Argentinean	204	0.19
Bolivian	14	0.01
Chilean	87	0.08
Colombian	349	0.32
Ecuadorian	123	0.11
Peruvian	226	0.21
Uruguayan	15	0.01
Venezuelan	52	0.05
Other South American	21	0.02
Other Hispanic or Latino	1,859	1.71

Race*	Population	%
African-American/Black (8,793)	10,600	9.77
Not Hispanic (8,416)	9,872	9.10
Hispanic (377)	728	0.67
American Indian/Alaska Native (641)	1,539	1.42
Not Hispanic (445)	1,114	1.03
Hispanic (196)	425	0.39
Alaska Athabascan *(Ala. Nat.)* (1)	1	<0.01
Aleut *(Alaska Native)* (8)	8	0.01
Apache (10)	55	0.05
Arapaho (2)	3	<0.01
Blackfeet (5)	31	0.03
Canadian/French Am. Ind. (0)	2	<0.01
Cherokee (58)	229	0.21
Chickasaw (4)	16	0.01
Chippewa (14)	32	0.03
Choctaw (11)	49	0.05
Colville (2)	4	<0.01
Comanche (1)	5	<0.01
Cree (2)	4	<0.01
Creek (8)	21	0.02
Crow (2)	2	<0.01
Delaware (2)	3	<0.01
Hopi (5)	7	0.01
Inupiat *(Alaska Native)* (2)	3	<0.01
Iroquois (4)	17	0.02
Kiowa (1)	2	<0.01
Lumbee (3)	3	<0.01
Menominee (0)	1	<0.01
Mexican American Ind. (20)	41	0.04
Navajo (87)	121	0.11
Osage (3)	5	<0.01
Paiute (7)	9	0.01
Pima (2)	2	<0.01
Potawatomi (3)	4	<0.01
Pueblo (19)	24	0.02
Puget Sound Salish (1)	1	<0.01
Seminole (0)	6	0.01
Shoshone (4)	10	0.01
Sioux (21)	50	0.05
South American Ind. (5)	11	0.01
Spanish American Ind. (1)	2	<0.01
Tlingit-Haida *(Alaska Native)* (3)	8	0.01
Tohono O'Odham (1)	4	<0.01
Tsimshian *(Alaska Native)* (0)	2	<0.01
Ute (1)	1	<0.01
Yakama (1)	1	<0.01
Yaqui (9)	14	0.01
Yuman (7)	9	0.01
Yup'ik *(Alaska Native)* (1)	3	<0.01
Asian (23,032)	26,600	24.52
Not Hispanic (22,774)	25,795	23.78
Hispanic (258)	805	0.74
Bangladeshi (24)	29	0.03
Burmese (57)	63	0.06
Cambodian (156)	211	0.19
Chinese, ex. Taiwanese (3,904)	4,857	4.48
Filipino (11,973)	14,074	12.97
Hmong (27)	36	0.03
Indian (873)	1,100	1.01
Indonesian (61)	102	0.09
Japanese (802)	1,647	1.52
Korean (1,621)	2,032	1.87
Laotian (229)	289	0.27
Malaysian (14)	24	0.02
Nepalese (1)	3	<0.01
Pakistani (117)	162	0.15
Sri Lankan (39)	54	0.05
Taiwanese (104)	144	0.13
Thai (579)	767	0.71
Vietnamese (1,462)	1,732	1.60
Hawaii Native/Pacific Islander (1,025)	2,004	1.85
Not Hispanic (940)	1,779	1.64
Hispanic (85)	225	0.21
Fijian (12)	19	0.02
Guamanian/Chamorro (255)	349	0.32
Marshallese (1)	1	<0.01
Native Hawaiian (388)	1,064	0.98
Samoan (222)	331	0.31
Tongan (21)	49	0.05
White (61,035)	66,316	61.13
Not Hispanic (52,166)	56,003	51.62
Hispanic (8,869)	10,313	9.51

Fallon

Place Type: City
County: Churchill
Population: 8,606†

Ancestry‡	Population	%
African, Sub-Saharan (4)	4	0.05
South African (4)	4	0.05
American (363)	363	4.24
Arab (0)	47	0.55
Syrian (0)	47	0.55
Austrian (7)	7	0.08
Basque (88)	125	1.46
Danish (16)	37	0.43
Dutch (0)	205	2.39
English (1,000)	1,795	20.97
European (34)	123	1.44
Finnish (40)	40	0.47
French, ex. Basque (49)	443	5.18
French Canadian (0)	12	0.14
German (305)	1,473	17.21
Greek (0)	43	0.50
Irish (331)	1,452	16.96
Italian (103)	588	6.87
Lithuanian (22)	22	0.26
Norwegian (18)	186	2.17
Polish (15)	143	1.67
Portuguese (64)	140	1.64
Russian (11)	29	0.34
Scandinavian (0)	47	0.55
Scotch-Irish (33)	116	1.36
Scottish (151)	357	4.17
Swedish (20)	155	1.81
Welsh (35)	272	3.18

Hispanic Origin	Population	%
Hispanic or Latino (of any race)	1,102	12.81
Central American, ex. Mexican	20	0.23
Guatemalan	2	0.02
Honduran	3	0.03
Nicaraguan	3	0.03
Salvadoran	12	0.14
Cuban	11	0.13
Dominican Republic	2	0.02
Mexican	874	10.16
Puerto Rican	54	0.63
South American	14	0.16
Argentinean	3	0.03
Colombian	1	0.01
Ecuadorian	3	0.03
Peruvian	6	0.07
Uruguayan	1	0.01
Other Hispanic or Latino	127	1.48

Race*	Population	%
African-American/Black (240)	375	4.36
Not Hispanic (223)	332	3.86
Hispanic (17)	43	0.50
American Indian/Alaska Native (251)	424	4.93
Not Hispanic (209)	337	3.92
Hispanic (42)	87	1.01
Alaska Athabascan *(Ala. Nat.)* (2)	8	0.09
Apache (5)	6	0.07
Blackfeet (6)	13	0.15
Canadian/French Am. Ind. (1)	1	0.01
Cherokee (14)	36	0.42
Cheyenne (1)	1	0.01
Chickasaw (0)	7	0.08
Chippewa (7)	7	0.08
Choctaw (2)	2	0.02
Cree (0)	1	0.01
Creek (2)	2	0.02
Crow (0)	2	0.02
Delaware (0)	1	0.01
Inupiat *(Alaska Native)* (5)	7	0.08
Lumbee (2)	2	0.02
Mexican American Ind. (8)	8	0.09
Navajo (13)	19	0.22
Paiute (17)	31	0.36
Pima (1)	2	0.02
Pueblo (7)	7	0.08
Shoshone (28)	37	0.43
Sioux (5)	15	0.17
Tlingit-Haida *(Alaska Native)* (0)	1	0.01
Ute (2)	4	0.05
Yaqui (0)	2	0.02
Yuman (2)	3	0.03
Asian (384)	580	6.74
Not Hispanic (368)	538	6.25
Hispanic (16)	42	0.49
Chinese, ex. Taiwanese (24)	41	0.48
Filipino (285)	427	4.96
Indian (31)	35	0.41
Indonesian (1)	1	0.01
Japanese (22)	63	0.73
Korean (3)	6	0.07
Thai (5)	13	0.15
Vietnamese (5)	9	0.10
Hawaii Native/Pacific Islander (17)	76	0.88
Not Hispanic (16)	72	0.84
Hispanic (1)	4	0.05
Guamanian/Chamorro (5)	21	0.24

*Notes: † The Census 2010 population figure is used to calculate the percentages in the Hispanic Origin and Race categories. Ancestry percentages are based on the 2006-2010 American Community Survey population (not shown); ‡ Numbers in parentheses indicate the number of people reporting a single ancestry; * Numbers in parentheses indicate the number of persons reporting this race alone, not in combination with any other race; Please refer to the Explanation of Data for more information.*

Native Hawaiian (3)	34	0.40
Samoan (9)	9	0.10
Tongan (0)	1	0.01
White (6,791)	7,202	83.69
Not Hispanic (6,299)	6,610	76.81
Hispanic (492)	592	6.88

Fernley

Place Type: City
County: Lyon
Population: 19,368†

Ancestry‡	Population	%
American (1,174)	1,174	6.39
Armenian (0)	24	0.13
Basque (61)	202	1.10
Belgian (0)	15	0.08
Canadian (162)	204	1.11
Celtic (98)	98	0.53
Czech (45)	45	0.24
Danish (19)	77	0.42
Dutch (47)	163	0.89
English (1,987)	3,524	19.18
European (26)	26	0.14
Finnish (35)	107	0.58
French, ex. Basque (0)	447	2.43
French Canadian (73)	169	0.92
German (1,063)	2,750	14.96
Greek (39)	39	0.21
Hungarian (17)	134	0.73
Icelander (62)	62	0.34
Irish (873)	2,520	13.71
Italian (504)	970	5.28
Macedonian (22)	22	0.12
Norwegian (218)	426	2.32
Polish (83)	215	1.17
Portuguese (22)	48	0.26
Russian (40)	132	0.72
Scotch-Irish (326)	648	3.53
Scottish (137)	490	2.67
Slavic (0)	9	0.05
Swedish (32)	172	0.94
Swiss (0)	12	0.07
Welsh (58)	193	1.05
West Indian, ex. Hispanic (94)	144	0.78
Jamaican (94)	144	0.78
Yugoslavian (20)	20	0.11

Hispanic Origin	Population	%
Hispanic or Latino (of any race)	2,785	14.38
Central American, ex. Mexican	135	0.70
Costa Rican	14	0.07
Guatemalan	37	0.19
Honduran	5	0.03
Nicaraguan	11	0.06
Salvadoran	66	0.34
Other Central American	2	0.01
Cuban	9	0.05
Mexican	2,254	11.64
Puerto Rican	98	0.51
South American	40	0.21
Argentinean	14	0.07
Chilean	1	0.01
Colombian	10	0.05
Ecuadorian	5	0.03
Peruvian	4	0.02
Venezuelan	6	0.03
Other Hispanic or Latino	249	1.29

Race*	Population	%
African-American/Black (202)	368	1.90
Not Hispanic (179)	324	1.67
Hispanic (23)	44	0.23
American Indian/Alaska Native (343)	702	3.62
Not Hispanic (283)	579	2.99
Hispanic (60)	123	0.64
Aleut *(Alaska Native)* (1)	1	0.01
Apache (5)	11	0.06
Blackfeet (0)	6	0.03
Canadian/French Am. Ind. (0)	5	0.03
Cherokee (22)	100	0.52
Chickasaw (1)	8	0.04
Chippewa (5)	9	0.05
Choctaw (9)	31	0.16
Colville (6)	6	0.03
Comanche (1)	1	0.01
Cree (0)	2	0.01
Creek (0)	2	0.01
Delaware (0)	1	0.01
Hopi (8)	8	0.04
Iroquois (2)	12	0.06
Lumbee (0)	3	0.02
Menominee (2)	2	0.01
Mexican American Ind. (0)	2	0.01
Navajo (11)	23	0.12
Osage (2)	3	0.02
Ottawa (0)	4	0.02
Paiute (79)	121	0.62
Pima (0)	1	0.01
Potawatomi (3)	11	0.06
Pueblo (5)	7	0.04
Seminole (0)	2	0.01
Shoshone (6)	14	0.07
Sioux (19)	43	0.22
South American Ind. (0)	1	0.01
Tohono O'Odham (3)	5	0.03
Ute (1)	2	0.01
Yaqui (7)	7	0.04
Asian (394)	586	3.03
Not Hispanic (386)	542	2.80
Hispanic (8)	44	0.23
Burmese (0)	2	0.01
Cambodian (2)	2	0.01
Chinese, ex. Taiwanese (36)	65	0.34
Filipino (183)	295	1.52
Indian (28)	35	0.18
Indonesian (1)	4	0.02
Japanese (51)	79	0.41
Korean (29)	42	0.22
Laotian (4)	7	0.04
Pakistani (4)	5	0.03
Taiwanese (7)	7	0.04
Thai (22)	28	0.14
Vietnamese (20)	30	0.15
Hawaii Native/Pacific Islander (69)	143	0.74
Not Hispanic (67)	137	0.71
Hispanic (2)	6	0.03
Fijian (2)	2	0.01
Guamanian/Chamorro (6)	22	0.11
Marshallese (4)	4	0.02
Native Hawaiian (18)	56	0.29
Samoan (17)	23	0.12
Tongan (12)	15	0.08
White (16,374)	17,178	88.69
Not Hispanic (15,024)	15,587	80.48
Hispanic (1,350)	1,591	8.21

Gardnerville Ranchos

Place Type: CDP
County: Douglas
Population: 11,312†

Ancestry‡	Population	%
American (631)	631	5.32
Austrian (0)	48	0.40
Basque (10)	40	0.34
Belgian (0)	76	0.64
Canadian (52)	88	0.74
Croatian (14)	37	0.31
Czech (0)	30	0.25
Czechoslovakian (17)	17	0.14
Danish (35)	203	1.71
Dutch (34)	321	2.71
Eastern European (7)	7	0.06
English (481)	2,043	17.23
European (201)	238	2.01
Finnish (39)	126	1.06
French, ex. Basque (115)	661	5.57
French Canadian (16)	70	0.59
German (557)	2,833	23.89
Greek (11)	28	0.24
Hungarian (0)	23	0.19
Icelander (13)	47	0.40
Irish (404)	2,499	21.08
Italian (349)	889	7.50
Latvian (0)	39	0.33
Lithuanian (40)	40	0.34
Norwegian (128)	525	4.43
Pennsylvania German (0)	12	0.10
Polish (135)	391	3.30
Portuguese (28)	198	1.67
Russian (35)	171	1.44
Scotch-Irish (63)	145	1.22
Scottish (172)	480	4.05
Slovak (0)	38	0.32
Swedish (72)	353	2.98
Swiss (0)	47	0.40
Ukrainian (0)	32	0.27
Welsh (45)	144	1.21

Hispanic Origin	Population	%
Hispanic or Latino (of any race)	1,444	12.77
Central American, ex. Mexican	55	0.49
Costa Rican	5	0.04
Guatemalan	10	0.09
Honduran	3	0.03
Nicaraguan	5	0.04
Salvadoran	32	0.28
Cuban	10	0.09
Mexican	1,077	9.52
Puerto Rican	81	0.72
South American	45	0.40
Argentinean	10	0.09
Chilean	3	0.03
Colombian	27	0.24
Ecuadorian	1	0.01
Peruvian	1	0.01
Venezuelan	3	0.03
Other Hispanic or Latino	176	1.56

Race*	Population	%
African-American/Black (53)	112	0.99
Not Hispanic (46)	83	0.73
Hispanic (7)	29	0.26
American Indian/Alaska Native (320)	508	4.49
Not Hispanic (258)	399	3.53
Hispanic (62)	109	0.96
Aleut *(Alaska Native)* (1)	1	0.01
Apache (2)	6	0.05
Arapaho (0)	2	0.02
Blackfeet (5)	15	0.13
Canadian/French Am. Ind. (1)	1	0.01
Cherokee (8)	27	0.24
Cheyenne (1)	3	0.03
Chickasaw (2)	5	0.04
Chippewa (1)	2	0.02
Choctaw (1)	4	0.04
Comanche (1)	1	0.01
Creek (0)	1	0.01
Crow (2)	2	0.02
Hopi (1)	1	0.01
Inupiat *(Alaska Native)* (1)	1	0.01
Iroquois (0)	3	0.03
Kiowa (1)	2	0.02
Mexican American Ind. (16)	18	0.16
Navajo (2)	3	0.03
Osage (0)	1	0.01
Paiute (15)	25	0.22
Pima (0)	2	0.02
Potawatomi (2)	2	0.02
Pueblo (3)	11	0.10
Shoshone (5)	15	0.13
Sioux (10)	18	0.16
South American Ind. (0)	1	0.01
Yaqui (0)	1	0.01
Yuman (2)	8	0.07
Asian (123)	263	2.32
Not Hispanic (116)	231	2.04

*Notes: † The Census 2010 population figure is used to calculate the percentages in the Hispanic Origin and Race categories. Ancestry percentages are based on the 2006-2010 American Community Survey population (not shown); ‡ Numbers in parentheses indicate the number of people reporting a single ancestry; * Numbers in parentheses indicate the number of persons reporting this race alone, not in combination with any other race; Please refer to the Explanation of Data for more information.*

Hispanic (7)	32	0.28
Burmese (0)	1	0.01
Chinese, ex. Taiwanese (15)	25	0.22
Filipino (49)	129	1.14
Indian (8)	15	0.13
Indonesian (1)	4	0.04
Japanese (33)	62	0.55
Korean (10)	23	0.20
Malaysian (1)	1	0.01
Pakistani (1)	1	0.01
Vietnamese (4)	5	0.04
Hawaii Native/Pacific Islander (21)	63	0.56
Not Hispanic (19)	50	0.44
Hispanic (2)	13	0.11
Guamanian/Chamorro (2)	13	0.11
Native Hawaiian (6)	18	0.16
Samoan (3)	13	0.11
Tongan (1)	6	0.05
White (9,888)	10,350	91.50
Not Hispanic (9,117)	9,416	83.24
Hispanic (771)	934	8.26

Henderson

Place Type: City
County: Clark
Population: 257,729†

Ancestry‡	Population	%
African, Sub-Saharan (1,002)	1,471	0.59
African (669)	1,034	0.41
Ethiopian (115)	175	0.07
Ghanaian (0)	14	0.01
Nigerian (58)	78	0.03
South African (97)	107	0.04
Sudanese (14)	14	0.01
Ugandan (11)	11	<0.01
Other Sub-Saharan African (38)	38	0.02
Albanian (14)	36	0.01
American (11,216)	11,216	4.50
Arab (1,262)	1,830	0.73
Arab (162)	273	0.11
Egyptian (311)	417	0.17
Iraqi (161)	169	0.07
Jordanian (30)	30	0.01
Lebanese (196)	358	0.14
Moroccan (63)	135	0.05
Palestinian (86)	86	0.03
Syrian (82)	191	0.08
Other Arab (171)	171	0.07
Armenian (555)	626	0.25
Assyrian/Chaldean/Syriac (78)	78	0.03
Australian (61)	131	0.05
Austrian (308)	847	0.34
Basque (39)	117	0.05
Belgian (129)	351	0.14
Brazilian (325)	381	0.15
British (635)	1,154	0.46
Bulgarian (114)	138	0.06
Cajun (23)	34	0.01
Canadian (846)	1,230	0.49
Carpatho Rusyn (5)	5	<0.01
Celtic (0)	34	0.01
Croatian (203)	518	0.21
Czech (347)	1,176	0.47
Czechoslovakian (194)	340	0.14
Danish (619)	2,803	1.12
Dutch (705)	4,574	1.84
Eastern European (311)	416	0.17
English (9,758)	29,502	11.84
Estonian (29)	35	0.01
European (2,501)	2,716	1.09
Finnish (222)	502	0.20
French, ex. Basque (1,402)	7,568	3.04
French Canadian (687)	1,654	0.66
German (13,309)	43,626	17.50
Greek (743)	1,492	0.60
Hungarian (784)	1,979	0.79
Icelander (0)	67	0.03
Iranian (898)	1,089	0.44
Irish (8,412)	31,572	12.67
Israeli (202)	273	0.11
Italian (9,968)	21,945	8.80
Latvian (16)	55	0.02
Lithuanian (265)	673	0.27
Luxemburger (9)	21	0.01
Macedonian (20)	87	0.03
Maltese (12)	37	0.01
New Zealander (78)	78	0.03
Northern European (222)	242	0.10
Norwegian (1,577)	4,967	1.99
Pennsylvania German (68)	68	0.03
Polish (2,601)	8,939	3.59
Portuguese (370)	1,368	0.55
Romanian (230)	454	0.18
Russian (1,888)	3,752	1.51
Scandinavian (257)	727	0.29
Scotch-Irish (1,492)	4,608	1.85
Scottish (1,998)	6,213	2.49
Serbian (41)	139	0.06
Slavic (34)	94	0.04
Slovak (153)	553	0.22
Slovene (25)	105	0.04
Swedish (1,030)	4,820	1.93
Swiss (186)	1,372	0.55
Turkish (43)	97	0.04
Ukrainian (258)	762	0.31
Welsh (242)	2,051	0.82
West Indian, ex. Hispanic (236)	504	0.20
Barbadian (0)	7	<0.01
Belizean (22)	61	0.02
British West Indian (15)	15	0.01
Haitian (16)	69	0.03
Jamaican (112)	225	0.09
Trinidadian/Tobagonian (38)	53	0.02
West Indian (33)	74	0.03
Yugoslavian (138)	265	0.11

Hispanic Origin	Population	%
Hispanic or Latino (of any race)	38,377	14.89
Central American, ex. Mexican	2,333	0.91
Costa Rican	119	0.05
Guatemalan	545	0.21
Honduran	173	0.07
Nicaraguan	315	0.12
Panamanian	171	0.07
Salvadoran	992	0.38
Other Central American	18	0.01
Cuban	1,550	0.60
Dominican Republic	201	0.08
Mexican	25,405	9.86
Puerto Rican	2,325	0.90
South American	2,157	0.84
Argentinean	437	0.17
Bolivian	69	0.03
Chilean	173	0.07
Colombian	592	0.23
Ecuadorian	199	0.08
Paraguayan	12	<0.01
Peruvian	493	0.19
Uruguayan	41	0.02
Venezuelan	122	0.05
Other South American	19	0.01
Other Hispanic or Latino	4,406	1.71

Race*	Population	%
African-American/Black (13,142)	16,439	6.38
Not Hispanic (12,471)	15,109	5.86
Hispanic (671)	1,330	0.52
American Indian/Alaska Native (1,683)	3,737	1.45
Not Hispanic (1,182)	2,708	1.05
Hispanic (501)	1,029	0.40
Alaska Athabascan *(Ala. Nat.)* (6)	7	<0.01
Aleut *(Alaska Native)* (6)	6	<0.01
Apache (66)	133	0.05
Arapaho (5)	7	<0.01
Blackfeet (15)	105	0.04
Canadian/French Am. Ind. (5)	9	<0.01
Central American Ind. (2)	3	<0.01
Cherokee (152)	571	0.22
Cheyenne (5)	10	<0.01
Chickasaw (27)	50	0.02
Chippewa (37)	72	0.03
Choctaw (74)	164	0.06
Comanche (5)	14	0.01
Cree (2)	4	<0.01
Creek (11)	32	0.01
Crow (1)	4	<0.01
Delaware (1)	3	<0.01
Hopi (7)	16	0.01
Houma (2)	2	<0.01
Inupiat *(Alaska Native)* (8)	12	<0.01
Iroquois (21)	61	0.02
Kiowa (0)	1	<0.01
Lumbee (5)	5	<0.01
Menominee (8)	10	<0.01
Mexican American Ind. (51)	90	0.03
Navajo (221)	307	0.12
Osage (6)	19	0.01
Ottawa (9)	16	0.01
Paiute (53)	70	0.03
Pima (0)	1	<0.01
Potawatomi (19)	31	0.01
Pueblo (37)	53	0.02
Puget Sound Salish (2)	2	<0.01
Seminole (1)	15	0.01
Shoshone (16)	25	0.01
Sioux (49)	110	0.04
South American Ind. (11)	25	0.01
Spanish American Ind. (17)	20	0.01
Tlingit-Haida *(Alaska Native)* (16)	21	0.01
Tohono O'Odham (1)	7	<0.01
Ute (4)	13	0.01
Yakama (8)	8	<0.01
Yaqui (10)	20	0.01
Yuman (10)	13	0.01
Yup'ik *(Alaska Native)* (3)	6	<0.01
Asian (18,614)	24,315	9.43
Not Hispanic (18,172)	23,003	8.93
Hispanic (442)	1,312	0.51
Bangladeshi (12)	13	0.01
Burmese (16)	21	0.01
Cambodian (61)	87	0.03
Chinese, ex. Taiwanese (2,283)	3,594	1.39
Filipino (8,641)	11,525	4.47
Hmong (21)	25	0.01
Indian (1,465)	1,726	0.67
Indonesian (68)	136	0.05
Japanese (1,616)	3,074	1.19
Korean (1,734)	2,338	0.91
Laotian (101)	127	0.05
Malaysian (9)	19	0.01
Nepalese (30)	30	0.01
Pakistani (209)	241	0.09
Sri Lankan (60)	69	0.03
Taiwanese (139)	174	0.07
Thai (430)	686	0.27
Vietnamese (877)	1,124	0.44
Hawaii Native/Pacific Islander (1,445)	3,287	1.28
Not Hispanic (1,354)	2,913	1.13
Hispanic (91)	374	0.15
Fijian (39)	69	0.03
Guamanian/Chamorro (199)	363	0.14
Native Hawaiian (636)	1,846	0.72
Samoan (304)	543	0.21
Tongan (90)	144	0.06
White (198,170)	208,655	80.96
Not Hispanic (177,039)	184,438	71.56
Hispanic (21,131)	24,217	9.40

Incline Village

Place Type: CDP
County: Washoe
Population: 8,777†

Ancestry‡	Population	%
American (230)	230	2.68
Arab (0)	18	0.21
Palestinian (0)	18	0.21

*Notes: † The Census 2010 population figure is used to calculate the percentages in the Hispanic Origin and Race categories. Ancestry percentages are based on the 2006-2010 American Community Survey population (not shown); ‡ Numbers in parentheses indicate the number of people reporting a single ancestry; * Numbers in parentheses indicate the number of persons reporting this race alone, not in combination with any other race; Please refer to the Explanation of Data for more information.*

Austrian (59)	74	0.86
Belgian (0)	48	0.56
British (47)	60	0.70
Canadian (18)	18	0.21
Croatian (0)	14	0.16
Czech (23)	54	0.63
Danish (9)	9	0.10
Dutch (0)	107	1.25
Eastern European (40)	40	0.47
English (187)	931	10.83
European (55)	55	0.64
Finnish (0)	53	0.62
French, ex. Basque (38)	269	3.13
French Canadian (61)	61	0.71
German (439)	1,302	15.15
Greek (6)	23	0.27
Hungarian (13)	30	0.35
Irish (258)	871	10.13
Italian (415)	693	8.06
Lithuanian (24)	54	0.63
Northern European (39)	39	0.45
Norwegian (212)	399	4.64
Polish (135)	338	3.93
Portuguese (0)	56	0.65
Romanian (64)	81	0.94
Russian (139)	234	2.72
Scandinavian (44)	104	1.21
Scotch-Irish (78)	210	2.44
Scottish (84)	344	4.00
Slovene (27)	27	0.31
Swedish (57)	208	2.42
Swiss (36)	131	1.52
Ukrainian (29)	29	0.34
Welsh (0)	76	0.88
West Indian, ex. Hispanic (0)	17	0.20
Jamaican (0)	17	0.20

Hispanic Origin	Population	%
Hispanic or Latino (of any race)	1,560	17.77
Central American, ex. Mexican	76	0.87
Costa Rican	7	0.08
Guatemalan	14	0.16
Honduran	3	0.03
Nicaraguan	9	0.10
Salvadoran	43	0.49
Cuban	7	0.08
Dominican Republic	3	0.03
Mexican	1,248	14.22
Puerto Rican	21	0.24
South American	44	0.50
Argentinean	1	0.01
Bolivian	24	0.27
Chilean	1	0.01
Colombian	2	0.02
Ecuadorian	1	0.01
Peruvian	13	0.15
Other South American	2	0.02
Other Hispanic or Latino	161	1.83

Race*	Population	%
African-American/Black (28)	53	0.60
Not Hispanic (23)	45	0.51
Hispanic (5)	8	0.09
American Indian/Alaska Native (28)	61	0.69
Not Hispanic (23)	49	0.56
Hispanic (5)	12	0.14
Apache (3)	6	0.07
Canadian/French Am. Ind. (1)	1	0.01
Cherokee (3)	13	0.15
Chickasaw (0)	3	0.03
Choctaw (2)	6	0.07
Mexican American Ind. (0)	1	0.01
Navajo (1)	1	0.01
Paiute (1)	1	0.01
Shoshone (0)	2	0.02
Asian (189)	267	3.04
Not Hispanic (182)	256	2.92
Hispanic (7)	11	0.13
Bhutanese (2)	2	0.02
Chinese, ex. Taiwanese (65)	85	0.97
Filipino (27)	54	0.62
Indian (20)	37	0.42
Japanese (24)	36	0.41
Korean (13)	16	0.18
Nepalese (1)	2	0.02
Taiwanese (7)	11	0.13
Thai (12)	17	0.19
Vietnamese (8)	10	0.11
Hawaii Native/Pacific Islander (7)	16	0.18
Not Hispanic (6)	13	0.15
Hispanic (1)	3	0.03
Guamanian/Chamorro (0)	2	0.02
Native Hawaiian (4)	9	0.10
Samoan (1)	1	0.01
White (7,631)	7,805	88.93
Not Hispanic (6,839)	6,960	79.30
Hispanic (792)	845	9.63

Las Vegas

Place Type: City
County: Clark
Population: 583,756†

Ancestry‡	Population	%
Afghan (75)	75	0.01
African, Sub-Saharan (6,588)	7,982	1.38
African (5,570)	6,715	1.16
Cape Verdean (0)	13	<0.01
Ethiopian (363)	431	0.07
Ghanaian (131)	131	0.02
Kenyan (86)	86	0.01
Nigerian (105)	122	0.02
Somalian (96)	96	0.02
South African (92)	103	0.02
Sudanese (28)	34	0.01
Ugandan (0)	44	0.01
Other Sub-Saharan African (117)	207	0.04
Albanian (281)	305	0.05
Alsatian (0)	23	<0.01
American (14,662)	14,662	2.53
Arab (1,990)	2,731	0.47
Arab (204)	220	0.04
Egyptian (349)	408	0.07
Iraqi (135)	147	0.03
Jordanian (44)	44	0.01
Lebanese (723)	1,259	0.22
Moroccan (79)	112	0.02
Palestinian (94)	94	0.02
Syrian (140)	189	0.03
Other Arab (222)	258	0.04
Armenian (1,103)	1,393	0.24
Assyrian/Chaldean/Syriac (162)	221	0.04
Australian (183)	241	0.04
Austrian (434)	1,545	0.27
Basque (59)	183	0.03
Belgian (133)	558	0.10
Brazilian (419)	552	0.10
British (929)	1,999	0.34
Bulgarian (420)	466	0.08
Cajun (10)	73	0.01
Canadian (777)	1,377	0.24
Celtic (16)	79	0.01
Croatian (345)	937	0.16
Czech (573)	2,336	0.40
Czechoslovakian (169)	483	0.08
Danish (836)	3,165	0.55
Dutch (1,663)	6,095	1.05
Eastern European (169)	245	0.04
English (13,556)	41,166	7.10
Estonian (16)	26	<0.01
European (4,311)	5,130	0.88
Finnish (210)	921	0.16
French, ex. Basque (2,774)	13,806	2.38
French Canadian (961)	2,086	0.36
German (20,033)	67,142	11.58
German Russian (32)	53	0.01
Greek (1,324)	2,578	0.44
Guyanese (52)	52	0.01
Hungarian (1,358)	3,106	0.54
Icelander (30)	132	0.02
Iranian (1,279)	1,319	0.23
Irish (15,709)	50,836	8.77
Israeli (341)	405	0.07
Italian (16,809)	38,013	6.56
Latvian (57)	135	0.02
Lithuanian (464)	1,029	0.18
Luxemburger (13)	98	0.02
Macedonian (102)	126	0.02
Maltese (285)	365	0.06
New Zealander (36)	36	0.01
Northern European (184)	278	0.05
Norwegian (2,157)	6,993	1.21
Pennsylvania German (89)	127	0.02
Polish (6,355)	15,542	2.68
Portuguese (561)	1,855	0.32
Romanian (537)	1,179	0.20
Russian (3,535)	7,526	1.30
Scandinavian (477)	1,029	0.18
Scotch-Irish (2,144)	6,246	1.08
Scottish (3,128)	9,277	1.60
Serbian (185)	398	0.07
Slavic (17)	232	0.04
Slovak (277)	715	0.12
Slovene (40)	121	0.02
Swedish (1,791)	6,296	1.09
Swiss (335)	1,327	0.23
Turkish (279)	408	0.07
Ukrainian (634)	1,333	0.23
Welsh (566)	3,194	0.55
West Indian, ex. Hispanic (905)	1,736	0.30
Barbadian (16)	43	0.01
Belizean (308)	335	0.06
British West Indian (42)	53	0.01
Dutch West Indian (0)	12	<0.01
Haitian (131)	276	0.05
Jamaican (296)	636	0.11
Trinidadian/Tobagonian (0)	30	0.01
West Indian (112)	351	0.06
Yugoslavian (422)	545	0.09

Hispanic Origin	Population	%
Hispanic or Latino (of any race)	183,859	31.50
Central American, ex. Mexican	15,318	2.62
Costa Rican	292	0.05
Guatemalan	3,592	0.62
Honduran	1,360	0.23
Nicaraguan	1,217	0.21
Panamanian	367	0.06
Salvadoran	8,392	1.44
Other Central American	98	0.02
Cuban	5,471	0.94
Dominican Republic	700	0.12
Mexican	140,104	24.00
Puerto Rican	5,209	0.89
South American	4,838	0.83
Argentinean	935	0.16
Bolivian	95	0.02
Chilean	467	0.08
Colombian	1,297	0.22
Ecuadorian	537	0.09
Paraguayan	30	0.01
Peruvian	1,068	0.18
Uruguayan	117	0.02
Venezuelan	230	0.04
Other South American	62	0.01
Other Hispanic or Latino	12,219	2.09

Race*	Population	%
African-American/Black (64,858)	74,093	12.69
Not Hispanic (62,008)	69,157	11.85
Hispanic (2,850)	4,936	0.85
American Indian/Alaska Native (4,125)	8,917	1.53
Not Hispanic (2,391)	5,708	0.98
Hispanic (1,734)	3,209	0.55
Alaska Athabascan *(Ala. Nat.)* (7)	18	<0.01
Aleut *(Alaska Native)* (9)	18	<0.01
Apache (117)	264	0.05
Arapaho (7)	13	<0.01
Blackfeet (45)	263	0.05

*Notes: † The Census 2010 population figure is used to calculate the percentages in the Hispanic Origin and Race categories. Ancestry percentages are based on the 2006-2010 American Community Survey population (not shown); ‡ Numbers in parentheses indicate the number of people reporting a single ancestry; * Numbers in parentheses indicate the number of persons reporting this race alone, not in combination with any other race; Please refer to the Explanation of Data for more information.*

Canadian/French Am. Ind. (10)	27	<0.01
Central American Ind. (18)	39	0.01
Cherokee (248)	1,213	0.21
Cheyenne (8)	24	<0.01
Chickasaw (24)	51	0.01
Chippewa (81)	135	0.02
Choctaw (81)	241	0.04
Colville (1)	3	<0.01
Comanche (20)	45	0.01
Cree (3)	22	<0.01
Creek (25)	78	0.01
Crow (4)	5	<0.01
Delaware (8)	25	<0.01
Hopi (15)	26	<0.01
Houma (0)	3	<0.01
Inupiat *(Alaska Native)* (8)	21	<0.01
Iroquois (42)	97	0.02
Kiowa (6)	9	<0.01
Lumbee (9)	12	<0.01
Menominee (5)	6	<0.01
Mexican American Ind. (272)	450	0.08
Navajo (406)	582	0.10
Osage (12)	29	<0.01
Ottawa (10)	15	<0.01
Paiute (101)	141	0.02
Pima (15)	32	0.01
Potawatomi (36)	58	0.01
Pueblo (56)	112	0.02
Puget Sound Salish (12)	17	<0.01
Seminole (22)	63	0.01
Shoshone (40)	79	0.01
Sioux (96)	202	0.03
South American Ind. (15)	44	0.01
Spanish American Ind. (38)	60	0.01
Tlingit-Haida *(Alaska Native)* (11)	29	<0.01
Tohono O'Odham (16)	27	<0.01
Tsimshian *(Alaska Native)* (2)	4	<0.01
Ute (11)	26	<0.01
Yakama (1)	7	<0.01
Yaqui (25)	63	0.01
Yuman (20)	24	<0.01
Yup'ik *(Alaska Native)* (1)	5	<0.01
Asian (35,620)	45,537	7.80
Not Hispanic (34,606)	42,871	7.34
Hispanic (1,014)	2,666	0.46
Bangladeshi (26)	30	0.01
Burmese (45)	58	0.01
Cambodian (225)	307	0.05
Chinese, ex. Taiwanese (3,801)	5,877	1.01
Filipino (19,042)	24,185	4.14
Hmong (17)	26	<0.01
Indian (2,064)	2,570	0.44
Indonesian (118)	220	0.04
Japanese (2,521)	4,685	0.80
Korean (2,627)	3,624	0.62
Laotian (356)	473	0.08
Malaysian (20)	48	0.01
Nepalese (12)	15	<0.01
Pakistani (305)	363	0.06
Sri Lankan (115)	141	0.02
Taiwanese (205)	288	0.05
Thai (1,030)	1,492	0.26
Vietnamese (1,420)	1,841	0.32
Hawaii Native/Pacific Islander (3,426)	6,856	1.17
Not Hispanic (3,103)	5,849	1.00
Hispanic (323)	1,007	0.17
Fijian (24)	41	0.01
Guamanian/Chamorro (643)	1,045	0.18
Marshallese (4)	10	<0.01
Native Hawaiian (1,585)	3,778	0.65
Samoan (674)	1,123	0.19
Tongan (61)	133	0.02
White (362,264)	385,348	66.01
Not Hispanic (279,703)	293,301	50.24
Hispanic (82,561)	92,047	15.77

Mesquite

Place Type: City
County: Clark
Population: 15,276†

Ancestry‡	Population	%
American (788)	788	5.39
Arab (0)	13	0.09
Other Arab (0)	13	0.09
Austrian (17)	26	0.18
Belgian (0)	9	0.06
British (11)	34	0.23
Canadian (80)	80	0.55
Czech (30)	102	0.70
Czechoslovakian (13)	13	0.09
Danish (55)	219	1.50
Dutch (48)	127	0.87
English (1,135)	2,609	17.86
European (280)	280	1.92
Finnish (11)	20	0.14
French, ex. Basque (86)	299	2.05
French Canadian (32)	51	0.35
German (708)	2,328	15.94
Greek (20)	43	0.29
Hungarian (22)	34	0.23
Iranian (0)	13	0.09
Irish (613)	1,617	11.07
Italian (311)	579	3.96
Lithuanian (0)	39	0.27
Norwegian (166)	309	2.12
Polish (96)	319	2.18
Portuguese (67)	77	0.53
Romanian (0)	11	0.08
Russian (30)	116	0.79
Scandinavian (0)	54	0.37
Scotch-Irish (212)	387	2.65
Scottish (162)	449	3.07
Serbian (0)	7	0.05
Slavic (9)	9	0.06
Slovene (0)	28	0.19
Swedish (138)	485	3.32
Swiss (19)	102	0.70
Ukrainian (0)	39	0.27
Welsh (78)	244	1.67
Yugoslavian (0)	25	0.17

Hispanic Origin	Population	%
Hispanic or Latino (of any race)	3,658	23.95
Central American, ex. Mexican	88	0.58
Costa Rican	2	0.01
Guatemalan	17	0.11
Honduran	19	0.12
Nicaraguan	11	0.07
Panamanian	1	0.01
Salvadoran	38	0.25
Cuban	6	0.04
Dominican Republic	5	0.03
Mexican	3,256	21.31
Puerto Rican	30	0.20
South American	34	0.22
Argentinean	4	0.03
Colombian	18	0.12
Peruvian	8	0.05
Uruguayan	3	0.02
Other South American	1	0.01
Other Hispanic or Latino	239	1.56

Race*	Population	%
African-American/Black (146)	178	1.17
Not Hispanic (137)	165	1.08
Hispanic (9)	13	0.09
American Indian/Alaska Native (143)	229	1.50
Not Hispanic (113)	170	1.11
Hispanic (30)	59	0.39
Alaska Athabascan *(Ala. Nat.)* (1)	1	0.01
Aleut *(Alaska Native)* (0)	1	0.01
Apache (6)	11	0.07
Arapaho (0)	1	0.01
Blackfeet (1)	5	0.03
Canadian/French Am. Ind. (0)	1	0.01
Cherokee (13)	27	0.18
Cheyenne (0)	1	0.01
Chippewa (2)	5	0.03
Choctaw (3)	4	0.03
Cree (2)	4	0.03
Creek (0)	2	0.01
Hopi (1)	4	0.03
Iroquois (1)	1	0.01
Kiowa (0)	1	0.01
Mexican American Ind. (3)	5	0.03
Navajo (49)	55	0.36
Ottawa (0)	1	0.01
Paiute (7)	8	0.05
Potawatomi (1)	2	0.01
Pueblo (0)	2	0.01
Sioux (2)	7	0.05
Spanish American Ind. (0)	1	0.01
Ute (4)	4	0.03
Asian (274)	361	2.36
Not Hispanic (265)	334	2.19
Hispanic (9)	27	0.18
Cambodian (7)	13	0.09
Chinese, ex. Taiwanese (26)	45	0.29
Filipino (99)	144	0.94
Indian (10)	17	0.11
Indonesian (2)	3	0.02
Japanese (36)	54	0.35
Korean (14)	14	0.09
Laotian (4)	6	0.04
Nepalese (1)	1	0.01
Pakistani (12)	12	0.08
Taiwanese (1)	1	0.01
Thai (12)	22	0.14
Vietnamese (36)	46	0.30
Hawaii Native/Pacific Islander (34)	73	0.48
Not Hispanic (34)	65	0.43
Hispanic (0)	8	0.05
Guamanian/Chamorro (3)	4	0.03
Native Hawaiian (12)	40	0.26
Samoan (11)	13	0.09
Tongan (7)	9	0.06
White (12,757)	13,026	85.27
Not Hispanic (10,896)	11,040	72.27
Hispanic (1,861)	1,986	13.00

North Las Vegas

Place Type: City
County: Clark
Population: 216,961†

Ancestry‡	Population	%
Afghan (73)	73	0.04
African, Sub-Saharan (1,245)	1,452	0.71
African (927)	1,134	0.56
Cape Verdean (24)	24	0.01
Ethiopian (74)	74	0.04
Ghanaian (42)	42	0.02
Kenyan (130)	130	0.06
Somalian (14)	14	0.01
Sudanese (34)	34	0.02
Albanian (32)	32	0.02
American (3,946)	3,946	1.93
Arab (285)	492	0.24
Arab (63)	81	0.04
Egyptian (22)	34	0.02
Iraqi (9)	9	<0.01
Jordanian (12)	12	0.01
Lebanese (45)	77	0.04
Moroccan (32)	120	0.06
Syrian (55)	112	0.05
Other Arab (47)	47	0.02
Armenian (149)	169	0.08
Assyrian/Chaldean/Syriac (18)	29	0.01
Australian (43)	78	0.04
Austrian (56)	240	0.12
Basque (21)	21	0.01
Belgian (48)	90	0.04
Brazilian (0)	11	0.01

SECTION TWO

*Notes: † The Census 2010 population figure is used to calculate the percentages in the Hispanic Origin and Race categories. Ancestry percentages are based on the 2006-2010 American Community Survey population (not shown); ‡ Numbers in parentheses indicate the number of people reporting a single ancestry; * Numbers in parentheses indicate the number of persons reporting this race alone, not in combination with any other race; Please refer to the Explanation of Data for more information.*

British (359)	435	0.21
Bulgarian (82)	82	0.04
Canadian (167)	402	0.20
Celtic (13)	13	0.01
Croatian (42)	92	0.05
Czech (74)	379	0.19
Czechoslovakian (17)	59	0.03
Danish (174)	597	0.29
Dutch (329)	1,502	0.74
Eastern European (35)	35	0.02
English (2,703)	9,206	4.51
European (1,098)	1,251	0.61
Finnish (0)	101	0.05
French, ex. Basque (643)	3,857	1.89
French Canadian (167)	544	0.27
German (4,687)	16,675	8.18
German Russian (0)	15	0.01
Greek (162)	253	0.12
Guyanese (25)	63	0.03
Hungarian (302)	703	0.34
Iranian (165)	201	0.10
Irish (3,102)	12,333	6.05
Italian (3,492)	8,310	4.07
Latvian (35)	47	0.02
Lithuanian (0)	111	0.05
Maltese (6)	6	<0.01
New Zealander (13)	13	0.01
Northern European (62)	71	0.03
Norwegian (499)	1,710	0.84
Pennsylvania German (28)	61	0.03
Polish (1,052)	3,035	1.49
Portuguese (320)	611	0.30
Romanian (79)	120	0.06
Russian (393)	1,083	0.53
Scandinavian (46)	207	0.10
Scotch-Irish (507)	1,359	0.67
Scottish (495)	1,784	0.87
Serbian (0)	38	0.02
Slavic (0)	6	<0.01
Slovak (38)	206	0.10
Slovene (5)	5	<0.01
Swedish (360)	1,297	0.64
Swiss (73)	460	0.23
Turkish (61)	84	0.04
Ukrainian (84)	172	0.08
Welsh (179)	765	0.38
West Indian, ex. Hispanic (591)	704	0.35
Bahamian (6)	6	<0.01
Barbadian (0)	9	<0.01
Belizean (120)	127	0.06
Haitian (32)	32	0.02
Jamaican (399)	465	0.23
Trinidadian/Tobagonian (11)	30	0.01
U.S. Virgin Islander (6)	6	<0.01
West Indian (17)	29	0.01
Yugoslavian (132)	235	0.12

Hispanic Origin	Population	%
Hispanic or Latino (of any race)	84,134	38.78
Central American, ex. Mexican	5,734	2.64
Costa Rican	102	0.05
Guatemalan	1,137	0.52
Honduran	507	0.23
Nicaraguan	375	0.17
Panamanian	244	0.11
Salvadoran	3,293	1.52
Other Central American	76	0.04
Cuban	1,151	0.53
Dominican Republic	236	0.11
Mexican	68,610	31.62
Puerto Rican	2,141	0.99
South American	1,220	0.56
Argentinean	221	0.10
Bolivian	17	0.01
Chilean	87	0.04
Colombian	316	0.15
Ecuadorian	187	0.09
Paraguayan	3	<0.01
Peruvian	273	0.13
Uruguayan	27	0.01
Venezuelan	73	0.03
Other South American	16	0.01
Other Hispanic or Latino	5,042	2.32

Race*	Population	%
African-American/Black (43,153)	47,802	22.03
Not Hispanic (41,561)	45,197	20.83
Hispanic (1,592)	2,605	1.20
American Indian/Alaska Native (1,680)	3,476	1.60
Not Hispanic (871)	2,179	1.00
Hispanic (809)	1,297	0.60
Alaska Athabascan *(Ala. Nat.)* (1)	1	<0.01
Aleut *(Alaska Native)* (1)	5	<0.01
Apache (81)	133	0.06
Arapaho (3)	3	<0.01
Blackfeet (8)	96	0.04
Canadian/French Am. Ind. (2)	7	<0.01
Central American Ind. (31)	40	0.02
Cherokee (92)	414	0.19
Cheyenne (6)	14	0.01
Chickasaw (19)	35	0.02
Chippewa (26)	50	0.02
Choctaw (33)	118	0.05
Comanche (1)	4	<0.01
Cree (8)	12	0.01
Creek (10)	27	0.01
Crow (1)	9	<0.01
Delaware (2)	4	<0.01
Hopi (8)	14	0.01
Inupiat *(Alaska Native)* (10)	17	0.01
Iroquois (13)	26	0.01
Kiowa (0)	3	<0.01
Lumbee (8)	12	0.01
Menominee (1)	1	<0.01
Mexican American Ind. (133)	219	0.10
Navajo (122)	172	0.08
Osage (2)	5	<0.01
Ottawa (4)	4	<0.01
Paiute (34)	48	0.02
Pima (3)	3	<0.01
Potawatomi (5)	11	0.01
Pueblo (24)	42	0.02
Puget Sound Salish (7)	12	0.01
Seminole (3)	24	0.01
Shoshone (25)	42	0.02
Sioux (23)	55	0.03
South American Ind. (9)	22	0.01
Spanish American Ind. (27)	31	0.01
Tlingit-Haida *(Alaska Native)* (4)	7	<0.01
Tohono O'Odham (4)	12	0.01
Tsimshian *(Alaska Native)* (0)	1	<0.01
Ute (4)	8	<0.01
Yaqui (3)	16	0.01
Yuman (4)	10	<0.01
Yup'ik *(Alaska Native)* (1)	1	<0.01
Asian (13,564)	18,046	8.32
Not Hispanic (13,122)	16,822	7.75
Hispanic (442)	1,224	0.56
Bangladeshi (2)	8	<0.01
Bhutanese (3)	3	<0.01
Burmese (7)	8	<0.01
Cambodian (108)	164	0.08
Chinese, ex. Taiwanese (888)	1,735	0.80
Filipino (9,174)	11,879	5.48
Hmong (22)	24	0.01
Indian (407)	561	0.26
Indonesian (47)	86	0.04
Japanese (579)	1,495	0.69
Korean (493)	934	0.43
Laotian (236)	365	0.17
Malaysian (14)	22	0.01
Nepalese (9)	9	<0.01
Pakistani (28)	31	0.01
Sri Lankan (25)	26	0.01
Taiwanese (28)	44	0.02
Thai (442)	726	0.33
Vietnamese (416)	580	0.27
Hawaii Native/Pacific Islander (1,822)	3,577	1.65
Not Hispanic (1,684)	3,074	1.42
Hispanic (138)	503	0.23
Fijian (33)	39	0.02
Guamanian/Chamorro (654)	978	0.45
Native Hawaiian (528)	1,567	0.72
Samoan (399)	642	0.30
Tongan (19)	42	0.02
White (102,829)	112,539	51.87
Not Hispanic (67,687)	73,328	33.80
Hispanic (35,142)	39,211	18.07

Pahrump

Place Type: CDP
County: Nye
Population: 36,441†

Ancestry‡	Population	%
African, Sub-Saharan (0)	18	0.05
African (0)	18	0.05
American (3,871)	3,871	10.73
Arab (12)	32	0.09
Lebanese (12)	32	0.09
Armenian (29)	35	0.10
Australian (12)	12	0.03
Austrian (32)	134	0.37
Basque (0)	13	0.04
British (27)	74	0.21
Canadian (13)	98	0.27
Celtic (0)	32	0.09
Croatian (13)	13	0.04
Czech (123)	280	0.78
Czechoslovakian (26)	136	0.38
Danish (111)	441	1.22
Dutch (248)	911	2.52
English (1,763)	5,403	14.97
European (451)	600	1.66
Finnish (46)	112	0.31
French, ex. Basque (244)	1,357	3.76
French Canadian (242)	343	0.95
German (2,386)	6,739	18.67
Greek (22)	218	0.60
Hungarian (84)	184	0.51
Iranian (25)	25	0.07
Irish (1,600)	5,162	14.30
Italian (833)	2,222	6.16
Lithuanian (16)	32	0.09
Maltese (13)	13	0.04
Norwegian (324)	707	1.96
Pennsylvania German (0)	14	0.04
Polish (364)	915	2.54
Portuguese (153)	259	0.72
Romanian (0)	23	0.06
Russian (69)	359	0.99
Scandinavian (23)	45	0.12
Scotch-Irish (403)	893	2.47
Scottish (373)	991	2.75
Serbian (0)	32	0.09
Slovak (24)	34	0.09
Soviet Union (0)	19	0.05
Swedish (152)	775	2.15
Swiss (16)	127	0.35
Turkish (0)	16	0.04
Ukrainian (0)	23	0.06
Welsh (54)	351	0.97
West Indian, ex. Hispanic (76)	76	0.21
Jamaican (76)	76	0.21
Yugoslavian (96)	96	0.27

Hispanic Origin	Population	%
Hispanic or Latino (of any race)	4,685	12.86
Central American, ex. Mexican	174	0.48
Costa Rican	19	0.05
Guatemalan	58	0.16
Honduran	16	0.04
Nicaraguan	6	0.02
Panamanian	7	0.02
Salvadoran	65	0.18
Other Central American	3	0.01
Cuban	83	0.23
Dominican Republic	24	0.07
Mexican	3,631	9.96

*Notes: † The Census 2010 population figure is used to calculate the percentages in the Hispanic Origin and Race categories. Ancestry percentages are based on the 2006-2010 American Community Survey population (not shown); ‡ Numbers in parentheses indicate the number of people reporting a single ancestry; * Numbers in parentheses indicate the number of persons reporting this race alone, not in combination with any other race; Please refer to the Explanation of Data for more information.*

Puerto Rican	207	0.57
South American	75	0.21
Argentinean	22	0.06
Bolivian	1	<0.01
Chilean	4	0.01
Colombian	13	0.04
Ecuadorian	9	0.02
Paraguayan	1	<0.01
Peruvian	23	0.06
Venezuelan	1	<0.01
Other South American	1	<0.01
Other Hispanic or Latino	491	1.35

Race*	Population	%
African-American/Black (783)	1,066	2.93
Not Hispanic (745)	995	2.73
Hispanic (38)	71	0.19
American Indian/Alaska Native (392)	886	2.43
Not Hispanic (318)	718	1.97
Hispanic (74)	168	0.46
Alaska Athabascan *(Ala. Nat.)* (1)	1	<0.01
Aleut *(Alaska Native)* (1)	1	<0.01
Apache (7)	20	0.05
Arapaho (0)	2	0.01
Blackfeet (6)	31	0.09
Canadian/French Am. Ind. (3)	7	0.02
Cherokee (52)	208	0.57
Cheyenne (3)	7	0.02
Chickasaw (4)	13	0.04
Chippewa (11)	23	0.06
Choctaw (10)	48	0.13
Comanche (1)	5	0.01
Cree (1)	3	0.01
Creek (0)	2	0.01
Delaware (1)	2	0.01
Hopi (0)	1	<0.01
Inupiat *(Alaska Native)* (2)	2	0.01
Iroquois (0)	4	0.01
Kiowa (0)	4	0.01
Lumbee (1)	1	<0.01
Mexican American Ind. (14)	28	0.08
Navajo (4)	17	0.05
Osage (3)	5	0.01
Ottawa (1)	1	<0.01
Paiute (35)	46	0.13
Pima (1)	2	0.01
Potawatomi (1)	2	0.01
Pueblo (1)	1	<0.01
Puget Sound Salish (0)	1	<0.01
Seminole (2)	9	0.02
Shoshone (17)	21	0.06
Sioux (12)	23	0.06
South American Ind. (1)	2	0.01
Spanish American Ind. (0)	4	0.01
Tohono O'Odham (1)	1	<0.01
Ute (0)	1	<0.01
Yaqui (2)	5	0.01
Yuman (1)	1	<0.01
Asian (519)	889	2.44
Not Hispanic (496)	815	2.24
Hispanic (23)	74	0.20
Burmese (1)	2	0.01
Cambodian (7)	7	0.02
Chinese, ex. Taiwanese (53)	106	0.29
Filipino (280)	476	1.31
Indian (22)	54	0.15
Indonesian (2)	5	0.01
Japanese (67)	153	0.42
Korean (31)	54	0.15
Laotian (2)	3	0.01
Thai (21)	25	0.07
Vietnamese (19)	20	0.05
Hawaii Native/Pacific Islander (201)	335	0.92
Not Hispanic (170)	278	0.76
Hispanic (31)	57	0.16
Fijian (0)	2	0.01
Guamanian/Chamorro (31)	37	0.10
Native Hawaiian (133)	249	0.68
Samoan (15)	35	0.10
Tongan (1)	1	<0.01
White (31,390)	32,557	89.34
Not Hispanic (29,055)	29,884	82.01
Hispanic (2,335)	2,673	7.34

Paradise

Place Type: CDP
County: Clark
Population: 223,167†

Ancestry‡	Population	%
Afghan (187)	215	0.10
African, Sub-Saharan (4,699)	5,153	2.36
African (2,240)	2,673	1.23
Ethiopian (1,735)	1,756	0.81
Liberian (221)	221	0.10
Nigerian (144)	144	0.07
Somalian (42)	42	0.02
South African (8)	8	<0.01
Sudanese (71)	71	0.03
Zimbabwean (26)	26	0.01
Other Sub-Saharan African (212)	212	0.10
Albanian (0)	27	0.01
American (4,773)	4,773	2.19
Arab (1,279)	1,992	0.91
Arab (170)	241	0.11
Egyptian (133)	139	0.06
Iraqi (184)	184	0.08
Lebanese (491)	836	0.38
Moroccan (173)	227	0.10
Palestinian (32)	42	0.02
Syrian (76)	235	0.11
Other Arab (20)	88	0.04
Armenian (354)	391	0.18
Assyrian/Chaldean/Syriac (18)	18	0.01
Australian (15)	15	0.01
Austrian (394)	758	0.35
Basque (77)	188	0.09
Belgian (29)	136	0.06
Brazilian (224)	301	0.14
British (401)	846	0.39
Bulgarian (196)	263	0.12
Cajun (0)	35	0.02
Canadian (247)	512	0.23
Celtic (29)	49	0.02
Croatian (247)	366	0.17
Czech (300)	1,062	0.49
Czechoslovakian (118)	196	0.09
Danish (318)	1,175	0.54
Dutch (512)	2,338	1.07
Eastern European (222)	222	0.10
English (4,723)	15,932	7.31
Estonian (12)	12	0.01
European (1,698)	2,019	0.93
Finnish (194)	358	0.16
French, ex. Basque (850)	4,821	2.21
French Canadian (573)	1,127	0.52
German (7,584)	24,104	11.06
German Russian (40)	40	0.02
Greek (629)	1,444	0.66
Guyanese (90)	90	0.04
Hungarian (619)	1,261	0.58
Iranian (509)	588	0.27
Irish (5,627)	19,493	8.94
Israeli (124)	146	0.07
Italian (5,880)	13,644	6.26
Latvian (16)	38	0.02
Lithuanian (210)	579	0.27
Macedonian (76)	76	0.03
Maltese (65)	79	0.04
New Zealander (9)	9	<0.01
Northern European (67)	67	0.03
Norwegian (1,077)	2,488	1.14
Pennsylvania German (8)	19	0.01
Polish (2,147)	5,507	2.53
Portuguese (503)	1,279	0.59
Romanian (332)	617	0.28
Russian (1,244)	2,457	1.13
Scandinavian (112)	278	0.13
Scotch-Irish (858)	2,348	1.08
Scottish (828)	3,987	1.83
Serbian (189)	255	0.12
Slavic (128)	288	0.13
Slovak (223)	392	0.18
Slovene (16)	44	0.02
Soviet Union (19)	19	0.01
Swedish (928)	2,574	1.18
Swiss (84)	370	0.17
Turkish (19)	42	0.02
Ukrainian (310)	523	0.24
Welsh (200)	1,144	0.52
West Indian, ex. Hispanic (630)	936	0.43
Barbadian (9)	9	<0.01
Belizean (125)	125	0.06
British West Indian (0)	9	<0.01
Haitian (251)	251	0.12
Jamaican (159)	362	0.17
Trinidadian/Tobagonian (25)	41	0.02
U.S. Virgin Islander (26)	26	0.01
West Indian (35)	113	0.05
Yugoslavian (344)	519	0.24

Hispanic Origin	Population	%
Hispanic or Latino (of any race)	69,599	31.19
Central American, ex. Mexican	6,648	2.98
Costa Rican	153	0.07
Guatemalan	1,669	0.75
Honduran	508	0.23
Nicaraguan	520	0.23
Panamanian	147	0.07
Salvadoran	3,578	1.60
Other Central American	73	0.03
Cuban	4,405	1.97
Dominican Republic	300	0.13
Mexican	48,022	21.52
Puerto Rican	2,213	0.99
South American	2,619	1.17
Argentinean	442	0.20
Bolivian	64	0.03
Chilean	202	0.09
Colombian	681	0.31
Ecuadorian	304	0.14
Paraguayan	14	0.01
Peruvian	719	0.32
Uruguayan	43	0.02
Venezuelan	111	0.05
Other South American	39	0.02
Other Hispanic or Latino	5,392	2.42

Race*	Population	%
African-American/Black (19,918)	23,422	10.50
Not Hispanic (18,659)	21,339	9.56
Hispanic (1,259)	2,083	0.93
American Indian/Alaska Native (1,721)	3,652	1.64
Not Hispanic (1,011)	2,343	1.05
Hispanic (710)	1,309	0.59
Alaska Athabascan *(Ala. Nat.)* (4)	11	<0.01
Aleut *(Alaska Native)* (7)	14	0.01
Apache (73)	139	0.06
Arapaho (3)	7	<0.01
Blackfeet (18)	89	0.04
Canadian/French Am. Ind. (4)	13	0.01
Central American Ind. (7)	17	0.01
Cherokee (116)	434	0.19
Cheyenne (2)	15	0.01
Chickasaw (18)	37	0.02
Chippewa (51)	74	0.03
Choctaw (44)	100	0.04
Colville (2)	2	<0.01
Comanche (5)	18	0.01
Cree (6)	12	0.01
Creek (8)	37	0.02
Crow (2)	5	<0.01
Delaware (3)	5	<0.01
Hopi (4)	13	0.01
Houma (0)	1	<0.01
Inupiat *(Alaska Native)* (3)	3	<0.01
Iroquois (14)	39	0.02
Kiowa (0)	1	<0.01
Lumbee (2)	6	<0.01

*Notes: † The Census 2010 population figure is used to calculate the percentages in the Hispanic Origin and Race categories. Ancestry percentages are based on the 2006-2010 American Community Survey population (not shown); ‡ Numbers in parentheses indicate the number of people reporting a single ancestry; * Numbers in parentheses indicate the number of persons reporting this race alone, not in combination with any other race; Please refer to the Explanation of Data for more information.*

Mexican American Ind. (105)	176	0.08
Navajo (164)	224	0.10
Osage (3)	3	<0.01
Ottawa (2)	3	<0.01
Paiute (18)	22	0.01
Pima (9)	17	0.01
Potawatomi (7)	25	0.01
Pueblo (18)	27	0.01
Puget Sound Salish (2)	3	<0.01
Seminole (2)	23	0.01
Shoshone (20)	29	0.01
Sioux (40)	86	0.04
South American Ind. (26)	32	0.01
Spanish American Ind. (7)	23	0.01
Tlingit-Haida *(Alaska Native)* (16)	21	0.01
Tohono O'Odham (9)	19	0.01
Ute (1)	6	<0.01
Yakama (5)	6	<0.01
Yaqui (9)	23	0.01
Yuman (13)	20	0.01
Yup'ik *(Alaska Native)* (0)	1	<0.01
Asian (21,106)	25,826	11.57
Not Hispanic (20,655)	24,583	11.02
Hispanic (451)	1,243	0.56
Bangladeshi (40)	53	0.02
Bhutanese (153)	160	0.07
Burmese (87)	88	0.04
Cambodian (122)	158	0.07
Chinese, ex. Taiwanese (2,160)	3,266	1.46
Filipino (11,087)	13,769	6.17
Hmong (21)	27	0.01
Indian (1,594)	1,912	0.86
Indonesian (97)	161	0.07
Japanese (1,137)	2,212	0.99
Korean (1,381)	1,836	0.82
Laotian (205)	257	0.12
Malaysian (12)	31	0.01
Nepalese (49)	65	0.03
Pakistani (89)	111	0.05
Sri Lankan (57)	64	0.03
Taiwanese (102)	123	0.06
Thai (584)	795	0.36
Vietnamese (1,054)	1,241	0.56
Hawaii Native/Pacific Islander (2,263)	4,287	1.92
Not Hispanic (2,098)	3,771	1.69
Hispanic (165)	516	0.23
Fijian (26)	50	0.02
Guamanian/Chamorro (433)	703	0.32
Marshallese (2)	2	<0.01
Native Hawaiian (1,041)	2,336	1.05
Samoan (477)	791	0.35
Tongan (72)	112	0.05
White (133,398)	143,067	64.11
Not Hispanic (103,257)	109,049	48.86
Hispanic (30,141)	34,018	15.24

Reno

Place Type: City
County: Washoe
Population: 225,221†

Ancestry‡	Population	%
Afghan (11)	11	<0.01
African, Sub-Saharan (984)	1,110	0.50
African (324)	401	0.18
Ethiopian (22)	22	0.01
Kenyan (12)	33	0.01
Nigerian (109)	109	0.05
Sierra Leonean (8)	8	<0.01
Somalian (6)	6	<0.01
South African (269)	297	0.13
Ugandan (5)	5	<0.01
Other Sub-Saharan African (229)	229	0.10
Alsatian (0)	24	0.01
American (10,284)	10,284	4.65
Arab (276)	917	0.41
Arab (0)	67	0.03
Iraqi (22)	22	0.01
Jordanian (0)	28	0.01
Lebanese (204)	568	0.26
Moroccan (0)	12	0.01
Syrian (0)	102	0.05
Other Arab (50)	118	0.05
Armenian (89)	245	0.11
Assyrian/Chaldean/Syriac (6)	6	<0.01
Australian (76)	236	0.11
Austrian (257)	998	0.45
Basque (542)	1,065	0.48
Belgian (61)	122	0.06
Brazilian (178)	391	0.18
British (674)	1,200	0.54
Bulgarian (0)	21	0.01
Canadian (481)	959	0.43
Celtic (68)	98	0.04
Croatian (199)	380	0.17
Czech (324)	840	0.38
Czechoslovakian (80)	198	0.09
Danish (652)	2,069	0.94
Dutch (819)	3,861	1.75
Eastern European (64)	102	0.05
English (6,071)	23,056	10.43
European (2,282)	2,903	1.31
Finnish (100)	452	0.20
French, ex. Basque (1,401)	7,226	3.27
French Canadian (529)	1,026	0.46
German (9,851)	35,389	16.01
Greek (470)	1,055	0.48
Hungarian (368)	786	0.36
Icelander (13)	44	0.02
Iranian (316)	354	0.16
Irish (7,122)	28,213	12.77
Israeli (18)	18	0.01
Italian (5,969)	16,423	7.43
Latvian (68)	109	0.05
Lithuanian (89)	284	0.13
Luxemburger (39)	53	0.02
Macedonian (0)	68	0.03
Maltese (21)	25	0.01
New Zealander (53)	53	0.02
Northern European (158)	167	0.08
Norwegian (1,621)	5,037	2.28
Pennsylvania German (55)	118	0.05
Polish (1,141)	4,122	1.87
Portuguese (1,313)	2,717	1.23
Romanian (66)	167	0.08
Russian (983)	2,458	1.11
Scandinavian (403)	760	0.34
Scotch-Irish (1,540)	4,901	2.22
Scottish (1,573)	5,267	2.38
Serbian (236)	539	0.24
Slavic (71)	98	0.04
Slovak (23)	212	0.10
Slovene (11)	28	0.01
Swedish (753)	3,513	1.59
Swiss (211)	1,057	0.48
Turkish (380)	380	0.17
Ukrainian (248)	538	0.24
Welsh (280)	1,524	0.69
West Indian, ex. Hispanic (143)	324	0.15
Belizean (0)	14	0.01
Jamaican (34)	201	0.09
Trinidadian/Tobagonian (8)	8	<0.01
West Indian (101)	101	0.05
Yugoslavian (171)	543	0.25

Hispanic Origin	Population	%
Hispanic or Latino (of any race)	54,640	24.26
Central American, ex. Mexican	5,366	2.38
Costa Rican	168	0.07
Guatemalan	1,825	0.81
Honduran	222	0.10
Nicaraguan	246	0.11
Panamanian	81	0.04
Salvadoran	2,783	1.24
Other Central American	41	0.02
Cuban	318	0.14
Dominican Republic	46	0.02
Mexican	42,271	18.77
Puerto Rican	1,015	0.45
South American	1,118	0.50
Argentinean	150	0.07
Bolivian	47	0.02
Chilean	162	0.07
Colombian	316	0.14
Ecuadorian	86	0.04
Paraguayan	5	<0.01
Peruvian	304	0.13
Uruguayan	9	<0.01
Venezuelan	31	0.01
Other South American	8	<0.01
Other Hispanic or Latino	4,506	2.00

Race*	Population	%
African-American/Black (6,429)	8,540	3.79
Not Hispanic (5,990)	7,685	3.41
Hispanic (439)	855	0.38
American Indian/Alaska Native (2,835)	4,938	2.19
Not Hispanic (2,066)	3,593	1.60
Hispanic (769)	1,345	0.60
Alaska Athabascan *(Ala. Nat.)* (14)	26	0.01
Aleut *(Alaska Native)* (6)	12	0.01
Apache (51)	124	0.06
Arapaho (12)	17	0.01
Blackfeet (20)	86	0.04
Canadian/French Am. Ind. (6)	15	0.01
Central American Ind. (3)	12	0.01
Cherokee (182)	510	0.23
Cheyenne (9)	17	0.01
Chickasaw (18)	38	0.02
Chippewa (46)	97	0.04
Choctaw (54)	139	0.06
Colville (2)	3	<0.01
Comanche (5)	17	0.01
Cree (1)	5	<0.01
Creek (26)	47	0.02
Crow (4)	14	0.01
Delaware (2)	11	<0.01
Hopi (9)	13	0.01
Inupiat *(Alaska Native)* (7)	16	0.01
Iroquois (27)	53	0.02
Kiowa (6)	8	<0.01
Lumbee (4)	8	<0.01
Menominee (4)	7	<0.01
Mexican American Ind. (128)	179	0.08
Navajo (65)	139	0.06
Osage (0)	6	<0.01
Ottawa (0)	2	<0.01
Paiute (367)	509	0.23
Pima (5)	17	0.01
Potawatomi (17)	24	0.01
Pueblo (21)	27	0.01
Puget Sound Salish (3)	4	<0.01
Seminole (1)	9	<0.01
Shoshone (128)	169	0.08
Sioux (71)	134	0.06
South American Ind. (8)	15	0.01
Spanish American Ind. (9)	12	0.01
Tlingit-Haida *(Alaska Native)* (17)	26	0.01
Tohono O'Odham (4)	5	<0.01
Tsimshian *(Alaska Native)* (1)	1	<0.01
Ute (9)	14	0.01
Yaqui (10)	16	0.01
Yuman (5)	13	0.01
Yup'ik *(Alaska Native)* (5)	6	<0.01
Asian (14,232)	17,700	7.86
Not Hispanic (13,913)	16,838	7.48
Hispanic (319)	862	0.38
Bangladeshi (273)	290	0.13
Burmese (18)	18	0.01
Cambodian (50)	77	0.03
Chinese, ex. Taiwanese (2,319)	3,027	1.34
Filipino (6,095)	7,769	3.45
Hmong (7)	9	<0.01
Indian (1,781)	2,028	0.90
Indonesian (42)	80	0.04
Japanese (822)	1,605	0.71
Korean (775)	1,034	0.46
Laotian (19)	37	0.02
Malaysian (10)	18	0.01

*Notes: † The Census 2010 population figure is used to calculate the percentages in the Hispanic Origin and Race categories. Ancestry percentages are based on the 2006-2010 American Community Survey population (not shown); ‡ Numbers in parentheses indicate the number of people reporting a single ancestry; * Numbers in parentheses indicate the number of persons reporting this race alone, not in combination with any other race; Please refer to the Explanation of Data for more information.*

Nepalese (83)	88	0.04
Pakistani (205)	241	0.11
Sri Lankan (34)	38	0.02
Taiwanese (82)	100	0.04
Thai (268)	365	0.16
Vietnamese (713)	934	0.41
Hawaii Native/Pacific Islander (1,624)	2,564	1.14
Not Hispanic (1,505)	2,266	1.01
Hispanic (119)	298	0.13
Fijian (23)	25	0.01
Guamanian/Chamorro (162)	272	0.12
Marshallese (35)	42	0.02
Native Hawaiian (373)	922	0.41
Samoan (193)	274	0.12
Tongan (425)	494	0.22
White (167,179)	175,322	77.84
Not Hispanic (140,752)	145,975	64.81
Hispanic (26,427)	29,347	13.03

Spanish Springs

Place Type: CDP
County: Washoe
Population: 15,064†

Ancestry‡	Population	%
American (949)	949	6.44
Australian (12)	37	0.25
Austrian (11)	116	0.79
Basque (49)	75	0.51
Belgian (0)	9	0.06
British (58)	98	0.66
Canadian (33)	62	0.42
Croatian (0)	10	0.07
Czech (7)	69	0.47
Czechoslovakian (9)	9	0.06
Danish (142)	466	3.16
Dutch (18)	98	0.66
Eastern European (0)	10	0.07
English (892)	2,033	13.79
European (154)	164	1.11
Finnish (27)	42	0.28
French, ex. Basque (109)	831	5.64
French Canadian (8)	53	0.36
German (1,012)	3,772	25.58
Greek (31)	166	1.13
Hungarian (12)	25	0.17
Icelander (0)	23	0.16
Irish (838)	2,546	17.26
Italian (422)	1,149	7.79
Lithuanian (0)	9	0.06
Norwegian (44)	304	2.06
Polish (57)	253	1.72
Portuguese (104)	285	1.93
Russian (31)	116	0.79
Scandinavian (20)	29	0.20
Scotch-Irish (82)	271	1.84
Scottish (89)	394	2.67
Swedish (50)	387	2.62
Swiss (0)	79	0.54
Ukrainian (0)	83	0.56
Welsh (0)	218	1.48
Yugoslavian (0)	7	0.05

Hispanic Origin	Population	%
Hispanic or Latino (of any race)	1,608	10.67
Central American, ex. Mexican	157	1.04
Costa Rican	18	0.12
Guatemalan	23	0.15
Honduran	6	0.04
Nicaraguan	16	0.11
Salvadoran	93	0.62
Other Central American	1	0.01
Cuban	17	0.11
Dominican Republic	1	0.01
Mexican	1,164	7.73
Puerto Rican	43	0.29
South American	24	0.16
Argentinean	7	0.05
Chilean	2	0.01
Colombian	6	0.04
Ecuadorian	1	0.01
Peruvian	7	0.05
Venezuelan	1	0.01
Other Hispanic or Latino	202	1.34

Race*	Population	%
African-American/Black (191)	291	1.93
Not Hispanic (175)	262	1.74
Hispanic (16)	29	0.19
American Indian/Alaska Native (200)	304	2.02
Not Hispanic (164)	251	1.67
Hispanic (36)	53	0.35
Alaska Athabascan *(Ala. Nat.)* (1)	2	0.01
Apache (0)	5	0.03
Blackfeet (1)	1	0.01
Cherokee (17)	38	0.25
Cheyenne (1)	2	0.01
Chickasaw (5)	5	0.03
Chippewa (7)	9	0.06
Choctaw (3)	5	0.03
Comanche (0)	1	0.01
Cree (0)	1	0.01
Creek (1)	4	0.03
Hopi (1)	1	0.01
Inupiat *(Alaska Native)* (0)	2	0.01
Iroquois (1)	2	0.01
Lumbee (1)	1	0.01
Mexican American Ind. (1)	5	0.03
Navajo (2)	5	0.03
Osage (1)	1	0.01
Ottawa (1)	1	0.01
Paiute (28)	35	0.23
Potawatomi (9)	11	0.07
Pueblo (1)	2	0.01
Shoshone (8)	11	0.07
Sioux (2)	5	0.03
Spanish American Ind. (1)	1	0.01
Tlingit-Haida *(Alaska Native)* (1)	1	0.01
Asian (322)	538	3.57
Not Hispanic (317)	490	3.25
Hispanic (5)	48	0.32
Chinese, ex. Taiwanese (30)	67	0.44
Filipino (163)	262	1.74
Indian (23)	31	0.21
Japanese (24)	58	0.39
Korean (27)	48	0.32
Malaysian (1)	1	0.01
Pakistani (3)	9	0.06
Sri Lankan (1)	1	0.01
Thai (10)	22	0.15
Vietnamese (18)	34	0.23
Hawaii Native/Pacific Islander (31)	86	0.57
Not Hispanic (27)	76	0.50
Hispanic (4)	10	0.07
Guamanian/Chamorro (0)	5	0.03
Native Hawaiian (18)	51	0.34
Samoan (8)	15	0.10
Tongan (4)	5	0.03
White (13,459)	13,873	92.09
Not Hispanic (12,430)	12,722	84.45
Hispanic (1,029)	1,151	7.64

Sparks

Place Type: City
County: Washoe
Population: 90,264†

Ancestry‡	Population	%
African, Sub-Saharan (234)	324	0.37
African (106)	134	0.15
Ethiopian (10)	10	0.01
Nigerian (70)	112	0.13
Somalian (0)	20	0.02
South African (27)	27	0.03
Other Sub-Saharan African (21)	21	0.02
Alsatian (0)	9	0.01
American (3,514)	3,514	4.03
Arab (67)	215	0.25
Arab (9)	9	0.01
Iraqi (31)	31	0.04
Lebanese (27)	109	0.12
Moroccan (0)	66	0.08
Armenian (23)	87	0.10
Assyrian/Chaldean/Syriac (0)	29	0.03
Australian (50)	50	0.06
Austrian (25)	147	0.17
Basque (108)	300	0.34
Belgian (0)	78	0.09
Brazilian (39)	39	0.04
British (161)	333	0.38
Canadian (65)	267	0.31
Celtic (62)	83	0.10
Croatian (92)	188	0.22
Czech (47)	261	0.30
Czechoslovakian (59)	144	0.16
Danish (195)	634	0.73
Dutch (347)	1,357	1.55
Eastern European (16)	27	0.03
English (2,964)	10,419	11.93
European (615)	699	0.80
Finnish (70)	178	0.20
French, ex. Basque (360)	2,523	2.89
French Canadian (194)	362	0.41
German (3,972)	13,947	15.98
Greek (189)	521	0.60
Hungarian (129)	530	0.61
Icelander (29)	41	0.05
Iranian (10)	10	0.01
Irish (2,301)	10,619	12.16
Israeli (22)	22	0.03
Italian (2,508)	6,098	6.99
Latvian (0)	7	0.01
Lithuanian (59)	280	0.32
Northern European (107)	197	0.23
Norwegian (716)	2,012	2.30
Pennsylvania German (16)	96	0.11
Polish (332)	1,410	1.62
Portuguese (396)	1,087	1.25
Romanian (116)	129	0.15
Russian (190)	561	0.64
Scandinavian (116)	241	0.28
Scotch-Irish (534)	1,518	1.74
Scottish (364)	1,674	1.92
Slavic (0)	56	0.06
Slovak (9)	103	0.12
Slovene (0)	26	0.03
Swedish (323)	1,856	2.13
Swiss (81)	363	0.42
Turkish (0)	13	0.01
Ukrainian (29)	123	0.14
Welsh (78)	905	1.04
West Indian, ex. Hispanic (22)	68	0.08
British West Indian (0)	46	0.05
Jamaican (22)	22	0.03
Yugoslavian (64)	140	0.16

Hispanic Origin	Population	%
Hispanic or Latino (of any race)	23,698	26.25
Central American, ex. Mexican	2,087	2.31
Costa Rican	77	0.09
Guatemalan	512	0.57
Honduran	62	0.07
Nicaraguan	104	0.12
Panamanian	32	0.04
Salvadoran	1,285	1.42
Other Central American	15	0.02
Cuban	116	0.13
Dominican Republic	27	0.03
Mexican	19,135	21.20
Puerto Rican	422	0.47
South American	383	0.42
Argentinean	32	0.04
Bolivian	32	0.04
Chilean	29	0.03
Colombian	83	0.09
Ecuadorian	25	0.03
Peruvian	144	0.16
Uruguayan	23	0.03

*Notes: † The Census 2010 population figure is used to calculate the percentages in the Hispanic Origin and Race categories. Ancestry percentages are based on the 2006-2010 American Community Survey population (not shown); ‡ Numbers in parentheses indicate the number of people reporting a single ancestry; * Numbers in parentheses indicate the number of persons reporting this race alone, not in combination with any other race; Please refer to the Explanation of Data for more information.*

SECTION TWO

Venezuelan	14	0.02
Other South American	1	<0.01
Other Hispanic or Latino	1,528	1.69

Race*	Population	%
African-American/Black (2,362)	3,247	3.60
Not Hispanic (2,151)	2,877	3.19
Hispanic (211)	370	0.41
American Indian/Alaska Native (1,121)	1,858	2.06
Not Hispanic (876)	1,416	1.57
Hispanic (245)	442	0.49
Alaska Athabascan *(Ala. Nat.)* (1)	1	<0.01
Aleut *(Alaska Native)* (7)	13	0.01
Apache (17)	33	0.04
Arapaho (2)	2	<0.01
Blackfeet (6)	35	0.04
Canadian/French Am. Ind. (2)	2	<0.01
Cherokee (74)	213	0.24
Cheyenne (1)	1	<0.01
Chickasaw (4)	9	0.01
Chippewa (13)	27	0.03
Choctaw (18)	46	0.05
Colville (1)	2	<0.01
Comanche (3)	8	0.01
Cree (0)	3	<0.01
Creek (4)	11	0.01
Delaware (2)	2	<0.01
Hopi (14)	22	0.02
Houma (0)	1	<0.01
Inupiat *(Alaska Native)* (4)	6	0.01
Iroquois (9)	19	0.02
Kiowa (4)	4	<0.01
Lumbee (3)	3	<0.01
Mexican American Ind. (23)	37	0.04
Navajo (25)	48	0.05
Osage (6)	11	0.01
Ottawa (1)	3	<0.01
Paiute (178)	238	0.26
Potawatomi (6)	12	0.01
Pueblo (11)	14	0.02
Puget Sound Salish (2)	8	0.01
Seminole (2)	4	<0.01
Shoshone (50)	70	0.08
Sioux (37)	59	0.07
South American Ind. (5)	8	0.01
Spanish American Ind. (2)	3	<0.01
Tlingit-Haida *(Alaska Native)* (3)	4	<0.01
Tohono O'Odham (1)	1	<0.01
Ute (3)	4	<0.01
Yaqui (7)	10	0.01
Yuman (2)	3	<0.01
Asian (5,283)	6,602	7.31
Not Hispanic (5,169)	6,280	6.96
Hispanic (114)	322	0.36
Bangladeshi (12)	14	0.02
Burmese (1)	3	<0.01
Cambodian (13)	15	0.02
Chinese, ex. Taiwanese (805)	1,042	1.15
Filipino (2,659)	3,340	3.70
Hmong (6)	6	0.01
Indian (493)	593	0.66
Indonesian (6)	22	0.02
Japanese (213)	447	0.50
Korean (382)	511	0.57
Laotian (4)	11	0.01
Malaysian (3)	4	<0.01
Pakistani (63)	75	0.08
Sri Lankan (6)	10	0.01
Taiwanese (16)	24	0.03
Thai (87)	126	0.14
Vietnamese (351)	448	0.50
Hawaii Native/Pacific Islander (586)	982	1.09
Not Hispanic (544)	860	0.95
Hispanic (42)	122	0.14
Fijian (19)	21	0.02
Guamanian/Chamorro (75)	117	0.13
Marshallese (18)	19	0.02
Native Hawaiian (99)	272	0.30
Samoan (116)	171	0.19
Tongan (136)	184	0.20
White (67,205)	70,309	77.89
Not Hispanic (55,410)	57,441	63.64
Hispanic (11,795)	12,868	14.26

Spring Creek

Place Type: CDP
County: Elko
Population: 12,361†

Ancestry‡	Population	%
American (2,989)	2,989	22.17
Armenian (10)	10	0.07
Austrian (0)	22	0.16
Basque (142)	201	1.49
British (14)	105	0.78
Celtic (0)	33	0.24
Czech (0)	8	0.06
Czechoslovakian (9)	23	0.17
Danish (52)	288	2.14
Dutch (21)	157	1.16
English (461)	1,357	10.07
European (353)	353	2.62
Finnish (41)	41	0.30
French, ex. Basque (104)	487	3.61
French Canadian (83)	182	1.35
German (976)	2,431	18.03
Hungarian (0)	22	0.16
Irish (436)	1,873	13.89
Italian (149)	646	4.79
Northern European (45)	45	0.33
Norwegian (138)	545	4.04
Pennsylvania German (19)	19	0.14
Polish (66)	136	1.01
Portuguese (64)	160	1.19
Romanian (18)	18	0.13
Russian (38)	54	0.40
Scandinavian (67)	116	0.86
Scotch-Irish (85)	420	3.12
Scottish (57)	249	1.85
Slavic (0)	24	0.18
Slovak (0)	11	0.08
Swedish (148)	369	2.74
Swiss (0)	63	0.47
Welsh (26)	195	1.45

Hispanic Origin	Population	%
Hispanic or Latino (of any race)	965	7.81
Central American, ex. Mexican	11	0.09
Guatemalan	2	0.02
Honduran	2	0.02
Salvadoran	7	0.06
Cuban	2	0.02
Mexican	741	5.99
Puerto Rican	25	0.20
South American	13	0.11
Bolivian	3	0.02
Chilean	1	0.01
Colombian	5	0.04
Peruvian	3	0.02
Uruguayan	1	0.01
Other Hispanic or Latino	173	1.40

Race*	Population	%
African-American/Black (43)	79	0.64
Not Hispanic (42)	70	0.57
Hispanic (1)	9	0.07
American Indian/Alaska Native (193)	350	2.83
Not Hispanic (166)	304	2.46
Hispanic (27)	46	0.37
Alaska Athabascan *(Ala. Nat.)* (2)	2	0.02
Aleut *(Alaska Native)* (1)	1	0.01
Apache (3)	3	0.02
Arapaho (1)	1	0.01
Blackfeet (1)	6	0.05
Cherokee (4)	39	0.32
Cheyenne (0)	1	0.01
Chickasaw (0)	2	0.02
Chippewa (3)	8	0.06
Choctaw (13)	31	0.25
Comanche (1)	7	0.06
Cree (0)	1	0.01
Creek (1)	1	0.01
Hopi (5)	5	0.04
Inupiat *(Alaska Native)* (1)	4	0.03
Mexican American Ind. (1)	1	0.01
Navajo (7)	8	0.06
Ottawa (10)	10	0.08
Paiute (10)	16	0.13
Potawatomi (0)	4	0.03
Pueblo (7)	7	0.06
Shoshone (32)	37	0.30
Sioux (3)	8	0.06
Spanish American Ind. (2)	2	0.02
Tlingit-Haida *(Alaska Native)* (0)	1	0.01
Tohono O'Odham (1)	1	0.01
Asian (76)	144	1.16
Not Hispanic (76)	140	1.13
Hispanic (0)	4	0.03
Chinese, ex. Taiwanese (14)	20	0.16
Filipino (32)	51	0.41
Indian (10)	11	0.09
Indonesian (2)	2	0.02
Japanese (6)	24	0.19
Korean (3)	21	0.17
Thai (0)	5	0.04
Vietnamese (9)	10	0.08
Hawaii Native/Pacific Islander (13)	30	0.24
Not Hispanic (12)	26	0.21
Hispanic (1)	4	0.03
Guamanian/Chamorro (1)	1	0.01
Marshallese (3)	3	0.02
Native Hawaiian (6)	16	0.13
Samoan (2)	4	0.03
Tongan (0)	3	0.02
White (11,428)	11,744	95.01
Not Hispanic (10,862)	11,091	89.73
Hispanic (566)	653	5.28

Spring Valley

Place Type: CDP
County: Clark
Population: 178,395†

Ancestry‡	Population	%
Afghan (265)	265	0.16
African, Sub-Saharan (3,148)	3,286	1.93
African (882)	997	0.58
Cape Verdean (300)	300	0.18
Ethiopian (1,712)	1,712	1.00
Ghanaian (20)	20	0.01
Nigerian (57)	57	0.03
Somalian (49)	49	0.03
South African (46)	69	0.04
Other Sub-Saharan African (82)	82	0.05
Albanian (345)	355	0.21
Alsatian (0)	55	0.03
American (3,736)	3,736	2.19
Arab (727)	1,080	0.63
Arab (181)	204	0.12
Egyptian (84)	96	0.06
Iraqi (72)	72	0.04
Jordanian (33)	33	0.02
Lebanese (238)	463	0.27
Moroccan (17)	71	0.04
Palestinian (17)	32	0.02
Syrian (20)	31	0.02
Other Arab (65)	78	0.05
Armenian (1,070)	1,199	0.70
Assyrian/Chaldean/Syriac (42)	42	0.02
Australian (69)	103	0.06
Austrian (145)	497	0.29
Basque (33)	99	0.06
Belgian (38)	132	0.08
Brazilian (87)	241	0.14
British (426)	576	0.34
Bulgarian (898)	898	0.53
Cajun (22)	22	0.01
Canadian (424)	687	0.40

*Notes: † The Census 2010 population figure is used to calculate the percentages in the Hispanic Origin and Race categories. Ancestry percentages are based on the 2006-2010 American Community Survey population (not shown); ‡ Numbers in parentheses indicate the number of people reporting a single ancestry; * Numbers in parentheses indicate the number of persons reporting this race alone, not in combination with any other race; Please refer to the Explanation of Data for more information.*

Croatian (159)	432	0.25
Czech (300)	651	0.38
Czechoslovakian (108)	128	0.08
Danish (223)	1,056	0.62
Dutch (446)	1,599	0.94
Eastern European (215)	297	0.17
English (3,642)	11,381	6.67
European (1,182)	1,517	0.89
Finnish (69)	275	0.16
French, ex. Basque (628)	3,971	2.33
French Canadian (394)	764	0.45
German (5,414)	17,726	10.39
Greek (778)	1,183	0.69
Hungarian (492)	1,049	0.61
Icelander (16)	35	0.02
Iranian (475)	537	0.31
Irish (4,594)	14,321	8.39
Israeli (142)	182	0.11
Italian (5,997)	11,913	6.98
Latvian (33)	148	0.09
Lithuanian (42)	200	0.12
Luxemburger (35)	67	0.04
Macedonian (16)	32	0.02
Maltese (0)	23	0.01
New Zealander (37)	96	0.06
Northern European (69)	69	0.04
Norwegian (679)	1,640	0.96
Pennsylvania German (26)	42	0.02
Polish (1,916)	4,638	2.72
Portuguese (101)	428	0.25
Romanian (311)	440	0.26
Russian (1,290)	2,346	1.37
Scandinavian (81)	170	0.10
Scotch-Irish (596)	1,516	0.89
Scottish (776)	2,224	1.30
Serbian (835)	941	0.55
Slavic (21)	121	0.07
Slovak (127)	267	0.16
Slovene (10)	61	0.04
Swedish (521)	1,712	1.00
Swiss (220)	457	0.27
Turkish (69)	90	0.05
Ukrainian (156)	450	0.26
Welsh (257)	795	0.47
West Indian, ex. Hispanic (313)	380	0.22
Barbadian (14)	14	0.01
Dutch West Indian (0)	9	0.01
Jamaican (109)	161	0.09
Trinidadian/Tobagonian (64)	70	0.04
West Indian (126)	126	0.07
Yugoslavian (664)	743	0.44

Hispanic Origin	Population	%
Hispanic or Latino (of any race)	36,691	20.57
Central American, ex. Mexican	3,447	1.93
Costa Rican	150	0.08
Guatemalan	810	0.45
Honduran	272	0.15
Nicaraguan	277	0.16
Panamanian	126	0.07
Salvadoran	1,776	1.00
Other Central American	36	0.02
Cuban	2,010	1.13
Dominican Republic	291	0.16
Mexican	23,871	13.38
Puerto Rican	1,589	0.89
South American	2,163	1.21
Argentinean	442	0.25
Bolivian	29	0.02
Chilean	200	0.11
Colombian	693	0.39
Ecuadorian	174	0.10
Paraguayan	16	0.01
Peruvian	475	0.27
Uruguayan	51	0.03
Venezuelan	71	0.04
Other South American	12	0.01
Other Hispanic or Latino	3,320	1.86

Race*	Population	%
African-American/Black (17,468)	20,084	11.26
Not Hispanic (16,767)	18,798	10.54
Hispanic (701)	1,286	0.72
American Indian/Alaska Native (1,087)	2,396	1.34
Not Hispanic (676)	1,626	0.91
Hispanic (411)	770	0.43
Alaska Athabascan *(Ala. Nat.)* (0)	1	<0.01
Aleut *(Alaska Native)* (2)	3	<0.01
Apache (32)	71	0.04
Arapaho (2)	2	<0.01
Blackfeet (7)	57	0.03
Canadian/French Am. Ind. (5)	10	0.01
Central American Ind. (6)	14	0.01
Cherokee (73)	333	0.19
Cheyenne (2)	8	<0.01
Chickasaw (6)	12	0.01
Chippewa (21)	29	0.02
Choctaw (27)	68	0.04
Colville (0)	1	<0.01
Comanche (6)	18	0.01
Cree (3)	6	<0.01
Creek (15)	33	0.02
Crow (0)	4	<0.01
Delaware (2)	9	0.01
Hopi (2)	13	0.01
Houma (1)	1	<0.01
Inupiat *(Alaska Native)* (1)	6	<0.01
Iroquois (13)	28	0.02
Kiowa (5)	6	<0.01
Lumbee (6)	10	0.01
Menominee (1)	2	<0.01
Mexican American Ind. (67)	108	0.06
Navajo (82)	117	0.07
Osage (4)	8	<0.01
Ottawa (2)	3	<0.01
Paiute (14)	31	0.02
Pima (7)	7	<0.01
Potawatomi (9)	10	0.01
Pueblo (9)	18	0.01
Puget Sound Salish (6)	8	<0.01
Seminole (2)	11	0.01
Shoshone (12)	26	0.01
Sioux (26)	61	0.03
South American Ind. (6)	21	0.01
Spanish American Ind. (12)	15	0.01
Tlingit-Haida *(Alaska Native)* (2)	4	<0.01
Tohono O'Odham (4)	10	0.01
Ute (11)	11	0.01
Yaqui (5)	12	0.01
Yuman (2)	12	0.01
Yup'ik *(Alaska Native)* (0)	1	<0.01
Asian (30,966)	35,247	19.76
Not Hispanic (30,527)	34,201	19.17
Hispanic (439)	1,046	0.59
Bangladeshi (20)	25	0.01
Burmese (49)	55	0.03
Cambodian (200)	244	0.14
Chinese, ex. Taiwanese (8,236)	9,578	5.37
Filipino (11,474)	13,813	7.74
Hmong (24)	34	0.02
Indian (1,074)	1,332	0.75
Indonesian (114)	159	0.09
Japanese (1,223)	2,171	1.22
Korean (2,881)	3,343	1.87
Laotian (216)	287	0.16
Malaysian (21)	38	0.02
Nepalese (3)	4	<0.01
Pakistani (238)	268	0.15
Sri Lankan (131)	150	0.08
Taiwanese (296)	370	0.21
Thai (978)	1,231	0.69
Vietnamese (2,326)	2,777	1.56
Hawaii Native/Pacific Islander (1,462)	2,774	1.55
Not Hispanic (1,368)	2,474	1.39
Hispanic (94)	300	0.17
Fijian (40)	47	0.03
Guamanian/Chamorro (339)	499	0.28
Marshallese (10)	14	0.01
Native Hawaiian (620)	1,439	0.81
Samoan (268)	426	0.24
Tongan (23)	48	0.03
White (103,235)	110,236	61.79
Not Hispanic (85,768)	90,750	50.87
Hispanic (17,467)	19,486	10.92

Summerlin South

Place Type: CDP
County: Clark
Population: 24,085†

Ancestry‡	Population	%
Afghan (321)	321	1.47
African, Sub-Saharan (27)	144	0.66
African (0)	67	0.31
Ethiopian (18)	56	0.26
South African (9)	21	0.10
American (633)	633	2.90
Arab (292)	338	1.55
Egyptian (88)	88	0.40
Iraqi (94)	94	0.43
Jordanian (7)	7	0.03
Lebanese (78)	115	0.53
Moroccan (12)	12	0.06
Syrian (13)	22	0.10
Armenian (208)	218	1.00
Assyrian/Chaldean/Syriac (12)	12	0.06
Austrian (34)	189	0.87
Basque (34)	111	0.51
Belgian (12)	20	0.09
British (61)	96	0.44
Bulgarian (7)	7	0.03
Canadian (71)	94	0.43
Croatian (41)	57	0.26
Czech (14)	69	0.32
Czechoslovakian (8)	8	0.04
Danish (38)	216	0.99
Dutch (46)	169	0.77
Eastern European (171)	171	0.78
English (983)	2,404	11.02
European (313)	359	1.65
Finnish (0)	71	0.33
French, ex. Basque (67)	740	3.39
French Canadian (62)	197	0.90
German (756)	2,648	12.14
Greek (55)	177	0.81
Hungarian (151)	315	1.44
Iranian (38)	38	0.17
Irish (851)	2,570	11.78
Israeli (151)	151	0.69
Italian (909)	1,968	9.02
Latvian (52)	81	0.37
Lithuanian (27)	132	0.61
New Zealander (0)	12	0.06
Norwegian (165)	401	1.84
Pennsylvania German (16)	16	0.07
Polish (392)	990	4.54
Portuguese (29)	79	0.36
Romanian (94)	134	0.61
Russian (147)	658	3.02
Scandinavian (106)	138	0.63
Scotch-Irish (47)	228	1.05
Scottish (132)	376	1.72
Serbian (40)	40	0.18
Slovak (14)	81	0.37
Swedish (85)	432	1.98
Swiss (33)	61	0.28
Turkish (50)	50	0.23
Ukrainian (21)	49	0.22
Welsh (0)	54	0.25
West Indian, ex. Hispanic (91)	100	0.46
Bahamian (67)	67	0.31
Dutch West Indian (24)	24	0.11
Jamaican (0)	9	0.04
Yugoslavian (0)	10	0.05

Hispanic Origin	Population	%
Hispanic or Latino (of any race)	2,066	8.58

*Notes: † The Census 2010 population figure is used to calculate the percentages in the Hispanic Origin and Race categories. Ancestry percentages are based on the 2006-2010 American Community Survey population (not shown); ‡ Numbers in parentheses indicate the number of people reporting a single ancestry; * Numbers in parentheses indicate the number of persons reporting this race alone, not in combination with any other race; Please refer to the Explanation of Data for more information.*

Central American, ex. Mexican	138	0.57
Costa Rican	10	0.04
Guatemalan	48	0.20
Honduran	13	0.05
Nicaraguan	8	0.03
Panamanian	11	0.05
Salvadoran	45	0.19
Other Central American	3	0.01
Cuban	94	0.39
Dominican Republic	16	0.07
Mexican	1,198	4.97
Puerto Rican	129	0.54
South American	206	0.86
Argentinean	42	0.17
Bolivian	1	<0.01
Chilean	8	0.03
Colombian	80	0.33
Ecuadorian	8	0.03
Paraguayan	5	0.02
Peruvian	40	0.17
Uruguayan	8	0.03
Venezuelan	14	0.06
Other Hispanic or Latino	285	1.18

Race*	Population	%
African-American/Black (1,071)	1,302	5.41
Not Hispanic (1,047)	1,244	5.17
Hispanic (24)	58	0.24
American Indian/Alaska Native (96)	231	0.96
Not Hispanic (64)	178	0.74
Hispanic (32)	53	0.22
Aleut *(Alaska Native)* (1)	4	0.02
Apache (3)	4	0.02
Blackfeet (3)	18	0.07
Cherokee (10)	39	0.16
Cheyenne (1)	1	<0.01
Chippewa (1)	3	0.01
Choctaw (1)	7	0.03
Creek (0)	7	0.03
Inupiat *(Alaska Native)* (1)	1	<0.01
Iroquois (0)	1	<0.01
Menominee (1)	1	<0.01
Mexican American Ind. (6)	8	0.03
Navajo (9)	10	0.04
Paiute (0)	3	0.01
Potawatomi (1)	2	0.01
Pueblo (2)	2	0.01
Sioux (3)	3	0.01
Asian (3,089)	3,627	15.06
Not Hispanic (3,047)	3,528	14.65
Hispanic (42)	99	0.41
Burmese (1)	2	0.01
Cambodian (6)	13	0.05
Chinese, ex. Taiwanese (643)	801	3.33
Filipino (1,164)	1,413	5.87
Hmong (5)	5	0.02
Indian (189)	234	0.97
Indonesian (5)	6	0.02
Japanese (264)	387	1.61
Korean (436)	508	2.11
Laotian (12)	29	0.12
Malaysian (2)	2	0.01
Nepalese (0)	3	0.01
Pakistani (46)	58	0.24
Taiwanese (48)	48	0.20
Thai (52)	78	0.32
Vietnamese (86)	119	0.49
Hawaii Native/Pacific Islander (89)	222	0.92
Not Hispanic (82)	198	0.82
Hispanic (7)	24	0.10
Guamanian/Chamorro (29)	43	0.18
Native Hawaiian (49)	133	0.55
Samoan (7)	12	0.05
White (18,363)	19,139	79.46
Not Hispanic (16,986)	17,608	73.11
Hispanic (1,377)	1,531	6.36

Sun Valley

Place Type: CDP
County: Washoe
Population: 19,299†

Ancestry‡	Population	%
American (679)	679	3.61
Arab (57)	57	0.30
Lebanese (57)	57	0.30
Basque (19)	19	0.10
British (0)	28	0.15
Canadian (44)	44	0.23
Czech (30)	196	1.04
Danish (36)	90	0.48
Dutch (28)	234	1.24
English (682)	2,354	12.51
European (261)	261	1.39
French, ex. Basque (52)	438	2.33
French Canadian (33)	103	0.55
German (491)	2,260	12.01
Greek (0)	11	0.06
Hungarian (26)	38	0.20
Irish (537)	2,317	12.31
Italian (267)	563	2.99
Northern European (65)	65	0.35
Norwegian (180)	500	2.66
Polish (32)	266	1.41
Portuguese (83)	121	0.64
Russian (0)	10	0.05
Scotch-Irish (162)	436	2.32
Scottish (28)	224	1.19
Slavic (0)	36	0.19
Slovak (13)	116	0.62
Swedish (26)	284	1.51
Swiss (21)	41	0.22
Welsh (21)	118	0.63

Hispanic Origin	Population	%
Hispanic or Latino (of any race)	7,032	36.44
Central American, ex. Mexican	461	2.39
Costa Rican	1	0.01
Guatemalan	138	0.72
Honduran	22	0.11
Nicaraguan	10	0.05
Panamanian	7	0.04
Salvadoran	283	1.47
Cuban	20	0.10
Dominican Republic	1	0.01
Mexican	6,032	31.26
Puerto Rican	78	0.40
South American	43	0.22
Bolivian	1	0.01
Chilean	12	0.06
Colombian	12	0.06
Ecuadorian	1	0.01
Peruvian	17	0.09
Other Hispanic or Latino	397	2.06

Race*	Population	%
African-American/Black (275)	414	2.15
Not Hispanic (243)	356	1.84
Hispanic (32)	58	0.30
American Indian/Alaska Native (355)	563	2.92
Not Hispanic (241)	387	2.01
Hispanic (114)	176	0.91
Alaska Athabascan *(Ala. Nat.)* (2)	4	0.02
Aleut *(Alaska Native)* (1)	1	0.01
Apache (5)	15	0.08
Blackfeet (2)	10	0.05
Canadian/French Am. Ind. (2)	3	0.02
Central American Ind. (1)	2	0.01
Cherokee (15)	68	0.35
Cheyenne (2)	2	0.01
Chickasaw (2)	4	0.02
Chippewa (8)	8	0.04
Choctaw (5)	19	0.10
Comanche (1)	1	0.01
Creek (3)	3	0.02
Delaware (0)	1	0.01
Hopi (0)	1	0.01
Iroquois (3)	5	0.03
Kiowa (1)	1	0.01
Mexican American Ind. (19)	39	0.20
Navajo (5)	8	0.04
Paiute (86)	109	0.56
Potawatomi (16)	20	0.10
Pueblo (1)	3	0.02
Seminole (2)	2	0.01
Shoshone (19)	25	0.13
Sioux (9)	11	0.06
Tlingit-Haida *(Alaska Native)* (2)	7	0.04
Tohono O'Odham (1)	1	0.01
Tsimshian *(Alaska Native)* (1)	1	0.01
Ute (1)	1	0.01
Yaqui (0)	1	0.01
Yuman (6)	6	0.03
Asian (385)	562	2.91
Not Hispanic (355)	498	2.58
Hispanic (30)	64	0.33
Chinese, ex. Taiwanese (30)	67	0.35
Filipino (198)	276	1.43
Hmong (0)	1	0.01
Indian (66)	70	0.36
Indonesian (2)	6	0.03
Japanese (22)	52	0.27
Korean (10)	21	0.11
Pakistani (9)	9	0.05
Sri Lankan (1)	1	0.01
Taiwanese (2)	5	0.03
Thai (9)	14	0.07
Vietnamese (21)	33	0.17
Hawaii Native/Pacific Islander (121)	208	1.08
Not Hispanic (108)	154	0.80
Hispanic (13)	54	0.28
Fijian (4)	5	0.03
Guamanian/Chamorro (13)	24	0.12
Marshallese (4)	4	0.02
Native Hawaiian (8)	57	0.30
Samoan (4)	16	0.08
Tongan (63)	66	0.34
White (13,763)	14,396	74.59
Not Hispanic (10,897)	11,253	58.31
Hispanic (2,866)	3,143	16.29

Sunrise Manor

Place Type: CDP
County: Clark
Population: 189,372†

Ancestry‡	Population	%
Afghan (67)	78	0.04
African, Sub-Saharan (1,930)	2,479	1.28
African (1,835)	2,303	1.19
Cape Verdean (11)	22	0.01
Nigerian (27)	27	0.01
Somalian (45)	115	0.06
Ugandan (12)	12	0.01
Albanian (55)	55	0.03
American (4,496)	4,496	2.31
Arab (201)	269	0.14
Arab (0)	19	0.01
Egyptian (37)	37	0.02
Iraqi (53)	70	0.04
Lebanese (53)	71	0.04
Moroccan (30)	30	0.02
Syrian (12)	22	0.01
Other Arab (16)	20	0.01
Armenian (49)	203	0.10
Assyrian/Chaldean/Syriac (87)	104	0.05
Australian (12)	32	0.02
Austrian (60)	176	0.09
Basque (31)	31	0.02
Belgian (26)	65	0.03
Brazilian (144)	144	0.07
British (278)	455	0.23
Bulgarian (0)	9	<0.01
Cajun (47)	93	0.05
Canadian (229)	359	0.18

*Notes: † The Census 2010 population figure is used to calculate the percentages in the Hispanic Origin and Race categories. Ancestry percentages are based on the 2006-2010 American Community Survey population (not shown); ‡ Numbers in parentheses indicate the number of people reporting a single ancestry; * Numbers in parentheses indicate the number of persons reporting this race alone, not in combination with any other race; Please refer to the Explanation of Data for more information.*

Celtic (12)	12	0.01
Croatian (21)	142	0.07
Czech (128)	566	0.29
Czechoslovakian (62)	89	0.05
Danish (159)	714	0.37
Dutch (327)	1,818	0.94
Eastern European (59)	59	0.03
English (3,362)	11,205	5.77
European (1,072)	1,650	0.85
Finnish (56)	148	0.08
French, ex. Basque (457)	3,106	1.60
French Canadian (221)	551	0.28
German (4,757)	15,052	7.75
Greek (40)	381	0.20
Hungarian (342)	673	0.35
Irish (4,506)	13,700	7.05
Israeli (9)	9	<0.01
Italian (3,099)	7,269	3.74
Latvian (19)	19	0.01
Lithuanian (44)	127	0.07
Luxemburger (11)	24	0.01
Macedonian (0)	35	0.02
Northern European (7)	7	<0.01
Norwegian (595)	1,618	0.83
Pennsylvania German (29)	29	0.01
Polish (958)	2,968	1.53
Portuguese (284)	673	0.35
Romanian (62)	75	0.04
Russian (229)	820	0.42
Scandinavian (118)	299	0.15
Scotch-Irish (566)	1,365	0.70
Scottish (550)	1,661	0.86
Slavic (0)	34	0.02
Slovak (128)	224	0.12
Slovene (18)	25	0.01
Swedish (395)	1,444	0.74
Swiss (71)	269	0.14
Turkish (13)	25	0.01
Ukrainian (133)	303	0.16
Welsh (183)	770	0.40
West Indian, ex. Hispanic (456)	735	0.38
Barbadian (8)	8	<0.01
Belizean (95)	95	0.05
Haitian (193)	204	0.11
Jamaican (113)	381	0.20
West Indian (47)	47	0.02
Yugoslavian (32)	69	0.04

Hispanic Origin	Population	%
Hispanic or Latino (of any race)	91,764	48.46
Central American, ex. Mexican	6,672	3.52
Costa Rican	68	0.04
Guatemalan	1,532	0.81
Honduran	741	0.39
Nicaraguan	458	0.24
Panamanian	142	0.07
Salvadoran	3,655	1.93
Other Central American	76	0.04
Cuban	2,604	1.38
Dominican Republic	199	0.11
Mexican	74,476	39.33
Puerto Rican	1,685	0.89
South American	1,001	0.53
Argentinean	219	0.12
Bolivian	23	0.01
Chilean	69	0.04
Colombian	216	0.11
Ecuadorian	169	0.09
Paraguayan	24	0.01
Peruvian	192	0.10
Uruguayan	26	0.01
Venezuelan	54	0.03
Other South American	9	<0.01
Other Hispanic or Latino	5,127	2.71

Race*	Population	%
African-American/Black (23,921)	27,084	14.30
Not Hispanic (22,615)	24,953	13.18
Hispanic (1,306)	2,131	1.13
American Indian/Alaska Native (1,633)	3,152	1.66
Not Hispanic (891)	1,903	1.00
Hispanic (742)	1,249	0.66
Alaska Athabascan *(Ala. Nat.)* (1)	1	<0.01
Aleut *(Alaska Native)* (6)	7	<0.01
Apache (49)	124	0.07
Arapaho (0)	1	<0.01
Blackfeet (22)	96	0.05
Canadian/French Am. Ind. (5)	9	<0.01
Central American Ind. (6)	16	0.01
Cherokee (98)	360	0.19
Cheyenne (2)	10	0.01
Chickasaw (4)	13	0.01
Chippewa (21)	57	0.03
Choctaw (23)	61	0.03
Colville (2)	2	<0.01
Comanche (7)	20	0.01
Cree (11)	16	0.01
Creek (3)	14	0.01
Crow (3)	3	<0.01
Delaware (1)	2	<0.01
Hopi (14)	22	0.01
Inupiat *(Alaska Native)* (8)	17	0.01
Iroquois (23)	37	0.02
Kiowa (5)	7	<0.01
Lumbee (3)	4	<0.01
Mexican American Ind. (124)	196	0.10
Navajo (149)	210	0.11
Osage (2)	3	<0.01
Ottawa (8)	10	0.01
Paiute (57)	84	0.04
Pima (0)	5	<0.01
Potawatomi (5)	7	<0.01
Pueblo (18)	37	0.02
Puget Sound Salish (2)	3	<0.01
Seminole (4)	15	0.01
Shoshone (25)	30	0.02
Sioux (42)	93	0.05
South American Ind. (14)	30	0.02
Spanish American Ind. (6)	8	<0.01
Tlingit-Haida *(Alaska Native)* (5)	9	<0.01
Tohono O'Odham (2)	5	<0.01
Tsimshian *(Alaska Native)* (1)	1	<0.01
Ute (2)	10	0.01
Yakama (2)	4	<0.01
Yaqui (22)	32	0.02
Yuman (29)	30	0.02
Yup'ik *(Alaska Native)* (7)	7	<0.01
Asian (10,883)	13,861	7.32
Not Hispanic (10,535)	12,857	6.79
Hispanic (348)	1,004	0.53
Bangladeshi (3)	3	<0.01
Burmese (1)	3	<0.01
Cambodian (170)	223	0.12
Chinese, ex. Taiwanese (464)	955	0.50
Filipino (7,090)	8,747	4.62
Hmong (4)	6	<0.01
Indian (343)	482	0.25
Indonesian (28)	36	0.02
Japanese (404)	870	0.46
Korean (462)	705	0.37
Laotian (442)	520	0.27
Malaysian (4)	13	0.01
Nepalese (3)	3	<0.01
Pakistani (53)	77	0.04
Sri Lankan (16)	21	0.01
Taiwanese (24)	36	0.02
Thai (560)	776	0.41
Vietnamese (360)	498	0.26
Hawaii Native/Pacific Islander (1,192)	2,214	1.17
Not Hispanic (1,019)	1,747	0.92
Hispanic (173)	467	0.25
Fijian (17)	28	0.01
Guamanian/Chamorro (371)	547	0.29
Marshallese (2)	2	<0.01
Native Hawaiian (379)	957	0.51
Samoan (254)	396	0.21
Tongan (53)	78	0.04
White (92,693)	100,290	52.96
Not Hispanic (57,218)	61,089	32.26
Hispanic (35,475)	39,201	20.70

Whitney

Place Type: CDP
County: Clark
Population: 38,585†

Ancestry‡	Population	%
African, Sub-Saharan (280)	280	0.78
African (244)	244	0.68
Kenyan (36)	36	0.10
Albanian (0)	18	0.05
American (1,506)	1,506	4.22
Arab (62)	62	0.17
Lebanese (23)	23	0.06
Other Arab (39)	39	0.11
Australian (0)	26	0.07
British (26)	81	0.23
Canadian (68)	186	0.52
Croatian (0)	29	0.08
Czech (0)	70	0.20
Danish (44)	216	0.60
Dutch (98)	322	0.90
Eastern European (0)	19	0.05
English (872)	1,752	4.90
European (220)	371	1.04
Finnish (9)	9	0.03
French, ex. Basque (101)	583	1.63
French Canadian (95)	122	0.34
German (998)	3,216	9.00
Greek (71)	135	0.38
Hungarian (103)	114	0.32
Iranian (0)	22	0.06
Irish (1,062)	2,635	7.38
Italian (708)	1,362	3.81
Latvian (0)	11	0.03
Lithuanian (111)	158	0.44
Luxemburger (0)	11	0.03
Norwegian (116)	287	0.80
Polish (212)	668	1.87
Portuguese (98)	271	0.76
Romanian (49)	59	0.17
Russian (20)	118	0.33
Scandinavian (0)	27	0.08
Scotch-Irish (129)	249	0.70
Scottish (151)	243	0.68
Serbian (0)	21	0.06
Slovak (11)	30	0.08
Swedish (145)	270	0.76
Swiss (11)	50	0.14
Turkish (0)	16	0.04
Ukrainian (0)	26	0.07
Welsh (90)	165	0.46
West Indian, ex. Hispanic (47)	159	0.45
Haitian (21)	21	0.06
Jamaican (0)	33	0.09
Trinidadian/Tobagonian (0)	56	0.16
West Indian (26)	49	0.14
Yugoslavian (10)	10	0.03

Hispanic Origin	Population	%
Hispanic or Latino (of any race)	13,960	36.18
Central American, ex. Mexican	1,427	3.70
Costa Rican	29	0.08
Guatemalan	288	0.75
Honduran	101	0.26
Nicaraguan	119	0.31
Panamanian	52	0.13
Salvadoran	834	2.16
Other Central American	4	0.01
Cuban	965	2.50
Dominican Republic	61	0.16
Mexican	9,597	24.87
Puerto Rican	386	1.00
South American	425	1.10
Argentinean	45	0.12
Bolivian	13	0.03
Chilean	28	0.07
Colombian	95	0.25
Ecuadorian	73	0.19
Peruvian	130	0.34

*Notes: † The Census 2010 population figure is used to calculate the percentages in the Hispanic Origin and Race categories. Ancestry percentages are based on the 2006-2010 American Community Survey population (not shown); ‡ Numbers in parentheses indicate the number of people reporting a single ancestry; * Numbers in parentheses indicate the number of persons reporting this race alone, not in combination with any other race; Please refer to the Explanation of Data for more information.*

Uruguayan	10	0.03
Venezuelan	24	0.06
Other South American	7	0.02
Other Hispanic or Latino	1,099	2.85

Race*	Population	%
African-American/Black (4,134)	4,889	12.67
Not Hispanic (3,824)	4,390	11.38
Hispanic (310)	499	1.29
American Indian/Alaska Native (306)	648	1.68
Not Hispanic (179)	425	1.10
Hispanic (127)	223	0.58
Alaska Athabascan *(Ala. Nat.)* (1)	3	0.01
Aleut *(Alaska Native)* (2)	2	0.01
Apache (10)	19	0.05
Arapaho (0)	1	<0.01
Blackfeet (7)	14	0.04
Canadian/French Am. Ind. (2)	3	0.01
Cherokee (17)	77	0.20
Cheyenne (0)	4	0.01
Chickasaw (1)	3	0.01
Chippewa (3)	5	0.01
Choctaw (9)	26	0.07
Creek (0)	1	<0.01
Iroquois (3)	6	0.02
Kiowa (0)	2	0.01
Lumbee (4)	6	0.02
Mexican American Ind. (26)	42	0.11
Navajo (43)	54	0.14
Osage (0)	1	<0.01
Paiute (9)	9	0.02
Potawatomi (1)	5	0.01
Pueblo (5)	7	0.02
Seminole (1)	2	0.01
Shoshone (3)	12	0.03
Sioux (10)	23	0.06
South American Ind. (1)	2	0.01
Spanish American Ind. (1)	1	<0.01
Tlingit-Haida *(Alaska Native)* (2)	3	0.01
Yaqui (2)	3	0.01
Yup'ik *(Alaska Native)* (0)	2	0.01
Asian (4,207)	4,991	12.94
Not Hispanic (4,135)	4,756	12.33
Hispanic (72)	235	0.61
Bangladeshi (7)	7	0.02
Burmese (4)	4	0.01
Cambodian (27)	38	0.10
Chinese, ex. Taiwanese (216)	396	1.03
Filipino (3,072)	3,540	9.17
Hmong (27)	31	0.08
Indian (144)	199	0.52
Indonesian (10)	20	0.05
Japanese (126)	303	0.79
Korean (105)	170	0.44
Laotian (32)	45	0.12
Malaysian (4)	4	0.01
Nepalese (7)	9	0.02
Pakistani (13)	17	0.04
Sri Lankan (10)	12	0.03
Taiwanese (3)	4	0.01
Thai (116)	174	0.45
Vietnamese (101)	125	0.32
Hawaii Native/Pacific Islander (299)	576	1.49
Not Hispanic (270)	494	1.28
Hispanic (29)	82	0.21
Guamanian/Chamorro (61)	103	0.27
Native Hawaiian (119)	289	0.75
Samoan (71)	125	0.32
Tongan (17)	34	0.09
White (20,832)	22,556	58.46
Not Hispanic (14,822)	15,872	41.14
Hispanic (6,010)	6,684	17.32

Winchester

Place Type: CDP
County: Clark
Population: 27,978†

Ancestry‡	Population	%
African, Sub-Saharan (964)	1,050	3.86
African (914)	1,000	3.68
Ethiopian (11)	11	0.04
South African (15)	15	0.06
Sudanese (24)	24	0.09
American (854)	854	3.14
Arab (74)	74	0.27
Jordanian (12)	12	0.04
Lebanese (62)	62	0.23
Armenian (0)	12	0.04
Austrian (37)	46	0.17
Belgian (44)	54	0.20
British (57)	90	0.33
Bulgarian (15)	15	0.06
Cajun (60)	60	0.22
Canadian (0)	20	0.07
Czech (14)	37	0.14
Czechoslovakian (0)	11	0.04
Danish (43)	103	0.38
Dutch (50)	277	1.02
Eastern European (17)	17	0.06
English (481)	1,321	4.86
European (222)	222	0.82
Finnish (32)	32	0.12
French, ex. Basque (180)	438	1.61
French Canadian (25)	40	0.15
German (794)	2,313	8.51
Greek (27)	51	0.19
Hungarian (35)	135	0.50
Iranian (23)	23	0.08
Irish (612)	2,142	7.88
Italian (666)	1,089	4.00
Latvian (0)	8	0.03
Lithuanian (19)	82	0.30
Norwegian (20)	116	0.43
Pennsylvania German (17)	17	0.06
Polish (288)	422	1.55
Portuguese (83)	124	0.46
Romanian (0)	24	0.09
Russian (95)	169	0.62
Scandinavian (15)	23	0.08
Scotch-Irish (89)	248	0.91
Scottish (129)	422	1.55
Serbian (9)	9	0.03
Slavic (0)	21	0.08
Slovak (9)	9	0.03
Slovene (15)	15	0.06
Swedish (11)	118	0.43
Swiss (13)	19	0.07
Ukrainian (43)	50	0.18
Welsh (19)	118	0.43
West Indian, ex. Hispanic (12)	12	0.04
Jamaican (12)	12	0.04
Yugoslavian (29)	90	0.33

Hispanic Origin	Population	%
Hispanic or Latino (of any race)	12,491	44.65
Central American, ex. Mexican	1,437	5.14
Costa Rican	13	0.05
Guatemalan	333	1.19
Honduran	135	0.48
Nicaraguan	74	0.26
Panamanian	23	0.08
Salvadoran	845	3.02
Other Central American	14	0.05
Cuban	985	3.52
Dominican Republic	55	0.20
Mexican	8,620	30.81
Puerto Rican	252	0.90
South American	326	1.17
Argentinean	61	0.22
Bolivian	3	0.01
Chilean	13	0.05
Colombian	64	0.23
Ecuadorian	41	0.15
Paraguayan	5	0.02
Peruvian	92	0.33
Uruguayan	26	0.09
Venezuelan	21	0.08
Other Hispanic or Latino	816	2.92

Race*	Population	%
African-American/Black (2,412)	2,769	9.90
Not Hispanic (2,190)	2,450	8.76
Hispanic (222)	319	1.14
American Indian/Alaska Native (312)	509	1.82
Not Hispanic (147)	264	0.94
Hispanic (165)	245	0.88
Alaska Athabascan *(Ala. Nat.)* (1)	1	<0.01
Aleut *(Alaska Native)* (1)	1	<0.01
Apache (11)	13	0.05
Blackfeet (0)	4	0.01
Canadian/French Am. Ind. (6)	6	0.02
Central American Ind. (4)	7	0.03
Cherokee (15)	50	0.18
Cheyenne (0)	1	<0.01
Chickasaw (4)	9	0.03
Chippewa (1)	7	0.03
Choctaw (0)	3	0.01
Comanche (2)	2	0.01
Creek (1)	2	0.01
Hopi (0)	1	<0.01
Inupiat *(Alaska Native)* (1)	1	<0.01
Iroquois (3)	6	0.02
Kiowa (1)	1	<0.01
Mexican American Ind. (26)	38	0.14
Navajo (37)	39	0.14
Ottawa (1)	1	<0.01
Paiute (2)	2	0.01
Pima (1)	1	<0.01
Potawatomi (1)	3	0.01
Pueblo (5)	7	0.03
Puget Sound Salish (0)	3	0.01
Sioux (10)	21	0.08
South American Ind. (0)	1	<0.01
Spanish American Ind. (3)	6	0.02
Tlingit-Haida *(Alaska Native)* (0)	1	<0.01
Tohono O'Odham (1)	1	<0.01
Ute (1)	6	0.02
Yaqui (2)	5	0.02
Yup'ik *(Alaska Native)* (1)	1	<0.01
Asian (1,950)	2,333	8.34
Not Hispanic (1,896)	2,200	7.86
Hispanic (54)	133	0.48
Burmese (2)	2	0.01
Cambodian (15)	17	0.06
Chinese, ex. Taiwanese (209)	276	0.99
Filipino (1,069)	1,308	4.68
Indian (116)	141	0.50
Indonesian (11)	13	0.05
Japanese (80)	162	0.58
Korean (137)	161	0.58
Laotian (31)	31	0.11
Pakistani (33)	39	0.14
Sri Lankan (4)	4	0.01
Taiwanese (10)	11	0.04
Thai (66)	82	0.29
Vietnamese (76)	85	0.30
Hawaii Native/Pacific Islander (164)	290	1.04
Not Hispanic (153)	250	0.89
Hispanic (11)	40	0.14
Fijian (3)	3	0.01
Guamanian/Chamorro (36)	44	0.16
Marshallese (1)	1	<0.01
Native Hawaiian (70)	151	0.54
Samoan (18)	40	0.14
Tongan (1)	5	0.02
White (15,670)	16,667	59.57
Not Hispanic (10,416)	10,951	39.14
Hispanic (5,254)	5,716	20.43

*Notes: † The Census 2010 population figure is used to calculate the percentages in the Hispanic Origin and Race categories. Ancestry percentages are based on the 2006-2010 American Community Survey population (not shown); ‡ Numbers in parentheses indicate the number of people reporting a single ancestry; * Numbers in parentheses indicate the number of persons reporting this race alone, not in combination with any other race; Please refer to the Explanation of Data for more information.*

NEW HAMPSHIRE

Place Type: State
Population: 1,316,470†

Ancestry‡	Population	%
African, Sub-Saharan (3,869)	4,912	0.37
African (1,153)	1,861	0.14
Cape Verdean (109)	311	0.02
Ethiopian (168)	168	0.01
Ghanaian (267)	267	0.02
Kenyan (198)	243	0.02
Liberian (199)	208	0.02
Nigerian (212)	220	0.02
South African (90)	96	0.01
Sudanese (843)	843	0.06
Ugandan (182)	182	0.01
Zimbabwean (170)	170	0.01
Other Sub-Saharan African (278)	343	0.03
Albanian (670)	1,385	0.11
Alsatian (3)	38	<0.01
American (56,844)	56,844	4.33
Arab (2,849)	7,578	0.58
Arab (305)	538	0.04
Egyptian (112)	250	0.02
Iraqi (28)	42	<0.01
Lebanese (1,866)	5,264	0.40
Moroccan (126)	200	0.02
Palestinian (4)	16	<0.01
Syrian (152)	930	0.07
Other Arab (256)	338	0.03
Armenian (1,234)	2,934	0.22
Assyrian/Chaldean/Syriac (0)	13	<0.01
Australian (205)	437	0.03
Austrian (474)	3,059	0.23
Basque (12)	46	<0.01
Belgian (411)	1,673	0.13
Brazilian (2,263)	2,783	0.21
British (4,449)	8,211	0.62
Bulgarian (109)	151	0.01
Cajun (69)	112	0.01
Canadian (9,438)	17,068	1.30
Celtic (171)	292	0.02
Croatian (299)	783	0.06
Czech (656)	3,311	0.25
Czechoslovakian (381)	1,016	0.08
Danish (931)	3,796	0.29
Dutch (2,364)	12,562	0.96
Eastern European (1,345)	1,520	0.12
English (79,852)	247,177	18.81
Estonian (77)	295	0.02
European (8,270)	9,595	0.73
Finnish (3,148)	8,741	0.67
French, ex. Basque (69,415)	217,353	16.54
French Canadian (65,471)	113,567	8.64
German (27,083)	124,609	9.48
German Russian (0)	13	<0.01
Greek (9,331)	21,025	1.60
Guyanese (0)	53	<0.01
Hungarian (1,078)	4,074	0.31
Icelander (39)	64	<0.01
Iranian (276)	500	0.04
Irish (87,186)	292,826	22.29
Israeli (342)	385	0.03
Italian (41,747)	137,298	10.45
Latvian (349)	521	0.04
Lithuanian (2,480)	8,433	0.64
Maltese (14)	157	0.01
New Zealander (50)	74	0.01
Northern European (868)	930	0.07
Norwegian (3,150)	12,016	0.91
Pennsylvania German (149)	446	0.03
Polish (16,319)	58,124	4.42
Portuguese (6,429)	18,526	1.41
Romanian (793)	1,641	0.12
Russian (4,452)	13,211	1.01
Scandinavian (1,039)	2,212	0.17
Scotch-Irish (12,795)	34,354	2.61
Scottish (15,218)	63,006	4.80
Serbian (127)	270	0.02
Slavic (73)	214	0.02
Slovak (528)	1,718	0.13
Slovene (60)	181	0.01
Swedish (6,418)	26,728	2.03
Swiss (715)	2,841	0.22
Turkish (305)	587	0.04
Ukrainian (1,684)	3,774	0.29
Welsh (1,525)	8,677	0.66
West Indian, ex. Hispanic (2,078)	3,499	0.27
Bahamian (0)	3	<0.01
Barbadian (15)	81	0.01
Belizean (0)	12	<0.01
Bermudan (9)	41	<0.01
British West Indian (21)	91	0.01
Dutch West Indian (1)	1	<0.01
Haitian (961)	1,591	0.12
Jamaican (884)	1,338	0.10
Trinidadian/Tobagonian (85)	123	0.01
U.S. Virgin Islander (0)	7	<0.01
West Indian (102)	199	0.02
Other West Indian (0)	12	<0.01
Yugoslavian (1,392)	1,620	0.12

Hispanic Origin	Population	%
Hispanic or Latino (of any race)	36,704	2.79
Central American, ex. Mexican	2,731	0.21
Costa Rican	233	0.02
Guatemalan	743	0.06
Honduran	506	0.04
Nicaraguan	174	0.01
Panamanian	214	0.02
Salvadoran	823	0.06
Other Central American	38	<0.01
Cuban	1,349	0.10
Dominican Republic	4,460	0.34
Mexican	7,822	0.59
Puerto Rican	11,729	0.89
South American	4,266	0.32
Argentinean	322	0.02
Bolivian	82	0.01
Chilean	224	0.02
Colombian	1,899	0.14
Ecuadorian	595	0.05
Paraguayan	28	<0.01
Peruvian	471	0.04
Uruguayan	351	0.03
Venezuelan	243	0.02
Other South American	51	<0.01
Other Hispanic or Latino	4,347	0.33

Race*	Population	%
African-American/Black (15,035)	21,736	1.65
Not Hispanic (13,625)	19,346	1.47
Hispanic (1,410)	2,390	0.18
American Indian/Alaska Native (3,150)	10,524	0.80
Not Hispanic (2,693)	9,527	0.72
Hispanic (457)	997	0.08
Alaska Athabascan *(Ala. Nat.)* (4)	10	<0.01
Aleut *(Alaska Native)* (14)	20	<0.01
Apache (36)	111	0.01
Arapaho (2)	11	<0.01
Blackfeet (101)	555	0.04
Canadian/French Am. Ind. (43)	155	0.01
Central American Ind. (14)	31	<0.01
Cherokee (259)	1,229	0.09
Cheyenne (3)	18	<0.01
Chickasaw (12)	28	<0.01
Chippewa (65)	169	0.01
Choctaw (40)	128	0.01
Colville (1)	2	<0.01
Comanche (6)	20	<0.01
Cree (11)	58	<0.01
Creek (14)	46	<0.01
Crow (3)	15	<0.01
Delaware (7)	24	<0.01
Hopi (5)	7	<0.01
Houma (0)	1	<0.01
Inupiat *(Alaska Native)* (27)	50	<0.01
Iroquois (137)	512	0.04
Kiowa (3)	7	<0.01
Lumbee (27)	49	<0.01
Menominee (2)	6	<0.01
Mexican American Ind. (93)	133	0.01
Navajo (48)	96	0.01
Osage (6)	19	<0.01
Ottawa (8)	12	<0.01
Paiute (6)	7	<0.01
Pima (0)	1	<0.01
Potawatomi (11)	24	<0.01
Pueblo (18)	38	<0.01
Puget Sound Salish (2)	4	<0.01
Seminole (7)	41	<0.01
Shoshone (2)	20	<0.01
Sioux (71)	294	0.02
South American Ind. (41)	84	0.01
Spanish American Ind. (9)	15	<0.01
Tlingit-Haida *(Alaska Native)* (5)	14	<0.01
Tohono O'Odham (1)	6	<0.01
Ute (1)	3	<0.01
Yakama (1)	2	<0.01
Yaqui (14)	17	<0.01
Yuman (3)	6	<0.01
Yup'ik *(Alaska Native)* (5)	8	<0.01
Asian (28,407)	34,522	2.62
Not Hispanic (28,241)	34,018	2.58
Hispanic (166)	504	0.04
Bangladeshi (121)	137	0.01
Bhutanese (651)	764	0.06
Burmese (54)	67	0.01
Cambodian (625)	807	0.06
Chinese, ex. Taiwanese (6,065)	7,327	0.56
Filipino (2,177)	3,369	0.26
Hmong (23)	27	<0.01
Indian (8,268)	9,075	0.69
Indonesian (1,056)	1,257	0.10
Japanese (841)	1,842	0.14
Korean (2,175)	3,021	0.23
Laotian (539)	673	0.05
Malaysian (38)	74	0.01
Nepalese (714)	829	0.06
Pakistani (496)	579	0.04
Sri Lankan (71)	79	0.01
Taiwanese (277)	339	0.03
Thai (451)	705	0.05
Vietnamese (2,472)	2,907	0.22
Hawaii Native/Pacific Islander (384)	1,160	0.09
Not Hispanic (329)	945	0.07
Hispanic (55)	215	0.02
Fijian (4)	6	<0.01
Guamanian/Chamorro (110)	195	0.01
Marshallese (15)	16	<0.01
Native Hawaiian (120)	385	0.03
Samoan (25)	69	0.01
Tongan (3)	8	<0.01
White (1,236,050)	1,255,950	95.40
Not Hispanic (1,215,050)	1,232,088	93.59
Hispanic (21,000)	23,862	1.81

*Notes: † The Census 2010 population figure is used to calculate the percentages in the Hispanic Origin and Race categories. Ancestry percentages are based on the 2006-2010 American Community Survey population (not shown); ‡ Numbers in parentheses indicate the number of people reporting a single ancestry; * Numbers in parentheses indicate the number of persons reporting this race alone, not in combination with any other race; Please refer to the Explanation of Data for more information.*

Amherst

Place Type: Town
County: Hillsborough
Population: 11,201†

Ancestry‡	Population	%
American (889)	889	7.94
Arab (8)	126	1.12
Arab (8)	26	0.23
Lebanese (0)	88	0.79
Syrian (0)	12	0.11
Armenian (28)	59	0.53
Austrian (22)	108	0.96
Belgian (0)	9	0.08
British (76)	98	0.87
Canadian (43)	109	0.97
Croatian (0)	7	0.06
Czech (30)	94	0.84
Czechoslovakian (0)	12	0.11
Danish (12)	24	0.21
Dutch (47)	256	2.29
Eastern European (7)	46	0.41
English (612)	2,168	19.36
European (70)	85	0.76
Finnish (9)	66	0.59
French, ex. Basque (109)	867	7.74
French Canadian (368)	594	5.30
German (184)	1,558	13.91
Greek (39)	179	1.60
Hungarian (35)	53	0.47
Irish (755)	2,987	26.67
Italian (785)	1,579	14.10
Lithuanian (61)	87	0.78
Norwegian (0)	53	0.47
Pennsylvania German (0)	24	0.21
Polish (162)	423	3.78
Portuguese (22)	91	0.81
Russian (30)	188	1.68
Scotch-Irish (71)	347	3.10
Scottish (148)	497	4.44
Slavic (0)	11	0.10
Slovak (13)	55	0.49
Swedish (52)	261	2.33
Swiss (9)	76	0.68
Ukrainian (23)	56	0.50
Welsh (18)	47	0.42

Hispanic Origin	Population	%
Hispanic or Latino (of any race)	218	1.95
Central American, ex. Mexican	17	0.15
Costa Rican	1	0.01
Guatemalan	7	0.06
Honduran	1	0.01
Nicaraguan	6	0.05
Panamanian	1	0.01
Salvadoran	1	0.01
Cuban	11	0.10
Dominican Republic	13	0.12
Mexican	53	0.47
Puerto Rican	53	0.47
South American	33	0.29
Argentinean	5	0.04
Bolivian	1	0.01
Chilean	4	0.04
Colombian	19	0.17
Ecuadorian	1	0.01
Peruvian	1	0.01
Venezuelan	2	0.02
Other Hispanic or Latino	38	0.34

Race*	Population	%
African-American/Black (55)	87	0.78
Not Hispanic (49)	76	0.68
Hispanic (6)	11	0.10
American Indian/Alaska Native (15)	54	0.48
Not Hispanic (14)	41	0.37
Hispanic (1)	13	0.12
Blackfeet (0)	5	0.04
Canadian/French Am. Ind. (1)	2	0.02
Cherokee (0)	5	0.04
Cree (0)	5	0.04
Creek (1)	1	0.01
Delaware (0)	1	0.01
Iroquois (3)	3	0.03
Seminole (0)	2	0.02
Shoshone (0)	1	0.01
Sioux (0)	1	0.01
Tohono O'Odham (0)	1	0.01
Asian (190)	278	2.48
Not Hispanic (188)	276	2.46
Hispanic (2)	2	0.02
Bangladeshi (2)	2	0.02
Cambodian (1)	1	0.01
Chinese, ex. Taiwanese (69)	103	0.92
Filipino (17)	30	0.27
Indian (30)	45	0.40
Japanese (9)	28	0.25
Korean (30)	40	0.36
Laotian (1)	4	0.04
Malaysian (2)	3	0.03
Sri Lankan (3)	3	0.03
Taiwanese (2)	2	0.02
Thai (5)	9	0.08
Vietnamese (5)	9	0.08
Hawaii Native/Pacific Islander (4)	14	0.12
Not Hispanic (4)	12	0.11
Hispanic (0)	2	0.02
Guamanian/Chamorro (0)	1	0.01
Native Hawaiian (3)	9	0.08
White (10,733)	10,891	97.23
Not Hispanic (10,580)	10,716	95.67
Hispanic (153)	175	1.56

Barrington

Place Type: Town
County: Strafford
Population: 8,576†

Ancestry‡	Population	%
American (409)	409	4.84
Arab (12)	52	0.62
Lebanese (12)	52	0.62
Armenian (44)	59	0.70
Austrian (0)	21	0.25
Belgian (0)	12	0.14
British (0)	15	0.18
Canadian (33)	46	0.54
Czechoslovakian (13)	13	0.15
Danish (0)	63	0.75
Dutch (13)	109	1.29
Eastern European (0)	16	0.19
English (570)	2,287	27.05
European (74)	74	0.88
Finnish (5)	18	0.21
French, ex. Basque (356)	1,702	20.13
French Canadian (332)	576	6.81
German (112)	778	9.20
Greek (0)	104	1.23
Hungarian (23)	37	0.44
Iranian (0)	12	0.14
Irish (541)	1,708	20.20
Italian (315)	903	10.68
Lithuanian (0)	19	0.22
Maltese (0)	32	0.38
Norwegian (26)	103	1.22
Pennsylvania German (14)	14	0.17
Polish (245)	530	6.27
Portuguese (15)	218	2.58
Russian (12)	32	0.38
Scotch-Irish (23)	334	3.95
Scottish (68)	463	5.48
Swedish (60)	259	3.06
Swiss (0)	86	1.02
Welsh (54)	61	0.72
West Indian, ex. Hispanic (0)	16	0.19
West Indian (0)	16	0.19

Hispanic Origin	Population	%
Hispanic or Latino (of any race)	112	1.31
Central American, ex. Mexican	4	0.05
Guatemalan	1	0.01
Salvadoran	3	0.03
Cuban	4	0.05
Dominican Republic	3	0.03
Mexican	36	0.42
Puerto Rican	17	0.20
South American	17	0.20
Argentinean	1	0.01
Chilean	9	0.10
Colombian	2	0.02
Ecuadorian	4	0.05
Venezuelan	1	0.01
Other Hispanic or Latino	31	0.36

Race*	Population	%
African-American/Black (40)	70	0.82
Not Hispanic (36)	63	0.73
Hispanic (4)	7	0.08
American Indian/Alaska Native (20)	58	0.68
Not Hispanic (15)	50	0.58
Hispanic (5)	8	0.09
Blackfeet (0)	3	0.03
Canadian/French Am. Ind. (2)	2	0.02
Cherokee (1)	9	0.10
Iroquois (0)	1	0.01
Mexican American Ind. (1)	1	0.01
Seminole (0)	1	0.01
Sioux (0)	2	0.02
South American Ind. (0)	3	0.03
Tlingit-Haida *(Alaska Native)* (0)	1	0.01
Asian (83)	110	1.28
Not Hispanic (82)	109	1.27
Hispanic (1)	1	0.01
Bhutanese (1)	1	0.01
Chinese, ex. Taiwanese (6)	8	0.09
Filipino (16)	26	0.30
Indian (6)	8	0.09
Indonesian (12)	14	0.16
Japanese (5)	7	0.08
Korean (5)	9	0.10
Laotian (5)	11	0.13
Nepalese (14)	15	0.17
Thai (6)	6	0.07
Vietnamese (4)	4	0.05
Hawaii Native/Pacific Islander (0)	1	0.01
Not Hispanic (0)	1	0.01
White (8,312)	8,412	98.09
Not Hispanic (8,231)	8,319	97.00
Hispanic (81)	93	1.08

Bedford

Place Type: Town
County: Hillsborough
Population: 21,203†

Ancestry‡	Population	%
Albanian (51)	51	0.25
American (700)	700	3.37
Arab (56)	251	1.21
Lebanese (23)	155	0.75
Moroccan (33)	49	0.24
Syrian (0)	47	0.23
Armenian (17)	54	0.26
Australian (10)	10	0.05
Austrian (0)	81	0.39
Belgian (0)	11	0.05
British (96)	141	0.68
Cajun (36)	36	0.17
Canadian (485)	564	2.71
Celtic (0)	13	0.06
Croatian (0)	39	0.19
Czech (16)	71	0.34
Czechoslovakian (0)	38	0.18
Danish (40)	114	0.55
Dutch (27)	263	1.26
Eastern European (27)	41	0.20

*Notes: † The Census 2010 population figure is used to calculate the percentages in the Hispanic Origin and Race categories. Ancestry percentages are based on the 2006-2010 American Community Survey population (not shown); ‡ Numbers in parentheses indicate the number of people reporting a single ancestry; * Numbers in parentheses indicate the number of persons reporting this race alone, not in combination with any other race; Please refer to the Explanation of Data for more information.*

English (945)	3,243	15.59
European (202)	219	1.05
Finnish (27)	162	0.78
French, ex. Basque (819)	2,505	12.04
French Canadian (1,117)	1,947	9.36
German (480)	1,937	9.31
Greek (245)	642	3.09
Hungarian (13)	13	0.06
Irish (1,491)	5,110	24.57
Israeli (0)	11	0.05
Italian (752)	2,586	12.43
Lithuanian (30)	121	0.58
Northern European (55)	55	0.26
Norwegian (40)	183	0.88
Polish (461)	1,238	5.95
Portuguese (25)	148	0.71
Romanian (0)	13	0.06
Russian (214)	410	1.97
Scotch-Irish (126)	497	2.39
Scottish (90)	876	4.21
Swedish (119)	410	1.97
Swiss (0)	227	1.09
Ukrainian (56)	72	0.35
Welsh (0)	108	0.52
West Indian, ex. Hispanic (30)	64	0.31
Haitian (30)	52	0.25
Jamaican (0)	12	0.06

Hispanic Origin	Population	%
Hispanic or Latino (of any race)	367	1.73
Central American, ex. Mexican	39	0.18
Costa Rican	3	0.01
Guatemalan	11	0.05
Honduran	4	0.02
Nicaraguan	5	0.02
Panamanian	7	0.03
Salvadoran	9	0.04
Cuban	29	0.14
Dominican Republic	21	0.10
Mexican	81	0.38
Puerto Rican	87	0.41
South American	52	0.25
Argentinean	9	0.04
Bolivian	4	0.02
Chilean	3	0.01
Colombian	13	0.06
Ecuadorian	2	0.01
Peruvian	6	0.03
Uruguayan	9	0.04
Venezuelan	6	0.03
Other Hispanic or Latino	58	0.27

Race*	Population	%
African-American/Black (135)	229	1.08
Not Hispanic (123)	207	0.98
Hispanic (12)	22	0.10
American Indian/Alaska Native (21)	92	0.43
Not Hispanic (20)	86	0.41
Hispanic (1)	6	0.03
Alaska Athabascan *(Ala. Nat.)* (0)	2	0.01
Blackfeet (0)	12	0.06
Central American Ind. (0)	1	<0.01
Cherokee (0)	11	0.05
Cheyenne (0)	2	0.01
Chickasaw (0)	2	0.01
Chippewa (0)	4	0.02
Cree (0)	1	<0.01
Creek (0)	2	0.01
Iroquois (1)	4	0.02
Mexican American Ind. (0)	1	<0.01
Navajo (1)	1	<0.01
Sioux (0)	5	0.02
Tlingit-Haida *(Alaska Native)* (0)	1	<0.01
Asian (615)	764	3.60
Not Hispanic (612)	752	3.55
Hispanic (3)	12	0.06
Bangladeshi (11)	12	0.06
Bhutanese (2)	2	0.01
Cambodian (12)	13	0.06
Chinese, ex. Taiwanese (144)	170	0.80
Filipino (36)	63	0.30
Indian (237)	256	1.21
Indonesian (1)	1	<0.01
Japanese (21)	42	0.20
Korean (66)	93	0.44
Laotian (2)	5	0.02
Malaysian (0)	1	<0.01
Pakistani (29)	33	0.16
Taiwanese (16)	18	0.08
Thai (1)	5	0.02
Vietnamese (13)	16	0.08
Hawaii Native/Pacific Islander (3)	4	0.02
Not Hispanic (3)	4	0.02
Guamanian/Chamorro (0)	1	<0.01
Native Hawaiian (2)	2	0.01
White (20,044)	20,328	95.87
Not Hispanic (19,788)	20,035	94.49
Hispanic (256)	293	1.38

Berlin

Place Type: City
County: Coos
Population: 10,051†

Ancestry‡	Population	%
African, Sub-Saharan (0)	9	0.09
African (0)	9	0.09
Albanian (0)	24	0.24
American (472)	472	4.62
Arab (7)	21	0.21
Lebanese (7)	7	0.07
Syrian (0)	14	0.14
Austrian (0)	25	0.24
Belgian (0)	19	0.19
British (64)	93	0.91
Canadian (121)	195	1.91
Celtic (0)	9	0.09
Czechoslovakian (9)	9	0.09
Danish (0)	8	0.08
Dutch (0)	16	0.16
Eastern European (0)	9	0.09
English (304)	1,006	9.86
Finnish (8)	8	0.08
French, ex. Basque (1,382)	2,840	27.82
French Canadian (2,281)	2,776	27.19
German (104)	469	4.59
Greek (9)	45	0.44
Irish (456)	1,603	15.70
Italian (185)	611	5.99
Lithuanian (0)	14	0.14
Norwegian (11)	310	3.04
Polish (60)	226	2.21
Portuguese (9)	17	0.17
Russian (22)	93	0.91
Scandinavian (7)	7	0.07
Scotch-Irish (32)	125	1.22
Scottish (48)	145	1.42
Swedish (39)	160	1.57
Turkish (6)	6	0.06
Welsh (0)	56	0.55

Hispanic Origin	Population	%
Hispanic or Latino (of any race)	152	1.51
Central American, ex. Mexican	4	0.04
Guatemalan	3	0.03
Honduran	1	0.01
Cuban	11	0.11
Dominican Republic	2	0.02
Mexican	47	0.47
Puerto Rican	49	0.49
South American	8	0.08
Peruvian	4	0.04
Uruguayan	1	0.01
Venezuelan	2	0.02
Other South American	1	0.01
Other Hispanic or Latino	31	0.31

Race*	Population	%
African-American/Black (81)	121	1.20
Not Hispanic (80)	115	1.14
Hispanic (1)	6	0.06
American Indian/Alaska Native (39)	144	1.43
Not Hispanic (33)	132	1.31
Hispanic (6)	12	0.12
Apache (0)	3	0.03
Blackfeet (5)	16	0.16
Canadian/French Am. Ind. (0)	4	0.04
Cherokee (0)	14	0.14
Chickasaw (1)	1	0.01
Chippewa (0)	5	0.05
Cree (0)	4	0.04
Crow (0)	1	0.01
Iroquois (2)	6	0.06
Ottawa (4)	4	0.04
Seminole (1)	1	0.01
South American Ind. (1)	3	0.03
Asian (28)	46	0.46
Not Hispanic (28)	45	0.45
Hispanic (0)	1	0.01
Chinese, ex. Taiwanese (4)	8	0.08
Filipino (6)	10	0.10
Indian (3)	7	0.07
Japanese (2)	6	0.06
Korean (4)	5	0.05
Thai (2)	3	0.03
Vietnamese (5)	5	0.05
White (9,703)	9,878	98.28
Not Hispanic (9,597)	9,749	97.00
Hispanic (106)	129	1.28

Bow

Place Type: Town
County: Merrimack
Population: 7,519†

Ancestry‡	Population	%
Albanian (21)	21	0.28
American (498)	498	6.58
Austrian (0)	11	0.15
British (108)	185	2.44
Canadian (39)	167	2.21
Celtic (14)	14	0.18
Czech (0)	53	0.70
Dutch (8)	82	1.08
Eastern European (13)	13	0.17
English (383)	1,307	17.27
European (87)	87	1.15
Finnish (20)	20	0.26
French, ex. Basque (275)	886	11.71
French Canadian (398)	815	10.77
German (160)	849	11.22
Greek (60)	172	2.27
Hungarian (0)	61	0.81
Irish (340)	1,500	19.82
Italian (366)	962	12.71
Latvian (11)	11	0.15
Lithuanian (25)	108	1.43
Norwegian (15)	146	1.93
Polish (53)	322	4.25
Portuguese (15)	33	0.44
Russian (38)	172	2.27
Scotch-Irish (82)	282	3.73
Scottish (120)	428	5.65
Swedish (108)	208	2.75
Swiss (20)	42	0.55
Ukrainian (18)	34	0.45
Welsh (0)	15	0.20

Hispanic Origin	Population	%
Hispanic or Latino (of any race)	105	1.40
Central American, ex. Mexican	13	0.17
Guatemalan	7	0.09
Nicaraguan	1	0.01
Panamanian	4	0.05
Salvadoran	1	0.01
Cuban	2	0.03
Mexican	35	0.47
Puerto Rican	16	0.21

*Notes: † The Census 2010 population figure is used to calculate the percentages in the Hispanic Origin and Race categories. Ancestry percentages are based on the 2006-2010 American Community Survey population (not shown); ‡ Numbers in parentheses indicate the number of people reporting a single ancestry; * Numbers in parentheses indicate the number of persons reporting this race alone, not in combination with any other race; Please refer to the Explanation of Data for more information.*

South American	18	0.24
Argentinean	4	0.05
Chilean	1	0.01
Colombian	9	0.12
Peruvian	4	0.05
Other Hispanic or Latino	21	0.28

Race*	Population	%
African-American/Black (7)	22	0.29
Not Hispanic (6)	20	0.27
Hispanic (1)	2	0.03
American Indian/Alaska Native (8)	27	0.36
Not Hispanic (7)	25	0.33
Hispanic (1)	2	0.03
Blackfeet (0)	1	0.01
Canadian/French Am. Ind. (0)	1	0.01
Cherokee (1)	2	0.03
Cheyenne (1)	1	0.01
Iroquois (0)	7	0.09
South American Ind. (1)	1	0.01
Asian (104)	131	1.74
Not Hispanic (104)	131	1.74
Burmese (1)	3	0.04
Cambodian (2)	4	0.05
Chinese, ex. Taiwanese (22)	29	0.39
Filipino (13)	18	0.24
Indian (36)	43	0.57
Japanese (8)	11	0.15
Korean (15)	17	0.23
Taiwanese (3)	3	0.04
Vietnamese (1)	1	0.01
Hawaii Native/Pacific Islander (0)	1	0.01
Not Hispanic (0)	1	0.01
White (7,310)	7,376	98.10
Not Hispanic (7,226)	7,287	96.91
Hispanic (84)	89	1.18

Claremont

Place Type: City
County: Sullivan
Population: 13,355†

Ancestry‡	Population	%
American (662)	662	4.91
Armenian (10)	10	0.07
Australian (48)	48	0.36
Austrian (0)	12	0.09
Basque (0)	17	0.13
Belgian (0)	15	0.11
British (75)	96	0.71
Canadian (220)	317	2.35
Czech (6)	45	0.33
Danish (0)	29	0.22
Dutch (0)	25	0.19
English (1,197)	2,557	18.98
European (34)	34	0.25
Finnish (0)	76	0.56
French, ex. Basque (1,550)	3,784	28.09
French Canadian (393)	748	5.55
German (255)	988	7.33
Greek (18)	47	0.35
Hungarian (0)	24	0.18
Irish (668)	1,989	14.77
Italian (347)	1,256	9.32
Lithuanian (41)	41	0.30
Northern European (11)	11	0.08
Norwegian (41)	101	0.75
Polish (474)	694	5.15
Portuguese (10)	52	0.39
Russian (52)	177	1.31
Scotch-Irish (105)	206	1.53
Scottish (155)	584	4.34
Swedish (47)	144	1.07
Swiss (0)	11	0.08
Ukrainian (0)	20	0.15
Welsh (9)	18	0.13
West Indian, ex. Hispanic (0)	42	0.31
Jamaican (0)	30	0.22
Other West Indian (0)	12	0.09

Hispanic Origin	Population	%
Hispanic or Latino (of any race)	171	1.28
Central American, ex. Mexican	13	0.10
Costa Rican	1	0.01
Guatemalan	5	0.04
Nicaraguan	2	0.01
Panamanian	2	0.01
Salvadoran	2	0.01
Other Central American	1	0.01
Cuban	3	0.02
Dominican Republic	6	0.04
Mexican	46	0.34
Puerto Rican	70	0.52
South American	2	0.01
Colombian	2	0.01
Other Hispanic or Latino	31	0.23

Race*	Population	%
African-American/Black (85)	167	1.25
Not Hispanic (81)	155	1.16
Hispanic (4)	12	0.09
American Indian/Alaska Native (44)	158	1.18
Not Hispanic (41)	148	1.11
Hispanic (3)	10	0.07
Apache (0)	2	0.01
Blackfeet (1)	14	0.10
Canadian/French Am. Ind. (1)	1	0.01
Cherokee (2)	16	0.12
Chippewa (2)	2	0.01
Crow (0)	1	0.01
Iroquois (3)	9	0.07
Navajo (0)	1	0.01
Seminole (1)	1	0.01
Sioux (0)	1	0.01
Asian (126)	167	1.25
Not Hispanic (126)	166	1.24
Hispanic (0)	1	0.01
Chinese, ex. Taiwanese (34)	40	0.30
Filipino (20)	28	0.21
Indian (22)	29	0.22
Indonesian (1)	1	0.01
Japanese (4)	8	0.06
Korean (10)	13	0.10
Laotian (1)	8	0.06
Pakistani (12)	16	0.12
Thai (1)	1	0.01
Vietnamese (8)	8	0.06
Hawaii Native/Pacific Islander (4)	6	0.04
Not Hispanic (3)	5	0.04
Hispanic (1)	1	0.01
Guamanian/Chamorro (1)	1	0.01
Native Hawaiian (3)	4	0.03
White (12,808)	13,038	97.63
Not Hispanic (12,713)	12,919	96.74
Hispanic (95)	119	0.89

Concord

Place Type: City
County: Merrimack
Population: 42,695†

Ancestry‡	Population	%
African, Sub-Saharan (191)	287	0.67
African (110)	206	0.48
Liberian (44)	44	0.10
Nigerian (37)	37	0.09
Albanian (59)	110	0.26
Alsatian (0)	9	0.02
American (1,795)	1,795	4.18
Arab (103)	406	0.95
Arab (49)	88	0.20
Lebanese (12)	188	0.44
Syrian (17)	88	0.20
Other Arab (25)	42	0.10
Armenian (39)	74	0.17
Austrian (0)	53	0.12
Belgian (0)	30	0.07
Brazilian (30)	31	0.07
British (95)	355	0.83
Canadian (153)	438	1.02
Croatian (13)	78	0.18
Czech (45)	99	0.23
Czechoslovakian (0)	12	0.03
Danish (35)	126	0.29
Dutch (85)	457	1.06
Eastern European (51)	51	0.12
English (2,699)	8,567	19.94
Estonian (0)	37	0.09
European (347)	424	0.99
Finnish (113)	203	0.47
French, ex. Basque (1,831)	6,341	14.76
French Canadian (2,047)	3,950	9.19
German (791)	4,120	9.59
Greek (445)	900	2.09
Hungarian (10)	232	0.54
Iranian (0)	15	0.03
Irish (2,547)	9,086	21.15
Italian (1,170)	3,949	9.19
Latvian (74)	91	0.21
Lithuanian (67)	140	0.33
Northern European (23)	23	0.05
Norwegian (49)	282	0.66
Pennsylvania German (0)	14	0.03
Polish (494)	1,654	3.85
Portuguese (164)	534	1.24
Romanian (9)	26	0.06
Russian (153)	303	0.71
Scandinavian (17)	46	0.11
Scotch-Irish (494)	1,165	2.71
Scottish (431)	2,368	5.51
Serbian (92)	110	0.26
Slovak (0)	61	0.14
Swedish (133)	869	2.02
Swiss (0)	55	0.13
Ukrainian (27)	67	0.16
Welsh (91)	569	1.32
West Indian, ex. Hispanic (120)	302	0.70
Barbadian (11)	48	0.11
Haitian (74)	219	0.51
Jamaican (28)	28	0.07
Trinidadian/Tobagonian (7)	7	0.02
Yugoslavian (41)	41	0.10

Hispanic Origin	Population	%
Hispanic or Latino (of any race)	878	2.06
Central American, ex. Mexican	49	0.11
Costa Rican	8	0.02
Guatemalan	16	0.04
Honduran	4	0.01
Nicaraguan	6	0.01
Panamanian	12	0.03
Salvadoran	3	0.01
Cuban	42	0.10
Dominican Republic	35	0.08
Mexican	164	0.38
Puerto Rican	298	0.70
South American	105	0.25
Argentinean	16	0.04
Bolivian	2	<0.01
Chilean	4	0.01
Colombian	42	0.10
Ecuadorian	4	0.01
Peruvian	8	0.02
Uruguayan	18	0.04
Venezuelan	9	0.02
Other South American	2	<0.01
Other Hispanic or Latino	185	0.43

Race*	Population	%
African-American/Black (950)	1,195	2.80
Not Hispanic (917)	1,133	2.65
Hispanic (33)	62	0.15
American Indian/Alaska Native (134)	409	0.96
Not Hispanic (118)	366	0.86
Hispanic (16)	43	0.10
Apache (7)	9	0.02
Arapaho (0)	1	<0.01
Blackfeet (8)	21	0.05
Canadian/French Am. Ind. (2)	2	<0.01

*Notes: † The Census 2010 population figure is used to calculate the percentages in the Hispanic Origin and Race categories. Ancestry percentages are based on the 2006-2010 American Community Survey population (not shown); ‡ Numbers in parentheses indicate the number of people reporting a single ancestry; * Numbers in parentheses indicate the number of persons reporting this race alone, not in combination with any other race; Please refer to the Explanation of Data for more information.*

Cherokee (11)	43	0.10
Cheyenne (0)	1	<0.01
Chippewa (4)	4	0.01
Choctaw (4)	5	0.01
Comanche (2)	5	0.01
Cree (0)	2	<0.01
Creek (0)	1	<0.01
Crow (0)	1	<0.01
Delaware (0)	1	<0.01
Hopi (2)	2	<0.01
Inupiat *(Alaska Native)* (0)	3	0.01
Iroquois (2)	12	0.03
Lumbee (0)	1	<0.01
Mexican American Ind. (2)	3	0.01
Navajo (0)	1	<0.01
Potawatomi (0)	1	<0.01
Seminole (1)	2	<0.01
Sioux (7)	16	0.04
South American Ind. (2)	10	0.02
Asian (1,451)	1,675	3.92
Not Hispanic (1,445)	1,657	3.88
Hispanic (6)	18	0.04
Bangladeshi (4)	4	0.01
Bhutanese (253)	288	0.67
Burmese (4)	5	0.01
Cambodian (6)	9	0.02
Chinese, ex. Taiwanese (184)	229	0.54
Filipino (155)	209	0.49
Indian (293)	335	0.78
Indonesian (4)	4	0.01
Japanese (18)	45	0.11
Korean (140)	175	0.41
Laotian (5)	6	0.01
Nepalese (184)	212	0.50
Pakistani (19)	22	0.05
Taiwanese (7)	8	0.02
Thai (21)	23	0.05
Vietnamese (58)	70	0.16
Hawaii Native/Pacific Islander (9)	34	0.08
Not Hispanic (8)	24	0.06
Hispanic (1)	10	0.02
Guamanian/Chamorro (1)	4	0.01
Marshallese (1)	1	<0.01
Native Hawaiian (5)	13	0.03
Samoan (1)	3	0.01
White (39,208)	39,895	93.44
Not Hispanic (38,630)	39,233	91.89
Hispanic (578)	662	1.55

Conway

Place Type: Town
County: Carroll
Population: 10,115†

Ancestry‡	Population	%
American (517)	517	5.17
Armenian (12)	32	0.32
Austrian (0)	10	0.10
British (34)	52	0.52
Canadian (28)	65	0.65
Czech (0)	5	0.05
Danish (0)	51	0.51
Dutch (41)	87	0.87
English (841)	3,058	30.60
Estonian (0)	63	0.63
European (0)	17	0.17
Finnish (0)	55	0.55
French, ex. Basque (503)	1,147	11.48
French Canadian (232)	482	4.82
German (199)	886	8.86
Greek (0)	8	0.08
Hungarian (0)	21	0.21
Irish (976)	3,055	30.57
Italian (117)	737	7.37
Lithuanian (0)	9	0.09
Norwegian (0)	8	0.08
Polish (22)	237	2.37
Portuguese (10)	55	0.55
Romanian (104)	114	1.14
Russian (43)	202	2.02
Scotch-Irish (257)	424	4.24
Scottish (265)	908	9.08
Slovak (5)	27	0.27
Swedish (53)	132	1.32
Welsh (34)	136	1.36
Yugoslavian (0)	5	0.05

Hispanic Origin	Population	%
Hispanic or Latino (of any race)	106	1.05
Central American, ex. Mexican	14	0.14
Costa Rican	8	0.08
Nicaraguan	1	0.01
Panamanian	1	0.01
Salvadoran	4	0.04
Cuban	2	0.02
Dominican Republic	2	0.02
Mexican	26	0.26
Puerto Rican	31	0.31
South American	16	0.16
Chilean	1	0.01
Colombian	1	0.01
Peruvian	4	0.04
Uruguayan	6	0.06
Other South American	4	0.04
Other Hispanic or Latino	15	0.15

Race*	Population	%
African-American/Black (33)	73	0.72
Not Hispanic (32)	67	0.66
Hispanic (1)	6	0.06
American Indian/Alaska Native (40)	93	0.92
Not Hispanic (39)	87	0.86
Hispanic (1)	6	0.06
Apache (2)	2	0.02
Blackfeet (3)	6	0.06
Cherokee (4)	8	0.08
Creek (1)	1	0.01
Iroquois (2)	3	0.03
Lumbee (1)	1	0.01
Seminole (2)	2	0.02
Sioux (0)	2	0.02
South American Ind. (1)	4	0.04
Asian (98)	120	1.19
Not Hispanic (95)	114	1.13
Hispanic (3)	6	0.06
Chinese, ex. Taiwanese (28)	33	0.33
Filipino (9)	13	0.13
Indian (29)	33	0.33
Japanese (5)	8	0.08
Korean (10)	11	0.11
Malaysian (2)	2	0.02
Thai (4)	8	0.08
Vietnamese (8)	10	0.10
Hawaii Native/Pacific Islander (4)	10	0.10
Not Hispanic (4)	9	0.09
Hispanic (0)	1	0.01
Native Hawaiian (4)	8	0.08
White (9,800)	9,912	97.99
Not Hispanic (9,728)	9,829	97.17
Hispanic (72)	83	0.82

Derry

Place Type: CDP
County: Rockingham
Population: 22,015†

Ancestry‡	Population	%
African, Sub-Saharan (135)	147	0.64
Cape Verdean (13)	25	0.11
Zimbabwean (122)	122	0.53
American (396)	396	1.73
Arab (22)	171	0.75
Arab (7)	7	0.03
Lebanese (15)	164	0.72
Armenian (42)	70	0.31
Australian (12)	33	0.14
Austrian (10)	34	0.15
Brazilian (59)	59	0.26
British (39)	73	0.32
Cajun (10)	10	0.04
Canadian (211)	323	1.41
Czech (0)	26	0.11
Danish (24)	24	0.10
Dutch (22)	147	0.64
English (827)	3,831	16.74
European (187)	187	0.82
Finnish (12)	101	0.44
French, ex. Basque (900)	3,762	16.44
French Canadian (1,058)	1,905	8.32
German (338)	2,389	10.44
Greek (84)	336	1.47
Hungarian (23)	62	0.27
Iranian (35)	35	0.15
Irish (1,558)	5,624	24.58
Italian (1,568)	3,794	16.58
Lithuanian (41)	210	0.92
Northern European (47)	47	0.21
Norwegian (79)	244	1.07
Polish (390)	903	3.95
Portuguese (294)	680	2.97
Romanian (0)	25	0.11
Russian (89)	229	1.00
Scandinavian (77)	77	0.34
Scotch-Irish (264)	572	2.50
Scottish (378)	946	4.13
Swedish (58)	295	1.29
Swiss (14)	14	0.06
Turkish (23)	53	0.23
Ukrainian (61)	167	0.73
Welsh (23)	94	0.41

Hispanic Origin	Population	%
Hispanic or Latino (of any race)	793	3.60
Central American, ex. Mexican	69	0.31
Costa Rican	8	0.04
Guatemalan	41	0.19
Honduran	7	0.03
Nicaraguan	6	0.03
Panamanian	2	0.01
Salvadoran	5	0.02
Cuban	25	0.11
Dominican Republic	94	0.43
Mexican	124	0.56
Puerto Rican	291	1.32
South American	87	0.40
Argentinean	15	0.07
Chilean	6	0.03
Colombian	36	0.16
Ecuadorian	20	0.09
Peruvian	4	0.02
Uruguayan	2	0.01
Venezuelan	3	0.01
Other South American	1	<0.01
Other Hispanic or Latino	103	0.47

Race*	Population	%
African-American/Black (215)	336	1.53
Not Hispanic (205)	309	1.40
Hispanic (10)	27	0.12
American Indian/Alaska Native (56)	196	0.89
Not Hispanic (45)	174	0.79
Hispanic (11)	22	0.10
Alaska Athabascan *(Ala. Nat.)* (0)	1	<0.01
Apache (1)	5	0.02
Blackfeet (2)	15	0.07
Canadian/French Am. Ind. (0)	1	<0.01
Cherokee (5)	36	0.16
Chickasaw (0)	1	<0.01
Chippewa (1)	2	0.01
Choctaw (0)	2	0.01
Inupiat *(Alaska Native)* (1)	1	<0.01
Iroquois (8)	14	0.06
Kiowa (0)	4	0.02
Lumbee (0)	2	0.01
Mexican American Ind. (5)	9	0.04
Navajo (1)	1	<0.01
Osage (1)	1	<0.01
Sioux (3)	4	0.02

*Notes: † The Census 2010 population figure is used to calculate the percentages in the Hispanic Origin and Race categories. Ancestry percentages are based on the 2006-2010 American Community Survey population (not shown); ‡ Numbers in parentheses indicate the number of people reporting a single ancestry; * Numbers in parentheses indicate the number of persons reporting this race alone, not in combination with any other race; Please refer to the Explanation of Data for more information.*

Spanish American Ind. (1)	1	<0.01
Asian (360)	450	2.04
Not Hispanic (354)	440	2.00
Hispanic (6)	10	0.05
Cambodian (11)	17	0.08
Chinese, ex. Taiwanese (70)	85	0.39
Filipino (41)	49	0.22
Indian (130)	143	0.65
Indonesian (2)	2	0.01
Japanese (14)	35	0.16
Korean (35)	47	0.21
Laotian (1)	1	<0.01
Nepalese (10)	11	0.05
Sri Lankan (2)	2	0.01
Taiwanese (3)	3	0.01
Thai (6)	8	0.04
Vietnamese (14)	24	0.11
Hawaii Native/Pacific Islander (11)	20	0.09
Not Hispanic (8)	16	0.07
Hispanic (3)	4	0.02
Guamanian/Chamorro (4)	4	0.02
Native Hawaiian (7)	12	0.05
Samoan (0)	1	<0.01
White (20,737)	21,108	95.88
Not Hispanic (20,243)	20,551	93.35
Hispanic (494)	557	2.53

Derry

Place Type: Town
County: Rockingham
Population: 33,109†

Ancestry‡	Population	%
African, Sub-Saharan (178)	202	0.60
African (26)	26	0.08
Cape Verdean (13)	25	0.07
Kenyan (17)	29	0.09
Zimbabwean (122)	122	0.36
American (730)	730	2.17
Arab (46)	226	0.67
Arab (7)	7	0.02
Lebanese (39)	188	0.56
Syrian (0)	31	0.09
Armenian (42)	81	0.24
Australian (12)	33	0.10
Austrian (10)	46	0.14
Brazilian (67)	67	0.20
British (39)	82	0.24
Cajun (10)	10	0.03
Canadian (295)	583	1.74
Czech (0)	26	0.08
Czechoslovakian (0)	9	0.03
Danish (24)	24	0.07
Dutch (22)	208	0.62
English (1,343)	5,591	16.66
European (266)	286	0.85
Finnish (22)	111	0.33
French, ex. Basque (1,241)	5,308	15.81
French Canadian (1,327)	2,399	7.15
German (472)	3,368	10.03
Greek (117)	500	1.49
Hungarian (42)	152	0.45
Iranian (35)	35	0.10
Irish (2,436)	8,455	25.19
Italian (2,030)	5,427	16.17
Lithuanian (66)	299	0.89
Northern European (47)	47	0.14
Norwegian (94)	259	0.77
Pennsylvania German (12)	55	0.16
Polish (470)	1,351	4.03
Portuguese (358)	1,011	3.01
Romanian (0)	25	0.07
Russian (97)	247	0.74
Scandinavian (77)	77	0.23
Scotch-Irish (471)	940	2.80
Scottish (620)	1,620	4.83
Slovak (0)	25	0.07
Slovene (22)	22	0.07
Swedish (205)	661	1.97
Swiss (14)	35	0.10
Turkish (23)	53	0.16
Ukrainian (115)	257	0.77
Welsh (23)	200	0.60
West Indian, ex. Hispanic (31)	71	0.21
Haitian (14)	33	0.10
Jamaican (0)	21	0.06
West Indian (17)	17	0.05

Hispanic Origin	Population	%
Hispanic or Latino (of any race)	1,080	3.26
Central American, ex. Mexican	111	0.34
Costa Rican	11	0.03
Guatemalan	57	0.17
Honduran	8	0.02
Nicaraguan	9	0.03
Panamanian	7	0.02
Salvadoran	19	0.06
Cuban	46	0.14
Dominican Republic	114	0.34
Mexican	177	0.53
Puerto Rican	372	1.12
South American	129	0.39
Argentinean	19	0.06
Chilean	7	0.02
Colombian	63	0.19
Ecuadorian	26	0.08
Peruvian	5	0.02
Uruguayan	2	0.01
Venezuelan	6	0.02
Other South American	1	<0.01
Other Hispanic or Latino	131	0.40

Race*	Population	%
African-American/Black (326)	507	1.53
Not Hispanic (312)	474	1.43
Hispanic (14)	33	0.10
American Indian/Alaska Native (80)	261	0.79
Not Hispanic (63)	233	0.70
Hispanic (17)	28	0.08
Alaska Athabascan *(Ala. Nat.)* (0)	1	<0.01
Apache (1)	5	0.02
Blackfeet (2)	20	0.06
Canadian/French Am. Ind. (0)	1	<0.01
Cherokee (8)	43	0.13
Chickasaw (0)	1	<0.01
Chippewa (1)	2	0.01
Choctaw (0)	4	0.01
Delaware (1)	2	0.01
Inupiat *(Alaska Native)* (1)	1	<0.01
Iroquois (9)	21	0.06
Kiowa (0)	4	0.01
Lumbee (0)	2	0.01
Mexican American Ind. (7)	11	0.03
Navajo (1)	1	<0.01
Osage (1)	1	<0.01
Sioux (4)	5	0.02
South American Ind. (2)	2	0.01
Spanish American Ind. (1)	1	<0.01
Asian (513)	659	1.99
Not Hispanic (507)	646	1.95
Hispanic (6)	13	0.04
Cambodian (12)	18	0.05
Chinese, ex. Taiwanese (114)	136	0.41
Filipino (51)	65	0.20
Indian (169)	187	0.56
Indonesian (3)	5	0.02
Japanese (21)	46	0.14
Korean (56)	87	0.26
Laotian (2)	3	0.01
Nepalese (13)	14	0.04
Pakistani (6)	6	0.02
Sri Lankan (2)	2	0.01
Taiwanese (5)	5	0.02
Thai (11)	14	0.04
Vietnamese (25)	41	0.12
Hawaii Native/Pacific Islander (12)	28	0.08
Not Hispanic (9)	24	0.07
Hispanic (3)	4	0.01
Guamanian/Chamorro (4)	5	0.02
Native Hawaiian (8)	17	0.05
Samoan (0)	1	<0.01
White (31,301)	31,846	96.19
Not Hispanic (30,599)	31,056	93.80
Hispanic (702)	790	2.39

Dover

Place Type: City
County: Strafford
Population: 29,987†

Ancestry‡	Population	%
African, Sub-Saharan (197)	309	1.04
African (0)	106	0.36
Ethiopian (43)	43	0.14
Ghanaian (78)	78	0.26
Kenyan (44)	44	0.15
South African (0)	6	0.02
Other Sub-Saharan African (32)	32	0.11
Albanian (19)	56	0.19
American (1,034)	1,034	3.48
Arab (216)	288	0.97
Arab (0)	13	0.04
Lebanese (216)	273	0.92
Syrian (0)	2	0.01
Armenian (34)	123	0.41
Australian (0)	65	0.22
Austrian (0)	30	0.10
Brazilian (40)	40	0.13
British (57)	125	0.42
Canadian (105)	212	0.71
Celtic (11)	11	0.04
Czech (23)	66	0.22
Czechoslovakian (0)	30	0.10
Danish (17)	75	0.25
Dutch (55)	262	0.88
Eastern European (33)	41	0.14
English (1,378)	4,842	16.31
Estonian (22)	22	0.07
European (182)	191	0.64
Finnish (38)	100	0.34
French, ex. Basque (1,547)	4,694	15.82
French Canadian (1,443)	2,633	8.87
German (592)	2,688	9.06
Greek (271)	543	1.83
Hungarian (35)	76	0.26
Irish (1,930)	6,367	21.45
Israeli (43)	43	0.14
Italian (758)	2,905	9.79
Lithuanian (0)	132	0.44
Maltese (0)	26	0.09
New Zealander (9)	9	0.03
Northern European (52)	52	0.18
Norwegian (37)	148	0.50
Pennsylvania German (0)	11	0.04
Polish (307)	920	3.10
Portuguese (39)	223	0.75
Romanian (31)	46	0.15
Russian (64)	181	0.61
Scandinavian (65)	65	0.22
Scotch-Irish (270)	601	2.03
Scottish (242)	1,327	4.47
Slovak (7)	39	0.13
Swedish (140)	728	2.45
Swiss (76)	192	0.65
Turkish (0)	19	0.06
Ukrainian (28)	103	0.35
Welsh (9)	243	0.82
West Indian, ex. Hispanic (15)	52	0.18
Haitian (15)	15	0.05
Jamaican (0)	37	0.12

Hispanic Origin	Population	%
Hispanic or Latino (of any race)	660	2.20
Central American, ex. Mexican	38	0.13
Costa Rican	3	0.01
Guatemalan	8	0.03
Honduran	8	0.03
Nicaraguan	4	0.01

*Notes: † The Census 2010 population figure is used to calculate the percentages in the Hispanic Origin and Race categories. Ancestry percentages are based on the 2006-2010 American Community Survey population (not shown); ‡ Numbers in parentheses indicate the number of people reporting a single ancestry; * Numbers in parentheses indicate the number of persons reporting this race alone, not in combination with any other race; Please refer to the Explanation of Data for more information.*

Panamanian	1	<0.01
Salvadoran	14	0.05
Cuban	29	0.10
Dominican Republic	79	0.26
Mexican	114	0.38
Puerto Rican	203	0.68
South American	77	0.26
Argentinean	6	0.02
Bolivian	3	0.01
Chilean	7	0.02
Colombian	34	0.11
Ecuadorian	8	0.03
Peruvian	12	0.04
Venezuelan	7	0.02
Other Hispanic or Latino	120	0.40

Race*	Population	%
African-American/Black (521)	802	2.67
Not Hispanic (475)	734	2.45
Hispanic (46)	68	0.23
American Indian/Alaska Native (59)	227	0.76
Not Hispanic (52)	212	0.71
Hispanic (7)	15	0.05
Alaska Athabascan *(Ala. Nat.)* (1)	2	0.01
Blackfeet (2)	9	0.03
Canadian/French Am. Ind. (1)	4	0.01
Central American Ind. (1)	1	<0.01
Cherokee (2)	21	0.07
Cheyenne (0)	1	<0.01
Chickasaw (0)	1	<0.01
Chippewa (1)	4	0.01
Choctaw (1)	9	0.03
Cree (0)	1	<0.01
Creek (0)	1	<0.01
Crow (0)	1	<0.01
Hopi (1)	1	<0.01
Iroquois (11)	18	0.06
Mexican American Ind. (1)	3	0.01
Navajo (1)	2	0.01
Ottawa (0)	1	<0.01
Sioux (0)	7	0.02
Tlingit-Haida *(Alaska Native)* (1)	1	<0.01
Asian (1,371)	1,618	5.40
Not Hispanic (1,365)	1,602	5.34
Hispanic (6)	16	0.05
Burmese (4)	4	0.01
Cambodian (41)	47	0.16
Chinese, ex. Taiwanese (145)	190	0.63
Filipino (77)	130	0.43
Hmong (2)	2	0.01
Indian (216)	246	0.82
Indonesian (503)	569	1.90
Japanese (24)	56	0.19
Korean (55)	89	0.30
Laotian (74)	87	0.29
Malaysian (8)	14	0.05
Nepalese (13)	15	0.05
Pakistani (5)	5	0.02
Sri Lankan (2)	2	0.01
Taiwanese (9)	9	0.03
Thai (20)	30	0.10
Vietnamese (69)	79	0.26
Hawaii Native/Pacific Islander (14)	49	0.16
Not Hispanic (12)	46	0.15
Hispanic (2)	3	0.01
Fijian (0)	1	<0.01
Guamanian/Chamorro (6)	6	0.02
Native Hawaiian (3)	13	0.04
Samoan (1)	1	<0.01
White (27,155)	27,771	92.61
Not Hispanic (26,769)	27,341	91.18
Hispanic (386)	430	1.43

Durham

Place Type: CDP
County: Strafford
Population: 10,345†

Ancestry‡	Population	%
African, Sub-Saharan (39)	65	0.73
African (0)	26	0.29
Kenyan (11)	11	0.12
Other Sub-Saharan African (28)	28	0.31
American (132)	132	1.48
Arab (39)	84	0.94
Arab (10)	21	0.23
Egyptian (7)	16	0.18
Lebanese (22)	35	0.39
Syrian (0)	12	0.13
Armenian (0)	19	0.21
Australian (0)	11	0.12
Austrian (0)	34	0.38
Belgian (0)	12	0.13
Brazilian (0)	8	0.09
British (43)	95	1.06
Canadian (0)	52	0.58
Czechoslovakian (0)	13	0.15
Danish (0)	8	0.09
Dutch (16)	121	1.35
Eastern European (0)	19	0.21
English (321)	1,357	15.18
European (12)	62	0.69
Finnish (0)	52	0.58
French, ex. Basque (93)	600	6.71
French Canadian (249)	660	7.38
German (146)	1,108	12.39
Greek (94)	189	2.11
Hungarian (0)	24	0.27
Iranian (38)	68	0.76
Irish (622)	2,330	26.06
Italian (282)	1,396	15.62
Lithuanian (58)	121	1.35
Northern European (11)	11	0.12
Norwegian (114)	210	2.35
Polish (21)	417	4.66
Portuguese (23)	84	0.94
Romanian (10)	10	0.11
Russian (41)	108	1.21
Scandinavian (31)	41	0.46
Scotch-Irish (36)	323	3.61
Scottish (89)	331	3.70
Slovak (35)	65	0.73
Swedish (23)	179	2.00
Swiss (0)	13	0.15
Turkish (9)	9	0.10
Ukrainian (31)	51	0.57
Welsh (13)	147	1.64

Hispanic Origin	Population	%
Hispanic or Latino (of any race)	235	2.27
Central American, ex. Mexican	17	0.16
Costa Rican	5	0.05
Guatemalan	3	0.03
Honduran	4	0.04
Nicaraguan	3	0.03
Panamanian	1	0.01
Salvadoran	1	0.01
Cuban	32	0.31
Dominican Republic	24	0.23
Mexican	38	0.37
Puerto Rican	45	0.43
South American	42	0.41
Argentinean	2	0.02
Bolivian	2	0.02
Chilean	5	0.05
Colombian	13	0.13
Ecuadorian	7	0.07
Paraguayan	1	0.01
Peruvian	12	0.12
Other Hispanic or Latino	37	0.36

Race*	Population	%
African-American/Black (107)	160	1.55
Not Hispanic (98)	146	1.41
Hispanic (9)	14	0.14
American Indian/Alaska Native (8)	38	0.37
Not Hispanic (6)	32	0.31
Hispanic (2)	6	0.06
Blackfeet (0)	4	0.04
Cherokee (2)	6	0.06
Choctaw (0)	2	0.02
Inupiat *(Alaska Native)* (1)	1	0.01
Iroquois (0)	3	0.03
Navajo (0)	1	0.01
Sioux (0)	1	0.01
South American Ind. (0)	1	0.01
Asian (377)	456	4.41
Not Hispanic (376)	452	4.37
Hispanic (1)	4	0.04
Cambodian (2)	2	0.02
Chinese, ex. Taiwanese (182)	200	1.93
Filipino (21)	38	0.37
Indian (78)	85	0.82
Indonesian (0)	1	0.01
Japanese (13)	27	0.26
Korean (38)	47	0.45
Malaysian (1)	1	0.01
Nepalese (1)	2	0.02
Pakistani (0)	2	0.02
Taiwanese (4)	6	0.06
Thai (2)	3	0.03
Vietnamese (27)	35	0.34
Hawaii Native/Pacific Islander (2)	14	0.14
Not Hispanic (2)	10	0.10
Hispanic (0)	4	0.04
Fijian (0)	1	0.01
Guamanian/Chamorro (0)	1	0.01
Native Hawaiian (0)	3	0.03
Samoan (2)	2	0.02
White (9,634)	9,783	94.57
Not Hispanic (9,472)	9,605	92.85
Hispanic (162)	178	1.72

Durham

Place Type: Town
County: Strafford
Population: 14,638†

Ancestry‡	Population	%
African, Sub-Saharan (39)	65	0.45
African (0)	26	0.18
Kenyan (11)	11	0.08
Other Sub-Saharan African (28)	28	0.20
American (304)	304	2.13
Arab (39)	117	0.82
Arab (10)	21	0.15
Egyptian (7)	16	0.11
Lebanese (22)	45	0.31
Palestinian (0)	6	0.04
Syrian (0)	23	0.16
Other Arab (0)	6	0.04
Armenian (9)	35	0.24
Australian (0)	11	0.08
Austrian (0)	42	0.29
Belgian (0)	48	0.34
Brazilian (0)	8	0.06
British (55)	128	0.90
Bulgarian (0)	10	0.07
Canadian (32)	94	0.66
Croatian (0)	4	0.03
Czech (8)	39	0.27
Czechoslovakian (0)	21	0.15
Danish (30)	81	0.57
Dutch (16)	143	1.00
Eastern European (0)	19	0.13
English (517)	2,457	17.20
European (106)	156	1.09
Finnish (0)	58	0.41
French, ex. Basque (181)	1,025	7.17
French Canadian (402)	1,086	7.60
German (298)	1,821	12.74
Greek (111)	211	1.48
Hungarian (0)	24	0.17
Iranian (48)	78	0.55
Irish (979)	3,485	24.39
Italian (534)	2,178	15.24
Lithuanian (69)	197	1.38

*Notes: † The Census 2010 population figure is used to calculate the percentages in the Hispanic Origin and Race categories. Ancestry percentages are based on the 2006-2010 American Community Survey population (not shown); ‡ Numbers in parentheses indicate the number of people reporting a single ancestry; * Numbers in parentheses indicate the number of persons reporting this race alone, not in combination with any other race; Please refer to the Explanation of Data for more information.*

Northern European (11)	11	0.08
Norwegian (154)	289	2.02
Polish (42)	532	3.72
Portuguese (28)	179	1.25
Romanian (10)	10	0.07
Russian (53)	232	1.62
Scandinavian (31)	41	0.29
Scotch-Irish (85)	493	3.45
Scottish (143)	705	4.93
Slovak (35)	65	0.45
Swedish (56)	293	2.05
Swiss (23)	36	0.25
Turkish (9)	9	0.06
Ukrainian (40)	72	0.50
Welsh (13)	213	1.49

Hispanic Origin	Population	%
Hispanic or Latino (of any race)	300	2.05
Central American, ex. Mexican	21	0.14
Costa Rican	6	0.04
Guatemalan	5	0.03
Honduran	4	0.03
Nicaraguan	3	0.02
Panamanian	2	0.01
Salvadoran	1	0.01
Cuban	40	0.27
Dominican Republic	28	0.19
Mexican	62	0.42
Puerto Rican	54	0.37
South American	50	0.34
Argentinean	4	0.03
Bolivian	2	0.01
Chilean	8	0.05
Colombian	14	0.10
Ecuadorian	9	0.06
Paraguayan	1	0.01
Peruvian	12	0.08
Other Hispanic or Latino	45	0.31

Race*	Population	%
African-American/Black (126)	196	1.34
Not Hispanic (115)	173	1.18
Hispanic (11)	23	0.16
American Indian/Alaska Native (10)	46	0.31
Not Hispanic (7)	39	0.27
Hispanic (3)	7	0.05
Apache (0)	1	0.01
Blackfeet (0)	5	0.03
Cherokee (2)	7	0.05
Choctaw (0)	2	0.01
Inupiat *(Alaska Native)* (1)	1	0.01
Iroquois (0)	4	0.03
Navajo (0)	1	0.01
Sioux (0)	1	0.01
South American Ind. (0)	1	0.01
Asian (474)	598	4.09
Not Hispanic (473)	593	4.05
Hispanic (1)	5	0.03
Burmese (7)	7	0.05
Cambodian (2)	2	0.01
Chinese, ex. Taiwanese (197)	232	1.58
Filipino (24)	42	0.29
Indian (112)	134	0.92
Indonesian (0)	1	0.01
Japanese (15)	32	0.22
Korean (56)	72	0.49
Laotian (7)	10	0.07
Malaysian (1)	1	0.01
Nepalese (1)	2	0.01
Pakistani (0)	2	0.01
Taiwanese (6)	9	0.06
Thai (3)	4	0.03
Vietnamese (32)	42	0.29
Hawaii Native/Pacific Islander (2)	18	0.12
Not Hispanic (2)	14	0.10
Hispanic (0)	4	0.03
Fijian (0)	1	0.01
Guamanian/Chamorro (0)	2	0.01
Native Hawaiian (0)	5	0.03
Samoan (2)	3	0.02
White (13,730)	13,944	95.26
Not Hispanic (13,522)	13,717	93.71
Hispanic (208)	227	1.55

Exeter

Place Type: CDP
County: Rockingham
Population: 9,242†

Ancestry‡	Population	%
American (293)	293	3.10
Armenian (15)	15	0.16
Austrian (0)	15	0.16
Belgian (0)	16	0.17
British (93)	132	1.40
Canadian (93)	119	1.26
Czech (0)	53	0.56
Czechoslovakian (0)	24	0.25
Danish (0)	24	0.25
Dutch (71)	123	1.30
Eastern European (14)	14	0.15
English (787)	2,454	25.97
European (161)	189	2.00
Finnish (39)	105	1.11
French, ex. Basque (228)	1,183	12.52
French Canadian (294)	464	4.91
German (218)	1,438	15.22
Greek (69)	132	1.40
Hungarian (0)	22	0.23
Icelander (13)	13	0.14
Irish (734)	2,263	23.95
Italian (429)	891	9.43
Latvian (8)	15	0.16
Lithuanian (11)	41	0.43
Northern European (46)	46	0.49
Norwegian (37)	193	2.04
Polish (102)	404	4.28
Portuguese (53)	133	1.41
Russian (57)	75	0.79
Scandinavian (0)	9	0.10
Scotch-Irish (147)	333	3.52
Scottish (75)	729	7.71
Swedish (42)	132	1.40
Swiss (10)	51	0.54
Ukrainian (7)	25	0.26
Welsh (11)	51	0.54
West Indian, ex. Hispanic (0)	31	0.33
Jamaican (0)	31	0.33

Hispanic Origin	Population	%
Hispanic or Latino (of any race)	148	1.60
Central American, ex. Mexican	2	0.02
Costa Rican	1	0.01
Guatemalan	1	0.01
Cuban	13	0.14
Dominican Republic	4	0.04
Mexican	21	0.23
Puerto Rican	35	0.38
South American	19	0.21
Argentinean	7	0.08
Chilean	2	0.02
Colombian	6	0.06
Ecuadorian	2	0.02
Venezuelan	2	0.02
Other Hispanic or Latino	54	0.58

Race*	Population	%
African-American/Black (59)	94	1.02
Not Hispanic (53)	82	0.89
Hispanic (6)	12	0.13
American Indian/Alaska Native (12)	70	0.76
Not Hispanic (12)	67	0.72
Hispanic (0)	3	0.03
Apache (0)	4	0.04
Blackfeet (0)	1	0.01
Cherokee (0)	13	0.14
Iroquois (0)	5	0.05
Mexican American Ind. (2)	2	0.02
Navajo (1)	1	0.01
Shoshone (0)	4	0.04
Sioux (2)	3	0.03
Asian (182)	248	2.68
Not Hispanic (179)	245	2.65
Hispanic (3)	3	0.03
Bangladeshi (2)	2	0.02
Chinese, ex. Taiwanese (80)	93	1.01
Filipino (10)	21	0.23
Indian (25)	34	0.37
Indonesian (4)	5	0.05
Japanese (15)	24	0.26
Korean (15)	31	0.34
Laotian (10)	10	0.11
Taiwanese (1)	1	0.01
Thai (4)	8	0.09
Vietnamese (6)	8	0.09
Hawaii Native/Pacific Islander (2)	3	0.03
Not Hispanic (2)	3	0.03
Native Hawaiian (1)	2	0.02
White (8,806)	8,960	96.95
Not Hispanic (8,695)	8,836	95.61
Hispanic (111)	124	1.34

Exeter

Place Type: Town
County: Rockingham
Population: 14,306†

Ancestry‡	Population	%
Albanian (0)	25	0.17
American (393)	393	2.73
Armenian (28)	28	0.19
Austrian (0)	15	0.10
Belgian (0)	16	0.11
Brazilian (15)	15	0.10
British (193)	232	1.61
Canadian (114)	167	1.16
Czech (0)	53	0.37
Czechoslovakian (0)	24	0.17
Danish (0)	24	0.17
Dutch (71)	133	0.92
Eastern European (14)	14	0.10
English (1,084)	3,558	24.72
European (239)	279	1.94
Finnish (52)	118	0.82
French, ex. Basque (409)	1,943	13.50
French Canadian (507)	797	5.54
German (359)	2,084	14.48
Greek (121)	249	1.73
Hungarian (0)	22	0.15
Icelander (13)	13	0.09
Irish (1,109)	3,423	23.78
Italian (574)	1,241	8.62
Latvian (8)	15	0.10
Lithuanian (28)	74	0.51
Northern European (55)	55	0.38
Norwegian (46)	219	1.52
Polish (140)	790	5.49
Portuguese (62)	238	1.65
Russian (92)	162	1.13
Scandinavian (0)	9	0.06
Scotch-Irish (157)	466	3.24
Scottish (160)	1,245	8.65
Slovak (9)	21	0.15
Swedish (86)	243	1.69
Swiss (10)	59	0.41
Ukrainian (23)	73	0.51
Welsh (27)	77	0.53
West Indian, ex. Hispanic (31)	119	0.83
Jamaican (31)	119	0.83

Hispanic Origin	Population	%
Hispanic or Latino (of any race)	240	1.68
Central American, ex. Mexican	5	0.03
Costa Rican	1	0.01
Guatemalan	2	0.01
Honduran	1	0.01
Nicaraguan	1	0.01
Cuban	27	0.19

*Notes: † The Census 2010 population figure is used to calculate the percentages in the Hispanic Origin and Race categories. Ancestry percentages are based on the 2006-2010 American Community Survey population (not shown); ‡ Numbers in parentheses indicate the number of people reporting a single ancestry; * Numbers in parentheses indicate the number of persons reporting this race alone, not in combination with any other race; Please refer to the Explanation of Data for more information.*

Dominican Republic	6	0.04
Mexican	47	0.33
Puerto Rican	54	0.38
South American	32	0.22
Argentinean	9	0.06
Bolivian	3	0.02
Chilean	3	0.02
Colombian	10	0.07
Ecuadorian	5	0.03
Venezuelan	2	0.01
Other Hispanic or Latino	69	0.48

Race*	Population	%
African-American/Black (79)	125	0.87
Not Hispanic (73)	113	0.79
Hispanic (6)	12	0.08
American Indian/Alaska Native (15)	82	0.57
Not Hispanic (14)	76	0.53
Hispanic (1)	6	0.04
Apache (0)	4	0.03
Blackfeet (0)	1	0.01
Cherokee (0)	13	0.09
Iroquois (1)	7	0.05
Mexican American Ind. (2)	2	0.01
Navajo (1)	1	0.01
Shoshone (0)	4	0.03
Sioux (2)	3	0.02
South American Ind. (1)	1	0.01
Asian (287)	396	2.77
Not Hispanic (284)	393	2.75
Hispanic (3)	3	0.02
Bangladeshi (2)	2	0.01
Cambodian (0)	3	0.02
Chinese, ex. Taiwanese (102)	124	0.87
Filipino (12)	32	0.22
Indian (53)	65	0.45
Indonesian (6)	7	0.05
Japanese (22)	44	0.31
Korean (34)	54	0.38
Laotian (19)	19	0.13
Pakistani (4)	4	0.03
Sri Lankan (5)	5	0.03
Taiwanese (1)	1	0.01
Thai (6)	14	0.10
Vietnamese (6)	8	0.06
Hawaii Native/Pacific Islander (2)	3	0.02
Not Hispanic (2)	3	0.02
Native Hawaiian (1)	2	0.01
White (13,659)	13,881	97.03
Not Hispanic (13,474)	13,673	95.58
Hispanic (185)	208	1.45

Franklin

Place Type: City
County: Merrimack
Population: 8,477†

Ancestry‡	Population	%
African, Sub-Saharan (113)	113	1.32
African (10)	10	0.12
Ghanaian (103)	103	1.20
Albanian (10)	18	0.21
American (606)	606	7.06
British (10)	34	0.40
Canadian (38)	105	1.22
Danish (0)	9	0.10
Dutch (17)	39	0.45
English (524)	1,309	15.25
European (37)	37	0.43
Finnish (19)	39	0.45
French, ex. Basque (645)	1,982	23.09
French Canadian (409)	835	9.73
German (224)	824	9.60
Greek (0)	37	0.43
Hungarian (0)	11	0.13
Irish (654)	1,711	19.94
Italian (180)	726	8.46
Lithuanian (0)	10	0.12
Norwegian (43)	96	1.12
Polish (79)	318	3.71
Portuguese (0)	52	0.61
Scotch-Irish (68)	162	1.89
Scottish (87)	382	4.45
Slovak (0)	8	0.09
Swedish (27)	63	0.73
Swiss (0)	9	0.10
Welsh (7)	46	0.54

Hispanic Origin	Population	%
Hispanic or Latino (of any race)	133	1.57
Central American, ex. Mexican	10	0.12
Honduran	3	0.04
Panamanian	1	0.01
Salvadoran	6	0.07
Cuban	7	0.08
Dominican Republic	8	0.09
Mexican	15	0.18
Puerto Rican	68	0.80
South American	9	0.11
Argentinean	1	0.01
Colombian	1	0.01
Ecuadorian	1	0.01
Peruvian	5	0.06
Uruguayan	1	0.01
Other Hispanic or Latino	16	0.19

Race*	Population	%
African-American/Black (42)	82	0.97
Not Hispanic (40)	73	0.86
Hispanic (2)	9	0.11
American Indian/Alaska Native (39)	127	1.50
Not Hispanic (37)	119	1.40
Hispanic (2)	8	0.09
Apache (0)	1	0.01
Blackfeet (1)	5	0.06
Canadian/French Am. Ind. (1)	1	0.01
Cherokee (1)	19	0.22
Chippewa (1)	1	0.01
Choctaw (0)	1	0.01
Crow (0)	2	0.02
Delaware (0)	1	0.01
Iroquois (0)	3	0.04
Mexican American Ind. (1)	1	0.01
Sioux (2)	6	0.07
Asian (66)	88	1.04
Not Hispanic (64)	81	0.96
Hispanic (2)	7	0.08
Cambodian (0)	3	0.04
Chinese, ex. Taiwanese (5)	9	0.11
Filipino (21)	21	0.25
Indian (12)	16	0.19
Japanese (3)	3	0.04
Korean (8)	13	0.15
Laotian (3)	3	0.04
Nepalese (1)	1	0.01
Pakistani (2)	4	0.05
Thai (1)	3	0.04
Vietnamese (8)	11	0.13
Hawaii Native/Pacific Islander (2)	10	0.12
Not Hispanic (2)	6	0.07
Hispanic (0)	4	0.05
Guamanian/Chamorro (1)	1	0.01
Native Hawaiian (0)	1	0.01
Samoan (0)	1	0.01
White (8,155)	8,299	97.90
Not Hispanic (8,072)	8,197	96.70
Hispanic (83)	102	1.20

Goffstown

Place Type: Town
County: Hillsborough
Population: 17,651†

Ancestry‡	Population	%
African, Sub-Saharan (34)	34	0.19
Ghanaian (34)	34	0.19
American (916)	916	5.19
Arab (0)	28	0.16
Lebanese (0)	28	0.16
Armenian (23)	63	0.36
Austrian (0)	13	0.07
Belgian (0)	27	0.15
British (120)	120	0.68
Canadian (241)	378	2.14
Celtic (21)	21	0.12
Czech (0)	13	0.07
Danish (17)	49	0.28
Dutch (32)	233	1.32
English (927)	2,774	15.73
European (26)	32	0.18
Finnish (65)	94	0.53
French, ex. Basque (1,900)	3,594	20.38
French Canadian (1,478)	2,402	13.62
German (467)	1,620	9.19
Greek (115)	301	1.71
Hungarian (0)	34	0.19
Irish (1,524)	4,400	24.95
Israeli (13)	13	0.07
Italian (520)	2,010	11.40
Lithuanian (25)	107	0.61
Maltese (0)	14	0.08
Norwegian (54)	126	0.71
Polish (302)	780	4.42
Portuguese (71)	209	1.19
Russian (29)	151	0.86
Scotch-Irish (201)	370	2.10
Scottish (151)	673	3.82
Slavic (0)	15	0.09
Swedish (88)	282	1.60
Ukrainian (29)	49	0.28
Welsh (45)	64	0.36
West Indian, ex. Hispanic (105)	128	0.73
Haitian (105)	128	0.73

Hispanic Origin	Population	%
Hispanic or Latino (of any race)	322	1.82
Central American, ex. Mexican	37	0.21
Costa Rican	1	0.01
Guatemalan	5	0.03
Honduran	4	0.02
Nicaraguan	2	0.01
Panamanian	6	0.03
Salvadoran	19	0.11
Cuban	21	0.12
Dominican Republic	23	0.13
Mexican	85	0.48
Puerto Rican	69	0.39
South American	50	0.28
Argentinean	6	0.03
Bolivian	1	0.01
Chilean	3	0.02
Colombian	11	0.06
Ecuadorian	8	0.05
Peruvian	8	0.05
Uruguayan	10	0.06
Venezuelan	3	0.02
Other Hispanic or Latino	37	0.21

Race*	Population	%
African-American/Black (151)	219	1.24
Not Hispanic (141)	200	1.13
Hispanic (10)	19	0.11
American Indian/Alaska Native (27)	91	0.52
Not Hispanic (23)	87	0.49
Hispanic (4)	4	0.02
Blackfeet (0)	2	0.01
Canadian/French Am. Ind. (0)	2	0.01
Cherokee (5)	11	0.06
Choctaw (0)	2	0.01
Cree (1)	2	0.01
Creek (0)	1	0.01
Iroquois (0)	7	0.04
Mexican American Ind. (4)	4	0.02
Osage (0)	1	0.01
Pueblo (2)	2	0.01
Seminole (0)	1	0.01
Sioux (0)	1	0.01
Asian (143)	205	1.16

*Notes: † The Census 2010 population figure is used to calculate the percentages in the Hispanic Origin and Race categories. Ancestry percentages are based on the 2006-2010 American Community Survey population (not shown); ‡ Numbers in parentheses indicate the number of people reporting a single ancestry; * Numbers in parentheses indicate the number of persons reporting this race alone, not in combination with any other race; Please refer to the Explanation of Data for more information.*

Not Hispanic (142)	201	1.14
Hispanic (1)	4	0.02
Bangladeshi (13)	13	0.07
Cambodian (1)	3	0.02
Chinese, ex. Taiwanese (50)	65	0.37
Filipino (27)	39	0.22
Indian (19)	30	0.17
Indonesian (1)	2	0.01
Japanese (3)	12	0.07
Korean (8)	18	0.10
Pakistani (1)	1	0.01
Taiwanese (5)	5	0.03
Thai (2)	2	0.01
Vietnamese (13)	17	0.10
Hawaii Native/Pacific Islander (6)	16	0.09
Not Hispanic (5)	15	0.08
Hispanic (1)	1	0.01
Native Hawaiian (2)	10	0.06
Samoan (1)	2	0.01
White (17,053)	17,249	97.72
Not Hispanic (16,813)	16,991	96.26
Hispanic (240)	258	1.46

Hampstead

Place Type: Town
County: Rockingham
Population: 8,523†

Ancestry‡	Population	%
American (307)	307	3.59
Arab (13)	34	0.40
Lebanese (13)	34	0.40
Armenian (0)	106	1.24
Austrian (12)	12	0.14
Belgian (10)	10	0.12
British (61)	113	1.32
Canadian (76)	172	2.01
Danish (47)	94	1.10
Dutch (0)	208	2.43
English (397)	1,353	15.81
European (116)	116	1.36
French, ex. Basque (406)	1,268	14.82
French Canadian (247)	632	7.38
German (47)	617	7.21
Greek (36)	96	1.12
Hungarian (13)	24	0.28
Irish (981)	2,590	30.26
Italian (645)	1,594	18.63
Lithuanian (18)	69	0.81
Norwegian (0)	112	1.31
Polish (119)	443	5.18
Portuguese (14)	82	0.96
Russian (37)	219	2.56
Scotch-Irish (220)	332	3.88
Scottish (203)	460	5.38
Slavic (12)	12	0.14
Swedish (77)	329	3.84
West Indian, ex. Hispanic (12)	12	0.14
Jamaican (12)	12	0.14

Hispanic Origin	Population	%
Hispanic or Latino (of any race)	84	0.99
Central American, ex. Mexican	2	0.02
Costa Rican	1	0.01
Guatemalan	1	0.01
Cuban	4	0.05
Dominican Republic	7	0.08
Mexican	27	0.32
Puerto Rican	20	0.23
South American	7	0.08
Argentinean	1	0.01
Colombian	4	0.05
Peruvian	1	0.01
Venezuelan	1	0.01
Other Hispanic or Latino	17	0.20

Race*	Population	%
African-American/Black (23)	56	0.66
Not Hispanic (20)	51	0.60
Hispanic (3)	5	0.06
American Indian/Alaska Native (7)	34	0.40
Not Hispanic (7)	34	0.40
Cherokee (2)	4	0.05
Chickasaw (0)	2	0.02
Chippewa (1)	1	0.01
Iroquois (0)	3	0.04
Seminole (0)	2	0.02
Asian (70)	96	1.13
Not Hispanic (68)	92	1.08
Hispanic (2)	4	0.05
Cambodian (1)	1	0.01
Chinese, ex. Taiwanese (21)	26	0.31
Filipino (7)	13	0.15
Indian (13)	16	0.19
Japanese (6)	10	0.12
Korean (13)	15	0.18
Thai (7)	13	0.15
Vietnamese (2)	2	0.02
Hawaii Native/Pacific Islander (1)	2	0.02
Not Hispanic (1)	2	0.02
Native Hawaiian (1)	2	0.02
White (8,320)	8,405	98.62
Not Hispanic (8,258)	8,336	97.81
Hispanic (62)	69	0.81

Hampton

Place Type: CDP
County: Rockingham
Population: 9,656†

Ancestry‡	Population	%
American (267)	267	3.01
Arab (0)	16	0.18
Lebanese (0)	16	0.18
Armenian (13)	13	0.15
Belgian (0)	14	0.16
Brazilian (25)	25	0.28
British (49)	85	0.96
Canadian (0)	61	0.69
Croatian (0)	52	0.59
Danish (0)	28	0.32
Dutch (0)	118	1.33
Eastern European (35)	35	0.39
English (686)	1,710	19.28
European (16)	16	0.18
French, ex. Basque (344)	1,211	13.65
French Canadian (371)	643	7.25
German (98)	676	7.62
Greek (44)	183	2.06
Hungarian (0)	26	0.29
Irish (1,088)	3,033	34.20
Israeli (13)	13	0.15
Italian (211)	1,026	11.57
Lithuanian (15)	38	0.43
Norwegian (17)	17	0.19
Polish (85)	440	4.96
Romanian (0)	8	0.09
Russian (111)	190	2.14
Scotch-Irish (213)	504	5.68
Scottish (53)	318	3.59
Slovak (0)	26	0.29
Swedish (85)	299	3.37
Swiss (20)	42	0.47
Turkish (0)	15	0.17
Welsh (39)	114	1.29

Hispanic Origin	Population	%
Hispanic or Latino (of any race)	175	1.81
Central American, ex. Mexican	13	0.13
Costa Rican	4	0.04
Guatemalan	4	0.04
Nicaraguan	1	0.01
Panamanian	1	0.01
Salvadoran	3	0.03
Cuban	8	0.08
Dominican Republic	45	0.47
Mexican	25	0.26
Puerto Rican	30	0.31
South American	14	0.14
Chilean	1	0.01
Colombian	5	0.05
Ecuadorian	3	0.03
Peruvian	2	0.02
Uruguayan	1	0.01
Venezuelan	1	0.01
Other South American	1	0.01
Other Hispanic or Latino	40	0.41

Race*	Population	%
African-American/Black (66)	96	0.99
Not Hispanic (59)	78	0.81
Hispanic (7)	18	0.19
American Indian/Alaska Native (14)	45	0.47
Not Hispanic (12)	43	0.45
Hispanic (2)	2	0.02
Apache (0)	1	0.01
Blackfeet (0)	3	0.03
Cherokee (1)	8	0.08
Chippewa (1)	1	0.01
Choctaw (0)	1	0.01
Comanche (0)	1	0.01
Iroquois (3)	4	0.04
Mexican American Ind. (2)	2	0.02
Navajo (1)	1	0.01
Asian (138)	176	1.82
Not Hispanic (138)	172	1.78
Hispanic (0)	4	0.04
Bangladeshi (0)	1	0.01
Cambodian (5)	5	0.05
Chinese, ex. Taiwanese (29)	33	0.34
Filipino (22)	32	0.33
Indian (23)	24	0.25
Indonesian (6)	8	0.08
Japanese (5)	11	0.11
Korean (22)	33	0.34
Malaysian (0)	1	0.01
Pakistani (0)	1	0.01
Taiwanese (1)	1	0.01
Thai (5)	9	0.09
Vietnamese (5)	6	0.06
Hawaii Native/Pacific Islander (6)	10	0.10
Not Hispanic (6)	9	0.09
Hispanic (0)	1	0.01
Native Hawaiian (4)	6	0.06
White (9,282)	9,386	97.20
Not Hispanic (9,172)	9,257	95.87
Hispanic (110)	129	1.34

Hampton

Place Type: Town
County: Rockingham
Population: 15,430†

Ancestry‡	Population	%
African, Sub-Saharan (50)	50	0.32
Nigerian (50)	50	0.32
Albanian (14)	14	0.09
American (424)	424	2.74
Arab (18)	77	0.50
Lebanese (18)	65	0.42
Syrian (0)	12	0.08
Armenian (24)	24	0.15
Austrian (0)	6	0.04
Belgian (0)	14	0.09
Brazilian (25)	25	0.16
British (59)	121	0.78
Bulgarian (0)	19	0.12
Canadian (30)	102	0.66
Croatian (0)	52	0.34
Czechoslovakian (12)	12	0.08
Danish (0)	51	0.33
Dutch (17)	175	1.13
Eastern European (35)	35	0.23
English (965)	3,032	19.58
European (47)	47	0.30
French, ex. Basque (589)	2,316	14.96
French Canadian (534)	933	6.03

*Notes: † The Census 2010 population figure is used to calculate the percentages in the Hispanic Origin and Race categories. Ancestry percentages are based on the 2006-2010 American Community Survey population (not shown); ‡ Numbers in parentheses indicate the number of people reporting a single ancestry; * Numbers in parentheses indicate the number of persons reporting this race alone, not in combination with any other race; Please refer to the Explanation of Data for more information.*

Ancestry	Population	%
German (199)	1,046	6.76
Greek (96)	235	1.52
Hungarian (0)	26	0.17
Irish (1,952)	5,240	33.84
Israeli (13)	13	0.08
Italian (622)	2,111	13.63
Lithuanian (26)	61	0.39
Northern European (13)	13	0.08
Norwegian (83)	103	0.67
Polish (247)	748	4.83
Portuguese (25)	79	0.51
Romanian (70)	78	0.50
Russian (210)	366	2.36
Scotch-Irish (309)	654	4.22
Scottish (142)	550	3.55
Slovak (0)	26	0.17
Swedish (85)	357	2.31
Swiss (20)	42	0.27
Turkish (0)	15	0.10
Ukrainian (0)	14	0.09
Welsh (101)	251	1.62
West Indian, ex. Hispanic (0)	13	0.08
Jamaican (0)	13	0.08

Hispanic Origin	Population	%
Hispanic or Latino (of any race)	264	1.71
Central American, ex. Mexican	22	0.14
Costa Rican	4	0.03
Guatemalan	4	0.03
Honduran	5	0.03
Nicaraguan	1	0.01
Panamanian	2	0.01
Salvadoran	6	0.04
Cuban	11	0.07
Dominican Republic	61	0.40
Mexican	42	0.27
Puerto Rican	53	0.34
South American	27	0.17
Argentinean	1	0.01
Chilean	1	0.01
Colombian	11	0.07
Ecuadorian	4	0.03
Peruvian	4	0.03
Uruguayan	1	0.01
Venezuelan	4	0.03
Other South American	1	0.01
Other Hispanic or Latino	48	0.31

Race*	Population	%
African-American/Black (89)	145	0.94
Not Hispanic (80)	122	0.79
Hispanic (9)	23	0.15
American Indian/Alaska Native (32)	104	0.67
Not Hispanic (27)	98	0.64
Hispanic (5)	6	0.04
Apache (0)	1	0.01
Blackfeet (1)	12	0.08
Canadian/French Am. Ind. (0)	1	0.01
Cherokee (2)	13	0.08
Chippewa (3)	4	0.03
Choctaw (0)	1	0.01
Comanche (0)	1	0.01
Creek (4)	4	0.03
Delaware (1)	1	0.01
Iroquois (4)	6	0.04
Mexican American Ind. (2)	2	0.01
Navajo (1)	3	0.02
Sioux (0)	3	0.02
Asian (191)	261	1.69
Not Hispanic (191)	257	1.67
Hispanic (0)	4	0.03
Bangladeshi (0)	1	0.01
Cambodian (8)	11	0.07
Chinese, ex. Taiwanese (41)	47	0.30
Filipino (29)	40	0.26
Indian (39)	43	0.28
Indonesian (7)	9	0.06
Japanese (8)	23	0.15
Korean (28)	43	0.28
Malaysian (0)	1	0.01
Pakistani (0)	1	0.01
Taiwanese (1)	1	0.01
Thai (6)	12	0.08
Vietnamese (7)	10	0.06
Hawaii Native/Pacific Islander (8)	16	0.10
Not Hispanic (8)	15	0.10
Hispanic (0)	1	0.01
Guamanian/Chamorro (0)	1	0.01
Native Hawaiian (6)	9	0.06
Samoan (0)	1	0.01
White (14,827)	15,024	97.37
Not Hispanic (14,671)	14,842	96.19
Hispanic (156)	182	1.18

Hanover

Place Type: CDP
County: Grafton
Population: 8,636†

Ancestry‡	Population	%
African, Sub-Saharan (93)	104	1.23
African (35)	35	0.41
Cape Verdean (0)	11	0.13
Ghanaian (27)	27	0.32
Nigerian (31)	31	0.37
American (179)	179	2.11
Arab (42)	103	1.21
Egyptian (0)	10	0.12
Iraqi (0)	9	0.11
Lebanese (32)	58	0.68
Moroccan (10)	10	0.12
Palestinian (0)	6	0.07
Other Arab (0)	10	0.12
Armenian (19)	32	0.38
Australian (0)	14	0.17
Austrian (42)	125	1.47
Belgian (34)	34	0.40
British (164)	257	3.03
Canadian (0)	42	0.50
Croatian (0)	10	0.12
Czech (0)	51	0.60
Czechoslovakian (13)	13	0.15
Danish (11)	38	0.45
Dutch (12)	64	0.75
Eastern European (123)	123	1.45
English (623)	1,414	16.67
European (107)	107	1.26
Finnish (10)	10	0.12
French, ex. Basque (48)	321	3.79
French Canadian (11)	84	0.99
German (369)	1,329	15.67
German Russian (0)	13	0.15
Greek (39)	95	1.12
Hungarian (26)	47	0.55
Iranian (18)	18	0.21
Irish (329)	1,082	12.76
Israeli (9)	9	0.11
Italian (233)	630	7.43
Latvian (50)	50	0.59
Lithuanian (0)	19	0.22
Northern European (27)	27	0.32
Norwegian (57)	325	3.83
Polish (73)	404	4.76
Portuguese (0)	16	0.19
Romanian (54)	66	0.78
Russian (108)	322	3.80
Scandinavian (0)	13	0.15
Scotch-Irish (27)	264	3.11
Scottish (42)	406	4.79
Serbian (0)	10	0.12
Slovak (11)	28	0.33
Swedish (153)	332	3.92
Swiss (11)	49	0.58
Turkish (11)	11	0.13
Ukrainian (9)	33	0.39
Welsh (10)	82	0.97
West Indian, ex. Hispanic (39)	74	0.87
Barbadian (0)	11	0.13
Haitian (0)	12	0.14
Jamaican (39)	51	0.60
Yugoslavian (0)	9	0.11

Hispanic Origin	Population	%
Hispanic or Latino (of any race)	399	4.62
Central American, ex. Mexican	33	0.38
Costa Rican	3	0.03
Guatemalan	4	0.05
Honduran	6	0.07
Nicaraguan	8	0.09
Panamanian	2	0.02
Salvadoran	10	0.12
Cuban	49	0.57
Dominican Republic	17	0.20
Mexican	99	1.15
Puerto Rican	31	0.36
South American	106	1.23
Argentinean	18	0.21
Bolivian	2	0.02
Chilean	8	0.09
Colombian	32	0.37
Ecuadorian	10	0.12
Paraguayan	2	0.02
Peruvian	24	0.28
Venezuelan	10	0.12
Other Hispanic or Latino	64	0.74

Race*	Population	%
African-American/Black (374)	459	5.31
Not Hispanic (359)	427	4.94
Hispanic (15)	32	0.37
American Indian/Alaska Native (87)	151	1.75
Not Hispanic (82)	140	1.62
Hispanic (5)	11	0.13
Alaska Athabascan *(Ala. Nat.)* (1)	2	0.02
Apache (1)	1	0.01
Blackfeet (1)	1	0.01
Cherokee (4)	13	0.15
Chippewa (5)	8	0.09
Choctaw (4)	9	0.10
Comanche (0)	1	0.01
Creek (1)	2	0.02
Crow (1)	1	0.01
Hopi (1)	1	0.01
Inupiat *(Alaska Native)* (3)	6	0.07
Iroquois (5)	9	0.10
Lumbee (2)	2	0.02
Mexican American Ind. (1)	2	0.02
Navajo (12)	16	0.19
Osage (2)	6	0.07
Paiute (1)	1	0.01
Potawatomi (2)	3	0.03
Pueblo (2)	5	0.06
Puget Sound Salish (1)	1	0.01
Sioux (4)	8	0.09
Yakama (0)	1	0.01
Yaqui (1)	2	0.02
Asian (1,074)	1,259	14.58
Not Hispanic (1,069)	1,249	14.46
Hispanic (5)	10	0.12
Bangladeshi (5)	5	0.06
Bhutanese (5)	6	0.07
Burmese (2)	3	0.03
Cambodian (2)	2	0.02
Chinese, ex. Taiwanese (475)	547	6.33
Filipino (22)	42	0.49
Indian (230)	261	3.02
Indonesian (2)	2	0.02
Japanese (38)	74	0.86
Korean (192)	216	2.50
Malaysian (1)	4	0.05
Nepalese (4)	4	0.05
Pakistani (18)	21	0.24
Sri Lankan (3)	4	0.05
Taiwanese (20)	20	0.23
Thai (12)	20	0.23
Vietnamese (19)	24	0.28
Hawaii Native/Pacific Islander (2)	7	0.08
Not Hispanic (2)	7	0.08
Guamanian/Chamorro (0)	1	0.01

SECTION TWO

*Notes: † The Census 2010 population figure is used to calculate the percentages in the Hispanic Origin and Race categories. Ancestry percentages are based on the 2006-2010 American Community Survey population (not shown); ‡ Numbers in parentheses indicate the number of people reporting a single ancestry; * Numbers in parentheses indicate the number of persons reporting this race alone, not in combination with any other race; Please refer to the Explanation of Data for more information.*

Native Hawaiian (1)	3	0.03
Samoan (0)	1	0.01
Tongan (1)	1	0.01
White (6,692)	6,996	81.01
Not Hispanic (6,412)	6,683	77.39
Hispanic (280)	313	3.62

Hanover

Place Type: Town
County: Grafton
Population: 11,260†

Ancestry‡	Population	%
African, Sub-Saharan (103)	114	1.01
African (35)	35	0.31
Cape Verdean (0)	11	0.10
Ghanaian (27)	27	0.24
Nigerian (31)	31	0.28
South African (10)	10	0.09
American (263)	263	2.34
Arab (56)	117	1.04
Egyptian (0)	10	0.09
Iraqi (0)	9	0.08
Lebanese (32)	58	0.51
Moroccan (10)	10	0.09
Palestinian (0)	6	0.05
Other Arab (14)	24	0.21
Armenian (19)	32	0.28
Australian (0)	14	0.12
Austrian (42)	140	1.24
Belgian (34)	34	0.30
British (195)	357	3.17
Canadian (0)	42	0.37
Croatian (0)	10	0.09
Czech (9)	60	0.53
Czechoslovakian (13)	13	0.12
Danish (11)	103	0.91
Dutch (24)	76	0.67
Eastern European (123)	123	1.09
English (1,028)	2,381	21.14
European (119)	119	1.06
Finnish (10)	10	0.09
French, ex. Basque (68)	400	3.55
French Canadian (41)	203	1.80
German (453)	1,878	16.67
German Russian (0)	13	0.12
Greek (39)	95	0.84
Hungarian (35)	70	0.62
Iranian (18)	18	0.16
Irish (454)	1,689	15.00
Israeli (9)	9	0.08
Italian (271)	764	6.78
Latvian (50)	50	0.44
Lithuanian (0)	43	0.38
Northern European (27)	27	0.24
Norwegian (57)	364	3.23
Polish (106)	487	4.32
Portuguese (0)	16	0.14
Romanian (63)	116	1.03
Russian (149)	477	4.24
Scandinavian (0)	23	0.20
Scotch-Irish (41)	308	2.73
Scottish (192)	719	6.38
Serbian (0)	10	0.09
Slovak (11)	28	0.25
Swedish (153)	351	3.12
Swiss (11)	49	0.44
Turkish (11)	11	0.10
Ukrainian (79)	114	1.01
Welsh (10)	110	0.98
West Indian, ex. Hispanic (39)	74	0.66
Barbadian (0)	11	0.10
Haitian (0)	12	0.11
Jamaican (39)	51	0.45
Yugoslavian (0)	9	0.08

Hispanic Origin	Population	%
Hispanic or Latino (of any race)	438	3.89
Central American, ex. Mexican	35	0.31
Costa Rican	5	0.04
Guatemalan	4	0.04
Honduran	6	0.05
Nicaraguan	8	0.07
Panamanian	2	0.02
Salvadoran	10	0.09
Cuban	51	0.45
Dominican Republic	18	0.16
Mexican	111	0.99
Puerto Rican	33	0.29
South American	112	0.99
Argentinean	19	0.17
Bolivian	2	0.02
Chilean	10	0.09
Colombian	34	0.30
Ecuadorian	10	0.09
Paraguayan	2	0.02
Peruvian	24	0.21
Venezuelan	11	0.10
Other Hispanic or Latino	78	0.69

Race*	Population	%
African-American/Black (386)	479	4.25
Not Hispanic (371)	447	3.97
Hispanic (15)	32	0.28
American Indian/Alaska Native (88)	154	1.37
Not Hispanic (83)	143	1.27
Hispanic (5)	11	0.10
Alaska Athabascan *(Ala. Nat.)* (1)	2	0.02
Apache (1)	1	0.01
Blackfeet (1)	1	0.01
Cherokee (4)	14	0.12
Chippewa (5)	8	0.07
Choctaw (4)	9	0.08
Comanche (0)	1	0.01
Creek (1)	2	0.02
Crow (1)	1	0.01
Hopi (1)	1	0.01
Inupiat *(Alaska Native)* (3)	6	0.05
Iroquois (5)	9	0.08
Lumbee (2)	2	0.02
Mexican American Ind. (1)	2	0.02
Navajo (12)	16	0.14
Osage (2)	6	0.05
Paiute (1)	1	0.01
Potawatomi (2)	3	0.03
Pueblo (2)	5	0.04
Puget Sound Salish (1)	1	0.01
Sioux (4)	8	0.07
Yakama (0)	1	0.01
Yaqui (1)	2	0.02
Asian (1,220)	1,426	12.66
Not Hispanic (1,215)	1,416	12.58
Hispanic (5)	10	0.09
Bangladeshi (5)	5	0.04
Bhutanese (5)	6	0.05
Burmese (2)	3	0.03
Cambodian (2)	2	0.02
Chinese, ex. Taiwanese (564)	647	5.75
Filipino (23)	43	0.38
Indian (261)	295	2.62
Indonesian (2)	6	0.05
Japanese (40)	81	0.72
Korean (201)	234	2.08
Malaysian (1)	4	0.04
Nepalese (5)	5	0.04
Pakistani (19)	22	0.20
Sri Lankan (3)	4	0.04
Taiwanese (21)	22	0.20
Thai (13)	21	0.19
Vietnamese (22)	28	0.25
Hawaii Native/Pacific Islander (3)	8	0.07
Not Hispanic (3)	8	0.07
Guamanian/Chamorro (1)	2	0.02
Native Hawaiian (1)	3	0.03
Samoan (0)	1	0.01
Tongan (1)	1	0.01
White (9,122)	9,456	83.98
Not Hispanic (8,803)	9,104	80.85
Hispanic (319)	352	3.13

Hollis

Place Type: Town
County: Hillsborough
Population: 7,684†

Ancestry‡	Population	%
Albanian (22)	131	1.72
Alsatian (0)	11	0.14
American (208)	208	2.73
Arab (13)	41	0.54
Lebanese (13)	27	0.35
Syrian (0)	14	0.18
Armenian (7)	7	0.09
Austrian (23)	176	2.31
British (170)	189	2.48
Canadian (19)	31	0.41
Croatian (0)	15	0.20
Czech (0)	49	0.64
Danish (0)	16	0.21
Dutch (50)	201	2.64
Eastern European (14)	14	0.18
English (450)	1,475	19.37
European (189)	201	2.64
French, ex. Basque (158)	799	10.49
French Canadian (361)	657	8.63
German (304)	1,371	18.00
Greek (62)	138	1.81
Hungarian (0)	48	0.63
Irish (320)	1,650	21.66
Italian (271)	875	11.49
Lithuanian (20)	57	0.75
Norwegian (40)	197	2.59
Pennsylvania German (19)	19	0.25
Polish (44)	515	6.76
Portuguese (39)	119	1.56
Russian (10)	67	0.88
Scotch-Irish (60)	124	1.63
Scottish (64)	338	4.44
Serbian (27)	42	0.55
Swedish (9)	104	1.37
Swiss (9)	9	0.12
Turkish (0)	10	0.13
West Indian, ex. Hispanic (8)	8	0.11
Jamaican (8)	8	0.11

Hispanic Origin	Population	%
Hispanic or Latino (of any race)	95	1.24
Central American, ex. Mexican	3	0.04
Guatemalan	3	0.04
Cuban	5	0.07
Dominican Republic	1	0.01
Mexican	24	0.31
Puerto Rican	25	0.33
South American	20	0.26
Argentinean	8	0.10
Colombian	2	0.03
Ecuadorian	2	0.03
Peruvian	5	0.07
Uruguayan	2	0.03
Venezuelan	1	0.01
Other Hispanic or Latino	17	0.22

Race*	Population	%
African-American/Black (40)	68	0.88
Not Hispanic (38)	63	0.82
Hispanic (2)	5	0.07
American Indian/Alaska Native (6)	45	0.59
Not Hispanic (5)	42	0.55
Hispanic (1)	3	0.04
Blackfeet (0)	4	0.05
Cherokee (2)	9	0.12
Choctaw (0)	1	0.01
Iroquois (0)	1	0.01
Lumbee (0)	1	0.01
Sioux (0)	5	0.07
South American Ind. (0)	1	0.01
Asian (187)	247	3.21
Not Hispanic (186)	244	3.18
Hispanic (1)	3	0.04

*Notes: † The Census 2010 population figure is used to calculate the percentages in the Hispanic Origin and Race categories. Ancestry percentages are based on the 2006-2010 American Community Survey population (not shown); ‡ Numbers in parentheses indicate the number of people reporting a single ancestry; * Numbers in parentheses indicate the number of persons reporting this race alone, not in combination with any other race; Please refer to the Explanation of Data for more information.*

Cambodian (1)	4	0.05
Chinese, ex. Taiwanese (76)	93	1.21
Filipino (10)	22	0.29
Hmong (3)	3	0.04
Indian (48)	58	0.75
Japanese (8)	20	0.26
Korean (18)	27	0.35
Pakistani (5)	5	0.07
Sri Lankan (1)	1	0.01
Taiwanese (3)	5	0.07
Thai (2)	7	0.09
Vietnamese (7)	7	0.09
Hawaii Native/Pacific Islander (1)	5	0.07
Not Hispanic (0)	4	0.05
Hispanic (1)	1	0.01
Guamanian/Chamorro (1)	1	0.01
White (7,315)	7,429	96.68
Not Hispanic (7,237)	7,347	95.61
Hispanic (78)	82	1.07

Hooksett

Place Type: Town
County: Merrimack
Population: 13,451†

Ancestry‡	Population	%
American (471)	471	3.53
Arab (78)	127	0.95
Lebanese (78)	127	0.95
Armenian (75)	106	0.80
Austrian (0)	30	0.23
Belgian (7)	7	0.05
British (20)	39	0.29
Canadian (197)	258	1.94
Croatian (0)	10	0.08
Czech (53)	53	0.40
Danish (0)	28	0.21
Dutch (4)	25	0.19
Eastern European (25)	25	0.19
English (508)	1,905	14.29
European (67)	67	0.50
Finnish (0)	9	0.07
French, ex. Basque (654)	2,199	16.50
French Canadian (1,607)	2,174	16.31
German (271)	1,004	7.53
Greek (86)	115	0.86
Irish (832)	2,433	18.25
Italian (306)	1,211	9.08
Lithuanian (12)	34	0.26
Norwegian (0)	88	0.66
Polish (316)	846	6.35
Portuguese (32)	117	0.88
Romanian (69)	69	0.52
Russian (68)	134	1.01
Scandinavian (58)	58	0.44
Scotch-Irish (65)	432	3.24
Scottish (56)	368	2.76
Slavic (0)	7	0.05
Swedish (38)	287	2.15
Swiss (0)	21	0.16
Turkish (9)	28	0.21
Ukrainian (0)	49	0.37
Welsh (11)	123	0.92
West Indian, ex. Hispanic (34)	34	0.26
Haitian (14)	14	0.11
Jamaican (20)	20	0.15
Yugoslavian (199)	208	1.56

Hispanic Origin	Population	%
Hispanic or Latino (of any race)	278	2.07
Central American, ex. Mexican	11	0.08
Guatemalan	6	0.04
Honduran	5	0.04
Cuban	7	0.05
Dominican Republic	20	0.15
Mexican	57	0.42
Puerto Rican	93	0.69
South American	51	0.38
Chilean	4	0.03
Colombian	9	0.07
Ecuadorian	13	0.10
Paraguayan	1	0.01
Peruvian	1	0.01
Uruguayan	17	0.13
Venezuelan	6	0.04
Other Hispanic or Latino	39	0.29

Race*	Population	%
African-American/Black (141)	212	1.58
Not Hispanic (129)	198	1.47
Hispanic (12)	14	0.10
American Indian/Alaska Native (23)	86	0.64
Not Hispanic (20)	76	0.57
Hispanic (3)	10	0.07
Blackfeet (2)	4	0.03
Central American Ind. (0)	1	0.01
Cherokee (3)	8	0.06
Chickasaw (1)	1	0.01
Chippewa (1)	1	0.01
Choctaw (0)	3	0.02
Iroquois (0)	2	0.01
Mexican American Ind. (1)	1	0.01
Navajo (0)	1	0.01
Pueblo (1)	1	0.01
Sioux (0)	3	0.02
Asian (265)	311	2.31
Not Hispanic (263)	307	2.28
Hispanic (2)	4	0.03
Cambodian (2)	2	0.01
Chinese, ex. Taiwanese (50)	60	0.45
Filipino (32)	43	0.32
Indian (64)	65	0.48
Indonesian (4)	5	0.04
Japanese (6)	13	0.10
Korean (20)	27	0.20
Nepalese (30)	30	0.22
Pakistani (11)	11	0.08
Taiwanese (8)	9	0.07
Thai (3)	8	0.06
Vietnamese (18)	26	0.19
Hawaii Native/Pacific Islander (7)	20	0.15
Not Hispanic (7)	20	0.15
Guamanian/Chamorro (1)	2	0.01
Native Hawaiian (2)	6	0.04
White (12,728)	12,910	95.98
Not Hispanic (12,574)	12,724	94.60
Hispanic (154)	186	1.38

Hudson

Place Type: Town
County: Hillsborough
Population: 24,467†

Ancestry‡	Population	%
African, Sub-Saharan (160)	160	0.66
African (122)	122	0.50
Kenyan (10)	10	0.04
Ugandan (28)	28	0.12
American (735)	735	3.02
Arab (53)	109	0.45
Lebanese (53)	109	0.45
Austrian (10)	58	0.24
Belgian (54)	68	0.28
Brazilian (113)	124	0.51
British (44)	127	0.52
Canadian (230)	347	1.43
Croatian (0)	25	0.10
Czech (13)	48	0.20
Danish (15)	15	0.06
Dutch (13)	167	0.69
Eastern European (13)	27	0.11
English (572)	2,630	10.81
European (47)	69	0.28
Finnish (5)	82	0.34
French, ex. Basque (1,144)	4,314	17.74
French Canadian (1,588)	2,735	11.24
German (361)	2,034	8.36
Greek (256)	702	2.89
Hungarian (11)	60	0.25
Irish (2,112)	6,673	27.43
Italian (1,040)	3,619	14.88
Latvian (31)	31	0.13
Lithuanian (84)	397	1.63
Maltese (14)	14	0.06
Northern European (18)	18	0.07
Norwegian (17)	132	0.54
Polish (236)	1,253	5.15
Portuguese (327)	935	3.84
Romanian (12)	12	0.05
Russian (11)	63	0.26
Scandinavian (15)	50	0.21
Scotch-Irish (230)	621	2.55
Scottish (127)	776	3.19
Slovak (0)	14	0.06
Slovene (15)	15	0.06
Swedish (61)	444	1.83
Swiss (0)	23	0.09
Ukrainian (16)	95	0.39
Welsh (0)	61	0.25
Yugoslavian (0)	15	0.06

Hispanic Origin	Population	%
Hispanic or Latino (of any race)	714	2.92
Central American, ex. Mexican	40	0.16
Costa Rican	2	0.01
Guatemalan	6	0.02
Honduran	11	0.04
Nicaraguan	1	<0.01
Panamanian	8	0.03
Salvadoran	12	0.05
Cuban	15	0.06
Dominican Republic	59	0.24
Mexican	117	0.48
Puerto Rican	275	1.12
South American	154	0.63
Argentinean	1	<0.01
Bolivian	23	0.09
Chilean	7	0.03
Colombian	64	0.26
Ecuadorian	23	0.09
Peruvian	28	0.11
Uruguayan	1	<0.01
Venezuelan	7	0.03
Other Hispanic or Latino	54	0.22

Race*	Population	%
African-American/Black (331)	443	1.81
Not Hispanic (311)	411	1.68
Hispanic (20)	32	0.13
American Indian/Alaska Native (33)	133	0.54
Not Hispanic (30)	128	0.52
Hispanic (3)	5	0.02
Apache (1)	1	<0.01
Blackfeet (0)	1	<0.01
Canadian/French Am. Ind. (2)	8	0.03
Central American Ind. (0)	3	0.01
Cherokee (7)	20	0.08
Cheyenne (0)	1	<0.01
Choctaw (0)	3	0.01
Creek (2)	5	0.02
Iroquois (4)	14	0.06
Mexican American Ind. (1)	1	<0.01
Potawatomi (1)	2	0.01
Sioux (0)	2	0.01
South American Ind. (0)	2	0.01
Asian (745)	869	3.55
Not Hispanic (745)	862	3.52
Hispanic (0)	7	0.03
Cambodian (20)	33	0.13
Chinese, ex. Taiwanese (108)	141	0.58
Filipino (55)	77	0.31
Indian (387)	410	1.68
Indonesian (4)	7	0.03
Japanese (10)	25	0.10
Korean (29)	47	0.19
Laotian (19)	19	0.08
Nepalese (12)	13	0.05
Pakistani (11)	11	0.04

*Notes: † The Census 2010 population figure is used to calculate the percentages in the Hispanic Origin and Race categories. Ancestry percentages are based on the 2006-2010 American Community Survey population (not shown); ‡ Numbers in parentheses indicate the number of people reporting a single ancestry; * Numbers in parentheses indicate the number of persons reporting this race alone, not in combination with any other race; Please refer to the Explanation of Data for more information.*

SECTION TWO

Sri Lankan (4)	4	0.02
Taiwanese (7)	7	0.03
Thai (8)	12	0.05
Vietnamese (40)	46	0.19
Hawaii Native/Pacific Islander (6)	18	0.07
Not Hispanic (6)	16	0.07
Hispanic (0)	2	0.01
Fijian (1)	1	<0.01
Native Hawaiian (2)	5	0.02
White (22,750)	23,099	94.41
Not Hispanic (22,310)	22,577	92.28
Hispanic (440)	522	2.13

Keene

Place Type: City
County: Cheshire
Population: 23,409†

Ancestry‡	Population	%
African, Sub-Saharan (10)	30	0.13
African (10)	30	0.13
American (1,129)	1,129	4.79
Arab (25)	60	0.25
Arab (10)	10	0.04
Lebanese (15)	50	0.21
Armenian (10)	58	0.25
Austrian (0)	22	0.09
Belgian (36)	36	0.15
British (71)	126	0.54
Canadian (106)	199	0.85
Celtic (0)	10	0.04
Croatian (0)	7	0.03
Czech (21)	97	0.41
Czechoslovakian (12)	12	0.05
Danish (8)	52	0.22
Dutch (62)	357	1.52
Eastern European (48)	48	0.20
English (1,287)	4,876	20.71
European (193)	200	0.85
Finnish (99)	329	1.40
French, ex. Basque (1,035)	3,194	13.56
French Canadian (900)	2,022	8.59
German (488)	3,128	13.28
Greek (121)	229	0.97
Hungarian (23)	76	0.32
Irish (1,333)	5,520	23.44
Italian (719)	2,273	9.65
Lithuanian (85)	181	0.77
New Zealander (25)	25	0.11
Northern European (15)	15	0.06
Norwegian (80)	323	1.37
Polish (225)	751	3.19
Portuguese (57)	209	0.89
Russian (49)	326	1.38
Scotch-Irish (162)	720	3.06
Scottish (249)	1,139	4.84
Slovak (23)	61	0.26
Swedish (121)	503	2.14
Swiss (7)	7	0.03
Ukrainian (19)	150	0.64
Welsh (20)	199	0.85

Hispanic Origin	Population	%
Hispanic or Latino (of any race)	372	1.59
Central American, ex. Mexican	38	0.16
Costa Rican	4	0.02
Guatemalan	17	0.07
Honduran	5	0.02
Nicaraguan	1	<0.01
Salvadoran	11	0.05
Cuban	19	0.08
Dominican Republic	4	0.02
Mexican	110	0.47
Puerto Rican	88	0.38
South American	59	0.25
Argentinean	3	0.01
Bolivian	1	<0.01
Chilean	3	0.01
Colombian	23	0.10
Ecuadorian	4	0.02
Peruvian	14	0.06
Uruguayan	2	0.01
Venezuelan	5	0.02
Other South American	4	0.02
Other Hispanic or Latino	54	0.23

Race*	Population	%
African-American/Black (144)	258	1.10
Not Hispanic (141)	239	1.02
Hispanic (3)	19	0.08
American Indian/Alaska Native (42)	151	0.65
Not Hispanic (38)	131	0.56
Hispanic (4)	20	0.09
Aleut *(Alaska Native)* (0)	1	<0.01
Apache (0)	3	0.01
Blackfeet (3)	8	0.03
Canadian/French Am. Ind. (0)	1	<0.01
Cherokee (4)	14	0.06
Chippewa (3)	10	0.04
Choctaw (0)	1	<0.01
Cree (1)	1	<0.01
Creek (0)	2	0.01
Iroquois (1)	7	0.03
Mexican American Ind. (1)	2	0.01
Navajo (0)	1	<0.01
Sioux (0)	5	0.02
South American Ind. (1)	3	0.01
Yuman (2)	4	0.02
Asian (474)	574	2.45
Not Hispanic (470)	559	2.39
Hispanic (4)	15	0.06
Cambodian (18)	25	0.11
Chinese, ex. Taiwanese (80)	99	0.42
Filipino (39)	55	0.23
Hmong (0)	2	0.01
Indian (213)	227	0.97
Indonesian (7)	7	0.03
Japanese (20)	46	0.20
Korean (47)	55	0.23
Laotian (1)	2	0.01
Malaysian (1)	1	<0.01
Pakistani (4)	6	0.03
Sri Lankan (1)	1	<0.01
Taiwanese (1)	1	<0.01
Thai (10)	12	0.05
Vietnamese (25)	32	0.14
Hawaii Native/Pacific Islander (1)	5	0.02
Not Hispanic (1)	4	0.02
Hispanic (0)	1	<0.01
Guamanian/Chamorro (0)	1	<0.01
Native Hawaiian (0)	1	<0.01
Samoan (0)	1	<0.01
White (22,314)	22,624	96.65
Not Hispanic (22,085)	22,352	95.48
Hispanic (229)	272	1.16

Laconia

Place Type: City
County: Belknap
Population: 15,951†

Ancestry‡	Population	%
African, Sub-Saharan (0)	8	0.05
African (0)	8	0.05
American (1,265)	1,265	7.80
Arab (0)	62	0.38
Lebanese (0)	62	0.38
Armenian (0)	32	0.20
Austrian (0)	157	0.97
Belgian (0)	121	0.75
Brazilian (145)	145	0.89
British (16)	54	0.33
Bulgarian (67)	67	0.41
Canadian (150)	195	1.20
Croatian (70)	84	0.52
Danish (0)	16	0.10
Dutch (13)	135	0.83
Eastern European (47)	47	0.29
English (1,040)	2,912	17.95
European (72)	72	0.44
Finnish (0)	68	0.42
French, ex. Basque (1,625)	3,261	20.11
French Canadian (991)	1,467	9.04
German (327)	1,036	6.39
Greek (55)	359	2.21
Hungarian (26)	26	0.16
Irish (872)	2,743	16.91
Italian (528)	1,255	7.74
Lithuanian (5)	43	0.27
Northern European (10)	10	0.06
Norwegian (20)	55	0.34
Polish (120)	508	3.13
Portuguese (64)	259	1.60
Russian (10)	54	0.33
Scotch-Irish (84)	266	1.64
Scottish (82)	593	3.66
Serbian (0)	14	0.09
Swedish (71)	219	1.35
Swiss (0)	9	0.06
Ukrainian (22)	33	0.20
Welsh (41)	79	0.49
West Indian, ex. Hispanic (32)	32	0.20
Jamaican (32)	32	0.20
Yugoslavian (15)	15	0.09

Hispanic Origin	Population	%
Hispanic or Latino (of any race)	250	1.57
Central American, ex. Mexican	14	0.09
Guatemalan	3	0.02
Nicaraguan	3	0.02
Panamanian	1	0.01
Salvadoran	7	0.04
Cuban	9	0.06
Dominican Republic	17	0.11
Mexican	70	0.44
Puerto Rican	93	0.58
South American	8	0.05
Argentinean	2	0.01
Colombian	2	0.01
Ecuadorian	2	0.01
Peruvian	2	0.01
Other Hispanic or Latino	39	0.24

Race*	Population	%
African-American/Black (150)	218	1.37
Not Hispanic (136)	192	1.20
Hispanic (14)	26	0.16
American Indian/Alaska Native (54)	161	1.01
Not Hispanic (54)	158	0.99
Hispanic (0)	3	0.02
Apache (0)	1	0.01
Blackfeet (5)	16	0.10
Canadian/French Am. Ind. (3)	5	0.03
Cherokee (3)	11	0.07
Chippewa (0)	1	0.01
Choctaw (0)	1	0.01
Cree (0)	2	0.01
Creek (0)	1	0.01
Delaware (0)	1	0.01
Inupiat *(Alaska Native)* (1)	3	0.02
Iroquois (3)	10	0.06
Lumbee (3)	3	0.02
Mexican American Ind. (1)	1	0.01
Navajo (0)	1	0.01
Sioux (2)	2	0.01
South American Ind. (1)	2	0.01
Asian (391)	440	2.76
Not Hispanic (389)	435	2.73
Hispanic (2)	5	0.03
Bhutanese (121)	128	0.80
Burmese (3)	3	0.02
Cambodian (7)	8	0.05
Chinese, ex. Taiwanese (41)	53	0.33
Filipino (45)	65	0.41
Indian (32)	33	0.21
Japanese (11)	17	0.11
Korean (13)	23	0.14
Laotian (53)	63	0.39

*Notes: † The Census 2010 population figure is used to calculate the percentages in the Hispanic Origin and Race categories. Ancestry percentages are based on the 2006-2010 American Community Survey population (not shown); ‡ Numbers in parentheses indicate the number of people reporting a single ancestry; * Numbers in parentheses indicate the number of persons reporting this race alone, not in combination with any other race; Please refer to the Explanation of Data for more information.*

Nepalese (5)	11	0.07
Pakistani (1)	1	0.01
Taiwanese (0)	2	0.01
Thai (9)	12	0.08
Vietnamese (30)	30	0.19
Hawaii Native/Pacific Islander (1)	5	0.03
Not Hispanic (0)	3	0.02
Hispanic (1)	2	0.01
Native Hawaiian (1)	1	0.01
White (15,073)	15,299	95.91
Not Hispanic (14,912)	15,106	94.70
Hispanic (161)	193	1.21

Lebanon

Place Type: City
County: Grafton
Population: 13,151†

Ancestry‡	Population	%
African, Sub-Saharan (0)	69	0.53
Cape Verdean (0)	69	0.53
Albanian (0)	11	0.08
American (776)	776	5.91
Arab (16)	33	0.25
Lebanese (16)	33	0.25
Australian (22)	38	0.29
Brazilian (0)	69	0.53
British (133)	163	1.24
Canadian (115)	195	1.49
Croatian (0)	15	0.11
Czech (0)	65	0.50
Czechoslovakian (14)	40	0.30
Danish (19)	71	0.54
Dutch (15)	41	0.31
Eastern European (75)	75	0.57
English (1,012)	2,541	19.36
European (159)	174	1.33
French, ex. Basque (516)	1,682	12.81
French Canadian (604)	843	6.42
German (304)	1,119	8.52
Greek (0)	52	0.40
Iranian (14)	14	0.11
Irish (827)	2,055	15.65
Israeli (39)	39	0.30
Italian (100)	443	3.37
Lithuanian (15)	27	0.21
Northern European (19)	32	0.24
Norwegian (71)	144	1.10
Polish (242)	597	4.55
Portuguese (69)	123	0.94
Romanian (133)	205	1.56
Russian (22)	22	0.17
Scotch-Irish (111)	226	1.72
Scottish (213)	638	4.86
Slovene (15)	39	0.30
Swedish (15)	193	1.47
Swiss (60)	60	0.46
Ukrainian (15)	46	0.35
Welsh (19)	48	0.37
West Indian, ex. Hispanic (270)	294	2.24
Haitian (100)	100	0.76
Jamaican (161)	161	1.23
Trinidadian/Tobagonian (9)	9	0.07
West Indian (0)	24	0.18
Yugoslavian (16)	16	0.12

Hispanic Origin	Population	%
Hispanic or Latino (of any race)	376	2.86
Central American, ex. Mexican	34	0.26
Guatemalan	20	0.15
Honduran	3	0.02
Nicaraguan	1	0.01
Panamanian	1	0.01
Salvadoran	8	0.06
Other Central American	1	0.01
Cuban	17	0.13
Dominican Republic	9	0.07
Mexican	117	0.89
Puerto Rican	60	0.46
South American	65	0.49
Argentinean	15	0.11
Chilean	3	0.02
Colombian	21	0.16
Ecuadorian	12	0.09
Peruvian	10	0.08
Uruguayan	2	0.02
Venezuelan	2	0.02
Other Hispanic or Latino	74	0.56

Race*	Population	%
African-American/Black (213)	279	2.12
Not Hispanic (201)	258	1.96
Hispanic (12)	21	0.16
American Indian/Alaska Native (36)	126	0.96
Not Hispanic (31)	114	0.87
Hispanic (5)	12	0.09
Apache (0)	3	0.02
Blackfeet (0)	2	0.02
Canadian/French Am. Ind. (1)	5	0.04
Cherokee (3)	20	0.15
Chickasaw (0)	1	0.01
Chippewa (1)	2	0.02
Choctaw (1)	1	0.01
Creek (1)	1	0.01
Delaware (0)	1	0.01
Iroquois (1)	8	0.06
Mexican American Ind. (3)	3	0.02
Navajo (0)	3	0.02
Paiute (1)	1	0.01
Sioux (0)	3	0.02
Tohono O'Odham (0)	3	0.02
Asian (900)	1,031	7.84
Not Hispanic (897)	1,025	7.79
Hispanic (3)	6	0.05
Bangladeshi (1)	1	0.01
Bhutanese (0)	8	0.06
Burmese (5)	5	0.04
Cambodian (12)	13	0.10
Chinese, ex. Taiwanese (266)	303	2.30
Filipino (63)	77	0.59
Indian (322)	347	2.64
Japanese (30)	54	0.41
Korean (91)	107	0.81
Laotian (9)	10	0.08
Nepalese (2)	10	0.08
Pakistani (14)	17	0.13
Taiwanese (15)	15	0.11
Thai (7)	8	0.06
Vietnamese (29)	30	0.23
Hawaii Native/Pacific Islander (1)	4	0.03
Not Hispanic (1)	4	0.03
Guamanian/Chamorro (0)	3	0.02
White (11,622)	11,859	90.18
Not Hispanic (11,372)	11,587	88.11
Hispanic (250)	272	2.07

Litchfield

Place Type: Town
County: Hillsborough
Population: 8,271†

Ancestry‡	Population	%
American (193)	193	2.37
Arab (12)	22	0.27
Lebanese (12)	22	0.27
Armenian (11)	11	0.13
Australian (13)	13	0.16
Austrian (0)	18	0.22
British (20)	51	0.63
Canadian (35)	35	0.43
Celtic (9)	27	0.33
Croatian (8)	8	0.10
Czech (0)	30	0.37
Czechoslovakian (0)	10	0.12
Dutch (0)	85	1.04
English (197)	1,338	16.42
European (79)	79	0.97
Finnish (0)	31	0.38
French, ex. Basque (253)	1,238	15.19
French Canadian (562)	872	10.70
German (151)	885	10.86
Greek (52)	90	1.10
Hungarian (14)	14	0.17
Irish (730)	2,391	29.34
Italian (430)	1,402	17.20
Lithuanian (48)	133	1.63
Norwegian (47)	83	1.02
Polish (69)	496	6.09
Portuguese (54)	185	2.27
Russian (0)	48	0.59
Scandinavian (0)	41	0.50
Scotch-Irish (82)	137	1.68
Scottish (98)	298	3.66
Swedish (12)	89	1.09
Swiss (0)	11	0.13
Ukrainian (48)	79	0.97
Welsh (0)	32	0.39
West Indian, ex. Hispanic (18)	36	0.44
Jamaican (18)	36	0.44

Hispanic Origin	Population	%
Hispanic or Latino (of any race)	162	1.96
Central American, ex. Mexican	24	0.29
Costa Rican	4	0.05
Guatemalan	11	0.13
Honduran	2	0.02
Nicaraguan	2	0.02
Panamanian	4	0.05
Salvadoran	1	0.01
Cuban	10	0.12
Dominican Republic	1	0.01
Mexican	21	0.25
Puerto Rican	60	0.73
South American	32	0.39
Argentinean	2	0.02
Bolivian	6	0.07
Chilean	5	0.06
Colombian	16	0.19
Ecuadorian	2	0.02
Venezuelan	1	0.01
Other Hispanic or Latino	14	0.17

Race*	Population	%
African-American/Black (59)	88	1.06
Not Hispanic (50)	74	0.89
Hispanic (9)	14	0.17
American Indian/Alaska Native (30)	55	0.66
Not Hispanic (22)	47	0.57
Hispanic (8)	8	0.10
Canadian/French Am. Ind. (1)	1	0.01
Chickasaw (1)	1	0.01
Chippewa (1)	1	0.01
Creek (0)	1	0.01
Mexican American Ind. (2)	2	0.02
Navajo (4)	4	0.05
Sioux (1)	2	0.02
Asian (70)	109	1.32
Not Hispanic (70)	108	1.31
Hispanic (0)	1	0.01
Cambodian (0)	4	0.05
Chinese, ex. Taiwanese (11)	16	0.19
Filipino (14)	18	0.22
Indian (7)	11	0.13
Japanese (3)	4	0.05
Korean (14)	32	0.39
Nepalese (3)	3	0.04
Pakistani (5)	5	0.06
Taiwanese (2)	5	0.06
Thai (3)	4	0.05
Vietnamese (2)	8	0.10
Hawaii Native/Pacific Islander (1)	6	0.07
Not Hispanic (1)	6	0.07
Guamanian/Chamorro (1)	1	0.01
Samoan (0)	5	0.06
White (7,973)	8,061	97.46
Not Hispanic (7,871)	7,950	96.12
Hispanic (102)	111	1.34

*Notes: † The Census 2010 population figure is used to calculate the percentages in the Hispanic Origin and Race categories. Ancestry percentages are based on the 2006-2010 American Community Survey population (not shown); ‡ Numbers in parentheses indicate the number of people reporting a single ancestry; * Numbers in parentheses indicate the number of persons reporting this race alone, not in combination with any other race; Please refer to the Explanation of Data for more information.*

Londonderry

Place Type: CDP
County: Rockingham
Population: 11,037†

Ancestry‡	Population	%
American (336)	336	3.08
Arab (0)	166	1.52
Arab (0)	36	0.33
Lebanese (0)	130	1.19
Armenian (14)	28	0.26
British (0)	21	0.19
Canadian (44)	158	1.45
Danish (0)	70	0.64
Dutch (9)	57	0.52
English (398)	1,663	15.24
European (32)	48	0.44
French, ex. Basque (775)	1,788	16.38
French Canadian (216)	668	6.12
German (289)	1,273	11.66
Greek (25)	25	0.23
Hungarian (10)	32	0.29
Icelander (9)	9	0.08
Iranian (13)	13	0.12
Irish (1,331)	3,463	31.73
Italian (439)	1,487	13.63
Lithuanian (44)	84	0.77
Norwegian (0)	45	0.41
Polish (116)	782	7.17
Portuguese (74)	208	1.91
Romanian (0)	44	0.40
Russian (43)	56	0.51
Scandinavian (92)	123	1.13
Scotch-Irish (22)	215	1.97
Scottish (47)	444	4.07
Slovak (29)	115	1.05
Swedish (28)	272	2.49
Turkish (15)	15	0.14
Ukrainian (5)	18	0.16
Welsh (0)	71	0.65
West Indian, ex. Hispanic (18)	36	0.33
Barbadian (0)	18	0.16
Trinidadian/Tobagonian (18)	18	0.16

Hispanic Origin	Population	%
Hispanic or Latino (of any race)	278	2.52
Central American, ex. Mexican	21	0.19
Costa Rican	3	0.03
Guatemalan	13	0.12
Panamanian	2	0.02
Salvadoran	3	0.03
Cuban	12	0.11
Dominican Republic	22	0.20
Mexican	43	0.39
Puerto Rican	117	1.06
South American	36	0.33
Chilean	4	0.04
Colombian	22	0.20
Ecuadorian	5	0.05
Uruguayan	1	0.01
Venezuelan	4	0.04
Other Hispanic or Latino	27	0.24

Race*	Population	%
African-American/Black (88)	116	1.05
Not Hispanic (72)	95	0.86
Hispanic (16)	21	0.19
American Indian/Alaska Native (7)	42	0.38
Not Hispanic (3)	33	0.30
Hispanic (4)	9	0.08
Blackfeet (0)	2	0.02
Canadian/French Am. Ind. (0)	1	0.01
Cherokee (0)	11	0.10
Chickasaw (1)	1	0.01
Choctaw (0)	1	0.01
Lumbee (0)	1	0.01
Mexican American Ind. (1)	1	0.01
Asian (167)	235	2.13
Not Hispanic (165)	227	2.06
Hispanic (2)	8	0.07
Bangladeshi (1)	3	0.03
Cambodian (10)	10	0.09
Chinese, ex. Taiwanese (57)	76	0.69
Filipino (18)	26	0.24
Hmong (1)	1	0.01
Indian (27)	35	0.32
Indonesian (1)	4	0.04
Japanese (5)	26	0.24
Korean (16)	23	0.21
Laotian (3)	3	0.03
Pakistani (16)	16	0.14
Thai (2)	2	0.02
Vietnamese (4)	11	0.10
Hawaii Native/Pacific Islander (3)	7	0.06
Not Hispanic (3)	7	0.06
Guamanian/Chamorro (1)	3	0.03
Native Hawaiian (2)	3	0.03
Samoan (0)	1	0.01
White (10,569)	10,713	97.06
Not Hispanic (10,385)	10,502	95.15
Hispanic (184)	211	1.91

Londonderry

Place Type: Town
County: Rockingham
Population: 24,129†

Ancestry‡	Population	%
African, Sub-Saharan (16)	16	0.07
Ethiopian (16)	16	0.07
Albanian (0)	41	0.17
American (641)	641	2.65
Arab (35)	201	0.83
Arab (0)	36	0.15
Lebanese (17)	147	0.61
Syrian (18)	18	0.07
Armenian (14)	28	0.12
Austrian (0)	26	0.11
Brazilian (0)	34	0.14
British (67)	114	0.47
Canadian (128)	481	1.99
Czech (15)	47	0.19
Czechoslovakian (15)	15	0.06
Danish (18)	145	0.60
Dutch (9)	125	0.52
Eastern European (12)	12	0.05
English (774)	4,009	16.57
European (60)	76	0.31
Finnish (13)	67	0.28
French, ex. Basque (1,181)	3,635	15.02
French Canadian (779)	1,916	7.92
German (461)	2,791	11.53
Greek (53)	283	1.17
Hungarian (10)	77	0.32
Icelander (9)	9	0.04
Iranian (13)	13	0.05
Irish (2,387)	7,647	31.60
Italian (1,084)	3,554	14.69
Latvian (13)	13	0.05
Lithuanian (78)	174	0.72
Northern European (27)	27	0.11
Norwegian (55)	227	0.94
Polish (250)	1,787	7.38
Portuguese (168)	601	2.48
Romanian (0)	44	0.18
Russian (201)	273	1.13
Scandinavian (112)	143	0.59
Scotch-Irish (106)	506	2.09
Scottish (118)	916	3.79
Serbian (0)	14	0.06
Slovak (29)	130	0.54
Swedish (57)	416	1.72
Swiss (14)	14	0.06
Turkish (15)	15	0.06
Ukrainian (5)	18	0.07
Welsh (12)	207	0.86
West Indian, ex. Hispanic (18)	36	0.15
Barbadian (0)	18	0.07
Trinidadian/Tobagonian (18)	18	0.07

Hispanic Origin	Population	%
Hispanic or Latino (of any race)	502	2.08
Central American, ex. Mexican	36	0.15
Costa Rican	4	0.02
Guatemalan	23	0.10
Honduran	1	<0.01
Nicaraguan	3	0.01
Panamanian	2	0.01
Salvadoran	3	0.01
Cuban	19	0.08
Dominican Republic	48	0.20
Mexican	80	0.33
Puerto Rican	204	0.85
South American	61	0.25
Argentinean	3	0.01
Chilean	4	0.02
Colombian	28	0.12
Ecuadorian	7	0.03
Uruguayan	1	<0.01
Venezuelan	17	0.07
Other South American	1	<0.01
Other Hispanic or Latino	54	0.22

Race*	Population	%
African-American/Black (180)	245	1.02
Not Hispanic (144)	204	0.85
Hispanic (36)	41	0.17
American Indian/Alaska Native (19)	102	0.42
Not Hispanic (12)	88	0.36
Hispanic (7)	14	0.06
Blackfeet (0)	2	0.01
Canadian/French Am. Ind. (0)	3	0.01
Cherokee (0)	12	0.05
Chickasaw (1)	1	<0.01
Choctaw (0)	1	<0.01
Cree (0)	3	0.01
Lumbee (0)	1	<0.01
Mexican American Ind. (1)	1	<0.01
Navajo (0)	1	<0.01
Osage (0)	5	0.02
Sioux (2)	2	0.01
Asian (418)	532	2.20
Not Hispanic (416)	524	2.17
Hispanic (2)	8	0.03
Bangladeshi (1)	3	0.01
Cambodian (17)	22	0.09
Chinese, ex. Taiwanese (150)	179	0.74
Filipino (40)	71	0.29
Hmong (1)	1	<0.01
Indian (83)	96	0.40
Indonesian (1)	4	0.02
Japanese (16)	42	0.17
Korean (51)	61	0.25
Laotian (3)	3	0.01
Pakistani (31)	31	0.13
Taiwanese (4)	4	0.02
Thai (5)	5	0.02
Vietnamese (5)	13	0.05
Hawaii Native/Pacific Islander (7)	13	0.05
Not Hispanic (7)	13	0.05
Guamanian/Chamorro (1)	3	0.01
Marshallese (1)	2	0.01
Native Hawaiian (2)	3	0.01
Samoan (0)	2	0.01
White (23,113)	23,402	96.99
Not Hispanic (22,768)	23,015	95.38
Hispanic (345)	387	1.60

Manchester

Place Type: City
County: Hillsborough
Population: 109,565†

Ancestry‡	Population	%
African, Sub-Saharan (1,707)	1,815	1.65
African (369)	410	0.37
Cape Verdean (21)	57	0.05

*Notes: † The Census 2010 population figure is used to calculate the percentages in the Hispanic Origin and Race categories. Ancestry percentages are based on the 2006-2010 American Community Survey population (not shown); ‡ Numbers in parentheses indicate the number of people reporting a single ancestry; * Numbers in parentheses indicate the number of persons reporting this race alone, not in combination with any other race; Please refer to the Explanation of Data for more information.*

Ethiopian (49)	49	0.04
Liberian (155)	164	0.15
Nigerian (48)	48	0.04
Sudanese (843)	843	0.77
Ugandan (55)	55	0.05
Zimbabwean (11)	11	0.01
Other Sub-Saharan African (156)	178	0.16
Albanian (352)	456	0.42
American (3,110)	3,110	2.83
Arab (382)	740	0.67
Arab (47)	87	0.08
Egyptian (37)	37	0.03
Iraqi (22)	22	0.02
Lebanese (215)	498	0.45
Syrian (0)	23	0.02
Other Arab (61)	73	0.07
Armenian (36)	149	0.14
Australian (20)	27	0.02
Austrian (48)	139	0.13
Belgian (50)	269	0.25
Brazilian (313)	342	0.31
British (127)	469	0.43
Bulgarian (12)	12	0.01
Canadian (1,006)	1,399	1.27
Celtic (0)	8	0.01
Croatian (130)	176	0.16
Czech (19)	126	0.11
Czechoslovakian (0)	40	0.04
Danish (64)	299	0.27
Dutch (27)	590	0.54
Eastern European (43)	43	0.04
English (3,208)	11,416	10.40
Estonian (15)	32	0.03
European (357)	517	0.47
Finnish (30)	156	0.14
French, ex. Basque (9,120)	23,578	21.48
French Canadian (8,370)	12,622	11.50
German (1,425)	6,967	6.35
Greek (1,863)	3,676	3.35
Hungarian (52)	235	0.21
Iranian (33)	33	0.03
Irish (6,508)	22,788	20.76
Italian (2,330)	9,684	8.82
Latvian (36)	36	0.03
Lithuanian (62)	423	0.39
Northern European (44)	44	0.04
Norwegian (78)	722	0.66
Polish (1,513)	5,660	5.16
Portuguese (440)	1,382	1.26
Romanian (64)	100	0.09
Russian (417)	1,027	0.94
Scandinavian (8)	57	0.05
Scotch-Irish (709)	2,296	2.09
Scottish (832)	3,642	3.32
Slovak (9)	29	0.03
Swedish (250)	1,942	1.77
Swiss (28)	92	0.08
Turkish (134)	191	0.17
Ukrainian (264)	386	0.35
Welsh (109)	397	0.36
West Indian, ex. Hispanic (705)	881	0.80
Belizean (0)	12	0.01
British West Indian (11)	20	0.02
Haitian (433)	503	0.46
Jamaican (244)	288	0.26
U.S. Virgin Islander (0)	7	0.01
West Indian (17)	51	0.05
Yugoslavian (869)	967	0.88

Hispanic Origin	Population	%
Hispanic or Latino (of any race)	8,883	8.11
Central American, ex. Mexican	862	0.79
Costa Rican	23	0.02
Guatemalan	134	0.12
Honduran	242	0.22
Nicaraguan	31	0.03
Panamanian	33	0.03
Salvadoran	386	0.35
Other Central American	13	0.01
Cuban	109	0.10
Dominican Republic	1,215	1.11
Mexican	1,914	1.75
Puerto Rican	3,315	3.03
South American	762	0.70
Argentinean	24	0.02
Bolivian	3	<0.01
Chilean	18	0.02
Colombian	334	0.30
Ecuadorian	64	0.06
Paraguayan	2	<0.01
Peruvian	67	0.06
Uruguayan	211	0.19
Venezuelan	24	0.02
Other South American	15	0.01
Other Hispanic or Latino	706	0.64

Race*	Population	%
African-American/Black (4,476)	5,751	5.25
Not Hispanic (4,063)	5,090	4.65
Hispanic (413)	661	0.60
American Indian/Alaska Native (346)	1,003	0.92
Not Hispanic (250)	811	0.74
Hispanic (96)	192	0.18
Aleut *(Alaska Native)* (1)	1	<0.01
Apache (4)	16	0.01
Arapaho (0)	6	0.01
Blackfeet (6)	58	0.05
Canadian/French Am. Ind. (5)	14	0.01
Central American Ind. (4)	7	0.01
Cherokee (28)	108	0.10
Cheyenne (1)	8	0.01
Chickasaw (2)	6	0.01
Chippewa (10)	16	0.01
Choctaw (1)	5	<0.01
Comanche (0)	1	<0.01
Cree (5)	16	0.01
Creek (1)	3	<0.01
Inupiat *(Alaska Native)* (4)	6	0.01
Iroquois (8)	30	0.03
Lumbee (3)	3	<0.01
Mexican American Ind. (10)	14	0.01
Navajo (4)	8	0.01
Osage (1)	1	<0.01
Ottawa (3)	3	<0.01
Pueblo (1)	1	<0.01
Seminole (1)	5	<0.01
Shoshone (0)	3	<0.01
Sioux (9)	40	0.04
South American Ind. (3)	4	<0.01
Spanish American Ind. (3)	3	<0.01
Ute (0)	1	<0.01
Yaqui (1)	1	<0.01
Yuman (0)	1	<0.01
Asian (4,014)	4,654	4.25
Not Hispanic (3,993)	4,579	4.18
Hispanic (21)	75	0.07
Bangladeshi (17)	18	0.02
Bhutanese (259)	316	0.29
Cambodian (66)	92	0.08
Chinese, ex. Taiwanese (749)	861	0.79
Filipino (261)	361	0.33
Hmong (3)	3	<0.01
Indian (543)	642	0.59
Indonesian (18)	25	0.02
Japanese (61)	155	0.14
Korean (153)	214	0.20
Laotian (30)	41	0.04
Malaysian (9)	20	0.02
Nepalese (258)	308	0.28
Pakistani (102)	125	0.11
Sri Lankan (1)	2	<0.01
Taiwanese (63)	69	0.06
Thai (52)	72	0.07
Vietnamese (1,134)	1,205	1.10
Hawaii Native/Pacific Islander (72)	205	0.19
Not Hispanic (41)	135	0.12
Hispanic (31)	70	0.06
Guamanian/Chamorro (39)	69	0.06
Native Hawaiian (15)	40	0.04
Samoan (1)	2	<0.01
Tongan (1)	1	<0.01
White (94,299)	96,908	88.45
Not Hispanic (89,893)	91,901	83.88
Hispanic (4,406)	5,007	4.57

Merrimack

Place Type: Town
County: Hillsborough
Population: 25,494†

Ancestry‡	Population	%
Albanian (17)	17	0.07
American (1,119)	1,119	4.37
Arab (33)	92	0.36
Lebanese (19)	66	0.26
Moroccan (14)	14	0.05
Syrian (0)	12	0.05
Armenian (24)	53	0.21
Austrian (13)	86	0.34
Belgian (14)	52	0.20
Brazilian (0)	25	0.10
British (39)	103	0.40
Canadian (136)	414	1.62
Croatian (0)	12	0.05
Czech (0)	21	0.08
Czechoslovakian (0)	31	0.12
Danish (5)	81	0.32
Dutch (81)	236	0.92
Eastern European (14)	46	0.18
English (1,293)	4,537	17.74
European (88)	101	0.39
Finnish (46)	147	0.57
French, ex. Basque (1,085)	4,752	18.58
French Canadian (1,180)	2,260	8.84
German (857)	3,176	12.42
Greek (239)	583	2.28
Hungarian (40)	156	0.61
Iranian (25)	25	0.10
Irish (1,822)	5,762	22.53
Italian (617)	2,848	11.13
Latvian (0)	6	0.02
Lithuanian (55)	187	0.73
Northern European (13)	13	0.05
Norwegian (10)	137	0.54
Pennsylvania German (13)	58	0.23
Polish (294)	1,321	5.16
Portuguese (303)	800	3.13
Romanian (6)	6	0.02
Russian (62)	178	0.70
Scandinavian (143)	143	0.56
Scotch-Irish (232)	525	2.05
Scottish (252)	1,379	5.39
Serbian (0)	39	0.15
Slavic (0)	10	0.04
Slovak (24)	107	0.42
Swedish (247)	748	2.92
Swiss (15)	109	0.43
Ukrainian (52)	87	0.34
Welsh (0)	150	0.59
West Indian, ex. Hispanic (23)	80	0.31
Haitian (0)	42	0.16
Jamaican (23)	38	0.15
Yugoslavian (15)	15	0.06

Hispanic Origin	Population	%
Hispanic or Latino (of any race)	546	2.14
Central American, ex. Mexican	49	0.19
Costa Rican	5	0.02
Guatemalan	14	0.05
Honduran	8	0.03
Nicaraguan	8	0.03
Panamanian	6	0.02
Salvadoran	8	0.03
Cuban	27	0.11
Dominican Republic	43	0.17
Mexican	126	0.49
Puerto Rican	169	0.66
South American	74	0.29
Argentinean	10	0.04

*Notes: † The Census 2010 population figure is used to calculate the percentages in the Hispanic Origin and Race categories. Ancestry percentages are based on the 2006-2010 American Community Survey population (not shown); ‡ Numbers in parentheses indicate the number of people reporting a single ancestry; * Numbers in parentheses indicate the number of persons reporting this race alone, not in combination with any other race; Please refer to the Explanation of Data for more information.*

Colombian	39	0.15
Ecuadorian	7	0.03
Peruvian	13	0.05
Uruguayan	1	<0.01
Venezuelan	1	<0.01
Other South American	3	0.01
Other Hispanic or Latino	58	0.23

Race*	Population	%
African-American/Black (192)	340	1.33
Not Hispanic (183)	317	1.24
Hispanic (9)	23	0.09
American Indian/Alaska Native (46)	138	0.54
Not Hispanic (44)	129	0.51
Hispanic (2)	9	0.04
Blackfeet (0)	1	<0.01
Canadian/French Am. Ind. (0)	1	<0.01
Cherokee (2)	10	0.04
Choctaw (3)	9	0.04
Cree (1)	1	<0.01
Creek (1)	1	<0.01
Iroquois (2)	4	0.02
Lumbee (2)	2	0.01
Mexican American Ind. (1)	1	<0.01
Osage (1)	1	<0.01
Sioux (0)	3	0.01
Asian (499)	642	2.52
Not Hispanic (498)	636	2.49
Hispanic (1)	6	0.02
Bangladeshi (1)	1	<0.01
Burmese (1)	1	<0.01
Cambodian (9)	13	0.05
Chinese, ex. Taiwanese (99)	127	0.50
Filipino (41)	68	0.27
Indian (195)	209	0.82
Indonesian (0)	3	0.01
Japanese (19)	51	0.20
Korean (46)	64	0.25
Laotian (2)	2	0.01
Malaysian (1)	1	<0.01
Nepalese (17)	17	0.07
Pakistani (9)	9	0.04
Sri Lankan (7)	7	0.03
Taiwanese (7)	7	0.03
Thai (6)	17	0.07
Vietnamese (26)	32	0.13
Hawaii Native/Pacific Islander (4)	21	0.08
Not Hispanic (4)	16	0.06
Hispanic (0)	5	0.02
Guamanian/Chamorro (1)	3	0.01
Native Hawaiian (2)	16	0.06
White (24,230)	24,618	96.56
Not Hispanic (23,828)	24,164	94.78
Hispanic (402)	454	1.78

Milford

Place Type: CDP
County: Hillsborough
Population: 8,835†

Ancestry‡	Population	%
African, Sub-Saharan (48)	48	0.53
African (16)	16	0.18
South African (32)	32	0.35
Albanian (0)	11	0.12
American (306)	306	3.38
Arab (16)	45	0.50
Lebanese (16)	45	0.50
Armenian (12)	12	0.13
Austrian (8)	22	0.24
Belgian (0)	9	0.10
Brazilian (136)	136	1.50
British (37)	89	0.98
Canadian (75)	119	1.31
Czech (13)	13	0.14
Dutch (22)	51	0.56
English (704)	1,852	20.44
European (62)	62	0.68
Finnish (58)	154	1.70
French, ex. Basque (322)	1,425	15.73
French Canadian (464)	916	10.11
German (157)	864	9.54
Greek (95)	227	2.51
Guyanese (0)	51	0.56
Hungarian (13)	24	0.26
Irish (508)	1,862	20.55
Italian (217)	650	7.17
Lithuanian (41)	100	1.10
Northern European (25)	25	0.28
Norwegian (30)	64	0.71
Polish (43)	213	2.35
Portuguese (12)	199	2.20
Romanian (0)	34	0.38
Russian (47)	133	1.47
Scandinavian (0)	42	0.46
Scotch-Irish (146)	369	4.07
Scottish (118)	337	3.72
Swedish (26)	144	1.59
Welsh (19)	98	1.08
Yugoslavian (106)	106	1.17

Hispanic Origin	Population	%
Hispanic or Latino (of any race)	217	2.46
Central American, ex. Mexican	23	0.26
Costa Rican	1	0.01
Guatemalan	13	0.15
Honduran	4	0.05
Salvadoran	5	0.06
Cuban	6	0.07
Dominican Republic	20	0.23
Mexican	47	0.53
Puerto Rican	62	0.70
South American	34	0.38
Argentinean	3	0.03
Chilean	3	0.03
Colombian	16	0.18
Ecuadorian	4	0.05
Peruvian	5	0.06
Uruguayan	3	0.03
Other Hispanic or Latino	25	0.28

Race*	Population	%
African-American/Black (121)	160	1.81
Not Hispanic (116)	150	1.70
Hispanic (5)	10	0.11
American Indian/Alaska Native (23)	72	0.81
Not Hispanic (22)	71	0.80
Hispanic (1)	1	0.01
Blackfeet (0)	1	0.01
Canadian/French Am. Ind. (0)	2	0.02
Cherokee (1)	13	0.15
Chippewa (0)	3	0.03
Choctaw (0)	1	0.01
Inupiat *(Alaska Native)* (0)	1	0.01
Iroquois (0)	6	0.07
Potawatomi (1)	1	0.01
Sioux (0)	1	0.01
Yup'ik *(Alaska Native)* (0)	1	0.01
Asian (122)	169	1.91
Not Hispanic (122)	164	1.86
Hispanic (0)	5	0.06
Bhutanese (1)	1	0.01
Cambodian (12)	14	0.16
Chinese, ex. Taiwanese (22)	26	0.29
Filipino (18)	33	0.37
Indian (18)	28	0.32
Japanese (5)	8	0.09
Korean (19)	31	0.35
Laotian (1)	3	0.03
Nepalese (6)	11	0.12
Pakistani (2)	2	0.02
Thai (6)	7	0.08
Vietnamese (3)	10	0.11
Hawaii Native/Pacific Islander (1)	3	0.03
Not Hispanic (1)	3	0.03
Guamanian/Chamorro (1)	1	0.01
Native Hawaiian (0)	1	0.01
White (8,340)	8,482	96.00
Not Hispanic (8,204)	8,321	94.18
Hispanic (136)	161	1.82

Milford

Place Type: Town
County: Hillsborough
Population: 15,115†

Ancestry‡	Population	%
African, Sub-Saharan (48)	48	0.32
African (16)	16	0.11
South African (32)	32	0.21
Albanian (0)	11	0.07
American (436)	436	2.92
Arab (16)	45	0.30
Lebanese (16)	45	0.30
Armenian (12)	12	0.08
Austrian (8)	52	0.35
Belgian (6)	15	0.10
Brazilian (136)	136	0.91
British (49)	101	0.68
Canadian (109)	233	1.56
Czech (28)	36	0.24
Danish (0)	20	0.13
Dutch (45)	116	0.78
English (1,142)	3,279	21.99
Estonian (9)	9	0.06
European (141)	141	0.95
Finnish (69)	243	1.63
French, ex. Basque (579)	2,324	15.58
French Canadian (841)	1,613	10.82
German (324)	1,511	10.13
Greek (128)	289	1.94
Guyanese (0)	51	0.34
Hungarian (21)	52	0.35
Irish (873)	3,161	21.19
Italian (453)	1,309	8.78
Lithuanian (66)	233	1.56
Northern European (25)	25	0.17
Norwegian (48)	122	0.82
Polish (105)	587	3.94
Portuguese (29)	216	1.45
Romanian (0)	34	0.23
Russian (56)	162	1.09
Scandinavian (16)	58	0.39
Scotch-Irish (285)	598	4.01
Scottish (148)	497	3.33
Swedish (88)	287	1.92
Swiss (0)	11	0.07
Turkish (0)	11	0.07
Ukrainian (7)	34	0.23
Welsh (19)	177	1.19
Yugoslavian (106)	106	0.71

Hispanic Origin	Population	%
Hispanic or Latino (of any race)	337	2.23
Central American, ex. Mexican	36	0.24
Costa Rican	1	0.01
Guatemalan	14	0.09
Honduran	5	0.03
Panamanian	6	0.04
Salvadoran	9	0.06
Other Central American	1	0.01
Cuban	20	0.13
Dominican Republic	25	0.17
Mexican	75	0.50
Puerto Rican	94	0.62
South American	48	0.32
Argentinean	8	0.05
Chilean	5	0.03
Colombian	18	0.12
Ecuadorian	7	0.05
Peruvian	5	0.03
Uruguayan	3	0.02
Other South American	2	0.01
Other Hispanic or Latino	39	0.26

Race*	Population	%
African-American/Black (193)	267	1.77
Not Hispanic (188)	255	1.69

*Notes: † The Census 2010 population figure is used to calculate the percentages in the Hispanic Origin and Race categories. Ancestry percentages are based on the 2006-2010 American Community Survey population (not shown); ‡ Numbers in parentheses indicate the number of people reporting a single ancestry; * Numbers in parentheses indicate the number of persons reporting this race alone, not in combination with any other race; Please refer to the Explanation of Data for more information.*

Hispanic (5)	12	0.08
American Indian/Alaska Native (35)	126	0.83
Not Hispanic (31)	119	0.79
Hispanic (4)	7	0.05
Apache (1)	1	0.01
Blackfeet (1)	7	0.05
Canadian/French Am. Ind. (0)	2	0.01
Cherokee (2)	24	0.16
Chippewa (0)	4	0.03
Choctaw (0)	1	0.01
Comanche (0)	2	0.01
Inupiat *(Alaska Native)* (0)	1	0.01
Iroquois (0)	8	0.05
Potawatomi (1)	1	0.01
Sioux (1)	4	0.03
South American Ind. (1)	1	0.01
Yup'ik *(Alaska Native)* (0)	1	0.01
Asian (200)	275	1.82
Not Hispanic (200)	268	1.77
Hispanic (0)	7	0.05
Bangladeshi (1)	1	0.01
Bhutanese (1)	1	0.01
Cambodian (18)	20	0.13
Chinese, ex. Taiwanese (38)	44	0.29
Filipino (27)	47	0.31
Indian (41)	58	0.38
Indonesian (0)	1	0.01
Japanese (6)	14	0.09
Korean (23)	35	0.23
Laotian (1)	3	0.02
Malaysian (1)	1	0.01
Nepalese (6)	11	0.07
Pakistani (3)	7	0.05
Thai (8)	11	0.07
Vietnamese (10)	22	0.15
Hawaii Native/Pacific Islander (1)	10	0.07
Not Hispanic (1)	4	0.03
Hispanic (0)	6	0.04
Guamanian/Chamorro (1)	1	0.01
Native Hawaiian (0)	1	0.01
White (14,334)	14,570	96.39
Not Hispanic (14,105)	14,310	94.67
Hispanic (229)	260	1.72

Nashua

Place Type: City
County: Hillsborough
Population: 86,494†

Ancestry‡	Population	%
African, Sub-Saharan (300)	449	0.52
African (134)	192	0.22
Cape Verdean (71)	96	0.11
Kenyan (95)	128	0.15
Other Sub-Saharan African (0)	33	0.04
Albanian (33)	46	0.05
American (2,707)	2,707	3.11
Arab (296)	636	0.73
Arab (75)	75	0.09
Egyptian (34)	65	0.07
Lebanese (139)	390	0.45
Moroccan (0)	14	0.02
Syrian (14)	58	0.07
Other Arab (34)	34	0.04
Armenian (165)	434	0.50
Australian (28)	65	0.07
Austrian (20)	316	0.36
Belgian (40)	125	0.14
Brazilian (1,071)	1,248	1.43
British (343)	562	0.65
Bulgarian (10)	10	0.01
Cajun (11)	21	0.02
Canadian (779)	1,290	1.48
Croatian (5)	5	0.01
Czech (79)	478	0.55
Czechoslovakian (9)	46	0.05
Danish (28)	187	0.21
Dutch (169)	842	0.97
Eastern European (70)	70	0.08
English (2,794)	10,754	12.35
Estonian (0)	9	0.01
European (408)	583	0.67
Finnish (112)	221	0.25
French, ex. Basque (3,907)	12,233	14.05
French Canadian (5,015)	8,465	9.73
German (1,554)	7,713	8.86
Greek (755)	1,698	1.95
Hungarian (67)	306	0.35
Iranian (48)	55	0.06
Irish (5,462)	20,134	23.13
Italian (2,355)	8,912	10.24
Latvian (0)	18	0.02
Lithuanian (402)	823	0.95
Maltese (0)	57	0.07
Norwegian (70)	456	0.52
Pennsylvania German (17)	30	0.03
Polish (794)	3,423	3.93
Portuguese (801)	1,878	2.16
Romanian (40)	185	0.21
Russian (357)	1,019	1.17
Scandinavian (43)	113	0.13
Scotch-Irish (744)	1,946	2.24
Scottish (875)	3,108	3.57
Serbian (0)	15	0.02
Slavic (6)	15	0.02
Slovak (58)	82	0.09
Slovene (0)	13	0.01
Swedish (209)	1,074	1.23
Swiss (0)	90	0.10
Ukrainian (134)	321	0.37
Welsh (84)	525	0.60
West Indian, ex. Hispanic (211)	459	0.53
British West Indian (0)	61	0.07
Haitian (102)	228	0.26
Jamaican (59)	85	0.10
Trinidadian/Tobagonian (38)	65	0.07
West Indian (12)	20	0.02
Yugoslavian (0)	14	0.02

Hispanic Origin	Population	%
Hispanic or Latino (of any race)	8,510	9.84
Central American, ex. Mexican	400	0.46
Costa Rican	28	0.03
Guatemalan	60	0.07
Honduran	110	0.13
Nicaraguan	13	0.02
Panamanian	36	0.04
Salvadoran	150	0.17
Other Central American	3	<0.01
Cuban	179	0.21
Dominican Republic	1,639	1.89
Mexican	1,825	2.11
Puerto Rican	2,577	2.98
South American	1,047	1.21
Argentinean	26	0.03
Bolivian	13	0.02
Chilean	10	0.01
Colombian	671	0.78
Ecuadorian	195	0.23
Paraguayan	5	0.01
Peruvian	67	0.08
Uruguayan	12	0.01
Venezuelan	45	0.05
Other South American	3	<0.01
Other Hispanic or Latino	843	0.97

Race*	Population	%
African-American/Black (2,346)	3,121	3.61
Not Hispanic (1,954)	2,506	2.90
Hispanic (392)	615	0.71
American Indian/Alaska Native (249)	679	0.79
Not Hispanic (167)	535	0.62
Hispanic (82)	144	0.17
Alaska Athabascan *(Ala. Nat.)* (1)	1	<0.01
Aleut *(Alaska Native)* (0)	4	<0.01
Apache (1)	4	<0.01
Blackfeet (4)	16	0.02
Canadian/French Am. Ind. (2)	9	0.01
Central American Ind. (5)	10	0.01
Cherokee (12)	98	0.11
Chickasaw (0)	2	<0.01
Chippewa (3)	6	0.01
Choctaw (1)	6	0.01
Colville (0)	1	<0.01
Cree (0)	3	<0.01
Creek (0)	3	<0.01
Crow (0)	1	<0.01
Houma (0)	1	<0.01
Inupiat *(Alaska Native)* (0)	4	<0.01
Iroquois (5)	31	0.04
Lumbee (0)	2	<0.01
Mexican American Ind. (12)	14	0.02
Navajo (2)	11	0.01
Osage (1)	1	<0.01
Potawatomi (0)	1	<0.01
Pueblo (3)	5	0.01
Seminole (0)	4	<0.01
Shoshone (0)	6	0.01
Sioux (3)	10	0.01
South American Ind. (6)	14	0.02
Spanish American Ind. (3)	4	<0.01
Tlingit-Haida *(Alaska Native)* (1)	4	<0.01
Yaqui (0)	2	<0.01
Asian (5,626)	6,180	7.15
Not Hispanic (5,600)	6,106	7.06
Hispanic (26)	74	0.09
Bangladeshi (41)	42	0.05
Bhutanese (1)	1	<0.01
Burmese (12)	15	0.02
Cambodian (113)	141	0.16
Chinese, ex. Taiwanese (931)	1,027	1.19
Filipino (195)	304	0.35
Hmong (2)	2	<0.01
Indian (3,181)	3,298	3.81
Indonesian (15)	25	0.03
Japanese (97)	173	0.20
Korean (239)	293	0.34
Laotian (26)	33	0.04
Malaysian (6)	7	0.01
Nepalese (83)	88	0.10
Pakistani (86)	100	0.12
Sri Lankan (18)	22	0.03
Taiwanese (38)	44	0.05
Thai (36)	58	0.07
Vietnamese (379)	420	0.49
Hawaii Native/Pacific Islander (26)	130	0.15
Not Hispanic (18)	71	0.08
Hispanic (8)	59	0.07
Fijian (2)	2	<0.01
Guamanian/Chamorro (7)	11	0.01
Marshallese (1)	1	<0.01
Native Hawaiian (5)	23	0.03
Samoan (1)	4	<0.01
Tongan (0)	5	0.01
White (72,120)	74,029	85.59
Not Hispanic (68,309)	69,656	80.53
Hispanic (3,811)	4,373	5.06

Newmarket

Place Type: Town
County: Rockingham
Population: 8,936†

Ancestry‡	Population	%
American (300)	300	3.39
Arab (0)	58	0.66
Lebanese (0)	58	0.66
Austrian (0)	23	0.26
Belgian (19)	31	0.35
British (83)	121	1.37
Canadian (34)	62	0.70
Celtic (0)	14	0.16
Danish (21)	92	1.04
Dutch (0)	102	1.15
English (313)	1,352	15.28
European (66)	93	1.05
Finnish (27)	43	0.49
French, ex. Basque (489)	1,827	20.64

*Notes: † The Census 2010 population figure is used to calculate the percentages in the Hispanic Origin and Race categories. Ancestry percentages are based on the 2006-2010 American Community Survey population (not shown); ‡ Numbers in parentheses indicate the number of people reporting a single ancestry; * Numbers in parentheses indicate the number of persons reporting this race alone, not in combination with any other race; Please refer to the Explanation of Data for more information.*

French Canadian (299)	805	9.10
German (209)	980	11.07
Greek (91)	255	2.88
Hungarian (0)	21	0.24
Irish (519)	2,445	27.63
Italian (209)	1,094	12.36
Latvian (9)	41	0.46
Lithuanian (0)	27	0.31
Norwegian (7)	38	0.43
Polish (164)	603	6.81
Portuguese (23)	91	1.03
Romanian (0)	14	0.16
Russian (8)	93	1.05
Scandinavian (0)	38	0.43
Scotch-Irish (82)	215	2.43
Scottish (169)	395	4.46
Slovak (15)	34	0.38
Swedish (20)	217	2.45
Swiss (8)	15	0.17
Ukrainian (9)	9	0.10
Welsh (14)	73	0.82
West Indian, ex. Hispanic (21)	21	0.24
Jamaican (21)	21	0.24

Hispanic Origin	Population	%
Hispanic or Latino (of any race)	202	2.26
Central American, ex. Mexican	7	0.08
Guatemalan	3	0.03
Honduran	1	0.01
Panamanian	3	0.03
Cuban	5	0.06
Dominican Republic	24	0.27
Mexican	35	0.39
Puerto Rican	83	0.93
South American	19	0.21
Argentinean	2	0.02
Bolivian	3	0.03
Chilean	4	0.04
Colombian	6	0.07
Ecuadorian	1	0.01
Peruvian	2	0.02
Uruguayan	1	0.01
Other Hispanic or Latino	29	0.32

Race*	Population	%
African-American/Black (90)	141	1.58
Not Hispanic (88)	132	1.48
Hispanic (2)	9	0.10
American Indian/Alaska Native (21)	73	0.82
Not Hispanic (15)	59	0.66
Hispanic (6)	14	0.16
Blackfeet (0)	5	0.06
Cherokee (2)	3	0.03
Chippewa (1)	1	0.01
Choctaw (3)	7	0.08
Iroquois (2)	4	0.04
Paiute (4)	4	0.04
Seminole (0)	1	0.01
Asian (358)	424	4.74
Not Hispanic (356)	422	4.72
Hispanic (2)	2	0.02
Cambodian (3)	6	0.07
Chinese, ex. Taiwanese (66)	78	0.87
Filipino (10)	30	0.34
Indian (55)	62	0.69
Indonesian (2)	5	0.06
Japanese (17)	29	0.32
Korean (8)	14	0.16
Laotian (156)	178	1.99
Malaysian (0)	1	0.01
Pakistani (4)	4	0.04
Taiwanese (1)	1	0.01
Thai (4)	8	0.09
Vietnamese (6)	8	0.09
Hawaii Native/Pacific Islander (9)	16	0.18
Not Hispanic (8)	15	0.17
Hispanic (1)	1	0.01
Guamanian/Chamorro (0)	1	0.01
Marshallese (1)	1	0.01
Native Hawaiian (1)	4	0.04
Samoan (6)	6	0.07
White (8,238)	8,389	93.88
Not Hispanic (8,112)	8,242	92.23
Hispanic (126)	147	1.65

Pelham

Place Type: Town
County: Hillsborough
Population: 12,897†

Ancestry‡	Population	%
Albanian (0)	19	0.15
American (453)	453	3.59
Arab (106)	480	3.81
Egyptian (0)	12	0.10
Lebanese (11)	196	1.55
Syrian (0)	150	1.19
Other Arab (95)	122	0.97
Armenian (24)	39	0.31
Belgian (12)	19	0.15
Brazilian (72)	72	0.57
British (29)	29	0.23
Canadian (81)	114	0.90
Czech (10)	10	0.08
Czechoslovakian (8)	8	0.06
Danish (0)	10	0.08
Dutch (25)	84	0.67
English (470)	1,801	14.28
European (106)	106	0.84
Finnish (0)	110	0.87
French, ex. Basque (634)	2,502	19.84
French Canadian (981)	1,779	14.10
German (172)	824	6.53
Greek (298)	579	4.59
Hungarian (53)	92	0.73
Iranian (22)	22	0.17
Irish (1,089)	3,806	30.18
Italian (450)	1,430	11.34
Latvian (23)	23	0.18
Lithuanian (11)	210	1.66
Norwegian (8)	38	0.30
Pennsylvania German (0)	8	0.06
Polish (180)	937	7.43
Portuguese (211)	270	2.14
Russian (42)	103	0.82
Scotch-Irish (70)	228	1.81
Scottish (88)	294	2.33
Swedish (10)	208	1.65
Ukrainian (12)	57	0.45
Yugoslavian (0)	8	0.06

Hispanic Origin	Population	%
Hispanic or Latino (of any race)	243	1.88
Central American, ex. Mexican	10	0.08
Guatemalan	6	0.05
Salvadoran	4	0.03
Cuban	15	0.12
Dominican Republic	19	0.15
Mexican	32	0.25
Puerto Rican	105	0.81
South American	36	0.28
Argentinean	1	0.01
Colombian	16	0.12
Ecuadorian	11	0.09
Peruvian	3	0.02
Uruguayan	3	0.02
Venezuelan	2	0.02
Other Hispanic or Latino	26	0.20

Race*	Population	%
African-American/Black (74)	108	0.84
Not Hispanic (70)	94	0.73
Hispanic (4)	14	0.11
American Indian/Alaska Native (18)	52	0.40
Not Hispanic (13)	47	0.36
Hispanic (5)	5	0.04
Apache (1)	1	0.01
Blackfeet (2)	5	0.04
Cherokee (1)	1	0.01
Chippewa (1)	2	0.02
Creek (0)	1	0.01
Crow (0)	1	0.01
Iroquois (4)	4	0.03
Mexican American Ind. (1)	1	0.01
Asian (225)	278	2.16
Not Hispanic (225)	278	2.16
Cambodian (43)	52	0.40
Chinese, ex. Taiwanese (17)	36	0.28
Filipino (7)	17	0.13
Indian (75)	78	0.60
Japanese (4)	13	0.10
Korean (22)	25	0.19
Laotian (7)	7	0.05
Malaysian (0)	1	0.01
Taiwanese (1)	2	0.02
Thai (10)	13	0.10
Vietnamese (29)	37	0.29
Hawaii Native/Pacific Islander (1)	6	0.05
Not Hispanic (1)	6	0.05
Guamanian/Chamorro (1)	1	0.01
White (12,387)	12,511	97.01
Not Hispanic (12,208)	12,315	95.49
Hispanic (179)	196	1.52

Plaistow

Place Type: Town
County: Rockingham
Population: 7,609†

Ancestry‡	Population	%
African, Sub-Saharan (17)	17	0.22
Kenyan (17)	17	0.22
American (156)	156	2.03
Arab (0)	139	1.80
Lebanese (0)	73	0.95
Syrian (0)	66	0.86
Armenian (0)	11	0.14
Austrian (32)	61	0.79
Belgian (0)	18	0.23
British (17)	17	0.22
Bulgarian (14)	27	0.35
Canadian (44)	94	1.22
Czech (0)	19	0.25
Danish (20)	50	0.65
Dutch (0)	26	0.34
English (533)	1,362	17.68
Finnish (35)	107	1.39
French, ex. Basque (388)	1,369	17.77
French Canadian (344)	816	10.59
German (150)	568	7.37
Greek (64)	162	2.10
Irish (641)	2,337	30.34
Italian (528)	1,275	16.55
Lithuanian (12)	127	1.65
Northern European (18)	18	0.23
Norwegian (24)	47	0.61
Polish (129)	286	3.71
Portuguese (172)	265	3.44
Russian (149)	197	2.56
Scandinavian (14)	14	0.18
Scotch-Irish (86)	173	2.25
Scottish (60)	225	2.92
Swedish (26)	102	1.32
Ukrainian (0)	9	0.12
Welsh (0)	14	0.18

Hispanic Origin	Population	%
Hispanic or Latino (of any race)	175	2.30
Central American, ex. Mexican	12	0.16
Costa Rican	1	0.01
Guatemalan	2	0.03
Honduran	3	0.04
Panamanian	3	0.04
Salvadoran	3	0.04
Cuban	6	0.08
Dominican Republic	17	0.22
Mexican	20	0.26
Puerto Rican	59	0.78

*Notes: † The Census 2010 population figure is used to calculate the percentages in the Hispanic Origin and Race categories. Ancestry percentages are based on the 2006-2010 American Community Survey population (not shown); ‡ Numbers in parentheses indicate the number of people reporting a single ancestry; * Numbers in parentheses indicate the number of persons reporting this race alone, not in combination with any other race; Please refer to the Explanation of Data for more information.*

South American	34	0.45
Argentinean	3	0.04
Chilean	6	0.08
Colombian	21	0.28
Ecuadorian	1	0.01
Peruvian	3	0.04
Other Hispanic or Latino	27	0.35

Race*	Population	%
African-American/Black (42)	62	0.81
Not Hispanic (41)	59	0.78
Hispanic (1)	3	0.04
American Indian/Alaska Native (13)	31	0.41
Not Hispanic (10)	26	0.34
Hispanic (3)	5	0.07
Blackfeet (2)	2	0.03
Cherokee (1)	6	0.08
Iroquois (0)	1	0.01
Asian (45)	55	0.72
Not Hispanic (44)	54	0.71
Hispanic (1)	1	0.01
Cambodian (4)	4	0.05
Chinese, ex. Taiwanese (16)	19	0.25
Filipino (5)	6	0.08
Indian (9)	11	0.14
Japanese (1)	3	0.04
Korean (8)	9	0.12
Thai (1)	1	0.01
Vietnamese (1)	1	0.01
Hawaii Native/Pacific Islander (0)	1	0.01
Hispanic (0)	1	0.01
White (7,426)	7,471	98.19
Not Hispanic (7,292)	7,330	96.33
Hispanic (134)	141	1.85

Portsmouth

Place Type: City
County: Rockingham
Population: 20,779†

Ancestry‡	Population	%
African, Sub-Saharan (115)	125	0.60
African (68)	78	0.37
Ethiopian (28)	28	0.13
Nigerian (16)	16	0.08
Other Sub-Saharan African (3)	3	0.01
American (915)	915	4.36
Arab (30)	50	0.24
Lebanese (0)	10	0.05
Syrian (30)	30	0.14
Other Arab (0)	10	0.05
Armenian (0)	9	0.04
Belgian (29)	29	0.14
Brazilian (20)	20	0.10
British (51)	152	0.73
Canadian (118)	266	1.27
Czech (6)	51	0.24
Czechoslovakian (0)	38	0.18
Danish (10)	66	0.31
Dutch (11)	159	0.76
Eastern European (97)	97	0.46
English (1,164)	4,416	21.07
Estonian (0)	28	0.13
European (239)	251	1.20
Finnish (0)	66	0.31
French, ex. Basque (662)	2,550	12.16
French Canadian (373)	806	3.84
German (611)	2,586	12.34
Greek (254)	558	2.66
Hungarian (9)	30	0.14
Irish (1,674)	5,456	26.03
Israeli (22)	22	0.10
Italian (839)	2,523	12.04
Lithuanian (31)	123	0.59
Northern European (10)	10	0.05
Norwegian (29)	181	0.86
Pennsylvania German (0)	19	0.09
Polish (387)	1,157	5.52
Portuguese (111)	144	0.69
Russian (76)	257	1.23
Scandinavian (22)	61	0.29
Scotch-Irish (273)	594	2.83
Scottish (147)	1,198	5.71
Slavic (0)	5	0.02
Slovak (9)	9	0.04
Swedish (55)	324	1.55
Swiss (0)	23	0.11
Ukrainian (52)	118	0.56
Welsh (34)	264	1.26
West Indian, ex. Hispanic (13)	23	0.11
Jamaican (0)	10	0.05
West Indian (13)	13	0.06

Hispanic Origin	Population	%
Hispanic or Latino (of any race)	573	2.76
Central American, ex. Mexican	53	0.26
Costa Rican	6	0.03
Guatemalan	19	0.09
Honduran	6	0.03
Nicaraguan	8	0.04
Panamanian	5	0.02
Salvadoran	9	0.04
Cuban	23	0.11
Dominican Republic	92	0.44
Mexican	139	0.67
Puerto Rican	143	0.69
South American	64	0.31
Argentinean	19	0.09
Chilean	9	0.04
Colombian	25	0.12
Ecuadorian	1	<0.01
Paraguayan	1	<0.01
Peruvian	4	0.02
Uruguayan	2	0.01
Venezuelan	3	0.01
Other Hispanic or Latino	59	0.28

Race*	Population	%
African-American/Black (359)	555	2.67
Not Hispanic (326)	504	2.43
Hispanic (33)	51	0.25
American Indian/Alaska Native (46)	194	0.93
Not Hispanic (40)	176	0.85
Hispanic (6)	18	0.09
Blackfeet (0)	15	0.07
Canadian/French Am. Ind. (1)	4	0.02
Central American Ind. (0)	1	<0.01
Cherokee (7)	36	0.17
Chickasaw (0)	2	0.01
Chippewa (2)	6	0.03
Choctaw (0)	2	0.01
Comanche (0)	1	<0.01
Cree (0)	3	0.01
Creek (0)	2	0.01
Delaware (2)	3	0.01
Inupiat *(Alaska Native)* (2)	2	0.01
Iroquois (2)	18	0.09
Kiowa (3)	3	0.01
Lumbee (3)	6	0.03
Mexican American Ind. (0)	1	<0.01
Navajo (0)	1	<0.01
Pueblo (0)	1	<0.01
Puget Sound Salish (0)	2	0.01
Shoshone (0)	1	<0.01
Sioux (5)	7	0.03
South American Ind. (0)	1	<0.01
Spanish American Ind. (0)	3	0.01
Yaqui (1)	1	<0.01
Asian (719)	874	4.21
Not Hispanic (718)	863	4.15
Hispanic (1)	11	0.05
Burmese (1)	1	<0.01
Cambodian (8)	11	0.05
Chinese, ex. Taiwanese (109)	150	0.72
Filipino (46)	76	0.37
Indian (248)	254	1.22
Indonesian (79)	89	0.43
Japanese (29)	54	0.26
Korean (57)	79	0.38
Laotian (12)	14	0.07
Malaysian (0)	1	<0.01
Nepalese (6)	6	0.03
Pakistani (12)	12	0.06
Sri Lankan (2)	2	0.01
Taiwanese (3)	7	0.03
Thai (11)	22	0.11
Vietnamese (73)	89	0.43
Hawaii Native/Pacific Islander (6)	23	0.11
Not Hispanic (5)	22	0.11
Hispanic (1)	1	<0.01
Guamanian/Chamorro (0)	3	0.01
Native Hawaiian (3)	10	0.05
White (19,017)	19,465	93.68
Not Hispanic (18,658)	19,050	91.68
Hispanic (359)	415	2.00

Raymond

Place Type: Town
County: Rockingham
Population: 10,138†

Ancestry‡	Population	%
American (598)	598	5.90
Arab (52)	68	0.67
Lebanese (52)	68	0.67
Armenian (13)	27	0.27
Assyrian/Chaldean/Syriac (0)	13	0.13
Australian (0)	15	0.15
Austrian (12)	12	0.12
British (27)	46	0.45
Canadian (65)	142	1.40
Danish (16)	16	0.16
Dutch (11)	35	0.35
English (753)	1,939	19.12
European (65)	65	0.64
Finnish (7)	37	0.36
French, ex. Basque (836)	2,318	22.86
French Canadian (489)	770	7.59
German (95)	767	7.56
Greek (27)	54	0.53
Hungarian (13)	13	0.13
Irish (525)	1,583	15.61
Italian (307)	1,057	10.42
Lithuanian (12)	64	0.63
Norwegian (62)	354	3.49
Polish (119)	623	6.14
Portuguese (63)	161	1.59
Russian (15)	81	0.80
Scotch-Irish (191)	376	3.71
Scottish (44)	301	2.97
Swedish (37)	149	1.47
Swiss (0)	8	0.08
Welsh (17)	83	0.82
West Indian, ex. Hispanic (9)	25	0.25
Bermudan (9)	25	0.25

Hispanic Origin	Population	%
Hispanic or Latino (of any race)	114	1.12
Central American, ex. Mexican	10	0.10
Guatemalan	5	0.05
Honduran	1	0.01
Salvadoran	3	0.03
Other Central American	1	0.01
Cuban	9	0.09
Dominican Republic	8	0.08
Mexican	26	0.26
Puerto Rican	44	0.43
South American	7	0.07
Chilean	1	0.01
Colombian	3	0.03
Peruvian	2	0.02
Venezuelan	1	0.01
Other Hispanic or Latino	10	0.10

Race*	Population	%
African-American/Black (68)	114	1.12
Not Hispanic (65)	111	1.09
Hispanic (3)	3	0.03

*Notes: † The Census 2010 population figure is used to calculate the percentages in the Hispanic Origin and Race categories. Ancestry percentages are based on the 2006-2010 American Community Survey population (not shown); ‡ Numbers in parentheses indicate the number of people reporting a single ancestry; * Numbers in parentheses indicate the number of persons reporting this race alone, not in combination with any other race; Please refer to the Explanation of Data for more information.*

American Indian/Alaska Native (17)	74	0.73
Not Hispanic (15)	71	0.70
Hispanic (2)	3	0.03
Alaska Athabascan *(Ala. Nat.)* (1)	1	0.01
Apache (0)	1	0.01
Blackfeet (0)	7	0.07
Canadian/French Am. Ind. (0)	2	0.02
Cherokee (2)	6	0.06
Chippewa (0)	1	0.01
Choctaw (0)	1	0.01
Iroquois (0)	2	0.02
Mexican American Ind. (1)	1	0.01
Sioux (0)	2	0.02
South American Ind. (0)	1	0.01
Asian (60)	96	0.95
Not Hispanic (60)	95	0.94
Hispanic (0)	1	0.01
Cambodian (0)	1	0.01
Chinese, ex. Taiwanese (12)	15	0.15
Filipino (17)	21	0.21
Indian (7)	10	0.10
Indonesian (0)	1	0.01
Japanese (4)	16	0.16
Korean (1)	8	0.08
Laotian (0)	1	0.01
Nepalese (3)	3	0.03
Pakistani (10)	10	0.10
Taiwanese (2)	2	0.02
Thai (1)	2	0.02
Vietnamese (3)	5	0.05
Hawaii Native/Pacific Islander (1)	4	0.04
Not Hispanic (1)	4	0.04
Native Hawaiian (1)	1	0.01
White (9,837)	9,969	98.33
Not Hispanic (9,751)	9,877	97.43
Hispanic (86)	92	0.91

Rochester

Place Type: City
County: Strafford
Population: 29,752†

Ancestry‡	Population	%
Albanian (0)	12	0.04
American (1,935)	1,935	6.49
Arab (10)	77	0.26
Egyptian (0)	19	0.06
Lebanese (10)	46	0.15
Syrian (0)	12	0.04
Armenian (0)	9	0.03
Austrian (0)	27	0.09
British (73)	143	0.48
Canadian (140)	218	0.73
Celtic (0)	7	0.02
Czech (0)	37	0.12
Danish (0)	73	0.24
Dutch (25)	390	1.31
Eastern European (28)	28	0.09
English (1,625)	5,106	17.13
European (94)	124	0.42
Finnish (0)	42	0.14
French, ex. Basque (1,850)	5,720	19.19
French Canadian (1,659)	2,488	8.35
German (672)	2,369	7.95
Greek (286)	573	1.92
Hungarian (7)	108	0.36
Irish (1,717)	5,178	17.38
Israeli (0)	11	0.04
Italian (635)	1,866	6.26
Latvian (22)	35	0.12
Lithuanian (32)	72	0.24
Northern European (0)	19	0.06
Norwegian (100)	266	0.89
Pennsylvania German (10)	18	0.06
Polish (132)	746	2.50
Portuguese (44)	251	0.84
Russian (22)	215	0.72
Scandinavian (12)	52	0.17
Scotch-Irish (267)	686	2.30
Scottish (359)	1,641	5.51
Slovak (0)	64	0.21
Swedish (59)	403	1.35
Turkish (0)	59	0.20
Ukrainian (43)	43	0.14
Welsh (11)	139	0.47

Hispanic Origin	Population	%
Hispanic or Latino (of any race)	547	1.84
Central American, ex. Mexican	15	0.05
Costa Rican	3	0.01
Guatemalan	3	0.01
Honduran	2	0.01
Panamanian	2	0.01
Salvadoran	5	0.02
Cuban	37	0.12
Dominican Republic	36	0.12
Mexican	137	0.46
Puerto Rican	191	0.64
South American	51	0.17
Argentinean	2	0.01
Bolivian	2	0.01
Chilean	6	0.02
Colombian	16	0.05
Ecuadorian	2	0.01
Paraguayan	1	<0.01
Peruvian	12	0.04
Venezuelan	9	0.03
Other South American	1	<0.01
Other Hispanic or Latino	80	0.27

Race*	Population	%
African-American/Black (251)	453	1.52
Not Hispanic (240)	414	1.39
Hispanic (11)	39	0.13
American Indian/Alaska Native (92)	264	0.89
Not Hispanic (87)	244	0.82
Hispanic (5)	20	0.07
Aleut *(Alaska Native)* (1)	2	0.01
Apache (0)	1	<0.01
Blackfeet (2)	13	0.04
Canadian/French Am. Ind. (1)	5	0.02
Central American Ind. (1)	1	<0.01
Cherokee (12)	33	0.11
Chickasaw (1)	1	<0.01
Chippewa (1)	2	0.01
Choctaw (0)	1	<0.01
Cree (0)	1	<0.01
Creek (1)	1	<0.01
Inupiat *(Alaska Native)* (0)	3	0.01
Iroquois (2)	13	0.04
Mexican American Ind. (0)	1	<0.01
Osage (0)	1	<0.01
Sioux (4)	10	0.03
South American Ind. (1)	1	<0.01
Spanish American Ind. (0)	1	<0.01
Asian (361)	491	1.65
Not Hispanic (353)	472	1.59
Hispanic (8)	19	0.06
Bhutanese (0)	2	0.01
Cambodian (13)	16	0.05
Chinese, ex. Taiwanese (53)	62	0.21
Filipino (46)	72	0.24
Indian (36)	42	0.14
Indonesian (75)	81	0.27
Japanese (14)	27	0.09
Korean (26)	62	0.21
Laotian (1)	4	0.01
Nepalese (19)	25	0.08
Pakistani (4)	4	0.01
Taiwanese (1)	2	0.01
Thai (14)	27	0.09
Vietnamese (33)	39	0.13
Hawaii Native/Pacific Islander (15)	29	0.10
Not Hispanic (14)	26	0.09
Hispanic (1)	3	0.01
Guamanian/Chamorro (3)	5	0.02
Native Hawaiian (1)	8	0.03
Samoan (2)	3	0.01
Tongan (1)	1	<0.01
White (28,388)	28,878	97.06
Not Hispanic (28,050)	28,464	95.67
Hispanic (338)	414	1.39

Salem

Place Type: Town
County: Rockingham
Population: 28,776†

Ancestry‡	Population	%
African, Sub-Saharan (157)	179	0.62
African (32)	44	0.15
Ghanaian (17)	17	0.06
Nigerian (9)	9	0.03
Ugandan (99)	99	0.34
Other Sub-Saharan African (0)	10	0.03
Albanian (34)	69	0.24
American (837)	837	2.90
Arab (346)	651	2.25
Arab (34)	96	0.33
Lebanese (270)	488	1.69
Syrian (25)	50	0.17
Other Arab (17)	17	0.06
Armenian (193)	220	0.76
Australian (11)	11	0.04
Austrian (0)	31	0.11
Belgian (0)	83	0.29
Brazilian (99)	209	0.72
British (47)	47	0.16
Canadian (296)	543	1.88
Czech (12)	12	0.04
Czechoslovakian (7)	15	0.05
Danish (0)	27	0.09
Dutch (0)	94	0.33
English (810)	3,466	11.99
Estonian (0)	8	0.03
European (51)	114	0.39
Finnish (14)	63	0.22
French, ex. Basque (740)	4,088	14.15
French Canadian (1,371)	2,500	8.65
German (550)	2,166	7.50
Greek (66)	324	1.12
Hungarian (77)	108	0.37
Iranian (0)	16	0.06
Irish (2,105)	7,887	27.29
Italian (2,369)	7,225	25.00
Lithuanian (110)	457	1.58
Northern European (11)	11	0.04
Norwegian (49)	71	0.25
Polish (471)	1,737	6.01
Portuguese (279)	762	2.64
Romanian (16)	32	0.11
Russian (101)	200	0.69
Scandinavian (6)	19	0.07
Scotch-Irish (123)	526	1.82
Scottish (76)	891	3.08
Slovak (0)	12	0.04
Swedish (94)	480	1.66
Swiss (15)	36	0.12
Turkish (68)	68	0.24
Ukrainian (21)	47	0.16
Welsh (10)	48	0.17

Hispanic Origin	Population	%
Hispanic or Latino (of any race)	1,270	4.41
Central American, ex. Mexican	124	0.43
Costa Rican	21	0.07
Guatemalan	54	0.19
Honduran	7	0.02
Nicaraguan	1	<0.01
Panamanian	6	0.02
Salvadoran	22	0.08
Other Central American	13	0.05
Cuban	56	0.19
Dominican Republic	371	1.29
Mexican	64	0.22
Puerto Rican	410	1.42
South American	113	0.39
Argentinean	9	0.03

*Notes: † The Census 2010 population figure is used to calculate the percentages in the Hispanic Origin and Race categories. Ancestry percentages are based on the 2006-2010 American Community Survey population (not shown); ‡ Numbers in parentheses indicate the number of people reporting a single ancestry; * Numbers in parentheses indicate the number of persons reporting this race alone, not in combination with any other race; Please refer to the Explanation of Data for more information.*

Chilean	4	0.01
Colombian	31	0.11
Ecuadorian	17	0.06
Peruvian	40	0.14
Uruguayan	4	0.01
Venezuelan	8	0.03
Other Hispanic or Latino	132	0.46

Race*	Population	%
African-American/Black (259)	357	1.24
Not Hispanic (212)	288	1.00
Hispanic (47)	69	0.24
American Indian/Alaska Native (42)	144	0.50
Not Hispanic (36)	130	0.45
Hispanic (6)	14	0.05
Blackfeet (0)	6	0.02
Cherokee (7)	29	0.10
Choctaw (2)	2	0.01
Cree (0)	1	<0.01
Crow (0)	1	<0.01
Delaware (0)	1	<0.01
Hopi (0)	1	<0.01
Iroquois (1)	1	<0.01
Mexican American Ind. (1)	1	<0.01
Sioux (0)	4	0.01
Asian (933)	1,079	3.75
Not Hispanic (925)	1,061	3.69
Hispanic (8)	18	0.06
Bangladeshi (0)	5	0.02
Burmese (4)	4	0.01
Cambodian (34)	39	0.14
Chinese, ex. Taiwanese (205)	242	0.84
Filipino (89)	118	0.41
Indian (309)	328	1.14
Indonesian (1)	1	<0.01
Japanese (26)	46	0.16
Korean (55)	76	0.26
Malaysian (0)	1	<0.01
Nepalese (7)	7	0.02
Pakistani (25)	26	0.09
Sri Lankan (7)	7	0.02
Taiwanese (9)	15	0.05
Thai (23)	28	0.10
Vietnamese (92)	102	0.35
Hawaii Native/Pacific Islander (9)	30	0.10
Not Hispanic (8)	23	0.08
Hispanic (1)	7	0.02
Native Hawaiian (4)	14	0.05
White (26,592)	26,974	93.74
Not Hispanic (25,958)	26,257	91.25
Hispanic (634)	717	2.49

Seabrook

Place Type: Town
County: Rockingham
Population: 8,693†

Ancestry‡	Population	%
American (534)	534	6.19
Arab (13)	66	0.77
Arab (13)	13	0.15
Lebanese (0)	53	0.61
Armenian (77)	110	1.28
British (8)	8	0.09
Canadian (55)	136	1.58
Czech (0)	76	0.88
Dutch (0)	8	0.09
English (837)	1,797	20.84
European (0)	17	0.20
French, ex. Basque (409)	1,005	11.66
French Canadian (145)	386	4.48
German (204)	591	6.85
Greek (98)	182	2.11
Hungarian (0)	12	0.14
Irish (868)	2,207	25.60
Italian (385)	668	7.75
Lithuanian (0)	46	0.53
Norwegian (117)	225	2.61
Polish (265)	570	6.61
Portuguese (23)	36	0.42
Russian (0)	35	0.41
Scotch-Irish (68)	68	0.79
Scottish (157)	241	2.80
Swedish (100)	160	1.86
Ukrainian (0)	14	0.16
West Indian, ex. Hispanic (87)	87	1.01
Jamaican (87)	87	1.01

Hispanic Origin	Population	%
Hispanic or Latino (of any race)	126	1.45
Central American, ex. Mexican	11	0.13
Guatemalan	5	0.06
Nicaraguan	1	0.01
Panamanian	1	0.01
Salvadoran	4	0.05
Cuban	3	0.03
Dominican Republic	7	0.08
Mexican	31	0.36
Puerto Rican	40	0.46
South American	15	0.17
Argentinean	2	0.02
Colombian	5	0.06
Ecuadorian	5	0.06
Peruvian	1	0.01
Other South American	2	0.02
Other Hispanic or Latino	19	0.22

Race*	Population	%
African-American/Black (46)	87	1.00
Not Hispanic (45)	84	0.97
Hispanic (1)	3	0.03
American Indian/Alaska Native (10)	61	0.70
Not Hispanic (9)	58	0.67
Hispanic (1)	3	0.03
Apache (1)	2	0.02
Blackfeet (1)	1	0.01
Cherokee (3)	9	0.10
Choctaw (1)	1	0.01
Delaware (0)	2	0.02
Hopi (0)	1	0.01
Iroquois (0)	1	0.01
Asian (92)	113	1.30
Not Hispanic (91)	112	1.29
Hispanic (1)	1	0.01
Bangladeshi (6)	6	0.07
Chinese, ex. Taiwanese (26)	29	0.33
Filipino (16)	27	0.31
Indian (23)	25	0.29
Japanese (3)	7	0.08
Korean (10)	10	0.12
Laotian (1)	1	0.01
Vietnamese (7)	7	0.08
White (8,373)	8,489	97.65
Not Hispanic (8,296)	8,401	96.64
Hispanic (77)	88	1.01

Somersworth

Place Type: City
County: Strafford
Population: 11,766†

Ancestry‡	Population	%
American (716)	716	6.06
Arab (0)	53	0.45
Lebanese (0)	53	0.45
Austrian (0)	63	0.53
Brazilian (12)	12	0.10
British (26)	38	0.32
Canadian (52)	194	1.64
Czech (0)	21	0.18
Danish (9)	9	0.08
Dutch (25)	79	0.67
English (439)	1,617	13.68
European (10)	10	0.08
Finnish (0)	23	0.19
French, ex. Basque (1,092)	2,125	17.97
French Canadian (736)	1,117	9.45
German (119)	617	5.22
Greek (9)	122	1.03
Hungarian (14)	14	0.12
Irish (584)	2,125	17.97
Italian (267)	1,221	10.33
Lithuanian (16)	28	0.24
Northern European (34)	34	0.29
Norwegian (6)	166	1.40
Polish (123)	330	2.79
Portuguese (43)	43	0.36
Romanian (9)	9	0.08
Russian (49)	143	1.21
Scotch-Irish (62)	224	1.89
Scottish (116)	559	4.73
Slovak (0)	16	0.14
Swedish (38)	113	0.96
Turkish (0)	22	0.19
Ukrainian (0)	14	0.12
Welsh (0)	85	0.72
West Indian, ex. Hispanic (14)	14	0.12
Haitian (14)	14	0.12

Hispanic Origin	Population	%
Hispanic or Latino (of any race)	296	2.52
Central American, ex. Mexican	27	0.23
Costa Rican	1	0.01
Guatemalan	9	0.08
Nicaraguan	6	0.05
Panamanian	2	0.02
Salvadoran	9	0.08
Cuban	12	0.10
Dominican Republic	33	0.28
Mexican	56	0.48
Puerto Rican	78	0.66
South American	48	0.41
Chilean	7	0.06
Colombian	17	0.14
Ecuadorian	23	0.20
Venezuelan	1	0.01
Other Hispanic or Latino	42	0.36

Race*	Population	%
African-American/Black (162)	289	2.46
Not Hispanic (145)	266	2.26
Hispanic (17)	23	0.20
American Indian/Alaska Native (40)	161	1.37
Not Hispanic (29)	139	1.18
Hispanic (11)	22	0.19
Alaska Athabascan *(Ala. Nat.)* (0)	1	0.01
Apache (0)	1	0.01
Blackfeet (0)	9	0.08
Canadian/French Am. Ind. (0)	1	0.01
Cherokee (8)	27	0.23
Choctaw (0)	1	0.01
Iroquois (2)	10	0.08
Lumbee (1)	2	0.02
Mexican American Ind. (2)	3	0.03
Navajo (1)	3	0.03
Sioux (1)	4	0.03
Ute (1)	1	0.01
Asian (621)	680	5.78
Not Hispanic (617)	673	5.72
Hispanic (4)	7	0.06
Bangladeshi (4)	4	0.03
Cambodian (14)	14	0.12
Chinese, ex. Taiwanese (69)	104	0.88
Filipino (28)	41	0.35
Indian (109)	112	0.95
Indonesian (272)	315	2.68
Japanese (4)	15	0.13
Korean (8)	16	0.14
Laotian (18)	19	0.16
Malaysian (0)	1	0.01
Nepalese (7)	8	0.07
Pakistani (8)	8	0.07
Taiwanese (2)	2	0.02
Thai (7)	11	0.09
Vietnamese (18)	26	0.22
Hawaii Native/Pacific Islander (2)	12	0.10
Not Hispanic (2)	12	0.10
Guamanian/Chamorro (1)	3	0.03

*Notes: † The Census 2010 population figure is used to calculate the percentages in the Hispanic Origin and Race categories. Ancestry percentages are based on the 2006-2010 American Community Survey population (not shown); ‡ Numbers in parentheses indicate the number of people reporting a single ancestry; * Numbers in parentheses indicate the number of persons reporting this race alone, not in combination with any other race; Please refer to the Explanation of Data for more information.*

	Population	%
Native Hawaiian (0)	1	0.01
Samoan (1)	3	0.03
White (10,523)	10,815	91.92
Not Hispanic (10,383)	10,647	90.49
Hispanic (140)	168	1.43

Weare

Place Type: Town
County: Hillsborough
Population: 8,785†

Ancestry‡	Population	%
American (311)	311	3.59
Arab (0)	33	0.38
Lebanese (0)	33	0.38
British (0)	15	0.17
Canadian (145)	224	2.59
Czech (0)	12	0.14
Czechoslovakian (0)	32	0.37
Danish (0)	29	0.33
Dutch (0)	25	0.29
English (749)	2,061	23.80
European (68)	68	0.79
Finnish (14)	14	0.16
French, ex. Basque (412)	1,882	21.73
French Canadian (419)	818	9.45
German (152)	603	6.96
Greek (112)	288	3.33
Irish (528)	1,878	21.69
Italian (174)	860	9.93
Lithuanian (11)	25	0.29
Norwegian (40)	55	0.64
Polish (198)	690	7.97
Portuguese (14)	84	0.97
Russian (0)	54	0.62
Scandinavian (14)	14	0.16
Scotch-Irish (176)	355	4.10
Scottish (182)	571	6.59
Slovak (0)	33	0.38
Swedish (0)	105	1.21
Welsh (0)	49	0.57
Yugoslavian (59)	59	0.68

Hispanic Origin	Population	%
Hispanic or Latino (of any race)	104	1.18
Central American, ex. Mexican	6	0.07
Guatemalan	5	0.06
Panamanian	1	0.01
Cuban	4	0.05
Dominican Republic	4	0.05
Mexican	23	0.26
Puerto Rican	39	0.44
South American	16	0.18
Argentinean	3	0.03
Colombian	6	0.07
Ecuadorian	4	0.05
Peruvian	1	0.01
Uruguayan	2	0.02
Other Hispanic or Latino	12	0.14

Race*	Population	%
African-American/Black (21)	39	0.44
Not Hispanic (20)	38	0.43
Hispanic (1)	1	0.01
American Indian/Alaska Native (27)	64	0.73
Not Hispanic (27)	64	0.73
Blackfeet (1)	2	0.02
Canadian/French Am. Ind. (0)	3	0.03
Cherokee (4)	9	0.10
Chickasaw (3)	3	0.03
Chippewa (1)	1	0.01
Iroquois (1)	6	0.07
Sioux (1)	2	0.02
Asian (36)	69	0.79
Not Hispanic (36)	68	0.77
Hispanic (0)	1	0.01
Cambodian (1)	1	0.01
Chinese, ex. Taiwanese (4)	9	0.10
Filipino (8)	12	0.14
Indian (12)	16	0.18
Indonesian (0)	5	0.06
Japanese (1)	7	0.08
Korean (5)	11	0.13
Thai (3)	4	0.05
Vietnamese (1)	5	0.06
Hawaii Native/Pacific Islander (2)	13	0.15
Not Hispanic (2)	13	0.15
Native Hawaiian (2)	7	0.08
Samoan (0)	1	0.01
White (8,586)	8,673	98.73
Not Hispanic (8,503)	8,587	97.75
Hispanic (83)	86	0.98

Windham

Place Type: Town
County: Rockingham
Population: 13,592†

Ancestry‡	Population	%
American (476)	476	3.61
Arab (167)	337	2.55
Lebanese (156)	282	2.14
Moroccan (11)	55	0.42
Armenian (23)	120	0.91
Austrian (0)	11	0.08
Canadian (71)	114	0.86
Czech (19)	19	0.14
Czechoslovakian (0)	59	0.45
Danish (15)	15	0.11
Dutch (12)	95	0.72
Eastern European (10)	10	0.08
English (475)	2,138	16.20
European (149)	149	1.13
Finnish (0)	101	0.77
French, ex. Basque (148)	1,456	11.04
French Canadian (270)	906	6.87
German (266)	960	7.28
Greek (27)	122	0.92
Hungarian (0)	43	0.33
Irish (1,188)	3,979	30.16
Italian (1,402)	3,034	23.00
Lithuanian (29)	95	0.72
Northern European (27)	27	0.20
Norwegian (8)	160	1.21
Polish (239)	826	6.26
Portuguese (122)	552	4.18
Romanian (10)	57	0.43
Russian (51)	199	1.51
Scotch-Irish (127)	439	3.33
Scottish (96)	415	3.15
Swedish (85)	281	2.13
Swiss (0)	15	0.11
Ukrainian (11)	34	0.26
Welsh (0)	30	0.23
West Indian, ex. Hispanic (12)	22	0.17
Jamaican (12)	22	0.17
Yugoslavian (0)	14	0.11

Hispanic Origin	Population	%
Hispanic or Latino (of any race)	218	1.60
Central American, ex. Mexican	32	0.24
Costa Rican	12	0.09
Guatemalan	11	0.08
Panamanian	3	0.02
Salvadoran	6	0.04
Cuban	31	0.23
Dominican Republic	13	0.10
Mexican	32	0.24
Puerto Rican	62	0.46
South American	27	0.20
Argentinean	4	0.03
Colombian	7	0.05
Ecuadorian	9	0.07
Peruvian	1	0.01
Venezuelan	5	0.04
Other South American	1	0.01
Other Hispanic or Latino	21	0.15

Race*	Population	%
African-American/Black (59)	88	0.65
Not Hispanic (57)	79	0.58
Hispanic (2)	9	0.07
American Indian/Alaska Native (26)	42	0.31
Not Hispanic (26)	40	0.29
Hispanic (0)	2	0.01
Blackfeet (2)	3	0.02
Cherokee (4)	6	0.04
Chippewa (1)	3	0.02
Choctaw (1)	4	0.03
Navajo (1)	1	0.01
Asian (392)	478	3.52
Not Hispanic (390)	470	3.46
Hispanic (2)	8	0.06
Bangladeshi (5)	8	0.06
Chinese, ex. Taiwanese (120)	149	1.10
Filipino (24)	47	0.35
Indian (123)	131	0.96
Indonesian (4)	4	0.03
Japanese (24)	37	0.27
Korean (32)	41	0.30
Laotian (0)	3	0.02
Pakistani (18)	18	0.13
Sri Lankan (4)	4	0.03
Taiwanese (10)	13	0.10
Thai (3)	8	0.06
Vietnamese (11)	21	0.15
Hawaii Native/Pacific Islander (8)	15	0.11
Not Hispanic (8)	15	0.11
Guamanian/Chamorro (3)	3	0.02
Native Hawaiian (0)	5	0.04
White (12,934)	13,072	96.17
Not Hispanic (12,763)	12,882	94.78
Hispanic (171)	190	1.40

*Notes: † The Census 2010 population figure is used to calculate the percentages in the Hispanic Origin and Race categories. Ancestry percentages are based on the 2006-2010 American Community Survey population (not shown); ‡ Numbers in parentheses indicate the number of people reporting a single ancestry; * Numbers in parentheses indicate the number of persons reporting this race alone, not in combination with any other race; Please refer to the Explanation of Data for more information.*

NEW JERSEY

Place Type: State
Population: 8,791,894†

Ancestry‡	Population	%
Afghan (2,741)	2,907	0.03
African, Sub-Saharan (77,524)	89,531	1.03
African (36,967)	45,134	0.52
Cape Verdean (1,044)	1,430	0.02
Ethiopian (1,240)	1,388	0.02
Ghanaian (8,535)	9,071	0.10
Kenyan (1,747)	1,953	0.02
Liberian (4,232)	4,445	0.05
Nigerian (15,677)	16,851	0.19
Senegalese (426)	474	0.01
Sierra Leonean (905)	947	0.01
Somalian (109)	233	<0.01
South African (1,635)	2,127	0.02
Sudanese (995)	1,075	0.01
Ugandan (234)	254	<0.01
Zimbabwean (121)	121	<0.01
Other Sub-Saharan African (3,657)	4,028	0.05
Albanian (8,722)	11,019	0.13
Alsatian (93)	492	0.01
American (280,724)	280,724	3.22
Arab (64,435)	84,528	0.97
Arab (9,522)	11,398	0.13
Egyptian (25,473)	28,164	0.32
Iraqi (372)	471	0.01
Jordanian (2,762)	3,112	0.04
Lebanese (7,052)	12,869	0.15
Moroccan (2,875)	4,481	0.05
Palestinian (3,873)	4,613	0.05
Syrian (7,771)	12,826	0.15
Other Arab (4,735)	6,594	0.08
Armenian (10,201)	15,816	0.18
Assyrian/Chaldean/Syriac (452)	891	0.01
Australian (866)	2,090	0.02
Austrian (10,022)	41,569	0.48
Basque (176)	520	0.01
Belgian (1,730)	6,706	0.08
Brazilian (30,003)	35,800	0.41
British (13,359)	25,400	0.29
Bulgarian (2,160)	2,697	0.03
Cajun (54)	176	<0.01
Canadian (5,409)	12,750	0.15
Carpatho Rusyn (197)	402	<0.01
Celtic (395)	1,079	0.01
Croatian (7,597)	13,154	0.15
Cypriot (577)	693	0.01
Czech (7,597)	32,426	0.37
Czechoslovakian (4,972)	12,038	0.14
Danish (4,190)	19,832	0.23
Dutch (24,880)	110,584	1.27
Eastern European (32,165)	35,149	0.40
English (105,187)	505,484	5.80
Estonian (1,087)	1,770	0.02
European (48,988)	55,373	0.63
Finnish (1,578)	6,396	0.07
French, ex. Basque (17,433)	120,116	1.38
French Canadian (7,399)	24,006	0.28
German (225,120)	1,069,417	12.26
German Russian (87)	199	<0.01
Greek (33,773)	65,156	0.75
Guyanese (15,337)	17,871	0.20
Hungarian (32,843)	109,305	1.25
Icelander (208)	698	0.01
Iranian (5,791)	7,366	0.08
Irish (380,173)	1,370,783	15.72
Israeli (7,358)	10,026	0.11
Italian (734,225)	1,521,527	17.45
Latvian (2,122)	3,946	0.05
Lithuanian (10,382)	35,622	0.41
Luxemburger (175)	515	0.01
Macedonian (4,250)	4,858	0.06
Maltese (472)	1,562	0.02
New Zealander (165)	316	<0.01
Northern European (2,629)	2,983	0.03
Norwegian (12,076)	42,793	0.49
Pennsylvania German (3,219)	6,854	0.08
Polish (215,510)	565,484	6.48
Portuguese (59,217)	79,514	0.91
Romanian (9,641)	20,608	0.24
Russian (83,945)	197,299	2.26
Scandinavian (2,155)	5,569	0.06
Scotch-Irish (29,886)	83,028	0.95
Scottish (25,982)	104,979	1.20
Serbian (2,412)	3,833	0.04
Slavic (2,395)	7,764	0.09
Slovak (15,119)	41,166	0.47
Slovene (617)	1,586	0.02
Soviet Union (353)	353	<0.01
Swedish (10,461)	54,488	0.62
Swiss (3,972)	18,304	0.21
Turkish (13,927)	16,830	0.19
Ukrainian (34,542)	71,894	0.82
Welsh (5,692)	38,268	0.44
West Indian, ex. Hispanic (125,438)	148,178	1.70
Bahamian (608)	867	0.01
Barbadian (2,730)	3,790	0.04
Belizean (760)	1,185	0.01
Bermudan (388)	452	0.01
British West Indian (4,481)	5,719	0.07
Dutch West Indian (320)	488	0.01
Haitian (50,565)	54,761	0.63
Jamaican (46,711)	55,938	0.64
Trinidadian/Tobagonian (8,969)	11,749	0.13
U.S. Virgin Islander (271)	392	<0.01
West Indian (9,358)	12,560	0.14
Other West Indian (277)	277	<0.01
Yugoslavian (5,230)	9,241	0.11

Hispanic Origin	Population	%
Hispanic or Latino (of any race)	1,555,144	17.69
Central American, ex. Mexican	176,611	2.01
Costa Rican	19,933	0.23
Guatemalan	48,869	0.56
Honduran	36,556	0.42
Nicaraguan	8,222	0.09
Panamanian	5,431	0.06
Salvadoran	56,532	0.64
Other Central American	1,068	0.01
Cuban	83,362	0.95
Dominican Republic	197,922	2.25
Mexican	217,715	2.48
Puerto Rican	434,092	4.94
South American	325,179	3.70
Argentinean	14,272	0.16
Bolivian	3,361	0.04
Chilean	8,100	0.09
Colombian	101,593	1.16
Ecuadorian	100,480	1.14
Paraguayan	1,964	0.02
Peruvian	75,869	0.86
Uruguayan	10,902	0.12
Venezuelan	6,950	0.08
Other South American	1,688	0.02
Other Hispanic or Latino	120,263	1.37

Race*	Population	%
African-American/Black (1,204,826)	1,300,363	14.79
Not Hispanic (1,125,401)	1,186,433	13.49
Hispanic (79,425)	113,930	1.30
American Indian/Alaska Native (29,026)	70,716	0.80
Not Hispanic (12,227)	40,487	0.46
Hispanic (16,799)	30,229	0.34
Alaska Athabascan *(Ala. Nat.)* (21)	53	<0.01
Aleut *(Alaska Native)* (24)	31	<0.01
Apache (103)	404	<0.01
Arapaho (10)	28	<0.01
Blackfeet (213)	1,987	0.02
Canadian/French Am. Ind. (64)	173	<0.01
Central American Ind. (776)	1,247	0.01
Cherokee (1,344)	7,716	0.09
Cheyenne (11)	73	<0.01
Chickasaw (42)	118	<0.01
Chippewa (130)	354	<0.01
Choctaw (78)	363	<0.01
Colville (1)	1	<0.01
Comanche (20)	98	<0.01
Cree (25)	120	<0.01
Creek (65)	243	<0.01
Crow (9)	53	<0.01
Delaware (901)	2,509	0.03
Hopi (20)	64	<0.01
Houma (19)	20	<0.01
Inupiat *(Alaska Native)* (17)	40	<0.01
Iroquois (326)	1,221	0.01
Kiowa (4)	21	<0.01
Lumbee (98)	200	<0.01
Menominee (4)	9	<0.01
Mexican American Ind. (2,140)	2,931	0.03
Navajo (110)	294	<0.01
Osage (19)	41	<0.01
Ottawa (11)	31	<0.01
Paiute (24)	41	<0.01
Pima (7)	22	<0.01
Potawatomi (45)	93	<0.01
Pueblo (125)	302	<0.01
Puget Sound Salish (8)	19	<0.01
Seminole (54)	419	<0.01
Shoshone (17)	62	<0.01
Sioux (174)	769	0.01
South American Ind. (1,998)	4,232	0.05
Spanish American Ind. (732)	1,073	0.01
Tlingit-Haida *(Alaska Native)* (23)	73	<0.01
Tohono O'Odham (11)	23	<0.01
Tsimshian *(Alaska Native)* (0)	1	<0.01
Ute (14)	24	<0.01
Yakama (2)	8	<0.01
Yaqui (19)	32	<0.01
Yuman (2)	11	<0.01
Yup'ik *(Alaska Native)* (7)	22	<0.01
Asian (725,726)	795,163	9.04
Not Hispanic (719,827)	780,769	8.88
Hispanic (5,899)	14,394	0.16
Bangladeshi (7,567)	8,680	0.10
Bhutanese (100)	126	<0.01
Burmese (1,058)	1,197	0.01
Cambodian (1,283)	1,667	0.02
Chinese, ex. Taiwanese (124,858)	139,699	1.59
Filipino (110,650)	126,793	1.44
Hmong (57)	83	<0.01
Indian (292,256)	311,310	3.54
Indonesian (1,635)	2,224	0.03
Japanese (13,146)	19,710	0.22
Korean (93,679)	100,334	1.14
Laotian (685)	973	0.01
Malaysian (538)	833	0.01
Nepalese (891)	989	0.01
Pakistani (26,006)	28,541	0.32
Sri Lankan (2,280)	2,656	0.03
Taiwanese (8,972)	10,317	0.12
Thai (2,879)	3,923	0.04
Vietnamese (20,628)	23,535	0.27
Hawaii Native/Pacific Islander (3,043)	12,999	0.15
Not Hispanic (1,963)	8,299	0.09
Hispanic (1,080)	4,700	0.05
Fijian (43)	74	<0.01
Guamanian/Chamorro (915)	1,447	0.02
Marshallese (20)	30	<0.01
Native Hawaiian (674)	2,066	0.02
Samoan (234)	642	0.01
Tongan (17)	27	<0.01
White (6,029,248)	6,210,995	70.64
Not Hispanic (5,214,878)	5,315,821	60.46
Hispanic (814,370)	895,174	10.18

*Notes: † The Census 2010 population figure is used to calculate the percentages in the Hispanic Origin and Race categories. Ancestry percentages are based on the 2006-2010 American Community Survey population (not shown); ‡ Numbers in parentheses indicate the number of people reporting a single ancestry; * Numbers in parentheses indicate the number of persons reporting this race alone, not in combination with any other race; Please refer to the Explanation of Data for more information.*

Aberdeen

Place Type: Township
County: Monmouth
Population: 18,210†

Ancestry‡	Population	%
African, Sub-Saharan (347)	347	1.92
Ghanaian (64)	64	0.35
Nigerian (231)	231	1.28
Senegalese (52)	52	0.29
Albanian (19)	19	0.10
American (509)	509	2.81
Arab (20)	65	0.36
Arab (9)	9	0.05
Egyptian (11)	34	0.19
Lebanese (0)	7	0.04
Moroccan (0)	7	0.04
Syrian (0)	8	0.04
Armenian (0)	9	0.05
Austrian (42)	117	0.65
Belgian (0)	14	0.08
Brazilian (161)	164	0.91
British (13)	31	0.17
Bulgarian (0)	7	0.04
Canadian (12)	12	0.07
Celtic (0)	8	0.04
Croatian (28)	28	0.15
Czech (26)	41	0.23
Czechoslovakian (13)	13	0.07
Danish (33)	87	0.48
Dutch (16)	102	0.56
Eastern European (148)	156	0.86
English (179)	938	5.18
European (21)	28	0.15
French, ex. Basque (0)	212	1.17
French Canadian (0)	54	0.30
German (582)	2,169	11.98
Greek (46)	147	0.81
Guyanese (12)	33	0.18
Hungarian (60)	368	2.03
Iranian (0)	8	0.04
Irish (1,144)	3,622	20.00
Italian (2,192)	4,530	25.02
Latvian (0)	28	0.15
Lithuanian (26)	50	0.28
Northern European (15)	15	0.08
Norwegian (42)	136	0.75
Pennsylvania German (5)	15	0.08
Polish (555)	1,466	8.10
Portuguese (140)	280	1.55
Romanian (28)	59	0.33
Russian (137)	384	2.12
Scandinavian (9)	9	0.05
Scotch-Irish (96)	177	0.98
Scottish (138)	262	1.45
Slavic (0)	51	0.28
Slovak (0)	60	0.33
Swedish (0)	82	0.45
Swiss (0)	32	0.18
Ukrainian (106)	230	1.27
Welsh (0)	46	0.25
West Indian, ex. Hispanic (297)	355	1.96
Haitian (46)	69	0.38
Jamaican (107)	142	0.78
Trinidadian/Tobagonian (8)	8	0.04
West Indian (136)	136	0.75
Yugoslavian (195)	195	1.08

Hispanic Origin	Population	%
Hispanic or Latino (of any race)	1,900	10.43
Central American, ex. Mexican	95	0.52
Costa Rican	22	0.12
Guatemalan	7	0.04
Honduran	15	0.08
Nicaraguan	4	0.02
Panamanian	25	0.14
Salvadoran	22	0.12
Cuban	154	0.85
Dominican Republic	104	0.57
Mexican	331	1.82
Puerto Rican	851	4.67
South American	280	1.54
Argentinean	26	0.14
Bolivian	4	0.02
Chilean	14	0.08
Colombian	97	0.53
Ecuadorian	47	0.26
Paraguayan	1	0.01
Peruvian	69	0.38
Uruguayan	11	0.06
Venezuelan	7	0.04
Other South American	4	0.02
Other Hispanic or Latino	85	0.47

Race*	Population	%
African-American/Black (2,161)	2,362	12.97
Not Hispanic (2,041)	2,198	12.07
Hispanic (120)	164	0.90
American Indian/Alaska Native (41)	106	0.58
Not Hispanic (14)	69	0.38
Hispanic (27)	37	0.20
Blackfeet (0)	5	0.03
Central American Ind. (0)	2	0.01
Cherokee (2)	18	0.10
Cheyenne (1)	1	0.01
Creek (0)	1	0.01
Delaware (0)	10	0.05
Iroquois (0)	1	0.01
Navajo (0)	1	0.01
Puget Sound Salish (0)	2	0.01
Sioux (0)	3	0.02
South American Ind. (16)	21	0.12
Asian (1,171)	1,283	7.05
Not Hispanic (1,162)	1,264	6.94
Hispanic (9)	19	0.10
Bangladeshi (10)	12	0.07
Cambodian (2)	2	0.01
Chinese, ex. Taiwanese (220)	248	1.36
Filipino (218)	255	1.40
Indian (511)	534	2.93
Indonesian (3)	3	0.02
Japanese (9)	18	0.10
Korean (59)	67	0.37
Laotian (0)	1	0.01
Nepalese (3)	3	0.02
Pakistani (58)	60	0.33
Sri Lankan (8)	10	0.05
Taiwanese (7)	8	0.04
Thai (5)	6	0.03
Vietnamese (32)	32	0.18
Hawaii Native/Pacific Islander (8)	16	0.09
Not Hispanic (7)	11	0.06
Hispanic (1)	5	0.03
Fijian (4)	4	0.02
Guamanian/Chamorro (1)	3	0.02
Native Hawaiian (3)	5	0.03
Samoan (0)	3	0.02
White (13,954)	14,240	78.20
Not Hispanic (12,757)	12,968	71.21
Hispanic (1,197)	1,272	6.99

Absecon

Place Type: City
County: Atlantic
Population: 8,411†

Ancestry‡	Population	%
African, Sub-Saharan (175)	210	2.51
African (74)	74	0.89
Ghanaian (101)	101	1.21
Nigerian (0)	35	0.42
American (478)	478	5.72
Arab (66)	66	0.79
Egyptian (23)	23	0.28
Lebanese (43)	43	0.51
Austrian (39)	52	0.62
Belgian (0)	14	0.17
British (12)	12	0.14
Czech (13)	13	0.16
Danish (25)	25	0.30
Dutch (49)	183	2.19
Eastern European (13)	13	0.16
English (177)	744	8.90
European (13)	28	0.34
French, ex. Basque (25)	242	2.90
French Canadian (0)	14	0.17
German (144)	1,294	15.48
Greek (14)	20	0.24
Hungarian (7)	79	0.95
Irish (567)	1,901	22.75
Italian (518)	1,404	16.80
Lithuanian (10)	40	0.48
Polish (81)	296	3.54
Romanian (0)	14	0.17
Russian (8)	148	1.77
Scotch-Irish (51)	62	0.74
Scottish (101)	221	2.64
Swedish (0)	35	0.42
Ukrainian (0)	44	0.53
Welsh (0)	10	0.12
West Indian, ex. Hispanic (154)	234	2.80
Haitian (65)	65	0.78
Jamaican (50)	102	1.22
West Indian (39)	67	0.80

Hispanic Origin	Population	%
Hispanic or Latino (of any race)	631	7.50
Central American, ex. Mexican	74	0.88
Guatemalan	4	0.05
Honduran	49	0.58
Nicaraguan	5	0.06
Panamanian	1	0.01
Salvadoran	15	0.18
Cuban	15	0.18
Dominican Republic	65	0.77
Mexican	93	1.11
Puerto Rican	208	2.47
South American	112	1.33
Argentinean	6	0.07
Bolivian	6	0.07
Chilean	3	0.04
Colombian	51	0.61
Ecuadorian	10	0.12
Peruvian	34	0.40
Venezuelan	2	0.02
Other Hispanic or Latino	64	0.76

Race*	Population	%
African-American/Black (832)	920	10.94
Not Hispanic (788)	848	10.08
Hispanic (44)	72	0.86
American Indian/Alaska Native (32)	69	0.82
Not Hispanic (16)	53	0.63
Hispanic (16)	16	0.19
Cherokee (1)	7	0.08
Chippewa (2)	2	0.02
Delaware (0)	1	0.01
Mexican American Ind. (6)	6	0.07
Sioux (1)	1	0.01
South American Ind. (1)	1	0.01
Asian (667)	745	8.86
Not Hispanic (662)	733	8.71
Hispanic (5)	12	0.14
Bangladeshi (61)	68	0.81
Cambodian (0)	1	0.01
Chinese, ex. Taiwanese (69)	73	0.87
Filipino (86)	98	1.17
Indian (322)	365	4.34
Japanese (4)	9	0.11
Korean (15)	16	0.19
Malaysian (0)	1	0.01
Nepalese (4)	5	0.06
Pakistani (37)	50	0.59
Taiwanese (6)	6	0.07
Thai (7)	7	0.08
Vietnamese (38)	39	0.46
Hawaii Native/Pacific Islander (0)	9	0.11
Not Hispanic (0)	5	0.06

*Notes: † The Census 2010 population figure is used to calculate the percentages in the Hispanic Origin and Race categories. Ancestry percentages are based on the 2006-2010 American Community Survey population (not shown); ‡ Numbers in parentheses indicate the number of people reporting a single ancestry; * Numbers in parentheses indicate the number of persons reporting this race alone, not in combination with any other race; Please refer to the Explanation of Data for more information.*

Hispanic (0)	4	0.05
White (6,430)	6,558	77.97
Not Hispanic (6,142)	6,244	74.24
Hispanic (288)	314	3.73

Asbury Park

Place Type: City
County: Monmouth
Population: 16,116†

Ancestry‡	Population	%
African, Sub-Saharan (114)	265	1.63
African (114)	233	1.43
Sierra Leonean (0)	32	0.20
American (152)	152	0.93
Armenian (18)	18	0.11
British (55)	60	0.37
Canadian (0)	8	0.05
Czech (0)	20	0.12
Danish (13)	29	0.18
Dutch (0)	18	0.11
English (118)	392	2.41
European (30)	51	0.31
Finnish (0)	9	0.06
French, ex. Basque (26)	103	0.63
French Canadian (9)	24	0.15
German (196)	726	4.46
Greek (23)	30	0.18
Guyanese (38)	38	0.23
Hungarian (0)	8	0.05
Irish (386)	909	5.59
Italian (468)	785	4.82
Lithuanian (0)	22	0.14
Norwegian (20)	20	0.12
Polish (77)	283	1.74
Portuguese (11)	11	0.07
Romanian (0)	13	0.08
Russian (59)	95	0.58
Scandinavian (13)	13	0.08
Scotch-Irish (0)	25	0.15
Scottish (0)	26	0.16
Swedish (43)	89	0.55
Turkish (0)	21	0.13
Ukrainian (0)	11	0.07
Welsh (0)	14	0.09
West Indian, ex. Hispanic (1,730)	1,964	12.07
Barbadian (85)	85	0.52
British West Indian (134)	183	1.12
Haitian (1,189)	1,265	7.77
Jamaican (217)	264	1.62
Trinidadian/Tobagonian (12)	12	0.07
West Indian (93)	155	0.95

Hispanic Origin	Population	%
Hispanic or Latino (of any race)	4,115	25.53
Central American, ex. Mexican	332	2.06
Costa Rican	14	0.09
Guatemalan	74	0.46
Honduran	60	0.37
Nicaraguan	138	0.86
Panamanian	9	0.06
Salvadoran	37	0.23
Cuban	34	0.21
Dominican Republic	61	0.38
Mexican	2,490	15.45
Puerto Rican	823	5.11
South American	174	1.08
Argentinean	15	0.09
Bolivian	4	0.02
Chilean	35	0.22
Colombian	37	0.23
Ecuadorian	23	0.14
Paraguayan	2	0.01
Peruvian	32	0.20
Uruguayan	7	0.04
Venezuelan	15	0.09
Other South American	4	0.02
Other Hispanic or Latino	201	1.25

Race*	Population	%
African-American/Black (8,275)	8,682	53.87
Not Hispanic (7,955)	8,257	51.23
Hispanic (320)	425	2.64
American Indian/Alaska Native (79)	233	1.45
Not Hispanic (40)	150	0.93
Hispanic (39)	83	0.52
Blackfeet (1)	6	0.04
Cherokee (5)	32	0.20
Chippewa (0)	1	0.01
Choctaw (1)	2	0.01
Cree (0)	5	0.03
Creek (1)	1	0.01
Delaware (1)	5	0.03
Iroquois (0)	3	0.02
Lumbee (1)	1	0.01
Mexican American Ind. (15)	22	0.14
Navajo (0)	1	0.01
Sioux (1)	1	0.01
South American Ind. (1)	3	0.02
Asian (77)	142	0.88
Not Hispanic (72)	113	0.70
Hispanic (5)	29	0.18
Chinese, ex. Taiwanese (22)	31	0.19
Filipino (7)	28	0.17
Indian (27)	42	0.26
Japanese (2)	2	0.01
Korean (7)	14	0.09
Pakistani (5)	8	0.05
Taiwanese (1)	1	0.01
Vietnamese (3)	4	0.02
Hawaii Native/Pacific Islander (20)	64	0.40
Not Hispanic (13)	51	0.32
Hispanic (7)	13	0.08
Guamanian/Chamorro (19)	22	0.14
Native Hawaiian (1)	6	0.04
White (5,875)	6,229	38.65
Not Hispanic (3,511)	3,727	23.13
Hispanic (2,364)	2,502	15.52

Ashland

Place Type: CDP
County: Camden
Population: 8,302†

Ancestry‡	Population	%
American (393)	393	4.55
Arab (83)	93	1.08
Egyptian (34)	34	0.39
Lebanese (0)	10	0.12
Other Arab (49)	49	0.57
Armenian (8)	67	0.78
Austrian (0)	26	0.30
Belgian (0)	11	0.13
British (0)	49	0.57
Canadian (9)	27	0.31
Czech (0)	19	0.22
Danish (13)	48	0.56
Dutch (17)	141	1.63
Eastern European (37)	46	0.53
English (209)	918	10.63
European (44)	44	0.51
French, ex. Basque (10)	101	1.17
French Canadian (0)	9	0.10
German (211)	1,367	15.82
Greek (0)	22	0.25
Hungarian (25)	72	0.83
Iranian (21)	21	0.24
Irish (539)	1,918	22.20
Israeli (94)	94	1.09
Italian (795)	1,888	21.85
Latvian (9)	9	0.10
Lithuanian (3)	34	0.39
Northern European (0)	17	0.20
Norwegian (10)	10	0.12
Polish (136)	416	4.81
Romanian (23)	92	1.06
Russian (348)	556	6.44
Scandinavian (7)	13	0.15
Scotch-Irish (38)	185	2.14
Scottish (11)	97	1.12
Serbian (47)	47	0.54
Slavic (0)	25	0.29
Slovak (10)	31	0.36
Swedish (17)	110	1.27
Swiss (0)	53	0.61
Ukrainian (17)	64	0.74
Welsh (10)	45	0.52
Yugoslavian (18)	73	0.84

Hispanic Origin	Population	%
Hispanic or Latino (of any race)	480	5.78
Central American, ex. Mexican	38	0.46
Costa Rican	4	0.05
Guatemalan	11	0.13
Honduran	4	0.05
Nicaraguan	2	0.02
Panamanian	8	0.10
Salvadoran	7	0.08
Other Central American	2	0.02
Cuban	28	0.34
Dominican Republic	41	0.49
Mexican	67	0.81
Puerto Rican	233	2.81
South American	52	0.63
Argentinean	1	0.01
Bolivian	2	0.02
Chilean	1	0.01
Colombian	26	0.31
Ecuadorian	13	0.16
Peruvian	3	0.04
Uruguayan	5	0.06
Venezuelan	1	0.01
Other Hispanic or Latino	21	0.25

Race*	Population	%
African-American/Black (584)	669	8.06
Not Hispanic (547)	614	7.40
Hispanic (37)	55	0.66
American Indian/Alaska Native (9)	52	0.63
Not Hispanic (7)	43	0.52
Hispanic (2)	9	0.11
Apache (0)	1	0.01
Blackfeet (2)	2	0.02
Cherokee (0)	6	0.07
Chickasaw (0)	1	0.01
Delaware (0)	1	0.01
Iroquois (1)	2	0.02
Sioux (0)	3	0.04
Asian (752)	830	10.00
Not Hispanic (752)	821	9.89
Hispanic (0)	9	0.11
Bangladeshi (9)	9	0.11
Cambodian (5)	7	0.08
Chinese, ex. Taiwanese (194)	215	2.59
Filipino (171)	205	2.47
Indian (116)	133	1.60
Japanese (15)	28	0.34
Korean (83)	90	1.08
Laotian (1)	2	0.02
Malaysian (1)	3	0.04
Pakistani (24)	26	0.31
Sri Lankan (2)	6	0.07
Taiwanese (8)	14	0.17
Thai (11)	11	0.13
Vietnamese (84)	94	1.13
Hawaii Native/Pacific Islander (0)	5	0.06
Not Hispanic (0)	5	0.06
Guamanian/Chamorro (0)	2	0.02
Native Hawaiian (0)	3	0.04
White (6,665)	6,824	82.20
Not Hispanic (6,363)	6,482	78.08
Hispanic (302)	342	4.12

SECTION TWO

*Notes: † The Census 2010 population figure is used to calculate the percentages in the Hispanic Origin and Race categories. Ancestry percentages are based on the 2006-2010 American Community Survey population (not shown); ‡ Numbers in parentheses indicate the number of people reporting a single ancestry; * Numbers in parentheses indicate the number of persons reporting this race alone, not in combination with any other race; Please refer to the Explanation of Data for more information.*

Atlantic City

Place Type: City
County: Atlantic
Population: 39,558†

Ancestry‡	Population	%
African, Sub-Saharan (1,916)	2,133	5.32
African (1,528)	1,745	4.35
Cape Verdean (10)	10	0.02
Ethiopian (19)	19	0.05
Ghanaian (19)	19	0.05
Liberian (172)	172	0.43
Nigerian (150)	150	0.37
Ugandan (18)	18	0.04
American (1,182)	1,182	2.95
Arab (133)	133	0.33
Arab (13)	13	0.03
Egyptian (65)	65	0.16
Lebanese (18)	18	0.04
Moroccan (37)	37	0.09
Australian (10)	10	0.02
Austrian (20)	35	0.09
Belgian (0)	20	0.05
Brazilian (32)	32	0.08
British (11)	43	0.11
Bulgarian (89)	89	0.22
Czech (27)	27	0.07
Danish (0)	12	0.03
Dutch (33)	56	0.14
Eastern European (35)	35	0.09
English (276)	628	1.57
European (46)	46	0.11
Finnish (0)	10	0.02
French, ex. Basque (21)	194	0.48
French Canadian (20)	31	0.08
German (243)	966	2.41
Greek (182)	245	0.61
Guyanese (11)	11	0.03
Hungarian (18)	41	0.10
Irish (732)	1,516	3.78
Italian (1,412)	2,052	5.12
Latvian (0)	11	0.03
Lithuanian (0)	57	0.14
Norwegian (0)	4	0.01
Polish (259)	449	1.12
Portuguese (19)	19	0.05
Romanian (0)	11	0.03
Russian (128)	250	0.62
Scotch-Irish (55)	69	0.17
Scottish (45)	157	0.39
Serbian (19)	19	0.05
Slovak (15)	55	0.14
Swedish (0)	28	0.07
Swiss (37)	37	0.09
Turkish (16)	23	0.06
Ukrainian (28)	68	0.17
Welsh (9)	36	0.09
West Indian, ex. Hispanic (183)	347	0.87
Bahamian (11)	11	0.03
Barbadian (10)	47	0.12
Haitian (20)	20	0.05
Jamaican (119)	196	0.49
West Indian (23)	73	0.18

Hispanic Origin	Population	%
Hispanic or Latino (of any race)	12,044	30.45
Central American, ex. Mexican	1,396	3.53
Costa Rican	13	0.03
Guatemalan	56	0.14
Honduran	857	2.17
Nicaraguan	46	0.12
Panamanian	44	0.11
Salvadoran	377	0.95
Other Central American	3	0.01
Cuban	234	0.59
Dominican Republic	1,419	3.59
Mexican	3,861	9.76
Puerto Rican	3,506	8.86
South American	910	2.30
Argentinean	25	0.06
Bolivian	5	0.01
Chilean	9	0.02
Colombian	495	1.25
Ecuadorian	110	0.28
Paraguayan	1	<0.01
Peruvian	240	0.61
Uruguayan	3	0.01
Venezuelan	15	0.04
Other South American	7	0.02
Other Hispanic or Latino	718	1.82

Race*	Population	%
African-American/Black (15,148)	15,908	40.21
Not Hispanic (14,100)	14,543	36.76
Hispanic (1,048)	1,365	3.45
American Indian/Alaska Native (242)	612	1.55
Not Hispanic (102)	368	0.93
Hispanic (140)	244	0.62
Apache (5)	7	0.02
Blackfeet (1)	13	0.03
Central American Ind. (5)	8	0.02
Cherokee (12)	54	0.14
Cheyenne (0)	3	0.01
Choctaw (0)	3	0.01
Creek (0)	3	0.01
Delaware (3)	4	0.01
Iroquois (2)	7	0.02
Mexican American Ind. (16)	19	0.05
Navajo (0)	3	0.01
Osage (0)	1	<0.01
Pueblo (0)	1	<0.01
Seminole (0)	2	0.01
Sioux (1)	2	0.01
South American Ind. (9)	16	0.04
Spanish American Ind. (3)	5	0.01
Asian (6,153)	6,556	16.57
Not Hispanic (6,132)	6,482	16.39
Hispanic (21)	74	0.19
Bangladeshi (885)	1,042	2.63
Bhutanese (1)	1	<0.01
Burmese (67)	67	0.17
Cambodian (14)	24	0.06
Chinese, ex. Taiwanese (1,295)	1,406	3.55
Filipino (456)	511	1.29
Indian (1,276)	1,507	3.81
Japanese (10)	32	0.08
Korean (84)	91	0.23
Laotian (15)	24	0.06
Malaysian (6)	9	0.02
Nepalese (1)	1	<0.01
Pakistani (380)	436	1.10
Sri Lankan (2)	2	0.01
Taiwanese (10)	10	0.03
Thai (19)	26	0.07
Vietnamese (1,305)	1,394	3.52
Hawaii Native/Pacific Islander (18)	83	0.21
Not Hispanic (8)	41	0.10
Hispanic (10)	42	0.11
Guamanian/Chamorro (1)	7	0.02
Marshallese (0)	3	0.01
Native Hawaiian (2)	11	0.03
Samoan (0)	5	0.01
White (10,543)	11,803	29.84
Not Hispanic (6,338)	6,770	17.11
Hispanic (4,205)	5,033	12.72

Audubon

Place Type: Borough
County: Camden
Population: 8,819†

Ancestry‡	Population	%
American (274)	274	3.08
Arab (76)	76	0.85
Iraqi (76)	76	0.85
Armenian (23)	40	0.45
Austrian (0)	50	0.56
British (11)	21	0.24
Croatian (0)	11	0.12
Czech (0)	11	0.12
Dutch (26)	75	0.84
English (115)	895	10.06
European (47)	56	0.63
Finnish (0)	42	0.47
French, ex. Basque (22)	190	2.13
French Canadian (11)	11	0.12
German (364)	2,427	27.27
Greek (0)	11	0.12
Hungarian (20)	67	0.75
Irish (943)	3,561	40.01
Italian (995)	2,085	23.43
Lithuanian (0)	15	0.17
Maltese (0)	35	0.39
Norwegian (0)	31	0.35
Pennsylvania German (13)	80	0.90
Polish (161)	792	8.90
Romanian (41)	41	0.46
Russian (32)	101	1.13
Scotch-Irish (82)	114	1.28
Scottish (64)	316	3.55
Slavic (11)	11	0.12
Slovak (22)	46	0.52
Swedish (0)	124	1.39
Swiss (0)	35	0.39
Ukrainian (12)	24	0.27
Welsh (10)	52	0.58
West Indian, ex. Hispanic (0)	14	0.16
Jamaican (0)	14	0.16

Hispanic Origin	Population	%
Hispanic or Latino (of any race)	290	3.29
Central American, ex. Mexican	38	0.43
Guatemalan	27	0.31
Nicaraguan	2	0.02
Panamanian	6	0.07
Salvadoran	3	0.03
Cuban	14	0.16
Dominican Republic	4	0.05
Mexican	91	1.03
Puerto Rican	96	1.09
South American	18	0.20
Argentinean	2	0.02
Chilean	2	0.02
Colombian	4	0.05
Ecuadorian	1	0.01
Paraguayan	1	0.01
Peruvian	7	0.08
Venezuelan	1	0.01
Other Hispanic or Latino	29	0.33

Race*	Population	%
African-American/Black (127)	164	1.86
Not Hispanic (117)	142	1.61
Hispanic (10)	22	0.25
American Indian/Alaska Native (12)	43	0.49
Not Hispanic (8)	23	0.26
Hispanic (4)	20	0.23
Apache (0)	1	0.01
Blackfeet (0)	4	0.05
Cherokee (0)	4	0.05
Delaware (1)	1	0.01
Mexican American Ind. (2)	6	0.07
Sioux (0)	1	0.01
South American Ind. (1)	3	0.03
Asian (100)	140	1.59
Not Hispanic (100)	132	1.50
Hispanic (0)	8	0.09
Burmese (11)	20	0.23
Cambodian (2)	2	0.02
Chinese, ex. Taiwanese (18)	26	0.29
Filipino (12)	24	0.27
Indian (6)	10	0.11
Indonesian (0)	1	0.01
Japanese (7)	13	0.15
Korean (23)	29	0.33
Nepalese (1)	1	0.01
Thai (2)	9	0.10
Vietnamese (8)	13	0.15

*Notes: † The Census 2010 population figure is used to calculate the percentages in the Hispanic Origin and Race categories. Ancestry percentages are based on the 2006-2010 American Community Survey population (not shown); ‡ Numbers in parentheses indicate the number of people reporting a single ancestry; * Numbers in parentheses indicate the number of persons reporting this race alone, not in combination with any other race; Please refer to the Explanation of Data for more information.*

Hawaii Native/Pacific Islander (1)	5	0.06
Not Hispanic (0)	4	0.05
Hispanic (1)	1	0.01
Native Hawaiian (1)	1	0.01
White (8,398)	8,493	96.30
Not Hispanic (8,231)	8,297	94.08
Hispanic (167)	196	2.22

Avenel

Place Type: CDP
County: Middlesex
Population: 17,011†

Ancestry‡	Population	%
Afghan (37)	37	0.22
African, Sub-Saharan (91)	119	0.70
African (74)	102	0.60
Ghanaian (17)	17	0.10
Albanian (0)	20	0.12
American (348)	348	2.04
Arab (285)	285	1.67
Arab (66)	66	0.39
Egyptian (211)	211	1.23
Jordanian (8)	8	0.05
Austrian (0)	14	0.08
Brazilian (151)	151	0.88
British (0)	20	0.12
Bulgarian (0)	12	0.07
Croatian (0)	7	0.04
Czech (0)	41	0.24
Czechoslovakian (25)	33	0.19
Danish (32)	45	0.26
Dutch (0)	117	0.68
English (19)	404	2.36
European (82)	82	0.48
French, ex. Basque (38)	145	0.85
German (195)	696	4.07
Greek (0)	25	0.15
Hungarian (118)	320	1.87
Irish (644)	1,909	11.17
Israeli (119)	119	0.70
Italian (854)	1,973	11.55
Lithuanian (13)	37	0.22
Norwegian (8)	8	0.05
Polish (445)	861	5.04
Portuguese (128)	142	0.83
Romanian (27)	27	0.16
Russian (76)	164	0.96
Scotch-Irish (21)	41	0.24
Scottish (12)	84	0.49
Slovak (29)	120	0.70
Slovene (0)	22	0.13
Swedish (39)	124	0.73
Swiss (0)	9	0.05
Turkish (57)	57	0.33
Ukrainian (46)	150	0.88
Welsh (15)	34	0.20
West Indian, ex. Hispanic (220)	273	1.60
Barbadian (0)	18	0.11
British West Indian (34)	52	0.30
Haitian (69)	69	0.40
Jamaican (27)	27	0.16
Trinidadian/Tobagonian (90)	90	0.53
U.S. Virgin Islander (0)	17	0.10
Yugoslavian (0)	19	0.11

Hispanic Origin	Population	%
Hispanic or Latino (of any race)	2,694	15.84
Central American, ex. Mexican	153	0.90
Costa Rican	21	0.12
Guatemalan	27	0.16
Honduran	17	0.10
Nicaraguan	3	0.02
Panamanian	7	0.04
Salvadoran	78	0.46
Cuban	127	0.75
Dominican Republic	271	1.59
Mexican	149	0.88
Puerto Rican	1,216	7.15
South American	575	3.38
Argentinean	18	0.11
Bolivian	5	0.03
Chilean	3	0.02
Colombian	156	0.92
Ecuadorian	99	0.58
Paraguayan	1	0.01
Peruvian	252	1.48
Uruguayan	33	0.19
Venezuelan	8	0.05
Other Hispanic or Latino	203	1.19

Race*	Population	%
African-American/Black (3,364)	3,594	21.13
Not Hispanic (3,129)	3,274	19.25
Hispanic (235)	320	1.88
American Indian/Alaska Native (88)	189	1.11
Not Hispanic (65)	140	0.82
Hispanic (23)	49	0.29
Apache (2)	2	0.01
Blackfeet (1)	3	0.02
Central American Ind. (5)	5	0.03
Cherokee (4)	20	0.12
Chippewa (1)	1	0.01
Cree (0)	2	0.01
Delaware (1)	4	0.02
Iroquois (1)	1	0.01
Mexican American Ind. (1)	2	0.01
Seminole (0)	1	0.01
Sioux (1)	4	0.02
South American Ind. (10)	28	0.16
Asian (3,893)	4,130	24.28
Not Hispanic (3,869)	4,089	24.04
Hispanic (24)	41	0.24
Bangladeshi (26)	30	0.18
Chinese, ex. Taiwanese (126)	131	0.77
Filipino (265)	287	1.69
Indian (2,786)	2,912	17.12
Indonesian (166)	174	1.02
Japanese (9)	13	0.08
Korean (79)	84	0.49
Laotian (1)	2	0.01
Malaysian (9)	17	0.10
Pakistani (320)	333	1.96
Sri Lankan (7)	8	0.05
Taiwanese (2)	2	0.01
Vietnamese (57)	57	0.34
Hawaii Native/Pacific Islander (12)	36	0.21
Not Hispanic (7)	22	0.13
Hispanic (5)	14	0.08
Guamanian/Chamorro (4)	4	0.02
Native Hawaiian (0)	1	0.01
Samoan (1)	1	0.01
Tongan (1)	1	0.01
White (8,146)	8,473	49.81
Not Hispanic (6,831)	7,019	41.26
Hispanic (1,315)	1,454	8.55

Barnegat

Place Type: Township
County: Ocean
Population: 20,936†

Ancestry‡	Population	%
African, Sub-Saharan (19)	19	0.09
Nigerian (19)	19	0.09
Albanian (0)	18	0.09
American (721)	721	3.59
Arab (57)	103	0.51
Arab (9)	20	0.10
Egyptian (31)	31	0.15
Moroccan (11)	11	0.05
Syrian (6)	41	0.20
Armenian (10)	10	0.05
Australian (0)	16	0.08
Austrian (22)	124	0.62
Belgian (0)	18	0.09
Brazilian (16)	16	0.08
British (143)	153	0.76
Croatian (0)	22	0.11
Czech (0)	54	0.27
Czechoslovakian (22)	65	0.32
Danish (8)	40	0.20
Dutch (46)	417	2.08
Eastern European (46)	46	0.23
English (415)	1,624	8.09
European (31)	31	0.15
French, ex. Basque (58)	350	1.74
French Canadian (23)	141	0.70
German (786)	3,653	18.20
Greek (25)	95	0.47
Hungarian (58)	277	1.38
Irish (1,603)	5,548	27.64
Italian (2,796)	5,912	29.45
Latvian (11)	11	0.05
Lithuanian (18)	67	0.33
Maltese (9)	27	0.13
Norwegian (36)	103	0.51
Polish (768)	1,962	9.77
Portuguese (73)	110	0.55
Romanian (9)	21	0.10
Russian (115)	311	1.55
Scandinavian (15)	15	0.07
Scotch-Irish (205)	528	2.63
Scottish (98)	383	1.91
Slavic (19)	28	0.14
Slovak (70)	95	0.47
Slovene (9)	9	0.04
Swedish (54)	254	1.27
Swiss (0)	72	0.36
Turkish (130)	130	0.65
Ukrainian (56)	109	0.54
Welsh (20)	105	0.52
West Indian, ex. Hispanic (165)	165	0.82
Barbadian (68)	68	0.34
Jamaican (69)	69	0.34
Trinidadian/Tobagonian (17)	17	0.08
West Indian (11)	11	0.05

Hispanic Origin	Population	%
Hispanic or Latino (of any race)	1,420	6.78
Central American, ex. Mexican	84	0.40
Costa Rican	11	0.05
Guatemalan	14	0.07
Honduran	39	0.19
Nicaraguan	4	0.02
Panamanian	11	0.05
Salvadoran	5	0.02
Cuban	119	0.57
Dominican Republic	24	0.11
Mexican	136	0.65
Puerto Rican	707	3.38
South American	200	0.96
Argentinean	24	0.11
Bolivian	6	0.03
Chilean	2	0.01
Colombian	67	0.32
Ecuadorian	28	0.13
Peruvian	45	0.21
Uruguayan	14	0.07
Venezuelan	13	0.06
Other South American	1	<0.01
Other Hispanic or Latino	150	0.72

Race*	Population	%
African-American/Black (681)	856	4.09
Not Hispanic (607)	764	3.65
Hispanic (74)	92	0.44
American Indian/Alaska Native (30)	109	0.52
Not Hispanic (24)	89	0.43
Hispanic (6)	20	0.10
Apache (0)	2	0.01
Blackfeet (0)	5	0.02
Canadian/French Am. Ind. (0)	1	<0.01
Cherokee (12)	27	0.13
Comanche (0)	3	0.01
Delaware (1)	7	0.03
Iroquois (0)	6	0.03
Mexican American Ind. (0)	1	<0.01

SECTION TWO

*Notes: † The Census 2010 population figure is used to calculate the percentages in the Hispanic Origin and Race categories. Ancestry percentages are based on the 2006-2010 American Community Survey population (not shown); ‡ Numbers in parentheses indicate the number of people reporting a single ancestry; * Numbers in parentheses indicate the number of persons reporting this race alone, not in combination with any other race; Please refer to the Explanation of Data for more information.*

Navajo (3)	3	0.01
Paiute (1)	1	<0.01
Potawatomi (0)	1	<0.01
Seminole (0)	6	0.03
Sioux (0)	4	0.02
South American Ind. (0)	1	<0.01
Asian (363)	460	2.20
Not Hispanic (360)	452	2.16
Hispanic (3)	8	0.04
Chinese, ex. Taiwanese (75)	82	0.39
Filipino (184)	233	1.11
Indian (55)	66	0.32
Indonesian (1)	1	<0.01
Japanese (11)	28	0.13
Korean (19)	25	0.12
Nepalese (0)	1	<0.01
Pakistani (2)	2	0.01
Thai (1)	3	0.01
Vietnamese (13)	15	0.07
Hawaii Native/Pacific Islander (1)	11	0.05
Not Hispanic (1)	11	0.05
Native Hawaiian (1)	6	0.03
Samoan (0)	1	<0.01
White (19,214)	19,546	93.36
Not Hispanic (18,215)	18,476	88.25
Hispanic (999)	1,070	5.11

Bayonne

Place Type: City
County: Hudson
Population: 63,024†

Ancestry‡	Population	%
Afghan (15)	15	0.02
African, Sub-Saharan (451)	470	0.76
African (165)	184	0.30
Kenyan (84)	84	0.14
Nigerian (74)	74	0.12
Senegalese (120)	120	0.19
Sierra Leonean (8)	8	0.01
Albanian (0)	9	0.01
American (1,443)	1,443	2.33
Arab (2,648)	2,773	4.47
Arab (8)	23	0.04
Egyptian (2,573)	2,608	4.20
Jordanian (19)	19	0.03
Lebanese (0)	50	0.08
Palestinian (0)	12	0.02
Syrian (12)	12	0.02
Other Arab (36)	49	0.08
Armenian (6)	15	0.02
Assyrian/Chaldean/Syriac (12)	12	0.02
Australian (0)	55	0.09
Austrian (56)	136	0.22
Brazilian (14)	14	0.02
British (82)	104	0.17
Canadian (86)	86	0.14
Celtic (0)	81	0.13
Croatian (25)	25	0.04
Czech (32)	148	0.24
Czechoslovakian (9)	30	0.05
Danish (16)	30	0.05
Dutch (135)	346	0.56
Eastern European (31)	31	0.05
English (158)	1,039	1.68
European (42)	42	0.07
Finnish (0)	15	0.02
French, ex. Basque (164)	380	0.61
French Canadian (32)	48	0.08
German (745)	3,237	5.22
Greek (162)	294	0.47
Guyanese (119)	140	0.23
Hungarian (181)	426	0.69
Iranian (16)	23	0.04
Irish (4,710)	11,169	18.01
Italian (5,555)	10,349	16.68
Lithuanian (85)	234	0.38
Macedonian (0)	9	0.01
Northern European (22)	22	0.04
Norwegian (34)	194	0.31
Pennsylvania German (13)	22	0.04
Polish (4,685)	8,533	13.76
Portuguese (60)	234	0.38
Romanian (15)	22	0.04
Russian (352)	756	1.22
Scandinavian (10)	38	0.06
Scotch-Irish (125)	361	0.58
Scottish (78)	205	0.33
Slavic (160)	347	0.56
Slovak (422)	782	1.26
Swedish (24)	196	0.32
Swiss (0)	31	0.05
Turkish (17)	17	0.03
Ukrainian (345)	589	0.95
Welsh (0)	53	0.09
West Indian, ex. Hispanic (627)	674	1.09
British West Indian (77)	77	0.12
Haitian (180)	180	0.29
Jamaican (222)	222	0.36
Trinidadian/Tobagonian (84)	110	0.18
West Indian (64)	85	0.14

Hispanic Origin	Population	%
Hispanic or Latino (of any race)	16,251	25.79
Central American, ex. Mexican	1,729	2.74
Costa Rican	29	0.05
Guatemalan	502	0.80
Honduran	489	0.78
Nicaraguan	103	0.16
Panamanian	107	0.17
Salvadoran	476	0.76
Other Central American	23	0.04
Cuban	553	0.88
Dominican Republic	2,464	3.91
Mexican	1,317	2.09
Puerto Rican	6,209	9.85
South American	2,116	3.36
Argentinean	124	0.20
Bolivian	81	0.13
Chilean	167	0.26
Colombian	618	0.98
Ecuadorian	709	1.12
Paraguayan	1	<0.01
Peruvian	284	0.45
Uruguayan	62	0.10
Venezuelan	51	0.08
Other South American	19	0.03
Other Hispanic or Latino	1,863	2.96

Race*	Population	%
African-American/Black (5,584)	6,600	10.47
Not Hispanic (4,730)	5,302	8.41
Hispanic (854)	1,298	2.06
American Indian/Alaska Native (194)	544	0.86
Not Hispanic (66)	249	0.40
Hispanic (128)	295	0.47
Alaska Athabascan *(Ala. Nat.)* (2)	3	<0.01
Apache (0)	4	0.01
Blackfeet (1)	3	<0.01
Canadian/French Am. Ind. (0)	4	0.01
Central American Ind. (1)	7	0.01
Cherokee (3)	45	0.07
Chippewa (0)	1	<0.01
Choctaw (0)	1	<0.01
Comanche (1)	2	<0.01
Cree (0)	5	0.01
Creek (2)	3	<0.01
Delaware (3)	4	0.01
Iroquois (0)	4	0.01
Lumbee (1)	5	0.01
Mexican American Ind. (9)	14	0.02
Pueblo (0)	2	<0.01
Seminole (0)	2	<0.01
Sioux (2)	5	0.01
South American Ind. (28)	49	0.08
Spanish American Ind. (3)	10	0.02
Asian (4,861)	5,364	8.51
Not Hispanic (4,803)	5,189	8.23
Hispanic (58)	175	0.28
Bangladeshi (42)	52	0.08
Chinese, ex. Taiwanese (361)	409	0.65
Filipino (2,168)	2,337	3.71
Hmong (2)	2	<0.01
Indian (1,099)	1,278	2.03
Indonesian (11)	12	0.02
Japanese (62)	87	0.14
Korean (228)	242	0.38
Laotian (1)	1	<0.01
Malaysian (6)	9	0.01
Nepalese (5)	5	0.01
Pakistani (584)	642	1.02
Sri Lankan (19)	19	0.03
Taiwanese (12)	13	0.02
Thai (19)	30	0.05
Vietnamese (84)	101	0.16
Hawaii Native/Pacific Islander (16)	139	0.22
Not Hispanic (10)	105	0.17
Hispanic (6)	34	0.05
Guamanian/Chamorro (3)	4	0.01
Native Hawaiian (7)	17	0.03
Samoan (1)	6	0.01
White (43,618)	45,473	72.15
Not Hispanic (35,821)	36,665	58.18
Hispanic (7,797)	8,808	13.98

Beachwood

Place Type: Borough
County: Ocean
Population: 11,045†

Ancestry‡	Population	%
Albanian (12)	48	0.44
American (323)	323	2.93
Arab (61)	107	0.97
Arab (18)	33	0.30
Egyptian (0)	17	0.15
Lebanese (43)	43	0.39
Syrian (0)	14	0.13
Austrian (0)	23	0.21
Belgian (0)	45	0.41
Czech (23)	117	1.06
Czechoslovakian (10)	20	0.18
Danish (0)	87	0.79
Dutch (21)	116	1.05
English (191)	1,165	10.58
European (159)	159	1.44
French, ex. Basque (0)	192	1.74
French Canadian (19)	41	0.37
German (357)	2,642	23.99
Greek (0)	93	0.84
Hungarian (68)	276	2.51
Irish (814)	3,561	32.33
Italian (1,078)	3,201	29.06
Lithuanian (0)	27	0.25
Norwegian (19)	120	1.09
Polish (318)	1,059	9.62
Portuguese (55)	91	0.83
Russian (33)	193	1.75
Scotch-Irish (18)	200	1.82
Scottish (10)	127	1.15
Slavic (10)	39	0.35
Slovak (48)	186	1.69
Swedish (11)	115	1.04
Swiss (0)	48	0.44
Ukrainian (9)	68	0.62
Welsh (69)	165	1.50
West Indian, ex. Hispanic (23)	39	0.35
Dutch West Indian (23)	23	0.21
Jamaican (0)	16	0.15
Yugoslavian (9)	46	0.42

Hispanic Origin	Population	%
Hispanic or Latino (of any race)	898	8.13
Central American, ex. Mexican	44	0.40
Costa Rican	10	0.09
Guatemalan	5	0.05
Honduran	7	0.06
Nicaraguan	3	0.03

*Notes: † The Census 2010 population figure is used to calculate the percentages in the Hispanic Origin and Race categories. Ancestry percentages are based on the 2006-2010 American Community Survey population (not shown); ‡ Numbers in parentheses indicate the number of people reporting a single ancestry; * Numbers in parentheses indicate the number of persons reporting this race alone, not in combination with any other race; Please refer to the Explanation of Data for more information.*

Panamanian	3	0.03
Salvadoran	15	0.14
Other Central American	1	0.01
Cuban	63	0.57
Dominican Republic	16	0.14
Mexican	345	3.12
Puerto Rican	276	2.50
South American	93	0.84
Argentinean	2	0.02
Chilean	3	0.03
Colombian	29	0.26
Ecuadorian	33	0.30
Peruvian	16	0.14
Uruguayan	5	0.05
Venezuelan	5	0.05
Other Hispanic or Latino	61	0.55

Race*	Population	%
African-American/Black (198)	253	2.29
Not Hispanic (185)	232	2.10
Hispanic (13)	21	0.19
American Indian/Alaska Native (8)	33	0.30
Not Hispanic (6)	26	0.24
Hispanic (2)	7	0.06
Cherokee (2)	6	0.05
Delaware (0)	4	0.04
Iroquois (4)	4	0.04
Paiute (0)	3	0.03
Ute (0)	1	0.01
Asian (166)	214	1.94
Not Hispanic (166)	213	1.93
Hispanic (0)	1	0.01
Chinese, ex. Taiwanese (21)	27	0.24
Filipino (69)	95	0.86
Indian (24)	27	0.24
Japanese (6)	12	0.11
Korean (24)	40	0.36
Malaysian (5)	7	0.06
Thai (3)	3	0.03
Vietnamese (5)	8	0.07
Hawaii Native/Pacific Islander (1)	3	0.03
Not Hispanic (0)	1	0.01
Hispanic (1)	2	0.02
Native Hawaiian (1)	2	0.02
White (10,251)	10,396	94.12
Not Hispanic (9,679)	9,785	88.59
Hispanic (572)	611	5.53

Bedminster

Place Type: Township
County: Somerset
Population: 8,165†

Ancestry‡	Population	%
Albanian (96)	108	1.32
American (881)	881	10.74
Arab (19)	19	0.23
Egyptian (9)	9	0.11
Lebanese (10)	10	0.12
Austrian (0)	71	0.87
Belgian (0)	15	0.18
Brazilian (7)	7	0.09
British (31)	103	1.26
Canadian (14)	14	0.17
Croatian (11)	11	0.13
Czech (67)	67	0.82
Danish (10)	20	0.24
Dutch (28)	258	3.15
Eastern European (56)	56	0.68
English (329)	1,022	12.46
Estonian (0)	12	0.15
European (81)	81	0.99
French, ex. Basque (56)	178	2.17
French Canadian (0)	13	0.16
German (344)	1,204	14.68
Greek (24)	49	0.60
Hungarian (17)	68	0.83
Irish (326)	1,279	15.60
Israeli (4)	16	0.20
Italian (633)	1,386	16.90
Lithuanian (0)	27	0.33
New Zealander (21)	21	0.26
Northern European (17)	17	0.21
Norwegian (25)	103	1.26
Polish (324)	541	6.60
Portuguese (26)	39	0.48
Romanian (0)	52	0.63
Russian (102)	223	2.72
Scandinavian (13)	13	0.16
Scotch-Irish (90)	126	1.54
Scottish (48)	282	3.44
Slavic (0)	7	0.09
Swedish (34)	202	2.46
Swiss (0)	60	0.73
Ukrainian (98)	285	3.48
Welsh (0)	55	0.67
West Indian, ex. Hispanic (32)	66	0.80
Jamaican (17)	17	0.21
West Indian (15)	49	0.60

Hispanic Origin	Population	%
Hispanic or Latino (of any race)	519	6.36
Central American, ex. Mexican	73	0.89
Costa Rican	27	0.33
Guatemalan	6	0.07
Honduran	26	0.32
Nicaraguan	1	0.01
Salvadoran	13	0.16
Cuban	43	0.53
Dominican Republic	26	0.32
Mexican	39	0.48
Puerto Rican	76	0.93
South American	194	2.38
Argentinean	31	0.38
Bolivian	4	0.05
Chilean	3	0.04
Colombian	37	0.45
Ecuadorian	16	0.20
Paraguayan	81	0.99
Peruvian	8	0.10
Uruguayan	7	0.09
Venezuelan	6	0.07
Other South American	1	0.01
Other Hispanic or Latino	68	0.83

Race*	Population	%
African-American/Black (168)	211	2.58
Not Hispanic (157)	195	2.39
Hispanic (11)	16	0.20
American Indian/Alaska Native (2)	22	0.27
Not Hispanic (1)	14	0.17
Hispanic (1)	8	0.10
Central American Ind. (1)	1	0.01
Cherokee (0)	7	0.09
Choctaw (0)	1	0.01
Delaware (0)	3	0.04
Iroquois (1)	1	0.01
South American Ind. (0)	2	0.02
Asian (709)	781	9.57
Not Hispanic (707)	778	9.53
Hispanic (2)	3	0.04
Chinese, ex. Taiwanese (234)	263	3.22
Filipino (77)	88	1.08
Indian (246)	259	3.17
Indonesian (0)	2	0.02
Japanese (25)	34	0.42
Korean (62)	66	0.81
Laotian (1)	1	0.01
Malaysian (3)	4	0.05
Nepalese (4)	4	0.05
Pakistani (17)	20	0.24
Sri Lankan (4)	4	0.05
Taiwanese (13)	13	0.16
Thai (2)	2	0.02
Vietnamese (10)	15	0.18
Hawaii Native/Pacific Islander (1)	3	0.04
Not Hispanic (0)	2	0.02
Hispanic (1)	1	0.01
Guamanian/Chamorro (1)	1	0.01
Native Hawaiian (0)	1	0.01
White (7,055)	7,190	88.06
Not Hispanic (6,646)	6,758	82.77
Hispanic (409)	432	5.29

Belleville

Place Type: Township
County: Essex
Population: 35,926†

Ancestry‡	Population	%
African, Sub-Saharan (265)	309	0.86
African (64)	108	0.30
Ghanaian (10)	10	0.03
Kenyan (17)	17	0.05
Nigerian (161)	161	0.45
Senegalese (13)	13	0.04
American (758)	758	2.12
Arab (534)	644	1.80
Arab (83)	83	0.23
Egyptian (280)	280	0.78
Jordanian (0)	22	0.06
Lebanese (0)	88	0.25
Moroccan (137)	137	0.38
Other Arab (34)	34	0.10
Austrian (4)	46	0.13
Belgian (31)	31	0.09
Brazilian (258)	326	0.91
British (61)	137	0.38
Canadian (0)	7	0.02
Croatian (14)	23	0.06
Czech (0)	21	0.06
Czechoslovakian (8)	16	0.04
Dutch (0)	81	0.23
Eastern European (11)	11	0.03
English (213)	676	1.89
European (65)	65	0.18
French, ex. Basque (44)	444	1.24
French Canadian (0)	38	0.11
German (313)	1,754	4.91
Greek (36)	48	0.13
Guyanese (123)	132	0.37
Hungarian (97)	229	0.64
Irish (894)	2,868	8.02
Italian (5,434)	7,500	20.98
Lithuanian (18)	41	0.11
Norwegian (0)	37	0.10
Polish (387)	736	2.06
Portuguese (410)	673	1.88
Romanian (13)	13	0.04
Russian (139)	241	0.67
Scotch-Irish (18)	144	0.40
Scottish (62)	253	0.71
Slovak (17)	69	0.19
Swedish (13)	66	0.18
Swiss (0)	149	0.42
Ukrainian (55)	74	0.21
Welsh (9)	41	0.11
West Indian, ex. Hispanic (314)	505	1.41
Haitian (77)	125	0.35
Jamaican (168)	229	0.64
Trinidadian/Tobagonian (55)	72	0.20
West Indian (14)	79	0.22
Yugoslavian (51)	51	0.14

Hispanic Origin	Population	%
Hispanic or Latino (of any race)	14,133	39.34
Central American, ex. Mexican	814	2.27
Costa Rican	89	0.25
Guatemalan	196	0.55
Honduran	192	0.53
Nicaraguan	55	0.15
Panamanian	30	0.08
Salvadoran	249	0.69
Other Central American	3	0.01
Cuban	500	1.39
Dominican Republic	1,352	3.76
Mexican	323	0.90
Puerto Rican	5,001	13.92

*Notes: † The Census 2010 population figure is used to calculate the percentages in the Hispanic Origin and Race categories. Ancestry percentages are based on the 2006-2010 American Community Survey population (not shown); ‡ Numbers in parentheses indicate the number of people reporting a single ancestry; * Numbers in parentheses indicate the number of persons reporting this race alone, not in combination with any other race; Please refer to the Explanation of Data for more information.*

South American	5,012	13.95
Argentinean	121	0.34
Bolivian	11	0.03
Chilean	44	0.12
Colombian	561	1.56
Ecuadorian	2,824	7.86
Paraguayan	2	0.01
Peruvian	1,239	3.45
Uruguayan	119	0.33
Venezuelan	60	0.17
Other South American	31	0.09
Other Hispanic or Latino	1,131	3.15

Race*	Population	%
African-American/Black (3,277)	3,794	10.56
Not Hispanic (2,794)	3,034	8.45
Hispanic (483)	760	2.12
American Indian/Alaska Native (126)	292	0.81
Not Hispanic (66)	132	0.37
Hispanic (60)	160	0.45
Alaska Athabascan *(Ala. Nat.)* (2)	2	0.01
Apache (1)	3	0.01
Blackfeet (0)	7	0.02
Central American Ind. (2)	7	0.02
Cherokee (5)	26	0.07
Chippewa (0)	1	<0.01
Delaware (2)	6	0.02
Iroquois (0)	3	0.01
Mexican American Ind. (3)	4	0.01
Navajo (1)	7	0.02
Pueblo (1)	6	0.02
Sioux (0)	2	0.01
South American Ind. (10)	30	0.08
Spanish American Ind. (6)	10	0.03
Tlingit-Haida *(Alaska Native)* (1)	4	0.01
Ute (6)	6	0.02
Asian (4,312)	4,620	12.86
Not Hispanic (4,251)	4,478	12.46
Hispanic (61)	142	0.40
Bangladeshi (2)	3	0.01
Burmese (5)	5	0.01
Chinese, ex. Taiwanese (209)	250	0.70
Filipino (2,596)	2,708	7.54
Indian (904)	996	2.77
Indonesian (5)	9	0.03
Japanese (43)	63	0.18
Korean (56)	70	0.19
Malaysian (1)	1	<0.01
Pakistani (47)	51	0.14
Sri Lankan (10)	10	0.03
Taiwanese (1)	1	<0.01
Thai (45)	49	0.14
Vietnamese (341)	360	1.00
Hawaii Native/Pacific Islander (18)	88	0.24
Not Hispanic (5)	41	0.11
Hispanic (13)	47	0.13
Guamanian/Chamorro (4)	17	0.05
Native Hawaiian (4)	17	0.05
Samoan (5)	7	0.02
White (21,753)	22,778	63.40
Not Hispanic (13,868)	14,202	39.53
Hispanic (7,885)	8,576	23.87

Bellmawr

Place Type: Borough
County: Camden
Population: 11,583†

Ancestry‡	Population	%
American (256)	256	2.20
Armenian (0)	28	0.24
Austrian (12)	29	0.25
Belgian (0)	6	0.05
Brazilian (26)	35	0.30
British (10)	29	0.25
Canadian (24)	24	0.21
Croatian (10)	10	0.09
Czech (0)	21	0.18
Danish (7)	7	0.06
Dutch (0)	43	0.37
English (171)	973	8.38
French, ex. Basque (36)	240	2.07
French Canadian (36)	88	0.76
German (537)	2,602	22.41
Greek (30)	80	0.69
Hungarian (29)	58	0.50
Irish (821)	3,482	29.99
Italian (1,732)	3,414	29.40
Lithuanian (5)	47	0.40
Norwegian (0)	26	0.22
Pennsylvania German (0)	13	0.11
Polish (328)	1,030	8.87
Russian (31)	229	1.97
Scotch-Irish (54)	180	1.55
Scottish (13)	156	1.34
Slovak (0)	10	0.09
Swedish (13)	88	0.76
Turkish (83)	83	0.71
Ukrainian (32)	141	1.21
Welsh (10)	62	0.53

Hispanic Origin	Population	%
Hispanic or Latino (of any race)	890	7.68
Central American, ex. Mexican	49	0.42
Guatemalan	35	0.30
Nicaraguan	3	0.03
Panamanian	4	0.03
Salvadoran	4	0.03
Other Central American	3	0.03
Cuban	22	0.19
Dominican Republic	32	0.28
Mexican	303	2.62
Puerto Rican	393	3.39
South American	28	0.24
Colombian	16	0.14
Ecuadorian	9	0.08
Peruvian	1	0.01
Uruguayan	2	0.02
Other Hispanic or Latino	63	0.54

Race*	Population	%
African-American/Black (285)	332	2.87
Not Hispanic (267)	299	2.58
Hispanic (18)	33	0.28
American Indian/Alaska Native (17)	61	0.53
Not Hispanic (11)	42	0.36
Hispanic (6)	19	0.16
Blackfeet (1)	3	0.03
Cherokee (0)	11	0.09
Creek (0)	1	0.01
Delaware (0)	1	0.01
Sioux (0)	1	0.01
South American Ind. (0)	1	0.01
Asian (679)	757	6.54
Not Hispanic (675)	743	6.41
Hispanic (4)	14	0.12
Bangladeshi (8)	8	0.07
Burmese (4)	4	0.03
Cambodian (1)	1	0.01
Chinese, ex. Taiwanese (44)	46	0.40
Filipino (63)	78	0.67
Indian (383)	403	3.48
Indonesian (4)	4	0.03
Japanese (6)	28	0.24
Korean (5)	10	0.09
Laotian (5)	5	0.04
Nepalese (18)	20	0.17
Pakistani (101)	105	0.91
Vietnamese (11)	20	0.17
Hawaii Native/Pacific Islander (7)	12	0.10
Not Hispanic (7)	11	0.09
Hispanic (0)	1	0.01
Guamanian/Chamorro (1)	1	0.01
Samoan (4)	4	0.03
White (10,012)	10,173	87.83
Not Hispanic (9,571)	9,671	83.49
Hispanic (441)	502	4.33

Bergenfield

Place Type: Borough
County: Bergen
Population: 26,764†

Ancestry‡	Population	%
Afghan (17)	17	0.06
African, Sub-Saharan (238)	238	0.90
African (126)	126	0.48
Ghanaian (59)	59	0.22
Nigerian (49)	49	0.18
Ugandan (4)	4	0.02
Albanian (0)	13	0.05
American (537)	537	2.03
Arab (209)	268	1.01
Arab (13)	13	0.05
Egyptian (155)	155	0.58
Lebanese (8)	18	0.07
Syrian (19)	68	0.26
Other Arab (14)	14	0.05
Armenian (158)	209	0.79
Australian (15)	15	0.06
Austrian (62)	99	0.37
Belgian (10)	35	0.13
British (12)	25	0.09
Czech (9)	65	0.25
Czechoslovakian (0)	9	0.03
Dutch (11)	118	0.44
Eastern European (270)	270	1.02
English (231)	607	2.29
European (33)	87	0.33
Finnish (0)	68	0.26
French, ex. Basque (61)	194	0.73
French Canadian (0)	42	0.16
German (470)	1,867	7.04
Greek (410)	453	1.71
Hungarian (27)	115	0.43
Iranian (12)	12	0.05
Irish (1,313)	2,983	11.25
Israeli (26)	26	0.10
Italian (1,514)	2,931	11.05
Latvian (21)	21	0.08
Lithuanian (8)	41	0.15
Maltese (15)	25	0.09
Norwegian (33)	166	0.63
Polish (379)	1,003	3.78
Portuguese (38)	38	0.14
Romanian (0)	54	0.20
Russian (71)	225	0.85
Scandinavian (0)	9	0.03
Scotch-Irish (36)	90	0.34
Scottish (76)	148	0.56
Slavic (0)	11	0.04
Slovak (73)	119	0.45
Swedish (72)	211	0.80
Swiss (20)	50	0.19
Turkish (30)	68	0.26
Ukrainian (68)	99	0.37
Welsh (9)	51	0.19
West Indian, ex. Hispanic (458)	819	3.09
British West Indian (62)	75	0.28
Dutch West Indian (0)	61	0.23
Haitian (61)	102	0.38
Jamaican (248)	427	1.61
Trinidadian/Tobagonian (0)	47	0.18
West Indian (87)	107	0.40

Hispanic Origin	Population	%
Hispanic or Latino (of any race)	7,097	26.52
Central American, ex. Mexican	631	2.36
Costa Rican	92	0.34
Guatemalan	105	0.39
Honduran	79	0.30
Nicaraguan	22	0.08
Panamanian	12	0.04
Salvadoran	313	1.17
Other Central American	8	0.03
Cuban	323	1.21
Dominican Republic	1,818	6.79

*Notes: † The Census 2010 population figure is used to calculate the percentages in the Hispanic Origin and Race categories. Ancestry percentages are based on the 2006-2010 American Community Survey population (not shown); ‡ Numbers in parentheses indicate the number of people reporting a single ancestry; * Numbers in parentheses indicate the number of persons reporting this race alone, not in combination with any other race; Please refer to the Explanation of Data for more information.*

Mexican	534	2.00
Puerto Rican	1,197	4.47
South American	2,143	8.01
Argentinean	71	0.27
Bolivian	20	0.07
Chilean	37	0.14
Colombian	1,566	5.85
Ecuadorian	280	1.05
Paraguayan	3	0.01
Peruvian	133	0.50
Uruguayan	9	0.03
Venezuelan	24	0.09
Other Hispanic or Latino	451	1.69

Race*	Population	%
African-American/Black (2,060)	2,447	9.14
Not Hispanic (1,724)	1,912	7.14
Hispanic (336)	535	2.00
American Indian/Alaska Native (84)	204	0.76
Not Hispanic (32)	115	0.43
Hispanic (52)	89	0.33
Apache (2)	3	0.01
Blackfeet (0)	3	0.01
Canadian/French Am. Ind. (0)	1	<0.01
Cherokee (2)	12	0.04
Choctaw (1)	4	0.01
Creek (1)	1	<0.01
Iroquois (0)	1	<0.01
Mexican American Ind. (4)	5	0.02
Osage (4)	4	0.01
Pueblo (1)	1	<0.01
Seminole (2)	2	0.01
Sioux (3)	4	0.01
South American Ind. (11)	18	0.07
Spanish American Ind. (0)	1	<0.01
Tlingit-Haida *(Alaska Native)* (0)	1	<0.01
Asian (6,851)	7,256	27.11
Not Hispanic (6,778)	7,123	26.61
Hispanic (73)	133	0.50
Bangladeshi (13)	13	0.05
Burmese (6)	6	0.02
Cambodian (5)	5	0.02
Chinese, ex. Taiwanese (237)	301	1.12
Filipino (4,569)	4,767	17.81
Indian (1,321)	1,421	5.31
Indonesian (4)	4	0.01
Japanese (44)	59	0.22
Korean (330)	356	1.33
Laotian (3)	3	0.01
Malaysian (0)	4	0.01
Nepalese (3)	3	0.01
Pakistani (162)	170	0.64
Sri Lankan (26)	26	0.10
Taiwanese (5)	5	0.02
Thai (28)	28	0.10
Vietnamese (21)	28	0.10
Hawaii Native/Pacific Islander (13)	55	0.21
Not Hispanic (9)	35	0.13
Hispanic (4)	20	0.07
Guamanian/Chamorro (0)	3	0.01
Native Hawaiian (6)	11	0.04
Samoan (0)	1	<0.01
White (14,029)	14,674	54.83
Not Hispanic (10,546)	10,840	40.50
Hispanic (3,483)	3,834	14.33

Berkeley Heights

Place Type: Township
County: Union
Population: 13,183†

Ancestry‡	Population	%
African, Sub-Saharan (8)	8	0.06
Nigerian (8)	8	0.06
American (286)	286	2.18
Arab (0)	11	0.08
Lebanese (0)	11	0.08
Austrian (0)	173	1.32
Brazilian (15)	15	0.11
British (100)	165	1.26
Celtic (40)	40	0.30
Croatian (0)	39	0.30
Czech (0)	186	1.42
Czechoslovakian (10)	23	0.18
Danish (0)	40	0.30
Dutch (28)	169	1.29
Eastern European (82)	109	0.83
English (204)	1,137	8.66
European (40)	64	0.49
French, ex. Basque (39)	229	1.74
German (495)	2,040	15.53
Hungarian (57)	253	1.93
Irish (672)	2,706	20.60
Italian (1,535)	3,709	28.24
Lithuanian (0)	122	0.93
Macedonian (11)	11	0.08
Norwegian (12)	108	0.82
Polish (232)	1,022	7.78
Portuguese (146)	181	1.38
Romanian (29)	60	0.46
Russian (234)	431	3.28
Scotch-Irish (67)	190	1.45
Scottish (59)	117	0.89
Slovak (80)	92	0.70
Swedish (16)	179	1.36
Swiss (0)	13	0.10
Turkish (21)	33	0.25
Ukrainian (53)	160	1.22
Welsh (13)	24	0.18
West Indian, ex. Hispanic (0)	16	0.12
Jamaican (0)	16	0.12
Yugoslavian (0)	68	0.52

Hispanic Origin	Population	%
Hispanic or Latino (of any race)	675	5.12
Central American, ex. Mexican	148	1.12
Costa Rican	98	0.74
Guatemalan	10	0.08
Honduran	2	0.02
Nicaraguan	12	0.09
Panamanian	2	0.02
Salvadoran	24	0.18
Cuban	93	0.71
Dominican Republic	16	0.12
Mexican	38	0.29
Puerto Rican	116	0.88
South American	162	1.23
Argentinean	14	0.11
Chilean	10	0.08
Colombian	47	0.36
Ecuadorian	30	0.23
Paraguayan	2	0.02
Peruvian	35	0.27
Uruguayan	18	0.14
Venezuelan	6	0.05
Other Hispanic or Latino	102	0.77

Race*	Population	%
African-American/Black (197)	234	1.78
Not Hispanic (186)	217	1.65
Hispanic (11)	17	0.13
American Indian/Alaska Native (3)	25	0.19
Not Hispanic (3)	20	0.15
Hispanic (0)	5	0.04
Blackfeet (0)	1	0.01
Canadian/French Am. Ind. (0)	3	0.02
Central American Ind. (1)	2	0.02
Cherokee (1)	3	0.02
Iroquois (0)	1	0.01
South American Ind. (0)	1	0.01
Asian (1,375)	1,521	11.54
Not Hispanic (1,372)	1,503	11.40
Hispanic (3)	18	0.14
Bangladeshi (8)	8	0.06
Cambodian (1)	1	0.01
Chinese, ex. Taiwanese (611)	694	5.26
Filipino (74)	101	0.77
Indian (381)	408	3.09
Indonesian (1)	1	0.01
Japanese (33)	48	0.36
Korean (118)	136	1.03
Laotian (0)	4	0.03
Malaysian (1)	2	0.02
Pakistani (12)	14	0.11
Sri Lankan (0)	1	0.01
Taiwanese (63)	76	0.58
Thai (6)	9	0.07
Vietnamese (21)	32	0.24
Hawaii Native/Pacific Islander (0)	6	0.05
Not Hispanic (0)	6	0.05
Native Hawaiian (0)	1	0.01
Samoan (0)	1	0.01
White (11,290)	11,472	87.02
Not Hispanic (10,760)	10,902	82.70
Hispanic (530)	570	4.32

Berkeley

Place Type: Township
County: Ocean
Population: 41,255†

Ancestry‡	Population	%
African, Sub-Saharan (27)	27	0.07
Cape Verdean (10)	10	0.02
Ethiopian (17)	17	0.04
Albanian (23)	44	0.11
Alsatian (0)	13	0.03
American (1,152)	1,152	2.78
Arab (87)	115	0.28
Arab (13)	13	0.03
Egyptian (45)	45	0.11
Lebanese (0)	9	0.02
Syrian (29)	48	0.12
Armenian (224)	236	0.57
Austrian (78)	255	0.62
Basque (13)	13	0.03
Belgian (0)	10	0.02
Brazilian (72)	72	0.17
British (31)	40	0.10
Canadian (19)	52	0.13
Carpatho Rusyn (12)	12	0.03
Celtic (9)	9	0.02
Croatian (57)	67	0.16
Cypriot (36)	36	0.09
Czech (56)	327	0.79
Czechoslovakian (107)	144	0.35
Danish (18)	146	0.35
Dutch (160)	667	1.61
English (829)	3,119	7.54
Estonian (11)	55	0.13
European (232)	282	0.68
Finnish (17)	31	0.07
French, ex. Basque (62)	957	2.31
French Canadian (12)	126	0.30
German (2,057)	7,425	17.95
Greek (186)	416	1.01
Guyanese (0)	8	0.02
Hungarian (317)	780	1.89
Irish (2,901)	9,422	22.77
Italian (8,802)	13,530	32.70
Lithuanian (135)	415	1.00
Maltese (21)	37	0.09
Norwegian (82)	328	0.79
Polish (2,303)	4,296	10.38
Portuguese (279)	536	1.30
Romanian (21)	21	0.05
Russian (298)	848	2.05
Scotch-Irish (246)	524	1.27
Scottish (307)	877	2.12
Slavic (20)	58	0.14
Slovak (140)	392	0.95
Swedish (106)	290	0.70
Swiss (25)	162	0.39
Ukrainian (217)	388	0.94
Welsh (37)	275	0.66
West Indian, ex. Hispanic (72)	72	0.17
Haitian (37)	37	0.09
Jamaican (35)	35	0.08

*Notes: † The Census 2010 population figure is used to calculate the percentages in the Hispanic Origin and Race categories. Ancestry percentages are based on the 2006-2010 American Community Survey population (not shown); ‡ Numbers in parentheses indicate the number of people reporting a single ancestry; * Numbers in parentheses indicate the number of persons reporting this race alone, not in combination with any other race; Please refer to the Explanation of Data for more information.*

Yugoslavian (38)	51	0.12

Hispanic Origin	Population	%
Hispanic or Latino (of any race)	2,028	4.92
Central American, ex. Mexican	80	0.19
Costa Rican	18	0.04
Guatemalan	31	0.08
Honduran	8	0.02
Nicaraguan	8	0.02
Panamanian	8	0.02
Salvadoran	7	0.02
Cuban	157	0.38
Dominican Republic	37	0.09
Mexican	479	1.16
Puerto Rican	863	2.09
South American	201	0.49
Argentinean	26	0.06
Bolivian	2	<0.01
Chilean	13	0.03
Colombian	78	0.19
Ecuadorian	25	0.06
Paraguayan	3	0.01
Peruvian	27	0.07
Uruguayan	24	0.06
Venezuelan	3	0.01
Other Hispanic or Latino	211	0.51

Race*	Population	%
African-American/Black (723)	869	2.11
Not Hispanic (681)	807	1.96
Hispanic (42)	62	0.15
American Indian/Alaska Native (46)	160	0.39
Not Hispanic (33)	137	0.33
Hispanic (13)	23	0.06
Apache (0)	1	<0.01
Blackfeet (4)	8	0.02
Cherokee (6)	26	0.06
Chippewa (1)	1	<0.01
Choctaw (0)	2	<0.01
Comanche (1)	1	<0.01
Creek (1)	1	<0.01
Delaware (0)	6	0.01
Iroquois (5)	8	0.02
Mexican American Ind. (1)	1	<0.01
Seminole (1)	3	0.01
South American Ind. (1)	4	0.01
Spanish American Ind. (1)	1	<0.01
Tlingit-Haida *(Alaska Native)* (0)	1	<0.01
Asian (466)	575	1.39
Not Hispanic (458)	554	1.34
Hispanic (8)	21	0.05
Burmese (5)	7	0.02
Chinese, ex. Taiwanese (64)	77	0.19
Filipino (202)	266	0.64
Indian (75)	86	0.21
Japanese (20)	31	0.08
Korean (46)	52	0.13
Laotian (1)	1	<0.01
Malaysian (0)	2	<0.01
Pakistani (1)	1	<0.01
Taiwanese (2)	2	<0.01
Thai (3)	3	0.01
Vietnamese (30)	35	0.08
Hawaii Native/Pacific Islander (5)	21	0.05
Not Hispanic (5)	19	0.05
Hispanic (0)	2	<0.01
Guamanian/Chamorro (1)	3	0.01
Native Hawaiian (3)	9	0.02
Samoan (1)	2	<0.01
White (39,129)	39,496	95.74
Not Hispanic (37,723)	37,984	92.07
Hispanic (1,406)	1,512	3.67

Berlin

Place Type: Borough
County: Camden
Population: 7,588†

Ancestry‡	Population	%
American (210)	210	2.85
Armenian (0)	10	0.14
Austrian (0)	14	0.19
British (9)	22	0.30
Canadian (0)	80	1.09
Croatian (46)	46	0.63
Czech (0)	39	0.53
Danish (0)	14	0.19
Dutch (17)	26	0.35
Eastern European (7)	7	0.10
English (115)	813	11.05
European (33)	33	0.45
French, ex. Basque (0)	391	5.31
French Canadian (23)	23	0.31
German (215)	1,431	19.45
Greek (90)	120	1.63
Hungarian (0)	20	0.27
Irish (516)	2,430	33.03
Italian (1,074)	2,298	31.24
Latvian (0)	10	0.14
Norwegian (0)	20	0.27
Polish (162)	672	9.13
Portuguese (14)	38	0.52
Russian (7)	140	1.90
Scotch-Irish (69)	107	1.45
Scottish (42)	163	2.22
Slovene (0)	10	0.14
Swedish (0)	22	0.30
Ukrainian (19)	75	1.02
Welsh (0)	113	1.54
West Indian, ex. Hispanic (74)	74	1.01
Haitian (74)	74	1.01

Hispanic Origin	Population	%
Hispanic or Latino (of any race)	237	3.12
Central American, ex. Mexican	16	0.21
Costa Rican	1	0.01
Guatemalan	1	0.01
Honduran	6	0.08
Panamanian	1	0.01
Salvadoran	7	0.09
Cuban	19	0.25
Dominican Republic	6	0.08
Mexican	49	0.65
Puerto Rican	112	1.48
South American	23	0.30
Argentinean	2	0.03
Chilean	1	0.01
Colombian	10	0.13
Ecuadorian	1	0.01
Peruvian	6	0.08
Venezuelan	3	0.04
Other Hispanic or Latino	12	0.16

Race*	Population	%
African-American/Black (318)	360	4.74
Not Hispanic (309)	349	4.60
Hispanic (9)	11	0.14
American Indian/Alaska Native (7)	42	0.55
Not Hispanic (6)	37	0.49
Hispanic (1)	5	0.07
Blackfeet (0)	3	0.04
Cherokee (0)	3	0.04
Delaware (1)	2	0.03
Lumbee (1)	1	0.01
Sioux (2)	2	0.03
Asian (211)	259	3.41
Not Hispanic (210)	256	3.37
Hispanic (1)	3	0.04
Bangladeshi (16)	16	0.21
Chinese, ex. Taiwanese (30)	38	0.50
Filipino (17)	37	0.49
Indian (109)	116	1.53
Japanese (2)	11	0.14
Korean (19)	22	0.29
Malaysian (0)	1	0.01
Pakistani (4)	4	0.05
Taiwanese (1)	1	0.01
Vietnamese (11)	12	0.16
Hawaii Native/Pacific Islander (3)	5	0.07
Not Hispanic (2)	4	0.05
Hispanic (1)	1	0.01
Guamanian/Chamorro (1)	1	0.01
Native Hawaiian (1)	1	0.01
White (6,865)	6,973	91.90
Not Hispanic (6,714)	6,814	89.80
Hispanic (151)	159	2.10

Bernards

Place Type: Township
County: Somerset
Population: 26,652†

Ancestry‡	Population	%
African, Sub-Saharan (41)	41	0.16
African (15)	15	0.06
Cape Verdean (15)	15	0.06
South African (11)	11	0.04
Albanian (23)	23	0.09
American (2,031)	2,031	7.72
Arab (63)	83	0.32
Egyptian (20)	20	0.08
Lebanese (17)	17	0.06
Syrian (0)	20	0.08
Other Arab (26)	26	0.10
Armenian (14)	39	0.15
Australian (39)	39	0.15
Austrian (24)	174	0.66
Belgian (8)	29	0.11
Brazilian (0)	26	0.10
British (37)	100	0.38
Canadian (50)	93	0.35
Croatian (16)	60	0.23
Czech (30)	231	0.88
Czechoslovakian (0)	14	0.05
Danish (47)	157	0.60
Dutch (260)	583	2.22
Eastern European (182)	182	0.69
English (488)	2,480	9.43
European (221)	232	0.88
Finnish (0)	21	0.08
French, ex. Basque (191)	576	2.19
French Canadian (51)	98	0.37
German (1,026)	4,309	16.38
Greek (81)	189	0.72
Hungarian (66)	224	0.85
Iranian (82)	82	0.31
Irish (1,602)	5,455	20.73
Italian (2,502)	5,600	21.28
Latvian (7)	7	0.03
Lithuanian (70)	274	1.04
Northern European (65)	65	0.25
Norwegian (21)	375	1.43
Pennsylvania German (16)	44	0.17
Polish (462)	1,213	4.61
Portuguese (61)	159	0.60
Romanian (18)	60	0.23
Russian (522)	871	3.31
Scandinavian (11)	21	0.08
Scotch-Irish (10)	206	0.78
Scottish (222)	695	2.64
Slavic (0)	12	0.05
Slovak (43)	137	0.52
Slovene (11)	11	0.04
Soviet Union (21)	21	0.08
Swedish (65)	411	1.56
Swiss (7)	57	0.22
Turkish (44)	44	0.17
Ukrainian (104)	227	0.86
Welsh (0)	142	0.54
West Indian, ex. Hispanic (49)	63	0.24
Jamaican (33)	47	0.18
Trinidadian/Tobagonian (16)	16	0.06
Yugoslavian (0)	12	0.05

Hispanic Origin	Population	%
Hispanic or Latino (of any race)	1,054	3.95
Central American, ex. Mexican	84	0.32

*Notes: † The Census 2010 population figure is used to calculate the percentages in the Hispanic Origin and Race categories. Ancestry percentages are based on the 2006-2010 American Community Survey population (not shown); ‡ Numbers in parentheses indicate the number of people reporting a single ancestry; * Numbers in parentheses indicate the number of persons reporting this race alone, not in combination with any other race; Please refer to the Explanation of Data for more information.*

Costa Rican	25	0.09
Guatemalan	30	0.11
Honduran	14	0.05
Nicaraguan	2	0.01
Panamanian	3	0.01
Salvadoran	10	0.04
Cuban	118	0.44
Dominican Republic	26	0.10
Mexican	135	0.51
Puerto Rican	233	0.87
South American	345	1.29
Argentinean	54	0.20
Chilean	34	0.13
Colombian	85	0.32
Ecuadorian	62	0.23
Paraguayan	37	0.14
Peruvian	39	0.15
Uruguayan	6	0.02
Venezuelan	24	0.09
Other South American	4	0.02
Other Hispanic or Latino	113	0.42

Race*	Population	%
African-American/Black (504)	594	2.23
Not Hispanic (478)	547	2.05
Hispanic (26)	47	0.18
American Indian/Alaska Native (20)	62	0.23
Not Hispanic (13)	52	0.20
Hispanic (7)	10	0.04
Cherokee (4)	7	0.03
Chippewa (1)	1	<0.01
Cree (0)	1	<0.01
Creek (0)	6	0.02
Delaware (0)	6	0.02
Iroquois (2)	6	0.02
Osage (1)	1	<0.01
Ottawa (0)	2	0.01
Sioux (0)	3	0.01
South American Ind. (6)	7	0.03
Asian (3,679)	4,032	15.13
Not Hispanic (3,670)	4,014	15.06
Hispanic (9)	18	0.07
Bangladeshi (7)	7	0.03
Chinese, ex. Taiwanese (1,530)	1,676	6.29
Filipino (143)	208	0.78
Indian (1,345)	1,416	5.31
Indonesian (7)	7	0.03
Japanese (58)	99	0.37
Korean (318)	363	1.36
Malaysian (0)	5	0.02
Nepalese (9)	9	0.03
Pakistani (89)	105	0.39
Sri Lankan (8)	9	0.03
Taiwanese (74)	83	0.31
Thai (5)	9	0.03
Vietnamese (24)	34	0.13
Hawaii Native/Pacific Islander (7)	13	0.05
Not Hispanic (7)	12	0.05
Hispanic (0)	1	<0.01
Guamanian/Chamorro (1)	2	0.01
Native Hawaiian (0)	1	<0.01
Samoan (0)	3	0.01
White (21,809)	22,251	83.49
Not Hispanic (20,946)	21,341	80.07
Hispanic (863)	910	3.41

Bernardsville

Place Type: Borough
County: Somerset
Population: 7,707†

Ancestry‡	Population	%
American (442)	442	5.78
Armenian (0)	24	0.31
Austrian (32)	32	0.42
British (61)	101	1.32
Czech (0)	14	0.18
Danish (95)	118	1.54
Dutch (12)	80	1.05
Eastern European (13)	13	0.17
English (115)	641	8.38
European (83)	83	1.08
French, ex. Basque (0)	120	1.57
French Canadian (37)	74	0.97
German (295)	1,327	17.34
Greek (16)	132	1.73
Hungarian (0)	86	1.12
Irish (355)	1,593	20.82
Italian (679)	1,838	24.02
Lithuanian (0)	59	0.77
Norwegian (69)	137	1.79
Polish (112)	398	5.20
Portuguese (35)	35	0.46
Romanian (0)	45	0.59
Russian (103)	211	2.76
Scotch-Irish (50)	89	1.16
Scottish (51)	173	2.26
Slavic (0)	9	0.12
Slovak (47)	109	1.42
Slovene (46)	46	0.60
Swedish (28)	153	2.00
Swiss (0)	66	0.86
Ukrainian (0)	25	0.33
Welsh (0)	78	1.02

Hispanic Origin	Population	%
Hispanic or Latino (of any race)	903	11.72
Central American, ex. Mexican	173	2.24
Costa Rican	11	0.14
Guatemalan	107	1.39
Honduran	21	0.27
Nicaraguan	1	0.01
Panamanian	4	0.05
Salvadoran	28	0.36
Other Central American	1	0.01
Cuban	11	0.14
Dominican Republic	12	0.16
Mexican	66	0.86
Puerto Rican	44	0.57
South American	482	6.25
Argentinean	16	0.21
Bolivian	1	0.01
Colombian	20	0.26
Ecuadorian	136	1.76
Paraguayan	266	3.45
Peruvian	28	0.36
Uruguayan	9	0.12
Venezuelan	3	0.04
Other South American	3	0.04
Other Hispanic or Latino	115	1.49

Race*	Population	%
African-American/Black (68)	94	1.22
Not Hispanic (58)	80	1.04
Hispanic (10)	14	0.18
American Indian/Alaska Native (11)	27	0.35
Not Hispanic (2)	9	0.12
Hispanic (9)	18	0.23
Central American Ind. (0)	4	0.05
Cherokee (0)	5	0.06
Navajo (2)	2	0.03
South American Ind. (5)	11	0.14
Asian (252)	312	4.05
Not Hispanic (248)	295	3.83
Hispanic (4)	17	0.22
Burmese (1)	1	0.01
Chinese, ex. Taiwanese (73)	102	1.32
Filipino (17)	22	0.29
Indian (80)	93	1.21
Japanese (5)	8	0.10
Korean (37)	46	0.60
Malaysian (0)	3	0.04
Nepalese (5)	7	0.09
Pakistani (3)	3	0.04
Sri Lankan (9)	11	0.14
Taiwanese (3)	5	0.06
Thai (5)	5	0.06
Vietnamese (3)	7	0.09
Hawaii Native/Pacific Islander (5)	7	0.09
Not Hispanic (5)	7	0.09
Guamanian/Chamorro (0)	1	0.01
White (7,043)	7,188	93.27
Not Hispanic (6,402)	6,485	84.14
Hispanic (641)	703	9.12

Bloomfield

Place Type: Township
County: Essex
Population: 47,315†

Ancestry‡	Population	%
African, Sub-Saharan (505)	600	1.27
African (211)	281	0.60
Cape Verdean (0)	13	0.03
Ghanaian (10)	10	0.02
Kenyan (18)	18	0.04
Liberian (9)	9	0.02
Nigerian (223)	235	0.50
Other Sub-Saharan African (34)	34	0.07
Albanian (149)	158	0.34
American (1,363)	1,363	2.89
Arab (414)	470	1.00
Arab (80)	80	0.17
Egyptian (173)	192	0.41
Jordanian (16)	16	0.03
Lebanese (104)	104	0.22
Moroccan (14)	20	0.04
Palestinian (4)	4	0.01
Syrian (0)	12	0.03
Other Arab (23)	42	0.09
Armenian (30)	38	0.08
Austrian (72)	126	0.27
Belgian (18)	75	0.16
Brazilian (65)	87	0.18
British (40)	69	0.15
Bulgarian (75)	75	0.16
Canadian (0)	36	0.08
Croatian (0)	9	0.02
Czech (4)	39	0.08
Czechoslovakian (38)	38	0.08
Danish (12)	38	0.08
Dutch (95)	424	0.90
Eastern European (126)	126	0.27
English (676)	2,254	4.79
European (156)	156	0.33
French, ex. Basque (46)	472	1.00
French Canadian (15)	77	0.16
German (612)	3,170	6.73
Greek (261)	503	1.07
Guyanese (204)	302	0.64
Hungarian (88)	349	0.74
Iranian (156)	156	0.33
Irish (1,305)	4,804	10.20
Italian (5,964)	9,588	20.36
Latvian (24)	24	0.05
Lithuanian (30)	98	0.21
Macedonian (63)	63	0.13
Maltese (22)	22	0.05
Northern European (37)	47	0.10
Norwegian (44)	93	0.20
Pennsylvania German (8)	13	0.03
Polish (881)	2,039	4.33
Portuguese (224)	368	0.78
Romanian (54)	75	0.16
Russian (397)	850	1.80
Scandinavian (8)	38	0.08
Scotch-Irish (158)	423	0.90
Scottish (111)	504	1.07
Slavic (23)	23	0.05
Slovak (80)	208	0.44
Slovene (27)	46	0.10
Swedish (233)	404	0.86
Swiss (0)	15	0.03
Turkish (6)	6	0.01
Ukrainian (44)	226	0.48
Welsh (18)	79	0.17
West Indian, ex. Hispanic (1,681)	2,204	4.68
Barbadian (60)	87	0.18

*Notes: † The Census 2010 population figure is used to calculate the percentages in the Hispanic Origin and Race categories. Ancestry percentages are based on the 2006-2010 American Community Survey population (not shown); ‡ Numbers in parentheses indicate the number of people reporting a single ancestry; * Numbers in parentheses indicate the number of persons reporting this race alone, not in combination with any other race; Please refer to the Explanation of Data for more information.*

Belizean (48)	48	0.10
Bermudan (40)	40	0.08
British West Indian (0)	10	0.02
Haitian (689)	797	1.69
Jamaican (682)	969	2.06
Trinidadian/Tobagonian (116)	187	0.40
West Indian (31)	51	0.11
Other West Indian (15)	15	0.03

Hispanic Origin	Population	%
Hispanic or Latino (of any race)	11,606	24.53
Central American, ex. Mexican	1,031	2.18
Costa Rican	319	0.67
Guatemalan	243	0.51
Honduran	115	0.24
Nicaraguan	57	0.12
Panamanian	42	0.09
Salvadoran	251	0.53
Other Central American	4	0.01
Cuban	427	0.90
Dominican Republic	1,340	2.83
Mexican	420	0.89
Puerto Rican	4,156	8.78
South American	3,347	7.07
Argentinean	134	0.28
Bolivian	30	0.06
Chilean	54	0.11
Colombian	521	1.10
Ecuadorian	1,635	3.46
Paraguayan	2	<0.01
Peruvian	820	1.73
Uruguayan	108	0.23
Venezuelan	26	0.05
Other South American	17	0.04
Other Hispanic or Latino	885	1.87

Race*	Population	%
African-American/Black (8,757)	9,532	20.15
Not Hispanic (8,092)	8,588	18.15
Hispanic (665)	944	2.00
American Indian/Alaska Native (193)	473	1.00
Not Hispanic (102)	263	0.56
Hispanic (91)	210	0.44
Apache (0)	1	<0.01
Blackfeet (2)	10	0.02
Canadian/French Am. Ind. (1)	2	<0.01
Central American Ind. (11)	19	0.04
Cherokee (2)	50	0.11
Cheyenne (0)	1	<0.01
Chippewa (1)	5	0.01
Choctaw (0)	1	<0.01
Delaware (2)	4	0.01
Hopi (0)	3	0.01
Iroquois (3)	13	0.03
Menominee (0)	1	<0.01
Mexican American Ind. (13)	20	0.04
Navajo (2)	8	0.02
Potawatomi (0)	1	<0.01
Pueblo (2)	2	<0.01
Puget Sound Salish (1)	1	<0.01
Seminole (0)	2	<0.01
Sioux (0)	4	0.01
South American Ind. (17)	37	0.08
Spanish American Ind. (4)	4	0.01
Asian (3,891)	4,401	9.30
Not Hispanic (3,846)	4,285	9.06
Hispanic (45)	116	0.25
Bangladeshi (43)	53	0.11
Burmese (10)	11	0.02
Cambodian (2)	2	<0.01
Chinese, ex. Taiwanese (437)	531	1.12
Filipino (1,769)	1,945	4.11
Hmong (1)	1	<0.01
Indian (1,112)	1,242	2.62
Indonesian (25)	31	0.07
Japanese (42)	66	0.14
Korean (139)	171	0.36
Malaysian (6)	6	0.01
Nepalese (5)	7	0.01
Pakistani (74)	87	0.18
Sri Lankan (10)	13	0.03
Taiwanese (11)	11	0.02
Thai (56)	63	0.13
Vietnamese (70)	89	0.19
Hawaii Native/Pacific Islander (21)	112	0.24
Not Hispanic (14)	81	0.17
Hispanic (7)	31	0.07
Guamanian/Chamorro (6)	8	0.02
Native Hawaiian (1)	8	0.02
Samoan (2)	3	0.01
Tongan (1)	1	<0.01
White (28,205)	29,479	62.30
Not Hispanic (22,291)	22,920	48.44
Hispanic (5,914)	6,559	13.86

Bloomingdale

Place Type: Borough
County: Passaic
Population: 7,656†

Ancestry‡	Population	%
Alsatian (0)	15	0.20
American (356)	356	4.70
Arab (83)	132	1.74
Arab (0)	20	0.26
Egyptian (14)	43	0.57
Jordanian (29)	29	0.38
Syrian (40)	40	0.53
Assyrian/Chaldean/Syriac (0)	13	0.17
Austrian (0)	14	0.18
Brazilian (37)	37	0.49
Czech (0)	36	0.47
Dutch (121)	499	6.58
English (169)	655	8.64
European (40)	59	0.78
French, ex. Basque (0)	237	3.13
French Canadian (0)	77	1.02
German (388)	1,755	23.15
Greek (21)	37	0.49
Hungarian (0)	66	0.87
Irish (179)	1,520	20.05
Italian (802)	1,887	24.89
Lithuanian (0)	47	0.62
Macedonian (372)	391	5.16
Norwegian (50)	81	1.07
Polish (105)	563	7.43
Portuguese (55)	55	0.73
Russian (0)	31	0.41
Scotch-Irish (17)	117	1.54
Scottish (43)	124	1.64
Serbian (0)	20	0.26
Slovak (0)	14	0.18
Swedish (0)	13	0.17
Swiss (0)	16	0.21
Welsh (17)	25	0.33
Yugoslavian (42)	62	0.82

Hispanic Origin	Population	%
Hispanic or Latino (of any race)	714	9.33
Central American, ex. Mexican	24	0.31
Costa Rican	2	0.03
Guatemalan	11	0.14
Honduran	4	0.05
Panamanian	1	0.01
Salvadoran	6	0.08
Cuban	44	0.57
Dominican Republic	29	0.38
Mexican	199	2.60
Puerto Rican	162	2.12
South American	168	2.19
Argentinean	17	0.22
Bolivian	2	0.03
Chilean	4	0.05
Colombian	58	0.76
Ecuadorian	37	0.48
Peruvian	38	0.50
Uruguayan	7	0.09
Venezuelan	5	0.07
Other Hispanic or Latino	88	1.15

Race*	Population	%
African-American/Black (87)	106	1.38
Not Hispanic (82)	100	1.31
Hispanic (5)	6	0.08
American Indian/Alaska Native (17)	29	0.38
Not Hispanic (15)	23	0.30
Hispanic (2)	6	0.08
Cherokee (1)	3	0.04
Delaware (4)	5	0.07
Mexican American Ind. (1)	1	0.01
Navajo (3)	3	0.04
South American Ind. (1)	1	0.01
Asian (188)	211	2.76
Not Hispanic (188)	211	2.76
Chinese, ex. Taiwanese (17)	19	0.25
Filipino (96)	104	1.36
Indian (40)	44	0.57
Japanese (4)	5	0.07
Korean (14)	15	0.20
Pakistani (3)	3	0.04
Thai (2)	2	0.03
Vietnamese (8)	8	0.10
Hawaii Native/Pacific Islander (0)	7	0.09
Not Hispanic (0)	7	0.09
Native Hawaiian (0)	2	0.03
White (7,041)	7,129	93.12
Not Hispanic (6,588)	6,642	86.76
Hispanic (453)	487	6.36

Bogota

Place Type: Borough
County: Bergen
Population: 8,187†

Ancestry‡	Population	%
American (63)	63	0.77
Arab (42)	42	0.51
Egyptian (42)	42	0.51
Armenian (33)	33	0.40
Canadian (14)	14	0.17
Czech (0)	38	0.47
Dutch (0)	32	0.39
English (53)	288	3.53
Estonian (13)	13	0.16
French, ex. Basque (13)	112	1.37
French Canadian (0)	13	0.16
German (303)	757	9.28
Guyanese (71)	166	2.03
Hungarian (35)	151	1.85
Irish (353)	1,214	14.88
Italian (773)	1,280	15.69
Lithuanian (0)	14	0.17
Polish (114)	241	2.95
Russian (19)	194	2.38
Scotch-Irish (21)	48	0.59
Scottish (12)	12	0.15
Swedish (24)	86	1.05
Ukrainian (0)	16	0.20
Welsh (0)	27	0.33
West Indian, ex. Hispanic (100)	110	1.35
British West Indian (44)	44	0.54
Jamaican (26)	36	0.44
West Indian (30)	30	0.37
Yugoslavian (12)	12	0.15

Hispanic Origin	Population	%
Hispanic or Latino (of any race)	3,169	38.71
Central American, ex. Mexican	218	2.66
Costa Rican	9	0.11
Guatemalan	43	0.53
Honduran	29	0.35
Nicaraguan	14	0.17
Panamanian	8	0.10
Salvadoran	115	1.40
Cuban	262	3.20
Dominican Republic	971	11.86
Mexican	108	1.32
Puerto Rican	550	6.72
South American	836	10.21

*Notes: † The Census 2010 population figure is used to calculate the percentages in the Hispanic Origin and Race categories. Ancestry percentages are based on the 2006-2010 American Community Survey population (not shown); ‡ Numbers in parentheses indicate the number of people reporting a single ancestry; * Numbers in parentheses indicate the number of persons reporting this race alone, not in combination with any other race; Please refer to the Explanation of Data for more information.*

Argentinean	23	0.28
Bolivian	11	0.13
Chilean	20	0.24
Colombian	344	4.20
Ecuadorian	298	3.64
Paraguayan	2	0.02
Peruvian	102	1.25
Uruguayan	13	0.16
Venezuelan	19	0.23
Other South American	4	0.05
Other Hispanic or Latino	224	2.74

Race*	Population	%
African-American/Black (771)	910	11.12
Not Hispanic (582)	647	7.90
Hispanic (189)	263	3.21
American Indian/Alaska Native (64)	96	1.17
Not Hispanic (30)	54	0.66
Hispanic (34)	42	0.51
Cherokee (0)	1	0.01
Pueblo (5)	5	0.06
South American Ind. (0)	4	0.05
Spanish American Ind. (4)	4	0.05
Asian (803)	893	10.91
Not Hispanic (795)	870	10.63
Hispanic (8)	23	0.28
Bangladeshi (10)	10	0.12
Cambodian (1)	1	0.01
Chinese, ex. Taiwanese (33)	46	0.56
Filipino (326)	347	4.24
Indian (244)	271	3.31
Japanese (20)	30	0.37
Korean (110)	117	1.43
Nepalese (1)	1	0.01
Pakistani (38)	40	0.49
Taiwanese (3)	3	0.04
Thai (3)	4	0.05
Vietnamese (2)	4	0.05
Hawaii Native/Pacific Islander (7)	17	0.21
Not Hispanic (7)	16	0.20
Hispanic (0)	1	0.01
White (4,994)	5,240	64.00
Not Hispanic (3,411)	3,497	42.71
Hispanic (1,583)	1,743	21.29

Boonton

Place Type: Town
County: Morris
Population: 8,347†

Ancestry‡	Population	%
American (408)	408	4.85
Arab (89)	89	1.06
Arab (20)	20	0.24
Moroccan (23)	23	0.27
Syrian (46)	46	0.55
Armenian (0)	11	0.13
Austrian (30)	38	0.45
British (23)	35	0.42
Canadian (22)	88	1.05
Croatian (8)	8	0.10
Czech (0)	12	0.14
Danish (0)	18	0.21
Dutch (23)	108	1.28
English (47)	468	5.57
European (92)	92	1.09
Finnish (0)	20	0.24
French, ex. Basque (9)	256	3.05
French Canadian (10)	32	0.38
German (195)	1,173	13.96
Greek (0)	25	0.30
Guyanese (49)	49	0.58
Hungarian (15)	56	0.67
Irish (360)	1,864	22.18
Italian (879)	1,837	21.86
Latvian (12)	36	0.43
Lithuanian (18)	28	0.33
Norwegian (0)	11	0.13
Polish (238)	420	5.00
Portuguese (8)	8	0.10
Romanian (0)	10	0.12
Russian (53)	122	1.45
Scotch-Irish (10)	38	0.45
Scottish (22)	120	1.43
Slavic (10)	21	0.25
Slovak (74)	147	1.75
Swedish (11)	34	0.40
Swiss (0)	46	0.55
Turkish (33)	33	0.39
Ukrainian (28)	28	0.33
Welsh (0)	39	0.46
West Indian, ex. Hispanic (549)	549	6.53
Jamaican (549)	549	6.53

Hispanic Origin	Population	%
Hispanic or Latino (of any race)	920	11.02
Central American, ex. Mexican	193	2.31
Costa Rican	16	0.19
Guatemalan	24	0.29
Honduran	123	1.47
Nicaraguan	3	0.04
Panamanian	4	0.05
Salvadoran	23	0.28
Cuban	25	0.30
Dominican Republic	48	0.58
Mexican	82	0.98
Puerto Rican	192	2.30
South American	322	3.86
Argentinean	20	0.24
Bolivian	8	0.10
Chilean	2	0.02
Colombian	185	2.22
Ecuadorian	17	0.20
Paraguayan	1	0.01
Peruvian	59	0.71
Uruguayan	18	0.22
Venezuelan	6	0.07
Other South American	6	0.07
Other Hispanic or Latino	58	0.69

Race*	Population	%
African-American/Black (402)	483	5.79
Not Hispanic (363)	416	4.98
Hispanic (39)	67	0.80
American Indian/Alaska Native (26)	73	0.87
Not Hispanic (8)	50	0.60
Hispanic (18)	23	0.28
Alaska Athabascan *(Ala. Nat.)* (0)	1	0.01
Blackfeet (0)	1	0.01
Cherokee (0)	7	0.08
Delaware (0)	5	0.06
Iroquois (0)	5	0.06
Lumbee (0)	1	0.01
Mexican American Ind. (4)	4	0.05
Shoshone (0)	1	0.01
Sioux (0)	4	0.05
South American Ind. (3)	5	0.06
Asian (839)	991	11.87
Not Hispanic (838)	980	11.74
Hispanic (1)	11	0.13
Bangladeshi (12)	12	0.14
Cambodian (1)	1	0.01
Chinese, ex. Taiwanese (83)	91	1.09
Filipino (63)	76	0.91
Indian (156)	182	2.18
Indonesian (1)	4	0.05
Japanese (9)	11	0.13
Korean (24)	27	0.32
Pakistani (410)	428	5.13
Sri Lankan (5)	5	0.06
Taiwanese (10)	10	0.12
Thai (1)	2	0.02
Vietnamese (25)	28	0.34
Hawaii Native/Pacific Islander (1)	17	0.20
Not Hispanic (0)	13	0.16
Hispanic (1)	4	0.05
Guamanian/Chamorro (1)	3	0.04
Native Hawaiian (0)	2	0.02
Samoan (0)	2	0.02
White (6,578)	6,810	81.59
Not Hispanic (5,968)	6,154	73.73
Hispanic (610)	656	7.86

Bordentown

Place Type: Township
County: Burlington
Population: 11,367†

Ancestry‡	Population	%
African, Sub-Saharan (110)	126	1.15
Nigerian (110)	126	1.15
Alsatian (0)	8	0.07
American (273)	273	2.50
Arab (46)	64	0.59
Egyptian (46)	46	0.42
Lebanese (0)	18	0.16
Austrian (0)	21	0.19
British (0)	12	0.11
Canadian (0)	6	0.05
Croatian (0)	16	0.15
Czech (12)	32	0.29
Czechoslovakian (11)	11	0.10
Danish (0)	56	0.51
Dutch (21)	93	0.85
Eastern European (35)	35	0.32
English (227)	1,164	10.64
European (11)	11	0.10
Finnish (0)	20	0.18
French, ex. Basque (12)	93	0.85
French Canadian (10)	10	0.09
German (337)	1,925	17.60
Greek (50)	86	0.79
Hungarian (197)	607	5.55
Irish (349)	1,851	16.92
Italian (1,025)	2,419	22.12
Lithuanian (0)	61	0.56
Norwegian (11)	47	0.43
Polish (539)	1,436	13.13
Portuguese (10)	17	0.16
Romanian (0)	27	0.25
Russian (61)	151	1.38
Scotch-Irish (68)	177	1.62
Scottish (30)	124	1.13
Slavic (6)	15	0.14
Slovak (57)	187	1.71
Swedish (13)	52	0.48
Swiss (0)	12	0.11
Turkish (12)	12	0.11
Ukrainian (102)	138	1.26
Welsh (18)	54	0.49
West Indian, ex. Hispanic (70)	137	1.25
Haitian (24)	24	0.22
Jamaican (46)	62	0.57
Trinidadian/Tobagonian (0)	51	0.47

Hispanic Origin	Population	%
Hispanic or Latino (of any race)	684	6.02
Central American, ex. Mexican	72	0.63
Costa Rican	19	0.17
Guatemalan	20	0.18
Honduran	2	0.02
Nicaraguan	4	0.04
Panamanian	17	0.15
Salvadoran	8	0.07
Other Central American	2	0.02
Cuban	30	0.26
Dominican Republic	52	0.46
Mexican	48	0.42
Puerto Rican	330	2.90
South American	85	0.75
Argentinean	3	0.03
Bolivian	1	0.01
Chilean	8	0.07
Colombian	25	0.22
Ecuadorian	27	0.24
Paraguayan	6	0.05
Peruvian	9	0.08
Uruguayan	2	0.02

*Notes: † The Census 2010 population figure is used to calculate the percentages in the Hispanic Origin and Race categories. Ancestry percentages are based on the 2006-2010 American Community Survey population (not shown); ‡ Numbers in parentheses indicate the number of people reporting a single ancestry; * Numbers in parentheses indicate the number of persons reporting this race alone, not in combination with any other race; Please refer to the Explanation of Data for more information.*

Venezuelan	1	0.01
Other South American	3	0.03
Other Hispanic or Latino	67	0.59

Race*	Population	%
African-American/Black (1,216)	1,328	11.68
Not Hispanic (1,166)	1,254	11.03
Hispanic (50)	74	0.65
American Indian/Alaska Native (30)	67	0.59
Not Hispanic (17)	52	0.46
Hispanic (13)	15	0.13
Blackfeet (0)	2	0.02
Canadian/French Am. Ind. (4)	4	0.04
Cherokee (2)	5	0.04
Chickasaw (3)	5	0.04
Iroquois (0)	1	0.01
Mexican American Ind. (3)	3	0.03
Potawatomi (1)	1	0.01
Seminole (0)	2	0.02
Sioux (0)	1	0.01
South American Ind. (6)	6	0.05
Asian (1,201)	1,304	11.47
Not Hispanic (1,182)	1,284	11.30
Hispanic (19)	20	0.18
Bangladeshi (2)	3	0.03
Chinese, ex. Taiwanese (97)	117	1.03
Filipino (153)	169	1.49
Indian (747)	762	6.70
Indonesian (4)	5	0.04
Japanese (8)	17	0.15
Korean (74)	83	0.73
Malaysian (0)	1	0.01
Pakistani (70)	75	0.66
Taiwanese (18)	18	0.16
Thai (1)	1	0.01
Vietnamese (16)	16	0.14
Hawaii Native/Pacific Islander (7)	19	0.17
Not Hispanic (7)	12	0.11
Hispanic (0)	7	0.06
Guamanian/Chamorro (5)	5	0.04
Native Hawaiian (1)	6	0.05
Samoan (1)	2	0.02
White (8,455)	8,670	76.27
Not Hispanic (8,065)	8,224	72.35
Hispanic (390)	446	3.92

Bound Brook

Place Type: Borough
County: Somerset
Population: 10,402†

Ancestry‡	Population	%
African, Sub-Saharan (5)	5	0.05
Ghanaian (5)	5	0.05
American (525)	525	5.05
Arab (34)	82	0.79
Lebanese (0)	21	0.20
Palestinian (34)	61	0.59
Armenian (0)	7	0.07
Austrian (0)	29	0.28
Brazilian (71)	71	0.68
Canadian (5)	32	0.31
Czech (0)	28	0.27
Czechoslovakian (7)	7	0.07
Dutch (0)	115	1.11
Eastern European (21)	21	0.20
English (105)	333	3.20
European (41)	50	0.48
Finnish (0)	10	0.10
French, ex. Basque (25)	58	0.56
French Canadian (7)	14	0.13
German (140)	812	7.81
Greek (34)	43	0.41
Hungarian (42)	111	1.07
Irish (138)	894	8.60
Italian (521)	1,204	11.58
Lithuanian (0)	52	0.50
Macedonian (0)	12	0.12
Pennsylvania German (0)	9	0.09
Polish (213)	612	5.89
Portuguese (39)	39	0.38
Russian (94)	125	1.20
Scotch-Irish (21)	45	0.43
Scottish (20)	94	0.90
Slovak (8)	41	0.39
Swedish (0)	8	0.08
Swiss (0)	5	0.05
Turkish (25)	25	0.24
Ukrainian (28)	75	0.72
Welsh (7)	75	0.72

Hispanic Origin	Population	%
Hispanic or Latino (of any race)	5,062	48.66
Central American, ex. Mexican	2,035	19.56
Costa Rican	1,229	11.82
Guatemalan	258	2.48
Honduran	119	1.14
Nicaraguan	20	0.19
Panamanian	11	0.11
Salvadoran	396	3.81
Other Central American	2	0.02
Cuban	51	0.49
Dominican Republic	91	0.87
Mexican	1,143	10.99
Puerto Rican	403	3.87
South American	1,021	9.82
Argentinean	37	0.36
Chilean	14	0.13
Colombian	456	4.38
Ecuadorian	186	1.79
Paraguayan	29	0.28
Peruvian	279	2.68
Uruguayan	5	0.05
Venezuelan	14	0.13
Other South American	1	0.01
Other Hispanic or Latino	318	3.06

Race*	Population	%
African-American/Black (597)	700	6.73
Not Hispanic (522)	588	5.65
Hispanic (75)	112	1.08
American Indian/Alaska Native (56)	103	0.99
Not Hispanic (19)	43	0.41
Hispanic (37)	60	0.58
Apache (0)	5	0.05
Cherokee (2)	14	0.13
Hopi (1)	2	0.02
Iroquois (0)	1	0.01
Lumbee (2)	2	0.02
Mexican American Ind. (14)	19	0.18
Pima (1)	1	0.01
South American Ind. (6)	16	0.15
Spanish American Ind. (3)	3	0.03
Asian (267)	328	3.15
Not Hispanic (264)	309	2.97
Hispanic (3)	19	0.18
Burmese (1)	1	0.01
Chinese, ex. Taiwanese (40)	51	0.49
Filipino (47)	63	0.61
Indian (118)	138	1.33
Indonesian (1)	2	0.02
Japanese (2)	7	0.07
Korean (11)	13	0.12
Laotian (4)	5	0.05
Pakistani (2)	2	0.02
Taiwanese (14)	14	0.13
Vietnamese (21)	23	0.22
Hawaii Native/Pacific Islander (5)	10	0.10
Not Hispanic (4)	8	0.08
Hispanic (1)	2	0.02
Guamanian/Chamorro (1)	2	0.02
Native Hawaiian (0)	1	0.01
White (7,253)	7,597	73.03
Not Hispanic (4,383)	4,478	43.05
Hispanic (2,870)	3,119	29.98

Bradley Gardens

Place Type: CDP
County: Somerset
Population: 14,206†

Ancestry‡	Population	%
Albanian (45)	45	0.31
American (743)	743	5.16
Arab (133)	160	1.11
Egyptian (77)	77	0.53
Iraqi (0)	14	0.10
Jordanian (39)	39	0.27
Lebanese (17)	30	0.21
Australian (0)	12	0.08
Austrian (0)	20	0.14
British (13)	13	0.09
Canadian (10)	10	0.07
Celtic (0)	11	0.08
Croatian (0)	13	0.09
Czech (0)	44	0.31
Czechoslovakian (0)	17	0.12
Dutch (0)	13	0.09
Eastern European (115)	154	1.07
English (211)	759	5.27
European (130)	170	1.18
French, ex. Basque (66)	151	1.05
French Canadian (10)	10	0.07
German (422)	1,650	11.46
Greek (72)	72	0.50
Hungarian (73)	197	1.37
Irish (377)	1,830	12.71
Italian (1,198)	2,499	17.36
Lithuanian (0)	120	0.83
Norwegian (18)	92	0.64
Polish (477)	1,405	9.76
Portuguese (211)	258	1.79
Romanian (12)	12	0.08
Russian (126)	372	2.58
Scotch-Irish (12)	80	0.56
Scottish (94)	341	2.37
Slavic (0)	13	0.09
Slovak (14)	52	0.36
Swedish (45)	211	1.47
Swiss (0)	14	0.10
Ukrainian (133)	201	1.40
Welsh (0)	32	0.22
West Indian, ex. Hispanic (0)	12	0.08
West Indian (0)	12	0.08

Hispanic Origin	Population	%
Hispanic or Latino (of any race)	713	5.02
Central American, ex. Mexican	105	0.74
Costa Rican	51	0.36
Guatemalan	22	0.15
Honduran	6	0.04
Nicaraguan	7	0.05
Panamanian	3	0.02
Salvadoran	16	0.11
Cuban	64	0.45
Dominican Republic	14	0.10
Mexican	46	0.32
Puerto Rican	161	1.13
South American	241	1.70
Argentinean	8	0.06
Bolivian	1	0.01
Chilean	18	0.13
Colombian	83	0.58
Ecuadorian	33	0.23
Paraguayan	33	0.23
Peruvian	55	0.39
Uruguayan	3	0.02
Venezuelan	4	0.03
Other South American	3	0.02
Other Hispanic or Latino	82	0.58

Race*	Population	%
African-American/Black (290)	344	2.42
Not Hispanic (271)	314	2.21
Hispanic (19)	30	0.21

*Notes: † The Census 2010 population figure is used to calculate the percentages in the Hispanic Origin and Race categories. Ancestry percentages are based on the 2006-2010 American Community Survey population (not shown); ‡ Numbers in parentheses indicate the number of people reporting a single ancestry; * Numbers in parentheses indicate the number of persons reporting this race alone, not in combination with any other race; Please refer to the Explanation of Data for more information.*

	Population	%
American Indian/Alaska Native (14)	48	0.34
Not Hispanic (11)	36	0.25
Hispanic (3)	12	0.08
Blackfeet (0)	3	0.02
Canadian/French Am. Ind. (0)	1	0.01
Cherokee (1)	7	0.05
Comanche (0)	2	0.01
Delaware (1)	1	0.01
Osage (4)	4	0.03
Sioux (0)	1	0.01
South American Ind. (0)	5	0.04
Asian (4,473)	4,638	32.65
Not Hispanic (4,468)	4,622	32.54
Hispanic (5)	16	0.11
Bangladeshi (13)	13	0.09
Burmese (5)	8	0.06
Chinese, ex. Taiwanese (1,374)	1,440	10.14
Filipino (258)	289	2.03
Indian (2,292)	2,353	16.56
Indonesian (3)	3	0.02
Japanese (14)	19	0.13
Korean (144)	157	1.11
Laotian (1)	1	0.01
Malaysian (0)	1	0.01
Pakistani (119)	129	0.91
Sri Lankan (27)	27	0.19
Taiwanese (71)	73	0.51
Thai (6)	6	0.04
Vietnamese (84)	99	0.70
Hawaii Native/Pacific Islander (2)	13	0.09
Not Hispanic (2)	9	0.06
Hispanic (0)	4	0.03
Fijian (1)	3	0.02
Guamanian/Chamorro (0)	3	0.02
Native Hawaiian (1)	5	0.04
Samoan (0)	4	0.03
White (9,004)	9,187	64.67
Not Hispanic (8,516)	8,654	60.92
Hispanic (488)	533	3.75

Branchburg

Place Type: Township
County: Somerset
Population: 14,459†

Ancestry‡	Population	%
Albanian (0)	14	0.10
American (641)	641	4.43
Arab (14)	86	0.59
Egyptian (14)	36	0.25
Lebanese (0)	14	0.10
Syrian (0)	14	0.10
Other Arab (0)	22	0.15
Austrian (12)	53	0.37
Belgian (13)	13	0.09
Brazilian (0)	14	0.10
British (135)	176	1.22
Canadian (28)	28	0.19
Czech (60)	90	0.62
Czechoslovakian (13)	31	0.21
Danish (14)	54	0.37
Dutch (74)	311	2.15
English (217)	1,269	8.76
European (218)	218	1.51
Finnish (22)	41	0.28
French, ex. Basque (84)	375	2.59
French Canadian (13)	64	0.44
German (689)	2,707	18.69
Greek (49)	154	1.06
Hungarian (173)	301	2.08
Irish (616)	2,484	17.15
Italian (1,158)	3,080	21.27
Lithuanian (18)	137	0.95
Norwegian (0)	94	0.65
Polish (548)	1,570	10.84
Portuguese (111)	208	1.44
Romanian (45)	55	0.38
Russian (98)	226	1.56
Scandinavian (15)	15	0.10
Scotch-Irish (32)	319	2.20
Scottish (117)	268	1.85
Slavic (0)	33	0.23
Slovak (48)	160	1.10
Swedish (24)	44	0.30
Swiss (0)	13	0.09
Ukrainian (200)	428	2.96
Welsh (58)	134	0.93
West Indian, ex. Hispanic (22)	22	0.15
Haitian (22)	22	0.15

Hispanic Origin	Population	%
Hispanic or Latino (of any race)	643	4.45
Central American, ex. Mexican	61	0.42
Costa Rican	33	0.23
Guatemalan	9	0.06
Honduran	8	0.06
Nicaraguan	2	0.01
Panamanian	1	0.01
Salvadoran	8	0.06
Cuban	88	0.61
Dominican Republic	22	0.15
Mexican	57	0.39
Puerto Rican	168	1.16
South American	171	1.18
Argentinean	17	0.12
Bolivian	2	0.01
Chilean	5	0.03
Colombian	64	0.44
Ecuadorian	27	0.19
Paraguayan	14	0.10
Peruvian	27	0.19
Uruguayan	6	0.04
Venezuelan	7	0.05
Other South American	2	0.01
Other Hispanic or Latino	76	0.53

Race*	Population	%
African-American/Black (326)	403	2.79
Not Hispanic (313)	374	2.59
Hispanic (13)	29	0.20
American Indian/Alaska Native (22)	75	0.52
Not Hispanic (18)	59	0.41
Hispanic (4)	16	0.11
Aleut *(Alaska Native)* (1)	1	0.01
Blackfeet (3)	4	0.03
Cherokee (1)	7	0.05
Chickasaw (2)	2	0.01
Chippewa (1)	1	0.01
Osage (0)	1	0.01
Seminole (0)	3	0.02
Sioux (1)	2	0.01
South American Ind. (1)	2	0.01
Spanish American Ind. (2)	2	0.01
Asian (1,215)	1,350	9.34
Not Hispanic (1,210)	1,340	9.27
Hispanic (5)	10	0.07
Cambodian (1)	3	0.02
Chinese, ex. Taiwanese (358)	399	2.76
Filipino (106)	149	1.03
Indian (574)	615	4.25
Japanese (24)	39	0.27
Korean (54)	70	0.48
Nepalese (2)	3	0.02
Pakistani (10)	11	0.08
Sri Lankan (1)	1	0.01
Taiwanese (26)	36	0.25
Thai (5)	7	0.05
Vietnamese (24)	27	0.19
Hawaii Native/Pacific Islander (5)	11	0.08
Not Hispanic (5)	10	0.07
Hispanic (0)	1	0.01
Native Hawaiian (1)	4	0.03
White (12,550)	12,748	88.17
Not Hispanic (12,036)	12,201	84.38
Hispanic (514)	547	3.78

Brick

Place Type: Township
County: Ocean
Population: 75,072†

Ancestry‡	Population	%
African, Sub-Saharan (9)	67	0.09
African (9)	67	0.09
Albanian (0)	51	0.07
American (2,449)	2,449	3.23
Arab (235)	353	0.47
Arab (21)	27	0.04
Egyptian (137)	150	0.20
Lebanese (20)	102	0.13
Moroccan (0)	17	0.02
Syrian (8)	8	0.01
Other Arab (49)	49	0.06
Armenian (50)	144	0.19
Australian (0)	10	0.01
Austrian (53)	493	0.65
Belgian (21)	46	0.06
Brazilian (118)	118	0.16
British (62)	305	0.40
Canadian (18)	97	0.13
Croatian (142)	187	0.25
Cypriot (27)	45	0.06
Czech (126)	469	0.62
Czechoslovakian (93)	236	0.31
Danish (31)	338	0.45
Dutch (315)	1,617	2.13
Eastern European (21)	21	0.03
English (1,169)	6,299	8.30
Estonian (23)	33	0.04
European (281)	311	0.41
Finnish (0)	90	0.12
French, ex. Basque (150)	1,744	2.30
French Canadian (75)	291	0.38
German (3,188)	15,685	20.66
Greek (306)	669	0.88
Hungarian (317)	1,333	1.76
Irish (6,682)	22,344	29.44
Italian (10,647)	24,022	31.65
Latvian (13)	52	0.07
Lithuanian (110)	427	0.56
Northern European (119)	119	0.16
Norwegian (219)	1,071	1.41
Pennsylvania German (57)	95	0.13
Polish (2,468)	7,418	9.77
Portuguese (158)	473	0.62
Romanian (9)	64	0.08
Russian (390)	1,308	1.72
Scandinavian (0)	40	0.05
Scotch-Irish (374)	1,096	1.44
Scottish (450)	1,567	2.06
Slavic (39)	88	0.12
Slovak (111)	470	0.62
Slovene (11)	23	0.03
Swedish (162)	821	1.08
Swiss (71)	191	0.25
Turkish (0)	17	0.02
Ukrainian (199)	698	0.92
Welsh (31)	380	0.50
West Indian, ex. Hispanic (373)	488	0.64
Belizean (0)	21	0.03
Jamaican (360)	412	0.54
Trinidadian/Tobagonian (13)	55	0.07
Yugoslavian (24)	89	0.12

Hispanic Origin	Population	%
Hispanic or Latino (of any race)	5,301	7.06
Central American, ex. Mexican	302	0.40
Costa Rican	92	0.12
Guatemalan	59	0.08
Honduran	49	0.07
Nicaraguan	20	0.03
Panamanian	14	0.02
Salvadoran	68	0.09
Cuban	298	0.40
Dominican Republic	148	0.20

SECTION TWO

*Notes: † The Census 2010 population figure is used to calculate the percentages in the Hispanic Origin and Race categories. Ancestry percentages are based on the 2006-2010 American Community Survey population (not shown); ‡ Numbers in parentheses indicate the number of people reporting a single ancestry; * Numbers in parentheses indicate the number of persons reporting this race alone, not in combination with any other race; Please refer to the Explanation of Data for more information.*

Mexican	1,260	1.68
Puerto Rican	1,902	2.53
South American	899	1.20
Argentinean	67	0.09
Bolivian	1	<0.01
Chilean	32	0.04
Colombian	369	0.49
Ecuadorian	157	0.21
Paraguayan	2	<0.01
Peruvian	238	0.32
Uruguayan	12	0.02
Venezuelan	16	0.02
Other South American	5	0.01
Other Hispanic or Latino	492	0.66

Race*	Population	%
African-American/Black (1,502)	1,923	2.56
Not Hispanic (1,374)	1,686	2.25
Hispanic (128)	237	0.32
American Indian/Alaska Native (104)	339	0.45
Not Hispanic (65)	253	0.34
Hispanic (39)	86	0.11
Apache (2)	7	0.01
Blackfeet (1)	9	0.01
Canadian/French Am. Ind. (0)	1	<0.01
Central American Ind. (1)	4	0.01
Cherokee (15)	60	0.08
Chippewa (1)	2	<0.01
Choctaw (1)	6	0.01
Comanche (0)	3	<0.01
Cree (0)	2	<0.01
Delaware (3)	10	0.01
Iroquois (6)	18	0.02
Lumbee (1)	1	<0.01
Mexican American Ind. (17)	22	0.03
Osage (0)	1	<0.01
Ottawa (1)	1	<0.01
Potawatomi (1)	4	0.01
Pueblo (0)	12	0.02
Seminole (1)	4	0.01
Shoshone (0)	1	<0.01
Sioux (3)	6	0.01
South American Ind. (4)	7	0.01
Spanish American Ind. (4)	4	0.01
Asian (1,173)	1,473	1.96
Not Hispanic (1,144)	1,399	1.86
Hispanic (29)	74	0.10
Bangladeshi (30)	31	0.04
Cambodian (2)	5	0.01
Chinese, ex. Taiwanese (199)	244	0.33
Filipino (339)	421	0.56
Indian (299)	344	0.46
Indonesian (3)	5	0.01
Japanese (17)	40	0.05
Korean (112)	148	0.20
Malaysian (1)	4	0.01
Pakistani (13)	13	0.02
Sri Lankan (5)	5	0.01
Taiwanese (14)	17	0.02
Thai (8)	13	0.02
Vietnamese (105)	134	0.18
Hawaii Native/Pacific Islander (27)	71	0.09
Not Hispanic (10)	44	0.06
Hispanic (17)	27	0.04
Guamanian/Chamorro (9)	12	0.02
Native Hawaiian (11)	23	0.03
Samoan (1)	2	<0.01
Tongan (5)	7	0.01
White (69,856)	70,803	94.31
Not Hispanic (66,372)	67,052	89.32
Hispanic (3,484)	3,751	5.00

Bridgeton

Place Type: City
County: Cumberland
Population: 25,349†

Ancestry‡	Population	%
African, Sub-Saharan (748)	802	3.20
African (745)	799	3.19
Liberian (3)	3	0.01
Albanian (8)	8	0.03
American (713)	713	2.85
Arab (8)	16	0.06
Arab (0)	8	0.03
Other Arab (8)	8	0.03
Belgian (8)	8	0.03
Brazilian (9)	9	0.04
British (0)	1	<0.01
Czech (0)	38	0.15
Czechoslovakian (0)	15	0.06
Dutch (13)	76	0.30
English (137)	556	2.22
Estonian (0)	15	0.06
European (37)	37	0.15
French, ex. Basque (2)	67	0.27
German (321)	1,316	5.26
Greek (44)	58	0.23
Hungarian (14)	54	0.22
Irish (219)	1,050	4.19
Italian (781)	1,604	6.41
Latvian (13)	13	0.05
Lithuanian (0)	2	0.01
Pennsylvania German (0)	21	0.08
Polish (106)	280	1.12
Portuguese (27)	43	0.17
Russian (29)	42	0.17
Scandinavian (0)	9	0.04
Scotch-Irish (0)	180	0.72
Scottish (8)	57	0.23
Slovak (21)	43	0.17
Swedish (7)	27	0.11
Swiss (0)	9	0.04
Ukrainian (0)	16	0.06
Welsh (2)	2	0.01
West Indian, ex. Hispanic (340)	374	1.49
Bahamian (11)	11	0.04
British West Indian (5)	11	0.04
Haitian (9)	9	0.04
Jamaican (213)	234	0.93
Trinidadian/Tobagonian (2)	2	0.01
West Indian (100)	107	0.43

Hispanic Origin	Population	%
Hispanic or Latino (of any race)	11,046	43.58
Central American, ex. Mexican	348	1.37
Costa Rican	2	0.01
Guatemalan	255	1.01
Honduran	43	0.17
Nicaraguan	9	0.04
Panamanian	6	0.02
Salvadoran	33	0.13
Cuban	40	0.16
Dominican Republic	56	0.22
Mexican	8,063	31.81
Puerto Rican	1,439	5.68
South American	90	0.36
Argentinean	3	0.01
Chilean	3	0.01
Colombian	46	0.18
Ecuadorian	14	0.06
Peruvian	20	0.08
Venezuelan	4	0.02
Other Hispanic or Latino	1,010	3.98

Race*	Population	%
African-American/Black (8,996)	9,526	37.58
Not Hispanic (8,617)	8,984	35.44
Hispanic (379)	542	2.14
American Indian/Alaska Native (350)	629	2.48
Not Hispanic (162)	371	1.46
Hispanic (188)	258	1.02
Apache (0)	1	<0.01
Blackfeet (1)	15	0.06
Central American Ind. (13)	13	0.05
Cherokee (7)	31	0.12
Delaware (35)	77	0.30
Mexican American Ind. (49)	57	0.22
Pueblo (2)	2	0.01
Seminole (1)	2	0.01
Sioux (2)	4	0.02
South American Ind. (2)	9	0.04
Spanish American Ind. (1)	1	<0.01
Yaqui (7)	7	0.03
Yup'ik *(Alaska Native)* (0)	1	<0.01
Asian (153)	210	0.83
Not Hispanic (141)	180	0.71
Hispanic (12)	30	0.12
Bangladeshi (2)	2	0.01
Cambodian (5)	8	0.03
Chinese, ex. Taiwanese (20)	23	0.09
Filipino (33)	39	0.15
Indian (49)	56	0.22
Japanese (21)	32	0.13
Korean (2)	2	0.01
Laotian (4)	4	0.02
Pakistani (0)	4	0.02
Thai (1)	2	0.01
Hawaii Native/Pacific Islander (12)	41	0.16
Not Hispanic (4)	10	0.04
Hispanic (8)	31	0.12
Fijian (2)	4	0.02
Guamanian/Chamorro (7)	11	0.04
Native Hawaiian (2)	3	0.01
Samoan (0)	1	<0.01
Tongan (0)	1	<0.01
White (8,274)	9,034	35.64
Not Hispanic (4,917)	5,179	20.43
Hispanic (3,357)	3,855	15.21

Bridgewater

Place Type: Township
County: Somerset
Population: 44,464†

Ancestry‡	Population	%
African, Sub-Saharan (21)	33	0.07
African (10)	22	0.05
Ghanaian (11)	11	0.02
Albanian (45)	45	0.10
American (3,211)	3,211	7.26
Arab (307)	367	0.83
Egyptian (185)	208	0.47
Iraqi (0)	14	0.03
Jordanian (39)	39	0.09
Lebanese (74)	87	0.20
Syrian (9)	19	0.04
Armenian (55)	84	0.19
Australian (0)	12	0.03
Austrian (50)	180	0.41
Belgian (16)	74	0.17
Brazilian (0)	42	0.09
British (88)	197	0.45
Canadian (27)	39	0.09
Celtic (0)	11	0.02
Croatian (11)	72	0.16
Czech (30)	270	0.61
Czechoslovakian (24)	122	0.28
Danish (21)	207	0.47
Dutch (80)	481	1.09
Eastern European (300)	339	0.77
English (768)	3,085	6.97
Estonian (11)	11	0.02
European (530)	570	1.29
Finnish (11)	11	0.02
French, ex. Basque (78)	852	1.93
French Canadian (21)	89	0.20
German (1,509)	6,373	14.41
Greek (226)	317	0.72
Guyanese (0)	25	0.06
Hungarian (248)	669	1.51
Iranian (21)	21	0.05
Irish (1,590)	6,931	15.67
Israeli (44)	44	0.10
Italian (3,999)	8,286	18.73
Latvian (17)	17	0.04
Lithuanian (13)	219	0.50
Norwegian (44)	225	0.51

*Notes: † The Census 2010 population figure is used to calculate the percentages in the Hispanic Origin and Race categories. Ancestry percentages are based on the 2006-2010 American Community Survey population (not shown); ‡ Numbers in parentheses indicate the number of people reporting a single ancestry; * Numbers in parentheses indicate the number of persons reporting this race alone, not in combination with any other race; Please refer to the Explanation of Data for more information.*

Pennsylvania German (26)	26	0.06
Polish (1,744)	4,603	10.41
Portuguese (401)	632	1.43
Romanian (22)	22	0.05
Russian (324)	1,124	2.54
Scotch-Irish (187)	498	1.13
Scottish (220)	762	1.72
Slavic (38)	65	0.15
Slovak (110)	332	0.75
Slovene (10)	10	0.02
Swedish (81)	386	0.87
Swiss (13)	109	0.25
Turkish (48)	48	0.11
Ukrainian (233)	570	1.29
Welsh (34)	251	0.57
West Indian, ex. Hispanic (140)	195	0.44
Belizean (8)	8	0.02
Jamaican (110)	110	0.25
Trinidadian/Tobagonian (22)	22	0.05
West Indian (0)	55	0.12

Hispanic Origin	Population	%
Hispanic or Latino (of any race)	3,004	6.76
Central American, ex. Mexican	744	1.67
Costa Rican	497	1.12
Guatemalan	124	0.28
Honduran	18	0.04
Nicaraguan	17	0.04
Panamanian	15	0.03
Salvadoran	72	0.16
Other Central American	1	<0.01
Cuban	224	0.50
Dominican Republic	62	0.14
Mexican	265	0.60
Puerto Rican	543	1.22
South American	853	1.92
Argentinean	59	0.13
Bolivian	1	<0.01
Chilean	30	0.07
Colombian	282	0.63
Ecuadorian	141	0.32
Paraguayan	82	0.18
Peruvian	210	0.47
Uruguayan	25	0.06
Venezuelan	19	0.04
Other South American	4	0.01
Other Hispanic or Latino	313	0.70

Race*	Population	%
African-American/Black (1,059)	1,241	2.79
Not Hispanic (978)	1,107	2.49
Hispanic (81)	134	0.30
American Indian/Alaska Native (46)	153	0.34
Not Hispanic (32)	114	0.26
Hispanic (14)	39	0.09
Blackfeet (0)	6	0.01
Canadian/French Am. Ind. (0)	1	<0.01
Central American Ind. (4)	4	0.01
Cherokee (3)	16	0.04
Chickasaw (0)	1	<0.01
Chippewa (0)	2	<0.01
Choctaw (0)	5	0.01
Comanche (0)	2	<0.01
Delaware (1)	6	0.01
Lumbee (0)	1	<0.01
Mexican American Ind. (2)	2	<0.01
Osage (4)	4	0.01
Sioux (0)	4	0.01
South American Ind. (5)	12	0.03
Asian (7,927)	8,382	18.85
Not Hispanic (7,901)	8,316	18.70
Hispanic (26)	66	0.15
Bangladeshi (16)	19	0.04
Burmese (5)	8	0.02
Chinese, ex. Taiwanese (2,417)	2,576	5.79
Filipino (552)	654	1.47
Indian (3,772)	3,917	8.81
Indonesian (5)	9	0.02
Japanese (50)	76	0.17
Korean (295)	344	0.77
Laotian (11)	15	0.03
Malaysian (2)	3	0.01
Nepalese (1)	1	<0.01
Pakistani (200)	223	0.50
Sri Lankan (37)	39	0.09
Taiwanese (218)	233	0.52
Thai (27)	28	0.06
Vietnamese (192)	225	0.51
Hawaii Native/Pacific Islander (2)	20	0.04
Not Hispanic (2)	11	0.02
Hispanic (0)	9	0.02
Fijian (1)	3	0.01
Guamanian/Chamorro (0)	3	0.01
Native Hawaiian (1)	6	0.01
Samoan (0)	4	0.01
White (33,996)	34,628	77.88
Not Hispanic (31,852)	32,333	72.72
Hispanic (2,144)	2,295	5.16

Brigantine

Place Type: City
County: Atlantic
Population: 9,450†

Ancestry‡	Population	%
Afghan (112)	112	1.11
African, Sub-Saharan (0)	36	0.36
African (0)	36	0.36
Albanian (10)	10	0.10
American (495)	495	4.89
Australian (0)	15	0.15
Austrian (0)	19	0.19
Belgian (0)	8	0.08
British (54)	54	0.53
Croatian (0)	13	0.13
Czechoslovakian (18)	72	0.71
Dutch (13)	104	1.03
English (141)	782	7.73
European (0)	31	0.31
French, ex. Basque (48)	296	2.93
German (254)	1,459	14.42
Greek (41)	168	1.66
Hungarian (42)	115	1.14
Irish (1,316)	3,044	30.09
Italian (1,327)	2,333	23.06
Lithuanian (72)	118	1.17
Norwegian (8)	22	0.22
Pennsylvania German (15)	15	0.15
Polish (171)	564	5.58
Portuguese (15)	15	0.15
Romanian (17)	33	0.33
Russian (87)	277	2.74
Scandinavian (59)	82	0.81
Scotch-Irish (17)	224	2.21
Scottish (63)	129	1.28
Serbian (11)	11	0.11
Slovak (14)	14	0.14
Swedish (0)	43	0.43
Swiss (0)	7	0.07
Ukrainian (35)	62	0.61
Welsh (8)	44	0.43
West Indian, ex. Hispanic (44)	54	0.53
Haitian (13)	13	0.13
West Indian (31)	41	0.41

Hispanic Origin	Population	%
Hispanic or Latino (of any race)	650	6.88
Central American, ex. Mexican	44	0.47
Costa Rican	2	0.02
Guatemalan	4	0.04
Honduran	9	0.10
Nicaraguan	4	0.04
Panamanian	3	0.03
Salvadoran	22	0.23
Cuban	25	0.26
Dominican Republic	25	0.26
Mexican	126	1.33
Puerto Rican	320	3.39
South American	75	0.79
Chilean	1	0.01
Colombian	60	0.63
Ecuadorian	4	0.04
Peruvian	9	0.10
Venezuelan	1	0.01
Other Hispanic or Latino	35	0.37

Race*	Population	%
African-American/Black (275)	361	3.82
Not Hispanic (244)	300	3.17
Hispanic (31)	61	0.65
American Indian/Alaska Native (16)	72	0.76
Not Hispanic (6)	52	0.55
Hispanic (10)	20	0.21
Apache (0)	1	0.01
Blackfeet (0)	3	0.03
Cherokee (0)	5	0.05
Comanche (0)	3	0.03
Delaware (0)	2	0.02
Iroquois (0)	1	0.01
Pima (0)	1	0.01
South American Ind. (8)	8	0.08
Asian (446)	520	5.50
Not Hispanic (442)	513	5.43
Hispanic (4)	7	0.07
Bangladeshi (25)	26	0.28
Cambodian (1)	1	0.01
Chinese, ex. Taiwanese (53)	63	0.67
Filipino (46)	60	0.63
Indian (175)	210	2.22
Japanese (6)	11	0.12
Korean (9)	14	0.15
Laotian (1)	2	0.02
Pakistani (56)	61	0.65
Taiwanese (2)	3	0.03
Thai (3)	5	0.05
Vietnamese (36)	38	0.40
Hawaii Native/Pacific Islander (3)	14	0.15
Not Hispanic (2)	8	0.08
Hispanic (1)	6	0.06
Native Hawaiian (1)	3	0.03
Samoan (2)	5	0.05
White (8,253)	8,413	89.03
Not Hispanic (7,939)	8,053	85.22
Hispanic (314)	360	3.81

Brookdale

Place Type: CDP
County: Essex
Population: 9,239†

Ancestry‡	Population	%
African, Sub-Saharan (0)	13	0.14
Cape Verdean (0)	13	0.14
Albanian (133)	133	1.45
American (195)	195	2.12
Arab (98)	98	1.07
Egyptian (75)	75	0.82
Other Arab (23)	23	0.25
Armenian (15)	15	0.16
Austrian (19)	55	0.60
Belgian (12)	27	0.29
Brazilian (25)	25	0.27
British (8)	16	0.17
Croatian (0)	9	0.10
Czech (0)	8	0.09
Czechoslovakian (38)	38	0.41
Danish (12)	38	0.41
Dutch (9)	121	1.32
Eastern European (70)	70	0.76
English (141)	670	7.29
European (10)	10	0.11
French, ex. Basque (0)	125	1.36
French Canadian (0)	11	0.12
German (191)	1,050	11.43
Greek (45)	119	1.30
Guyanese (21)	53	0.58
Hungarian (19)	149	1.62
Iranian (11)	11	0.12

*Notes: † The Census 2010 population figure is used to calculate the percentages in the Hispanic Origin and Race categories. Ancestry percentages are based on the 2006-2010 American Community Survey population (not shown); ‡ Numbers in parentheses indicate the number of people reporting a single ancestry; * Numbers in parentheses indicate the number of persons reporting this race alone, not in combination with any other race; Please refer to the Explanation of Data for more information.*

Irish (313)	1,762	19.18
Italian (1,763)	3,122	33.99
Latvian (24)	24	0.26
Lithuanian (9)	18	0.20
Macedonian (15)	15	0.16
Norwegian (26)	58	0.63
Polish (231)	601	6.54
Portuguese (22)	51	0.56
Russian (126)	302	3.29
Scotch-Irish (101)	228	2.48
Scottish (38)	195	2.12
Slavic (8)	8	0.09
Slovak (10)	65	0.71
Slovene (27)	27	0.29
Swedish (75)	152	1.65
Swiss (0)	15	0.16
Ukrainian (11)	95	1.03
Welsh (18)	18	0.20
West Indian, ex. Hispanic (56)	56	0.61
Haitian (22)	22	0.24
Jamaican (22)	22	0.24
West Indian (12)	12	0.13

Hispanic Origin	Population	%
Hispanic or Latino (of any race)	1,085	11.74
Central American, ex. Mexican	76	0.82
Costa Rican	18	0.19
Guatemalan	25	0.27
Honduran	12	0.13
Nicaraguan	5	0.05
Panamanian	8	0.09
Salvadoran	8	0.09
Cuban	117	1.27
Dominican Republic	107	1.16
Mexican	69	0.75
Puerto Rican	359	3.89
South American	264	2.86
Argentinean	18	0.19
Bolivian	4	0.04
Chilean	16	0.17
Colombian	53	0.57
Ecuadorian	82	0.89
Paraguayan	1	0.01
Peruvian	69	0.75
Uruguayan	17	0.18
Venezuelan	3	0.03
Other South American	1	0.01
Other Hispanic or Latino	93	1.01

Race*	Population	%
African-American/Black (458)	561	6.07
Not Hispanic (409)	469	5.08
Hispanic (49)	92	1.00
American Indian/Alaska Native (10)	26	0.28
Not Hispanic (4)	17	0.18
Hispanic (6)	9	0.10
Central American Ind. (0)	1	0.01
Mexican American Ind. (0)	1	0.01
South American Ind. (1)	1	0.01
Spanish American Ind. (1)	1	0.01
Asian (1,132)	1,254	13.57
Not Hispanic (1,121)	1,223	13.24
Hispanic (11)	31	0.34
Burmese (3)	3	0.03
Chinese, ex. Taiwanese (164)	200	2.16
Filipino (575)	624	6.75
Indian (268)	284	3.07
Indonesian (10)	10	0.11
Japanese (12)	18	0.19
Korean (38)	47	0.51
Malaysian (4)	4	0.04
Pakistani (10)	17	0.18
Sri Lankan (9)	12	0.13
Taiwanese (3)	3	0.03
Thai (7)	11	0.12
Vietnamese (10)	11	0.12
Hawaii Native/Pacific Islander (2)	7	0.08
Not Hispanic (2)	7	0.08
Native Hawaiian (1)	3	0.03
Tongan (1)	1	0.01
White (7,064)	7,297	78.98
Not Hispanic (6,415)	6,547	70.86
Hispanic (649)	750	8.12

Browns Mills

Place Type: CDP
County: Burlington
Population: 11,223†

Ancestry‡	Population	%
African, Sub-Saharan (268)	268	2.41
African (245)	245	2.20
Nigerian (23)	23	0.21
American (353)	353	3.17
Armenian (0)	15	0.13
Austrian (17)	17	0.15
British (40)	49	0.44
Croatian (0)	13	0.12
Czech (10)	36	0.32
Czechoslovakian (0)	10	0.09
Dutch (0)	96	0.86
English (340)	1,108	9.96
European (47)	47	0.42
French, ex. Basque (67)	335	3.01
French Canadian (0)	20	0.18
German (559)	2,216	19.91
Hungarian (14)	75	0.67
Irish (347)	1,803	16.20
Italian (472)	1,356	12.18
Lithuanian (0)	30	0.27
Northern European (10)	10	0.09
Norwegian (0)	108	0.97
Pennsylvania German (20)	20	0.18
Polish (151)	461	4.14
Portuguese (87)	97	0.87
Russian (13)	38	0.34
Scandinavian (23)	23	0.21
Scotch-Irish (46)	189	1.70
Scottish (0)	177	1.59
Slovak (38)	38	0.34
Swedish (16)	241	2.17
Swiss (14)	14	0.13
Ukrainian (0)	12	0.11
Welsh (0)	67	0.60
West Indian, ex. Hispanic (181)	181	1.63
Jamaican (181)	181	1.63

Hispanic Origin	Population	%
Hispanic or Latino (of any race)	1,336	11.90
Central American, ex. Mexican	104	0.93
Costa Rican	6	0.05
Guatemalan	10	0.09
Honduran	3	0.03
Nicaraguan	1	0.01
Panamanian	68	0.61
Salvadoran	15	0.13
Other Central American	1	0.01
Cuban	36	0.32
Dominican Republic	35	0.31
Mexican	235	2.09
Puerto Rican	792	7.06
South American	58	0.52
Argentinean	4	0.04
Chilean	4	0.04
Colombian	15	0.13
Ecuadorian	15	0.13
Peruvian	18	0.16
Venezuelan	2	0.02
Other Hispanic or Latino	76	0.68

Race*	Population	%
African-American/Black (2,320)	2,755	24.55
Not Hispanic (2,158)	2,509	22.36
Hispanic (162)	246	2.19
American Indian/Alaska Native (60)	192	1.71
Not Hispanic (47)	145	1.29
Hispanic (13)	47	0.42
Blackfeet (1)	9	0.08
Central American Ind. (3)	3	0.03
Cherokee (10)	52	0.46
Chippewa (0)	3	0.03
Choctaw (0)	3	0.03
Delaware (0)	8	0.07
Iroquois (5)	5	0.04
Lumbee (1)	3	0.03
Mexican American Ind. (1)	4	0.04
Pueblo (1)	1	0.01
Seminole (1)	1	0.01
Sioux (1)	4	0.04
South American Ind. (3)	7	0.06
Spanish American Ind. (1)	1	0.01
Asian (393)	609	5.43
Not Hispanic (381)	579	5.16
Hispanic (12)	30	0.27
Cambodian (2)	2	0.02
Chinese, ex. Taiwanese (14)	19	0.17
Filipino (109)	170	1.51
Indian (33)	40	0.36
Indonesian (0)	2	0.02
Japanese (49)	107	0.95
Korean (131)	180	1.60
Malaysian (3)	3	0.03
Pakistani (7)	7	0.06
Taiwanese (3)	4	0.04
Thai (21)	45	0.40
Vietnamese (7)	17	0.15
Hawaii Native/Pacific Islander (7)	24	0.21
Not Hispanic (3)	13	0.12
Hispanic (4)	11	0.10
Guamanian/Chamorro (3)	3	0.03
Native Hawaiian (4)	12	0.11
White (7,452)	8,037	71.61
Not Hispanic (6,755)	7,208	64.23
Hispanic (697)	829	7.39

Budd Lake

Place Type: CDP
County: Morris
Population: 8,968†

Ancestry‡	Population	%
African, Sub-Saharan (17)	17	0.20
Nigerian (17)	17	0.20
American (136)	136	1.62
Arab (10)	10	0.12
Iraqi (10)	10	0.12
Armenian (13)	13	0.16
Austrian (0)	25	0.30
Belgian (0)	24	0.29
Brazilian (39)	105	1.25
Czech (0)	93	1.11
Czechoslovakian (14)	30	0.36
Danish (0)	11	0.13
Dutch (58)	146	1.74
English (166)	802	9.58
Estonian (6)	6	0.07
European (14)	260	3.10
French, ex. Basque (38)	255	3.05
French Canadian (0)	56	0.67
German (120)	1,421	16.97
Greek (0)	13	0.16
Guyanese (6)	6	0.07
Hungarian (14)	108	1.29
Irish (396)	1,995	23.82
Italian (737)	2,054	24.53
Lithuanian (0)	13	0.16
Norwegian (0)	41	0.49
Polish (107)	428	5.11
Russian (147)	383	4.57
Scandinavian (27)	52	0.62
Scotch-Irish (12)	53	0.63
Scottish (55)	204	2.44
Slavic (15)	15	0.18
Slovak (0)	36	0.43
Swedish (27)	39	0.47
Swiss (0)	61	0.73
Ukrainian (0)	28	0.33
Welsh (0)	27	0.32

*Notes: † The Census 2010 population figure is used to calculate the percentages in the Hispanic Origin and Race categories. Ancestry percentages are based on the 2006-2010 American Community Survey population (not shown); ‡ Numbers in parentheses indicate the number of people reporting a single ancestry; * Numbers in parentheses indicate the number of persons reporting this race alone, not in combination with any other race; Please refer to the Explanation of Data for more information.*

	Population	%
West Indian, ex. Hispanic (12)	32	0.38
Haitian (12)	12	0.14
Jamaican (0)	20	0.24
Yugoslavian (48)	48	0.57

Hispanic Origin	Population	%
Hispanic or Latino (of any race)	1,173	13.08
Central American, ex. Mexican	86	0.96
Costa Rican	34	0.38
Guatemalan	20	0.22
Honduran	10	0.11
Panamanian	4	0.04
Salvadoran	18	0.20
Cuban	44	0.49
Dominican Republic	74	0.83
Mexican	71	0.79
Puerto Rican	329	3.67
South American	459	5.12
Argentinean	23	0.26
Chilean	40	0.45
Colombian	199	2.22
Ecuadorian	57	0.64
Paraguayan	3	0.03
Peruvian	94	1.05
Uruguayan	40	0.45
Venezuelan	3	0.03
Other Hispanic or Latino	110	1.23

Race*	Population	%
African-American/Black (573)	653	7.28
Not Hispanic (537)	584	6.51
Hispanic (36)	69	0.77
American Indian/Alaska Native (14)	51	0.57
Not Hispanic (9)	33	0.37
Hispanic (5)	18	0.20
Blackfeet (1)	4	0.04
Cherokee (3)	15	0.17
Chippewa (1)	1	0.01
Delaware (0)	1	0.01
Iroquois (0)	3	0.03
Navajo (1)	1	0.01
Seminole (0)	3	0.03
South American Ind. (5)	7	0.08
Asian (691)	766	8.54
Not Hispanic (690)	758	8.45
Hispanic (1)	8	0.09
Bangladeshi (4)	4	0.04
Chinese, ex. Taiwanese (81)	117	1.30
Filipino (115)	138	1.54
Hmong (0)	2	0.02
Indian (261)	274	3.06
Japanese (2)	2	0.02
Korean (52)	58	0.65
Laotian (1)	1	0.01
Nepalese (5)	5	0.06
Pakistani (99)	104	1.16
Sri Lankan (2)	2	0.02
Taiwanese (3)	3	0.03
Thai (5)	10	0.11
Vietnamese (32)	40	0.45
Hawaii Native/Pacific Islander (8)	27	0.30
Not Hispanic (5)	22	0.25
Hispanic (3)	5	0.06
Fijian (0)	1	0.01
Guamanian/Chamorro (1)	1	0.01
Native Hawaiian (0)	1	0.01
White (7,253)	7,417	82.71
Not Hispanic (6,405)	6,512	72.61
Hispanic (848)	905	10.09

Buena Vista

Place Type: Township
County: Atlantic
Population: 7,570†

Ancestry‡	Population	%
African, Sub-Saharan (41)	116	1.52
African (14)	89	1.17
Nigerian (27)	27	0.35
American (247)	247	3.24
Austrian (0)	32	0.42
Czechoslovakian (15)	15	0.20
Danish (0)	11	0.14
Dutch (11)	197	2.59
English (79)	495	6.50
European (6)	6	0.08
Finnish (0)	11	0.14
French, ex. Basque (11)	116	1.52
French Canadian (0)	17	0.22
German (467)	1,816	23.84
Hungarian (28)	28	0.37
Irish (376)	1,255	16.48
Italian (1,493)	2,621	34.41
Lithuanian (42)	105	1.38
Norwegian (27)	66	0.87
Polish (73)	380	4.99
Russian (56)	155	2.03
Scotch-Irish (77)	120	1.58
Scottish (15)	99	1.30
Slovak (0)	48	0.63
Swedish (7)	50	0.66
Swiss (0)	11	0.14
Ukrainian (50)	50	0.66
Welsh (0)	54	0.71

Hispanic Origin	Population	%
Hispanic or Latino (of any race)	869	11.48
Central American, ex. Mexican	5	0.07
Guatemalan	2	0.03
Honduran	1	0.01
Nicaraguan	1	0.01
Panamanian	1	0.01
Cuban	16	0.21
Dominican Republic	20	0.26
Mexican	134	1.77
Puerto Rican	645	8.52
South American	12	0.16
Colombian	10	0.13
Venezuelan	2	0.03
Other Hispanic or Latino	37	0.49

Race*	Population	%
African-American/Black (1,018)	1,127	14.89
Not Hispanic (969)	1,041	13.75
Hispanic (49)	86	1.14
American Indian/Alaska Native (35)	80	1.06
Not Hispanic (21)	52	0.69
Hispanic (14)	28	0.37
Blackfeet (1)	3	0.04
Cherokee (3)	12	0.16
Delaware (1)	2	0.03
Mexican American Ind. (0)	2	0.03
Seminole (0)	1	0.01
South American Ind. (0)	1	0.01
Spanish American Ind. (0)	2	0.03
Asian (80)	114	1.51
Not Hispanic (76)	102	1.35
Hispanic (4)	12	0.16
Chinese, ex. Taiwanese (19)	23	0.30
Filipino (13)	23	0.30
Indian (23)	26	0.34
Japanese (3)	7	0.09
Korean (5)	8	0.11
Laotian (4)	4	0.05
Pakistani (0)	8	0.11
Vietnamese (12)	13	0.17
Hawaii Native/Pacific Islander (3)	18	0.24
Not Hispanic (3)	13	0.17
Hispanic (0)	5	0.07
Native Hawaiian (2)	2	0.03
Samoan (1)	2	0.03
White (5,918)	6,075	80.25
Not Hispanic (5,509)	5,604	74.03
Hispanic (409)	471	6.22

Burlington

Place Type: City
County: Burlington
Population: 9,920†

Ancestry‡	Population	%
African, Sub-Saharan (19)	37	0.37
African (19)	37	0.37
American (385)	385	3.87
Arab (23)	23	0.23
Egyptian (23)	23	0.23
Austrian (0)	7	0.07
British (36)	44	0.44
Canadian (10)	10	0.10
Croatian (8)	8	0.08
Czech (0)	22	0.22
Czechoslovakian (0)	7	0.07
Dutch (67)	161	1.62
English (186)	792	7.96
European (70)	83	0.83
French, ex. Basque (18)	132	1.33
French Canadian (0)	16	0.16
German (276)	1,389	13.96
Greek (18)	27	0.27
Hungarian (0)	72	0.72
Irish (310)	1,454	14.61
Israeli (0)	14	0.14
Italian (650)	1,725	17.33
Lithuanian (72)	126	1.27
Norwegian (11)	43	0.43
Pennsylvania German (6)	6	0.06
Polish (224)	635	6.38
Portuguese (33)	33	0.33
Romanian (29)	29	0.29
Russian (15)	89	0.89
Scotch-Irish (27)	69	0.69
Scottish (26)	80	0.80
Slovene (0)	12	0.12
Swedish (19)	65	0.65
Swiss (0)	15	0.15
Ukrainian (25)	34	0.34
Welsh (0)	35	0.35
West Indian, ex. Hispanic (145)	185	1.86
Haitian (41)	41	0.41
Jamaican (104)	104	1.04
Trinidadian/Tobagonian (0)	40	0.40

Hispanic Origin	Population	%
Hispanic or Latino (of any race)	645	6.50
Central American, ex. Mexican	98	0.99
Costa Rican	10	0.10
Guatemalan	11	0.11
Honduran	17	0.17
Nicaraguan	16	0.16
Panamanian	29	0.29
Salvadoran	12	0.12
Other Central American	3	0.03
Cuban	16	0.16
Dominican Republic	51	0.51
Mexican	61	0.61
Puerto Rican	338	3.41
South American	32	0.32
Argentinean	1	0.01
Bolivian	1	0.01
Colombian	19	0.19
Ecuadorian	3	0.03
Peruvian	5	0.05
Venezuelan	2	0.02
Other South American	1	0.01
Other Hispanic or Latino	49	0.49

Race*	Population	%
African-American/Black (3,272)	3,560	35.89
Not Hispanic (3,165)	3,389	34.16
Hispanic (107)	171	1.72
American Indian/Alaska Native (18)	120	1.21
Not Hispanic (16)	91	0.92
Hispanic (2)	29	0.29
Apache (1)	1	0.01

SECTION TWO

*Notes: † The Census 2010 population figure is used to calculate the percentages in the Hispanic Origin and Race categories. Ancestry percentages are based on the 2006-2010 American Community Survey population (not shown); ‡ Numbers in parentheses indicate the number of people reporting a single ancestry; * Numbers in parentheses indicate the number of persons reporting this race alone, not in combination with any other race; Please refer to the Explanation of Data for more information.*

Blackfeet (0)	10	0.10
Cherokee (2)	46	0.46
Chippewa (2)	2	0.02
Crow (1)	1	0.01
Delaware (1)	4	0.04
Navajo (0)	1	0.01
Seminole (0)	1	0.01
Shoshone (1)	1	0.01
Sioux (0)	1	0.01
Tlingit-Haida *(Alaska Native)* (0)	2	0.02
Yaqui (1)	1	0.01
Asian (201)	240	2.42
Not Hispanic (197)	230	2.32
Hispanic (4)	10	0.10
Bangladeshi (19)	26	0.26
Burmese (1)	1	0.01
Chinese, ex. Taiwanese (14)	18	0.18
Filipino (16)	28	0.28
Indian (119)	132	1.33
Japanese (1)	8	0.08
Korean (10)	17	0.17
Pakistani (7)	7	0.07
Taiwanese (1)	1	0.01
Thai (2)	4	0.04
Vietnamese (2)	4	0.04
Hawaii Native/Pacific Islander (4)	8	0.08
Not Hispanic (4)	6	0.06
Hispanic (0)	2	0.02
Guamanian/Chamorro (1)	1	0.01
Native Hawaiian (3)	3	0.03
White (5,845)	6,102	61.51
Not Hispanic (5,579)	5,802	58.49
Hispanic (266)	300	3.02

Burlington

Place Type: Township
County: Burlington
Population: 22,594†

Ancestry‡	Population	%
African, Sub-Saharan (680)	724	3.24
African (251)	273	1.22
Ghanaian (60)	60	0.27
Liberian (300)	322	1.44
Nigerian (69)	69	0.31
Albanian (6)	29	0.13
American (380)	380	1.70
Arab (43)	43	0.19
Egyptian (43)	43	0.19
Armenian (16)	27	0.12
Austrian (11)	26	0.12
Belgian (0)	34	0.15
Brazilian (74)	101	0.45
British (0)	31	0.14
Canadian (12)	22	0.10
Czech (9)	76	0.34
Danish (5)	5	0.02
Dutch (16)	110	0.49
English (472)	1,779	7.95
European (11)	60	0.27
Finnish (0)	40	0.18
French, ex. Basque (22)	335	1.50
French Canadian (0)	26	0.12
German (650)	3,347	14.96
Greek (167)	186	0.83
Guyanese (29)	29	0.13
Hungarian (98)	233	1.04
Irish (805)	4,108	18.36
Italian (1,120)	3,707	16.57
Lithuanian (79)	129	0.58
Norwegian (11)	90	0.40
Pennsylvania German (25)	25	0.11
Polish (299)	1,428	6.38
Portuguese (6)	122	0.55
Romanian (39)	165	0.74
Russian (28)	187	0.84
Scandinavian (0)	22	0.10
Scotch-Irish (68)	325	1.45
Scottish (78)	230	1.03
Slavic (0)	63	0.28
Slovak (59)	193	0.86
Swedish (46)	157	0.70
Swiss (0)	42	0.19
Ukrainian (102)	152	0.68
Welsh (0)	113	0.51
West Indian, ex. Hispanic (682)	852	3.81
Barbadian (101)	127	0.57
Haitian (177)	177	0.79
Jamaican (302)	395	1.77
West Indian (102)	153	0.68
Yugoslavian (8)	8	0.04

Hispanic Origin	Population	%
Hispanic or Latino (of any race)	1,593	7.05
Central American, ex. Mexican	168	0.74
Costa Rican	8	0.04
Guatemalan	33	0.15
Honduran	39	0.17
Nicaraguan	4	0.02
Panamanian	69	0.31
Salvadoran	15	0.07
Cuban	39	0.17
Dominican Republic	89	0.39
Mexican	117	0.52
Puerto Rican	834	3.69
South American	210	0.93
Argentinean	16	0.07
Bolivian	9	0.04
Chilean	3	0.01
Colombian	70	0.31
Ecuadorian	32	0.14
Paraguayan	2	0.01
Peruvian	62	0.27
Uruguayan	1	<0.01
Venezuelan	9	0.04
Other South American	6	0.03
Other Hispanic or Latino	136	0.60

Race*	Population	%
African-American/Black (6,322)	6,824	30.20
Not Hispanic (6,088)	6,477	28.67
Hispanic (234)	347	1.54
American Indian/Alaska Native (35)	210	0.93
Not Hispanic (19)	164	0.73
Hispanic (16)	46	0.20
Arapaho (0)	2	0.01
Blackfeet (1)	16	0.07
Central American Ind. (5)	9	0.04
Cherokee (4)	42	0.19
Cheyenne (0)	2	0.01
Choctaw (1)	1	<0.01
Cree (0)	2	0.01
Crow (0)	3	0.01
Delaware (0)	2	0.01
Iroquois (0)	3	0.01
Lumbee (0)	1	<0.01
Mexican American Ind. (1)	1	<0.01
Osage (1)	1	<0.01
Pima (0)	4	0.02
Sioux (1)	1	<0.01
South American Ind. (1)	3	0.01
Asian (1,590)	1,815	8.03
Not Hispanic (1,582)	1,781	7.88
Hispanic (8)	34	0.15
Bangladeshi (13)	13	0.06
Burmese (0)	2	0.01
Cambodian (1)	2	0.01
Chinese, ex. Taiwanese (135)	163	0.72
Filipino (210)	267	1.18
Indian (895)	932	4.12
Japanese (10)	60	0.27
Korean (88)	119	0.53
Laotian (4)	6	0.03
Malaysian (3)	5	0.02
Pakistani (124)	127	0.56
Sri Lankan (1)	1	<0.01
Taiwanese (2)	2	0.01
Thai (1)	3	0.01
Vietnamese (74)	78	0.35
Hawaii Native/Pacific Islander (9)	36	0.16
Not Hispanic (9)	27	0.12
Hispanic (0)	9	0.04
Guamanian/Chamorro (0)	1	<0.01
Native Hawaiian (3)	7	0.03
White (13,331)	13,857	61.33
Not Hispanic (12,580)	12,990	57.49
Hispanic (751)	867	3.84

Butler

Place Type: Borough
County: Morris
Population: 7,539†

Ancestry‡	Population	%
African, Sub-Saharan (0)	24	0.32
African (0)	24	0.32
American (201)	201	2.67
Arab (13)	81	1.08
Arab (13)	63	0.84
Lebanese (0)	18	0.24
Austrian (20)	84	1.12
Canadian (45)	67	0.89
Croatian (12)	12	0.16
Czech (0)	13	0.17
Czechoslovakian (0)	15	0.20
Dutch (126)	440	5.85
Eastern European (8)	8	0.11
English (82)	539	7.17
European (56)	56	0.75
Finnish (0)	11	0.15
French, ex. Basque (30)	177	2.36
French Canadian (12)	26	0.35
German (259)	1,333	17.74
Greek (22)	29	0.39
Guyanese (29)	34	0.45
Hungarian (27)	201	2.67
Irish (434)	1,598	21.26
Italian (1,004)	2,356	31.35
Latvian (16)	16	0.21
Lithuanian (19)	19	0.25
Macedonian (29)	40	0.53
Northern European (32)	32	0.43
Norwegian (0)	15	0.20
Polish (346)	832	11.07
Portuguese (9)	21	0.28
Russian (33)	268	3.57
Scotch-Irish (20)	50	0.67
Scottish (104)	259	3.45
Slovak (22)	22	0.29
Swedish (27)	81	1.08
Swiss (10)	48	0.64
Ukrainian (10)	21	0.28
Welsh (0)	108	1.44
West Indian, ex. Hispanic (0)	9	0.12
Haitian (0)	9	0.12
Yugoslavian (31)	54	0.72

Hispanic Origin	Population	%
Hispanic or Latino (of any race)	860	11.41
Central American, ex. Mexican	76	1.01
Costa Rican	14	0.19
Guatemalan	30	0.40
Honduran	20	0.27
Panamanian	2	0.03
Salvadoran	4	0.05
Other Central American	6	0.08
Cuban	43	0.57
Dominican Republic	39	0.52
Mexican	343	4.55
Puerto Rican	159	2.11
South American	154	2.04
Argentinean	13	0.17
Bolivian	3	0.04
Chilean	2	0.03
Colombian	57	0.76
Ecuadorian	38	0.50
Paraguayan	2	0.03
Peruvian	36	0.48

*Notes: † The Census 2010 population figure is used to calculate the percentages in the Hispanic Origin and Race categories. Ancestry percentages are based on the 2006-2010 American Community Survey population (not shown); ‡ Numbers in parentheses indicate the number of people reporting a single ancestry; * Numbers in parentheses indicate the number of persons reporting this race alone, not in combination with any other race; Please refer to the Explanation of Data for more information.*

Uruguayan	3	0.04
Other Hispanic or Latino	46	0.61

Race*	Population	%
African-American/Black (84)	131	1.74
Not Hispanic (78)	114	1.51
Hispanic (6)	17	0.23
American Indian/Alaska Native (12)	34	0.45
Not Hispanic (8)	23	0.31
Hispanic (4)	11	0.15
Central American Ind. (1)	1	0.01
Cherokee (3)	8	0.11
Delaware (2)	4	0.05
Iroquois (0)	3	0.04
Sioux (0)	1	0.01
South American Ind. (1)	1	0.01
Spanish American Ind. (2)	2	0.03
Asian (228)	267	3.54
Not Hispanic (228)	263	3.49
Hispanic (0)	4	0.05
Chinese, ex. Taiwanese (41)	53	0.70
Filipino (61)	76	1.01
Indian (76)	82	1.09
Japanese (7)	12	0.16
Korean (15)	19	0.25
Malaysian (0)	4	0.05
Pakistani (9)	9	0.12
Taiwanese (1)	3	0.04
Thai (0)	1	0.01
Vietnamese (5)	5	0.07
Hawaii Native/Pacific Islander (0)	6	0.08
Not Hispanic (0)	5	0.07
Hispanic (0)	1	0.01
White (6,706)	6,827	90.56
Not Hispanic (6,266)	6,345	84.16
Hispanic (440)	482	6.39

Byram

Place Type: Township
County: Sussex
Population: 8,350†

Ancestry‡	Population	%
Albanian (0)	8	0.09
American (338)	338	4.00
Armenian (19)	71	0.84
Austrian (0)	55	0.65
Belgian (10)	30	0.36
Brazilian (0)	15	0.18
British (17)	66	0.78
Canadian (48)	48	0.57
Czech (18)	110	1.30
Czechoslovakian (8)	8	0.09
Danish (9)	55	0.65
Dutch (40)	248	2.94
Eastern European (28)	28	0.33
English (88)	955	11.31
European (105)	105	1.24
Finnish (11)	52	0.62
French, ex. Basque (11)	180	2.13
French Canadian (15)	28	0.33
German (476)	1,826	21.62
Greek (72)	159	1.88
Hungarian (38)	276	3.27
Iranian (23)	23	0.27
Irish (375)	1,783	21.11
Italian (722)	2,049	24.26
Latvian (36)	36	0.43
Lithuanian (0)	83	0.98
Luxemburger (13)	13	0.15
Norwegian (30)	117	1.39
Polish (325)	979	11.59
Portuguese (43)	43	0.51
Russian (28)	120	1.42
Scandinavian (0)	13	0.15
Scotch-Irish (18)	145	1.72
Scottish (61)	321	3.80
Slavic (0)	40	0.47
Slovak (31)	104	1.23
Swedish (35)	88	1.04
Swiss (0)	23	0.27
Ukrainian (99)	137	1.62
Welsh (0)	106	1.26
Yugoslavian (0)	9	0.11

Hispanic Origin	Population	%
Hispanic or Latino (of any race)	417	4.99
Central American, ex. Mexican	38	0.46
Costa Rican	8	0.10
Guatemalan	4	0.05
Honduran	12	0.14
Nicaraguan	1	0.01
Panamanian	5	0.06
Salvadoran	8	0.10
Cuban	63	0.75
Dominican Republic	22	0.26
Mexican	30	0.36
Puerto Rican	147	1.76
South American	78	0.93
Argentinean	10	0.12
Chilean	9	0.11
Colombian	31	0.37
Ecuadorian	12	0.14
Peruvian	14	0.17
Uruguayan	1	0.01
Venezuelan	1	0.01
Other Hispanic or Latino	39	0.47

Race*	Population	%
African-American/Black (123)	150	1.80
Not Hispanic (113)	136	1.63
Hispanic (10)	14	0.17
American Indian/Alaska Native (10)	35	0.42
Not Hispanic (2)	24	0.29
Hispanic (8)	11	0.13
Cherokee (0)	11	0.13
Chickasaw (1)	1	0.01
Cree (0)	2	0.02
Iroquois (0)	3	0.04
Mexican American Ind. (1)	1	0.01
South American Ind. (3)	3	0.04
Asian (179)	220	2.63
Not Hispanic (173)	207	2.48
Hispanic (6)	13	0.16
Cambodian (2)	2	0.02
Chinese, ex. Taiwanese (42)	63	0.75
Filipino (43)	47	0.56
Indian (51)	52	0.62
Japanese (4)	10	0.12
Korean (8)	8	0.10
Malaysian (1)	1	0.01
Pakistani (7)	7	0.08
Sri Lankan (1)	1	0.01
Taiwanese (1)	1	0.01
Thai (4)	5	0.06
Vietnamese (8)	11	0.13
Hawaii Native/Pacific Islander (1)	3	0.04
Not Hispanic (1)	2	0.02
Hispanic (0)	1	0.01
Guamanian/Chamorro (0)	1	0.01
Native Hawaiian (0)	1	0.01
White (7,878)	7,982	95.59
Not Hispanic (7,553)	7,627	91.34
Hispanic (325)	355	4.25

Caldwell

Place Type: Borough
County: Essex
Population: 7,822†

Ancestry‡	Population	%
African, Sub-Saharan (12)	12	0.15
Nigerian (12)	12	0.15
American (129)	129	1.67
Arab (0)	35	0.45
Lebanese (0)	12	0.15
Palestinian (0)	12	0.15
Syrian (0)	11	0.14
Austrian (69)	69	0.89
Brazilian (12)	12	0.15
British (16)	16	0.21
Canadian (0)	17	0.22
Croatian (20)	20	0.26
Czech (0)	42	0.54
Dutch (14)	127	1.64
Eastern European (53)	78	1.01
English (73)	423	5.46
European (14)	14	0.18
French, ex. Basque (20)	98	1.27
French Canadian (17)	53	0.68
German (177)	1,217	15.71
Greek (13)	50	0.65
Hungarian (98)	131	1.69
Iranian (46)	46	0.59
Irish (739)	2,320	29.95
Italian (1,247)	2,457	31.72
Latvian (4)	4	0.05
Lithuanian (15)	27	0.35
Norwegian (12)	55	0.71
Pennsylvania German (4)	4	0.05
Polish (173)	602	7.77
Russian (77)	155	2.00
Scandinavian (14)	14	0.18
Scotch-Irish (17)	59	0.76
Scottish (17)	197	2.54
Slovak (0)	11	0.14
Swedish (89)	203	2.62
Swiss (0)	31	0.40
Turkish (17)	17	0.22
Ukrainian (16)	16	0.21
Welsh (0)	13	0.17
West Indian, ex. Hispanic (10)	10	0.13
Haitian (10)	10	0.13

Hispanic Origin	Population	%
Hispanic or Latino (of any race)	786	10.05
Central American, ex. Mexican	104	1.33
Costa Rican	66	0.84
Guatemalan	24	0.31
Honduran	3	0.04
Salvadoran	11	0.14
Cuban	50	0.64
Dominican Republic	55	0.70
Mexican	118	1.51
Puerto Rican	182	2.33
South American	150	1.92
Argentinean	10	0.13
Bolivian	1	0.01
Chilean	11	0.14
Colombian	37	0.47
Ecuadorian	26	0.33
Peruvian	54	0.69
Uruguayan	8	0.10
Venezuelan	3	0.04
Other Hispanic or Latino	127	1.62

Race*	Population	%
African-American/Black (260)	303	3.87
Not Hispanic (233)	268	3.43
Hispanic (27)	35	0.45
American Indian/Alaska Native (8)	33	0.42
Not Hispanic (4)	22	0.28
Hispanic (4)	11	0.14
Blackfeet (1)	1	0.01
Canadian/French Am. Ind. (0)	1	0.01
Cherokee (1)	4	0.05
Choctaw (0)	1	0.01
Cree (0)	2	0.03
Creek (0)	1	0.01
Iroquois (1)	1	0.01
South American Ind. (1)	2	0.03
Asian (369)	434	5.55
Not Hispanic (366)	426	5.45
Hispanic (3)	8	0.10
Cambodian (3)	3	0.04
Chinese, ex. Taiwanese (88)	100	1.28
Filipino (37)	54	0.69
Indian (106)	119	1.52

*Notes: † The Census 2010 population figure is used to calculate the percentages in the Hispanic Origin and Race categories. Ancestry percentages are based on the 2006-2010 American Community Survey population (not shown); ‡ Numbers in parentheses indicate the number of people reporting a single ancestry; * Numbers in parentheses indicate the number of persons reporting this race alone, not in combination with any other race; Please refer to the Explanation of Data for more information.*

Indonesian (1)	3	0.04
Japanese (14)	23	0.29
Korean (51)	56	0.72
Nepalese (22)	22	0.28
Pakistani (6)	6	0.08
Sri Lankan (5)	5	0.06
Taiwanese (6)	6	0.08
Thai (3)	3	0.04
Vietnamese (13)	14	0.18
Hawaii Native/Pacific Islander (3)	14	0.18
Not Hispanic (3)	5	0.06
Hispanic (0)	9	0.12
Native Hawaiian (0)	1	0.01
Samoan (3)	3	0.04
White (6,788)	6,908	88.32
Not Hispanic (6,306)	6,403	81.86
Hispanic (482)	505	6.46

Camden

Place Type: City
County: Camden
Population: 77,344†

Ancestry‡	Population	%
African, Sub-Saharan (679)	853	1.09
African (544)	718	0.92
Ghanaian (53)	53	0.07
Kenyan (11)	11	0.01
Liberian (33)	33	0.04
Sierra Leonean (35)	35	0.04
Other Sub-Saharan African (3)	3	<0.01
American (521)	521	0.67
Arab (157)	340	0.44
Egyptian (71)	71	0.09
Lebanese (0)	80	0.10
Moroccan (53)	137	0.18
Syrian (33)	52	0.07
Austrian (0)	12	0.02
British (55)	65	0.08
Canadian (0)	9	0.01
Czech (0)	51	0.07
Dutch (57)	190	0.24
English (80)	347	0.44
European (37)	43	0.06
French, ex. Basque (16)	143	0.18
French Canadian (23)	35	0.04
German (143)	1,039	1.33
Greek (23)	48	0.06
Hungarian (30)	73	0.09
Icelander (13)	13	0.02
Iranian (9)	9	0.01
Irish (302)	1,257	1.61
Israeli (9)	9	0.01
Italian (595)	1,409	1.81
Norwegian (0)	2	<0.01
Polish (195)	496	0.64
Portuguese (41)	41	0.05
Russian (0)	48	0.06
Scotch-Irish (19)	75	0.10
Scottish (0)	23	0.03
Swedish (0)	31	0.04
Swiss (14)	31	0.04
Ukrainian (20)	56	0.07
Welsh (0)	22	0.03
West Indian, ex. Hispanic (793)	1,020	1.31
Barbadian (0)	13	0.02
Haitian (114)	165	0.21
Jamaican (556)	639	0.82
Trinidadian/Tobagonian (40)	97	0.12
U.S. Virgin Islander (0)	9	0.01
West Indian (83)	97	0.12
Yugoslavian (0)	67	0.09

Hispanic Origin	Population	%
Hispanic or Latino (of any race)	36,379	47.04
Central American, ex. Mexican	1,737	2.25
Costa Rican	59	0.08
Guatemalan	439	0.57
Honduran	110	0.14
Nicaraguan	880	1.14
Panamanian	54	0.07
Salvadoran	188	0.24
Other Central American	7	0.01
Cuban	218	0.28
Dominican Republic	4,006	5.18
Mexican	5,035	6.51
Puerto Rican	23,759	30.72
South American	279	0.36
Argentinean	24	0.03
Bolivian	3	<0.01
Chilean	3	<0.01
Colombian	65	0.08
Ecuadorian	118	0.15
Paraguayan	1	<0.01
Peruvian	34	0.04
Uruguayan	3	<0.01
Venezuelan	21	0.03
Other South American	7	0.01
Other Hispanic or Latino	1,345	1.74

Race*	Population	%
African-American/Black (37,180)	38,960	50.37
Not Hispanic (34,277)	35,088	45.37
Hispanic (2,903)	3,872	5.01
American Indian/Alaska Native (588)	1,127	1.46
Not Hispanic (235)	534	0.69
Hispanic (353)	593	0.77
Aleut *(Alaska Native)* (0)	1	<0.01
Apache (0)	5	0.01
Blackfeet (1)	31	0.04
Canadian/French Am. Ind. (0)	1	<0.01
Central American Ind. (23)	24	0.03
Cherokee (44)	130	0.17
Chickasaw (0)	1	<0.01
Chippewa (1)	1	<0.01
Choctaw (1)	4	0.01
Crow (0)	1	<0.01
Delaware (11)	19	0.02
Hopi (0)	4	0.01
Iroquois (1)	13	0.02
Lumbee (1)	2	<0.01
Mexican American Ind. (17)	21	0.03
Navajo (0)	1	<0.01
Osage (1)	1	<0.01
Paiute (2)	7	0.01
Pueblo (1)	2	<0.01
Seminole (4)	10	0.01
Shoshone (0)	5	0.01
Sioux (3)	12	0.02
South American Ind. (42)	74	0.10
Spanish American Ind. (13)	20	0.03
Tlingit-Haida *(Alaska Native)* (1)	2	<0.01
Yaqui (2)	2	<0.01
Asian (1,637)	1,942	2.51
Not Hispanic (1,599)	1,768	2.29
Hispanic (38)	174	0.22
Bangladeshi (1)	1	<0.01
Burmese (4)	4	0.01
Cambodian (229)	300	0.39
Chinese, ex. Taiwanese (146)	188	0.24
Filipino (56)	119	0.15
Indian (98)	176	0.23
Indonesian (1)	2	<0.01
Japanese (17)	46	0.06
Korean (50)	78	0.10
Laotian (10)	10	0.01
Pakistani (19)	31	0.04
Taiwanese (2)	2	<0.01
Vietnamese (901)	988	1.28
Hawaii Native/Pacific Islander (48)	188	0.24
Not Hispanic (15)	60	0.08
Hispanic (33)	128	0.17
Guamanian/Chamorro (11)	16	0.02
Native Hawaiian (17)	32	0.04
Samoan (3)	4	0.01
White (13,602)	15,318	19.81
Not Hispanic (3,792)	4,351	5.63
Hispanic (9,810)	10,967	14.18

Carneys Point

Place Type: Township
County: Salem
Population: 8,049†

Ancestry‡	Population	%
African, Sub-Saharan (87)	87	1.09
African (87)	87	1.09
Albanian (12)	12	0.15
American (473)	473	5.90
Austrian (0)	18	0.22
British (12)	51	0.64
Celtic (31)	31	0.39
Danish (0)	97	1.21
Dutch (9)	52	0.65
English (227)	828	10.33
European (10)	10	0.12
French, ex. Basque (33)	238	2.97
French Canadian (48)	87	1.09
German (472)	1,803	22.50
Greek (16)	48	0.60
Hungarian (0)	32	0.40
Irish (353)	1,391	17.36
Italian (571)	1,299	16.21
Lithuanian (66)	152	1.90
Norwegian (10)	10	0.12
Pennsylvania German (0)	25	0.31
Polish (93)	304	3.79
Portuguese (13)	13	0.16
Romanian (10)	37	0.46
Russian (0)	43	0.54
Scandinavian (10)	10	0.12
Scotch-Irish (28)	171	2.13
Scottish (10)	88	1.10
Slovak (12)	30	0.37
Swedish (15)	43	0.54
Swiss (0)	9	0.11
Ukrainian (0)	43	0.54
Welsh (26)	83	1.04

Hispanic Origin	Population	%
Hispanic or Latino (of any race)	900	11.18
Central American, ex. Mexican	86	1.07
Costa Rican	2	0.02
Guatemalan	66	0.82
Honduran	2	0.02
Nicaraguan	1	0.01
Panamanian	8	0.10
Salvadoran	7	0.09
Cuban	6	0.07
Dominican Republic	14	0.17
Mexican	315	3.91
Puerto Rican	401	4.98
South American	28	0.35
Colombian	10	0.12
Ecuadorian	3	0.04
Paraguayan	5	0.06
Peruvian	9	0.11
Uruguayan	1	0.01
Other Hispanic or Latino	50	0.62

Race*	Population	%
African-American/Black (1,361)	1,488	18.49
Not Hispanic (1,309)	1,414	17.57
Hispanic (52)	74	0.92
American Indian/Alaska Native (17)	55	0.68
Not Hispanic (13)	41	0.51
Hispanic (4)	14	0.17
Canadian/French Am. Ind. (0)	1	0.01
Cherokee (1)	2	0.02
Cheyenne (0)	1	0.01
Chippewa (0)	1	0.01
Delaware (1)	9	0.11
Lumbee (0)	2	0.02
Pueblo (0)	1	0.01
Sioux (0)	1	0.01
Asian (65)	78	0.97
Not Hispanic (65)	78	0.97
Chinese, ex. Taiwanese (5)	6	0.07

*Notes: † The Census 2010 population figure is used to calculate the percentages in the Hispanic Origin and Race categories. Ancestry percentages are based on the 2006-2010 American Community Survey population (not shown); ‡ Numbers in parentheses indicate the number of people reporting a single ancestry; * Numbers in parentheses indicate the number of persons reporting this race alone, not in combination with any other race; Please refer to the Explanation of Data for more information.*

Filipino (24)	25	0.31
Indian (6)	6	0.07
Indonesian (2)	3	0.04
Japanese (5)	14	0.17
Korean (9)	10	0.12
Pakistani (2)	2	0.02
Thai (0)	1	0.01
Vietnamese (4)	4	0.05
Hawaii Native/Pacific Islander (0)	1	0.01
Not Hispanic (0)	1	0.01
White (5,963)	6,118	76.01
Not Hispanic (5,626)	5,746	71.39
Hispanic (337)	372	4.62

Carteret

Place Type: Borough
County: Middlesex
Population: 22,844†

Ancestry‡	Population	%
African, Sub-Saharan (133)	155	0.69
African (71)	93	0.41
Ghanaian (62)	62	0.28
American (83)	83	0.37
Arab (199)	258	1.15
Arab (20)	79	0.35
Egyptian (179)	179	0.80
Austrian (0)	34	0.15
Brazilian (69)	69	0.31
Canadian (10)	10	0.04
Croatian (0)	18	0.08
Czech (9)	42	0.19
Czechoslovakian (47)	47	0.21
Danish (0)	18	0.08
Dutch (11)	30	0.13
English (28)	206	0.92
European (41)	68	0.30
Finnish (11)	11	0.05
French, ex. Basque (0)	68	0.30
French Canadian (0)	61	0.27
German (317)	1,551	6.91
Greek (14)	55	0.25
Guyanese (104)	104	0.46
Hungarian (359)	604	2.69
Iranian (13)	13	0.06
Irish (425)	2,314	10.31
Italian (1,018)	3,153	14.05
Lithuanian (14)	74	0.33
Norwegian (0)	45	0.20
Polish (816)	1,730	7.71
Portuguese (158)	263	1.17
Romanian (50)	68	0.30
Russian (40)	159	0.71
Scotch-Irish (24)	59	0.26
Scottish (30)	139	0.62
Serbian (0)	18	0.08
Slavic (11)	44	0.20
Slovak (160)	497	2.21
Swedish (0)	16	0.07
Ukrainian (338)	621	2.77
Welsh (0)	27	0.12
West Indian, ex. Hispanic (346)	388	1.73
Barbadian (60)	60	0.27
Haitian (156)	156	0.70
Jamaican (24)	38	0.17
Trinidadian/Tobagonian (0)	14	0.06
West Indian (106)	120	0.53

Hispanic Origin	Population	%
Hispanic or Latino (of any race)	7,066	30.93
Central American, ex. Mexican	364	1.59
Costa Rican	66	0.29
Guatemalan	22	0.10
Honduran	104	0.46
Nicaraguan	29	0.13
Panamanian	14	0.06
Salvadoran	124	0.54
Other Central American	5	0.02
Cuban	298	1.30
Dominican Republic	856	3.75
Mexican	298	1.30
Puerto Rican	3,135	13.72
South American	1,615	7.07
Argentinean	78	0.34
Bolivian	17	0.07
Chilean	52	0.23
Colombian	226	0.99
Ecuadorian	259	1.13
Paraguayan	1	<0.01
Peruvian	896	3.92
Uruguayan	69	0.30
Venezuelan	15	0.07
Other South American	2	0.01
Other Hispanic or Latino	500	2.19

Race*	Population	%
African-American/Black (3,393)	3,739	16.37
Not Hispanic (3,056)	3,235	14.16
Hispanic (337)	504	2.21
American Indian/Alaska Native (80)	255	1.12
Not Hispanic (37)	157	0.69
Hispanic (43)	98	0.43
Blackfeet (0)	4	0.02
Central American Ind. (1)	3	0.01
Cherokee (2)	33	0.14
Chickasaw (0)	1	<0.01
Delaware (2)	2	0.01
Iroquois (0)	3	0.01
Lumbee (0)	1	<0.01
Mexican American Ind. (1)	1	<0.01
Pueblo (1)	1	<0.01
Seminole (0)	1	<0.01
Sioux (1)	3	0.01
South American Ind. (5)	8	0.04
Spanish American Ind. (7)	14	0.06
Tlingit-Haida *(Alaska Native)* (1)	3	0.01
Asian (4,349)	4,653	20.37
Not Hispanic (4,308)	4,543	19.89
Hispanic (41)	110	0.48
Bangladeshi (26)	27	0.12
Chinese, ex. Taiwanese (69)	98	0.43
Filipino (420)	458	2.00
Indian (3,113)	3,284	14.38
Indonesian (7)	8	0.04
Japanese (13)	20	0.09
Korean (57)	61	0.27
Malaysian (0)	1	<0.01
Nepalese (3)	3	0.01
Pakistani (519)	551	2.41
Sri Lankan (6)	17	0.07
Thai (5)	9	0.04
Vietnamese (44)	52	0.23
Hawaii Native/Pacific Islander (12)	40	0.18
Not Hispanic (6)	20	0.09
Hispanic (6)	20	0.09
Guamanian/Chamorro (0)	1	<0.01
Native Hawaiian (0)	1	<0.01
White (11,577)	12,101	52.97
Not Hispanic (7,812)	8,040	35.20
Hispanic (3,765)	4,061	17.78

Cedar Grove

Place Type: Township
County: Essex
Population: 12,411†

Ancestry‡	Population	%
African, Sub-Saharan (16)	16	0.13
African (8)	8	0.06
Nigerian (8)	8	0.06
Albanian (16)	35	0.28
American (138)	138	1.12
Arab (227)	474	3.85
Arab (123)	166	1.35
Egyptian (55)	92	0.75
Syrian (49)	216	1.75
Austrian (0)	54	0.44
Belgian (9)	22	0.18
Brazilian (38)	38	0.31
British (25)	37	0.30
Czech (0)	11	0.09
Danish (0)	18	0.15
Dutch (76)	197	1.60
Eastern European (33)	33	0.27
English (49)	498	4.04
European (170)	212	1.72
French, ex. Basque (19)	260	2.11
French Canadian (44)	44	0.36
German (316)	1,931	15.68
Greek (29)	37	0.30
Hungarian (47)	100	0.81
Irish (659)	2,193	17.81
Italian (2,495)	4,411	35.83
Lithuanian (26)	37	0.30
Norwegian (9)	47	0.38
Polish (317)	876	7.12
Portuguese (118)	134	1.09
Russian (81)	250	2.03
Scandinavian (12)	12	0.10
Scotch-Irish (65)	131	1.06
Scottish (28)	208	1.69
Slavic (0)	49	0.40
Slovak (0)	149	1.21
Swedish (15)	112	0.91
Swiss (0)	29	0.24
Turkish (13)	13	0.11
Ukrainian (85)	214	1.74
Welsh (0)	26	0.21
West Indian, ex. Hispanic (110)	110	0.89
Haitian (47)	47	0.38
Jamaican (63)	63	0.51

Hispanic Origin	Population	%
Hispanic or Latino (of any race)	727	5.86
Central American, ex. Mexican	42	0.34
Costa Rican	8	0.06
Guatemalan	11	0.09
Honduran	1	0.01
Nicaraguan	13	0.10
Panamanian	5	0.04
Salvadoran	4	0.03
Cuban	82	0.66
Dominican Republic	43	0.35
Mexican	46	0.37
Puerto Rican	223	1.80
South American	210	1.69
Argentinean	27	0.22
Bolivian	2	0.02
Chilean	3	0.02
Colombian	54	0.44
Ecuadorian	37	0.30
Paraguayan	1	0.01
Peruvian	69	0.56
Uruguayan	9	0.07
Venezuelan	7	0.06
Other South American	1	0.01
Other Hispanic or Latino	81	0.65

Race*	Population	%
African-American/Black (306)	326	2.63
Not Hispanic (294)	313	2.52
Hispanic (12)	13	0.10
American Indian/Alaska Native (6)	17	0.14
Not Hispanic (3)	14	0.11
Hispanic (3)	3	0.02
Cherokee (3)	4	0.03
Asian (811)	881	7.10
Not Hispanic (800)	861	6.94
Hispanic (11)	20	0.16
Chinese, ex. Taiwanese (156)	178	1.43
Filipino (197)	221	1.78
Indian (266)	280	2.26
Indonesian (1)	3	0.02
Japanese (28)	35	0.28
Korean (42)	49	0.39
Laotian (2)	2	0.02
Malaysian (0)	2	0.02
Pakistani (28)	28	0.23

*Notes: † The Census 2010 population figure is used to calculate the percentages in the Hispanic Origin and Race categories. Ancestry percentages are based on the 2006-2010 American Community Survey population (not shown); ‡ Numbers in parentheses indicate the number of people reporting a single ancestry; * Numbers in parentheses indicate the number of persons reporting this race alone, not in combination with any other race; Please refer to the Explanation of Data for more information.*

	Population	%
Sri Lankan (2)	2	0.02
Taiwanese (35)	35	0.28
Thai (5)	5	0.04
Vietnamese (14)	16	0.13
Hawaii Native/Pacific Islander (1)	5	0.04
Not Hispanic (1)	5	0.04
Native Hawaiian (1)	1	0.01
White (11,047)	11,159	89.91
Not Hispanic (10,475)	10,556	85.05
Hispanic (572)	603	4.86

Chatham

Place Type: Borough
County: Morris
Population: 8,962†

Ancestry‡	Population	%
Albanian (11)	22	0.25
American (92)	92	1.03
Arab (22)	37	0.42
Lebanese (12)	27	0.30
Moroccan (10)	10	0.11
Australian (4)	4	0.04
Austrian (25)	81	0.91
Belgian (0)	48	0.54
British (18)	54	0.61
Canadian (0)	31	0.35
Croatian (91)	107	1.20
Czech (0)	52	0.58
Czechoslovakian (0)	9	0.10
Danish (23)	129	1.45
Dutch (29)	163	1.83
Eastern European (12)	22	0.25
English (176)	1,011	11.37
European (77)	88	0.99
Finnish (28)	41	0.46
French, ex. Basque (66)	253	2.85
French Canadian (0)	15	0.17
German (274)	1,986	22.33
Greek (23)	136	1.53
Hungarian (60)	133	1.50
Irish (728)	3,144	35.36
Italian (862)	2,344	26.36
Lithuanian (13)	101	1.14
Macedonian (25)	34	0.38
Northern European (56)	56	0.63
Norwegian (10)	79	0.89
Pennsylvania German (0)	11	0.12
Polish (130)	644	7.24
Portuguese (55)	84	0.94
Romanian (0)	9	0.10
Russian (22)	161	1.81
Scandinavian (0)	12	0.13
Scotch-Irish (60)	95	1.07
Scottish (43)	93	1.05
Swedish (8)	109	1.23
Swiss (0)	18	0.20
Ukrainian (45)	72	0.81
Welsh (18)	145	1.63
Yugoslavian (45)	45	0.51

Hispanic Origin	Population	%
Hispanic or Latino (of any race)	457	5.10
Central American, ex. Mexican	84	0.94
Costa Rican	46	0.51
Guatemalan	20	0.22
Honduran	9	0.10
Nicaraguan	3	0.03
Panamanian	5	0.06
Salvadoran	1	0.01
Cuban	23	0.26
Dominican Republic	1	0.01
Mexican	59	0.66
Puerto Rican	64	0.71
South American	172	1.92
Argentinean	6	0.07
Bolivian	4	0.04
Chilean	7	0.08
Colombian	119	1.33
Ecuadorian	16	0.18
Paraguayan	2	0.02
Peruvian	9	0.10
Uruguayan	1	0.01
Venezuelan	6	0.07
Other South American	2	0.02
Other Hispanic or Latino	54	0.60

Race*	Population	%
African-American/Black (89)	129	1.44
Not Hispanic (85)	114	1.27
Hispanic (4)	15	0.17
American Indian/Alaska Native (18)	29	0.32
Not Hispanic (14)	23	0.26
Hispanic (4)	6	0.07
Apache (0)	2	0.02
Blackfeet (0)	1	0.01
Canadian/French Am. Ind. (0)	1	0.01
Cherokee (3)	4	0.04
Choctaw (4)	4	0.04
Delaware (0)	1	0.01
Iroquois (0)	2	0.02
Mexican American Ind. (1)	1	0.01
Tlingit-Haida *(Alaska Native)* (2)	2	0.02
Asian (435)	543	6.06
Not Hispanic (433)	532	5.94
Hispanic (2)	11	0.12
Chinese, ex. Taiwanese (174)	200	2.23
Filipino (42)	64	0.71
Indian (95)	113	1.26
Indonesian (1)	1	0.01
Japanese (10)	22	0.25
Korean (65)	79	0.88
Pakistani (13)	14	0.16
Sri Lankan (1)	1	0.01
Taiwanese (15)	20	0.22
Thai (2)	4	0.04
Vietnamese (4)	8	0.09
Hawaii Native/Pacific Islander (0)	4	0.04
Not Hispanic (0)	4	0.04
White (8,167)	8,317	92.80
Not Hispanic (7,825)	7,946	88.66
Hispanic (342)	371	4.14

Chatham

Place Type: Township
County: Morris
Population: 10,452†

Ancestry‡	Population	%
African, Sub-Saharan (12)	12	0.12
South African (12)	12	0.12
American (264)	264	2.53
Arab (80)	109	1.05
Egyptian (34)	34	0.33
Iraqi (17)	17	0.16
Lebanese (29)	29	0.28
Syrian (0)	29	0.28
Armenian (57)	57	0.55
Austrian (37)	202	1.94
British (130)	243	2.33
Canadian (29)	29	0.28
Czech (43)	86	0.82
Danish (27)	43	0.41
Dutch (54)	130	1.25
Eastern European (42)	42	0.40
English (370)	1,472	14.12
European (196)	196	1.88
Finnish (18)	28	0.27
French, ex. Basque (74)	212	2.03
French Canadian (0)	38	0.36
German (500)	2,177	20.88
Greek (53)	211	2.02
Hungarian (49)	83	0.80
Iranian (0)	51	0.49
Irish (868)	3,026	29.02
Italian (934)	2,306	22.12
Lithuanian (66)	143	1.37
Luxemburger (8)	16	0.15
New Zealander (0)	31	0.30
Norwegian (0)	45	0.43
Polish (223)	656	6.29
Portuguese (10)	22	0.21
Russian (130)	255	2.45
Scandinavian (0)	11	0.11
Scotch-Irish (66)	218	2.09
Scottish (54)	172	1.65
Serbian (12)	12	0.12
Slovak (29)	83	0.80
Swedish (19)	139	1.33
Swiss (34)	74	0.71
Turkish (30)	30	0.29
Ukrainian (0)	54	0.52
Welsh (0)	34	0.33
West Indian, ex. Hispanic (66)	66	0.63
Trinidadian/Tobagonian (66)	66	0.63

Hispanic Origin	Population	%
Hispanic or Latino (of any race)	349	3.34
Central American, ex. Mexican	36	0.34
Costa Rican	23	0.22
Guatemalan	6	0.06
Honduran	1	0.01
Nicaraguan	5	0.05
Salvadoran	1	0.01
Cuban	51	0.49
Dominican Republic	14	0.13
Mexican	68	0.65
Puerto Rican	48	0.46
South American	96	0.92
Argentinean	7	0.07
Chilean	2	0.02
Colombian	42	0.40
Ecuadorian	20	0.19
Peruvian	19	0.18
Venezuelan	6	0.06
Other Hispanic or Latino	36	0.34

Race*	Population	%
African-American/Black (78)	99	0.95
Not Hispanic (69)	88	0.84
Hispanic (9)	11	0.11
American Indian/Alaska Native (8)	19	0.18
Not Hispanic (6)	17	0.16
Hispanic (2)	2	0.02
Apache (0)	3	0.03
Cherokee (5)	11	0.11
Asian (665)	803	7.68
Not Hispanic (657)	794	7.60
Hispanic (8)	9	0.09
Bangladeshi (7)	7	0.07
Chinese, ex. Taiwanese (239)	301	2.88
Filipino (44)	67	0.64
Indian (216)	248	2.37
Japanese (17)	29	0.28
Korean (76)	93	0.89
Malaysian (1)	1	0.01
Pakistani (28)	30	0.29
Sri Lankan (1)	1	0.01
Taiwanese (9)	11	0.11
Thai (3)	6	0.06
Vietnamese (2)	5	0.05
Hawaii Native/Pacific Islander (1)	7	0.07
Not Hispanic (1)	7	0.07
Guamanian/Chamorro (1)	1	0.01
Native Hawaiian (0)	2	0.02
White (9,495)	9,653	92.36
Not Hispanic (9,197)	9,350	89.46
Hispanic (298)	303	2.90

Cherry Hill Mall

Place Type: CDP
County: Camden
Population: 14,171†

Ancestry‡	Population	%
African, Sub-Saharan (24)	52	0.37
African (9)	37	0.26

*Notes: † The Census 2010 population figure is used to calculate the percentages in the Hispanic Origin and Race categories. Ancestry percentages are based on the 2006-2010 American Community Survey population (not shown); ‡ Numbers in parentheses indicate the number of people reporting a single ancestry; * Numbers in parentheses indicate the number of persons reporting this race alone, not in combination with any other race; Please refer to the Explanation of Data for more information.*

Cape Verdean (15)	15	0.11
Albanian (46)	46	0.33
American (567)	567	4.06
Arab (224)	310	2.22
Arab (48)	48	0.34
Egyptian (23)	23	0.16
Moroccan (0)	52	0.37
Syrian (15)	32	0.23
Other Arab (138)	155	1.11
Austrian (31)	54	0.39
Belgian (0)	13	0.09
British (34)	59	0.42
Czech (15)	15	0.11
Czechoslovakian (0)	29	0.21
Danish (0)	63	0.45
Dutch (10)	138	0.99
Eastern European (93)	183	1.31
English (180)	759	5.43
European (122)	122	0.87
French, ex. Basque (0)	144	1.03
French Canadian (26)	26	0.19
German (397)	2,319	16.60
Greek (145)	168	1.20
Hungarian (19)	88	0.63
Irish (652)	2,543	18.20
Italian (1,161)	2,500	17.89
Latvian (0)	16	0.11
Lithuanian (32)	103	0.74
Luxemburger (0)	11	0.08
Northern European (30)	30	0.21
Norwegian (13)	26	0.19
Polish (503)	1,300	9.30
Portuguese (17)	17	0.12
Romanian (58)	83	0.59
Russian (487)	1,089	7.79
Scandinavian (28)	28	0.20
Scotch-Irish (51)	222	1.59
Scottish (30)	156	1.12
Slovak (42)	59	0.42
Slovene (14)	14	0.10
Swedish (0)	60	0.43
Swiss (12)	12	0.09
Ukrainian (115)	172	1.23
Welsh (0)	108	0.77

Hispanic Origin	Population	%
Hispanic or Latino (of any race)	1,014	7.16
Central American, ex. Mexican	93	0.66
Costa Rican	5	0.04
Guatemalan	20	0.14
Honduran	3	0.02
Nicaraguan	25	0.18
Panamanian	12	0.08
Salvadoran	18	0.13
Other Central American	10	0.07
Cuban	31	0.22
Dominican Republic	73	0.52
Mexican	167	1.18
Puerto Rican	455	3.21
South American	104	0.73
Argentinean	10	0.07
Bolivian	1	0.01
Chilean	8	0.06
Colombian	32	0.23
Ecuadorian	12	0.08
Paraguayan	2	0.01
Peruvian	18	0.13
Uruguayan	11	0.08
Venezuelan	8	0.06
Other South American	2	0.01
Other Hispanic or Latino	91	0.64

Race*	Population	%
African-American/Black (1,090)	1,225	8.64
Not Hispanic (1,039)	1,126	7.95
Hispanic (51)	99	0.70
American Indian/Alaska Native (22)	71	0.50
Not Hispanic (13)	56	0.40
Hispanic (9)	15	0.11
Blackfeet (0)	1	0.01
Central American Ind. (0)	2	0.01
Cherokee (5)	12	0.08
Delaware (0)	2	0.01
Iroquois (2)	2	0.01
South American Ind. (1)	1	0.01
Asian (1,832)	2,039	14.39
Not Hispanic (1,822)	2,013	14.21
Hispanic (10)	26	0.18
Bangladeshi (0)	1	0.01
Burmese (0)	1	0.01
Cambodian (42)	46	0.32
Chinese, ex. Taiwanese (321)	373	2.63
Filipino (311)	362	2.55
Indian (357)	388	2.74
Indonesian (5)	5	0.04
Japanese (16)	30	0.21
Korean (374)	399	2.82
Laotian (0)	2	0.01
Pakistani (48)	49	0.35
Taiwanese (26)	28	0.20
Thai (6)	6	0.04
Vietnamese (276)	302	2.13
Hawaii Native/Pacific Islander (2)	14	0.10
Not Hispanic (1)	8	0.06
Hispanic (1)	6	0.04
Guamanian/Chamorro (1)	3	0.02
Native Hawaiian (1)	3	0.02
White (10,515)	10,803	76.23
Not Hispanic (9,972)	10,196	71.95
Hispanic (543)	607	4.28

Cherry Hill

Place Type: Township
County: Camden
Population: 71,045†

Ancestry‡	Population	%
African, Sub-Saharan (204)	242	0.34
African (42)	78	0.11
Cape Verdean (15)	15	0.02
Ghanaian (9)	9	0.01
Kenyan (70)	70	0.10
Nigerian (15)	15	0.02
Other Sub-Saharan African (53)	55	0.08
Albanian (46)	46	0.06
American (2,809)	2,809	3.96
Arab (376)	561	0.79
Arab (48)	48	0.07
Egyptian (57)	57	0.08
Lebanese (0)	10	0.01
Moroccan (50)	149	0.21
Syrian (34)	51	0.07
Other Arab (187)	246	0.35
Armenian (150)	248	0.35
Australian (0)	20	0.03
Austrian (162)	720	1.01
Belgian (46)	85	0.12
Brazilian (116)	156	0.22
British (122)	365	0.51
Canadian (102)	162	0.23
Celtic (0)	35	0.05
Croatian (9)	45	0.06
Czech (36)	163	0.23
Czechoslovakian (0)	55	0.08
Danish (26)	210	0.30
Dutch (77)	583	0.82
Eastern European (816)	931	1.31
English (903)	5,050	7.12
European (478)	498	0.70
Finnish (11)	23	0.03
French, ex. Basque (124)	941	1.33
French Canadian (95)	232	0.33
German (2,208)	11,149	15.71
Greek (408)	524	0.74
Guyanese (121)	121	0.17
Hungarian (188)	668	0.94
Iranian (41)	41	0.06
Irish (3,568)	13,556	19.10
Israeli (330)	344	0.48
Italian (5,999)	12,695	17.89
Latvian (24)	61	0.09
Lithuanian (81)	343	0.48
Luxemburger (0)	11	0.02
Northern European (30)	47	0.07
Norwegian (71)	242	0.34
Pennsylvania German (35)	84	0.12
Polish (1,921)	5,334	7.52
Portuguese (91)	130	0.18
Romanian (222)	509	0.72
Russian (2,773)	5,175	7.29
Scandinavian (35)	126	0.18
Scotch-Irish (340)	895	1.26
Scottish (258)	833	1.17
Serbian (47)	47	0.07
Slavic (0)	54	0.08
Slovak (88)	199	0.28
Slovene (14)	28	0.04
Swedish (79)	471	0.66
Swiss (22)	130	0.18
Turkish (0)	15	0.02
Ukrainian (352)	637	0.90
Welsh (89)	487	0.69
West Indian, ex. Hispanic (202)	322	0.45
British West Indian (19)	45	0.06
Haitian (83)	107	0.15
Jamaican (70)	116	0.16
Trinidadian/Tobagonian (20)	44	0.06
U.S. Virgin Islander (10)	10	0.01
Yugoslavian (18)	73	0.10

Hispanic Origin	Population	%
Hispanic or Latino (of any race)	4,005	5.64
Central American, ex. Mexican	277	0.39
Costa Rican	23	0.03
Guatemalan	66	0.09
Honduran	27	0.04
Nicaraguan	61	0.09
Panamanian	41	0.06
Salvadoran	43	0.06
Other Central American	16	0.02
Cuban	155	0.22
Dominican Republic	270	0.38
Mexican	818	1.15
Puerto Rican	1,716	2.42
South American	455	0.64
Argentinean	61	0.09
Bolivian	6	0.01
Chilean	30	0.04
Colombian	156	0.22
Ecuadorian	70	0.10
Paraguayan	8	0.01
Peruvian	52	0.07
Uruguayan	24	0.03
Venezuelan	45	0.06
Other South American	3	<0.01
Other Hispanic or Latino	314	0.44

Race*	Population	%
African-American/Black (4,360)	4,957	6.98
Not Hispanic (4,161)	4,617	6.50
Hispanic (199)	340	0.48
American Indian/Alaska Native (78)	334	0.47
Not Hispanic (56)	261	0.37
Hispanic (22)	73	0.10
Apache (0)	3	<0.01
Blackfeet (2)	9	0.01
Canadian/French Am. Ind. (0)	6	0.01
Central American Ind. (0)	2	<0.01
Cherokee (11)	51	0.07
Chickasaw (0)	1	<0.01
Chippewa (2)	3	<0.01
Choctaw (0)	4	0.01
Delaware (1)	8	0.01
Iroquois (3)	8	0.01
Mexican American Ind. (0)	4	0.01
Pima (0)	1	<0.01
Potawatomi (1)	1	<0.01
Pueblo (1)	1	<0.01
Seminole (0)	2	<0.01

*Notes: † The Census 2010 population figure is used to calculate the percentages in the Hispanic Origin and Race categories. Ancestry percentages are based on the 2006-2010 American Community Survey population (not shown); ‡ Numbers in parentheses indicate the number of people reporting a single ancestry; * Numbers in parentheses indicate the number of persons reporting this race alone, not in combination with any other race; Please refer to the Explanation of Data for more information.*

Sioux (0)	5	0.01
South American Ind. (1)	2	<0.01
Spanish American Ind. (0)	1	<0.01
Asian (8,304)	9,049	12.74
Not Hispanic (8,259)	8,947	12.59
Hispanic (45)	102	0.14
Bangladeshi (74)	80	0.11
Burmese (2)	3	<0.01
Cambodian (98)	120	0.17
Chinese, ex. Taiwanese (1,975)	2,172	3.06
Filipino (1,423)	1,627	2.29
Hmong (1)	1	<0.01
Indian (1,861)	2,017	2.84
Indonesian (12)	15	0.02
Japanese (104)	178	0.25
Korean (1,352)	1,463	2.06
Laotian (2)	5	0.01
Malaysian (2)	4	0.01
Nepalese (3)	3	<0.01
Pakistani (170)	191	0.27
Sri Lankan (12)	16	0.02
Taiwanese (148)	178	0.25
Thai (35)	42	0.06
Vietnamese (799)	879	1.24
Hawaii Native/Pacific Islander (13)	67	0.09
Not Hispanic (9)	53	0.07
Hispanic (4)	14	0.02
Guamanian/Chamorro (4)	8	0.01
Native Hawaiian (6)	23	0.03
Samoan (0)	1	<0.01
White (55,459)	56,681	79.78
Not Hispanic (53,283)	54,244	76.35
Hispanic (2,176)	2,437	3.43

Chester

Place Type: Township
County: Morris
Population: 7,838†

Ancestry‡	Population	%
American (246)	246	3.17
Armenian (25)	47	0.61
Austrian (14)	40	0.52
Brazilian (3)	9	0.12
British (95)	144	1.86
Czech (51)	113	1.46
Czechoslovakian (40)	40	0.52
Danish (0)	6	0.08
Dutch (12)	196	2.53
Eastern European (67)	67	0.86
English (182)	974	12.55
European (84)	90	1.16
French, ex. Basque (101)	384	4.95
French Canadian (17)	42	0.54
German (306)	1,548	19.95
Greek (29)	99	1.28
Hungarian (14)	64	0.82
Irish (621)	1,993	25.69
Italian (942)	2,057	26.51
Lithuanian (0)	13	0.17
Maltese (0)	32	0.41
Norwegian (15)	133	1.71
Pennsylvania German (13)	13	0.17
Polish (63)	327	4.22
Portuguese (128)	173	2.23
Romanian (15)	26	0.34
Russian (95)	277	3.57
Scotch-Irish (30)	89	1.15
Scottish (0)	98	1.26
Serbian (0)	10	0.13
Slavic (0)	3	0.04
Slovak (58)	71	0.92
Swedish (39)	94	1.21
Swiss (14)	52	0.67
Ukrainian (27)	63	0.81
Welsh (15)	33	0.43
Yugoslavian (12)	12	0.15

Hispanic Origin	Population	%
Hispanic or Latino (of any race)	341	4.35
Central American, ex. Mexican	47	0.60
Costa Rican	11	0.14
Guatemalan	27	0.34
Honduran	8	0.10
Nicaraguan	1	0.01
Cuban	49	0.63
Dominican Republic	1	0.01
Mexican	57	0.73
Puerto Rican	53	0.68
South American	70	0.89
Argentinean	15	0.19
Bolivian	1	0.01
Chilean	2	0.03
Colombian	25	0.32
Ecuadorian	12	0.15
Paraguayan	6	0.08
Peruvian	3	0.04
Uruguayan	2	0.03
Venezuelan	3	0.04
Other South American	1	0.01
Other Hispanic or Latino	64	0.82

Race*	Population	%
African-American/Black (82)	107	1.37
Not Hispanic (77)	100	1.28
Hispanic (5)	7	0.09
American Indian/Alaska Native (2)	24	0.31
Not Hispanic (1)	20	0.26
Hispanic (1)	4	0.05
Cherokee (0)	2	0.03
Iroquois (1)	1	0.01
Mexican American Ind. (1)	1	0.01
Navajo (0)	3	0.04
Seminole (0)	1	0.01
Asian (274)	339	4.33
Not Hispanic (268)	333	4.25
Hispanic (6)	6	0.08
Cambodian (6)	6	0.08
Chinese, ex. Taiwanese (83)	115	1.47
Filipino (30)	38	0.48
Indian (73)	91	1.16
Indonesian (1)	1	0.01
Japanese (3)	6	0.08
Korean (31)	41	0.52
Malaysian (1)	1	0.01
Pakistani (19)	20	0.26
Sri Lankan (4)	5	0.06
Taiwanese (9)	9	0.11
Thai (1)	1	0.01
Vietnamese (4)	6	0.08
Hawaii Native/Pacific Islander (1)	4	0.05
Not Hispanic (1)	3	0.04
Hispanic (0)	1	0.01
Guamanian/Chamorro (0)	1	0.01
Native Hawaiian (0)	2	0.03
Samoan (1)	1	0.01
White (7,314)	7,428	94.77
Not Hispanic (7,034)	7,131	90.98
Hispanic (280)	297	3.79

Chesterfield

Place Type: Township
County: Burlington
Population: 7,699†

Ancestry‡	Population	%
African, Sub-Saharan (90)	115	1.55
African (65)	74	1.00
Kenyan (4)	13	0.18
Liberian (9)	9	0.12
South African (12)	19	0.26
American (94)	94	1.27
Arab (0)	8	0.11
Lebanese (0)	8	0.11
Armenian (9)	17	0.23
Austrian (104)	104	1.40
Basque (4)	4	0.05
Belgian (0)	5	0.07
British (11)	24	0.32
Croatian (0)	6	0.08
Czech (11)	55	0.74
Czechoslovakian (8)	8	0.11
Dutch (11)	81	1.09
English (38)	563	7.60
European (20)	36	0.49
French, ex. Basque (9)	83	1.12
French Canadian (8)	25	0.34
German (88)	644	8.69
Greek (7)	20	0.27
Guyanese (8)	8	0.11
Hungarian (24)	122	1.65
Irish (198)	846	11.41
Italian (192)	928	12.52
Lithuanian (0)	12	0.16
Polish (100)	401	5.41
Romanian (0)	23	0.31
Russian (5)	111	1.50
Scotch-Irish (15)	72	0.97
Scottish (22)	135	1.82
Slavic (5)	43	0.58
Slovak (5)	54	0.73
Swedish (0)	30	0.40
Swiss (0)	9	0.12
Ukrainian (21)	39	0.53
Welsh (0)	5	0.07
West Indian, ex. Hispanic (86)	158	2.13
Barbadian (0)	9	0.12
Jamaican (58)	121	1.63
Trinidadian/Tobagonian (19)	19	0.26
West Indian (9)	9	0.12

Hispanic Origin	Population	%
Hispanic or Latino (of any race)	1,007	13.08
Central American, ex. Mexican	71	0.92
Costa Rican	11	0.14
Guatemalan	16	0.21
Honduran	21	0.27
Nicaraguan	6	0.08
Panamanian	5	0.06
Salvadoran	12	0.16
Cuban	35	0.45
Dominican Republic	123	1.60
Mexican	123	1.60
Puerto Rican	511	6.64
South American	62	0.81
Argentinean	9	0.12
Colombian	22	0.29
Ecuadorian	19	0.25
Peruvian	11	0.14
Venezuelan	1	0.01
Other Hispanic or Latino	82	1.07

Race*	Population	%
African-American/Black (2,242)	2,385	30.98
Not Hispanic (2,053)	2,137	27.76
Hispanic (189)	248	3.22
American Indian/Alaska Native (39)	120	1.56
Not Hispanic (11)	68	0.88
Hispanic (28)	52	0.68
Apache (1)	1	0.01
Blackfeet (0)	1	0.01
Canadian/French Am. Ind. (3)	4	0.05
Cherokee (1)	6	0.08
Chippewa (0)	4	0.05
Choctaw (0)	1	0.01
Delaware (1)	1	0.01
Mexican American Ind. (2)	2	0.03
South American Ind. (5)	11	0.14
Spanish American Ind. (1)	1	0.01
Asian (643)	699	9.08
Not Hispanic (634)	679	8.82
Hispanic (9)	20	0.26
Bangladeshi (1)	1	0.01
Chinese, ex. Taiwanese (31)	47	0.61
Filipino (80)	90	1.17
Indian (460)	469	6.09
Japanese (1)	8	0.10

*Notes: † The Census 2010 population figure is used to calculate the percentages in the Hispanic Origin and Race categories. Ancestry percentages are based on the 2006-2010 American Community Survey population (not shown); ‡ Numbers in parentheses indicate the number of people reporting a single ancestry; * Numbers in parentheses indicate the number of persons reporting this race alone, not in combination with any other race; Please refer to the Explanation of Data for more information.*

Korean (32)	35	0.45
Laotian (4)	7	0.09
Pakistani (18)	19	0.25
Taiwanese (6)	6	0.08
Thai (0)	1	0.01
Vietnamese (6)	6	0.08
Hawaii Native/Pacific Islander (2)	13	0.17
Not Hispanic (0)	4	0.05
Hispanic (2)	9	0.12
Guamanian/Chamorro (2)	3	0.04
Native Hawaiian (0)	5	0.06
Samoan (0)	1	0.01
White (4,156)	4,291	55.73
Not Hispanic (3,851)	3,925	50.98
Hispanic (305)	366	4.75

Cinnaminson

Place Type: Township
County: Burlington
Population: 15,569†

Ancestry‡	Population	%
African, Sub-Saharan (38)	75	0.48
African (0)	37	0.24
Ethiopian (11)	11	0.07
Nigerian (27)	27	0.17
American (258)	258	1.66
Arab (8)	8	0.05
Lebanese (8)	8	0.05
Austrian (0)	74	0.48
British (8)	49	0.32
Canadian (8)	33	0.21
Croatian (0)	11	0.07
Czechoslovakian (0)	10	0.06
Danish (0)	19	0.12
Dutch (32)	151	0.97
English (337)	1,743	11.22
European (12)	12	0.08
Finnish (11)	35	0.23
French, ex. Basque (22)	314	2.02
German (701)	3,826	24.63
Greek (4)	23	0.15
Guyanese (0)	11	0.07
Hungarian (38)	145	0.93
Iranian (0)	57	0.37
Irish (1,264)	5,052	32.52
Italian (1,400)	3,866	24.89
Latvian (0)	73	0.47
Lithuanian (52)	236	1.52
Luxemburger (0)	3	0.02
New Zealander (0)	9	0.06
Norwegian (0)	19	0.12
Pennsylvania German (0)	30	0.19
Polish (273)	1,344	8.65
Portuguese (131)	131	0.84
Romanian (25)	35	0.23
Russian (18)	268	1.73
Scandinavian (0)	14	0.09
Scotch-Irish (138)	379	2.44
Scottish (32)	223	1.44
Slovak (38)	84	0.54
Slovene (0)	11	0.07
Swedish (33)	57	0.37
Swiss (0)	10	0.06
Turkish (195)	202	1.30
Ukrainian (61)	181	1.17
Welsh (36)	209	1.35
Yugoslavian (64)	97	0.62

Hispanic Origin	Population	%
Hispanic or Latino (of any race)	478	3.07
Central American, ex. Mexican	34	0.22
Costa Rican	3	0.02
Guatemalan	10	0.06
Honduran	8	0.05
Nicaraguan	2	0.01
Panamanian	3	0.02
Salvadoran	8	0.05
Cuban	35	0.22
Dominican Republic	11	0.07
Mexican	48	0.31
Puerto Rican	268	1.72
South American	41	0.26
Argentinean	2	0.01
Bolivian	1	0.01
Chilean	3	0.02
Colombian	14	0.09
Ecuadorian	6	0.04
Peruvian	13	0.08
Other South American	2	0.01
Other Hispanic or Latino	41	0.26

Race*	Population	%
African-American/Black (855)	954	6.13
Not Hispanic (832)	918	5.90
Hispanic (23)	36	0.23
American Indian/Alaska Native (13)	67	0.43
Not Hispanic (10)	60	0.39
Hispanic (3)	7	0.04
Apache (0)	4	0.03
Blackfeet (3)	3	0.02
Cherokee (4)	17	0.11
Chippewa (0)	1	0.01
Delaware (0)	1	0.01
Iroquois (1)	2	0.01
Mexican American Ind. (0)	2	0.01
Seminole (0)	1	0.01
Tlingit-Haida *(Alaska Native)* (0)	1	0.01
Asian (370)	454	2.92
Not Hispanic (365)	444	2.85
Hispanic (5)	10	0.06
Burmese (3)	3	0.02
Cambodian (1)	1	0.01
Chinese, ex. Taiwanese (76)	81	0.52
Filipino (44)	64	0.41
Indian (119)	127	0.82
Japanese (7)	24	0.15
Korean (61)	71	0.46
Pakistani (3)	7	0.04
Sri Lankan (11)	12	0.08
Taiwanese (6)	7	0.04
Thai (5)	7	0.04
Vietnamese (33)	34	0.22
Hawaii Native/Pacific Islander (3)	10	0.06
Not Hispanic (3)	10	0.06
Fijian (0)	1	0.01
Guamanian/Chamorro (0)	4	0.03
Native Hawaiian (2)	4	0.03
Samoan (0)	1	0.01
White (13,931)	14,140	90.82
Not Hispanic (13,628)	13,817	88.75
Hispanic (303)	323	2.07

City of Orange

Place Type: Township
County: Essex
Population: 30,134†

Ancestry‡	Population	%
African, Sub-Saharan (2,432)	2,755	9.07
African (693)	834	2.74
Cape Verdean (53)	53	0.17
Ethiopian (46)	46	0.15
Ghanaian (604)	604	1.99
Kenyan (23)	23	0.08
Liberian (22)	22	0.07
Nigerian (778)	910	2.99
Sudanese (85)	85	0.28
Other Sub-Saharan African (128)	178	0.59
American (578)	578	1.90
Brazilian (21)	21	0.07
Danish (0)	10	0.03
Dutch (0)	36	0.12
English (54)	321	1.06
French, ex. Basque (13)	52	0.17
German (134)	409	1.35
Greek (0)	89	0.29
Guyanese (280)	481	1.58
Hungarian (15)	15	0.05
Irish (128)	340	1.12
Italian (345)	662	2.18
Lithuanian (11)	11	0.04
Polish (40)	202	0.66
Portuguese (11)	11	0.04
Russian (20)	48	0.16
Scotch-Irish (11)	42	0.14
Scottish (0)	12	0.04
Swedish (0)	28	0.09
West Indian, ex. Hispanic (5,690)	6,099	20.07
Barbadian (80)	80	0.26
Belizean (16)	16	0.05
British West Indian (100)	100	0.33
Dutch West Indian (33)	33	0.11
Haitian (2,822)	3,013	9.91
Jamaican (2,141)	2,334	7.68
Trinidadian/Tobagonian (258)	283	0.93
West Indian (240)	240	0.79

Hispanic Origin	Population	%
Hispanic or Latino (of any race)	6,531	21.67
Central American, ex. Mexican	1,514	5.02
Costa Rican	79	0.26
Guatemalan	434	1.44
Honduran	144	0.48
Nicaraguan	11	0.04
Panamanian	32	0.11
Salvadoran	809	2.68
Other Central American	5	0.02
Cuban	74	0.25
Dominican Republic	509	1.69
Mexican	856	2.84
Puerto Rican	523	1.74
South American	2,375	7.88
Argentinean	39	0.13
Bolivian	72	0.24
Chilean	2	0.01
Colombian	77	0.26
Ecuadorian	1,210	4.02
Paraguayan	1	<0.01
Peruvian	491	1.63
Uruguayan	445	1.48
Venezuelan	9	0.03
Other South American	29	0.10
Other Hispanic or Latino	680	2.26

Race*	Population	%
African-American/Black (21,645)	22,223	73.75
Not Hispanic (21,067)	21,461	71.22
Hispanic (578)	762	2.53
American Indian/Alaska Native (173)	352	1.17
Not Hispanic (114)	247	0.82
Hispanic (59)	105	0.35
Alaska Athabascan *(Ala. Nat.)* (1)	1	<0.01
Apache (1)	6	0.02
Arapaho (0)	1	<0.01
Blackfeet (2)	20	0.07
Central American Ind. (5)	8	0.03
Cherokee (14)	49	0.16
Creek (0)	2	0.01
Delaware (1)	1	<0.01
Iroquois (1)	1	<0.01
Lumbee (0)	2	0.01
Mexican American Ind. (8)	11	0.04
Seminole (1)	2	0.01
Sioux (1)	5	0.02
South American Ind. (6)	20	0.07
Spanish American Ind. (6)	6	0.02
Asian (455)	558	1.85
Not Hispanic (448)	510	1.69
Hispanic (7)	48	0.16
Bangladeshi (7)	7	0.02
Burmese (1)	1	<0.01
Chinese, ex. Taiwanese (24)	42	0.14
Filipino (156)	170	0.56
Indian (221)	269	0.89
Indonesian (2)	2	0.01
Japanese (1)	5	0.02
Korean (23)	28	0.09

*Notes: † The Census 2010 population figure is used to calculate the percentages in the Hispanic Origin and Race categories. Ancestry percentages are based on the 2006-2010 American Community Survey population (not shown); ‡ Numbers in parentheses indicate the number of people reporting a single ancestry; * Numbers in parentheses indicate the number of persons reporting this race alone, not in combination with any other race; Please refer to the Explanation of Data for more information.*

Laotian (1)	1	<0.01
Pakistani (10)	10	0.03
Sri Lankan (2)	2	0.01
Vietnamese (3)	3	0.01
Hawaii Native/Pacific Islander (6)	79	0.26
Not Hispanic (3)	61	0.20
Hispanic (3)	18	0.06
Guamanian/Chamorro (3)	6	0.02
Native Hawaiian (1)	3	0.01
Samoan (0)	1	<0.01
White (3,857)	4,482	14.87
Not Hispanic (1,357)	1,551	5.15
Hispanic (2,500)	2,931	9.73

Clark

Place Type: Township
County: Union
Population: 14,756†

Ancestry‡	Population	%
Albanian (0)	31	0.21
American (940)	940	6.44
Arab (93)	93	0.64
Egyptian (31)	31	0.21
Lebanese (62)	62	0.42
Armenian (53)	63	0.43
Australian (0)	10	0.07
Austrian (32)	41	0.28
British (0)	11	0.08
Canadian (10)	10	0.07
Croatian (0)	15	0.10
Czech (88)	125	0.86
Czechoslovakian (31)	96	0.66
Danish (0)	42	0.29
Dutch (34)	150	1.03
Eastern European (0)	20	0.14
English (81)	587	4.02
European (44)	44	0.30
Finnish (0)	13	0.09
French, ex. Basque (0)	151	1.03
French Canadian (14)	71	0.49
German (536)	2,293	15.71
Greek (139)	203	1.39
Hungarian (43)	121	0.83
Iranian (36)	36	0.25
Irish (695)	2,867	19.64
Israeli (10)	10	0.07
Italian (1,952)	4,306	29.50
Lithuanian (92)	164	1.12
Luxemburger (13)	13	0.09
Norwegian (0)	47	0.32
Pennsylvania German (22)	22	0.15
Polish (954)	2,350	16.10
Portuguese (520)	594	4.07
Russian (137)	273	1.87
Scotch-Irish (32)	186	1.27
Scottish (45)	156	1.07
Slavic (15)	15	0.10
Slovak (101)	267	1.83
Swedish (0)	134	0.92
Ukrainian (229)	358	2.45
Welsh (0)	15	0.10
West Indian, ex. Hispanic (0)	11	0.08
West Indian (0)	11	0.08

Hispanic Origin	Population	%
Hispanic or Latino (of any race)	1,107	7.50
Central American, ex. Mexican	62	0.42
Costa Rican	8	0.05
Guatemalan	18	0.12
Honduran	18	0.12
Nicaraguan	5	0.03
Salvadoran	13	0.09
Cuban	202	1.37
Dominican Republic	45	0.30
Mexican	41	0.28
Puerto Rican	237	1.61
South American	316	2.14
Argentinean	51	0.35
Chilean	10	0.07
Colombian	110	0.75
Ecuadorian	59	0.40
Paraguayan	4	0.03
Peruvian	46	0.31
Uruguayan	31	0.21
Venezuelan	5	0.03
Other Hispanic or Latino	204	1.38

Race*	Population	%
African-American/Black (124)	153	1.04
Not Hispanic (116)	135	0.91
Hispanic (8)	18	0.12
American Indian/Alaska Native (15)	42	0.28
Not Hispanic (7)	27	0.18
Hispanic (8)	15	0.10
Apache (1)	4	0.03
Blackfeet (1)	2	0.01
Cherokee (0)	3	0.02
Comanche (0)	3	0.02
Delaware (0)	1	0.01
Iroquois (1)	1	0.01
Mexican American Ind. (1)	1	0.01
Pueblo (2)	2	0.01
Sioux (0)	1	0.01
South American Ind. (0)	3	0.02
Asian (547)	590	4.00
Not Hispanic (527)	565	3.83
Hispanic (20)	25	0.17
Cambodian (1)	3	0.02
Chinese, ex. Taiwanese (142)	157	1.06
Filipino (148)	160	1.08
Indian (151)	156	1.06
Japanese (4)	6	0.04
Korean (65)	69	0.47
Laotian (2)	4	0.03
Pakistani (8)	8	0.05
Sri Lankan (5)	5	0.03
Taiwanese (1)	2	0.01
Vietnamese (13)	14	0.09
Hawaii Native/Pacific Islander (5)	9	0.06
Not Hispanic (4)	8	0.05
Hispanic (1)	1	0.01
Guamanian/Chamorro (1)	1	0.01
Native Hawaiian (0)	2	0.01
White (13,766)	13,890	94.13
Not Hispanic (12,874)	12,965	87.86
Hispanic (892)	925	6.27

Clayton

Place Type: Borough
County: Gloucester
Population: 8,179†

Ancestry‡	Population	%
American (172)	172	2.13
British (0)	14	0.17
Canadian (15)	29	0.36
Czechoslovakian (19)	19	0.24
Dutch (0)	76	0.94
English (87)	759	9.41
European (14)	14	0.17
French, ex. Basque (0)	81	1.00
German (371)	2,248	27.88
Irish (400)	2,215	27.47
Italian (1,184)	2,012	24.95
Lithuanian (0)	63	0.78
Norwegian (0)	14	0.17
Polish (194)	549	6.81
Romanian (0)	13	0.16
Russian (11)	56	0.69
Scotch-Irish (0)	42	0.52
Scottish (55)	204	2.53
Slovak (22)	22	0.27
Swedish (0)	13	0.16
Turkish (171)	171	2.12
Ukrainian (0)	11	0.14
Welsh (0)	38	0.47
West Indian, ex. Hispanic (53)	53	0.66
Barbadian (14)	14	0.17
Jamaican (39)	39	0.48

Hispanic Origin	Population	%
Hispanic or Latino (of any race)	487	5.95
Central American, ex. Mexican	17	0.21
Honduran	2	0.02
Panamanian	3	0.04
Salvadoran	12	0.15
Cuban	10	0.12
Dominican Republic	10	0.12
Mexican	88	1.08
Puerto Rican	306	3.74
South American	21	0.26
Argentinean	1	0.01
Chilean	2	0.02
Colombian	10	0.12
Ecuadorian	2	0.02
Peruvian	5	0.06
Venezuelan	1	0.01
Other Hispanic or Latino	35	0.43

Race*	Population	%
African-American/Black (1,473)	1,660	20.30
Not Hispanic (1,392)	1,554	19.00
Hispanic (81)	106	1.30
American Indian/Alaska Native (30)	81	0.99
Not Hispanic (23)	69	0.84
Hispanic (7)	12	0.15
Blackfeet (5)	8	0.10
Cherokee (3)	19	0.23
Chippewa (0)	1	0.01
Delaware (0)	1	0.01
Inupiat *(Alaska Native)* (0)	1	0.01
Iroquois (0)	2	0.02
Navajo (0)	2	0.02
Pueblo (1)	1	0.01
Seminole (0)	2	0.02
South American Ind. (1)	1	0.01
Asian (147)	223	2.73
Not Hispanic (145)	214	2.62
Hispanic (2)	9	0.11
Chinese, ex. Taiwanese (31)	38	0.46
Filipino (57)	83	1.01
Indian (38)	43	0.53
Japanese (3)	18	0.22
Korean (5)	10	0.12
Pakistani (7)	7	0.09
Taiwanese (0)	1	0.01
Thai (0)	3	0.04
Vietnamese (6)	12	0.15
Hawaii Native/Pacific Islander (2)	4	0.05
Not Hispanic (2)	4	0.05
Native Hawaiian (2)	2	0.02
White (6,120)	6,356	77.71
Not Hispanic (5,876)	6,087	74.42
Hispanic (244)	269	3.29

Cliffside Park

Place Type: Borough
County: Bergen
Population: 23,594†

Ancestry‡	Population	%
African, Sub-Saharan (47)	47	0.20
African (47)	47	0.20
Albanian (102)	102	0.44
American (564)	564	2.41
Arab (523)	579	2.48
Arab (33)	33	0.14
Egyptian (192)	220	0.94
Iraqi (0)	16	0.07
Lebanese (14)	14	0.06
Palestinian (215)	215	0.92
Syrian (69)	81	0.35
Armenian (408)	425	1.82
Australian (13)	13	0.06
Austrian (0)	56	0.24
Brazilian (77)	77	0.33

*Notes: † The Census 2010 population figure is used to calculate the percentages in the Hispanic Origin and Race categories. Ancestry percentages are based on the 2006-2010 American Community Survey population (not shown); ‡ Numbers in parentheses indicate the number of people reporting a single ancestry; * Numbers in parentheses indicate the number of persons reporting this race alone, not in combination with any other race; Please refer to the Explanation of Data for more information.*

British (0)	76	0.33
Croatian (612)	750	3.21
Czech (25)	39	0.17
Danish (13)	33	0.14
Dutch (18)	32	0.14
Eastern European (78)	78	0.33
English (54)	315	1.35
European (38)	38	0.16
French, ex. Basque (141)	214	0.92
French Canadian (0)	15	0.06
German (275)	1,115	4.77
Greek (516)	598	2.56
Guyanese (0)	17	0.07
Hungarian (100)	230	0.98
Iranian (46)	46	0.20
Irish (608)	1,650	7.06
Israeli (62)	88	0.38
Italian (2,885)	4,246	18.17
Lithuanian (37)	50	0.21
Maltese (0)	18	0.08
Norwegian (12)	24	0.10
Polish (342)	948	4.06
Portuguese (264)	264	1.13
Romanian (45)	95	0.41
Russian (958)	1,139	4.87
Scotch-Irish (0)	49	0.21
Scottish (33)	65	0.28
Serbian (0)	7	0.03
Swedish (0)	39	0.17
Swiss (0)	17	0.07
Turkish (360)	360	1.54
Ukrainian (166)	184	0.79
West Indian, ex. Hispanic (9)	9	0.04
Jamaican (9)	9	0.04
Yugoslavian (42)	54	0.23

Hispanic Origin	Population	%
Hispanic or Latino (of any race)	6,704	28.41
Central American, ex. Mexican	2,011	8.52
Costa Rican	17	0.07
Guatemalan	1,044	4.42
Honduran	88	0.37
Nicaraguan	26	0.11
Panamanian	18	0.08
Salvadoran	802	3.40
Other Central American	16	0.07
Cuban	765	3.24
Dominican Republic	852	3.61
Mexican	191	0.81
Puerto Rican	846	3.59
South American	1,458	6.18
Argentinean	66	0.28
Bolivian	6	0.03
Chilean	95	0.40
Colombian	652	2.76
Ecuadorian	414	1.75
Paraguayan	3	0.01
Peruvian	154	0.65
Uruguayan	25	0.11
Venezuelan	41	0.17
Other South American	2	0.01
Other Hispanic or Latino	581	2.46

Race*	Population	%
African-American/Black (776)	964	4.09
Not Hispanic (584)	669	2.84
Hispanic (192)	295	1.25
American Indian/Alaska Native (75)	186	0.79
Not Hispanic (24)	63	0.27
Hispanic (51)	123	0.52
Central American Ind. (3)	5	0.02
Cherokee (0)	8	0.03
Chippewa (0)	3	0.01
Creek (0)	1	<0.01
Mexican American Ind. (15)	39	0.17
Navajo (5)	5	0.02
Seminole (1)	1	<0.01
Sioux (1)	4	0.02
South American Ind. (4)	22	0.09
Spanish American Ind. (0)	3	0.01
Asian (3,252)	3,535	14.98
Not Hispanic (3,219)	3,448	14.61
Hispanic (33)	87	0.37
Bangladeshi (10)	12	0.05
Burmese (8)	8	0.03
Cambodian (4)	5	0.02
Chinese, ex. Taiwanese (489)	527	2.23
Filipino (191)	220	0.93
Indian (328)	361	1.53
Indonesian (5)	5	0.02
Japanese (253)	278	1.18
Korean (1,797)	1,828	7.75
Laotian (1)	3	0.01
Malaysian (2)	2	0.01
Pakistani (38)	42	0.18
Sri Lankan (1)	1	<0.01
Taiwanese (40)	48	0.20
Thai (14)	14	0.06
Vietnamese (20)	25	0.11
Hawaii Native/Pacific Islander (11)	38	0.16
Not Hispanic (10)	28	0.12
Hispanic (1)	10	0.04
Guamanian/Chamorro (6)	8	0.03
Samoan (0)	1	<0.01
White (16,541)	17,302	73.33
Not Hispanic (12,434)	12,816	54.32
Hispanic (4,107)	4,486	19.01

Clifton

Place Type: City
County: Passaic
Population: 84,136†

Ancestry‡	Population	%
African, Sub-Saharan (309)	342	0.41
African (205)	238	0.29
Cape Verdean (26)	26	0.03
Ethiopian (22)	22	0.03
Ghanaian (17)	17	0.02
Sudanese (39)	39	0.05
Albanian (532)	543	0.66
American (1,736)	1,736	2.10
Arab (3,492)	3,816	4.61
Arab (1,177)	1,177	1.42
Egyptian (356)	502	0.61
Jordanian (135)	135	0.16
Lebanese (140)	169	0.20
Palestinian (345)	356	0.43
Syrian (463)	601	0.73
Other Arab (876)	876	1.06
Armenian (176)	215	0.26
Australian (9)	9	0.01
Austrian (136)	433	0.52
Belgian (0)	71	0.09
Brazilian (73)	124	0.15
British (15)	37	0.04
Bulgarian (107)	107	0.13
Canadian (0)	23	0.03
Carpatho Rusyn (0)	34	0.04
Croatian (103)	124	0.15
Czech (102)	310	0.37
Czechoslovakian (169)	220	0.27
Danish (8)	71	0.09
Dutch (222)	1,091	1.32
Eastern European (112)	122	0.15
English (441)	2,406	2.91
European (325)	485	0.59
Finnish (0)	22	0.03
French, ex. Basque (118)	588	0.71
French Canadian (21)	107	0.13
German (1,353)	4,521	5.46
German Russian (0)	16	0.02
Greek (238)	391	0.47
Hungarian (358)	1,249	1.51
Iranian (131)	141	0.17
Irish (2,490)	7,107	8.59
Israeli (76)	111	0.13
Italian (7,150)	12,158	14.69
Latvian (0)	19	0.02
Lithuanian (11)	118	0.14
Macedonian (230)	230	0.28
Northern European (14)	14	0.02
Norwegian (8)	161	0.19
Pennsylvania German (41)	41	0.05
Polish (6,187)	8,833	10.67
Portuguese (209)	316	0.38
Romanian (99)	122	0.15
Russian (956)	1,923	2.32
Scandinavian (0)	8	0.01
Scotch-Irish (110)	562	0.68
Scottish (134)	752	0.91
Serbian (149)	182	0.22
Slavic (48)	95	0.11
Slovak (589)	913	1.10
Slovene (0)	22	0.03
Soviet Union (23)	23	0.03
Swedish (53)	463	0.56
Swiss (18)	82	0.10
Turkish (1,078)	1,122	1.36
Ukrainian (1,073)	1,493	1.80
Welsh (21)	156	0.19
West Indian, ex. Hispanic (392)	456	0.55
Barbadian (17)	17	0.02
British West Indian (15)	26	0.03
Haitian (104)	138	0.17
Jamaican (180)	199	0.24
Trinidadian/Tobagonian (60)	60	0.07
West Indian (16)	16	0.02
Yugoslavian (328)	364	0.44

Hispanic Origin	Population	%
Hispanic or Latino (of any race)	26,854	31.92
Central American, ex. Mexican	1,036	1.23
Costa Rican	163	0.19
Guatemalan	227	0.27
Honduran	215	0.26
Nicaraguan	50	0.06
Panamanian	28	0.03
Salvadoran	345	0.41
Other Central American	8	0.01
Cuban	754	0.90
Dominican Republic	4,561	5.42
Mexican	3,538	4.21
Puerto Rican	5,969	7.09
South American	9,347	11.11
Argentinean	243	0.29
Bolivian	255	0.30
Chilean	149	0.18
Colombian	2,973	3.53
Ecuadorian	993	1.18
Paraguayan	14	0.02
Peruvian	4,473	5.32
Uruguayan	78	0.09
Venezuelan	153	0.18
Other South American	16	0.02
Other Hispanic or Latino	1,649	1.96

Race*	Population	%
African-American/Black (4,137)	4,938	5.87
Not Hispanic (3,235)	3,538	4.21
Hispanic (902)	1,400	1.66
American Indian/Alaska Native (419)	698	0.83
Not Hispanic (105)	237	0.28
Hispanic (314)	461	0.55
Apache (1)	1	<0.01
Blackfeet (0)	8	0.01
Canadian/French Am. Ind. (3)	4	<0.01
Central American Ind. (15)	20	0.02
Cherokee (7)	27	0.03
Chickasaw (2)	2	<0.01
Choctaw (5)	5	0.01
Comanche (1)	1	<0.01
Creek (3)	3	<0.01
Delaware (8)	14	0.02
Hopi (1)	1	<0.01
Iroquois (6)	6	0.01
Kiowa (0)	1	<0.01
Mexican American Ind. (50)	59	0.07
Navajo (1)	3	<0.01

*Notes: † The Census 2010 population figure is used to calculate the percentages in the Hispanic Origin and Race categories. Ancestry percentages are based on the 2006-2010 American Community Survey population (not shown); ‡ Numbers in parentheses indicate the number of people reporting a single ancestry; * Numbers in parentheses indicate the number of persons reporting this race alone, not in combination with any other race; Please refer to the Explanation of Data for more information.*

Pueblo (3)	3	<0.01
Seminole (1)	3	<0.01
Sioux (2)	4	<0.01
South American Ind. (57)	83	0.10
Spanish American Ind. (18)	24	0.03
Asian (7,488)	8,502	10.11
Not Hispanic (7,401)	8,268	9.83
Hispanic (87)	234	0.28
Bangladeshi (159)	173	0.21
Burmese (4)	4	<0.01
Cambodian (2)	2	<0.01
Chinese, ex. Taiwanese (555)	680	0.81
Filipino (2,045)	2,224	2.64
Indian (3,702)	3,899	4.63
Indonesian (29)	33	0.04
Japanese (132)	188	0.22
Korean (405)	433	0.51
Laotian (4)	5	0.01
Malaysian (1)	2	<0.01
Pakistani (136)	163	0.19
Sri Lankan (11)	12	0.01
Taiwanese (23)	27	0.03
Thai (28)	48	0.06
Vietnamese (46)	53	0.06
Hawaii Native/Pacific Islander (22)	145	0.17
Not Hispanic (11)	71	0.08
Hispanic (11)	74	0.09
Guamanian/Chamorro (7)	14	0.02
Native Hawaiian (0)	11	0.01
Samoan (0)	1	<0.01
White (58,588)	60,942	72.43
Not Hispanic (44,870)	45,898	54.55
Hispanic (13,718)	15,044	17.88

Clinton

Place Type: Township
County: Hunterdon
Population: 13,478†

Ancestry‡	Population	%
Afghan (5)	5	0.04
African, Sub-Saharan (8)	34	0.25
African (8)	34	0.25
Albanian (13)	13	0.10
American (345)	345	2.55
Arab (96)	102	0.75
Egyptian (83)	83	0.61
Lebanese (0)	6	0.04
Other Arab (13)	13	0.10
Armenian (8)	8	0.06
Austrian (34)	110	0.81
Brazilian (19)	19	0.14
British (75)	129	0.95
Croatian (0)	15	0.11
Czech (12)	94	0.70
Czechoslovakian (0)	20	0.15
Danish (0)	143	1.06
Dutch (29)	241	1.78
Eastern European (37)	37	0.27
English (367)	1,606	11.88
European (107)	107	0.79
Finnish (5)	21	0.16
French, ex. Basque (87)	429	3.17
French Canadian (25)	66	0.49
German (679)	3,264	24.14
Greek (93)	195	1.44
Guyanese (8)	8	0.06
Hungarian (31)	365	2.70
Irish (597)	3,038	22.47
Israeli (13)	13	0.10
Italian (870)	2,581	19.09
Latvian (9)	9	0.07
Lithuanian (27)	94	0.70
Maltese (10)	33	0.24
Norwegian (24)	75	0.55
Pennsylvania German (15)	23	0.17
Polish (289)	1,390	10.28
Portuguese (13)	28	0.21
Romanian (56)	65	0.48
Russian (104)	337	2.49
Scandinavian (13)	37	0.27
Scotch-Irish (66)	275	2.03
Scottish (75)	303	2.24
Slovak (82)	240	1.78
Slovene (14)	57	0.42
Swedish (11)	95	0.70
Swiss (0)	8	0.06
Turkish (7)	11	0.08
Ukrainian (41)	175	1.29
Welsh (6)	107	0.79
West Indian, ex. Hispanic (30)	57	0.42
Haitian (0)	13	0.10
Jamaican (16)	16	0.12
Trinidadian/Tobagonian (0)	14	0.10
West Indian (14)	14	0.10
Yugoslavian (0)	7	0.05

Hispanic Origin	Population	%
Hispanic or Latino (of any race)	755	5.60
Central American, ex. Mexican	72	0.53
Costa Rican	26	0.19
Guatemalan	6	0.04
Honduran	14	0.10
Nicaraguan	2	0.01
Panamanian	6	0.04
Salvadoran	18	0.13
Cuban	54	0.40
Dominican Republic	60	0.45
Mexican	112	0.83
Puerto Rican	290	2.15
South American	94	0.70
Argentinean	14	0.10
Bolivian	3	0.02
Chilean	13	0.10
Colombian	32	0.24
Ecuadorian	15	0.11
Paraguayan	1	0.01
Peruvian	8	0.06
Uruguayan	6	0.04
Venezuelan	2	0.01
Other Hispanic or Latino	73	0.54

Race*	Population	%
African-American/Black (810)	873	6.48
Not Hispanic (734)	783	5.81
Hispanic (76)	90	0.67
American Indian/Alaska Native (27)	69	0.51
Not Hispanic (18)	55	0.41
Hispanic (9)	14	0.10
Cherokee (2)	9	0.07
Chippewa (0)	1	0.01
Choctaw (4)	4	0.03
Iroquois (0)	1	0.01
Lumbee (0)	3	0.02
Mexican American Ind. (2)	3	0.02
Potawatomi (0)	1	0.01
Puget Sound Salish (0)	1	0.01
Seminole (1)	1	0.01
Sioux (0)	1	0.01
Asian (525)	633	4.70
Not Hispanic (523)	621	4.61
Hispanic (2)	12	0.09
Bangladeshi (4)	4	0.03
Cambodian (1)	1	0.01
Chinese, ex. Taiwanese (176)	214	1.59
Filipino (34)	54	0.40
Indian (180)	206	1.53
Indonesian (1)	1	0.01
Japanese (11)	24	0.18
Korean (39)	41	0.30
Laotian (6)	6	0.04
Pakistani (26)	28	0.21
Taiwanese (28)	29	0.22
Thai (1)	4	0.03
Vietnamese (11)	16	0.12
Hawaii Native/Pacific Islander (6)	20	0.15
Not Hispanic (6)	16	0.12
Hispanic (0)	4	0.03
Guamanian/Chamorro (0)	1	0.01
Native Hawaiian (0)	7	0.05
Samoan (0)	1	0.01
White (11,649)	11,831	87.78
Not Hispanic (11,239)	11,383	84.46
Hispanic (410)	448	3.32

Closter

Place Type: Borough
County: Bergen
Population: 8,373†

Ancestry‡	Population	%
Albanian (45)	45	0.54
American (336)	336	4.04
Arab (56)	73	0.88
Lebanese (48)	48	0.58
Moroccan (8)	25	0.30
Armenian (33)	40	0.48
Austrian (26)	102	1.23
Belgian (9)	9	0.11
Brazilian (11)	22	0.26
British (22)	22	0.26
Canadian (12)	12	0.14
Croatian (87)	105	1.26
Czechoslovakian (0)	10	0.12
Dutch (14)	27	0.32
Eastern European (192)	209	2.51
English (171)	407	4.89
European (96)	96	1.15
French, ex. Basque (39)	75	0.90
French Canadian (8)	8	0.10
German (353)	791	9.51
Greek (44)	69	0.83
Hungarian (0)	10	0.12
Irish (288)	798	9.59
Israeli (103)	103	1.24
Italian (449)	1,017	12.23
Latvian (0)	9	0.11
Lithuanian (9)	16	0.19
Norwegian (10)	49	0.59
Polish (122)	342	4.11
Romanian (11)	20	0.24
Russian (180)	471	5.66
Scotch-Irish (12)	52	0.63
Scottish (26)	61	0.73
Slovak (8)	28	0.34
Swedish (23)	30	0.36
Swiss (43)	82	0.99
Turkish (45)	45	0.54
Ukrainian (21)	47	0.57
Welsh (0)	10	0.12
Yugoslavian (7)	7	0.08

Hispanic Origin	Population	%
Hispanic or Latino (of any race)	501	5.98
Central American, ex. Mexican	80	0.96
Costa Rican	20	0.24
Guatemalan	23	0.27
Nicaraguan	4	0.05
Panamanian	4	0.05
Salvadoran	29	0.35
Cuban	85	1.02
Dominican Republic	45	0.54
Mexican	40	0.48
Puerto Rican	96	1.15
South American	112	1.34
Argentinean	14	0.17
Bolivian	1	0.01
Chilean	1	0.01
Colombian	60	0.72
Ecuadorian	16	0.19
Peruvian	10	0.12
Venezuelan	10	0.12
Other Hispanic or Latino	43	0.51

Race*	Population	%
African-American/Black (110)	123	1.47
Not Hispanic (100)	111	1.33
Hispanic (10)	12	0.14

*Notes: † The Census 2010 population figure is used to calculate the percentages in the Hispanic Origin and Race categories. Ancestry percentages are based on the 2006-2010 American Community Survey population (not shown); ‡ Numbers in parentheses indicate the number of people reporting a single ancestry; * Numbers in parentheses indicate the number of persons reporting this race alone, not in combination with any other race; Please refer to the Explanation of Data for more information.*

American Indian/Alaska Native (4)	16	0.19
Not Hispanic (1)	11	0.13
Hispanic (3)	5	0.06
South American Ind. (0)	2	0.02
Asian (2,650)	2,731	32.62
Not Hispanic (2,649)	2,725	32.55
Hispanic (1)	6	0.07
Burmese (0)	1	0.01
Chinese, ex. Taiwanese (273)	303	3.62
Filipino (116)	142	1.70
Indian (323)	339	4.05
Indonesian (4)	4	0.05
Japanese (73)	87	1.04
Korean (1,771)	1,787	21.34
Malaysian (1)	2	0.02
Pakistani (28)	32	0.38
Taiwanese (30)	30	0.36
Vietnamese (1)	4	0.05
Hawaii Native/Pacific Islander (1)	1	0.01
Not Hispanic (1)	1	0.01
White (5,373)	5,458	65.19
Not Hispanic (5,019)	5,093	60.83
Hispanic (354)	365	4.36

Collingswood

Place Type: Borough
County: Camden
Population: 13,926†

Ancestry‡	Population	%
African, Sub-Saharan (10)	10	0.07
African (10)	10	0.07
American (249)	249	1.78
Arab (24)	39	0.28
Lebanese (0)	15	0.11
Syrian (12)	12	0.09
Other Arab (12)	12	0.09
Armenian (9)	35	0.25
Austrian (31)	82	0.58
Belgian (9)	55	0.39
British (46)	167	1.19
Canadian (0)	27	0.19
Croatian (10)	23	0.16
Czech (59)	59	0.42
Czechoslovakian (13)	54	0.39
Dutch (20)	146	1.04
Eastern European (12)	12	0.09
English (320)	1,662	11.85
European (54)	66	0.47
Finnish (0)	32	0.23
French, ex. Basque (33)	581	4.14
French Canadian (0)	28	0.20
German (317)	2,844	20.28
Greek (23)	75	0.53
Hungarian (9)	106	0.76
Irish (1,102)	4,060	28.95
Italian (1,085)	2,736	19.51
Lithuanian (0)	74	0.53
Norwegian (54)	208	1.48
Pennsylvania German (49)	49	0.35
Polish (175)	901	6.42
Portuguese (0)	104	0.74
Romanian (28)	38	0.27
Russian (89)	304	2.17
Scotch-Irish (85)	332	2.37
Scottish (116)	231	1.65
Serbian (13)	26	0.19
Slavic (0)	20	0.14
Slovak (10)	86	0.61
Swedish (21)	151	1.08
Swiss (22)	63	0.45
Ukrainian (56)	116	0.83
Welsh (19)	114	0.81
West Indian, ex. Hispanic (24)	89	0.63
Haitian (0)	19	0.14
Jamaican (24)	43	0.31
Trinidadian/Tobagonian (0)	27	0.19

Hispanic Origin	Population	%
Hispanic or Latino (of any race)	1,347	9.67
Central American, ex. Mexican	75	0.54
Costa Rican	17	0.12
Guatemalan	6	0.04
Honduran	5	0.04
Nicaraguan	26	0.19
Panamanian	7	0.05
Salvadoran	14	0.10
Cuban	46	0.33
Dominican Republic	103	0.74
Mexican	250	1.80
Puerto Rican	727	5.22
South American	69	0.50
Argentinean	6	0.04
Chilean	13	0.09
Colombian	19	0.14
Ecuadorian	15	0.11
Peruvian	9	0.06
Uruguayan	2	0.01
Venezuelan	5	0.04
Other Hispanic or Latino	77	0.55

Race*	Population	%
African-American/Black (1,268)	1,447	10.39
Not Hispanic (1,190)	1,330	9.55
Hispanic (78)	117	0.84
American Indian/Alaska Native (45)	121	0.87
Not Hispanic (14)	77	0.55
Hispanic (31)	44	0.32
Apache (1)	7	0.05
Blackfeet (0)	1	0.01
Cherokee (1)	15	0.11
Creek (0)	1	0.01
Delaware (3)	5	0.04
Iroquois (1)	4	0.03
Kiowa (0)	1	0.01
Mexican American Ind. (6)	6	0.04
Navajo (0)	1	0.01
Shoshone (0)	1	0.01
Sioux (0)	6	0.04
South American Ind. (1)	1	0.01
Asian (307)	405	2.91
Not Hispanic (304)	395	2.84
Hispanic (3)	10	0.07
Burmese (7)	7	0.05
Cambodian (1)	1	0.01
Chinese, ex. Taiwanese (70)	104	0.75
Filipino (51)	70	0.50
Indian (49)	74	0.53
Indonesian (1)	5	0.04
Japanese (8)	17	0.12
Korean (27)	37	0.27
Laotian (0)	1	0.01
Pakistani (4)	4	0.03
Sri Lankan (0)	1	0.01
Taiwanese (3)	3	0.02
Thai (5)	12	0.09
Vietnamese (58)	75	0.54
Hawaii Native/Pacific Islander (2)	15	0.11
Not Hispanic (2)	7	0.05
Hispanic (0)	8	0.06
Fijian (1)	1	0.01
Guamanian/Chamorro (0)	1	0.01
Native Hawaiian (1)	2	0.01
White (11,388)	11,696	83.99
Not Hispanic (10,792)	11,017	79.11
Hispanic (596)	679	4.88

Colonia

Place Type: CDP
County: Middlesex
Population: 17,795†

Ancestry‡	Population	%
African, Sub-Saharan (36)	36	0.20
Ghanaian (36)	36	0.20
American (278)	278	1.54
Arab (171)	182	1.01
Arab (61)	61	0.34
Egyptian (100)	100	0.55
Jordanian (10)	10	0.06
Palestinian (0)	11	0.06
Armenian (0)	10	0.06
Austrian (20)	128	0.71
Brazilian (0)	17	0.09
British (0)	55	0.30
Canadian (0)	37	0.20
Croatian (0)	35	0.19
Czech (10)	58	0.32
Czechoslovakian (11)	11	0.06
Danish (25)	48	0.27
Dutch (41)	61	0.34
Eastern European (81)	81	0.45
English (147)	700	3.87
European (9)	9	0.05
French, ex. Basque (13)	212	1.17
French Canadian (21)	34	0.19
German (374)	2,760	15.25
Greek (38)	119	0.66
Guyanese (17)	17	0.09
Hungarian (163)	394	2.18
Iranian (11)	19	0.10
Irish (723)	3,033	16.76
Italian (2,106)	4,125	22.79
Latvian (0)	15	0.08
Lithuanian (82)	195	1.08
Maltese (0)	36	0.20
Norwegian (4)	73	0.40
Polish (1,253)	2,524	13.94
Portuguese (649)	812	4.49
Romanian (39)	39	0.22
Russian (146)	413	2.28
Scandinavian (13)	13	0.07
Scotch-Irish (33)	135	0.75
Scottish (55)	261	1.44
Slovak (30)	170	0.94
Slovene (16)	34	0.19
Swedish (0)	143	0.79
Swiss (0)	24	0.13
Ukrainian (330)	474	2.62
Welsh (30)	71	0.39
West Indian, ex. Hispanic (164)	242	1.34
British West Indian (46)	78	0.43
Haitian (66)	66	0.36
Jamaican (0)	32	0.18
Trinidadian/Tobagonian (17)	17	0.09
West Indian (35)	49	0.27
Yugoslavian (0)	15	0.08

Hispanic Origin	Population	%
Hispanic or Latino (of any race)	1,649	9.27
Central American, ex. Mexican	86	0.48
Costa Rican	16	0.09
Guatemalan	15	0.08
Honduran	22	0.12
Nicaraguan	4	0.02
Panamanian	7	0.04
Salvadoran	22	0.12
Cuban	171	0.96
Dominican Republic	111	0.62
Mexican	53	0.30
Puerto Rican	589	3.31
South American	444	2.50
Argentinean	48	0.27
Bolivian	2	0.01
Chilean	4	0.02
Colombian	161	0.90
Ecuadorian	105	0.59
Peruvian	73	0.41
Uruguayan	22	0.12
Venezuelan	21	0.12
Other South American	8	0.04
Other Hispanic or Latino	195	1.10

Race*	Population	%
African-American/Black (936)	1,046	5.88
Not Hispanic (888)	949	5.33
Hispanic (48)	97	0.55

*Notes: † The Census 2010 population figure is used to calculate the percentages in the Hispanic Origin and Race categories. Ancestry percentages are based on the 2006-2010 American Community Survey population (not shown); ‡ Numbers in parentheses indicate the number of people reporting a single ancestry; * Numbers in parentheses indicate the number of persons reporting this race alone, not in combination with any other race; Please refer to the Explanation of Data for more information.*

Race* (continued)	Population	%
American Indian/Alaska Native (21)	64	0.36
Not Hispanic (16)	40	0.22
Hispanic (5)	24	0.13
Cherokee (0)	5	0.03
Choctaw (0)	2	0.01
Potawatomi (3)	3	0.02
South American Ind. (0)	5	0.03
Asian (1,904)	2,061	11.58
Not Hispanic (1,892)	2,030	11.41
Hispanic (12)	31	0.17
Bangladeshi (9)	9	0.05
Burmese (7)	7	0.04
Chinese, ex. Taiwanese (176)	207	1.16
Filipino (431)	491	2.76
Indian (1,017)	1,067	6.00
Japanese (5)	6	0.03
Korean (77)	84	0.47
Pakistani (89)	91	0.51
Sri Lankan (5)	5	0.03
Taiwanese (7)	9	0.05
Thai (1)	3	0.02
Vietnamese (54)	59	0.33
Hawaii Native/Pacific Islander (8)	21	0.12
Not Hispanic (2)	10	0.06
Hispanic (6)	11	0.06
Guamanian/Chamorro (1)	1	0.01
Native Hawaiian (0)	4	0.02
White (14,302)	14,567	81.86
Not Hispanic (13,084)	13,246	74.44
Hispanic (1,218)	1,321	7.42

Colts Neck

Place Type: Township
County: Monmouth
Population: 10,142†

Ancestry‡	Population	%
African, Sub-Saharan (21)	30	0.29
African (7)	16	0.16
Liberian (9)	9	0.09
South African (5)	5	0.05
Alsatian (0)	8	0.08
American (1,523)	1,523	14.97
Arab (29)	88	0.87
Arab (11)	11	0.11
Lebanese (18)	50	0.49
Syrian (0)	27	0.27
Australian (0)	6	0.06
Austrian (0)	65	0.64
British (8)	19	0.19
Canadian (10)	10	0.10
Croatian (0)	12	0.12
Czech (0)	51	0.50
Czechoslovakian (0)	29	0.29
Danish (23)	44	0.43
Dutch (17)	148	1.45
Eastern European (24)	35	0.34
English (84)	548	5.39
European (33)	42	0.41
Finnish (8)	28	0.28
French, ex. Basque (10)	123	1.21
French Canadian (15)	15	0.15
German (292)	1,216	11.95
Greek (65)	100	0.98
Hungarian (27)	112	1.10
Icelander (14)	49	0.48
Irish (820)	2,594	25.50
Israeli (16)	16	0.16
Italian (1,776)	3,179	31.25
Lithuanian (10)	10	0.10
Maltese (38)	140	1.38
Norwegian (10)	74	0.73
Polish (133)	765	7.52
Portuguese (23)	68	0.67
Romanian (8)	32	0.31
Russian (37)	220	2.16
Scotch-Irish (51)	100	0.98
Scottish (21)	105	1.03
Serbian (0)	9	0.09
Slavic (0)	30	0.29
Slovak (0)	39	0.38
Swedish (11)	51	0.50
Swiss (0)	19	0.19
Turkish (56)	56	0.55
Ukrainian (31)	74	0.73
West Indian, ex. Hispanic (39)	48	0.47
Barbadian (9)	9	0.09
Haitian (30)	30	0.29
West Indian (0)	9	0.09

Hispanic Origin	Population	%
Hispanic or Latino (of any race)	359	3.54
Central American, ex. Mexican	21	0.21
Costa Rican	7	0.07
Guatemalan	3	0.03
Honduran	9	0.09
Nicaraguan	1	0.01
Salvadoran	1	0.01
Cuban	35	0.35
Dominican Republic	13	0.13
Mexican	90	0.89
Puerto Rican	104	1.03
South American	48	0.47
Argentinean	13	0.13
Chilean	11	0.11
Colombian	9	0.09
Ecuadorian	2	0.02
Peruvian	11	0.11
Uruguayan	1	0.01
Venezuelan	1	0.01
Other Hispanic or Latino	48	0.47

Race*	Population	%
African-American/Black (169)	193	1.90
Not Hispanic (163)	182	1.79
Hispanic (6)	11	0.11
American Indian/Alaska Native (1)	22	0.22
Not Hispanic (1)	16	0.16
Hispanic (0)	6	0.06
Cherokee (0)	3	0.03
Iroquois (0)	2	0.02
Potawatomi (0)	3	0.03
Asian (464)	544	5.36
Not Hispanic (463)	535	5.28
Hispanic (1)	9	0.09
Bangladeshi (3)	3	0.03
Chinese, ex. Taiwanese (142)	150	1.48
Filipino (49)	63	0.62
Indian (160)	178	1.76
Indonesian (2)	2	0.02
Japanese (8)	21	0.21
Korean (34)	45	0.44
Pakistani (8)	19	0.19
Taiwanese (19)	21	0.21
Thai (1)	1	0.01
Vietnamese (27)	36	0.35
Hawaii Native/Pacific Islander (0)	3	0.03
Not Hispanic (0)	2	0.02
Hispanic (0)	1	0.01
Native Hawaiian (0)	3	0.03
White (9,348)	9,456	93.24
Not Hispanic (9,042)	9,136	90.08
Hispanic (306)	320	3.16

Cranford

Place Type: Township
County: Union
Population: 22,625†

Ancestry‡	Population	%
African, Sub-Saharan (0)	15	0.07
Ethiopian (0)	15	0.07
Albanian (0)	31	0.14
American (1,221)	1,221	5.45
Arab (40)	168	0.75
Lebanese (40)	109	0.49
Syrian (0)	59	0.26
Armenian (0)	45	0.20
Austrian (44)	163	0.73
Belgian (0)	46	0.21
Brazilian (0)	15	0.07
British (21)	64	0.29
Canadian (0)	22	0.10
Czech (42)	97	0.43
Czechoslovakian (8)	57	0.25
Danish (45)	95	0.42
Dutch (0)	219	0.98
Eastern European (124)	124	0.55
English (316)	1,579	7.04
European (174)	211	0.94
Finnish (0)	9	0.04
French, ex. Basque (10)	433	1.93
French Canadian (16)	53	0.24
German (585)	3,450	15.39
Greek (184)	296	1.32
Guyanese (5)	5	0.02
Hungarian (95)	350	1.56
Irish (1,669)	6,290	28.06
Israeli (10)	10	0.04
Italian (2,274)	5,505	24.56
Lithuanian (48)	234	1.04
Norwegian (20)	162	0.72
Pennsylvania German (18)	40	0.18
Polish (812)	2,749	12.26
Portuguese (165)	294	1.31
Romanian (74)	123	0.55
Russian (175)	578	2.58
Scandinavian (19)	19	0.08
Scotch-Irish (157)	295	1.32
Scottish (47)	283	1.26
Slavic (35)	85	0.38
Slovak (87)	171	0.76
Swedish (80)	309	1.38
Swiss (25)	83	0.37
Turkish (14)	24	0.11
Ukrainian (134)	439	1.96
Welsh (28)	81	0.36
West Indian, ex. Hispanic (189)	231	1.03
Bermudan (0)	7	0.03
Haitian (35)	35	0.16
Jamaican (62)	97	0.43
Trinidadian/Tobagonian (8)	8	0.04
West Indian (84)	84	0.37

Hispanic Origin	Population	%
Hispanic or Latino (of any race)	1,474	6.51
Central American, ex. Mexican	108	0.48
Costa Rican	10	0.04
Guatemalan	20	0.09
Honduran	16	0.07
Nicaraguan	7	0.03
Panamanian	3	0.01
Salvadoran	52	0.23
Cuban	276	1.22
Dominican Republic	53	0.23
Mexican	85	0.38
Puerto Rican	386	1.71
South American	369	1.63
Argentinean	38	0.17
Bolivian	9	0.04
Chilean	10	0.04
Colombian	158	0.70
Ecuadorian	49	0.22
Paraguayan	1	<0.01
Peruvian	51	0.23
Uruguayan	26	0.11
Venezuelan	27	0.12
Other Hispanic or Latino	197	0.87

Race*	Population	%
African-American/Black (592)	703	3.11
Not Hispanic (563)	638	2.82
Hispanic (29)	65	0.29
American Indian/Alaska Native (18)	82	0.36
Not Hispanic (10)	58	0.26
Hispanic (8)	24	0.11
Arapaho (0)	1	<0.01
Blackfeet (1)	7	0.03

*Notes: † The Census 2010 population figure is used to calculate the percentages in the Hispanic Origin and Race categories. Ancestry percentages are based on the 2006-2010 American Community Survey population (not shown); ‡ Numbers in parentheses indicate the number of people reporting a single ancestry; * Numbers in parentheses indicate the number of persons reporting this race alone, not in combination with any other race; Please refer to the Explanation of Data for more information.*

Canadian/French Am. Ind. (0)	3	0.01
Cherokee (0)	13	0.06
Houma (4)	4	0.02
Inupiat *(Alaska Native)* (0)	1	<0.01
Iroquois (0)	6	0.03
Potawatomi (0)	3	0.01
Shoshone (0)	1	<0.01
South American Ind. (1)	5	0.02
Asian (643)	809	3.58
Not Hispanic (635)	778	3.44
Hispanic (8)	31	0.14
Bangladeshi (3)	5	0.02
Chinese, ex. Taiwanese (210)	261	1.15
Filipino (149)	210	0.93
Indian (136)	160	0.71
Indonesian (2)	2	0.01
Japanese (18)	35	0.15
Korean (62)	73	0.32
Pakistani (18)	18	0.08
Sri Lankan (3)	6	0.03
Taiwanese (11)	16	0.07
Thai (5)	7	0.03
Vietnamese (14)	17	0.08
Hawaii Native/Pacific Islander (4)	15	0.07
Not Hispanic (3)	10	0.04
Hispanic (1)	5	0.02
Guamanian/Chamorro (2)	3	0.01
Native Hawaiian (1)	5	0.02
White (20,781)	21,091	93.22
Not Hispanic (19,635)	19,866	87.81
Hispanic (1,146)	1,225	5.41

Cresskill

Place Type: Borough
County: Bergen
Population: 8,573†

Ancestry‡	Population	%
Albanian (274)	274	3.27
American (167)	167	1.99
Arab (95)	155	1.85
Egyptian (91)	91	1.09
Lebanese (4)	37	0.44
Palestinian (0)	13	0.16
Syrian (0)	14	0.17
Armenian (100)	115	1.37
Austrian (33)	182	2.17
Belgian (0)	13	0.16
British (14)	14	0.17
Canadian (19)	19	0.23
Carpatho Rusyn (0)	15	0.18
Czechoslovakian (0)	78	0.93
Danish (0)	14	0.17
Dutch (38)	56	0.67
Eastern European (18)	18	0.21
English (98)	514	6.13
European (59)	59	0.70
Finnish (18)	33	0.39
French, ex. Basque (0)	70	0.84
French Canadian (0)	19	0.23
German (42)	737	8.79
Greek (54)	117	1.40
Hungarian (34)	74	0.88
Irish (324)	1,209	14.43
Israeli (13)	54	0.64
Italian (1,014)	1,784	21.29
Lithuanian (0)	17	0.20
Norwegian (15)	35	0.42
Polish (251)	330	3.94
Portuguese (15)	48	0.57
Romanian (0)	17	0.20
Russian (139)	306	3.65
Scandinavian (0)	15	0.18
Scotch-Irish (99)	194	2.32
Scottish (30)	49	0.58
Slovak (17)	62	0.74
Swedish (0)	49	0.58
Ukrainian (33)	98	1.17
Welsh (0)	41	0.49

Hispanic Origin	Population	%
Hispanic or Latino (of any race)	537	6.26
Central American, ex. Mexican	25	0.29
Costa Rican	2	0.02
Guatemalan	12	0.14
Honduran	2	0.02
Nicaraguan	1	0.01
Panamanian	2	0.02
Salvadoran	5	0.06
Other Central American	1	0.01
Cuban	108	1.26
Dominican Republic	53	0.62
Mexican	29	0.34
Puerto Rican	117	1.36
South American	133	1.55
Argentinean	11	0.13
Chilean	5	0.06
Colombian	78	0.91
Ecuadorian	16	0.19
Peruvian	13	0.15
Uruguayan	6	0.07
Venezuelan	4	0.05
Other Hispanic or Latino	72	0.84

Race*	Population	%
African-American/Black (63)	83	0.97
Not Hispanic (57)	73	0.85
Hispanic (6)	10	0.12
American Indian/Alaska Native (3)	9	0.10
Not Hispanic (2)	6	0.07
Hispanic (1)	3	0.03
Cherokee (0)	1	0.01
Mexican American Ind. (1)	1	0.01
South American Ind. (0)	2	0.02
Asian (2,370)	2,471	28.82
Not Hispanic (2,367)	2,454	28.62
Hispanic (3)	17	0.20
Bangladeshi (2)	2	0.02
Cambodian (2)	2	0.02
Chinese, ex. Taiwanese (255)	292	3.41
Filipino (88)	125	1.46
Indian (210)	220	2.57
Indonesian (0)	1	0.01
Japanese (180)	200	2.33
Korean (1,522)	1,560	18.20
Malaysian (1)	5	0.06
Nepalese (1)	1	0.01
Pakistani (10)	10	0.12
Sri Lankan (1)	1	0.01
Taiwanese (43)	51	0.59
Thai (5)	5	0.06
Vietnamese (2)	2	0.02
Hawaii Native/Pacific Islander (1)	5	0.06
Not Hispanic (1)	5	0.06
White (5,911)	6,027	70.30
Not Hispanic (5,500)	5,590	65.20
Hispanic (411)	437	5.10

Crestwood Village

Place Type: CDP
County: Ocean
Population: 7,907†

Ancestry‡	Population	%
Alsatian (0)	12	0.15
American (203)	203	2.50
Austrian (49)	132	1.62
British (27)	40	0.49
Canadian (15)	15	0.18
Czech (13)	51	0.63
Czechoslovakian (52)	82	1.01
Danish (12)	52	0.64
Dutch (119)	333	4.09
English (246)	1,032	12.68
European (28)	42	0.52
French, ex. Basque (55)	232	2.85
French Canadian (0)	36	0.44
German (731)	1,756	21.58
Hungarian (50)	105	1.29
Irish (842)	1,901	23.37
Italian (1,455)	1,864	22.91
Latvian (27)	27	0.33
Lithuanian (13)	13	0.16
Norwegian (80)	117	1.44
Pennsylvania German (25)	54	0.66
Polish (448)	785	9.65
Portuguese (0)	13	0.16
Romanian (12)	43	0.53
Russian (29)	83	1.02
Scotch-Irish (129)	196	2.41
Scottish (66)	217	2.67
Serbian (0)	13	0.16
Slavic (0)	13	0.16
Slovak (12)	25	0.31
Swedish (14)	69	0.85
Swiss (53)	97	1.19
Turkish (13)	13	0.16
Ukrainian (43)	89	1.09
Welsh (13)	91	1.12

Hispanic Origin	Population	%
Hispanic or Latino (of any race)	169	2.14
Central American, ex. Mexican	9	0.11
Guatemalan	4	0.05
Honduran	3	0.04
Nicaraguan	1	0.01
Panamanian	1	0.01
Cuban	12	0.15
Dominican Republic	4	0.05
Mexican	6	0.08
Puerto Rican	87	1.10
South American	23	0.29
Argentinean	3	0.04
Chilean	2	0.03
Colombian	4	0.05
Ecuadorian	4	0.05
Peruvian	1	0.01
Uruguayan	7	0.09
Venezuelan	1	0.01
Other South American	1	0.01
Other Hispanic or Latino	28	0.35

Race*	Population	%
African-American/Black (116)	124	1.57
Not Hispanic (114)	121	1.53
Hispanic (2)	3	0.04
American Indian/Alaska Native (8)	38	0.48
Not Hispanic (8)	37	0.47
Hispanic (0)	1	0.01
Cherokee (2)	10	0.13
Delaware (3)	6	0.08
Iroquois (0)	1	0.01
Sioux (1)	2	0.03
South American Ind. (0)	1	0.01
Asian (51)	59	0.75
Not Hispanic (51)	59	0.75
Chinese, ex. Taiwanese (9)	11	0.14
Filipino (20)	24	0.30
Indian (6)	9	0.11
Japanese (2)	2	0.03
Korean (8)	8	0.10
Taiwanese (2)	2	0.03
Thai (2)	2	0.03
Hawaii Native/Pacific Islander (1)	3	0.04
Not Hispanic (1)	3	0.04
Guamanian/Chamorro (0)	1	0.01
Native Hawaiian (1)	2	0.03
White (7,664)	7,713	97.55
Not Hispanic (7,512)	7,556	95.56
Hispanic (152)	157	1.99

Delran

Place Type: Township
County: Burlington
Population: 16,896†

Ancestry‡	Population	%
African, Sub-Saharan (81)	98	0.58

*Notes: † The Census 2010 population figure is used to calculate the percentages in the Hispanic Origin and Race categories. Ancestry percentages are based on the 2006-2010 American Community Survey population (not shown); ‡ Numbers in parentheses indicate the number of people reporting a single ancestry; * Numbers in parentheses indicate the number of persons reporting this race alone, not in combination with any other race; Please refer to the Explanation of Data for more information.*

Ancestry	Population	%
African (0)	17	0.10
Liberian (17)	17	0.10
Nigerian (33)	33	0.20
Other Sub-Saharan African (31)	31	0.18
Albanian (9)	9	0.05
American (545)	545	3.25
Arab (37)	37	0.22
Arab (37)	37	0.22
Armenian (15)	15	0.09
Australian (12)	12	0.07
Belgian (30)	30	0.18
Brazilian (223)	314	1.87
British (21)	21	0.13
Canadian (0)	15	0.09
Croatian (24)	24	0.14
Czech (7)	195	1.16
Czechoslovakian (0)	11	0.07
Dutch (0)	135	0.80
English (184)	1,358	8.10
European (83)	83	0.49
French, ex. Basque (34)	448	2.67
French Canadian (13)	72	0.43
German (777)	3,821	22.78
Greek (22)	39	0.23
Hungarian (12)	205	1.22
Irish (968)	3,974	23.69
Italian (1,184)	3,462	20.64
Lithuanian (95)	290	1.73
Norwegian (0)	31	0.18
Pennsylvania German (0)	9	0.05
Polish (410)	1,960	11.69
Portuguese (192)	266	1.59
Romanian (0)	14	0.08
Russian (32)	120	0.72
Scotch-Irish (139)	235	1.40
Scottish (36)	96	0.57
Slovak (0)	10	0.06
Swedish (19)	91	0.54
Swiss (18)	33	0.20
Turkish (258)	258	1.54
Ukrainian (8)	121	0.72
Welsh (0)	51	0.30
West Indian, ex. Hispanic (99)	99	0.59
Barbadian (99)	99	0.59
Yugoslavian (0)	11	0.07

Hispanic Origin	Population	%
Hispanic or Latino (of any race)	779	4.61
Central American, ex. Mexican	81	0.48
Costa Rican	5	0.03
Guatemalan	22	0.13
Honduran	20	0.12
Nicaraguan	6	0.04
Panamanian	7	0.04
Salvadoran	21	0.12
Cuban	33	0.20
Dominican Republic	28	0.17
Mexican	66	0.39
Puerto Rican	382	2.26
South American	78	0.46
Argentinean	2	0.01
Bolivian	6	0.04
Colombian	26	0.15
Ecuadorian	14	0.08
Peruvian	23	0.14
Uruguayan	1	0.01
Other South American	6	0.04
Other Hispanic or Latino	111	0.66

Race*	Population	%
African-American/Black (1,616)	1,800	10.65
Not Hispanic (1,565)	1,706	10.10
Hispanic (51)	94	0.56
American Indian/Alaska Native (33)	116	0.69
Not Hispanic (26)	95	0.56
Hispanic (7)	21	0.12
Blackfeet (0)	2	0.01
Cherokee (6)	15	0.09
Chippewa (1)	1	0.01
Delaware (0)	3	0.02
Iroquois (0)	1	0.01
Puget Sound Salish (1)	1	0.01
Seminole (2)	2	0.01
Sioux (1)	4	0.02
South American Ind. (2)	6	0.04
Asian (683)	799	4.73
Not Hispanic (673)	786	4.65
Hispanic (10)	13	0.08
Burmese (3)	3	0.02
Cambodian (5)	10	0.06
Chinese, ex. Taiwanese (63)	83	0.49
Filipino (76)	102	0.60
Indian (340)	371	2.20
Indonesian (0)	3	0.02
Japanese (10)	32	0.19
Korean (88)	102	0.60
Pakistani (52)	57	0.34
Taiwanese (3)	3	0.02
Vietnamese (16)	20	0.12
Hawaii Native/Pacific Islander (7)	21	0.12
Not Hispanic (7)	21	0.12
Native Hawaiian (2)	11	0.07
White (13,688)	14,021	82.98
Not Hispanic (13,261)	13,550	80.20
Hispanic (427)	471	2.79

Denville

Place Type: Township
County: Morris
Population: 16,635†

Ancestry‡	Population	%
African, Sub-Saharan (40)	40	0.24
African (25)	25	0.15
Nigerian (15)	15	0.09
American (267)	267	1.61
Arab (0)	20	0.12
Syrian (0)	20	0.12
Armenian (4)	58	0.35
Austrian (0)	99	0.60
Belgian (18)	29	0.18
British (38)	57	0.34
Canadian (0)	30	0.18
Celtic (16)	47	0.28
Czech (53)	135	0.82
Czechoslovakian (29)	40	0.24
Danish (0)	47	0.28
Dutch (26)	359	2.17
Eastern European (151)	151	0.91
English (526)	1,817	10.99
European (131)	131	0.79
French, ex. Basque (26)	338	2.04
French Canadian (0)	40	0.24
German (701)	3,787	22.90
Greek (179)	261	1.58
Guyanese (4)	4	0.02
Hungarian (87)	252	1.52
Irish (1,115)	5,335	32.26
Italian (1,495)	4,012	24.26
Latvian (24)	24	0.15
Lithuanian (0)	40	0.24
Luxemburger (0)	12	0.07
Norwegian (154)	320	1.94
Polish (424)	1,187	7.18
Romanian (13)	13	0.08
Russian (129)	373	2.26
Scotch-Irish (68)	229	1.38
Scottish (29)	410	2.48
Serbian (0)	12	0.07
Slavic (80)	80	0.48
Slovak (49)	217	1.31
Swedish (21)	219	1.32
Swiss (0)	84	0.51
Ukrainian (86)	236	1.43
Welsh (12)	247	1.49
West Indian, ex. Hispanic (7)	52	0.31
Bahamian (4)	4	0.02
Barbadian (0)	45	0.27
British West Indian (3)	3	0.02
Yugoslavian (0)	39	0.24

Hispanic Origin	Population	%
Hispanic or Latino (of any race)	883	5.31
Central American, ex. Mexican	82	0.49
Costa Rican	12	0.07
Guatemalan	18	0.11
Honduran	26	0.16
Nicaraguan	5	0.03
Panamanian	2	0.01
Salvadoran	19	0.11
Cuban	78	0.47
Dominican Republic	47	0.28
Mexican	80	0.48
Puerto Rican	225	1.35
South American	284	1.71
Argentinean	25	0.15
Bolivian	6	0.04
Chilean	10	0.06
Colombian	117	0.70
Ecuadorian	44	0.26
Peruvian	45	0.27
Uruguayan	7	0.04
Venezuelan	21	0.13
Other South American	9	0.05
Other Hispanic or Latino	87	0.52

Race*	Population	%
African-American/Black (236)	318	1.91
Not Hispanic (220)	286	1.72
Hispanic (16)	32	0.19
American Indian/Alaska Native (20)	76	0.46
Not Hispanic (16)	69	0.41
Hispanic (4)	7	0.04
Blackfeet (0)	8	0.05
Cherokee (1)	14	0.08
Iroquois (4)	11	0.07
Mexican American Ind. (2)	2	0.01
Osage (0)	1	0.01
Sioux (0)	1	0.01
South American Ind. (4)	5	0.03
Tlingit-Haida *(Alaska Native)* (0)	1	0.01
Asian (1,084)	1,224	7.36
Not Hispanic (1,081)	1,213	7.29
Hispanic (3)	11	0.07
Bangladeshi (2)	3	0.02
Burmese (1)	1	0.01
Chinese, ex. Taiwanese (323)	371	2.23
Filipino (108)	141	0.85
Indian (351)	380	2.28
Indonesian (1)	1	0.01
Japanese (24)	43	0.26
Korean (99)	118	0.71
Malaysian (1)	1	0.01
Pakistani (39)	51	0.31
Sri Lankan (1)	3	0.02
Taiwanese (42)	55	0.33
Thai (12)	15	0.09
Vietnamese (40)	49	0.29
Hawaii Native/Pacific Islander (1)	5	0.03
Not Hispanic (0)	4	0.02
Hispanic (1)	1	0.01
Guamanian/Chamorro (1)	1	0.01
White (14,887)	15,133	90.97
Not Hispanic (14,186)	14,398	86.55
Hispanic (701)	735	4.42

Deptford

Place Type: Township
County: Gloucester
Population: 30,561†

Ancestry‡	Population	%
African, Sub-Saharan (91)	128	0.42
African (42)	64	0.21
Ethiopian (41)	56	0.19
South African (8)	8	0.03
American (959)	959	3.18
Arab (95)	110	0.36

*Notes: † The Census 2010 population figure is used to calculate the percentages in the Hispanic Origin and Race categories. Ancestry percentages are based on the 2006-2010 American Community Survey population (not shown); ‡ Numbers in parentheses indicate the number of people reporting a single ancestry; * Numbers in parentheses indicate the number of persons reporting this race alone, not in combination with any other race; Please refer to the Explanation of Data for more information.*

Egyptian (84)	84	0.28
Lebanese (11)	26	0.09
Armenian (10)	10	0.03
Austrian (10)	78	0.26
Belgian (11)	38	0.13
British (40)	40	0.13
Bulgarian (8)	8	0.03
Celtic (0)	11	0.04
Croatian (17)	26	0.09
Czech (0)	82	0.27
Czechoslovakian (8)	62	0.21
Danish (12)	82	0.27
Dutch (118)	341	1.13
Eastern European (20)	20	0.07
English (597)	2,834	9.39
European (97)	97	0.32
French, ex. Basque (19)	557	1.85
French Canadian (12)	43	0.14
German (1,028)	5,856	19.41
Greek (108)	179	0.59
Hungarian (22)	120	0.40
Iranian (0)	11	0.04
Irish (2,280)	8,255	27.36
Italian (3,802)	7,533	24.96
Lithuanian (18)	74	0.25
Norwegian (16)	80	0.27
Pennsylvania German (24)	50	0.17
Polish (610)	1,914	6.34
Portuguese (93)	101	0.33
Romanian (0)	45	0.15
Russian (75)	371	1.23
Scotch-Irish (61)	338	1.12
Scottish (44)	454	1.50
Slovak (61)	61	0.20
Swedish (54)	345	1.14
Swiss (0)	47	0.16
Turkish (54)	76	0.25
Ukrainian (51)	175	0.58
Welsh (40)	168	0.56
West Indian, ex. Hispanic (84)	174	0.58
Barbadian (19)	31	0.10
Dutch West Indian (0)	48	0.16
Jamaican (33)	51	0.17
Trinidadian/Tobagonian (32)	32	0.11
West Indian (0)	12	0.04
Yugoslavian (26)	26	0.09

Hispanic Origin	Population	%
Hispanic or Latino (of any race)	1,830	5.99
Central American, ex. Mexican	180	0.59
Costa Rican	19	0.06
Guatemalan	105	0.34
Honduran	9	0.03
Nicaraguan	18	0.06
Panamanian	14	0.05
Salvadoran	11	0.04
Other Central American	4	0.01
Cuban	52	0.17
Dominican Republic	51	0.17
Mexican	265	0.87
Puerto Rican	1,002	3.28
South American	152	0.50
Argentinean	24	0.08
Bolivian	1	<0.01
Chilean	12	0.04
Colombian	52	0.17
Ecuadorian	31	0.10
Peruvian	13	0.04
Venezuelan	18	0.06
Other South American	1	<0.01
Other Hispanic or Latino	128	0.42

Race*	Population	%
African-American/Black (3,717)	4,093	13.39
Not Hispanic (3,578)	3,905	12.78
Hispanic (139)	188	0.62
American Indian/Alaska Native (73)	226	0.74
Not Hispanic (44)	185	0.61
Hispanic (29)	41	0.13
Apache (0)	1	<0.01
Blackfeet (0)	16	0.05
Canadian/French Am. Ind. (0)	1	<0.01
Central American Ind. (0)	1	<0.01
Cherokee (8)	39	0.13
Chickasaw (0)	1	<0.01
Delaware (8)	19	0.06
Inupiat *(Alaska Native)* (0)	1	<0.01
Iroquois (3)	5	0.02
Lumbee (3)	3	0.01
Mexican American Ind. (0)	1	<0.01
Navajo (1)	4	0.01
Sioux (0)	4	0.01
South American Ind. (3)	6	0.02
Asian (1,361)	1,497	4.90
Not Hispanic (1,350)	1,466	4.80
Hispanic (11)	31	0.10
Bangladeshi (37)	45	0.15
Cambodian (16)	16	0.05
Chinese, ex. Taiwanese (214)	237	0.78
Filipino (476)	523	1.71
Indian (344)	369	1.21
Indonesian (1)	3	0.01
Japanese (12)	29	0.09
Korean (80)	94	0.31
Laotian (1)	1	<0.01
Malaysian (1)	1	<0.01
Pakistani (31)	33	0.11
Sri Lankan (3)	3	0.01
Thai (7)	12	0.04
Vietnamese (82)	103	0.34
Hawaii Native/Pacific Islander (12)	42	0.14
Not Hispanic (9)	25	0.08
Hispanic (3)	17	0.06
Guamanian/Chamorro (3)	3	0.01
Native Hawaiian (4)	8	0.03
Samoan (1)	3	0.01
White (24,082)	24,656	80.68
Not Hispanic (23,190)	23,629	77.32
Hispanic (892)	1,027	3.36

Dover

Place Type: Town
County: Morris
Population: 18,157†

Ancestry‡	Population	%
Afghan (48)	48	0.26
African, Sub-Saharan (52)	52	0.29
Ghanaian (42)	42	0.23
Nigerian (10)	10	0.05
American (371)	371	2.04
Arab (53)	64	0.35
Iraqi (42)	42	0.23
Lebanese (0)	11	0.06
Syrian (11)	11	0.06
Austrian (11)	40	0.22
Brazilian (38)	38	0.21
Canadian (0)	9	0.05
Celtic (9)	9	0.05
Czech (41)	150	0.82
Danish (0)	14	0.08
Dutch (26)	56	0.31
Eastern European (14)	14	0.08
English (175)	412	2.26
European (11)	11	0.06
French, ex. Basque (0)	45	0.25
French Canadian (0)	12	0.07
German (127)	587	3.22
Greek (233)	247	1.36
Hungarian (7)	95	0.52
Irish (176)	735	4.03
Italian (381)	738	4.05
Lithuanian (0)	6	0.03
Norwegian (9)	21	0.12
Polish (176)	381	2.09
Romanian (44)	44	0.24
Russian (8)	47	0.26
Scotch-Irish (32)	83	0.46
Scottish (11)	125	0.69
Slovak (37)	66	0.36
Swedish (12)	12	0.07
Swiss (0)	8	0.04
Turkish (11)	11	0.06
Ukrainian (23)	23	0.13
Welsh (0)	31	0.17
West Indian, ex. Hispanic (83)	83	0.46
Jamaican (83)	83	0.46
Yugoslavian (9)	9	0.05

Hispanic Origin	Population	%
Hispanic or Latino (of any race)	12,598	69.38
Central American, ex. Mexican	1,568	8.64
Costa Rican	315	1.73
Guatemalan	156	0.86
Honduran	860	4.74
Nicaraguan	15	0.08
Panamanian	10	0.06
Salvadoran	212	1.17
Cuban	74	0.41
Dominican Republic	319	1.76
Mexican	2,707	14.91
Puerto Rican	2,012	11.08
South American	4,978	27.42
Argentinean	70	0.39
Bolivian	2	0.01
Chilean	281	1.55
Colombian	2,767	15.24
Ecuadorian	1,016	5.60
Paraguayan	2	0.01
Peruvian	505	2.78
Uruguayan	307	1.69
Venezuelan	26	0.14
Other South American	2	0.01
Other Hispanic or Latino	940	5.18

Race*	Population	%
African-American/Black (1,108)	1,355	7.46
Not Hispanic (845)	931	5.13
Hispanic (263)	424	2.34
American Indian/Alaska Native (114)	206	1.13
Not Hispanic (13)	45	0.25
Hispanic (101)	161	0.89
Alaska Athabascan *(Ala. Nat.)* (1)	1	0.01
Blackfeet (2)	5	0.03
Central American Ind. (0)	8	0.04
Cherokee (5)	17	0.09
Chickasaw (0)	4	0.02
Delaware (0)	3	0.02
Iroquois (0)	1	0.01
Mexican American Ind. (4)	6	0.03
Navajo (3)	5	0.03
Potawatomi (0)	1	0.01
Pueblo (0)	1	0.01
Seminole (0)	1	0.01
Sioux (0)	1	0.01
South American Ind. (14)	20	0.11
Spanish American Ind. (1)	1	0.01
Tlingit-Haida *(Alaska Native)* (0)	1	0.01
Tohono O'Odham (0)	2	0.01
Asian (461)	551	3.03
Not Hispanic (447)	506	2.79
Hispanic (14)	45	0.25
Bangladeshi (8)	8	0.04
Burmese (5)	5	0.03
Chinese, ex. Taiwanese (86)	93	0.51
Filipino (133)	158	0.87
Indian (110)	130	0.72
Indonesian (2)	2	0.01
Japanese (9)	13	0.07
Korean (23)	29	0.16
Nepalese (2)	2	0.01
Pakistani (32)	34	0.19
Taiwanese (9)	9	0.05
Thai (2)	5	0.03
Vietnamese (35)	42	0.23
Hawaii Native/Pacific Islander (9)	21	0.12
Not Hispanic (5)	11	0.06
Hispanic (4)	10	0.06
Guamanian/Chamorro (5)	5	0.03

*Notes: † The Census 2010 population figure is used to calculate the percentages in the Hispanic Origin and Race categories. Ancestry percentages are based on the 2006-2010 American Community Survey population (not shown); ‡ Numbers in parentheses indicate the number of people reporting a single ancestry; * Numbers in parentheses indicate the number of persons reporting this race alone, not in combination with any other race; Please refer to the Explanation of Data for more information.*

Native Hawaiian (4)	5	0.03
White (12,083)	12,703	69.96
Not Hispanic (4,071)	4,173	22.98
Hispanic (8,012)	8,530	46.98

Dumont

Place Type: Borough
County: Bergen
Population: 17,479†

Ancestry‡	Population	%
African, Sub-Saharan (17)	17	0.10
South African (17)	17	0.10
Albanian (13)	25	0.14
American (311)	311	1.79
Arab (359)	359	2.06
Lebanese (227)	227	1.31
Syrian (132)	132	0.76
Armenian (11)	36	0.21
Austrian (59)	94	0.54
Belgian (0)	28	0.16
Brazilian (0)	15	0.09
British (11)	19	0.11
Bulgarian (12)	12	0.07
Canadian (17)	30	0.17
Celtic (0)	13	0.07
Croatian (30)	42	0.24
Czech (20)	41	0.24
Czechoslovakian (24)	24	0.14
Dutch (13)	182	1.05
Eastern European (68)	68	0.39
English (122)	684	3.93
Estonian (12)	12	0.07
European (54)	54	0.31
Finnish (14)	14	0.08
French, ex. Basque (16)	194	1.12
French Canadian (13)	24	0.14
German (494)	1,969	11.33
Greek (181)	385	2.21
Hungarian (13)	127	0.73
Irish (1,466)	3,754	21.59
Israeli (77)	77	0.44
Italian (2,219)	4,210	24.21
Lithuanian (16)	29	0.17
Northern European (50)	50	0.29
Norwegian (19)	117	0.67
Pennsylvania German (7)	7	0.04
Polish (231)	657	3.78
Portuguese (57)	115	0.66
Romanian (6)	31	0.18
Russian (135)	227	1.31
Scandinavian (4)	4	0.02
Scotch-Irish (24)	219	1.26
Scottish (0)	99	0.57
Slovak (0)	22	0.13
Swedish (0)	118	0.68
Swiss (6)	28	0.16
Ukrainian (46)	83	0.48
Welsh (13)	56	0.32
West Indian, ex. Hispanic (21)	59	0.34
Jamaican (21)	36	0.21
Trinidadian/Tobagonian (0)	23	0.13
Yugoslavian (33)	33	0.19

Hispanic Origin	Population	%
Hispanic or Latino (of any race)	2,580	14.76
Central American, ex. Mexican	192	1.10
Costa Rican	32	0.18
Guatemalan	46	0.26
Honduran	19	0.11
Nicaraguan	6	0.03
Panamanian	7	0.04
Salvadoran	79	0.45
Other Central American	3	0.02
Cuban	257	1.47
Dominican Republic	501	2.87
Mexican	166	0.95
Puerto Rican	560	3.20
South American	726	4.15
Argentinean	22	0.13
Bolivian	16	0.09
Chilean	12	0.07
Colombian	465	2.66
Ecuadorian	101	0.58
Paraguayan	4	0.02
Peruvian	93	0.53
Uruguayan	2	0.01
Venezuelan	9	0.05
Other South American	2	0.01
Other Hispanic or Latino	178	1.02

Race*	Population	%
African-American/Black (445)	559	3.20
Not Hispanic (375)	437	2.50
Hispanic (70)	122	0.70
American Indian/Alaska Native (32)	72	0.41
Not Hispanic (17)	43	0.25
Hispanic (15)	29	0.17
Blackfeet (0)	1	0.01
Canadian/French Am. Ind. (1)	1	0.01
Central American Ind. (0)	1	0.01
Cherokee (0)	3	0.02
Mexican American Ind. (2)	3	0.02
Navajo (4)	4	0.02
South American Ind. (0)	4	0.02
Yakama (1)	1	0.01
Asian (2,620)	2,810	16.08
Not Hispanic (2,599)	2,755	15.76
Hispanic (21)	55	0.31
Bangladeshi (3)	3	0.02
Burmese (4)	4	0.02
Cambodian (5)	5	0.03
Chinese, ex. Taiwanese (198)	247	1.41
Filipino (1,159)	1,246	7.13
Indian (604)	660	3.78
Indonesian (1)	1	0.01
Japanese (89)	120	0.69
Korean (460)	471	2.69
Pakistani (21)	33	0.19
Sri Lankan (5)	5	0.03
Taiwanese (3)	8	0.05
Thai (10)	11	0.06
Vietnamese (12)	19	0.11
Hawaii Native/Pacific Islander (3)	27	0.15
Not Hispanic (3)	15	0.09
Hispanic (0)	12	0.07
Native Hawaiian (1)	1	0.01
White (13,268)	13,559	77.57
Not Hispanic (11,641)	11,815	67.60
Hispanic (1,627)	1,744	9.98

East Brunswick

Place Type: Township
County: Middlesex
Population: 47,512†

Ancestry‡	Population	%
African, Sub-Saharan (180)	180	0.38
African (60)	60	0.13
Ethiopian (14)	14	0.03
Ghanaian (37)	37	0.08
Kenyan (17)	17	0.04
South African (52)	52	0.11
Albanian (42)	42	0.09
American (1,306)	1,306	2.75
Arab (1,929)	2,092	4.41
Arab (33)	33	0.07
Egyptian (1,776)	1,893	3.99
Lebanese (39)	54	0.11
Syrian (73)	73	0.15
Other Arab (8)	39	0.08
Armenian (64)	76	0.16
Austrian (71)	241	0.51
Belgian (0)	30	0.06
Brazilian (59)	130	0.27
British (35)	58	0.12
Bulgarian (7)	7	0.01
Canadian (34)	43	0.09
Croatian (0)	11	0.02
Cypriot (9)	9	0.02
Czech (0)	195	0.41
Czechoslovakian (18)	103	0.22
Danish (0)	100	0.21
Dutch (78)	309	0.65
Eastern European (635)	669	1.41
English (273)	1,642	3.46
Estonian (19)	36	0.08
European (402)	433	0.91
French, ex. Basque (50)	581	1.23
French Canadian (41)	118	0.25
German (1,191)	4,683	9.88
Greek (195)	532	1.12
Guyanese (66)	104	0.22
Hungarian (322)	1,255	2.65
Iranian (99)	99	0.21
Irish (1,430)	5,660	11.94
Israeli (358)	397	0.84
Italian (2,984)	7,016	14.80
Latvian (35)	73	0.15
Lithuanian (72)	275	0.58
Maltese (17)	62	0.13
Norwegian (19)	156	0.33
Polish (1,633)	5,322	11.23
Portuguese (56)	245	0.52
Romanian (99)	409	0.86
Russian (1,796)	3,518	7.42
Scandinavian (11)	11	0.02
Scotch-Irish (107)	368	0.78
Scottish (75)	281	0.59
Slavic (22)	52	0.11
Slovak (106)	271	0.57
Slovene (6)	6	0.01
Soviet Union (27)	27	0.06
Swedish (10)	119	0.25
Swiss (22)	91	0.19
Turkish (29)	52	0.11
Ukrainian (495)	768	1.62
Welsh (0)	46	0.10
West Indian, ex. Hispanic (320)	374	0.79
British West Indian (48)	48	0.10
Haitian (17)	28	0.06
Jamaican (236)	236	0.50
Trinidadian/Tobagonian (19)	19	0.04
West Indian (0)	43	0.09
Yugoslavian (125)	136	0.29

Hispanic Origin	Population	%
Hispanic or Latino (of any race)	3,184	6.70
Central American, ex. Mexican	229	0.48
Costa Rican	27	0.06
Guatemalan	54	0.11
Honduran	45	0.09
Nicaraguan	24	0.05
Panamanian	42	0.09
Salvadoran	32	0.07
Other Central American	5	0.01
Cuban	272	0.57
Dominican Republic	247	0.52
Mexican	310	0.65
Puerto Rican	1,069	2.25
South American	731	1.54
Argentinean	83	0.17
Bolivian	19	0.04
Chilean	31	0.07
Colombian	200	0.42
Ecuadorian	141	0.30
Paraguayan	5	0.01
Peruvian	182	0.38
Uruguayan	20	0.04
Venezuelan	36	0.08
Other South American	14	0.03
Other Hispanic or Latino	326	0.69

Race*	Population	%
African-American/Black (1,890)	2,183	4.59
Not Hispanic (1,741)	1,939	4.08
Hispanic (149)	244	0.51
American Indian/Alaska Native (48)	165	0.35

*Notes: † The Census 2010 population figure is used to calculate the percentages in the Hispanic Origin and Race categories. Ancestry percentages are based on the 2006-2010 American Community Survey population (not shown); ‡ Numbers in parentheses indicate the number of people reporting a single ancestry; * Numbers in parentheses indicate the number of persons reporting this race alone, not in combination with any other race; Please refer to the Explanation of Data for more information.*

Not Hispanic (33)	112	0.24
Hispanic (15)	53	0.11
Blackfeet (0)	2	<0.01
Cherokee (8)	18	0.04
Chickasaw (0)	1	<0.01
Choctaw (0)	1	<0.01
Cree (0)	4	0.01
Creek (1)	1	<0.01
Delaware (0)	2	<0.01
Iroquois (1)	9	0.02
Lumbee (2)	2	<0.01
Mexican American Ind. (1)	1	<0.01
Navajo (0)	1	<0.01
Sioux (1)	7	0.01
South American Ind. (3)	20	0.04
Spanish American Ind. (1)	1	<0.01
Asian (10,835)	11,334	23.86
Not Hispanic (10,812)	11,269	23.72
Hispanic (23)	65	0.14
Bangladeshi (70)	74	0.16
Burmese (62)	63	0.13
Cambodian (2)	2	<0.01
Chinese, ex. Taiwanese (4,160)	4,378	9.21
Filipino (842)	936	1.97
Indian (3,603)	3,772	7.94
Indonesian (16)	18	0.04
Japanese (52)	81	0.17
Korean (929)	976	2.05
Laotian (1)	1	<0.01
Malaysian (4)	8	0.02
Nepalese (6)	6	0.01
Pakistani (358)	390	0.82
Sri Lankan (66)	75	0.16
Taiwanese (333)	393	0.83
Thai (14)	23	0.05
Vietnamese (86)	105	0.22
Hawaii Native/Pacific Islander (6)	62	0.13
Not Hispanic (6)	51	0.11
Hispanic (0)	11	0.02
Guamanian/Chamorro (0)	3	0.01
Native Hawaiian (1)	3	0.01
Samoan (0)	1	<0.01
White (32,954)	33,683	70.89
Not Hispanic (30,887)	31,413	66.12
Hispanic (2,067)	2,270	4.78

East Franklin

Place Type: CDP
County: Somerset
Population: 8,669†

Ancestry‡	Population	%
African, Sub-Saharan (228)	228	2.96
African (121)	121	1.57
Ethiopian (6)	6	0.08
Sierra Leonean (67)	67	0.87
Other Sub-Saharan African (34)	34	0.44
American (33)	33	0.43
Arab (43)	67	0.87
Lebanese (43)	55	0.71
Syrian (0)	12	0.16
Austrian (14)	14	0.18
Canadian (5)	5	0.06
Czechoslovakian (5)	5	0.06
English (11)	89	1.15
French, ex. Basque (0)	12	0.16
German (84)	332	4.31
Greek (13)	19	0.25
Hungarian (185)	226	2.93
Irish (14)	255	3.31
Italian (143)	396	5.14
Maltese (16)	16	0.21
Norwegian (0)	87	1.13
Polish (92)	127	1.65
Romanian (8)	8	0.10
Russian (0)	25	0.32
Scotch-Irish (0)	25	0.32
Scottish (12)	50	0.65
Slovak (49)	84	1.09
Ukrainian (35)	58	0.75
Welsh (0)	12	0.16
West Indian, ex. Hispanic (191)	227	2.94
Haitian (7)	7	0.09
Jamaican (176)	212	2.75
West Indian (8)	8	0.10

Hispanic Origin	Population	%
Hispanic or Latino (of any race)	3,565	41.12
Central American, ex. Mexican	549	6.33
Costa Rican	19	0.22
Guatemalan	56	0.65
Honduran	377	4.35
Nicaraguan	50	0.58
Panamanian	12	0.14
Salvadoran	34	0.39
Other Central American	1	0.01
Cuban	17	0.20
Dominican Republic	938	10.82
Mexican	1,166	13.45
Puerto Rican	491	5.66
South American	189	2.18
Argentinean	5	0.06
Chilean	1	0.01
Colombian	43	0.50
Ecuadorian	64	0.74
Peruvian	64	0.74
Uruguayan	3	0.03
Venezuelan	8	0.09
Other South American	1	0.01
Other Hispanic or Latino	215	2.48

Race*	Population	%
African-American/Black (3,379)	3,582	41.32
Not Hispanic (3,166)	3,311	38.19
Hispanic (213)	271	3.13
American Indian/Alaska Native (57)	130	1.50
Not Hispanic (35)	90	1.04
Hispanic (22)	40	0.46
Cherokee (2)	12	0.14
Chippewa (1)	2	0.02
Delaware (0)	3	0.03
Mexican American Ind. (3)	3	0.03
Navajo (0)	1	0.01
Seminole (0)	1	0.01
Sioux (5)	5	0.06
South American Ind. (10)	13	0.15
Spanish American Ind. (0)	1	0.01
Asian (453)	526	6.07
Not Hispanic (446)	499	5.76
Hispanic (7)	27	0.31
Bangladeshi (3)	3	0.03
Chinese, ex. Taiwanese (46)	53	0.61
Filipino (143)	154	1.78
Indian (158)	177	2.04
Indonesian (1)	1	0.01
Japanese (4)	10	0.12
Korean (10)	13	0.15
Pakistani (32)	34	0.39
Taiwanese (13)	13	0.15
Vietnamese (11)	11	0.13
Hawaii Native/Pacific Islander (3)	33	0.38
Not Hispanic (3)	16	0.18
Hispanic (0)	17	0.20
Native Hawaiian (0)	1	0.01
White (2,554)	2,831	32.66
Not Hispanic (1,209)	1,317	15.19
Hispanic (1,345)	1,514	17.46

East Greenwich

Place Type: Township
County: Gloucester
Population: 9,555†

Ancestry‡	Population	%
American (170)	170	1.91
Austrian (0)	14	0.16
British (0)	23	0.26
Canadian (0)	17	0.19
Czech (0)	27	0.30
Czechoslovakian (11)	11	0.12
Danish (19)	19	0.21
Dutch (0)	97	1.09
English (186)	1,109	12.45
European (76)	76	0.85
French, ex. Basque (44)	170	1.91
French Canadian (13)	26	0.29
German (494)	2,207	24.77
Greek (52)	52	0.58
Hungarian (0)	16	0.18
Irish (601)	2,387	26.79
Italian (1,000)	2,336	26.22
Lithuanian (0)	29	0.33
Norwegian (0)	22	0.25
Pennsylvania German (0)	13	0.15
Polish (118)	738	8.28
Portuguese (62)	62	0.70
Russian (21)	87	0.98
Scotch-Irish (50)	232	2.60
Scottish (14)	113	1.27
Slovak (0)	92	1.03
Swedish (0)	112	1.26
Ukrainian (40)	70	0.79
Welsh (0)	58	0.65
Yugoslavian (0)	9	0.10

Hispanic Origin	Population	%
Hispanic or Latino (of any race)	289	3.02
Central American, ex. Mexican	12	0.13
Costa Rican	1	0.01
Guatemalan	2	0.02
Honduran	3	0.03
Nicaraguan	4	0.04
Panamanian	1	0.01
Salvadoran	1	0.01
Cuban	15	0.16
Dominican Republic	16	0.17
Mexican	35	0.37
Puerto Rican	147	1.54
South American	41	0.43
Argentinean	3	0.03
Chilean	10	0.10
Colombian	15	0.16
Ecuadorian	6	0.06
Peruvian	4	0.04
Venezuelan	3	0.03
Other Hispanic or Latino	23	0.24

Race*	Population	%
African-American/Black (560)	616	6.45
Not Hispanic (538)	586	6.13
Hispanic (22)	30	0.31
American Indian/Alaska Native (13)	39	0.41
Not Hispanic (10)	25	0.26
Hispanic (3)	14	0.15
Apache (0)	1	0.01
Blackfeet (0)	1	0.01
Cherokee (5)	6	0.06
Cheyenne (0)	1	0.01
Crow (0)	1	0.01
Delaware (0)	2	0.02
Iroquois (1)	1	0.01
Lumbee (2)	3	0.03
Seminole (0)	1	0.01
South American Ind. (0)	3	0.03
Asian (345)	401	4.20
Not Hispanic (343)	395	4.13
Hispanic (2)	6	0.06
Cambodian (8)	8	0.08
Chinese, ex. Taiwanese (59)	76	0.80
Filipino (61)	71	0.74
Indian (122)	137	1.43
Japanese (7)	8	0.08
Korean (15)	28	0.29
Malaysian (1)	1	0.01
Pakistani (7)	7	0.07
Sri Lankan (5)	5	0.05
Taiwanese (3)	3	0.03
Thai (6)	13	0.14

*Notes: † The Census 2010 population figure is used to calculate the percentages in the Hispanic Origin and Race categories. Ancestry percentages are based on the 2006-2010 American Community Survey population (not shown); ‡ Numbers in parentheses indicate the number of people reporting a single ancestry; * Numbers in parentheses indicate the number of persons reporting this race alone, not in combination with any other race; Please refer to the Explanation of Data for more information.*

Vietnamese (39)	44	0.46
Hawaii Native/Pacific Islander (5)	6	0.06
Not Hispanic (2)	3	0.03
Hispanic (3)	3	0.03
Guamanian/Chamorro (3)	4	0.04
Native Hawaiian (2)	2	0.02
White (8,451)	8,552	89.50
Not Hispanic (8,266)	8,351	87.40
Hispanic (185)	201	2.10

East Hanover

Place Type: Township
County: Morris
Population: 11,157†

Ancestry‡	Population	%
American (115)	115	1.02
Armenian (23)	114	1.01
Austrian (10)	146	1.30
Belgian (0)	10	0.09
Brazilian (14)	14	0.12
Canadian (0)	19	0.17
Croatian (0)	8	0.07
Czech (0)	25	0.22
Czechoslovakian (9)	28	0.25
Danish (11)	20	0.18
Dutch (51)	241	2.15
English (116)	358	3.19
Estonian (0)	19	0.17
French, ex. Basque (17)	46	0.41
French Canadian (54)	114	1.01
German (243)	1,301	11.58
Greek (215)	261	2.32
Guyanese (72)	72	0.64
Hungarian (0)	65	0.58
Irish (177)	1,450	12.91
Israeli (12)	12	0.11
Italian (4,243)	5,463	48.64
Lithuanian (0)	9	0.08
Norwegian (8)	85	0.76
Polish (275)	784	6.98
Portuguese (109)	147	1.31
Romanian (8)	15	0.13
Russian (72)	203	1.81
Scotch-Irish (24)	47	0.42
Scottish (3)	32	0.28
Slovak (0)	120	1.07
Swedish (0)	32	0.28
Swiss (0)	26	0.23
Ukrainian (62)	82	0.73
Yugoslavian (10)	10	0.09

Hispanic Origin	Population	%
Hispanic or Latino (of any race)	600	5.38
Central American, ex. Mexican	32	0.29
Costa Rican	5	0.04
Guatemalan	9	0.08
Honduran	7	0.06
Panamanian	1	0.01
Salvadoran	10	0.09
Cuban	84	0.75
Dominican Republic	31	0.28
Mexican	73	0.65
Puerto Rican	119	1.07
South American	167	1.50
Argentinean	15	0.13
Chilean	4	0.04
Colombian	52	0.47
Ecuadorian	39	0.35
Paraguayan	1	0.01
Peruvian	42	0.38
Uruguayan	13	0.12
Other South American	1	0.01
Other Hispanic or Latino	94	0.84

Race*	Population	%
African-American/Black (93)	121	1.08
Not Hispanic (90)	104	0.93
Hispanic (3)	17	0.15
American Indian/Alaska Native (9)	19	0.17
Not Hispanic (4)	10	0.09
Hispanic (5)	9	0.08
Blackfeet (0)	2	0.02
Delaware (1)	1	0.01
Iroquois (0)	1	0.01
Asian (1,330)	1,400	12.55
Not Hispanic (1,322)	1,383	12.40
Hispanic (8)	17	0.15
Burmese (3)	3	0.03
Chinese, ex. Taiwanese (418)	439	3.93
Filipino (136)	160	1.43
Indian (428)	445	3.99
Japanese (1)	2	0.02
Korean (109)	116	1.04
Pakistani (21)	24	0.22
Taiwanese (131)	140	1.25
Thai (3)	3	0.03
Vietnamese (54)	56	0.50
Hawaii Native/Pacific Islander (0)	9	0.08
Not Hispanic (0)	8	0.07
Hispanic (0)	1	0.01
Guamanian/Chamorro (0)	1	0.01
White (9,496)	9,597	86.02
Not Hispanic (9,042)	9,110	81.65
Hispanic (454)	487	4.36

East Orange

Place Type: City
County: Essex
Population: 64,270†

Ancestry‡	Population	%
African, Sub-Saharan (2,192)	2,343	3.61
African (608)	733	1.13
Cape Verdean (0)	14	0.02
Ghanaian (345)	345	0.53
Kenyan (75)	75	0.12
Liberian (185)	197	0.30
Nigerian (493)	493	0.76
Sierra Leonean (160)	160	0.25
South African (44)	44	0.07
Other Sub-Saharan African (282)	282	0.43
American (1,033)	1,033	1.59
Arab (53)	53	0.08
Arab (24)	24	0.04
Moroccan (29)	29	0.04
Brazilian (164)	193	0.30
British (0)	2	<0.01
Croatian (0)	6	0.01
Czech (0)	16	0.02
Dutch (72)	153	0.24
Eastern European (33)	33	0.05
English (35)	121	0.19
European (22)	22	0.03
French, ex. Basque (41)	169	0.26
French Canadian (0)	13	0.02
German (29)	102	0.16
Greek (0)	17	0.03
Guyanese (2,590)	2,746	4.23
Hungarian (27)	39	0.06
Irish (165)	413	0.64
Italian (544)	627	0.97
Norwegian (11)	11	0.02
Polish (19)	46	0.07
Portuguese (0)	38	0.06
Russian (7)	7	0.01
Scotch-Irish (0)	22	0.03
Scottish (13)	39	0.06
Swedish (11)	11	0.02
Ukrainian (82)	91	0.14
Welsh (0)	6	0.01
West Indian, ex. Hispanic (8,721)	9,005	13.87
Barbadian (141)	141	0.22
Bermudan (27)	28	0.04
British West Indian (282)	310	0.48
Haitian (3,642)	3,699	5.70
Jamaican (3,047)	3,176	4.89
Trinidadian/Tobagonian (1,114)	1,131	1.74
U.S. Virgin Islander (8)	8	0.01
West Indian (452)	504	0.78
Other West Indian (8)	8	0.01

Hispanic Origin	Population	%
Hispanic or Latino (of any race)	5,095	7.93
Central American, ex. Mexican	606	0.94
Costa Rican	36	0.06
Guatemalan	209	0.33
Honduran	146	0.23
Nicaraguan	30	0.05
Panamanian	80	0.12
Salvadoran	97	0.15
Other Central American	8	0.01
Cuban	172	0.27
Dominican Republic	1,212	1.89
Mexican	360	0.56
Puerto Rican	1,715	2.67
South American	467	0.73
Argentinean	17	0.03
Bolivian	8	0.01
Chilean	16	0.02
Colombian	61	0.09
Ecuadorian	154	0.24
Paraguayan	6	0.01
Peruvian	97	0.15
Uruguayan	75	0.12
Venezuelan	17	0.03
Other South American	16	0.02
Other Hispanic or Latino	563	0.88

Race*	Population	%
African-American/Black (56,887)	58,193	90.54
Not Hispanic (55,702)	56,704	88.23
Hispanic (1,185)	1,489	2.32
American Indian/Alaska Native (248)	681	1.06
Not Hispanic (186)	566	0.88
Hispanic (62)	115	0.18
Blackfeet (4)	39	0.06
Central American Ind. (4)	10	0.02
Cherokee (34)	128	0.20
Chippewa (0)	2	<0.01
Choctaw (0)	1	<0.01
Creek (0)	3	<0.01
Delaware (2)	6	0.01
Iroquois (4)	6	0.01
Lumbee (0)	2	<0.01
Mexican American Ind. (11)	22	0.03
Navajo (0)	4	0.01
Pueblo (4)	6	0.01
Seminole (0)	6	0.01
Shoshone (0)	1	<0.01
Sioux (0)	6	0.01
South American Ind. (1)	12	0.02
Spanish American Ind. (2)	3	<0.01
Tlingit-Haida *(Alaska Native)* (0)	1	<0.01
Yuman (1)	2	<0.01
Asian (465)	619	0.96
Not Hispanic (436)	573	0.89
Hispanic (29)	46	0.07
Chinese, ex. Taiwanese (44)	89	0.14
Filipino (122)	138	0.21
Indian (237)	284	0.44
Indonesian (3)	3	<0.01
Japanese (9)	14	0.02
Korean (9)	29	0.05
Laotian (0)	2	<0.01
Pakistani (8)	13	0.02
Taiwanese (2)	2	<0.01
Thai (1)	6	0.01
Vietnamese (7)	9	0.01
Hawaii Native/Pacific Islander (38)	174	0.27
Not Hispanic (29)	130	0.20
Hispanic (9)	44	0.07
Guamanian/Chamorro (21)	28	0.04
Native Hawaiian (5)	12	0.02
Samoan (2)	5	0.01
White (2,657)	3,306	5.14
Not Hispanic (1,422)	1,788	2.78
Hispanic (1,235)	1,518	2.36

*Notes: † The Census 2010 population figure is used to calculate the percentages in the Hispanic Origin and Race categories. Ancestry percentages are based on the 2006-2010 American Community Survey population (not shown); ‡ Numbers in parentheses indicate the number of people reporting a single ancestry; * Numbers in parentheses indicate the number of persons reporting this race alone, not in combination with any other race; Please refer to the Explanation of Data for more information.*

East Rutherford

Place Type: Borough
County: Bergen
Population: 8,913†

Ancestry‡	Population	%
African, Sub-Saharan (36)	73	0.83
African (36)	73	0.83
American (317)	317	3.59
Arab (21)	64	0.72
Egyptian (21)	40	0.45
Syrian (0)	24	0.27
Brazilian (29)	29	0.33
British (7)	26	0.29
Bulgarian (37)	37	0.42
Canadian (18)	75	0.85
Croatian (0)	35	0.40
Czech (0)	12	0.14
Dutch (0)	58	0.66
Eastern European (29)	44	0.50
English (43)	149	1.69
European (0)	8	0.09
French, ex. Basque (20)	32	0.36
French Canadian (0)	16	0.18
German (62)	555	6.29
Greek (92)	169	1.91
Guyanese (0)	18	0.20
Hungarian (69)	94	1.06
Irish (368)	931	10.54
Israeli (12)	12	0.14
Italian (924)	1,900	21.52
Lithuanian (0)	25	0.28
Norwegian (0)	45	0.51
Polish (988)	1,372	15.54
Portuguese (0)	26	0.29
Romanian (8)	15	0.17
Russian (64)	133	1.51
Scotch-Irish (0)	94	1.06
Scottish (85)	172	1.95
Slovak (15)	15	0.17
Turkish (18)	18	0.20
West Indian, ex. Hispanic (22)	42	0.48
Jamaican (0)	20	0.23
Trinidadian/Tobagonian (22)	22	0.25

Hispanic Origin	Population	%
Hispanic or Latino (of any race)	1,563	17.54
Central American, ex. Mexican	62	0.70
Costa Rican	5	0.06
Guatemalan	19	0.21
Honduran	11	0.12
Nicaraguan	1	0.01
Panamanian	4	0.04
Salvadoran	22	0.25
Cuban	106	1.19
Dominican Republic	177	1.99
Mexican	169	1.90
Puerto Rican	360	4.04
South American	521	5.85
Argentinean	28	0.31
Bolivian	31	0.35
Chilean	8	0.09
Colombian	189	2.12
Ecuadorian	122	1.37
Peruvian	112	1.26
Uruguayan	5	0.06
Venezuelan	7	0.08
Other South American	19	0.21
Other Hispanic or Latino	168	1.88

Race*	Population	%
African-American/Black (401)	470	5.27
Not Hispanic (336)	388	4.35
Hispanic (65)	82	0.92
American Indian/Alaska Native (20)	56	0.63
Not Hispanic (5)	32	0.36
Hispanic (15)	24	0.27
Blackfeet (1)	2	0.02
Cherokee (1)	6	0.07
Iroquois (1)	4	0.04
Mexican American Ind. (3)	3	0.03
South American Ind. (6)	8	0.09
Asian (1,242)	1,318	14.79
Not Hispanic (1,237)	1,293	14.51
Hispanic (5)	25	0.28
Bangladeshi (1)	1	0.01
Chinese, ex. Taiwanese (136)	147	1.65
Filipino (114)	130	1.46
Indian (464)	479	5.37
Indonesian (1)	3	0.03
Japanese (13)	19	0.21
Korean (405)	412	4.62
Laotian (8)	8	0.09
Nepalese (6)	6	0.07
Pakistani (32)	33	0.37
Sri Lankan (8)	8	0.09
Taiwanese (13)	14	0.16
Thai (16)	17	0.19
Vietnamese (7)	7	0.08
Hawaii Native/Pacific Islander (3)	5	0.06
Not Hispanic (2)	4	0.04
Hispanic (1)	1	0.01
Native Hawaiian (1)	1	0.01
White (6,510)	6,684	74.99
Not Hispanic (5,616)	5,722	64.20
Hispanic (894)	962	10.79

East Windsor

Place Type: Township
County: Mercer
Population: 27,190†

Ancestry‡	Population	%
Afghan (81)	81	0.30
African, Sub-Saharan (520)	560	2.09
African (287)	327	1.22
Ghanaian (60)	60	0.22
Liberian (38)	38	0.14
Senegalese (14)	14	0.05
Sierra Leonean (121)	121	0.45
Albanian (15)	15	0.06
American (797)	797	2.97
Arab (60)	198	0.74
Egyptian (35)	35	0.13
Lebanese (8)	146	0.54
Palestinian (17)	17	0.06
Armenian (12)	12	0.04
Austrian (33)	122	0.45
Belgian (18)	38	0.14
British (56)	124	0.46
Bulgarian (13)	13	0.05
Canadian (0)	53	0.20
Celtic (0)	16	0.06
Croatian (0)	55	0.21
Czech (17)	104	0.39
Czechoslovakian (19)	19	0.07
Danish (7)	37	0.14
Dutch (42)	269	1.00
Eastern European (70)	81	0.30
English (304)	1,395	5.20
Estonian (17)	17	0.06
European (272)	417	1.55
Finnish (28)	28	0.10
French, ex. Basque (59)	288	1.07
French Canadian (17)	58	0.22
German (660)	2,759	10.29
German Russian (4)	4	0.01
Greek (114)	114	0.43
Hungarian (161)	556	2.07
Irish (624)	2,946	10.99
Israeli (30)	30	0.11
Italian (1,486)	3,456	12.89
Lithuanian (51)	185	0.69
New Zealander (0)	14	0.05
Norwegian (0)	31	0.12
Polish (835)	1,993	7.43
Portuguese (85)	154	0.57
Romanian (0)	107	0.40
Russian (667)	1,186	4.42
Scandinavian (13)	54	0.20
Scotch-Irish (39)	203	0.76
Scottish (58)	190	0.71
Slavic (10)	10	0.04
Slovak (15)	49	0.18
Swedish (21)	103	0.38
Swiss (0)	54	0.20
Turkish (11)	11	0.04
Ukrainian (81)	135	0.50
Welsh (25)	68	0.25
West Indian, ex. Hispanic (353)	430	1.60
British West Indian (12)	12	0.04
Haitian (114)	114	0.43
Jamaican (183)	260	0.97
Trinidadian/Tobagonian (44)	44	0.16

Hispanic Origin	Population	%
Hispanic or Latino (of any race)	5,340	19.64
Central American, ex. Mexican	813	2.99
Costa Rican	27	0.10
Guatemalan	600	2.21
Honduran	41	0.15
Nicaraguan	42	0.15
Panamanian	23	0.08
Salvadoran	72	0.26
Other Central American	8	0.03
Cuban	117	0.43
Dominican Republic	210	0.77
Mexican	532	1.96
Puerto Rican	696	2.56
South American	2,448	9.00
Argentinean	21	0.08
Bolivian	14	0.05
Chilean	12	0.04
Colombian	369	1.36
Ecuadorian	1,780	6.55
Peruvian	211	0.78
Uruguayan	11	0.04
Venezuelan	16	0.06
Other South American	14	0.05
Other Hispanic or Latino	524	1.93

Race*	Population	%
African-American/Black (2,343)	2,576	9.47
Not Hispanic (2,220)	2,396	8.81
Hispanic (123)	180	0.66
American Indian/Alaska Native (145)	268	0.99
Not Hispanic (25)	108	0.40
Hispanic (120)	160	0.59
Apache (0)	3	0.01
Blackfeet (1)	6	0.02
Canadian/French Am. Ind. (1)	1	<0.01
Cherokee (1)	22	0.08
Choctaw (0)	1	<0.01
Creek (1)	1	<0.01
Delaware (1)	3	0.01
Iroquois (0)	6	0.02
Lumbee (0)	1	<0.01
Mexican American Ind. (14)	14	0.05
Osage (0)	1	<0.01
Seminole (1)	2	0.01
South American Ind. (10)	19	0.07
Spanish American Ind. (7)	7	0.03
Asian (4,802)	5,068	18.64
Not Hispanic (4,786)	5,027	18.49
Hispanic (16)	41	0.15
Bangladeshi (36)	37	0.14
Burmese (4)	4	0.01
Chinese, ex. Taiwanese (625)	678	2.49
Filipino (333)	386	1.42
Indian (3,332)	3,448	12.68
Indonesian (5)	14	0.05
Japanese (25)	48	0.18
Korean (132)	146	0.54
Laotian (1)	2	0.01
Malaysian (5)	5	0.02
Pakistani (164)	174	0.64
Sri Lankan (14)	18	0.07
Taiwanese (28)	29	0.11

*Notes: † The Census 2010 population figure is used to calculate the percentages in the Hispanic Origin and Race categories. Ancestry percentages are based on the 2006-2010 American Community Survey population (not shown); ‡ Numbers in parentheses indicate the number of people reporting a single ancestry; * Numbers in parentheses indicate the number of persons reporting this race alone, not in combination with any other race; Please refer to the Explanation of Data for more information.*

Thai (6)	10	0.04
Vietnamese (43)	49	0.18
Hawaii Native/Pacific Islander (16)	50	0.18
Not Hispanic (3)	26	0.10
Hispanic (13)	24	0.09
Guamanian/Chamorro (10)	11	0.04
Native Hawaiian (0)	5	0.02
Samoan (1)	3	0.01
White (16,880)	17,443	64.15
Not Hispanic (14,301)	14,609	53.73
Hispanic (2,579)	2,834	10.42

Eatontown

Place Type: Borough
County: Monmouth
Population: 12,709†

Ancestry‡	Population	%
African, Sub-Saharan (20)	44	0.34
African (0)	24	0.19
South African (20)	20	0.15
American (291)	291	2.25
Arab (150)	185	1.43
Egyptian (150)	150	1.16
Lebanese (0)	12	0.09
Syrian (0)	23	0.18
Armenian (12)	12	0.09
Austrian (17)	39	0.30
Brazilian (256)	256	1.98
Canadian (35)	83	0.64
Croatian (59)	59	0.46
Czech (0)	17	0.13
Czechoslovakian (14)	21	0.16
Danish (0)	2	0.02
Dutch (12)	70	0.54
Eastern European (47)	55	0.43
English (215)	860	6.65
European (70)	70	0.54
French, ex. Basque (24)	291	2.25
French Canadian (38)	47	0.36
German (354)	1,601	12.37
Greek (65)	203	1.57
Hungarian (8)	128	0.99
Irish (573)	1,917	14.82
Israeli (11)	62	0.48
Italian (1,406)	2,677	20.69
Lithuanian (30)	38	0.29
Norwegian (0)	27	0.21
Pennsylvania German (0)	9	0.07
Polish (289)	698	5.39
Portuguese (22)	22	0.17
Romanian (0)	23	0.18
Russian (112)	229	1.77
Scotch-Irish (93)	192	1.48
Scottish (30)	194	1.50
Slavic (0)	6	0.05
Slovak (18)	36	0.28
Slovene (0)	9	0.07
Swedish (14)	81	0.63
Swiss (0)	48	0.37
Turkish (133)	184	1.42
Ukrainian (17)	54	0.42
Welsh (27)	88	0.68
West Indian, ex. Hispanic (97)	112	0.87
Haitian (30)	30	0.23
Trinidadian/Tobagonian (44)	59	0.46
West Indian (23)	23	0.18

Hispanic Origin	Population	%
Hispanic or Latino (of any race)	1,571	12.36
Central American, ex. Mexican	161	1.27
Costa Rican	22	0.17
Guatemalan	18	0.14
Honduran	17	0.13
Nicaraguan	13	0.10
Panamanian	15	0.12
Salvadoran	70	0.55
Other Central American	6	0.05
Cuban	65	0.51
Dominican Republic	57	0.45
Mexican	364	2.86
Puerto Rican	575	4.52
South American	234	1.84
Argentinean	9	0.07
Bolivian	13	0.10
Chilean	10	0.08
Colombian	72	0.57
Ecuadorian	32	0.25
Peruvian	66	0.52
Uruguayan	2	0.02
Venezuelan	30	0.24
Other Hispanic or Latino	115	0.90

Race*	Population	%
African-American/Black (1,577)	1,831	14.41
Not Hispanic (1,475)	1,661	13.07
Hispanic (102)	170	1.34
American Indian/Alaska Native (36)	129	1.02
Not Hispanic (32)	97	0.76
Hispanic (4)	32	0.25
Apache (4)	4	0.03
Blackfeet (2)	7	0.06
Cherokee (3)	14	0.11
Chickasaw (4)	4	0.03
Creek (0)	1	0.01
Delaware (1)	6	0.05
Iroquois (5)	5	0.04
Mexican American Ind. (1)	4	0.03
Navajo (0)	1	0.01
Seminole (0)	1	0.01
Sioux (1)	6	0.05
South American Ind. (3)	5	0.04
Asian (1,102)	1,249	9.83
Not Hispanic (1,097)	1,216	9.57
Hispanic (5)	33	0.26
Bangladeshi (5)	5	0.04
Burmese (2)	2	0.02
Cambodian (4)	4	0.03
Chinese, ex. Taiwanese (195)	243	1.91
Filipino (219)	243	1.91
Hmong (1)	3	0.02
Indian (253)	271	2.13
Indonesian (13)	13	0.10
Japanese (13)	48	0.38
Korean (129)	165	1.30
Malaysian (0)	5	0.04
Pakistani (14)	15	0.12
Sri Lankan (1)	1	0.01
Taiwanese (24)	27	0.21
Thai (8)	9	0.07
Vietnamese (190)	197	1.55
Hawaii Native/Pacific Islander (11)	35	0.28
Not Hispanic (10)	27	0.21
Hispanic (1)	8	0.06
Fijian (1)	1	0.01
Guamanian/Chamorro (4)	4	0.03
Native Hawaiian (4)	15	0.12
Samoan (2)	2	0.02
White (9,060)	9,433	74.22
Not Hispanic (8,129)	8,398	66.08
Hispanic (931)	1,035	8.14

Echelon

Place Type: CDP
County: Camden
Population: 10,743†

Ancestry‡	Population	%
African, Sub-Saharan (7)	7	0.07
African (7)	7	0.07
American (241)	241	2.40
Arab (39)	129	1.28
Egyptian (0)	59	0.59
Lebanese (0)	13	0.13
Moroccan (39)	39	0.39
Syrian (0)	18	0.18
British (69)	69	0.69
Canadian (10)	10	0.10
Czech (0)	14	0.14
Dutch (18)	60	0.60
Eastern European (26)	26	0.26
English (108)	951	9.46
European (0)	16	0.16
Finnish (0)	45	0.45
French, ex. Basque (0)	243	2.42
French Canadian (0)	22	0.22
German (270)	1,559	15.51
Greek (0)	33	0.33
Hungarian (94)	161	1.60
Irish (365)	1,587	15.79
Israeli (25)	25	0.25
Italian (852)	1,911	19.02
Latvian (0)	67	0.67
Lithuanian (0)	58	0.58
Norwegian (0)	37	0.37
Pennsylvania German (12)	68	0.68
Polish (196)	715	7.12
Portuguese (38)	57	0.57
Romanian (0)	30	0.30
Russian (75)	429	4.27
Scotch-Irish (59)	94	0.94
Scottish (0)	82	0.82
Slovak (0)	77	0.77
Swedish (10)	157	1.56
Swiss (0)	7	0.07
Turkish (65)	65	0.65
Ukrainian (68)	91	0.91
Welsh (17)	58	0.58
West Indian, ex. Hispanic (27)	27	0.27
British West Indian (14)	14	0.14
West Indian (13)	13	0.13

Hispanic Origin	Population	%
Hispanic or Latino (of any race)	476	4.43
Central American, ex. Mexican	18	0.17
Costa Rican	1	0.01
Guatemalan	1	0.01
Honduran	3	0.03
Nicaraguan	1	0.01
Panamanian	4	0.04
Salvadoran	8	0.07
Cuban	25	0.23
Dominican Republic	21	0.20
Mexican	103	0.96
Puerto Rican	192	1.79
South American	78	0.73
Argentinean	3	0.03
Bolivian	1	0.01
Chilean	2	0.02
Colombian	28	0.26
Ecuadorian	18	0.17
Peruvian	10	0.09
Uruguayan	1	0.01
Venezuelan	15	0.14
Other Hispanic or Latino	39	0.36

Race*	Population	%
African-American/Black (1,291)	1,418	13.20
Not Hispanic (1,244)	1,362	12.68
Hispanic (47)	56	0.52
American Indian/Alaska Native (26)	92	0.86
Not Hispanic (19)	73	0.68
Hispanic (7)	19	0.18
Blackfeet (0)	1	0.01
Cherokee (2)	12	0.11
Comanche (1)	3	0.03
Creek (1)	1	0.01
Delaware (1)	3	0.03
Iroquois (0)	1	0.01
Mexican American Ind. (0)	1	0.01
Navajo (0)	1	0.01
South American Ind. (2)	5	0.05
Asian (2,094)	2,274	21.17
Not Hispanic (2,086)	2,258	21.02
Hispanic (8)	16	0.15
Bangladeshi (20)	21	0.20
Cambodian (8)	8	0.07
Chinese, ex. Taiwanese (274)	301	2.80

*Notes: † The Census 2010 population figure is used to calculate the percentages in the Hispanic Origin and Race categories. Ancestry percentages are based on the 2006-2010 American Community Survey population (not shown); ‡ Numbers in parentheses indicate the number of people reporting a single ancestry; * Numbers in parentheses indicate the number of persons reporting this race alone, not in combination with any other race; Please refer to the Explanation of Data for more information.*

Filipino (228)	281	2.62
Indian (1,132)	1,190	11.08
Indonesian (1)	2	0.02
Japanese (11)	24	0.22
Korean (242)	271	2.52
Malaysian (1)	1	0.01
Nepalese (2)	2	0.02
Pakistani (57)	63	0.59
Sri Lankan (1)	1	0.01
Taiwanese (6)	8	0.07
Thai (4)	4	0.04
Vietnamese (38)	50	0.47
Hawaii Native/Pacific Islander (6)	22	0.20
Not Hispanic (6)	14	0.13
Hispanic (0)	8	0.07
Native Hawaiian (1)	6	0.06
Samoan (0)	2	0.02
Tongan (3)	3	0.03
White (6,860)	7,067	65.78
Not Hispanic (6,597)	6,781	63.12
Hispanic (263)	286	2.66

Edgewater Park

Place Type: Township
County: Burlington
Population: 8,881†

Ancestry‡	Population	%
African, Sub-Saharan (166)	177	2.02
African (133)	144	1.65
Liberian (33)	33	0.38
American (202)	202	2.31
Arab (10)	27	0.31
Lebanese (10)	27	0.31
Australian (0)	27	0.31
Austrian (0)	9	0.10
Belgian (8)	8	0.09
Brazilian (262)	262	3.00
British (25)	50	0.57
Czech (0)	12	0.14
Dutch (17)	173	1.98
Eastern European (12)	37	0.42
English (149)	783	8.95
Estonian (0)	16	0.18
European (26)	26	0.30
French, ex. Basque (22)	74	0.85
German (318)	1,293	14.79
Greek (24)	85	0.97
Hungarian (10)	50	0.57
Irish (329)	1,300	14.87
Italian (304)	870	9.95
Lithuanian (7)	42	0.48
Norwegian (9)	54	0.62
Pennsylvania German (15)	15	0.17
Polish (107)	506	5.79
Portuguese (0)	10	0.11
Romanian (0)	17	0.19
Russian (13)	150	1.72
Scotch-Irish (27)	75	0.86
Scottish (87)	171	1.96
Slavic (0)	9	0.10
Slovak (22)	64	0.73
Swedish (0)	19	0.22
Swiss (0)	8	0.09
Turkish (180)	180	2.06
Ukrainian (9)	57	0.65
Welsh (0)	131	1.50
West Indian, ex. Hispanic (38)	52	0.59
British West Indian (15)	15	0.17
Haitian (0)	14	0.16
Jamaican (14)	14	0.16
West Indian (9)	9	0.10

Hispanic Origin	Population	%
Hispanic or Latino (of any race)	970	10.92
Central American, ex. Mexican	320	3.60
Costa Rican	3	0.03
Guatemalan	26	0.29
Honduran	246	2.77
Nicaraguan	4	0.05
Panamanian	13	0.15
Salvadoran	13	0.15
Other Central American	15	0.17
Cuban	15	0.17
Dominican Republic	48	0.54
Mexican	121	1.36
Puerto Rican	339	3.82
South American	40	0.45
Argentinean	1	0.01
Chilean	3	0.03
Colombian	10	0.11
Ecuadorian	7	0.08
Peruvian	11	0.12
Venezuelan	7	0.08
Other South American	1	0.01
Other Hispanic or Latino	87	0.98

Race*	Population	%
African-American/Black (2,426)	2,666	30.02
Not Hispanic (2,320)	2,518	28.35
Hispanic (106)	148	1.67
American Indian/Alaska Native (30)	115	1.29
Not Hispanic (20)	93	1.05
Hispanic (10)	22	0.25
Apache (0)	1	0.01
Blackfeet (0)	1	0.01
Central American Ind. (3)	3	0.03
Cherokee (0)	17	0.19
Choctaw (0)	4	0.05
Iroquois (1)	2	0.02
Pima (2)	2	0.02
Seminole (0)	1	0.01
South American Ind. (3)	3	0.03
Spanish American Ind. (0)	1	0.01
Yup'ik *(Alaska Native)* (0)	1	0.01
Asian (283)	392	4.41
Not Hispanic (282)	386	4.35
Hispanic (1)	6	0.07
Bangladeshi (5)	10	0.11
Burmese (3)	3	0.03
Chinese, ex. Taiwanese (22)	31	0.35
Filipino (24)	37	0.42
Indian (129)	151	1.70
Japanese (5)	30	0.34
Korean (26)	35	0.39
Pakistani (47)	57	0.64
Taiwanese (1)	1	0.01
Thai (1)	4	0.05
Vietnamese (6)	13	0.15
Hawaii Native/Pacific Islander (2)	18	0.20
Not Hispanic (2)	12	0.14
Hispanic (0)	6	0.07
Guamanian/Chamorro (1)	1	0.01
Native Hawaiian (1)	5	0.06
Samoan (0)	1	0.01
White (5,125)	5,468	61.57
Not Hispanic (4,758)	5,038	56.73
Hispanic (367)	430	4.84

Edgewater

Place Type: Borough
County: Bergen
Population: 11,513†

Ancestry‡	Population	%
African, Sub-Saharan (69)	80	0.74
African (10)	21	0.20
Nigerian (59)	59	0.55
American (205)	205	1.90
Arab (60)	60	0.56
Egyptian (13)	13	0.12
Lebanese (47)	47	0.44
Armenian (66)	75	0.70
Assyrian/Chaldean/Syriac (14)	14	0.13
Austrian (0)	45	0.42
Brazilian (52)	52	0.48
British (13)	28	0.26
Czech (0)	30	0.28
Czechoslovakian (0)	11	0.10
Danish (12)	12	0.11
Dutch (20)	89	0.83
Eastern European (49)	78	0.72
English (35)	252	2.34
European (71)	85	0.79
French, ex. Basque (21)	216	2.01
French Canadian (12)	56	0.52
German (179)	890	8.27
Greek (65)	100	0.93
Hungarian (103)	163	1.51
Iranian (60)	73	0.68
Irish (284)	1,084	10.07
Israeli (14)	27	0.25
Italian (312)	775	7.20
Latvian (38)	124	1.15
Lithuanian (0)	52	0.48
Northern European (15)	15	0.14
Norwegian (0)	24	0.22
Polish (112)	345	3.20
Portuguese (80)	80	0.74
Romanian (15)	29	0.27
Russian (393)	579	5.38
Scotch-Irish (0)	140	1.30
Scottish (15)	140	1.30
Serbian (23)	52	0.48
Swedish (12)	25	0.23
Swiss (33)	113	1.05
Turkish (239)	249	2.31
Ukrainian (78)	78	0.72
Welsh (16)	26	0.24
West Indian, ex. Hispanic (42)	42	0.39
Jamaican (42)	42	0.39
Yugoslavian (9)	29	0.27

Hispanic Origin	Population	%
Hispanic or Latino (of any race)	1,278	11.10
Central American, ex. Mexican	80	0.69
Costa Rican	7	0.06
Guatemalan	14	0.12
Honduran	7	0.06
Nicaraguan	4	0.03
Panamanian	8	0.07
Salvadoran	40	0.35
Cuban	180	1.56
Dominican Republic	245	2.13
Mexican	51	0.44
Puerto Rican	299	2.60
South American	324	2.81
Argentinean	30	0.26
Bolivian	8	0.07
Chilean	15	0.13
Colombian	124	1.08
Ecuadorian	72	0.63
Paraguayan	3	0.03
Peruvian	26	0.23
Uruguayan	24	0.21
Venezuelan	22	0.19
Other Hispanic or Latino	99	0.86

Race*	Population	%
African-American/Black (570)	671	5.83
Not Hispanic (519)	589	5.12
Hispanic (51)	82	0.71
American Indian/Alaska Native (16)	53	0.46
Not Hispanic (8)	30	0.26
Hispanic (8)	23	0.20
Blackfeet (0)	1	0.01
Cherokee (0)	10	0.09
Iroquois (1)	2	0.02
Mexican American Ind. (1)	3	0.03
Navajo (1)	2	0.02
Shoshone (0)	1	0.01
South American Ind. (1)	7	0.06
Asian (4,084)	4,247	36.89
Not Hispanic (4,076)	4,226	36.71
Hispanic (8)	21	0.18
Bangladeshi (3)	3	0.03
Burmese (3)	3	0.03
Chinese, ex. Taiwanese (488)	543	4.72

*Notes: † The Census 2010 population figure is used to calculate the percentages in the Hispanic Origin and Race categories. Ancestry percentages are based on the 2006-2010 American Community Survey population (not shown); ‡ Numbers in parentheses indicate the number of people reporting a single ancestry; * Numbers in parentheses indicate the number of persons reporting this race alone, not in combination with any other race; Please refer to the Explanation of Data for more information.*

Filipino (137)	152	1.32
Indian (450)	481	4.18
Indonesian (2)	2	0.02
Japanese (560)	608	5.28
Korean (2,258)	2,316	20.12
Malaysian (1)	6	0.05
Nepalese (3)	3	0.03
Pakistani (22)	24	0.21
Sri Lankan (7)	8	0.07
Taiwanese (38)	41	0.36
Thai (17)	17	0.15
Vietnamese (11)	15	0.13
Hawaii Native/Pacific Islander (7)	13	0.11
Not Hispanic (6)	9	0.08
Hispanic (1)	4	0.03
Guamanian/Chamorro (1)	1	0.01
Native Hawaiian (2)	6	0.05
Samoan (0)	1	0.01
White (6,135)	6,394	55.54
Not Hispanic (5,343)	5,544	48.15
Hispanic (792)	850	7.38

Edison

Place Type: Township
County: Middlesex
Population: 99,967†

Ancestry‡	Population	%
Afghan (183)	209	0.21
African, Sub-Saharan (677)	907	0.91
African (185)	344	0.35
Ethiopian (24)	24	0.02
Ghanaian (84)	84	0.08
Kenyan (79)	79	0.08
Nigerian (225)	296	0.30
Sierra Leonean (39)	39	0.04
South African (29)	29	0.03
Zimbabwean (12)	12	0.01
Albanian (18)	18	0.02
American (3,284)	3,284	3.30
Arab (798)	1,046	1.05
Arab (204)	204	0.20
Egyptian (214)	304	0.31
Jordanian (233)	233	0.23
Lebanese (75)	207	0.21
Moroccan (47)	47	0.05
Palestinian (9)	9	0.01
Syrian (16)	25	0.03
Other Arab (0)	17	0.02
Armenian (8)	43	0.04
Austrian (48)	346	0.35
Belgian (9)	9	0.01
Brazilian (59)	92	0.09
British (46)	102	0.10
Canadian (51)	262	0.26
Carpatho Rusyn (0)	7	0.01
Celtic (11)	11	0.01
Croatian (0)	22	0.02
Czech (38)	220	0.22
Czechoslovakian (108)	203	0.20
Danish (120)	423	0.42
Dutch (110)	335	0.34
Eastern European (606)	677	0.68
English (330)	2,256	2.27
European (272)	454	0.46
Finnish (16)	58	0.06
French, ex. Basque (235)	932	0.94
French Canadian (105)	365	0.37
German (1,466)	6,757	6.79
Greek (384)	733	0.74
Guyanese (175)	221	0.22
Hungarian (839)	2,322	2.33
Iranian (233)	233	0.23
Irish (1,972)	7,996	8.03
Israeli (56)	65	0.07
Italian (5,014)	10,197	10.24
Latvian (75)	75	0.08
Lithuanian (89)	270	0.27
Norwegian (25)	204	0.20
Pennsylvania German (8)	8	0.01
Polish (2,093)	5,536	5.56
Portuguese (320)	612	0.61
Romanian (101)	184	0.18
Russian (1,072)	2,079	2.09
Scandinavian (0)	10	0.01
Scotch-Irish (70)	315	0.32
Scottish (104)	449	0.45
Serbian (24)	24	0.02
Slavic (39)	147	0.15
Slovak (330)	662	0.66
Slovene (11)	26	0.03
Swedish (81)	399	0.40
Swiss (0)	59	0.06
Turkish (203)	240	0.24
Ukrainian (236)	490	0.49
Welsh (10)	123	0.12
West Indian, ex. Hispanic (986)	1,145	1.15
British West Indian (16)	36	0.04
Haitian (226)	226	0.23
Jamaican (519)	631	0.63
Trinidadian/Tobagonian (59)	81	0.08
U.S. Virgin Islander (10)	10	0.01
West Indian (156)	161	0.16
Yugoslavian (7)	26	0.03

Hispanic Origin	Population	%
Hispanic or Latino (of any race)	8,112	8.11
Central American, ex. Mexican	589	0.59
Costa Rican	63	0.06
Guatemalan	112	0.11
Honduran	141	0.14
Nicaraguan	53	0.05
Panamanian	53	0.05
Salvadoran	158	0.16
Other Central American	9	0.01
Cuban	555	0.56
Dominican Republic	726	0.73
Mexican	1,183	1.18
Puerto Rican	2,591	2.59
South American	1,727	1.73
Argentinean	119	0.12
Bolivian	14	0.01
Chilean	72	0.07
Colombian	740	0.74
Ecuadorian	285	0.29
Paraguayan	4	<0.01
Peruvian	389	0.39
Uruguayan	54	0.05
Venezuelan	45	0.05
Other South American	5	0.01
Other Hispanic or Latino	741	0.74

Race*	Population	%
African-American/Black (7,046)	7,713	7.72
Not Hispanic (6,631)	7,089	7.09
Hispanic (415)	624	0.62
American Indian/Alaska Native (229)	694	0.69
Not Hispanic (186)	589	0.59
Hispanic (43)	105	0.11
Apache (1)	6	0.01
Blackfeet (2)	15	0.02
Central American Ind. (0)	5	0.01
Cherokee (8)	47	0.05
Chippewa (0)	2	<0.01
Choctaw (0)	2	<0.01
Cree (2)	2	<0.01
Creek (0)	1	<0.01
Crow (2)	2	<0.01
Delaware (3)	9	0.01
Inupiat *(Alaska Native)* (1)	1	<0.01
Iroquois (3)	8	0.01
Lumbee (1)	1	<0.01
Mexican American Ind. (6)	8	0.01
Navajo (2)	2	<0.01
Seminole (3)	3	<0.01
Sioux (0)	4	<0.01
South American Ind. (17)	27	0.03
Spanish American Ind. (1)	1	<0.01
Asian (43,177)	44,924	44.94
Not Hispanic (43,092)	44,748	44.76
Hispanic (85)	176	0.18
Bangladeshi (152)	162	0.16
Bhutanese (1)	1	<0.01
Burmese (15)	17	0.02
Cambodian (9)	9	0.01
Chinese, ex. Taiwanese (7,182)	7,486	7.49
Filipino (2,475)	2,758	2.76
Hmong (10)	10	0.01
Indian (28,286)	29,277	29.29
Indonesian (242)	282	0.28
Japanese (98)	144	0.14
Korean (1,603)	1,669	1.67
Laotian (0)	4	<0.01
Malaysian (12)	28	0.03
Nepalese (44)	52	0.05
Pakistani (1,194)	1,274	1.27
Sri Lankan (129)	147	0.15
Taiwanese (682)	759	0.76
Thai (88)	101	0.10
Vietnamese (438)	478	0.48
Hawaii Native/Pacific Islander (36)	150	0.15
Not Hispanic (31)	127	0.13
Hispanic (5)	23	0.02
Fijian (3)	3	<0.01
Guamanian/Chamorro (6)	14	0.01
Native Hawaiian (6)	10	0.01
Samoan (2)	14	0.01
White (44,084)	45,379	45.39
Not Hispanic (39,577)	40,477	40.49
Hispanic (4,507)	4,902	4.90

Egg Harbor

Place Type: Township
County: Atlantic
Population: 43,323†

Ancestry‡	Population	%
African, Sub-Saharan (487)	508	1.23
African (273)	294	0.71
Nigerian (214)	214	0.52
American (1,636)	1,636	3.95
Arab (172)	194	0.47
Egyptian (104)	104	0.25
Lebanese (16)	27	0.07
Syrian (52)	52	0.13
Other Arab (0)	11	0.03
Armenian (12)	30	0.07
Australian (0)	11	0.03
Austrian (14)	147	0.36
British (13)	49	0.12
Canadian (0)	25	0.06
Croatian (237)	237	0.57
Czech (0)	78	0.19
Czechoslovakian (11)	37	0.09
Danish (14)	30	0.07
Dutch (79)	411	0.99
Eastern European (121)	121	0.29
English (863)	3,270	7.90
Estonian (0)	11	0.03
European (241)	256	0.62
Finnish (18)	103	0.25
French, ex. Basque (67)	662	1.60
French Canadian (101)	260	0.63
German (1,052)	6,520	15.75
Greek (174)	534	1.29
Hungarian (17)	371	0.90
Iranian (9)	9	0.02
Irish (2,228)	8,594	20.76
Israeli (0)	39	0.09
Italian (2,866)	7,862	18.99
Latvian (0)	11	0.03
Lithuanian (22)	134	0.32
Macedonian (68)	68	0.16
Northern European (21)	21	0.05
Norwegian (97)	128	0.31
Pennsylvania German (0)	29	0.07
Polish (523)	1,543	3.73
Portuguese (46)	110	0.27

*Notes: † The Census 2010 population figure is used to calculate the percentages in the Hispanic Origin and Race categories. Ancestry percentages are based on the 2006-2010 American Community Survey population (not shown); ‡ Numbers in parentheses indicate the number of people reporting a single ancestry; * Numbers in parentheses indicate the number of persons reporting this race alone, not in combination with any other race; Please refer to the Explanation of Data for more information.*

Romanian (0)	15	0.04
Russian (163)	641	1.55
Scandinavian (0)	16	0.04
Scotch-Irish (241)	490	1.18
Scottish (226)	671	1.62
Slavic (0)	9	0.02
Slovak (0)	76	0.18
Swedish (31)	316	0.76
Swiss (12)	47	0.11
Ukrainian (169)	329	0.79
Welsh (33)	245	0.59
West Indian, ex. Hispanic (450)	533	1.29
British West Indian (20)	20	0.05
Haitian (59)	59	0.14
Jamaican (337)	420	1.01
Trinidadian/Tobagonian (26)	26	0.06
West Indian (8)	8	0.02
Yugoslavian (0)	22	0.05

Hispanic Origin	Population	%
Hispanic or Latino (of any race)	5,630	13.00
Central American, ex. Mexican	571	1.32
Costa Rican	21	0.05
Guatemalan	26	0.06
Honduran	299	0.69
Nicaraguan	38	0.09
Panamanian	17	0.04
Salvadoran	170	0.39
Cuban	100	0.23
Dominican Republic	626	1.44
Mexican	801	1.85
Puerto Rican	2,357	5.44
South American	840	1.94
Argentinean	33	0.08
Bolivian	1	<0.01
Chilean	18	0.04
Colombian	413	0.95
Ecuadorian	53	0.12
Peruvian	292	0.67
Uruguayan	6	0.01
Venezuelan	20	0.05
Other South American	4	0.01
Other Hispanic or Latino	335	0.77

Race*	Population	%
African-American/Black (4,152)	4,712	10.88
Not Hispanic (3,838)	4,237	9.78
Hispanic (314)	475	1.10
American Indian/Alaska Native (163)	446	1.03
Not Hispanic (69)	298	0.69
Hispanic (94)	148	0.34
Apache (1)	5	0.01
Blackfeet (6)	26	0.06
Central American Ind. (4)	5	0.01
Cherokee (10)	59	0.14
Chippewa (5)	10	0.02
Choctaw (0)	2	<0.01
Comanche (2)	5	0.01
Delaware (1)	13	0.03
Houma (3)	3	0.01
Iroquois (2)	11	0.03
Mexican American Ind. (4)	4	0.01
Navajo (0)	2	<0.01
Potawatomi (5)	5	0.01
Seminole (0)	1	<0.01
Shoshone (1)	1	<0.01
Sioux (1)	15	0.03
South American Ind. (17)	27	0.06
Spanish American Ind. (7)	7	0.02
Tlingit-Haida *(Alaska Native)* (0)	2	<0.01
Asian (5,096)	5,587	12.90
Not Hispanic (5,041)	5,479	12.65
Hispanic (55)	108	0.25
Bangladeshi (216)	254	0.59
Burmese (1)	1	<0.01
Cambodian (23)	25	0.06
Chinese, ex. Taiwanese (1,234)	1,353	3.12
Filipino (920)	1,079	2.49
Indian (871)	982	2.27
Indonesian (3)	4	0.01
Japanese (30)	53	0.12
Korean (238)	297	0.69
Laotian (62)	81	0.19
Malaysian (2)	2	<0.01
Pakistani (224)	243	0.56
Sri Lankan (6)	8	0.02
Taiwanese (28)	30	0.07
Thai (36)	59	0.14
Vietnamese (1,016)	1,109	2.56
Hawaii Native/Pacific Islander (8)	48	0.11
Not Hispanic (8)	40	0.09
Hispanic (0)	8	0.02
Fijian (0)	1	<0.01
Guamanian/Chamorro (1)	1	<0.01
Native Hawaiian (2)	10	0.02
Samoan (1)	2	<0.01
White (30,230)	31,368	72.40
Not Hispanic (27,743)	28,503	65.79
Hispanic (2,487)	2,865	6.61

Elizabeth

Place Type: City
County: Union
Population: 124,969†

Ancestry‡	Population	%
African, Sub-Saharan (1,547)	1,736	1.41
African (868)	1,019	0.83
Ghanaian (224)	224	0.18
Kenyan (39)	39	0.03
Nigerian (270)	270	0.22
Somalian (7)	7	0.01
South African (29)	29	0.02
Sudanese (7)	45	0.04
Other Sub-Saharan African (103)	103	0.08
Alsatian (13)	13	0.01
American (2,128)	2,128	1.73
Arab (587)	668	0.54
Arab (48)	48	0.04
Egyptian (290)	290	0.24
Lebanese (39)	62	0.05
Palestinian (170)	170	0.14
Syrian (0)	58	0.05
Other Arab (40)	40	0.03
Armenian (9)	46	0.04
Australian (0)	64	0.05
Austrian (54)	97	0.08
Brazilian (2,039)	2,462	2.00
British (0)	48	0.04
Canadian (0)	22	0.02
Croatian (0)	12	0.01
Czech (41)	105	0.09
Czechoslovakian (22)	33	0.03
Danish (0)	7	0.01
Dutch (17)	71	0.06
Eastern European (85)	85	0.07
English (76)	778	0.63
European (67)	106	0.09
French, ex. Basque (71)	376	0.31
French Canadian (12)	12	0.01
German (603)	2,172	1.76
Greek (78)	100	0.08
Guyanese (335)	381	0.31
Hungarian (80)	226	0.18
Iranian (15)	15	0.01
Irish (1,140)	3,561	2.89
Israeli (6)	44	0.04
Italian (2,391)	4,467	3.63
Lithuanian (162)	427	0.35
Norwegian (8)	131	0.11
Pennsylvania German (0)	10	0.01
Polish (1,384)	2,597	2.11
Portuguese (6,402)	7,274	5.91
Romanian (43)	109	0.09
Russian (433)	1,016	0.82
Scotch-Irish (48)	175	0.14
Scottish (58)	157	0.13
Serbian (0)	59	0.05
Slavic (0)	13	0.01
Slovak (167)	253	0.21
Swedish (14)	80	0.06
Swiss (0)	15	0.01
Ukrainian (341)	531	0.43
Welsh (0)	74	0.06
West Indian, ex. Hispanic (4,455)	5,042	4.09
Barbadian (35)	38	0.03
Belizean (51)	175	0.14
British West Indian (101)	101	0.08
Dutch West Indian (27)	27	0.02
Haitian (3,665)	3,811	3.09
Jamaican (373)	455	0.37
Trinidadian/Tobagonian (54)	155	0.13
U.S. Virgin Islander (32)	49	0.04
West Indian (117)	231	0.19
Yugoslavian (59)	106	0.09

Hispanic Origin	Population	%
Hispanic or Latino (of any race)	74,353	59.50
Central American, ex. Mexican	12,097	9.68
Costa Rican	660	0.53
Guatemalan	1,131	0.91
Honduran	2,338	1.87
Nicaraguan	407	0.33
Panamanian	127	0.10
Salvadoran	7,364	5.89
Other Central American	70	0.06
Cuban	6,570	5.26
Dominican Republic	7,073	5.66
Mexican	4,126	3.30
Puerto Rican	13,488	10.79
South American	25,649	20.52
Argentinean	557	0.45
Bolivian	164	0.13
Chilean	212	0.17
Colombian	10,692	8.56
Ecuadorian	5,591	4.47
Paraguayan	23	0.02
Peruvian	5,419	4.34
Uruguayan	2,553	2.04
Venezuelan	389	0.31
Other South American	49	0.04
Other Hispanic or Latino	5,350	4.28

Race*	Population	%
African-American/Black (26,343)	28,113	22.50
Not Hispanic (23,072)	23,815	19.06
Hispanic (3,271)	4,298	3.44
American Indian/Alaska Native (1,036)	1,732	1.39
Not Hispanic (138)	346	0.28
Hispanic (898)	1,386	1.11
Aleut *(Alaska Native)* (1)	2	<0.01
Arapaho (6)	6	<0.01
Blackfeet (4)	17	0.01
Central American Ind. (31)	47	0.04
Cherokee (9)	62	0.05
Cheyenne (0)	1	<0.01
Chippewa (0)	2	<0.01
Choctaw (0)	1	<0.01
Delaware (4)	5	<0.01
Iroquois (3)	7	0.01
Lumbee (4)	7	0.01
Mexican American Ind. (25)	44	0.04
Navajo (1)	2	<0.01
Pueblo (4)	8	0.01
Puget Sound Salish (5)	5	<0.01
Seminole (3)	4	<0.01
Sioux (1)	1	<0.01
South American Ind. (131)	197	0.16
Spanish American Ind. (112)	124	0.10
Tlingit-Haida *(Alaska Native)* (0)	4	<0.01
Asian (2,604)	3,131	2.51
Not Hispanic (2,521)	2,855	2.28
Hispanic (83)	276	0.22
Bangladeshi (110)	123	0.10
Bhutanese (51)	74	0.06
Burmese (29)	30	0.02
Cambodian (2)	4	<0.01
Chinese, ex. Taiwanese (304)	388	0.31
Filipino (755)	850	0.68

*Notes: † The Census 2010 population figure is used to calculate the percentages in the Hispanic Origin and Race categories. Ancestry percentages are based on the 2006-2010 American Community Survey population (not shown); ‡ Numbers in parentheses indicate the number of people reporting a single ancestry; * Numbers in parentheses indicate the number of persons reporting this race alone, not in combination with any other race; Please refer to the Explanation of Data for more information.*

Indian (865)	1,090	0.87
Indonesian (9)	20	0.02
Japanese (33)	76	0.06
Korean (83)	93	0.07
Laotian (0)	1	<0.01
Malaysian (5)	5	<0.01
Nepalese (5)	10	0.01
Pakistani (152)	188	0.15
Sri Lankan (2)	8	0.01
Taiwanese (3)	3	<0.01
Thai (19)	23	0.02
Vietnamese (23)	32	0.03
Hawaii Native/Pacific Islander (52)	278	0.22
Not Hispanic (31)	143	0.11
Hispanic (21)	135	0.11
Fijian (0)	3	<0.01
Guamanian/Chamorro (9)	20	0.02
Native Hawaiian (14)	28	0.02
Samoan (0)	11	0.01
White (68,292)	72,788	58.24
Not Hispanic (22,705)	23,615	18.90
Hispanic (45,587)	49,173	39.35

Elmwood Park

Place Type: Borough
County: Bergen
Population: 19,403†

Ancestry‡	Population	%
African, Sub-Saharan (66)	84	0.44
African (9)	18	0.09
Kenyan (0)	9	0.05
Nigerian (57)	57	0.30
Albanian (123)	149	0.78
American (428)	428	2.23
Arab (183)	269	1.40
Arab (0)	50	0.26
Egyptian (59)	59	0.31
Lebanese (7)	7	0.04
Moroccan (19)	19	0.10
Syrian (89)	125	0.65
Other Arab (9)	9	0.05
Austrian (9)	78	0.41
Brazilian (92)	92	0.48
British (49)	62	0.32
Czech (17)	111	0.58
Czechoslovakian (0)	35	0.18
Dutch (6)	172	0.90
Eastern European (17)	17	0.09
English (48)	247	1.29
European (176)	176	0.92
French, ex. Basque (106)	352	1.83
French Canadian (0)	8	0.04
German (224)	1,744	9.08
Greek (234)	271	1.41
Guyanese (47)	81	0.42
Hungarian (96)	267	1.39
Irish (483)	2,230	11.61
Israeli (27)	42	0.22
Italian (3,384)	5,172	26.92
Latvian (17)	17	0.09
Lithuanian (29)	36	0.19
Macedonian (224)	224	1.17
Norwegian (0)	18	0.09
Pennsylvania German (0)	33	0.17
Polish (1,747)	2,470	12.86
Portuguese (24)	24	0.12
Romanian (19)	19	0.10
Russian (171)	319	1.66
Scandinavian (18)	42	0.22
Scotch-Irish (28)	39	0.20
Scottish (27)	60	0.31
Slovak (63)	152	0.79
Swedish (0)	61	0.32
Swiss (0)	49	0.26
Turkish (66)	66	0.34
Ukrainian (99)	149	0.78
Welsh (0)	21	0.11
West Indian, ex. Hispanic (229)	246	1.28
British West Indian (21)	21	0.11
Haitian (180)	180	0.94
Jamaican (9)	26	0.14
Trinidadian/Tobagonian (10)	10	0.05
West Indian (9)	9	0.05
Yugoslavian (0)	14	0.07

Hispanic Origin	Population	%
Hispanic or Latino (of any race)	4,117	21.22
Central American, ex. Mexican	166	0.86
Costa Rican	57	0.29
Guatemalan	33	0.17
Honduran	11	0.06
Nicaraguan	14	0.07
Panamanian	10	0.05
Salvadoran	41	0.21
Cuban	221	1.14
Dominican Republic	701	3.61
Mexican	105	0.54
Puerto Rican	928	4.78
South American	1,677	8.64
Argentinean	68	0.35
Bolivian	12	0.06
Chilean	65	0.33
Colombian	637	3.28
Ecuadorian	274	1.41
Paraguayan	1	0.01
Peruvian	568	2.93
Uruguayan	27	0.14
Venezuelan	21	0.11
Other South American	4	0.02
Other Hispanic or Latino	319	1.64

Race*	Population	%
African-American/Black (1,019)	1,193	6.15
Not Hispanic (884)	973	5.01
Hispanic (135)	220	1.13
American Indian/Alaska Native (65)	127	0.65
Not Hispanic (19)	60	0.31
Hispanic (46)	67	0.35
Blackfeet (0)	1	0.01
Central American Ind. (1)	1	0.01
Cherokee (0)	15	0.08
Delaware (1)	1	0.01
Sioux (1)	2	0.01
South American Ind. (14)	24	0.12
Spanish American Ind. (1)	1	0.01
Asian (2,080)	2,281	11.76
Not Hispanic (2,055)	2,230	11.49
Hispanic (25)	51	0.26
Bangladeshi (42)	44	0.23
Chinese, ex. Taiwanese (151)	180	0.93
Filipino (409)	458	2.36
Indian (1,145)	1,201	6.19
Indonesian (5)	10	0.05
Japanese (23)	31	0.16
Korean (75)	86	0.44
Pakistani (153)	160	0.82
Taiwanese (1)	6	0.03
Thai (9)	9	0.05
Vietnamese (22)	24	0.12
Hawaii Native/Pacific Islander (4)	27	0.14
Not Hispanic (3)	16	0.08
Hispanic (1)	11	0.06
Guamanian/Chamorro (1)	4	0.02
Native Hawaiian (1)	4	0.02
White (14,624)	15,033	77.48
Not Hispanic (11,957)	12,154	62.64
Hispanic (2,667)	2,879	14.84

Englewood

Place Type: City
County: Bergen
Population: 27,147†

Ancestry‡	Population	%
African, Sub-Saharan (645)	768	2.86
African (502)	549	2.05
Ethiopian (41)	41	0.15
Liberian (16)	16	0.06
Nigerian (59)	126	0.47
South African (0)	9	0.03
Other Sub-Saharan African (27)	27	0.10
Albanian (134)	134	0.50
American (692)	692	2.58
Arab (131)	213	0.79
Arab (21)	84	0.31
Egyptian (0)	19	0.07
Lebanese (20)	20	0.07
Moroccan (32)	32	0.12
Other Arab (58)	58	0.22
Armenian (32)	44	0.16
Australian (0)	13	0.05
Austrian (78)	187	0.70
Belgian (33)	142	0.53
Brazilian (0)	16	0.06
British (27)	58	0.22
Canadian (68)	68	0.25
Czech (0)	43	0.16
Czechoslovakian (0)	10	0.04
Danish (11)	25	0.09
Dutch (56)	162	0.60
Eastern European (243)	243	0.91
English (198)	605	2.26
Estonian (42)	42	0.16
European (107)	131	0.49
French, ex. Basque (35)	65	0.24
French Canadian (0)	31	0.12
German (298)	1,361	5.07
Greek (76)	132	0.49
Guyanese (85)	120	0.45
Hungarian (96)	328	1.22
Iranian (0)	39	0.15
Irish (358)	1,487	5.54
Israeli (111)	146	0.54
Italian (341)	838	3.12
Latvian (0)	11	0.04
Lithuanian (11)	11	0.04
Luxemburger (18)	85	0.32
Norwegian (26)	105	0.39
Polish (422)	962	3.59
Portuguese (0)	8	0.03
Romanian (52)	52	0.19
Russian (272)	606	2.26
Scotch-Irish (10)	19	0.07
Scottish (15)	51	0.19
Slovak (20)	20	0.07
Swedish (0)	46	0.17
Swiss (0)	9	0.03
Turkish (14)	27	0.10
Ukrainian (40)	108	0.40
Welsh (22)	42	0.16
West Indian, ex. Hispanic (1,544)	1,933	7.21
Barbadian (0)	33	0.12
Belizean (16)	16	0.06
Bermudan (0)	25	0.09
British West Indian (24)	24	0.09
Haitian (258)	274	1.02
Jamaican (927)	1,046	3.90
Trinidadian/Tobagonian (50)	176	0.66
West Indian (269)	339	1.26
Yugoslavian (57)	57	0.21

Hispanic Origin	Population	%
Hispanic or Latino (of any race)	7,460	27.48
Central American, ex. Mexican	1,042	3.84
Costa Rican	33	0.12
Guatemalan	282	1.04
Honduran	148	0.55
Nicaraguan	24	0.09
Panamanian	47	0.17
Salvadoran	488	1.80
Other Central American	20	0.07
Cuban	259	0.95
Dominican Republic	1,180	4.35
Mexican	728	2.68
Puerto Rican	854	3.15
South American	2,767	10.19
Argentinean	59	0.22

*Notes: † The Census 2010 population figure is used to calculate the percentages in the Hispanic Origin and Race categories. Ancestry percentages are based on the 2006-2010 American Community Survey population (not shown); ‡ Numbers in parentheses indicate the number of people reporting a single ancestry; * Numbers in parentheses indicate the number of persons reporting this race alone, not in combination with any other race; Please refer to the Explanation of Data for more information.*

Bolivian	12	0.04
Chilean	27	0.10
Colombian	2,306	8.49
Ecuadorian	204	0.75
Peruvian	111	0.41
Uruguayan	12	0.04
Venezuelan	26	0.10
Other South American	10	0.04
Other Hispanic or Latino	630	2.32

Race*	Population	%
African-American/Black (8,845)	9,423	34.71
Not Hispanic (8,373)	8,725	32.14
Hispanic (472)	698	2.57
American Indian/Alaska Native (147)	351	1.29
Not Hispanic (79)	224	0.83
Hispanic (68)	127	0.47
Alaska Athabascan *(Ala. Nat.)* (1)	1	<0.01
Apache (0)	1	<0.01
Blackfeet (2)	32	0.12
Central American Ind. (2)	7	0.03
Cherokee (18)	72	0.27
Cheyenne (0)	5	0.02
Crow (0)	1	<0.01
Delaware (8)	16	0.06
Mexican American Ind. (19)	21	0.08
Navajo (0)	2	0.01
Paiute (1)	1	<0.01
Potawatomi (3)	3	0.01
Seminole (1)	2	0.01
Shoshone (2)	2	0.01
Sioux (1)	2	0.01
South American Ind. (4)	14	0.05
Spanish American Ind. (5)	11	0.04
Ute (0)	1	<0.01
Asian (2,199)	2,419	8.91
Not Hispanic (2,169)	2,340	8.62
Hispanic (30)	79	0.29
Bangladeshi (15)	15	0.06
Bhutanese (1)	1	<0.01
Cambodian (2)	3	0.01
Chinese, ex. Taiwanese (165)	201	0.74
Filipino (502)	537	1.98
Indian (397)	480	1.77
Indonesian (9)	9	0.03
Japanese (70)	104	0.38
Korean (867)	891	3.28
Laotian (0)	3	0.01
Malaysian (1)	1	<0.01
Nepalese (3)	6	0.02
Pakistani (63)	80	0.29
Sri Lankan (20)	24	0.09
Taiwanese (12)	12	0.04
Thai (7)	7	0.03
Vietnamese (15)	17	0.06
Hawaii Native/Pacific Islander (12)	52	0.19
Not Hispanic (11)	31	0.11
Hispanic (1)	21	0.08
Fijian (2)	2	0.01
Guamanian/Chamorro (5)	5	0.02
Native Hawaiian (1)	4	0.01
Samoan (0)	7	0.03
White (12,292)	12,931	47.63
Not Hispanic (8,474)	8,744	32.21
Hispanic (3,818)	4,187	15.42

Evesham

Place Type: Township
County: Burlington
Population: 45,538†

Ancestry‡	Population	%
African, Sub-Saharan (40)	40	0.09
Ghanaian (40)	40	0.09
Albanian (9)	26	0.06
American (1,439)	1,439	3.17
Arab (133)	181	0.40
Lebanese (120)	144	0.32
Moroccan (13)	13	0.03
Syrian (0)	24	0.05
Armenian (20)	67	0.15
Austrian (60)	259	0.57
Belgian (26)	26	0.06
Brazilian (0)	45	0.10
British (90)	185	0.41
Canadian (21)	61	0.13
Croatian (13)	45	0.10
Czech (8)	175	0.39
Czechoslovakian (26)	33	0.07
Danish (0)	56	0.12
Dutch (27)	471	1.04
Eastern European (109)	135	0.30
English (618)	4,342	9.58
Estonian (0)	30	0.07
European (245)	245	0.54
Finnish (11)	11	0.02
French, ex. Basque (138)	868	1.91
French Canadian (56)	291	0.64
German (1,922)	10,239	22.58
Greek (279)	489	1.08
Guyanese (12)	33	0.07
Hungarian (121)	482	1.06
Iranian (56)	56	0.12
Irish (3,043)	12,453	27.46
Israeli (48)	58	0.13
Italian (5,202)	11,983	26.43
Lithuanian (52)	290	0.64
Northern European (13)	13	0.03
Norwegian (50)	362	0.80
Pennsylvania German (34)	91	0.20
Polish (1,143)	4,014	8.85
Portuguese (52)	208	0.46
Romanian (36)	109	0.24
Russian (815)	1,762	3.89
Scandinavian (0)	12	0.03
Scotch-Irish (330)	606	1.34
Scottish (143)	981	2.16
Slavic (10)	131	0.29
Slovak (31)	158	0.35
Slovene (0)	10	0.02
Swedish (99)	356	0.79
Swiss (9)	93	0.21
Turkish (92)	92	0.20
Ukrainian (256)	617	1.36
Welsh (17)	374	0.82
West Indian, ex. Hispanic (71)	112	0.25
Belizean (0)	14	0.03
British West Indian (15)	15	0.03
Jamaican (33)	47	0.10
Trinidadian/Tobagonian (23)	23	0.05
West Indian (0)	13	0.03
Yugoslavian (15)	59	0.13

Hispanic Origin	Population	%
Hispanic or Latino (of any race)	1,542	3.39
Central American, ex. Mexican	96	0.21
Costa Rican	10	0.02
Guatemalan	25	0.05
Honduran	14	0.03
Nicaraguan	10	0.02
Panamanian	26	0.06
Salvadoran	11	0.02
Cuban	90	0.20
Dominican Republic	68	0.15
Mexican	290	0.64
Puerto Rican	653	1.43
South American	192	0.42
Argentinean	30	0.07
Bolivian	1	<0.01
Chilean	12	0.03
Colombian	57	0.13
Ecuadorian	19	0.04
Paraguayan	1	<0.01
Peruvian	42	0.09
Uruguayan	7	0.02
Venezuelan	20	0.04
Other South American	3	0.01
Other Hispanic or Latino	153	0.34

Race*	Population	%
African-American/Black (1,910)	2,247	4.93
Not Hispanic (1,817)	2,092	4.59
Hispanic (93)	155	0.34
American Indian/Alaska Native (54)	227	0.50
Not Hispanic (41)	196	0.43
Hispanic (13)	31	0.07
Blackfeet (1)	4	0.01
Central American Ind. (2)	2	<0.01
Cherokee (0)	50	0.11
Chippewa (0)	1	<0.01
Choctaw (0)	6	0.01
Cree (1)	1	<0.01
Creek (0)	1	<0.01
Crow (0)	1	<0.01
Delaware (0)	11	0.02
Hopi (1)	1	<0.01
Inupiat *(Alaska Native)* (5)	5	0.01
Iroquois (1)	13	0.03
Lumbee (3)	8	0.02
Mexican American Ind. (3)	3	0.01
Navajo (2)	2	<0.01
Pueblo (0)	3	0.01
Sioux (0)	4	0.01
South American Ind. (3)	3	0.01
Asian (2,804)	3,147	6.91
Not Hispanic (2,787)	3,099	6.81
Hispanic (17)	48	0.11
Bangladeshi (9)	10	0.02
Cambodian (14)	19	0.04
Chinese, ex. Taiwanese (537)	600	1.32
Filipino (362)	467	1.03
Indian (1,049)	1,107	2.43
Indonesian (4)	5	0.01
Japanese (65)	116	0.25
Korean (478)	522	1.15
Nepalese (2)	2	<0.01
Pakistani (58)	60	0.13
Sri Lankan (17)	19	0.04
Taiwanese (39)	59	0.13
Thai (12)	18	0.04
Vietnamese (95)	107	0.23
Hawaii Native/Pacific Islander (9)	25	0.05
Not Hispanic (8)	24	0.05
Hispanic (1)	1	<0.01
Guamanian/Chamorro (4)	5	0.01
Native Hawaiian (1)	7	0.02
White (39,609)	40,263	88.42
Not Hispanic (38,658)	39,191	86.06
Hispanic (951)	1,072	2.35

Ewing

Place Type: Township
County: Mercer
Population: 35,790†

Ancestry‡	Population	%
African, Sub-Saharan (865)	876	2.44
African (481)	492	1.37
Ghanaian (164)	164	0.46
Kenyan (17)	17	0.05
Liberian (160)	160	0.45
Nigerian (24)	24	0.07
Sierra Leonean (19)	19	0.05
Albanian (11)	44	0.12
Alsatian (0)	24	0.07
American (1,319)	1,319	3.68
Arab (54)	84	0.23
Arab (8)	8	0.02
Egyptian (14)	14	0.04
Iraqi (15)	15	0.04
Lebanese (0)	15	0.04
Syrian (0)	15	0.04
Other Arab (17)	17	0.05
Assyrian/Chaldean/Syriac (10)	10	0.03
Austrian (35)	95	0.27
Belgian (0)	11	0.03
Brazilian (23)	23	0.06

*Notes: † The Census 2010 population figure is used to calculate the percentages in the Hispanic Origin and Race categories. Ancestry percentages are based on the 2006-2010 American Community Survey population (not shown); ‡ Numbers in parentheses indicate the number of people reporting a single ancestry; * Numbers in parentheses indicate the number of persons reporting this race alone, not in combination with any other race; Please refer to the Explanation of Data for more information.*

British (65)	169	0.47
Canadian (0)	49	0.14
Croatian (8)	18	0.05
Cypriot (15)	15	0.04
Czech (0)	236	0.66
Czechoslovakian (30)	40	0.11
Danish (10)	130	0.36
Dutch (124)	606	1.69
Eastern European (122)	185	0.52
English (565)	3,046	8.50
European (74)	99	0.28
French, ex. Basque (50)	499	1.39
French Canadian (7)	94	0.26
German (913)	4,723	13.18
Greek (46)	144	0.40
Guyanese (14)	39	0.11
Hungarian (299)	925	2.58
Iranian (14)	57	0.16
Irish (1,666)	5,819	16.23
Israeli (7)	7	0.02
Italian (2,150)	5,620	15.68
Latvian (7)	21	0.06
Lithuanian (36)	146	0.41
Norwegian (0)	102	0.28
Pennsylvania German (8)	8	0.02
Polish (1,077)	2,723	7.60
Portuguese (0)	54	0.15
Romanian (7)	22	0.06
Russian (222)	678	1.89
Scandinavian (0)	22	0.06
Scotch-Irish (254)	464	1.29
Scottish (122)	468	1.31
Slavic (20)	108	0.30
Slovak (141)	446	1.24
Swedish (66)	131	0.37
Swiss (11)	44	0.12
Turkish (36)	36	0.10
Ukrainian (71)	187	0.52
Welsh (62)	206	0.57
West Indian, ex. Hispanic (898)	1,200	3.35
British West Indian (0)	12	0.03
Haitian (603)	603	1.68
Jamaican (271)	536	1.50
Trinidadian/Tobagonian (24)	49	0.14

Hispanic Origin	Population	%
Hispanic or Latino (of any race)	2,727	7.62
Central American, ex. Mexican	468	1.31
Costa Rican	71	0.20
Guatemalan	287	0.80
Honduran	25	0.07
Nicaraguan	9	0.03
Panamanian	41	0.11
Salvadoran	34	0.09
Other Central American	1	<0.01
Cuban	86	0.24
Dominican Republic	156	0.44
Mexican	318	0.89
Puerto Rican	1,155	3.23
South American	267	0.75
Argentinean	23	0.06
Bolivian	2	0.01
Chilean	10	0.03
Colombian	99	0.28
Ecuadorian	62	0.17
Paraguayan	1	<0.01
Peruvian	33	0.09
Uruguayan	10	0.03
Venezuelan	25	0.07
Other South American	2	0.01
Other Hispanic or Latino	277	0.77

Race*	Population	%
African-American/Black (9,885)	10,403	29.07
Not Hispanic (9,586)	9,992	27.92
Hispanic (299)	411	1.15
American Indian/Alaska Native (109)	291	0.81
Not Hispanic (73)	215	0.60
Hispanic (36)	76	0.21
Blackfeet (3)	13	0.04
Canadian/French Am. Ind. (2)	2	0.01
Central American Ind. (1)	1	<0.01
Cherokee (10)	48	0.13
Chickasaw (0)	1	<0.01
Choctaw (1)	1	<0.01
Cree (0)	1	<0.01
Creek (1)	1	<0.01
Delaware (1)	12	0.03
Iroquois (2)	4	0.01
Lumbee (6)	6	0.02
Mexican American Ind. (2)	3	0.01
Seminole (0)	4	0.01
Sioux (7)	8	0.02
South American Ind. (2)	9	0.03
Spanish American Ind. (0)	1	<0.01
Asian (1,538)	1,771	4.95
Not Hispanic (1,520)	1,736	4.85
Hispanic (18)	35	0.10
Bangladeshi (5)	5	0.01
Burmese (1)	1	<0.01
Cambodian (17)	18	0.05
Chinese, ex. Taiwanese (238)	287	0.80
Filipino (219)	281	0.79
Indian (655)	714	1.99
Indonesian (7)	7	0.02
Japanese (27)	50	0.14
Korean (106)	134	0.37
Laotian (3)	5	0.01
Malaysian (3)	4	0.01
Nepalese (1)	1	<0.01
Pakistani (93)	108	0.30
Sri Lankan (1)	1	<0.01
Taiwanese (26)	30	0.08
Thai (8)	9	0.03
Vietnamese (57)	63	0.18
Hawaii Native/Pacific Islander (15)	57	0.16
Not Hispanic (12)	48	0.13
Hispanic (3)	9	0.03
Guamanian/Chamorro (3)	6	0.02
Native Hawaiian (1)	10	0.03
Samoan (1)	1	<0.01
White (22,598)	23,219	64.88
Not Hispanic (21,188)	21,657	60.51
Hispanic (1,410)	1,562	4.36

Fair Lawn

Place Type: Borough
County: Bergen
Population: 32,457†

Ancestry‡	Population	%
African, Sub-Saharan (53)	203	0.63
African (41)	149	0.46
Kenyan (0)	34	0.11
Nigerian (12)	20	0.06
Albanian (262)	330	1.03
Alsatian (0)	41	0.13
American (803)	803	2.50
Arab (344)	459	1.43
Egyptian (167)	167	0.52
Jordanian (142)	142	0.44
Lebanese (0)	9	0.03
Moroccan (0)	11	0.03
Syrian (0)	9	0.03
Other Arab (35)	121	0.38
Armenian (128)	177	0.55
Assyrian/Chaldean/Syriac (11)	11	0.03
Austrian (63)	297	0.92
Basque (0)	15	0.05
Belgian (0)	39	0.12
Brazilian (0)	16	0.05
British (43)	43	0.13
Bulgarian (28)	28	0.09
Canadian (0)	18	0.06
Celtic (0)	15	0.05
Croatian (13)	48	0.15
Czech (65)	207	0.64
Czechoslovakian (29)	40	0.12
Danish (0)	11	0.03
Dutch (201)	891	2.77
Eastern European (462)	531	1.65
English (131)	893	2.78
European (1,274)	1,469	4.57
French, ex. Basque (101)	311	0.97
French Canadian (0)	10	0.03
German (947)	3,793	11.80
Greek (329)	329	1.02
Hungarian (87)	401	1.25
Iranian (0)	15	0.05
Irish (819)	3,876	12.06
Israeli (719)	746	2.32
Italian (2,876)	5,733	17.83
Latvian (36)	56	0.17
Lithuanian (72)	225	0.70
Macedonian (23)	23	0.07
Northern European (13)	13	0.04
Norwegian (13)	134	0.42
Polish (861)	2,345	7.29
Portuguese (93)	117	0.36
Romanian (242)	359	1.12
Russian (1,932)	3,083	9.59
Scotch-Irish (46)	167	0.52
Scottish (38)	222	0.69
Serbian (0)	24	0.07
Slavic (0)	32	0.10
Slovak (7)	50	0.16
Soviet Union (43)	43	0.13
Swedish (47)	150	0.47
Swiss (0)	29	0.09
Ukrainian (747)	952	2.96
Welsh (0)	33	0.10
West Indian, ex. Hispanic (88)	124	0.39
Jamaican (13)	49	0.15
West Indian (75)	75	0.23
Yugoslavian (0)	7	0.02

Hispanic Origin	Population	%
Hispanic or Latino (of any race)	3,296	10.15
Central American, ex. Mexican	207	0.64
Costa Rican	74	0.23
Guatemalan	33	0.10
Honduran	30	0.09
Nicaraguan	11	0.03
Panamanian	14	0.04
Salvadoran	45	0.14
Cuban	286	0.88
Dominican Republic	601	1.85
Mexican	71	0.22
Puerto Rican	821	2.53
South American	1,001	3.08
Argentinean	58	0.18
Bolivian	14	0.04
Chilean	64	0.20
Colombian	397	1.22
Ecuadorian	190	0.59
Paraguayan	3	0.01
Peruvian	238	0.73
Uruguayan	23	0.07
Venezuelan	13	0.04
Other South American	1	<0.01
Other Hispanic or Latino	309	0.95

Race*	Population	%
African-American/Black (567)	741	2.28
Not Hispanic (464)	564	1.74
Hispanic (103)	177	0.55
American Indian/Alaska Native (20)	114	0.35
Not Hispanic (14)	69	0.21
Hispanic (6)	45	0.14
Blackfeet (0)	4	0.01
Cherokee (0)	11	0.03
Choctaw (4)	6	0.02
Delaware (0)	4	0.01
Iroquois (1)	2	0.01
Mexican American Ind. (1)	2	0.01
Sioux (0)	1	<0.01
South American Ind. (2)	9	0.03
Asian (3,154)	3,399	10.47
Not Hispanic (3,130)	3,338	10.28

*Notes: † The Census 2010 population figure is used to calculate the percentages in the Hispanic Origin and Race categories. Ancestry percentages are based on the 2006-2010 American Community Survey population (not shown); ‡ Numbers in parentheses indicate the number of people reporting a single ancestry; * Numbers in parentheses indicate the number of persons reporting this race alone, not in combination with any other race; Please refer to the Explanation of Data for more information.*

Hispanic (24)	61	0.19
Bangladeshi (39)	47	0.14
Chinese, ex. Taiwanese (490)	545	1.68
Filipino (626)	690	2.13
Indian (1,189)	1,271	3.92
Indonesian (7)	7	0.02
Japanese (73)	91	0.28
Korean (389)	402	1.24
Laotian (1)	1	<0.01
Malaysian (2)	4	0.01
Nepalese (3)	4	0.01
Pakistani (133)	139	0.43
Sri Lankan (4)	6	0.02
Taiwanese (29)	33	0.10
Thai (10)	13	0.04
Vietnamese (92)	106	0.33
Hawaii Native/Pacific Islander (1)	15	0.05
Not Hispanic (1)	9	0.03
Hispanic (0)	6	0.02
Fijian (1)	1	<0.01
Samoan (0)	1	<0.01
White (27,380)	27,833	85.75
Not Hispanic (25,151)	25,408	78.28
Hispanic (2,229)	2,425	7.47

Fairview

Place Type: Borough
County: Bergen
Population: 13,835†

Ancestry‡	Population	%
African, Sub-Saharan (14)	31	0.23
African (0)	17	0.12
Nigerian (14)	14	0.10
American (206)	206	1.51
Arab (484)	484	3.54
Arab (70)	70	0.51
Egyptian (39)	39	0.29
Palestinian (291)	291	2.13
Syrian (84)	84	0.62
Armenian (74)	115	0.84
Australian (7)	10	0.07
Austrian (12)	26	0.19
Brazilian (285)	285	2.09
Croatian (508)	594	4.35
Czech (13)	13	0.10
Dutch (11)	11	0.08
English (45)	96	0.70
European (18)	18	0.13
French, ex. Basque (0)	84	0.62
French Canadian (0)	12	0.09
German (111)	463	3.39
Greek (177)	246	1.80
Hungarian (11)	45	0.33
Irish (69)	320	2.34
Israeli (62)	62	0.45
Italian (1,291)	1,894	13.87
Polish (62)	169	1.24
Portuguese (32)	32	0.23
Romanian (0)	12	0.09
Russian (48)	48	0.35
Scottish (0)	13	0.10
Slovak (25)	25	0.18
Swedish (39)	49	0.36
Turkish (297)	297	2.17
West Indian, ex. Hispanic (30)	54	0.40
Haitian (17)	17	0.12
Jamaican (13)	37	0.27
Yugoslavian (25)	41	0.30

Hispanic Origin	Population	%
Hispanic or Latino (of any race)	7,558	54.63
Central American, ex. Mexican	3,433	24.81
Costa Rican	17	0.12
Guatemalan	2,191	15.84
Honduran	120	0.87
Nicaraguan	27	0.20
Panamanian	4	0.03
Salvadoran	1,063	7.68
Other Central American	11	0.08
Cuban	709	5.12
Dominican Republic	647	4.68
Mexican	207	1.50
Puerto Rican	522	3.77
South American	1,430	10.34
Argentinean	46	0.33
Bolivian	6	0.04
Chilean	58	0.42
Colombian	607	4.39
Ecuadorian	517	3.74
Peruvian	141	1.02
Uruguayan	25	0.18
Venezuelan	27	0.20
Other South American	3	0.02
Other Hispanic or Latino	610	4.41

Race*	Population	%
African-American/Black (407)	538	3.89
Not Hispanic (286)	347	2.51
Hispanic (121)	191	1.38
American Indian/Alaska Native (92)	181	1.31
Not Hispanic (22)	43	0.31
Hispanic (70)	138	1.00
Blackfeet (0)	1	0.01
Central American Ind. (10)	15	0.11
Cherokee (10)	13	0.09
Crow (0)	2	0.01
Delaware (0)	1	0.01
Mexican American Ind. (28)	52	0.38
Navajo (0)	2	0.01
South American Ind. (3)	10	0.07
Spanish American Ind. (0)	2	0.01
Asian (640)	774	5.59
Not Hispanic (612)	725	5.24
Hispanic (28)	49	0.35
Chinese, ex. Taiwanese (80)	102	0.74
Filipino (51)	58	0.42
Indian (125)	142	1.03
Indonesian (6)	6	0.04
Japanese (34)	49	0.35
Korean (306)	312	2.26
Pakistani (21)	24	0.17
Sri Lankan (4)	4	0.03
Vietnamese (3)	3	0.02
Hawaii Native/Pacific Islander (4)	13	0.09
Not Hispanic (0)	5	0.04
Hispanic (4)	8	0.06
Guamanian/Chamorro (2)	6	0.04
White (9,186)	9,851	71.20
Not Hispanic (4,945)	5,124	37.04
Hispanic (4,241)	4,727	34.17

Florence

Place Type: Township
County: Burlington
Population: 12,109†

Ancestry‡	Population	%
African, Sub-Saharan (17)	35	0.29
African (17)	35	0.29
American (384)	384	3.20
Arab (41)	60	0.50
Egyptian (41)	60	0.50
Austrian (11)	42	0.35
British (11)	61	0.51
Canadian (0)	23	0.19
Czech (0)	14	0.12
Czechoslovakian (17)	17	0.14
Danish (0)	113	0.94
Dutch (10)	226	1.89
English (473)	1,423	11.87
European (18)	18	0.15
Finnish (0)	8	0.07
French, ex. Basque (0)	218	1.82
French Canadian (48)	80	0.67
German (353)	2,138	17.84
Greek (15)	45	0.38
Guyanese (0)	50	0.42
Hungarian (439)	962	8.03
Irish (688)	2,907	24.26
Italian (897)	2,414	20.14
Lithuanian (13)	19	0.16
Norwegian (7)	43	0.36
Pennsylvania German (0)	11	0.09
Polish (417)	1,226	10.23
Portuguese (0)	66	0.55
Romanian (0)	71	0.59
Russian (47)	179	1.49
Scandinavian (0)	32	0.27
Scotch-Irish (10)	56	0.47
Scottish (30)	131	1.09
Slavic (0)	96	0.80
Slovak (58)	215	1.79
Swedish (0)	50	0.42
Swiss (0)	10	0.08
Turkish (44)	44	0.37
Ukrainian (21)	104	0.87
Welsh (0)	61	0.51
West Indian, ex. Hispanic (53)	53	0.44
Jamaican (44)	44	0.37
West Indian (9)	9	0.08
Yugoslavian (0)	52	0.43

Hispanic Origin	Population	%
Hispanic or Latino (of any race)	576	4.76
Central American, ex. Mexican	61	0.50
Costa Rican	14	0.12
Guatemalan	28	0.23
Honduran	3	0.02
Panamanian	11	0.09
Salvadoran	4	0.03
Other Central American	1	0.01
Cuban	16	0.13
Dominican Republic	24	0.20
Mexican	64	0.53
Puerto Rican	336	2.77
South American	47	0.39
Argentinean	3	0.02
Colombian	23	0.19
Ecuadorian	9	0.07
Paraguayan	2	0.02
Peruvian	6	0.05
Uruguayan	1	0.01
Venezuelan	3	0.02
Other Hispanic or Latino	28	0.23

Race*	Population	%
African-American/Black (1,481)	1,663	13.73
Not Hispanic (1,421)	1,582	13.06
Hispanic (60)	81	0.67
American Indian/Alaska Native (23)	101	0.83
Not Hispanic (9)	79	0.65
Hispanic (14)	22	0.18
Blackfeet (1)	4	0.03
Cherokee (2)	17	0.14
Choctaw (0)	1	0.01
Iroquois (0)	1	0.01
Mexican American Ind. (1)	1	0.01
Seminole (0)	2	0.02
Shoshone (1)	2	0.02
Sioux (1)	6	0.05
South American Ind. (5)	5	0.04
Asian (610)	738	6.09
Not Hispanic (608)	730	6.03
Hispanic (2)	8	0.07
Bangladeshi (68)	87	0.72
Chinese, ex. Taiwanese (36)	43	0.36
Filipino (51)	72	0.59
Indian (361)	420	3.47
Indonesian (1)	1	0.01
Japanese (8)	22	0.18
Korean (23)	33	0.27
Pakistani (22)	26	0.21
Taiwanese (4)	4	0.03
Thai (2)	10	0.08
Vietnamese (2)	4	0.03
Hawaii Native/Pacific Islander (7)	14	0.12
Not Hispanic (5)	9	0.07

*Notes: † The Census 2010 population figure is used to calculate the percentages in the Hispanic Origin and Race categories. Ancestry percentages are based on the 2006-2010 American Community Survey population (not shown); ‡ Numbers in parentheses indicate the number of people reporting a single ancestry; * Numbers in parentheses indicate the number of persons reporting this race alone, not in combination with any other race; Please refer to the Explanation of Data for more information.*

Hispanic (2)	5	0.04
Native Hawaiian (0)	1	0.01
Samoan (2)	4	0.03
White (9,497)	9,796	80.90
Not Hispanic (9,153)	9,407	77.69
Hispanic (344)	389	3.21

Florham Park

Place Type: Borough
County: Morris
Population: 11,696†

Ancestry‡	Population	%
American (342)	342	2.98
Arab (42)	65	0.57
Egyptian (42)	42	0.37
Lebanese (0)	23	0.20
Armenian (0)	8	0.07
Austrian (34)	86	0.75
Belgian (7)	7	0.06
Brazilian (26)	55	0.48
British (0)	66	0.57
Danish (7)	44	0.38
Dutch (15)	30	0.26
Eastern European (36)	36	0.31
English (145)	883	7.68
European (107)	107	0.93
French, ex. Basque (21)	137	1.19
French Canadian (8)	30	0.26
German (527)	2,265	19.71
Greek (106)	189	1.64
Hungarian (0)	61	0.53
Irish (808)	2,656	23.11
Israeli (21)	21	0.18
Italian (1,943)	3,173	27.61
Lithuanian (0)	124	1.08
Northern European (8)	8	0.07
Norwegian (8)	132	1.15
Polish (159)	570	4.96
Portuguese (37)	54	0.47
Romanian (0)	36	0.31
Russian (78)	339	2.95
Scotch-Irish (39)	101	0.88
Scottish (28)	306	2.66
Slavic (0)	13	0.11
Slovak (59)	91	0.79
Swedish (17)	88	0.77
Swiss (0)	16	0.14
Turkish (11)	35	0.30
Ukrainian (49)	58	0.50
Welsh (0)	39	0.34
Yugoslavian (32)	32	0.28

Hispanic Origin	Population	%
Hispanic or Latino (of any race)	594	5.08
Central American, ex. Mexican	44	0.38
Costa Rican	7	0.06
Guatemalan	16	0.14
Honduran	6	0.05
Nicaraguan	5	0.04
Panamanian	2	0.02
Salvadoran	7	0.06
Other Central American	1	0.01
Cuban	82	0.70
Dominican Republic	47	0.40
Mexican	50	0.43
Puerto Rican	154	1.32
South American	154	1.32
Argentinean	15	0.13
Chilean	3	0.03
Colombian	69	0.59
Ecuadorian	14	0.12
Paraguayan	5	0.04
Peruvian	25	0.21
Uruguayan	3	0.03
Venezuelan	18	0.15
Other South American	2	0.02
Other Hispanic or Latino	63	0.54

Race*	Population	%
African-American/Black (509)	583	4.98
Not Hispanic (488)	552	4.72
Hispanic (21)	31	0.27
American Indian/Alaska Native (8)	33	0.28
Not Hispanic (7)	29	0.25
Hispanic (1)	4	0.03
Apache (1)	1	0.01
Blackfeet (0)	1	0.01
Cherokee (1)	8	0.07
Choctaw (1)	3	0.03
Delaware (1)	3	0.03
South American Ind. (0)	1	0.01
Tlingit-Haida *(Alaska Native)* (0)	2	0.02
Asian (745)	848	7.25
Not Hispanic (743)	836	7.15
Hispanic (2)	12	0.10
Bangladeshi (5)	5	0.04
Cambodian (1)	1	0.01
Chinese, ex. Taiwanese (248)	265	2.27
Filipino (26)	43	0.37
Indian (243)	272	2.33
Indonesian (6)	9	0.08
Japanese (50)	63	0.54
Korean (79)	87	0.74
Malaysian (6)	9	0.08
Nepalese (1)	1	0.01
Pakistani (30)	32	0.27
Sri Lankan (2)	2	0.02
Taiwanese (20)	25	0.21
Vietnamese (13)	17	0.15
Hawaii Native/Pacific Islander (8)	17	0.15
Not Hispanic (8)	16	0.14
Hispanic (0)	1	0.01
Guamanian/Chamorro (1)	1	0.01
Native Hawaiian (0)	1	0.01
Samoan (1)	1	0.01
White (10,099)	10,259	87.71
Not Hispanic (9,664)	9,802	83.81
Hispanic (435)	457	3.91

Fords

Place Type: CDP
County: Middlesex
Population: 15,187†

Ancestry‡	Population	%
African, Sub-Saharan (397)	397	2.63
African (172)	172	1.14
Ghanaian (101)	101	0.67
Kenyan (62)	62	0.41
Nigerian (62)	62	0.41
American (720)	720	4.77
Arab (23)	47	0.31
Egyptian (0)	2	0.01
Moroccan (23)	23	0.15
Syrian (0)	22	0.15
Armenian (10)	10	0.07
Austrian (0)	32	0.21
Brazilian (0)	10	0.07
British (0)	9	0.06
Canadian (0)	22	0.15
Czech (22)	22	0.15
Czechoslovakian (32)	79	0.52
Danish (9)	216	1.43
Dutch (12)	37	0.25
Eastern European (8)	8	0.05
English (39)	401	2.66
European (93)	132	0.88
French, ex. Basque (0)	120	0.80
French Canadian (0)	24	0.16
German (273)	1,326	8.79
Greek (97)	126	0.84
Guyanese (34)	34	0.23
Hungarian (371)	900	5.97
Iranian (77)	77	0.51
Irish (455)	1,691	11.21
Israeli (56)	56	0.37
Italian (1,170)	2,406	15.95
Lithuanian (0)	22	0.15
Norwegian (9)	9	0.06
Polish (810)	1,777	11.78
Portuguese (270)	284	1.88
Romanian (8)	8	0.05
Russian (32)	242	1.60
Scotch-Irish (58)	153	1.01
Scottish (44)	252	1.67
Slavic (20)	20	0.13
Slovak (95)	199	1.32
Swedish (0)	28	0.19
Swiss (0)	21	0.14
Turkish (8)	17	0.11
Ukrainian (37)	199	1.32
Welsh (22)	62	0.41
West Indian, ex. Hispanic (282)	282	1.87
Dutch West Indian (9)	9	0.06
Jamaican (131)	131	0.87
West Indian (142)	142	0.94
Yugoslavian (0)	22	0.15

Hispanic Origin	Population	%
Hispanic or Latino (of any race)	2,643	17.40
Central American, ex. Mexican	201	1.32
Costa Rican	44	0.29
Guatemalan	29	0.19
Honduran	60	0.40
Nicaraguan	13	0.09
Panamanian	5	0.03
Salvadoran	50	0.33
Cuban	146	0.96
Dominican Republic	405	2.67
Mexican	125	0.82
Puerto Rican	1,059	6.97
South American	553	3.64
Argentinean	58	0.38
Bolivian	8	0.05
Chilean	9	0.06
Colombian	107	0.70
Ecuadorian	122	0.80
Paraguayan	1	0.01
Peruvian	173	1.14
Uruguayan	37	0.24
Venezuelan	24	0.16
Other South American	14	0.09
Other Hispanic or Latino	154	1.01

Race*	Population	%
African-American/Black (1,399)	1,518	10.00
Not Hispanic (1,302)	1,385	9.12
Hispanic (97)	133	0.88
American Indian/Alaska Native (43)	120	0.79
Not Hispanic (24)	80	0.53
Hispanic (19)	40	0.26
Cherokee (0)	7	0.05
Chippewa (0)	1	0.01
Delaware (2)	3	0.02
Iroquois (0)	1	0.01
Mexican American Ind. (4)	6	0.04
Potawatomi (0)	1	0.01
Seminole (0)	2	0.01
South American Ind. (2)	9	0.06
Asian (3,143)	3,352	22.07
Not Hispanic (3,119)	3,304	21.76
Hispanic (24)	48	0.32
Bangladeshi (2)	5	0.03
Chinese, ex. Taiwanese (217)	243	1.60
Filipino (767)	814	5.36
Indian (1,792)	1,884	12.41
Indonesian (25)	29	0.19
Japanese (2)	9	0.06
Korean (50)	53	0.35
Malaysian (0)	1	0.01
Nepalese (3)	3	0.02
Pakistani (159)	168	1.11
Sri Lankan (38)	46	0.30
Taiwanese (11)	16	0.11
Thai (1)	4	0.03
Vietnamese (34)	34	0.22

*Notes: † The Census 2010 population figure is used to calculate the percentages in the Hispanic Origin and Race categories. Ancestry percentages are based on the 2006-2010 American Community Survey population (not shown); ‡ Numbers in parentheses indicate the number of people reporting a single ancestry; * Numbers in parentheses indicate the number of persons reporting this race alone, not in combination with any other race; Please refer to the Explanation of Data for more information.*

Hawaii Native/Pacific Islander (1)	17	0.11
Not Hispanic (1)	12	0.08
Hispanic (0)	5	0.03
Native Hawaiian (1)	3	0.02
Samoan (0)	1	0.01
White (9,263)	9,535	62.78
Not Hispanic (7,782)	7,920	52.15
Hispanic (1,481)	1,615	10.63

Fort Dix

Place Type: CDP
County: Burlington
Population: 7,716†

Ancestry‡	Population	%
African, Sub-Saharan (140)	156	3.00
African (112)	128	2.46
Nigerian (28)	28	0.54
American (44)	44	0.85
Arab (0)	18	0.35
Lebanese (0)	18	0.35
Belgian (0)	9	0.17
British (9)	9	0.17
Cajun (0)	10	0.19
Celtic (10)	10	0.19
Czech (0)	8	0.15
Dutch (0)	10	0.19
Eastern European (9)	9	0.17
English (141)	240	4.61
European (16)	16	0.31
Finnish (0)	21	0.40
French, ex. Basque (24)	124	2.38
French Canadian (0)	27	0.52
German (51)	336	6.45
Greek (5)	5	0.10
Guyanese (10)	10	0.19
Hungarian (0)	10	0.19
Iranian (11)	11	0.21
Irish (160)	557	10.70
Italian (161)	319	6.13
Norwegian (23)	23	0.44
Polish (52)	223	4.28
Portuguese (57)	66	1.27
Russian (26)	36	0.69
Scotch-Irish (7)	51	0.98
Scottish (68)	86	1.65
Serbian (0)	9	0.17
Swedish (0)	5	0.10
Ukrainian (18)	18	0.35
Welsh (0)	10	0.19
West Indian, ex. Hispanic (109)	129	2.48
Haitian (8)	8	0.15
Jamaican (73)	82	1.58
Trinidadian/Tobagonian (20)	20	0.38
West Indian (8)	19	0.36

Hispanic Origin	Population	%
Hispanic or Latino (of any race)	1,657	21.47
Central American, ex. Mexican	63	0.82
Costa Rican	5	0.06
Guatemalan	1	0.01
Honduran	30	0.39
Nicaraguan	1	0.01
Panamanian	14	0.18
Salvadoran	12	0.16
Cuban	80	1.04
Dominican Republic	211	2.73
Mexican	347	4.50
Puerto Rican	668	8.66
South American	197	2.55
Argentinean	7	0.09
Bolivian	3	0.04
Colombian	144	1.87
Ecuadorian	25	0.32
Peruvian	1	0.01
Venezuelan	10	0.13
Other South American	7	0.09
Other Hispanic or Latino	91	1.18

Race*	Population	%
African-American/Black (2,660)	2,803	36.33
Not Hispanic (2,457)	2,536	32.87
Hispanic (203)	267	3.46
American Indian/Alaska Native (52)	108	1.40
Not Hispanic (39)	76	0.98
Hispanic (13)	32	0.41
Apache (0)	2	0.03
Blackfeet (1)	7	0.09
Cherokee (0)	11	0.14
Chippewa (2)	2	0.03
Choctaw (1)	3	0.04
Delaware (2)	2	0.03
Mexican American Ind. (1)	3	0.04
Navajo (1)	1	0.01
Ottawa (1)	1	0.01
Potawatomi (1)	1	0.01
Sioux (1)	4	0.05
South American Ind. (4)	6	0.08
Yaqui (3)	3	0.04
Asian (147)	217	2.81
Not Hispanic (145)	212	2.75
Hispanic (2)	5	0.06
Chinese, ex. Taiwanese (22)	34	0.44
Filipino (40)	63	0.82
Indian (50)	52	0.67
Indonesian (0)	3	0.04
Japanese (5)	16	0.21
Korean (3)	10	0.13
Pakistani (1)	3	0.04
Thai (0)	2	0.03
Vietnamese (11)	11	0.14
Hawaii Native/Pacific Islander (23)	38	0.49
Not Hispanic (17)	32	0.41
Hispanic (6)	6	0.08
Guamanian/Chamorro (6)	6	0.08
Native Hawaiian (3)	8	0.10
Samoan (1)	1	0.01
White (4,056)	4,285	55.53
Not Hispanic (3,220)	3,361	43.56
Hispanic (836)	924	11.98

Fort Lee

Place Type: Borough
County: Bergen
Population: 35,345†

Ancestry‡	Population	%
African, Sub-Saharan (112)	129	0.37
African (77)	77	0.22
South African (35)	52	0.15
Albanian (116)	116	0.33
American (575)	575	1.64
Arab (245)	342	0.97
Arab (14)	14	0.04
Egyptian (73)	82	0.23
Lebanese (39)	86	0.24
Syrian (39)	48	0.14
Other Arab (80)	112	0.32
Armenian (371)	385	1.09
Assyrian/Chaldean/Syriac (11)	11	0.03
Austrian (144)	331	0.94
Belgian (0)	11	0.03
Brazilian (76)	149	0.42
British (121)	138	0.39
Bulgarian (60)	71	0.20
Canadian (82)	82	0.23
Croatian (138)	220	0.63
Cypriot (10)	10	0.03
Czech (14)	130	0.37
Czechoslovakian (12)	26	0.07
Dutch (101)	185	0.53
Eastern European (171)	232	0.66
English (148)	734	2.09
Estonian (12)	12	0.03
European (172)	187	0.53
Finnish (0)	19	0.05
French, ex. Basque (48)	341	0.97
French Canadian (0)	35	0.10
German (544)	1,784	5.07
Greek (795)	933	2.65
Guyanese (0)	101	0.29
Hungarian (179)	458	1.30
Iranian (121)	121	0.34
Irish (474)	1,406	4.00
Israeli (226)	245	0.70
Italian (2,202)	3,350	9.53
Latvian (13)	13	0.04
Lithuanian (68)	93	0.26
Luxemburger (61)	61	0.17
Norwegian (32)	86	0.24
Polish (409)	1,085	3.09
Portuguese (14)	129	0.37
Romanian (238)	326	0.93
Russian (1,747)	2,695	7.66
Scottish (39)	156	0.44
Serbian (197)	197	0.56
Slavic (39)	39	0.11
Slovak (7)	49	0.14
Swedish (40)	103	0.29
Swiss (12)	40	0.11
Turkish (75)	75	0.21
Ukrainian (327)	370	1.05
Welsh (0)	42	0.12
West Indian, ex. Hispanic (57)	152	0.43
British West Indian (0)	45	0.13
Haitian (17)	67	0.19
Jamaican (40)	40	0.11
Yugoslavian (32)	49	0.14

Hispanic Origin	Population	%
Hispanic or Latino (of any race)	3,877	10.97
Central American, ex. Mexican	385	1.09
Costa Rican	9	0.03
Guatemalan	58	0.16
Honduran	14	0.04
Nicaraguan	26	0.07
Panamanian	18	0.05
Salvadoran	259	0.73
Other Central American	1	<0.01
Cuban	476	1.35
Dominican Republic	968	2.74
Mexican	102	0.29
Puerto Rican	656	1.86
South American	878	2.48
Argentinean	122	0.35
Bolivian	10	0.03
Chilean	37	0.10
Colombian	382	1.08
Ecuadorian	141	0.40
Paraguayan	5	0.01
Peruvian	135	0.38
Uruguayan	12	0.03
Venezuelan	30	0.08
Other South American	4	0.01
Other Hispanic or Latino	412	1.17

Race*	Population	%
African-American/Black (973)	1,172	3.32
Not Hispanic (805)	910	2.57
Hispanic (168)	262	0.74
American Indian/Alaska Native (50)	115	0.33
Not Hispanic (29)	55	0.16
Hispanic (21)	60	0.17
Blackfeet (0)	3	0.01
Central American Ind. (0)	1	<0.01
Cherokee (0)	2	0.01
Chippewa (1)	1	<0.01
Choctaw (0)	1	<0.01
Creek (0)	1	<0.01
Delaware (1)	2	0.01
Mexican American Ind. (1)	1	<0.01
South American Ind. (2)	11	0.03
Spanish American Ind. (0)	1	<0.01
Asian (13,587)	13,964	39.51
Not Hispanic (13,552)	13,893	39.31
Hispanic (35)	71	0.20
Bangladeshi (22)	29	0.08

SECTION TWO

*Notes: † The Census 2010 population figure is used to calculate the percentages in the Hispanic Origin and Race categories. Ancestry percentages are based on the 2006-2010 American Community Survey population (not shown); ‡ Numbers in parentheses indicate the number of people reporting a single ancestry; * Numbers in parentheses indicate the number of persons reporting this race alone, not in combination with any other race; Please refer to the Explanation of Data for more information.*

Burmese (18)	20	0.06
Cambodian (1)	2	0.01
Chinese, ex. Taiwanese (2,513)	2,633	7.45
Filipino (410)	464	1.31
Indian (558)	615	1.74
Indonesian (13)	14	0.04
Japanese (1,302)	1,397	3.95
Korean (8,318)	8,437	23.87
Malaysian (24)	31	0.09
Nepalese (20)	21	0.06
Pakistani (48)	53	0.15
Sri Lankan (2)	2	0.01
Taiwanese (130)	148	0.42
Thai (16)	22	0.06
Vietnamese (35)	46	0.13
Hawaii Native/Pacific Islander (7)	40	0.11
Not Hispanic (7)	26	0.07
Hispanic (0)	14	0.04
Guamanian/Chamorro (1)	1	<0.01
Native Hawaiian (4)	9	0.03
White (18,905)	19,486	55.13
Not Hispanic (16,514)	16,895	47.80
Hispanic (2,391)	2,591	7.33

Franklin Lakes

Place Type: Borough
County: Bergen
Population: 10,590†

Ancestry‡	Population	%
Albanian (11)	33	0.31
American (328)	328	3.12
Arab (229)	229	2.18
Arab (22)	22	0.21
Egyptian (80)	80	0.76
Lebanese (22)	22	0.21
Syrian (105)	105	1.00
Armenian (243)	243	2.31
Austrian (22)	95	0.90
British (43)	60	0.57
Canadian (0)	18	0.17
Croatian (78)	78	0.74
Czech (5)	49	0.47
Dutch (203)	574	5.46
Eastern European (119)	119	1.13
English (124)	578	5.50
Estonian (9)	9	0.09
European (142)	208	1.98
French, ex. Basque (0)	86	0.82
French Canadian (8)	50	0.48
German (335)	1,396	13.29
Greek (54)	133	1.27
Hungarian (20)	191	1.82
Iranian (177)	177	1.68
Irish (281)	1,310	12.47
Israeli (18)	46	0.44
Italian (1,798)	2,903	27.63
Lithuanian (0)	10	0.10
Norwegian (10)	42	0.40
Polish (340)	987	9.39
Romanian (26)	26	0.25
Russian (169)	514	4.89
Scotch-Irish (27)	57	0.54
Scottish (0)	27	0.26
Slovak (9)	9	0.09
Swedish (15)	67	0.64
Swiss (0)	19	0.18
Turkish (26)	132	1.26
Ukrainian (56)	67	0.64
Welsh (0)	75	0.71
Yugoslavian (31)	31	0.30

Hispanic Origin	Population	%
Hispanic or Latino (of any race)	525	4.96
Central American, ex. Mexican	36	0.34
Costa Rican	5	0.05
Guatemalan	8	0.08
Honduran	3	0.03
Nicaraguan	6	0.06
Panamanian	3	0.03
Salvadoran	11	0.10
Cuban	101	0.95
Dominican Republic	63	0.59
Mexican	43	0.41
Puerto Rican	73	0.69
South American	129	1.22
Argentinean	9	0.08
Bolivian	3	0.03
Chilean	3	0.03
Colombian	47	0.44
Ecuadorian	32	0.30
Paraguayan	1	0.01
Peruvian	27	0.25
Venezuelan	7	0.07
Other Hispanic or Latino	80	0.76

Race*	Population	%
African-American/Black (149)	175	1.65
Not Hispanic (136)	152	1.44
Hispanic (13)	23	0.22
American Indian/Alaska Native (4)	9	0.08
Not Hispanic (3)	8	0.08
Hispanic (1)	1	0.01
Spanish American Ind. (1)	1	0.01
Asian (777)	883	8.34
Not Hispanic (777)	873	8.24
Hispanic (0)	10	0.09
Chinese, ex. Taiwanese (133)	154	1.45
Filipino (56)	65	0.61
Indian (204)	216	2.04
Indonesian (1)	1	0.01
Japanese (32)	43	0.41
Korean (278)	288	2.72
Malaysian (0)	3	0.03
Pakistani (26)	27	0.25
Sri Lankan (1)	8	0.08
Taiwanese (20)	23	0.22
Thai (9)	14	0.13
Vietnamese (7)	18	0.17
Hawaii Native/Pacific Islander (0)	1	0.01
Not Hispanic (0)	1	0.01
White (9,417)	9,563	90.30
Not Hispanic (9,017)	9,133	86.24
Hispanic (400)	430	4.06

Franklin Park

Place Type: CDP
County: Somerset
Population: 13,295†

Ancestry‡	Population	%
African, Sub-Saharan (260)	347	2.75
African (21)	21	0.17
Ghanaian (16)	53	0.42
Nigerian (223)	273	2.16
Albanian (0)	10	0.08
American (182)	182	1.44
Arab (56)	67	0.53
Arab (0)	11	0.09
Egyptian (22)	22	0.17
Lebanese (23)	23	0.18
Moroccan (11)	11	0.09
Armenian (15)	15	0.12
Austrian (16)	33	0.26
British (90)	90	0.71
Cajun (8)	8	0.06
Czechoslovakian (0)	13	0.10
Danish (32)	32	0.25
Dutch (0)	80	0.63
Eastern European (13)	13	0.10
English (73)	299	2.37
Estonian (0)	12	0.10
French, ex. Basque (9)	176	1.39
German (90)	491	3.89
Greek (0)	34	0.27
Guyanese (26)	89	0.71
Hungarian (89)	135	1.07
Irish (143)	497	3.94
Italian (468)	816	6.46
Lithuanian (0)	13	0.10
Norwegian (26)	46	0.36
Polish (125)	422	3.34
Romanian (31)	55	0.44
Russian (42)	175	1.39
Scotch-Irish (33)	64	0.51
Scottish (16)	25	0.20
Swedish (0)	12	0.10
Swiss (11)	23	0.18
Turkish (0)	21	0.17
Ukrainian (12)	35	0.28
West Indian, ex. Hispanic (271)	371	2.94
British West Indian (24)	87	0.69
Jamaican (157)	157	1.24
Trinidadian/Tobagonian (26)	26	0.21
West Indian (64)	101	0.80

Hispanic Origin	Population	%
Hispanic or Latino (of any race)	1,040	7.82
Central American, ex. Mexican	87	0.65
Costa Rican	15	0.11
Guatemalan	6	0.05
Honduran	28	0.21
Nicaraguan	1	0.01
Panamanian	17	0.13
Salvadoran	20	0.15
Cuban	56	0.42
Dominican Republic	161	1.21
Mexican	87	0.65
Puerto Rican	390	2.93
South American	199	1.50
Argentinean	16	0.12
Bolivian	2	0.02
Chilean	3	0.02
Colombian	98	0.74
Ecuadorian	23	0.17
Peruvian	32	0.24
Uruguayan	9	0.07
Venezuelan	16	0.12
Other Hispanic or Latino	60	0.45

Race*	Population	%
African-American/Black (3,635)	3,838	28.87
Not Hispanic (3,527)	3,673	27.63
Hispanic (108)	165	1.24
American Indian/Alaska Native (44)	134	1.01
Not Hispanic (27)	91	0.68
Hispanic (17)	43	0.32
Alaska Athabascan *(Ala. Nat.)* (3)	3	0.02
Blackfeet (0)	5	0.04
Central American Ind. (0)	1	0.01
Cherokee (0)	21	0.16
Delaware (2)	2	0.02
Iroquois (0)	1	0.01
Lumbee (0)	2	0.02
Paiute (0)	1	0.01
Pueblo (2)	2	0.02
Sioux (1)	1	0.01
South American Ind. (5)	11	0.08
Spanish American Ind. (2)	2	0.02
Asian (4,591)	4,867	36.61
Not Hispanic (4,581)	4,829	36.32
Hispanic (10)	38	0.29
Bangladeshi (23)	28	0.21
Burmese (8)	8	0.06
Cambodian (0)	11	0.08
Chinese, ex. Taiwanese (367)	389	2.93
Filipino (313)	351	2.64
Indian (3,415)	3,528	26.54
Indonesian (9)	12	0.09
Japanese (32)	48	0.36
Korean (63)	72	0.54
Nepalese (7)	7	0.05
Pakistani (240)	248	1.87
Sri Lankan (19)	26	0.20
Taiwanese (24)	32	0.24
Thai (1)	3	0.02
Vietnamese (27)	30	0.23
Hawaii Native/Pacific Islander (0)	15	0.11

*Notes: † The Census 2010 population figure is used to calculate the percentages in the Hispanic Origin and Race categories. Ancestry percentages are based on the 2006-2010 American Community Survey population (not shown); ‡ Numbers in parentheses indicate the number of people reporting a single ancestry; * Numbers in parentheses indicate the number of persons reporting this race alone, not in combination with any other race; Please refer to the Explanation of Data for more information.*

Not Hispanic (0)	10	0.08
Hispanic (0)	5	0.04
Guamanian/Chamorro (0)	2	0.02
Native Hawaiian (0)	4	0.03
Samoan (0)	1	0.01
White (4,237)	4,500	33.85
Not Hispanic (3,691)	3,900	29.33
Hispanic (546)	600	4.51

Franklin

Place Type: Township
County: Gloucester
Population: 16,820†

Ancestry‡	Population	%
African, Sub-Saharan (30)	54	0.32
African (30)	54	0.32
Albanian (0)	34	0.20
American (826)	826	4.93
Austrian (0)	43	0.26
British (0)	19	0.11
Czech (19)	67	0.40
Czechoslovakian (7)	7	0.04
Danish (10)	31	0.19
Dutch (0)	106	0.63
English (228)	1,820	10.87
European (135)	159	0.95
French, ex. Basque (107)	566	3.38
French Canadian (0)	132	0.79
German (738)	4,227	25.24
Greek (28)	102	0.61
Hungarian (18)	279	1.67
Irish (877)	4,377	26.14
Italian (2,009)	5,046	30.14
Lithuanian (41)	41	0.24
Norwegian (27)	116	0.69
Pennsylvania German (0)	15	0.09
Polish (708)	1,601	9.56
Portuguese (0)	35	0.21
Russian (49)	186	1.11
Scotch-Irish (63)	237	1.42
Scottish (92)	346	2.07
Slovak (5)	44	0.26
Swedish (14)	71	0.42
Swiss (12)	12	0.07
Ukrainian (42)	196	1.17
Welsh (35)	102	0.61
West Indian, ex. Hispanic (63)	63	0.38
Jamaican (13)	13	0.08
West Indian (50)	50	0.30
Yugoslavian (39)	53	0.32

Hispanic Origin	Population	%
Hispanic or Latino (of any race)	755	4.49
Central American, ex. Mexican	18	0.11
Guatemalan	1	0.01
Honduran	10	0.06
Nicaraguan	1	0.01
Panamanian	1	0.01
Salvadoran	5	0.03
Cuban	20	0.12
Dominican Republic	11	0.07
Mexican	172	1.02
Puerto Rican	431	2.56
South American	24	0.14
Argentinean	9	0.05
Bolivian	2	0.01
Colombian	1	0.01
Ecuadorian	2	0.01
Peruvian	8	0.05
Uruguayan	2	0.01
Other Hispanic or Latino	79	0.47

Race*	Population	%
African-American/Black (1,208)	1,368	8.13
Not Hispanic (1,162)	1,301	7.73
Hispanic (46)	67	0.40
American Indian/Alaska Native (34)	146	0.87
Not Hispanic (26)	131	0.78
Hispanic (8)	15	0.09
Apache (0)	6	0.04
Arapaho (0)	1	0.01
Blackfeet (1)	5	0.03
Cherokee (5)	25	0.15
Chippewa (0)	2	0.01
Delaware (1)	10	0.06
Houma (3)	3	0.02
Iroquois (1)	2	0.01
Mexican American Ind. (3)	5	0.03
Osage (0)	1	0.01
Seminole (0)	2	0.01
Sioux (3)	9	0.05
South American Ind. (2)	2	0.01
Asian (213)	267	1.59
Not Hispanic (206)	250	1.49
Hispanic (7)	17	0.10
Cambodian (11)	11	0.07
Chinese, ex. Taiwanese (24)	31	0.18
Filipino (37)	46	0.27
Indian (43)	47	0.28
Indonesian (1)	1	0.01
Japanese (2)	10	0.06
Korean (45)	54	0.32
Laotian (4)	5	0.03
Thai (4)	4	0.02
Vietnamese (25)	27	0.16
Hawaii Native/Pacific Islander (5)	11	0.07
Not Hispanic (5)	9	0.05
Hispanic (0)	2	0.01
Native Hawaiian (5)	8	0.05
White (14,876)	15,142	90.02
Not Hispanic (14,405)	14,626	86.96
Hispanic (471)	516	3.07

Franklin

Place Type: Township
County: Somerset
Population: 62,300†

Ancestry‡	Population	%
African, Sub-Saharan (1,733)	1,894	3.14
African (1,012)	1,075	1.78
Ethiopian (6)	6	0.01
Ghanaian (107)	144	0.24
Liberian (0)	11	0.02
Nigerian (440)	490	0.81
Sierra Leonean (120)	120	0.20
Somalian (14)	14	0.02
Other Sub-Saharan African (34)	34	0.06
Albanian (0)	10	0.02
American (933)	933	1.55
Arab (775)	1,018	1.69
Arab (53)	75	0.12
Egyptian (211)	242	0.40
Lebanese (129)	279	0.46
Moroccan (298)	298	0.49
Palestinian (51)	79	0.13
Syrian (0)	12	0.02
Other Arab (33)	33	0.05
Armenian (116)	138	0.23
Australian (24)	45	0.07
Austrian (129)	324	0.54
Basque (39)	39	0.06
Belgian (9)	9	0.01
Brazilian (15)	15	0.02
British (141)	204	0.34
Cajun (8)	8	0.01
Canadian (15)	40	0.07
Carpatho Rusyn (0)	17	0.03
Celtic (0)	26	0.04
Croatian (11)	58	0.10
Cypriot (8)	8	0.01
Czech (113)	161	0.27
Czechoslovakian (5)	30	0.05
Danish (42)	108	0.18
Dutch (101)	538	0.89
Eastern European (102)	111	0.18
English (374)	1,852	3.07
Estonian (0)	12	0.02
European (271)	321	0.53
French, ex. Basque (30)	480	0.80
French Canadian (61)	118	0.20
German (855)	4,362	7.23
Greek (100)	184	0.30
Guyanese (55)	148	0.25
Hungarian (701)	1,295	2.15
Icelander (0)	19	0.03
Iranian (98)	98	0.16
Irish (1,028)	4,325	7.17
Italian (2,897)	5,802	9.61
Latvian (8)	8	0.01
Lithuanian (42)	159	0.26
Maltese (16)	16	0.03
Norwegian (250)	453	0.75
Pennsylvania German (10)	23	0.04
Polish (1,153)	2,957	4.90
Portuguese (8)	65	0.11
Romanian (65)	154	0.26
Russian (515)	1,302	2.16
Scandinavian (0)	28	0.05
Scotch-Irish (172)	426	0.71
Scottish (92)	455	0.75
Slavic (10)	19	0.03
Slovak (102)	379	0.63
Swedish (48)	299	0.50
Swiss (11)	121	0.20
Turkish (68)	89	0.15
Ukrainian (223)	562	0.93
Welsh (44)	170	0.28
West Indian, ex. Hispanic (1,413)	1,739	2.88
Bahamian (18)	18	0.03
Barbadian (59)	59	0.10
British West Indian (119)	182	0.30
Haitian (98)	98	0.16
Jamaican (846)	1,022	1.69
Trinidadian/Tobagonian (38)	38	0.06
U.S. Virgin Islander (8)	8	0.01
West Indian (214)	301	0.50
Other West Indian (13)	13	0.02

Hispanic Origin	Population	%
Hispanic or Latino (of any race)	8,050	12.92
Central American, ex. Mexican	1,092	1.75
Costa Rican	97	0.16
Guatemalan	136	0.22
Honduran	541	0.87
Nicaraguan	118	0.19
Panamanian	84	0.13
Salvadoran	112	0.18
Other Central American	4	0.01
Cuban	266	0.43
Dominican Republic	1,456	2.34
Mexican	1,710	2.74
Puerto Rican	2,031	3.26
South American	950	1.52
Argentinean	52	0.08
Bolivian	4	0.01
Chilean	24	0.04
Colombian	375	0.60
Ecuadorian	210	0.34
Paraguayan	3	<0.01
Peruvian	213	0.34
Uruguayan	17	0.03
Venezuelan	43	0.07
Other South American	9	0.01
Other Hispanic or Latino	545	0.87

Race*	Population	%
African-American/Black (16,539)	17,500	28.09
Not Hispanic (15,888)	16,573	26.60
Hispanic (651)	927	1.49
American Indian/Alaska Native (183)	548	0.88
Not Hispanic (102)	372	0.60
Hispanic (81)	176	0.28
Alaska Athabascan *(Ala. Nat.)* (3)	3	<0.01
Apache (2)	3	<0.01
Blackfeet (0)	13	0.02
Central American Ind. (0)	3	<0.01

SECTION TWO

*Notes: † The Census 2010 population figure is used to calculate the percentages in the Hispanic Origin and Race categories. Ancestry percentages are based on the 2006-2010 American Community Survey population (not shown); ‡ Numbers in parentheses indicate the number of people reporting a single ancestry; * Numbers in parentheses indicate the number of persons reporting this race alone, not in combination with any other race; Please refer to the Explanation of Data for more information.*

Cherokee (10)	70	0.11
Chippewa (1)	2	<0.01
Choctaw (0)	4	0.01
Delaware (2)	9	0.01
Hopi (0)	2	<0.01
Iroquois (0)	2	<0.01
Lumbee (0)	3	<0.01
Mexican American Ind. (15)	19	0.03
Navajo (1)	2	<0.01
Paiute (0)	1	<0.01
Potawatomi (2)	2	<0.01
Pueblo (2)	3	<0.01
Seminole (0)	8	0.01
Sioux (6)	6	0.01
South American Ind. (20)	43	0.07
Spanish American Ind. (8)	9	0.01
Asian (12,450)	13,281	21.32
Not Hispanic (12,410)	13,158	21.12
Hispanic (40)	123	0.20
Bangladeshi (74)	84	0.13
Burmese (8)	8	0.01
Cambodian (2)	13	0.02
Chinese, ex. Taiwanese (1,566)	1,730	2.78
Filipino (1,498)	1,687	2.71
Hmong (1)	1	<0.01
Indian (7,703)	7,998	12.84
Indonesian (29)	39	0.06
Japanese (86)	128	0.21
Korean (374)	416	0.67
Laotian (4)	9	0.01
Malaysian (1)	3	<0.01
Nepalese (22)	22	0.04
Pakistani (573)	609	0.98
Sri Lankan (32)	39	0.06
Taiwanese (151)	179	0.29
Thai (17)	28	0.04
Vietnamese (118)	128	0.21
Hawaii Native/Pacific Islander (9)	102	0.16
Not Hispanic (8)	75	0.12
Hispanic (1)	27	0.04
Guamanian/Chamorro (1)	5	0.01
Native Hawaiian (1)	7	0.01
Samoan (0)	1	<0.01
White (27,887)	29,217	46.90
Not Hispanic (24,198)	25,084	40.26
Hispanic (3,689)	4,133	6.63

Freehold

Place Type: Borough
County: Monmouth
Population: 12,052†

Ancestry‡	Population	%
African, Sub-Saharan (89)	89	0.75
African (35)	35	0.29
Ghanaian (9)	9	0.08
Nigerian (45)	45	0.38
American (491)	491	4.12
Arab (11)	20	0.17
Egyptian (11)	11	0.09
Lebanese (0)	9	0.08
Australian (0)	13	0.11
Austrian (0)	14	0.12
Czech (10)	23	0.19
Czechoslovakian (0)	31	0.26
Dutch (41)	61	0.51
English (219)	716	6.01
European (32)	32	0.27
French, ex. Basque (23)	164	1.38
French Canadian (22)	53	0.45
German (348)	1,158	9.72
Greek (8)	26	0.22
Hungarian (38)	74	0.62
Irish (591)	1,693	14.21
Italian (380)	1,040	8.73
Lithuanian (0)	42	0.35
Norwegian (10)	27	0.23
Polish (110)	615	5.16
Portuguese (30)	40	0.34
Romanian (0)	13	0.11
Russian (68)	201	1.69
Scandinavian (16)	16	0.13
Scotch-Irish (45)	141	1.18
Scottish (24)	71	0.60
Slovak (0)	10	0.08
Swedish (0)	44	0.37
Ukrainian (37)	158	1.33
Welsh (0)	28	0.24
West Indian, ex. Hispanic (70)	70	0.59
Jamaican (27)	27	0.23
Trinidadian/Tobagonian (43)	43	0.36
Yugoslavian (0)	26	0.22

Hispanic Origin	Population	%
Hispanic or Latino (of any race)	5,167	42.87
Central American, ex. Mexican	273	2.27
Costa Rican	13	0.11
Guatemalan	147	1.22
Honduran	49	0.41
Nicaraguan	3	0.02
Panamanian	3	0.02
Salvadoran	53	0.44
Other Central American	5	0.04
Cuban	61	0.51
Dominican Republic	67	0.56
Mexican	3,565	29.58
Puerto Rican	605	5.02
South American	427	3.54
Argentinean	7	0.06
Bolivian	2	0.02
Chilean	4	0.03
Colombian	28	0.23
Ecuadorian	54	0.45
Peruvian	322	2.67
Uruguayan	4	0.03
Venezuelan	6	0.05
Other Hispanic or Latino	169	1.40

Race*	Population	%
African-American/Black (1,515)	1,657	13.75
Not Hispanic (1,391)	1,485	12.32
Hispanic (124)	172	1.43
American Indian/Alaska Native (63)	119	0.99
Not Hispanic (13)	43	0.36
Hispanic (50)	76	0.63
Arapaho (0)	1	0.01
Blackfeet (0)	1	0.01
Cherokee (3)	12	0.10
Delaware (0)	2	0.02
Iroquois (1)	6	0.05
Mexican American Ind. (9)	17	0.14
Navajo (1)	3	0.02
Potawatomi (0)	1	0.01
Pueblo (5)	5	0.04
Sioux (0)	1	0.01
South American Ind. (6)	8	0.07
Spanish American Ind. (0)	3	0.02
Tohono O'Odham (1)	1	0.01
Ute (3)	3	0.02
Asian (348)	411	3.41
Not Hispanic (342)	396	3.29
Hispanic (6)	15	0.12
Bangladeshi (4)	4	0.03
Cambodian (0)	2	0.02
Chinese, ex. Taiwanese (117)	133	1.10
Filipino (77)	85	0.71
Indian (70)	85	0.71
Indonesian (1)	1	0.01
Japanese (8)	15	0.12
Korean (21)	24	0.20
Laotian (0)	6	0.05
Malaysian (3)	3	0.02
Pakistani (2)	4	0.03
Taiwanese (6)	7	0.06
Thai (2)	4	0.03
Vietnamese (28)	32	0.27
Hawaii Native/Pacific Islander (8)	19	0.16
Not Hispanic (8)	9	0.07
Hispanic (0)	10	0.08
Guamanian/Chamorro (8)	9	0.07
White (7,920)	8,213	68.15
Not Hispanic (4,957)	5,090	42.23
Hispanic (2,963)	3,123	25.91

Freehold

Place Type: Township
County: Monmouth
Population: 36,184†

Ancestry‡	Population	%
African, Sub-Saharan (62)	71	0.20
African (8)	17	0.05
Ghanaian (30)	30	0.08
South African (24)	24	0.07
Albanian (127)	147	0.41
American (2,948)	2,948	8.32
Arab (125)	317	0.89
Arab (0)	13	0.04
Egyptian (29)	29	0.08
Lebanese (26)	46	0.13
Moroccan (2)	2	0.01
Palestinian (16)	31	0.09
Syrian (52)	164	0.46
Other Arab (0)	32	0.09
Austrian (32)	342	0.97
Belgian (0)	15	0.04
Brazilian (179)	188	0.53
British (64)	91	0.26
Canadian (15)	57	0.16
Croatian (25)	43	0.12
Cypriot (8)	8	0.02
Czech (13)	127	0.36
Czechoslovakian (26)	33	0.09
Danish (15)	199	0.56
Dutch (54)	229	0.65
Eastern European (299)	350	0.99
English (458)	1,869	5.28
European (291)	291	0.82
French, ex. Basque (69)	416	1.17
French Canadian (100)	277	0.78
German (868)	4,232	11.94
Greek (239)	430	1.21
Hungarian (92)	649	1.83
Iranian (0)	10	0.03
Irish (1,883)	6,666	18.81
Israeli (102)	102	0.29
Italian (5,338)	10,701	30.20
Latvian (9)	9	0.03
Lithuanian (53)	294	0.83
Maltese (0)	14	0.04
Norwegian (41)	267	0.75
Pennsylvania German (0)	11	0.03
Polish (688)	2,446	6.90
Portuguese (190)	251	0.71
Romanian (55)	245	0.69
Russian (559)	1,148	3.24
Scotch-Irish (167)	405	1.14
Scottish (74)	465	1.31
Slavic (12)	25	0.07
Slovak (28)	127	0.36
Swedish (0)	189	0.53
Swiss (0)	72	0.20
Turkish (97)	150	0.42
Ukrainian (116)	251	0.71
Welsh (0)	125	0.35
West Indian, ex. Hispanic (499)	526	1.48
Barbadian (8)	8	0.02
Haitian (45)	53	0.15
Jamaican (256)	261	0.74
Trinidadian/Tobagonian (82)	89	0.25
U.S. Virgin Islander (8)	8	0.02
West Indian (100)	107	0.30
Yugoslavian (11)	22	0.06

Hispanic Origin	Population	%
Hispanic or Latino (of any race)	2,808	7.76
Central American, ex. Mexican	126	0.35
Costa Rican	17	0.05

*Notes: † The Census 2010 population figure is used to calculate the percentages in the Hispanic Origin and Race categories. Ancestry percentages are based on the 2006-2010 American Community Survey population (not shown); ‡ Numbers in parentheses indicate the number of people reporting a single ancestry; * Numbers in parentheses indicate the number of persons reporting this race alone, not in combination with any other race; Please refer to the Explanation of Data for more information.*

Guatemalan	33	0.09
Honduran	19	0.05
Nicaraguan	9	0.02
Panamanian	17	0.05
Salvadoran	31	0.09
Cuban	257	0.71
Dominican Republic	118	0.33
Mexican	757	2.09
Puerto Rican	947	2.62
South American	417	1.15
Argentinean	35	0.10
Bolivian	7	0.02
Chilean	23	0.06
Colombian	144	0.40
Ecuadorian	53	0.15
Paraguayan	2	0.01
Peruvian	123	0.34
Uruguayan	14	0.04
Venezuelan	12	0.03
Other South American	4	0.01
Other Hispanic or Latino	186	0.51

Race*	Population	%
African-American/Black (1,931)	2,114	5.84
Not Hispanic (1,860)	1,990	5.50
Hispanic (71)	124	0.34
American Indian/Alaska Native (47)	117	0.32
Not Hispanic (26)	75	0.21
Hispanic (21)	42	0.12
Apache (0)	1	<0.01
Blackfeet (2)	6	0.02
Canadian/French Am. Ind. (1)	3	0.01
Cherokee (2)	10	0.03
Chippewa (0)	1	<0.01
Cree (0)	2	0.01
Delaware (0)	1	<0.01
Iroquois (0)	2	0.01
Mexican American Ind. (12)	12	0.03
Sioux (4)	5	0.01
South American Ind. (6)	10	0.03
Asian (2,544)	2,851	7.88
Not Hispanic (2,530)	2,820	7.79
Hispanic (14)	31	0.09
Bangladeshi (9)	9	0.02
Burmese (0)	3	0.01
Cambodian (0)	1	<0.01
Chinese, ex. Taiwanese (698)	801	2.21
Filipino (479)	599	1.66
Indian (943)	1,003	2.77
Indonesian (3)	5	0.01
Japanese (14)	30	0.08
Korean (170)	196	0.54
Laotian (2)	5	0.01
Malaysian (4)	6	0.02
Nepalese (0)	1	<0.01
Pakistani (74)	81	0.22
Sri Lankan (1)	1	<0.01
Taiwanese (16)	17	0.05
Thai (4)	8	0.02
Vietnamese (55)	62	0.17
Hawaii Native/Pacific Islander (7)	39	0.11
Not Hispanic (7)	32	0.09
Hispanic (0)	7	0.02
Fijian (1)	1	<0.01
Guamanian/Chamorro (2)	5	0.01
Native Hawaiian (1)	5	0.01
Samoan (2)	8	0.02
Tongan (1)	1	<0.01
White (30,509)	31,031	85.76
Not Hispanic (28,427)	28,823	79.66
Hispanic (2,082)	2,208	6.10

Galloway

Place Type: Township
County: Atlantic
Population: 37,349†

Ancestry‡	Population	%
African, Sub-Saharan (258)	296	0.81
African (196)	225	0.62
Liberian (11)	11	0.03
Nigerian (51)	60	0.16
Albanian (60)	60	0.16
American (897)	897	2.45
Arab (214)	252	0.69
Arab (0)	29	0.08
Egyptian (141)	150	0.41
Lebanese (50)	50	0.14
Syrian (23)	23	0.06
Armenian (25)	58	0.16
Australian (8)	32	0.09
Austrian (34)	105	0.29
Belgian (6)	14	0.04
British (55)	98	0.27
Bulgarian (69)	69	0.19
Canadian (0)	61	0.17
Croatian (80)	80	0.22
Czech (18)	263	0.72
Czechoslovakian (41)	41	0.11
Danish (53)	287	0.79
Dutch (25)	187	0.51
Eastern European (42)	42	0.11
English (690)	2,591	7.09
European (135)	247	0.68
Finnish (27)	119	0.33
French, ex. Basque (60)	775	2.12
French Canadian (23)	101	0.28
German (1,081)	5,764	15.77
Greek (180)	506	1.38
Hungarian (50)	307	0.84
Icelander (0)	7	0.02
Iranian (34)	34	0.09
Irish (1,914)	8,517	23.30
Israeli (0)	83	0.23
Italian (3,191)	8,862	24.25
Latvian (8)	8	0.02
Lithuanian (26)	109	0.30
Macedonian (25)	43	0.12
New Zealander (7)	7	0.02
Northern European (13)	13	0.04
Norwegian (63)	241	0.66
Pennsylvania German (10)	22	0.06
Polish (653)	2,372	6.49
Portuguese (10)	20	0.05
Romanian (0)	34	0.09
Russian (246)	793	2.17
Scandinavian (10)	20	0.05
Scotch-Irish (50)	178	0.49
Scottish (33)	454	1.24
Serbian (0)	61	0.17
Slavic (0)	31	0.08
Slovak (0)	107	0.29
Slovene (0)	8	0.02
Swedish (12)	210	0.57
Swiss (0)	139	0.38
Ukrainian (44)	126	0.34
Welsh (17)	364	1.00
West Indian, ex. Hispanic (47)	61	0.17
British West Indian (9)	9	0.02
Haitian (8)	8	0.02
Jamaican (23)	23	0.06
Trinidadian/Tobagonian (0)	14	0.04
West Indian (7)	7	0.02
Yugoslavian (0)	10	0.03

Hispanic Origin	Population	%
Hispanic or Latino (of any race)	3,752	10.05
Central American, ex. Mexican	261	0.70
Costa Rican	8	0.02
Guatemalan	24	0.06
Honduran	67	0.18
Nicaraguan	38	0.10
Panamanian	6	0.02
Salvadoran	91	0.24
Other Central American	27	0.07
Cuban	85	0.23
Dominican Republic	295	0.79
Mexican	407	1.09
Puerto Rican	1,770	4.74
South American	636	1.70
Argentinean	24	0.06
Bolivian	3	0.01
Chilean	14	0.04
Colombian	225	0.60
Ecuadorian	40	0.11
Peruvian	302	0.81
Uruguayan	6	0.02
Venezuelan	16	0.04
Other South American	6	0.02
Other Hispanic or Latino	298	0.80

Race*	Population	%
African-American/Black (4,271)	4,750	12.72
Not Hispanic (3,955)	4,291	11.49
Hispanic (316)	459	1.23
American Indian/Alaska Native (99)	337	0.90
Not Hispanic (73)	263	0.70
Hispanic (26)	74	0.20
Apache (3)	5	0.01
Arapaho (0)	2	0.01
Blackfeet (2)	6	0.02
Central American Ind. (3)	3	0.01
Cherokee (7)	56	0.15
Chippewa (1)	5	0.01
Choctaw (0)	1	<0.01
Comanche (0)	3	0.01
Cree (0)	3	0.01
Creek (0)	1	<0.01
Delaware (6)	15	0.04
Iroquois (1)	3	0.01
Mexican American Ind. (1)	1	<0.01
Navajo (1)	9	0.02
Ottawa (0)	1	<0.01
Seminole (0)	2	0.01
Shoshone (1)	3	0.01
Sioux (1)	8	0.02
South American Ind. (0)	4	0.01
Spanish American Ind. (1)	1	<0.01
Asian (3,744)	4,132	11.06
Not Hispanic (3,720)	4,077	10.92
Hispanic (24)	55	0.15
Bangladeshi (75)	81	0.22
Cambodian (8)	9	0.02
Chinese, ex. Taiwanese (620)	687	1.84
Filipino (466)	555	1.49
Indian (1,544)	1,669	4.47
Indonesian (2)	3	0.01
Japanese (27)	77	0.21
Korean (183)	216	0.58
Laotian (17)	23	0.06
Pakistani (319)	345	0.92
Sri Lankan (0)	2	0.01
Taiwanese (13)	14	0.04
Thai (32)	39	0.10
Vietnamese (339)	374	1.00
Hawaii Native/Pacific Islander (9)	37	0.10
Not Hispanic (7)	28	0.07
Hispanic (2)	9	0.02
Fijian (1)	3	0.01
Guamanian/Chamorro (1)	3	0.01
Native Hawaiian (4)	10	0.03
Samoan (3)	8	0.02
White (26,860)	27,713	74.20
Not Hispanic (24,964)	25,574	68.47
Hispanic (1,896)	2,139	5.73

Garfield

Place Type: City
County: Bergen
Population: 30,487†

Ancestry‡	Population	%
Albanian (764)	826	2.74
Alsatian (0)	10	0.03
American (844)	844	2.80
Arab (316)	324	1.07
Arab (142)	142	0.47
Egyptian (33)	33	0.11

*Notes: † The Census 2010 population figure is used to calculate the percentages in the Hispanic Origin and Race categories. Ancestry percentages are based on the 2006-2010 American Community Survey population (not shown); ‡ Numbers in parentheses indicate the number of people reporting a single ancestry; * Numbers in parentheses indicate the number of persons reporting this race alone, not in combination with any other race; Please refer to the Explanation of Data for more information.*

Ancestry	Population	%
Moroccan (21)	21	0.07
Syrian (120)	128	0.42
Austrian (0)	72	0.24
Brazilian (192)	192	0.64
British (14)	14	0.05
Bulgarian (169)	169	0.56
Canadian (0)	21	0.07
Cypriot (12)	12	0.04
Czech (52)	144	0.48
Czechoslovakian (130)	172	0.57
Danish (0)	27	0.09
Dutch (4)	255	0.84
Eastern European (30)	30	0.10
English (81)	400	1.32
European (59)	78	0.26
French, ex. Basque (8)	146	0.48
French Canadian (6)	13	0.04
German (224)	967	3.20
Greek (64)	132	0.44
Guyanese (72)	72	0.24
Hungarian (274)	598	1.98
Irish (258)	1,103	3.65
Italian (2,937)	4,727	15.66
Macedonian (795)	826	2.74
Maltese (0)	9	0.03
Northern European (13)	13	0.04
Norwegian (41)	74	0.25
Polish (5,111)	6,403	21.21
Portuguese (160)	199	0.66
Romanian (13)	23	0.08
Russian (50)	210	0.70
Scotch-Irish (0)	141	0.47
Scottish (37)	229	0.76
Serbian (20)	28	0.09
Slavic (0)	8	0.03
Slovak (68)	192	0.64
Swedish (0)	136	0.45
Turkish (54)	109	0.36
Ukrainian (294)	451	1.49
Welsh (0)	58	0.19
West Indian, ex. Hispanic (184)	250	0.83
British West Indian (0)	7	0.02
Haitian (18)	34	0.11
Jamaican (113)	113	0.37
Trinidadian/Tobagonian (18)	61	0.20
Other West Indian (35)	35	0.12
Yugoslavian (140)	140	0.46

Hispanic Origin	Population	%
Hispanic or Latino (of any race)	9,830	32.24
Central American, ex. Mexican	498	1.63
Costa Rican	58	0.19
Guatemalan	87	0.29
Honduran	109	0.36
Nicaraguan	44	0.14
Panamanian	5	0.02
Salvadoran	186	0.61
Other Central American	9	0.03
Cuban	216	0.71
Dominican Republic	2,057	6.75
Mexican	852	2.79
Puerto Rican	2,210	7.25
South American	3,338	10.95
Argentinean	151	0.50
Bolivian	102	0.33
Chilean	39	0.13
Colombian	880	2.89
Ecuadorian	619	2.03
Paraguayan	2	0.01
Peruvian	1,462	4.80
Uruguayan	35	0.11
Venezuelan	30	0.10
Other South American	18	0.06
Other Hispanic or Latino	659	2.16

Race*	Population	%
African-American/Black (1,981)	2,341	7.68
Not Hispanic (1,564)	1,750	5.74
Hispanic (417)	591	1.94
American Indian/Alaska Native (132)	278	0.91
Not Hispanic (16)	66	0.22
Hispanic (116)	212	0.70
Alaska Athabascan *(Ala. Nat.)* (1)	1	<0.01
Apache (0)	1	<0.01
Arapaho (0)	1	<0.01
Blackfeet (0)	10	0.03
Central American Ind. (2)	2	0.01
Cherokee (1)	14	0.05
Creek (1)	1	<0.01
Iroquois (1)	2	0.01
Mexican American Ind. (2)	2	0.01
Potawatomi (0)	3	0.01
South American Ind. (16)	33	0.11
Spanish American Ind. (1)	4	0.01
Asian (678)	842	2.76
Not Hispanic (659)	784	2.57
Hispanic (19)	58	0.19
Bangladeshi (13)	13	0.04
Chinese, ex. Taiwanese (73)	98	0.32
Filipino (141)	178	0.58
Indian (231)	261	0.86
Indonesian (12)	12	0.04
Japanese (21)	27	0.09
Korean (49)	58	0.19
Laotian (0)	3	0.01
Pakistani (89)	90	0.30
Sri Lankan (3)	3	0.01
Taiwanese (2)	3	0.01
Thai (3)	3	0.01
Vietnamese (18)	18	0.06
Hawaii Native/Pacific Islander (2)	44	0.14
Not Hispanic (2)	21	0.07
Hispanic (0)	23	0.08
Native Hawaiian (0)	10	0.03
Samoan (0)	5	0.02
White (23,393)	24,181	79.32
Not Hispanic (17,972)	18,241	59.83
Hispanic (5,421)	5,940	19.48

Glassboro

Place Type: Borough
County: Gloucester
Population: 18,579†

Ancestry‡	Population	%
African, Sub-Saharan (214)	288	1.53
African (214)	251	1.33
Other Sub-Saharan African (0)	37	0.20
American (623)	623	3.31
Arab (108)	117	0.62
Egyptian (108)	108	0.57
Lebanese (0)	9	0.05
Armenian (9)	20	0.11
Australian (11)	42	0.22
Austrian (18)	35	0.19
Brazilian (10)	38	0.20
British (25)	52	0.28
Canadian (29)	39	0.21
Celtic (0)	40	0.21
Croatian (0)	17	0.09
Czech (30)	54	0.29
Czechoslovakian (0)	10	0.05
Danish (0)	11	0.06
Dutch (39)	163	0.87
Eastern European (9)	9	0.05
English (278)	1,535	8.16
European (7)	7	0.04
Finnish (0)	25	0.13
French, ex. Basque (10)	278	1.48
French Canadian (7)	15	0.08
German (708)	3,356	17.84
Greek (11)	370	1.97
Guyanese (0)	11	0.06
Hungarian (0)	81	0.43
Irish (1,162)	4,595	24.43
Italian (1,914)	3,981	21.16
Lithuanian (7)	48	0.26
Northern European (31)	31	0.16
Norwegian (7)	16	0.09
Pennsylvania German (9)	31	0.16
Polish (216)	986	5.24
Portuguese (233)	281	1.49
Romanian (28)	43	0.23
Russian (118)	546	2.90
Scandinavian (0)	17	0.09
Scotch-Irish (86)	217	1.15
Scottish (37)	212	1.13
Serbian (13)	13	0.07
Slovak (13)	13	0.07
Swedish (10)	46	0.24
Turkish (158)	169	0.90
Ukrainian (122)	200	1.06
Welsh (67)	175	0.93
West Indian, ex. Hispanic (72)	105	0.56
British West Indian (14)	14	0.07
Haitian (7)	17	0.09
Jamaican (25)	48	0.26
West Indian (26)	26	0.14

Hispanic Origin	Population	%
Hispanic or Latino (of any race)	1,378	7.42
Central American, ex. Mexican	53	0.29
Costa Rican	11	0.06
Guatemalan	20	0.11
Honduran	2	0.01
Nicaraguan	1	0.01
Panamanian	8	0.04
Salvadoran	11	0.06
Cuban	63	0.34
Dominican Republic	35	0.19
Mexican	354	1.91
Puerto Rican	685	3.69
South American	60	0.32
Argentinean	7	0.04
Chilean	5	0.03
Colombian	22	0.12
Ecuadorian	14	0.08
Peruvian	10	0.05
Venezuelan	2	0.01
Other Hispanic or Latino	128	0.69

Race*	Population	%
African-American/Black (3,469)	3,804	20.47
Not Hispanic (3,340)	3,597	19.36
Hispanic (129)	207	1.11
American Indian/Alaska Native (21)	136	0.73
Not Hispanic (12)	107	0.58
Hispanic (9)	29	0.16
Blackfeet (0)	8	0.04
Canadian/French Am. Ind. (1)	1	0.01
Central American Ind. (1)	1	0.01
Cherokee (0)	25	0.13
Cheyenne (0)	2	0.01
Chippewa (0)	2	0.01
Choctaw (0)	3	0.02
Delaware (0)	6	0.03
Iroquois (1)	4	0.02
Lumbee (2)	2	0.01
Mexican American Ind. (0)	1	0.01
South American Ind. (4)	5	0.03
Asian (534)	649	3.49
Not Hispanic (529)	622	3.35
Hispanic (5)	27	0.15
Bangladeshi (3)	3	0.02
Cambodian (20)	24	0.13
Chinese, ex. Taiwanese (160)	181	0.97
Filipino (88)	120	0.65
Indian (97)	114	0.61
Japanese (9)	22	0.12
Korean (43)	59	0.32
Laotian (15)	19	0.10
Nepalese (1)	1	0.01
Pakistani (36)	37	0.20
Sri Lankan (5)	5	0.03
Taiwanese (9)	9	0.05
Thai (3)	3	0.02
Vietnamese (31)	41	0.22
Hawaii Native/Pacific Islander (10)	16	0.09
Not Hispanic (8)	14	0.08

*Notes: † The Census 2010 population figure is used to calculate the percentages in the Hispanic Origin and Race categories. Ancestry percentages are based on the 2006-2010 American Community Survey population (not shown); ‡ Numbers in parentheses indicate the number of people reporting a single ancestry; * Numbers in parentheses indicate the number of persons reporting this race alone, not in combination with any other race; Please refer to the Explanation of Data for more information.*

Hispanic (2)	2	0.01
Guamanian/Chamorro (1)	1	0.01
Native Hawaiian (5)	7	0.04
Samoan (0)	2	0.01
White (13,423)	13,861	74.61
Not Hispanic (12,899)	13,221	71.16
Hispanic (524)	640	3.44

Glen Ridge

Place Type: Borough
County: Essex
Population: 7,527†

Ancestry‡	Population	%
American (290)	290	3.90
Arab (13)	92	1.24
Lebanese (13)	92	1.24
Armenian (13)	42	0.56
Australian (0)	11	0.15
Austrian (14)	48	0.65
Brazilian (12)	12	0.16
British (130)	163	2.19
Canadian (10)	10	0.13
Croatian (20)	20	0.27
Czech (11)	56	0.75
Czechoslovakian (10)	10	0.13
Dutch (0)	24	0.32
Eastern European (78)	78	1.05
English (108)	1,205	16.19
European (152)	152	2.04
French, ex. Basque (8)	129	1.73
French Canadian (0)	36	0.48
German (61)	935	12.57
Greek (50)	50	0.67
Hungarian (11)	50	0.67
Icelander (10)	38	0.51
Iranian (10)	31	0.42
Irish (444)	1,895	25.47
Italian (554)	1,374	18.47
Lithuanian (0)	133	1.79
Northern European (37)	70	0.94
Norwegian (0)	30	0.40
Polish (174)	891	11.97
Portuguese (30)	38	0.51
Romanian (0)	8	0.11
Russian (84)	245	3.29
Scandinavian (51)	62	0.83
Scotch-Irish (31)	136	1.83
Scottish (43)	141	1.89
Slovak (15)	15	0.20
Swedish (16)	161	2.16
Swiss (8)	16	0.22
Welsh (0)	42	0.56
West Indian, ex. Hispanic (355)	405	5.44
Haitian (46)	58	0.78
Jamaican (309)	347	4.66

Hispanic Origin	Population	%
Hispanic or Latino (of any race)	377	5.01
Central American, ex. Mexican	22	0.29
Costa Rican	4	0.05
Guatemalan	3	0.04
Honduran	2	0.03
Panamanian	6	0.08
Salvadoran	7	0.09
Cuban	49	0.65
Dominican Republic	31	0.41
Mexican	25	0.33
Puerto Rican	94	1.25
South American	101	1.34
Argentinean	10	0.13
Bolivian	6	0.08
Chilean	2	0.03
Colombian	25	0.33
Ecuadorian	26	0.35
Peruvian	19	0.25
Uruguayan	4	0.05
Venezuelan	4	0.05
Other South American	5	0.07
Other Hispanic or Latino	55	0.73

Race*	Population	%
African-American/Black (379)	431	5.73
Not Hispanic (356)	397	5.27
Hispanic (23)	34	0.45
American Indian/Alaska Native (3)	28	0.37
Not Hispanic (2)	24	0.32
Hispanic (1)	4	0.05
Blackfeet (0)	5	0.07
Cherokee (0)	3	0.04
Cree (0)	2	0.03
Puget Sound Salish (0)	2	0.03
Asian (350)	472	6.27
Not Hispanic (348)	463	6.15
Hispanic (2)	9	0.12
Chinese, ex. Taiwanese (81)	116	1.54
Filipino (68)	93	1.24
Indian (112)	133	1.77
Indonesian (1)	1	0.01
Japanese (43)	74	0.98
Korean (28)	46	0.61
Sri Lankan (1)	2	0.03
Taiwanese (3)	5	0.07
Vietnamese (2)	6	0.08
Hawaii Native/Pacific Islander (0)	1	0.01
Not Hispanic (0)	1	0.01
Guamanian/Chamorro (0)	1	0.01
White (6,489)	6,671	88.63
Not Hispanic (6,253)	6,400	85.03
Hispanic (236)	271	3.60

Glen Rock

Place Type: Borough
County: Bergen
Population: 11,601†

Ancestry‡	Population	%
African, Sub-Saharan (0)	34	0.29
African (0)	18	0.16
Nigerian (0)	16	0.14
American (366)	366	3.17
Arab (12)	105	0.91
Jordanian (0)	42	0.36
Syrian (12)	63	0.55
Armenian (88)	164	1.42
Austrian (20)	249	2.16
Belgian (12)	30	0.26
British (0)	14	0.12
Canadian (0)	53	0.46
Croatian (146)	146	1.26
Czech (0)	23	0.20
Danish (0)	84	0.73
Dutch (45)	238	2.06
Eastern European (124)	124	1.07
English (146)	752	6.51
European (295)	348	3.01
Finnish (0)	14	0.12
French, ex. Basque (45)	198	1.72
French Canadian (5)	107	0.93
German (340)	1,864	16.15
Greek (43)	135	1.17
Guyanese (17)	17	0.15
Hungarian (61)	157	1.36
Irish (724)	2,528	21.90
Italian (1,073)	2,923	25.32
Lithuanian (30)	79	0.68
Norwegian (32)	66	0.57
Polish (272)	742	6.43
Romanian (52)	52	0.45
Russian (198)	530	4.59
Scandinavian (0)	12	0.10
Scotch-Irish (185)	388	3.36
Scottish (50)	231	2.00
Slavic (0)	15	0.13
Slovak (31)	45	0.39
Swedish (45)	275	2.38
Swiss (17)	91	0.79
Turkish (16)	47	0.41
Ukrainian (14)	59	0.51
Welsh (0)	52	0.45
West Indian, ex. Hispanic (36)	80	0.69
Haitian (12)	29	0.25
Jamaican (24)	51	0.44
Yugoslavian (40)	127	1.10

Hispanic Origin	Population	%
Hispanic or Latino (of any race)	527	4.54
Central American, ex. Mexican	44	0.38
Costa Rican	6	0.05
Guatemalan	12	0.10
Honduran	6	0.05
Nicaraguan	3	0.03
Panamanian	5	0.04
Salvadoran	12	0.10
Cuban	90	0.78
Dominican Republic	41	0.35
Mexican	36	0.31
Puerto Rican	127	1.09
South American	111	0.96
Argentinean	12	0.10
Bolivian	6	0.05
Chilean	14	0.12
Colombian	35	0.30
Ecuadorian	11	0.09
Paraguayan	1	0.01
Peruvian	22	0.19
Uruguayan	5	0.04
Venezuelan	5	0.04
Other Hispanic or Latino	78	0.67

Race*	Population	%
African-American/Black (159)	196	1.69
Not Hispanic (151)	178	1.53
Hispanic (8)	18	0.16
American Indian/Alaska Native (10)	25	0.22
Not Hispanic (5)	17	0.15
Hispanic (5)	8	0.07
Central American Ind. (0)	3	0.03
Cherokee (0)	6	0.05
Delaware (3)	3	0.03
Iroquois (0)	1	0.01
Mexican American Ind. (1)	1	0.01
Sioux (1)	1	0.01
South American Ind. (1)	1	0.01
Asian (1,054)	1,174	10.12
Not Hispanic (1,050)	1,158	9.98
Hispanic (4)	16	0.14
Chinese, ex. Taiwanese (184)	224	1.93
Filipino (73)	97	0.84
Indian (161)	171	1.47
Indonesian (0)	3	0.03
Japanese (141)	155	1.34
Korean (428)	471	4.06
Malaysian (1)	1	0.01
Pakistani (6)	6	0.05
Taiwanese (22)	29	0.25
Thai (19)	21	0.18
Vietnamese (2)	4	0.03
Hawaii Native/Pacific Islander (3)	8	0.07
Not Hispanic (3)	7	0.06
Hispanic (0)	1	0.01
Native Hawaiian (3)	5	0.04
Samoan (0)	2	0.02
White (10,111)	10,295	88.74
Not Hispanic (9,691)	9,835	84.78
Hispanic (420)	460	3.97

Gloucester City

Place Type: City
County: Camden
Population: 11,456†

Ancestry‡	Population	%
American (520)	520	4.53
Arab (41)	139	1.21
Egyptian (23)	23	0.20
Lebanese (0)	80	0.70

*Notes: † The Census 2010 population figure is used to calculate the percentages in the Hispanic Origin and Race categories. Ancestry percentages are based on the 2006-2010 American Community Survey population (not shown); ‡ Numbers in parentheses indicate the number of people reporting a single ancestry; * Numbers in parentheses indicate the number of persons reporting this race alone, not in combination with any other race; Please refer to the Explanation of Data for more information.*

Moroccan (9)	9	0.08
Other Arab (9)	27	0.24
Armenian (13)	13	0.11
Austrian (0)	35	0.30
Belgian (0)	27	0.24
British (9)	9	0.08
Croatian (0)	7	0.06
Czechoslovakian (17)	17	0.15
Danish (0)	38	0.33
Dutch (13)	179	1.56
English (330)	1,434	12.49
European (33)	33	0.29
French, ex. Basque (0)	129	1.12
French Canadian (15)	15	0.13
German (574)	2,984	26.00
Greek (0)	56	0.49
Hungarian (35)	64	0.56
Icelander (0)	24	0.21
Irish (1,243)	4,447	38.74
Italian (807)	2,276	19.83
Lithuanian (27)	72	0.63
Norwegian (33)	57	0.50
Pennsylvania German (0)	9	0.08
Polish (281)	742	6.46
Portuguese (82)	102	0.89
Russian (9)	27	0.24
Scotch-Irish (66)	175	1.52
Scottish (17)	129	1.12
Slovak (0)	10	0.09
Swedish (0)	54	0.47
Ukrainian (0)	18	0.16
Welsh (12)	156	1.36
West Indian, ex. Hispanic (56)	62	0.54
Haitian (15)	21	0.18
Jamaican (30)	30	0.26
West Indian (11)	11	0.10

Hispanic Origin	Population	%
Hispanic or Latino (of any race)	767	6.70
Central American, ex. Mexican	24	0.21
Costa Rican	4	0.03
Guatemalan	4	0.03
Honduran	9	0.08
Nicaraguan	1	0.01
Panamanian	5	0.04
Salvadoran	1	0.01
Cuban	16	0.14
Dominican Republic	26	0.23
Mexican	166	1.45
Puerto Rican	419	3.66
South American	38	0.33
Argentinean	6	0.05
Chilean	6	0.05
Colombian	11	0.10
Ecuadorian	6	0.05
Peruvian	1	0.01
Venezuelan	2	0.02
Other South American	6	0.05
Other Hispanic or Latino	78	0.68

Race*	Population	%
African-American/Black (352)	452	3.95
Not Hispanic (328)	400	3.49
Hispanic (24)	52	0.45
American Indian/Alaska Native (16)	57	0.50
Not Hispanic (8)	47	0.41
Hispanic (8)	10	0.09
Blackfeet (0)	1	0.01
Canadian/French Am. Ind. (0)	1	0.01
Cherokee (4)	15	0.13
Creek (0)	1	0.01
Delaware (1)	7	0.06
Sioux (0)	2	0.02
Asian (307)	330	2.88
Not Hispanic (307)	328	2.86
Hispanic (0)	2	0.02
Bangladeshi (20)	20	0.17
Cambodian (1)	3	0.03
Chinese, ex. Taiwanese (117)	123	1.07
Filipino (33)	48	0.42
Indian (50)	54	0.47
Indonesian (2)	2	0.02
Japanese (1)	2	0.02
Korean (15)	17	0.15
Laotian (4)	5	0.04
Nepalese (3)	3	0.03
Pakistani (20)	20	0.17
Thai (3)	4	0.03
Vietnamese (27)	33	0.29
Hawaii Native/Pacific Islander (0)	5	0.04
Not Hispanic (0)	3	0.03
Hispanic (0)	2	0.02
Native Hawaiian (0)	2	0.02
White (10,370)	10,559	92.17
Not Hispanic (9,896)	10,028	87.53
Hispanic (474)	531	4.64

Gloucester

Place Type: Township
County: Camden
Population: 64,634†

Ancestry‡	Population	%
African, Sub-Saharan (777)	887	1.38
African (430)	489	0.76
Ghanaian (29)	29	0.04
Liberian (27)	56	0.09
Nigerian (266)	266	0.41
Sudanese (25)	47	0.07
Albanian (0)	14	0.02
American (1,270)	1,270	1.97
Arab (171)	197	0.31
Arab (23)	23	0.04
Egyptian (62)	62	0.10
Lebanese (64)	76	0.12
Palestinian (22)	22	0.03
Other Arab (0)	14	0.02
Armenian (44)	58	0.09
Australian (0)	32	0.05
Austrian (46)	183	0.28
Belgian (0)	21	0.03
Brazilian (80)	129	0.20
British (76)	124	0.19
Canadian (11)	54	0.08
Celtic (25)	56	0.09
Croatian (55)	116	0.18
Czech (7)	61	0.09
Czechoslovakian (3)	57	0.09
Danish (9)	63	0.10
Dutch (71)	521	0.81
Eastern European (54)	54	0.08
English (995)	5,124	7.95
European (190)	255	0.40
Finnish (24)	79	0.12
French, ex. Basque (119)	1,162	1.80
French Canadian (35)	228	0.35
German (2,064)	12,288	19.06
Greek (256)	331	0.51
Guyanese (22)	44	0.07
Hungarian (34)	393	0.61
Iranian (18)	18	0.03
Irish (4,163)	18,330	28.42
Israeli (33)	33	0.05
Italian (8,314)	18,256	28.31
Latvian (0)	16	0.02
Lithuanian (70)	369	0.57
Maltese (11)	35	0.05
Norwegian (30)	154	0.24
Pennsylvania German (44)	128	0.20
Polish (1,291)	4,537	7.04
Portuguese (45)	166	0.26
Romanian (10)	39	0.06
Russian (240)	861	1.34
Scotch-Irish (199)	871	1.35
Scottish (110)	473	0.73
Serbian (0)	13	0.02
Slavic (0)	11	0.02
Slovak (60)	131	0.20
Swedish (97)	443	0.69
Swiss (0)	41	0.06
Turkish (9)	9	0.01
Ukrainian (242)	644	1.00
Welsh (17)	505	0.78
West Indian, ex. Hispanic (258)	380	0.59
Bahamian (138)	138	0.21
Barbadian (7)	7	0.01
Belizean (0)	19	0.03
Haitian (0)	35	0.05
Jamaican (92)	160	0.25
West Indian (21)	21	0.03
Yugoslavian (6)	36	0.06

Hispanic Origin	Population	%
Hispanic or Latino (of any race)	3,650	5.65
Central American, ex. Mexican	229	0.35
Costa Rican	19	0.03
Guatemalan	56	0.09
Honduran	29	0.04
Nicaraguan	36	0.06
Panamanian	16	0.02
Salvadoran	71	0.11
Other Central American	2	<0.01
Cuban	94	0.15
Dominican Republic	181	0.28
Mexican	492	0.76
Puerto Rican	2,118	3.28
South American	252	0.39
Argentinean	43	0.07
Bolivian	1	<0.01
Chilean	16	0.02
Colombian	85	0.13
Ecuadorian	38	0.06
Paraguayan	2	<0.01
Peruvian	42	0.06
Uruguayan	5	0.01
Venezuelan	17	0.03
Other South American	3	<0.01
Other Hispanic or Latino	284	0.44

Race*	Population	%
African-American/Black (10,464)	11,412	17.66
Not Hispanic (10,069)	10,792	16.70
Hispanic (395)	620	0.96
American Indian/Alaska Native (129)	460	0.71
Not Hispanic (88)	344	0.53
Hispanic (41)	116	0.18
Apache (3)	6	0.01
Blackfeet (0)	8	0.01
Central American Ind. (1)	1	<0.01
Cherokee (12)	81	0.13
Chickasaw (0)	3	<0.01
Chippewa (0)	3	<0.01
Choctaw (4)	6	0.01
Comanche (0)	1	<0.01
Cree (0)	5	0.01
Creek (4)	7	0.01
Delaware (2)	28	0.04
Iroquois (1)	13	0.02
Kiowa (0)	6	0.01
Lumbee (1)	1	<0.01
Mexican American Ind. (4)	5	0.01
Navajo (2)	5	0.01
Pueblo (0)	1	<0.01
Seminole (0)	9	0.01
Sioux (1)	11	0.02
South American Ind. (3)	18	0.03
Tohono O'Odham (5)	5	0.01
Asian (2,374)	2,709	4.19
Not Hispanic (2,360)	2,659	4.11
Hispanic (14)	50	0.08
Bangladeshi (105)	122	0.19
Cambodian (22)	27	0.04
Chinese, ex. Taiwanese (278)	351	0.54
Filipino (794)	947	1.47
Hmong (5)	5	0.01
Indian (549)	610	0.94
Indonesian (5)	5	0.01
Japanese (31)	62	0.10
Korean (133)	160	0.25

*Notes: † The Census 2010 population figure is used to calculate the percentages in the Hispanic Origin and Race categories. Ancestry percentages are based on the 2006-2010 American Community Survey population (not shown); ‡ Numbers in parentheses indicate the number of people reporting a single ancestry; * Numbers in parentheses indicate the number of persons reporting this race alone, not in combination with any other race; Please refer to the Explanation of Data for more information.*

Laotian (10)	14	0.02
Malaysian (1)	3	<0.01
Pakistani (110)	119	0.18
Sri Lankan (3)	4	0.01
Taiwanese (3)	6	0.01
Thai (14)	22	0.03
Vietnamese (207)	257	0.40
Hawaii Native/Pacific Islander (20)	65	0.10
Not Hispanic (13)	45	0.07
Hispanic (7)	20	0.03
Guamanian/Chamorro (8)	8	0.01
Native Hawaiian (4)	10	0.02
Samoan (2)	4	0.01
White (48,993)	50,146	77.58
Not Hispanic (47,297)	48,166	74.52
Hispanic (1,696)	1,980	3.06

Greentree

Place Type: CDP
County: Camden
Population: 11,367†

Ancestry‡	Population	%
American (503)	503	4.39
Arab (13)	56	0.49
Moroccan (13)	56	0.49
Armenian (69)	82	0.72
Austrian (60)	231	2.02
Belgian (46)	46	0.40
British (11)	100	0.87
Canadian (44)	54	0.47
Croatian (0)	25	0.22
Czech (0)	14	0.12
Czechoslovakian (0)	13	0.11
Danish (13)	49	0.43
Dutch (12)	49	0.43
Eastern European (40)	40	0.35
English (96)	745	6.50
European (98)	98	0.86
French, ex. Basque (25)	172	1.50
French Canadian (0)	4	0.03
German (328)	1,834	16.00
Greek (78)	78	0.68
Guyanese (121)	121	1.06
Hungarian (38)	135	1.18
Iranian (20)	20	0.17
Irish (328)	1,857	16.20
Israeli (13)	13	0.11
Italian (1,058)	2,131	18.60
Latvian (0)	13	0.11
Lithuanian (0)	36	0.31
Norwegian (0)	65	0.57
Polish (171)	426	3.72
Portuguese (0)	22	0.19
Romanian (88)	88	0.77
Russian (385)	804	7.02
Scotch-Irish (81)	125	1.09
Scottish (0)	74	0.65
Slavic (0)	12	0.10
Slovak (25)	35	0.31
Swedish (0)	12	0.10
Ukrainian (32)	80	0.70
Welsh (26)	113	0.99
West Indian, ex. Hispanic (31)	57	0.50
British West Indian (13)	39	0.34
Jamaican (18)	18	0.16

Hispanic Origin	Population	%
Hispanic or Latino (of any race)	345	3.04
Central American, ex. Mexican	32	0.28
Costa Rican	5	0.04
Guatemalan	2	0.02
Honduran	9	0.08
Nicaraguan	9	0.08
Panamanian	6	0.05
Salvadoran	1	0.01
Cuban	17	0.15
Dominican Republic	12	0.11
Mexican	19	0.17
Puerto Rican	140	1.23
South American	74	0.65
Argentinean	9	0.08
Chilean	8	0.07
Colombian	24	0.21
Ecuadorian	14	0.12
Paraguayan	4	0.04
Peruvian	5	0.04
Uruguayan	4	0.04
Venezuelan	6	0.05
Other Hispanic or Latino	51	0.45

Race*	Population	%
African-American/Black (743)	822	7.23
Not Hispanic (721)	790	6.95
Hispanic (22)	32	0.28
American Indian/Alaska Native (9)	36	0.32
Not Hispanic (8)	27	0.24
Hispanic (1)	9	0.08
Blackfeet (0)	1	0.01
Cherokee (0)	11	0.10
Delaware (1)	4	0.04
Pima (0)	1	0.01
Pueblo (1)	1	0.01
Sioux (0)	1	0.01
Spanish American Ind. (0)	1	0.01
Asian (1,971)	2,090	18.39
Not Hispanic (1,960)	2,072	18.23
Hispanic (11)	18	0.16
Bangladeshi (13)	13	0.11
Burmese (2)	2	0.02
Cambodian (6)	9	0.08
Chinese, ex. Taiwanese (570)	589	5.18
Filipino (199)	224	1.97
Indian (603)	633	5.57
Indonesian (0)	1	0.01
Japanese (29)	46	0.40
Korean (342)	358	3.15
Pakistani (20)	20	0.18
Sri Lankan (7)	7	0.06
Taiwanese (60)	65	0.57
Thai (2)	2	0.02
Vietnamese (86)	101	0.89
Hawaii Native/Pacific Islander (0)	6	0.05
Not Hispanic (0)	6	0.05
White (8,357)	8,547	75.19
Not Hispanic (8,139)	8,301	73.03
Hispanic (218)	246	2.16

Guttenberg

Place Type: Town
County: Hudson
Population: 11,176†

Ancestry‡	Population	%
African, Sub-Saharan (64)	64	0.58
African (48)	48	0.44
South African (16)	16	0.15
Albanian (137)	137	1.25
American (52)	52	0.47
Arab (14)	67	0.61
Lebanese (0)	35	0.32
Moroccan (14)	32	0.29
Austrian (15)	30	0.27
Basque (0)	38	0.35
Brazilian (74)	88	0.80
Canadian (29)	29	0.26
Croatian (101)	111	1.01
Dutch (0)	34	0.31
Eastern European (8)	8	0.07
English (63)	133	1.21
European (83)	98	0.89
French, ex. Basque (73)	139	1.27
German (220)	466	4.25
Greek (31)	31	0.28
Hungarian (16)	43	0.39
Irish (73)	429	3.91
Italian (304)	565	5.16
Norwegian (0)	15	0.14
Polish (25)	147	1.34
Portuguese (0)	16	0.15
Romanian (32)	32	0.29
Russian (58)	175	1.60
Slovak (0)	15	0.14
Swedish (0)	29	0.26
Turkish (84)	99	0.90
Ukrainian (17)	17	0.16
West Indian, ex. Hispanic (136)	160	1.46
Jamaican (15)	15	0.14
Trinidadian/Tobagonian (65)	65	0.59
West Indian (56)	80	0.73
Yugoslavian (8)	23	0.21

Hispanic Origin	Population	%
Hispanic or Latino (of any race)	7,245	64.83
Central American, ex. Mexican	1,340	11.99
Costa Rican	22	0.20
Guatemalan	410	3.67
Honduran	233	2.08
Nicaraguan	44	0.39
Panamanian	9	0.08
Salvadoran	618	5.53
Other Central American	4	0.04
Cuban	1,011	9.05
Dominican Republic	878	7.86
Mexican	455	4.07
Puerto Rican	669	5.99
South American	2,340	20.94
Argentinean	125	1.12
Bolivian	38	0.34
Chilean	87	0.78
Colombian	921	8.24
Ecuadorian	849	7.60
Paraguayan	3	0.03
Peruvian	224	2.00
Uruguayan	33	0.30
Venezuelan	59	0.53
Other South American	1	0.01
Other Hispanic or Latino	552	4.94

Race*	Population	%
African-American/Black (537)	712	6.37
Not Hispanic (330)	370	3.31
Hispanic (207)	342	3.06
American Indian/Alaska Native (102)	171	1.53
Not Hispanic (13)	31	0.28
Hispanic (89)	140	1.25
Blackfeet (0)	1	0.01
Central American Ind. (9)	11	0.10
Cherokee (0)	1	0.01
Mexican American Ind. (12)	14	0.13
South American Ind. (8)	10	0.09
Spanish American Ind. (1)	3	0.03
Asian (818)	903	8.08
Not Hispanic (803)	866	7.75
Hispanic (15)	37	0.33
Bangladeshi (5)	5	0.04
Burmese (0)	2	0.02
Chinese, ex. Taiwanese (179)	200	1.79
Filipino (76)	85	0.76
Hmong (1)	1	0.01
Indian (353)	377	3.37
Indonesian (3)	3	0.03
Japanese (48)	62	0.55
Korean (104)	112	1.00
Malaysian (5)	5	0.04
Pakistani (6)	6	0.05
Sri Lankan (10)	10	0.09
Taiwanese (4)	6	0.05
Thai (5)	7	0.06
Vietnamese (7)	9	0.08
Hawaii Native/Pacific Islander (4)	22	0.20
Not Hispanic (4)	11	0.10
Hispanic (0)	11	0.10
Native Hawaiian (1)	3	0.03
Samoan (0)	2	0.02
White (7,537)	8,034	71.89
Not Hispanic (2,622)	2,701	24.17
Hispanic (4,915)	5,333	47.72

*Notes: † The Census 2010 population figure is used to calculate the percentages in the Hispanic Origin and Race categories. Ancestry percentages are based on the 2006-2010 American Community Survey population (not shown); ‡ Numbers in parentheses indicate the number of people reporting a single ancestry; * Numbers in parentheses indicate the number of persons reporting this race alone, not in combination with any other race; Please refer to the Explanation of Data for more information.*

Hackensack

Place Type: City
County: Bergen
Population: 43,010†

Ancestry‡	Population	%
Afghan (58)	107	0.25
African, Sub-Saharan (990)	1,210	2.83
African (909)	1,112	2.60
Ghanaian (18)	18	0.04
Liberian (14)	14	0.03
Sudanese (12)	12	0.03
Other Sub-Saharan African (37)	54	0.13
Albanian (111)	111	0.26
American (429)	429	1.00
Arab (1,094)	1,226	2.87
Arab (617)	617	1.44
Egyptian (201)	256	0.60
Lebanese (88)	153	0.36
Palestinian (104)	116	0.27
Syrian (45)	45	0.11
Other Arab (39)	39	0.09
Armenian (160)	160	0.37
Austrian (15)	152	0.36
Belgian (0)	2	<0.01
Brazilian (233)	249	0.58
British (27)	76	0.18
Bulgarian (4)	4	0.01
Cajun (0)	24	0.06
Canadian (16)	128	0.30
Croatian (12)	47	0.11
Czech (42)	113	0.26
Czechoslovakian (0)	39	0.09
Danish (0)	75	0.18
Dutch (101)	363	0.85
Eastern European (39)	39	0.09
English (238)	779	1.82
Estonian (21)	74	0.17
European (62)	86	0.20
French, ex. Basque (161)	447	1.05
French Canadian (12)	20	0.05
German (533)	2,040	4.78
Greek (81)	149	0.35
Guyanese (12)	19	0.04
Hungarian (34)	94	0.22
Iranian (101)	185	0.43
Irish (757)	2,461	5.76
Israeli (15)	15	0.04
Italian (2,429)	4,102	9.60
Latvian (9)	9	0.02
Lithuanian (18)	85	0.20
Macedonian (31)	69	0.16
Norwegian (35)	98	0.23
Polish (469)	1,474	3.45
Portuguese (0)	30	0.07
Romanian (229)	331	0.77
Russian (245)	653	1.53
Scandinavian (8)	26	0.06
Scotch-Irish (23)	98	0.23
Scottish (17)	100	0.23
Serbian (0)	13	0.03
Slavic (18)	32	0.07
Slovak (72)	104	0.24
Slovene (6)	6	0.01
Swedish (7)	74	0.17
Swiss (28)	111	0.26
Turkish (118)	118	0.28
Ukrainian (53)	90	0.21
Welsh (10)	144	0.34
West Indian, ex. Hispanic (1,405)	1,714	4.01
Barbadian (55)	66	0.15
Bermudan (64)	64	0.15
British West Indian (159)	171	0.40
Haitian (0)	59	0.14
Jamaican (664)	780	1.83
Trinidadian/Tobagonian (286)	349	0.82
West Indian (177)	225	0.53

Hispanic Origin	Population	%
Hispanic or Latino (of any race)	15,186	35.31
Central American, ex. Mexican	884	2.06
Costa Rican	75	0.17
Guatemalan	158	0.37
Honduran	103	0.24
Nicaraguan	56	0.13
Panamanian	62	0.14
Salvadoran	417	0.97
Other Central American	13	0.03
Cuban	339	0.79
Dominican Republic	3,021	7.02
Mexican	827	1.92
Puerto Rican	1,658	3.85
South American	6,917	16.08
Argentinean	83	0.19
Bolivian	74	0.17
Chilean	66	0.15
Colombian	1,835	4.27
Ecuadorian	4,291	9.98
Paraguayan	3	0.01
Peruvian	483	1.12
Uruguayan	27	0.06
Venezuelan	40	0.09
Other South American	15	0.03
Other Hispanic or Latino	1,540	3.58

Race*	Population	%
African-American/Black (10,511)	11,190	26.02
Not Hispanic (9,693)	10,033	23.33
Hispanic (818)	1,157	2.69
American Indian/Alaska Native (241)	559	1.30
Not Hispanic (67)	223	0.52
Hispanic (174)	336	0.78
Apache (0)	1	<0.01
Blackfeet (0)	14	0.03
Canadian/French Am. Ind. (1)	1	<0.01
Central American Ind. (9)	13	0.03
Cherokee (18)	64	0.15
Choctaw (0)	1	<0.01
Comanche (0)	2	<0.01
Cree (0)	1	<0.01
Creek (1)	1	<0.01
Delaware (1)	8	0.02
Iroquois (2)	2	<0.01
Lumbee (1)	1	<0.01
Mexican American Ind. (16)	23	0.05
Navajo (2)	3	0.01
Seminole (0)	7	0.02
Shoshone (0)	1	<0.01
Sioux (1)	4	0.01
South American Ind. (19)	58	0.13
Spanish American Ind. (16)	17	0.04
Asian (4,432)	4,814	11.19
Not Hispanic (4,372)	4,682	10.89
Hispanic (60)	132	0.31
Bangladeshi (49)	70	0.16
Burmese (5)	5	0.01
Cambodian (3)	4	0.01
Chinese, ex. Taiwanese (375)	449	1.04
Filipino (1,050)	1,125	2.62
Indian (1,850)	1,960	4.56
Indonesian (22)	26	0.06
Japanese (110)	136	0.32
Korean (630)	648	1.51
Laotian (0)	1	<0.01
Malaysian (9)	10	0.02
Nepalese (15)	15	0.03
Pakistani (95)	109	0.25
Sri Lankan (15)	20	0.05
Taiwanese (29)	38	0.09
Thai (46)	50	0.12
Vietnamese (31)	39	0.09
Hawaii Native/Pacific Islander (10)	120	0.28
Not Hispanic (5)	59	0.14
Hispanic (5)	61	0.14
Guamanian/Chamorro (2)	12	0.03
Native Hawaiian (0)	10	0.02
Samoan (1)	6	0.01
White (20,072)	21,432	49.83
Not Hispanic (12,845)	13,256	30.82
Hispanic (7,227)	8,176	19.01

Hacketts

Place Type: Town
County: Warren
Population: 9,724†

Ancestry‡	Population	%
American (623)	623	6.42
Arab (0)	12	0.12
Syrian (0)	12	0.12
Armenian (5)	62	0.64
Assyrian/Chaldean/Syriac (0)	8	0.08
Australian (0)	23	0.24
Austrian (0)	11	0.11
Brazilian (54)	72	0.74
British (5)	52	0.54
Canadian (0)	10	0.10
Czech (0)	40	0.41
Czechoslovakian (27)	27	0.28
Danish (0)	23	0.24
Dutch (13)	198	2.04
Eastern European (5)	5	0.05
English (212)	749	7.72
European (20)	20	0.21
Finnish (9)	20	0.21
French, ex. Basque (27)	255	2.63
French Canadian (41)	95	0.98
German (318)	1,643	16.93
Greek (0)	26	0.27
Hungarian (88)	128	1.32
Irish (449)	1,786	18.40
Italian (984)	2,032	20.94
Lithuanian (0)	10	0.10
Northern European (45)	45	0.46
Norwegian (11)	137	1.41
Pennsylvania German (11)	22	0.23
Polish (180)	634	6.53
Portuguese (0)	43	0.44
Russian (16)	92	0.95
Scotch-Irish (34)	46	0.47
Scottish (68)	282	2.91
Slovak (17)	72	0.74
Swedish (8)	90	0.93
Swiss (0)	35	0.36
Ukrainian (55)	84	0.87
Welsh (10)	119	1.23
West Indian, ex. Hispanic (18)	34	0.35
Haitian (18)	34	0.35
Yugoslavian (28)	37	0.38

Hispanic Origin	Population	%
Hispanic or Latino (of any race)	1,474	15.16
Central American, ex. Mexican	406	4.18
Costa Rican	104	1.07
Guatemalan	186	1.91
Honduran	95	0.98
Nicaraguan	2	0.02
Panamanian	3	0.03
Salvadoran	15	0.15
Other Central American	1	0.01
Cuban	51	0.52
Dominican Republic	33	0.34
Mexican	195	2.01
Puerto Rican	252	2.59
South American	400	4.11
Argentinean	8	0.08
Chilean	16	0.16
Colombian	107	1.10
Ecuadorian	193	1.98
Peruvian	54	0.56
Uruguayan	17	0.17
Venezuelan	5	0.05
Other Hispanic or Latino	137	1.41

Race*	Population	%
African-American/Black (239)	300	3.09
Not Hispanic (210)	250	2.57

*Notes: † The Census 2010 population figure is used to calculate the percentages in the Hispanic Origin and Race categories. Ancestry percentages are based on the 2006-2010 American Community Survey population (not shown); ‡ Numbers in parentheses indicate the number of people reporting a single ancestry; * Numbers in parentheses indicate the number of persons reporting this race alone, not in combination with any other race; Please refer to the Explanation of Data for more information.*

Hispanic (29)	50	0.51
American Indian/Alaska Native (23)	56	0.58
Not Hispanic (12)	34	0.35
Hispanic (11)	22	0.23
Cherokee (1)	4	0.04
Delaware (0)	6	0.06
Iroquois (0)	5	0.05
Lumbee (1)	1	0.01
Mexican American Ind. (2)	2	0.02
Navajo (0)	2	0.02
Sioux (0)	1	0.01
South American Ind. (4)	4	0.04
Asian (483)	547	5.63
Not Hispanic (478)	531	5.46
Hispanic (5)	16	0.16
Bangladeshi (1)	3	0.03
Cambodian (1)	1	0.01
Chinese, ex. Taiwanese (118)	127	1.31
Filipino (72)	81	0.83
Indian (167)	189	1.94
Indonesian (1)	1	0.01
Japanese (17)	27	0.28
Korean (52)	60	0.62
Laotian (7)	9	0.09
Pakistani (11)	16	0.16
Sri Lankan (1)	4	0.04
Vietnamese (18)	22	0.23
Hawaii Native/Pacific Islander (5)	18	0.19
Not Hispanic (0)	3	0.03
Hispanic (5)	15	0.15
Guamanian/Chamorro (0)	1	0.01
Native Hawaiian (0)	2	0.02
White (8,273)	8,422	86.61
Not Hispanic (7,407)	7,491	77.04
Hispanic (866)	931	9.57

Haddon

Place Type: Township
County: Camden
Population: 14,707†

Ancestry‡	Population	%
African, Sub-Saharan (0)	12	0.08
African (0)	12	0.08
American (362)	362	2.46
Arab (6)	21	0.14
Lebanese (6)	6	0.04
Syrian (0)	15	0.10
Armenian (29)	58	0.39
Austrian (7)	54	0.37
British (11)	80	0.54
Canadian (11)	11	0.07
Croatian (23)	45	0.31
Czech (0)	96	0.65
Czechoslovakian (0)	22	0.15
Danish (0)	10	0.07
Dutch (24)	141	0.96
English (413)	1,984	13.46
European (108)	108	0.73
French, ex. Basque (0)	206	1.40
French Canadian (10)	37	0.25
German (863)	4,160	28.22
Greek (122)	218	1.48
Hungarian (9)	75	0.51
Iranian (0)	12	0.08
Irish (1,245)	5,181	35.15
Italian (1,331)	3,360	22.80
Lithuanian (23)	102	0.69
Maltese (7)	7	0.05
Northern European (8)	8	0.05
Norwegian (0)	87	0.59
Pennsylvania German (28)	37	0.25
Polish (292)	1,222	8.29
Portuguese (13)	41	0.28
Russian (89)	272	1.85
Scotch-Irish (194)	350	2.37
Scottish (190)	412	2.80
Slovak (25)	169	1.15
Slovene (0)	22	0.15
Swedish (28)	192	1.30
Swiss (25)	25	0.17
Ukrainian (0)	44	0.30
Welsh (55)	169	1.15

Hispanic Origin	Population	%
Hispanic or Latino (of any race)	581	3.95
Central American, ex. Mexican	46	0.31
Guatemalan	17	0.12
Honduran	7	0.05
Nicaraguan	12	0.08
Panamanian	5	0.03
Salvadoran	5	0.03
Cuban	39	0.27
Dominican Republic	19	0.13
Mexican	129	0.88
Puerto Rican	280	1.90
South American	30	0.20
Argentinean	2	0.01
Bolivian	4	0.03
Chilean	1	0.01
Colombian	6	0.04
Ecuadorian	5	0.03
Peruvian	11	0.07
Uruguayan	1	0.01
Other Hispanic or Latino	38	0.26

Race*	Population	%
African-American/Black (220)	285	1.94
Not Hispanic (189)	239	1.63
Hispanic (31)	46	0.31
American Indian/Alaska Native (23)	58	0.39
Not Hispanic (22)	45	0.31
Hispanic (1)	13	0.09
Alaska Athabascan *(Ala. Nat.)* (0)	1	0.01
Arapaho (0)	1	0.01
Blackfeet (0)	4	0.03
Canadian/French Am. Ind. (1)	1	0.01
Cherokee (1)	6	0.04
Chickasaw (6)	6	0.04
Chippewa (0)	1	0.01
Mexican American Ind. (0)	2	0.01
Seminole (0)	2	0.01
Sioux (0)	4	0.03
Spanish American Ind. (0)	1	0.01
Asian (398)	477	3.24
Not Hispanic (392)	466	3.17
Hispanic (6)	11	0.07
Burmese (10)	10	0.07
Chinese, ex. Taiwanese (105)	129	0.88
Filipino (45)	60	0.41
Indian (99)	112	0.76
Indonesian (1)	1	0.01
Japanese (9)	14	0.10
Korean (41)	52	0.35
Laotian (6)	6	0.04
Pakistani (24)	26	0.18
Taiwanese (1)	5	0.03
Thai (1)	1	0.01
Vietnamese (42)	47	0.32
Hawaii Native/Pacific Islander (2)	9	0.06
Not Hispanic (2)	7	0.05
Hispanic (0)	2	0.01
Native Hawaiian (0)	4	0.03
Samoan (1)	4	0.03
White (13,701)	13,883	94.40
Not Hispanic (13,365)	13,502	91.81
Hispanic (336)	381	2.59

Haddonfield

Place Type: Borough
County: Camden
Population: 11,593†

Ancestry‡	Population	%
African, Sub-Saharan (8)	8	0.07
African (8)	8	0.07
American (125)	125	1.08
Arab (52)	52	0.45
Egyptian (19)	19	0.16
Other Arab (33)	33	0.28
Austrian (0)	181	1.56
Belgian (0)	26	0.22
British (48)	93	0.80
Croatian (0)	29	0.25
Czech (24)	82	0.71
Dutch (47)	192	1.65
Eastern European (27)	27	0.23
English (492)	2,216	19.09
Estonian (0)	13	0.11
European (50)	50	0.43
French, ex. Basque (27)	459	3.95
French Canadian (0)	99	0.85
German (676)	2,883	24.84
Greek (10)	30	0.26
Hungarian (28)	74	0.64
Irish (817)	3,294	28.38
Italian (1,106)	2,965	25.54
Latvian (15)	39	0.34
Lithuanian (16)	45	0.39
Northern European (90)	90	0.78
Norwegian (47)	156	1.34
Pennsylvania German (16)	16	0.14
Polish (153)	1,127	9.71
Portuguese (9)	9	0.08
Romanian (47)	58	0.50
Russian (188)	460	3.96
Scandinavian (0)	3	0.03
Scotch-Irish (95)	414	3.57
Scottish (34)	282	2.43
Slavic (0)	29	0.25
Slovak (23)	23	0.20
Swedish (10)	262	2.26
Swiss (0)	20	0.17
Turkish (27)	27	0.23
Ukrainian (42)	138	1.19
Welsh (51)	169	1.46
Yugoslavian (0)	7	0.06

Hispanic Origin	Population	%
Hispanic or Latino (of any race)	248	2.14
Central American, ex. Mexican	17	0.15
Guatemalan	1	0.01
Honduran	3	0.03
Nicaraguan	1	0.01
Panamanian	10	0.09
Other Central American	2	0.02
Cuban	20	0.17
Dominican Republic	2	0.02
Mexican	50	0.43
Puerto Rican	86	0.74
South American	43	0.37
Argentinean	3	0.03
Bolivian	11	0.09
Chilean	3	0.03
Colombian	10	0.09
Ecuadorian	7	0.06
Paraguayan	1	0.01
Peruvian	8	0.07
Other Hispanic or Latino	30	0.26

Race*	Population	%
African-American/Black (129)	184	1.59
Not Hispanic (115)	160	1.38
Hispanic (14)	24	0.21
American Indian/Alaska Native (4)	25	0.22
Not Hispanic (2)	21	0.18
Hispanic (2)	4	0.03
Alaska Athabascan *(Ala. Nat.)* (0)	1	0.01
Cherokee (0)	3	0.03
Iroquois (0)	4	0.03
Potawatomi (0)	1	0.01
Sioux (0)	5	0.04
Yup'ik *(Alaska Native)* (0)	1	0.01
Asian (215)	296	2.55
Not Hispanic (215)	295	2.54
Hispanic (0)	1	0.01
Chinese, ex. Taiwanese (71)	87	0.75
Filipino (27)	49	0.42

*Notes: † The Census 2010 population figure is used to calculate the percentages in the Hispanic Origin and Race categories. Ancestry percentages are based on the 2006-2010 American Community Survey population (not shown); ‡ Numbers in parentheses indicate the number of people reporting a single ancestry; * Numbers in parentheses indicate the number of persons reporting this race alone, not in combination with any other race; Please refer to the Explanation of Data for more information.*

Indian (21)	32	0.28
Japanese (24)	38	0.33
Korean (36)	49	0.42
Malaysian (1)	1	0.01
Nepalese (1)	1	0.01
Pakistani (13)	13	0.11
Taiwanese (3)	3	0.03
Thai (2)	2	0.02
Vietnamese (5)	6	0.05
White (11,040)	11,191	96.53
Not Hispanic (10,856)	10,991	94.81
Hispanic (184)	200	1.73

Haledon

Place Type: Borough
County: Passaic
Population: 8,318†

Ancestry‡	Population	%
African, Sub-Saharan (12)	21	0.25
African (12)	12	0.15
South African (0)	9	0.11
Albanian (43)	43	0.52
American (23)	23	0.28
Arab (162)	162	1.96
Arab (47)	47	0.57
Jordanian (44)	44	0.53
Syrian (71)	71	0.86
Belgian (0)	23	0.28
Czech (0)	8	0.10
Dutch (168)	430	5.22
English (59)	294	3.57
European (68)	68	0.82
French, ex. Basque (0)	83	1.01
German (92)	558	6.77
Hungarian (4)	35	0.42
Irish (40)	549	6.66
Italian (358)	1,111	13.47
Lithuanian (0)	3	0.04
Pennsylvania German (29)	29	0.35
Polish (63)	185	2.24
Portuguese (49)	49	0.59
Russian (148)	203	2.46
Scotch-Irish (15)	53	0.64
Scottish (0)	20	0.24
Serbian (66)	66	0.80
Slavic (0)	36	0.44
Ukrainian (8)	8	0.10
Welsh (0)	13	0.16
West Indian, ex. Hispanic (70)	70	0.85
Haitian (70)	70	0.85

Hispanic Origin	Population	%
Hispanic or Latino (of any race)	3,460	41.60
Central American, ex. Mexican	249	2.99
Costa Rican	95	1.14
Guatemalan	67	0.81
Honduran	19	0.23
Nicaraguan	21	0.25
Panamanian	4	0.05
Salvadoran	43	0.52
Cuban	64	0.77
Dominican Republic	634	7.62
Mexican	132	1.59
Puerto Rican	1,185	14.25
South American	952	11.45
Argentinean	36	0.43
Bolivian	1	0.01
Chilean	14	0.17
Colombian	218	2.62
Ecuadorian	91	1.09
Paraguayan	1	0.01
Peruvian	557	6.70
Uruguayan	15	0.18
Venezuelan	13	0.16
Other South American	6	0.07
Other Hispanic or Latino	244	2.93

Race*	Population	%
African-American/Black (979)	1,085	13.04
Not Hispanic (806)	846	10.17
Hispanic (173)	239	2.87
American Indian/Alaska Native (44)	80	0.96
Not Hispanic (8)	26	0.31
Hispanic (36)	54	0.65
Apache (0)	1	0.01
Central American Ind. (1)	1	0.01
Cherokee (0)	6	0.07
Cheyenne (1)	1	0.01
Delaware (1)	2	0.02
Hopi (1)	1	0.01
Iroquois (0)	1	0.01
Mexican American Ind. (0)	3	0.04
South American Ind. (0)	1	0.01
Spanish American Ind. (2)	2	0.02
Asian (528)	610	7.33
Not Hispanic (505)	577	6.94
Hispanic (23)	33	0.40
Bangladeshi (138)	149	1.79
Chinese, ex. Taiwanese (49)	49	0.59
Filipino (108)	127	1.53
Indian (146)	161	1.94
Indonesian (1)	2	0.02
Japanese (1)	4	0.05
Korean (13)	19	0.23
Laotian (0)	1	0.01
Pakistani (31)	32	0.38
Taiwanese (1)	1	0.01
Thai (2)	3	0.04
Vietnamese (13)	13	0.16
Hawaii Native/Pacific Islander (8)	16	0.19
Not Hispanic (0)	2	0.02
Hispanic (8)	14	0.17
Guamanian/Chamorro (6)	6	0.07
Samoan (2)	2	0.02
White (5,189)	5,470	65.76
Not Hispanic (3,393)	3,496	42.03
Hispanic (1,796)	1,974	23.73

Hamilton Square

Place Type: CDP
County: Mercer
Population: 12,784†

Ancestry‡	Population	%
Afghan (7)	7	0.05
American (613)	613	4.56
Arab (103)	114	0.85
Egyptian (14)	14	0.10
Lebanese (11)	22	0.16
Syrian (78)	78	0.58
Australian (11)	34	0.25
Austrian (30)	117	0.87
Belgian (0)	22	0.16
British (31)	106	0.79
Canadian (15)	42	0.31
Croatian (24)	34	0.25
Czech (11)	96	0.71
Czechoslovakian (12)	45	0.33
Danish (0)	9	0.07
Dutch (12)	272	2.02
Eastern European (12)	12	0.09
English (346)	1,523	11.33
Estonian (12)	12	0.09
European (0)	12	0.09
Finnish (10)	10	0.07
French, ex. Basque (7)	149	1.11
French Canadian (50)	95	0.71
German (633)	2,384	17.74
Greek (260)	295	2.19
Hungarian (68)	274	2.04
Iranian (11)	11	0.08
Irish (1,177)	3,481	25.90
Israeli (48)	48	0.36
Italian (1,731)	3,760	27.97
Lithuanian (8)	87	0.65
Norwegian (0)	17	0.13
Pennsylvania German (0)	43	0.32
Polish (570)	1,591	11.84
Romanian (11)	53	0.39
Russian (46)	116	0.86
Scandinavian (0)	18	0.13
Scotch-Irish (35)	130	0.97
Scottish (98)	267	1.99
Slavic (8)	68	0.51
Slovak (48)	315	2.34
Swedish (40)	170	1.26
Swiss (0)	9	0.07
Ukrainian (99)	129	0.96
Welsh (0)	47	0.35
West Indian, ex. Hispanic (168)	168	1.25
Haitian (168)	168	1.25
Yugoslavian (23)	36	0.27

Hispanic Origin	Population	%
Hispanic or Latino (of any race)	487	3.81
Central American, ex. Mexican	47	0.37
Costa Rican	13	0.10
Guatemalan	19	0.15
Honduran	5	0.04
Nicaraguan	4	0.03
Panamanian	2	0.02
Salvadoran	4	0.03
Cuban	23	0.18
Dominican Republic	16	0.13
Mexican	40	0.31
Puerto Rican	217	1.70
South American	83	0.65
Argentinean	5	0.04
Chilean	4	0.03
Colombian	25	0.20
Ecuadorian	31	0.24
Peruvian	6	0.05
Uruguayan	2	0.02
Venezuelan	10	0.08
Other Hispanic or Latino	61	0.48

Race*	Population	%
African-American/Black (223)	268	2.10
Not Hispanic (216)	251	1.96
Hispanic (7)	17	0.13
American Indian/Alaska Native (10)	40	0.31
Not Hispanic (9)	32	0.25
Hispanic (1)	8	0.06
Blackfeet (0)	4	0.03
Cherokee (3)	9	0.07
Sioux (0)	2	0.02
South American Ind. (0)	4	0.03
Asian (457)	530	4.15
Not Hispanic (455)	520	4.07
Hispanic (2)	10	0.08
Bangladeshi (4)	4	0.03
Cambodian (4)	5	0.04
Chinese, ex. Taiwanese (101)	111	0.87
Filipino (82)	101	0.79
Indian (133)	147	1.15
Indonesian (0)	1	0.01
Japanese (6)	11	0.09
Korean (68)	82	0.64
Nepalese (4)	4	0.03
Pakistani (28)	30	0.23
Taiwanese (7)	7	0.05
Thai (3)	3	0.02
Vietnamese (9)	14	0.11
Hawaii Native/Pacific Islander (3)	7	0.05
Not Hispanic (3)	7	0.05
Guamanian/Chamorro (0)	1	0.01
Native Hawaiian (1)	2	0.02
White (11,858)	11,981	93.72
Not Hispanic (11,495)	11,592	90.68
Hispanic (363)	389	3.04

*Notes: † The Census 2010 population figure is used to calculate the percentages in the Hispanic Origin and Race categories. Ancestry percentages are based on the 2006-2010 American Community Survey population (not shown); ‡ Numbers in parentheses indicate the number of people reporting a single ancestry; * Numbers in parentheses indicate the number of persons reporting this race alone, not in combination with any other race; Please refer to the Explanation of Data for more information.*

Hamilton

Place Type: Township
County: Atlantic
Population: 26,503†

Ancestry‡	Population	%
African, Sub-Saharan (274)	337	1.31
African (133)	196	0.76
Nigerian (141)	141	0.55
American (701)	701	2.73
Arab (173)	206	0.80
Arab (21)	21	0.08
Egyptian (125)	125	0.49
Lebanese (20)	46	0.18
Moroccan (7)	7	0.03
Syrian (0)	7	0.03
Austrian (0)	77	0.30
Brazilian (6)	6	0.02
British (0)	9	0.04
Canadian (22)	39	0.15
Croatian (114)	124	0.48
Czech (11)	42	0.16
Czechoslovakian (14)	28	0.11
Danish (40)	57	0.22
Dutch (39)	198	0.77
Eastern European (53)	53	0.21
English (367)	2,191	8.54
European (49)	49	0.19
Finnish (0)	35	0.14
French, ex. Basque (105)	509	1.98
French Canadian (0)	46	0.18
German (1,121)	4,827	18.82
Greek (56)	177	0.69
Hungarian (30)	203	0.79
Iranian (0)	17	0.07
Irish (1,406)	5,143	20.06
Italian (1,664)	4,923	19.20
Lithuanian (37)	112	0.44
Northern European (23)	23	0.09
Norwegian (29)	185	0.72
Pennsylvania German (0)	9	0.04
Polish (526)	1,201	4.68
Portuguese (15)	52	0.20
Romanian (0)	49	0.19
Russian (212)	433	1.69
Scandinavian (14)	21	0.08
Scotch-Irish (126)	270	1.05
Scottish (95)	383	1.49
Serbian (11)	11	0.04
Slavic (0)	9	0.04
Slovak (35)	139	0.54
Swedish (36)	271	1.06
Swiss (10)	41	0.16
Turkish (33)	33	0.13
Ukrainian (27)	120	0.47
Welsh (26)	209	0.82
West Indian, ex. Hispanic (158)	186	0.73
Bahamian (36)	48	0.19
Haitian (110)	110	0.43
Jamaican (0)	16	0.06
West Indian (12)	12	0.05
Yugoslavian (0)	28	0.11

Hispanic Origin	Population	%
Hispanic or Latino (of any race)	3,390	12.79
Central American, ex. Mexican	195	0.74
Costa Rican	6	0.02
Guatemalan	15	0.06
Honduran	86	0.32
Nicaraguan	30	0.11
Panamanian	9	0.03
Salvadoran	49	0.18
Cuban	62	0.23
Dominican Republic	382	1.44
Mexican	322	1.21
Puerto Rican	1,684	6.35
South American	429	1.62
Argentinean	25	0.09
Bolivian	4	0.02
Chilean	6	0.02
Colombian	184	0.69
Ecuadorian	60	0.23
Paraguayan	1	<0.01
Peruvian	138	0.52
Venezuelan	11	0.04
Other Hispanic or Latino	316	1.19

Race*	Population	%
African-American/Black (4,916)	5,436	20.51
Not Hispanic (4,592)	4,987	18.82
Hispanic (324)	449	1.69
American Indian/Alaska Native (68)	343	1.29
Not Hispanic (37)	250	0.94
Hispanic (31)	93	0.35
Apache (0)	4	0.02
Blackfeet (1)	11	0.04
Central American Ind. (1)	4	0.02
Cherokee (7)	46	0.17
Chippewa (3)	7	0.03
Creek (3)	4	0.02
Delaware (1)	27	0.10
Hopi (0)	3	0.01
Iroquois (4)	24	0.09
Mexican American Ind. (7)	15	0.06
Navajo (2)	9	0.03
Potawatomi (0)	4	0.02
Seminole (0)	5	0.02
Sioux (0)	2	0.01
South American Ind. (3)	16	0.06
Spanish American Ind. (3)	4	0.02
Asian (1,435)	1,637	6.18
Not Hispanic (1,417)	1,594	6.01
Hispanic (18)	43	0.16
Bangladeshi (20)	23	0.09
Burmese (3)	3	0.01
Cambodian (7)	7	0.03
Chinese, ex. Taiwanese (283)	321	1.21
Filipino (370)	438	1.65
Indian (210)	259	0.98
Japanese (12)	36	0.14
Korean (90)	112	0.42
Laotian (60)	78	0.29
Nepalese (10)	10	0.04
Pakistani (61)	61	0.23
Sri Lankan (17)	23	0.09
Taiwanese (6)	14	0.05
Thai (18)	27	0.10
Vietnamese (182)	212	0.80
Hawaii Native/Pacific Islander (16)	36	0.14
Not Hispanic (6)	23	0.09
Hispanic (10)	13	0.05
Guamanian/Chamorro (1)	6	0.02
Native Hawaiian (5)	8	0.03
Samoan (3)	4	0.02
White (18,011)	18,790	70.90
Not Hispanic (16,347)	16,901	63.77
Hispanic (1,664)	1,889	7.13

Hamilton

Place Type: Township
County: Mercer
Population: 88,464†

Ancestry‡	Population	%
Afghan (49)	49	0.06
African, Sub-Saharan (1,618)	1,655	1.87
African (437)	474	0.54
Ethiopian (23)	23	0.03
Ghanaian (182)	182	0.21
Liberian (495)	495	0.56
Nigerian (470)	470	0.53
Other Sub-Saharan African (11)	11	0.01
Albanian (11)	44	0.05
Alsatian (17)	44	0.05
American (2,988)	2,988	3.38
Arab (563)	610	0.69
Arab (15)	15	0.02
Egyptian (242)	242	0.27
Lebanese (71)	105	0.12
Moroccan (10)	10	0.01
Palestinian (127)	127	0.14
Syrian (98)	98	0.11
Other Arab (0)	13	0.01
Armenian (11)	30	0.03
Australian (11)	64	0.07
Austrian (92)	318	0.36
Basque (0)	22	0.02
Belgian (13)	61	0.07
Brazilian (70)	101	0.11
British (84)	205	0.23
Canadian (58)	101	0.11
Carpatho Rusyn (6)	6	0.01
Croatian (88)	231	0.26
Cypriot (12)	12	0.01
Czech (91)	478	0.54
Czechoslovakian (78)	340	0.38
Danish (0)	105	0.12
Dutch (132)	927	1.05
Eastern European (50)	61	0.07
English (1,604)	7,985	9.03
Estonian (12)	12	0.01
European (158)	170	0.19
Finnish (10)	25	0.03
French, ex. Basque (181)	1,180	1.33
French Canadian (101)	391	0.44
German (3,512)	14,921	16.88
Greek (574)	833	0.94
Guyanese (10)	10	0.01
Hungarian (968)	2,948	3.33
Iranian (23)	36	0.04
Irish (4,509)	16,955	19.18
Israeli (48)	48	0.05
Italian (10,198)	21,077	23.84
Lithuanian (128)	408	0.46
Macedonian (9)	27	0.03
Maltese (0)	40	0.05
Norwegian (32)	209	0.24
Pennsylvania German (25)	112	0.13
Polish (3,921)	9,949	11.25
Portuguese (35)	119	0.13
Romanian (72)	278	0.31
Russian (513)	1,386	1.57
Scandinavian (0)	25	0.03
Scotch-Irish (291)	1,013	1.15
Scottish (236)	1,159	1.31
Serbian (0)	9	0.01
Slavic (32)	286	0.32
Slovak (478)	1,508	1.71
Slovene (0)	9	0.01
Swedish (49)	647	0.73
Swiss (0)	91	0.10
Turkish (22)	22	0.02
Ukrainian (540)	944	1.07
Welsh (125)	384	0.43
West Indian, ex. Hispanic (1,867)	1,978	2.24
Barbadian (18)	18	0.02
Belizean (24)	24	0.03
Haitian (1,392)	1,494	1.69
Jamaican (376)	385	0.44
West Indian (57)	57	0.06
Yugoslavian (74)	132	0.15

Hispanic Origin	Population	%
Hispanic or Latino (of any race)	9,613	10.87
Central American, ex. Mexican	2,143	2.42
Costa Rican	355	0.40
Guatemalan	1,547	1.75
Honduran	79	0.09
Nicaraguan	32	0.04
Panamanian	26	0.03
Salvadoran	92	0.10
Other Central American	12	0.01
Cuban	194	0.22
Dominican Republic	702	0.79
Mexican	614	0.69
Puerto Rican	3,902	4.41
South American	1,237	1.40
Argentinean	55	0.06

*Notes: † The Census 2010 population figure is used to calculate the percentages in the Hispanic Origin and Race categories. Ancestry percentages are based on the 2006-2010 American Community Survey population (not shown); ‡ Numbers in parentheses indicate the number of people reporting a single ancestry; * Numbers in parentheses indicate the number of persons reporting this race alone, not in combination with any other race; Please refer to the Explanation of Data for more information.*

Bolivian	3	<0.01
Chilean	32	0.04
Colombian	293	0.33
Ecuadorian	650	0.73
Paraguayan	1	<0.01
Peruvian	81	0.09
Uruguayan	34	0.04
Venezuelan	75	0.08
Other South American	13	0.01
Other Hispanic or Latino	821	0.93

Race*	Population	%
African-American/Black (10,419)	11,261	12.73
Not Hispanic (10,042)	10,688	12.08
Hispanic (377)	573	0.65
American Indian/Alaska Native (149)	475	0.54
Not Hispanic (93)	344	0.39
Hispanic (56)	131	0.15
Aleut *(Alaska Native)* (1)	1	<0.01
Apache (1)	3	<0.01
Blackfeet (1)	23	0.03
Canadian/French Am. Ind. (0)	4	<0.01
Central American Ind. (1)	1	<0.01
Cherokee (22)	93	0.11
Cheyenne (0)	1	<0.01
Chippewa (1)	2	<0.01
Choctaw (0)	1	<0.01
Cree (0)	4	<0.01
Delaware (0)	14	0.02
Houma (2)	2	<0.01
Iroquois (3)	11	0.01
Lumbee (1)	1	<0.01
Mexican American Ind. (10)	13	0.01
Navajo (1)	2	<0.01
Seminole (0)	2	<0.01
Sioux (4)	19	0.02
South American Ind. (11)	26	0.03
Tlingit-Haida *(Alaska Native)* (0)	2	<0.01
Asian (2,914)	3,361	3.80
Not Hispanic (2,890)	3,296	3.73
Hispanic (24)	65	0.07
Bangladeshi (58)	70	0.08
Bhutanese (8)	8	0.01
Burmese (16)	17	0.02
Cambodian (32)	34	0.04
Chinese, ex. Taiwanese (471)	525	0.59
Filipino (411)	494	0.56
Indian (1,000)	1,112	1.26
Indonesian (6)	9	0.01
Japanese (43)	85	0.10
Korean (283)	327	0.37
Laotian (0)	5	0.01
Malaysian (1)	2	<0.01
Nepalese (12)	12	0.01
Pakistani (321)	380	0.43
Sri Lankan (8)	8	0.01
Taiwanese (12)	19	0.02
Thai (12)	23	0.03
Vietnamese (116)	134	0.15
Hawaii Native/Pacific Islander (79)	188	0.21
Not Hispanic (41)	129	0.15
Hispanic (38)	59	0.07
Guamanian/Chamorro (62)	80	0.09
Native Hawaiian (11)	17	0.02
Samoan (0)	1	<0.01
Tongan (0)	1	<0.01
White (69,340)	70,723	79.95
Not Hispanic (64,530)	65,422	73.95
Hispanic (4,810)	5,301	5.99

Hammonton

Place Type: Town
County: Atlantic
Population: 14,791†

Ancestry‡	Population	%
American (189)	189	1.29
Arab (123)	123	0.84
Syrian (123)	123	0.84
Armenian (29)	78	0.53
Austrian (0)	16	0.11
British (0)	39	0.27
Carpatho Rusyn (0)	15	0.10
Czechoslovakian (7)	38	0.26
Dutch (10)	232	1.58
English (131)	952	6.50
European (41)	41	0.28
French, ex. Basque (19)	97	0.66
French Canadian (0)	15	0.10
German (337)	2,326	15.87
Greek (31)	106	0.72
Hungarian (0)	13	0.09
Irish (434)	2,276	15.53
Italian (3,952)	6,599	45.03
Lithuanian (0)	27	0.18
Norwegian (0)	99	0.68
Polish (140)	355	2.42
Russian (60)	101	0.69
Scotch-Irish (40)	163	1.11
Scottish (16)	316	2.16
Slovak (9)	43	0.29
Swedish (0)	140	0.96
Swiss (0)	9	0.06
Ukrainian (16)	57	0.39
Welsh (15)	32	0.22
West Indian, ex. Hispanic (5)	5	0.03
Trinidadian/Tobagonian (5)	5	0.03
Yugoslavian (0)	11	0.08

Hispanic Origin	Population	%
Hispanic or Latino (of any race)	3,096	20.93
Central American, ex. Mexican	220	1.49
Costa Rican	2	0.01
Guatemalan	45	0.30
Honduran	153	1.03
Nicaraguan	4	0.03
Panamanian	6	0.04
Salvadoran	10	0.07
Cuban	12	0.08
Dominican Republic	60	0.41
Mexican	1,490	10.07
Puerto Rican	1,166	7.88
South American	70	0.47
Argentinean	11	0.07
Bolivian	1	0.01
Chilean	2	0.01
Colombian	30	0.20
Ecuadorian	10	0.07
Paraguayan	3	0.02
Peruvian	13	0.09
Other Hispanic or Latino	78	0.53

Race*	Population	%
African-American/Black (444)	569	3.85
Not Hispanic (382)	457	3.09
Hispanic (62)	112	0.76
American Indian/Alaska Native (42)	115	0.78
Not Hispanic (10)	51	0.34
Hispanic (32)	64	0.43
Blackfeet (0)	9	0.06
Cherokee (2)	17	0.11
Chickasaw (0)	1	0.01
Delaware (0)	4	0.03
Iroquois (0)	2	0.01
Lumbee (1)	1	0.01
Mexican American Ind. (1)	2	0.01
Paiute (1)	1	0.01
Seminole (0)	1	0.01
Sioux (0)	1	0.01
South American Ind. (0)	8	0.05
Spanish American Ind. (1)	1	0.01
Asian (203)	270	1.83
Not Hispanic (196)	255	1.72
Hispanic (7)	15	0.10
Cambodian (4)	6	0.04
Chinese, ex. Taiwanese (65)	76	0.51
Filipino (75)	88	0.59
Hmong (2)	2	0.01
Indian (34)	40	0.27
Indonesian (1)	1	0.01
Japanese (2)	12	0.08
Korean (10)	26	0.18
Taiwanese (6)	8	0.05
Vietnamese (2)	6	0.04
Hawaii Native/Pacific Islander (2)	15	0.10
Not Hispanic (0)	8	0.05
Hispanic (2)	7	0.05
Guamanian/Chamorro (1)	1	0.01
Native Hawaiian (0)	2	0.01
Samoan (1)	1	0.01
White (12,080)	12,453	84.19
Not Hispanic (10,938)	11,089	74.97
Hispanic (1,142)	1,364	9.22

Hanover

Place Type: Township
County: Morris
Population: 13,712†

Ancestry‡	Population	%
American (304)	304	2.23
Arab (138)	248	1.82
Egyptian (128)	166	1.22
Lebanese (0)	45	0.33
Syrian (10)	37	0.27
Austrian (0)	41	0.30
Brazilian (36)	54	0.40
British (18)	35	0.26
Bulgarian (8)	8	0.06
Canadian (0)	10	0.07
Croatian (0)	8	0.06
Czech (19)	148	1.09
Czechoslovakian (36)	47	0.35
Danish (0)	17	0.12
Dutch (44)	202	1.48
Eastern European (56)	74	0.54
English (233)	788	5.78
European (8)	8	0.06
French, ex. Basque (21)	190	1.39
French Canadian (0)	38	0.28
German (430)	2,044	15.01
Greek (70)	145	1.06
Hungarian (37)	141	1.04
Irish (742)	2,622	19.25
Italian (2,266)	4,084	29.98
Lithuanian (0)	39	0.29
Northern European (36)	36	0.26
Norwegian (18)	18	0.13
Pennsylvania German (0)	9	0.07
Polish (364)	1,367	10.04
Portuguese (198)	198	1.45
Russian (148)	352	2.58
Scandinavian (10)	32	0.23
Scotch-Irish (46)	228	1.67
Scottish (52)	245	1.80
Slavic (0)	9	0.07
Slovak (55)	93	0.68
Swedish (10)	146	1.07
Swiss (19)	64	0.47
Turkish (236)	236	1.73
Ukrainian (241)	554	4.07
Welsh (0)	9	0.07
West Indian, ex. Hispanic (23)	50	0.37
Jamaican (23)	50	0.37

Hispanic Origin	Population	%
Hispanic or Latino (of any race)	630	4.59
Central American, ex. Mexican	56	0.41
Costa Rican	10	0.07
Guatemalan	1	0.01
Honduran	18	0.13
Nicaraguan	1	0.01
Salvadoran	26	0.19
Cuban	89	0.65
Dominican Republic	19	0.14
Mexican	96	0.70
Puerto Rican	89	0.65
South American	195	1.42

*Notes: † The Census 2010 population figure is used to calculate the percentages in the Hispanic Origin and Race categories. Ancestry percentages are based on the 2006-2010 American Community Survey population (not shown); ‡ Numbers in parentheses indicate the number of people reporting a single ancestry; * Numbers in parentheses indicate the number of persons reporting this race alone, not in combination with any other race; Please refer to the Explanation of Data for more information.*

Argentinean	6	0.04
Chilean	4	0.03
Colombian	91	0.66
Ecuadorian	53	0.39
Paraguayan	4	0.03
Peruvian	32	0.23
Uruguayan	3	0.02
Venezuelan	2	0.01
Other Hispanic or Latino	86	0.63

Race*	Population	%
African-American/Black (138)	178	1.30
Not Hispanic (134)	169	1.23
Hispanic (4)	9	0.07
American Indian/Alaska Native (6)	35	0.26
Not Hispanic (5)	28	0.20
Hispanic (1)	7	0.05
Blackfeet (1)	2	0.01
Cherokee (0)	1	0.01
Choctaw (0)	1	0.01
Creek (0)	5	0.04
Hopi (1)	1	0.01
Iroquois (2)	6	0.04
Navajo (1)	2	0.01
Asian (1,481)	1,570	11.45
Not Hispanic (1,480)	1,562	11.39
Hispanic (1)	8	0.06
Burmese (8)	8	0.06
Chinese, ex. Taiwanese (604)	635	4.63
Filipino (87)	109	0.79
Indian (385)	409	2.98
Japanese (14)	18	0.13
Korean (121)	131	0.96
Laotian (3)	3	0.02
Malaysian (3)	7	0.05
Pakistani (20)	21	0.15
Sri Lankan (1)	1	0.01
Taiwanese (149)	159	1.16
Thai (4)	10	0.07
Vietnamese (55)	62	0.45
Hawaii Native/Pacific Islander (1)	7	0.05
Not Hispanic (1)	7	0.05
Samoan (1)	1	0.01
White (11,728)	11,874	86.60
Not Hispanic (11,297)	11,408	83.20
Hispanic (431)	466	3.40

Hardyston

Place Type: Township
County: Sussex
Population: 8,213†

Ancestry‡	Population	%
Albanian (0)	9	0.11
Alsatian (0)	9	0.11
American (161)	161	2.03
Arab (25)	25	0.32
Lebanese (14)	14	0.18
Syrian (11)	11	0.14
Austrian (0)	38	0.48
Belgian (0)	8	0.10
British (24)	24	0.30
Canadian (13)	13	0.16
Czech (19)	148	1.87
Czechoslovakian (0)	9	0.11
Danish (0)	20	0.25
Dutch (93)	566	7.14
English (117)	696	8.78
European (60)	60	0.76
French, ex. Basque (0)	135	1.70
French Canadian (12)	21	0.26
German (412)	1,951	24.61
Greek (16)	105	1.32
Hungarian (38)	133	1.68
Irish (516)	2,175	27.44
Italian (888)	2,324	29.32
Lithuanian (0)	62	0.78
Macedonian (0)	11	0.14
Norwegian (0)	100	1.26
Pennsylvania German (0)	38	0.48
Polish (171)	624	7.87
Portuguese (8)	8	0.10
Russian (29)	78	0.98
Scandinavian (0)	12	0.15
Scotch-Irish (0)	19	0.24
Scottish (23)	174	2.20
Slovak (13)	138	1.74
Swedish (0)	32	0.40
Swiss (0)	38	0.48
Ukrainian (22)	50	0.63
Welsh (0)	19	0.24
West Indian, ex. Hispanic (0)	31	0.39
British West Indian (0)	13	0.16
Jamaican (0)	5	0.06
West Indian (0)	13	0.16

Hispanic Origin	Population	%
Hispanic or Latino (of any race)	457	5.56
Central American, ex. Mexican	24	0.29
Costa Rican	6	0.07
Guatemalan	4	0.05
Honduran	7	0.09
Nicaraguan	1	0.01
Panamanian	1	0.01
Salvadoran	5	0.06
Cuban	65	0.79
Dominican Republic	26	0.32
Mexican	26	0.32
Puerto Rican	174	2.12
South American	78	0.95
Argentinean	4	0.05
Chilean	2	0.02
Colombian	36	0.44
Ecuadorian	13	0.16
Peruvian	11	0.13
Uruguayan	5	0.06
Venezuelan	7	0.09
Other Hispanic or Latino	64	0.78

Race*	Population	%
African-American/Black (214)	257	3.13
Not Hispanic (200)	235	2.86
Hispanic (14)	22	0.27
American Indian/Alaska Native (14)	47	0.57
Not Hispanic (8)	41	0.50
Hispanic (6)	6	0.07
Cherokee (3)	11	0.13
Cheyenne (0)	4	0.05
Choctaw (0)	3	0.04
Delaware (1)	6	0.07
Iroquois (0)	1	0.01
Potawatomi (1)	2	0.02
Sioux (1)	3	0.04
Asian (247)	276	3.36
Not Hispanic (243)	271	3.30
Hispanic (4)	5	0.06
Bangladeshi (5)	5	0.06
Burmese (1)	1	0.01
Chinese, ex. Taiwanese (45)	57	0.69
Filipino (24)	29	0.35
Indian (62)	63	0.77
Indonesian (5)	5	0.06
Japanese (13)	16	0.19
Korean (66)	67	0.82
Pakistani (5)	6	0.07
Sri Lankan (1)	1	0.01
Taiwanese (6)	7	0.09
Thai (3)	3	0.04
Vietnamese (5)	5	0.06
Hawaii Native/Pacific Islander (1)	3	0.04
Not Hispanic (1)	3	0.04
Guamanian/Chamorro (1)	1	0.01
White (7,527)	7,628	92.88
Not Hispanic (7,199)	7,276	88.59
Hispanic (328)	352	4.29

Harrison

Place Type: Town
County: Hudson
Population: 13,620†

Ancestry‡	Population	%
African, Sub-Saharan (39)	39	0.29
African (28)	28	0.21
Other Sub-Saharan African (11)	11	0.08
American (162)	162	1.19
Arab (124)	124	0.91
Arab (42)	42	0.31
Egyptian (28)	28	0.21
Moroccan (54)	54	0.40
Brazilian (616)	692	5.10
British (22)	22	0.16
Czech (20)	32	0.24
Dutch (21)	21	0.15
English (16)	118	0.87
French, ex. Basque (19)	41	0.30
German (33)	305	2.25
Greek (11)	11	0.08
Irish (587)	1,164	8.58
Italian (220)	654	4.82
Polish (497)	590	4.35
Portuguese (1,362)	1,362	10.04
Russian (87)	87	0.64
Scotch-Irish (79)	90	0.66
Scottish (115)	146	1.08
Slovak (11)	11	0.08
Swedish (0)	11	0.08

Hispanic Origin	Population	%
Hispanic or Latino (of any race)	6,017	44.18
Central American, ex. Mexican	424	3.11
Costa Rican	18	0.13
Guatemalan	148	1.09
Honduran	95	0.70
Nicaraguan	58	0.43
Panamanian	9	0.07
Salvadoran	96	0.70
Cuban	299	2.20
Dominican Republic	339	2.49
Mexican	312	2.29
Puerto Rican	764	5.61
South American	3,193	23.44
Argentinean	42	0.31
Chilean	38	0.28
Colombian	230	1.69
Ecuadorian	1,056	7.75
Paraguayan	1	0.01
Peruvian	1,651	12.12
Uruguayan	137	1.01
Venezuelan	37	0.27
Other South American	1	0.01
Other Hispanic or Latino	686	5.04

Race*	Population	%
African-American/Black (297)	388	2.85
Not Hispanic (173)	214	1.57
Hispanic (124)	174	1.28
American Indian/Alaska Native (76)	152	1.12
Not Hispanic (6)	18	0.13
Hispanic (70)	134	0.98
Cherokee (0)	4	0.03
Iroquois (1)	1	0.01
Mexican American Ind. (7)	12	0.09
Sioux (0)	1	0.01
South American Ind. (6)	30	0.22
Asian (2,217)	2,313	16.98
Not Hispanic (2,198)	2,252	16.53
Hispanic (19)	61	0.45
Bangladeshi (8)	12	0.09
Chinese, ex. Taiwanese (1,041)	1,076	7.90
Filipino (49)	54	0.40
Hmong (1)	1	0.01
Indian (910)	945	6.94
Japanese (14)	32	0.23
Korean (5)	8	0.06

*Notes: † The Census 2010 population figure is used to calculate the percentages in the Hispanic Origin and Race categories. Ancestry percentages are based on the 2006-2010 American Community Survey population (not shown); ‡ Numbers in parentheses indicate the number of people reporting a single ancestry; * Numbers in parentheses indicate the number of persons reporting this race alone, not in combination with any other race; Please refer to the Explanation of Data for more information.*

Nepalese (12)	12	0.09
Pakistani (67)	74	0.54
Sri Lankan (5)	11	0.08
Taiwanese (46)	49	0.36
Thai (4)	7	0.05
Vietnamese (9)	9	0.07
Hawaii Native/Pacific Islander (2)	17	0.12
Not Hispanic (2)	5	0.04
Hispanic (0)	12	0.09
Guamanian/Chamorro (0)	1	0.01
Native Hawaiian (1)	4	0.03
White (7,941)	8,400	61.67
Not Hispanic (4,818)	4,960	36.42
Hispanic (3,123)	3,440	25.26

Harrison

Place Type: Township
County: Gloucester
Population: 12,417†

Ancestry‡	Population	%
African, Sub-Saharan (8)	8	0.07
African (8)	8	0.07
American (261)	261	2.20
Arab (0)	13	0.11
Lebanese (0)	13	0.11
Austrian (25)	58	0.49
British (34)	58	0.49
Canadian (0)	7	0.06
Croatian (0)	66	0.56
Czechoslovakian (25)	25	0.21
Dutch (79)	405	3.41
English (179)	1,264	10.65
European (78)	78	0.66
Finnish (0)	9	0.08
French, ex. Basque (29)	381	3.21
French Canadian (0)	65	0.55
German (414)	2,800	23.60
Greek (14)	33	0.28
Hungarian (0)	71	0.60
Iranian (15)	45	0.38
Irish (1,219)	3,915	32.99
Italian (1,209)	3,317	27.95
Latvian (16)	49	0.41
Lithuanian (0)	58	0.49
Norwegian (39)	77	0.65
Pennsylvania German (47)	106	0.89
Polish (107)	604	5.09
Portuguese (10)	52	0.44
Romanian (0)	82	0.69
Russian (51)	177	1.49
Scandinavian (0)	33	0.28
Scotch-Irish (70)	138	1.16
Scottish (30)	320	2.70
Slovak (12)	114	0.96
Swedish (78)	233	1.96
Ukrainian (40)	85	0.72
Welsh (16)	224	1.89
West Indian, ex. Hispanic (51)	65	0.55
Jamaican (51)	65	0.55

Hispanic Origin	Population	%
Hispanic or Latino (of any race)	374	3.01
Central American, ex. Mexican	27	0.22
Guatemalan	19	0.15
Honduran	3	0.02
Panamanian	4	0.03
Salvadoran	1	0.01
Cuban	27	0.22
Dominican Republic	4	0.03
Mexican	70	0.56
Puerto Rican	161	1.30
South American	46	0.37
Chilean	6	0.05
Colombian	21	0.17
Ecuadorian	12	0.10
Paraguayan	3	0.02
Peruvian	1	0.01
Venezuelan	3	0.02
Other Hispanic or Latino	39	0.31

Race*	Population	%
African-American/Black (475)	561	4.52
Not Hispanic (452)	518	4.17
Hispanic (23)	43	0.35
American Indian/Alaska Native (11)	52	0.42
Not Hispanic (10)	47	0.38
Hispanic (1)	5	0.04
Blackfeet (0)	1	0.01
Cherokee (0)	1	0.01
Choctaw (0)	4	0.03
Cree (0)	1	0.01
Delaware (0)	1	0.01
Pueblo (0)	5	0.04
Sioux (0)	1	0.01
Asian (420)	493	3.97
Not Hispanic (407)	479	3.86
Hispanic (13)	14	0.11
Bangladeshi (1)	2	0.02
Cambodian (0)	6	0.05
Chinese, ex. Taiwanese (63)	72	0.58
Filipino (63)	83	0.67
Indian (151)	157	1.26
Indonesian (0)	1	0.01
Japanese (3)	14	0.11
Korean (30)	44	0.35
Laotian (1)	2	0.02
Pakistani (29)	31	0.25
Sri Lankan (1)	3	0.02
Taiwanese (1)	1	0.01
Vietnamese (56)	64	0.52
Hawaii Native/Pacific Islander (0)	1	0.01
Not Hispanic (0)	1	0.01
White (11,246)	11,427	92.03
Not Hispanic (10,998)	11,138	89.70
Hispanic (248)	289	2.33

Hasbrouck Heights

Place Type: Borough
County: Bergen
Population: 11,842†

Ancestry‡	Population	%
African, Sub-Saharan (0)	32	0.27
African (0)	16	0.14
Liberian (0)	16	0.14
Albanian (124)	124	1.06
American (654)	654	5.57
Arab (278)	308	2.62
Arab (74)	74	0.63
Egyptian (43)	43	0.37
Lebanese (147)	162	1.38
Syrian (14)	29	0.25
Armenian (43)	43	0.37
Austrian (14)	88	0.75
Belgian (0)	13	0.11
Brazilian (0)	16	0.14
British (0)	11	0.09
Canadian (0)	14	0.12
Croatian (0)	28	0.24
Cypriot (14)	14	0.12
Czech (16)	45	0.38
Czechoslovakian (16)	16	0.14
Danish (0)	11	0.09
Dutch (29)	185	1.58
English (23)	287	2.44
French, ex. Basque (0)	13	0.11
German (336)	1,366	11.63
Greek (0)	283	2.41
Hungarian (61)	141	1.20
Irish (468)	1,872	15.94
Italian (2,072)	4,027	34.30
Lithuanian (13)	13	0.11
Macedonian (50)	50	0.43
Norwegian (27)	84	0.72
Polish (262)	613	5.22
Portuguese (45)	60	0.51
Romanian (0)	15	0.13
Russian (0)	78	0.66
Scotch-Irish (69)	107	0.91
Scottish (0)	63	0.54
Slovak (32)	52	0.44
Swedish (0)	106	0.90
Swiss (96)	96	0.82
Turkish (81)	81	0.69
Ukrainian (14)	31	0.26
Welsh (15)	15	0.13
West Indian, ex. Hispanic (33)	33	0.28
Jamaican (33)	33	0.28

Hispanic Origin	Population	%
Hispanic or Latino (of any race)	1,760	14.86
Central American, ex. Mexican	73	0.62
Costa Rican	9	0.08
Guatemalan	10	0.08
Honduran	13	0.11
Nicaraguan	11	0.09
Panamanian	4	0.03
Salvadoran	25	0.21
Other Central American	1	0.01
Cuban	306	2.58
Dominican Republic	192	1.62
Mexican	55	0.46
Puerto Rican	426	3.60
South American	507	4.28
Argentinean	41	0.35
Bolivian	8	0.07
Chilean	12	0.10
Colombian	171	1.44
Ecuadorian	138	1.17
Paraguayan	1	0.01
Peruvian	104	0.88
Uruguayan	9	0.08
Venezuelan	14	0.12
Other South American	9	0.08
Other Hispanic or Latino	201	1.70

Race*	Population	%
African-American/Black (339)	392	3.31
Not Hispanic (293)	320	2.70
Hispanic (46)	72	0.61
American Indian/Alaska Native (9)	23	0.19
Not Hispanic (7)	17	0.14
Hispanic (2)	6	0.05
Apache (1)	2	0.02
Blackfeet (0)	1	0.01
Cherokee (0)	1	0.01
Chippewa (4)	4	0.03
Creek (1)	1	0.01
Crow (0)	2	0.02
Mexican American Ind. (0)	1	0.01
Navajo (0)	1	0.01
South American Ind. (0)	2	0.02
Asian (1,183)	1,300	10.98
Not Hispanic (1,169)	1,274	10.76
Hispanic (14)	26	0.22
Cambodian (3)	3	0.03
Chinese, ex. Taiwanese (165)	190	1.60
Filipino (250)	283	2.39
Indian (444)	467	3.94
Indonesian (6)	6	0.05
Japanese (29)	37	0.31
Korean (189)	203	1.71
Laotian (5)	6	0.05
Nepalese (4)	4	0.03
Pakistani (30)	31	0.26
Sri Lankan (6)	8	0.07
Taiwanese (9)	9	0.08
Thai (9)	15	0.13
Vietnamese (14)	17	0.14
Hawaii Native/Pacific Islander (2)	7	0.06
Not Hispanic (2)	5	0.04
Hispanic (0)	2	0.02
Fijian (0)	2	0.02
Guamanian/Chamorro (0)	1	0.01
Native Hawaiian (1)	1	0.01
White (9,632)	9,835	83.05
Not Hispanic (8,445)	8,559	72.28

*Notes: † The Census 2010 population figure is used to calculate the percentages in the Hispanic Origin and Race categories. Ancestry percentages are based on the 2006-2010 American Community Survey population (not shown); ‡ Numbers in parentheses indicate the number of people reporting a single ancestry; * Numbers in parentheses indicate the number of persons reporting this race alone, not in combination with any other race; Please refer to the Explanation of Data for more information.*

Hispanic (1,187)	1,276	10.78

Hawthorne

Place Type: Borough
County: Passaic
Population: 18,791†

Ancestry‡	Population	%
African, Sub-Saharan (15)	32	0.17
African (0)	17	0.09
Ghanaian (15)	15	0.08
Albanian (266)	317	1.71
American (259)	259	1.39
Arab (438)	571	3.07
Arab (136)	136	0.73
Egyptian (36)	36	0.19
Jordanian (14)	14	0.08
Lebanese (119)	119	0.64
Palestinian (0)	14	0.08
Syrian (47)	137	0.74
Other Arab (86)	115	0.62
Armenian (11)	62	0.33
Austrian (28)	93	0.50
Belgian (9)	35	0.19
Canadian (0)	75	0.40
Czech (66)	108	0.58
Danish (0)	60	0.32
Dutch (896)	1,699	9.15
English (201)	1,388	7.47
European (0)	29	0.16
French, ex. Basque (34)	227	1.22
German (602)	2,652	14.28
Greek (23)	23	0.12
Hungarian (105)	350	1.88
Iranian (42)	42	0.23
Irish (784)	3,776	20.33
Israeli (0)	26	0.14
Italian (3,118)	5,860	31.55
Lithuanian (15)	54	0.29
Norwegian (74)	74	0.40
Polish (592)	1,275	6.86
Portuguese (104)	132	0.71
Romanian (0)	50	0.27
Russian (75)	267	1.44
Scotch-Irish (100)	252	1.36
Scottish (82)	294	1.58
Slovak (12)	34	0.18
Swedish (17)	190	1.02
Swiss (13)	194	1.04
Turkish (96)	96	0.52
Ukrainian (10)	48	0.26
Welsh (31)	117	0.63
West Indian, ex. Hispanic (43)	56	0.30
Haitian (0)	13	0.07
West Indian (43)	43	0.23
Yugoslavian (0)	31	0.17

Hispanic Origin	Population	%
Hispanic or Latino (of any race)	2,897	15.42
Central American, ex. Mexican	357	1.90
Costa Rican	154	0.82
Guatemalan	51	0.27
Honduran	14	0.07
Nicaraguan	13	0.07
Salvadoran	115	0.61
Other Central American	10	0.05
Cuban	152	0.81
Dominican Republic	361	1.92
Mexican	136	0.72
Puerto Rican	754	4.01
South American	898	4.78
Argentinean	37	0.20
Bolivian	8	0.04
Chilean	39	0.21
Colombian	256	1.36
Ecuadorian	157	0.84
Peruvian	375	2.00
Uruguayan	17	0.09
Venezuelan	6	0.03
Other South American	3	0.02
Other Hispanic or Latino	239	1.27

Race*	Population	%
African-American/Black (426)	535	2.85
Not Hispanic (355)	416	2.21
Hispanic (71)	119	0.63
American Indian/Alaska Native (40)	98	0.52
Not Hispanic (17)	62	0.33
Hispanic (23)	36	0.19
Apache (1)	1	0.01
Blackfeet (0)	1	0.01
Central American Ind. (0)	5	0.03
Cherokee (1)	9	0.05
Chippewa (1)	1	0.01
Choctaw (0)	1	0.01
Delaware (0)	2	0.01
Inupiat *(Alaska Native)* (1)	1	0.01
Iroquois (0)	1	0.01
Lumbee (1)	1	0.01
Sioux (0)	1	0.01
South American Ind. (2)	2	0.01
Yup'ik *(Alaska Native)* (1)	1	0.01
Asian (530)	623	3.32
Not Hispanic (524)	598	3.18
Hispanic (6)	25	0.13
Bangladeshi (8)	8	0.04
Chinese, ex. Taiwanese (75)	106	0.56
Filipino (84)	116	0.62
Indian (172)	191	1.02
Indonesian (0)	1	0.01
Japanese (9)	14	0.07
Korean (104)	111	0.59
Laotian (1)	1	0.01
Pakistani (29)	34	0.18
Taiwanese (2)	2	0.01
Thai (1)	1	0.01
Vietnamese (23)	27	0.14
Hawaii Native/Pacific Islander (0)	7	0.04
Not Hispanic (0)	6	0.03
Hispanic (0)	1	0.01
White (16,652)	16,941	90.15
Not Hispanic (14,792)	14,929	79.45
Hispanic (1,860)	2,012	10.71

Hazlet

Place Type: Township
County: Monmouth
Population: 20,334†

Ancestry‡	Population	%
American (534)	534	2.60
Arab (120)	144	0.70
Egyptian (113)	113	0.55
Lebanese (0)	8	0.04
Moroccan (0)	3	0.01
Syrian (7)	20	0.10
Armenian (2)	5	0.02
Austrian (10)	54	0.26
Belgian (0)	10	0.05
Brazilian (0)	9	0.04
British (22)	22	0.11
Canadian (0)	14	0.07
Croatian (131)	147	0.72
Czech (12)	91	0.44
Czechoslovakian (8)	67	0.33
Danish (12)	108	0.53
Dutch (6)	216	1.05
Eastern European (7)	7	0.03
English (112)	1,170	5.70
European (27)	46	0.22
Finnish (21)	34	0.17
French, ex. Basque (0)	199	0.97
French Canadian (12)	23	0.11
German (398)	3,631	17.68
Greek (101)	255	1.24
Hungarian (45)	272	1.32
Irish (2,134)	6,871	33.45
Italian (3,387)	7,344	35.75
Lithuanian (59)	162	0.79
Maltese (8)	23	0.11
Norwegian (63)	228	1.11
Pennsylvania German (0)	69	0.34
Polish (482)	1,657	8.07
Portuguese (124)	170	0.83
Russian (113)	388	1.89
Scandinavian (27)	27	0.13
Scotch-Irish (78)	206	1.00
Scottish (58)	157	0.76
Slovak (55)	158	0.77
Swedish (8)	33	0.16
Swiss (13)	42	0.20
Turkish (0)	8	0.04
Ukrainian (134)	250	1.22
Welsh (0)	52	0.25
West Indian, ex. Hispanic (0)	4	0.02
Jamaican (0)	4	0.02

Hispanic Origin	Population	%
Hispanic or Latino (of any race)	1,601	7.87
Central American, ex. Mexican	57	0.28
Costa Rican	6	0.03
Guatemalan	13	0.06
Honduran	10	0.05
Nicaraguan	9	0.04
Panamanian	7	0.03
Salvadoran	12	0.06
Cuban	129	0.63
Dominican Republic	64	0.31
Mexican	141	0.69
Puerto Rican	806	3.96
South American	227	1.12
Argentinean	34	0.17
Chilean	9	0.04
Colombian	61	0.30
Ecuadorian	56	0.28
Paraguayan	2	0.01
Peruvian	47	0.23
Uruguayan	10	0.05
Venezuelan	7	0.03
Other South American	1	<0.01
Other Hispanic or Latino	177	0.87

Race*	Population	%
African-American/Black (301)	395	1.94
Not Hispanic (279)	350	1.72
Hispanic (22)	45	0.22
American Indian/Alaska Native (15)	64	0.31
Not Hispanic (6)	41	0.20
Hispanic (9)	23	0.11
Blackfeet (0)	11	0.05
Canadian/French Am. Ind. (0)	1	<0.01
Cherokee (1)	6	0.03
Delaware (0)	3	0.01
Iroquois (0)	3	0.01
Mexican American Ind. (2)	2	0.01
Sioux (0)	2	0.01
South American Ind. (1)	3	0.01
Spanish American Ind. (1)	1	<0.01
Asian (691)	809	3.98
Not Hispanic (675)	770	3.79
Hispanic (16)	39	0.19
Bangladeshi (2)	5	0.02
Burmese (3)	3	0.01
Chinese, ex. Taiwanese (273)	310	1.52
Filipino (155)	195	0.96
Indian (160)	180	0.89
Indonesian (1)	1	<0.01
Japanese (5)	14	0.07
Korean (19)	37	0.18
Laotian (1)	2	0.01
Pakistani (16)	18	0.09
Sri Lankan (4)	4	0.02
Taiwanese (0)	3	0.01
Thai (6)	6	0.03
Vietnamese (18)	19	0.09
Hawaii Native/Pacific Islander (3)	10	0.05
Not Hispanic (2)	6	0.03
Hispanic (1)	4	0.02

*Notes: † The Census 2010 population figure is used to calculate the percentages in the Hispanic Origin and Race categories. Ancestry percentages are based on the 2006-2010 American Community Survey population (not shown); ‡ Numbers in parentheses indicate the number of people reporting a single ancestry; * Numbers in parentheses indicate the number of persons reporting this race alone, not in combination with any other race; Please refer to the Explanation of Data for more information.*

Guamanian/Chamorro (1)	1	<0.01
Samoan (2)	2	0.01
White (18,694)	18,957	93.23
Not Hispanic (17,550)	17,721	87.15
Hispanic (1,144)	1,236	6.08

Highland Park

Place Type: Borough
County: Middlesex
Population: 13,982†

Ancestry‡	Population	%
African, Sub-Saharan (113)	113	0.81
African (63)	63	0.45
Cape Verdean (10)	10	0.07
Nigerian (40)	40	0.29
Albanian (74)	74	0.53
American (268)	268	1.92
Arab (58)	136	0.97
Arab (33)	33	0.24
Lebanese (10)	15	0.11
Moroccan (15)	68	0.49
Syrian (0)	20	0.14
Armenian (14)	28	0.20
Austrian (14)	73	0.52
Basque (0)	10	0.07
Belgian (36)	36	0.26
Brazilian (6)	16	0.11
British (42)	118	0.84
Bulgarian (103)	103	0.74
Canadian (0)	81	0.58
Croatian (0)	13	0.09
Czech (39)	39	0.28
Czechoslovakian (15)	15	0.11
Danish (30)	195	1.39
Dutch (14)	168	1.20
Eastern European (1,117)	1,124	8.03
English (115)	715	5.11
European (159)	159	1.14
Finnish (29)	29	0.21
French, ex. Basque (93)	189	1.35
German (334)	1,265	9.04
Greek (44)	62	0.44
Hungarian (198)	465	3.32
Icelander (10)	19	0.14
Iranian (19)	51	0.36
Irish (382)	1,069	7.64
Israeli (45)	124	0.89
Italian (493)	905	6.47
Latvian (49)	49	0.35
Lithuanian (79)	126	0.90
Northern European (32)	32	0.23
Norwegian (0)	39	0.28
Polish (261)	908	6.49
Portuguese (11)	59	0.42
Romanian (272)	323	2.31
Russian (478)	1,135	8.11
Scotch-Irish (41)	166	1.19
Scottish (9)	179	1.28
Slavic (0)	21	0.15
Slovak (29)	42	0.30
Swedish (44)	152	1.09
Swiss (0)	26	0.19
Turkish (104)	152	1.09
Ukrainian (94)	164	1.17
Welsh (2)	15	0.11
West Indian, ex. Hispanic (100)	141	1.01
Jamaican (40)	81	0.58
Trinidadian/Tobagonian (6)	6	0.04
West Indian (54)	54	0.39

Hispanic Origin	Population	%
Hispanic or Latino (of any race)	1,252	8.95
Central American, ex. Mexican	139	0.99
Costa Rican	19	0.14
Guatemalan	37	0.26
Honduran	23	0.16
Nicaraguan	10	0.07
Panamanian	14	0.10
Salvadoran	34	0.24
Other Central American	2	0.01
Cuban	57	0.41
Dominican Republic	109	0.78
Mexican	277	1.98
Puerto Rican	304	2.17
South American	276	1.97
Argentinean	27	0.19
Bolivian	10	0.07
Chilean	27	0.19
Colombian	80	0.57
Ecuadorian	53	0.38
Peruvian	63	0.45
Uruguayan	7	0.05
Venezuelan	6	0.04
Other South American	3	0.02
Other Hispanic or Latino	90	0.64

Race*	Population	%
African-American/Black (1,095)	1,254	8.97
Not Hispanic (1,018)	1,145	8.19
Hispanic (77)	109	0.78
American Indian/Alaska Native (20)	82	0.59
Not Hispanic (11)	60	0.43
Hispanic (9)	22	0.16
Apache (0)	2	0.01
Blackfeet (0)	1	0.01
Cherokee (1)	18	0.13
Chippewa (0)	2	0.01
Choctaw (0)	1	0.01
Comanche (0)	3	0.02
Iroquois (2)	2	0.01
Mexican American Ind. (1)	1	0.01
Sioux (1)	5	0.04
South American Ind. (1)	6	0.04
Spanish American Ind. (2)	3	0.02
Asian (2,495)	2,659	19.02
Not Hispanic (2,494)	2,645	18.92
Hispanic (1)	14	0.10
Bangladeshi (5)	5	0.04
Burmese (2)	2	0.01
Chinese, ex. Taiwanese (969)	1,003	7.17
Filipino (107)	139	0.99
Indian (745)	779	5.57
Indonesian (14)	18	0.13
Japanese (50)	72	0.51
Korean (348)	369	2.64
Laotian (0)	5	0.04
Malaysian (9)	10	0.07
Nepalese (2)	2	0.01
Pakistani (71)	82	0.59
Sri Lankan (12)	13	0.09
Taiwanese (45)	48	0.34
Thai (30)	36	0.26
Vietnamese (35)	49	0.35
Hawaii Native/Pacific Islander (4)	26	0.19
Not Hispanic (3)	20	0.14
Hispanic (1)	6	0.04
Guamanian/Chamorro (2)	2	0.01
Native Hawaiian (2)	3	0.02
Samoan (0)	3	0.02
White (9,544)	9,830	70.30
Not Hispanic (8,886)	9,104	65.11
Hispanic (658)	726	5.19

Hillsborough

Place Type: Township
County: Somerset
Population: 38,303†

Ancestry‡	Population	%
Afghan (107)	107	0.28
African, Sub-Saharan (262)	396	1.04
African (55)	107	0.28
Ghanaian (207)	207	0.54
South African (0)	82	0.22
American (897)	897	2.36
Arab (154)	326	0.86
Arab (0)	9	0.02
Egyptian (68)	106	0.28
Lebanese (72)	148	0.39
Syrian (14)	43	0.11
Other Arab (0)	20	0.05
Armenian (89)	139	0.37
Australian (0)	44	0.12
Austrian (32)	256	0.67
Basque (0)	18	0.05
Belgian (14)	52	0.14
British (111)	180	0.47
Canadian (13)	45	0.12
Carpatho Rusyn (17)	17	0.04
Croatian (6)	80	0.21
Czech (47)	204	0.54
Czechoslovakian (12)	194	0.51
Danish (25)	259	0.68
Dutch (117)	810	2.13
Eastern European (104)	104	0.27
English (291)	2,251	5.92
Estonian (0)	40	0.11
European (323)	364	0.96
Finnish (0)	7	0.02
French, ex. Basque (35)	456	1.20
French Canadian (130)	272	0.71
German (1,077)	6,040	15.87
Greek (207)	420	1.10
Guyanese (130)	130	0.34
Hungarian (207)	1,056	2.78
Iranian (39)	97	0.25
Irish (1,240)	6,150	16.16
Israeli (11)	11	0.03
Italian (2,711)	7,041	18.50
Latvian (14)	14	0.04
Lithuanian (21)	305	0.80
Macedonian (31)	59	0.16
Maltese (0)	10	0.03
Northern European (11)	21	0.06
Norwegian (27)	91	0.24
Polish (1,934)	4,740	12.46
Portuguese (117)	209	0.55
Romanian (32)	92	0.24
Russian (562)	1,519	3.99
Scandinavian (17)	17	0.04
Scotch-Irish (107)	423	1.11
Scottish (179)	566	1.49
Slavic (18)	51	0.13
Slovak (64)	417	1.10
Slovene (0)	7	0.02
Swedish (34)	344	0.90
Swiss (29)	68	0.18
Turkish (29)	59	0.16
Ukrainian (342)	700	1.84
Welsh (6)	254	0.67
West Indian, ex. Hispanic (183)	207	0.54
Haitian (93)	93	0.24
Jamaican (90)	114	0.30

Hispanic Origin	Population	%
Hispanic or Latino (of any race)	2,893	7.55
Central American, ex. Mexican	418	1.09
Costa Rican	291	0.76
Guatemalan	39	0.10
Honduran	21	0.05
Nicaraguan	10	0.03
Panamanian	18	0.05
Salvadoran	37	0.10
Other Central American	2	0.01
Cuban	197	0.51
Dominican Republic	94	0.25
Mexican	632	1.65
Puerto Rican	575	1.50
South American	727	1.90
Argentinean	55	0.14
Bolivian	2	0.01
Chilean	27	0.07
Colombian	321	0.84
Ecuadorian	107	0.28
Paraguayan	15	0.04
Peruvian	163	0.43
Uruguayan	11	0.03

*Notes: † The Census 2010 population figure is used to calculate the percentages in the Hispanic Origin and Race categories. Ancestry percentages are based on the 2006-2010 American Community Survey population (not shown); ‡ Numbers in parentheses indicate the number of people reporting a single ancestry; * Numbers in parentheses indicate the number of persons reporting this race alone, not in combination with any other race; Please refer to the Explanation of Data for more information.*

Venezuelan	22	0.06
Other South American	4	0.01
Other Hispanic or Latino	250	0.65

Race*	Population	%
African-American/Black (1,757)	2,013	5.26
Not Hispanic (1,674)	1,850	4.83
Hispanic (83)	163	0.43
American Indian/Alaska Native (46)	160	0.42
Not Hispanic (22)	106	0.28
Hispanic (24)	54	0.14
Apache (1)	3	0.01
Blackfeet (0)	6	0.02
Canadian/French Am. Ind. (0)	1	<0.01
Cherokee (12)	37	0.10
Chickasaw (0)	1	<0.01
Chippewa (0)	1	<0.01
Choctaw (1)	1	<0.01
Creek (1)	1	<0.01
Delaware (0)	4	0.01
Houma (1)	1	<0.01
Iroquois (0)	2	0.01
Mexican American Ind. (9)	11	0.03
Navajo (0)	4	0.01
Seminole (0)	1	<0.01
South American Ind. (8)	12	0.03
Asian (4,743)	5,124	13.38
Not Hispanic (4,723)	5,067	13.23
Hispanic (20)	57	0.15
Bangladeshi (27)	27	0.07
Burmese (1)	1	<0.01
Cambodian (4)	4	0.01
Chinese, ex. Taiwanese (1,124)	1,237	3.23
Filipino (461)	563	1.47
Indian (2,237)	2,348	6.13
Indonesian (2)	11	0.03
Japanese (33)	65	0.17
Korean (185)	224	0.58
Laotian (2)	4	0.01
Malaysian (0)	1	<0.01
Nepalese (6)	6	0.02
Pakistani (293)	312	0.81
Sri Lankan (12)	12	0.03
Taiwanese (120)	130	0.34
Thai (23)	30	0.08
Vietnamese (92)	117	0.31
Hawaii Native/Pacific Islander (15)	42	0.11
Not Hispanic (14)	31	0.08
Hispanic (1)	11	0.03
Guamanian/Chamorro (5)	5	0.01
Marshallese (2)	2	0.01
Native Hawaiian (4)	8	0.02
Samoan (0)	1	<0.01
White (30,109)	30,776	80.35
Not Hispanic (28,369)	28,832	75.27
Hispanic (1,740)	1,944	5.08

Hillsdale

Place Type: Borough
County: Bergen
Population: 10,219†

Ancestry‡	Population	%
American (390)	390	3.85
Arab (0)	52	0.51
Lebanese (0)	38	0.37
Moroccan (0)	14	0.14
Armenian (31)	56	0.55
Austrian (45)	193	1.90
British (16)	32	0.32
Canadian (0)	43	0.42
Celtic (8)	8	0.08
Croatian (74)	74	0.73
Czech (9)	57	0.56
Czechoslovakian (11)	11	0.11
Dutch (0)	258	2.54
Eastern European (66)	73	0.72
English (79)	657	6.48
European (256)	256	2.52
Finnish (0)	10	0.10
French, ex. Basque (16)	250	2.47
French Canadian (36)	44	0.43
German (249)	1,777	17.52
Greek (64)	242	2.39
Hungarian (35)	78	0.77
Irish (645)	2,450	24.16
Israeli (18)	18	0.18
Italian (1,141)	2,940	28.99
Lithuanian (9)	22	0.22
Norwegian (20)	98	0.97
Polish (160)	746	7.36
Portuguese (80)	80	0.79
Romanian (110)	117	1.15
Russian (220)	502	4.95
Scotch-Irish (83)	199	1.96
Scottish (65)	226	2.23
Slovak (7)	22	0.22
Swedish (30)	149	1.47
Swiss (0)	11	0.11
Turkish (0)	14	0.14
Ukrainian (0)	13	0.13
Welsh (0)	8	0.08
West Indian, ex. Hispanic (19)	19	0.19
Jamaican (19)	19	0.19

Hispanic Origin	Population	%
Hispanic or Latino (of any race)	794	7.77
Central American, ex. Mexican	66	0.65
Costa Rican	40	0.39
Guatemalan	6	0.06
Honduran	10	0.10
Nicaraguan	1	0.01
Panamanian	3	0.03
Salvadoran	6	0.06
Cuban	108	1.06
Dominican Republic	57	0.56
Mexican	204	2.00
Puerto Rican	154	1.51
South American	156	1.53
Argentinean	21	0.21
Chilean	2	0.02
Colombian	53	0.52
Ecuadorian	60	0.59
Peruvian	15	0.15
Uruguayan	2	0.02
Venezuelan	3	0.03
Other Hispanic or Latino	49	0.48

Race*	Population	%
African-American/Black (103)	140	1.37
Not Hispanic (93)	117	1.14
Hispanic (10)	23	0.23
American Indian/Alaska Native (12)	33	0.32
Not Hispanic (8)	26	0.25
Hispanic (4)	7	0.07
Alaska Athabascan *(Ala. Nat.)* (0)	1	0.01
Blackfeet (0)	2	0.02
Cherokee (0)	2	0.02
Creek (0)	1	0.01
Delaware (0)	1	0.01
Iroquois (0)	2	0.02
Mexican American Ind. (4)	4	0.04
South American Ind. (0)	1	0.01
Asian (640)	690	6.75
Not Hispanic (638)	684	6.69
Hispanic (2)	6	0.06
Cambodian (3)	3	0.03
Chinese, ex. Taiwanese (191)	210	2.05
Filipino (59)	74	0.72
Indian (117)	131	1.28
Indonesian (3)	3	0.03
Japanese (32)	46	0.45
Korean (183)	187	1.83
Malaysian (1)	1	0.01
Sri Lankan (2)	2	0.02
Taiwanese (19)	19	0.19
Thai (2)	3	0.03
Vietnamese (9)	12	0.12
Hawaii Native/Pacific Islander (5)	6	0.06
Not Hispanic (2)	2	0.02
Hispanic (3)	4	0.04
Guamanian/Chamorro (5)	5	0.05
White (9,138)	9,235	90.37
Not Hispanic (8,590)	8,653	84.68
Hispanic (548)	582	5.70

Hillside

Place Type: Township
County: Union
Population: 21,404†

Ancestry‡	Population	%
African, Sub-Saharan (1,264)	1,318	6.20
African (474)	528	2.48
Cape Verdean (146)	146	0.69
Ghanaian (117)	117	0.55
Kenyan (127)	127	0.60
Liberian (22)	22	0.10
Nigerian (378)	378	1.78
Albanian (9)	18	0.08
American (410)	410	1.93
Arab (46)	70	0.33
Egyptian (36)	36	0.17
Moroccan (10)	34	0.16
Brazilian (682)	734	3.45
Croatian (0)	13	0.06
Czech (0)	68	0.32
Czechoslovakian (11)	11	0.05
Dutch (22)	38	0.18
English (47)	158	0.74
European (121)	121	0.57
French, ex. Basque (0)	52	0.24
French Canadian (15)	31	0.15
German (241)	572	2.69
Greek (12)	29	0.14
Guyanese (103)	103	0.48
Hungarian (0)	30	0.14
Irish (55)	316	1.49
Italian (328)	548	2.58
Lithuanian (8)	8	0.04
Polish (58)	195	0.92
Portuguese (1,276)	1,385	6.51
Romanian (8)	20	0.09
Russian (8)	63	0.30
Scottish (9)	17	0.08
Serbian (15)	15	0.07
Slavic (13)	13	0.06
Slovak (14)	33	0.16
Ukrainian (53)	53	0.25
Welsh (10)	74	0.35
West Indian, ex. Hispanic (1,616)	1,789	8.41
Barbadian (30)	30	0.14
British West Indian (10)	10	0.05
Haitian (1,029)	1,090	5.12
Jamaican (262)	311	1.46
Trinidadian/Tobagonian (36)	36	0.17
West Indian (249)	312	1.47

Hispanic Origin	Population	%
Hispanic or Latino (of any race)	3,774	17.63
Central American, ex. Mexican	451	2.11
Costa Rican	40	0.19
Guatemalan	78	0.36
Honduran	57	0.27
Nicaraguan	32	0.15
Panamanian	34	0.16
Salvadoran	208	0.97
Other Central American	2	0.01
Cuban	310	1.45
Dominican Republic	328	1.53
Mexican	111	0.52
Puerto Rican	978	4.57
South American	1,242	5.80
Argentinean	34	0.16
Bolivian	23	0.11
Chilean	45	0.21
Colombian	306	1.43
Ecuadorian	461	2.15

*Notes: † The Census 2010 population figure is used to calculate the percentages in the Hispanic Origin and Race categories. Ancestry percentages are based on the 2006-2010 American Community Survey population (not shown); ‡ Numbers in parentheses indicate the number of people reporting a single ancestry; * Numbers in parentheses indicate the number of persons reporting this race alone, not in combination with any other race; Please refer to the Explanation of Data for more information.*

Paraguayan	4	0.02
Peruvian	222	1.04
Uruguayan	125	0.58
Venezuelan	17	0.08
Other South American	5	0.02
Other Hispanic or Latino	354	1.65

Race*	Population	%
African-American/Black (11,384)	11,692	54.63
Not Hispanic (11,091)	11,320	52.89
Hispanic (293)	372	1.74
American Indian/Alaska Native (47)	145	0.68
Not Hispanic (33)	101	0.47
Hispanic (14)	44	0.21
Blackfeet (0)	10	0.05
Cherokee (4)	24	0.11
Chippewa (1)	1	<0.01
Iroquois (1)	3	0.01
Mexican American Ind. (0)	2	0.01
Seminole (0)	5	0.02
South American Ind. (2)	9	0.04
Spanish American Ind. (4)	4	0.02
Tlingit-Haida *(Alaska Native)* (2)	2	0.01
Asian (585)	685	3.20
Not Hispanic (571)	657	3.07
Hispanic (14)	28	0.13
Bangladeshi (2)	4	0.02
Chinese, ex. Taiwanese (60)	74	0.35
Filipino (316)	346	1.62
Hmong (1)	1	<0.01
Indian (144)	177	0.83
Indonesian (1)	4	0.02
Japanese (6)	14	0.07
Korean (2)	3	0.01
Laotian (0)	2	0.01
Malaysian (1)	1	<0.01
Pakistani (19)	19	0.09
Sri Lankan (3)	8	0.04
Taiwanese (2)	2	0.01
Thai (1)	1	<0.01
Vietnamese (13)	14	0.07
Hawaii Native/Pacific Islander (7)	55	0.26
Not Hispanic (5)	37	0.17
Hispanic (2)	18	0.08
Guamanian/Chamorro (2)	2	0.01
Native Hawaiian (1)	5	0.02
Samoan (0)	6	0.03
White (7,438)	7,825	36.56
Not Hispanic (5,374)	5,561	25.98
Hispanic (2,064)	2,264	10.58

Hoboken

Place Type: City
County: Hudson
Population: 50,005†

Ancestry‡	Population	%
African, Sub-Saharan (87)	97	0.20
African (17)	17	0.04
Ghanaian (9)	9	0.02
South African (61)	61	0.13
Other Sub-Saharan African (0)	10	0.02
Albanian (0)	64	0.14
American (618)	618	1.30
Arab (177)	463	0.98
Arab (0)	23	0.05
Egyptian (59)	59	0.12
Lebanese (35)	168	0.35
Palestinian (9)	9	0.02
Syrian (0)	39	0.08
Other Arab (74)	165	0.35
Armenian (19)	101	0.21
Australian (64)	145	0.31
Austrian (9)	373	0.79
Belgian (65)	109	0.23
Brazilian (60)	95	0.20
British (256)	440	0.93
Bulgarian (43)	114	0.24
Canadian (40)	111	0.23
Celtic (13)	13	0.03
Croatian (146)	239	0.50
Cypriot (8)	8	0.02
Czech (19)	161	0.34
Czechoslovakian (31)	78	0.16
Danish (8)	88	0.19
Dutch (252)	499	1.05
Eastern European (856)	991	2.09
English (627)	2,708	5.72
European (333)	380	0.80
Finnish (18)	18	0.04
French, ex. Basque (364)	1,141	2.41
French Canadian (23)	123	0.26
German (1,332)	6,114	12.90
Greek (260)	599	1.26
Guyanese (24)	24	0.05
Hungarian (82)	419	0.88
Icelander (26)	41	0.09
Iranian (24)	67	0.14
Irish (3,360)	9,815	20.71
Israeli (166)	298	0.63
Italian (4,941)	10,654	22.48
Latvian (16)	75	0.16
Lithuanian (54)	204	0.43
New Zealander (7)	21	0.04
Norwegian (27)	274	0.58
Polish (682)	2,916	6.15
Portuguese (45)	138	0.29
Romanian (47)	156	0.33
Russian (649)	1,772	3.74
Scandinavian (39)	85	0.18
Scotch-Irish (145)	628	1.33
Scottish (89)	639	1.35
Serbian (61)	61	0.13
Slavic (0)	101	0.21
Slovak (11)	68	0.14
Slovene (0)	11	0.02
Swedish (37)	163	0.34
Swiss (14)	155	0.33
Turkish (95)	150	0.32
Ukrainian (197)	689	1.45
Welsh (194)	311	0.66
West Indian, ex. Hispanic (118)	185	0.39
British West Indian (22)	22	0.05
Jamaican (45)	93	0.20
Trinidadian/Tobagonian (0)	12	0.03
West Indian (51)	58	0.12
Yugoslavian (130)	176	0.37

Hispanic Origin	Population	%
Hispanic or Latino (of any race)	7,602	15.20
Central American, ex. Mexican	262	0.52
Costa Rican	19	0.04
Guatemalan	45	0.09
Honduran	77	0.15
Nicaraguan	17	0.03
Panamanian	18	0.04
Salvadoran	82	0.16
Other Central American	4	0.01
Cuban	577	1.15
Dominican Republic	681	1.36
Mexican	421	0.84
Puerto Rican	4,110	8.22
South American	1,028	2.06
Argentinean	129	0.26
Bolivian	25	0.05
Chilean	51	0.10
Colombian	270	0.54
Ecuadorian	334	0.67
Paraguayan	4	0.01
Peruvian	147	0.29
Uruguayan	13	0.03
Venezuelan	41	0.08
Other South American	14	0.03
Other Hispanic or Latino	523	1.05

Race*	Population	%
African-American/Black (1,767)	2,154	4.31
Not Hispanic (1,289)	1,480	2.96
Hispanic (478)	674	1.35
American Indian/Alaska Native (73)	215	0.43
Not Hispanic (33)	121	0.24
Hispanic (40)	94	0.19
Apache (0)	1	<0.01
Blackfeet (1)	7	0.01
Cherokee (2)	30	0.06
Chippewa (0)	2	<0.01
Choctaw (0)	1	<0.01
Creek (1)	9	0.02
Delaware (2)	8	0.02
Inupiat *(Alaska Native)* (0)	1	<0.01
Iroquois (0)	4	0.01
Lumbee (0)	1	<0.01
Mexican American Ind. (3)	3	0.01
Navajo (2)	3	0.01
Pima (2)	2	<0.01
Pueblo (1)	2	<0.01
Seminole (1)	2	<0.01
Shoshone (1)	2	<0.01
Sioux (1)	2	<0.01
South American Ind. (11)	30	0.06
Spanish American Ind. (3)	3	0.01
Asian (3,558)	4,187	8.37
Not Hispanic (3,516)	4,092	8.18
Hispanic (42)	95	0.19
Bangladeshi (8)	8	0.02
Burmese (5)	6	0.01
Cambodian (3)	4	0.01
Chinese, ex. Taiwanese (946)	1,121	2.24
Filipino (346)	461	0.92
Hmong (0)	1	<0.01
Indian (1,235)	1,375	2.75
Indonesian (16)	19	0.04
Japanese (132)	227	0.45
Korean (423)	502	1.00
Laotian (3)	3	0.01
Malaysian (54)	57	0.11
Nepalese (5)	5	0.01
Pakistani (69)	86	0.17
Sri Lankan (18)	20	0.04
Taiwanese (92)	103	0.21
Thai (46)	51	0.10
Vietnamese (60)	85	0.17
Hawaii Native/Pacific Islander (15)	76	0.15
Not Hispanic (11)	47	0.09
Hispanic (4)	29	0.06
Fijian (0)	2	<0.01
Guamanian/Chamorro (0)	1	<0.01
Native Hawaiian (5)	14	0.03
Samoan (0)	2	<0.01
White (41,124)	42,234	84.46
Not Hispanic (36,607)	37,342	74.68
Hispanic (4,517)	4,892	9.78

Holiday City-Berkeley

Place Type: CDP
County: Ocean
Population: 12,831†

Ancestry‡	Population	%
African, Sub-Saharan (17)	17	0.14
Ethiopian (17)	17	0.14
American (334)	334	2.65
Arab (26)	26	0.21
Arab (13)	13	0.10
Syrian (13)	13	0.10
Armenian (9)	9	0.07
Austrian (10)	126	1.00
British (15)	15	0.12
Celtic (9)	9	0.07
Czech (23)	49	0.39
Czechoslovakian (66)	66	0.52
Danish (18)	53	0.42
Dutch (80)	229	1.82
English (319)	1,007	8.00
Estonian (11)	11	0.09
European (27)	27	0.21
Finnish (17)	17	0.14
French, ex. Basque (12)	246	1.96

*Notes: † The Census 2010 population figure is used to calculate the percentages in the Hispanic Origin and Race categories. Ancestry percentages are based on the 2006-2010 American Community Survey population (not shown); ‡ Numbers in parentheses indicate the number of people reporting a single ancestry; * Numbers in parentheses indicate the number of persons reporting this race alone, not in combination with any other race; Please refer to the Explanation of Data for more information.*

French Canadian (0)	28	0.22
German (756)	1,996	15.87
Greek (56)	97	0.77
Hungarian (215)	265	2.11
Irish (753)	2,214	17.60
Italian (3,697)	4,467	35.51
Lithuanian (10)	108	0.86
Norwegian (35)	129	1.03
Polish (994)	1,344	10.68
Portuguese (97)	120	0.95
Russian (164)	274	2.18
Scotch-Irish (65)	173	1.38
Scottish (73)	157	1.25
Slavic (20)	39	0.31
Slovak (85)	154	1.22
Swedish (34)	120	0.95
Swiss (11)	91	0.72
Ukrainian (140)	186	1.48
Welsh (27)	74	0.59
West Indian, ex. Hispanic (35)	35	0.28
Jamaican (35)	35	0.28
Yugoslavian (14)	27	0.21

Hispanic Origin	Population	%
Hispanic or Latino (of any race)	308	2.40
Central American, ex. Mexican	22	0.17
Costa Rican	6	0.05
Guatemalan	8	0.06
Honduran	1	0.01
Nicaraguan	1	0.01
Panamanian	5	0.04
Salvadoran	1	0.01
Cuban	27	0.21
Dominican Republic	7	0.05
Mexican	21	0.16
Puerto Rican	131	1.02
South American	49	0.38
Argentinean	6	0.05
Chilean	5	0.04
Colombian	13	0.10
Ecuadorian	9	0.07
Peruvian	5	0.04
Uruguayan	10	0.08
Venezuelan	1	0.01
Other Hispanic or Latino	51	0.40

Race*	Population	%
African-American/Black (92)	98	0.76
Not Hispanic (87)	91	0.71
Hispanic (5)	7	0.05
American Indian/Alaska Native (9)	29	0.23
Not Hispanic (8)	27	0.21
Hispanic (1)	2	0.02
Cherokee (2)	4	0.03
Chippewa (1)	1	0.01
Iroquois (1)	3	0.02
Seminole (1)	1	0.01
Asian (93)	103	0.80
Not Hispanic (92)	101	0.79
Hispanic (1)	2	0.02
Chinese, ex. Taiwanese (13)	14	0.11
Filipino (43)	48	0.37
Indian (5)	6	0.05
Japanese (11)	12	0.09
Korean (16)	17	0.13
Laotian (1)	1	0.01
Taiwanese (2)	2	0.02
Thai (1)	1	0.01
Vietnamese (0)	3	0.02
Hawaii Native/Pacific Islander (0)	5	0.04
Not Hispanic (0)	5	0.04
Native Hawaiian (0)	1	0.01
Samoan (0)	1	0.01
White (12,545)	12,600	98.20
Not Hispanic (12,287)	12,329	96.09
Hispanic (258)	271	2.11

Holmdel

Place Type: Township
County: Monmouth
Population: 16,773†

Ancestry‡	Population	%
African, Sub-Saharan (46)	46	0.28
African (39)	39	0.23
Cape Verdean (7)	7	0.04
Albanian (45)	45	0.27
American (628)	628	3.78
Arab (101)	124	0.75
Arab (7)	10	0.06
Egyptian (32)	32	0.19
Lebanese (41)	41	0.25
Syrian (21)	41	0.25
Armenian (12)	12	0.07
Austrian (44)	172	1.04
Brazilian (68)	115	0.69
British (68)	68	0.41
Canadian (14)	24	0.14
Croatian (101)	144	0.87
Cypriot (83)	83	0.50
Czech (0)	52	0.31
Czechoslovakian (0)	34	0.20
Danish (0)	7	0.04
Dutch (55)	222	1.34
Eastern European (104)	104	0.63
English (301)	965	5.81
Estonian (8)	8	0.05
Finnish (0)	77	0.46
French, ex. Basque (43)	361	2.17
German (231)	1,652	9.95
Greek (219)	378	2.28
Hungarian (105)	350	2.11
Iranian (92)	92	0.55
Irish (1,047)	2,964	17.86
Italian (2,722)	4,774	28.76
Lithuanian (35)	48	0.29
Norwegian (55)	215	1.30
Polish (251)	1,299	7.83
Portuguese (29)	122	0.73
Romanian (25)	25	0.15
Russian (176)	470	2.83
Scandinavian (0)	9	0.05
Scotch-Irish (51)	178	1.07
Scottish (24)	122	0.73
Serbian (0)	14	0.08
Slavic (22)	78	0.47
Slovak (10)	62	0.37
Swedish (23)	190	1.14
Swiss (0)	19	0.11
Turkish (191)	191	1.15
Ukrainian (55)	92	0.55
Welsh (0)	123	0.74
Yugoslavian (4)	4	0.02

Hispanic Origin	Population	%
Hispanic or Latino (of any race)	621	3.70
Central American, ex. Mexican	20	0.12
Costa Rican	1	0.01
Guatemalan	11	0.07
Honduran	3	0.02
Panamanian	1	0.01
Salvadoran	4	0.02
Cuban	85	0.51
Dominican Republic	38	0.23
Mexican	56	0.33
Puerto Rican	187	1.11
South American	146	0.87
Argentinean	10	0.06
Bolivian	2	0.01
Chilean	7	0.04
Colombian	63	0.38
Ecuadorian	29	0.17
Peruvian	24	0.14
Uruguayan	3	0.02
Venezuelan	8	0.05
Other Hispanic or Latino	89	0.53

Race*	Population	%
African-American/Black (145)	184	1.10
Not Hispanic (135)	167	1.00
Hispanic (10)	17	0.10
American Indian/Alaska Native (11)	39	0.23
Not Hispanic (11)	33	0.20
Hispanic (0)	6	0.04
Aleut *(Alaska Native)* (0)	1	0.01
Cherokee (1)	2	0.01
Choctaw (3)	3	0.02
Crow (1)	1	0.01
Delaware (0)	1	0.01
Asian (3,213)	3,453	20.59
Not Hispanic (3,201)	3,424	20.41
Hispanic (12)	29	0.17
Bangladeshi (5)	5	0.03
Chinese, ex. Taiwanese (1,588)	1,678	10.00
Filipino (136)	201	1.20
Indian (774)	824	4.91
Indonesian (0)	1	0.01
Japanese (25)	37	0.22
Korean (285)	308	1.84
Laotian (2)	4	0.02
Malaysian (1)	5	0.03
Pakistani (37)	43	0.26
Sri Lankan (16)	22	0.13
Taiwanese (256)	274	1.63
Thai (7)	12	0.07
Vietnamese (15)	21	0.13
Hawaii Native/Pacific Islander (2)	29	0.17
Not Hispanic (1)	28	0.17
Hispanic (1)	1	0.01
Guamanian/Chamorro (1)	1	0.01
Samoan (1)	1	0.01
White (13,007)	13,262	79.07
Not Hispanic (12,498)	12,727	75.88
Hispanic (509)	535	3.19

Hopatcong

Place Type: Borough
County: Sussex
Population: 15,147†

Ancestry‡	Population	%
African, Sub-Saharan (233)	245	1.59
African (233)	245	1.59
Albanian (2)	2	0.01
American (617)	617	4.00
Arab (45)	55	0.36
Arab (36)	36	0.23
Egyptian (9)	9	0.06
Lebanese (0)	10	0.06
Armenian (0)	25	0.16
Austrian (20)	126	0.82
Brazilian (87)	188	1.22
British (18)	18	0.12
Canadian (95)	95	0.62
Celtic (0)	25	0.16
Czech (33)	111	0.72
Czechoslovakian (0)	37	0.24
Danish (6)	6	0.04
Dutch (25)	470	3.04
Eastern European (8)	8	0.05
English (243)	1,431	9.27
European (120)	131	0.85
Finnish (0)	13	0.08
French, ex. Basque (81)	455	2.95
French Canadian (47)	47	0.30
German (561)	3,209	20.78
Greek (123)	183	1.19
Hungarian (98)	295	1.91
Irish (808)	3,941	25.52
Israeli (23)	23	0.15
Italian (1,511)	3,985	25.81
Lithuanian (0)	29	0.19
Macedonian (57)	57	0.37
Norwegian (56)	138	0.89
Polish (331)	1,170	7.58

SECTION TWO

*Notes: † The Census 2010 population figure is used to calculate the percentages in the Hispanic Origin and Race categories. Ancestry percentages are based on the 2006-2010 American Community Survey population (not shown); ‡ Numbers in parentheses indicate the number of people reporting a single ancestry; * Numbers in parentheses indicate the number of persons reporting this race alone, not in combination with any other race; Please refer to the Explanation of Data for more information.*

Ancestry	Population	%
Romanian (46)	46	0.30
Russian (138)	325	2.10
Scotch-Irish (31)	88	0.57
Scottish (48)	162	1.05
Slovak (35)	153	0.99
Swedish (63)	281	1.82
Swiss (0)	9	0.06
Ukrainian (42)	158	1.02
Welsh (16)	74	0.48
West Indian, ex. Hispanic (81)	81	0.52
Jamaican (63)	63	0.41
Trinidadian/Tobagonian (7)	7	0.05
U.S. Virgin Islander (11)	11	0.07
Yugoslavian (24)	36	0.23

Hispanic Origin	Population	%
Hispanic or Latino (of any race)	1,714	11.32
Central American, ex. Mexican	143	0.94
Costa Rican	26	0.17
Guatemalan	26	0.17
Honduran	49	0.32
Nicaraguan	5	0.03
Panamanian	2	0.01
Salvadoran	32	0.21
Other Central American	3	0.02
Cuban	129	0.85
Dominican Republic	86	0.57
Mexican	50	0.33
Puerto Rican	597	3.94
South American	556	3.67
Argentinean	54	0.36
Bolivian	1	0.01
Chilean	68	0.45
Colombian	196	1.29
Ecuadorian	103	0.68
Peruvian	78	0.51
Uruguayan	45	0.30
Venezuelan	6	0.04
Other South American	5	0.03
Other Hispanic or Latino	153	1.01

Race*	Population	%
African-American/Black (441)	537	3.55
Not Hispanic (401)	473	3.12
Hispanic (40)	64	0.42
American Indian/Alaska Native (16)	72	0.48
Not Hispanic (11)	57	0.38
Hispanic (5)	15	0.10
Apache (0)	1	0.01
Blackfeet (0)	6	0.04
Cherokee (1)	12	0.08
Delaware (0)	1	0.01
Iroquois (2)	4	0.03
Mexican American Ind. (1)	1	0.01
Seminole (0)	4	0.03
Sioux (1)	1	0.01
South American Ind. (0)	4	0.03
Asian (341)	417	2.75
Not Hispanic (334)	396	2.61
Hispanic (7)	21	0.14
Burmese (1)	1	0.01
Cambodian (6)	6	0.04
Chinese, ex. Taiwanese (61)	72	0.48
Filipino (102)	124	0.82
Indian (81)	105	0.69
Japanese (4)	14	0.09
Korean (22)	30	0.20
Laotian (4)	4	0.03
Malaysian (1)	1	0.01
Pakistani (29)	34	0.22
Thai (2)	2	0.01
Vietnamese (22)	23	0.15
Hawaii Native/Pacific Islander (3)	13	0.09
Not Hispanic (3)	11	0.07
Hispanic (0)	2	0.01
Guamanian/Chamorro (1)	1	0.01
Native Hawaiian (1)	1	0.01
White (13,794)	14,045	92.72
Not Hispanic (12,490)	12,653	83.53
Hispanic (1,304)	1,392	9.19

Hopewell

Place Type: Township
County: Mercer
Population: 17,304†

Ancestry‡	Population	%
African, Sub-Saharan (26)	48	0.28
African (26)	48	0.28
Albanian (0)	44	0.26
American (511)	511	2.98
Arab (65)	125	0.73
Lebanese (17)	27	0.16
Moroccan (0)	20	0.12
Palestinian (16)	46	0.27
Other Arab (32)	32	0.19
Armenian (22)	56	0.33
Austrian (37)	89	0.52
Belgian (0)	80	0.47
British (226)	299	1.74
Bulgarian (12)	12	0.07
Canadian (30)	30	0.18
Croatian (6)	6	0.04
Czech (19)	150	0.88
Czechoslovakian (9)	21	0.12
Dutch (200)	473	2.76
Eastern European (91)	91	0.53
English (620)	2,351	13.72
European (194)	225	1.31
French, ex. Basque (10)	433	2.53
French Canadian (8)	62	0.36
German (604)	3,168	18.49
Greek (96)	265	1.55
Guyanese (0)	18	0.11
Hungarian (130)	562	3.28
Irish (797)	3,530	20.60
Italian (1,315)	2,931	17.10
Lithuanian (54)	76	0.44
Northern European (47)	47	0.27
Norwegian (21)	86	0.50
Pennsylvania German (62)	62	0.36
Polish (454)	1,339	7.81
Portuguese (38)	71	0.41
Romanian (0)	20	0.12
Russian (244)	571	3.33
Scotch-Irish (76)	295	1.72
Scottish (133)	418	2.44
Slavic (0)	12	0.07
Slovak (49)	114	0.67
Swedish (10)	142	0.83
Swiss (0)	43	0.25
Ukrainian (78)	284	1.66
Welsh (12)	123	0.72
West Indian, ex. Hispanic (42)	82	0.48
Haitian (24)	39	0.23
Jamaican (10)	35	0.20
West Indian (8)	8	0.05
Yugoslavian (11)	11	0.06

Hispanic Origin	Population	%
Hispanic or Latino (of any race)	573	3.31
Central American, ex. Mexican	62	0.36
Costa Rican	9	0.05
Guatemalan	31	0.18
Honduran	6	0.03
Nicaraguan	3	0.02
Panamanian	10	0.06
Salvadoran	3	0.02
Cuban	48	0.28
Dominican Republic	19	0.11
Mexican	95	0.55
Puerto Rican	132	0.76
South American	156	0.90
Argentinean	18	0.10
Bolivian	2	0.01
Chilean	12	0.07
Colombian	75	0.43
Ecuadorian	25	0.14
Paraguayan	2	0.01
Peruvian	16	0.09
Venezuelan	6	0.03
Other Hispanic or Latino	61	0.35

Race*	Population	%
African-American/Black (364)	438	2.53
Not Hispanic (354)	413	2.39
Hispanic (10)	25	0.14
American Indian/Alaska Native (12)	46	0.27
Not Hispanic (11)	38	0.22
Hispanic (1)	8	0.05
Blackfeet (0)	2	0.01
Cherokee (0)	8	0.05
Chickasaw (0)	1	0.01
Choctaw (0)	1	0.01
Delaware (0)	2	0.01
Iroquois (1)	1	0.01
Osage (1)	1	0.01
South American Ind. (0)	3	0.02
Spanish American Ind. (1)	1	0.01
Asian (1,539)	1,735	10.03
Not Hispanic (1,532)	1,722	9.95
Hispanic (7)	13	0.08
Bangladeshi (7)	7	0.04
Cambodian (3)	3	0.02
Chinese, ex. Taiwanese (465)	518	2.99
Filipino (72)	99	0.57
Indian (632)	689	3.98
Indonesian (3)	3	0.02
Japanese (60)	80	0.46
Korean (149)	159	0.92
Malaysian (3)	3	0.02
Nepalese (7)	7	0.04
Pakistani (56)	67	0.39
Sri Lankan (6)	6	0.03
Taiwanese (22)	25	0.14
Thai (4)	5	0.03
Vietnamese (19)	30	0.17
Hawaii Native/Pacific Islander (1)	10	0.06
Not Hispanic (1)	10	0.06
Native Hawaiian (0)	4	0.02
White (15,010)	15,279	88.30
Not Hispanic (14,551)	14,794	85.49
Hispanic (459)	485	2.80

Howell

Place Type: Township
County: Monmouth
Population: 51,075†

Ancestry‡	Population	%
African, Sub-Saharan (98)	129	0.25
African (43)	43	0.08
Cape Verdean (0)	17	0.03
Ethiopian (0)	14	0.03
Ghanaian (30)	30	0.06
Nigerian (25)	25	0.05
Albanian (344)	344	0.68
American (1,799)	1,799	3.54
Arab (265)	402	0.79
Arab (0)	28	0.06
Egyptian (170)	181	0.36
Jordanian (7)	7	0.01
Lebanese (88)	165	0.32
Syrian (0)	13	0.03
Other Arab (0)	8	0.02
Armenian (0)	14	0.03
Austrian (128)	304	0.60
Belgian (0)	60	0.12
Brazilian (45)	153	0.30
British (76)	229	0.45
Canadian (45)	67	0.13
Celtic (13)	13	0.03
Croatian (81)	138	0.27
Czech (83)	219	0.43
Czechoslovakian (24)	94	0.19
Danish (0)	100	0.20
Dutch (100)	755	1.49
Eastern European (102)	102	0.20
English (622)	3,106	6.12

*Notes: † The Census 2010 population figure is used to calculate the percentages in the Hispanic Origin and Race categories. Ancestry percentages are based on the 2006-2010 American Community Survey population (not shown); ‡ Numbers in parentheses indicate the number of people reporting a single ancestry; * Numbers in parentheses indicate the number of persons reporting this race alone, not in combination with any other race; Please refer to the Explanation of Data for more information.*

European (222)	245	0.48
French, ex. Basque (47)	1,041	2.05
French Canadian (81)	252	0.50
German (1,280)	8,137	16.03
Greek (122)	305	0.60
Hungarian (255)	1,024	2.02
Irish (3,114)	12,477	24.57
Israeli (9)	19	0.04
Italian (7,696)	16,618	32.73
Latvian (34)	60	0.12
Lithuanian (106)	226	0.45
Maltese (0)	72	0.14
Norwegian (166)	503	0.99
Pennsylvania German (0)	47	0.09
Polish (1,429)	4,554	8.97
Portuguese (309)	557	1.10
Romanian (70)	109	0.21
Russian (436)	1,524	3.00
Scandinavian (11)	23	0.05
Scotch-Irish (277)	852	1.68
Scottish (110)	687	1.35
Serbian (0)	15	0.03
Slavic (20)	20	0.04
Slovak (122)	372	0.73
Swedish (42)	219	0.43
Swiss (0)	51	0.10
Turkish (110)	243	0.48
Ukrainian (81)	442	0.87
Welsh (57)	253	0.50
West Indian, ex. Hispanic (110)	182	0.36
Haitian (25)	54	0.11
Jamaican (28)	39	0.08
West Indian (57)	89	0.18
Yugoslavian (46)	137	0.27

Hispanic Origin	Population	%
Hispanic or Latino (of any race)	4,153	8.13
Central American, ex. Mexican	263	0.51
Costa Rican	98	0.19
Guatemalan	56	0.11
Honduran	44	0.09
Nicaraguan	7	0.01
Panamanian	15	0.03
Salvadoran	42	0.08
Other Central American	1	<0.01
Cuban	287	0.56
Dominican Republic	135	0.26
Mexican	570	1.12
Puerto Rican	1,889	3.70
South American	644	1.26
Argentinean	39	0.08
Bolivian	3	0.01
Chilean	34	0.07
Colombian	243	0.48
Ecuadorian	138	0.27
Peruvian	158	0.31
Uruguayan	15	0.03
Venezuelan	10	0.02
Other South American	4	0.01
Other Hispanic or Latino	365	0.71

Race*	Population	%
African-American/Black (1,865)	2,175	4.26
Not Hispanic (1,767)	1,988	3.89
Hispanic (98)	187	0.37
American Indian/Alaska Native (79)	213	0.42
Not Hispanic (53)	142	0.28
Hispanic (26)	71	0.14
Apache (1)	2	<0.01
Blackfeet (4)	9	0.02
Canadian/French Am. Ind. (0)	2	<0.01
Central American Ind. (1)	4	0.01
Cherokee (5)	23	0.05
Chickasaw (0)	3	0.01
Chippewa (0)	2	<0.01
Creek (3)	3	0.01
Delaware (0)	8	0.02
Hopi (0)	2	<0.01
Inupiat *(Alaska Native)* (0)	1	<0.01
Iroquois (4)	20	0.04
Lumbee (1)	1	<0.01
Mexican American Ind. (7)	9	0.02
Navajo (0)	3	0.01
Potawatomi (6)	6	0.01
Seminole (0)	2	<0.01
Shoshone (3)	3	0.01
Sioux (1)	4	0.01
South American Ind. (7)	16	0.03
Asian (2,309)	2,702	5.29
Not Hispanic (2,283)	2,638	5.16
Hispanic (26)	64	0.13
Bangladeshi (15)	15	0.03
Burmese (2)	5	0.01
Cambodian (6)	6	0.01
Chinese, ex. Taiwanese (479)	570	1.12
Filipino (549)	672	1.32
Indian (643)	715	1.40
Indonesian (3)	15	0.03
Japanese (16)	27	0.05
Korean (152)	198	0.39
Laotian (3)	6	0.01
Malaysian (3)	3	0.01
Pakistani (80)	85	0.17
Sri Lankan (4)	4	0.01
Taiwanese (21)	32	0.06
Thai (9)	21	0.04
Vietnamese (172)	197	0.39
Hawaii Native/Pacific Islander (23)	56	0.11
Not Hispanic (18)	43	0.08
Hispanic (5)	13	0.03
Guamanian/Chamorro (10)	13	0.03
Native Hawaiian (5)	14	0.03
Samoan (4)	6	0.01
White (45,100)	45,867	89.80
Not Hispanic (42,088)	42,656	83.52
Hispanic (3,012)	3,211	6.29

Irvington

Place Type: Township
County: Essex
Population: 53,926†

Ancestry‡	Population	%
African, Sub-Saharan (2,704)	3,030	5.53
African (764)	904	1.65
Ghanaian (594)	692	1.26
Kenyan (76)	76	0.14
Liberian (48)	48	0.09
Nigerian (812)	832	1.52
Senegalese (10)	10	0.02
South African (43)	43	0.08
Other Sub-Saharan African (357)	425	0.78
American (772)	772	1.41
Arab (27)	42	0.08
Egyptian (11)	11	0.02
Syrian (16)	20	0.04
Other Arab (0)	11	0.02
Austrian (0)	12	0.02
Canadian (22)	22	0.04
Croatian (20)	20	0.04
Czech (10)	10	0.02
Danish (0)	11	0.02
Dutch (13)	13	0.02
English (9)	104	0.19
European (56)	56	0.10
French, ex. Basque (95)	196	0.36
German (57)	122	0.22
Greek (0)	14	0.03
Guyanese (878)	993	1.81
Hungarian (0)	17	0.03
Irish (93)	385	0.70
Italian (161)	355	0.65
Latvian (9)	9	0.02
Lithuanian (0)	22	0.04
Polish (214)	267	0.49
Portuguese (192)	214	0.39
Russian (31)	45	0.08
Scotch-Irish (13)	20	0.04
Scottish (0)	36	0.07
Slovak (0)	9	0.02
Ukrainian (106)	119	0.22
Welsh (0)	47	0.09
West Indian, ex. Hispanic (10,954)	11,355	20.71
Barbadian (139)	160	0.29
British West Indian (272)	300	0.55
Dutch West Indian (29)	34	0.06
Haitian (7,276)	7,341	13.39
Jamaican (2,334)	2,472	4.51
Trinidadian/Tobagonian (525)	635	1.16
U.S. Virgin Islander (16)	16	0.03
West Indian (363)	397	0.72

Hispanic Origin	Population	%
Hispanic or Latino (of any race)	5,716	10.60
Central American, ex. Mexican	1,001	1.86
Costa Rican	195	0.36
Guatemalan	362	0.67
Honduran	119	0.22
Nicaraguan	29	0.05
Panamanian	51	0.09
Salvadoran	231	0.43
Other Central American	14	0.03
Cuban	108	0.20
Dominican Republic	590	1.09
Mexican	724	1.34
Puerto Rican	1,599	2.97
South American	1,157	2.15
Argentinean	21	0.04
Bolivian	1	<0.01
Colombian	63	0.12
Ecuadorian	993	1.84
Paraguayan	7	0.01
Peruvian	42	0.08
Uruguayan	8	0.01
Venezuelan	13	0.02
Other South American	9	0.02
Other Hispanic or Latino	537	1.00

Race*	Population	%
African-American/Black (46,058)	46,928	87.02
Not Hispanic (45,285)	45,917	85.15
Hispanic (773)	1,011	1.87
American Indian/Alaska Native (204)	463	0.86
Not Hispanic (125)	324	0.60
Hispanic (79)	139	0.26
Apache (0)	8	0.01
Arapaho (0)	1	<0.01
Blackfeet (3)	24	0.04
Central American Ind. (1)	1	<0.01
Cherokee (6)	59	0.11
Comanche (0)	1	<0.01
Crow (0)	5	0.01
Delaware (3)	8	0.01
Inupiat *(Alaska Native)* (0)	1	<0.01
Iroquois (1)	7	0.01
Lumbee (1)	1	<0.01
Mexican American Ind. (16)	23	0.04
Navajo (0)	2	<0.01
Sioux (0)	7	0.01
South American Ind. (16)	28	0.05
Spanish American Ind. (2)	3	0.01
Tlingit-Haida *(Alaska Native)* (0)	4	0.01
Asian (471)	618	1.15
Not Hispanic (462)	585	1.08
Hispanic (9)	33	0.06
Bangladeshi (3)	3	0.01
Chinese, ex. Taiwanese (38)	80	0.15
Filipino (140)	156	0.29
Indian (174)	230	0.43
Japanese (7)	12	0.02
Korean (9)	14	0.03
Laotian (5)	5	0.01
Nepalese (3)	3	0.01
Pakistani (17)	17	0.03
Sri Lankan (14)	14	0.03
Vietnamese (45)	50	0.09
Hawaii Native/Pacific Islander (38)	203	0.38
Not Hispanic (18)	158	0.29
Hispanic (20)	45	0.08

*Notes: † The Census 2010 population figure is used to calculate the percentages in the Hispanic Origin and Race categories. Ancestry percentages are based on the 2006-2010 American Community Survey population (not shown); ‡ Numbers in parentheses indicate the number of people reporting a single ancestry; * Numbers in parentheses indicate the number of persons reporting this race alone, not in combination with any other race; Please refer to the Explanation of Data for more information.*

Guamanian/Chamorro (22)	24	0.04
Marshallese (1)	1	<0.01
Native Hawaiian (3)	16	0.03
Samoan (0)	4	0.01
White (3,042)	3,570	6.62
Not Hispanic (1,429)	1,654	3.07
Hispanic (1,613)	1,916	3.55

Iselin

Place Type: CDP
County: Middlesex
Population: 18,695†

Ancestry‡	Population	%
African, Sub-Saharan (77)	77	0.41
African (77)	77	0.41
Albanian (32)	61	0.33
American (317)	317	1.69
Arab (0)	61	0.33
Egyptian (0)	51	0.27
Lebanese (0)	10	0.05
Armenian (62)	73	0.39
Austrian (0)	27	0.14
Brazilian (126)	126	0.67
British (0)	9	0.05
Canadian (0)	34	0.18
Croatian (0)	13	0.07
Czech (13)	76	0.41
Czechoslovakian (34)	34	0.18
Danish (0)	12	0.06
Dutch (15)	23	0.12
Eastern European (36)	36	0.19
English (59)	485	2.59
European (27)	27	0.14
French, ex. Basque (17)	256	1.37
French Canadian (51)	51	0.27
German (190)	998	5.33
Greek (15)	123	0.66
Guyanese (18)	18	0.10
Hungarian (47)	281	1.50
Irish (533)	2,118	11.31
Israeli (0)	10	0.05
Italian (1,371)	2,478	13.23
Lithuanian (31)	97	0.52
Norwegian (16)	48	0.26
Polish (584)	1,187	6.34
Portuguese (89)	137	0.73
Russian (151)	439	2.34
Scotch-Irish (7)	26	0.14
Scottish (66)	202	1.08
Slovak (61)	140	0.75
Swedish (0)	19	0.10
Ukrainian (41)	96	0.51
West Indian, ex. Hispanic (91)	110	0.59
Bermudan (27)	27	0.14
Haitian (24)	43	0.23
Jamaican (40)	40	0.21

Hispanic Origin	Population	%
Hispanic or Latino (of any race)	1,332	7.12
Central American, ex. Mexican	80	0.43
Costa Rican	10	0.05
Guatemalan	18	0.10
Honduran	14	0.07
Nicaraguan	2	0.01
Panamanian	7	0.04
Salvadoran	28	0.15
Other Central American	1	0.01
Cuban	91	0.49
Dominican Republic	88	0.47
Mexican	168	0.90
Puerto Rican	523	2.80
South American	255	1.36
Argentinean	15	0.08
Bolivian	2	0.01
Chilean	1	0.01
Colombian	102	0.55
Ecuadorian	62	0.33
Paraguayan	1	0.01
Peruvian	61	0.33
Uruguayan	4	0.02
Venezuelan	3	0.02
Other South American	4	0.02
Other Hispanic or Latino	127	0.68

Race*	Population	%
African-American/Black (1,257)	1,363	7.29
Not Hispanic (1,193)	1,269	6.79
Hispanic (64)	94	0.50
American Indian/Alaska Native (62)	198	1.06
Not Hispanic (49)	163	0.87
Hispanic (13)	35	0.19
Aleut *(Alaska Native)* (3)	3	0.02
Apache (0)	4	0.02
Blackfeet (0)	2	0.01
Canadian/French Am. Ind. (0)	3	0.02
Central American Ind. (4)	4	0.02
Cherokee (1)	8	0.04
Iroquois (8)	12	0.06
Mexican American Ind. (1)	6	0.03
Pueblo (0)	1	0.01
South American Ind. (0)	3	0.02
Asian (8,623)	9,018	48.24
Not Hispanic (8,599)	8,969	47.98
Hispanic (24)	49	0.26
Bangladeshi (65)	72	0.39
Chinese, ex. Taiwanese (264)	298	1.59
Filipino (476)	511	2.73
Indian (6,997)	7,273	38.90
Indonesian (22)	22	0.12
Japanese (14)	21	0.11
Korean (86)	88	0.47
Laotian (1)	1	0.01
Malaysian (5)	5	0.03
Nepalese (24)	24	0.13
Pakistani (491)	538	2.88
Sri Lankan (30)	34	0.18
Taiwanese (8)	13	0.07
Thai (6)	7	0.04
Vietnamese (34)	47	0.25
Hawaii Native/Pacific Islander (0)	12	0.06
Not Hispanic (0)	5	0.03
Hispanic (0)	7	0.04
White (7,753)	7,996	42.77
Not Hispanic (7,001)	7,161	38.30
Hispanic (752)	835	4.47

Jackson

Place Type: Township
County: Ocean
Population: 54,856†

Ancestry‡	Population	%
African, Sub-Saharan (274)	384	0.72
African (263)	373	0.70
Nigerian (11)	11	0.02
Albanian (89)	100	0.19
American (1,610)	1,610	3.03
Arab (169)	291	0.55
Egyptian (42)	48	0.09
Lebanese (43)	111	0.21
Palestinian (52)	52	0.10
Syrian (22)	70	0.13
Other Arab (10)	10	0.02
Armenian (13)	24	0.05
Australian (0)	34	0.06
Austrian (28)	176	0.33
Belgian (0)	24	0.05
Brazilian (125)	165	0.31
British (52)	138	0.26
Canadian (11)	174	0.33
Croatian (14)	28	0.05
Czech (54)	371	0.70
Czechoslovakian (5)	66	0.12
Danish (10)	116	0.22
Dutch (89)	721	1.36
Eastern European (41)	41	0.08
English (785)	4,476	8.43
Estonian (43)	90	0.17
European (353)	432	0.81
Finnish (0)	42	0.08
French, ex. Basque (193)	1,020	1.92
French Canadian (65)	228	0.43
German (1,474)	9,585	18.05
Greek (172)	351	0.66
Guyanese (58)	58	0.11
Hungarian (256)	1,365	2.57
Icelander (0)	22	0.04
Irish (2,898)	13,227	24.90
Israeli (0)	17	0.03
Italian (6,411)	15,576	29.33
Latvian (0)	68	0.13
Lithuanian (75)	415	0.78
Maltese (17)	50	0.09
Northern European (0)	8	0.02
Norwegian (52)	533	1.00
Pennsylvania German (0)	14	0.03
Polish (1,402)	5,676	10.69
Portuguese (426)	578	1.09
Romanian (157)	251	0.47
Russian (774)	2,206	4.15
Scandinavian (8)	58	0.11
Scotch-Irish (230)	566	1.07
Scottish (226)	849	1.60
Serbian (0)	22	0.04
Slavic (8)	58	0.11
Slovak (130)	348	0.66
Slovene (0)	29	0.05
Swedish (78)	455	0.86
Swiss (28)	138	0.26
Turkish (81)	88	0.17
Ukrainian (236)	696	1.31
Welsh (30)	364	0.69
West Indian, ex. Hispanic (142)	255	0.48
Haitian (41)	41	0.08
Jamaican (57)	128	0.24
Trinidadian/Tobagonian (0)	42	0.08
West Indian (44)	44	0.08
Yugoslavian (0)	44	0.08

Hispanic Origin	Population	%
Hispanic or Latino (of any race)	4,295	7.83
Central American, ex. Mexican	236	0.43
Costa Rican	49	0.09
Guatemalan	42	0.08
Honduran	49	0.09
Nicaraguan	20	0.04
Panamanian	27	0.05
Salvadoran	48	0.09
Other Central American	1	<0.01
Cuban	316	0.58
Dominican Republic	144	0.26
Mexican	447	0.81
Puerto Rican	2,257	4.11
South American	527	0.96
Argentinean	59	0.11
Bolivian	6	0.01
Chilean	20	0.04
Colombian	217	0.40
Ecuadorian	112	0.20
Paraguayan	5	0.01
Peruvian	75	0.14
Uruguayan	17	0.03
Venezuelan	12	0.02
Other South American	4	0.01
Other Hispanic or Latino	368	0.67

Race*	Population	%
African-American/Black (2,664)	3,104	5.66
Not Hispanic (2,460)	2,786	5.08
Hispanic (204)	318	0.58
American Indian/Alaska Native (57)	310	0.57
Not Hispanic (40)	242	0.44
Hispanic (17)	68	0.12
Apache (3)	3	0.01
Blackfeet (1)	15	0.03
Canadian/French Am. Ind. (2)	3	0.01
Central American Ind. (1)	1	<0.01

*Notes: † The Census 2010 population figure is used to calculate the percentages in the Hispanic Origin and Race categories. Ancestry percentages are based on the 2006-2010 American Community Survey population (not shown); ‡ Numbers in parentheses indicate the number of people reporting a single ancestry; * Numbers in parentheses indicate the number of persons reporting this race alone, not in combination with any other race; Please refer to the Explanation of Data for more information.*

Cherokee (6)	52	0.09
Chippewa (3)	3	0.01
Comanche (0)	2	<0.01
Creek (0)	2	<0.01
Crow (0)	1	<0.01
Delaware (1)	19	0.03
Iroquois (1)	13	0.02
Kiowa (0)	2	<0.01
Mexican American Ind. (4)	5	0.01
Navajo (0)	3	0.01
Seminole (0)	5	0.01
Sioux (0)	6	0.01
South American Ind. (3)	11	0.02
Asian (1,616)	1,939	3.53
Not Hispanic (1,592)	1,877	3.42
Hispanic (24)	62	0.11
Bangladeshi (0)	1	<0.01
Burmese (1)	1	<0.01
Chinese, ex. Taiwanese (261)	340	0.62
Filipino (443)	535	0.98
Indian (502)	583	1.06
Indonesian (12)	12	0.02
Japanese (20)	45	0.08
Korean (167)	208	0.38
Laotian (0)	3	0.01
Malaysian (2)	6	0.01
Pakistani (39)	46	0.08
Sri Lankan (14)	15	0.03
Taiwanese (12)	13	0.02
Thai (19)	22	0.04
Vietnamese (57)	79	0.14
Hawaii Native/Pacific Islander (18)	56	0.10
Not Hispanic (14)	49	0.09
Hispanic (4)	7	0.01
Guamanian/Chamorro (7)	9	0.02
Native Hawaiian (2)	8	0.01
White (48,765)	49,647	90.50
Not Hispanic (45,632)	46,275	84.36
Hispanic (3,133)	3,372	6.15

Jefferson

Place Type: Township
County: Morris
Population: 21,314†

Ancestry‡	Population	%
African, Sub-Saharan (36)	36	0.17
Ghanaian (36)	36	0.17
Albanian (47)	57	0.27
American (434)	434	2.06
Arab (14)	66	0.31
Arab (0)	13	0.06
Jordanian (14)	14	0.07
Lebanese (0)	39	0.18
Armenian (81)	102	0.48
Austrian (0)	112	0.53
Brazilian (27)	43	0.20
British (51)	79	0.37
Canadian (17)	17	0.08
Croatian (13)	13	0.06
Czech (35)	187	0.89
Czechoslovakian (42)	42	0.20
Danish (21)	132	0.63
Dutch (195)	1,051	4.98
Eastern European (37)	37	0.18
English (372)	2,081	9.87
Estonian (10)	10	0.05
European (85)	85	0.40
Finnish (8)	42	0.20
French, ex. Basque (2)	220	1.04
French Canadian (12)	91	0.43
German (777)	4,546	21.55
Greek (100)	241	1.14
Hungarian (110)	600	2.84
Irish (1,197)	5,208	24.69
Israeli (9)	9	0.04
Italian (1,848)	5,271	24.99
Lithuanian (22)	99	0.47
Maltese (27)	27	0.13
Norwegian (86)	258	1.22
Pennsylvania German (12)	20	0.09
Polish (582)	2,185	10.36
Portuguese (56)	124	0.59
Romanian (29)	38	0.18
Russian (214)	623	2.95
Scandinavian (0)	8	0.04
Scotch-Irish (140)	349	1.65
Scottish (86)	420	1.99
Slovak (154)	261	1.24
Slovene (27)	27	0.13
Swedish (24)	176	0.83
Swiss (22)	124	0.59
Turkish (12)	22	0.10
Ukrainian (51)	138	0.65
Welsh (0)	63	0.30
West Indian, ex. Hispanic (122)	122	0.58
Bahamian (30)	30	0.14
Jamaican (92)	92	0.44
Yugoslavian (32)	67	0.32

Hispanic Origin	Population	%
Hispanic or Latino (of any race)	1,382	6.48
Central American, ex. Mexican	93	0.44
Costa Rican	21	0.10
Guatemalan	23	0.11
Honduran	25	0.12
Nicaraguan	7	0.03
Panamanian	3	0.01
Salvadoran	14	0.07
Cuban	120	0.56
Dominican Republic	73	0.34
Mexican	107	0.50
Puerto Rican	468	2.20
South American	377	1.77
Argentinean	33	0.15
Bolivian	2	0.01
Chilean	32	0.15
Colombian	163	0.76
Ecuadorian	58	0.27
Paraguayan	1	<0.01
Peruvian	53	0.25
Uruguayan	19	0.09
Venezuelan	11	0.05
Other South American	5	0.02
Other Hispanic or Latino	144	0.68

Race*	Population	%
African-American/Black (332)	431	2.02
Not Hispanic (305)	391	1.83
Hispanic (27)	40	0.19
American Indian/Alaska Native (18)	99	0.46
Not Hispanic (16)	84	0.39
Hispanic (2)	15	0.07
Blackfeet (0)	5	0.02
Canadian/French Am. Ind. (1)	1	<0.01
Cherokee (1)	10	0.05
Chippewa (2)	2	0.01
Choctaw (0)	1	<0.01
Delaware (5)	9	0.04
Iroquois (0)	10	0.05
Mexican American Ind. (1)	1	<0.01
Navajo (0)	2	0.01
Ottawa (0)	2	0.01
Sioux (2)	4	0.02
Spanish American Ind. (0)	1	<0.01
Asian (981)	1,084	5.09
Not Hispanic (977)	1,066	5.00
Hispanic (4)	18	0.08
Bangladeshi (4)	4	0.02
Cambodian (1)	3	0.01
Chinese, ex. Taiwanese (157)	179	0.84
Filipino (185)	205	0.96
Indian (465)	495	2.32
Indonesian (5)	5	0.02
Japanese (11)	24	0.11
Korean (63)	74	0.35
Pakistani (34)	35	0.16
Sri Lankan (9)	9	0.04
Taiwanese (2)	3	0.01
Thai (5)	8	0.04
Vietnamese (28)	36	0.17
Hawaii Native/Pacific Islander (4)	17	0.08
Not Hispanic (3)	13	0.06
Hispanic (1)	4	0.02
Guamanian/Chamorro (1)	1	<0.01
Native Hawaiian (0)	2	0.01
White (19,318)	19,635	92.12
Not Hispanic (18,373)	18,593	87.23
Hispanic (945)	1,042	4.89

Jersey City

Place Type: City
County: Hudson
Population: 247,597†

Ancestry‡	Population	%
Afghan (109)	109	0.04
African, Sub-Saharan (4,107)	4,569	1.88
African (1,289)	1,581	0.65
Cape Verdean (352)	435	0.18
Ethiopian (112)	112	0.05
Ghanaian (624)	624	0.26
Kenyan (252)	252	0.10
Liberian (123)	123	0.05
Nigerian (772)	822	0.34
Senegalese (90)	90	0.04
Somalian (0)	12	<0.01
South African (27)	52	0.02
Sudanese (203)	203	0.08
Ugandan (7)	7	<0.01
Zimbabwean (9)	9	<0.01
Other Sub-Saharan African (247)	247	0.10
Albanian (51)	68	0.03
American (2,044)	2,044	0.84
Arab (6,178)	6,852	2.82
Arab (318)	341	0.14
Egyptian (4,316)	4,507	1.85
Iraqi (37)	37	0.02
Jordanian (111)	198	0.08
Lebanese (45)	154	0.06
Moroccan (663)	716	0.29
Palestinian (11)	38	0.02
Syrian (67)	118	0.05
Other Arab (610)	743	0.31
Armenian (25)	43	0.02
Australian (126)	255	0.10
Austrian (72)	257	0.11
Belgian (65)	217	0.09
Brazilian (227)	370	0.15
British (430)	667	0.27
Bulgarian (119)	131	0.05
Cajun (13)	13	0.01
Canadian (73)	237	0.10
Croatian (146)	260	0.11
Cypriot (27)	27	0.01
Czech (123)	312	0.13
Czechoslovakian (95)	142	0.06
Danish (0)	57	0.02
Dutch (95)	553	0.23
Eastern European (413)	441	0.18
English (970)	3,797	1.56
Estonian (56)	67	0.03
European (530)	594	0.24
Finnish (8)	70	0.03
French, ex. Basque (374)	1,291	0.53
French Canadian (80)	273	0.11
German (2,081)	8,698	3.58
Greek (417)	612	0.25
Guyanese (2,822)	3,025	1.24
Hungarian (220)	615	0.25
Icelander (0)	33	0.01
Iranian (121)	150	0.06
Irish (4,150)	12,691	5.22
Israeli (184)	216	0.09
Italian (6,960)	12,466	5.12
Latvian (180)	216	0.09
Lithuanian (69)	236	0.10
Luxemburger (0)	33	0.01

*Notes: † The Census 2010 population figure is used to calculate the percentages in the Hispanic Origin and Race categories. Ancestry percentages are based on the 2006-2010 American Community Survey population (not shown); ‡ Numbers in parentheses indicate the number of people reporting a single ancestry; * Numbers in parentheses indicate the number of persons reporting this race alone, not in combination with any other race; Please refer to the Explanation of Data for more information.*

Macedonian (21)	81	0.03
Maltese (10)	10	<0.01
Northern European (70)	70	0.03
Norwegian (93)	379	0.16
Pennsylvania German (5)	14	0.01
Polish (3,382)	6,577	2.70
Portuguese (161)	384	0.16
Romanian (238)	344	0.14
Russian (1,206)	2,439	1.00
Scandinavian (32)	69	0.03
Scotch-Irish (285)	647	0.27
Scottish (274)	855	0.35
Serbian (4)	43	0.02
Slavic (23)	71	0.03
Slovak (187)	275	0.11
Slovene (0)	13	0.01
Swedish (186)	529	0.22
Swiss (34)	105	0.04
Turkish (410)	453	0.19
Ukrainian (540)	883	0.36
Welsh (56)	373	0.15
West Indian, ex. Hispanic (6,460)	7,300	3.00
Bahamian (19)	19	0.01
Barbadian (187)	239	0.10
Belizean (165)	195	0.08
British West Indian (628)	638	0.26
Dutch West Indian (0)	27	0.01
Haitian (2,312)	2,371	0.97
Jamaican (1,384)	1,670	0.69
Trinidadian/Tobagonian (996)	1,140	0.47
West Indian (743)	975	0.40
Other West Indian (26)	26	0.01
Yugoslavian (61)	61	0.03

Hispanic Origin	Population	%
Hispanic or Latino (of any race)	68,256	27.57
Central American, ex. Mexican	6,838	2.76
Costa Rican	229	0.09
Guatemalan	1,148	0.46
Honduran	3,041	1.23
Nicaraguan	528	0.21
Panamanian	384	0.16
Salvadoran	1,427	0.58
Other Central American	81	0.03
Cuban	1,641	0.66
Dominican Republic	13,512	5.46
Mexican	4,535	1.83
Puerto Rican	25,677	10.37
South American	11,034	4.46
Argentinean	558	0.23
Bolivian	337	0.14
Chilean	316	0.13
Colombian	2,246	0.91
Ecuadorian	5,754	2.32
Paraguayan	26	0.01
Peruvian	1,221	0.49
Uruguayan	149	0.06
Venezuelan	303	0.12
Other South American	124	0.05
Other Hispanic or Latino	5,019	2.03

Race*	Population	%
African-American/Black (64,002)	68,694	27.74
Not Hispanic (59,060)	61,622	24.89
Hispanic (4,942)	7,072	2.86
American Indian/Alaska Native (1,272)	2,910	1.18
Not Hispanic (586)	1,653	0.67
Hispanic (686)	1,257	0.51
Alaska Athabascan *(Ala. Nat.)* (0)	6	<0.01
Apache (0)	2	<0.01
Blackfeet (3)	32	0.01
Canadian/French Am. Ind. (6)	7	<0.01
Central American Ind. (34)	58	0.02
Cherokee (45)	241	0.10
Chickasaw (0)	1	<0.01
Chippewa (4)	5	<0.01
Choctaw (0)	4	<0.01
Comanche (1)	1	<0.01
Cree (1)	3	<0.01
Creek (1)	7	<0.01
Crow (1)	2	<0.01
Delaware (6)	8	<0.01
Hopi (1)	4	<0.01
Inupiat *(Alaska Native)* (0)	4	<0.01
Iroquois (8)	20	0.01
Lumbee (2)	2	<0.01
Mexican American Ind. (54)	71	0.03
Navajo (1)	3	<0.01
Paiute (0)	1	<0.01
Pueblo (6)	15	0.01
Seminole (0)	14	0.01
Shoshone (0)	2	<0.01
Sioux (7)	16	0.01
South American Ind. (95)	228	0.09
Spanish American Ind. (21)	33	0.01
Tlingit-Haida *(Alaska Native)* (0)	2	<0.01
Tohono O'Odham (0)	1	<0.01
Yup'ik *(Alaska Native)* (0)	1	<0.01
Asian (58,595)	62,449	25.22
Not Hispanic (58,106)	61,418	24.81
Hispanic (489)	1,031	0.42
Bangladeshi (278)	332	0.13
Bhutanese (3)	6	<0.01
Burmese (13)	22	0.01
Cambodian (16)	21	0.01
Chinese, ex. Taiwanese (5,262)	5,886	2.38
Filipino (16,213)	17,268	6.97
Hmong (2)	3	<0.01
Indian (27,111)	28,688	11.59
Indonesian (49)	74	0.03
Japanese (480)	660	0.27
Korean (2,308)	2,482	1.00
Laotian (19)	33	0.01
Malaysian (30)	43	0.02
Nepalese (146)	155	0.06
Pakistani (3,269)	3,490	1.41
Sri Lankan (87)	95	0.04
Taiwanese (362)	406	0.16
Thai (142)	181	0.07
Vietnamese (1,607)	1,753	0.71
Hawaii Native/Pacific Islander (161)	781	0.32
Not Hispanic (95)	500	0.20
Hispanic (66)	281	0.11
Fijian (0)	3	<0.01
Guamanian/Chamorro (38)	49	0.02
Native Hawaiian (30)	65	0.03
Samoan (16)	30	0.01
White (80,885)	87,208	35.22
Not Hispanic (53,236)	56,100	22.66
Hispanic (27,649)	31,108	12.56

Keansburg

Place Type: Borough
County: Monmouth
Population: 10,105†

Ancestry‡	Population	%
Albanian (86)	86	0.84
American (317)	317	3.10
Arab (58)	82	0.80
Lebanese (58)	82	0.80
Austrian (0)	42	0.41
Canadian (51)	169	1.65
Czech (0)	10	0.10
Danish (0)	29	0.28
Dutch (12)	183	1.79
English (137)	461	4.51
European (10)	10	0.10
French, ex. Basque (0)	104	1.02
German (405)	1,662	16.25
Greek (0)	101	0.99
Hungarian (63)	195	1.91
Irish (1,050)	3,129	30.60
Italian (1,028)	2,327	22.75
Macedonian (29)	29	0.28
Norwegian (0)	58	0.57
Pennsylvania German (6)	6	0.06
Polish (211)	655	6.40
Portuguese (150)	190	1.86
Russian (12)	132	1.29
Scotch-Irish (278)	297	2.90
Scottish (52)	170	1.66
Slavic (22)	22	0.22
Slovak (0)	23	0.22
Swedish (29)	86	0.84
Swiss (0)	17	0.17
Turkish (9)	9	0.09
Ukrainian (48)	84	0.82
Welsh (8)	25	0.24
West Indian, ex. Hispanic (0)	138	1.35
Barbadian (0)	138	1.35
Yugoslavian (37)	76	0.74

Hispanic Origin	Population	%
Hispanic or Latino (of any race)	1,493	14.77
Central American, ex. Mexican	76	0.75
Costa Rican	18	0.18
Guatemalan	4	0.04
Honduran	12	0.12
Nicaraguan	5	0.05
Panamanian	15	0.15
Salvadoran	22	0.22
Cuban	79	0.78
Dominican Republic	83	0.82
Mexican	302	2.99
Puerto Rican	693	6.86
South American	168	1.66
Argentinean	11	0.11
Chilean	3	0.03
Colombian	62	0.61
Ecuadorian	38	0.38
Paraguayan	3	0.03
Peruvian	36	0.36
Uruguayan	13	0.13
Venezuelan	2	0.02
Other Hispanic or Latino	92	0.91

Race*	Population	%
African-American/Black (664)	832	8.23
Not Hispanic (582)	710	7.03
Hispanic (82)	122	1.21
American Indian/Alaska Native (23)	87	0.86
Not Hispanic (13)	57	0.56
Hispanic (10)	30	0.30
Blackfeet (0)	1	0.01
Cherokee (4)	10	0.10
Chickasaw (1)	1	0.01
Chippewa (0)	2	0.02
Creek (0)	1	0.01
Delaware (0)	4	0.04
Iroquois (0)	3	0.03
Mexican American Ind. (0)	1	0.01
Navajo (1)	3	0.03
Pueblo (0)	1	0.01
Sioux (1)	1	0.01
South American Ind. (7)	8	0.08
Asian (172)	227	2.25
Not Hispanic (169)	219	2.17
Hispanic (3)	8	0.08
Chinese, ex. Taiwanese (23)	28	0.28
Filipino (54)	87	0.86
Indian (33)	35	0.35
Japanese (7)	14	0.14
Korean (14)	20	0.20
Laotian (0)	1	0.01
Nepalese (3)	3	0.03
Pakistani (30)	30	0.30
Vietnamese (6)	6	0.06
Hawaii Native/Pacific Islander (8)	16	0.16
Not Hispanic (8)	13	0.13
Hispanic (0)	3	0.03
Guamanian/Chamorro (1)	1	0.01
Native Hawaiian (0)	1	0.01
Samoan (5)	5	0.05
White (8,505)	8,795	87.04
Not Hispanic (7,616)	7,815	77.34
Hispanic (889)	980	9.70

*Notes: † The Census 2010 population figure is used to calculate the percentages in the Hispanic Origin and Race categories. Ancestry percentages are based on the 2006-2010 American Community Survey population (not shown); ‡ Numbers in parentheses indicate the number of people reporting a single ancestry; * Numbers in parentheses indicate the number of persons reporting this race alone, not in combination with any other race; Please refer to the Explanation of Data for more information.*

Kearny

Place Type: Town
County: Hudson
Population: 40,684†

Ancestry‡	Population	%
African, Sub-Saharan (116)	130	0.32
African (74)	88	0.22
Nigerian (42)	42	0.10
American (908)	908	2.26
Arab (191)	391	0.97
Arab (0)	155	0.39
Egyptian (185)	194	0.48
Lebanese (6)	42	0.10
Armenian (10)	19	0.05
Australian (0)	10	0.02
Austrian (0)	17	0.04
Brazilian (1,908)	2,074	5.16
British (22)	49	0.12
Bulgarian (53)	53	0.13
Canadian (0)	11	0.03
Czech (0)	19	0.05
Czechoslovakian (5)	16	0.04
Danish (0)	48	0.12
Dutch (31)	67	0.17
Eastern European (13)	33	0.08
English (161)	743	1.85
European (53)	53	0.13
Finnish (0)	7	0.02
French, ex. Basque (16)	450	1.12
French Canadian (16)	21	0.05
German (269)	1,763	4.38
Greek (97)	205	0.51
Guyanese (125)	235	0.58
Hungarian (41)	110	0.27
Irish (1,646)	3,561	8.86
Italian (1,747)	3,189	7.93
Lithuanian (142)	247	0.61
Macedonian (8)	8	0.02
Norwegian (10)	60	0.15
Polish (1,308)	2,683	6.67
Portuguese (3,566)	3,917	9.74
Romanian (30)	30	0.07
Russian (92)	312	0.78
Scotch-Irish (413)	594	1.48
Scottish (407)	763	1.90
Slavic (0)	17	0.04
Slovak (11)	36	0.09
Swedish (39)	147	0.37
Turkish (10)	69	0.17
Ukrainian (37)	108	0.27
Welsh (0)	76	0.19
West Indian, ex. Hispanic (122)	191	0.48
Barbadian (8)	8	0.02
Belizean (0)	46	0.11
British West Indian (0)	23	0.06
Haitian (86)	86	0.21
Jamaican (28)	28	0.07
Yugoslavian (10)	10	0.02

Hispanic Origin	Population	%
Hispanic or Latino (of any race)	16,253	39.95
Central American, ex. Mexican	1,041	2.56
Costa Rican	96	0.24
Guatemalan	264	0.65
Honduran	183	0.45
Nicaraguan	58	0.14
Panamanian	8	0.02
Salvadoran	432	1.06
Cuban	719	1.77
Dominican Republic	1,009	2.48
Mexican	913	2.24
Puerto Rican	2,730	6.71
South American	7,015	17.24
Argentinean	177	0.44
Bolivian	24	0.06
Chilean	97	0.24
Colombian	623	1.53
Ecuadorian	2,230	5.48
Paraguayan	7	0.02
Peruvian	3,315	8.15
Uruguayan	418	1.03
Venezuelan	104	0.26
Other South American	20	0.05
Other Hispanic or Latino	2,826	6.95

Race*	Population	%
African-American/Black (2,186)	2,533	6.23
Not Hispanic (1,721)	1,887	4.64
Hispanic (465)	646	1.59
American Indian/Alaska Native (163)	324	0.80
Not Hispanic (43)	100	0.25
Hispanic (120)	224	0.55
Canadian/French Am. Ind. (1)	3	0.01
Central American Ind. (11)	15	0.04
Cherokee (4)	7	0.02
Choctaw (1)	1	<0.01
Delaware (0)	1	<0.01
Iroquois (0)	2	<0.01
Mexican American Ind. (13)	17	0.04
Pueblo (0)	2	<0.01
Sioux (0)	1	<0.01
South American Ind. (41)	111	0.27
Spanish American Ind. (6)	7	0.02
Asian (1,793)	2,013	4.95
Not Hispanic (1,746)	1,903	4.68
Hispanic (47)	110	0.27
Bangladeshi (10)	10	0.02
Burmese (1)	1	<0.01
Chinese, ex. Taiwanese (654)	696	1.71
Filipino (343)	376	0.92
Indian (518)	592	1.46
Indonesian (4)	8	0.02
Japanese (32)	55	0.14
Korean (50)	58	0.14
Malaysian (2)	2	<0.01
Nepalese (6)	9	0.02
Pakistani (58)	72	0.18
Sri Lankan (10)	10	0.02
Taiwanese (29)	29	0.07
Thai (3)	8	0.02
Vietnamese (27)	27	0.07
Hawaii Native/Pacific Islander (32)	111	0.27
Not Hispanic (22)	65	0.16
Hispanic (10)	46	0.11
Guamanian/Chamorro (7)	7	0.02
Native Hawaiian (4)	9	0.02
Samoan (1)	1	<0.01
White (29,933)	31,165	76.60
Not Hispanic (19,816)	20,277	49.84
Hispanic (10,117)	10,888	26.76

Kendall Park

Place Type: CDP
County: Middlesex
Population: 9,339†

Ancestry‡	Population	%
African, Sub-Saharan (297)	297	3.37
African (8)	8	0.09
Ghanaian (289)	289	3.28
American (227)	227	2.58
Arab (61)	86	0.98
Egyptian (8)	8	0.09
Jordanian (8)	8	0.09
Lebanese (12)	37	0.42
Syrian (33)	33	0.37
Armenian (0)	17	0.19
Austrian (73)	159	1.81
Canadian (0)	39	0.44
Czech (0)	48	0.55
Czechoslovakian (28)	70	0.80
Danish (12)	183	2.08
Dutch (0)	64	0.73
Eastern European (33)	33	0.37
English (57)	460	5.22
Estonian (14)	14	0.16
European (50)	50	0.57
French, ex. Basque (0)	167	1.90
French Canadian (0)	41	0.47
German (174)	1,312	14.90
Greek (11)	35	0.40
Hungarian (79)	272	3.09
Irish (170)	1,402	15.92
Italian (815)	1,964	22.31
Lithuanian (0)	69	0.78
Norwegian (29)	56	0.64
Polish (256)	590	6.70
Portuguese (8)	34	0.39
Romanian (27)	27	0.31
Russian (30)	115	1.31
Scotch-Irish (16)	135	1.53
Scottish (16)	165	1.87
Slavic (0)	9	0.10
Slovak (9)	56	0.64
Swedish (11)	39	0.44
Swiss (8)	8	0.09
Turkish (11)	35	0.40
Ukrainian (34)	51	0.58
Welsh (0)	21	0.24

Hispanic Origin	Population	%
Hispanic or Latino (of any race)	633	6.78
Central American, ex. Mexican	62	0.66
Costa Rican	5	0.05
Guatemalan	27	0.29
Honduran	3	0.03
Nicaraguan	13	0.14
Panamanian	6	0.06
Salvadoran	8	0.09
Cuban	50	0.54
Dominican Republic	62	0.66
Mexican	70	0.75
Puerto Rican	232	2.48
South American	102	1.09
Argentinean	6	0.06
Bolivian	4	0.04
Chilean	4	0.04
Colombian	41	0.44
Ecuadorian	14	0.15
Paraguayan	4	0.04
Peruvian	16	0.17
Uruguayan	8	0.09
Venezuelan	4	0.04
Other South American	1	0.01
Other Hispanic or Latino	55	0.59

Race*	Population	%
African-American/Black (487)	568	6.08
Not Hispanic (463)	536	5.74
Hispanic (24)	32	0.34
American Indian/Alaska Native (17)	57	0.61
Not Hispanic (17)	51	0.55
Hispanic (0)	6	0.06
Blackfeet (1)	3	0.03
Cherokee (0)	6	0.06
Delaware (0)	5	0.05
Iroquois (0)	1	0.01
Sioux (0)	1	0.01
South American Ind. (0)	1	0.01
Asian (2,342)	2,438	26.11
Not Hispanic (2,340)	2,424	25.96
Hispanic (2)	14	0.15
Bangladeshi (13)	13	0.14
Chinese, ex. Taiwanese (398)	424	4.54
Filipino (170)	200	2.14
Indian (1,431)	1,460	15.63
Japanese (8)	13	0.14
Korean (58)	73	0.78
Malaysian (4)	4	0.04
Pakistani (129)	129	1.38
Sri Lankan (48)	52	0.56
Taiwanese (42)	44	0.47
Thai (4)	7	0.07
Vietnamese (12)	16	0.17
Hawaii Native/Pacific Islander (2)	11	0.12
Not Hispanic (1)	4	0.04
Hispanic (1)	7	0.07

*Notes: † The Census 2010 population figure is used to calculate the percentages in the Hispanic Origin and Race categories. Ancestry percentages are based on the 2006-2010 American Community Survey population (not shown); ‡ Numbers in parentheses indicate the number of people reporting a single ancestry; * Numbers in parentheses indicate the number of persons reporting this race alone, not in combination with any other race; Please refer to the Explanation of Data for more information.*

Guamanian/Chamorro (1)	1	0.01
Marshallese (0)	1	0.01
Samoan (1)	1	0.01
White (6,115)	6,285	67.30
Not Hispanic (5,700)	5,846	62.60
Hispanic (415)	439	4.70

Kenilworth

Place Type: Borough
County: Union
Population: 7,914†

Ancestry‡	Population	%
African, Sub-Saharan (8)	8	0.10
Nigerian (8)	8	0.10
American (593)	593	7.59
Arab (13)	25	0.32
Lebanese (13)	13	0.17
Syrian (0)	12	0.15
Austrian (11)	90	1.15
Czech (31)	93	1.19
Czechoslovakian (15)	15	0.19
Danish (0)	22	0.28
Dutch (12)	12	0.15
Eastern European (15)	15	0.19
English (59)	291	3.73
French, ex. Basque (28)	34	0.44
French Canadian (0)	13	0.17
German (194)	796	10.19
Greek (47)	80	1.02
Hungarian (25)	51	0.65
Irish (131)	1,279	16.38
Italian (1,756)	2,613	33.46
Polish (199)	804	10.29
Portuguese (452)	464	5.94
Romanian (80)	94	1.20
Russian (63)	144	1.84
Scottish (9)	62	0.79
Slovak (29)	66	0.85
Swedish (0)	59	0.76
Swiss (0)	13	0.17
Turkish (0)	12	0.15
Ukrainian (64)	133	1.70
West Indian, ex. Hispanic (129)	158	2.02
Haitian (110)	139	1.78
Jamaican (19)	19	0.24

Hispanic Origin	Population	%
Hispanic or Latino (of any race)	1,228	15.52
Central American, ex. Mexican	89	1.12
Costa Rican	30	0.38
Guatemalan	16	0.20
Honduran	10	0.13
Nicaraguan	21	0.27
Panamanian	4	0.05
Salvadoran	8	0.10
Cuban	151	1.91
Dominican Republic	21	0.27
Mexican	180	2.27
Puerto Rican	231	2.92
South American	412	5.21
Argentinean	69	0.87
Chilean	18	0.23
Colombian	158	2.00
Ecuadorian	74	0.94
Paraguayan	1	0.01
Peruvian	58	0.73
Uruguayan	25	0.32
Venezuelan	3	0.04
Other South American	6	0.08
Other Hispanic or Latino	144	1.82

Race*	Population	%
African-American/Black (230)	269	3.40
Not Hispanic (213)	242	3.06
Hispanic (17)	27	0.34
American Indian/Alaska Native (11)	23	0.29
Not Hispanic (9)	18	0.23
Hispanic (2)	5	0.06
Apache (0)	1	0.01
Cherokee (0)	1	0.01
Mexican American Ind. (0)	1	0.01
South American Ind. (2)	2	0.03
Asian (304)	366	4.62
Not Hispanic (303)	357	4.51
Hispanic (1)	9	0.11
Chinese, ex. Taiwanese (40)	49	0.62
Filipino (119)	140	1.77
Indian (92)	108	1.36
Indonesian (1)	2	0.03
Japanese (13)	25	0.32
Korean (20)	22	0.28
Pakistani (8)	8	0.10
Thai (3)	3	0.04
Vietnamese (2)	2	0.03
Hawaii Native/Pacific Islander (2)	7	0.09
Not Hispanic (2)	5	0.06
Hispanic (0)	2	0.03
Guamanian/Chamorro (0)	1	0.01
Samoan (2)	2	0.03
White (6,970)	7,077	89.42
Not Hispanic (6,047)	6,111	77.22
Hispanic (923)	966	12.21

Kinnelon

Place Type: Borough
County: Morris
Population: 10,248†

Ancestry‡	Population	%
Albanian (79)	79	0.78
American (244)	244	2.40
Arab (47)	114	1.12
Palestinian (0)	9	0.09
Syrian (47)	105	1.03
Armenian (41)	69	0.68
Austrian (27)	95	0.93
British (27)	44	0.43
Canadian (0)	11	0.11
Croatian (13)	13	0.13
Cypriot (22)	22	0.22
Czech (61)	148	1.45
Danish (0)	17	0.17
Dutch (255)	567	5.57
Eastern European (26)	88	0.86
English (163)	1,039	10.21
European (109)	124	1.22
French, ex. Basque (46)	458	4.50
French Canadian (18)	81	0.80
German (383)	1,687	16.58
Greek (75)	165	1.62
Hungarian (87)	212	2.08
Iranian (20)	20	0.20
Irish (780)	2,500	24.57
Israeli (9)	9	0.09
Italian (1,036)	2,606	25.61
Latvian (0)	6	0.06
Lithuanian (20)	112	1.10
Macedonian (80)	80	0.79
Norwegian (78)	143	1.41
Polish (561)	1,145	11.25
Portuguese (0)	11	0.11
Romanian (42)	42	0.41
Russian (199)	517	5.08
Scotch-Irish (83)	159	1.56
Scottish (49)	191	1.88
Slavic (11)	11	0.11
Slovak (25)	48	0.47
Swedish (14)	230	2.26
Swiss (25)	87	0.85
Turkish (32)	32	0.31
Ukrainian (96)	164	1.61
Welsh (11)	65	0.64
Yugoslavian (0)	26	0.26

Hispanic Origin	Population	%
Hispanic or Latino (of any race)	418	4.08
Central American, ex. Mexican	16	0.16
Costa Rican	2	0.02
Guatemalan	2	0.02
Honduran	2	0.02
Panamanian	7	0.07
Salvadoran	3	0.03
Cuban	90	0.88
Dominican Republic	19	0.19
Mexican	40	0.39
Puerto Rican	110	1.07
South American	97	0.95
Argentinean	10	0.10
Bolivian	2	0.02
Chilean	3	0.03
Colombian	56	0.55
Ecuadorian	8	0.08
Peruvian	8	0.08
Uruguayan	1	0.01
Venezuelan	9	0.09
Other Hispanic or Latino	46	0.45

Race*	Population	%
African-American/Black (93)	125	1.22
Not Hispanic (86)	106	1.03
Hispanic (7)	19	0.19
American Indian/Alaska Native (5)	31	0.30
Not Hispanic (4)	21	0.20
Hispanic (1)	10	0.10
Cherokee (0)	5	0.05
Delaware (0)	1	0.01
Menominee (1)	1	0.01
Sioux (0)	5	0.05
Asian (437)	499	4.87
Not Hispanic (433)	492	4.80
Hispanic (4)	7	0.07
Bangladeshi (3)	3	0.03
Burmese (1)	1	0.01
Chinese, ex. Taiwanese (87)	103	1.01
Filipino (45)	73	0.71
Indian (176)	191	1.86
Japanese (9)	9	0.09
Korean (65)	73	0.71
Pakistani (19)	23	0.22
Sri Lankan (4)	4	0.04
Taiwanese (8)	8	0.08
Thai (4)	5	0.05
Vietnamese (10)	10	0.10
Hawaii Native/Pacific Islander (0)	2	0.02
Not Hispanic (0)	2	0.02
White (9,536)	9,652	94.18
Not Hispanic (9,204)	9,288	90.63
Hispanic (332)	364	3.55

Lacey

Place Type: Township
County: Ocean
Population: 27,644†

Ancestry‡	Population	%
Albanian (0)	11	0.04
American (631)	631	2.30
Arab (26)	26	0.09
Egyptian (26)	26	0.09
Armenian (38)	49	0.18
Austrian (29)	90	0.33
Basque (14)	14	0.05
Belgian (0)	37	0.13
British (9)	9	0.03
Canadian (50)	136	0.50
Croatian (0)	7	0.03
Czech (102)	213	0.78
Czechoslovakian (0)	31	0.11
Danish (11)	96	0.35
Dutch (99)	584	2.13
English (542)	2,821	10.27
Estonian (0)	11	0.04
European (208)	221	0.80
Finnish (15)	60	0.22
French, ex. Basque (22)	806	2.93
French Canadian (57)	109	0.40

*Notes: † The Census 2010 population figure is used to calculate the percentages in the Hispanic Origin and Race categories. Ancestry percentages are based on the 2006-2010 American Community Survey population (not shown); ‡ Numbers in parentheses indicate the number of people reporting a single ancestry; * Numbers in parentheses indicate the number of persons reporting this race alone, not in combination with any other race; Please refer to the Explanation of Data for more information.*

German (978)	6,687	24.34
Greek (241)	512	1.86
Hungarian (109)	710	2.58
Icelander (0)	97	0.35
Irish (2,038)	8,038	29.26
Italian (3,466)	8,890	32.36
Latvian (11)	11	0.04
Lithuanian (14)	124	0.45
Luxemburger (0)	19	0.07
Norwegian (89)	199	0.72
Polish (825)	2,601	9.47
Portuguese (96)	273	0.99
Russian (99)	563	2.05
Scandinavian (0)	19	0.07
Scotch-Irish (102)	362	1.32
Scottish (194)	625	2.28
Serbian (14)	14	0.05
Slavic (16)	54	0.20
Slovak (83)	258	0.94
Swedish (115)	317	1.15
Swiss (0)	54	0.20
Turkish (40)	40	0.15
Ukrainian (72)	240	0.87
Welsh (44)	233	0.85
West Indian, ex. Hispanic (15)	45	0.16
Dutch West Indian (0)	17	0.06
Jamaican (0)	13	0.05
Other West Indian (15)	15	0.05
Yugoslavian (0)	17	0.06

Hispanic Origin	Population	%
Hispanic or Latino (of any race)	1,310	4.74
Central American, ex. Mexican	59	0.21
Costa Rican	13	0.05
Guatemalan	21	0.08
Nicaraguan	3	0.01
Panamanian	2	0.01
Salvadoran	17	0.06
Other Central American	3	0.01
Cuban	101	0.37
Dominican Republic	26	0.09
Mexican	378	1.37
Puerto Rican	481	1.74
South American	126	0.46
Argentinean	6	0.02
Chilean	15	0.05
Colombian	49	0.18
Ecuadorian	18	0.07
Paraguayan	1	<0.01
Peruvian	29	0.10
Uruguayan	2	0.01
Venezuelan	6	0.02
Other Hispanic or Latino	139	0.50

Race*	Population	%
African-American/Black (167)	255	0.92
Not Hispanic (150)	214	0.77
Hispanic (17)	41	0.15
American Indian/Alaska Native (38)	141	0.51
Not Hispanic (24)	108	0.39
Hispanic (14)	33	0.12
Apache (0)	5	0.02
Blackfeet (3)	9	0.03
Central American Ind. (0)	2	0.01
Cherokee (3)	14	0.05
Chippewa (0)	1	<0.01
Choctaw (4)	4	0.01
Cree (1)	1	<0.01
Creek (0)	2	0.01
Delaware (2)	13	0.05
Iroquois (0)	1	<0.01
Mexican American Ind. (5)	5	0.02
Navajo (0)	2	0.01
Pima (1)	1	<0.01
Seminole (1)	4	0.01
South American Ind. (0)	6	0.02
Tlingit-Haida *(Alaska Native)* (2)	2	0.01
Asian (222)	326	1.18
Not Hispanic (221)	317	1.15
Hispanic (1)	9	0.03
Chinese, ex. Taiwanese (58)	63	0.23
Filipino (81)	121	0.44
Indian (33)	36	0.13
Indonesian (1)	2	0.01
Japanese (3)	20	0.07
Korean (23)	31	0.11
Laotian (1)	2	0.01
Malaysian (2)	2	0.01
Pakistani (2)	3	0.01
Taiwanese (1)	3	0.01
Thai (1)	1	<0.01
Vietnamese (12)	16	0.06
Hawaii Native/Pacific Islander (6)	19	0.07
Not Hispanic (6)	18	0.07
Hispanic (0)	1	<0.01
Guamanian/Chamorro (0)	1	<0.01
Native Hawaiian (6)	10	0.04
White (26,581)	26,878	97.23
Not Hispanic (25,659)	25,890	93.66
Hispanic (922)	988	3.57

Lake Mohawk

Place Type: CDP
County: Sussex
Population: 9,916†

Ancestry‡	Population	%
African, Sub-Saharan (13)	13	0.13
Ghanaian (13)	13	0.13
American (700)	700	6.98
Arab (0)	40	0.40
Egyptian (0)	11	0.11
Syrian (0)	29	0.29
Armenian (0)	12	0.12
Austrian (0)	32	0.32
Brazilian (36)	36	0.36
British (11)	31	0.31
Canadian (21)	30	0.30
Croatian (0)	23	0.23
Czech (18)	80	0.80
Czechoslovakian (35)	70	0.70
Danish (25)	67	0.67
Dutch (66)	378	3.77
Eastern European (28)	28	0.28
English (264)	1,333	13.28
European (58)	58	0.58
Finnish (35)	47	0.47
French, ex. Basque (30)	293	2.92
French Canadian (12)	41	0.41
German (531)	2,595	25.86
Greek (49)	172	1.71
Hungarian (44)	110	1.10
Iranian (23)	23	0.23
Irish (661)	2,410	24.02
Italian (816)	2,285	22.77
Lithuanian (21)	68	0.68
Luxemburger (13)	13	0.13
Norwegian (13)	94	0.94
Polish (460)	1,126	11.22
Portuguese (6)	15	0.15
Romanian (32)	44	0.44
Russian (54)	101	1.01
Scandinavian (0)	32	0.32
Scotch-Irish (86)	172	1.71
Scottish (42)	290	2.89
Slavic (0)	50	0.50
Slovak (27)	48	0.48
Swedish (26)	54	0.54
Swiss (27)	43	0.43
Ukrainian (24)	59	0.59
Welsh (16)	67	0.67

Hispanic Origin	Population	%
Hispanic or Latino (of any race)	473	4.77
Central American, ex. Mexican	31	0.31
Costa Rican	10	0.10
Guatemalan	11	0.11
Honduran	8	0.08
Salvadoran	2	0.02
Cuban	61	0.62
Dominican Republic	19	0.19
Mexican	53	0.53
Puerto Rican	155	1.56
South American	101	1.02
Argentinean	7	0.07
Bolivian	5	0.05
Chilean	5	0.05
Colombian	33	0.33
Ecuadorian	21	0.21
Paraguayan	1	0.01
Peruvian	20	0.20
Uruguayan	5	0.05
Venezuelan	4	0.04
Other Hispanic or Latino	53	0.53

Race*	Population	%
African-American/Black (60)	90	0.91
Not Hispanic (53)	73	0.74
Hispanic (7)	17	0.17
American Indian/Alaska Native (5)	39	0.39
Not Hispanic (5)	34	0.34
Hispanic (0)	5	0.05
Cherokee (0)	6	0.06
Comanche (0)	1	0.01
Crow (0)	1	0.01
Delaware (0)	1	0.01
Iroquois (1)	3	0.03
Sioux (0)	1	0.01
Ute (0)	2	0.02
Asian (151)	231	2.33
Not Hispanic (148)	218	2.20
Hispanic (3)	13	0.13
Cambodian (1)	1	0.01
Chinese, ex. Taiwanese (50)	71	0.72
Filipino (29)	53	0.53
Indian (27)	35	0.35
Indonesian (0)	1	0.01
Japanese (2)	12	0.12
Korean (22)	32	0.32
Malaysian (1)	1	0.01
Nepalese (1)	1	0.01
Taiwanese (1)	3	0.03
Thai (2)	2	0.02
Vietnamese (7)	10	0.10
Hawaii Native/Pacific Islander (0)	6	0.06
Not Hispanic (0)	4	0.04
Hispanic (0)	2	0.02
Native Hawaiian (0)	1	0.01
White (9,510)	9,647	97.29
Not Hispanic (9,115)	9,220	92.98
Hispanic (395)	427	4.31

Lakewood

Place Type: CDP
County: Ocean
Population: 53,805†

Ancestry‡	Population	%
African, Sub-Saharan (112)	172	0.35
African (40)	100	0.20
Nigerian (22)	22	0.04
South African (50)	50	0.10
Albanian (26)	26	0.05
American (6,834)	6,834	13.72
Arab (387)	994	2.00
Egyptian (194)	259	0.52
Moroccan (29)	466	0.94
Syrian (85)	124	0.25
Other Arab (79)	145	0.29
Australian (6)	6	0.01
Austrian (86)	107	0.21
Belgian (0)	23	0.05
British (28)	46	0.09
Canadian (281)	313	0.63
Czech (89)	239	0.48
Czechoslovakian (95)	129	0.26
Danish (11)	59	0.12
Dutch (33)	225	0.45

*Notes: † The Census 2010 population figure is used to calculate the percentages in the Hispanic Origin and Race categories. Ancestry percentages are based on the 2006-2010 American Community Survey population (not shown); ‡ Numbers in parentheses indicate the number of people reporting a single ancestry; * Numbers in parentheses indicate the number of persons reporting this race alone, not in combination with any other race; Please refer to the Explanation of Data for more information.*

Eastern European (1,410)	1,442	2.90
English (719)	967	1.94
Estonian (53)	53	0.11
European (2,339)	2,375	4.77
French, ex. Basque (111)	654	1.31
German (449)	1,726	3.47
Greek (17)	17	0.03
Guyanese (245)	245	0.49
Hungarian (1,402)	2,502	5.02
Iranian (0)	60	0.12
Irish (228)	788	1.58
Israeli (420)	589	1.18
Italian (497)	1,043	2.09
Latvian (25)	57	0.11
Lithuanian (407)	800	1.61
Norwegian (16)	56	0.11
Polish (2,671)	4,539	9.11
Portuguese (44)	132	0.27
Romanian (52)	168	0.34
Russian (695)	1,450	2.91
Scotch-Irish (1)	85	0.17
Scottish (37)	170	0.34
Swedish (7)	59	0.12
Swiss (21)	30	0.06
Ukrainian (327)	454	0.91
Welsh (0)	60	0.12
West Indian, ex. Hispanic (6)	23	0.05
Jamaican (6)	23	0.05
Yugoslavian (0)	16	0.03

Hispanic Origin	Population	%
Hispanic or Latino (of any race)	9,546	17.74
Central American, ex. Mexican	681	1.27
Costa Rican	134	0.25
Guatemalan	108	0.20
Honduran	103	0.19
Nicaraguan	38	0.07
Panamanian	19	0.04
Salvadoran	262	0.49
Other Central American	17	0.03
Cuban	64	0.12
Dominican Republic	187	0.35
Mexican	6,348	11.80
Puerto Rican	1,489	2.77
South American	401	0.75
Argentinean	30	0.06
Chilean	5	0.01
Colombian	120	0.22
Ecuadorian	112	0.21
Peruvian	100	0.19
Uruguayan	15	0.03
Venezuelan	16	0.03
Other South American	3	0.01
Other Hispanic or Latino	376	0.70

Race*	Population	%
African-American/Black (2,556)	2,783	5.17
Not Hispanic (2,262)	2,371	4.41
Hispanic (294)	412	0.77
American Indian/Alaska Native (149)	232	0.43
Not Hispanic (21)	67	0.12
Hispanic (128)	165	0.31
Blackfeet (1)	5	0.01
Canadian/French Am. Ind. (0)	1	<0.01
Cherokee (1)	6	0.01
Delaware (0)	1	<0.01
Hopi (1)	1	<0.01
Iroquois (0)	1	<0.01
Mexican American Ind. (51)	54	0.10
Pueblo (2)	2	<0.01
Sioux (2)	2	<0.01
South American Ind. (12)	15	0.03
Spanish American Ind. (3)	6	0.01
Asian (270)	344	0.64
Not Hispanic (249)	308	0.57
Hispanic (21)	36	0.07
Chinese, ex. Taiwanese (24)	38	0.07
Filipino (78)	86	0.16
Indian (97)	114	0.21
Japanese (10)	21	0.04
Korean (0)	4	0.01
Malaysian (1)	1	<0.01
Pakistani (13)	14	0.03
Thai (7)	7	0.01
Vietnamese (1)	4	0.01
Hawaii Native/Pacific Islander (14)	40	0.07
Not Hispanic (6)	20	0.04
Hispanic (8)	20	0.04
Native Hawaiian (7)	13	0.02
Samoan (4)	5	0.01
White (46,160)	46,725	86.84
Not Hispanic (41,438)	41,621	77.36
Hispanic (4,722)	5,104	9.49

Lakewood

Place Type: Township
County: Ocean
Population: 92,843†

Ancestry‡	Population	%
African, Sub-Saharan (361)	590	0.67
African (238)	339	0.39
Cape Verdean (0)	116	0.13
Nigerian (64)	64	0.07
Sierra Leonean (9)	9	0.01
South African (50)	62	0.07
Albanian (26)	35	0.04
American (10,480)	10,480	11.95
Arab (507)	1,312	1.50
Arab (0)	34	0.04
Egyptian (213)	339	0.39
Moroccan (41)	532	0.61
Palestinian (18)	60	0.07
Syrian (100)	139	0.16
Other Arab (135)	208	0.24
Armenian (10)	27	0.03
Australian (6)	31	0.04
Austrian (155)	235	0.27
Belgian (0)	126	0.14
Brazilian (0)	40	0.05
British (54)	72	0.08
Canadian (293)	430	0.49
Croatian (20)	20	0.02
Czech (144)	402	0.46
Czechoslovakian (168)	269	0.31
Danish (36)	123	0.14
Dutch (109)	463	0.53
Eastern European (1,733)	1,765	2.01
English (1,118)	2,861	3.26
Estonian (53)	53	0.06
European (3,040)	3,076	3.51
French, ex. Basque (111)	913	1.04
French Canadian (35)	97	0.11
German (1,484)	4,841	5.52
Greek (127)	189	0.22
Guyanese (245)	245	0.28
Hungarian (2,135)	3,772	4.30
Iranian (0)	60	0.07
Irish (1,857)	4,844	5.52
Israeli (489)	777	0.89
Italian (4,064)	6,450	7.36
Latvian (25)	57	0.07
Lithuanian (623)	1,181	1.35
Northern European (13)	13	0.01
Norwegian (29)	149	0.17
Polish (3,835)	6,788	7.74
Portuguese (55)	178	0.20
Romanian (148)	319	0.36
Russian (1,164)	2,742	3.13
Scotch-Irish (75)	288	0.33
Scottish (174)	555	0.63
Slavic (7)	7	0.01
Slovak (24)	139	0.16
Swedish (61)	153	0.17
Swiss (34)	99	0.11
Ukrainian (517)	755	0.86
Welsh (44)	145	0.17
West Indian, ex. Hispanic (210)	320	0.36
Haitian (36)	101	0.12
Jamaican (174)	219	0.25
Yugoslavian (0)	16	0.02

Hispanic Origin	Population	%
Hispanic or Latino (of any race)	16,062	17.30
Central American, ex. Mexican	1,147	1.24
Costa Rican	258	0.28
Guatemalan	142	0.15
Honduran	137	0.15
Nicaraguan	66	0.07
Panamanian	36	0.04
Salvadoran	474	0.51
Other Central American	34	0.04
Cuban	166	0.18
Dominican Republic	379	0.41
Mexican	9,661	10.41
Puerto Rican	3,127	3.37
South American	921	0.99
Argentinean	52	0.06
Chilean	16	0.02
Colombian	324	0.35
Ecuadorian	226	0.24
Paraguayan	1	<0.01
Peruvian	232	0.25
Uruguayan	30	0.03
Venezuelan	30	0.03
Other South American	10	0.01
Other Hispanic or Latino	661	0.71

Race*	Population	%
African-American/Black (5,898)	6,480	6.98
Not Hispanic (5,346)	5,692	6.13
Hispanic (552)	788	0.85
American Indian/Alaska Native (276)	500	0.54
Not Hispanic (39)	175	0.19
Hispanic (237)	325	0.35
Blackfeet (1)	18	0.02
Canadian/French Am. Ind. (0)	1	<0.01
Central American Ind. (0)	3	<0.01
Cherokee (6)	46	0.05
Cheyenne (0)	1	<0.01
Chippewa (0)	6	0.01
Choctaw (0)	1	<0.01
Delaware (1)	14	0.02
Hopi (1)	1	<0.01
Iroquois (0)	1	<0.01
Lumbee (0)	1	<0.01
Mexican American Ind. (75)	78	0.08
Navajo (1)	2	<0.01
Pueblo (2)	2	<0.01
Sioux (4)	5	0.01
South American Ind. (14)	17	0.02
Spanish American Ind. (3)	6	0.01
Asian (777)	963	1.04
Not Hispanic (737)	882	0.95
Hispanic (40)	81	0.09
Burmese (4)	4	<0.01
Cambodian (1)	2	<0.01
Chinese, ex. Taiwanese (88)	109	0.12
Filipino (297)	340	0.37
Indian (228)	259	0.28
Indonesian (2)	5	0.01
Japanese (21)	39	0.04
Korean (30)	48	0.05
Laotian (1)	2	<0.01
Malaysian (1)	1	<0.01
Pakistani (24)	25	0.03
Sri Lankan (0)	1	<0.01
Taiwanese (3)	5	0.01
Thai (14)	19	0.02
Vietnamese (20)	28	0.03
Hawaii Native/Pacific Islander (14)	73	0.08
Not Hispanic (6)	33	0.04
Hispanic (8)	40	0.04
Guamanian/Chamorro (0)	1	<0.01
Native Hawaiian (7)	29	0.03
Samoan (4)	11	0.01
White (78,290)	79,428	85.55
Not Hispanic (70,005)	70,460	75.89
Hispanic (8,285)	8,968	9.66

*Notes: † The Census 2010 population figure is used to calculate the percentages in the Hispanic Origin and Race categories. Ancestry percentages are based on the 2006-2010 American Community Survey population (not shown); ‡ Numbers in parentheses indicate the number of people reporting a single ancestry; * Numbers in parentheses indicate the number of persons reporting this race alone, not in combination with any other race; Please refer to the Explanation of Data for more information.*

Lawrence

Place Type: Township
County: Mercer
Population: 33,472†

Ancestry‡	Population	%
African, Sub-Saharan (241)	371	1.13
African (101)	179	0.55
Nigerian (42)	42	0.13
Senegalese (54)	80	0.24
South African (16)	16	0.05
Other Sub-Saharan African (28)	54	0.16
American (996)	996	3.04
Arab (103)	163	0.50
Egyptian (62)	62	0.19
Iraqi (11)	11	0.03
Lebanese (15)	48	0.15
Syrian (15)	15	0.05
Other Arab (0)	27	0.08
Austrian (82)	226	0.69
Belgian (0)	10	0.03
British (209)	304	0.93
Canadian (0)	25	0.08
Croatian (0)	22	0.07
Cypriot (79)	116	0.35
Czech (10)	105	0.32
Czechoslovakian (10)	38	0.12
Danish (14)	69	0.21
Dutch (112)	410	1.25
Eastern European (338)	356	1.09
English (508)	2,535	7.74
Estonian (19)	76	0.23
European (171)	190	0.58
Finnish (35)	35	0.11
French, ex. Basque (42)	416	1.27
French Canadian (25)	123	0.38
German (956)	3,839	11.72
Greek (40)	130	0.40
Hungarian (202)	524	1.60
Iranian (51)	51	0.16
Irish (738)	3,945	12.04
Israeli (52)	62	0.19
Italian (2,253)	5,307	16.20
Lithuanian (35)	233	0.71
Northern European (0)	26	0.08
Norwegian (116)	162	0.49
Pennsylvania German (14)	90	0.27
Polish (2,450)	4,120	12.58
Portuguese (0)	46	0.14
Romanian (29)	56	0.17
Russian (527)	1,126	3.44
Scandinavian (0)	51	0.16
Scotch-Irish (106)	381	1.16
Scottish (91)	460	1.40
Serbian (0)	10	0.03
Slavic (13)	99	0.30
Slovak (105)	326	1.00
Slovene (0)	13	0.04
Swedish (64)	220	0.67
Swiss (14)	44	0.13
Ukrainian (387)	533	1.63
Welsh (18)	225	0.69
West Indian, ex. Hispanic (239)	368	1.12
Bahamian (0)	8	0.02
Barbadian (0)	27	0.08
British West Indian (8)	8	0.02
Haitian (174)	252	0.77
Jamaican (27)	43	0.13
Trinidadian/Tobagonian (15)	15	0.05
West Indian (15)	15	0.05
Yugoslavian (0)	24	0.07

Hispanic Origin	Population	%
Hispanic or Latino (of any race)	2,503	7.48
Central American, ex. Mexican	578	1.73
Costa Rican	23	0.07
Guatemalan	500	1.49
Honduran	24	0.07
Nicaraguan	3	0.01
Panamanian	13	0.04
Salvadoran	15	0.04
Cuban	103	0.31
Dominican Republic	119	0.36
Mexican	505	1.51
Puerto Rican	635	1.90
South American	342	1.02
Argentinean	33	0.10
Bolivian	8	0.02
Chilean	19	0.06
Colombian	128	0.38
Ecuadorian	65	0.19
Paraguayan	1	<0.01
Peruvian	49	0.15
Uruguayan	12	0.04
Venezuelan	23	0.07
Other South American	4	0.01
Other Hispanic or Latino	221	0.66

Race*	Population	%
African-American/Black (3,602)	3,903	11.66
Not Hispanic (3,493)	3,726	11.13
Hispanic (109)	177	0.53
American Indian/Alaska Native (66)	185	0.55
Not Hispanic (55)	141	0.42
Hispanic (11)	44	0.13
Apache (1)	1	<0.01
Blackfeet (0)	6	0.02
Cherokee (1)	26	0.08
Chippewa (0)	1	<0.01
Creek (0)	2	0.01
Crow (1)	1	<0.01
Delaware (1)	3	0.01
Iroquois (0)	3	0.01
Lumbee (0)	5	0.01
Mexican American Ind. (2)	5	0.01
Osage (2)	2	0.01
Pima (0)	1	<0.01
Pueblo (0)	3	0.01
Seminole (0)	1	<0.01
Shoshone (0)	1	<0.01
Sioux (0)	2	0.01
South American Ind. (5)	12	0.04
Spanish American Ind. (3)	3	0.01
Asian (4,721)	5,104	15.25
Not Hispanic (4,711)	5,069	15.14
Hispanic (10)	35	0.10
Bangladeshi (34)	46	0.14
Burmese (6)	6	0.02
Cambodian (2)	3	0.01
Chinese, ex. Taiwanese (911)	995	2.97
Filipino (371)	415	1.24
Indian (2,541)	2,661	7.95
Indonesian (3)	4	0.01
Japanese (76)	116	0.35
Korean (250)	278	0.83
Malaysian (8)	8	0.02
Pakistani (217)	234	0.70
Sri Lankan (32)	38	0.11
Taiwanese (72)	81	0.24
Thai (9)	11	0.03
Vietnamese (67)	81	0.24
Hawaii Native/Pacific Islander (29)	142	0.42
Not Hispanic (29)	132	0.39
Hispanic (0)	10	0.03
Guamanian/Chamorro (0)	4	0.01
Native Hawaiian (4)	8	0.02
Samoan (1)	6	0.02
Tongan (1)	2	0.01
White (23,322)	23,883	71.35
Not Hispanic (22,003)	22,416	66.97
Hispanic (1,319)	1,467	4.38

Leonia

Place Type: Borough
County: Bergen
Population: 8,937†

Ancestry‡	Population	%
American (115)	115	1.29
Arab (78)	88	0.99
Egyptian (69)	69	0.78
Syrian (0)	10	0.11
Other Arab (9)	9	0.10
Armenian (32)	52	0.58
Austrian (0)	26	0.29
Brazilian (17)	17	0.19
British (14)	23	0.26
Bulgarian (37)	37	0.42
Croatian (46)	99	1.11
Czech (7)	23	0.26
Czechoslovakian (0)	10	0.11
Danish (0)	13	0.15
Dutch (11)	53	0.60
Eastern European (61)	61	0.69
English (77)	433	4.87
European (43)	51	0.57
French, ex. Basque (71)	125	1.41
French Canadian (0)	30	0.34
German (169)	489	5.50
Greek (76)	123	1.38
Hungarian (24)	52	0.58
Iranian (62)	70	0.79
Irish (235)	708	7.96
Italian (560)	997	11.21
Latvian (12)	12	0.13
Lithuanian (31)	50	0.56
Norwegian (0)	27	0.30
Polish (63)	287	3.23
Romanian (11)	11	0.12
Russian (163)	571	6.42
Scandinavian (0)	8	0.09
Scotch-Irish (12)	70	0.79
Scottish (8)	115	1.29
Slovak (75)	75	0.84
Swedish (8)	36	0.40
Turkish (19)	19	0.21
Ukrainian (15)	25	0.28
Welsh (0)	15	0.17
West Indian, ex. Hispanic (5)	26	0.29
West Indian (5)	26	0.29

Hispanic Origin	Population	%
Hispanic or Latino (of any race)	1,489	16.66
Central American, ex. Mexican	203	2.27
Costa Rican	10	0.11
Guatemalan	80	0.90
Honduran	6	0.07
Nicaraguan	7	0.08
Panamanian	3	0.03
Salvadoran	95	1.06
Other Central American	2	0.02
Cuban	240	2.69
Dominican Republic	222	2.48
Mexican	59	0.66
Puerto Rican	234	2.62
South American	422	4.72
Argentinean	39	0.44
Bolivian	5	0.06
Chilean	17	0.19
Colombian	199	2.23
Ecuadorian	101	1.13
Paraguayan	4	0.04
Peruvian	45	0.50
Uruguayan	3	0.03
Venezuelan	9	0.10
Other Hispanic or Latino	109	1.22

Race*	Population	%
African-American/Black (209)	296	3.31
Not Hispanic (169)	225	2.52
Hispanic (40)	71	0.79
American Indian/Alaska Native (14)	63	0.70
Not Hispanic (6)	38	0.43
Hispanic (8)	25	0.28
Blackfeet (0)	4	0.04
Central American Ind. (3)	3	0.03
Cherokee (1)	10	0.11

SECTION TWO

*Notes: † The Census 2010 population figure is used to calculate the percentages in the Hispanic Origin and Race categories. Ancestry percentages are based on the 2006-2010 American Community Survey population (not shown); ‡ Numbers in parentheses indicate the number of people reporting a single ancestry; * Numbers in parentheses indicate the number of persons reporting this race alone, not in combination with any other race; Please refer to the Explanation of Data for more information.*

Choctaw (0)	4	0.04
Creek (0)	3	0.03
Delaware (3)	3	0.03
Iroquois (1)	1	0.01
Mexican American Ind. (0)	1	0.01
Seminole (0)	2	0.02
Sioux (0)	1	0.01
South American Ind. (2)	6	0.07
Spanish American Ind. (0)	4	0.04
Yaqui (0)	3	0.03
Asian (3,139)	3,273	36.62
Not Hispanic (3,122)	3,241	36.26
Hispanic (17)	32	0.36
Bangladeshi (8)	8	0.09
Burmese (11)	11	0.12
Cambodian (2)	3	0.03
Chinese, ex. Taiwanese (215)	239	2.67
Filipino (135)	159	1.78
Indian (159)	176	1.97
Indonesian (7)	7	0.08
Japanese (126)	160	1.79
Korean (2,369)	2,426	27.15
Malaysian (3)	4	0.04
Nepalese (5)	5	0.06
Pakistani (13)	14	0.16
Sri Lankan (9)	10	0.11
Taiwanese (21)	24	0.27
Thai (1)	3	0.03
Vietnamese (8)	12	0.13
Hawaii Native/Pacific Islander (1)	9	0.10
Not Hispanic (0)	3	0.03
Hispanic (1)	6	0.07
Guamanian/Chamorro (1)	1	0.01
White (4,935)	5,194	58.12
Not Hispanic (3,941)	4,090	45.76
Hispanic (994)	1,104	12.35

Lincoln Park

Place Type: Borough
County: Morris
Population: 10,521†

Ancestry‡	Population	%
African, Sub-Saharan (40)	47	0.44
South African (40)	47	0.44
Albanian (147)	195	1.83
American (104)	104	0.98
Arab (72)	84	0.79
Egyptian (32)	32	0.30
Syrian (40)	52	0.49
Armenian (18)	18	0.17
Austrian (28)	153	1.44
Belgian (0)	19	0.18
Brazilian (0)	9	0.08
British (28)	45	0.42
Czech (18)	69	0.65
Danish (0)	94	0.88
Dutch (148)	478	4.50
Eastern European (9)	9	0.08
English (87)	631	5.94
European (25)	51	0.48
French, ex. Basque (15)	152	1.43
French Canadian (67)	149	1.40
German (378)	1,405	13.22
Greek (11)	97	0.91
Hungarian (21)	232	2.18
Irish (515)	2,189	20.59
Italian (1,311)	2,921	27.48
Latvian (0)	26	0.24
Lithuanian (16)	38	0.36
Macedonian (84)	93	0.87
Norwegian (0)	51	0.48
Polish (427)	1,111	10.45
Portuguese (19)	105	0.99
Romanian (7)	46	0.43
Russian (86)	339	3.19
Scotch-Irish (11)	85	0.80
Scottish (30)	253	2.38
Serbian (109)	109	1.03
Slavic (0)	11	0.10
Slovak (0)	41	0.39
Swedish (25)	33	0.31
Swiss (0)	27	0.25
Turkish (25)	25	0.24
Ukrainian (13)	56	0.53
Welsh (0)	46	0.43
Yugoslavian (52)	61	0.57

Hispanic Origin	Population	%
Hispanic or Latino (of any race)	1,009	9.59
Central American, ex. Mexican	40	0.38
Costa Rican	7	0.07
Guatemalan	13	0.12
Honduran	1	0.01
Nicaraguan	1	0.01
Panamanian	3	0.03
Salvadoran	15	0.14
Cuban	118	1.12
Dominican Republic	61	0.58
Mexican	72	0.68
Puerto Rican	374	3.55
South American	279	2.65
Argentinean	20	0.19
Chilean	12	0.11
Colombian	78	0.74
Ecuadorian	55	0.52
Peruvian	90	0.86
Uruguayan	11	0.10
Venezuelan	13	0.12
Other Hispanic or Latino	65	0.62

Race*	Population	%
African-American/Black (193)	258	2.45
Not Hispanic (165)	200	1.90
Hispanic (28)	58	0.55
American Indian/Alaska Native (21)	56	0.53
Not Hispanic (15)	45	0.43
Hispanic (6)	11	0.10
Cherokee (3)	15	0.14
Inupiat *(Alaska Native)* (2)	2	0.02
Iroquois (1)	2	0.02
Potawatomi (0)	1	0.01
Sioux (1)	3	0.03
South American Ind. (0)	2	0.02
Asian (776)	870	8.27
Not Hispanic (775)	861	8.18
Hispanic (1)	9	0.09
Bangladeshi (4)	4	0.04
Cambodian (0)	3	0.03
Chinese, ex. Taiwanese (110)	130	1.24
Filipino (266)	288	2.74
Indian (229)	253	2.40
Japanese (19)	28	0.27
Korean (75)	80	0.76
Pakistani (34)	35	0.33
Taiwanese (13)	14	0.13
Vietnamese (8)	19	0.18
Hawaii Native/Pacific Islander (0)	11	0.10
Not Hispanic (0)	9	0.09
Hispanic (0)	2	0.02
Guamanian/Chamorro (0)	1	0.01
Native Hawaiian (0)	3	0.03
White (9,075)	9,264	88.05
Not Hispanic (8,399)	8,528	81.06
Hispanic (676)	736	7.00

Linden

Place Type: City
County: Union
Population: 40,499†

Ancestry‡	Population	%
Afghan (10)	10	0.03
African, Sub-Saharan (253)	297	0.74
African (117)	149	0.37
Kenyan (0)	12	0.03
Nigerian (136)	136	0.34
Albanian (72)	82	0.21
Alsatian (36)	36	0.09
American (1,261)	1,261	3.16
Arab (12)	12	0.03
Moroccan (12)	12	0.03
Armenian (9)	19	0.05
Austrian (20)	84	0.21
Brazilian (336)	351	0.88
British (115)	115	0.29
Canadian (25)	25	0.06
Croatian (11)	11	0.03
Czech (69)	201	0.50
Czechoslovakian (118)	130	0.33
Danish (10)	16	0.04
Dutch (12)	108	0.27
Eastern European (9)	9	0.02
English (197)	633	1.58
European (79)	90	0.23
Finnish (0)	11	0.03
French, ex. Basque (30)	175	0.44
French Canadian (0)	11	0.03
German (623)	2,163	5.41
Greek (184)	300	0.75
Guyanese (258)	277	0.69
Hungarian (125)	228	0.57
Irish (683)	2,724	6.82
Italian (1,673)	3,524	8.82
Lithuanian (184)	354	0.89
Northern European (62)	62	0.16
Norwegian (12)	33	0.08
Polish (4,734)	6,086	15.23
Portuguese (1,013)	1,077	2.69
Romanian (16)	36	0.09
Russian (91)	338	0.85
Scotch-Irish (103)	174	0.44
Scottish (65)	159	0.40
Serbian (9)	9	0.02
Slavic (0)	10	0.03
Slovak (617)	900	2.25
Swedish (0)	108	0.27
Swiss (0)	10	0.03
Turkish (27)	27	0.07
Ukrainian (431)	660	1.65
Welsh (0)	49	0.12
West Indian, ex. Hispanic (2,118)	2,184	5.46
Haitian (1,671)	1,682	4.21
Jamaican (318)	355	0.89
Trinidadian/Tobagonian (0)	18	0.05
West Indian (116)	116	0.29
Other West Indian (13)	13	0.03

Hispanic Origin	Population	%
Hispanic or Latino (of any race)	10,095	24.93
Central American, ex. Mexican	1,019	2.52
Costa Rican	109	0.27
Guatemalan	137	0.34
Honduran	199	0.49
Nicaraguan	82	0.20
Panamanian	29	0.07
Salvadoran	457	1.13
Other Central American	6	0.01
Cuban	780	1.93
Dominican Republic	957	2.36
Mexican	295	0.73
Puerto Rican	2,484	6.13
South American	3,608	8.91
Argentinean	149	0.37
Bolivian	12	0.03
Chilean	43	0.11
Colombian	1,652	4.08
Ecuadorian	563	1.39
Paraguayan	1	<0.01
Peruvian	906	2.24
Uruguayan	209	0.52
Venezuelan	53	0.13
Other South American	20	0.05
Other Hispanic or Latino	952	2.35

Race*	Population	%
African-American/Black (10,888)	11,487	28.36
Not Hispanic (10,403)	10,788	26.64

*Notes: † The Census 2010 population figure is used to calculate the percentages in the Hispanic Origin and Race categories. Ancestry percentages are based on the 2006-2010 American Community Survey population (not shown); ‡ Numbers in parentheses indicate the number of people reporting a single ancestry; * Numbers in parentheses indicate the number of persons reporting this race alone, not in combination with any other race; Please refer to the Explanation of Data for more information.*

Hispanic (485)	699	1.73
American Indian/Alaska Native (118)	358	0.88
Not Hispanic (58)	223	0.55
Hispanic (60)	135	0.33
Apache (0)	2	<0.01
Blackfeet (1)	7	0.02
Central American Ind. (3)	9	0.02
Cherokee (5)	53	0.13
Cree (0)	2	<0.01
Delaware (10)	24	0.06
Iroquois (4)	13	0.03
Lumbee (2)	2	<0.01
Mexican American Ind. (5)	6	0.01
Osage (0)	3	0.01
Potawatomi (1)	1	<0.01
Shoshone (0)	1	<0.01
Sioux (0)	3	0.01
South American Ind. (13)	22	0.05
Spanish American Ind. (3)	9	0.02
Asian (1,099)	1,308	3.23
Not Hispanic (1,066)	1,226	3.03
Hispanic (33)	82	0.20
Bangladeshi (6)	6	0.01
Burmese (2)	2	<0.01
Cambodian (1)	1	<0.01
Chinese, ex. Taiwanese (129)	155	0.38
Filipino (374)	426	1.05
Indian (349)	399	0.99
Indonesian (0)	5	0.01
Japanese (22)	27	0.07
Korean (37)	49	0.12
Laotian (0)	2	<0.01
Malaysian (0)	2	<0.01
Pakistani (63)	74	0.18
Sri Lankan (11)	11	0.03
Taiwanese (2)	2	<0.01
Thai (4)	7	0.02
Vietnamese (52)	58	0.14
Hawaii Native/Pacific Islander (8)	79	0.20
Not Hispanic (8)	59	0.15
Hispanic (0)	20	0.05
Guamanian/Chamorro (5)	16	0.04
Native Hawaiian (2)	10	0.02
Samoan (0)	3	0.01
White (23,957)	24,976	61.67
Not Hispanic (18,089)	18,507	45.70
Hispanic (5,868)	6,469	15.97

Lindenwold

Place Type: Borough
County: Camden
Population: 17,613†

Ancestry‡	Population	%
African, Sub-Saharan (216)	226	1.28
African (151)	161	0.91
Ghanaian (52)	52	0.30
Sierra Leonean (13)	13	0.07
Albanian (0)	46	0.26
American (333)	333	1.89
Arab (82)	82	0.47
Egyptian (42)	42	0.24
Palestinian (25)	25	0.14
Other Arab (15)	15	0.09
Austrian (0)	20	0.11
Brazilian (26)	26	0.15
British (7)	7	0.04
Canadian (21)	35	0.20
Czech (6)	12	0.07
Danish (0)	14	0.08
Dutch (8)	32	0.18
English (237)	869	4.94
European (14)	14	0.08
French, ex. Basque (2)	226	1.28
French Canadian (0)	34	0.19
German (569)	2,501	14.21
German Russian (25)	25	0.14
Greek (0)	46	0.26
Hungarian (15)	118	0.67
Irish (450)	2,177	12.37
Italian (551)	1,570	8.92
Latvian (3)	3	0.02
Lithuanian (10)	17	0.10
Norwegian (5)	118	0.67
Pennsylvania German (0)	74	0.42
Polish (142)	471	2.68
Portuguese (102)	118	0.67
Romanian (51)	62	0.35
Russian (26)	177	1.01
Scotch-Irish (64)	169	0.96
Scottish (69)	262	1.49
Swedish (18)	75	0.43
Turkish (52)	63	0.36
Ukrainian (21)	47	0.27
Welsh (0)	22	0.12
West Indian, ex. Hispanic (146)	198	1.12
Haitian (70)	70	0.40
Jamaican (12)	51	0.29
Trinidadian/Tobagonian (45)	45	0.26
U.S. Virgin Islander (10)	10	0.06
West Indian (9)	22	0.12
Yugoslavian (0)	10	0.06

Hispanic Origin	Population	%
Hispanic or Latino (of any race)	3,673	20.85
Central American, ex. Mexican	1,233	7.00
Costa Rican	2	0.01
Guatemalan	22	0.12
Honduran	302	1.71
Nicaraguan	18	0.10
Panamanian	24	0.14
Salvadoran	849	4.82
Other Central American	16	0.09
Cuban	35	0.20
Dominican Republic	89	0.51
Mexican	1,070	6.08
Puerto Rican	955	5.42
South American	63	0.36
Argentinean	10	0.06
Bolivian	1	0.01
Chilean	2	0.01
Colombian	19	0.11
Ecuadorian	8	0.05
Paraguayan	3	0.02
Peruvian	12	0.07
Uruguayan	1	0.01
Venezuelan	7	0.04
Other Hispanic or Latino	228	1.29

Race*	Population	%
African-American/Black (6,104)	6,516	37.00
Not Hispanic (5,847)	6,161	34.98
Hispanic (257)	355	2.02
American Indian/Alaska Native (78)	240	1.36
Not Hispanic (27)	142	0.81
Hispanic (51)	98	0.56
Blackfeet (0)	4	0.02
Cherokee (4)	24	0.14
Cheyenne (0)	1	0.01
Chippewa (0)	1	0.01
Creek (0)	1	0.01
Delaware (1)	3	0.02
Menominee (1)	1	0.01
Mexican American Ind. (5)	17	0.10
Ottawa (0)	1	0.01
Sioux (0)	4	0.02
South American Ind. (5)	7	0.04
Spanish American Ind. (22)	32	0.18
Asian (493)	578	3.28
Not Hispanic (484)	563	3.20
Hispanic (9)	15	0.09
Bangladeshi (1)	3	0.02
Cambodian (5)	5	0.03
Chinese, ex. Taiwanese (61)	77	0.44
Filipino (122)	146	0.83
Indian (171)	194	1.10
Indonesian (7)	8	0.05
Japanese (4)	19	0.11
Korean (38)	40	0.23
Malaysian (1)	1	0.01
Pakistani (37)	38	0.22
Taiwanese (2)	2	0.01
Thai (2)	2	0.01
Vietnamese (36)	43	0.24
Hawaii Native/Pacific Islander (4)	30	0.17
Not Hispanic (4)	22	0.12
Hispanic (0)	8	0.05
Guamanian/Chamorro (1)	2	0.01
Native Hawaiian (2)	6	0.03
Samoan (1)	6	0.03
White (8,469)	8,929	50.70
Not Hispanic (7,123)	7,436	42.22
Hispanic (1,346)	1,493	8.48

Little Egg Harbor

Place Type: Township
County: Ocean
Population: 20,065†

Ancestry‡	Population	%
Albanian (0)	24	0.12
American (439)	439	2.25
Arab (10)	69	0.35
Arab (0)	28	0.14
Lebanese (0)	31	0.16
Syrian (10)	10	0.05
Armenian (17)	60	0.31
Austrian (12)	124	0.64
Belgian (13)	37	0.19
British (31)	83	0.43
Bulgarian (6)	6	0.03
Canadian (0)	21	0.11
Croatian (37)	98	0.50
Czech (7)	34	0.17
Czechoslovakian (21)	34	0.17
Danish (13)	21	0.11
Dutch (71)	356	1.83
English (314)	1,873	9.61
Estonian (17)	17	0.09
European (10)	10	0.05
Finnish (0)	64	0.33
French, ex. Basque (52)	453	2.33
French Canadian (23)	117	0.60
German (1,044)	4,876	25.03
Greek (83)	196	1.01
Hungarian (83)	399	2.05
Irish (1,596)	5,720	29.36
Italian (2,574)	5,785	29.70
Latvian (0)	7	0.04
Lithuanian (1)	95	0.49
Norwegian (86)	355	1.82
Pennsylvania German (26)	49	0.25
Polish (831)	2,410	12.37
Portuguese (36)	96	0.49
Romanian (0)	4	0.02
Russian (183)	323	1.66
Scandinavian (0)	38	0.20
Scotch-Irish (70)	282	1.45
Scottish (45)	369	1.89
Slavic (0)	10	0.05
Slovak (69)	204	1.05
Swedish (34)	103	0.53
Swiss (0)	69	0.35
Ukrainian (32)	60	0.31
Welsh (13)	139	0.71
West Indian, ex. Hispanic (0)	42	0.22
Haitian (0)	42	0.22
Yugoslavian (0)	12	0.06

Hispanic Origin	Population	%
Hispanic or Latino (of any race)	1,047	5.22
Central American, ex. Mexican	65	0.32
Costa Rican	6	0.03
Guatemalan	7	0.03
Honduran	29	0.14
Nicaraguan	3	0.01
Panamanian	6	0.03
Salvadoran	11	0.05

*Notes: † The Census 2010 population figure is used to calculate the percentages in the Hispanic Origin and Race categories. Ancestry percentages are based on the 2006-2010 American Community Survey population (not shown); ‡ Numbers in parentheses indicate the number of people reporting a single ancestry; * Numbers in parentheses indicate the number of persons reporting this race alone, not in combination with any other race; Please refer to the Explanation of Data for more information.*

Other Central American	3	0.01
Cuban	64	0.32
Dominican Republic	26	0.13
Mexican	241	1.20
Puerto Rican	445	2.22
South American	110	0.55
Argentinean	10	0.05
Bolivian	2	0.01
Colombian	35	0.17
Ecuadorian	22	0.11
Peruvian	41	0.20
Other Hispanic or Latino	96	0.48

Race*	Population	%
African-American/Black (271)	368	1.83
Not Hispanic (259)	342	1.70
Hispanic (12)	26	0.13
American Indian/Alaska Native (33)	98	0.49
Not Hispanic (26)	81	0.40
Hispanic (7)	17	0.08
Apache (0)	2	0.01
Blackfeet (0)	7	0.03
Canadian/French Am. Ind. (1)	1	<0.01
Cherokee (8)	25	0.12
Comanche (1)	1	<0.01
Delaware (2)	6	0.03
Hopi (2)	2	0.01
Iroquois (1)	6	0.03
Lumbee (2)	2	0.01
Ottawa (1)	1	<0.01
Seminole (0)	3	0.01
South American Ind. (4)	10	0.05
Asian (249)	316	1.57
Not Hispanic (249)	311	1.55
Hispanic (0)	5	0.02
Cambodian (3)	3	0.01
Chinese, ex. Taiwanese (48)	56	0.28
Filipino (106)	131	0.65
Indian (26)	26	0.13
Indonesian (0)	1	<0.01
Japanese (8)	20	0.10
Korean (29)	47	0.23
Laotian (1)	3	0.01
Pakistani (14)	14	0.07
Sri Lankan (1)	1	<0.01
Taiwanese (1)	1	<0.01
Thai (2)	6	0.03
Vietnamese (4)	4	0.02
Hawaii Native/Pacific Islander (2)	7	0.03
Not Hispanic (1)	5	0.02
Hispanic (1)	2	0.01
Guamanian/Chamorro (1)	1	<0.01
Native Hawaiian (1)	1	<0.01
White (18,899)	19,197	95.67
Not Hispanic (18,272)	18,471	92.06
Hispanic (627)	726	3.62

Little Falls

Place Type: Township
County: Passaic
Population: 14,432†

Ancestry‡	Population	%
Albanian (142)	217	1.56
American (209)	209	1.51
Arab (919)	1,000	7.21
Egyptian (108)	108	0.78
Lebanese (128)	153	1.10
Palestinian (115)	154	1.11
Syrian (560)	577	4.16
Other Arab (8)	8	0.06
Armenian (0)	16	0.12
Assyrian/Chaldean/Syriac (0)	17	0.12
Austrian (0)	33	0.24
Belgian (15)	26	0.19
Brazilian (10)	10	0.07
Canadian (0)	14	0.10
Carpatho Rusyn (13)	13	0.09
Croatian (0)	19	0.14
Czech (0)	44	0.32
Danish (13)	46	0.33
Dutch (113)	491	3.54
Eastern European (13)	13	0.09
English (114)	505	3.64
European (64)	64	0.46
French, ex. Basque (47)	169	1.22
French Canadian (21)	66	0.48
German (420)	1,648	11.88
Greek (15)	25	0.18
Guyanese (8)	8	0.06
Hungarian (36)	189	1.36
Irish (1,161)	2,522	18.18
Italian (2,127)	4,048	29.17
Lithuanian (0)	31	0.22
Macedonian (31)	31	0.22
Norwegian (14)	49	0.35
Polish (344)	883	6.36
Portuguese (173)	351	2.53
Romanian (0)	27	0.19
Russian (133)	403	2.90
Scotch-Irish (74)	198	1.43
Scottish (0)	122	0.88
Serbian (30)	30	0.22
Slovak (35)	71	0.51
Swedish (0)	111	0.80
Swiss (0)	74	0.53
Ukrainian (30)	106	0.76
Welsh (0)	16	0.12
West Indian, ex. Hispanic (0)	13	0.09
West Indian (0)	13	0.09
Yugoslavian (0)	30	0.22

Hispanic Origin	Population	%
Hispanic or Latino (of any race)	1,428	9.89
Central American, ex. Mexican	95	0.66
Costa Rican	20	0.14
Guatemalan	18	0.12
Honduran	24	0.17
Nicaraguan	6	0.04
Panamanian	4	0.03
Salvadoran	20	0.14
Other Central American	3	0.02
Cuban	115	0.80
Dominican Republic	127	0.88
Mexican	99	0.69
Puerto Rican	406	2.81
South American	383	2.65
Argentinean	27	0.19
Chilean	25	0.17
Colombian	153	1.06
Ecuadorian	53	0.37
Paraguayan	1	0.01
Peruvian	110	0.76
Uruguayan	5	0.03
Venezuelan	6	0.04
Other South American	3	0.02
Other Hispanic or Latino	203	1.41

Race*	Population	%
African-American/Black (593)	670	4.64
Not Hispanic (549)	605	4.19
Hispanic (44)	65	0.45
American Indian/Alaska Native (22)	61	0.42
Not Hispanic (13)	45	0.31
Hispanic (9)	16	0.11
Blackfeet (0)	4	0.03
Central American Ind. (6)	6	0.04
Cherokee (2)	13	0.09
Choctaw (0)	3	0.02
Creek (0)	2	0.01
Delaware (2)	5	0.03
Iroquois (1)	1	0.01
Mexican American Ind. (2)	5	0.03
Seminole (0)	1	0.01
South American Ind. (1)	1	0.01
Asian (658)	793	5.49
Not Hispanic (652)	778	5.39
Hispanic (6)	15	0.10
Bangladeshi (9)	15	0.10
Cambodian (0)	1	0.01
Chinese, ex. Taiwanese (106)	124	0.86
Filipino (121)	152	1.05
Indian (252)	268	1.86
Japanese (6)	24	0.17
Korean (74)	78	0.54
Pakistani (31)	32	0.22
Sri Lankan (0)	4	0.03
Taiwanese (7)	7	0.05
Thai (3)	4	0.03
Vietnamese (38)	40	0.28
Hawaii Native/Pacific Islander (1)	15	0.10
Not Hispanic (1)	15	0.10
Samoan (1)	3	0.02
White (12,510)	12,763	88.44
Not Hispanic (11,530)	11,716	81.18
Hispanic (980)	1,047	7.25

Little Ferry

Place Type: Borough
County: Bergen
Population: 10,626†

Ancestry‡	Population	%
African, Sub-Saharan (9)	51	0.48
African (9)	42	0.40
Other Sub-Saharan African (0)	9	0.08
Albanian (28)	28	0.26
American (46)	46	0.43
Arab (198)	198	1.87
Jordanian (114)	114	1.08
Lebanese (48)	48	0.45
Palestinian (36)	36	0.34
Armenian (24)	24	0.23
Croatian (100)	113	1.07
Czech (54)	201	1.90
Czechoslovakian (12)	12	0.11
Danish (12)	22	0.21
Dutch (0)	23	0.22
Eastern European (25)	38	0.36
English (30)	173	1.63
European (84)	84	0.79
Finnish (0)	11	0.10
French, ex. Basque (0)	182	1.72
French Canadian (9)	30	0.28
German (149)	622	5.87
Greek (163)	163	1.54
Hungarian (96)	120	1.13
Irish (245)	912	8.60
Italian (1,559)	2,253	21.25
Lithuanian (11)	22	0.21
Norwegian (0)	20	0.19
Polish (74)	320	3.02
Portuguese (30)	30	0.28
Russian (12)	35	0.33
Scotch-Irish (24)	40	0.38
Scottish (0)	19	0.18
Slovak (10)	32	0.30
Swedish (0)	20	0.19
Turkish (143)	143	1.35
Ukrainian (20)	31	0.29
Welsh (0)	14	0.13
West Indian, ex. Hispanic (24)	54	0.51
West Indian (24)	54	0.51
Yugoslavian (0)	13	0.12

Hispanic Origin	Population	%
Hispanic or Latino (of any race)	2,442	22.98
Central American, ex. Mexican	182	1.71
Costa Rican	23	0.22
Guatemalan	29	0.27
Honduran	23	0.22
Nicaraguan	10	0.09
Panamanian	3	0.03
Salvadoran	91	0.86
Other Central American	3	0.03
Cuban	258	2.43
Dominican Republic	420	3.95
Mexican	101	0.95

*Notes: † The Census 2010 population figure is used to calculate the percentages in the Hispanic Origin and Race categories. Ancestry percentages are based on the 2006-2010 American Community Survey population (not shown); ‡ Numbers in parentheses indicate the number of people reporting a single ancestry; * Numbers in parentheses indicate the number of persons reporting this race alone, not in combination with any other race; Please refer to the Explanation of Data for more information.*

Puerto Rican	448	4.22
South American	802	7.55
Argentinean	34	0.32
Bolivian	2	0.02
Chilean	3	0.03
Colombian	380	3.58
Ecuadorian	268	2.52
Peruvian	87	0.82
Uruguayan	17	0.16
Venezuelan	6	0.06
Other South American	5	0.05
Other Hispanic or Latino	231	2.17

Race*	Population	%
African-American/Black (419)	499	4.70
Not Hispanic (366)	413	3.89
Hispanic (53)	86	0.81
American Indian/Alaska Native (32)	91	0.86
Not Hispanic (22)	53	0.50
Hispanic (10)	38	0.36
Cherokee (0)	4	0.04
Delaware (3)	5	0.05
Houma (3)	3	0.03
Iroquois (1)	1	0.01
Mexican American Ind. (1)	1	0.01
Sioux (2)	2	0.02
South American Ind. (1)	7	0.07
Asian (2,576)	2,735	25.74
Not Hispanic (2,550)	2,695	25.36
Hispanic (26)	40	0.38
Bangladeshi (0)	5	0.05
Chinese, ex. Taiwanese (72)	82	0.77
Filipino (473)	500	4.71
Indian (428)	493	4.64
Indonesian (1)	1	0.01
Japanese (125)	139	1.31
Korean (1,271)	1,315	12.38
Malaysian (0)	2	0.02
Nepalese (3)	3	0.03
Pakistani (105)	132	1.24
Taiwanese (2)	3	0.03
Thai (2)	2	0.02
Vietnamese (22)	25	0.24
Hawaii Native/Pacific Islander (4)	7	0.07
Not Hispanic (2)	4	0.04
Hispanic (2)	3	0.03
Native Hawaiian (2)	2	0.02
White (6,458)	6,745	63.48
Not Hispanic (5,016)	5,143	48.40
Hispanic (1,442)	1,602	15.08

Livingston

Place Type: Township
County: Essex
Population: 29,366†

Ancestry‡	Population	%
Albanian (51)	51	0.18
American (1,659)	1,659	5.76
Arab (61)	158	0.55
Egyptian (32)	49	0.17
Lebanese (11)	22	0.08
Syrian (18)	74	0.26
Other Arab (0)	13	0.05
Armenian (18)	52	0.18
Austrian (142)	536	1.86
Belgian (8)	19	0.07
Brazilian (46)	46	0.16
British (21)	33	0.11
Canadian (49)	74	0.26
Croatian (0)	48	0.17
Czech (50)	136	0.47
Czechoslovakian (20)	45	0.16
Danish (0)	51	0.18
Dutch (23)	113	0.39
Eastern European (1,284)	1,284	4.46
English (275)	900	3.12
European (366)	407	1.41
French, ex. Basque (22)	128	0.44
French Canadian (0)	12	0.04
German (407)	2,122	7.37
Greek (103)	187	0.65
Hungarian (166)	309	1.07
Iranian (66)	66	0.23
Irish (853)	2,763	9.59
Israeli (256)	311	1.08
Italian (2,617)	4,546	15.78
Latvian (64)	64	0.22
Lithuanian (18)	52	0.18
Maltese (0)	9	0.03
New Zealander (0)	9	0.03
Northern European (0)	12	0.04
Norwegian (73)	116	0.40
Polish (832)	2,427	8.42
Portuguese (161)	167	0.58
Romanian (80)	270	0.94
Russian (1,355)	2,881	10.00
Scotch-Irish (36)	113	0.39
Scottish (93)	136	0.47
Slovak (46)	55	0.19
Swedish (34)	110	0.38
Swiss (0)	10	0.03
Ukrainian (327)	444	1.54
Welsh (0)	36	0.12
West Indian, ex. Hispanic (23)	23	0.08
Haitian (12)	12	0.04
Jamaican (11)	11	0.04
Yugoslavian (18)	29	0.10

Hispanic Origin	Population	%
Hispanic or Latino (of any race)	1,192	4.06
Central American, ex. Mexican	51	0.17
Costa Rican	15	0.05
Guatemalan	8	0.03
Honduran	3	0.01
Nicaraguan	1	<0.01
Panamanian	3	0.01
Salvadoran	21	0.07
Cuban	114	0.39
Dominican Republic	62	0.21
Mexican	105	0.36
Puerto Rican	200	0.68
South American	485	1.65
Argentinean	44	0.15
Bolivian	7	0.02
Chilean	10	0.03
Colombian	86	0.29
Ecuadorian	94	0.32
Paraguayan	4	0.01
Peruvian	185	0.63
Uruguayan	39	0.13
Venezuelan	11	0.04
Other South American	5	0.02
Other Hispanic or Latino	175	0.60

Race*	Population	%
African-American/Black (663)	738	2.51
Not Hispanic (632)	687	2.34
Hispanic (31)	51	0.17
American Indian/Alaska Native (20)	58	0.20
Not Hispanic (9)	43	0.15
Hispanic (11)	15	0.05
Cherokee (4)	9	0.03
Cree (0)	2	0.01
Creek (0)	1	<0.01
Delaware (1)	5	0.02
Mexican American Ind. (2)	3	0.01
Seminole (0)	4	0.01
Sioux (0)	1	<0.01
South American Ind. (3)	5	0.02
Ute (2)	2	0.01
Asian (5,642)	5,912	20.13
Not Hispanic (5,609)	5,862	19.96
Hispanic (33)	50	0.17
Bangladeshi (1)	1	<0.01
Burmese (1)	1	<0.01
Cambodian (1)	3	0.01
Chinese, ex. Taiwanese (2,590)	2,722	9.27
Filipino (602)	677	2.31
Indian (1,230)	1,282	4.37
Indonesian (17)	22	0.07
Japanese (36)	66	0.22
Korean (603)	633	2.16
Malaysian (4)	6	0.02
Nepalese (3)	3	0.01
Pakistani (77)	83	0.28
Sri Lankan (7)	7	0.02
Taiwanese (286)	313	1.07
Thai (24)	33	0.11
Vietnamese (36)	48	0.16
Hawaii Native/Pacific Islander (5)	18	0.06
Not Hispanic (5)	18	0.06
Native Hawaiian (1)	6	0.02
Samoan (1)	2	0.01
White (22,367)	22,709	77.33
Not Hispanic (21,535)	21,813	74.28
Hispanic (832)	896	3.05

Lodi

Place Type: Borough
County: Bergen
Population: 24,136†

Ancestry‡	Population	%
African, Sub-Saharan (77)	132	0.55
African (40)	95	0.40
South African (37)	37	0.15
Albanian (409)	436	1.82
American (307)	307	1.28
Arab (935)	960	4.01
Arab (382)	382	1.59
Egyptian (93)	93	0.39
Iraqi (4)	4	0.02
Jordanian (228)	234	0.98
Lebanese (136)	136	0.57
Syrian (11)	30	0.13
Other Arab (81)	81	0.34
Armenian (25)	94	0.39
Assyrian/Chaldean/Syriac (0)	39	0.16
Austrian (0)	19	0.08
Belgian (0)	6	0.03
Brazilian (11)	11	0.05
British (15)	15	0.06
Croatian (49)	156	0.65
Czech (10)	61	0.25
Danish (0)	10	0.04
Dutch (29)	137	0.57
English (132)	274	1.14
Estonian (0)	41	0.17
French, ex. Basque (173)	219	0.91
French Canadian (9)	42	0.18
German (250)	1,210	5.05
Greek (254)	346	1.44
Hungarian (56)	162	0.68
Iranian (0)	15	0.06
Irish (526)	1,708	7.13
Israeli (5)	5	0.02
Italian (4,785)	6,652	27.75
Macedonian (26)	53	0.22
Norwegian (0)	44	0.18
Polish (1,683)	2,229	9.30
Portuguese (663)	796	3.32
Russian (100)	294	1.23
Scotch-Irish (56)	247	1.03
Scottish (0)	32	0.13
Serbian (9)	9	0.04
Slovak (31)	41	0.17
Swedish (0)	54	0.23
Swiss (21)	49	0.20
Turkish (248)	286	1.19
Ukrainian (12)	95	0.40
Welsh (0)	4	0.02
West Indian, ex. Hispanic (228)	228	0.95
Barbadian (16)	16	0.07
Belizean (19)	19	0.08
British West Indian (2)	2	0.01
Haitian (30)	30	0.13
Jamaican (121)	121	0.50

*Notes: † The Census 2010 population figure is used to calculate the percentages in the Hispanic Origin and Race categories. Ancestry percentages are based on the 2006-2010 American Community Survey population (not shown); ‡ Numbers in parentheses indicate the number of people reporting a single ancestry; * Numbers in parentheses indicate the number of persons reporting this race alone, not in combination with any other race; Please refer to the Explanation of Data for more information.*

Trinidadian/Tobagonian (33)	33	0.14
West Indian (7)	7	0.03
Yugoslavian (87)	133	0.55

Hispanic Origin	Population	%
Hispanic or Latino (of any race)	7,360	30.49
Central American, ex. Mexican	438	1.81
Costa Rican	72	0.30
Guatemalan	46	0.19
Honduran	57	0.24
Nicaraguan	17	0.07
Panamanian	15	0.06
Salvadoran	225	0.93
Other Central American	6	0.02
Cuban	256	1.06
Dominican Republic	1,396	5.78
Mexican	444	1.84
Puerto Rican	1,442	5.97
South American	2,824	11.70
Argentinean	128	0.53
Bolivian	26	0.11
Chilean	24	0.10
Colombian	1,197	4.96
Ecuadorian	682	2.83
Paraguayan	1	<0.01
Peruvian	705	2.92
Uruguayan	18	0.07
Venezuelan	37	0.15
Other South American	6	0.02
Other Hispanic or Latino	560	2.32

Race*	Population	%
African-American/Black (1,816)	2,082	8.63
Not Hispanic (1,589)	1,715	7.11
Hispanic (227)	367	1.52
American Indian/Alaska Native (101)	200	0.83
Not Hispanic (31)	81	0.34
Hispanic (70)	119	0.49
Blackfeet (5)	7	0.03
Central American Ind. (1)	2	0.01
Cherokee (4)	13	0.05
Chippewa (0)	1	<0.01
Creek (0)	1	<0.01
Delaware (5)	5	0.02
Mexican American Ind. (7)	10	0.04
Osage (0)	1	<0.01
South American Ind. (5)	23	0.10
Spanish American Ind. (2)	2	0.01
Tohono O'Odham (2)	2	0.01
Asian (2,069)	2,363	9.79
Not Hispanic (2,036)	2,276	9.43
Hispanic (33)	87	0.36
Bangladeshi (20)	20	0.08
Burmese (0)	1	<0.01
Cambodian (1)	1	<0.01
Chinese, ex. Taiwanese (110)	138	0.57
Filipino (583)	642	2.66
Indian (1,068)	1,136	4.71
Japanese (30)	49	0.20
Korean (84)	95	0.39
Laotian (14)	16	0.07
Pakistani (92)	103	0.43
Sri Lankan (8)	8	0.03
Taiwanese (8)	9	0.04
Thai (9)	11	0.05
Vietnamese (8)	10	0.04
Hawaii Native/Pacific Islander (15)	53	0.22
Not Hispanic (10)	32	0.13
Hispanic (5)	21	0.09
Guamanian/Chamorro (3)	4	0.02
Native Hawaiian (10)	13	0.05
Samoan (0)	1	<0.01
White (16,459)	17,179	71.18
Not Hispanic (12,592)	12,921	53.53
Hispanic (3,867)	4,258	17.64

Long Branch

Place Type: City
County: Monmouth
Population: 30,719†

Ancestry‡	Population	%
African, Sub-Saharan (32)	71	0.23
African (18)	57	0.18
Nigerian (14)	14	0.05
Albanian (17)	17	0.06
American (1,099)	1,099	3.56
Arab (406)	507	1.64
Arab (27)	27	0.09
Egyptian (46)	46	0.15
Lebanese (32)	56	0.18
Moroccan (91)	115	0.37
Syrian (198)	251	0.81
Other Arab (12)	12	0.04
Austrian (58)	167	0.54
Basque (0)	17	0.06
Brazilian (2,396)	2,702	8.76
British (54)	54	0.18
Croatian (0)	10	0.03
Czech (0)	18	0.06
Czechoslovakian (0)	21	0.07
Dutch (71)	206	0.67
Eastern European (31)	31	0.10
English (118)	816	2.64
European (45)	45	0.15
French, ex. Basque (53)	272	0.88
French Canadian (36)	54	0.18
German (483)	1,907	6.18
Greek (59)	98	0.32
Hungarian (25)	186	0.60
Iranian (41)	41	0.13
Irish (891)	3,025	9.80
Israeli (34)	34	0.11
Italian (3,017)	4,837	15.68
Lithuanian (56)	66	0.21
Norwegian (10)	72	0.23
Polish (436)	1,254	4.06
Portuguese (585)	756	2.45
Romanian (11)	43	0.14
Russian (203)	498	1.61
Scotch-Irish (117)	176	0.57
Scottish (57)	191	0.62
Swedish (37)	179	0.58
Swiss (13)	27	0.09
Turkish (25)	25	0.08
Ukrainian (79)	90	0.29
Welsh (10)	92	0.30
West Indian, ex. Hispanic (167)	167	0.54
Belizean (14)	14	0.05
Haitian (95)	95	0.31
Trinidadian/Tobagonian (18)	18	0.06
West Indian (40)	40	0.13

Hispanic Origin	Population	%
Hispanic or Latino (of any race)	8,624	28.07
Central American, ex. Mexican	1,499	4.88
Costa Rican	88	0.29
Guatemalan	479	1.56
Honduran	147	0.48
Nicaraguan	35	0.11
Panamanian	14	0.05
Salvadoran	733	2.39
Other Central American	3	0.01
Cuban	103	0.34
Dominican Republic	215	0.70
Mexican	3,496	11.38
Puerto Rican	2,187	7.12
South American	655	2.13
Argentinean	48	0.16
Bolivian	7	0.02
Chilean	87	0.28
Colombian	231	0.75
Ecuadorian	166	0.54
Paraguayan	5	0.02
Peruvian	84	0.27
Uruguayan	8	0.03
Venezuelan	13	0.04
Other South American	6	0.02
Other Hispanic or Latino	469	1.53

Race*	Population	%
African-American/Black (4,364)	4,869	15.85
Not Hispanic (3,946)	4,330	14.10
Hispanic (418)	539	1.75
American Indian/Alaska Native (170)	423	1.38
Not Hispanic (55)	162	0.53
Hispanic (115)	261	0.85
Apache (0)	2	0.01
Blackfeet (2)	15	0.05
Cherokee (9)	35	0.11
Chippewa (0)	1	<0.01
Choctaw (0)	1	<0.01
Cree (0)	1	<0.01
Creek (0)	1	<0.01
Delaware (2)	5	0.02
Mexican American Ind. (32)	39	0.13
Navajo (1)	1	<0.01
Osage (0)	1	<0.01
Ottawa (0)	1	<0.01
Paiute (3)	3	0.01
Potawatomi (0)	1	<0.01
Seminole (0)	1	<0.01
Sioux (0)	5	0.02
South American Ind. (6)	8	0.03
Spanish American Ind. (8)	14	0.05
Tlingit-Haida *(Alaska Native)* (0)	1	<0.01
Asian (655)	815	2.65
Not Hispanic (633)	770	2.51
Hispanic (22)	45	0.15
Burmese (3)	3	0.01
Cambodian (6)	6	0.02
Chinese, ex. Taiwanese (111)	139	0.45
Filipino (166)	200	0.65
Hmong (1)	1	<0.01
Indian (239)	279	0.91
Indonesian (0)	3	0.01
Japanese (13)	31	0.10
Korean (70)	91	0.30
Pakistani (16)	18	0.06
Sri Lankan (0)	1	<0.01
Taiwanese (4)	5	0.02
Thai (1)	4	0.01
Vietnamese (5)	14	0.05
Hawaii Native/Pacific Islander (24)	73	0.24
Not Hispanic (19)	45	0.15
Hispanic (5)	28	0.09
Guamanian/Chamorro (0)	1	<0.01
Native Hawaiian (10)	22	0.07
Samoan (1)	3	0.01
White (20,060)	21,241	69.15
Not Hispanic (15,939)	16,581	53.98
Hispanic (4,121)	4,660	15.17

Long Hill

Place Type: Township
County: Morris
Population: 8,702†

Ancestry‡	Population	%
Alsatian (0)	22	0.25
American (359)	359	4.11
Arab (20)	30	0.34
Jordanian (20)	20	0.23
Lebanese (0)	10	0.11
Austrian (34)	114	1.30
Belgian (0)	18	0.21
Brazilian (13)	37	0.42
British (0)	18	0.21
Bulgarian (69)	69	0.79
Canadian (0)	61	0.70
Celtic (0)	29	0.33
Czech (61)	233	2.67
Czechoslovakian (0)	69	0.79
Danish (10)	41	0.47

*Notes: † The Census 2010 population figure is used to calculate the percentages in the Hispanic Origin and Race categories. Ancestry percentages are based on the 2006-2010 American Community Survey population (not shown); ‡ Numbers in parentheses indicate the number of people reporting a single ancestry; * Numbers in parentheses indicate the number of persons reporting this race alone, not in combination with any other race; Please refer to the Explanation of Data for more information.*

Dutch (0)	47	0.54
Eastern European (10)	10	0.11
English (158)	838	9.59
European (124)	124	1.42
French, ex. Basque (26)	295	3.38
French Canadian (9)	27	0.31
German (451)	1,490	17.05
Greek (0)	16	0.18
Hungarian (34)	90	1.03
Irish (547)	2,003	22.92
Italian (744)	2,075	23.74
Lithuanian (18)	94	1.08
Maltese (0)	17	0.19
Norwegian (23)	132	1.51
Polish (69)	653	7.47
Portuguese (153)	177	2.03
Romanian (18)	28	0.32
Russian (120)	376	4.30
Scotch-Irish (66)	147	1.68
Scottish (88)	177	2.03
Serbian (68)	68	0.78
Slavic (9)	27	0.31
Slovak (15)	24	0.27
Slovene (0)	16	0.18
Swedish (0)	62	0.71
Swiss (0)	43	0.49
Ukrainian (23)	76	0.87
Welsh (0)	13	0.15
West Indian, ex. Hispanic (16)	16	0.18
Jamaican (16)	16	0.18
Yugoslavian (0)	39	0.45

Hispanic Origin	Population	%
Hispanic or Latino (of any race)	614	7.06
Central American, ex. Mexican	176	2.02
Costa Rican	113	1.30
Guatemalan	14	0.16
Honduran	12	0.14
Nicaraguan	2	0.02
Panamanian	1	0.01
Salvadoran	32	0.37
Other Central American	2	0.02
Cuban	59	0.68
Dominican Republic	12	0.14
Mexican	58	0.67
Puerto Rican	77	0.88
South American	161	1.85
Argentinean	21	0.24
Chilean	11	0.13
Colombian	48	0.55
Ecuadorian	22	0.25
Paraguayan	40	0.46
Peruvian	10	0.11
Uruguayan	3	0.03
Venezuelan	4	0.05
Other South American	2	0.02
Other Hispanic or Latino	71	0.82

Race*	Population	%
African-American/Black (54)	82	0.94
Not Hispanic (48)	64	0.74
Hispanic (6)	18	0.21
American Indian/Alaska Native (8)	29	0.33
Not Hispanic (4)	22	0.25
Hispanic (4)	7	0.08
Apache (0)	1	0.01
Blackfeet (0)	1	0.01
Cherokee (0)	2	0.02
Creek (0)	1	0.01
Iroquois (1)	1	0.01
Lumbee (1)	1	0.01
Mexican American Ind. (0)	2	0.02
Seminole (0)	1	0.01
Sioux (0)	1	0.01
South American Ind. (0)	3	0.03
Asian (520)	607	6.98
Not Hispanic (520)	603	6.93
Hispanic (0)	4	0.05
Chinese, ex. Taiwanese (222)	245	2.82
Filipino (34)	57	0.66
Indian (175)	191	2.19
Indonesian (0)	1	0.01
Japanese (6)	12	0.14
Korean (45)	54	0.62
Pakistani (1)	4	0.05
Taiwanese (30)	33	0.38
Hawaii Native/Pacific Islander (1)	4	0.05
Not Hispanic (1)	2	0.02
Hispanic (0)	2	0.02
Native Hawaiian (1)	2	0.02
White (7,885)	8,017	92.13
Not Hispanic (7,385)	7,491	86.08
Hispanic (500)	526	6.04

Lopatcong

Place Type: Township
County: Warren
Population: 8,014†

Ancestry‡	Population	%
African, Sub-Saharan (32)	47	0.61
African (19)	19	0.25
South African (0)	15	0.19
Other Sub-Saharan African (13)	13	0.17
American (252)	252	3.27
Austrian (0)	84	1.09
British (19)	34	0.44
Canadian (0)	30	0.39
Czech (36)	109	1.42
Dutch (81)	361	4.69
English (221)	735	9.54
European (103)	103	1.34
Finnish (0)	43	0.56
French, ex. Basque (51)	180	2.34
French Canadian (18)	18	0.23
German (446)	1,741	22.61
Greek (12)	142	1.84
Hungarian (67)	182	2.36
Iranian (7)	7	0.09
Irish (368)	1,394	18.10
Italian (601)	1,442	18.72
Lithuanian (0)	55	0.71
Norwegian (0)	11	0.14
Pennsylvania German (42)	51	0.66
Polish (226)	527	6.84
Portuguese (69)	123	1.60
Romanian (0)	13	0.17
Russian (29)	83	1.08
Scotch-Irish (31)	62	0.81
Scottish (18)	182	2.36
Slavic (18)	35	0.45
Slovak (82)	130	1.69
Swedish (52)	111	1.44
Swiss (0)	14	0.18
Ukrainian (70)	81	1.05
Welsh (0)	32	0.42
West Indian, ex. Hispanic (163)	163	2.12
Dutch West Indian (12)	12	0.16
Jamaican (151)	151	1.96
Yugoslavian (0)	13	0.17

Hispanic Origin	Population	%
Hispanic or Latino (of any race)	480	5.99
Central American, ex. Mexican	30	0.37
Costa Rican	12	0.15
Guatemalan	2	0.02
Honduran	7	0.09
Nicaraguan	2	0.02
Panamanian	2	0.02
Salvadoran	5	0.06
Cuban	58	0.72
Dominican Republic	38	0.47
Mexican	25	0.31
Puerto Rican	196	2.45
South American	104	1.30
Argentinean	19	0.24
Chilean	5	0.06
Colombian	23	0.29
Ecuadorian	35	0.44
Peruvian	13	0.16
Venezuelan	9	0.11
Other Hispanic or Latino	29	0.36

Race*	Population	%
African-American/Black (483)	537	6.70
Not Hispanic (458)	494	6.16
Hispanic (25)	43	0.54
American Indian/Alaska Native (11)	27	0.34
Not Hispanic (8)	20	0.25
Hispanic (3)	7	0.09
Cherokee (0)	6	0.07
Delaware (1)	1	0.01
Mexican American Ind. (1)	1	0.01
Asian (335)	383	4.78
Not Hispanic (334)	378	4.72
Hispanic (1)	5	0.06
Cambodian (1)	2	0.02
Chinese, ex. Taiwanese (78)	88	1.10
Filipino (80)	98	1.22
Indian (124)	138	1.72
Japanese (1)	4	0.05
Korean (26)	31	0.39
Laotian (0)	2	0.02
Pakistani (6)	12	0.15
Taiwanese (0)	1	0.01
Thai (1)	1	0.01
Vietnamese (7)	7	0.09
Hawaii Native/Pacific Islander (1)	10	0.12
Not Hispanic (1)	6	0.07
Hispanic (0)	4	0.05
Guamanian/Chamorro (1)	2	0.02
White (6,990)	7,085	88.41
Not Hispanic (6,630)	6,707	83.69
Hispanic (360)	378	4.72

Lower

Place Type: Township
County: Cape May
Population: 22,866†

Ancestry‡	Population	%
African, Sub-Saharan (44)	48	0.21
African (44)	48	0.21
American (924)	924	4.06
Arab (0)	18	0.08
Lebanese (0)	18	0.08
Armenian (19)	51	0.22
Austrian (0)	11	0.05
Belgian (0)	26	0.11
Brazilian (44)	44	0.19
British (35)	76	0.33
Croatian (0)	11	0.05
Czech (33)	63	0.28
Danish (13)	35	0.15
Dutch (21)	277	1.22
Eastern European (0)	18	0.08
English (754)	3,109	13.67
European (80)	87	0.38
French, ex. Basque (27)	593	2.61
French Canadian (0)	19	0.08
German (1,292)	5,699	25.07
Greek (33)	85	0.37
Hungarian (36)	47	0.21
Irish (2,735)	8,399	36.94
Italian (1,978)	4,411	19.40
Latvian (0)	6	0.03
Lithuanian (0)	74	0.33
Macedonian (150)	150	0.66
Norwegian (46)	108	0.48
Pennsylvania German (71)	108	0.48
Polish (610)	1,659	7.30
Portuguese (45)	75	0.33
Romanian (14)	14	0.06
Russian (0)	87	0.38
Scandinavian (0)	13	0.06
Scotch-Irish (134)	454	2.00
Scottish (139)	424	1.86
Slavic (14)	62	0.27

SECTION TWO

*Notes: † The Census 2010 population figure is used to calculate the percentages in the Hispanic Origin and Race categories. Ancestry percentages are based on the 2006-2010 American Community Survey population (not shown); ‡ Numbers in parentheses indicate the number of people reporting a single ancestry; * Numbers in parentheses indicate the number of persons reporting this race alone, not in combination with any other race; Please refer to the Explanation of Data for more information.*

Slovak (25)	36	0.16
Slovene (8)	18	0.08
Swedish (78)	501	2.20
Swiss (0)	43	0.19
Ukrainian (122)	208	0.91
Welsh (83)	255	1.12
West Indian, ex. Hispanic (0)	12	0.05
Jamaican (0)	12	0.05
Yugoslavian (2)	38	0.17

Hispanic Origin	Population	%
Hispanic or Latino (of any race)	969	4.24
Central American, ex. Mexican	43	0.19
Costa Rican	4	0.02
Guatemalan	11	0.05
Nicaraguan	2	0.01
Panamanian	20	0.09
Salvadoran	6	0.03
Cuban	35	0.15
Dominican Republic	5	0.02
Mexican	313	1.37
Puerto Rican	436	1.91
South American	72	0.31
Argentinean	26	0.11
Colombian	21	0.09
Ecuadorian	4	0.02
Paraguayan	1	<0.01
Peruvian	17	0.07
Uruguayan	3	0.01
Other Hispanic or Latino	65	0.28

Race*	Population	%
African-American/Black (456)	653	2.86
Not Hispanic (423)	586	2.56
Hispanic (33)	67	0.29
American Indian/Alaska Native (37)	121	0.53
Not Hispanic (32)	113	0.49
Hispanic (5)	8	0.03
Apache (0)	1	<0.01
Blackfeet (2)	9	0.04
Cherokee (4)	17	0.07
Chippewa (2)	2	0.01
Choctaw (1)	8	0.03
Creek (0)	4	0.02
Delaware (3)	5	0.02
Iroquois (3)	9	0.04
Potawatomi (1)	1	<0.01
Seminole (0)	1	<0.01
Sioux (2)	8	0.03
South American Ind. (4)	4	0.02
Asian (142)	209	0.91
Not Hispanic (140)	204	0.89
Hispanic (2)	5	0.02
Chinese, ex. Taiwanese (35)	41	0.18
Filipino (40)	73	0.32
Indian (16)	20	0.09
Indonesian (1)	4	0.02
Japanese (6)	14	0.06
Korean (12)	18	0.08
Laotian (1)	1	<0.01
Nepalese (1)	1	<0.01
Pakistani (2)	2	0.01
Thai (5)	6	0.03
Vietnamese (23)	26	0.11
Hawaii Native/Pacific Islander (10)	38	0.17
Not Hispanic (10)	27	0.12
Hispanic (0)	11	0.05
Guamanian/Chamorro (0)	2	0.01
Native Hawaiian (1)	14	0.06
Samoan (1)	4	0.02
White (21,549)	21,919	95.86
Not Hispanic (20,978)	21,271	93.02
Hispanic (571)	648	2.83

Lumberton

Place Type: Township
County: Burlington
Population: 12,559†

Ancestry‡	Population	%
African, Sub-Saharan (203)	226	1.84
African (27)	50	0.41
Nigerian (176)	176	1.43
American (413)	413	3.36
Arab (55)	55	0.45
Jordanian (55)	55	0.45
Armenian (15)	36	0.29
Austrian (15)	15	0.12
Belgian (0)	9	0.07
Bulgarian (17)	17	0.14
Canadian (0)	19	0.15
Croatian (9)	9	0.07
Czech (0)	61	0.50
Danish (71)	134	1.09
Dutch (7)	111	0.90
Eastern European (21)	21	0.17
English (241)	1,320	10.75
European (88)	88	0.72
Finnish (39)	85	0.69
French, ex. Basque (41)	225	1.83
French Canadian (22)	68	0.55
German (532)	2,026	16.51
Greek (37)	37	0.30
Hungarian (39)	249	2.03
Irish (696)	2,724	22.19
Italian (635)	1,824	14.86
Lithuanian (11)	41	0.33
Norwegian (0)	45	0.37
Polish (190)	943	7.68
Portuguese (0)	132	1.08
Romanian (16)	47	0.38
Russian (39)	143	1.16
Scotch-Irish (40)	100	0.81
Scottish (30)	269	2.19
Slavic (0)	19	0.15
Swedish (0)	118	0.96
Swiss (0)	18	0.15
Ukrainian (29)	29	0.24
Welsh (9)	101	0.82
West Indian, ex. Hispanic (224)	277	2.26
Barbadian (19)	19	0.15
Haitian (0)	53	0.43
Jamaican (205)	205	1.67

Hispanic Origin	Population	%
Hispanic or Latino (of any race)	736	5.86
Central American, ex. Mexican	81	0.64
Costa Rican	3	0.02
Guatemalan	8	0.06
Honduran	6	0.05
Nicaraguan	1	0.01
Panamanian	58	0.46
Salvadoran	3	0.02
Other Central American	2	0.02
Cuban	20	0.16
Dominican Republic	24	0.19
Mexican	58	0.46
Puerto Rican	408	3.25
South American	89	0.71
Argentinean	1	0.01
Chilean	7	0.06
Colombian	23	0.18
Ecuadorian	14	0.11
Paraguayan	2	0.02
Peruvian	34	0.27
Uruguayan	1	0.01
Venezuelan	1	0.01
Other South American	6	0.05
Other Hispanic or Latino	56	0.45

Race*	Population	%
African-American/Black (2,378)	2,664	21.21
Not Hispanic (2,305)	2,529	20.14
Hispanic (73)	135	1.07
American Indian/Alaska Native (30)	124	0.99
Not Hispanic (15)	83	0.66
Hispanic (15)	41	0.33
Apache (0)	1	0.01
Blackfeet (0)	3	0.02
Cherokee (5)	22	0.18
Chickasaw (0)	2	0.02
Comanche (0)	1	0.01
Delaware (2)	3	0.02
Iroquois (0)	1	0.01
Navajo (1)	4	0.03
Seminole (0)	1	0.01
Sioux (0)	2	0.02
South American Ind. (1)	6	0.05
Spanish American Ind. (2)	2	0.02
Asian (591)	741	5.90
Not Hispanic (581)	728	5.80
Hispanic (10)	13	0.10
Bangladeshi (21)	21	0.17
Chinese, ex. Taiwanese (80)	101	0.80
Filipino (119)	150	1.19
Indian (240)	256	2.04
Japanese (14)	37	0.29
Korean (64)	117	0.93
Pakistani (23)	23	0.18
Thai (1)	7	0.06
Vietnamese (16)	22	0.18
Hawaii Native/Pacific Islander (5)	19	0.15
Not Hispanic (3)	10	0.08
Hispanic (2)	9	0.07
Guamanian/Chamorro (5)	10	0.08
Native Hawaiian (0)	2	0.02
Samoan (0)	2	0.02
White (8,916)	9,248	73.64
Not Hispanic (8,556)	8,823	70.25
Hispanic (360)	425	3.38

Lyndhurst

Place Type: Township
County: Bergen
Population: 20,554†

Ancestry‡	Population	%
African, Sub-Saharan (25)	40	0.20
African (25)	25	0.12
Cape Verdean (0)	15	0.07
American (330)	330	1.63
Arab (48)	129	0.64
Egyptian (32)	65	0.32
Lebanese (5)	42	0.21
Syrian (11)	22	0.11
Armenian (13)	23	0.11
Australian (0)	32	0.16
Austrian (0)	43	0.21
Belgian (7)	7	0.03
Brazilian (177)	283	1.40
Canadian (0)	11	0.05
Croatian (37)	37	0.18
Czech (0)	91	0.45
Czechoslovakian (29)	37	0.18
Danish (0)	107	0.53
Dutch (0)	89	0.44
English (78)	745	3.68
Estonian (7)	7	0.03
European (34)	34	0.17
French, ex. Basque (0)	272	1.34
French Canadian (12)	32	0.16
German (186)	2,002	9.89
Greek (110)	209	1.03
Hungarian (100)	245	1.21
Irish (993)	3,125	15.44
Israeli (29)	29	0.14
Italian (4,015)	6,819	33.69
Lithuanian (24)	77	0.38
Norwegian (12)	34	0.17
Pennsylvania German (10)	10	0.05
Polish (1,037)	2,002	9.89
Portuguese (260)	362	1.79
Romanian (16)	31	0.15
Russian (92)	227	1.12
Scandinavian (0)	20	0.10
Scotch-Irish (72)	318	1.57
Scottish (193)	453	2.24
Slovak (14)	28	0.14

*Notes: † The Census 2010 population figure is used to calculate the percentages in the Hispanic Origin and Race categories. Ancestry percentages are based on the 2006-2010 American Community Survey population (not shown); ‡ Numbers in parentheses indicate the number of people reporting a single ancestry; * Numbers in parentheses indicate the number of persons reporting this race alone, not in combination with any other race; Please refer to the Explanation of Data for more information.*

Swedish (21)	21	0.10
Swiss (12)	71	0.35
Turkish (362)	362	1.79
Ukrainian (68)	126	0.62
Welsh (12)	29	0.14
West Indian, ex. Hispanic (58)	129	0.64
Barbadian (0)	15	0.07
British West Indian (0)	15	0.07
Haitian (0)	11	0.05
Jamaican (42)	72	0.36
West Indian (16)	16	0.08

Hispanic Origin	Population	%
Hispanic or Latino (of any race)	3,769	18.34
Central American, ex. Mexican	210	1.02
Costa Rican	26	0.13
Guatemalan	38	0.18
Honduran	36	0.18
Nicaraguan	7	0.03
Panamanian	6	0.03
Salvadoran	96	0.47
Other Central American	1	<0.01
Cuban	461	2.24
Dominican Republic	331	1.61
Mexican	232	1.13
Puerto Rican	844	4.11
South American	1,238	6.02
Argentinean	63	0.31
Bolivian	14	0.07
Chilean	45	0.22
Colombian	292	1.42
Ecuadorian	403	1.96
Peruvian	334	1.62
Uruguayan	56	0.27
Venezuelan	29	0.14
Other South American	2	0.01
Other Hispanic or Latino	453	2.20

Race*	Population	%
African-American/Black (406)	512	2.49
Not Hispanic (325)	388	1.89
Hispanic (81)	124	0.60
American Indian/Alaska Native (34)	108	0.53
Not Hispanic (10)	56	0.27
Hispanic (24)	52	0.25
Central American Ind. (0)	3	0.01
Cherokee (0)	14	0.07
Chippewa (0)	4	0.02
Creek (0)	1	<0.01
Delaware (3)	3	0.01
Iroquois (1)	6	0.03
Navajo (0)	1	<0.01
Potawatomi (0)	1	<0.01
Pueblo (0)	1	<0.01
Seminole (0)	1	<0.01
South American Ind. (1)	9	0.04
Spanish American Ind. (0)	2	0.01
Asian (1,355)	1,515	7.37
Not Hispanic (1,333)	1,472	7.16
Hispanic (22)	43	0.21
Bangladeshi (0)	2	0.01
Burmese (3)	4	0.02
Cambodian (1)	2	0.01
Chinese, ex. Taiwanese (194)	218	1.06
Filipino (262)	301	1.46
Indian (371)	398	1.94
Indonesian (1)	7	0.03
Japanese (39)	54	0.26
Korean (363)	379	1.84
Laotian (11)	12	0.06
Nepalese (4)	4	0.02
Pakistani (10)	10	0.05
Sri Lankan (4)	4	0.02
Taiwanese (4)	6	0.03
Thai (31)	33	0.16
Vietnamese (21)	27	0.13
Hawaii Native/Pacific Islander (6)	16	0.08
Not Hispanic (6)	12	0.06
Hispanic (0)	4	0.02
Guamanian/Chamorro (0)	1	<0.01
Native Hawaiian (0)	3	0.01
White (17,053)	17,532	85.30
Not Hispanic (14,709)	14,948	72.73
Hispanic (2,344)	2,584	12.57

Madison

Place Type: Borough
County: Morris
Population: 15,845†

Ancestry‡	Population	%
African, Sub-Saharan (32)	32	0.20
Kenyan (32)	32	0.20
Albanian (54)	54	0.34
American (297)	297	1.87
Arab (102)	155	0.98
Egyptian (23)	48	0.30
Lebanese (20)	35	0.22
Moroccan (41)	41	0.26
Other Arab (18)	31	0.20
Armenian (0)	24	0.15
Austrian (20)	113	0.71
Brazilian (15)	15	0.09
British (56)	86	0.54
Canadian (0)	11	0.07
Croatian (26)	26	0.16
Czech (33)	59	0.37
Danish (14)	111	0.70
Dutch (32)	155	0.98
Eastern European (23)	23	0.15
English (321)	1,332	8.41
European (65)	65	0.41
Finnish (11)	21	0.13
French, ex. Basque (11)	309	1.95
French Canadian (12)	96	0.61
German (636)	2,806	17.71
Greek (111)	161	1.02
Guyanese (11)	11	0.07
Hungarian (34)	67	0.42
Irish (899)	3,308	20.88
Italian (2,640)	4,695	29.63
Latvian (20)	20	0.13
Lithuanian (17)	62	0.39
Norwegian (114)	237	1.50
Polish (241)	892	5.63
Portuguese (12)	76	0.48
Romanian (0)	15	0.09
Russian (111)	419	2.64
Scandinavian (49)	49	0.31
Scotch-Irish (51)	265	1.67
Scottish (63)	489	3.09
Slovak (10)	99	0.62
Slovene (25)	25	0.16
Swedish (28)	116	0.73
Swiss (0)	42	0.27
Turkish (56)	56	0.35
Ukrainian (48)	90	0.57
Welsh (21)	78	0.49
West Indian, ex. Hispanic (8)	65	0.41
British West Indian (8)	8	0.05
Jamaican (0)	37	0.23
Trinidadian/Tobagonian (0)	10	0.06
West Indian (0)	10	0.06
Yugoslavian (39)	75	0.47

Hispanic Origin	Population	%
Hispanic or Latino (of any race)	1,406	8.87
Central American, ex. Mexican	187	1.18
Costa Rican	82	0.52
Guatemalan	16	0.10
Honduran	51	0.32
Nicaraguan	10	0.06
Panamanian	6	0.04
Salvadoran	22	0.14
Cuban	73	0.46
Dominican Republic	40	0.25
Mexican	79	0.50
Puerto Rican	130	0.82
South American	763	4.82
Argentinean	12	0.08
Bolivian	8	0.05
Chilean	5	0.03
Colombian	646	4.08
Ecuadorian	26	0.16
Paraguayan	13	0.08
Peruvian	47	0.30
Uruguayan	1	0.01
Venezuelan	3	0.02
Other South American	2	0.01
Other Hispanic or Latino	134	0.85

Race*	Population	%
African-American/Black (469)	598	3.77
Not Hispanic (441)	537	3.39
Hispanic (28)	61	0.38
American Indian/Alaska Native (19)	62	0.39
Not Hispanic (7)	35	0.22
Hispanic (12)	27	0.17
Cherokee (2)	13	0.08
Chippewa (0)	1	0.01
Choctaw (1)	1	0.01
Cree (0)	3	0.02
Delaware (3)	4	0.03
Mexican American Ind. (1)	2	0.01
Seminole (0)	1	0.01
Sioux (1)	1	0.01
South American Ind. (1)	3	0.02
Spanish American Ind. (4)	4	0.03
Asian (873)	1,041	6.57
Not Hispanic (869)	1,029	6.49
Hispanic (4)	12	0.08
Chinese, ex. Taiwanese (254)	293	1.85
Filipino (82)	123	0.78
Indian (212)	242	1.53
Indonesian (2)	5	0.03
Japanese (31)	53	0.33
Korean (214)	236	1.49
Laotian (4)	4	0.03
Nepalese (10)	10	0.06
Pakistani (18)	18	0.11
Sri Lankan (4)	5	0.03
Taiwanese (13)	15	0.09
Thai (5)	6	0.04
Vietnamese (11)	18	0.11
Hawaii Native/Pacific Islander (2)	7	0.04
Not Hispanic (2)	4	0.03
Hispanic (0)	3	0.02
Native Hawaiian (1)	3	0.02
Samoan (1)	1	0.01
White (13,746)	14,078	88.85
Not Hispanic (12,840)	13,075	82.52
Hispanic (906)	1,003	6.33

Mahwah

Place Type: Township
County: Bergen
Population: 25,890†

Ancestry‡	Population	%
African, Sub-Saharan (55)	65	0.26
African (38)	38	0.15
Cape Verdean (0)	10	0.04
Other Sub-Saharan African (17)	17	0.07
American (506)	506	1.99
Arab (265)	436	1.72
Arab (34)	67	0.26
Egyptian (76)	116	0.46
Lebanese (53)	53	0.21
Moroccan (22)	43	0.17
Syrian (21)	98	0.39
Other Arab (59)	59	0.23
Armenian (43)	122	0.48
Assyrian/Chaldean/Syriac (13)	13	0.05
Austrian (11)	148	0.58
Basque (13)	13	0.05
Belgian (27)	39	0.15
Brazilian (27)	27	0.11
British (18)	52	0.20

*Notes: † The Census 2010 population figure is used to calculate the percentages in the Hispanic Origin and Race categories. Ancestry percentages are based on the 2006-2010 American Community Survey population (not shown); ‡ Numbers in parentheses indicate the number of people reporting a single ancestry; * Numbers in parentheses indicate the number of persons reporting this race alone, not in combination with any other race; Please refer to the Explanation of Data for more information.*

Bulgarian (15)	15	0.06
Canadian (0)	63	0.25
Croatian (53)	53	0.21
Cypriot (3)	3	0.01
Czech (12)	121	0.48
Czechoslovakian (0)	44	0.17
Danish (0)	50	0.20
Dutch (271)	826	3.25
Eastern European (409)	418	1.64
English (365)	1,961	7.71
European (954)	954	3.75
Finnish (0)	12	0.05
French, ex. Basque (109)	493	1.94
French Canadian (26)	62	0.24
German (577)	3,494	13.74
Greek (183)	412	1.62
Guyanese (0)	12	0.05
Hungarian (126)	226	0.89
Iranian (123)	209	0.82
Irish (1,372)	5,485	21.58
Israeli (28)	40	0.16
Italian (3,359)	6,930	27.26
Lithuanian (14)	115	0.45
Luxemburger (0)	39	0.15
Northern European (12)	12	0.05
Norwegian (97)	283	1.11
Polish (544)	2,004	7.88
Portuguese (69)	87	0.34
Romanian (23)	30	0.12
Russian (362)	1,082	4.26
Scandinavian (12)	35	0.14
Scotch-Irish (112)	199	0.78
Scottish (76)	403	1.59
Serbian (6)	8	0.03
Slavic (107)	168	0.66
Slovak (31)	103	0.41
Swedish (39)	225	0.89
Swiss (10)	116	0.46
Turkish (6)	6	0.02
Ukrainian (102)	162	0.64
Welsh (2)	105	0.41
West Indian, ex. Hispanic (59)	70	0.28
Barbadian (1)	1	<0.01
Haitian (40)	40	0.16
Jamaican (18)	29	0.11
Yugoslavian (0)	10	0.04

Hispanic Origin	Population	%
Hispanic or Latino (of any race)	1,622	6.26
Central American, ex. Mexican	130	0.50
Costa Rican	11	0.04
Guatemalan	19	0.07
Honduran	19	0.07
Nicaraguan	5	0.02
Panamanian	3	0.01
Salvadoran	73	0.28
Cuban	142	0.55
Dominican Republic	138	0.53
Mexican	214	0.83
Puerto Rican	310	1.20
South American	345	1.33
Argentinean	27	0.10
Bolivian	4	0.02
Chilean	10	0.04
Colombian	130	0.50
Ecuadorian	47	0.18
Peruvian	112	0.43
Uruguayan	2	0.01
Venezuelan	13	0.05
Other Hispanic or Latino	343	1.32

Race*	Population	%
African-American/Black (678)	781	3.02
Not Hispanic (616)	681	2.63
Hispanic (62)	100	0.39
American Indian/Alaska Native (146)	247	0.95
Not Hispanic (121)	206	0.80
Hispanic (25)	41	0.16
Alaska Athabascan *(Ala. Nat.)* (0)	1	<0.01
Central American Ind. (0)	1	<0.01
Cherokee (3)	3	0.01
Chickasaw (3)	3	0.01
Chippewa (0)	1	<0.01
Cree (1)	1	<0.01
Delaware (74)	121	0.47
Iroquois (4)	5	0.02
Lumbee (1)	1	<0.01
Mexican American Ind. (1)	1	<0.01
Sioux (0)	4	0.02
South American Ind. (5)	8	0.03
Spanish American Ind. (2)	2	0.01
Asian (2,021)	2,328	8.99
Not Hispanic (2,014)	2,305	8.90
Hispanic (7)	23	0.09
Burmese (5)	5	0.02
Chinese, ex. Taiwanese (359)	402	1.55
Filipino (132)	165	0.64
Indian (888)	919	3.55
Indonesian (1)	2	0.01
Japanese (109)	120	0.46
Korean (326)	361	1.39
Laotian (2)	4	0.02
Malaysian (1)	1	<0.01
Nepalese (3)	3	0.01
Pakistani (108)	115	0.44
Sri Lankan (19)	20	0.08
Taiwanese (17)	24	0.09
Thai (7)	10	0.04
Vietnamese (10)	14	0.05
Hawaii Native/Pacific Islander (2)	142	0.55
Not Hispanic (0)	136	0.53
Hispanic (2)	6	0.02
Guamanian/Chamorro (0)	1	<0.01
Native Hawaiian (0)	1	<0.01
White (22,180)	22,469	86.79
Not Hispanic (21,088)	21,318	82.34
Hispanic (1,092)	1,151	4.45

Manalapan

Place Type: Township
County: Monmouth
Population: 38,872†

Ancestry‡	Population	%
African, Sub-Saharan (110)	110	0.29
African (97)	97	0.26
Nigerian (13)	13	0.03
American (4,256)	4,256	11.22
Arab (154)	281	0.74
Arab (0)	16	0.04
Egyptian (37)	37	0.10
Iraqi (0)	23	0.06
Lebanese (117)	148	0.39
Moroccan (0)	35	0.09
Syrian (0)	22	0.06
Armenian (0)	32	0.08
Australian (0)	11	0.03
Austrian (235)	584	1.54
Belgian (0)	25	0.07
Brazilian (95)	132	0.35
British (86)	94	0.25
Bulgarian (20)	20	0.05
Canadian (11)	36	0.09
Czech (71)	183	0.48
Czechoslovakian (30)	38	0.10
Danish (17)	45	0.12
Dutch (48)	176	0.46
Eastern European (449)	487	1.28
English (282)	1,045	2.75
European (395)	411	1.08
Finnish (0)	68	0.18
French, ex. Basque (37)	298	0.79
French Canadian (0)	43	0.11
German (515)	2,889	7.62
Greek (301)	529	1.39
Hungarian (154)	704	1.86
Irish (2,004)	5,851	15.42
Israeli (151)	174	0.46
Italian (5,991)	9,871	26.02
Latvian (7)	7	0.02
Lithuanian (78)	222	0.59
Maltese (17)	52	0.14
Norwegian (50)	114	0.30
Pennsylvania German (0)	9	0.02
Polish (1,050)	3,372	8.89
Portuguese (172)	215	0.57
Romanian (87)	286	0.75
Russian (1,531)	3,099	8.17
Scandinavian (22)	44	0.12
Scotch-Irish (97)	307	0.81
Scottish (104)	335	0.88
Slavic (14)	24	0.06
Slovak (53)	196	0.52
Swedish (9)	163	0.43
Swiss (11)	82	0.22
Turkish (14)	53	0.14
Ukrainian (346)	381	1.00
Welsh (26)	103	0.27
West Indian, ex. Hispanic (89)	89	0.23
West Indian (89)	89	0.23

Hispanic Origin	Population	%
Hispanic or Latino (of any race)	2,202	5.66
Central American, ex. Mexican	99	0.25
Costa Rican	10	0.03
Guatemalan	37	0.10
Honduran	12	0.03
Nicaraguan	10	0.03
Panamanian	13	0.03
Salvadoran	15	0.04
Other Central American	2	0.01
Cuban	231	0.59
Dominican Republic	74	0.19
Mexican	257	0.66
Puerto Rican	931	2.40
South American	383	0.99
Argentinean	81	0.21
Bolivian	7	0.02
Chilean	17	0.04
Colombian	136	0.35
Ecuadorian	56	0.14
Peruvian	50	0.13
Uruguayan	11	0.03
Venezuelan	21	0.05
Other South American	4	0.01
Other Hispanic or Latino	227	0.58

Race*	Population	%
African-American/Black (925)	1,054	2.71
Not Hispanic (872)	964	2.48
Hispanic (53)	90	0.23
American Indian/Alaska Native (18)	64	0.16
Not Hispanic (15)	52	0.13
Hispanic (3)	12	0.03
Blackfeet (1)	1	<0.01
Cherokee (5)	9	0.02
Choctaw (0)	1	<0.01
Delaware (0)	3	0.01
Iroquois (0)	4	0.01
Seminole (0)	4	0.01
Sioux (0)	1	<0.01
South American Ind. (1)	4	0.01
Asian (2,682)	2,935	7.55
Not Hispanic (2,670)	2,909	7.48
Hispanic (12)	26	0.07
Bangladeshi (10)	10	0.03
Burmese (3)	5	0.01
Cambodian (2)	2	0.01
Chinese, ex. Taiwanese (856)	949	2.44
Filipino (256)	343	0.88
Indian (1,069)	1,120	2.88
Indonesian (5)	6	0.02
Japanese (14)	39	0.10
Korean (228)	251	0.65
Laotian (0)	1	<0.01
Malaysian (1)	8	0.02
Nepalese (1)	1	<0.01
Pakistani (85)	94	0.24
Sri Lankan (2)	9	0.02

*Notes: † The Census 2010 population figure is used to calculate the percentages in the Hispanic Origin and Race categories. Ancestry percentages are based on the 2006-2010 American Community Survey population (not shown); ‡ Numbers in parentheses indicate the number of people reporting a single ancestry; * Numbers in parentheses indicate the number of persons reporting this race alone, not in combination with any other race; Please refer to the Explanation of Data for more information.*

Taiwanese (38)	51	0.13
Thai (8)	8	0.02
Vietnamese (32)	33	0.08
Hawaii Native/Pacific Islander (7)	31	0.08
Not Hispanic (7)	31	0.08
Guamanian/Chamorro (1)	2	0.01
Native Hawaiian (1)	8	0.02
White (34,423)	34,807	89.54
Not Hispanic (32,685)	32,988	84.86
Hispanic (1,738)	1,819	4.68

Manchester

Place Type: Township
County: Ocean
Population: 43,070†

Ancestry‡	Population	%
African, Sub-Saharan (12)	90	0.21
African (12)	90	0.21
Albanian (0)	14	0.03
Alsatian (0)	12	0.03
American (1,570)	1,570	3.68
Arab (10)	29	0.07
Lebanese (0)	5	0.01
Syrian (10)	24	0.06
Armenian (38)	38	0.09
Austrian (91)	399	0.94
Belgian (16)	53	0.12
Brazilian (10)	10	0.02
British (86)	123	0.29
Canadian (79)	140	0.33
Croatian (0)	26	0.06
Czech (35)	143	0.34
Czechoslovakian (137)	177	0.41
Danish (43)	157	0.37
Dutch (302)	935	2.19
Eastern European (59)	59	0.14
English (960)	3,597	8.43
European (97)	111	0.26
Finnish (0)	6	0.01
French, ex. Basque (139)	829	1.94
French Canadian (46)	214	0.50
German (2,501)	8,198	19.22
Greek (145)	303	0.71
Hungarian (517)	827	1.94
Irish (3,495)	9,697	22.73
Italian (6,823)	11,566	27.11
Latvian (63)	63	0.15
Lithuanian (187)	243	0.57
Northern European (56)	66	0.15
Norwegian (235)	517	1.21
Pennsylvania German (104)	166	0.39
Polish (2,018)	4,202	9.85
Portuguese (167)	375	0.88
Romanian (19)	118	0.28
Russian (458)	992	2.33
Scandinavian (14)	14	0.03
Scotch-Irish (220)	546	1.28
Scottish (221)	737	1.73
Serbian (0)	13	0.03
Slavic (9)	74	0.17
Slovak (141)	285	0.67
Slovene (8)	8	0.02
Swedish (145)	521	1.22
Swiss (53)	116	0.27
Turkish (44)	44	0.10
Ukrainian (272)	476	1.12
Welsh (57)	496	1.16
West Indian, ex. Hispanic (80)	162	0.38
Bahamian (0)	12	0.03
Haitian (31)	81	0.19
Trinidadian/Tobagonian (26)	26	0.06
West Indian (23)	43	0.10
Yugoslavian (0)	35	0.08

Hispanic Origin	Population	%
Hispanic or Latino (of any race)	2,062	4.79
Central American, ex. Mexican	88	0.20
Costa Rican	22	0.05
Guatemalan	16	0.04
Honduran	9	0.02
Nicaraguan	16	0.04
Panamanian	12	0.03
Salvadoran	9	0.02
Other Central American	4	0.01
Cuban	99	0.23
Dominican Republic	69	0.16
Mexican	223	0.52
Puerto Rican	1,095	2.54
South American	268	0.62
Argentinean	20	0.05
Bolivian	2	<0.01
Chilean	8	0.02
Colombian	64	0.15
Ecuadorian	85	0.20
Paraguayan	1	<0.01
Peruvian	66	0.15
Uruguayan	17	0.04
Venezuelan	3	0.01
Other South American	2	<0.01
Other Hispanic or Latino	220	0.51

Race*	Population	%
African-American/Black (1,654)	1,851	4.30
Not Hispanic (1,572)	1,735	4.03
Hispanic (82)	116	0.27
American Indian/Alaska Native (38)	183	0.42
Not Hispanic (30)	156	0.36
Hispanic (8)	27	0.06
Apache (0)	3	0.01
Blackfeet (0)	6	0.01
Cherokee (5)	31	0.07
Chippewa (1)	1	<0.01
Colville (1)	1	<0.01
Delaware (3)	12	0.03
Inupiat *(Alaska Native)* (1)	1	<0.01
Iroquois (0)	11	0.03
Mexican American Ind. (0)	1	<0.01
Navajo (1)	1	<0.01
Ottawa (0)	1	<0.01
Potawatomi (1)	1	<0.01
Shoshone (0)	1	<0.01
Sioux (1)	4	0.01
South American Ind. (2)	3	0.01
Spanish American Ind. (1)	1	<0.01
Asian (768)	894	2.08
Not Hispanic (754)	872	2.02
Hispanic (14)	22	0.05
Cambodian (1)	1	<0.01
Chinese, ex. Taiwanese (107)	115	0.27
Filipino (394)	451	1.05
Indian (99)	111	0.26
Indonesian (2)	5	0.01
Japanese (21)	36	0.08
Korean (63)	76	0.18
Laotian (6)	7	0.02
Pakistani (7)	7	0.02
Taiwanese (2)	2	<0.01
Thai (23)	28	0.07
Vietnamese (24)	26	0.06
Hawaii Native/Pacific Islander (10)	43	0.10
Not Hispanic (10)	38	0.09
Hispanic (0)	5	0.01
Fijian (0)	2	<0.01
Guamanian/Chamorro (2)	5	0.01
Native Hawaiian (6)	14	0.03
Samoan (1)	5	0.01
White (39,623)	40,049	92.99
Not Hispanic (38,215)	38,556	89.52
Hispanic (1,408)	1,493	3.47

Mansfield

Place Type: Township
County: Burlington
Population: 8,544†

Ancestry‡	Population	%
African, Sub-Saharan (15)	27	0.34
African (15)	27	0.34
American (190)	190	2.38
Arab (115)	232	2.90
Egyptian (21)	21	0.26
Lebanese (55)	55	0.69
Other Arab (39)	156	1.95
Armenian (12)	24	0.30
Austrian (7)	55	0.69
Belgian (0)	13	0.16
British (8)	35	0.44
Czech (9)	16	0.20
Czechoslovakian (0)	9	0.11
Danish (0)	7	0.09
Dutch (0)	38	0.48
Eastern European (15)	15	0.19
English (237)	942	11.78
European (140)	140	1.75
Finnish (28)	36	0.45
French, ex. Basque (27)	138	1.73
French Canadian (0)	8	0.10
German (453)	1,489	18.62
Greek (60)	72	0.90
Guyanese (19)	19	0.24
Hungarian (63)	333	4.16
Irish (402)	1,379	17.24
Italian (717)	1,283	16.04
Lithuanian (12)	64	0.80
Northern European (26)	26	0.33
Norwegian (6)	49	0.61
Pennsylvania German (0)	5	0.06
Polish (174)	674	8.43
Portuguese (74)	97	1.21
Romanian (0)	115	1.44
Russian (92)	188	2.35
Scotch-Irish (27)	65	0.81
Scottish (16)	38	0.48
Slavic (0)	47	0.59
Slovak (62)	109	1.36
Swedish (10)	19	0.24
Swiss (9)	21	0.26
Ukrainian (20)	52	0.65
Welsh (0)	7	0.09
West Indian, ex. Hispanic (71)	165	2.06
Jamaican (71)	132	1.65
West Indian (0)	33	0.41
Yugoslavian (10)	10	0.13

Hispanic Origin	Population	%
Hispanic or Latino (of any race)	428	5.01
Central American, ex. Mexican	37	0.43
Costa Rican	7	0.08
Guatemalan	9	0.11
Honduran	4	0.05
Panamanian	17	0.20
Cuban	24	0.28
Dominican Republic	19	0.22
Mexican	46	0.54
Puerto Rican	191	2.24
South American	69	0.81
Argentinean	9	0.11
Bolivian	2	0.02
Chilean	5	0.06
Colombian	20	0.23
Ecuadorian	13	0.15
Paraguayan	1	0.01
Peruvian	11	0.13
Uruguayan	3	0.04
Venezuelan	3	0.04
Other South American	2	0.02
Other Hispanic or Latino	42	0.49

Race*	Population	%
African-American/Black (890)	957	11.20
Not Hispanic (847)	889	10.40
Hispanic (43)	68	0.80
American Indian/Alaska Native (14)	52	0.61
Not Hispanic (11)	44	0.51
Hispanic (3)	8	0.09
Apache (1)	1	0.01
Blackfeet (0)	3	0.04

*Notes: † The Census 2010 population figure is used to calculate the percentages in the Hispanic Origin and Race categories. Ancestry percentages are based on the 2006-2010 American Community Survey population (not shown); ‡ Numbers in parentheses indicate the number of people reporting a single ancestry; * Numbers in parentheses indicate the number of persons reporting this race alone, not in combination with any other race; Please refer to the Explanation of Data for more information.*

Cherokee (1)	16	0.19
Iroquois (0)	1	0.01
Lumbee (0)	8	0.09
Mexican American Ind. (2)	2	0.02
Navajo (2)	2	0.02
South American Ind. (1)	2	0.02
Asian (657)	725	8.49
Not Hispanic (652)	714	8.36
Hispanic (5)	11	0.13
Chinese, ex. Taiwanese (52)	72	0.84
Filipino (128)	142	1.66
Indian (328)	347	4.06
Japanese (4)	13	0.15
Korean (47)	52	0.61
Malaysian (2)	5	0.06
Pakistani (58)	63	0.74
Taiwanese (3)	3	0.04
Thai (0)	1	0.01
Vietnamese (8)	10	0.12
Hawaii Native/Pacific Islander (5)	18	0.21
Not Hispanic (5)	18	0.21
Fijian (5)	5	0.06
Native Hawaiian (0)	6	0.07
White (6,753)	6,876	80.48
Not Hispanic (6,470)	6,555	76.72
Hispanic (283)	321	3.76

Mansfield

Place Type: Township
County: Warren
Population: 7,725†

Ancestry‡	Population	%
African, Sub-Saharan (112)	112	1.42
Ethiopian (112)	112	1.42
Albanian (36)	36	0.46
American (492)	492	6.24
Arab (31)	31	0.39
Arab (31)	31	0.39
Brazilian (52)	68	0.86
Canadian (0)	42	0.53
Czech (0)	53	0.67
Danish (15)	56	0.71
Dutch (39)	172	2.18
Eastern European (23)	50	0.63
English (103)	745	9.44
European (61)	61	0.77
French, ex. Basque (0)	128	1.62
French Canadian (0)	19	0.24
German (440)	1,621	20.55
Greek (0)	12	0.15
Hungarian (13)	13	0.16
Irish (156)	1,397	17.71
Italian (437)	1,481	18.77
Latvian (0)	13	0.16
Lithuanian (91)	267	3.38
Norwegian (31)	152	1.93
Pennsylvania German (28)	68	0.86
Polish (176)	568	7.20
Portuguese (26)	103	1.31
Romanian (20)	34	0.43
Russian (9)	93	1.18
Scotch-Irish (27)	147	1.86
Scottish (13)	125	1.58
Slovak (0)	49	0.62
Swedish (13)	100	1.27
Swiss (13)	25	0.32
Ukrainian (157)	224	2.84
Welsh (24)	77	0.98
West Indian, ex. Hispanic (0)	41	0.52
Trinidadian/Tobagonian (0)	22	0.28
West Indian (0)	19	0.24
Yugoslavian (57)	57	0.72

Hispanic Origin	Population	%
Hispanic or Latino (of any race)	845	10.94
Central American, ex. Mexican	130	1.68
Costa Rican	27	0.35
Guatemalan	37	0.48
Honduran	54	0.70
Nicaraguan	1	0.01
Panamanian	2	0.03
Salvadoran	9	0.12
Cuban	31	0.40
Dominican Republic	39	0.50
Mexican	62	0.80
Puerto Rican	201	2.60
South American	328	4.25
Argentinean	11	0.14
Chilean	24	0.31
Colombian	81	1.05
Ecuadorian	84	1.09
Paraguayan	12	0.16
Peruvian	75	0.97
Uruguayan	37	0.48
Venezuelan	3	0.04
Other South American	1	0.01
Other Hispanic or Latino	54	0.70

Race*	Population	%
African-American/Black (378)	440	5.70
Not Hispanic (355)	408	5.28
Hispanic (23)	32	0.41
American Indian/Alaska Native (14)	41	0.53
Not Hispanic (12)	37	0.48
Hispanic (2)	4	0.05
Aleut *(Alaska Native)* (4)	5	0.06
Arapaho (2)	2	0.03
Blackfeet (1)	2	0.03
Cherokee (1)	12	0.16
Chickasaw (0)	2	0.03
Cree (0)	1	0.01
Delaware (0)	1	0.01
South American Ind. (2)	2	0.03
Asian (248)	296	3.83
Not Hispanic (248)	286	3.70
Hispanic (0)	10	0.13
Bangladeshi (4)	4	0.05
Chinese, ex. Taiwanese (27)	34	0.44
Filipino (37)	47	0.61
Indian (89)	96	1.24
Indonesian (2)	2	0.03
Japanese (1)	10	0.13
Korean (16)	19	0.25
Pakistani (26)	26	0.34
Thai (3)	4	0.05
Vietnamese (40)	42	0.54
Hawaii Native/Pacific Islander (2)	2	0.03
Not Hispanic (1)	1	0.01
Hispanic (1)	1	0.01
Native Hawaiian (1)	1	0.01
White (6,700)	6,818	88.26
Not Hispanic (6,138)	6,231	80.66
Hispanic (562)	587	7.60

Mantua

Place Type: Township
County: Gloucester
Population: 15,217†

Ancestry‡	Population	%
African, Sub-Saharan (33)	73	0.48
African (20)	20	0.13
South African (13)	53	0.35
Albanian (0)	13	0.09
American (402)	402	2.65
Arab (0)	12	0.08
Lebanese (0)	12	0.08
Armenian (0)	32	0.21
Austrian (0)	221	1.46
British (45)	45	0.30
Canadian (0)	14	0.09
Croatian (0)	14	0.09
Czech (0)	54	0.36
Czechoslovakian (17)	33	0.22
Danish (0)	19	0.13
Dutch (82)	464	3.06
English (298)	1,906	12.55
European (78)	78	0.51
French, ex. Basque (0)	389	2.56
French Canadian (0)	10	0.07
German (863)	4,471	29.45
Greek (70)	335	2.21
Guyanese (101)	101	0.67
Hungarian (49)	144	0.95
Iranian (44)	44	0.29
Irish (1,117)	4,606	30.34
Italian (1,424)	3,510	23.12
Lithuanian (27)	186	1.23
Norwegian (0)	112	0.74
Pennsylvania German (0)	17	0.11
Polish (365)	1,394	9.18
Portuguese (59)	72	0.47
Romanian (15)	15	0.10
Russian (153)	306	2.02
Scandinavian (0)	11	0.07
Scotch-Irish (187)	385	2.54
Scottish (66)	357	2.35
Slovak (26)	93	0.61
Swedish (52)	138	0.91
Swiss (0)	14	0.09
Turkish (45)	106	0.70
Ukrainian (21)	187	1.23
Welsh (17)	203	1.34
West Indian, ex. Hispanic (25)	25	0.16
British West Indian (13)	13	0.09
Trinidadian/Tobagonian (12)	12	0.08

Hispanic Origin	Population	%
Hispanic or Latino (of any race)	449	2.95
Central American, ex. Mexican	17	0.11
Guatemalan	2	0.01
Honduran	4	0.03
Nicaraguan	9	0.06
Panamanian	2	0.01
Cuban	13	0.09
Dominican Republic	6	0.04
Mexican	72	0.47
Puerto Rican	228	1.50
South American	53	0.35
Argentinean	6	0.04
Bolivian	1	0.01
Chilean	1	0.01
Colombian	32	0.21
Ecuadorian	6	0.04
Paraguayan	1	0.01
Peruvian	1	0.01
Uruguayan	2	0.01
Venezuelan	3	0.02
Other Hispanic or Latino	60	0.39

Race*	Population	%
African-American/Black (380)	459	3.02
Not Hispanic (363)	430	2.83
Hispanic (17)	29	0.19
American Indian/Alaska Native (31)	79	0.52
Not Hispanic (23)	68	0.45
Hispanic (8)	11	0.07
Blackfeet (0)	5	0.03
Cherokee (0)	4	0.03
Chippewa (0)	1	0.01
Choctaw (1)	1	0.01
Delaware (0)	9	0.06
Inupiat *(Alaska Native)* (1)	1	0.01
Iroquois (5)	6	0.04
Lumbee (1)	1	0.01
Mexican American Ind. (2)	2	0.01
Potawatomi (1)	1	0.01
Sioux (0)	8	0.05
Asian (168)	224	1.47
Not Hispanic (167)	221	1.45
Hispanic (1)	3	0.02
Cambodian (1)	4	0.03
Chinese, ex. Taiwanese (36)	48	0.32
Filipino (35)	54	0.35
Indian (29)	35	0.23
Indonesian (1)	5	0.03
Japanese (5)	14	0.09

*Notes: † The Census 2010 population figure is used to calculate the percentages in the Hispanic Origin and Race categories. Ancestry percentages are based on the 2006-2010 American Community Survey population (not shown); ‡ Numbers in parentheses indicate the number of people reporting a single ancestry; * Numbers in parentheses indicate the number of persons reporting this race alone, not in combination with any other race; Please refer to the Explanation of Data for more information.*

Korean (24)	26	0.17
Malaysian (0)	1	0.01
Nepalese (1)	1	0.01
Pakistani (7)	7	0.05
Thai (1)	2	0.01
Vietnamese (18)	21	0.14
Hawaii Native/Pacific Islander (1)	22	0.14
Not Hispanic (1)	15	0.10
Hispanic (0)	7	0.05
Native Hawaiian (0)	7	0.05
Samoan (1)	1	0.01
White (14,340)	14,516	95.39
Not Hispanic (14,051)	14,194	93.28
Hispanic (289)	322	2.12

Manville

Place Type: Borough
County: Somerset
Population: 10,344†

Ancestry‡	Population	%
American (307)	307	2.96
Austrian (0)	65	0.63
Belgian (8)	8	0.08
Brazilian (9)	9	0.09
Canadian (0)	37	0.36
Carpatho Rusyn (26)	46	0.44
Czech (35)	120	1.16
Czechoslovakian (14)	23	0.22
Dutch (0)	105	1.01
Eastern European (25)	25	0.24
English (48)	280	2.70
French, ex. Basque (14)	98	0.95
French Canadian (10)	10	0.10
German (254)	1,226	11.83
Hungarian (129)	406	3.92
Iranian (0)	11	0.11
Irish (241)	1,156	11.15
Italian (673)	1,785	17.22
Lithuanian (9)	31	0.30
Maltese (0)	15	0.14
Norwegian (0)	9	0.09
Pennsylvania German (13)	13	0.13
Polish (1,038)	2,226	21.48
Portuguese (10)	19	0.18
Romanian (17)	17	0.16
Russian (98)	345	3.33
Scotch-Irish (11)	74	0.71
Scottish (0)	18	0.17
Slavic (17)	27	0.26
Slovak (104)	378	3.65
Slovene (20)	20	0.19
Swedish (0)	20	0.19
Ukrainian (155)	344	3.32
Welsh (18)	36	0.35
West Indian, ex. Hispanic (0)	23	0.22
Haitian (0)	9	0.09
Jamaican (0)	14	0.14

Hispanic Origin	Population	%
Hispanic or Latino (of any race)	1,963	18.98
Central American, ex. Mexican	779	7.53
Costa Rican	576	5.57
Guatemalan	73	0.71
Honduran	29	0.28
Nicaraguan	7	0.07
Panamanian	4	0.04
Salvadoran	90	0.87
Cuban	19	0.18
Dominican Republic	57	0.55
Mexican	175	1.69
Puerto Rican	239	2.31
South American	432	4.18
Argentinean	22	0.21
Chilean	5	0.05
Colombian	168	1.62
Ecuadorian	52	0.50
Paraguayan	49	0.47
Peruvian	130	1.26
Uruguayan	2	0.02
Venezuelan	3	0.03
Other South American	1	0.01
Other Hispanic or Latino	262	2.53

Race*	Population	%
African-American/Black (281)	344	3.33
Not Hispanic (259)	306	2.96
Hispanic (22)	38	0.37
American Indian/Alaska Native (10)	48	0.46
Not Hispanic (6)	31	0.30
Hispanic (4)	17	0.16
Apache (1)	1	0.01
Blackfeet (0)	3	0.03
Cherokee (3)	14	0.14
Iroquois (0)	2	0.02
Lumbee (1)	1	0.01
Sioux (0)	1	0.01
South American Ind. (0)	3	0.03
Asian (206)	262	2.53
Not Hispanic (205)	249	2.41
Hispanic (1)	13	0.13
Cambodian (1)	4	0.04
Chinese, ex. Taiwanese (50)	57	0.55
Filipino (48)	59	0.57
Indian (42)	50	0.48
Indonesian (0)	2	0.02
Japanese (2)	7	0.07
Korean (4)	12	0.12
Laotian (8)	10	0.10
Nepalese (8)	12	0.12
Pakistani (2)	2	0.02
Vietnamese (31)	34	0.33
Hawaii Native/Pacific Islander (0)	3	0.03
Not Hispanic (0)	3	0.03
White (8,932)	9,154	88.50
Not Hispanic (7,755)	7,860	75.99
Hispanic (1,177)	1,294	12.51

Maple Shade

Place Type: Township
County: Burlington
Population: 19,131†

Ancestry‡	Population	%
African, Sub-Saharan (34)	61	0.32
African (34)	61	0.32
American (430)	430	2.23
Arab (16)	16	0.08
Other Arab (16)	16	0.08
Armenian (11)	30	0.16
Austrian (0)	13	0.07
Belgian (14)	30	0.16
British (0)	7	0.04
Bulgarian (47)	47	0.24
Czech (23)	83	0.43
Danish (14)	27	0.14
Dutch (54)	158	0.82
English (197)	1,760	9.13
European (40)	40	0.21
French, ex. Basque (24)	278	1.44
French Canadian (16)	42	0.22
German (981)	4,199	21.79
Greek (10)	24	0.12
Hungarian (0)	60	0.31
Irish (1,122)	5,597	29.05
Italian (1,649)	3,956	20.53
Lithuanian (94)	284	1.47
Norwegian (0)	40	0.21
Pennsylvania German (16)	79	0.41
Polish (550)	1,753	9.10
Portuguese (0)	27	0.14
Romanian (0)	22	0.11
Russian (120)	352	1.83
Scotch-Irish (149)	306	1.59
Scottish (120)	398	2.07
Serbian (0)	43	0.22
Slavic (0)	11	0.06
Slovak (0)	29	0.15
Swedish (48)	166	0.86
Swiss (0)	24	0.12
Turkish (17)	17	0.09
Ukrainian (28)	55	0.29
Welsh (12)	100	0.52
West Indian, ex. Hispanic (57)	108	0.56
Haitian (57)	108	0.56

Hispanic Origin	Population	%
Hispanic or Latino (of any race)	1,591	8.32
Central American, ex. Mexican	94	0.49
Guatemalan	12	0.06
Honduran	12	0.06
Nicaraguan	26	0.14
Panamanian	11	0.06
Salvadoran	31	0.16
Other Central American	2	0.01
Cuban	49	0.26
Dominican Republic	69	0.36
Mexican	295	1.54
Puerto Rican	801	4.19
South American	159	0.83
Argentinean	6	0.03
Bolivian	3	0.02
Chilean	15	0.08
Colombian	27	0.14
Ecuadorian	81	0.42
Peruvian	15	0.08
Uruguayan	2	0.01
Venezuelan	8	0.04
Other South American	2	0.01
Other Hispanic or Latino	124	0.65

Race*	Population	%
African-American/Black (1,826)	2,072	10.83
Not Hispanic (1,678)	1,871	9.78
Hispanic (148)	201	1.05
American Indian/Alaska Native (31)	248	1.30
Not Hispanic (24)	214	1.12
Hispanic (7)	34	0.18
Blackfeet (0)	8	0.04
Cherokee (3)	20	0.10
Delaware (0)	5	0.03
Iroquois (1)	5	0.03
Lumbee (1)	1	0.01
Potawatomi (0)	2	0.01
Seminole (0)	3	0.02
Sioux (0)	2	0.01
South American Ind. (1)	6	0.03
Asian (1,080)	1,199	6.27
Not Hispanic (1,076)	1,174	6.14
Hispanic (4)	25	0.13
Bangladeshi (18)	27	0.14
Burmese (2)	2	0.01
Cambodian (3)	3	0.02
Chinese, ex. Taiwanese (70)	85	0.44
Filipino (129)	170	0.89
Hmong (1)	3	0.02
Indian (522)	562	2.94
Japanese (14)	30	0.16
Korean (147)	165	0.86
Nepalese (4)	8	0.04
Pakistani (37)	39	0.20
Sri Lankan (3)	3	0.02
Taiwanese (7)	7	0.04
Thai (6)	12	0.06
Vietnamese (62)	65	0.34
Hawaii Native/Pacific Islander (5)	26	0.14
Not Hispanic (5)	21	0.11
Hispanic (0)	5	0.03
Guamanian/Chamorro (1)	1	0.01
Native Hawaiian (3)	17	0.09
Samoan (1)	2	0.01
White (15,040)	15,480	80.92
Not Hispanic (14,288)	14,618	76.41
Hispanic (752)	862	4.51

*Notes: † The Census 2010 population figure is used to calculate the percentages in the Hispanic Origin and Race categories. Ancestry percentages are based on the 2006-2010 American Community Survey population (not shown); ‡ Numbers in parentheses indicate the number of people reporting a single ancestry; * Numbers in parentheses indicate the number of persons reporting this race alone, not in combination with any other race; Please refer to the Explanation of Data for more information.*

Maplewood

Place Type: Township
County: Essex
Population: 23,867†

Ancestry‡	Population	%
Afghan (7)	14	0.06
African, Sub-Saharan (1,096)	1,197	5.04
African (281)	365	1.54
Ethiopian (63)	63	0.27
Ghanaian (81)	81	0.34
Liberian (25)	25	0.11
Nigerian (349)	349	1.47
Somalian (8)	25	0.11
South African (216)	216	0.91
Ugandan (73)	73	0.31
American (579)	579	2.44
Arab (38)	89	0.38
Arab (0)	27	0.11
Egyptian (15)	15	0.06
Lebanese (12)	12	0.05
Syrian (11)	35	0.15
Armenian (41)	54	0.23
Australian (0)	33	0.14
Austrian (26)	139	0.59
Belgian (0)	35	0.15
Brazilian (28)	36	0.15
British (74)	101	0.43
Canadian (6)	74	0.31
Czech (7)	154	0.65
Danish (0)	5	0.02
Dutch (33)	114	0.48
Eastern European (253)	325	1.37
English (361)	1,603	6.75
Estonian (0)	8	0.03
European (153)	354	1.49
French, ex. Basque (26)	368	1.55
French Canadian (0)	107	0.45
German (493)	2,881	12.14
German Russian (14)	14	0.06
Greek (33)	119	0.50
Guyanese (59)	59	0.25
Hungarian (27)	219	0.92
Irish (821)	3,140	13.23
Italian (1,143)	2,412	10.16
Latvian (8)	8	0.03
Lithuanian (33)	124	0.52
Northern European (0)	11	0.05
Norwegian (46)	149	0.63
Pennsylvania German (0)	18	0.08
Polish (357)	1,368	5.76
Portuguese (0)	21	0.09
Romanian (36)	81	0.34
Russian (452)	1,262	5.32
Scandinavian (0)	12	0.05
Scotch-Irish (61)	192	0.81
Scottish (101)	379	1.60
Slovak (39)	101	0.43
Slovene (17)	17	0.07
Swedish (46)	285	1.20
Swiss (0)	45	0.19
Turkish (11)	56	0.24
Ukrainian (151)	327	1.38
Welsh (38)	262	1.10
West Indian, ex. Hispanic (2,025)	2,332	9.83
Barbadian (0)	10	0.04
British West Indian (150)	168	0.71
Haitian (973)	1,070	4.51
Jamaican (648)	744	3.13
Trinidadian/Tobagonian (178)	207	0.87
West Indian (76)	133	0.56

Hispanic Origin	Population	%
Hispanic or Latino (of any race)	1,595	6.68
Central American, ex. Mexican	275	1.15
Costa Rican	58	0.24
Guatemalan	61	0.26
Honduran	65	0.27
Nicaraguan	14	0.06
Panamanian	36	0.15
Salvadoran	39	0.16
Other Central American	2	0.01
Cuban	135	0.57
Dominican Republic	93	0.39
Mexican	147	0.62
Puerto Rican	458	1.92
South American	328	1.37
Argentinean	48	0.20
Bolivian	5	0.02
Chilean	19	0.08
Colombian	101	0.42
Ecuadorian	57	0.24
Peruvian	45	0.19
Uruguayan	33	0.14
Venezuelan	15	0.06
Other South American	5	0.02
Other Hispanic or Latino	159	0.67

Race*	Population	%
African-American/Black (8,426)	8,895	37.27
Not Hispanic (8,189)	8,554	35.84
Hispanic (237)	341	1.43
American Indian/Alaska Native (44)	188	0.79
Not Hispanic (17)	123	0.52
Hispanic (27)	65	0.27
Apache (2)	3	0.01
Blackfeet (1)	5	0.02
Central American Ind. (1)	3	0.01
Cherokee (2)	18	0.08
Chickasaw (0)	1	<0.01
Chippewa (0)	1	<0.01
Choctaw (0)	11	0.05
Comanche (0)	1	<0.01
Delaware (0)	7	0.03
Iroquois (1)	6	0.03
Mexican American Ind. (6)	8	0.03
Navajo (1)	4	0.02
Osage (0)	4	0.02
Ottawa (1)	3	0.01
Seminole (0)	4	0.02
South American Ind. (5)	16	0.07
Spanish American Ind. (0)	6	0.03
Yuman (0)	1	<0.01
Asian (725)	1,042	4.37
Not Hispanic (722)	1,006	4.22
Hispanic (3)	36	0.15
Bangladeshi (5)	5	0.02
Burmese (0)	3	0.01
Chinese, ex. Taiwanese (183)	266	1.11
Filipino (164)	230	0.96
Hmong (3)	3	0.01
Indian (189)	272	1.14
Indonesian (2)	2	0.01
Japanese (34)	87	0.36
Korean (38)	65	0.27
Laotian (1)	1	<0.01
Malaysian (0)	2	0.01
Pakistani (3)	7	0.03
Sri Lankan (7)	10	0.04
Taiwanese (11)	16	0.07
Thai (6)	7	0.03
Vietnamese (38)	54	0.23
Hawaii Native/Pacific Islander (6)	50	0.21
Not Hispanic (4)	48	0.20
Hispanic (2)	2	0.01
Fijian (2)	2	0.01
Guamanian/Chamorro (2)	4	0.02
Native Hawaiian (0)	4	0.02
Samoan (0)	3	0.01
White (13,430)	14,015	58.72
Not Hispanic (12,585)	13,056	54.70
Hispanic (845)	959	4.02

Marlboro

Place Type: Township
County: Monmouth
Population: 40,191†

Ancestry‡	Population	%
African, Sub-Saharan (40)	116	0.29
African (11)	29	0.07
Ghanaian (15)	15	0.04
Kenyan (0)	31	0.08
Nigerian (14)	41	0.10
American (3,017)	3,017	7.65
Arab (307)	393	1.00
Arab (101)	123	0.31
Egyptian (180)	199	0.50
Lebanese (7)	18	0.05
Moroccan (19)	33	0.08
Syrian (0)	20	0.05
Armenian (76)	88	0.22
Austrian (64)	402	1.02
Basque (21)	21	0.05
Belgian (5)	5	0.01
Brazilian (8)	8	0.02
British (53)	97	0.25
Canadian (13)	21	0.05
Celtic (14)	14	0.04
Croatian (33)	49	0.12
Czech (25)	170	0.43
Czechoslovakian (30)	30	0.08
Danish (0)	94	0.24
Dutch (26)	171	0.43
Eastern European (324)	324	0.82
English (360)	1,008	2.56
European (386)	449	1.14
Finnish (0)	24	0.06
French, ex. Basque (8)	209	0.53
French Canadian (16)	58	0.15
German (571)	2,601	6.60
Greek (358)	611	1.55
Guyanese (0)	7	0.02
Hungarian (122)	487	1.24
Iranian (0)	36	0.09
Irish (967)	3,620	9.18
Israeli (61)	221	0.56
Italian (4,870)	8,390	21.28
Lithuanian (11)	181	0.46
Maltese (24)	38	0.10
Northern European (7)	7	0.02
Norwegian (69)	166	0.42
Pennsylvania German (7)	7	0.02
Polish (1,304)	4,053	10.28
Portuguese (93)	338	0.86
Romanian (195)	338	0.86
Russian (2,024)	3,591	9.11
Scandinavian (12)	26	0.07
Scotch-Irish (72)	139	0.35
Scottish (11)	107	0.27
Slavic (0)	8	0.02
Slovak (48)	83	0.21
Soviet Union (16)	16	0.04
Swedish (5)	44	0.11
Swiss (6)	31	0.08
Turkish (48)	115	0.29
Ukrainian (168)	353	0.90
Welsh (8)	107	0.27
West Indian, ex. Hispanic (210)	241	0.61
Haitian (158)	158	0.40
Jamaican (36)	67	0.17
Trinidadian/Tobagonian (16)	16	0.04
Yugoslavian (0)	43	0.11

Hispanic Origin	Population	%
Hispanic or Latino (of any race)	1,619	4.03
Central American, ex. Mexican	59	0.15
Costa Rican	9	0.02
Guatemalan	28	0.07
Honduran	12	0.03
Nicaraguan	2	<0.01
Panamanian	4	0.01
Salvadoran	4	0.01
Cuban	206	0.51
Dominican Republic	78	0.19
Mexican	193	0.48
Puerto Rican	569	1.42
South American	319	0.79

*Notes: † The Census 2010 population figure is used to calculate the percentages in the Hispanic Origin and Race categories. Ancestry percentages are based on the 2006-2010 American Community Survey population (not shown); ‡ Numbers in parentheses indicate the number of people reporting a single ancestry; * Numbers in parentheses indicate the number of persons reporting this race alone, not in combination with any other race; Please refer to the Explanation of Data for more information.*

Argentinean	54	0.13
Bolivian	7	0.02
Chilean	23	0.06
Colombian	127	0.32
Ecuadorian	55	0.14
Paraguayan	3	0.01
Peruvian	39	0.10
Uruguayan	2	<0.01
Venezuelan	4	0.01
Other South American	5	0.01
Other Hispanic or Latino	195	0.49

Race*	Population	%
African-American/Black (841)	965	2.40
Not Hispanic (814)	896	2.23
Hispanic (27)	69	0.17
American Indian/Alaska Native (25)	90	0.22
Not Hispanic (19)	50	0.12
Hispanic (6)	40	0.10
Central American Ind. (0)	3	0.01
Cherokee (3)	17	0.04
Delaware (1)	1	<0.01
Iroquois (3)	3	0.01
Mexican American Ind. (5)	7	0.02
Navajo (1)	1	<0.01
Seminole (0)	2	<0.01
South American Ind. (0)	2	<0.01
Asian (6,939)	7,261	18.07
Not Hispanic (6,921)	7,215	17.95
Hispanic (18)	46	0.11
Bangladeshi (52)	53	0.13
Bhutanese (2)	2	<0.01
Burmese (0)	1	<0.01
Cambodian (1)	1	<0.01
Chinese, ex. Taiwanese (2,805)	2,943	7.32
Filipino (360)	406	1.01
Indian (2,798)	2,903	7.22
Indonesian (8)	16	0.04
Japanese (18)	25	0.06
Korean (444)	477	1.19
Malaysian (4)	11	0.03
Nepalese (6)	7	0.02
Pakistani (121)	133	0.33
Sri Lankan (13)	15	0.04
Taiwanese (124)	154	0.38
Thai (11)	15	0.04
Vietnamese (74)	85	0.21
Hawaii Native/Pacific Islander (2)	25	0.06
Not Hispanic (2)	25	0.06
Guamanian/Chamorro (1)	2	<0.01
Native Hawaiian (0)	1	<0.01
White (31,587)	32,005	79.63
Not Hispanic (30,362)	30,679	76.33
Hispanic (1,225)	1,326	3.30

Marlton

Place Type: CDP
County: Burlington
Population: 10,133†

Ancestry‡	Population	%
Albanian (9)	9	0.09
American (162)	162	1.57
Arab (13)	45	0.44
Lebanese (13)	37	0.36
Syrian (0)	8	0.08
Austrian (25)	67	0.65
Belgian (8)	8	0.08
Brazilian (0)	45	0.44
British (20)	102	0.99
Czech (0)	60	0.58
Dutch (0)	160	1.55
English (86)	919	8.91
European (9)	9	0.09
French, ex. Basque (41)	179	1.74
French Canadian (0)	18	0.17
German (350)	2,321	22.51
Greek (42)	57	0.55
Guyanese (12)	12	0.12
Hungarian (29)	113	1.10
Irish (919)	3,137	30.43
Italian (1,113)	2,986	28.96
Lithuanian (0)	37	0.36
Norwegian (0)	46	0.45
Pennsylvania German (10)	20	0.19
Polish (259)	886	8.59
Portuguese (0)	20	0.19
Romanian (0)	22	0.21
Russian (298)	530	5.14
Scotch-Irish (77)	154	1.49
Scottish (31)	306	2.97
Slavic (10)	10	0.10
Slovak (0)	26	0.25
Swedish (0)	30	0.29
Swiss (0)	9	0.09
Ukrainian (58)	81	0.79
Welsh (0)	34	0.33

Hispanic Origin	Population	%
Hispanic or Latino (of any race)	447	4.41
Central American, ex. Mexican	22	0.22
Guatemalan	11	0.11
Honduran	4	0.04
Panamanian	4	0.04
Salvadoran	3	0.03
Cuban	25	0.25
Dominican Republic	7	0.07
Mexican	112	1.11
Puerto Rican	178	1.76
South American	54	0.53
Argentinean	6	0.06
Bolivian	1	0.01
Chilean	1	0.01
Colombian	14	0.14
Ecuadorian	14	0.14
Peruvian	13	0.13
Venezuelan	5	0.05
Other Hispanic or Latino	49	0.48

Race*	Population	%
African-American/Black (433)	485	4.79
Not Hispanic (416)	465	4.59
Hispanic (17)	20	0.20
American Indian/Alaska Native (15)	68	0.67
Not Hispanic (13)	61	0.60
Hispanic (2)	7	0.07
Blackfeet (1)	3	0.03
Cherokee (0)	8	0.08
Delaware (0)	4	0.04
Inupiat *(Alaska Native)* (5)	5	0.05
Iroquois (0)	3	0.03
Mexican American Ind. (1)	1	0.01
Pueblo (0)	3	0.03
Sioux (0)	3	0.03
South American Ind. (1)	1	0.01
Asian (618)	689	6.80
Not Hispanic (613)	680	6.71
Hispanic (5)	9	0.09
Bangladeshi (4)	4	0.04
Chinese, ex. Taiwanese (126)	142	1.40
Filipino (93)	109	1.08
Indian (234)	248	2.45
Japanese (17)	29	0.29
Korean (84)	96	0.95
Nepalese (2)	2	0.02
Pakistani (5)	6	0.06
Taiwanese (15)	18	0.18
Thai (7)	9	0.09
Vietnamese (8)	11	0.11
Hawaii Native/Pacific Islander (1)	3	0.03
Not Hispanic (1)	3	0.03
Guamanian/Chamorro (1)	1	0.01
Native Hawaiian (0)	1	0.01
White (8,772)	8,900	87.83
Not Hispanic (8,494)	8,599	84.86
Hispanic (278)	301	2.97

Martinsville

Place Type: CDP
County: Somerset
Population: 11,980†

Ancestry‡	Population	%
American (766)	766	6.68
Arab (9)	9	0.08
Syrian (9)	9	0.08
Armenian (8)	8	0.07
Austrian (14)	101	0.88
Brazilian (0)	42	0.37
British (48)	114	0.99
Canadian (10)	10	0.09
Croatian (11)	34	0.30
Czech (0)	95	0.83
Czechoslovakian (24)	84	0.73
Danish (7)	42	0.37
Dutch (25)	255	2.22
Eastern European (163)	163	1.42
English (181)	891	7.77
European (301)	301	2.63
Finnish (11)	11	0.10
French, ex. Basque (12)	329	2.87
French Canadian (0)	11	0.10
German (516)	2,442	21.31
Greek (53)	66	0.58
Guyanese (0)	13	0.11
Hungarian (78)	186	1.62
Iranian (21)	21	0.18
Irish (408)	2,168	18.92
Italian (1,365)	2,693	23.50
Lithuanian (13)	37	0.32
Norwegian (0)	27	0.24
Polish (324)	1,077	9.40
Portuguese (58)	154	1.34
Romanian (10)	10	0.09
Russian (75)	324	2.83
Scotch-Irish (122)	245	2.14
Scottish (18)	172	1.50
Slavic (21)	35	0.31
Slovak (23)	75	0.65
Swedish (28)	108	0.94
Swiss (13)	60	0.52
Turkish (48)	48	0.42
Ukrainian (54)	241	2.10
Welsh (24)	87	0.76
West Indian, ex. Hispanic (0)	13	0.11
West Indian (0)	13	0.11

Hispanic Origin	Population	%
Hispanic or Latino (of any race)	457	3.81
Central American, ex. Mexican	68	0.57
Costa Rican	42	0.35
Guatemalan	10	0.08
Honduran	1	0.01
Panamanian	3	0.03
Salvadoran	12	0.10
Cuban	64	0.53
Dominican Republic	8	0.07
Mexican	37	0.31
Puerto Rican	98	0.82
South American	105	0.88
Argentinean	14	0.12
Chilean	3	0.03
Colombian	35	0.29
Ecuadorian	26	0.22
Paraguayan	8	0.07
Peruvian	4	0.03
Uruguayan	7	0.06
Venezuelan	7	0.06
Other South American	1	0.01
Other Hispanic or Latino	77	0.64

Race*	Population	%
African-American/Black (157)	182	1.52
Not Hispanic (147)	166	1.39
Hispanic (10)	16	0.13
American Indian/Alaska Native (5)	29	0.24

*Notes: † The Census 2010 population figure is used to calculate the percentages in the Hispanic Origin and Race categories. Ancestry percentages are based on the 2006-2010 American Community Survey population (not shown); ‡ Numbers in parentheses indicate the number of people reporting a single ancestry; * Numbers in parentheses indicate the number of persons reporting this race alone, not in combination with any other race; Please refer to the Explanation of Data for more information.*

Not Hispanic (5)	25	0.21
Hispanic (0)	4	0.03
Cherokee (1)	2	0.02
Chickasaw (0)	1	0.01
Choctaw (0)	4	0.03
Delaware (0)	3	0.03
South American Ind. (0)	1	0.01
Asian (982)	1,116	9.32
Not Hispanic (980)	1,105	9.22
Hispanic (2)	11	0.09
Chinese, ex. Taiwanese (364)	409	3.41
Filipino (76)	99	0.83
Indian (338)	373	3.11
Indonesian (0)	4	0.03
Japanese (8)	15	0.13
Korean (59)	78	0.65
Laotian (1)	1	0.01
Pakistani (12)	13	0.11
Sri Lankan (4)	4	0.03
Taiwanese (68)	79	0.66
Thai (13)	13	0.11
Vietnamese (20)	31	0.26
Hawaii Native/Pacific Islander (0)	1	0.01
Not Hispanic (0)	1	0.01
Native Hawaiian (0)	1	0.01
White (10,596)	10,770	89.90
Not Hispanic (10,206)	10,358	86.46
Hispanic (390)	412	3.44

Matawan

Place Type: Borough
County: Monmouth
Population: 8,810†

Ancestry‡	Population	%
African, Sub-Saharan (8)	8	0.09
African (8)	8	0.09
American (197)	197	2.24
Arab (157)	157	1.79
Egyptian (157)	157	1.79
Austrian (14)	61	0.69
British (7)	7	0.08
Danish (0)	73	0.83
Dutch (0)	14	0.16
Eastern European (53)	86	0.98
English (58)	504	5.74
European (56)	56	0.64
French, ex. Basque (0)	116	1.32
French Canadian (31)	46	0.52
German (129)	938	10.68
Greek (39)	70	0.80
Hungarian (0)	99	1.13
Irish (426)	1,734	19.74
Israeli (17)	17	0.19
Italian (944)	2,332	26.54
Lithuanian (14)	78	0.89
Maltese (0)	20	0.23
Norwegian (0)	48	0.55
Polish (218)	800	9.11
Portuguese (197)	221	2.52
Russian (30)	177	2.01
Scandinavian (9)	26	0.30
Scotch-Irish (181)	206	2.34
Scottish (110)	213	2.42
Serbian (98)	98	1.12
Slovak (0)	12	0.14
Swedish (0)	58	0.66
Ukrainian (49)	72	0.82
Welsh (0)	46	0.52
West Indian, ex. Hispanic (78)	158	1.80
Haitian (63)	63	0.72
Jamaican (0)	55	0.63
Trinidadian/Tobagonian (15)	29	0.33
West Indian (0)	11	0.13

Hispanic Origin	Population	%
Hispanic or Latino (of any race)	949	10.77
Central American, ex. Mexican	49	0.56
Costa Rican	7	0.08
Guatemalan	23	0.26
Honduran	5	0.06
Nicaraguan	1	0.01
Panamanian	3	0.03
Salvadoran	6	0.07
Other Central American	4	0.05
Cuban	66	0.75
Dominican Republic	39	0.44
Mexican	268	3.04
Puerto Rican	326	3.70
South American	136	1.54
Argentinean	20	0.23
Chilean	2	0.02
Colombian	45	0.51
Ecuadorian	18	0.20
Peruvian	43	0.49
Uruguayan	5	0.06
Other South American	3	0.03
Other Hispanic or Latino	65	0.74

Race*	Population	%
African-American/Black (620)	732	8.31
Not Hispanic (576)	667	7.57
Hispanic (44)	65	0.74
American Indian/Alaska Native (10)	59	0.67
Not Hispanic (3)	44	0.50
Hispanic (7)	15	0.17
Blackfeet (0)	5	0.06
Cherokee (0)	14	0.16
Chippewa (0)	3	0.03
Delaware (3)	7	0.08
Mexican American Ind. (5)	6	0.07
South American Ind. (1)	2	0.02
Asian (565)	651	7.39
Not Hispanic (557)	640	7.26
Hispanic (8)	11	0.12
Bangladeshi (3)	3	0.03
Burmese (0)	8	0.09
Cambodian (1)	1	0.01
Chinese, ex. Taiwanese (128)	140	1.59
Filipino (72)	94	1.07
Indian (246)	273	3.10
Japanese (9)	12	0.14
Korean (23)	23	0.26
Malaysian (13)	15	0.17
Pakistani (35)	39	0.44
Sri Lankan (1)	1	0.01
Taiwanese (5)	8	0.09
Thai (2)	3	0.03
Vietnamese (14)	15	0.17
Hawaii Native/Pacific Islander (1)	10	0.11
Not Hispanic (1)	7	0.08
Hispanic (0)	3	0.03
Native Hawaiian (0)	2	0.02
White (7,134)	7,312	83.00
Not Hispanic (6,524)	6,661	75.61
Hispanic (610)	651	7.39

Maurice River

Place Type: Township
County: Cumberland
Population: 7,976†

Ancestry‡	Population	%
African, Sub-Saharan (97)	114	1.42
African (97)	114	1.42
American (608)	608	7.59
Arab (16)	16	0.20
Arab (8)	8	0.10
Moroccan (8)	8	0.10
British (0)	23	0.29
Celtic (0)	29	0.36
Czech (0)	28	0.35
Danish (9)	49	0.61
Dutch (23)	48	0.60
Eastern European (9)	9	0.11
English (368)	980	12.24
European (39)	39	0.49
French, ex. Basque (8)	142	1.77
German (186)	866	10.82
Greek (24)	24	0.30
Guyanese (9)	9	0.11
Hungarian (8)	16	0.20
Irish (336)	949	11.85
Italian (330)	938	11.72
Norwegian (0)	9	0.11
Pennsylvania German (5)	5	0.06
Polish (151)	284	3.55
Portuguese (36)	36	0.45
Romanian (8)	8	0.10
Russian (0)	16	0.20
Scandinavian (0)	14	0.17
Scotch-Irish (192)	254	3.17
Scottish (0)	203	2.54
Swedish (8)	21	0.26
Swiss (0)	13	0.16
Welsh (0)	17	0.21
West Indian, ex. Hispanic (41)	75	0.94
Barbadian (8)	16	0.20
Haitian (17)	17	0.21
Jamaican (7)	25	0.31
West Indian (9)	17	0.21

Hispanic Origin	Population	%
Hispanic or Latino (of any race)	919	11.52
Central American, ex. Mexican	9	0.11
Guatemalan	3	0.04
Honduran	2	0.03
Panamanian	4	0.05
Cuban	24	0.30
Dominican Republic	29	0.36
Mexican	63	0.79
Puerto Rican	379	4.75
South American	12	0.15
Colombian	8	0.10
Ecuadorian	2	0.03
Peruvian	1	0.01
Venezuelan	1	0.01
Other Hispanic or Latino	403	5.05

Race*	Population	%
African-American/Black (2,874)	2,941	36.87
Not Hispanic (2,737)	2,781	34.87
Hispanic (137)	160	2.01
American Indian/Alaska Native (35)	81	1.02
Not Hispanic (16)	55	0.69
Hispanic (19)	26	0.33
Blackfeet (1)	4	0.05
Central American Ind. (1)	1	0.01
Cherokee (2)	8	0.10
Choctaw (0)	2	0.03
Delaware (2)	7	0.09
Iroquois (2)	2	0.03
Mexican American Ind. (1)	1	0.01
Seminole (0)	1	0.01
South American Ind. (3)	4	0.05
Asian (28)	52	0.65
Not Hispanic (26)	43	0.54
Hispanic (2)	9	0.11
Chinese, ex. Taiwanese (2)	4	0.05
Filipino (6)	9	0.11
Indian (4)	6	0.08
Japanese (2)	7	0.09
Korean (4)	6	0.08
Pakistani (1)	2	0.03
Vietnamese (3)	8	0.10
Hawaii Native/Pacific Islander (2)	6	0.08
Not Hispanic (2)	5	0.06
Hispanic (0)	1	0.01
Guamanian/Chamorro (0)	1	0.01
Samoan (1)	1	0.01
White (4,629)	4,722	59.20
Not Hispanic (4,182)	4,244	53.21
Hispanic (447)	478	5.99

*Notes: † The Census 2010 population figure is used to calculate the percentages in the Hispanic Origin and Race categories. Ancestry percentages are based on the 2006-2010 American Community Survey population (not shown); ‡ Numbers in parentheses indicate the number of people reporting a single ancestry; * Numbers in parentheses indicate the number of persons reporting this race alone, not in combination with any other race; Please refer to the Explanation of Data for more information.*

Maywood

Place Type: Borough
County: Bergen
Population: 9,555†

Ancestry‡	Population	%
American (165)	165	1.74
Armenian (10)	10	0.11
Austrian (16)	49	0.52
Brazilian (25)	42	0.44
British (13)	140	1.47
Canadian (0)	15	0.16
Czech (0)	12	0.13
Dutch (0)	61	0.64
English (70)	496	5.22
French, ex. Basque (13)	168	1.77
French Canadian (0)	10	0.11
German (449)	1,520	15.99
Greek (17)	137	1.44
Guyanese (0)	22	0.23
Hungarian (13)	110	1.16
Irish (643)	1,717	18.07
Israeli (9)	19	0.20
Italian (1,537)	3,028	31.86
Latvian (0)	9	0.09
Maltese (0)	11	0.12
Norwegian (22)	51	0.54
Polish (294)	632	6.65
Portuguese (0)	9	0.09
Romanian (14)	14	0.15
Russian (133)	255	2.68
Scandinavian (5)	5	0.05
Scotch-Irish (56)	117	1.23
Scottish (10)	128	1.35
Slovak (0)	18	0.19
Swedish (0)	39	0.41
Swiss (0)	63	0.66
Turkish (52)	52	0.55
Ukrainian (8)	22	0.23
Welsh (0)	40	0.42
West Indian, ex. Hispanic (93)	93	0.98
British West Indian (79)	79	0.83
Jamaican (14)	14	0.15
Yugoslavian (0)	13	0.14

Hispanic Origin	Population	%
Hispanic or Latino (of any race)	1,785	18.68
Central American, ex. Mexican	89	0.93
Costa Rican	17	0.18
Guatemalan	15	0.16
Honduran	12	0.13
Nicaraguan	7	0.07
Panamanian	1	0.01
Salvadoran	37	0.39
Cuban	139	1.45
Dominican Republic	378	3.96
Mexican	59	0.62
Puerto Rican	413	4.32
South American	550	5.76
Argentinean	51	0.53
Bolivian	5	0.05
Chilean	11	0.12
Colombian	251	2.63
Ecuadorian	140	1.47
Paraguayan	2	0.02
Peruvian	69	0.72
Uruguayan	11	0.12
Venezuelan	10	0.10
Other Hispanic or Latino	157	1.64

Race*	Population	%
African-American/Black (510)	608	6.36
Not Hispanic (460)	517	5.41
Hispanic (50)	91	0.95
American Indian/Alaska Native (17)	48	0.50
Not Hispanic (5)	30	0.31
Hispanic (12)	18	0.19
Blackfeet (0)	1	0.01
Chippewa (0)	1	0.01
Creek (0)	3	0.03
Pueblo (3)	3	0.03
Tlingit-Haida *(Alaska Native)* (0)	1	0.01
Asian (1,049)	1,132	11.85
Not Hispanic (1,042)	1,111	11.63
Hispanic (7)	21	0.22
Bangladeshi (5)	5	0.05
Burmese (8)	9	0.09
Cambodian (1)	2	0.02
Chinese, ex. Taiwanese (118)	134	1.40
Filipino (299)	335	3.51
Indian (455)	472	4.94
Indonesian (5)	5	0.05
Japanese (11)	16	0.17
Korean (98)	104	1.09
Laotian (4)	5	0.05
Pakistani (11)	13	0.14
Taiwanese (2)	2	0.02
Thai (4)	4	0.04
Vietnamese (8)	10	0.10
Hawaii Native/Pacific Islander (2)	11	0.12
Not Hispanic (2)	9	0.09
Hispanic (0)	2	0.02
Native Hawaiian (0)	3	0.03
White (7,145)	7,329	76.70
Not Hispanic (6,081)	6,190	64.78
Hispanic (1,064)	1,139	11.92

Medford

Place Type: Township
County: Burlington
Population: 23,033†

Ancestry‡	Population	%
African, Sub-Saharan (7)	19	0.08
Cape Verdean (7)	7	0.03
Ethiopian (0)	12	0.05
Albanian (10)	10	0.04
Alsatian (0)	9	0.04
American (797)	797	3.45
Arab (55)	55	0.24
Lebanese (55)	55	0.24
Armenian (0)	14	0.06
Australian (0)	13	0.06
Austrian (9)	84	0.36
Belgian (16)	30	0.13
Brazilian (0)	32	0.14
British (31)	61	0.26
Canadian (0)	11	0.05
Croatian (11)	54	0.23
Czech (0)	40	0.17
Czechoslovakian (0)	12	0.05
Danish (11)	23	0.10
Dutch (132)	518	2.24
Eastern European (141)	141	0.61
English (764)	4,047	17.53
European (209)	236	1.02
Finnish (0)	115	0.50
French, ex. Basque (40)	614	2.66
French Canadian (19)	73	0.32
German (970)	5,754	24.93
Greek (86)	332	1.44
Hungarian (28)	250	1.08
Irish (1,705)	6,692	28.99
Italian (1,863)	5,235	22.68
Lithuanian (20)	71	0.31
Macedonian (0)	16	0.07
Norwegian (27)	176	0.76
Pennsylvania German (0)	14	0.06
Polish (507)	1,582	6.85
Portuguese (0)	21	0.09
Romanian (21)	109	0.47
Russian (170)	451	1.95
Scandinavian (0)	16	0.07
Scotch-Irish (167)	383	1.66
Scottish (180)	597	2.59
Serbian (43)	43	0.19
Slavic (11)	40	0.17
Slovak (8)	84	0.36
Slovene (0)	19	0.08
Swedish (104)	303	1.31
Swiss (48)	109	0.47
Turkish (0)	14	0.06
Ukrainian (118)	207	0.90
Welsh (120)	451	1.95
West Indian, ex. Hispanic (71)	71	0.31
Haitian (52)	52	0.23
West Indian (19)	19	0.08

Hispanic Origin	Population	%
Hispanic or Latino (of any race)	600	2.60
Central American, ex. Mexican	93	0.40
Costa Rican	7	0.03
Guatemalan	64	0.28
Honduran	5	0.02
Nicaraguan	6	0.03
Panamanian	2	0.01
Salvadoran	9	0.04
Cuban	31	0.13
Dominican Republic	13	0.06
Mexican	138	0.60
Puerto Rican	205	0.89
South American	54	0.23
Argentinean	10	0.04
Chilean	1	<0.01
Colombian	22	0.10
Ecuadorian	5	0.02
Peruvian	12	0.05
Venezuelan	4	0.02
Other Hispanic or Latino	66	0.29

Race*	Population	%
African-American/Black (353)	437	1.90
Not Hispanic (338)	417	1.81
Hispanic (15)	20	0.09
American Indian/Alaska Native (36)	107	0.46
Not Hispanic (15)	76	0.33
Hispanic (21)	31	0.13
Apache (1)	1	<0.01
Blackfeet (0)	5	0.02
Cherokee (1)	12	0.05
Choctaw (0)	5	0.02
Comanche (0)	3	0.01
Creek (3)	5	0.02
Delaware (0)	2	0.01
Iroquois (2)	5	0.02
Lumbee (1)	1	<0.01
Mexican American Ind. (12)	12	0.05
Potawatomi (0)	2	0.01
Seminole (0)	1	<0.01
Sioux (0)	3	0.01
South American Ind. (1)	1	<0.01
Spanish American Ind. (1)	1	<0.01
Asian (467)	627	2.72
Not Hispanic (460)	613	2.66
Hispanic (7)	14	0.06
Burmese (5)	6	0.03
Cambodian (1)	1	<0.01
Chinese, ex. Taiwanese (120)	147	0.64
Filipino (42)	84	0.36
Indian (123)	137	0.59
Indonesian (0)	1	<0.01
Japanese (37)	70	0.30
Korean (102)	132	0.57
Laotian (0)	1	<0.01
Pakistani (6)	6	0.03
Taiwanese (4)	6	0.03
Vietnamese (15)	24	0.10
Hawaii Native/Pacific Islander (6)	25	0.11
Not Hispanic (4)	19	0.08
Hispanic (2)	6	0.03
Guamanian/Chamorro (2)	2	0.01
Native Hawaiian (0)	9	0.04
Samoan (4)	7	0.03
White (21,726)	22,017	95.59
Not Hispanic (21,330)	21,582	93.70
Hispanic (396)	435	1.89

*Notes: † The Census 2010 population figure is used to calculate the percentages in the Hispanic Origin and Race categories. Ancestry percentages are based on the 2006-2010 American Community Survey population (not shown); ‡ Numbers in parentheses indicate the number of people reporting a single ancestry; * Numbers in parentheses indicate the number of persons reporting this race alone, not in combination with any other race; Please refer to the Explanation of Data for more information.*

Mercerville

Place Type: CDP
County: Mercer
Population: 13,230†

Ancestry‡	Population	%
African, Sub-Saharan (45)	45	0.36
African (45)	45	0.36
Albanian (11)	34	0.27
American (261)	261	2.06
Arab (20)	20	0.16
Egyptian (20)	20	0.16
Armenian (11)	30	0.24
Australian (0)	30	0.24
Austrian (0)	9	0.07
Belgian (0)	15	0.12
British (12)	36	0.28
Canadian (18)	18	0.14
Carpatho Rusyn (6)	6	0.05
Czech (13)	41	0.32
Czechoslovakian (43)	79	0.62
Danish (0)	14	0.11
Dutch (27)	160	1.26
English (449)	1,613	12.74
French, ex. Basque (75)	264	2.08
French Canadian (13)	55	0.43
German (681)	2,465	19.47
Greek (37)	171	1.35
Hungarian (120)	440	3.47
Irish (614)	2,484	19.62
Italian (1,744)	3,628	28.65
Lithuanian (26)	59	0.47
Norwegian (0)	78	0.62
Polish (791)	1,584	12.51
Portuguese (12)	25	0.20
Romanian (10)	39	0.31
Russian (39)	160	1.26
Scandinavian (0)	7	0.06
Scotch-Irish (4)	131	1.03
Scottish (40)	152	1.20
Slavic (0)	31	0.24
Slovak (46)	100	0.79
Swedish (0)	167	1.32
Ukrainian (27)	100	0.79
Welsh (22)	79	0.62
West Indian, ex. Hispanic (275)	275	2.17
Haitian (261)	261	2.06
Jamaican (14)	14	0.11
Yugoslavian (0)	24	0.19

Hispanic Origin	Population	%
Hispanic or Latino (of any race)	907	6.86
Central American, ex. Mexican	112	0.85
Costa Rican	16	0.12
Guatemalan	86	0.65
Honduran	2	0.02
Panamanian	1	0.01
Other Central American	7	0.05
Cuban	23	0.17
Dominican Republic	55	0.42
Mexican	78	0.59
Puerto Rican	393	2.97
South American	170	1.28
Argentinean	7	0.05
Chilean	8	0.06
Colombian	45	0.34
Ecuadorian	72	0.54
Peruvian	16	0.12
Uruguayan	3	0.02
Venezuelan	11	0.08
Other South American	8	0.06
Other Hispanic or Latino	76	0.57

Race*	Population	%
African-American/Black (527)	596	4.50
Not Hispanic (491)	539	4.07
Hispanic (36)	57	0.43
American Indian/Alaska Native (29)	69	0.52
Not Hispanic (15)	46	0.35
Hispanic (14)	23	0.17
Aleut *(Alaska Native)* (1)	1	0.01
Apache (0)	1	0.01
Blackfeet (0)	4	0.03
Cherokee (1)	5	0.04
Chippewa (1)	1	0.01
Cree (0)	4	0.03
Delaware (0)	3	0.02
Iroquois (1)	6	0.05
Mexican American Ind. (5)	7	0.05
Sioux (0)	5	0.04
South American Ind. (9)	9	0.07
Tlingit-Haida *(Alaska Native)* (0)	1	0.01
Asian (486)	547	4.13
Not Hispanic (486)	543	4.10
Hispanic (0)	4	0.03
Bangladeshi (13)	14	0.11
Burmese (4)	4	0.03
Chinese, ex. Taiwanese (72)	83	0.63
Filipino (61)	74	0.56
Indian (170)	197	1.49
Indonesian (0)	1	0.01
Japanese (5)	9	0.07
Korean (37)	42	0.32
Pakistani (90)	103	0.78
Taiwanese (2)	4	0.03
Thai (0)	3	0.02
Vietnamese (16)	17	0.13
Hawaii Native/Pacific Islander (5)	17	0.13
Not Hispanic (0)	9	0.07
Hispanic (5)	8	0.06
Guamanian/Chamorro (5)	7	0.05
White (11,749)	11,898	89.93
Not Hispanic (11,189)	11,293	85.36
Hispanic (560)	605	4.57

Metuchen

Place Type: Borough
County: Middlesex
Population: 13,574†

Ancestry‡	Population	%
African, Sub-Saharan (102)	102	0.76
African (102)	102	0.76
Albanian (35)	35	0.26
American (693)	693	5.16
Arab (57)	72	0.54
Egyptian (57)	57	0.42
Syrian (0)	15	0.11
Austrian (30)	78	0.58
Belgian (9)	9	0.07
Brazilian (6)	6	0.04
British (83)	143	1.06
Canadian (4)	16	0.12
Celtic (0)	8	0.06
Croatian (15)	64	0.48
Czech (0)	206	1.53
Danish (25)	146	1.09
Dutch (47)	276	2.05
Eastern European (208)	233	1.73
English (178)	1,087	8.09
European (245)	290	2.16
Finnish (0)	9	0.07
French, ex. Basque (25)	167	1.24
French Canadian (23)	23	0.17
German (462)	1,930	14.37
Greek (45)	97	0.72
Hungarian (131)	301	2.24
Icelander (0)	12	0.09
Irish (711)	2,203	16.40
Israeli (74)	101	0.75
Italian (1,061)	2,623	19.53
Lithuanian (11)	25	0.19
Maltese (0)	11	0.08
Northern European (65)	65	0.48
Norwegian (12)	93	0.69
Polish (399)	1,091	8.12
Portuguese (47)	58	0.43
Romanian (50)	58	0.43
Russian (171)	476	3.54
Scandinavian (17)	32	0.24
Scotch-Irish (51)	174	1.30
Scottish (48)	207	1.54
Slavic (23)	97	0.72
Slovak (74)	106	0.79
Swedish (0)	154	1.15
Swiss (10)	25	0.19
Turkish (0)	9	0.07
Ukrainian (74)	166	1.24
Welsh (11)	75	0.56
West Indian, ex. Hispanic (50)	58	0.43
Dutch West Indian (10)	10	0.07
Haitian (19)	19	0.14
Jamaican (0)	8	0.06
Trinidadian/Tobagonian (12)	12	0.09
West Indian (9)	9	0.07

Hispanic Origin	Population	%
Hispanic or Latino (of any race)	935	6.89
Central American, ex. Mexican	65	0.48
Costa Rican	12	0.09
Guatemalan	19	0.14
Honduran	11	0.08
Nicaraguan	4	0.03
Panamanian	7	0.05
Salvadoran	12	0.09
Cuban	106	0.78
Dominican Republic	72	0.53
Mexican	69	0.51
Puerto Rican	341	2.51
South American	190	1.40
Argentinean	46	0.34
Bolivian	4	0.03
Chilean	9	0.07
Colombian	47	0.35
Ecuadorian	30	0.22
Paraguayan	3	0.02
Peruvian	30	0.22
Uruguayan	3	0.02
Venezuelan	18	0.13
Other Hispanic or Latino	92	0.68

Race*	Population	%
African-American/Black (662)	803	5.92
Not Hispanic (617)	725	5.34
Hispanic (45)	78	0.57
American Indian/Alaska Native (10)	62	0.46
Not Hispanic (8)	50	0.37
Hispanic (2)	12	0.09
Apache (0)	2	0.01
Central American Ind. (0)	3	0.02
Cherokee (1)	8	0.06
Creek (1)	1	0.01
Delaware (1)	1	0.01
Mexican American Ind. (1)	1	0.01
Seminole (0)	3	0.02
Sioux (2)	2	0.01
Asian (1,759)	1,968	14.50
Not Hispanic (1,744)	1,924	14.17
Hispanic (15)	44	0.32
Bangladeshi (5)	5	0.04
Chinese, ex. Taiwanese (445)	511	3.76
Filipino (197)	232	1.71
Indian (622)	671	4.94
Indonesian (58)	65	0.48
Japanese (41)	71	0.52
Korean (164)	195	1.44
Malaysian (1)	7	0.05
Nepalese (10)	11	0.08
Pakistani (48)	68	0.50
Sri Lankan (15)	17	0.13
Taiwanese (33)	35	0.26
Thai (5)	9	0.07
Vietnamese (65)	68	0.50
Hawaii Native/Pacific Islander (3)	8	0.06
Not Hispanic (3)	7	0.05
Hispanic (0)	1	0.01
Marshallese (1)	2	0.01
White (10,577)	10,871	80.09

*Notes: † The Census 2010 population figure is used to calculate the percentages in the Hispanic Origin and Race categories. Ancestry percentages are based on the 2006-2010 American Community Survey population (not shown); ‡ Numbers in parentheses indicate the number of people reporting a single ancestry; * Numbers in parentheses indicate the number of persons reporting this race alone, not in combination with any other race; Please refer to the Explanation of Data for more information.*

Not Hispanic (9,952)	10,168	74.91
Hispanic (625)	703	5.18

Middle

Place Type: Township
County: Cape May
Population: 18,911†

Ancestry‡	Population	%
African, Sub-Saharan (104)	104	0.57
African (86)	86	0.47
South African (18)	18	0.10
Albanian (7)	7	0.04
American (1,755)	1,755	9.55
Arab (0)	14	0.08
Lebanese (0)	14	0.08
Austrian (0)	16	0.09
Belgian (0)	10	0.05
British (31)	87	0.47
Canadian (0)	29	0.16
Croatian (9)	9	0.05
Czech (22)	40	0.22
Czechoslovakian (15)	15	0.08
Danish (4)	93	0.51
Dutch (14)	551	3.00
English (671)	2,424	13.19
European (105)	105	0.57
Finnish (20)	43	0.23
French, ex. Basque (50)	364	1.98
French Canadian (0)	15	0.08
German (1,076)	4,161	22.65
Greek (34)	38	0.21
Hungarian (7)	162	0.88
Icelander (0)	13	0.07
Irish (1,694)	4,857	26.43
Italian (941)	2,846	15.49
Lithuanian (37)	111	0.60
Norwegian (31)	131	0.71
Pennsylvania German (29)	29	0.16
Polish (298)	1,006	5.48
Portuguese (30)	43	0.23
Romanian (8)	18	0.10
Russian (48)	174	0.95
Scandinavian (17)	42	0.23
Scotch-Irish (189)	345	1.88
Scottish (123)	398	2.17
Serbian (13)	13	0.07
Slavic (6)	53	0.29
Slovak (30)	93	0.51
Swedish (54)	323	1.76
Swiss (13)	45	0.24
Ukrainian (14)	94	0.51
Welsh (34)	142	0.77
West Indian, ex. Hispanic (134)	143	0.78
Bahamian (47)	56	0.30
Jamaican (39)	39	0.21
West Indian (48)	48	0.26

Hispanic Origin	Population	%
Hispanic or Latino (of any race)	962	5.09
Central American, ex. Mexican	66	0.35
Costa Rican	8	0.04
Guatemalan	37	0.20
Honduran	1	0.01
Nicaraguan	2	0.01
Panamanian	16	0.08
Salvadoran	2	0.01
Cuban	24	0.13
Dominican Republic	14	0.07
Mexican	239	1.26
Puerto Rican	473	2.50
South American	43	0.23
Argentinean	19	0.10
Chilean	4	0.02
Colombian	13	0.07
Paraguayan	1	0.01
Peruvian	4	0.02
Venezuelan	2	0.01
Other Hispanic or Latino	103	0.54

Race*	Population	%
African-American/Black (1,969)	2,273	12.02
Not Hispanic (1,885)	2,139	11.31
Hispanic (84)	134	0.71
American Indian/Alaska Native (34)	170	0.90
Not Hispanic (29)	150	0.79
Hispanic (5)	20	0.11
Apache (1)	4	0.02
Blackfeet (1)	18	0.10
Central American Ind. (1)	1	0.01
Cherokee (3)	30	0.16
Cheyenne (1)	1	0.01
Creek (1)	1	0.01
Delaware (1)	6	0.03
Iroquois (4)	5	0.03
Lumbee (1)	2	0.01
Mexican American Ind. (1)	1	0.01
Navajo (2)	2	0.01
Sioux (0)	1	0.01
Yakama (0)	6	0.03
Asian (339)	410	2.17
Not Hispanic (338)	400	2.12
Hispanic (1)	10	0.05
Cambodian (0)	2	0.01
Chinese, ex. Taiwanese (42)	51	0.27
Filipino (104)	125	0.66
Indian (101)	121	0.64
Indonesian (4)	4	0.02
Japanese (0)	8	0.04
Korean (20)	34	0.18
Nepalese (1)	1	0.01
Pakistani (3)	3	0.02
Taiwanese (8)	8	0.04
Thai (2)	3	0.02
Vietnamese (42)	42	0.22
Hawaii Native/Pacific Islander (9)	13	0.07
Not Hispanic (7)	8	0.04
Hispanic (2)	5	0.03
Guamanian/Chamorro (2)	2	0.01
Native Hawaiian (1)	3	0.02
Samoan (1)	1	0.01
White (15,716)	16,121	85.25
Not Hispanic (15,276)	15,608	82.53
Hispanic (440)	513	2.71

Middlesex

Place Type: Borough
County: Middlesex
Population: 13,635†

Ancestry‡	Population	%
African, Sub-Saharan (349)	367	2.69
African (149)	167	1.22
Other Sub-Saharan African (200)	200	1.46
American (588)	588	4.31
Arab (66)	81	0.59
Egyptian (66)	66	0.48
Syrian (0)	15	0.11
Armenian (0)	13	0.10
Austrian (0)	85	0.62
Belgian (0)	13	0.10
Brazilian (0)	6	0.04
Canadian (55)	83	0.61
Czech (38)	105	0.77
Czechoslovakian (15)	57	0.42
Danish (70)	124	0.91
Dutch (35)	185	1.36
English (133)	955	7.00
European (55)	55	0.40
Finnish (0)	13	0.10
French, ex. Basque (32)	313	2.29
French Canadian (50)	62	0.45
German (438)	2,351	17.22
Greek (56)	95	0.70
Hungarian (13)	503	3.68
Irish (509)	2,517	18.44
Italian (1,554)	2,941	21.54
Latvian (0)	23	0.17
Lithuanian (0)	15	0.11
Norwegian (15)	83	0.61
Pennsylvania German (40)	51	0.37
Polish (861)	1,617	11.84
Portuguese (0)	6	0.04
Romanian (248)	248	1.82
Russian (202)	450	3.30
Scotch-Irish (0)	123	0.90
Scottish (30)	171	1.25
Serbian (0)	25	0.18
Slavic (13)	13	0.10
Slovak (58)	120	0.88
Swiss (0)	53	0.39
Ukrainian (139)	183	1.34
Welsh (0)	107	0.78
West Indian, ex. Hispanic (13)	13	0.10
Jamaican (13)	13	0.10

Hispanic Origin	Population	%
Hispanic or Latino (of any race)	2,246	16.47
Central American, ex. Mexican	495	3.63
Costa Rican	161	1.18
Guatemalan	92	0.67
Honduran	21	0.15
Nicaraguan	19	0.14
Panamanian	8	0.06
Salvadoran	194	1.42
Cuban	49	0.36
Dominican Republic	102	0.75
Mexican	110	0.81
Puerto Rican	428	3.14
South American	874	6.41
Argentinean	36	0.26
Bolivian	6	0.04
Chilean	8	0.06
Colombian	344	2.52
Ecuadorian	193	1.42
Paraguayan	7	0.05
Peruvian	262	1.92
Uruguayan	9	0.07
Venezuelan	5	0.04
Other South American	4	0.03
Other Hispanic or Latino	188	1.38

Race*	Population	%
African-American/Black (699)	817	5.99
Not Hispanic (645)	714	5.24
Hispanic (54)	103	0.76
American Indian/Alaska Native (24)	72	0.53
Not Hispanic (8)	39	0.29
Hispanic (16)	33	0.24
Arapaho (0)	1	0.01
Blackfeet (1)	1	0.01
Canadian/French Am. Ind. (5)	5	0.04
Cherokee (0)	4	0.03
Delaware (1)	1	0.01
Iroquois (1)	1	0.01
Lumbee (1)	1	0.01
Mexican American Ind. (1)	1	0.01
South American Ind. (4)	10	0.07
Asian (818)	889	6.52
Not Hispanic (804)	864	6.34
Hispanic (14)	25	0.18
Bangladeshi (8)	8	0.06
Burmese (0)	2	0.01
Chinese, ex. Taiwanese (113)	135	0.99
Filipino (172)	200	1.47
Hmong (1)	1	0.01
Indian (216)	238	1.75
Japanese (6)	9	0.07
Korean (20)	25	0.18
Laotian (9)	9	0.07
Pakistani (14)	14	0.10
Sri Lankan (2)	8	0.06
Taiwanese (4)	4	0.03
Thai (6)	10	0.07
Vietnamese (226)	231	1.69
Hawaii Native/Pacific Islander (10)	14	0.10
Not Hispanic (5)	6	0.04
Hispanic (5)	8	0.06

*Notes: † The Census 2010 population figure is used to calculate the percentages in the Hispanic Origin and Race categories. Ancestry percentages are based on the 2006-2010 American Community Survey population (not shown); ‡ Numbers in parentheses indicate the number of people reporting a single ancestry; * Numbers in parentheses indicate the number of persons reporting this race alone, not in combination with any other race; Please refer to the Explanation of Data for more information.*

Guamanian/Chamorro (2)	2	0.01
Samoan (4)	4	0.03
White (11,077)	11,303	82.90
Not Hispanic (9,748)	9,878	72.45
Hispanic (1,329)	1,425	10.45

Middletown

Place Type: Township
County: Monmouth
Population: 66,522†

Ancestry‡	Population	%
African, Sub-Saharan (148)	184	0.28
African (54)	90	0.13
Ghanaian (47)	47	0.07
South African (47)	47	0.07
Albanian (27)	85	0.13
Alsatian (0)	15	0.02
American (2,419)	2,419	3.63
Arab (260)	365	0.55
Arab (8)	15	0.02
Egyptian (140)	140	0.21
Jordanian (42)	42	0.06
Lebanese (63)	94	0.14
Moroccan (0)	13	0.02
Syrian (7)	28	0.04
Other Arab (0)	33	0.05
Armenian (104)	191	0.29
Austrian (110)	550	0.82
Belgian (0)	70	0.10
Brazilian (42)	62	0.09
British (187)	347	0.52
Canadian (128)	307	0.46
Celtic (11)	11	0.02
Croatian (11)	60	0.09
Czech (13)	520	0.78
Czechoslovakian (32)	147	0.22
Danish (150)	416	0.62
Dutch (86)	989	1.48
Eastern European (104)	118	0.18
English (791)	4,987	7.48
European (435)	458	0.69
Finnish (12)	217	0.33
French, ex. Basque (128)	1,158	1.74
French Canadian (111)	232	0.35
German (2,305)	11,682	17.51
Greek (128)	516	0.77
Guyanese (210)	236	0.35
Hungarian (260)	1,180	1.77
Iranian (38)	38	0.06
Irish (7,267)	23,587	35.36
Israeli (12)	23	0.03
Italian (8,216)	20,292	30.42
Latvian (36)	36	0.05
Lithuanian (62)	262	0.39
Northern European (19)	19	0.03
Norwegian (201)	740	1.11
Polish (1,573)	5,449	8.17
Portuguese (202)	424	0.64
Romanian (0)	92	0.14
Russian (634)	1,446	2.17
Scandinavian (15)	93	0.14
Scotch-Irish (577)	1,237	1.85
Scottish (310)	1,126	1.69
Slavic (7)	63	0.09
Slovak (108)	382	0.57
Slovene (9)	9	0.01
Swedish (150)	993	1.49
Swiss (106)	294	0.44
Turkish (173)	173	0.26
Ukrainian (224)	666	1.00
Welsh (21)	267	0.40
West Indian, ex. Hispanic (262)	408	0.61
Barbadian (78)	78	0.12
British West Indian (17)	25	0.04
Haitian (9)	9	0.01
Jamaican (25)	35	0.05
Trinidadian/Tobagonian (0)	9	0.01
West Indian (133)	252	0.38
Yugoslavian (28)	75	0.11

Hispanic Origin	Population	%
Hispanic or Latino (of any race)	3,569	5.37
Central American, ex. Mexican	143	0.21
Costa Rican	17	0.03
Guatemalan	28	0.04
Honduran	18	0.03
Nicaraguan	10	0.02
Panamanian	13	0.02
Salvadoran	56	0.08
Other Central American	1	<0.01
Cuban	342	0.51
Dominican Republic	146	0.22
Mexican	411	0.62
Puerto Rican	1,545	2.32
South American	564	0.85
Argentinean	59	0.09
Bolivian	16	0.02
Chilean	36	0.05
Colombian	158	0.24
Ecuadorian	156	0.23
Paraguayan	10	0.02
Peruvian	86	0.13
Uruguayan	12	0.02
Venezuelan	23	0.03
Other South American	8	0.01
Other Hispanic or Latino	418	0.63

Race*	Population	%
African-American/Black (869)	1,171	1.76
Not Hispanic (814)	1,047	1.57
Hispanic (55)	124	0.19
American Indian/Alaska Native (67)	214	0.32
Not Hispanic (44)	172	0.26
Hispanic (23)	42	0.06
Apache (0)	1	<0.01
Blackfeet (0)	11	0.02
Central American Ind. (1)	4	0.01
Cherokee (6)	30	0.05
Cheyenne (0)	1	<0.01
Chickasaw (1)	1	<0.01
Cree (1)	1	<0.01
Creek (2)	3	<0.01
Delaware (2)	20	0.03
Iroquois (6)	8	0.01
Mexican American Ind. (2)	6	0.01
Navajo (0)	1	<0.01
Potawatomi (1)	2	<0.01
Pueblo (4)	4	0.01
Seminole (0)	5	0.01
Sioux (0)	1	<0.01
South American Ind. (2)	3	<0.01
Spanish American Ind. (1)	1	<0.01
Yup'ik *(Alaska Native)* (0)	1	<0.01
Asian (1,730)	2,095	3.15
Not Hispanic (1,717)	2,028	3.05
Hispanic (13)	67	0.10
Bangladeshi (11)	11	0.02
Burmese (2)	2	<0.01
Cambodian (2)	2	<0.01
Chinese, ex. Taiwanese (538)	638	0.96
Filipino (305)	410	0.62
Indian (449)	494	0.74
Indonesian (5)	8	0.01
Japanese (35)	88	0.13
Korean (168)	198	0.30
Pakistani (40)	44	0.07
Taiwanese (44)	50	0.08
Thai (7)	9	0.01
Vietnamese (66)	88	0.13
Hawaii Native/Pacific Islander (8)	31	0.05
Not Hispanic (6)	25	0.04
Hispanic (2)	6	0.01
Fijian (0)	3	<0.01
Guamanian/Chamorro (3)	6	0.01
Marshallese (2)	4	0.01
Native Hawaiian (0)	5	0.01
Samoan (0)	1	<0.01
Tongan (1)	1	<0.01
White (62,456)	63,218	95.03
Not Hispanic (59,702)	60,242	90.56
Hispanic (2,754)	2,976	4.47

Millburn

Place Type: Township
County: Essex
Population: 20,149†

Ancestry‡	Population	%
African, Sub-Saharan (87)	132	0.66
African (36)	36	0.18
Nigerian (11)	11	0.06
South African (22)	67	0.34
Zimbabwean (18)	18	0.09
Albanian (25)	103	0.52
American (1,297)	1,297	6.50
Arab (50)	207	1.04
Egyptian (0)	73	0.37
Lebanese (32)	67	0.34
Palestinian (7)	22	0.11
Syrian (11)	28	0.14
Other Arab (0)	17	0.09
Armenian (42)	46	0.23
Australian (39)	39	0.20
Austrian (146)	350	1.75
Basque (32)	32	0.16
Brazilian (60)	102	0.51
British (50)	149	0.75
Bulgarian (55)	55	0.28
Canadian (31)	31	0.16
Croatian (0)	21	0.11
Czech (44)	111	0.56
Czechoslovakian (10)	10	0.05
Dutch (25)	210	1.05
Eastern European (913)	945	4.73
English (261)	1,208	6.05
European (417)	455	2.28
Finnish (9)	38	0.19
French, ex. Basque (33)	157	0.79
French Canadian (52)	172	0.86
German (623)	2,243	11.24
Greek (43)	103	0.52
Hungarian (104)	388	1.94
Iranian (94)	94	0.47
Irish (531)	2,025	10.15
Israeli (40)	89	0.45
Italian (1,178)	2,583	12.94
Latvian (20)	38	0.19
Lithuanian (60)	177	0.89
Northern European (38)	38	0.19
Norwegian (19)	93	0.47
Polish (473)	1,289	6.46
Portuguese (51)	58	0.29
Romanian (39)	88	0.44
Russian (907)	1,963	9.84
Scotch-Irish (64)	149	0.75
Scottish (100)	290	1.45
Serbian (48)	60	0.30
Slovak (40)	67	0.34
Swedish (89)	196	0.98
Swiss (18)	132	0.66
Turkish (10)	27	0.14
Ukrainian (149)	315	1.58
Welsh (11)	78	0.39
West Indian, ex. Hispanic (39)	49	0.25
Bermudan (12)	12	0.06
Dutch West Indian (0)	10	0.05
Jamaican (10)	10	0.05
Trinidadian/Tobagonian (17)	17	0.09
Yugoslavian (10)	10	0.05

Hispanic Origin	Population	%
Hispanic or Latino (of any race)	703	3.49
Central American, ex. Mexican	108	0.54
Costa Rican	46	0.23
Guatemalan	26	0.13
Honduran	16	0.08
Nicaraguan	5	0.02

*Notes: † The Census 2010 population figure is used to calculate the percentages in the Hispanic Origin and Race categories. Ancestry percentages are based on the 2006-2010 American Community Survey population (not shown); ‡ Numbers in parentheses indicate the number of people reporting a single ancestry; * Numbers in parentheses indicate the number of persons reporting this race alone, not in combination with any other race; Please refer to the Explanation of Data for more information.*

Panamanian	6	0.03
Salvadoran	8	0.04
Other Central American	1	<0.01
Cuban	64	0.32
Dominican Republic	24	0.12
Mexican	77	0.38
Puerto Rican	100	0.50
South American	231	1.15
Argentinean	58	0.29
Bolivian	11	0.05
Chilean	16	0.08
Colombian	69	0.34
Ecuadorian	37	0.18
Paraguayan	4	0.02
Peruvian	25	0.12
Uruguayan	3	0.01
Venezuelan	7	0.03
Other South American	1	<0.01
Other Hispanic or Latino	99	0.49

Race*	Population	%
African-American/Black (329)	361	1.79
Not Hispanic (303)	331	1.64
Hispanic (26)	30	0.15
American Indian/Alaska Native (6)	32	0.16
Not Hispanic (5)	26	0.13
Hispanic (1)	6	0.03
Blackfeet (0)	1	<0.01
Cherokee (1)	6	0.03
Creek (1)	1	<0.01
Mexican American Ind. (1)	2	0.01
South American Ind. (0)	1	<0.01
Asian (3,155)	3,487	17.31
Not Hispanic (3,149)	3,470	17.22
Hispanic (6)	17	0.08
Burmese (2)	5	0.02
Cambodian (2)	2	0.01
Chinese, ex. Taiwanese (1,430)	1,584	7.86
Filipino (145)	181	0.90
Indian (915)	981	4.87
Indonesian (2)	3	0.01
Japanese (63)	109	0.54
Korean (341)	393	1.95
Laotian (1)	1	<0.01
Malaysian (12)	14	0.07
Nepalese (9)	9	0.04
Pakistani (35)	38	0.19
Sri Lankan (3)	3	0.01
Taiwanese (93)	118	0.59
Thai (10)	12	0.06
Vietnamese (8)	16	0.08
Hawaii Native/Pacific Islander (5)	17	0.08
Not Hispanic (5)	17	0.08
Guamanian/Chamorro (1)	3	0.01
Native Hawaiian (2)	8	0.04
White (16,154)	16,506	81.92
Not Hispanic (15,587)	15,919	79.01
Hispanic (567)	587	2.91

Millstone

Place Type: Township
County: Monmouth
Population: 10,566†

Ancestry‡	Population	%
American (1,541)	1,541	14.97
Arab (102)	167	1.62
Egyptian (78)	78	0.76
Lebanese (13)	37	0.36
Syrian (11)	52	0.51
Austrian (13)	41	0.40
Brazilian (68)	68	0.66
British (35)	87	0.85
Bulgarian (11)	22	0.21
Croatian (110)	134	1.30
Czech (13)	61	0.59
Danish (0)	17	0.17
Dutch (38)	110	1.07
Eastern European (11)	11	0.11
English (29)	637	6.19
European (84)	84	0.82
French, ex. Basque (16)	218	2.12
German (189)	1,175	11.42
Greek (56)	115	1.12
Hungarian (36)	296	2.88
Irish (847)	2,307	22.41
Italian (1,491)	2,722	26.45
Lithuanian (0)	14	0.14
Northern European (37)	37	0.36
Norwegian (9)	40	0.39
Polish (215)	1,046	10.16
Portuguese (99)	99	0.96
Romanian (0)	14	0.14
Russian (289)	547	5.31
Scandinavian (0)	11	0.11
Scotch-Irish (106)	156	1.52
Scottish (75)	102	0.99
Slovak (30)	42	0.41
Slovene (0)	11	0.11
Swedish (0)	41	0.40
Ukrainian (15)	39	0.38
Welsh (0)	13	0.13

Hispanic Origin	Population	%
Hispanic or Latino (of any race)	579	5.48
Central American, ex. Mexican	32	0.30
Costa Rican	1	0.01
Guatemalan	16	0.15
Honduran	2	0.02
Nicaraguan	4	0.04
Panamanian	3	0.03
Salvadoran	6	0.06
Cuban	84	0.80
Dominican Republic	13	0.12
Mexican	83	0.79
Puerto Rican	225	2.13
South American	81	0.77
Argentinean	11	0.10
Bolivian	6	0.06
Chilean	2	0.02
Colombian	28	0.27
Ecuadorian	10	0.09
Peruvian	11	0.10
Uruguayan	6	0.06
Venezuelan	2	0.02
Other South American	5	0.05
Other Hispanic or Latino	61	0.58

Race*	Population	%
African-American/Black (379)	424	4.01
Not Hispanic (363)	397	3.76
Hispanic (16)	27	0.26
American Indian/Alaska Native (18)	68	0.64
Not Hispanic (11)	56	0.53
Hispanic (7)	12	0.11
Apache (0)	3	0.03
Central American Ind. (0)	1	0.01
Cherokee (7)	12	0.11
Creek (0)	3	0.03
Delaware (0)	13	0.12
Kiowa (0)	1	0.01
Lumbee (1)	4	0.04
Pueblo (0)	3	0.03
Asian (476)	551	5.21
Not Hispanic (472)	544	5.15
Hispanic (4)	7	0.07
Bangladeshi (2)	2	0.02
Chinese, ex. Taiwanese (105)	130	1.23
Filipino (67)	93	0.88
Indian (234)	246	2.33
Indonesian (0)	4	0.04
Japanese (5)	15	0.14
Korean (33)	35	0.33
Pakistani (11)	13	0.12
Thai (1)	1	0.01
Vietnamese (8)	10	0.09
Hawaii Native/Pacific Islander (0)	4	0.04
Not Hispanic (0)	4	0.04
Native Hawaiian (0)	2	0.02
White (9,450)	9,593	90.79
Not Hispanic (8,993)	9,111	86.23
Hispanic (457)	482	4.56

Millville

Place Type: City
County: Cumberland
Population: 28,400†

Ancestry‡	Population	%
African, Sub-Saharan (528)	580	2.06
African (528)	538	1.91
Ghanaian (0)	21	0.07
Other Sub-Saharan African (0)	21	0.07
American (1,787)	1,787	6.35
Arab (98)	98	0.35
Egyptian (84)	84	0.30
Lebanese (14)	14	0.05
Austrian (48)	144	0.51
British (38)	106	0.38
Canadian (8)	8	0.03
Czech (0)	55	0.20
Czechoslovakian (19)	57	0.20
Danish (0)	34	0.12
Dutch (69)	320	1.14
Eastern European (8)	8	0.03
English (939)	3,056	10.86
European (99)	125	0.44
Finnish (0)	14	0.05
French, ex. Basque (82)	639	2.27
French Canadian (16)	55	0.20
German (1,091)	4,879	17.34
Greek (0)	25	0.09
Guyanese (42)	42	0.15
Hungarian (15)	65	0.23
Irish (679)	3,406	12.11
Italian (1,963)	3,622	12.87
Lithuanian (14)	28	0.10
Norwegian (23)	99	0.35
Pennsylvania German (71)	97	0.34
Polish (363)	1,074	3.82
Portuguese (12)	65	0.23
Romanian (5)	11	0.04
Russian (176)	381	1.35
Scandinavian (46)	46	0.16
Scotch-Irish (115)	348	1.24
Scottish (128)	457	1.62
Serbian (0)	37	0.13
Slavic (10)	10	0.04
Slovak (0)	26	0.09
Swedish (11)	354	1.26
Swiss (0)	16	0.06
Turkish (0)	25	0.09
Ukrainian (334)	398	1.41
Welsh (12)	120	0.43
West Indian, ex. Hispanic (198)	369	1.31
Belizean (20)	20	0.07
Haitian (56)	101	0.36
Jamaican (70)	132	0.47
Trinidadian/Tobagonian (0)	64	0.23
West Indian (52)	52	0.18

Hispanic Origin	Population	%
Hispanic or Latino (of any race)	4,239	14.93
Central American, ex. Mexican	42	0.15
Costa Rican	14	0.05
Guatemalan	7	0.02
Honduran	11	0.04
Nicaraguan	4	0.01
Panamanian	4	0.01
Salvadoran	2	0.01
Cuban	62	0.22
Dominican Republic	78	0.27
Mexican	263	0.93
Puerto Rican	3,538	12.46
South American	74	0.26
Argentinean	6	0.02
Bolivian	2	0.01
Chilean	3	0.01

SECTION TWO

*Notes: † The Census 2010 population figure is used to calculate the percentages in the Hispanic Origin and Race categories. Ancestry percentages are based on the 2006-2010 American Community Survey population (not shown); ‡ Numbers in parentheses indicate the number of people reporting a single ancestry; * Numbers in parentheses indicate the number of persons reporting this race alone, not in combination with any other race; Please refer to the Explanation of Data for more information.*

Colombian	27	0.10
Ecuadorian	6	0.02
Peruvian	17	0.06
Uruguayan	9	0.03
Venezuelan	3	0.01
Other South American	1	<0.01
Other Hispanic or Latino	182	0.64

Race*	Population	%
African-American/Black (5,631)	6,316	22.24
Not Hispanic (5,228)	5,715	20.12
Hispanic (403)	601	2.12
American Indian/Alaska Native (266)	573	2.02
Not Hispanic (177)	442	1.56
Hispanic (89)	131	0.46
Apache (0)	1	<0.01
Blackfeet (1)	9	0.03
Central American Ind. (4)	5	0.02
Cherokee (10)	70	0.25
Choctaw (0)	4	0.01
Comanche (0)	1	<0.01
Crow (0)	2	0.01
Delaware (37)	93	0.33
Iroquois (1)	4	0.01
Lumbee (2)	2	0.01
Mexican American Ind. (1)	1	<0.01
Navajo (0)	4	0.01
Shoshone (0)	1	<0.01
Sioux (2)	8	0.03
South American Ind. (13)	16	0.06
Spanish American Ind. (1)	2	0.01
Asian (338)	443	1.56
Not Hispanic (329)	412	1.45
Hispanic (9)	31	0.11
Bangladeshi (1)	1	<0.01
Cambodian (2)	6	0.02
Chinese, ex. Taiwanese (74)	95	0.33
Filipino (104)	135	0.48
Indian (59)	81	0.29
Japanese (13)	38	0.13
Korean (41)	46	0.16
Laotian (4)	12	0.04
Nepalese (3)	3	0.01
Pakistani (10)	13	0.05
Sri Lankan (0)	1	<0.01
Thai (2)	5	0.02
Vietnamese (11)	18	0.06
Hawaii Native/Pacific Islander (18)	53	0.19
Not Hispanic (7)	23	0.08
Hispanic (11)	30	0.11
Guamanian/Chamorro (6)	8	0.03
Native Hawaiian (2)	16	0.06
Samoan (6)	7	0.02
White (19,608)	20,379	71.76
Not Hispanic (17,720)	18,243	64.24
Hispanic (1,888)	2,136	7.52

Monroe

Place Type: Township
County: Gloucester
Population: 36,129†

Ancestry‡	Population	%
African, Sub-Saharan (286)	291	0.83
African (226)	226	0.64
Ghanaian (60)	65	0.18
Albanian (12)	35	0.10
American (1,204)	1,204	3.42
Arab (18)	49	0.14
Lebanese (18)	32	0.09
Palestinian (0)	17	0.05
Armenian (14)	14	0.04
Austrian (22)	86	0.24
Belgian (0)	10	0.03
Brazilian (88)	132	0.38
British (10)	60	0.17
Canadian (0)	8	0.02
Croatian (0)	37	0.11
Czech (0)	91	0.26
Czechoslovakian (22)	34	0.10
Danish (26)	166	0.47
Dutch (51)	376	1.07
Eastern European (11)	11	0.03
English (595)	3,165	8.99
Estonian (10)	10	0.03
European (196)	211	0.60
Finnish (0)	15	0.04
French, ex. Basque (46)	851	2.42
French Canadian (0)	76	0.22
German (1,332)	7,759	22.05
Greek (85)	274	0.78
Guyanese (25)	48	0.14
Hungarian (24)	132	0.38
Irish (2,366)	9,890	28.10
Italian (4,281)	9,446	26.84
Lithuanian (31)	162	0.46
Norwegian (23)	87	0.25
Pennsylvania German (14)	62	0.18
Polish (767)	3,057	8.69
Portuguese (27)	72	0.20
Romanian (24)	100	0.28
Russian (12)	348	0.99
Scandinavian (0)	25	0.07
Scotch-Irish (148)	423	1.20
Scottish (90)	592	1.68
Slovak (13)	94	0.27
Swedish (44)	192	0.55
Swiss (0)	64	0.18
Turkish (13)	13	0.04
Ukrainian (136)	316	0.90
Welsh (11)	215	0.61
West Indian, ex. Hispanic (123)	218	0.62
British West Indian (33)	57	0.16
Haitian (0)	16	0.05
Jamaican (44)	68	0.19
Trinidadian/Tobagonian (23)	23	0.07
West Indian (23)	54	0.15
Yugoslavian (0)	54	0.15

Hispanic Origin	Population	%
Hispanic or Latino (of any race)	1,795	4.97
Central American, ex. Mexican	60	0.17
Costa Rican	11	0.03
Guatemalan	25	0.07
Honduran	5	0.01
Nicaraguan	5	0.01
Panamanian	8	0.02
Salvadoran	6	0.02
Cuban	67	0.19
Dominican Republic	44	0.12
Mexican	268	0.74
Puerto Rican	1,014	2.81
South American	185	0.51
Argentinean	8	0.02
Chilean	8	0.02
Colombian	43	0.12
Ecuadorian	99	0.27
Peruvian	24	0.07
Venezuelan	3	0.01
Other Hispanic or Latino	157	0.43

Race*	Population	%
African-American/Black (5,060)	5,583	15.45
Not Hispanic (4,935)	5,369	14.86
Hispanic (125)	214	0.59
American Indian/Alaska Native (73)	306	0.85
Not Hispanic (60)	269	0.74
Hispanic (13)	37	0.10
Apache (0)	5	0.01
Blackfeet (2)	12	0.03
Canadian/French Am. Ind. (0)	1	<0.01
Central American Ind. (3)	4	0.01
Cherokee (12)	61	0.17
Chippewa (0)	5	0.01
Crow (0)	2	0.01
Delaware (2)	18	0.05
Iroquois (2)	7	0.02
Lumbee (1)	3	0.01
Mexican American Ind. (0)	1	<0.01
Navajo (0)	1	<0.01
Seminole (0)	7	0.02
Sioux (3)	8	0.02
South American Ind. (1)	2	0.01
Asian (875)	1,053	2.91
Not Hispanic (862)	1,015	2.81
Hispanic (13)	38	0.11
Bangladeshi (4)	4	0.01
Cambodian (26)	29	0.08
Chinese, ex. Taiwanese (136)	174	0.48
Filipino (305)	379	1.05
Indian (228)	249	0.69
Indonesian (12)	12	0.03
Japanese (16)	43	0.12
Korean (45)	62	0.17
Malaysian (0)	8	0.02
Pakistani (23)	30	0.08
Taiwanese (0)	2	0.01
Thai (1)	3	0.01
Vietnamese (50)	66	0.18
Hawaii Native/Pacific Islander (5)	41	0.11
Not Hispanic (4)	37	0.10
Hispanic (1)	4	0.01
Guamanian/Chamorro (1)	2	0.01
Native Hawaiian (3)	14	0.04
Samoan (1)	4	0.01
White (28,689)	29,375	81.31
Not Hispanic (27,765)	28,313	78.37
Hispanic (924)	1,062	2.94

Monroe

Place Type: Township
County: Middlesex
Population: 39,132†

Ancestry‡	Population	%
African, Sub-Saharan (39)	64	0.17
African (29)	54	0.15
Nigerian (10)	10	0.03
Albanian (79)	79	0.21
American (1,328)	1,328	3.57
Arab (257)	307	0.83
Arab (0)	14	0.04
Egyptian (248)	248	0.67
Iraqi (2)	2	0.01
Palestinian (7)	7	0.02
Syrian (0)	36	0.10
Armenian (0)	47	0.13
Austrian (223)	522	1.40
Belgian (7)	28	0.08
Brazilian (174)	174	0.47
British (10)	66	0.18
Bulgarian (0)	23	0.06
Canadian (0)	17	0.05
Croatian (13)	46	0.12
Czech (26)	83	0.22
Czechoslovakian (23)	87	0.23
Danish (14)	99	0.27
Dutch (39)	238	0.64
Eastern European (214)	214	0.58
English (527)	1,929	5.19
Estonian (28)	28	0.08
European (359)	398	1.07
Finnish (0)	76	0.20
French, ex. Basque (105)	355	0.96
French Canadian (20)	106	0.29
German (1,000)	3,517	9.46
Greek (200)	405	1.09
Guyanese (21)	21	0.06
Hungarian (480)	1,053	2.83
Icelander (7)	17	0.05
Irish (1,680)	5,027	13.52
Israeli (29)	29	0.08
Italian (4,601)	7,672	20.64
Latvian (0)	11	0.03
Lithuanian (40)	107	0.29
Maltese (0)	20	0.05
Norwegian (155)	319	0.86
Pennsylvania German (0)	12	0.03

*Notes: † The Census 2010 population figure is used to calculate the percentages in the Hispanic Origin and Race categories. Ancestry percentages are based on the 2006-2010 American Community Survey population (not shown); ‡ Numbers in parentheses indicate the number of people reporting a single ancestry; * Numbers in parentheses indicate the number of persons reporting this race alone, not in combination with any other race; Please refer to the Explanation of Data for more information.*

Polish (2,453)	4,666	12.55
Portuguese (241)	294	0.79
Romanian (141)	229	0.62
Russian (1,581)	2,769	7.45
Scotch-Irish (61)	183	0.49
Scottish (64)	313	0.84
Serbian (11)	11	0.03
Slavic (0)	24	0.06
Slovak (180)	340	0.91
Slovene (23)	37	0.10
Swedish (75)	250	0.67
Swiss (0)	48	0.13
Turkish (23)	36	0.10
Ukrainian (216)	475	1.28
Welsh (0)	95	0.26
West Indian, ex. Hispanic (83)	221	0.59
Barbadian (0)	14	0.04
Haitian (56)	154	0.41
Jamaican (14)	28	0.08
West Indian (13)	25	0.07
Yugoslavian (0)	15	0.04

Hispanic Origin	Population	%
Hispanic or Latino (of any race)	1,673	4.28
Central American, ex. Mexican	91	0.23
Costa Rican	11	0.03
Guatemalan	14	0.04
Honduran	22	0.06
Nicaraguan	20	0.05
Panamanian	4	0.01
Salvadoran	13	0.03
Other Central American	7	0.02
Cuban	246	0.63
Dominican Republic	91	0.23
Mexican	102	0.26
Puerto Rican	647	1.65
South American	324	0.83
Argentinean	42	0.11
Bolivian	3	0.01
Chilean	9	0.02
Colombian	105	0.27
Ecuadorian	60	0.15
Peruvian	67	0.17
Uruguayan	20	0.05
Venezuelan	12	0.03
Other South American	6	0.02
Other Hispanic or Latino	172	0.44

Race*	Population	%
African-American/Black (1,533)	1,672	4.27
Not Hispanic (1,486)	1,601	4.09
Hispanic (47)	71	0.18
American Indian/Alaska Native (33)	120	0.31
Not Hispanic (24)	104	0.27
Hispanic (9)	16	0.04
Blackfeet (0)	1	<0.01
Cherokee (1)	11	0.03
Cree (0)	1	<0.01
Delaware (3)	11	0.03
Iroquois (0)	4	0.01
Pueblo (1)	1	<0.01
Seminole (0)	2	0.01
Sioux (0)	1	<0.01
South American Ind. (4)	5	0.01
Asian (4,930)	5,206	13.30
Not Hispanic (4,911)	5,170	13.21
Hispanic (19)	36	0.09
Bangladeshi (22)	28	0.07
Chinese, ex. Taiwanese (788)	869	2.22
Filipino (561)	623	1.59
Indian (2,850)	2,952	7.54
Japanese (26)	43	0.11
Korean (270)	287	0.73
Malaysian (2)	2	0.01
Nepalese (5)	5	0.01
Pakistani (209)	226	0.58
Sri Lankan (20)	20	0.05
Taiwanese (41)	49	0.13
Thai (8)	12	0.03
Vietnamese (67)	80	0.20
Hawaii Native/Pacific Islander (4)	9	0.02
Not Hispanic (4)	9	0.02
Guamanian/Chamorro (2)	2	0.01
Samoan (2)	2	0.01
White (31,913)	32,268	82.46
Not Hispanic (30,576)	30,872	78.89
Hispanic (1,337)	1,396	3.57

Montclair

Place Type: Township
County: Essex
Population: 37,669†

Ancestry‡	Population	%
African, Sub-Saharan (205)	304	0.81
African (86)	185	0.49
Cape Verdean (39)	39	0.10
Ethiopian (18)	18	0.05
Nigerian (36)	36	0.10
South African (20)	20	0.05
Other Sub-Saharan African (6)	6	0.02
Alsatian (0)	7	0.02
American (2,547)	2,547	6.77
Arab (156)	273	0.73
Arab (9)	52	0.14
Egyptian (42)	62	0.16
Lebanese (22)	33	0.09
Palestinian (6)	12	0.03
Syrian (64)	101	0.27
Other Arab (13)	13	0.03
Armenian (104)	130	0.35
Australian (9)	25	0.07
Austrian (46)	275	0.73
Belgian (0)	89	0.24
Brazilian (49)	89	0.24
British (222)	356	0.95
Bulgarian (35)	49	0.13
Canadian (139)	164	0.44
Croatian (0)	41	0.11
Czech (13)	96	0.26
Czechoslovakian (50)	61	0.16
Danish (20)	97	0.26
Dutch (20)	327	0.87
Eastern European (561)	649	1.72
English (584)	2,738	7.27
European (649)	733	1.95
Finnish (7)	40	0.11
French, ex. Basque (102)	835	2.22
French Canadian (7)	101	0.27
German (651)	3,518	9.35
Greek (197)	341	0.91
Guyanese (32)	42	0.11
Hungarian (32)	320	0.85
Icelander (0)	19	0.05
Iranian (0)	22	0.06
Irish (1,682)	5,209	13.84
Israeli (76)	116	0.31
Italian (1,976)	4,370	11.61
Latvian (11)	11	0.03
Lithuanian (72)	185	0.49
Macedonian (12)	12	0.03
Maltese (13)	38	0.10
New Zealander (40)	40	0.11
Northern European (26)	26	0.07
Norwegian (101)	245	0.65
Pennsylvania German (0)	8	0.02
Polish (579)	2,203	5.85
Portuguese (80)	122	0.32
Romanian (19)	155	0.41
Russian (786)	2,154	5.72
Scandinavian (7)	60	0.16
Scotch-Irish (107)	537	1.43
Scottish (148)	601	1.60
Serbian (0)	8	0.02
Slavic (0)	33	0.09
Slovak (16)	157	0.42
Swedish (28)	291	0.77
Swiss (142)	265	0.70
Turkish (34)	43	0.11
Ukrainian (147)	320	0.85
Welsh (18)	253	0.67
West Indian, ex. Hispanic (1,102)	1,746	4.64
Barbadian (29)	83	0.22
British West Indian (45)	114	0.30
Haitian (477)	508	1.35
Jamaican (404)	718	1.91
Trinidadian/Tobagonian (88)	252	0.67
West Indian (59)	71	0.19
Yugoslavian (54)	62	0.16

Hispanic Origin	Population	%
Hispanic or Latino (of any race)	2,810	7.46
Central American, ex. Mexican	296	0.79
Costa Rican	97	0.26
Guatemalan	80	0.21
Honduran	34	0.09
Nicaraguan	17	0.05
Panamanian	35	0.09
Salvadoran	33	0.09
Cuban	241	0.64
Dominican Republic	206	0.55
Mexican	371	0.98
Puerto Rican	761	2.02
South American	632	1.68
Argentinean	75	0.20
Bolivian	20	0.05
Chilean	21	0.06
Colombian	207	0.55
Ecuadorian	83	0.22
Paraguayan	2	0.01
Peruvian	139	0.37
Uruguayan	33	0.09
Venezuelan	43	0.11
Other South American	9	0.02
Other Hispanic or Latino	303	0.80

Race*	Population	%
African-American/Black (10,230)	11,241	29.84
Not Hispanic (9,902)	10,697	28.40
Hispanic (328)	544	1.44
American Indian/Alaska Native (59)	393	1.04
Not Hispanic (39)	295	0.78
Hispanic (20)	98	0.26
Alaska Athabascan *(Ala. Nat.)* (0)	1	<0.01
Apache (0)	2	0.01
Blackfeet (2)	18	0.05
Canadian/French Am. Ind. (1)	2	0.01
Central American Ind. (0)	3	0.01
Cherokee (3)	56	0.15
Chickasaw (0)	2	0.01
Choctaw (0)	9	0.02
Creek (0)	5	0.01
Delaware (1)	10	0.03
Hopi (0)	1	<0.01
Iroquois (0)	6	0.02
Lumbee (0)	2	0.01
Mexican American Ind. (0)	1	<0.01
Seminole (0)	7	0.02
Sioux (2)	2	0.01
South American Ind. (9)	36	0.10
Spanish American Ind. (1)	1	<0.01
Tlingit-Haida *(Alaska Native)* (0)	1	<0.01
Yup'ik *(Alaska Native)* (0)	1	<0.01
Asian (1,434)	2,036	5.40
Not Hispanic (1,416)	1,964	5.21
Hispanic (18)	72	0.19
Bangladeshi (37)	42	0.11
Burmese (2)	3	0.01
Cambodian (4)	4	0.01
Chinese, ex. Taiwanese (348)	514	1.36
Filipino (186)	291	0.77
Indian (460)	608	1.61
Indonesian (6)	17	0.05
Japanese (79)	148	0.39
Korean (168)	265	0.70
Laotian (2)	4	0.01
Malaysian (1)	2	0.01
Nepalese (2)	2	0.01
Pakistani (40)	54	0.14

SECTION TWO

*Notes: † The Census 2010 population figure is used to calculate the percentages in the Hispanic Origin and Race categories. Ancestry percentages are based on the 2006-2010 American Community Survey population (not shown); ‡ Numbers in parentheses indicate the number of people reporting a single ancestry; * Numbers in parentheses indicate the number of persons reporting this race alone, not in combination with any other race; Please refer to the Explanation of Data for more information.*

Sri Lankan (1)	1	<0.01
Taiwanese (9)	13	0.03
Thai (13)	20	0.05
Vietnamese (24)	41	0.11
Hawaii Native/Pacific Islander (9)	78	0.21
Not Hispanic (8)	69	0.18
Hispanic (1)	9	0.02
Guamanian/Chamorro (1)	4	0.01
Native Hawaiian (5)	12	0.03
White (23,416)	24,689	65.54
Not Hispanic (21,920)	22,938	60.89
Hispanic (1,496)	1,751	4.65

Montgomery

Place Type: Township
County: Somerset
Population: 22,254†

Ancestry‡	Population	%
African, Sub-Saharan (116)	157	0.73
African (0)	26	0.12
Nigerian (80)	80	0.37
South African (22)	22	0.10
Other Sub-Saharan African (14)	29	0.14
Albanian (0)	18	0.08
American (888)	888	4.14
Arab (74)	100	0.47
Egyptian (59)	59	0.28
Lebanese (0)	26	0.12
Syrian (15)	15	0.07
Armenian (10)	62	0.29
Austrian (9)	69	0.32
Belgian (94)	111	0.52
Brazilian (26)	137	0.64
British (76)	121	0.56
Canadian (20)	49	0.23
Czech (18)	74	0.35
Czechoslovakian (0)	35	0.16
Danish (66)	109	0.51
Dutch (24)	387	1.81
Eastern European (48)	48	0.22
English (233)	1,535	7.16
European (202)	202	0.94
French, ex. Basque (14)	292	1.36
French Canadian (86)	103	0.48
German (570)	3,297	15.38
German Russian (0)	7	0.03
Greek (47)	105	0.49
Hungarian (79)	337	1.57
Iranian (0)	10	0.05
Irish (578)	3,028	14.13
Israeli (19)	19	0.09
Italian (1,234)	3,235	15.09
Latvian (17)	17	0.08
Lithuanian (22)	63	0.29
Northern European (14)	14	0.07
Norwegian (112)	290	1.35
Polish (267)	1,476	6.89
Portuguese (12)	74	0.35
Romanian (17)	106	0.49
Russian (112)	491	2.29
Scandinavian (10)	10	0.05
Scotch-Irish (43)	216	1.01
Scottish (82)	482	2.25
Serbian (0)	22	0.10
Slavic (11)	73	0.34
Slovak (0)	208	0.97
Slovene (0)	9	0.04
Swedish (22)	96	0.45
Swiss (15)	45	0.21
Turkish (62)	62	0.29
Ukrainian (92)	156	0.73
Welsh (23)	79	0.37
West Indian, ex. Hispanic (160)	202	0.94
Barbadian (64)	95	0.44
British West Indian (17)	17	0.08
Haitian (45)	45	0.21
Jamaican (21)	21	0.10
West Indian (13)	24	0.11

Hispanic Origin	Population	%
Hispanic or Latino (of any race)	1,017	4.57
Central American, ex. Mexican	138	0.62
Costa Rican	33	0.15
Guatemalan	80	0.36
Nicaraguan	2	0.01
Panamanian	13	0.06
Salvadoran	9	0.04
Other Central American	1	<0.01
Cuban	101	0.45
Dominican Republic	26	0.12
Mexican	206	0.93
Puerto Rican	213	0.96
South American	215	0.97
Argentinean	39	0.18
Bolivian	3	0.01
Chilean	9	0.04
Colombian	72	0.32
Ecuadorian	27	0.12
Peruvian	37	0.17
Uruguayan	5	0.02
Venezuelan	18	0.08
Other South American	5	0.02
Other Hispanic or Latino	118	0.53

Race*	Population	%
African-American/Black (633)	763	3.43
Not Hispanic (586)	701	3.15
Hispanic (47)	62	0.28
American Indian/Alaska Native (19)	82	0.37
Not Hispanic (12)	68	0.31
Hispanic (7)	14	0.06
Apache (0)	1	<0.01
Blackfeet (0)	1	<0.01
Cherokee (4)	21	0.09
Chippewa (1)	1	<0.01
Delaware (0)	4	0.02
Inupiat *(Alaska Native)* (0)	1	<0.01
Mexican American Ind. (4)	4	0.02
Sioux (0)	1	<0.01
South American Ind. (2)	5	0.02
Asian (5,700)	6,084	27.34
Not Hispanic (5,689)	6,041	27.15
Hispanic (11)	43	0.19
Bangladeshi (10)	13	0.06
Burmese (1)	4	0.02
Cambodian (4)	4	0.02
Chinese, ex. Taiwanese (2,267)	2,407	10.82
Filipino (165)	206	0.93
Indian (2,416)	2,519	11.32
Indonesian (8)	12	0.05
Japanese (78)	134	0.60
Korean (393)	445	2.00
Malaysian (3)	4	0.02
Nepalese (1)	1	<0.01
Pakistani (63)	78	0.35
Sri Lankan (36)	40	0.18
Taiwanese (150)	174	0.78
Thai (8)	13	0.06
Vietnamese (16)	31	0.14
Hawaii Native/Pacific Islander (2)	15	0.07
Not Hispanic (2)	15	0.07
Guamanian/Chamorro (2)	5	0.02
White (15,057)	15,479	69.56
Not Hispanic (14,436)	14,797	66.49
Hispanic (621)	682	3.06

Montvale

Place Type: Borough
County: Bergen
Population: 7,844†

Ancestry‡	Population	%
African, Sub-Saharan (24)	24	0.31
Ghanaian (24)	24	0.31
American (353)	353	4.61
Armenian (56)	56	0.73
Austrian (46)	140	1.83
Belgian (0)	21	0.27
Brazilian (0)	10	0.13
British (51)	93	1.21
Czech (0)	74	0.97
Danish (28)	36	0.47
Dutch (0)	50	0.65
Eastern European (36)	36	0.47
English (25)	394	5.14
Estonian (0)	18	0.23
European (79)	79	1.03
French, ex. Basque (34)	306	3.99
French Canadian (42)	60	0.78
German (167)	1,283	16.74
Greek (240)	331	4.32
Hungarian (0)	46	0.60
Iranian (48)	48	0.63
Irish (330)	1,570	20.49
Israeli (7)	7	0.09
Italian (957)	1,838	23.99
Latvian (21)	21	0.27
Lithuanian (0)	15	0.20
Maltese (29)	29	0.38
Norwegian (19)	62	0.81
Polish (106)	450	5.87
Portuguese (24)	93	1.21
Romanian (0)	32	0.42
Russian (47)	202	2.64
Scandinavian (0)	10	0.13
Scotch-Irish (45)	67	0.87
Scottish (0)	185	2.41
Swedish (28)	48	0.63
Swiss (23)	77	1.00
Ukrainian (30)	30	0.39
Welsh (12)	36	0.47
West Indian, ex. Hispanic (36)	36	0.47
Haitian (36)	36	0.47

Hispanic Origin	Population	%
Hispanic or Latino (of any race)	419	5.34
Central American, ex. Mexican	41	0.52
Costa Rican	8	0.10
Guatemalan	3	0.04
Honduran	7	0.09
Nicaraguan	4	0.05
Panamanian	5	0.06
Salvadoran	14	0.18
Cuban	44	0.56
Dominican Republic	25	0.32
Mexican	97	1.24
Puerto Rican	72	0.92
South American	95	1.21
Argentinean	7	0.09
Chilean	3	0.04
Colombian	55	0.70
Ecuadorian	17	0.22
Paraguayan	1	0.01
Peruvian	8	0.10
Venezuelan	4	0.05
Other Hispanic or Latino	45	0.57

Race*	Population	%
African-American/Black (81)	100	1.27
Not Hispanic (70)	80	1.02
Hispanic (11)	20	0.25
American Indian/Alaska Native (6)	26	0.33
Not Hispanic (4)	16	0.20
Hispanic (2)	10	0.13
Delaware (2)	3	0.04
Iroquois (1)	1	0.01
Mexican American Ind. (1)	1	0.01
Spanish American Ind. (0)	5	0.06
Asian (866)	928	11.83
Not Hispanic (861)	917	11.69
Hispanic (5)	11	0.14
Chinese, ex. Taiwanese (239)	261	3.33
Filipino (51)	71	0.91
Indian (295)	304	3.88
Japanese (22)	26	0.33
Korean (203)	219	2.79
Malaysian (1)	1	0.01
Nepalese (1)	1	0.01

*Notes: † The Census 2010 population figure is used to calculate the percentages in the Hispanic Origin and Race categories. Ancestry percentages are based on the 2006-2010 American Community Survey population (not shown); ‡ Numbers in parentheses indicate the number of people reporting a single ancestry; * Numbers in parentheses indicate the number of persons reporting this race alone, not in combination with any other race; Please refer to the Explanation of Data for more information.*

	Population	%
Pakistani (26)	29	0.37
Taiwanese (15)	15	0.19
Thai (1)	1	0.01
Vietnamese (1)	1	0.01
Hawaii Native/Pacific Islander (0)	3	0.04
Not Hispanic (0)	3	0.04
White (6,654)	6,745	85.99
Not Hispanic (6,395)	6,465	82.42
Hispanic (259)	280	3.57

Montville

Place Type: Township
County: Morris
Population: 21,528†

Ancestry‡	Population	%
African, Sub-Saharan (14)	25	0.12
African (0)	11	0.05
Ethiopian (14)	14	0.07
American (691)	691	3.22
Arab (30)	90	0.42
Arab (9)	9	0.04
Lebanese (14)	41	0.19
Moroccan (7)	7	0.03
Syrian (0)	33	0.15
Armenian (0)	13	0.06
Austrian (171)	272	1.27
Belgian (10)	10	0.05
Brazilian (12)	12	0.06
British (23)	75	0.35
Canadian (52)	70	0.33
Carpatho Rusyn (9)	9	0.04
Czech (83)	213	0.99
Czechoslovakian (11)	52	0.24
Danish (35)	46	0.21
Dutch (92)	707	3.29
Eastern European (147)	168	0.78
English (214)	1,064	4.96
Estonian (0)	11	0.05
European (167)	198	0.92
Finnish (10)	10	0.05
French, ex. Basque (31)	299	1.39
French Canadian (0)	9	0.04
German (796)	3,132	14.59
Greek (158)	263	1.23
Guyanese (0)	25	0.12
Hungarian (79)	422	1.97
Iranian (95)	95	0.44
Irish (609)	2,720	12.67
Israeli (14)	33	0.15
Italian (3,527)	6,432	29.96
Latvian (41)	41	0.19
Lithuanian (13)	128	0.60
Norwegian (7)	50	0.23
Polish (675)	1,728	8.05
Portuguese (73)	199	0.93
Romanian (59)	88	0.41
Russian (555)	1,210	5.64
Scandinavian (18)	18	0.08
Scotch-Irish (58)	165	0.77
Scottish (74)	349	1.63
Slavic (0)	22	0.10
Slovak (32)	141	0.66
Swedish (9)	76	0.35
Swiss (29)	83	0.39
Turkish (90)	100	0.47
Ukrainian (106)	191	0.89
Welsh (0)	42	0.20
Yugoslavian (0)	13	0.06

Hispanic Origin	Population	%
Hispanic or Latino (of any race)	900	4.18
Central American, ex. Mexican	52	0.24
Costa Rican	5	0.02
Guatemalan	16	0.07
Honduran	10	0.05
Nicaraguan	2	0.01
Panamanian	4	0.02
Salvadoran	14	0.07
Other Central American	1	<0.01
Cuban	100	0.46
Dominican Republic	52	0.24
Mexican	137	0.64
Puerto Rican	281	1.31
South American	194	0.90
Argentinean	10	0.05
Bolivian	2	0.01
Chilean	11	0.05
Colombian	98	0.46
Ecuadorian	24	0.11
Peruvian	42	0.20
Uruguayan	2	0.01
Venezuelan	3	0.01
Other South American	2	0.01
Other Hispanic or Latino	84	0.39

Race*	Population	%
African-American/Black (275)	355	1.65
Not Hispanic (252)	316	1.47
Hispanic (23)	39	0.18
American Indian/Alaska Native (22)	49	0.23
Not Hispanic (6)	25	0.12
Hispanic (16)	24	0.11
Canadian/French Am. Ind. (0)	1	<0.01
Cherokee (1)	4	0.02
Iroquois (0)	4	0.02
Mexican American Ind. (1)	5	0.02
Potawatomi (1)	1	<0.01
South American Ind. (5)	7	0.03
Asian (3,890)	4,129	19.18
Not Hispanic (3,885)	4,115	19.11
Hispanic (5)	14	0.07
Bangladeshi (4)	4	0.02
Cambodian (4)	5	0.02
Chinese, ex. Taiwanese (1,209)	1,269	5.89
Filipino (130)	173	0.80
Indian (1,529)	1,567	7.28
Indonesian (5)	7	0.03
Japanese (35)	55	0.26
Korean (573)	593	2.75
Malaysian (1)	1	<0.01
Nepalese (5)	5	0.02
Pakistani (153)	161	0.75
Sri Lankan (11)	11	0.05
Taiwanese (166)	176	0.82
Thai (10)	10	0.05
Vietnamese (12)	19	0.09
Hawaii Native/Pacific Islander (2)	13	0.06
Not Hispanic (2)	13	0.06
Native Hawaiian (2)	2	0.01
White (16,800)	17,086	79.37
Not Hispanic (16,134)	16,384	76.11
Hispanic (666)	702	3.26

Moorestown

Place Type: Township
County: Burlington
Population: 20,726†

Ancestry‡	Population	%
African, Sub-Saharan (11)	23	0.11
African (11)	11	0.05
Ethiopian (0)	12	0.06
American (386)	386	1.88
Arab (20)	65	0.32
Lebanese (0)	45	0.22
Palestinian (13)	13	0.06
Other Arab (7)	7	0.03
Armenian (10)	29	0.14
Australian (18)	18	0.09
Austrian (48)	182	0.88
Belgian (0)	7	0.03
British (162)	231	1.12
Canadian (54)	114	0.55
Croatian (0)	29	0.14
Czech (0)	83	0.40
Danish (0)	47	0.23
Dutch (91)	560	2.72
Eastern European (165)	176	0.86
English (709)	3,104	15.08
Estonian (14)	14	0.07
European (507)	507	2.46
French, ex. Basque (56)	337	1.64
French Canadian (20)	145	0.70
German (1,007)	4,080	19.83
Greek (118)	217	1.05
Hungarian (41)	113	0.55
Iranian (39)	39	0.19
Irish (1,325)	5,291	25.71
Israeli (13)	13	0.06
Italian (1,469)	3,571	17.35
Latvian (8)	24	0.12
Lithuanian (36)	133	0.65
Norwegian (59)	191	0.93
Pennsylvania German (16)	27	0.13
Polish (270)	964	4.68
Portuguese (0)	53	0.26
Romanian (24)	117	0.57
Russian (246)	609	2.96
Scotch-Irish (162)	409	1.99
Scottish (190)	662	3.22
Serbian (37)	37	0.18
Slovak (9)	169	0.82
Swedish (42)	156	0.76
Swiss (9)	66	0.32
Turkish (19)	33	0.16
Ukrainian (12)	43	0.21
Welsh (69)	298	1.45
West Indian, ex. Hispanic (41)	68	0.33
West Indian (41)	68	0.33
Yugoslavian (0)	22	0.11

Hispanic Origin	Population	%
Hispanic or Latino (of any race)	721	3.48
Central American, ex. Mexican	42	0.20
Costa Rican	2	0.01
Guatemalan	12	0.06
Honduran	8	0.04
Nicaraguan	4	0.02
Panamanian	9	0.04
Salvadoran	7	0.03
Cuban	40	0.19
Dominican Republic	24	0.12
Mexican	115	0.55
Puerto Rican	303	1.46
South American	127	0.61
Argentinean	17	0.08
Bolivian	9	0.04
Chilean	21	0.10
Colombian	24	0.12
Ecuadorian	16	0.08
Paraguayan	1	<0.01
Peruvian	32	0.15
Uruguayan	2	0.01
Venezuelan	5	0.02
Other Hispanic or Latino	70	0.34

Race*	Population	%
African-American/Black (1,331)	1,524	7.35
Not Hispanic (1,278)	1,443	6.96
Hispanic (53)	81	0.39
American Indian/Alaska Native (18)	133	0.64
Not Hispanic (14)	112	0.54
Hispanic (4)	21	0.10
Blackfeet (0)	1	<0.01
Cherokee (0)	20	0.10
Choctaw (0)	1	<0.01
Creek (0)	1	<0.01
Delaware (1)	3	0.01
Iroquois (0)	2	0.01
Lumbee (1)	1	<0.01
Seminole (0)	2	0.01
Sioux (0)	2	0.01
South American Ind. (3)	6	0.03
Asian (1,244)	1,439	6.94
Not Hispanic (1,229)	1,421	6.86
Hispanic (15)	18	0.09
Burmese (1)	1	<0.01

*Notes: † The Census 2010 population figure is used to calculate the percentages in the Hispanic Origin and Race categories. Ancestry percentages are based on the 2006-2010 American Community Survey population (not shown); ‡ Numbers in parentheses indicate the number of people reporting a single ancestry; * Numbers in parentheses indicate the number of persons reporting this race alone, not in combination with any other race; Please refer to the Explanation of Data for more information.*

Cambodian (9)	11	0.05
Chinese, ex. Taiwanese (296)	373	1.80
Filipino (77)	120	0.58
Indian (432)	482	2.33
Indonesian (3)	8	0.04
Japanese (29)	61	0.29
Korean (183)	215	1.04
Laotian (2)	2	0.01
Nepalese (0)	1	<0.01
Pakistani (73)	91	0.44
Sri Lankan (7)	10	0.05
Taiwanese (19)	19	0.09
Thai (1)	6	0.03
Vietnamese (34)	43	0.21
Hawaii Native/Pacific Islander (5)	14	0.07
Not Hispanic (4)	13	0.06
Hispanic (1)	1	<0.01
Guamanian/Chamorro (1)	2	0.01
Native Hawaiian (1)	3	0.01
White (17,513)	17,892	86.33
Not Hispanic (17,045)	17,386	83.88
Hispanic (468)	506	2.44

Moorestown-Lenola

Place Type: CDP
County: Burlington
Population: 14,217†

Ancestry‡	Population	%
African, Sub-Saharan (11)	23	0.17
African (11)	11	0.08
Ethiopian (0)	12	0.09
American (190)	190	1.39
Arab (7)	31	0.23
Lebanese (0)	24	0.18
Other Arab (7)	7	0.05
Armenian (10)	29	0.21
Australian (18)	18	0.13
Austrian (36)	110	0.80
British (152)	194	1.42
Canadian (0)	21	0.15
Croatian (0)	8	0.06
Czech (0)	73	0.53
Danish (0)	36	0.26
Dutch (85)	523	3.82
Eastern European (59)	59	0.43
English (354)	2,329	17.02
Estonian (14)	14	0.10
European (216)	216	1.58
French, ex. Basque (44)	226	1.65
French Canadian (0)	50	0.37
German (745)	3,074	22.47
Greek (11)	33	0.24
Hungarian (31)	57	0.42
Iranian (7)	7	0.05
Irish (930)	3,752	27.42
Italian (991)	2,556	18.68
Latvian (8)	24	0.18
Lithuanian (25)	81	0.59
Norwegian (59)	150	1.10
Pennsylvania German (6)	17	0.12
Polish (186)	576	4.21
Portuguese (0)	28	0.20
Romanian (12)	94	0.69
Russian (121)	278	2.03
Scotch-Irish (130)	349	2.55
Scottish (158)	386	2.82
Slovak (9)	154	1.13
Swedish (21)	111	0.81
Swiss (9)	18	0.13
Turkish (19)	33	0.24
Ukrainian (12)	24	0.18
Welsh (48)	255	1.86
West Indian, ex. Hispanic (0)	27	0.20
West Indian (0)	27	0.20

Hispanic Origin	Population	%
Hispanic or Latino (of any race)	587	4.13
Central American, ex. Mexican	32	0.23
Costa Rican	1	0.01
Guatemalan	9	0.06
Honduran	6	0.04
Nicaraguan	4	0.03
Panamanian	9	0.06
Salvadoran	3	0.02
Cuban	34	0.24
Dominican Republic	24	0.17
Mexican	92	0.65
Puerto Rican	269	1.89
South American	78	0.55
Argentinean	8	0.06
Bolivian	1	0.01
Chilean	12	0.08
Colombian	18	0.13
Ecuadorian	14	0.10
Paraguayan	1	0.01
Peruvian	22	0.15
Uruguayan	2	0.01
Other Hispanic or Latino	58	0.41

Race*	Population	%
African-American/Black (1,178)	1,350	9.50
Not Hispanic (1,127)	1,272	8.95
Hispanic (51)	78	0.55
American Indian/Alaska Native (16)	127	0.89
Not Hispanic (13)	107	0.75
Hispanic (3)	20	0.14
Blackfeet (0)	1	0.01
Cherokee (0)	17	0.12
Choctaw (0)	1	0.01
Creek (0)	1	0.01
Delaware (1)	3	0.02
Iroquois (0)	2	0.01
Seminole (0)	2	0.01
Sioux (0)	2	0.01
South American Ind. (2)	5	0.04
Asian (447)	569	4.00
Not Hispanic (440)	560	3.94
Hispanic (7)	9	0.06
Burmese (1)	1	0.01
Cambodian (4)	4	0.03
Chinese, ex. Taiwanese (112)	159	1.12
Filipino (47)	82	0.58
Indian (95)	122	0.86
Japanese (20)	42	0.30
Korean (59)	75	0.53
Laotian (2)	2	0.01
Nepalese (0)	1	0.01
Pakistani (38)	50	0.35
Sri Lankan (3)	4	0.03
Taiwanese (3)	3	0.02
Thai (1)	4	0.03
Vietnamese (21)	30	0.21
Hawaii Native/Pacific Islander (5)	14	0.10
Not Hispanic (4)	13	0.09
Hispanic (1)	1	0.01
Guamanian/Chamorro (1)	2	0.01
Native Hawaiian (1)	3	0.02
White (12,074)	12,363	86.96
Not Hispanic (11,713)	11,969	84.19
Hispanic (361)	394	2.77

Morris

Place Type: Township
County: Morris
Population: 22,306†

Ancestry‡	Population	%
African, Sub-Saharan (93)	173	0.78
African (45)	125	0.56
Nigerian (48)	48	0.22
Albanian (0)	9	0.04
American (938)	938	4.22
Arab (23)	61	0.27
Egyptian (0)	11	0.05
Jordanian (10)	10	0.04
Lebanese (13)	28	0.13
Syrian (0)	12	0.05
Austrian (38)	256	1.15
Belgian (0)	54	0.24
British (98)	130	0.58
Bulgarian (17)	17	0.08
Canadian (8)	28	0.13
Croatian (10)	22	0.10
Czech (73)	257	1.16
Czechoslovakian (0)	19	0.09
Danish (31)	126	0.57
Dutch (103)	559	2.52
Eastern European (187)	210	0.94
English (566)	2,175	9.79
Estonian (9)	9	0.04
European (420)	432	1.94
Finnish (0)	19	0.09
French, ex. Basque (79)	668	3.01
French Canadian (28)	61	0.27
German (711)	3,000	13.50
Greek (24)	111	0.50
Hungarian (54)	338	1.52
Irish (1,628)	5,382	24.22
Israeli (11)	11	0.05
Italian (2,095)	4,494	20.22
Latvian (8)	26	0.12
Lithuanian (67)	161	0.72
Northern European (58)	108	0.49
Norwegian (80)	215	0.97
Polish (507)	1,436	6.46
Portuguese (38)	57	0.26
Romanian (0)	25	0.11
Russian (425)	972	4.37
Scandinavian (13)	26	0.12
Scotch-Irish (176)	320	1.44
Scottish (137)	515	2.32
Serbian (1)	3	0.01
Slavic (0)	10	0.04
Slovak (13)	140	0.63
Slovene (47)	83	0.37
Swedish (74)	298	1.34
Swiss (21)	50	0.22
Ukrainian (66)	106	0.48
Welsh (48)	155	0.70
West Indian, ex. Hispanic (100)	148	0.67
Bahamian (0)	9	0.04
Barbadian (0)	9	0.04
Jamaican (100)	119	0.54
Trinidadian/Tobagonian (0)	11	0.05
Yugoslavian (0)	25	0.11

Hispanic Origin	Population	%
Hispanic or Latino (of any race)	1,683	7.55
Central American, ex. Mexican	423	1.90
Costa Rican	16	0.07
Guatemalan	53	0.24
Honduran	282	1.26
Nicaraguan	1	<0.01
Panamanian	3	0.01
Salvadoran	62	0.28
Other Central American	6	0.03
Cuban	95	0.43
Dominican Republic	55	0.25
Mexican	110	0.49
Puerto Rican	271	1.21
South American	540	2.42
Argentinean	63	0.28
Chilean	14	0.06
Colombian	280	1.26
Ecuadorian	71	0.32
Paraguayan	9	0.04
Peruvian	66	0.30
Uruguayan	16	0.07
Venezuelan	20	0.09
Other South American	1	<0.01
Other Hispanic or Latino	189	0.85

Race*	Population	%
African-American/Black (1,261)	1,404	6.29
Not Hispanic (1,216)	1,327	5.95
Hispanic (45)	77	0.35
American Indian/Alaska Native (23)	87	0.39

*Notes: † The Census 2010 population figure is used to calculate the percentages in the Hispanic Origin and Race categories. Ancestry percentages are based on the 2006-2010 American Community Survey population (not shown); ‡ Numbers in parentheses indicate the number of people reporting a single ancestry; * Numbers in parentheses indicate the number of persons reporting this race alone, not in combination with any other race; Please refer to the Explanation of Data for more information.*

Not Hispanic (9)	63	0.28
Hispanic (14)	24	0.11
Canadian/French Am. Ind. (0)	3	0.01
Cherokee (3)	10	0.04
Chickasaw (1)	1	<0.01
Chippewa (0)	1	<0.01
Choctaw (1)	1	<0.01
Creek (0)	2	0.01
Iroquois (1)	7	0.03
Mexican American Ind. (2)	2	0.01
Sioux (1)	2	0.01
South American Ind. (2)	4	0.02
Spanish American Ind. (0)	1	<0.01
Asian (1,141)	1,323	5.93
Not Hispanic (1,136)	1,309	5.87
Hispanic (5)	14	0.06
Cambodian (1)	1	<0.01
Chinese, ex. Taiwanese (370)	415	1.86
Filipino (131)	170	0.76
Indian (371)	412	1.85
Indonesian (4)	4	0.02
Japanese (39)	66	0.30
Korean (105)	130	0.58
Pakistani (8)	9	0.04
Sri Lankan (7)	8	0.04
Taiwanese (37)	43	0.19
Thai (5)	7	0.03
Vietnamese (27)	33	0.15
Hawaii Native/Pacific Islander (6)	15	0.07
Not Hispanic (6)	14	0.06
Hispanic (0)	1	<0.01
Guamanian/Chamorro (1)	6	0.03
Marshallese (1)	1	<0.01
Native Hawaiian (0)	2	0.01
Samoan (3)	3	0.01
White (19,022)	19,380	86.88
Not Hispanic (17,893)	18,168	81.45
Hispanic (1,129)	1,212	5.43

Morris

Place Type: Town
County: Morris
Population: 18,411†

Ancestry‡	Population	%
African, Sub-Saharan (168)	168	0.91
African (132)	132	0.72
Ghanaian (36)	36	0.20
American (122)	122	0.66
Arab (98)	123	0.67
Egyptian (51)	51	0.28
Lebanese (47)	60	0.33
Syrian (0)	12	0.07
Austrian (13)	48	0.26
British (36)	118	0.64
Cajun (0)	12	0.07
Canadian (17)	17	0.09
Celtic (14)	14	0.08
Croatian (0)	16	0.09
Czech (0)	53	0.29
Czechoslovakian (0)	12	0.07
Danish (0)	19	0.10
Dutch (15)	146	0.79
Eastern European (45)	45	0.24
English (253)	959	5.20
Estonian (14)	14	0.08
European (71)	71	0.38
Finnish (0)	16	0.09
French, ex. Basque (67)	364	1.97
French Canadian (36)	89	0.48
German (361)	2,075	11.24
Greek (60)	142	0.77
Hungarian (100)	225	1.22
Iranian (0)	7	0.04
Irish (764)	2,522	13.66
Italian (842)	2,021	10.95
Latvian (13)	13	0.07
Lithuanian (0)	11	0.06
Northern European (2)	2	0.01
Norwegian (0)	77	0.42
Pennsylvania German (0)	12	0.07
Polish (147)	709	3.84
Portuguese (16)	45	0.24
Russian (245)	353	1.91
Scandinavian (9)	9	0.05
Scotch-Irish (67)	156	0.85
Scottish (79)	367	1.99
Serbian (0)	13	0.07
Slovak (13)	39	0.21
Swedish (12)	142	0.77
Swiss (0)	5	0.03
Turkish (11)	11	0.06
Ukrainian (37)	37	0.20
Welsh (0)	12	0.07
West Indian, ex. Hispanic (550)	678	3.67
Barbadian (21)	21	0.11
British West Indian (9)	9	0.05
Haitian (33)	33	0.18
Jamaican (464)	587	3.18
Trinidadian/Tobagonian (5)	10	0.05
West Indian (18)	18	0.10
Yugoslavian (37)	37	0.20

Hispanic Origin	Population	%
Hispanic or Latino (of any race)	6,277	34.09
Central American, ex. Mexican	3,067	16.66
Costa Rican	30	0.16
Guatemalan	809	4.39
Honduran	1,840	9.99
Nicaraguan	15	0.08
Panamanian	9	0.05
Salvadoran	346	1.88
Other Central American	18	0.10
Cuban	78	0.42
Dominican Republic	79	0.43
Mexican	206	1.12
Puerto Rican	247	1.34
South American	2,015	10.94
Argentinean	21	0.11
Bolivian	4	0.02
Chilean	13	0.07
Colombian	1,267	6.88
Ecuadorian	537	2.92
Paraguayan	10	0.05
Peruvian	113	0.61
Uruguayan	15	0.08
Venezuelan	22	0.12
Other South American	13	0.07
Other Hispanic or Latino	585	3.18

Race*	Population	%
African-American/Black (2,572)	2,756	14.97
Not Hispanic (2,479)	2,586	14.05
Hispanic (93)	170	0.92
American Indian/Alaska Native (117)	233	1.27
Not Hispanic (14)	62	0.34
Hispanic (103)	171	0.93
Apache (0)	1	0.01
Blackfeet (1)	8	0.04
Central American Ind. (18)	22	0.12
Cherokee (3)	25	0.14
Choctaw (2)	3	0.02
Cree (0)	1	0.01
Delaware (0)	1	0.01
Mexican American Ind. (28)	33	0.18
Navajo (0)	1	0.01
Pueblo (0)	2	0.01
Puget Sound Salish (1)	1	0.01
Sioux (0)	1	0.01
South American Ind. (12)	24	0.13
Spanish American Ind. (2)	2	0.01
Asian (799)	939	5.10
Not Hispanic (794)	916	4.98
Hispanic (5)	23	0.12
Cambodian (3)	5	0.03
Chinese, ex. Taiwanese (174)	211	1.15
Filipino (196)	213	1.16
Indian (278)	340	1.85
Indonesian (2)	2	0.01
Japanese (20)	31	0.17
Korean (42)	54	0.29
Laotian (11)	11	0.06
Malaysian (2)	2	0.01
Nepalese (2)	2	0.01
Pakistani (8)	15	0.08
Sri Lankan (3)	3	0.02
Taiwanese (13)	16	0.09
Thai (5)	8	0.04
Vietnamese (13)	19	0.10
Hawaii Native/Pacific Islander (11)	31	0.17
Not Hispanic (8)	20	0.11
Hispanic (3)	11	0.06
Fijian (1)	1	0.01
Guamanian/Chamorro (7)	14	0.08
Native Hawaiian (0)	13	0.07
Samoan (0)	7	0.04
White (11,507)	12,059	65.50
Not Hispanic (8,561)	8,747	47.51
Hispanic (2,946)	3,312	17.99

Mount Holly

Place Type: Township
County: Burlington
Population: 9,536†

Ancestry‡	Population	%
African, Sub-Saharan (27)	27	0.27
African (27)	27	0.27
American (336)	336	3.42
Arab (13)	22	0.22
Egyptian (13)	22	0.22
Australian (0)	5	0.05
Austrian (0)	28	0.28
Belgian (0)	14	0.14
British (14)	25	0.25
Czech (0)	45	0.46
Czechoslovakian (14)	14	0.14
Dutch (30)	188	1.91
Eastern European (0)	6	0.06
English (196)	1,063	10.81
European (20)	31	0.32
Finnish (0)	8	0.08
French, ex. Basque (82)	300	3.05
French Canadian (40)	122	1.24
German (233)	1,763	17.93
Greek (18)	38	0.39
Hungarian (14)	79	0.80
Irish (340)	1,654	16.82
Israeli (0)	17	0.17
Italian (276)	1,214	12.35
Lithuanian (0)	10	0.10
Norwegian (11)	21	0.21
Polish (215)	641	6.52
Portuguese (159)	168	1.71
Russian (0)	124	1.26
Scotch-Irish (76)	167	1.70
Scottish (41)	302	3.07
Serbian (4)	4	0.04
Slovak (0)	44	0.45
Swedish (34)	102	1.04
Swiss (0)	20	0.20
Ukrainian (0)	22	0.22
Welsh (0)	35	0.36
West Indian, ex. Hispanic (110)	120	1.22
Bermudan (12)	12	0.12
Haitian (37)	37	0.38
Jamaican (61)	64	0.65
West Indian (0)	7	0.07

Hispanic Origin	Population	%
Hispanic or Latino (of any race)	1,210	12.69
Central American, ex. Mexican	99	1.04
Costa Rican	7	0.07
Guatemalan	3	0.03
Honduran	20	0.21
Nicaraguan	4	0.04
Panamanian	36	0.38
Salvadoran	29	0.30

*Notes: † The Census 2010 population figure is used to calculate the percentages in the Hispanic Origin and Race categories. Ancestry percentages are based on the 2006-2010 American Community Survey population (not shown); ‡ Numbers in parentheses indicate the number of people reporting a single ancestry; * Numbers in parentheses indicate the number of persons reporting this race alone, not in combination with any other race; Please refer to the Explanation of Data for more information.*

Cuban	25	0.26
Dominican Republic	83	0.87
Mexican	137	1.44
Puerto Rican	749	7.85
South American	79	0.83
Argentinean	2	0.02
Bolivian	2	0.02
Chilean	9	0.09
Colombian	26	0.27
Ecuadorian	19	0.20
Peruvian	16	0.17
Venezuelan	3	0.03
Other South American	2	0.02
Other Hispanic or Latino	38	0.40

Race*	Population	%
African-American/Black (2,203)	2,543	26.67
Not Hispanic (2,037)	2,312	24.24
Hispanic (166)	231	2.42
American Indian/Alaska Native (35)	155	1.63
Not Hispanic (22)	122	1.28
Hispanic (13)	33	0.35
Blackfeet (0)	4	0.04
Canadian/French Am. Ind. (0)	1	0.01
Cherokee (7)	37	0.39
Chickasaw (0)	2	0.02
Chippewa (0)	1	0.01
Choctaw (0)	1	0.01
Delaware (2)	7	0.07
Iroquois (1)	5	0.05
Mexican American Ind. (3)	4	0.04
Seminole (0)	2	0.02
South American Ind. (0)	3	0.03
Asian (140)	231	2.42
Not Hispanic (139)	226	2.37
Hispanic (1)	5	0.05
Bangladeshi (3)	3	0.03
Cambodian (1)	1	0.01
Chinese, ex. Taiwanese (15)	27	0.28
Filipino (25)	45	0.47
Hmong (1)	1	0.01
Indian (29)	30	0.31
Japanese (7)	28	0.29
Korean (28)	50	0.52
Pakistani (8)	8	0.08
Taiwanese (3)	3	0.03
Thai (2)	5	0.05
Vietnamese (8)	8	0.08
Hawaii Native/Pacific Islander (7)	24	0.25
Not Hispanic (5)	22	0.23
Hispanic (2)	2	0.02
Guamanian/Chamorro (1)	2	0.02
Native Hawaiian (4)	18	0.19
Samoan (2)	2	0.02
White (6,253)	6,645	69.68
Not Hispanic (5,731)	6,026	63.19
Hispanic (522)	619	6.49

Mount Laurel

Place Type: Township
County: Burlington
Population: 41,864†

Ancestry‡	Population	%
African, Sub-Saharan (73)	95	0.23
African (15)	15	0.04
Nigerian (58)	58	0.14
Sudanese (0)	17	0.04
Other Sub-Saharan African (0)	5	0.01
American (1,250)	1,250	2.98
Arab (74)	148	0.35
Arab (29)	29	0.07
Egyptian (45)	45	0.11
Lebanese (0)	35	0.08
Moroccan (0)	12	0.03
Palestinian (0)	8	0.02
Syrian (0)	7	0.02
Other Arab (0)	12	0.03
Armenian (86)	109	0.26
Austrian (17)	228	0.54
British (165)	268	0.64
Canadian (32)	58	0.14
Croatian (19)	43	0.10
Czech (20)	90	0.21
Czechoslovakian (13)	60	0.14
Danish (0)	26	0.06
Dutch (28)	449	1.07
Eastern European (192)	220	0.52
English (762)	4,884	11.65
European (396)	426	1.02
Finnish (0)	14	0.03
French, ex. Basque (60)	620	1.48
French Canadian (0)	88	0.21
German (1,390)	7,924	18.90
Greek (20)	309	0.74
Hungarian (92)	492	1.17
Iranian (54)	54	0.13
Irish (2,657)	9,717	23.18
Italian (4,239)	9,559	22.80
Latvian (0)	16	0.04
Lithuanian (80)	404	0.96
Norwegian (73)	210	0.50
Pennsylvania German (53)	83	0.20
Polish (918)	3,590	8.56
Portuguese (26)	131	0.31
Romanian (25)	136	0.32
Russian (502)	1,254	2.99
Scandinavian (12)	12	0.03
Scotch-Irish (131)	484	1.15
Scottish (165)	766	1.83
Serbian (119)	119	0.28
Slavic (0)	13	0.03
Slovak (82)	190	0.45
Slovene (0)	15	0.04
Swedish (118)	601	1.43
Swiss (109)	221	0.53
Turkish (48)	73	0.17
Ukrainian (155)	534	1.27
Welsh (51)	445	1.06
West Indian, ex. Hispanic (143)	267	0.64
Barbadian (0)	46	0.11
Haitian (65)	65	0.16
Jamaican (60)	138	0.33
West Indian (18)	18	0.04
Yugoslavian (0)	14	0.03

Hispanic Origin	Population	%
Hispanic or Latino (of any race)	1,907	4.56
Central American, ex. Mexican	126	0.30
Costa Rican	16	0.04
Guatemalan	40	0.10
Honduran	13	0.03
Nicaraguan	15	0.04
Panamanian	26	0.06
Salvadoran	16	0.04
Cuban	131	0.31
Dominican Republic	84	0.20
Mexican	202	0.48
Puerto Rican	934	2.23
South American	299	0.71
Argentinean	41	0.10
Bolivian	12	0.03
Chilean	13	0.03
Colombian	96	0.23
Ecuadorian	41	0.10
Paraguayan	2	<0.01
Peruvian	59	0.14
Uruguayan	4	0.01
Venezuelan	30	0.07
Other South American	1	<0.01
Other Hispanic or Latino	131	0.31

Race*	Population	%
African-American/Black (4,061)	4,606	11.00
Not Hispanic (3,881)	4,319	10.32
Hispanic (180)	287	0.69
American Indian/Alaska Native (67)	251	0.60
Not Hispanic (50)	220	0.53
Hispanic (17)	31	0.07
Aleut *(Alaska Native)* (1)	1	<0.01
Apache (2)	2	<0.01
Blackfeet (2)	18	0.04
Canadian/French Am. Ind. (0)	1	<0.01
Cherokee (5)	38	0.09
Chippewa (3)	4	0.01
Cree (0)	1	<0.01
Delaware (1)	13	0.03
Iroquois (1)	2	<0.01
Lumbee (1)	4	0.01
Mexican American Ind. (2)	2	<0.01
Navajo (0)	1	<0.01
Seminole (1)	2	<0.01
Sioux (0)	1	<0.01
South American Ind. (3)	5	0.01
Asian (3,040)	3,469	8.29
Not Hispanic (3,028)	3,420	8.17
Hispanic (12)	49	0.12
Bangladeshi (15)	22	0.05
Burmese (1)	2	<0.01
Cambodian (9)	13	0.03
Chinese, ex. Taiwanese (679)	766	1.83
Filipino (309)	431	1.03
Hmong (1)	1	<0.01
Indian (1,226)	1,302	3.11
Indonesian (6)	8	0.02
Japanese (45)	109	0.26
Korean (375)	425	1.02
Laotian (1)	1	<0.01
Nepalese (3)	3	0.01
Pakistani (96)	112	0.27
Sri Lankan (25)	25	0.06
Taiwanese (52)	61	0.15
Thai (14)	30	0.07
Vietnamese (112)	132	0.32
Hawaii Native/Pacific Islander (17)	61	0.15
Not Hispanic (17)	53	0.13
Hispanic (0)	8	0.02
Guamanian/Chamorro (6)	11	0.03
Native Hawaiian (5)	22	0.05
Samoan (1)	5	0.01
Tongan (1)	2	<0.01
White (33,249)	34,014	81.25
Not Hispanic (32,118)	32,753	78.24
Hispanic (1,131)	1,261	3.01

Mount Olive

Place Type: Township
County: Morris
Population: 28,117†

Ancestry‡	Population	%
African, Sub-Saharan (168)	168	0.61
African (70)	70	0.25
Nigerian (17)	17	0.06
South African (29)	29	0.11
Ugandan (52)	52	0.19
Albanian (105)	113	0.41
American (1,027)	1,027	3.74
Arab (261)	328	1.19
Arab (135)	135	0.49
Egyptian (0)	15	0.05
Iraqi (10)	10	0.04
Lebanese (13)	13	0.05
Palestinian (103)	103	0.37
Syrian (0)	52	0.19
Armenian (32)	32	0.12
Austrian (50)	104	0.38
Belgian (0)	24	0.09
Brazilian (39)	241	0.88
British (26)	26	0.09
Bulgarian (0)	38	0.14
Croatian (61)	61	0.22
Czech (0)	145	0.53
Czechoslovakian (31)	57	0.21
Danish (0)	41	0.15
Dutch (188)	791	2.88
Eastern European (130)	130	0.47
English (438)	2,167	7.89

*Notes: † The Census 2010 population figure is used to calculate the percentages in the Hispanic Origin and Race categories. Ancestry percentages are based on the 2006-2010 American Community Survey population (not shown); ‡ Numbers in parentheses indicate the number of people reporting a single ancestry; * Numbers in parentheses indicate the number of persons reporting this race alone, not in combination with any other race; Please refer to the Explanation of Data for more information.*

Ancestry	Population	%
Estonian (6)	6	0.02
European (98)	360	1.31
Finnish (16)	16	0.06
French, ex. Basque (140)	841	3.06
French Canadian (16)	139	0.51
German (528)	4,389	15.97
Greek (143)	225	0.82
Guyanese (6)	6	0.02
Hungarian (43)	290	1.06
Iranian (71)	103	0.37
Irish (1,013)	6,320	23.00
Israeli (19)	19	0.07
Italian (2,136)	6,180	22.49
Lithuanian (33)	60	0.22
Maltese (19)	54	0.20
Norwegian (154)	240	0.87
Pennsylvania German (17)	17	0.06
Polish (403)	1,933	7.03
Portuguese (45)	255	0.93
Romanian (30)	30	0.11
Russian (312)	820	2.98
Scandinavian (27)	52	0.19
Scotch-Irish (105)	284	1.03
Scottish (87)	416	1.51
Slavic (15)	42	0.15
Slovak (0)	53	0.19
Swedish (75)	248	0.90
Swiss (35)	197	0.72
Turkish (0)	21	0.08
Ukrainian (120)	231	0.84
Welsh (51)	206	0.75
West Indian, ex. Hispanic (192)	290	1.06
Barbadian (17)	17	0.06
Belizean (0)	78	0.28
Haitian (40)	40	0.15
Jamaican (122)	142	0.52
West Indian (13)	13	0.05
Yugoslavian (152)	193	0.70

Hispanic Origin	Population	%
Hispanic or Latino (of any race)	3,237	11.51
Central American, ex. Mexican	279	0.99
Costa Rican	97	0.34
Guatemalan	59	0.21
Honduran	68	0.24
Nicaraguan	8	0.03
Panamanian	11	0.04
Salvadoran	35	0.12
Other Central American	1	<0.01
Cuban	164	0.58
Dominican Republic	185	0.66
Mexican	212	0.75
Puerto Rican	967	3.44
South American	1,166	4.15
Argentinean	60	0.21
Bolivian	2	0.01
Chilean	85	0.30
Colombian	474	1.69
Ecuadorian	174	0.62
Paraguayan	27	0.10
Peruvian	218	0.78
Uruguayan	88	0.31
Venezuelan	27	0.10
Other South American	11	0.04
Other Hispanic or Latino	264	0.94

Race*	Population	%
African-American/Black (1,614)	1,836	6.53
Not Hispanic (1,514)	1,673	5.95
Hispanic (100)	163	0.58
American Indian/Alaska Native (55)	144	0.51
Not Hispanic (40)	101	0.36
Hispanic (15)	43	0.15
Arapaho (0)	2	0.01
Blackfeet (4)	9	0.03
Central American Ind. (1)	1	<0.01
Cherokee (9)	29	0.10
Chippewa (2)	2	0.01
Delaware (0)	7	0.02
Iroquois (1)	10	0.04
Mexican American Ind. (2)	3	0.01
Navajo (1)	1	<0.01
Seminole (0)	3	0.01
Sioux (1)	1	<0.01
South American Ind. (6)	10	0.04
Yup'ik *(Alaska Native)* (1)	1	<0.01
Asian (2,315)	2,562	9.11
Not Hispanic (2,297)	2,519	8.96
Hispanic (18)	43	0.15
Bangladeshi (5)	5	0.02
Burmese (6)	6	0.02
Cambodian (0)	1	<0.01
Chinese, ex. Taiwanese (298)	358	1.27
Filipino (338)	396	1.41
Hmong (0)	2	0.01
Indian (1,107)	1,146	4.08
Indonesian (6)	18	0.06
Japanese (27)	61	0.22
Korean (171)	192	0.68
Laotian (5)	5	0.02
Malaysian (0)	2	0.01
Nepalese (10)	12	0.04
Pakistani (160)	168	0.60
Sri Lankan (3)	3	0.01
Taiwanese (9)	10	0.04
Thai (25)	36	0.13
Vietnamese (99)	115	0.41
Hawaii Native/Pacific Islander (12)	52	0.18
Not Hispanic (5)	41	0.15
Hispanic (7)	11	0.04
Fijian (0)	1	<0.01
Guamanian/Chamorro (3)	6	0.02
Native Hawaiian (0)	3	0.01
Samoan (2)	2	0.01
White (22,679)	23,185	82.46
Not Hispanic (20,522)	20,869	74.22
Hispanic (2,157)	2,316	8.24

Mystic Island

Place Type: CDP
County: Ocean
Population: 8,493†

Ancestry‡	Population	%
American (162)	162	1.90
Arab (10)	41	0.48
Lebanese (0)	31	0.36
Syrian (10)	10	0.12
Armenian (12)	55	0.64
Austrian (0)	10	0.12
Belgian (13)	37	0.43
British (0)	23	0.27
Canadian (0)	21	0.25
Croatian (26)	65	0.76
Czech (7)	25	0.29
Czechoslovakian (21)	29	0.34
Danish (0)	8	0.09
Dutch (22)	167	1.96
English (193)	821	9.62
European (10)	10	0.12
French, ex. Basque (24)	201	2.36
French Canadian (12)	89	1.04
German (526)	2,285	26.78
Greek (44)	111	1.30
Hungarian (12)	64	0.75
Irish (630)	2,171	25.44
Italian (1,244)	2,400	28.13
Lithuanian (1)	12	0.14
Norwegian (51)	180	2.11
Pennsylvania German (11)	11	0.13
Polish (555)	1,233	14.45
Portuguese (30)	75	0.88
Russian (29)	94	1.10
Scandinavian (0)	38	0.45
Scotch-Irish (20)	96	1.13
Scottish (23)	156	1.83
Slovak (10)	62	0.73
Swedish (25)	74	0.87
Swiss (0)	24	0.28
Ukrainian (11)	11	0.13
Welsh (0)	35	0.41

Hispanic Origin	Population	%
Hispanic or Latino (of any race)	425	5.00
Central American, ex. Mexican	24	0.28
Costa Rican	1	0.01
Guatemalan	3	0.04
Honduran	10	0.12
Nicaraguan	1	0.01
Panamanian	5	0.06
Salvadoran	4	0.05
Cuban	26	0.31
Dominican Republic	13	0.15
Mexican	70	0.82
Puerto Rican	195	2.30
South American	48	0.57
Argentinean	8	0.09
Colombian	18	0.21
Ecuadorian	5	0.06
Peruvian	17	0.20
Other Hispanic or Latino	49	0.58

Race*	Population	%
African-American/Black (80)	114	1.34
Not Hispanic (77)	101	1.19
Hispanic (3)	13	0.15
American Indian/Alaska Native (16)	47	0.55
Not Hispanic (12)	39	0.46
Hispanic (4)	8	0.09
Apache (0)	2	0.02
Blackfeet (0)	5	0.06
Cherokee (2)	11	0.13
Delaware (1)	3	0.04
Iroquois (1)	2	0.02
Lumbee (2)	2	0.02
Ottawa (1)	1	0.01
Seminole (0)	3	0.04
South American Ind. (1)	1	0.01
Asian (93)	113	1.33
Not Hispanic (93)	109	1.28
Hispanic (0)	4	0.05
Cambodian (1)	1	0.01
Chinese, ex. Taiwanese (16)	22	0.26
Filipino (34)	41	0.48
Indian (8)	8	0.09
Japanese (5)	8	0.09
Korean (18)	22	0.26
Laotian (1)	3	0.04
Sri Lankan (1)	1	0.01
Thai (1)	1	0.01
Vietnamese (2)	2	0.02
Hawaii Native/Pacific Islander (1)	3	0.04
Not Hispanic (1)	3	0.04
Native Hawaiian (1)	1	0.01
White (8,073)	8,169	96.19
Not Hispanic (7,810)	7,879	92.77
Hispanic (263)	290	3.41

Neptune

Place Type: Township
County: Monmouth
Population: 27,935†

Ancestry‡	Population	%
African, Sub-Saharan (530)	559	2.00
African (399)	428	1.53
Ghanaian (27)	27	0.10
Nigerian (104)	104	0.37
American (730)	730	2.61
Arab (66)	66	0.24
Lebanese (22)	22	0.08
Palestinian (34)	34	0.12
Syrian (10)	10	0.04
Armenian (36)	36	0.13
Australian (0)	8	0.03
Austrian (0)	87	0.31
Brazilian (20)	30	0.11
British (78)	82	0.29

*Notes: † The Census 2010 population figure is used to calculate the percentages in the Hispanic Origin and Race categories. Ancestry percentages are based on the 2006-2010 American Community Survey population (not shown); ‡ Numbers in parentheses indicate the number of people reporting a single ancestry; * Numbers in parentheses indicate the number of persons reporting this race alone, not in combination with any other race; Please refer to the Explanation of Data for more information.*

Canadian (22)	101	0.36
Croatian (8)	8	0.03
Czech (0)	84	0.30
Czechoslovakian (0)	9	0.03
Danish (12)	63	0.23
Dutch (43)	244	0.87
Eastern European (42)	42	0.15
English (321)	1,683	6.03
European (70)	94	0.34
Finnish (10)	38	0.14
French, ex. Basque (54)	428	1.53
French Canadian (21)	54	0.19
German (623)	3,027	10.84
Greek (31)	173	0.62
Guyanese (36)	36	0.13
Hungarian (94)	285	1.02
Irish (1,636)	4,774	17.10
Israeli (0)	8	0.03
Italian (1,451)	3,454	12.37
Latvian (14)	14	0.05
Lithuanian (42)	84	0.30
Northern European (12)	12	0.04
Norwegian (132)	303	1.09
Pennsylvania German (16)	49	0.18
Polish (411)	1,289	4.62
Portuguese (94)	125	0.45
Romanian (0)	11	0.04
Russian (72)	314	1.12
Scandinavian (9)	30	0.11
Scotch-Irish (155)	397	1.42
Scottish (120)	550	1.97
Serbian (21)	21	0.08
Slavic (32)	43	0.15
Slovak (48)	78	0.28
Slovene (0)	12	0.04
Swedish (90)	248	0.89
Swiss (27)	64	0.23
Turkish (23)	23	0.08
Ukrainian (20)	101	0.36
Welsh (33)	116	0.42
West Indian, ex. Hispanic (1,200)	1,357	4.86
British West Indian (22)	22	0.08
Haitian (372)	493	1.77
Jamaican (707)	727	2.60
Trinidadian/Tobagonian (77)	87	0.31
West Indian (22)	28	0.10
Yugoslavian (0)	11	0.04

Hispanic Origin	Population	%
Hispanic or Latino (of any race)	2,607	9.33
Central American, ex. Mexican	239	0.86
Costa Rican	20	0.07
Guatemalan	20	0.07
Honduran	9	0.03
Nicaraguan	66	0.24
Panamanian	39	0.14
Salvadoran	83	0.30
Other Central American	2	0.01
Cuban	54	0.19
Dominican Republic	66	0.24
Mexican	805	2.88
Puerto Rican	1,099	3.93
South American	203	0.73
Argentinean	14	0.05
Bolivian	9	0.03
Chilean	24	0.09
Colombian	60	0.21
Ecuadorian	54	0.19
Paraguayan	5	0.02
Peruvian	29	0.10
Venezuelan	3	0.01
Other South American	5	0.02
Other Hispanic or Latino	141	0.50

Race*	Population	%
African-American/Black (10,772)	11,423	40.89
Not Hispanic (10,377)	10,890	38.98
Hispanic (395)	533	1.91
American Indian/Alaska Native (94)	342	1.22
Not Hispanic (62)	262	0.94
Hispanic (32)	80	0.29
Blackfeet (1)	13	0.05
Central American Ind. (1)	1	<0.01
Cherokee (10)	63	0.23
Chippewa (0)	1	<0.01
Choctaw (0)	4	0.01
Creek (0)	1	<0.01
Delaware (8)	21	0.08
Iroquois (0)	4	0.01
Navajo (3)	3	0.01
Potawatomi (1)	1	<0.01
Seminole (0)	3	0.01
Shoshone (0)	1	<0.01
Sioux (1)	4	0.01
South American Ind. (2)	10	0.04
Asian (632)	776	2.78
Not Hispanic (628)	745	2.67
Hispanic (4)	31	0.11
Bangladeshi (6)	11	0.04
Burmese (0)	1	<0.01
Chinese, ex. Taiwanese (54)	85	0.30
Filipino (332)	387	1.39
Indian (121)	142	0.51
Indonesian (1)	1	<0.01
Japanese (17)	44	0.16
Korean (64)	84	0.30
Malaysian (1)	1	<0.01
Pakistani (3)	8	0.03
Sri Lankan (1)	3	0.01
Taiwanese (3)	3	0.01
Thai (1)	4	0.01
Vietnamese (8)	11	0.04
Hawaii Native/Pacific Islander (9)	31	0.11
Not Hispanic (5)	22	0.08
Hispanic (4)	9	0.03
Guamanian/Chamorro (4)	6	0.02
Native Hawaiian (1)	9	0.03
Samoan (1)	4	0.01
White (14,855)	15,458	55.34
Not Hispanic (13,578)	14,008	50.14
Hispanic (1,277)	1,450	5.19

New Brunswick

Place Type: City
County: Middlesex
Population: 55,181†

Ancestry‡	Population	%
African, Sub-Saharan (331)	421	0.78
African (183)	210	0.39
Cape Verdean (0)	15	0.03
Ethiopian (9)	9	0.02
Ghanaian (6)	6	0.01
Kenyan (43)	59	0.11
Nigerian (90)	90	0.17
South African (0)	15	0.03
Other Sub-Saharan African (0)	17	0.03
American (1,321)	1,321	2.45
Arab (246)	318	0.59
Arab (83)	83	0.15
Egyptian (57)	57	0.11
Jordanian (7)	7	0.01
Lebanese (70)	94	0.17
Palestinian (5)	5	0.01
Syrian (0)	40	0.07
Other Arab (24)	32	0.06
Australian (20)	20	0.04
Austrian (9)	62	0.11
Brazilian (70)	70	0.13
British (69)	143	0.27
Canadian (49)	49	0.09
Croatian (6)	40	0.07
Czech (12)	77	0.14
Czechoslovakian (25)	87	0.16
Danish (9)	23	0.04
Dutch (43)	149	0.28
Eastern European (143)	143	0.27
English (114)	910	1.69
Estonian (16)	16	0.03
European (82)	94	0.17
French, ex. Basque (67)	278	0.52
French Canadian (42)	58	0.11
German (282)	1,854	3.44
Greek (153)	210	0.39
Guyanese (103)	103	0.19
Hungarian (219)	613	1.14
Icelander (0)	8	0.01
Iranian (24)	24	0.04
Irish (1,275)	3,134	5.81
Israeli (18)	54	0.10
Italian (1,924)	3,969	7.36
Latvian (9)	24	0.04
Lithuanian (8)	65	0.12
Norwegian (10)	124	0.23
Pennsylvania German (0)	10	0.02
Polish (509)	1,245	2.31
Portuguese (13)	51	0.09
Romanian (62)	62	0.11
Russian (414)	754	1.40
Scotch-Irish (53)	121	0.22
Scottish (54)	122	0.23
Serbian (0)	15	0.03
Slovak (17)	71	0.13
Swedish (37)	103	0.19
Swiss (39)	46	0.09
Turkish (70)	80	0.15
Ukrainian (133)	374	0.69
Welsh (0)	29	0.05
West Indian, ex. Hispanic (551)	625	1.16
Bahamian (21)	21	0.04
Barbadian (0)	8	0.01
Belizean (23)	23	0.04
Haitian (16)	16	0.03
Jamaican (381)	439	0.81
Trinidadian/Tobagonian (34)	34	0.06
U.S. Virgin Islander (35)	35	0.06
West Indian (41)	49	0.09

Hispanic Origin	Population	%
Hispanic or Latino (of any race)	27,553	49.93
Central American, ex. Mexican	3,761	6.82
Costa Rican	44	0.08
Guatemalan	353	0.64
Honduran	2,772	5.02
Nicaraguan	244	0.44
Panamanian	27	0.05
Salvadoran	313	0.57
Other Central American	8	0.01
Cuban	273	0.49
Dominican Republic	4,139	7.50
Mexican	14,104	25.56
Puerto Rican	2,832	5.13
South American	1,103	2.00
Argentinean	40	0.07
Bolivian	9	0.02
Chilean	27	0.05
Colombian	274	0.50
Ecuadorian	334	0.61
Paraguayan	6	0.01
Peruvian	335	0.61
Uruguayan	23	0.04
Venezuelan	50	0.09
Other South American	5	0.01
Other Hispanic or Latino	1,341	2.43

Race*	Population	%
African-American/Black (8,852)	9,695	17.57
Not Hispanic (7,743)	8,097	14.67
Hispanic (1,109)	1,598	2.90
American Indian/Alaska Native (498)	1,018	1.84
Not Hispanic (50)	202	0.37
Hispanic (448)	816	1.48
Apache (0)	1	<0.01
Blackfeet (0)	12	0.02
Canadian/French Am. Ind. (1)	4	0.01
Central American Ind. (4)	18	0.03
Cherokee (4)	36	0.07
Creek (1)	2	<0.01
Crow (0)	1	<0.01

*Notes: † The Census 2010 population figure is used to calculate the percentages in the Hispanic Origin and Race categories. Ancestry percentages are based on the 2006-2010 American Community Survey population (not shown); ‡ Numbers in parentheses indicate the number of people reporting a single ancestry; * Numbers in parentheses indicate the number of persons reporting this race alone, not in combination with any other race; Please refer to the Explanation of Data for more information.*

Delaware (0)	1	<0.01
Iroquois (0)	2	<0.01
Mexican American Ind. (79)	120	0.22
Paiute (0)	1	<0.01
Potawatomi (0)	2	<0.01
Pueblo (2)	4	0.01
Seminole (0)	6	0.01
Sioux (0)	3	0.01
South American Ind. (22)	46	0.08
Spanish American Ind. (9)	16	0.03
Asian (4,195)	4,621	8.37
Not Hispanic (4,122)	4,442	8.05
Hispanic (73)	179	0.32
Bangladeshi (29)	31	0.06
Burmese (8)	9	0.02
Cambodian (6)	6	0.01
Chinese, ex. Taiwanese (1,015)	1,117	2.02
Filipino (396)	465	0.84
Indian (1,594)	1,727	3.13
Indonesian (13)	14	0.03
Japanese (69)	106	0.19
Korean (561)	605	1.10
Laotian (1)	5	0.01
Malaysian (11)	12	0.02
Pakistani (131)	144	0.26
Sri Lankan (14)	16	0.03
Taiwanese (92)	115	0.21
Thai (18)	23	0.04
Vietnamese (91)	102	0.18
Hawaii Native/Pacific Islander (19)	112	0.20
Not Hispanic (12)	40	0.07
Hispanic (7)	72	0.13
Guamanian/Chamorro (1)	4	0.01
Native Hawaiian (4)	24	0.04
Samoan (0)	3	0.01
White (25,071)	26,904	48.76
Not Hispanic (14,761)	15,279	27.69
Hispanic (10,310)	11,625	21.07

New Milford

Place Type: Borough
County: Bergen
Population: 16,341†

Ancestry‡	Population	%
Afghan (77)	77	0.47
African, Sub-Saharan (81)	81	0.50
African (81)	81	0.50
Albanian (34)	53	0.33
American (213)	213	1.31
Arab (235)	298	1.83
Arab (19)	29	0.18
Egyptian (98)	98	0.60
Jordanian (29)	29	0.18
Lebanese (10)	44	0.27
Moroccan (0)	19	0.12
Syrian (79)	79	0.49
Armenian (46)	46	0.28
Assyrian/Chaldean/Syriac (183)	183	1.13
Austrian (10)	29	0.18
Belgian (0)	10	0.06
Bulgarian (100)	115	0.71
Croatian (59)	84	0.52
Czech (18)	105	0.65
Czechoslovakian (0)	11	0.07
Danish (0)	25	0.15
Dutch (20)	104	0.64
Eastern European (10)	10	0.06
English (140)	808	4.97
European (94)	94	0.58
French, ex. Basque (19)	81	0.50
French Canadian (0)	8	0.05
German (340)	1,721	10.58
Greek (143)	265	1.63
Hungarian (0)	109	0.67
Iranian (118)	118	0.73
Irish (1,322)	2,960	18.20
Israeli (23)	23	0.14
Italian (1,666)	3,201	19.69
Latvian (0)	23	0.14
Lithuanian (7)	47	0.29
Norwegian (0)	61	0.38
Pennsylvania German (0)	62	0.38
Polish (143)	491	3.02
Portuguese (0)	23	0.14
Romanian (35)	46	0.28
Russian (320)	514	3.16
Scotch-Irish (0)	11	0.07
Scottish (0)	135	0.83
Slovak (43)	113	0.69
Swedish (25)	90	0.55
Swiss (0)	52	0.32
Turkish (35)	64	0.39
Ukrainian (49)	49	0.30
Welsh (0)	39	0.24
West Indian, ex. Hispanic (215)	215	1.32
British West Indian (13)	13	0.08
Jamaican (133)	133	0.82
Trinidadian/Tobagonian (34)	34	0.21
West Indian (35)	35	0.22
Yugoslavian (12)	36	0.22

Hispanic Origin	Population	%
Hispanic or Latino (of any race)	2,227	13.63
Central American, ex. Mexican	136	0.83
Costa Rican	34	0.21
Guatemalan	18	0.11
Honduran	23	0.14
Nicaraguan	9	0.06
Panamanian	6	0.04
Salvadoran	46	0.28
Cuban	272	1.66
Dominican Republic	478	2.93
Mexican	88	0.54
Puerto Rican	472	2.89
South American	615	3.76
Argentinean	36	0.22
Bolivian	7	0.04
Chilean	5	0.03
Colombian	317	1.94
Ecuadorian	129	0.79
Paraguayan	1	0.01
Peruvian	80	0.49
Uruguayan	23	0.14
Venezuelan	12	0.07
Other South American	5	0.03
Other Hispanic or Latino	166	1.02

Race*	Population	%
African-American/Black (608)	754	4.61
Not Hispanic (507)	575	3.52
Hispanic (101)	179	1.10
American Indian/Alaska Native (20)	62	0.38
Not Hispanic (14)	43	0.26
Hispanic (6)	19	0.12
Blackfeet (0)	4	0.02
Central American Ind. (0)	1	0.01
Cherokee (2)	10	0.06
Chickasaw (1)	1	0.01
Chippewa (1)	1	0.01
Delaware (1)	2	0.01
Mexican American Ind. (2)	2	0.01
Shoshone (0)	1	0.01
South American Ind. (2)	11	0.07
Asian (3,169)	3,350	20.50
Not Hispanic (3,163)	3,317	20.30
Hispanic (6)	33	0.20
Bangladeshi (4)	7	0.04
Burmese (1)	1	0.01
Cambodian (1)	3	0.02
Chinese, ex. Taiwanese (222)	263	1.61
Filipino (1,519)	1,594	9.75
Hmong (0)	1	0.01
Indian (856)	923	5.65
Indonesian (7)	9	0.06
Japanese (81)	96	0.59
Korean (315)	320	1.96
Nepalese (3)	3	0.02
Pakistani (45)	45	0.28
Sri Lankan (10)	14	0.09
Taiwanese (29)	33	0.20
Thai (23)	27	0.17
Vietnamese (3)	7	0.04
Hawaii Native/Pacific Islander (4)	16	0.10
Not Hispanic (2)	12	0.07
Hispanic (2)	4	0.02
Guamanian/Chamorro (1)	1	0.01
Native Hawaiian (1)	3	0.02
White (11,522)	11,835	72.43
Not Hispanic (10,160)	10,308	63.08
Hispanic (1,362)	1,527	9.34

New Providence

Place Type: Borough
County: Union
Population: 12,171†

Ancestry‡	Population	%
American (205)	205	1.71
Arab (47)	47	0.39
Egyptian (47)	47	0.39
Armenian (12)	20	0.17
Assyrian/Chaldean/Syriac (0)	8	0.07
Australian (0)	8	0.07
Austrian (0)	68	0.57
Basque (7)	7	0.06
Belgian (28)	28	0.23
Brazilian (27)	53	0.44
British (23)	40	0.33
Canadian (15)	33	0.27
Celtic (0)	8	0.07
Czech (17)	77	0.64
Dutch (9)	112	0.93
Eastern European (107)	107	0.89
English (242)	1,441	11.99
European (100)	100	0.83
Finnish (0)	12	0.10
French, ex. Basque (78)	253	2.11
French Canadian (0)	61	0.51
German (344)	2,209	18.38
Greek (0)	19	0.16
Hungarian (16)	72	0.60
Icelander (0)	12	0.10
Irish (714)	2,691	22.39
Italian (1,239)	2,517	20.94
Lithuanian (38)	83	0.69
Norwegian (50)	147	1.22
Polish (231)	939	7.81
Portuguese (292)	292	2.43
Romanian (15)	24	0.20
Russian (341)	518	4.31
Scotch-Irish (163)	284	2.36
Scottish (54)	330	2.75
Serbian (0)	22	0.18
Slavic (44)	44	0.37
Slovak (24)	61	0.51
Swedish (0)	68	0.57
Swiss (11)	60	0.50
Ukrainian (91)	129	1.07
Welsh (11)	93	0.77
West Indian, ex. Hispanic (16)	30	0.25
Jamaican (16)	30	0.25
Yugoslavian (0)	8	0.07

Hispanic Origin	Population	%
Hispanic or Latino (of any race)	783	6.43
Central American, ex. Mexican	274	2.25
Costa Rican	218	1.79
Guatemalan	25	0.21
Honduran	7	0.06
Nicaraguan	5	0.04
Panamanian	1	0.01
Salvadoran	18	0.15
Cuban	62	0.51
Dominican Republic	18	0.15
Mexican	70	0.58
Puerto Rican	98	0.81
South American	189	1.55

*Notes: † The Census 2010 population figure is used to calculate the percentages in the Hispanic Origin and Race categories. Ancestry percentages are based on the 2006-2010 American Community Survey population (not shown); ‡ Numbers in parentheses indicate the number of people reporting a single ancestry; * Numbers in parentheses indicate the number of persons reporting this race alone, not in combination with any other race; Please refer to the Explanation of Data for more information.*

Argentinean	20	0.16
Bolivian	1	0.01
Chilean	21	0.17
Colombian	57	0.47
Ecuadorian	25	0.21
Paraguayan	7	0.06
Peruvian	29	0.24
Uruguayan	6	0.05
Venezuelan	15	0.12
Other South American	8	0.07
Other Hispanic or Latino	72	0.59

Race*	Population	%
African-American/Black (155)	192	1.58
Not Hispanic (153)	181	1.49
Hispanic (2)	11	0.09
American Indian/Alaska Native (12)	34	0.28
Not Hispanic (9)	16	0.13
Hispanic (3)	18	0.15
Apache (0)	2	0.02
Central American Ind. (0)	4	0.03
Cherokee (1)	4	0.03
Chippewa (1)	1	0.01
Cree (0)	1	0.01
Iroquois (4)	4	0.03
Navajo (0)	1	0.01
South American Ind. (1)	7	0.06
Spanish American Ind. (2)	2	0.02
Asian (1,190)	1,323	10.87
Not Hispanic (1,187)	1,307	10.74
Hispanic (3)	16	0.13
Chinese, ex. Taiwanese (447)	493	4.05
Filipino (87)	109	0.90
Indian (418)	442	3.63
Indonesian (0)	3	0.02
Japanese (51)	69	0.57
Korean (86)	96	0.79
Malaysian (4)	4	0.03
Nepalese (10)	10	0.08
Pakistani (27)	29	0.24
Taiwanese (33)	39	0.32
Thai (3)	7	0.06
Vietnamese (13)	13	0.11
Hawaii Native/Pacific Islander (5)	10	0.08
Not Hispanic (0)	5	0.04
Hispanic (5)	5	0.04
Guamanian/Chamorro (5)	5	0.04
White (10,465)	10,639	87.41
Not Hispanic (9,870)	10,004	82.20
Hispanic (595)	635	5.22

Newark

Place Type: City
County: Essex
Population: 277,140†

Ancestry‡	Population	%
Afghan (505)	505	0.18
African, Sub-Saharan (10,169)	10,842	3.95
African (3,689)	4,089	1.49
Cape Verdean (111)	132	0.05
Ethiopian (8)	20	0.01
Ghanaian (1,334)	1,420	0.52
Kenyan (11)	11	<0.01
Liberian (902)	918	0.33
Nigerian (2,614)	2,732	0.99
Sierra Leonean (123)	123	0.04
Somalian (30)	30	0.01
Sudanese (29)	29	0.01
Ugandan (14)	14	0.01
Other Sub-Saharan African (1,304)	1,324	0.48
Albanian (12)	24	0.01
American (6,326)	6,326	2.30
Arab (513)	657	0.24
Arab (26)	45	0.02
Egyptian (186)	186	0.07
Lebanese (22)	22	0.01
Moroccan (204)	289	0.11
Syrian (36)	53	0.02
Other Arab (39)	62	0.02
Austrian (10)	55	0.02
Brazilian (8,505)	9,232	3.36
British (15)	24	0.01
Bulgarian (23)	23	0.01
Canadian (134)	134	0.05
Czech (9)	36	0.01
Czechoslovakian (14)	42	0.02
Danish (0)	10	<0.01
Dutch (19)	98	0.04
Eastern European (11)	11	<0.01
English (401)	1,229	0.45
European (151)	161	0.06
French, ex. Basque (32)	508	0.18
French Canadian (58)	84	0.03
German (515)	2,147	0.78
Greek (84)	196	0.07
Guyanese (2,092)	2,202	0.80
Hungarian (114)	262	0.10
Icelander (0)	7	<0.01
Iranian (143)	143	0.05
Irish (996)	3,424	1.25
Israeli (80)	88	0.03
Italian (3,892)	6,170	2.25
Lithuanian (13)	13	<0.01
Norwegian (34)	62	0.02
Polish (939)	1,714	0.62
Portuguese (13,132)	14,175	5.16
Romanian (29)	71	0.03
Russian (223)	394	0.14
Scotch-Irish (32)	67	0.02
Scottish (85)	247	0.09
Serbian (12)	12	<0.01
Slovak (0)	46	0.02
Swedish (14)	73	0.03
Swiss (0)	13	<0.01
Turkish (22)	22	0.01
Ukrainian (300)	385	0.14
Welsh (11)	111	0.04
West Indian, ex. Hispanic (8,254)	9,871	3.59
Bahamian (9)	37	0.01
Barbadian (475)	590	0.21
Bermudan (70)	70	0.03
British West Indian (137)	291	0.11
Haitian (2,743)	3,138	1.14
Jamaican (2,977)	3,448	1.26
Trinidadian/Tobagonian (1,141)	1,399	0.51
U.S. Virgin Islander (0)	21	0.01
West Indian (690)	865	0.31
Other West Indian (12)	12	<0.01

Hispanic Origin	Population	%
Hispanic or Latino (of any race)	93,746	33.83
Central American, ex. Mexican	7,497	2.71
Costa Rican	444	0.16
Guatemalan	1,375	0.50
Honduran	2,126	0.77
Nicaraguan	285	0.10
Panamanian	220	0.08
Salvadoran	3,000	1.08
Other Central American	47	0.02
Cuban	2,241	0.81
Dominican Republic	12,527	4.52
Mexican	4,336	1.56
Puerto Rican	35,993	12.99
South American	22,413	8.09
Argentinean	351	0.13
Bolivian	105	0.04
Chilean	125	0.05
Colombian	1,393	0.50
Ecuadorian	16,847	6.08
Paraguayan	21	0.01
Peruvian	2,448	0.88
Uruguayan	634	0.23
Venezuelan	299	0.11
Other South American	190	0.07
Other Hispanic or Latino	8,739	3.15

Race*	Population	%
African-American/Black (145,085)	149,512	53.95
Not Hispanic (138,074)	140,365	50.65
Hispanic (7,011)	9,147	3.30
American Indian/Alaska Native (1,697)	3,258	1.18
Not Hispanic (713)	1,623	0.59
Hispanic (984)	1,635	0.59
Alaska Athabascan *(Ala. Nat.)* (1)	2	<0.01
Apache (5)	22	0.01
Blackfeet (10)	72	0.03
Canadian/French Am. Ind. (3)	9	<0.01
Central American Ind. (55)	74	0.03
Cherokee (62)	265	0.10
Chippewa (2)	7	<0.01
Choctaw (4)	13	<0.01
Comanche (0)	3	<0.01
Cree (0)	3	<0.01
Creek (0)	7	<0.01
Delaware (8)	17	0.01
Hopi (0)	5	<0.01
Inupiat *(Alaska Native)* (0)	1	<0.01
Iroquois (2)	24	0.01
Lumbee (3)	4	<0.01
Mexican American Ind. (52)	72	0.03
Navajo (1)	3	<0.01
Pueblo (20)	40	0.01
Seminole (4)	36	0.01
Shoshone (0)	1	<0.01
Sioux (1)	9	<0.01
South American Ind. (117)	230	0.08
Spanish American Ind. (31)	59	0.02
Tlingit-Haida *(Alaska Native)* (2)	3	<0.01
Yuman (0)	1	<0.01
Asian (4,485)	5,388	1.94
Not Hispanic (4,318)	4,996	1.80
Hispanic (167)	392	0.14
Bangladeshi (102)	113	0.04
Cambodian (9)	9	<0.01
Chinese, ex. Taiwanese (697)	847	0.31
Filipino (605)	732	0.26
Indian (1,848)	2,129	0.77
Indonesian (7)	10	<0.01
Japanese (80)	177	0.06
Korean (237)	272	0.10
Laotian (18)	23	0.01
Malaysian (4)	8	<0.01
Nepalese (4)	4	<0.01
Pakistani (308)	335	0.12
Sri Lankan (132)	152	0.05
Taiwanese (30)	32	0.01
Thai (28)	36	0.01
Vietnamese (129)	172	0.06
Hawaii Native/Pacific Islander (118)	661	0.24
Not Hispanic (68)	337	0.12
Hispanic (50)	324	0.12
Guamanian/Chamorro (41)	60	0.02
Native Hawaiian (18)	53	0.02
Samoan (12)	25	0.01
White (72,914)	80,339	28.99
Not Hispanic (32,122)	34,774	12.55
Hispanic (40,792)	45,565	16.44

Newton

Place Type: Town
County: Sussex
Population: 7,997†

Ancestry‡	Population	%
African, Sub-Saharan (162)	162	1.99
African (162)	162	1.99
Albanian (19)	51	0.63
American (298)	298	3.67
Arab (17)	17	0.21
Lebanese (9)	9	0.11
Syrian (8)	8	0.10
Austrian (16)	81	1.00
British (19)	56	0.69
Canadian (27)	146	1.80
Croatian (11)	30	0.37
Czech (0)	72	0.89
Czechoslovakian (21)	34	0.42

*Notes: † The Census 2010 population figure is used to calculate the percentages in the Hispanic Origin and Race categories. Ancestry percentages are based on the 2006-2010 American Community Survey population (not shown); ‡ Numbers in parentheses indicate the number of people reporting a single ancestry; * Numbers in parentheses indicate the number of persons reporting this race alone, not in combination with any other race; Please refer to the Explanation of Data for more information.*

Danish (7)	14	0.17
Dutch (100)	484	5.96
English (318)	1,049	12.92
European (19)	25	0.31
French, ex. Basque (8)	321	3.95
French Canadian (18)	52	0.64
German (329)	1,990	24.50
Greek (40)	233	2.87
Hungarian (9)	62	0.76
Irish (415)	2,072	25.51
Italian (477)	1,466	18.05
Lithuanian (11)	11	0.14
Norwegian (20)	66	0.81
Pennsylvania German (11)	40	0.49
Polish (79)	306	3.77
Portuguese (11)	19	0.23
Russian (27)	85	1.05
Scotch-Irish (21)	112	1.38
Scottish (37)	306	3.77
Slovak (8)	42	0.52
Swedish (7)	17	0.21
Swiss (0)	47	0.58
Ukrainian (10)	40	0.49
Welsh (0)	79	0.97
West Indian, ex. Hispanic (7)	7	0.09
Haitian (7)	7	0.09
Yugoslavian (12)	12	0.15

Hispanic Origin	Population	%
Hispanic or Latino (of any race)	987	12.34
Central American, ex. Mexican	84	1.05
Costa Rican	9	0.11
Guatemalan	26	0.33
Honduran	23	0.29
Nicaraguan	7	0.09
Panamanian	1	0.01
Salvadoran	18	0.23
Cuban	29	0.36
Dominican Republic	57	0.71
Mexican	325	4.06
Puerto Rican	261	3.26
South American	161	2.01
Argentinean	2	0.03
Chilean	11	0.14
Colombian	50	0.63
Ecuadorian	43	0.54
Paraguayan	2	0.03
Peruvian	19	0.24
Uruguayan	32	0.40
Venezuelan	2	0.03
Other Hispanic or Latino	70	0.88

Race*	Population	%
African-American/Black (390)	479	5.99
Not Hispanic (361)	431	5.39
Hispanic (29)	48	0.60
American Indian/Alaska Native (39)	67	0.84
Not Hispanic (27)	51	0.64
Hispanic (12)	16	0.20
Blackfeet (1)	1	0.01
Central American Ind. (2)	2	0.03
Cherokee (1)	7	0.09
Cree (4)	4	0.05
Lumbee (4)	4	0.05
Mexican American Ind. (2)	2	0.03
Navajo (3)	3	0.04
Ottawa (0)	4	0.05
Sioux (0)	1	0.01
Yup'ik *(Alaska Native)* (1)	1	0.01
Asian (238)	273	3.41
Not Hispanic (233)	263	3.29
Hispanic (5)	10	0.13
Bangladeshi (4)	4	0.05
Chinese, ex. Taiwanese (34)	40	0.50
Filipino (88)	106	1.33
Indian (53)	59	0.74
Indonesian (2)	5	0.06
Japanese (2)	2	0.03
Korean (21)	21	0.26
Pakistani (20)	20	0.25
Taiwanese (1)	1	0.01
Thai (3)	4	0.05
Vietnamese (1)	1	0.01
Hawaii Native/Pacific Islander (4)	9	0.11
Not Hispanic (3)	6	0.08
Hispanic (1)	3	0.04
Guamanian/Chamorro (1)	2	0.03
Native Hawaiian (0)	1	0.01
White (6,801)	6,964	87.08
Not Hispanic (6,257)	6,368	79.63
Hispanic (544)	596	7.45

North Arlington

Place Type: Borough
County: Bergen
Population: 15,392†

Ancestry‡	Population	%
American (155)	155	1.01
Arab (298)	354	2.32
Egyptian (58)	101	0.66
Moroccan (90)	90	0.59
Palestinian (150)	150	0.98
Syrian (0)	13	0.09
Austrian (0)	51	0.33
Brazilian (324)	324	2.12
British (0)	14	0.09
Croatian (0)	12	0.08
Czech (12)	12	0.08
Dutch (0)	42	0.28
English (12)	428	2.80
European (8)	99	0.65
French, ex. Basque (54)	193	1.26
French Canadian (24)	24	0.16
German (177)	1,019	6.67
Greek (142)	242	1.58
Guyanese (10)	10	0.07
Hungarian (10)	75	0.49
Irish (797)	2,764	18.10
Italian (1,956)	3,679	24.09
Latvian (0)	10	0.07
Lithuanian (14)	90	0.59
Norwegian (0)	12	0.08
Polish (936)	2,220	14.54
Portuguese (691)	901	5.90
Russian (32)	55	0.36
Scotch-Irish (56)	153	1.00
Scottish (146)	544	3.56
Slavic (0)	13	0.09
Slovak (14)	65	0.43
Slovene (0)	11	0.07
Swedish (12)	77	0.50
Swiss (0)	8	0.05
Turkish (8)	8	0.05
Ukrainian (25)	75	0.49
Welsh (0)	23	0.15
West Indian, ex. Hispanic (11)	11	0.07
Jamaican (11)	11	0.07

Hispanic Origin	Population	%
Hispanic or Latino (of any race)	3,211	20.86
Central American, ex. Mexican	160	1.04
Costa Rican	28	0.18
Guatemalan	32	0.21
Honduran	30	0.19
Nicaraguan	12	0.08
Panamanian	6	0.04
Salvadoran	52	0.34
Cuban	303	1.97
Dominican Republic	295	1.92
Mexican	81	0.53
Puerto Rican	782	5.08
South American	1,100	7.15
Argentinean	30	0.19
Bolivian	7	0.05
Chilean	27	0.18
Colombian	243	1.58
Ecuadorian	357	2.32
Peruvian	369	2.40
Uruguayan	38	0.25
Venezuelan	28	0.18
Other South American	1	0.01
Other Hispanic or Latino	490	3.18

Race*	Population	%
African-American/Black (220)	281	1.83
Not Hispanic (148)	181	1.18
Hispanic (72)	100	0.65
American Indian/Alaska Native (36)	65	0.42
Not Hispanic (19)	39	0.25
Hispanic (17)	26	0.17
Cherokee (0)	3	0.02
Delaware (3)	3	0.02
Iroquois (1)	1	0.01
Seminole (0)	1	0.01
South American Ind. (4)	8	0.05
Asian (1,211)	1,302	8.46
Not Hispanic (1,201)	1,275	8.28
Hispanic (10)	27	0.18
Chinese, ex. Taiwanese (185)	200	1.30
Filipino (252)	282	1.83
Indian (562)	583	3.79
Indonesian (1)	1	0.01
Japanese (8)	10	0.06
Korean (135)	142	0.92
Pakistani (17)	19	0.12
Sri Lankan (14)	14	0.09
Taiwanese (4)	4	0.03
Thai (22)	27	0.18
Vietnamese (6)	10	0.06
Hawaii Native/Pacific Islander (2)	15	0.10
Not Hispanic (2)	11	0.07
Hispanic (0)	4	0.03
Guamanian/Chamorro (1)	5	0.03
Native Hawaiian (0)	1	0.01
White (12,712)	12,956	84.17
Not Hispanic (10,567)	10,698	69.50
Hispanic (2,145)	2,258	14.67

North Bergen

Place Type: Township
County: Hudson
Population: 60,773†

Ancestry‡	Population	%
African, Sub-Saharan (181)	222	0.37
African (0)	41	0.07
Cape Verdean (35)	35	0.06
Kenyan (71)	71	0.12
Nigerian (11)	11	0.02
South African (3)	3	0.01
Zimbabwean (33)	33	0.06
Other Sub-Saharan African (28)	28	0.05
American (476)	476	0.80
Arab (1,146)	1,502	2.52
Arab (102)	115	0.19
Egyptian (152)	163	0.27
Jordanian (6)	6	0.01
Lebanese (310)	337	0.57
Moroccan (55)	55	0.09
Palestinian (422)	422	0.71
Syrian (99)	152	0.26
Other Arab (0)	252	0.42
Armenian (136)	216	0.36
Assyrian/Chaldean/Syriac (7)	7	0.01
Australian (0)	15	0.03
Austrian (31)	62	0.10
Basque (0)	49	0.08
Belgian (0)	10	0.02
Brazilian (145)	215	0.36
British (0)	21	0.04
Bulgarian (23)	23	0.04
Canadian (0)	7	0.01
Celtic (9)	9	0.02
Croatian (133)	223	0.37
Czech (34)	58	0.10
Czechoslovakian (7)	37	0.06
Danish (17)	40	0.07

SECTION TWO

*Notes: † The Census 2010 population figure is used to calculate the percentages in the Hispanic Origin and Race categories. Ancestry percentages are based on the 2006-2010 American Community Survey population (not shown); ‡ Numbers in parentheses indicate the number of people reporting a single ancestry; * Numbers in parentheses indicate the number of persons reporting this race alone, not in combination with any other race; Please refer to the Explanation of Data for more information.*

Dutch (0)	56	0.09
Eastern European (12)	12	0.02
English (196)	654	1.10
European (64)	74	0.12
Finnish (0)	43	0.07
French, ex. Basque (12)	358	0.60
French Canadian (23)	39	0.07
German (566)	1,769	2.97
Greek (276)	533	0.89
Guyanese (127)	134	0.22
Hungarian (101)	208	0.35
Iranian (10)	57	0.10
Irish (708)	2,180	3.66
Israeli (11)	35	0.06
Italian (2,706)	4,622	7.76
Latvian (17)	17	0.03
Lithuanian (7)	23	0.04
Norwegian (11)	48	0.08
Polish (305)	494	0.83
Portuguese (20)	72	0.12
Romanian (121)	141	0.24
Russian (168)	545	0.92
Scotch-Irish (14)	66	0.11
Scottish (19)	120	0.20
Serbian (14)	14	0.02
Slavic (10)	41	0.07
Slovak (21)	55	0.09
Slovene (0)	14	0.02
Swedish (0)	41	0.07
Swiss (30)	65	0.11
Turkish (110)	159	0.27
Ukrainian (71)	107	0.18
Welsh (0)	16	0.03
West Indian, ex. Hispanic (126)	182	0.31
Barbadian (44)	44	0.07
British West Indian (10)	10	0.02
Jamaican (39)	61	0.10
Trinidadian/Tobagonian (0)	18	0.03
West Indian (33)	49	0.08
Yugoslavian (41)	65	0.11

Hispanic Origin	Population	%
Hispanic or Latino (of any race)	41,569	68.40
Central American, ex. Mexican	5,991	9.86
Costa Rican	167	0.27
Guatemalan	1,596	2.63
Honduran	1,081	1.78
Nicaraguan	240	0.39
Panamanian	71	0.12
Salvadoran	2,825	4.65
Other Central American	11	0.02
Cuban	7,248	11.93
Dominican Republic	5,999	9.87
Mexican	1,440	2.37
Puerto Rican	5,090	8.38
South American	13,026	21.43
Argentinean	494	0.81
Bolivian	92	0.15
Chilean	472	0.78
Colombian	4,784	7.87
Ecuadorian	5,064	8.33
Paraguayan	16	0.03
Peruvian	1,590	2.62
Uruguayan	201	0.33
Venezuelan	267	0.44
Other South American	46	0.08
Other Hispanic or Latino	2,775	4.57

Race*	Population	%
African-American/Black (2,456)	3,134	5.16
Not Hispanic (1,065)	1,217	2.00
Hispanic (1,391)	1,917	3.15
American Indian/Alaska Native (535)	918	1.51
Not Hispanic (62)	160	0.26
Hispanic (473)	758	1.25
Apache (0)	1	<0.01
Blackfeet (0)	5	0.01
Central American Ind. (26)	32	0.05
Cherokee (3)	19	0.03
Chickasaw (0)	1	<0.01
Chippewa (2)	5	0.01
Choctaw (0)	1	<0.01
Creek (0)	4	0.01
Delaware (1)	1	<0.01
Lumbee (0)	1	<0.01
Mexican American Ind. (44)	73	0.12
Navajo (1)	5	0.01
Pueblo (0)	1	<0.01
Sioux (2)	3	<0.01
South American Ind. (46)	73	0.12
Spanish American Ind. (19)	21	0.03
Tohono O'Odham (0)	2	<0.01
Asian (3,979)	4,497	7.40
Not Hispanic (3,835)	4,220	6.94
Hispanic (144)	277	0.46
Bangladeshi (19)	20	0.03
Burmese (4)	4	0.01
Cambodian (0)	1	<0.01
Chinese, ex. Taiwanese (453)	541	0.89
Filipino (317)	391	0.64
Hmong (0)	3	<0.01
Indian (2,271)	2,424	3.99
Indonesian (10)	19	0.03
Japanese (138)	172	0.28
Korean (490)	512	0.84
Laotian (4)	6	0.01
Malaysian (0)	3	<0.01
Nepalese (9)	9	0.01
Pakistani (75)	85	0.14
Sri Lankan (3)	3	<0.01
Taiwanese (13)	16	0.03
Thai (21)	26	0.04
Vietnamese (43)	55	0.09
Hawaii Native/Pacific Islander (49)	165	0.27
Not Hispanic (18)	53	0.09
Hispanic (31)	112	0.18
Guamanian/Chamorro (5)	13	0.02
Native Hawaiian (15)	25	0.04
Samoan (8)	8	0.01
White (40,705)	43,023	70.79
Not Hispanic (13,370)	13,803	22.71
Hispanic (27,335)	29,220	48.08

North Brunswick

Place Type: Township
County: Middlesex
Population: 40,742[†]

Ancestry[‡]	Population	%
African, Sub-Saharan (1,637)	1,879	4.71
African (574)	585	1.47
Ethiopian (38)	38	0.10
Ghanaian (366)	385	0.96
Kenyan (31)	126	0.32
Liberian (16)	16	0.04
Nigerian (56)	56	0.14
Senegalese (0)	22	0.06
Sierra Leonean (15)	15	0.04
Somalian (37)	132	0.33
South African (23)	23	0.06
Sudanese (481)	481	1.20
Albanian (0)	13	0.03
American (886)	886	2.22
Arab (510)	707	1.77
Arab (17)	17	0.04
Egyptian (338)	338	0.85
Lebanese (134)	307	0.77
Syrian (21)	34	0.09
Other Arab (0)	11	0.03
Austrian (22)	156	0.39
Brazilian (103)	135	0.34
British (15)	23	0.06
Bulgarian (80)	80	0.20
Canadian (96)	96	0.24
Celtic (15)	42	0.11
Croatian (0)	6	0.02
Czech (0)	15	0.04
Czechoslovakian (10)	10	0.03
Danish (27)	140	0.35
Dutch (19)	215	0.54
Eastern European (137)	212	0.53
English (235)	1,297	3.25
European (140)	140	0.35
Finnish (0)	6	0.02
French, ex. Basque (0)	222	0.56
French Canadian (14)	97	0.24
German (351)	2,851	7.14
Greek (94)	252	0.63
Guyanese (73)	73	0.18
Hungarian (362)	1,021	2.56
Iranian (10)	10	0.03
Irish (883)	3,273	8.20
Israeli (0)	38	0.10
Italian (1,929)	4,337	10.86
Latvian (22)	32	0.08
Lithuanian (67)	124	0.31
Maltese (0)	21	0.05
Norwegian (0)	27	0.07
Polish (826)	2,014	5.05
Portuguese (98)	152	0.38
Romanian (160)	205	0.51
Russian (257)	688	1.72
Scandinavian (0)	8	0.02
Scotch-Irish (0)	281	0.70
Scottish (47)	266	0.67
Slavic (0)	12	0.03
Slovak (119)	215	0.54
Swedish (20)	152	0.38
Swiss (0)	23	0.06
Turkish (52)	67	0.17
Ukrainian (332)	558	1.40
Welsh (20)	44	0.11
West Indian, ex. Hispanic (452)	615	1.54
British West Indian (20)	20	0.05
Haitian (24)	24	0.06
Jamaican (366)	483	1.21
Trinidadian/Tobagonian (42)	42	0.11
West Indian (0)	46	0.12
Yugoslavian (0)	55	0.14

Hispanic Origin	Population	%
Hispanic or Latino (of any race)	7,223	17.73
Central American, ex. Mexican	861	2.11
Costa Rican	19	0.05
Guatemalan	118	0.29
Honduran	475	1.17
Nicaraguan	137	0.34
Panamanian	46	0.11
Salvadoran	62	0.15
Other Central American	4	0.01
Cuban	204	0.50
Dominican Republic	1,300	3.19
Mexican	1,507	3.70
Puerto Rican	1,811	4.45
South American	947	2.32
Argentinean	46	0.11
Bolivian	6	0.01
Chilean	14	0.03
Colombian	280	0.69
Ecuadorian	338	0.83
Peruvian	203	0.50
Uruguayan	14	0.03
Venezuelan	44	0.11
Other South American	2	<0.01
Other Hispanic or Latino	593	1.46

Race*	Population	%
African-American/Black (7,116)	7,614	18.69
Not Hispanic (6,625)	6,921	16.99
Hispanic (491)	693	1.70
American Indian/Alaska Native (171)	358	0.88
Not Hispanic (72)	220	0.54
Hispanic (99)	138	0.34
Blackfeet (0)	9	0.02
Central American Ind. (5)	5	0.01
Cherokee (3)	27	0.07
Chippewa (1)	1	<0.01
Choctaw (0)	1	<0.01
Cree (0)	1	<0.01

*Notes: † The Census 2010 population figure is used to calculate the percentages in the Hispanic Origin and Race categories. Ancestry percentages are based on the 2006-2010 American Community Survey population (not shown); ‡ Numbers in parentheses indicate the number of people reporting a single ancestry; * Numbers in parentheses indicate the number of persons reporting this race alone, not in combination with any other race; Please refer to the Explanation of Data for more information.*

	Population	%
Creek (1)	3	0.01
Crow (0)	1	<0.01
Delaware (0)	1	<0.01
Hopi (0)	1	<0.01
Iroquois (0)	4	0.01
Lumbee (0)	3	0.01
Mexican American Ind. (29)	31	0.08
Navajo (1)	5	0.01
Sioux (2)	7	0.02
South American Ind. (4)	15	0.04
Spanish American Ind. (6)	6	0.01
Asian (9,888)	10,439	25.62
Not Hispanic (9,865)	10,381	25.48
Hispanic (23)	58	0.14
Bangladeshi (72)	75	0.18
Burmese (6)	7	0.02
Cambodian (1)	1	<0.01
Chinese, ex. Taiwanese (866)	963	2.36
Filipino (551)	620	1.52
Indian (6,952)	7,197	17.66
Indonesian (10)	12	0.03
Japanese (45)	61	0.15
Korean (523)	541	1.33
Laotian (1)	1	<0.01
Malaysian (1)	3	0.01
Nepalese (5)	5	0.01
Pakistani (544)	586	1.44
Sri Lankan (52)	53	0.13
Taiwanese (96)	119	0.29
Thai (6)	7	0.02
Vietnamese (45)	50	0.12
Hawaii Native/Pacific Islander (15)	63	0.15
Not Hispanic (10)	38	0.09
Hispanic (5)	25	0.06
Guamanian/Chamorro (4)	5	0.01
Native Hawaiian (1)	3	0.01
White (18,991)	19,759	48.50
Not Hispanic (15,946)	16,432	40.33
Hispanic (3,045)	3,327	8.17

North Haledon

Place Type: Borough
County: Passaic
Population: 8,417†

Ancestry‡	Population	%
Albanian (115)	115	1.40
American (181)	181	2.21
Arab (130)	130	1.59
Syrian (130)	130	1.59
Armenian (0)	10	0.12
Austrian (7)	32	0.39
Brazilian (26)	26	0.32
British (0)	20	0.24
Croatian (0)	10	0.12
Czech (0)	22	0.27
Danish (0)	10	0.12
Dutch (774)	1,213	14.82
Eastern European (18)	18	0.22
English (24)	425	5.19
European (6)	6	0.07
Finnish (11)	11	0.13
French, ex. Basque (0)	50	0.61
French Canadian (19)	19	0.23
German (315)	1,238	15.12
Greek (0)	111	1.36
Guyanese (3)	3	0.04
Hungarian (0)	23	0.28
Irish (266)	1,208	14.76
Italian (1,333)	2,541	31.04
Lithuanian (8)	25	0.31
Norwegian (0)	12	0.15
Polish (266)	685	8.37
Portuguese (0)	36	0.44
Romanian (15)	15	0.18
Russian (48)	180	2.20
Scotch-Irish (0)	43	0.53
Scottish (11)	110	1.34
Slovak (18)	29	0.35
Slovene (0)	10	0.12
Swedish (11)	53	0.65
Swiss (0)	33	0.40
Ukrainian (30)	106	1.29
Welsh (0)	42	0.51
West Indian, ex. Hispanic (15)	15	0.18
Jamaican (15)	15	0.18
Yugoslavian (10)	55	0.67

Hispanic Origin	Population	%
Hispanic or Latino (of any race)	628	7.46
Central American, ex. Mexican	39	0.46
Costa Rican	18	0.21
Guatemalan	6	0.07
Honduran	4	0.05
Panamanian	4	0.05
Salvadoran	5	0.06
Other Central American	2	0.02
Cuban	66	0.78
Dominican Republic	60	0.71
Mexican	28	0.33
Puerto Rican	165	1.96
South American	171	2.03
Argentinean	13	0.15
Chilean	4	0.05
Colombian	57	0.68
Ecuadorian	22	0.26
Peruvian	74	0.88
Venezuelan	1	0.01
Other Hispanic or Latino	99	1.18

Race*	Population	%
African-American/Black (148)	190	2.26
Not Hispanic (136)	150	1.78
Hispanic (12)	40	0.48
American Indian/Alaska Native (2)	20	0.24
Not Hispanic (2)	14	0.17
Hispanic (0)	6	0.07
Blackfeet (0)	4	0.05
Cherokee (0)	1	0.01
Iroquois (2)	3	0.04
Sioux (0)	1	0.01
South American Ind. (0)	1	0.01
Asian (318)	373	4.43
Not Hispanic (318)	364	4.32
Hispanic (0)	9	0.11
Chinese, ex. Taiwanese (57)	66	0.78
Filipino (58)	75	0.89
Indian (93)	105	1.25
Japanese (7)	9	0.11
Korean (88)	89	1.06
Pakistani (5)	6	0.07
Sri Lankan (0)	1	0.01
Vietnamese (2)	2	0.02
White (7,704)	7,828	93.00
Not Hispanic (7,248)	7,310	86.85
Hispanic (456)	518	6.15

North Hanover

Place Type: Township
County: Burlington
Population: 7,678†

Ancestry‡	Population	%
African, Sub-Saharan (19)	19	0.26
Ghanaian (19)	19	0.26
American (264)	264	3.57
Arab (0)	26	0.35
Lebanese (0)	26	0.35
Austrian (0)	30	0.41
British (0)	49	0.66
Czechoslovakian (0)	33	0.45
Danish (0)	23	0.31
Dutch (0)	136	1.84
English (281)	1,306	17.64
European (10)	10	0.14
French, ex. Basque (40)	313	4.23
French Canadian (0)	12	0.16
German (281)	1,735	23.43
Hungarian (146)	331	4.47
Irish (248)	1,638	22.12
Italian (421)	1,300	17.56
Lithuanian (35)	35	0.47
Norwegian (14)	69	0.93
Pennsylvania German (0)	15	0.20
Polish (386)	1,193	16.11
Russian (0)	36	0.49
Scotch-Irish (36)	105	1.42
Scottish (112)	448	6.05
Serbian (0)	31	0.42
Slovak (0)	37	0.50
Swedish (0)	148	2.00
Ukrainian (14)	31	0.42
Welsh (0)	12	0.16

Hispanic Origin	Population	%
Hispanic or Latino (of any race)	801	10.43
Central American, ex. Mexican	40	0.52
Costa Rican	10	0.13
Guatemalan	1	0.01
Honduran	3	0.04
Nicaraguan	9	0.12
Panamanian	17	0.22
Cuban	21	0.27
Dominican Republic	24	0.31
Mexican	284	3.70
Puerto Rican	331	4.31
South American	39	0.51
Argentinean	2	0.03
Bolivian	1	0.01
Colombian	16	0.21
Ecuadorian	6	0.08
Peruvian	7	0.09
Uruguayan	1	0.01
Venezuelan	6	0.08
Other Hispanic or Latino	62	0.81

Race*	Population	%
African-American/Black (716)	902	11.75
Not Hispanic (675)	826	10.76
Hispanic (41)	76	0.99
American Indian/Alaska Native (31)	91	1.19
Not Hispanic (20)	65	0.85
Hispanic (11)	26	0.34
Blackfeet (0)	12	0.16
Cherokee (6)	13	0.17
Chippewa (1)	2	0.03
Delaware (0)	1	0.01
Mexican American Ind. (0)	2	0.03
Navajo (1)	1	0.01
Ute (0)	1	0.01
Yup'ik *(Alaska Native)* (1)	3	0.04
Asian (145)	253	3.30
Not Hispanic (141)	237	3.09
Hispanic (4)	16	0.21
Chinese, ex. Taiwanese (12)	35	0.46
Filipino (54)	99	1.29
Indian (15)	24	0.31
Japanese (21)	45	0.59
Korean (20)	37	0.48
Laotian (3)	3	0.04
Malaysian (0)	1	0.01
Thai (6)	12	0.16
Vietnamese (4)	5	0.07
Hawaii Native/Pacific Islander (32)	58	0.76
Not Hispanic (31)	53	0.69
Hispanic (1)	5	0.07
Guamanian/Chamorro (24)	36	0.47
Native Hawaiian (7)	17	0.22
White (6,156)	6,469	84.25
Not Hispanic (5,741)	5,981	77.90
Hispanic (415)	488	6.36

North Plainfield

Place Type: Borough
County: Somerset
Population: 21,936†

*Notes: † The Census 2010 population figure is used to calculate the percentages in the Hispanic Origin and Race categories. Ancestry percentages are based on the 2006-2010 American Community Survey population (not shown); ‡ Numbers in parentheses indicate the number of people reporting a single ancestry; * Numbers in parentheses indicate the number of persons reporting this race alone, not in combination with any other race; Please refer to the Explanation of Data for more information.*

Ancestry‡	Population	%
African, Sub-Saharan (292)	318	1.45
African (103)	129	0.59
Kenyan (101)	101	0.46
Nigerian (88)	88	0.40
American (1,638)	1,638	7.47
Arab (190)	221	1.01
Arab (119)	119	0.54
Egyptian (31)	31	0.14
Jordanian (17)	17	0.08
Moroccan (0)	13	0.06
Palestinian (23)	23	0.10
Syrian (0)	18	0.08
Austrian (41)	144	0.66
Brazilian (94)	136	0.62
Cajun (0)	8	0.04
Croatian (0)	13	0.06
Czech (23)	61	0.28
Czechoslovakian (12)	12	0.05
Danish (20)	41	0.19
Dutch (19)	168	0.77
English (157)	785	3.58
European (34)	34	0.16
French, ex. Basque (10)	161	0.73
French Canadian (62)	101	0.46
German (260)	1,496	6.82
Greek (127)	180	0.82
Guyanese (6)	6	0.03
Hungarian (25)	207	0.94
Irish (260)	1,405	6.41
Italian (1,039)	2,116	9.65
Lithuanian (32)	43	0.20
Norwegian (53)	120	0.55
Polish (316)	740	3.37
Portuguese (167)	202	0.92
Romanian (12)	107	0.49
Russian (66)	136	0.62
Scandinavian (0)	33	0.15
Scotch-Irish (19)	100	0.46
Scottish (17)	198	0.90
Slovak (9)	19	0.09
Swedish (21)	65	0.30
Swiss (0)	53	0.24
Turkish (17)	17	0.08
Ukrainian (30)	125	0.57
Welsh (8)	101	0.46
West Indian, ex. Hispanic (343)	372	1.70
British West Indian (41)	41	0.19
Haitian (97)	97	0.44
Jamaican (192)	208	0.95
Trinidadian/Tobagonian (13)	26	0.12
Yugoslavian (0)	15	0.07

Hispanic Origin	Population	%
Hispanic or Latino (of any race)	9,699	44.21
Central American, ex. Mexican	2,920	13.31
Costa Rican	119	0.54
Guatemalan	1,089	4.96
Honduran	446	2.03
Nicaraguan	57	0.26
Panamanian	14	0.06
Salvadoran	1,167	5.32
Other Central American	28	0.13
Cuban	122	0.56
Dominican Republic	363	1.65
Mexican	677	3.09
Puerto Rican	948	4.32
South American	3,653	16.65
Argentinean	73	0.33
Bolivian	4	0.02
Chilean	38	0.17
Colombian	941	4.29
Ecuadorian	2,063	9.40
Paraguayan	1	<0.01
Peruvian	474	2.16
Uruguayan	22	0.10
Venezuelan	35	0.16
Other South American	2	0.01
Other Hispanic or Latino	1,016	4.63

Race*	Population	%
African-American/Black (4,134)	4,417	20.14
Not Hispanic (3,848)	4,012	18.29
Hispanic (286)	405	1.85
American Indian/Alaska Native (63)	182	0.83
Not Hispanic (17)	75	0.34
Hispanic (46)	107	0.49
Aleut *(Alaska Native)* (0)	1	<0.01
Apache (0)	1	<0.01
Blackfeet (1)	2	0.01
Central American Ind. (0)	1	<0.01
Cherokee (7)	17	0.08
Chippewa (0)	2	0.01
Choctaw (3)	4	0.02
Delaware (2)	5	0.02
Mexican American Ind. (7)	16	0.07
Pueblo (1)	1	<0.01
Seminole (0)	3	0.01
Sioux (3)	3	0.01
South American Ind. (7)	17	0.08
Spanish American Ind. (9)	9	0.04
Asian (1,275)	1,403	6.40
Not Hispanic (1,260)	1,357	6.19
Hispanic (15)	46	0.21
Bangladeshi (3)	3	0.01
Burmese (2)	2	0.01
Cambodian (3)	3	0.01
Chinese, ex. Taiwanese (218)	233	1.06
Filipino (232)	270	1.23
Indian (302)	342	1.56
Indonesian (3)	4	0.02
Japanese (6)	8	0.04
Korean (25)	31	0.14
Laotian (17)	20	0.09
Malaysian (0)	1	<0.01
Nepalese (2)	3	0.01
Pakistani (275)	287	1.31
Sri Lankan (37)	37	0.17
Taiwanese (1)	1	<0.01
Thai (15)	19	0.09
Vietnamese (91)	100	0.46
Hawaii Native/Pacific Islander (12)	30	0.14
Not Hispanic (10)	14	0.06
Hispanic (2)	16	0.07
Guamanian/Chamorro (3)	4	0.02
Native Hawaiian (2)	8	0.04
White (12,066)	12,798	58.34
Not Hispanic (6,735)	6,948	31.67
Hispanic (5,331)	5,850	26.67

Northfield

Place Type: City
County: Atlantic
Population: 8,624†

Ancestry‡	Population	%
African, Sub-Saharan (24)	32	0.37
African (19)	27	0.32
Ghanaian (5)	5	0.06
Albanian (0)	41	0.48
American (303)	303	3.54
Arab (61)	137	1.60
Arab (19)	19	0.22
Egyptian (42)	42	0.49
Lebanese (0)	76	0.89
Austrian (15)	40	0.47
Brazilian (0)	7	0.08
British (11)	39	0.46
Bulgarian (9)	19	0.22
Croatian (0)	18	0.21
Czech (0)	69	0.81
Dutch (0)	34	0.40
English (191)	890	10.40
European (24)	24	0.28
French, ex. Basque (0)	252	2.94
French Canadian (0)	32	0.37
German (338)	1,856	21.68
Greek (56)	56	0.65
Hungarian (84)	145	1.69
Irish (966)	2,866	33.49
Italian (779)	1,739	20.32
Lithuanian (9)	18	0.21
Norwegian (0)	27	0.32
Pennsylvania German (0)	35	0.41
Polish (116)	384	4.49
Portuguese (0)	8	0.09
Romanian (39)	83	0.97
Russian (212)	376	4.39
Scotch-Irish (103)	127	1.48
Scottish (48)	209	2.44
Slovak (9)	9	0.11
Swedish (9)	30	0.35
Swiss (0)	7	0.08
Ukrainian (22)	138	1.61
Welsh (12)	164	1.92

Hispanic Origin	Population	%
Hispanic or Latino (of any race)	690	8.00
Central American, ex. Mexican	61	0.71
Costa Rican	1	0.01
Guatemalan	5	0.06
Honduran	29	0.34
Nicaraguan	5	0.06
Panamanian	5	0.06
Salvadoran	16	0.19
Cuban	10	0.12
Dominican Republic	131	1.52
Mexican	105	1.22
Puerto Rican	181	2.10
South American	126	1.46
Argentinean	6	0.07
Chilean	1	0.01
Colombian	51	0.59
Ecuadorian	8	0.09
Peruvian	55	0.64
Uruguayan	1	0.01
Venezuelan	4	0.05
Other Hispanic or Latino	76	0.88

Race*	Population	%
African-American/Black (279)	335	3.88
Not Hispanic (247)	280	3.25
Hispanic (32)	55	0.64
American Indian/Alaska Native (16)	44	0.51
Not Hispanic (10)	38	0.44
Hispanic (6)	6	0.07
Central American Ind. (1)	1	0.01
Cherokee (0)	3	0.03
Creek (0)	1	0.01
Delaware (1)	2	0.02
Iroquois (1)	5	0.06
Asian (388)	456	5.29
Not Hispanic (384)	447	5.18
Hispanic (4)	9	0.10
Bangladeshi (45)	47	0.54
Burmese (12)	12	0.14
Chinese, ex. Taiwanese (83)	103	1.19
Filipino (84)	108	1.25
Indian (50)	65	0.75
Japanese (7)	9	0.10
Korean (39)	42	0.49
Laotian (3)	3	0.03
Pakistani (1)	1	0.01
Taiwanese (2)	2	0.02
Vietnamese (53)	65	0.75
Hawaii Native/Pacific Islander (1)	6	0.07
Not Hispanic (0)	1	0.01
Hispanic (1)	5	0.06
Samoan (0)	1	0.01
White (7,515)	7,657	88.79
Not Hispanic (7,153)	7,258	84.16
Hispanic (362)	399	4.63

Nutley

Place Type: Township
County: Essex
Population: 28,370†

*Notes: † The Census 2010 population figure is used to calculate the percentages in the Hispanic Origin and Race categories. Ancestry percentages are based on the 2006-2010 American Community Survey population (not shown); ‡ Numbers in parentheses indicate the number of people reporting a single ancestry; * Numbers in parentheses indicate the number of persons reporting this race alone, not in combination with any other race; Please refer to the Explanation of Data for more information.*

Ancestry‡	Population	%
Afghan (97)	97	0.35
African, Sub-Saharan (32)	32	0.11
African (32)	32	0.11
Albanian (200)	212	0.76
Alsatian (0)	13	0.05
American (839)	839	2.99
Arab (73)	171	0.61
Egyptian (49)	80	0.29
Lebanese (15)	15	0.05
Moroccan (0)	53	0.19
Syrian (9)	23	0.08
Armenian (150)	183	0.65
Austrian (15)	77	0.27
Basque (0)	11	0.04
Belgian (0)	25	0.09
Brazilian (43)	109	0.39
British (36)	101	0.36
Canadian (39)	54	0.19
Croatian (9)	33	0.12
Czech (33)	204	0.73
Czechoslovakian (0)	69	0.25
Danish (8)	48	0.17
Dutch (30)	336	1.20
Eastern European (21)	46	0.16
English (249)	957	3.42
European (176)	176	0.63
Finnish (9)	9	0.03
French, ex. Basque (68)	379	1.35
French Canadian (0)	65	0.23
German (568)	3,089	11.02
Greek (124)	238	0.85
Hungarian (78)	189	0.67
Iranian (31)	55	0.20
Irish (1,016)	4,197	14.98
Israeli (15)	15	0.05
Italian (7,090)	10,739	38.33
Latvian (14)	27	0.10
Lithuanian (25)	92	0.33
Norwegian (11)	88	0.31
Pennsylvania German (0)	13	0.05
Polish (657)	1,788	6.38
Portuguese (257)	392	1.40
Romanian (197)	281	1.00
Russian (208)	358	1.28
Scandinavian (0)	23	0.08
Scotch-Irish (74)	287	1.02
Scottish (151)	408	1.46
Serbian (30)	55	0.20
Slovak (37)	146	0.52
Slovene (0)	10	0.04
Swedish (97)	176	0.63
Swiss (9)	22	0.08
Turkish (53)	53	0.19
Ukrainian (149)	266	0.95
Welsh (19)	118	0.42
West Indian, ex. Hispanic (63)	77	0.27
Bermudan (8)	8	0.03
British West Indian (8)	8	0.03
Haitian (15)	29	0.10
Jamaican (32)	32	0.11
Yugoslavian (99)	99	0.35

Hispanic Origin	Population	%
Hispanic or Latino (of any race)	3,354	11.82
Central American, ex. Mexican	185	0.65
Costa Rican	18	0.06
Guatemalan	39	0.14
Honduran	27	0.10
Nicaraguan	16	0.06
Panamanian	15	0.05
Salvadoran	70	0.25
Cuban	322	1.14
Dominican Republic	358	1.26
Mexican	124	0.44
Puerto Rican	1,059	3.73
South American	951	3.35
Argentinean	45	0.16
Bolivian	17	0.06
Chilean	22	0.08
Colombian	228	0.80
Ecuadorian	382	1.35
Paraguayan	6	0.02
Peruvian	187	0.66
Uruguayan	28	0.10
Venezuelan	30	0.11
Other South American	6	0.02
Other Hispanic or Latino	355	1.25

Race*	Population	%
African-American/Black (628)	784	2.76
Not Hispanic (541)	636	2.24
Hispanic (87)	148	0.52
American Indian/Alaska Native (36)	82	0.29
Not Hispanic (12)	35	0.12
Hispanic (24)	47	0.17
Blackfeet (0)	1	<0.01
Central American Ind. (1)	2	0.01
Cherokee (1)	6	0.02
Chippewa (0)	2	0.01
Hopi (0)	1	<0.01
Iroquois (0)	1	<0.01
Lumbee (2)	3	0.01
Mexican American Ind. (2)	2	0.01
Seminole (2)	3	0.01
South American Ind. (7)	13	0.05
Spanish American Ind. (0)	1	<0.01
Asian (2,824)	3,123	11.01
Not Hispanic (2,789)	3,054	10.76
Hispanic (35)	69	0.24
Bangladeshi (16)	18	0.06
Burmese (5)	6	0.02
Chinese, ex. Taiwanese (518)	583	2.05
Filipino (780)	865	3.05
Indian (909)	962	3.39
Indonesian (5)	6	0.02
Japanese (94)	138	0.49
Korean (179)	192	0.68
Malaysian (1)	1	<0.01
Pakistani (63)	71	0.25
Sri Lankan (3)	3	0.01
Taiwanese (42)	48	0.17
Thai (57)	61	0.22
Vietnamese (97)	118	0.42
Hawaii Native/Pacific Islander (4)	30	0.11
Not Hispanic (1)	24	0.08
Hispanic (3)	6	0.02
Guamanian/Chamorro (1)	6	0.02
Native Hawaiian (0)	3	0.01
Samoan (0)	2	0.01
White (23,405)	23,929	84.35
Not Hispanic (21,196)	21,512	75.83
Hispanic (2,209)	2,417	8.52

Oakland

Place Type: Borough
County: Bergen
Population: 12,754†

Ancestry‡	Population	%
American (261)	261	2.06
Arab (142)	151	1.19
Arab (42)	42	0.33
Egyptian (19)	19	0.15
Lebanese (0)	9	0.07
Syrian (81)	81	0.64
Assyrian/Chaldean/Syriac (0)	10	0.08
Australian (0)	10	0.08
Austrian (30)	103	0.81
Belgian (0)	11	0.09
Brazilian (0)	19	0.15
British (21)	21	0.17
Bulgarian (17)	33	0.26
Canadian (9)	35	0.28
Croatian (0)	17	0.13
Czech (0)	88	0.70
Czechoslovakian (0)	9	0.07
Danish (0)	8	0.06
Dutch (146)	413	3.27
Eastern European (161)	192	1.52
English (183)	914	7.23
Estonian (0)	14	0.11
European (190)	220	1.74
Finnish (8)	27	0.21
French, ex. Basque (38)	183	1.45
French Canadian (17)	32	0.25
German (491)	2,385	18.87
Greek (70)	169	1.34
Hungarian (39)	193	1.53
Iranian (12)	12	0.09
Irish (1,058)	3,536	27.97
Israeli (47)	47	0.37
Italian (1,498)	3,819	30.21
Latvian (0)	14	0.11
Lithuanian (38)	46	0.36
Northern European (12)	12	0.09
Norwegian (53)	165	1.31
Polish (236)	1,159	9.17
Portuguese (22)	65	0.51
Russian (207)	557	4.41
Scandinavian (22)	42	0.33
Scotch-Irish (18)	174	1.38
Scottish (20)	190	1.50
Slavic (0)	8	0.06
Slovak (13)	56	0.44
Swedish (19)	115	0.91
Swiss (30)	52	0.41
Ukrainian (73)	170	1.34
Welsh (0)	24	0.19
West Indian, ex. Hispanic (23)	23	0.18
Haitian (12)	12	0.09
Jamaican (11)	11	0.09
Yugoslavian (9)	9	0.07

Hispanic Origin	Population	%
Hispanic or Latino (of any race)	681	5.34
Central American, ex. Mexican	39	0.31
Costa Rican	8	0.06
Guatemalan	5	0.04
Honduran	7	0.05
Nicaraguan	5	0.04
Panamanian	1	0.01
Salvadoran	13	0.10
Cuban	104	0.82
Dominican Republic	73	0.57
Mexican	83	0.65
Puerto Rican	162	1.27
South American	166	1.30
Argentinean	31	0.24
Chilean	14	0.11
Colombian	59	0.46
Ecuadorian	23	0.18
Peruvian	23	0.18
Uruguayan	4	0.03
Venezuelan	12	0.09
Other Hispanic or Latino	54	0.42

Race*	Population	%
African-American/Black (113)	153	1.20
Not Hispanic (104)	133	1.04
Hispanic (9)	20	0.16
American Indian/Alaska Native (24)	72	0.56
Not Hispanic (18)	53	0.42
Hispanic (6)	19	0.15
Blackfeet (0)	6	0.05
Canadian/French Am. Ind. (0)	2	0.02
Cherokee (0)	16	0.13
Creek (1)	1	0.01
Delaware (10)	10	0.08
Iroquois (0)	3	0.02
Mexican American Ind. (1)	2	0.02
Seminole (0)	1	0.01
Sioux (0)	3	0.02
South American Ind. (0)	3	0.02
Asian (532)	620	4.86
Not Hispanic (532)	613	4.81
Hispanic (0)	7	0.05
Chinese, ex. Taiwanese (118)	145	1.14
Filipino (93)	130	1.02

*Notes: † The Census 2010 population figure is used to calculate the percentages in the Hispanic Origin and Race categories. Ancestry percentages are based on the 2006-2010 American Community Survey population (not shown); ‡ Numbers in parentheses indicate the number of people reporting a single ancestry; * Numbers in parentheses indicate the number of persons reporting this race alone, not in combination with any other race; Please refer to the Explanation of Data for more information.*

Indian (129)	142	1.11
Indonesian (1)	1	0.01
Japanese (21)	28	0.22
Korean (113)	124	0.97
Nepalese (1)	1	0.01
Pakistani (1)	4	0.03
Taiwanese (13)	13	0.10
Thai (7)	10	0.08
Vietnamese (7)	7	0.05
Hawaii Native/Pacific Islander (1)	7	0.05
Not Hispanic (1)	6	0.05
Hispanic (0)	1	0.01
Native Hawaiian (0)	3	0.02
White (11,824)	12,006	94.14
Not Hispanic (11,273)	11,398	89.37
Hispanic (551)	608	4.77

Ocean Acres

Place Type: CDP
County: Ocean
Population: 16,142†

Ancestry‡	Population	%
American (391)	391	2.48
Arab (48)	91	0.58
Lebanese (0)	10	0.06
Syrian (48)	66	0.42
Other Arab (0)	15	0.10
Armenian (0)	15	0.10
Austrian (25)	37	0.23
Belgian (15)	44	0.28
Brazilian (0)	12	0.08
British (0)	22	0.14
Bulgarian (15)	15	0.10
Czech (24)	93	0.59
Czechoslovakian (0)	94	0.60
Danish (34)	157	1.00
Dutch (39)	333	2.11
English (315)	1,594	10.11
European (110)	126	0.80
French, ex. Basque (37)	363	2.30
French Canadian (0)	214	1.36
German (629)	3,723	23.61
Greek (15)	101	0.64
Hungarian (111)	280	1.78
Irish (1,077)	5,025	31.86
Italian (2,663)	5,997	38.02
Lithuanian (0)	69	0.44
Maltese (9)	27	0.17
Norwegian (0)	109	0.69
Polish (419)	1,666	10.56
Portuguese (83)	208	1.32
Romanian (14)	44	0.28
Russian (13)	65	0.41
Scotch-Irish (58)	145	0.92
Scottish (54)	343	2.17
Slovak (38)	268	1.70
Slovene (0)	43	0.27
Swedish (41)	130	0.82
Swiss (0)	36	0.23
Ukrainian (0)	69	0.44
Welsh (11)	66	0.42
West Indian, ex. Hispanic (14)	14	0.09
British West Indian (14)	14	0.09
Yugoslavian (0)	39	0.25

Hispanic Origin	Population	%
Hispanic or Latino (of any race)	936	5.80
Central American, ex. Mexican	74	0.46
Costa Rican	16	0.10
Guatemalan	5	0.03
Honduran	24	0.15
Nicaraguan	4	0.02
Panamanian	10	0.06
Salvadoran	15	0.09
Cuban	88	0.55
Dominican Republic	27	0.17
Mexican	204	1.26
Puerto Rican	365	2.26
South American	105	0.65
Argentinean	19	0.12
Chilean	5	0.03
Colombian	24	0.15
Ecuadorian	26	0.16
Peruvian	26	0.16
Uruguayan	2	0.01
Venezuelan	3	0.02
Other Hispanic or Latino	73	0.45

Race*	Population	%
African-American/Black (224)	288	1.78
Not Hispanic (197)	244	1.51
Hispanic (27)	44	0.27
American Indian/Alaska Native (20)	71	0.44
Not Hispanic (14)	55	0.34
Hispanic (6)	16	0.10
Canadian/French Am. Ind. (0)	1	0.01
Central American Ind. (2)	2	0.01
Cherokee (4)	13	0.08
Cheyenne (0)	5	0.03
Delaware (0)	4	0.02
Iroquois (0)	2	0.01
Navajo (0)	2	0.01
Shoshone (1)	1	0.01
Sioux (0)	1	0.01
Asian (234)	306	1.90
Not Hispanic (234)	296	1.83
Hispanic (0)	10	0.06
Burmese (0)	1	0.01
Cambodian (1)	1	0.01
Chinese, ex. Taiwanese (40)	44	0.27
Filipino (84)	121	0.75
Indian (40)	48	0.30
Japanese (5)	17	0.11
Korean (30)	41	0.25
Nepalese (0)	1	0.01
Pakistani (6)	6	0.04
Thai (2)	2	0.01
Vietnamese (20)	22	0.14
Hawaii Native/Pacific Islander (8)	17	0.11
Not Hispanic (8)	12	0.07
Hispanic (0)	5	0.03
Guamanian/Chamorro (0)	3	0.02
Native Hawaiian (0)	1	0.01
Samoan (2)	5	0.03
White (15,190)	15,375	95.25
Not Hispanic (14,595)	14,725	91.22
Hispanic (595)	650	4.03

Ocean City

Place Type: City
County: Cape May
Population: 11,701†

Ancestry‡	Population	%
African, Sub-Saharan (0)	29	0.24
African (0)	29	0.24
Albanian (19)	31	0.25
American (526)	526	4.28
Arab (0)	37	0.30
Lebanese (0)	37	0.30
Austrian (20)	50	0.41
Belgian (0)	21	0.17
British (12)	26	0.21
Bulgarian (20)	20	0.16
Canadian (12)	12	0.10
Croatian (12)	12	0.10
Czechoslovakian (6)	6	0.05
Dutch (58)	323	2.63
English (380)	2,006	16.32
European (89)	89	0.72
French, ex. Basque (0)	254	2.07
French Canadian (0)	30	0.24
German (807)	3,322	27.03
Greek (42)	42	0.34
Hungarian (29)	184	1.50
Irish (1,533)	4,152	33.79
Italian (1,232)	2,073	16.87
Latvian (35)	35	0.28
Lithuanian (18)	48	0.39
Norwegian (9)	67	0.55
Pennsylvania German (42)	138	1.12
Polish (102)	398	3.24
Portuguese (0)	12	0.10
Romanian (0)	47	0.38
Russian (41)	206	1.68
Scotch-Irish (153)	329	2.68
Scottish (74)	300	2.44
Serbian (0)	36	0.29
Slovak (23)	48	0.39
Swedish (39)	223	1.81
Swiss (7)	53	0.43
Ukrainian (19)	59	0.48
Welsh (44)	138	1.12
West Indian, ex. Hispanic (24)	53	0.43
Jamaican (24)	53	0.43
Yugoslavian (0)	11	0.09

Hispanic Origin	Population	%
Hispanic or Latino (of any race)	643	5.50
Central American, ex. Mexican	12	0.10
Costa Rican	2	0.02
Guatemalan	2	0.02
Honduran	3	0.03
Nicaraguan	1	0.01
Panamanian	3	0.03
Salvadoran	1	0.01
Cuban	24	0.21
Dominican Republic	4	0.03
Mexican	412	3.52
Puerto Rican	134	1.15
South American	27	0.23
Argentinean	3	0.03
Chilean	2	0.02
Colombian	13	0.11
Ecuadorian	4	0.03
Peruvian	3	0.03
Uruguayan	2	0.02
Other Hispanic or Latino	30	0.26

Race*	Population	%
African-American/Black (410)	525	4.49
Not Hispanic (359)	455	3.89
Hispanic (51)	70	0.60
American Indian/Alaska Native (15)	62	0.53
Not Hispanic (8)	51	0.44
Hispanic (7)	11	0.09
Blackfeet (0)	4	0.03
Cherokee (1)	14	0.12
Delaware (0)	11	0.09
Mexican American Ind. (1)	1	0.01
Sioux (0)	1	0.01
South American Ind. (2)	4	0.03
Asian (83)	112	0.96
Not Hispanic (80)	109	0.93
Hispanic (3)	3	0.03
Burmese (4)	4	0.03
Cambodian (0)	4	0.03
Chinese, ex. Taiwanese (31)	34	0.29
Filipino (16)	25	0.21
Indian (6)	7	0.06
Indonesian (1)	4	0.03
Japanese (5)	9	0.08
Korean (9)	12	0.10
Pakistani (2)	2	0.02
Thai (0)	1	0.01
Vietnamese (6)	6	0.05
Hawaii Native/Pacific Islander (3)	12	0.10
Not Hispanic (3)	8	0.07
Hispanic (0)	4	0.03
Native Hawaiian (0)	1	0.01
White (10,771)	10,938	93.48
Not Hispanic (10,455)	10,582	90.44
Hispanic (316)	356	3.04

*Notes: † The Census 2010 population figure is used to calculate the percentages in the Hispanic Origin and Race categories. Ancestry percentages are based on the 2006-2010 American Community Survey population (not shown); ‡ Numbers in parentheses indicate the number of people reporting a single ancestry; * Numbers in parentheses indicate the number of persons reporting this race alone, not in combination with any other race; Please refer to the Explanation of Data for more information.*

Ocean

Place Type: Township
County: Monmouth
Population: 27,291†

Ancestry‡	Population	%
African, Sub-Saharan (76)	130	0.48
African (26)	26	0.10
Ghanaian (19)	29	0.11
Liberian (31)	65	0.24
Other Sub-Saharan African (0)	10	0.04
American (1,063)	1,063	3.90
Arab (548)	727	2.67
Egyptian (36)	70	0.26
Lebanese (35)	104	0.38
Moroccan (24)	24	0.09
Syrian (334)	410	1.50
Other Arab (119)	119	0.44
Armenian (49)	102	0.37
Austrian (33)	210	0.77
Belgian (9)	9	0.03
Brazilian (195)	195	0.72
British (63)	63	0.23
Bulgarian (0)	11	0.04
Canadian (16)	60	0.22
Croatian (0)	28	0.10
Czech (0)	54	0.20
Czechoslovakian (27)	27	0.10
Danish (33)	140	0.51
Dutch (98)	242	0.89
Eastern European (168)	195	0.72
English (426)	1,815	6.66
Estonian (78)	100	0.37
European (366)	385	1.41
Finnish (0)	34	0.12
French, ex. Basque (54)	324	1.19
French Canadian (17)	29	0.11
German (726)	3,762	13.80
Greek (347)	498	1.83
Guyanese (0)	9	0.03
Hungarian (52)	202	0.74
Iranian (28)	28	0.10
Irish (1,612)	5,449	19.99
Israeli (140)	140	0.51
Italian (3,607)	6,625	24.30
Latvian (0)	6	0.02
Lithuanian (64)	155	0.57
Luxemburger (0)	20	0.07
Norwegian (24)	256	0.94
Pennsylvania German (4)	4	0.01
Polish (386)	1,518	5.57
Portuguese (69)	69	0.25
Romanian (66)	149	0.55
Russian (504)	1,072	3.93
Scotch-Irish (136)	373	1.37
Scottish (83)	450	1.65
Slavic (0)	23	0.08
Slovak (0)	32	0.12
Slovene (0)	8	0.03
Swedish (20)	183	0.67
Swiss (25)	95	0.35
Turkish (9)	9	0.03
Ukrainian (59)	69	0.25
Welsh (28)	117	0.43
West Indian, ex. Hispanic (918)	992	3.64
British West Indian (45)	89	0.33
Haitian (714)	714	2.62
Jamaican (129)	159	0.58
Trinidadian/Tobagonian (30)	30	0.11
Yugoslavian (0)	56	0.21

Hispanic Origin	Population	%
Hispanic or Latino (of any race)	2,453	8.99
Central American, ex. Mexican	271	0.99
Costa Rican	30	0.11
Guatemalan	44	0.16
Honduran	19	0.07
Nicaraguan	44	0.16
Panamanian	16	0.06
Salvadoran	112	0.41
Other Central American	6	0.02
Cuban	112	0.41
Dominican Republic	120	0.44
Mexican	691	2.53
Puerto Rican	552	2.02
South American	532	1.95
Argentinean	17	0.06
Bolivian	6	0.02
Chilean	74	0.27
Colombian	236	0.86
Ecuadorian	41	0.15
Paraguayan	4	0.01
Peruvian	89	0.33
Uruguayan	9	0.03
Venezuelan	54	0.20
Other South American	2	0.01
Other Hispanic or Latino	175	0.64

Race*	Population	%
African-American/Black (2,173)	2,451	8.98
Not Hispanic (2,038)	2,239	8.20
Hispanic (135)	212	0.78
American Indian/Alaska Native (54)	157	0.58
Not Hispanic (41)	110	0.40
Hispanic (13)	47	0.17
Blackfeet (0)	3	0.01
Central American Ind. (0)	2	0.01
Cherokee (7)	28	0.10
Cheyenne (0)	1	<0.01
Chippewa (0)	1	<0.01
Cree (0)	1	<0.01
Delaware (1)	6	0.02
Hopi (1)	1	<0.01
Iroquois (1)	1	<0.01
Mexican American Ind. (1)	1	<0.01
Navajo (0)	1	<0.01
Paiute (13)	13	0.05
Sioux (0)	1	<0.01
South American Ind. (0)	4	0.01
Spanish American Ind. (2)	5	0.02
Asian (1,791)	2,029	7.43
Not Hispanic (1,775)	2,002	7.34
Hispanic (16)	27	0.10
Bangladeshi (48)	50	0.18
Burmese (3)	3	0.01
Cambodian (3)	3	0.01
Chinese, ex. Taiwanese (271)	301	1.10
Filipino (312)	374	1.37
Indian (674)	741	2.72
Indonesian (2)	6	0.02
Japanese (18)	35	0.13
Korean (230)	264	0.97
Pakistani (101)	108	0.40
Sri Lankan (4)	4	0.01
Taiwanese (18)	24	0.09
Thai (7)	9	0.03
Vietnamese (67)	72	0.26
Hawaii Native/Pacific Islander (13)	45	0.16
Not Hispanic (13)	44	0.16
Hispanic (0)	1	<0.01
Guamanian/Chamorro (1)	2	0.01
Native Hawaiian (6)	7	0.03
Samoan (1)	1	<0.01
White (22,013)	22,543	82.60
Not Hispanic (20,447)	20,819	76.29
Hispanic (1,566)	1,724	6.32

Ocean

Place Type: Township
County: Ocean
Population: 8,332†

Ancestry‡	Population	%
American (488)	488	6.06
Arab (0)	11	0.14
Syrian (0)	11	0.14
Austrian (17)	17	0.21
Belgian (0)	43	0.53
British (14)	14	0.17
Canadian (0)	12	0.15
Croatian (26)	26	0.32
Czech (0)	40	0.50
Czechoslovakian (0)	29	0.36
Danish (14)	14	0.17
Dutch (84)	250	3.10
Eastern European (7)	26	0.32
English (160)	916	11.37
European (31)	31	0.38
French, ex. Basque (13)	79	0.98
French Canadian (8)	19	0.24
German (307)	1,609	19.98
Greek (0)	14	0.17
Hungarian (84)	212	2.63
Iranian (0)	13	0.16
Irish (932)	2,380	29.55
Italian (885)	1,652	20.51
Lithuanian (14)	54	0.67
Maltese (16)	16	0.20
Norwegian (37)	97	1.20
Pennsylvania German (13)	13	0.16
Polish (356)	842	10.45
Portuguese (32)	56	0.70
Romanian (36)	72	0.89
Russian (40)	88	1.09
Scotch-Irish (48)	105	1.30
Scottish (84)	268	3.33
Slavic (42)	42	0.52
Slovak (69)	69	0.86
Swedish (0)	59	0.73
Swiss (0)	54	0.67
Ukrainian (31)	64	0.79
Welsh (13)	118	1.46
West Indian, ex. Hispanic (66)	84	1.04
Bermudan (10)	10	0.12
Jamaican (56)	74	0.92

Hispanic Origin	Population	%
Hispanic or Latino (of any race)	230	2.76
Central American, ex. Mexican	6	0.07
Costa Rican	3	0.04
Guatemalan	2	0.02
Nicaraguan	1	0.01
Cuban	23	0.28
Dominican Republic	5	0.06
Mexican	27	0.32
Puerto Rican	124	1.49
South American	23	0.28
Argentinean	1	0.01
Colombian	5	0.06
Ecuadorian	5	0.06
Peruvian	6	0.07
Uruguayan	1	0.01
Venezuelan	3	0.04
Other South American	2	0.02
Other Hispanic or Latino	22	0.26

Race*	Population	%
African-American/Black (49)	80	0.96
Not Hispanic (49)	77	0.92
Hispanic (0)	3	0.04
American Indian/Alaska Native (11)	42	0.50
Not Hispanic (7)	33	0.40
Hispanic (4)	9	0.11
Apache (0)	3	0.04
Blackfeet (0)	2	0.02
Central American Ind. (2)	2	0.02
Cherokee (0)	6	0.07
Comanche (0)	2	0.02
Creek (1)	1	0.01
Delaware (1)	1	0.01
Iroquois (1)	1	0.01
Sioux (2)	2	0.02
Asian (90)	107	1.28
Not Hispanic (89)	106	1.27
Hispanic (1)	1	0.01
Chinese, ex. Taiwanese (13)	14	0.17
Filipino (29)	38	0.46
Indian (17)	22	0.26

SECTION TWO

*Notes: † The Census 2010 population figure is used to calculate the percentages in the Hispanic Origin and Race categories. Ancestry percentages are based on the 2006-2010 American Community Survey population (not shown); ‡ Numbers in parentheses indicate the number of people reporting a single ancestry; * Numbers in parentheses indicate the number of persons reporting this race alone, not in combination with any other race; Please refer to the Explanation of Data for more information.*

Japanese (5)	6	0.07
Korean (21)	23	0.28
Taiwanese (1)	1	0.01
Vietnamese (3)	4	0.05
Hawaii Native/Pacific Islander (1)	7	0.08
Not Hispanic (1)	7	0.08
Native Hawaiian (1)	6	0.07
Samoan (0)	1	0.01
White (8,061)	8,137	97.66
Not Hispanic (7,879)	7,940	95.30
Hispanic (182)	197	2.36

Old Bridge

Place Type: CDP
County: Middlesex
Population: 23,753†

Ancestry‡	Population	%
African, Sub-Saharan (118)	137	0.59
African (36)	55	0.24
Ghanaian (82)	82	0.35
Albanian (25)	42	0.18
Alsatian (9)	9	0.04
American (1,206)	1,206	5.17
Arab (405)	496	2.13
Arab (0)	9	0.04
Egyptian (259)	283	1.21
Lebanese (0)	11	0.05
Moroccan (67)	82	0.35
Palestinian (11)	11	0.05
Other Arab (68)	100	0.43
Armenian (12)	23	0.10
Austrian (0)	152	0.65
Brazilian (68)	110	0.47
British (0)	32	0.14
Canadian (0)	9	0.04
Croatian (13)	13	0.06
Czech (0)	99	0.42
Czechoslovakian (23)	23	0.10
Danish (0)	11	0.05
Dutch (19)	114	0.49
Eastern European (127)	145	0.62
English (195)	974	4.18
European (26)	26	0.11
Finnish (0)	8	0.03
French, ex. Basque (14)	163	0.70
French Canadian (29)	91	0.39
German (331)	2,234	9.58
Greek (112)	186	0.80
Hungarian (112)	364	1.56
Irish (1,605)	4,824	20.68
Italian (4,096)	7,045	30.20
Lithuanian (20)	113	0.48
Macedonian (13)	13	0.06
Maltese (6)	27	0.12
Norwegian (10)	184	0.79
Pennsylvania German (0)	41	0.18
Polish (766)	1,858	7.97
Portuguese (83)	172	0.74
Romanian (42)	42	0.18
Russian (435)	738	3.16
Scandinavian (0)	30	0.13
Scotch-Irish (49)	144	0.62
Scottish (22)	161	0.69
Slavic (0)	10	0.04
Slovak (10)	53	0.23
Swedish (9)	187	0.80
Swiss (17)	61	0.26
Turkish (89)	89	0.38
Ukrainian (40)	201	0.86
Welsh (0)	57	0.24
West Indian, ex. Hispanic (144)	163	0.70
Bermudan (10)	10	0.04
Haitian (23)	23	0.10
Jamaican (12)	12	0.05
Trinidadian/Tobagonian (56)	56	0.24
West Indian (43)	62	0.27
Yugoslavian (0)	41	0.18

Hispanic Origin	Population	%
Hispanic or Latino (of any race)	2,606	10.97
Central American, ex. Mexican	121	0.51
Costa Rican	8	0.03
Guatemalan	24	0.10
Honduran	39	0.16
Nicaraguan	8	0.03
Panamanian	15	0.06
Salvadoran	27	0.11
Cuban	204	0.86
Dominican Republic	173	0.73
Mexican	182	0.77
Puerto Rican	1,350	5.68
South American	438	1.84
Argentinean	49	0.21
Bolivian	4	0.02
Chilean	17	0.07
Colombian	131	0.55
Ecuadorian	124	0.52
Paraguayan	1	<0.01
Peruvian	79	0.33
Uruguayan	14	0.06
Venezuelan	19	0.08
Other Hispanic or Latino	138	0.58

Race*	Population	%
African-American/Black (1,041)	1,169	4.92
Not Hispanic (964)	1,045	4.40
Hispanic (77)	124	0.52
American Indian/Alaska Native (43)	104	0.44
Not Hispanic (28)	78	0.33
Hispanic (15)	26	0.11
Blackfeet (0)	1	<0.01
Canadian/French Am. Ind. (1)	1	<0.01
Central American Ind. (0)	1	<0.01
Cherokee (4)	5	0.02
Cree (1)	1	<0.01
Crow (0)	1	<0.01
Hopi (1)	1	<0.01
Iroquois (4)	7	0.03
Mexican American Ind. (1)	1	<0.01
South American Ind. (5)	10	0.04
Asian (2,630)	2,904	12.23
Not Hispanic (2,615)	2,862	12.05
Hispanic (15)	42	0.18
Bangladeshi (7)	11	0.05
Burmese (3)	4	0.02
Cambodian (5)	5	0.02
Chinese, ex. Taiwanese (501)	562	2.37
Filipino (634)	737	3.10
Indian (1,114)	1,201	5.06
Indonesian (9)	15	0.06
Japanese (12)	30	0.13
Korean (110)	135	0.57
Malaysian (1)	1	<0.01
Nepalese (9)	9	0.04
Pakistani (103)	125	0.53
Sri Lankan (0)	3	0.01
Taiwanese (3)	3	0.01
Thai (18)	19	0.08
Vietnamese (33)	51	0.21
Hawaii Native/Pacific Islander (5)	28	0.12
Not Hispanic (5)	24	0.10
Hispanic (0)	4	0.02
Fijian (0)	2	0.01
Guamanian/Chamorro (1)	4	0.02
Native Hawaiian (0)	1	<0.01
Samoan (1)	1	<0.01
White (18,897)	19,293	81.22
Not Hispanic (17,091)	17,347	73.03
Hispanic (1,806)	1,946	8.19

Old Bridge

Place Type: Township
County: Middlesex
Population: 65,375†

Ancestry‡	Population	%
Afghan (100)	100	0.16
African, Sub-Saharan (675)	694	1.08
African (93)	112	0.17
Ghanaian (197)	197	0.31
Nigerian (231)	231	0.36
Sierra Leonean (138)	138	0.21
South African (16)	16	0.02
Albanian (341)	367	0.57
Alsatian (9)	9	0.01
American (2,450)	2,450	3.80
Arab (1,374)	1,562	2.42
Arab (0)	9	0.01
Egyptian (1,142)	1,204	1.87
Iraqi (0)	8	0.01
Jordanian (38)	38	0.06
Lebanese (26)	68	0.11
Moroccan (77)	92	0.14
Palestinian (11)	11	0.02
Other Arab (80)	132	0.20
Armenian (25)	47	0.07
Australian (0)	11	0.02
Austrian (59)	369	0.57
Belgian (14)	14	0.02
Brazilian (72)	168	0.26
British (6)	95	0.15
Bulgarian (7)	7	0.01
Canadian (8)	39	0.06
Croatian (13)	24	0.04
Czech (15)	238	0.37
Czechoslovakian (41)	69	0.11
Danish (35)	171	0.27
Dutch (165)	442	0.69
Eastern European (232)	250	0.39
English (577)	2,469	3.83
European (89)	100	0.16
Finnish (0)	8	0.01
French, ex. Basque (147)	609	0.94
French Canadian (46)	150	0.23
German (1,262)	5,727	8.88
Greek (415)	638	0.99
Guyanese (50)	50	0.08
Hungarian (254)	918	1.42
Iranian (0)	11	0.02
Irish (3,982)	10,776	16.71
Italian (9,083)	15,376	23.84
Lithuanian (72)	236	0.37
Macedonian (22)	22	0.03
Maltese (20)	59	0.09
Norwegian (221)	576	0.89
Pennsylvania German (0)	41	0.06
Polish (2,571)	5,356	8.31
Portuguese (365)	584	0.91
Romanian (42)	87	0.13
Russian (1,612)	2,361	3.66
Scandinavian (0)	42	0.07
Scotch-Irish (119)	468	0.73
Scottish (88)	516	0.80
Serbian (10)	10	0.02
Slavic (21)	88	0.14
Slovak (92)	487	0.76
Soviet Union (43)	43	0.07
Swedish (93)	394	0.61
Swiss (50)	94	0.15
Turkish (89)	89	0.14
Ukrainian (444)	717	1.11
Welsh (0)	137	0.21
West Indian, ex. Hispanic (776)	816	1.27
Bermudan (10)	10	0.02
British West Indian (87)	87	0.13
Haitian (164)	164	0.25
Jamaican (202)	213	0.33
Trinidadian/Tobagonian (114)	114	0.18
West Indian (98)	127	0.20
Other West Indian (101)	101	0.16
Yugoslavian (6)	56	0.09

Hispanic Origin	Population	%
Hispanic or Latino (of any race)	7,064	10.81
Central American, ex. Mexican	380	0.58
Costa Rican	56	0.09
Guatemalan	74	0.11

*Notes: † The Census 2010 population figure is used to calculate the percentages in the Hispanic Origin and Race categories. Ancestry percentages are based on the 2006-2010 American Community Survey population (not shown); ‡ Numbers in parentheses indicate the number of people reporting a single ancestry; * Numbers in parentheses indicate the number of persons reporting this race alone, not in combination with any other race; Please refer to the Explanation of Data for more information.*

Honduran	77	0.12
Nicaraguan	24	0.04
Panamanian	52	0.08
Salvadoran	97	0.15
Cuban	519	0.79
Dominican Republic	526	0.80
Mexican	607	0.93
Puerto Rican	3,435	5.25
South American	1,160	1.77
Argentinean	120	0.18
Bolivian	13	0.02
Chilean	33	0.05
Colombian	401	0.61
Ecuadorian	276	0.42
Paraguayan	12	0.02
Peruvian	197	0.30
Uruguayan	62	0.09
Venezuelan	44	0.07
Other South American	2	<0.01
Other Hispanic or Latino	437	0.67

Race*	Population	%
African-American/Black (4,063)	4,499	6.88
Not Hispanic (3,770)	4,062	6.21
Hispanic (293)	437	0.67
American Indian/Alaska Native (129)	345	0.53
Not Hispanic (89)	262	0.40
Hispanic (40)	83	0.13
Apache (0)	4	0.01
Blackfeet (0)	10	0.02
Canadian/French Am. Ind. (1)	1	<0.01
Central American Ind. (0)	1	<0.01
Cherokee (6)	31	0.05
Chippewa (2)	4	0.01
Cree (1)	1	<0.01
Crow (0)	1	<0.01
Delaware (4)	6	0.01
Hopi (1)	1	<0.01
Houma (0)	1	<0.01
Iroquois (9)	13	0.02
Mexican American Ind. (3)	3	<0.01
Osage (0)	1	<0.01
Puget Sound Salish (0)	1	<0.01
Sioux (1)	4	0.01
South American Ind. (9)	19	0.03
Asian (9,374)	10,202	15.61
Not Hispanic (9,319)	10,064	15.39
Hispanic (55)	138	0.21
Bangladeshi (65)	80	0.12
Burmese (14)	15	0.02
Cambodian (5)	5	0.01
Chinese, ex. Taiwanese (1,397)	1,538	2.35
Filipino (1,553)	1,758	2.69
Indian (4,738)	5,110	7.82
Indonesian (20)	30	0.05
Japanese (30)	65	0.10
Korean (319)	379	0.58
Malaysian (2)	5	0.01
Nepalese (14)	14	0.02
Pakistani (803)	926	1.42
Sri Lankan (13)	18	0.03
Taiwanese (19)	24	0.04
Thai (24)	32	0.05
Vietnamese (100)	134	0.20
Hawaii Native/Pacific Islander (10)	55	0.08
Not Hispanic (9)	50	0.08
Hispanic (1)	5	0.01
Fijian (0)	2	<0.01
Guamanian/Chamorro (2)	6	0.01
Native Hawaiian (1)	3	<0.01
Samoan (3)	4	0.01
White (48,418)	49,577	75.83
Not Hispanic (43,782)	44,549	68.14
Hispanic (4,636)	5,028	7.69

Oradell

Place Type: Borough
County: Bergen
Population: 7,978†

Ancestry‡	Population	%
African, Sub-Saharan (25)	25	0.32
South African (25)	25	0.32
American (135)	135	1.70
Arab (46)	46	0.58
Arab (46)	46	0.58
Armenian (204)	204	2.57
Austrian (22)	80	1.01
British (11)	11	0.14
Croatian (34)	102	1.29
Czech (13)	59	0.74
Czechoslovakian (16)	26	0.33
Danish (10)	10	0.13
Dutch (0)	84	1.06
English (57)	324	4.08
European (73)	73	0.92
French, ex. Basque (18)	176	2.22
French Canadian (0)	8	0.10
German (229)	1,021	12.87
Greek (93)	178	2.24
Hungarian (22)	127	1.60
Iranian (55)	55	0.69
Irish (783)	2,056	25.91
Italian (1,181)	2,067	26.05
Lithuanian (0)	40	0.50
Polish (133)	628	7.91
Romanian (38)	87	1.10
Russian (159)	313	3.94
Scotch-Irish (17)	101	1.27
Scottish (25)	74	0.93
Swedish (0)	13	0.16
Swiss (0)	28	0.35
Ukrainian (0)	12	0.15
West Indian, ex. Hispanic (0)	37	0.47
Jamaican (0)	17	0.21
West Indian (0)	20	0.25
Yugoslavian (0)	18	0.23

Hispanic Origin	Population	%
Hispanic or Latino (of any race)	397	4.98
Central American, ex. Mexican	16	0.20
Guatemalan	4	0.05
Nicaraguan	6	0.08
Panamanian	1	0.01
Salvadoran	5	0.06
Cuban	120	1.50
Dominican Republic	66	0.83
Mexican	14	0.18
Puerto Rican	93	1.17
South American	63	0.79
Argentinean	5	0.06
Colombian	23	0.29
Ecuadorian	21	0.26
Paraguayan	2	0.03
Peruvian	10	0.13
Uruguayan	2	0.03
Other Hispanic or Latino	25	0.31

Race*	Population	%
African-American/Black (54)	84	1.05
Not Hispanic (46)	62	0.78
Hispanic (8)	22	0.28
American Indian/Alaska Native (6)	13	0.16
Not Hispanic (5)	8	0.10
Hispanic (1)	5	0.06
Canadian/French Am. Ind. (0)	1	0.01
Delaware (0)	1	0.01
Mexican American Ind. (1)	1	0.01
Navajo (0)	2	0.03
South American Ind. (0)	3	0.04
Asian (898)	959	12.02
Not Hispanic (895)	955	11.97
Hispanic (3)	4	0.05
Burmese (4)	4	0.05
Chinese, ex. Taiwanese (216)	234	2.93
Filipino (120)	128	1.60
Indian (94)	110	1.38
Indonesian (1)	1	0.01
Japanese (70)	77	0.97
Korean (354)	368	4.61
Pakistani (9)	11	0.14
Taiwanese (17)	17	0.21
Thai (1)	1	0.01
Vietnamese (4)	4	0.05
Hawaii Native/Pacific Islander (0)	2	0.03
Not Hispanic (0)	2	0.03
Native Hawaiian (0)	1	0.01
White (6,844)	6,944	87.04
Not Hispanic (6,537)	6,625	83.04
Hispanic (307)	319	4.00

Palisades Park

Place Type: Borough
County: Bergen
Population: 19,622†

Ancestry‡	Population	%
African, Sub-Saharan (0)	17	0.09
African (0)	17	0.09
American (127)	127	0.67
Arab (184)	184	0.97
Egyptian (89)	89	0.47
Lebanese (38)	38	0.20
Palestinian (13)	13	0.07
Other Arab (44)	44	0.23
Armenian (203)	203	1.06
Australian (16)	29	0.15
Austrian (15)	15	0.08
Brazilian (86)	86	0.45
Canadian (0)	12	0.06
Croatian (244)	279	1.46
Czech (0)	43	0.23
Czechoslovakian (0)	39	0.20
Danish (27)	27	0.14
Dutch (0)	47	0.25
English (26)	79	0.41
European (19)	36	0.19
French, ex. Basque (10)	22	0.12
German (187)	510	2.68
Greek (266)	302	1.58
Hungarian (0)	38	0.20
Irish (273)	548	2.87
Italian (1,074)	1,438	7.54
Lithuanian (0)	7	0.04
Norwegian (58)	58	0.30
Pennsylvania German (11)	11	0.06
Polish (64)	133	0.70
Russian (104)	196	1.03
Scottish (55)	72	0.38
Slovak (0)	22	0.12
Swedish (0)	27	0.14
Turkish (32)	32	0.17
Ukrainian (0)	34	0.18
Welsh (0)	20	0.10
West Indian, ex. Hispanic (0)	19	0.10
British West Indian (0)	19	0.10
Yugoslavian (110)	110	0.58

Hispanic Origin	Population	%
Hispanic or Latino (of any race)	3,575	18.22
Central American, ex. Mexican	1,333	6.79
Costa Rican	4	0.02
Guatemalan	1,159	5.91
Honduran	36	0.18
Nicaraguan	16	0.08
Panamanian	6	0.03
Salvadoran	111	0.57
Other Central American	1	0.01
Cuban	207	1.05
Dominican Republic	518	2.64
Mexican	120	0.61
Puerto Rican	354	1.80
South American	767	3.91
Argentinean	20	0.10
Chilean	22	0.11
Colombian	459	2.34
Ecuadorian	193	0.98
Paraguayan	6	0.03
Peruvian	55	0.28

*Notes: † The Census 2010 population figure is used to calculate the percentages in the Hispanic Origin and Race categories. Ancestry percentages are based on the 2006-2010 American Community Survey population (not shown); ‡ Numbers in parentheses indicate the number of people reporting a single ancestry; * Numbers in parentheses indicate the number of persons reporting this race alone, not in combination with any other race; Please refer to the Explanation of Data for more information.*

Uruguayan	2	0.01
Venezuelan	10	0.05
Other Hispanic or Latino	276	1.41

Race*	Population	%
African-American/Black (385)	446	2.27
Not Hispanic (283)	308	1.57
Hispanic (102)	138	0.70
American Indian/Alaska Native (60)	93	0.47
Not Hispanic (7)	26	0.13
Hispanic (53)	67	0.34
Apache (1)	1	0.01
Blackfeet (0)	1	0.01
Cherokee (1)	7	0.04
Iroquois (1)	1	0.01
Mexican American Ind. (16)	22	0.11
Navajo (2)	2	0.01
Pueblo (6)	6	0.03
South American Ind. (0)	3	0.02
Asian (11,350)	11,498	58.60
Not Hispanic (11,312)	11,445	58.33
Hispanic (38)	53	0.27
Burmese (3)	3	0.02
Cambodian (4)	7	0.04
Chinese, ex. Taiwanese (652)	710	3.62
Filipino (105)	119	0.61
Indian (177)	195	0.99
Indonesian (1)	3	0.02
Japanese (115)	125	0.64
Korean (10,115)	10,259	52.28
Laotian (0)	5	0.03
Nepalese (5)	5	0.03
Pakistani (27)	28	0.14
Taiwanese (35)	36	0.18
Thai (4)	4	0.02
Vietnamese (13)	14	0.07
Hawaii Native/Pacific Islander (10)	15	0.08
Not Hispanic (3)	3	0.02
Hispanic (7)	12	0.06
Guamanian/Chamorro (6)	6	0.03
Native Hawaiian (0)	2	0.01
Samoan (2)	2	0.01
White (5,670)	5,986	30.51
Not Hispanic (4,213)	4,348	22.16
Hispanic (1,457)	1,638	8.35

Paramus

Place Type: Borough
County: Bergen
Population: 26,342†

Ancestry‡	Population	%
African, Sub-Saharan (0)	25	0.10
African (0)	25	0.10
Albanian (15)	44	0.17
American (646)	646	2.48
Arab (775)	879	3.37
Arab (166)	174	0.67
Egyptian (99)	99	0.38
Jordanian (125)	125	0.48
Lebanese (246)	262	1.00
Palestinian (20)	20	0.08
Syrian (91)	163	0.62
Other Arab (28)	36	0.14
Armenian (337)	510	1.96
Assyrian/Chaldean/Syriac (0)	22	0.08
Austrian (7)	156	0.60
Belgian (0)	10	0.04
British (12)	12	0.05
Bulgarian (11)	75	0.29
Cajun (0)	34	0.13
Canadian (24)	31	0.12
Celtic (15)	31	0.12
Croatian (129)	182	0.70
Czech (37)	81	0.31
Czechoslovakian (14)	14	0.05
Danish (6)	39	0.15
Dutch (38)	224	0.86
Eastern European (148)	148	0.57
English (164)	907	3.48
European (478)	555	2.13
Finnish (0)	24	0.09
French, ex. Basque (35)	130	0.50
French Canadian (17)	103	0.39
German (837)	3,042	11.66
Greek (250)	399	1.53
Hungarian (50)	252	0.97
Iranian (196)	196	0.75
Irish (1,089)	3,892	14.92
Israeli (50)	50	0.19
Italian (3,304)	5,830	22.35
Lithuanian (20)	64	0.25
Maltese (0)	9	0.03
Norwegian (15)	76	0.29
Polish (564)	1,671	6.41
Portuguese (23)	60	0.23
Romanian (58)	128	0.49
Russian (390)	887	3.40
Scandinavian (11)	33	0.13
Scotch-Irish (106)	186	0.71
Scottish (53)	155	0.59
Slavic (7)	7	0.03
Slovak (38)	133	0.51
Slovene (7)	7	0.03
Swedish (7)	159	0.61
Swiss (38)	90	0.35
Turkish (42)	42	0.16
Ukrainian (63)	267	1.02
Welsh (9)	84	0.32
West Indian, ex. Hispanic (77)	90	0.35
Haitian (68)	68	0.26
West Indian (9)	22	0.08
Yugoslavian (65)	65	0.25

Hispanic Origin	Population	%
Hispanic or Latino (of any race)	1,913	7.26
Central American, ex. Mexican	59	0.22
Costa Rican	12	0.05
Guatemalan	7	0.03
Honduran	12	0.05
Nicaraguan	3	0.01
Panamanian	5	0.02
Salvadoran	20	0.08
Cuban	339	1.29
Dominican Republic	317	1.20
Mexican	73	0.28
Puerto Rican	373	1.42
South American	531	2.02
Argentinean	44	0.17
Bolivian	3	0.01
Chilean	12	0.05
Colombian	240	0.91
Ecuadorian	134	0.51
Paraguayan	1	<0.01
Peruvian	83	0.32
Uruguayan	3	0.01
Venezuelan	9	0.03
Other South American	2	0.01
Other Hispanic or Latino	221	0.84

Race*	Population	%
African-American/Black (374)	477	1.81
Not Hispanic (335)	392	1.49
Hispanic (39)	85	0.32
American Indian/Alaska Native (28)	68	0.26
Not Hispanic (11)	45	0.17
Hispanic (17)	23	0.09
Aleut *(Alaska Native)* (1)	1	<0.01
Blackfeet (0)	4	0.02
Canadian/French Am. Ind. (0)	3	0.01
Central American Ind. (7)	7	0.03
Chickasaw (0)	3	0.01
Delaware (1)	1	<0.01
Mexican American Ind. (0)	1	<0.01
South American Ind. (2)	7	0.03
Spanish American Ind. (3)	4	0.02
Ute (0)	1	<0.01
Asian (5,869)	6,344	24.08
Not Hispanic (5,850)	6,306	23.94
Hispanic (19)	38	0.14
Bangladeshi (1)	5	0.02
Chinese, ex. Taiwanese (823)	901	3.42
Filipino (762)	829	3.15
Indian (1,664)	1,856	7.05
Indonesian (7)	10	0.04
Japanese (305)	322	1.22
Korean (1,813)	1,859	7.06
Malaysian (2)	2	0.01
Nepalese (1)	3	0.01
Pakistani (185)	205	0.78
Sri Lankan (3)	3	0.01
Taiwanese (141)	160	0.61
Thai (9)	12	0.05
Vietnamese (22)	22	0.08
Hawaii Native/Pacific Islander (13)	134	0.51
Not Hispanic (13)	134	0.51
Native Hawaiian (2)	3	0.01
Samoan (4)	4	0.02
White (19,042)	19,434	73.78
Not Hispanic (17,626)	17,935	68.09
Hispanic (1,416)	1,499	5.69

Park Ridge

Place Type: Borough
County: Bergen
Population: 8,645†

Ancestry‡	Population	%
American (310)	310	3.60
Arab (36)	97	1.13
Egyptian (0)	9	0.10
Lebanese (28)	53	0.62
Syrian (0)	12	0.14
Other Arab (8)	23	0.27
Armenian (78)	101	1.17
Australian (8)	8	0.09
Austrian (0)	11	0.13
British (30)	30	0.35
Canadian (7)	17	0.20
Croatian (114)	114	1.32
Czech (0)	8	0.09
Czechoslovakian (11)	21	0.24
Danish (12)	39	0.45
Dutch (21)	53	0.62
Eastern European (21)	21	0.24
English (87)	492	5.71
Estonian (0)	10	0.12
European (110)	110	1.28
Finnish (11)	23	0.27
French, ex. Basque (36)	220	2.55
French Canadian (11)	27	0.31
German (325)	1,398	16.23
Greek (94)	270	3.13
Hungarian (19)	130	1.51
Iranian (44)	44	0.51
Irish (790)	2,250	26.12
Italian (1,054)	2,136	24.79
Lithuanian (11)	22	0.26
Norwegian (28)	140	1.63
Polish (325)	775	9.00
Portuguese (53)	53	0.62
Romanian (8)	8	0.09
Russian (66)	237	2.75
Scandinavian (0)	17	0.20
Scotch-Irish (33)	155	1.80
Scottish (50)	186	2.16
Slovak (0)	19	0.22
Swedish (18)	72	0.84
Swiss (8)	81	0.94
Ukrainian (47)	66	0.77
Welsh (0)	23	0.27
West Indian, ex. Hispanic (10)	10	0.12
Barbadian (10)	10	0.12
Yugoslavian (9)	26	0.30

Hispanic Origin	Population	%
Hispanic or Latino (of any race)	669	7.74
Central American, ex. Mexican	14	0.16

*Notes: † The Census 2010 population figure is used to calculate the percentages in the Hispanic Origin and Race categories. Ancestry percentages are based on the 2006-2010 American Community Survey population (not shown); ‡ Numbers in parentheses indicate the number of people reporting a single ancestry; * Numbers in parentheses indicate the number of persons reporting this race alone, not in combination with any other race; Please refer to the Explanation of Data for more information.*

Costa Rican	1	0.01
Guatemalan	3	0.03
Honduran	6	0.07
Panamanian	1	0.01
Salvadoran	3	0.03
Cuban	65	0.75
Dominican Republic	48	0.56
Mexican	318	3.68
Puerto Rican	75	0.87
South American	102	1.18
Argentinean	14	0.16
Chilean	8	0.09
Colombian	34	0.39
Ecuadorian	30	0.35
Paraguayan	5	0.06
Peruvian	9	0.10
Venezuelan	1	0.01
Other South American	1	0.01
Other Hispanic or Latino	47	0.54

Race*	Population	%
African-American/Black (90)	108	1.25
Not Hispanic (80)	91	1.05
Hispanic (10)	17	0.20
American Indian/Alaska Native (19)	26	0.30
Not Hispanic (5)	9	0.10
Hispanic (14)	17	0.20
Canadian/French Am. Ind. (0)	1	0.01
Cherokee (0)	1	0.01
Mexican American Ind. (8)	10	0.12
Asian (525)	575	6.65
Not Hispanic (524)	569	6.58
Hispanic (1)	6	0.07
Bangladeshi (4)	4	0.05
Chinese, ex. Taiwanese (118)	137	1.58
Filipino (40)	55	0.64
Indian (201)	204	2.36
Japanese (30)	44	0.51
Korean (107)	116	1.34
Taiwanese (6)	6	0.07
Thai (1)	1	0.01
Vietnamese (4)	10	0.12
Hawaii Native/Pacific Islander (2)	3	0.03
Not Hispanic (2)	3	0.03
Native Hawaiian (2)	3	0.03
White (7,706)	7,783	90.03
Not Hispanic (7,288)	7,350	85.02
Hispanic (418)	433	5.01

Parsippany-Troy Hills

Place Type: Township
County: Morris
Population: 53,238†

Ancestry‡	Population	%
Afghan (588)	588	1.11
African, Sub-Saharan (162)	210	0.40
African (53)	101	0.19
Ghanaian (38)	38	0.07
Kenyan (12)	12	0.02
Nigerian (59)	59	0.11
Albanian (7)	22	0.04
Alsatian (0)	11	0.02
American (701)	701	1.33
Arab (352)	455	0.86
Arab (52)	63	0.12
Egyptian (155)	155	0.29
Lebanese (0)	26	0.05
Palestinian (10)	21	0.04
Syrian (126)	181	0.34
Other Arab (9)	9	0.02
Armenian (10)	78	0.15
Australian (52)	52	0.10
Austrian (132)	361	0.68
Belgian (0)	18	0.03
Brazilian (74)	174	0.33
British (19)	36	0.07
Canadian (26)	75	0.14
Carpatho Rusyn (14)	14	0.03
Croatian (0)	33	0.06
Cypriot (23)	23	0.04
Czech (42)	282	0.53
Czechoslovakian (11)	56	0.11
Danish (19)	69	0.13
Dutch (169)	843	1.59
Eastern European (211)	211	0.40
English (537)	2,785	5.27
European (231)	247	0.47
Finnish (14)	32	0.06
French, ex. Basque (63)	507	0.96
French Canadian (19)	185	0.35
German (1,328)	5,585	10.57
Greek (280)	416	0.79
Guyanese (70)	70	0.13
Hungarian (188)	792	1.50
Iranian (51)	51	0.10
Irish (1,934)	7,466	14.13
Israeli (32)	74	0.14
Italian (5,279)	9,985	18.89
Latvian (11)	48	0.09
Lithuanian (83)	252	0.48
Macedonian (146)	146	0.28
Northern European (45)	45	0.09
Norwegian (41)	199	0.38
Polish (1,386)	3,520	6.66
Portuguese (181)	269	0.51
Romanian (119)	205	0.39
Russian (717)	1,297	2.45
Scandinavian (9)	41	0.08
Scotch-Irish (159)	486	0.92
Scottish (172)	685	1.30
Serbian (0)	10	0.02
Slovak (224)	403	0.76
Swedish (72)	357	0.68
Swiss (7)	200	0.38
Turkish (102)	183	0.35
Ukrainian (229)	397	0.75
Welsh (37)	302	0.57
West Indian, ex. Hispanic (343)	391	0.74
Barbadian (0)	6	0.01
Haitian (138)	162	0.31
Jamaican (197)	215	0.41
West Indian (8)	8	0.02
Yugoslavian (76)	141	0.27

Hispanic Origin	Population	%
Hispanic or Latino (of any race)	4,430	8.32
Central American, ex. Mexican	475	0.89
Costa Rican	55	0.10
Guatemalan	176	0.33
Honduran	116	0.22
Nicaraguan	12	0.02
Panamanian	5	0.01
Salvadoran	107	0.20
Other Central American	4	0.01
Cuban	259	0.49
Dominican Republic	314	0.59
Mexican	581	1.09
Puerto Rican	931	1.75
South American	1,495	2.81
Argentinean	56	0.11
Bolivian	11	0.02
Chilean	58	0.11
Colombian	822	1.54
Ecuadorian	169	0.32
Paraguayan	10	0.02
Peruvian	251	0.47
Uruguayan	64	0.12
Venezuelan	46	0.09
Other South American	8	0.02
Other Hispanic or Latino	375	0.70

Race*	Population	%
African-American/Black (1,874)	2,176	4.09
Not Hispanic (1,741)	1,974	3.71
Hispanic (133)	202	0.38
American Indian/Alaska Native (92)	255	0.48
Not Hispanic (81)	205	0.39
Hispanic (11)	50	0.09
Alaska Athabascan *(Ala. Nat.)* (1)	1	<0.01
Apache (1)	5	0.01
Blackfeet (0)	1	<0.01
Central American Ind. (2)	2	<0.01
Cherokee (2)	13	0.02
Cheyenne (0)	1	<0.01
Chippewa (0)	1	<0.01
Choctaw (0)	1	<0.01
Crow (0)	1	<0.01
Delaware (1)	3	0.01
Hopi (0)	1	<0.01
Iroquois (2)	9	0.02
Mexican American Ind. (3)	6	0.01
Ottawa (1)	1	<0.01
Seminole (0)	2	<0.01
Sioux (0)	3	0.01
South American Ind. (6)	11	0.02
Spanish American Ind. (0)	5	0.01
Asian (15,487)	16,491	30.98
Not Hispanic (15,443)	16,392	30.79
Hispanic (44)	99	0.19
Bangladeshi (56)	58	0.11
Cambodian (9)	9	0.02
Chinese, ex. Taiwanese (3,001)	3,205	6.02
Filipino (1,057)	1,183	2.22
Indian (9,250)	9,576	17.99
Indonesian (11)	26	0.05
Japanese (49)	77	0.14
Korean (541)	580	1.09
Laotian (1)	1	<0.01
Malaysian (8)	12	0.02
Nepalese (13)	23	0.04
Pakistani (442)	462	0.87
Sri Lankan (20)	23	0.04
Taiwanese (466)	526	0.99
Thai (28)	34	0.06
Vietnamese (293)	327	0.61
Hawaii Native/Pacific Islander (8)	45	0.08
Not Hispanic (4)	38	0.07
Hispanic (4)	7	0.01
Guamanian/Chamorro (4)	7	0.01
Native Hawaiian (1)	11	0.02
White (33,204)	34,277	64.38
Not Hispanic (30,214)	31,056	58.33
Hispanic (2,990)	3,221	6.05

Passaic

Place Type: City
County: Passaic
Population: 69,781†

Ancestry‡	Population	%
African, Sub-Saharan (262)	339	0.49
African (136)	177	0.26
Ghanaian (41)	59	0.09
Nigerian (12)	30	0.04
South African (57)	57	0.08
Zimbabwean (16)	16	0.02
American (1,157)	1,157	1.68
Arab (263)	263	0.38
Arab (119)	119	0.17
Jordanian (5)	5	0.01
Moroccan (36)	36	0.05
Syrian (103)	103	0.15
Austrian (61)	140	0.20
Belgian (34)	34	0.05
Brazilian (0)	25	0.04
British (15)	51	0.07
Czech (20)	32	0.05
Czechoslovakian (15)	15	0.02
Dutch (21)	49	0.07
Eastern European (410)	410	0.59
English (176)	386	0.56
European (466)	466	0.68
French, ex. Basque (74)	121	0.18
German (412)	874	1.27
Greek (48)	64	0.09
Hungarian (223)	454	0.66
Iranian (83)	83	0.12

*Notes: † The Census 2010 population figure is used to calculate the percentages in the Hispanic Origin and Race categories. Ancestry percentages are based on the 2006-2010 American Community Survey population (not shown); ‡ Numbers in parentheses indicate the number of people reporting a single ancestry; * Numbers in parentheses indicate the number of persons reporting this race alone, not in combination with any other race; Please refer to the Explanation of Data for more information.*

Irish (250)	788	1.14
Israeli (0)	14	0.02
Italian (1,008)	1,575	2.28
Lithuanian (33)	245	0.36
Macedonian (76)	76	0.11
Polish (1,308)	2,175	3.15
Portuguese (26)	51	0.07
Romanian (11)	126	0.18
Russian (411)	1,121	1.63
Scotch-Irish (0)	14	0.02
Scottish (0)	25	0.04
Slavic (0)	61	0.09
Slovak (29)	56	0.08
Swiss (0)	37	0.05
Ukrainian (246)	409	0.59
West Indian, ex. Hispanic (443)	480	0.70
Barbadian (23)	23	0.03
British West Indian (35)	35	0.05
Jamaican (296)	333	0.48
Trinidadian/Tobagonian (61)	61	0.09
West Indian (28)	28	0.04
Yugoslavian (206)	206	0.30

Hispanic Origin	Population	%
Hispanic or Latino (of any race)	49,557	71.02
Central American, ex. Mexican	1,372	1.97
Costa Rican	78	0.11
Guatemalan	409	0.59
Honduran	499	0.72
Nicaraguan	42	0.06
Panamanian	26	0.04
Salvadoran	318	0.46
Cuban	481	0.69
Dominican Republic	12,340	17.68
Mexican	21,123	30.27
Puerto Rican	7,368	10.56
South American	4,723	6.77
Argentinean	133	0.19
Bolivian	139	0.20
Chilean	60	0.09
Colombian	1,251	1.79
Ecuadorian	761	1.09
Paraguayan	2	<0.01
Peruvian	2,228	3.19
Uruguayan	73	0.10
Venezuelan	64	0.09
Other South American	12	0.02
Other Hispanic or Latino	2,150	3.08

Race*	Population	%
African-American/Black (7,425)	8,597	12.32
Not Hispanic (5,221)	5,476	7.85
Hispanic (2,204)	3,121	4.47
American Indian/Alaska Native (745)	1,277	1.83
Not Hispanic (57)	157	0.22
Hispanic (688)	1,120	1.61
Apache (0)	7	0.01
Blackfeet (1)	12	0.02
Central American Ind. (26)	61	0.09
Cherokee (5)	21	0.03
Chippewa (2)	2	<0.01
Choctaw (0)	2	<0.01
Comanche (3)	3	<0.01
Delaware (6)	22	0.03
Iroquois (3)	5	0.01
Lumbee (0)	8	0.01
Mexican American Ind. (125)	162	0.23
Paiute (1)	1	<0.01
Pueblo (1)	19	0.03
Sioux (0)	1	<0.01
South American Ind. (46)	113	0.16
Spanish American Ind. (27)	47	0.07
Asian (3,040)	3,507	5.03
Not Hispanic (2,924)	3,232	4.63
Hispanic (116)	275	0.39
Bangladeshi (45)	47	0.07
Burmese (1)	1	<0.01
Cambodian (1)	1	<0.01
Chinese, ex. Taiwanese (179)	225	0.32
Filipino (587)	648	0.93
Indian (2,007)	2,215	3.17
Indonesian (16)	16	0.02
Japanese (35)	64	0.09
Korean (26)	32	0.05
Malaysian (7)	7	0.01
Pakistani (45)	49	0.07
Sri Lankan (7)	7	0.01
Taiwanese (1)	1	<0.01
Thai (9)	15	0.02
Vietnamese (15)	17	0.02
Hawaii Native/Pacific Islander (27)	180	0.26
Not Hispanic (3)	18	0.03
Hispanic (24)	162	0.23
Guamanian/Chamorro (3)	4	0.01
Marshallese (0)	1	<0.01
Native Hawaiian (5)	12	0.02
Samoan (0)	9	0.01
White (31,440)	34,059	48.81
Not Hispanic (11,241)	11,524	16.51
Hispanic (20,199)	22,535	32.29

Paterson

Place Type: City
County: Passaic
Population: 146,199†

Ancestry‡	Population	%
African, Sub-Saharan (899)	1,168	0.80
African (759)	975	0.67
Ghanaian (102)	127	0.09
Nigerian (10)	38	0.03
Sudanese (28)	28	0.02
Albanian (197)	197	0.14
American (11,070)	11,070	7.59
Arab (2,396)	2,774	1.90
Arab (942)	1,083	0.74
Jordanian (561)	596	0.41
Lebanese (129)	153	0.10
Moroccan (17)	17	0.01
Palestinian (292)	323	0.22
Syrian (189)	336	0.23
Other Arab (266)	266	0.18
Armenian (13)	35	0.02
Austrian (14)	31	0.02
Belgian (22)	47	0.03
Brazilian (14)	23	0.02
British (23)	37	0.03
Canadian (23)	40	0.03
Carpatho Rusyn (0)	19	0.01
Croatian (13)	86	0.06
Czech (0)	32	0.02
Dutch (62)	406	0.28
Eastern European (12)	12	0.01
English (574)	1,168	0.80
European (15)	15	0.01
French, ex. Basque (70)	192	0.13
French Canadian (15)	51	0.03
German (257)	1,141	0.78
German Russian (18)	18	0.01
Greek (21)	31	0.02
Guyanese (82)	107	0.07
Hungarian (0)	217	0.15
Irish (577)	1,953	1.34
Israeli (130)	130	0.09
Italian (3,473)	5,128	3.52
Lithuanian (0)	40	0.03
Macedonian (175)	175	0.12
Northern European (0)	5	<0.01
Norwegian (35)	44	0.03
Polish (434)	769	0.53
Portuguese (31)	86	0.06
Romanian (29)	29	0.02
Russian (273)	380	0.26
Scandinavian (244)	244	0.17
Scotch-Irish (46)	311	0.21
Scottish (10)	126	0.09
Serbian (271)	271	0.19
Slavic (47)	65	0.04
Slovak (28)	49	0.03
Slovene (14)	30	0.02
Swedish (12)	60	0.04
Swiss (22)	71	0.05
Turkish (1,148)	1,148	0.79
Ukrainian (26)	60	0.04
West Indian, ex. Hispanic (4,753)	5,356	3.67
Bahamian (0)	8	0.01
British West Indian (5)	13	0.01
Haitian (322)	388	0.27
Jamaican (4,299)	4,741	3.25
Trinidadian/Tobagonian (35)	61	0.04
West Indian (92)	145	0.10
Yugoslavian (89)	168	0.12

Hispanic Origin	Population	%
Hispanic or Latino (of any race)	84,254	57.63
Central American, ex. Mexican	4,281	2.93
Costa Rican	1,241	0.85
Guatemalan	879	0.60
Honduran	453	0.31
Nicaraguan	339	0.23
Panamanian	70	0.05
Salvadoran	1,292	0.88
Other Central American	7	<0.01
Cuban	783	0.54
Dominican Republic	27,426	18.76
Mexican	8,136	5.57
Puerto Rican	21,015	14.37
South American	17,383	11.89
Argentinean	327	0.22
Bolivian	60	0.04
Chilean	101	0.07
Colombian	5,204	3.56
Ecuadorian	1,243	0.85
Paraguayan	11	0.01
Peruvian	9,943	6.80
Uruguayan	204	0.14
Venezuelan	273	0.19
Other South American	17	0.01
Other Hispanic or Latino	5,230	3.58

Race*	Population	%
African-American/Black (46,314)	49,340	33.75
Not Hispanic (41,431)	42,328	28.95
Hispanic (4,883)	7,012	4.80
American Indian/Alaska Native (1,547)	2,769	1.89
Not Hispanic (217)	598	0.41
Hispanic (1,330)	2,171	1.48
Apache (1)	2	<0.01
Blackfeet (2)	26	0.02
Canadian/French Am. Ind. (1)	2	<0.01
Central American Ind. (61)	100	0.07
Cherokee (20)	108	0.07
Cheyenne (0)	1	<0.01
Chippewa (0)	2	<0.01
Choctaw (1)	2	<0.01
Delaware (27)	54	0.04
Iroquois (1)	2	<0.01
Mexican American Ind. (82)	99	0.07
Navajo (3)	4	<0.01
Pima (0)	1	<0.01
Pueblo (10)	16	0.01
Seminole (0)	5	<0.01
Shoshone (0)	1	<0.01
Sioux (0)	4	<0.01
South American Ind. (105)	208	0.14
Spanish American Ind. (84)	111	0.08
Tlingit-Haida *(Alaska Native)* (0)	1	<0.01
Yaqui (0)	4	<0.01
Asian (4,878)	5,873	4.02
Not Hispanic (4,663)	5,370	3.67
Hispanic (215)	503	0.34
Bangladeshi (1,823)	2,119	1.45
Burmese (0)	1	<0.01
Cambodian (1)	1	<0.01
Chinese, ex. Taiwanese (158)	245	0.17
Filipino (228)	294	0.20
Hmong (1)	1	<0.01
Indian (1,960)	2,375	1.62
Indonesian (6)	13	0.01

*Notes: † The Census 2010 population figure is used to calculate the percentages in the Hispanic Origin and Race categories. Ancestry percentages are based on the 2006-2010 American Community Survey population (not shown); ‡ Numbers in parentheses indicate the number of people reporting a single ancestry; * Numbers in parentheses indicate the number of persons reporting this race alone, not in combination with any other race; Please refer to the Explanation of Data for more information.*

Japanese (46)	112	0.08
Korean (44)	65	0.04
Laotian (23)	23	0.02
Pakistani (99)	108	0.07
Sri Lankan (1)	3	<0.01
Taiwanese (1)	1	<0.01
Thai (16)	20	0.01
Vietnamese (21)	27	0.02
Hawaii Native/Pacific Islander (60)	490	0.34
Not Hispanic (21)	157	0.11
Hispanic (39)	333	0.23
Guamanian/Chamorro (10)	19	0.01
Native Hawaiian (15)	39	0.03
Samoan (4)	10	0.01
White (50,706)	56,369	38.56
Not Hispanic (13,426)	14,643	10.02
Hispanic (37,280)	41,726	28.54

Pemberton

Place Type: Township
County: Burlington
Population: 27,912†

Ancestry‡	Population	%
African, Sub-Saharan (349)	364	1.29
African (259)	274	0.97
Nigerian (90)	90	0.32
American (935)	935	3.31
Armenian (9)	24	0.08
Austrian (17)	36	0.13
Belgian (0)	5	0.02
British (52)	72	0.25
Croatian (11)	84	0.30
Czech (16)	42	0.15
Czechoslovakian (0)	10	0.04
Danish (48)	55	0.19
Dutch (39)	267	0.94
English (694)	2,505	8.86
European (199)	323	1.14
Finnish (0)	35	0.12
French, ex. Basque (202)	918	3.25
French Canadian (46)	190	0.67
German (1,160)	5,652	20.00
Greek (19)	67	0.24
Guyanese (10)	32	0.11
Hungarian (40)	301	1.06
Irish (1,097)	4,932	17.45
Italian (922)	3,303	11.69
Lithuanian (0)	38	0.13
Northern European (10)	10	0.04
Norwegian (20)	202	0.71
Pennsylvania German (30)	54	0.19
Polish (344)	1,479	5.23
Portuguese (157)	213	0.75
Romanian (27)	42	0.15
Russian (21)	90	0.32
Scandinavian (23)	23	0.08
Scotch-Irish (147)	565	2.00
Scottish (47)	436	1.54
Slavic (0)	27	0.10
Slovak (38)	76	0.27
Swedish (16)	279	0.99
Swiss (14)	47	0.17
Ukrainian (62)	117	0.41
Welsh (0)	143	0.51
West Indian, ex. Hispanic (407)	474	1.68
Bahamian (44)	44	0.16
Haitian (91)	91	0.32
Jamaican (181)	181	0.64
Trinidadian/Tobagonian (13)	80	0.28
West Indian (78)	78	0.28

Hispanic Origin	Population	%
Hispanic or Latino (of any race)	3,326	11.92
Central American, ex. Mexican	243	0.87
Costa Rican	13	0.05
Guatemalan	20	0.07
Honduran	24	0.09
Nicaraguan	3	0.01
Panamanian	156	0.56
Salvadoran	25	0.09
Other Central American	2	0.01
Cuban	87	0.31
Dominican Republic	134	0.48
Mexican	595	2.13
Puerto Rican	1,895	6.79
South American	167	0.60
Argentinean	9	0.03
Bolivian	3	0.01
Chilean	7	0.03
Colombian	54	0.19
Ecuadorian	56	0.20
Peruvian	33	0.12
Venezuelan	5	0.02
Other Hispanic or Latino	205	0.73

Race*	Population	%
African-American/Black (5,719)	6,702	24.01
Not Hispanic (5,332)	6,123	21.94
Hispanic (387)	579	2.07
American Indian/Alaska Native (104)	415	1.49
Not Hispanic (77)	327	1.17
Hispanic (27)	88	0.32
Apache (1)	5	0.02
Blackfeet (1)	20	0.07
Canadian/French Am. Ind. (1)	1	<0.01
Central American Ind. (3)	3	0.01
Cherokee (12)	98	0.35
Cheyenne (0)	2	0.01
Chippewa (3)	9	0.03
Choctaw (0)	5	0.02
Comanche (1)	1	<0.01
Creek (1)	3	0.01
Crow (0)	1	<0.01
Delaware (3)	18	0.06
Iroquois (5)	7	0.03
Lumbee (1)	3	0.01
Menominee (0)	2	0.01
Mexican American Ind. (4)	7	0.03
Pueblo (1)	1	<0.01
Seminole (1)	2	0.01
Sioux (3)	10	0.04
South American Ind. (7)	11	0.04
Spanish American Ind. (1)	1	<0.01
Yaqui (3)	3	0.01
Asian (806)	1,281	4.59
Not Hispanic (778)	1,213	4.35
Hispanic (28)	68	0.24
Cambodian (5)	7	0.03
Chinese, ex. Taiwanese (35)	55	0.20
Filipino (223)	352	1.26
Indian (72)	96	0.34
Indonesian (2)	9	0.03
Japanese (109)	224	0.80
Korean (222)	325	1.16
Laotian (2)	2	0.01
Malaysian (3)	3	0.01
Pakistani (24)	24	0.09
Taiwanese (3)	6	0.02
Thai (38)	95	0.34
Vietnamese (32)	53	0.19
Hawaii Native/Pacific Islander (37)	86	0.31
Not Hispanic (30)	70	0.25
Hispanic (7)	16	0.06
Guamanian/Chamorro (10)	10	0.04
Native Hawaiian (15)	37	0.13
Samoan (2)	3	0.01
White (18,848)	20,115	72.07
Not Hispanic (17,124)	18,115	64.90
Hispanic (1,724)	2,000	7.17

Pennsauken

Place Type: Township
County: Camden
Population: 35,885†

Ancestry‡	Population	%
Afghan (41)	41	0.11
African, Sub-Saharan (310)	433	1.21
African (89)	185	0.51
Nigerian (126)	143	0.40
Sierra Leonean (60)	70	0.19
Other Sub-Saharan African (35)	35	0.10
Albanian (0)	11	0.03
American (1,487)	1,487	4.14
Arab (229)	262	0.73
Arab (49)	49	0.14
Egyptian (15)	15	0.04
Lebanese (150)	150	0.42
Moroccan (0)	15	0.04
Syrian (15)	33	0.09
Armenian (12)	30	0.08
Austrian (30)	182	0.51
Belgian (0)	25	0.07
Brazilian (14)	27	0.08
British (25)	33	0.09
Canadian (17)	29	0.08
Croatian (0)	10	0.03
Czech (64)	188	0.52
Czechoslovakian (11)	20	0.06
Danish (0)	17	0.05
Dutch (24)	244	0.68
Eastern European (66)	66	0.18
English (450)	1,966	5.47
European (117)	117	0.33
Finnish (25)	39	0.11
French, ex. Basque (0)	414	1.15
French Canadian (17)	60	0.17
German (815)	3,854	10.73
Greek (196)	228	0.63
Guyanese (124)	135	0.38
Hungarian (69)	124	0.35
Irish (1,444)	5,530	15.39
Italian (1,564)	3,352	9.33
Lithuanian (0)	106	0.30
New Zealander (21)	21	0.06
Northern European (9)	9	0.03
Norwegian (14)	69	0.19
Pennsylvania German (21)	42	0.12
Polish (470)	1,686	4.69
Portuguese (87)	142	0.40
Romanian (60)	70	0.19
Russian (132)	247	0.69
Scotch-Irish (62)	187	0.52
Scottish (30)	206	0.57
Slavic (0)	13	0.04
Slovak (0)	18	0.05
Swedish (23)	138	0.38
Ukrainian (18)	90	0.25
Welsh (0)	135	0.38
West Indian, ex. Hispanic (298)	363	1.01
Belizean (0)	19	0.05
Haitian (11)	11	0.03
Jamaican (193)	228	0.63
Trinidadian/Tobagonian (18)	18	0.05
West Indian (76)	87	0.24
Yugoslavian (8)	8	0.02

Hispanic Origin	Population	%
Hispanic or Latino (of any race)	9,657	26.91
Central American, ex. Mexican	650	1.81
Costa Rican	19	0.05
Guatemalan	123	0.34
Honduran	50	0.14
Nicaraguan	336	0.94
Panamanian	45	0.13
Salvadoran	77	0.21
Cuban	101	0.28
Dominican Republic	1,347	3.75
Mexican	822	2.29
Puerto Rican	6,038	16.83
South American	312	0.87
Argentinean	8	0.02
Chilean	13	0.04
Colombian	107	0.30
Ecuadorian	86	0.24
Paraguayan	3	0.01
Peruvian	56	0.16

*Notes: † The Census 2010 population figure is used to calculate the percentages in the Hispanic Origin and Race categories. Ancestry percentages are based on the 2006-2010 American Community Survey population (not shown); ‡ Numbers in parentheses indicate the number of people reporting a single ancestry; * Numbers in parentheses indicate the number of persons reporting this race alone, not in combination with any other race; Please refer to the Explanation of Data for more information.*

Uruguayan	2	0.01
Venezuelan	36	0.10
Other South American	1	<0.01
Other Hispanic or Latino	387	1.08

Race*	Population	%
African-American/Black (9,644)	10,397	28.97
Not Hispanic (8,984)	9,456	26.35
Hispanic (660)	941	2.62
American Indian/Alaska Native (210)	481	1.34
Not Hispanic (100)	304	0.85
Hispanic (110)	177	0.49
Blackfeet (0)	23	0.06
Cherokee (7)	56	0.16
Chippewa (4)	5	0.01
Choctaw (0)	1	<0.01
Delaware (7)	20	0.06
Iroquois (0)	3	0.01
Lumbee (0)	2	0.01
Mexican American Ind. (7)	9	0.03
Navajo (0)	1	<0.01
Paiute (1)	1	<0.01
Seminole (0)	1	<0.01
Sioux (1)	9	0.03
South American Ind. (17)	27	0.08
Asian (2,770)	3,009	8.39
Not Hispanic (2,743)	2,935	8.18
Hispanic (27)	74	0.21
Bangladeshi (20)	22	0.06
Burmese (0)	1	<0.01
Cambodian (186)	249	0.69
Chinese, ex. Taiwanese (277)	342	0.95
Filipino (304)	366	1.02
Hmong (0)	1	<0.01
Indian (140)	175	0.49
Indonesian (0)	1	<0.01
Japanese (16)	24	0.07
Korean (64)	85	0.24
Laotian (0)	3	0.01
Pakistani (33)	40	0.11
Taiwanese (5)	7	0.02
Thai (8)	10	0.03
Vietnamese (1,580)	1,687	4.70
Hawaii Native/Pacific Islander (15)	61	0.17
Not Hispanic (7)	29	0.08
Hispanic (8)	32	0.09
Guamanian/Chamorro (4)	9	0.03
Native Hawaiian (2)	8	0.02
White (17,081)	17,964	50.06
Not Hispanic (13,645)	14,125	39.36
Hispanic (3,436)	3,839	10.70

Pennsville

Place Type: CDP
County: Salem
Population: 11,888†

Ancestry‡	Population	%
African, Sub-Saharan (12)	12	0.10
Liberian (12)	12	0.10
American (555)	555	4.66
Austrian (10)	10	0.08
Belgian (17)	28	0.23
Brazilian (53)	53	0.44
British (25)	33	0.28
Canadian (10)	18	0.15
Danish (0)	13	0.11
Dutch (104)	425	3.56
English (408)	1,699	14.25
European (76)	88	0.74
French, ex. Basque (57)	390	3.27
French Canadian (96)	145	1.22
German (588)	3,313	27.79
Greek (48)	63	0.53
Hungarian (43)	79	0.66
Iranian (21)	21	0.18
Irish (1,024)	3,153	26.45
Italian (1,099)	2,316	19.43
Lithuanian (0)	23	0.19
Norwegian (12)	43	0.36
Pennsylvania German (20)	28	0.23
Polish (157)	571	4.79
Portuguese (48)	117	0.98
Russian (27)	81	0.68
Scandinavian (0)	15	0.13
Scotch-Irish (155)	306	2.57
Scottish (40)	290	2.43
Serbian (0)	21	0.18
Slovak (25)	25	0.21
Swedish (42)	247	2.07
Ukrainian (21)	58	0.49
Welsh (94)	199	1.67

Hispanic Origin	Population	%
Hispanic or Latino (of any race)	337	2.83
Central American, ex. Mexican	24	0.20
Costa Rican	5	0.04
Guatemalan	17	0.14
Panamanian	1	0.01
Salvadoran	1	0.01
Cuban	13	0.11
Dominican Republic	2	0.02
Mexican	86	0.72
Puerto Rican	161	1.35
South American	16	0.13
Argentinean	1	0.01
Chilean	1	0.01
Colombian	5	0.04
Ecuadorian	2	0.02
Peruvian	1	0.01
Uruguayan	1	0.01
Venezuelan	1	0.01
Other South American	4	0.03
Other Hispanic or Latino	35	0.29

Race*	Population	%
African-American/Black (159)	211	1.77
Not Hispanic (147)	199	1.67
Hispanic (12)	12	0.10
American Indian/Alaska Native (27)	58	0.49
Not Hispanic (22)	50	0.42
Hispanic (5)	8	0.07
Blackfeet (1)	5	0.04
Central American Ind. (1)	1	0.01
Cherokee (7)	14	0.12
Chickasaw (4)	5	0.04
Chippewa (1)	2	0.02
Comanche (0)	3	0.03
Creek (1)	1	0.01
Delaware (2)	5	0.04
Lumbee (2)	2	0.02
South American Ind. (2)	2	0.02
Yup'ik *(Alaska Native)* (3)	3	0.03
Asian (160)	191	1.61
Not Hispanic (159)	187	1.57
Hispanic (1)	4	0.03
Cambodian (1)	1	0.01
Chinese, ex. Taiwanese (26)	29	0.24
Filipino (14)	25	0.21
Indian (80)	80	0.67
Japanese (6)	13	0.11
Korean (14)	19	0.16
Laotian (1)	1	0.01
Nepalese (4)	4	0.03
Sri Lankan (4)	4	0.03
Taiwanese (1)	1	0.01
Thai (2)	5	0.04
Vietnamese (1)	1	0.01
Hawaii Native/Pacific Islander (2)	9	0.08
Not Hispanic (2)	8	0.07
Hispanic (0)	1	0.01
Native Hawaiian (1)	5	0.04
Samoan (1)	1	0.01
White (11,302)	11,427	96.12
Not Hispanic (11,106)	11,208	94.28
Hispanic (196)	219	1.84

Pennsville

Place Type: Township
County: Salem
Population: 13,409†

Ancestry‡	Population	%
African, Sub-Saharan (35)	35	0.26
African (23)	23	0.17
Liberian (12)	12	0.09
American (677)	677	5.05
Arab (11)	11	0.08
Egyptian (11)	11	0.08
Austrian (10)	10	0.07
Belgian (17)	28	0.21
Brazilian (53)	53	0.40
British (25)	47	0.35
Canadian (10)	18	0.13
Danish (0)	13	0.10
Dutch (104)	425	3.17
English (501)	2,037	15.19
European (103)	115	0.86
French, ex. Basque (70)	436	3.25
French Canadian (96)	145	1.08
German (658)	3,455	25.76
Greek (48)	63	0.47
Hungarian (43)	79	0.59
Iranian (21)	21	0.16
Irish (1,084)	3,442	25.67
Italian (1,251)	2,497	18.62
Lithuanian (0)	23	0.17
Norwegian (23)	54	0.40
Pennsylvania German (20)	28	0.21
Polish (200)	653	4.87
Portuguese (48)	117	0.87
Russian (27)	81	0.60
Scandinavian (12)	27	0.20
Scotch-Irish (171)	400	2.98
Scottish (90)	340	2.54
Serbian (0)	21	0.16
Slovak (34)	34	0.25
Swedish (42)	298	2.22
Ukrainian (32)	69	0.51
Welsh (94)	199	1.48

Hispanic Origin	Population	%
Hispanic or Latino (of any race)	411	3.07
Central American, ex. Mexican	29	0.22
Costa Rican	5	0.04
Guatemalan	20	0.15
Panamanian	3	0.02
Salvadoran	1	0.01
Cuban	14	0.10
Dominican Republic	4	0.03
Mexican	96	0.72
Puerto Rican	192	1.43
South American	26	0.19
Argentinean	1	0.01
Chilean	2	0.01
Colombian	11	0.08
Ecuadorian	5	0.04
Peruvian	1	0.01
Uruguayan	1	0.01
Venezuelan	1	0.01
Other South American	4	0.03
Other Hispanic or Latino	50	0.37

Race*	Population	%
African-American/Black (206)	273	2.04
Not Hispanic (192)	257	1.92
Hispanic (14)	16	0.12
American Indian/Alaska Native (31)	66	0.49
Not Hispanic (26)	58	0.43
Hispanic (5)	8	0.06
Blackfeet (1)	7	0.05
Central American Ind. (1)	1	0.01
Cherokee (8)	15	0.11
Chickasaw (4)	5	0.04
Chippewa (1)	2	0.01
Comanche (0)	3	0.02

*Notes: † The Census 2010 population figure is used to calculate the percentages in the Hispanic Origin and Race categories. Ancestry percentages are based on the 2006-2010 American Community Survey population (not shown); ‡ Numbers in parentheses indicate the number of people reporting a single ancestry; * Numbers in parentheses indicate the number of persons reporting this race alone, not in combination with any other race; Please refer to the Explanation of Data for more information.*

Creek (1)	1	0.01
Delaware (2)	5	0.04
Lumbee (2)	2	0.01
South American Ind. (2)	2	0.01
Yup'ik *(Alaska Native)* (3)	3	0.02
Asian (190)	227	1.69
Not Hispanic (189)	223	1.66
Hispanic (1)	4	0.03
Cambodian (1)	1	0.01
Chinese, ex. Taiwanese (32)	37	0.28
Filipino (16)	31	0.23
Indian (96)	96	0.72
Japanese (6)	13	0.10
Korean (18)	23	0.17
Laotian (1)	1	0.01
Nepalese (4)	4	0.03
Sri Lankan (4)	4	0.03
Taiwanese (1)	1	0.01
Thai (3)	6	0.04
Vietnamese (2)	2	0.01
Hawaii Native/Pacific Islander (2)	9	0.07
Not Hispanic (2)	8	0.06
Hispanic (0)	1	0.01
Native Hawaiian (1)	5	0.04
Samoan (1)	1	0.01
White (12,696)	12,845	95.79
Not Hispanic (12,450)	12,573	93.77
Hispanic (246)	272	2.03

Pequannock

Place Type: Township
County: Morris
Population: 15,540†

Ancestry‡	Population	%
African, Sub-Saharan (4)	8	0.05
African (4)	8	0.05
Albanian (17)	17	0.11
Alsatian (0)	17	0.11
American (489)	489	3.21
Arab (57)	82	0.54
Egyptian (15)	15	0.10
Lebanese (0)	13	0.09
Syrian (42)	54	0.35
Armenian (10)	35	0.23
Austrian (37)	85	0.56
Belgian (0)	38	0.25
Brazilian (15)	15	0.10
British (69)	69	0.45
Canadian (17)	17	0.11
Croatian (0)	9	0.06
Czech (15)	15	0.10
Czechoslovakian (28)	125	0.82
Danish (11)	66	0.43
Dutch (290)	888	5.82
Eastern European (11)	11	0.07
English (215)	1,284	8.42
European (25)	25	0.16
French, ex. Basque (10)	251	1.65
French Canadian (16)	59	0.39
German (747)	2,659	17.44
Greek (49)	107	0.70
Hungarian (26)	76	0.50
Irish (1,428)	4,404	28.89
Italian (2,127)	5,105	33.49
Latvian (11)	11	0.07
Lithuanian (0)	14	0.09
Macedonian (15)	15	0.10
Norwegian (0)	162	1.06
Polish (623)	1,434	9.41
Portuguese (16)	130	0.85
Romanian (10)	10	0.07
Russian (186)	422	2.77
Scotch-Irish (41)	309	2.03
Scottish (145)	395	2.59
Slovak (15)	88	0.58
Slovene (0)	9	0.06
Swedish (23)	167	1.10
Swiss (0)	79	0.52
Ukrainian (138)	201	1.32
Welsh (18)	86	0.56
West Indian, ex. Hispanic (20)	20	0.13
Jamaican (20)	20	0.13
Yugoslavian (186)	186	1.22

Hispanic Origin	Population	%
Hispanic or Latino (of any race)	703	4.52
Central American, ex. Mexican	44	0.28
Costa Rican	10	0.06
Guatemalan	21	0.14
Honduran	4	0.03
Nicaraguan	1	0.01
Panamanian	1	0.01
Salvadoran	7	0.05
Cuban	76	0.49
Dominican Republic	41	0.26
Mexican	92	0.59
Puerto Rican	203	1.31
South American	160	1.03
Argentinean	9	0.06
Bolivian	3	0.02
Chilean	2	0.01
Colombian	70	0.45
Ecuadorian	31	0.20
Paraguayan	1	0.01
Peruvian	36	0.23
Uruguayan	3	0.02
Venezuelan	5	0.03
Other Hispanic or Latino	87	0.56

Race*	Population	%
African-American/Black (75)	113	0.73
Not Hispanic (72)	105	0.68
Hispanic (3)	8	0.05
American Indian/Alaska Native (14)	45	0.29
Not Hispanic (13)	41	0.26
Hispanic (1)	4	0.03
Blackfeet (0)	2	0.01
Cherokee (0)	2	0.01
Chippewa (4)	4	0.03
Delaware (1)	7	0.05
Lumbee (1)	1	0.01
Sioux (0)	3	0.02
South American Ind. (0)	2	0.01
Asian (302)	347	2.23
Not Hispanic (291)	331	2.13
Hispanic (11)	16	0.10
Bangladeshi (0)	3	0.02
Chinese, ex. Taiwanese (66)	83	0.53
Filipino (111)	131	0.84
Indian (45)	53	0.34
Japanese (6)	13	0.08
Korean (41)	41	0.26
Pakistani (0)	4	0.03
Taiwanese (9)	9	0.06
Thai (1)	2	0.01
Vietnamese (11)	11	0.07
Hawaii Native/Pacific Islander (0)	1	0.01
Not Hispanic (0)	1	0.01
White (14,881)	15,005	96.56
Not Hispanic (14,342)	14,443	92.94
Hispanic (539)	562	3.62

Perth Amboy

Place Type: City
County: Middlesex
Population: 50,814†

Ancestry‡	Population	%
African, Sub-Saharan (428)	498	0.99
African (414)	433	0.86
Nigerian (14)	65	0.13
American (748)	748	1.49
Arab (155)	181	0.36
Arab (19)	32	0.06
Lebanese (0)	13	0.03
Palestinian (136)	136	0.27
Armenian (0)	18	0.04
Austrian (0)	13	0.03
Brazilian (282)	282	0.56
British (10)	21	0.04
Czech (59)	132	0.26
Czechoslovakian (0)	14	0.03
Danish (35)	80	0.16
Dutch (0)	36	0.07
English (0)	275	0.55
Estonian (29)	29	0.06
European (59)	59	0.12
French, ex. Basque (0)	70	0.14
French Canadian (0)	29	0.06
German (106)	395	0.79
Greek (25)	33	0.07
Guyanese (79)	79	0.16
Hungarian (379)	553	1.10
Irish (352)	1,113	2.22
Italian (416)	1,176	2.34
Lithuanian (37)	72	0.14
Polish (855)	1,281	2.55
Portuguese (437)	445	0.89
Romanian (65)	79	0.16
Russian (61)	153	0.30
Scotch-Irish (9)	159	0.32
Scottish (0)	34	0.07
Slavic (14)	14	0.03
Slovak (134)	326	0.65
Ukrainian (182)	240	0.48
West Indian, ex. Hispanic (988)	999	1.99
British West Indian (724)	735	1.46
Jamaican (107)	107	0.21
Trinidadian/Tobagonian (50)	50	0.10
West Indian (107)	107	0.21

Hispanic Origin	Population	%
Hispanic or Latino (of any race)	39,685	78.10
Central American, ex. Mexican	1,441	2.84
Costa Rican	87	0.17
Guatemalan	181	0.36
Honduran	404	0.80
Nicaraguan	52	0.10
Panamanian	47	0.09
Salvadoran	670	1.32
Cuban	824	1.62
Dominican Republic	14,773	29.07
Mexican	5,183	10.20
Puerto Rican	12,090	23.79
South American	3,538	6.96
Argentinean	427	0.84
Bolivian	30	0.06
Chilean	44	0.09
Colombian	530	1.04
Ecuadorian	366	0.72
Paraguayan	4	0.01
Peruvian	1,979	3.89
Uruguayan	76	0.15
Venezuelan	65	0.13
Other South American	17	0.03
Other Hispanic or Latino	1,836	3.61

Race*	Population	%
African-American/Black (5,358)	6,316	12.43
Not Hispanic (3,742)	3,913	7.70
Hispanic (1,616)	2,403	4.73
American Indian/Alaska Native (561)	887	1.75
Not Hispanic (51)	107	0.21
Hispanic (510)	780	1.54
Alaska Athabascan *(Ala. Nat.)* (1)	1	<0.01
Apache (1)	1	<0.01
Blackfeet (0)	5	0.01
Central American Ind. (51)	61	0.12
Cherokee (4)	18	0.04
Chippewa (2)	2	<0.01
Creek (0)	2	<0.01
Delaware (1)	1	<0.01
Iroquois (1)	2	<0.01
Mexican American Ind. (38)	45	0.09
Pueblo (7)	8	0.02
South American Ind. (65)	112	0.22
Spanish American Ind. (7)	27	0.05

*Notes: † The Census 2010 population figure is used to calculate the percentages in the Hispanic Origin and Race categories. Ancestry percentages are based on the 2006-2010 American Community Survey population (not shown); ‡ Numbers in parentheses indicate the number of people reporting a single ancestry; * Numbers in parentheses indicate the number of persons reporting this race alone, not in combination with any other race; Please refer to the Explanation of Data for more information.*

Asian (859)	1,051	2.07
Not Hispanic (806)	888	1.75
Hispanic (53)	163	0.32
Bangladeshi (7)	7	0.01
Chinese, ex. Taiwanese (155)	183	0.36
Filipino (210)	242	0.48
Indian (347)	389	0.77
Indonesian (0)	1	<0.01
Japanese (5)	16	0.03
Korean (27)	30	0.06
Laotian (0)	3	0.01
Malaysian (2)	2	<0.01
Pakistani (25)	35	0.07
Sri Lankan (1)	1	<0.01
Taiwanese (1)	1	<0.01
Thai (1)	2	<0.01
Vietnamese (60)	62	0.12
Hawaii Native/Pacific Islander (27)	170	0.33
Not Hispanic (2)	23	0.05
Hispanic (25)	147	0.29
Guamanian/Chamorro (1)	1	<0.01
Native Hawaiian (1)	9	0.02
Samoan (1)	3	0.01
White (25,541)	27,633	54.38
Not Hispanic (6,104)	6,300	12.40
Hispanic (19,437)	21,333	41.98

Phillipsburg

Place Type: Town
County: Warren
Population: 14,950†

Ancestry‡	Population	%
Albanian (0)	55	0.36
American (1,126)	1,126	7.41
Arab (52)	59	0.39
Lebanese (7)	7	0.05
Moroccan (21)	21	0.14
Syrian (24)	31	0.20
Austrian (0)	47	0.31
Brazilian (57)	57	0.38
British (17)	30	0.20
Canadian (19)	94	0.62
Croatian (0)	10	0.07
Czech (0)	31	0.20
Danish (0)	26	0.17
Dutch (132)	616	4.05
Eastern European (75)	75	0.49
English (253)	1,328	8.74
European (52)	52	0.34
Finnish (0)	37	0.24
French, ex. Basque (27)	302	1.99
French Canadian (16)	49	0.32
German (1,082)	3,697	24.33
Greek (0)	67	0.44
Hungarian (122)	499	3.28
Irish (670)	2,961	19.48
Italian (1,187)	2,958	19.46
Lithuanian (25)	60	0.39
Maltese (15)	15	0.10
Norwegian (0)	26	0.17
Pennsylvania German (121)	232	1.53
Polish (316)	837	5.51
Portuguese (88)	100	0.66
Romanian (0)	38	0.25
Russian (23)	57	0.38
Scandinavian (0)	17	0.11
Scotch-Irish (77)	84	0.55
Scottish (13)	225	1.48
Slavic (7)	7	0.05
Slovak (18)	37	0.24
Swedish (0)	30	0.20
Swiss (7)	28	0.18
Turkish (0)	27	0.18
Ukrainian (54)	131	0.86
Welsh (35)	185	1.22
West Indian, ex. Hispanic (206)	258	1.70
Haitian (29)	29	0.19
Jamaican (170)	179	1.18
West Indian (7)	50	0.33
Yugoslavian (11)	61	0.40

Hispanic Origin	Population	%
Hispanic or Latino (of any race)	1,767	11.82
Central American, ex. Mexican	263	1.76
Costa Rican	43	0.29
Guatemalan	50	0.33
Honduran	69	0.46
Nicaraguan	28	0.19
Panamanian	2	0.01
Salvadoran	71	0.47
Cuban	79	0.53
Dominican Republic	56	0.37
Mexican	320	2.14
Puerto Rican	665	4.45
South American	244	1.63
Argentinean	7	0.05
Bolivian	1	0.01
Chilean	4	0.03
Colombian	80	0.54
Ecuadorian	39	0.26
Paraguayan	8	0.05
Peruvian	94	0.63
Uruguayan	8	0.05
Venezuelan	2	0.01
Other South American	1	0.01
Other Hispanic or Latino	140	0.94

Race*	Population	%
African-American/Black (1,120)	1,415	9.46
Not Hispanic (1,037)	1,273	8.52
Hispanic (83)	142	0.95
American Indian/Alaska Native (26)	135	0.90
Not Hispanic (16)	100	0.67
Hispanic (10)	35	0.23
Apache (1)	1	0.01
Blackfeet (1)	10	0.07
Cherokee (1)	17	0.11
Chippewa (0)	4	0.03
Cree (0)	3	0.02
Delaware (0)	7	0.05
Iroquois (4)	14	0.09
Lumbee (0)	1	0.01
Shoshone (0)	1	0.01
South American Ind. (1)	7	0.05
Asian (228)	279	1.87
Not Hispanic (222)	265	1.77
Hispanic (6)	14	0.09
Burmese (4)	4	0.03
Chinese, ex. Taiwanese (42)	46	0.31
Filipino (30)	42	0.28
Indian (84)	94	0.63
Indonesian (6)	11	0.07
Japanese (9)	17	0.11
Korean (6)	13	0.09
Laotian (14)	14	0.09
Pakistani (5)	13	0.09
Sri Lankan (3)	3	0.02
Taiwanese (1)	1	0.01
Thai (3)	3	0.02
Vietnamese (8)	11	0.07
Hawaii Native/Pacific Islander (8)	29	0.19
Not Hispanic (8)	20	0.13
Hispanic (0)	9	0.06
Guamanian/Chamorro (2)	2	0.01
Marshallese (5)	5	0.03
Native Hawaiian (1)	5	0.03
Samoan (0)	1	0.01
White (12,475)	12,923	86.44
Not Hispanic (11,555)	11,857	79.31
Hispanic (920)	1,066	7.13

Pine Hill

Place Type: Borough
County: Camden
Population: 10,233†

Ancestry‡	Population	%
African, Sub-Saharan (59)	59	0.57
African (51)	51	0.49
Other Sub-Saharan African (8)	8	0.08
American (235)	235	2.27
Arab (9)	49	0.47
Lebanese (9)	49	0.47
Armenian (8)	8	0.08
British (9)	45	0.43
Croatian (0)	9	0.09
Czech (11)	43	0.42
Dutch (24)	131	1.27
English (153)	1,112	10.74
European (56)	56	0.54
French, ex. Basque (0)	262	2.53
French Canadian (8)	36	0.35
German (503)	2,460	23.76
Greek (14)	25	0.24
Hungarian (26)	63	0.61
Irish (735)	2,667	25.76
Italian (522)	1,798	17.37
Norwegian (19)	37	0.36
Polish (65)	549	5.30
Portuguese (9)	9	0.09
Russian (0)	35	0.34
Scotch-Irish (94)	220	2.12
Scottish (50)	280	2.70
Slavic (13)	13	0.13
Slovak (21)	21	0.20
Swedish (0)	24	0.23
Ukrainian (14)	56	0.54
Welsh (0)	130	1.26
West Indian, ex. Hispanic (23)	66	0.64
Haitian (15)	31	0.30
Jamaican (8)	35	0.34

Hispanic Origin	Population	%
Hispanic or Latino (of any race)	690	6.74
Central American, ex. Mexican	20	0.20
Costa Rican	4	0.04
Guatemalan	2	0.02
Nicaraguan	8	0.08
Panamanian	1	0.01
Salvadoran	5	0.05
Cuban	16	0.16
Dominican Republic	16	0.16
Mexican	85	0.83
Puerto Rican	500	4.89
South American	21	0.21
Argentinean	1	0.01
Chilean	2	0.02
Colombian	11	0.11
Ecuadorian	4	0.04
Peruvian	3	0.03
Other Hispanic or Latino	32	0.31

Race*	Population	%
African-American/Black (2,463)	2,698	26.37
Not Hispanic (2,362)	2,552	24.94
Hispanic (101)	146	1.43
American Indian/Alaska Native (27)	110	1.07
Not Hispanic (26)	96	0.94
Hispanic (1)	14	0.14
Apache (1)	3	0.03
Blackfeet (2)	10	0.10
Cherokee (5)	30	0.29
Cheyenne (0)	2	0.02
Comanche (0)	1	0.01
Delaware (3)	4	0.04
Iroquois (1)	2	0.02
Shoshone (0)	2	0.02
Sioux (0)	2	0.02
Asian (217)	277	2.71
Not Hispanic (213)	263	2.57
Hispanic (4)	14	0.14
Bangladeshi (8)	8	0.08
Chinese, ex. Taiwanese (36)	42	0.41
Filipino (81)	112	1.09
Indian (28)	45	0.44
Japanese (2)	10	0.10

*Notes: † The Census 2010 population figure is used to calculate the percentages in the Hispanic Origin and Race categories. Ancestry percentages are based on the 2006-2010 American Community Survey population (not shown); ‡ Numbers in parentheses indicate the number of people reporting a single ancestry; * Numbers in parentheses indicate the number of persons reporting this race alone, not in combination with any other race; Please refer to the Explanation of Data for more information.*

	Population	%
Korean (21)	30	0.29
Pakistani (2)	2	0.02
Sri Lankan (3)	3	0.03
Taiwanese (2)	2	0.02
Thai (6)	6	0.06
Vietnamese (16)	24	0.23
Hawaii Native/Pacific Islander (5)	29	0.28
Not Hispanic (5)	25	0.24
Hispanic (0)	4	0.04
Native Hawaiian (2)	19	0.19
Samoan (1)	3	0.03
White (6,904)	7,201	70.37
Not Hispanic (6,653)	6,883	67.26
Hispanic (251)	318	3.11

Pine Lake Park

Place Type: CDP
County: Ocean
Population: 8,707†

Ancestry‡	Population	%
African, Sub-Saharan (0)	7	0.09
African (0)	7	0.09
American (297)	297	3.65
Austrian (0)	13	0.16
Canadian (20)	41	0.50
Czech (0)	11	0.14
Danish (0)	19	0.23
Dutch (19)	106	1.30
English (55)	292	3.59
European (60)	60	0.74
French, ex. Basque (33)	145	1.78
French Canadian (0)	11	0.14
German (308)	1,581	19.43
Greek (14)	14	0.17
Hungarian (129)	213	2.62
Irish (385)	2,007	24.66
Italian (989)	2,667	32.77
Lithuanian (13)	39	0.48
Northern European (56)	66	0.81
Norwegian (41)	108	1.33
Pennsylvania German (42)	61	0.75
Polish (314)	1,099	13.50
Portuguese (10)	42	0.52
Russian (44)	188	2.31
Scotch-Irish (16)	65	0.80
Scottish (43)	141	1.73
Slovak (0)	23	0.28
Swedish (13)	124	1.52
Turkish (31)	31	0.38
Ukrainian (23)	50	0.61
Welsh (0)	22	0.27
West Indian, ex. Hispanic (54)	136	1.67
Bahamian (0)	12	0.15
Haitian (31)	81	1.00
West Indian (23)	43	0.53
Yugoslavian (0)	22	0.27

Hispanic Origin	Population	%
Hispanic or Latino (of any race)	810	9.30
Central American, ex. Mexican	35	0.40
Costa Rican	15	0.17
Guatemalan	4	0.05
Honduran	3	0.03
Nicaraguan	5	0.06
Panamanian	1	0.01
Salvadoran	3	0.03
Other Central American	4	0.05
Cuban	31	0.36
Dominican Republic	31	0.36
Mexican	102	1.17
Puerto Rican	420	4.82
South American	124	1.42
Argentinean	8	0.09
Bolivian	2	0.02
Chilean	3	0.03
Colombian	32	0.37
Ecuadorian	50	0.57
Peruvian	26	0.30
Uruguayan	2	0.02
Other South American	1	0.01
Other Hispanic or Latino	67	0.77

Race*	Population	%
African-American/Black (478)	557	6.40
Not Hispanic (453)	514	5.90
Hispanic (25)	43	0.49
American Indian/Alaska Native (10)	46	0.53
Not Hispanic (9)	39	0.45
Hispanic (1)	7	0.08
Apache (0)	1	0.01
Cherokee (0)	5	0.06
Colville (1)	1	0.01
Inupiat *(Alaska Native)* (1)	1	0.01
Iroquois (0)	2	0.02
Potawatomi (1)	1	0.01
Asian (356)	410	4.71
Not Hispanic (354)	405	4.65
Hispanic (2)	5	0.06
Chinese, ex. Taiwanese (31)	32	0.37
Filipino (222)	249	2.86
Indian (35)	38	0.44
Japanese (5)	9	0.10
Korean (13)	22	0.25
Laotian (6)	7	0.08
Pakistani (6)	6	0.07
Thai (9)	11	0.13
Vietnamese (17)	19	0.22
Hawaii Native/Pacific Islander (4)	15	0.17
Not Hispanic (4)	15	0.17
Guamanian/Chamorro (0)	1	0.01
Native Hawaiian (4)	5	0.06
Samoan (0)	3	0.03
White (7,450)	7,600	87.29
Not Hispanic (6,930)	7,044	80.90
Hispanic (520)	556	6.39

Piscataway

Place Type: Township
County: Middlesex
Population: 56,044†

Ancestry‡	Population	%
African, Sub-Saharan (722)	798	1.45
African (396)	434	0.79
Cape Verdean (40)	40	0.07
Ghanaian (108)	108	0.20
Nigerian (10)	48	0.09
Other Sub-Saharan African (168)	168	0.31
American (1,615)	1,615	2.94
Arab (396)	520	0.95
Arab (96)	96	0.17
Egyptian (170)	206	0.37
Iraqi (18)	18	0.03
Lebanese (38)	72	0.13
Moroccan (64)	88	0.16
Syrian (0)	30	0.05
Other Arab (10)	10	0.02
Austrian (0)	131	0.24
Basque (7)	7	0.01
Belgian (0)	11	0.02
Brazilian (76)	94	0.17
British (26)	26	0.05
Canadian (33)	76	0.14
Croatian (0)	6	0.01
Czech (0)	167	0.30
Czechoslovakian (11)	40	0.07
Danish (34)	130	0.24
Dutch (30)	241	0.44
Eastern European (0)	33	0.06
English (242)	1,619	2.94
Estonian (13)	13	0.02
European (141)	156	0.28
Finnish (0)	11	0.02
French, ex. Basque (8)	317	0.58
French Canadian (20)	199	0.36
German (830)	4,135	7.52
Greek (171)	294	0.53
Guyanese (158)	169	0.31
Hungarian (133)	874	1.59
Icelander (0)	28	0.05
Iranian (11)	11	0.02
Irish (759)	3,711	6.75
Italian (2,216)	4,834	8.79
Latvian (6)	6	0.01
Lithuanian (20)	83	0.15
Northern European (19)	19	0.03
Norwegian (28)	203	0.37
Polish (1,052)	2,767	5.03
Portuguese (19)	55	0.10
Romanian (15)	15	0.03
Russian (371)	689	1.25
Scandinavian (0)	6	0.01
Scotch-Irish (74)	246	0.45
Scottish (39)	197	0.36
Serbian (0)	11	0.02
Slavic (28)	56	0.10
Slovak (77)	169	0.31
Slovene (6)	6	0.01
Swedish (40)	310	0.56
Swiss (13)	45	0.08
Turkish (20)	76	0.14
Ukrainian (308)	455	0.83
Welsh (30)	134	0.24
West Indian, ex. Hispanic (1,164)	1,333	2.42
Barbadian (63)	63	0.11
British West Indian (9)	9	0.02
Haitian (450)	488	0.89
Jamaican (378)	422	0.77
Trinidadian/Tobagonian (23)	41	0.07
West Indian (241)	310	0.56
Yugoslavian (0)	36	0.07

Hispanic Origin	Population	%
Hispanic or Latino (of any race)	6,289	11.22
Central American, ex. Mexican	1,025	1.83
Costa Rican	135	0.24
Guatemalan	243	0.43
Honduran	80	0.14
Nicaraguan	69	0.12
Panamanian	81	0.14
Salvadoran	393	0.70
Other Central American	24	0.04
Cuban	265	0.47
Dominican Republic	499	0.89
Mexican	337	0.60
Puerto Rican	1,661	2.96
South American	1,864	3.33
Argentinean	58	0.10
Bolivian	5	0.01
Chilean	39	0.07
Colombian	933	1.66
Ecuadorian	352	0.63
Paraguayan	3	0.01
Peruvian	408	0.73
Uruguayan	27	0.05
Venezuelan	32	0.06
Other South American	7	0.01
Other Hispanic or Latino	638	1.14

Race*	Population	%
African-American/Black (11,596)	12,312	21.97
Not Hispanic (11,053)	11,583	20.67
Hispanic (543)	729	1.30
American Indian/Alaska Native (173)	487	0.87
Not Hispanic (100)	358	0.64
Hispanic (73)	129	0.23
Apache (0)	1	<0.01
Blackfeet (0)	18	0.03
Central American Ind. (12)	16	0.03
Cherokee (4)	39	0.07
Chippewa (0)	1	<0.01
Choctaw (0)	6	0.01
Delaware (2)	9	0.02
Iroquois (3)	7	0.01
Mexican American Ind. (10)	13	0.02
Sioux (2)	3	0.01
South American Ind. (8)	17	0.03

*Notes: † The Census 2010 population figure is used to calculate the percentages in the Hispanic Origin and Race categories. Ancestry percentages are based on the 2006-2010 American Community Survey population (not shown); ‡ Numbers in parentheses indicate the number of people reporting a single ancestry; * Numbers in parentheses indicate the number of persons reporting this race alone, not in combination with any other race; Please refer to the Explanation of Data for more information.*

SECTION TWO

Spanish American Ind. (1)	1	<0.01
Asian (18,744)	19,733	35.21
Not Hispanic (18,654)	19,583	34.94
Hispanic (90)	150	0.27
Bangladeshi (120)	135	0.24
Burmese (23)	29	0.05
Cambodian (4)	7	0.01
Chinese, ex. Taiwanese (2,252)	2,482	4.43
Filipino (2,377)	2,585	4.61
Hmong (0)	4	0.01
Indian (10,662)	11,189	19.96
Indonesian (39)	46	0.08
Japanese (61)	101	0.18
Korean (956)	996	1.78
Laotian (4)	8	0.01
Malaysian (1)	4	0.01
Nepalese (22)	23	0.04
Pakistani (821)	920	1.64
Sri Lankan (80)	98	0.17
Taiwanese (209)	259	0.46
Thai (18)	27	0.05
Vietnamese (682)	726	1.30
Hawaii Native/Pacific Islander (13)	100	0.18
Not Hispanic (8)	77	0.14
Hispanic (5)	23	0.04
Guamanian/Chamorro (6)	9	0.02
Native Hawaiian (4)	16	0.03
Samoan (0)	9	0.02
White (21,554)	22,716	40.53
Not Hispanic (18,271)	19,049	33.99
Hispanic (3,283)	3,667	6.54

Pitman

Place Type: Borough
County: Gloucester
Population: 9,011†

Ancestry‡	Population	%
American (330)	330	3.60
Arab (19)	19	0.21
Egyptian (19)	19	0.21
Austrian (9)	59	0.64
British (84)	95	1.04
Czech (7)	58	0.63
Czechoslovakian (0)	17	0.19
Danish (14)	26	0.28
Dutch (34)	159	1.74
English (283)	1,499	16.38
Estonian (11)	11	0.12
European (36)	36	0.39
Finnish (0)	29	0.32
French, ex. Basque (78)	371	4.05
French Canadian (0)	7	0.08
German (770)	3,102	33.89
Guyanese (5)	5	0.05
Hungarian (0)	71	0.78
Irish (825)	2,865	31.30
Israeli (12)	12	0.13
Italian (414)	1,541	16.83
Lithuanian (0)	53	0.58
Northern European (93)	93	1.02
Norwegian (64)	75	0.82
Pennsylvania German (62)	62	0.68
Polish (241)	724	7.91
Portuguese (0)	12	0.13
Romanian (11)	11	0.12
Russian (29)	55	0.60
Scandinavian (23)	23	0.25
Scotch-Irish (62)	191	2.09
Scottish (40)	247	2.70
Slovak (0)	22	0.24
Swedish (27)	106	1.16
Swiss (10)	39	0.43
Turkish (11)	11	0.12
Ukrainian (9)	95	1.04
Welsh (11)	146	1.59

Hispanic Origin	Population	%
Hispanic or Latino (of any race)	222	2.46
Central American, ex. Mexican	7	0.08
Guatemalan	2	0.02
Honduran	3	0.03
Salvadoran	2	0.02
Cuban	9	0.10
Dominican Republic	1	0.01
Mexican	48	0.53
Puerto Rican	84	0.93
South American	25	0.28
Argentinean	11	0.12
Chilean	2	0.02
Colombian	6	0.07
Paraguayan	4	0.04
Peruvian	1	0.01
Venezuelan	1	0.01
Other Hispanic or Latino	48	0.53

Race*	Population	%
African-American/Black (103)	146	1.62
Not Hispanic (100)	137	1.52
Hispanic (3)	9	0.10
American Indian/Alaska Native (8)	35	0.39
Not Hispanic (7)	31	0.34
Hispanic (1)	4	0.04
Arapaho (1)	1	0.01
Blackfeet (1)	3	0.03
Cherokee (1)	9	0.10
Choctaw (0)	5	0.06
Delaware (0)	1	0.01
Asian (56)	101	1.12
Not Hispanic (56)	99	1.10
Hispanic (0)	2	0.02
Chinese, ex. Taiwanese (9)	16	0.18
Filipino (10)	23	0.26
Indian (7)	10	0.11
Indonesian (2)	2	0.02
Japanese (2)	9	0.10
Korean (13)	26	0.29
Pakistani (6)	9	0.10
Thai (3)	4	0.04
Vietnamese (2)	3	0.03
Hawaii Native/Pacific Islander (3)	7	0.08
Not Hispanic (3)	4	0.04
Hispanic (0)	3	0.03
Guamanian/Chamorro (3)	3	0.03
Samoan (0)	1	0.01
White (8,658)	8,773	97.36
Not Hispanic (8,505)	8,600	95.44
Hispanic (153)	173	1.92

Pittsgrove

Place Type: Township
County: Salem
Population: 9,393†

Ancestry‡	Population	%
American (363)	363	3.89
Basque (0)	14	0.15
Belgian (0)	9	0.10
British (11)	24	0.26
Canadian (13)	25	0.27
Czech (0)	13	0.14
Dutch (0)	115	1.23
Eastern European (13)	13	0.14
English (358)	1,222	13.09
European (67)	106	1.14
French, ex. Basque (22)	191	2.05
French Canadian (20)	61	0.65
German (681)	2,623	28.09
Greek (0)	39	0.42
Hungarian (22)	44	0.47
Irish (477)	2,146	22.98
Italian (1,016)	2,112	22.62
Lithuanian (30)	30	0.32
Northern European (10)	10	0.11
Norwegian (6)	36	0.39
Pennsylvania German (25)	44	0.47
Polish (192)	512	5.48
Portuguese (0)	46	0.49
Romanian (15)	15	0.16
Russian (84)	134	1.44
Scandinavian (0)	47	0.50
Scotch-Irish (29)	161	1.72
Scottish (0)	110	1.18
Swedish (13)	56	0.60
Swiss (0)	81	0.87
Ukrainian (40)	98	1.05
Welsh (4)	31	0.33
West Indian, ex. Hispanic (55)	55	0.59
Jamaican (55)	55	0.59

Hispanic Origin	Population	%
Hispanic or Latino (of any race)	451	4.80
Central American, ex. Mexican	9	0.10
Guatemalan	3	0.03
Nicaraguan	1	0.01
Panamanian	2	0.02
Salvadoran	3	0.03
Cuban	16	0.17
Dominican Republic	6	0.06
Mexican	83	0.88
Puerto Rican	281	2.99
South American	17	0.18
Argentinean	1	0.01
Chilean	4	0.04
Colombian	2	0.02
Ecuadorian	3	0.03
Peruvian	5	0.05
Venezuelan	2	0.02
Other Hispanic or Latino	39	0.42

Race*	Population	%
African-American/Black (655)	736	7.84
Not Hispanic (638)	705	7.51
Hispanic (17)	31	0.33
American Indian/Alaska Native (39)	115	1.22
Not Hispanic (33)	103	1.10
Hispanic (6)	12	0.13
Apache (1)	1	0.01
Blackfeet (1)	5	0.05
Cherokee (0)	17	0.18
Comanche (0)	1	0.01
Delaware (13)	27	0.29
Iroquois (0)	4	0.04
Mexican American Ind. (3)	3	0.03
Navajo (1)	1	0.01
Potawatomi (1)	1	0.01
Sioux (0)	3	0.03
Spanish American Ind. (0)	1	0.01
Asian (88)	119	1.27
Not Hispanic (88)	119	1.27
Chinese, ex. Taiwanese (6)	9	0.10
Filipino (10)	20	0.21
Indian (33)	33	0.35
Japanese (19)	32	0.34
Korean (12)	17	0.18
Pakistani (2)	2	0.02
Taiwanese (4)	4	0.04
Thai (1)	1	0.01
Vietnamese (1)	1	0.01
Hawaii Native/Pacific Islander (1)	6	0.06
Not Hispanic (1)	6	0.06
Guamanian/Chamorro (0)	1	0.01
Native Hawaiian (1)	3	0.03
White (8,282)	8,455	90.01
Not Hispanic (8,019)	8,161	86.88
Hispanic (263)	294	3.13

Plainfield

Place Type: City
County: Union
Population: 49,808†

Ancestry‡	Population	%
African, Sub-Saharan (747)	886	1.81
African (578)	717	1.46
Ghanaian (44)	44	0.09
Nigerian (51)	51	0.10

*Notes: † The Census 2010 population figure is used to calculate the percentages in the Hispanic Origin and Race categories. Ancestry percentages are based on the 2006-2010 American Community Survey population (not shown); ‡ Numbers in parentheses indicate the number of people reporting a single ancestry; * Numbers in parentheses indicate the number of persons reporting this race alone, not in combination with any other race; Please refer to the Explanation of Data for more information.*

Other Sub-Saharan African (74)	74	0.15
Albanian (17)	67	0.14
American (1,368)	1,368	2.79
Arab (165)	215	0.44
Egyptian (72)	72	0.15
Lebanese (60)	110	0.22
Syrian (33)	33	0.07
Austrian (0)	50	0.10
Belgian (10)	32	0.07
Brazilian (17)	17	0.03
British (25)	85	0.17
Canadian (61)	117	0.24
Czech (0)	12	0.02
Danish (0)	14	0.03
Dutch (0)	52	0.11
Eastern European (27)	27	0.06
English (168)	457	0.93
European (52)	67	0.14
French, ex. Basque (13)	104	0.21
French Canadian (23)	32	0.07
German (77)	767	1.56
German Russian (13)	13	0.03
Greek (17)	17	0.03
Guyanese (287)	321	0.65
Hungarian (123)	179	0.36
Irish (162)	551	1.12
Italian (464)	895	1.82
Lithuanian (0)	15	0.03
Polish (113)	224	0.46
Portuguese (0)	62	0.13
Russian (49)	76	0.15
Scotch-Irish (27)	141	0.29
Scottish (8)	119	0.24
Slavic (0)	13	0.03
Slovak (35)	48	0.10
Swedish (39)	107	0.22
Swiss (11)	23	0.05
Ukrainian (95)	164	0.33
Welsh (0)	11	0.02
West Indian, ex. Hispanic (2,042)	2,945	6.00
Barbadian (109)	174	0.35
Bermudan (42)	42	0.09
Haitian (197)	431	0.88
Jamaican (1,299)	1,690	3.45
Trinidadian/Tobagonian (132)	287	0.59
West Indian (263)	321	0.65

Hispanic Origin	Population	%
Hispanic or Latino (of any race)	20,105	40.37
Central American, ex. Mexican	9,822	19.72
Costa Rican	128	0.26
Guatemalan	4,302	8.64
Honduran	1,493	3.00
Nicaraguan	78	0.16
Panamanian	91	0.18
Salvadoran	3,684	7.40
Other Central American	46	0.09
Cuban	168	0.34
Dominican Republic	1,601	3.21
Mexican	1,568	3.15
Puerto Rican	1,822	3.66
South American	3,400	6.83
Argentinean	18	0.04
Bolivian	11	0.02
Chilean	18	0.04
Colombian	748	1.50
Ecuadorian	2,061	4.14
Paraguayan	15	0.03
Peruvian	450	0.90
Uruguayan	26	0.05
Venezuelan	47	0.09
Other South American	6	0.01
Other Hispanic or Latino	1,724	3.46

Race*	Population	%
African-American/Black (25,006)	25,952	52.10
Not Hispanic (24,069)	24,695	49.58
Hispanic (937)	1,257	2.52
American Indian/Alaska Native (455)	943	1.89
Not Hispanic (97)	371	0.74
Hispanic (358)	572	1.15
Apache (1)	6	0.01
Blackfeet (2)	23	0.05
Canadian/French Am. Ind. (1)	1	<0.01
Central American Ind. (23)	40	0.08
Cherokee (7)	84	0.17
Chickasaw (1)	1	<0.01
Choctaw (1)	4	0.01
Creek (0)	1	<0.01
Crow (0)	1	<0.01
Delaware (1)	6	0.01
Iroquois (0)	5	0.01
Lumbee (2)	2	<0.01
Mexican American Ind. (24)	31	0.06
Pima (0)	1	<0.01
Pueblo (5)	14	0.03
Seminole (0)	4	0.01
Sioux (1)	3	0.01
South American Ind. (10)	29	0.06
Spanish American Ind. (16)	33	0.07
Ute (0)	1	<0.01
Yuman (0)	4	0.01
Asian (474)	683	1.37
Not Hispanic (439)	595	1.19
Hispanic (35)	88	0.18
Bangladeshi (5)	5	0.01
Burmese (0)	1	<0.01
Chinese, ex. Taiwanese (53)	97	0.19
Filipino (99)	133	0.27
Indian (183)	248	0.50
Indonesian (3)	4	0.01
Japanese (8)	20	0.04
Korean (12)	19	0.04
Malaysian (1)	1	<0.01
Nepalese (4)	4	0.01
Pakistani (20)	24	0.05
Taiwanese (5)	6	0.01
Thai (4)	4	0.01
Vietnamese (44)	54	0.11
Hawaii Native/Pacific Islander (26)	109	0.22
Not Hispanic (18)	54	0.11
Hispanic (8)	55	0.11
Guamanian/Chamorro (16)	25	0.05
Native Hawaiian (1)	14	0.03
Samoan (0)	7	0.01
White (11,724)	13,180	26.46
Not Hispanic (4,139)	4,556	9.15
Hispanic (7,585)	8,624	17.31

Plainsboro

Place Type: Township
County: Middlesex
Population: 22,999†

Ancestry‡	Population	%
African, Sub-Saharan (398)	434	1.93
African (34)	58	0.26
Ethiopian (13)	13	0.06
Ghanaian (58)	58	0.26
Nigerian (279)	279	1.24
Senegalese (14)	14	0.06
Other Sub-Saharan African (0)	12	0.05
Albanian (15)	15	0.07
American (161)	161	0.72
Arab (480)	605	2.69
Arab (84)	157	0.70
Egyptian (17)	17	0.08
Lebanese (103)	155	0.69
Syrian (233)	233	1.04
Other Arab (43)	43	0.19
Armenian (49)	49	0.22
Austrian (27)	186	0.83
Brazilian (53)	53	0.24
British (48)	80	0.36
Czech (6)	20	0.09
Danish (14)	98	0.44
Dutch (63)	103	0.46
Eastern European (164)	164	0.73
English (322)	1,106	4.92
Estonian (9)	9	0.04
European (101)	135	0.60
Finnish (85)	85	0.38
French, ex. Basque (144)	437	1.94
French Canadian (16)	102	0.45
German (429)	1,916	8.52
Greek (23)	122	0.54
Hungarian (43)	237	1.05
Iranian (0)	40	0.18
Irish (663)	2,424	10.77
Israeli (11)	11	0.05
Italian (1,010)	2,149	9.55
Latvian (14)	14	0.06
Lithuanian (60)	146	0.65
Macedonian (103)	103	0.46
Norwegian (0)	77	0.34
Pennsylvania German (16)	32	0.14
Polish (213)	760	3.38
Portuguese (0)	88	0.39
Romanian (91)	103	0.46
Russian (251)	484	2.15
Scandinavian (15)	30	0.13
Scotch-Irish (35)	196	0.87
Scottish (47)	134	0.60
Slovak (30)	96	0.43
Slovene (18)	18	0.08
Swedish (19)	163	0.72
Swiss (20)	56	0.25
Turkish (72)	72	0.32
Ukrainian (87)	226	1.00
Welsh (21)	71	0.32
West Indian, ex. Hispanic (205)	295	1.31
Haitian (27)	72	0.32
Jamaican (145)	190	0.84
West Indian (33)	33	0.15

Hispanic Origin	Population	%
Hispanic or Latino (of any race)	1,429	6.21
Central American, ex. Mexican	238	1.03
Costa Rican	16	0.07
Guatemalan	165	0.72
Honduran	15	0.07
Nicaraguan	8	0.03
Panamanian	25	0.11
Salvadoran	9	0.04
Cuban	95	0.41
Dominican Republic	77	0.33
Mexican	131	0.57
Puerto Rican	437	1.90
South American	326	1.42
Argentinean	31	0.13
Bolivian	7	0.03
Chilean	41	0.18
Colombian	112	0.49
Ecuadorian	47	0.20
Paraguayan	1	<0.01
Peruvian	50	0.22
Uruguayan	6	0.03
Venezuelan	29	0.13
Other South American	2	0.01
Other Hispanic or Latino	125	0.54

Race*	Population	%
African-American/Black (1,847)	2,026	8.81
Not Hispanic (1,749)	1,889	8.21
Hispanic (98)	137	0.60
American Indian/Alaska Native (69)	143	0.62
Not Hispanic (52)	108	0.47
Hispanic (17)	35	0.15
Blackfeet (0)	2	0.01
Central American Ind. (3)	3	0.01
Cherokee (5)	17	0.07
Chippewa (1)	5	0.02
Choctaw (0)	4	0.02
Comanche (0)	1	<0.01
Iroquois (0)	2	0.01
Kiowa (0)	1	<0.01
Mexican American Ind. (7)	7	0.03
Navajo (1)	2	0.01
South American Ind. (3)	5	0.02

SECTION TWO

*Notes: † The Census 2010 population figure is used to calculate the percentages in the Hispanic Origin and Race categories. Ancestry percentages are based on the 2006-2010 American Community Survey population (not shown); ‡ Numbers in parentheses indicate the number of people reporting a single ancestry; * Numbers in parentheses indicate the number of persons reporting this race alone, not in combination with any other race; Please refer to the Explanation of Data for more information.*

Spanish American Ind. (1)	2	0.01
Yuman (0)	1	<0.01
Asian (10,630)	11,001	47.83
Not Hispanic (10,608)	10,949	47.61
Hispanic (22)	52	0.23
Bangladeshi (59)	60	0.26
Burmese (4)	4	0.02
Chinese, ex. Taiwanese (2,435)	2,529	11.00
Filipino (294)	340	1.48
Indian (6,818)	6,957	30.25
Indonesian (9)	9	0.04
Japanese (113)	142	0.62
Korean (385)	408	1.77
Laotian (1)	1	<0.01
Malaysian (10)	13	0.06
Nepalese (7)	9	0.04
Pakistani (181)	192	0.83
Sri Lankan (49)	50	0.22
Taiwanese (121)	136	0.59
Thai (13)	15	0.07
Vietnamese (36)	48	0.21
Hawaii Native/Pacific Islander (4)	34	0.15
Not Hispanic (3)	23	0.10
Hispanic (1)	11	0.05
Guamanian/Chamorro (0)	3	0.01
Native Hawaiian (1)	13	0.06
Samoan (2)	4	0.02
White (9,445)	9,803	42.62
Not Hispanic (8,615)	8,902	38.71
Hispanic (830)	901	3.92

Pleasantville

Place Type: City
County: Atlantic
Population: 20,249†

Ancestry‡	Population	%
African, Sub-Saharan (362)	406	2.01
African (314)	314	1.55
Liberian (0)	22	0.11
Nigerian (48)	70	0.35
Albanian (41)	41	0.20
American (517)	517	2.56
Arab (7)	7	0.03
Palestinian (7)	7	0.03
Austrian (0)	21	0.10
British (0)	7	0.03
Canadian (0)	10	0.05
Dutch (25)	99	0.49
English (93)	457	2.26
French, ex. Basque (33)	109	0.54
German (192)	739	3.66
German Russian (0)	13	0.06
Greek (8)	8	0.04
Hungarian (0)	10	0.05
Irish (284)	903	4.47
Italian (300)	690	3.41
Norwegian (12)	43	0.21
Polish (116)	153	0.76
Russian (18)	51	0.25
Scandinavian (0)	23	0.11
Scotch-Irish (27)	87	0.43
Scottish (32)	71	0.35
Slovak (0)	15	0.07
Swedish (0)	39	0.19
Welsh (0)	22	0.11
West Indian, ex. Hispanic (1,212)	1,341	6.64
Bahamian (32)	98	0.48
Barbadian (10)	10	0.05
British West Indian (24)	24	0.12
Haitian (1,026)	1,026	5.08
Jamaican (29)	29	0.14
Trinidadian/Tobagonian (91)	91	0.45
West Indian (0)	63	0.31

Hispanic Origin	Population	%
Hispanic or Latino (of any race)	8,314	41.06
Central American, ex. Mexican	1,055	5.21
Costa Rican	8	0.04
Guatemalan	36	0.18
Honduran	598	2.95
Nicaraguan	45	0.22
Panamanian	12	0.06
Salvadoran	348	1.72
Other Central American	8	0.04
Cuban	107	0.53
Dominican Republic	1,461	7.22
Mexican	1,966	9.71
Puerto Rican	2,637	13.02
South American	612	3.02
Argentinean	10	0.05
Chilean	7	0.03
Colombian	328	1.62
Ecuadorian	76	0.38
Peruvian	174	0.86
Venezuelan	15	0.07
Other South American	2	0.01
Other Hispanic or Latino	476	2.35

Race*	Population	%
African-American/Black (9,303)	9,857	48.68
Not Hispanic (8,615)	8,924	44.07
Hispanic (688)	933	4.61
American Indian/Alaska Native (168)	334	1.65
Not Hispanic (48)	157	0.78
Hispanic (120)	177	0.87
Blackfeet (1)	4	0.02
Central American Ind. (6)	7	0.03
Cherokee (4)	39	0.19
Chippewa (1)	1	<0.01
Delaware (2)	9	0.04
Iroquois (5)	7	0.03
Lumbee (1)	1	<0.01
Mexican American Ind. (16)	20	0.10
Seminole (0)	5	0.02
Sioux (2)	3	0.01
South American Ind. (6)	13	0.06
Spanish American Ind. (11)	13	0.06
Yaqui (6)	6	0.03
Asian (490)	637	3.15
Not Hispanic (480)	585	2.89
Hispanic (10)	52	0.26
Bangladeshi (23)	24	0.12
Burmese (1)	1	<0.01
Chinese, ex. Taiwanese (59)	74	0.37
Filipino (88)	128	0.63
Hmong (0)	1	<0.01
Indian (94)	121	0.60
Japanese (10)	16	0.08
Korean (39)	48	0.24
Laotian (27)	38	0.19
Pakistani (23)	26	0.13
Taiwanese (0)	1	<0.01
Thai (10)	16	0.08
Vietnamese (94)	104	0.51
Hawaii Native/Pacific Islander (6)	40	0.20
Not Hispanic (2)	17	0.08
Hispanic (4)	23	0.11
Native Hawaiian (0)	5	0.02
Samoan (0)	5	0.02
White (4,926)	5,515	27.24
Not Hispanic (2,332)	2,575	12.72
Hispanic (2,594)	2,940	14.52

Plumsted

Place Type: Township
County: Ocean
Population: 8,421†

Ancestry‡	Population	%
American (293)	293	3.54
Arab (43)	43	0.52
Other Arab (43)	43	0.52
Austrian (16)	24	0.29
British (14)	14	0.17
Canadian (27)	27	0.33
Croatian (0)	14	0.17
Czech (0)	13	0.16
Czechoslovakian (0)	15	0.18
Danish (0)	17	0.21
Dutch (62)	173	2.09
English (158)	1,131	13.65
French, ex. Basque (31)	280	3.38
French Canadian (16)	54	0.65
German (591)	2,463	29.74
Greek (0)	14	0.17
Hungarian (70)	194	2.34
Irish (367)	2,107	25.44
Italian (888)	2,246	27.12
Lithuanian (0)	41	0.49
Norwegian (0)	13	0.16
Pennsylvania German (12)	12	0.14
Polish (134)	765	9.24
Portuguese (0)	92	1.11
Romanian (17)	17	0.21
Russian (27)	224	2.70
Scotch-Irish (9)	86	1.04
Scottish (58)	192	2.32
Slavic (16)	16	0.19
Slovak (0)	30	0.36
Swedish (13)	65	0.78
Ukrainian (0)	36	0.43
Welsh (0)	63	0.76
Yugoslavian (0)	13	0.16

Hispanic Origin	Population	%
Hispanic or Latino (of any race)	498	5.91
Central American, ex. Mexican	14	0.17
Costa Rican	9	0.11
Guatemalan	1	0.01
Honduran	3	0.04
Panamanian	1	0.01
Cuban	22	0.26
Dominican Republic	4	0.05
Mexican	198	2.35
Puerto Rican	190	2.26
South American	38	0.45
Argentinean	1	0.01
Chilean	3	0.04
Colombian	14	0.17
Ecuadorian	4	0.05
Peruvian	13	0.15
Venezuelan	3	0.04
Other Hispanic or Latino	32	0.38

Race*	Population	%
African-American/Black (152)	179	2.13
Not Hispanic (131)	152	1.81
Hispanic (21)	27	0.32
American Indian/Alaska Native (27)	85	1.01
Not Hispanic (19)	64	0.76
Hispanic (8)	21	0.25
Apache (1)	1	0.01
Blackfeet (0)	7	0.08
Canadian/French Am. Ind. (1)	1	0.01
Cherokee (7)	14	0.17
Chippewa (1)	1	0.01
Delaware (0)	5	0.06
Iroquois (1)	1	0.01
Navajo (0)	1	0.01
Paiute (0)	1	0.01
South American Ind. (1)	4	0.05
Asian (73)	109	1.29
Not Hispanic (73)	107	1.27
Hispanic (0)	2	0.02
Burmese (2)	2	0.02
Chinese, ex. Taiwanese (34)	36	0.43
Filipino (15)	23	0.27
Indian (4)	6	0.07
Japanese (5)	21	0.25
Korean (5)	7	0.08
Pakistani (3)	3	0.04
Thai (0)	2	0.02
Vietnamese (4)	6	0.07
Hawaii Native/Pacific Islander (2)	10	0.12
Not Hispanic (2)	10	0.12
Guamanian/Chamorro (1)	1	0.01
Native Hawaiian (0)	6	0.07

*Notes: † The Census 2010 population figure is used to calculate the percentages in the Hispanic Origin and Race categories. Ancestry percentages are based on the 2006-2010 American Community Survey population (not shown); ‡ Numbers in parentheses indicate the number of people reporting a single ancestry; * Numbers in parentheses indicate the number of persons reporting this race alone, not in combination with any other race; Please refer to the Explanation of Data for more information.*

Samoan (0)	2	0.02
White (7,932)	8,059	95.70
Not Hispanic (7,591)	7,686	91.27
Hispanic (341)	373	4.43

Point Pleasant

Place Type: Borough
County: Ocean
Population: 18,392†

Ancestry‡	Population	%
Albanian (0)	9	0.05
Alsatian (0)	13	0.07
American (840)	840	4.49
Arab (0)	30	0.16
Arab (0)	10	0.05
Lebanese (0)	11	0.06
Other Arab (0)	9	0.05
Armenian (0)	42	0.22
Austrian (35)	172	0.92
Brazilian (7)	69	0.37
British (24)	49	0.26
Bulgarian (13)	13	0.07
Canadian (7)	7	0.04
Czech (30)	214	1.14
Czechoslovakian (13)	126	0.67
Danish (0)	42	0.22
Dutch (191)	530	2.83
English (314)	2,207	11.80
Estonian (0)	16	0.09
European (25)	25	0.13
French, ex. Basque (35)	402	2.15
French Canadian (33)	106	0.57
German (687)	4,844	25.90
Greek (0)	153	0.82
Hungarian (154)	576	3.08
Icelander (0)	20	0.11
Irish (1,829)	6,824	36.48
Italian (2,071)	4,804	25.68
Latvian (12)	12	0.06
Lithuanian (15)	128	0.68
Luxemburger (0)	32	0.17
Norwegian (45)	329	1.76
Pennsylvania German (40)	40	0.21
Polish (458)	1,794	9.59
Portuguese (0)	90	0.48
Russian (153)	330	1.76
Scandinavian (14)	29	0.16
Scotch-Irish (142)	416	2.22
Scottish (155)	428	2.29
Slavic (9)	29	0.16
Slovak (42)	210	1.12
Slovene (0)	21	0.11
Swedish (0)	116	0.62
Swiss (0)	89	0.48
Ukrainian (73)	254	1.36
Welsh (32)	124	0.66
Yugoslavian (20)	20	0.11

Hispanic Origin	Population	%
Hispanic or Latino (of any race)	935	5.08
Central American, ex. Mexican	55	0.30
Costa Rican	6	0.03
Guatemalan	24	0.13
Honduran	14	0.08
Nicaraguan	3	0.02
Salvadoran	8	0.04
Cuban	44	0.24
Dominican Republic	16	0.09
Mexican	411	2.23
Puerto Rican	185	1.01
South American	115	0.63
Argentinean	5	0.03
Bolivian	4	0.02
Chilean	8	0.04
Colombian	27	0.15
Ecuadorian	38	0.21
Paraguayan	1	0.01
Peruvian	25	0.14
Uruguayan	3	0.02
Venezuelan	4	0.02
Other Hispanic or Latino	109	0.59

Race*	Population	%
African-American/Black (75)	109	0.59
Not Hispanic (56)	80	0.43
Hispanic (19)	29	0.16
American Indian/Alaska Native (24)	66	0.36
Not Hispanic (12)	45	0.24
Hispanic (12)	21	0.11
Apache (0)	1	0.01
Cherokee (1)	16	0.09
Cheyenne (2)	2	0.01
Choctaw (0)	2	0.01
Delaware (1)	1	0.01
Hopi (1)	1	0.01
Iroquois (6)	7	0.04
Mexican American Ind. (1)	3	0.02
Navajo (1)	1	0.01
Seminole (0)	4	0.02
Sioux (0)	2	0.01
South American Ind. (2)	5	0.03
Spanish American Ind. (0)	1	0.01
Asian (133)	189	1.03
Not Hispanic (129)	181	0.98
Hispanic (4)	8	0.04
Cambodian (1)	2	0.01
Chinese, ex. Taiwanese (53)	57	0.31
Filipino (18)	34	0.18
Indian (6)	12	0.07
Indonesian (4)	4	0.02
Japanese (2)	14	0.08
Korean (25)	36	0.20
Pakistani (8)	8	0.04
Taiwanese (1)	3	0.02
Thai (0)	2	0.01
Vietnamese (7)	7	0.04
Hawaii Native/Pacific Islander (6)	8	0.04
Not Hispanic (6)	7	0.04
Hispanic (0)	1	0.01
Native Hawaiian (1)	1	0.01
Samoan (3)	3	0.02
White (17,666)	17,843	97.02
Not Hispanic (17,133)	17,242	93.75
Hispanic (533)	601	3.27

Pompton Lakes

Place Type: Borough
County: Passaic
Population: 11,097†

Ancestry‡	Population	%
Albanian (54)	54	0.49
American (91)	91	0.83
Arab (180)	298	2.72
Arab (41)	41	0.37
Jordanian (123)	123	1.12
Syrian (16)	134	1.22
Armenian (16)	51	0.47
Austrian (60)	189	1.72
Belgian (0)	27	0.25
Brazilian (143)	195	1.78
Canadian (48)	48	0.44
Croatian (27)	54	0.49
Czech (67)	75	0.68
Czechoslovakian (0)	12	0.11
Dutch (210)	559	5.10
Eastern European (39)	39	0.36
English (27)	626	5.71
European (129)	139	1.27
French, ex. Basque (32)	277	2.53
French Canadian (0)	21	0.19
German (290)	1,718	15.67
Greek (143)	170	1.55
Guyanese (0)	11	0.10
Hungarian (65)	206	1.88
Irish (567)	2,433	22.19
Italian (1,237)	2,782	25.37
Lithuanian (0)	76	0.69
Macedonian (81)	81	0.74
Norwegian (0)	90	0.82
Polish (350)	938	8.55
Portuguese (14)	81	0.74
Romanian (0)	16	0.15
Russian (125)	220	2.01
Scotch-Irish (99)	147	1.34
Scottish (11)	142	1.29
Slavic (9)	40	0.36
Swedish (0)	95	0.87
Swiss (0)	29	0.26
Ukrainian (8)	110	1.00
Welsh (0)	17	0.16
West Indian, ex. Hispanic (0)	22	0.20
U.S. Virgin Islander (0)	22	0.20

Hispanic Origin	Population	%
Hispanic or Latino (of any race)	1,209	10.89
Central American, ex. Mexican	56	0.50
Costa Rican	15	0.14
Guatemalan	10	0.09
Honduran	9	0.08
Panamanian	7	0.06
Salvadoran	15	0.14
Cuban	63	0.57
Dominican Republic	59	0.53
Mexican	313	2.82
Puerto Rican	296	2.67
South American	329	2.96
Argentinean	18	0.16
Bolivian	1	0.01
Chilean	20	0.18
Colombian	116	1.05
Ecuadorian	53	0.48
Peruvian	106	0.96
Uruguayan	5	0.05
Venezuelan	10	0.09
Other Hispanic or Latino	93	0.84

Race*	Population	%
African-American/Black (157)	231	2.08
Not Hispanic (127)	177	1.60
Hispanic (30)	54	0.49
American Indian/Alaska Native (12)	56	0.50
Not Hispanic (6)	28	0.25
Hispanic (6)	28	0.25
Blackfeet (0)	4	0.04
Central American Ind. (1)	1	0.01
Cherokee (1)	7	0.06
Comanche (1)	1	0.01
Delaware (0)	5	0.05
Iroquois (2)	4	0.04
Mexican American Ind. (1)	6	0.05
South American Ind. (0)	2	0.02
Asian (598)	660	5.95
Not Hispanic (595)	643	5.79
Hispanic (3)	17	0.15
Bangladeshi (0)	3	0.03
Chinese, ex. Taiwanese (79)	91	0.82
Filipino (265)	281	2.53
Indian (166)	172	1.55
Indonesian (2)	2	0.02
Japanese (10)	21	0.19
Korean (44)	53	0.48
Pakistani (8)	9	0.08
Taiwanese (2)	2	0.02
Thai (5)	7	0.06
Vietnamese (8)	8	0.07
Hawaii Native/Pacific Islander (2)	3	0.03
Hispanic (2)	3	0.03
White (9,758)	9,919	89.38
Not Hispanic (9,019)	9,120	82.18
Hispanic (739)	799	7.20

Princeton Meadows

Place Type: CDP
County: Middlesex
Population: 13,834†

SECTION TWO

*Notes: † The Census 2010 population figure is used to calculate the percentages in the Hispanic Origin and Race categories. Ancestry percentages are based on the 2006-2010 American Community Survey population (not shown); ‡ Numbers in parentheses indicate the number of people reporting a single ancestry; * Numbers in parentheses indicate the number of persons reporting this race alone, not in combination with any other race; Please refer to the Explanation of Data for more information.*

Ancestry‡	Population	%
African, Sub-Saharan (371)	371	2.70
African (34)	34	0.25
Ghanaian (58)	58	0.42
Nigerian (279)	279	2.03
Albanian (15)	15	0.11
American (121)	121	0.88
Arab (370)	470	3.42
Arab (0)	73	0.53
Egyptian (17)	17	0.12
Lebanese (77)	104	0.76
Syrian (233)	233	1.70
Other Arab (43)	43	0.31
Armenian (49)	49	0.36
Austrian (0)	39	0.28
Brazilian (39)	39	0.28
British (12)	27	0.20
Czech (0)	14	0.10
Danish (14)	98	0.71
Dutch (0)	25	0.18
Eastern European (102)	102	0.74
English (201)	685	4.99
European (31)	31	0.23
French, ex. Basque (125)	300	2.18
French Canadian (16)	93	0.68
German (185)	1,076	7.83
Greek (15)	97	0.71
Hungarian (43)	188	1.37
Iranian (0)	40	0.29
Irish (274)	1,270	9.25
Israeli (11)	11	0.08
Italian (620)	1,313	9.56
Latvian (14)	14	0.10
Lithuanian (0)	18	0.13
Macedonian (103)	103	0.75
Norwegian (0)	50	0.36
Pennsylvania German (0)	16	0.12
Polish (81)	261	1.90
Portuguese (0)	58	0.42
Romanian (30)	42	0.31
Russian (127)	231	1.68
Scotch-Irish (17)	153	1.11
Scottish (19)	68	0.50
Slovak (20)	51	0.37
Swedish (19)	114	0.83
Swiss (0)	16	0.12
Turkish (22)	22	0.16
Ukrainian (68)	153	1.11
Welsh (12)	40	0.29
West Indian, ex. Hispanic (197)	287	2.09
Haitian (19)	64	0.47
Jamaican (145)	190	1.38
West Indian (33)	33	0.24

Hispanic Origin	Population	%
Hispanic or Latino (of any race)	1,059	7.66
Central American, ex. Mexican	209	1.51
Costa Rican	8	0.06
Guatemalan	155	1.12
Honduran	14	0.10
Nicaraguan	7	0.05
Panamanian	16	0.12
Salvadoran	9	0.07
Cuban	53	0.38
Dominican Republic	70	0.51
Mexican	91	0.66
Puerto Rican	327	2.36
South American	227	1.64
Argentinean	19	0.14
Bolivian	2	0.01
Chilean	21	0.15
Colombian	81	0.59
Ecuadorian	36	0.26
Paraguayan	1	0.01
Peruvian	41	0.30
Uruguayan	1	0.01
Venezuelan	23	0.17
Other South American	2	0.01
Other Hispanic or Latino	82	0.59

Race*	Population	%
African-American/Black (1,426)	1,547	11.18
Not Hispanic (1,342)	1,432	10.35
Hispanic (84)	115	0.83
American Indian/Alaska Native (48)	102	0.74
Not Hispanic (37)	75	0.54
Hispanic (11)	27	0.20
Blackfeet (0)	2	0.01
Central American Ind. (3)	3	0.02
Cherokee (1)	10	0.07
Chippewa (1)	4	0.03
Choctaw (0)	4	0.03
Comanche (0)	1	0.01
Iroquois (0)	2	0.01
Mexican American Ind. (7)	7	0.05
South American Ind. (0)	2	0.01
Spanish American Ind. (1)	2	0.01
Asian (6,343)	6,576	47.54
Not Hispanic (6,330)	6,540	47.27
Hispanic (13)	36	0.26
Bangladeshi (38)	39	0.28
Burmese (3)	3	0.02
Chinese, ex. Taiwanese (1,195)	1,257	9.09
Filipino (188)	224	1.62
Indian (4,352)	4,428	32.01
Indonesian (9)	9	0.07
Japanese (39)	53	0.38
Korean (209)	229	1.66
Laotian (1)	1	0.01
Malaysian (10)	13	0.09
Nepalese (6)	8	0.06
Pakistani (113)	123	0.89
Sri Lankan (36)	36	0.26
Taiwanese (53)	61	0.44
Thai (7)	8	0.06
Vietnamese (23)	34	0.25
Hawaii Native/Pacific Islander (3)	15	0.11
Not Hispanic (2)	7	0.05
Hispanic (1)	8	0.06
Native Hawaiian (1)	3	0.02
Samoan (2)	3	0.02
White (5,300)	5,557	40.17
Not Hispanic (4,718)	4,911	35.50
Hispanic (582)	646	4.67

Princeton

Place Type: Borough
County: Mercer
Population: 12,307†

Ancestry‡	Population	%
African, Sub-Saharan (123)	147	1.17
African (13)	37	0.30
Ethiopian (20)	20	0.16
Ghanaian (14)	14	0.11
Nigerian (44)	44	0.35
Sierra Leonean (14)	14	0.11
Somalian (13)	13	0.10
Other Sub-Saharan African (5)	5	0.04
Albanian (42)	42	0.34
American (149)	149	1.19
Arab (185)	381	3.04
Arab (0)	47	0.38
Egyptian (22)	65	0.52
Iraqi (45)	45	0.36
Lebanese (53)	147	1.17
Moroccan (29)	29	0.23
Palestinian (36)	36	0.29
Other Arab (0)	12	0.10
Armenian (32)	32	0.26
Austrian (9)	208	1.66
Belgian (0)	29	0.23
British (176)	360	2.87
Bulgarian (14)	14	0.11
Canadian (11)	91	0.73
Croatian (0)	53	0.42
Czech (0)	56	0.45
Czechoslovakian (0)	27	0.22
Danish (48)	64	0.51
Dutch (65)	271	2.16
Eastern European (147)	147	1.17
English (386)	1,736	13.85
European (145)	209	1.67
Finnish (0)	5	0.04
French, ex. Basque (100)	303	2.42
French Canadian (0)	41	0.33
German (392)	1,834	14.63
Greek (24)	95	0.76
Hungarian (17)	192	1.53
Iranian (40)	40	0.32
Irish (244)	1,776	14.17
Israeli (33)	33	0.26
Italian (564)	1,384	11.04
Lithuanian (0)	58	0.46
New Zealander (14)	26	0.21
Northern European (50)	50	0.40
Norwegian (63)	206	1.64
Pennsylvania German (0)	13	0.10
Polish (107)	725	5.78
Romanian (73)	73	0.58
Russian (273)	766	6.11
Scandinavian (0)	17	0.14
Scotch-Irish (133)	394	3.14
Scottish (205)	528	4.21
Slavic (0)	13	0.10
Slovak (29)	56	0.45
Slovene (0)	10	0.08
Swedish (0)	208	1.66
Swiss (22)	138	1.10
Turkish (13)	27	0.22
Ukrainian (175)	358	2.86
Welsh (0)	211	1.68
West Indian, ex. Hispanic (60)	74	0.59
British West Indian (14)	14	0.11
Haitian (13)	13	0.10
Jamaican (20)	20	0.16
West Indian (13)	27	0.22
Yugoslavian (0)	14	0.11

Hispanic Origin	Population	%
Hispanic or Latino (of any race)	1,268	10.30
Central American, ex. Mexican	401	3.26
Costa Rican	5	0.04
Guatemalan	361	2.93
Honduran	12	0.10
Nicaraguan	6	0.05
Panamanian	11	0.09
Salvadoran	5	0.04
Other Central American	1	0.01
Cuban	69	0.56
Dominican Republic	13	0.11
Mexican	355	2.88
Puerto Rican	100	0.81
South American	153	1.24
Argentinean	37	0.30
Bolivian	3	0.02
Chilean	11	0.09
Colombian	46	0.37
Ecuadorian	11	0.09
Paraguayan	6	0.05
Peruvian	21	0.17
Uruguayan	5	0.04
Venezuelan	13	0.11
Other Hispanic or Latino	177	1.44

Race*	Population	%
African-American/Black (793)	924	7.51
Not Hispanic (761)	881	7.16
Hispanic (32)	43	0.35
American Indian/Alaska Native (22)	74	0.60
Not Hispanic (13)	57	0.46
Hispanic (9)	17	0.14
Apache (0)	1	0.01
Blackfeet (0)	4	0.03
Central American Ind. (2)	2	0.02
Cherokee (0)	11	0.09
Chippewa (0)	1	0.01
Choctaw (0)	2	0.02

*Notes: † The Census 2010 population figure is used to calculate the percentages in the Hispanic Origin and Race categories. Ancestry percentages are based on the 2006-2010 American Community Survey population (not shown); ‡ Numbers in parentheses indicate the number of people reporting a single ancestry; * Numbers in parentheses indicate the number of persons reporting this race alone, not in combination with any other race; Please refer to the Explanation of Data for more information.*

Comanche (1)	1	0.01
Creek (1)	2	0.02
Crow (0)	1	0.01
Delaware (3)	4	0.03
Inupiat *(Alaska Native)* (0)	1	0.01
Iroquois (0)	3	0.02
Mexican American Ind. (1)	2	0.02
Navajo (0)	1	0.01
Potawatomi (1)	2	0.02
Seminole (0)	1	0.01
Sioux (1)	2	0.02
South American Ind. (4)	5	0.04
Asian (1,663)	1,910	15.52
Not Hispanic (1,655)	1,891	15.37
Hispanic (8)	19	0.15
Bangladeshi (6)	6	0.05
Burmese (6)	6	0.05
Cambodian (0)	1	0.01
Chinese, ex. Taiwanese (863)	980	7.96
Filipino (30)	47	0.38
Indian (245)	281	2.28
Indonesian (2)	2	0.02
Japanese (48)	99	0.80
Korean (158)	192	1.56
Laotian (0)	1	0.01
Malaysian (4)	10	0.08
Nepalese (4)	4	0.03
Pakistani (12)	14	0.11
Sri Lankan (5)	7	0.06
Taiwanese (84)	96	0.78
Thai (10)	13	0.11
Vietnamese (17)	26	0.21
Hawaii Native/Pacific Islander (20)	34	0.28
Not Hispanic (20)	32	0.26
Hispanic (0)	2	0.02
Guamanian/Chamorro (3)	3	0.02
Native Hawaiian (3)	13	0.11
Samoan (1)	1	0.01
White (8,870)	9,250	75.16
Not Hispanic (8,199)	8,514	69.18
Hispanic (671)	736	5.98

Princeton

Place Type: Township
County: Mercer
Population: 16,265†

Ancestry‡	Population	%
African, Sub-Saharan (34)	60	0.37
African (0)	15	0.09
Ghanaian (13)	13	0.08
Kenyan (12)	12	0.07
Other Sub-Saharan African (9)	20	0.12
American (422)	422	2.57
Arab (235)	312	1.90
Arab (164)	174	1.06
Egyptian (15)	75	0.46
Lebanese (56)	63	0.38
Armenian (42)	42	0.26
Australian (39)	52	0.32
Austrian (48)	121	0.74
Basque (0)	30	0.18
Belgian (0)	69	0.42
Brazilian (46)	76	0.46
British (86)	301	1.84
Bulgarian (35)	35	0.21
Canadian (64)	86	0.52
Celtic (0)	13	0.08
Croatian (14)	14	0.09
Czech (115)	203	1.24
Czechoslovakian (24)	24	0.15
Danish (83)	168	1.03
Dutch (30)	115	0.70
Eastern European (383)	464	2.83
English (363)	1,600	9.76
European (337)	387	2.36
Finnish (23)	23	0.14
French, ex. Basque (63)	320	1.95
French Canadian (32)	134	0.82
German (660)	2,204	13.45
Greek (101)	140	0.85
Hungarian (44)	158	0.96
Iranian (133)	147	0.90
Irish (646)	2,164	13.20
Israeli (34)	70	0.43
Italian (657)	1,318	8.04
Lithuanian (33)	63	0.38
New Zealander (8)	8	0.05
Northern European (61)	85	0.52
Norwegian (9)	90	0.55
Pennsylvania German (6)	17	0.10
Polish (171)	747	4.56
Portuguese (0)	34	0.21
Romanian (26)	62	0.38
Russian (404)	1,014	6.19
Scandinavian (0)	57	0.35
Scotch-Irish (112)	320	1.95
Scottish (90)	609	3.72
Serbian (12)	30	0.18
Slovak (27)	89	0.54
Slovene (0)	55	0.34
Swedish (94)	236	1.44
Swiss (47)	89	0.54
Turkish (67)	81	0.49
Ukrainian (89)	165	1.01
Welsh (0)	170	1.04
West Indian, ex. Hispanic (102)	337	2.06
Barbadian (7)	7	0.04
British West Indian (12)	179	1.09
Haitian (83)	83	0.51
Jamaican (0)	68	0.41
Yugoslavian (75)	84	0.51

Hispanic Origin	Population	%
Hispanic or Latino (of any race)	1,124	6.91
Central American, ex. Mexican	334	2.05
Costa Rican	9	0.06
Guatemalan	290	1.78
Honduran	8	0.05
Nicaraguan	10	0.06
Panamanian	10	0.06
Salvadoran	7	0.04
Cuban	28	0.17
Dominican Republic	12	0.07
Mexican	285	1.75
Puerto Rican	101	0.62
South American	224	1.38
Argentinean	55	0.34
Bolivian	2	0.01
Chilean	30	0.18
Colombian	81	0.50
Ecuadorian	10	0.06
Peruvian	18	0.11
Uruguayan	1	0.01
Venezuelan	27	0.17
Other Hispanic or Latino	140	0.86

Race*	Population	%
African-American/Black (810)	933	5.74
Not Hispanic (786)	893	5.49
Hispanic (24)	40	0.25
American Indian/Alaska Native (22)	101	0.62
Not Hispanic (10)	69	0.42
Hispanic (12)	32	0.20
Cherokee (1)	21	0.13
Cheyenne (1)	2	0.01
Chickasaw (1)	1	0.01
Choctaw (3)	6	0.04
Delaware (0)	1	0.01
Iroquois (0)	1	0.01
Mexican American Ind. (1)	6	0.04
Navajo (3)	3	0.02
Pima (0)	1	0.01
South American Ind. (4)	10	0.06
Spanish American Ind. (0)	1	0.01
Asian (2,305)	2,581	15.87
Not Hispanic (2,300)	2,568	15.79
Hispanic (5)	13	0.08
Bangladeshi (5)	7	0.04
Burmese (15)	16	0.10
Cambodian (3)	3	0.02
Chinese, ex. Taiwanese (1,024)	1,119	6.88
Filipino (83)	108	0.66
Indian (506)	565	3.47
Indonesian (2)	2	0.01
Japanese (101)	140	0.86
Korean (285)	333	2.05
Laotian (2)	2	0.01
Malaysian (4)	6	0.04
Nepalese (8)	8	0.05
Pakistani (87)	97	0.60
Sri Lankan (8)	9	0.06
Taiwanese (101)	103	0.63
Thai (8)	11	0.07
Vietnamese (19)	24	0.15
Hawaii Native/Pacific Islander (4)	14	0.09
Not Hispanic (0)	9	0.06
Hispanic (4)	5	0.03
Guamanian/Chamorro (4)	5	0.03
Native Hawaiian (0)	4	0.02
Samoan (0)	1	0.01
White (12,283)	12,703	78.10
Not Hispanic (11,595)	11,949	73.46
Hispanic (688)	754	4.64

Rahway

Place Type: City
County: Union
Population: 27,346†

Ancestry‡	Population	%
African, Sub-Saharan (232)	446	1.65
African (108)	230	0.85
Liberian (29)	29	0.11
Nigerian (95)	187	0.69
Albanian (0)	9	0.03
American (1,678)	1,678	6.22
Arab (341)	386	1.43
Arab (44)	44	0.16
Egyptian (297)	328	1.22
Syrian (0)	14	0.05
Armenian (0)	9	0.03
Austrian (0)	63	0.23
Belgian (0)	17	0.06
Brazilian (20)	28	0.10
British (29)	29	0.11
Canadian (0)	15	0.06
Croatian (14)	14	0.05
Czech (9)	54	0.20
Czechoslovakian (21)	21	0.08
Danish (0)	26	0.10
Dutch (0)	121	0.45
English (66)	533	1.98
Estonian (10)	10	0.04
European (159)	159	0.59
French, ex. Basque (0)	174	0.65
French Canadian (54)	74	0.27
German (392)	1,588	5.89
Greek (115)	186	0.69
Guyanese (20)	40	0.15
Hungarian (0)	97	0.36
Irish (658)	2,478	9.19
Israeli (11)	11	0.04
Italian (1,202)	2,800	10.38
Lithuanian (8)	107	0.40
Northern European (16)	16	0.06
Norwegian (12)	25	0.09
Polish (859)	1,559	5.78
Portuguese (267)	326	1.21
Romanian (35)	78	0.29
Russian (225)	545	2.02
Scotch-Irish (34)	97	0.36
Scottish (159)	533	1.98
Slavic (0)	27	0.10
Slovak (174)	312	1.16
Swedish (20)	81	0.30
Swiss (0)	20	0.07
Turkish (0)	10	0.04

*Notes: † The Census 2010 population figure is used to calculate the percentages in the Hispanic Origin and Race categories. Ancestry percentages are based on the 2006-2010 American Community Survey population (not shown); ‡ Numbers in parentheses indicate the number of people reporting a single ancestry; * Numbers in parentheses indicate the number of persons reporting this race alone, not in combination with any other race; Please refer to the Explanation of Data for more information.*

Ukrainian (100)	144	0.53
Welsh (54)	78	0.29
West Indian, ex. Hispanic (811)	863	3.20
Bahamian (19)	19	0.07
Barbadian (18)	18	0.07
British West Indian (23)	23	0.09
Haitian (488)	494	1.83
Jamaican (214)	236	0.88
Trinidadian/Tobagonian (49)	73	0.27
Yugoslavian (0)	8	0.03

Hispanic Origin	Population	%
Hispanic or Latino (of any race)	6,433	23.52
Central American, ex. Mexican	1,081	3.95
Costa Rican	57	0.21
Guatemalan	121	0.44
Honduran	149	0.54
Nicaraguan	28	0.10
Panamanian	34	0.12
Salvadoran	681	2.49
Other Central American	11	0.04
Cuban	345	1.26
Dominican Republic	567	2.07
Mexican	745	2.72
Puerto Rican	1,653	6.04
South American	1,572	5.75
Argentinean	61	0.22
Bolivian	10	0.04
Chilean	21	0.08
Colombian	525	1.92
Ecuadorian	227	0.83
Paraguayan	1	<0.01
Peruvian	644	2.36
Uruguayan	37	0.14
Venezuelan	43	0.16
Other South American	3	0.01
Other Hispanic or Latino	470	1.72

Race*	Population	%
African-American/Black (8,457)	8,999	32.91
Not Hispanic (8,104)	8,461	30.94
Hispanic (353)	538	1.97
American Indian/Alaska Native (84)	344	1.26
Not Hispanic (42)	209	0.76
Hispanic (42)	135	0.49
Apache (0)	2	0.01
Blackfeet (1)	13	0.05
Central American Ind. (0)	5	0.02
Cherokee (7)	47	0.17
Chickasaw (0)	1	<0.01
Chippewa (1)	2	0.01
Choctaw (0)	2	0.01
Delaware (0)	1	<0.01
Iroquois (0)	2	0.01
Lumbee (0)	2	0.01
Mexican American Ind. (6)	13	0.05
Navajo (1)	1	<0.01
Potawatomi (0)	2	0.01
Pueblo (0)	2	0.01
Puget Sound Salish (0)	1	<0.01
Seminole (3)	4	0.01
Sioux (0)	8	0.03
South American Ind. (3)	26	0.10
Spanish American Ind. (0)	2	0.01
Tlingit-Haida *(Alaska Native)* (0)	1	<0.01
Tsimshian *(Alaska Native)* (0)	1	<0.01
Asian (1,175)	1,348	4.93
Not Hispanic (1,148)	1,282	4.69
Hispanic (27)	66	0.24
Cambodian (1)	3	0.01
Chinese, ex. Taiwanese (131)	167	0.61
Filipino (482)	539	1.97
Indian (361)	401	1.47
Indonesian (4)	4	0.01
Japanese (19)	39	0.14
Korean (38)	44	0.16
Nepalese (5)	5	0.02
Pakistani (34)	35	0.13
Sri Lankan (5)	5	0.02
Taiwanese (3)	4	0.01
Thai (3)	6	0.02
Vietnamese (64)	68	0.25
Hawaii Native/Pacific Islander (5)	64	0.23
Not Hispanic (3)	40	0.15
Hispanic (2)	24	0.09
Fijian (1)	1	<0.01
Guamanian/Chamorro (1)	2	0.01
Native Hawaiian (0)	2	0.01
White (14,301)	14,999	54.85
Not Hispanic (11,013)	11,345	41.49
Hispanic (3,288)	3,654	13.36

Ramsey

Place Type: Borough
County: Bergen
Population: 14,473†

Ancestry‡	Population	%
African, Sub-Saharan (89)	134	0.93
African (89)	134	0.93
American (336)	336	2.34
Arab (12)	12	0.08
Other Arab (12)	12	0.08
Armenian (125)	185	1.29
Austrian (0)	97	0.67
British (40)	108	0.75
Croatian (13)	54	0.38
Czech (25)	145	1.01
Czechoslovakian (15)	15	0.10
Danish (0)	50	0.35
Dutch (168)	739	5.14
Eastern European (103)	103	0.72
English (249)	1,222	8.50
European (185)	185	1.29
French, ex. Basque (0)	215	1.50
French Canadian (40)	40	0.28
German (644)	2,771	19.28
Greek (56)	161	1.12
Hungarian (40)	175	1.22
Irish (1,293)	3,578	24.89
Italian (2,163)	4,367	30.38
Lithuanian (14)	14	0.10
Norwegian (0)	19	0.13
Pennsylvania German (17)	33	0.23
Polish (198)	754	5.24
Portuguese (105)	146	1.02
Romanian (0)	14	0.10
Russian (143)	276	1.92
Scotch-Irish (12)	185	1.29
Scottish (80)	388	2.70
Slavic (0)	52	0.36
Slovak (54)	121	0.84
Swedish (28)	214	1.49
Swiss (39)	156	1.09
Ukrainian (201)	241	1.68
Welsh (0)	111	0.77
West Indian, ex. Hispanic (17)	17	0.12
Trinidadian/Tobagonian (17)	17	0.12

Hispanic Origin	Population	%
Hispanic or Latino (of any race)	866	5.98
Central American, ex. Mexican	187	1.29
Costa Rican	13	0.09
Guatemalan	16	0.11
Honduran	7	0.05
Nicaraguan	1	0.01
Panamanian	1	0.01
Salvadoran	143	0.99
Other Central American	6	0.04
Cuban	66	0.46
Dominican Republic	55	0.38
Mexican	213	1.47
Puerto Rican	120	0.83
South American	153	1.06
Argentinean	18	0.12
Bolivian	8	0.06
Chilean	7	0.05
Colombian	32	0.22
Ecuadorian	37	0.26
Paraguayan	1	0.01
Peruvian	33	0.23
Uruguayan	4	0.03
Venezuelan	13	0.09
Other Hispanic or Latino	72	0.50

Race*	Population	%
African-American/Black (94)	129	0.89
Not Hispanic (90)	119	0.82
Hispanic (4)	10	0.07
American Indian/Alaska Native (17)	45	0.31
Not Hispanic (9)	31	0.21
Hispanic (8)	14	0.10
Cherokee (3)	4	0.03
Delaware (0)	1	0.01
Iroquois (0)	1	0.01
Mexican American Ind. (1)	3	0.02
Asian (964)	1,052	7.27
Not Hispanic (959)	1,044	7.21
Hispanic (5)	8	0.06
Chinese, ex. Taiwanese (212)	255	1.76
Filipino (72)	95	0.66
Indian (205)	217	1.50
Japanese (74)	95	0.66
Korean (301)	311	2.15
Pakistani (38)	41	0.28
Sri Lankan (8)	9	0.06
Taiwanese (16)	22	0.15
Thai (9)	10	0.07
Vietnamese (6)	9	0.06
Hawaii Native/Pacific Islander (0)	11	0.08
Not Hispanic (0)	11	0.08
Native Hawaiian (0)	3	0.02
White (12,946)	13,106	90.55
Not Hispanic (12,391)	12,515	86.47
Hispanic (555)	591	4.08

Randolph

Place Type: Township
County: Morris
Population: 25,734†

Ancestry‡	Population	%
African, Sub-Saharan (228)	228	0.89
African (74)	74	0.29
Nigerian (144)	144	0.56
South African (10)	10	0.04
Albanian (0)	24	0.09
American (722)	722	2.81
Arab (40)	76	0.30
Egyptian (5)	5	0.02
Lebanese (25)	41	0.16
Moroccan (10)	30	0.12
Armenian (0)	8	0.03
Assyrian/Chaldean/Syriac (15)	30	0.12
Austrian (0)	117	0.46
British (80)	119	0.46
Canadian (12)	12	0.05
Croatian (11)	11	0.04
Czech (44)	248	0.97
Czechoslovakian (0)	51	0.20
Danish (40)	120	0.47
Dutch (41)	488	1.90
Eastern European (167)	180	0.70
English (454)	2,009	7.83
Estonian (20)	20	0.08
European (275)	301	1.17
Finnish (12)	22	0.09
French, ex. Basque (125)	672	2.62
French Canadian (45)	119	0.46
German (736)	4,857	18.94
Greek (121)	326	1.27
Guyanese (62)	62	0.24
Hungarian (45)	427	1.66
Iranian (18)	18	0.07
Irish (1,305)	5,395	21.03
Israeli (60)	69	0.27
Italian (2,120)	5,725	22.32
Lithuanian (10)	73	0.28

*Notes: † The Census 2010 population figure is used to calculate the percentages in the Hispanic Origin and Race categories. Ancestry percentages are based on the 2006-2010 American Community Survey population (not shown); ‡ Numbers in parentheses indicate the number of people reporting a single ancestry; * Numbers in parentheses indicate the number of persons reporting this race alone, not in combination with any other race; Please refer to the Explanation of Data for more information.*

Maltese (0)	13	0.05
Norwegian (87)	168	0.65
Pennsylvania German (35)	71	0.28
Polish (513)	1,979	7.72
Portuguese (111)	359	1.40
Romanian (110)	158	0.62
Russian (398)	1,293	5.04
Scandinavian (10)	28	0.11
Scotch-Irish (180)	263	1.03
Scottish (64)	528	2.06
Slavic (0)	18	0.07
Slovak (62)	146	0.57
Slovene (9)	9	0.04
Swedish (111)	537	2.09
Swiss (0)	68	0.27
Turkish (10)	10	0.04
Ukrainian (21)	122	0.48
Welsh (59)	144	0.56
West Indian, ex. Hispanic (69)	85	0.33
Haitian (51)	51	0.20
Trinidadian/Tobagonian (18)	34	0.13
Yugoslavian (20)	55	0.21

Hispanic Origin	Population	%
Hispanic or Latino (of any race)	2,616	10.17
Central American, ex. Mexican	278	1.08
Costa Rican	63	0.24
Guatemalan	63	0.24
Honduran	79	0.31
Nicaraguan	10	0.04
Panamanian	9	0.03
Salvadoran	51	0.20
Other Central American	3	0.01
Cuban	138	0.54
Dominican Republic	104	0.40
Mexican	232	0.90
Puerto Rican	458	1.78
South American	1,156	4.49
Argentinean	43	0.17
Chilean	39	0.15
Colombian	716	2.78
Ecuadorian	159	0.62
Paraguayan	8	0.03
Peruvian	79	0.31
Uruguayan	68	0.26
Venezuelan	36	0.14
Other South American	8	0.03
Other Hispanic or Latino	250	0.97

Race*	Population	%
African-American/Black (690)	897	3.49
Not Hispanic (638)	777	3.02
Hispanic (52)	120	0.47
American Indian/Alaska Native (28)	74	0.29
Not Hispanic (11)	41	0.16
Hispanic (17)	33	0.13
Blackfeet (0)	1	<0.01
Central American Ind. (1)	5	0.02
Cherokee (0)	5	0.02
Cheyenne (0)	1	<0.01
Delaware (0)	1	<0.01
Iroquois (0)	1	<0.01
Mexican American Ind. (2)	3	0.01
Sioux (2)	4	0.02
South American Ind. (2)	8	0.03
Asian (2,691)	2,937	11.41
Not Hispanic (2,674)	2,900	11.27
Hispanic (17)	37	0.14
Bangladeshi (16)	20	0.08
Cambodian (1)	1	<0.01
Chinese, ex. Taiwanese (559)	644	2.50
Filipino (195)	251	0.98
Indian (1,473)	1,537	5.97
Indonesian (3)	3	0.01
Japanese (24)	48	0.19
Korean (227)	239	0.93
Malaysian (2)	4	0.02
Nepalese (2)	2	0.01
Pakistani (49)	54	0.21
Sri Lankan (8)	8	0.03
Taiwanese (43)	45	0.17
Thai (1)	3	0.01
Vietnamese (30)	38	0.15
Hawaii Native/Pacific Islander (3)	14	0.05
Not Hispanic (3)	12	0.05
Hispanic (0)	2	0.01
Fijian (2)	5	0.02
Guamanian/Chamorro (0)	3	0.01
Native Hawaiian (1)	1	<0.01
White (21,215)	21,637	84.08
Not Hispanic (19,376)	19,672	76.44
Hispanic (1,839)	1,965	7.64

Raritan

Place Type: Township
County: Hunterdon
Population: 22,185†

Ancestry‡	Population	%
Afghan (56)	56	0.25
African, Sub-Saharan (47)	47	0.21
South African (47)	47	0.21
Albanian (18)	28	0.13
Alsatian (0)	9	0.04
American (882)	882	4.01
Arab (54)	81	0.37
Egyptian (43)	43	0.20
Lebanese (11)	38	0.17
Armenian (7)	7	0.03
Austrian (74)	306	1.39
Basque (0)	9	0.04
Brazilian (21)	63	0.29
British (97)	125	0.57
Canadian (9)	54	0.25
Croatian (42)	120	0.55
Cypriot (24)	24	0.11
Czech (32)	187	0.85
Czechoslovakian (33)	52	0.24
Danish (16)	121	0.55
Dutch (272)	574	2.61
Eastern European (42)	42	0.19
English (396)	2,033	9.25
European (323)	373	1.70
Finnish (0)	28	0.13
French, ex. Basque (75)	470	2.14
French Canadian (29)	41	0.19
German (867)	4,224	19.21
Greek (244)	359	1.63
Guyanese (14)	14	0.06
Hungarian (85)	669	3.04
Iranian (12)	39	0.18
Irish (1,107)	5,261	23.93
Italian (1,899)	5,534	25.17
Lithuanian (86)	265	1.21
Luxemburger (0)	19	0.09
Northern European (67)	67	0.30
Norwegian (119)	262	1.19
Pennsylvania German (13)	13	0.06
Polish (517)	1,924	8.75
Portuguese (4)	146	0.66
Romanian (8)	33	0.15
Russian (292)	868	3.95
Scandinavian (7)	62	0.28
Scotch-Irish (96)	280	1.27
Scottish (123)	429	1.95
Serbian (0)	25	0.11
Slavic (0)	14	0.06
Slovak (53)	289	1.31
Slovene (0)	25	0.11
Swedish (40)	209	0.95
Swiss (17)	61	0.28
Turkish (0)	6	0.03
Ukrainian (55)	224	1.02
Welsh (25)	212	0.96
West Indian, ex. Hispanic (10)	15	0.07
Jamaican (10)	10	0.05
West Indian (0)	5	0.02
Yugoslavian (12)	12	0.05

Hispanic Origin	Population	%
Hispanic or Latino (of any race)	1,138	5.13
Central American, ex. Mexican	186	0.84
Costa Rican	74	0.33
Guatemalan	35	0.16
Honduran	40	0.18
Panamanian	1	<0.01
Salvadoran	31	0.14
Other Central American	5	0.02
Cuban	119	0.54
Dominican Republic	51	0.23
Mexican	179	0.81
Puerto Rican	268	1.21
South American	220	0.99
Argentinean	27	0.12
Bolivian	1	<0.01
Chilean	7	0.03
Colombian	94	0.42
Ecuadorian	41	0.18
Paraguayan	4	0.02
Peruvian	27	0.12
Uruguayan	1	<0.01
Venezuelan	18	0.08
Other Hispanic or Latino	115	0.52

Race*	Population	%
African-American/Black (459)	548	2.47
Not Hispanic (438)	510	2.30
Hispanic (21)	38	0.17
American Indian/Alaska Native (23)	86	0.39
Not Hispanic (9)	49	0.22
Hispanic (14)	37	0.17
Apache (0)	1	<0.01
Blackfeet (0)	4	0.02
Central American Ind. (3)	3	0.01
Cherokee (3)	13	0.06
Cheyenne (1)	1	<0.01
Delaware (0)	1	<0.01
Iroquois (0)	5	0.02
Lumbee (1)	1	<0.01
Mexican American Ind. (3)	8	0.04
Navajo (0)	1	<0.01
Shoshone (0)	3	0.01
Sioux (0)	1	<0.01
South American Ind. (2)	2	0.01
Asian (1,319)	1,482	6.68
Not Hispanic (1,315)	1,473	6.64
Hispanic (4)	9	0.04
Bangladeshi (5)	6	0.03
Chinese, ex. Taiwanese (347)	392	1.77
Filipino (104)	144	0.65
Indian (665)	704	3.17
Indonesian (3)	5	0.02
Japanese (7)	14	0.06
Korean (71)	99	0.45
Malaysian (1)	1	<0.01
Pakistani (43)	45	0.20
Sri Lankan (4)	4	0.02
Taiwanese (11)	11	0.05
Thai (2)	3	0.01
Vietnamese (31)	34	0.15
Hawaii Native/Pacific Islander (9)	10	0.05
Not Hispanic (2)	2	0.01
Hispanic (7)	8	0.04
Native Hawaiian (7)	7	0.03
Samoan (1)	1	<0.01
White (19,870)	20,164	90.89
Not Hispanic (18,993)	19,234	86.70
Hispanic (877)	930	4.19

Readington

Place Type: Township
County: Hunterdon
Population: 16,126†

Ancestry‡	Population	%
African, Sub-Saharan (112)	112	0.69
African (9)	9	0.06
Ethiopian (103)	103	0.63

SECTION TWO

*Notes: † The Census 2010 population figure is used to calculate the percentages in the Hispanic Origin and Race categories. Ancestry percentages are based on the 2006-2010 American Community Survey population (not shown); ‡ Numbers in parentheses indicate the number of people reporting a single ancestry; * Numbers in parentheses indicate the number of persons reporting this race alone, not in combination with any other race; Please refer to the Explanation of Data for more information.*

American (647)	647	3.99
Arab (62)	251	1.55
Egyptian (41)	117	0.72
Lebanese (15)	77	0.47
Palestinian (6)	20	0.12
Syrian (0)	37	0.23
Armenian (12)	28	0.17
Australian (15)	15	0.09
Austrian (87)	289	1.78
Belgian (16)	16	0.10
Brazilian (12)	12	0.07
British (86)	86	0.53
Czech (21)	111	0.68
Czechoslovakian (22)	55	0.34
Danish (11)	72	0.44
Dutch (31)	147	0.91
Eastern European (42)	42	0.26
English (271)	1,627	10.02
European (142)	183	1.13
Finnish (9)	19	0.12
French, ex. Basque (79)	318	1.96
French Canadian (12)	12	0.07
German (773)	3,634	22.38
Greek (23)	170	1.05
Hungarian (104)	639	3.94
Irish (909)	4,154	25.59
Israeli (12)	12	0.07
Italian (1,934)	4,447	27.39
Latvian (0)	13	0.08
Lithuanian (35)	60	0.37
New Zealander (0)	9	0.06
Norwegian (13)	92	0.57
Pennsylvania German (27)	37	0.23
Polish (499)	1,538	9.47
Portuguese (70)	261	1.61
Romanian (18)	58	0.36
Russian (197)	320	1.97
Scotch-Irish (91)	262	1.61
Scottish (134)	373	2.30
Serbian (0)	13	0.08
Slavic (14)	14	0.09
Slovak (83)	244	1.50
Slovene (0)	20	0.12
Swedish (11)	226	1.39
Swiss (0)	32	0.20
Turkish (14)	44	0.27
Ukrainian (87)	263	1.62
Welsh (30)	154	0.95

Hispanic Origin	Population	%
Hispanic or Latino (of any race)	633	3.93
Central American, ex. Mexican	104	0.64
Costa Rican	33	0.20
Guatemalan	27	0.17
Honduran	12	0.07
Nicaraguan	1	0.01
Panamanian	3	0.02
Salvadoran	26	0.16
Other Central American	2	0.01
Cuban	75	0.47
Dominican Republic	32	0.20
Mexican	66	0.41
Puerto Rican	135	0.84
South American	154	0.95
Argentinean	13	0.08
Bolivian	4	0.02
Chilean	5	0.03
Colombian	56	0.35
Ecuadorian	22	0.14
Paraguayan	6	0.04
Peruvian	34	0.21
Uruguayan	5	0.03
Venezuelan	7	0.04
Other South American	2	0.01
Other Hispanic or Latino	67	0.42

Race*	Population	%
African-American/Black (214)	255	1.58
Not Hispanic (205)	244	1.51
Hispanic (9)	11	0.07
American Indian/Alaska Native (18)	45	0.28
Not Hispanic (17)	43	0.27
Hispanic (1)	2	0.01
Blackfeet (3)	5	0.03
Cherokee (3)	7	0.04
Cheyenne (1)	1	0.01
Iroquois (0)	3	0.02
Potawatomi (1)	1	0.01
Sioux (0)	1	0.01
Tlingit-Haida *(Alaska Native)* (1)	1	0.01
Asian (581)	676	4.19
Not Hispanic (578)	668	4.14
Hispanic (3)	8	0.05
Bangladeshi (4)	4	0.02
Cambodian (5)	5	0.03
Chinese, ex. Taiwanese (153)	183	1.13
Filipino (59)	90	0.56
Indian (263)	290	1.80
Indonesian (1)	2	0.01
Japanese (14)	15	0.09
Korean (37)	46	0.29
Malaysian (3)	3	0.02
Pakistani (6)	6	0.04
Taiwanese (13)	18	0.11
Thai (4)	6	0.04
Vietnamese (3)	8	0.05
Hawaii Native/Pacific Islander (1)	9	0.06
Not Hispanic (0)	8	0.05
Hispanic (1)	1	0.01
Guamanian/Chamorro (1)	3	0.02
Native Hawaiian (0)	1	0.01
White (15,011)	15,180	94.13
Not Hispanic (14,530)	14,678	91.02
Hispanic (481)	502	3.11

Red Bank

Place Type: Borough
County: Monmouth
Population: 12,206†

Ancestry‡	Population	%
African, Sub-Saharan (59)	59	0.49
African (23)	23	0.19
Kenyan (36)	36	0.30
American (193)	193	1.59
Arab (0)	12	0.10
Lebanese (0)	12	0.10
Armenian (34)	49	0.40
Austrian (0)	19	0.16
British (37)	37	0.31
Canadian (0)	13	0.11
Croatian (0)	30	0.25
Czech (20)	56	0.46
Czechoslovakian (13)	41	0.34
Danish (14)	108	0.89
Dutch (17)	121	1.00
Eastern European (28)	28	0.23
English (201)	850	7.01
Estonian (25)	25	0.21
European (30)	30	0.25
French, ex. Basque (5)	161	1.33
French Canadian (14)	72	0.59
German (216)	1,614	13.30
Greek (29)	49	0.40
Hungarian (9)	104	0.86
Irish (780)	2,942	24.25
Israeli (29)	37	0.31
Italian (767)	2,227	18.36
Lithuanian (0)	16	0.13
Norwegian (38)	88	0.73
Polish (105)	438	3.61
Portuguese (0)	12	0.10
Romanian (0)	19	0.16
Russian (49)	130	1.07
Scotch-Irish (50)	129	1.06
Scottish (54)	112	0.92
Slovak (18)	44	0.36
Swedish (0)	51	0.42
Swiss (18)	18	0.15
Ukrainian (38)	65	0.54
Welsh (0)	27	0.22
West Indian, ex. Hispanic (47)	55	0.45
Bermudan (5)	5	0.04
British West Indian (5)	5	0.04
Jamaican (37)	45	0.37

Hispanic Origin	Population	%
Hispanic or Latino (of any race)	4,198	34.39
Central American, ex. Mexican	572	4.69
Costa Rican	85	0.70
Guatemalan	34	0.28
Nicaraguan	10	0.08
Panamanian	10	0.08
Salvadoran	433	3.55
Cuban	41	0.34
Dominican Republic	30	0.25
Mexican	3,064	25.10
Puerto Rican	242	1.98
South American	116	0.95
Argentinean	11	0.09
Bolivian	4	0.03
Chilean	3	0.02
Colombian	38	0.31
Ecuadorian	25	0.20
Peruvian	25	0.20
Uruguayan	1	0.01
Venezuelan	9	0.07
Other Hispanic or Latino	133	1.09

Race*	Population	%
African-American/Black (1,516)	1,671	13.69
Not Hispanic (1,408)	1,522	12.47
Hispanic (108)	149	1.22
American Indian/Alaska Native (118)	259	2.12
Not Hispanic (7)	59	0.48
Hispanic (111)	200	1.64
Blackfeet (1)	4	0.03
Central American Ind. (2)	3	0.02
Cherokee (0)	8	0.07
Creek (0)	1	0.01
Delaware (1)	4	0.03
Iroquois (0)	2	0.02
Mexican American Ind. (32)	43	0.35
Sioux (0)	3	0.02
Asian (226)	263	2.15
Not Hispanic (223)	254	2.08
Hispanic (3)	9	0.07
Chinese, ex. Taiwanese (53)	68	0.56
Filipino (73)	82	0.67
Indian (36)	41	0.34
Indonesian (0)	1	0.01
Japanese (7)	15	0.12
Korean (19)	24	0.20
Nepalese (1)	1	0.01
Sri Lankan (1)	1	0.01
Taiwanese (2)	2	0.02
Thai (11)	12	0.10
Vietnamese (13)	17	0.14
Hawaii Native/Pacific Islander (13)	25	0.20
Not Hispanic (10)	21	0.17
Hispanic (3)	4	0.03
Guamanian/Chamorro (7)	7	0.06
Marshallese (5)	7	0.06
Native Hawaiian (0)	1	0.01
Samoan (1)	5	0.04
White (7,714)	7,983	65.40
Not Hispanic (6,147)	6,271	51.38
Hispanic (1,567)	1,712	14.03

Ridgefield Park

Place Type: Village
County: Bergen
Population: 12,729†

Ancestry‡	Population	%
Afghan (125)	125	0.99
African, Sub-Saharan (39)	50	0.39
African (26)	26	0.20

*Notes: † The Census 2010 population figure is used to calculate the percentages in the Hispanic Origin and Race categories. Ancestry percentages are based on the 2006-2010 American Community Survey population (not shown); ‡ Numbers in parentheses indicate the number of people reporting a single ancestry; * Numbers in parentheses indicate the number of persons reporting this race alone, not in combination with any other race; Please refer to the Explanation of Data for more information.*

Cape Verdean (0)	11	0.09
Kenyan (13)	13	0.10
American (149)	149	1.17
Arab (506)	506	3.99
Arab (137)	137	1.08
Egyptian (294)	294	2.32
Jordanian (16)	16	0.13
Lebanese (19)	19	0.15
Other Arab (40)	40	0.32
Armenian (79)	109	0.86
Austrian (0)	31	0.24
British (20)	20	0.16
Bulgarian (28)	28	0.22
Croatian (49)	49	0.39
Czech (0)	40	0.32
Dutch (28)	89	0.70
Eastern European (10)	10	0.08
English (11)	387	3.05
Estonian (12)	12	0.09
European (31)	31	0.24
Finnish (0)	38	0.30
French, ex. Basque (0)	151	1.19
French Canadian (0)	53	0.42
German (264)	1,255	9.89
Greek (84)	172	1.36
Hungarian (23)	23	0.18
Iranian (48)	48	0.38
Irish (686)	1,738	13.70
Israeli (31)	31	0.24
Italian (681)	1,591	12.54
Lithuanian (0)	12	0.09
Norwegian (10)	67	0.53
Polish (136)	464	3.66
Portuguese (55)	76	0.60
Romanian (0)	22	0.17
Russian (166)	249	1.96
Scandinavian (0)	18	0.14
Scotch-Irish (31)	164	1.29
Scottish (39)	89	0.70
Slavic (12)	12	0.09
Swedish (14)	23	0.18
Swiss (0)	56	0.44
Turkish (11)	23	0.18
Welsh (0)	37	0.29
West Indian, ex. Hispanic (62)	175	1.38
Belizean (0)	34	0.27
Haitian (0)	16	0.13
Jamaican (40)	40	0.32
Trinidadian/Tobagonian (22)	56	0.44
West Indian (0)	29	0.23

Hispanic Origin	Population	%
Hispanic or Latino (of any race)	4,605	36.18
Central American, ex. Mexican	353	2.77
Costa Rican	56	0.44
Guatemalan	71	0.56
Honduran	51	0.40
Nicaraguan	12	0.09
Panamanian	13	0.10
Salvadoran	146	1.15
Other Central American	4	0.03
Cuban	612	4.81
Dominican Republic	1,105	8.68
Mexican	91	0.71
Puerto Rican	801	6.29
South American	1,298	10.20
Argentinean	54	0.42
Bolivian	24	0.19
Chilean	34	0.27
Colombian	587	4.61
Ecuadorian	415	3.26
Paraguayan	4	0.03
Peruvian	147	1.15
Uruguayan	22	0.17
Venezuelan	11	0.09
Other Hispanic or Latino	345	2.71

Race*	Population	%
African-American/Black (815)	1,004	7.89
Not Hispanic (581)	650	5.11
Hispanic (234)	354	2.78
American Indian/Alaska Native (44)	109	0.86
Not Hispanic (15)	43	0.34
Hispanic (29)	66	0.52
Blackfeet (0)	3	0.02
Cherokee (0)	8	0.06
Cheyenne (0)	1	0.01
Creek (0)	3	0.02
Iroquois (4)	8	0.06
Mexican American Ind. (0)	1	0.01
South American Ind. (1)	16	0.13
Asian (1,461)	1,574	12.37
Not Hispanic (1,447)	1,527	12.00
Hispanic (14)	47	0.37
Bangladeshi (12)	12	0.09
Bhutanese (3)	3	0.02
Burmese (5)	5	0.04
Chinese, ex. Taiwanese (93)	116	0.91
Filipino (274)	300	2.36
Indian (235)	261	2.05
Indonesian (5)	5	0.04
Japanese (62)	68	0.53
Korean (670)	686	5.39
Nepalese (2)	2	0.02
Pakistani (60)	69	0.54
Sri Lankan (2)	2	0.02
Taiwanese (1)	1	0.01
Thai (5)	5	0.04
Vietnamese (2)	4	0.03
Hawaii Native/Pacific Islander (1)	23	0.18
Not Hispanic (1)	11	0.09
Hispanic (0)	12	0.09
White (8,413)	8,800	69.13
Not Hispanic (5,882)	6,002	47.15
Hispanic (2,531)	2,798	21.98

Ridgefield

Place Type: Borough
County: Bergen
Population: 11,032†

Ancestry‡	Population	%
Albanian (53)	53	0.48
American (150)	150	1.37
Arab (187)	268	2.45
Egyptian (108)	108	0.99
Syrian (37)	37	0.34
Other Arab (42)	123	1.12
Armenian (243)	274	2.50
Assyrian/Chaldean/Syriac (12)	12	0.11
Austrian (0)	42	0.38
Belgian (15)	15	0.14
Canadian (0)	24	0.22
Croatian (136)	289	2.64
Czech (30)	45	0.41
Czechoslovakian (0)	14	0.13
Danish (15)	15	0.14
Dutch (11)	64	0.59
English (17)	236	2.16
European (11)	11	0.10
Finnish (13)	13	0.12
French, ex. Basque (28)	57	0.52
German (161)	927	8.47
Greek (168)	245	2.24
Hungarian (52)	109	1.00
Iranian (118)	118	1.08
Irish (123)	722	6.60
Italian (1,373)	2,381	21.77
Norwegian (0)	13	0.12
Polish (133)	403	3.68
Russian (76)	158	1.44
Scotch-Irish (15)	86	0.79
Scottish (16)	43	0.39
Slovak (0)	10	0.09
Swiss (13)	151	1.38
Turkish (42)	42	0.38
Ukrainian (26)	26	0.24
Welsh (0)	106	0.97
Yugoslavian (12)	12	0.11

Hispanic Origin	Population	%
Hispanic or Latino (of any race)	2,362	21.41
Central American, ex. Mexican	187	1.70
Costa Rican	5	0.05
Guatemalan	69	0.63
Honduran	16	0.15
Nicaraguan	11	0.10
Panamanian	1	0.01
Salvadoran	85	0.77
Cuban	575	5.21
Dominican Republic	383	3.47
Mexican	75	0.68
Puerto Rican	335	3.04
South American	585	5.30
Argentinean	40	0.36
Bolivian	4	0.04
Chilean	11	0.10
Colombian	241	2.18
Ecuadorian	199	1.80
Paraguayan	2	0.02
Peruvian	67	0.61
Uruguayan	12	0.11
Venezuelan	8	0.07
Other South American	1	0.01
Other Hispanic or Latino	222	2.01

Race*	Population	%
African-American/Black (132)	196	1.78
Not Hispanic (95)	115	1.04
Hispanic (37)	81	0.73
American Indian/Alaska Native (20)	48	0.44
Not Hispanic (4)	27	0.24
Hispanic (16)	21	0.19
Canadian/French Am. Ind. (0)	1	0.01
Cherokee (0)	3	0.03
Choctaw (0)	1	0.01
Cree (0)	1	0.01
Iroquois (2)	2	0.02
Mexican American Ind. (7)	7	0.06
Pueblo (0)	2	0.02
Shoshone (0)	1	0.01
South American Ind. (2)	5	0.05
Asian (3,206)	3,313	30.03
Not Hispanic (3,199)	3,285	29.78
Hispanic (7)	28	0.25
Bangladeshi (1)	1	0.01
Chinese, ex. Taiwanese (161)	178	1.61
Filipino (45)	49	0.44
Indian (75)	86	0.78
Indonesian (4)	4	0.04
Japanese (19)	39	0.35
Korean (2,835)	2,886	26.16
Malaysian (1)	1	0.01
Pakistani (18)	20	0.18
Sri Lankan (1)	1	0.01
Taiwanese (9)	9	0.08
Thai (3)	4	0.04
Vietnamese (7)	8	0.07
Hawaii Native/Pacific Islander (2)	7	0.06
Not Hispanic (0)	3	0.03
Hispanic (2)	4	0.04
Native Hawaiian (2)	3	0.03
White (6,874)	7,112	64.47
Not Hispanic (5,215)	5,319	48.21
Hispanic (1,659)	1,793	16.25

Ridgewood

Place Type: Village
County: Bergen
Population: 24,958†

Ancestry‡	Population	%
African, Sub-Saharan (186)	186	0.75
African (186)	186	0.75
American (571)	571	2.30
Arab (75)	271	1.09
Arab (0)	10	0.04
Egyptian (43)	50	0.20
Lebanese (32)	102	0.41

*Notes: † The Census 2010 population figure is used to calculate the percentages in the Hispanic Origin and Race categories. Ancestry percentages are based on the 2006-2010 American Community Survey population (not shown); ‡ Numbers in parentheses indicate the number of people reporting a single ancestry; * Numbers in parentheses indicate the number of persons reporting this race alone, not in combination with any other race; Please refer to the Explanation of Data for more information.*

Ancestry	Population	%
Syrian (0)	109	0.44
Armenian (55)	119	0.48
Australian (40)	40	0.16
Austrian (23)	191	0.77
Belgian (0)	59	0.24
Brazilian (29)	29	0.12
British (79)	98	0.39
Bulgarian (18)	18	0.07
Canadian (52)	76	0.31
Celtic (0)	16	0.06
Croatian (52)	141	0.57
Czech (0)	80	0.32
Czechoslovakian (9)	17	0.07
Danish (0)	21	0.08
Dutch (198)	459	1.85
Eastern European (272)	295	1.19
English (279)	2,005	8.08
European (420)	436	1.76
Finnish (7)	7	0.03
French, ex. Basque (92)	622	2.51
French Canadian (31)	130	0.52
German (702)	3,915	15.77
Greek (121)	364	1.47
Hungarian (57)	199	0.80
Irish (2,165)	5,973	24.06
Israeli (44)	44	0.18
Italian (1,683)	4,913	19.79
Latvian (0)	8	0.03
Lithuanian (34)	82	0.33
Maltese (10)	28	0.11
Northern European (30)	30	0.12
Norwegian (63)	144	0.58
Pennsylvania German (13)	13	0.05
Polish (540)	1,557	6.27
Portuguese (20)	81	0.33
Romanian (0)	44	0.18
Russian (449)	1,204	4.85
Scandinavian (10)	39	0.16
Scotch-Irish (279)	601	2.42
Scottish (142)	551	2.22
Serbian (32)	50	0.20
Slovak (43)	111	0.45
Swedish (114)	401	1.62
Swiss (45)	156	0.63
Turkish (46)	53	0.21
Ukrainian (199)	258	1.04
Welsh (28)	127	0.51
West Indian, ex. Hispanic (45)	108	0.44
Barbadian (0)	11	0.04
Belizean (11)	11	0.04
British West Indian (0)	11	0.04
Jamaican (22)	51	0.21
Trinidadian/Tobagonian (12)	24	0.10
Yugoslavian (0)	5	0.02

Hispanic Origin	Population	%
Hispanic or Latino (of any race)	1,316	5.27
Central American, ex. Mexican	157	0.63
Costa Rican	73	0.29
Guatemalan	7	0.03
Honduran	4	0.02
Nicaraguan	7	0.03
Panamanian	5	0.02
Salvadoran	61	0.24
Cuban	211	0.85
Dominican Republic	90	0.36
Mexican	126	0.50
Puerto Rican	215	0.86
South American	371	1.49
Argentinean	65	0.26
Bolivian	8	0.03
Chilean	9	0.04
Colombian	96	0.38
Ecuadorian	81	0.32
Paraguayan	4	0.02
Peruvian	66	0.26
Uruguayan	4	0.02
Venezuelan	38	0.15
Other Hispanic or Latino	146	0.58

Race*	Population	%
African-American/Black (398)	508	2.04
Not Hispanic (373)	465	1.86
Hispanic (25)	43	0.17
American Indian/Alaska Native (16)	73	0.29
Not Hispanic (10)	48	0.19
Hispanic (6)	25	0.10
Blackfeet (0)	4	0.02
Canadian/French Am. Ind. (0)	1	<0.01
Central American Ind. (1)	1	<0.01
Cherokee (2)	7	0.03
Creek (0)	1	<0.01
Delaware (1)	1	<0.01
Iroquois (0)	4	0.02
Mexican American Ind. (0)	2	0.01
Pima (1)	3	0.01
Sioux (0)	2	0.01
South American Ind. (0)	1	<0.01
Yup'ik *(Alaska Native)* (0)	1	<0.01
Asian (3,242)	3,589	14.38
Not Hispanic (3,237)	3,557	14.25
Hispanic (5)	32	0.13
Bangladeshi (7)	9	0.04
Chinese, ex. Taiwanese (594)	714	2.86
Filipino (231)	308	1.23
Indian (512)	554	2.22
Indonesian (2)	2	0.01
Japanese (327)	384	1.54
Korean (1,370)	1,441	5.77
Malaysian (0)	4	0.02
Nepalese (2)	2	0.01
Pakistani (31)	39	0.16
Sri Lankan (22)	27	0.11
Taiwanese (39)	44	0.18
Thai (19)	23	0.09
Vietnamese (18)	20	0.08
Hawaii Native/Pacific Islander (4)	12	0.05
Not Hispanic (3)	9	0.04
Hispanic (1)	3	0.01
Samoan (3)	3	0.01
Tongan (0)	1	<0.01
White (20,518)	20,986	84.09
Not Hispanic (19,561)	19,955	79.95
Hispanic (957)	1,031	4.13

Ringwood

Place Type: Borough
County: Passaic
Population: 12,228†

Ancestry‡	Population	%
African, Sub-Saharan (28)	28	0.23
African (2)	2	0.02
Cape Verdean (26)	26	0.21
Albanian (0)	26	0.21
American (320)	320	2.63
Arab (130)	209	1.72
Egyptian (54)	54	0.44
Lebanese (12)	38	0.31
Syrian (0)	53	0.44
Other Arab (64)	64	0.53
Assyrian/Chaldean/Syriac (0)	9	0.07
Austrian (12)	90	0.74
Belgian (38)	94	0.77
Brazilian (27)	40	0.33
British (0)	10	0.08
Canadian (34)	34	0.28
Croatian (0)	40	0.33
Czech (48)	63	0.52
Czechoslovakian (0)	14	0.12
Danish (0)	22	0.18
Dutch (86)	397	3.26
English (199)	1,183	9.73
European (94)	94	0.77
Finnish (28)	67	0.55
French, ex. Basque (16)	360	2.96
French Canadian (8)	36	0.30
German (472)	3,092	25.42
Greek (69)	145	1.19
Hungarian (38)	249	2.05
Irish (1,028)	3,739	30.74
Italian (1,424)	3,563	29.29
Latvian (0)	39	0.32
Lithuanian (14)	52	0.43
Maltese (0)	26	0.21
Norwegian (0)	78	0.64
Polish (233)	608	5.00
Portuguese (0)	37	0.30
Russian (135)	253	2.08
Scandinavian (37)	170	1.40
Scotch-Irish (11)	52	0.43
Scottish (35)	228	1.87
Serbian (0)	11	0.09
Slavic (11)	11	0.09
Slovak (27)	64	0.53
Swedish (27)	98	0.81
Swiss (10)	118	0.97
Ukrainian (18)	61	0.50
Welsh (20)	20	0.16
West Indian, ex. Hispanic (20)	53	0.44
Jamaican (20)	53	0.44
Yugoslavian (0)	24	0.20

Hispanic Origin	Population	%
Hispanic or Latino (of any race)	707	5.78
Central American, ex. Mexican	26	0.21
Costa Rican	4	0.03
Guatemalan	6	0.05
Honduran	4	0.03
Nicaraguan	1	0.01
Panamanian	4	0.03
Salvadoran	7	0.06
Cuban	84	0.69
Dominican Republic	46	0.38
Mexican	55	0.45
Puerto Rican	259	2.12
South American	154	1.26
Argentinean	10	0.08
Bolivian	1	0.01
Chilean	5	0.04
Colombian	80	0.65
Ecuadorian	26	0.21
Paraguayan	3	0.02
Peruvian	18	0.15
Uruguayan	4	0.03
Venezuelan	7	0.06
Other Hispanic or Latino	83	0.68

Race*	Population	%
African-American/Black (166)	263	2.15
Not Hispanic (148)	230	1.88
Hispanic (18)	33	0.27
American Indian/Alaska Native (152)	275	2.25
Not Hispanic (132)	250	2.04
Hispanic (20)	25	0.20
Apache (0)	6	0.05
Blackfeet (0)	12	0.10
Canadian/French Am. Ind. (0)	1	0.01
Cherokee (1)	8	0.07
Creek (0)	3	0.02
Delaware (94)	155	1.27
Iroquois (0)	4	0.03
Sioux (4)	6	0.05
South American Ind. (0)	3	0.02
Spanish American Ind. (3)	4	0.03
Asian (213)	265	2.17
Not Hispanic (209)	255	2.09
Hispanic (4)	10	0.08
Chinese, ex. Taiwanese (49)	57	0.47
Filipino (43)	54	0.44
Indian (65)	69	0.56
Indonesian (0)	2	0.02
Japanese (7)	12	0.10
Korean (33)	40	0.33
Malaysian (1)	3	0.02
Thai (6)	10	0.08
Vietnamese (5)	7	0.06
Hawaii Native/Pacific Islander (2)	5	0.04

*Notes: † The Census 2010 population figure is used to calculate the percentages in the Hispanic Origin and Race categories. Ancestry percentages are based on the 2006-2010 American Community Survey population (not shown); ‡ Numbers in parentheses indicate the number of people reporting a single ancestry; * Numbers in parentheses indicate the number of persons reporting this race alone, not in combination with any other race; Please refer to the Explanation of Data for more information.*

	Population	%
Not Hispanic (1)	4	0.03
Hispanic (1)	1	0.01
Guamanian/Chamorro (1)	1	0.01
Native Hawaiian (1)	2	0.02
White (11,321)	11,493	93.99
Not Hispanic (10,800)	10,943	89.49
Hispanic (521)	550	4.50

River Edge

Place Type: Borough
County: Bergen
Population: 11,340†

Ancestry‡	Population	%
American (207)	207	1.85
Arab (28)	108	0.96
Lebanese (18)	85	0.76
Syrian (10)	23	0.21
Armenian (23)	36	0.32
Austrian (80)	97	0.87
Belgian (0)	7	0.06
British (10)	52	0.46
Canadian (14)	30	0.27
Croatian (71)	127	1.13
Czech (0)	93	0.83
Danish (14)	54	0.48
Dutch (10)	154	1.38
Eastern European (74)	80	0.71
English (65)	492	4.39
European (12)	12	0.11
Finnish (11)	38	0.34
French, ex. Basque (15)	200	1.79
French Canadian (0)	24	0.21
German (279)	1,591	14.21
Greek (130)	184	1.64
Hungarian (9)	229	2.04
Irish (851)	2,751	24.56
Italian (1,143)	2,710	24.20
Latvian (0)	12	0.11
Lithuanian (5)	28	0.25
Macedonian (15)	15	0.13
Norwegian (31)	78	0.70
Polish (256)	537	4.80
Portuguese (0)	14	0.13
Romanian (30)	67	0.60
Russian (126)	351	3.13
Scotch-Irish (47)	106	0.95
Scottish (27)	82	0.73
Slovak (12)	34	0.30
Swedish (0)	31	0.28
Swiss (8)	8	0.07
Ukrainian (43)	74	0.66
Welsh (0)	44	0.39

Hispanic Origin	Population	%
Hispanic or Latino (of any race)	869	7.66
Central American, ex. Mexican	35	0.31
Costa Rican	10	0.09
Guatemalan	7	0.06
Honduran	4	0.04
Nicaraguan	1	0.01
Salvadoran	13	0.11
Cuban	139	1.23
Dominican Republic	102	0.90
Mexican	56	0.49
Puerto Rican	211	1.86
South American	246	2.17
Argentinean	32	0.28
Chilean	12	0.11
Colombian	111	0.98
Ecuadorian	41	0.36
Peruvian	26	0.23
Uruguayan	4	0.04
Venezuelan	13	0.11
Other South American	7	0.06
Other Hispanic or Latino	80	0.71

Race*	Population	%
African-American/Black (172)	209	1.84
Not Hispanic (156)	178	1.57
Hispanic (16)	31	0.27
American Indian/Alaska Native (6)	28	0.25
Not Hispanic (5)	18	0.16
Hispanic (1)	10	0.09
Cherokee (0)	5	0.04
South American Ind. (0)	7	0.06
Tlingit-Haida *(Alaska Native)* (1)	1	0.01
Asian (2,516)	2,617	23.08
Not Hispanic (2,505)	2,592	22.86
Hispanic (11)	25	0.22
Bangladeshi (4)	4	0.04
Chinese, ex. Taiwanese (452)	484	4.27
Filipino (254)	280	2.47
Indian (266)	306	2.70
Indonesian (5)	5	0.04
Japanese (119)	132	1.16
Korean (1,264)	1,313	11.58
Pakistani (27)	27	0.24
Sri Lankan (5)	6	0.05
Taiwanese (29)	29	0.26
Thai (26)	30	0.26
Vietnamese (16)	16	0.14
Hawaii Native/Pacific Islander (9)	16	0.14
Not Hispanic (9)	15	0.13
Hispanic (0)	1	0.01
White (8,326)	8,466	74.66
Not Hispanic (7,669)	7,767	68.49
Hispanic (657)	699	6.16

River Vale

Place Type: Township
County: Bergen
Population: 9,659†

Ancestry‡	Population	%
American (439)	439	4.58
Arab (135)	169	1.77
Arab (12)	12	0.13
Egyptian (26)	26	0.27
Lebanese (77)	100	1.04
Palestinian (7)	7	0.07
Syrian (13)	24	0.25
Armenian (93)	121	1.26
Australian (8)	8	0.08
Austrian (73)	188	1.96
Belgian (8)	18	0.19
British (9)	9	0.09
Canadian (0)	15	0.16
Croatian (11)	29	0.30
Czech (12)	12	0.13
Czechoslovakian (9)	21	0.22
Danish (0)	10	0.10
Dutch (0)	279	2.91
Eastern European (23)	23	0.24
English (55)	485	5.07
European (140)	166	1.73
Finnish (0)	27	0.28
French, ex. Basque (17)	238	2.49
French Canadian (8)	28	0.29
German (348)	1,697	17.72
Greek (173)	337	3.52
Hungarian (38)	199	2.08
Iranian (37)	70	0.73
Irish (593)	1,896	19.80
Israeli (45)	83	0.87
Italian (1,104)	2,262	23.62
Lithuanian (0)	7	0.07
Norwegian (119)	157	1.64
Polish (224)	883	9.22
Romanian (7)	59	0.62
Russian (130)	561	5.86
Scotch-Irish (15)	76	0.79
Scottish (0)	33	0.34
Slovak (8)	17	0.18
Slovene (9)	9	0.09
Swedish (0)	9	0.09
Swiss (12)	37	0.39
Turkish (0)	12	0.13
Ukrainian (19)	91	0.95
Welsh (0)	68	0.71
West Indian, ex. Hispanic (9)	9	0.09
Haitian (9)	9	0.09
Yugoslavian (0)	42	0.44

Hispanic Origin	Population	%
Hispanic or Latino (of any race)	481	4.98
Central American, ex. Mexican	25	0.26
Costa Rican	3	0.03
Guatemalan	7	0.07
Nicaraguan	1	0.01
Panamanian	1	0.01
Salvadoran	13	0.13
Cuban	122	1.26
Dominican Republic	58	0.60
Mexican	53	0.55
Puerto Rican	96	0.99
South American	87	0.90
Argentinean	9	0.09
Bolivian	1	0.01
Chilean	1	0.01
Colombian	47	0.49
Ecuadorian	14	0.14
Peruvian	11	0.11
Uruguayan	2	0.02
Venezuelan	2	0.02
Other Hispanic or Latino	40	0.41

Race*	Population	%
African-American/Black (68)	106	1.10
Not Hispanic (64)	89	0.92
Hispanic (4)	17	0.18
American Indian/Alaska Native (4)	24	0.25
Not Hispanic (2)	17	0.18
Hispanic (2)	7	0.07
Blackfeet (0)	2	0.02
Central American Ind. (2)	2	0.02
Cherokee (0)	4	0.04
Mexican American Ind. (0)	3	0.03
Asian (813)	884	9.15
Not Hispanic (809)	877	9.08
Hispanic (4)	7	0.07
Cambodian (1)	1	0.01
Chinese, ex. Taiwanese (144)	188	1.95
Filipino (52)	68	0.70
Indian (111)	115	1.19
Indonesian (1)	1	0.01
Japanese (55)	64	0.66
Korean (406)	422	4.37
Pakistani (4)	4	0.04
Taiwanese (22)	28	0.29
Thai (5)	5	0.05
Vietnamese (1)	1	0.01
Hawaii Native/Pacific Islander (0)	9	0.09
Not Hispanic (0)	8	0.08
Hispanic (0)	1	0.01
Guamanian/Chamorro (0)	3	0.03
Native Hawaiian (0)	5	0.05
White (8,582)	8,713	90.21
Not Hispanic (8,186)	8,287	85.80
Hispanic (396)	426	4.41

Riverside

Place Type: Township
County: Burlington
Population: 8,079†

Ancestry‡	Population	%
African, Sub-Saharan (13)	13	0.16
Other Sub-Saharan African (13)	13	0.16
American (164)	164	2.02
Armenian (88)	98	1.21
Austrian (12)	23	0.28
Brazilian (740)	764	9.40
British (39)	48	0.59
Croatian (12)	53	0.65
Dutch (10)	89	1.10
Eastern European (0)	19	0.23

*Notes: † The Census 2010 population figure is used to calculate the percentages in the Hispanic Origin and Race categories. Ancestry percentages are based on the 2006-2010 American Community Survey population (not shown); ‡ Numbers in parentheses indicate the number of people reporting a single ancestry; * Numbers in parentheses indicate the number of persons reporting this race alone, not in combination with any other race; Please refer to the Explanation of Data for more information.*

Ancestry	Population	%
English (104)	829	10.20
French, ex. Basque (0)	26	0.32
French Canadian (6)	51	0.63
German (237)	1,733	21.33
Greek (0)	47	0.58
Hungarian (30)	196	2.41
Irish (491)	2,154	26.51
Italian (588)	1,845	22.71
Norwegian (9)	9	0.11
Polish (201)	901	11.09
Portuguese (272)	308	3.79
Romanian (0)	21	0.26
Russian (0)	12	0.15
Scandinavian (18)	53	0.65
Scotch-Irish (38)	93	1.14
Scottish (49)	124	1.53
Slovak (10)	26	0.32
Swedish (0)	30	0.37
Ukrainian (5)	5	0.06
Welsh (22)	47	0.58
West Indian, ex. Hispanic (19)	19	0.23
West Indian (19)	19	0.23

Hispanic Origin	Population	%
Hispanic or Latino (of any race)	916	11.34
Central American, ex. Mexican	119	1.47
Costa Rican	6	0.07
Guatemalan	16	0.20
Honduran	78	0.97
Nicaraguan	1	0.01
Panamanian	10	0.12
Salvadoran	8	0.10
Cuban	22	0.27
Dominican Republic	23	0.28
Mexican	95	1.18
Puerto Rican	285	3.53
South American	232	2.87
Argentinean	8	0.10
Chilean	4	0.05
Colombian	12	0.15
Ecuadorian	190	2.35
Peruvian	15	0.19
Other South American	3	0.04
Other Hispanic or Latino	140	1.73

Race*	Population	%
African-American/Black (516)	694	8.59
Not Hispanic (481)	628	7.77
Hispanic (35)	66	0.82
American Indian/Alaska Native (21)	166	2.05
Not Hispanic (12)	135	1.67
Hispanic (9)	31	0.38
Blackfeet (1)	1	0.01
Central American Ind. (8)	8	0.10
Cherokee (3)	16	0.20
Chickasaw (0)	1	0.01
Delaware (3)	6	0.07
Mexican American Ind. (0)	3	0.04
Sioux (0)	1	0.01
Asian (77)	132	1.63
Not Hispanic (74)	127	1.57
Hispanic (3)	5	0.06
Burmese (2)	2	0.02
Chinese, ex. Taiwanese (7)	7	0.09
Filipino (12)	23	0.28
Indian (25)	40	0.50
Indonesian (1)	2	0.02
Japanese (1)	8	0.10
Korean (14)	25	0.31
Pakistani (7)	7	0.09
Thai (2)	4	0.05
Vietnamese (2)	2	0.02
Hawaii Native/Pacific Islander (4)	11	0.14
Not Hispanic (4)	11	0.14
Native Hawaiian (4)	8	0.10
White (6,480)	6,807	84.26
Not Hispanic (6,076)	6,312	78.13
Hispanic (404)	495	6.13

Robbinsville

Place Type: Township
County: Mercer
Population: 13,642†

Ancestry‡	Population	%
African, Sub-Saharan (133)	157	1.21
Ethiopian (84)	108	0.83
South African (49)	49	0.38
American (419)	419	3.22
Arab (251)	406	3.12
Egyptian (134)	193	1.48
Iraqi (0)	34	0.26
Lebanese (117)	179	1.38
Armenian (0)	18	0.14
Austrian (0)	48	0.37
Brazilian (18)	18	0.14
British (80)	150	1.15
Bulgarian (18)	18	0.14
Canadian (17)	17	0.13
Croatian (34)	34	0.26
Czech (13)	13	0.10
Czechoslovakian (0)	78	0.60
Dutch (0)	112	0.86
Eastern European (89)	118	0.91
English (225)	1,263	9.70
European (90)	125	0.96
Finnish (16)	16	0.12
French, ex. Basque (19)	196	1.51
French Canadian (17)	56	0.43
German (381)	1,985	15.25
Greek (73)	148	1.14
Guyanese (0)	61	0.47
Hungarian (73)	325	2.50
Irish (533)	2,164	16.63
Italian (1,329)	2,972	22.83
Lithuanian (20)	54	0.41
Norwegian (10)	132	1.01
Pennsylvania German (19)	19	0.15
Polish (804)	1,564	12.02
Portuguese (35)	35	0.27
Romanian (0)	86	0.66
Russian (31)	202	1.55
Scotch-Irish (72)	97	0.75
Scottish (94)	267	2.05
Slavic (38)	110	0.85
Slovak (31)	72	0.55
Slovene (10)	42	0.32
Swedish (18)	67	0.51
Swiss (0)	15	0.12
Turkish (56)	67	0.51
Ukrainian (127)	266	2.04
Welsh (15)	31	0.24
West Indian, ex. Hispanic (18)	18	0.14
Jamaican (18)	18	0.14
Yugoslavian (14)	14	0.11

Hispanic Origin	Population	%
Hispanic or Latino (of any race)	564	4.13
Central American, ex. Mexican	61	0.45
Costa Rican	4	0.03
Guatemalan	19	0.14
Honduran	21	0.15
Panamanian	8	0.06
Salvadoran	9	0.07
Cuban	58	0.43
Dominican Republic	30	0.22
Mexican	35	0.26
Puerto Rican	196	1.44
South American	121	0.89
Argentinean	6	0.04
Bolivian	3	0.02
Chilean	5	0.04
Colombian	67	0.49
Ecuadorian	25	0.18
Peruvian	7	0.05
Uruguayan	1	0.01
Venezuelan	6	0.04
Other South American	1	0.01
Other Hispanic or Latino	63	0.46

Race*	Population	%
African-American/Black (426)	499	3.66
Not Hispanic (407)	459	3.36
Hispanic (19)	40	0.29
American Indian/Alaska Native (13)	35	0.26
Not Hispanic (12)	32	0.23
Hispanic (1)	3	0.02
Apache (0)	1	0.01
Blackfeet (0)	2	0.01
Cherokee (1)	4	0.03
Chickasaw (0)	2	0.01
Delaware (1)	3	0.02
Shoshone (3)	3	0.02
Sioux (0)	2	0.01
Tohono O'Odham (1)	1	0.01
Asian (1,729)	1,878	13.77
Not Hispanic (1,728)	1,865	13.67
Hispanic (1)	13	0.10
Bangladeshi (1)	1	0.01
Cambodian (3)	6	0.04
Chinese, ex. Taiwanese (259)	300	2.20
Filipino (178)	216	1.58
Indian (1,019)	1,038	7.61
Indonesian (4)	6	0.04
Japanese (25)	48	0.35
Korean (91)	101	0.74
Malaysian (0)	2	0.01
Nepalese (2)	2	0.01
Pakistani (64)	65	0.48
Sri Lankan (4)	6	0.04
Taiwanese (11)	11	0.08
Thai (2)	4	0.03
Vietnamese (34)	47	0.34
Hawaii Native/Pacific Islander (0)	3	0.02
Not Hispanic (0)	3	0.02
White (11,131)	11,331	83.06
Not Hispanic (10,708)	10,866	79.65
Hispanic (423)	465	3.41

Robertsville

Place Type: CDP
County: Monmouth
Population: 11,297†

Ancestry‡	Population	%
American (1,093)	1,093	9.90
Arab (126)	154	1.40
Egyptian (126)	145	1.31
Syrian (0)	9	0.08
Armenian (0)	12	0.11
Austrian (0)	62	0.56
British (35)	35	0.32
Czech (0)	30	0.27
Czechoslovakian (11)	11	0.10
Dutch (0)	82	0.74
Eastern European (97)	97	0.88
English (103)	364	3.30
European (206)	269	2.44
Finnish (0)	24	0.22
French, ex. Basque (0)	72	0.65
French Canadian (0)	35	0.32
German (161)	846	7.66
Greek (144)	219	1.98
Hungarian (62)	145	1.31
Irish (183)	965	8.74
Israeli (11)	30	0.27
Italian (1,467)	2,519	22.82
Lithuanian (0)	24	0.22
Maltese (14)	28	0.25
Norwegian (37)	85	0.77
Polish (456)	1,268	11.49
Portuguese (15)	46	0.42
Romanian (90)	100	0.91
Russian (738)	1,346	12.19
Scottish (0)	8	0.07
Slavic (0)	8	0.07
Slovak (14)	14	0.13

*Notes: † The Census 2010 population figure is used to calculate the percentages in the Hispanic Origin and Race categories. Ancestry percentages are based on the 2006-2010 American Community Survey population (not shown); ‡ Numbers in parentheses indicate the number of people reporting a single ancestry; * Numbers in parentheses indicate the number of persons reporting this race alone, not in combination with any other race; Please refer to the Explanation of Data for more information.*

	Population	%
Swedish (0)	11	0.10
Turkish (0)	26	0.24
Ukrainian (21)	46	0.42
Welsh (8)	23	0.21
West Indian, ex. Hispanic (35)	35	0.32
Jamaican (19)	19	0.17
Trinidadian/Tobagonian (16)	16	0.14
Yugoslavian (0)	19	0.17

Hispanic Origin	Population	%
Hispanic or Latino (of any race)	458	4.05
Central American, ex. Mexican	12	0.11
Costa Rican	1	0.01
Guatemalan	5	0.04
Honduran	1	0.01
Nicaraguan	1	0.01
Salvadoran	4	0.04
Cuban	64	0.57
Dominican Republic	16	0.14
Mexican	36	0.32
Puerto Rican	180	1.59
South American	99	0.88
Argentinean	22	0.19
Chilean	5	0.04
Colombian	34	0.30
Ecuadorian	16	0.14
Paraguayan	1	0.01
Peruvian	14	0.12
Uruguayan	1	0.01
Venezuelan	3	0.03
Other South American	3	0.03
Other Hispanic or Latino	51	0.45

Race*	Population	%
African-American/Black (270)	309	2.74
Not Hispanic (261)	285	2.52
Hispanic (9)	24	0.21
American Indian/Alaska Native (3)	20	0.18
Not Hispanic (2)	13	0.12
Hispanic (1)	7	0.06
Cherokee (1)	2	0.02
Mexican American Ind. (0)	2	0.02
Navajo (1)	1	0.01
Asian (1,324)	1,390	12.30
Not Hispanic (1,320)	1,377	12.19
Hispanic (4)	13	0.12
Bangladeshi (6)	7	0.06
Cambodian (1)	1	0.01
Chinese, ex. Taiwanese (572)	603	5.34
Filipino (97)	105	0.93
Indian (420)	449	3.97
Indonesian (3)	7	0.06
Japanese (1)	1	0.01
Korean (118)	125	1.11
Malaysian (0)	5	0.04
Nepalese (0)	1	0.01
Pakistani (22)	24	0.21
Taiwanese (34)	40	0.35
Thai (4)	6	0.05
Vietnamese (16)	16	0.14
Hawaii Native/Pacific Islander (1)	4	0.04
Not Hispanic (1)	4	0.04
Guamanian/Chamorro (1)	2	0.02
White (9,513)	9,597	84.95
Not Hispanic (9,145)	9,211	81.53
Hispanic (368)	386	3.42

Rockaway

Place Type: Township
County: Morris
Population: 24,156†

Ancestry‡	Population	%
African, Sub-Saharan (119)	140	0.58
African (119)	140	0.58
Albanian (0)	9	0.04
American (781)	781	3.25
Arab (66)	93	0.39
Arab (22)	22	0.09
Egyptian (10)	10	0.04
Lebanese (19)	19	0.08
Syrian (15)	42	0.17
Armenian (0)	14	0.06
Australian (12)	12	0.05
Austrian (29)	204	0.85
Belgian (0)	39	0.16
British (24)	40	0.17
Canadian (164)	231	0.96
Celtic (9)	9	0.04
Czech (128)	333	1.39
Czechoslovakian (0)	57	0.24
Danish (15)	98	0.41
Dutch (90)	364	1.52
Eastern European (160)	160	0.67
English (330)	1,496	6.23
European (220)	220	0.92
Finnish (25)	25	0.10
French, ex. Basque (75)	381	1.59
French Canadian (19)	73	0.30
German (839)	3,603	15.00
Greek (83)	163	0.68
Hungarian (104)	387	1.61
Irish (1,300)	4,647	19.35
Italian (2,486)	5,689	23.68
Latvian (25)	25	0.10
Lithuanian (37)	169	0.70
Macedonian (18)	18	0.07
Norwegian (159)	374	1.56
Pennsylvania German (11)	11	0.05
Polish (740)	2,366	9.85
Portuguese (104)	188	0.78
Romanian (78)	184	0.77
Russian (550)	1,276	5.31
Scandinavian (0)	14	0.06
Scotch-Irish (69)	230	0.96
Scottish (66)	292	1.22
Slavic (26)	26	0.11
Slovak (61)	251	1.04
Swedish (36)	130	0.54
Swiss (32)	206	0.86
Turkish (25)	67	0.28
Ukrainian (117)	273	1.14
Welsh (0)	153	0.64
West Indian, ex. Hispanic (230)	276	1.15
British West Indian (0)	12	0.05
Haitian (205)	205	0.85
Jamaican (9)	43	0.18
Trinidadian/Tobagonian (16)	16	0.07
Yugoslavian (0)	17	0.07

Hispanic Origin	Population	%
Hispanic or Latino (of any race)	2,705	11.20
Central American, ex. Mexican	242	1.00
Costa Rican	42	0.17
Guatemalan	59	0.24
Honduran	91	0.38
Nicaraguan	13	0.05
Panamanian	9	0.04
Salvadoran	28	0.12
Cuban	155	0.64
Dominican Republic	144	0.60
Mexican	185	0.77
Puerto Rican	711	2.94
South American	1,030	4.26
Argentinean	20	0.08
Bolivian	3	0.01
Chilean	75	0.31
Colombian	566	2.34
Ecuadorian	165	0.68
Paraguayan	6	0.02
Peruvian	134	0.55
Uruguayan	42	0.17
Venezuelan	18	0.07
Other South American	1	<0.01
Other Hispanic or Latino	238	0.99

Race*	Population	%
African-American/Black (616)	788	3.26
Not Hispanic (552)	667	2.76
Hispanic (64)	121	0.50
American Indian/Alaska Native (28)	106	0.44
Not Hispanic (12)	55	0.23
Hispanic (16)	51	0.21
Central American Ind. (5)	10	0.04
Cherokee (0)	8	0.03
Delaware (2)	12	0.05
Hopi (3)	3	0.01
Iroquois (0)	1	<0.01
Mexican American Ind. (2)	2	0.01
Navajo (1)	2	0.01
Seminole (1)	2	0.01
South American Ind. (1)	16	0.07
Spanish American Ind. (0)	2	0.01
Asian (1,611)	1,786	7.39
Not Hispanic (1,605)	1,771	7.33
Hispanic (6)	15	0.06
Bangladeshi (8)	8	0.03
Chinese, ex. Taiwanese (285)	333	1.38
Filipino (294)	338	1.40
Indian (764)	802	3.32
Japanese (23)	50	0.21
Korean (74)	83	0.34
Nepalese (7)	7	0.03
Pakistani (37)	44	0.18
Sri Lankan (5)	6	0.02
Taiwanese (27)	29	0.12
Thai (12)	13	0.05
Vietnamese (44)	54	0.22
Hawaii Native/Pacific Islander (4)	16	0.07
Not Hispanic (4)	16	0.07
Guamanian/Chamorro (1)	6	0.02
Native Hawaiian (0)	5	0.02
White (20,878)	21,293	88.15
Not Hispanic (18,919)	19,200	79.48
Hispanic (1,959)	2,093	8.66

Roselle Park

Place Type: Borough
County: Union
Population: 13,297†

Ancestry‡	Population	%
African, Sub-Saharan (99)	112	0.85
African (40)	40	0.30
Nigerian (0)	13	0.10
Senegalese (59)	59	0.45
Albanian (237)	237	1.80
American (237)	237	1.80
Arab (79)	79	0.60
Lebanese (12)	12	0.09
Syrian (9)	9	0.07
Other Arab (58)	58	0.44
Austrian (22)	71	0.54
Brazilian (0)	16	0.12
British (31)	31	0.24
Canadian (14)	19	0.14
Croatian (9)	25	0.19
Czech (36)	44	0.33
Czechoslovakian (11)	11	0.08
Danish (11)	25	0.19
Dutch (0)	41	0.31
Eastern European (0)	12	0.09
English (72)	285	2.16
Estonian (18)	42	0.32
European (34)	44	0.33
French, ex. Basque (0)	65	0.49
German (222)	1,224	9.29
Greek (34)	34	0.26
Hungarian (107)	218	1.65
Icelander (10)	10	0.08
Irish (501)	1,511	11.47
Italian (1,372)	2,360	17.91
Lithuanian (0)	78	0.59
Macedonian (51)	51	0.39
Norwegian (0)	12	0.09
Polish (469)	989	7.50
Portuguese (329)	386	2.93
Romanian (34)	71	0.54

*Notes: † The Census 2010 population figure is used to calculate the percentages in the Hispanic Origin and Race categories. Ancestry percentages are based on the 2006-2010 American Community Survey population (not shown); ‡ Numbers in parentheses indicate the number of people reporting a single ancestry; * Numbers in parentheses indicate the number of persons reporting this race alone, not in combination with any other race; Please refer to the Explanation of Data for more information.*

Russian (14)	188	1.43
Scotch-Irish (30)	50	0.38
Scottish (25)	75	0.57
Slavic (25)	25	0.19
Slovak (23)	45	0.34
Swedish (0)	34	0.26
Swiss (0)	40	0.30
Ukrainian (47)	60	0.46
West Indian, ex. Hispanic (173)	187	1.42
Barbadian (11)	25	0.19
Haitian (162)	162	1.23

Hispanic Origin	Population	%
Hispanic or Latino (of any race)	3,809	28.65
Central American, ex. Mexican	240	1.80
Costa Rican	47	0.35
Guatemalan	48	0.36
Honduran	55	0.41
Nicaraguan	4	0.03
Panamanian	17	0.13
Salvadoran	69	0.52
Cuban	309	2.32
Dominican Republic	227	1.71
Mexican	556	4.18
Puerto Rican	660	4.96
South American	1,488	11.19
Argentinean	85	0.64
Bolivian	27	0.20
Chilean	40	0.30
Colombian	726	5.46
Ecuadorian	297	2.23
Paraguayan	1	0.01
Peruvian	201	1.51
Uruguayan	86	0.65
Venezuelan	5	0.04
Other South American	20	0.15
Other Hispanic or Latino	329	2.47

Race*	Population	%
African-American/Black (783)	894	6.72
Not Hispanic (697)	758	5.70
Hispanic (86)	136	1.02
American Indian/Alaska Native (20)	59	0.44
Not Hispanic (7)	33	0.25
Hispanic (13)	26	0.20
Apache (0)	1	0.01
Blackfeet (0)	4	0.03
Cherokee (2)	12	0.09
Mexican American Ind. (1)	1	0.01
South American Ind. (3)	5	0.04
Asian (1,354)	1,456	10.95
Not Hispanic (1,337)	1,433	10.78
Hispanic (17)	23	0.17
Bangladeshi (4)	4	0.03
Chinese, ex. Taiwanese (138)	157	1.18
Filipino (289)	322	2.42
Indian (820)	850	6.39
Indonesian (1)	1	0.01
Japanese (21)	30	0.23
Korean (22)	26	0.20
Malaysian (5)	5	0.04
Pakistani (24)	24	0.18
Sri Lankan (6)	6	0.05
Taiwanese (2)	2	0.02
Thai (6)	8	0.06
Vietnamese (7)	10	0.08
Hawaii Native/Pacific Islander (2)	8	0.06
Not Hispanic (0)	2	0.02
Hispanic (2)	6	0.05
Guamanian/Chamorro (1)	1	0.01
Native Hawaiian (0)	1	0.01
White (9,802)	10,072	75.75
Not Hispanic (7,261)	7,375	55.46
Hispanic (2,541)	2,697	20.28

Roselle

Place Type: Borough
County: Union
Population: 21,085†

Ancestry‡	Population	%
African, Sub-Saharan (634)	661	3.15
African (356)	383	1.83
Ghanaian (94)	94	0.45
Kenyan (56)	56	0.27
Nigerian (116)	116	0.55
Sierra Leonean (12)	12	0.06
Albanian (0)	19	0.09
American (248)	248	1.18
Arab (78)	78	0.37
Arab (66)	66	0.31
Moroccan (12)	12	0.06
Assyrian/Chaldean/Syriac (11)	11	0.05
Austrian (0)	23	0.11
Brazilian (144)	144	0.69
British (9)	14	0.07
Celtic (8)	8	0.04
Czech (0)	19	0.09
Czechoslovakian (19)	19	0.09
Dutch (9)	90	0.43
English (46)	221	1.05
European (11)	11	0.05
French, ex. Basque (0)	128	0.61
German (110)	698	3.33
Greek (11)	23	0.11
Guyanese (85)	85	0.41
Hungarian (53)	131	0.63
Irish (330)	787	3.76
Italian (419)	626	2.99
Latvian (12)	12	0.06
Northern European (9)	19	0.09
Norwegian (14)	14	0.07
Polish (227)	347	1.66
Portuguese (197)	199	0.95
Romanian (0)	7	0.03
Russian (23)	35	0.17
Scotch-Irish (26)	41	0.20
Scottish (15)	61	0.29
Slavic (5)	5	0.02
Slovak (12)	12	0.06
Swedish (0)	36	0.17
Ukrainian (63)	99	0.47
Welsh (8)	33	0.16
West Indian, ex. Hispanic (2,782)	2,851	13.61
Barbadian (11)	11	0.05
Haitian (2,237)	2,264	10.80
Jamaican (417)	433	2.07
Trinidadian/Tobagonian (15)	15	0.07
West Indian (102)	128	0.61

Hispanic Origin	Population	%
Hispanic or Latino (of any race)	5,644	26.77
Central American, ex. Mexican	514	2.44
Costa Rican	33	0.16
Guatemalan	39	0.18
Honduran	73	0.35
Nicaraguan	37	0.18
Panamanian	53	0.25
Salvadoran	279	1.32
Cuban	247	1.17
Dominican Republic	438	2.08
Mexican	963	4.57
Puerto Rican	1,242	5.89
South American	1,771	8.40
Argentinean	59	0.28
Bolivian	6	0.03
Chilean	25	0.12
Colombian	767	3.64
Ecuadorian	242	1.15
Paraguayan	3	0.01
Peruvian	506	2.40
Uruguayan	124	0.59
Venezuelan	27	0.13
Other South American	12	0.06
Other Hispanic or Latino	469	2.22

Race*	Population	%
African-American/Black (11,610)	11,978	56.81
Not Hispanic (11,148)	11,394	54.04
Hispanic (462)	584	2.77
American Indian/Alaska Native (65)	204	0.97
Not Hispanic (25)	121	0.57
Hispanic (40)	83	0.39
Apache (1)	1	<0.01
Blackfeet (3)	3	0.01
Central American Ind. (0)	1	<0.01
Cherokee (1)	23	0.11
Delaware (0)	1	<0.01
Iroquois (0)	1	<0.01
Mexican American Ind. (3)	3	0.01
Seminole (0)	4	0.02
Sioux (0)	2	0.01
South American Ind. (7)	17	0.08
Tohono O'Odham (0)	4	0.02
Asian (471)	577	2.74
Not Hispanic (464)	539	2.56
Hispanic (7)	38	0.18
Chinese, ex. Taiwanese (45)	67	0.32
Filipino (209)	231	1.10
Indian (126)	170	0.81
Indonesian (4)	4	0.02
Japanese (4)	15	0.07
Korean (23)	24	0.11
Laotian (1)	4	0.02
Pakistani (20)	23	0.11
Taiwanese (3)	3	0.01
Thai (2)	5	0.02
Vietnamese (20)	25	0.12
Hawaii Native/Pacific Islander (5)	45	0.21
Not Hispanic (0)	33	0.16
Hispanic (5)	12	0.06
Guamanian/Chamorro (0)	1	<0.01
Native Hawaiian (5)	5	0.02
Samoan (0)	1	<0.01
White (6,240)	6,677	31.67
Not Hispanic (3,389)	3,548	16.83
Hispanic (2,851)	3,129	14.84

Roxbury

Place Type: Township
County: Morris
Population: 23,324†

Ancestry‡	Population	%
African, Sub-Saharan (157)	371	1.59
African (14)	142	0.61
Ghanaian (133)	219	0.94
Sierra Leonean (10)	10	0.04
Albanian (65)	65	0.28
American (913)	913	3.90
Arab (279)	353	1.51
Egyptian (240)	250	1.07
Lebanese (20)	35	0.15
Syrian (19)	68	0.29
Armenian (64)	64	0.27
Australian (10)	10	0.04
Austrian (23)	289	1.24
Belgian (11)	11	0.05
Brazilian (0)	22	0.09
British (23)	43	0.18
Bulgarian (37)	37	0.16
Canadian (0)	28	0.12
Czech (16)	109	0.47
Czechoslovakian (21)	47	0.20
Danish (39)	54	0.23
Dutch (53)	292	1.25
Eastern European (129)	146	0.62
English (373)	2,075	8.87
European (109)	109	0.47
Finnish (14)	39	0.17
French, ex. Basque (101)	483	2.07
French Canadian (126)	240	1.03
German (660)	3,727	15.94
Greek (8)	307	1.31
Guyanese (0)	12	0.05
Hungarian (193)	577	2.47
Irish (783)	4,142	17.71
Italian (2,790)	5,853	25.03
Latvian (0)	30	0.13

*Notes: † The Census 2010 population figure is used to calculate the percentages in the Hispanic Origin and Race categories. Ancestry percentages are based on the 2006-2010 American Community Survey population (not shown); ‡ Numbers in parentheses indicate the number of people reporting a single ancestry; * Numbers in parentheses indicate the number of persons reporting this race alone, not in combination with any other race; Please refer to the Explanation of Data for more information.*

Lithuanian (32)	41	0.18
Macedonian (0)	10	0.04
Norwegian (84)	268	1.15
Pennsylvania German (0)	9	0.04
Polish (507)	1,874	8.01
Portuguese (163)	228	0.97
Romanian (19)	59	0.25
Russian (240)	600	2.57
Scandinavian (0)	9	0.04
Scotch-Irish (93)	283	1.21
Scottish (74)	491	2.10
Slavic (21)	67	0.29
Slovak (57)	121	0.52
Slovene (0)	10	0.04
Swedish (92)	264	1.13
Swiss (0)	68	0.29
Turkish (50)	76	0.32
Ukrainian (134)	221	0.94
Welsh (10)	147	0.63
West Indian, ex. Hispanic (121)	121	0.52
Bahamian (9)	9	0.04
Haitian (42)	42	0.18
Jamaican (70)	70	0.30
Yugoslavian (16)	26	0.11

Hispanic Origin	Population	%
Hispanic or Latino (of any race)	2,083	8.93
Central American, ex. Mexican	220	0.94
Costa Rican	51	0.22
Guatemalan	49	0.21
Honduran	77	0.33
Nicaraguan	11	0.05
Panamanian	2	0.01
Salvadoran	30	0.13
Cuban	156	0.67
Dominican Republic	61	0.26
Mexican	173	0.74
Puerto Rican	628	2.69
South American	647	2.77
Argentinean	39	0.17
Bolivian	6	0.03
Chilean	36	0.15
Colombian	327	1.40
Ecuadorian	124	0.53
Paraguayan	5	0.02
Peruvian	57	0.24
Uruguayan	36	0.15
Venezuelan	16	0.07
Other South American	1	<0.01
Other Hispanic or Latino	198	0.85

Race*	Population	%
African-American/Black (546)	700	3.00
Not Hispanic (496)	627	2.69
Hispanic (50)	73	0.31
American Indian/Alaska Native (22)	92	0.39
Not Hispanic (6)	61	0.26
Hispanic (16)	31	0.13
Blackfeet (0)	1	<0.01
Central American Ind. (1)	1	<0.01
Cherokee (2)	8	0.03
Cree (0)	1	<0.01
Iroquois (0)	4	0.02
Mexican American Ind. (1)	1	<0.01
Ottawa (1)	2	0.01
Pueblo (1)	8	0.03
Sioux (0)	4	0.02
South American Ind. (1)	3	0.01
Asian (1,346)	1,509	6.47
Not Hispanic (1,330)	1,474	6.32
Hispanic (16)	35	0.15
Bangladeshi (7)	7	0.03
Cambodian (1)	3	0.01
Chinese, ex. Taiwanese (249)	288	1.23
Filipino (268)	306	1.31
Indian (551)	591	2.53
Indonesian (2)	2	0.01
Japanese (14)	22	0.09
Korean (88)	109	0.47
Malaysian (3)	3	0.01
Pakistani (21)	24	0.10
Sri Lankan (12)	18	0.08
Taiwanese (15)	20	0.09
Thai (6)	6	0.03
Vietnamese (81)	97	0.42
Hawaii Native/Pacific Islander (12)	22	0.09
Not Hispanic (3)	12	0.05
Hispanic (9)	10	0.04
Guamanian/Chamorro (4)	4	0.02
Native Hawaiian (5)	7	0.03
Samoan (0)	1	<0.01
White (20,573)	20,996	90.02
Not Hispanic (19,041)	19,346	82.94
Hispanic (1,532)	1,650	7.07

Runnemede

Place Type: Borough
County: Camden
Population: 8,468†

Ancestry‡	Population	%
Albanian (22)	22	0.26
American (189)	189	2.23
Arab (13)	13	0.15
Lebanese (13)	13	0.15
Austrian (13)	30	0.35
Canadian (8)	8	0.09
Czech (0)	41	0.48
Danish (0)	11	0.13
Dutch (0)	123	1.45
English (282)	1,079	12.71
European (21)	21	0.25
Finnish (0)	8	0.09
French, ex. Basque (9)	118	1.39
French Canadian (0)	14	0.16
German (403)	1,987	23.41
Greek (11)	42	0.49
Hungarian (0)	89	1.05
Irish (584)	2,661	31.35
Israeli (0)	19	0.22
Italian (1,253)	2,587	30.48
Lithuanian (0)	69	0.81
Northern European (13)	41	0.48
Norwegian (0)	14	0.16
Pennsylvania German (0)	15	0.18
Polish (294)	828	9.76
Portuguese (40)	65	0.77
Russian (13)	108	1.27
Scotch-Irish (28)	96	1.13
Scottish (76)	176	2.07
Slavic (9)	24	0.28
Slovak (0)	69	0.81
Swedish (0)	41	0.48
Turkish (17)	17	0.20
Ukrainian (11)	30	0.35
Welsh (0)	33	0.39
West Indian, ex. Hispanic (18)	18	0.21
Jamaican (18)	18	0.21

Hispanic Origin	Population	%
Hispanic or Latino (of any race)	516	6.09
Central American, ex. Mexican	21	0.25
Costa Rican	4	0.05
Guatemalan	11	0.13
Salvadoran	6	0.07
Cuban	8	0.09
Dominican Republic	8	0.09
Mexican	126	1.49
Puerto Rican	302	3.57
South American	23	0.27
Argentinean	3	0.04
Colombian	12	0.14
Ecuadorian	2	0.02
Peruvian	1	0.01
Venezuelan	5	0.06
Other Hispanic or Latino	28	0.33

Race*	Population	%
African-American/Black (400)	456	5.38
Not Hispanic (386)	428	5.05
Hispanic (14)	28	0.33
American Indian/Alaska Native (25)	56	0.66
Not Hispanic (13)	39	0.46
Hispanic (12)	17	0.20
Blackfeet (0)	1	0.01
Cherokee (2)	11	0.13
Delaware (1)	1	0.01
Iroquois (0)	4	0.05
Mexican American Ind. (1)	1	0.01
South American Ind. (4)	4	0.05
Asian (223)	264	3.12
Not Hispanic (221)	257	3.03
Hispanic (2)	7	0.08
Bangladeshi (6)	6	0.07
Chinese, ex. Taiwanese (23)	32	0.38
Filipino (26)	49	0.58
Indian (95)	97	1.15
Japanese (2)	5	0.06
Korean (20)	27	0.32
Pakistani (14)	14	0.17
Vietnamese (29)	33	0.39
Hawaii Native/Pacific Islander (0)	4	0.05
Not Hispanic (0)	2	0.02
Hispanic (0)	2	0.02
Guamanian/Chamorro (0)	1	0.01
White (7,496)	7,612	89.89
Not Hispanic (7,221)	7,306	86.28
Hispanic (275)	306	3.61

Rutherford

Place Type: Borough
County: Bergen
Population: 18,061†

Ancestry‡	Population	%
African, Sub-Saharan (238)	250	1.39
African (218)	230	1.28
Kenyan (20)	20	0.11
Albanian (0)	25	0.14
American (314)	314	1.75
Arab (109)	135	0.75
Egyptian (95)	95	0.53
Lebanese (14)	40	0.22
Armenian (15)	62	0.35
Australian (0)	9	0.05
Austrian (28)	162	0.90
Belgian (14)	14	0.08
Brazilian (29)	50	0.28
British (0)	12	0.07
Canadian (0)	54	0.30
Croatian (16)	37	0.21
Czech (0)	44	0.24
Czechoslovakian (9)	39	0.22
Danish (0)	14	0.08
Dutch (37)	266	1.48
Eastern European (10)	10	0.06
English (174)	1,035	5.76
Estonian (0)	9	0.05
European (143)	143	0.80
Finnish (0)	32	0.18
French, ex. Basque (10)	180	1.00
French Canadian (13)	13	0.07
German (332)	2,218	12.34
Greek (175)	339	1.89
Hungarian (29)	192	1.07
Iranian (151)	151	0.84
Irish (1,164)	4,213	23.44
Israeli (40)	86	0.48
Italian (2,070)	4,354	24.23
Lithuanian (80)	127	0.71
Norwegian (9)	39	0.22
Polish (504)	1,454	8.09
Portuguese (28)	90	0.50
Romanian (0)	20	0.11
Russian (137)	444	2.47
Scotch-Irish (134)	218	1.21
Scottish (47)	246	1.37
Serbian (0)	30	0.17

*Notes: † The Census 2010 population figure is used to calculate the percentages in the Hispanic Origin and Race categories. Ancestry percentages are based on the 2006-2010 American Community Survey population (not shown); ‡ Numbers in parentheses indicate the number of people reporting a single ancestry; * Numbers in parentheses indicate the number of persons reporting this race alone, not in combination with any other race; Please refer to the Explanation of Data for more information.*

Slavic (14)	28	0.16
Slovak (15)	72	0.40
Swedish (23)	85	0.47
Swiss (0)	70	0.39
Turkish (84)	84	0.47
Ukrainian (277)	309	1.72
Welsh (9)	41	0.23
West Indian, ex. Hispanic (69)	123	0.68
Haitian (0)	5	0.03
Jamaican (0)	49	0.27
Trinidadian/Tobagonian (69)	69	0.38
Yugoslavian (11)	51	0.28

Hispanic Origin	Population	%
Hispanic or Latino (of any race)	2,543	14.08
Central American, ex. Mexican	132	0.73
Costa Rican	12	0.07
Guatemalan	31	0.17
Honduran	25	0.14
Nicaraguan	7	0.04
Panamanian	17	0.09
Salvadoran	40	0.22
Cuban	422	2.34
Dominican Republic	238	1.32
Mexican	147	0.81
Puerto Rican	641	3.55
South American	672	3.72
Argentinean	74	0.41
Bolivian	12	0.07
Chilean	34	0.19
Colombian	232	1.28
Ecuadorian	119	0.66
Paraguayan	2	0.01
Peruvian	161	0.89
Uruguayan	9	0.05
Venezuelan	18	0.10
Other South American	11	0.06
Other Hispanic or Latino	291	1.61

Race*	Population	%
African-American/Black (527)	665	3.68
Not Hispanic (454)	538	2.98
Hispanic (73)	127	0.70
American Indian/Alaska Native (13)	59	0.33
Not Hispanic (12)	43	0.24
Hispanic (1)	16	0.09
Apache (1)	2	0.01
Blackfeet (0)	1	0.01
Central American Ind. (0)	1	0.01
Cherokee (1)	7	0.04
Comanche (3)	3	0.02
Delaware (0)	1	0.01
Iroquois (0)	2	0.01
Mexican American Ind. (0)	1	0.01
Potawatomi (0)	1	0.01
Shoshone (1)	1	0.01
Sioux (0)	3	0.02
South American Ind. (0)	1	0.01
Asian (2,362)	2,607	14.43
Not Hispanic (2,340)	2,566	14.21
Hispanic (22)	41	0.23
Bangladeshi (5)	10	0.06
Chinese, ex. Taiwanese (279)	329	1.82
Filipino (246)	289	1.60
Indian (700)	740	4.10
Indonesian (3)	4	0.02
Japanese (40)	74	0.41
Korean (889)	921	5.10
Laotian (1)	3	0.02
Malaysian (1)	1	0.01
Pakistani (47)	51	0.28
Sri Lankan (3)	3	0.02
Taiwanese (4)	4	0.02
Thai (59)	69	0.38
Vietnamese (26)	38	0.21
Hawaii Native/Pacific Islander (1)	7	0.04
Not Hispanic (0)	5	0.03
Hispanic (1)	2	0.01
Guamanian/Chamorro (1)	2	0.01
White (14,010)	14,419	79.84
Not Hispanic (12,298)	12,597	69.75
Hispanic (1,712)	1,822	10.09

Saddle Brook

Place Type: Township
County: Bergen
Population: 13,659†

Ancestry‡	Population	%
African, Sub-Saharan (0)	12	0.09
African (0)	12	0.09
American (448)	448	3.32
Arab (102)	180	1.33
Lebanese (102)	139	1.03
Syrian (0)	41	0.30
Armenian (62)	134	0.99
Austrian (81)	127	0.94
British (14)	14	0.10
Carpatho Rusyn (18)	18	0.13
Croatian (63)	63	0.47
Czech (12)	27	0.20
Czechoslovakian (10)	53	0.39
Danish (0)	18	0.13
Dutch (0)	319	2.37
English (25)	397	2.94
Finnish (16)	16	0.12
French, ex. Basque (22)	102	0.76
German (419)	1,661	12.32
Greek (52)	52	0.39
Hungarian (86)	230	1.71
Iranian (36)	36	0.27
Irish (715)	2,020	14.98
Italian (3,286)	5,201	38.56
Latvian (0)	9	0.07
Macedonian (12)	12	0.09
Norwegian (72)	90	0.67
Pennsylvania German (0)	9	0.07
Polish (691)	1,456	10.80
Portuguese (12)	24	0.18
Romanian (39)	39	0.29
Russian (162)	345	2.56
Scotch-Irish (13)	68	0.50
Scottish (41)	182	1.35
Slavic (16)	16	0.12
Slovak (59)	145	1.08
Swedish (0)	43	0.32
Swiss (0)	36	0.27
Ukrainian (196)	378	2.80
Welsh (16)	41	0.30
Yugoslavian (46)	70	0.52

Hispanic Origin	Population	%
Hispanic or Latino (of any race)	1,666	12.20
Central American, ex. Mexican	89	0.65
Costa Rican	4	0.03
Guatemalan	37	0.27
Honduran	6	0.04
Nicaraguan	13	0.10
Panamanian	6	0.04
Salvadoran	19	0.14
Other Central American	4	0.03
Cuban	125	0.92
Dominican Republic	204	1.49
Mexican	40	0.29
Puerto Rican	411	3.01
South American	671	4.91
Argentinean	62	0.45
Bolivian	7	0.05
Chilean	29	0.21
Colombian	236	1.73
Ecuadorian	147	1.08
Peruvian	163	1.19
Uruguayan	18	0.13
Venezuelan	8	0.06
Other South American	1	0.01
Other Hispanic or Latino	126	0.92

Race*	Population	%
African-American/Black (316)	359	2.63
Not Hispanic (268)	294	2.15
Hispanic (48)	65	0.48
American Indian/Alaska Native (22)	60	0.44
Not Hispanic (8)	39	0.29
Hispanic (14)	21	0.15
Blackfeet (0)	3	0.02
Cherokee (0)	1	0.01
Creek (0)	1	0.01
Delaware (0)	5	0.04
Iroquois (1)	2	0.01
Mexican American Ind. (2)	2	0.01
Navajo (1)	1	0.01
South American Ind. (1)	4	0.03
Asian (1,121)	1,240	9.08
Not Hispanic (1,102)	1,202	8.80
Hispanic (19)	38	0.28
Bangladeshi (0)	4	0.03
Cambodian (1)	1	0.01
Chinese, ex. Taiwanese (134)	153	1.12
Filipino (217)	242	1.77
Indian (547)	568	4.16
Indonesian (9)	12	0.09
Japanese (12)	23	0.17
Korean (113)	126	0.92
Pakistani (33)	33	0.24
Sri Lankan (10)	10	0.07
Taiwanese (1)	2	0.01
Thai (2)	4	0.03
Vietnamese (28)	32	0.23
Hawaii Native/Pacific Islander (0)	12	0.09
Not Hispanic (0)	9	0.07
Hispanic (0)	3	0.02
Guamanian/Chamorro (0)	2	0.01
Native Hawaiian (0)	4	0.03
Samoan (0)	1	0.01
White (11,521)	11,722	85.82
Not Hispanic (10,418)	10,548	77.22
Hispanic (1,103)	1,174	8.60

Sayreville

Place Type: Borough
County: Middlesex
Population: 42,704†

Ancestry‡	Population	%
African, Sub-Saharan (792)	812	1.92
African (310)	310	0.73
Ethiopian (13)	13	0.03
Ghanaian (155)	155	0.37
Kenyan (103)	103	0.24
Liberian (46)	46	0.11
Nigerian (90)	90	0.21
Ugandan (48)	68	0.16
Other Sub-Saharan African (27)	27	0.06
Albanian (73)	104	0.25
American (1,347)	1,347	3.19
Arab (626)	746	1.76
Arab (181)	229	0.54
Egyptian (298)	333	0.79
Jordanian (90)	90	0.21
Lebanese (12)	19	0.04
Syrian (0)	30	0.07
Other Arab (45)	45	0.11
Austrian (17)	80	0.19
Belgian (9)	30	0.07
Brazilian (148)	148	0.35
British (10)	18	0.04
Bulgarian (0)	9	0.02
Canadian (0)	11	0.03
Croatian (0)	12	0.03
Czech (27)	105	0.25
Czechoslovakian (22)	89	0.21
Danish (18)	245	0.58
Dutch (28)	193	0.46
Eastern European (26)	26	0.06
English (370)	1,038	2.46
European (120)	147	0.35
French, ex. Basque (61)	473	1.12
French Canadian (12)	102	0.24

*Notes: † The Census 2010 population figure is used to calculate the percentages in the Hispanic Origin and Race categories. Ancestry percentages are based on the 2006-2010 American Community Survey population (not shown); ‡ Numbers in parentheses indicate the number of people reporting a single ancestry; * Numbers in parentheses indicate the number of persons reporting this race alone, not in combination with any other race; Please refer to the Explanation of Data for more information.*

German (1,007)	4,434	10.49
Greek (243)	413	0.98
Guyanese (37)	37	0.09
Hungarian (186)	605	1.43
Irish (2,086)	6,176	14.61
Italian (4,172)	7,370	17.43
Lithuanian (8)	83	0.20
Macedonian (22)	22	0.05
Maltese (0)	10	0.02
Norwegian (109)	197	0.47
Pennsylvania German (0)	8	0.02
Polish (3,673)	6,405	15.15
Portuguese (259)	421	1.00
Romanian (55)	66	0.16
Russian (518)	880	2.08
Scotch-Irish (40)	166	0.39
Scottish (37)	137	0.32
Slavic (23)	114	0.27
Slovak (306)	592	1.40
Slovene (7)	7	0.02
Swedish (22)	140	0.33
Swiss (10)	40	0.09
Turkish (65)	65	0.15
Ukrainian (253)	447	1.06
Welsh (17)	135	0.32
West Indian, ex. Hispanic (690)	720	1.70
Barbadian (12)	12	0.03
British West Indian (60)	60	0.14
Haitian (90)	100	0.24
Jamaican (174)	174	0.41
Trinidadian/Tobagonian (212)	232	0.55
U.S. Virgin Islander (108)	108	0.26
West Indian (34)	34	0.08

Hispanic Origin	Population	%
Hispanic or Latino (of any race)	5,258	12.31
Central American, ex. Mexican	332	0.78
Costa Rican	23	0.05
Guatemalan	44	0.10
Honduran	88	0.21
Nicaraguan	39	0.09
Panamanian	62	0.15
Salvadoran	75	0.18
Other Central American	1	<0.01
Cuban	341	0.80
Dominican Republic	482	1.13
Mexican	302	0.71
Puerto Rican	2,298	5.38
South American	1,077	2.52
Argentinean	110	0.26
Bolivian	36	0.08
Chilean	33	0.08
Colombian	298	0.70
Ecuadorian	246	0.58
Paraguayan	1	<0.01
Peruvian	226	0.53
Uruguayan	55	0.13
Venezuelan	58	0.14
Other South American	14	0.03
Other Hispanic or Latino	426	1.00

Race*	Population	%
African-American/Black (4,573)	4,937	11.56
Not Hispanic (4,287)	4,535	10.62
Hispanic (286)	402	0.94
American Indian/Alaska Native (100)	211	0.49
Not Hispanic (72)	149	0.35
Hispanic (28)	62	0.15
Blackfeet (1)	5	0.01
Canadian/French Am. Ind. (1)	1	<0.01
Central American Ind. (1)	2	<0.01
Cherokee (7)	10	0.02
Chippewa (2)	3	0.01
Choctaw (0)	2	<0.01
Creek (0)	1	<0.01
Delaware (8)	11	0.03
Iroquois (2)	2	<0.01
Mexican American Ind. (1)	1	<0.01
Pueblo (2)	4	0.01
Seminole (0)	6	0.01
Sioux (0)	5	0.01
South American Ind. (3)	11	0.03
Spanish American Ind. (2)	2	<0.01
Tlingit-Haida *(Alaska Native)* (4)	5	0.01
Asian (6,882)	7,311	17.12
Not Hispanic (6,841)	7,231	16.93
Hispanic (41)	80	0.19
Bangladeshi (62)	77	0.18
Cambodian (0)	2	<0.01
Chinese, ex. Taiwanese (548)	613	1.44
Filipino (940)	1,024	2.40
Indian (4,240)	4,483	10.50
Indonesian (3)	9	0.02
Japanese (26)	39	0.09
Korean (213)	221	0.52
Laotian (5)	9	0.02
Malaysian (7)	8	0.02
Nepalese (29)	29	0.07
Pakistani (519)	595	1.39
Sri Lankan (16)	20	0.05
Taiwanese (6)	16	0.04
Thai (9)	11	0.03
Vietnamese (89)	100	0.23
Hawaii Native/Pacific Islander (18)	66	0.15
Not Hispanic (17)	54	0.13
Hispanic (1)	12	0.03
Fijian (3)	3	0.01
Guamanian/Chamorro (0)	7	0.02
Native Hawaiian (5)	9	0.02
White (28,630)	29,300	68.61
Not Hispanic (25,350)	25,773	60.35
Hispanic (3,280)	3,527	8.26

Scotch Plains

Place Type: Township
County: Union
Population: 23,510†

Ancestry‡	Population	%
African, Sub-Saharan (188)	198	0.85
African (41)	51	0.22
Kenyan (3)	3	0.01
Liberian (36)	36	0.16
Nigerian (108)	108	0.47
Albanian (12)	46	0.20
American (1,027)	1,027	4.43
Arab (266)	298	1.29
Egyptian (226)	241	1.04
Lebanese (32)	32	0.14
Other Arab (8)	25	0.11
Armenian (28)	28	0.12
Austrian (40)	329	1.42
Belgian (0)	6	0.03
Brazilian (0)	39	0.17
British (69)	130	0.56
Canadian (38)	73	0.32
Celtic (23)	23	0.10
Croatian (11)	11	0.05
Czech (45)	205	0.88
Czechoslovakian (0)	46	0.20
Danish (9)	36	0.16
Dutch (59)	192	0.83
Eastern European (278)	323	1.39
English (240)	1,422	6.14
Estonian (8)	8	0.03
European (357)	357	1.54
French, ex. Basque (93)	526	2.27
French Canadian (113)	147	0.63
German (589)	2,318	10.00
Greek (86)	313	1.35
Hungarian (202)	511	2.21
Irish (1,179)	3,761	16.23
Italian (2,858)	5,766	24.88
Latvian (8)	8	0.03
Lithuanian (71)	254	1.10
Norwegian (41)	191	0.82
Polish (484)	1,856	8.01
Portuguese (71)	161	0.69
Romanian (57)	80	0.35
Russian (272)	1,082	4.67
Scotch-Irish (199)	343	1.48
Scottish (36)	285	1.23
Serbian (16)	16	0.07
Slavic (14)	50	0.22
Slovak (55)	97	0.42
Swedish (69)	214	0.92
Swiss (0)	13	0.06
Ukrainian (168)	394	1.70
Welsh (11)	141	0.61
West Indian, ex. Hispanic (132)	142	0.61
Haitian (10)	10	0.04
Jamaican (75)	75	0.32
Trinidadian/Tobagonian (26)	36	0.16
West Indian (21)	21	0.09
Yugoslavian (0)	11	0.05

Hispanic Origin	Population	%
Hispanic or Latino (of any race)	1,582	6.73
Central American, ex. Mexican	173	0.74
Costa Rican	51	0.22
Guatemalan	48	0.20
Honduran	15	0.06
Nicaraguan	1	<0.01
Panamanian	10	0.04
Salvadoran	48	0.20
Cuban	195	0.83
Dominican Republic	101	0.43
Mexican	81	0.34
Puerto Rican	399	1.70
South American	459	1.95
Argentinean	45	0.19
Bolivian	10	0.04
Chilean	21	0.09
Colombian	175	0.74
Ecuadorian	91	0.39
Paraguayan	8	0.03
Peruvian	82	0.35
Uruguayan	12	0.05
Venezuelan	9	0.04
Other South American	6	0.03
Other Hispanic or Latino	174	0.74

Race*	Population	%
African-American/Black (2,605)	2,857	12.15
Not Hispanic (2,519)	2,714	11.54
Hispanic (86)	143	0.61
American Indian/Alaska Native (29)	108	0.46
Not Hispanic (23)	89	0.38
Hispanic (6)	19	0.08
Apache (0)	1	<0.01
Blackfeet (0)	3	0.01
Canadian/French Am. Ind. (1)	1	<0.01
Central American Ind. (1)	3	0.01
Cherokee (0)	9	0.04
Choctaw (0)	3	0.01
Creek (1)	7	0.03
Delaware (0)	1	<0.01
Hopi (0)	2	0.01
Iroquois (4)	8	0.03
Mexican American Ind. (0)	5	0.02
Sioux (2)	5	0.02
South American Ind. (2)	3	0.01
Asian (1,799)	2,017	8.58
Not Hispanic (1,795)	1,995	8.49
Hispanic (4)	22	0.09
Cambodian (1)	1	<0.01
Chinese, ex. Taiwanese (536)	612	2.60
Filipino (287)	332	1.41
Indian (689)	749	3.19
Indonesian (8)	11	0.05
Japanese (12)	25	0.11
Korean (142)	167	0.71
Malaysian (1)	2	0.01
Pakistani (22)	24	0.10
Sri Lankan (1)	1	<0.01
Taiwanese (27)	29	0.12
Thai (19)	23	0.10
Vietnamese (29)	36	0.15
Hawaii Native/Pacific Islander (2)	25	0.11

*Notes: † The Census 2010 population figure is used to calculate the percentages in the Hispanic Origin and Race categories. Ancestry percentages are based on the 2006-2010 American Community Survey population (not shown); ‡ Numbers in parentheses indicate the number of people reporting a single ancestry; * Numbers in parentheses indicate the number of persons reporting this race alone, not in combination with any other race; Please refer to the Explanation of Data for more information.*

Not Hispanic (2)	18	0.08
Hispanic (0)	7	0.03
Native Hawaiian (1)	2	0.01
White (18,203)	18,627	79.23
Not Hispanic (17,121)	17,434	74.16
Hispanic (1,082)	1,193	5.07

Secaucus

Place Type: Town
County: Hudson
Population: 16,264†

Ancestry‡	Population	%
African, Sub-Saharan (74)	74	0.46
African (28)	28	0.17
Ethiopian (23)	23	0.14
Nigerian (23)	23	0.14
American (362)	362	2.26
Arab (27)	44	0.27
Egyptian (7)	7	0.04
Syrian (0)	17	0.11
Other Arab (20)	20	0.12
Armenian (103)	125	0.78
Austrian (16)	29	0.18
Belgian (0)	13	0.08
Brazilian (12)	12	0.07
Bulgarian (28)	28	0.17
Canadian (0)	14	0.09
Croatian (10)	10	0.06
Czech (10)	40	0.25
Czechoslovakian (20)	20	0.12
Danish (11)	51	0.32
Dutch (10)	76	0.47
Eastern European (41)	41	0.26
English (115)	343	2.14
Estonian (17)	17	0.11
European (38)	38	0.24
Finnish (0)	3	0.02
French, ex. Basque (36)	250	1.56
French Canadian (26)	26	0.16
German (533)	2,268	14.17
Greek (148)	378	2.36
Guyanese (33)	33	0.21
Hungarian (13)	100	0.62
Irish (806)	2,651	16.56
Italian (2,086)	3,189	19.92
Lithuanian (0)	49	0.31
Northern European (24)	24	0.15
Norwegian (0)	54	0.34
Polish (223)	666	4.16
Romanian (45)	45	0.28
Russian (38)	148	0.92
Scandinavian (7)	7	0.04
Scotch-Irish (19)	37	0.23
Scottish (18)	47	0.29
Swedish (10)	51	0.32
Swiss (0)	18	0.11
Turkish (0)	14	0.09
Ukrainian (115)	281	1.76
West Indian, ex. Hispanic (117)	157	0.98
British West Indian (18)	24	0.15
Haitian (32)	40	0.25
Jamaican (0)	20	0.12
Trinidadian/Tobagonian (44)	44	0.27
West Indian (23)	29	0.18
Yugoslavian (0)	68	0.42

Hispanic Origin	Population	%
Hispanic or Latino (of any race)	3,025	18.60
Central American, ex. Mexican	205	1.26
Costa Rican	20	0.12
Guatemalan	28	0.17
Honduran	54	0.33
Nicaraguan	22	0.14
Panamanian	3	0.02
Salvadoran	78	0.48
Cuban	554	3.41
Dominican Republic	340	2.09
Mexican	95	0.58
Puerto Rican	728	4.48
South American	831	5.11
Argentinean	56	0.34
Bolivian	5	0.03
Chilean	57	0.35
Colombian	232	1.43
Ecuadorian	283	1.74
Paraguayan	1	0.01
Peruvian	143	0.88
Uruguayan	5	0.03
Venezuelan	35	0.22
Other South American	14	0.09
Other Hispanic or Latino	272	1.67

Race*	Population	%
African-American/Black (668)	766	4.71
Not Hispanic (575)	626	3.85
Hispanic (93)	140	0.86
American Indian/Alaska Native (32)	82	0.50
Not Hispanic (23)	66	0.41
Hispanic (9)	16	0.10
Apache (0)	2	0.01
Blackfeet (1)	3	0.02
Cherokee (1)	6	0.04
Iroquois (0)	4	0.02
Lumbee (2)	2	0.01
South American Ind. (0)	4	0.02
Asian (3,318)	3,513	21.60
Not Hispanic (3,269)	3,437	21.13
Hispanic (49)	76	0.47
Bangladeshi (2)	2	0.01
Chinese, ex. Taiwanese (578)	627	3.86
Filipino (579)	619	3.81
Indian (1,596)	1,662	10.22
Indonesian (14)	16	0.10
Japanese (39)	56	0.34
Korean (202)	214	1.32
Laotian (1)	1	0.01
Nepalese (24)	26	0.16
Pakistani (82)	95	0.58
Sri Lankan (7)	7	0.04
Taiwanese (14)	20	0.12
Thai (10)	13	0.08
Vietnamese (96)	104	0.64
Hawaii Native/Pacific Islander (6)	22	0.14
Not Hispanic (1)	14	0.09
Hispanic (5)	8	0.05
Guamanian/Chamorro (6)	7	0.04
Native Hawaiian (0)	1	0.01
Samoan (0)	1	0.01
White (11,125)	11,407	70.14
Not Hispanic (9,091)	9,245	56.84
Hispanic (2,034)	2,162	13.29

Short Hills

Place Type: CDP
County: Essex
Population: 13,165†

Ancestry‡	Population	%
African, Sub-Saharan (65)	110	0.83
African (25)	25	0.19
South African (22)	67	0.51
Zimbabwean (18)	18	0.14
Albanian (25)	103	0.78
American (917)	917	6.94
Arab (50)	207	1.57
Egyptian (0)	73	0.55
Lebanese (32)	67	0.51
Palestinian (7)	22	0.17
Syrian (11)	28	0.21
Other Arab (0)	17	0.13
Armenian (26)	30	0.23
Australian (39)	39	0.30
Austrian (113)	256	1.94
Basque (32)	32	0.24
Brazilian (51)	93	0.70
British (50)	110	0.83
Canadian (21)	21	0.16
Czech (10)	46	0.35
Dutch (7)	63	0.48
Eastern European (517)	549	4.16
English (198)	931	7.05
European (341)	379	2.87
Finnish (0)	8	0.06
French, ex. Basque (33)	131	0.99
French Canadian (52)	172	1.30
German (306)	1,414	10.70
Greek (15)	46	0.35
Hungarian (77)	276	2.09
Irish (352)	1,335	10.11
Israeli (22)	63	0.48
Italian (768)	1,902	14.40
Latvian (20)	38	0.29
Lithuanian (60)	131	0.99
Northern European (38)	38	0.29
Norwegian (19)	61	0.46
Polish (289)	804	6.09
Portuguese (51)	51	0.39
Romanian (0)	24	0.18
Russian (656)	1,416	10.72
Scotch-Irish (50)	81	0.61
Scottish (49)	160	1.21
Serbian (18)	30	0.23
Slovak (40)	40	0.30
Swedish (77)	184	1.39
Swiss (18)	132	1.00
Turkish (0)	17	0.13
Ukrainian (91)	205	1.55
Welsh (11)	58	0.44
West Indian, ex. Hispanic (29)	39	0.30
Bermudan (12)	12	0.09
Dutch West Indian (0)	10	0.08
Trinidadian/Tobagonian (17)	17	0.13
Yugoslavian (10)	10	0.08

Hispanic Origin	Population	%
Hispanic or Latino (of any race)	316	2.40
Central American, ex. Mexican	22	0.17
Costa Rican	4	0.03
Guatemalan	4	0.03
Honduran	7	0.05
Salvadoran	6	0.05
Other Central American	1	0.01
Cuban	41	0.31
Dominican Republic	10	0.08
Mexican	45	0.34
Puerto Rican	34	0.26
South American	106	0.81
Argentinean	40	0.30
Bolivian	6	0.05
Chilean	9	0.07
Colombian	26	0.20
Ecuadorian	7	0.05
Paraguayan	3	0.02
Peruvian	10	0.08
Venezuelan	5	0.04
Other Hispanic or Latino	58	0.44

Race*	Population	%
African-American/Black (127)	140	1.06
Not Hispanic (121)	132	1.00
Hispanic (6)	8	0.06
American Indian/Alaska Native (1)	13	0.10
Not Hispanic (0)	8	0.06
Hispanic (1)	5	0.04
Cherokee (0)	3	0.02
Mexican American Ind. (1)	2	0.02
Asian (2,038)	2,247	17.07
Not Hispanic (2,033)	2,237	16.99
Hispanic (5)	10	0.08
Burmese (0)	3	0.02
Chinese, ex. Taiwanese (884)	979	7.44
Filipino (80)	95	0.72
Indian (663)	704	5.35
Indonesian (1)	1	0.01
Japanese (41)	71	0.54
Korean (205)	239	1.82
Malaysian (4)	4	0.03

*Notes: † The Census 2010 population figure is used to calculate the percentages in the Hispanic Origin and Race categories. Ancestry percentages are based on the 2006-2010 American Community Survey population (not shown); ‡ Numbers in parentheses indicate the number of people reporting a single ancestry; * Numbers in parentheses indicate the number of persons reporting this race alone, not in combination with any other race; Please refer to the Explanation of Data for more information.*

Nepalese (5)	5	0.04
Pakistani (28)	29	0.22
Sri Lankan (3)	3	0.02
Taiwanese (70)	86	0.65
Thai (7)	7	0.05
Vietnamese (6)	10	0.08
Hawaii Native/Pacific Islander (2)	14	0.11
Not Hispanic (2)	14	0.11
Guamanian/Chamorro (0)	2	0.02
Native Hawaiian (0)	6	0.05
White (10,721)	10,939	83.09
Not Hispanic (10,449)	10,657	80.95
Hispanic (272)	282	2.14

Somers Point

Place Type: City
County: Atlantic
Population: 10,795†

Ancestry‡	Population	%
African, Sub-Saharan (194)	194	1.76
African (194)	194	1.76
American (395)	395	3.58
Armenian (3)	3	0.03
Austrian (12)	52	0.47
Belgian (0)	12	0.11
British (0)	32	0.29
Canadian (0)	6	0.05
Celtic (0)	21	0.19
Croatian (0)	9	0.08
Czech (0)	8	0.07
Czechoslovakian (17)	27	0.24
Danish (10)	10	0.09
Dutch (0)	84	0.76
Eastern European (11)	21	0.19
English (191)	1,167	10.57
European (47)	104	0.94
Finnish (0)	58	0.53
French, ex. Basque (29)	327	2.96
French Canadian (8)	32	0.29
German (595)	2,086	18.90
Greek (10)	37	0.34
Hungarian (0)	17	0.15
Irish (886)	3,062	27.74
Italian (1,027)	2,271	20.57
Lithuanian (35)	67	0.61
Macedonian (20)	30	0.27
Norwegian (12)	33	0.30
Pennsylvania German (11)	11	0.10
Polish (199)	715	6.48
Russian (54)	187	1.69
Scandinavian (13)	13	0.12
Scotch-Irish (55)	180	1.63
Scottish (36)	150	1.36
Serbian (0)	29	0.26
Slovak (19)	30	0.27
Swedish (10)	120	1.09
Swiss (26)	36	0.33
Ukrainian (16)	64	0.58
Welsh (8)	74	0.67
West Indian, ex. Hispanic (263)	273	2.47
Bermudan (0)	10	0.09
Haitian (187)	187	1.69
Trinidadian/Tobagonian (28)	28	0.25
West Indian (48)	48	0.43

Hispanic Origin	Population	%
Hispanic or Latino (of any race)	1,024	9.49
Central American, ex. Mexican	38	0.35
Costa Rican	1	0.01
Guatemalan	15	0.14
Honduran	4	0.04
Nicaraguan	4	0.04
Panamanian	4	0.04
Salvadoran	10	0.09
Cuban	26	0.24
Dominican Republic	55	0.51
Mexican	347	3.21
Puerto Rican	399	3.70
South American	96	0.89
Argentinean	6	0.06
Bolivian	1	0.01
Colombian	43	0.40
Ecuadorian	7	0.06
Peruvian	37	0.34
Uruguayan	2	0.02
Other Hispanic or Latino	63	0.58

Race*	Population	%
African-American/Black (1,153)	1,346	12.47
Not Hispanic (1,087)	1,243	11.51
Hispanic (66)	103	0.95
American Indian/Alaska Native (27)	95	0.88
Not Hispanic (23)	84	0.78
Hispanic (4)	11	0.10
Apache (0)	2	0.02
Blackfeet (1)	10	0.09
Central American Ind. (1)	1	0.01
Cherokee (0)	13	0.12
Chippewa (1)	2	0.02
Choctaw (0)	1	0.01
Comanche (0)	1	0.01
Cree (0)	1	0.01
Creek (0)	2	0.02
Delaware (4)	4	0.04
Hopi (2)	4	0.04
Potawatomi (0)	2	0.02
Sioux (2)	4	0.04
Asian (332)	380	3.52
Not Hispanic (321)	360	3.33
Hispanic (11)	20	0.19
Burmese (5)	6	0.06
Cambodian (1)	1	0.01
Chinese, ex. Taiwanese (82)	99	0.92
Filipino (98)	107	0.99
Indian (83)	97	0.90
Indonesian (1)	2	0.02
Japanese (3)	11	0.10
Korean (9)	9	0.08
Laotian (6)	6	0.06
Pakistani (18)	19	0.18
Taiwanese (4)	5	0.05
Thai (2)	5	0.05
Vietnamese (11)	16	0.15
Hawaii Native/Pacific Islander (6)	14	0.13
Not Hispanic (6)	13	0.12
Hispanic (0)	1	0.01
Native Hawaiian (3)	5	0.05
Samoan (2)	2	0.02
White (8,501)	8,777	81.31
Not Hispanic (8,091)	8,298	76.87
Hispanic (410)	479	4.44

Somerset

Place Type: CDP
County: Somerset
Population: 22,083†

Ancestry‡	Population	%
African, Sub-Saharan (728)	790	3.53
African (651)	702	3.14
Liberian (0)	11	0.05
Nigerian (63)	63	0.28
Somalian (14)	14	0.06
American (282)	282	1.26
Arab (400)	543	2.43
Arab (53)	53	0.24
Egyptian (81)	112	0.50
Lebanese (31)	126	0.56
Moroccan (187)	187	0.84
Palestinian (15)	32	0.14
Other Arab (33)	33	0.15
Armenian (91)	91	0.41
Australian (11)	32	0.14
Austrian (36)	150	0.67
Basque (9)	9	0.04
Belgian (9)	9	0.04
Brazilian (15)	15	0.07
British (17)	80	0.36
Canadian (10)	18	0.08
Carpatho Rusyn (0)	17	0.08
Croatian (0)	25	0.11
Cypriot (8)	8	0.04
Danish (0)	33	0.15
Dutch (28)	222	0.99
Eastern European (71)	71	0.32
English (132)	681	3.04
European (167)	167	0.75
French, ex. Basque (0)	95	0.42
French Canadian (53)	73	0.33
German (237)	1,597	7.13
Greek (15)	59	0.26
Guyanese (29)	59	0.26
Hungarian (300)	499	2.23
Iranian (27)	27	0.12
Irish (493)	1,892	8.45
Italian (1,159)	2,405	10.74
Lithuanian (12)	35	0.16
Norwegian (25)	76	0.34
Pennsylvania German (10)	23	0.10
Polish (528)	1,333	5.95
Romanian (0)	41	0.18
Russian (98)	418	1.87
Scandinavian (0)	8	0.04
Scotch-Irish (27)	105	0.47
Scottish (28)	144	0.64
Slavic (10)	10	0.04
Slovak (9)	160	0.71
Swedish (13)	100	0.45
Swiss (0)	60	0.27
Turkish (59)	59	0.26
Ukrainian (108)	189	0.84
Welsh (33)	118	0.53
West Indian, ex. Hispanic (735)	925	4.13
Barbadian (59)	59	0.26
British West Indian (52)	52	0.23
Haitian (9)	9	0.04
Jamaican (440)	580	2.59
Trinidadian/Tobagonian (12)	12	0.05
U.S. Virgin Islander (8)	8	0.04
West Indian (142)	192	0.86
Other West Indian (13)	13	0.06

Hispanic Origin	Population	%
Hispanic or Latino (of any race)	2,092	9.47
Central American, ex. Mexican	264	1.20
Costa Rican	19	0.09
Guatemalan	45	0.20
Honduran	84	0.38
Nicaraguan	40	0.18
Panamanian	34	0.15
Salvadoran	42	0.19
Cuban	125	0.57
Dominican Republic	197	0.89
Mexican	251	1.14
Puerto Rican	726	3.29
South American	379	1.72
Argentinean	14	0.06
Bolivian	1	<0.01
Chilean	19	0.09
Colombian	149	0.67
Ecuadorian	87	0.39
Paraguayan	1	<0.01
Peruvian	89	0.40
Uruguayan	3	0.01
Venezuelan	10	0.05
Other South American	6	0.03
Other Hispanic or Latino	150	0.68

Race*	Population	%
African-American/Black (6,378)	6,783	30.72
Not Hispanic (6,161)	6,444	29.18
Hispanic (217)	339	1.54
American Indian/Alaska Native (50)	189	0.86
Not Hispanic (27)	130	0.59
Hispanic (23)	59	0.27
Blackfeet (0)	2	0.01
Cherokee (6)	20	0.09

*Notes: † The Census 2010 population figure is used to calculate the percentages in the Hispanic Origin and Race categories. Ancestry percentages are based on the 2006-2010 American Community Survey population (not shown); ‡ Numbers in parentheses indicate the number of people reporting a single ancestry; * Numbers in parentheses indicate the number of persons reporting this race alone, not in combination with any other race; Please refer to the Explanation of Data for more information.*

Choctaw (0)	3	0.01
Delaware (0)	4	0.02
Hopi (0)	2	0.01
Iroquois (0)	1	<0.01
Lumbee (0)	1	<0.01
Mexican American Ind. (3)	6	0.03
Navajo (1)	1	<0.01
Pueblo (0)	1	<0.01
Seminole (0)	7	0.03
South American Ind. (5)	15	0.07
Spanish American Ind. (2)	2	0.01
Asian (3,885)	4,147	18.78
Not Hispanic (3,874)	4,115	18.63
Hispanic (11)	32	0.14
Bangladeshi (27)	29	0.13
Cambodian (2)	2	0.01
Chinese, ex. Taiwanese (678)	765	3.46
Filipino (670)	746	3.38
Indian (2,017)	2,106	9.54
Indonesian (14)	16	0.07
Japanese (21)	35	0.16
Korean (138)	155	0.70
Laotian (2)	4	0.02
Malaysian (1)	2	0.01
Nepalese (8)	8	0.04
Pakistani (121)	129	0.58
Sri Lankan (7)	7	0.03
Taiwanese (67)	80	0.36
Thai (14)	22	0.10
Vietnamese (38)	41	0.19
Hawaii Native/Pacific Islander (3)	38	0.17
Not Hispanic (2)	33	0.15
Hispanic (1)	5	0.02
Guamanian/Chamorro (1)	2	0.01
White (10,387)	10,891	49.32
Not Hispanic (9,314)	9,661	43.75
Hispanic (1,073)	1,230	5.57

Somerville

Place Type: Borough
County: Somerset
Population: 12,098†

Ancestry‡	Population	%
African, Sub-Saharan (132)	132	1.08
African (20)	20	0.16
Nigerian (31)	31	0.25
Other Sub-Saharan African (81)	81	0.66
American (762)	762	6.25
Arab (21)	29	0.24
Egyptian (4)	12	0.10
Lebanese (17)	17	0.14
Armenian (14)	41	0.34
Austrian (12)	37	0.30
British (0)	63	0.52
Bulgarian (14)	14	0.11
Czech (9)	45	0.37
Czechoslovakian (11)	61	0.50
Danish (0)	31	0.25
Dutch (37)	195	1.60
Eastern European (30)	30	0.25
English (206)	654	5.37
Estonian (13)	13	0.11
European (28)	28	0.23
Finnish (0)	19	0.16
French, ex. Basque (25)	131	1.07
French Canadian (22)	22	0.18
German (144)	1,188	9.75
Greek (23)	23	0.19
Guyanese (0)	24	0.20
Hungarian (212)	333	2.73
Iranian (6)	6	0.05
Irish (274)	1,251	10.26
Israeli (0)	36	0.30
Italian (644)	1,621	13.30
Latvian (0)	8	0.07
Lithuanian (0)	35	0.29
Northern European (9)	9	0.07
Norwegian (14)	66	0.54
Pennsylvania German (0)	5	0.04
Polish (196)	764	6.27
Portuguese (0)	10	0.08
Romanian (0)	10	0.08
Russian (25)	113	0.93
Scotch-Irish (39)	60	0.49
Scottish (67)	141	1.16
Slovak (22)	71	0.58
Swedish (19)	31	0.25
Swiss (0)	33	0.27
Ukrainian (30)	93	0.76
Welsh (18)	66	0.54
West Indian, ex. Hispanic (159)	234	1.92
British West Indian (13)	13	0.11
Jamaican (29)	104	0.85
Trinidadian/Tobagonian (117)	117	0.96
Yugoslavian (0)	12	0.10

Hispanic Origin	Population	%
Hispanic or Latino (of any race)	2,873	23.75
Central American, ex. Mexican	854	7.06
Costa Rican	627	5.18
Guatemalan	117	0.97
Honduran	28	0.23
Nicaraguan	10	0.08
Panamanian	9	0.07
Salvadoran	58	0.48
Other Central American	5	0.04
Cuban	59	0.49
Dominican Republic	84	0.69
Mexican	516	4.27
Puerto Rican	412	3.41
South American	672	5.55
Argentinean	20	0.17
Bolivian	9	0.07
Chilean	8	0.07
Colombian	206	1.70
Ecuadorian	100	0.83
Paraguayan	114	0.94
Peruvian	183	1.51
Uruguayan	6	0.05
Venezuelan	20	0.17
Other South American	6	0.05
Other Hispanic or Latino	276	2.28

Race*	Population	%
African-American/Black (1,470)	1,707	14.11
Not Hispanic (1,389)	1,557	12.87
Hispanic (81)	150	1.24
American Indian/Alaska Native (41)	114	0.94
Not Hispanic (14)	60	0.50
Hispanic (27)	54	0.45
Blackfeet (0)	2	0.02
Central American Ind. (1)	1	0.01
Cherokee (5)	17	0.14
Delaware (1)	3	0.02
Mexican American Ind. (1)	4	0.03
Potawatomi (2)	2	0.02
Sioux (0)	5	0.04
South American Ind. (8)	14	0.12
Spanish American Ind. (1)	1	0.01
Asian (1,375)	1,493	12.34
Not Hispanic (1,359)	1,463	12.09
Hispanic (16)	30	0.25
Bangladeshi (5)	6	0.05
Burmese (8)	8	0.07
Chinese, ex. Taiwanese (133)	162	1.34
Filipino (481)	512	4.23
Hmong (1)	1	0.01
Indian (591)	624	5.16
Indonesian (7)	11	0.09
Japanese (13)	20	0.17
Korean (14)	14	0.12
Laotian (1)	1	0.01
Malaysian (8)	9	0.07
Pakistani (24)	26	0.21
Sri Lankan (1)	1	0.01
Taiwanese (4)	7	0.06
Thai (27)	35	0.29
Vietnamese (33)	33	0.27
Hawaii Native/Pacific Islander (9)	13	0.11
Not Hispanic (9)	12	0.10
Hispanic (0)	1	0.01
Guamanian/Chamorro (1)	1	0.01
Native Hawaiian (0)	1	0.01
Samoan (1)	1	0.01
Tongan (1)	1	0.01
White (7,941)	8,358	69.09
Not Hispanic (6,152)	6,361	52.58
Hispanic (1,789)	1,997	16.51

South Amboy

Place Type: City
County: Middlesex
Population: 8,631†

Ancestry‡	Population	%
American (608)	608	7.15
Austrian (19)	29	0.34
Canadian (0)	17	0.20
Croatian (59)	59	0.69
Czech (108)	121	1.42
Czechoslovakian (9)	9	0.11
Danish (0)	18	0.21
Dutch (9)	145	1.71
Eastern European (66)	66	0.78
English (131)	407	4.79
European (10)	10	0.12
French, ex. Basque (0)	81	0.95
French Canadian (0)	28	0.33
German (181)	708	8.33
Greek (15)	58	0.68
Guyanese (10)	10	0.12
Hungarian (27)	190	2.23
Irish (619)	1,577	18.55
Italian (833)	1,441	16.95
Lithuanian (7)	54	0.64
Norwegian (10)	28	0.33
Polish (767)	1,601	18.83
Portuguese (43)	53	0.62
Russian (19)	150	1.76
Scotch-Irish (78)	123	1.45
Scottish (0)	37	0.44
Serbian (114)	114	1.34
Slavic (0)	9	0.11
Slovak (87)	131	1.54
Slovene (31)	31	0.36
Swedish (0)	8	0.09
Turkish (40)	40	0.47
Ukrainian (7)	89	1.05
Welsh (13)	61	0.72

Hispanic Origin	Population	%
Hispanic or Latino (of any race)	1,158	13.42
Central American, ex. Mexican	52	0.60
Costa Rican	3	0.03
Guatemalan	5	0.06
Honduran	28	0.32
Panamanian	8	0.09
Salvadoran	6	0.07
Other Central American	2	0.02
Cuban	42	0.49
Dominican Republic	149	1.73
Mexican	76	0.88
Puerto Rican	519	6.01
South American	240	2.78
Argentinean	43	0.50
Bolivian	29	0.34
Chilean	3	0.03
Colombian	44	0.51
Ecuadorian	33	0.38
Paraguayan	1	0.01
Peruvian	70	0.81
Uruguayan	11	0.13
Venezuelan	6	0.07
Other Hispanic or Latino	80	0.93

Race*	Population	%
African-American/Black (382)	450	5.21

*Notes: † The Census 2010 population figure is used to calculate the percentages in the Hispanic Origin and Race categories. Ancestry percentages are based on the 2006-2010 American Community Survey population (not shown); ‡ Numbers in parentheses indicate the number of people reporting a single ancestry; * Numbers in parentheses indicate the number of persons reporting this race alone, not in combination with any other race; Please refer to the Explanation of Data for more information.*

Not Hispanic (347)	403	4.67
Hispanic (35)	47	0.54
American Indian/Alaska Native (9)	47	0.54
Not Hispanic (5)	34	0.39
Hispanic (4)	13	0.15
Blackfeet (0)	1	0.01
Cherokee (3)	7	0.08
Cheyenne (0)	1	0.01
Navajo (0)	1	0.01
Pueblo (0)	1	0.01
Sioux (0)	3	0.03
South American Ind. (4)	4	0.05
Asian (348)	394	4.56
Not Hispanic (345)	388	4.50
Hispanic (3)	6	0.07
Bangladeshi (5)	5	0.06
Cambodian (0)	1	0.01
Chinese, ex. Taiwanese (68)	75	0.87
Filipino (97)	114	1.32
Indian (102)	110	1.27
Japanese (2)	3	0.03
Korean (20)	24	0.28
Nepalese (1)	2	0.02
Pakistani (33)	35	0.41
Taiwanese (5)	12	0.14
Thai (3)	4	0.05
Vietnamese (5)	6	0.07
Hawaii Native/Pacific Islander (0)	9	0.10
Not Hispanic (0)	9	0.10
Native Hawaiian (0)	3	0.03
White (7,459)	7,613	88.21
Not Hispanic (6,638)	6,746	78.16
Hispanic (821)	867	10.05

South Brunswick

Place Type: Township
County: Middlesex
Population: 43,417†

Ancestry‡	Population	%
African, Sub-Saharan (635)	635	1.50
African (179)	179	0.42
Ghanaian (342)	342	0.81
Nigerian (114)	114	0.27
American (1,022)	1,022	2.41
Arab (628)	787	1.86
Arab (103)	103	0.24
Egyptian (423)	472	1.11
Jordanian (8)	8	0.02
Lebanese (42)	100	0.24
Moroccan (0)	15	0.04
Palestinian (0)	15	0.04
Syrian (52)	74	0.17
Armenian (10)	27	0.06
Austrian (93)	379	0.89
Brazilian (21)	21	0.05
British (0)	66	0.16
Canadian (31)	100	0.24
Croatian (15)	15	0.04
Cypriot (33)	33	0.08
Czech (30)	150	0.35
Czechoslovakian (69)	135	0.32
Danish (46)	400	0.94
Dutch (69)	655	1.55
Eastern European (341)	448	1.06
English (405)	2,150	5.07
Estonian (14)	14	0.03
European (229)	262	0.62
Finnish (0)	14	0.03
French, ex. Basque (20)	549	1.30
French Canadian (0)	49	0.12
German (916)	4,697	11.08
Greek (128)	208	0.49
Guyanese (41)	41	0.10
Hungarian (351)	835	1.97
Iranian (39)	49	0.12
Irish (1,112)	4,938	11.65
Israeli (54)	107	0.25
Italian (2,459)	5,719	13.49
Latvian (0)	13	0.03
Lithuanian (0)	174	0.41
Maltese (0)	12	0.03
Norwegian (182)	373	0.88
Pennsylvania German (0)	35	0.08
Polish (713)	2,410	5.69
Portuguese (61)	109	0.26
Romanian (75)	133	0.31
Russian (713)	1,482	3.50
Scandinavian (32)	67	0.16
Scotch-Irish (181)	452	1.07
Scottish (96)	587	1.38
Slavic (0)	9	0.02
Slovak (24)	131	0.31
Swedish (63)	245	0.58
Swiss (8)	90	0.21
Turkish (35)	59	0.14
Ukrainian (220)	476	1.12
Welsh (0)	171	0.40
West Indian, ex. Hispanic (353)	426	1.01
Bahamian (14)	14	0.03
Belizean (198)	198	0.47
British West Indian (0)	8	0.02
Jamaican (102)	125	0.29
West Indian (39)	81	0.19
Yugoslavian (55)	55	0.13

Hispanic Origin	Population	%
Hispanic or Latino (of any race)	2,624	6.04
Central American, ex. Mexican	275	0.63
Costa Rican	19	0.04
Guatemalan	115	0.26
Honduran	55	0.13
Nicaraguan	21	0.05
Panamanian	22	0.05
Salvadoran	37	0.09
Other Central American	6	0.01
Cuban	189	0.44
Dominican Republic	176	0.41
Mexican	270	0.62
Puerto Rican	991	2.28
South American	498	1.15
Argentinean	41	0.09
Bolivian	5	0.01
Chilean	27	0.06
Colombian	206	0.47
Ecuadorian	71	0.16
Paraguayan	8	0.02
Peruvian	70	0.16
Uruguayan	25	0.06
Venezuelan	37	0.09
Other South American	8	0.02
Other Hispanic or Latino	225	0.52

Race*	Population	%
African-American/Black (3,348)	3,745	8.63
Not Hispanic (3,172)	3,499	8.06
Hispanic (176)	246	0.57
American Indian/Alaska Native (72)	276	0.64
Not Hispanic (64)	230	0.53
Hispanic (8)	46	0.11
Alaska Athabascan *(Ala. Nat.)* (0)	1	<0.01
Blackfeet (2)	16	0.04
Central American Ind. (1)	6	0.01
Cherokee (6)	39	0.09
Chippewa (1)	1	<0.01
Choctaw (0)	2	<0.01
Crow (0)	2	<0.01
Delaware (0)	8	0.02
Iroquois (1)	4	0.01
Mexican American Ind. (2)	6	0.01
Navajo (0)	1	<0.01
Seminole (1)	1	<0.01
Sioux (0)	3	0.01
South American Ind. (2)	6	0.01
Tlingit-Haida *(Alaska Native)* (0)	2	<0.01
Asian (15,592)	16,194	37.30
Not Hispanic (15,571)	16,135	37.16
Hispanic (21)	59	0.14
Bangladeshi (106)	116	0.27
Burmese (10)	14	0.03
Chinese, ex. Taiwanese (1,892)	2,015	4.64
Filipino (751)	851	1.96
Indian (11,040)	11,344	26.13
Indonesian (3)	9	0.02
Japanese (46)	78	0.18
Korean (418)	472	1.09
Laotian (1)	3	0.01
Malaysian (10)	11	0.03
Nepalese (3)	4	0.01
Pakistani (736)	766	1.76
Sri Lankan (133)	157	0.36
Taiwanese (142)	149	0.34
Thai (30)	41	0.09
Vietnamese (95)	110	0.25
Hawaii Native/Pacific Islander (8)	50	0.12
Not Hispanic (7)	31	0.07
Hispanic (1)	19	0.04
Guamanian/Chamorro (1)	1	<0.01
Marshallese (0)	1	<0.01
Native Hawaiian (0)	5	0.01
Samoan (2)	7	0.02
White (22,611)	23,325	53.72
Not Hispanic (20,978)	21,540	49.61
Hispanic (1,633)	1,785	4.11

South Orange Village

Place Type: Township
County: Essex
Population: 16,198†

Ancestry‡	Population	%
African, Sub-Saharan (171)	229	1.41
African (91)	123	0.76
Ghanaian (16)	35	0.22
Liberian (42)	42	0.26
Nigerian (9)	16	0.10
Other Sub-Saharan African (13)	13	0.08
Albanian (11)	11	0.07
American (588)	588	3.63
Arab (29)	92	0.57
Arab (15)	15	0.09
Lebanese (14)	40	0.25
Moroccan (0)	37	0.23
Australian (11)	11	0.07
Austrian (90)	166	1.02
Belgian (9)	29	0.18
Brazilian (117)	152	0.94
British (47)	113	0.70
Canadian (27)	61	0.38
Croatian (12)	12	0.07
Czech (8)	76	0.47
Czechoslovakian (22)	53	0.33
Danish (0)	13	0.08
Dutch (20)	96	0.59
Eastern European (314)	347	2.14
English (130)	852	5.25
European (206)	221	1.36
Finnish (0)	23	0.14
French, ex. Basque (83)	200	1.23
French Canadian (44)	110	0.68
German (318)	1,690	10.42
Greek (115)	162	1.00
Guyanese (187)	195	1.20
Hungarian (42)	210	1.29
Irish (960)	2,393	14.75
Israeli (0)	22	0.14
Italian (973)	1,912	11.79
Lithuanian (43)	113	0.70
Maltese (0)	8	0.05
Norwegian (49)	65	0.40
Polish (305)	814	5.02
Portuguese (29)	91	0.56
Romanian (82)	121	0.75
Russian (254)	766	4.72
Scandinavian (0)	18	0.11
Scotch-Irish (17)	119	0.73
Scottish (34)	261	1.61
Slovak (0)	20	0.12

*Notes: † The Census 2010 population figure is used to calculate the percentages in the Hispanic Origin and Race categories. Ancestry percentages are based on the 2006-2010 American Community Survey population (not shown); ‡ Numbers in parentheses indicate the number of people reporting a single ancestry; * Numbers in parentheses indicate the number of persons reporting this race alone, not in combination with any other race; Please refer to the Explanation of Data for more information.*

Slovene (0)	10	0.06
Swedish (14)	187	1.15
Swiss (10)	76	0.47
Ukrainian (30)	133	0.82
Welsh (19)	143	0.88
West Indian, ex. Hispanic (588)	766	4.72
Barbadian (21)	21	0.13
Belizean (6)	6	0.04
Bermudan (0)	8	0.05
British West Indian (20)	28	0.17
Haitian (237)	321	1.98
Jamaican (277)	326	2.01
Trinidadian/Tobagonian (13)	23	0.14
West Indian (14)	33	0.20
Yugoslavian (79)	79	0.49

Hispanic Origin	Population	%
Hispanic or Latino (of any race)	993	6.13
Central American, ex. Mexican	65	0.40
Costa Rican	7	0.04
Guatemalan	8	0.05
Honduran	13	0.08
Nicaraguan	6	0.04
Panamanian	18	0.11
Salvadoran	13	0.08
Cuban	100	0.62
Dominican Republic	64	0.40
Mexican	119	0.73
Puerto Rican	296	1.83
South American	212	1.31
Argentinean	25	0.15
Chilean	20	0.12
Colombian	66	0.41
Ecuadorian	46	0.28
Paraguayan	3	0.02
Peruvian	33	0.20
Uruguayan	10	0.06
Venezuelan	5	0.03
Other South American	4	0.02
Other Hispanic or Latino	137	0.85

Race*	Population	%
African-American/Black (4,642)	5,024	31.02
Not Hispanic (4,484)	4,809	29.69
Hispanic (158)	215	1.33
American Indian/Alaska Native (23)	155	0.96
Not Hispanic (18)	126	0.78
Hispanic (5)	29	0.18
Blackfeet (0)	3	0.02
Central American Ind. (0)	3	0.02
Cherokee (2)	29	0.18
Choctaw (0)	4	0.02
Creek (0)	1	0.01
Delaware (0)	2	0.01
Iroquois (1)	15	0.09
Mexican American Ind. (0)	1	0.01
Navajo (0)	1	0.01
Sioux (0)	3	0.02
South American Ind. (1)	8	0.05
Asian (836)	1,104	6.82
Not Hispanic (829)	1,077	6.65
Hispanic (7)	27	0.17
Bangladeshi (12)	14	0.09
Burmese (3)	3	0.02
Cambodian (3)	5	0.03
Chinese, ex. Taiwanese (221)	291	1.80
Filipino (126)	182	1.12
Indian (258)	329	2.03
Indonesian (0)	6	0.04
Japanese (43)	80	0.49
Korean (74)	113	0.70
Malaysian (0)	1	0.01
Pakistani (13)	13	0.08
Sri Lankan (3)	10	0.06
Taiwanese (21)	29	0.18
Thai (4)	9	0.06
Vietnamese (18)	23	0.14
Hawaii Native/Pacific Islander (1)	21	0.13
Not Hispanic (1)	19	0.12
Hispanic (0)	2	0.01
Guamanian/Chamorro (0)	2	0.01
Native Hawaiian (0)	4	0.02
White (9,750)	10,249	63.27
Not Hispanic (9,231)	9,653	59.59
Hispanic (519)	596	3.68

South Plainfield

Place Type: Borough
County: Middlesex
Population: 23,385†

Ancestry‡	Population	%
African, Sub-Saharan (52)	93	0.40
African (0)	41	0.18
Liberian (52)	52	0.23
American (1,311)	1,311	5.68
Arab (91)	153	0.66
Arab (11)	36	0.16
Egyptian (65)	65	0.28
Lebanese (0)	37	0.16
Palestinian (15)	15	0.06
Armenian (0)	15	0.06
Austrian (0)	96	0.42
Brazilian (17)	38	0.16
British (25)	70	0.30
Bulgarian (11)	11	0.05
Canadian (0)	9	0.04
Croatian (0)	9	0.04
Czech (17)	244	1.06
Czechoslovakian (23)	50	0.22
Danish (23)	160	0.69
Dutch (111)	313	1.36
Eastern European (182)	182	0.79
English (150)	1,095	4.74
European (88)	157	0.68
Finnish (6)	13	0.06
French, ex. Basque (21)	309	1.34
French Canadian (49)	118	0.51
German (694)	3,020	13.08
Greek (54)	97	0.42
Guyanese (293)	413	1.79
Hungarian (28)	218	0.94
Icelander (27)	43	0.19
Irish (1,101)	3,235	14.01
Israeli (0)	30	0.13
Italian (2,007)	4,465	19.34
Latvian (0)	8	0.03
Lithuanian (63)	205	0.89
Macedonian (26)	37	0.16
Norwegian (65)	101	0.44
Pennsylvania German (11)	11	0.05
Polish (497)	1,483	6.42
Portuguese (37)	93	0.40
Romanian (4)	15	0.06
Russian (85)	402	1.74
Scandinavian (0)	12	0.05
Scotch-Irish (127)	307	1.33
Scottish (38)	191	0.83
Serbian (0)	6	0.03
Slavic (0)	8	0.03
Slovak (33)	103	0.45
Slovene (4)	8	0.03
Swedish (38)	62	0.27
Swiss (11)	11	0.05
Turkish (13)	13	0.06
Ukrainian (93)	244	1.06
Welsh (10)	78	0.34
West Indian, ex. Hispanic (220)	288	1.25
British West Indian (1)	1	<0.01
Haitian (11)	11	0.05
Jamaican (155)	195	0.84
Trinidadian/Tobagonian (14)	26	0.11
West Indian (39)	55	0.24
Yugoslavian (0)	11	0.05

Hispanic Origin	Population	%
Hispanic or Latino (of any race)	3,097	13.24
Central American, ex. Mexican	642	2.75
Costa Rican	17	0.07
Guatemalan	164	0.70
Honduran	121	0.52
Nicaraguan	20	0.09
Panamanian	37	0.16
Salvadoran	282	1.21
Other Central American	1	<0.01
Cuban	119	0.51
Dominican Republic	163	0.70
Mexican	142	0.61
Puerto Rican	799	3.42
South American	959	4.10
Argentinean	39	0.17
Chilean	8	0.03
Colombian	376	1.61
Ecuadorian	346	1.48
Paraguayan	1	<0.01
Peruvian	158	0.68
Uruguayan	10	0.04
Venezuelan	9	0.04
Other South American	12	0.05
Other Hispanic or Latino	273	1.17

Race*	Population	%
African-American/Black (2,361)	2,650	11.33
Not Hispanic (2,266)	2,452	10.49
Hispanic (95)	198	0.85
American Indian/Alaska Native (87)	216	0.92
Not Hispanic (76)	166	0.71
Hispanic (11)	50	0.21
Apache (0)	4	0.02
Blackfeet (1)	3	0.01
Cherokee (1)	25	0.11
Cheyenne (0)	1	<0.01
Comanche (0)	4	0.02
Delaware (0)	13	0.06
Iroquois (0)	1	<0.01
Navajo (1)	1	<0.01
Seminole (3)	5	0.02
Sioux (1)	4	0.02
South American Ind. (6)	17	0.07
Asian (3,433)	3,739	15.99
Not Hispanic (3,422)	3,706	15.85
Hispanic (11)	33	0.14
Bangladeshi (12)	12	0.05
Cambodian (4)	10	0.04
Chinese, ex. Taiwanese (303)	334	1.43
Filipino (557)	605	2.59
Indian (1,952)	2,048	8.76
Indonesian (19)	19	0.08
Japanese (9)	13	0.06
Korean (84)	101	0.43
Malaysian (2)	2	0.01
Pakistani (39)	39	0.17
Sri Lankan (5)	7	0.03
Taiwanese (21)	21	0.09
Thai (3)	3	0.01
Vietnamese (364)	381	1.63
Hawaii Native/Pacific Islander (8)	45	0.19
Not Hispanic (8)	38	0.16
Hispanic (0)	7	0.03
Native Hawaiian (1)	3	0.01
Samoan (3)	5	0.02
White (15,607)	16,108	68.88
Not Hispanic (13,850)	14,126	60.41
Hispanic (1,757)	1,982	8.48

South River

Place Type: Borough
County: Middlesex
Population: 16,008†

Ancestry‡	Population	%
African, Sub-Saharan (0)	9	0.06
African (0)	9	0.06
American (360)	360	2.27
Arab (315)	323	2.04
Egyptian (315)	315	1.99
Syrian (0)	8	0.05
Austrian (0)	16	0.10

*Notes: † The Census 2010 population figure is used to calculate the percentages in the Hispanic Origin and Race categories. Ancestry percentages are based on the 2006-2010 American Community Survey population (not shown); ‡ Numbers in parentheses indicate the number of people reporting a single ancestry; * Numbers in parentheses indicate the number of persons reporting this race alone, not in combination with any other race; Please refer to the Explanation of Data for more information.*

Brazilian (657)	709	4.47
British (12)	12	0.08
Czech (0)	51	0.32
Czechoslovakian (0)	10	0.06
Danish (65)	111	0.70
Dutch (11)	73	0.46
English (41)	588	3.71
European (62)	62	0.39
French, ex. Basque (59)	226	1.42
French Canadian (0)	60	0.38
German (242)	1,508	9.51
Greek (14)	42	0.26
Hungarian (191)	464	2.93
Irish (403)	1,644	10.36
Italian (872)	1,924	12.13
Lithuanian (80)	80	0.50
Macedonian (137)	137	0.86
Norwegian (0)	92	0.58
Pennsylvania German (0)	17	0.11
Polish (1,558)	2,728	17.20
Portuguese (1,489)	1,679	10.59
Romanian (0)	13	0.08
Russian (213)	472	2.98
Scandinavian (15)	15	0.09
Scotch-Irish (60)	106	0.67
Scottish (12)	105	0.66
Slovak (75)	98	0.62
Swedish (11)	74	0.47
Turkish (24)	24	0.15
Ukrainian (83)	228	1.44
West Indian, ex. Hispanic (311)	384	2.42
British West Indian (0)	12	0.08
Haitian (54)	54	0.34
Jamaican (257)	271	1.71
West Indian (0)	47	0.30

Hispanic Origin	Population	%
Hispanic or Latino (of any race)	2,913	18.20
Central American, ex. Mexican	267	1.67
Costa Rican	5	0.03
Guatemalan	32	0.20
Honduran	164	1.02
Nicaraguan	37	0.23
Panamanian	10	0.06
Salvadoran	19	0.12
Cuban	76	0.47
Dominican Republic	134	0.84
Mexican	889	5.55
Puerto Rican	646	4.04
South American	653	4.08
Argentinean	48	0.30
Bolivian	10	0.06
Chilean	19	0.12
Colombian	135	0.84
Ecuadorian	253	1.58
Paraguayan	10	0.06
Peruvian	90	0.56
Uruguayan	21	0.13
Venezuelan	44	0.27
Other South American	23	0.14
Other Hispanic or Latino	248	1.55

Race*	Population	%
African-American/Black (1,142)	1,294	8.08
Not Hispanic (1,028)	1,136	7.10
Hispanic (114)	158	0.99
American Indian/Alaska Native (50)	96	0.60
Not Hispanic (20)	51	0.32
Hispanic (30)	45	0.28
Blackfeet (0)	1	0.01
Canadian/French Am. Ind. (1)	1	0.01
Cherokee (0)	15	0.09
Iroquois (4)	6	0.04
Mexican American Ind. (17)	18	0.11
South American Ind. (1)	3	0.02
Asian (775)	867	5.42
Not Hispanic (758)	837	5.23
Hispanic (17)	30	0.19
Bangladeshi (1)	1	0.01
Chinese, ex. Taiwanese (176)	213	1.33
Filipino (202)	229	1.43
Hmong (1)	1	0.01
Indian (251)	274	1.71
Indonesian (8)	8	0.05
Japanese (3)	9	0.06
Korean (14)	18	0.11
Malaysian (2)	2	0.01
Pakistani (63)	63	0.39
Sri Lankan (1)	1	0.01
Taiwanese (14)	15	0.09
Thai (3)	3	0.02
Vietnamese (7)	8	0.05
Hawaii Native/Pacific Islander (9)	26	0.16
Not Hispanic (4)	14	0.09
Hispanic (5)	12	0.07
Native Hawaiian (5)	6	0.04
White (12,195)	12,658	79.07
Not Hispanic (10,737)	11,019	68.83
Hispanic (1,458)	1,639	10.24

Southampton

Place Type: Township
County: Burlington
Population: 10,464†

Ancestry‡	Population	%
American (474)	474	4.49
Australian (0)	17	0.16
Austrian (13)	61	0.58
British (23)	23	0.22
Canadian (0)	15	0.14
Celtic (15)	15	0.14
Croatian (28)	28	0.27
Czech (11)	23	0.22
Czechoslovakian (20)	64	0.61
Danish (13)	53	0.50
Dutch (112)	270	2.56
English (406)	1,660	15.74
European (48)	48	0.46
Finnish (17)	31	0.29
French, ex. Basque (34)	316	3.00
French Canadian (10)	97	0.92
German (631)	2,852	27.04
Greek (0)	58	0.55
Guyanese (162)	162	1.54
Hungarian (41)	183	1.74
Irish (919)	2,947	27.94
Italian (647)	1,540	14.60
Latvian (14)	14	0.13
Lithuanian (27)	27	0.26
Norwegian (56)	99	0.94
Pennsylvania German (69)	69	0.65
Polish (218)	734	6.96
Portuguese (0)	36	0.34
Romanian (8)	61	0.58
Russian (29)	139	1.32
Scotch-Irish (52)	104	0.99
Scottish (50)	131	1.24
Slovak (12)	26	0.25
Swedish (51)	137	1.30
Swiss (33)	33	0.31
Ukrainian (8)	8	0.08
Welsh (85)	186	1.76

Hispanic Origin	Population	%
Hispanic or Latino (of any race)	225	2.15
Central American, ex. Mexican	17	0.16
Costa Rican	1	0.01
Guatemalan	5	0.05
Honduran	1	0.01
Nicaraguan	4	0.04
Panamanian	5	0.05
Salvadoran	1	0.01
Cuban	17	0.16
Dominican Republic	3	0.03
Mexican	43	0.41
Puerto Rican	102	0.97
South American	17	0.16
Argentinean	1	0.01
Bolivian	4	0.04
Colombian	6	0.06
Ecuadorian	5	0.05
Peruvian	1	0.01
Other Hispanic or Latino	26	0.25

Race*	Population	%
African-American/Black (231)	287	2.74
Not Hispanic (224)	272	2.60
Hispanic (7)	15	0.14
American Indian/Alaska Native (12)	46	0.44
Not Hispanic (11)	40	0.38
Hispanic (1)	6	0.06
Blackfeet (0)	1	0.01
Cherokee (2)	7	0.07
Delaware (2)	2	0.02
South American Ind. (0)	3	0.03
Asian (139)	180	1.72
Not Hispanic (139)	180	1.72
Bangladeshi (4)	4	0.04
Chinese, ex. Taiwanese (15)	22	0.21
Filipino (18)	24	0.23
Indian (19)	23	0.22
Indonesian (4)	4	0.04
Japanese (8)	20	0.19
Korean (50)	60	0.57
Malaysian (1)	1	0.01
Thai (3)	7	0.07
Vietnamese (11)	12	0.11
Hawaii Native/Pacific Islander (1)	11	0.11
Not Hispanic (1)	11	0.11
Native Hawaiian (1)	7	0.07
White (9,888)	10,015	95.71
Not Hispanic (9,742)	9,851	94.14
Hispanic (146)	164	1.57

Sparta

Place Type: Township
County: Sussex
Population: 19,722†

Ancestry‡	Population	%
African, Sub-Saharan (13)	28	0.14
African (0)	15	0.08
Ghanaian (13)	13	0.07
American (1,180)	1,180	6.01
Arab (55)	126	0.64
Egyptian (0)	11	0.06
Lebanese (10)	19	0.10
Palestinian (35)	35	0.18
Syrian (10)	61	0.31
Armenian (42)	94	0.48
Austrian (11)	126	0.64
Basque (14)	14	0.07
Belgian (0)	11	0.06
Brazilian (42)	42	0.21
British (32)	78	0.40
Canadian (0)	20	0.10
Croatian (19)	59	0.30
Czech (33)	89	0.45
Czechoslovakian (55)	105	0.53
Danish (35)	106	0.54
Dutch (106)	669	3.41
Eastern European (8)	24	0.12
English (571)	2,619	13.33
European (165)	165	0.84
Finnish (24)	46	0.23
French, ex. Basque (34)	500	2.55
French Canadian (42)	140	0.71
German (730)	4,858	24.73
Greek (43)	177	0.90
Hungarian (45)	159	0.81
Irish (1,256)	5,138	26.16
Italian (1,912)	4,932	25.11
Lithuanian (53)	187	0.95
Norwegian (64)	249	1.27
Pennsylvania German (0)	13	0.07
Polish (759)	1,974	10.05
Portuguese (19)	103	0.52

SECTION TWO

*Notes: † The Census 2010 population figure is used to calculate the percentages in the Hispanic Origin and Race categories. Ancestry percentages are based on the 2006-2010 American Community Survey population (not shown); ‡ Numbers in parentheses indicate the number of people reporting a single ancestry; * Numbers in parentheses indicate the number of persons reporting this race alone, not in combination with any other race; Please refer to the Explanation of Data for more information.*

Ancestry	Population	%
Romanian (44)	80	0.41
Russian (118)	293	1.49
Scandinavian (0)	37	0.19
Scotch-Irish (92)	211	1.07
Scottish (71)	477	2.43
Serbian (10)	10	0.05
Slavic (0)	10	0.05
Slovak (49)	174	0.89
Swedish (34)	237	1.21
Swiss (44)	76	0.39
Turkish (8)	24	0.12
Ukrainian (24)	150	0.76
Welsh (16)	74	0.38

Hispanic Origin	Population	%
Hispanic or Latino (of any race)	1,054	5.34
Central American, ex. Mexican	68	0.34
Costa Rican	9	0.05
Guatemalan	22	0.11
Honduran	12	0.06
Nicaraguan	9	0.05
Panamanian	1	0.01
Salvadoran	15	0.08
Cuban	139	0.70
Dominican Republic	72	0.37
Mexican	111	0.56
Puerto Rican	277	1.40
South American	266	1.35
Argentinean	12	0.06
Bolivian	7	0.04
Chilean	5	0.03
Colombian	87	0.44
Ecuadorian	76	0.39
Paraguayan	1	0.01
Peruvian	59	0.30
Uruguayan	13	0.07
Venezuelan	5	0.03
Other South American	1	0.01
Other Hispanic or Latino	121	0.61

Race*	Population	%
African-American/Black (198)	267	1.35
Not Hispanic (187)	237	1.20
Hispanic (11)	30	0.15
American Indian/Alaska Native (22)	80	0.41
Not Hispanic (12)	60	0.30
Hispanic (10)	20	0.10
Arapaho (0)	1	0.01
Blackfeet (0)	3	0.02
Cherokee (1)	13	0.07
Chickasaw (3)	3	0.02
Comanche (0)	1	0.01
Crow (0)	1	0.01
Delaware (0)	1	0.01
Iroquois (1)	3	0.02
Mexican American Ind. (1)	3	0.02
Pueblo (0)	5	0.03
Seminole (0)	1	0.01
Sioux (0)	1	0.01
South American Ind. (4)	5	0.03
Tohono O'Odham (0)	1	0.01
Ute (0)	2	0.01
Asian (491)	650	3.30
Not Hispanic (490)	641	3.25
Hispanic (1)	9	0.05
Bangladeshi (1)	2	0.01
Cambodian (1)	1	0.01
Chinese, ex. Taiwanese (111)	150	0.76
Filipino (93)	146	0.74
Indian (157)	178	0.90
Indonesian (0)	1	0.01
Japanese (3)	18	0.09
Korean (81)	108	0.55
Nepalese (1)	1	0.01
Pakistani (13)	13	0.07
Taiwanese (1)	3	0.02
Thai (1)	1	0.01
Vietnamese (18)	22	0.11
Hawaii Native/Pacific Islander (4)	23	0.12
Not Hispanic (3)	15	0.08
Hispanic (1)	8	0.04
Guamanian/Chamorro (1)	1	0.01
Native Hawaiian (1)	6	0.03
White (18,569)	18,833	95.49
Not Hispanic (17,715)	17,930	90.91
Hispanic (854)	903	4.58

Spotswood

Place Type: Borough
County: Middlesex
Population: 8,257†

Ancestry‡	Population	%
American (504)	504	6.15
Arab (132)	132	1.61
Egyptian (132)	132	1.61
Austrian (14)	14	0.17
British (13)	26	0.32
Canadian (12)	12	0.15
Celtic (0)	9	0.11
Croatian (0)	7	0.09
Czech (4)	12	0.15
Danish (0)	39	0.48
Dutch (0)	75	0.92
Eastern European (61)	61	0.74
English (73)	414	5.05
European (9)	9	0.11
Finnish (0)	12	0.15
French, ex. Basque (15)	126	1.54
French Canadian (10)	58	0.71
German (316)	1,556	18.98
Greek (11)	32	0.39
Hungarian (36)	254	3.10
Irish (541)	1,892	23.08
Italian (911)	1,915	23.37
Latvian (51)	51	0.62
Lithuanian (0)	44	0.54
Norwegian (22)	126	1.54
Polish (520)	1,542	18.81
Portuguese (81)	149	1.82
Romanian (12)	12	0.15
Russian (30)	188	2.29
Scotch-Irish (21)	67	0.82
Scottish (15)	85	1.04
Slavic (0)	11	0.13
Slovak (28)	131	1.60
Swedish (41)	63	0.77
Swiss (0)	10	0.12
Turkish (30)	30	0.37
Ukrainian (110)	196	2.39
Welsh (22)	87	1.06
West Indian, ex. Hispanic (65)	71	0.87
Trinidadian/Tobagonian (65)	71	0.87
Yugoslavian (31)	31	0.38

Hispanic Origin	Population	%
Hispanic or Latino (of any race)	687	8.32
Central American, ex. Mexican	41	0.50
Costa Rican	6	0.07
Guatemalan	3	0.04
Honduran	19	0.23
Nicaraguan	7	0.08
Panamanian	2	0.02
Salvadoran	4	0.05
Cuban	56	0.68
Dominican Republic	66	0.80
Mexican	78	0.94
Puerto Rican	269	3.26
South American	103	1.25
Argentinean	7	0.08
Colombian	37	0.45
Ecuadorian	36	0.44
Peruvian	15	0.18
Uruguayan	2	0.02
Venezuelan	6	0.07
Other Hispanic or Latino	74	0.90

Race*	Population	%
African-American/Black (246)	312	3.78
Not Hispanic (227)	281	3.40
Hispanic (19)	31	0.38
American Indian/Alaska Native (9)	48	0.58
Not Hispanic (8)	38	0.46
Hispanic (1)	10	0.12
Blackfeet (0)	1	0.01
Cherokee (1)	13	0.16
Iroquois (1)	7	0.08
Osage (0)	1	0.01
South American Ind. (0)	5	0.06
Asian (424)	473	5.73
Not Hispanic (419)	461	5.58
Hispanic (5)	12	0.15
Bangladeshi (3)	3	0.04
Burmese (0)	2	0.02
Chinese, ex. Taiwanese (84)	97	1.17
Filipino (70)	78	0.94
Indian (205)	223	2.70
Japanese (8)	14	0.17
Korean (17)	20	0.24
Pakistani (23)	23	0.28
Taiwanese (1)	1	0.01
Thai (0)	2	0.02
Vietnamese (5)	6	0.07
Hawaii Native/Pacific Islander (1)	5	0.06
Not Hispanic (1)	4	0.05
Hispanic (0)	1	0.01
Native Hawaiian (1)	1	0.01
White (7,318)	7,456	90.30
Not Hispanic (6,800)	6,899	83.55
Hispanic (518)	557	6.75

Springdale

Place Type: CDP
County: Camden
Population: 14,518†

Ancestry‡	Population	%
African, Sub-Saharan (138)	148	1.01
African (33)	41	0.28
Kenyan (70)	70	0.48
Nigerian (15)	15	0.10
Other Sub-Saharan African (20)	22	0.15
American (604)	604	4.11
Arab (56)	60	0.41
Moroccan (37)	41	0.28
Syrian (19)	19	0.13
Armenian (60)	60	0.41
Australian (0)	11	0.07
Austrian (45)	301	2.05
Belgian (0)	15	0.10
Brazilian (0)	40	0.27
British (68)	139	0.95
Canadian (39)	51	0.35
Celtic (0)	35	0.24
Croatian (0)	11	0.07
Czech (11)	22	0.15
Czechoslovakian (0)	13	0.09
Danish (0)	25	0.17
Dutch (0)	62	0.42
Eastern European (550)	550	3.74
English (170)	819	5.57
European (181)	192	1.31
French, ex. Basque (17)	128	0.87
French Canadian (25)	25	0.17
German (637)	1,830	12.45
Greek (88)	102	0.69
Hungarian (38)	145	0.99
Irish (549)	1,739	11.83
Israeli (203)	217	1.48
Italian (710)	1,656	11.27
Latvian (0)	8	0.05
Lithuanian (9)	58	0.39
Norwegian (0)	52	0.35
Pennsylvania German (0)	12	0.08
Polish (695)	1,587	10.80
Romanian (53)	207	1.41
Russian (1,104)	1,859	12.65
Scandinavian (0)	51	0.35

*Notes: † The Census 2010 population figure is used to calculate the percentages in the Hispanic Origin and Race categories. Ancestry percentages are based on the 2006-2010 American Community Survey population (not shown); ‡ Numbers in parentheses indicate the number of people reporting a single ancestry; * Numbers in parentheses indicate the number of persons reporting this race alone, not in combination with any other race; Please refer to the Explanation of Data for more information.*

Scotch-Irish (77)	117	0.80
Scottish (106)	231	1.57
Slovak (0)	13	0.09
Slovene (0)	14	0.10
Swedish (37)	150	1.02
Swiss (0)	42	0.29
Ukrainian (106)	164	1.12
Welsh (0)	23	0.16
West Indian, ex. Hispanic (6)	24	0.16
British West Indian (6)	6	0.04
Jamaican (0)	18	0.12

Hispanic Origin	Population	%
Hispanic or Latino (of any race)	337	2.32
Central American, ex. Mexican	22	0.15
Guatemalan	10	0.07
Honduran	1	0.01
Nicaraguan	5	0.03
Panamanian	6	0.04
Cuban	28	0.19
Dominican Republic	16	0.11
Mexican	35	0.24
Puerto Rican	146	1.01
South American	57	0.39
Argentinean	17	0.12
Bolivian	1	0.01
Colombian	16	0.11
Ecuadorian	2	0.01
Peruvian	1	0.01
Venezuelan	19	0.13
Other South American	1	0.01
Other Hispanic or Latino	33	0.23

Race*	Population	%
African-American/Black (509)	596	4.11
Not Hispanic (494)	570	3.93
Hispanic (15)	26	0.18
American Indian/Alaska Native (10)	45	0.31
Not Hispanic (10)	40	0.28
Hispanic (0)	5	0.03
Apache (0)	2	0.01
Cherokee (4)	7	0.05
Chippewa (1)	1	0.01
Choctaw (0)	4	0.03
Delaware (0)	1	0.01
Mexican American Ind. (0)	4	0.03
Asian (1,662)	1,809	12.46
Not Hispanic (1,659)	1,804	12.43
Hispanic (3)	5	0.03
Bangladeshi (5)	5	0.03
Cambodian (6)	6	0.04
Chinese, ex. Taiwanese (537)	578	3.98
Filipino (119)	148	1.02
Hmong (1)	1	0.01
Indian (421)	446	3.07
Indonesian (6)	7	0.05
Japanese (25)	37	0.25
Korean (389)	430	2.96
Malaysian (1)	1	0.01
Pakistani (23)	23	0.16
Sri Lankan (3)	3	0.02
Taiwanese (43)	52	0.36
Vietnamese (49)	60	0.41
Hawaii Native/Pacific Islander (2)	9	0.06
Not Hispanic (2)	9	0.06
Native Hawaiian (2)	5	0.03
White (12,021)	12,229	84.23
Not Hispanic (11,779)	11,965	82.41
Hispanic (242)	264	1.82

Springfield

Place Type: Township
County: Union
Population: 15,817†

Ancestry‡	Population	%
African, Sub-Saharan (73)	73	0.47
African (17)	17	0.11
South African (21)	21	0.14
Ugandan (18)	18	0.12
Other Sub-Saharan African (17)	17	0.11
American (925)	925	5.98
Arab (41)	74	0.48
Iraqi (30)	30	0.19
Other Arab (11)	44	0.28
Armenian (71)	71	0.46
Austrian (0)	23	0.15
Brazilian (47)	58	0.37
British (69)	139	0.90
Canadian (9)	9	0.06
Czech (0)	33	0.21
Czechoslovakian (47)	61	0.39
Danish (0)	10	0.06
Dutch (18)	198	1.28
Eastern European (201)	234	1.51
English (103)	640	4.13
European (149)	267	1.72
French, ex. Basque (26)	157	1.01
French Canadian (21)	42	0.27
German (345)	1,704	11.01
Greek (216)	266	1.72
Hungarian (80)	172	1.11
Irish (438)	1,539	9.94
Italian (1,354)	2,474	15.98
Lithuanian (43)	129	0.83
Norwegian (13)	61	0.39
Pennsylvania German (23)	23	0.15
Polish (638)	1,643	10.61
Portuguese (96)	96	0.62
Romanian (34)	82	0.53
Russian (948)	1,474	9.52
Scotch-Irish (100)	171	1.10
Scottish (127)	329	2.13
Swedish (12)	106	0.68
Swiss (0)	60	0.39
Turkish (8)	15	0.10
Ukrainian (281)	360	2.33
Welsh (0)	66	0.43
West Indian, ex. Hispanic (107)	119	0.77
Haitian (85)	85	0.55
Jamaican (15)	27	0.17
West Indian (7)	7	0.05

Hispanic Origin	Population	%
Hispanic or Latino (of any race)	1,502	9.50
Central American, ex. Mexican	342	2.16
Costa Rican	262	1.66
Guatemalan	23	0.15
Honduran	27	0.17
Nicaraguan	1	0.01
Panamanian	10	0.06
Salvadoran	19	0.12
Cuban	126	0.80
Dominican Republic	49	0.31
Mexican	90	0.57
Puerto Rican	244	1.54
South American	443	2.80
Argentinean	32	0.20
Bolivian	5	0.03
Chilean	17	0.11
Colombian	157	0.99
Ecuadorian	95	0.60
Paraguayan	3	0.02
Peruvian	72	0.46
Uruguayan	34	0.21
Venezuelan	19	0.12
Other South American	9	0.06
Other Hispanic or Latino	208	1.32

Race*	Population	%
African-American/Black (989)	1,066	6.74
Not Hispanic (968)	1,034	6.54
Hispanic (21)	32	0.20
American Indian/Alaska Native (10)	49	0.31
Not Hispanic (8)	42	0.27
Hispanic (2)	7	0.04
Apache (0)	1	0.01
Arapaho (0)	1	0.01
Blackfeet (0)	3	0.02
Cherokee (2)	9	0.06
Creek (1)	1	0.01
South American Ind. (0)	1	0.01
Asian (1,218)	1,335	8.44
Not Hispanic (1,196)	1,300	8.22
Hispanic (22)	35	0.22
Bangladeshi (11)	14	0.09
Burmese (1)	1	0.01
Chinese, ex. Taiwanese (285)	311	1.97
Filipino (230)	258	1.63
Indian (540)	569	3.60
Indonesian (1)	3	0.02
Japanese (14)	25	0.16
Korean (45)	55	0.35
Pakistani (8)	10	0.06
Sri Lankan (4)	4	0.03
Taiwanese (7)	8	0.05
Thai (4)	6	0.04
Vietnamese (31)	32	0.20
Hawaii Native/Pacific Islander (2)	14	0.09
Not Hispanic (0)	9	0.06
Hispanic (2)	5	0.03
Guamanian/Chamorro (2)	4	0.03
Native Hawaiian (0)	1	0.01
White (13,042)	13,284	83.99
Not Hispanic (11,922)	12,092	76.45
Hispanic (1,120)	1,192	7.54

Stafford

Place Type: Township
County: Ocean
Population: 26,535†

Ancestry‡	Population	%
African, Sub-Saharan (0)	17	0.07
African (0)	17	0.07
American (795)	795	3.05
Arab (48)	91	0.35
Lebanese (0)	10	0.04
Syrian (48)	66	0.25
Other Arab (0)	15	0.06
Armenian (0)	15	0.06
Austrian (41)	84	0.32
Belgian (15)	44	0.17
Brazilian (0)	12	0.05
British (44)	124	0.48
Bulgarian (15)	15	0.06
Canadian (17)	17	0.07
Croatian (0)	15	0.06
Czech (24)	116	0.45
Czechoslovakian (16)	110	0.42
Danish (55)	190	0.73
Dutch (39)	460	1.77
English (574)	2,643	10.15
European (225)	241	0.93
Finnish (0)	19	0.07
French, ex. Basque (55)	429	1.65
French Canadian (0)	231	0.89
German (1,267)	6,153	23.64
Greek (31)	132	0.51
Hungarian (142)	416	1.60
Irish (1,849)	7,351	28.24
Italian (4,432)	9,068	34.84
Lithuanian (81)	202	0.78
Norwegian (49)	223	0.86
Pennsylvania German (0)	20	0.08
Polish (679)	2,319	8.91
Portuguese (98)	308	1.18
Romanian (23)	53	0.20
Russian (60)	182	0.70
Scandinavian (0)	15	0.06
Scotch-Irish (190)	389	1.49
Scottish (103)	689	2.65
Slavic (0)	112	0.43
Slovak (133)	481	1.85
Slovene (0)	43	0.17
Swedish (69)	274	1.05
Swiss (0)	49	0.19
Ukrainian (58)	257	0.99

*Notes: † The Census 2010 population figure is used to calculate the percentages in the Hispanic Origin and Race categories. Ancestry percentages are based on the 2006-2010 American Community Survey population (not shown); ‡ Numbers in parentheses indicate the number of people reporting a single ancestry; * Numbers in parentheses indicate the number of persons reporting this race alone, not in combination with any other race; Please refer to the Explanation of Data for more information.*

Welsh (11)	115	0.44
West Indian, ex. Hispanic (14)	14	0.05
British West Indian (14)	14	0.05
Yugoslavian (0)	39	0.15

Hispanic Origin	Population	%
Hispanic or Latino (of any race)	1,410	5.31
Central American, ex. Mexican	117	0.44
Costa Rican	19	0.07
Guatemalan	5	0.02
Honduran	56	0.21
Nicaraguan	9	0.03
Panamanian	11	0.04
Salvadoran	17	0.06
Cuban	127	0.48
Dominican Republic	35	0.13
Mexican	459	1.73
Puerto Rican	443	1.67
South American	128	0.48
Argentinean	22	0.08
Chilean	9	0.03
Colombian	35	0.13
Ecuadorian	28	0.11
Peruvian	26	0.10
Uruguayan	4	0.02
Venezuelan	4	0.02
Other Hispanic or Latino	101	0.38

Race*	Population	%
African-American/Black (278)	351	1.32
Not Hispanic (243)	300	1.13
Hispanic (35)	51	0.19
American Indian/Alaska Native (42)	113	0.43
Not Hispanic (22)	86	0.32
Hispanic (20)	27	0.10
Aleut *(Alaska Native)* (1)	1	<0.01
Canadian/French Am. Ind. (0)	1	<0.01
Central American Ind. (2)	2	0.01
Cherokee (6)	21	0.08
Cheyenne (0)	5	0.02
Chippewa (0)	1	<0.01
Delaware (0)	4	0.02
Iroquois (0)	2	0.01
Lumbee (1)	1	<0.01
Mexican American Ind. (10)	12	0.05
Navajo (0)	2	0.01
Shoshone (1)	1	<0.01
Sioux (0)	7	0.03
South American Ind. (5)	5	0.02
Asian (394)	506	1.91
Not Hispanic (393)	494	1.86
Hispanic (1)	12	0.05
Burmese (0)	1	<0.01
Cambodian (1)	1	<0.01
Chinese, ex. Taiwanese (81)	96	0.36
Filipino (101)	159	0.60
Indian (101)	107	0.40
Japanese (8)	24	0.09
Korean (42)	63	0.24
Pakistani (6)	6	0.02
Taiwanese (0)	5	0.02
Thai (3)	3	0.01
Vietnamese (36)	42	0.16
Hawaii Native/Pacific Islander (8)	21	0.08
Not Hispanic (8)	16	0.06
Hispanic (0)	5	0.02
Guamanian/Chamorro (0)	3	0.01
Native Hawaiian (0)	2	0.01
Samoan (2)	5	0.02
White (25,077)	25,347	95.52
Not Hispanic (24,228)	24,431	92.07
Hispanic (849)	916	3.45

Succasunna

Place Type: CDP
County: Morris
Population: 9,152†

Ancestry‡	Population	%
African, Sub-Saharan (133)	305	3.40
African (0)	86	0.96
Ghanaian (133)	219	2.44
Albanian (65)	65	0.72
American (143)	143	1.59
Arab (6)	35	0.39
Lebanese (6)	21	0.23
Syrian (0)	14	0.16
Armenian (64)	64	0.71
Australian (10)	10	0.11
Austrian (14)	136	1.51
Brazilian (0)	10	0.11
British (0)	20	0.22
Bulgarian (37)	37	0.41
Canadian (0)	28	0.31
Czech (9)	39	0.43
Dutch (14)	109	1.21
Eastern European (24)	24	0.27
English (254)	945	10.53
European (27)	27	0.30
Finnish (14)	39	0.43
French, ex. Basque (62)	208	2.32
French Canadian (0)	31	0.35
German (349)	1,548	17.24
Greek (0)	236	2.63
Hungarian (21)	173	1.93
Irish (381)	1,591	17.72
Italian (1,384)	2,619	29.17
Latvian (0)	21	0.23
Lithuanian (12)	12	0.13
Macedonian (0)	10	0.11
Norwegian (60)	136	1.51
Polish (264)	791	8.81
Portuguese (89)	111	1.24
Romanian (10)	39	0.43
Russian (132)	323	3.60
Scotch-Irish (42)	59	0.66
Scottish (21)	259	2.89
Slavic (21)	67	0.75
Slovak (7)	26	0.29
Swedish (72)	209	2.33
Swiss (0)	15	0.17
Ukrainian (84)	136	1.51
Welsh (10)	47	0.52
West Indian, ex. Hispanic (21)	21	0.23
Haitian (21)	21	0.23
Yugoslavian (16)	26	0.29

Hispanic Origin	Population	%
Hispanic or Latino (of any race)	536	5.86
Central American, ex. Mexican	38	0.42
Costa Rican	16	0.17
Guatemalan	3	0.03
Honduran	10	0.11
Nicaraguan	1	0.01
Panamanian	1	0.01
Salvadoran	7	0.08
Cuban	61	0.67
Dominican Republic	23	0.25
Mexican	38	0.42
Puerto Rican	176	1.92
South American	140	1.53
Argentinean	15	0.16
Chilean	9	0.10
Colombian	80	0.87
Ecuadorian	10	0.11
Peruvian	16	0.17
Uruguayan	5	0.05
Venezuelan	5	0.05
Other Hispanic or Latino	60	0.66

Race*	Population	%
African-American/Black (135)	162	1.77
Not Hispanic (123)	147	1.61
Hispanic (12)	15	0.16
American Indian/Alaska Native (4)	17	0.19
Not Hispanic (2)	14	0.15
Hispanic (2)	3	0.03
Central American Ind. (1)	1	0.01
Cherokee (1)	2	0.02
Cree (0)	1	0.01
Ottawa (0)	1	0.01
South American Ind. (1)	2	0.02
Asian (449)	506	5.53
Not Hispanic (445)	491	5.36
Hispanic (4)	15	0.16
Chinese, ex. Taiwanese (94)	112	1.22
Filipino (83)	100	1.09
Indian (167)	179	1.96
Japanese (6)	6	0.07
Korean (40)	50	0.55
Pakistani (4)	4	0.04
Sri Lankan (3)	3	0.03
Taiwanese (6)	9	0.10
Thai (1)	1	0.01
Vietnamese (37)	41	0.45
White (8,365)	8,480	92.66
Not Hispanic (7,948)	8,031	87.75
Hispanic (417)	449	4.91

Summit

Place Type: City
County: Union
Population: 21,457†

Ancestry‡	Population	%
African, Sub-Saharan (6)	6	0.03
African (6)	6	0.03
American (726)	726	3.42
Arab (86)	140	0.66
Egyptian (86)	110	0.52
Lebanese (0)	10	0.05
Syrian (0)	20	0.09
Armenian (35)	44	0.21
Australian (10)	10	0.05
Austrian (38)	145	0.68
Belgian (0)	35	0.16
Brazilian (12)	12	0.06
British (125)	163	0.77
Canadian (54)	66	0.31
Celtic (0)	45	0.21
Croatian (34)	174	0.82
Czech (12)	19	0.09
Danish (10)	108	0.51
Dutch (39)	160	0.75
Eastern European (196)	233	1.10
English (567)	2,213	10.43
European (368)	378	1.78
Finnish (0)	84	0.40
French, ex. Basque (45)	421	1.98
French Canadian (36)	198	0.93
German (486)	2,713	12.79
Greek (120)	263	1.24
Hungarian (147)	313	1.48
Irish (1,509)	4,228	19.93
Israeli (65)	82	0.39
Italian (1,731)	3,374	15.90
Latvian (0)	6	0.03
Lithuanian (35)	64	0.30
Macedonian (13)	35	0.16
Norwegian (29)	132	0.62
Polish (172)	912	4.30
Portuguese (151)	151	0.71
Romanian (0)	9	0.04
Russian (155)	440	2.07
Scandinavian (0)	38	0.18
Scotch-Irish (122)	298	1.40
Scottish (136)	528	2.49
Slovak (28)	123	0.58
Slovene (4)	8	0.04
Swedish (43)	200	0.94
Swiss (29)	162	0.76
Turkish (8)	33	0.16
Ukrainian (48)	135	0.64
Welsh (19)	106	0.50
West Indian, ex. Hispanic (74)	104	0.49
Barbadian (8)	23	0.11
Haitian (66)	66	0.31

*Notes: † The Census 2010 population figure is used to calculate the percentages in the Hispanic Origin and Race categories. Ancestry percentages are based on the 2006-2010 American Community Survey population (not shown); ‡ Numbers in parentheses indicate the number of people reporting a single ancestry; * Numbers in parentheses indicate the number of persons reporting this race alone, not in combination with any other race; Please refer to the Explanation of Data for more information.*

Ancestry‡	Population	%
Trinidadian/Tobagonian (0)	15	0.07
Yugoslavian (0)	10	0.05

Hispanic Origin	Population	%
Hispanic or Latino (of any race)	2,851	13.29
Central American, ex. Mexican	1,236	5.76
Costa Rican	990	4.61
Guatemalan	92	0.43
Honduran	82	0.38
Nicaraguan	15	0.07
Panamanian	10	0.05
Salvadoran	40	0.19
Other Central American	7	0.03
Cuban	122	0.57
Dominican Republic	34	0.16
Mexican	348	1.62
Puerto Rican	279	1.30
South American	564	2.63
Argentinean	48	0.22
Bolivian	2	0.01
Chilean	41	0.19
Colombian	235	1.10
Ecuadorian	87	0.41
Peruvian	117	0.55
Uruguayan	7	0.03
Venezuelan	27	0.13
Other Hispanic or Latino	268	1.25

Race*	Population	%
African-American/Black (970)	1,089	5.08
Not Hispanic (933)	1,016	4.74
Hispanic (37)	73	0.34
American Indian/Alaska Native (30)	93	0.43
Not Hispanic (7)	37	0.17
Hispanic (23)	56	0.26
Apache (1)	4	0.02
Blackfeet (0)	3	0.01
Canadian/French Am. Ind. (0)	1	<0.01
Central American Ind. (1)	4	0.02
Cherokee (0)	8	0.04
Creek (0)	2	0.01
Iroquois (1)	5	0.02
Mexican American Ind. (9)	10	0.05
Potawatomi (1)	1	<0.01
Shoshone (1)	1	<0.01
South American Ind. (0)	1	<0.01
Ute (0)	1	<0.01
Yuman (0)	1	<0.01
Asian (1,368)	1,641	7.65
Not Hispanic (1,367)	1,621	7.55
Hispanic (1)	20	0.09
Burmese (1)	1	<0.01
Cambodian (0)	2	0.01
Chinese, ex. Taiwanese (457)	545	2.54
Filipino (186)	251	1.17
Indian (383)	439	2.05
Indonesian (2)	2	0.01
Japanese (53)	92	0.43
Korean (131)	164	0.76
Malaysian (4)	7	0.03
Nepalese (4)	4	0.02
Pakistani (50)	53	0.25
Sri Lankan (11)	15	0.07
Taiwanese (22)	26	0.12
Thai (7)	11	0.05
Vietnamese (16)	23	0.11
Hawaii Native/Pacific Islander (3)	14	0.07
Not Hispanic (0)	8	0.04
Hispanic (3)	6	0.03
Guamanian/Chamorro (3)	5	0.02
Native Hawaiian (0)	4	0.02
White (17,926)	18,404	85.77
Not Hispanic (15,897)	16,218	75.58
Hispanic (2,029)	2,186	10.19

Teaneck

Place Type: Township
County: Bergen
Population: 39,776†

Ancestry‡	Population	%
Afghan (113)	149	0.38
African, Sub-Saharan (932)	1,112	2.82
African (600)	745	1.89
Ghanaian (23)	23	0.06
Kenyan (10)	10	0.03
Nigerian (227)	227	0.57
Sierra Leonean (9)	9	0.02
South African (58)	93	0.24
Other Sub-Saharan African (5)	5	0.01
American (1,209)	1,209	3.06
Arab (417)	556	1.41
Arab (9)	9	0.02
Egyptian (66)	74	0.19
Jordanian (50)	50	0.13
Lebanese (24)	103	0.26
Moroccan (148)	167	0.42
Syrian (10)	28	0.07
Other Arab (110)	125	0.32
Armenian (54)	147	0.37
Assyrian/Chaldean/Syriac (14)	76	0.19
Austrian (91)	343	0.87
Belgian (13)	43	0.11
Brazilian (11)	27	0.07
British (178)	189	0.48
Canadian (97)	126	0.32
Croatian (47)	99	0.25
Czech (46)	88	0.22
Czechoslovakian (26)	38	0.10
Dutch (194)	284	0.72
Eastern European (923)	1,026	2.60
English (194)	861	2.18
European (696)	713	1.81
French, ex. Basque (57)	296	0.75
French Canadian (0)	35	0.09
German (636)	2,097	5.31
Greek (69)	119	0.30
Guyanese (87)	98	0.25
Hungarian (165)	593	1.50
Icelander (15)	15	0.04
Iranian (31)	43	0.11
Irish (532)	1,859	4.71
Israeli (250)	378	0.96
Italian (868)	2,089	5.29
Latvian (14)	58	0.15
Lithuanian (80)	149	0.38
Luxemburger (0)	11	0.03
Maltese (0)	20	0.05
Norwegian (61)	293	0.74
Polish (1,167)	2,503	6.34
Portuguese (96)	155	0.39
Romanian (48)	125	0.32
Russian (878)	1,837	4.65
Scotch-Irish (11)	160	0.41
Scottish (0)	144	0.36
Serbian (10)	63	0.16
Slovak (26)	37	0.09
Swedish (31)	179	0.45
Swiss (51)	157	0.40
Turkish (70)	84	0.21
Ukrainian (79)	159	0.40
Welsh (0)	38	0.10
West Indian, ex. Hispanic (2,341)	2,628	6.66
Barbadian (48)	74	0.19
Belizean (79)	79	0.20
British West Indian (86)	86	0.22
Haitian (348)	421	1.07
Jamaican (1,513)	1,680	4.26
Trinidadian/Tobagonian (100)	111	0.28
West Indian (141)	151	0.38
Other West Indian (26)	26	0.07

Hispanic Origin	Population	%
Hispanic or Latino (of any race)	6,575	16.53
Central American, ex. Mexican	389	0.98
Costa Rican	44	0.11
Guatemalan	49	0.12
Honduran	56	0.14
Nicaraguan	30	0.08
Panamanian	61	0.15
Salvadoran	149	0.37
Cuban	366	0.92
Dominican Republic	1,981	4.98
Mexican	428	1.08
Puerto Rican	1,556	3.91
South American	1,294	3.25
Argentinean	110	0.28
Bolivian	21	0.05
Chilean	43	0.11
Colombian	664	1.67
Ecuadorian	252	0.63
Paraguayan	4	0.01
Peruvian	135	0.34
Uruguayan	6	0.02
Venezuelan	38	0.10
Other South American	21	0.05
Other Hispanic or Latino	561	1.41

Race*	Population	%
African-American/Black (11,013)	11,809	29.69
Not Hispanic (10,266)	10,741	27.00
Hispanic (747)	1,068	2.69
American Indian/Alaska Native (113)	341	0.86
Not Hispanic (47)	199	0.50
Hispanic (66)	142	0.36
Apache (1)	1	<0.01
Blackfeet (0)	6	0.02
Canadian/French Am. Ind. (2)	5	0.01
Central American Ind. (4)	9	0.02
Cherokee (4)	35	0.09
Chippewa (2)	5	0.01
Choctaw (0)	5	0.01
Cree (0)	1	<0.01
Delaware (6)	9	0.02
Iroquois (0)	8	0.02
Mexican American Ind. (15)	16	0.04
Navajo (0)	1	<0.01
Pueblo (0)	1	<0.01
Seminole (5)	9	0.02
Shoshone (0)	1	<0.01
Sioux (0)	5	0.01
South American Ind. (8)	26	0.07
Spanish American Ind. (5)	5	0.01
Yaqui (0)	2	0.01
Asian (3,622)	4,055	10.19
Not Hispanic (3,574)	3,952	9.94
Hispanic (48)	103	0.26
Bangladeshi (45)	45	0.11
Burmese (13)	14	0.04
Cambodian (0)	1	<0.01
Chinese, ex. Taiwanese (321)	389	0.98
Filipino (1,005)	1,113	2.80
Indian (1,229)	1,399	3.52
Indonesian (2)	4	0.01
Japanese (83)	112	0.28
Korean (389)	399	1.00
Malaysian (8)	9	0.02
Pakistani (332)	376	0.95
Sri Lankan (11)	11	0.03
Taiwanese (17)	24	0.06
Thai (22)	24	0.06
Vietnamese (28)	45	0.11
Hawaii Native/Pacific Islander (25)	70	0.18
Not Hispanic (21)	44	0.11
Hispanic (4)	26	0.07
Guamanian/Chamorro (0)	2	0.01
Native Hawaiian (11)	15	0.04
Samoan (0)	2	0.01
White (21,214)	22,159	55.71
Not Hispanic (18,346)	18,860	47.42
Hispanic (2,868)	3,299	8.29

Tenafly

Place Type: Borough
County: Bergen
Population: 14,488†

Ancestry‡	Population	%
African, Sub-Saharan (37)	67	0.47

*Notes: † The Census 2010 population figure is used to calculate the percentages in the Hispanic Origin and Race categories. Ancestry percentages are based on the 2006-2010 American Community Survey population (not shown); ‡ Numbers in parentheses indicate the number of people reporting a single ancestry; * Numbers in parentheses indicate the number of persons reporting this race alone, not in combination with any other race; Please refer to the Explanation of Data for more information.*

Ethiopian (37)	67	0.47
Albanian (87)	87	0.61
Alsatian (0)	15	0.11
American (346)	346	2.42
Arab (120)	206	1.44
Lebanese (0)	38	0.27
Palestinian (18)	18	0.13
Syrian (0)	32	0.22
Other Arab (102)	118	0.83
Armenian (89)	102	0.71
Austrian (114)	229	1.60
British (12)	36	0.25
Bulgarian (15)	15	0.11
Canadian (13)	46	0.32
Croatian (13)	13	0.09
Czech (0)	16	0.11
Czechoslovakian (0)	12	0.08
Danish (0)	8	0.06
Eastern European (653)	653	4.57
English (22)	467	3.27
European (273)	298	2.09
Finnish (0)	13	0.09
French, ex. Basque (89)	240	1.68
French Canadian (90)	125	0.88
German (329)	1,183	8.29
Greek (357)	451	3.16
Hungarian (137)	157	1.10
Iranian (67)	103	0.72
Irish (277)	1,144	8.01
Israeli (467)	498	3.49
Italian (525)	1,163	8.15
Lithuanian (16)	80	0.56
Polish (177)	994	6.96
Portuguese (0)	36	0.25
Romanian (53)	124	0.87
Russian (486)	1,503	10.53
Scotch-Irish (12)	12	0.08
Scottish (19)	60	0.42
Slovene (22)	110	0.77
Soviet Union (180)	180	1.26
Swedish (25)	59	0.41
Swiss (0)	41	0.29
Turkish (0)	30	0.21
Ukrainian (24)	36	0.25
Welsh (0)	27	0.19
West Indian, ex. Hispanic (102)	102	0.71
British West Indian (34)	34	0.24
Jamaican (68)	68	0.48

Hispanic Origin	Population	%
Hispanic or Latino (of any race)	776	5.36
Central American, ex. Mexican	74	0.51
Costa Rican	4	0.03
Guatemalan	34	0.23
Honduran	6	0.04
Nicaraguan	6	0.04
Panamanian	5	0.03
Salvadoran	19	0.13
Cuban	102	0.70
Dominican Republic	84	0.58
Mexican	69	0.48
Puerto Rican	143	0.99
South American	238	1.64
Argentinean	42	0.29
Bolivian	1	0.01
Chilean	27	0.19
Colombian	104	0.72
Ecuadorian	22	0.15
Peruvian	28	0.19
Uruguayan	3	0.02
Venezuelan	11	0.08
Other Hispanic or Latino	66	0.46

Race*	Population	%
African-American/Black (128)	188	1.30
Not Hispanic (123)	174	1.20
Hispanic (5)	14	0.10
American Indian/Alaska Native (5)	22	0.15
Not Hispanic (2)	14	0.10
Hispanic (3)	8	0.06
Cherokee (1)	6	0.04
Cree (1)	2	0.01
Sioux (0)	1	0.01
South American Ind. (1)	1	0.01
Spanish American Ind. (0)	1	0.01
Asian (3,799)	4,048	27.94
Not Hispanic (3,794)	4,026	27.79
Hispanic (5)	22	0.15
Burmese (1)	2	0.01
Chinese, ex. Taiwanese (777)	861	5.94
Filipino (154)	189	1.30
Indian (211)	244	1.68
Indonesian (5)	10	0.07
Japanese (242)	313	2.16
Korean (2,236)	2,308	15.93
Malaysian (1)	2	0.01
Nepalese (4)	4	0.03
Pakistani (24)	27	0.19
Sri Lankan (5)	6	0.04
Taiwanese (58)	67	0.46
Thai (4)	4	0.03
Vietnamese (19)	24	0.17
Hawaii Native/Pacific Islander (0)	18	0.12
Not Hispanic (0)	18	0.12
Samoan (0)	3	0.02
White (10,041)	10,318	71.22
Not Hispanic (9,475)	9,710	67.02
Hispanic (566)	608	4.20

Tinton Falls

Place Type: Borough
County: Monmouth
Population: 17,892†

Ancestry‡	Population	%
African, Sub-Saharan (85)	111	0.63
African (85)	111	0.63
American (455)	455	2.60
Arab (11)	39	0.22
Egyptian (11)	11	0.06
Lebanese (0)	28	0.16
Armenian (61)	90	0.51
Austrian (54)	222	1.27
Belgian (18)	18	0.10
Brazilian (15)	18	0.10
British (42)	112	0.64
Canadian (0)	20	0.11
Croatian (0)	7	0.04
Czech (24)	135	0.77
Czechoslovakian (41)	41	0.23
Danish (0)	9	0.05
Dutch (61)	170	0.97
Eastern European (76)	76	0.43
English (341)	1,060	6.05
Estonian (12)	12	0.07
European (122)	163	0.93
French, ex. Basque (135)	334	1.91
French Canadian (9)	16	0.09
German (561)	2,545	14.52
Greek (39)	215	1.23
Hungarian (45)	199	1.14
Iranian (47)	47	0.27
Irish (993)	3,866	22.05
Italian (2,480)	4,804	27.40
Lithuanian (76)	175	1.00
Northern European (19)	19	0.11
Norwegian (72)	304	1.73
Polish (395)	1,286	7.34
Portuguese (33)	54	0.31
Romanian (47)	146	0.83
Russian (379)	862	4.92
Scotch-Irish (59)	197	1.12
Scottish (150)	348	1.98
Serbian (0)	9	0.05
Slavic (0)	10	0.06
Slovak (23)	153	0.87
Swedish (14)	272	1.55
Swiss (31)	100	0.57
Turkish (15)	45	0.26
Ukrainian (68)	239	1.36
Welsh (0)	57	0.33
West Indian, ex. Hispanic (118)	150	0.86
Belizean (0)	14	0.08
Haitian (65)	65	0.37
Jamaican (53)	62	0.35
Trinidadian/Tobagonian (0)	9	0.05

Hispanic Origin	Population	%
Hispanic or Latino (of any race)	1,118	6.25
Central American, ex. Mexican	115	0.64
Costa Rican	12	0.07
Guatemalan	26	0.15
Honduran	8	0.04
Nicaraguan	6	0.03
Panamanian	13	0.07
Salvadoran	50	0.28
Cuban	66	0.37
Dominican Republic	30	0.17
Mexican	219	1.22
Puerto Rican	387	2.16
South American	193	1.08
Argentinean	9	0.05
Bolivian	7	0.04
Chilean	14	0.08
Colombian	79	0.44
Ecuadorian	24	0.13
Paraguayan	1	0.01
Peruvian	43	0.24
Uruguayan	3	0.02
Venezuelan	13	0.07
Other Hispanic or Latino	108	0.60

Race*	Population	%
African-American/Black (1,672)	1,869	10.45
Not Hispanic (1,610)	1,775	9.92
Hispanic (62)	94	0.53
American Indian/Alaska Native (23)	108	0.60
Not Hispanic (15)	88	0.49
Hispanic (8)	20	0.11
Apache (0)	2	0.01
Blackfeet (0)	9	0.05
Canadian/French Am. Ind. (0)	3	0.02
Central American Ind. (2)	2	0.01
Cherokee (3)	10	0.06
Chickasaw (1)	1	0.01
Creek (0)	1	0.01
Delaware (2)	8	0.04
Iroquois (0)	2	0.01
Mexican American Ind. (2)	8	0.04
Navajo (1)	1	0.01
Potawatomi (0)	1	0.01
Seminole (0)	1	0.01
Sioux (0)	2	0.01
South American Ind. (2)	4	0.02
Asian (835)	987	5.52
Not Hispanic (829)	971	5.43
Hispanic (6)	16	0.09
Bangladeshi (7)	7	0.04
Burmese (0)	3	0.02
Chinese, ex. Taiwanese (180)	212	1.18
Filipino (173)	213	1.19
Indian (191)	220	1.23
Japanese (16)	32	0.18
Korean (149)	179	1.00
Malaysian (0)	1	0.01
Pakistani (16)	18	0.10
Taiwanese (9)	11	0.06
Thai (1)	2	0.01
Vietnamese (67)	71	0.40
Hawaii Native/Pacific Islander (4)	19	0.11
Not Hispanic (4)	15	0.08
Hispanic (0)	4	0.02
Guamanian/Chamorro (0)	3	0.02
Native Hawaiian (4)	10	0.06
Samoan (0)	2	0.01
White (14,741)	15,045	84.09
Not Hispanic (14,003)	14,247	79.63
Hispanic (738)	798	4.46

*Notes: † The Census 2010 population figure is used to calculate the percentages in the Hispanic Origin and Race categories. Ancestry percentages are based on the 2006-2010 American Community Survey population (not shown); ‡ Numbers in parentheses indicate the number of people reporting a single ancestry; * Numbers in parentheses indicate the number of persons reporting this race alone, not in combination with any other race; Please refer to the Explanation of Data for more information.*

Toms River

Place Type: CDP
County: Ocean
Population: 88,791†

Ancestry‡	Population	%
African, Sub-Saharan (82)	285	0.32
African (12)	126	0.14
Nigerian (70)	122	0.14
South African (0)	37	0.04
Albanian (12)	26	0.03
American (2,182)	2,182	2.46
Arab (258)	405	0.46
Arab (13)	57	0.06
Egyptian (131)	140	0.16
Lebanese (59)	78	0.09
Palestinian (19)	58	0.07
Syrian (27)	63	0.07
Other Arab (9)	9	0.01
Armenian (14)	91	0.10
Assyrian/Chaldean/Syriac (17)	17	0.02
Australian (14)	66	0.07
Austrian (120)	602	0.68
Basque (0)	11	0.01
Belgian (8)	247	0.28
Brazilian (135)	135	0.15
British (92)	239	0.27
Bulgarian (0)	24	0.03
Canadian (24)	114	0.13
Croatian (162)	162	0.18
Czech (221)	647	0.73
Czechoslovakian (80)	345	0.39
Danish (152)	529	0.60
Dutch (209)	1,307	1.47
Eastern European (162)	162	0.18
English (1,194)	6,713	7.56
Estonian (10)	39	0.04
European (534)	578	0.65
Finnish (17)	115	0.13
French, ex. Basque (212)	1,848	2.08
French Canadian (108)	273	0.31
German (3,315)	16,601	18.69
Greek (569)	976	1.10
Hungarian (292)	1,568	1.76
Icelander (31)	31	0.03
Iranian (26)	39	0.04
Irish (5,299)	21,555	24.26
Israeli (16)	32	0.04
Italian (14,640)	29,313	32.99
Latvian (83)	91	0.10
Lithuanian (161)	658	0.74
Luxemburger (10)	10	0.01
Maltese (23)	41	0.05
Norwegian (329)	870	0.98
Pennsylvania German (70)	81	0.09
Polish (2,561)	9,250	10.41
Portuguese (815)	1,467	1.65
Romanian (9)	50	0.06
Russian (638)	2,174	2.45
Scandinavian (8)	8	0.01
Scotch-Irish (489)	1,276	1.44
Scottish (348)	1,634	1.84
Serbian (10)	24	0.03
Slavic (64)	95	0.11
Slovak (120)	367	0.41
Slovene (10)	27	0.03
Swedish (132)	738	0.83
Swiss (23)	197	0.22
Turkish (117)	131	0.15
Ukrainian (209)	965	1.09
Welsh (108)	334	0.38
West Indian, ex. Hispanic (318)	400	0.45
Dutch West Indian (10)	10	0.01
Haitian (204)	204	0.23
Jamaican (80)	80	0.09
Trinidadian/Tobagonian (24)	106	0.12
Yugoslavian (9)	22	0.02

Hispanic Origin	Population	%
Hispanic or Latino (of any race)	7,136	8.04
Central American, ex. Mexican	326	0.37
Costa Rican	113	0.13
Guatemalan	64	0.07
Honduran	49	0.06
Nicaraguan	27	0.03
Panamanian	13	0.01
Salvadoran	57	0.06
Other Central American	3	<0.01
Cuban	507	0.57
Dominican Republic	189	0.21
Mexican	1,752	1.97
Puerto Rican	2,597	2.92
South American	1,040	1.17
Argentinean	70	0.08
Bolivian	5	0.01
Chilean	27	0.03
Colombian	360	0.41
Ecuadorian	149	0.17
Paraguayan	7	0.01
Peruvian	352	0.40
Uruguayan	36	0.04
Venezuelan	24	0.03
Other South American	10	0.01
Other Hispanic or Latino	725	0.82

Race*	Population	%
African-American/Black (2,459)	2,990	3.37
Not Hispanic (2,210)	2,643	2.98
Hispanic (249)	347	0.39
American Indian/Alaska Native (151)	503	0.57
Not Hispanic (78)	371	0.42
Hispanic (73)	132	0.15
Alaska Athabascan *(Ala. Nat.)* (0)	1	<0.01
Apache (0)	5	0.01
Blackfeet (1)	12	0.01
Central American Ind. (7)	7	0.01
Cherokee (13)	67	0.08
Chickasaw (1)	1	<0.01
Chippewa (2)	10	0.01
Choctaw (0)	1	<0.01
Comanche (0)	2	<0.01
Creek (0)	2	<0.01
Delaware (5)	29	0.03
Hopi (0)	2	<0.01
Houma (3)	3	<0.01
Iroquois (6)	29	0.03
Lumbee (0)	1	<0.01
Mexican American Ind. (22)	26	0.03
Navajo (1)	2	<0.01
Osage (1)	1	<0.01
Puget Sound Salish (0)	4	<0.01
Seminole (0)	4	<0.01
Sioux (2)	6	0.01
South American Ind. (16)	18	0.02
Spanish American Ind. (0)	2	<0.01
Tlingit-Haida *(Alaska Native)* (0)	4	<0.01
Asian (3,260)	3,688	4.15
Not Hispanic (3,231)	3,612	4.07
Hispanic (29)	76	0.09
Bangladeshi (13)	13	0.01
Burmese (1)	1	<0.01
Chinese, ex. Taiwanese (328)	401	0.45
Filipino (1,475)	1,671	1.88
Indian (793)	860	0.97
Indonesian (2)	4	<0.01
Japanese (39)	70	0.08
Korean (190)	223	0.25
Laotian (3)	3	<0.01
Malaysian (7)	10	0.01
Nepalese (2)	2	<0.01
Pakistani (105)	117	0.13
Sri Lankan (10)	10	0.01
Taiwanese (9)	16	0.02
Thai (19)	30	0.03
Vietnamese (188)	209	0.24
Hawaii Native/Pacific Islander (17)	58	0.07
Not Hispanic (15)	50	0.06
Hispanic (2)	8	0.01
Guamanian/Chamorro (14)	18	0.02
Native Hawaiian (2)	16	0.02
Samoan (0)	1	<0.01
White (79,653)	80,981	91.20
Not Hispanic (74,921)	75,899	85.48
Hispanic (4,732)	5,082	5.72

Toms River

Place Type: Township
County: Ocean
Population: 91,239†

Ancestry‡	Population	%
African, Sub-Saharan (82)	285	0.31
African (12)	126	0.14
Nigerian (70)	122	0.13
South African (0)	37	0.04
Albanian (12)	26	0.03
American (2,259)	2,259	2.46
Arab (258)	405	0.44
Arab (13)	57	0.06
Egyptian (131)	140	0.15
Lebanese (59)	78	0.09
Palestinian (19)	58	0.06
Syrian (27)	63	0.07
Other Arab (9)	9	0.01
Armenian (25)	102	0.11
Assyrian/Chaldean/Syriac (17)	17	0.02
Australian (14)	66	0.07
Austrian (120)	602	0.66
Basque (0)	11	0.01
Belgian (8)	247	0.27
Brazilian (135)	135	0.15
British (92)	274	0.30
Bulgarian (0)	24	0.03
Canadian (24)	114	0.12
Celtic (19)	19	0.02
Croatian (162)	162	0.18
Czech (221)	737	0.80
Czechoslovakian (90)	355	0.39
Danish (163)	540	0.59
Dutch (219)	1,344	1.47
Eastern European (162)	162	0.18
English (1,255)	6,966	7.60
Estonian (10)	39	0.04
European (534)	578	0.63
Finnish (17)	115	0.13
French, ex. Basque (212)	1,916	2.09
French Canadian (108)	273	0.30
German (3,510)	17,231	18.79
Greek (579)	986	1.08
Hungarian (313)	1,678	1.83
Icelander (31)	31	0.03
Iranian (26)	39	0.04
Irish (5,652)	22,448	24.48
Israeli (16)	32	0.03
Italian (15,075)	30,325	33.07
Latvian (83)	101	0.11
Lithuanian (171)	701	0.76
Luxemburger (10)	10	0.01
Maltese (23)	41	0.04
Norwegian (329)	870	0.95
Pennsylvania German (70)	81	0.09
Polish (2,699)	9,531	10.39
Portuguese (836)	1,488	1.62
Romanian (9)	59	0.06
Russian (647)	2,192	2.39
Scandinavian (8)	8	0.01
Scotch-Irish (507)	1,315	1.43
Scottish (359)	1,682	1.83
Serbian (10)	24	0.03
Slavic (64)	95	0.10
Slovak (140)	410	0.45
Slovene (10)	27	0.03
Swedish (132)	784	0.86
Swiss (23)	206	0.22
Turkish (117)	131	0.14
Ukrainian (209)	986	1.08
Welsh (108)	344	0.38

*Notes: † The Census 2010 population figure is used to calculate the percentages in the Hispanic Origin and Race categories. Ancestry percentages are based on the 2006-2010 American Community Survey population (not shown); ‡ Numbers in parentheses indicate the number of people reporting a single ancestry; * Numbers in parentheses indicate the number of persons reporting this race alone, not in combination with any other race; Please refer to the Explanation of Data for more information.*

	Population	%
West Indian, ex. Hispanic (318)	400	0.44
Dutch West Indian (10)	10	0.01
Haitian (204)	204	0.22
Jamaican (80)	80	0.09
Trinidadian/Tobagonian (24)	106	0.12
Yugoslavian (9)	22	0.02

Hispanic Origin	Population	%
Hispanic or Latino (of any race)	7,231	7.93
Central American, ex. Mexican	333	0.36
Costa Rican	113	0.12
Guatemalan	67	0.07
Honduran	49	0.05
Nicaraguan	27	0.03
Panamanian	13	0.01
Salvadoran	61	0.07
Other Central American	3	<0.01
Cuban	511	0.56
Dominican Republic	191	0.21
Mexican	1,782	1.95
Puerto Rican	2,622	2.87
South American	1,052	1.15
Argentinean	70	0.08
Bolivian	5	0.01
Chilean	27	0.03
Colombian	368	0.40
Ecuadorian	153	0.17
Paraguayan	7	0.01
Peruvian	352	0.39
Uruguayan	36	0.04
Venezuelan	24	0.03
Other South American	10	0.01
Other Hispanic or Latino	740	0.81

Race*	Population	%
African-American/Black (2,465)	3,006	3.29
Not Hispanic (2,213)	2,656	2.91
Hispanic (252)	350	0.38
American Indian/Alaska Native (156)	515	0.56
Not Hispanic (83)	383	0.42
Hispanic (73)	132	0.14
Alaska Athabascan *(Ala. Nat.)* (0)	1	<0.01
Apache (0)	5	0.01
Blackfeet (1)	12	0.01
Central American Ind. (7)	7	0.01
Cherokee (14)	68	0.07
Chickasaw (1)	2	<0.01
Chippewa (2)	10	0.01
Choctaw (0)	1	<0.01
Comanche (0)	2	<0.01
Creek (0)	2	<0.01
Delaware (5)	29	0.03
Hopi (0)	2	<0.01
Houma (3)	3	<0.01
Iroquois (6)	29	0.03
Lumbee (0)	1	<0.01
Mexican American Ind. (22)	26	0.03
Navajo (5)	6	0.01
Osage (1)	1	<0.01
Puget Sound Salish (0)	4	<0.01
Seminole (0)	4	<0.01
Sioux (2)	6	0.01
South American Ind. (16)	18	0.02
Spanish American Ind. (0)	2	<0.01
Tlingit-Haida *(Alaska Native)* (0)	4	<0.01
Asian (3,266)	3,697	4.05
Not Hispanic (3,237)	3,621	3.97
Hispanic (29)	76	0.08
Bangladeshi (13)	13	0.01
Burmese (1)	1	<0.01
Chinese, ex. Taiwanese (330)	403	0.44
Filipino (1,476)	1,672	1.83
Indian (793)	860	0.94
Indonesian (2)	4	<0.01
Japanese (40)	74	0.08
Korean (192)	225	0.25
Laotian (3)	3	<0.01
Malaysian (7)	10	0.01
Nepalese (2)	2	<0.01
Pakistani (105)	117	0.13
Sri Lankan (10)	10	0.01
Taiwanese (9)	16	0.02
Thai (19)	30	0.03
Vietnamese (188)	209	0.23
Hawaii Native/Pacific Islander (17)	58	0.06
Not Hispanic (15)	50	0.05
Hispanic (2)	8	0.01
Guamanian/Chamorro (14)	18	0.02
Native Hawaiian (2)	16	0.02
Samoan (0)	1	<0.01
White (82,035)	83,387	91.39
Not Hispanic (77,241)	78,234	85.75
Hispanic (4,794)	5,153	5.65

Totowa

Place Type: Borough
County: Passaic
Population: 10,804†

Ancestry‡	Population	%
American (336)	336	3.17
Arab (292)	403	3.80
Arab (8)	26	0.25
Egyptian (44)	44	0.42
Jordanian (13)	13	0.12
Lebanese (0)	13	0.12
Syrian (208)	288	2.72
Other Arab (19)	19	0.18
Armenian (0)	28	0.26
Austrian (11)	45	0.42
Belgian (0)	36	0.34
British (19)	19	0.18
Canadian (8)	25	0.24
Dutch (153)	465	4.39
Eastern European (16)	16	0.15
English (29)	255	2.41
European (50)	50	0.47
French, ex. Basque (12)	69	0.65
German (75)	698	6.59
Greek (0)	27	0.25
Hungarian (13)	35	0.33
Irish (398)	1,146	10.82
Italian (3,239)	4,411	41.64
Lithuanian (0)	70	0.66
Macedonian (100)	100	0.94
Norwegian (13)	13	0.12
Polish (236)	466	4.40
Romanian (0)	20	0.19
Russian (14)	102	0.96
Scotch-Irish (57)	145	1.37
Scottish (14)	74	0.70
Serbian (82)	89	0.84
Slovak (26)	56	0.53
Swedish (0)	30	0.28
Swiss (0)	13	0.12
Turkish (89)	89	0.84
Ukrainian (21)	48	0.45
Yugoslavian (31)	58	0.55

Hispanic Origin	Population	%
Hispanic or Latino (of any race)	1,550	14.35
Central American, ex. Mexican	76	0.70
Costa Rican	36	0.33
Guatemalan	13	0.12
Honduran	8	0.07
Nicaraguan	7	0.06
Panamanian	4	0.04
Salvadoran	8	0.07
Cuban	73	0.68
Dominican Republic	179	1.66
Mexican	58	0.54
Puerto Rican	502	4.65
South American	569	5.27
Argentinean	20	0.19
Chilean	8	0.07
Colombian	177	1.64
Ecuadorian	44	0.41
Paraguayan	1	0.01
Peruvian	294	2.72
Uruguayan	12	0.11
Venezuelan	12	0.11
Other South American	1	0.01
Other Hispanic or Latino	93	0.86

Race*	Population	%
African-American/Black (248)	291	2.69
Not Hispanic (220)	243	2.25
Hispanic (28)	48	0.44
American Indian/Alaska Native (11)	29	0.27
Not Hispanic (4)	15	0.14
Hispanic (7)	14	0.13
Apache (2)	3	0.03
Blackfeet (0)	1	0.01
Cherokee (0)	6	0.06
Delaware (1)	1	0.01
South American Ind. (3)	3	0.03
Asian (640)	726	6.72
Not Hispanic (639)	714	6.61
Hispanic (1)	12	0.11
Bangladeshi (63)	70	0.65
Cambodian (3)	3	0.03
Chinese, ex. Taiwanese (84)	97	0.90
Filipino (86)	100	0.93
Indian (192)	211	1.95
Japanese (2)	4	0.04
Korean (136)	145	1.34
Malaysian (1)	1	0.01
Nepalese (1)	1	0.01
Pakistani (24)	25	0.23
Taiwanese (6)	6	0.06
Thai (1)	1	0.01
Vietnamese (10)	11	0.10
Hawaii Native/Pacific Islander (0)	3	0.03
Not Hispanic (0)	3	0.03
Native Hawaiian (0)	1	0.01
White (9,231)	9,423	87.22
Not Hispanic (8,249)	8,357	77.35
Hispanic (982)	1,066	9.87

Trenton

Place Type: City
County: Mercer
Population: 84,913†

Ancestry‡	Population	%
African, Sub-Saharan (2,471)	3,208	3.77
African (1,427)	2,000	2.35
Ethiopian (41)	41	0.05
Ghanaian (197)	300	0.35
Liberian (726)	755	0.89
Nigerian (59)	81	0.10
Zimbabwean (8)	8	0.01
Other Sub-Saharan African (13)	23	0.03
Alsatian (7)	7	0.01
American (2,520)	2,520	2.96
Arab (48)	77	0.09
Egyptian (4)	4	<0.01
Lebanese (12)	41	0.05
Moroccan (32)	32	0.04
Austrian (19)	26	0.03
British (9)	37	0.04
Canadian (0)	7	0.01
Carpatho Rusyn (8)	8	0.01
Celtic (0)	40	0.05
Croatian (24)	56	0.07
Czech (36)	52	0.06
Czechoslovakian (15)	30	0.04
Dutch (23)	250	0.29
Eastern European (11)	11	0.01
English (677)	1,565	1.84
European (60)	73	0.09
Finnish (0)	22	0.03
French, ex. Basque (19)	164	0.19
French Canadian (0)	21	0.02
German (537)	2,431	2.85
Greek (58)	139	0.16
Guyanese (37)	37	0.04
Hungarian (167)	530	0.62

*Notes: † The Census 2010 population figure is used to calculate the percentages in the Hispanic Origin and Race categories. Ancestry percentages are based on the 2006-2010 American Community Survey population (not shown); ‡ Numbers in parentheses indicate the number of people reporting a single ancestry; * Numbers in parentheses indicate the number of persons reporting this race alone, not in combination with any other race; Please refer to the Explanation of Data for more information.*

Irish (967)	3,075	3.61
Italian (1,939)	3,367	3.95
Lithuanian (10)	97	0.11
Norwegian (19)	40	0.05
Polish (1,695)	2,617	3.07
Portuguese (179)	190	0.22
Romanian (37)	166	0.19
Russian (52)	291	0.34
Scotch-Irish (18)	160	0.19
Scottish (53)	245	0.29
Slavic (0)	41	0.05
Slovak (74)	147	0.17
Swedish (80)	149	0.17
Swiss (20)	32	0.04
Turkish (51)	51	0.06
Ukrainian (83)	254	0.30
Welsh (0)	144	0.17
West Indian, ex. Hispanic (2,366)	3,010	3.53
Bahamian (12)	59	0.07
British West Indian (28)	39	0.05
Haitian (801)	1,054	1.24
Jamaican (1,315)	1,571	1.84
Trinidadian/Tobagonian (115)	126	0.15
West Indian (90)	156	0.18
Other West Indian (5)	5	0.01

Hispanic Origin	Population	%
Hispanic or Latino (of any race)	28,621	33.71
Central American, ex. Mexican	11,346	13.36
Costa Rican	1,279	1.51
Guatemalan	8,691	10.24
Honduran	820	0.97
Nicaraguan	65	0.08
Panamanian	47	0.06
Salvadoran	414	0.49
Other Central American	30	0.04
Cuban	250	0.29
Dominican Republic	1,707	2.01
Mexican	2,337	2.75
Puerto Rican	9,746	11.48
South American	1,238	1.46
Argentinean	26	0.03
Bolivian	1	<0.01
Chilean	11	0.01
Colombian	250	0.29
Ecuadorian	802	0.94
Peruvian	87	0.10
Uruguayan	34	0.04
Venezuelan	13	0.02
Other South American	14	0.02
Other Hispanic or Latino	1,997	2.35

Race*	Population	%
African-American/Black (44,160)	45,846	53.99
Not Hispanic (42,286)	43,372	51.08
Hispanic (1,874)	2,474	2.91
American Indian/Alaska Native (598)	1,262	1.49
Not Hispanic (219)	631	0.74
Hispanic (379)	631	0.74
Alaska Athabascan *(Ala. Nat.)* (0)	2	<0.01
Apache (2)	4	<0.01
Blackfeet (11)	48	0.06
Central American Ind. (33)	44	0.05
Cherokee (37)	163	0.19
Cheyenne (0)	3	<0.01
Chippewa (4)	4	<0.01
Choctaw (0)	3	<0.01
Cree (2)	2	<0.01
Creek (1)	2	<0.01
Delaware (9)	12	0.01
Hopi (1)	1	<0.01
Inupiat *(Alaska Native)* (0)	3	<0.01
Iroquois (4)	13	0.02
Lumbee (0)	1	<0.01
Mexican American Ind. (72)	103	0.12
Navajo (2)	3	<0.01
Ottawa (1)	1	<0.01
Pueblo (3)	3	<0.01
Seminole (1)	3	<0.01
Sioux (3)	8	0.01
South American Ind. (49)	86	0.10
Spanish American Ind. (24)	32	0.04
Tlingit-Haida *(Alaska Native)* (0)	2	<0.01
Yuman (1)	1	<0.01
Asian (1,013)	1,330	1.57
Not Hispanic (923)	1,140	1.34
Hispanic (90)	190	0.22
Bangladeshi (20)	25	0.03
Bhutanese (29)	29	0.03
Burmese (188)	205	0.24
Cambodian (25)	27	0.03
Chinese, ex. Taiwanese (112)	135	0.16
Filipino (68)	107	0.13
Hmong (6)	6	0.01
Indian (238)	343	0.40
Indonesian (7)	14	0.02
Japanese (8)	41	0.05
Korean (48)	62	0.07
Laotian (1)	5	0.01
Malaysian (1)	1	<0.01
Nepalese (6)	20	0.02
Pakistani (89)	106	0.12
Sri Lankan (2)	2	<0.01
Thai (50)	52	0.06
Vietnamese (41)	57	0.07
Hawaii Native/Pacific Islander (110)	315	0.37
Not Hispanic (30)	126	0.15
Hispanic (80)	189	0.22
Guamanian/Chamorro (89)	103	0.12
Native Hawaiian (3)	19	0.02
Samoan (7)	10	0.01
Tongan (1)	2	<0.01
White (22,549)	24,968	29.40
Not Hispanic (11,442)	12,235	14.41
Hispanic (11,107)	12,733	15.00

Union City

Place Type: City
County: Hudson
Population: 66,455†

Ancestry‡	Population	%
Afghan (0)	9	0.01
African, Sub-Saharan (262)	401	0.61
African (153)	272	0.41
Ethiopian (9)	9	0.01
Ghanaian (17)	17	0.03
Nigerian (0)	20	0.03
Sudanese (83)	83	0.13
American (734)	734	1.12
Arab (238)	408	0.62
Arab (105)	159	0.24
Iraqi (13)	13	0.02
Lebanese (19)	52	0.08
Moroccan (24)	107	0.16
Palestinian (12)	12	0.02
Syrian (54)	54	0.08
Other Arab (11)	11	0.02
Armenian (10)	10	0.02
Austrian (16)	45	0.07
Brazilian (32)	32	0.05
British (0)	20	0.03
Bulgarian (0)	8	0.01
Canadian (36)	36	0.05
Croatian (99)	99	0.15
Czech (19)	39	0.06
Czechoslovakian (35)	58	0.09
Danish (21)	21	0.03
Dutch (0)	28	0.04
Eastern European (22)	22	0.03
English (71)	279	0.42
European (27)	73	0.11
French, ex. Basque (134)	366	0.56
French Canadian (11)	22	0.03
German (122)	783	1.19
Greek (70)	93	0.14
Guyanese (0)	18	0.03
Hungarian (42)	286	0.43
Iranian (0)	13	0.02
Irish (464)	1,180	1.79
Israeli (52)	52	0.08
Italian (1,361)	2,046	3.11
Lithuanian (15)	15	0.02
Macedonian (0)	8	0.01
Maltese (9)	18	0.03
Northern European (9)	9	0.01
Norwegian (14)	37	0.06
Polish (112)	575	0.87
Portuguese (8)	17	0.03
Romanian (18)	18	0.03
Russian (18)	62	0.09
Scandinavian (15)	15	0.02
Scotch-Irish (17)	45	0.07
Scottish (11)	42	0.06
Slavic (8)	8	0.01
Slovak (0)	10	0.02
Swedish (0)	42	0.06
Swiss (0)	10	0.02
Turkish (160)	160	0.24
Ukrainian (25)	25	0.04
Welsh (10)	29	0.04
West Indian, ex. Hispanic (141)	187	0.28
Barbadian (13)	13	0.02
Haitian (79)	90	0.14
Jamaican (40)	75	0.11
Trinidadian/Tobagonian (9)	9	0.01
Yugoslavian (66)	66	0.10

Hispanic Origin	Population	%
Hispanic or Latino (of any race)	56,291	84.71
Central American, ex. Mexican	9,159	13.78
Costa Rican	82	0.12
Guatemalan	1,097	1.65
Honduran	2,533	3.81
Nicaraguan	294	0.44
Panamanian	47	0.07
Salvadoran	5,060	7.61
Other Central American	46	0.07
Cuban	7,510	11.30
Dominican Republic	10,020	15.08
Mexican	5,189	7.81
Puerto Rican	6,643	10.00
South American	13,923	20.95
Argentinean	448	0.67
Bolivian	145	0.22
Chilean	372	0.56
Colombian	3,224	4.85
Ecuadorian	6,135	9.23
Paraguayan	11	0.02
Peruvian	3,111	4.68
Uruguayan	181	0.27
Venezuelan	266	0.40
Other South American	30	0.05
Other Hispanic or Latino	3,847	5.79

Race*	Population	%
African-American/Black (3,487)	4,440	6.68
Not Hispanic (1,070)	1,207	1.82
Hispanic (2,417)	3,233	4.86
American Indian/Alaska Native (819)	1,259	1.89
Not Hispanic (48)	96	0.14
Hispanic (771)	1,163	1.75
Alaska Athabascan *(Ala. Nat.)* (1)	1	<0.01
Apache (0)	2	<0.01
Blackfeet (0)	3	<0.01
Canadian/French Am. Ind. (1)	5	0.01
Central American Ind. (29)	55	0.08
Cherokee (3)	20	0.03
Choctaw (0)	2	<0.01
Cree (0)	5	0.01
Inupiat *(Alaska Native)* (1)	1	<0.01
Iroquois (1)	3	<0.01
Lumbee (0)	1	<0.01
Mexican American Ind. (77)	99	0.15
Navajo (1)	2	<0.01
Osage (0)	1	<0.01
Pima (0)	1	<0.01
Pueblo (1)	11	0.02
Sioux (0)	5	0.01

*Notes: † The Census 2010 population figure is used to calculate the percentages in the Hispanic Origin and Race categories. Ancestry percentages are based on the 2006-2010 American Community Survey population (not shown); ‡ Numbers in parentheses indicate the number of people reporting a single ancestry; * Numbers in parentheses indicate the number of persons reporting this race alone, not in combination with any other race; Please refer to the Explanation of Data for more information.*

Race*	Population	%
South American Ind. (80)	129	0.19
Spanish American Ind. (49)	72	0.11
Yaqui (0)	1	<0.01
Asian (1,587)	1,916	2.88
Not Hispanic (1,447)	1,592	2.40
Hispanic (140)	324	0.49
Bangladeshi (31)	37	0.06
Chinese, ex. Taiwanese (300)	363	0.55
Filipino (218)	259	0.39
Indian (693)	783	1.18
Indonesian (2)	2	<0.01
Japanese (52)	74	0.11
Korean (105)	121	0.18
Laotian (1)	1	<0.01
Malaysian (3)	4	0.01
Pakistani (24)	28	0.04
Sri Lankan (65)	71	0.11
Taiwanese (11)	14	0.02
Thai (14)	20	0.03
Vietnamese (13)	14	0.02
Hawaii Native/Pacific Islander (33)	185	0.28
Not Hispanic (9)	23	0.03
Hispanic (24)	162	0.24
Guamanian/Chamorro (11)	13	0.02
Native Hawaiian (7)	16	0.02
Samoan (1)	3	<0.01
White (38,549)	41,520	62.48
Not Hispanic (7,040)	7,306	10.99
Hispanic (31,509)	34,214	51.48

Union

Place Type: Township
County: Union
Population: 56,642†

Ancestry‡	Population	%
African, Sub-Saharan (2,022)	2,262	4.06
African (509)	628	1.13
Cape Verdean (8)	69	0.12
Ethiopian (0)	14	0.03
Ghanaian (21)	21	0.04
Liberian (34)	34	0.06
Nigerian (1,396)	1,428	2.56
Other Sub-Saharan African (54)	68	0.12
Alsatian (0)	14	0.03
American (1,546)	1,546	2.77
Arab (231)	250	0.45
Arab (210)	210	0.38
Egyptian (21)	21	0.04
Other Arab (0)	19	0.03
Armenian (21)	32	0.06
Austrian (78)	146	0.26
Belgian (18)	18	0.03
Brazilian (697)	774	1.39
British (68)	100	0.18
Canadian (0)	37	0.07
Cypriot (12)	38	0.07
Czech (44)	83	0.15
Czechoslovakian (40)	50	0.09
Danish (15)	103	0.18
Dutch (89)	343	0.62
Eastern European (105)	105	0.19
English (213)	1,132	2.03
European (296)	397	0.71
Finnish (0)	10	0.02
French, ex. Basque (107)	324	0.58
French Canadian (32)	75	0.13
German (1,034)	3,431	6.16
Greek (444)	550	0.99
Guyanese (88)	108	0.19
Hungarian (51)	346	0.62
Irish (1,062)	3,941	7.07
Israeli (117)	152	0.27
Italian (4,590)	7,911	14.19
Lithuanian (122)	229	0.41
Norwegian (43)	83	0.15
Polish (1,709)	3,116	5.59
Portuguese (3,676)	4,077	7.32
Romanian (23)	60	0.11
Russian (414)	852	1.53
Scotch-Irish (44)	251	0.45
Scottish (50)	199	0.36
Slovak (78)	153	0.27
Swedish (18)	186	0.33
Swiss (14)	51	0.09
Ukrainian (283)	624	1.12
Welsh (25)	112	0.20
West Indian, ex. Hispanic (3,504)	3,727	6.69
Belizean (52)	52	0.09
Bermudan (10)	10	0.02
British West Indian (23)	23	0.04
Haitian (2,505)	2,530	4.54
Jamaican (680)	756	1.36
Trinidadian/Tobagonian (200)	200	0.36
West Indian (26)	148	0.27
Other West Indian (8)	8	0.01
Yugoslavian (34)	57	0.10

Hispanic Origin	Population	%
Hispanic or Latino (of any race)	8,465	14.94
Central American, ex. Mexican	912	1.61
Costa Rican	409	0.72
Guatemalan	120	0.21
Honduran	62	0.11
Nicaraguan	75	0.13
Panamanian	46	0.08
Salvadoran	196	0.35
Other Central American	4	0.01
Cuban	793	1.40
Dominican Republic	656	1.16
Mexican	243	0.43
Puerto Rican	2,122	3.75
South American	2,678	4.73
Argentinean	113	0.20
Bolivian	20	0.04
Chilean	64	0.11
Colombian	972	1.72
Ecuadorian	846	1.49
Paraguayan	20	0.04
Peruvian	442	0.78
Uruguayan	131	0.23
Venezuelan	47	0.08
Other South American	23	0.04
Other Hispanic or Latino	1,061	1.87

Race*	Population	%
African-American/Black (16,417)	16,991	30.00
Not Hispanic (15,979)	16,380	28.92
Hispanic (438)	611	1.08
American Indian/Alaska Native (80)	270	0.48
Not Hispanic (44)	183	0.32
Hispanic (36)	87	0.15
Blackfeet (0)	11	0.02
Central American Ind. (2)	3	0.01
Cherokee (0)	21	0.04
Chippewa (0)	1	<0.01
Choctaw (0)	5	0.01
Cree (1)	1	<0.01
Creek (1)	3	0.01
Delaware (2)	5	0.01
Iroquois (1)	5	0.01
Lumbee (0)	3	0.01
Mexican American Ind. (5)	5	0.01
Navajo (0)	2	<0.01
Pueblo (1)	3	0.01
Seminole (0)	5	0.01
Sioux (2)	7	0.01
South American Ind. (12)	28	0.05
Spanish American Ind. (2)	2	<0.01
Asian (6,003)	6,461	11.41
Not Hispanic (5,959)	6,358	11.22
Hispanic (44)	103	0.18
Bangladeshi (5)	8	0.01
Cambodian (16)	20	0.04
Chinese, ex. Taiwanese (493)	559	0.99
Filipino (3,422)	3,602	6.36
Hmong (1)	3	0.01
Indian (1,367)	1,466	2.59
Indonesian (1)	5	0.01
Japanese (18)	40	0.07
Korean (72)	94	0.17
Laotian (0)	1	<0.01
Malaysian (2)	2	<0.01
Nepalese (1)	4	0.01
Pakistani (178)	193	0.34
Sri Lankan (16)	20	0.04
Taiwanese (13)	13	0.02
Thai (13)	16	0.03
Vietnamese (260)	275	0.49
Hawaii Native/Pacific Islander (24)	129	0.23
Not Hispanic (20)	118	0.21
Hispanic (4)	11	0.02
Guamanian/Chamorro (2)	8	0.01
Native Hawaiian (1)	18	0.03
Samoan (4)	8	0.01
White (30,464)	31,370	55.38
Not Hispanic (24,973)	25,503	45.02
Hispanic (5,491)	5,867	10.36

Upper Deerfield

Place Type: Township
County: Cumberland
Population: 7,660†

Ancestry‡	Population	%
American (973)	973	12.74
Arab (7)	149	1.95
Arab (0)	64	0.84
Egyptian (7)	85	1.11
Austrian (0)	27	0.35
British (15)	15	0.20
Czechoslovakian (22)	42	0.55
Dutch (12)	53	0.69
English (203)	703	9.20
Estonian (34)	34	0.45
European (33)	33	0.43
French, ex. Basque (12)	162	2.12
German (387)	1,408	18.43
Greek (0)	15	0.20
Hungarian (13)	45	0.59
Irish (348)	1,244	16.29
Italian (494)	1,000	13.09
Pennsylvania German (32)	32	0.42
Polish (157)	436	5.71
Russian (13)	109	1.43
Scotch-Irish (94)	155	2.03
Scottish (24)	37	0.48
Slovak (10)	10	0.13
Swedish (48)	113	1.48
Turkish (58)	58	0.76
Ukrainian (26)	96	1.26
Welsh (0)	60	0.79

Hispanic Origin	Population	%
Hispanic or Latino (of any race)	722	9.43
Central American, ex. Mexican	8	0.10
Guatemalan	7	0.09
Honduran	1	0.01
Cuban	13	0.17
Dominican Republic	3	0.04
Mexican	246	3.21
Puerto Rican	383	5.00
South American	16	0.21
Argentinean	1	0.01
Chilean	1	0.01
Colombian	7	0.09
Ecuadorian	2	0.03
Paraguayan	1	0.01
Peruvian	3	0.04
Uruguayan	1	0.01
Other Hispanic or Latino	53	0.69

Race*	Population	%
African-American/Black (993)	1,145	14.95
Not Hispanic (953)	1,058	13.81
Hispanic (40)	87	1.14
American Indian/Alaska Native (97)	174	2.27
Not Hispanic (70)	138	1.80

*Notes: † The Census 2010 population figure is used to calculate the percentages in the Hispanic Origin and Race categories. Ancestry percentages are based on the 2006-2010 American Community Survey population (not shown); ‡ Numbers in parentheses indicate the number of people reporting a single ancestry; * Numbers in parentheses indicate the number of persons reporting this race alone, not in combination with any other race; Please refer to the Explanation of Data for more information.*

Hispanic (27)	36	0.47
Blackfeet (0)	4	0.05
Cherokee (5)	22	0.29
Delaware (9)	14	0.18
Iroquois (0)	3	0.04
Mexican American Ind. (4)	4	0.05
Navajo (0)	6	0.08
Seminole (0)	2	0.03
Sioux (0)	3	0.04
Asian (203)	246	3.21
Not Hispanic (202)	242	3.16
Hispanic (1)	4	0.05
Cambodian (1)	2	0.03
Chinese, ex. Taiwanese (24)	24	0.31
Filipino (30)	33	0.43
Indian (34)	44	0.57
Japanese (94)	112	1.46
Korean (6)	10	0.13
Pakistani (5)	6	0.08
Thai (1)	3	0.04
Vietnamese (4)	6	0.08
Hawaii Native/Pacific Islander (0)	4	0.05
Not Hispanic (0)	3	0.04
Hispanic (0)	1	0.01
Native Hawaiian (0)	2	0.03
White (5,720)	5,873	76.67
Not Hispanic (5,530)	5,665	73.96
Hispanic (190)	208	2.72

Upper Montclair

Place Type: CDP
County: Essex
Population: 11,565†

Ancestry‡	Population	%
African, Sub-Saharan (18)	18	0.16
African (9)	9	0.08
South African (9)	9	0.08
Alsatian (0)	7	0.06
American (468)	468	4.03
Arab (42)	86	0.74
Arab (9)	37	0.32
Egyptian (14)	30	0.26
Lebanese (12)	12	0.10
Syrian (7)	7	0.06
Armenian (33)	49	0.42
Australian (9)	16	0.14
Austrian (25)	122	1.05
Belgian (0)	54	0.47
British (177)	244	2.10
Canadian (47)	57	0.49
Croatian (0)	15	0.13
Czech (0)	42	0.36
Czechoslovakian (10)	21	0.18
Danish (20)	72	0.62
Dutch (13)	121	1.04
Eastern European (310)	354	3.05
English (332)	1,092	9.41
European (285)	369	3.18
Finnish (7)	31	0.27
French, ex. Basque (50)	313	2.70
German (219)	1,298	11.19
Greek (73)	146	1.26
Hungarian (16)	90	0.78
Irish (632)	1,817	15.67
Israeli (33)	47	0.41
Italian (623)	1,413	12.18
Lithuanian (57)	134	1.16
Maltese (13)	13	0.11
Northern European (5)	5	0.04
Norwegian (63)	152	1.31
Pennsylvania German (0)	8	0.07
Polish (375)	1,312	11.31
Portuguese (26)	35	0.30
Romanian (19)	30	0.26
Russian (413)	899	7.75
Scandinavian (7)	21	0.18
Scotch-Irish (57)	209	1.80
Scottish (65)	205	1.77
Slavic (0)	8	0.07
Slovak (16)	119	1.03
Swedish (20)	150	1.29
Swiss (142)	235	2.03
Turkish (9)	18	0.16
Ukrainian (77)	139	1.20
Welsh (11)	66	0.57
West Indian, ex. Hispanic (185)	354	3.05
British West Indian (22)	68	0.59
Haitian (118)	118	1.02
Jamaican (45)	168	1.45

Hispanic Origin	Population	%
Hispanic or Latino (of any race)	649	5.61
Central American, ex. Mexican	59	0.51
Costa Rican	7	0.06
Guatemalan	26	0.22
Honduran	7	0.06
Nicaraguan	6	0.05
Panamanian	8	0.07
Salvadoran	5	0.04
Cuban	66	0.57
Dominican Republic	35	0.30
Mexican	71	0.61
Puerto Rican	183	1.58
South American	168	1.45
Argentinean	26	0.22
Bolivian	2	0.02
Chilean	9	0.08
Colombian	40	0.35
Ecuadorian	21	0.18
Paraguayan	2	0.02
Peruvian	34	0.29
Uruguayan	14	0.12
Venezuelan	19	0.16
Other South American	1	0.01
Other Hispanic or Latino	67	0.58

Race*	Population	%
African-American/Black (747)	950	8.21
Not Hispanic (715)	873	7.55
Hispanic (32)	77	0.67
American Indian/Alaska Native (12)	63	0.54
Not Hispanic (9)	48	0.42
Hispanic (3)	15	0.13
Alaska Athabascan *(Ala. Nat.)* (0)	1	0.01
Blackfeet (0)	1	0.01
Cherokee (1)	12	0.10
Choctaw (0)	1	0.01
Creek (0)	5	0.04
Delaware (1)	2	0.02
Iroquois (0)	1	0.01
South American Ind. (3)	15	0.13
Spanish American Ind. (1)	1	0.01
Yup'ik *(Alaska Native)* (0)	1	0.01
Asian (483)	728	6.29
Not Hispanic (479)	707	6.11
Hispanic (4)	21	0.18
Bangladeshi (1)	1	0.01
Burmese (2)	2	0.02
Cambodian (1)	1	0.01
Chinese, ex. Taiwanese (157)	230	1.99
Filipino (46)	84	0.73
Indian (139)	186	1.61
Indonesian (3)	3	0.03
Japanese (43)	77	0.67
Korean (60)	97	0.84
Malaysian (1)	1	0.01
Nepalese (1)	1	0.01
Pakistani (6)	9	0.08
Taiwanese (2)	6	0.05
Thai (1)	4	0.03
Vietnamese (3)	13	0.11
Hawaii Native/Pacific Islander (0)	15	0.13
Not Hispanic (0)	14	0.12
Hispanic (0)	1	0.01
Guamanian/Chamorro (0)	2	0.02
Native Hawaiian (0)	5	0.04
White (9,713)	10,117	87.48
Not Hispanic (9,264)	9,606	83.06
Hispanic (449)	511	4.42

Upper Saddle River

Place Type: Borough
County: Bergen
Population: 8,208†

Ancestry‡	Population	%
Afghan (13)	39	0.48
African, Sub-Saharan (27)	131	1.62
African (14)	118	1.46
South African (13)	13	0.16
American (202)	202	2.50
Arab (32)	82	1.01
Arab (16)	66	0.82
Lebanese (16)	16	0.20
Armenian (81)	81	1.00
Assyrian/Chaldean/Syriac (19)	19	0.24
Austrian (0)	188	2.33
British (38)	161	1.99
Canadian (34)	92	1.14
Croatian (28)	96	1.19
Czech (13)	58	0.72
Danish (12)	40	0.49
Dutch (0)	64	0.79
Eastern European (126)	126	1.56
English (21)	346	4.28
European (482)	482	5.96
Finnish (0)	14	0.17
French, ex. Basque (0)	128	1.58
German (164)	701	8.67
Greek (251)	358	4.43
Hungarian (13)	77	0.95
Iranian (43)	69	0.85
Irish (469)	1,325	16.39
Italian (848)	1,584	19.59
Latvian (65)	65	0.80
Lithuanian (0)	14	0.17
Norwegian (53)	103	1.27
Polish (281)	560	6.93
Romanian (0)	28	0.35
Russian (136)	442	5.47
Scandinavian (36)	36	0.45
Scotch-Irish (33)	76	0.94
Scottish (12)	49	0.61
Slovak (14)	14	0.17
Slovene (26)	40	0.49
Swedish (12)	36	0.45
Swiss (13)	27	0.33
Turkish (0)	14	0.17
Ukrainian (135)	222	2.75
Welsh (10)	76	0.94
West Indian, ex. Hispanic (24)	24	0.30
West Indian (24)	24	0.30
Yugoslavian (16)	87	1.08

Hispanic Origin	Population	%
Hispanic or Latino (of any race)	355	4.33
Central American, ex. Mexican	12	0.15
Guatemalan	6	0.07
Honduran	4	0.05
Salvadoran	2	0.02
Cuban	55	0.67
Dominican Republic	33	0.40
Mexican	25	0.30
Puerto Rican	61	0.74
South American	130	1.58
Argentinean	15	0.18
Bolivian	3	0.04
Chilean	2	0.02
Colombian	56	0.68
Ecuadorian	30	0.37
Peruvian	10	0.12
Venezuelan	12	0.15
Other South American	2	0.02
Other Hispanic or Latino	39	0.48

Race*	Population	%
African-American/Black (118)	143	1.74

*Notes: † The Census 2010 population figure is used to calculate the percentages in the Hispanic Origin and Race categories. Ancestry percentages are based on the 2006-2010 American Community Survey population (not shown); ‡ Numbers in parentheses indicate the number of people reporting a single ancestry; * Numbers in parentheses indicate the number of persons reporting this race alone, not in combination with any other race; Please refer to the Explanation of Data for more information.*

Not Hispanic (108)	132	1.61
Hispanic (10)	11	0.13
American Indian/Alaska Native (11)	18	0.22
Not Hispanic (10)	15	0.18
Hispanic (1)	3	0.04
Central American Ind. (1)	1	0.01
Cherokee (1)	3	0.04
Choctaw (0)	2	0.02
South American Ind. (6)	6	0.07
Asian (828)	904	11.01
Not Hispanic (822)	888	10.82
Hispanic (6)	16	0.19
Chinese, ex. Taiwanese (165)	191	2.33
Filipino (72)	92	1.12
Hmong (1)	1	0.01
Indian (212)	227	2.77
Japanese (24)	37	0.45
Korean (261)	284	3.46
Pakistani (43)	48	0.58
Sri Lankan (4)	5	0.06
Taiwanese (7)	7	0.09
Thai (3)	4	0.05
Vietnamese (6)	6	0.07
Hawaii Native/Pacific Islander (1)	4	0.05
Not Hispanic (1)	4	0.05
Guamanian/Chamorro (1)	4	0.05
White (7,104)	7,193	87.63
Not Hispanic (6,809)	6,887	83.91
Hispanic (295)	306	3.73

Upper

Place Type: Township
County: Cape May
Population: 12,373†

Ancestry‡	Population	%
American (598)	598	4.88
Armenian (0)	24	0.20
Austrian (21)	52	0.42
Belgian (7)	7	0.06
British (31)	39	0.32
Canadian (3)	18	0.15
Celtic (8)	8	0.07
Croatian (20)	20	0.16
Czech (64)	126	1.03
Danish (0)	61	0.50
Dutch (74)	186	1.52
Eastern European (19)	19	0.16
English (198)	1,697	13.85
European (148)	148	1.21
Finnish (0)	19	0.16
French, ex. Basque (42)	166	1.35
French Canadian (3)	25	0.20
German (919)	3,632	29.63
Greek (11)	49	0.40
Hungarian (20)	122	1.00
Irish (1,047)	3,669	29.93
Italian (1,215)	3,047	24.86
Lithuanian (21)	95	0.78
Luxemburger (16)	16	0.13
Norwegian (37)	137	1.12
Pennsylvania German (8)	8	0.07
Polish (237)	916	7.47
Portuguese (0)	9	0.07
Russian (19)	130	1.06
Scandinavian (0)	10	0.08
Scotch-Irish (83)	197	1.61
Scottish (111)	274	2.24
Slavic (0)	23	0.19
Swedish (160)	259	2.11
Swiss (0)	19	0.16
Ukrainian (65)	105	0.86
Welsh (13)	245	2.00

Hispanic Origin	Population	%
Hispanic or Latino (of any race)	292	2.36
Central American, ex. Mexican	9	0.07
Costa Rican	3	0.02
Guatemalan	1	0.01
Honduran	5	0.04
Cuban	21	0.17
Dominican Republic	6	0.05
Mexican	90	0.73
Puerto Rican	107	0.86
South American	23	0.19
Argentinean	4	0.03
Chilean	2	0.02
Colombian	7	0.06
Ecuadorian	1	0.01
Peruvian	6	0.05
Uruguayan	3	0.02
Other Hispanic or Latino	36	0.29

Race*	Population	%
African-American/Black (72)	139	1.12
Not Hispanic (69)	136	1.10
Hispanic (3)	3	0.02
American Indian/Alaska Native (16)	67	0.54
Not Hispanic (15)	63	0.51
Hispanic (1)	4	0.03
Apache (1)	1	0.01
Blackfeet (0)	7	0.06
Cherokee (1)	20	0.16
Chippewa (3)	3	0.02
Cree (0)	3	0.02
Creek (0)	3	0.02
Delaware (1)	5	0.04
Iroquois (0)	1	0.01
Pueblo (0)	3	0.02
Seminole (0)	1	0.01
Sioux (0)	4	0.03
Asian (92)	125	1.01
Not Hispanic (92)	119	0.96
Hispanic (0)	6	0.05
Chinese, ex. Taiwanese (19)	20	0.16
Filipino (24)	38	0.31
Indian (18)	18	0.15
Japanese (4)	19	0.15
Korean (15)	18	0.15
Pakistani (7)	7	0.06
Taiwanese (1)	1	0.01
Thai (3)	3	0.02
Vietnamese (1)	1	0.01
Hawaii Native/Pacific Islander (1)	8	0.06
Not Hispanic (0)	7	0.06
Hispanic (1)	1	0.01
Guamanian/Chamorro (1)	1	0.01
Native Hawaiian (0)	6	0.05
White (11,954)	12,095	97.75
Not Hispanic (11,763)	11,895	96.14
Hispanic (191)	200	1.62

Ventnor City

Place Type: City
County: Atlantic
Population: 10,650†

Ancestry‡	Population	%
African, Sub-Saharan (32)	32	0.29
African (13)	13	0.12
Liberian (19)	19	0.17
Albanian (48)	48	0.43
American (625)	625	5.60
Arab (62)	266	2.39
Jordanian (0)	53	0.48
Lebanese (43)	70	0.63
Moroccan (19)	58	0.52
Palestinian (0)	53	0.48
Syrian (0)	32	0.29
Armenian (0)	62	0.56
Austrian (31)	44	0.39
Belgian (0)	17	0.15
Brazilian (12)	12	0.11
Canadian (0)	41	0.37
Czech (0)	12	0.11
Czechoslovakian (17)	17	0.15
Danish (16)	16	0.14
Dutch (0)	15	0.13
Eastern European (66)	66	0.59
English (55)	902	8.09
European (57)	57	0.51
French, ex. Basque (13)	90	0.81
German (316)	880	7.89
Greek (0)	23	0.21
Hungarian (0)	56	0.50
Irish (539)	1,821	16.33
Italian (1,627)	2,525	22.64
Latvian (18)	18	0.16
Lithuanian (11)	89	0.80
Maltese (14)	14	0.13
Norwegian (29)	44	0.39
Pennsylvania German (0)	9	0.08
Polish (166)	456	4.09
Portuguese (30)	30	0.27
Russian (203)	344	3.08
Scotch-Irish (66)	108	0.97
Scottish (82)	272	2.44
Slovak (0)	17	0.15
Swedish (0)	33	0.30
Turkish (34)	82	0.74
Ukrainian (0)	16	0.14
Welsh (0)	110	0.99
West Indian, ex. Hispanic (149)	149	1.34
Dutch West Indian (149)	149	1.34

Hispanic Origin	Population	%
Hispanic or Latino (of any race)	1,922	18.05
Central American, ex. Mexican	115	1.08
Costa Rican	6	0.06
Guatemalan	3	0.03
Honduran	52	0.49
Nicaraguan	11	0.10
Panamanian	7	0.07
Salvadoran	35	0.33
Other Central American	1	0.01
Cuban	33	0.31
Dominican Republic	241	2.26
Mexican	447	4.20
Puerto Rican	529	4.97
South American	443	4.16
Argentinean	7	0.07
Chilean	14	0.13
Colombian	284	2.67
Ecuadorian	24	0.23
Peruvian	105	0.99
Uruguayan	1	0.01
Venezuelan	5	0.05
Other South American	3	0.03
Other Hispanic or Latino	114	1.07

Race*	Population	%
African-American/Black (453)	570	5.35
Not Hispanic (384)	455	4.27
Hispanic (69)	115	1.08
American Indian/Alaska Native (50)	104	0.98
Not Hispanic (22)	62	0.58
Hispanic (28)	42	0.39
Apache (0)	1	0.01
Blackfeet (1)	5	0.05
Cherokee (5)	6	0.06
Choctaw (0)	2	0.02
Crow (0)	2	0.02
Delaware (0)	1	0.01
Iroquois (1)	3	0.03
Mexican American Ind. (4)	7	0.07
Navajo (0)	1	0.01
South American Ind. (3)	7	0.07
Asian (924)	1,001	9.40
Not Hispanic (922)	992	9.31
Hispanic (2)	9	0.08
Bangladeshi (138)	180	1.69
Burmese (5)	5	0.05
Cambodian (3)	6	0.06
Chinese, ex. Taiwanese (123)	137	1.29
Filipino (79)	98	0.92
Indian (274)	316	2.97
Japanese (2)	6	0.06
Korean (13)	19	0.18

*Notes: † The Census 2010 population figure is used to calculate the percentages in the Hispanic Origin and Race categories. Ancestry percentages are based on the 2006-2010 American Community Survey population (not shown); ‡ Numbers in parentheses indicate the number of people reporting a single ancestry; * Numbers in parentheses indicate the number of persons reporting this race alone, not in combination with any other race; Please refer to the Explanation of Data for more information.*

Laotian (2)	2	0.02
Pakistani (72)	73	0.69
Sri Lankan (5)	5	0.05
Taiwanese (0)	2	0.02
Vietnamese (152)	163	1.53
Hawaii Native/Pacific Islander (5)	16	0.15
Not Hispanic (5)	9	0.08
Hispanic (0)	7	0.07
Fijian (4)	4	0.04
Guamanian/Chamorro (1)	2	0.02
Native Hawaiian (0)	6	0.06
Samoan (0)	1	0.01
White (8,076)	8,289	77.83
Not Hispanic (7,224)	7,339	68.91
Hispanic (852)	950	8.92

Vernon

Place Type: Township
County: Sussex
Population: 23,943†

Ancestry‡	Population	%
African, Sub-Saharan (69)	69	0.28
Ethiopian (11)	11	0.05
Ghanaian (58)	58	0.24
American (775)	775	3.18
Arab (19)	125	0.51
Arab (0)	24	0.10
Egyptian (0)	10	0.04
Lebanese (9)	46	0.19
Syrian (10)	45	0.18
Armenian (0)	40	0.16
Assyrian/Chaldean/Syriac (0)	8	0.03
Austrian (11)	217	0.89
Belgian (0)	13	0.05
Brazilian (14)	69	0.28
British (22)	239	0.98
Canadian (0)	86	0.35
Czech (64)	256	1.05
Czechoslovakian (15)	50	0.21
Danish (34)	145	0.59
Dutch (272)	1,651	6.77
Eastern European (13)	26	0.11
English (332)	2,586	10.61
Estonian (12)	12	0.05
European (219)	219	0.90
French, ex. Basque (14)	560	2.30
French Canadian (0)	48	0.20
German (1,208)	6,452	26.47
Greek (0)	114	0.47
Guyanese (32)	32	0.13
Hungarian (267)	781	3.20
Iranian (13)	24	0.10
Irish (1,746)	7,540	30.93
Italian (2,363)	6,750	27.69
Lithuanian (0)	75	0.31
Northern European (21)	21	0.09
Norwegian (74)	263	1.08
Polish (750)	2,251	9.23
Portuguese (46)	68	0.28
Romanian (16)	77	0.32
Russian (78)	541	2.22
Scandinavian (8)	8	0.03
Scotch-Irish (104)	409	1.68
Scottish (132)	595	2.44
Slavic (22)	46	0.19
Slovak (10)	77	0.32
Swedish (15)	175	0.72
Swiss (10)	168	0.69
Ukrainian (53)	218	0.89
Welsh (44)	190	0.78
West Indian, ex. Hispanic (13)	20	0.08
Trinidadian/Tobagonian (13)	13	0.05
West Indian (0)	7	0.03

Hispanic Origin	Population	%
Hispanic or Latino (of any race)	1,534	6.41
Central American, ex. Mexican	84	0.35
Costa Rican	30	0.13
Guatemalan	22	0.09
Honduran	9	0.04
Nicaraguan	2	0.01
Panamanian	1	<0.01
Salvadoran	20	0.08
Cuban	148	0.62
Dominican Republic	141	0.59
Mexican	121	0.51
Puerto Rican	569	2.38
South American	302	1.26
Argentinean	35	0.15
Bolivian	10	0.04
Chilean	13	0.05
Colombian	86	0.36
Ecuadorian	84	0.35
Peruvian	58	0.24
Uruguayan	4	0.02
Venezuelan	6	0.03
Other South American	6	0.03
Other Hispanic or Latino	169	0.71

Race*	Population	%
African-American/Black (332)	442	1.85
Not Hispanic (292)	379	1.58
Hispanic (40)	63	0.26
American Indian/Alaska Native (40)	140	0.58
Not Hispanic (29)	108	0.45
Hispanic (11)	32	0.13
Alaska Athabascan *(Ala. Nat.)* (0)	1	<0.01
Blackfeet (3)	7	0.03
Cherokee (3)	16	0.07
Chippewa (1)	1	<0.01
Choctaw (0)	2	0.01
Cree (0)	1	<0.01
Delaware (8)	10	0.04
Iroquois (1)	7	0.03
Mexican American Ind. (1)	2	0.01
Osage (0)	3	0.01
Pueblo (1)	4	0.02
Sioux (0)	3	0.01
South American Ind. (7)	12	0.05
Spanish American Ind. (0)	1	<0.01
Asian (186)	277	1.16
Not Hispanic (185)	261	1.09
Hispanic (1)	16	0.07
Burmese (0)	3	0.01
Chinese, ex. Taiwanese (24)	43	0.18
Filipino (45)	66	0.28
Indian (38)	41	0.17
Japanese (6)	20	0.08
Korean (36)	61	0.25
Laotian (1)	1	<0.01
Malaysian (1)	1	<0.01
Pakistani (3)	8	0.03
Taiwanese (1)	1	<0.01
Thai (6)	8	0.03
Vietnamese (18)	21	0.09
Hawaii Native/Pacific Islander (8)	19	0.08
Not Hispanic (7)	17	0.07
Hispanic (1)	2	0.01
Guamanian/Chamorro (2)	3	0.01
Native Hawaiian (2)	5	0.02
Samoan (1)	3	0.01
White (22,790)	23,092	96.45
Not Hispanic (21,624)	21,850	91.26
Hispanic (1,166)	1,242	5.19

Verona

Place Type: Township
County: Essex
Population: 13,332†

Ancestry‡	Population	%
African, Sub-Saharan (0)	7	0.05
African (0)	7	0.05
Albanian (0)	10	0.08
American (419)	419	3.15
Arab (43)	139	1.05
Egyptian (25)	25	0.19
Lebanese (11)	35	0.26
Syrian (0)	47	0.35
Other Arab (7)	32	0.24
Armenian (0)	11	0.08
Austrian (56)	147	1.11
Brazilian (9)	9	0.07
British (7)	71	0.53
Bulgarian (44)	44	0.33
Celtic (15)	15	0.11
Czech (39)	148	1.11
Czechoslovakian (12)	24	0.18
Danish (0)	35	0.26
Dutch (14)	239	1.80
Eastern European (82)	137	1.03
English (208)	874	6.57
European (99)	99	0.74
Finnish (0)	27	0.20
French, ex. Basque (0)	69	0.52
French Canadian (34)	41	0.31
German (270)	1,591	11.97
Greek (45)	96	0.72
Hungarian (0)	172	1.29
Iranian (29)	29	0.22
Irish (1,150)	3,633	27.32
Israeli (9)	9	0.07
Italian (1,920)	3,882	29.19
Latvian (0)	7	0.05
Lithuanian (9)	165	1.24
Maltese (0)	10	0.08
Norwegian (20)	70	0.53
Polish (385)	1,039	7.81
Romanian (22)	43	0.32
Russian (361)	813	6.11
Scandinavian (0)	23	0.17
Scotch-Irish (42)	205	1.54
Scottish (90)	299	2.25
Slovak (22)	133	1.00
Swedish (0)	115	0.86
Swiss (71)	71	0.53
Turkish (9)	18	0.14
Ukrainian (137)	283	2.13
Welsh (8)	33	0.25
West Indian, ex. Hispanic (139)	147	1.11
Haitian (96)	96	0.72
Jamaican (17)	17	0.13
West Indian (26)	34	0.26

Hispanic Origin	Population	%
Hispanic or Latino (of any race)	795	5.96
Central American, ex. Mexican	57	0.43
Costa Rican	16	0.12
Guatemalan	5	0.04
Honduran	4	0.03
Panamanian	9	0.07
Salvadoran	23	0.17
Cuban	96	0.72
Dominican Republic	33	0.25
Mexican	66	0.50
Puerto Rican	258	1.94
South American	198	1.49
Argentinean	23	0.17
Bolivian	4	0.03
Chilean	14	0.11
Colombian	55	0.41
Ecuadorian	39	0.29
Peruvian	46	0.35
Uruguayan	10	0.08
Venezuelan	5	0.04
Other South American	2	0.02
Other Hispanic or Latino	87	0.65

Race*	Population	%
African-American/Black (262)	311	2.33
Not Hispanic (239)	274	2.06
Hispanic (23)	37	0.28
American Indian/Alaska Native (4)	38	0.29
Not Hispanic (2)	27	0.20
Hispanic (2)	11	0.08
Canadian/French Am. Ind. (0)	2	0.02
Central American Ind. (0)	1	0.01

*Notes: † The Census 2010 population figure is used to calculate the percentages in the Hispanic Origin and Race categories. Ancestry percentages are based on the 2006-2010 American Community Survey population (not shown); ‡ Numbers in parentheses indicate the number of people reporting a single ancestry; * Numbers in parentheses indicate the number of persons reporting this race alone, not in combination with any other race; Please refer to the Explanation of Data for more information.*

Cherokee (0)	7	0.05
Iroquois (0)	1	0.01
Mexican American Ind. (1)	3	0.02
Seminole (0)	1	0.01
Sioux (0)	3	0.02
South American Ind. (0)	2	0.02
Asian (537)	654	4.91
Not Hispanic (535)	637	4.78
Hispanic (2)	17	0.13
Cambodian (3)	3	0.02
Chinese, ex. Taiwanese (187)	226	1.70
Filipino (84)	112	0.84
Indian (174)	193	1.45
Indonesian (1)	1	0.01
Japanese (9)	23	0.17
Korean (30)	47	0.35
Malaysian (1)	1	0.01
Nepalese (2)	2	0.02
Pakistani (7)	9	0.07
Sri Lankan (1)	3	0.02
Taiwanese (15)	19	0.14
Thai (1)	2	0.02
Vietnamese (3)	6	0.05
Hawaii Native/Pacific Islander (1)	8	0.06
Not Hispanic (1)	7	0.05
Hispanic (0)	1	0.01
Guamanian/Chamorro (0)	5	0.04
Native Hawaiian (0)	1	0.01
White (12,164)	12,346	92.60
Not Hispanic (11,569)	11,713	87.86
Hispanic (595)	633	4.75

Villas

Place Type: CDP
County: Cape May
Population: 9,483†

Ancestry‡	Population	%
American (368)	368	3.90
Austrian (0)	11	0.12
Belgian (0)	11	0.12
British (9)	22	0.23
Czech (33)	35	0.37
Danish (13)	25	0.26
Dutch (0)	86	0.91
English (244)	1,121	11.87
French, ex. Basque (15)	221	2.34
French Canadian (0)	10	0.11
German (319)	2,126	22.52
Irish (1,381)	3,552	37.62
Italian (784)	1,878	19.89
Lithuanian (0)	36	0.38
Macedonian (150)	150	1.59
Norwegian (14)	63	0.67
Pennsylvania German (23)	40	0.42
Polish (310)	760	8.05
Portuguese (34)	34	0.36
Russian (0)	10	0.11
Scandinavian (0)	13	0.14
Scotch-Irish (78)	245	2.59
Scottish (11)	181	1.92
Slavic (0)	16	0.17
Slovak (0)	11	0.12
Slovene (8)	8	0.08
Swedish (21)	68	0.72
Swiss (0)	24	0.25
Ukrainian (40)	52	0.55
Welsh (69)	119	1.26
West Indian, ex. Hispanic (0)	12	0.13
Jamaican (0)	12	0.13

Hispanic Origin	Population	%
Hispanic or Latino (of any race)	586	6.18
Central American, ex. Mexican	16	0.17
Costa Rican	2	0.02
Guatemalan	5	0.05
Nicaraguan	2	0.02
Panamanian	6	0.06
Salvadoran	1	0.01
Cuban	15	0.16
Dominican Republic	3	0.03
Mexican	161	1.70
Puerto Rican	313	3.30
South American	45	0.47
Argentinean	17	0.18
Colombian	14	0.15
Ecuadorian	2	0.02
Peruvian	12	0.13
Other Hispanic or Latino	33	0.35

Race*	Population	%
African-American/Black (185)	300	3.16
Not Hispanic (175)	269	2.84
Hispanic (10)	31	0.33
American Indian/Alaska Native (16)	54	0.57
Not Hispanic (11)	49	0.52
Hispanic (5)	5	0.05
Apache (0)	1	0.01
Blackfeet (0)	2	0.02
Cherokee (0)	5	0.05
Chippewa (2)	2	0.02
Choctaw (1)	7	0.07
Delaware (1)	1	0.01
Iroquois (0)	3	0.03
Sioux (0)	3	0.03
South American Ind. (4)	4	0.04
Asian (31)	57	0.60
Not Hispanic (31)	56	0.59
Hispanic (0)	1	0.01
Chinese, ex. Taiwanese (7)	9	0.09
Filipino (7)	24	0.25
Indian (4)	6	0.06
Indonesian (1)	2	0.02
Japanese (5)	7	0.07
Korean (4)	4	0.04
Nepalese (1)	1	0.01
Thai (2)	2	0.02
Hawaii Native/Pacific Islander (6)	25	0.26
Not Hispanic (6)	15	0.16
Hispanic (0)	10	0.11
Guamanian/Chamorro (0)	1	0.01
Native Hawaiian (1)	7	0.07
White (8,866)	9,062	95.56
Not Hispanic (8,509)	8,663	91.35
Hispanic (357)	399	4.21

Vineland

Place Type: City
County: Cumberland
Population: 60,724†

Ancestry‡	Population	%
African, Sub-Saharan (793)	823	1.37
African (681)	711	1.19
Ghanaian (58)	58	0.10
Nigerian (54)	54	0.09
American (1,654)	1,654	2.76
Armenian (0)	11	0.02
Australian (15)	15	0.03
Austrian (108)	232	0.39
Basque (0)	57	0.10
Brazilian (144)	144	0.24
British (14)	63	0.11
Bulgarian (0)	47	0.08
Canadian (21)	43	0.07
Carpatho Rusyn (0)	15	0.03
Croatian (0)	8	0.01
Czech (12)	55	0.09
Czechoslovakian (14)	31	0.05
Danish (10)	115	0.19
Dutch (79)	605	1.01
Eastern European (82)	82	0.14
English (902)	3,244	5.41
Estonian (11)	11	0.02
European (187)	193	0.32
Finnish (11)	43	0.07
French, ex. Basque (65)	838	1.40
French Canadian (0)	57	0.10
German (1,794)	6,774	11.31
Greek (263)	371	0.62
Guyanese (23)	23	0.04
Hungarian (69)	96	0.16
Irish (1,364)	5,996	10.01
Italian (7,461)	12,932	21.59
Latvian (37)	37	0.06
Lithuanian (29)	120	0.20
Norwegian (29)	114	0.19
Pennsylvania German (58)	108	0.18
Polish (699)	2,144	3.58
Portuguese (22)	22	0.04
Romanian (7)	44	0.07
Russian (490)	788	1.32
Scandinavian (44)	61	0.10
Scotch-Irish (124)	478	0.80
Scottish (178)	476	0.79
Slavic (19)	19	0.03
Slovak (0)	48	0.08
Slovene (5)	5	0.01
Swedish (98)	332	0.55
Turkish (0)	9	0.02
Ukrainian (329)	454	0.76
Welsh (47)	362	0.60
West Indian, ex. Hispanic (377)	503	0.84
Bahamian (14)	14	0.02
Haitian (29)	78	0.13
Jamaican (193)	270	0.45
West Indian (141)	141	0.24
Yugoslavian (0)	18	0.03

Hispanic Origin	Population	%
Hispanic or Latino (of any race)	23,093	38.03
Central American, ex. Mexican	407	0.67
Costa Rican	30	0.05
Guatemalan	126	0.21
Honduran	86	0.14
Nicaraguan	11	0.02
Panamanian	27	0.04
Salvadoran	124	0.20
Other Central American	3	<0.01
Cuban	200	0.33
Dominican Republic	819	1.35
Mexican	4,383	7.22
Puerto Rican	16,236	26.74
South American	402	0.66
Argentinean	42	0.07
Bolivian	7	0.01
Chilean	21	0.03
Colombian	170	0.28
Ecuadorian	69	0.11
Paraguayan	2	<0.01
Peruvian	70	0.12
Uruguayan	7	0.01
Venezuelan	11	0.02
Other South American	3	<0.01
Other Hispanic or Latino	646	1.06

Race*	Population	%
African-American/Black (8,600)	9,680	15.94
Not Hispanic (7,384)	7,992	13.16
Hispanic (1,216)	1,688	2.78
American Indian/Alaska Native (406)	844	1.39
Not Hispanic (165)	471	0.78
Hispanic (241)	373	0.61
Alaska Athabascan *(Ala. Nat.)* (1)	1	<0.01
Apache (3)	3	<0.01
Blackfeet (0)	24	0.04
Central American Ind. (3)	7	0.01
Cherokee (16)	93	0.15
Choctaw (1)	1	<0.01
Cree (2)	2	<0.01
Creek (6)	6	0.01
Delaware (24)	60	0.10
Hopi (1)	1	<0.01
Iroquois (5)	10	0.02
Mexican American Ind. (39)	55	0.09
Navajo (1)	2	<0.01
Ottawa (1)	1	<0.01
Pueblo (2)	2	<0.01

*Notes: † The Census 2010 population figure is used to calculate the percentages in the Hispanic Origin and Race categories. Ancestry percentages are based on the 2006-2010 American Community Survey population (not shown); ‡ Numbers in parentheses indicate the number of people reporting a single ancestry; * Numbers in parentheses indicate the number of persons reporting this race alone, not in combination with any other race; Please refer to the Explanation of Data for more information.*

Seminole (0)	2	<0.01
Sioux (0)	5	0.01
South American Ind. (34)	67	0.11
Spanish American Ind. (5)	5	0.01
Tlingit-Haida *(Alaska Native)* (1)	1	<0.01
Yakama (1)	1	<0.01
Asian (1,036)	1,294	2.13
Not Hispanic (1,011)	1,206	1.99
Hispanic (25)	88	0.14
Bangladeshi (5)	8	0.01
Cambodian (2)	6	0.01
Chinese, ex. Taiwanese (177)	209	0.34
Filipino (182)	265	0.44
Indian (436)	512	0.84
Indonesian (1)	2	<0.01
Japanese (20)	50	0.08
Korean (46)	62	0.10
Laotian (2)	3	<0.01
Pakistani (70)	81	0.13
Taiwanese (0)	1	<0.01
Thai (8)	10	0.02
Vietnamese (41)	52	0.09
Hawaii Native/Pacific Islander (24)	106	0.17
Not Hispanic (15)	51	0.08
Hispanic (9)	55	0.09
Guamanian/Chamorro (7)	13	0.02
Marshallese (1)	1	<0.01
Native Hawaiian (11)	27	0.04
Samoan (0)	4	0.01
White (40,703)	42,283	69.63
Not Hispanic (28,087)	28,758	47.36
Hispanic (12,616)	13,525	22.27

Voorhees

Place Type: Township
County: Camden
Population: 29,131†

Ancestry‡	Population	%
African, Sub-Saharan (53)	72	0.25
African (24)	43	0.15
Nigerian (29)	29	0.10
American (889)	889	3.06
Arab (152)	275	0.95
Arab (35)	35	0.12
Egyptian (13)	84	0.29
Lebanese (0)	13	0.04
Moroccan (52)	52	0.18
Palestinian (0)	21	0.07
Syrian (0)	18	0.06
Other Arab (52)	52	0.18
Armenian (22)	61	0.21
Austrian (13)	145	0.50
British (110)	178	0.61
Bulgarian (38)	38	0.13
Canadian (25)	41	0.14
Croatian (8)	8	0.03
Czech (7)	83	0.29
Danish (0)	10	0.03
Dutch (38)	175	0.60
Eastern European (275)	275	0.95
English (281)	1,963	6.76
European (215)	386	1.33
Finnish (0)	45	0.15
French, ex. Basque (111)	510	1.76
French Canadian (11)	33	0.11
German (1,048)	4,137	14.24
Greek (11)	90	0.31
Hungarian (206)	521	1.79
Irish (957)	3,986	13.72
Israeli (33)	33	0.11
Italian (2,245)	4,759	16.38
Latvian (0)	67	0.23
Lithuanian (12)	105	0.36
Norwegian (22)	149	0.51
Pennsylvania German (12)	68	0.23
Polish (583)	1,980	6.82
Portuguese (53)	85	0.29
Romanian (35)	143	0.49
Russian (622)	1,533	5.28
Scandinavian (39)	39	0.13
Scotch-Irish (138)	257	0.88
Scottish (105)	505	1.74
Slavic (0)	18	0.06
Slovak (16)	121	0.42
Swedish (27)	240	0.83
Swiss (0)	39	0.13
Turkish (80)	89	0.31
Ukrainian (218)	319	1.10
Welsh (41)	159	0.55
West Indian, ex. Hispanic (57)	73	0.25
British West Indian (14)	14	0.05
Haitian (30)	46	0.16
West Indian (13)	13	0.04
Yugoslavian (0)	7	0.02

Hispanic Origin	Population	%
Hispanic or Latino (of any race)	998	3.43
Central American, ex. Mexican	53	0.18
Costa Rican	3	0.01
Guatemalan	14	0.05
Honduran	5	0.02
Nicaraguan	11	0.04
Panamanian	7	0.02
Salvadoran	13	0.04
Cuban	73	0.25
Dominican Republic	35	0.12
Mexican	190	0.65
Puerto Rican	389	1.34
South American	164	0.56
Argentinean	16	0.05
Bolivian	3	0.01
Chilean	9	0.03
Colombian	66	0.23
Ecuadorian	23	0.08
Paraguayan	2	0.01
Peruvian	11	0.04
Uruguayan	1	<0.01
Venezuelan	33	0.11
Other Hispanic or Latino	94	0.32

Race*	Population	%
African-American/Black (2,534)	2,838	9.74
Not Hispanic (2,468)	2,724	9.35
Hispanic (66)	114	0.39
American Indian/Alaska Native (44)	167	0.57
Not Hispanic (31)	133	0.46
Hispanic (13)	34	0.12
Blackfeet (0)	1	<0.01
Cherokee (2)	22	0.08
Choctaw (0)	2	0.01
Comanche (1)	3	0.01
Creek (1)	1	<0.01
Delaware (1)	10	0.03
Iroquois (0)	1	<0.01
Mexican American Ind. (4)	6	0.02
Navajo (0)	1	<0.01
Seminole (0)	3	0.01
Sioux (0)	1	<0.01
South American Ind. (2)	5	0.02
Asian (4,700)	5,042	17.31
Not Hispanic (4,677)	5,010	17.20
Hispanic (23)	32	0.11
Bangladeshi (58)	59	0.20
Burmese (3)	3	0.01
Cambodian (12)	13	0.04
Chinese, ex. Taiwanese (648)	701	2.41
Filipino (483)	568	1.95
Indian (2,397)	2,497	8.57
Indonesian (2)	3	0.01
Japanese (24)	58	0.20
Korean (648)	700	2.40
Malaysian (5)	6	0.02
Nepalese (6)	6	0.02
Pakistani (131)	150	0.51
Sri Lankan (5)	5	0.02
Taiwanese (62)	67	0.23
Thai (8)	9	0.03
Vietnamese (78)	95	0.33
Hawaii Native/Pacific Islander (11)	41	0.14
Not Hispanic (10)	29	0.10
Hispanic (1)	12	0.04
Guamanian/Chamorro (1)	3	0.01
Native Hawaiian (5)	18	0.06
Samoan (0)	2	0.01
Tongan (3)	3	0.01
White (20,908)	21,387	73.42
Not Hispanic (20,308)	20,724	71.14
Hispanic (600)	663	2.28

Waldwick

Place Type: Borough
County: Bergen
Population: 9,625†

Ancestry‡	Population	%
African, Sub-Saharan (10)	10	0.10
South African (10)	10	0.10
American (225)	225	2.35
Arab (80)	223	2.33
Arab (56)	77	0.80
Lebanese (10)	80	0.84
Syrian (14)	54	0.56
Other Arab (0)	12	0.13
Armenian (30)	58	0.61
Austrian (8)	39	0.41
British (10)	17	0.18
Canadian (0)	17	0.18
Czech (11)	38	0.40
Czechoslovakian (0)	8	0.08
Danish (8)	8	0.08
Dutch (156)	526	5.49
English (113)	610	6.37
European (114)	125	1.30
Finnish (11)	60	0.63
French, ex. Basque (12)	176	1.84
French Canadian (0)	53	0.55
German (412)	1,996	20.84
Greek (72)	158	1.65
Hungarian (22)	144	1.50
Iranian (5)	5	0.05
Irish (805)	2,881	30.07
Italian (1,131)	2,928	30.56
Latvian (51)	51	0.53
Lithuanian (0)	45	0.47
Maltese (0)	13	0.14
Norwegian (0)	32	0.33
Polish (28)	415	4.33
Portuguese (13)	13	0.14
Romanian (0)	15	0.16
Russian (25)	149	1.56
Scotch-Irish (49)	126	1.32
Scottish (12)	168	1.75
Slavic (0)	10	0.10
Slovak (29)	83	0.87
Swedish (23)	70	0.73
Swiss (0)	9	0.09
Turkish (30)	30	0.31
Ukrainian (12)	153	1.60
Welsh (0)	40	0.42

Hispanic Origin	Population	%
Hispanic or Latino (of any race)	830	8.62
Central American, ex. Mexican	219	2.28
Costa Rican	11	0.11
Guatemalan	2	0.02
Honduran	10	0.10
Panamanian	1	0.01
Salvadoran	195	2.03
Cuban	77	0.80
Dominican Republic	41	0.43
Mexican	73	0.76
Puerto Rican	168	1.75
South American	151	1.57
Argentinean	16	0.17
Bolivian	8	0.08
Chilean	3	0.03
Colombian	78	0.81

*Notes: † The Census 2010 population figure is used to calculate the percentages in the Hispanic Origin and Race categories. Ancestry percentages are based on the 2006-2010 American Community Survey population (not shown); ‡ Numbers in parentheses indicate the number of people reporting a single ancestry; * Numbers in parentheses indicate the number of persons reporting this race alone, not in combination with any other race; Please refer to the Explanation of Data for more information.*

Ecuadorian	12	0.12
Peruvian	23	0.24
Uruguayan	5	0.05
Venezuelan	5	0.05
Other South American	1	0.01
Other Hispanic or Latino	101	1.05

Race*	Population	%
African-American/Black (104)	146	1.52
Not Hispanic (74)	101	1.05
Hispanic (30)	45	0.47
American Indian/Alaska Native (11)	29	0.30
Not Hispanic (9)	22	0.23
Hispanic (2)	7	0.07
Cherokee (0)	4	0.04
Creek (0)	1	0.01
Osage (0)	1	0.01
Potawatomi (3)	3	0.03
Seminole (0)	3	0.03
Sioux (0)	1	0.01
South American Ind. (3)	8	0.08
Asian (480)	544	5.65
Not Hispanic (478)	539	5.60
Hispanic (2)	5	0.05
Bangladeshi (4)	4	0.04
Chinese, ex. Taiwanese (112)	127	1.32
Filipino (66)	84	0.87
Indian (90)	110	1.14
Indonesian (0)	1	0.01
Japanese (70)	81	0.84
Korean (89)	95	0.99
Nepalese (1)	2	0.02
Pakistani (4)	7	0.07
Taiwanese (3)	3	0.03
Thai (12)	16	0.17
Vietnamese (4)	4	0.04
Hawaii Native/Pacific Islander (0)	4	0.04
Not Hispanic (0)	1	0.01
Hispanic (0)	3	0.03
Samoan (0)	1	0.01
White (8,723)	8,849	91.94
Not Hispanic (8,122)	8,219	85.39
Hispanic (601)	630	6.55

Wall

Place Type: Township
County: Monmouth
Population: 26,164†

Ancestry‡	Population	%
Albanian (41)	41	0.16
American (769)	769	2.96
Arab (122)	193	0.74
Egyptian (30)	30	0.12
Jordanian (0)	12	0.05
Lebanese (60)	74	0.28
Syrian (32)	77	0.30
Armenian (42)	80	0.31
Assyrian/Chaldean/Syriac (0)	9	0.03
Austrian (0)	130	0.50
Belgian (12)	100	0.38
Brazilian (0)	54	0.21
British (13)	24	0.09
Canadian (19)	33	0.13
Carpatho Rusyn (0)	31	0.12
Celtic (0)	10	0.04
Croatian (10)	35	0.13
Czech (29)	63	0.24
Czechoslovakian (0)	81	0.31
Danish (62)	92	0.35
Dutch (190)	494	1.90
English (529)	3,159	12.14
European (80)	80	0.31
Finnish (0)	13	0.05
French, ex. Basque (73)	501	1.93
French Canadian (14)	114	0.44
German (868)	5,266	20.25
Greek (253)	422	1.62
Hungarian (117)	345	1.33
Irish (2,815)	8,480	32.60
Italian (3,326)	7,558	29.06
Latvian (12)	22	0.08
Lithuanian (33)	104	0.40
Luxemburger (36)	36	0.14
Northern European (16)	16	0.06
Norwegian (117)	196	0.75
Polish (634)	2,099	8.07
Portuguese (42)	86	0.33
Romanian (0)	77	0.30
Russian (192)	462	1.78
Scotch-Irish (219)	633	2.43
Scottish (264)	640	2.46
Slavic (10)	30	0.12
Slovak (67)	253	0.97
Slovene (14)	14	0.05
Swedish (122)	353	1.36
Swiss (0)	28	0.11
Turkish (22)	22	0.08
Ukrainian (143)	251	0.96
Welsh (0)	111	0.43
West Indian, ex. Hispanic (139)	173	0.67
British West Indian (0)	12	0.05
Haitian (139)	139	0.53
West Indian (0)	22	0.08
Yugoslavian (92)	135	0.52

Hispanic Origin	Population	%
Hispanic or Latino (of any race)	908	3.47
Central American, ex. Mexican	79	0.30
Costa Rican	25	0.10
Guatemalan	16	0.06
Honduran	12	0.05
Nicaraguan	1	<0.01
Salvadoran	24	0.09
Other Central American	1	<0.01
Cuban	50	0.19
Dominican Republic	26	0.10
Mexican	292	1.12
Puerto Rican	243	0.93
South American	117	0.45
Argentinean	11	0.04
Chilean	6	0.02
Colombian	52	0.20
Ecuadorian	20	0.08
Peruvian	19	0.07
Venezuelan	8	0.03
Other South American	1	<0.01
Other Hispanic or Latino	101	0.39

Race*	Population	%
African-American/Black (639)	725	2.77
Not Hispanic (611)	687	2.63
Hispanic (28)	38	0.15
American Indian/Alaska Native (41)	115	0.44
Not Hispanic (26)	92	0.35
Hispanic (15)	23	0.09
Apache (0)	1	<0.01
Blackfeet (0)	11	0.04
Canadian/French Am. Ind. (0)	1	<0.01
Cherokee (5)	16	0.06
Chickasaw (3)	13	0.05
Chippewa (1)	1	<0.01
Choctaw (0)	2	0.01
Comanche (0)	1	<0.01
Creek (0)	2	0.01
Delaware (3)	6	0.02
Iroquois (1)	7	0.03
Mexican American Ind. (5)	5	0.02
Navajo (0)	1	<0.01
Paiute (0)	2	0.01
Asian (421)	540	2.06
Not Hispanic (420)	535	2.04
Hispanic (1)	5	0.02
Cambodian (0)	1	<0.01
Chinese, ex. Taiwanese (79)	110	0.42
Filipino (79)	115	0.44
Indian (140)	154	0.59
Japanese (5)	14	0.05
Korean (46)	56	0.21
Laotian (1)	1	<0.01
Pakistani (4)	6	0.02
Taiwanese (2)	2	0.01
Thai (3)	3	0.01
Vietnamese (48)	54	0.21
Hawaii Native/Pacific Islander (2)	17	0.06
Not Hispanic (2)	16	0.06
Hispanic (0)	1	<0.01
Native Hawaiian (0)	8	0.03
Tongan (1)	3	0.01
White (24,521)	24,790	94.75
Not Hispanic (23,925)	24,151	92.31
Hispanic (596)	639	2.44

Wallington

Place Type: Borough
County: Bergen
Population: 11,335†

Ancestry‡	Population	%
African, Sub-Saharan (75)	75	0.66
African (54)	54	0.48
Kenyan (21)	21	0.19
American (427)	427	3.77
Arab (408)	476	4.20
Arab (18)	34	0.30
Egyptian (255)	255	2.25
Jordanian (10)	10	0.09
Palestinian (26)	78	0.69
Syrian (99)	99	0.87
British (17)	17	0.15
Croatian (53)	53	0.47
Czech (0)	23	0.20
Danish (6)	6	0.05
Dutch (50)	159	1.40
English (39)	128	1.13
French, ex. Basque (8)	18	0.16
German (81)	504	4.45
Hungarian (73)	201	1.77
Irish (136)	591	5.22
Italian (333)	1,044	9.22
Lithuanian (18)	39	0.34
Norwegian (0)	10	0.09
Polish (4,731)	5,307	46.85
Romanian (22)	42	0.37
Russian (75)	153	1.35
Scandinavian (0)	9	0.08
Scotch-Irish (18)	24	0.21
Scottish (19)	19	0.17
Slavic (0)	12	0.11
Slovak (60)	162	1.43
Swedish (26)	44	0.39
Ukrainian (107)	107	0.94
Welsh (14)	14	0.12
West Indian, ex. Hispanic (36)	84	0.74
Jamaican (21)	21	0.19
Trinidadian/Tobagonian (0)	48	0.42
U.S. Virgin Islander (15)	15	0.13
Yugoslavian (39)	39	0.34

Hispanic Origin	Population	%
Hispanic or Latino (of any race)	1,225	10.81
Central American, ex. Mexican	64	0.56
Costa Rican	15	0.13
Guatemalan	15	0.13
Honduran	15	0.13
Panamanian	3	0.03
Salvadoran	16	0.14
Cuban	66	0.58
Dominican Republic	201	1.77
Mexican	30	0.26
Puerto Rican	350	3.09
South American	441	3.89
Argentinean	4	0.04
Bolivian	5	0.04
Chilean	4	0.04
Colombian	133	1.17
Ecuadorian	103	0.91
Paraguayan	8	0.07

*Notes: † The Census 2010 population figure is used to calculate the percentages in the Hispanic Origin and Race categories. Ancestry percentages are based on the 2006-2010 American Community Survey population (not shown); ‡ Numbers in parentheses indicate the number of people reporting a single ancestry; * Numbers in parentheses indicate the number of persons reporting this race alone, not in combination with any other race; Please refer to the Explanation of Data for more information.*

Peruvian	149	1.31
Uruguayan	8	0.07
Venezuelan	23	0.20
Other South American	4	0.04
Other Hispanic or Latino	73	0.64

Race*	Population	%
African-American/Black (366)	422	3.72
Not Hispanic (303)	340	3.00
Hispanic (63)	82	0.72
American Indian/Alaska Native (18)	42	0.37
Not Hispanic (14)	32	0.28
Hispanic (4)	10	0.09
Cherokee (1)	4	0.04
Iroquois (0)	2	0.02
Ottawa (0)	1	0.01
South American Ind. (0)	7	0.06
Asian (631)	696	6.14
Not Hispanic (610)	669	5.90
Hispanic (21)	27	0.24
Bangladeshi (1)	1	0.01
Chinese, ex. Taiwanese (26)	30	0.26
Filipino (69)	78	0.69
Indian (430)	454	4.01
Japanese (20)	21	0.19
Korean (67)	70	0.62
Nepalese (1)	1	0.01
Pakistani (6)	6	0.05
Sri Lankan (1)	1	0.01
Taiwanese (1)	1	0.01
Thai (3)	5	0.04
Vietnamese (3)	6	0.05
Hawaii Native/Pacific Islander (0)	15	0.13
Not Hispanic (0)	13	0.11
Hispanic (0)	2	0.02
White (9,689)	9,838	86.79
Not Hispanic (9,048)	9,132	80.56
Hispanic (641)	706	6.23

Wanaque

Place Type: Borough
County: Passaic
Population: 11,116†

Ancestry‡	Population	%
American (255)	255	2.34
Arab (204)	292	2.68
Arab (0)	18	0.17
Egyptian (29)	29	0.27
Lebanese (12)	12	0.11
Syrian (163)	184	1.69
Other Arab (0)	49	0.45
Armenian (19)	19	0.17
Assyrian/Chaldean/Syriac (11)	11	0.10
Austrian (28)	53	0.49
Brazilian (67)	67	0.62
British (0)	4	0.04
Canadian (20)	51	0.47
Czech (12)	15	0.14
Czechoslovakian (12)	12	0.11
Danish (0)	4	0.04
Dutch (29)	636	5.84
Eastern European (42)	42	0.39
English (101)	1,037	9.52
European (79)	79	0.73
Finnish (0)	17	0.16
French, ex. Basque (19)	288	2.64
French Canadian (10)	21	0.19
German (405)	1,698	15.59
Greek (49)	146	1.34
Hungarian (17)	110	1.01
Irish (615)	2,380	21.85
Italian (1,377)	2,685	24.65
Lithuanian (0)	11	0.10
Macedonian (33)	94	0.86
Polish (411)	1,145	10.51
Portuguese (19)	19	0.17
Russian (116)	362	3.32
Scotch-Irish (24)	91	0.84
Scottish (20)	179	1.64
Serbian (57)	145	1.33
Swedish (0)	50	0.46
Swiss (33)	98	0.90
Turkish (7)	23	0.21
Ukrainian (31)	31	0.28
Welsh (0)	293	2.69
West Indian, ex. Hispanic (27)	102	0.94
Haitian (27)	102	0.94
Yugoslavian (11)	11	0.10

Hispanic Origin	Population	%
Hispanic or Latino (of any race)	1,075	9.67
Central American, ex. Mexican	45	0.40
Costa Rican	3	0.03
Guatemalan	16	0.14
Honduran	16	0.14
Nicaraguan	3	0.03
Panamanian	4	0.04
Salvadoran	3	0.03
Cuban	59	0.53
Dominican Republic	56	0.50
Mexican	152	1.37
Puerto Rican	367	3.30
South American	257	2.31
Argentinean	13	0.12
Bolivian	3	0.03
Chilean	6	0.05
Colombian	81	0.73
Ecuadorian	39	0.35
Peruvian	100	0.90
Uruguayan	11	0.10
Venezuelan	4	0.04
Other Hispanic or Latino	139	1.25

Race*	Population	%
African-American/Black (341)	424	3.81
Not Hispanic (305)	362	3.26
Hispanic (36)	62	0.56
American Indian/Alaska Native (45)	123	1.11
Not Hispanic (33)	104	0.94
Hispanic (12)	19	0.17
Apache (3)	3	0.03
Blackfeet (1)	5	0.04
Cherokee (7)	18	0.16
Chippewa (1)	3	0.03
Delaware (16)	44	0.40
Iroquois (0)	3	0.03
Pueblo (1)	1	0.01
Sioux (1)	1	0.01
South American Ind. (9)	10	0.09
Spanish American Ind. (0)	1	0.01
Asian (517)	577	5.19
Not Hispanic (508)	561	5.05
Hispanic (9)	16	0.14
Chinese, ex. Taiwanese (52)	60	0.54
Filipino (321)	349	3.14
Indian (87)	93	0.84
Japanese (10)	10	0.09
Korean (21)	25	0.22
Pakistani (5)	5	0.04
Sri Lankan (1)	1	0.01
Taiwanese (1)	1	0.01
Thai (6)	11	0.10
Vietnamese (1)	2	0.02
Hawaii Native/Pacific Islander (1)	7	0.06
Not Hispanic (1)	6	0.05
Hispanic (0)	1	0.01
Native Hawaiian (0)	2	0.02
White (9,724)	9,929	89.32
Not Hispanic (9,014)	9,160	82.40
Hispanic (710)	769	6.92

Wantage

Place Type: Township
County: Sussex
Population: 11,358†

Ancestry‡	Population	%
American (316)	316	2.80
Armenian (20)	37	0.33
Austrian (12)	56	0.50
British (10)	10	0.09
Bulgarian (20)	77	0.68
Canadian (0)	27	0.24
Carpatho Rusyn (10)	10	0.09
Czech (72)	195	1.73
Czechoslovakian (0)	13	0.12
Danish (0)	66	0.58
Dutch (520)	1,107	9.80
English (155)	1,155	10.22
European (48)	48	0.42
Finnish (14)	14	0.12
French, ex. Basque (38)	304	2.69
French Canadian (11)	116	1.03
German (589)	3,395	30.04
Greek (6)	20	0.18
Hungarian (26)	288	2.55
Irish (369)	2,794	24.73
Italian (997)	2,867	25.37
Latvian (19)	19	0.17
Lithuanian (48)	164	1.45
Norwegian (21)	127	1.12
Pennsylvania German (0)	14	0.12
Polish (313)	1,063	9.41
Portuguese (0)	12	0.11
Russian (19)	263	2.33
Scotch-Irish (41)	183	1.62
Scottish (10)	293	2.59
Slavic (0)	12	0.11
Slovak (19)	126	1.12
Swedish (0)	138	1.22
Swiss (0)	141	1.25
Ukrainian (11)	25	0.22
Welsh (0)	55	0.49

Hispanic Origin	Population	%
Hispanic or Latino (of any race)	594	5.23
Central American, ex. Mexican	58	0.51
Costa Rican	27	0.24
Guatemalan	17	0.15
Honduran	6	0.05
Panamanian	1	0.01
Salvadoran	7	0.06
Cuban	57	0.50
Dominican Republic	19	0.17
Mexican	39	0.34
Puerto Rican	252	2.22
South American	107	0.94
Argentinean	5	0.04
Chilean	4	0.04
Colombian	32	0.28
Ecuadorian	30	0.26
Peruvian	23	0.20
Venezuelan	13	0.11
Other Hispanic or Latino	62	0.55

Race*	Population	%
African-American/Black (137)	179	1.58
Not Hispanic (126)	166	1.46
Hispanic (11)	13	0.11
American Indian/Alaska Native (13)	71	0.63
Not Hispanic (7)	59	0.52
Hispanic (6)	12	0.11
Apache (0)	1	0.01
Blackfeet (0)	4	0.04
Cherokee (0)	5	0.04
Chippewa (0)	2	0.02
Comanche (1)	1	0.01
Delaware (0)	1	0.01
Iroquois (0)	16	0.14
Mexican American Ind. (3)	3	0.03
Ottawa (1)	1	0.01
South American Ind. (0)	2	0.02
Asian (113)	182	1.60
Not Hispanic (112)	175	1.54
Hispanic (1)	7	0.06
Cambodian (1)	1	0.01

SECTION TWO

*Notes: † The Census 2010 population figure is used to calculate the percentages in the Hispanic Origin and Race categories. Ancestry percentages are based on the 2006-2010 American Community Survey population (not shown); ‡ Numbers in parentheses indicate the number of people reporting a single ancestry; * Numbers in parentheses indicate the number of persons reporting this race alone, not in combination with any other race; Please refer to the Explanation of Data for more information.*

Chinese, ex. Taiwanese (34)	46	0.41
Filipino (25)	41	0.36
Indian (21)	32	0.28
Japanese (1)	9	0.08
Korean (27)	49	0.43
Vietnamese (2)	3	0.03
White (10,816)	10,981	96.68
Not Hispanic (10,368)	10,510	92.53
Hispanic (448)	471	4.15

Warren

Place Type: Township
County: Somerset
Population: 15,311†

Ancestry‡	Population	%
Alsatian (11)	11	0.07
American (920)	920	6.07
Arab (24)	34	0.22
Egyptian (8)	8	0.05
Moroccan (16)	16	0.11
Syrian (0)	10	0.07
Armenian (11)	22	0.15
Austrian (0)	146	0.96
Belgian (9)	19	0.13
British (100)	109	0.72
Canadian (13)	13	0.09
Czech (14)	103	0.68
Czechoslovakian (0)	51	0.34
Danish (30)	93	0.61
Dutch (86)	329	2.17
Eastern European (224)	224	1.48
English (116)	1,014	6.69
European (155)	155	1.02
French, ex. Basque (46)	182	1.20
French Canadian (14)	14	0.09
German (575)	2,363	15.59
Greek (118)	128	0.84
Hungarian (70)	332	2.19
Iranian (38)	54	0.36
Irish (477)	2,355	15.54
Italian (1,572)	3,107	20.50
Lithuanian (15)	71	0.47
Northern European (9)	9	0.06
Norwegian (30)	179	1.18
Pennsylvania German (0)	6	0.04
Polish (414)	1,221	8.06
Portuguese (519)	675	4.45
Romanian (23)	109	0.72
Russian (378)	674	4.45
Scandinavian (36)	47	0.31
Scotch-Irish (28)	85	0.56
Scottish (51)	348	2.30
Slavic (0)	8	0.05
Slovak (61)	181	1.19
Slovene (0)	12	0.08
Swedish (30)	137	0.90
Swiss (19)	52	0.34
Ukrainian (129)	153	1.01
Welsh (0)	40	0.26
West Indian, ex. Hispanic (0)	23	0.15
Barbadian (0)	11	0.07
West Indian (0)	12	0.08

Hispanic Origin	Population	%
Hispanic or Latino (of any race)	820	5.36
Central American, ex. Mexican	100	0.65
Costa Rican	32	0.21
Guatemalan	14	0.09
Honduran	22	0.14
Nicaraguan	5	0.03
Panamanian	2	0.01
Salvadoran	20	0.13
Other Central American	5	0.03
Cuban	146	0.95
Dominican Republic	33	0.22
Mexican	38	0.25
Puerto Rican	98	0.64
South American	220	1.44
Argentinean	21	0.14
Bolivian	6	0.04
Chilean	8	0.05
Colombian	44	0.29
Ecuadorian	63	0.41
Paraguayan	24	0.16
Peruvian	29	0.19
Uruguayan	13	0.08
Venezuelan	5	0.03
Other South American	7	0.05
Other Hispanic or Latino	185	1.21

Race*	Population	%
African-American/Black (233)	265	1.73
Not Hispanic (225)	249	1.63
Hispanic (8)	16	0.10
American Indian/Alaska Native (7)	31	0.20
Not Hispanic (6)	29	0.19
Hispanic (1)	2	0.01
Blackfeet (0)	4	0.03
Cherokee (0)	11	0.07
Cree (4)	4	0.03
Delaware (1)	1	0.01
Iroquois (0)	1	0.01
Mexican American Ind. (1)	1	0.01
Asian (2,307)	2,492	16.28
Not Hispanic (2,304)	2,479	16.19
Hispanic (3)	13	0.08
Bangladeshi (9)	9	0.06
Burmese (5)	5	0.03
Cambodian (1)	1	0.01
Chinese, ex. Taiwanese (890)	977	6.38
Filipino (110)	151	0.99
Indian (835)	881	5.75
Indonesian (1)	9	0.06
Japanese (21)	39	0.25
Korean (182)	198	1.29
Nepalese (4)	4	0.03
Pakistani (43)	44	0.29
Sri Lankan (8)	8	0.05
Taiwanese (116)	129	0.84
Thai (4)	9	0.06
Vietnamese (33)	36	0.24
Hawaii Native/Pacific Islander (15)	19	0.12
Not Hispanic (3)	7	0.05
Hispanic (12)	12	0.08
Guamanian/Chamorro (1)	1	0.01
Native Hawaiian (2)	2	0.01
Samoan (0)	2	0.01
White (12,392)	12,624	82.45
Not Hispanic (11,704)	11,908	77.77
Hispanic (688)	716	4.68

Washington

Place Type: Township
County: Bergen
Population: 9,102†

Ancestry‡	Population	%
Alsatian (0)	14	0.16
American (338)	338	3.75
Arab (266)	271	3.01
Arab (120)	120	1.33
Lebanese (67)	72	0.80
Syrian (31)	31	0.34
Other Arab (48)	48	0.53
Armenian (125)	125	1.39
Assyrian/Chaldean/Syriac (12)	47	0.52
Austrian (37)	170	1.89
Brazilian (0)	6	0.07
British (17)	62	0.69
Canadian (13)	33	0.37
Croatian (30)	30	0.33
Czech (0)	51	0.57
Czechoslovakian (20)	37	0.41
Danish (0)	7	0.08
Dutch (22)	145	1.61
Eastern European (53)	53	0.59
English (107)	432	4.79
European (59)	59	0.65
French, ex. Basque (0)	70	0.78
French Canadian (13)	93	1.03
German (333)	1,641	18.20
Greek (35)	68	0.75
Hungarian (42)	127	1.41
Iranian (0)	9	0.10
Irish (430)	1,833	20.33
Italian (1,319)	2,504	27.77
Latvian (23)	23	0.26
Lithuanian (40)	40	0.44
Norwegian (11)	21	0.23
Polish (148)	613	6.80
Romanian (0)	65	0.72
Russian (109)	352	3.90
Scotch-Irish (24)	34	0.38
Scottish (22)	62	0.69
Slovak (0)	29	0.32
Swedish (0)	113	1.25
Swiss (0)	61	0.68
Turkish (0)	35	0.39
Ukrainian (47)	122	1.35
Yugoslavian (0)	10	0.11

Hispanic Origin	Population	%
Hispanic or Latino (of any race)	495	5.44
Central American, ex. Mexican	17	0.19
Costa Rican	3	0.03
Guatemalan	3	0.03
Honduran	1	0.01
Nicaraguan	1	0.01
Panamanian	2	0.02
Salvadoran	4	0.04
Other Central American	3	0.03
Cuban	110	1.21
Dominican Republic	48	0.53
Mexican	32	0.35
Puerto Rican	104	1.14
South American	126	1.38
Argentinean	10	0.11
Chilean	16	0.18
Colombian	51	0.56
Ecuadorian	26	0.29
Peruvian	11	0.12
Uruguayan	2	0.02
Venezuelan	10	0.11
Other Hispanic or Latino	58	0.64

Race*	Population	%
African-American/Black (98)	131	1.44
Not Hispanic (93)	116	1.27
Hispanic (5)	15	0.16
American Indian/Alaska Native (1)	20	0.22
Not Hispanic (0)	11	0.12
Hispanic (1)	9	0.10
Apache (0)	2	0.02
Cherokee (0)	3	0.03
Comanche (0)	1	0.01
Delaware (0)	3	0.03
South American Ind. (1)	3	0.03
Asian (589)	639	7.02
Not Hispanic (581)	627	6.89
Hispanic (8)	12	0.13
Chinese, ex. Taiwanese (126)	131	1.44
Filipino (67)	78	0.86
Indian (114)	126	1.38
Indonesian (3)	3	0.03
Japanese (48)	54	0.59
Korean (180)	189	2.08
Pakistani (23)	25	0.27
Sri Lankan (3)	3	0.03
Taiwanese (12)	12	0.13
Thai (1)	1	0.01
Vietnamese (4)	6	0.07
Hawaii Native/Pacific Islander (2)	5	0.05
Not Hispanic (1)	3	0.03
Hispanic (1)	2	0.02
Guamanian/Chamorro (1)	1	0.01
Native Hawaiian (0)	1	0.01
White (8,237)	8,344	91.67

*Notes: † The Census 2010 population figure is used to calculate the percentages in the Hispanic Origin and Race categories. Ancestry percentages are based on the 2006-2010 American Community Survey population (not shown); ‡ Numbers in parentheses indicate the number of people reporting a single ancestry; * Numbers in parentheses indicate the number of persons reporting this race alone, not in combination with any other race; Please refer to the Explanation of Data for more information.*

Not Hispanic (7,839)	7,918	86.99
Hispanic (398)	426	4.68

Washington

Place Type: Township
County: Gloucester
Population: 48,559†

Ancestry‡	Population	%
African, Sub-Saharan (128)	137	0.28
African (128)	137	0.28
Albanian (46)	46	0.09
American (758)	758	1.55
Arab (135)	195	0.40
Arab (47)	57	0.12
Lebanese (58)	94	0.19
Palestinian (30)	30	0.06
Syrian (0)	14	0.03
Armenian (8)	34	0.07
Austrian (29)	243	0.50
Brazilian (45)	56	0.11
British (52)	123	0.25
Canadian (34)	44	0.09
Croatian (10)	48	0.10
Czech (9)	108	0.22
Czechoslovakian (34)	96	0.20
Danish (32)	112	0.23
Dutch (84)	570	1.16
Eastern European (74)	74	0.15
English (682)	4,071	8.31
Estonian (12)	12	0.02
European (171)	191	0.39
Finnish (32)	70	0.14
French, ex. Basque (63)	794	1.62
French Canadian (22)	82	0.17
German (1,857)	10,188	20.79
German Russian (0)	10	0.02
Greek (228)	575	1.17
Guyanese (12)	12	0.02
Hungarian (121)	433	0.88
Iranian (63)	70	0.14
Irish (3,878)	14,730	30.05
Italian (8,819)	17,036	34.76
Latvian (19)	58	0.12
Lithuanian (78)	359	0.73
Northern European (0)	25	0.05
Norwegian (18)	120	0.24
Pennsylvania German (55)	73	0.15
Polish (949)	3,502	7.14
Portuguese (39)	84	0.17
Romanian (0)	32	0.07
Russian (348)	818	1.67
Scandinavian (9)	35	0.07
Scotch-Irish (161)	519	1.06
Scottish (109)	431	0.88
Serbian (14)	30	0.06
Slavic (0)	14	0.03
Slovak (20)	109	0.22
Swedish (39)	294	0.60
Swiss (11)	39	0.08
Turkish (44)	44	0.09
Ukrainian (55)	252	0.51
Welsh (28)	285	0.58
West Indian, ex. Hispanic (114)	238	0.49
Haitian (35)	79	0.16
Jamaican (63)	95	0.19
U.S. Virgin Islander (0)	9	0.02
West Indian (16)	55	0.11
Yugoslavian (41)	83	0.17

Hispanic Origin	Population	%
Hispanic or Latino (of any race)	1,774	3.65
Central American, ex. Mexican	103	0.21
Costa Rican	6	0.01
Guatemalan	22	0.05
Honduran	16	0.03
Nicaraguan	20	0.04
Panamanian	11	0.02
Salvadoran	25	0.05
Other Central American	3	0.01
Cuban	94	0.19
Dominican Republic	59	0.12
Mexican	217	0.45
Puerto Rican	972	2.00
South American	183	0.38
Argentinean	43	0.09
Bolivian	6	0.01
Chilean	11	0.02
Colombian	46	0.09
Ecuadorian	24	0.05
Paraguayan	1	<0.01
Peruvian	27	0.06
Uruguayan	8	0.02
Venezuelan	13	0.03
Other South American	4	0.01
Other Hispanic or Latino	146	0.30

Race*	Population	%
African-American/Black (2,825)	3,199	6.59
Not Hispanic (2,724)	3,024	6.23
Hispanic (101)	175	0.36
American Indian/Alaska Native (52)	240	0.49
Not Hispanic (39)	190	0.39
Hispanic (13)	50	0.10
Alaska Athabascan *(Ala. Nat.)* (0)	6	0.01
Aleut *(Alaska Native)* (0)	1	<0.01
Blackfeet (2)	14	0.03
Central American Ind. (0)	1	<0.01
Cherokee (16)	63	0.13
Chickasaw (0)	1	<0.01
Chippewa (0)	3	0.01
Choctaw (1)	3	0.01
Delaware (5)	25	0.05
Iroquois (0)	7	0.01
Lumbee (1)	1	<0.01
Mexican American Ind. (3)	3	0.01
Seminole (0)	3	0.01
Sioux (0)	2	<0.01
South American Ind. (0)	4	0.01
Asian (1,836)	2,152	4.43
Not Hispanic (1,827)	2,105	4.33
Hispanic (9)	47	0.10
Bangladeshi (9)	9	0.02
Cambodian (28)	35	0.07
Chinese, ex. Taiwanese (251)	318	0.65
Filipino (690)	804	1.66
Indian (449)	504	1.04
Indonesian (0)	4	0.01
Japanese (19)	60	0.12
Korean (127)	157	0.32
Laotian (10)	13	0.03
Malaysian (4)	5	0.01
Nepalese (2)	2	<0.01
Pakistani (22)	24	0.05
Sri Lankan (5)	5	0.01
Taiwanese (19)	19	0.04
Thai (21)	24	0.05
Vietnamese (94)	150	0.31
Hawaii Native/Pacific Islander (9)	29	0.06
Not Hispanic (8)	26	0.05
Hispanic (1)	3	0.01
Guamanian/Chamorro (5)	8	0.02
Native Hawaiian (2)	10	0.02
Samoan (0)	3	0.01
White (42,588)	43,292	89.15
Not Hispanic (41,506)	42,067	86.63
Hispanic (1,082)	1,225	2.52

Washington

Place Type: Township
County: Morris
Population: 18,533†

Ancestry‡	Population	%
American (699)	699	3.79
Arab (35)	54	0.29
Lebanese (35)	47	0.26
Syrian (0)	7	0.04
Armenian (0)	30	0.16
Assyrian/Chaldean/Syriac (0)	10	0.05
Austrian (6)	145	0.79
Belgian (18)	82	0.45
Brazilian (5)	11	0.06
British (76)	115	0.62
Canadian (0)	90	0.49
Croatian (9)	19	0.10
Czech (62)	272	1.48
Czechoslovakian (27)	36	0.20
Danish (0)	71	0.39
Dutch (131)	554	3.01
English (386)	2,312	12.55
European (229)	229	1.24
Finnish (15)	23	0.12
French, ex. Basque (141)	572	3.10
French Canadian (40)	129	0.70
German (911)	4,371	23.73
Greek (97)	326	1.77
Guyanese (0)	6	0.03
Hungarian (21)	264	1.43
Irish (1,250)	4,860	26.38
Israeli (33)	33	0.18
Italian (2,030)	4,981	27.04
Lithuanian (28)	107	0.58
Luxemburger (0)	12	0.07
Northern European (12)	12	0.07
Norwegian (38)	177	0.96
Pennsylvania German (31)	44	0.24
Polish (479)	1,458	7.91
Portuguese (51)	94	0.51
Romanian (0)	29	0.16
Russian (140)	383	2.08
Scandinavian (11)	25	0.14
Scotch-Irish (82)	254	1.38
Scottish (89)	407	2.21
Slavic (17)	61	0.33
Slovak (39)	106	0.58
Swedish (82)	175	0.95
Swiss (10)	63	0.34
Ukrainian (37)	201	1.09
Welsh (32)	152	0.83
West Indian, ex. Hispanic (91)	91	0.49
Haitian (80)	80	0.43
Trinidadian/Tobagonian (11)	11	0.06
Yugoslavian (11)	34	0.18

Hispanic Origin	Population	%
Hispanic or Latino (of any race)	847	4.57
Central American, ex. Mexican	97	0.52
Costa Rican	5	0.03
Guatemalan	53	0.29
Honduran	17	0.09
Panamanian	2	0.01
Salvadoran	20	0.11
Cuban	116	0.63
Dominican Republic	64	0.35
Mexican	104	0.56
Puerto Rican	185	1.00
South American	178	0.96
Argentinean	31	0.17
Bolivian	2	0.01
Chilean	11	0.06
Colombian	48	0.26
Ecuadorian	26	0.14
Paraguayan	23	0.12
Peruvian	22	0.12
Uruguayan	4	0.02
Venezuelan	10	0.05
Other South American	1	0.01
Other Hispanic or Latino	103	0.56

Race*	Population	%
African-American/Black (257)	366	1.97
Not Hispanic (239)	328	1.77
Hispanic (18)	38	0.21
American Indian/Alaska Native (11)	54	0.29
Not Hispanic (4)	44	0.24
Hispanic (7)	10	0.05
Blackfeet (0)	1	0.01

SECTION TWO

*Notes: † The Census 2010 population figure is used to calculate the percentages in the Hispanic Origin and Race categories. Ancestry percentages are based on the 2006-2010 American Community Survey population (not shown); ‡ Numbers in parentheses indicate the number of people reporting a single ancestry; * Numbers in parentheses indicate the number of persons reporting this race alone, not in combination with any other race; Please refer to the Explanation of Data for more information.*

Cherokee (1)	13	0.07
Delaware (0)	5	0.03
Iroquois (0)	2	0.01
Mexican American Ind. (5)	5	0.03
Pueblo (1)	5	0.03
Seminole (0)	1	0.01
Sioux (0)	1	0.01
Spanish American Ind. (1)	1	0.01
Asian (612)	728	3.93
Not Hispanic (607)	717	3.87
Hispanic (5)	11	0.06
Bangladeshi (6)	6	0.03
Cambodian (1)	1	0.01
Chinese, ex. Taiwanese (159)	194	1.05
Filipino (84)	114	0.62
Indian (227)	246	1.33
Japanese (8)	14	0.08
Korean (64)	77	0.42
Malaysian (1)	1	0.01
Pakistani (21)	21	0.11
Sri Lankan (3)	4	0.02
Taiwanese (13)	13	0.07
Thai (3)	8	0.04
Vietnamese (14)	19	0.10
Hawaii Native/Pacific Islander (2)	6	0.03
Not Hispanic (2)	6	0.03
Guamanian/Chamorro (0)	1	0.01
Samoan (2)	2	0.01
White (17,247)	17,509	94.47
Not Hispanic (16,590)	16,802	90.66
Hispanic (657)	707	3.81

Waterford

Place Type: Township
County: Camden
Population: 10,649†

Ancestry‡	Population	%
African, Sub-Saharan (31)	31	0.29
African (31)	31	0.29
American (214)	214	2.01
Arab (0)	10	0.09
Lebanese (0)	10	0.09
Austrian (13)	52	0.49
Belgian (0)	13	0.12
Brazilian (0)	14	0.13
British (0)	31	0.29
Canadian (14)	67	0.63
Danish (0)	21	0.20
Dutch (0)	232	2.17
Eastern European (11)	11	0.10
English (146)	1,163	10.90
European (24)	24	0.22
French, ex. Basque (45)	159	1.49
French Canadian (11)	25	0.23
German (548)	3,440	32.24
Hungarian (14)	70	0.66
Irish (551)	3,587	33.62
Italian (1,215)	2,896	27.14
Lithuanian (30)	166	1.56
Norwegian (11)	82	0.77
Polish (349)	1,181	11.07
Russian (34)	115	1.08
Scotch-Irish (33)	157	1.47
Scottish (49)	161	1.51
Serbian (10)	19	0.18
Slovak (0)	61	0.57
Swedish (0)	46	0.43
Swiss (10)	23	0.22
Ukrainian (29)	50	0.47
Welsh (29)	61	0.57
West Indian, ex. Hispanic (47)	47	0.44
West Indian (47)	47	0.44
Yugoslavian (9)	9	0.08

Hispanic Origin	Population	%
Hispanic or Latino (of any race)	467	4.39
Central American, ex. Mexican	20	0.19
Costa Rican	8	0.08
Honduran	1	0.01
Nicaraguan	4	0.04
Panamanian	6	0.06
Salvadoran	1	0.01
Cuban	25	0.23
Dominican Republic	9	0.08
Mexican	120	1.13
Puerto Rican	221	2.08
South American	34	0.32
Argentinean	6	0.06
Bolivian	1	0.01
Colombian	8	0.08
Ecuadorian	1	0.01
Peruvian	12	0.11
Uruguayan	1	0.01
Venezuelan	5	0.05
Other Hispanic or Latino	38	0.36

Race*	Population	%
African-American/Black (514)	598	5.62
Not Hispanic (501)	574	5.39
Hispanic (13)	24	0.23
American Indian/Alaska Native (11)	49	0.46
Not Hispanic (8)	43	0.40
Hispanic (3)	6	0.06
Blackfeet (0)	2	0.02
Canadian/French Am. Ind. (1)	1	0.01
Cherokee (1)	7	0.07
Seminole (0)	4	0.04
South American Ind. (0)	1	0.01
Tlingit-Haida *(Alaska Native)* (1)	1	0.01
Asian (124)	169	1.59
Not Hispanic (124)	168	1.58
Hispanic (0)	1	0.01
Chinese, ex. Taiwanese (12)	18	0.17
Filipino (22)	43	0.40
Indian (53)	58	0.54
Indonesian (1)	5	0.05
Japanese (3)	6	0.06
Korean (18)	22	0.21
Nepalese (1)	1	0.01
Taiwanese (2)	2	0.02
Vietnamese (3)	5	0.05
Hawaii Native/Pacific Islander (3)	10	0.09
Not Hispanic (3)	9	0.08
Hispanic (0)	1	0.01
Fijian (1)	1	0.01
Native Hawaiian (2)	4	0.04
White (9,647)	9,809	92.11
Not Hispanic (9,398)	9,521	89.41
Hispanic (249)	288	2.70

Wayne

Place Type: Township
County: Passaic
Population: 54,717†

Ancestry‡	Population	%
Afghan (86)	86	0.16
African, Sub-Saharan (41)	63	0.12
African (22)	38	0.07
Nigerian (19)	19	0.03
South African (0)	6	0.01
Albanian (393)	417	0.77
American (1,523)	1,523	2.80
Arab (1,829)	2,206	4.06
Arab (282)	282	0.52
Egyptian (347)	351	0.65
Jordanian (69)	88	0.16
Lebanese (151)	169	0.31
Moroccan (20)	36	0.07
Palestinian (376)	476	0.88
Syrian (545)	715	1.32
Other Arab (39)	89	0.16
Armenian (152)	152	0.28
Assyrian/Chaldean/Syriac (11)	11	0.02
Australian (11)	24	0.04
Austrian (42)	343	0.63
Belgian (0)	105	0.19
Brazilian (42)	42	0.08
British (104)	197	0.36
Canadian (48)	99	0.18
Carpatho Rusyn (31)	31	0.06
Croatian (57)	122	0.22
Cypriot (40)	40	0.07
Czech (121)	324	0.60
Czechoslovakian (11)	53	0.10
Danish (14)	95	0.17
Dutch (546)	2,235	4.11
Eastern European (452)	452	0.83
English (461)	2,779	5.11
European (285)	318	0.59
Finnish (15)	15	0.03
French, ex. Basque (261)	992	1.83
French Canadian (77)	271	0.50
German (1,396)	6,445	11.86
Greek (247)	388	0.71
Guyanese (8)	24	0.04
Hungarian (175)	670	1.23
Iranian (196)	208	0.38
Irish (2,593)	8,874	16.33
Israeli (54)	54	0.10
Italian (8,208)	14,760	27.16
Latvian (0)	10	0.02
Lithuanian (47)	192	0.35
Macedonian (461)	461	0.85
New Zealander (0)	53	0.10
Northern European (8)	20	0.04
Norwegian (311)	639	1.18
Pennsylvania German (0)	9	0.02
Polish (1,700)	4,248	7.82
Portuguese (134)	236	0.43
Romanian (51)	110	0.20
Russian (1,065)	2,027	3.73
Scandinavian (17)	74	0.14
Scotch-Irish (159)	529	0.97
Scottish (62)	754	1.39
Serbian (35)	35	0.06
Slavic (0)	38	0.07
Slovak (51)	274	0.50
Slovene (9)	9	0.02
Swedish (51)	432	0.80
Swiss (9)	158	0.29
Turkish (474)	569	1.05
Ukrainian (130)	532	0.98
Welsh (18)	144	0.27
West Indian, ex. Hispanic (55)	106	0.20
Haitian (0)	12	0.02
Jamaican (55)	94	0.17
Yugoslavian (48)	84	0.15

Hispanic Origin	Population	%
Hispanic or Latino (of any race)	4,335	7.92
Central American, ex. Mexican	233	0.43
Costa Rican	77	0.14
Guatemalan	44	0.08
Honduran	26	0.05
Nicaraguan	17	0.03
Panamanian	16	0.03
Salvadoran	52	0.10
Other Central American	1	<0.01
Cuban	440	0.80
Dominican Republic	360	0.66
Mexican	256	0.47
Puerto Rican	1,270	2.32
South American	1,299	2.37
Argentinean	131	0.24
Bolivian	8	0.01
Chilean	31	0.06
Colombian	444	0.81
Ecuadorian	182	0.33
Paraguayan	3	0.01
Peruvian	423	0.77
Uruguayan	23	0.04
Venezuelan	41	0.07
Other South American	13	0.02
Other Hispanic or Latino	477	0.87

*Notes: † The Census 2010 population figure is used to calculate the percentages in the Hispanic Origin and Race categories. Ancestry percentages are based on the 2006-2010 American Community Survey population (not shown); ‡ Numbers in parentheses indicate the number of people reporting a single ancestry; * Numbers in parentheses indicate the number of persons reporting this race alone, not in combination with any other race; Please refer to the Explanation of Data for more information.*

Race*	Population	%
African-American/Black (1,247)	1,418	2.59
Not Hispanic (1,124)	1,257	2.30
Hispanic (123)	161	0.29
American Indian/Alaska Native (51)	147	0.27
Not Hispanic (34)	115	0.21
Hispanic (17)	32	0.06
Apache (0)	1	<0.01
Blackfeet (1)	1	<0.01
Cherokee (5)	32	0.06
Chickasaw (0)	2	<0.01
Chippewa (0)	8	0.01
Choctaw (0)	4	0.01
Crow (0)	1	<0.01
Delaware (3)	6	0.01
Iroquois (4)	6	0.01
Lumbee (0)	1	<0.01
Mexican American Ind. (0)	1	<0.01
Seminole (0)	1	<0.01
South American Ind. (5)	14	0.03
Asian (4,478)	4,941	9.03
Not Hispanic (4,441)	4,879	8.92
Hispanic (37)	62	0.11
Bangladeshi (60)	60	0.11
Burmese (5)	5	0.01
Cambodian (1)	1	<0.01
Chinese, ex. Taiwanese (721)	796	1.45
Filipino (555)	642	1.17
Hmong (5)	5	0.01
Indian (1,634)	1,702	3.11
Indonesian (2)	9	0.02
Japanese (76)	114	0.21
Korean (1,106)	1,158	2.12
Malaysian (1)	5	0.01
Pakistani (65)	73	0.13
Sri Lankan (13)	16	0.03
Taiwanese (50)	58	0.11
Thai (12)	15	0.03
Vietnamese (73)	81	0.15
Hawaii Native/Pacific Islander (11)	46	0.08
Not Hispanic (9)	36	0.07
Hispanic (2)	10	0.02
Guamanian/Chamorro (1)	1	<0.01
Native Hawaiian (2)	5	0.01
Samoan (2)	3	0.01
White (47,097)	47,837	87.43
Not Hispanic (44,030)	44,592	81.50
Hispanic (3,067)	3,245	5.93

Weehawken

Place Type: Township
County: Hudson
Population: 12,554†

Ancestry‡	Population	%
African, Sub-Saharan (17)	17	0.13
African (17)	17	0.13
Albanian (0)	6	0.05
American (478)	478	3.79
Arab (42)	42	0.33
Iraqi (9)	9	0.07
Lebanese (24)	24	0.19
Palestinian (9)	9	0.07
Armenian (75)	141	1.12
Australian (0)	54	0.43
Austrian (7)	73	0.58
Brazilian (156)	156	1.24
British (36)	82	0.65
Canadian (0)	84	0.67
Croatian (14)	14	0.11
Czech (0)	12	0.10
Czechoslovakian (0)	39	0.31
Danish (0)	9	0.07
Dutch (0)	16	0.13
English (84)	318	2.52
Estonian (6)	6	0.05
European (72)	72	0.57
French, ex. Basque (48)	176	1.40
French Canadian (11)	11	0.09
German (129)	716	5.68
Greek (46)	70	0.56
Hungarian (28)	37	0.29
Iranian (5)	5	0.04
Irish (444)	1,261	10.00
Italian (985)	1,811	14.37
Lithuanian (0)	25	0.20
New Zealander (8)	8	0.06
Northern European (11)	11	0.09
Norwegian (23)	58	0.46
Polish (91)	215	1.71
Portuguese (0)	4	0.03
Romanian (14)	14	0.11
Russian (110)	190	1.51
Scandinavian (0)	60	0.48
Scotch-Irish (51)	71	0.56
Scottish (27)	80	0.63
Serbian (7)	7	0.06
Slovak (6)	13	0.10
Swedish (7)	26	0.21
Swiss (67)	81	0.64
Turkish (64)	70	0.56
Ukrainian (38)	90	0.71
Welsh (0)	13	0.10
West Indian, ex. Hispanic (119)	172	1.36
Barbadian (14)	14	0.11
Haitian (29)	29	0.23
Jamaican (33)	86	0.68
Trinidadian/Tobagonian (43)	43	0.34
Yugoslavian (23)	47	0.37

Hispanic Origin	Population	%
Hispanic or Latino (of any race)	5,055	40.27
Central American, ex. Mexican	318	2.53
Costa Rican	15	0.12
Guatemalan	29	0.23
Honduran	99	0.79
Nicaraguan	17	0.14
Panamanian	6	0.05
Salvadoran	150	1.19
Other Central American	2	0.02
Cuban	980	7.81
Dominican Republic	950	7.57
Mexican	269	2.14
Puerto Rican	815	6.49
South American	1,360	10.83
Argentinean	57	0.45
Bolivian	13	0.10
Chilean	72	0.57
Colombian	493	3.93
Ecuadorian	410	3.27
Paraguayan	5	0.04
Peruvian	232	1.85
Uruguayan	33	0.26
Venezuelan	32	0.25
Other South American	13	0.10
Other Hispanic or Latino	363	2.89

Race*	Population	%
African-American/Black (606)	754	6.01
Not Hispanic (412)	461	3.67
Hispanic (194)	293	2.33
American Indian/Alaska Native (61)	120	0.96
Not Hispanic (14)	38	0.30
Hispanic (47)	82	0.65
Apache (0)	1	0.01
Central American Ind. (1)	3	0.02
Cherokee (1)	4	0.03
Choctaw (1)	1	0.01
Cree (1)	1	0.01
Delaware (0)	2	0.02
Iroquois (0)	1	0.01
Lumbee (2)	4	0.03
Mexican American Ind. (1)	11	0.09
Sioux (1)	2	0.02
South American Ind. (10)	21	0.17
Spanish American Ind. (1)	5	0.04
Asian (1,024)	1,144	9.11
Not Hispanic (1,010)	1,113	8.87
Hispanic (14)	31	0.25
Bangladeshi (4)	4	0.03
Cambodian (1)	1	0.01
Chinese, ex. Taiwanese (205)	239	1.90
Filipino (100)	123	0.98
Indian (387)	402	3.20
Indonesian (4)	7	0.06
Japanese (58)	79	0.63
Korean (121)	140	1.12
Laotian (1)	1	0.01
Malaysian (5)	5	0.04
Pakistani (44)	52	0.41
Sri Lankan (3)	3	0.02
Taiwanese (13)	24	0.19
Thai (7)	9	0.07
Vietnamese (16)	19	0.15
Hawaii Native/Pacific Islander (1)	12	0.10
Not Hispanic (1)	11	0.09
Hispanic (0)	1	0.01
Guamanian/Chamorro (0)	1	0.01
Native Hawaiian (1)	1	0.01
White (9,020)	9,435	75.16
Not Hispanic (5,850)	5,999	47.79
Hispanic (3,170)	3,436	27.37

West Caldwell

Place Type: Township
County: Essex
Population: 10,759†

Ancestry‡	Population	%
African, Sub-Saharan (20)	20	0.19
Kenyan (20)	20	0.19
Albanian (25)	25	0.23
American (537)	537	4.99
Arab (10)	26	0.24
Syrian (10)	26	0.24
Austrian (13)	75	0.70
Brazilian (23)	23	0.21
British (10)	42	0.39
Czech (0)	22	0.20
Czechoslovakian (9)	21	0.19
Danish (12)	52	0.48
Dutch (25)	136	1.26
English (172)	1,168	10.84
European (62)	62	0.58
Finnish (0)	11	0.10
French, ex. Basque (0)	90	0.84
French Canadian (0)	37	0.34
German (294)	1,735	16.11
Greek (58)	114	1.06
Hungarian (57)	215	2.00
Irish (637)	2,881	26.75
Italian (1,880)	3,819	35.45
Latvian (10)	10	0.09
Lithuanian (40)	93	0.86
Northern European (0)	10	0.09
Norwegian (0)	38	0.35
Polish (196)	652	6.05
Portuguese (65)	97	0.90
Romanian (25)	45	0.42
Russian (183)	452	4.20
Scandinavian (15)	31	0.29
Scotch-Irish (48)	213	1.98
Scottish (48)	213	1.98
Slovak (11)	46	0.43
Swedish (10)	97	0.90
Swiss (0)	65	0.60
Turkish (43)	43	0.40
Ukrainian (170)	329	3.05
Welsh (0)	34	0.32

Hispanic Origin	Population	%
Hispanic or Latino (of any race)	523	4.86
Central American, ex. Mexican	47	0.44
Costa Rican	10	0.09
Guatemalan	11	0.10
Honduran	7	0.07
Nicaraguan	1	0.01

SECTION TWO

*Notes: † The Census 2010 population figure is used to calculate the percentages in the Hispanic Origin and Race categories. Ancestry percentages are based on the 2006-2010 American Community Survey population (not shown); ‡ Numbers in parentheses indicate the number of people reporting a single ancestry; * Numbers in parentheses indicate the number of persons reporting this race alone, not in combination with any other race; Please refer to the Explanation of Data for more information.*

Salvadoran	14	0.13
Other Central American	4	0.04
Cuban	97	0.90
Dominican Republic	28	0.26
Mexican	33	0.31
Puerto Rican	146	1.36
South American	121	1.12
Argentinean	20	0.19
Bolivian	1	0.01
Chilean	12	0.11
Colombian	41	0.38
Ecuadorian	18	0.17
Paraguayan	2	0.02
Peruvian	14	0.13
Uruguayan	7	0.07
Venezuelan	6	0.06
Other Hispanic or Latino	51	0.47

Race*	Population	%
African-American/Black (136)	164	1.52
Not Hispanic (122)	149	1.38
Hispanic (14)	15	0.14
American Indian/Alaska Native (5)	15	0.14
Not Hispanic (5)	12	0.11
Hispanic (0)	3	0.03
Blackfeet (1)	2	0.02
Cherokee (0)	4	0.04
Iroquois (0)	1	0.01
Potawatomi (0)	1	0.01
Sioux (3)	3	0.03
Spanish American Ind. (0)	1	0.01
Asian (421)	479	4.45
Not Hispanic (418)	474	4.41
Hispanic (3)	5	0.05
Chinese, ex. Taiwanese (146)	151	1.40
Filipino (81)	99	0.92
Indian (122)	134	1.25
Japanese (8)	14	0.13
Korean (31)	35	0.33
Pakistani (1)	2	0.02
Taiwanese (15)	15	0.14
Thai (2)	2	0.02
Vietnamese (6)	7	0.07
Hawaii Native/Pacific Islander (2)	7	0.07
Not Hispanic (2)	7	0.07
Guamanian/Chamorro (1)	3	0.03
Native Hawaiian (1)	1	0.01
Samoan (0)	3	0.03
White (9,996)	10,105	93.92
Not Hispanic (9,574)	9,670	89.88
Hispanic (422)	435	4.04

West Deptford

Place Type: Township
County: Gloucester
Population: 21,677†

Ancestry‡	Population	%
African, Sub-Saharan (33)	57	0.27
African (19)	34	0.16
Ghanaian (14)	23	0.11
American (989)	989	4.61
Arab (52)	95	0.44
Arab (31)	31	0.14
Egyptian (21)	21	0.10
Lebanese (0)	43	0.20
Austrian (0)	44	0.21
Belgian (11)	57	0.27
Brazilian (0)	9	0.04
British (88)	130	0.61
Czech (30)	64	0.30
Danish (14)	52	0.24
Dutch (75)	307	1.43
Eastern European (50)	50	0.23
English (420)	2,139	9.97
European (111)	118	0.55
French, ex. Basque (104)	628	2.93
French Canadian (16)	51	0.24
German (936)	4,823	22.49
Greek (60)	87	0.41
Hungarian (12)	118	0.55
Iranian (0)	26	0.12
Irish (1,762)	6,726	31.36
Italian (2,378)	5,340	24.90
Latvian (7)	7	0.03
Lithuanian (48)	242	1.13
Luxemburger (0)	11	0.05
Norwegian (107)	154	0.72
Pennsylvania German (0)	39	0.18
Polish (337)	1,477	6.89
Portuguese (38)	38	0.18
Romanian (0)	12	0.06
Russian (58)	186	0.87
Scandinavian (13)	24	0.11
Scotch-Irish (243)	470	2.19
Scottish (83)	436	2.03
Slovak (0)	23	0.11
Swedish (25)	353	1.65
Swiss (12)	26	0.12
Ukrainian (9)	21	0.10
Welsh (69)	329	1.53
West Indian, ex. Hispanic (42)	344	1.60
British West Indian (0)	151	0.70
Trinidadian/Tobagonian (42)	193	0.90
Yugoslavian (13)	24	0.11

Hispanic Origin	Population	%
Hispanic or Latino (of any race)	731	3.37
Central American, ex. Mexican	47	0.22
Costa Rican	2	0.01
Guatemalan	14	0.06
Honduran	5	0.02
Nicaraguan	9	0.04
Panamanian	3	0.01
Salvadoran	14	0.06
Cuban	16	0.07
Dominican Republic	11	0.05
Mexican	88	0.41
Puerto Rican	419	1.93
South American	79	0.36
Argentinean	20	0.09
Chilean	2	0.01
Colombian	21	0.10
Ecuadorian	20	0.09
Peruvian	4	0.02
Uruguayan	6	0.03
Venezuelan	6	0.03
Other Hispanic or Latino	71	0.33

Race*	Population	%
African-American/Black (1,414)	1,599	7.38
Not Hispanic (1,356)	1,501	6.92
Hispanic (58)	98	0.45
American Indian/Alaska Native (25)	111	0.51
Not Hispanic (22)	97	0.45
Hispanic (3)	14	0.06
Blackfeet (0)	5	0.02
Cherokee (5)	31	0.14
Chippewa (0)	1	<0.01
Delaware (0)	7	0.03
Iroquois (3)	4	0.02
Lumbee (2)	5	0.02
Navajo (0)	1	<0.01
Sioux (2)	4	0.02
Asian (415)	493	2.27
Not Hispanic (410)	485	2.24
Hispanic (5)	8	0.04
Cambodian (14)	16	0.07
Chinese, ex. Taiwanese (72)	81	0.37
Filipino (117)	141	0.65
Indian (117)	128	0.59
Indonesian (1)	4	0.02
Japanese (2)	19	0.09
Korean (38)	53	0.24
Nepalese (2)	2	0.01
Pakistani (4)	5	0.02
Taiwanese (1)	1	<0.01
Thai (3)	4	0.02
Vietnamese (25)	26	0.12
Hawaii Native/Pacific Islander (3)	25	0.12
Not Hispanic (3)	22	0.10
Hispanic (0)	3	0.01
Native Hawaiian (3)	16	0.07
Samoan (0)	1	<0.01
White (19,283)	19,581	90.33
Not Hispanic (18,867)	19,091	88.07
Hispanic (416)	490	2.26

West Freehold

Place Type: CDP
County: Monmouth
Population: 13,613†

Ancestry‡	Population	%
African, Sub-Saharan (24)	24	0.17
South African (24)	24	0.17
American (1,689)	1,689	12.14
Arab (100)	115	0.83
Egyptian (16)	16	0.11
Lebanese (16)	16	0.11
Palestinian (16)	31	0.22
Syrian (52)	52	0.37
Austrian (6)	216	1.55
Belgian (0)	15	0.11
Brazilian (0)	9	0.06
British (51)	78	0.56
Croatian (18)	36	0.26
Czech (0)	79	0.57
Czechoslovakian (26)	26	0.19
Danish (0)	29	0.21
Dutch (31)	98	0.70
Eastern European (231)	282	2.03
English (92)	580	4.17
European (163)	163	1.17
French, ex. Basque (10)	143	1.03
French Canadian (0)	72	0.52
German (307)	1,545	11.10
Greek (89)	161	1.16
Hungarian (59)	325	2.34
Irish (1,039)	3,264	23.45
Israeli (102)	102	0.73
Italian (1,947)	4,467	32.10
Latvian (9)	9	0.06
Lithuanian (10)	76	0.55
Norwegian (23)	143	1.03
Polish (338)	819	5.88
Portuguese (67)	79	0.57
Romanian (32)	48	0.34
Russian (246)	438	3.15
Scotch-Irish (30)	126	0.91
Scottish (16)	98	0.70
Slavic (0)	13	0.09
Slovak (14)	40	0.29
Swedish (0)	28	0.20
Swiss (0)	13	0.09
Turkish (61)	84	0.60
Ukrainian (22)	54	0.39
Welsh (0)	36	0.26
West Indian, ex. Hispanic (72)	77	0.55
Jamaican (54)	59	0.42
Trinidadian/Tobagonian (18)	18	0.13

Hispanic Origin	Population	%
Hispanic or Latino (of any race)	1,107	8.13
Central American, ex. Mexican	42	0.31
Costa Rican	3	0.02
Guatemalan	20	0.15
Honduran	1	0.01
Nicaraguan	1	0.01
Panamanian	3	0.02
Salvadoran	14	0.10
Cuban	73	0.54
Dominican Republic	50	0.37
Mexican	347	2.55
Puerto Rican	349	2.56
South American	154	1.13
Argentinean	17	0.12
Chilean	4	0.03

*Notes: † The Census 2010 population figure is used to calculate the percentages in the Hispanic Origin and Race categories. Ancestry percentages are based on the 2006-2010 American Community Survey population (not shown); ‡ Numbers in parentheses indicate the number of people reporting a single ancestry; * Numbers in parentheses indicate the number of persons reporting this race alone, not in combination with any other race; Please refer to the Explanation of Data for more information.*

Colombian	45	0.33
Ecuadorian	17	0.12
Paraguayan	1	0.01
Peruvian	58	0.43
Uruguayan	6	0.04
Venezuelan	6	0.04
Other Hispanic or Latino	92	0.68

Race*	Population	%
African-American/Black (431)	502	3.69
Not Hispanic (409)	454	3.34
Hispanic (22)	48	0.35
American Indian/Alaska Native (30)	61	0.45
Not Hispanic (13)	30	0.22
Hispanic (17)	31	0.23
Canadian/French Am. Ind. (1)	1	0.01
Cherokee (1)	2	0.01
Chippewa (0)	1	0.01
Iroquois (0)	2	0.01
Mexican American Ind. (11)	11	0.08
Sioux (3)	3	0.02
South American Ind. (3)	4	0.03
Asian (842)	958	7.04
Not Hispanic (836)	946	6.95
Hispanic (6)	12	0.09
Bangladeshi (1)	1	0.01
Burmese (0)	3	0.02
Cambodian (0)	1	0.01
Chinese, ex. Taiwanese (247)	294	2.16
Filipino (193)	249	1.83
Indian (261)	277	2.03
Indonesian (0)	2	0.01
Japanese (5)	13	0.10
Korean (48)	59	0.43
Laotian (1)	2	0.01
Malaysian (4)	6	0.04
Nepalese (0)	1	0.01
Pakistani (26)	30	0.22
Sri Lankan (1)	1	0.01
Taiwanese (11)	11	0.08
Thai (3)	7	0.05
Vietnamese (17)	21	0.15
Hawaii Native/Pacific Islander (1)	17	0.12
Not Hispanic (1)	12	0.09
Hispanic (0)	5	0.04
Native Hawaiian (1)	1	0.01
White (11,851)	12,047	88.50
Not Hispanic (11,043)	11,196	82.24
Hispanic (808)	851	6.25

West Long Branch

Place Type: Borough
County: Monmouth
Population: 8,097†

Ancestry‡	Population	%
American (392)	392	4.83
Arab (339)	540	6.65
Egyptian (94)	94	1.16
Lebanese (0)	19	0.23
Syrian (245)	427	5.26
Austrian (16)	47	0.58
Brazilian (176)	176	2.17
British (0)	30	0.37
Czech (9)	50	0.62
Dutch (0)	175	2.16
English (38)	426	5.25
European (42)	42	0.52
Finnish (0)	11	0.14
French, ex. Basque (13)	216	2.66
German (382)	1,573	19.38
Greek (66)	221	2.72
Hungarian (43)	218	2.69
Irish (406)	2,060	25.39
Italian (1,041)	2,077	25.59
Lithuanian (0)	63	0.78
Maltese (11)	11	0.14
Northern European (0)	17	0.21
Norwegian (48)	72	0.89
Polish (197)	744	9.17
Portuguese (116)	146	1.80
Russian (76)	242	2.98
Scotch-Irish (83)	134	1.65
Scottish (13)	62	0.76
Slavic (0)	15	0.18
Slovak (8)	70	0.86
Swedish (10)	87	1.07
Turkish (11)	11	0.14
Ukrainian (16)	106	1.31
Welsh (0)	47	0.58
West Indian, ex. Hispanic (15)	37	0.46
Belizean (0)	11	0.14
Jamaican (15)	26	0.32

Hispanic Origin	Population	%
Hispanic or Latino (of any race)	407	5.03
Central American, ex. Mexican	33	0.41
Costa Rican	3	0.04
Guatemalan	6	0.07
Honduran	6	0.07
Nicaraguan	1	0.01
Salvadoran	17	0.21
Cuban	39	0.48
Dominican Republic	15	0.19
Mexican	64	0.79
Puerto Rican	110	1.36
South American	81	1.00
Argentinean	5	0.06
Bolivian	11	0.14
Chilean	7	0.09
Colombian	29	0.36
Ecuadorian	14	0.17
Peruvian	11	0.14
Venezuelan	4	0.05
Other Hispanic or Latino	65	0.80

Race*	Population	%
African-American/Black (179)	205	2.53
Not Hispanic (163)	188	2.32
Hispanic (16)	17	0.21
American Indian/Alaska Native (5)	22	0.27
Not Hispanic (5)	19	0.23
Hispanic (0)	3	0.04
Blackfeet (0)	2	0.02
Cherokee (1)	4	0.05
Chippewa (1)	2	0.02
Cree (0)	1	0.01
Delaware (0)	1	0.01
Iroquois (1)	1	0.01
Asian (96)	128	1.58
Not Hispanic (95)	125	1.54
Hispanic (1)	3	0.04
Cambodian (1)	2	0.02
Chinese, ex. Taiwanese (24)	25	0.31
Filipino (18)	34	0.42
Indian (34)	37	0.46
Japanese (3)	5	0.06
Korean (8)	12	0.15
Pakistani (1)	3	0.04
Sri Lankan (1)	1	0.01
Vietnamese (6)	6	0.07
Hawaii Native/Pacific Islander (1)	5	0.06
Not Hispanic (1)	5	0.06
Native Hawaiian (1)	2	0.02
White (7,648)	7,727	95.43
Not Hispanic (7,339)	7,400	91.39
Hispanic (309)	327	4.04

West Milford

Place Type: Township
County: Passaic
Population: 25,850†

Ancestry‡	Population	%
Afghan (9)	9	0.03
African, Sub-Saharan (40)	86	0.33
South African (40)	86	0.33
Albanian (8)	37	0.14
American (716)	716	2.78
Arab (48)	93	0.36
Arab (33)	49	0.19
Jordanian (7)	7	0.03
Palestinian (8)	8	0.03
Syrian (0)	29	0.11
Armenian (20)	47	0.18
Assyrian/Chaldean/Syriac (0)	9	0.03
Austrian (23)	97	0.38
Belgian (0)	17	0.07
British (0)	39	0.15
Canadian (17)	45	0.17
Croatian (16)	47	0.18
Czech (0)	162	0.63
Czechoslovakian (6)	48	0.19
Danish (34)	151	0.59
Dutch (610)	2,396	9.30
Eastern European (38)	79	0.31
English (416)	2,585	10.04
European (294)	304	1.18
French, ex. Basque (70)	640	2.49
French Canadian (13)	140	0.54
German (1,163)	5,931	23.03
Greek (0)	18	0.07
Guyanese (13)	36	0.14
Hungarian (84)	429	1.67
Iranian (12)	12	0.05
Irish (1,714)	7,685	29.84
Italian (2,783)	7,742	30.06
Latvian (0)	11	0.04
Lithuanian (16)	194	0.75
Macedonian (87)	87	0.34
New Zealander (28)	28	0.11
Northern European (17)	17	0.07
Norwegian (73)	343	1.33
Pennsylvania German (16)	70	0.27
Polish (457)	1,982	7.70
Portuguese (20)	98	0.38
Romanian (25)	86	0.33
Russian (169)	933	3.62
Scotch-Irish (122)	439	1.70
Scottish (171)	601	2.33
Slavic (0)	42	0.16
Slovak (76)	274	1.06
Swedish (55)	286	1.11
Swiss (19)	218	0.85
Turkish (23)	34	0.13
Ukrainian (38)	236	0.92
Welsh (27)	92	0.36
Yugoslavian (0)	8	0.03

Hispanic Origin	Population	%
Hispanic or Latino (of any race)	1,512	5.85
Central American, ex. Mexican	124	0.48
Costa Rican	38	0.15
Guatemalan	26	0.10
Honduran	17	0.07
Nicaraguan	8	0.03
Panamanian	2	0.01
Salvadoran	33	0.13
Cuban	154	0.60
Dominican Republic	98	0.38
Mexican	153	0.59
Puerto Rican	528	2.04
South American	314	1.21
Argentinean	37	0.14
Chilean	25	0.10
Colombian	124	0.48
Ecuadorian	37	0.14
Peruvian	76	0.29
Uruguayan	8	0.03
Venezuelan	2	0.01
Other South American	5	0.02
Other Hispanic or Latino	141	0.55

Race*	Population	%
African-American/Black (362)	524	2.03
Not Hispanic (327)	454	1.76
Hispanic (35)	70	0.27
American Indian/Alaska Native (134)	282	1.09

SECTION TWO

*Notes: † The Census 2010 population figure is used to calculate the percentages in the Hispanic Origin and Race categories. Ancestry percentages are based on the 2006-2010 American Community Survey population (not shown); ‡ Numbers in parentheses indicate the number of people reporting a single ancestry; * Numbers in parentheses indicate the number of persons reporting this race alone, not in combination with any other race; Please refer to the Explanation of Data for more information.*

Not Hispanic (104)	233	0.90
Hispanic (30)	49	0.19
Apache (0)	3	0.01
Arapaho (0)	1	<0.01
Blackfeet (2)	7	0.03
Canadian/French Am. Ind. (0)	1	<0.01
Central American Ind. (1)	1	<0.01
Cherokee (5)	19	0.07
Choctaw (0)	1	<0.01
Delaware (45)	56	0.22
Iroquois (6)	17	0.07
Mexican American Ind. (6)	7	0.03
Pueblo (1)	1	<0.01
Seminole (1)	1	<0.01
Shoshone (1)	2	0.01
Sioux (1)	2	0.01
South American Ind. (16)	19	0.07
Asian (334)	459	1.78
Not Hispanic (319)	435	1.68
Hispanic (15)	24	0.09
Burmese (0)	1	<0.01
Chinese, ex. Taiwanese (73)	96	0.37
Filipino (97)	136	0.53
Indian (57)	76	0.29
Indonesian (7)	12	0.05
Japanese (13)	27	0.10
Korean (53)	66	0.26
Nepalese (0)	1	<0.01
Pakistani (2)	3	0.01
Taiwanese (1)	1	<0.01
Thai (8)	14	0.05
Vietnamese (4)	11	0.04
Hawaii Native/Pacific Islander (4)	11	0.04
Not Hispanic (2)	8	0.03
Hispanic (2)	3	0.01
Guamanian/Chamorro (2)	5	0.02
Samoan (0)	2	0.01
White (24,315)	24,681	95.48
Not Hispanic (23,232)	23,521	90.99
Hispanic (1,083)	1,160	4.49

West New York

Place Type: Town
County: Hudson
Population: 49,708†

Ancestry‡	Population	%
African, Sub-Saharan (184)	184	0.38
African (86)	86	0.18
Ghanaian (73)	73	0.15
Zimbabwean (25)	25	0.05
American (345)	345	0.71
Arab (351)	407	0.84
Arab (0)	38	0.08
Egyptian (54)	54	0.11
Jordanian (171)	180	0.37
Palestinian (8)	17	0.04
Syrian (9)	9	0.02
Other Arab (109)	109	0.23
Armenian (159)	178	0.37
Australian (39)	39	0.08
Austrian (48)	89	0.18
Brazilian (103)	103	0.21
British (31)	46	0.10
Canadian (14)	17	0.04
Croatian (8)	24	0.05
Czech (0)	31	0.06
Czechoslovakian (0)	26	0.05
Danish (0)	25	0.05
Eastern European (93)	93	0.19
English (60)	260	0.54
European (103)	128	0.26
Finnish (33)	33	0.07
French, ex. Basque (91)	241	0.50
French Canadian (30)	45	0.09
German (258)	912	1.88
Greek (0)	133	0.27
Hungarian (0)	54	0.11
Icelander (10)	10	0.02
Iranian (26)	26	0.05
Irish (241)	821	1.70
Italian (899)	1,460	3.02
Lithuanian (13)	42	0.09
Northern European (9)	9	0.02
Norwegian (0)	30	0.06
Polish (218)	432	0.89
Portuguese (0)	43	0.09
Romanian (33)	57	0.12
Russian (223)	386	0.80
Scotch-Irish (18)	29	0.06
Scottish (36)	58	0.12
Slovak (9)	9	0.02
Swedish (27)	62	0.13
Swiss (10)	14	0.03
Turkish (256)	308	0.64
Ukrainian (43)	43	0.09
West Indian, ex. Hispanic (322)	335	0.69
British West Indian (0)	13	0.03
Haitian (222)	222	0.46
Jamaican (28)	28	0.06
Trinidadian/Tobagonian (57)	57	0.12
West Indian (15)	15	0.03
Yugoslavian (71)	106	0.22

Hispanic Origin	Population	%
Hispanic or Latino (of any race)	38,812	78.08
Central American, ex. Mexican	7,421	14.93
Costa Rican	114	0.23
Guatemalan	1,594	3.21
Honduran	970	1.95
Nicaraguan	182	0.37
Panamanian	35	0.07
Salvadoran	4,504	9.06
Other Central American	22	0.04
Cuban	7,514	15.12
Dominican Republic	4,935	9.93
Mexican	4,944	9.95
Puerto Rican	2,849	5.73
South American	8,700	17.50
Argentinean	312	0.63
Bolivian	87	0.18
Chilean	279	0.56
Colombian	3,077	6.19
Ecuadorian	3,348	6.74
Paraguayan	7	0.01
Peruvian	1,205	2.42
Uruguayan	127	0.26
Venezuelan	243	0.49
Other South American	15	0.03
Other Hispanic or Latino	2,449	4.93

Race*	Population	%
African-American/Black (2,289)	3,013	6.06
Not Hispanic (873)	995	2.00
Hispanic (1,416)	2,018	4.06
American Indian/Alaska Native (744)	1,114	2.24
Not Hispanic (39)	109	0.22
Hispanic (705)	1,005	2.02
Apache (1)	3	0.01
Central American Ind. (45)	60	0.12
Cherokee (1)	13	0.03
Chippewa (5)	5	0.01
Choctaw (0)	2	<0.01
Creek (0)	1	<0.01
Delaware (1)	1	<0.01
Iroquois (3)	7	0.01
Mexican American Ind. (141)	166	0.33
Pueblo (0)	8	0.02
Seminole (0)	1	<0.01
Sioux (1)	3	0.01
South American Ind. (48)	80	0.16
Spanish American Ind. (17)	23	0.05
Asian (2,986)	3,317	6.67
Not Hispanic (2,904)	3,108	6.25
Hispanic (82)	209	0.42
Bangladeshi (3)	4	0.01
Burmese (3)	3	0.01
Cambodian (1)	1	<0.01
Chinese, ex. Taiwanese (541)	633	1.27
Filipino (228)	276	0.56
Indian (938)	1,023	2.06
Japanese (317)	353	0.71
Korean (755)	787	1.58
Malaysian (3)	3	0.01
Nepalese (16)	17	0.03
Pakistani (58)	61	0.12
Sri Lankan (3)	3	0.01
Taiwanese (27)	30	0.06
Thai (22)	26	0.05
Vietnamese (11)	14	0.03
Hawaii Native/Pacific Islander (24)	81	0.16
Not Hispanic (3)	13	0.03
Hispanic (21)	68	0.14
Guamanian/Chamorro (12)	15	0.03
Native Hawaiian (10)	10	0.02
Samoan (0)	1	<0.01
White (30,839)	33,095	66.58
Not Hispanic (6,571)	6,863	13.81
Hispanic (24,268)	26,232	52.77

West Orange

Place Type: Township
County: Essex
Population: 46,207†

Ancestry‡	Population	%
Afghan (61)	61	0.13
African, Sub-Saharan (1,241)	1,396	3.05
African (401)	556	1.22
Cape Verdean (87)	87	0.19
Ethiopian (210)	210	0.46
Ghanaian (23)	23	0.05
Liberian (10)	10	0.02
Nigerian (404)	404	0.88
Other Sub-Saharan African (106)	106	0.23
American (1,172)	1,172	2.56
Arab (199)	438	0.96
Arab (16)	118	0.26
Egyptian (131)	179	0.39
Jordanian (33)	33	0.07
Lebanese (0)	32	0.07
Moroccan (0)	30	0.07
Palestinian (0)	14	0.03
Syrian (0)	13	0.03
Other Arab (19)	19	0.04
Armenian (39)	39	0.09
Austrian (151)	469	1.03
Belgian (0)	11	0.02
Brazilian (80)	80	0.17
British (117)	231	0.51
Bulgarian (28)	28	0.06
Canadian (0)	13	0.03
Czech (14)	67	0.15
Czechoslovakian (0)	14	0.03
Danish (37)	64	0.14
Dutch (14)	154	0.34
Eastern European (581)	623	1.36
English (289)	1,429	3.12
European (185)	276	0.60
Finnish (13)	22	0.05
French, ex. Basque (134)	689	1.51
French Canadian (0)	41	0.09
German (688)	3,015	6.59
Greek (209)	290	0.63
Guyanese (241)	260	0.57
Hungarian (182)	431	0.94
Iranian (170)	170	0.37
Irish (1,788)	4,263	9.32
Israeli (46)	95	0.21
Italian (3,633)	6,091	13.32
Lithuanian (15)	29	0.06
Northern European (20)	20	0.04
Norwegian (57)	97	0.21
Polish (887)	2,210	4.83
Portuguese (244)	267	0.58
Romanian (74)	166	0.36
Russian (1,007)	1,920	4.20
Scandinavian (39)	75	0.16

*Notes: † The Census 2010 population figure is used to calculate the percentages in the Hispanic Origin and Race categories. Ancestry percentages are based on the 2006-2010 American Community Survey population (not shown); ‡ Numbers in parentheses indicate the number of people reporting a single ancestry; * Numbers in parentheses indicate the number of persons reporting this race alone, not in combination with any other race; Please refer to the Explanation of Data for more information.*

Scotch-Irish (141)	407	0.89
Scottish (108)	376	0.82
Serbian (10)	10	0.02
Slovak (50)	70	0.15
Swedish (9)	146	0.32
Swiss (41)	129	0.28
Ukrainian (121)	241	0.53
Welsh (11)	44	0.10
West Indian, ex. Hispanic (2,334)	2,506	5.48
British West Indian (131)	156	0.34
Haitian (1,258)	1,327	2.90
Jamaican (628)	671	1.47
Trinidadian/Tobagonian (180)	215	0.47
West Indian (137)	137	0.30
Yugoslavian (0)	53	0.12

Hispanic Origin	Population	%
Hispanic or Latino (of any race)	7,487	16.20
Central American, ex. Mexican	992	2.15
Costa Rican	121	0.26
Guatemalan	192	0.42
Honduran	115	0.25
Nicaraguan	14	0.03
Panamanian	35	0.08
Salvadoran	492	1.06
Other Central American	23	0.05
Cuban	291	0.63
Dominican Republic	473	1.02
Mexican	675	1.46
Puerto Rican	1,011	2.19
South American	3,398	7.35
Argentinean	116	0.25
Bolivian	47	0.10
Chilean	34	0.07
Colombian	418	0.90
Ecuadorian	599	1.30
Paraguayan	7	0.02
Peruvian	1,382	2.99
Uruguayan	733	1.59
Venezuelan	43	0.09
Other South American	19	0.04
Other Hispanic or Latino	647	1.40

Race*	Population	%
African-American/Black (12,284)	13,007	28.15
Not Hispanic (11,841)	12,371	26.77
Hispanic (443)	636	1.38
American Indian/Alaska Native (174)	378	0.82
Not Hispanic (80)	210	0.45
Hispanic (94)	168	0.36
Apache (2)	3	0.01
Blackfeet (1)	6	0.01
Central American Ind. (3)	6	0.01
Cherokee (8)	49	0.11
Choctaw (0)	2	<0.01
Creek (0)	1	<0.01
Crow (3)	3	0.01
Delaware (0)	2	<0.01
Hopi (1)	1	<0.01
Iroquois (3)	6	0.01
Mexican American Ind. (8)	13	0.03
Navajo (1)	1	<0.01
Seminole (0)	1	<0.01
Sioux (0)	1	<0.01
South American Ind. (6)	22	0.05
Spanish American Ind. (21)	22	0.05
Tlingit-Haida *(Alaska Native)* (0)	3	0.01
Asian (3,680)	4,112	8.90
Not Hispanic (3,641)	4,042	8.75
Hispanic (39)	70	0.15
Bangladeshi (9)	13	0.03
Burmese (14)	14	0.03
Cambodian (1)	1	<0.01
Chinese, ex. Taiwanese (641)	765	1.66
Filipino (1,009)	1,132	2.45
Indian (1,377)	1,537	3.33
Indonesian (5)	10	0.02
Japanese (33)	70	0.15
Korean (262)	305	0.66
Laotian (3)	3	0.01
Malaysian (6)	12	0.03
Nepalese (7)	8	0.02
Pakistani (49)	59	0.13
Sri Lankan (12)	21	0.05
Taiwanese (59)	62	0.13
Thai (15)	22	0.05
Vietnamese (77)	90	0.19
Hawaii Native/Pacific Islander (10)	71	0.15
Not Hispanic (9)	52	0.11
Hispanic (1)	19	0.04
Fijian (1)	1	<0.01
Guamanian/Chamorro (2)	2	<0.01
Marshallese (1)	1	<0.01
Native Hawaiian (3)	13	0.03
Samoan (1)	1	<0.01
White (26,406)	27,436	59.38
Not Hispanic (22,140)	22,727	49.19
Hispanic (4,266)	4,709	10.19

West Windsor

Place Type: Township
County: Mercer
Population: 27,165†

Ancestry‡	Population	%
African, Sub-Saharan (201)	201	0.76
African (169)	169	0.64
Kenyan (12)	12	0.05
South African (11)	11	0.04
Other Sub-Saharan African (9)	9	0.03
American (465)	465	1.77
Arab (194)	194	0.74
Egyptian (119)	119	0.45
Lebanese (64)	64	0.24
Syrian (11)	11	0.04
Armenian (0)	14	0.05
Austrian (13)	169	0.64
Belgian (17)	32	0.12
Brazilian (14)	23	0.09
British (128)	175	0.67
Bulgarian (34)	58	0.22
Canadian (0)	21	0.08
Czech (68)	276	1.05
Czechoslovakian (59)	97	0.37
Danish (38)	91	0.35
Dutch (77)	171	0.65
Eastern European (335)	343	1.31
English (440)	1,912	7.27
European (227)	270	1.03
Finnish (14)	43	0.16
French, ex. Basque (71)	225	0.86
French Canadian (0)	84	0.32
German (447)	2,676	10.18
Greek (30)	72	0.27
Guyanese (7)	7	0.03
Hungarian (120)	331	1.26
Iranian (35)	35	0.13
Irish (745)	3,185	12.12
Israeli (0)	13	0.05
Italian (1,182)	2,958	11.25
Latvian (0)	15	0.06
Lithuanian (6)	73	0.28
Norwegian (46)	195	0.74
Polish (596)	1,790	6.81
Portuguese (5)	41	0.16
Romanian (26)	148	0.56
Russian (649)	1,584	6.03
Scandinavian (0)	13	0.05
Scotch-Irish (65)	155	0.59
Scottish (71)	452	1.72
Serbian (24)	32	0.12
Slavic (0)	17	0.06
Slovak (33)	84	0.32
Swedish (86)	306	1.16
Swiss (0)	9	0.03
Turkish (110)	110	0.42
Ukrainian (128)	271	1.03
Welsh (42)	209	0.80
West Indian, ex. Hispanic (228)	386	1.47
Barbadian (37)	37	0.14
British West Indian (8)	8	0.03
Dutch West Indian (18)	18	0.07
Haitian (12)	12	0.05
Jamaican (90)	161	0.61
Trinidadian/Tobagonian (22)	93	0.35
West Indian (41)	57	0.22
Yugoslavian (9)	33	0.13

Hispanic Origin	Population	%
Hispanic or Latino (of any race)	1,213	4.47
Central American, ex. Mexican	115	0.42
Costa Rican	13	0.05
Guatemalan	68	0.25
Honduran	10	0.04
Nicaraguan	5	0.02
Panamanian	9	0.03
Salvadoran	10	0.04
Cuban	73	0.27
Dominican Republic	55	0.20
Mexican	136	0.50
Puerto Rican	263	0.97
South American	403	1.48
Argentinean	47	0.17
Bolivian	6	0.02
Chilean	21	0.08
Colombian	160	0.59
Ecuadorian	59	0.22
Paraguayan	5	0.02
Peruvian	45	0.17
Uruguayan	6	0.02
Venezuelan	54	0.20
Other Hispanic or Latino	168	0.62

Race*	Population	%
African-American/Black (998)	1,162	4.28
Not Hispanic (956)	1,080	3.98
Hispanic (42)	82	0.30
American Indian/Alaska Native (25)	74	0.27
Not Hispanic (15)	50	0.18
Hispanic (10)	24	0.09
Apache (0)	1	<0.01
Arapaho (1)	1	<0.01
Canadian/French Am. Ind. (1)	1	<0.01
Central American Ind. (0)	1	<0.01
Cherokee (3)	10	0.04
Choctaw (0)	1	<0.01
Comanche (0)	1	<0.01
Creek (0)	1	<0.01
Delaware (1)	2	0.01
Iroquois (1)	1	<0.01
Mexican American Ind. (3)	3	0.01
Ottawa (0)	2	0.01
Potawatomi (0)	1	<0.01
Seminole (0)	1	<0.01
South American Ind. (3)	3	0.01
Asian (10,245)	10,743	39.55
Not Hispanic (10,223)	10,702	39.40
Hispanic (22)	41	0.15
Bangladeshi (53)	58	0.21
Burmese (9)	13	0.05
Chinese, ex. Taiwanese (3,106)	3,267	12.03
Filipino (178)	255	0.94
Indian (5,109)	5,280	19.44
Indonesian (4)	8	0.03
Japanese (298)	376	1.38
Korean (746)	798	2.94
Malaysian (6)	15	0.06
Nepalese (10)	10	0.04
Pakistani (229)	240	0.88
Sri Lankan (36)	38	0.14
Taiwanese (254)	282	1.04
Thai (12)	17	0.06
Vietnamese (34)	44	0.16
Hawaii Native/Pacific Islander (10)	24	0.09
Not Hispanic (6)	19	0.07
Hispanic (4)	5	0.02
Fijian (0)	1	<0.01
Guamanian/Chamorro (3)	3	0.01
Native Hawaiian (5)	6	0.02

*Notes: † The Census 2010 population figure is used to calculate the percentages in the Hispanic Origin and Race categories. Ancestry percentages are based on the 2006-2010 American Community Survey population (not shown); ‡ Numbers in parentheses indicate the number of people reporting a single ancestry; * Numbers in parentheses indicate the number of persons reporting this race alone, not in combination with any other race; Please refer to the Explanation of Data for more information.*

Samoan (1)	1	<0.01
White (14,924)	15,471	56.95
Not Hispanic (14,086)	14,544	53.54
Hispanic (838)	927	3.41

Westampton

Place Type: Township
County: Burlington
Population: 8,813†

Ancestry‡	Population	%
African, Sub-Saharan (100)	100	1.16
African (83)	83	0.97
Ghanaian (17)	17	0.20
American (210)	210	2.44
Arab (0)	14	0.16
Syrian (0)	14	0.16
Austrian (31)	67	0.78
Belgian (0)	20	0.23
British (0)	18	0.21
Czech (0)	44	0.51
Czechoslovakian (0)	15	0.17
Danish (0)	45	0.52
Dutch (34)	105	1.22
English (404)	1,150	13.38
European (33)	33	0.38
Finnish (0)	76	0.88
French, ex. Basque (32)	86	1.00
French Canadian (7)	7	0.08
German (393)	1,692	19.69
Greek (7)	7	0.08
Hungarian (0)	48	0.56
Irish (480)	1,469	17.09
Italian (353)	1,120	13.03
Lithuanian (21)	36	0.42
Norwegian (6)	6	0.07
Pennsylvania German (21)	21	0.24
Polish (234)	696	8.10
Portuguese (0)	8	0.09
Romanian (0)	23	0.27
Russian (47)	90	1.05
Scandinavian (0)	15	0.17
Scotch-Irish (111)	120	1.40
Scottish (66)	148	1.72
Slovak (0)	17	0.20
Swiss (18)	18	0.21
Welsh (0)	79	0.92
West Indian, ex. Hispanic (61)	76	0.88
Jamaican (17)	17	0.20
Trinidadian/Tobagonian (11)	11	0.13
West Indian (33)	48	0.56

Hispanic Origin	Population	%
Hispanic or Latino (of any race)	779	8.84
Central American, ex. Mexican	88	1.00
Costa Rican	6	0.07
Guatemalan	9	0.10
Honduran	11	0.12
Nicaraguan	1	0.01
Panamanian	33	0.37
Salvadoran	28	0.32
Cuban	17	0.19
Dominican Republic	40	0.45
Mexican	44	0.50
Puerto Rican	452	5.13
South American	83	0.94
Argentinean	5	0.06
Colombian	22	0.25
Ecuadorian	39	0.44
Peruvian	11	0.12
Uruguayan	1	0.01
Venezuelan	5	0.06
Other Hispanic or Latino	55	0.62

Race*	Population	%
African-American/Black (2,243)	2,476	28.09
Not Hispanic (2,128)	2,310	26.21
Hispanic (115)	166	1.88
American Indian/Alaska Native (17)	96	1.09
Not Hispanic (11)	73	0.83
Hispanic (6)	23	0.26
Apache (1)	2	0.02
Blackfeet (0)	3	0.03
Cherokee (1)	21	0.24
Delaware (0)	2	0.02
Mexican American Ind. (4)	4	0.05
Pueblo (1)	1	0.01
Sioux (1)	2	0.02
South American Ind. (0)	5	0.06
Asian (608)	713	8.09
Not Hispanic (602)	698	7.92
Hispanic (6)	15	0.17
Bangladeshi (16)	18	0.20
Chinese, ex. Taiwanese (52)	64	0.73
Filipino (94)	131	1.49
Indian (303)	322	3.65
Japanese (12)	31	0.35
Korean (67)	90	1.02
Malaysian (1)	2	0.02
Pakistani (21)	23	0.26
Sri Lankan (2)	2	0.02
Taiwanese (7)	7	0.08
Thai (11)	18	0.20
Vietnamese (11)	12	0.14
Hawaii Native/Pacific Islander (3)	6	0.07
Not Hispanic (3)	6	0.07
Guamanian/Chamorro (1)	2	0.02
Native Hawaiian (1)	1	0.01
White (5,376)	5,654	64.16
Not Hispanic (4,992)	5,202	59.03
Hispanic (384)	452	5.13

Westfield

Place Type: Town
County: Union
Population: 30,316†

Ancestry‡	Population	%
African, Sub-Saharan (10)	43	0.14
African (0)	18	0.06
South African (0)	15	0.05
Other Sub-Saharan African (10)	10	0.03
Albanian (0)	27	0.09
American (1,821)	1,821	6.08
Arab (112)	194	0.65
Egyptian (13)	24	0.08
Lebanese (43)	114	0.38
Other Arab (56)	56	0.19
Austrian (103)	252	0.84
Belgian (84)	96	0.32
Brazilian (21)	30	0.10
British (155)	208	0.69
Canadian (10)	56	0.19
Croatian (0)	12	0.04
Cypriot (13)	13	0.04
Czech (67)	232	0.77
Czechoslovakian (33)	48	0.16
Danish (29)	29	0.10
Dutch (25)	263	0.88
Eastern European (426)	489	1.63
English (810)	2,497	8.34
European (322)	367	1.23
Finnish (52)	107	0.36
French, ex. Basque (229)	601	2.01
French Canadian (48)	128	0.43
German (1,017)	5,493	18.34
Greek (126)	435	1.45
Guyanese (0)	12	0.04
Hungarian (80)	451	1.51
Irish (1,902)	6,612	22.08
Israeli (44)	44	0.15
Italian (2,978)	6,331	21.14
Latvian (0)	84	0.28
Lithuanian (35)	270	0.90
Northern European (76)	76	0.25
Norwegian (60)	408	1.36
Pennsylvania German (10)	51	0.17
Polish (579)	2,161	7.22
Portuguese (158)	287	0.96
Romanian (12)	55	0.18
Russian (916)	1,723	5.75
Scandinavian (0)	10	0.03
Scotch-Irish (81)	334	1.12
Scottish (50)	511	1.71
Serbian (0)	10	0.03
Slavic (0)	13	0.04
Slovak (80)	160	0.53
Swedish (15)	82	0.27
Swiss (30)	85	0.28
Turkish (60)	77	0.26
Ukrainian (217)	446	1.49
Welsh (17)	151	0.50
West Indian, ex. Hispanic (44)	80	0.27
Trinidadian/Tobagonian (44)	56	0.19
West Indian (0)	24	0.08
Yugoslavian (0)	14	0.05

Hispanic Origin	Population	%
Hispanic or Latino (of any race)	1,492	4.92
Central American, ex. Mexican	76	0.25
Costa Rican	25	0.08
Guatemalan	27	0.09
Honduran	2	0.01
Nicaraguan	12	0.04
Panamanian	2	0.01
Salvadoran	8	0.03
Cuban	151	0.50
Dominican Republic	50	0.16
Mexican	229	0.76
Puerto Rican	308	1.02
South American	469	1.55
Argentinean	61	0.20
Bolivian	7	0.02
Chilean	13	0.04
Colombian	166	0.55
Ecuadorian	87	0.29
Paraguayan	1	<0.01
Peruvian	104	0.34
Uruguayan	19	0.06
Venezuelan	9	0.03
Other South American	2	0.01
Other Hispanic or Latino	209	0.69

Race*	Population	%
African-American/Black (984)	1,136	3.75
Not Hispanic (940)	1,049	3.46
Hispanic (44)	87	0.29
American Indian/Alaska Native (36)	102	0.34
Not Hispanic (20)	66	0.22
Hispanic (16)	36	0.12
Apache (0)	1	<0.01
Blackfeet (0)	2	0.01
Cherokee (2)	17	0.06
Chippewa (1)	1	<0.01
Choctaw (0)	1	<0.01
Delaware (0)	2	0.01
Inupiat *(Alaska Native)* (4)	4	0.01
Iroquois (0)	4	0.01
Mexican American Ind. (8)	10	0.03
Seminole (0)	2	0.01
Sioux (0)	1	<0.01
South American Ind. (0)	6	0.02
Asian (1,718)	2,061	6.80
Not Hispanic (1,708)	2,034	6.71
Hispanic (10)	27	0.09
Bangladeshi (2)	3	0.01
Burmese (0)	3	0.01
Cambodian (2)	2	0.01
Chinese, ex. Taiwanese (735)	857	2.83
Filipino (137)	198	0.65
Hmong (1)	3	0.01
Indian (385)	441	1.45
Indonesian (3)	10	0.03
Japanese (55)	100	0.33
Korean (233)	284	0.94
Laotian (0)	2	0.01
Malaysian (4)	6	0.02
Pakistani (19)	25	0.08

*Notes: † The Census 2010 population figure is used to calculate the percentages in the Hispanic Origin and Race categories. Ancestry percentages are based on the 2006-2010 American Community Survey population (not shown); ‡ Numbers in parentheses indicate the number of people reporting a single ancestry; * Numbers in parentheses indicate the number of persons reporting this race alone, not in combination with any other race; Please refer to the Explanation of Data for more information.*

Sri Lankan (10)	10	0.03
Taiwanese (56)	63	0.21
Thai (11)	15	0.05
Vietnamese (21)	40	0.13
Hawaii Native/Pacific Islander (10)	29	0.10
Not Hispanic (10)	28	0.09
Hispanic (0)	1	<0.01
Guamanian/Chamorro (5)	11	0.04
Native Hawaiian (0)	8	0.03
White (26,729)	27,278	89.98
Not Hispanic (25,629)	26,059	85.96
Hispanic (1,100)	1,219	4.02

Westwood

Place Type: Borough
County: Bergen
Population: 10,908†

Ancestry‡	Population	%
African, Sub-Saharan (0)	6	0.06
African (0)	6	0.06
American (150)	150	1.38
Arab (27)	43	0.40
Other Arab (27)	43	0.40
Australian (17)	32	0.29
Austrian (57)	274	2.52
British (27)	62	0.57
Croatian (66)	66	0.61
Czech (14)	127	1.17
Czechoslovakian (0)	50	0.46
Danish (27)	27	0.25
Dutch (125)	228	2.10
Eastern European (65)	65	0.60
English (105)	559	5.14
European (440)	467	4.30
Finnish (0)	27	0.25
French, ex. Basque (27)	209	1.92
French Canadian (0)	61	0.56
German (472)	1,904	17.51
Greek (77)	103	0.95
Hungarian (64)	248	2.28
Irish (731)	2,390	21.98
Italian (1,545)	3,036	27.92
Lithuanian (18)	18	0.17
Norwegian (0)	42	0.39
Polish (174)	469	4.31
Portuguese (45)	45	0.41
Russian (84)	180	1.66
Scotch-Irish (7)	206	1.89
Scottish (30)	206	1.89
Slavic (8)	8	0.07
Slovak (27)	65	0.60
Swedish (41)	97	0.89
Swiss (13)	68	0.63
Turkish (26)	89	0.82
Ukrainian (0)	14	0.13
Welsh (15)	52	0.48
West Indian, ex. Hispanic (12)	12	0.11
West Indian (12)	12	0.11

Hispanic Origin	Population	%
Hispanic or Latino (of any race)	1,263	11.58
Central American, ex. Mexican	181	1.66
Costa Rican	132	1.21
Guatemalan	11	0.10
Honduran	7	0.06
Nicaraguan	4	0.04
Panamanian	5	0.05
Salvadoran	22	0.20
Cuban	106	0.97
Dominican Republic	65	0.60
Mexican	398	3.65
Puerto Rican	190	1.74
South American	215	1.97
Argentinean	18	0.17
Bolivian	1	0.01
Chilean	8	0.07
Colombian	95	0.87
Ecuadorian	56	0.51
Peruvian	21	0.19
Uruguayan	9	0.08
Venezuelan	7	0.06
Other Hispanic or Latino	108	0.99

Race*	Population	%
African-American/Black (504)	561	5.14
Not Hispanic (466)	501	4.59
Hispanic (38)	60	0.55
American Indian/Alaska Native (34)	70	0.64
Not Hispanic (5)	24	0.22
Hispanic (29)	46	0.42
Blackfeet (0)	2	0.02
Central American Ind. (1)	4	0.04
Cherokee (1)	4	0.04
Comanche (1)	3	0.03
Delaware (0)	4	0.04
Mexican American Ind. (5)	5	0.05
Navajo (0)	3	0.03
Seminole (0)	1	0.01
South American Ind. (0)	3	0.03
Asian (805)	891	8.17
Not Hispanic (802)	880	8.07
Hispanic (3)	11	0.10
Bangladeshi (0)	2	0.02
Burmese (3)	3	0.03
Cambodian (0)	1	0.01
Chinese, ex. Taiwanese (129)	158	1.45
Filipino (105)	135	1.24
Indian (340)	349	3.20
Indonesian (2)	2	0.02
Japanese (35)	48	0.44
Korean (150)	162	1.49
Pakistani (11)	13	0.12
Taiwanese (10)	10	0.09
Thai (2)	2	0.02
Vietnamese (5)	7	0.06
Hawaii Native/Pacific Islander (0)	6	0.06
Not Hispanic (0)	5	0.05
Hispanic (0)	1	0.01
Native Hawaiian (0)	5	0.05
White (9,052)	9,242	84.73
Not Hispanic (8,245)	8,360	76.64
Hispanic (807)	882	8.09

White Horse

Place Type: CDP
County: Mercer
Population: 9,494†

Ancestry‡	Population	%
African, Sub-Saharan (42)	42	0.46
African (42)	42	0.46
American (162)	162	1.77
Arab (127)	153	1.67
Lebanese (0)	13	0.14
Palestinian (127)	127	1.39
Other Arab (0)	13	0.14
Austrian (8)	48	0.53
British (0)	10	0.11
Canadian (0)	16	0.18
Croatian (0)	9	0.10
Czech (24)	94	1.03
Czechoslovakian (12)	65	0.71
Danish (0)	24	0.26
Dutch (0)	32	0.35
Eastern European (26)	37	0.40
English (110)	769	8.41
European (33)	33	0.36
French, ex. Basque (0)	72	0.79
French Canadian (27)	56	0.61
German (575)	1,898	20.76
Greek (13)	13	0.14
Hungarian (359)	615	6.73
Irish (462)	1,782	19.49
Italian (1,100)	2,227	24.36
Norwegian (11)	23	0.25
Pennsylvania German (16)	16	0.18
Polish (565)	1,426	15.60
Portuguese (8)	17	0.19
Romanian (12)	12	0.13
Russian (75)	252	2.76
Scotch-Irish (68)	156	1.71
Scottish (0)	180	1.97
Slavic (0)	30	0.33
Slovak (103)	177	1.94
Slovene (0)	9	0.10
Swedish (0)	104	1.14
Ukrainian (28)	65	0.71
Welsh (51)	88	0.96

Hispanic Origin	Population	%
Hispanic or Latino (of any race)	812	8.55
Central American, ex. Mexican	156	1.64
Costa Rican	16	0.17
Guatemalan	113	1.19
Honduran	5	0.05
Nicaraguan	3	0.03
Panamanian	4	0.04
Salvadoran	15	0.16
Cuban	17	0.18
Dominican Republic	48	0.51
Mexican	51	0.54
Puerto Rican	385	4.06
South American	93	0.98
Argentinean	7	0.07
Bolivian	1	0.01
Chilean	4	0.04
Colombian	22	0.23
Ecuadorian	37	0.39
Peruvian	9	0.09
Uruguayan	7	0.07
Venezuelan	5	0.05
Other South American	1	0.01
Other Hispanic or Latino	62	0.65

Race*	Population	%
African-American/Black (531)	593	6.25
Not Hispanic (500)	540	5.69
Hispanic (31)	53	0.56
American Indian/Alaska Native (7)	34	0.36
Not Hispanic (6)	27	0.28
Hispanic (1)	7	0.07
Canadian/French Am. Ind. (0)	1	0.01
Cherokee (1)	4	0.04
Iroquois (1)	1	0.01
Mexican American Ind. (1)	1	0.01
Sioux (0)	4	0.04
Asian (208)	249	2.62
Not Hispanic (206)	237	2.50
Hispanic (2)	12	0.13
Bangladeshi (5)	5	0.05
Burmese (0)	1	0.01
Cambodian (6)	6	0.06
Chinese, ex. Taiwanese (49)	55	0.58
Filipino (54)	57	0.60
Indian (48)	49	0.52
Japanese (3)	8	0.08
Korean (12)	17	0.18
Pakistani (11)	13	0.14
Sri Lankan (1)	1	0.01
Taiwanese (3)	4	0.04
Thai (0)	6	0.06
Vietnamese (15)	17	0.18
Hawaii Native/Pacific Islander (9)	12	0.13
Not Hispanic (9)	12	0.13
Guamanian/Chamorro (6)	6	0.06
Native Hawaiian (3)	3	0.03
White (8,346)	8,463	89.14
Not Hispanic (7,872)	7,938	83.61
Hispanic (474)	525	5.53

White Meadow Lake

Place Type: CDP
County: Morris
Population: 8,836†

*Notes: † The Census 2010 population figure is used to calculate the percentages in the Hispanic Origin and Race categories. Ancestry percentages are based on the 2006-2010 American Community Survey population (not shown); ‡ Numbers in parentheses indicate the number of people reporting a single ancestry; * Numbers in parentheses indicate the number of persons reporting this race alone, not in combination with any other race; Please refer to the Explanation of Data for more information.*

Ancestry‡	Population	%
Albanian (0)	9	0.11
American (321)	321	3.83
Arab (47)	65	0.78
Arab (22)	22	0.26
Egyptian (10)	10	0.12
Syrian (15)	33	0.39
Armenian (0)	14	0.17
Australian (12)	12	0.14
Austrian (19)	48	0.57
Canadian (33)	100	1.19
Czech (18)	115	1.37
Czechoslovakian (0)	33	0.39
Danish (5)	26	0.31
Dutch (0)	54	0.64
Eastern European (101)	101	1.21
English (158)	455	5.43
European (88)	88	1.05
French, ex. Basque (11)	136	1.62
French Canadian (8)	8	0.10
German (229)	1,241	14.81
Greek (8)	25	0.30
Hungarian (18)	148	1.77
Irish (491)	1,955	23.34
Italian (635)	1,752	20.91
Latvian (25)	25	0.30
Lithuanian (12)	58	0.69
Macedonian (18)	18	0.21
Norwegian (31)	106	1.27
Polish (347)	1,045	12.47
Portuguese (93)	106	1.27
Romanian (33)	114	1.36
Russian (307)	832	9.93
Scotch-Irish (13)	86	1.03
Scottish (24)	105	1.25
Slovak (16)	69	0.82
Swedish (13)	30	0.36
Swiss (0)	42	0.50
Turkish (10)	19	0.23
Ukrainian (21)	123	1.47
Welsh (0)	64	0.76
West Indian, ex. Hispanic (16)	29	0.35
Jamaican (0)	13	0.16
Trinidadian/Tobagonian (16)	16	0.19
Yugoslavian (0)	17	0.20

Hispanic Origin	Population	%
Hispanic or Latino (of any race)	812	9.19
Central American, ex. Mexican	82	0.93
Costa Rican	21	0.24
Guatemalan	19	0.22
Honduran	20	0.23
Nicaraguan	9	0.10
Salvadoran	13	0.15
Cuban	64	0.72
Dominican Republic	60	0.68
Mexican	31	0.35
Puerto Rican	281	3.18
South American	231	2.61
Argentinean	12	0.14
Bolivian	3	0.03
Chilean	19	0.22
Colombian	82	0.93
Ecuadorian	58	0.66
Paraguayan	6	0.07
Peruvian	39	0.44
Uruguayan	6	0.07
Venezuelan	5	0.06
Other South American	1	0.01
Other Hispanic or Latino	63	0.71

Race*	Population	%
African-American/Black (149)	217	2.46
Not Hispanic (135)	174	1.97
Hispanic (14)	43	0.49
American Indian/Alaska Native (3)	24	0.27
Not Hispanic (1)	13	0.15
Hispanic (2)	11	0.12
Cherokee (0)	3	0.03
Delaware (0)	6	0.07
Mexican American Ind. (2)	2	0.02
Navajo (1)	2	0.02
South American Ind. (0)	8	0.09
Asian (520)	571	6.46
Not Hispanic (520)	570	6.45
Hispanic (0)	1	0.01
Bangladeshi (8)	8	0.09
Chinese, ex. Taiwanese (86)	94	1.06
Filipino (119)	135	1.53
Indian (225)	233	2.64
Japanese (4)	16	0.18
Korean (17)	21	0.24
Pakistani (18)	24	0.27
Sri Lankan (5)	6	0.07
Taiwanese (9)	11	0.12
Thai (4)	4	0.05
Vietnamese (14)	14	0.16
Hawaii Native/Pacific Islander (4)	4	0.05
Not Hispanic (4)	4	0.05
Guamanian/Chamorro (1)	1	0.01
White (7,871)	8,021	90.78
Not Hispanic (7,248)	7,346	83.14
Hispanic (623)	675	7.64

Williamstown

Place Type: CDP
County: Gloucester
Population: 15,567†

Ancestry‡	Population	%
African, Sub-Saharan (115)	115	0.81
African (115)	115	0.81
American (446)	446	3.13
Arab (18)	49	0.34
Lebanese (18)	32	0.22
Palestinian (0)	17	0.12
Austrian (22)	63	0.44
British (10)	36	0.25
Canadian (0)	8	0.06
Croatian (0)	37	0.26
Czech (0)	13	0.09
Dutch (32)	249	1.75
English (331)	1,288	9.05
European (44)	44	0.31
French, ex. Basque (0)	428	3.01
French Canadian (0)	31	0.22
German (561)	2,996	21.05
Greek (0)	165	1.16
Guyanese (25)	48	0.34
Hungarian (13)	24	0.17
Irish (1,147)	4,416	31.03
Italian (1,703)	3,483	24.47
Lithuanian (13)	66	0.46
Norwegian (0)	42	0.30
Pennsylvania German (14)	30	0.21
Polish (393)	1,293	9.09
Portuguese (15)	37	0.26
Romanian (24)	79	0.56
Russian (12)	221	1.55
Scotch-Irish (75)	221	1.55
Scottish (42)	183	1.29
Slovak (0)	21	0.15
Swedish (10)	42	0.30
Swiss (0)	15	0.11
Ukrainian (72)	135	0.95
Welsh (0)	48	0.34
West Indian, ex. Hispanic (59)	138	0.97
British West Indian (33)	57	0.40
Jamaican (14)	38	0.27
Trinidadian/Tobagonian (12)	12	0.08
West Indian (0)	31	0.22
Yugoslavian (0)	43	0.30

Hispanic Origin	Population	%
Hispanic or Latino (of any race)	820	5.27
Central American, ex. Mexican	24	0.15
Costa Rican	4	0.03
Guatemalan	11	0.07
Nicaraguan	3	0.02
Panamanian	5	0.03
Salvadoran	1	0.01
Cuban	30	0.19
Dominican Republic	20	0.13
Mexican	126	0.81
Puerto Rican	431	2.77
South American	126	0.81
Argentinean	2	0.01
Chilean	2	0.01
Colombian	32	0.21
Ecuadorian	82	0.53
Peruvian	5	0.03
Venezuelan	3	0.02
Other Hispanic or Latino	63	0.40

Race*	Population	%
African-American/Black (2,036)	2,265	14.55
Not Hispanic (1,989)	2,187	14.05
Hispanic (47)	78	0.50
American Indian/Alaska Native (29)	110	0.71
Not Hispanic (24)	99	0.64
Hispanic (5)	11	0.07
Apache (0)	1	0.01
Blackfeet (2)	3	0.02
Central American Ind. (2)	3	0.02
Cherokee (3)	20	0.13
Chippewa (0)	5	0.03
Delaware (0)	7	0.04
Iroquois (1)	4	0.03
Lumbee (0)	1	0.01
Mexican American Ind. (0)	1	0.01
Seminole (0)	2	0.01
Asian (318)	389	2.50
Not Hispanic (316)	378	2.43
Hispanic (2)	11	0.07
Cambodian (8)	11	0.07
Chinese, ex. Taiwanese (54)	66	0.42
Filipino (94)	115	0.74
Indian (99)	104	0.67
Indonesian (12)	12	0.08
Japanese (9)	28	0.18
Korean (10)	15	0.10
Malaysian (0)	3	0.02
Pakistani (7)	10	0.06
Vietnamese (18)	25	0.16
Hawaii Native/Pacific Islander (2)	11	0.07
Not Hispanic (2)	11	0.07
Native Hawaiian (1)	4	0.03
Samoan (1)	4	0.03
White (12,521)	12,835	82.45
Not Hispanic (12,106)	12,366	79.44
Hispanic (415)	469	3.01

Willingboro

Place Type: Township
County: Burlington
Population: 31,629†

Ancestry‡	Population	%
African, Sub-Saharan (1,502)	1,643	5.11
African (768)	829	2.58
Ghanaian (40)	40	0.12
Kenyan (79)	79	0.25
Liberian (435)	435	1.35
Nigerian (138)	201	0.62
Other Sub-Saharan African (42)	59	0.18
American (769)	769	2.39
Arab (54)	65	0.20
Iraqi (11)	11	0.03
Jordanian (21)	21	0.07
Palestinian (0)	11	0.03
Other Arab (22)	22	0.07
Austrian (9)	41	0.13
Brazilian (23)	23	0.07
British (38)	53	0.16
Canadian (50)	105	0.33
Czech (5)	16	0.05
Dutch (0)	59	0.18
English (258)	927	2.88

*Notes: † The Census 2010 population figure is used to calculate the percentages in the Hispanic Origin and Race categories. Ancestry percentages are based on the 2006-2010 American Community Survey population (not shown); ‡ Numbers in parentheses indicate the number of people reporting a single ancestry; * Numbers in parentheses indicate the number of persons reporting this race alone, not in combination with any other race; Please refer to the Explanation of Data for more information.*

Estonian (11)	11	0.03
European (6)	6	0.02
Finnish (0)	5	0.02
French, ex. Basque (26)	190	0.59
French Canadian (0)	18	0.06
German (565)	1,910	5.94
Greek (13)	13	0.04
Guyanese (13)	30	0.09
Hungarian (21)	98	0.30
Iranian (16)	16	0.05
Irish (268)	1,413	4.39
Italian (298)	761	2.37
Latvian (13)	29	0.09
Lithuanian (8)	20	0.06
Pennsylvania German (9)	9	0.03
Polish (169)	601	1.87
Romanian (13)	64	0.20
Russian (90)	256	0.80
Scandinavian (9)	9	0.03
Scotch-Irish (26)	146	0.45
Scottish (0)	85	0.26
Slovak (3)	20	0.06
Swedish (18)	41	0.13
Swiss (9)	28	0.09
Turkish (71)	87	0.27
Ukrainian (48)	69	0.21
Welsh (32)	127	0.39
West Indian, ex. Hispanic (1,876)	2,365	7.35
Barbadian (57)	126	0.39
British West Indian (0)	6	0.02
Haitian (838)	979	3.04
Jamaican (892)	1,130	3.51
Trinidadian/Tobagonian (26)	34	0.11
West Indian (63)	90	0.28

Hispanic Origin	Population	%
Hispanic or Latino (of any race)	2,737	8.65
Central American, ex. Mexican	414	1.31
Costa Rican	17	0.05
Guatemalan	32	0.10
Honduran	112	0.35
Nicaraguan	18	0.06
Panamanian	185	0.58
Salvadoran	42	0.13
Other Central American	8	0.03
Cuban	96	0.30
Dominican Republic	205	0.65
Mexican	118	0.37
Puerto Rican	1,547	4.89
South American	167	0.53
Argentinean	7	0.02
Chilean	14	0.04
Colombian	65	0.21
Ecuadorian	43	0.14
Peruvian	31	0.10
Uruguayan	1	<0.01
Venezuelan	5	0.02
Other South American	1	<0.01
Other Hispanic or Latino	190	0.60

Race*	Population	%
African-American/Black (23,007)	24,215	76.56
Not Hispanic (22,325)	23,262	73.55
Hispanic (682)	953	3.01
American Indian/Alaska Native (117)	541	1.71
Not Hispanic (82)	445	1.41
Hispanic (35)	96	0.30
Apache (1)	3	0.01
Blackfeet (1)	51	0.16
Central American Ind. (2)	4	0.01
Cherokee (19)	112	0.35
Cheyenne (0)	1	<0.01
Chippewa (1)	11	0.03
Choctaw (0)	6	0.02
Creek (1)	5	0.02
Delaware (4)	6	0.02
Inupiat *(Alaska Native)* (0)	1	<0.01
Iroquois (0)	9	0.03
Kiowa (3)	3	0.01
Lumbee (0)	1	<0.01
Mexican American Ind. (1)	1	<0.01
Navajo (0)	2	0.01
Pueblo (0)	4	0.01
Seminole (0)	6	0.02
Sioux (5)	18	0.06
South American Ind. (3)	12	0.04
Spanish American Ind. (1)	2	0.01
Asian (635)	854	2.70
Not Hispanic (618)	810	2.56
Hispanic (17)	44	0.14
Bangladeshi (10)	10	0.03
Burmese (9)	9	0.03
Cambodian (12)	18	0.06
Chinese, ex. Taiwanese (30)	59	0.19
Filipino (105)	172	0.54
Indian (148)	189	0.60
Indonesian (6)	6	0.02
Japanese (36)	71	0.22
Korean (38)	51	0.16
Malaysian (0)	2	0.01
Pakistani (96)	110	0.35
Sri Lankan (3)	3	0.01
Taiwanese (0)	1	<0.01
Thai (10)	17	0.05
Vietnamese (104)	112	0.35
Hawaii Native/Pacific Islander (10)	45	0.14
Not Hispanic (10)	37	0.12
Hispanic (0)	8	0.03
Guamanian/Chamorro (1)	5	0.02
Native Hawaiian (5)	15	0.05
Samoan (1)	6	0.02
White (5,475)	6,302	19.92
Not Hispanic (4,690)	5,338	16.88
Hispanic (785)	964	3.05

Winslow

Place Type: Township
County: Camden
Population: 39,499†

Ancestry‡	Population	%
African, Sub-Saharan (401)	534	1.38
African (175)	286	0.74
Ghanaian (61)	61	0.16
Liberian (0)	22	0.06
Nigerian (165)	165	0.43
American (696)	696	1.80
Arab (64)	126	0.33
Arab (28)	28	0.07
Egyptian (0)	20	0.05
Lebanese (0)	11	0.03
Moroccan (36)	67	0.17
Armenian (8)	8	0.02
Austrian (18)	88	0.23
Belgian (53)	58	0.15
Brazilian (0)	14	0.04
British (23)	32	0.08
Bulgarian (9)	9	0.02
Canadian (57)	205	0.53
Croatian (0)	7	0.02
Czech (0)	47	0.12
Czechoslovakian (11)	41	0.11
Danish (0)	23	0.06
Dutch (44)	249	0.65
Eastern European (107)	122	0.32
English (349)	2,548	6.61
European (92)	103	0.27
Finnish (0)	51	0.13
French, ex. Basque (101)	606	1.57
French Canadian (97)	226	0.59
German (1,054)	5,568	14.44
German Russian (13)	13	0.03
Greek (136)	161	0.42
Guyanese (29)	29	0.08
Hungarian (36)	270	0.70
Icelander (15)	15	0.04
Irish (1,424)	6,105	15.83
Italian (3,449)	6,788	17.60
Latvian (9)	9	0.02
Lithuanian (35)	131	0.34
Macedonian (59)	59	0.15
Norwegian (0)	93	0.24
Pennsylvania German (34)	68	0.18
Polish (407)	1,717	4.45
Portuguese (5)	16	0.04
Romanian (129)	129	0.33
Russian (91)	506	1.31
Scandinavian (13)	40	0.10
Scotch-Irish (36)	382	0.99
Scottish (110)	361	0.94
Slavic (0)	7	0.02
Slovak (6)	39	0.10
Swedish (72)	214	0.55
Swiss (42)	77	0.20
Ukrainian (91)	237	0.61
Welsh (0)	109	0.28
West Indian, ex. Hispanic (826)	1,217	3.16
Barbadian (124)	124	0.32
Belizean (0)	15	0.04
British West Indian (41)	41	0.11
Haitian (259)	339	0.88
Jamaican (335)	585	1.52
Trinidadian/Tobagonian (56)	63	0.16
West Indian (11)	50	0.13
Yugoslavian (12)	12	0.03

Hispanic Origin	Population	%
Hispanic or Latino (of any race)	3,200	8.10
Central American, ex. Mexican	177	0.45
Costa Rican	16	0.04
Guatemalan	41	0.10
Honduran	25	0.06
Nicaraguan	35	0.09
Panamanian	34	0.09
Salvadoran	26	0.07
Cuban	95	0.24
Dominican Republic	110	0.28
Mexican	794	2.01
Puerto Rican	1,670	4.23
South American	165	0.42
Argentinean	19	0.05
Chilean	4	0.01
Colombian	57	0.14
Ecuadorian	23	0.06
Peruvian	45	0.11
Uruguayan	2	0.01
Venezuelan	15	0.04
Other Hispanic or Latino	189	0.48

Race*	Population	%
African-American/Black (14,287)	15,128	38.30
Not Hispanic (13,822)	14,439	36.56
Hispanic (465)	689	1.74
American Indian/Alaska Native (113)	442	1.12
Not Hispanic (81)	358	0.91
Hispanic (32)	84	0.21
Aleut *(Alaska Native)* (1)	1	<0.01
Apache (6)	7	0.02
Blackfeet (1)	22	0.06
Canadian/French Am. Ind. (1)	2	0.01
Central American Ind. (4)	4	0.01
Cherokee (12)	85	0.22
Cheyenne (0)	1	<0.01
Chippewa (0)	3	0.01
Choctaw (0)	3	0.01
Creek (0)	3	0.01
Delaware (2)	12	0.03
Iroquois (3)	9	0.02
Lumbee (0)	4	0.01
Mexican American Ind. (1)	1	<0.01
Navajo (0)	4	0.01
Pueblo (0)	2	0.01
Seminole (0)	2	0.01
Sioux (1)	4	0.01
South American Ind. (6)	16	0.04
Asian (1,224)	1,459	3.69
Not Hispanic (1,208)	1,410	3.57
Hispanic (16)	49	0.12
Bangladeshi (13)	18	0.05

*Notes: † The Census 2010 population figure is used to calculate the percentages in the Hispanic Origin and Race categories. Ancestry percentages are based on the 2006-2010 American Community Survey population (not shown); ‡ Numbers in parentheses indicate the number of people reporting a single ancestry; * Numbers in parentheses indicate the number of persons reporting this race alone, not in combination with any other race; Please refer to the Explanation of Data for more information.*

Burmese (1)	1	<0.01
Cambodian (33)	39	0.10
Chinese, ex. Taiwanese (186)	211	0.53
Filipino (388)	471	1.19
Indian (294)	329	0.83
Indonesian (10)	11	0.03
Japanese (12)	42	0.11
Korean (117)	146	0.37
Laotian (3)	7	0.02
Malaysian (2)	7	0.02
Pakistani (33)	46	0.12
Taiwanese (8)	8	0.02
Thai (6)	10	0.03
Vietnamese (72)	98	0.25
Hawaii Native/Pacific Islander (14)	37	0.09
Not Hispanic (12)	30	0.08
Hispanic (2)	7	0.02
Guamanian/Chamorro (6)	9	0.02
Marshallese (1)	1	<0.01
Native Hawaiian (6)	8	0.02
White (21,491)	22,299	56.45
Not Hispanic (20,281)	20,895	52.90
Hispanic (1,210)	1,404	3.55

Wood-Ridge

Place Type: Borough
County: Bergen
Population: 7,626†

Ancestry‡	Population	%
American (134)	134	1.77
Arab (110)	150	1.98
Egyptian (66)	66	0.87
Lebanese (12)	12	0.16
Syrian (32)	72	0.95
Armenian (28)	28	0.37
Brazilian (13)	13	0.17
Czech (0)	15	0.20
Czechoslovakian (0)	20	0.26
Dutch (0)	13	0.17
Eastern European (14)	14	0.18
English (170)	387	5.11
European (18)	18	0.24
Finnish (0)	12	0.16
French, ex. Basque (15)	45	0.59
French Canadian (0)	93	1.23
German (235)	933	12.32
Greek (0)	55	0.73
Hungarian (13)	50	0.66
Irish (499)	1,230	16.24
Italian (1,560)	2,692	35.55
Latvian (16)	16	0.21
Lithuanian (0)	27	0.36
Norwegian (0)	54	0.71
Pennsylvania German (12)	12	0.16
Polish (272)	595	7.86
Romanian (15)	154	2.03
Russian (114)	219	2.89
Scotch-Irish (13)	25	0.33
Serbian (109)	155	2.05
Slavic (0)	40	0.53
Slovak (40)	66	0.87
Swedish (0)	15	0.20
Swiss (13)	13	0.17
Ukrainian (31)	58	0.77
Welsh (0)	29	0.38
West Indian, ex. Hispanic (40)	40	0.53
Haitian (40)	40	0.53
Yugoslavian (40)	59	0.78

Hispanic Origin	Population	%
Hispanic or Latino (of any race)	1,000	13.11
Central American, ex. Mexican	44	0.58
Costa Rican	10	0.13
Guatemalan	13	0.17
Honduran	4	0.05
Nicaraguan	2	0.03
Salvadoran	15	0.20
Cuban	172	2.26
Dominican Republic	94	1.23
Mexican	24	0.31
Puerto Rican	253	3.32
South American	329	4.31
Argentinean	25	0.33
Bolivian	6	0.08
Chilean	14	0.18
Colombian	126	1.65
Ecuadorian	80	1.05
Peruvian	67	0.88
Venezuelan	6	0.08
Other South American	5	0.07
Other Hispanic or Latino	84	1.10

Race*	Population	%
African-American/Black (109)	132	1.73
Not Hispanic (95)	106	1.39
Hispanic (14)	26	0.34
American Indian/Alaska Native (16)	36	0.47
Not Hispanic (9)	19	0.25
Hispanic (7)	17	0.22
Blackfeet (1)	3	0.04
Cherokee (2)	2	0.03
Delaware (1)	1	0.01
Iroquois (0)	3	0.04
Mexican American Ind. (1)	1	0.01
South American Ind. (0)	3	0.04
Asian (544)	588	7.71
Not Hispanic (538)	580	7.61
Hispanic (6)	8	0.10
Bangladeshi (4)	4	0.05
Burmese (1)	3	0.04
Chinese, ex. Taiwanese (59)	69	0.90
Filipino (74)	80	1.05
Indian (166)	180	2.36
Japanese (29)	31	0.41
Korean (134)	136	1.78
Pakistani (24)	28	0.37
Sri Lankan (9)	10	0.13
Taiwanese (9)	9	0.12
Thai (4)	4	0.05
Vietnamese (15)	19	0.25
Hawaii Native/Pacific Islander (1)	8	0.10
Not Hispanic (0)	5	0.07
Hispanic (1)	3	0.04
Guamanian/Chamorro (1)	1	0.01
Native Hawaiian (0)	1	0.01
White (6,652)	6,747	88.47
Not Hispanic (5,898)	5,950	78.02
Hispanic (754)	797	10.45

Woodbridge

Place Type: CDP
County: Middlesex
Population: 19,265†

Ancestry‡	Population	%
African, Sub-Saharan (50)	66	0.34
African (30)	46	0.24
Kenyan (20)	20	0.10
Albanian (0)	15	0.08
American (557)	557	2.90
Arab (74)	107	0.56
Egyptian (63)	96	0.50
Other Arab (11)	11	0.06
Armenian (8)	20	0.10
Austrian (0)	44	0.23
Bulgarian (35)	35	0.18
Canadian (0)	9	0.05
Croatian (11)	39	0.20
Czech (0)	59	0.31
Czechoslovakian (0)	39	0.20
Danish (47)	174	0.90
Dutch (0)	62	0.32
Eastern European (45)	45	0.23
English (124)	657	3.42
European (81)	81	0.42
Finnish (12)	39	0.20
French, ex. Basque (35)	105	0.55
French Canadian (0)	24	0.12
German (155)	1,459	7.59
Greek (183)	209	1.09
Guyanese (77)	77	0.40
Hungarian (265)	735	3.82
Icelander (0)	6	0.03
Iranian (22)	22	0.11
Irish (708)	2,707	14.07
Italian (1,496)	3,343	17.38
Lithuanian (40)	112	0.58
Norwegian (0)	61	0.32
Polish (813)	1,834	9.54
Portuguese (180)	204	1.06
Romanian (8)	29	0.15
Russian (145)	304	1.58
Scotch-Irish (34)	117	0.61
Scottish (27)	203	1.06
Slavic (12)	24	0.12
Slovak (178)	276	1.43
Swedish (35)	42	0.22
Swiss (0)	29	0.15
Turkish (0)	15	0.08
Ukrainian (97)	243	1.26
Welsh (0)	52	0.27
West Indian, ex. Hispanic (146)	159	0.83
Haitian (91)	91	0.47
Jamaican (30)	30	0.16
West Indian (25)	38	0.20
Yugoslavian (115)	115	0.60

Hispanic Origin	Population	%
Hispanic or Latino (of any race)	3,506	18.20
Central American, ex. Mexican	204	1.06
Costa Rican	49	0.25
Guatemalan	42	0.22
Honduran	51	0.26
Nicaraguan	13	0.07
Panamanian	13	0.07
Salvadoran	31	0.16
Other Central American	5	0.03
Cuban	178	0.92
Dominican Republic	444	2.30
Mexican	433	2.25
Puerto Rican	1,324	6.87
South American	673	3.49
Argentinean	52	0.27
Bolivian	6	0.03
Chilean	13	0.07
Colombian	245	1.27
Ecuadorian	122	0.63
Paraguayan	4	0.02
Peruvian	161	0.84
Uruguayan	45	0.23
Venezuelan	20	0.10
Other South American	5	0.03
Other Hispanic or Latino	250	1.30

Race*	Population	%
African-American/Black (1,804)	1,985	10.30
Not Hispanic (1,645)	1,751	9.09
Hispanic (159)	234	1.21
American Indian/Alaska Native (73)	158	0.82
Not Hispanic (30)	77	0.40
Hispanic (43)	81	0.42
Blackfeet (0)	7	0.04
Cherokee (0)	25	0.13
Mexican American Ind. (11)	11	0.06
Navajo (0)	1	0.01
South American Ind. (5)	15	0.08
Spanish American Ind. (1)	1	0.01
Asian (4,012)	4,189	21.74
Not Hispanic (3,979)	4,135	21.46
Hispanic (33)	54	0.28
Bangladeshi (22)	24	0.12
Cambodian (1)	1	0.01
Chinese, ex. Taiwanese (219)	256	1.33
Filipino (347)	397	2.06
Hmong (2)	4	0.02
Indian (2,843)	2,932	15.22
Indonesian (23)	23	0.12

*Notes: † The Census 2010 population figure is used to calculate the percentages in the Hispanic Origin and Race categories. Ancestry percentages are based on the 2006-2010 American Community Survey population (not shown); ‡ Numbers in parentheses indicate the number of people reporting a single ancestry; * Numbers in parentheses indicate the number of persons reporting this race alone, not in combination with any other race; Please refer to the Explanation of Data for more information.*

Japanese (14)	20	0.10
Korean (103)	112	0.58
Laotian (0)	2	0.01
Nepalese (4)	4	0.02
Pakistani (256)	273	1.42
Sri Lankan (27)	28	0.15
Taiwanese (12)	14	0.07
Thai (15)	19	0.10
Vietnamese (42)	52	0.27
Hawaii Native/Pacific Islander (12)	20	0.10
Not Hispanic (5)	9	0.05
Hispanic (7)	11	0.06
Guamanian/Chamorro (7)	7	0.04
Native Hawaiian (1)	3	0.02
White (11,497)	11,912	61.83
Not Hispanic (9,773)	9,954	51.67
Hispanic (1,724)	1,958	10.16

Woodbridge

Place Type: Township
County: Middlesex
Population: 99,585†

Ancestry‡	Population	%
Afghan (37)	37	0.04
African, Sub-Saharan (690)	734	0.74
African (392)	436	0.44
Ghanaian (154)	154	0.16
Kenyan (82)	82	0.08
Nigerian (62)	62	0.06
Albanian (32)	96	0.10
American (2,580)	2,580	2.60
Arab (553)	682	0.69
Arab (127)	127	0.13
Egyptian (374)	460	0.46
Jordanian (18)	18	0.02
Lebanese (0)	10	0.01
Moroccan (23)	23	0.02
Palestinian (0)	11	0.01
Syrian (0)	22	0.02
Other Arab (11)	11	0.01
Armenian (80)	113	0.11
Austrian (20)	275	0.28
Brazilian (277)	304	0.31
British (11)	104	0.10
Bulgarian (35)	47	0.05
Canadian (17)	119	0.12
Croatian (11)	94	0.09
Czech (54)	305	0.31
Czechoslovakian (123)	230	0.23
Danish (124)	599	0.60
Dutch (80)	345	0.35
Eastern European (170)	170	0.17
English (403)	2,845	2.87
European (304)	343	0.35
Finnish (12)	39	0.04
French, ex. Basque (123)	994	1.00
French Canadian (72)	133	0.13
German (1,351)	7,961	8.03
Greek (369)	638	0.64
Guyanese (248)	248	0.25
Hungarian (1,249)	3,418	3.45
Icelander (0)	6	0.01
Iranian (119)	127	0.13
Irish (3,438)	12,841	12.96
Israeli (175)	185	0.19
Italian (7,960)	16,422	16.57
Latvian (0)	15	0.02
Lithuanian (174)	522	0.53
Maltese (0)	36	0.04
Norwegian (59)	232	0.23
Polish (4,318)	9,183	9.26
Portuguese (1,412)	1,723	1.74
Romanian (82)	103	0.10
Russian (592)	1,683	1.70
Scandinavian (13)	13	0.01
Scotch-Irish (239)	576	0.58
Scottish (247)	1,100	1.11
Slavic (60)	115	0.12
Slovak (482)	1,139	1.15
Slovene (16)	56	0.06
Swedish (74)	356	0.36
Swiss (18)	101	0.10
Turkish (65)	89	0.09
Ukrainian (702)	1,370	1.38
Welsh (67)	230	0.23
West Indian, ex. Hispanic (969)	1,202	1.21
Barbadian (0)	18	0.02
Bermudan (27)	27	0.03
British West Indian (92)	142	0.14
Dutch West Indian (9)	9	0.01
Haitian (262)	294	0.30
Jamaican (234)	280	0.28
Trinidadian/Tobagonian (143)	143	0.14
U.S. Virgin Islander (0)	43	0.04
West Indian (202)	246	0.25
Yugoslavian (115)	185	0.19

Hispanic Origin	Population	%
Hispanic or Latino (of any race)	15,562	15.63
Central American, ex. Mexican	843	0.85
Costa Rican	148	0.15
Guatemalan	141	0.14
Honduran	203	0.20
Nicaraguan	38	0.04
Panamanian	41	0.04
Salvadoran	266	0.27
Other Central American	6	0.01
Cuban	884	0.89
Dominican Republic	2,406	2.42
Mexican	1,066	1.07
Puerto Rican	6,063	6.09
South American	3,127	3.14
Argentinean	216	0.22
Bolivian	47	0.05
Chilean	52	0.05
Colombian	873	0.88
Ecuadorian	599	0.60
Paraguayan	7	0.01
Peruvian	1,043	1.05
Uruguayan	166	0.17
Venezuelan	88	0.09
Other South American	36	0.04
Other Hispanic or Latino	1,173	1.18

Race*	Population	%
African-American/Black (9,810)	10,711	10.76
Not Hispanic (9,038)	9,572	9.61
Hispanic (772)	1,139	1.14
American Indian/Alaska Native (321)	834	0.84
Not Hispanic (200)	555	0.56
Hispanic (121)	279	0.28
Aleut *(Alaska Native)* (3)	3	<0.01
Apache (2)	6	0.01
Blackfeet (1)	12	0.01
Canadian/French Am. Ind. (0)	3	<0.01
Central American Ind. (9)	13	0.01
Cherokee (5)	74	0.07
Chickasaw (0)	1	<0.01
Chippewa (1)	2	<0.01
Choctaw (0)	3	<0.01
Comanche (1)	7	0.01
Cree (0)	2	<0.01
Creek (0)	3	<0.01
Delaware (5)	10	0.01
Iroquois (10)	18	0.02
Mexican American Ind. (18)	26	0.03
Navajo (0)	2	<0.01
Potawatomi (3)	4	<0.01
Pueblo (0)	1	<0.01
Seminole (0)	3	<0.01
Sioux (6)	9	0.01
South American Ind. (21)	66	0.07
Spanish American Ind. (1)	2	<0.01
Asian (22,324)	23,571	23.67
Not Hispanic (22,193)	23,312	23.41
Hispanic (131)	259	0.26
Bangladeshi (127)	146	0.15
Burmese (13)	13	0.01
Cambodian (1)	1	<0.01
Chinese, ex. Taiwanese (1,075)	1,222	1.23
Filipino (2,438)	2,680	2.69
Hmong (2)	4	<0.01
Indian (15,827)	16,495	16.56
Indonesian (238)	250	0.25
Japanese (44)	69	0.07
Korean (404)	431	0.43
Laotian (2)	5	0.01
Malaysian (14)	23	0.02
Nepalese (31)	31	0.03
Pakistani (1,382)	1,481	1.49
Sri Lankan (107)	121	0.12
Taiwanese (40)	54	0.05
Thai (24)	34	0.03
Vietnamese (247)	275	0.28
Hawaii Native/Pacific Islander (39)	143	0.14
Not Hispanic (16)	60	0.06
Hispanic (23)	83	0.08
Guamanian/Chamorro (12)	12	0.01
Native Hawaiian (7)	20	0.02
Samoan (1)	2	<0.01
Tongan (1)	1	<0.01
White (58,935)	60,773	61.03
Not Hispanic (50,531)	51,480	51.69
Hispanic (8,404)	9,293	9.33

Woodbury

Place Type: City
County: Gloucester
Population: 10,174†

Ancestry‡	Population	%
American (293)	293	2.85
Austrian (14)	40	0.39
Basque (0)	21	0.20
British (11)	25	0.24
Croatian (0)	15	0.15
Czech (20)	30	0.29
Dutch (12)	72	0.70
English (253)	1,168	11.36
European (37)	37	0.36
French, ex. Basque (0)	195	1.90
French Canadian (0)	10	0.10
German (413)	2,233	21.72
Greek (16)	56	0.54
Hungarian (0)	5	0.05
Irish (443)	2,408	23.42
Italian (567)	1,779	17.31
Lithuanian (0)	66	0.64
Northern European (0)	12	0.12
Norwegian (0)	16	0.16
Pennsylvania German (8)	24	0.23
Polish (81)	594	5.78
Portuguese (12)	12	0.12
Russian (25)	175	1.70
Scotch-Irish (43)	219	2.13
Scottish (60)	272	2.65
Slovak (14)	14	0.14
Swedish (0)	97	0.94
Swiss (0)	13	0.13
Ukrainian (27)	49	0.48
Welsh (0)	98	0.95
West Indian, ex. Hispanic (125)	215	2.09
Bahamian (103)	103	1.00
Bermudan (10)	10	0.10
Jamaican (0)	90	0.88
West Indian (12)	12	0.12

Hispanic Origin	Population	%
Hispanic or Latino (of any race)	1,085	10.66
Central American, ex. Mexican	234	2.30
Costa Rican	1	0.01
Guatemalan	192	1.89
Nicaraguan	6	0.06
Panamanian	4	0.04
Salvadoran	31	0.30
Cuban	15	0.15
Dominican Republic	31	0.30

*Notes: † The Census 2010 population figure is used to calculate the percentages in the Hispanic Origin and Race categories. Ancestry percentages are based on the 2006-2010 American Community Survey population (not shown); ‡ Numbers in parentheses indicate the number of people reporting a single ancestry; * Numbers in parentheses indicate the number of persons reporting this race alone, not in combination with any other race; Please refer to the Explanation of Data for more information.*

SECTION TWO

Mexican	118	1.16
Puerto Rican	548	5.39
South American	36	0.35
Argentinean	5	0.05
Bolivian	4	0.04
Chilean	1	0.01
Colombian	10	0.10
Ecuadorian	4	0.04
Peruvian	9	0.09
Venezuelan	3	0.03
Other Hispanic or Latino	103	1.01

Race*	Population	%
African-American/Black (2,534)	2,844	27.95
Not Hispanic (2,419)	2,658	26.13
Hispanic (115)	186	1.83
American Indian/Alaska Native (23)	127	1.25
Not Hispanic (14)	90	0.88
Hispanic (9)	37	0.36
Apache (1)	1	0.01
Blackfeet (0)	7	0.07
Central American Ind. (0)	1	0.01
Cherokee (1)	24	0.24
Delaware (6)	15	0.15
Lumbee (1)	1	0.01
Navajo (0)	6	0.06
Sioux (0)	1	0.01
Asian (130)	169	1.66
Not Hispanic (125)	158	1.55
Hispanic (5)	11	0.11
Cambodian (3)	3	0.03
Chinese, ex. Taiwanese (31)	41	0.40
Filipino (30)	41	0.40
Indian (15)	23	0.23
Indonesian (1)	1	0.01
Japanese (7)	16	0.16
Korean (10)	15	0.15
Nepalese (8)	8	0.08
Pakistani (1)	1	0.01
Sri Lankan (1)	1	0.01
Thai (4)	4	0.04
Vietnamese (4)	5	0.05
Hawaii Native/Pacific Islander (28)	36	0.35
Not Hispanic (8)	10	0.10
Hispanic (20)	26	0.26
Guamanian/Chamorro (23)	23	0.23
Native Hawaiian (3)	5	0.05
White (6,716)	7,061	69.40
Not Hispanic (6,226)	6,459	63.49
Hispanic (490)	602	5.92

Woodland Park

Place Type: Borough
County: Passaic
Population: 11,819†

Ancestry‡	Population	%
African, Sub-Saharan (21)	21	0.18
Ghanaian (21)	21	0.18
Albanian (43)	43	0.37
American (291)	291	2.51
Arab (669)	716	6.17
Arab (401)	401	3.45
Lebanese (80)	95	0.82
Syrian (188)	220	1.90
Armenian (16)	16	0.14
Austrian (10)	23	0.20
Croatian (17)	17	0.15
Czech (111)	150	1.29
Danish (13)	42	0.36
Dutch (68)	266	2.29
English (39)	327	2.82
European (0)	43	0.37
French, ex. Basque (12)	12	0.10
French Canadian (0)	9	0.08
German (164)	830	7.15
Greek (165)	165	1.42
Hungarian (60)	113	0.97
Iranian (9)	9	0.08
Irish (355)	919	7.92
Israeli (0)	33	0.28
Italian (2,204)	3,257	28.06
Lithuanian (0)	9	0.08
Norwegian (12)	12	0.10
Polish (140)	473	4.07
Portuguese (26)	82	0.71
Romanian (38)	82	0.71
Russian (83)	231	1.99
Scotch-Irish (16)	57	0.49
Scottish (12)	62	0.53
Serbian (48)	48	0.41
Slavic (108)	108	0.93
Slovak (129)	161	1.39
Swedish (0)	27	0.23
Swiss (0)	38	0.33
Turkish (275)	275	2.37
Ukrainian (187)	303	2.61
Welsh (0)	66	0.57
West Indian, ex. Hispanic (53)	53	0.46
West Indian (53)	53	0.46

Hispanic Origin	Population	%
Hispanic or Latino (of any race)	2,442	20.66
Central American, ex. Mexican	90	0.76
Costa Rican	27	0.23
Guatemalan	24	0.20
Honduran	12	0.10
Nicaraguan	5	0.04
Panamanian	2	0.02
Salvadoran	20	0.17
Cuban	76	0.64
Dominican Republic	392	3.32
Mexican	95	0.80
Puerto Rican	775	6.56
South American	819	6.93
Argentinean	43	0.36
Bolivian	7	0.06
Chilean	15	0.13
Colombian	262	2.22
Ecuadorian	50	0.42
Paraguayan	3	0.03
Peruvian	396	3.35
Uruguayan	28	0.24
Venezuelan	10	0.08
Other South American	5	0.04
Other Hispanic or Latino	195	1.65

Race*	Population	%
African-American/Black (500)	600	5.08
Not Hispanic (398)	434	3.67
Hispanic (102)	166	1.40
American Indian/Alaska Native (19)	62	0.52
Not Hispanic (9)	33	0.28
Hispanic (10)	29	0.25
Apache (0)	1	0.01
Blackfeet (0)	1	0.01
Cherokee (2)	12	0.10
Delaware (0)	2	0.02
Iroquois (0)	1	0.01
Potawatomi (0)	1	0.01
South American Ind. (3)	4	0.03
Asian (496)	640	5.42
Not Hispanic (494)	623	5.27
Hispanic (2)	17	0.14
Bangladeshi (16)	16	0.14
Burmese (1)	1	0.01
Chinese, ex. Taiwanese (35)	45	0.38
Filipino (79)	91	0.77
Indian (223)	248	2.10
Japanese (2)	4	0.03
Korean (77)	82	0.69
Nepalese (2)	2	0.02
Pakistani (30)	39	0.33
Taiwanese (4)	6	0.05
Thai (8)	8	0.07
Vietnamese (2)	2	0.02
Hawaii Native/Pacific Islander (12)	19	0.16
Not Hispanic (2)	6	0.05
Hispanic (10)	13	0.11
Fijian (0)	1	0.01
Guamanian/Chamorro (6)	6	0.05
Native Hawaiian (4)	4	0.03
Samoan (1)	1	0.01
White (9,730)	10,025	84.82
Not Hispanic (8,233)	8,406	71.12
Hispanic (1,497)	1,619	13.70

Woolwich

Place Type: Township
County: Gloucester
Population: 10,200†

Ancestry‡	Population	%
African, Sub-Saharan (92)	100	1.11
African (54)	54	0.60
Ethiopian (38)	38	0.42
Nigerian (0)	8	0.09
American (238)	238	2.65
Arab (23)	40	0.45
Egyptian (23)	23	0.26
Lebanese (0)	17	0.19
Austrian (10)	10	0.11
British (8)	54	0.60
Bulgarian (0)	8	0.09
Croatian (0)	7	0.08
Czech (31)	120	1.34
Dutch (16)	95	1.06
Eastern European (9)	9	0.10
English (219)	908	10.11
European (27)	27	0.30
Finnish (0)	13	0.14
French, ex. Basque (17)	240	2.67
French Canadian (14)	14	0.16
German (281)	1,704	18.96
Greek (75)	115	1.28
Hungarian (20)	51	0.57
Irish (669)	2,425	26.99
Italian (925)	2,472	27.51
Latvian (10)	10	0.11
Lithuanian (18)	74	0.82
Macedonian (0)	8	0.09
Norwegian (0)	10	0.11
Pennsylvania German (0)	70	0.78
Polish (169)	1,055	11.74
Russian (15)	93	1.04
Scandinavian (0)	8	0.09
Scotch-Irish (24)	112	1.25
Scottish (9)	99	1.10
Slovak (7)	70	0.78
Swedish (19)	104	1.16
Swiss (8)	17	0.19
Turkish (24)	24	0.27
Ukrainian (34)	108	1.20
Welsh (0)	43	0.48
West Indian, ex. Hispanic (45)	93	1.04
Jamaican (27)	54	0.60
Trinidadian/Tobagonian (18)	39	0.43
Yugoslavian (0)	14	0.16

Hispanic Origin	Population	%
Hispanic or Latino (of any race)	365	3.58
Central American, ex. Mexican	26	0.25
Costa Rican	4	0.04
Guatemalan	6	0.06
Honduran	3	0.03
Nicaraguan	4	0.04
Panamanian	3	0.03
Salvadoran	6	0.06
Cuban	22	0.22
Dominican Republic	12	0.12
Mexican	73	0.72
Puerto Rican	170	1.67
South American	32	0.31
Argentinean	4	0.04
Bolivian	2	0.02
Chilean	4	0.04
Colombian	11	0.11
Ecuadorian	1	0.01

*Notes: † The Census 2010 population figure is used to calculate the percentages in the Hispanic Origin and Race categories. Ancestry percentages are based on the 2006-2010 American Community Survey population (not shown); ‡ Numbers in parentheses indicate the number of people reporting a single ancestry; * Numbers in parentheses indicate the number of persons reporting this race alone, not in combination with any other race; Please refer to the Explanation of Data for more information.*

Peruvian	3	0.03
Venezuelan	7	0.07
Other Hispanic or Latino	30	0.29

Race*	Population	%
African-American/Black (1,017)	1,117	10.95
Not Hispanic (989)	1,071	10.50
Hispanic (28)	46	0.45
American Indian/Alaska Native (13)	70	0.69
Not Hispanic (8)	54	0.53
Hispanic (5)	16	0.16
Blackfeet (0)	6	0.06
Cherokee (0)	12	0.12
Delaware (0)	5	0.05
Iroquois (1)	3	0.03
Mexican American Ind. (3)	6	0.06
South American Ind. (0)	7	0.07
Asian (614)	687	6.74
Not Hispanic (614)	681	6.68
Hispanic (0)	6	0.06
Cambodian (5)	5	0.05
Chinese, ex. Taiwanese (89)	113	1.11
Filipino (45)	58	0.57
Indian (314)	333	3.26
Indonesian (1)	2	0.02
Japanese (3)	12	0.12
Korean (40)	60	0.59
Laotian (1)	2	0.02
Malaysian (0)	4	0.04
Pakistani (50)	56	0.55
Taiwanese (0)	1	0.01
Vietnamese (36)	49	0.48
Hawaii Native/Pacific Islander (0)	4	0.04
Not Hispanic (0)	4	0.04
White (8,276)	8,443	82.77
Not Hispanic (8,043)	8,185	80.25
Hispanic (233)	258	2.53

Wyckoff

Place Type: Township
County: Bergen
Population: 16,696†

Ancestry‡	Population	%
African, Sub-Saharan (54)	54	0.33
South African (54)	54	0.33
American (621)	621	3.75
Arab (85)	183	1.10
Arab (34)	34	0.21
Egyptian (33)	72	0.43
Lebanese (0)	11	0.07
Syrian (5)	14	0.08
Other Arab (13)	52	0.31
Armenian (132)	208	1.25
Assyrian/Chaldean/Syriac (22)	22	0.13
Australian (10)	10	0.06
Austrian (42)	237	1.43
Belgian (0)	33	0.20
British (27)	118	0.71
Bulgarian (0)	11	0.07
Canadian (23)	23	0.14
Croatian (26)	26	0.16
Czech (0)	190	1.15
Czechoslovakian (0)	13	0.08
Danish (10)	180	1.09
Dutch (308)	908	5.48
Eastern European (111)	111	0.67
English (423)	1,715	10.35
European (240)	240	1.45
Finnish (8)	72	0.43
French, ex. Basque (23)	232	1.40
French Canadian (19)	88	0.53
German (460)	2,493	15.04
Greek (216)	270	1.63
Hungarian (150)	384	2.32
Iranian (8)	32	0.19
Irish (922)	3,476	20.97
Italian (2,240)	4,987	30.09
Latvian (37)	37	0.22
Lithuanian (9)	38	0.23
Northern European (56)	56	0.34
Norwegian (15)	166	1.00
Polish (294)	992	5.99
Portuguese (8)	90	0.54
Romanian (22)	33	0.20
Russian (136)	567	3.42
Scandinavian (21)	31	0.19
Scotch-Irish (64)	279	1.68
Scottish (35)	306	1.85
Slavic (0)	21	0.13
Slovak (4)	67	0.40
Slovene (0)	11	0.07
Swedish (33)	170	1.03
Swiss (30)	107	0.65
Turkish (15)	59	0.36
Ukrainian (34)	183	1.10
Welsh (23)	100	0.60
West Indian, ex. Hispanic (11)	11	0.07
Jamaican (11)	11	0.07
Yugoslavian (0)	11	0.07

Hispanic Origin	Population	%
Hispanic or Latino (of any race)	737	4.41
Central American, ex. Mexican	34	0.20
Costa Rican	8	0.05
Guatemalan	8	0.05
Honduran	4	0.02
Nicaraguan	1	0.01
Panamanian	2	0.01
Salvadoran	11	0.07
Cuban	113	0.68
Dominican Republic	71	0.43
Mexican	65	0.39
Puerto Rican	179	1.07
South American	168	1.01
Argentinean	19	0.11
Bolivian	4	0.02
Chilean	9	0.05
Colombian	69	0.41
Ecuadorian	28	0.17
Paraguayan	1	0.01
Peruvian	26	0.16
Uruguayan	3	0.02
Venezuelan	9	0.05
Other Hispanic or Latino	107	0.64

Race*	Population	%
African-American/Black (94)	128	0.77
Not Hispanic (81)	104	0.62
Hispanic (13)	24	0.14
American Indian/Alaska Native (7)	21	0.13
Not Hispanic (5)	16	0.10
Hispanic (2)	5	0.03
Cherokee (0)	1	0.01
Choctaw (2)	2	0.01
South American Ind. (1)	1	0.01
Asian (706)	835	5.00
Not Hispanic (705)	820	4.91
Hispanic (1)	15	0.09
Chinese, ex. Taiwanese (165)	209	1.25
Filipino (58)	111	0.66
Indian (64)	71	0.43
Indonesian (1)	2	0.01
Japanese (37)	53	0.32
Korean (342)	357	2.14
Pakistani (3)	3	0.02
Taiwanese (2)	3	0.02
Thai (6)	10	0.06
Vietnamese (2)	2	0.01
Hawaii Native/Pacific Islander (0)	4	0.02
Not Hispanic (0)	3	0.02
Hispanic (0)	1	0.01
Native Hawaiian (0)	3	0.02
White (15,616)	15,799	94.63
Not Hispanic (15,005)	15,152	90.75
Hispanic (611)	647	3.88

*Notes: † The Census 2010 population figure is used to calculate the percentages in the Hispanic Origin and Race categories. Ancestry percentages are based on the 2006-2010 American Community Survey population (not shown); ‡ Numbers in parentheses indicate the number of people reporting a single ancestry; * Numbers in parentheses indicate the number of persons reporting this race alone, not in combination with any other race; Please refer to the Explanation of Data for more information.*

NEW MEXICO

Place Type: State
Population: 2,059,179†

Ancestry‡	Population	%
Afghan (145)	179	0.01
African, Sub-Saharan (2,705)	3,951	0.20
African (2,047)	3,102	0.15
Cape Verdean (52)	52	<0.01
Ethiopian (142)	175	0.01
Ghanaian (40)	40	<0.01
Kenyan (24)	35	<0.01
Liberian (0)	11	<0.01
Nigerian (205)	276	0.01
South African (142)	163	0.01
Ugandan (0)	12	<0.01
Other Sub-Saharan African (53)	85	<0.01
Albanian (206)	258	0.01
Alsatian (21)	72	<0.01
American (67,803)	67,803	3.37
Arab (2,409)	4,972	0.25
Arab (344)	708	0.04
Egyptian (181)	295	0.01
Iraqi (202)	202	0.01
Jordanian (131)	150	0.01
Lebanese (847)	2,338	0.12
Moroccan (58)	105	0.01
Palestinian (85)	114	0.01
Syrian (78)	373	0.02
Other Arab (483)	687	0.03
Armenian (331)	739	0.04
Assyrian/Chaldean/Syriac (0)	118	0.01
Australian (236)	503	0.02
Austrian (871)	2,966	0.15
Basque (245)	685	0.03
Belgian (388)	1,452	0.07
Brazilian (197)	443	0.02
British (3,642)	7,049	0.35
Bulgarian (186)	275	0.01
Cajun (129)	355	0.02
Canadian (1,458)	2,667	0.13
Celtic (590)	939	0.05
Croatian (553)	1,298	0.06
Cypriot (25)	25	<0.01
Czech (1,830)	5,868	0.29
Czechoslovakian (834)	1,685	0.08
Danish (2,166)	7,207	0.36
Dutch (5,568)	23,258	1.16
Eastern European (1,480)	1,723	0.09
English (61,349)	160,177	7.96
Estonian (120)	185	0.01
European (14,930)	17,217	0.86
Finnish (814)	2,510	0.12
French, ex. Basque (7,503)	43,256	2.15
French Canadian (2,482)	6,320	0.31
German (67,184)	209,559	10.41
German Russian (26)	44	<0.01
Greek (2,165)	5,103	0.25
Guyanese (63)	81	<0.01
Hungarian (1,331)	4,935	0.25
Icelander (151)	233	0.01
Iranian (881)	1,146	0.06
Irish (42,334)	151,945	7.55
Israeli (194)	439	0.02
Italian (17,687)	50,703	2.52
Latvian (206)	411	0.02
Lithuanian (523)	2,154	0.11
Luxemburger (70)	109	0.01
Macedonian (63)	238	0.01
Maltese (3)	20	<0.01
New Zealander (103)	140	0.01
Northern European (1,802)	2,060	0.10
Norwegian (7,120)	19,139	0.95
Pennsylvania German (420)	511	0.03
Polish (7,340)	23,528	1.17
Portuguese (1,137)	3,975	0.20
Romanian (363)	1,016	0.05
Russian (3,367)	9,662	0.48
Scandinavian (1,711)	3,757	0.19
Scotch-Irish (12,617)	32,039	1.59
Scottish (10,716)	34,572	1.72
Serbian (150)	440	0.02
Slavic (316)	955	0.05
Slovak (634)	1,836	0.09
Slovene (133)	527	0.03
Swedish (5,037)	18,667	0.93
Swiss (1,133)	4,417	0.22
Turkish (489)	712	0.04
Ukrainian (898)	2,259	0.11
Welsh (2,398)	11,089	0.55
West Indian, ex. Hispanic (959)	2,284	0.11
Bahamian (41)	50	<0.01
Barbadian (0)	28	<0.01
Belizean (10)	30	<0.01
Bermudan (0)	20	<0.01
British West Indian (55)	107	0.01
Dutch West Indian (195)	908	0.05
Haitian (82)	218	0.01
Jamaican (369)	645	0.03
Trinidadian/Tobagonian (64)	77	<0.01
West Indian (143)	201	0.01
Yugoslavian (446)	1,166	0.06

Hispanic Origin	Population	%
Hispanic or Latino (of any race)	953,403	46.30
Central American, ex. Mexican	6,621	0.32
Costa Rican	342	0.02
Guatemalan	2,386	0.12
Honduran	657	0.03
Nicaraguan	493	0.02
Panamanian	625	0.03
Salvadoran	2,051	0.10
Other Central American	67	<0.01
Cuban	4,298	0.21
Dominican Republic	492	0.02
Mexican	590,890	28.70
Puerto Rican	7,964	0.39
South American	4,841	0.24
Argentinean	653	0.03
Bolivian	229	0.01
Chilean	569	0.03
Colombian	1,347	0.07
Ecuadorian	548	0.03
Paraguayan	53	<0.01
Peruvian	913	0.04
Uruguayan	81	<0.01
Venezuelan	394	0.02
Other South American	54	<0.01
Other Hispanic or Latino	338,297	16.43

Race*	Population	%
African-American/Black (42,550)	57,040	2.77
Not Hispanic (35,462)	44,273	2.15
Hispanic (7,088)	12,767	0.62
American Indian/Alaska Native (193,222)	219,512	10.66
Not Hispanic (175,368)	190,050	9.23
Hispanic (17,854)	29,462	1.43
Alaska Athabascan *(Ala. Nat.)* (65)	95	<0.01
Aleut *(Alaska Native)* (40)	69	<0.01
Apache (7,778)	9,926	0.48
Arapaho (89)	141	0.01
Blackfeet (165)	463	0.02
Canadian/French Am. Ind. (42)	99	<0.01
Central American Ind. (61)	103	0.01
Cherokee (1,221)	4,358	0.21
Cheyenne (184)	354	0.02
Chickasaw (235)	498	0.02
Chippewa (430)	696	0.03
Choctaw (792)	1,679	0.08
Colville (25)	36	<0.01
Comanche (240)	454	0.02
Cree (21)	83	<0.01
Creek (242)	475	0.02
Crow (99)	135	0.01
Delaware (61)	127	0.01
Hopi (417)	891	0.04
Houma (5)	11	<0.01
Inupiat *(Alaska Native)* (77)	123	0.01
Iroquois (205)	448	0.02
Kiowa (1,202)	1,343	0.07
Lumbee (43)	74	<0.01
Menominee (32)	49	<0.01
Mexican American Ind. (1,160)	1,757	0.09
Navajo (108,306)	116,157	5.64
Osage (100)	234	0.01
Ottawa (23)	40	<0.01
Paiute (58)	127	0.01
Pima (138)	218	0.01
Potawatomi (142)	246	0.01
Pueblo (38,321)	42,481	2.06
Puget Sound Salish (50)	73	<0.01
Seminole (93)	213	0.01
Shoshone (97)	182	0.01
Sioux (1,136)	1,885	0.09
South American Ind. (71)	151	0.01
Spanish American Ind. (336)	540	0.03
Tlingit-Haida *(Alaska Native)* (99)	152	0.01
Tohono O'Odham (171)	207	0.01
Tsimshian *(Alaska Native)* (8)	16	<0.01
Ute (308)	546	0.03
Yakama (33)	44	<0.01
Yaqui (117)	238	0.01
Yuman (91)	138	0.01
Yup'ik *(Alaska Native)* (37)	51	<0.01
Asian (28,208)	40,456	1.96
Not Hispanic (26,305)	34,771	1.69
Hispanic (1,903)	5,685	0.28
Bangladeshi (77)	83	<0.01
Bhutanese (49)	49	<0.01
Burmese (73)	89	<0.01
Cambodian (110)	154	0.01
Chinese, ex. Taiwanese (5,418)	7,335	0.36
Filipino (4,963)	8,535	0.41
Hmong (20)	28	<0.01
Indian (4,550)	5,727	0.28
Indonesian (103)	238	0.01
Japanese (2,208)	4,889	0.24
Korean (2,423)	3,760	0.18
Laotian (518)	673	0.03
Malaysian (36)	61	<0.01
Nepalese (222)	237	0.01
Pakistani (405)	498	0.02
Sri Lankan (105)	122	0.01
Taiwanese (281)	366	0.02
Thai (567)	944	0.05
Vietnamese (4,726)	5,403	0.26
Hawaii Native/Pacific Islander (1,810)	4,698	0.23
Not Hispanic (1,246)	2,841	0.14
Hispanic (564)	1,857	0.09
Fijian (22)	31	<0.01
Guamanian/Chamorro (420)	805	0.04
Marshallese (14)	17	<0.01
Native Hawaiian (660)	1,854	0.09
Samoan (302)	624	0.03
Tongan (16)	50	<0.01
White (1,407,876)	1,473,005	71.53
Not Hispanic (833,810)	859,633	41.75
Hispanic (574,066)	613,372	29.79

*Notes: † The Census 2010 population figure is used to calculate the percentages in the Hispanic Origin and Race categories. Ancestry percentages are based on the 2006-2010 American Community Survey population (not shown); ‡ Numbers in parentheses indicate the number of people reporting a single ancestry; * Numbers in parentheses indicate the number of persons reporting this race alone, not in combination with any other race; Please refer to the Explanation of Data for more information.*

Alamogordo

Place Type: City
County: Otero
Population: 30,403†

Ancestry‡	Population	%
African, Sub-Saharan (14)	14	0.05
African (14)	14	0.05
American (1,195)	1,195	4.02
Arab (0)	69	0.23
Arab (0)	52	0.17
Syrian (0)	17	0.06
Australian (3)	6	0.02
Austrian (27)	41	0.14
Belgian (15)	84	0.28
British (120)	229	0.77
Cajun (0)	48	0.16
Canadian (0)	15	0.05
Croatian (0)	12	0.04
Czech (30)	64	0.22
Czechoslovakian (0)	15	0.05
Dutch (78)	568	1.91
Eastern European (7)	7	0.02
English (1,177)	2,357	7.92
European (328)	342	1.15
Finnish (0)	53	0.18
French, ex. Basque (40)	446	1.50
French Canadian (85)	128	0.43
German (2,505)	5,165	17.36
German Russian (4)	4	0.01
Greek (5)	31	0.10
Hungarian (0)	42	0.14
Irish (861)	2,656	8.93
Israeli (0)	52	0.17
Italian (433)	977	3.28
Lithuanian (12)	49	0.16
Northern European (18)	18	0.06
Norwegian (82)	322	1.08
Polish (86)	442	1.49
Portuguese (38)	54	0.18
Russian (6)	41	0.14
Scotch-Irish (200)	770	2.59
Scottish (159)	513	1.72
Slavic (19)	19	0.06
Slovak (0)	8	0.03
Slovene (15)	15	0.05
Swedish (153)	411	1.38
Ukrainian (7)	13	0.04
Welsh (70)	235	0.79
West Indian, ex. Hispanic (0)	4	0.01
Dutch West Indian (0)	4	0.01
Yugoslavian (15)	29	0.10

Hispanic Origin	Population	%
Hispanic or Latino (of any race)	9,271	30.49
Central American, ex. Mexican	60	0.20
Costa Rican	8	0.03
Guatemalan	12	0.04
Honduran	12	0.04
Nicaraguan	2	0.01
Panamanian	13	0.04
Salvadoran	13	0.04
Cuban	48	0.16
Dominican Republic	6	0.02
Mexican	7,061	23.22
Puerto Rican	243	0.80
South American	48	0.16
Argentinean	3	0.01
Bolivian	7	0.02
Chilean	3	0.01
Colombian	8	0.03
Ecuadorian	5	0.02
Peruvian	19	0.06
Uruguayan	1	<0.01
Venezuelan	1	<0.01
Other South American	1	<0.01
Other Hispanic or Latino	1,805	5.94

Race*	Population	%
African-American/Black (1,648)	2,096	6.89
Not Hispanic (1,511)	1,842	6.06
Hispanic (137)	254	0.84
American Indian/Alaska Native (431)	817	2.69
Not Hispanic (295)	556	1.83
Hispanic (136)	261	0.86
Alaska Athabascan *(Ala. Nat.)* (1)	1	<0.01
Aleut *(Alaska Native)* (2)	6	0.02
Apache (102)	151	0.50
Blackfeet (1)	2	0.01
Canadian/French Am. Ind. (0)	1	<0.01
Cherokee (18)	97	0.32
Cheyenne (1)	2	0.01
Chickasaw (6)	8	0.03
Chippewa (0)	2	0.01
Choctaw (5)	13	0.04
Comanche (1)	8	0.03
Creek (5)	10	0.03
Hopi (0)	1	<0.01
Inupiat *(Alaska Native)* (0)	3	0.01
Iroquois (6)	11	0.04
Mexican American Ind. (8)	18	0.06
Navajo (57)	95	0.31
Paiute (1)	3	0.01
Pima (1)	1	<0.01
Potawatomi (1)	2	0.01
Pueblo (31)	59	0.19
Seminole (0)	1	<0.01
Sioux (11)	22	0.07
Spanish American Ind. (1)	2	0.01
Tlingit-Haida *(Alaska Native)* (1)	3	0.01
Ute (2)	2	0.01
Asian (523)	871	2.86
Not Hispanic (499)	778	2.56
Hispanic (24)	93	0.31
Cambodian (5)	5	0.02
Chinese, ex. Taiwanese (58)	90	0.30
Filipino (208)	337	1.11
Indian (30)	54	0.18
Indonesian (3)	5	0.02
Japanese (58)	110	0.36
Korean (74)	140	0.46
Pakistani (2)	5	0.02
Sri Lankan (1)	1	<0.01
Taiwanese (4)	6	0.02
Thai (35)	60	0.20
Vietnamese (32)	39	0.13
Hawaii Native/Pacific Islander (102)	203	0.67
Not Hispanic (88)	163	0.54
Hispanic (14)	40	0.13
Fijian (1)	2	0.01
Guamanian/Chamorro (59)	71	0.23
Native Hawaiian (14)	61	0.20
Samoan (10)	21	0.07
Tongan (0)	6	0.02
White (23,363)	24,662	81.12
Not Hispanic (17,887)	18,602	61.18
Hispanic (5,476)	6,060	19.93

Albuquerque

Place Type: City
County: Bernalillo
Population: 545,852†

Ancestry‡	Population	%
Afghan (129)	129	0.02
African, Sub-Saharan (927)	1,405	0.26
African (704)	1,025	0.19
Cape Verdean (13)	13	<0.01
Ethiopian (49)	71	0.01
Kenyan (0)	11	<0.01
Liberian (0)	11	<0.01
Nigerian (100)	171	0.03
South African (32)	53	0.01
Ugandan (0)	12	<0.01
Other Sub-Saharan African (29)	38	0.01
Albanian (206)	249	0.05
Alsatian (0)	8	<0.01
American (13,911)	13,911	2.62
Arab (1,104)	2,393	0.45
Arab (173)	317	0.06
Egyptian (54)	131	0.02
Iraqi (191)	191	0.04
Jordanian (35)	35	0.01
Lebanese (331)	999	0.19
Moroccan (33)	80	0.02
Palestinian (14)	24	<0.01
Syrian (33)	232	0.04
Other Arab (240)	384	0.07
Armenian (166)	396	0.07
Australian (184)	366	0.07
Austrian (209)	1,155	0.22
Basque (63)	181	0.03
Belgian (73)	401	0.08
Brazilian (109)	170	0.03
British (1,171)	2,194	0.41
Bulgarian (105)	144	0.03
Cajun (32)	32	0.01
Canadian (530)	894	0.17
Celtic (45)	192	0.04
Croatian (152)	367	0.07
Cypriot (12)	12	<0.01
Czech (480)	1,642	0.31
Czechoslovakian (182)	473	0.09
Danish (593)	2,273	0.43
Dutch (1,454)	6,233	1.17
Eastern European (367)	526	0.10
English (12,210)	40,798	7.68
Estonian (75)	124	0.02
European (5,538)	6,436	1.21
Finnish (344)	985	0.19
French, ex. Basque (2,057)	12,304	2.32
French Canadian (867)	2,420	0.46
German (18,258)	63,293	11.91
German Russian (13)	13	<0.01
Greek (895)	1,797	0.34
Guyanese (10)	25	<0.01
Hungarian (540)	1,798	0.34
Icelander (53)	89	0.02
Iranian (619)	672	0.13
Irish (12,309)	46,146	8.68
Israeli (141)	249	0.05
Italian (5,838)	18,032	3.39
Latvian (75)	140	0.03
Lithuanian (141)	889	0.17
Luxemburger (8)	22	<0.01
Macedonian (63)	183	0.03
Maltese (0)	17	<0.01
New Zealander (10)	10	<0.01
Northern European (791)	949	0.18
Norwegian (2,437)	7,108	1.34
Pennsylvania German (313)	333	0.06
Polish (2,695)	8,841	1.66
Portuguese (273)	1,358	0.26
Romanian (144)	346	0.07
Russian (1,169)	3,282	0.62
Scandinavian (612)	1,442	0.27
Scotch-Irish (3,508)	9,382	1.77
Scottish (2,930)	10,368	1.95
Serbian (59)	212	0.04
Slavic (89)	194	0.04
Slovak (110)	472	0.09
Slovene (40)	156	0.03
Swedish (1,287)	6,215	1.17
Swiss (208)	1,201	0.23
Turkish (324)	460	0.09
Ukrainian (330)	791	0.15
Welsh (665)	3,720	0.70
West Indian, ex. Hispanic (306)	517	0.10
Bahamian (41)	41	0.01
Barbadian (0)	28	0.01
Belizean (10)	10	<0.01
British West Indian (14)	14	<0.01
Dutch West Indian (0)	14	<0.01
Haitian (32)	43	0.01
Jamaican (127)	249	0.05
Trinidadian/Tobagonian (14)	14	<0.01

*Notes: † The Census 2010 population figure is used to calculate the percentages in the Hispanic Origin and Race categories. Ancestry percentages are based on the 2006-2010 American Community Survey population (not shown); ‡ Numbers in parentheses indicate the number of people reporting a single ancestry; * Numbers in parentheses indicate the number of persons reporting this race alone, not in combination with any other race; Please refer to the Explanation of Data for more information.*

Ancestry (cont.)	Population	%
West Indian (68)	104	0.02
Yugoslavian (56)	208	0.04

Hispanic Origin	Population	%
Hispanic or Latino (of any race)	255,055	46.73
Central American, ex. Mexican	2,310	0.42
Costa Rican	136	0.02
Guatemalan	724	0.13
Honduran	202	0.04
Nicaraguan	205	0.04
Panamanian	306	0.06
Salvadoran	723	0.13
Other Central American	14	<0.01
Cuban	2,915	0.53
Dominican Republic	183	0.03
Mexican	146,035	26.75
Puerto Rican	2,802	0.51
South American	2,220	0.41
Argentinean	250	0.05
Bolivian	88	0.02
Chilean	282	0.05
Colombian	627	0.11
Ecuadorian	309	0.06
Paraguayan	19	<0.01
Peruvian	426	0.08
Uruguayan	24	<0.01
Venezuelan	171	0.03
Other South American	24	<0.01
Other Hispanic or Latino	98,590	18.06

Race*	Population	%
African-American/Black (17,933)	23,683	4.34
Not Hispanic (14,878)	18,235	3.34
Hispanic (3,055)	5,448	1.00
American Indian/Alaska Native (25,087)	32,571	5.97
Not Hispanic (20,627)	24,591	4.51
Hispanic (4,460)	7,980	1.46
Alaska Athabascan *(Ala. Nat.)* (40)	53	0.01
Aleut *(Alaska Native)* (9)	22	<0.01
Apache (672)	1,095	0.20
Arapaho (34)	49	0.01
Blackfeet (60)	141	0.03
Canadian/French Am. Ind. (11)	30	0.01
Central American Ind. (11)	30	0.01
Cherokee (284)	1,113	0.20
Cheyenne (70)	120	0.02
Chickasaw (65)	142	0.03
Chippewa (152)	253	0.05
Choctaw (199)	442	0.08
Colville (7)	16	<0.01
Comanche (71)	128	0.02
Cree (4)	25	<0.01
Creek (66)	131	0.02
Crow (40)	51	0.01
Delaware (19)	39	0.01
Hopi (153)	276	0.05
Houma (0)	3	<0.01
Inupiat *(Alaska Native)* (18)	33	0.01
Iroquois (70)	156	0.03
Kiowa (93)	141	0.03
Lumbee (17)	30	0.01
Menominee (16)	27	<0.01
Mexican American Ind. (312)	495	0.09
Navajo (10,907)	12,768	2.34
Osage (23)	56	0.01
Ottawa (5)	12	<0.01
Paiute (19)	38	0.01
Pima (44)	62	0.01
Potawatomi (34)	46	0.01
Pueblo (4,808)	6,137	1.12
Puget Sound Salish (18)	22	<0.01
Seminole (33)	64	0.01
Shoshone (26)	43	0.01
Sioux (461)	726	0.13
South American Ind. (29)	67	0.01
Spanish American Ind. (72)	136	0.02
Tlingit-Haida *(Alaska Native)* (24)	37	0.01
Tohono O'Odham (52)	64	0.01
Tsimshian *(Alaska Native)* (0)	1	<0.01
Ute (72)	102	0.02
Yakama (9)	12	<0.01
Yaqui (31)	63	0.01
Yuman (31)	51	0.01
Yup'ik *(Alaska Native)* (12)	23	<0.01
Asian (14,450)	19,631	3.60
Not Hispanic (13,674)	17,372	3.18
Hispanic (776)	2,259	0.41
Bangladeshi (67)	71	0.01
Bhutanese (46)	46	0.01
Burmese (33)	43	0.01
Cambodian (61)	92	0.02
Chinese, ex. Taiwanese (2,732)	3,566	0.65
Filipino (1,799)	3,130	0.57
Hmong (9)	13	<0.01
Indian (2,143)	2,635	0.48
Indonesian (39)	79	0.01
Japanese (921)	2,085	0.38
Korean (1,143)	1,693	0.31
Laotian (410)	500	0.09
Malaysian (6)	18	<0.01
Nepalese (75)	76	0.01
Pakistani (251)	293	0.05
Sri Lankan (43)	45	0.01
Taiwanese (138)	168	0.03
Thai (235)	392	0.07
Vietnamese (3,649)	4,059	0.74
Hawaii Native/Pacific Islander (613)	1,579	0.29
Not Hispanic (418)	971	0.18
Hispanic (195)	608	0.11
Fijian (4)	5	<0.01
Guamanian/Chamorro (142)	294	0.05
Marshallese (6)	6	<0.01
Native Hawaiian (249)	688	0.13
Samoan (71)	163	0.03
Tongan (8)	10	<0.01
White (380,552)	401,578	73.57
Not Hispanic (229,933)	238,484	43.69
Hispanic (150,619)	163,094	29.88

Anthony

Place Type: CDP
County: Do±a Ana
Population: 9,360†

Ancestry‡	Population	%
American (28)	28	0.34
Arab (36)	73	0.88
Lebanese (36)	73	0.88
French, ex. Basque (0)	14	0.17
German (0)	38	0.46
Irish (0)	81	0.98
Italian (0)	19	0.23
Norwegian (0)	24	0.29
Scottish (0)	14	0.17

Hispanic Origin	Population	%
Hispanic or Latino (of any race)	9,120	97.44
Central American, ex. Mexican	25	0.27
Guatemalan	14	0.15
Honduran	2	0.02
Panamanian	1	0.01
Salvadoran	7	0.07
Other Central American	1	0.01
Cuban	2	0.02
Mexican	8,618	92.07
Puerto Rican	11	0.12
South American	4	0.04
Chilean	1	0.01
Ecuadorian	1	0.01
Peruvian	1	0.01
Uruguayan	1	0.01
Other Hispanic or Latino	460	4.91

Race*	Population	%
African-American/Black (76)	98	1.05
Not Hispanic (10)	15	0.16
Hispanic (66)	83	0.89
American Indian/Alaska Native (51)	78	0.83
Not Hispanic (8)	14	0.15
Hispanic (43)	64	0.68
Apache (3)	7	0.07
Cherokee (0)	1	0.01
Comanche (1)	1	0.01
Mexican American Ind. (1)	4	0.04
Navajo (7)	11	0.12
Osage (0)	1	0.01
Pueblo (1)	2	0.02
Shoshone (1)	1	0.01
Asian (8)	27	0.29
Not Hispanic (2)	6	0.06
Hispanic (6)	21	0.22
Chinese, ex. Taiwanese (0)	10	0.11
Filipino (2)	6	0.06
Indian (5)	9	0.10
Laotian (0)	1	0.01
Vietnamese (0)	5	0.05
Hawaii Native/Pacific Islander (5)	11	0.12
Not Hispanic (0)	1	0.01
Hispanic (5)	10	0.11
Guamanian/Chamorro (4)	5	0.05
Native Hawaiian (1)	4	0.04
White (5,758)	5,954	63.61
Not Hispanic (202)	216	2.31
Hispanic (5,556)	5,738	61.30

Artesia

Place Type: City
County: Eddy
Population: 11,301†

Ancestry‡	Population	%
American (629)	629	5.69
British (11)	31	0.28
Danish (9)	9	0.08
Dutch (29)	175	1.58
English (300)	630	5.70
European (66)	66	0.60
French, ex. Basque (74)	179	1.62
French Canadian (0)	33	0.30
German (504)	1,201	10.86
Greek (0)	16	0.14
Irish (257)	801	7.24
Italian (45)	92	0.83
Norwegian (246)	314	2.84
Polish (15)	15	0.14
Portuguese (45)	157	1.42
Scandinavian (15)	15	0.14
Scotch-Irish (66)	122	1.10
Scottish (101)	138	1.25
Swedish (63)	73	0.66
Swiss (13)	13	0.12
Welsh (16)	72	0.65
West Indian, ex. Hispanic (20)	87	0.79
Dutch West Indian (20)	87	0.79

Hispanic Origin	Population	%
Hispanic or Latino (of any race)	5,858	51.84
Central American, ex. Mexican	2	0.02
Honduran	1	0.01
Salvadoran	1	0.01
Cuban	4	0.04
Mexican	4,755	42.08
Puerto Rican	47	0.42
South American	19	0.17
Colombian	17	0.15
Peruvian	1	0.01
Venezuelan	1	0.01
Other Hispanic or Latino	1,031	9.12

Race*	Population	%
African-American/Black (133)	176	1.56
Not Hispanic (105)	132	1.17
Hispanic (28)	44	0.39
American Indian/Alaska Native (177)	286	2.53
Not Hispanic (78)	127	1.12
Hispanic (99)	159	1.41
Apache (15)	38	0.34
Blackfeet (4)	9	0.08

*Notes: † The Census 2010 population figure is used to calculate the percentages in the Hispanic Origin and Race categories. Ancestry percentages are based on the 2006-2010 American Community Survey population (not shown); ‡ Numbers in parentheses indicate the number of people reporting a single ancestry; * Numbers in parentheses indicate the number of persons reporting this race alone, not in combination with any other race; Please refer to the Explanation of Data for more information.*

Cherokee (14)	26	0.23
Chickasaw (2)	2	0.02
Choctaw (11)	20	0.18
Comanche (1)	1	0.01
Creek (2)	2	0.02
Crow (0)	3	0.03
Inupiat *(Alaska Native)* (1)	1	0.01
Mexican American Ind. (11)	11	0.10
Navajo (30)	52	0.46
Osage (0)	2	0.02
Pueblo (17)	20	0.18
Seminole (5)	5	0.04
Sioux (4)	5	0.04
Spanish American Ind. (2)	3	0.03
Tohono O'Odham (1)	4	0.04
Ute (1)	1	0.01
Asian (43)	75	0.66
Not Hispanic (27)	47	0.42
Hispanic (16)	28	0.25
Chinese, ex. Taiwanese (5)	5	0.04
Filipino (10)	13	0.12
Indian (8)	9	0.08
Japanese (7)	15	0.13
Korean (7)	19	0.17
Laotian (1)	2	0.02
Thai (1)	1	0.01
Vietnamese (0)	3	0.03
Hawaii Native/Pacific Islander (5)	23	0.20
Not Hispanic (3)	8	0.07
Hispanic (2)	15	0.13
Guamanian/Chamorro (1)	1	0.01
Native Hawaiian (4)	14	0.12
White (8,422)	8,744	77.37
Not Hispanic (5,110)	5,209	46.09
Hispanic (3,312)	3,535	31.28

Bernalillo

Place Type: Town
County: Sandoval
Population: 8,320†

Ancestry‡	Population	%
American (103)	103	1.28
Arab (0)	7	0.09
Lebanese (0)	7	0.09
Austrian (0)	20	0.25
Canadian (40)	40	0.50
Danish (0)	2	0.02
Dutch (10)	50	0.62
Eastern European (9)	9	0.11
English (154)	326	4.04
Estonian (0)	6	0.07
Finnish (0)	2	0.02
French, ex. Basque (37)	109	1.35
French Canadian (7)	46	0.57
German (118)	352	4.36
Hungarian (0)	9	0.11
Irish (58)	291	3.60
Italian (21)	83	1.03
Norwegian (30)	33	0.41
Polish (32)	74	0.92
Romanian (3)	3	0.04
Russian (0)	26	0.32
Scandinavian (0)	20	0.25
Scotch-Irish (72)	82	1.02
Scottish (40)	112	1.39
Slavic (0)	44	0.55
Slovak (5)	5	0.06
Swedish (0)	7	0.09
Welsh (2)	6	0.07

Hispanic Origin	Population	%
Hispanic or Latino (of any race)	5,804	69.76
Central American, ex. Mexican	20	0.24
Guatemalan	4	0.05
Honduran	1	0.01
Nicaraguan	2	0.02
Panamanian	2	0.02
Salvadoran	11	0.13
Cuban	3	0.04
Dominican Republic	5	0.06
Mexican	2,506	30.12
Puerto Rican	14	0.17
South American	5	0.06
Bolivian	1	0.01
Colombian	1	0.01
Venezuelan	3	0.04
Other Hispanic or Latino	3,251	39.07

Race*	Population	%
African-American/Black (74)	95	1.14
Not Hispanic (55)	64	0.77
Hispanic (19)	31	0.37
American Indian/Alaska Native (439)	486	5.84
Not Hispanic (386)	409	4.92
Hispanic (53)	77	0.93
Apache (12)	13	0.16
Blackfeet (0)	3	0.04
Cherokee (3)	9	0.11
Cheyenne (5)	7	0.08
Choctaw (3)	5	0.06
Comanche (1)	1	0.01
Cree (1)	1	0.01
Creek (0)	2	0.02
Hopi (0)	1	0.01
Iroquois (1)	1	0.01
Kiowa (24)	24	0.29
Mexican American Ind. (2)	2	0.02
Navajo (66)	77	0.93
Pueblo (161)	175	2.10
Seminole (6)	7	0.08
Sioux (1)	1	0.01
South American Ind. (0)	1	0.01
Spanish American Ind. (1)	1	0.01
Ute (2)	4	0.05
Yaqui (0)	1	0.01
Asian (41)	62	0.75
Not Hispanic (31)	48	0.58
Hispanic (10)	14	0.17
Cambodian (1)	1	0.01
Chinese, ex. Taiwanese (16)	19	0.23
Filipino (12)	15	0.18
Indian (3)	4	0.05
Indonesian (1)	1	0.01
Japanese (2)	15	0.18
Korean (5)	8	0.10
Taiwanese (0)	1	0.01
Hawaii Native/Pacific Islander (9)	23	0.28
Not Hispanic (9)	17	0.20
Hispanic (0)	6	0.07
Guamanian/Chamorro (1)	5	0.06
Marshallese (1)	1	0.01
Native Hawaiian (3)	5	0.06
Samoan (0)	1	0.01
White (5,255)	5,409	65.01
Not Hispanic (1,955)	2,012	24.18
Hispanic (3,300)	3,397	40.83

Bloomfield

Place Type: City
County: San Juan
Population: 8,112†

Ancestry‡	Population	%
American (169)	169	2.14
British (14)	14	0.18
Czech (0)	16	0.20
Danish (28)	165	2.09
Dutch (0)	55	0.70
English (909)	1,537	19.49
European (34)	34	0.43
Finnish (13)	13	0.16
French, ex. Basque (5)	59	0.75
French Canadian (0)	53	0.67
German (267)	755	9.57
Hungarian (41)	41	0.52
Irish (114)	445	5.64
Italian (38)	100	1.27
Norwegian (0)	34	0.43
Polish (8)	91	1.15
Portuguese (0)	29	0.37
Romanian (0)	30	0.38
Russian (0)	15	0.19
Scotch-Irish (31)	63	0.80
Scottish (55)	67	0.85
Slovak (14)	14	0.18
Swedish (47)	81	1.03
Swiss (0)	77	0.98
Welsh (0)	12	0.15

Hispanic Origin	Population	%
Hispanic or Latino (of any race)	2,571	31.69
Central American, ex. Mexican	8	0.10
Guatemalan	1	0.01
Honduran	4	0.05
Nicaraguan	2	0.02
Salvadoran	1	0.01
Cuban	3	0.04
Mexican	1,342	16.54
Puerto Rican	8	0.10
South American	3	0.04
Colombian	1	0.01
Other South American	2	0.02
Other Hispanic or Latino	1,207	14.88

Race*	Population	%
African-American/Black (50)	82	1.01
Not Hispanic (33)	53	0.65
Hispanic (17)	29	0.36
American Indian/Alaska Native (1,482)	1,644	20.27
Not Hispanic (1,401)	1,522	18.76
Hispanic (81)	122	1.50
Apache (18)	29	0.36
Cherokee (7)	20	0.25
Chickasaw (1)	1	0.01
Chippewa (1)	1	0.01
Choctaw (5)	18	0.22
Comanche (0)	1	0.01
Cree (2)	2	0.02
Creek (0)	1	0.01
Iroquois (0)	4	0.05
Lumbee (0)	1	0.01
Navajo (1,224)	1,346	16.59
Osage (1)	2	0.02
Potawatomi (0)	1	0.01
Pueblo (5)	8	0.10
Seminole (3)	3	0.04
Sioux (3)	15	0.18
Tohono O'Odham (2)	2	0.02
Ute (7)	8	0.10
Yaqui (3)	3	0.04
Yuman (2)	3	0.04
Asian (36)	57	0.70
Not Hispanic (31)	48	0.59
Hispanic (5)	9	0.11
Chinese, ex. Taiwanese (10)	11	0.14
Filipino (5)	6	0.07
Indian (1)	9	0.11
Japanese (7)	13	0.16
Korean (2)	2	0.02
Pakistani (1)	1	0.01
Thai (7)	10	0.12
Hawaii Native/Pacific Islander (2)	9	0.11
Not Hispanic (1)	4	0.05
Hispanic (1)	5	0.06
Native Hawaiian (1)	7	0.09
Samoan (1)	2	0.02
White (5,461)	5,718	70.49
Not Hispanic (3,917)	4,052	49.95
Hispanic (1,544)	1,666	20.54

Carlsbad

Place Type: City
County: Eddy
Population: 26,138†

*Notes: † The Census 2010 population figure is used to calculate the percentages in the Hispanic Origin and Race categories. Ancestry percentages are based on the 2006-2010 American Community Survey population (not shown); ‡ Numbers in parentheses indicate the number of people reporting a single ancestry; * Numbers in parentheses indicate the number of persons reporting this race alone, not in combination with any other race; Please refer to the Explanation of Data for more information.*

Ancestry‡	Population	%
African, Sub-Saharan (49)	259	1.01
African (49)	259	1.01
American (1,444)	1,444	5.62
Arab (8)	27	0.11
Egyptian (8)	27	0.11
Austrian (19)	34	0.13
Belgian (0)	27	0.11
British (44)	107	0.42
Canadian (10)	10	0.04
Croatian (0)	12	0.05
Czech (62)	113	0.44
Czechoslovakian (17)	17	0.07
Danish (23)	33	0.13
Dutch (55)	553	2.15
English (1,078)	2,302	8.96
European (251)	265	1.03
Finnish (37)	92	0.36
French, ex. Basque (145)	739	2.88
French Canadian (9)	97	0.38
German (702)	2,732	10.63
Greek (10)	10	0.04
Hungarian (10)	16	0.06
Irish (648)	2,836	11.04
Italian (239)	543	2.11
Lithuanian (0)	9	0.04
Norwegian (121)	183	0.71
Polish (53)	149	0.58
Portuguese (18)	18	0.07
Russian (0)	244	0.95
Scandinavian (11)	30	0.12
Scotch-Irish (273)	552	2.15
Scottish (88)	415	1.61
Swedish (72)	152	0.59
Swiss (0)	15	0.06
Welsh (33)	135	0.53
West Indian, ex. Hispanic (0)	58	0.23
Dutch West Indian (0)	46	0.18
Jamaican (0)	12	0.05
Yugoslavian (0)	12	0.05

Hispanic Origin	Population	%
Hispanic or Latino (of any race)	11,105	42.49
Central American, ex. Mexican	17	0.07
Costa Rican	4	0.02
Guatemalan	4	0.02
Nicaraguan	1	<0.01
Panamanian	1	<0.01
Salvadoran	7	0.03
Cuban	13	0.05
Dominican Republic	2	0.01
Mexican	8,803	33.68
Puerto Rican	46	0.18
South American	29	0.11
Argentinean	1	<0.01
Chilean	2	0.01
Colombian	15	0.06
Peruvian	9	0.03
Venezuelan	2	0.01
Other Hispanic or Latino	2,195	8.40

Race*	Population	%
African-American/Black (498)	658	2.52
Not Hispanic (411)	507	1.94
Hispanic (87)	151	0.58
American Indian/Alaska Native (335)	556	2.13
Not Hispanic (170)	307	1.17
Hispanic (165)	249	0.95
Apache (16)	38	0.15
Blackfeet (0)	2	0.01
Cherokee (21)	75	0.29
Cheyenne (3)	4	0.02
Chickasaw (11)	16	0.06
Chippewa (0)	2	0.01
Choctaw (25)	38	0.15
Colville (1)	1	<0.01
Comanche (0)	2	0.01
Cree (2)	8	0.03
Creek (4)	11	0.04
Hopi (1)	3	0.01
Iroquois (0)	4	0.02
Kiowa (3)	4	0.02
Mexican American Ind. (13)	20	0.08
Navajo (29)	60	0.23
Ottawa (3)	4	0.02
Potawatomi (4)	4	0.02
Pueblo (22)	29	0.11
Seminole (0)	1	<0.01
Shoshone (1)	1	<0.01
Sioux (4)	6	0.02
Yaqui (5)	6	0.02
Yup'ik *(Alaska Native)* (1)	1	<0.01
Asian (262)	334	1.28
Not Hispanic (252)	301	1.15
Hispanic (10)	33	0.13
Burmese (6)	6	0.02
Chinese, ex. Taiwanese (35)	43	0.16
Filipino (62)	83	0.32
Indian (87)	95	0.36
Indonesian (0)	1	<0.01
Japanese (18)	30	0.11
Korean (23)	38	0.15
Laotian (0)	1	<0.01
Malaysian (8)	8	0.03
Pakistani (2)	7	0.03
Taiwanese (2)	2	0.01
Thai (1)	2	0.01
Vietnamese (7)	10	0.04
Hawaii Native/Pacific Islander (12)	47	0.18
Not Hispanic (10)	28	0.11
Hispanic (2)	19	0.07
Guamanian/Chamorro (1)	2	0.01
Native Hawaiian (8)	27	0.10
Samoan (1)	1	<0.01
White (20,236)	20,943	80.12
Not Hispanic (13,870)	14,133	54.07
Hispanic (6,366)	6,810	26.05

Chaparral

Place Type: CDP
County: Otero
Population: 14,631†

Ancestry‡	Population	%
African, Sub-Saharan (182)	182	1.34
African (182)	182	1.34
American (148)	148	1.09
Austrian (0)	13	0.10
British (0)	30	0.22
Czech (0)	11	0.08
Danish (0)	13	0.10
Dutch (40)	40	0.30
English (67)	211	1.56
European (15)	15	0.11
French, ex. Basque (0)	83	0.61
French Canadian (0)	15	0.11
German (308)	613	4.53
Greek (0)	13	0.10
Irish (139)	325	2.40
Italian (49)	91	0.67
Northern European (25)	25	0.18
Norwegian (0)	71	0.52
Portuguese (13)	13	0.10
Scandinavian (0)	13	0.10
Scotch-Irish (63)	126	0.93
Scottish (59)	91	0.67
Yugoslavian (0)	22	0.16

Hispanic Origin	Population	%
Hispanic or Latino (of any race)	12,303	84.09
Central American, ex. Mexican	24	0.16
Guatemalan	5	0.03
Honduran	4	0.03
Nicaraguan	6	0.04
Panamanian	1	0.01
Salvadoran	8	0.05
Cuban	3	0.02
Dominican Republic	8	0.05
Mexican	11,703	79.99
Puerto Rican	95	0.65
South American	4	0.03
Colombian	2	0.01
Ecuadorian	2	0.01
Other Hispanic or Latino	466	3.19

Race*	Population	%
African-American/Black (165)	212	1.45
Not Hispanic (117)	139	0.95
Hispanic (48)	73	0.50
American Indian/Alaska Native (109)	211	1.44
Not Hispanic (47)	74	0.51
Hispanic (62)	137	0.94
Apache (7)	19	0.13
Blackfeet (0)	2	0.01
Cherokee (4)	13	0.09
Chickasaw (0)	3	0.02
Chippewa (1)	1	0.01
Choctaw (2)	3	0.02
Delaware (1)	3	0.02
Iroquois (0)	1	0.01
Mexican American Ind. (19)	24	0.16
Navajo (12)	23	0.16
Ottawa (1)	1	0.01
Pueblo (2)	11	0.08
Seminole (0)	1	0.01
Sioux (0)	3	0.02
Spanish American Ind. (0)	1	0.01
Asian (25)	70	0.48
Not Hispanic (20)	48	0.33
Hispanic (5)	22	0.15
Chinese, ex. Taiwanese (2)	12	0.08
Filipino (7)	17	0.12
Indian (1)	11	0.08
Japanese (1)	11	0.08
Korean (8)	16	0.11
Thai (3)	6	0.04
Vietnamese (2)	3	0.02
Hawaii Native/Pacific Islander (5)	22	0.15
Not Hispanic (4)	11	0.08
Hispanic (1)	11	0.08
Guamanian/Chamorro (2)	4	0.03
Native Hawaiian (1)	10	0.07
Samoan (1)	3	0.02
White (8,565)	8,964	61.27
Not Hispanic (2,041)	2,111	14.43
Hispanic (6,524)	6,853	46.84

Clovis

Place Type: City
County: Curry
Population: 37,775†

Ancestry‡	Population	%
African, Sub-Saharan (78)	78	0.22
African (78)	78	0.22
American (3,922)	3,922	10.83
Arab (36)	36	0.10
Egyptian (36)	36	0.10
Austrian (0)	16	0.04
Basque (15)	15	0.04
British (68)	231	0.64
Canadian (73)	83	0.23
Croatian (17)	17	0.05
Czech (39)	79	0.22
Czechoslovakian (111)	127	0.35
Danish (30)	30	0.08
Dutch (95)	267	0.74
English (1,227)	2,472	6.83
European (304)	347	0.96
Finnish (14)	14	0.04
French, ex. Basque (66)	662	1.83
French Canadian (59)	70	0.19
German (1,305)	3,849	10.63
Greek (0)	49	0.14
Hungarian (0)	28	0.08
Iranian (14)	14	0.04
Irish (731)	2,778	7.67
Italian (192)	662	1.83

*Notes: † The Census 2010 population figure is used to calculate the percentages in the Hispanic Origin and Race categories. Ancestry percentages are based on the 2006-2010 American Community Survey population (not shown); ‡ Numbers in parentheses indicate the number of people reporting a single ancestry; * Numbers in parentheses indicate the number of persons reporting this race alone, not in combination with any other race; Please refer to the Explanation of Data for more information.*

Northern European (52)	52	0.14
Norwegian (72)	195	0.54
Polish (100)	279	0.77
Portuguese (24)	47	0.13
Russian (33)	38	0.10
Scandinavian (0)	38	0.10
Scotch-Irish (162)	309	0.85
Scottish (149)	452	1.25
Slovak (0)	17	0.05
Swedish (82)	223	0.62
Swiss (6)	17	0.05
Welsh (12)	83	0.23
West Indian, ex. Hispanic (22)	63	0.17
Dutch West Indian (13)	54	0.15
Jamaican (9)	9	0.02

Hispanic Origin	Population	%
Hispanic or Latino (of any race)	15,804	41.84
Central American, ex. Mexican	142	0.38
Guatemalan	14	0.04
Honduran	56	0.15
Nicaraguan	22	0.06
Panamanian	34	0.09
Salvadoran	15	0.04
Other Central American	1	<0.01
Cuban	33	0.09
Dominican Republic	10	0.03
Mexican	10,901	28.86
Puerto Rican	265	0.70
South American	44	0.12
Argentinean	11	0.03
Colombian	16	0.04
Ecuadorian	6	0.02
Peruvian	5	0.01
Venezuelan	6	0.02
Other Hispanic or Latino	4,409	11.67

Race*	Population	%
African-American/Black (2,625)	3,150	8.34
Not Hispanic (2,366)	2,718	7.20
Hispanic (259)	432	1.14
American Indian/Alaska Native (423)	792	2.10
Not Hispanic (209)	455	1.20
Hispanic (214)	337	0.89
Apache (32)	63	0.17
Arapaho (3)	6	0.02
Blackfeet (0)	5	0.01
Cherokee (37)	120	0.32
Cheyenne (0)	6	0.02
Chickasaw (5)	10	0.03
Chippewa (0)	3	0.01
Choctaw (17)	27	0.07
Comanche (1)	12	0.03
Cree (1)	2	0.01
Creek (8)	10	0.03
Hopi (0)	2	0.01
Iroquois (0)	2	0.01
Kiowa (6)	10	0.03
Lumbee (1)	4	0.01
Menominee (0)	1	<0.01
Mexican American Ind. (10)	18	0.05
Navajo (48)	68	0.18
Osage (0)	1	<0.01
Potawatomi (1)	1	<0.01
Pueblo (16)	30	0.08
Seminole (2)	5	0.01
Sioux (1)	7	0.02
South American Ind. (0)	1	<0.01
Spanish American Ind. (14)	16	0.04
Ute (1)	1	<0.01
Asian (536)	853	2.26
Not Hispanic (490)	721	1.91
Hispanic (46)	132	0.35
Chinese, ex. Taiwanese (45)	88	0.23
Filipino (144)	257	0.68
Indian (65)	83	0.22
Indonesian (0)	6	0.02
Japanese (57)	138	0.37
Korean (61)	103	0.27
Laotian (36)	54	0.14
Sri Lankan (0)	4	0.01
Taiwanese (2)	2	0.01
Thai (42)	66	0.17
Vietnamese (46)	52	0.14
Hawaii Native/Pacific Islander (43)	90	0.24
Not Hispanic (21)	51	0.14
Hispanic (22)	39	0.10
Guamanian/Chamorro (7)	11	0.03
Native Hawaiian (17)	42	0.11
Samoan (7)	13	0.03
White (25,858)	27,180	71.95
Not Hispanic (18,081)	18,732	49.59
Hispanic (7,777)	8,448	22.36

Corrales

Place Type: Village
County: Sandoval
Population: 8,329†

Ancestry‡	Population	%
Alsatian (7)	21	0.26
American (265)	265	3.25
Arab (10)	53	0.65
Lebanese (10)	23	0.28
Other Arab (0)	30	0.37
Australian (0)	8	0.10
Austrian (9)	18	0.22
Brazilian (0)	30	0.37
British (89)	166	2.04
Canadian (10)	52	0.64
Czech (0)	61	0.75
Czechoslovakian (27)	27	0.33
Danish (0)	9	0.11
Dutch (21)	107	1.31
Eastern European (15)	15	0.18
English (282)	1,198	14.69
European (80)	121	1.48
Finnish (0)	10	0.12
French, ex. Basque (30)	421	5.16
German (415)	1,712	20.99
Greek (10)	113	1.39
Hungarian (0)	58	0.71
Irish (353)	1,269	15.56
Italian (136)	435	5.33
Latvian (11)	11	0.13
Lithuanian (0)	16	0.20
Macedonian (0)	22	0.27
Norwegian (7)	220	2.70
Polish (58)	244	2.99
Portuguese (0)	17	0.21
Romanian (0)	13	0.16
Russian (28)	97	1.19
Scandinavian (28)	58	0.71
Scotch-Irish (98)	227	2.78
Scottish (66)	425	5.21
Swedish (42)	126	1.54
Swiss (0)	46	0.56
Ukrainian (8)	8	0.10
Welsh (0)	100	1.23
Yugoslavian (0)	19	0.23

Hispanic Origin	Population	%
Hispanic or Latino (of any race)	2,252	27.04
Central American, ex. Mexican	24	0.29
Costa Rican	4	0.05
Guatemalan	10	0.12
Nicaraguan	6	0.07
Panamanian	3	0.04
Salvadoran	1	0.01
Cuban	10	0.12
Dominican Republic	1	0.01
Mexican	774	9.29
Puerto Rican	21	0.25
South American	34	0.41
Argentinean	6	0.07
Bolivian	1	0.01
Chilean	2	0.02
Colombian	14	0.17
Ecuadorian	1	0.01
Peruvian	6	0.07
Venezuelan	3	0.04
Other South American	1	0.01
Other Hispanic or Latino	1,388	16.66

Race*	Population	%
African-American/Black (88)	129	1.55
Not Hispanic (79)	104	1.25
Hispanic (9)	25	0.30
American Indian/Alaska Native (137)	214	2.57
Not Hispanic (107)	155	1.86
Hispanic (30)	59	0.71
Apache (5)	8	0.10
Cherokee (10)	27	0.32
Chickasaw (1)	2	0.02
Chippewa (6)	7	0.08
Choctaw (2)	2	0.02
Comanche (5)	7	0.08
Creek (0)	1	0.01
Delaware (1)	3	0.04
Hopi (0)	2	0.02
Iroquois (0)	1	0.01
Mexican American Ind. (6)	9	0.11
Navajo (45)	57	0.68
Potawatomi (5)	5	0.06
Pueblo (21)	28	0.34
Seminole (6)	6	0.07
Sioux (2)	4	0.05
South American Ind. (2)	4	0.05
Yuman (0)	2	0.02
Asian (105)	163	1.96
Not Hispanic (90)	133	1.60
Hispanic (15)	30	0.36
Chinese, ex. Taiwanese (21)	42	0.50
Filipino (21)	34	0.41
Indian (20)	26	0.31
Japanese (15)	28	0.34
Korean (15)	17	0.20
Laotian (0)	1	0.01
Taiwanese (2)	2	0.02
Thai (0)	4	0.05
Vietnamese (4)	6	0.07
Hawaii Native/Pacific Islander (0)	2	0.02
Not Hispanic (0)	1	0.01
Hispanic (0)	1	0.01
White (7,195)	7,429	89.19
Not Hispanic (5,669)	5,771	69.29
Hispanic (1,526)	1,658	19.91

Deming

Place Type: City
County: Luna
Population: 14,855†

Ancestry‡	Population	%
American (150)	150	1.01
Austrian (0)	10	0.07
Belgian (0)	49	0.33
Cajun (0)	25	0.17
Canadian (9)	9	0.06
Czech (40)	55	0.37
Czechoslovakian (4)	4	0.03
Dutch (12)	142	0.95
English (304)	750	5.04
European (25)	25	0.17
French, ex. Basque (45)	181	1.22
French Canadian (11)	22	0.15
German (417)	1,243	8.36
Hungarian (0)	51	0.34
Irish (282)	870	5.85
Italian (107)	182	1.22
Lithuanian (15)	15	0.10
Northern European (12)	12	0.08
Norwegian (27)	110	0.74
Pennsylvania German (0)	10	0.07
Polish (52)	67	0.45
Romanian (0)	21	0.14
Russian (0)	10	0.07
Scandinavian (11)	11	0.07

*Notes: † The Census 2010 population figure is used to calculate the percentages in the Hispanic Origin and Race categories. Ancestry percentages are based on the 2006-2010 American Community Survey population (not shown); ‡ Numbers in parentheses indicate the number of people reporting a single ancestry; * Numbers in parentheses indicate the number of persons reporting this race alone, not in combination with any other race; Please refer to the Explanation of Data for more information.*

Ancestry	Population	%
Scotch-Irish (31)	294	1.98
Scottish (53)	139	0.93
Swedish (11)	21	0.14
Swiss (27)	64	0.43
Ukrainian (11)	11	0.07
Welsh (0)	30	0.20
West Indian, ex. Hispanic (0)	11	0.07
Dutch West Indian (0)	11	0.07
Yugoslavian (0)	9	0.06

Hispanic Origin	Population	%
Hispanic or Latino (of any race)	10,190	68.60
Central American, ex. Mexican	36	0.24
Costa Rican	4	0.03
Guatemalan	7	0.05
Honduran	6	0.04
Nicaraguan	3	0.02
Panamanian	8	0.05
Salvadoran	8	0.05
Cuban	8	0.05
Dominican Republic	1	0.01
Mexican	8,953	60.27
Puerto Rican	74	0.50
South American	14	0.09
Argentinean	2	0.01
Chilean	3	0.02
Colombian	7	0.05
Ecuadorian	1	0.01
Peruvian	1	0.01
Other Hispanic or Latino	1,104	7.43

Race*	Population	%
African-American/Black (230)	286	1.93
Not Hispanic (139)	160	1.08
Hispanic (91)	126	0.85
American Indian/Alaska Native (197)	298	2.01
Not Hispanic (65)	118	0.79
Hispanic (132)	180	1.21
Aleut *(Alaska Native)* (1)	1	0.01
Apache (11)	23	0.15
Blackfeet (0)	1	0.01
Cherokee (5)	17	0.11
Chippewa (0)	1	0.01
Choctaw (6)	13	0.09
Comanche (2)	2	0.01
Creek (0)	2	0.01
Delaware (1)	1	0.01
Hopi (0)	5	0.03
Iroquois (0)	2	0.01
Kiowa (0)	1	0.01
Mexican American Ind. (18)	25	0.17
Navajo (6)	17	0.11
Osage (1)	1	0.01
Potawatomi (1)	2	0.01
Pueblo (21)	28	0.19
Seminole (0)	1	0.01
Sioux (1)	2	0.01
Asian (85)	125	0.84
Not Hispanic (80)	103	0.69
Hispanic (5)	22	0.15
Chinese, ex. Taiwanese (26)	29	0.20
Filipino (34)	46	0.31
Indian (16)	18	0.12
Indonesian (1)	2	0.01
Japanese (2)	7	0.05
Korean (1)	2	0.01
Nepalese (1)	1	0.01
Thai (1)	1	0.01
Vietnamese (0)	6	0.04
Hawaii Native/Pacific Islander (17)	31	0.21
Not Hispanic (1)	1	0.01
Hispanic (16)	30	0.20
Guamanian/Chamorro (1)	1	0.01
Native Hawaiian (2)	4	0.03
Samoan (13)	14	0.09
White (11,383)	11,722	78.91
Not Hispanic (4,275)	4,348	29.27
Hispanic (7,108)	7,374	49.64

Espanola

Place Type: City
County: Rio Arriba
Population: 10,224†

Ancestry‡	Population	%
American (65)	65	0.64
Arab (32)	37	0.36
Arab (3)	8	0.08
Lebanese (29)	29	0.28
Celtic (0)	8	0.08
Czech (0)	4	0.04
Danish (0)	23	0.23
Eastern European (3)	3	0.03
English (29)	131	1.29
European (13)	13	0.13
French, ex. Basque (27)	188	1.85
German (81)	382	3.75
Greek (0)	6	0.06
Irish (14)	155	1.52
Italian (20)	105	1.03
Latvian (0)	4	0.04
Lithuanian (0)	4	0.04
Norwegian (3)	37	0.36
Pennsylvania German (3)	3	0.03
Polish (19)	54	0.53
Russian (0)	14	0.14
Scotch-Irish (0)	20	0.20
Scottish (7)	59	0.58
Slovak (0)	9	0.09
Swedish (0)	72	0.71
Welsh (0)	26	0.26
West Indian, ex. Hispanic (4)	8	0.08
Dutch West Indian (0)	4	0.04
Jamaican (4)	4	0.04
Yugoslavian (6)	11	0.11

Hispanic Origin	Population	%
Hispanic or Latino (of any race)	8,910	87.15
Central American, ex. Mexican	7	0.07
Guatemalan	4	0.04
Salvadoran	3	0.03
Cuban	9	0.09
Dominican Republic	2	0.02
Mexican	3,102	30.34
Puerto Rican	19	0.19
South American	9	0.09
Argentinean	2	0.02
Bolivian	1	0.01
Colombian	4	0.04
Ecuadorian	2	0.02
Other Hispanic or Latino	5,762	56.36

Race*	Population	%
African-American/Black (54)	79	0.77
Not Hispanic (31)	39	0.38
Hispanic (23)	40	0.39
American Indian/Alaska Native (345)	404	3.95
Not Hispanic (237)	252	2.46
Hispanic (108)	152	1.49
Apache (14)	14	0.14
Cherokee (1)	2	0.02
Cheyenne (2)	2	0.02
Chickasaw (0)	1	0.01
Choctaw (1)	1	0.01
Hopi (1)	1	0.01
Kiowa (3)	3	0.03
Navajo (35)	35	0.34
Pueblo (116)	132	1.29
Sioux (2)	4	0.04
Spanish American Ind. (1)	2	0.02
Ute (2)	2	0.02
Yaqui (1)	1	0.01
Asian (116)	137	1.34
Not Hispanic (105)	121	1.18
Hispanic (11)	16	0.16
Chinese, ex. Taiwanese (2)	4	0.04
Filipino (71)	84	0.82
Indian (29)	33	0.32
Japanese (1)	4	0.04
Korean (8)	8	0.08
Nepalese (2)	2	0.02
Vietnamese (2)	5	0.05
Hawaii Native/Pacific Islander (5)	13	0.13
Hispanic (5)	13	0.13
Native Hawaiian (0)	2	0.02
White (6,939)	7,132	69.76
Not Hispanic (896)	928	9.08
Hispanic (6,043)	6,204	60.68

Farmington

Place Type: City
County: San Juan
Population: 45,877†

Ancestry‡	Population	%
African, Sub-Saharan (62)	62	0.14
African (32)	32	0.07
Nigerian (30)	30	0.07
American (2,120)	2,120	4.75
Arab (0)	42	0.09
Lebanese (0)	42	0.09
Armenian (25)	25	0.06
Austrian (0)	14	0.03
Basque (10)	10	0.02
Belgian (0)	72	0.16
Brazilian (0)	7	0.02
British (77)	160	0.36
Bulgarian (48)	48	0.11
Cajun (0)	7	0.02
Canadian (88)	142	0.32
Croatian (14)	14	0.03
Czech (85)	184	0.41
Czechoslovakian (22)	26	0.06
Danish (24)	111	0.25
Dutch (86)	332	0.74
Eastern European (6)	6	0.01
English (4,127)	6,930	15.52
European (201)	246	0.55
Finnish (10)	113	0.25
French, ex. Basque (239)	1,062	2.38
French Canadian (41)	41	0.09
German (2,131)	5,448	12.20
Greek (0)	26	0.06
Hungarian (0)	18	0.04
Irish (838)	3,225	7.22
Italian (274)	902	2.02
Lithuanian (0)	26	0.06
Northern European (9)	9	0.02
Norwegian (122)	358	0.80
Polish (114)	303	0.68
Portuguese (9)	72	0.16
Russian (27)	142	0.32
Scandinavian (10)	20	0.04
Scotch-Irish (306)	923	2.07
Scottish (225)	524	1.17
Serbian (9)	9	0.02
Slavic (11)	71	0.16
Slovak (39)	89	0.20
Slovene (0)	6	0.01
Swedish (180)	674	1.51
Swiss (7)	47	0.11
Ukrainian (0)	22	0.05
Welsh (101)	333	0.75
West Indian, ex. Hispanic (19)	19	0.04
Dutch West Indian (11)	11	0.02
Jamaican (8)	8	0.02
Yugoslavian (0)	30	0.07

Hispanic Origin	Population	%
Hispanic or Latino (of any race)	10,298	22.45
Central American, ex. Mexican	77	0.17
Costa Rican	4	0.01
Guatemalan	29	0.06
Honduran	6	0.01
Nicaraguan	8	0.02
Panamanian	6	0.01
Salvadoran	24	0.05

*Notes: † The Census 2010 population figure is used to calculate the percentages in the Hispanic Origin and Race categories. Ancestry percentages are based on the 2006-2010 American Community Survey population (not shown); ‡ Numbers in parentheses indicate the number of people reporting a single ancestry; * Numbers in parentheses indicate the number of persons reporting this race alone, not in combination with any other race; Please refer to the Explanation of Data for more information.*

Cuban	21	0.05
Dominican Republic	3	0.01
Mexican	6,054	13.20
Puerto Rican	64	0.14
South American	83	0.18
Argentinean	4	0.01
Bolivian	3	0.01
Chilean	5	0.01
Colombian	10	0.02
Ecuadorian	7	0.02
Peruvian	23	0.05
Venezuelan	31	0.07
Other Hispanic or Latino	3,996	8.71

Race*	Population	%
African-American/Black (438)	716	1.56
Not Hispanic (377)	584	1.27
Hispanic (61)	132	0.29
American Indian/Alaska Native (10,168)	11,230	24.48
Not Hispanic (9,793)	10,561	23.02
Hispanic (375)	669	1.46
Alaska Athabascan *(Ala. Nat.)* (1)	1	<0.01
Aleut *(Alaska Native)* (1)	1	<0.01
Apache (138)	189	0.41
Arapaho (2)	2	<0.01
Blackfeet (6)	20	0.04
Canadian/French Am. Ind. (0)	4	0.01
Cherokee (25)	113	0.25
Cheyenne (8)	15	0.03
Chickasaw (10)	26	0.06
Chippewa (10)	16	0.03
Choctaw (22)	53	0.12
Colville (1)	1	<0.01
Comanche (15)	20	0.04
Cree (0)	1	<0.01
Creek (12)	21	0.05
Crow (4)	5	0.01
Delaware (0)	2	<0.01
Hopi (17)	61	0.13
Inupiat *(Alaska Native)* (6)	7	0.02
Iroquois (5)	7	0.02
Kiowa (10)	15	0.03
Menominee (0)	2	<0.01
Mexican American Ind. (21)	24	0.05
Navajo (8,708)	9,522	20.76
Osage (3)	8	0.02
Ottawa (5)	5	0.01
Paiute (1)	4	0.01
Pima (3)	5	0.01
Potawatomi (5)	15	0.03
Pueblo (115)	165	0.36
Puget Sound Salish (4)	4	0.01
Seminole (1)	1	<0.01
Shoshone (2)	8	0.02
Sioux (37)	73	0.16
South American Ind. (5)	5	0.01
Spanish American Ind. (3)	8	0.02
Tlingit-Haida *(Alaska Native)* (3)	9	0.02
Tohono O'Odham (5)	6	0.01
Tsimshian *(Alaska Native)* (0)	3	0.01
Ute (38)	84	0.18
Yuman (2)	6	0.01
Yup'ik *(Alaska Native)* (2)	2	<0.01
Asian (272)	459	1.00
Not Hispanic (260)	402	0.88
Hispanic (12)	57	0.12
Burmese (1)	1	<0.01
Cambodian (0)	1	<0.01
Chinese, ex. Taiwanese (51)	76	0.17
Filipino (55)	123	0.27
Indian (31)	42	0.09
Indonesian (2)	4	0.01
Japanese (21)	61	0.13
Korean (17)	42	0.09
Laotian (1)	4	0.01
Malaysian (2)	2	<0.01
Pakistani (4)	4	0.01
Sri Lankan (2)	2	<0.01
Thai (1)	9	0.02
Vietnamese (64)	74	0.16
Hawaii Native/Pacific Islander (31)	84	0.18
Not Hispanic (28)	61	0.13
Hispanic (3)	23	0.05
Fijian (0)	1	<0.01
Guamanian/Chamorro (12)	22	0.05
Native Hawaiian (9)	32	0.07
Samoan (3)	8	0.02
Tongan (0)	1	<0.01
White (28,824)	30,471	66.42
Not Hispanic (24,059)	24,935	54.35
Hispanic (4,765)	5,536	12.07

Gallup

Place Type: City
County: McKinley
Population: 21,678†

Ancestry‡	Population	%
African, Sub-Saharan (0)	34	0.16
African (0)	34	0.16
American (424)	424	2.01
Arab (95)	95	0.45
Arab (74)	74	0.35
Palestinian (21)	21	0.10
Austrian (77)	99	0.47
British (20)	20	0.09
Canadian (0)	22	0.10
Croatian (5)	23	0.11
Czech (10)	10	0.05
Czechoslovakian (21)	21	0.10
Dutch (193)	348	1.65
English (156)	832	3.95
Estonian (14)	14	0.07
European (55)	55	0.26
Finnish (14)	14	0.07
French, ex. Basque (23)	131	0.62
French Canadian (14)	24	0.11
German (367)	882	4.18
Greek (61)	61	0.29
Hungarian (13)	41	0.19
Irish (264)	825	3.91
Italian (224)	497	2.36
Northern European (23)	23	0.11
Norwegian (12)	141	0.67
Pennsylvania German (0)	19	0.09
Polish (6)	92	0.44
Romanian (20)	20	0.09
Russian (16)	81	0.38
Scotch-Irish (46)	141	0.67
Scottish (59)	188	0.89
Slavic (17)	17	0.08
Slovak (14)	25	0.12
Swedish (41)	154	0.73
Swiss (0)	35	0.17
Welsh (0)	43	0.20
West Indian, ex. Hispanic (76)	76	0.36
Jamaican (76)	76	0.36
Yugoslavian (31)	31	0.15

Hispanic Origin	Population	%
Hispanic or Latino (of any race)	6,864	31.66
Central American, ex. Mexican	12	0.06
Costa Rican	1	<0.01
Guatemalan	4	0.02
Honduran	1	<0.01
Nicaraguan	2	0.01
Salvadoran	4	0.02
Cuban	6	0.03
Dominican Republic	2	0.01
Mexican	4,563	21.05
Puerto Rican	69	0.32
South American	34	0.16
Argentinean	2	0.01
Bolivian	9	0.04
Colombian	10	0.05
Ecuadorian	3	0.01
Paraguayan	1	<0.01
Peruvian	7	0.03
Venezuelan	2	0.01
Other Hispanic or Latino	2,178	10.05

Race*	Population	%
African-American/Black (257)	444	2.05
Not Hispanic (223)	361	1.67
Hispanic (34)	83	0.38
American Indian/Alaska Native (9,498)	10,343	47.71
Not Hispanic (8,748)	9,235	42.60
Hispanic (750)	1,108	5.11
Alaska Athabascan *(Ala. Nat.)* (1)	1	<0.01
Aleut *(Alaska Native)* (0)	1	<0.01
Apache (19)	46	0.21
Arapaho (1)	3	0.01
Blackfeet (7)	8	0.04
Canadian/French Am. Ind. (0)	1	<0.01
Cherokee (19)	47	0.22
Cheyenne (10)	13	0.06
Chickasaw (6)	9	0.04
Chippewa (9)	10	0.05
Choctaw (14)	29	0.13
Comanche (2)	4	0.02
Cree (1)	5	0.02
Creek (11)	16	0.07
Crow (2)	2	0.01
Hopi (29)	63	0.29
Inupiat *(Alaska Native)* (2)	3	0.01
Iroquois (1)	7	0.03
Kiowa (8)	10	0.05
Menominee (1)	2	0.01
Mexican American Ind. (11)	17	0.08
Navajo (7,389)	8,119	37.45
Osage (5)	10	0.05
Paiute (4)	5	0.02
Pima (6)	6	0.03
Potawatomi (3)	7	0.03
Pueblo (484)	675	3.11
Puget Sound Salish (1)	1	<0.01
Seminole (3)	3	0.01
Shoshone (4)	8	0.04
Sioux (20)	34	0.16
South American Ind. (0)	4	0.02
Spanish American Ind. (2)	3	0.01
Tlingit-Haida *(Alaska Native)* (0)	1	<0.01
Tohono O'Odham (16)	16	0.07
Ute (7)	15	0.07
Yuman (3)	5	0.02
Yup'ik *(Alaska Native)* (0)	1	<0.01
Asian (434)	574	2.65
Not Hispanic (410)	511	2.36
Hispanic (24)	63	0.29
Bangladeshi (1)	1	<0.01
Chinese, ex. Taiwanese (68)	79	0.36
Filipino (156)	209	0.96
Indian (63)	76	0.35
Indonesian (1)	5	0.02
Japanese (39)	91	0.42
Korean (31)	37	0.17
Laotian (3)	4	0.02
Malaysian (1)	1	<0.01
Nepalese (14)	14	0.06
Pakistani (9)	13	0.06
Sri Lankan (1)	1	<0.01
Taiwanese (6)	7	0.03
Thai (0)	1	<0.01
Vietnamese (20)	24	0.11
Hawaii Native/Pacific Islander (11)	43	0.20
Not Hispanic (6)	31	0.14
Hispanic (5)	12	0.06
Guamanian/Chamorro (5)	8	0.04
Native Hawaiian (1)	10	0.05
Samoan (5)	8	0.04
White (7,631)	8,510	39.26
Not Hispanic (4,783)	5,235	24.15
Hispanic (2,848)	3,275	15.11

Grants

Place Type: City
County: Cibola
Population: 9,182†

*Notes: † The Census 2010 population figure is used to calculate the percentages in the Hispanic Origin and Race categories. Ancestry percentages are based on the 2006-2010 American Community Survey population (not shown); ‡ Numbers in parentheses indicate the number of people reporting a single ancestry; * Numbers in parentheses indicate the number of persons reporting this race alone, not in combination with any other race; Please refer to the Explanation of Data for more information.*

Ancestry‡	Population	%
American (210)	210	2.28
Arab (2)	2	0.02
Lebanese (2)	2	0.02
Basque (10)	13	0.14
Czech (0)	11	0.12
Czechoslovakian (10)	10	0.11
Dutch (9)	35	0.38
English (73)	355	3.85
European (17)	17	0.18
Finnish (0)	14	0.15
French, ex. Basque (55)	220	2.39
German (171)	524	5.69
Greek (9)	9	0.10
Hungarian (28)	28	0.30
Irish (153)	605	6.57
Italian (50)	113	1.23
Norwegian (30)	79	0.86
Scandinavian (11)	44	0.48
Scotch-Irish (142)	150	1.63
Scottish (76)	137	1.49
Swedish (0)	46	0.50
Swiss (13)	26	0.28
Welsh (15)	15	0.16
West Indian, ex. Hispanic (0)	9	0.10
Bahamian (0)	9	0.10

Hispanic Origin	Population	%
Hispanic or Latino (of any race)	4,782	52.08
Central American, ex. Mexican	7	0.08
Honduran	1	0.01
Nicaraguan	1	0.01
Salvadoran	5	0.05
Cuban	6	0.07
Mexican	2,238	24.37
Puerto Rican	19	0.21
South American	14	0.15
Argentinean	2	0.02
Chilean	3	0.03
Colombian	6	0.07
Peruvian	3	0.03
Other Hispanic or Latino	2,498	27.21

Race*	Population	%
African-American/Black (159)	200	2.18
Not Hispanic (124)	145	1.58
Hispanic (35)	55	0.60
American Indian/Alaska Native (1,553)	1,710	18.62
Not Hispanic (1,402)	1,497	16.30
Hispanic (151)	213	2.32
Aleut *(Alaska Native)* (1)	1	0.01
Apache (6)	15	0.16
Arapaho (0)	1	0.01
Blackfeet (0)	1	0.01
Cherokee (4)	25	0.27
Cheyenne (0)	1	0.01
Chippewa (1)	2	0.02
Choctaw (12)	16	0.17
Comanche (1)	1	0.01
Creek (2)	2	0.02
Delaware (2)	2	0.02
Hopi (6)	14	0.15
Houma (0)	1	0.01
Inupiat *(Alaska Native)* (0)	1	0.01
Mexican American Ind. (8)	8	0.09
Navajo (776)	861	9.38
Osage (2)	2	0.02
Pima (5)	5	0.05
Pueblo (398)	462	5.03
Shoshone (1)	3	0.03
Sioux (0)	3	0.03
Spanish American Ind. (1)	2	0.02
Tohono O'Odham (6)	8	0.09
Ute (4)	5	0.05
Yup'ik *(Alaska Native)* (1)	1	0.01
Asian (78)	106	1.15
Not Hispanic (71)	88	0.96
Hispanic (7)	18	0.20
Cambodian (0)	1	0.01
Chinese, ex. Taiwanese (14)	16	0.17
Filipino (32)	42	0.46
Indian (14)	19	0.21
Indonesian (0)	1	0.01
Japanese (4)	7	0.08
Korean (4)	9	0.10
Thai (0)	1	0.01
Vietnamese (8)	8	0.09
Hawaii Native/Pacific Islander (20)	29	0.32
Not Hispanic (14)	20	0.22
Hispanic (6)	9	0.10
Guamanian/Chamorro (1)	1	0.01
Native Hawaiian (10)	15	0.16
Samoan (3)	3	0.03
Tongan (0)	3	0.03
White (5,273)	5,598	60.97
Not Hispanic (2,651)	2,755	30.00
Hispanic (2,622)	2,843	30.96

Hobbs

Place Type: City
County: Lea
Population: 34,122†

Ancestry‡	Population	%
African, Sub-Saharan (109)	128	0.39
African (84)	103	0.31
Ethiopian (11)	11	0.03
Ghanaian (14)	14	0.04
American (2,051)	2,051	6.23
Arab (0)	24	0.07
Lebanese (0)	24	0.07
Belgian (0)	18	0.05
British (33)	78	0.24
Canadian (0)	19	0.06
Czech (0)	32	0.10
Danish (0)	46	0.14
Dutch (33)	433	1.31
English (1,210)	2,550	7.74
European (136)	136	0.41
French, ex. Basque (115)	249	0.76
French Canadian (95)	95	0.29
German (773)	2,317	7.03
Greek (22)	46	0.14
Hungarian (0)	61	0.19
Irish (463)	2,070	6.28
Italian (88)	181	0.55
Norwegian (54)	125	0.38
Polish (39)	203	0.62
Russian (0)	42	0.13
Scandinavian (5)	5	0.02
Scotch-Irish (76)	247	0.75
Scottish (93)	208	0.63
Serbian (0)	10	0.03
Slovak (0)	90	0.27
Swedish (14)	62	0.19
Swiss (11)	11	0.03
Ukrainian (0)	9	0.03
Welsh (101)	112	0.34
West Indian, ex. Hispanic (0)	69	0.21
Dutch West Indian (0)	59	0.18
West Indian (0)	10	0.03

Hispanic Origin	Population	%
Hispanic or Latino (of any race)	18,317	53.68
Central American, ex. Mexican	45	0.13
Costa Rican	3	0.01
Guatemalan	9	0.03
Honduran	8	0.02
Nicaraguan	2	0.01
Panamanian	1	<0.01
Salvadoran	22	0.06
Cuban	19	0.06
Dominican Republic	9	0.03
Mexican	16,023	46.96
Puerto Rican	63	0.18
South American	32	0.09
Argentinean	2	0.01
Bolivian	2	0.01
Colombian	15	0.04
Ecuadorian	1	<0.01
Peruvian	5	0.01
Venezuelan	7	0.02
Other Hispanic or Latino	2,126	6.23

Race*	Population	%
African-American/Black (2,082)	2,377	6.97
Not Hispanic (1,924)	2,098	6.15
Hispanic (158)	279	0.82
American Indian/Alaska Native (443)	665	1.95
Not Hispanic (270)	400	1.17
Hispanic (173)	265	0.78
Apache (10)	26	0.08
Arapaho (0)	4	0.01
Blackfeet (2)	4	0.01
Cherokee (24)	65	0.19
Chickasaw (9)	16	0.05
Chippewa (2)	2	0.01
Choctaw (16)	25	0.07
Comanche (2)	3	0.01
Creek (10)	12	0.04
Crow (2)	2	0.01
Delaware (1)	1	<0.01
Hopi (0)	1	<0.01
Iroquois (2)	2	0.01
Kiowa (3)	3	0.01
Mexican American Ind. (26)	32	0.09
Navajo (80)	97	0.28
Osage (1)	2	0.01
Potawatomi (5)	7	0.02
Pueblo (22)	28	0.08
Seminole (0)	4	0.01
Shoshone (2)	9	0.03
Sioux (5)	6	0.02
South American Ind. (1)	1	<0.01
Spanish American Ind. (1)	11	0.03
Asian (204)	252	0.74
Not Hispanic (199)	225	0.66
Hispanic (5)	27	0.08
Burmese (2)	2	0.01
Chinese, ex. Taiwanese (23)	36	0.11
Filipino (39)	55	0.16
Indian (48)	54	0.16
Indonesian (3)	3	0.01
Japanese (2)	10	0.03
Korean (16)	23	0.07
Nepalese (9)	9	0.03
Pakistani (7)	7	0.02
Sri Lankan (1)	4	0.01
Taiwanese (0)	2	0.01
Thai (3)	3	0.01
Vietnamese (38)	40	0.12
Hawaii Native/Pacific Islander (25)	51	0.15
Not Hispanic (14)	29	0.08
Hispanic (11)	22	0.06
Fijian (5)	5	0.01
Guamanian/Chamorro (5)	13	0.04
Native Hawaiian (8)	13	0.04
Samoan (1)	2	0.01
Tongan (1)	3	0.01
White (24,897)	25,703	75.33
Not Hispanic (13,059)	13,326	39.05
Hispanic (11,838)	12,377	36.27

Kirtland

Place Type: CDP
County: San Juan
Population: 7,875†

Ancestry‡	Population	%
American (70)	70	1.09
Belgian (0)	83	1.29
Canadian (0)	16	0.25
Czech (0)	16	0.25
Dutch (0)	109	1.70
English (464)	789	12.29
European (43)	73	1.14
French, ex. Basque (240)	466	7.26
French Canadian (0)	13	0.20

*Notes: † The Census 2010 population figure is used to calculate the percentages in the Hispanic Origin and Race categories. Ancestry percentages are based on the 2006-2010 American Community Survey population (not shown); ‡ Numbers in parentheses indicate the number of people reporting a single ancestry; * Numbers in parentheses indicate the number of persons reporting this race alone, not in combination with any other race; Please refer to the Explanation of Data for more information.*

German (264)	802	12.50
Hungarian (0)	16	0.25
Irish (47)	358	5.58
Italian (7)	36	0.56
Norwegian (0)	54	0.84
Russian (0)	18	0.28
Scotch-Irish (34)	59	0.92
Scottish (77)	278	4.33
Swedish (0)	190	2.96
Welsh (18)	18	0.28
Yugoslavian (0)	17	0.26

Hispanic Origin	Population	%
Hispanic or Latino (of any race)	887	11.26
Central American, ex. Mexican	5	0.06
Guatemalan	1	0.01
Honduran	1	0.01
Nicaraguan	1	0.01
Panamanian	2	0.03
Cuban	1	0.01
Mexican	558	7.09
Puerto Rican	8	0.10
South American	1	0.01
Colombian	1	0.01
Other Hispanic or Latino	314	3.99

Race*	Population	%
African-American/Black (33)	72	0.91
Not Hispanic (29)	58	0.74
Hispanic (4)	14	0.18
American Indian/Alaska Native (4,104)	4,369	55.48
Not Hispanic (3,989)	4,181	53.09
Hispanic (115)	188	2.39
Aleut *(Alaska Native)* (2)	2	0.03
Apache (13)	31	0.39
Blackfeet (1)	1	0.01
Cherokee (8)	13	0.17
Cheyenne (2)	3	0.04
Chickasaw (0)	3	0.04
Chippewa (3)	5	0.06
Choctaw (11)	19	0.24
Comanche (2)	3	0.04
Cree (1)	1	0.01
Crow (1)	1	0.01
Delaware (1)	1	0.01
Hopi (0)	3	0.04
Inupiat *(Alaska Native)* (0)	1	0.01
Iroquois (2)	2	0.03
Mexican American Ind. (3)	5	0.06
Navajo (3,739)	3,975	50.48
Osage (1)	1	0.01
Paiute (2)	2	0.03
Pima (1)	1	0.01
Potawatomi (8)	17	0.22
Pueblo (25)	38	0.48
Shoshone (1)	2	0.03
Sioux (14)	25	0.32
Spanish American Ind. (2)	2	0.03
Tlingit-Haida *(Alaska Native)* (2)	3	0.04
Tsimshian *(Alaska Native)* (0)	3	0.04
Ute (11)	34	0.43
Yakama (3)	3	0.04
Yuman (1)	4	0.05
Asian (21)	59	0.75
Not Hispanic (20)	55	0.70
Hispanic (1)	4	0.05
Chinese, ex. Taiwanese (3)	13	0.17
Filipino (10)	20	0.25
Indian (0)	2	0.03
Japanese (1)	4	0.05
Korean (3)	9	0.11
Vietnamese (4)	7	0.09
Hawaii Native/Pacific Islander (20)	26	0.33
Not Hispanic (20)	26	0.33
Native Hawaiian (19)	21	0.27
Samoan (1)	4	0.05
White (3,041)	3,326	42.23
Not Hispanic (2,694)	2,906	36.90
Hispanic (347)	420	5.33

Las Cruces

Place Type: City
County: Do±a Ana
Population: 97,618[†]

Ancestry[‡]	Population	%
African, Sub-Saharan (220)	291	0.31
African (143)	203	0.22
Ethiopian (20)	31	0.03
Kenyan (17)	17	0.02
Nigerian (14)	14	0.02
South African (10)	10	0.01
Other Sub-Saharan African (16)	16	0.02
American (2,593)	2,593	2.79
Arab (171)	262	0.28
Arab (0)	5	0.01
Egyptian (69)	69	0.07
Lebanese (53)	128	0.14
Moroccan (12)	12	0.01
Syrian (27)	38	0.04
Other Arab (10)	10	0.01
Armenian (43)	43	0.05
Australian (0)	6	0.01
Austrian (47)	159	0.17
Basque (18)	18	0.02
Belgian (0)	44	0.05
Brazilian (10)	10	0.01
British (113)	252	0.27
Canadian (66)	142	0.15
Celtic (18)	18	0.02
Croatian (0)	24	0.03
Czech (27)	100	0.11
Czechoslovakian (90)	115	0.12
Danish (246)	420	0.45
Dutch (230)	696	0.75
Eastern European (43)	43	0.05
English (2,112)	5,698	6.13
Estonian (11)	11	0.01
European (357)	397	0.43
Finnish (42)	54	0.06
French, ex. Basque (326)	1,524	1.64
French Canadian (115)	233	0.25
German (3,473)	8,507	9.16
Greek (89)	98	0.11
Guyanese (10)	13	0.01
Hungarian (40)	141	0.15
Irish (1,603)	5,353	5.76
Italian (1,132)	2,111	2.27
Latvian (33)	44	0.05
Lithuanian (37)	72	0.08
Luxemburger (14)	14	0.02
Norwegian (219)	717	0.77
Pennsylvania German (0)	11	0.01
Polish (318)	805	0.87
Portuguese (104)	214	0.23
Romanian (37)	74	0.08
Russian (186)	376	0.40
Scandinavian (62)	127	0.14
Scotch-Irish (331)	878	0.95
Scottish (459)	1,166	1.26
Slavic (11)	33	0.04
Slovak (96)	109	0.12
Slovene (32)	59	0.06
Swedish (284)	797	0.86
Swiss (28)	213	0.23
Turkish (0)	54	0.06
Ukrainian (45)	101	0.11
Welsh (101)	406	0.44
West Indian, ex. Hispanic (0)	43	0.05
Jamaican (0)	43	0.05
Yugoslavian (0)	56	0.06

Hispanic Origin	Population	%
Hispanic or Latino (of any race)	55,443	56.80
Central American, ex. Mexican	232	0.24
Costa Rican	20	0.02
Guatemalan	50	0.05
Honduran	20	0.02
Nicaraguan	36	0.04
Panamanian	37	0.04
Salvadoran	63	0.06
Other Central American	6	0.01
Cuban	115	0.12
Dominican Republic	37	0.04
Mexican	45,747	46.86
Puerto Rican	594	0.61
South American	262	0.27
Argentinean	38	0.04
Bolivian	14	0.01
Chilean	12	0.01
Colombian	95	0.10
Ecuadorian	31	0.03
Paraguayan	7	0.01
Peruvian	40	0.04
Uruguayan	1	<0.01
Venezuelan	23	0.02
Other South American	1	<0.01
Other Hispanic or Latino	8,456	8.66

Race*	Population	%
African-American/Black (2,385)	3,178	3.26
Not Hispanic (1,915)	2,361	2.42
Hispanic (470)	817	0.84
American Indian/Alaska Native (1,706)	2,655	2.72
Not Hispanic (861)	1,264	1.29
Hispanic (845)	1,391	1.42
Alaska Athabascan *(Ala. Nat.)* (4)	4	<0.01
Aleut *(Alaska Native)* (0)	1	<0.01
Apache (134)	270	0.28
Arapaho (1)	1	<0.01
Blackfeet (3)	16	0.02
Canadian/French Am. Ind. (1)	4	<0.01
Central American Ind. (0)	2	<0.01
Cherokee (56)	186	0.19
Cheyenne (3)	8	0.01
Chickasaw (10)	23	0.02
Chippewa (9)	19	0.02
Choctaw (18)	54	0.06
Comanche (1)	5	0.01
Creek (6)	7	0.01
Crow (0)	1	<0.01
Delaware (0)	2	<0.01
Hopi (2)	5	0.01
Inupiat *(Alaska Native)* (2)	2	<0.01
Iroquois (3)	8	0.01
Kiowa (3)	3	<0.01
Lumbee (1)	4	<0.01
Mexican American Ind. (91)	128	0.13
Navajo (271)	365	0.37
Osage (7)	13	0.01
Paiute (1)	4	<0.01
Pima (5)	9	0.01
Potawatomi (9)	10	0.01
Pueblo (317)	413	0.42
Seminole (0)	7	0.01
Shoshone (3)	3	<0.01
Sioux (28)	38	0.04
South American Ind. (3)	4	<0.01
Spanish American Ind. (9)	20	0.02
Tlingit-Haida *(Alaska Native)* (10)	11	0.01
Tohono O'Odham (5)	5	0.01
Tsimshian *(Alaska Native)* (3)	3	<0.01
Ute (14)	20	0.02
Yaqui (4)	13	0.01
Yuman (3)	5	0.01
Asian (1,541)	2,159	2.21
Not Hispanic (1,421)	1,819	1.86
Hispanic (120)	340	0.35
Bangladeshi (3)	3	<0.01
Burmese (7)	8	0.01
Cambodian (1)	5	0.01
Chinese, ex. Taiwanese (354)	447	0.46
Filipino (250)	436	0.45
Hmong (0)	1	<0.01
Indian (334)	392	0.40
Indonesian (4)	14	0.01
Japanese (121)	275	0.28
Korean (148)	208	0.21
Laotian (2)	3	<0.01

*Notes: † The Census 2010 population figure is used to calculate the percentages in the Hispanic Origin and Race categories. Ancestry percentages are based on the 2006-2010 American Community Survey population (not shown); ‡ Numbers in parentheses indicate the number of people reporting a single ancestry; * Numbers in parentheses indicate the number of persons reporting this race alone, not in combination with any other race; Please refer to the Explanation of Data for more information.*

Malaysian (6)	8	0.01
Nepalese (39)	42	0.04
Pakistani (49)	56	0.06
Sri Lankan (32)	34	0.03
Taiwanese (19)	25	0.03
Thai (32)	64	0.07
Vietnamese (72)	98	0.10
Hawaii Native/Pacific Islander (106)	253	0.26
Not Hispanic (77)	147	0.15
Hispanic (29)	106	0.11
Fijian (2)	2	<0.01
Guamanian/Chamorro (28)	37	0.04
Native Hawaiian (34)	90	0.09
Samoan (15)	25	0.03
Tongan (1)	7	0.01
White (73,513)	76,498	78.36
Not Hispanic (36,577)	37,641	38.56
Hispanic (36,936)	38,857	39.81

Las Vegas

Place Type: City
County: San Miguel
Population: 13,753†

Ancestry‡	Population	%
American (181)	181	1.31
Arab (10)	22	0.16
Egyptian (0)	12	0.09
Lebanese (10)	10	0.07
Basque (12)	12	0.09
British (13)	13	0.09
Czech (0)	20	0.14
Czechoslovakian (0)	19	0.14
Danish (0)	6	0.04
Dutch (0)	9	0.07
English (238)	567	4.10
European (0)	9	0.07
Finnish (7)	7	0.05
French, ex. Basque (20)	332	2.40
French Canadian (31)	31	0.22
German (163)	701	5.06
Irish (33)	581	4.20
Italian (231)	329	2.38
Lithuanian (14)	14	0.10
Norwegian (0)	8	0.06
Pennsylvania German (10)	10	0.07
Polish (20)	51	0.37
Portuguese (0)	11	0.08
Russian (20)	32	0.23
Scotch-Irish (44)	79	0.57
Scottish (59)	78	0.56
Slavic (0)	10	0.07
Slovene (0)	10	0.07
Swedish (0)	19	0.14
Ukrainian (0)	17	0.12
Welsh (0)	43	0.31
West Indian, ex. Hispanic (25)	34	0.25
Jamaican (25)	34	0.25

Hispanic Origin	Population	%
Hispanic or Latino (of any race)	11,069	80.48
Central American, ex. Mexican	12	0.09
Honduran	2	0.01
Panamanian	1	0.01
Salvadoran	9	0.07
Cuban	19	0.14
Mexican	3,907	28.41
Puerto Rican	21	0.15
South American	8	0.06
Colombian	1	0.01
Peruvian	6	0.04
Other South American	1	0.01
Other Hispanic or Latino	7,102	51.64

Race*	Population	%
African-American/Black (265)	334	2.43
Not Hispanic (227)	257	1.87
Hispanic (38)	77	0.56
American Indian/Alaska Native (294)	434	3.16
Not Hispanic (156)	200	1.45
Hispanic (138)	234	1.70
Apache (9)	23	0.17
Arapaho (0)	1	0.01
Cherokee (5)	10	0.07
Cheyenne (0)	1	0.01
Chippewa (6)	7	0.05
Choctaw (4)	7	0.05
Colville (0)	1	0.01
Comanche (1)	1	0.01
Hopi (1)	2	0.01
Iroquois (2)	5	0.04
Mexican American Ind. (7)	16	0.12
Navajo (61)	74	0.54
Osage (0)	2	0.01
Pueblo (26)	32	0.23
Seminole (0)	1	0.01
Shoshone (2)	2	0.01
Sioux (2)	7	0.05
Spanish American Ind. (10)	10	0.07
Tlingit-Haida *(Alaska Native)* (0)	2	0.01
Tsimshian *(Alaska Native)* (2)	2	0.01
Asian (130)	179	1.30
Not Hispanic (106)	131	0.95
Hispanic (24)	48	0.35
Chinese, ex. Taiwanese (17)	26	0.19
Filipino (12)	15	0.11
Indian (48)	59	0.43
Japanese (8)	15	0.11
Korean (6)	10	0.07
Nepalese (5)	5	0.04
Vietnamese (24)	26	0.19
Hawaii Native/Pacific Islander (22)	36	0.26
Not Hispanic (18)	24	0.17
Hispanic (4)	12	0.09
Guamanian/Chamorro (2)	2	0.01
Native Hawaiian (9)	13	0.09
Samoan (7)	11	0.08
Tongan (3)	3	0.02
White (8,923)	9,361	68.07
Not Hispanic (2,051)	2,130	15.49
Hispanic (6,872)	7,231	52.58

Los Alamos

Place Type: CDP
County: Los Alamos
Population: 12,019†

Ancestry‡	Population	%
American (914)	914	7.60
Australian (22)	22	0.18
Austrian (17)	71	0.59
Basque (11)	11	0.09
Belgian (19)	30	0.25
British (105)	165	1.37
Canadian (34)	50	0.42
Celtic (28)	46	0.38
Croatian (11)	11	0.09
Czech (46)	86	0.71
Czechoslovakian (23)	23	0.19
Danish (21)	195	1.62
Dutch (64)	228	1.90
Eastern European (11)	11	0.09
English (651)	1,797	14.94
European (403)	453	3.77
Finnish (0)	12	0.10
French, ex. Basque (97)	615	5.11
French Canadian (0)	142	1.18
German (461)	2,097	17.43
Greek (13)	13	0.11
Hungarian (0)	23	0.19
Iranian (11)	11	0.09
Irish (235)	1,417	11.78
Italian (98)	548	4.56
Lithuanian (17)	43	0.36
Macedonian (0)	12	0.10
New Zealander (0)	37	0.31
Northern European (25)	25	0.21
Norwegian (63)	286	2.38
Polish (113)	229	1.90
Portuguese (38)	59	0.49
Romanian (47)	47	0.39
Russian (206)	419	3.48
Scandinavian (0)	16	0.13
Scotch-Irish (310)	461	3.83
Scottish (141)	598	4.97
Slavic (18)	108	0.90
Slovak (35)	69	0.57
Swedish (108)	283	2.35
Swiss (99)	332	2.76
Turkish (70)	70	0.58
Ukrainian (59)	66	0.55
Welsh (15)	130	1.08

Hispanic Origin	Population	%
Hispanic or Latino (of any race)	1,757	14.62
Central American, ex. Mexican	27	0.22
Costa Rican	10	0.08
Guatemalan	6	0.05
Honduran	7	0.06
Nicaraguan	3	0.02
Panamanian	1	0.01
Cuban	17	0.14
Dominican Republic	7	0.06
Mexican	756	6.29
Puerto Rican	36	0.30
South American	65	0.54
Argentinean	38	0.32
Bolivian	2	0.02
Colombian	9	0.07
Ecuadorian	5	0.04
Peruvian	7	0.06
Venezuelan	4	0.03
Other Hispanic or Latino	849	7.06

Race*	Population	%
African-American/Black (75)	131	1.09
Not Hispanic (73)	116	0.97
Hispanic (2)	15	0.12
American Indian/Alaska Native (102)	220	1.83
Not Hispanic (82)	159	1.32
Hispanic (20)	61	0.51
Apache (3)	7	0.06
Arapaho (1)	1	0.01
Blackfeet (4)	4	0.03
Cherokee (10)	26	0.22
Cheyenne (1)	1	0.01
Chickasaw (0)	1	0.01
Chippewa (2)	5	0.04
Choctaw (5)	12	0.10
Crow (0)	1	0.01
Delaware (0)	2	0.02
Hopi (4)	4	0.03
Inupiat *(Alaska Native)* (1)	1	0.01
Iroquois (0)	2	0.02
Kiowa (1)	1	0.01
Mexican American Ind. (3)	18	0.15
Navajo (15)	19	0.16
Osage (0)	1	0.01
Ottawa (0)	1	0.01
Potawatomi (1)	6	0.05
Pueblo (20)	34	0.28
Sioux (1)	6	0.05
South American Ind. (0)	2	0.02
Spanish American Ind. (0)	1	0.01
Asian (862)	988	8.22
Not Hispanic (858)	974	8.10
Hispanic (4)	14	0.12
Cambodian (1)	1	0.01
Chinese, ex. Taiwanese (379)	429	3.57
Filipino (28)	43	0.36
Indian (174)	192	1.60
Indonesian (5)	5	0.04
Japanese (63)	96	0.80
Korean (117)	130	1.08
Laotian (0)	1	0.01
Nepalese (11)	11	0.09
Pakistani (1)	1	0.01
Sri Lankan (1)	1	0.01

*Notes: † The Census 2010 population figure is used to calculate the percentages in the Hispanic Origin and Race categories. Ancestry percentages are based on the 2006-2010 American Community Survey population (not shown); ‡ Numbers in parentheses indicate the number of people reporting a single ancestry; * Numbers in parentheses indicate the number of persons reporting this race alone, not in combination with any other race; Please refer to the Explanation of Data for more information.*

SECTION TWO

	Population	%
Taiwanese (23)	26	0.22
Thai (2)	9	0.07
Vietnamese (34)	47	0.39
Hawaii Native/Pacific Islander (8)	23	0.19
Not Hispanic (7)	19	0.16
Hispanic (1)	4	0.03
Guamanian/Chamorro (2)	2	0.02
Native Hawaiian (1)	10	0.08
Samoan (2)	3	0.02
White (10,326)	10,645	88.57
Not Hispanic (8,992)	9,208	76.61
Hispanic (1,334)	1,437	11.96

Los Lunas

Place Type: Village
County: Valencia
Population: 14,835†

Ancestry‡	Population	%
American (570)	570	4.11
Armenian (0)	19	0.14
Austrian (28)	28	0.20
British (36)	36	0.26
Canadian (17)	17	0.12
Celtic (78)	78	0.56
Czech (22)	66	0.48
Dutch (15)	81	0.58
Eastern European (10)	10	0.07
English (335)	890	6.41
European (69)	96	0.69
Finnish (0)	31	0.22
French, ex. Basque (26)	171	1.23
French Canadian (12)	29	0.21
German (277)	1,695	12.22
Greek (0)	26	0.19
Hungarian (0)	25	0.18
Iranian (0)	29	0.21
Irish (127)	570	4.11
Italian (89)	355	2.56
Northern European (13)	13	0.09
Norwegian (115)	179	1.29
Polish (18)	93	0.67
Scandinavian (79)	79	0.57
Scotch-Irish (66)	278	2.00
Scottish (14)	152	1.10
Swedish (43)	76	0.55
Swiss (11)	11	0.08
Turkish (14)	35	0.25
Ukrainian (0)	4	0.03
Welsh (0)	55	0.40
West Indian, ex. Hispanic (0)	74	0.53
Haitian (0)	74	0.53
Yugoslavian (16)	25	0.18

Hispanic Origin	Population	%
Hispanic or Latino (of any race)	8,593	57.92
Central American, ex. Mexican	28	0.19
Costa Rican	2	0.01
Guatemalan	2	0.01
Nicaraguan	4	0.03
Panamanian	1	0.01
Salvadoran	19	0.13
Cuban	20	0.13
Dominican Republic	2	0.01
Mexican	3,925	26.46
Puerto Rican	81	0.55
South American	35	0.24
Bolivian	1	0.01
Chilean	2	0.01
Colombian	15	0.10
Ecuadorian	1	0.01
Peruvian	16	0.11
Other Hispanic or Latino	4,502	30.35

Race*	Population	%
African-American/Black (293)	405	2.73
Not Hispanic (236)	294	1.98
Hispanic (57)	111	0.75
American Indian/Alaska Native (373)	566	3.82
Not Hispanic (252)	328	2.21
Hispanic (121)	238	1.60
Aleut *(Alaska Native)* (1)	1	0.01
Apache (12)	18	0.12
Arapaho (2)	3	0.02
Blackfeet (2)	8	0.05
Cherokee (12)	36	0.24
Cheyenne (1)	1	0.01
Chippewa (5)	5	0.03
Choctaw (8)	12	0.08
Comanche (1)	1	0.01
Creek (5)	7	0.05
Delaware (1)	2	0.01
Hopi (2)	2	0.01
Iroquois (0)	2	0.01
Mexican American Ind. (4)	19	0.13
Navajo (80)	101	0.68
Osage (1)	1	0.01
Potawatomi (1)	2	0.01
Pueblo (112)	160	1.08
Sioux (5)	6	0.04
South American Ind. (2)	4	0.03
Spanish American Ind. (2)	5	0.03
Ute (2)	3	0.02
Yaqui (6)	7	0.05
Yuman (1)	1	0.01
Asian (121)	229	1.54
Not Hispanic (92)	150	1.01
Hispanic (29)	79	0.53
Chinese, ex. Taiwanese (9)	14	0.09
Filipino (51)	91	0.61
Indian (19)	30	0.20
Japanese (20)	44	0.30
Korean (10)	16	0.11
Laotian (2)	5	0.03
Pakistani (0)	1	0.01
Sri Lankan (1)	1	0.01
Thai (4)	5	0.03
Vietnamese (2)	3	0.02
Hawaii Native/Pacific Islander (18)	44	0.30
Not Hispanic (13)	25	0.17
Hispanic (5)	19	0.13
Guamanian/Chamorro (3)	11	0.07
Native Hawaiian (7)	17	0.11
Samoan (3)	11	0.07
Tongan (0)	2	0.01
White (10,700)	11,239	75.76
Not Hispanic (5,437)	5,592	37.69
Hispanic (5,263)	5,647	38.07

Lovington

Place Type: City
County: Lea
Population: 11,009†

Ancestry‡	Population	%
American (518)	518	4.87
Czech (29)	63	0.59
Dutch (74)	186	1.75
English (102)	292	2.74
European (7)	7	0.07
French, ex. Basque (0)	201	1.89
German (246)	587	5.51
Irish (70)	474	4.45
Italian (10)	10	0.09
Norwegian (16)	16	0.15
Polish (56)	56	0.53
Scotch-Irish (22)	88	0.83
Scottish (27)	49	0.46

Hispanic Origin	Population	%
Hispanic or Latino (of any race)	7,076	64.27
Central American, ex. Mexican	18	0.16
Guatemalan	2	0.02
Honduran	1	0.01
Nicaraguan	4	0.04
Salvadoran	11	0.10
Mexican	6,419	58.31
Puerto Rican	10	0.09
South American	2	0.02
Bolivian	1	0.01
Colombian	1	0.01
Other Hispanic or Latino	627	5.70

Race*	Population	%
African-American/Black (261)	310	2.82
Not Hispanic (220)	250	2.27
Hispanic (41)	60	0.55
American Indian/Alaska Native (163)	222	2.02
Not Hispanic (83)	128	1.16
Hispanic (80)	94	0.85
Apache (10)	12	0.11
Central American Ind. (0)	1	0.01
Cherokee (5)	23	0.21
Cheyenne (1)	2	0.02
Chickasaw (5)	11	0.10
Choctaw (7)	13	0.12
Hopi (1)	1	0.01
Mexican American Ind. (16)	17	0.15
Navajo (18)	25	0.23
Osage (5)	5	0.05
Paiute (1)	1	0.01
Pueblo (1)	2	0.02
Sioux (10)	10	0.09
Spanish American Ind. (0)	3	0.03
Asian (44)	72	0.65
Not Hispanic (38)	51	0.46
Hispanic (6)	21	0.19
Chinese, ex. Taiwanese (0)	1	0.01
Filipino (25)	29	0.26
Indian (7)	11	0.10
Japanese (3)	3	0.03
Korean (1)	5	0.05
Pakistani (7)	8	0.07
Hawaii Native/Pacific Islander (4)	6	0.05
Hispanic (4)	6	0.05
Native Hawaiian (2)	2	0.02
Samoan (2)	2	0.02
White (7,368)	7,623	69.24
Not Hispanic (3,487)	3,570	32.43
Hispanic (3,881)	4,053	36.82

North Valley

Place Type: CDP
County: Bernalillo
Population: 11,333†

Ancestry‡	Population	%
American (359)	359	3.07
Armenian (25)	25	0.21
British (32)	74	0.63
Bulgarian (15)	15	0.13
Canadian (0)	43	0.37
Czech (22)	22	0.19
Danish (0)	17	0.15
Dutch (27)	171	1.46
English (230)	1,082	9.24
European (24)	58	0.50
French, ex. Basque (0)	398	3.40
French Canadian (51)	51	0.44
German (293)	1,113	9.51
Greek (0)	30	0.26
Iranian (9)	26	0.22
Irish (358)	894	7.64
Italian (233)	561	4.79
Latvian (0)	12	0.10
Luxemburger (10)	10	0.09
Norwegian (83)	90	0.77
Polish (33)	139	1.19
Russian (9)	42	0.36
Scotch-Irish (78)	218	1.86
Scottish (23)	102	0.87
Slovak (37)	78	0.67
Swedish (14)	28	0.24
Swiss (16)	51	0.44
Welsh (15)	36	0.31

*Notes: † The Census 2010 population figure is used to calculate the percentages in the Hispanic Origin and Race categories. Ancestry percentages are based on the 2006-2010 American Community Survey population (not shown); ‡ Numbers in parentheses indicate the number of people reporting a single ancestry; * Numbers in parentheses indicate the number of persons reporting this race alone, not in combination with any other race; Please refer to the Explanation of Data for more information.*

Hispanic Origin	Population	%
Hispanic or Latino (of any race)	6,708	59.19
Central American, ex. Mexican	22	0.19
Guatemalan	17	0.15
Nicaraguan	1	0.01
Salvadoran	4	0.04
Cuban	8	0.07
Mexican	3,189	28.14
Puerto Rican	40	0.35
South American	21	0.19
Argentinean	6	0.05
Bolivian	1	0.01
Chilean	5	0.04
Colombian	3	0.03
Ecuadorian	4	0.04
Peruvian	2	0.02
Other Hispanic or Latino	3,428	30.25

Race*	Population	%
African-American/Black (71)	120	1.06
Not Hispanic (49)	80	0.71
Hispanic (22)	40	0.35
American Indian/Alaska Native (338)	441	3.89
Not Hispanic (253)	296	2.61
Hispanic (85)	145	1.28
Apache (12)	14	0.12
Cherokee (3)	10	0.09
Cheyenne (1)	3	0.03
Chickasaw (0)	1	0.01
Chippewa (5)	6	0.05
Choctaw (3)	5	0.04
Comanche (1)	1	0.01
Creek (2)	2	0.02
Delaware (1)	1	0.01
Hopi (1)	11	0.10
Inupiat *(Alaska Native)* (1)	1	0.01
Iroquois (1)	1	0.01
Kiowa (1)	3	0.03
Mexican American Ind. (2)	8	0.07
Navajo (165)	178	1.57
Paiute (1)	1	0.01
Pima (0)	8	0.07
Potawatomi (0)	3	0.03
Pueblo (48)	61	0.54
Shoshone (1)	1	0.01
Sioux (7)	12	0.11
South American Ind. (1)	2	0.02
Spanish American Ind. (3)	4	0.04
Ute (3)	4	0.04
Yaqui (1)	1	0.01
Yuman (4)	4	0.04
Yup'ik *(Alaska Native)* (1)	1	0.01
Asian (68)	123	1.09
Not Hispanic (53)	87	0.77
Hispanic (15)	36	0.32
Burmese (1)	1	0.01
Cambodian (1)	1	0.01
Chinese, ex. Taiwanese (16)	27	0.24
Filipino (21)	37	0.33
Indian (2)	3	0.03
Indonesian (1)	1	0.01
Japanese (10)	22	0.19
Korean (5)	9	0.08
Thai (5)	8	0.07
Vietnamese (6)	10	0.09
Hawaii Native/Pacific Islander (7)	18	0.16
Not Hispanic (2)	8	0.07
Hispanic (5)	10	0.09
Guamanian/Chamorro (2)	2	0.02
Native Hawaiian (5)	9	0.08
White (8,033)	8,458	74.63
Not Hispanic (4,147)	4,245	37.46
Hispanic (3,886)	4,213	37.17

Portales

Place Type: City
County: Roosevelt
Population: 12,280†

Ancestry‡	Population	%
American (882)	882	7.34
Belgian (0)	15	0.12
British (7)	24	0.20
Czech (0)	47	0.39
Danish (27)	27	0.22
Dutch (54)	170	1.41
Eastern European (17)	17	0.14
English (387)	956	7.96
European (84)	84	0.70
French, ex. Basque (19)	361	3.00
French Canadian (76)	76	0.63
German (604)	1,459	12.14
Greek (0)	69	0.57
Irish (247)	1,037	8.63
Italian (52)	133	1.11
New Zealander (37)	37	0.31
Norwegian (0)	67	0.56
Polish (7)	48	0.40
Portuguese (0)	16	0.13
Russian (0)	21	0.17
Scandinavian (0)	17	0.14
Scotch-Irish (57)	135	1.12
Scottish (72)	138	1.15
Slavic (0)	11	0.09
Swedish (11)	17	0.14
Ukrainian (0)	10	0.08
Welsh (0)	47	0.39
West Indian, ex. Hispanic (0)	14	0.12
Dutch West Indian (0)	14	0.12

Hispanic Origin	Population	%
Hispanic or Latino (of any race)	5,278	42.98
Central American, ex. Mexican	21	0.17
Costa Rican	2	0.02
Guatemalan	10	0.08
Honduran	4	0.03
Panamanian	3	0.02
Salvadoran	2	0.02
Cuban	8	0.07
Dominican Republic	5	0.04
Mexican	3,679	29.96
Puerto Rican	47	0.38
South American	8	0.07
Colombian	5	0.04
Peruvian	1	0.01
Venezuelan	2	0.02
Other Hispanic or Latino	1,510	12.30

Race*	Population	%
African-American/Black (313)	410	3.34
Not Hispanic (263)	338	2.75
Hispanic (50)	72	0.59
American Indian/Alaska Native (191)	332	2.70
Not Hispanic (143)	232	1.89
Hispanic (48)	100	0.81
Apache (5)	17	0.14
Blackfeet (0)	3	0.02
Canadian/French Am. Ind. (0)	1	0.01
Cherokee (8)	26	0.21
Cheyenne (0)	1	0.01
Chickasaw (1)	2	0.02
Chippewa (2)	2	0.02
Choctaw (10)	15	0.12
Comanche (0)	3	0.02
Creek (0)	3	0.02
Iroquois (0)	2	0.02
Mexican American Ind. (1)	13	0.11
Navajo (93)	112	0.91
Paiute (1)	3	0.02
Potawatomi (0)	2	0.02
Pueblo (14)	18	0.15
Seminole (0)	1	0.01
Sioux (1)	3	0.02
Spanish American Ind. (4)	7	0.06
Tohono O'Odham (2)	2	0.02
Ute (1)	1	0.01
Yaqui (0)	1	0.01
Asian (152)	199	1.62
Not Hispanic (141)	174	1.42
Hispanic (11)	25	0.20
Chinese, ex. Taiwanese (80)	83	0.68
Filipino (36)	50	0.41
Indian (14)	18	0.15
Japanese (5)	16	0.13
Korean (3)	7	0.06
Taiwanese (0)	5	0.04
Thai (4)	8	0.07
Vietnamese (6)	8	0.07
Hawaii Native/Pacific Islander (5)	26	0.21
Not Hispanic (3)	12	0.10
Hispanic (2)	14	0.11
Guamanian/Chamorro (2)	2	0.02
Native Hawaiian (1)	8	0.07
Samoan (1)	3	0.02
White (9,171)	9,583	78.04
Not Hispanic (6,255)	6,429	52.35
Hispanic (2,916)	3,154	25.68

Rio Rancho

Place Type: City
County: Sandoval
Population: 87,521†

Ancestry‡	Population	%
African, Sub-Saharan (209)	240	0.30
African (198)	219	0.27
Ethiopian (11)	11	0.01
Other Sub-Saharan African (0)	10	0.01
Albanian (0)	9	0.01
American (3,247)	3,247	4.01
Arab (103)	333	0.41
Egyptian (14)	14	0.02
Lebanese (77)	282	0.35
Palestinian (12)	23	0.03
Syrian (0)	14	0.02
Australian (0)	11	0.01
Austrian (55)	220	0.27
Belgian (46)	80	0.10
British (190)	436	0.54
Cajun (32)	32	0.04
Canadian (105)	133	0.16
Celtic (34)	45	0.06
Croatian (44)	81	0.10
Czech (126)	417	0.51
Czechoslovakian (51)	103	0.13
Danish (265)	691	0.85
Dutch (178)	1,164	1.44
Eastern European (39)	39	0.05
English (2,616)	7,530	9.29
European (764)	1,103	1.36
Finnish (68)	302	0.37
French, ex. Basque (470)	2,617	3.23
French Canadian (243)	668	0.82
German (3,515)	12,598	15.54
Greek (226)	340	0.42
Guyanese (43)	43	0.05
Hungarian (118)	342	0.42
Icelander (0)	27	0.03
Iranian (36)	153	0.19
Irish (2,758)	8,758	10.80
Israeli (34)	64	0.08
Italian (1,709)	4,324	5.33
Latvian (17)	25	0.03
Lithuanian (62)	233	0.29
Northern European (28)	28	0.03
Norwegian (379)	976	1.20
Pennsylvania German (28)	28	0.03
Polish (419)	1,736	2.14
Portuguese (56)	314	0.39
Romanian (12)	23	0.03
Russian (112)	391	0.48
Scandinavian (80)	123	0.15
Scotch-Irish (848)	1,945	2.40
Scottish (614)	1,741	2.15
Serbian (30)	93	0.11
Slavic (12)	34	0.04
Slovak (55)	176	0.22
Slovene (0)	15	0.02

*Notes: † The Census 2010 population figure is used to calculate the percentages in the Hispanic Origin and Race categories. Ancestry percentages are based on the 2006-2010 American Community Survey population (not shown); ‡ Numbers in parentheses indicate the number of people reporting a single ancestry; * Numbers in parentheses indicate the number of persons reporting this race alone, not in combination with any other race; Please refer to the Explanation of Data for more information.*

Swedish (271)	1,046	1.29
Swiss (41)	209	0.26
Turkish (10)	16	0.02
Ukrainian (66)	188	0.23
Welsh (29)	571	0.70
West Indian, ex. Hispanic (45)	110	0.14
Dutch West Indian (0)	11	0.01
Haitian (22)	59	0.07
Jamaican (0)	17	0.02
West Indian (23)	23	0.03
Yugoslavian (0)	25	0.03

Hispanic Origin	Population	%
Hispanic or Latino (of any race)	32,153	36.74
Central American, ex. Mexican	451	0.52
Costa Rican	28	0.03
Guatemalan	108	0.12
Honduran	37	0.04
Nicaraguan	48	0.05
Panamanian	47	0.05
Salvadoran	180	0.21
Other Central American	3	<0.01
Cuban	160	0.18
Dominican Republic	63	0.07
Mexican	16,070	18.36
Puerto Rican	783	0.89
South American	389	0.44
Argentinean	39	0.04
Bolivian	13	0.01
Chilean	57	0.07
Colombian	111	0.13
Ecuadorian	45	0.05
Paraguayan	8	0.01
Peruvian	92	0.11
Uruguayan	6	0.01
Venezuelan	17	0.02
Other South American	1	<0.01
Other Hispanic or Latino	14,237	16.27

Race*	Population	%
African-American/Black (2,533)	3,484	3.98
Not Hispanic (2,236)	2,856	3.26
Hispanic (297)	628	0.72
American Indian/Alaska Native (2,830)	4,066	4.65
Not Hispanic (2,242)	2,935	3.35
Hispanic (588)	1,131	1.29
Alaska Athabascan *(Ala. Nat.)* (4)	8	0.01
Aleut *(Alaska Native)* (1)	1	<0.01
Apache (78)	136	0.16
Arapaho (12)	23	0.03
Blackfeet (5)	31	0.04
Canadian/French Am. Ind. (2)	3	<0.01
Central American Ind. (6)	7	0.01
Cherokee (61)	191	0.22
Cheyenne (6)	10	0.01
Chickasaw (8)	19	0.02
Chippewa (21)	34	0.04
Choctaw (36)	79	0.09
Colville (1)	2	<0.01
Comanche (14)	30	0.03
Cree (0)	5	0.01
Creek (8)	14	0.02
Crow (3)	4	<0.01
Delaware (3)	9	0.01
Hopi (15)	31	0.04
Inupiat *(Alaska Native)* (2)	5	0.01
Iroquois (12)	26	0.03
Kiowa (8)	11	0.01
Lumbee (2)	3	<0.01
Mexican American Ind. (35)	61	0.07
Navajo (1,002)	1,234	1.41
Osage (2)	5	0.01
Ottawa (3)	5	0.01
Paiute (2)	2	<0.01
Pima (7)	7	0.01
Potawatomi (8)	13	0.01
Pueblo (603)	800	0.91
Puget Sound Salish (7)	7	0.01
Seminole (3)	16	0.02
Shoshone (2)	5	0.01
Sioux (50)	77	0.09
South American Ind. (2)	6	0.01
Spanish American Ind. (16)	26	0.03
Tlingit-Haida *(Alaska Native)* (12)	16	0.02
Tohono O'Odham (8)	9	0.01
Ute (23)	30	0.03
Yakama (6)	6	0.01
Yaqui (16)	24	0.03
Yup'ik *(Alaska Native)* (1)	1	<0.01
Asian (1,656)	2,536	2.90
Not Hispanic (1,538)	2,141	2.45
Hispanic (118)	395	0.45
Cambodian (12)	14	0.02
Chinese, ex. Taiwanese (218)	370	0.42
Filipino (481)	855	0.98
Hmong (4)	4	<0.01
Indian (134)	168	0.19
Indonesian (7)	29	0.03
Japanese (137)	323	0.37
Korean (135)	232	0.27
Laotian (41)	52	0.06
Malaysian (3)	10	0.01
Nepalese (10)	10	0.01
Pakistani (22)	28	0.03
Sri Lankan (8)	9	0.01
Taiwanese (18)	31	0.04
Thai (50)	68	0.08
Vietnamese (288)	326	0.37
Hawaii Native/Pacific Islander (153)	359	0.41
Not Hispanic (122)	285	0.33
Hispanic (31)	74	0.08
Fijian (2)	3	<0.01
Guamanian/Chamorro (29)	60	0.07
Native Hawaiian (74)	186	0.21
Samoan (20)	59	0.07
Tongan (0)	4	<0.01
White (66,534)	70,057	80.05
Not Hispanic (47,124)	48,827	55.79
Hispanic (19,410)	21,230	24.26

Roswell

Place Type: City
County: Chaves
Population: 48,366†

Ancestry‡	Population	%
African, Sub-Saharan (43)	234	0.49
African (43)	234	0.49
American (2,104)	2,104	4.44
Arab (0)	10	0.02
Lebanese (0)	10	0.02
Austrian (24)	46	0.10
Basque (0)	20	0.04
Belgian (0)	25	0.05
British (47)	147	0.31
Cajun (15)	15	0.03
Canadian (0)	43	0.09
Celtic (12)	12	0.03
Czech (16)	54	0.11
Czechoslovakian (22)	99	0.21
Danish (20)	84	0.18
Dutch (125)	485	1.02
English (1,757)	4,350	9.17
European (207)	309	0.65
Finnish (76)	76	0.16
French, ex. Basque (70)	699	1.47
French Canadian (74)	125	0.26
German (1,396)	4,665	9.84
German Russian (0)	18	0.04
Greek (16)	32	0.07
Hungarian (10)	39	0.08
Irish (1,032)	4,523	9.54
Italian (264)	821	1.73
Latvian (16)	16	0.03
Lithuanian (0)	14	0.03
Northern European (19)	19	0.04
Norwegian (146)	464	0.98
Polish (284)	682	1.44
Portuguese (20)	20	0.04
Russian (12)	105	0.22
Scandinavian (19)	100	0.21
Scotch-Irish (366)	922	1.94
Scottish (114)	514	1.08
Slovak (10)	10	0.02
Swedish (83)	525	1.11
Swiss (36)	100	0.21
Turkish (17)	17	0.04
Ukrainian (0)	70	0.15
Welsh (60)	161	0.34
West Indian, ex. Hispanic (17)	17	0.04
West Indian (17)	17	0.04

Hispanic Origin	Population	%
Hispanic or Latino (of any race)	25,832	53.41
Central American, ex. Mexican	161	0.33
Costa Rican	6	0.01
Guatemalan	68	0.14
Honduran	17	0.04
Nicaraguan	15	0.03
Panamanian	11	0.02
Salvadoran	41	0.08
Other Central American	3	0.01
Cuban	39	0.08
Dominican Republic	3	0.01
Mexican	20,586	42.56
Puerto Rican	155	0.32
South American	32	0.07
Bolivian	1	<0.01
Chilean	7	0.01
Colombian	13	0.03
Ecuadorian	5	0.01
Paraguayan	1	<0.01
Peruvian	4	0.01
Uruguayan	1	<0.01
Other Hispanic or Latino	4,856	10.04

Race*	Population	%
African-American/Black (1,189)	1,494	3.09
Not Hispanic (980)	1,114	2.30
Hispanic (209)	380	0.79
American Indian/Alaska Native (588)	997	2.06
Not Hispanic (313)	533	1.10
Hispanic (275)	464	0.96
Apache (55)	105	0.22
Blackfeet (1)	5	0.01
Cherokee (33)	130	0.27
Cheyenne (5)	9	0.02
Chickasaw (9)	16	0.03
Chippewa (1)	4	0.01
Choctaw (21)	49	0.10
Comanche (6)	11	0.02
Creek (9)	14	0.03
Crow (3)	3	0.01
Delaware (1)	1	<0.01
Iroquois (2)	3	0.01
Kiowa (3)	3	0.01
Lumbee (4)	4	0.01
Mexican American Ind. (14)	24	0.05
Navajo (68)	99	0.20
Osage (0)	1	<0.01
Pima (2)	2	<0.01
Potawatomi (2)	6	0.01
Pueblo (49)	55	0.11
Puget Sound Salish (2)	3	0.01
Seminole (3)	3	0.01
Sioux (12)	14	0.03
South American Ind. (3)	4	0.01
Spanish American Ind. (6)	13	0.03
Tlingit-Haida *(Alaska Native)* (0)	4	0.01
Tohono O'Odham (1)	1	<0.01
Tsimshian *(Alaska Native)* (1)	1	<0.01
Ute (3)	3	0.01
Yakama (1)	2	<0.01
Yaqui (4)	9	0.02
Yuman (0)	1	<0.01
Yup'ik *(Alaska Native)* (0)	1	<0.01
Asian (355)	574	1.19
Not Hispanic (321)	450	0.93
Hispanic (34)	124	0.26

*Notes: † The Census 2010 population figure is used to calculate the percentages in the Hispanic Origin and Race categories. Ancestry percentages are based on the 2006-2010 American Community Survey population (not shown); ‡ Numbers in parentheses indicate the number of people reporting a single ancestry; * Numbers in parentheses indicate the number of persons reporting this race alone, not in combination with any other race; Please refer to the Explanation of Data for more information.*

Chinese, ex. Taiwanese (49)	78	0.16
Filipino (77)	127	0.26
Indian (64)	86	0.18
Indonesian (0)	3	0.01
Japanese (37)	85	0.18
Korean (32)	45	0.09
Laotian (4)	8	0.02
Pakistani (15)	18	0.04
Sri Lankan (1)	1	<0.01
Taiwanese (2)	2	<0.01
Thai (16)	22	0.05
Vietnamese (42)	58	0.12
Hawaii Native/Pacific Islander (41)	114	0.24
Not Hispanic (29)	52	0.11
Hispanic (12)	62	0.13
Fijian (1)	1	<0.01
Guamanian/Chamorro (1)	8	0.02
Native Hawaiian (2)	22	0.05
Samoan (27)	32	0.07
White (33,827)	35,227	72.83
Not Hispanic (20,296)	20,747	42.90
Hispanic (13,531)	14,480	29.94

Ruidoso

Place Type: Village
County: Lincoln
Population: 8,029†

Ancestry‡	Population	%
American (452)	452	5.54
British (0)	40	0.49
Canadian (16)	35	0.43
Czech (43)	57	0.70
Dutch (12)	144	1.77
English (550)	1,011	12.40
European (15)	15	0.18
French, ex. Basque (46)	329	4.03
German (765)	1,433	17.57
Greek (20)	20	0.25
Hungarian (0)	14	0.17
Irish (723)	1,829	22.43
Italian (73)	180	2.21
Norwegian (66)	66	0.81
Polish (85)	134	1.64
Russian (0)	17	0.21
Scandinavian (0)	75	0.92
Scotch-Irish (293)	493	6.05
Scottish (144)	236	2.89
Serbian (12)	12	0.15
Swedish (39)	94	1.15
Ukrainian (0)	19	0.23
Welsh (0)	52	0.64
West Indian, ex. Hispanic (48)	226	2.77
Dutch West Indian (48)	226	2.77
Yugoslavian (25)	25	0.31

Hispanic Origin	Population	%
Hispanic or Latino (of any race)	2,176	27.10
Central American, ex. Mexican	2	0.02
Guatemalan	1	0.01
Nicaraguan	1	0.01
Cuban	10	0.12
Mexican	1,777	22.13
Puerto Rican	12	0.15
South American	9	0.11
Chilean	3	0.04
Ecuadorian	2	0.02
Peruvian	4	0.05
Other Hispanic or Latino	366	4.56

Race*	Population	%
African-American/Black (32)	66	0.82
Not Hispanic (26)	45	0.56
Hispanic (6)	21	0.26
American Indian/Alaska Native (241)	321	4.00
Not Hispanic (207)	261	3.25
Hispanic (34)	60	0.75
Apache (71)	81	1.01
Blackfeet (1)	1	0.01
Canadian/French Am. Ind. (0)	1	0.01
Central American Ind. (0)	1	0.01
Cherokee (6)	24	0.30
Chickasaw (1)	1	0.01
Chippewa (1)	1	0.01
Choctaw (9)	16	0.20
Comanche (1)	1	0.01
Delaware (1)	2	0.02
Kiowa (4)	4	0.05
Navajo (37)	42	0.52
Osage (1)	7	0.09
Paiute (1)	4	0.05
Potawatomi (1)	1	0.01
Pueblo (12)	13	0.16
Seminole (1)	1	0.01
Sioux (10)	10	0.12
Spanish American Ind. (1)	1	0.01
Tlingit-Haida *(Alaska Native)* (2)	2	0.02
Asian (46)	68	0.85
Not Hispanic (41)	53	0.66
Hispanic (5)	15	0.19
Chinese, ex. Taiwanese (10)	15	0.19
Filipino (15)	20	0.25
Indian (7)	10	0.12
Japanese (2)	5	0.06
Korean (3)	4	0.05
Thai (2)	5	0.06
Vietnamese (7)	7	0.09
Hawaii Native/Pacific Islander (3)	12	0.15
Not Hispanic (3)	7	0.09
Hispanic (0)	5	0.06
Fijian (0)	1	0.01
Marshallese (0)	2	0.02
Native Hawaiian (2)	7	0.09
Samoan (1)	1	0.01
White (6,898)	7,060	87.93
Not Hispanic (5,478)	5,555	69.19
Hispanic (1,420)	1,505	18.74

Santa Fe

Place Type: City
County: Santa Fe
Population: 67,947†

Ancestry‡	Population	%
Afghan (0)	28	0.04
African, Sub-Saharan (102)	115	0.17
African (5)	5	0.01
Ethiopian (51)	51	0.08
Nigerian (37)	37	0.05
South African (9)	9	0.01
Other Sub-Saharan African (0)	13	0.02
American (1,689)	1,689	2.50
Arab (168)	314	0.46
Arab (9)	12	0.02
Egyptian (0)	6	0.01
Lebanese (47)	143	0.21
Moroccan (13)	13	0.02
Palestinian (38)	38	0.06
Syrian (0)	23	0.03
Other Arab (61)	79	0.12
Armenian (26)	56	0.08
Assyrian/Chaldean/Syriac (0)	98	0.14
Australian (10)	27	0.04
Austrian (32)	180	0.27
Basque (26)	160	0.24
Belgian (12)	63	0.09
Brazilian (20)	35	0.05
British (324)	435	0.64
Bulgarian (18)	68	0.10
Cajun (0)	33	0.05
Canadian (46)	84	0.12
Celtic (27)	36	0.05
Croatian (19)	96	0.14
Czech (33)	217	0.32
Czechoslovakian (13)	13	0.02
Danish (158)	415	0.61
Dutch (190)	588	0.87
Eastern European (437)	455	0.67
English (1,776)	6,964	10.30
European (781)	834	1.23
Finnish (59)	162	0.24
French, ex. Basque (337)	2,462	3.64
French Canadian (57)	219	0.32
German (2,014)	7,770	11.50
Greek (96)	386	0.57
Hungarian (91)	323	0.48
Icelander (17)	17	0.03
Iranian (10)	27	0.04
Irish (1,141)	5,514	8.16
Israeli (12)	12	0.02
Italian (812)	2,433	3.60
Latvian (0)	41	0.06
Lithuanian (81)	287	0.42
New Zealander (12)	12	0.02
Northern European (107)	132	0.20
Norwegian (246)	703	1.04
Pennsylvania German (0)	3	<0.01
Polish (398)	1,420	2.10
Portuguese (71)	202	0.30
Romanian (9)	174	0.26
Russian (396)	1,154	1.71
Scandinavian (147)	203	0.30
Scotch-Irish (647)	1,806	2.67
Scottish (474)	2,100	3.11
Serbian (10)	49	0.07
Slavic (14)	46	0.07
Slovak (14)	43	0.06
Swedish (185)	862	1.28
Swiss (153)	460	0.68
Turkish (10)	16	0.02
Ukrainian (47)	185	0.27
Welsh (38)	631	0.93
West Indian, ex. Hispanic (97)	115	0.17
British West Indian (41)	41	0.06
Haitian (0)	5	0.01
Jamaican (56)	56	0.08
Trinidadian/Tobagonian (0)	13	0.02
Yugoslavian (23)	86	0.13

Hispanic Origin	Population	%
Hispanic or Latino (of any race)	33,089	48.70
Central American, ex. Mexican	1,190	1.75
Costa Rican	21	0.03
Guatemalan	648	0.95
Honduran	95	0.14
Nicaraguan	17	0.03
Panamanian	13	0.02
Salvadoran	369	0.54
Other Central American	27	0.04
Cuban	107	0.16
Dominican Republic	26	0.04
Mexican	14,084	20.73
Puerto Rican	205	0.30
South American	384	0.57
Argentinean	73	0.11
Bolivian	21	0.03
Chilean	62	0.09
Colombian	75	0.11
Ecuadorian	26	0.04
Paraguayan	3	<0.01
Peruvian	45	0.07
Uruguayan	24	0.04
Venezuelan	46	0.07
Other South American	9	0.01
Other Hispanic or Latino	17,093	25.16

Race*	Population	%
African-American/Black (689)	1,056	1.55
Not Hispanic (530)	767	1.13
Hispanic (159)	289	0.43
American Indian/Alaska Native (1,422)	2,219	3.27
Not Hispanic (891)	1,293	1.90
Hispanic (531)	926	1.36
Alaska Athabascan *(Ala. Nat.)* (2)	5	0.01
Aleut *(Alaska Native)* (2)	3	<0.01
Apache (52)	97	0.14
Arapaho (7)	7	0.01
Blackfeet (7)	21	0.03

SECTION TWO

*Notes: † The Census 2010 population figure is used to calculate the percentages in the Hispanic Origin and Race categories. Ancestry percentages are based on the 2006-2010 American Community Survey population (not shown); ‡ Numbers in parentheses indicate the number of people reporting a single ancestry; * Numbers in parentheses indicate the number of persons reporting this race alone, not in combination with any other race; Please refer to the Explanation of Data for more information.*

Canadian/French Am. Ind. (6)	12	0.02
Central American Ind. (16)	20	0.03
Cherokee (29)	105	0.15
Cheyenne (6)	13	0.02
Chickasaw (5)	8	0.01
Chippewa (27)	41	0.06
Choctaw (14)	35	0.05
Comanche (4)	12	0.02
Cree (0)	2	<0.01
Creek (10)	20	0.03
Delaware (1)	9	0.01
Hopi (12)	18	0.03
Inupiat *(Alaska Native)* (4)	8	0.01
Iroquois (13)	24	0.04
Kiowa (15)	21	0.03
Lumbee (1)	1	<0.01
Menominee (5)	5	0.01
Mexican American Ind. (64)	97	0.14
Navajo (214)	292	0.43
Osage (1)	11	0.02
Ottawa (0)	2	<0.01
Paiute (2)	3	<0.01
Pima (1)	3	<0.01
Potawatomi (4)	10	0.01
Pueblo (342)	462	0.68
Seminole (3)	11	0.02
Shoshone (7)	11	0.02
Sioux (38)	51	0.08
South American Ind. (4)	14	0.02
Spanish American Ind. (8)	16	0.02
Tlingit-Haida *(Alaska Native)* (2)	2	<0.01
Tohono O'Odham (2)	2	<0.01
Ute (2)	3	<0.01
Yakama (1)	1	<0.01
Yaqui (5)	7	0.01
Yuman (2)	2	<0.01
Yup'ik *(Alaska Native)* (1)	2	<0.01
Asian (980)	1,373	2.02
Not Hispanic (927)	1,218	1.79
Hispanic (53)	155	0.23
Bangladeshi (0)	1	<0.01
Bhutanese (2)	2	<0.01
Burmese (13)	16	0.02
Cambodian (1)	1	<0.01
Chinese, ex. Taiwanese (222)	294	0.43
Filipino (100)	202	0.30
Indian (270)	329	0.48
Indonesian (10)	19	0.03
Japanese (118)	182	0.27
Korean (85)	134	0.20
Laotian (2)	2	<0.01
Malaysian (0)	2	<0.01
Nepalese (23)	30	0.04
Pakistani (3)	3	<0.01
Sri Lankan (3)	4	0.01
Taiwanese (14)	14	0.02
Thai (18)	31	0.05
Vietnamese (41)	54	0.08
Hawaii Native/Pacific Islander (47)	137	0.20
Not Hispanic (25)	73	0.11
Hispanic (22)	64	0.09
Fijian (2)	2	<0.01
Guamanian/Chamorro (6)	18	0.03
Marshallese (1)	1	<0.01
Native Hawaiian (25)	64	0.09
Samoan (9)	19	0.03
Tongan (0)	3	<0.01
White (53,607)	55,865	82.22
Not Hispanic (31,412)	32,213	47.41
Hispanic (22,195)	23,652	34.81

Shiprock

Place Type: CDP
County: San Juan
Population: 8,295†

Ancestry‡	Population	%
English (0)	57	0.60
Irish (72)	92	0.96

Hispanic Origin	Population	%
Hispanic or Latino (of any race)	132	1.59
Mexican	88	1.06
Puerto Rican	2	0.02
Other Hispanic or Latino	42	0.51

Race*	Population	%
African-American/Black (9)	43	0.52
Not Hispanic (7)	40	0.48
Hispanic (2)	3	0.04
American Indian/Alaska Native (7,979)	8,131	98.02
Not Hispanic (7,891)	8,018	96.66
Hispanic (88)	113	1.36
Apache (8)	16	0.19
Arapaho (4)	4	0.05
Blackfeet (0)	6	0.07
Cherokee (3)	8	0.10
Cheyenne (2)	5	0.06
Chickasaw (0)	2	0.02
Choctaw (2)	9	0.11
Comanche (2)	4	0.05
Creek (0)	8	0.10
Hopi (7)	24	0.29
Kiowa (0)	1	0.01
Lumbee (1)	3	0.04
Mexican American Ind. (1)	1	0.01
Navajo (7,371)	7,603	91.66
Osage (0)	1	0.01
Paiute (2)	12	0.14
Pima (1)	1	0.01
Pueblo (19)	37	0.45
Puget Sound Salish (2)	4	0.05
Seminole (0)	12	0.14
Sioux (4)	21	0.25
Ute (5)	14	0.17
Yuman (1)	1	0.01
Asian (17)	30	0.36
Not Hispanic (17)	28	0.34
Hispanic (0)	2	0.02
Chinese, ex. Taiwanese (5)	5	0.06
Filipino (5)	8	0.10
Indian (1)	5	0.06
Indonesian (2)	4	0.05
Japanese (0)	1	0.01
Korean (1)	3	0.04
Nepalese (1)	1	0.01
Thai (1)	1	0.01
Vietnamese (0)	1	0.01
Hawaii Native/Pacific Islander (1)	5	0.06
Not Hispanic (1)	5	0.06
Samoan (1)	4	0.05
White (124)	217	2.62
Not Hispanic (115)	201	2.42
Hispanic (9)	16	0.19

Silver City

Place Type: Town
County: Grant
Population: 10,315†

Ancestry‡	Population	%
African, Sub-Saharan (16)	43	0.42
African (1)	28	0.27
South African (15)	15	0.15
American (591)	591	5.71
Belgian (11)	11	0.11
Brazilian (0)	43	0.42
British (90)	106	1.02
Canadian (17)	40	0.39
Croatian (35)	35	0.34
Czech (15)	24	0.23
Danish (18)	75	0.73
Dutch (29)	194	1.88
English (240)	1,147	11.09
European (214)	214	2.07
Finnish (0)	29	0.28
French, ex. Basque (87)	357	3.45
French Canadian (41)	68	0.66
German (403)	1,375	13.29
Hungarian (20)	58	0.56
Irish (132)	1,067	10.32
Italian (15)	134	1.30
New Zealander (16)	16	0.15
Norwegian (41)	106	1.02
Polish (39)	89	0.86
Portuguese (0)	10	0.10
Russian (29)	43	0.42
Scandinavian (34)	69	0.67
Scotch-Irish (71)	267	2.58
Scottish (39)	161	1.56
Swedish (0)	92	0.89
Swiss (0)	29	0.28
Ukrainian (0)	10	0.10
Welsh (23)	23	0.22
West Indian, ex. Hispanic (16)	16	0.15
Haitian (16)	16	0.15

Hispanic Origin	Population	%
Hispanic or Latino (of any race)	5,405	52.40
Central American, ex. Mexican	19	0.18
Costa Rican	3	0.03
Guatemalan	2	0.02
Nicaraguan	4	0.04
Panamanian	3	0.03
Salvadoran	7	0.07
Cuban	9	0.09
Dominican Republic	5	0.05
Mexican	4,236	41.07
Puerto Rican	17	0.16
South American	20	0.19
Argentinean	8	0.08
Bolivian	2	0.02
Chilean	2	0.02
Colombian	4	0.04
Peruvian	1	0.01
Venezuelan	3	0.03
Other Hispanic or Latino	1,099	10.65

Race*	Population	%
African-American/Black (133)	165	1.60
Not Hispanic (103)	130	1.26
Hispanic (30)	35	0.34
American Indian/Alaska Native (148)	245	2.38
Not Hispanic (65)	118	1.14
Hispanic (83)	127	1.23
Apache (16)	39	0.38
Blackfeet (0)	1	0.01
Cherokee (1)	13	0.13
Chippewa (1)	1	0.01
Choctaw (2)	5	0.05
Creek (1)	3	0.03
Hopi (0)	2	0.02
Mexican American Ind. (2)	3	0.03
Navajo (28)	37	0.36
Osage (0)	1	0.01
Paiute (3)	3	0.03
Pima (2)	2	0.02
Potawatomi (1)	6	0.06
Pueblo (7)	10	0.10
Shoshone (1)	3	0.03
Sioux (2)	2	0.02
Spanish American Ind. (3)	5	0.05
Tohono O'Odham (5)	5	0.05
Asian (74)	105	1.02
Not Hispanic (67)	89	0.86
Hispanic (7)	16	0.16
Bangladeshi (1)	1	0.01
Cambodian (2)	2	0.02
Chinese, ex. Taiwanese (35)	40	0.39
Filipino (15)	21	0.20
Indian (7)	11	0.11
Japanese (4)	11	0.11
Korean (3)	7	0.07
Laotian (1)	2	0.02
Vietnamese (4)	4	0.04
Hawaii Native/Pacific Islander (14)	23	0.22
Not Hispanic (14)	21	0.20
Hispanic (0)	2	0.02
Native Hawaiian (1)	11	0.11

*Notes: † The Census 2010 population figure is used to calculate the percentages in the Hispanic Origin and Race categories. Ancestry percentages are based on the 2006-2010 American Community Survey population (not shown); ‡ Numbers in parentheses indicate the number of people reporting a single ancestry; * Numbers in parentheses indicate the number of persons reporting this race alone, not in combination with any other race; Please refer to the Explanation of Data for more information.*

Samoan (9)	10	0.10
Tongan (1)	3	0.03
White (8,418)	8,644	83.80
Not Hispanic (4,526)	4,624	44.83
Hispanic (3,892)	4,020	38.97

Socorro

Place Type: City
County: Socorro
Population: 9,051†

Ancestry‡	Population	%
African, Sub-Saharan (26)	26	0.29
Ghanaian (26)	26	0.29
American (279)	279	3.08
Arab (137)	145	1.60
Lebanese (0)	8	0.09
Other Arab (137)	137	1.51
Basque (0)	8	0.09
British (26)	51	0.56
Canadian (0)	28	0.31
Celtic (0)	43	0.47
Croatian (0)	19	0.21
Czech (4)	4	0.04
Danish (16)	16	0.18
Dutch (35)	223	2.46
Eastern European (26)	26	0.29
English (212)	711	7.85
European (71)	90	0.99
French, ex. Basque (7)	129	1.42
German (165)	666	7.35
German Russian (9)	9	0.10
Greek (0)	27	0.30
Hungarian (10)	10	0.11
Irish (78)	402	4.44
Italian (67)	132	1.46
Lithuanian (23)	23	0.25
Norwegian (0)	19	0.21
Polish (14)	50	0.55
Portuguese (11)	11	0.12
Russian (17)	24	0.26
Scotch-Irish (26)	144	1.59
Scottish (38)	64	0.71
Swedish (47)	73	0.81
Swiss (31)	40	0.44
Welsh (31)	76	0.84
West Indian, ex. Hispanic (15)	67	0.74
Dutch West Indian (0)	20	0.22
Jamaican (15)	47	0.52

Hispanic Origin	Population	%
Hispanic or Latino (of any race)	4,885	53.97
Central American, ex. Mexican	14	0.15
Costa Rican	2	0.02
Guatemalan	3	0.03
Honduran	2	0.02
Nicaraguan	2	0.02
Panamanian	4	0.04
Salvadoran	1	0.01
Cuban	8	0.09
Dominican Republic	1	0.01
Mexican	2,977	32.89
Puerto Rican	22	0.24
South American	27	0.30
Argentinean	2	0.02
Chilean	12	0.13
Colombian	8	0.09
Ecuadorian	1	0.01
Peruvian	4	0.04
Other Hispanic or Latino	1,836	20.29

Race*	Population	%
African-American/Black (139)	181	2.00
Not Hispanic (103)	125	1.38
Hispanic (36)	56	0.62
American Indian/Alaska Native (351)	456	5.04
Not Hispanic (277)	324	3.58
Hispanic (74)	132	1.46
Apache (5)	18	0.20
Blackfeet (0)	5	0.06
Cherokee (6)	14	0.15
Cheyenne (2)	3	0.03
Chippewa (2)	2	0.02
Choctaw (0)	3	0.03
Comanche (3)	4	0.04
Creek (0)	1	0.01
Hopi (0)	2	0.02
Inupiat *(Alaska Native)* (0)	1	0.01
Iroquois (0)	2	0.02
Lumbee (1)	1	0.01
Mexican American Ind. (2)	2	0.02
Navajo (225)	258	2.85
Paiute (2)	2	0.02
Pueblo (24)	34	0.38
Sioux (2)	2	0.02
Spanish American Ind. (3)	3	0.03
Tlingit-Haida *(Alaska Native)* (2)	2	0.02
Asian (187)	262	2.89
Not Hispanic (181)	231	2.55
Hispanic (6)	31	0.34
Chinese, ex. Taiwanese (80)	86	0.95
Filipino (9)	18	0.20
Indian (59)	62	0.69
Indonesian (0)	1	0.01
Japanese (10)	24	0.27
Korean (12)	16	0.18
Nepalese (1)	1	0.01
Sri Lankan (2)	2	0.02
Thai (3)	5	0.06
Vietnamese (9)	9	0.10
Hawaii Native/Pacific Islander (6)	18	0.20
Not Hispanic (2)	4	0.04
Hispanic (4)	14	0.15
Guamanian/Chamorro (5)	9	0.10
Native Hawaiian (0)	3	0.03
Samoan (1)	1	0.01
White (7,307)	7,589	83.85
Not Hispanic (3,461)	3,568	39.42
Hispanic (3,846)	4,021	44.43

South Valley

Place Type: CDP
County: Bernalillo
Population: 40,976†

Ancestry‡	Population	%
American (673)	673	1.60
Arab (20)	32	0.08
Iraqi (11)	11	0.03
Lebanese (9)	9	0.02
Other Arab (0)	12	0.03
Armenian (0)	39	0.09
Austrian (12)	47	0.11
British (35)	69	0.16
Canadian (27)	43	0.10
Croatian (0)	13	0.03
Czech (13)	89	0.21
Czechoslovakian (0)	27	0.06
Danish (9)	9	0.02
Dutch (19)	100	0.24
English (477)	1,259	3.00
European (74)	140	0.33
French, ex. Basque (42)	381	0.91
French Canadian (63)	112	0.27
German (505)	1,848	4.40
Greek (0)	10	0.02
Hungarian (0)	14	0.03
Irish (341)	1,226	2.92
Israeli (0)	12	0.03
Italian (160)	679	1.62
Northern European (42)	42	0.10
Norwegian (70)	104	0.25
Pennsylvania German (0)	17	0.04
Polish (10)	410	0.98
Portuguese (28)	85	0.20
Russian (8)	49	0.12
Scandinavian (0)	15	0.04
Scotch-Irish (108)	291	0.69
Scottish (93)	412	0.98
Slavic (10)	10	0.02
Slovak (11)	84	0.20
Slovene (0)	7	0.02
Swedish (26)	191	0.45
Swiss (0)	8	0.02
Turkish (31)	31	0.07
Ukrainian (0)	38	0.09
Welsh (46)	155	0.37
Yugoslavian (0)	6	0.01

Hispanic Origin	Population	%
Hispanic or Latino (of any race)	32,860	80.19
Central American, ex. Mexican	92	0.22
Costa Rican	3	0.01
Guatemalan	34	0.08
Honduran	20	0.05
Nicaraguan	4	0.01
Panamanian	3	0.01
Salvadoran	28	0.07
Cuban	98	0.24
Dominican Republic	12	0.03
Mexican	21,189	51.71
Puerto Rican	119	0.29
South American	50	0.12
Argentinean	3	0.01
Chilean	9	0.02
Colombian	16	0.04
Ecuadorian	6	0.01
Paraguayan	1	<0.01
Peruvian	10	0.02
Venezuelan	3	0.01
Other South American	2	<0.01
Other Hispanic or Latino	11,300	27.58

Race*	Population	%
African-American/Black (496)	718	1.75
Not Hispanic (346)	453	1.11
Hispanic (150)	265	0.65
American Indian/Alaska Native (898)	1,306	3.19
Not Hispanic (493)	633	1.54
Hispanic (405)	673	1.64
Apache (36)	82	0.20
Arapaho (0)	3	0.01
Blackfeet (1)	5	0.01
Central American Ind. (4)	4	0.01
Cherokee (8)	39	0.10
Chickasaw (1)	1	<0.01
Chippewa (2)	3	0.01
Choctaw (7)	18	0.04
Colville (5)	5	0.01
Comanche (2)	2	<0.01
Creek (3)	3	0.01
Delaware (1)	1	<0.01
Hopi (9)	12	0.03
Iroquois (9)	10	0.02
Kiowa (3)	3	0.01
Lumbee (1)	1	<0.01
Mexican American Ind. (43)	55	0.13
Navajo (182)	249	0.61
Osage (1)	3	0.01
Pima (0)	1	<0.01
Potawatomi (0)	2	<0.01
Pueblo (204)	276	0.67
Puget Sound Salish (0)	1	<0.01
Seminole (0)	1	<0.01
Sioux (9)	16	0.04
South American Ind. (1)	2	<0.01
Spanish American Ind. (11)	16	0.04
Tlingit-Haida *(Alaska Native)* (0)	1	<0.01
Ute (7)	11	0.03
Yaqui (0)	2	<0.01
Yuman (1)	1	<0.01
Yup'ik *(Alaska Native)* (2)	2	<0.01
Asian (170)	308	0.75
Not Hispanic (109)	160	0.39
Hispanic (61)	148	0.36
Bangladeshi (0)	1	<0.01
Chinese, ex. Taiwanese (20)	27	0.07
Filipino (56)	95	0.23

*Notes: † The Census 2010 population figure is used to calculate the percentages in the Hispanic Origin and Race categories. Ancestry percentages are based on the 2006-2010 American Community Survey population (not shown); ‡ Numbers in parentheses indicate the number of people reporting a single ancestry; * Numbers in parentheses indicate the number of persons reporting this race alone, not in combination with any other race; Please refer to the Explanation of Data for more information.*

Indian (18)	33	0.08
Indonesian (0)	1	<0.01
Japanese (21)	51	0.12
Korean (18)	32	0.08
Laotian (3)	5	0.01
Nepalese (1)	1	<0.01
Taiwanese (2)	2	<0.01
Thai (5)	7	0.02
Vietnamese (14)	17	0.04
Hawaii Native/Pacific Islander (10)	65	0.16
Not Hispanic (5)	24	0.06
Hispanic (5)	41	0.10
Fijian (2)	3	0.01
Guamanian/Chamorro (0)	2	<0.01
Native Hawaiian (5)	17	0.04
Samoan (1)	2	<0.01
White (24,379)	25,761	62.87
Not Hispanic (6,763)	7,010	17.11
Hispanic (17,616)	18,751	45.76

Sunland Park

Place Type: City
County: Do±a Ana
Population: 14,106[†]

Ancestry[‡]	Population	%
American (50)	50	0.36
Czech (10)	10	0.07
Dutch (0)	10	0.07
French, ex. Basque (10)	26	0.19
German (99)	99	0.72
Irish (0)	23	0.17
Italian (16)	37	0.27
Latvian (10)	10	0.07
Polish (0)	10	0.07
Scottish (28)	28	0.20
Ukrainian (0)	12	0.09

Hispanic Origin	Population	%
Hispanic or Latino (of any race)	13,434	95.24
Central American, ex. Mexican	22	0.16
Costa Rican	4	0.03
Guatemalan	7	0.05
Honduran	2	0.01
Nicaraguan	4	0.03
Panamanian	3	0.02
Salvadoran	2	0.01
Cuban	2	0.01
Dominican Republic	1	0.01
Mexican	12,294	87.15
Puerto Rican	37	0.26
South American	10	0.07
Argentinean	1	0.01
Chilean	1	0.01
Colombian	1	0.01
Ecuadorian	3	0.02
Peruvian	3	0.02
Venezuelan	1	0.01
Other Hispanic or Latino	1,068	7.57

Race*	Population	%
African-American/Black (86)	122	0.86
Not Hispanic (41)	47	0.33
Hispanic (45)	75	0.53
American Indian/Alaska Native (74)	99	0.70
Not Hispanic (3)	7	0.05
Hispanic (71)	92	0.65
Apache (2)	5	0.04
Cherokee (1)	3	0.02
Mexican American Ind. (6)	7	0.05
Navajo (4)	4	0.03
Pueblo (1)	2	0.01
South American Ind. (1)	1	0.01
Spanish American Ind. (0)	2	0.01
Yaqui (0)	1	0.01
Asian (22)	46	0.33
Not Hispanic (15)	22	0.16
Hispanic (7)	24	0.17
Chinese, ex. Taiwanese (4)	10	0.07
Filipino (1)	7	0.05
Indian (4)	8	0.06
Japanese (5)	9	0.06
Korean (1)	2	0.01
Malaysian (2)	2	0.01
Hawaii Native/Pacific Islander (9)	19	0.13
Not Hispanic (3)	5	0.04
Hispanic (6)	14	0.10
Guamanian/Chamorro (2)	2	0.01
Native Hawaiian (2)	7	0.05
White (10,486)	10,724	76.02
Not Hispanic (578)	598	4.24
Hispanic (9,908)	10,126	71.79

*Notes: † The Census 2010 population figure is used to calculate the percentages in the Hispanic Origin and Race categories. Ancestry percentages are based on the 2006-2010 American Community Survey population (not shown); ‡ Numbers in parentheses indicate the number of people reporting a single ancestry; * Numbers in parentheses indicate the number of persons reporting this race alone, not in combination with any other race; Please refer to the Explanation of Data for more information.*

NEW YORK

Place Type: State
Population: 19,378,102†

Ancestry‡	Population	%
Afghan (9,904)	10,755	0.06
African, Sub-Saharan (178,451)	240,909	1.25
African (90,390)	142,623	0.74
Cape Verdean (463)	844	<0.01
Ethiopian (4,371)	5,107	0.03
Ghanaian (22,113)	23,006	0.12
Kenyan (1,138)	1,324	0.01
Liberian (2,675)	3,006	0.02
Nigerian (25,852)	28,991	0.15
Senegalese (2,893)	3,166	0.02
Sierra Leonean (1,672)	1,711	0.01
Somalian (2,764)	3,053	0.02
South African (2,838)	3,993	0.02
Sudanese (1,819)	2,137	0.01
Ugandan (388)	464	<0.01
Zimbabwean (607)	646	<0.01
Other Sub-Saharan African (18,468)	20,838	0.11
Albanian (41,939)	46,223	0.24
Alsatian (202)	882	<0.01
American (689,298)	689,298	3.58
Arab (103,238)	145,746	0.76
Arab (20,874)	25,231	0.13
Egyptian (21,344)	25,478	0.13
Iraqi (1,882)	3,013	0.02
Jordanian (3,956)	4,623	0.02
Lebanese (16,431)	32,642	0.17
Moroccan (9,220)	12,364	0.06
Palestinian (4,397)	5,501	0.03
Syrian (7,544)	14,535	0.08
Other Arab (17,590)	22,359	0.12
Armenian (15,331)	24,803	0.13
Assyrian/Chaldean/Syriac (384)	644	<0.01
Australian (4,252)	7,418	0.04
Austrian (22,923)	91,260	0.47
Basque (570)	1,514	0.01
Belgian (4,380)	13,929	0.07
Brazilian (19,433)	26,401	0.14
British (29,032)	58,548	0.30
Bulgarian (6,409)	8,210	0.04
Cajun (295)	897	<0.01
Canadian (23,228)	50,059	0.26
Carpatho Rusyn (474)	741	<0.01
Celtic (1,106)	2,324	0.01
Croatian (15,221)	26,607	0.14
Cypriot (1,402)	1,721	0.01
Czech (13,656)	57,264	0.30
Czechoslovakian (9,727)	22,547	0.12
Danish (8,961)	35,247	0.18
Dutch (50,011)	277,731	1.44
Eastern European (82,212)	89,540	0.47
English (307,176)	1,180,365	6.14
Estonian (1,710)	3,462	0.02
European (142,136)	157,939	0.82
Finnish (5,117)	16,941	0.09
French, ex. Basque (93,941)	505,680	2.63
French Canadian (52,040)	134,420	0.70
German (532,432)	2,238,521	11.64
German Russian (196)	587	<0.01
Greek (102,342)	163,796	0.85
Guyanese (109,285)	123,809	0.64
Hungarian (61,925)	154,481	0.80
Icelander (753)	1,528	0.01
Iranian (23,356)	27,773	0.14
Irish (763,450)	2,565,928	13.34
Israeli (25,337)	36,808	0.19
Italian (1,405,357)	2,731,316	14.20
Latvian (4,261)	9,194	0.05
Lithuanian (15,565)	48,825	0.25
Luxemburger (158)	582	<0.01
Macedonian (6,414)	7,783	0.04
Maltese (3,431)	7,645	0.04
New Zealander (484)	1,002	0.01
Northern European (8,610)	10,116	0.05
Norwegian (23,292)	85,859	0.45
Pennsylvania German (8,537)	13,519	0.07
Polish (396,502)	1,007,597	5.24
Portuguese (28,735)	52,967	0.28
Romanian (28,352)	56,605	0.29
Russian (241,898)	474,184	2.47
Scandinavian (4,984)	12,891	0.07
Scotch-Irish (58,045)	164,725	0.86
Scottish (53,369)	227,255	1.18
Serbian (5,585)	8,499	0.04
Slavic (3,865)	9,898	0.05
Slovak (14,038)	35,389	0.18
Slovene (1,922)	4,802	0.02
Soviet Union (317)	458	<0.01
Swedish (29,980)	132,781	0.69
Swiss (9,956)	39,241	0.20
Turkish (22,814)	29,907	0.16
Ukrainian (73,876)	133,633	0.69
Welsh (15,842)	88,255	0.46
West Indian, ex. Hispanic (665,395)	790,170	4.11
Bahamian (1,110)	1,796	0.01
Barbadian (22,928)	27,200	0.14
Belizean (5,612)	7,037	0.04
Bermudan (433)	672	<0.01
British West Indian (42,984)	49,916	0.26
Dutch West Indian (1,177)	1,887	0.01
Haitian (164,815)	179,024	0.93
Jamaican (265,516)	300,094	1.56
Trinidadian/Tobagonian (76,788)	89,490	0.47
U.S. Virgin Islander (2,037)	2,873	0.01
West Indian (80,923)	128,763	0.67
Other West Indian (1,072)	1,418	0.01
Yugoslavian (20,521)	28,253	0.15

Hispanic Origin	Population	%
Hispanic or Latino (of any race)	3,416,922	17.63
Central American, ex. Mexican	353,589	1.82
Costa Rican	11,576	0.06
Guatemalan	73,806	0.38
Honduran	71,919	0.37
Nicaraguan	13,006	0.07
Panamanian	28,200	0.15
Salvadoran	152,130	0.79
Other Central American	2,952	0.02
Cuban	70,803	0.37
Dominican Republic	674,787	3.48
Mexican	457,288	2.36
Puerto Rican	1,070,558	5.52
South American	513,417	2.65
Argentinean	24,969	0.13
Bolivian	7,122	0.04
Chilean	15,050	0.08
Colombian	141,879	0.73
Ecuadorian	228,216	1.18
Paraguayan	5,940	0.03
Peruvian	66,318	0.34
Uruguayan	6,021	0.03
Venezuelan	13,910	0.07
Other South American	3,992	0.02
Other Hispanic or Latino	276,480	1.43

Race*	Population	%
African-American/Black (3,073,800)	3,334,550	17.21
Not Hispanic (2,783,857)	2,946,880	15.21
Hispanic (289,943)	387,670	2.00
American Indian/Alaska Native (106,906)	221,058	1.14
Not Hispanic (53,908)	128,049	0.66
Hispanic (52,998)	93,009	0.48
Alaska Athabascan *(Ala. Nat.)* (57)	116	<0.01
Aleut *(Alaska Native)* (48)	82	<0.01
Apache (337)	1,080	0.01
Arapaho (24)	65	<0.01
Blackfeet (606)	4,496	0.02
Canadian/French Am. Ind. (530)	1,022	0.01
Central American Ind. (4,475)	8,602	0.04
Cherokee (2,714)	16,947	0.09
Cheyenne (47)	163	<0.01
Chickasaw (68)	215	<0.01
Chippewa (548)	1,125	0.01
Choctaw (263)	1,052	0.01
Colville (11)	22	<0.01
Comanche (69)	199	<0.01
Cree (50)	263	<0.01
Creek (155)	624	<0.01
Crow (52)	181	<0.01
Delaware (598)	1,384	0.01
Hopi (39)	115	<0.01
Houma (35)	48	<0.01
Inupiat *(Alaska Native)* (91)	169	<0.01
Iroquois (16,957)	26,567	0.14
Kiowa (24)	44	<0.01
Lumbee (127)	304	<0.01
Menominee (19)	41	<0.01
Mexican American Ind. (5,344)	7,439	0.04
Navajo (347)	788	<0.01
Osage (31)	86	<0.01
Ottawa (24)	52	<0.01
Paiute (25)	49	<0.01
Pima (13)	40	<0.01
Potawatomi (83)	166	<0.01
Pueblo (556)	1,096	0.01
Puget Sound Salish (14)	33	<0.01
Seminole (107)	848	<0.01
Shoshone (22)	96	<0.01
Sioux (628)	1,758	0.01
South American Ind. (6,294)	13,078	0.07
Spanish American Ind. (2,563)	3,506	0.02
Tlingit-Haida *(Alaska Native)* (60)	169	<0.01
Tohono O'Odham (59)	103	<0.01
Tsimshian *(Alaska Native)* (4)	5	<0.01
Ute (13)	36	<0.01
Yakama (8)	18	<0.01
Yaqui (48)	104	<0.01
Yuman (24)	45	<0.01
Yup'ik *(Alaska Native)* (20)	39	<0.01
Asian (1,420,244)	1,579,494	8.15
Not Hispanic (1,406,194)	1,545,106	7.97
Hispanic (14,050)	34,388	0.18
Bangladeshi (57,761)	67,063	0.35
Bhutanese (1,534)	1,824	0.01
Burmese (11,214)	12,174	0.06
Cambodian (4,212)	5,114	0.03
Chinese, ex. Taiwanese (559,516)	598,597	3.09
Filipino (104,287)	126,129	0.65
Hmong (227)	296	<0.01
Indian (313,620)	368,767	1.90
Indonesian (4,568)	6,122	0.03
Japanese (37,780)	51,781	0.27
Korean (140,994)	153,609	0.79
Laotian (3,420)	4,471	0.02
Malaysian (2,537)	3,908	0.02
Nepalese (6,844)	7,625	0.04
Pakistani (63,696)	70,622	0.36
Sri Lankan (5,196)	6,153	0.03
Taiwanese (16,023)	18,868	0.10
Thai (9,258)	11,763	0.06
Vietnamese (28,764)	34,510	0.18
Hawaii Native/Pacific Islander (8,766)	36,423	0.19
Not Hispanic (5,320)	21,768	0.11
Hispanic (3,446)	14,655	0.08
Fijian (157)	321	<0.01
Guamanian/Chamorro (2,235)	3,407	0.02
Marshallese (32)	37	<0.01
Native Hawaiian (1,802)	5,108	0.03
Samoan (685)	1,654	0.01
Tongan (80)	138	<0.01
White (12,740,974)	13,155,274	67.89
Not Hispanic (11,304,247)	11,534,988	59.53
Hispanic (1,436,727)	1,620,286	8.36

*Notes: † The Census 2010 population figure is used to calculate the percentages in the Hispanic Origin and Race categories. Ancestry percentages are based on the 2006-2010 American Community Survey population (not shown); ‡ Numbers in parentheses indicate the number of people reporting a single ancestry; * Numbers in parentheses indicate the number of persons reporting this race alone, not in combination with any other race; Please refer to the Explanation of Data for more information.*

Airmont

Place Type: Village
County: Rockland
Population: 8,628†

Ancestry‡	Population	%
African, Sub-Saharan (75)	75	0.89
African (75)	75	0.89
American (397)	397	4.71
Arab (157)	167	1.98
Egyptian (16)	16	0.19
Jordanian (10)	10	0.12
Lebanese (9)	9	0.11
Moroccan (109)	109	1.29
Other Arab (13)	23	0.27
Austrian (30)	109	1.29
Belgian (15)	15	0.18
British (10)	53	0.63
Canadian (25)	25	0.30
Czech (0)	38	0.45
Czechoslovakian (29)	29	0.34
Danish (10)	20	0.24
Dutch (0)	44	0.52
Eastern European (22)	22	0.26
English (31)	366	4.34
European (136)	144	1.71
French, ex. Basque (9)	142	1.69
French Canadian (12)	12	0.14
German (290)	1,150	13.65
Greek (83)	203	2.41
Guyanese (13)	26	0.31
Hungarian (28)	98	1.16
Irish (454)	1,354	16.07
Italian (1,051)	1,654	19.63
Latvian (87)	132	1.57
Lithuanian (23)	80	0.95
Norwegian (23)	35	0.42
Polish (89)	524	6.22
Portuguese (0)	33	0.39
Romanian (116)	219	2.60
Russian (255)	715	8.49
Scotch-Irish (0)	33	0.39
Scottish (18)	58	0.69
Slavic (9)	19	0.23
Swedish (0)	35	0.42
Swiss (0)	21	0.25
Turkish (0)	43	0.51
Ukrainian (22)	58	0.69
Welsh (0)	12	0.14
West Indian, ex. Hispanic (88)	88	1.04
Haitian (88)	88	1.04

Hispanic Origin	Population	%
Hispanic or Latino (of any race)	710	8.23
Central American, ex. Mexican	53	0.61
Costa Rican	2	0.02
Guatemalan	35	0.41
Honduran	1	0.01
Nicaraguan	2	0.02
Panamanian	6	0.07
Salvadoran	7	0.08
Cuban	22	0.25
Dominican Republic	58	0.67
Mexican	86	1.00
Puerto Rican	307	3.56
South American	125	1.45
Argentinean	26	0.30
Chilean	3	0.03
Colombian	25	0.29
Ecuadorian	47	0.54
Peruvian	19	0.22
Venezuelan	4	0.05
Other South American	1	0.01
Other Hispanic or Latino	59	0.68

Race*	Population	%
African-American/Black (396)	482	5.59
Not Hispanic (365)	418	4.84
Hispanic (31)	64	0.74
American Indian/Alaska Native (30)	77	0.89
Not Hispanic (28)	55	0.64
Hispanic (2)	22	0.25
Blackfeet (0)	4	0.05
Central American Ind. (0)	2	0.02
Cherokee (2)	13	0.15
Delaware (14)	15	0.17
Iroquois (2)	3	0.03
Lumbee (0)	2	0.02
South American Ind. (0)	8	0.09
Asian (435)	511	5.92
Not Hispanic (434)	502	5.82
Hispanic (1)	9	0.10
Bangladeshi (5)	5	0.06
Cambodian (13)	13	0.15
Chinese, ex. Taiwanese (79)	97	1.12
Filipino (63)	79	0.92
Indian (147)	177	2.05
Indonesian (0)	2	0.02
Japanese (13)	22	0.25
Korean (36)	41	0.48
Malaysian (0)	2	0.02
Nepalese (3)	3	0.03
Pakistani (39)	41	0.48
Taiwanese (7)	7	0.08
Thai (4)	4	0.05
Vietnamese (7)	11	0.13
Hawaii Native/Pacific Islander (4)	11	0.13
Not Hispanic (4)	11	0.13
Samoan (4)	4	0.05
White (7,450)	7,604	88.13
Not Hispanic (6,946)	7,051	81.72
Hispanic (504)	553	6.41

Albany

Place Type: City
County: Albany
Population: 97,856†

Ancestry‡	Population	%
African, Sub-Saharan (1,142)	1,533	1.57
African (656)	975	1.00
Cape Verdean (0)	13	0.01
Ethiopian (21)	21	0.02
Ghanaian (143)	143	0.15
Kenyan (101)	101	0.10
Nigerian (132)	191	0.19
Sudanese (25)	25	0.03
Other Sub-Saharan African (64)	64	0.07
Albanian (318)	384	0.39
Alsatian (19)	51	0.05
American (1,531)	1,531	1.56
Arab (181)	525	0.54
Arab (105)	116	0.12
Egyptian (41)	124	0.13
Lebanese (23)	138	0.14
Palestinian (12)	25	0.03
Syrian (0)	104	0.11
Other Arab (0)	18	0.02
Armenian (26)	75	0.08
Australian (30)	88	0.09
Austrian (31)	247	0.25
Belgian (53)	78	0.08
Brazilian (45)	45	0.05
British (132)	255	0.26
Bulgarian (0)	9	0.01
Canadian (80)	128	0.13
Carpatho Rusyn (12)	12	0.01
Croatian (32)	54	0.06
Czech (153)	392	0.40
Czechoslovakian (11)	35	0.04
Danish (89)	303	0.31
Dutch (321)	1,664	1.70
Eastern European (220)	253	0.26
English (1,100)	5,315	5.43
European (1,163)	1,362	1.39
Finnish (0)	35	0.04
French, ex. Basque (458)	3,690	3.77
French Canadian (329)	1,061	1.08
German (1,888)	10,150	10.36
Greek (368)	755	0.77
Guyanese (466)	483	0.49
Hungarian (183)	405	0.41
Iranian (50)	60	0.06
Irish (5,251)	17,818	18.19
Italian (4,932)	12,860	13.13
Latvian (15)	24	0.02
Lithuanian (38)	217	0.22
Luxemburger (9)	9	0.01
Maltese (11)	24	0.02
Northern European (56)	160	0.16
Norwegian (146)	406	0.41
Pennsylvania German (0)	12	0.01
Polish (1,282)	4,476	4.57
Portuguese (116)	266	0.27
Romanian (0)	182	0.19
Russian (483)	1,487	1.52
Scandinavian (31)	313	0.32
Scotch-Irish (229)	842	0.86
Scottish (311)	1,162	1.19
Serbian (19)	19	0.02
Slavic (28)	94	0.10
Slovak (110)	351	0.36
Slovene (12)	70	0.07
Swedish (57)	444	0.45
Swiss (15)	125	0.13
Turkish (14)	39	0.04
Ukrainian (85)	496	0.51
Welsh (103)	597	0.61
West Indian, ex. Hispanic (2,407)	3,298	3.37
Barbadian (14)	29	0.03
Bermudan (36)	36	0.04
British West Indian (133)	210	0.21
Dutch West Indian (39)	79	0.08
Haitian (421)	446	0.46
Jamaican (1,228)	1,636	1.67
Trinidadian/Tobagonian (193)	219	0.22
West Indian (276)	576	0.59
Other West Indian (67)	67	0.07
Yugoslavian (36)	48	0.05

Hispanic Origin	Population	%
Hispanic or Latino (of any race)	8,396	8.58
Central American, ex. Mexican	343	0.35
Costa Rican	35	0.04
Guatemalan	54	0.06
Honduran	70	0.07
Nicaraguan	28	0.03
Panamanian	81	0.08
Salvadoran	65	0.07
Other Central American	10	0.01
Cuban	298	0.30
Dominican Republic	1,095	1.12
Mexican	616	0.63
Puerto Rican	4,654	4.76
South American	626	0.64
Argentinean	38	0.04
Bolivian	5	0.01
Chilean	38	0.04
Colombian	196	0.20
Ecuadorian	184	0.19
Paraguayan	6	0.01
Peruvian	89	0.09
Uruguayan	15	0.02
Venezuelan	39	0.04
Other South American	16	0.02
Other Hispanic or Latino	764	0.78

Race*	Population	%
African-American/Black (30,110)	32,569	33.28
Not Hispanic (28,479)	30,376	31.04
Hispanic (1,631)	2,193	2.24
American Indian/Alaska Native (295)	1,120	1.14
Not Hispanic (191)	856	0.87
Hispanic (104)	264	0.27
Alaska Athabascan *(Ala. Nat.)* (0)	1	<0.01
Apache (0)	5	0.01
Blackfeet (6)	57	0.06
Canadian/French Am. Ind. (0)	5	0.01

*Notes: † The Census 2010 population figure is used to calculate the percentages in the Hispanic Origin and Race categories. Ancestry percentages are based on the 2006-2010 American Community Survey population (not shown); ‡ Numbers in parentheses indicate the number of people reporting a single ancestry; * Numbers in parentheses indicate the number of persons reporting this race alone, not in combination with any other race; Please refer to the Explanation of Data for more information.*

Central American Ind. (5)	10	0.01
Cherokee (23)	205	0.21
Chickasaw (2)	2	<0.01
Chippewa (0)	3	<0.01
Choctaw (2)	8	0.01
Cree (1)	4	<0.01
Creek (0)	6	0.01
Delaware (2)	11	0.01
Inupiat *(Alaska Native)* (1)	1	<0.01
Iroquois (26)	102	0.10
Mexican American Ind. (10)	13	0.01
Navajo (1)	2	<0.01
Ottawa (0)	1	<0.01
Potawatomi (1)	2	<0.01
Pueblo (1)	1	<0.01
Seminole (1)	7	0.01
Shoshone (0)	1	<0.01
Sioux (5)	11	0.01
South American Ind. (24)	49	0.05
Spanish American Ind. (6)	10	0.01
Tlingit-Haida *(Alaska Native)* (1)	3	<0.01
Yakama (1)	1	<0.01
Yup'ik *(Alaska Native)* (1)	1	<0.01
Asian (4,890)	5,588	5.71
Not Hispanic (4,850)	5,482	5.60
Hispanic (40)	106	0.11
Bangladeshi (148)	171	0.17
Bhutanese (62)	62	0.06
Burmese (294)	322	0.33
Cambodian (8)	12	0.01
Chinese, ex. Taiwanese (1,219)	1,349	1.38
Filipino (645)	746	0.76
Indian (1,009)	1,198	1.22
Indonesian (10)	12	0.01
Japanese (109)	200	0.20
Korean (368)	426	0.44
Laotian (0)	3	<0.01
Malaysian (2)	8	0.01
Nepalese (48)	55	0.06
Pakistani (425)	483	0.49
Sri Lankan (13)	13	0.01
Taiwanese (61)	69	0.07
Thai (35)	46	0.05
Vietnamese (197)	231	0.24
Hawaii Native/Pacific Islander (55)	180	0.18
Not Hispanic (47)	158	0.16
Hispanic (8)	22	0.02
Fijian (0)	1	<0.01
Guamanian/Chamorro (7)	15	0.02
Native Hawaiian (8)	38	0.04
Samoan (9)	15	0.02
Tongan (0)	1	<0.01
White (55,783)	58,605	59.89
Not Hispanic (52,857)	55,044	56.25
Hispanic (2,926)	3,561	3.64

Albion

Place Type: Town
County: Orleans
Population: 8,468†

Ancestry‡	Population	%
African, Sub-Saharan (8)	8	0.09
Nigerian (8)	8	0.09
American (299)	299	3.46
Arab (0)	18	0.21
Egyptian (0)	11	0.13
Lebanese (0)	7	0.08
Belgian (0)	13	0.15
Brazilian (8)	8	0.09
British (19)	55	0.64
Canadian (51)	51	0.59
Danish (0)	13	0.15
Dutch (0)	322	3.73
English (380)	1,281	14.82
European (47)	47	0.54
French, ex. Basque (8)	385	4.45
French Canadian (31)	31	0.36
German (199)	1,216	14.07
Greek (0)	6	0.07
Hungarian (0)	7	0.08
Irish (216)	1,203	13.92
Italian (632)	1,402	16.22
Lithuanian (15)	15	0.17
Pennsylvania German (0)	24	0.28
Polish (232)	619	7.16
Scotch-Irish (46)	86	1.00
Scottish (0)	291	3.37
Ukrainian (7)	26	0.30
Welsh (13)	151	1.75
West Indian, ex. Hispanic (147)	155	1.79
Haitian (13)	13	0.15
Jamaican (114)	122	1.41
Trinidadian/Tobagonian (14)	14	0.16
West Indian (6)	6	0.07

Hispanic Origin	Population	%
Hispanic or Latino (of any race)	626	7.39
Central American, ex. Mexican	33	0.39
Costa Rican	1	0.01
Guatemalan	4	0.05
Honduran	6	0.07
Nicaraguan	3	0.04
Panamanian	8	0.09
Salvadoran	11	0.13
Cuban	20	0.24
Dominican Republic	41	0.48
Mexican	204	2.41
Puerto Rican	257	3.03
South American	21	0.25
Colombian	9	0.11
Ecuadorian	5	0.06
Peruvian	7	0.08
Other Hispanic or Latino	50	0.59

Race*	Population	%
African-American/Black (1,494)	1,629	19.24
Not Hispanic (1,405)	1,530	18.07
Hispanic (89)	99	1.17
American Indian/Alaska Native (53)	97	1.15
Not Hispanic (43)	81	0.96
Hispanic (10)	16	0.19
Apache (0)	1	0.01
Blackfeet (0)	4	0.05
Central American Ind. (2)	2	0.02
Cherokee (1)	5	0.06
Cheyenne (0)	1	0.01
Chippewa (0)	4	0.05
Iroquois (9)	18	0.21
Mexican American Ind. (2)	4	0.05
South American Ind. (1)	3	0.04
Spanish American Ind. (3)	3	0.04
Asian (46)	62	0.73
Not Hispanic (40)	56	0.66
Hispanic (6)	6	0.07
Chinese, ex. Taiwanese (2)	2	0.02
Filipino (9)	20	0.24
Indian (1)	1	0.01
Japanese (1)	3	0.04
Korean (2)	2	0.02
Pakistani (10)	10	0.12
Thai (5)	8	0.09
Hawaii Native/Pacific Islander (2)	8	0.09
Not Hispanic (2)	8	0.09
Guamanian/Chamorro (1)	2	0.02
Native Hawaiian (1)	2	0.02
White (6,459)	6,662	78.67
Not Hispanic (6,159)	6,325	74.69
Hispanic (300)	337	3.98

Alden

Place Type: Town
County: Erie
Population: 10,865†

Ancestry‡	Population	%
African, Sub-Saharan (6)	6	0.06
Ghanaian (6)	6	0.06
American (453)	453	4.20
Arab (8)	41	0.38
Lebanese (8)	41	0.38
Austrian (7)	19	0.18
British (0)	10	0.09
Canadian (17)	72	0.67
Czechoslovakian (6)	17	0.16
Dutch (4)	40	0.37
English (163)	763	7.07
French, ex. Basque (102)	509	4.72
French Canadian (34)	49	0.45
German (1,313)	4,180	38.75
Greek (8)	107	0.99
Hungarian (35)	206	1.91
Irish (343)	1,484	13.76
Italian (381)	1,210	11.22
Norwegian (0)	21	0.19
Pennsylvania German (0)	6	0.06
Polish (1,651)	3,165	29.34
Russian (0)	134	1.24
Scandinavian (0)	52	0.48
Scotch-Irish (52)	75	0.70
Scottish (20)	113	1.05
Slovak (36)	36	0.33
Swedish (0)	54	0.50
Swiss (23)	52	0.48
Ukrainian (33)	70	0.65
Welsh (0)	30	0.28
West Indian, ex. Hispanic (72)	82	0.76
Jamaican (72)	82	0.76
Yugoslavian (73)	73	0.68

Hispanic Origin	Population	%
Hispanic or Latino (of any race)	285	2.62
Central American, ex. Mexican	21	0.19
Guatemalan	3	0.03
Nicaraguan	2	0.02
Panamanian	12	0.11
Salvadoran	4	0.04
Cuban	14	0.13
Dominican Republic	19	0.17
Mexican	19	0.17
Puerto Rican	177	1.63
South American	1	0.01
Colombian	1	0.01
Other Hispanic or Latino	34	0.31

Race*	Population	%
African-American/Black (1,164)	1,191	10.96
Not Hispanic (1,118)	1,143	10.52
Hispanic (46)	48	0.44
American Indian/Alaska Native (33)	58	0.53
Not Hispanic (32)	57	0.52
Hispanic (1)	1	0.01
Chippewa (2)	2	0.02
Iroquois (8)	22	0.20
Sioux (0)	1	0.01
Asian (45)	52	0.48
Not Hispanic (45)	52	0.48
Chinese, ex. Taiwanese (23)	23	0.21
Filipino (2)	2	0.02
Indian (2)	3	0.03
Japanese (6)	7	0.06
Korean (6)	13	0.12
Pakistani (1)	1	0.01
Thai (1)	1	0.01
Hawaii Native/Pacific Islander (0)	3	0.03
Not Hispanic (0)	2	0.02
Hispanic (0)	1	0.01
Samoan (0)	1	0.01
White (9,433)	9,495	87.39
Not Hispanic (9,295)	9,353	86.08
Hispanic (138)	142	1.31

Allegany

Place Type: Town
County: Cattaraugus
Population: 8,004†

*Notes: † The Census 2010 population figure is used to calculate the percentages in the Hispanic Origin and Race categories. Ancestry percentages are based on the 2006-2010 American Community Survey population (not shown); ‡ Numbers in parentheses indicate the number of people reporting a single ancestry; * Numbers in parentheses indicate the number of persons reporting this race alone, not in combination with any other race; Please refer to the Explanation of Data for more information.*

Ancestry‡	Population	%
African, Sub-Saharan (0)	11	0.14
African (0)	11	0.14
American (430)	430	5.36
Arab (17)	62	0.77
Arab (7)	7	0.09
Lebanese (10)	55	0.69
Austrian (3)	19	0.24
Belgian (3)	7	0.09
British (19)	52	0.65
Canadian (24)	33	0.41
Croatian (15)	15	0.19
Czech (0)	5	0.06
Danish (11)	27	0.34
Dutch (13)	106	1.32
Eastern European (7)	7	0.09
English (186)	749	9.33
European (17)	47	0.59
Finnish (9)	9	0.11
French, ex. Basque (0)	143	1.78
French Canadian (3)	19	0.24
German (761)	2,312	28.80
Greek (19)	44	0.55
Guyanese (0)	13	0.16
Hungarian (23)	59	0.73
Irish (424)	1,934	24.09
Italian (713)	1,716	21.37
Lithuanian (8)	31	0.39
Macedonian (8)	8	0.10
Pennsylvania German (18)	46	0.57
Polish (182)	863	10.75
Romanian (34)	46	0.57
Russian (29)	70	0.87
Scandinavian (0)	13	0.16
Scotch-Irish (37)	55	0.69
Scottish (41)	145	1.81
Swedish (45)	183	2.28
Swiss (0)	43	0.54
Ukrainian (0)	24	0.30
Welsh (0)	50	0.62
West Indian, ex. Hispanic (20)	20	0.25
Haitian (11)	11	0.14
Jamaican (9)	9	0.11
Yugoslavian (3)	3	0.04

Hispanic Origin	Population	%
Hispanic or Latino (of any race)	151	1.89
Central American, ex. Mexican	5	0.06
Costa Rican	1	0.01
Guatemalan	1	0.01
Panamanian	1	0.01
Salvadoran	2	0.02
Cuban	8	0.10
Dominican Republic	14	0.17
Mexican	36	0.45
Puerto Rican	53	0.66
South American	11	0.14
Argentinean	1	0.01
Chilean	1	0.01
Colombian	3	0.04
Ecuadorian	2	0.02
Uruguayan	1	0.01
Venezuelan	3	0.04
Other Hispanic or Latino	24	0.30

Race*	Population	%
African-American/Black (151)	202	2.52
Not Hispanic (138)	186	2.32
Hispanic (13)	16	0.20
American Indian/Alaska Native (25)	53	0.66
Not Hispanic (25)	51	0.64
Hispanic (0)	2	0.02
Blackfeet (1)	1	0.01
Cherokee (2)	3	0.04
Iroquois (14)	27	0.34
Kiowa (1)	1	0.01
Menominee (2)	2	0.02
Sioux (0)	1	0.01
Asian (154)	175	2.19
Not Hispanic (153)	174	2.17
Hispanic (1)	1	0.01
Bangladeshi (1)	1	0.01
Chinese, ex. Taiwanese (30)	37	0.46
Filipino (4)	8	0.10
Indian (82)	85	1.06
Japanese (0)	1	0.01
Korean (14)	17	0.21
Laotian (0)	2	0.02
Pakistani (10)	10	0.12
Sri Lankan (1)	1	0.01
Taiwanese (2)	2	0.02
Thai (2)	2	0.02
Vietnamese (7)	7	0.09
Hawaii Native/Pacific Islander (1)	3	0.04
Not Hispanic (1)	3	0.04
Native Hawaiian (0)	1	0.01
Samoan (0)	1	0.01
White (7,528)	7,627	95.29
Not Hispanic (7,447)	7,529	94.07
Hispanic (81)	98	1.22

Amherst

Place Type: Town
County: Erie
Population: 122,366†

Ancestry‡	Population	%
Afghan (144)	144	0.12
African, Sub-Saharan (897)	1,095	0.91
African (481)	625	0.52
Ethiopian (71)	71	0.06
Ghanaian (15)	15	0.01
Kenyan (12)	12	0.01
Nigerian (167)	167	0.14
South African (22)	35	0.03
Other Sub-Saharan African (129)	170	0.14
Albanian (26)	114	0.09
Alsatian (9)	32	0.03
American (3,077)	3,077	2.54
Arab (818)	1,530	1.27
Arab (46)	90	0.07
Egyptian (8)	8	0.01
Jordanian (84)	84	0.07
Lebanese (342)	985	0.81
Moroccan (13)	13	0.01
Palestinian (18)	18	0.01
Syrian (48)	62	0.05
Other Arab (259)	270	0.22
Armenian (157)	203	0.17
Australian (29)	47	0.04
Austrian (367)	1,014	0.84
Belgian (11)	38	0.03
Brazilian (223)	223	0.18
British (194)	438	0.36
Bulgarian (68)	98	0.08
Canadian (282)	589	0.49
Celtic (10)	10	0.01
Croatian (114)	393	0.32
Czech (105)	255	0.21
Czechoslovakian (46)	82	0.07
Danish (55)	199	0.16
Dutch (148)	1,690	1.40
Eastern European (507)	575	0.48
English (3,188)	11,840	9.79
Estonian (10)	25	0.02
European (915)	981	0.81
Finnish (35)	196	0.16
French, ex. Basque (438)	3,549	2.93
French Canadian (283)	983	0.81
German (8,678)	30,579	25.28
Greek (323)	802	0.66
Guyanese (43)	43	0.04
Hungarian (420)	1,194	0.99
Iranian (174)	188	0.16
Irish (5,285)	22,106	18.28
Israeli (75)	122	0.10
Italian (11,256)	23,615	19.53
Latvian (26)	64	0.05
Lithuanian (82)	182	0.15
Macedonian (0)	14	0.01
New Zealander (0)	26	0.02
Northern European (29)	101	0.08
Norwegian (114)	400	0.33
Pennsylvania German (0)	43	0.04
Polish (6,777)	17,104	14.14
Portuguese (90)	144	0.12
Romanian (169)	324	0.27
Russian (1,684)	3,468	2.87
Scandinavian (11)	116	0.10
Scotch-Irish (504)	1,527	1.26
Scottish (333)	1,736	1.44
Serbian (81)	158	0.13
Slavic (25)	153	0.13
Slovak (40)	141	0.12
Slovene (40)	53	0.04
Swedish (139)	902	0.75
Swiss (67)	222	0.18
Turkish (138)	164	0.14
Ukrainian (545)	1,074	0.89
Welsh (218)	798	0.66
West Indian, ex. Hispanic (282)	440	0.36
Barbadian (12)	12	0.01
British West Indian (13)	13	0.01
Haitian (45)	45	0.04
Jamaican (169)	226	0.19
Trinidadian/Tobagonian (5)	19	0.02
West Indian (38)	125	0.10
Yugoslavian (52)	52	0.04

Hispanic Origin	Population	%
Hispanic or Latino (of any race)	2,870	2.35
Central American, ex. Mexican	189	0.15
Costa Rican	20	0.02
Guatemalan	49	0.04
Honduran	23	0.02
Nicaraguan	8	0.01
Panamanian	39	0.03
Salvadoran	49	0.04
Other Central American	1	<0.01
Cuban	120	0.10
Dominican Republic	194	0.16
Mexican	478	0.39
Puerto Rican	1,108	0.91
South American	436	0.36
Argentinean	57	0.05
Bolivian	14	0.01
Chilean	40	0.03
Colombian	163	0.13
Ecuadorian	63	0.05
Paraguayan	5	<0.01
Peruvian	52	0.04
Uruguayan	7	0.01
Venezuelan	33	0.03
Other South American	2	<0.01
Other Hispanic or Latino	345	0.28

Race*	Population	%
African-American/Black (7,009)	7,946	6.49
Not Hispanic (6,765)	7,563	6.18
Hispanic (244)	383	0.31
American Indian/Alaska Native (220)	616	0.50
Not Hispanic (196)	531	0.43
Hispanic (24)	85	0.07
Alaska Athabascan *(Ala. Nat.)* (0)	1	<0.01
Blackfeet (2)	14	0.01
Canadian/French Am. Ind. (9)	11	0.01
Central American Ind. (0)	1	<0.01
Cherokee (7)	67	0.05
Chippewa (1)	7	0.01
Choctaw (1)	3	<0.01
Creek (0)	2	<0.01
Crow (2)	2	<0.01
Delaware (1)	2	<0.01
Inupiat *(Alaska Native)* (0)	3	<0.01
Iroquois (84)	155	0.13
Lumbee (1)	1	<0.01
Mexican American Ind. (11)	22	0.02
Navajo (0)	1	<0.01
Osage (1)	1	<0.01

*Notes: † The Census 2010 population figure is used to calculate the percentages in the Hispanic Origin and Race categories. Ancestry percentages are based on the 2006-2010 American Community Survey population (not shown); ‡ Numbers in parentheses indicate the number of people reporting a single ancestry; * Numbers in parentheses indicate the number of persons reporting this race alone, not in combination with any other race; Please refer to the Explanation of Data for more information.*

Pueblo (2)	5	<0.01
Seminole (0)	10	0.01
Sioux (0)	1	<0.01
South American Ind. (4)	13	0.01
Tlingit-Haida *(Alaska Native)* (0)	1	<0.01
Tohono O'Odham (1)	1	<0.01
Yup'ik *(Alaska Native)* (0)	1	<0.01
Asian (9,675)	10,683	8.73
Not Hispanic (9,643)	10,590	8.65
Hispanic (32)	93	0.08
Bangladeshi (42)	45	0.04
Burmese (28)	32	0.03
Cambodian (16)	17	0.01
Chinese, ex. Taiwanese (2,925)	3,146	2.57
Filipino (273)	396	0.32
Indian (3,263)	3,491	2.85
Indonesian (26)	42	0.03
Japanese (215)	294	0.24
Korean (1,377)	1,493	1.22
Laotian (19)	25	0.02
Malaysian (41)	47	0.04
Nepalese (12)	12	0.01
Pakistani (515)	592	0.48
Sri Lankan (122)	130	0.11
Taiwanese (180)	202	0.17
Thai (36)	52	0.04
Vietnamese (307)	362	0.30
Hawaii Native/Pacific Islander (26)	94	0.08
Not Hispanic (26)	86	0.07
Hispanic (0)	8	0.01
Fijian (3)	3	<0.01
Guamanian/Chamorro (8)	10	0.01
Marshallese (1)	1	<0.01
Native Hawaiian (9)	24	0.02
Samoan (3)	12	0.01
White (102,558)	104,439	85.35
Not Hispanic (100,778)	102,429	83.71
Hispanic (1,780)	2,010	1.64

Amityville

Place Type: Village
County: Suffolk
Population: 9,523†

Ancestry‡	Population	%
Albanian (18)	18	0.19
American (140)	140	1.47
Armenian (0)	10	0.10
Austrian (0)	33	0.35
Brazilian (10)	10	0.10
British (9)	37	0.39
Canadian (0)	34	0.36
Czech (15)	27	0.28
Czechoslovakian (9)	9	0.09
Danish (0)	17	0.18
Dutch (42)	85	0.89
Eastern European (12)	12	0.13
English (215)	800	8.39
French, ex. Basque (19)	155	1.63
French Canadian (0)	11	0.12
German (282)	2,103	22.05
Greek (17)	81	0.85
Hungarian (16)	46	0.48
Irish (731)	2,556	26.80
Israeli (0)	11	0.12
Italian (979)	1,833	19.22
Lithuanian (9)	22	0.23
Maltese (11)	11	0.12
Norwegian (33)	99	1.04
Polish (267)	550	5.77
Portuguese (0)	92	0.96
Russian (35)	141	1.48
Scandinavian (0)	11	0.12
Scotch-Irish (8)	148	1.55
Scottish (8)	105	1.10
Slavic (0)	25	0.26
Swedish (0)	34	0.36
Swiss (0)	126	1.32
Turkish (26)	26	0.27
Ukrainian (0)	22	0.23
Welsh (0)	53	0.56
West Indian, ex. Hispanic (456)	503	5.27
Haitian (14)	14	0.15
Jamaican (433)	480	5.03
Trinidadian/Tobagonian (9)	9	0.09

Hispanic Origin	Population	%
Hispanic or Latino (of any race)	1,249	13.12
Central American, ex. Mexican	338	3.55
Costa Rican	3	0.03
Guatemalan	39	0.41
Honduran	48	0.50
Nicaraguan	3	0.03
Panamanian	8	0.08
Salvadoran	218	2.29
Other Central American	19	0.20
Cuban	13	0.14
Dominican Republic	290	3.05
Mexican	74	0.78
Puerto Rican	269	2.82
South American	140	1.47
Argentinean	9	0.09
Chilean	7	0.07
Colombian	76	0.80
Ecuadorian	26	0.27
Peruvian	16	0.17
Uruguayan	1	0.01
Venezuelan	5	0.05
Other Hispanic or Latino	125	1.31

Race*	Population	%
African-American/Black (922)	1,022	10.73
Not Hispanic (874)	929	9.76
Hispanic (48)	93	0.98
American Indian/Alaska Native (26)	79	0.83
Not Hispanic (23)	42	0.44
Hispanic (3)	37	0.39
Cherokee (0)	7	0.07
Iroquois (5)	7	0.07
Mexican American Ind. (1)	1	0.01
South American Ind. (0)	8	0.08
Asian (169)	225	2.36
Not Hispanic (166)	211	2.22
Hispanic (3)	14	0.15
Chinese, ex. Taiwanese (34)	48	0.50
Filipino (19)	27	0.28
Indian (76)	81	0.85
Japanese (9)	15	0.16
Korean (18)	26	0.27
Pakistani (5)	9	0.09
Sri Lankan (0)	3	0.03
Taiwanese (1)	1	0.01
Thai (2)	4	0.04
Hawaii Native/Pacific Islander (0)	10	0.11
Not Hispanic (0)	2	0.02
Hispanic (0)	8	0.08
Native Hawaiian (0)	1	0.01
White (7,784)	7,972	83.71
Not Hispanic (7,096)	7,189	75.49
Hispanic (688)	783	8.22

Amsterdam

Place Type: City
County: Montgomery
Population: 18,620†

Ancestry‡	Population	%
African, Sub-Saharan (11)	11	0.06
South African (11)	11	0.06
American (1,350)	1,350	7.29
Arab (22)	62	0.33
Arab (0)	18	0.10
Lebanese (22)	44	0.24
Armenian (0)	66	0.36
Austrian (22)	39	0.21
Belgian (0)	11	0.06
British (8)	15	0.08
Canadian (0)	21	0.11
Czech (17)	45	0.24
Danish (23)	110	0.59
Dutch (37)	505	2.73
English (720)	1,692	9.14
European (33)	41	0.22
French, ex. Basque (56)	703	3.80
French Canadian (53)	158	0.85
German (494)	2,096	11.32
Greek (25)	125	0.68
Hungarian (0)	3	0.02
Irish (380)	2,597	14.03
Italian (1,997)	3,797	20.51
Lithuanian (156)	344	1.86
Norwegian (0)	21	0.11
Polish (1,476)	2,678	14.47
Portuguese (4)	12	0.06
Romanian (8)	19	0.10
Russian (0)	75	0.41
Scotch-Irish (56)	130	0.70
Scottish (68)	230	1.24
Slovak (0)	29	0.16
Swedish (0)	43	0.23
Swiss (0)	11	0.06
Ukrainian (22)	33	0.18
Welsh (0)	40	0.22
West Indian, ex. Hispanic (49)	127	0.69
Jamaican (49)	127	0.69

Hispanic Origin	Population	%
Hispanic or Latino (of any race)	4,873	26.17
Central American, ex. Mexican	185	0.99
Costa Rican	102	0.55
Guatemalan	29	0.16
Honduran	10	0.05
Nicaraguan	5	0.03
Panamanian	9	0.05
Salvadoran	30	0.16
Cuban	80	0.43
Dominican Republic	239	1.28
Mexican	102	0.55
Puerto Rican	3,923	21.07
South American	107	0.57
Argentinean	5	0.03
Bolivian	1	0.01
Colombian	30	0.16
Ecuadorian	51	0.27
Peruvian	16	0.09
Venezuelan	3	0.02
Other South American	1	0.01
Other Hispanic or Latino	237	1.27

Race*	Population	%
African-American/Black (712)	1,058	5.68
Not Hispanic (496)	716	3.85
Hispanic (216)	342	1.84
American Indian/Alaska Native (103)	219	1.18
Not Hispanic (53)	137	0.74
Hispanic (50)	82	0.44
Apache (0)	2	0.01
Blackfeet (0)	11	0.06
Canadian/French Am. Ind. (0)	1	0.01
Central American Ind. (1)	1	0.01
Cherokee (7)	24	0.13
Choctaw (0)	2	0.01
Cree (1)	1	0.01
Delaware (3)	7	0.04
Iroquois (12)	43	0.23
Mexican American Ind. (1)	1	0.01
Navajo (0)	1	0.01
Sioux (0)	3	0.02
South American Ind. (9)	16	0.09
Spanish American Ind. (2)	2	0.01
Tlingit-Haida *(Alaska Native)* (1)	2	0.01
Asian (165)	212	1.14
Not Hispanic (153)	185	0.99
Hispanic (12)	27	0.15
Chinese, ex. Taiwanese (23)	33	0.18
Filipino (20)	28	0.15
Indian (69)	75	0.40
Japanese (1)	8	0.04

*Notes: † The Census 2010 population figure is used to calculate the percentages in the Hispanic Origin and Race categories. Ancestry percentages are based on the 2006-2010 American Community Survey population (not shown); ‡ Numbers in parentheses indicate the number of people reporting a single ancestry; * Numbers in parentheses indicate the number of persons reporting this race alone, not in combination with any other race; Please refer to the Explanation of Data for more information.*

Korean (15)	24	0.13
Pakistani (10)	15	0.08
Taiwanese (1)	1	0.01
Thai (3)	5	0.03
Vietnamese (2)	10	0.05
Hawaii Native/Pacific Islander (7)	30	0.16
Not Hispanic (2)	7	0.04
Hispanic (5)	23	0.12
Guamanian/Chamorro (4)	5	0.03
Native Hawaiian (3)	6	0.03
White (14,963)	15,512	83.31
Not Hispanic (12,681)	12,983	69.73
Hispanic (2,282)	2,529	13.58

Arcadia

Place Type: Town
County: Wayne
Population: 14,244†

Ancestry‡	Population	%
American (801)	801	5.58
Arab (19)	19	0.13
Moroccan (19)	19	0.13
Austrian (8)	31	0.22
Belgian (11)	34	0.24
Brazilian (0)	8	0.06
British (24)	24	0.17
Canadian (56)	56	0.39
Czech (14)	14	0.10
Danish (13)	52	0.36
Dutch (813)	2,484	17.31
English (562)	2,031	14.16
European (51)	51	0.36
French, ex. Basque (67)	471	3.28
French Canadian (211)	493	3.44
German (693)	3,568	24.87
Greek (16)	28	0.20
Guyanese (19)	19	0.13
Hungarian (38)	50	0.35
Irish (441)	2,288	15.95
Italian (1,030)	2,102	14.65
Latvian (7)	7	0.05
Lithuanian (11)	30	0.21
Norwegian (0)	13	0.09
Pennsylvania German (16)	16	0.11
Polish (190)	510	3.55
Russian (12)	47	0.33
Scotch-Irish (26)	150	1.05
Scottish (48)	278	1.94
Slovak (13)	40	0.28
Slovene (0)	9	0.06
Swedish (11)	87	0.61
Swiss (0)	28	0.20
Ukrainian (0)	80	0.56
Welsh (22)	126	0.88
West Indian, ex. Hispanic (47)	79	0.55
Haitian (47)	79	0.55
Yugoslavian (0)	31	0.22

Hispanic Origin	Population	%
Hispanic or Latino (of any race)	962	6.75
Central American, ex. Mexican	48	0.34
Guatemalan	1	0.01
Honduran	37	0.26
Panamanian	6	0.04
Salvadoran	4	0.03
Cuban	9	0.06
Dominican Republic	18	0.13
Mexican	99	0.70
Puerto Rican	727	5.10
South American	12	0.08
Argentinean	4	0.03
Colombian	3	0.02
Ecuadorian	2	0.01
Peruvian	2	0.01
Venezuelan	1	0.01
Other Hispanic or Latino	49	0.34

Race*	Population	%
African-American/Black (649)	919	6.45
Not Hispanic (591)	822	5.77
Hispanic (58)	97	0.68
American Indian/Alaska Native (48)	132	0.93
Not Hispanic (34)	106	0.74
Hispanic (14)	26	0.18
Apache (1)	1	0.01
Blackfeet (4)	4	0.03
Cherokee (4)	15	0.11
Chippewa (2)	2	0.01
Comanche (1)	1	0.01
Cree (0)	4	0.03
Delaware (1)	1	0.01
Iroquois (11)	25	0.18
Mexican American Ind. (3)	3	0.02
Seminole (0)	1	0.01
Sioux (0)	3	0.02
Asian (78)	110	0.77
Not Hispanic (75)	104	0.73
Hispanic (3)	6	0.04
Bangladeshi (1)	1	0.01
Cambodian (5)	5	0.04
Chinese, ex. Taiwanese (17)	25	0.18
Filipino (13)	17	0.12
Indian (7)	10	0.07
Japanese (2)	7	0.05
Korean (15)	20	0.14
Laotian (2)	4	0.03
Malaysian (1)	1	0.01
Thai (3)	5	0.04
Vietnamese (4)	5	0.04
Hawaii Native/Pacific Islander (9)	17	0.12
Not Hispanic (9)	17	0.12
Native Hawaiian (1)	5	0.04
White (12,723)	13,119	92.10
Not Hispanic (12,242)	12,549	88.10
Hispanic (481)	570	4.00

Attica

Place Type: Town
County: Wyoming
Population: 7,702†

Ancestry‡	Population	%
African, Sub-Saharan (135)	144	1.86
African (126)	135	1.74
Nigerian (9)	9	0.12
American (222)	222	2.86
Arab (8)	17	0.22
Egyptian (0)	9	0.12
Lebanese (8)	8	0.10
Austrian (0)	11	0.14
British (0)	8	0.10
Cajun (0)	9	0.12
Canadian (0)	9	0.12
Danish (0)	11	0.14
Dutch (5)	184	2.37
English (185)	731	9.43
European (4)	13	0.17
French, ex. Basque (40)	255	3.29
French Canadian (24)	37	0.48
German (524)	1,573	20.30
Guyanese (8)	8	0.10
Hungarian (0)	6	0.08
Irish (156)	611	7.88
Italian (80)	322	4.16
Lithuanian (0)	6	0.08
Norwegian (0)	21	0.27
Polish (121)	409	5.28
Russian (0)	5	0.06
Scotch-Irish (12)	75	0.97
Scottish (9)	111	1.43
Slovak (0)	8	0.10
Swedish (0)	55	0.71
Swiss (23)	43	0.55
Ukrainian (2)	2	0.03
Welsh (0)	38	0.49
West Indian, ex. Hispanic (92)	118	1.52
Belizean (9)	9	0.12
Haitian (16)	25	0.32
Jamaican (41)	41	0.53
Trinidadian/Tobagonian (8)	16	0.21
U.S. Virgin Islander (10)	10	0.13
West Indian (8)	17	0.22

Hispanic Origin	Population	%
Hispanic or Latino (of any race)	653	8.48
Central American, ex. Mexican	37	0.48
Costa Rican	1	0.01
Guatemalan	10	0.13
Honduran	6	0.08
Nicaraguan	2	0.03
Panamanian	12	0.16
Salvadoran	6	0.08
Cuban	35	0.45
Dominican Republic	86	1.12
Mexican	50	0.65
Puerto Rican	383	4.97
South American	21	0.27
Argentinean	1	0.01
Chilean	1	0.01
Colombian	13	0.17
Ecuadorian	4	0.05
Uruguayan	1	0.01
Venezuelan	1	0.01
Other Hispanic or Latino	41	0.53

Race*	Population	%
African-American/Black (2,284)	2,293	29.77
Not Hispanic (2,153)	2,162	28.07
Hispanic (131)	131	1.70
American Indian/Alaska Native (43)	62	0.80
Not Hispanic (36)	55	0.71
Hispanic (7)	7	0.09
Central American Ind. (1)	1	0.01
Cherokee (0)	3	0.04
Iroquois (2)	9	0.12
South American Ind. (3)	3	0.04
Asian (37)	42	0.55
Not Hispanic (35)	40	0.52
Hispanic (2)	2	0.03
Chinese, ex. Taiwanese (8)	8	0.10
Filipino (2)	6	0.08
Indian (3)	3	0.04
Japanese (1)	2	0.03
Korean (5)	6	0.08
Taiwanese (1)	1	0.01
Vietnamese (6)	6	0.08
Hawaii Native/Pacific Islander (1)	2	0.03
Not Hispanic (1)	1	0.01
Hispanic (0)	1	0.01
Native Hawaiian (1)	1	0.01
White (4,963)	4,999	64.91
Not Hispanic (4,718)	4,752	61.70
Hispanic (245)	247	3.21

Auburn

Place Type: City
County: Cayuga
Population: 27,687†

Ancestry‡	Population	%
African, Sub-Saharan (28)	57	0.20
African (28)	39	0.14
Other Sub-Saharan African (0)	18	0.06
American (839)	839	3.01
Arab (20)	66	0.24
Lebanese (10)	41	0.15
Syrian (0)	15	0.05
Other Arab (10)	10	0.04
Austrian (24)	75	0.27
Brazilian (31)	31	0.11
British (9)	23	0.08
Canadian (36)	48	0.17
Czech (11)	68	0.24
Czechoslovakian (32)	32	0.11

*Notes: † The Census 2010 population figure is used to calculate the percentages in the Hispanic Origin and Race categories. Ancestry percentages are based on the 2006-2010 American Community Survey population (not shown); ‡ Numbers in parentheses indicate the number of people reporting a single ancestry; * Numbers in parentheses indicate the number of persons reporting this race alone, not in combination with any other race; Please refer to the Explanation of Data for more information.*

Ancestry	Population	%
Danish (16)	24	0.09
Dutch (110)	680	2.44
English (1,334)	4,314	15.48
European (28)	39	0.14
Finnish (10)	10	0.04
French, ex. Basque (164)	891	3.20
French Canadian (84)	444	1.59
German (634)	3,821	13.71
Greek (6)	31	0.11
Guyanese (12)	12	0.04
Hungarian (12)	74	0.27
Irish (2,738)	7,141	25.63
Italian (2,537)	5,392	19.35
Northern European (8)	8	0.03
Norwegian (35)	229	0.82
Polish (856)	2,199	7.89
Portuguese (0)	47	0.17
Russian (59)	219	0.79
Scandinavian (0)	12	0.04
Scotch-Irish (142)	342	1.23
Scottish (205)	606	2.17
Slavic (24)	24	0.09
Slovak (0)	38	0.14
Swedish (36)	209	0.75
Swiss (0)	23	0.08
Turkish (0)	20	0.07
Ukrainian (546)	1,247	4.48
Welsh (58)	231	0.83
West Indian, ex. Hispanic (47)	81	0.29
Barbadian (0)	8	0.03
British West Indian (0)	1	<0.01
Haitian (8)	15	0.05
Jamaican (22)	40	0.14
West Indian (17)	17	0.06

Hispanic Origin	Population	%
Hispanic or Latino (of any race)	991	3.58
Central American, ex. Mexican	105	0.38
Costa Rican	5	0.02
Guatemalan	52	0.19
Honduran	13	0.05
Nicaraguan	10	0.04
Panamanian	21	0.08
Salvadoran	4	0.01
Cuban	30	0.11
Dominican Republic	49	0.18
Mexican	147	0.53
Puerto Rican	519	1.87
South American	37	0.13
Bolivian	1	<0.01
Chilean	6	0.02
Colombian	8	0.03
Ecuadorian	8	0.03
Paraguayan	1	<0.01
Peruvian	6	0.02
Uruguayan	1	<0.01
Venezuelan	6	0.02
Other Hispanic or Latino	104	0.38

Race*	Population	%
African-American/Black (2,346)	2,985	10.78
Not Hispanic (2,214)	2,789	10.07
Hispanic (132)	196	0.71
American Indian/Alaska Native (107)	277	1.00
Not Hispanic (99)	254	0.92
Hispanic (8)	23	0.08
Apache (0)	3	0.01
Blackfeet (0)	10	0.04
Canadian/French Am. Ind. (1)	2	0.01
Cherokee (6)	23	0.08
Cheyenne (0)	1	<0.01
Chippewa (0)	6	0.02
Choctaw (7)	8	0.03
Creek (1)	1	<0.01
Iroquois (34)	84	0.30
Lumbee (2)	2	0.01
Mexican American Ind. (0)	3	0.01
Navajo (1)	1	<0.01
Ottawa (5)	5	0.02
Sioux (2)	6	0.02
South American Ind. (1)	5	0.02
Asian (168)	222	0.80
Not Hispanic (166)	213	0.77
Hispanic (2)	9	0.03
Chinese, ex. Taiwanese (38)	46	0.17
Filipino (14)	30	0.11
Indian (45)	54	0.20
Japanese (0)	1	<0.01
Korean (19)	24	0.09
Laotian (14)	15	0.05
Thai (6)	9	0.03
Vietnamese (19)	30	0.11
Hawaii Native/Pacific Islander (9)	30	0.11
Not Hispanic (9)	24	0.09
Hispanic (0)	6	0.02
Fijian (1)	1	<0.01
Guamanian/Chamorro (1)	2	0.01
Native Hawaiian (3)	10	0.04
Samoan (4)	9	0.03
White (23,889)	24,684	89.15
Not Hispanic (23,404)	24,105	87.06
Hispanic (485)	579	2.09

Aurora

Place Type: Town
County: Erie
Population: 13,782†

Ancestry‡	Population	%
Alsatian (0)	21	0.15
American (255)	255	1.85
Arab (11)	66	0.48
Arab (0)	12	0.09
Lebanese (0)	9	0.07
Syrian (0)	24	0.17
Other Arab (11)	21	0.15
Australian (9)	9	0.07
Austrian (25)	120	0.87
Belgian (0)	41	0.30
Brazilian (42)	52	0.38
British (0)	13	0.09
Canadian (77)	77	0.56
Celtic (27)	27	0.20
Croatian (0)	40	0.29
Czech (0)	20	0.15
Danish (20)	87	0.63
Dutch (71)	304	2.21
Eastern European (10)	10	0.07
English (373)	1,771	12.87
European (64)	64	0.47
Finnish (15)	46	0.33
French, ex. Basque (50)	430	3.12
French Canadian (14)	53	0.39
German (1,692)	5,590	40.62
Greek (9)	36	0.26
Hungarian (46)	188	1.37
Irish (781)	3,454	25.10
Italian (643)	2,155	15.66
Lithuanian (15)	56	0.41
Northern European (12)	12	0.09
Norwegian (14)	26	0.19
Polish (1,011)	2,573	18.70
Russian (17)	79	0.57
Scandinavian (10)	52	0.38
Scotch-Irish (79)	214	1.55
Scottish (53)	526	3.82
Slavic (0)	14	0.10
Slovak (0)	41	0.30
Swedish (6)	276	2.01
Swiss (0)	24	0.17
Turkish (29)	29	0.21
Ukrainian (0)	110	0.80
Welsh (50)	262	1.90
Yugoslavian (0)	33	0.24

Hispanic Origin	Population	%
Hispanic or Latino (of any race)	143	1.04
Central American, ex. Mexican	12	0.09
Guatemalan	11	0.08
Salvadoran	1	0.01
Cuban	6	0.04
Dominican Republic	8	0.06
Mexican	46	0.33
Puerto Rican	39	0.28
South American	16	0.12
Chilean	5	0.04
Colombian	6	0.04
Ecuadorian	2	0.01
Peruvian	1	0.01
Venezuelan	2	0.01
Other Hispanic or Latino	16	0.12

Race*	Population	%
African-American/Black (41)	76	0.55
Not Hispanic (40)	74	0.54
Hispanic (1)	2	0.01
American Indian/Alaska Native (10)	44	0.32
Not Hispanic (8)	35	0.25
Hispanic (2)	9	0.07
Cherokee (1)	6	0.04
Iroquois (4)	11	0.08
Mexican American Ind. (2)	2	0.01
Ottawa (0)	3	0.02
Asian (83)	127	0.92
Not Hispanic (83)	127	0.92
Cambodian (0)	1	0.01
Chinese, ex. Taiwanese (18)	24	0.17
Filipino (8)	11	0.08
Indian (16)	22	0.16
Japanese (3)	13	0.09
Korean (18)	29	0.21
Laotian (1)	1	0.01
Malaysian (0)	3	0.02
Thai (3)	3	0.02
Vietnamese (15)	15	0.11
Hawaii Native/Pacific Islander (2)	8	0.06
Not Hispanic (0)	5	0.04
Hispanic (2)	3	0.02
Guamanian/Chamorro (2)	2	0.01
Samoan (0)	2	0.01
White (13,500)	13,609	98.74
Not Hispanic (13,394)	13,495	97.92
Hispanic (106)	114	0.83

Babylon

Place Type: Town
County: Suffolk
Population: 213,603†

Ancestry‡	Population	%
Afghan (219)	219	0.10
African, Sub-Saharan (1,803)	2,217	1.04
African (734)	1,071	0.50
Cape Verdean (0)	9	<0.01
Ethiopian (0)	11	0.01
Ghanaian (64)	64	0.03
Liberian (300)	309	0.14
Nigerian (670)	707	0.33
Other Sub-Saharan African (35)	46	0.02
Albanian (139)	210	0.10
American (3,343)	3,343	1.56
Arab (595)	842	0.39
Arab (236)	259	0.12
Egyptian (30)	79	0.04
Lebanese (20)	79	0.04
Moroccan (142)	209	0.10
Palestinian (114)	114	0.05
Syrian (0)	49	0.02
Other Arab (53)	53	0.02
Armenian (69)	188	0.09
Australian (0)	20	0.01
Austrian (149)	808	0.38
Basque (15)	15	0.01
Belgian (22)	41	0.02
Brazilian (30)	166	0.08
British (149)	348	0.16
Bulgarian (8)	20	0.01
Canadian (80)	581	0.27

*Notes: † The Census 2010 population figure is used to calculate the percentages in the Hispanic Origin and Race categories. Ancestry percentages are based on the 2006-2010 American Community Survey population (not shown); ‡ Numbers in parentheses indicate the number of people reporting a single ancestry; * Numbers in parentheses indicate the number of persons reporting this race alone, not in combination with any other race; Please refer to the Explanation of Data for more information.*

Celtic (33)	64	0.03
Croatian (144)	207	0.10
Czech (61)	578	0.27
Czechoslovakian (296)	438	0.21
Danish (107)	384	0.18
Dutch (218)	1,653	0.77
Eastern European (253)	270	0.13
English (1,368)	8,596	4.02
Estonian (10)	33	0.02
European (342)	416	0.19
Finnish (26)	190	0.09
French, ex. Basque (203)	2,679	1.25
French Canadian (445)	939	0.44
German (5,375)	31,578	14.78
Greek (964)	2,182	1.02
Guyanese (602)	747	0.35
Hungarian (188)	989	0.46
Icelander (22)	22	0.01
Iranian (53)	69	0.03
Irish (10,079)	42,364	19.83
Israeli (28)	172	0.08
Italian (32,274)	61,852	28.95
Latvian (11)	35	0.02
Lithuanian (287)	642	0.30
Macedonian (11)	33	0.02
Maltese (61)	378	0.18
Northern European (45)	61	0.03
Norwegian (303)	1,701	0.80
Pennsylvania German (18)	18	0.01
Polish (5,564)	12,444	5.82
Portuguese (168)	676	0.32
Romanian (230)	316	0.15
Russian (845)	3,774	1.77
Scandinavian (17)	48	0.02
Scotch-Irish (570)	1,863	0.87
Scottish (225)	1,548	0.72
Serbian (16)	19	0.01
Slavic (6)	64	0.03
Slovak (134)	367	0.17
Slovene (14)	14	0.01
Swedish (205)	1,400	0.66
Swiss (57)	361	0.17
Turkish (826)	939	0.44
Ukrainian (329)	905	0.42
Welsh (103)	423	0.20
West Indian, ex. Hispanic (9,910)	11,187	5.24
Bahamian (35)	88	0.04
Barbadian (105)	183	0.09
Belizean (0)	12	0.01
British West Indian (64)	119	0.06
Dutch West Indian (6)	6	<0.01
Haitian (3,585)	3,789	1.77
Jamaican (4,141)	4,758	2.23
Trinidadian/Tobagonian (842)	854	0.40
West Indian (1,132)	1,378	0.64
Yugoslavian (14)	156	0.07

Hispanic Origin	Population	%
Hispanic or Latino (of any race)	35,793	16.76
Central American, ex. Mexican	11,096	5.19
Costa Rican	146	0.07
Guatemalan	884	0.41
Honduran	1,756	0.82
Nicaraguan	112	0.05
Panamanian	305	0.14
Salvadoran	7,805	3.65
Other Central American	88	0.04
Cuban	550	0.26
Dominican Republic	6,543	3.06
Mexican	1,145	0.54
Puerto Rican	7,562	3.54
South American	5,576	2.61
Argentinean	336	0.16
Bolivian	78	0.04
Chilean	226	0.11
Colombian	2,036	0.95
Ecuadorian	1,348	0.63
Paraguayan	37	0.02
Peruvian	1,313	0.61
Uruguayan	64	0.03
Venezuelan	104	0.05
Other South American	34	0.02
Other Hispanic or Latino	3,321	1.55

Race*	Population	%
African-American/Black (34,881)	37,421	17.52
Not Hispanic (33,147)	34,993	16.38
Hispanic (1,734)	2,428	1.14
American Indian/Alaska Native (719)	1,894	0.89
Not Hispanic (447)	1,351	0.63
Hispanic (272)	543	0.25
Aleut *(Alaska Native)* (2)	2	<0.01
Apache (1)	11	0.01
Blackfeet (4)	44	0.02
Canadian/French Am. Ind. (7)	10	<0.01
Central American Ind. (14)	22	0.01
Cherokee (51)	250	0.12
Cheyenne (1)	1	<0.01
Chippewa (6)	7	<0.01
Choctaw (1)	5	<0.01
Comanche (1)	2	<0.01
Cree (1)	2	<0.01
Creek (0)	13	0.01
Crow (0)	1	<0.01
Delaware (2)	2	<0.01
Hopi (3)	5	<0.01
Inupiat *(Alaska Native)* (0)	1	<0.01
Iroquois (34)	65	0.03
Lumbee (3)	12	0.01
Mexican American Ind. (15)	25	0.01
Navajo (1)	6	<0.01
Pueblo (9)	9	<0.01
Seminole (2)	13	0.01
Sioux (8)	16	0.01
South American Ind. (47)	82	0.04
Spanish American Ind. (8)	17	0.01
Tlingit-Haida *(Alaska Native)* (0)	1	<0.01
Tohono O'Odham (0)	1	<0.01
Asian (6,524)	7,919	3.71
Not Hispanic (6,411)	7,577	3.55
Hispanic (113)	342	0.16
Bangladeshi (271)	341	0.16
Burmese (4)	7	<0.01
Cambodian (3)	5	<0.01
Chinese, ex. Taiwanese (1,108)	1,357	0.64
Filipino (765)	1,046	0.49
Indian (2,582)	2,940	1.38
Indonesian (16)	22	0.01
Japanese (88)	186	0.09
Korean (388)	477	0.22
Laotian (6)	9	<0.01
Malaysian (2)	3	<0.01
Nepalese (4)	4	<0.01
Pakistani (678)	739	0.35
Sri Lankan (25)	32	0.01
Taiwanese (24)	26	0.01
Thai (41)	67	0.03
Vietnamese (257)	297	0.14
Hawaii Native/Pacific Islander (51)	272	0.13
Not Hispanic (31)	153	0.07
Hispanic (20)	119	0.06
Guamanian/Chamorro (11)	22	0.01
Native Hawaiian (13)	45	0.02
Samoan (3)	10	<0.01
White (153,067)	157,336	73.66
Not Hispanic (133,961)	136,259	63.79
Hispanic (19,106)	21,077	9.87

Babylon

Place Type: Village
County: Suffolk
Population: 12,166†

Ancestry‡	Population	%
African, Sub-Saharan (0)	10	0.08
African (0)	10	0.08
Albanian (0)	10	0.08
American (127)	127	1.04
Arab (38)	38	0.31
Lebanese (10)	10	0.08
Other Arab (28)	28	0.23
Austrian (10)	142	1.16
Brazilian (9)	18	0.15
British (22)	32	0.26
Canadian (0)	43	0.35
Croatian (0)	8	0.07
Czech (0)	24	0.20
Czechoslovakian (13)	40	0.33
Danish (22)	73	0.60
Dutch (11)	256	2.09
English (224)	1,104	9.00
European (39)	39	0.32
Finnish (12)	32	0.26
French, ex. Basque (20)	301	2.45
French Canadian (12)	57	0.46
German (407)	2,928	23.87
Greek (37)	139	1.13
Guyanese (0)	12	0.10
Hungarian (12)	37	0.30
Irish (1,379)	4,264	34.77
Italian (1,656)	3,837	31.29
Lithuanian (9)	16	0.13
Macedonian (11)	33	0.27
Maltese (0)	28	0.23
Northern European (28)	28	0.23
Norwegian (33)	255	2.08
Polish (131)	747	6.09
Portuguese (0)	45	0.37
Romanian (0)	11	0.09
Russian (35)	271	2.21
Scandinavian (9)	9	0.07
Scotch-Irish (79)	128	1.04
Scottish (50)	204	1.66
Slovak (0)	17	0.14
Swedish (0)	195	1.59
Swiss (0)	21	0.17
Ukrainian (0)	89	0.73
Welsh (0)	43	0.35
West Indian, ex. Hispanic (11)	11	0.09
Trinidadian/Tobagonian (11)	11	0.09
Yugoslavian (0)	71	0.58

Hispanic Origin	Population	%
Hispanic or Latino (of any race)	817	6.72
Central American, ex. Mexican	139	1.14
Costa Rican	1	0.01
Guatemalan	10	0.08
Honduran	25	0.21
Nicaraguan	5	0.04
Panamanian	6	0.05
Salvadoran	91	0.75
Other Central American	1	0.01
Cuban	33	0.27
Dominican Republic	59	0.48
Mexican	44	0.36
Puerto Rican	233	1.92
South American	194	1.59
Argentinean	6	0.05
Bolivian	6	0.05
Chilean	19	0.16
Colombian	77	0.63
Ecuadorian	54	0.44
Paraguayan	1	0.01
Peruvian	25	0.21
Uruguayan	6	0.05
Other Hispanic or Latino	115	0.95

Race*	Population	%
African-American/Black (245)	328	2.70
Not Hispanic (221)	289	2.38
Hispanic (24)	39	0.32
American Indian/Alaska Native (15)	43	0.35
Not Hispanic (11)	33	0.27
Hispanic (4)	10	0.08
Blackfeet (0)	2	0.02
Cherokee (0)	7	0.06
Comanche (1)	1	0.01
Iroquois (4)	4	0.03
South American Ind. (0)	3	0.02

*Notes: † The Census 2010 population figure is used to calculate the percentages in the Hispanic Origin and Race categories. Ancestry percentages are based on the 2006-2010 American Community Survey population (not shown); ‡ Numbers in parentheses indicate the number of people reporting a single ancestry; * Numbers in parentheses indicate the number of persons reporting this race alone, not in combination with any other race; Please refer to the Explanation of Data for more information.*

Asian (264)	366	3.01
Not Hispanic (263)	353	2.90
Hispanic (1)	13	0.11
Bangladeshi (6)	6	0.05
Chinese, ex. Taiwanese (35)	53	0.44
Filipino (29)	38	0.31
Indian (94)	121	0.99
Japanese (12)	31	0.25
Korean (37)	42	0.35
Laotian (1)	3	0.02
Pakistani (30)	30	0.25
Sri Lankan (4)	5	0.04
Thai (1)	8	0.07
Vietnamese (9)	11	0.09
Hawaii Native/Pacific Islander (0)	3	0.02
Not Hispanic (0)	2	0.02
Hispanic (0)	1	0.01
Guamanian/Chamorro (0)	1	0.01
Samoan (0)	1	0.01
White (11,185)	11,380	93.54
Not Hispanic (10,658)	10,793	88.71
Hispanic (527)	587	4.82

Baldwin

Place Type: CDP
County: Nassau
Population: 24,033†

Ancestry‡	Population	%
African, Sub-Saharan (127)	187	0.79
African (88)	148	0.62
Nigerian (28)	28	0.12
Sierra Leonean (11)	11	0.05
Alsatian (0)	9	0.04
American (508)	508	2.14
Arab (146)	275	1.16
Arab (22)	22	0.09
Egyptian (62)	162	0.68
Lebanese (17)	46	0.19
Palestinian (45)	45	0.19
Armenian (31)	31	0.13
Australian (0)	18	0.08
Austrian (28)	147	0.62
Belgian (0)	28	0.12
Brazilian (0)	13	0.05
Croatian (9)	9	0.04
Czech (0)	116	0.49
Danish (0)	8	0.03
Dutch (11)	77	0.32
Eastern European (61)	95	0.40
English (105)	566	2.39
European (69)	99	0.42
French, ex. Basque (40)	238	1.00
French Canadian (0)	13	0.05
German (492)	2,307	9.73
Greek (57)	134	0.57
Guyanese (81)	81	0.34
Hungarian (54)	146	0.62
Irish (1,306)	3,623	15.28
Italian (2,180)	3,987	16.81
Latvian (10)	32	0.13
Lithuanian (15)	32	0.13
Norwegian (44)	95	0.40
Polish (180)	689	2.91
Portuguese (90)	204	0.86
Romanian (58)	133	0.56
Russian (148)	416	1.75
Scotch-Irish (25)	92	0.39
Scottish (12)	64	0.27
Slovak (0)	12	0.05
Swedish (8)	151	0.64
Swiss (11)	48	0.20
Turkish (9)	9	0.04
Ukrainian (33)	207	0.87
Welsh (0)	70	0.30
West Indian, ex. Hispanic (3,239)	3,673	15.49
Barbadian (68)	79	0.33
British West Indian (74)	96	0.40
Haitian (1,243)	1,323	5.58
Jamaican (1,340)	1,531	6.46
Trinidadian/Tobagonian (177)	195	0.82
West Indian (337)	449	1.89
Yugoslavian (0)	13	0.05

Hispanic Origin	Population	%
Hispanic or Latino (of any race)	4,862	20.23
Central American, ex. Mexican	1,311	5.45
Costa Rican	39	0.16
Guatemalan	202	0.84
Honduran	177	0.74
Nicaraguan	34	0.14
Panamanian	104	0.43
Salvadoran	737	3.07
Other Central American	18	0.07
Cuban	137	0.57
Dominican Republic	1,032	4.29
Mexican	90	0.37
Puerto Rican	1,012	4.21
South American	874	3.64
Argentinean	39	0.16
Bolivian	3	0.01
Chilean	12	0.05
Colombian	287	1.19
Ecuadorian	238	0.99
Paraguayan	3	0.01
Peruvian	249	1.04
Uruguayan	9	0.04
Venezuelan	27	0.11
Other South American	7	0.03
Other Hispanic or Latino	406	1.69

Race*	Population	%
African-American/Black (8,306)	8,849	36.82
Not Hispanic (7,886)	8,249	34.32
Hispanic (420)	600	2.50
American Indian/Alaska Native (99)	226	0.94
Not Hispanic (47)	140	0.58
Hispanic (52)	86	0.36
Apache (2)	2	0.01
Blackfeet (3)	12	0.05
Canadian/French Am. Ind. (1)	1	<0.01
Central American Ind. (0)	1	<0.01
Cherokee (2)	29	0.12
Choctaw (1)	2	0.01
Creek (0)	1	<0.01
Crow (0)	1	<0.01
Iroquois (4)	11	0.05
Mexican American Ind. (8)	11	0.05
Seminole (0)	2	0.01
Sioux (1)	4	0.02
South American Ind. (10)	19	0.08
Spanish American Ind. (3)	3	0.01
Tlingit-Haida *(Alaska Native)* (2)	2	0.01
Asian (1,003)	1,222	5.08
Not Hispanic (979)	1,162	4.84
Hispanic (24)	60	0.25
Bangladeshi (4)	4	0.02
Cambodian (6)	6	0.02
Chinese, ex. Taiwanese (207)	264	1.10
Filipino (186)	233	0.97
Indian (420)	483	2.01
Indonesian (2)	2	0.01
Japanese (6)	20	0.08
Korean (35)	44	0.18
Laotian (1)	1	<0.01
Pakistani (92)	107	0.45
Sri Lankan (6)	8	0.03
Taiwanese (7)	7	0.03
Thai (8)	8	0.03
Vietnamese (7)	14	0.06
Hawaii Native/Pacific Islander (5)	30	0.12
Not Hispanic (5)	19	0.08
Hispanic (0)	11	0.05
Native Hawaiian (5)	7	0.03
Samoan (0)	1	<0.01
White (11,717)	12,358	51.42
Not Hispanic (9,555)	9,882	41.12
Hispanic (2,162)	2,476	10.30

Baldwin Harbor

Place Type: CDP
County: Nassau
Population: 8,102†

Ancestry‡	Population	%
African, Sub-Saharan (0)	12	0.14
African (0)	12	0.14
American (395)	395	4.54
Arab (140)	159	1.83
Egyptian (35)	35	0.40
Lebanese (0)	9	0.10
Moroccan (0)	10	0.12
Other Arab (105)	105	1.21
Armenian (0)	10	0.12
Australian (7)	20	0.23
Austrian (0)	82	0.94
Brazilian (40)	62	0.71
British (8)	8	0.09
Croatian (0)	31	0.36
Dutch (0)	23	0.26
Eastern European (36)	36	0.41
English (54)	366	4.21
European (65)	65	0.75
French, ex. Basque (7)	235	2.70
French Canadian (24)	33	0.38
German (262)	900	10.35
Greek (11)	93	1.07
Guyanese (13)	26	0.30
Hungarian (18)	68	0.78
Iranian (0)	9	0.10
Irish (566)	1,218	14.01
Israeli (0)	22	0.25
Italian (616)	1,342	15.44
Lithuanian (0)	20	0.23
Polish (187)	611	7.03
Portuguese (15)	15	0.17
Romanian (8)	31	0.36
Russian (190)	394	4.53
Scotch-Irish (9)	24	0.28
Scottish (15)	80	0.92
Swedish (0)	28	0.32
Swiss (0)	17	0.20
Ukrainian (0)	10	0.12
West Indian, ex. Hispanic (724)	771	8.87
Barbadian (68)	68	0.78
Haitian (434)	468	5.38
Jamaican (131)	144	1.66
Trinidadian/Tobagonian (39)	39	0.45
West Indian (52)	52	0.60

Hispanic Origin	Population	%
Hispanic or Latino (of any race)	959	11.84
Central American, ex. Mexican	151	1.86
Costa Rican	2	0.02
Guatemalan	9	0.11
Honduran	18	0.22
Nicaraguan	1	0.01
Panamanian	19	0.23
Salvadoran	102	1.26
Cuban	63	0.78
Dominican Republic	169	2.09
Mexican	27	0.33
Puerto Rican	255	3.15
South American	221	2.73
Argentinean	13	0.16
Bolivian	9	0.11
Chilean	8	0.10
Colombian	93	1.15
Ecuadorian	62	0.77
Peruvian	28	0.35
Uruguayan	2	0.02
Venezuelan	6	0.07
Other Hispanic or Latino	73	0.90

Race*	Population	%
African-American/Black (2,153)	2,309	28.50
Not Hispanic (2,055)	2,169	26.77
Hispanic (98)	140	1.73

*Notes: † The Census 2010 population figure is used to calculate the percentages in the Hispanic Origin and Race categories. Ancestry percentages are based on the 2006-2010 American Community Survey population (not shown); ‡ Numbers in parentheses indicate the number of people reporting a single ancestry; * Numbers in parentheses indicate the number of persons reporting this race alone, not in combination with any other race; Please refer to the Explanation of Data for more information.*

American Indian/Alaska Native (11)	33	0.41
Not Hispanic (8)	23	0.28
Hispanic (3)	10	0.12
Central American Ind. (0)	1	0.01
Cherokee (3)	4	0.05
Seminole (0)	3	0.04
Sioux (1)	1	0.01
Asian (395)	482	5.95
Not Hispanic (392)	473	5.84
Hispanic (3)	9	0.11
Chinese, ex. Taiwanese (77)	94	1.16
Filipino (87)	99	1.22
Indian (172)	196	2.42
Japanese (6)	7	0.09
Korean (11)	21	0.26
Nepalese (1)	1	0.01
Pakistani (21)	24	0.30
Sri Lankan (1)	1	0.01
Taiwanese (4)	7	0.09
Thai (5)	5	0.06
Vietnamese (2)	2	0.02
Hawaii Native/Pacific Islander (0)	23	0.28
Not Hispanic (0)	15	0.19
Hispanic (0)	8	0.10
Native Hawaiian (0)	4	0.05
White (4,963)	5,133	63.35
Not Hispanic (4,449)	4,562	56.31
Hispanic (514)	571	7.05

Ballston

Place Type: Town
County: Saratoga
Population: 9,776†

Ancestry‡	Population	%
American (822)	822	8.53
Arab (0)	20	0.21
Egyptian (0)	10	0.10
Other Arab (0)	10	0.10
Austrian (69)	78	0.81
Belgian (22)	48	0.50
British (155)	155	1.61
Canadian (10)	10	0.10
Czech (0)	22	0.23
Czechoslovakian (0)	10	0.10
Danish (0)	38	0.39
Dutch (49)	287	2.98
English (343)	1,284	13.32
European (47)	60	0.62
French, ex. Basque (173)	1,036	10.75
French Canadian (86)	313	3.25
German (570)	1,908	19.79
Greek (16)	66	0.68
Hungarian (16)	41	0.43
Irish (630)	2,373	24.62
Italian (515)	1,388	14.40
Lithuanian (0)	36	0.37
Norwegian (0)	37	0.38
Polish (173)	649	6.73
Portuguese (0)	23	0.24
Russian (34)	140	1.45
Scandinavian (14)	14	0.15
Scotch-Irish (83)	180	1.87
Scottish (92)	264	2.74
Slovak (0)	11	0.11
Swedish (12)	34	0.35
Swiss (6)	63	0.65
Ukrainian (21)	108	1.12
Welsh (0)	132	1.37

Hispanic Origin	Population	%
Hispanic or Latino (of any race)	189	1.93
Central American, ex. Mexican	15	0.15
Costa Rican	8	0.08
Guatemalan	3	0.03
Honduran	1	0.01
Panamanian	2	0.02
Other Central American	1	0.01
Cuban	9	0.09
Dominican Republic	16	0.16
Mexican	31	0.32
Puerto Rican	69	0.71
South American	16	0.16
Chilean	2	0.02
Colombian	4	0.04
Ecuadorian	2	0.02
Peruvian	6	0.06
Venezuelan	2	0.02
Other Hispanic or Latino	33	0.34

Race*	Population	%
African-American/Black (111)	176	1.80
Not Hispanic (101)	155	1.59
Hispanic (10)	21	0.21
American Indian/Alaska Native (18)	59	0.60
Not Hispanic (17)	55	0.56
Hispanic (1)	4	0.04
Blackfeet (0)	1	0.01
Cherokee (2)	7	0.07
Iroquois (9)	19	0.19
Mexican American Ind. (1)	1	0.01
South American Ind. (0)	1	0.01
Asian (98)	124	1.27
Not Hispanic (97)	123	1.26
Hispanic (1)	1	0.01
Chinese, ex. Taiwanese (21)	24	0.25
Filipino (7)	12	0.12
Indian (3)	7	0.07
Indonesian (1)	2	0.02
Japanese (9)	13	0.13
Korean (7)	10	0.10
Taiwanese (3)	3	0.03
Thai (3)	4	0.04
Vietnamese (43)	45	0.46
Hawaii Native/Pacific Islander (1)	6	0.06
Not Hispanic (1)	6	0.06
Native Hawaiian (1)	2	0.02
White (9,393)	9,530	97.48
Not Hispanic (9,249)	9,364	95.79
Hispanic (144)	166	1.70

Barton

Place Type: Town
County: Tioga
Population: 8,858†

Ancestry‡	Population	%
African, Sub-Saharan (25)	25	0.28
South African (25)	25	0.28
American (815)	815	9.15
Austrian (7)	17	0.19
Brazilian (34)	34	0.38
British (46)	46	0.52
Czech (0)	17	0.19
Dutch (68)	302	3.39
English (734)	1,493	16.75
European (77)	83	0.93
Finnish (7)	26	0.29
French, ex. Basque (7)	137	1.54
French Canadian (47)	84	0.94
German (817)	2,045	22.95
Greek (0)	9	0.10
Hungarian (29)	44	0.49
Irish (559)	1,818	20.40
Italian (428)	1,004	11.27
Northern European (7)	7	0.08
Norwegian (57)	147	1.65
Pennsylvania German (74)	104	1.17
Polish (84)	323	3.62
Russian (17)	46	0.52
Scotch-Irish (58)	189	2.12
Scottish (63)	162	1.82
Slovak (0)	8	0.09
Swedish (44)	176	1.98
Swiss (0)	23	0.26
Ukrainian (74)	129	1.45
Welsh (17)	195	2.19

Hispanic Origin	Population	%
Hispanic or Latino (of any race)	122	1.38
Central American, ex. Mexican	23	0.26
Guatemalan	2	0.02
Panamanian	1	0.01
Salvadoran	20	0.23
Cuban	9	0.10
Mexican	34	0.38
Puerto Rican	36	0.41
South American	12	0.14
Colombian	8	0.09
Ecuadorian	4	0.05
Other Hispanic or Latino	8	0.09

Race*	Population	%
African-American/Black (46)	83	0.94
Not Hispanic (45)	78	0.88
Hispanic (1)	5	0.06
American Indian/Alaska Native (25)	78	0.88
Not Hispanic (18)	66	0.75
Hispanic (7)	12	0.14
Blackfeet (2)	3	0.03
Canadian/French Am. Ind. (1)	2	0.02
Cherokee (2)	5	0.06
Crow (1)	1	0.01
Iroquois (5)	17	0.19
Mexican American Ind. (2)	2	0.02
Navajo (1)	2	0.02
Sioux (1)	6	0.07
South American Ind. (1)	1	0.01
Tohono O'Odham (1)	1	0.01
Asian (31)	33	0.37
Not Hispanic (31)	33	0.37
Chinese, ex. Taiwanese (10)	10	0.11
Filipino (6)	7	0.08
Indian (7)	8	0.09
Japanese (2)	2	0.02
Korean (4)	4	0.05
Thai (1)	1	0.01
Vietnamese (0)	1	0.01
Hawaii Native/Pacific Islander (0)	1	0.01
Not Hispanic (0)	1	0.01
Native Hawaiian (0)	1	0.01
White (8,645)	8,748	98.76
Not Hispanic (8,557)	8,641	97.55
Hispanic (88)	107	1.21

Batavia

Place Type: City
County: Genesee
Population: 15,465†

Ancestry‡	Population	%
African, Sub-Saharan (46)	132	0.85
African (46)	132	0.85
American (574)	574	3.68
Arab (27)	41	0.26
Arab (17)	31	0.20
Other Arab (10)	10	0.06
Belgian (9)	9	0.06
British (7)	7	0.04
Canadian (19)	29	0.19
Croatian (0)	11	0.07
Czech (0)	97	0.62
Czechoslovakian (0)	10	0.06
Danish (35)	43	0.28
Dutch (29)	436	2.80
English (670)	2,543	16.32
European (40)	40	0.26
Finnish (10)	10	0.06
French, ex. Basque (88)	730	4.68
French Canadian (83)	154	0.99
German (1,294)	4,634	29.73
Greek (73)	73	0.47
Hungarian (0)	131	0.84
Irish (660)	2,838	18.21
Italian (1,515)	3,313	21.26
Lithuanian (0)	10	0.06
Norwegian (0)	48	0.31

*Notes: † The Census 2010 population figure is used to calculate the percentages in the Hispanic Origin and Race categories. Ancestry percentages are based on the 2006-2010 American Community Survey population (not shown); ‡ Numbers in parentheses indicate the number of people reporting a single ancestry; * Numbers in parentheses indicate the number of persons reporting this race alone, not in combination with any other race; Please refer to the Explanation of Data for more information.*

Pennsylvania German (0)	8	0.05
Polish (605)	1,735	11.13
Russian (0)	7	0.04
Scotch-Irish (113)	265	1.70
Scottish (65)	302	1.94
Slovak (59)	70	0.45
Swedish (47)	177	1.14
Swiss (0)	12	0.08
Ukrainian (17)	71	0.46
Welsh (20)	96	0.62
West Indian, ex. Hispanic (45)	45	0.29
West Indian (45)	45	0.29

Hispanic Origin	Population	%
Hispanic or Latino (of any race)	466	3.01
Central American, ex. Mexican	8	0.05
Guatemalan	7	0.05
Nicaraguan	1	0.01
Cuban	2	0.01
Dominican Republic	27	0.17
Mexican	103	0.67
Puerto Rican	266	1.72
South American	22	0.14
Argentinean	2	0.01
Bolivian	7	0.05
Chilean	3	0.02
Colombian	1	0.01
Ecuadorian	4	0.03
Venezuelan	5	0.03
Other Hispanic or Latino	38	0.25

Race*	Population	%
African-American/Black (837)	1,190	7.69
Not Hispanic (764)	1,067	6.90
Hispanic (73)	123	0.80
American Indian/Alaska Native (64)	194	1.25
Not Hispanic (63)	174	1.13
Hispanic (1)	20	0.13
Apache (0)	3	0.02
Blackfeet (0)	10	0.06
Canadian/French Am. Ind. (0)	2	0.01
Cherokee (6)	26	0.17
Chippewa (2)	4	0.03
Iroquois (29)	50	0.32
Seminole (0)	10	0.06
Sioux (1)	1	0.01
Asian (126)	173	1.12
Not Hispanic (125)	168	1.09
Hispanic (1)	5	0.03
Bangladeshi (2)	4	0.03
Chinese, ex. Taiwanese (25)	33	0.21
Filipino (21)	33	0.21
Indian (36)	44	0.28
Japanese (8)	17	0.11
Korean (22)	31	0.20
Laotian (3)	5	0.03
Pakistani (5)	5	0.03
Vietnamese (2)	3	0.02
Hawaii Native/Pacific Islander (4)	12	0.08
Not Hispanic (2)	4	0.03
Hispanic (2)	8	0.05
Guamanian/Chamorro (2)	4	0.03
Native Hawaiian (2)	3	0.02
White (13,831)	14,297	92.45
Not Hispanic (13,601)	14,007	90.57
Hispanic (230)	290	1.88

Bath

Place Type: Town
County: Steuben
Population: 12,379†

Ancestry‡	Population	%
Alsatian (0)	8	0.07
American (1,134)	1,134	9.22
Austrian (10)	45	0.37
Belgian (0)	12	0.10
British (21)	34	0.28
Canadian (4)	4	0.03
Czech (54)	63	0.51
Danish (34)	36	0.29
Dutch (153)	845	6.87
Eastern European (55)	55	0.45
English (731)	2,326	18.91
European (20)	20	0.16
Finnish (10)	22	0.18
French, ex. Basque (111)	284	2.31
French Canadian (39)	95	0.77
German (653)	2,545	20.69
Greek (0)	14	0.11
Hungarian (11)	11	0.09
Irish (577)	2,143	17.42
Italian (340)	906	7.36
Northern European (21)	21	0.17
Norwegian (40)	74	0.60
Pennsylvania German (44)	98	0.80
Polish (442)	990	8.05
Portuguese (13)	18	0.15
Russian (0)	27	0.22
Scandinavian (11)	11	0.09
Scotch-Irish (99)	202	1.64
Scottish (52)	244	1.98
Swedish (23)	114	0.93
Swiss (0)	5	0.04
Ukrainian (43)	79	0.64
Welsh (23)	109	0.89
West Indian, ex. Hispanic (0)	22	0.18
Jamaican (0)	11	0.09
West Indian (0)	11	0.09

Hispanic Origin	Population	%
Hispanic or Latino (of any race)	153	1.24
Central American, ex. Mexican	12	0.10
Guatemalan	3	0.02
Honduran	5	0.04
Panamanian	2	0.02
Salvadoran	2	0.02
Dominican Republic	3	0.02
Mexican	47	0.38
Puerto Rican	60	0.48
South American	12	0.10
Chilean	1	0.01
Colombian	4	0.03
Ecuadorian	1	0.01
Paraguayan	1	0.01
Peruvian	5	0.04
Other Hispanic or Latino	19	0.15

Race*	Population	%
African-American/Black (353)	435	3.51
Not Hispanic (346)	425	3.43
Hispanic (7)	10	0.08
American Indian/Alaska Native (32)	89	0.72
Not Hispanic (29)	85	0.69
Hispanic (3)	4	0.03
Apache (0)	2	0.02
Blackfeet (1)	7	0.06
Cherokee (4)	13	0.11
Choctaw (0)	2	0.02
Crow (1)	1	0.01
Iroquois (5)	13	0.11
Mexican American Ind. (1)	1	0.01
Shoshone (0)	1	0.01
Sioux (1)	2	0.02
Tlingit-Haida *(Alaska Native)* (1)	1	0.01
Yup'ik *(Alaska Native)* (1)	1	0.01
Asian (59)	65	0.53
Not Hispanic (59)	65	0.53
Chinese, ex. Taiwanese (11)	11	0.09
Filipino (9)	10	0.08
Indian (27)	27	0.22
Japanese (2)	4	0.03
Korean (1)	3	0.02
Taiwanese (3)	3	0.02
Vietnamese (2)	3	0.02
Hawaii Native/Pacific Islander (2)	4	0.03
Not Hispanic (2)	4	0.03
Native Hawaiian (2)	4	0.03
White (11,747)	11,900	96.13
Not Hispanic (11,642)	11,783	95.19
Hispanic (105)	117	0.95

Bay Shore

Place Type: CDP
County: Suffolk
Population: 26,337†

Ancestry‡	Population	%
African, Sub-Saharan (100)	157	0.56
African (100)	157	0.56
American (260)	260	0.93
Arab (65)	86	0.31
Lebanese (65)	76	0.27
Syrian (0)	10	0.04
Armenian (14)	14	0.05
Austrian (26)	164	0.59
Belgian (13)	13	0.05
Brazilian (39)	72	0.26
British (33)	68	0.24
Czech (23)	106	0.38
Czechoslovakian (8)	60	0.21
Danish (0)	22	0.08
Dutch (0)	129	0.46
Eastern European (17)	17	0.06
English (121)	955	3.42
European (104)	104	0.37
Finnish (11)	24	0.09
French, ex. Basque (25)	417	1.49
French Canadian (41)	170	0.61
German (439)	2,657	9.52
Greek (37)	120	0.43
Guyanese (157)	157	0.56
Hungarian (89)	324	1.16
Irish (984)	4,374	15.67
Italian (2,289)	5,065	18.14
Lithuanian (55)	71	0.25
Norwegian (67)	238	0.85
Polish (502)	1,246	4.46
Portuguese (132)	255	0.91
Romanian (0)	7	0.03
Russian (79)	370	1.33
Scandinavian (0)	33	0.12
Scotch-Irish (62)	196	0.70
Scottish (24)	178	0.64
Slovak (0)	15	0.05
Swedish (47)	194	0.69
Swiss (0)	178	0.64
Turkish (43)	43	0.15
Ukrainian (12)	41	0.15
Welsh (0)	77	0.28
West Indian, ex. Hispanic (855)	1,196	4.28
Barbadian (5)	5	0.02
British West Indian (117)	253	0.91
Haitian (323)	398	1.43
Jamaican (392)	472	1.69
Trinidadian/Tobagonian (18)	53	0.19
West Indian (0)	15	0.05

Hispanic Origin	Population	%
Hispanic or Latino (of any race)	8,101	30.76
Central American, ex. Mexican	1,992	7.56
Costa Rican	60	0.23
Guatemalan	159	0.60
Honduran	239	0.91
Nicaraguan	25	0.09
Panamanian	27	0.10
Salvadoran	1,477	5.61
Other Central American	5	0.02
Cuban	77	0.29
Dominican Republic	806	3.06
Mexican	336	1.28
Puerto Rican	2,245	8.52
South American	1,997	7.58
Argentinean	60	0.23
Bolivian	3	0.01
Chilean	23	0.09
Colombian	500	1.90
Ecuadorian	1,038	3.94

SECTION TWO

*Notes: † The Census 2010 population figure is used to calculate the percentages in the Hispanic Origin and Race categories. Ancestry percentages are based on the 2006-2010 American Community Survey population (not shown); ‡ Numbers in parentheses indicate the number of people reporting a single ancestry; * Numbers in parentheses indicate the number of persons reporting this race alone, not in combination with any other race; Please refer to the Explanation of Data for more information.*

Peruvian	305	1.16
Uruguayan	19	0.07
Venezuelan	35	0.13
Other South American	14	0.05
Other Hispanic or Latino	648	2.46

Race*	Population	%
African-American/Black (5,170)	5,777	21.93
Not Hispanic (4,590)	4,998	18.98
Hispanic (580)	779	2.96
American Indian/Alaska Native (173)	424	1.61
Not Hispanic (94)	278	1.06
Hispanic (79)	146	0.55
Aleut *(Alaska Native)* (1)	1	<0.01
Apache (1)	5	0.02
Blackfeet (5)	17	0.06
Cherokee (3)	40	0.15
Chippewa (1)	1	<0.01
Crow (0)	1	<0.01
Inupiat *(Alaska Native)* (0)	1	<0.01
Iroquois (10)	14	0.05
Mexican American Ind. (5)	5	0.02
Potawatomi (1)	1	<0.01
Pueblo (0)	1	<0.01
Shoshone (0)	3	0.01
Sioux (3)	8	0.03
South American Ind. (20)	33	0.13
Spanish American Ind. (2)	4	0.02
Tlingit-Haida *(Alaska Native)* (1)	2	0.01
Asian (855)	1,033	3.92
Not Hispanic (845)	981	3.72
Hispanic (10)	52	0.20
Bangladeshi (60)	74	0.28
Chinese, ex. Taiwanese (136)	176	0.67
Filipino (97)	122	0.46
Indian (262)	326	1.24
Indonesian (4)	6	0.02
Japanese (9)	16	0.06
Korean (35)	43	0.16
Laotian (1)	4	0.02
Malaysian (0)	2	0.01
Nepalese (2)	2	0.01
Pakistani (136)	165	0.63
Sri Lankan (0)	4	0.02
Taiwanese (3)	3	0.01
Thai (4)	6	0.02
Vietnamese (24)	36	0.14
Hawaii Native/Pacific Islander (11)	41	0.16
Not Hispanic (4)	20	0.08
Hispanic (7)	21	0.08
Fijian (0)	2	0.01
Guamanian/Chamorro (1)	2	0.01
Native Hawaiian (1)	2	0.01
White (16,058)	16,866	64.04
Not Hispanic (12,055)	12,452	47.28
Hispanic (4,003)	4,414	16.76

Bayport

Place Type: CDP
County: Suffolk
Population: 8,896†

Ancestry‡	Population	%
African, Sub-Saharan (29)	29	0.33
African (29)	29	0.33
American (233)	233	2.61
Armenian (11)	22	0.25
Austrian (11)	120	1.35
Belgian (11)	11	0.12
Canadian (0)	24	0.27
Croatian (0)	5	0.06
Czech (25)	52	0.58
Czechoslovakian (38)	82	0.92
Danish (0)	65	0.73
Dutch (9)	122	1.37
Eastern European (26)	37	0.41
English (242)	1,024	11.48
European (12)	12	0.13
Finnish (0)	39	0.44
French, ex. Basque (0)	92	1.03
French Canadian (21)	68	0.76
German (371)	2,056	23.06
Greek (61)	115	1.29
Hungarian (0)	91	1.02
Irish (818)	2,972	33.33
Italian (1,580)	3,375	37.85
Lithuanian (12)	12	0.13
Northern European (10)	10	0.11
Norwegian (50)	108	1.21
Polish (51)	232	2.60
Romanian (30)	59	0.66
Russian (8)	31	0.35
Scotch-Irish (13)	108	1.21
Scottish (10)	133	1.49
Slovak (0)	15	0.17
Swedish (0)	137	1.54
Swiss (0)	24	0.27
Turkish (14)	14	0.16
Ukrainian (28)	69	0.77
Welsh (9)	37	0.41
West Indian, ex. Hispanic (19)	35	0.39
Haitian (12)	12	0.13
Trinidadian/Tobagonian (7)	23	0.26

Hispanic Origin	Population	%
Hispanic or Latino (of any race)	470	5.28
Central American, ex. Mexican	38	0.43
Costa Rican	3	0.03
Guatemalan	8	0.09
Honduran	10	0.11
Nicaraguan	4	0.04
Panamanian	2	0.02
Salvadoran	11	0.12
Cuban	31	0.35
Dominican Republic	14	0.16
Mexican	28	0.31
Puerto Rican	214	2.41
South American	93	1.05
Argentinean	16	0.18
Chilean	4	0.04
Colombian	31	0.35
Ecuadorian	26	0.29
Peruvian	16	0.18
Other Hispanic or Latino	52	0.58

Race*	Population	%
African-American/Black (128)	177	1.99
Not Hispanic (115)	159	1.79
Hispanic (13)	18	0.20
American Indian/Alaska Native (8)	21	0.24
Not Hispanic (5)	18	0.20
Hispanic (3)	3	0.03
Blackfeet (0)	1	0.01
Cherokee (0)	3	0.03
Iroquois (1)	3	0.03
South American Ind. (1)	1	0.01
Asian (151)	180	2.02
Not Hispanic (151)	179	2.01
Hispanic (0)	1	0.01
Bangladeshi (2)	2	0.02
Burmese (2)	2	0.02
Chinese, ex. Taiwanese (10)	17	0.19
Filipino (19)	19	0.21
Indian (78)	79	0.89
Japanese (2)	2	0.02
Korean (15)	21	0.24
Laotian (0)	1	0.01
Malaysian (0)	1	0.01
Pakistani (15)	16	0.18
Taiwanese (1)	1	0.01
Thai (3)	4	0.04
Hawaii Native/Pacific Islander (1)	5	0.06
Not Hispanic (0)	4	0.04
Hispanic (1)	1	0.01
Guamanian/Chamorro (1)	2	0.02
White (8,419)	8,498	95.53
Not Hispanic (8,072)	8,130	91.39
Hispanic (347)	368	4.14

Beacon

Place Type: City
County: Dutchess
Population: 15,541†

Ancestry‡	Population	%
African, Sub-Saharan (37)	179	1.16
African (29)	171	1.10
Nigerian (8)	8	0.05
Albanian (6)	6	0.04
American (265)	265	1.71
Arab (26)	84	0.54
Lebanese (26)	84	0.54
Australian (14)	14	0.09
Austrian (0)	94	0.61
Belgian (13)	28	0.18
Brazilian (0)	12	0.08
British (15)	28	0.18
Canadian (6)	6	0.04
Czech (0)	42	0.27
Czechoslovakian (14)	14	0.09
Danish (0)	19	0.12
Dutch (5)	203	1.31
English (292)	1,033	6.67
European (49)	74	0.48
French, ex. Basque (51)	344	2.22
French Canadian (11)	89	0.57
German (246)	1,674	10.80
Greek (26)	160	1.03
Guyanese (15)	22	0.14
Hungarian (85)	122	0.79
Iranian (6)	6	0.04
Irish (1,093)	3,231	20.85
Italian (880)	2,355	15.20
Lithuanian (6)	23	0.15
New Zealander (13)	13	0.08
Norwegian (0)	104	0.67
Polish (135)	709	4.58
Russian (28)	229	1.48
Scandinavian (9)	26	0.17
Scotch-Irish (8)	108	0.70
Scottish (133)	333	2.15
Slavic (8)	19	0.12
Slovak (0)	43	0.28
Swedish (69)	244	1.57
Swiss (8)	85	0.55
Turkish (0)	27	0.17
Ukrainian (9)	34	0.22
Welsh (13)	134	0.86
West Indian, ex. Hispanic (318)	423	2.73
Barbadian (0)	10	0.06
Haitian (14)	24	0.15
Jamaican (246)	288	1.86
Trinidadian/Tobagonian (0)	8	0.05
U.S. Virgin Islander (7)	7	0.05
West Indian (51)	86	0.56
Yugoslavian (0)	13	0.08

Hispanic Origin	Population	%
Hispanic or Latino (of any race)	3,219	20.71
Central American, ex. Mexican	123	0.79
Costa Rican	13	0.08
Guatemalan	29	0.19
Honduran	23	0.15
Nicaraguan	3	0.02
Panamanian	21	0.14
Salvadoran	32	0.21
Other Central American	2	0.01
Cuban	95	0.61
Dominican Republic	283	1.82
Mexican	320	2.06
Puerto Rican	1,726	11.11
South American	483	3.11
Argentinean	22	0.14
Bolivian	3	0.02
Chilean	12	0.08
Colombian	198	1.27
Ecuadorian	158	1.02
Paraguayan	1	0.01

*Notes: † The Census 2010 population figure is used to calculate the percentages in the Hispanic Origin and Race categories. Ancestry percentages are based on the 2006-2010 American Community Survey population (not shown); ‡ Numbers in parentheses indicate the number of people reporting a single ancestry; * Numbers in parentheses indicate the number of persons reporting this race alone, not in combination with any other race; Please refer to the Explanation of Data for more information.*

Peruvian	48	0.31
Uruguayan	25	0.16
Venezuelan	12	0.08
Other South American	4	0.03
Other Hispanic or Latino	189	1.22

Race*	Population	%
African-American/Black (3,612)	4,073	26.21
Not Hispanic (3,232)	3,514	22.61
Hispanic (380)	559	3.60
American Indian/Alaska Native (54)	212	1.36
Not Hispanic (26)	140	0.90
Hispanic (28)	72	0.46
Apache (1)	3	0.02
Blackfeet (2)	9	0.06
Central American Ind. (1)	2	0.01
Cherokee (2)	38	0.24
Chippewa (0)	1	0.01
Choctaw (0)	2	0.01
Creek (0)	1	0.01
Crow (0)	1	0.01
Delaware (0)	2	0.01
Iroquois (8)	16	0.10
Mexican American Ind. (1)	3	0.02
Pueblo (0)	5	0.03
Seminole (0)	3	0.02
Sioux (1)	3	0.02
South American Ind. (9)	15	0.10
Tohono O'Odham (0)	1	0.01
Asian (253)	340	2.19
Not Hispanic (250)	321	2.07
Hispanic (3)	19	0.12
Bangladeshi (2)	2	0.01
Cambodian (1)	1	0.01
Chinese, ex. Taiwanese (65)	88	0.57
Filipino (35)	55	0.35
Indian (74)	85	0.55
Indonesian (3)	3	0.02
Japanese (16)	22	0.14
Korean (12)	16	0.10
Malaysian (0)	1	0.01
Nepalese (1)	1	0.01
Pakistani (9)	10	0.06
Sri Lankan (2)	5	0.03
Taiwanese (1)	2	0.01
Thai (7)	16	0.10
Vietnamese (5)	14	0.09
Hawaii Native/Pacific Islander (0)	16	0.10
Not Hispanic (0)	1	0.01
Hispanic (0)	15	0.10
Samoan (0)	1	0.01
White (9,887)	10,437	67.16
Not Hispanic (8,333)	8,684	55.88
Hispanic (1,554)	1,753	11.28

Bedford

Place Type: Town
County: Westchester
Population: 17,335†

Ancestry‡	Population	%
African, Sub-Saharan (58)	137	0.79
Ethiopian (38)	117	0.67
Ghanaian (20)	20	0.11
Albanian (0)	23	0.13
American (932)	932	5.36
Arab (121)	136	0.78
Egyptian (55)	55	0.32
Lebanese (20)	35	0.20
Palestinian (34)	34	0.20
Other Arab (12)	12	0.07
Armenian (0)	7	0.04
Australian (12)	12	0.07
Austrian (28)	232	1.33
Belgian (11)	37	0.21
British (64)	112	0.64
Bulgarian (105)	105	0.60
Canadian (0)	56	0.32
Celtic (15)	22	0.13
Croatian (14)	36	0.21
Czech (47)	186	1.07
Czechoslovakian (0)	32	0.18
Danish (20)	64	0.37
Dutch (10)	185	1.06
Eastern European (197)	213	1.22
English (234)	1,554	8.93
European (451)	451	2.59
Finnish (0)	12	0.07
French, ex. Basque (105)	585	3.36
French Canadian (26)	121	0.70
German (502)	2,098	12.06
Greek (126)	213	1.22
Guyanese (0)	8	0.05
Hungarian (107)	242	1.39
Iranian (0)	12	0.07
Irish (983)	3,393	19.50
Italian (1,889)	3,266	18.77
Lithuanian (18)	56	0.32
Northern European (23)	23	0.13
Norwegian (43)	247	1.42
Polish (139)	803	4.62
Portuguese (14)	32	0.18
Romanian (0)	45	0.26
Russian (345)	1,008	5.79
Scandinavian (6)	23	0.13
Scotch-Irish (279)	402	2.31
Scottish (91)	457	2.63
Slavic (6)	6	0.03
Slovak (0)	22	0.13
Slovene (28)	96	0.55
Swedish (25)	180	1.03
Swiss (0)	26	0.15
Turkish (0)	9	0.05
Ukrainian (116)	155	0.89
Welsh (21)	81	0.47
West Indian, ex. Hispanic (94)	131	0.75
British West Indian (6)	6	0.03
Haitian (20)	28	0.16
Jamaican (42)	50	0.29
Trinidadian/Tobagonian (18)	18	0.10
West Indian (8)	29	0.17
Yugoslavian (9)	9	0.05

Hispanic Origin	Population	%
Hispanic or Latino (of any race)	2,104	12.14
Central American, ex. Mexican	638	3.68
Costa Rican	3	0.02
Guatemalan	491	2.83
Honduran	65	0.37
Nicaraguan	6	0.03
Panamanian	13	0.07
Salvadoran	60	0.35
Cuban	51	0.29
Dominican Republic	82	0.47
Mexican	188	1.08
Puerto Rican	328	1.89
South American	607	3.50
Argentinean	37	0.21
Bolivian	3	0.02
Chilean	15	0.09
Colombian	163	0.94
Ecuadorian	227	1.31
Paraguayan	63	0.36
Peruvian	89	0.51
Uruguayan	4	0.02
Venezuelan	6	0.03
Other Hispanic or Latino	210	1.21

Race*	Population	%
African-American/Black (937)	1,042	6.01
Not Hispanic (855)	935	5.39
Hispanic (82)	107	0.62
American Indian/Alaska Native (34)	85	0.49
Not Hispanic (19)	59	0.34
Hispanic (15)	26	0.15
Apache (1)	2	0.01
Cherokee (3)	13	0.07
Crow (1)	1	0.01
Iroquois (1)	2	0.01
Mexican American Ind. (4)	6	0.03
Seminole (1)	1	0.01
Sioux (0)	2	0.01
South American Ind. (2)	3	0.02
Spanish American Ind. (0)	1	0.01
Yaqui (0)	1	0.01
Asian (509)	632	3.65
Not Hispanic (507)	619	3.57
Hispanic (2)	13	0.07
Bangladeshi (0)	3	0.02
Chinese, ex. Taiwanese (145)	176	1.02
Filipino (115)	138	0.80
Indian (133)	161	0.93
Japanese (19)	46	0.27
Korean (54)	69	0.40
Laotian (0)	1	0.01
Nepalese (2)	2	0.01
Pakistani (2)	7	0.04
Sri Lankan (9)	10	0.06
Taiwanese (4)	4	0.02
Thai (1)	1	0.01
Vietnamese (5)	7	0.04
Hawaii Native/Pacific Islander (0)	3	0.02
Not Hispanic (0)	2	0.01
Hispanic (0)	1	0.01
White (14,858)	15,126	87.26
Not Hispanic (13,617)	13,781	79.50
Hispanic (1,241)	1,345	7.76

Beekman

Place Type: Town
County: Dutchess
Population: 14,621†

Ancestry‡	Population	%
African, Sub-Saharan (10)	18	0.12
African (10)	18	0.12
American (508)	508	3.50
Arab (0)	31	0.21
Syrian (0)	19	0.13
Other Arab (0)	12	0.08
Austrian (99)	203	1.40
Belgian (13)	13	0.09
British (0)	77	0.53
Bulgarian (0)	7	0.05
Canadian (30)	49	0.34
Czech (32)	271	1.87
Czechoslovakian (5)	12	0.08
Dutch (36)	216	1.49
Eastern European (77)	99	0.68
English (115)	832	5.73
Estonian (15)	15	0.10
European (28)	28	0.19
Finnish (0)	8	0.06
French, ex. Basque (19)	216	1.49
French Canadian (57)	143	0.98
German (363)	2,393	16.47
Greek (0)	19	0.13
Guyanese (17)	17	0.12
Hungarian (38)	251	1.73
Iranian (33)	33	0.23
Irish (966)	3,287	22.63
Italian (2,257)	4,301	29.61
Lithuanian (62)	102	0.70
Norwegian (0)	63	0.43
Polish (231)	774	5.33
Portuguese (6)	92	0.63
Romanian (0)	9	0.06
Russian (169)	357	2.46
Scandinavian (18)	53	0.36
Scotch-Irish (185)	279	1.92
Scottish (56)	285	1.96
Slavic (0)	6	0.04
Slovak (91)	91	0.63
Swedish (14)	206	1.42
Swiss (22)	42	0.29
Turkish (0)	10	0.07
Ukrainian (9)	171	1.18
Welsh (0)	64	0.44

*Notes: † The Census 2010 population figure is used to calculate the percentages in the Hispanic Origin and Race categories. Ancestry percentages are based on the 2006-2010 American Community Survey population (not shown); ‡ Numbers in parentheses indicate the number of people reporting a single ancestry; * Numbers in parentheses indicate the number of persons reporting this race alone, not in combination with any other race; Please refer to the Explanation of Data for more information.*

West Indian, ex. Hispanic (182)	271	1.87
Haitian (25)	25	0.17
Jamaican (73)	82	0.56
Trinidadian/Tobagonian (0)	8	0.06
West Indian (84)	156	1.07

Hispanic Origin	Population	%
Hispanic or Latino (of any race)	1,332	9.11
Central American, ex. Mexican	63	0.43
Costa Rican	5	0.03
Guatemalan	10	0.07
Honduran	17	0.12
Nicaraguan	3	0.02
Panamanian	11	0.08
Salvadoran	17	0.12
Cuban	42	0.29
Dominican Republic	165	1.13
Mexican	86	0.59
Puerto Rican	717	4.90
South American	171	1.17
Argentinean	11	0.08
Bolivian	14	0.10
Chilean	2	0.01
Colombian	46	0.31
Ecuadorian	41	0.28
Paraguayan	2	0.01
Peruvian	40	0.27
Uruguayan	8	0.05
Venezuelan	5	0.03
Other South American	2	0.01
Other Hispanic or Latino	88	0.60

Race*	Population	%
African-American/Black (1,719)	1,811	12.39
Not Hispanic (1,559)	1,627	11.13
Hispanic (160)	184	1.26
American Indian/Alaska Native (34)	91	0.62
Not Hispanic (28)	84	0.57
Hispanic (6)	7	0.05
Blackfeet (0)	4	0.03
Cherokee (1)	17	0.12
Chippewa (1)	1	0.01
Creek (2)	2	0.01
Delaware (0)	1	0.01
Iroquois (5)	8	0.05
South American Ind. (2)	2	0.01
Asian (400)	485	3.32
Not Hispanic (387)	468	3.20
Hispanic (13)	17	0.12
Cambodian (1)	2	0.01
Chinese, ex. Taiwanese (134)	163	1.11
Filipino (36)	43	0.29
Indian (113)	134	0.92
Japanese (13)	18	0.12
Korean (43)	49	0.34
Malaysian (0)	3	0.02
Pakistani (14)	16	0.11
Sri Lankan (1)	1	0.01
Taiwanese (2)	3	0.02
Thai (1)	1	0.01
Vietnamese (15)	20	0.14
Hawaii Native/Pacific Islander (2)	7	0.05
Not Hispanic (2)	7	0.05
Native Hawaiian (2)	3	0.02
White (11,851)	12,063	82.50
Not Hispanic (11,067)	11,233	76.83
Hispanic (784)	830	5.68

Bellmore

Place Type: CDP
County: Nassau
Population: 16,218†

Ancestry‡	Population	%
Afghan (50)	50	0.31
Albanian (0)	36	0.22
American (808)	808	4.99
Austrian (42)	137	0.85
Belgian (17)	27	0.17
Brazilian (9)	65	0.40
British (10)	41	0.25
Croatian (9)	9	0.06
Czech (75)	178	1.10
Czechoslovakian (31)	31	0.19
Danish (0)	10	0.06
Dutch (0)	10	0.06
Eastern European (199)	199	1.23
English (77)	571	3.53
European (130)	170	1.05
Finnish (0)	11	0.07
French, ex. Basque (11)	255	1.58
French Canadian (0)	20	0.12
German (561)	2,670	16.49
Greek (438)	627	3.87
Hungarian (81)	228	1.41
Irish (904)	3,566	22.03
Israeli (22)	42	0.26
Italian (2,490)	4,938	30.50
Lithuanian (0)	37	0.23
Northern European (62)	62	0.38
Norwegian (13)	95	0.59
Polish (370)	1,262	7.80
Portuguese (9)	24	0.15
Romanian (0)	59	0.36
Russian (418)	1,015	6.27
Scotch-Irish (40)	119	0.74
Scottish (25)	95	0.59
Slovak (0)	16	0.10
Swedish (24)	132	0.82
Swiss (13)	13	0.08
Turkish (0)	10	0.06
Ukrainian (0)	21	0.13
Welsh (0)	74	0.46
West Indian, ex. Hispanic (13)	13	0.08
Jamaican (13)	13	0.08
Yugoslavian (0)	14	0.09

Hispanic Origin	Population	%
Hispanic or Latino (of any race)	922	5.69
Central American, ex. Mexican	129	0.80
Costa Rican	5	0.03
Guatemalan	9	0.06
Honduran	11	0.07
Nicaraguan	5	0.03
Panamanian	2	0.01
Salvadoran	97	0.60
Cuban	71	0.44
Dominican Republic	98	0.60
Mexican	41	0.25
Puerto Rican	276	1.70
South American	214	1.32
Argentinean	28	0.17
Bolivian	8	0.05
Chilean	14	0.09
Colombian	76	0.47
Ecuadorian	55	0.34
Paraguayan	2	0.01
Peruvian	25	0.15
Uruguayan	3	0.02
Other South American	3	0.02
Other Hispanic or Latino	93	0.57

Race*	Population	%
African-American/Black (166)	218	1.34
Not Hispanic (158)	190	1.17
Hispanic (8)	28	0.17
American Indian/Alaska Native (16)	48	0.30
Not Hispanic (9)	36	0.22
Hispanic (7)	12	0.07
Blackfeet (0)	3	0.02
Cherokee (0)	6	0.04
Choctaw (2)	3	0.02
Creek (0)	1	0.01
Mexican American Ind. (1)	1	0.01
Sioux (4)	4	0.02
South American Ind. (1)	1	0.01
Spanish American Ind. (1)	1	0.01
Asian (482)	564	3.48
Not Hispanic (477)	554	3.42
Hispanic (5)	10	0.06
Cambodian (0)	3	0.02
Chinese, ex. Taiwanese (182)	214	1.32
Filipino (31)	48	0.30
Indian (140)	165	1.02
Indonesian (1)	1	0.01
Japanese (10)	12	0.07
Korean (43)	50	0.31
Malaysian (0)	1	0.01
Pakistani (42)	48	0.30
Sri Lankan (2)	3	0.02
Taiwanese (3)	3	0.02
Thai (7)	7	0.04
Vietnamese (5)	9	0.06
Hawaii Native/Pacific Islander (0)	5	0.03
Not Hispanic (0)	3	0.02
Hispanic (0)	2	0.01
Native Hawaiian (0)	1	0.01
White (15,144)	15,334	94.55
Not Hispanic (14,478)	14,609	90.08
Hispanic (666)	725	4.47

Bethlehem

Place Type: Town
County: Albany
Population: 33,656†

Ancestry‡	Population	%
African, Sub-Saharan (29)	52	0.16
African (0)	15	0.04
Nigerian (29)	29	0.09
Zimbabwean (0)	8	0.02
American (1,269)	1,269	3.80
Arab (161)	183	0.55
Arab (15)	15	0.04
Jordanian (67)	67	0.20
Lebanese (32)	32	0.10
Palestinian (12)	12	0.04
Syrian (35)	57	0.17
Armenian (0)	52	0.16
Austrian (11)	133	0.40
Brazilian (33)	77	0.23
British (154)	253	0.76
Canadian (66)	153	0.46
Croatian (0)	14	0.04
Czech (0)	61	0.18
Czechoslovakian (0)	37	0.11
Danish (26)	112	0.34
Dutch (241)	1,495	4.48
Eastern European (248)	260	0.78
English (988)	4,443	13.31
European (499)	552	1.65
Finnish (0)	104	0.31
French, ex. Basque (212)	1,716	5.14
French Canadian (180)	562	1.68
German (1,294)	6,696	20.06
Greek (164)	303	0.91
Guyanese (0)	10	0.03
Hungarian (107)	349	1.05
Iranian (50)	50	0.15
Irish (2,628)	8,696	26.05
Israeli (20)	53	0.16
Italian (2,506)	6,392	19.15
Latvian (12)	22	0.07
Lithuanian (0)	198	0.59
Northern European (128)	128	0.38
Norwegian (96)	319	0.96
Polish (455)	2,141	6.41
Portuguese (13)	93	0.28
Romanian (15)	49	0.15
Russian (418)	965	2.89
Scandinavian (9)	42	0.13
Scotch-Irish (182)	558	1.67
Scottish (150)	810	2.43
Slovak (0)	9	0.03
Slovene (0)	26	0.08
Swedish (125)	590	1.77
Swiss (66)	186	0.56
Ukrainian (109)	174	0.52

*Notes: † The Census 2010 population figure is used to calculate the percentages in the Hispanic Origin and Race categories. Ancestry percentages are based on the 2006-2010 American Community Survey population (not shown); ‡ Numbers in parentheses indicate the number of people reporting a single ancestry; * Numbers in parentheses indicate the number of persons reporting this race alone, not in combination with any other race; Please refer to the Explanation of Data for more information.*

Welsh (44)	376	1.13
West Indian, ex. Hispanic (147)	203	0.61
Haitian (91)	91	0.27
Jamaican (56)	56	0.17
Trinidadian/Tobagonian (0)	56	0.17
Yugoslavian (13)	29	0.09

Hispanic Origin	Population	%
Hispanic or Latino (of any race)	896	2.66
Central American, ex. Mexican	53	0.16
Costa Rican	9	0.03
Guatemalan	16	0.05
Honduran	2	0.01
Nicaraguan	1	<0.01
Panamanian	13	0.04
Salvadoran	10	0.03
Other Central American	2	0.01
Cuban	31	0.09
Dominican Republic	45	0.13
Mexican	143	0.42
Puerto Rican	328	0.97
South American	124	0.37
Argentinean	20	0.06
Bolivian	5	0.01
Chilean	8	0.02
Colombian	56	0.17
Ecuadorian	3	0.01
Peruvian	17	0.05
Uruguayan	2	0.01
Venezuelan	12	0.04
Other South American	1	<0.01
Other Hispanic or Latino	172	0.51

Race*	Population	%
African-American/Black (884)	1,088	3.23
Not Hispanic (828)	1,005	2.99
Hispanic (56)	83	0.25
American Indian/Alaska Native (46)	180	0.53
Not Hispanic (39)	157	0.47
Hispanic (7)	23	0.07
Blackfeet (1)	12	0.04
Canadian/French Am. Ind. (2)	2	0.01
Central American Ind. (0)	1	<0.01
Cherokee (0)	9	0.03
Delaware (0)	1	<0.01
Iroquois (11)	42	0.12
Mexican American Ind. (2)	2	0.01
Navajo (1)	4	0.01
Shoshone (0)	2	0.01
Sioux (0)	1	<0.01
South American Ind. (3)	4	0.01
Asian (1,067)	1,307	3.88
Not Hispanic (1,060)	1,282	3.81
Hispanic (7)	25	0.07
Bangladeshi (7)	8	0.02
Cambodian (4)	5	0.01
Chinese, ex. Taiwanese (377)	422	1.25
Filipino (50)	88	0.26
Indian (324)	392	1.16
Indonesian (1)	6	0.02
Japanese (54)	80	0.24
Korean (83)	106	0.31
Laotian (1)	1	<0.01
Malaysian (2)	2	0.01
Pakistani (75)	83	0.25
Taiwanese (21)	21	0.06
Thai (6)	14	0.04
Vietnamese (25)	32	0.10
Hawaii Native/Pacific Islander (4)	18	0.05
Not Hispanic (4)	14	0.04
Hispanic (0)	4	0.01
Guamanian/Chamorro (0)	3	0.01
Native Hawaiian (3)	8	0.02
White (30,943)	31,426	93.37
Not Hispanic (30,314)	30,738	91.33
Hispanic (629)	688	2.04

Bethpage

Place Type: CDP
County: Nassau
Population: 16,429†

Ancestry‡	Population	%
Afghan (0)	109	0.66
Albanian (0)	44	0.26
American (265)	265	1.59
Arab (50)	113	0.68
Arab (0)	12	0.07
Egyptian (35)	74	0.45
Lebanese (0)	12	0.07
Syrian (15)	15	0.09
Armenian (33)	33	0.20
Austrian (73)	163	0.98
Brazilian (68)	68	0.41
Bulgarian (10)	10	0.06
Cajun (0)	27	0.16
Canadian (13)	24	0.14
Croatian (110)	204	1.23
Czech (22)	62	0.37
Czechoslovakian (20)	30	0.18
Danish (0)	102	0.61
Dutch (38)	63	0.38
English (50)	437	2.63
Estonian (0)	20	0.12
European (47)	47	0.28
Finnish (0)	32	0.19
French, ex. Basque (20)	255	1.53
French Canadian (0)	114	0.69
German (616)	3,335	20.06
Greek (469)	574	3.45
Hungarian (32)	47	0.28
Iranian (28)	75	0.45
Irish (1,236)	4,387	26.38
Italian (3,424)	5,861	35.25
Latvian (0)	12	0.07
Lithuanian (13)	75	0.45
Maltese (0)	12	0.07
Norwegian (23)	167	1.00
Polish (282)	889	5.35
Romanian (0)	54	0.32
Russian (185)	450	2.71
Scandinavian (0)	10	0.06
Scotch-Irish (49)	116	0.70
Scottish (32)	70	0.42
Serbian (0)	67	0.40
Slovak (0)	35	0.21
Swedish (13)	184	1.11
Swiss (18)	56	0.34
Turkish (71)	178	1.07
Ukrainian (37)	114	0.69
Welsh (0)	9	0.05
West Indian, ex. Hispanic (16)	16	0.10
Trinidadian/Tobagonian (16)	16	0.10
Yugoslavian (0)	25	0.15

Hispanic Origin	Population	%
Hispanic or Latino (of any race)	1,152	7.01
Central American, ex. Mexican	156	0.95
Costa Rican	2	0.01
Guatemalan	28	0.17
Honduran	16	0.10
Nicaraguan	5	0.03
Panamanian	4	0.02
Salvadoran	101	0.61
Cuban	36	0.22
Dominican Republic	67	0.41
Mexican	107	0.65
Puerto Rican	336	2.05
South American	340	2.07
Argentinean	20	0.12
Bolivian	11	0.07
Chilean	15	0.09
Colombian	159	0.97
Ecuadorian	94	0.57
Peruvian	33	0.20
Uruguayan	2	0.01
Venezuelan	6	0.04
Other Hispanic or Latino	110	0.67

Race*	Population	%
African-American/Black (101)	151	0.92
Not Hispanic (90)	117	0.71
Hispanic (11)	34	0.21
American Indian/Alaska Native (24)	48	0.29
Not Hispanic (14)	28	0.17
Hispanic (10)	20	0.12
Central American Ind. (5)	5	0.03
Choctaw (1)	1	0.01
Iroquois (7)	11	0.07
South American Ind. (4)	6	0.04
Asian (897)	1,025	6.24
Not Hispanic (895)	1,018	6.20
Hispanic (2)	7	0.04
Bangladeshi (6)	6	0.04
Cambodian (2)	2	0.01
Chinese, ex. Taiwanese (180)	204	1.24
Filipino (86)	115	0.70
Indian (312)	346	2.11
Indonesian (1)	1	0.01
Japanese (16)	19	0.12
Korean (192)	197	1.20
Pakistani (54)	61	0.37
Taiwanese (5)	5	0.03
Thai (9)	11	0.07
Vietnamese (13)	15	0.09
Hawaii Native/Pacific Islander (0)	11	0.07
Not Hispanic (0)	5	0.03
Hispanic (0)	6	0.04
Native Hawaiian (0)	5	0.03
White (14,916)	15,114	92.00
Not Hispanic (14,095)	14,221	86.56
Hispanic (821)	893	5.44

Big Flats

Place Type: Town
County: Chemung
Population: 7,731†

Ancestry‡	Population	%
African, Sub-Saharan (36)	36	0.47
African (36)	36	0.47
American (581)	581	7.65
Arab (16)	16	0.21
Lebanese (16)	16	0.21
Armenian (0)	37	0.49
Austrian (43)	55	0.72
British (0)	11	0.14
Canadian (0)	20	0.26
Dutch (28)	289	3.80
English (313)	1,067	14.05
European (13)	13	0.17
Finnish (41)	52	0.68
French, ex. Basque (13)	326	4.29
French Canadian (0)	142	1.87
German (870)	2,168	28.54
Greek (0)	23	0.30
Hungarian (0)	12	0.16
Irish (422)	1,380	18.17
Italian (367)	1,157	15.23
Norwegian (0)	30	0.39
Pennsylvania German (12)	50	0.66
Polish (218)	475	6.25
Russian (0)	28	0.37
Scotch-Irish (0)	181	2.38
Scottish (0)	169	2.22
Slovak (0)	12	0.16
Swedish (61)	174	2.29
Swiss (0)	9	0.12
Ukrainian (132)	199	2.62
Welsh (71)	185	2.44
West Indian, ex. Hispanic (28)	82	1.08
British West Indian (14)	41	0.54
Jamaican (14)	41	0.54
Yugoslavian (18)	41	0.54

*Notes: † The Census 2010 population figure is used to calculate the percentages in the Hispanic Origin and Race categories. Ancestry percentages are based on the 2006-2010 American Community Survey population (not shown); ‡ Numbers in parentheses indicate the number of people reporting a single ancestry; * Numbers in parentheses indicate the number of persons reporting this race alone, not in combination with any other race; Please refer to the Explanation of Data for more information.*

Hispanic Origin	Population	%
Hispanic or Latino (of any race)	98	1.27
Central American, ex. Mexican	5	0.06
Guatemalan	2	0.03
Panamanian	3	0.04
Cuban	14	0.18
Dominican Republic	2	0.03
Mexican	24	0.31
Puerto Rican	27	0.35
South American	18	0.23
Argentinean	3	0.04
Bolivian	1	0.01
Colombian	7	0.09
Ecuadorian	1	0.01
Other South American	6	0.08
Other Hispanic or Latino	8	0.10

Race*	Population	%
African-American/Black (131)	151	1.95
Not Hispanic (129)	148	1.91
Hispanic (2)	3	0.04
American Indian/Alaska Native (13)	44	0.57
Not Hispanic (13)	42	0.54
Hispanic (0)	2	0.03
Blackfeet (0)	3	0.04
Cherokee (0)	2	0.03
Iroquois (12)	12	0.16
South American Ind. (0)	2	0.03
Asian (207)	248	3.21
Not Hispanic (203)	244	3.16
Hispanic (4)	4	0.05
Bangladeshi (3)	3	0.04
Chinese, ex. Taiwanese (31)	43	0.56
Filipino (10)	20	0.26
Indian (82)	96	1.24
Indonesian (4)	5	0.06
Japanese (2)	3	0.04
Korean (12)	19	0.25
Nepalese (3)	3	0.04
Pakistani (38)	45	0.58
Sri Lankan (1)	1	0.01
Taiwanese (3)	7	0.09
Vietnamese (7)	9	0.12
Hawaii Native/Pacific Islander (2)	8	0.10
Not Hispanic (2)	8	0.10
Samoan (1)	3	0.04
Tongan (0)	1	0.01
White (7,273)	7,355	95.14
Not Hispanic (7,197)	7,274	94.09
Hispanic (76)	81	1.05

Binghamton

Place Type: City
County: Broome
Population: 47,376†

Ancestry‡	Population	%
African, Sub-Saharan (80)	217	0.46
African (76)	199	0.42
Nigerian (4)	4	0.01
South African (0)	14	0.03
American (1,356)	1,356	2.86
Arab (611)	789	1.66
Arab (8)	24	0.05
Egyptian (38)	46	0.10
Jordanian (12)	12	0.03
Lebanese (62)	177	0.37
Moroccan (0)	8	0.02
Syrian (0)	1	<0.01
Other Arab (491)	521	1.10
Armenian (35)	54	0.11
Austrian (10)	61	0.13
British (52)	252	0.53
Bulgarian (7)	7	0.01
Canadian (35)	64	0.14
Carpatho Rusyn (0)	7	0.01
Celtic (0)	10	0.02
Czech (97)	447	0.94
Czechoslovakian (36)	66	0.14
Danish (20)	20	0.04
Dutch (360)	1,525	3.22
Eastern European (10)	26	0.05
English (1,476)	4,619	9.75
European (289)	380	0.80
Finnish (0)	27	0.06
French, ex. Basque (144)	1,771	3.74
French Canadian (77)	220	0.46
German (1,775)	7,716	16.28
Greek (250)	425	0.90
Guyanese (23)	23	0.05
Hungarian (17)	183	0.39
Icelander (46)	46	0.10
Iranian (12)	35	0.07
Irish (3,627)	10,657	22.49
Italian (2,725)	6,312	13.32
Latvian (23)	74	0.16
Lithuanian (102)	286	0.60
Northern European (11)	11	0.02
Norwegian (38)	162	0.34
Pennsylvania German (50)	134	0.28
Polish (730)	2,313	4.88
Romanian (65)	99	0.21
Russian (454)	1,175	2.48
Scandinavian (0)	60	0.13
Scotch-Irish (102)	468	0.99
Scottish (223)	858	1.81
Slavic (78)	130	0.27
Slovak (447)	1,334	2.81
Slovene (16)	31	0.07
Swedish (110)	313	0.66
Swiss (50)	90	0.19
Turkish (73)	73	0.15
Ukrainian (340)	517	1.09
Welsh (80)	483	1.02
West Indian, ex. Hispanic (311)	408	0.86
Belizean (5)	5	0.01
British West Indian (26)	26	0.05
Haitian (76)	76	0.16
Jamaican (137)	206	0.43
Trinidadian/Tobagonian (47)	47	0.10
West Indian (20)	48	0.10
Yugoslavian (161)	161	0.34

Hispanic Origin	Population	%
Hispanic or Latino (of any race)	3,051	6.44
Central American, ex. Mexican	137	0.29
Costa Rican	15	0.03
Guatemalan	22	0.05
Honduran	41	0.09
Nicaraguan	6	0.01
Panamanian	19	0.04
Salvadoran	34	0.07
Cuban	157	0.33
Dominican Republic	240	0.51
Mexican	281	0.59
Puerto Rican	1,754	3.70
South American	205	0.43
Argentinean	29	0.06
Bolivian	6	0.01
Chilean	24	0.05
Colombian	58	0.12
Ecuadorian	38	0.08
Paraguayan	1	<0.01
Peruvian	33	0.07
Uruguayan	1	<0.01
Venezuelan	14	0.03
Other South American	1	<0.01
Other Hispanic or Latino	277	0.58

Race*	Population	%
African-American/Black (5,406)	6,808	14.37
Not Hispanic (4,932)	6,101	12.88
Hispanic (474)	707	1.49
American Indian/Alaska Native (150)	579	1.22
Not Hispanic (126)	492	1.04
Hispanic (24)	87	0.18
Alaska Athabascan *(Ala. Nat.)* (1)	3	0.01
Apache (2)	4	0.01
Blackfeet (2)	30	0.06
Canadian/French Am. Ind. (0)	2	<0.01
Cherokee (14)	99	0.21
Chippewa (4)	8	0.02
Choctaw (1)	3	0.01
Comanche (0)	2	<0.01
Cree (1)	2	<0.01
Creek (0)	1	<0.01
Delaware (1)	6	0.01
Iroquois (14)	79	0.17
Mexican American Ind. (2)	9	0.02
Navajo (0)	6	0.01
Osage (0)	1	<0.01
Seminole (0)	2	<0.01
Sioux (4)	15	0.03
South American Ind. (8)	15	0.03
Spanish American Ind. (1)	1	<0.01
Asian (1,978)	2,336	4.93
Not Hispanic (1,947)	2,274	4.80
Hispanic (31)	62	0.13
Bangladeshi (18)	23	0.05
Burmese (0)	2	<0.01
Cambodian (3)	6	0.01
Chinese, ex. Taiwanese (554)	619	1.31
Filipino (83)	144	0.30
Indian (417)	475	1.00
Indonesian (3)	4	0.01
Japanese (32)	56	0.12
Korean (148)	172	0.36
Laotian (153)	211	0.45
Malaysian (3)	4	0.01
Nepalese (1)	3	0.01
Pakistani (61)	62	0.13
Sri Lankan (3)	3	0.01
Taiwanese (11)	17	0.04
Thai (10)	18	0.04
Vietnamese (418)	467	0.99
Hawaii Native/Pacific Islander (18)	91	0.19
Not Hispanic (14)	76	0.16
Hispanic (4)	15	0.03
Fijian (0)	1	<0.01
Guamanian/Chamorro (7)	17	0.04
Native Hawaiian (1)	10	0.02
Samoan (4)	4	0.01
White (36,773)	38,620	81.52
Not Hispanic (35,518)	37,042	78.19
Hispanic (1,255)	1,578	3.33

Blooming Grove

Place Type: Town
County: Orange
Population: 18,028†

Ancestry‡	Population	%
African, Sub-Saharan (57)	192	1.06
African (0)	135	0.75
Ghanaian (57)	57	0.32
Albanian (55)	55	0.30
American (1,174)	1,174	6.50
Arab (13)	115	0.64
Egyptian (13)	13	0.07
Syrian (0)	89	0.49
Other Arab (0)	13	0.07
Austrian (26)	120	0.66
British (20)	59	0.33
Canadian (27)	109	0.60
Celtic (7)	7	0.04
Croatian (0)	26	0.14
Czech (0)	97	0.54
Czechoslovakian (14)	45	0.25
Danish (0)	27	0.15
Dutch (98)	481	2.66
Eastern European (70)	70	0.39
English (120)	1,147	6.35
European (81)	157	0.87
Finnish (0)	68	0.38
French, ex. Basque (13)	392	2.17
French Canadian (12)	105	0.58
German (401)	2,903	16.08
Greek (37)	100	0.55

*Notes: † The Census 2010 population figure is used to calculate the percentages in the Hispanic Origin and Race categories. Ancestry percentages are based on the 2006-2010 American Community Survey population (not shown); ‡ Numbers in parentheses indicate the number of people reporting a single ancestry; * Numbers in parentheses indicate the number of persons reporting this race alone, not in combination with any other race; Please refer to the Explanation of Data for more information.*

Hungarian (0)	54	0.30
Icelander (16)	62	0.34
Irish (1,685)	4,809	26.64
Italian (1,892)	3,917	21.69
Latvian (36)	49	0.27
Lithuanian (9)	67	0.37
Norwegian (33)	247	1.37
Polish (245)	1,041	5.77
Portuguese (0)	33	0.18
Romanian (11)	31	0.17
Russian (42)	275	1.52
Scotch-Irish (78)	171	0.95
Scottish (36)	216	1.20
Slavic (0)	15	0.08
Slovak (0)	36	0.20
Swedish (146)	237	1.31
Swiss (50)	75	0.42
Ukrainian (223)	307	1.70
Welsh (14)	203	1.12
West Indian, ex. Hispanic (304)	569	3.15
Barbadian (0)	46	0.25
Haitian (0)	14	0.08
Jamaican (227)	270	1.50
U.S. Virgin Islander (0)	11	0.06
West Indian (77)	228	1.26

Hispanic Origin	Population	%
Hispanic or Latino (of any race)	2,709	15.03
Central American, ex. Mexican	144	0.80
Costa Rican	15	0.08
Guatemalan	30	0.17
Honduran	31	0.17
Nicaraguan	6	0.03
Panamanian	21	0.12
Salvadoran	41	0.23
Cuban	115	0.64
Dominican Republic	304	1.69
Mexican	147	0.82
Puerto Rican	1,598	8.86
South American	244	1.35
Argentinean	11	0.06
Bolivian	5	0.03
Chilean	5	0.03
Colombian	100	0.55
Ecuadorian	73	0.40
Paraguayan	2	0.01
Peruvian	21	0.12
Uruguayan	9	0.05
Venezuelan	17	0.09
Other South American	1	0.01
Other Hispanic or Latino	157	0.87

Race*	Population	%
African-American/Black (1,121)	1,346	7.47
Not Hispanic (953)	1,096	6.08
Hispanic (168)	250	1.39
American Indian/Alaska Native (96)	238	1.32
Not Hispanic (59)	173	0.96
Hispanic (37)	65	0.36
Apache (0)	5	0.03
Blackfeet (1)	6	0.03
Canadian/French Am. Ind. (1)	4	0.02
Cherokee (6)	17	0.09
Chippewa (0)	2	0.01
Delaware (29)	51	0.28
Inupiat *(Alaska Native)* (2)	2	0.01
Iroquois (9)	18	0.10
Mexican American Ind. (4)	5	0.03
Navajo (0)	2	0.01
Sioux (0)	1	0.01
South American Ind. (12)	22	0.12
Asian (405)	527	2.92
Not Hispanic (392)	496	2.75
Hispanic (13)	31	0.17
Cambodian (1)	1	0.01
Chinese, ex. Taiwanese (97)	134	0.74
Filipino (98)	124	0.69
Indian (87)	101	0.56
Indonesian (4)	9	0.05
Japanese (14)	33	0.18
Korean (51)	62	0.34
Nepalese (1)	1	0.01
Pakistani (14)	14	0.08
Sri Lankan (0)	1	0.01
Thai (4)	6	0.03
Vietnamese (21)	28	0.16
Hawaii Native/Pacific Islander (1)	6	0.03
Not Hispanic (1)	2	0.01
Hispanic (0)	4	0.02
Native Hawaiian (0)	2	0.01
White (15,239)	15,637	86.74
Not Hispanic (13,577)	13,833	76.73
Hispanic (1,662)	1,804	10.01

Bohemia

Place Type: CDP
County: Suffolk
Population: 10,180†

Ancestry‡	Population	%
African, Sub-Saharan (0)	13	0.13
African (0)	13	0.13
American (157)	157	1.59
Arab (41)	73	0.74
Arab (0)	15	0.15
Lebanese (10)	10	0.10
Other Arab (31)	48	0.48
Armenian (0)	16	0.16
Austrian (49)	63	0.64
Belgian (0)	24	0.24
Canadian (0)	20	0.20
Czech (56)	271	2.74
Czechoslovakian (48)	106	1.07
Dutch (14)	130	1.31
Eastern European (13)	13	0.13
English (124)	399	4.03
Estonian (55)	55	0.56
European (12)	12	0.12
Finnish (0)	15	0.15
French, ex. Basque (0)	244	2.47
French Canadian (0)	26	0.26
German (415)	2,662	26.89
Greek (18)	30	0.30
Hungarian (14)	192	1.94
Irish (595)	2,906	29.36
Italian (1,458)	3,670	37.08
Latvian (13)	27	0.27
Lithuanian (15)	64	0.65
Maltese (14)	63	0.64
Norwegian (11)	34	0.34
Polish (150)	863	8.72
Portuguese (66)	66	0.67
Russian (51)	320	3.23
Scandinavian (0)	38	0.38
Scotch-Irish (31)	189	1.91
Scottish (30)	236	2.38
Slovak (24)	93	0.94
Swedish (30)	274	2.77
Swiss (0)	46	0.46
Ukrainian (28)	100	1.01
Welsh (0)	15	0.15
West Indian, ex. Hispanic (29)	47	0.47
Jamaican (13)	31	0.31
West Indian (16)	16	0.16

Hispanic Origin	Population	%
Hispanic or Latino (of any race)	723	7.10
Central American, ex. Mexican	85	0.83
Costa Rican	2	0.02
Guatemalan	15	0.15
Honduran	9	0.09
Panamanian	12	0.12
Salvadoran	47	0.46
Cuban	29	0.28
Dominican Republic	30	0.29
Mexican	38	0.37
Puerto Rican	326	3.20
South American	158	1.55
Argentinean	13	0.13
Bolivian	4	0.04
Chilean	8	0.08
Colombian	36	0.35
Ecuadorian	43	0.42
Peruvian	44	0.43
Uruguayan	3	0.03
Venezuelan	7	0.07
Other Hispanic or Latino	57	0.56

Race*	Population	%
African-American/Black (102)	137	1.35
Not Hispanic (91)	116	1.14
Hispanic (11)	21	0.21
American Indian/Alaska Native (9)	30	0.29
Not Hispanic (7)	22	0.22
Hispanic (2)	8	0.08
Cherokee (0)	3	0.03
Mexican American Ind. (2)	5	0.05
South American Ind. (1)	1	0.01
Asian (232)	269	2.64
Not Hispanic (232)	260	2.55
Hispanic (0)	9	0.09
Bangladeshi (4)	4	0.04
Burmese (0)	1	0.01
Cambodian (1)	1	0.01
Chinese, ex. Taiwanese (62)	71	0.70
Filipino (8)	16	0.16
Indian (99)	114	1.12
Japanese (2)	2	0.02
Korean (4)	4	0.04
Pakistani (33)	47	0.46
Taiwanese (1)	3	0.03
Thai (1)	1	0.01
Vietnamese (9)	10	0.10
Hawaii Native/Pacific Islander (1)	1	0.01
Hispanic (1)	1	0.01
White (9,561)	9,685	95.14
Not Hispanic (9,061)	9,116	89.55
Hispanic (500)	569	5.59

Boston

Place Type: Town
County: Erie
Population: 8,023†

Ancestry‡	Population	%
Albanian (0)	9	0.11
American (163)	163	2.05
Armenian (0)	11	0.14
Austrian (11)	20	0.25
British (11)	11	0.14
Canadian (14)	27	0.34
Croatian (0)	44	0.55
Czech (14)	53	0.67
Dutch (0)	91	1.14
English (35)	1,106	13.89
European (19)	19	0.24
French, ex. Basque (0)	213	2.67
French Canadian (37)	72	0.90
German (978)	3,177	39.89
Greek (0)	13	0.16
Hungarian (55)	104	1.31
Irish (329)	2,078	26.09
Italian (221)	981	12.32
Macedonian (9)	9	0.11
Northern European (24)	24	0.30
Norwegian (0)	45	0.57
Polish (855)	1,848	23.20
Portuguese (0)	39	0.49
Russian (0)	57	0.72
Scotch-Irish (84)	172	2.16
Scottish (46)	188	2.36
Serbian (10)	10	0.13
Slovak (8)	54	0.68
Swedish (0)	71	0.89
Ukrainian (0)	61	0.77
Welsh (28)	180	2.26
West Indian, ex. Hispanic (13)	13	0.16
Jamaican (13)	13	0.16

SECTION TWO

*Notes: † The Census 2010 population figure is used to calculate the percentages in the Hispanic Origin and Race categories. Ancestry percentages are based on the 2006-2010 American Community Survey population (not shown); ‡ Numbers in parentheses indicate the number of people reporting a single ancestry; * Numbers in parentheses indicate the number of persons reporting this race alone, not in combination with any other race; Please refer to the Explanation of Data for more information.*

Hispanic Origin	Population	%
Hispanic or Latino (of any race)	78	0.97
Central American, ex. Mexican	2	0.02
Guatemalan	1	0.01
Nicaraguan	1	0.01
Cuban	4	0.05
Dominican Republic	2	0.02
Mexican	20	0.25
Puerto Rican	26	0.32
South American	11	0.14
Bolivian	1	0.01
Colombian	9	0.11
Peruvian	1	0.01
Other Hispanic or Latino	13	0.16

Race*	Population	%
African-American/Black (10)	29	0.36
Not Hispanic (10)	28	0.35
Hispanic (0)	1	0.01
American Indian/Alaska Native (19)	38	0.47
Not Hispanic (18)	37	0.46
Hispanic (1)	1	0.01
Blackfeet (0)	1	0.01
Cherokee (0)	1	0.01
Iroquois (15)	21	0.26
Navajo (1)	5	0.06
Asian (25)	36	0.45
Not Hispanic (25)	36	0.45
Cambodian (2)	2	0.02
Chinese, ex. Taiwanese (4)	4	0.05
Filipino (3)	3	0.04
Indian (4)	4	0.05
Japanese (4)	10	0.12
Korean (1)	1	0.01
Pakistani (5)	5	0.06
Thai (2)	6	0.07
Hawaii Native/Pacific Islander (2)	2	0.02
Not Hispanic (2)	2	0.02
Guamanian/Chamorro (1)	1	0.01
Samoan (1)	1	0.01
White (7,894)	7,946	99.04
Not Hispanic (7,835)	7,881	98.23
Hispanic (59)	65	0.81

Brentwood

Place Type: CDP
County: Suffolk
Population: 60,664†

Ancestry‡	Population	%
Afghan (50)	68	0.12
African, Sub-Saharan (301)	336	0.61
African (86)	106	0.19
Ghanaian (45)	45	0.08
Nigerian (90)	105	0.19
Other Sub-Saharan African (80)	80	0.15
American (588)	588	1.07
Arab (82)	92	0.17
Arab (25)	25	0.05
Egyptian (20)	20	0.04
Lebanese (0)	10	0.02
Other Arab (37)	37	0.07
Australian (0)	8	0.01
Austrian (19)	80	0.15
Belgian (0)	9	0.02
Brazilian (418)	418	0.76
British (46)	78	0.14
Canadian (0)	8	0.01
Czech (0)	38	0.07
Czechoslovakian (8)	25	0.05
Dutch (0)	96	0.18
English (338)	850	1.55
Estonian (0)	17	0.03
European (32)	43	0.08
Finnish (8)	11	0.02
French, ex. Basque (57)	181	0.33
French Canadian (10)	48	0.09
German (310)	1,994	3.64
Greek (37)	59	0.11
Guyanese (126)	138	0.25
Hungarian (16)	42	0.08
Irish (934)	2,578	4.70
Italian (1,517)	3,236	5.90
Lithuanian (9)	25	0.05
Maltese (17)	17	0.03
Norwegian (24)	72	0.13
Polish (164)	623	1.14
Portuguese (504)	524	0.96
Russian (61)	180	0.33
Scandinavian (7)	29	0.05
Scotch-Irish (39)	161	0.29
Scottish (20)	92	0.17
Serbian (0)	10	0.02
Slovak (8)	8	0.01
Swedish (39)	210	0.38
Swiss (0)	14	0.03
Turkish (0)	5	0.01
Ukrainian (0)	10	0.02
West Indian, ex. Hispanic (3,143)	3,472	6.33
Barbadian (5)	5	0.01
British West Indian (37)	58	0.11
Haitian (2,072)	2,162	3.94
Jamaican (622)	771	1.41
Trinidadian/Tobagonian (104)	152	0.28
West Indian (303)	324	0.59
Yugoslavian (0)	10	0.02

Hispanic Origin	Population	%
Hispanic or Latino (of any race)	41,529	68.46
Central American, ex. Mexican	19,957	32.90
Costa Rican	85	0.14
Guatemalan	1,553	2.56
Honduran	2,062	3.40
Nicaraguan	87	0.14
Panamanian	148	0.24
Salvadoran	15,946	26.29
Other Central American	76	0.13
Cuban	223	0.37
Dominican Republic	4,205	6.93
Mexican	1,193	1.97
Puerto Rican	6,125	10.10
South American	6,350	10.47
Argentinean	203	0.33
Bolivian	79	0.13
Chilean	153	0.25
Colombian	2,083	3.43
Ecuadorian	1,985	3.27
Paraguayan	36	0.06
Peruvian	1,610	2.65
Uruguayan	80	0.13
Venezuelan	113	0.19
Other South American	8	0.01
Other Hispanic or Latino	3,476	5.73

Race*	Population	%
African-American/Black (9,934)	11,026	18.18
Not Hispanic (8,344)	8,888	14.65
Hispanic (1,590)	2,138	3.52
American Indian/Alaska Native (710)	1,135	1.87
Not Hispanic (132)	326	0.54
Hispanic (578)	809	1.33
Alaska Athabascan *(Ala. Nat.)* (0)	1	<0.01
Blackfeet (5)	6	0.01
Central American Ind. (27)	36	0.06
Cherokee (16)	76	0.13
Chippewa (4)	5	0.01
Comanche (0)	7	0.01
Crow (11)	11	0.02
Iroquois (14)	17	0.03
Lumbee (2)	2	<0.01
Mexican American Ind. (48)	72	0.12
Navajo (3)	4	0.01
Osage (0)	1	<0.01
Pima (1)	1	<0.01
Pueblo (4)	5	0.01
Sioux (2)	2	<0.01
South American Ind. (63)	87	0.14
Spanish American Ind. (41)	52	0.09
Tlingit-Haida *(Alaska Native)* (3)	3	<0.01
Yaqui (1)	1	<0.01
Asian (1,193)	1,544	2.55
Not Hispanic (1,101)	1,349	2.22
Hispanic (92)	195	0.32
Bangladeshi (33)	37	0.06
Burmese (1)	1	<0.01
Cambodian (5)	5	0.01
Chinese, ex. Taiwanese (95)	141	0.23
Filipino (120)	163	0.27
Indian (516)	647	1.07
Indonesian (10)	12	0.02
Japanese (3)	15	0.02
Korean (11)	17	0.03
Laotian (8)	8	0.01
Malaysian (1)	3	<0.01
Pakistani (246)	268	0.44
Sri Lankan (6)	10	0.02
Taiwanese (4)	4	0.01
Thai (30)	38	0.06
Vietnamese (47)	57	0.09
Hawaii Native/Pacific Islander (29)	134	0.22
Not Hispanic (11)	59	0.10
Hispanic (18)	75	0.12
Fijian (0)	1	<0.01
Guamanian/Chamorro (8)	8	0.01
Native Hawaiian (8)	17	0.03
Samoan (1)	4	0.01
Tongan (0)	2	<0.01
White (29,344)	31,986	52.73
Not Hispanic (8,554)	8,973	14.79
Hispanic (20,790)	23,013	37.94

Briarcliff Manor

Place Type: Village
County: Westchester
Population: 7,867†

Ancestry‡	Population	%
African, Sub-Saharan (14)	14	0.17
African (14)	14	0.17
Albanian (59)	59	0.74
American (413)	413	5.15
Arab (162)	222	2.77
Arab (113)	113	1.41
Egyptian (0)	11	0.14
Lebanese (0)	24	0.30
Syrian (0)	12	0.15
Other Arab (49)	62	0.77
Austrian (19)	238	2.97
Belgian (0)	11	0.14
Brazilian (64)	64	0.80
British (115)	159	1.98
Bulgarian (34)	34	0.42
Canadian (0)	26	0.32
Czech (0)	47	0.59
Czechoslovakian (7)	7	0.09
Danish (0)	9	0.11
Dutch (0)	21	0.26
Eastern European (209)	225	2.80
English (145)	517	6.44
Estonian (0)	12	0.15
European (46)	71	0.89
Finnish (11)	26	0.32
French, ex. Basque (46)	138	1.72
German (157)	799	9.96
Greek (48)	48	0.60
Hungarian (82)	125	1.56
Irish (469)	1,711	21.33
Israeli (42)	42	0.52
Italian (775)	1,839	22.92
Latvian (0)	23	0.29
Lithuanian (0)	15	0.19
Macedonian (0)	25	0.31
Northern European (6)	6	0.07
Norwegian (0)	20	0.25
Pennsylvania German (0)	10	0.12
Polish (327)	690	8.60
Romanian (30)	104	1.30
Russian (324)	730	9.10

*Notes: † The Census 2010 population figure is used to calculate the percentages in the Hispanic Origin and Race categories. Ancestry percentages are based on the 2006-2010 American Community Survey population (not shown); ‡ Numbers in parentheses indicate the number of people reporting a single ancestry; * Numbers in parentheses indicate the number of persons reporting this race alone, not in combination with any other race; Please refer to the Explanation of Data for more information.*

Ancestry	Population	%
Scotch-Irish (54)	159	1.98
Scottish (29)	110	1.37
Slavic (0)	27	0.34
Slovak (0)	24	0.30
Swedish (0)	26	0.32
Swiss (7)	95	1.18
Ukrainian (15)	26	0.32
Welsh (0)	32	0.40
West Indian, ex. Hispanic (55)	55	0.69
British West Indian (12)	12	0.15
Jamaican (43)	43	0.54

Hispanic Origin	Population	%
Hispanic or Latino (of any race)	414	5.26
Central American, ex. Mexican	19	0.24
Costa Rican	1	0.01
Guatemalan	8	0.10
Honduran	2	0.03
Nicaraguan	4	0.05
Panamanian	3	0.04
Salvadoran	1	0.01
Cuban	37	0.47
Dominican Republic	44	0.56
Mexican	24	0.31
Puerto Rican	113	1.44
South American	116	1.47
Argentinean	10	0.13
Bolivian	3	0.04
Chilean	14	0.18
Colombian	32	0.41
Ecuadorian	42	0.53
Paraguayan	1	0.01
Peruvian	6	0.08
Uruguayan	2	0.03
Venezuelan	6	0.08
Other Hispanic or Latino	61	0.78

Race*	Population	%
African-American/Black (265)	317	4.03
Not Hispanic (247)	284	3.61
Hispanic (18)	33	0.42
American Indian/Alaska Native (6)	15	0.19
Not Hispanic (3)	8	0.10
Hispanic (3)	7	0.09
Central American Ind. (0)	1	0.01
Cherokee (0)	1	0.01
Mexican American Ind. (1)	1	0.01
Sioux (0)	2	0.03
Asian (546)	620	7.88
Not Hispanic (541)	603	7.66
Hispanic (5)	17	0.22
Chinese, ex. Taiwanese (195)	224	2.85
Filipino (26)	41	0.52
Indian (167)	179	2.28
Indonesian (1)	3	0.04
Japanese (27)	38	0.48
Korean (75)	84	1.07
Malaysian (1)	1	0.01
Pakistani (23)	24	0.31
Taiwanese (10)	10	0.13
Thai (1)	3	0.04
Vietnamese (4)	5	0.06
Hawaii Native/Pacific Islander (2)	6	0.08
Not Hispanic (2)	6	0.08
Guamanian/Chamorro (1)	1	0.01
Native Hawaiian (1)	1	0.01
White (6,796)	6,924	88.01
Not Hispanic (6,543)	6,638	84.38
Hispanic (253)	286	3.64

Brighton

Place Type: CDP/Town
County: Monroe
Population: 36,609†

Ancestry‡	Population	%
African, Sub-Saharan (334)	350	0.96
African (37)	53	0.15
Ethiopian (79)	79	0.22
South African (58)	58	0.16
Sudanese (47)	47	0.13
Other Sub-Saharan African (113)	113	0.31
Albanian (32)	49	0.13
Alsatian (0)	22	0.06
American (1,266)	1,266	3.48
Arab (234)	346	0.95
Egyptian (22)	22	0.06
Iraqi (0)	40	0.11
Lebanese (0)	43	0.12
Moroccan (154)	154	0.42
Palestinian (50)	79	0.22
Other Arab (8)	8	0.02
Armenian (9)	70	0.19
Australian (12)	12	0.03
Austrian (46)	208	0.57
Belgian (23)	68	0.19
Brazilian (0)	11	0.03
British (142)	242	0.67
Canadian (60)	194	0.53
Czech (12)	130	0.36
Czechoslovakian (14)	99	0.27
Danish (62)	113	0.31
Dutch (201)	1,100	3.02
Eastern European (343)	419	1.15
English (1,570)	5,361	14.73
Estonian (0)	17	0.05
European (574)	638	1.75
Finnish (14)	70	0.19
French, ex. Basque (91)	970	2.67
French Canadian (97)	210	0.58
German (1,313)	6,519	17.92
Greek (174)	436	1.20
Hungarian (67)	339	0.93
Iranian (36)	36	0.10
Irish (1,487)	6,457	17.75
Israeli (143)	204	0.56
Italian (2,092)	4,756	13.07
Latvian (35)	73	0.20
Lithuanian (77)	257	0.71
Maltese (0)	12	0.03
Northern European (13)	13	0.04
Norwegian (73)	266	0.73
Pennsylvania German (26)	49	0.13
Polish (620)	2,293	6.30
Portuguese (10)	86	0.24
Romanian (131)	275	0.76
Russian (970)	1,915	5.26
Scandinavian (8)	60	0.16
Scotch-Irish (179)	570	1.57
Scottish (145)	741	2.04
Slavic (0)	12	0.03
Slovak (64)	100	0.27
Slovene (0)	11	0.03
Swedish (76)	381	1.05
Swiss (10)	160	0.44
Turkish (154)	239	0.66
Ukrainian (493)	940	2.58
Welsh (67)	317	0.87
West Indian, ex. Hispanic (134)	244	0.67
Haitian (67)	84	0.23
Jamaican (0)	81	0.22
Trinidadian/Tobagonian (17)	17	0.05
West Indian (50)	62	0.17
Yugoslavian (105)	105	0.29

Hispanic Origin	Population	%
Hispanic or Latino (of any race)	1,199	3.28
Central American, ex. Mexican	83	0.23
Costa Rican	16	0.04
Guatemalan	22	0.06
Honduran	11	0.03
Nicaraguan	21	0.06
Panamanian	3	0.01
Salvadoran	10	0.03
Cuban	71	0.19
Dominican Republic	58	0.16
Mexican	156	0.43
Puerto Rican	452	1.23
South American	262	0.72
Argentinean	29	0.08
Bolivian	6	0.02
Chilean	26	0.07
Colombian	74	0.20
Ecuadorian	34	0.09
Paraguayan	8	0.02
Peruvian	63	0.17
Uruguayan	1	<0.01
Venezuelan	20	0.05
Other South American	1	<0.01
Other Hispanic or Latino	117	0.32

Race*	Population	%
African-American/Black (1,860)	2,177	5.95
Not Hispanic (1,802)	2,065	5.64
Hispanic (58)	112	0.31
American Indian/Alaska Native (53)	210	0.57
Not Hispanic (43)	161	0.44
Hispanic (10)	49	0.13
Alaska Athabascan (*Ala. Nat.*) (1)	5	0.01
Blackfeet (0)	7	0.02
Cherokee (1)	25	0.07
Chippewa (0)	3	0.01
Choctaw (0)	2	0.01
Cree (1)	4	0.01
Creek (0)	1	<0.01
Iroquois (9)	23	0.06
Mexican American Ind. (1)	9	0.02
Navajo (3)	5	0.01
Pueblo (1)	1	<0.01
Seminole (1)	1	<0.01
Shoshone (0)	1	<0.01
Sioux (1)	6	0.02
South American Ind. (2)	18	0.05
Asian (4,337)	4,813	13.15
Not Hispanic (4,324)	4,781	13.06
Hispanic (13)	32	0.09
Bangladeshi (23)	31	0.08
Burmese (12)	12	0.03
Cambodian (14)	16	0.04
Chinese, ex. Taiwanese (1,268)	1,380	3.77
Filipino (89)	123	0.34
Indian (1,861)	1,977	5.40
Indonesian (11)	19	0.05
Japanese (153)	196	0.54
Korean (405)	449	1.23
Laotian (24)	31	0.08
Malaysian (18)	18	0.05
Nepalese (14)	15	0.04
Pakistani (117)	120	0.33
Sri Lankan (40)	46	0.13
Taiwanese (76)	96	0.26
Thai (12)	17	0.05
Vietnamese (93)	111	0.30
Hawaii Native/Pacific Islander (12)	29	0.08
Not Hispanic (12)	28	0.08
Hispanic (0)	1	<0.01
Guamanian/Chamorro (0)	3	0.01
Native Hawaiian (2)	10	0.03
Samoan (0)	1	<0.01
Tongan (1)	1	<0.01
White (29,203)	29,937	81.77
Not Hispanic (28,400)	29,032	79.30
Hispanic (803)	905	2.47

Brockport

Place Type: Village
County: Monroe
Population: 8,366†

Ancestry‡	Population	%
African, Sub-Saharan (54)	136	1.62
African (54)	136	1.62
American (322)	322	3.83
Arab (7)	39	0.46
Egyptian (7)	7	0.08
Moroccan (0)	19	0.23
Other Arab (0)	13	0.15
Austrian (0)	32	0.38

*Notes: † The Census 2010 population figure is used to calculate the percentages in the Hispanic Origin and Race categories. Ancestry percentages are based on the 2006-2010 American Community Survey population (not shown); ‡ Numbers in parentheses indicate the number of people reporting a single ancestry; * Numbers in parentheses indicate the number of persons reporting this race alone, not in combination with any other race; Please refer to the Explanation of Data for more information.*

Brazilian (22)	22	0.26
Bulgarian (11)	24	0.29
Canadian (68)	112	1.33
Czech (0)	28	0.33
Danish (38)	38	0.45
Dutch (16)	205	2.44
Eastern European (10)	10	0.12
English (329)	1,245	14.81
European (94)	94	1.12
Finnish (0)	13	0.15
French, ex. Basque (28)	296	3.52
French Canadian (76)	160	1.90
German (336)	2,044	24.31
Greek (0)	73	0.87
Hungarian (0)	120	1.43
Irish (338)	1,757	20.90
Italian (617)	1,704	20.27
Norwegian (17)	59	0.70
Polish (119)	600	7.14
Portuguese (0)	16	0.19
Romanian (16)	22	0.26
Russian (0)	93	1.11
Scotch-Irish (63)	151	1.80
Scottish (43)	294	3.50
Swedish (0)	65	0.77
Swiss (0)	18	0.21
Ukrainian (55)	143	1.70
Welsh (0)	83	0.99
West Indian, ex. Hispanic (49)	61	0.73
Belizean (19)	19	0.23
Jamaican (30)	42	0.50
Yugoslavian (11)	36	0.43

Hispanic Origin	Population	%
Hispanic or Latino (of any race)	319	3.81
Central American, ex. Mexican	10	0.12
Costa Rican	2	0.02
Guatemalan	4	0.05
Honduran	1	0.01
Nicaraguan	1	0.01
Salvadoran	2	0.02
Cuban	14	0.17
Dominican Republic	26	0.31
Mexican	96	1.15
Puerto Rican	108	1.29
South American	34	0.41
Argentinean	2	0.02
Bolivian	2	0.02
Chilean	3	0.04
Colombian	14	0.17
Ecuadorian	7	0.08
Paraguayan	1	0.01
Peruvian	4	0.05
Uruguayan	1	0.01
Other Hispanic or Latino	31	0.37

Race*	Population	%
African-American/Black (322)	408	4.88
Not Hispanic (302)	373	4.46
Hispanic (20)	35	0.42
American Indian/Alaska Native (24)	70	0.84
Not Hispanic (14)	58	0.69
Hispanic (10)	12	0.14
Blackfeet (0)	3	0.04
Canadian/French Am. Ind. (4)	4	0.05
Cherokee (1)	8	0.10
Cheyenne (1)	1	0.01
Creek (0)	1	0.01
Inupiat *(Alaska Native)* (0)	1	0.01
Iroquois (10)	14	0.17
Mexican American Ind. (1)	1	0.01
Navajo (0)	1	0.01
Seminole (0)	1	0.01
South American Ind. (0)	1	0.01
Asian (107)	141	1.69
Not Hispanic (105)	136	1.63
Hispanic (2)	5	0.06
Chinese, ex. Taiwanese (20)	23	0.27
Filipino (7)	15	0.18
Indian (25)	34	0.41
Indonesian (2)	2	0.02
Japanese (11)	13	0.16
Korean (30)	35	0.42
Laotian (1)	1	0.01
Vietnamese (5)	5	0.06
Hawaii Native/Pacific Islander (5)	14	0.17
Not Hispanic (5)	13	0.16
Hispanic (0)	1	0.01
Guamanian/Chamorro (1)	2	0.02
Marshallese (0)	1	0.01
Native Hawaiian (3)	6	0.07
Samoan (0)	1	0.01
Tongan (1)	1	0.01
White (7,674)	7,803	93.27
Not Hispanic (7,487)	7,594	90.77
Hispanic (187)	209	2.50

Bronx

Place Type: Borough
County: Bronx
Population: 1,385,108†

Ancestry‡	Population	%
Afghan (14)	14	<0.01
African, Sub-Saharan (50,131)	55,928	4.10
African (19,345)	22,647	1.66
Cape Verdean (49)	108	0.01
Ethiopian (790)	945	0.07
Ghanaian (13,163)	13,490	0.99
Kenyan (12)	24	<0.01
Liberian (365)	450	0.03
Nigerian (4,896)	5,538	0.41
Senegalese (956)	1,068	0.08
Sierra Leonean (759)	759	0.06
Somalian (11)	35	<0.01
South African (29)	68	<0.01
Sudanese (88)	149	0.01
Zimbabwean (108)	108	0.01
Other Sub-Saharan African (9,560)	10,539	0.77
Albanian (7,460)	7,835	0.57
American (16,297)	16,297	1.19
Arab (4,063)	5,008	0.37
Arab (1,481)	1,719	0.13
Egyptian (495)	718	0.05
Iraqi (64)	73	0.01
Jordanian (8)	8	<0.01
Lebanese (229)	347	0.03
Moroccan (526)	667	0.05
Palestinian (28)	28	<0.01
Syrian (44)	192	0.01
Other Arab (1,188)	1,256	0.09
Armenian (128)	237	0.02
Assyrian/Chaldean/Syriac (0)	18	<0.01
Australian (8)	21	<0.01
Austrian (539)	1,868	0.14
Basque (66)	109	0.01
Belgian (52)	131	0.01
Brazilian (276)	397	0.03
British (517)	1,115	0.08
Bulgarian (506)	521	0.04
Canadian (197)	375	0.03
Carpatho Rusyn (0)	12	<0.01
Celtic (1)	13	<0.01
Croatian (91)	219	0.02
Cypriot (12)	38	<0.01
Czech (99)	388	0.03
Czechoslovakian (90)	226	0.02
Danish (17)	385	0.03
Dutch (314)	1,920	0.14
Eastern European (1,425)	1,646	0.12
English (1,821)	7,038	0.52
Estonian (70)	85	0.01
European (1,845)	2,270	0.17
Finnish (89)	291	0.02
French, ex. Basque (909)	4,971	0.36
French Canadian (102)	403	0.03
German (3,729)	16,487	1.21
German Russian (7)	30	<0.01
Greek (2,499)	3,607	0.26
Guyanese (10,276)	11,837	0.87
Hungarian (966)	2,427	0.18
Icelander (6)	6	<0.01
Iranian (187)	248	0.02
Irish (18,712)	38,479	2.82
Israeli (427)	618	0.05
Italian (38,592)	57,527	4.21
Latvian (92)	103	0.01
Lithuanian (167)	547	0.04
Macedonian (628)	628	0.05
Maltese (16)	45	<0.01
New Zealander (23)	23	<0.01
Northern European (25)	25	<0.01
Norwegian (260)	773	0.06
Polish (3,429)	7,834	0.57
Portuguese (474)	1,113	0.08
Romanian (691)	1,164	0.09
Russian (4,351)	8,064	0.59
Scandinavian (102)	155	0.01
Scotch-Irish (516)	1,601	0.12
Scottish (388)	1,570	0.11
Serbian (154)	187	0.01
Slavic (15)	90	0.01
Slovak (87)	226	0.02
Slovene (10)	45	<0.01
Soviet Union (12)	12	<0.01
Swedish (119)	549	0.04
Swiss (24)	166	0.01
Turkish (589)	686	0.05
Ukrainian (970)	1,608	0.12
Welsh (101)	530	0.04
West Indian, ex. Hispanic (93,323)	107,527	7.87
Bahamian (165)	208	0.02
Barbadian (1,285)	1,612	0.12
Belizean (1,253)	1,493	0.11
Bermudan (101)	198	0.01
British West Indian (5,959)	7,136	0.52
Dutch West Indian (127)	172	0.01
Haitian (3,891)	4,652	0.34
Jamaican (58,387)	64,222	4.70
Trinidadian/Tobagonian (3,695)	4,811	0.35
U.S. Virgin Islander (737)	952	0.07
West Indian (17,683)	21,941	1.61
Other West Indian (40)	130	0.01
Yugoslavian (1,275)	1,480	0.11

Hispanic Origin	Population	%
Hispanic or Latino (of any race)	741,413	53.53
Central American, ex. Mexican	34,492	2.49
Costa Rican	1,095	0.08
Guatemalan	4,645	0.34
Honduran	17,990	1.30
Nicaraguan	2,342	0.17
Panamanian	2,372	0.17
Salvadoran	5,469	0.39
Other Central American	579	0.04
Cuban	8,785	0.63
Dominican Republic	240,987	17.40
Mexican	71,194	5.14
Puerto Rican	298,921	21.58
South American	35,463	2.56
Argentinean	1,117	0.08
Bolivian	227	0.02
Chilean	646	0.05
Colombian	4,635	0.33
Ecuadorian	23,206	1.68
Paraguayan	223	0.02
Peruvian	3,596	0.26
Uruguayan	148	0.01
Venezuelan	1,296	0.09
Other South American	369	0.03
Other Hispanic or Latino	51,571	3.72

Race*	Population	%
African-American/Black (505,200)	541,622	39.10
Not Hispanic (416,695)	427,134	30.84
Hispanic (88,505)	114,488	8.27
American Indian/Alaska Native (18,260)	32,011	2.31
Not Hispanic (3,460)	7,638	0.55
Hispanic (14,800)	24,373	1.76

*Notes: † The Census 2010 population figure is used to calculate the percentages in the Hispanic Origin and Race categories. Ancestry percentages are based on the 2006-2010 American Community Survey population (not shown); ‡ Numbers in parentheses indicate the number of people reporting a single ancestry; * Numbers in parentheses indicate the number of persons reporting this race alone, not in combination with any other race; Please refer to the Explanation of Data for more information.*

Alaska Athabascan *(Ala. Nat.)* (4)	8	<0.01
Aleut *(Alaska Native)* (0)	3	<0.01
Apache (30)	99	0.01
Arapaho (2)	3	<0.01
Blackfeet (43)	310	0.02
Canadian/French Am. Ind. (13)	25	<0.01
Central American Ind. (2,274)	4,520	0.33
Cherokee (247)	1,312	0.09
Cheyenne (2)	5	<0.01
Chickasaw (6)	16	<0.01
Chippewa (25)	38	<0.01
Choctaw (4)	43	<0.01
Colville (0)	2	<0.01
Comanche (8)	26	<0.01
Cree (1)	16	<0.01
Creek (7)	47	<0.01
Crow (1)	16	<0.01
Delaware (1)	10	<0.01
Hopi (0)	2	<0.01
Houma (12)	12	<0.01
Inupiat *(Alaska Native)* (11)	15	<0.01
Iroquois (81)	170	0.01
Kiowa (1)	1	<0.01
Lumbee (3)	6	<0.01
Menominee (1)	3	<0.01
Mexican American Ind. (714)	963	0.07
Navajo (24)	42	<0.01
Osage (2)	3	<0.01
Ottawa (0)	1	<0.01
Paiute (0)	5	<0.01
Pima (0)	1	<0.01
Potawatomi (1)	2	<0.01
Pueblo (177)	382	0.03
Seminole (6)	50	<0.01
Shoshone (0)	8	<0.01
Sioux (46)	82	0.01
South American Ind. (1,568)	2,938	0.21
Spanish American Ind. (709)	992	0.07
Tlingit-Haida *(Alaska Native)* (1)	11	<0.01
Tohono O'Odham (4)	9	<0.01
Ute (2)	5	<0.01
Yakama (3)	3	<0.01
Yaqui (4)	5	<0.01
Yuman (1)	2	<0.01
Yup'ik *(Alaska Native)* (1)	6	<0.01
Asian (49,609)	59,085	4.27
Not Hispanic (47,335)	53,458	3.86
Hispanic (2,274)	5,627	0.41
Bangladeshi (7,323)	8,623	0.62
Bhutanese (74)	104	0.01
Burmese (71)	81	0.01
Cambodian (1,055)	1,188	0.09
Chinese, ex. Taiwanese (6,644)	8,112	0.59
Filipino (5,576)	6,456	0.47
Hmong (1)	3	<0.01
Indian (15,865)	20,357	1.47
Indonesian (50)	96	0.01
Japanese (562)	1,027	0.07
Korean (2,840)	3,101	0.22
Laotian (99)	148	0.01
Malaysian (11)	30	<0.01
Nepalese (129)	159	0.01
Pakistani (2,399)	2,728	0.20
Sri Lankan (174)	234	0.02
Taiwanese (98)	130	0.01
Thai (326)	414	0.03
Vietnamese (3,215)	3,526	0.25
Hawaii Native/Pacific Islander (1,288)	6,213	0.45
Not Hispanic (398)	1,854	0.13
Hispanic (890)	4,359	0.31
Fijian (13)	13	<0.01
Guamanian/Chamorro (251)	376	0.03
Marshallese (3)	3	<0.01
Native Hawaiian (371)	669	0.05
Samoan (70)	160	0.01
Tongan (5)	7	<0.01
White (386,497)	427,659	30.88
Not Hispanic (151,209)	158,245	11.42
Hispanic (235,288)	269,414	19.45

Brookhaven

Place Type: Town
County: Suffolk
Population: 486,040†

Ancestry‡	Population	%
African, Sub-Saharan (2,475)	2,832	0.59
African (2,224)	2,533	0.53
Ghanaian (57)	57	0.01
Liberian (9)	9	<0.01
Nigerian (163)	179	0.04
South African (6)	24	<0.01
Sudanese (0)	14	<0.01
Other Sub-Saharan African (16)	16	<0.01
Albanian (59)	133	0.03
Alsatian (0)	12	<0.01
American (10,016)	10,016	2.09
Arab (797)	1,321	0.28
Arab (164)	191	0.04
Egyptian (317)	435	0.09
Jordanian (100)	178	0.04
Lebanese (29)	98	0.02
Moroccan (15)	15	<0.01
Palestinian (0)	13	<0.01
Syrian (12)	220	0.05
Other Arab (160)	171	0.04
Armenian (254)	643	0.13
Australian (31)	79	0.02
Austrian (603)	2,867	0.60
Basque (9)	23	<0.01
Belgian (61)	401	0.08
Brazilian (314)	436	0.09
British (605)	1,235	0.26
Bulgarian (101)	128	0.03
Canadian (432)	999	0.21
Celtic (0)	31	0.01
Croatian (317)	588	0.12
Cypriot (51)	51	0.01
Czech (697)	3,121	0.65
Czechoslovakian (344)	917	0.19
Danish (180)	1,229	0.26
Dutch (554)	4,038	0.84
Eastern European (604)	728	0.15
English (4,862)	30,089	6.27
Estonian (14)	102	0.02
European (1,893)	2,098	0.44
Finnish (144)	706	0.15
French, ex. Basque (933)	8,961	1.87
French Canadian (665)	2,478	0.52
German (16,000)	89,711	18.69
German Russian (0)	40	0.01
Greek (2,196)	5,703	1.19
Guyanese (373)	441	0.09
Hungarian (814)	4,390	0.91
Icelander (18)	45	0.01
Iranian (353)	398	0.08
Irish (29,544)	122,200	25.45
Israeli (355)	545	0.11
Italian (72,814)	155,749	32.44
Latvian (120)	182	0.04
Lithuanian (674)	1,898	0.40
Luxemburger (0)	36	0.01
Maltese (235)	686	0.14
New Zealander (10)	23	<0.01
Northern European (233)	249	0.05
Norwegian (1,381)	5,078	1.06
Pennsylvania German (45)	66	0.01
Polish (7,478)	27,233	5.67
Portuguese (2,684)	3,802	0.79
Romanian (472)	1,216	0.25
Russian (4,331)	12,073	2.51
Scandinavian (127)	388	0.08
Scotch-Irish (1,789)	5,102	1.06
Scottish (1,051)	5,703	1.19
Slavic (22)	91	0.02
Slovak (304)	690	0.14
Slovene (5)	76	0.02
Swedish (519)	4,045	0.84
Swiss (319)	1,356	0.28
Turkish (1,572)	1,935	0.40
Ukrainian (779)	2,350	0.49
Welsh (195)	1,189	0.25
West Indian, ex. Hispanic (4,567)	6,377	1.33
Bahamian (0)	47	0.01
Barbadian (44)	44	0.01
Bermudan (0)	34	0.01
British West Indian (59)	59	0.01
Dutch West Indian (20)	20	<0.01
Haitian (1,544)	2,077	0.43
Jamaican (998)	1,546	0.32
Trinidadian/Tobagonian (922)	1,200	0.25
West Indian (980)	1,323	0.28
Other West Indian (0)	27	0.01
Yugoslavian (145)	518	0.11

Hispanic Origin	Population	%
Hispanic or Latino (of any race)	60,270	12.40
Central American, ex. Mexican	9,259	1.90
Costa Rican	198	0.04
Guatemalan	1,411	0.29
Honduran	1,195	0.25
Nicaraguan	159	0.03
Panamanian	291	0.06
Salvadoran	5,899	1.21
Other Central American	106	0.02
Cuban	1,500	0.31
Dominican Republic	4,781	0.98
Mexican	4,926	1.01
Puerto Rican	21,429	4.41
South American	12,182	2.51
Argentinean	653	0.13
Bolivian	148	0.03
Chilean	363	0.07
Colombian	2,970	0.61
Ecuadorian	6,437	1.32
Paraguayan	50	0.01
Peruvian	1,074	0.22
Uruguayan	87	0.02
Venezuelan	302	0.06
Other South American	98	0.02
Other Hispanic or Latino	6,193	1.27

Race*	Population	%
African-American/Black (26,639)	31,615	6.50
Not Hispanic (24,428)	28,098	5.78
Hispanic (2,211)	3,517	0.72
American Indian/Alaska Native (1,368)	3,782	0.78
Not Hispanic (847)	2,586	0.53
Hispanic (521)	1,196	0.25
Alaska Athabascan *(Ala. Nat.)* (1)	4	<0.01
Aleut *(Alaska Native)* (2)	3	<0.01
Apache (4)	18	<0.01
Arapaho (0)	1	<0.01
Blackfeet (12)	164	0.03
Canadian/French Am. Ind. (4)	15	<0.01
Central American Ind. (27)	53	0.01
Cherokee (82)	546	0.11
Cheyenne (1)	6	<0.01
Chickasaw (0)	3	<0.01
Chippewa (8)	19	<0.01
Choctaw (7)	34	0.01
Comanche (0)	4	<0.01
Cree (1)	4	<0.01
Creek (1)	12	<0.01
Crow (0)	1	<0.01
Delaware (3)	12	<0.01
Hopi (0)	1	<0.01
Inupiat *(Alaska Native)* (1)	2	<0.01
Iroquois (39)	116	0.02
Lumbee (2)	7	<0.01
Mexican American Ind. (37)	64	0.01
Navajo (3)	15	<0.01
Osage (0)	2	<0.01
Ottawa (0)	3	<0.01
Paiute (2)	4	<0.01
Potawatomi (6)	6	<0.01
Pueblo (2)	2	<0.01
Puget Sound Salish (5)	6	<0.01

SECTION TWO

*Notes: † The Census 2010 population figure is used to calculate the percentages in the Hispanic Origin and Race categories. Ancestry percentages are based on the 2006-2010 American Community Survey population (not shown); ‡ Numbers in parentheses indicate the number of people reporting a single ancestry; * Numbers in parentheses indicate the number of persons reporting this race alone, not in combination with any other race; Please refer to the Explanation of Data for more information.*

Seminole (7)	33	0.01
Shoshone (0)	4	<0.01
Sioux (16)	42	0.01
South American Ind. (47)	136	0.03
Spanish American Ind. (26)	34	0.01
Tlingit-Haida *(Alaska Native)* (0)	5	<0.01
Ute (0)	1	<0.01
Yakama (0)	1	<0.01
Yaqui (1)	5	<0.01
Yuman (1)	1	<0.01
Asian (19,082)	21,849	4.50
Not Hispanic (18,880)	21,257	4.37
Hispanic (202)	592	0.12
Bangladeshi (528)	621	0.13
Burmese (36)	40	0.01
Cambodian (14)	29	0.01
Chinese, ex. Taiwanese (5,433)	6,107	1.26
Filipino (2,117)	2,705	0.56
Hmong (1)	4	<0.01
Indian (5,078)	5,745	1.18
Indonesian (38)	63	0.01
Japanese (339)	605	0.12
Korean (1,728)	2,025	0.42
Laotian (42)	54	0.01
Malaysian (9)	18	<0.01
Nepalese (43)	44	0.01
Pakistani (1,867)	2,081	0.43
Sri Lankan (85)	100	0.02
Taiwanese (181)	213	0.04
Thai (150)	211	0.04
Vietnamese (544)	620	0.13
Hawaii Native/Pacific Islander (152)	447	0.09
Not Hispanic (98)	306	0.06
Hispanic (54)	141	0.03
Fijian (3)	10	<0.01
Guamanian/Chamorro (40)	51	0.01
Native Hawaiian (31)	100	0.02
Samoan (6)	15	<0.01
Tongan (0)	2	<0.01
White (410,649)	419,725	86.36
Not Hispanic (373,782)	379,158	78.01
Hispanic (36,867)	40,567	8.35

Brooklyn

Place Type: Borough
County: Kings
Population: 2,504,700†

Ancestry‡	Population	%
Afghan (335)	344	0.01
African, Sub-Saharan (30,768)	63,004	2.55
African (17,256)	48,168	1.95
Cape Verdean (106)	153	0.01
Ethiopian (283)	330	0.01
Ghanaian (3,692)	3,898	0.16
Kenyan (65)	77	<0.01
Liberian (392)	452	0.02
Nigerian (5,499)	6,033	0.24
Senegalese (401)	401	0.02
Sierra Leonean (147)	147	0.01
Somalian (234)	260	0.01
South African (204)	320	0.01
Sudanese (693)	731	0.03
Ugandan (29)	54	<0.01
Zimbabwean (99)	99	<0.01
Other Sub-Saharan African (1,668)	1,881	0.08
Albanian (6,490)	6,871	0.28
Alsatian (0)	27	<0.01
American (78,858)	78,858	3.20
Arab (29,346)	34,840	1.41
Arab (6,779)	7,609	0.31
Egyptian (4,705)	5,231	0.21
Iraqi (71)	134	0.01
Jordanian (714)	752	0.03
Lebanese (3,425)	4,757	0.19
Moroccan (2,156)	2,648	0.11
Palestinian (1,372)	1,482	0.06
Syrian (4,854)	5,890	0.24
Other Arab (5,270)	6,337	0.26
Armenian (1,798)	2,300	0.09
Assyrian/Chaldean/Syriac (22)	44	<0.01
Australian (539)	832	0.03
Austrian (1,677)	5,123	0.21
Basque (69)	129	0.01
Belgian (498)	1,012	0.04
Brazilian (1,257)	1,719	0.07
British (2,002)	4,749	0.19
Bulgarian (970)	1,128	0.05
Cajun (99)	175	0.01
Canadian (1,814)	3,116	0.13
Carpatho Rusyn (46)	53	<0.01
Celtic (16)	32	<0.01
Croatian (488)	998	0.04
Cypriot (37)	62	<0.01
Czech (759)	3,393	0.14
Czechoslovakian (793)	1,684	0.07
Danish (380)	1,267	0.05
Dutch (1,616)	5,664	0.23
Eastern European (11,912)	12,941	0.52
English (9,927)	32,407	1.31
Estonian (209)	340	0.01
European (25,194)	27,499	1.11
Finnish (303)	692	0.03
French, ex. Basque (3,484)	14,137	0.57
French Canadian (1,082)	2,974	0.12
German (12,299)	52,798	2.14
German Russian (29)	55	<0.01
Greek (10,688)	14,075	0.57
Guyanese (36,322)	38,963	1.58
Hungarian (17,858)	26,607	1.08
Icelander (69)	103	<0.01
Iranian (1,520)	1,822	0.07
Irish (32,255)	84,945	3.44
Israeli (7,062)	9,707	0.39
Italian (108,743)	152,814	6.19
Latvian (418)	667	0.03
Lithuanian (938)	2,676	0.11
Luxemburger (41)	58	<0.01
Macedonian (389)	498	0.02
Maltese (197)	362	0.01
New Zealander (71)	140	0.01
Northern European (905)	961	0.04
Norwegian (2,042)	5,982	0.24
Pennsylvania German (19)	59	<0.01
Polish (41,882)	66,792	2.71
Portuguese (1,106)	2,882	0.12
Romanian (4,537)	8,046	0.33
Russian (69,188)	88,579	3.59
Scandinavian (512)	882	0.04
Scotch-Irish (1,997)	6,090	0.25
Scottish (2,407)	8,809	0.36
Serbian (288)	520	0.02
Slavic (289)	564	0.02
Slovak (1,164)	1,826	0.07
Slovene (55)	160	0.01
Soviet Union (185)	219	0.01
Swedish (1,240)	5,185	0.21
Swiss (473)	1,491	0.06
Turkish (4,449)	5,164	0.21
Ukrainian (21,703)	25,046	1.02
Welsh (345)	2,606	0.11
West Indian, ex. Hispanic (257,579)	306,541	12.43
Bahamian (195)	266	0.01
Barbadian (13,358)	14,916	0.60
Belizean (1,610)	2,026	0.08
Bermudan (16)	16	<0.01
British West Indian (28,123)	30,607	1.24
Dutch West Indian (289)	424	0.02
Haitian (67,083)	69,941	2.84
Jamaican (74,216)	80,999	3.28
Trinidadian/Tobagonian (42,450)	46,490	1.88
U.S. Virgin Islander (470)	558	0.02
West Indian (29,404)	59,844	2.43
Other West Indian (365)	454	0.02
Yugoslavian (2,305)	2,800	0.11

Hispanic Origin	Population	%
Hispanic or Latino (of any race)	496,285	19.81
Central American, ex. Mexican	46,119	1.84
Costa Rican	2,576	0.10
Guatemalan	9,160	0.37
Honduran	10,071	0.40
Nicaraguan	2,407	0.10
Panamanian	13,681	0.55
Salvadoran	7,737	0.31
Other Central American	487	0.02
Cuban	7,581	0.30
Dominican Republic	86,764	3.46
Mexican	94,585	3.78
Puerto Rican	176,528	7.05
South American	49,003	1.96
Argentinean	2,760	0.11
Bolivian	310	0.01
Chilean	1,026	0.04
Colombian	8,861	0.35
Ecuadorian	28,684	1.15
Paraguayan	230	0.01
Peruvian	4,222	0.17
Uruguayan	488	0.02
Venezuelan	1,916	0.08
Other South American	506	0.02
Other Hispanic or Latino	35,705	1.43

Race*	Population	%
African-American/Black (860,083)	896,165	35.78
Not Hispanic (799,066)	820,437	32.76
Hispanic (61,017)	75,728	3.02
American Indian/Alaska Native (13,524)	26,571	1.06
Not Hispanic (4,638)	12,062	0.48
Hispanic (8,886)	14,509	0.58
Alaska Athabascan *(Ala. Nat.)* (1)	5	<0.01
Aleut *(Alaska Native)* (4)	8	<0.01
Apache (46)	122	<0.01
Arapaho (2)	10	<0.01
Blackfeet (89)	531	0.02
Canadian/French Am. Ind. (42)	62	<0.01
Central American Ind. (616)	1,263	0.05
Cherokee (289)	1,903	0.08
Cheyenne (0)	10	<0.01
Chickasaw (9)	30	<0.01
Chippewa (23)	65	<0.01
Choctaw (30)	104	<0.01
Colville (1)	1	<0.01
Comanche (5)	19	<0.01
Cree (3)	15	<0.01
Creek (20)	81	<0.01
Crow (5)	19	<0.01
Delaware (5)	35	<0.01
Hopi (7)	12	<0.01
Houma (1)	3	<0.01
Inupiat *(Alaska Native)* (7)	21	<0.01
Iroquois (194)	381	0.02
Kiowa (1)	2	<0.01
Lumbee (6)	24	<0.01
Menominee (1)	4	<0.01
Mexican American Ind. (1,022)	1,363	0.05
Navajo (41)	93	<0.01
Osage (1)	3	<0.01
Ottawa (2)	5	<0.01
Paiute (0)	1	<0.01
Pima (0)	2	<0.01
Potawatomi (3)	11	<0.01
Pueblo (93)	169	0.01
Puget Sound Salish (1)	1	<0.01
Seminole (18)	92	<0.01
Shoshone (6)	23	<0.01
Sioux (29)	121	<0.01
South American Ind. (874)	1,855	0.07
Spanish American Ind. (290)	382	0.02
Tlingit-Haida *(Alaska Native)* (4)	28	<0.01
Tohono O'Odham (9)	10	<0.01
Ute (0)	4	<0.01
Yakama (1)	3	<0.01
Yaqui (11)	19	<0.01
Yuman (5)	8	<0.01
Yup'ik *(Alaska Native)* (0)	1	<0.01
Asian (262,276)	284,489	11.36
Not Hispanic (260,129)	279,499	11.16
Hispanic (2,147)	4,990	0.20

*Notes: † The Census 2010 population figure is used to calculate the percentages in the Hispanic Origin and Race categories. Ancestry percentages are based on the 2006-2010 American Community Survey population (not shown); ‡ Numbers in parentheses indicate the number of people reporting a single ancestry; * Numbers in parentheses indicate the number of persons reporting this race alone, not in combination with any other race; Please refer to the Explanation of Data for more information.*

Bangladeshi (10,667)	12,408	0.50
Bhutanese (5)	8	<0.01
Burmese (1,055)	1,260	0.05
Cambodian (613)	751	0.03
Chinese, ex. Taiwanese (171,214)	178,214	7.12
Filipino (7,930)	10,208	0.41
Hmong (14)	22	<0.01
Indian (26,144)	33,490	1.34
Indonesian (383)	564	0.02
Japanese (3,938)	5,917	0.24
Korean (6,904)	8,201	0.33
Laotian (82)	131	0.01
Malaysian (478)	708	0.03
Nepalese (355)	393	0.02
Pakistani (18,296)	19,840	0.79
Sri Lankan (219)	270	0.01
Taiwanese (857)	1,075	0.04
Thai (636)	883	0.04
Vietnamese (3,944)	5,041	0.20
Hawaii Native/Pacific Islander (1,243)	5,784	0.23
Not Hispanic (633)	3,463	0.14
Hispanic (610)	2,321	0.09
Fijian (20)	45	<0.01
Guamanian/Chamorro (386)	568	0.02
Marshallese (1)	2	<0.01
Native Hawaiian (208)	564	0.02
Samoan (72)	216	0.01
Tongan (5)	10	<0.01
White (1,072,041)	1,120,592	44.74
Not Hispanic (893,306)	917,717	36.64
Hispanic (178,735)	202,875	8.10

Brunswick

Place Type: Town
County: Rensselaer
Population: 11,941†

Ancestry‡	Population	%
African, Sub-Saharan (12)	12	0.10
Ghanaian (12)	12	0.10
American (567)	567	4.75
Armenian (43)	102	0.85
Austrian (0)	26	0.22
British (13)	24	0.20
Canadian (36)	56	0.47
Danish (17)	237	1.99
Dutch (70)	445	3.73
Eastern European (10)	10	0.08
English (287)	1,404	11.76
European (92)	107	0.90
French, ex. Basque (245)	1,522	12.75
French Canadian (152)	415	3.48
German (482)	2,483	20.81
Greek (60)	85	0.71
Hungarian (0)	15	0.13
Irish (1,281)	3,925	32.89
Italian (930)	2,603	21.81
Lithuanian (0)	118	0.99
Norwegian (0)	13	0.11
Polish (109)	725	6.08
Russian (12)	98	0.82
Scandinavian (0)	30	0.25
Scotch-Irish (45)	264	2.21
Scottish (74)	312	2.61
Slavic (0)	9	0.08
Slovak (25)	36	0.30
Swedish (20)	68	0.57
Swiss (12)	77	0.65
Turkish (0)	16	0.13
Ukrainian (104)	185	1.55
Welsh (0)	88	0.74
West Indian, ex. Hispanic (20)	29	0.24
Haitian (20)	29	0.24

Hispanic Origin	Population	%
Hispanic or Latino (of any race)	198	1.66
Central American, ex. Mexican	13	0.11
Guatemalan	7	0.06
Honduran	1	0.01
Nicaraguan	1	0.01
Panamanian	3	0.03
Salvadoran	1	0.01
Cuban	13	0.11
Dominican Republic	8	0.07
Mexican	48	0.40
Puerto Rican	82	0.69
South American	6	0.05
Argentinean	1	0.01
Chilean	1	0.01
Colombian	3	0.03
Peruvian	1	0.01
Other Hispanic or Latino	28	0.23

Race*	Population	%
African-American/Black (214)	295	2.47
Not Hispanic (205)	273	2.29
Hispanic (9)	22	0.18
American Indian/Alaska Native (24)	62	0.52
Not Hispanic (18)	56	0.47
Hispanic (6)	6	0.05
Blackfeet (0)	1	0.01
Cherokee (3)	9	0.08
Chippewa (2)	2	0.02
Choctaw (0)	1	0.01
Cree (0)	1	0.01
Iroquois (10)	18	0.15
Sioux (0)	1	0.01
Asian (194)	250	2.09
Not Hispanic (191)	247	2.07
Hispanic (3)	3	0.03
Bangladeshi (1)	1	0.01
Cambodian (0)	3	0.03
Chinese, ex. Taiwanese (58)	61	0.51
Filipino (19)	32	0.27
Indian (40)	55	0.46
Indonesian (0)	1	0.01
Japanese (7)	8	0.07
Korean (40)	46	0.39
Pakistani (3)	3	0.03
Taiwanese (5)	5	0.04
Thai (5)	7	0.06
Vietnamese (6)	10	0.08
Hawaii Native/Pacific Islander (2)	4	0.03
Not Hispanic (2)	4	0.03
Guamanian/Chamorro (2)	2	0.02
Native Hawaiian (0)	1	0.01
White (11,289)	11,452	95.90
Not Hispanic (11,161)	11,305	94.67
Hispanic (128)	147	1.23

Buffalo

Place Type: City
County: Erie
Population: 261,310†

Ancestry‡	Population	%
Afghan (178)	178	0.07
African, Sub-Saharan (5,618)	6,085	2.29
African (3,925)	4,177	1.57
Cape Verdean (95)	95	0.04
Ethiopian (223)	223	0.08
Ghanaian (43)	43	0.02
Kenyan (38)	38	0.01
Liberian (74)	74	0.03
Nigerian (94)	105	0.04
Sierra Leonean (17)	17	0.01
Somalian (706)	858	0.32
Sudanese (259)	268	0.10
Ugandan (24)	33	0.01
Zimbabwean (45)	45	0.02
Other Sub-Saharan African (75)	109	0.04
Albanian (360)	369	0.14
Alsatian (12)	12	<0.01
American (6,386)	6,386	2.40
Arab (1,374)	1,815	0.68
Arab (586)	644	0.24
Egyptian (27)	39	0.01
Iraqi (286)	288	0.11
Jordanian (2)	4	<0.01
Lebanese (165)	481	0.18
Moroccan (21)	57	0.02
Syrian (17)	32	0.01
Other Arab (270)	270	0.10
Armenian (39)	67	0.03
Australian (0)	14	0.01
Austrian (244)	799	0.30
Basque (9)	9	<0.01
Belgian (21)	21	0.01
Brazilian (25)	25	0.01
British (306)	722	0.27
Bulgarian (114)	201	0.08
Cajun (0)	11	<0.01
Canadian (264)	558	0.21
Celtic (0)	13	<0.01
Croatian (249)	487	0.18
Czech (13)	310	0.12
Czechoslovakian (76)	231	0.09
Danish (41)	152	0.06
Dutch (224)	1,451	0.55
Eastern European (189)	198	0.07
English (2,703)	11,203	4.21
Estonian (0)	11	<0.01
European (884)	1,016	0.38
Finnish (56)	248	0.09
French, ex. Basque (446)	4,110	1.55
French Canadian (420)	1,376	0.52
German (7,601)	35,760	13.44
German Russian (16)	41	0.02
Greek (305)	769	0.29
Guyanese (517)	529	0.20
Hungarian (748)	2,201	0.83
Iranian (82)	125	0.05
Irish (9,009)	34,103	12.82
Israeli (104)	180	0.07
Italian (13,524)	30,606	11.51
Latvian (13)	22	0.01
Lithuanian (121)	358	0.13
Luxemburger (0)	24	0.01
Macedonian (40)	52	0.02
Maltese (0)	8	<0.01
Northern European (31)	31	0.01
Norwegian (78)	586	0.22
Pennsylvania German (0)	159	0.06
Polish (12,089)	28,108	10.57
Portuguese (169)	474	0.18
Romanian (30)	122	0.05
Russian (616)	1,883	0.71
Scandinavian (0)	76	0.03
Scotch-Irish (902)	2,324	0.87
Scottish (437)	2,816	1.06
Serbian (115)	291	0.11
Slavic (15)	35	0.01
Slovak (27)	174	0.07
Slovene (23)	100	0.04
Swedish (309)	1,596	0.60
Swiss (41)	308	0.12
Turkish (251)	350	0.13
Ukrainian (899)	1,739	0.65
Welsh (90)	729	0.27
West Indian, ex. Hispanic (2,330)	2,773	1.04
Bahamian (13)	13	<0.01
Barbadian (18)	44	0.02
British West Indian (102)	115	0.04
Dutch West Indian (0)	17	0.01
Haitian (480)	626	0.24
Jamaican (1,260)	1,420	0.53
Trinidadian/Tobagonian (196)	200	0.08
West Indian (261)	338	0.13
Yugoslavian (187)	282	0.11

Hispanic Origin	Population	%
Hispanic or Latino (of any race)	27,519	10.53
Central American, ex. Mexican	386	0.15
Costa Rican	27	0.01
Guatemalan	72	0.03
Honduran	76	0.03
Nicaraguan	25	0.01
Panamanian	89	0.03

*Notes: † The Census 2010 population figure is used to calculate the percentages in the Hispanic Origin and Race categories. Ancestry percentages are based on the 2006-2010 American Community Survey population (not shown); ‡ Numbers in parentheses indicate the number of people reporting a single ancestry; * Numbers in parentheses indicate the number of persons reporting this race alone, not in combination with any other race; Please refer to the Explanation of Data for more information.*

Salvadoran	92	0.04
Other Central American	5	<0.01
Cuban	795	0.30
Dominican Republic	707	0.27
Mexican	1,382	0.53
Puerto Rican	22,076	8.45
South American	679	0.26
Argentinean	117	0.04
Bolivian	35	0.01
Chilean	35	0.01
Colombian	215	0.08
Ecuadorian	106	0.04
Paraguayan	8	<0.01
Peruvian	105	0.04
Uruguayan	2	<0.01
Venezuelan	44	0.02
Other South American	12	<0.01
Other Hispanic or Latino	1,494	0.57

Race*	Population	%
African-American/Black (100,774)	106,107	40.61
Not Hispanic (97,637)	101,817	38.96
Hispanic (3,137)	4,290	1.64
American Indian/Alaska Native (2,009)	4,019	1.54
Not Hispanic (1,597)	3,229	1.24
Hispanic (412)	790	0.30
Alaska Athabascan *(Ala. Nat.)* (1)	1	<0.01
Apache (5)	11	<0.01
Arapaho (0)	1	<0.01
Blackfeet (10)	104	0.04
Canadian/French Am. Ind. (29)	57	0.02
Central American Ind. (9)	17	0.01
Cherokee (37)	294	0.11
Chickasaw (2)	2	<0.01
Chippewa (24)	42	0.02
Choctaw (3)	21	0.01
Comanche (1)	4	<0.01
Cree (1)	4	<0.01
Creek (0)	7	<0.01
Crow (0)	1	<0.01
Delaware (6)	10	<0.01
Hopi (0)	5	<0.01
Houma (1)	2	<0.01
Inupiat *(Alaska Native)* (2)	4	<0.01
Iroquois (935)	1,316	0.50
Kiowa (1)	1	<0.01
Lumbee (1)	1	<0.01
Menominee (2)	2	<0.01
Mexican American Ind. (19)	27	0.01
Navajo (8)	16	0.01
Pima (1)	1	<0.01
Pueblo (3)	4	<0.01
Seminole (3)	23	0.01
Sioux (24)	46	0.02
South American Ind. (24)	60	0.02
Spanish American Ind. (11)	14	0.01
Tlingit-Haida *(Alaska Native)* (2)	3	<0.01
Tohono O'Odham (1)	3	<0.01
Yaqui (2)	2	<0.01
Yuman (1)	1	<0.01
Asian (8,409)	9,698	3.71
Not Hispanic (8,313)	9,459	3.62
Hispanic (96)	239	0.09
Bangladeshi (167)	206	0.08
Bhutanese (298)	370	0.14
Burmese (2,267)	2,361	0.90
Cambodian (43)	48	0.02
Chinese, ex. Taiwanese (919)	1,065	0.41
Filipino (214)	417	0.16
Hmong (5)	6	<0.01
Indian (1,576)	1,889	0.72
Indonesian (17)	22	0.01
Japanese (128)	243	0.09
Korean (350)	447	0.17
Laotian (248)	288	0.11
Malaysian (19)	21	0.01
Nepalese (115)	160	0.06
Pakistani (320)	362	0.14
Sri Lankan (45)	54	0.02
Taiwanese (31)	43	0.02
Thai (59)	107	0.04
Vietnamese (1,128)	1,220	0.47
Hawaii Native/Pacific Islander (119)	357	0.14
Not Hispanic (79)	252	0.10
Hispanic (40)	105	0.04
Guamanian/Chamorro (10)	30	0.01
Native Hawaiian (21)	75	0.03
Samoan (32)	63	0.02
Tongan (3)	3	<0.01
White (131,753)	138,013	52.82
Not Hispanic (119,801)	124,612	47.69
Hispanic (11,952)	13,401	5.13

Camillus

Place Type: Town
County: Onondaga
Population: 24,167†

Ancestry‡	Population	%
African, Sub-Saharan (41)	41	0.17
African (41)	41	0.17
American (664)	664	2.78
Arab (172)	268	1.12
Arab (108)	108	0.45
Lebanese (0)	92	0.38
Palestinian (64)	64	0.27
Syrian (0)	4	0.02
Armenian (9)	29	0.12
Austrian (91)	340	1.42
Belgian (0)	17	0.07
Brazilian (19)	19	0.08
Canadian (46)	117	0.49
Croatian (25)	25	0.10
Czech (0)	61	0.26
Czechoslovakian (26)	55	0.23
Danish (25)	39	0.16
Dutch (72)	463	1.94
Eastern European (0)	5	0.02
English (693)	3,085	12.90
European (95)	95	0.40
Finnish (0)	22	0.09
French, ex. Basque (173)	1,223	5.12
French Canadian (116)	486	2.03
German (676)	5,134	21.47
Greek (59)	107	0.45
Guyanese (16)	16	0.07
Hungarian (36)	201	0.84
Irish (2,175)	7,994	33.43
Italian (2,351)	5,050	21.12
Latvian (25)	29	0.12
Lithuanian (0)	9	0.04
Norwegian (10)	59	0.25
Polish (849)	2,531	10.59
Portuguese (54)	94	0.39
Romanian (49)	60	0.25
Russian (97)	296	1.24
Scandinavian (10)	10	0.04
Scotch-Irish (117)	395	1.65
Scottish (45)	543	2.27
Serbian (63)	63	0.26
Slavic (0)	12	0.05
Slovak (30)	45	0.19
Swedish (25)	117	0.49
Swiss (9)	112	0.47
Turkish (24)	24	0.10
Ukrainian (744)	975	4.08
Welsh (32)	123	0.51
West Indian, ex. Hispanic (17)	17	0.07
British West Indian (17)	17	0.07
Yugoslavian (42)	42	0.18

Hispanic Origin	Population	%
Hispanic or Latino (of any race)	432	1.79
Central American, ex. Mexican	13	0.05
Costa Rican	1	<0.01
Guatemalan	3	0.01
Honduran	6	0.02
Nicaraguan	1	<0.01
Panamanian	2	0.01
Cuban	19	0.08
Dominican Republic	16	0.07
Mexican	85	0.35
Puerto Rican	196	0.81
South American	50	0.21
Argentinean	3	0.01
Chilean	2	0.01
Colombian	25	0.10
Ecuadorian	2	0.01
Paraguayan	1	<0.01
Peruvian	12	0.05
Venezuelan	5	0.02
Other Hispanic or Latino	53	0.22

Race*	Population	%
African-American/Black (441)	589	2.44
Not Hispanic (431)	554	2.29
Hispanic (10)	35	0.14
American Indian/Alaska Native (115)	242	1.00
Not Hispanic (104)	221	0.91
Hispanic (11)	21	0.09
Blackfeet (0)	1	<0.01
Canadian/French Am. Ind. (1)	2	0.01
Cherokee (5)	21	0.09
Cheyenne (0)	1	<0.01
Iroquois (71)	121	0.50
Mexican American Ind. (5)	5	0.02
Shoshone (0)	1	<0.01
Asian (341)	405	1.68
Not Hispanic (341)	398	1.65
Hispanic (0)	7	0.03
Cambodian (7)	13	0.05
Chinese, ex. Taiwanese (62)	88	0.36
Filipino (25)	29	0.12
Indian (87)	99	0.41
Japanese (7)	14	0.06
Korean (64)	71	0.29
Laotian (1)	1	<0.01
Malaysian (1)	1	<0.01
Pakistani (19)	21	0.09
Sri Lankan (5)	5	0.02
Taiwanese (6)	6	0.02
Thai (3)	3	0.01
Vietnamese (32)	39	0.16
Hawaii Native/Pacific Islander (10)	26	0.11
Not Hispanic (7)	17	0.07
Hispanic (3)	9	0.04
Fijian (0)	3	0.01
Guamanian/Chamorro (3)	3	0.01
Native Hawaiian (4)	12	0.05
Samoan (1)	1	<0.01
White (22,820)	23,131	95.71
Not Hispanic (22,547)	22,821	94.43
Hispanic (273)	310	1.28

Canandaigua

Place Type: City
County: Ontario
Population: 10,545†

Ancestry‡	Population	%
African, Sub-Saharan (9)	9	0.08
African (9)	9	0.08
Albanian (48)	48	0.45
American (315)	315	2.95
Arab (0)	9	0.08
Lebanese (0)	9	0.08
Armenian (0)	10	0.09
Austrian (23)	23	0.22
Belgian (10)	40	0.37
British (0)	29	0.27
Canadian (47)	95	0.89
Croatian (10)	10	0.09
Czech (0)	15	0.14
Czechoslovakian (0)	9	0.08
Danish (0)	35	0.33
Dutch (148)	713	6.68
English (594)	2,220	20.79
European (9)	9	0.08

*Notes: † The Census 2010 population figure is used to calculate the percentages in the Hispanic Origin and Race categories. Ancestry percentages are based on the 2006-2010 American Community Survey population (not shown); ‡ Numbers in parentheses indicate the number of people reporting a single ancestry; * Numbers in parentheses indicate the number of persons reporting this race alone, not in combination with any other race; Please refer to the Explanation of Data for more information.*

Finnish (0)	11	0.10
French, ex. Basque (78)	414	3.88
French Canadian (63)	273	2.56
German (622)	2,683	25.13
Greek (0)	57	0.53
Hungarian (28)	28	0.26
Irish (770)	2,417	22.64
Italian (586)	1,544	14.46
Lithuanian (0)	49	0.46
Maltese (20)	20	0.19
Northern European (36)	36	0.34
Norwegian (22)	76	0.71
Pennsylvania German (0)	19	0.18
Polish (160)	532	4.98
Portuguese (0)	33	0.31
Russian (10)	23	0.22
Scandinavian (16)	24	0.22
Scotch-Irish (101)	328	3.07
Scottish (91)	340	3.18
Serbian (10)	44	0.41
Slavic (0)	11	0.10
Slovak (11)	23	0.22
Swedish (0)	73	0.68
Swiss (8)	18	0.17
Turkish (0)	9	0.08
Ukrainian (32)	67	0.63
Welsh (14)	141	1.32
Yugoslavian (8)	8	0.07

Hispanic Origin	Population	%
Hispanic or Latino (of any race)	215	2.04
Central American, ex. Mexican	21	0.20
Costa Rican	5	0.05
Guatemalan	2	0.02
Honduran	6	0.06
Nicaraguan	3	0.03
Salvadoran	5	0.05
Cuban	3	0.03
Dominican Republic	5	0.05
Mexican	48	0.46
Puerto Rican	105	1.00
South American	13	0.12
Argentinean	3	0.03
Bolivian	1	0.01
Colombian	3	0.03
Peruvian	6	0.06
Other Hispanic or Latino	20	0.19

Race*	Population	%
African-American/Black (190)	280	2.66
Not Hispanic (181)	261	2.48
Hispanic (9)	19	0.18
American Indian/Alaska Native (33)	83	0.79
Not Hispanic (30)	78	0.74
Hispanic (3)	5	0.05
Apache (1)	3	0.03
Blackfeet (0)	1	0.01
Cherokee (1)	8	0.08
Chickasaw (1)	1	0.01
Chippewa (5)	5	0.05
Houma (1)	1	0.01
Inupiat *(Alaska Native)* (0)	1	0.01
Iroquois (10)	30	0.28
Ottawa (1)	1	0.01
Sioux (1)	3	0.03
South American Ind. (1)	1	0.01
Yup'ik *(Alaska Native)* (1)	1	0.01
Asian (70)	106	1.01
Not Hispanic (68)	101	0.96
Hispanic (2)	5	0.05
Burmese (4)	4	0.04
Chinese, ex. Taiwanese (11)	19	0.18
Filipino (9)	21	0.20
Indian (6)	8	0.08
Indonesian (1)	1	0.01
Japanese (8)	11	0.10
Korean (12)	17	0.16
Laotian (2)	3	0.03
Pakistani (9)	9	0.09
Vietnamese (5)	5	0.05
Hawaii Native/Pacific Islander (0)	14	0.13
Not Hispanic (0)	14	0.13
Guamanian/Chamorro (0)	4	0.04
Native Hawaiian (0)	7	0.07
White (10,031)	10,204	96.77
Not Hispanic (9,889)	10,040	95.21
Hispanic (142)	164	1.56

Canandaigua

Place Type: Town
County: Ontario
Population: 10,020†

Ancestry‡	Population	%
American (550)	550	5.74
Arab (16)	16	0.17
Lebanese (16)	16	0.17
Austrian (0)	13	0.14
British (42)	86	0.90
Canadian (28)	28	0.29
Czech (18)	78	0.81
Czechoslovakian (0)	48	0.50
Danish (14)	47	0.49
Dutch (55)	461	4.81
English (471)	2,169	22.64
European (159)	186	1.94
Finnish (0)	19	0.20
French, ex. Basque (72)	329	3.43
French Canadian (22)	114	1.19
German (734)	2,808	29.30
Greek (15)	81	0.85
Hungarian (0)	11	0.11
Irish (516)	2,290	23.90
Italian (513)	1,251	13.06
Lithuanian (0)	12	0.13
Norwegian (0)	96	1.00
Pennsylvania German (0)	16	0.17
Polish (70)	595	6.21
Portuguese (12)	12	0.13
Russian (0)	65	0.68
Scotch-Irish (24)	99	1.03
Scottish (160)	425	4.44
Swedish (92)	172	1.80
Swiss (0)	11	0.11
Ukrainian (13)	33	0.34
Welsh (25)	74	0.77
West Indian, ex. Hispanic (70)	70	0.73
Jamaican (70)	70	0.73

Hispanic Origin	Population	%
Hispanic or Latino (of any race)	187	1.87
Central American, ex. Mexican	14	0.14
Guatemalan	8	0.08
Nicaraguan	2	0.02
Panamanian	2	0.02
Salvadoran	2	0.02
Cuban	4	0.04
Dominican Republic	3	0.03
Mexican	43	0.43
Puerto Rican	96	0.96
South American	11	0.11
Colombian	6	0.06
Ecuadorian	1	0.01
Venezuelan	4	0.04
Other Hispanic or Latino	16	0.16

Race*	Population	%
African-American/Black (98)	127	1.27
Not Hispanic (97)	124	1.24
Hispanic (1)	3	0.03
American Indian/Alaska Native (24)	52	0.52
Not Hispanic (19)	43	0.43
Hispanic (5)	9	0.09
Apache (0)	3	0.03
Blackfeet (1)	1	0.01
Canadian/French Am. Ind. (1)	1	0.01
Central American Ind. (1)	1	0.01
Cherokee (1)	6	0.06
Iroquois (13)	19	0.19
Sioux (0)	1	0.01
Asian (118)	164	1.64
Not Hispanic (116)	161	1.61
Hispanic (2)	3	0.03
Burmese (1)	1	0.01
Chinese, ex. Taiwanese (31)	40	0.40
Filipino (29)	45	0.45
Indian (19)	22	0.22
Japanese (1)	4	0.04
Korean (26)	34	0.34
Pakistani (1)	3	0.03
Taiwanese (4)	4	0.04
Thai (3)	3	0.03
Vietnamese (2)	3	0.03
Hawaii Native/Pacific Islander (0)	1	0.01
Not Hispanic (0)	1	0.01
White (9,629)	9,737	97.18
Not Hispanic (9,505)	9,594	95.75
Hispanic (124)	143	1.43

Canton

Place Type: Town
County: St. Lawrence
Population: 10,995†

Ancestry‡	Population	%
Afghan (13)	13	0.12
African, Sub-Saharan (28)	28	0.26
Kenyan (15)	15	0.14
Zimbabwean (13)	13	0.12
American (658)	658	6.04
Austrian (0)	21	0.19
British (67)	78	0.72
Canadian (31)	63	0.58
Croatian (13)	13	0.12
Czech (0)	11	0.10
Czechoslovakian (10)	10	0.09
Danish (0)	46	0.42
Dutch (33)	298	2.73
Eastern European (7)	7	0.06
English (974)	1,956	17.95
European (45)	45	0.41
Finnish (0)	13	0.12
French, ex. Basque (523)	1,320	12.11
French Canadian (173)	473	4.34
German (268)	1,026	9.42
Greek (0)	16	0.15
Hungarian (0)	56	0.51
Icelander (0)	13	0.12
Irish (544)	1,661	15.24
Italian (267)	839	7.70
Latvian (0)	14	0.13
Lithuanian (6)	37	0.34
Northern European (6)	6	0.06
Norwegian (14)	125	1.15
Polish (67)	344	3.16
Portuguese (0)	7	0.06
Russian (15)	84	0.77
Scandinavian (3)	3	0.03
Scotch-Irish (73)	187	1.72
Scottish (263)	734	6.74
Slovak (13)	20	0.18
Swedish (0)	52	0.48
Ukrainian (72)	192	1.76
Welsh (53)	75	0.69
West Indian, ex. Hispanic (49)	50	0.46
Barbadian (4)	4	0.04
Haitian (17)	17	0.16
West Indian (28)	29	0.27
Yugoslavian (6)	6	0.06

Hispanic Origin	Population	%
Hispanic or Latino (of any race)	319	2.90
Central American, ex. Mexican	16	0.15
Honduran	4	0.04
Panamanian	3	0.03
Salvadoran	8	0.07
Other Central American	1	0.01
Cuban	12	0.11

*Notes: † The Census 2010 population figure is used to calculate the percentages in the Hispanic Origin and Race categories. Ancestry percentages are based on the 2006-2010 American Community Survey population (not shown); ‡ Numbers in parentheses indicate the number of people reporting a single ancestry; * Numbers in parentheses indicate the number of persons reporting this race alone, not in combination with any other race; Please refer to the Explanation of Data for more information.*

Dominican Republic	41	0.37
Mexican	63	0.57
Puerto Rican	116	1.06
South American	32	0.29
Argentinean	1	0.01
Bolivian	1	0.01
Chilean	2	0.02
Colombian	11	0.10
Ecuadorian	6	0.05
Paraguayan	1	0.01
Peruvian	3	0.03
Uruguayan	5	0.05
Venezuelan	2	0.02
Other Hispanic or Latino	39	0.35

Race*	Population	%
African-American/Black (408)	484	4.40
Not Hispanic (373)	436	3.97
Hispanic (35)	48	0.44
American Indian/Alaska Native (46)	123	1.12
Not Hispanic (41)	105	0.95
Hispanic (5)	18	0.16
Blackfeet (0)	3	0.03
Cherokee (0)	12	0.11
Chippewa (4)	4	0.04
Inupiat *(Alaska Native)* (0)	1	0.01
Iroquois (20)	33	0.30
Mexican American Ind. (0)	2	0.02
Navajo (2)	2	0.02
South American Ind. (2)	2	0.02
Yup'ik *(Alaska Native)* (0)	3	0.03
Asian (136)	193	1.76
Not Hispanic (133)	184	1.67
Hispanic (3)	9	0.08
Bangladeshi (1)	2	0.02
Chinese, ex. Taiwanese (39)	55	0.50
Filipino (8)	21	0.19
Hmong (1)	2	0.02
Indian (23)	31	0.28
Indonesian (0)	4	0.04
Japanese (11)	16	0.15
Korean (20)	29	0.26
Laotian (1)	1	0.01
Pakistani (1)	2	0.02
Sri Lankan (2)	2	0.02
Taiwanese (5)	5	0.05
Thai (2)	2	0.02
Vietnamese (14)	16	0.15
Hawaii Native/Pacific Islander (0)	11	0.10
Not Hispanic (0)	7	0.06
Hispanic (0)	4	0.04
Native Hawaiian (0)	3	0.03
Samoan (0)	2	0.02
White (10,105)	10,280	93.50
Not Hispanic (9,962)	10,105	91.91
Hispanic (143)	175	1.59

Carmel

Place Type: Town
County: Putnam
Population: 34,305†

Ancestry‡	Population	%
African, Sub-Saharan (90)	105	0.31
African (0)	15	0.04
Ethiopian (26)	26	0.08
Senegalese (64)	64	0.19
Albanian (334)	361	1.05
American (949)	949	2.77
Arab (38)	152	0.44
Arab (0)	61	0.18
Egyptian (9)	9	0.03
Lebanese (29)	61	0.18
Palestinian (0)	21	0.06
Armenian (0)	20	0.06
Australian (0)	41	0.12
Austrian (78)	389	1.14
Basque (0)	14	0.04
Belgian (12)	12	0.04
Brazilian (13)	39	0.11
British (62)	87	0.25
Bulgarian (35)	35	0.10
Canadian (0)	46	0.13
Celtic (0)	6	0.02
Croatian (105)	155	0.45
Czech (11)	126	0.37
Czechoslovakian (63)	124	0.36
Danish (4)	53	0.15
Dutch (54)	178	0.52
Eastern European (64)	64	0.19
English (272)	1,918	5.60
Estonian (0)	40	0.12
European (329)	329	0.96
Finnish (20)	74	0.22
French, ex. Basque (30)	505	1.47
French Canadian (27)	149	0.44
German (1,087)	5,998	17.52
Greek (140)	449	1.31
Hungarian (30)	193	0.56
Irish (2,637)	9,039	26.40
Italian (6,437)	12,369	36.13
Lithuanian (34)	239	0.70
Maltese (6)	6	0.02
Northern European (22)	62	0.18
Norwegian (64)	105	0.31
Polish (828)	2,295	6.70
Portuguese (238)	464	1.36
Romanian (46)	116	0.34
Russian (278)	864	2.52
Scandinavian (0)	32	0.09
Scotch-Irish (86)	346	1.01
Scottish (94)	312	0.91
Slavic (17)	17	0.05
Slovak (42)	103	0.30
Slovene (0)	27	0.08
Swedish (59)	360	1.05
Swiss (0)	62	0.18
Turkish (9)	9	0.03
Ukrainian (138)	292	0.85
Welsh (73)	271	0.79
West Indian, ex. Hispanic (37)	129	0.38
Haitian (22)	56	0.16
Jamaican (0)	18	0.05
Trinidadian/Tobagonian (15)	55	0.16
Yugoslavian (58)	150	0.44

Hispanic Origin	Population	%
Hispanic or Latino (of any race)	3,469	10.11
Central American, ex. Mexican	498	1.45
Costa Rican	17	0.05
Guatemalan	277	0.81
Honduran	15	0.04
Nicaraguan	5	0.01
Panamanian	11	0.03
Salvadoran	171	0.50
Other Central American	2	0.01
Cuban	132	0.38
Dominican Republic	226	0.66
Mexican	326	0.95
Puerto Rican	1,288	3.75
South American	629	1.83
Argentinean	54	0.16
Bolivian	11	0.03
Chilean	29	0.08
Colombian	128	0.37
Ecuadorian	271	0.79
Paraguayan	12	0.03
Peruvian	85	0.25
Uruguayan	13	0.04
Venezuelan	25	0.07
Other South American	1	<0.01
Other Hispanic or Latino	370	1.08

Race*	Population	%
African-American/Black (671)	848	2.47
Not Hispanic (545)	653	1.90
Hispanic (126)	195	0.57
American Indian/Alaska Native (37)	126	0.37
Not Hispanic (24)	89	0.26
Hispanic (13)	37	0.11
Apache (0)	1	<0.01
Blackfeet (0)	7	0.02
Canadian/French Am. Ind. (2)	3	0.01
Central American Ind. (6)	8	0.02
Cherokee (0)	15	0.04
Choctaw (2)	2	0.01
Creek (1)	1	<0.01
Iroquois (1)	5	0.01
Mexican American Ind. (0)	6	0.02
Seminole (0)	2	0.01
South American Ind. (6)	12	0.03
Spanish American Ind. (1)	1	<0.01
Asian (608)	772	2.25
Not Hispanic (588)	731	2.13
Hispanic (20)	41	0.12
Bangladeshi (1)	1	<0.01
Cambodian (2)	2	0.01
Chinese, ex. Taiwanese (160)	217	0.63
Filipino (84)	117	0.34
Indian (200)	226	0.66
Japanese (27)	36	0.10
Korean (55)	66	0.19
Malaysian (2)	2	0.01
Nepalese (1)	1	<0.01
Pakistani (24)	29	0.08
Sri Lankan (1)	1	<0.01
Taiwanese (2)	4	0.01
Thai (16)	22	0.06
Vietnamese (12)	19	0.06
Hawaii Native/Pacific Islander (5)	32	0.09
Not Hispanic (5)	17	0.05
Hispanic (0)	15	0.04
Guamanian/Chamorro (0)	8	0.02
Native Hawaiian (0)	1	<0.01
White (31,600)	32,102	93.58
Not Hispanic (29,303)	29,587	86.25
Hispanic (2,297)	2,515	7.33

Catskill

Place Type: Town
County: Greene
Population: 11,775†

Ancestry‡	Population	%
African, Sub-Saharan (40)	40	0.34
African (40)	40	0.34
Albanian (80)	80	0.67
American (312)	312	2.62
Arab (9)	9	0.08
Syrian (9)	9	0.08
Austrian (37)	141	1.19
Brazilian (10)	10	0.08
British (156)	168	1.41
Cajun (0)	62	0.52
Canadian (0)	31	0.26
Croatian (36)	78	0.66
Czech (4)	20	0.17
Danish (0)	12	0.10
Dutch (100)	838	7.05
Eastern European (0)	9	0.08
English (219)	899	7.56
European (298)	383	3.22
French, ex. Basque (37)	273	2.30
French Canadian (12)	172	1.45
German (464)	2,166	18.21
Greek (95)	172	1.45
Hungarian (85)	158	1.33
Irish (691)	2,377	19.98
Italian (1,279)	3,026	25.44
Lithuanian (33)	60	0.50
Norwegian (40)	72	0.61
Pennsylvania German (0)	13	0.11
Polish (235)	614	5.16
Portuguese (0)	15	0.13
Russian (23)	114	0.96
Scotch-Irish (11)	120	1.01
Scottish (65)	171	1.44
Slavic (0)	53	0.45

*Notes: † The Census 2010 population figure is used to calculate the percentages in the Hispanic Origin and Race categories. Ancestry percentages are based on the 2006-2010 American Community Survey population (not shown); ‡ Numbers in parentheses indicate the number of people reporting a single ancestry; * Numbers in parentheses indicate the number of persons reporting this race alone, not in combination with any other race; Please refer to the Explanation of Data for more information.*

Slovak (65)	65	0.55
Swedish (45)	74	0.62
Ukrainian (31)	79	0.66
Welsh (0)	83	0.70
West Indian, ex. Hispanic (8)	8	0.07
Jamaican (8)	8	0.07
Yugoslavian (0)	28	0.24

Hispanic Origin	Population	%
Hispanic or Latino (of any race)	695	5.90
Central American, ex. Mexican	74	0.63
Costa Rican	2	0.02
Guatemalan	9	0.08
Honduran	8	0.07
Nicaraguan	4	0.03
Salvadoran	51	0.43
Cuban	12	0.10
Dominican Republic	14	0.12
Mexican	104	0.88
Puerto Rican	404	3.43
South American	32	0.27
Argentinean	2	0.02
Chilean	8	0.07
Colombian	12	0.10
Ecuadorian	1	0.01
Paraguayan	1	0.01
Peruvian	6	0.05
Venezuelan	2	0.02
Other Hispanic or Latino	55	0.47

Race*	Population	%
African-American/Black (719)	948	8.05
Not Hispanic (673)	883	7.50
Hispanic (46)	65	0.55
American Indian/Alaska Native (42)	129	1.10
Not Hispanic (32)	110	0.93
Hispanic (10)	19	0.16
Apache (2)	5	0.04
Blackfeet (0)	2	0.02
Cherokee (2)	11	0.09
Chippewa (0)	1	0.01
Choctaw (1)	3	0.03
Creek (0)	1	0.01
Delaware (1)	2	0.02
Iroquois (2)	12	0.10
Lumbee (1)	2	0.02
Mexican American Ind. (5)	5	0.04
Navajo (1)	1	0.01
Seminole (1)	1	0.01
Sioux (0)	2	0.02
Asian (113)	157	1.33
Not Hispanic (108)	149	1.27
Hispanic (5)	8	0.07
Burmese (1)	1	0.01
Chinese, ex. Taiwanese (24)	30	0.25
Filipino (20)	37	0.31
Indian (27)	36	0.31
Japanese (4)	11	0.09
Korean (5)	7	0.06
Pakistani (15)	19	0.16
Thai (3)	4	0.03
Vietnamese (11)	12	0.10
Hawaii Native/Pacific Islander (1)	9	0.08
Not Hispanic (1)	9	0.08
Guamanian/Chamorro (0)	1	0.01
Native Hawaiian (0)	1	0.01
Samoan (1)	2	0.02
White (10,354)	10,679	90.69
Not Hispanic (9,937)	10,217	86.77
Hispanic (417)	462	3.92

Center Moriches

Place Type: CDP
County: Suffolk
Population: 7,580†

Ancestry‡	Population	%
African, Sub-Saharan (16)	16	0.20
African (16)	16	0.20
American (284)	284	3.49
Arab (0)	15	0.18
Lebanese (0)	15	0.18
Austrian (0)	37	0.45
Brazilian (28)	28	0.34
British (14)	14	0.17
Canadian (0)	13	0.16
Czech (0)	28	0.34
Dutch (25)	171	2.10
Eastern European (10)	19	0.23
English (77)	897	11.03
European (28)	41	0.50
French, ex. Basque (0)	264	3.25
French Canadian (25)	121	1.49
German (152)	1,780	21.89
Hungarian (9)	83	1.02
Icelander (0)	14	0.17
Irish (463)	2,368	29.12
Italian (1,176)	2,378	29.24
Lithuanian (39)	39	0.48
Northern European (30)	30	0.37
Norwegian (9)	51	0.63
Polish (152)	787	9.68
Portuguese (0)	16	0.20
Romanian (0)	44	0.54
Russian (0)	161	1.98
Scandinavian (16)	28	0.34
Scotch-Irish (0)	55	0.68
Scottish (31)	100	1.23
Swedish (0)	83	1.02
Ukrainian (0)	14	0.17
Welsh (0)	12	0.15
West Indian, ex. Hispanic (15)	15	0.18
Haitian (15)	15	0.18
Yugoslavian (5)	5	0.06

Hispanic Origin	Population	%
Hispanic or Latino (of any race)	776	10.24
Central American, ex. Mexican	195	2.57
Costa Rican	10	0.13
Guatemalan	98	1.29
Honduran	5	0.07
Panamanian	1	0.01
Salvadoran	81	1.07
Cuban	11	0.15
Dominican Republic	15	0.20
Mexican	80	1.06
Puerto Rican	232	3.06
South American	150	1.98
Argentinean	17	0.22
Bolivian	2	0.03
Chilean	4	0.05
Colombian	23	0.30
Ecuadorian	78	1.03
Paraguayan	7	0.09
Peruvian	14	0.18
Uruguayan	3	0.04
Venezuelan	2	0.03
Other Hispanic or Latino	93	1.23

Race*	Population	%
African-American/Black (263)	368	4.85
Not Hispanic (248)	333	4.39
Hispanic (15)	35	0.46
American Indian/Alaska Native (15)	49	0.65
Not Hispanic (5)	28	0.37
Hispanic (10)	21	0.28
Apache (0)	3	0.04
Blackfeet (0)	1	0.01
Central American Ind. (6)	6	0.08
Cherokee (0)	3	0.04
Hopi (0)	1	0.01
Iroquois (2)	2	0.03
Mexican American Ind. (3)	4	0.05
South American Ind. (0)	1	0.01
Ute (0)	1	0.01
Asian (108)	151	1.99
Not Hispanic (105)	135	1.78
Hispanic (3)	16	0.21
Chinese, ex. Taiwanese (40)	47	0.62
Filipino (8)	12	0.16
Indian (6)	17	0.22
Japanese (7)	10	0.13
Korean (21)	25	0.33
Pakistani (13)	13	0.17
Thai (3)	8	0.11
Vietnamese (7)	7	0.09
Hawaii Native/Pacific Islander (1)	6	0.08
Not Hispanic (1)	5	0.07
Hispanic (0)	1	0.01
Samoan (0)	1	0.01
White (6,787)	6,945	91.62
Not Hispanic (6,313)	6,420	84.70
Hispanic (474)	525	6.93

Centereach

Place Type: CDP
County: Suffolk
Population: 31,578†

Ancestry‡	Population	%
American (654)	654	2.06
Arab (0)	22	0.07
Arab (0)	11	0.03
Syrian (0)	11	0.03
Armenian (0)	14	0.04
Austrian (65)	198	0.62
British (48)	99	0.31
Bulgarian (0)	27	0.09
Canadian (0)	116	0.37
Croatian (0)	82	0.26
Czech (8)	182	0.57
Czechoslovakian (6)	49	0.15
Danish (13)	94	0.30
Dutch (11)	220	0.69
Eastern European (16)	16	0.05
English (196)	1,677	5.29
Estonian (0)	12	0.04
European (97)	116	0.37
French, ex. Basque (28)	905	2.86
French Canadian (17)	239	0.75
German (875)	5,397	17.03
Greek (94)	360	1.14
Hungarian (75)	257	0.81
Iranian (21)	21	0.07
Irish (1,298)	7,442	23.49
Israeli (0)	20	0.06
Italian (5,272)	11,413	36.02
Lithuanian (6)	66	0.21
Luxemburger (0)	18	0.06
Maltese (0)	5	0.02
Norwegian (42)	270	0.85
Pennsylvania German (13)	13	0.04
Polish (632)	2,082	6.57
Portuguese (257)	312	0.98
Romanian (29)	66	0.21
Russian (425)	1,056	3.33
Scotch-Irish (26)	252	0.80
Scottish (51)	346	1.09
Slovak (127)	135	0.43
Swedish (9)	210	0.66
Swiss (22)	187	0.59
Turkish (30)	57	0.18
Ukrainian (27)	174	0.55
Welsh (0)	18	0.06
West Indian, ex. Hispanic (266)	580	1.83
Bermudan (0)	34	0.11
Haitian (179)	358	1.13
Jamaican (49)	96	0.30
West Indian (38)	77	0.24
Other West Indian (0)	15	0.05
Yugoslavian (60)	86	0.27

Hispanic Origin	Population	%
Hispanic or Latino (of any race)	3,575	11.32
Central American, ex. Mexican	637	2.02
Costa Rican	15	0.05
Guatemalan	45	0.14
Honduran	158	0.50

*Notes: † The Census 2010 population figure is used to calculate the percentages in the Hispanic Origin and Race categories. Ancestry percentages are based on the 2006-2010 American Community Survey population (not shown); ‡ Numbers in parentheses indicate the number of people reporting a single ancestry; * Numbers in parentheses indicate the number of persons reporting this race alone, not in combination with any other race; Please refer to the Explanation of Data for more information.*

Nicaraguan	16	0.05
Panamanian	13	0.04
Salvadoran	385	1.22
Other Central American	5	0.02
Cuban	96	0.30
Dominican Republic	275	0.87
Mexican	276	0.87
Puerto Rican	1,312	4.15
South American	615	1.95
Argentinean	46	0.15
Bolivian	23	0.07
Chilean	20	0.06
Colombian	210	0.67
Ecuadorian	217	0.69
Paraguayan	1	<0.01
Peruvian	43	0.14
Uruguayan	11	0.03
Venezuelan	30	0.10
Other South American	14	0.04
Other Hispanic or Latino	364	1.15

Race*	Population	%
African-American/Black (970)	1,192	3.77
Not Hispanic (834)	1,001	3.17
Hispanic (136)	191	0.60
American Indian/Alaska Native (37)	153	0.48
Not Hispanic (23)	118	0.37
Hispanic (14)	35	0.11
Arapaho (0)	1	<0.01
Blackfeet (0)	12	0.04
Cherokee (0)	17	0.05
Chippewa (0)	1	<0.01
Creek (0)	1	<0.01
Delaware (0)	1	<0.01
Iroquois (1)	4	0.01
Lumbee (0)	1	<0.01
Navajo (0)	2	0.01
Seminole (1)	3	0.01
Shoshone (0)	1	<0.01
South American Ind. (7)	14	0.04
Asian (1,956)	2,176	6.89
Not Hispanic (1,950)	2,137	6.77
Hispanic (6)	39	0.12
Bangladeshi (78)	82	0.26
Burmese (5)	5	0.02
Chinese, ex. Taiwanese (613)	681	2.16
Filipino (248)	280	0.89
Indian (523)	558	1.77
Indonesian (1)	5	0.02
Japanese (18)	34	0.11
Korean (121)	139	0.44
Nepalese (4)	4	0.01
Pakistani (196)	224	0.71
Sri Lankan (19)	30	0.10
Taiwanese (20)	20	0.06
Thai (14)	21	0.07
Vietnamese (25)	35	0.11
Hawaii Native/Pacific Islander (7)	30	0.10
Not Hispanic (7)	25	0.08
Hispanic (0)	5	0.02
Fijian (1)	1	<0.01
Guamanian/Chamorro (2)	3	0.01
Native Hawaiian (3)	10	0.03
White (26,956)	27,487	87.04
Not Hispanic (24,749)	25,079	79.42
Hispanic (2,207)	2,408	7.63

Central Islip

Place Type: CDP
County: Suffolk
Population: 34,450†

Ancestry‡	Population	%
Afghan (17)	17	0.05
African, Sub-Saharan (243)	277	0.77
African (104)	124	0.35
Ghanaian (15)	15	0.04
Nigerian (49)	63	0.18
Other Sub-Saharan African (75)	75	0.21
American (489)	489	1.36
Arab (146)	189	0.53
Egyptian (28)	53	0.15
Moroccan (41)	59	0.16
Palestinian (77)	77	0.21
Austrian (0)	5	0.01
Basque (18)	18	0.05
Brazilian (77)	158	0.44
British (34)	50	0.14
Canadian (47)	47	0.13
Celtic (28)	28	0.08
Czech (34)	129	0.36
Czechoslovakian (19)	32	0.09
Danish (0)	15	0.04
Dutch (0)	13	0.04
English (30)	480	1.34
French, ex. Basque (28)	172	0.48
French Canadian (0)	25	0.07
German (346)	1,742	4.85
Greek (199)	234	0.65
Guyanese (106)	112	0.31
Hungarian (21)	29	0.08
Iranian (19)	19	0.05
Irish (628)	2,344	6.53
Israeli (5)	5	0.01
Italian (1,210)	2,379	6.62
Lithuanian (21)	67	0.19
Norwegian (10)	111	0.31
Polish (113)	694	1.93
Portuguese (68)	80	0.22
Russian (24)	196	0.55
Scotch-Irish (28)	199	0.55
Scottish (11)	68	0.19
Slavic (0)	35	0.10
Slovak (0)	12	0.03
Slovene (7)	7	0.02
Swedish (37)	93	0.26
Swiss (8)	34	0.09
Ukrainian (16)	37	0.10
Welsh (0)	32	0.09
West Indian, ex. Hispanic (2,122)	2,523	7.03
Barbadian (0)	20	0.06
Belizean (17)	17	0.05
British West Indian (27)	85	0.24
Dutch West Indian (16)	16	0.04
Haitian (1,382)	1,538	4.28
Jamaican (390)	485	1.35
Trinidadian/Tobagonian (273)	289	0.80
West Indian (17)	73	0.20

Hispanic Origin	Population	%
Hispanic or Latino (of any race)	17,938	52.07
Central American, ex. Mexican	8,487	24.64
Costa Rican	43	0.12
Guatemalan	677	1.97
Honduran	1,118	3.25
Nicaraguan	69	0.20
Panamanian	134	0.39
Salvadoran	6,381	18.52
Other Central American	65	0.19
Cuban	146	0.42
Dominican Republic	1,261	3.66
Mexican	598	1.74
Puerto Rican	3,452	10.02
South American	2,327	6.75
Argentinean	116	0.34
Bolivian	64	0.19
Chilean	99	0.29
Colombian	711	2.06
Ecuadorian	676	1.96
Paraguayan	13	0.04
Peruvian	558	1.62
Uruguayan	23	0.07
Venezuelan	63	0.18
Other South American	4	0.01
Other Hispanic or Latino	1,667	4.84

Race*	Population	%
African-American/Black (8,600)	9,450	27.43
Not Hispanic (7,740)	8,255	23.96
Hispanic (860)	1,195	3.47
American Indian/Alaska Native (303)	651	1.89
Not Hispanic (110)	292	0.85
Hispanic (193)	359	1.04
Apache (0)	2	0.01
Blackfeet (1)	13	0.04
Central American Ind. (22)	31	0.09
Cherokee (5)	73	0.21
Chickasaw (0)	2	0.01
Delaware (1)	6	0.02
Houma (1)	1	<0.01
Iroquois (2)	6	0.02
Lumbee (2)	2	0.01
Mexican American Ind. (16)	26	0.08
Navajo (0)	1	<0.01
Pueblo (0)	1	<0.01
Seminole (1)	1	<0.01
South American Ind. (28)	49	0.14
Spanish American Ind. (17)	23	0.07
Tlingit-Haida *(Alaska Native)* (1)	1	<0.01
Yuman (0)	1	<0.01
Asian (1,158)	1,436	4.17
Not Hispanic (1,112)	1,333	3.87
Hispanic (46)	103	0.30
Bangladeshi (27)	29	0.08
Chinese, ex. Taiwanese (109)	148	0.43
Filipino (111)	133	0.39
Indian (531)	660	1.92
Indonesian (1)	2	0.01
Japanese (6)	26	0.08
Korean (44)	50	0.15
Laotian (3)	3	0.01
Malaysian (1)	1	<0.01
Nepalese (8)	8	0.02
Pakistani (177)	186	0.54
Sri Lankan (3)	3	0.01
Thai (5)	7	0.02
Vietnamese (91)	98	0.28
Hawaii Native/Pacific Islander (13)	90	0.26
Not Hispanic (5)	32	0.09
Hispanic (8)	58	0.17
Fijian (0)	1	<0.01
Guamanian/Chamorro (7)	16	0.05
Native Hawaiian (3)	20	0.06
Samoan (0)	1	<0.01
White (15,037)	16,480	47.84
Not Hispanic (6,683)	7,108	20.63
Hispanic (8,354)	9,372	27.20

Cheektowaga

Place Type: CDP
County: Erie
Population: 75,178†

Ancestry‡	Population	%
African, Sub-Saharan (178)	178	0.23
African (145)	145	0.19
Other Sub-Saharan African (33)	33	0.04
Albanian (15)	21	0.03
American (1,642)	1,642	2.17
Arab (498)	611	0.81
Arab (208)	224	0.30
Iraqi (30)	30	0.04
Lebanese (260)	338	0.45
Syrian (0)	13	0.02
Other Arab (0)	6	0.01
Armenian (0)	13	0.02
Austrian (33)	202	0.27
Belgian (0)	29	0.04
British (51)	217	0.29
Bulgarian (30)	30	0.04
Canadian (63)	193	0.25
Carpatho Rusyn (6)	6	0.01
Croatian (21)	90	0.12
Czech (0)	249	0.33
Czechoslovakian (10)	10	0.01
Danish (0)	53	0.07
Dutch (59)	763	1.01
English (753)	4,258	5.62

*Notes: † The Census 2010 population figure is used to calculate the percentages in the Hispanic Origin and Race categories. Ancestry percentages are based on the 2006-2010 American Community Survey population (not shown); ‡ Numbers in parentheses indicate the number of people reporting a single ancestry; * Numbers in parentheses indicate the number of persons reporting this race alone, not in combination with any other race; Please refer to the Explanation of Data for more information.*

Ancestry	Population	%
Estonian (78)	78	0.10
European (101)	122	0.16
Finnish (12)	28	0.04
French, ex. Basque (123)	2,246	2.96
French Canadian (122)	608	0.80
German (6,860)	21,843	28.83
German Russian (12)	12	0.02
Greek (116)	188	0.25
Guyanese (23)	23	0.03
Hungarian (132)	542	0.72
Irish (2,376)	11,306	14.92
Italian (5,350)	12,314	16.26
Latvian (16)	16	0.02
Lithuanian (12)	84	0.11
Macedonian (21)	35	0.05
New Zealander (11)	11	0.01
Norwegian (15)	247	0.33
Pennsylvania German (15)	24	0.03
Polish (15,029)	26,237	34.63
Portuguese (11)	75	0.10
Romanian (38)	51	0.07
Russian (173)	411	0.54
Scandinavian (0)	15	0.02
Scotch-Irish (268)	861	1.14
Scottish (183)	788	1.04
Serbian (82)	100	0.13
Slavic (11)	45	0.06
Slovak (71)	229	0.30
Slovene (0)	16	0.02
Swedish (143)	418	0.55
Swiss (14)	63	0.08
Turkish (0)	42	0.06
Ukrainian (268)	499	0.66
Welsh (8)	327	0.43
West Indian, ex. Hispanic (240)	315	0.42
Barbadian (8)	8	0.01
British West Indian (13)	13	0.02
Haitian (7)	7	0.01
Jamaican (129)	182	0.24
Trinidadian/Tobagonian (33)	55	0.07
West Indian (50)	50	0.07
Yugoslavian (69)	69	0.09

Hispanic Origin	Population	%
Hispanic or Latino (of any race)	1,672	2.22
Central American, ex. Mexican	55	0.07
Costa Rican	5	0.01
Guatemalan	11	0.01
Honduran	6	0.01
Nicaraguan	1	<0.01
Panamanian	13	0.02
Salvadoran	14	0.02
Other Central American	5	0.01
Cuban	47	0.06
Dominican Republic	55	0.07
Mexican	244	0.32
Puerto Rican	1,011	1.34
South American	105	0.14
Argentinean	7	0.01
Bolivian	6	0.01
Chilean	4	0.01
Colombian	39	0.05
Ecuadorian	22	0.03
Paraguayan	2	<0.01
Peruvian	10	0.01
Uruguayan	2	<0.01
Venezuelan	11	0.01
Other South American	2	<0.01
Other Hispanic or Latino	155	0.21

Race*	Population	%
African-American/Black (6,881)	7,619	10.13
Not Hispanic (6,716)	7,368	9.80
Hispanic (165)	251	0.33
American Indian/Alaska Native (189)	469	0.62
Not Hispanic (171)	416	0.55
Hispanic (18)	53	0.07
Apache (1)	6	0.01
Blackfeet (0)	12	0.02
Canadian/French Am. Ind. (5)	5	0.01
Central American Ind. (1)	1	<0.01
Cherokee (6)	45	0.06
Cheyenne (0)	1	<0.01
Chippewa (5)	6	0.01
Choctaw (2)	3	<0.01
Cree (0)	1	<0.01
Creek (1)	1	<0.01
Delaware (2)	2	<0.01
Hopi (2)	2	<0.01
Iroquois (95)	179	0.24
Mexican American Ind. (5)	7	0.01
Navajo (1)	3	<0.01
Pueblo (0)	3	<0.01
Sioux (1)	6	0.01
South American Ind. (0)	4	0.01
Asian (1,252)	1,476	1.96
Not Hispanic (1,249)	1,455	1.94
Hispanic (3)	21	0.03
Bangladeshi (2)	2	<0.01
Burmese (6)	8	0.01
Cambodian (9)	11	0.01
Chinese, ex. Taiwanese (100)	134	0.18
Filipino (68)	112	0.15
Hmong (0)	1	<0.01
Indian (499)	529	0.70
Indonesian (6)	10	0.01
Japanese (16)	37	0.05
Korean (61)	89	0.12
Laotian (58)	65	0.09
Malaysian (12)	12	0.02
Nepalese (5)	5	0.01
Pakistani (37)	52	0.07
Sri Lankan (0)	2	<0.01
Taiwanese (4)	4	0.01
Thai (5)	10	0.01
Vietnamese (297)	326	0.43
Hawaii Native/Pacific Islander (12)	39	0.05
Not Hispanic (9)	30	0.04
Hispanic (3)	9	0.01
Fijian (2)	2	<0.01
Guamanian/Chamorro (2)	7	0.01
Native Hawaiian (5)	14	0.02
Samoan (1)	2	<0.01
White (65,225)	66,265	88.14
Not Hispanic (64,288)	65,180	86.70
Hispanic (937)	1,085	1.44

Cheektowaga

Place Type: Town
County: Erie
Population: 88,226†

Ancestry‡	Population	%
African, Sub-Saharan (178)	178	0.20
African (145)	145	0.16
Other Sub-Saharan African (33)	33	0.04
Albanian (15)	30	0.03
American (1,927)	1,927	2.17
Arab (768)	905	1.02
Arab (231)	247	0.28
Iraqi (30)	30	0.03
Lebanese (260)	350	0.39
Palestinian (9)	9	0.01
Syrian (0)	25	0.03
Other Arab (238)	244	0.27
Armenian (0)	13	0.01
Austrian (33)	225	0.25
Belgian (0)	29	0.03
British (84)	277	0.31
Bulgarian (73)	73	0.08
Canadian (72)	202	0.23
Carpatho Rusyn (6)	6	0.01
Croatian (21)	90	0.10
Czech (29)	312	0.35
Czechoslovakian (48)	60	0.07
Danish (0)	53	0.06
Dutch (125)	935	1.05
English (852)	4,818	5.42
Estonian (78)	78	0.09
European (123)	144	0.16
Finnish (12)	28	0.03
French, ex. Basque (132)	2,577	2.90
French Canadian (122)	701	0.79
German (7,899)	26,125	29.39
German Russian (12)	12	0.01
Greek (169)	249	0.28
Guyanese (23)	23	0.03
Hungarian (132)	575	0.65
Irish (2,677)	13,325	14.99
Italian (6,376)	14,630	16.46
Latvian (16)	16	0.02
Lithuanian (12)	99	0.11
Macedonian (21)	35	0.04
New Zealander (11)	11	0.01
Northern European (130)	130	0.15
Norwegian (15)	256	0.29
Pennsylvania German (24)	33	0.04
Polish (18,227)	31,456	35.39
Portuguese (11)	84	0.09
Romanian (38)	61	0.07
Russian (182)	430	0.48
Scandinavian (0)	44	0.05
Scotch-Irish (291)	969	1.09
Scottish (232)	954	1.07
Serbian (82)	100	0.11
Slavic (11)	45	0.05
Slovak (71)	229	0.26
Slovene (0)	16	0.02
Swedish (228)	542	0.61
Swiss (26)	85	0.10
Turkish (0)	42	0.05
Ukrainian (295)	556	0.63
Welsh (8)	383	0.43
West Indian, ex. Hispanic (240)	315	0.35
Barbadian (8)	8	0.01
British West Indian (13)	13	0.01
Haitian (7)	7	0.01
Jamaican (129)	182	0.20
Trinidadian/Tobagonian (33)	55	0.06
West Indian (50)	50	0.06
Yugoslavian (69)	69	0.08

Hispanic Origin	Population	%
Hispanic or Latino (of any race)	1,900	2.15
Central American, ex. Mexican	78	0.09
Costa Rican	5	0.01
Guatemalan	21	0.02
Honduran	6	0.01
Nicaraguan	4	<0.01
Panamanian	13	0.01
Salvadoran	21	0.02
Other Central American	8	0.01
Cuban	51	0.06
Dominican Republic	59	0.07
Mexican	285	0.32
Puerto Rican	1,138	1.29
South American	112	0.13
Argentinean	7	0.01
Bolivian	6	0.01
Chilean	4	<0.01
Colombian	41	0.05
Ecuadorian	26	0.03
Paraguayan	2	<0.01
Peruvian	10	0.01
Uruguayan	2	<0.01
Venezuelan	12	0.01
Other South American	2	<0.01
Other Hispanic or Latino	177	0.20

Race*	Population	%
African-American/Black (7,069)	7,879	8.93
Not Hispanic (6,898)	7,611	8.63
Hispanic (171)	268	0.30
American Indian/Alaska Native (223)	546	0.62
Not Hispanic (200)	482	0.55
Hispanic (23)	64	0.07
Apache (1)	6	0.01
Arapaho (1)	1	<0.01
Blackfeet (0)	15	0.02

*Notes: † The Census 2010 population figure is used to calculate the percentages in the Hispanic Origin and Race categories. Ancestry percentages are based on the 2006-2010 American Community Survey population (not shown); ‡ Numbers in parentheses indicate the number of people reporting a single ancestry; * Numbers in parentheses indicate the number of persons reporting this race alone, not in combination with any other race; Please refer to the Explanation of Data for more information.*

Race (continued)	Population	%
Canadian/French Am. Ind. (5)	5	0.01
Central American Ind. (3)	4	<0.01
Cherokee (6)	52	0.06
Cheyenne (0)	1	<0.01
Chippewa (5)	6	0.01
Choctaw (2)	3	<0.01
Cree (0)	1	<0.01
Creek (1)	2	<0.01
Delaware (2)	2	<0.01
Hopi (2)	2	<0.01
Iroquois (110)	194	0.22
Lumbee (0)	4	<0.01
Mexican American Ind. (7)	9	0.01
Navajo (1)	3	<0.01
Pueblo (0)	3	<0.01
Sioux (1)	6	0.01
South American Ind. (0)	4	<0.01
Asian (1,336)	1,598	1.81
Not Hispanic (1,333)	1,576	1.79
Hispanic (3)	22	0.02
Bangladeshi (4)	4	<0.01
Burmese (6)	8	0.01
Cambodian (10)	15	0.02
Chinese, ex. Taiwanese (111)	146	0.17
Filipino (77)	128	0.15
Hmong (0)	1	<0.01
Indian (530)	568	0.64
Indonesian (6)	10	0.01
Japanese (17)	38	0.04
Korean (69)	106	0.12
Laotian (58)	65	0.07
Malaysian (13)	13	0.01
Nepalese (5)	5	0.01
Pakistani (37)	52	0.06
Sri Lankan (0)	2	<0.01
Taiwanese (4)	4	<0.01
Thai (5)	10	0.01
Vietnamese (315)	344	0.39
Hawaii Native/Pacific Islander (14)	43	0.05
Not Hispanic (10)	33	0.04
Hispanic (4)	10	0.01
Fijian (2)	2	<0.01
Guamanian/Chamorro (3)	8	0.01
Native Hawaiian (5)	16	0.02
Samoan (1)	5	0.01
White (77,769)	78,958	89.50
Not Hispanic (76,673)	77,687	88.05
Hispanic (1,096)	1,271	1.44

Chenango

Place Type: Town
County: Broome
Population: 11,252†

Ancestry‡	Population	%
African, Sub-Saharan (49)	49	0.43
Other Sub-Saharan African (49)	49	0.43
American (562)	562	4.98
Arab (50)	59	0.52
Arab (22)	22	0.20
Lebanese (28)	37	0.33
Armenian (0)	106	0.94
Austrian (37)	102	0.90
British (19)	107	0.95
Canadian (18)	38	0.34
Celtic (30)	30	0.27
Croatian (9)	29	0.26
Czech (103)	207	1.84
Czechoslovakian (82)	119	1.06
Dutch (39)	197	1.75
Eastern European (11)	11	0.10
English (550)	1,757	15.58
Estonian (11)	32	0.28
European (31)	31	0.27
Finnish (0)	18	0.16
French, ex. Basque (12)	256	2.27
French Canadian (26)	52	0.46
German (626)	2,126	18.85
Greek (54)	54	0.48
Hungarian (33)	71	0.63
Irish (818)	2,893	25.65
Italian (518)	1,420	12.59
Lithuanian (40)	126	1.12
Norwegian (10)	36	0.32
Pennsylvania German (0)	60	0.53
Polish (342)	973	8.63
Portuguese (11)	11	0.10
Romanian (0)	11	0.10
Russian (97)	178	1.58
Scotch-Irish (80)	192	1.70
Scottish (71)	223	1.98
Slavic (8)	8	0.07
Slovak (145)	401	3.56
Swedish (17)	140	1.24
Swiss (14)	40	0.35
Ukrainian (113)	165	1.46
Welsh (89)	419	3.72

Hispanic Origin	Population	%
Hispanic or Latino (of any race)	166	1.48
Central American, ex. Mexican	22	0.20
Costa Rican	3	0.03
Guatemalan	5	0.04
Honduran	2	0.02
Nicaraguan	3	0.03
Salvadoran	9	0.08
Cuban	6	0.05
Mexican	24	0.21
Puerto Rican	69	0.61
South American	15	0.13
Argentinean	1	0.01
Colombian	5	0.04
Ecuadorian	4	0.04
Peruvian	3	0.03
Uruguayan	2	0.02
Other Hispanic or Latino	30	0.27

Race*	Population	%
African-American/Black (91)	174	1.55
Not Hispanic (79)	159	1.41
Hispanic (12)	15	0.13
American Indian/Alaska Native (24)	85	0.76
Not Hispanic (23)	79	0.70
Hispanic (1)	6	0.05
Apache (0)	2	0.02
Blackfeet (2)	5	0.04
Cherokee (2)	12	0.11
Chickasaw (0)	1	0.01
Chippewa (0)	1	0.01
Iroquois (8)	15	0.13
Mexican American Ind. (1)	1	0.01
Potawatomi (1)	1	0.01
Pueblo (0)	2	0.02
Sioux (2)	5	0.04
South American Ind. (5)	5	0.04
Asian (93)	144	1.28
Not Hispanic (93)	143	1.27
Hispanic (0)	1	0.01
Bangladeshi (0)	4	0.04
Chinese, ex. Taiwanese (33)	44	0.39
Filipino (5)	9	0.08
Indian (12)	22	0.20
Japanese (3)	8	0.07
Korean (12)	26	0.23
Laotian (3)	4	0.04
Malaysian (0)	1	0.01
Taiwanese (0)	1	0.01
Thai (4)	6	0.05
Vietnamese (14)	22	0.20
Hawaii Native/Pacific Islander (0)	8	0.07
Not Hispanic (0)	8	0.07
Native Hawaiian (0)	4	0.04
Samoan (0)	1	0.01
White (10,812)	10,986	97.64
Not Hispanic (10,711)	10,872	96.62
Hispanic (101)	114	1.01

Chester

Place Type: Town
County: Orange
Population: 11,981†

Ancestry‡	Population	%
African, Sub-Saharan (66)	66	0.54
Nigerian (66)	66	0.54
American (553)	553	4.56
Arab (0)	10	0.08
Lebanese (0)	10	0.08
Austrian (39)	52	0.43
Belgian (0)	86	0.71
British (54)	54	0.44
Canadian (0)	69	0.57
Czech (0)	25	0.21
Czechoslovakian (0)	34	0.28
Danish (0)	10	0.08
Dutch (19)	147	1.21
Eastern European (24)	24	0.20
English (112)	611	5.04
European (219)	219	1.80
French, ex. Basque (0)	339	2.79
French Canadian (47)	71	0.59
German (489)	1,990	16.40
Greek (0)	91	0.75
Hungarian (25)	36	0.30
Iranian (11)	11	0.09
Irish (1,065)	3,179	26.20
Italian (1,510)	3,264	26.90
Lithuanian (36)	96	0.79
Norwegian (21)	146	1.20
Polish (185)	850	7.00
Portuguese (76)	171	1.41
Romanian (0)	11	0.09
Russian (102)	197	1.62
Scotch-Irish (0)	58	0.48
Scottish (26)	271	2.23
Slovak (24)	24	0.20
Swedish (0)	46	0.38
Ukrainian (140)	171	1.41
Welsh (11)	29	0.24
West Indian, ex. Hispanic (359)	463	3.82
Haitian (220)	324	2.67
Jamaican (89)	89	0.73
West Indian (50)	50	0.41
Yugoslavian (0)	32	0.26

Hispanic Origin	Population	%
Hispanic or Latino (of any race)	1,669	13.93
Central American, ex. Mexican	42	0.35
Guatemalan	12	0.10
Honduran	6	0.05
Nicaraguan	1	0.01
Panamanian	12	0.10
Salvadoran	11	0.09
Cuban	66	0.55
Dominican Republic	192	1.60
Mexican	154	1.29
Puerto Rican	977	8.15
South American	143	1.19
Argentinean	5	0.04
Chilean	3	0.03
Colombian	40	0.33
Ecuadorian	65	0.54
Paraguayan	3	0.03
Peruvian	20	0.17
Venezuelan	7	0.06
Other Hispanic or Latino	95	0.79

Race*	Population	%
African-American/Black (911)	1,060	8.85
Not Hispanic (812)	923	7.70
Hispanic (99)	137	1.14
American Indian/Alaska Native (49)	130	1.09
Not Hispanic (38)	108	0.90
Hispanic (11)	22	0.18
Blackfeet (0)	4	0.03
Cherokee (2)	9	0.08

*Notes: † The Census 2010 population figure is used to calculate the percentages in the Hispanic Origin and Race categories. Ancestry percentages are based on the 2006-2010 American Community Survey population (not shown); ‡ Numbers in parentheses indicate the number of people reporting a single ancestry; * Numbers in parentheses indicate the number of persons reporting this race alone, not in combination with any other race; Please refer to the Explanation of Data for more information.*

Delaware (8)	17	0.14
Iroquois (5)	18	0.15
Navajo (2)	2	0.02
Sioux (0)	1	0.01
South American Ind. (0)	2	0.02
Tohono O'Odham (0)	3	0.03
Asian (492)	613	5.12
Not Hispanic (490)	602	5.02
Hispanic (2)	11	0.09
Bangladeshi (8)	8	0.07
Cambodian (4)	6	0.05
Chinese, ex. Taiwanese (114)	145	1.21
Filipino (81)	110	0.92
Indian (140)	165	1.38
Indonesian (3)	8	0.07
Japanese (9)	20	0.17
Korean (41)	56	0.47
Pakistani (30)	33	0.28
Sri Lankan (0)	3	0.03
Taiwanese (4)	4	0.03
Thai (2)	3	0.03
Vietnamese (39)	52	0.43
Hawaii Native/Pacific Islander (1)	9	0.08
Not Hispanic (1)	5	0.04
Hispanic (0)	4	0.03
Guamanian/Chamorro (1)	1	0.01
White (9,660)	9,938	82.95
Not Hispanic (8,695)	8,899	74.28
Hispanic (965)	1,039	8.67

Chestnut Ridge

Place Type: Village
County: Rockland
Population: 7,916†

Ancestry‡	Population	%
African, Sub-Saharan (49)	49	0.62
African (22)	22	0.28
Nigerian (27)	27	0.34
American (233)	233	2.97
Austrian (19)	55	0.70
Belgian (0)	8	0.10
British (0)	7	0.09
Bulgarian (8)	8	0.10
Canadian (0)	8	0.10
Czech (50)	75	0.96
Czechoslovakian (10)	19	0.24
Danish (0)	9	0.11
Dutch (13)	31	0.39
Eastern European (63)	63	0.80
English (38)	280	3.57
European (297)	297	3.78
French, ex. Basque (24)	98	1.25
French Canadian (0)	9	0.11
German (253)	696	8.87
Greek (99)	125	1.59
Hungarian (54)	110	1.40
Iranian (24)	121	1.54
Irish (374)	780	9.94
Israeli (78)	78	0.99
Italian (868)	1,277	16.27
Lithuanian (28)	28	0.36
Polish (249)	431	5.49
Portuguese (20)	20	0.25
Romanian (0)	4	0.05
Russian (115)	239	3.04
Scotch-Irish (59)	127	1.62
Scottish (59)	101	1.29
Swedish (7)	55	0.70
Swiss (34)	43	0.55
Turkish (10)	20	0.25
Ukrainian (76)	76	0.97
Welsh (0)	46	0.59
West Indian, ex. Hispanic (666)	775	9.87
Barbadian (0)	24	0.31
Belizean (12)	35	0.45
Haitian (562)	570	7.26
Jamaican (52)	87	1.11
Trinidadian/Tobagonian (0)	9	0.11
West Indian (40)	50	0.64
Yugoslavian (42)	78	0.99

Hispanic Origin	Population	%
Hispanic or Latino (of any race)	875	11.05
Central American, ex. Mexican	92	1.16
Costa Rican	1	0.01
Guatemalan	65	0.82
Honduran	3	0.04
Panamanian	9	0.11
Salvadoran	14	0.18
Cuban	50	0.63
Dominican Republic	98	1.24
Mexican	63	0.80
Puerto Rican	316	3.99
South American	187	2.36
Argentinean	14	0.18
Bolivian	4	0.05
Chilean	3	0.04
Colombian	32	0.40
Ecuadorian	105	1.33
Peruvian	26	0.33
Venezuelan	3	0.04
Other Hispanic or Latino	69	0.87

Race*	Population	%
African-American/Black (1,387)	1,485	18.76
Not Hispanic (1,337)	1,410	17.81
Hispanic (50)	75	0.95
American Indian/Alaska Native (5)	30	0.38
Not Hispanic (3)	17	0.21
Hispanic (2)	13	0.16
Central American Ind. (0)	2	0.03
Cherokee (1)	5	0.06
Iroquois (1)	1	0.01
Mexican American Ind. (0)	3	0.04
South American Ind. (0)	5	0.06
Asian (644)	698	8.82
Not Hispanic (626)	671	8.48
Hispanic (18)	27	0.34
Bangladeshi (5)	5	0.06
Cambodian (7)	7	0.09
Chinese, ex. Taiwanese (108)	131	1.65
Filipino (158)	173	2.19
Indian (219)	236	2.98
Indonesian (0)	1	0.01
Japanese (31)	37	0.47
Korean (37)	43	0.54
Nepalese (6)	6	0.08
Pakistani (31)	32	0.40
Taiwanese (2)	3	0.04
Thai (8)	12	0.15
Vietnamese (11)	18	0.23
Hawaii Native/Pacific Islander (6)	12	0.15
Not Hispanic (6)	11	0.14
Hispanic (0)	1	0.01
Guamanian/Chamorro (2)	2	0.03
Native Hawaiian (4)	4	0.05
White (5,438)	5,605	70.81
Not Hispanic (4,922)	5,022	63.44
Hispanic (516)	583	7.36

Chili

Place Type: Town
County: Monroe
Population: 28,625†

Ancestry‡	Population	%
African, Sub-Saharan (71)	148	0.52
African (71)	118	0.42
Nigerian (0)	30	0.11
American (1,297)	1,297	4.57
Arab (14)	49	0.17
Lebanese (14)	49	0.17
Armenian (10)	10	0.04
Australian (13)	13	0.05
Austrian (0)	72	0.25
Belgian (0)	50	0.18
British (32)	108	0.38
Bulgarian (26)	26	0.09
Canadian (76)	268	0.94
Croatian (5)	5	0.02
Czech (0)	49	0.17
Danish (12)	21	0.07
Dutch (201)	958	3.38
Eastern European (35)	35	0.12
English (965)	4,079	14.38
European (222)	222	0.78
Finnish (0)	12	0.04
French, ex. Basque (73)	924	3.26
French Canadian (198)	461	1.62
German (1,734)	8,136	28.68
German Russian (7)	7	0.02
Greek (318)	400	1.41
Guyanese (34)	34	0.12
Hungarian (79)	145	0.51
Irish (1,297)	5,883	20.74
Italian (3,089)	6,341	22.35
Lithuanian (22)	64	0.23
Macedonian (42)	45	0.16
Northern European (33)	33	0.12
Norwegian (0)	129	0.45
Polish (553)	1,424	5.02
Portuguese (57)	57	0.20
Romanian (41)	51	0.18
Russian (14)	84	0.30
Scotch-Irish (176)	594	2.09
Scottish (120)	668	2.35
Slovak (35)	54	0.19
Swedish (79)	363	1.28
Swiss (0)	11	0.04
Ukrainian (109)	254	0.90
Welsh (86)	313	1.10
West Indian, ex. Hispanic (203)	241	0.85
Barbadian (10)	10	0.04
Belizean (47)	85	0.30
Haitian (52)	52	0.18
Jamaican (94)	94	0.33
Yugoslavian (12)	25	0.09

Hispanic Origin	Population	%
Hispanic or Latino (of any race)	796	2.78
Central American, ex. Mexican	49	0.17
Costa Rican	2	0.01
Guatemalan	13	0.05
Honduran	7	0.02
Nicaraguan	3	0.01
Panamanian	13	0.05
Salvadoran	11	0.04
Cuban	44	0.15
Dominican Republic	26	0.09
Mexican	93	0.32
Puerto Rican	488	1.70
South American	47	0.16
Argentinean	9	0.03
Chilean	3	0.01
Colombian	18	0.06
Ecuadorian	5	0.02
Paraguayan	2	0.01
Peruvian	5	0.02
Venezuelan	4	0.01
Other South American	1	<0.01
Other Hispanic or Latino	49	0.17

Race*	Population	%
African-American/Black (2,177)	2,413	8.43
Not Hispanic (2,110)	2,311	8.07
Hispanic (67)	102	0.36
American Indian/Alaska Native (66)	158	0.55
Not Hispanic (63)	151	0.53
Hispanic (3)	7	0.02
Cherokee (3)	23	0.08
Chippewa (2)	4	0.01
Choctaw (0)	2	0.01
Creek (0)	2	0.01
Inupiat *(Alaska Native)* (1)	1	<0.01
Iroquois (28)	61	0.21
Mexican American Ind. (1)	1	<0.01
Navajo (1)	1	<0.01

*Notes: † The Census 2010 population figure is used to calculate the percentages in the Hispanic Origin and Race categories. Ancestry percentages are based on the 2006-2010 American Community Survey population (not shown); ‡ Numbers in parentheses indicate the number of people reporting a single ancestry; * Numbers in parentheses indicate the number of persons reporting this race alone, not in combination with any other race; Please refer to the Explanation of Data for more information.*

Seminole (0)	1	<0.01
Asian (609)	726	2.54
Not Hispanic (604)	716	2.50
Hispanic (5)	10	0.03
Burmese (1)	2	0.01
Cambodian (13)	16	0.06
Chinese, ex. Taiwanese (76)	98	0.34
Filipino (40)	60	0.21
Indian (142)	162	0.57
Indonesian (1)	1	<0.01
Japanese (11)	28	0.10
Korean (69)	95	0.33
Laotian (45)	59	0.21
Malaysian (1)	1	<0.01
Pakistani (24)	30	0.10
Sri Lankan (5)	5	0.02
Thai (7)	13	0.05
Vietnamese (143)	153	0.53
Hawaii Native/Pacific Islander (11)	22	0.08
Not Hispanic (11)	18	0.06
Hispanic (0)	4	0.01
Fijian (0)	1	<0.01
Native Hawaiian (1)	7	0.02
Samoan (4)	4	0.01
White (25,063)	25,458	88.94
Not Hispanic (24,603)	24,927	87.08
Hispanic (460)	531	1.86

Cicero

Place Type: Town
County: Onondaga
Population: 31,632†

Ancestry‡	Population	%
African, Sub-Saharan (0)	13	0.04
African (0)	13	0.04
American (975)	975	3.16
Arab (60)	224	0.73
Arab (22)	35	0.11
Egyptian (19)	74	0.24
Lebanese (11)	99	0.32
Syrian (8)	16	0.05
Armenian (0)	77	0.25
Australian (0)	8	0.03
Austrian (20)	69	0.22
Belgian (0)	74	0.24
British (46)	46	0.15
Cajun (0)	10	0.03
Canadian (21)	129	0.42
Croatian (0)	35	0.11
Czech (0)	23	0.07
Czechoslovakian (0)	24	0.08
Danish (4)	101	0.33
Dutch (101)	871	2.82
Eastern European (29)	78	0.25
English (1,192)	4,990	16.17
European (120)	157	0.51
Finnish (23)	94	0.30
French, ex. Basque (255)	2,604	8.44
French Canadian (304)	966	3.13
German (1,628)	7,533	24.40
Greek (103)	256	0.83
Hungarian (40)	183	0.59
Icelander (13)	13	0.04
Irish (1,660)	8,202	26.57
Italian (2,755)	6,405	20.75
Latvian (10)	28	0.09
Lithuanian (23)	85	0.28
Macedonian (11)	11	0.04
Maltese (16)	36	0.12
Northern European (32)	32	0.10
Norwegian (41)	154	0.50
Pennsylvania German (22)	31	0.10
Polish (1,091)	3,474	11.25
Portuguese (0)	11	0.04
Romanian (31)	59	0.19
Russian (47)	225	0.73
Scotch-Irish (253)	524	1.70
Scottish (169)	659	2.13
Slovak (14)	108	0.35
Slovene (9)	17	0.06
Swedish (31)	235	0.76
Swiss (12)	127	0.41
Turkish (128)	128	0.41
Ukrainian (87)	507	1.64
Welsh (66)	448	1.45
West Indian, ex. Hispanic (24)	41	0.13
Haitian (12)	12	0.04
Jamaican (12)	29	0.09
Yugoslavian (92)	100	0.32

Hispanic Origin	Population	%
Hispanic or Latino (of any race)	517	1.63
Central American, ex. Mexican	24	0.08
Costa Rican	2	0.01
Guatemalan	18	0.06
Honduran	2	0.01
Panamanian	2	0.01
Cuban	46	0.15
Dominican Republic	10	0.03
Mexican	125	0.40
Puerto Rican	211	0.67
South American	37	0.12
Argentinean	3	0.01
Bolivian	1	<0.01
Colombian	15	0.05
Ecuadorian	9	0.03
Peruvian	3	0.01
Venezuelan	6	0.02
Other Hispanic or Latino	64	0.20

Race*	Population	%
African-American/Black (527)	717	2.27
Not Hispanic (501)	664	2.10
Hispanic (26)	53	0.17
American Indian/Alaska Native (105)	240	0.76
Not Hispanic (96)	219	0.69
Hispanic (9)	21	0.07
Aleut *(Alaska Native)* (1)	1	<0.01
Apache (3)	4	0.01
Canadian/French Am. Ind. (1)	6	0.02
Cherokee (2)	11	0.03
Chippewa (0)	1	<0.01
Choctaw (1)	5	0.02
Iroquois (63)	119	0.38
Mexican American Ind. (2)	2	0.01
Asian (312)	402	1.27
Not Hispanic (311)	395	1.25
Hispanic (1)	7	0.02
Cambodian (16)	16	0.05
Chinese, ex. Taiwanese (49)	63	0.20
Filipino (25)	48	0.15
Hmong (12)	12	0.04
Indian (64)	79	0.25
Indonesian (1)	1	<0.01
Japanese (14)	39	0.12
Korean (36)	51	0.16
Laotian (1)	1	<0.01
Pakistani (10)	19	0.06
Sri Lankan (3)	4	0.01
Taiwanese (2)	2	0.01
Thai (7)	12	0.04
Vietnamese (47)	58	0.18
Hawaii Native/Pacific Islander (12)	25	0.08
Not Hispanic (3)	15	0.05
Hispanic (9)	10	0.03
Guamanian/Chamorro (10)	12	0.04
Native Hawaiian (2)	5	0.02
Samoan (0)	2	0.01
White (30,121)	30,505	96.44
Not Hispanic (29,804)	30,139	95.28
Hispanic (317)	366	1.16

Clarence

Place Type: Town
County: Erie
Population: 30,673†

Ancestry‡	Population	%
Albanian (0)	104	0.35
Alsatian (11)	26	0.09
American (885)	885	2.98
Arab (104)	186	0.63
Arab (63)	63	0.21
Lebanese (41)	69	0.23
Syrian (0)	5	0.02
Other Arab (0)	49	0.16
Armenian (0)	11	0.04
Australian (11)	11	0.04
Austrian (11)	137	0.46
British (91)	166	0.56
Bulgarian (0)	12	0.04
Canadian (47)	128	0.43
Croatian (11)	38	0.13
Cypriot (17)	17	0.06
Czech (15)	110	0.37
Czechoslovakian (8)	8	0.03
Danish (12)	27	0.09
Dutch (43)	353	1.19
Eastern European (30)	30	0.10
English (647)	2,995	10.07
Estonian (0)	78	0.26
European (288)	301	1.01
Finnish (0)	23	0.08
French, ex. Basque (31)	1,105	3.72
French Canadian (43)	228	0.77
German (3,189)	10,368	34.87
Greek (262)	389	1.31
Hungarian (123)	465	1.56
Icelander (14)	14	0.05
Iranian (0)	28	0.09
Irish (1,314)	5,636	18.95
Italian (3,046)	6,492	21.83
Latvian (48)	48	0.16
Lithuanian (0)	50	0.17
Luxemburger (0)	21	0.07
Macedonian (10)	30	0.10
Northern European (13)	13	0.04
Norwegian (48)	132	0.44
Pennsylvania German (8)	8	0.03
Polish (1,776)	4,414	14.84
Portuguese (9)	66	0.22
Russian (169)	255	0.86
Scotch-Irish (112)	465	1.56
Scottish (195)	766	2.58
Serbian (0)	17	0.06
Slavic (27)	50	0.17
Slovak (0)	36	0.12
Slovene (12)	39	0.13
Swedish (109)	609	2.05
Swiss (49)	182	0.61
Turkish (14)	14	0.05
Ukrainian (136)	292	0.98
Welsh (28)	205	0.69
West Indian, ex. Hispanic (32)	32	0.11
Haitian (32)	32	0.11
Yugoslavian (14)	22	0.07

Hispanic Origin	Population	%
Hispanic or Latino (of any race)	418	1.36
Central American, ex. Mexican	27	0.09
Costa Rican	6	0.02
Guatemalan	19	0.06
Panamanian	2	0.01
Cuban	24	0.08
Dominican Republic	14	0.05
Mexican	107	0.35
Puerto Rican	126	0.41
South American	65	0.21
Argentinean	10	0.03
Chilean	5	0.02
Colombian	24	0.08
Ecuadorian	10	0.03
Paraguayan	1	<0.01
Peruvian	4	0.01
Venezuelan	11	0.04
Other Hispanic or Latino	55	0.18

*Notes: † The Census 2010 population figure is used to calculate the percentages in the Hispanic Origin and Race categories. Ancestry percentages are based on the 2006-2010 American Community Survey population (not shown); ‡ Numbers in parentheses indicate the number of people reporting a single ancestry; * Numbers in parentheses indicate the number of persons reporting this race alone, not in combination with any other race; Please refer to the Explanation of Data for more information.*

Race*	Population	%
African-American/Black (350)	446	1.45
Not Hispanic (345)	432	1.41
Hispanic (5)	14	0.05
American Indian/Alaska Native (31)	96	0.31
Not Hispanic (30)	91	0.30
Hispanic (1)	5	0.02
Blackfeet (0)	1	<0.01
Cherokee (0)	3	0.01
Chippewa (1)	1	<0.01
Delaware (1)	1	<0.01
Iroquois (21)	44	0.14
Lumbee (0)	1	<0.01
Mexican American Ind. (1)	1	<0.01
South American Ind. (0)	4	0.01
Asian (1,093)	1,276	4.16
Not Hispanic (1,089)	1,259	4.10
Hispanic (4)	17	0.06
Burmese (2)	2	0.01
Chinese, ex. Taiwanese (288)	336	1.10
Filipino (34)	61	0.20
Indian (452)	517	1.69
Indonesian (2)	2	0.01
Japanese (22)	30	0.10
Korean (124)	136	0.44
Laotian (0)	1	<0.01
Malaysian (1)	1	<0.01
Pakistani (77)	80	0.26
Sri Lankan (13)	14	0.05
Taiwanese (2)	2	0.01
Thai (4)	6	0.02
Vietnamese (51)	52	0.17
Hawaii Native/Pacific Islander (6)	18	0.06
Not Hispanic (6)	15	0.05
Hispanic (0)	3	0.01
Native Hawaiian (2)	12	0.04
Samoan (2)	2	0.01
White (28,785)	29,088	94.83
Not Hispanic (28,451)	28,727	93.66
Hispanic (334)	361	1.18

Clarkstown

Place Type: Town
County: Rockland
Population: 84,187†

Ancestry‡	Population	%
African, Sub-Saharan (248)	283	0.34
African (149)	184	0.22
Ghanaian (99)	99	0.12
Albanian (317)	328	0.39
Alsatian (0)	3	<0.01
American (4,138)	4,138	4.96
Arab (440)	705	0.85
Arab (8)	29	0.03
Egyptian (229)	254	0.30
Iraqi (7)	24	0.03
Jordanian (9)	9	0.01
Lebanese (138)	252	0.30
Syrian (0)	88	0.11
Other Arab (49)	49	0.06
Armenian (84)	99	0.12
Assyrian/Chaldean/Syriac (11)	51	0.06
Australian (12)	18	0.02
Austrian (199)	827	0.99
Belgian (0)	42	0.05
Brazilian (69)	203	0.24
British (105)	190	0.23
Canadian (78)	112	0.13
Croatian (54)	111	0.13
Czech (65)	292	0.35
Czechoslovakian (75)	123	0.15
Danish (20)	91	0.11
Dutch (130)	487	0.58
Eastern European (1,163)	1,282	1.54
English (620)	2,751	3.30
European (659)	690	0.83
Finnish (50)	119	0.14
French, ex. Basque (154)	874	1.05
French Canadian (98)	288	0.35
German (1,752)	7,742	9.28
Greek (204)	613	0.74
Guyanese (77)	95	0.11
Hungarian (301)	1,008	1.21
Iranian (100)	146	0.18
Irish (7,258)	15,823	18.97
Israeli (99)	247	0.30
Italian (9,086)	16,766	20.10
Latvian (64)	87	0.10
Lithuanian (129)	286	0.34
Macedonian (24)	24	0.03
Maltese (0)	8	0.01
New Zealander (0)	3	<0.01
Northern European (15)	28	0.03
Norwegian (214)	464	0.56
Polish (1,491)	4,159	4.99
Portuguese (165)	216	0.26
Romanian (167)	544	0.65
Russian (2,652)	5,317	6.38
Scandinavian (12)	16	0.02
Scotch-Irish (228)	499	0.60
Scottish (102)	591	0.71
Serbian (11)	19	0.02
Slavic (11)	40	0.05
Slovak (179)	310	0.37
Swedish (65)	359	0.43
Swiss (39)	85	0.10
Turkish (66)	72	0.09
Ukrainian (387)	690	0.83
Welsh (0)	212	0.25
West Indian, ex. Hispanic (2,635)	2,834	3.40
Barbadian (10)	10	0.01
Belizean (9)	9	0.01
Bermudan (0)	3	<0.01
British West Indian (21)	45	0.05
Haitian (2,003)	2,077	2.49
Jamaican (382)	432	0.52
Trinidadian/Tobagonian (90)	117	0.14
West Indian (120)	141	0.17
Yugoslavian (43)	53	0.06

Hispanic Origin	Population	%
Hispanic or Latino (of any race)	9,831	11.68
Central American, ex. Mexican	1,656	1.97
Costa Rican	40	0.05
Guatemalan	802	0.95
Honduran	80	0.10
Nicaraguan	10	0.01
Panamanian	41	0.05
Salvadoran	662	0.79
Other Central American	21	0.02
Cuban	421	0.50
Dominican Republic	939	1.12
Mexican	897	1.07
Puerto Rican	3,427	4.07
South American	1,708	2.03
Argentinean	113	0.13
Bolivian	31	0.04
Chilean	73	0.09
Colombian	281	0.33
Ecuadorian	1,051	1.25
Paraguayan	5	0.01
Peruvian	119	0.14
Uruguayan	14	0.02
Venezuelan	14	0.02
Other South American	7	0.01
Other Hispanic or Latino	783	0.93

Race*	Population	%
African-American/Black (8,091)	8,965	10.65
Not Hispanic (7,598)	8,194	9.73
Hispanic (493)	771	0.92
American Indian/Alaska Native (193)	459	0.55
Not Hispanic (111)	308	0.37
Hispanic (82)	151	0.18
Apache (0)	2	<0.01
Blackfeet (1)	8	0.01
Central American Ind. (1)	2	<0.01
Cherokee (1)	42	0.05
Chippewa (1)	1	<0.01
Choctaw (1)	6	0.01
Cree (0)	1	<0.01
Creek (0)	3	<0.01
Delaware (12)	16	0.02
Iroquois (8)	13	0.02
Lumbee (2)	2	<0.01
Mexican American Ind. (6)	8	0.01
Navajo (0)	1	<0.01
Paiute (1)	1	<0.01
Potawatomi (1)	1	<0.01
Pueblo (1)	4	<0.01
Seminole (0)	4	<0.01
Sioux (1)	2	<0.01
South American Ind. (22)	38	0.05
Tlingit-Haida *(Alaska Native)* (0)	1	<0.01
Asian (8,800)	9,614	11.42
Not Hispanic (8,748)	9,462	11.24
Hispanic (52)	152	0.18
Bangladeshi (73)	85	0.10
Burmese (4)	8	0.01
Cambodian (59)	68	0.08
Chinese, ex. Taiwanese (1,132)	1,326	1.58
Filipino (2,079)	2,320	2.76
Indian (3,576)	3,874	4.60
Indonesian (5)	14	0.02
Japanese (73)	110	0.13
Korean (994)	1,026	1.22
Malaysian (3)	6	0.01
Nepalese (2)	2	<0.01
Pakistani (322)	346	0.41
Sri Lankan (43)	55	0.07
Taiwanese (49)	58	0.07
Thai (109)	121	0.14
Vietnamese (129)	164	0.19
Hawaii Native/Pacific Islander (22)	106	0.13
Not Hispanic (5)	77	0.09
Hispanic (17)	29	0.03
Guamanian/Chamorro (13)	21	0.02
Native Hawaiian (1)	5	0.01
Samoan (1)	2	<0.01
White (62,210)	63,664	75.62
Not Hispanic (56,369)	57,290	68.05
Hispanic (5,841)	6,374	7.57

Clay

Place Type: Town
County: Onondaga
Population: 58,206†

Ancestry‡	Population	%
African, Sub-Saharan (172)	216	0.37
African (107)	145	0.25
Cape Verdean (0)	6	0.01
Ghanaian (65)	65	0.11
Albanian (10)	31	0.05
American (1,975)	1,975	3.40
Arab (153)	417	0.72
Arab (58)	136	0.23
Egyptian (7)	7	0.01
Lebanese (47)	213	0.37
Palestinian (0)	13	0.02
Syrian (0)	7	0.01
Other Arab (41)	41	0.07
Austrian (49)	113	0.19
Belgian (57)	68	0.12
Brazilian (43)	43	0.07
British (33)	118	0.20
Canadian (176)	345	0.59
Celtic (0)	47	0.08
Czech (35)	312	0.54
Czechoslovakian (0)	34	0.06
Danish (0)	68	0.12
Dutch (106)	1,704	2.93
Eastern European (25)	40	0.07
English (1,748)	8,266	14.23
European (505)	550	0.95
Finnish (20)	55	0.09

*Notes: † The Census 2010 population figure is used to calculate the percentages in the Hispanic Origin and Race categories. Ancestry percentages are based on the 2006-2010 American Community Survey population (not shown); ‡ Numbers in parentheses indicate the number of people reporting a single ancestry; * Numbers in parentheses indicate the number of persons reporting this race alone, not in combination with any other race; Please refer to the Explanation of Data for more information.*

French, ex. Basque (420)	3,175	5.47
French Canadian (432)	1,241	2.14
German (2,624)	14,237	24.51
Greek (203)	475	0.82
Guyanese (17)	17	0.03
Hungarian (170)	353	0.61
Iranian (78)	99	0.17
Irish (3,324)	14,197	24.44
Italian (5,434)	13,235	22.78
Lithuanian (78)	143	0.25
Luxemburger (0)	26	0.04
Macedonian (177)	185	0.32
Northern European (35)	35	0.06
Norwegian (55)	221	0.38
Pennsylvania German (20)	38	0.07
Polish (1,694)	4,728	8.14
Portuguese (0)	37	0.06
Romanian (0)	29	0.05
Russian (60)	276	0.48
Scandinavian (8)	8	0.01
Scotch-Irish (380)	1,162	2.00
Scottish (302)	1,377	2.37
Serbian (0)	9	0.02
Slavic (8)	93	0.16
Slovak (78)	150	0.26
Slovene (0)	9	0.02
Swedish (114)	625	1.08
Swiss (22)	175	0.30
Turkish (11)	11	0.02
Ukrainian (136)	650	1.12
Welsh (52)	496	0.85
West Indian, ex. Hispanic (380)	494	0.85
Barbadian (9)	40	0.07
Haitian (157)	157	0.27
Jamaican (162)	245	0.42
Trinidadian/Tobagonian (40)	40	0.07
West Indian (12)	12	0.02
Yugoslavian (108)	132	0.23

Hispanic Origin	Population	%
Hispanic or Latino (of any race)	1,472	2.53
Central American, ex. Mexican	94	0.16
Costa Rican	3	0.01
Guatemalan	35	0.06
Honduran	16	0.03
Nicaraguan	12	0.02
Panamanian	21	0.04
Salvadoran	7	0.01
Cuban	91	0.16
Dominican Republic	61	0.10
Mexican	283	0.49
Puerto Rican	633	1.09
South American	161	0.28
Argentinean	7	0.01
Bolivian	8	0.01
Chilean	16	0.03
Colombian	65	0.11
Ecuadorian	10	0.02
Paraguayan	6	0.01
Peruvian	29	0.05
Uruguayan	2	<0.01
Venezuelan	16	0.03
Other South American	2	<0.01
Other Hispanic or Latino	149	0.26

Race*	Population	%
African-American/Black (2,524)	3,202	5.50
Not Hispanic (2,398)	3,014	5.18
Hispanic (126)	188	0.32
American Indian/Alaska Native (266)	627	1.08
Not Hispanic (228)	557	0.96
Hispanic (38)	70	0.12
Apache (1)	3	0.01
Blackfeet (0)	11	0.02
Canadian/French Am. Ind. (9)	16	0.03
Cherokee (8)	42	0.07
Chippewa (5)	11	0.02
Choctaw (1)	5	0.01
Comanche (1)	1	<0.01
Cree (1)	1	<0.01
Creek (0)	1	<0.01
Delaware (0)	1	<0.01
Hopi (0)	2	<0.01
Houma (1)	1	<0.01
Inupiat *(Alaska Native)* (0)	1	<0.01
Iroquois (130)	252	0.43
Lumbee (0)	3	0.01
Mexican American Ind. (5)	9	0.02
Navajo (3)	4	0.01
Osage (1)	1	<0.01
Ottawa (1)	1	<0.01
Potawatomi (0)	1	<0.01
Seminole (0)	3	0.01
Sioux (2)	4	0.01
South American Ind. (1)	4	0.01
Spanish American Ind. (8)	8	0.01
Asian (1,430)	1,754	3.01
Not Hispanic (1,426)	1,733	2.98
Hispanic (4)	21	0.04
Bangladeshi (0)	1	<0.01
Burmese (5)	5	0.01
Cambodian (28)	29	0.05
Chinese, ex. Taiwanese (259)	299	0.51
Filipino (123)	192	0.33
Hmong (61)	75	0.13
Indian (367)	398	0.68
Indonesian (1)	2	<0.01
Japanese (21)	66	0.11
Korean (130)	190	0.33
Laotian (47)	52	0.09
Malaysian (0)	1	<0.01
Nepalese (4)	4	0.01
Pakistani (47)	52	0.09
Sri Lankan (2)	2	<0.01
Taiwanese (11)	12	0.02
Thai (14)	18	0.03
Vietnamese (246)	265	0.46
Hawaii Native/Pacific Islander (20)	44	0.08
Not Hispanic (17)	40	0.07
Hispanic (3)	4	0.01
Guamanian/Chamorro (6)	7	0.01
Native Hawaiian (7)	18	0.03
Samoan (0)	1	<0.01
White (52,324)	53,514	91.94
Not Hispanic (51,459)	52,515	90.22
Hispanic (865)	999	1.72

Clifton Park

Place Type: Town
County: Saratoga
Population: 36,705†

Ancestry‡	Population	%
Afghan (198)	214	0.59
African, Sub-Saharan (61)	61	0.17
Ghanaian (61)	61	0.17
American (1,816)	1,816	5.02
Arab (34)	231	0.64
Lebanese (34)	216	0.60
Syrian (0)	15	0.04
Armenian (9)	47	0.13
Australian (0)	26	0.07
Austrian (81)	184	0.51
Belgian (0)	9	0.02
Brazilian (69)	80	0.22
British (184)	343	0.95
Bulgarian (20)	20	0.06
Canadian (20)	136	0.38
Celtic (0)	8	0.02
Croatian (29)	57	0.16
Czech (54)	204	0.56
Danish (24)	283	0.78
Dutch (86)	965	2.67
Eastern European (66)	66	0.18
English (1,252)	4,952	13.68
Estonian (10)	35	0.10
European (247)	247	0.68
Finnish (12)	109	0.30
French, ex. Basque (269)	2,227	6.15
French Canadian (324)	769	2.12
German (1,407)	7,144	19.73
German Russian (0)	26	0.07
Greek (147)	232	0.64
Guyanese (113)	113	0.31
Hungarian (84)	351	0.97
Iranian (48)	64	0.18
Irish (2,558)	9,185	25.37
Italian (2,974)	7,530	20.80
Latvian (0)	23	0.06
Lithuanian (24)	212	0.59
Macedonian (11)	11	0.03
Norwegian (66)	478	1.32
Polish (819)	3,161	8.73
Portuguese (46)	96	0.27
Romanian (39)	79	0.22
Russian (407)	1,091	3.01
Scandinavian (9)	9	0.02
Scotch-Irish (200)	712	1.97
Scottish (200)	937	2.59
Slovak (9)	64	0.18
Slovene (0)	19	0.05
Swedish (67)	449	1.24
Swiss (12)	91	0.25
Turkish (17)	17	0.05
Ukrainian (163)	431	1.19
Welsh (50)	277	0.77
West Indian, ex. Hispanic (53)	169	0.47
Haitian (0)	13	0.04
Jamaican (26)	129	0.36
West Indian (27)	27	0.07

Hispanic Origin	Population	%
Hispanic or Latino (of any race)	1,002	2.73
Central American, ex. Mexican	76	0.21
Costa Rican	4	0.01
Guatemalan	24	0.07
Honduran	10	0.03
Nicaraguan	2	0.01
Panamanian	5	0.01
Salvadoran	31	0.08
Cuban	48	0.13
Dominican Republic	53	0.14
Mexican	241	0.66
Puerto Rican	347	0.95
South American	144	0.39
Argentinean	18	0.05
Bolivian	9	0.02
Chilean	19	0.05
Colombian	59	0.16
Ecuadorian	11	0.03
Paraguayan	1	<0.01
Peruvian	16	0.04
Uruguayan	2	0.01
Venezuelan	9	0.02
Other Hispanic or Latino	93	0.25

Race*	Population	%
African-American/Black (682)	873	2.38
Not Hispanic (646)	814	2.22
Hispanic (36)	59	0.16
American Indian/Alaska Native (39)	155	0.42
Not Hispanic (34)	137	0.37
Hispanic (5)	18	0.05
Apache (4)	6	0.02
Blackfeet (0)	6	0.02
Canadian/French Am. Ind. (1)	3	0.01
Central American Ind. (0)	2	0.01
Cherokee (2)	22	0.06
Chippewa (0)	1	<0.01
Choctaw (2)	2	0.01
Comanche (1)	1	<0.01
Cree (0)	1	<0.01
Creek (0)	1	<0.01
Iroquois (3)	11	0.03
Lumbee (0)	3	0.01
Mexican American Ind. (0)	1	<0.01
Navajo (0)	3	0.01
Sioux (2)	3	0.01
South American Ind. (0)	8	0.02

*Notes: † The Census 2010 population figure is used to calculate the percentages in the Hispanic Origin and Race categories. Ancestry percentages are based on the 2006-2010 American Community Survey population (not shown); ‡ Numbers in parentheses indicate the number of people reporting a single ancestry; * Numbers in parentheses indicate the number of persons reporting this race alone, not in combination with any other race; Please refer to the Explanation of Data for more information.*

Asian (1,679)	1,990	5.42
Not Hispanic (1,668)	1,960	5.34
Hispanic (11)	30	0.08
Bangladeshi (21)	21	0.06
Cambodian (1)	1	<0.01
Chinese, ex. Taiwanese (474)	540	1.47
Filipino (82)	144	0.39
Indian (621)	689	1.88
Indonesian (0)	5	0.01
Japanese (54)	87	0.24
Korean (156)	200	0.54
Laotian (2)	5	0.01
Malaysian (0)	2	0.01
Nepalese (2)	2	0.01
Pakistani (104)	119	0.32
Sri Lankan (5)	6	0.02
Taiwanese (28)	34	0.09
Thai (5)	12	0.03
Vietnamese (58)	61	0.17
Hawaii Native/Pacific Islander (2)	20	0.05
Not Hispanic (1)	15	0.04
Hispanic (1)	5	0.01
Native Hawaiian (2)	14	0.04
White (33,416)	33,988	92.60
Not Hispanic (32,734)	33,236	90.55
Hispanic (682)	752	2.05

Cohoes

Place Type: City
County: Albany
Population: 16,168†

Ancestry‡	Population	%
Afghan (14)	14	0.09
African, Sub-Saharan (21)	21	0.13
Other Sub-Saharan African (21)	21	0.13
American (475)	475	2.95
Arab (0)	70	0.43
Lebanese (0)	70	0.43
Armenian (21)	30	0.19
Austrian (0)	12	0.07
Brazilian (0)	10	0.06
British (0)	49	0.30
Canadian (11)	45	0.28
Czech (0)	45	0.28
Czechoslovakian (0)	12	0.07
Danish (16)	64	0.40
Dutch (29)	534	3.31
English (352)	1,399	8.68
European (102)	170	1.05
Finnish (0)	15	0.09
French, ex. Basque (761)	3,016	18.71
French Canadian (318)	545	3.38
German (449)	2,214	13.74
Greek (35)	129	0.80
Guyanese (18)	18	0.11
Hungarian (0)	112	0.69
Irish (1,284)	4,383	27.20
Italian (813)	2,465	15.30
Latvian (0)	11	0.07
Lithuanian (0)	11	0.07
Norwegian (13)	26	0.16
Pennsylvania German (29)	29	0.18
Polish (716)	1,848	11.47
Russian (108)	273	1.69
Scandinavian (18)	29	0.18
Scotch-Irish (79)	212	1.32
Scottish (14)	256	1.59
Slavic (0)	21	0.13
Slovak (10)	10	0.06
Swedish (27)	98	0.61
Swiss (14)	14	0.09
Ukrainian (423)	642	3.98
Welsh (0)	75	0.47
West Indian, ex. Hispanic (177)	272	1.69
Haitian (97)	192	1.19
West Indian (80)	80	0.50

Hispanic Origin	Population	%
Hispanic or Latino (of any race)	606	3.75
Central American, ex. Mexican	47	0.29
Guatemalan	2	0.01
Honduran	4	0.02
Panamanian	6	0.04
Salvadoran	35	0.22
Cuban	9	0.06
Dominican Republic	46	0.28
Mexican	41	0.25
Puerto Rican	372	2.30
South American	21	0.13
Argentinean	2	0.01
Chilean	1	0.01
Colombian	9	0.06
Ecuadorian	2	0.01
Peruvian	3	0.02
Venezuelan	4	0.02
Other Hispanic or Latino	70	0.43

Race*	Population	%
African-American/Black (754)	1,034	6.40
Not Hispanic (691)	941	5.82
Hispanic (63)	93	0.58
American Indian/Alaska Native (39)	143	0.88
Not Hispanic (30)	117	0.72
Hispanic (9)	26	0.16
Blackfeet (0)	9	0.06
Canadian/French Am. Ind. (2)	5	0.03
Cherokee (3)	17	0.11
Comanche (0)	4	0.02
Iroquois (4)	11	0.07
Mexican American Ind. (0)	1	0.01
Seminole (0)	1	0.01
Sioux (1)	1	0.01
South American Ind. (0)	2	0.01
Asian (142)	237	1.47
Not Hispanic (141)	229	1.42
Hispanic (1)	8	0.05
Bangladeshi (1)	1	0.01
Cambodian (2)	3	0.02
Chinese, ex. Taiwanese (19)	25	0.15
Filipino (26)	43	0.27
Indian (25)	35	0.22
Japanese (7)	12	0.07
Korean (17)	30	0.19
Laotian (0)	1	0.01
Pakistani (24)	27	0.17
Thai (7)	7	0.04
Vietnamese (9)	9	0.06
Hawaii Native/Pacific Islander (0)	16	0.10
Not Hispanic (0)	12	0.07
Hispanic (0)	4	0.02
Native Hawaiian (0)	7	0.04
White (14,582)	15,019	92.89
Not Hispanic (14,269)	14,650	90.61
Hispanic (313)	369	2.28

Colonie

Place Type: Town
County: Albany
Population: 81,591†

Ancestry‡	Population	%
African, Sub-Saharan (408)	482	0.59
African (259)	310	0.38
Ethiopian (13)	13	0.02
Ghanaian (11)	11	0.01
Nigerian (80)	80	0.10
South African (9)	32	0.04
Other Sub-Saharan African (36)	36	0.04
Albanian (405)	405	0.50
American (2,133)	2,133	2.62
Arab (561)	863	1.06
Arab (0)	17	0.02
Egyptian (125)	125	0.15
Lebanese (144)	267	0.33
Moroccan (64)	111	0.14
Palestinian (72)	72	0.09
Syrian (27)	116	0.14
Other Arab (129)	155	0.19
Armenian (142)	244	0.30
Australian (10)	10	0.01
Austrian (112)	470	0.58
Belgian (0)	25	0.03
Brazilian (13)	13	0.02
British (140)	240	0.29
Bulgarian (9)	9	0.01
Canadian (114)	321	0.39
Celtic (11)	11	0.01
Croatian (16)	74	0.09
Czech (134)	453	0.56
Czechoslovakian (26)	124	0.15
Danish (35)	195	0.24
Dutch (627)	3,334	4.09
Eastern European (46)	83	0.10
English (1,400)	8,332	10.22
European (492)	544	0.67
Finnish (6)	68	0.08
French, ex. Basque (786)	5,795	7.11
French Canadian (545)	1,591	1.95
German (2,908)	14,495	17.78
Greek (238)	563	0.69
Guyanese (116)	137	0.17
Hungarian (124)	542	0.66
Iranian (0)	9	0.01
Irish (6,490)	23,049	28.27
Israeli (42)	42	0.05
Italian (6,582)	16,393	20.11
Latvian (34)	34	0.04
Lithuanian (55)	377	0.46
Luxemburger (0)	13	0.02
Northern European (39)	39	0.05
Norwegian (159)	598	0.73
Pennsylvania German (17)	25	0.03
Polish (2,206)	6,915	8.48
Portuguese (0)	80	0.10
Romanian (55)	228	0.28
Russian (690)	1,626	1.99
Scandinavian (27)	39	0.05
Scotch-Irish (468)	1,261	1.55
Scottish (263)	1,526	1.87
Slavic (18)	28	0.03
Slovak (72)	185	0.23
Swedish (217)	944	1.16
Swiss (17)	145	0.18
Turkish (10)	10	0.01
Ukrainian (212)	860	1.05
Welsh (41)	704	0.86
West Indian, ex. Hispanic (372)	580	0.71
Haitian (60)	83	0.10
Jamaican (235)	373	0.46
Trinidadian/Tobagonian (0)	4	<0.01
West Indian (77)	120	0.15
Yugoslavian (143)	143	0.18

Hispanic Origin	Population	%
Hispanic or Latino (of any race)	2,526	3.10
Central American, ex. Mexican	159	0.19
Costa Rican	24	0.03
Guatemalan	25	0.03
Honduran	20	0.02
Nicaraguan	17	0.02
Panamanian	13	0.02
Salvadoran	59	0.07
Other Central American	1	<0.01
Cuban	114	0.14
Dominican Republic	224	0.27
Mexican	462	0.57
Puerto Rican	1,001	1.23
South American	278	0.34
Argentinean	26	0.03
Bolivian	9	0.01
Chilean	12	0.01
Colombian	94	0.12
Ecuadorian	35	0.04
Paraguayan	3	<0.01
Peruvian	76	0.09
Uruguayan	1	<0.01

*Notes: † The Census 2010 population figure is used to calculate the percentages in the Hispanic Origin and Race categories. Ancestry percentages are based on the 2006-2010 American Community Survey population (not shown); ‡ Numbers in parentheses indicate the number of people reporting a single ancestry; * Numbers in parentheses indicate the number of persons reporting this race alone, not in combination with any other race; Please refer to the Explanation of Data for more information.*

Venezuelan	19	0.02
Other South American	3	<0.01
Other Hispanic or Latino	288	0.35

Race*	Population	%
African-American/Black (4,288)	5,091	6.24
Not Hispanic (4,061)	4,752	5.82
Hispanic (227)	339	0.42
American Indian/Alaska Native (121)	397	0.49
Not Hispanic (79)	318	0.39
Hispanic (42)	79	0.10
Alaska Athabascan *(Ala. Nat.)* (1)	1	<0.01
Blackfeet (1)	11	0.01
Canadian/French Am. Ind. (6)	10	0.01
Central American Ind. (3)	3	<0.01
Cherokee (6)	32	0.04
Chippewa (0)	1	<0.01
Choctaw (0)	1	<0.01
Cree (0)	2	<0.01
Crow (1)	1	<0.01
Iroquois (15)	50	0.06
Mexican American Ind. (28)	29	0.04
Navajo (0)	1	<0.01
Osage (0)	1	<0.01
Potawatomi (0)	1	<0.01
Seminole (0)	3	<0.01
Sioux (3)	7	0.01
South American Ind. (5)	10	0.01
Spanish American Ind. (0)	2	<0.01
Tlingit-Haida *(Alaska Native)* (1)	1	<0.01
Asian (5,353)	5,892	7.22
Not Hispanic (5,342)	5,866	7.19
Hispanic (11)	26	0.03
Bangladeshi (78)	80	0.10
Burmese (3)	4	<0.01
Cambodian (2)	3	<0.01
Chinese, ex. Taiwanese (1,186)	1,284	1.57
Filipino (306)	397	0.49
Indian (1,969)	2,099	2.57
Indonesian (11)	13	0.02
Japanese (58)	90	0.11
Korean (471)	531	0.65
Laotian (2)	4	<0.01
Malaysian (3)	5	0.01
Nepalese (13)	13	0.02
Pakistani (680)	736	0.90
Sri Lankan (24)	30	0.04
Taiwanese (48)	60	0.07
Thai (30)	40	0.05
Vietnamese (313)	360	0.44
Hawaii Native/Pacific Islander (15)	66	0.08
Not Hispanic (14)	47	0.06
Hispanic (1)	19	0.02
Fijian (1)	1	<0.01
Guamanian/Chamorro (2)	6	0.01
Native Hawaiian (2)	10	0.01
Samoan (4)	9	0.01
Tongan (1)	5	0.01
White (69,541)	70,917	86.92
Not Hispanic (68,088)	69,290	84.92
Hispanic (1,453)	1,627	1.99

Colonie

Place Type: Village
County: Albany
Population: 7,793†

Ancestry‡	Population	%
African, Sub-Saharan (79)	79	1.01
Ethiopian (13)	13	0.17
Nigerian (66)	66	0.84
Albanian (161)	161	2.05
American (242)	242	3.09
Austrian (0)	49	0.63
Czech (0)	11	0.14
Danish (14)	25	0.32
Dutch (47)	304	3.88
English (119)	789	10.07
European (0)	13	0.17
French, ex. Basque (23)	419	5.35
French Canadian (38)	114	1.45
German (362)	1,490	19.01
Greek (0)	41	0.52
Hungarian (0)	36	0.46
Irish (573)	2,357	30.07
Italian (778)	1,574	20.08
Lithuanian (35)	211	2.69
Norwegian (19)	75	0.96
Polish (305)	663	8.46
Portuguese (0)	25	0.32
Romanian (10)	24	0.31
Russian (49)	109	1.39
Scotch-Irish (27)	123	1.57
Scottish (10)	135	1.72
Slovak (0)	11	0.14
Swedish (18)	97	1.24
Swiss (0)	9	0.11
Ukrainian (15)	26	0.33
Welsh (0)	67	0.85
West Indian, ex. Hispanic (22)	22	0.28
Jamaican (22)	22	0.28

Hispanic Origin	Population	%
Hispanic or Latino (of any race)	203	2.60
Central American, ex. Mexican	18	0.23
Costa Rican	2	0.03
Guatemalan	4	0.05
Nicaraguan	3	0.04
Panamanian	7	0.09
Salvadoran	2	0.03
Cuban	5	0.06
Dominican Republic	13	0.17
Mexican	39	0.50
Puerto Rican	93	1.19
South American	12	0.15
Argentinean	2	0.03
Colombian	5	0.06
Paraguayan	2	0.03
Peruvian	3	0.04
Other Hispanic or Latino	23	0.30

Race*	Population	%
African-American/Black (359)	435	5.58
Not Hispanic (344)	406	5.21
Hispanic (15)	29	0.37
American Indian/Alaska Native (6)	33	0.42
Not Hispanic (5)	29	0.37
Hispanic (1)	4	0.05
Blackfeet (0)	1	0.01
Central American Ind. (1)	1	0.01
Cherokee (0)	2	0.03
Iroquois (2)	3	0.04
Asian (508)	545	6.99
Not Hispanic (508)	545	6.99
Chinese, ex. Taiwanese (209)	220	2.82
Filipino (13)	20	0.26
Indian (129)	139	1.78
Indonesian (0)	1	0.01
Japanese (11)	16	0.21
Korean (36)	37	0.47
Laotian (0)	2	0.03
Pakistani (37)	43	0.55
Sri Lankan (4)	4	0.05
Taiwanese (3)	3	0.04
Thai (4)	7	0.09
Vietnamese (44)	55	0.71
Hawaii Native/Pacific Islander (0)	1	0.01
Not Hispanic (0)	1	0.01
White (6,759)	6,876	88.23
Not Hispanic (6,627)	6,715	86.17
Hispanic (132)	161	2.07

Commack

Place Type: CDP
County: Suffolk
Population: 36,124†

Ancestry‡	Population	%
African, Sub-Saharan (61)	79	0.22
Nigerian (61)	79	0.22
Albanian (9)	9	0.02
American (1,282)	1,282	3.55
Arab (73)	158	0.44
Arab (52)	52	0.14
Egyptian (14)	14	0.04
Lebanese (0)	39	0.11
Moroccan (7)	14	0.04
Syrian (0)	12	0.03
Other Arab (0)	27	0.07
Armenian (0)	30	0.08
Australian (0)	22	0.06
Austrian (58)	300	0.83
Belgian (0)	8	0.02
Brazilian (18)	26	0.07
British (52)	82	0.23
Canadian (21)	21	0.06
Croatian (154)	253	0.70
Czech (37)	130	0.36
Czechoslovakian (13)	36	0.10
Danish (0)	42	0.12
Dutch (119)	403	1.11
Eastern European (336)	336	0.93
English (165)	1,535	4.25
Estonian (12)	12	0.03
European (516)	554	1.53
Finnish (0)	32	0.09
French, ex. Basque (10)	431	1.19
French Canadian (50)	97	0.27
German (1,047)	6,179	17.09
Greek (787)	1,230	3.40
Guyanese (8)	8	0.02
Hungarian (155)	494	1.37
Iranian (8)	8	0.02
Irish (1,908)	7,653	21.17
Israeli (102)	153	0.42
Italian (6,390)	13,261	36.68
Lithuanian (76)	191	0.53
Maltese (0)	64	0.18
Norwegian (82)	257	0.71
Pennsylvania German (6)	6	0.02
Polish (957)	3,270	9.04
Portuguese (31)	45	0.12
Romanian (84)	297	0.82
Russian (985)	2,576	7.13
Scotch-Irish (90)	205	0.57
Scottish (41)	278	0.77
Slovak (7)	14	0.04
Slovene (150)	150	0.41
Swedish (9)	265	0.73
Swiss (0)	83	0.23
Turkish (176)	211	0.58
Ukrainian (24)	167	0.46
Welsh (0)	89	0.25
West Indian, ex. Hispanic (22)	41	0.11
Jamaican (22)	41	0.11
Yugoslavian (35)	106	0.29

Hispanic Origin	Population	%
Hispanic or Latino (of any race)	1,722	4.77
Central American, ex. Mexican	202	0.56
Costa Rican	6	0.02
Guatemalan	14	0.04
Honduran	71	0.20
Nicaraguan	7	0.02
Panamanian	9	0.02
Salvadoran	85	0.24
Other Central American	10	0.03
Cuban	129	0.36
Dominican Republic	103	0.29
Mexican	123	0.34
Puerto Rican	541	1.50
South American	443	1.23
Argentinean	51	0.14
Bolivian	2	0.01
Chilean	42	0.12
Colombian	176	0.49
Ecuadorian	76	0.21

*Notes: † The Census 2010 population figure is used to calculate the percentages in the Hispanic Origin and Race categories. Ancestry percentages are based on the 2006-2010 American Community Survey population (not shown); ‡ Numbers in parentheses indicate the number of people reporting a single ancestry; * Numbers in parentheses indicate the number of persons reporting this race alone, not in combination with any other race; Please refer to the Explanation of Data for more information.*

Paraguayan	10	0.03
Peruvian	63	0.17
Uruguayan	9	0.02
Venezuelan	11	0.03
Other South American	3	0.01
Other Hispanic or Latino	181	0.50

Race*	Population	%
African-American/Black (325)	393	1.09
Not Hispanic (297)	353	0.98
Hispanic (28)	40	0.11
American Indian/Alaska Native (35)	88	0.24
Not Hispanic (19)	56	0.16
Hispanic (16)	32	0.09
Cherokee (1)	11	0.03
Chippewa (0)	2	0.01
Choctaw (0)	2	0.01
Creek (0)	4	0.01
Iroquois (1)	1	<0.01
Mexican American Ind. (1)	1	<0.01
South American Ind. (12)	17	0.05
Asian (1,963)	2,211	6.12
Not Hispanic (1,951)	2,170	6.01
Hispanic (12)	41	0.11
Bangladeshi (7)	7	0.02
Chinese, ex. Taiwanese (464)	538	1.49
Filipino (130)	188	0.52
Indian (568)	612	1.69
Indonesian (2)	3	0.01
Japanese (24)	40	0.11
Korean (582)	610	1.69
Malaysian (0)	1	<0.01
Nepalese (5)	5	0.01
Pakistani (68)	81	0.22
Taiwanese (43)	53	0.15
Thai (4)	5	0.01
Vietnamese (17)	20	0.06
Hawaii Native/Pacific Islander (4)	16	0.04
Not Hispanic (2)	10	0.03
Hispanic (2)	6	0.02
Guamanian/Chamorro (0)	1	<0.01
Native Hawaiian (3)	11	0.03
White (33,080)	33,453	92.61
Not Hispanic (31,750)	32,030	88.67
Hispanic (1,330)	1,423	3.94

Concord

Place Type: Town
County: Erie
Population: 8,494†

Ancestry‡	Population	%
American (182)	182	2.15
Austrian (18)	28	0.33
British (29)	45	0.53
Canadian (46)	46	0.54
Czech (9)	9	0.11
Dutch (37)	293	3.45
English (416)	1,356	15.98
European (13)	13	0.15
Finnish (8)	8	0.09
French, ex. Basque (79)	257	3.03
French Canadian (28)	71	0.84
German (1,314)	3,370	39.72
Greek (15)	29	0.34
Hungarian (0)	37	0.44
Irish (486)	1,571	18.52
Italian (274)	1,050	12.38
Macedonian (32)	32	0.38
Northern European (11)	11	0.13
Norwegian (8)	18	0.21
Pennsylvania German (8)	16	0.19
Polish (489)	1,209	14.25
Scotch-Irish (44)	129	1.52
Scottish (42)	262	3.09
Slovak (13)	13	0.15
Slovene (0)	16	0.19
Swedish (52)	203	2.39
Swiss (0)	17	0.20
Ukrainian (7)	59	0.70
Welsh (22)	102	1.20

Hispanic Origin	Population	%
Hispanic or Latino (of any race)	151	1.78
Central American, ex. Mexican	3	0.04
Guatemalan	2	0.02
Panamanian	1	0.01
Cuban	5	0.06
Mexican	59	0.69
Puerto Rican	60	0.71
South American	5	0.06
Chilean	1	0.01
Colombian	1	0.01
Ecuadorian	1	0.01
Peruvian	2	0.02
Other Hispanic or Latino	19	0.22

Race*	Population	%
African-American/Black (55)	85	1.00
Not Hispanic (49)	72	0.85
Hispanic (6)	13	0.15
American Indian/Alaska Native (42)	74	0.87
Not Hispanic (32)	56	0.66
Hispanic (10)	18	0.21
Blackfeet (0)	1	0.01
Canadian/French Am. Ind. (0)	1	0.01
Central American Ind. (1)	1	0.01
Cherokee (0)	3	0.04
Cheyenne (0)	1	0.01
Iroquois (23)	35	0.41
Mexican American Ind. (1)	1	0.01
Asian (36)	53	0.62
Not Hispanic (36)	53	0.62
Chinese, ex. Taiwanese (10)	16	0.19
Filipino (4)	13	0.15
Indian (11)	12	0.14
Japanese (0)	1	0.01
Korean (8)	8	0.09
Thai (1)	1	0.01
Hawaii Native/Pacific Islander (1)	11	0.13
Not Hispanic (1)	11	0.13
Guamanian/Chamorro (0)	3	0.04
Native Hawaiian (0)	5	0.06
Samoan (1)	3	0.04
White (8,268)	8,340	98.19
Not Hispanic (8,160)	8,221	96.79
Hispanic (108)	119	1.40

Congers

Place Type: CDP
County: Rockland
Population: 8,363†

Ancestry‡	Population	%
African, Sub-Saharan (0)	11	0.14
African (0)	11	0.14
Albanian (63)	63	0.80
American (314)	314	3.97
Arab (0)	10	0.13
Lebanese (0)	10	0.13
Armenian (12)	27	0.34
Assyrian/Chaldean/Syriac (11)	34	0.43
Austrian (28)	92	1.16
Brazilian (23)	72	0.91
British (18)	18	0.23
Croatian (4)	13	0.16
Czech (5)	28	0.35
Czechoslovakian (9)	37	0.47
Danish (0)	20	0.25
Dutch (11)	30	0.38
Eastern European (33)	33	0.42
English (31)	299	3.78
European (35)	35	0.44
Finnish (0)	8	0.10
French, ex. Basque (37)	78	0.99
French Canadian (9)	22	0.28
German (207)	1,007	12.74
Greek (0)	53	0.67
Hungarian (52)	166	2.10
Irish (907)	2,015	25.49
Italian (1,119)	2,152	27.23
Lithuanian (63)	73	0.92
Norwegian (53)	97	1.23
Polish (88)	412	5.21
Portuguese (47)	78	0.99
Romanian (10)	36	0.46
Russian (74)	344	4.35
Scotch-Irish (29)	68	0.86
Scottish (25)	107	1.35
Slovak (19)	50	0.63
Swedish (18)	59	0.75
Ukrainian (10)	81	1.02
Welsh (0)	62	0.78
West Indian, ex. Hispanic (33)	33	0.42
Jamaican (33)	33	0.42

Hispanic Origin	Population	%
Hispanic or Latino (of any race)	954	11.41
Central American, ex. Mexican	131	1.57
Costa Rican	5	0.06
Guatemalan	41	0.49
Honduran	3	0.04
Panamanian	2	0.02
Salvadoran	80	0.96
Cuban	56	0.67
Dominican Republic	73	0.87
Mexican	75	0.90
Puerto Rican	448	5.36
South American	96	1.15
Argentinean	11	0.13
Bolivian	1	0.01
Chilean	15	0.18
Colombian	30	0.36
Ecuadorian	22	0.26
Peruvian	11	0.13
Uruguayan	1	0.01
Venezuelan	5	0.06
Other Hispanic or Latino	75	0.90

Race*	Population	%
African-American/Black (273)	323	3.86
Not Hispanic (240)	275	3.29
Hispanic (33)	48	0.57
American Indian/Alaska Native (33)	58	0.69
Not Hispanic (25)	39	0.47
Hispanic (8)	19	0.23
Cherokee (0)	8	0.10
Chippewa (1)	1	0.01
Delaware (6)	6	0.07
Iroquois (2)	3	0.04
Potawatomi (1)	1	0.01
South American Ind. (0)	7	0.08
Asian (982)	1,068	12.77
Not Hispanic (978)	1,059	12.66
Hispanic (4)	9	0.11
Bangladeshi (16)	16	0.19
Burmese (0)	3	0.04
Cambodian (6)	6	0.07
Chinese, ex. Taiwanese (68)	99	1.18
Filipino (207)	224	2.68
Indian (514)	543	6.49
Japanese (3)	8	0.10
Korean (87)	91	1.09
Malaysian (3)	3	0.04
Pakistani (18)	18	0.22
Sri Lankan (9)	10	0.12
Taiwanese (2)	6	0.07
Thai (18)	18	0.22
Vietnamese (11)	20	0.24
Hawaii Native/Pacific Islander (1)	6	0.07
Not Hispanic (1)	6	0.07
Guamanian/Chamorro (1)	4	0.05
White (6,721)	6,857	81.99
Not Hispanic (6,016)	6,113	73.10
Hispanic (705)	744	8.90

SECTION TWO

*Notes: † The Census 2010 population figure is used to calculate the percentages in the Hispanic Origin and Race categories. Ancestry percentages are based on the 2006-2010 American Community Survey population (not shown); ‡ Numbers in parentheses indicate the number of people reporting a single ancestry; * Numbers in parentheses indicate the number of persons reporting this race alone, not in combination with any other race; Please refer to the Explanation of Data for more information.*

Copiague

Place Type: CDP
County: Suffolk
Population: 22,993†

Ancestry‡	Population	%
African, Sub-Saharan (0)	20	0.10
Cape Verdean (0)	9	0.04
Ethiopian (0)	11	0.05
Albanian (0)	48	0.23
American (286)	286	1.39
Arab (18)	54	0.26
Egyptian (0)	36	0.17
Other Arab (18)	18	0.09
Armenian (0)	99	0.48
Austrian (27)	163	0.79
Basque (15)	15	0.07
British (11)	21	0.10
Bulgarian (0)	12	0.06
Canadian (10)	113	0.55
Celtic (19)	19	0.09
Croatian (10)	28	0.14
Czech (26)	39	0.19
Czechoslovakian (115)	136	0.66
Danish (0)	17	0.08
Dutch (38)	326	1.58
English (96)	667	3.23
European (30)	30	0.15
French, ex. Basque (20)	243	1.18
French Canadian (21)	36	0.17
German (653)	3,337	16.18
Greek (40)	135	0.65
Guyanese (0)	79	0.38
Hungarian (0)	100	0.48
Irish (693)	3,328	16.14
Israeli (0)	97	0.47
Italian (3,452)	5,892	28.57
Maltese (11)	24	0.12
Norwegian (49)	75	0.36
Pennsylvania German (18)	18	0.09
Polish (1,481)	2,280	11.06
Portuguese (13)	60	0.29
Russian (69)	234	1.13
Scandinavian (0)	10	0.05
Scotch-Irish (123)	320	1.55
Scottish (10)	61	0.30
Slovak (0)	20	0.10
Swedish (15)	59	0.29
Swiss (0)	15	0.07
Turkish (45)	45	0.22
Ukrainian (29)	51	0.25
West Indian, ex. Hispanic (230)	422	2.05
Barbadian (11)	36	0.17
Haitian (87)	111	0.54
Jamaican (75)	109	0.53
Trinidadian/Tobagonian (18)	18	0.09
West Indian (39)	148	0.72
Yugoslavian (0)	10	0.05

Hispanic Origin	Population	%
Hispanic or Latino (of any race)	7,523	32.72
Central American, ex. Mexican	2,199	9.56
Costa Rican	17	0.07
Guatemalan	234	1.02
Honduran	412	1.79
Nicaraguan	48	0.21
Panamanian	23	0.10
Salvadoran	1,457	6.34
Other Central American	8	0.03
Cuban	65	0.28
Dominican Republic	2,846	12.38
Mexican	117	0.51
Puerto Rican	858	3.73
South American	769	3.34
Argentinean	54	0.23
Bolivian	4	0.02
Chilean	26	0.11
Colombian	369	1.60
Ecuadorian	184	0.80
Paraguayan	1	<0.01
Peruvian	107	0.47
Uruguayan	8	0.03
Venezuelan	16	0.07
Other Hispanic or Latino	669	2.91

Race*	Population	%
African-American/Black (1,736)	1,988	8.65
Not Hispanic (1,455)	1,594	6.93
Hispanic (281)	394	1.71
American Indian/Alaska Native (74)	173	0.75
Not Hispanic (43)	110	0.48
Hispanic (31)	63	0.27
Blackfeet (0)	3	0.01
Central American Ind. (2)	3	0.01
Cherokee (4)	18	0.08
Cree (1)	1	<0.01
Delaware (1)	1	<0.01
Iroquois (0)	4	0.02
Lumbee (2)	4	0.02
Mexican American Ind. (3)	3	0.01
Seminole (0)	1	<0.01
Sioux (1)	1	<0.01
South American Ind. (5)	8	0.03
Spanish American Ind. (7)	7	0.03
Asian (507)	647	2.81
Not Hispanic (464)	559	2.43
Hispanic (43)	88	0.38
Bangladeshi (4)	6	0.03
Burmese (3)	5	0.02
Chinese, ex. Taiwanese (97)	134	0.58
Filipino (111)	151	0.66
Indian (198)	226	0.98
Indonesian (1)	1	<0.01
Japanese (0)	18	0.08
Korean (24)	31	0.13
Laotian (0)	1	<0.01
Pakistani (31)	38	0.17
Sri Lankan (3)	3	0.01
Thai (6)	8	0.03
Vietnamese (7)	9	0.04
Hawaii Native/Pacific Islander (1)	38	0.17
Not Hispanic (0)	12	0.05
Hispanic (1)	26	0.11
Guamanian/Chamorro (0)	1	<0.01
Native Hawaiian (1)	12	0.05
Samoan (0)	1	<0.01
White (16,892)	17,553	76.34
Not Hispanic (13,167)	13,413	58.34
Hispanic (3,725)	4,140	18.01

Coram

Place Type: CDP
County: Suffolk
Population: 39,113†

Ancestry‡	Population	%
African, Sub-Saharan (186)	254	0.66
African (55)	93	0.24
Nigerian (115)	131	0.34
Sudanese (0)	14	0.04
Other Sub-Saharan African (16)	16	0.04
American (664)	664	1.72
Arab (28)	96	0.25
Arab (28)	28	0.07
Egyptian (0)	61	0.16
Other Arab (0)	7	0.02
Armenian (0)	153	0.40
Austrian (26)	207	0.54
Basque (9)	9	0.02
Belgian (0)	23	0.06
Brazilian (0)	26	0.07
British (35)	130	0.34
Canadian (57)	143	0.37
Celtic (0)	18	0.05
Croatian (0)	18	0.05
Czech (40)	146	0.38
Czechoslovakian (22)	48	0.12
Danish (28)	96	0.25
Dutch (30)	275	0.71
Eastern European (82)	89	0.23
English (252)	1,724	4.46
European (99)	157	0.41
Finnish (15)	66	0.17
French, ex. Basque (23)	396	1.03
French Canadian (0)	126	0.33
German (1,214)	6,423	16.63
Greek (155)	394	1.02
Guyanese (46)	68	0.18
Hungarian (100)	622	1.61
Icelander (18)	18	0.05
Iranian (11)	11	0.03
Irish (1,520)	7,661	19.84
Israeli (132)	132	0.34
Italian (5,333)	11,675	30.23
Latvian (0)	15	0.04
Lithuanian (27)	96	0.25
Maltese (23)	53	0.14
Northern European (9)	9	0.02
Norwegian (100)	391	1.01
Polish (551)	2,377	6.16
Portuguese (84)	192	0.50
Romanian (59)	198	0.51
Russian (405)	1,334	3.45
Scandinavian (16)	50	0.13
Scotch-Irish (160)	455	1.18
Scottish (54)	229	0.59
Slovak (24)	39	0.10
Swedish (42)	366	0.95
Swiss (6)	83	0.21
Turkish (59)	74	0.19
Ukrainian (113)	230	0.60
Welsh (28)	66	0.17
West Indian, ex. Hispanic (1,037)	1,380	3.57
Barbadian (11)	11	0.03
Haitian (85)	132	0.34
Jamaican (220)	480	1.24
Trinidadian/Tobagonian (116)	116	0.30
West Indian (605)	641	1.66

Hispanic Origin	Population	%
Hispanic or Latino (of any race)	5,307	13.57
Central American, ex. Mexican	469	1.20
Costa Rican	13	0.03
Guatemalan	84	0.21
Honduran	89	0.23
Nicaraguan	24	0.06
Panamanian	41	0.10
Salvadoran	218	0.56
Cuban	135	0.35
Dominican Republic	870	2.22
Mexican	404	1.03
Puerto Rican	1,895	4.84
South American	998	2.55
Argentinean	69	0.18
Bolivian	10	0.03
Chilean	61	0.16
Colombian	407	1.04
Ecuadorian	274	0.70
Paraguayan	7	0.02
Peruvian	125	0.32
Uruguayan	10	0.03
Venezuelan	26	0.07
Other South American	9	0.02
Other Hispanic or Latino	536	1.37

Race*	Population	%
African-American/Black (4,127)	4,767	12.19
Not Hispanic (3,842)	4,352	11.13
Hispanic (285)	415	1.06
American Indian/Alaska Native (73)	318	0.81
Not Hispanic (51)	235	0.60
Hispanic (22)	83	0.21
Apache (0)	3	0.01
Blackfeet (1)	15	0.04
Central American Ind. (4)	4	0.01
Cherokee (15)	52	0.13
Chickasaw (0)	2	0.01
Chippewa (2)	3	0.01

*Notes: † The Census 2010 population figure is used to calculate the percentages in the Hispanic Origin and Race categories. Ancestry percentages are based on the 2006-2010 American Community Survey population (not shown); ‡ Numbers in parentheses indicate the number of people reporting a single ancestry; * Numbers in parentheses indicate the number of persons reporting this race alone, not in combination with any other race; Please refer to the Explanation of Data for more information.*

Choctaw (3)	8	0.02
Comanche (0)	1	<0.01
Cree (0)	2	0.01
Crow (0)	1	<0.01
Delaware (0)	1	<0.01
Inupiat *(Alaska Native)* (1)	1	<0.01
Iroquois (0)	4	0.01
Lumbee (1)	2	0.01
Mexican American Ind. (1)	1	<0.01
Pueblo (1)	1	<0.01
Sioux (0)	4	0.01
South American Ind. (4)	12	0.03
Spanish American Ind. (1)	1	<0.01
Asian (1,975)	2,274	5.81
Not Hispanic (1,952)	2,209	5.65
Hispanic (23)	65	0.17
Bangladeshi (68)	78	0.20
Burmese (1)	2	0.01
Chinese, ex. Taiwanese (401)	475	1.21
Filipino (241)	302	0.77
Indian (658)	739	1.89
Indonesian (12)	14	0.04
Japanese (17)	43	0.11
Korean (161)	177	0.45
Laotian (1)	1	<0.01
Malaysian (2)	4	0.01
Nepalese (8)	8	0.02
Pakistani (273)	311	0.80
Sri Lankan (4)	4	0.01
Taiwanese (6)	8	0.02
Thai (9)	17	0.04
Vietnamese (41)	48	0.12
Hawaii Native/Pacific Islander (10)	33	0.08
Not Hispanic (8)	24	0.06
Hispanic (2)	9	0.02
Guamanian/Chamorro (2)	4	0.01
Native Hawaiian (4)	13	0.03
Samoan (0)	1	<0.01
White (30,260)	31,182	79.72
Not Hispanic (27,073)	27,653	70.70
Hispanic (3,187)	3,529	9.02

Corning

Place Type: City
County: Steuben
Population: 11,183†

Ancestry‡	Population	%
American (655)	655	5.90
Austrian (0)	51	0.46
Basque (0)	13	0.12
British (63)	153	1.38
Croatian (0)	6	0.05
Czech (10)	82	0.74
Czechoslovakian (13)	13	0.12
Dutch (64)	638	5.75
Eastern European (17)	17	0.15
English (526)	1,838	16.56
Estonian (5)	5	0.05
European (42)	42	0.38
Finnish (0)	16	0.14
French, ex. Basque (71)	360	3.24
French Canadian (13)	22	0.20
German (498)	2,485	22.39
Greek (20)	20	0.18
Guyanese (31)	31	0.28
Hungarian (0)	22	0.20
Irish (1,184)	2,523	22.74
Italian (650)	1,608	14.49
Latvian (0)	16	0.14
Lithuanian (0)	17	0.15
Northern European (24)	24	0.22
Norwegian (25)	56	0.50
Pennsylvania German (52)	52	0.47
Polish (114)	458	4.13
Portuguese (0)	18	0.16
Romanian (9)	9	0.08
Russian (11)	32	0.29
Scandinavian (0)	10	0.09
Scotch-Irish (45)	139	1.25
Scottish (50)	363	3.27
Slovak (11)	20	0.18
Slovene (0)	8	0.07
Swedish (35)	119	1.07
Swiss (12)	43	0.39
Turkish (25)	46	0.41
Ukrainian (18)	59	0.53
Welsh (69)	175	1.58

Hispanic Origin	Population	%
Hispanic or Latino (of any race)	271	2.42
Central American, ex. Mexican	25	0.22
Costa Rican	1	0.01
Guatemalan	8	0.07
Honduran	10	0.09
Panamanian	2	0.02
Salvadoran	4	0.04
Cuban	6	0.05
Dominican Republic	16	0.14
Mexican	58	0.52
Puerto Rican	121	1.08
South American	18	0.16
Chilean	1	0.01
Colombian	9	0.08
Paraguayan	1	0.01
Peruvian	3	0.03
Venezuelan	2	0.02
Other South American	2	0.02
Other Hispanic or Latino	27	0.24

Race*	Population	%
African-American/Black (356)	507	4.53
Not Hispanic (346)	485	4.34
Hispanic (10)	22	0.20
American Indian/Alaska Native (32)	110	0.98
Not Hispanic (23)	85	0.76
Hispanic (9)	25	0.22
Blackfeet (2)	4	0.04
Canadian/French Am. Ind. (0)	3	0.03
Cherokee (1)	8	0.07
Iroquois (8)	17	0.15
Mexican American Ind. (4)	4	0.04
Asian (202)	236	2.11
Not Hispanic (197)	230	2.06
Hispanic (5)	6	0.05
Burmese (1)	1	0.01
Chinese, ex. Taiwanese (64)	69	0.62
Filipino (15)	19	0.17
Indian (71)	81	0.72
Indonesian (2)	2	0.02
Japanese (12)	14	0.13
Korean (16)	24	0.21
Laotian (4)	5	0.04
Nepalese (1)	1	0.01
Pakistani (2)	2	0.02
Sri Lankan (4)	4	0.04
Taiwanese (4)	4	0.04
Thai (2)	3	0.03
Vietnamese (3)	3	0.03
Hawaii Native/Pacific Islander (1)	9	0.08
Not Hispanic (0)	8	0.07
Hispanic (1)	1	0.01
Guamanian/Chamorro (1)	1	0.01
Native Hawaiian (0)	7	0.06
White (10,269)	10,519	94.06
Not Hispanic (10,113)	10,324	92.32
Hispanic (156)	195	1.74

Cornwall

Place Type: Town
County: Orange
Population: 12,646†

Ancestry‡	Population	%
American (1,502)	1,502	11.82
Arab (8)	74	0.58
Lebanese (8)	74	0.58
Armenian (29)	42	0.33
Austrian (31)	115	0.91
British (48)	144	1.13
Canadian (17)	17	0.13
Croatian (52)	116	0.91
Czech (8)	19	0.15
Czechoslovakian (0)	7	0.06
Danish (0)	26	0.20
Dutch (122)	396	3.12
Eastern European (55)	55	0.43
English (177)	1,076	8.47
European (102)	102	0.80
French, ex. Basque (29)	214	1.68
French Canadian (15)	39	0.31
German (443)	2,084	16.40
Greek (31)	152	1.20
Hungarian (52)	124	0.98
Irish (1,397)	4,238	33.36
Italian (1,198)	3,371	26.53
Latvian (0)	7	0.06
Lithuanian (34)	59	0.46
Maltese (14)	27	0.21
Norwegian (136)	279	2.20
Polish (62)	595	4.68
Portuguese (7)	36	0.28
Romanian (22)	31	0.24
Russian (147)	265	2.09
Scandinavian (0)	21	0.17
Scotch-Irish (56)	185	1.46
Scottish (115)	341	2.68
Slovak (30)	96	0.76
Swedish (17)	85	0.67
Ukrainian (49)	87	0.68
Welsh (14)	29	0.23
West Indian, ex. Hispanic (31)	42	0.33
Barbadian (0)	11	0.09
Haitian (31)	31	0.24

Hispanic Origin	Population	%
Hispanic or Latino (of any race)	1,046	8.27
Central American, ex. Mexican	39	0.31
Costa Rican	6	0.05
Guatemalan	6	0.05
Honduran	9	0.07
Nicaraguan	5	0.04
Panamanian	3	0.02
Salvadoran	10	0.08
Cuban	39	0.31
Dominican Republic	83	0.66
Mexican	89	0.70
Puerto Rican	573	4.53
South American	105	0.83
Argentinean	5	0.04
Chilean	5	0.04
Colombian	42	0.33
Ecuadorian	20	0.16
Paraguayan	1	0.01
Peruvian	23	0.18
Uruguayan	5	0.04
Other South American	4	0.03
Other Hispanic or Latino	118	0.93

Race*	Population	%
African-American/Black (250)	349	2.76
Not Hispanic (221)	280	2.21
Hispanic (29)	69	0.55
American Indian/Alaska Native (35)	102	0.81
Not Hispanic (28)	71	0.56
Hispanic (7)	31	0.25
Aleut *(Alaska Native)* (1)	1	0.01
Blackfeet (2)	3	0.02
Canadian/French Am. Ind. (0)	1	0.01
Cherokee (3)	17	0.13
Chippewa (0)	1	0.01
Delaware (5)	10	0.08
Hopi (0)	3	0.02
Houma (2)	2	0.02
Iroquois (2)	8	0.06
Mexican American Ind. (1)	1	0.01
Navajo (2)	6	0.05
Sioux (0)	2	0.02

SECTION TWO

*Notes: † The Census 2010 population figure is used to calculate the percentages in the Hispanic Origin and Race categories. Ancestry percentages are based on the 2006-2010 American Community Survey population (not shown); ‡ Numbers in parentheses indicate the number of people reporting a single ancestry; * Numbers in parentheses indicate the number of persons reporting this race alone, not in combination with any other race; Please refer to the Explanation of Data for more information.*

South American Ind. (0)	6	0.05
Asian (219)	347	2.74
Not Hispanic (212)	326	2.58
Hispanic (7)	21	0.17
Cambodian (2)	7	0.06
Chinese, ex. Taiwanese (25)	34	0.27
Filipino (32)	59	0.47
Indian (79)	98	0.77
Indonesian (1)	1	0.01
Japanese (14)	37	0.29
Korean (29)	39	0.31
Malaysian (1)	1	0.01
Nepalese (0)	3	0.02
Pakistani (17)	29	0.23
Taiwanese (3)	3	0.02
Thai (4)	13	0.10
Vietnamese (1)	5	0.04
Hawaii Native/Pacific Islander (7)	15	0.12
Not Hispanic (5)	9	0.07
Hispanic (2)	6	0.05
Guamanian/Chamorro (5)	5	0.04
Native Hawaiian (0)	1	0.01
White (11,635)	11,912	94.20
Not Hispanic (10,916)	11,104	87.81
Hispanic (719)	808	6.39

Cortland

Place Type: City
County: Cortland
Population: 19,204†

Ancestry‡	Population	%
American (643)	643	3.34
Arab (78)	150	0.78
Lebanese (78)	150	0.78
Austrian (0)	37	0.19
British (25)	44	0.23
Celtic (8)	19	0.10
Czech (8)	20	0.10
Czechoslovakian (0)	11	0.06
Danish (0)	13	0.07
Dutch (97)	611	3.17
Eastern European (12)	12	0.06
English (989)	2,567	13.33
Estonian (7)	7	0.04
European (239)	239	1.24
Finnish (0)	79	0.41
French, ex. Basque (137)	627	3.26
French Canadian (54)	153	0.79
German (639)	2,792	14.50
Greek (36)	98	0.51
Hungarian (8)	72	0.37
Irish (1,077)	3,789	19.68
Italian (936)	2,562	13.30
Lithuanian (0)	13	0.07
Northern European (92)	92	0.48
Norwegian (38)	118	0.61
Pennsylvania German (25)	34	0.18
Polish (179)	634	3.29
Portuguese (10)	10	0.05
Romanian (35)	75	0.39
Russian (27)	193	1.00
Scotch-Irish (57)	207	1.07
Scottish (118)	468	2.43
Slavic (16)	31	0.16
Slovak (0)	25	0.13
Swedish (7)	132	0.69
Swiss (0)	8	0.04
Turkish (42)	42	0.22
Ukrainian (61)	87	0.45
Welsh (52)	162	0.84
West Indian, ex. Hispanic (12)	34	0.18
Haitian (12)	25	0.13
Trinidadian/Tobagonian (0)	9	0.05

Hispanic Origin	Population	%
Hispanic or Latino (of any race)	623	3.24
Central American, ex. Mexican	29	0.15
Costa Rican	2	0.01
Guatemalan	9	0.05
Honduran	3	0.02
Nicaraguan	1	0.01
Panamanian	3	0.02
Salvadoran	10	0.05
Other Central American	1	0.01
Cuban	40	0.21
Dominican Republic	47	0.24
Mexican	79	0.41
Puerto Rican	285	1.48
South American	63	0.33
Argentinean	3	0.02
Bolivian	2	0.01
Chilean	2	0.01
Colombian	32	0.17
Ecuadorian	15	0.08
Peruvian	4	0.02
Uruguayan	3	0.02
Venezuelan	2	0.01
Other Hispanic or Latino	80	0.42

Race*	Population	%
African-American/Black (547)	770	4.01
Not Hispanic (503)	697	3.63
Hispanic (44)	73	0.38
American Indian/Alaska Native (48)	197	1.03
Not Hispanic (47)	177	0.92
Hispanic (1)	20	0.10
Blackfeet (0)	6	0.03
Canadian/French Am. Ind. (1)	5	0.03
Cherokee (1)	26	0.14
Cree (0)	1	0.01
Delaware (0)	2	0.01
Iroquois (10)	44	0.23
Sioux (1)	4	0.02
Asian (180)	239	1.24
Not Hispanic (178)	231	1.20
Hispanic (2)	8	0.04
Bangladeshi (4)	4	0.02
Chinese, ex. Taiwanese (54)	61	0.32
Filipino (22)	43	0.22
Indian (23)	28	0.15
Indonesian (4)	4	0.02
Japanese (8)	21	0.11
Korean (35)	42	0.22
Laotian (8)	9	0.05
Malaysian (0)	1	0.01
Pakistani (2)	2	0.01
Sri Lankan (2)	2	0.01
Taiwanese (0)	1	0.01
Vietnamese (8)	10	0.05
Hawaii Native/Pacific Islander (4)	13	0.07
Not Hispanic (2)	9	0.05
Hispanic (2)	4	0.02
Guamanian/Chamorro (1)	1	0.01
Native Hawaiian (0)	3	0.02
Samoan (0)	1	0.01
Tongan (0)	1	0.01
White (17,820)	18,236	94.96
Not Hispanic (17,479)	17,837	92.88
Hispanic (341)	399	2.08

Cortlandt

Place Type: Town
County: Westchester
Population: 41,592†

Ancestry‡	Population	%
African, Sub-Saharan (136)	221	0.54
African (55)	115	0.28
Ghanaian (26)	26	0.06
South African (55)	80	0.20
American (1,668)	1,668	4.08
Arab (40)	150	0.37
Egyptian (12)	48	0.12
Lebanese (7)	81	0.20
Palestinian (21)	21	0.05
Armenian (37)	72	0.18
Assyrian/Chaldean/Syriac (0)	45	0.11
Austrian (66)	481	1.18
Basque (31)	42	0.10
Belgian (0)	9	0.02
Brazilian (100)	112	0.27
British (103)	251	0.61
Canadian (104)	251	0.61
Croatian (8)	32	0.08
Czech (130)	350	0.86
Czechoslovakian (64)	138	0.34
Danish (30)	116	0.28
Dutch (93)	518	1.27
Eastern European (365)	425	1.04
English (451)	2,110	5.17
Estonian (5)	5	0.01
European (649)	820	2.01
Finnish (25)	99	0.24
French, ex. Basque (226)	1,083	2.65
French Canadian (161)	381	0.93
German (791)	4,939	12.09
Greek (93)	206	0.50
Guyanese (78)	78	0.19
Hungarian (121)	463	1.13
Icelander (0)	19	0.05
Iranian (10)	10	0.02
Irish (2,734)	8,786	21.51
Israeli (33)	49	0.12
Italian (5,131)	10,979	26.88
Lithuanian (33)	127	0.31
Maltese (6)	6	0.01
Northern European (38)	46	0.11
Norwegian (29)	244	0.60
Polish (469)	2,371	5.81
Portuguese (287)	380	0.93
Romanian (171)	383	0.94
Russian (467)	1,599	3.92
Scandinavian (0)	58	0.14
Scotch-Irish (214)	594	1.45
Scottish (205)	823	2.02
Serbian (0)	12	0.03
Slavic (19)	19	0.05
Slovak (188)	368	0.90
Slovene (10)	39	0.10
Swedish (7)	354	0.87
Swiss (58)	198	0.48
Turkish (7)	53	0.13
Ukrainian (38)	244	0.60
Welsh (20)	102	0.25
West Indian, ex. Hispanic (233)	342	0.84
Barbadian (7)	18	0.04
Belizean (14)	14	0.03
British West Indian (40)	47	0.12
Jamaican (126)	133	0.33
Trinidadian/Tobagonian (23)	59	0.14
West Indian (23)	61	0.15
Other West Indian (0)	10	0.02
Yugoslavian (0)	52	0.13

Hispanic Origin	Population	%
Hispanic or Latino (of any race)	5,324	12.80
Central American, ex. Mexican	418	1.01
Costa Rican	22	0.05
Guatemalan	177	0.43
Honduran	59	0.14
Nicaraguan	16	0.04
Panamanian	9	0.02
Salvadoran	132	0.32
Other Central American	3	0.01
Cuban	206	0.50
Dominican Republic	407	0.98
Mexican	336	0.81
Puerto Rican	1,698	4.08
South American	1,721	4.14
Argentinean	66	0.16
Bolivian	6	0.01
Chilean	84	0.20
Colombian	269	0.65
Ecuadorian	903	2.17
Paraguayan	34	0.08
Peruvian	180	0.43
Uruguayan	140	0.34

*Notes: † The Census 2010 population figure is used to calculate the percentages in the Hispanic Origin and Race categories. Ancestry percentages are based on the 2006-2010 American Community Survey population (not shown); ‡ Numbers in parentheses indicate the number of people reporting a single ancestry; * Numbers in parentheses indicate the number of persons reporting this race alone, not in combination with any other race; Please refer to the Explanation of Data for more information.*

	Population	%
Venezuelan	16	0.04
Other South American	23	0.06
Other Hispanic or Latino	538	1.29

Race*	Population	%
African-American/Black (2,229)	2,661	6.40
Not Hispanic (1,994)	2,275	5.47
Hispanic (235)	386	0.93
American Indian/Alaska Native (64)	284	0.68
Not Hispanic (30)	174	0.42
Hispanic (34)	110	0.26
Blackfeet (0)	1	<0.01
Cherokee (2)	32	0.08
Chippewa (0)	1	<0.01
Choctaw (0)	3	0.01
Creek (0)	1	<0.01
Delaware (0)	6	0.01
Iroquois (10)	20	0.05
Lumbee (0)	1	<0.01
Mexican American Ind. (1)	4	0.01
Navajo (1)	2	<0.01
Potawatomi (0)	3	0.01
Seminole (0)	5	0.01
Sioux (1)	3	0.01
South American Ind. (4)	34	0.08
Spanish American Ind. (4)	4	0.01
Tlingit-Haida *(Alaska Native)* (1)	1	<0.01
Tohono O'Odham (1)	1	<0.01
Asian (1,504)	1,855	4.46
Not Hispanic (1,479)	1,767	4.25
Hispanic (25)	88	0.21
Bangladeshi (0)	2	<0.01
Burmese (3)	3	0.01
Cambodian (4)	5	0.01
Chinese, ex. Taiwanese (404)	520	1.25
Filipino (158)	212	0.51
Indian (562)	647	1.56
Indonesian (6)	8	0.02
Japanese (71)	105	0.25
Korean (130)	161	0.39
Laotian (2)	6	0.01
Nepalese (5)	6	0.01
Pakistani (63)	68	0.16
Sri Lankan (10)	10	0.02
Taiwanese (23)	29	0.07
Thai (13)	16	0.04
Vietnamese (15)	23	0.06
Hawaii Native/Pacific Islander (8)	50	0.12
Not Hispanic (7)	28	0.07
Hispanic (1)	22	0.05
Fijian (0)	1	<0.01
Guamanian/Chamorro (3)	9	0.02
Native Hawaiian (0)	11	0.03
Samoan (1)	3	0.01
White (35,143)	36,108	86.81
Not Hispanic (31,976)	32,570	78.31
Hispanic (3,167)	3,538	8.51

Cortlandville

Place Type: Town
County: Cortland
Population: 8,509†

Ancestry‡	Population	%
American (331)	331	3.92
Arab (0)	10	0.12
Syrian (0)	10	0.12
Austrian (0)	13	0.15
Canadian (25)	30	0.36
Croatian (0)	33	0.39
Czech (0)	35	0.41
Czechoslovakian (0)	11	0.13
Danish (9)	9	0.11
Dutch (43)	267	3.16
Eastern European (18)	18	0.21
English (598)	1,426	16.88
European (389)	400	4.74
Finnish (0)	3	0.04
French, ex. Basque (0)	259	3.07
French Canadian (66)	172	2.04
German (704)	1,627	19.26
Greek (10)	47	0.56
Hungarian (0)	14	0.17
Irish (445)	1,642	19.44
Italian (601)	1,370	16.22
Lithuanian (0)	26	0.31
Maltese (0)	22	0.26
Northern European (61)	61	0.72
Norwegian (0)	61	0.72
Polish (113)	387	4.58
Russian (31)	98	1.16
Scandinavian (10)	10	0.12
Scotch-Irish (0)	46	0.54
Scottish (46)	121	1.43
Swedish (30)	54	0.64
Ukrainian (33)	59	0.70
Welsh (0)	24	0.28

Hispanic Origin	Population	%
Hispanic or Latino (of any race)	128	1.50
Central American, ex. Mexican	7	0.08
Costa Rican	1	0.01
Guatemalan	4	0.05
Panamanian	1	0.01
Salvadoran	1	0.01
Cuban	9	0.11
Dominican Republic	1	0.01
Mexican	19	0.22
Puerto Rican	66	0.78
South American	12	0.14
Bolivian	2	0.02
Colombian	3	0.04
Ecuadorian	3	0.04
Peruvian	3	0.04
Uruguayan	1	0.01
Other Hispanic or Latino	14	0.16

Race*	Population	%
African-American/Black (108)	166	1.95
Not Hispanic (101)	154	1.81
Hispanic (7)	12	0.14
American Indian/Alaska Native (31)	83	0.98
Not Hispanic (29)	79	0.93
Hispanic (2)	4	0.05
Blackfeet (1)	4	0.05
Canadian/French Am. Ind. (1)	2	0.02
Cherokee (0)	5	0.06
Choctaw (0)	2	0.02
Delaware (0)	2	0.02
Iroquois (15)	19	0.22
Mexican American Ind. (2)	2	0.02
Navajo (1)	1	0.01
Sioux (1)	1	0.01
Asian (126)	172	2.02
Not Hispanic (126)	171	2.01
Hispanic (0)	1	0.01
Chinese, ex. Taiwanese (20)	37	0.43
Filipino (3)	10	0.12
Indian (66)	67	0.79
Indonesian (1)	5	0.06
Japanese (4)	12	0.14
Korean (7)	13	0.15
Laotian (1)	1	0.01
Pakistani (4)	4	0.05
Taiwanese (2)	2	0.02
Thai (1)	3	0.04
Vietnamese (14)	14	0.16
Hawaii Native/Pacific Islander (0)	1	0.01
Not Hispanic (0)	1	0.01
White (8,068)	8,199	96.36
Not Hispanic (7,985)	8,109	95.30
Hispanic (83)	90	1.06

Coxsackie

Place Type: Town
County: Greene
Population: 8,918†

Ancestry‡	Population	%
African, Sub-Saharan (44)	51	0.57
African (0)	7	0.08
Ghanaian (44)	44	0.49
American (646)	646	7.20
Arab (24)	24	0.27
Syrian (24)	24	0.27
Austrian (40)	40	0.45
British (0)	9	0.10
Canadian (8)	8	0.09
Croatian (0)	11	0.12
Czech (0)	39	0.43
Czechoslovakian (23)	45	0.50
Danish (0)	24	0.27
Dutch (90)	343	3.82
English (92)	795	8.86
European (41)	41	0.46
French, ex. Basque (45)	372	4.15
French Canadian (34)	87	0.97
German (354)	1,318	14.69
Greek (27)	27	0.30
Guyanese (8)	8	0.09
Hungarian (35)	66	0.74
Irish (218)	1,288	14.35
Italian (489)	1,292	14.40
Northern European (0)	6	0.07
Norwegian (10)	30	0.33
Polish (90)	436	4.86
Portuguese (0)	52	0.58
Russian (0)	11	0.12
Scandinavian (0)	33	0.37
Scotch-Irish (20)	76	0.85
Scottish (6)	49	0.55
Slovak (0)	13	0.14
Swedish (18)	89	0.99
Swiss (8)	8	0.09
Ukrainian (0)	48	0.53
Welsh (0)	57	0.64
West Indian, ex. Hispanic (34)	34	0.38
Haitian (8)	8	0.09
Jamaican (9)	9	0.10
Trinidadian/Tobagonian (17)	17	0.19
Yugoslavian (8)	8	0.09

Hispanic Origin	Population	%
Hispanic or Latino (of any race)	759	8.51
Central American, ex. Mexican	65	0.73
Costa Rican	5	0.06
Guatemalan	14	0.16
Honduran	14	0.16
Nicaraguan	1	0.01
Panamanian	10	0.11
Salvadoran	21	0.24
Cuban	26	0.29
Dominican Republic	102	1.14
Mexican	95	1.07
Puerto Rican	392	4.40
South American	56	0.63
Argentinean	2	0.02
Chilean	3	0.03
Colombian	23	0.26
Ecuadorian	17	0.19
Peruvian	4	0.04
Venezuelan	7	0.08
Other Hispanic or Latino	23	0.26

Race*	Population	%
African-American/Black (1,782)	1,827	20.49
Not Hispanic (1,649)	1,689	18.94
Hispanic (133)	138	1.55
American Indian/Alaska Native (40)	70	0.78
Not Hispanic (35)	63	0.71
Hispanic (5)	7	0.08
Apache (0)	1	0.01
Central American Ind. (1)	2	0.02
Cherokee (0)	7	0.08
Choctaw (0)	2	0.02
Inupiat *(Alaska Native)* (1)	2	0.02
Iroquois (1)	1	0.01
Sioux (4)	6	0.07

*Notes: † The Census 2010 population figure is used to calculate the percentages in the Hispanic Origin and Race categories. Ancestry percentages are based on the 2006-2010 American Community Survey population (not shown); ‡ Numbers in parentheses indicate the number of people reporting a single ancestry; * Numbers in parentheses indicate the number of persons reporting this race alone, not in combination with any other race; Please refer to the Explanation of Data for more information.*

Yakama (0)	1	0.01
Asian (68)	79	0.89
Not Hispanic (66)	77	0.86
Hispanic (2)	2	0.02
Chinese, ex. Taiwanese (18)	21	0.24
Filipino (5)	5	0.06
Indian (7)	11	0.12
Japanese (1)	1	0.01
Korean (1)	1	0.01
Pakistani (1)	3	0.03
Taiwanese (1)	1	0.01
Thai (0)	1	0.01
Hawaii Native/Pacific Islander (4)	5	0.06
Not Hispanic (4)	5	0.06
Guamanian/Chamorro (2)	3	0.03
White (6,742)	6,816	76.43
Not Hispanic (6,277)	6,337	71.06
Hispanic (465)	479	5.37

Crawford

Place Type: Town
County: Orange
Population: 9,316†

Ancestry‡	Population	%
American (1,162)	1,162	12.72
Austrian (0)	35	0.38
British (0)	23	0.25
Czech (0)	25	0.27
Czechoslovakian (0)	10	0.11
Dutch (142)	554	6.06
English (93)	791	8.66
European (0)	51	0.56
Finnish (26)	67	0.73
French, ex. Basque (15)	152	1.66
French Canadian (0)	14	0.15
German (438)	1,878	20.55
Greek (99)	177	1.94
Guyanese (15)	15	0.16
Hungarian (54)	137	1.50
Irish (849)	2,500	27.36
Italian (582)	1,786	19.55
Lithuanian (14)	112	1.23
Norwegian (21)	66	0.72
Polish (160)	539	5.90
Portuguese (203)	245	2.68
Russian (61)	127	1.39
Scotch-Irish (19)	102	1.12
Scottish (36)	221	2.42
Slovak (14)	27	0.30
Swedish (0)	23	0.25
Ukrainian (0)	144	1.58
Welsh (0)	30	0.33
West Indian, ex. Hispanic (34)	34	0.37
Haitian (7)	7	0.08
Jamaican (15)	15	0.16
West Indian (12)	12	0.13

Hispanic Origin	Population	%
Hispanic or Latino (of any race)	924	9.92
Central American, ex. Mexican	36	0.39
Costa Rican	1	0.01
Guatemalan	6	0.06
Honduran	10	0.11
Panamanian	10	0.11
Salvadoran	9	0.10
Cuban	48	0.52
Dominican Republic	34	0.36
Mexican	158	1.70
Puerto Rican	512	5.50
South American	63	0.68
Argentinean	4	0.04
Chilean	6	0.06
Colombian	24	0.26
Ecuadorian	13	0.14
Peruvian	16	0.17
Other Hispanic or Latino	73	0.78

Race*	Population	%
African-American/Black (362)	464	4.98
Not Hispanic (303)	385	4.13
Hispanic (59)	79	0.85
American Indian/Alaska Native (22)	85	0.91
Not Hispanic (16)	69	0.74
Hispanic (6)	16	0.17
Aleut *(Alaska Native)* (0)	1	0.01
Apache (0)	1	0.01
Blackfeet (1)	1	0.01
Cherokee (1)	10	0.11
Chippewa (5)	9	0.10
Delaware (1)	4	0.04
Iroquois (0)	1	0.01
Mexican American Ind. (0)	4	0.04
South American Ind. (2)	2	0.02
Spanish American Ind. (3)	3	0.03
Asian (146)	206	2.21
Not Hispanic (139)	185	1.99
Hispanic (7)	21	0.23
Cambodian (1)	1	0.01
Chinese, ex. Taiwanese (40)	65	0.70
Filipino (20)	31	0.33
Indian (42)	44	0.47
Japanese (3)	5	0.05
Korean (16)	32	0.34
Laotian (1)	1	0.01
Nepalese (1)	1	0.01
Pakistani (7)	9	0.10
Vietnamese (12)	14	0.15
Hawaii Native/Pacific Islander (6)	8	0.09
Not Hispanic (6)	8	0.09
White (8,317)	8,528	91.54
Not Hispanic (7,736)	7,890	84.69
Hispanic (581)	638	6.85

Croton-on-Hudson

Place Type: Village
County: Westchester
Population: 8,070†

Ancestry‡	Population	%
American (181)	181	2.29
Arab (12)	33	0.42
Egyptian (12)	12	0.15
Lebanese (0)	21	0.27
Armenian (10)	10	0.13
Austrian (0)	191	2.42
Basque (31)	42	0.53
Brazilian (36)	48	0.61
British (45)	109	1.38
Canadian (10)	80	1.01
Czech (0)	54	0.68
Czechoslovakian (28)	28	0.35
Danish (21)	49	0.62
Dutch (0)	58	0.73
Eastern European (139)	146	1.85
English (161)	638	8.08
Estonian (5)	5	0.06
European (206)	257	3.25
Finnish (0)	25	0.32
French, ex. Basque (50)	158	2.00
French Canadian (32)	66	0.84
German (180)	990	12.54
Greek (10)	24	0.30
Hungarian (37)	104	1.32
Icelander (0)	19	0.24
Irish (670)	1,792	22.70
Italian (797)	1,842	23.33
Lithuanian (8)	27	0.34
Northern European (9)	17	0.22
Norwegian (0)	71	0.90
Polish (127)	353	4.47
Portuguese (26)	58	0.73
Romanian (37)	83	1.05
Russian (107)	477	6.04
Scandinavian (0)	33	0.42
Scotch-Irish (89)	219	2.77
Scottish (42)	120	1.52
Slavic (10)	10	0.13
Slovak (0)	25	0.32
Slovene (10)	39	0.49
Swedish (0)	97	1.23
Swiss (10)	42	0.53
Turkish (0)	28	0.35
Ukrainian (18)	95	1.20
Welsh (11)	53	0.67
West Indian, ex. Hispanic (32)	32	0.41
Jamaican (9)	9	0.11
Trinidadian/Tobagonian (23)	23	0.29

Hispanic Origin	Population	%
Hispanic or Latino (of any race)	921	11.41
Central American, ex. Mexican	48	0.59
Costa Rican	1	0.01
Guatemalan	23	0.29
Honduran	15	0.19
Nicaraguan	3	0.04
Salvadoran	6	0.07
Cuban	41	0.51
Dominican Republic	59	0.73
Mexican	82	1.02
Puerto Rican	190	2.35
South American	424	5.25
Argentinean	13	0.16
Bolivian	3	0.04
Chilean	18	0.22
Colombian	60	0.74
Ecuadorian	257	3.18
Paraguayan	2	0.02
Peruvian	33	0.41
Uruguayan	23	0.29
Venezuelan	10	0.12
Other South American	5	0.06
Other Hispanic or Latino	77	0.95

Race*	Population	%
African-American/Black (234)	305	3.78
Not Hispanic (201)	248	3.07
Hispanic (33)	57	0.71
American Indian/Alaska Native (19)	60	0.74
Not Hispanic (7)	35	0.43
Hispanic (12)	25	0.31
Cherokee (0)	4	0.05
Iroquois (5)	6	0.07
Mexican American Ind. (0)	1	0.01
Navajo (0)	1	0.01
Potawatomi (0)	2	0.02
Seminole (0)	5	0.06
South American Ind. (0)	5	0.06
Spanish American Ind. (3)	3	0.04
Tohono O'Odham (1)	1	0.01
Asian (297)	392	4.86
Not Hispanic (296)	378	4.68
Hispanic (1)	14	0.17
Bangladeshi (0)	1	0.01
Chinese, ex. Taiwanese (119)	155	1.92
Filipino (19)	33	0.41
Indian (63)	88	1.09
Indonesian (2)	2	0.02
Japanese (16)	24	0.30
Korean (37)	45	0.56
Pakistani (11)	11	0.14
Sri Lankan (2)	2	0.02
Taiwanese (11)	13	0.16
Thai (6)	7	0.09
Vietnamese (0)	1	0.01
Hawaii Native/Pacific Islander (1)	12	0.15
Not Hispanic (0)	2	0.02
Hispanic (1)	10	0.12
Guamanian/Chamorro (1)	3	0.04
Native Hawaiian (0)	4	0.05
White (6,991)	7,200	89.22
Not Hispanic (6,458)	6,601	81.80
Hispanic (533)	599	7.42

*Notes: † The Census 2010 population figure is used to calculate the percentages in the Hispanic Origin and Race categories. Ancestry percentages are based on the 2006-2010 American Community Survey population (not shown); ‡ Numbers in parentheses indicate the number of people reporting a single ancestry; * Numbers in parentheses indicate the number of persons reporting this race alone, not in combination with any other race; Please refer to the Explanation of Data for more information.*

De Witt

Place Type: Town
County: Onondaga
Population: 25,838†

Ancestry‡	Population	%
African, Sub-Saharan (76)	86	0.34
African (76)	86	0.34
Albanian (0)	18	0.07
Alsatian (39)	39	0.15
American (747)	747	2.92
Arab (117)	214	0.84
Arab (11)	11	0.04
Egyptian (19)	28	0.11
Lebanese (41)	95	0.37
Palestinian (8)	17	0.07
Syrian (0)	25	0.10
Other Arab (38)	38	0.15
Armenian (102)	118	0.46
Assyrian/Chaldean/Syriac (0)	10	0.04
Austrian (13)	179	0.70
Belgian (0)	36	0.14
Brazilian (11)	11	0.04
British (5)	113	0.44
Canadian (14)	63	0.25
Celtic (6)	6	0.02
Czech (12)	54	0.21
Czechoslovakian (11)	11	0.04
Danish (0)	21	0.08
Dutch (111)	720	2.82
Eastern European (125)	152	0.59
English (950)	3,165	12.39
European (446)	459	1.80
Finnish (0)	30	0.12
French, ex. Basque (172)	1,202	4.70
French Canadian (70)	403	1.58
German (1,086)	4,903	19.19
Greek (205)	315	1.23
Hungarian (119)	216	0.85
Iranian (24)	24	0.09
Irish (1,395)	5,643	22.09
Israeli (12)	12	0.05
Italian (2,261)	4,839	18.94
Latvian (28)	53	0.21
Lithuanian (20)	52	0.20
Macedonian (10)	10	0.04
Northern European (16)	16	0.06
Norwegian (10)	76	0.30
Pennsylvania German (0)	9	0.04
Polish (612)	1,917	7.50
Portuguese (191)	201	0.79
Romanian (0)	10	0.04
Russian (468)	719	2.81
Scandinavian (22)	51	0.20
Scotch-Irish (105)	374	1.46
Scottish (119)	464	1.82
Serbian (10)	40	0.16
Slovak (0)	25	0.10
Slovene (0)	17	0.07
Swedish (73)	245	0.96
Swiss (15)	119	0.47
Ukrainian (171)	411	1.61
Welsh (83)	306	1.20
West Indian, ex. Hispanic (205)	248	0.97
Haitian (0)	14	0.05
Jamaican (142)	171	0.67
Trinidadian/Tobagonian (52)	52	0.20
West Indian (11)	11	0.04
Yugoslavian (289)	298	1.17

Hispanic Origin	Population	%
Hispanic or Latino (of any race)	761	2.95
Central American, ex. Mexican	33	0.13
Costa Rican	2	0.01
Guatemalan	11	0.04
Honduran	7	0.03
Nicaraguan	1	<0.01
Panamanian	5	0.02
Salvadoran	6	0.02
Other Central American	1	<0.01
Cuban	139	0.54
Dominican Republic	54	0.21
Mexican	126	0.49
Puerto Rican	246	0.95
South American	72	0.28
Argentinean	10	0.04
Bolivian	1	<0.01
Chilean	12	0.05
Colombian	23	0.09
Ecuadorian	8	0.03
Paraguayan	1	<0.01
Peruvian	7	0.03
Uruguayan	3	0.01
Venezuelan	4	0.02
Other South American	3	0.01
Other Hispanic or Latino	91	0.35

Race*	Population	%
African-American/Black (1,521)	1,815	7.02
Not Hispanic (1,448)	1,698	6.57
Hispanic (73)	117	0.45
American Indian/Alaska Native (149)	302	1.17
Not Hispanic (136)	271	1.05
Hispanic (13)	31	0.12
Apache (0)	1	<0.01
Blackfeet (0)	8	0.03
Canadian/French Am. Ind. (8)	14	0.05
Central American Ind. (0)	5	0.02
Cherokee (2)	15	0.06
Chippewa (2)	4	0.02
Choctaw (1)	2	0.01
Cree (0)	1	<0.01
Creek (0)	3	0.01
Delaware (1)	1	<0.01
Iroquois (89)	149	0.58
Kiowa (1)	1	<0.01
Mexican American Ind. (7)	8	0.03
Sioux (0)	1	<0.01
South American Ind. (0)	2	0.01
Yuman (1)	4	0.02
Asian (1,054)	1,231	4.76
Not Hispanic (1,047)	1,213	4.69
Hispanic (7)	18	0.07
Bangladeshi (6)	10	0.04
Burmese (2)	2	0.01
Cambodian (6)	6	0.02
Chinese, ex. Taiwanese (269)	293	1.13
Filipino (51)	69	0.27
Indian (357)	395	1.53
Indonesian (4)	9	0.03
Japanese (25)	50	0.19
Korean (134)	159	0.62
Laotian (2)	2	0.01
Nepalese (8)	8	0.03
Pakistani (34)	34	0.13
Sri Lankan (1)	2	0.01
Taiwanese (12)	15	0.06
Thai (14)	17	0.07
Vietnamese (82)	105	0.41
Hawaii Native/Pacific Islander (8)	19	0.07
Not Hispanic (8)	18	0.07
Hispanic (0)	1	<0.01
Native Hawaiian (3)	7	0.03
Samoan (1)	3	0.01
White (22,334)	22,840	88.40
Not Hispanic (21,890)	22,345	86.48
Hispanic (444)	495	1.92

Deer Park

Place Type: CDP
County: Suffolk
Population: 27,745†

Ancestry‡	Population	%
Afghan (56)	56	0.20
African, Sub-Saharan (52)	137	0.48
African (52)	137	0.48
American (685)	685	2.42
Arab (149)	168	0.59
Arab (95)	95	0.34
Lebanese (10)	17	0.06
Palestinian (44)	44	0.16
Syrian (0)	12	0.04
Armenian (20)	20	0.07
Austrian (6)	43	0.15
Brazilian (0)	69	0.24
British (26)	37	0.13
Canadian (0)	25	0.09
Croatian (10)	10	0.04
Czech (0)	265	0.94
Czechoslovakian (106)	138	0.49
Danish (22)	61	0.22
Dutch (12)	139	0.49
Eastern European (0)	17	0.06
English (195)	1,057	3.74
European (84)	84	0.30
Finnish (14)	52	0.18
French, ex. Basque (54)	430	1.52
French Canadian (42)	160	0.57
German (572)	3,800	13.43
Greek (90)	351	1.24
Guyanese (159)	164	0.58
Hungarian (42)	177	0.63
Irish (1,136)	5,364	18.96
Israeli (10)	10	0.04
Italian (5,597)	10,193	36.03
Lithuanian (71)	146	0.52
Maltese (0)	28	0.10
Norwegian (19)	57	0.20
Polish (407)	969	3.42
Portuguese (25)	106	0.37
Romanian (102)	108	0.38
Russian (155)	604	2.13
Scotch-Irish (28)	304	1.07
Scottish (11)	203	0.72
Slavic (0)	6	0.02
Slovak (0)	20	0.07
Slovene (14)	14	0.05
Swedish (0)	84	0.30
Swiss (0)	14	0.05
Turkish (270)	308	1.09
Ukrainian (83)	150	0.53
Welsh (14)	80	0.28
West Indian, ex. Hispanic (1,190)	1,344	4.75
Haitian (470)	558	1.97
Jamaican (457)	498	1.76
Trinidadian/Tobagonian (154)	154	0.54
West Indian (109)	134	0.47

Hispanic Origin	Population	%
Hispanic or Latino (of any race)	3,364	12.12
Central American, ex. Mexican	682	2.46
Costa Rican	20	0.07
Guatemalan	94	0.34
Honduran	98	0.35
Nicaraguan	16	0.06
Panamanian	31	0.11
Salvadoran	422	1.52
Other Central American	1	<0.01
Cuban	64	0.23
Dominican Republic	304	1.10
Mexican	103	0.37
Puerto Rican	1,122	4.04
South American	770	2.78
Argentinean	52	0.19
Bolivian	3	0.01
Chilean	50	0.18
Colombian	241	0.87
Ecuadorian	181	0.65
Paraguayan	12	0.04
Peruvian	202	0.73
Uruguayan	12	0.04
Venezuelan	15	0.05
Other South American	2	0.01
Other Hispanic or Latino	319	1.15

Race*	Population	%
African-American/Black (3,340)	3,672	13.23

*Notes: † The Census 2010 population figure is used to calculate the percentages in the Hispanic Origin and Race categories. Ancestry percentages are based on the 2006-2010 American Community Survey population (not shown); ‡ Numbers in parentheses indicate the number of people reporting a single ancestry; * Numbers in parentheses indicate the number of persons reporting this race alone, not in combination with any other race; Please refer to the Explanation of Data for more information.*

Not Hispanic (3,182)	3,424	12.34
Hispanic (158)	248	0.89
American Indian/Alaska Native (65)	195	0.70
Not Hispanic (37)	145	0.52
Hispanic (28)	50	0.18
Aleut *(Alaska Native)* (2)	2	0.01
Blackfeet (0)	5	0.02
Canadian/French Am. Ind. (4)	4	0.01
Central American Ind. (3)	7	0.03
Cherokee (7)	35	0.13
Creek (0)	1	<0.01
Iroquois (5)	6	0.02
South American Ind. (3)	10	0.04
Spanish American Ind. (0)	1	<0.01
Asian (1,877)	2,106	7.59
Not Hispanic (1,871)	2,071	7.46
Hispanic (6)	35	0.13
Bangladeshi (170)	224	0.81
Cambodian (1)	3	0.01
Chinese, ex. Taiwanese (231)	267	0.96
Filipino (129)	173	0.62
Indian (782)	877	3.16
Indonesian (1)	2	0.01
Japanese (13)	13	0.05
Korean (120)	139	0.50
Nepalese (1)	1	<0.01
Pakistani (273)	296	1.07
Sri Lankan (5)	6	0.02
Thai (11)	14	0.05
Vietnamese (41)	45	0.16
Hawaii Native/Pacific Islander (2)	24	0.09
Not Hispanic (0)	16	0.06
Hispanic (2)	8	0.03
Guamanian/Chamorro (0)	1	<0.01
Native Hawaiian (2)	5	0.02
White (20,786)	21,337	76.90
Not Hispanic (18,755)	19,096	68.83
Hispanic (2,031)	2,241	8.08

Deerpark

Place Type: Town
County: Orange
Population: 7,901†

Ancestry‡	Population	%
African, Sub-Saharan (216)	216	2.72
Ghanaian (20)	20	0.25
Nigerian (196)	196	2.47
American (421)	421	5.30
Arab (0)	12	0.15
Lebanese (0)	12	0.15
Armenian (12)	12	0.15
Austrian (0)	66	0.83
Canadian (0)	75	0.94
Czech (11)	25	0.31
Dutch (51)	325	4.09
Eastern European (12)	12	0.15
English (86)	680	8.56
European (12)	12	0.15
French, ex. Basque (9)	277	3.49
French Canadian (15)	15	0.19
German (463)	2,153	27.10
Greek (25)	48	0.60
Hungarian (23)	54	0.68
Irish (420)	1,802	22.68
Italian (515)	1,400	17.62
Lithuanian (0)	9	0.11
New Zealander (0)	35	0.44
Northern European (10)	38	0.48
Norwegian (0)	14	0.18
Polish (150)	593	7.46
Portuguese (0)	30	0.38
Russian (0)	124	1.56
Scotch-Irish (30)	75	0.94
Scottish (14)	112	1.41
Slovak (0)	54	0.68
Swedish (14)	168	2.11
Swiss (0)	46	0.58
Ukrainian (46)	251	3.16
Welsh (0)	77	0.97
West Indian, ex. Hispanic (25)	66	0.83
Jamaican (25)	66	0.83
Yugoslavian (0)	66	0.83

Hispanic Origin	Population	%
Hispanic or Latino (of any race)	547	6.92
Central American, ex. Mexican	8	0.10
Honduran	2	0.03
Nicaraguan	2	0.03
Panamanian	2	0.03
Salvadoran	2	0.03
Cuban	20	0.25
Dominican Republic	37	0.47
Mexican	47	0.59
Puerto Rican	339	4.29
South American	39	0.49
Argentinean	5	0.06
Chilean	2	0.03
Colombian	14	0.18
Ecuadorian	9	0.11
Peruvian	6	0.08
Uruguayan	1	0.01
Venezuelan	2	0.03
Other Hispanic or Latino	57	0.72

Race*	Population	%
African-American/Black (201)	315	3.99
Not Hispanic (174)	262	3.32
Hispanic (27)	53	0.67
American Indian/Alaska Native (40)	119	1.51
Not Hispanic (27)	96	1.22
Hispanic (13)	23	0.29
Apache (0)	1	0.01
Blackfeet (0)	9	0.11
Central American Ind. (1)	1	0.01
Cherokee (4)	19	0.24
Chippewa (0)	1	0.01
Comanche (1)	1	0.01
Crow (0)	1	0.01
Delaware (7)	13	0.16
Iroquois (1)	4	0.05
Mexican American Ind. (1)	1	0.01
Pueblo (1)	2	0.03
Seminole (0)	2	0.03
South American Ind. (4)	5	0.06
Yuman (1)	4	0.05
Asian (92)	120	1.52
Not Hispanic (89)	114	1.44
Hispanic (3)	6	0.08
Cambodian (5)	5	0.06
Chinese, ex. Taiwanese (24)	32	0.41
Filipino (12)	19	0.24
Indian (20)	25	0.32
Japanese (4)	10	0.13
Korean (3)	3	0.04
Pakistani (10)	11	0.14
Taiwanese (1)	1	0.01
Vietnamese (10)	14	0.18
Hawaii Native/Pacific Islander (3)	4	0.05
Not Hispanic (1)	2	0.03
Hispanic (2)	2	0.03
Guamanian/Chamorro (2)	2	0.03
Native Hawaiian (1)	2	0.03
White (7,237)	7,427	94.00
Not Hispanic (6,899)	7,046	89.18
Hispanic (338)	381	4.82

Depew

Place Type: Village
County: Erie
Population: 15,303†

Ancestry‡	Population	%
American (492)	492	3.18
Arab (335)	359	2.32
Arab (23)	23	0.15
Lebanese (0)	12	0.08
Palestinian (9)	9	0.06
Syrian (0)	12	0.08
Other Arab (303)	303	1.96
Austrian (13)	55	0.36
British (33)	60	0.39
Bulgarian (43)	43	0.28
Canadian (10)	24	0.16
Czech (0)	43	0.28
Czechoslovakian (38)	50	0.32
Dutch (66)	147	0.95
English (165)	815	5.27
European (13)	13	0.08
Finnish (14)	14	0.09
French, ex. Basque (9)	358	2.32
French Canadian (9)	132	0.85
German (1,360)	5,426	35.11
Greek (79)	137	0.89
Hungarian (0)	43	0.28
Irish (268)	2,306	14.92
Italian (1,184)	2,943	19.04
Lithuanian (12)	27	0.17
Northern European (130)	130	0.84
Norwegian (0)	6	0.04
Polish (3,252)	5,979	38.69
Portuguese (0)	9	0.06
Romanian (0)	10	0.06
Russian (48)	76	0.49
Scotch-Irish (13)	171	1.11
Scottish (56)	193	1.25
Serbian (0)	10	0.06
Slovak (9)	9	0.06
Swedish (15)	157	1.02
Swiss (12)	12	0.08
Ukrainian (31)	61	0.39
Welsh (0)	82	0.53

Hispanic Origin	Population	%
Hispanic or Latino (of any race)	261	1.71
Central American, ex. Mexican	19	0.12
Guatemalan	5	0.03
Nicaraguan	3	0.02
Panamanian	1	0.01
Salvadoran	7	0.05
Other Central American	3	0.02
Cuban	3	0.02
Dominican Republic	2	0.01
Mexican	53	0.35
Puerto Rican	150	0.98
South American	19	0.12
Argentinean	1	0.01
Colombian	7	0.05
Ecuadorian	4	0.03
Peruvian	2	0.01
Venezuelan	5	0.03
Other Hispanic or Latino	15	0.10

Race*	Population	%
African-American/Black (184)	267	1.74
Not Hispanic (179)	249	1.63
Hispanic (5)	18	0.12
American Indian/Alaska Native (34)	69	0.45
Not Hispanic (31)	58	0.38
Hispanic (3)	11	0.07
Arapaho (1)	1	0.01
Blackfeet (4)	6	0.04
Canadian/French Am. Ind. (1)	1	0.01
Central American Ind. (2)	3	0.02
Cherokee (0)	5	0.03
Iroquois (18)	20	0.13
South American Ind. (0)	3	0.02
Tlingit-Haida *(Alaska Native)* (0)	1	0.01
Asian (101)	162	1.06
Not Hispanic (101)	160	1.05
Hispanic (0)	2	0.01
Bangladeshi (2)	2	0.01
Cambodian (1)	4	0.03
Chinese, ex. Taiwanese (13)	18	0.12
Filipino (13)	30	0.20
Indian (38)	48	0.31
Indonesian (0)	1	0.01
Japanese (1)	3	0.02

*Notes: † The Census 2010 population figure is used to calculate the percentages in the Hispanic Origin and Race categories. Ancestry percentages are based on the 2006-2010 American Community Survey population (not shown); ‡ Numbers in parentheses indicate the number of people reporting a single ancestry; * Numbers in parentheses indicate the number of persons reporting this race alone, not in combination with any other race; Please refer to the Explanation of Data for more information.*

Korean (12)	20	0.13
Malaysian (1)	1	0.01
Taiwanese (1)	1	0.01
Thai (4)	7	0.05
Vietnamese (10)	14	0.09
Hawaii Native/Pacific Islander (1)	10	0.07
Not Hispanic (1)	7	0.05
Hispanic (0)	3	0.02
Native Hawaiian (0)	5	0.03
Samoan (0)	3	0.02
White (14,763)	14,927	97.54
Not Hispanic (14,575)	14,709	96.12
Hispanic (188)	218	1.42

Dix Hills

Place Type: CDP
County: Suffolk
Population: 26,892†

Ancestry‡	Population	%
Afghan (25)	25	0.09
African, Sub-Saharan (16)	16	0.06
Nigerian (16)	16	0.06
American (1,042)	1,042	3.92
Arab (220)	375	1.41
Arab (13)	13	0.05
Egyptian (118)	118	0.44
Iraqi (42)	166	0.63
Other Arab (47)	78	0.29
Armenian (63)	123	0.46
Austrian (175)	322	1.21
British (0)	7	0.03
Canadian (58)	115	0.43
Croatian (0)	7	0.03
Czech (28)	158	0.60
Czechoslovakian (14)	79	0.30
Danish (0)	8	0.03
Dutch (9)	148	0.56
Eastern European (395)	424	1.60
English (206)	864	3.25
Estonian (0)	32	0.12
European (277)	290	1.09
Finnish (0)	12	0.05
French, ex. Basque (73)	233	0.88
French Canadian (14)	46	0.17
German (774)	3,025	11.39
Greek (518)	659	2.48
Guyanese (39)	39	0.15
Hungarian (254)	954	3.59
Iranian (232)	232	0.87
Irish (758)	3,412	12.85
Israeli (64)	106	0.40
Italian (4,526)	7,358	27.72
Latvian (38)	38	0.14
Lithuanian (26)	56	0.21
Norwegian (26)	45	0.17
Polish (560)	1,961	7.39
Portuguese (0)	31	0.12
Romanian (222)	565	2.13
Russian (494)	1,928	7.26
Scandinavian (0)	21	0.08
Scotch-Irish (62)	101	0.38
Scottish (0)	39	0.15
Serbian (0)	37	0.14
Swedish (54)	199	0.75
Swiss (0)	37	0.14
Turkish (45)	53	0.20
Ukrainian (198)	329	1.24
Welsh (0)	11	0.04
West Indian, ex. Hispanic (294)	382	1.44
Haitian (161)	175	0.66
Jamaican (98)	166	0.63
West Indian (35)	41	0.15
Yugoslavian (113)	288	1.08

Hispanic Origin	Population	%
Hispanic or Latino (of any race)	1,533	5.70
Central American, ex. Mexican	175	0.65
Costa Rican	7	0.03
Guatemalan	31	0.12
Honduran	15	0.06
Nicaraguan	1	<0.01
Panamanian	17	0.06
Salvadoran	104	0.39
Cuban	122	0.45
Dominican Republic	162	0.60
Mexican	62	0.23
Puerto Rican	410	1.52
South American	408	1.52
Argentinean	45	0.17
Bolivian	11	0.04
Chilean	27	0.10
Colombian	167	0.62
Ecuadorian	66	0.25
Paraguayan	2	0.01
Peruvian	68	0.25
Uruguayan	12	0.04
Venezuelan	7	0.03
Other South American	3	0.01
Other Hispanic or Latino	194	0.72

Race*	Population	%
African-American/Black (1,480)	1,652	6.14
Not Hispanic (1,385)	1,523	5.66
Hispanic (95)	129	0.48
American Indian/Alaska Native (28)	115	0.43
Not Hispanic (23)	84	0.31
Hispanic (5)	31	0.12
Apache (1)	1	<0.01
Canadian/French Am. Ind. (5)	5	0.02
Central American Ind. (1)	1	<0.01
Cherokee (1)	21	0.08
Cheyenne (0)	3	0.01
Chippewa (1)	2	0.01
Choctaw (0)	3	0.01
Cree (0)	3	0.01
Delaware (0)	4	0.01
Mexican American Ind. (0)	5	0.02
Navajo (1)	5	0.02
South American Ind. (1)	3	0.01
Spanish American Ind. (0)	3	0.01
Asian (3,010)	3,345	12.44
Not Hispanic (2,990)	3,297	12.26
Hispanic (20)	48	0.18
Bangladeshi (71)	74	0.28
Burmese (6)	6	0.02
Chinese, ex. Taiwanese (555)	650	2.42
Filipino (174)	224	0.83
Indian (1,129)	1,227	4.56
Indonesian (0)	3	0.01
Japanese (13)	28	0.10
Korean (561)	595	2.21
Laotian (1)	1	<0.01
Malaysian (2)	3	0.01
Pakistani (302)	325	1.21
Sri Lankan (8)	9	0.03
Taiwanese (52)	53	0.20
Thai (3)	5	0.02
Vietnamese (48)	57	0.21
Hawaii Native/Pacific Islander (3)	12	0.04
Not Hispanic (3)	9	0.03
Hispanic (0)	3	0.01
Guamanian/Chamorro (0)	1	<0.01
Native Hawaiian (3)	3	0.01
White (21,478)	21,929	81.54
Not Hispanic (20,433)	20,781	77.28
Hispanic (1,045)	1,148	4.27

Dobbs Ferry

Place Type: Village
County: Westchester
Population: 10,875†

Ancestry‡	Population	%
African, Sub-Saharan (9)	134	1.24
African (6)	118	1.09
Ghanaian (3)	3	0.03
South African (0)	13	0.12
American (427)	427	3.96
Arab (56)	68	0.63
Jordanian (26)	26	0.24
Lebanese (16)	16	0.15
Syrian (14)	26	0.24
Austrian (13)	98	0.91
Belgian (0)	18	0.17
British (97)	150	1.39
Bulgarian (54)	54	0.50
Canadian (4)	12	0.11
Croatian (102)	175	1.62
Czech (32)	93	0.86
Czechoslovakian (8)	28	0.26
Dutch (33)	125	1.16
Eastern European (261)	323	3.00
English (214)	541	5.02
European (233)	270	2.50
French, ex. Basque (17)	206	1.91
French Canadian (23)	64	0.59
German (139)	914	8.48
German Russian (0)	13	0.12
Greek (128)	145	1.34
Hungarian (49)	155	1.44
Irish (633)	1,705	15.81
Italian (1,714)	2,903	26.92
Latvian (0)	32	0.30
Lithuanian (0)	27	0.25
Norwegian (16)	60	0.56
Polish (264)	702	6.51
Portuguese (12)	12	0.11
Romanian (56)	56	0.52
Russian (193)	550	5.10
Scandinavian (0)	7	0.06
Scotch-Irish (38)	79	0.73
Scottish (40)	148	1.37
Slovak (9)	65	0.60
Swedish (12)	27	0.25
Swiss (0)	24	0.22
Turkish (0)	34	0.32
Ukrainian (40)	112	1.04
Welsh (0)	50	0.46
West Indian, ex. Hispanic (152)	221	2.05
Haitian (3)	36	0.33
Jamaican (128)	164	1.52
Trinidadian/Tobagonian (21)	21	0.19
Yugoslavian (13)	13	0.12

Hispanic Origin	Population	%
Hispanic or Latino (of any race)	1,141	10.49
Central American, ex. Mexican	181	1.66
Guatemalan	125	1.15
Honduran	9	0.08
Nicaraguan	6	0.06
Panamanian	12	0.11
Salvadoran	23	0.21
Other Central American	6	0.06
Cuban	58	0.53
Dominican Republic	107	0.98
Mexican	136	1.25
Puerto Rican	386	3.55
South American	151	1.39
Argentinean	28	0.26
Bolivian	2	0.02
Chilean	14	0.13
Colombian	23	0.21
Ecuadorian	43	0.40
Paraguayan	4	0.04
Peruvian	31	0.29
Uruguayan	4	0.04
Venezuelan	2	0.02
Other Hispanic or Latino	122	1.12

Race*	Population	%
African-American/Black (788)	887	8.16
Not Hispanic (702)	775	7.13
Hispanic (86)	112	1.03
American Indian/Alaska Native (9)	60	0.55
Not Hispanic (3)	37	0.34
Hispanic (6)	23	0.21
Cherokee (0)	13	0.12

*Notes: † The Census 2010 population figure is used to calculate the percentages in the Hispanic Origin and Race categories. Ancestry percentages are based on the 2006-2010 American Community Survey population (not shown); ‡ Numbers in parentheses indicate the number of people reporting a single ancestry; * Numbers in parentheses indicate the number of persons reporting this race alone, not in combination with any other race; Please refer to the Explanation of Data for more information.*

Chippewa (0)	1	0.01
Delaware (1)	1	0.01
Iroquois (0)	7	0.06
Mexican American Ind. (0)	7	0.06
Sioux (0)	1	0.01
South American Ind. (1)	3	0.03
Spanish American Ind. (1)	1	0.01
Asian (932)	1,055	9.70
Not Hispanic (921)	1,027	9.44
Hispanic (11)	28	0.26
Bangladeshi (3)	3	0.03
Burmese (3)	3	0.03
Cambodian (1)	1	0.01
Chinese, ex. Taiwanese (208)	243	2.23
Filipino (82)	107	0.98
Indian (259)	283	2.60
Japanese (96)	124	1.14
Korean (172)	183	1.68
Pakistani (51)	58	0.53
Sri Lankan (1)	1	0.01
Taiwanese (9)	10	0.09
Thai (11)	13	0.12
Vietnamese (4)	5	0.05
Hawaii Native/Pacific Islander (11)	25	0.23
Not Hispanic (7)	16	0.15
Hispanic (4)	9	0.08
Guamanian/Chamorro (6)	7	0.06
White (8,548)	8,775	80.69
Not Hispanic (7,883)	8,050	74.02
Hispanic (665)	725	6.67

Dover

Place Type: Town
County: Dutchess
Population: 8,699†

Ancestry‡	Population	%
African, Sub-Saharan (0)	59	0.68
African (0)	59	0.68
Albanian (15)	44	0.50
American (569)	569	6.53
Arab (8)	8	0.09
Moroccan (8)	8	0.09
Austrian (11)	39	0.45
British (0)	40	0.46
Czech (0)	29	0.33
Czechoslovakian (0)	9	0.10
Danish (0)	218	2.50
Dutch (30)	380	4.36
Eastern European (7)	7	0.08
English (185)	864	9.91
European (69)	69	0.79
French, ex. Basque (72)	269	3.09
French Canadian (18)	99	1.14
German (392)	1,721	19.75
Greek (25)	72	0.83
Guyanese (33)	33	0.38
Hungarian (0)	97	1.11
Irish (631)	2,636	30.24
Israeli (0)	17	0.20
Italian (626)	1,888	21.66
Lithuanian (35)	51	0.59
Polish (53)	382	4.38
Portuguese (1)	1	0.01
Romanian (0)	35	0.40
Russian (28)	126	1.45
Scandinavian (0)	21	0.24
Scotch-Irish (85)	169	1.94
Scottish (25)	183	2.10
Slovak (27)	40	0.46
Swedish (5)	278	3.19
Ukrainian (51)	71	0.81
West Indian, ex. Hispanic (27)	86	0.99
Jamaican (14)	14	0.16
Trinidadian/Tobagonian (13)	13	0.15
West Indian (0)	59	0.68
Yugoslavian (14)	21	0.24

Hispanic Origin	Population	%
Hispanic or Latino (of any race)	1,199	13.78
Central American, ex. Mexican	356	4.09
Costa Rican	6	0.07
Guatemalan	283	3.25
Honduran	19	0.22
Nicaraguan	7	0.08
Panamanian	1	0.01
Salvadoran	40	0.46
Cuban	29	0.33
Dominican Republic	58	0.67
Mexican	128	1.47
Puerto Rican	296	3.40
South American	190	2.18
Argentinean	20	0.23
Chilean	8	0.09
Colombian	28	0.32
Ecuadorian	93	1.07
Paraguayan	1	0.01
Peruvian	37	0.43
Uruguayan	1	0.01
Venezuelan	1	0.01
Other South American	1	0.01
Other Hispanic or Latino	142	1.63

Race*	Population	%
African-American/Black (426)	521	5.99
Not Hispanic (379)	457	5.25
Hispanic (47)	64	0.74
American Indian/Alaska Native (21)	84	0.97
Not Hispanic (17)	75	0.86
Hispanic (4)	9	0.10
Blackfeet (1)	5	0.06
Central American Ind. (1)	1	0.01
Cherokee (0)	7	0.08
Chippewa (1)	1	0.01
Creek (0)	2	0.02
Iroquois (3)	10	0.11
Mexican American Ind. (1)	1	0.01
Sioux (0)	3	0.03
Asian (115)	151	1.74
Not Hispanic (115)	144	1.66
Hispanic (0)	7	0.08
Burmese (10)	10	0.11
Chinese, ex. Taiwanese (30)	37	0.43
Filipino (15)	32	0.37
Indian (16)	17	0.20
Japanese (1)	1	0.01
Korean (7)	11	0.13
Pakistani (15)	15	0.17
Sri Lankan (3)	6	0.07
Taiwanese (0)	1	0.01
Thai (3)	3	0.03
Vietnamese (13)	15	0.17
Hawaii Native/Pacific Islander (1)	11	0.13
Not Hispanic (0)	6	0.07
Hispanic (1)	5	0.06
Guamanian/Chamorro (1)	2	0.02
Native Hawaiian (0)	2	0.02
Samoan (0)	1	0.01
White (7,482)	7,704	88.56
Not Hispanic (6,828)	6,969	80.11
Hispanic (654)	735	8.45

Dryden

Place Type: Town
County: Tompkins
Population: 14,435†

Ancestry‡	Population	%
African, Sub-Saharan (84)	88	0.62
African (42)	42	0.29
Kenyan (20)	20	0.14
Sierra Leonean (22)	22	0.15
South African (0)	4	0.03
American (1,219)	1,219	8.55
Arab (0)	31	0.22
Lebanese (0)	31	0.22
Austrian (0)	119	0.83
British (73)	118	0.83
Canadian (27)	34	0.24
Celtic (6)	6	0.04
Croatian (16)	16	0.11
Czech (15)	68	0.48
Czechoslovakian (0)	28	0.20
Danish (16)	27	0.19
Dutch (174)	583	4.09
Eastern European (17)	17	0.12
English (666)	2,411	16.91
European (301)	328	2.30
Finnish (79)	254	1.78
French, ex. Basque (95)	717	5.03
French Canadian (48)	73	0.51
German (546)	2,552	17.90
Greek (14)	16	0.11
Hungarian (93)	148	1.04
Icelander (0)	15	0.11
Irish (562)	2,392	16.77
Italian (468)	1,365	9.57
Lithuanian (0)	24	0.17
Northern European (18)	18	0.13
Norwegian (64)	127	0.89
Pennsylvania German (12)	28	0.20
Polish (155)	577	4.05
Portuguese (0)	5	0.04
Romanian (6)	17	0.12
Russian (187)	360	2.52
Scandinavian (10)	20	0.14
Scotch-Irish (160)	340	2.38
Scottish (95)	264	1.85
Slovak (12)	69	0.48
Swedish (12)	157	1.10
Swiss (11)	28	0.20
Turkish (0)	2	0.01
Ukrainian (64)	73	0.51
Welsh (65)	157	1.10
West Indian, ex. Hispanic (0)	14	0.10
Jamaican (0)	14	0.10

Hispanic Origin	Population	%
Hispanic or Latino (of any race)	441	3.06
Central American, ex. Mexican	31	0.21
Costa Rican	1	0.01
Guatemalan	12	0.08
Honduran	4	0.03
Nicaraguan	4	0.03
Panamanian	3	0.02
Salvadoran	7	0.05
Cuban	9	0.06
Dominican Republic	37	0.26
Mexican	66	0.46
Puerto Rican	144	1.00
South American	71	0.49
Argentinean	7	0.05
Bolivian	5	0.03
Chilean	5	0.03
Colombian	20	0.14
Ecuadorian	10	0.07
Paraguayan	2	0.01
Peruvian	8	0.06
Uruguayan	6	0.04
Venezuelan	5	0.03
Other South American	3	0.02
Other Hispanic or Latino	83	0.57

Race*	Population	%
African-American/Black (424)	602	4.17
Not Hispanic (390)	548	3.80
Hispanic (34)	54	0.37
American Indian/Alaska Native (46)	168	1.16
Not Hispanic (35)	141	0.98
Hispanic (11)	27	0.19
Apache (4)	6	0.04
Blackfeet (1)	17	0.12
Canadian/French Am. Ind. (1)	5	0.03
Cherokee (5)	19	0.13
Chippewa (0)	1	0.01
Crow (1)	1	0.01
Iroquois (3)	24	0.17

*Notes: † The Census 2010 population figure is used to calculate the percentages in the Hispanic Origin and Race categories. Ancestry percentages are based on the 2006-2010 American Community Survey population (not shown); ‡ Numbers in parentheses indicate the number of people reporting a single ancestry; * Numbers in parentheses indicate the number of persons reporting this race alone, not in combination with any other race; Please refer to the Explanation of Data for more information.*

Lumbee (1)	1	0.01
Mexican American Ind. (0)	6	0.04
Seminole (0)	1	0.01
Sioux (4)	4	0.03
South American Ind. (2)	6	0.04
Spanish American Ind. (0)	1	0.01
Yaqui (1)	1	0.01
Asian (276)	392	2.72
Not Hispanic (272)	379	2.63
Hispanic (4)	13	0.09
Bangladeshi (2)	2	0.01
Burmese (12)	13	0.09
Cambodian (6)	6	0.04
Chinese, ex. Taiwanese (101)	132	0.91
Filipino (6)	13	0.09
Indian (37)	66	0.46
Indonesian (3)	4	0.03
Japanese (11)	34	0.24
Korean (40)	48	0.33
Laotian (6)	10	0.07
Malaysian (0)	1	0.01
Nepalese (0)	1	0.01
Pakistani (2)	3	0.02
Sri Lankan (1)	1	0.01
Taiwanese (4)	9	0.06
Thai (2)	4	0.03
Vietnamese (23)	27	0.19
Hawaii Native/Pacific Islander (5)	15	0.10
Not Hispanic (5)	13	0.09
Hispanic (0)	2	0.01
Fijian (0)	2	0.01
Guamanian/Chamorro (1)	3	0.02
Native Hawaiian (1)	3	0.02
Samoan (1)	3	0.02
White (13,138)	13,522	93.68
Not Hispanic (12,914)	13,246	91.76
Hispanic (224)	276	1.91

Dunkirk

Place Type: City
County: Chautauqua
Population: 12,563†

Ancestry‡	Population	%
African, Sub-Saharan (0)	60	0.48
African (0)	60	0.48
American (126)	126	1.00
Arab (22)	136	1.08
Arab (0)	44	0.35
Lebanese (22)	36	0.29
Syrian (0)	56	0.44
Armenian (23)	23	0.18
Austrian (0)	23	0.18
Brazilian (19)	19	0.15
British (0)	19	0.15
Canadian (0)	12	0.10
Croatian (0)	10	0.08
Danish (0)	44	0.35
Dutch (50)	218	1.73
English (241)	869	6.89
Finnish (0)	20	0.16
French, ex. Basque (15)	161	1.28
French Canadian (34)	62	0.49
German (697)	2,394	18.98
Greek (9)	9	0.07
Hungarian (55)	133	1.05
Irish (319)	1,276	10.12
Italian (957)	2,009	15.93
Lithuanian (0)	14	0.11
Norwegian (11)	11	0.09
Polish (1,807)	3,610	28.63
Russian (17)	116	0.92
Scotch-Irish (38)	97	0.77
Scottish (21)	192	1.52
Slovak (12)	37	0.29
Swedish (36)	203	1.61
Swiss (0)	23	0.18
Welsh (0)	43	0.34
West Indian, ex. Hispanic (0)	14	0.11
Jamaican (0)	14	0.11

Hispanic Origin	Population	%
Hispanic or Latino (of any race)	3,322	26.44
Central American, ex. Mexican	30	0.24
Guatemalan	22	0.18
Honduran	3	0.02
Panamanian	1	0.01
Salvadoran	4	0.03
Cuban	25	0.20
Dominican Republic	19	0.15
Mexican	317	2.52
Puerto Rican	2,782	22.14
South American	19	0.15
Argentinean	4	0.03
Chilean	1	0.01
Colombian	7	0.06
Ecuadorian	2	0.02
Peruvian	2	0.02
Venezuelan	3	0.02
Other Hispanic or Latino	130	1.03

Race*	Population	%
African-American/Black (770)	1,028	8.18
Not Hispanic (635)	803	6.39
Hispanic (135)	225	1.79
American Indian/Alaska Native (125)	195	1.55
Not Hispanic (69)	124	0.99
Hispanic (56)	71	0.57
Apache (0)	1	0.01
Blackfeet (4)	5	0.04
Cherokee (2)	12	0.10
Chippewa (1)	1	0.01
Creek (1)	1	0.01
Iroquois (47)	70	0.56
Mexican American Ind. (14)	14	0.11
South American Ind. (1)	1	0.01
Asian (47)	69	0.55
Not Hispanic (47)	59	0.47
Hispanic (0)	10	0.08
Chinese, ex. Taiwanese (18)	18	0.14
Filipino (10)	15	0.12
Indian (5)	8	0.06
Indonesian (1)	2	0.02
Japanese (2)	5	0.04
Korean (3)	4	0.03
Laotian (0)	1	0.01
Taiwanese (1)	1	0.01
Vietnamese (7)	7	0.06
Hawaii Native/Pacific Islander (4)	17	0.14
Not Hispanic (3)	7	0.06
Hispanic (1)	10	0.08
Guamanian/Chamorro (2)	2	0.02
Native Hawaiian (1)	3	0.02
White (9,740)	10,143	80.74
Not Hispanic (8,255)	8,467	67.40
Hispanic (1,485)	1,676	13.34

East Fishkill

Place Type: Town
County: Dutchess
Population: 29,029†

Ancestry‡	Population	%
African, Sub-Saharan (107)	163	0.57
African (39)	95	0.33
Ghanaian (38)	38	0.13
Nigerian (30)	30	0.10
Albanian (236)	236	0.83
American (478)	478	1.67
Arab (153)	362	1.27
Arab (0)	75	0.26
Egyptian (43)	82	0.29
Jordanian (110)	110	0.38
Lebanese (0)	9	0.03
Syrian (0)	11	0.04
Other Arab (0)	75	0.26
Armenian (10)	31	0.11
Austrian (27)	115	0.40
Belgian (0)	61	0.21
British (36)	113	0.40
Bulgarian (63)	63	0.22
Canadian (0)	42	0.15
Croatian (6)	17	0.06
Czech (64)	316	1.11
Czechoslovakian (10)	80	0.28
Danish (0)	23	0.08
Dutch (21)	180	0.63
Eastern European (47)	47	0.16
English (412)	2,426	8.49
European (94)	94	0.33
Finnish (37)	64	0.22
French, ex. Basque (103)	818	2.86
French Canadian (97)	287	1.00
German (882)	4,879	17.07
Greek (188)	397	1.39
Hungarian (18)	233	0.82
Irish (2,424)	8,662	30.30
Israeli (0)	29	0.10
Italian (4,550)	9,947	34.80
Latvian (0)	27	0.09
Lithuanian (13)	62	0.22
Maltese (8)	8	0.03
Norwegian (55)	300	1.05
Polish (334)	1,592	5.57
Portuguese (160)	182	0.64
Russian (157)	686	2.40
Scandinavian (8)	21	0.07
Scotch-Irish (69)	280	0.98
Scottish (31)	416	1.46
Slavic (0)	8	0.03
Slovak (71)	211	0.74
Slovene (9)	9	0.03
Swedish (49)	209	0.73
Swiss (30)	173	0.61
Ukrainian (70)	145	0.51
Welsh (13)	93	0.33
West Indian, ex. Hispanic (136)	239	0.84
British West Indian (16)	16	0.06
Haitian (7)	7	0.02
Jamaican (75)	75	0.26
West Indian (38)	141	0.49
Yugoslavian (12)	12	0.04

Hispanic Origin	Population	%
Hispanic or Latino (of any race)	2,224	7.66
Central American, ex. Mexican	116	0.40
Costa Rican	3	0.01
Guatemalan	43	0.15
Honduran	31	0.11
Nicaraguan	4	0.01
Panamanian	10	0.03
Salvadoran	24	0.08
Other Central American	1	<0.01
Cuban	107	0.37
Dominican Republic	129	0.44
Mexican	160	0.55
Puerto Rican	1,014	3.49
South American	404	1.39
Argentinean	17	0.06
Bolivian	5	0.02
Chilean	24	0.08
Colombian	93	0.32
Ecuadorian	154	0.53
Paraguayan	1	<0.01
Peruvian	70	0.24
Uruguayan	27	0.09
Venezuelan	10	0.03
Other South American	3	0.01
Other Hispanic or Latino	294	1.01

Race*	Population	%
African-American/Black (1,000)	1,182	4.07
Not Hispanic (918)	1,043	3.59
Hispanic (82)	139	0.48
American Indian/Alaska Native (35)	154	0.53
Not Hispanic (21)	107	0.37
Hispanic (14)	47	0.16
Apache (0)	1	<0.01

SECTION TWO

*Notes: † The Census 2010 population figure is used to calculate the percentages in the Hispanic Origin and Race categories. Ancestry percentages are based on the 2006-2010 American Community Survey population (not shown); ‡ Numbers in parentheses indicate the number of people reporting a single ancestry; * Numbers in parentheses indicate the number of persons reporting this race alone, not in combination with any other race; Please refer to the Explanation of Data for more information.*

Blackfeet (0)	1	<0.01
Canadian/French Am. Ind. (2)	2	0.01
Central American Ind. (0)	6	0.02
Cherokee (5)	24	0.08
Iroquois (2)	12	0.04
Lumbee (0)	2	0.01
Seminole (0)	3	0.01
Sioux (3)	7	0.02
South American Ind. (5)	11	0.04
Asian (1,179)	1,344	4.63
Not Hispanic (1,162)	1,300	4.48
Hispanic (17)	44	0.15
Bangladeshi (3)	3	0.01
Cambodian (1)	6	0.02
Chinese, ex. Taiwanese (338)	373	1.28
Filipino (61)	80	0.28
Indian (462)	523	1.80
Indonesian (0)	3	0.01
Japanese (25)	39	0.13
Korean (128)	143	0.49
Malaysian (3)	3	0.01
Nepalese (3)	3	0.01
Pakistani (60)	67	0.23
Sri Lankan (11)	11	0.04
Taiwanese (20)	20	0.07
Thai (4)	7	0.02
Vietnamese (27)	28	0.10
Hawaii Native/Pacific Islander (9)	30	0.10
Not Hispanic (4)	24	0.08
Hispanic (5)	6	0.02
Native Hawaiian (0)	3	0.01
Samoan (2)	2	0.01
White (25,713)	26,143	90.06
Not Hispanic (24,295)	24,581	84.68
Hispanic (1,418)	1,562	5.38

East Greenbush

Place Type: Town
County: Rensselaer
Population: 16,473†

Ancestry‡	Population	%
African, Sub-Saharan (0)	24	0.15
African (0)	24	0.15
Albanian (15)	15	0.09
Alsatian (13)	13	0.08
American (583)	583	3.57
Arab (85)	177	1.09
Egyptian (21)	91	0.56
Lebanese (48)	48	0.29
Syrian (16)	38	0.23
Armenian (0)	36	0.22
Austrian (22)	36	0.22
Belgian (0)	7	0.04
British (10)	42	0.26
Canadian (13)	37	0.23
Czech (15)	69	0.42
Czechoslovakian (31)	59	0.36
Danish (9)	46	0.28
Dutch (79)	787	4.82
Eastern European (52)	84	0.51
English (259)	2,215	13.58
European (128)	128	0.78
Finnish (12)	27	0.17
French, ex. Basque (178)	1,441	8.83
French Canadian (126)	563	3.45
German (580)	3,598	22.06
Greek (23)	83	0.51
Guyanese (0)	9	0.06
Hungarian (23)	120	0.74
Irish (1,310)	4,940	30.28
Italian (735)	2,842	17.42
Lithuanian (15)	42	0.26
Norwegian (16)	89	0.55
Polish (398)	1,857	11.38
Portuguese (24)	94	0.58
Romanian (0)	24	0.15
Russian (159)	383	2.35
Scandinavian (0)	15	0.09
Scotch-Irish (73)	283	1.73
Scottish (111)	595	3.65
Slavic (0)	13	0.08
Slovak (9)	42	0.26
Slovene (0)	15	0.09
Swedish (35)	215	1.32
Swiss (0)	103	0.63
Ukrainian (17)	128	0.78
Welsh (27)	80	0.49
West Indian, ex. Hispanic (191)	200	1.23
Jamaican (45)	45	0.28
Trinidadian/Tobagonian (13)	13	0.08
West Indian (133)	142	0.87
Yugoslavian (0)	15	0.09

Hispanic Origin	Population	%
Hispanic or Latino (of any race)	391	2.37
Central American, ex. Mexican	17	0.10
Costa Rican	2	0.01
Guatemalan	7	0.04
Honduran	1	0.01
Panamanian	1	0.01
Salvadoran	3	0.02
Other Central American	3	0.02
Cuban	23	0.14
Dominican Republic	28	0.17
Mexican	39	0.24
Puerto Rican	197	1.20
South American	32	0.19
Argentinean	6	0.04
Chilean	1	0.01
Colombian	7	0.04
Ecuadorian	8	0.05
Peruvian	1	0.01
Venezuelan	5	0.03
Other South American	4	0.02
Other Hispanic or Latino	55	0.33

Race*	Population	%
African-American/Black (515)	687	4.17
Not Hispanic (499)	640	3.89
Hispanic (16)	47	0.29
American Indian/Alaska Native (25)	93	0.56
Not Hispanic (21)	75	0.46
Hispanic (4)	18	0.11
Blackfeet (0)	7	0.04
Canadian/French Am. Ind. (0)	3	0.02
Cherokee (1)	9	0.05
Choctaw (0)	1	0.01
Iroquois (3)	7	0.04
Lumbee (1)	1	0.01
Mexican American Ind. (1)	1	0.01
Seminole (0)	3	0.02
South American Ind. (3)	4	0.02
Asian (523)	603	3.66
Not Hispanic (521)	598	3.63
Hispanic (2)	5	0.03
Bangladeshi (14)	18	0.11
Burmese (4)	4	0.02
Cambodian (1)	1	0.01
Chinese, ex. Taiwanese (103)	119	0.72
Filipino (41)	56	0.34
Hmong (1)	2	0.01
Indian (197)	222	1.35
Japanese (14)	28	0.17
Korean (37)	43	0.26
Nepalese (1)	2	0.01
Pakistani (47)	56	0.34
Sri Lankan (2)	2	0.01
Taiwanese (2)	2	0.01
Thai (3)	5	0.03
Vietnamese (26)	29	0.18
Hawaii Native/Pacific Islander (1)	14	0.08
Not Hispanic (0)	11	0.07
Hispanic (1)	3	0.02
Guamanian/Chamorro (0)	5	0.03
Native Hawaiian (0)	4	0.02
White (15,043)	15,310	92.94
Not Hispanic (14,770)	14,995	91.03
Hispanic (273)	315	1.91

East Hampton

Place Type: Town
County: Suffolk
Population: 21,457†

Ancestry‡	Population	%
African, Sub-Saharan (6)	31	0.15
African (6)	31	0.15
American (549)	549	2.59
Arab (9)	44	0.21
Lebanese (0)	26	0.12
Other Arab (9)	18	0.09
Armenian (23)	58	0.27
Austrian (45)	228	1.08
Belgian (0)	18	0.09
British (65)	143	0.68
Canadian (31)	58	0.27
Croatian (32)	40	0.19
Czech (0)	89	0.42
Czechoslovakian (40)	40	0.19
Danish (34)	95	0.45
Dutch (91)	162	0.77
Eastern European (96)	113	0.53
English (760)	2,653	12.53
European (159)	206	0.97
Finnish (33)	44	0.21
French, ex. Basque (212)	729	3.44
French Canadian (20)	67	0.32
German (608)	2,729	12.89
Greek (55)	157	0.74
Hungarian (73)	178	0.84
Iranian (9)	9	0.04
Irish (1,155)	3,399	16.06
Italian (1,267)	2,956	13.96
Lithuanian (62)	140	0.66
Northern European (35)	35	0.17
Norwegian (31)	149	0.70
Polish (367)	969	4.58
Portuguese (63)	75	0.35
Romanian (3)	34	0.16
Russian (325)	899	4.25
Scandinavian (0)	17	0.08
Scotch-Irish (93)	172	0.81
Scottish (153)	589	2.78
Slovak (11)	11	0.05
Slovene (0)	16	0.08
Soviet Union (3)	3	0.01
Swedish (26)	327	1.54
Swiss (19)	69	0.33
Turkish (29)	29	0.14
Ukrainian (63)	136	0.64
Welsh (40)	132	0.62
West Indian, ex. Hispanic (113)	130	0.61
British West Indian (0)	17	0.08
Jamaican (113)	113	0.53
Yugoslavian (17)	65	0.31

Hispanic Origin	Population	%
Hispanic or Latino (of any race)	5,660	26.38
Central American, ex. Mexican	502	2.34
Costa Rican	216	1.01
Guatemalan	137	0.64
Honduran	21	0.10
Nicaraguan	16	0.07
Panamanian	5	0.02
Salvadoran	106	0.49
Other Central American	1	<0.01
Cuban	47	0.22
Dominican Republic	242	1.13
Mexican	637	2.97
Puerto Rican	172	0.80
South American	3,513	16.37
Argentinean	39	0.18
Bolivian	5	0.02
Chilean	66	0.31
Colombian	987	4.60
Ecuadorian	2,319	10.81
Peruvian	33	0.15
Uruguayan	13	0.06

*Notes: † The Census 2010 population figure is used to calculate the percentages in the Hispanic Origin and Race categories. Ancestry percentages are based on the 2006-2010 American Community Survey population (not shown); ‡ Numbers in parentheses indicate the number of people reporting a single ancestry; * Numbers in parentheses indicate the number of persons reporting this race alone, not in combination with any other race; Please refer to the Explanation of Data for more information.*

Venezuelan	18	0.08
Other South American	33	0.15
Other Hispanic or Latino	547	2.55

Race*	Population	%
African-American/Black (722)	864	4.03
Not Hispanic (678)	779	3.63
Hispanic (44)	85	0.40
American Indian/Alaska Native (129)	197	0.92
Not Hispanic (45)	94	0.44
Hispanic (84)	103	0.48
Apache (1)	1	<0.01
Arapaho (0)	1	<0.01
Blackfeet (3)	3	0.01
Canadian/French Am. Ind. (1)	1	<0.01
Central American Ind. (3)	5	0.02
Cherokee (16)	30	0.14
Choctaw (1)	9	0.04
Comanche (0)	2	0.01
Iroquois (0)	3	0.01
Mexican American Ind. (5)	5	0.02
Pueblo (4)	4	0.02
Seminole (0)	2	0.01
Sioux (1)	5	0.02
South American Ind. (30)	30	0.14
Spanish American Ind. (7)	7	0.03
Asian (284)	354	1.65
Not Hispanic (278)	338	1.58
Hispanic (6)	16	0.07
Burmese (2)	2	0.01
Chinese, ex. Taiwanese (59)	68	0.32
Filipino (32)	46	0.21
Indian (44)	59	0.27
Indonesian (1)	5	0.02
Japanese (22)	30	0.14
Korean (15)	30	0.14
Laotian (4)	4	0.02
Malaysian (1)	5	0.02
Pakistani (8)	8	0.04
Taiwanese (4)	4	0.02
Thai (9)	12	0.06
Vietnamese (71)	74	0.34
Hawaii Native/Pacific Islander (16)	18	0.08
Not Hispanic (8)	10	0.05
Hispanic (8)	8	0.04
Guamanian/Chamorro (13)	13	0.06
Native Hawaiian (0)	1	<0.01
Samoan (1)	1	<0.01
White (18,197)	18,460	86.03
Not Hispanic (14,564)	14,730	68.65
Hispanic (3,633)	3,730	17.38

East Islip

Place Type: CDP
County: Suffolk
Population: 14,475†

Ancestry‡	Population	%
Afghan (30)	93	0.67
American (263)	263	1.89
Arab (36)	84	0.60
Lebanese (0)	11	0.08
Syrian (36)	73	0.52
Austrian (0)	22	0.16
Brazilian (0)	7	0.05
Canadian (0)	73	0.52
Czech (70)	188	1.35
Czechoslovakian (0)	16	0.11
Danish (0)	50	0.36
Dutch (29)	95	0.68
Eastern European (59)	59	0.42
English (185)	1,308	9.38
Estonian (0)	18	0.13
European (91)	98	0.70
Finnish (0)	17	0.12
French, ex. Basque (47)	220	1.58
French Canadian (0)	91	0.65
German (377)	2,792	20.03
Greek (30)	259	1.86
Hungarian (0)	19	0.14
Irish (1,116)	4,821	34.59
Israeli (10)	30	0.22
Italian (2,037)	5,173	37.11
Lithuanian (20)	69	0.50
Northern European (10)	10	0.07
Norwegian (141)	509	3.65
Polish (174)	655	4.70
Portuguese (18)	93	0.67
Romanian (9)	9	0.06
Russian (61)	303	2.17
Scotch-Irish (38)	247	1.77
Scottish (10)	228	1.64
Serbian (0)	10	0.07
Slavic (0)	12	0.09
Slovak (10)	44	0.32
Swedish (0)	98	0.70
Swiss (10)	22	0.16
Ukrainian (0)	62	0.44
Welsh (58)	58	0.42
West Indian, ex. Hispanic (0)	21	0.15
Barbadian (0)	21	0.15
Yugoslavian (0)	14	0.10

Hispanic Origin	Population	%
Hispanic or Latino (of any race)	903	6.24
Central American, ex. Mexican	77	0.53
Costa Rican	4	0.03
Guatemalan	12	0.08
Honduran	2	0.01
Nicaraguan	1	0.01
Panamanian	4	0.03
Salvadoran	54	0.37
Cuban	30	0.21
Dominican Republic	52	0.36
Mexican	41	0.28
Puerto Rican	461	3.18
South American	138	0.95
Argentinean	7	0.05
Bolivian	2	0.01
Chilean	1	0.01
Colombian	62	0.43
Ecuadorian	31	0.21
Paraguayan	1	0.01
Peruvian	24	0.17
Uruguayan	2	0.01
Venezuelan	6	0.04
Other South American	2	0.01
Other Hispanic or Latino	104	0.72

Race*	Population	%
African-American/Black (149)	203	1.40
Not Hispanic (143)	182	1.26
Hispanic (6)	21	0.15
American Indian/Alaska Native (8)	67	0.46
Not Hispanic (6)	38	0.26
Hispanic (2)	29	0.20
Blackfeet (0)	1	0.01
Central American Ind. (0)	1	0.01
Cherokee (0)	14	0.10
Choctaw (0)	4	0.03
Creek (1)	1	0.01
Hopi (1)	1	0.01
Iroquois (0)	4	0.03
Lumbee (2)	2	0.01
Mexican American Ind. (1)	1	0.01
South American Ind. (0)	2	0.01
Asian (230)	292	2.02
Not Hispanic (223)	282	1.95
Hispanic (7)	10	0.07
Chinese, ex. Taiwanese (76)	85	0.59
Filipino (21)	39	0.27
Indian (58)	64	0.44
Indonesian (3)	3	0.02
Japanese (4)	9	0.06
Korean (34)	34	0.23
Pakistani (12)	14	0.10
Taiwanese (1)	1	0.01
Thai (3)	3	0.02
Vietnamese (12)	19	0.13
Hawaii Native/Pacific Islander (0)	7	0.05
Not Hispanic (0)	6	0.04
Hispanic (0)	1	0.01
Native Hawaiian (0)	1	0.01
White (13,683)	13,849	95.68
Not Hispanic (13,053)	13,173	91.01
Hispanic (630)	676	4.67

East Massapequa

Place Type: CDP
County: Nassau
Population: 19,069†

Ancestry‡	Population	%
African, Sub-Saharan (25)	37	0.21
African (25)	37	0.21
American (197)	197	1.10
Arab (20)	87	0.49
Arab (8)	26	0.15
Egyptian (12)	12	0.07
Lebanese (0)	49	0.27
Armenian (47)	164	0.92
Austrian (0)	104	0.58
Canadian (0)	74	0.41
Celtic (27)	27	0.15
Croatian (7)	33	0.19
Czech (20)	80	0.45
Czechoslovakian (10)	29	0.16
Danish (0)	43	0.24
Dutch (8)	56	0.31
Eastern European (18)	18	0.10
English (58)	968	5.43
European (48)	48	0.27
Finnish (0)	11	0.06
French, ex. Basque (29)	225	1.26
French Canadian (42)	42	0.24
German (552)	3,729	20.91
Greek (146)	238	1.33
Guyanese (12)	12	0.07
Hungarian (19)	299	1.68
Iranian (0)	5	0.03
Irish (1,392)	5,035	28.23
Israeli (11)	60	0.34
Italian (2,880)	5,539	31.06
Lithuanian (8)	47	0.26
Maltese (0)	33	0.19
Norwegian (66)	125	0.70
Polish (314)	951	5.33
Portuguese (9)	31	0.17
Romanian (21)	21	0.12
Russian (99)	400	2.24
Scotch-Irish (28)	112	0.63
Scottish (118)	271	1.52
Slovak (11)	25	0.14
Swedish (11)	170	0.95
Swiss (0)	8	0.04
Turkish (56)	212	1.19
Ukrainian (0)	30	0.17
Welsh (0)	49	0.27
West Indian, ex. Hispanic (1,072)	1,128	6.33
Barbadian (0)	12	0.07
Belizean (16)	16	0.09
British West Indian (0)	19	0.11
Haitian (481)	481	2.70
Jamaican (575)	600	3.36
Yugoslavian (0)	54	0.30

Hispanic Origin	Population	%
Hispanic or Latino (of any race)	1,929	10.12
Central American, ex. Mexican	454	2.38
Costa Rican	13	0.07
Guatemalan	71	0.37
Honduran	72	0.38
Nicaraguan	5	0.03
Panamanian	27	0.14
Salvadoran	261	1.37
Other Central American	5	0.03
Cuban	79	0.41
Dominican Republic	233	1.22

*Notes: † The Census 2010 population figure is used to calculate the percentages in the Hispanic Origin and Race categories. Ancestry percentages are based on the 2006-2010 American Community Survey population (not shown); ‡ Numbers in parentheses indicate the number of people reporting a single ancestry; * Numbers in parentheses indicate the number of persons reporting this race alone, not in combination with any other race; Please refer to the Explanation of Data for more information.*

Mexican	73	0.38
Puerto Rican	463	2.43
South American	420	2.20
Argentinean	18	0.09
Bolivian	10	0.05
Chilean	20	0.10
Colombian	155	0.81
Ecuadorian	98	0.51
Paraguayan	3	0.02
Peruvian	81	0.42
Uruguayan	13	0.07
Venezuelan	19	0.10
Other South American	3	0.02
Other Hispanic or Latino	207	1.09

Race*	Population	%
African-American/Black (2,426)	2,622	13.75
Not Hispanic (2,298)	2,435	12.77
Hispanic (128)	187	0.98
American Indian/Alaska Native (50)	141	0.74
Not Hispanic (21)	86	0.45
Hispanic (29)	55	0.29
Apache (1)	1	0.01
Blackfeet (0)	7	0.04
Central American Ind. (1)	1	0.01
Cherokee (0)	10	0.05
Chippewa (2)	2	0.01
Iroquois (1)	9	0.05
Mexican American Ind. (9)	14	0.07
Sioux (1)	1	0.01
South American Ind. (1)	3	0.02
Spanish American Ind. (0)	1	0.01
Asian (406)	546	2.86
Not Hispanic (404)	532	2.79
Hispanic (2)	14	0.07
Burmese (1)	1	0.01
Cambodian (7)	9	0.05
Chinese, ex. Taiwanese (135)	177	0.93
Filipino (73)	101	0.53
Indian (107)	126	0.66
Japanese (3)	16	0.08
Korean (33)	43	0.23
Pakistani (19)	23	0.12
Sri Lankan (2)	5	0.03
Taiwanese (7)	7	0.04
Vietnamese (12)	24	0.13
Hawaii Native/Pacific Islander (7)	19	0.10
Not Hispanic (3)	5	0.03
Hispanic (4)	14	0.07
Native Hawaiian (0)	1	0.01
Samoan (0)	1	0.01
White (15,268)	15,553	81.56
Not Hispanic (14,098)	14,293	74.95
Hispanic (1,170)	1,260	6.61

East Meadow

Place Type: CDP
County: Nassau
Population: 38,132†

Ancestry‡	Population	%
African, Sub-Saharan (169)	169	0.45
African (136)	136	0.36
Sudanese (33)	33	0.09
American (1,130)	1,130	3.02
Arab (63)	105	0.28
Arab (31)	73	0.19
Egyptian (18)	18	0.05
Syrian (14)	14	0.04
Armenian (61)	61	0.16
Australian (10)	10	0.03
Austrian (87)	402	1.07
Brazilian (12)	67	0.18
British (48)	67	0.18
Canadian (0)	72	0.19
Croatian (46)	74	0.20
Czech (14)	47	0.13
Czechoslovakian (26)	77	0.21
Danish (0)	38	0.10
Dutch (0)	73	0.19
Eastern European (320)	320	0.85
English (101)	991	2.64
Estonian (18)	35	0.09
European (106)	163	0.43
Finnish (17)	26	0.07
French, ex. Basque (74)	465	1.24
French Canadian (8)	22	0.06
German (564)	3,813	10.17
Greek (295)	834	2.23
Guyanese (134)	134	0.36
Hungarian (124)	473	1.26
Iranian (0)	37	0.10
Irish (1,652)	6,315	16.85
Israeli (24)	49	0.13
Italian (4,664)	9,120	24.33
Latvian (36)	54	0.14
Lithuanian (37)	135	0.36
Maltese (12)	24	0.06
Northern European (11)	11	0.03
Norwegian (103)	166	0.44
Polish (1,040)	2,511	6.70
Portuguese (758)	1,048	2.80
Romanian (23)	133	0.35
Russian (623)	1,571	4.19
Scandinavian (16)	25	0.07
Scotch-Irish (185)	376	1.00
Scottish (62)	175	0.47
Slovak (0)	66	0.18
Swedish (92)	249	0.66
Swiss (33)	33	0.09
Turkish (39)	39	0.10
Ukrainian (71)	183	0.49
Welsh (10)	34	0.09
West Indian, ex. Hispanic (273)	297	0.79
Haitian (26)	26	0.07
Jamaican (167)	191	0.51
West Indian (80)	80	0.21
Yugoslavian (29)	29	0.08

Hispanic Origin	Population	%
Hispanic or Latino (of any race)	4,653	12.20
Central American, ex. Mexican	1,249	3.28
Costa Rican	26	0.07
Guatemalan	88	0.23
Honduran	218	0.57
Nicaraguan	2	0.01
Panamanian	16	0.04
Salvadoran	881	2.31
Other Central American	18	0.05
Cuban	179	0.47
Dominican Republic	349	0.92
Mexican	215	0.56
Puerto Rican	1,005	2.64
South American	1,177	3.09
Argentinean	71	0.19
Bolivian	12	0.03
Chilean	50	0.13
Colombian	529	1.39
Ecuadorian	317	0.83
Paraguayan	6	0.02
Peruvian	128	0.34
Uruguayan	30	0.08
Venezuelan	23	0.06
Other South American	11	0.03
Other Hispanic or Latino	479	1.26

Race*	Population	%
African-American/Black (1,975)	2,172	5.70
Not Hispanic (1,867)	2,008	5.27
Hispanic (108)	164	0.43
American Indian/Alaska Native (42)	124	0.33
Not Hispanic (24)	89	0.23
Hispanic (18)	35	0.09
Blackfeet (1)	3	0.01
Canadian/French Am. Ind. (0)	1	<0.01
Central American Ind. (1)	2	0.01
Cherokee (1)	14	0.04
Chippewa (0)	1	<0.01
Choctaw (0)	3	0.01
Cree (0)	1	<0.01
Creek (1)	4	0.01
Iroquois (5)	8	0.02
Seminole (0)	1	<0.01
South American Ind. (9)	18	0.05
Spanish American Ind. (6)	6	0.02
Asian (4,429)	4,776	12.52
Not Hispanic (4,400)	4,697	12.32
Hispanic (29)	79	0.21
Bangladeshi (70)	72	0.19
Burmese (12)	13	0.03
Cambodian (2)	2	0.01
Chinese, ex. Taiwanese (568)	632	1.66
Filipino (565)	648	1.70
Indian (2,018)	2,188	5.74
Japanese (15)	34	0.09
Korean (286)	294	0.77
Laotian (1)	1	<0.01
Nepalese (11)	11	0.03
Pakistani (640)	708	1.86
Sri Lankan (14)	16	0.04
Taiwanese (8)	10	0.03
Thai (6)	8	0.02
Vietnamese (81)	89	0.23
Hawaii Native/Pacific Islander (7)	32	0.08
Not Hispanic (5)	21	0.06
Hispanic (2)	11	0.03
Guamanian/Chamorro (6)	9	0.02
Native Hawaiian (1)	2	0.01
Samoan (0)	1	<0.01
White (29,489)	30,043	78.79
Not Hispanic (26,628)	26,941	70.65
Hispanic (2,861)	3,102	8.13

East Northport

Place Type: CDP
County: Suffolk
Population: 20,217†

Ancestry‡	Population	%
Albanian (20)	20	0.10
American (278)	278	1.33
Arab (12)	36	0.17
Lebanese (0)	12	0.06
Moroccan (0)	12	0.06
Syrian (3)	3	0.01
Other Arab (9)	9	0.04
Armenian (23)	73	0.35
Austrian (17)	195	0.93
Brazilian (31)	31	0.15
British (24)	57	0.27
Canadian (55)	89	0.42
Croatian (66)	253	1.21
Czech (49)	125	0.60
Czechoslovakian (10)	117	0.56
Danish (20)	121	0.58
Dutch (0)	99	0.47
Eastern European (30)	30	0.14
English (316)	1,685	8.04
Estonian (11)	11	0.05
European (97)	118	0.56
Finnish (0)	33	0.16
French, ex. Basque (42)	347	1.66
French Canadian (37)	202	0.96
German (763)	5,216	24.89
Greek (136)	317	1.51
Guyanese (29)	29	0.14
Hungarian (18)	173	0.83
Irish (2,072)	7,238	34.54
Italian (3,020)	7,443	35.52
Latvian (8)	8	0.04
Lithuanian (14)	204	0.97
Norwegian (87)	276	1.32
Polish (202)	1,312	6.26
Portuguese (27)	91	0.43
Romanian (10)	59	0.28
Russian (214)	757	3.61
Scandinavian (16)	31	0.15
Scotch-Irish (154)	334	1.59

*Notes: † The Census 2010 population figure is used to calculate the percentages in the Hispanic Origin and Race categories. Ancestry percentages are based on the 2006-2010 American Community Survey population (not shown); ‡ Numbers in parentheses indicate the number of people reporting a single ancestry; * Numbers in parentheses indicate the number of persons reporting this race alone, not in combination with any other race; Please refer to the Explanation of Data for more information.*

Scottish (79)	344	1.64
Slovak (7)	42	0.20
Slovene (0)	10	0.05
Swedish (54)	340	1.62
Swiss (0)	48	0.23
Turkish (80)	80	0.38
Ukrainian (19)	211	1.01
Welsh (0)	66	0.31
West Indian, ex. Hispanic (10)	61	0.29
West Indian (10)	61	0.29

Hispanic Origin	Population	%
Hispanic or Latino (of any race)	1,354	6.70
Central American, ex. Mexican	362	1.79
Costa Rican	9	0.04
Guatemalan	45	0.22
Honduran	172	0.85
Nicaraguan	2	0.01
Panamanian	6	0.03
Salvadoran	127	0.63
Other Central American	1	<0.01
Cuban	64	0.32
Dominican Republic	46	0.23
Mexican	85	0.42
Puerto Rican	377	1.86
South American	251	1.24
Argentinean	14	0.07
Bolivian	20	0.10
Chilean	26	0.13
Colombian	80	0.40
Ecuadorian	35	0.17
Paraguayan	5	0.02
Peruvian	58	0.29
Uruguayan	1	<0.01
Venezuelan	9	0.04
Other South American	3	0.01
Other Hispanic or Latino	169	0.84

Race*	Population	%
African-American/Black (170)	242	1.20
Not Hispanic (158)	215	1.06
Hispanic (12)	27	0.13
American Indian/Alaska Native (10)	63	0.31
Not Hispanic (5)	47	0.23
Hispanic (5)	16	0.08
Canadian/French Am. Ind. (0)	1	<0.01
Central American Ind. (1)	4	0.02
Cherokee (0)	11	0.05
Chippewa (0)	2	0.01
Choctaw (0)	4	0.02
Creek (1)	5	0.02
Delaware (0)	4	0.02
Iroquois (1)	5	0.02
Mexican American Ind. (1)	1	<0.01
Seminole (0)	1	<0.01
South American Ind. (2)	2	0.01
Spanish American Ind. (1)	1	<0.01
Asian (575)	703	3.48
Not Hispanic (564)	674	3.33
Hispanic (11)	29	0.14
Burmese (1)	3	0.01
Chinese, ex. Taiwanese (142)	195	0.96
Filipino (37)	52	0.26
Indian (79)	107	0.53
Indonesian (1)	1	<0.01
Japanese (21)	32	0.16
Korean (195)	201	0.99
Pakistani (44)	53	0.26
Sri Lankan (1)	2	0.01
Taiwanese (8)	8	0.04
Thai (11)	11	0.05
Vietnamese (10)	16	0.08
Hawaii Native/Pacific Islander (10)	19	0.09
Not Hispanic (4)	11	0.05
Hispanic (6)	8	0.04
Guamanian/Chamorro (6)	6	0.03
Native Hawaiian (4)	4	0.02
White (18,822)	19,085	94.40
Not Hispanic (17,888)	18,083	89.44
Hispanic (934)	1,002	4.96

East Patchogue

Place Type: CDP
County: Suffolk
Population: 22,469†

Ancestry‡	Population	%
African, Sub-Saharan (193)	193	0.92
African (193)	193	0.92
Albanian (10)	10	0.05
American (399)	399	1.89
Arab (0)	14	0.07
Syrian (0)	14	0.07
Armenian (66)	66	0.31
Australian (0)	11	0.05
Austrian (13)	34	0.16
British (23)	41	0.19
Bulgarian (12)	12	0.06
Canadian (0)	14	0.07
Cypriot (12)	12	0.06
Czech (31)	208	0.99
Czechoslovakian (24)	24	0.11
Danish (0)	30	0.14
Dutch (44)	381	1.81
Eastern European (23)	23	0.11
English (196)	1,278	6.06
European (33)	48	0.23
Finnish (12)	12	0.06
French, ex. Basque (62)	361	1.71
French Canadian (65)	150	0.71
German (856)	3,485	16.53
Greek (0)	47	0.22
Hungarian (0)	54	0.26
Irish (2,153)	6,046	28.68
Italian (2,903)	5,938	28.17
Lithuanian (12)	23	0.11
Maltese (77)	220	1.04
Norwegian (33)	230	1.09
Pennsylvania German (0)	12	0.06
Polish (327)	1,113	5.28
Portuguese (17)	83	0.39
Romanian (11)	23	0.11
Russian (150)	271	1.29
Scotch-Irish (106)	238	1.13
Scottish (73)	313	1.48
Slavic (0)	15	0.07
Slovak (12)	12	0.06
Swedish (13)	191	0.91
Swiss (13)	19	0.09
Turkish (364)	388	1.84
Ukrainian (13)	66	0.31
Welsh (13)	59	0.28
West Indian, ex. Hispanic (78)	134	0.64
Haitian (1)	1	<0.01
Jamaican (51)	79	0.37
Trinidadian/Tobagonian (26)	54	0.26

Hispanic Origin	Population	%
Hispanic or Latino (of any race)	3,951	17.58
Central American, ex. Mexican	896	3.99
Costa Rican	6	0.03
Guatemalan	65	0.29
Honduran	39	0.17
Nicaraguan	11	0.05
Panamanian	13	0.06
Salvadoran	758	3.37
Other Central American	4	0.02
Cuban	54	0.24
Dominican Republic	93	0.41
Mexican	248	1.10
Puerto Rican	1,098	4.89
South American	1,270	5.65
Argentinean	33	0.15
Bolivian	4	0.02
Chilean	8	0.04
Colombian	114	0.51
Ecuadorian	1,057	4.70
Paraguayan	2	0.01
Peruvian	32	0.14
Uruguayan	4	0.02
Venezuelan	14	0.06
Other South American	2	0.01
Other Hispanic or Latino	292	1.30

Race*	Population	%
African-American/Black (991)	1,200	5.34
Not Hispanic (903)	1,063	4.73
Hispanic (88)	137	0.61
American Indian/Alaska Native (76)	187	0.83
Not Hispanic (44)	119	0.53
Hispanic (32)	68	0.30
Blackfeet (2)	3	0.01
Central American Ind. (0)	4	0.02
Cherokee (1)	18	0.08
Iroquois (2)	5	0.02
Mexican American Ind. (5)	5	0.02
Seminole (0)	4	0.02
South American Ind. (0)	8	0.04
Spanish American Ind. (7)	8	0.04
Asian (524)	640	2.85
Not Hispanic (518)	612	2.72
Hispanic (6)	28	0.12
Cambodian (0)	2	0.01
Chinese, ex. Taiwanese (110)	135	0.60
Filipino (106)	123	0.55
Indian (135)	163	0.73
Japanese (11)	26	0.12
Korean (41)	51	0.23
Laotian (1)	6	0.03
Pakistani (63)	80	0.36
Sri Lankan (6)	6	0.03
Taiwanese (0)	1	<0.01
Thai (9)	16	0.07
Vietnamese (18)	19	0.08
Hawaii Native/Pacific Islander (5)	29	0.13
Not Hispanic (3)	13	0.06
Hispanic (2)	16	0.07
Guamanian/Chamorro (3)	3	0.01
Native Hawaiian (0)	1	<0.01
White (18,933)	19,399	86.34
Not Hispanic (16,713)	16,947	75.42
Hispanic (2,220)	2,452	10.91

East Rockaway

Place Type: Village
County: Nassau
Population: 9,818†

Ancestry‡	Population	%
Albanian (90)	90	0.92
American (807)	807	8.20
Arab (66)	96	0.98
Egyptian (50)	65	0.66
Palestinian (16)	31	0.32
Armenian (14)	14	0.14
Austrian (31)	84	0.85
Canadian (16)	36	0.37
Czech (0)	26	0.26
Dutch (14)	80	0.81
Eastern European (349)	349	3.55
English (153)	467	4.75
European (176)	188	1.91
Finnish (9)	30	0.31
French, ex. Basque (8)	100	1.02
French Canadian (11)	193	1.96
German (336)	1,102	11.20
Greek (127)	175	1.78
Hungarian (0)	33	0.34
Irish (1,083)	2,610	26.54
Italian (2,005)	3,374	34.30
Lithuanian (13)	26	0.26
Norwegian (11)	66	0.67
Polish (195)	594	6.04
Romanian (0)	20	0.20
Russian (90)	373	3.79
Scotch-Irish (9)	31	0.32
Scottish (11)	57	0.58
Slovak (10)	27	0.27
Swedish (0)	32	0.33

*Notes: † The Census 2010 population figure is used to calculate the percentages in the Hispanic Origin and Race categories. Ancestry percentages are based on the 2006-2010 American Community Survey population (not shown); ‡ Numbers in parentheses indicate the number of people reporting a single ancestry; * Numbers in parentheses indicate the number of persons reporting this race alone, not in combination with any other race; Please refer to the Explanation of Data for more information.*

Swiss (0)	5	0.05
Turkish (33)	59	0.60
Ukrainian (11)	42	0.43
Welsh (15)	52	0.53

Hispanic Origin	Population	%
Hispanic or Latino (of any race)	788	8.03
Central American, ex. Mexican	105	1.07
Costa Rican	4	0.04
Guatemalan	16	0.16
Honduran	10	0.10
Panamanian	2	0.02
Salvadoran	73	0.74
Cuban	48	0.49
Dominican Republic	73	0.74
Mexican	29	0.30
Puerto Rican	211	2.15
South American	241	2.45
Argentinean	30	0.31
Bolivian	31	0.32
Chilean	24	0.24
Colombian	87	0.89
Ecuadorian	36	0.37
Paraguayan	1	0.01
Peruvian	29	0.30
Uruguayan	1	0.01
Venezuelan	2	0.02
Other Hispanic or Latino	81	0.83

Race*	Population	%
African-American/Black (136)	171	1.74
Not Hispanic (127)	147	1.50
Hispanic (9)	24	0.24
American Indian/Alaska Native (5)	8	0.08
Not Hispanic (4)	6	0.06
Hispanic (1)	2	0.02
Cherokee (0)	1	0.01
Choctaw (3)	3	0.03
Asian (206)	249	2.54
Not Hispanic (200)	239	2.43
Hispanic (6)	10	0.10
Bangladeshi (3)	5	0.05
Chinese, ex. Taiwanese (54)	65	0.66
Filipino (50)	59	0.60
Indian (34)	45	0.46
Indonesian (2)	5	0.05
Japanese (9)	11	0.11
Korean (16)	19	0.19
Pakistani (13)	14	0.14
Taiwanese (4)	4	0.04
Vietnamese (8)	9	0.09
Hawaii Native/Pacific Islander (1)	1	0.01
Not Hispanic (1)	1	0.01
Guamanian/Chamorro (1)	1	0.01
White (9,146)	9,238	94.09
Not Hispanic (8,617)	8,672	88.33
Hispanic (529)	566	5.76

Eastchester

Place Type: CDP
County: Westchester
Population: 19,554†

Ancestry‡	Population	%
African, Sub-Saharan (49)	49	0.25
Ethiopian (49)	49	0.25
Albanian (58)	58	0.30
American (685)	685	3.55
Arab (32)	45	0.23
Egyptian (11)	11	0.06
Lebanese (7)	20	0.10
Moroccan (14)	14	0.07
Armenian (12)	22	0.11
Australian (17)	20	0.10
Austrian (42)	155	0.80
Belgian (20)	36	0.19
British (39)	68	0.35
Bulgarian (13)	26	0.13
Croatian (31)	45	0.23
Cypriot (12)	12	0.06
Czech (0)	56	0.29
Czechoslovakian (0)	11	0.06
Danish (0)	17	0.09
Dutch (10)	74	0.38
Eastern European (139)	139	0.72
English (363)	1,015	5.26
Estonian (0)	10	0.05
European (130)	130	0.67
Finnish (0)	10	0.05
French, ex. Basque (82)	395	2.05
French Canadian (37)	101	0.52
German (481)	2,075	10.75
Greek (476)	664	3.44
Hungarian (48)	219	1.13
Iranian (25)	42	0.22
Irish (1,375)	3,512	18.19
Israeli (29)	29	0.15
Italian (5,637)	8,201	42.49
Latvian (70)	70	0.36
Lithuanian (0)	17	0.09
Maltese (23)	23	0.12
Norwegian (0)	24	0.12
Polish (242)	673	3.49
Portuguese (139)	268	1.39
Romanian (45)	72	0.37
Russian (340)	636	3.29
Scotch-Irish (15)	131	0.68
Scottish (12)	105	0.54
Slovak (9)	15	0.08
Swedish (25)	137	0.71
Swiss (0)	34	0.18
Turkish (0)	10	0.05
Ukrainian (15)	75	0.39
Welsh (0)	33	0.17

Hispanic Origin	Population	%
Hispanic or Latino (of any race)	1,275	6.52
Central American, ex. Mexican	86	0.44
Costa Rican	7	0.04
Guatemalan	42	0.21
Honduran	18	0.09
Nicaraguan	3	0.02
Panamanian	7	0.04
Salvadoran	9	0.05
Cuban	66	0.34
Dominican Republic	64	0.33
Mexican	169	0.86
Puerto Rican	403	2.06
South American	349	1.78
Argentinean	34	0.17
Bolivian	8	0.04
Chilean	15	0.08
Colombian	72	0.37
Ecuadorian	119	0.61
Paraguayan	21	0.11
Peruvian	53	0.27
Uruguayan	7	0.04
Venezuelan	20	0.10
Other Hispanic or Latino	138	0.71

Race*	Population	%
African-American/Black (252)	293	1.50
Not Hispanic (222)	251	1.28
Hispanic (30)	42	0.21
American Indian/Alaska Native (25)	71	0.36
Not Hispanic (10)	45	0.23
Hispanic (15)	26	0.13
Central American Ind. (1)	2	0.01
Cherokee (0)	4	0.02
Choctaw (5)	6	0.03
Iroquois (0)	3	0.02
Mexican American Ind. (2)	3	0.02
Pueblo (0)	1	0.01
South American Ind. (2)	10	0.05
Yuman (0)	1	0.01
Asian (1,500)	1,674	8.56
Not Hispanic (1,494)	1,662	8.50
Hispanic (6)	12	0.06
Bangladeshi (3)	3	0.02
Burmese (4)	4	0.02
Chinese, ex. Taiwanese (300)	356	1.82
Filipino (96)	129	0.66
Indian (239)	257	1.31
Indonesian (1)	4	0.02
Japanese (555)	610	3.12
Korean (190)	211	1.08
Nepalese (2)	4	0.02
Pakistani (20)	20	0.10
Sri Lankan (2)	2	0.01
Taiwanese (12)	15	0.08
Thai (23)	30	0.15
Vietnamese (13)	23	0.12
Hawaii Native/Pacific Islander (1)	3	0.02
Not Hispanic (1)	3	0.02
Native Hawaiian (1)	3	0.02
White (17,262)	17,509	89.54
Not Hispanic (16,284)	16,492	84.34
Hispanic (978)	1,017	5.20

Eastchester

Place Type: Town
County: Westchester
Population: 32,363†

Ancestry‡	Population	%
African, Sub-Saharan (60)	60	0.19
Ethiopian (49)	49	0.15
South African (11)	11	0.03
Albanian (58)	58	0.18
American (971)	971	3.03
Arab (38)	80	0.25
Egyptian (17)	24	0.07
Lebanese (7)	29	0.09
Moroccan (14)	14	0.04
Syrian (0)	13	0.04
Armenian (34)	44	0.14
Australian (17)	46	0.14
Austrian (66)	204	0.64
Belgian (20)	36	0.11
Brazilian (11)	33	0.10
British (199)	346	1.08
Bulgarian (13)	26	0.08
Canadian (11)	11	0.03
Croatian (70)	146	0.46
Cypriot (12)	12	0.04
Czech (0)	108	0.34
Czechoslovakian (0)	11	0.03
Danish (20)	84	0.26
Dutch (52)	189	0.59
Eastern European (271)	313	0.98
English (571)	2,302	7.18
Estonian (0)	10	0.03
European (287)	305	0.95
Finnish (0)	54	0.17
French, ex. Basque (91)	734	2.29
French Canadian (50)	147	0.46
German (769)	4,015	12.53
Greek (568)	835	2.61
Hungarian (85)	322	1.00
Iranian (25)	42	0.13
Irish (2,662)	6,768	21.12
Israeli (29)	29	0.09
Italian (7,389)	10,979	34.27
Latvian (70)	70	0.22
Lithuanian (44)	146	0.46
Maltese (23)	23	0.07
Norwegian (12)	121	0.38
Pennsylvania German (21)	21	0.07
Polish (343)	1,010	3.15
Portuguese (139)	268	0.84
Romanian (45)	72	0.22
Russian (382)	954	2.98
Scandinavian (7)	32	0.10
Scotch-Irish (92)	307	0.96
Scottish (83)	358	1.12
Slovak (9)	46	0.14
Swedish (25)	223	0.70
Swiss (0)	77	0.24

*Notes: † The Census 2010 population figure is used to calculate the percentages in the Hispanic Origin and Race categories. Ancestry percentages are based on the 2006-2010 American Community Survey population (not shown); ‡ Numbers in parentheses indicate the number of people reporting a single ancestry; * Numbers in parentheses indicate the number of persons reporting this race alone, not in combination with any other race; Please refer to the Explanation of Data for more information.*

Ancestry	Population	%
Turkish (11)	43	0.13
Ukrainian (27)	96	0.30
Welsh (0)	88	0.27
West Indian, ex. Hispanic (27)	27	0.08
Jamaican (27)	27	0.08
Yugoslavian (0)	9	0.03

Hispanic Origin	Population	%
Hispanic or Latino (of any race)	2,335	7.22
Central American, ex. Mexican	150	0.46
Costa Rican	16	0.05
Guatemalan	65	0.20
Honduran	27	0.08
Nicaraguan	8	0.02
Panamanian	9	0.03
Salvadoran	25	0.08
Cuban	151	0.47
Dominican Republic	158	0.49
Mexican	279	0.86
Puerto Rican	738	2.28
South American	612	1.89
Argentinean	53	0.16
Bolivian	16	0.05
Chilean	29	0.09
Colombian	128	0.40
Ecuadorian	218	0.67
Paraguayan	25	0.08
Peruvian	100	0.31
Uruguayan	9	0.03
Venezuelan	34	0.11
Other Hispanic or Latino	247	0.76

Race*	Population	%
African-American/Black (1,055)	1,191	3.68
Not Hispanic (967)	1,044	3.23
Hispanic (88)	147	0.45
American Indian/Alaska Native (36)	136	0.42
Not Hispanic (16)	79	0.24
Hispanic (20)	57	0.18
Blackfeet (1)	2	0.01
Central American Ind. (1)	2	0.01
Cherokee (1)	9	0.03
Chippewa (1)	5	0.02
Choctaw (5)	6	0.02
Iroquois (0)	4	0.01
Mexican American Ind. (3)	8	0.02
Pueblo (0)	1	<0.01
Puget Sound Salish (0)	3	0.01
South American Ind. (2)	15	0.05
Yuman (0)	1	<0.01
Asian (2,366)	2,715	8.39
Not Hispanic (2,355)	2,670	8.25
Hispanic (11)	45	0.14
Bangladeshi (9)	9	0.03
Burmese (4)	4	0.01
Cambodian (2)	2	0.01
Chinese, ex. Taiwanese (461)	568	1.76
Filipino (163)	218	0.67
Indian (367)	399	1.23
Indonesian (1)	4	0.01
Japanese (822)	903	2.79
Korean (334)	375	1.16
Laotian (1)	4	0.01
Nepalese (3)	5	0.02
Pakistani (41)	41	0.13
Sri Lankan (4)	4	0.01
Taiwanese (30)	36	0.11
Thai (39)	48	0.15
Vietnamese (18)	33	0.10
Hawaii Native/Pacific Islander (1)	7	0.02
Not Hispanic (1)	6	0.02
Hispanic (0)	1	<0.01
Native Hawaiian (1)	3	0.01
White (27,806)	28,345	87.58
Not Hispanic (26,166)	26,573	82.11
Hispanic (1,640)	1,772	5.48

Eden

Place Type: Town
County: Erie
Population: 7,688†

Ancestry‡	Population	%
Albanian (0)	11	0.14
American (268)	268	3.47
Arab (0)	25	0.32
Lebanese (0)	10	0.13
Syrian (0)	15	0.19
Armenian (0)	21	0.27
Austrian (14)	35	0.45
Belgian (9)	20	0.26
British (11)	48	0.62
Canadian (39)	66	0.85
Croatian (19)	64	0.83
Czech (0)	18	0.23
Czechoslovakian (12)	22	0.28
Dutch (54)	225	2.91
English (217)	996	12.90
European (38)	53	0.69
French, ex. Basque (27)	295	3.82
French Canadian (15)	64	0.83
German (927)	3,307	42.83
Greek (0)	31	0.40
Hungarian (31)	84	1.09
Irish (244)	1,706	22.10
Italian (286)	808	10.46
Macedonian (11)	11	0.14
Pennsylvania German (8)	8	0.10
Polish (787)	1,696	21.97
Russian (0)	8	0.10
Scandinavian (10)	10	0.13
Scotch-Irish (111)	253	3.28
Scottish (42)	131	1.70
Swedish (37)	156	2.02
Swiss (0)	13	0.17
Ukrainian (0)	36	0.47
Welsh (0)	67	0.87
West Indian, ex. Hispanic (0)	8	0.10
Jamaican (0)	8	0.10

Hispanic Origin	Population	%
Hispanic or Latino (of any race)	136	1.77
Central American, ex. Mexican	3	0.04
Guatemalan	3	0.04
Cuban	6	0.08
Mexican	73	0.95
Puerto Rican	32	0.42
South American	10	0.13
Argentinean	1	0.01
Chilean	1	0.01
Colombian	7	0.09
Ecuadorian	1	0.01
Other Hispanic or Latino	12	0.16

Race*	Population	%
African-American/Black (32)	48	0.62
Not Hispanic (32)	46	0.60
Hispanic (0)	2	0.03
American Indian/Alaska Native (23)	41	0.53
Not Hispanic (23)	41	0.53
Cherokee (0)	1	0.01
Choctaw (1)	3	0.04
Iroquois (17)	23	0.30
Asian (19)	30	0.39
Not Hispanic (18)	29	0.38
Hispanic (1)	1	0.01
Cambodian (1)	1	0.01
Chinese, ex. Taiwanese (6)	7	0.09
Filipino (5)	5	0.07
Indian (1)	7	0.09
Japanese (0)	2	0.03
Korean (2)	4	0.05
Taiwanese (3)	3	0.04
Thai (1)	1	0.01
Hawaii Native/Pacific Islander (2)	3	0.04
Not Hispanic (1)	2	0.03
Hispanic (1)	1	0.01
Guamanian/Chamorro (2)	3	0.04
White (7,534)	7,572	98.49
Not Hispanic (7,440)	7,472	97.19
Hispanic (94)	100	1.30

Eggertsville

Place Type: CDP
County: Erie
Population: 15,019†

Ancestry‡	Population	%
African, Sub-Saharan (120)	180	1.19
African (50)	110	0.73
Nigerian (70)	70	0.46
Albanian (0)	67	0.44
American (311)	311	2.06
Arab (33)	162	1.07
Arab (0)	33	0.22
Lebanese (15)	111	0.74
Palestinian (18)	18	0.12
Armenian (57)	89	0.59
Austrian (13)	113	0.75
Belgian (0)	15	0.10
Brazilian (34)	34	0.23
British (13)	24	0.16
Bulgarian (37)	37	0.25
Canadian (0)	61	0.40
Croatian (0)	52	0.34
Czech (0)	14	0.09
Danish (14)	26	0.17
Dutch (0)	244	1.62
Eastern European (24)	24	0.16
English (253)	1,410	9.34
Estonian (0)	15	0.10
European (118)	118	0.78
French, ex. Basque (26)	319	2.11
French Canadian (89)	184	1.22
German (1,170)	3,430	22.72
Greek (20)	20	0.13
Hungarian (54)	130	0.86
Iranian (80)	80	0.53
Irish (490)	2,545	16.86
Italian (1,263)	2,706	17.93
Latvian (0)	13	0.09
Lithuanian (29)	59	0.39
New Zealander (0)	26	0.17
Northern European (9)	9	0.06
Norwegian (0)	64	0.42
Polish (765)	1,967	13.03
Romanian (12)	26	0.17
Russian (365)	510	3.38
Scotch-Irish (22)	167	1.11
Scottish (29)	229	1.52
Serbian (61)	61	0.40
Slavic (0)	11	0.07
Slovene (0)	13	0.09
Swedish (0)	110	0.73
Swiss (10)	72	0.48
Ukrainian (94)	133	0.88
Welsh (15)	76	0.50
West Indian, ex. Hispanic (74)	88	0.58
Jamaican (64)	78	0.52
Trinidadian/Tobagonian (5)	5	0.03
West Indian (5)	5	0.03
Yugoslavian (14)	14	0.09

Hispanic Origin	Population	%
Hispanic or Latino (of any race)	429	2.86
Central American, ex. Mexican	19	0.13
Guatemalan	1	0.01
Honduran	2	0.01
Nicaraguan	4	0.03
Panamanian	8	0.05
Salvadoran	4	0.03
Cuban	22	0.15
Dominican Republic	21	0.14
Mexican	44	0.29
Puerto Rican	210	1.40

SECTION TWO

*Notes: † The Census 2010 population figure is used to calculate the percentages in the Hispanic Origin and Race categories. Ancestry percentages are based on the 2006-2010 American Community Survey population (not shown); ‡ Numbers in parentheses indicate the number of people reporting a single ancestry; * Numbers in parentheses indicate the number of persons reporting this race alone, not in combination with any other race; Please refer to the Explanation of Data for more information.*

South American	56	0.37
Argentinean	6	0.04
Bolivian	1	0.01
Chilean	6	0.04
Colombian	19	0.13
Ecuadorian	16	0.11
Paraguayan	3	0.02
Peruvian	4	0.03
Venezuelan	1	0.01
Other Hispanic or Latino	57	0.38

Race*	Population	%
African-American/Black (1,828)	2,076	13.82
Not Hispanic (1,778)	1,981	13.19
Hispanic (50)	95	0.63
American Indian/Alaska Native (31)	111	0.74
Not Hispanic (30)	98	0.65
Hispanic (1)	13	0.09
Blackfeet (1)	3	0.02
Canadian/French Am. Ind. (2)	3	0.02
Cherokee (0)	19	0.13
Chippewa (0)	1	0.01
Crow (1)	1	0.01
Delaware (1)	2	0.01
Iroquois (10)	18	0.12
Mexican American Ind. (0)	1	0.01
Seminole (0)	5	0.03
Sioux (0)	1	0.01
Asian (1,091)	1,208	8.04
Not Hispanic (1,083)	1,188	7.91
Hispanic (8)	20	0.13
Bangladeshi (8)	8	0.05
Burmese (5)	6	0.04
Cambodian (0)	1	0.01
Chinese, ex. Taiwanese (361)	387	2.58
Filipino (20)	26	0.17
Indian (455)	479	3.19
Indonesian (1)	1	0.01
Japanese (19)	26	0.17
Korean (60)	76	0.51
Laotian (1)	1	0.01
Malaysian (5)	6	0.04
Pakistani (40)	50	0.33
Sri Lankan (23)	23	0.15
Taiwanese (9)	10	0.07
Thai (4)	4	0.03
Vietnamese (54)	62	0.41
Hawaii Native/Pacific Islander (1)	9	0.06
Not Hispanic (1)	3	0.02
Hispanic (0)	6	0.04
Guamanian/Chamorro (1)	1	0.01
Native Hawaiian (0)	1	0.01
White (11,592)	11,930	79.43
Not Hispanic (11,351)	11,643	77.52
Hispanic (241)	287	1.91

Ellicott

Place Type: Town
County: Chautauqua
Population: 8,714†

Ancestry‡	Population	%
Albanian (6)	6	0.07
American (252)	252	2.87
Arab (0)	5	0.06
Lebanese (0)	5	0.06
Armenian (0)	9	0.10
Australian (0)	3	0.03
Austrian (12)	12	0.14
Belgian (10)	10	0.11
British (0)	36	0.41
Canadian (6)	68	0.78
Croatian (7)	7	0.08
Czech (0)	15	0.17
Danish (25)	44	0.50
Dutch (45)	290	3.31
Eastern European (14)	14	0.16
English (447)	1,730	19.72
European (42)	42	0.48
Finnish (0)	6	0.07
French, ex. Basque (7)	125	1.43
French Canadian (21)	30	0.34
German (562)	1,918	21.87
Greek (0)	4	0.05
Hungarian (19)	48	0.55
Irish (374)	1,438	16.39
Italian (656)	1,324	15.10
Northern European (13)	13	0.15
Norwegian (34)	78	0.89
Pennsylvania German (19)	24	0.27
Polish (189)	563	6.42
Romanian (0)	9	0.10
Russian (23)	32	0.36
Scandinavian (8)	25	0.29
Scotch-Irish (68)	171	1.95
Scottish (45)	183	2.09
Swedish (1,007)	2,238	25.52
Swiss (10)	23	0.26
Ukrainian (12)	12	0.14
Welsh (7)	74	0.84
West Indian, ex. Hispanic (0)	24	0.27
Haitian (0)	22	0.25
West Indian (0)	2	0.02

Hispanic Origin	Population	%
Hispanic or Latino (of any race)	147	1.69
Central American, ex. Mexican	2	0.02
Honduran	1	0.01
Salvadoran	1	0.01
Cuban	3	0.03
Dominican Republic	7	0.08
Mexican	27	0.31
Puerto Rican	90	1.03
South American	5	0.06
Colombian	3	0.03
Peruvian	1	0.01
Venezuelan	1	0.01
Other Hispanic or Latino	13	0.15

Race*	Population	%
African-American/Black (59)	100	1.15
Not Hispanic (55)	89	1.02
Hispanic (4)	11	0.13
American Indian/Alaska Native (11)	29	0.33
Not Hispanic (11)	28	0.32
Hispanic (0)	1	0.01
Cherokee (1)	4	0.05
Cheyenne (0)	2	0.02
Iroquois (5)	7	0.08
Sioux (1)	2	0.02
Asian (56)	65	0.75
Not Hispanic (56)	65	0.75
Cambodian (2)	2	0.02
Chinese, ex. Taiwanese (14)	14	0.16
Filipino (3)	5	0.06
Indian (22)	23	0.26
Indonesian (0)	2	0.02
Japanese (0)	3	0.03
Korean (7)	8	0.09
Vietnamese (6)	6	0.07
Hawaii Native/Pacific Islander (0)	1	0.01
Not Hispanic (0)	1	0.01
Samoan (0)	1	0.01
White (8,486)	8,555	98.18
Not Hispanic (8,386)	8,441	96.87
Hispanic (100)	114	1.31

Elma

Place Type: Town
County: Erie
Population: 11,317†

Ancestry‡	Population	%
American (355)	355	3.16
Arab (63)	63	0.56
Lebanese (46)	46	0.41
Other Arab (17)	17	0.15
Austrian (17)	30	0.27
British (13)	13	0.12
Cajun (15)	15	0.13
Canadian (0)	17	0.15
Croatian (0)	84	0.75
Czech (21)	21	0.19
Danish (0)	32	0.28
Dutch (31)	151	1.34
English (434)	1,439	12.81
European (101)	101	0.90
Finnish (0)	29	0.26
French, ex. Basque (15)	339	3.02
French Canadian (0)	69	0.61
German (1,805)	4,435	39.49
Greek (203)	232	2.07
Hungarian (11)	78	0.69
Irish (410)	2,084	18.56
Italian (644)	1,746	15.55
Norwegian (14)	14	0.12
Pennsylvania German (24)	24	0.21
Polish (1,095)	2,306	20.53
Romanian (17)	17	0.15
Russian (25)	73	0.65
Scandinavian (0)	32	0.28
Scotch-Irish (12)	47	0.42
Scottish (29)	149	1.33
Slavic (0)	13	0.12
Slovak (0)	8	0.07
Swedish (42)	116	1.03
Swiss (0)	10	0.09
Turkish (0)	14	0.12
Ukrainian (69)	143	1.27
Welsh (0)	61	0.54

Hispanic Origin	Population	%
Hispanic or Latino (of any race)	72	0.64
Central American, ex. Mexican	7	0.06
Guatemalan	3	0.03
Honduran	1	0.01
Panamanian	1	0.01
Salvadoran	2	0.02
Cuban	7	0.06
Mexican	20	0.18
Puerto Rican	25	0.22
South American	6	0.05
Colombian	3	0.03
Ecuadorian	1	0.01
Peruvian	2	0.02
Other Hispanic or Latino	7	0.06

Race*	Population	%
African-American/Black (19)	41	0.36
Not Hispanic (19)	37	0.33
Hispanic (0)	4	0.04
American Indian/Alaska Native (13)	21	0.19
Not Hispanic (10)	18	0.16
Hispanic (3)	3	0.03
Cherokee (0)	1	0.01
Iroquois (7)	10	0.09
Asian (32)	37	0.33
Not Hispanic (31)	36	0.32
Hispanic (1)	1	0.01
Chinese, ex. Taiwanese (9)	9	0.08
Filipino (5)	7	0.06
Indonesian (1)	2	0.02
Japanese (7)	8	0.07
Korean (9)	9	0.08
Vietnamese (1)	2	0.02
Hawaii Native/Pacific Islander (5)	5	0.04
Not Hispanic (4)	4	0.04
Hispanic (1)	1	0.01
White (11,192)	11,232	99.25
Not Hispanic (11,149)	11,179	98.78
Hispanic (43)	53	0.47

Elmira

Place Type: City
County: Chemung
Population: 29,200†

*Notes: † The Census 2010 population figure is used to calculate the percentages in the Hispanic Origin and Race categories. Ancestry percentages are based on the 2006-2010 American Community Survey population (not shown); ‡ Numbers in parentheses indicate the number of people reporting a single ancestry; * Numbers in parentheses indicate the number of persons reporting this race alone, not in combination with any other race; Please refer to the Explanation of Data for more information.*

Ancestry‡	Population	%
African, Sub-Saharan (159)	159	0.54
African (136)	136	0.46
Ethiopian (11)	11	0.04
Ghanaian (11)	11	0.04
Nigerian (1)	1	<0.01
Alsatian (0)	10	0.03
American (2,010)	2,010	6.85
Arab (44)	90	0.31
Lebanese (32)	78	0.27
Other Arab (12)	12	0.04
Austrian (6)	45	0.15
British (21)	38	0.13
Bulgarian (12)	12	0.04
Canadian (68)	68	0.23
Croatian (0)	24	0.08
Czech (21)	84	0.29
Czechoslovakian (23)	31	0.11
Danish (38)	98	0.33
Dutch (356)	1,087	3.70
English (751)	2,789	9.50
European (13)	13	0.04
Finnish (0)	36	0.12
French, ex. Basque (75)	654	2.23
French Canadian (164)	344	1.17
German (1,168)	4,872	16.60
Greek (58)	115	0.39
Hungarian (52)	68	0.23
Iranian (12)	12	0.04
Irish (1,881)	5,746	19.57
Israeli (0)	12	0.04
Italian (1,493)	3,363	11.46
Latvian (0)	11	0.04
Lithuanian (18)	68	0.23
Northern European (10)	10	0.03
Norwegian (36)	172	0.59
Pennsylvania German (55)	109	0.37
Polish (590)	1,846	6.29
Portuguese (11)	45	0.15
Romanian (0)	15	0.05
Russian (0)	141	0.48
Scotch-Irish (75)	271	0.92
Scottish (140)	386	1.31
Serbian (11)	11	0.04
Slavic (0)	25	0.09
Slovak (7)	59	0.20
Swedish (70)	276	0.94
Swiss (0)	31	0.11
Turkish (10)	10	0.03
Ukrainian (225)	496	1.69
Welsh (29)	221	0.75
West Indian, ex. Hispanic (159)	159	0.54
Bahamian (31)	31	0.11
Barbadian (26)	26	0.09
Haitian (51)	51	0.17
Jamaican (28)	28	0.10
West Indian (23)	23	0.08
Yugoslavian (121)	152	0.52

Hispanic Origin	Population	%
Hispanic or Latino (of any race)	1,251	4.28
Central American, ex. Mexican	55	0.19
Costa Rican	7	0.02
Guatemalan	7	0.02
Honduran	9	0.03
Nicaraguan	1	<0.01
Panamanian	18	0.06
Salvadoran	13	0.04
Cuban	38	0.13
Dominican Republic	64	0.22
Mexican	163	0.56
Puerto Rican	758	2.60
South American	43	0.15
Argentinean	4	0.01
Bolivian	3	0.01
Chilean	1	<0.01
Colombian	10	0.03
Ecuadorian	7	0.02
Peruvian	10	0.03
Uruguayan	2	0.01
Venezuelan	3	0.01
Other South American	3	0.01
Other Hispanic or Latino	130	0.45

Race*	Population	%
African-American/Black (4,268)	5,424	18.58
Not Hispanic (4,049)	5,085	17.41
Hispanic (219)	339	1.16
American Indian/Alaska Native (121)	410	1.40
Not Hispanic (101)	351	1.20
Hispanic (20)	59	0.20
Apache (0)	1	<0.01
Blackfeet (2)	17	0.06
Cherokee (9)	68	0.23
Chickasaw (0)	1	<0.01
Chippewa (1)	2	0.01
Cree (0)	2	0.01
Creek (0)	1	<0.01
Houma (1)	1	<0.01
Iroquois (23)	64	0.22
Mexican American Ind. (2)	3	0.01
Navajo (0)	4	0.01
Seminole (0)	2	0.01
Sioux (0)	3	0.01
South American Ind. (3)	5	0.02
Spanish American Ind. (0)	1	<0.01
Tlingit-Haida *(Alaska Native)* (3)	3	0.01
Yakama (0)	1	<0.01
Asian (179)	261	0.89
Not Hispanic (178)	249	0.85
Hispanic (1)	12	0.04
Chinese, ex. Taiwanese (31)	36	0.12
Filipino (24)	42	0.14
Indian (31)	45	0.15
Japanese (16)	35	0.12
Korean (22)	33	0.11
Laotian (8)	20	0.07
Malaysian (2)	2	0.01
Pakistani (5)	7	0.02
Taiwanese (3)	3	0.01
Thai (3)	3	0.01
Vietnamese (15)	18	0.06
Hawaii Native/Pacific Islander (11)	32	0.11
Not Hispanic (5)	20	0.07
Hispanic (6)	12	0.04
Guamanian/Chamorro (1)	5	0.02
Native Hawaiian (8)	15	0.05
Samoan (2)	2	0.01
White (22,850)	24,235	83.00
Not Hispanic (22,304)	23,521	80.55
Hispanic (546)	714	2.45

Elmont

Place Type: CDP
County: Nassau
Population: 33,198†

Ancestry‡	Population	%
African, Sub-Saharan (562)	661	1.92
African (439)	519	1.50
Nigerian (92)	92	0.27
Other Sub-Saharan African (31)	50	0.14
American (497)	497	1.44
Arab (147)	156	0.45
Lebanese (12)	12	0.03
Moroccan (8)	17	0.05
Other Arab (127)	127	0.37
Austrian (37)	37	0.11
British (0)	16	0.05
Canadian (0)	9	0.03
Czech (0)	22	0.06
Czechoslovakian (7)	18	0.05
Danish (0)	39	0.11
Dutch (10)	93	0.27
English (78)	371	1.08
European (9)	18	0.05
Finnish (0)	31	0.09
French, ex. Basque (40)	189	0.55
German (314)	1,294	3.75
Greek (44)	77	0.22
Guyanese (388)	581	1.68
Hungarian (39)	67	0.19
Irish (460)	1,763	5.11
Italian (2,312)	3,902	11.31
Lithuanian (0)	12	0.03
Maltese (93)	93	0.27
Norwegian (7)	73	0.21
Polish (332)	600	1.74
Portuguese (68)	81	0.23
Romanian (23)	23	0.07
Russian (88)	137	0.40
Scotch-Irish (28)	79	0.23
Scottish (15)	206	0.60
Slavic (30)	91	0.26
Slovak (12)	12	0.03
Swedish (0)	17	0.05
Swiss (23)	23	0.07
Turkish (13)	13	0.04
Ukrainian (48)	90	0.26
Welsh (0)	8	0.02
West Indian, ex. Hispanic (7,500)	9,499	27.54
Barbadian (32)	60	0.17
British West Indian (23)	59	0.17
Haitian (4,770)	5,587	16.20
Jamaican (2,308)	2,968	8.61
Trinidadian/Tobagonian (215)	474	1.37
West Indian (152)	351	1.02

Hispanic Origin	Population	%
Hispanic or Latino (of any race)	7,236	21.80
Central American, ex. Mexican	1,681	5.06
Costa Rican	27	0.08
Guatemalan	340	1.02
Honduran	289	0.87
Nicaraguan	7	0.02
Panamanian	143	0.43
Salvadoran	862	2.60
Other Central American	13	0.04
Cuban	143	0.43
Dominican Republic	772	2.33
Mexican	811	2.44
Puerto Rican	1,250	3.77
South American	1,941	5.85
Argentinean	122	0.37
Bolivian	22	0.07
Chilean	119	0.36
Colombian	698	2.10
Ecuadorian	426	1.28
Paraguayan	6	0.02
Peruvian	465	1.40
Uruguayan	13	0.04
Venezuelan	51	0.15
Other South American	19	0.06
Other Hispanic or Latino	638	1.92

Race*	Population	%
African-American/Black (15,109)	15,744	47.42
Not Hispanic (14,587)	15,005	45.20
Hispanic (522)	739	2.23
American Indian/Alaska Native (172)	405	1.22
Not Hispanic (98)	244	0.73
Hispanic (74)	161	0.48
Apache (0)	5	0.02
Blackfeet (0)	5	0.02
Canadian/French Am. Ind. (0)	2	0.01
Central American Ind. (0)	6	0.02
Cherokee (1)	26	0.08
Choctaw (0)	1	<0.01
Colville (1)	1	<0.01
Iroquois (3)	8	0.02
Mexican American Ind. (4)	4	0.01
Seminole (0)	2	0.01
South American Ind. (6)	22	0.07
Spanish American Ind. (4)	5	0.02
Asian (3,635)	4,067	12.25
Not Hispanic (3,609)	3,997	12.04
Hispanic (26)	70	0.21
Bangladeshi (50)	63	0.19
Burmese (1)	1	<0.01

*Notes: † The Census 2010 population figure is used to calculate the percentages in the Hispanic Origin and Race categories. Ancestry percentages are based on the 2006-2010 American Community Survey population (not shown); ‡ Numbers in parentheses indicate the number of people reporting a single ancestry; * Numbers in parentheses indicate the number of persons reporting this race alone, not in combination with any other race; Please refer to the Explanation of Data for more information.*

Chinese, ex. Taiwanese (157)	241	0.73
Filipino (449)	494	1.49
Indian (2,122)	2,355	7.09
Indonesian (0)	2	0.01
Japanese (7)	18	0.05
Korean (29)	30	0.09
Nepalese (1)	1	<0.01
Pakistani (596)	650	1.96
Sri Lankan (29)	33	0.10
Taiwanese (14)	14	0.04
Thai (25)	36	0.11
Vietnamese (9)	15	0.05
Hawaii Native/Pacific Islander (14)	88	0.27
Not Hispanic (8)	68	0.20
Hispanic (6)	20	0.06
Guamanian/Chamorro (3)	4	0.01
Native Hawaiian (1)	4	0.01
Samoan (0)	3	0.01
White (9,446)	10,227	30.81
Not Hispanic (6,494)	6,775	20.41
Hispanic (2,952)	3,452	10.40

Elwood

Place Type: CDP
County: Suffolk
Population: 11,177†

Ancestry‡	Population	%
African, Sub-Saharan (0)	23	0.21
African (0)	8	0.07
Ethiopian (0)	15	0.13
American (356)	356	3.20
Armenian (57)	71	0.64
Austrian (0)	66	0.59
British (27)	40	0.36
Bulgarian (44)	65	0.58
Canadian (13)	27	0.24
Celtic (24)	24	0.22
Croatian (46)	46	0.41
Czech (0)	11	0.10
Czechoslovakian (9)	9	0.08
Danish (0)	13	0.12
Dutch (32)	227	2.04
Eastern European (37)	37	0.33
English (51)	476	4.27
European (39)	39	0.35
Finnish (0)	31	0.28
French, ex. Basque (37)	142	1.28
French Canadian (13)	78	0.70
German (231)	1,899	17.05
Greek (169)	218	1.96
Hungarian (38)	203	1.82
Iranian (8)	8	0.07
Irish (707)	2,841	25.51
Italian (1,536)	3,432	30.82
Lithuanian (17)	42	0.38
Norwegian (13)	82	0.74
Polish (218)	745	6.69
Portuguese (6)	16	0.14
Romanian (14)	22	0.20
Russian (164)	365	3.28
Scotch-Irish (39)	139	1.25
Scottish (15)	119	1.07
Slavic (0)	38	0.34
Slovak (9)	23	0.21
Swedish (0)	49	0.44
Swiss (17)	26	0.23
Turkish (11)	11	0.10
Ukrainian (66)	192	1.72
Welsh (0)	11	0.10
West Indian, ex. Hispanic (38)	38	0.34
Haitian (23)	23	0.21
Jamaican (15)	15	0.13
Yugoslavian (0)	24	0.22

Hispanic Origin	Population	%
Hispanic or Latino (of any race)	918	8.21
Central American, ex. Mexican	242	2.17
Costa Rican	9	0.08
Guatemalan	55	0.49
Honduran	17	0.15
Panamanian	3	0.03
Salvadoran	158	1.41
Cuban	37	0.33
Dominican Republic	37	0.33
Mexican	31	0.28
Puerto Rican	251	2.25
South American	202	1.81
Argentinean	21	0.19
Bolivian	5	0.04
Chilean	8	0.07
Colombian	57	0.51
Ecuadorian	68	0.61
Paraguayan	14	0.13
Peruvian	27	0.24
Uruguayan	1	0.01
Venezuelan	1	0.01
Other Hispanic or Latino	118	1.06

Race*	Population	%
African-American/Black (697)	770	6.89
Not Hispanic (674)	733	6.56
Hispanic (23)	37	0.33
American Indian/Alaska Native (12)	53	0.47
Not Hispanic (9)	41	0.37
Hispanic (3)	12	0.11
Cherokee (0)	4	0.04
Comanche (0)	2	0.02
Delaware (0)	1	0.01
Lumbee (1)	3	0.03
Asian (890)	950	8.50
Not Hispanic (887)	941	8.42
Hispanic (3)	9	0.08
Bangladeshi (1)	4	0.04
Chinese, ex. Taiwanese (154)	166	1.49
Filipino (30)	38	0.34
Indian (178)	204	1.83
Indonesian (1)	2	0.02
Japanese (9)	12	0.11
Korean (348)	360	3.22
Laotian (4)	4	0.04
Malaysian (1)	1	0.01
Pakistani (135)	149	1.33
Taiwanese (6)	6	0.05
Thai (2)	2	0.02
Vietnamese (8)	8	0.07
Hawaii Native/Pacific Islander (4)	14	0.13
Not Hispanic (3)	4	0.04
Hispanic (1)	10	0.09
Guamanian/Chamorro (3)	3	0.03
Native Hawaiian (1)	1	0.01
White (9,179)	9,303	83.23
Not Hispanic (8,544)	8,631	77.22
Hispanic (635)	672	6.01

Endicott

Place Type: Village
County: Broome
Population: 13,392†

Ancestry‡	Population	%
African, Sub-Saharan (30)	30	0.23
Ghanaian (30)	30	0.23
American (454)	454	3.41
Arab (14)	23	0.17
Iraqi (6)	6	0.05
Lebanese (0)	9	0.07
Other Arab (8)	8	0.06
Austrian (12)	68	0.51
Belgian (0)	17	0.13
British (40)	135	1.01
Canadian (8)	19	0.14
Czech (67)	297	2.23
Czechoslovakian (30)	30	0.23
Danish (8)	18	0.14
Dutch (42)	297	2.23
English (359)	1,497	11.24
European (44)	83	0.62
French, ex. Basque (19)	278	2.09
French Canadian (40)	80	0.60
German (756)	2,546	19.11
Greek (87)	139	1.04
Guyanese (80)	121	0.91
Hungarian (7)	33	0.25
Iranian (0)	11	0.08
Irish (548)	2,792	20.96
Italian (1,007)	2,591	19.45
Lithuanian (13)	68	0.51
Norwegian (0)	59	0.44
Pennsylvania German (9)	23	0.17
Polish (171)	772	5.80
Portuguese (0)	11	0.08
Romanian (8)	8	0.06
Russian (88)	352	2.64
Scotch-Irish (19)	111	0.83
Scottish (48)	315	2.36
Serbian (0)	11	0.08
Slavic (16)	16	0.12
Slovak (178)	634	4.76
Slovene (0)	11	0.08
Swedish (10)	62	0.47
Swiss (0)	26	0.20
Turkish (0)	11	0.08
Ukrainian (81)	146	1.10
Welsh (96)	352	2.64
West Indian, ex. Hispanic (0)	11	0.08
Jamaican (0)	11	0.08

Hispanic Origin	Population	%
Hispanic or Latino (of any race)	594	4.44
Central American, ex. Mexican	52	0.39
Costa Rican	5	0.04
Guatemalan	17	0.13
Honduran	11	0.08
Nicaraguan	10	0.07
Panamanian	5	0.04
Salvadoran	4	0.03
Cuban	17	0.13
Dominican Republic	31	0.23
Mexican	73	0.55
Puerto Rican	314	2.34
South American	37	0.28
Argentinean	14	0.10
Colombian	6	0.04
Ecuadorian	9	0.07
Peruvian	4	0.03
Venezuelan	3	0.02
Other South American	1	0.01
Other Hispanic or Latino	70	0.52

Race*	Population	%
African-American/Black (932)	1,226	9.15
Not Hispanic (846)	1,084	8.09
Hispanic (86)	142	1.06
American Indian/Alaska Native (28)	142	1.06
Not Hispanic (21)	116	0.87
Hispanic (7)	26	0.19
Apache (1)	2	0.01
Blackfeet (0)	3	0.02
Canadian/French Am. Ind. (3)	3	0.02
Cherokee (2)	14	0.10
Choctaw (0)	2	0.01
Delaware (0)	2	0.01
Iroquois (5)	17	0.13
Mexican American Ind. (0)	1	0.01
Navajo (0)	1	0.01
Potawatomi (0)	2	0.01
Seminole (0)	2	0.01
Sioux (1)	3	0.02
Spanish American Ind. (2)	3	0.02
Asian (235)	294	2.20
Not Hispanic (234)	282	2.11
Hispanic (1)	12	0.09
Chinese, ex. Taiwanese (33)	44	0.33
Filipino (21)	32	0.24
Indian (41)	48	0.36
Indonesian (3)	3	0.02
Japanese (9)	14	0.10

*Notes: † The Census 2010 population figure is used to calculate the percentages in the Hispanic Origin and Race categories. Ancestry percentages are based on the 2006-2010 American Community Survey population (not shown); ‡ Numbers in parentheses indicate the number of people reporting a single ancestry; * Numbers in parentheses indicate the number of persons reporting this race alone, not in combination with any other race; Please refer to the Explanation of Data for more information.*

Korean (7)	11	0.08
Laotian (42)	54	0.40
Malaysian (1)	2	0.01
Pakistani (1)	2	0.01
Taiwanese (2)	2	0.01
Thai (0)	1	0.01
Vietnamese (70)	79	0.59
Hawaii Native/Pacific Islander (18)	28	0.21
Not Hispanic (8)	15	0.11
Hispanic (10)	13	0.10
Guamanian/Chamorro (10)	10	0.07
Native Hawaiian (1)	3	0.02
White (11,603)	12,010	89.68
Not Hispanic (11,300)	11,640	86.92
Hispanic (303)	370	2.76

Endwell

Place Type: CDP
County: Broome
Population: 11,446†

Ancestry‡	Population	%
African, Sub-Saharan (24)	24	0.21
Cape Verdean (11)	11	0.09
Nigerian (13)	13	0.11
Albanian (0)	7	0.06
American (303)	303	2.59
Arab (30)	30	0.26
Arab (12)	12	0.10
Lebanese (18)	18	0.15
Austrian (14)	164	1.40
Belgian (0)	14	0.12
British (14)	28	0.24
Canadian (11)	54	0.46
Carpatho Rusyn (11)	11	0.09
Croatian (0)	21	0.18
Czech (20)	205	1.75
Czechoslovakian (63)	98	0.84
Danish (7)	7	0.06
Dutch (31)	270	2.31
Eastern European (11)	33	0.28
English (533)	1,809	15.47
European (146)	146	1.25
French, ex. Basque (12)	368	3.15
French Canadian (21)	111	0.95
German (481)	2,244	19.19
Greek (11)	44	0.38
Hungarian (30)	70	0.60
Irish (683)	2,556	21.86
Italian (957)	2,236	19.13
Lithuanian (11)	89	0.76
Norwegian (13)	96	0.82
Pennsylvania German (10)	10	0.09
Polish (442)	1,110	9.49
Portuguese (33)	48	0.41
Russian (97)	431	3.69
Scandinavian (0)	9	0.08
Scotch-Irish (47)	291	2.49
Scottish (15)	345	2.95
Serbian (10)	54	0.46
Slovak (363)	740	6.33
Slovene (18)	18	0.15
Swedish (68)	142	1.21
Swiss (8)	26	0.22
Ukrainian (50)	181	1.55
Welsh (25)	383	3.28
West Indian, ex. Hispanic (47)	47	0.40
West Indian (47)	47	0.40

Hispanic Origin	Population	%
Hispanic or Latino (of any race)	301	2.63
Central American, ex. Mexican	25	0.22
Costa Rican	8	0.07
Guatemalan	8	0.07
Honduran	1	0.01
Nicaraguan	5	0.04
Salvadoran	3	0.03
Cuban	18	0.16
Dominican Republic	20	0.17
Mexican	33	0.29
Puerto Rican	121	1.06
South American	27	0.24
Argentinean	2	0.02
Bolivian	2	0.02
Chilean	2	0.02
Colombian	13	0.11
Ecuadorian	4	0.03
Peruvian	2	0.02
Uruguayan	1	0.01
Venezuelan	1	0.01
Other Hispanic or Latino	57	0.50

Race*	Population	%
African-American/Black (271)	381	3.33
Not Hispanic (257)	355	3.10
Hispanic (14)	26	0.23
American Indian/Alaska Native (24)	63	0.55
Not Hispanic (23)	56	0.49
Hispanic (1)	7	0.06
Apache (1)	1	0.01
Blackfeet (0)	1	0.01
Cherokee (5)	10	0.09
Chippewa (1)	1	0.01
Choctaw (0)	1	0.01
Delaware (1)	1	0.01
Houma (0)	1	0.01
Iroquois (1)	6	0.05
Sioux (1)	3	0.03
Asian (227)	292	2.55
Not Hispanic (224)	284	2.48
Hispanic (3)	8	0.07
Bangladeshi (1)	1	0.01
Burmese (4)	4	0.03
Chinese, ex. Taiwanese (71)	94	0.82
Filipino (28)	40	0.35
Indian (21)	25	0.22
Japanese (3)	5	0.04
Korean (23)	34	0.30
Laotian (6)	8	0.07
Pakistani (17)	17	0.15
Taiwanese (5)	7	0.06
Thai (1)	3	0.03
Vietnamese (33)	43	0.38
Hawaii Native/Pacific Islander (10)	14	0.12
Not Hispanic (10)	14	0.12
Native Hawaiian (1)	2	0.02
White (10,652)	10,835	94.66
Not Hispanic (10,443)	10,603	92.63
Hispanic (209)	232	2.03

Erwin

Place Type: Town
County: Steuben
Population: 8,037†

Ancestry‡	Population	%
American (692)	692	8.80
Arab (4)	4	0.05
Syrian (4)	4	0.05
Armenian (7)	7	0.09
Austrian (0)	6	0.08
Belgian (4)	4	0.05
British (59)	65	0.83
Canadian (0)	6	0.08
Carpatho Rusyn (23)	23	0.29
Croatian (0)	3	0.04
Czech (13)	43	0.55
Czechoslovakian (0)	3	0.04
Danish (27)	35	0.44
Dutch (31)	312	3.97
Eastern European (13)	13	0.17
English (447)	1,265	16.08
European (97)	97	1.23
Finnish (2)	2	0.03
French, ex. Basque (66)	271	3.44
French Canadian (20)	89	1.13
German (416)	1,447	18.39
Greek (0)	9	0.11
Hungarian (65)	132	1.68
Irish (256)	1,140	14.49
Italian (246)	715	9.09
Latvian (6)	18	0.23
Norwegian (13)	27	0.34
Pennsylvania German (21)	39	0.50
Polish (84)	378	4.80
Portuguese (5)	5	0.06
Romanian (11)	11	0.14
Russian (39)	105	1.33
Scandinavian (9)	9	0.11
Scotch-Irish (36)	245	3.11
Scottish (60)	215	2.73
Slovak (6)	17	0.22
Slovene (0)	10	0.13
Swedish (73)	165	2.10
Swiss (0)	9	0.11
Ukrainian (10)	42	0.53
Welsh (28)	161	2.05
West Indian, ex. Hispanic (10)	10	0.13
Jamaican (10)	10	0.13

Hispanic Origin	Population	%
Hispanic or Latino (of any race)	115	1.43
Central American, ex. Mexican	9	0.11
Guatemalan	1	0.01
Honduran	2	0.02
Panamanian	5	0.06
Salvadoran	1	0.01
Cuban	1	0.01
Dominican Republic	2	0.02
Mexican	37	0.46
Puerto Rican	39	0.49
South American	15	0.19
Chilean	5	0.06
Colombian	2	0.02
Paraguayan	5	0.06
Peruvian	1	0.01
Uruguayan	1	0.01
Venezuelan	1	0.01
Other Hispanic or Latino	12	0.15

Race*	Population	%
African-American/Black (207)	257	3.20
Not Hispanic (195)	243	3.02
Hispanic (12)	14	0.17
American Indian/Alaska Native (17)	55	0.68
Not Hispanic (16)	52	0.65
Hispanic (1)	3	0.04
Cherokee (0)	2	0.02
Choctaw (3)	3	0.04
Crow (2)	3	0.04
Inupiat *(Alaska Native)* (1)	3	0.04
Iroquois (2)	6	0.07
Sioux (0)	1	0.01
Asian (590)	635	7.90
Not Hispanic (587)	632	7.86
Hispanic (3)	3	0.04
Bangladeshi (9)	9	0.11
Chinese, ex. Taiwanese (199)	213	2.65
Filipino (25)	33	0.41
Indian (234)	251	3.12
Indonesian (4)	4	0.05
Japanese (16)	25	0.31
Korean (39)	47	0.58
Malaysian (2)	2	0.02
Nepalese (8)	8	0.10
Pakistani (10)	10	0.12
Taiwanese (20)	20	0.25
Thai (7)	7	0.09
Vietnamese (5)	5	0.06
Hawaii Native/Pacific Islander (0)	1	0.01
Hispanic (0)	1	0.01
White (7,049)	7,169	89.20
Not Hispanic (6,982)	7,095	88.28
Hispanic (67)	74	0.92

SECTION TWO

*Notes: † The Census 2010 population figure is used to calculate the percentages in the Hispanic Origin and Race categories. Ancestry percentages are based on the 2006-2010 American Community Survey population (not shown); ‡ Numbers in parentheses indicate the number of people reporting a single ancestry; * Numbers in parentheses indicate the number of persons reporting this race alone, not in combination with any other race; Please refer to the Explanation of Data for more information.*

Esopus

Place Type: Town
County: Ulster
Population: 9,041†

Ancestry‡	Population	%
African, Sub-Saharan (8)	8	0.09
African (8)	8	0.09
Alsatian (0)	20	0.22
American (1,000)	1,000	10.93
Austrian (38)	175	1.91
Brazilian (7)	7	0.08
British (38)	67	0.73
Canadian (0)	11	0.12
Croatian (0)	14	0.15
Czech (16)	68	0.74
Danish (11)	102	1.12
Dutch (83)	660	7.22
Eastern European (7)	7	0.08
English (170)	936	10.24
European (155)	165	1.80
Finnish (8)	8	0.09
French, ex. Basque (21)	222	2.43
French Canadian (10)	98	1.07
German (406)	2,609	28.53
Greek (0)	36	0.39
Hungarian (5)	59	0.65
Icelander (0)	15	0.16
Irish (557)	2,523	27.59
Israeli (10)	10	0.11
Italian (507)	1,592	17.41
Lithuanian (0)	10	0.11
Norwegian (46)	124	1.36
Polish (129)	439	4.80
Portuguese (0)	12	0.13
Romanian (0)	8	0.09
Russian (28)	283	3.09
Scandinavian (0)	19	0.21
Scotch-Irish (19)	109	1.19
Scottish (57)	145	1.59
Slovak (0)	27	0.30
Swedish (15)	85	0.93
Swiss (0)	29	0.32
Ukrainian (36)	130	1.42
Welsh (0)	38	0.42
Yugoslavian (44)	52	0.57

Hispanic Origin	Population	%
Hispanic or Latino (of any race)	487	5.39
Central American, ex. Mexican	29	0.32
Costa Rican	1	0.01
Guatemalan	17	0.19
Honduran	3	0.03
Panamanian	5	0.06
Salvadoran	2	0.02
Other Central American	1	0.01
Cuban	6	0.07
Dominican Republic	19	0.21
Mexican	72	0.80
Puerto Rican	248	2.74
South American	65	0.72
Argentinean	7	0.08
Chilean	9	0.10
Colombian	9	0.10
Ecuadorian	20	0.22
Paraguayan	7	0.08
Peruvian	9	0.10
Venezuelan	3	0.03
Other South American	1	0.01
Other Hispanic or Latino	48	0.53

Race*	Population	%
African-American/Black (453)	579	6.40
Not Hispanic (395)	507	5.61
Hispanic (58)	72	0.80
American Indian/Alaska Native (33)	104	1.15
Not Hispanic (26)	94	1.04
Hispanic (7)	10	0.11
Apache (0)	1	0.01
Arapaho (1)	1	0.01
Blackfeet (0)	2	0.02
Canadian/French Am. Ind. (0)	3	0.03
Central American Ind. (1)	1	0.01
Cherokee (5)	16	0.18
Cheyenne (1)	1	0.01
Delaware (4)	8	0.09
Iroquois (1)	10	0.11
Mexican American Ind. (2)	2	0.02
Sioux (0)	2	0.02
South American Ind. (3)	4	0.04
Asian (128)	175	1.94
Not Hispanic (125)	167	1.85
Hispanic (3)	8	0.09
Bangladeshi (0)	1	0.01
Cambodian (2)	2	0.02
Chinese, ex. Taiwanese (42)	54	0.60
Filipino (15)	18	0.20
Indian (28)	46	0.51
Japanese (9)	10	0.11
Korean (10)	12	0.13
Malaysian (1)	1	0.01
Pakistani (1)	8	0.09
Sri Lankan (0)	9	0.10
Taiwanese (2)	2	0.02
Thai (4)	8	0.09
Vietnamese (7)	9	0.10
Hawaii Native/Pacific Islander (1)	8	0.09
Not Hispanic (1)	5	0.06
Hispanic (0)	3	0.03
Native Hawaiian (0)	3	0.03
Samoan (1)	1	0.01
White (8,060)	8,273	91.51
Not Hispanic (7,794)	7,977	88.23
Hispanic (266)	296	3.27

Evans

Place Type: Town
County: Erie
Population: 16,356†

Ancestry‡	Population	%
American (429)	429	2.60
Arab (98)	112	0.68
Lebanese (68)	68	0.41
Syrian (0)	14	0.08
Other Arab (30)	30	0.18
Austrian (0)	16	0.10
Belgian (0)	11	0.07
British (14)	35	0.21
Bulgarian (0)	11	0.07
Canadian (12)	18	0.11
Croatian (0)	107	0.65
Czech (0)	22	0.13
Czechoslovakian (8)	21	0.13
Dutch (31)	268	1.62
English (209)	1,236	7.48
European (16)	16	0.10
French, ex. Basque (77)	534	3.23
French Canadian (47)	126	0.76
German (1,446)	5,576	33.76
Greek (18)	47	0.28
Hungarian (42)	134	0.81
Irish (946)	3,802	23.02
Italian (1,219)	3,156	19.11
Lithuanian (7)	25	0.15
Macedonian (26)	26	0.16
Norwegian (33)	98	0.59
Pennsylvania German (22)	22	0.13
Polish (1,542)	4,024	24.36
Romanian (7)	44	0.27
Russian (21)	93	0.56
Scotch-Irish (64)	187	1.13
Scottish (199)	540	3.27
Serbian (14)	33	0.20
Slavic (18)	35	0.21
Slovak (0)	12	0.07
Swedish (46)	88	0.53
Ukrainian (39)	112	0.68
Welsh (30)	170	1.03
Yugoslavian (55)	67	0.41

Hispanic Origin	Population	%
Hispanic or Latino (of any race)	299	1.83
Central American, ex. Mexican	8	0.05
Costa Rican	2	0.01
Guatemalan	5	0.03
Salvadoran	1	0.01
Dominican Republic	1	0.01
Mexican	70	0.43
Puerto Rican	162	0.99
South American	5	0.03
Chilean	1	0.01
Ecuadorian	1	0.01
Peruvian	1	0.01
Other South American	2	0.01
Other Hispanic or Latino	53	0.32

Race*	Population	%
African-American/Black (115)	180	1.10
Not Hispanic (106)	165	1.01
Hispanic (9)	15	0.09
American Indian/Alaska Native (202)	318	1.94
Not Hispanic (186)	290	1.77
Hispanic (16)	28	0.17
Apache (0)	2	0.01
Blackfeet (0)	5	0.03
Canadian/French Am. Ind. (4)	5	0.03
Cherokee (4)	16	0.10
Cheyenne (0)	3	0.02
Chippewa (2)	5	0.03
Inupiat *(Alaska Native)* (0)	1	0.01
Iroquois (139)	184	1.12
Menominee (0)	1	0.01
Mexican American Ind. (5)	6	0.04
Osage (1)	1	0.01
Potawatomi (2)	3	0.02
South American Ind. (0)	1	0.01
Asian (34)	48	0.29
Not Hispanic (34)	47	0.29
Hispanic (0)	1	0.01
Chinese, ex. Taiwanese (20)	22	0.13
Filipino (3)	7	0.04
Indian (3)	3	0.02
Indonesian (0)	1	0.01
Japanese (1)	5	0.03
Korean (4)	6	0.04
Nepalese (2)	2	0.01
Vietnamese (1)	1	0.01
Hawaii Native/Pacific Islander (5)	15	0.09
Not Hispanic (4)	14	0.09
Hispanic (1)	1	0.01
Guamanian/Chamorro (3)	6	0.04
Native Hawaiian (1)	7	0.04
Samoan (1)	1	0.01
White (15,762)	15,951	97.52
Not Hispanic (15,547)	15,713	96.07
Hispanic (215)	238	1.46

Fairmount

Place Type: CDP
County: Onondaga
Population: 10,224†

Ancestry‡	Population	%
American (340)	340	3.38
Arab (108)	108	1.07
Arab (108)	108	1.07
Austrian (65)	218	2.17
Belgian (0)	17	0.17
Canadian (26)	49	0.49
Croatian (15)	15	0.15
Czech (0)	28	0.28
Danish (12)	17	0.17
Dutch (49)	236	2.35
English (250)	1,025	10.19
European (73)	73	0.73
French, ex. Basque (104)	555	5.52

*Notes: † The Census 2010 population figure is used to calculate the percentages in the Hispanic Origin and Race categories. Ancestry percentages are based on the 2006-2010 American Community Survey population (not shown); ‡ Numbers in parentheses indicate the number of people reporting a single ancestry; * Numbers in parentheses indicate the number of persons reporting this race alone, not in combination with any other race; Please refer to the Explanation of Data for more information.*

French Canadian (49)	144	1.43
German (217)	2,079	20.67
Guyanese (16)	16	0.16
Hungarian (23)	112	1.11
Irish (974)	3,011	29.94
Italian (928)	2,223	22.11
Latvian (25)	25	0.25
Norwegian (0)	18	0.18
Polish (333)	939	9.34
Portuguese (10)	26	0.26
Romanian (49)	60	0.60
Russian (52)	166	1.65
Scotch-Irish (53)	122	1.21
Scottish (23)	245	2.44
Serbian (63)	63	0.63
Slavic (0)	12	0.12
Slovak (11)	11	0.11
Swedish (0)	33	0.33
Swiss (0)	35	0.35
Ukrainian (487)	578	5.75
Welsh (0)	6	0.06
West Indian, ex. Hispanic (17)	17	0.17
British West Indian (17)	17	0.17
Yugoslavian (42)	42	0.42

Hispanic Origin	Population	%
Hispanic or Latino (of any race)	209	2.04
Central American, ex. Mexican	5	0.05
Guatemalan	1	0.01
Honduran	3	0.03
Nicaraguan	1	0.01
Cuban	13	0.13
Dominican Republic	3	0.03
Mexican	39	0.38
Puerto Rican	95	0.93
South American	23	0.22
Argentinean	2	0.02
Chilean	1	0.01
Colombian	8	0.08
Ecuadorian	2	0.02
Peruvian	8	0.08
Venezuelan	2	0.02
Other Hispanic or Latino	31	0.30

Race*	Population	%
African-American/Black (229)	310	3.03
Not Hispanic (226)	291	2.85
Hispanic (3)	19	0.19
American Indian/Alaska Native (57)	135	1.32
Not Hispanic (51)	119	1.16
Hispanic (6)	16	0.16
Blackfeet (0)	1	0.01
Canadian/French Am. Ind. (1)	1	0.01
Cherokee (1)	13	0.13
Cheyenne (0)	1	0.01
Iroquois (39)	73	0.71
Asian (170)	201	1.97
Not Hispanic (170)	197	1.93
Hispanic (0)	4	0.04
Cambodian (5)	5	0.05
Chinese, ex. Taiwanese (38)	52	0.51
Filipino (10)	12	0.12
Indian (39)	46	0.45
Japanese (2)	4	0.04
Korean (37)	40	0.39
Malaysian (1)	1	0.01
Pakistani (5)	6	0.06
Sri Lankan (5)	5	0.05
Taiwanese (1)	1	0.01
Thai (1)	1	0.01
Vietnamese (15)	16	0.16
Hawaii Native/Pacific Islander (7)	19	0.19
Not Hispanic (6)	12	0.12
Hispanic (1)	7	0.07
Fijian (0)	3	0.03
Native Hawaiian (4)	8	0.08
Samoan (1)	1	0.01
White (9,529)	9,689	94.77
Not Hispanic (9,404)	9,546	93.37
Hispanic (125)	143	1.40

Fallsburg

Place Type: Town
County: Sullivan
Population: 12,870†

Ancestry‡	Population	%
African, Sub-Saharan (50)	74	0.57
African (18)	42	0.33
Liberian (18)	18	0.14
Nigerian (14)	14	0.11
American (312)	312	2.42
Arab (32)	45	0.35
Egyptian (20)	20	0.16
Syrian (12)	25	0.19
Austrian (37)	74	0.57
Brazilian (0)	8	0.06
British (31)	40	0.31
Canadian (87)	204	1.58
Czechoslovakian (8)	8	0.06
Danish (0)	6	0.05
Dutch (32)	241	1.87
Eastern European (141)	141	1.09
English (242)	926	7.18
European (98)	98	0.76
French, ex. Basque (11)	249	1.93
French Canadian (39)	57	0.44
German (345)	1,387	10.75
Greek (85)	156	1.21
Hungarian (83)	232	1.80
Iranian (5)	5	0.04
Irish (622)	1,890	14.65
Israeli (0)	14	0.11
Italian (346)	1,016	7.88
Latvian (19)	35	0.27
Lithuanian (58)	82	0.64
Macedonian (8)	8	0.06
Norwegian (110)	118	0.91
Polish (238)	739	5.73
Portuguese (7)	15	0.12
Romanian (23)	41	0.32
Russian (261)	546	4.23
Scandinavian (0)	22	0.17
Scotch-Irish (5)	36	0.28
Scottish (145)	191	1.48
Swedish (0)	75	0.58
Swiss (95)	117	0.91
Turkish (7)	29	0.22
Ukrainian (54)	139	1.08
Welsh (0)	3	0.02
West Indian, ex. Hispanic (210)	323	2.50
Barbadian (0)	72	0.56
Haitian (8)	8	0.06
Jamaican (149)	163	1.26
Trinidadian/Tobagonian (16)	16	0.12
West Indian (37)	64	0.50

Hispanic Origin	Population	%
Hispanic or Latino (of any race)	2,823	21.93
Central American, ex. Mexican	805	6.25
Costa Rican	12	0.09
Guatemalan	95	0.74
Honduran	305	2.37
Nicaraguan	18	0.14
Panamanian	18	0.14
Salvadoran	353	2.74
Other Central American	4	0.03
Cuban	63	0.49
Dominican Republic	170	1.32
Mexican	292	2.27
Puerto Rican	1,200	9.32
South American	144	1.12
Argentinean	16	0.12
Bolivian	1	0.01
Chilean	11	0.09
Colombian	54	0.42
Ecuadorian	21	0.16
Paraguayan	8	0.06
Peruvian	24	0.19
Uruguayan	3	0.02
Venezuelan	5	0.04
Other South American	1	0.01
Other Hispanic or Latino	149	1.16

Race*	Population	%
African-American/Black (1,853)	2,107	16.37
Not Hispanic (1,654)	1,833	14.24
Hispanic (199)	274	2.13
American Indian/Alaska Native (74)	178	1.38
Not Hispanic (48)	126	0.98
Hispanic (26)	52	0.40
Blackfeet (2)	2	0.02
Central American Ind. (2)	2	0.02
Cherokee (10)	33	0.26
Chippewa (2)	5	0.04
Choctaw (0)	1	0.01
Cree (0)	2	0.02
Creek (0)	1	0.01
Delaware (2)	4	0.03
Iroquois (6)	17	0.13
Mexican American Ind. (7)	8	0.06
Pima (0)	2	0.02
Sioux (0)	1	0.01
South American Ind. (2)	2	0.02
Spanish American Ind. (1)	1	0.01
Asian (191)	247	1.92
Not Hispanic (176)	212	1.65
Hispanic (15)	35	0.27
Chinese, ex. Taiwanese (30)	36	0.28
Filipino (25)	36	0.28
Indian (75)	81	0.63
Indonesian (0)	1	0.01
Japanese (5)	14	0.11
Korean (17)	31	0.24
Pakistani (19)	20	0.16
Vietnamese (2)	2	0.02
Hawaii Native/Pacific Islander (11)	22	0.17
Not Hispanic (3)	6	0.05
Hispanic (8)	16	0.12
Guamanian/Chamorro (9)	10	0.08
Native Hawaiian (1)	2	0.02
Samoan (1)	2	0.02
White (9,384)	9,791	76.08
Not Hispanic (7,864)	8,098	62.92
Hispanic (1,520)	1,693	13.15

Farmingdale

Place Type: Village
County: Nassau
Population: 8,189†

Ancestry‡	Population	%
African, Sub-Saharan (21)	21	0.26
Nigerian (13)	13	0.16
South African (8)	8	0.10
American (193)	193	2.36
Arab (88)	242	2.96
Lebanese (15)	63	0.77
Moroccan (29)	58	0.71
Palestinian (29)	58	0.71
Other Arab (15)	63	0.77
Armenian (0)	10	0.12
Austrian (11)	102	1.25
Czech (0)	32	0.39
Czechoslovakian (18)	68	0.83
Danish (18)	18	0.22
Dutch (0)	11	0.13
Eastern European (9)	9	0.11
English (79)	577	7.06
European (28)	28	0.34
Finnish (0)	33	0.40
French, ex. Basque (0)	108	1.32
French Canadian (0)	33	0.40
German (240)	1,511	18.50
Greek (153)	332	4.06
Hungarian (38)	38	0.47
Iranian (0)	42	0.51
Irish (451)	1,897	23.22
Italian (1,503)	2,750	33.66

*Notes: † The Census 2010 population figure is used to calculate the percentages in the Hispanic Origin and Race categories. Ancestry percentages are based on the 2006-2010 American Community Survey population (not shown); ‡ Numbers in parentheses indicate the number of people reporting a single ancestry; * Numbers in parentheses indicate the number of persons reporting this race alone, not in combination with any other race; Please refer to the Explanation of Data for more information.*

Ancestry	Population	%
Norwegian (9)	40	0.49
Polish (126)	456	5.58
Portuguese (0)	11	0.13
Romanian (0)	10	0.12
Russian (92)	275	3.37
Scotch-Irish (28)	98	1.20
Scottish (37)	97	1.19
Slovak (0)	22	0.27
Slovene (0)	19	0.23
Swedish (32)	152	1.86
Ukrainian (0)	32	0.39
Welsh (14)	14	0.17
West Indian, ex. Hispanic (11)	11	0.13
Haitian (11)	11	0.13
Yugoslavian (21)	21	0.26

Hispanic Origin	Population	%
Hispanic or Latino (of any race)	1,122	13.70
Central American, ex. Mexican	427	5.21
Costa Rican	2	0.02
Guatemalan	20	0.24
Honduran	161	1.97
Nicaraguan	5	0.06
Panamanian	3	0.04
Salvadoran	236	2.88
Cuban	22	0.27
Dominican Republic	32	0.39
Mexican	124	1.51
Puerto Rican	203	2.48
South American	216	2.64
Argentinean	10	0.12
Bolivian	11	0.13
Chilean	16	0.20
Colombian	75	0.92
Ecuadorian	60	0.73
Paraguayan	2	0.02
Peruvian	25	0.31
Uruguayan	16	0.20
Venezuelan	1	0.01
Other Hispanic or Latino	98	1.20

Race*	Population	%
African-American/Black (210)	258	3.15
Not Hispanic (199)	238	2.91
Hispanic (11)	20	0.24
American Indian/Alaska Native (30)	50	0.61
Not Hispanic (6)	19	0.23
Hispanic (24)	31	0.38
Cherokee (0)	4	0.05
Choctaw (0)	1	0.01
Creek (1)	1	0.01
Iroquois (1)	5	0.06
South American Ind. (5)	8	0.10
Spanish American Ind. (14)	14	0.17
Asian (448)	489	5.97
Not Hispanic (445)	485	5.92
Hispanic (3)	4	0.05
Bangladeshi (3)	3	0.04
Burmese (1)	1	0.01
Chinese, ex. Taiwanese (102)	109	1.33
Filipino (70)	75	0.92
Indian (166)	178	2.17
Indonesian (8)	8	0.10
Japanese (7)	15	0.18
Korean (29)	41	0.50
Pakistani (19)	19	0.23
Sri Lankan (15)	15	0.18
Taiwanese (5)	6	0.07
Vietnamese (4)	5	0.06
Hawaii Native/Pacific Islander (1)	3	0.04
Not Hispanic (0)	1	0.01
Hispanic (1)	2	0.02
Guamanian/Chamorro (1)	1	0.01
White (6,975)	7,090	86.58
Not Hispanic (6,315)	6,374	77.84
Hispanic (660)	716	8.74

Farmington

Place Type: Town
County: Ontario
Population: 11,825†

Ancestry‡	Population	%
Albanian (388)	388	3.35
American (594)	594	5.13
Arab (0)	12	0.10
Lebanese (0)	12	0.10
Austrian (0)	24	0.21
Belgian (0)	35	0.30
British (51)	89	0.77
Canadian (36)	117	1.01
Czech (0)	12	0.10
Danish (19)	160	1.38
Dutch (103)	709	6.12
English (660)	2,296	19.82
European (50)	50	0.43
Finnish (26)	44	0.38
French, ex. Basque (43)	522	4.51
French Canadian (47)	282	2.43
German (838)	3,475	30.00
Guyanese (90)	90	0.78
Hungarian (76)	88	0.76
Irish (485)	2,332	20.13
Italian (498)	1,317	11.37
Lithuanian (43)	57	0.49
Macedonian (10)	35	0.30
Norwegian (16)	66	0.57
Pennsylvania German (9)	9	0.08
Polish (196)	536	4.63
Portuguese (0)	17	0.15
Romanian (56)	100	0.86
Russian (0)	17	0.15
Scandinavian (29)	29	0.25
Scotch-Irish (96)	211	1.82
Scottish (102)	318	2.75
Serbian (0)	11	0.09
Slovak (0)	22	0.19
Swedish (38)	81	0.70
Swiss (0)	24	0.21
Ukrainian (23)	89	0.77
Welsh (11)	165	1.42
West Indian, ex. Hispanic (258)	302	2.61
British West Indian (0)	27	0.23
Jamaican (224)	224	1.93
Trinidadian/Tobagonian (0)	17	0.15
West Indian (34)	34	0.29
Yugoslavian (17)	61	0.53

Hispanic Origin	Population	%
Hispanic or Latino (of any race)	363	3.07
Central American, ex. Mexican	26	0.22
Costa Rican	5	0.04
Guatemalan	8	0.07
Honduran	1	0.01
Panamanian	9	0.08
Salvadoran	3	0.03
Cuban	24	0.20
Dominican Republic	14	0.12
Mexican	62	0.52
Puerto Rican	194	1.64
South American	18	0.15
Argentinean	5	0.04
Chilean	1	0.01
Colombian	3	0.03
Ecuadorian	3	0.03
Peruvian	5	0.04
Venezuelan	1	0.01
Other Hispanic or Latino	25	0.21

Race*	Population	%
African-American/Black (184)	264	2.23
Not Hispanic (179)	249	2.11
Hispanic (5)	15	0.13
American Indian/Alaska Native (31)	74	0.63
Not Hispanic (28)	68	0.58
Hispanic (3)	6	0.05
Cherokee (5)	16	0.14
Chippewa (2)	2	0.02
Choctaw (1)	4	0.03
Iroquois (12)	18	0.15
Kiowa (1)	1	0.01
Mexican American Ind. (1)	1	0.01
Seminole (0)	1	0.01
Ute (0)	2	0.02
Asian (152)	203	1.72
Not Hispanic (147)	198	1.67
Hispanic (5)	5	0.04
Cambodian (6)	6	0.05
Chinese, ex. Taiwanese (30)	44	0.37
Filipino (21)	37	0.31
Indian (33)	39	0.33
Indonesian (0)	1	0.01
Japanese (3)	5	0.04
Korean (13)	14	0.12
Laotian (14)	18	0.15
Nepalese (2)	2	0.02
Thai (5)	9	0.08
Vietnamese (17)	21	0.18
Hawaii Native/Pacific Islander (4)	8	0.07
Not Hispanic (3)	7	0.06
Hispanic (1)	1	0.01
Guamanian/Chamorro (1)	4	0.03
Native Hawaiian (2)	2	0.02
White (11,198)	11,369	96.14
Not Hispanic (10,954)	11,095	93.83
Hispanic (244)	274	2.32

Farmingville

Place Type: CDP
County: Suffolk
Population: 15,481†

Ancestry‡	Population	%
American (83)	83	0.52
Arab (51)	51	0.32
Egyptian (51)	51	0.32
Austrian (0)	113	0.71
Belgian (0)	40	0.25
British (35)	35	0.22
Czech (0)	115	0.72
Czechoslovakian (15)	66	0.41
Dutch (0)	56	0.35
Eastern European (0)	39	0.24
English (36)	511	3.19
European (8)	8	0.05
Finnish (0)	9	0.06
French, ex. Basque (13)	190	1.19
French Canadian (14)	60	0.37
German (637)	2,963	18.50
Greek (91)	161	1.01
Hungarian (19)	91	0.57
Icelander (0)	13	0.08
Irish (813)	3,752	23.43
Italian (2,975)	6,818	42.57
Latvian (12)	12	0.07
Lithuanian (0)	8	0.05
Maltese (11)	40	0.25
Norwegian (97)	271	1.69
Polish (155)	1,172	7.32
Portuguese (1,049)	1,109	6.92
Russian (99)	318	1.99
Scotch-Irish (63)	78	0.49
Scottish (23)	162	1.01
Slovak (8)	58	0.36
Swedish (14)	78	0.49
Swiss (11)	97	0.61
Turkish (92)	111	0.69
Ukrainian (59)	209	1.30
West Indian, ex. Hispanic (87)	87	0.54
Trinidadian/Tobagonian (87)	87	0.54
Yugoslavian (0)	14	0.09

Hispanic Origin	Population	%
Hispanic or Latino (of any race)	1,942	12.54
Central American, ex. Mexican	193	1.25

*Notes: † The Census 2010 population figure is used to calculate the percentages in the Hispanic Origin and Race categories. Ancestry percentages are based on the 2006-2010 American Community Survey population (not shown); ‡ Numbers in parentheses indicate the number of people reporting a single ancestry; * Numbers in parentheses indicate the number of persons reporting this race alone, not in combination with any other race; Please refer to the Explanation of Data for more information.*

Hispanic Origin	Population	%
Costa Rican	13	0.08
Guatemalan	37	0.24
Honduran	36	0.23
Panamanian	8	0.05
Salvadoran	99	0.64
Cuban	46	0.30
Dominican Republic	84	0.54
Mexican	425	2.75
Puerto Rican	728	4.70
South American	305	1.97
Argentinean	19	0.12
Chilean	7	0.05
Colombian	95	0.61
Ecuadorian	125	0.81
Paraguayan	4	0.03
Peruvian	40	0.26
Uruguayan	2	0.01
Venezuelan	13	0.08
Other Hispanic or Latino	161	1.04

Race*	Population	%
African-American/Black (370)	481	3.11
Not Hispanic (339)	431	2.78
Hispanic (31)	50	0.32
American Indian/Alaska Native (43)	124	0.80
Not Hispanic (22)	79	0.51
Hispanic (21)	45	0.29
Blackfeet (1)	2	0.01
Cherokee (4)	30	0.19
Iroquois (1)	3	0.02
Mexican American Ind. (3)	3	0.02
Sioux (0)	5	0.03
South American Ind. (4)	10	0.06
Asian (578)	675	4.36
Not Hispanic (571)	652	4.21
Hispanic (7)	23	0.15
Bangladeshi (34)	43	0.28
Burmese (3)	3	0.02
Chinese, ex. Taiwanese (80)	95	0.61
Filipino (47)	61	0.39
Indian (149)	178	1.15
Japanese (6)	9	0.06
Korean (34)	40	0.26
Laotian (2)	2	0.01
Pakistani (149)	158	1.02
Thai (4)	5	0.03
Vietnamese (32)	35	0.23
Hawaii Native/Pacific Islander (6)	9	0.06
Not Hispanic (5)	8	0.05
Hispanic (1)	1	0.01
Native Hawaiian (3)	3	0.02
White (13,656)	13,918	89.90
Not Hispanic (12,364)	12,526	80.91
Hispanic (1,292)	1,392	8.99

Fishkill

Place Type: Town
County: Dutchess
Population: 22,107†

Ancestry‡	Population	%
African, Sub-Saharan (109)	109	0.50
African (21)	21	0.10
Ghanaian (70)	70	0.32
Nigerian (18)	18	0.08
Albanian (133)	133	0.61
American (255)	255	1.17
Arab (124)	212	0.98
Arab (43)	101	0.47
Lebanese (81)	111	0.51
Armenian (13)	40	0.18
Austrian (22)	70	0.32
Brazilian (52)	69	0.32
British (38)	93	0.43
Canadian (9)	31	0.14
Croatian (0)	73	0.34
Czech (0)	14	0.06
Czechoslovakian (0)	94	0.43
Danish (11)	41	0.19
Dutch (48)	224	1.03
Eastern European (13)	13	0.06
English (241)	1,461	6.73
European (218)	221	1.02
Finnish (38)	93	0.43
French, ex. Basque (117)	347	1.60
French Canadian (30)	91	0.42
German (581)	3,622	16.68
Greek (80)	234	1.08
Guyanese (16)	16	0.07
Hungarian (63)	175	0.81
Iranian (5)	5	0.02
Irish (1,545)	4,917	22.64
Italian (2,776)	6,104	28.11
Latvian (78)	95	0.44
Lithuanian (8)	46	0.21
Northern European (0)	14	0.06
Norwegian (35)	88	0.41
Pennsylvania German (0)	40	0.18
Polish (298)	1,014	4.67
Portuguese (29)	169	0.78
Romanian (0)	35	0.16
Russian (130)	322	1.48
Scandinavian (0)	13	0.06
Scotch-Irish (235)	483	2.22
Scottish (96)	353	1.63
Slavic (18)	18	0.08
Slovak (0)	37	0.17
Slovene (17)	17	0.08
Swedish (49)	185	0.85
Swiss (12)	40	0.18
Turkish (6)	6	0.03
Ukrainian (26)	84	0.39
Welsh (0)	24	0.11
West Indian, ex. Hispanic (512)	636	2.93
British West Indian (9)	9	0.04
Haitian (14)	20	0.09
Jamaican (419)	427	1.97
Trinidadian/Tobagonian (25)	34	0.16
U.S. Virgin Islander (0)	6	0.03
West Indian (45)	140	0.64
Yugoslavian (16)	33	0.15

Hispanic Origin	Population	%
Hispanic or Latino (of any race)	2,420	10.95
Central American, ex. Mexican	124	0.56
Costa Rican	24	0.11
Guatemalan	36	0.16
Honduran	17	0.08
Nicaraguan	2	0.01
Panamanian	14	0.06
Salvadoran	31	0.14
Cuban	102	0.46
Dominican Republic	192	0.87
Mexican	208	0.94
Puerto Rican	1,253	5.67
South American	377	1.71
Argentinean	12	0.05
Bolivian	10	0.05
Chilean	37	0.17
Colombian	109	0.49
Ecuadorian	119	0.54
Paraguayan	1	<0.01
Peruvian	48	0.22
Uruguayan	13	0.06
Venezuelan	26	0.12
Other South American	2	0.01
Other Hispanic or Latino	164	0.74

Race*	Population	%
African-American/Black (2,297)	2,518	11.39
Not Hispanic (2,083)	2,250	10.18
Hispanic (214)	268	1.21
American Indian/Alaska Native (52)	123	0.56
Not Hispanic (45)	98	0.44
Hispanic (7)	25	0.11
Apache (0)	3	0.01
Blackfeet (4)	5	0.02
Central American Ind. (1)	1	<0.01
Cherokee (2)	27	0.12
Creek (1)	1	<0.01
Iroquois (10)	14	0.06
Mexican American Ind. (1)	2	0.01
Navajo (3)	5	0.02
Potawatomi (0)	2	0.01
Seminole (0)	1	<0.01
Shoshone (0)	1	<0.01
Sioux (2)	3	0.01
South American Ind. (1)	3	0.01
Asian (1,700)	1,850	8.37
Not Hispanic (1,695)	1,822	8.24
Hispanic (5)	28	0.13
Bangladeshi (19)	21	0.09
Cambodian (4)	4	0.02
Chinese, ex. Taiwanese (452)	499	2.26
Filipino (116)	131	0.59
Indian (565)	601	2.72
Indonesian (9)	9	0.04
Japanese (133)	143	0.65
Korean (296)	302	1.37
Laotian (1)	3	0.01
Malaysian (2)	2	0.01
Nepalese (11)	12	0.05
Pakistani (32)	34	0.15
Sri Lankan (2)	3	0.01
Taiwanese (17)	22	0.10
Thai (10)	13	0.06
Vietnamese (13)	17	0.08
Hawaii Native/Pacific Islander (13)	37	0.17
Not Hispanic (10)	23	0.10
Hispanic (3)	14	0.06
Native Hawaiian (3)	11	0.05
White (17,022)	17,400	78.71
Not Hispanic (15,479)	15,736	71.18
Hispanic (1,543)	1,664	7.53

Floral Park

Place Type: Village
County: Nassau
Population: 15,863†

Ancestry‡	Population	%
African, Sub-Saharan (14)	14	0.09
African (14)	14	0.09
American (330)	330	2.06
Arab (0)	54	0.34
Lebanese (0)	29	0.18
Syrian (0)	25	0.16
Armenian (9)	20	0.12
Austrian (0)	89	0.56
Belgian (0)	10	0.06
British (0)	8	0.05
Canadian (0)	11	0.07
Croatian (25)	69	0.43
Czech (13)	60	0.37
Czechoslovakian (32)	60	0.37
Danish (0)	79	0.49
Dutch (12)	163	1.02
Eastern European (77)	77	0.48
English (89)	698	4.36
European (68)	75	0.47
French, ex. Basque (28)	159	0.99
French Canadian (30)	76	0.47
German (464)	3,235	20.20
Greek (17)	78	0.49
Guyanese (167)	167	1.04
Hungarian (0)	15	0.09
Iranian (12)	24	0.15
Irish (2,399)	5,928	37.02
Italian (2,429)	4,793	29.93
Lithuanian (9)	79	0.49
Norwegian (14)	155	0.97
Polish (475)	1,230	7.68
Romanian (45)	45	0.28
Russian (135)	248	1.55
Scotch-Irish (114)	260	1.62
Scottish (44)	207	1.29
Slovak (0)	3	0.02
Swedish (49)	219	1.37

*Notes: † The Census 2010 population figure is used to calculate the percentages in the Hispanic Origin and Race categories. Ancestry percentages are based on the 2006-2010 American Community Survey population (not shown); ‡ Numbers in parentheses indicate the number of people reporting a single ancestry; * Numbers in parentheses indicate the number of persons reporting this race alone, not in combination with any other race; Please refer to the Explanation of Data for more information.*

SECTION TWO

Ancestry	Population	%
Swiss (0)	21	0.13
Turkish (15)	15	0.09
Ukrainian (64)	125	0.78
West Indian, ex. Hispanic (327)	327	2.04
Belizean (25)	25	0.16
British West Indian (20)	20	0.12
Haitian (15)	15	0.09
Jamaican (267)	267	1.67
Yugoslavian (10)	10	0.06

Hispanic Origin	Population	%
Hispanic or Latino (of any race)	1,391	8.77
Central American, ex. Mexican	149	0.94
Costa Rican	7	0.04
Guatemalan	40	0.25
Honduran	48	0.30
Nicaraguan	5	0.03
Panamanian	7	0.04
Salvadoran	42	0.26
Cuban	77	0.49
Dominican Republic	144	0.91
Mexican	43	0.27
Puerto Rican	356	2.24
South American	479	3.02
Argentinean	39	0.25
Bolivian	8	0.05
Chilean	28	0.18
Colombian	186	1.17
Ecuadorian	98	0.62
Paraguayan	6	0.04
Peruvian	86	0.54
Uruguayan	6	0.04
Venezuelan	22	0.14
Other Hispanic or Latino	143	0.90

Race*	Population	%
African-American/Black (214)	285	1.80
Not Hispanic (198)	246	1.55
Hispanic (16)	39	0.25
American Indian/Alaska Native (13)	60	0.38
Not Hispanic (10)	45	0.28
Hispanic (3)	15	0.09
Cherokee (0)	9	0.06
Mexican American Ind. (0)	2	0.01
South American Ind. (0)	2	0.01
Spanish American Ind. (3)	3	0.02
Tlingit-Haida *(Alaska Native)* (1)	1	0.01
Asian (1,096)	1,240	7.82
Not Hispanic (1,086)	1,197	7.55
Hispanic (10)	43	0.27
Bangladeshi (20)	20	0.13
Burmese (5)	6	0.04
Chinese, ex. Taiwanese (181)	219	1.38
Filipino (121)	145	0.91
Indian (545)	618	3.90
Indonesian (1)	1	0.01
Japanese (8)	13	0.08
Korean (78)	86	0.54
Nepalese (2)	2	0.01
Pakistani (71)	86	0.54
Sri Lankan (8)	8	0.05
Taiwanese (13)	16	0.10
Thai (2)	2	0.01
Vietnamese (2)	4	0.03
Hawaii Native/Pacific Islander (3)	8	0.05
Not Hispanic (3)	7	0.04
Hispanic (0)	1	0.01
Guamanian/Chamorro (0)	1	0.01
Samoan (3)	3	0.02
White (13,806)	14,056	88.61
Not Hispanic (12,938)	13,076	82.43
Hispanic (868)	980	6.18

Fort Drum

Place Type: CDP
County: Jefferson
Population: 12,955†

Ancestry‡	Population	%
African, Sub-Saharan (69)	95	0.78
African (54)	79	0.65
Ghanaian (15)	15	0.12
South African (0)	1	0.01
American (432)	432	3.53
Arab (125)	125	1.02
Egyptian (76)	76	0.62
Lebanese (2)	2	0.02
Moroccan (47)	47	0.38
Armenian (6)	6	0.05
Australian (25)	25	0.20
Belgian (41)	185	1.51
British (5)	45	0.37
Czech (17)	111	0.91
Czechoslovakian (77)	77	0.63
Dutch (4)	53	0.43
English (181)	841	6.88
European (13)	14	0.11
French, ex. Basque (119)	460	3.76
French Canadian (121)	303	2.48
German (761)	2,788	22.81
German Russian (17)	17	0.14
Greek (28)	75	0.61
Irish (826)	2,327	19.04
Italian (358)	952	7.79
Norwegian (0)	1	0.01
Polish (102)	187	1.53
Portuguese (0)	11	0.09
Romanian (56)	56	0.46
Russian (76)	76	0.62
Scotch-Irish (22)	223	1.82
Scottish (212)	327	2.68
Swedish (63)	176	1.44
Turkish (31)	31	0.25
Ukrainian (29)	29	0.24
Welsh (0)	93	0.76
West Indian, ex. Hispanic (130)	204	1.67
Belizean (1)	1	0.01
British West Indian (2)	2	0.02
Haitian (46)	46	0.38
Jamaican (66)	97	0.79
Trinidadian/Tobagonian (15)	51	0.42
West Indian (0)	7	0.06

Hispanic Origin	Population	%
Hispanic or Latino (of any race)	2,012	15.53
Central American, ex. Mexican	125	0.96
Costa Rican	5	0.04
Guatemalan	14	0.11
Honduran	16	0.12
Nicaraguan	22	0.17
Panamanian	44	0.34
Salvadoran	24	0.19
Cuban	58	0.45
Dominican Republic	68	0.52
Mexican	820	6.33
Puerto Rican	692	5.34
South American	69	0.53
Argentinean	5	0.04
Bolivian	2	0.02
Chilean	5	0.04
Colombian	23	0.18
Ecuadorian	14	0.11
Peruvian	16	0.12
Venezuelan	3	0.02
Other South American	1	0.01
Other Hispanic or Latino	180	1.39

Race*	Population	%
African-American/Black (1,682)	2,017	15.57
Not Hispanic (1,549)	1,789	13.81
Hispanic (133)	228	1.76
American Indian/Alaska Native (130)	315	2.43
Not Hispanic (105)	240	1.85
Hispanic (25)	75	0.58
Alaska Athabascan *(Ala. Nat.)* (0)	1	0.01
Aleut *(Alaska Native)* (2)	2	0.02
Apache (4)	12	0.09
Blackfeet (6)	15	0.12
Cherokee (16)	84	0.65
Chickasaw (2)	2	0.02
Chippewa (1)	6	0.05
Choctaw (6)	14	0.11
Crow (0)	1	0.01
Inupiat *(Alaska Native)* (3)	4	0.03
Iroquois (13)	17	0.13
Lumbee (2)	2	0.02
Menominee (1)	1	0.01
Mexican American Ind. (2)	10	0.08
Navajo (11)	23	0.18
Potawatomi (5)	5	0.04
Pueblo (6)	10	0.08
Sioux (5)	6	0.05
South American Ind. (1)	6	0.05
Spanish American Ind. (1)	1	0.01
Tlingit-Haida *(Alaska Native)* (0)	2	0.02
Yup'ik *(Alaska Native)* (3)	3	0.02
Asian (348)	529	4.08
Not Hispanic (322)	471	3.64
Hispanic (26)	58	0.45
Cambodian (4)	9	0.07
Chinese, ex. Taiwanese (22)	40	0.31
Filipino (151)	235	1.81
Hmong (1)	1	0.01
Indian (12)	24	0.19
Indonesian (1)	1	0.01
Japanese (27)	58	0.45
Korean (90)	129	1.00
Laotian (3)	6	0.05
Pakistani (1)	1	0.01
Thai (6)	21	0.16
Vietnamese (13)	26	0.20
Hawaii Native/Pacific Islander (161)	226	1.74
Not Hispanic (147)	196	1.51
Hispanic (14)	30	0.23
Fijian (1)	1	0.01
Guamanian/Chamorro (60)	70	0.54
Marshallese (5)	5	0.04
Native Hawaiian (20)	49	0.38
Samoan (39)	49	0.38
Tongan (2)	2	0.02
White (9,378)	10,028	77.41
Not Hispanic (8,307)	8,759	67.61
Hispanic (1,071)	1,269	9.80

Fort Salonga

Place Type: CDP
County: Suffolk
Population: 10,008†

Ancestry‡	Population	%
Albanian (121)	121	1.15
American (440)	440	4.19
Arab (33)	33	0.31
Iraqi (33)	33	0.31
Armenian (9)	33	0.31
Austrian (0)	5	0.05
British (18)	18	0.17
Canadian (53)	178	1.70
Croatian (5)	87	0.83
Czech (26)	77	0.73
Danish (0)	86	0.82
Dutch (0)	60	0.57
Eastern European (14)	14	0.13
English (146)	915	8.72
Estonian (14)	14	0.13
European (141)	141	1.34
Finnish (0)	44	0.42
French, ex. Basque (0)	192	1.83
French Canadian (0)	56	0.53
German (475)	1,888	17.99
Greek (58)	217	2.07
Hungarian (44)	119	1.13
Irish (1,115)	3,105	29.59
Italian (1,328)	2,611	24.88
Lithuanian (28)	75	0.71
Norwegian (10)	122	1.16
Pennsylvania German (0)	17	0.16

*Notes: † The Census 2010 population figure is used to calculate the percentages in the Hispanic Origin and Race categories. Ancestry percentages are based on the 2006-2010 American Community Survey population (not shown); ‡ Numbers in parentheses indicate the number of people reporting a single ancestry; * Numbers in parentheses indicate the number of persons reporting this race alone, not in combination with any other race; Please refer to the Explanation of Data for more information.*

Ancestry	Population	%
Polish (178)	571	5.44
Portuguese (0)	18	0.17
Romanian (0)	32	0.30
Russian (103)	268	2.55
Scandinavian (0)	15	0.14
Scotch-Irish (142)	211	2.01
Scottish (25)	110	1.05
Slovak (54)	54	0.51
Slovene (17)	17	0.16
Swedish (26)	144	1.37
Swiss (0)	8	0.08
Ukrainian (5)	25	0.24
Welsh (18)	40	0.38
West Indian, ex. Hispanic (13)	13	0.12
Jamaican (13)	13	0.12
Yugoslavian (37)	61	0.58

Hispanic Origin	Population	%
Hispanic or Latino (of any race)	388	3.88
Central American, ex. Mexican	27	0.27
Guatemalan	5	0.05
Honduran	12	0.12
Nicaraguan	4	0.04
Panamanian	2	0.02
Salvadoran	3	0.03
Other Central American	1	0.01
Cuban	32	0.32
Dominican Republic	23	0.23
Mexican	35	0.35
Puerto Rican	130	1.30
South American	88	0.88
Argentinean	16	0.16
Bolivian	1	0.01
Chilean	10	0.10
Colombian	30	0.30
Ecuadorian	19	0.19
Peruvian	11	0.11
Venezuelan	1	0.01
Other Hispanic or Latino	53	0.53

Race*	Population	%
African-American/Black (91)	107	1.07
Not Hispanic (84)	96	0.96
Hispanic (7)	11	0.11
American Indian/Alaska Native (13)	30	0.30
Not Hispanic (11)	28	0.28
Hispanic (2)	2	0.02
Apache (1)	1	0.01
Central American Ind. (1)	1	0.01
Cherokee (1)	10	0.10
Cheyenne (0)	1	0.01
Crow (0)	3	0.03
Iroquois (0)	2	0.02
South American Ind. (1)	1	0.01
Asian (216)	263	2.63
Not Hispanic (216)	261	2.61
Hispanic (0)	2	0.02
Chinese, ex. Taiwanese (62)	80	0.80
Filipino (22)	25	0.25
Indian (47)	57	0.57
Japanese (11)	18	0.18
Korean (30)	37	0.37
Pakistani (21)	21	0.21
Taiwanese (8)	8	0.08
Thai (2)	2	0.02
Vietnamese (5)	6	0.06
Hawaii Native/Pacific Islander (6)	6	0.06
Not Hispanic (6)	6	0.06
Samoan (6)	6	0.06
White (9,528)	9,608	96.00
Not Hispanic (9,214)	9,284	92.77
Hispanic (314)	324	3.24

Frankfort

Place Type: Town
County: Herkimer
Population: 7,636†

Ancestry‡	Population	%
American (225)	225	2.97
Arab (19)	34	0.45
Lebanese (19)	34	0.45
Armenian (0)	7	0.09
Australian (0)	17	0.22
Austrian (0)	78	1.03
Czech (0)	17	0.22
Czechoslovakian (0)	33	0.44
Danish (0)	8	0.11
Dutch (24)	132	1.74
English (368)	845	11.16
French, ex. Basque (68)	542	7.16
French Canadian (15)	128	1.69
German (418)	1,163	15.36
Hungarian (26)	56	0.74
Irish (341)	1,287	16.99
Israeli (0)	7	0.09
Italian (1,865)	2,823	37.28
Pennsylvania German (16)	16	0.21
Polish (197)	587	7.75
Russian (5)	42	0.55
Scotch-Irish (0)	57	0.75
Scottish (0)	81	1.07
Swedish (0)	28	0.37
Swiss (22)	26	0.34
Ukrainian (17)	52	0.69
Welsh (44)	271	3.58
West Indian, ex. Hispanic (0)	18	0.24
Jamaican (0)	18	0.24
Yugoslavian (42)	42	0.55

Hispanic Origin	Population	%
Hispanic or Latino (of any race)	100	1.31
Central American, ex. Mexican	5	0.07
Guatemalan	3	0.04
Panamanian	2	0.03
Cuban	2	0.03
Mexican	17	0.22
Puerto Rican	53	0.69
South American	10	0.13
Ecuadorian	8	0.10
Peruvian	2	0.03
Other Hispanic or Latino	13	0.17

Race*	Population	%
African-American/Black (52)	102	1.34
Not Hispanic (50)	100	1.31
Hispanic (2)	2	0.03
American Indian/Alaska Native (9)	21	0.28
Not Hispanic (6)	16	0.21
Hispanic (3)	5	0.07
Canadian/French Am. Ind. (0)	1	0.01
Cherokee (0)	3	0.04
Chippewa (0)	1	0.01
Delaware (1)	1	0.01
Iroquois (0)	3	0.04
Mexican American Ind. (1)	1	0.01
Navajo (1)	1	0.01
Spanish American Ind. (0)	1	0.01
Asian (34)	57	0.75
Not Hispanic (32)	52	0.68
Hispanic (2)	5	0.07
Chinese, ex. Taiwanese (2)	4	0.05
Filipino (13)	26	0.34
Indian (6)	8	0.10
Japanese (5)	12	0.16
Korean (2)	3	0.04
Pakistani (1)	1	0.01
Vietnamese (0)	1	0.01
Hawaii Native/Pacific Islander (0)	1	0.01
Not Hispanic (0)	1	0.01
White (7,418)	7,518	98.45
Not Hispanic (7,364)	7,442	97.46
Hispanic (54)	76	1.00

Franklin Square

Place Type: CDP
County: Nassau
Population: 29,320†

Ancestry‡	Population	%
Afghan (97)	97	0.33
African, Sub-Saharan (78)	78	0.26
African (65)	65	0.22
Nigerian (13)	13	0.04
Albanian (46)	205	0.69
American (521)	521	1.76
Arab (115)	130	0.44
Egyptian (20)	20	0.07
Moroccan (30)	45	0.15
Other Arab (65)	65	0.22
Australian (0)	22	0.07
Austrian (48)	250	0.84
Belgian (21)	89	0.30
Brazilian (31)	31	0.10
British (8)	56	0.19
Croatian (69)	88	0.30
Cypriot (19)	67	0.23
Czech (10)	67	0.23
Czechoslovakian (0)	43	0.14
Danish (0)	15	0.05
Dutch (9)	101	0.34
Eastern European (17)	45	0.15
English (65)	453	1.53
European (22)	22	0.07
Finnish (0)	10	0.03
French, ex. Basque (31)	221	0.74
French Canadian (17)	77	0.26
German (886)	3,164	10.66
Greek (568)	788	2.66
Guyanese (214)	234	0.79
Hungarian (66)	268	0.90
Iranian (0)	45	0.15
Irish (1,285)	4,711	15.87
Israeli (22)	42	0.14
Italian (9,351)	13,514	45.54
Lithuanian (0)	77	0.26
Macedonian (0)	10	0.03
Maltese (25)	110	0.37
Norwegian (39)	162	0.55
Pennsylvania German (11)	11	0.04
Polish (335)	1,278	4.31
Portuguese (95)	137	0.46
Romanian (20)	70	0.24
Russian (282)	627	2.11
Scotch-Irish (122)	184	0.62
Scottish (52)	183	0.62
Slovak (0)	12	0.04
Slovene (0)	28	0.09
Swedish (32)	156	0.53
Swiss (0)	12	0.04
Turkish (124)	124	0.42
Ukrainian (47)	118	0.40
Welsh (0)	52	0.18
West Indian, ex. Hispanic (297)	433	1.46
Barbadian (0)	34	0.11
Haitian (0)	11	0.04
Jamaican (158)	192	0.65
West Indian (139)	196	0.66

Hispanic Origin	Population	%
Hispanic or Latino (of any race)	3,885	13.25
Central American, ex. Mexican	517	1.76
Costa Rican	15	0.05
Guatemalan	118	0.40
Honduran	54	0.18
Nicaraguan	8	0.03
Panamanian	16	0.05
Salvadoran	299	1.02
Other Central American	7	0.02
Cuban	166	0.57
Dominican Republic	370	1.26
Mexican	162	0.55
Puerto Rican	879	3.00

SECTION TWO

*Notes: † The Census 2010 population figure is used to calculate the percentages in the Hispanic Origin and Race categories. Ancestry percentages are based on the 2006-2010 American Community Survey population (not shown); ‡ Numbers in parentheses indicate the number of people reporting a single ancestry; * Numbers in parentheses indicate the number of persons reporting this race alone, not in combination with any other race; Please refer to the Explanation of Data for more information.*

South American	1,366	4.66
Argentinean	101	0.34
Bolivian	22	0.08
Chilean	40	0.14
Colombian	469	1.60
Ecuadorian	395	1.35
Paraguayan	19	0.06
Peruvian	256	0.87
Uruguayan	32	0.11
Venezuelan	21	0.07
Other South American	11	0.04
Other Hispanic or Latino	425	1.45

Race*	Population	%
African-American/Black (934)	1,046	3.57
Not Hispanic (845)	909	3.10
Hispanic (89)	137	0.47
American Indian/Alaska Native (80)	154	0.53
Not Hispanic (45)	75	0.26
Hispanic (35)	79	0.27
Central American Ind. (4)	10	0.03
Cherokee (2)	6	0.02
Choctaw (4)	4	0.01
Iroquois (8)	8	0.03
Lumbee (1)	3	0.01
Pueblo (2)	2	0.01
Seminole (0)	2	0.01
South American Ind. (14)	32	0.11
Spanish American Ind. (3)	3	0.01
Asian (2,113)	2,330	7.95
Not Hispanic (2,100)	2,295	7.83
Hispanic (13)	35	0.12
Bangladeshi (8)	10	0.03
Cambodian (3)	7	0.02
Chinese, ex. Taiwanese (326)	369	1.26
Filipino (262)	298	1.02
Indian (922)	989	3.37
Indonesian (1)	2	0.01
Japanese (23)	35	0.12
Korean (127)	140	0.48
Malaysian (1)	7	0.02
Pakistani (322)	341	1.16
Sri Lankan (6)	6	0.02
Taiwanese (14)	21	0.07
Thai (6)	6	0.02
Vietnamese (39)	39	0.13
Hawaii Native/Pacific Islander (4)	20	0.07
Not Hispanic (3)	18	0.06
Hispanic (1)	2	0.01
Guamanian/Chamorro (1)	1	<0.01
Native Hawaiian (3)	8	0.03
White (24,424)	24,878	84.85
Not Hispanic (22,012)	22,214	75.76
Hispanic (2,412)	2,664	9.09

Fredonia

Place Type: Village
County: Chautauqua
Population: 11,230†

Ancestry‡	Population	%
African, Sub-Saharan (0)	20	0.18
African (0)	20	0.18
American (204)	204	1.83
Arab (38)	63	0.57
Egyptian (11)	36	0.32
Lebanese (27)	27	0.24
Austrian (0)	84	0.76
British (0)	27	0.24
Bulgarian (13)	13	0.12
Canadian (0)	17	0.15
Croatian (23)	23	0.21
Czech (0)	33	0.30
Czechoslovakian (15)	77	0.69
Danish (0)	45	0.40
Dutch (8)	288	2.59
English (459)	1,506	13.54
European (26)	45	0.40
French, ex. Basque (14)	302	2.71
French Canadian (21)	82	0.74
German (823)	3,281	29.49
Greek (16)	49	0.44
Hungarian (24)	55	0.49
Irish (334)	1,943	17.47
Italian (1,398)	2,987	26.85
Latvian (0)	12	0.11
Norwegian (0)	98	0.88
Polish (816)	2,212	19.88
Romanian (0)	48	0.43
Russian (27)	235	2.11
Scandinavian (0)	27	0.24
Scotch-Irish (64)	188	1.69
Scottish (24)	208	1.87
Slavic (10)	10	0.09
Slovak (0)	28	0.25
Swedish (128)	206	1.85
Swiss (0)	88	0.79
Ukrainian (52)	62	0.56
Welsh (0)	114	1.02
West Indian, ex. Hispanic (37)	37	0.33
Haitian (14)	14	0.13
Trinidadian/Tobagonian (23)	23	0.21

Hispanic Origin	Population	%
Hispanic or Latino (of any race)	439	3.91
Central American, ex. Mexican	10	0.09
Costa Rican	2	0.02
Guatemalan	2	0.02
Honduran	4	0.04
Salvadoran	2	0.02
Cuban	9	0.08
Dominican Republic	12	0.11
Mexican	76	0.68
Puerto Rican	262	2.33
South American	40	0.36
Argentinean	2	0.02
Chilean	2	0.02
Colombian	10	0.09
Ecuadorian	16	0.14
Peruvian	7	0.06
Venezuelan	3	0.03
Other Hispanic or Latino	30	0.27

Race*	Population	%
African-American/Black (202)	269	2.40
Not Hispanic (177)	233	2.07
Hispanic (25)	36	0.32
American Indian/Alaska Native (30)	61	0.54
Not Hispanic (27)	52	0.46
Hispanic (3)	9	0.08
Blackfeet (0)	2	0.02
Central American Ind. (1)	1	0.01
Cherokee (1)	6	0.05
Iroquois (16)	27	0.24
Sioux (1)	1	0.01
South American Ind. (1)	4	0.04
Asian (181)	221	1.97
Not Hispanic (181)	218	1.94
Hispanic (0)	3	0.03
Bangladeshi (1)	1	0.01
Chinese, ex. Taiwanese (55)	63	0.56
Filipino (15)	22	0.20
Indian (14)	20	0.18
Japanese (11)	14	0.12
Korean (43)	55	0.49
Pakistani (27)	28	0.25
Taiwanese (2)	3	0.03
Thai (5)	7	0.06
Vietnamese (5)	6	0.05
Hawaii Native/Pacific Islander (4)	7	0.06
Not Hispanic (4)	7	0.06
Samoan (2)	3	0.03
White (10,536)	10,663	94.95
Not Hispanic (10,279)	10,384	92.47
Hispanic (257)	279	2.48

Freeport

Place Type: Village
County: Nassau
Population: 42,860†

Ancestry‡	Population	%
African, Sub-Saharan (545)	654	1.53
African (414)	519	1.22
Ghanaian (58)	58	0.14
South African (0)	4	0.01
Other Sub-Saharan African (73)	73	0.17
American (801)	801	1.88
Arab (9)	150	0.35
Arab (9)	18	0.04
Lebanese (0)	101	0.24
Moroccan (0)	10	0.02
Syrian (0)	21	0.05
Armenian (0)	14	0.03
Australian (0)	20	0.05
Austrian (0)	39	0.09
Brazilian (6)	13	0.03
British (0)	12	0.03
Czech (45)	62	0.15
Czechoslovakian (0)	50	0.12
Danish (0)	14	0.03
Dutch (43)	118	0.28
Eastern European (35)	35	0.08
English (109)	1,010	2.37
European (121)	121	0.28
Finnish (24)	24	0.06
French, ex. Basque (56)	510	1.19
French Canadian (8)	46	0.11
German (476)	2,821	6.61
Greek (229)	283	0.66
Guyanese (324)	324	0.76
Hungarian (21)	76	0.18
Icelander (0)	18	0.04
Iranian (8)	8	0.02
Irish (918)	3,098	7.25
Israeli (44)	56	0.13
Italian (2,131)	3,576	8.37
Latvian (41)	41	0.10
Lithuanian (0)	10	0.02
Maltese (13)	13	0.03
Northern European (0)	19	0.04
Norwegian (85)	196	0.46
Pennsylvania German (24)	24	0.06
Polish (168)	552	1.29
Portuguese (24)	69	0.16
Romanian (17)	37	0.09
Russian (264)	567	1.33
Scandinavian (21)	21	0.05
Scotch-Irish (28)	137	0.32
Scottish (16)	141	0.33
Slovak (0)	9	0.02
Swedish (21)	123	0.29
Swiss (0)	22	0.05
Ukrainian (71)	92	0.22
Welsh (9)	26	0.06
West Indian, ex. Hispanic (3,548)	3,970	9.30
Barbadian (437)	447	1.05
Belizean (0)	14	0.03
British West Indian (72)	90	0.21
Haitian (789)	818	1.92
Jamaican (1,647)	1,840	4.31
Trinidadian/Tobagonian (220)	333	0.78
West Indian (366)	411	0.96
Other West Indian (17)	17	0.04
Yugoslavian (0)	10	0.02

Hispanic Origin	Population	%
Hispanic or Latino (of any race)	17,858	41.67
Central American, ex. Mexican	6,668	15.56
Costa Rican	108	0.25
Guatemalan	1,070	2.50
Honduran	785	1.83
Nicaraguan	93	0.22
Panamanian	149	0.35
Salvadoran	4,439	10.36

*Notes: † The Census 2010 population figure is used to calculate the percentages in the Hispanic Origin and Race categories. Ancestry percentages are based on the 2006-2010 American Community Survey population (not shown); ‡ Numbers in parentheses indicate the number of people reporting a single ancestry; * Numbers in parentheses indicate the number of persons reporting this race alone, not in combination with any other race; Please refer to the Explanation of Data for more information.*

Other Central American	24	0.06
Cuban	379	0.88
Dominican Republic	5,539	12.92
Mexican	408	0.95
Puerto Rican	1,626	3.79
South American	1,604	3.74
Argentinean	52	0.12
Bolivian	14	0.03
Chilean	32	0.07
Colombian	692	1.61
Ecuadorian	432	1.01
Paraguayan	19	0.04
Peruvian	275	0.64
Uruguayan	13	0.03
Venezuelan	60	0.14
Other South American	15	0.03
Other Hispanic or Latino	1,634	3.81

Race*	Population	%
African-American/Black (14,259)	15,199	35.46
Not Hispanic (13,226)	13,809	32.22
Hispanic (1,033)	1,390	3.24
American Indian/Alaska Native (322)	717	1.67
Not Hispanic (94)	295	0.69
Hispanic (228)	422	0.98
Blackfeet (4)	20	0.05
Canadian/French Am. Ind. (0)	1	<0.01
Central American Ind. (5)	18	0.04
Cherokee (13)	77	0.18
Choctaw (0)	4	0.01
Comanche (0)	3	0.01
Creek (4)	5	0.01
Delaware (0)	1	<0.01
Inupiat *(Alaska Native)* (0)	3	0.01
Iroquois (2)	14	0.03
Lumbee (0)	1	<0.01
Mexican American Ind. (19)	32	0.07
Ottawa (1)	1	<0.01
Pueblo (1)	1	<0.01
Seminole (0)	2	<0.01
Sioux (2)	2	<0.01
South American Ind. (2)	11	0.03
Spanish American Ind. (16)	25	0.06
Tohono O'Odham (1)	1	<0.01
Asian (705)	963	2.25
Not Hispanic (669)	853	1.99
Hispanic (36)	110	0.26
Bangladeshi (5)	5	0.01
Chinese, ex. Taiwanese (147)	211	0.49
Filipino (109)	132	0.31
Indian (233)	340	0.79
Indonesian (0)	1	<0.01
Japanese (15)	26	0.06
Korean (61)	83	0.19
Nepalese (1)	1	<0.01
Pakistani (81)	91	0.21
Sri Lankan (3)	8	0.02
Thai (14)	14	0.03
Vietnamese (4)	11	0.03
Hawaii Native/Pacific Islander (23)	109	0.25
Not Hispanic (9)	40	0.09
Hispanic (14)	69	0.16
Guamanian/Chamorro (3)	5	0.01
Native Hawaiian (6)	10	0.02
Samoan (0)	1	<0.01
White (17,352)	18,830	43.93
Not Hispanic (10,113)	10,538	24.59
Hispanic (7,239)	8,292	19.35

Fulton

Place Type: City
County: Oswego
Population: 11,896†

Ancestry‡	Population	%
American (469)	469	3.94
Arab (22)	97	0.81
Lebanese (22)	42	0.35
Syrian (0)	55	0.46
Austrian (9)	12	0.10
British (33)	44	0.37
Canadian (11)	50	0.42
Croatian (7)	7	0.06
Czech (0)	12	0.10
Danish (10)	15	0.13
Dutch (39)	374	3.14
English (519)	1,675	14.07
European (81)	89	0.75
French, ex. Basque (237)	1,037	8.71
French Canadian (122)	224	1.88
German (562)	2,175	18.27
Greek (21)	43	0.36
Irish (820)	2,418	20.32
Israeli (39)	39	0.33
Italian (711)	1,828	15.36
Lithuanian (44)	55	0.46
Maltese (12)	12	0.10
Northern European (47)	47	0.39
Norwegian (0)	11	0.09
Polish (233)	928	7.80
Russian (53)	59	0.50
Scotch-Irish (48)	173	1.45
Scottish (67)	319	2.68
Slovene (0)	9	0.08
Swedish (28)	135	1.13
Swiss (12)	70	0.59
Ukrainian (268)	318	2.67
Welsh (0)	39	0.33
Yugoslavian (0)	42	0.35

Hispanic Origin	Population	%
Hispanic or Latino (of any race)	371	3.12
Central American, ex. Mexican	42	0.35
Costa Rican	3	0.03
Guatemalan	32	0.27
Salvadoran	7	0.06
Cuban	5	0.04
Dominican Republic	2	0.02
Mexican	129	1.08
Puerto Rican	158	1.33
South American	3	0.03
Argentinean	1	0.01
Ecuadorian	2	0.02
Other Hispanic or Latino	32	0.27

Race*	Population	%
African-American/Black (118)	198	1.66
Not Hispanic (107)	181	1.52
Hispanic (11)	17	0.14
American Indian/Alaska Native (55)	130	1.09
Not Hispanic (54)	119	1.00
Hispanic (1)	11	0.09
Apache (0)	3	0.03
Blackfeet (0)	2	0.02
Cherokee (8)	12	0.10
Cheyenne (0)	1	0.01
Chippewa (0)	2	0.02
Iroquois (21)	37	0.31
Seminole (0)	1	0.01
Sioux (0)	1	0.01
South American Ind. (0)	3	0.03
Asian (60)	79	0.66
Not Hispanic (60)	79	0.66
Bangladeshi (2)	2	0.02
Chinese, ex. Taiwanese (15)	16	0.13
Filipino (15)	19	0.16
Indian (13)	16	0.13
Japanese (2)	5	0.04
Korean (8)	10	0.08
Thai (2)	7	0.06
Vietnamese (3)	4	0.03
Hawaii Native/Pacific Islander (3)	8	0.07
Not Hispanic (3)	8	0.07
Native Hawaiian (1)	3	0.03
White (11,356)	11,548	97.07
Not Hispanic (11,127)	11,279	94.81
Hispanic (229)	269	2.26

Garden City Park

Place Type: CDP
County: Nassau
Population: 7,806†

Ancestry‡	Population	%
Albanian (62)	62	0.79
American (242)	242	3.10
Austrian (11)	45	0.58
British (0)	12	0.15
Bulgarian (37)	37	0.47
Croatian (11)	11	0.14
Czech (15)	26	0.33
Danish (0)	20	0.26
Dutch (0)	31	0.40
English (0)	91	1.17
European (99)	99	1.27
German (229)	746	9.55
German Russian (0)	26	0.33
Greek (238)	288	3.69
Hungarian (7)	31	0.40
Irish (411)	858	10.98
Italian (766)	1,261	16.14
Lithuanian (10)	35	0.45
Norwegian (0)	27	0.35
Polish (212)	445	5.70
Portuguese (93)	93	1.19
Romanian (0)	11	0.14
Russian (139)	231	2.96
Scottish (7)	126	1.61
Ukrainian (14)	70	0.90

Hispanic Origin	Population	%
Hispanic or Latino (of any race)	942	12.07
Central American, ex. Mexican	273	3.50
Costa Rican	7	0.09
Guatemalan	27	0.35
Honduran	51	0.65
Nicaraguan	1	0.01
Panamanian	1	0.01
Salvadoran	184	2.36
Other Central American	2	0.03
Cuban	19	0.24
Dominican Republic	91	1.17
Mexican	38	0.49
Puerto Rican	131	1.68
South American	283	3.63
Argentinean	14	0.18
Bolivian	2	0.03
Chilean	22	0.28
Colombian	118	1.51
Ecuadorian	64	0.82
Paraguayan	2	0.03
Peruvian	47	0.60
Uruguayan	2	0.03
Venezuelan	5	0.06
Other South American	7	0.09
Other Hispanic or Latino	107	1.37

Race*	Population	%
African-American/Black (293)	333	4.27
Not Hispanic (282)	316	4.05
Hispanic (11)	17	0.22
American Indian/Alaska Native (23)	53	0.68
Not Hispanic (20)	49	0.63
Hispanic (3)	4	0.05
Central American Ind. (0)	1	0.01
Cherokee (0)	1	0.01
Chippewa (0)	3	0.04
Choctaw (0)	3	0.04
Inupiat *(Alaska Native)* (2)	2	0.03
Iroquois (5)	5	0.06
Sioux (2)	2	0.03
South American Ind. (3)	4	0.05
Asian (2,586)	2,698	34.56
Not Hispanic (2,578)	2,670	34.20
Hispanic (8)	28	0.36
Bangladeshi (47)	55	0.70
Chinese, ex. Taiwanese (492)	530	6.79

SECTION TWO

*Notes: † The Census 2010 population figure is used to calculate the percentages in the Hispanic Origin and Race categories. Ancestry percentages are based on the 2006-2010 American Community Survey population (not shown); ‡ Numbers in parentheses indicate the number of people reporting a single ancestry; * Numbers in parentheses indicate the number of persons reporting this race alone, not in combination with any other race; Please refer to the Explanation of Data for more information.*

Filipino (155)	175	2.24
Indian (1,413)	1,487	19.05
Indonesian (0)	4	0.05
Japanese (36)	41	0.53
Korean (201)	201	2.57
Malaysian (1)	1	0.01
Pakistani (115)	124	1.59
Sri Lankan (18)	22	0.28
Taiwanese (37)	38	0.49
Thai (6)	6	0.08
Vietnamese (4)	4	0.05
Hawaii Native/Pacific Islander (0)	13	0.17
Not Hispanic (0)	8	0.10
Hispanic (0)	5	0.06
Native Hawaiian (0)	3	0.04
Samoan (0)	1	0.01
White (4,404)	4,529	58.02
Not Hispanic (3,790)	3,870	49.58
Hispanic (614)	659	8.44

Garden City

Place Type: Village
County: Nassau
Population: 22,371†

Ancestry‡	Population	%
Albanian (9)	20	0.09
American (1,075)	1,075	4.86
Arab (103)	170	0.77
Lebanese (72)	72	0.33
Syrian (31)	98	0.44
Armenian (61)	86	0.39
Austrian (77)	148	0.67
Brazilian (23)	23	0.10
Bulgarian (16)	16	0.07
Canadian (65)	173	0.78
Croatian (27)	86	0.39
Czech (25)	36	0.16
Czechoslovakian (16)	61	0.28
Danish (44)	210	0.95
Dutch (0)	172	0.78
Eastern European (8)	8	0.04
English (286)	1,653	7.47
European (224)	224	1.01
Finnish (0)	18	0.08
French, ex. Basque (43)	487	2.20
French Canadian (35)	162	0.73
German (601)	3,295	14.90
Greek (405)	596	2.69
Guyanese (17)	29	0.13
Hungarian (56)	175	0.79
Iranian (16)	16	0.07
Irish (3,100)	8,078	36.52
Italian (2,909)	6,456	29.19
Latvian (19)	67	0.30
Lithuanian (55)	182	0.82
Macedonian (26)	26	0.12
Maltese (13)	13	0.06
Northern European (56)	76	0.34
Norwegian (53)	175	0.79
Polish (237)	1,205	5.45
Portuguese (0)	11	0.05
Romanian (28)	81	0.37
Russian (154)	283	1.28
Scandinavian (12)	30	0.14
Scotch-Irish (55)	297	1.34
Scottish (104)	241	1.09
Serbian (14)	14	0.06
Slovak (11)	33	0.15
Swedish (13)	48	0.22
Swiss (0)	196	0.89
Ukrainian (20)	142	0.64
Welsh (9)	53	0.24
West Indian, ex. Hispanic (94)	112	0.51
Barbadian (0)	18	0.08
Jamaican (94)	94	0.42
Yugoslavian (0)	5	0.02

Hispanic Origin	Population	%
Hispanic or Latino (of any race)	1,003	4.48
Central American, ex. Mexican	82	0.37
Costa Rican	5	0.02
Guatemalan	14	0.06
Honduran	12	0.05
Nicaraguan	4	0.02
Panamanian	13	0.06
Salvadoran	28	0.13
Other Central American	6	0.03
Cuban	128	0.57
Dominican Republic	63	0.28
Mexican	62	0.28
Puerto Rican	236	1.05
South American	266	1.19
Argentinean	28	0.13
Bolivian	18	0.08
Chilean	13	0.06
Colombian	93	0.42
Ecuadorian	59	0.26
Paraguayan	3	0.01
Peruvian	39	0.17
Uruguayan	6	0.03
Venezuelan	5	0.02
Other South American	2	0.01
Other Hispanic or Latino	166	0.74

Race*	Population	%
African-American/Black (304)	365	1.63
Not Hispanic (294)	340	1.52
Hispanic (10)	25	0.11
American Indian/Alaska Native (17)	64	0.29
Not Hispanic (6)	50	0.22
Hispanic (11)	14	0.06
Blackfeet (0)	1	<0.01
Cherokee (0)	13	0.06
Iroquois (1)	1	<0.01
Mexican American Ind. (1)	1	<0.01
South American Ind. (1)	1	<0.01
Asian (797)	940	4.20
Not Hispanic (792)	921	4.12
Hispanic (5)	19	0.08
Bangladeshi (1)	2	0.01
Burmese (1)	4	0.02
Cambodian (3)	3	0.01
Chinese, ex. Taiwanese (311)	363	1.62
Filipino (95)	134	0.60
Indian (193)	205	0.92
Indonesian (2)	2	0.01
Japanese (27)	35	0.16
Korean (89)	104	0.46
Laotian (0)	1	<0.01
Pakistani (18)	18	0.08
Sri Lankan (6)	6	0.03
Taiwanese (18)	21	0.09
Thai (5)	9	0.04
Vietnamese (8)	17	0.08
Hawaii Native/Pacific Islander (2)	10	0.04
Not Hispanic (1)	6	0.03
Hispanic (1)	4	0.02
Guamanian/Chamorro (1)	2	0.01
Native Hawaiian (1)	3	0.01
Samoan (0)	1	<0.01
White (20,812)	21,053	94.11
Not Hispanic (20,034)	20,229	90.43
Hispanic (778)	824	3.68

Gates

Place Type: Town
County: Monroe
Population: 28,400†

Ancestry‡	Population	%
African, Sub-Saharan (53)	53	0.19
African (53)	53	0.19
Albanian (61)	61	0.21
American (892)	892	3.13
Arab (437)	497	1.75
Arab (40)	40	0.14
Egyptian (15)	15	0.05
Lebanese (91)	151	0.53
Other Arab (291)	291	1.02
Austrian (12)	84	0.30
Belgian (15)	15	0.05
British (46)	100	0.35
Canadian (104)	310	1.09
Croatian (13)	13	0.05
Czech (0)	113	0.40
Czechoslovakian (0)	33	0.12
Danish (0)	24	0.08
Dutch (68)	625	2.20
English (562)	2,745	9.64
European (280)	360	1.26
Finnish (7)	21	0.07
French, ex. Basque (61)	1,045	3.67
French Canadian (78)	220	0.77
German (1,363)	6,609	23.21
Greek (166)	257	0.90
Guyanese (34)	34	0.12
Hungarian (64)	108	0.38
Irish (1,032)	4,946	17.37
Italian (5,107)	9,171	32.21
Lithuanian (0)	34	0.12
Macedonian (9)	9	0.03
Norwegian (32)	48	0.17
Pennsylvania German (28)	40	0.14
Polish (454)	1,518	5.33
Portuguese (64)	139	0.49
Russian (30)	75	0.26
Scotch-Irish (87)	343	1.20
Scottish (71)	453	1.59
Slovak (0)	28	0.10
Slovene (0)	9	0.03
Swedish (13)	202	0.71
Swiss (0)	63	0.22
Turkish (26)	106	0.37
Ukrainian (310)	536	1.88
Welsh (102)	195	0.68
West Indian, ex. Hispanic (651)	761	2.67
Barbadian (68)	68	0.24
Haitian (108)	183	0.64
Jamaican (384)	419	1.47
West Indian (91)	91	0.32

Hispanic Origin	Population	%
Hispanic or Latino (of any race)	1,464	5.15
Central American, ex. Mexican	46	0.16
Costa Rican	3	0.01
Guatemalan	6	0.02
Honduran	13	0.05
Nicaraguan	4	0.01
Panamanian	11	0.04
Salvadoran	9	0.03
Cuban	123	0.43
Dominican Republic	49	0.17
Mexican	102	0.36
Puerto Rican	1,012	3.56
South American	68	0.24
Argentinean	9	0.03
Bolivian	1	<0.01
Chilean	18	0.06
Colombian	18	0.06
Ecuadorian	5	0.02
Paraguayan	1	<0.01
Peruvian	6	0.02
Venezuelan	9	0.03
Other South American	1	<0.01
Other Hispanic or Latino	64	0.23

Race*	Population	%
African-American/Black (2,809)	3,161	11.13
Not Hispanic (2,698)	2,991	10.53
Hispanic (111)	170	0.60
American Indian/Alaska Native (78)	197	0.69
Not Hispanic (69)	168	0.59
Hispanic (9)	29	0.10
Canadian/French Am. Ind. (0)	1	<0.01
Cherokee (0)	18	0.06
Chippewa (6)	7	0.02

*Notes: † The Census 2010 population figure is used to calculate the percentages in the Hispanic Origin and Race categories. Ancestry percentages are based on the 2006-2010 American Community Survey population (not shown); ‡ Numbers in parentheses indicate the number of people reporting a single ancestry; * Numbers in parentheses indicate the number of persons reporting this race alone, not in combination with any other race; Please refer to the Explanation of Data for more information.*

Choctaw (2)	9	0.03
Delaware (0)	4	0.01
Iroquois (35)	62	0.22
Navajo (1)	1	<0.01
Puget Sound Salish (1)	1	<0.01
Sioux (2)	3	0.01
South American Ind. (1)	4	0.01
Ute (0)	1	<0.01
Asian (920)	1,040	3.66
Not Hispanic (916)	1,031	3.63
Hispanic (4)	9	0.03
Burmese (2)	2	0.01
Cambodian (3)	11	0.04
Chinese, ex. Taiwanese (107)	137	0.48
Filipino (49)	69	0.24
Indian (88)	109	0.38
Indonesian (1)	3	0.01
Japanese (13)	32	0.11
Korean (88)	109	0.38
Laotian (80)	93	0.33
Pakistani (37)	47	0.17
Sri Lankan (1)	6	0.02
Taiwanese (6)	6	0.02
Thai (18)	20	0.07
Vietnamese (366)	411	1.45
Hawaii Native/Pacific Islander (8)	40	0.14
Not Hispanic (8)	32	0.11
Hispanic (0)	8	0.03
Guamanian/Chamorro (3)	4	0.01
Native Hawaiian (3)	9	0.03
Samoan (0)	1	<0.01
White (23,581)	24,137	84.99
Not Hispanic (22,726)	23,172	81.59
Hispanic (855)	965	3.40

Geddes

Place Type: Town
County: Onondaga
Population: 17,118†

Ancestry‡	Population	%
African, Sub-Saharan (0)	12	0.07
Nigerian (0)	12	0.07
American (399)	399	2.32
Arab (11)	38	0.22
Lebanese (7)	19	0.11
Palestinian (4)	4	0.02
Syrian (0)	15	0.09
Armenian (32)	32	0.19
Austrian (110)	341	1.99
British (11)	19	0.11
Bulgarian (16)	16	0.09
Canadian (69)	79	0.46
Czech (0)	127	0.74
Czechoslovakian (9)	47	0.27
Danish (34)	44	0.26
Dutch (21)	407	2.37
English (317)	1,897	11.05
European (40)	40	0.23
Finnish (0)	34	0.20
French, ex. Basque (133)	1,001	5.83
French Canadian (111)	322	1.88
German (487)	3,619	21.08
Greek (58)	77	0.45
Hungarian (22)	60	0.35
Iranian (10)	10	0.06
Irish (1,338)	4,999	29.12
Italian (2,442)	5,123	29.84
Lithuanian (0)	89	0.52
Macedonian (15)	15	0.09
Northern European (36)	36	0.21
Norwegian (0)	36	0.21
Polish (966)	2,336	13.61
Portuguese (40)	75	0.44
Russian (125)	299	1.74
Scandinavian (8)	19	0.11
Scotch-Irish (61)	139	0.81
Scottish (96)	329	1.92
Slavic (0)	25	0.15
Slovak (8)	70	0.41
Swedish (22)	55	0.32
Swiss (36)	36	0.21
Ukrainian (606)	780	4.54
Welsh (16)	47	0.27

Hispanic Origin	Population	%
Hispanic or Latino (of any race)	485	2.83
Central American, ex. Mexican	31	0.18
Guatemalan	14	0.08
Honduran	4	0.02
Nicaraguan	1	0.01
Panamanian	4	0.02
Salvadoran	8	0.05
Cuban	33	0.19
Dominican Republic	7	0.04
Mexican	79	0.46
Puerto Rican	243	1.42
South American	27	0.16
Argentinean	3	0.02
Chilean	1	0.01
Colombian	9	0.05
Ecuadorian	4	0.02
Paraguayan	1	0.01
Peruvian	1	0.01
Venezuelan	8	0.05
Other Hispanic or Latino	65	0.38

Race*	Population	%
African-American/Black (197)	321	1.88
Not Hispanic (173)	279	1.63
Hispanic (24)	42	0.25
American Indian/Alaska Native (131)	258	1.51
Not Hispanic (117)	225	1.31
Hispanic (14)	33	0.19
Alaska Athabascan *(Ala. Nat.)* (0)	2	0.01
Blackfeet (0)	5	0.03
Central American Ind. (0)	2	0.01
Cherokee (1)	8	0.05
Chippewa (1)	1	0.01
Delaware (3)	3	0.02
Iroquois (78)	143	0.84
Mexican American Ind. (3)	9	0.05
Potawatomi (1)	1	0.01
Seminole (1)	1	0.01
Sioux (0)	2	0.01
Asian (106)	144	0.84
Not Hispanic (104)	142	0.83
Hispanic (2)	2	0.01
Chinese, ex. Taiwanese (17)	24	0.14
Filipino (15)	26	0.15
Indian (25)	30	0.18
Japanese (5)	5	0.03
Korean (27)	31	0.18
Laotian (1)	2	0.01
Thai (1)	5	0.03
Vietnamese (10)	17	0.10
Hawaii Native/Pacific Islander (5)	12	0.07
Not Hispanic (5)	8	0.05
Hispanic (0)	4	0.02
Guamanian/Chamorro (4)	4	0.02
Native Hawaiian (0)	1	0.01
White (16,275)	16,554	96.71
Not Hispanic (15,978)	16,220	94.75
Hispanic (297)	334	1.95

Geneseo

Place Type: Town
County: Livingston
Population: 10,483†

Ancestry‡	Population	%
African, Sub-Saharan (12)	13	0.13
Senegalese (12)	12	0.12
Other Sub-Saharan African (0)	1	0.01
American (114)	114	1.10
Arab (0)	78	0.75
Lebanese (0)	59	0.57
Syrian (0)	19	0.18
Austrian (0)	30	0.29
Belgian (8)	19	0.18
British (12)	46	0.44
Canadian (12)	70	0.67
Czech (0)	12	0.12
Danish (8)	34	0.33
Dutch (25)	232	2.23
Eastern European (30)	30	0.29
English (403)	1,750	16.85
European (101)	101	0.97
Finnish (0)	14	0.13
French, ex. Basque (48)	375	3.61
French Canadian (36)	102	0.98
German (600)	2,238	21.55
Greek (10)	12	0.12
Guyanese (14)	14	0.13
Hungarian (15)	52	0.50
Irish (719)	2,617	25.20
Italian (744)	2,002	19.28
Latvian (0)	11	0.11
Lithuanian (0)	97	0.93
Maltese (0)	13	0.13
Norwegian (9)	50	0.48
Polish (175)	634	6.11
Portuguese (12)	82	0.79
Romanian (19)	44	0.42
Russian (40)	208	2.00
Scandinavian (9)	9	0.09
Scotch-Irish (54)	117	1.13
Scottish (109)	318	3.06
Serbian (0)	14	0.13
Slovak (0)	43	0.41
Swedish (0)	108	1.04
Swiss (0)	52	0.50
Ukrainian (33)	89	0.86
Welsh (11)	55	0.53
West Indian, ex. Hispanic (38)	50	0.48
Haitian (13)	14	0.13
Jamaican (25)	36	0.35
Yugoslavian (0)	10	0.10

Hispanic Origin	Population	%
Hispanic or Latino (of any race)	358	3.42
Central American, ex. Mexican	16	0.15
Costa Rican	2	0.02
Guatemalan	2	0.02
Honduran	6	0.06
Nicaraguan	2	0.02
Panamanian	2	0.02
Salvadoran	2	0.02
Cuban	16	0.15
Dominican Republic	21	0.20
Mexican	61	0.58
Puerto Rican	155	1.48
South American	54	0.52
Argentinean	3	0.03
Bolivian	1	0.01
Chilean	10	0.10
Colombian	22	0.21
Ecuadorian	8	0.08
Paraguayan	3	0.03
Peruvian	7	0.07
Other Hispanic or Latino	35	0.33

Race*	Population	%
African-American/Black (205)	289	2.76
Not Hispanic (193)	261	2.49
Hispanic (12)	28	0.27
American Indian/Alaska Native (17)	68	0.65
Not Hispanic (15)	57	0.54
Hispanic (2)	11	0.10
Blackfeet (0)	3	0.03
Cherokee (1)	6	0.06
Choctaw (1)	1	0.01
Iroquois (5)	16	0.15
Navajo (0)	1	0.01
Seminole (0)	2	0.02
Sioux (0)	3	0.03
South American Ind. (0)	5	0.05
Asian (451)	544	5.19

*Notes: † The Census 2010 population figure is used to calculate the percentages in the Hispanic Origin and Race categories. Ancestry percentages are based on the 2006-2010 American Community Survey population (not shown); ‡ Numbers in parentheses indicate the number of people reporting a single ancestry; * Numbers in parentheses indicate the number of persons reporting this race alone, not in combination with any other race; Please refer to the Explanation of Data for more information.*

Not Hispanic (448)	527	5.03
Hispanic (3)	17	0.16
Bangladeshi (1)	1	0.01
Burmese (3)	3	0.03
Cambodian (2)	2	0.02
Chinese, ex. Taiwanese (123)	155	1.48
Filipino (18)	35	0.33
Hmong (1)	1	0.01
Indian (50)	68	0.65
Indonesian (0)	1	0.01
Japanese (32)	43	0.41
Korean (125)	148	1.41
Nepalese (3)	4	0.04
Pakistani (27)	28	0.27
Sri Lankan (8)	8	0.08
Taiwanese (4)	5	0.05
Thai (0)	1	0.01
Vietnamese (31)	37	0.35
Hawaii Native/Pacific Islander (2)	13	0.12
Not Hispanic (2)	8	0.08
Hispanic (0)	5	0.05
Fijian (0)	1	0.01
Guamanian/Chamorro (1)	3	0.03
Native Hawaiian (1)	4	0.04
Samoan (0)	1	0.01
White (9,484)	9,677	92.31
Not Hispanic (9,282)	9,439	90.04
Hispanic (202)	238	2.27

Geneseo

Place Type: Village
County: Livingston
Population: 8,031†

Ancestry‡	Population	%
African, Sub-Saharan (12)	13	0.16
Senegalese (12)	12	0.15
Other Sub-Saharan African (0)	1	0.01
American (79)	79	1.00
Arab (0)	59	0.74
Lebanese (0)	59	0.74
Austrian (0)	30	0.38
Belgian (8)	8	0.10
British (12)	35	0.44
Canadian (12)	60	0.76
Czech (0)	12	0.15
Danish (8)	34	0.43
Dutch (7)	168	2.12
Eastern European (30)	30	0.38
English (213)	1,130	14.26
European (101)	101	1.27
Finnish (0)	14	0.18
French, ex. Basque (34)	281	3.55
French Canadian (17)	72	0.91
German (508)	1,607	20.28
Greek (0)	2	0.03
Guyanese (14)	14	0.18
Hungarian (15)	52	0.66
Irish (515)	1,935	24.41
Italian (505)	1,570	19.81
Latvian (0)	11	0.14
Lithuanian (0)	14	0.18
Maltese (0)	13	0.16
Norwegian (9)	41	0.52
Polish (116)	471	5.94
Portuguese (0)	36	0.45
Romanian (12)	37	0.47
Russian (40)	208	2.62
Scandinavian (9)	9	0.11
Scotch-Irish (42)	105	1.32
Scottish (97)	283	3.57
Serbian (0)	14	0.18
Slovak (0)	43	0.54
Swedish (0)	73	0.92
Swiss (0)	9	0.11
Ukrainian (22)	78	0.98
Welsh (11)	41	0.52
West Indian, ex. Hispanic (38)	50	0.63
Haitian (13)	14	0.18
Jamaican (25)	36	0.45

Hispanic Origin	Population	%
Hispanic or Latino (of any race)	313	3.90
Central American, ex. Mexican	15	0.19
Costa Rican	2	0.02
Guatemalan	2	0.02
Honduran	5	0.06
Nicaraguan	2	0.02
Panamanian	2	0.02
Salvadoran	2	0.02
Cuban	14	0.17
Dominican Republic	21	0.26
Mexican	50	0.62
Puerto Rican	136	1.69
South American	48	0.60
Argentinean	3	0.04
Bolivian	1	0.01
Chilean	10	0.12
Colombian	20	0.25
Ecuadorian	8	0.10
Paraguayan	2	0.02
Peruvian	4	0.05
Other Hispanic or Latino	29	0.36

Race*	Population	%
African-American/Black (183)	250	3.11
Not Hispanic (171)	223	2.78
Hispanic (12)	27	0.34
American Indian/Alaska Native (13)	48	0.60
Not Hispanic (11)	37	0.46
Hispanic (2)	11	0.14
Blackfeet (0)	3	0.04
Cherokee (1)	6	0.07
Choctaw (1)	1	0.01
Iroquois (3)	8	0.10
Navajo (0)	1	0.01
Seminole (0)	2	0.02
South American Ind. (0)	5	0.06
Asian (425)	510	6.35
Not Hispanic (423)	494	6.15
Hispanic (2)	16	0.20
Bangladeshi (1)	1	0.01
Cambodian (2)	2	0.02
Chinese, ex. Taiwanese (118)	150	1.87
Filipino (16)	33	0.41
Hmong (1)	1	0.01
Indian (49)	65	0.81
Indonesian (0)	1	0.01
Japanese (30)	38	0.47
Korean (123)	142	1.77
Nepalese (3)	4	0.05
Pakistani (19)	19	0.24
Sri Lankan (8)	8	0.10
Taiwanese (4)	5	0.06
Thai (0)	1	0.01
Vietnamese (30)	36	0.45
Hawaii Native/Pacific Islander (1)	11	0.14
Not Hispanic (1)	7	0.09
Hispanic (0)	4	0.05
Fijian (0)	1	0.01
Guamanian/Chamorro (1)	3	0.04
Native Hawaiian (0)	2	0.02
Samoan (0)	1	0.01
White (7,134)	7,289	90.76
Not Hispanic (6,963)	7,084	88.21
Hispanic (171)	205	2.55

Geneva

Place Type: City
County: Ontario
Population: 13,261†

Ancestry‡	Population	%
African, Sub-Saharan (0)	59	0.44
African (0)	59	0.44
American (368)	368	2.76
Arab (57)	167	1.25
Lebanese (0)	12	0.09
Syrian (57)	155	1.16
Austrian (11)	19	0.14
British (52)	135	1.01
Bulgarian (0)	49	0.37
Canadian (43)	57	0.43
Czech (0)	6	0.05
Czechoslovakian (7)	16	0.12
Danish (41)	157	1.18
Dutch (49)	428	3.21
Eastern European (17)	17	0.13
English (365)	1,599	12.00
European (172)	189	1.42
Finnish (19)	19	0.14
French, ex. Basque (35)	347	2.60
French Canadian (110)	265	1.99
German (606)	1,894	14.21
Greek (5)	29	0.22
Guyanese (12)	12	0.09
Hungarian (39)	77	0.58
Icelander (0)	10	0.08
Irish (684)	2,947	22.11
Italian (1,531)	3,549	26.63
Lithuanian (11)	11	0.08
Northern European (9)	9	0.07
Norwegian (24)	44	0.33
Pennsylvania German (8)	8	0.06
Polish (92)	444	3.33
Romanian (31)	36	0.27
Russian (50)	147	1.10
Scandinavian (0)	8	0.06
Scotch-Irish (38)	157	1.18
Scottish (61)	203	1.52
Slovak (0)	31	0.23
Swedish (43)	128	0.96
Swiss (0)	7	0.05
Ukrainian (0)	26	0.20
Welsh (0)	72	0.54
West Indian, ex. Hispanic (36)	49	0.37
Jamaican (7)	20	0.15
Trinidadian/Tobagonian (29)	29	0.22

Hispanic Origin	Population	%
Hispanic or Latino (of any race)	1,746	13.17
Central American, ex. Mexican	47	0.35
Costa Rican	5	0.04
Guatemalan	15	0.11
Honduran	17	0.13
Nicaraguan	2	0.02
Panamanian	5	0.04
Salvadoran	3	0.02
Cuban	26	0.20
Dominican Republic	67	0.51
Mexican	289	2.18
Puerto Rican	1,214	9.15
South American	38	0.29
Argentinean	9	0.07
Bolivian	1	0.01
Chilean	2	0.02
Colombian	12	0.09
Ecuadorian	9	0.07
Peruvian	3	0.02
Venezuelan	2	0.02
Other Hispanic or Latino	65	0.49

Race*	Population	%
African-American/Black (1,388)	1,837	13.85
Not Hispanic (1,220)	1,584	11.94
Hispanic (168)	253	1.91
American Indian/Alaska Native (42)	167	1.26
Not Hispanic (32)	122	0.92
Hispanic (10)	45	0.34
Apache (2)	6	0.05
Blackfeet (0)	8	0.06
Canadian/French Am. Ind. (0)	1	0.01
Cherokee (4)	26	0.20
Cheyenne (0)	3	0.02
Chippewa (7)	7	0.05
Choctaw (0)	1	0.01
Comanche (0)	1	0.01
Crow (0)	4	0.03

*Notes: † The Census 2010 population figure is used to calculate the percentages in the Hispanic Origin and Race categories. Ancestry percentages are based on the 2006-2010 American Community Survey population (not shown); ‡ Numbers in parentheses indicate the number of people reporting a single ancestry; * Numbers in parentheses indicate the number of persons reporting this race alone, not in combination with any other race; Please refer to the Explanation of Data for more information.*

Hopi (2)	2	0.02
Iroquois (5)	14	0.11
Seminole (0)	4	0.03
Sioux (1)	6	0.05
South American Ind. (0)	6	0.05
Asian (225)	286	2.16
Not Hispanic (224)	280	2.11
Hispanic (1)	6	0.05
Bangladeshi (3)	3	0.02
Chinese, ex. Taiwanese (115)	137	1.03
Filipino (5)	14	0.11
Indian (33)	46	0.35
Indonesian (6)	7	0.05
Japanese (11)	19	0.14
Korean (18)	26	0.20
Laotian (7)	7	0.05
Malaysian (0)	1	0.01
Nepalese (1)	2	0.02
Pakistani (1)	2	0.02
Sri Lankan (4)	4	0.03
Taiwanese (2)	4	0.03
Thai (4)	4	0.03
Vietnamese (4)	8	0.06
Hawaii Native/Pacific Islander (5)	22	0.17
Not Hispanic (3)	11	0.08
Hispanic (2)	11	0.08
Guamanian/Chamorro (2)	11	0.08
Native Hawaiian (1)	5	0.04
White (10,248)	10,802	81.46
Not Hispanic (9,561)	9,986	75.30
Hispanic (687)	816	6.15

German Flatts

Place Type: Town
County: Herkimer
Population: 13,258†

Ancestry‡	Population	%
African, Sub-Saharan (0)	23	0.17
African (0)	23	0.17
American (466)	466	3.51
Arab (0)	66	0.50
Lebanese (0)	47	0.35
Syrian (0)	19	0.14
Austrian (0)	15	0.11
British (26)	34	0.26
Canadian (0)	35	0.26
Czech (56)	82	0.62
Czechoslovakian (32)	53	0.40
Danish (23)	78	0.59
Dutch (46)	727	5.47
English (556)	2,086	15.69
European (23)	23	0.17
French, ex. Basque (190)	1,028	7.73
French Canadian (173)	429	3.23
German (595)	3,085	23.21
Greek (90)	90	0.68
Hungarian (14)	39	0.29
Irish (1,091)	3,383	25.45
Italian (903)	2,134	16.05
Lithuanian (16)	16	0.12
Norwegian (0)	4	0.03
Polish (270)	875	6.58
Russian (16)	69	0.52
Scotch-Irish (28)	70	0.53
Scottish (34)	138	1.04
Slavic (14)	14	0.11
Slovene (0)	32	0.24
Swedish (6)	20	0.15
Swiss (8)	25	0.19
Ukrainian (33)	130	0.98
Welsh (101)	351	2.64
West Indian, ex. Hispanic (0)	20	0.15
Haitian (0)	20	0.15
Yugoslavian (5)	5	0.04

Hispanic Origin	Population	%
Hispanic or Latino (of any race)	267	2.01
Central American, ex. Mexican	12	0.09
Costa Rican	7	0.05
Honduran	1	0.01
Nicaraguan	2	0.02
Panamanian	1	0.01
Salvadoran	1	0.01
Cuban	8	0.06
Dominican Republic	7	0.05
Mexican	37	0.28
Puerto Rican	156	1.18
South American	12	0.09
Argentinean	5	0.04
Bolivian	1	0.01
Colombian	3	0.02
Ecuadorian	2	0.02
Peruvian	1	0.01
Other Hispanic or Latino	35	0.26

Race*	Population	%
African-American/Black (158)	262	1.98
Not Hispanic (147)	241	1.82
Hispanic (11)	21	0.16
American Indian/Alaska Native (41)	99	0.75
Not Hispanic (39)	90	0.68
Hispanic (2)	9	0.07
Apache (0)	1	0.01
Blackfeet (2)	3	0.02
Cherokee (0)	2	0.02
Creek (2)	2	0.02
Delaware (0)	4	0.03
Iroquois (11)	24	0.18
Navajo (2)	2	0.02
Sioux (1)	6	0.05
Asian (69)	99	0.75
Not Hispanic (68)	98	0.74
Hispanic (1)	1	0.01
Cambodian (0)	5	0.04
Chinese, ex. Taiwanese (11)	13	0.10
Filipino (17)	22	0.17
Indian (20)	29	0.22
Japanese (4)	7	0.05
Korean (5)	7	0.05
Laotian (4)	6	0.05
Thai (6)	9	0.07
Vietnamese (0)	3	0.02
Hawaii Native/Pacific Islander (0)	1	0.01
Not Hispanic (0)	1	0.01
Native Hawaiian (0)	1	0.01
White (12,757)	12,939	97.59
Not Hispanic (12,571)	12,724	95.97
Hispanic (186)	215	1.62

Glen Cove

Place Type: City
County: Nassau
Population: 26,964†

Ancestry‡	Population	%
Afghan (10)	10	0.04
African, Sub-Saharan (28)	28	0.10
South African (28)	28	0.10
Albanian (0)	10	0.04
American (490)	490	1.83
Arab (17)	43	0.16
Egyptian (17)	17	0.06
Moroccan (0)	26	0.10
Armenian (38)	38	0.14
Austrian (52)	191	0.71
Belgian (22)	22	0.08
British (53)	83	0.31
Canadian (8)	49	0.18
Croatian (34)	54	0.20
Czech (59)	139	0.52
Czechoslovakian (0)	20	0.07
Danish (19)	109	0.41
Dutch (11)	126	0.47
Eastern European (140)	147	0.55
English (260)	1,332	4.98
Estonian (7)	7	0.03
European (110)	110	0.41
Finnish (15)	15	0.06
French, ex. Basque (114)	401	1.50
French Canadian (13)	114	0.43
German (533)	2,319	8.68
Greek (429)	601	2.25
Guyanese (11)	41	0.15
Hungarian (79)	231	0.86
Iranian (60)	60	0.22
Irish (901)	4,188	15.67
Israeli (118)	118	0.44
Italian (3,940)	6,466	24.19
Latvian (14)	14	0.05
Lithuanian (20)	101	0.38
Norwegian (78)	152	0.57
Polish (745)	1,643	6.15
Romanian (30)	78	0.29
Russian (405)	690	2.58
Scandinavian (12)	21	0.08
Scotch-Irish (35)	182	0.68
Scottish (122)	382	1.43
Slovak (23)	23	0.09
Slovene (10)	30	0.11
Swedish (29)	171	0.64
Swiss (31)	85	0.32
Turkish (0)	35	0.13
Ukrainian (111)	137	0.51
Welsh (11)	35	0.13
West Indian, ex. Hispanic (316)	358	1.34
British West Indian (7)	7	0.03
Haitian (181)	181	0.68
Jamaican (110)	110	0.41
Trinidadian/Tobagonian (7)	49	0.18
West Indian (11)	11	0.04

Hispanic Origin	Population	%
Hispanic or Latino (of any race)	7,513	27.86
Central American, ex. Mexican	3,158	11.71
Costa Rican	71	0.26
Guatemalan	142	0.53
Honduran	364	1.35
Nicaraguan	11	0.04
Panamanian	10	0.04
Salvadoran	2,544	9.43
Other Central American	16	0.06
Cuban	114	0.42
Dominican Republic	194	0.72
Mexican	318	1.18
Puerto Rican	924	3.43
South American	1,715	6.36
Argentinean	75	0.28
Bolivian	4	0.01
Chilean	217	0.80
Colombian	351	1.30
Ecuadorian	108	0.40
Paraguayan	14	0.05
Peruvian	883	3.27
Uruguayan	15	0.06
Venezuelan	40	0.15
Other South American	8	0.03
Other Hispanic or Latino	1,090	4.04

Race*	Population	%
African-American/Black (1,936)	2,236	8.29
Not Hispanic (1,728)	1,906	7.07
Hispanic (208)	330	1.22
American Indian/Alaska Native (96)	250	0.93
Not Hispanic (31)	96	0.36
Hispanic (65)	154	0.57
Blackfeet (0)	7	0.03
Central American Ind. (9)	12	0.04
Cherokee (2)	32	0.12
Cheyenne (2)	2	0.01
Iroquois (2)	6	0.02
Mexican American Ind. (5)	9	0.03
Pueblo (2)	2	0.01
South American Ind. (5)	8	0.03
Spanish American Ind. (5)	12	0.04
Asian (1,247)	1,427	5.29
Not Hispanic (1,235)	1,380	5.12
Hispanic (12)	47	0.17

*Notes: † The Census 2010 population figure is used to calculate the percentages in the Hispanic Origin and Race categories. Ancestry percentages are based on the 2006-2010 American Community Survey population (not shown); ‡ Numbers in parentheses indicate the number of people reporting a single ancestry; * Numbers in parentheses indicate the number of persons reporting this race alone, not in combination with any other race; Please refer to the Explanation of Data for more information.*

Bangladeshi (3)	6	0.02
Burmese (4)	4	0.01
Chinese, ex. Taiwanese (328)	365	1.35
Filipino (192)	228	0.85
Indian (364)	398	1.48
Indonesian (1)	2	0.01
Japanese (54)	65	0.24
Korean (198)	206	0.76
Malaysian (1)	1	<0.01
Pakistani (35)	41	0.15
Sri Lankan (7)	7	0.03
Taiwanese (17)	24	0.09
Thai (11)	14	0.05
Vietnamese (10)	14	0.05
Hawaii Native/Pacific Islander (26)	68	0.25
Not Hispanic (20)	44	0.16
Hispanic (6)	24	0.09
Guamanian/Chamorro (11)	11	0.04
Native Hawaiian (5)	10	0.04
Samoan (4)	8	0.03
White (20,006)	20,661	76.62
Not Hispanic (16,013)	16,286	60.40
Hispanic (3,993)	4,375	16.23

Glens Falls North

Place Type: CDP
County: Warren
Population: 8,443†

Ancestry‡	Population	%
American (394)	394	4.50
Arab (14)	28	0.32
Syrian (14)	28	0.32
Armenian (16)	39	0.45
Austrian (0)	60	0.69
British (12)	27	0.31
Bulgarian (0)	12	0.14
Canadian (233)	245	2.80
Czech (12)	12	0.14
Dutch (8)	194	2.22
English (277)	1,055	12.05
European (15)	15	0.17
Finnish (0)	14	0.16
French, ex. Basque (360)	1,309	14.95
French Canadian (103)	203	2.32
German (333)	1,411	16.12
Hungarian (33)	69	0.79
Iranian (5)	14	0.16
Irish (827)	2,552	29.16
Italian (552)	1,424	16.27
Lithuanian (14)	47	0.54
Norwegian (22)	69	0.79
Polish (68)	424	4.84
Russian (12)	86	0.98
Scandinavian (17)	17	0.19
Scotch-Irish (100)	188	2.15
Scottish (174)	390	4.46
Serbian (17)	17	0.19
Slovak (37)	67	0.77
Swedish (0)	26	0.30
Swiss (0)	8	0.09
Ukrainian (11)	104	1.19
Welsh (30)	164	1.87

Hispanic Origin	Population	%
Hispanic or Latino (of any race)	162	1.92
Central American, ex. Mexican	6	0.07
Costa Rican	1	0.01
Guatemalan	4	0.05
Salvadoran	1	0.01
Cuban	4	0.05
Dominican Republic	2	0.02
Mexican	27	0.32
Puerto Rican	88	1.04
South American	17	0.20
Argentinean	1	0.01
Chilean	2	0.02
Colombian	8	0.09
Peruvian	3	0.04
Venezuelan	3	0.04
Other Hispanic or Latino	18	0.21

Race*	Population	%
African-American/Black (89)	130	1.54
Not Hispanic (86)	126	1.49
Hispanic (3)	4	0.05
American Indian/Alaska Native (17)	57	0.68
Not Hispanic (13)	49	0.58
Hispanic (4)	8	0.09
Alaska Athabascan *(Ala. Nat.)* (1)	1	0.01
Blackfeet (0)	5	0.06
Cherokee (1)	4	0.05
Chippewa (0)	1	0.01
Choctaw (0)	1	0.01
Iroquois (0)	4	0.05
Sioux (0)	3	0.04
Asian (117)	134	1.59
Not Hispanic (116)	132	1.56
Hispanic (1)	2	0.02
Cambodian (0)	1	0.01
Chinese, ex. Taiwanese (37)	43	0.51
Filipino (21)	24	0.28
Indian (16)	21	0.25
Korean (9)	9	0.11
Pakistani (9)	14	0.17
Sri Lankan (1)	1	0.01
Thai (3)	3	0.04
Vietnamese (15)	15	0.18
Hawaii Native/Pacific Islander (6)	9	0.11
Not Hispanic (3)	6	0.07
Hispanic (3)	3	0.04
Guamanian/Chamorro (1)	3	0.04
Native Hawaiian (3)	3	0.04
Samoan (2)	2	0.02
White (8,090)	8,177	96.85
Not Hispanic (7,974)	8,050	95.35
Hispanic (116)	127	1.50

Glens Falls

Place Type: City
County: Warren
Population: 14,700†

Ancestry‡	Population	%
African, Sub-Saharan (0)	27	0.18
African (0)	27	0.18
American (1,431)	1,431	9.70
Arab (45)	53	0.36
Lebanese (17)	17	0.12
Syrian (28)	36	0.24
Australian (9)	9	0.06
Austrian (15)	36	0.24
Belgian (0)	17	0.12
Canadian (44)	96	0.65
Czech (10)	10	0.07
Czechoslovakian (0)	12	0.08
Danish (0)	39	0.26
Dutch (106)	545	3.70
Eastern European (18)	18	0.12
English (433)	2,219	15.05
Estonian (18)	18	0.12
European (7)	7	0.05
Finnish (0)	19	0.13
French, ex. Basque (635)	2,398	16.26
French Canadian (235)	695	4.71
German (308)	1,613	10.94
Greek (0)	6	0.04
Guyanese (17)	17	0.12
Hungarian (7)	72	0.49
Irish (950)	3,290	22.31
Italian (708)	1,682	11.41
Latvian (22)	22	0.15
Lithuanian (7)	14	0.09
Norwegian (0)	78	0.53
Polish (116)	767	5.20
Portuguese (12)	25	0.17
Romanian (18)	18	0.12
Russian (52)	257	1.74
Scandinavian (12)	20	0.14
Scotch-Irish (104)	286	1.94
Scottish (80)	510	3.46
Slavic (0)	5	0.03
Slovak (0)	17	0.12
Swedish (74)	283	1.92
Swiss (7)	24	0.16
Ukrainian (38)	51	0.35
Welsh (63)	234	1.59
West Indian, ex. Hispanic (50)	67	0.45
Jamaican (50)	50	0.34
West Indian (0)	17	0.12

Hispanic Origin	Population	%
Hispanic or Latino (of any race)	334	2.27
Central American, ex. Mexican	21	0.14
Costa Rican	2	0.01
Guatemalan	3	0.02
Panamanian	10	0.07
Salvadoran	6	0.04
Cuban	13	0.09
Dominican Republic	7	0.05
Mexican	42	0.29
Puerto Rican	181	1.23
South American	19	0.13
Argentinean	3	0.02
Chilean	1	0.01
Colombian	5	0.03
Paraguayan	1	0.01
Peruvian	5	0.03
Uruguayan	3	0.02
Venezuelan	1	0.01
Other Hispanic or Latino	51	0.35

Race*	Population	%
African-American/Black (260)	437	2.97
Not Hispanic (236)	383	2.61
Hispanic (24)	54	0.37
American Indian/Alaska Native (38)	151	1.03
Not Hispanic (30)	128	0.87
Hispanic (8)	23	0.16
Apache (1)	4	0.03
Blackfeet (6)	13	0.09
Canadian/French Am. Ind. (0)	1	0.01
Cherokee (5)	15	0.10
Chippewa (3)	4	0.03
Iroquois (2)	16	0.11
Menominee (0)	3	0.02
Mexican American Ind. (2)	3	0.02
Ottawa (1)	1	0.01
Potawatomi (0)	1	0.01
Seminole (1)	4	0.03
Sioux (1)	5	0.03
South American Ind. (3)	4	0.03
Asian (95)	154	1.05
Not Hispanic (94)	149	1.01
Hispanic (1)	5	0.03
Chinese, ex. Taiwanese (28)	35	0.24
Filipino (16)	33	0.22
Indian (5)	20	0.14
Indonesian (1)	1	0.01
Japanese (2)	8	0.05
Korean (18)	29	0.20
Malaysian (1)	2	0.01
Pakistani (6)	8	0.05
Thai (1)	1	0.01
Vietnamese (13)	17	0.12
Hawaii Native/Pacific Islander (0)	6	0.04
Not Hispanic (0)	3	0.02
Hispanic (0)	3	0.02
Guamanian/Chamorro (0)	1	0.01
Native Hawaiian (0)	2	0.01
White (13,916)	14,236	96.84
Not Hispanic (13,721)	13,994	95.20
Hispanic (195)	242	1.65

*Notes: † The Census 2010 population figure is used to calculate the percentages in the Hispanic Origin and Race categories. Ancestry percentages are based on the 2006-2010 American Community Survey population (not shown); ‡ Numbers in parentheses indicate the number of people reporting a single ancestry; * Numbers in parentheses indicate the number of persons reporting this race alone, not in combination with any other race; Please refer to the Explanation of Data for more information.*

Glenville

Place Type: Town
County: Schenectady
Population: 29,480†

Ancestry‡	Population	%
African, Sub-Saharan (0)	5	0.02
African (0)	5	0.02
Albanian (10)	41	0.14
American (2,025)	2,025	6.92
Arab (26)	99	0.34
Arab (0)	18	0.06
Lebanese (26)	54	0.18
Syrian (0)	27	0.09
Armenian (19)	41	0.14
Austrian (47)	115	0.39
British (107)	193	0.66
Canadian (63)	192	0.66
Czech (37)	197	0.67
Czechoslovakian (42)	77	0.26
Danish (86)	287	0.98
Dutch (238)	1,562	5.34
Eastern European (50)	50	0.17
English (1,027)	4,035	13.80
European (177)	177	0.61
French, ex. Basque (226)	1,925	6.58
French Canadian (357)	783	2.68
German (1,069)	5,586	19.10
Greek (32)	108	0.37
Hungarian (36)	240	0.82
Irish (2,023)	6,411	21.92
Italian (2,733)	6,079	20.79
Latvian (0)	24	0.08
Lithuanian (55)	150	0.51
Maltese (0)	9	0.03
Northern European (120)	120	0.41
Norwegian (64)	219	0.75
Pennsylvania German (0)	14	0.05
Polish (1,254)	3,197	10.93
Portuguese (80)	103	0.35
Romanian (2)	57	0.19
Russian (114)	352	1.20
Scandinavian (11)	84	0.29
Scotch-Irish (239)	594	2.03
Scottish (316)	1,068	3.65
Slavic (0)	23	0.08
Slovak (36)	167	0.57
Swedish (114)	284	0.97
Swiss (22)	101	0.35
Ukrainian (80)	210	0.72
Welsh (52)	251	0.86
West Indian, ex. Hispanic (38)	60	0.21
Jamaican (24)	24	0.08
Trinidadian/Tobagonian (6)	28	0.10
West Indian (8)	8	0.03

Hispanic Origin	Population	%
Hispanic or Latino (of any race)	576	1.95
Central American, ex. Mexican	51	0.17
Costa Rican	5	0.02
Guatemalan	13	0.04
Honduran	9	0.03
Panamanian	11	0.04
Salvadoran	13	0.04
Cuban	29	0.10
Dominican Republic	35	0.12
Mexican	76	0.26
Puerto Rican	214	0.73
South American	100	0.34
Argentinean	11	0.04
Bolivian	1	<0.01
Chilean	4	0.01
Colombian	30	0.10
Ecuadorian	16	0.05
Peruvian	21	0.07
Uruguayan	3	0.01
Venezuelan	14	0.05
Other Hispanic or Latino	71	0.24

Race*	Population	%
African-American/Black (301)	449	1.52
Not Hispanic (280)	395	1.34
Hispanic (21)	54	0.18
American Indian/Alaska Native (24)	102	0.35
Not Hispanic (18)	78	0.26
Hispanic (6)	24	0.08
Apache (2)	2	0.01
Canadian/French Am. Ind. (2)	2	0.01
Cherokee (2)	9	0.03
Chippewa (0)	1	<0.01
Choctaw (1)	1	<0.01
Cree (0)	1	<0.01
Inupiat *(Alaska Native)* (1)	1	<0.01
Iroquois (5)	21	0.07
Mexican American Ind. (0)	3	0.01
Navajo (0)	2	0.01
Potawatomi (1)	1	<0.01
Sioux (0)	1	<0.01
South American Ind. (0)	2	0.01
Asian (418)	539	1.83
Not Hispanic (414)	531	1.80
Hispanic (4)	8	0.03
Cambodian (2)	2	0.01
Chinese, ex. Taiwanese (87)	107	0.36
Filipino (40)	64	0.22
Indian (149)	176	0.60
Indonesian (1)	1	<0.01
Japanese (19)	27	0.09
Korean (62)	81	0.27
Laotian (0)	5	0.02
Nepalese (2)	2	0.01
Pakistani (15)	15	0.05
Sri Lankan (6)	6	0.02
Taiwanese (1)	2	0.01
Thai (4)	8	0.03
Vietnamese (25)	34	0.12
Hawaii Native/Pacific Islander (5)	17	0.06
Not Hispanic (5)	17	0.06
Native Hawaiian (0)	4	0.01
White (28,260)	28,588	96.97
Not Hispanic (27,867)	28,143	95.46
Hispanic (393)	445	1.51

Gloversville

Place Type: City
County: Fulton
Population: 15,665†

Ancestry‡	Population	%
American (1,578)	1,578	10.10
Arab (7)	22	0.14
Lebanese (0)	15	0.10
Other Arab (7)	7	0.04
Armenian (9)	29	0.19
Belgian (0)	9	0.06
Bulgarian (0)	7	0.04
Canadian (29)	44	0.28
Czech (11)	31	0.20
Czechoslovakian (24)	34	0.22
Danish (0)	29	0.19
Dutch (55)	795	5.09
Eastern European (26)	26	0.17
English (609)	1,593	10.20
European (25)	25	0.16
French, ex. Basque (56)	1,107	7.09
French Canadian (27)	157	1.01
German (723)	3,697	23.67
Greek (0)	50	0.32
Hungarian (8)	64	0.41
Irish (772)	3,177	20.34
Italian (1,185)	2,615	16.74
Latvian (0)	10	0.06
Lithuanian (40)	119	0.76
Norwegian (25)	79	0.51
Pennsylvania German (0)	27	0.17
Polish (134)	532	3.41
Portuguese (11)	11	0.07
Russian (0)	18	0.12
Scotch-Irish (49)	100	0.64
Scottish (0)	206	1.32
Slovak (37)	57	0.36
Swedish (47)	130	0.83
Swiss (0)	33	0.21
Ukrainian (15)	94	0.60
Welsh (0)	57	0.36
West Indian, ex. Hispanic (0)	19	0.12
Trinidadian/Tobagonian (0)	19	0.12

Hispanic Origin	Population	%
Hispanic or Latino (of any race)	531	3.39
Central American, ex. Mexican	12	0.08
Costa Rican	8	0.05
Panamanian	3	0.02
Salvadoran	1	0.01
Cuban	7	0.04
Dominican Republic	25	0.16
Mexican	44	0.28
Puerto Rican	365	2.33
South American	32	0.20
Bolivian	1	0.01
Colombian	10	0.06
Ecuadorian	12	0.08
Peruvian	8	0.05
Venezuelan	1	0.01
Other Hispanic or Latino	46	0.29

Race*	Population	%
African-American/Black (445)	653	4.17
Not Hispanic (416)	600	3.83
Hispanic (29)	53	0.34
American Indian/Alaska Native (44)	119	0.76
Not Hispanic (41)	114	0.73
Hispanic (3)	5	0.03
Apache (1)	2	0.01
Blackfeet (2)	4	0.03
Cherokee (0)	7	0.04
Delaware (1)	1	0.01
Iroquois (14)	29	0.19
Mexican American Ind. (3)	3	0.02
Navajo (3)	6	0.04
Sioux (0)	2	0.01
Asian (77)	111	0.71
Not Hispanic (76)	106	0.68
Hispanic (1)	5	0.03
Chinese, ex. Taiwanese (11)	15	0.10
Filipino (27)	43	0.27
Indian (13)	16	0.10
Japanese (11)	15	0.10
Korean (9)	13	0.08
Pakistani (0)	2	0.01
Taiwanese (1)	1	0.01
Vietnamese (5)	8	0.05
Hawaii Native/Pacific Islander (2)	26	0.17
Not Hispanic (2)	18	0.11
Hispanic (0)	8	0.05
Native Hawaiian (1)	17	0.11
Samoan (0)	5	0.03
White (14,635)	14,939	95.37
Not Hispanic (14,298)	14,568	93.00
Hispanic (337)	371	2.37

Goshen

Place Type: Town
County: Orange
Population: 13,687†

Ancestry‡	Population	%
African, Sub-Saharan (0)	60	0.44
African (0)	52	0.38
South African (0)	8	0.06
American (538)	538	3.93
Arab (20)	26	0.19
Syrian (20)	26	0.19
Armenian (0)	15	0.11
Austrian (12)	91	0.67
British (12)	48	0.35

*Notes: † The Census 2010 population figure is used to calculate the percentages in the Hispanic Origin and Race categories. Ancestry percentages are based on the 2006-2010 American Community Survey population (not shown); ‡ Numbers in parentheses indicate the number of people reporting a single ancestry; * Numbers in parentheses indicate the number of persons reporting this race alone, not in combination with any other race; Please refer to the Explanation of Data for more information.*

Bulgarian (36)	36	0.26
Canadian (64)	79	0.58
Croatian (9)	9	0.07
Czech (0)	24	0.18
Danish (7)	35	0.26
Dutch (78)	264	1.93
Eastern European (14)	14	0.10
English (181)	1,150	8.41
European (40)	40	0.29
Finnish (40)	47	0.34
French, ex. Basque (15)	239	1.75
French Canadian (17)	120	0.88
German (385)	2,139	15.64
Greek (23)	53	0.39
Guyanese (26)	26	0.19
Hungarian (4)	123	0.90
Icelander (7)	7	0.05
Irish (793)	2,671	19.52
Israeli (11)	11	0.08
Italian (1,104)	2,408	17.60
Lithuanian (17)	29	0.21
Maltese (10)	21	0.15
Norwegian (74)	224	1.64
Polish (371)	885	6.47
Portuguese (0)	39	0.29
Romanian (0)	52	0.38
Russian (267)	612	4.47
Scandinavian (7)	26	0.19
Scotch-Irish (68)	230	1.68
Scottish (19)	80	0.58
Slavic (9)	9	0.07
Slovak (25)	34	0.25
Swedish (29)	213	1.56
Swiss (23)	72	0.53
Ukrainian (37)	138	1.01
Welsh (12)	40	0.29
West Indian, ex. Hispanic (276)	448	3.27
Haitian (122)	222	1.62
Jamaican (11)	31	0.23
Trinidadian/Tobagonian (111)	111	0.81
West Indian (32)	84	0.61
Yugoslavian (0)	31	0.23

Hispanic Origin	Population	%
Hispanic or Latino (of any race)	1,867	13.64
Central American, ex. Mexican	69	0.50
Costa Rican	3	0.02
Guatemalan	28	0.20
Honduran	12	0.09
Nicaraguan	2	0.01
Panamanian	6	0.04
Salvadoran	18	0.13
Cuban	48	0.35
Dominican Republic	90	0.66
Mexican	557	4.07
Puerto Rican	641	4.68
South American	151	1.10
Argentinean	10	0.07
Bolivian	7	0.05
Chilean	9	0.07
Colombian	47	0.34
Ecuadorian	53	0.39
Paraguayan	3	0.02
Peruvian	8	0.06
Uruguayan	6	0.04
Venezuelan	5	0.04
Other South American	3	0.02
Other Hispanic or Latino	311	2.27

Race*	Population	%
African-American/Black (970)	1,087	7.94
Not Hispanic (888)	968	7.07
Hispanic (82)	119	0.87
American Indian/Alaska Native (53)	142	1.04
Not Hispanic (42)	104	0.76
Hispanic (11)	38	0.28
Blackfeet (0)	5	0.04
Cherokee (2)	19	0.14
Choctaw (2)	2	0.01
Delaware (12)	26	0.19
Inupiat *(Alaska Native)* (0)	2	0.01
Iroquois (5)	13	0.09
Mexican American Ind. (0)	4	0.03
Navajo (0)	1	0.01
Sioux (1)	2	0.01
South American Ind. (2)	4	0.03
Asian (355)	435	3.18
Not Hispanic (347)	418	3.05
Hispanic (8)	17	0.12
Bangladeshi (4)	4	0.03
Burmese (4)	4	0.03
Cambodian (1)	1	0.01
Chinese, ex. Taiwanese (55)	64	0.47
Filipino (62)	76	0.56
Indian (111)	128	0.94
Indonesian (2)	4	0.03
Japanese (10)	16	0.12
Korean (46)	63	0.46
Pakistani (20)	21	0.15
Sri Lankan (3)	6	0.04
Taiwanese (1)	1	0.01
Thai (1)	1	0.01
Vietnamese (6)	14	0.10
Hawaii Native/Pacific Islander (11)	22	0.16
Not Hispanic (9)	20	0.15
Hispanic (2)	2	0.01
Guamanian/Chamorro (2)	3	0.02
Native Hawaiian (0)	2	0.01
White (11,280)	11,538	84.30
Not Hispanic (10,317)	10,486	76.61
Hispanic (963)	1,052	7.69

Grand Island

Place Type: Town
County: Erie
Population: 20,374†

Ancestry‡	Population	%
African, Sub-Saharan (8)	8	0.04
African (8)	8	0.04
American (432)	432	2.16
Arab (37)	185	0.93
Egyptian (0)	52	0.26
Lebanese (23)	105	0.53
Syrian (14)	28	0.14
Armenian (0)	77	0.39
Australian (0)	26	0.13
Austrian (10)	23	0.12
Belgian (0)	23	0.12
British (41)	69	0.35
Canadian (54)	123	0.62
Croatian (79)	213	1.07
Czech (40)	185	0.93
Czechoslovakian (40)	40	0.20
Danish (0)	27	0.14
Dutch (86)	409	2.05
Eastern European (39)	39	0.20
English (584)	2,602	13.03
European (38)	69	0.35
Finnish (7)	7	0.04
French, ex. Basque (53)	600	3.00
French Canadian (23)	92	0.46
German (1,993)	6,365	31.87
Greek (30)	60	0.30
Hungarian (40)	199	1.00
Irish (811)	3,836	19.20
Italian (1,899)	4,267	21.36
Lithuanian (0)	11	0.06
Maltese (0)	11	0.06
Norwegian (99)	153	0.77
Polish (1,103)	3,086	15.45
Russian (27)	184	0.92
Scotch-Irish (131)	498	2.49
Scottish (149)	563	2.82
Slavic (0)	10	0.05
Slovak (14)	22	0.11
Slovene (11)	11	0.06
Swedish (24)	430	2.15
Swiss (0)	23	0.12
Turkish (14)	14	0.07
Ukrainian (44)	260	1.30
Welsh (39)	208	1.04
West Indian, ex. Hispanic (88)	98	0.49
Trinidadian/Tobagonian (35)	45	0.23
West Indian (53)	53	0.27

Hispanic Origin	Population	%
Hispanic or Latino (of any race)	363	1.78
Central American, ex. Mexican	21	0.10
Guatemalan	6	0.03
Honduran	10	0.05
Panamanian	3	0.01
Salvadoran	1	<0.01
Other Central American	1	<0.01
Cuban	11	0.05
Dominican Republic	4	0.02
Mexican	99	0.49
Puerto Rican	151	0.74
South American	34	0.17
Argentinean	1	<0.01
Chilean	2	0.01
Colombian	14	0.07
Ecuadorian	2	0.01
Paraguayan	2	0.01
Peruvian	7	0.03
Venezuelan	6	0.03
Other Hispanic or Latino	43	0.21

Race*	Population	%
African-American/Black (441)	514	2.52
Not Hispanic (431)	498	2.44
Hispanic (10)	16	0.08
American Indian/Alaska Native (99)	169	0.83
Not Hispanic (95)	158	0.78
Hispanic (4)	11	0.05
Blackfeet (0)	1	<0.01
Canadian/French Am. Ind. (5)	15	0.07
Cherokee (5)	13	0.06
Chickasaw (0)	1	<0.01
Chippewa (0)	3	0.01
Choctaw (4)	4	0.02
Delaware (0)	1	<0.01
Iroquois (54)	66	0.32
Mexican American Ind. (0)	3	0.01
Potawatomi (1)	1	<0.01
Seminole (0)	1	<0.01
Sioux (4)	4	0.02
South American Ind. (1)	1	<0.01
Yuman (1)	1	<0.01
Asian (459)	533	2.62
Not Hispanic (453)	527	2.59
Hispanic (6)	6	0.03
Bangladeshi (1)	1	<0.01
Cambodian (5)	6	0.03
Chinese, ex. Taiwanese (74)	86	0.42
Filipino (52)	61	0.30
Indian (240)	263	1.29
Indonesian (1)	2	0.01
Japanese (6)	12	0.06
Korean (31)	41	0.20
Laotian (0)	1	<0.01
Nepalese (3)	3	0.01
Pakistani (17)	17	0.08
Sri Lankan (6)	7	0.03
Taiwanese (3)	4	0.02
Thai (3)	4	0.02
Vietnamese (7)	14	0.07
Hawaii Native/Pacific Islander (3)	8	0.04
Not Hispanic (3)	8	0.04
Native Hawaiian (2)	5	0.02
White (19,069)	19,275	94.61
Not Hispanic (18,805)	18,994	93.23
Hispanic (264)	281	1.38

Great Neck

Place Type: Village
County: Nassau
Population: 9,989†

*Notes: † The Census 2010 population figure is used to calculate the percentages in the Hispanic Origin and Race categories. Ancestry percentages are based on the 2006-2010 American Community Survey population (not shown); ‡ Numbers in parentheses indicate the number of people reporting a single ancestry; * Numbers in parentheses indicate the number of persons reporting this race alone, not in combination with any other race; Please refer to the Explanation of Data for more information.*

Ancestry‡	Population	%
Afghan (0)	9	0.09
American (480)	480	4.88
Arab (131)	141	1.43
Egyptian (58)	58	0.59
Iraqi (20)	20	0.20
Syrian (10)	10	0.10
Other Arab (43)	53	0.54
Austrian (45)	154	1.56
Belgian (11)	45	0.46
Brazilian (20)	20	0.20
British (6)	41	0.42
Canadian (0)	14	0.14
Czechoslovakian (8)	39	0.40
Danish (10)	10	0.10
Dutch (0)	18	0.18
Eastern European (366)	396	4.02
English (56)	156	1.59
European (76)	76	0.77
French Canadian (0)	10	0.10
German (96)	396	4.02
Hungarian (82)	174	1.77
Iranian (2,323)	2,382	24.20
Irish (150)	427	4.34
Israeli (311)	326	3.31
Italian (142)	511	5.19
Latvian (0)	11	0.11
Lithuanian (68)	153	1.55
Norwegian (11)	11	0.11
Polish (343)	1,188	12.07
Romanian (73)	192	1.95
Russian (444)	1,371	13.93
Scandinavian (11)	11	0.11
Scotch-Irish (13)	29	0.29
Slavic (11)	11	0.11
Slovak (0)	11	0.11
Swedish (0)	32	0.33
Ukrainian (0)	11	0.11
Welsh (0)	10	0.10
West Indian, ex. Hispanic (13)	13	0.13
West Indian (13)	13	0.13

Hispanic Origin	Population	%
Hispanic or Latino (of any race)	1,015	10.16
Central American, ex. Mexican	415	4.15
Costa Rican	10	0.10
Guatemalan	56	0.56
Honduran	11	0.11
Nicaraguan	4	0.04
Salvadoran	319	3.19
Other Central American	15	0.15
Cuban	5	0.05
Dominican Republic	49	0.49
Mexican	200	2.00
Puerto Rican	58	0.58
South American	144	1.44
Argentinean	21	0.21
Bolivian	1	0.01
Chilean	4	0.04
Colombian	39	0.39
Ecuadorian	19	0.19
Paraguayan	1	0.01
Peruvian	58	0.58
Uruguayan	1	0.01
Other Hispanic or Latino	144	1.44

Race*	Population	%
African-American/Black (195)	228	2.28
Not Hispanic (176)	196	1.96
Hispanic (19)	32	0.32
American Indian/Alaska Native (24)	41	0.41
Not Hispanic (2)	12	0.12
Hispanic (22)	29	0.29
South American Ind. (2)	2	0.02
Asian (722)	1,006	10.07
Not Hispanic (721)	1,002	10.03
Hispanic (1)	4	0.04
Burmese (5)	5	0.05
Chinese, ex. Taiwanese (375)	389	3.89
Filipino (18)	30	0.30
Indian (66)	89	0.89
Japanese (30)	32	0.32
Korean (130)	136	1.36
Laotian (0)	1	0.01
Pakistani (4)	9	0.09
Taiwanese (38)	39	0.39
Thai (5)	6	0.06
Vietnamese (5)	9	0.09
Hawaii Native/Pacific Islander (0)	9	0.09
Not Hispanic (0)	9	0.09
Samoan (0)	1	0.01
White (8,270)	8,635	86.45
Not Hispanic (7,749)	8,045	80.54
Hispanic (521)	590	5.91

Greece

Place Type: CDP
County: Monroe
Population: 14,519†

Ancestry‡	Population	%
African, Sub-Saharan (94)	108	0.76
African (94)	108	0.76
American (297)	297	2.09
Arab (0)	8	0.06
Lebanese (0)	8	0.06
Austrian (26)	128	0.90
Belgian (26)	69	0.49
British (52)	109	0.77
Bulgarian (16)	16	0.11
Canadian (9)	49	0.35
Czech (33)	75	0.53
Czechoslovakian (0)	17	0.12
Danish (10)	58	0.41
Dutch (147)	559	3.94
Eastern European (32)	32	0.23
English (557)	1,787	12.60
European (88)	116	0.82
French, ex. Basque (48)	457	3.22
French Canadian (51)	226	1.59
German (1,227)	4,079	28.76
Greek (48)	48	0.34
Guyanese (40)	40	0.28
Hungarian (0)	54	0.38
Irish (668)	3,149	22.21
Italian (2,319)	4,021	28.35
Latvian (0)	32	0.23
Lithuanian (0)	39	0.28
Macedonian (30)	30	0.21
Norwegian (0)	21	0.15
Pennsylvania German (13)	13	0.09
Polish (263)	739	5.21
Portuguese (55)	100	0.71
Russian (9)	42	0.30
Scotch-Irish (113)	221	1.56
Scottish (123)	229	1.61
Slavic (0)	10	0.07
Slovak (10)	10	0.07
Swedish (0)	40	0.28
Swiss (9)	31	0.22
Turkish (63)	63	0.44
Ukrainian (94)	165	1.16
Welsh (10)	61	0.43
West Indian, ex. Hispanic (44)	52	0.37
Haitian (21)	21	0.15
Jamaican (23)	31	0.22

Hispanic Origin	Population	%
Hispanic or Latino (of any race)	781	5.38
Central American, ex. Mexican	24	0.17
Guatemalan	2	0.01
Honduran	2	0.01
Nicaraguan	6	0.04
Panamanian	3	0.02
Salvadoran	11	0.08
Cuban	60	0.41
Dominican Republic	48	0.33
Mexican	57	0.39
Puerto Rican	514	3.54
South American	37	0.25
Chilean	18	0.12
Colombian	9	0.06
Ecuadorian	3	0.02
Peruvian	2	0.01
Uruguayan	1	0.01
Venezuelan	3	0.02
Other South American	1	0.01
Other Hispanic or Latino	41	0.28

Race*	Population	%
African-American/Black (780)	944	6.50
Not Hispanic (736)	871	6.00
Hispanic (44)	73	0.50
American Indian/Alaska Native (38)	96	0.66
Not Hispanic (30)	80	0.55
Hispanic (8)	16	0.11
Blackfeet (0)	3	0.02
Canadian/French Am. Ind. (1)	1	0.01
Central American Ind. (1)	2	0.01
Cherokee (0)	11	0.08
Chippewa (4)	4	0.03
Choctaw (2)	4	0.03
Delaware (0)	1	0.01
Iroquois (13)	16	0.11
Navajo (1)	1	0.01
Sioux (0)	1	0.01
South American Ind. (3)	6	0.04
Yuman (1)	1	0.01
Asian (343)	406	2.80
Not Hispanic (343)	402	2.77
Hispanic (0)	4	0.03
Cambodian (15)	16	0.11
Chinese, ex. Taiwanese (62)	70	0.48
Filipino (38)	52	0.36
Indian (57)	64	0.44
Indonesian (0)	1	0.01
Japanese (5)	13	0.09
Korean (32)	39	0.27
Laotian (38)	42	0.29
Nepalese (1)	1	0.01
Pakistani (9)	9	0.06
Sri Lankan (1)	1	0.01
Thai (3)	3	0.02
Vietnamese (71)	81	0.56
Hawaii Native/Pacific Islander (2)	9	0.06
Not Hispanic (2)	5	0.03
Hispanic (0)	4	0.03
Native Hawaiian (2)	2	0.01
Samoan (0)	1	0.01
White (12,810)	13,087	90.14
Not Hispanic (12,369)	12,576	86.62
Hispanic (441)	511	3.52

Greece

Place Type: Town
County: Monroe
Population: 96,095†

Ancestry‡	Population	%
African, Sub-Saharan (373)	434	0.45
African (217)	244	0.26
Ethiopian (49)	49	0.05
South African (38)	48	0.05
Sudanese (27)	51	0.05
Other Sub-Saharan African (42)	42	0.04
Albanian (113)	113	0.12
American (2,361)	2,361	2.47
Arab (161)	384	0.40
Arab (0)	42	0.04
Lebanese (98)	214	0.22
Palestinian (0)	31	0.03
Syrian (63)	97	0.10
Australian (29)	87	0.09
Austrian (36)	225	0.24
Belgian (57)	254	0.27
Brazilian (23)	23	0.02
British (178)	387	0.41
Bulgarian (25)	25	0.03

*Notes: † The Census 2010 population figure is used to calculate the percentages in the Hispanic Origin and Race categories. Ancestry percentages are based on the 2006-2010 American Community Survey population (not shown); ‡ Numbers in parentheses indicate the number of people reporting a single ancestry; * Numbers in parentheses indicate the number of persons reporting this race alone, not in combination with any other race; Please refer to the Explanation of Data for more information.*

Canadian (228)	525	0.55
Celtic (12)	12	0.01
Croatian (0)	13	0.01
Czech (77)	507	0.53
Czechoslovakian (55)	151	0.16
Danish (40)	144	0.15
Dutch (571)	2,890	3.03
Eastern European (81)	115	0.12
English (3,011)	12,568	13.17
Estonian (0)	40	0.04
European (406)	451	0.47
Finnish (15)	62	0.06
French, ex. Basque (553)	3,655	3.83
French Canadian (346)	1,220	1.28
German (6,357)	25,631	26.85
Greek (153)	610	0.64
Guyanese (40)	40	0.04
Hungarian (85)	397	0.42
Iranian (14)	14	0.01
Irish (4,177)	19,015	19.92
Italian (15,156)	26,121	27.36
Latvian (12)	71	0.07
Lithuanian (183)	543	0.57
Luxemburger (0)	15	0.02
Macedonian (92)	119	0.12
Norwegian (139)	434	0.45
Pennsylvania German (46)	145	0.15
Polish (1,797)	5,879	6.16
Portuguese (111)	314	0.33
Romanian (16)	60	0.06
Russian (229)	654	0.69
Scandinavian (10)	88	0.09
Scotch-Irish (524)	1,469	1.54
Scottish (452)	1,843	1.93
Serbian (10)	10	0.01
Slavic (156)	240	0.25
Slovak (81)	236	0.25
Slovene (31)	31	0.03
Swedish (31)	447	0.47
Swiss (16)	116	0.12
Turkish (489)	561	0.59
Ukrainian (993)	1,758	1.84
Welsh (36)	564	0.59
West Indian, ex. Hispanic (285)	447	0.47
Barbadian (16)	16	0.02
Haitian (114)	114	0.12
Jamaican (144)	243	0.25
Trinidadian/Tobagonian (11)	27	0.03
West Indian (0)	47	0.05
Yugoslavian (77)	91	0.10

Hispanic Origin	Population	%
Hispanic or Latino (of any race)	4,625	4.81
Central American, ex. Mexican	159	0.17
Costa Rican	11	0.01
Guatemalan	27	0.03
Honduran	12	0.01
Nicaraguan	22	0.02
Panamanian	18	0.02
Salvadoran	68	0.07
Other Central American	1	<0.01
Cuban	312	0.32
Dominican Republic	194	0.20
Mexican	338	0.35
Puerto Rican	3,072	3.20
South American	257	0.27
Argentinean	7	0.01
Bolivian	1	<0.01
Chilean	63	0.07
Colombian	89	0.09
Ecuadorian	21	0.02
Paraguayan	4	<0.01
Peruvian	33	0.03
Uruguayan	4	<0.01
Venezuelan	27	0.03
Other South American	8	0.01
Other Hispanic or Latino	293	0.30

Race*	Population	%
African-American/Black (5,743)	6,728	7.00
Not Hispanic (5,446)	6,227	6.48
Hispanic (297)	501	0.52
American Indian/Alaska Native (263)	658	0.68
Not Hispanic (212)	545	0.57
Hispanic (51)	113	0.12
Apache (1)	3	<0.01
Arapaho (0)	4	<0.01
Blackfeet (1)	9	0.01
Canadian/French Am. Ind. (8)	14	0.01
Central American Ind. (5)	6	0.01
Cherokee (7)	75	0.08
Chippewa (10)	13	0.01
Choctaw (3)	8	0.01
Comanche (0)	1	<0.01
Cree (3)	4	<0.01
Creek (2)	2	<0.01
Delaware (0)	1	<0.01
Houma (2)	2	<0.01
Inupiat *(Alaska Native)* (0)	1	<0.01
Iroquois (114)	181	0.19
Mexican American Ind. (4)	7	0.01
Navajo (2)	2	<0.01
Seminole (1)	4	<0.01
Shoshone (0)	1	<0.01
Sioux (3)	11	0.01
South American Ind. (7)	16	0.02
Spanish American Ind. (1)	5	0.01
Tlingit-Haida *(Alaska Native)* (0)	1	<0.01
Yuman (1)	1	<0.01
Asian (1,664)	2,054	2.14
Not Hispanic (1,643)	2,014	2.10
Hispanic (21)	40	0.04
Bangladeshi (6)	9	0.01
Cambodian (33)	47	0.05
Chinese, ex. Taiwanese (294)	351	0.37
Filipino (141)	213	0.22
Indian (283)	330	0.34
Indonesian (3)	5	0.01
Japanese (28)	71	0.07
Korean (209)	261	0.27
Laotian (112)	139	0.14
Nepalese (3)	3	<0.01
Pakistani (25)	32	0.03
Sri Lankan (5)	5	0.01
Taiwanese (10)	11	0.01
Thai (21)	24	0.02
Vietnamese (433)	473	0.49
Hawaii Native/Pacific Islander (14)	59	0.06
Not Hispanic (12)	40	0.04
Hispanic (2)	19	0.02
Guamanian/Chamorro (4)	7	0.01
Native Hawaiian (5)	18	0.02
Samoan (2)	5	0.01
White (85,220)	86,829	90.36
Not Hispanic (82,634)	83,902	87.31
Hispanic (2,586)	2,927	3.05

Greenburgh

Place Type: Town
County: Westchester
Population: 88,400†

Ancestry‡	Population	%
African, Sub-Saharan (642)	914	1.04
African (287)	536	0.61
Ethiopian (39)	39	0.04
Ghanaian (16)	16	0.02
Kenyan (55)	55	0.06
Nigerian (231)	231	0.26
Sierra Leonean (14)	14	0.02
South African (0)	23	0.03
Albanian (80)	80	0.09
American (3,324)	3,324	3.79
Arab (306)	485	0.55
Arab (0)	22	0.03
Egyptian (9)	37	0.04
Jordanian (45)	45	0.05
Lebanese (213)	224	0.26
Moroccan (0)	35	0.04
Palestinian (0)	8	0.01
Syrian (32)	107	0.12
Other Arab (7)	7	0.01
Armenian (109)	175	0.20
Assyrian/Chaldean/Syriac (15)	29	0.03
Australian (0)	24	0.03
Austrian (267)	1,117	1.27
Basque (0)	8	0.01
Belgian (21)	93	0.11
Brazilian (74)	123	0.14
British (358)	519	0.59
Bulgarian (54)	54	0.06
Canadian (53)	282	0.32
Celtic (0)	7	0.01
Croatian (384)	609	0.69
Czech (40)	415	0.47
Czechoslovakian (72)	172	0.20
Danish (10)	130	0.15
Dutch (174)	580	0.66
Eastern European (1,840)	2,009	2.29
English (1,185)	4,118	4.70
Estonian (15)	57	0.07
European (1,275)	1,360	1.55
Finnish (34)	85	0.10
French, ex. Basque (225)	1,496	1.71
French Canadian (166)	483	0.55
German (1,568)	7,526	8.58
German Russian (0)	13	0.01
Greek (762)	1,202	1.37
Guyanese (52)	226	0.26
Hungarian (520)	1,242	1.42
Iranian (248)	267	0.30
Irish (4,736)	11,358	12.95
Israeli (172)	225	0.26
Italian (9,180)	16,339	18.64
Latvian (48)	153	0.17
Lithuanian (51)	328	0.37
Macedonian (24)	24	0.03
Maltese (0)	11	0.01
Northern European (47)	65	0.07
Norwegian (204)	530	0.60
Polish (1,541)	4,636	5.29
Portuguese (534)	718	0.82
Romanian (234)	489	0.56
Russian (2,209)	5,042	5.75
Scandinavian (46)	79	0.09
Scotch-Irish (336)	741	0.85
Scottish (258)	987	1.13
Serbian (8)	8	0.01
Slavic (6)	6	0.01
Slovak (117)	388	0.44
Swedish (33)	374	0.43
Swiss (46)	211	0.24
Turkish (85)	172	0.20
Ukrainian (263)	652	0.74
Welsh (0)	81	0.09
West Indian, ex. Hispanic (2,889)	3,562	4.06
Barbadian (143)	155	0.18
Belizean (10)	19	0.02
British West Indian (65)	76	0.09
Haitian (469)	516	0.59
Jamaican (1,753)	2,150	2.45
Trinidadian/Tobagonian (159)	201	0.23
West Indian (290)	445	0.51
Yugoslavian (123)	130	0.15

Hispanic Origin	Population	%
Hispanic or Latino (of any race)	12,366	13.99
Central American, ex. Mexican	878	0.99
Costa Rican	34	0.04
Guatemalan	434	0.49
Honduran	90	0.10
Nicaraguan	50	0.06
Panamanian	73	0.08
Salvadoran	185	0.21
Other Central American	12	0.01
Cuban	565	0.64
Dominican Republic	1,400	1.58
Mexican	1,711	1.94
Puerto Rican	2,629	2.97

*Notes: † The Census 2010 population figure is used to calculate the percentages in the Hispanic Origin and Race categories. Ancestry percentages are based on the 2006-2010 American Community Survey population (not shown); ‡ Numbers in parentheses indicate the number of people reporting a single ancestry; * Numbers in parentheses indicate the number of persons reporting this race alone, not in combination with any other race; Please refer to the Explanation of Data for more information.*

South American	4,004	4.53
Argentinean	188	0.21
Bolivian	48	0.05
Chilean	192	0.22
Colombian	845	0.96
Ecuadorian	1,434	1.62
Paraguayan	144	0.16
Peruvian	962	1.09
Uruguayan	65	0.07
Venezuelan	94	0.11
Other South American	32	0.04
Other Hispanic or Latino	1,179	1.33

Race*	Population	%
African-American/Black (11,103)	12,045	13.63
Not Hispanic (10,377)	11,022	12.47
Hispanic (726)	1,023	1.16
American Indian/Alaska Native (201)	630	0.71
Not Hispanic (64)	334	0.38
Hispanic (137)	296	0.33
Aleut *(Alaska Native)* (0)	1	<0.01
Apache (1)	6	0.01
Blackfeet (0)	7	0.01
Canadian/French Am. Ind. (0)	2	<0.01
Central American Ind. (1)	4	<0.01
Cherokee (5)	90	0.10
Cheyenne (0)	5	0.01
Chickasaw (0)	1	<0.01
Chippewa (0)	4	<0.01
Choctaw (0)	3	<0.01
Comanche (0)	5	0.01
Cree (0)	3	<0.01
Delaware (3)	5	0.01
Inupiat *(Alaska Native)* (1)	1	<0.01
Iroquois (6)	19	0.02
Lumbee (1)	1	<0.01
Mexican American Ind. (10)	25	0.03
Navajo (0)	3	<0.01
Seminole (0)	3	<0.01
Sioux (1)	8	0.01
South American Ind. (30)	72	0.08
Spanish American Ind. (14)	23	0.03
Asian (9,210)	10,180	11.52
Not Hispanic (9,155)	10,025	11.34
Hispanic (55)	155	0.18
Bangladeshi (37)	44	0.05
Bhutanese (8)	8	0.01
Burmese (28)	28	0.03
Cambodian (4)	4	<0.01
Chinese, ex. Taiwanese (1,910)	2,225	2.52
Filipino (826)	959	1.08
Indian (3,241)	3,518	3.98
Indonesian (18)	24	0.03
Japanese (1,018)	1,230	1.39
Korean (1,328)	1,452	1.64
Laotian (3)	5	0.01
Malaysian (6)	11	0.01
Nepalese (48)	55	0.06
Pakistani (212)	244	0.28
Sri Lankan (14)	20	0.02
Taiwanese (113)	142	0.16
Thai (62)	77	0.09
Vietnamese (81)	95	0.11
Hawaii Native/Pacific Islander (33)	116	0.13
Not Hispanic (23)	88	0.10
Hispanic (10)	28	0.03
Guamanian/Chamorro (11)	16	0.02
Marshallese (1)	1	<0.01
Native Hawaiian (1)	10	0.01
Samoan (1)	5	0.01
White (61,185)	63,005	71.27
Not Hispanic (54,539)	55,731	63.04
Hispanic (6,646)	7,274	8.23

Greenfield

Place Type: Town
County: Saratoga
Population: 7,775†

Ancestry‡	Population	%
American (1,602)	1,602	20.71
Arab (0)	15	0.19
Lebanese (0)	15	0.19
Australian (31)	31	0.40
Austrian (20)	47	0.61
Canadian (0)	50	0.65
Croatian (9)	9	0.12
Czech (0)	7	0.09
Czechoslovakian (15)	40	0.52
Dutch (117)	348	4.50
English (383)	1,016	13.13
European (17)	69	0.89
Finnish (0)	12	0.16
French, ex. Basque (37)	482	6.23
French Canadian (107)	204	2.64
German (326)	1,229	15.88
Greek (26)	46	0.59
Hungarian (17)	34	0.44
Irish (516)	1,407	18.19
Italian (271)	697	9.01
Lithuanian (45)	102	1.32
Norwegian (18)	18	0.23
Polish (77)	346	4.47
Russian (73)	73	0.94
Scandinavian (0)	22	0.28
Scotch-Irish (75)	98	1.27
Scottish (54)	148	1.91
Slavic (12)	12	0.16
Slovak (26)	55	0.71
Swedish (26)	84	1.09
Swiss (13)	37	0.48
Ukrainian (33)	67	0.87
Welsh (6)	11	0.14
West Indian, ex. Hispanic (47)	47	0.61
Jamaican (47)	47	0.61
Yugoslavian (0)	14	0.18

Hispanic Origin	Population	%
Hispanic or Latino (of any race)	139	1.79
Central American, ex. Mexican	15	0.19
Costa Rican	2	0.03
Guatemalan	7	0.09
Honduran	4	0.05
Salvadoran	2	0.03
Cuban	4	0.05
Dominican Republic	3	0.04
Mexican	39	0.50
Puerto Rican	51	0.66
South American	12	0.15
Chilean	1	0.01
Colombian	1	0.01
Ecuadorian	7	0.09
Peruvian	1	0.01
Venezuelan	2	0.03
Other Hispanic or Latino	15	0.19

Race*	Population	%
African-American/Black (53)	98	1.26
Not Hispanic (52)	96	1.23
Hispanic (1)	2	0.03
American Indian/Alaska Native (6)	50	0.64
Not Hispanic (4)	47	0.60
Hispanic (2)	3	0.04
Blackfeet (0)	1	0.01
Cherokee (0)	7	0.09
Iroquois (0)	6	0.08
Sioux (0)	1	0.01
Asian (26)	56	0.72
Not Hispanic (26)	56	0.72
Chinese, ex. Taiwanese (6)	12	0.15
Filipino (3)	6	0.08
Indian (4)	11	0.14
Indonesian (1)	1	0.01
Japanese (3)	9	0.12
Korean (4)	8	0.10
Thai (1)	1	0.01
Vietnamese (3)	3	0.04
Hawaii Native/Pacific Islander (2)	7	0.09
Not Hispanic (2)	7	0.09
Native Hawaiian (1)	6	0.08
Samoan (1)	1	0.01
White (7,542)	7,659	98.51
Not Hispanic (7,432)	7,540	96.98
Hispanic (110)	119	1.53

Greenlawn

Place Type: CDP
County: Suffolk
Population: 13,742†

Ancestry‡	Population	%
African, Sub-Saharan (42)	56	0.43
African (27)	41	0.32
South African (15)	15	0.12
American (224)	224	1.74
Arab (7)	28	0.22
Lebanese (7)	17	0.13
Other Arab (0)	11	0.09
Armenian (22)	22	0.17
Austrian (30)	136	1.06
Belgian (15)	15	0.12
British (36)	80	0.62
Canadian (0)	32	0.25
Croatian (11)	37	0.29
Cypriot (56)	56	0.43
Czech (28)	46	0.36
Czechoslovakian (8)	15	0.12
Danish (8)	16	0.12
Dutch (27)	111	0.86
Eastern European (216)	216	1.68
English (303)	1,089	8.45
Estonian (0)	11	0.09
European (33)	48	0.37
Finnish (21)	21	0.16
French, ex. Basque (33)	148	1.15
French Canadian (0)	21	0.16
German (415)	2,004	15.55
Greek (83)	144	1.12
Guyanese (22)	22	0.17
Hungarian (17)	188	1.46
Iranian (7)	21	0.16
Irish (909)	2,819	21.88
Israeli (21)	21	0.16
Italian (1,340)	2,930	22.74
Latvian (0)	22	0.17
Lithuanian (9)	22	0.17
Northern European (10)	10	0.08
Norwegian (13)	46	0.36
Polish (114)	790	6.13
Portuguese (8)	26	0.20
Romanian (11)	54	0.42
Russian (230)	561	4.35
Scandinavian (0)	27	0.21
Scotch-Irish (29)	159	1.23
Scottish (5)	91	0.71
Serbian (0)	26	0.20
Swedish (100)	248	1.92
Swiss (24)	24	0.19
Turkish (18)	26	0.20
Ukrainian (10)	69	0.54
Welsh (0)	32	0.25
West Indian, ex. Hispanic (395)	420	3.26
Haitian (81)	81	0.63
Jamaican (243)	254	1.97
Trinidadian/Tobagonian (13)	13	0.10
West Indian (58)	72	0.56

Hispanic Origin	Population	%
Hispanic or Latino (of any race)	1,724	12.55
Central American, ex. Mexican	770	5.60
Costa Rican	5	0.04
Guatemalan	141	1.03
Honduran	71	0.52
Nicaraguan	7	0.05
Panamanian	7	0.05
Salvadoran	538	3.92
Other Central American	1	0.01
Cuban	41	0.30

*Notes: † The Census 2010 population figure is used to calculate the percentages in the Hispanic Origin and Race categories. Ancestry percentages are based on the 2006-2010 American Community Survey population (not shown); ‡ Numbers in parentheses indicate the number of people reporting a single ancestry; * Numbers in parentheses indicate the number of persons reporting this race alone, not in combination with any other race; Please refer to the Explanation of Data for more information.*

Dominican Republic	77	0.56
Mexican	80	0.58
Puerto Rican	337	2.45
South American	248	1.80
Argentinean	20	0.15
Bolivian	1	0.01
Chilean	22	0.16
Colombian	48	0.35
Ecuadorian	80	0.58
Paraguayan	13	0.09
Peruvian	52	0.38
Venezuelan	12	0.09
Other Hispanic or Latino	171	1.24

Race*	Population	%
African-American/Black (1,915)	2,094	15.24
Not Hispanic (1,841)	1,971	14.34
Hispanic (74)	123	0.90
American Indian/Alaska Native (52)	152	1.11
Not Hispanic (34)	106	0.77
Hispanic (18)	46	0.33
Apache (6)	8	0.06
Blackfeet (0)	8	0.06
Cherokee (3)	15	0.11
Chickasaw (0)	1	0.01
Chippewa (1)	1	0.01
Comanche (5)	5	0.04
Delaware (0)	1	0.01
Iroquois (7)	7	0.05
Lumbee (1)	2	0.01
Mexican American Ind. (3)	3	0.02
Navajo (0)	1	0.01
Seminole (0)	1	0.01
Sioux (0)	4	0.03
South American Ind. (2)	17	0.12
Asian (564)	661	4.81
Not Hispanic (555)	645	4.69
Hispanic (9)	16	0.12
Burmese (1)	3	0.02
Cambodian (1)	1	0.01
Chinese, ex. Taiwanese (136)	164	1.19
Filipino (45)	63	0.46
Indian (146)	158	1.15
Indonesian (1)	1	0.01
Japanese (12)	15	0.11
Korean (101)	116	0.84
Malaysian (1)	1	0.01
Pakistani (71)	77	0.56
Taiwanese (9)	10	0.07
Thai (6)	8	0.06
Vietnamese (13)	13	0.09
Hawaii Native/Pacific Islander (2)	12	0.09
Not Hispanic (2)	6	0.04
Hispanic (0)	6	0.04
Native Hawaiian (0)	1	0.01
White (10,168)	10,468	76.18
Not Hispanic (9,338)	9,522	69.29
Hispanic (830)	946	6.88

Guilderland

Place Type: Town
County: Albany
Population: 35,303†

Ancestry‡	Population	%
African, Sub-Saharan (115)	115	0.33
African (102)	102	0.29
Ghanaian (13)	13	0.04
Albanian (211)	211	0.60
American (1,442)	1,442	4.10
Arab (109)	172	0.49
Egyptian (24)	24	0.07
Jordanian (9)	9	0.03
Lebanese (23)	49	0.14
Palestinian (3)	3	0.01
Syrian (2)	39	0.11
Other Arab (48)	48	0.14
Armenian (50)	59	0.17
Austrian (23)	279	0.79
Basque (0)	38	0.11
British (133)	224	0.64
Bulgarian (13)	13	0.04
Canadian (66)	132	0.38
Carpatho Rusyn (0)	14	0.04
Croatian (0)	12	0.03
Czech (16)	154	0.44
Danish (21)	92	0.26
Dutch (144)	1,551	4.41
Eastern European (107)	107	0.30
English (1,060)	4,213	11.99
European (501)	577	1.64
Finnish (37)	37	0.11
French, ex. Basque (248)	1,792	5.10
French Canadian (293)	774	2.20
German (1,399)	7,009	19.94
Greek (50)	324	0.92
Guyanese (116)	116	0.33
Hungarian (67)	274	0.78
Icelander (10)	10	0.03
Iranian (70)	84	0.24
Irish (2,599)	8,494	24.17
Italian (3,172)	7,406	21.07
Latvian (50)	80	0.23
Lithuanian (23)	105	0.30
Norwegian (50)	152	0.43
Pennsylvania German (0)	6	0.02
Polish (771)	2,755	7.84
Portuguese (47)	90	0.26
Romanian (11)	11	0.03
Russian (356)	901	2.56
Scandinavian (21)	30	0.09
Scotch-Irish (205)	432	1.23
Scottish (223)	746	2.12
Slavic (26)	26	0.07
Slovak (7)	104	0.30
Slovene (28)	28	0.08
Swedish (28)	512	1.46
Swiss (30)	51	0.15
Turkish (11)	35	0.10
Ukrainian (65)	330	0.94
Welsh (16)	297	0.85
West Indian, ex. Hispanic (41)	98	0.28
Barbadian (0)	16	0.05
Haitian (0)	13	0.04
Jamaican (13)	13	0.04
Trinidadian/Tobagonian (14)	42	0.12
West Indian (14)	14	0.04
Yugoslavian (53)	53	0.15

Hispanic Origin	Population	%
Hispanic or Latino (of any race)	1,132	3.21
Central American, ex. Mexican	86	0.24
Costa Rican	8	0.02
Guatemalan	16	0.05
Honduran	15	0.04
Nicaraguan	9	0.03
Panamanian	11	0.03
Salvadoran	27	0.08
Cuban	54	0.15
Dominican Republic	118	0.33
Mexican	127	0.36
Puerto Rican	420	1.19
South American	170	0.48
Argentinean	30	0.08
Bolivian	3	0.01
Chilean	9	0.03
Colombian	60	0.17
Ecuadorian	24	0.07
Paraguayan	2	0.01
Peruvian	26	0.07
Uruguayan	2	0.01
Venezuelan	7	0.02
Other South American	7	0.02
Other Hispanic or Latino	157	0.44

Race*	Population	%
African-American/Black (1,204)	1,489	4.22
Not Hispanic (1,127)	1,353	3.83
Hispanic (77)	136	0.39
American Indian/Alaska Native (56)	170	0.48
Not Hispanic (42)	130	0.37
Hispanic (14)	40	0.11
Apache (0)	2	0.01
Blackfeet (0)	5	0.01
Canadian/French Am. Ind. (1)	1	<0.01
Central American Ind. (2)	5	0.01
Cherokee (3)	18	0.05
Chickasaw (3)	3	0.01
Chippewa (1)	1	<0.01
Choctaw (0)	3	0.01
Comanche (0)	1	<0.01
Cree (0)	1	<0.01
Creek (0)	1	<0.01
Iroquois (9)	23	0.07
Mexican American Ind. (1)	5	0.01
Seminole (2)	2	0.01
Sioux (1)	1	<0.01
South American Ind. (3)	10	0.03
Spanish American Ind. (1)	1	<0.01
Asian (2,643)	2,878	8.15
Not Hispanic (2,631)	2,847	8.06
Hispanic (12)	31	0.09
Bangladeshi (30)	34	0.10
Cambodian (2)	4	0.01
Chinese, ex. Taiwanese (677)	736	2.08
Filipino (87)	129	0.37
Indian (1,180)	1,237	3.50
Indonesian (8)	9	0.03
Japanese (65)	95	0.27
Korean (322)	351	0.99
Laotian (2)	5	0.01
Malaysian (1)	2	0.01
Nepalese (8)	9	0.03
Pakistani (71)	84	0.24
Sri Lankan (27)	28	0.08
Taiwanese (26)	33	0.09
Thai (12)	14	0.04
Vietnamese (53)	60	0.17
Hawaii Native/Pacific Islander (14)	26	0.07
Not Hispanic (14)	22	0.06
Hispanic (0)	4	0.01
Fijian (2)	2	0.01
Guamanian/Chamorro (3)	3	0.01
Native Hawaiian (1)	4	0.01
Samoan (3)	3	0.01
White (30,434)	30,965	87.71
Not Hispanic (29,813)	30,242	85.66
Hispanic (621)	723	2.05

Halfmoon

Place Type: Town
County: Saratoga
Population: 21,535†

Ancestry‡	Population	%
Afghan (17)	42	0.20
Albanian (101)	134	0.64
American (1,572)	1,572	7.46
Arab (86)	112	0.53
Egyptian (76)	76	0.36
Lebanese (10)	36	0.17
Armenian (24)	30	0.14
Austrian (18)	83	0.39
Belgian (0)	13	0.06
British (0)	61	0.29
Bulgarian (0)	19	0.09
Canadian (90)	129	0.61
Celtic (11)	11	0.05
Czech (12)	54	0.26
Czechoslovakian (6)	53	0.25
Danish (51)	129	0.61
Dutch (116)	681	3.23
Eastern European (24)	31	0.15
English (602)	2,561	12.15
European (31)	38	0.18
Finnish (0)	89	0.42
French, ex. Basque (469)	2,627	12.47
French Canadian (277)	645	3.06

*Notes: † The Census 2010 population figure is used to calculate the percentages in the Hispanic Origin and Race categories. Ancestry percentages are based on the 2006-2010 American Community Survey population (not shown); ‡ Numbers in parentheses indicate the number of people reporting a single ancestry; * Numbers in parentheses indicate the number of persons reporting this race alone, not in combination with any other race; Please refer to the Explanation of Data for more information.*

Ancestry	Population	%
German (824)	4,046	19.20
Greek (20)	45	0.21
Guyanese (44)	44	0.21
Hungarian (10)	137	0.65
Iranian (16)	16	0.08
Irish (1,173)	5,127	24.33
Italian (1,404)	3,521	16.71
Latvian (0)	55	0.26
Lithuanian (31)	109	0.52
Norwegian (13)	122	0.58
Pennsylvania German (26)	26	0.12
Polish (613)	1,870	8.87
Portuguese (23)	92	0.44
Romanian (0)	14	0.07
Russian (172)	398	1.89
Scandinavian (14)	61	0.29
Scotch-Irish (21)	319	1.51
Scottish (41)	429	2.04
Serbian (42)	42	0.20
Slavic (0)	11	0.05
Slovak (18)	114	0.54
Swedish (50)	290	1.38
Swiss (0)	19	0.09
Ukrainian (75)	227	1.08
Welsh (24)	135	0.64
West Indian, ex. Hispanic (54)	174	0.83
Bahamian (0)	13	0.06
Barbadian (24)	24	0.11
Jamaican (19)	126	0.60
West Indian (11)	11	0.05

Hispanic Origin	Population	%
Hispanic or Latino (of any race)	612	2.84
Central American, ex. Mexican	46	0.21
Costa Rican	7	0.03
Guatemalan	1	<0.01
Honduran	2	0.01
Nicaraguan	7	0.03
Panamanian	10	0.05
Salvadoran	19	0.09
Cuban	22	0.10
Dominican Republic	68	0.32
Mexican	107	0.50
Puerto Rican	229	1.06
South American	80	0.37
Argentinean	9	0.04
Bolivian	2	0.01
Chilean	9	0.04
Colombian	13	0.06
Ecuadorian	17	0.08
Peruvian	20	0.09
Venezuelan	7	0.03
Other South American	3	0.01
Other Hispanic or Latino	60	0.28

Race*	Population	%
African-American/Black (416)	580	2.69
Not Hispanic (379)	521	2.42
Hispanic (37)	59	0.27
American Indian/Alaska Native (49)	128	0.59
Not Hispanic (48)	119	0.55
Hispanic (1)	9	0.04
Alaska Athabascan *(Ala. Nat.)* (1)	1	<0.01
Blackfeet (2)	6	0.03
Canadian/French Am. Ind. (0)	2	0.01
Cherokee (3)	18	0.08
Iroquois (13)	21	0.10
Lumbee (1)	1	<0.01
Navajo (6)	6	0.03
Potawatomi (0)	3	0.01
Sioux (0)	2	0.01
South American Ind. (3)	5	0.02
Asian (714)	901	4.18
Not Hispanic (712)	899	4.17
Hispanic (2)	2	0.01
Cambodian (2)	2	0.01
Chinese, ex. Taiwanese (161)	180	0.84
Filipino (28)	59	0.27
Indian (246)	266	1.24
Indonesian (2)	3	0.01
Japanese (31)	43	0.20
Korean (76)	97	0.45
Laotian (0)	3	0.01
Malaysian (4)	4	0.02
Nepalese (4)	4	0.02
Pakistani (93)	103	0.48
Sri Lankan (0)	3	0.01
Taiwanese (4)	6	0.03
Thai (2)	7	0.03
Vietnamese (27)	40	0.19
Hawaii Native/Pacific Islander (11)	24	0.11
Not Hispanic (8)	20	0.09
Hispanic (3)	4	0.02
Guamanian/Chamorro (5)	5	0.02
Native Hawaiian (4)	16	0.07
Samoan (1)	1	<0.01
White (19,730)	20,134	93.49
Not Hispanic (19,359)	19,726	91.60
Hispanic (371)	408	1.89

Hamburg

Place Type: Town
County: Erie
Population: 56,936†

Ancestry‡	Population	%
African, Sub-Saharan (57)	57	0.10
South African (57)	57	0.10
Alsatian (9)	27	0.05
American (1,835)	1,835	3.24
Arab (93)	325	0.57
Arab (23)	70	0.12
Egyptian (38)	38	0.07
Jordanian (0)	11	0.02
Lebanese (17)	136	0.24
Moroccan (0)	26	0.05
Palestinian (15)	15	0.03
Other Arab (0)	29	0.05
Austrian (35)	216	0.38
Belgian (0)	25	0.04
British (66)	154	0.27
Bulgarian (183)	192	0.34
Canadian (180)	368	0.65
Celtic (43)	43	0.08
Croatian (37)	246	0.43
Czech (45)	144	0.25
Czechoslovakian (27)	57	0.10
Danish (32)	66	0.12
Dutch (69)	660	1.17
Eastern European (37)	45	0.08
English (1,093)	5,284	9.34
European (223)	250	0.44
Finnish (0)	9	0.02
French, ex. Basque (199)	2,079	3.67
French Canadian (153)	586	1.04
German (5,209)	19,590	34.62
Greek (61)	186	0.33
Guyanese (33)	33	0.06
Hungarian (200)	761	1.34
Iranian (44)	44	0.08
Irish (3,944)	15,679	27.71
Italian (3,775)	10,185	18.00
Latvian (0)	11	0.02
Lithuanian (26)	63	0.11
Macedonian (119)	149	0.26
Norwegian (9)	52	0.09
Pennsylvania German (39)	103	0.18
Polish (5,175)	13,189	23.31
Portuguese (0)	45	0.08
Russian (39)	385	0.68
Scandinavian (0)	8	0.01
Scotch-Irish (164)	542	0.96
Scottish (159)	836	1.48
Serbian (55)	279	0.49
Slavic (0)	57	0.10
Slovak (24)	182	0.32
Slovene (0)	16	0.03
Swedish (188)	948	1.68
Swiss (17)	57	0.10
Ukrainian (185)	664	1.17
Welsh (105)	292	0.52
West Indian, ex. Hispanic (200)	230	0.41
Bahamian (21)	21	0.04
Belizean (0)	30	0.05
Jamaican (144)	144	0.25
Trinidadian/Tobagonian (13)	13	0.02
West Indian (22)	22	0.04
Yugoslavian (43)	70	0.12

Hispanic Origin	Population	%
Hispanic or Latino (of any race)	1,214	2.13
Central American, ex. Mexican	38	0.07
Costa Rican	7	0.01
Guatemalan	20	0.04
Honduran	2	<0.01
Nicaraguan	4	0.01
Salvadoran	5	0.01
Cuban	29	0.05
Dominican Republic	32	0.06
Mexican	296	0.52
Puerto Rican	551	0.97
South American	72	0.13
Argentinean	4	0.01
Bolivian	7	0.01
Chilean	8	0.01
Colombian	37	0.06
Ecuadorian	2	<0.01
Paraguayan	2	<0.01
Peruvian	10	0.02
Venezuelan	2	<0.01
Other Hispanic or Latino	196	0.34

Race*	Population	%
African-American/Black (433)	664	1.17
Not Hispanic (404)	608	1.07
Hispanic (29)	56	0.10
American Indian/Alaska Native (179)	319	0.56
Not Hispanic (158)	290	0.51
Hispanic (21)	29	0.05
Apache (1)	1	<0.01
Blackfeet (1)	2	<0.01
Canadian/French Am. Ind. (8)	12	0.02
Cherokee (9)	19	0.03
Chippewa (2)	7	0.01
Comanche (1)	1	<0.01
Crow (0)	2	<0.01
Delaware (0)	1	<0.01
Iroquois (100)	159	0.28
Lumbee (0)	1	<0.01
Mexican American Ind. (4)	5	0.01
Paiute (0)	2	<0.01
Seminole (0)	1	<0.01
Sioux (1)	3	0.01
South American Ind. (1)	1	<0.01
Spanish American Ind. (2)	2	<0.01
Asian (325)	431	0.76
Not Hispanic (322)	423	0.74
Hispanic (3)	8	0.01
Cambodian (3)	3	0.01
Chinese, ex. Taiwanese (63)	80	0.14
Filipino (31)	52	0.09
Indian (72)	85	0.15
Indonesian (3)	5	0.01
Japanese (7)	19	0.03
Korean (43)	61	0.11
Laotian (3)	9	0.02
Pakistani (11)	11	0.02
Taiwanese (2)	2	<0.01
Thai (26)	32	0.06
Vietnamese (31)	35	0.06
Hawaii Native/Pacific Islander (6)	18	0.03
Not Hispanic (4)	14	0.02
Hispanic (2)	4	0.01
Guamanian/Chamorro (4)	8	0.01
Native Hawaiian (0)	4	0.01
White (55,242)	55,749	97.92
Not Hispanic (54,366)	54,789	96.23
Hispanic (876)	960	1.69

*Notes: † The Census 2010 population figure is used to calculate the percentages in the Hispanic Origin and Race categories. Ancestry percentages are based on the 2006-2010 American Community Survey population (not shown); ‡ Numbers in parentheses indicate the number of people reporting a single ancestry; * Numbers in parentheses indicate the number of persons reporting this race alone, not in combination with any other race; Please refer to the Explanation of Data for more information.*

Hamburg

Place Type: Village
County: Erie
Population: 9,409†

Ancestry‡	Population	%
African, Sub-Saharan (57)	57	0.60
South African (57)	57	0.60
American (240)	240	2.52
Arab (55)	66	0.69
Egyptian (38)	38	0.40
Jordanian (0)	11	0.12
Lebanese (17)	17	0.18
Austrian (0)	58	0.61
British (22)	61	0.64
Canadian (52)	104	1.09
Celtic (30)	30	0.32
Croatian (8)	64	0.67
Czech (0)	9	0.09
Czechoslovakian (0)	13	0.14
Danish (19)	19	0.20
Dutch (16)	108	1.14
Eastern European (16)	16	0.17
English (306)	1,016	10.68
European (36)	36	0.38
Finnish (0)	9	0.09
French, ex. Basque (11)	307	3.23
French Canadian (28)	152	1.60
German (992)	3,438	36.14
Hungarian (16)	84	0.88
Iranian (44)	44	0.46
Irish (625)	2,796	29.39
Italian (638)	1,613	16.96
Norwegian (9)	9	0.09
Polish (581)	1,455	15.29
Russian (0)	65	0.68
Scotch-Irish (60)	169	1.78
Scottish (63)	127	1.34
Serbian (12)	66	0.69
Slavic (0)	16	0.17
Slovak (14)	90	0.95
Slovene (0)	16	0.17
Swedish (61)	187	1.97
Ukrainian (35)	114	1.20
Welsh (32)	42	0.44

Hispanic Origin	Population	%
Hispanic or Latino (of any race)	135	1.43
Central American, ex. Mexican	4	0.04
Guatemalan	3	0.03
Salvadoran	1	0.01
Cuban	2	0.02
Dominican Republic	1	0.01
Mexican	28	0.30
Puerto Rican	53	0.56
South American	16	0.17
Argentinean	1	0.01
Bolivian	2	0.02
Chilean	4	0.04
Colombian	7	0.07
Peruvian	2	0.02
Other Hispanic or Latino	31	0.33

Race*	Population	%
African-American/Black (36)	49	0.52
Not Hispanic (33)	46	0.49
Hispanic (3)	3	0.03
American Indian/Alaska Native (16)	39	0.41
Not Hispanic (14)	37	0.39
Hispanic (2)	2	0.02
Cherokee (1)	2	0.02
Chippewa (1)	3	0.03
Delaware (0)	1	0.01
Iroquois (7)	19	0.20
Spanish American Ind. (2)	2	0.02
Asian (40)	57	0.61
Not Hispanic (40)	57	0.61
Cambodian (3)	3	0.03
Chinese, ex. Taiwanese (9)	10	0.11
Filipino (8)	13	0.14
Indian (8)	11	0.12
Indonesian (1)	1	0.01
Japanese (1)	2	0.02
Korean (4)	6	0.06
Laotian (0)	1	0.01
Pakistani (1)	1	0.01
Taiwanese (1)	1	0.01
Thai (1)	2	0.02
Vietnamese (2)	5	0.05
White (9,235)	9,297	98.81
Not Hispanic (9,135)	9,185	97.62
Hispanic (100)	112	1.19

Hamlin

Place Type: Town
County: Monroe
Population: 9,045†

Ancestry‡	Population	%
African, Sub-Saharan (0)	16	0.18
African (0)	16	0.18
American (324)	324	3.57
Australian (0)	4	0.04
Belgian (0)	17	0.19
British (10)	20	0.22
Canadian (0)	23	0.25
Croatian (0)	11	0.12
Danish (0)	43	0.47
Dutch (113)	380	4.19
English (433)	1,653	18.22
Estonian (10)	10	0.11
European (174)	181	1.99
Finnish (61)	79	0.87
French, ex. Basque (33)	188	2.07
French Canadian (101)	270	2.98
German (757)	2,937	32.37
Greek (8)	15	0.17
Hungarian (30)	71	0.78
Irish (441)	2,049	22.58
Italian (486)	1,421	15.66
Lithuanian (50)	206	2.27
Norwegian (0)	34	0.37
Polish (127)	543	5.98
Romanian (0)	7	0.08
Russian (9)	9	0.10
Scotch-Irish (9)	83	0.91
Scottish (57)	154	1.70
Swedish (26)	115	1.27
Swiss (0)	10	0.11
Ukrainian (26)	218	2.40
Welsh (18)	68	0.75

Hispanic Origin	Population	%
Hispanic or Latino (of any race)	236	2.61
Central American, ex. Mexican	7	0.08
Guatemalan	3	0.03
Honduran	1	0.01
Panamanian	2	0.02
Salvadoran	1	0.01
Cuban	5	0.06
Mexican	65	0.72
Puerto Rican	131	1.45
South American	7	0.08
Argentinean	1	0.01
Ecuadorian	1	0.01
Peruvian	4	0.04
Venezuelan	1	0.01
Other Hispanic or Latino	21	0.23

Race*	Population	%
African-American/Black (94)	164	1.81
Not Hispanic (87)	150	1.66
Hispanic (7)	14	0.15
American Indian/Alaska Native (44)	91	1.01
Not Hispanic (42)	85	0.94
Hispanic (2)	6	0.07
Canadian/French Am. Ind. (0)	2	0.02
Cherokee (1)	3	0.03
Chippewa (1)	2	0.02
Cree (0)	3	0.03
Delaware (4)	4	0.04
Iroquois (7)	14	0.15
Seminole (0)	4	0.04
Sioux (2)	3	0.03
Asian (35)	61	0.67
Not Hispanic (35)	58	0.64
Hispanic (0)	3	0.03
Cambodian (0)	3	0.03
Chinese, ex. Taiwanese (6)	7	0.08
Filipino (3)	6	0.07
Indian (3)	12	0.13
Indonesian (0)	2	0.02
Japanese (4)	9	0.10
Korean (6)	14	0.15
Laotian (4)	4	0.04
Thai (0)	4	0.04
Vietnamese (4)	4	0.04
Hawaii Native/Pacific Islander (1)	4	0.04
Not Hispanic (1)	3	0.03
Hispanic (0)	1	0.01
Guamanian/Chamorro (1)	1	0.01
White (8,651)	8,808	97.38
Not Hispanic (8,514)	8,641	95.53
Hispanic (137)	167	1.85

Hampton Bays

Place Type: CDP
County: Suffolk
Population: 13,603†

Ancestry‡	Population	%
American (187)	187	1.37
Arab (20)	38	0.28
Arab (20)	20	0.15
Moroccan (0)	18	0.13
Austrian (0)	120	0.88
Belgian (18)	18	0.13
Brazilian (71)	97	0.71
British (11)	11	0.08
Bulgarian (29)	29	0.21
Canadian (13)	37	0.27
Croatian (0)	11	0.08
Czech (15)	15	0.11
Czechoslovakian (41)	41	0.30
Danish (11)	46	0.34
Dutch (22)	127	0.93
English (374)	1,355	9.96
European (72)	72	0.53
French, ex. Basque (10)	340	2.50
French Canadian (0)	6	0.04
German (442)	2,120	15.58
Greek (118)	198	1.46
Hungarian (22)	110	0.81
Irish (1,370)	3,525	25.91
Italian (993)	2,275	16.72
Lithuanian (0)	44	0.32
Macedonian (11)	11	0.08
Norwegian (45)	118	0.87
Polish (628)	1,006	7.39
Portuguese (28)	40	0.29
Russian (113)	361	2.65
Scotch-Irish (73)	275	2.02
Scottish (30)	209	1.54
Slovak (35)	58	0.43
Swedish (25)	114	0.84
Swiss (0)	89	0.65
Ukrainian (101)	224	1.65
Welsh (0)	14	0.10

Hispanic Origin	Population	%
Hispanic or Latino (of any race)	3,895	28.63
Central American, ex. Mexican	1,042	7.66
Costa Rican	406	2.98
Guatemalan	287	2.11
Honduran	76	0.56
Nicaraguan	9	0.07
Panamanian	3	0.02

*Notes: † The Census 2010 population figure is used to calculate the percentages in the Hispanic Origin and Race categories. Ancestry percentages are based on the 2006-2010 American Community Survey population (not shown); ‡ Numbers in parentheses indicate the number of people reporting a single ancestry; * Numbers in parentheses indicate the number of persons reporting this race alone, not in combination with any other race; Please refer to the Explanation of Data for more information.*

Salvadoran	254	1.87
Other Central American	7	0.05
Cuban	22	0.16
Dominican Republic	55	0.40
Mexican	1,025	7.54
Puerto Rican	154	1.13
South American	1,106	8.13
Argentinean	44	0.32
Chilean	11	0.08
Colombian	614	4.51
Ecuadorian	393	2.89
Paraguayan	4	0.03
Peruvian	30	0.22
Uruguayan	1	0.01
Venezuelan	7	0.05
Other South American	2	0.01
Other Hispanic or Latino	491	3.61

Race*	Population	%
African-American/Black (203)	269	1.98
Not Hispanic (161)	213	1.57
Hispanic (42)	56	0.41
American Indian/Alaska Native (35)	65	0.48
Not Hispanic (24)	46	0.34
Hispanic (11)	19	0.14
Blackfeet (2)	2	0.01
Cherokee (3)	5	0.04
Choctaw (1)	2	0.01
Creek (2)	2	0.01
Iroquois (3)	6	0.04
Mexican American Ind. (3)	6	0.04
Pueblo (0)	5	0.04
Sioux (0)	1	0.01
Asian (109)	147	1.08
Not Hispanic (108)	144	1.06
Hispanic (1)	3	0.02
Chinese, ex. Taiwanese (17)	20	0.15
Filipino (35)	44	0.32
Indian (12)	16	0.12
Japanese (7)	15	0.11
Korean (19)	26	0.19
Laotian (0)	1	0.01
Malaysian (1)	1	0.01
Pakistani (1)	1	0.01
Taiwanese (2)	2	0.01
Thai (1)	1	0.01
Vietnamese (7)	18	0.13
Hawaii Native/Pacific Islander (21)	32	0.24
Not Hispanic (5)	10	0.07
Hispanic (16)	22	0.16
Guamanian/Chamorro (14)	14	0.10
Native Hawaiian (6)	12	0.09
White (11,470)	11,675	85.83
Not Hispanic (9,274)	9,373	68.90
Hispanic (2,196)	2,302	16.92

Harrison

Place Type: Town/Village
County: Westchester
Population: 27,472†

Ancestry‡	Population	%
African, Sub-Saharan (90)	90	0.34
Ethiopian (31)	31	0.12
Nigerian (46)	46	0.17
Sudanese (13)	13	0.05
Albanian (115)	115	0.43
American (3,246)	3,246	12.12
Arab (171)	209	0.78
Arab (0)	14	0.05
Egyptian (5)	15	0.06
Jordanian (20)	20	0.07
Lebanese (131)	145	0.54
Syrian (15)	15	0.06
Armenian (13)	13	0.05
Australian (0)	29	0.11
Austrian (27)	271	1.01
Belgian (9)	29	0.11
Brazilian (363)	450	1.68
British (70)	175	0.65
Canadian (0)	22	0.08
Celtic (10)	24	0.09
Czech (46)	128	0.48
Czechoslovakian (22)	46	0.17
Danish (10)	10	0.04
Dutch (42)	233	0.87
Eastern European (482)	507	1.89
English (237)	769	2.87
European (99)	99	0.37
French, ex. Basque (309)	574	2.14
French Canadian (0)	72	0.27
German (313)	1,812	6.77
Greek (184)	232	0.87
Hungarian (59)	163	0.61
Iranian (11)	11	0.04
Irish (740)	3,159	11.80
Israeli (12)	18	0.07
Italian (5,219)	7,683	28.69
Latvian (7)	55	0.21
Lithuanian (0)	77	0.29
Maltese (0)	11	0.04
Northern European (70)	70	0.26
Norwegian (59)	132	0.49
Polish (218)	1,057	3.95
Portuguese (230)	448	1.67
Romanian (12)	103	0.38
Russian (527)	1,014	3.79
Scandinavian (8)	23	0.09
Scotch-Irish (38)	238	0.89
Scottish (58)	274	1.02
Slavic (8)	8	0.03
Slovak (0)	29	0.11
Slovene (0)	30	0.11
Swedish (2)	155	0.58
Swiss (0)	60	0.22
Turkish (27)	39	0.15
Ukrainian (28)	89	0.33
Welsh (44)	85	0.32
West Indian, ex. Hispanic (46)	150	0.56
Haitian (46)	49	0.18
Jamaican (0)	69	0.26
West Indian (0)	32	0.12

Hispanic Origin	Population	%
Hispanic or Latino (of any race)	3,202	11.66
Central American, ex. Mexican	266	0.97
Costa Rican	21	0.08
Guatemalan	133	0.48
Honduran	32	0.12
Nicaraguan	15	0.05
Panamanian	11	0.04
Salvadoran	53	0.19
Other Central American	1	<0.01
Cuban	107	0.39
Dominican Republic	270	0.98
Mexican	459	1.67
Puerto Rican	633	2.30
South American	1,186	4.32
Argentinean	107	0.39
Bolivian	30	0.11
Chilean	35	0.13
Colombian	361	1.31
Ecuadorian	103	0.37
Paraguayan	235	0.86
Peruvian	261	0.95
Uruguayan	28	0.10
Venezuelan	23	0.08
Other South American	3	0.01
Other Hispanic or Latino	281	1.02

Race*	Population	%
African-American/Black (673)	869	3.16
Not Hispanic (563)	705	2.57
Hispanic (110)	164	0.60
American Indian/Alaska Native (58)	143	0.52
Not Hispanic (15)	72	0.26
Hispanic (43)	71	0.26
Blackfeet (1)	7	0.03
Canadian/French Am. Ind. (1)	1	<0.01
Central American Ind. (0)	1	<0.01
Cherokee (3)	21	0.08
Chickasaw (0)	1	<0.01
Chippewa (0)	3	0.01
Delaware (1)	1	<0.01
Iroquois (2)	3	0.01
Mexican American Ind. (3)	4	0.01
Navajo (0)	1	<0.01
Pima (2)	2	0.01
Potawatomi (1)	1	<0.01
Sioux (0)	4	0.01
South American Ind. (4)	11	0.04
Spanish American Ind. (4)	4	0.01
Asian (2,072)	2,326	8.47
Not Hispanic (2,062)	2,285	8.32
Hispanic (10)	41	0.15
Bhutanese (8)	8	0.03
Burmese (7)	7	0.03
Cambodian (4)	4	0.01
Chinese, ex. Taiwanese (232)	305	1.11
Filipino (73)	115	0.42
Indian (229)	264	0.96
Indonesian (3)	6	0.02
Japanese (1,182)	1,239	4.51
Korean (181)	206	0.75
Laotian (0)	1	<0.01
Malaysian (5)	5	0.02
Nepalese (6)	7	0.03
Pakistani (77)	82	0.30
Sri Lankan (1)	1	<0.01
Taiwanese (16)	17	0.06
Thai (7)	11	0.04
Vietnamese (14)	20	0.07
Hawaii Native/Pacific Islander (10)	46	0.17
Not Hispanic (8)	36	0.13
Hispanic (2)	10	0.04
Guamanian/Chamorro (1)	5	0.02
Native Hawaiian (4)	7	0.03
Samoan (1)	3	0.01
White (23,095)	23,690	86.23
Not Hispanic (21,133)	21,511	78.30
Hispanic (1,962)	2,179	7.93

Hastings

Place Type: Town
County: Oswego
Population: 9,450†

Ancestry‡	Population	%
African, Sub-Saharan (10)	10	0.11
African (10)	10	0.11
American (608)	608	6.52
Arab (10)	10	0.11
Lebanese (10)	10	0.11
Belgian (0)	3	0.03
Canadian (24)	83	0.89
Croatian (0)	22	0.24
Czech (0)	14	0.15
Czechoslovakian (2)	2	0.02
Danish (11)	70	0.75
Dutch (55)	460	4.93
Eastern European (30)	30	0.32
English (457)	1,487	15.95
European (75)	75	0.80
Finnish (0)	37	0.40
French, ex. Basque (160)	661	7.09
French Canadian (78)	249	2.67
German (555)	2,068	22.18
Greek (19)	105	1.13
Hungarian (25)	76	0.82
Irish (671)	1,959	21.01
Italian (555)	1,462	15.68
Latvian (0)	10	0.11
Lithuanian (6)	24	0.26
Macedonian (0)	6	0.06
Norwegian (30)	48	0.51
Polish (390)	914	9.80
Portuguese (0)	15	0.16
Russian (26)	94	1.01

*Notes: † The Census 2010 population figure is used to calculate the percentages in the Hispanic Origin and Race categories. Ancestry percentages are based on the 2006-2010 American Community Survey population (not shown); ‡ Numbers in parentheses indicate the number of people reporting a single ancestry; * Numbers in parentheses indicate the number of persons reporting this race alone, not in combination with any other race; Please refer to the Explanation of Data for more information.*

Scandinavian (2)	2	0.02
Scotch-Irish (29)	113	1.21
Scottish (40)	245	2.63
Serbian (0)	22	0.24
Slovak (5)	8	0.09
Swedish (4)	136	1.46
Swiss (0)	28	0.30
Ukrainian (9)	32	0.34
Welsh (15)	135	1.45

Hispanic Origin	Population	%
Hispanic or Latino (of any race)	83	0.88
Central American, ex. Mexican	3	0.03
Guatemalan	1	0.01
Salvadoran	2	0.02
Cuban	3	0.03
Dominican Republic	1	0.01
Mexican	18	0.19
Puerto Rican	50	0.53
South American	3	0.03
Argentinean	1	0.01
Chilean	1	0.01
Peruvian	1	0.01
Other Hispanic or Latino	5	0.05

Race*	Population	%
African-American/Black (30)	60	0.63
Not Hispanic (28)	58	0.61
Hispanic (2)	2	0.02
American Indian/Alaska Native (49)	107	1.13
Not Hispanic (49)	105	1.11
Hispanic (0)	2	0.02
Apache (0)	1	0.01
Blackfeet (1)	2	0.02
Canadian/French Am. Ind. (1)	1	0.01
Cherokee (3)	5	0.05
Cheyenne (1)	1	0.01
Chippewa (1)	2	0.02
Delaware (1)	1	0.01
Iroquois (30)	61	0.65
Mexican American Ind. (0)	1	0.01
Ute (0)	1	0.01
Asian (30)	42	0.44
Not Hispanic (30)	42	0.44
Chinese, ex. Taiwanese (10)	12	0.13
Filipino (7)	8	0.08
Indian (2)	2	0.02
Indonesian (1)	1	0.01
Japanese (1)	3	0.03
Korean (6)	8	0.08
Vietnamese (3)	4	0.04
Hawaii Native/Pacific Islander (0)	1	0.01
Not Hispanic (0)	1	0.01
Guamanian/Chamorro (0)	1	0.01
White (9,207)	9,315	98.57
Not Hispanic (9,151)	9,249	97.87
Hispanic (56)	66	0.70

Hastings-on-Hudson

Place Type: Village
County: Westchester
Population: 7,849†

Ancestry‡	Population	%
African, Sub-Saharan (0)	10	0.13
South African (0)	10	0.13
American (321)	321	4.12
Arab (154)	225	2.89
Arab (0)	9	0.12
Egyptian (0)	9	0.12
Jordanian (19)	19	0.24
Lebanese (117)	117	1.50
Moroccan (0)	35	0.45
Syrian (18)	36	0.46
Armenian (0)	11	0.14
Australian (0)	24	0.31
Austrian (7)	144	1.85
Brazilian (44)	81	1.04
British (66)	100	1.29
Canadian (0)	56	0.72
Czech (0)	40	0.51
Dutch (0)	57	0.73
Eastern European (282)	316	4.06
English (159)	602	7.74
European (140)	140	1.80
French, ex. Basque (57)	291	3.74
French Canadian (54)	101	1.30
German (146)	1,035	13.30
Greek (277)	288	3.70
Hungarian (46)	109	1.40
Iranian (25)	25	0.32
Irish (523)	1,424	18.30
Israeli (10)	26	0.33
Italian (572)	1,273	16.36
Latvian (16)	16	0.21
Lithuanian (9)	86	1.11
Northern European (13)	13	0.17
Norwegian (10)	69	0.89
Polish (210)	590	7.58
Portuguese (77)	106	1.36
Romanian (20)	48	0.62
Russian (277)	808	10.38
Scandinavian (0)	9	0.12
Scotch-Irish (32)	99	1.27
Scottish (62)	89	1.14
Slavic (6)	6	0.08
Slovak (21)	62	0.80
Swedish (3)	32	0.41
Swiss (13)	49	0.63
Ukrainian (59)	88	1.13
Welsh (0)	10	0.13
West Indian, ex. Hispanic (42)	42	0.54
British West Indian (7)	7	0.09
Haitian (35)	35	0.45

Hispanic Origin	Population	%
Hispanic or Latino (of any race)	710	9.05
Central American, ex. Mexican	95	1.21
Guatemalan	20	0.25
Honduran	11	0.14
Nicaraguan	13	0.17
Panamanian	5	0.06
Salvadoran	44	0.56
Other Central American	2	0.03
Cuban	40	0.51
Dominican Republic	67	0.85
Mexican	74	0.94
Puerto Rican	211	2.69
South American	145	1.85
Argentinean	9	0.11
Chilean	28	0.36
Colombian	21	0.27
Ecuadorian	47	0.60
Paraguayan	6	0.08
Peruvian	25	0.32
Uruguayan	1	0.01
Venezuelan	7	0.09
Other South American	1	0.01
Other Hispanic or Latino	78	0.99

Race*	Population	%
African-American/Black (362)	429	5.47
Not Hispanic (303)	355	4.52
Hispanic (59)	74	0.94
American Indian/Alaska Native (18)	55	0.70
Not Hispanic (11)	39	0.50
Hispanic (7)	16	0.20
Cherokee (3)	8	0.10
Chippewa (0)	3	0.04
Cree (0)	3	0.04
Iroquois (0)	1	0.01
Lumbee (1)	1	0.01
South American Ind. (3)	5	0.06
Asian (369)	455	5.80
Not Hispanic (367)	446	5.68
Hispanic (2)	9	0.11
Bangladeshi (3)	3	0.04
Chinese, ex. Taiwanese (112)	134	1.71
Filipino (42)	54	0.69
Indian (73)	99	1.26
Indonesian (1)	1	0.01
Japanese (37)	51	0.65
Korean (67)	74	0.94
Nepalese (3)	3	0.04
Pakistani (1)	2	0.03
Sri Lankan (1)	5	0.06
Taiwanese (5)	7	0.09
Thai (1)	3	0.04
Vietnamese (6)	6	0.08
Hawaii Native/Pacific Islander (0)	1	0.01
Not Hispanic (0)	1	0.01
Native Hawaiian (0)	1	0.01
White (6,687)	6,876	87.60
Not Hispanic (6,272)	6,407	81.63
Hispanic (415)	469	5.98

Hauppauge

Place Type: CDP
County: Suffolk
Population: 20,882†

Ancestry‡	Population	%
Albanian (0)	3	0.01
American (823)	823	3.93
Arab (34)	147	0.70
Arab (0)	41	0.20
Egyptian (34)	34	0.16
Lebanese (0)	22	0.11
Syrian (0)	50	0.24
Armenian (16)	16	0.08
Austrian (83)	289	1.38
Belgian (0)	34	0.16
Brazilian (7)	7	0.03
British (7)	19	0.09
Canadian (32)	49	0.23
Carpatho Rusyn (26)	26	0.12
Croatian (0)	50	0.24
Czech (46)	123	0.59
Czechoslovakian (6)	81	0.39
Danish (9)	99	0.47
Dutch (49)	191	0.91
Eastern European (76)	76	0.36
English (133)	774	3.70
European (93)	93	0.44
Finnish (0)	24	0.11
French, ex. Basque (43)	363	1.74
French Canadian (41)	68	0.33
German (1,094)	4,367	20.87
Greek (128)	311	1.49
Hungarian (28)	263	1.26
Iranian (50)	50	0.24
Irish (1,371)	4,810	22.99
Italian (4,034)	7,401	35.37
Lithuanian (67)	100	0.48
Northern European (21)	21	0.10
Norwegian (115)	398	1.90
Polish (413)	1,683	8.04
Portuguese (17)	75	0.36
Romanian (21)	38	0.18
Russian (368)	972	4.65
Scandinavian (9)	9	0.04
Scotch-Irish (106)	243	1.16
Scottish (11)	200	0.96
Slavic (0)	11	0.05
Slovak (13)	13	0.06
Swedish (16)	280	1.34
Swiss (16)	16	0.08
Turkish (95)	95	0.45
Ukrainian (0)	128	0.61
Welsh (0)	30	0.14
West Indian, ex. Hispanic (63)	119	0.57
Haitian (24)	24	0.11
Jamaican (32)	49	0.23
West Indian (7)	46	0.22

Hispanic Origin	Population	%
Hispanic or Latino (of any race)	1,479	7.08
Central American, ex. Mexican	159	0.76

*Notes: † The Census 2010 population figure is used to calculate the percentages in the Hispanic Origin and Race categories. Ancestry percentages are based on the 2006-2010 American Community Survey population (not shown); ‡ Numbers in parentheses indicate the number of people reporting a single ancestry; * Numbers in parentheses indicate the number of persons reporting this race alone, not in combination with any other race; Please refer to the Explanation of Data for more information.*

Costa Rican	1	<0.01
Guatemalan	22	0.11
Honduran	22	0.11
Nicaraguan	2	0.01
Panamanian	7	0.03
Salvadoran	105	0.50
Cuban	56	0.27
Dominican Republic	97	0.46
Mexican	87	0.42
Puerto Rican	631	3.02
South American	317	1.52
Argentinean	29	0.14
Chilean	13	0.06
Colombian	158	0.76
Ecuadorian	55	0.26
Paraguayan	2	0.01
Peruvian	42	0.20
Uruguayan	6	0.03
Venezuelan	9	0.04
Other South American	3	0.01
Other Hispanic or Latino	132	0.63

Race*	Population	%
African-American/Black (457)	525	2.51
Not Hispanic (389)	442	2.12
Hispanic (68)	83	0.40
American Indian/Alaska Native (28)	87	0.42
Not Hispanic (11)	46	0.22
Hispanic (17)	41	0.20
Cherokee (0)	18	0.09
Iroquois (0)	5	0.02
Mexican American Ind. (2)	13	0.06
Navajo (0)	3	0.01
South American Ind. (0)	3	0.01
Asian (1,236)	1,343	6.43
Not Hispanic (1,226)	1,325	6.35
Hispanic (10)	18	0.09
Bangladeshi (4)	4	0.02
Bhutanese (2)	2	0.01
Burmese (2)	2	0.01
Chinese, ex. Taiwanese (284)	297	1.42
Filipino (53)	70	0.34
Indian (526)	548	2.62
Indonesian (1)	2	0.01
Japanese (15)	27	0.13
Korean (221)	232	1.11
Malaysian (1)	1	<0.01
Nepalese (3)	3	0.01
Pakistani (47)	50	0.24
Taiwanese (20)	20	0.10
Thai (4)	5	0.02
Vietnamese (33)	35	0.17
Hawaii Native/Pacific Islander (1)	9	0.04
Not Hispanic (1)	8	0.04
Hispanic (0)	1	<0.01
Native Hawaiian (0)	2	0.01
Samoan (1)	1	<0.01
White (18,618)	18,851	90.27
Not Hispanic (17,548)	17,711	84.81
Hispanic (1,070)	1,140	5.46

Haverstraw

Place Type: Town
County: Rockland
Population: 36,634†

Ancestry‡	Population	%
Afghan (61)	61	0.17
African, Sub-Saharan (369)	633	1.76
African (68)	260	0.72
Ethiopian (14)	31	0.09
Ghanaian (149)	149	0.42
Kenyan (60)	60	0.17
Nigerian (0)	55	0.15
Senegalese (52)	52	0.14
Other Sub-Saharan African (26)	26	0.07
American (1,436)	1,436	4.00
Arab (12)	31	0.09
Egyptian (12)	12	0.03
Syrian (0)	19	0.05
Armenian (10)	26	0.07
Austrian (32)	195	0.54
Belgian (40)	49	0.14
British (11)	19	0.05
Canadian (28)	62	0.17
Czech (0)	81	0.23
Czechoslovakian (37)	80	0.22
Danish (0)	70	0.20
Dutch (7)	248	0.69
Eastern European (265)	265	0.74
English (183)	1,140	3.18
European (159)	159	0.44
Finnish (0)	20	0.06
French, ex. Basque (85)	595	1.66
French Canadian (0)	44	0.12
German (440)	2,248	6.27
German Russian (12)	12	0.03
Greek (112)	181	0.50
Guyanese (16)	16	0.04
Hungarian (73)	219	0.61
Iranian (74)	74	0.21
Irish (1,859)	4,554	12.69
Israeli (57)	67	0.19
Italian (2,434)	4,912	13.69
Latvian (48)	48	0.13
Lithuanian (69)	86	0.24
Maltese (19)	58	0.16
Norwegian (29)	75	0.21
Pennsylvania German (0)	11	0.03
Polish (403)	1,039	2.90
Portuguese (15)	29	0.08
Romanian (6)	53	0.15
Russian (269)	443	1.23
Scandinavian (11)	11	0.03
Scotch-Irish (30)	110	0.31
Scottish (116)	337	0.94
Slavic (0)	6	0.02
Slovak (88)	235	0.66
Swedish (73)	307	0.86
Swiss (0)	37	0.10
Turkish (0)	8	0.02
Ukrainian (18)	53	0.15
Welsh (14)	14	0.04
West Indian, ex. Hispanic (1,570)	1,791	4.99
Haitian (1,017)	1,200	3.34
Jamaican (470)	497	1.39
West Indian (83)	94	0.26
Yugoslavian (0)	16	0.04

Hispanic Origin	Population	%
Hispanic or Latino (of any race)	15,012	40.98
Central American, ex. Mexican	1,009	2.75
Costa Rican	42	0.11
Guatemalan	325	0.89
Honduran	36	0.10
Nicaraguan	39	0.11
Panamanian	29	0.08
Salvadoran	532	1.45
Other Central American	6	0.02
Cuban	152	0.41
Dominican Republic	6,277	17.13
Mexican	1,425	3.89
Puerto Rican	4,061	11.09
South American	1,067	2.91
Argentinean	28	0.08
Bolivian	7	0.02
Chilean	28	0.08
Colombian	174	0.47
Ecuadorian	669	1.83
Peruvian	134	0.37
Uruguayan	13	0.04
Venezuelan	10	0.03
Other South American	4	0.01
Other Hispanic or Latino	1,021	2.79

Race*	Population	%
African-American/Black (5,380)	6,152	16.79
Not Hispanic (4,627)	4,975	13.58
Hispanic (753)	1,177	3.21
American Indian/Alaska Native (166)	472	1.29
Not Hispanic (54)	194	0.53
Hispanic (112)	278	0.76
Alaska Athabascan *(Ala. Nat.)* (1)	1	<0.01
Blackfeet (1)	11	0.03
Central American Ind. (7)	12	0.03
Cherokee (6)	34	0.09
Cheyenne (0)	1	<0.01
Delaware (5)	32	0.09
Iroquois (4)	18	0.05
Lumbee (0)	1	<0.01
Mexican American Ind. (2)	9	0.02
Pueblo (3)	4	0.01
Seminole (0)	2	0.01
Sioux (3)	11	0.03
South American Ind. (14)	71	0.19
Spanish American Ind. (5)	7	0.02
Asian (1,602)	1,906	5.20
Not Hispanic (1,559)	1,785	4.87
Hispanic (43)	121	0.33
Bangladeshi (10)	13	0.04
Burmese (1)	1	<0.01
Cambodian (25)	28	0.08
Chinese, ex. Taiwanese (195)	243	0.66
Filipino (341)	410	1.12
Indian (644)	740	2.02
Indonesian (1)	6	0.02
Japanese (18)	27	0.07
Korean (111)	130	0.35
Laotian (0)	1	<0.01
Nepalese (0)	1	<0.01
Pakistani (73)	88	0.24
Sri Lankan (9)	9	0.02
Taiwanese (5)	8	0.02
Thai (10)	14	0.04
Vietnamese (88)	108	0.29
Hawaii Native/Pacific Islander (36)	115	0.31
Not Hispanic (5)	26	0.07
Hispanic (31)	89	0.24
Guamanian/Chamorro (15)	17	0.05
Native Hawaiian (2)	10	0.03
White (21,697)	23,040	62.89
Not Hispanic (14,706)	15,174	41.42
Hispanic (6,991)	7,866	21.47

Haverstraw

Place Type: Village
County: Rockland
Population: 11,910†

Ancestry‡	Population	%
African, Sub-Saharan (120)	141	1.22
African (68)	89	0.77
Senegalese (52)	52	0.45
American (274)	274	2.38
Arab (0)	8	0.07
Syrian (0)	8	0.07
Austrian (8)	8	0.07
Canadian (21)	21	0.18
Czech (0)	55	0.48
Czechoslovakian (15)	50	0.43
Dutch (7)	20	0.17
Eastern European (5)	5	0.04
English (9)	85	0.74
European (23)	23	0.20
Finnish (0)	11	0.10
French, ex. Basque (31)	91	0.79
German (98)	239	2.07
German Russian (12)	12	0.10
Guyanese (10)	10	0.09
Hungarian (9)	26	0.23
Irish (207)	488	4.24
Israeli (0)	10	0.09
Italian (406)	610	5.29
Lithuanian (3)	3	0.03
Norwegian (0)	10	0.09
Polish (80)	155	1.35
Russian (33)	48	0.42
Scotch-Irish (0)	23	0.20

*Notes: † The Census 2010 population figure is used to calculate the percentages in the Hispanic Origin and Race categories. Ancestry percentages are based on the 2006-2010 American Community Survey population (not shown); ‡ Numbers in parentheses indicate the number of people reporting a single ancestry; * Numbers in parentheses indicate the number of persons reporting this race alone, not in combination with any other race; Please refer to the Explanation of Data for more information.*

Scottish (40)	44	0.38
Slavic (0)	6	0.05
Slovak (26)	34	0.30
Swedish (11)	55	0.48
West Indian, ex. Hispanic (527)	548	4.76
Haitian (419)	419	3.64
Jamaican (101)	111	0.96
West Indian (7)	18	0.16

Hispanic Origin	Population	%
Hispanic or Latino (of any race)	7,993	67.11
Central American, ex. Mexican	422	3.54
Costa Rican	26	0.22
Guatemalan	125	1.05
Honduran	9	0.08
Nicaraguan	5	0.04
Panamanian	17	0.14
Salvadoran	240	2.02
Cuban	28	0.24
Dominican Republic	3,847	32.30
Mexican	1,112	9.34
Puerto Rican	1,427	11.98
South American	620	5.21
Argentinean	5	0.04
Bolivian	3	0.03
Chilean	10	0.08
Colombian	53	0.45
Ecuadorian	474	3.98
Peruvian	62	0.52
Uruguayan	9	0.08
Venezuelan	4	0.03
Other Hispanic or Latino	537	4.51

Race*	Population	%
African-American/Black (1,512)	1,844	15.48
Not Hispanic (1,154)	1,270	10.66
Hispanic (358)	574	4.82
American Indian/Alaska Native (96)	231	1.94
Not Hispanic (24)	71	0.60
Hispanic (72)	160	1.34
Blackfeet (1)	7	0.06
Central American Ind. (6)	10	0.08
Cherokee (5)	13	0.11
Delaware (4)	10	0.08
Iroquois (1)	6	0.05
Mexican American Ind. (2)	9	0.08
Pueblo (2)	3	0.03
Seminole (0)	1	0.01
Sioux (0)	1	0.01
South American Ind. (6)	32	0.27
Spanish American Ind. (5)	7	0.06
Asian (269)	342	2.87
Not Hispanic (262)	299	2.51
Hispanic (7)	43	0.36
Cambodian (10)	10	0.08
Chinese, ex. Taiwanese (39)	52	0.44
Filipino (91)	110	0.92
Indian (60)	90	0.76
Japanese (1)	3	0.03
Korean (21)	23	0.19
Laotian (0)	1	0.01
Pakistani (9)	14	0.12
Thai (5)	7	0.06
Vietnamese (20)	23	0.19
Hawaii Native/Pacific Islander (22)	76	0.64
Not Hispanic (2)	10	0.08
Hispanic (20)	66	0.55
Guamanian/Chamorro (5)	5	0.04
Native Hawaiian (0)	7	0.06
White (5,708)	6,339	53.22
Not Hispanic (2,299)	2,425	20.36
Hispanic (3,409)	3,914	32.86

Hempstead

Place Type: Town
County: Nassau
Population: 759,757†

Ancestry‡	Population	%
Afghan (260)	399	0.05
African, Sub-Saharan (4,323)	5,844	0.78
African (2,716)	3,879	0.51
Ethiopian (38)	106	0.01
Ghanaian (239)	306	0.04
Nigerian (952)	1,115	0.15
Sierra Leonean (11)	11	<0.01
Somalian (15)	15	<0.01
South African (72)	104	0.01
Sudanese (33)	33	<0.01
Other Sub-Saharan African (247)	275	0.04
Albanian (733)	1,052	0.14
Alsatian (0)	30	<0.01
American (23,869)	23,869	3.17
Arab (2,403)	4,218	0.56
Arab (232)	319	0.04
Egyptian (787)	1,227	0.16
Iraqi (149)	284	0.04
Jordanian (66)	66	0.01
Lebanese (270)	657	0.09
Moroccan (163)	376	0.05
Palestinian (64)	113	0.01
Syrian (103)	512	0.07
Other Arab (569)	664	0.09
Armenian (922)	1,451	0.19
Assyrian/Chaldean/Syriac (3)	19	<0.01
Australian (98)	236	0.03
Austrian (1,518)	4,963	0.66
Basque (2)	43	0.01
Belgian (136)	405	0.05
Brazilian (208)	479	0.06
British (540)	1,197	0.16
Bulgarian (158)	181	0.02
Canadian (321)	1,084	0.14
Carpatho Rusyn (4)	36	<0.01
Celtic (13)	24	<0.01
Croatian (536)	1,033	0.14
Cypriot (197)	254	0.03
Czech (615)	2,447	0.32
Czechoslovakian (357)	1,054	0.14
Danish (150)	1,023	0.14
Dutch (387)	3,142	0.42
Eastern European (5,468)	5,775	0.77
English (3,407)	21,808	2.89
Estonian (120)	175	0.02
European (5,191)	5,650	0.75
Finnish (105)	647	0.09
French, ex. Basque (1,119)	8,239	1.09
French Canadian (440)	1,779	0.24
German (15,495)	78,518	10.42
German Russian (0)	17	<0.01
Greek (6,061)	10,033	1.33
Guyanese (2,705)	3,520	0.47
Hungarian (2,954)	6,992	0.93
Icelander (19)	92	0.01
Iranian (290)	539	0.07
Irish (41,161)	125,911	16.71
Israeli (1,902)	2,558	0.34
Italian (90,988)	164,467	21.82
Latvian (193)	438	0.06
Lithuanian (826)	2,538	0.34
Macedonian (41)	51	0.01
Maltese (254)	540	0.07
Northern European (433)	514	0.07
Norwegian (826)	3,371	0.45
Pennsylvania German (82)	143	0.02
Polish (11,210)	35,774	4.75
Portuguese (1,774)	2,805	0.37
Romanian (1,090)	2,811	0.37
Russian (11,619)	26,754	3.55
Scandinavian (171)	360	0.05
Scotch-Irish (1,797)	4,788	0.64
Scottish (822)	3,831	0.51
Serbian (23)	38	0.01
Slavic (62)	166	0.02
Slovak (182)	702	0.09
Slovene (6)	89	0.01
Soviet Union (0)	10	<0.01
Swedish (601)	3,930	0.52
Swiss (173)	1,183	0.16
Turkish (820)	1,202	0.16
Ukrainian (1,249)	2,806	0.37
Welsh (84)	865	0.11
West Indian, ex. Hispanic (37,978)	45,733	6.07
Bahamian (5)	51	0.01
Barbadian (1,031)	1,279	0.17
Belizean (85)	118	0.02
Bermudan (52)	52	0.01
British West Indian (635)	972	0.13
Dutch West Indian (165)	199	0.03
Haitian (15,396)	17,422	2.31
Jamaican (15,060)	17,690	2.35
Trinidadian/Tobagonian (2,092)	3,155	0.42
U.S. Virgin Islander (0)	30	<0.01
West Indian (3,440)	4,748	0.63
Other West Indian (17)	17	<0.01
Yugoslavian (227)	649	0.09

Hispanic Origin	Population	%
Hispanic or Latino (of any race)	132,154	17.39
Central American, ex. Mexican	49,236	6.48
Costa Rican	664	0.09
Guatemalan	5,948	0.78
Honduran	7,842	1.03
Nicaraguan	656	0.09
Panamanian	1,163	0.15
Salvadoran	32,681	4.30
Other Central American	282	0.04
Cuban	3,597	0.47
Dominican Republic	16,914	2.23
Mexican	5,000	0.66
Puerto Rican	20,508	2.70
South American	23,626	3.11
Argentinean	1,500	0.20
Bolivian	494	0.07
Chilean	1,415	0.19
Colombian	8,522	1.12
Ecuadorian	5,881	0.77
Paraguayan	185	0.02
Peruvian	4,510	0.59
Uruguayan	359	0.05
Venezuelan	517	0.07
Other South American	243	0.03
Other Hispanic or Latino	13,273	1.75

Race*	Population	%
African-American/Black (125,724)	133,280	17.54
Not Hispanic (119,480)	124,525	16.39
Hispanic (6,244)	8,755	1.15
American Indian/Alaska Native (2,092)	5,363	0.71
Not Hispanic (913)	2,835	0.37
Hispanic (1,179)	2,528	0.33
Aleut *(Alaska Native)* (1)	2	<0.01
Apache (5)	21	<0.01
Blackfeet (16)	117	0.02
Canadian/French Am. Ind. (5)	9	<0.01
Central American Ind. (36)	87	0.01
Cherokee (59)	572	0.08
Cheyenne (0)	2	<0.01
Chickasaw (0)	5	<0.01
Chippewa (4)	7	<0.01
Choctaw (10)	36	<0.01
Colville (1)	1	<0.01
Comanche (7)	11	<0.01
Cree (0)	2	<0.01
Creek (6)	29	<0.01
Crow (0)	2	<0.01
Delaware (4)	11	<0.01
Hopi (0)	2	<0.01
Inupiat *(Alaska Native)* (0)	3	<0.01
Iroquois (66)	145	0.02
Lumbee (9)	22	<0.01
Mexican American Ind. (85)	143	0.02
Navajo (2)	13	<0.01
Osage (0)	2	<0.01
Ottawa (1)	1	<0.01
Pueblo (9)	13	<0.01
Seminole (2)	28	<0.01

*Notes: † The Census 2010 population figure is used to calculate the percentages in the Hispanic Origin and Race categories. Ancestry percentages are based on the 2006-2010 American Community Survey population (not shown); ‡ Numbers in parentheses indicate the number of people reporting a single ancestry; * Numbers in parentheses indicate the number of persons reporting this race alone, not in combination with any other race; Please refer to the Explanation of Data for more information.*

Shoshone (1)	3	<0.01
Sioux (12)	33	<0.01
South American Ind. (147)	294	0.04
Spanish American Ind. (111)	137	0.02
Tlingit-Haida *(Alaska Native)* (3)	6	<0.01
Tohono O'Odham (7)	7	<0.01
Ute (1)	1	<0.01
Asian (39,495)	45,112	5.94
Not Hispanic (39,084)	43,880	5.78
Hispanic (411)	1,232	0.16
Bangladeshi (530)	582	0.08
Burmese (37)	61	0.01
Cambodian (46)	65	0.01
Chinese, ex. Taiwanese (6,491)	7,849	1.03
Filipino (6,252)	7,212	0.95
Hmong (0)	2	<0.01
Indian (15,861)	17,802	2.34
Indonesian (37)	66	0.01
Japanese (360)	657	0.09
Korean (2,720)	3,074	0.40
Laotian (21)	32	<0.01
Malaysian (12)	29	<0.01
Nepalese (41)	45	0.01
Pakistani (4,581)	4,976	0.65
Sri Lankan (180)	201	0.03
Taiwanese (367)	438	0.06
Thai (213)	278	0.04
Vietnamese (492)	617	0.08
Hawaii Native/Pacific Islander (229)	1,001	0.13
Not Hispanic (117)	599	0.08
Hispanic (112)	402	0.05
Fijian (9)	10	<0.01
Guamanian/Chamorro (88)	110	0.01
Marshallese (1)	1	<0.01
Native Hawaiian (34)	114	0.02
Samoan (12)	36	<0.01
White (518,756)	532,650	70.11
Not Hispanic (454,883)	460,994	60.68
Hispanic (63,873)	71,656	9.43

Hempstead

Place Type: Village
County: Nassau
Population: 53,891†

Ancestry‡	Population	%
African, Sub-Saharan (1,102)	1,285	2.41
African (682)	850	1.59
Ghanaian (8)	8	0.01
Nigerian (412)	427	0.80
American (471)	471	0.88
Arab (54)	54	0.10
Arab (12)	12	0.02
Moroccan (42)	42	0.08
Australian (9)	9	0.02
Austrian (28)	64	0.12
Brazilian (0)	41	0.08
British (0)	90	0.17
Canadian (0)	143	0.27
Cypriot (0)	9	0.02
Czech (7)	7	0.01
Dutch (6)	6	0.01
Eastern European (34)	34	0.06
English (47)	124	0.23
French, ex. Basque (0)	82	0.15
French Canadian (0)	9	0.02
German (130)	594	1.11
Greek (203)	231	0.43
Guyanese (259)	307	0.58
Hungarian (32)	41	0.08
Irish (278)	659	1.23
Italian (333)	641	1.20
Latvian (0)	6	0.01
Lithuanian (28)	36	0.07
Polish (203)	351	0.66
Portuguese (13)	69	0.13
Russian (44)	129	0.24
Scotch-Irish (17)	47	0.09
Scottish (21)	103	0.19
Slovak (0)	9	0.02
Swedish (23)	102	0.19
Swiss (9)	47	0.09
Ukrainian (62)	90	0.17
Welsh (0)	71	0.13
West Indian, ex. Hispanic (5,489)	6,463	12.11
Barbadian (153)	153	0.29
Bermudan (9)	9	0.02
British West Indian (228)	250	0.47
Dutch West Indian (31)	31	0.06
Haitian (1,796)	2,104	3.94
Jamaican (2,500)	2,809	5.26
Trinidadian/Tobagonian (203)	322	0.60
West Indian (569)	785	1.47

Hispanic Origin	Population	%
Hispanic or Latino (of any race)	23,823	44.21
Central American, ex. Mexican	16,171	30.01
Costa Rican	44	0.08
Guatemalan	1,402	2.60
Honduran	3,758	6.97
Nicaraguan	56	0.10
Panamanian	138	0.26
Salvadoran	10,707	19.87
Other Central American	66	0.12
Cuban	174	0.32
Dominican Republic	1,398	2.59
Mexican	752	1.40
Puerto Rican	1,144	2.12
South American	1,575	2.92
Argentinean	25	0.05
Bolivian	23	0.04
Chilean	21	0.04
Colombian	506	0.94
Ecuadorian	641	1.19
Paraguayan	16	0.03
Peruvian	279	0.52
Uruguayan	4	0.01
Venezuelan	37	0.07
Other South American	23	0.04
Other Hispanic or Latino	2,609	4.84

Race*	Population	%
African-American/Black (26,016)	27,076	50.24
Not Hispanic (24,724)	25,388	47.11
Hispanic (1,292)	1,688	3.13
American Indian/Alaska Native (316)	997	1.85
Not Hispanic (96)	404	0.75
Hispanic (220)	593	1.10
Apache (2)	5	0.01
Blackfeet (1)	27	0.05
Central American Ind. (5)	15	0.03
Cherokee (17)	109	0.20
Cheyenne (0)	1	<0.01
Chippewa (1)	1	<0.01
Choctaw (0)	3	0.01
Comanche (0)	1	<0.01
Creek (1)	2	<0.01
Delaware (0)	4	0.01
Hopi (0)	2	<0.01
Iroquois (13)	19	0.04
Lumbee (0)	1	<0.01
Mexican American Ind. (17)	27	0.05
Navajo (1)	2	<0.01
Pueblo (4)	6	0.01
Seminole (0)	5	0.01
Sioux (1)	6	0.01
South American Ind. (9)	18	0.03
Spanish American Ind. (42)	47	0.09
Tlingit-Haida *(Alaska Native)* (0)	2	<0.01
Asian (751)	977	1.81
Not Hispanic (704)	842	1.56
Hispanic (47)	135	0.25
Bangladeshi (11)	11	0.02
Chinese, ex. Taiwanese (135)	177	0.33
Filipino (150)	171	0.32
Indian (282)	383	0.71
Indonesian (3)	5	0.01
Japanese (6)	14	0.03
Korean (24)	29	0.05
Laotian (3)	4	0.01
Malaysian (1)	1	<0.01
Nepalese (7)	9	0.02
Pakistani (48)	60	0.11
Sri Lankan (15)	15	0.03
Taiwanese (1)	1	<0.01
Thai (5)	10	0.02
Vietnamese (6)	9	0.02
Hawaii Native/Pacific Islander (23)	117	0.22
Not Hispanic (13)	57	0.11
Hispanic (10)	60	0.11
Fijian (1)	1	<0.01
Guamanian/Chamorro (9)	13	0.02
Native Hawaiian (1)	9	0.02
Samoan (0)	3	0.01
White (11,788)	13,665	25.36
Not Hispanic (3,548)	3,892	7.22
Hispanic (8,240)	9,773	18.13

Henrietta

Place Type: Town
County: Monroe
Population: 42,581†

Ancestry‡	Population	%
African, Sub-Saharan (305)	364	0.87
African (109)	168	0.40
Ethiopian (177)	177	0.42
Nigerian (19)	19	0.05
Albanian (69)	83	0.20
American (1,335)	1,335	3.18
Arab (165)	395	0.94
Arab (144)	321	0.76
Egyptian (0)	6	0.01
Iraqi (0)	16	0.04
Lebanese (21)	44	0.10
Other Arab (0)	8	0.02
Armenian (93)	163	0.39
Australian (12)	12	0.03
Austrian (17)	86	0.20
Belgian (14)	67	0.16
Brazilian (0)	4	0.01
British (57)	137	0.33
Canadian (173)	283	0.67
Croatian (13)	25	0.06
Czech (14)	124	0.30
Czechoslovakian (12)	12	0.03
Danish (17)	73	0.17
Dutch (135)	1,110	2.64
Eastern European (29)	29	0.07
English (1,392)	5,950	14.17
European (487)	511	1.22
Finnish (0)	18	0.04
French, ex. Basque (251)	1,401	3.34
French Canadian (149)	569	1.35
German (2,003)	9,369	22.31
Greek (113)	184	0.44
Guyanese (36)	111	0.26
Hungarian (22)	232	0.55
Icelander (12)	12	0.03
Irish (1,713)	8,275	19.70
Israeli (12)	12	0.03
Italian (2,820)	6,557	15.61
Latvian (11)	35	0.08
Lithuanian (29)	51	0.12
Macedonian (16)	39	0.09
Northern European (36)	48	0.11
Norwegian (46)	142	0.34
Pennsylvania German (28)	42	0.10
Polish (690)	2,743	6.53
Portuguese (25)	67	0.16
Romanian (82)	128	0.30
Russian (276)	745	1.77
Scandinavian (13)	13	0.03
Scotch-Irish (277)	676	1.61
Scottish (159)	899	2.14
Slavic (16)	20	0.05
Slovak (0)	19	0.05
Slovene (0)	51	0.12

SECTION TWO

*Notes: † The Census 2010 population figure is used to calculate the percentages in the Hispanic Origin and Race categories. Ancestry percentages are based on the 2006-2010 American Community Survey population (not shown); ‡ Numbers in parentheses indicate the number of people reporting a single ancestry; * Numbers in parentheses indicate the number of persons reporting this race alone, not in combination with any other race; Please refer to the Explanation of Data for more information.*

Ancestry (continued)	Population	%
Swedish (177)	361	0.86
Swiss (11)	142	0.34
Turkish (190)	209	0.50
Ukrainian (153)	296	0.70
Welsh (31)	207	0.49
West Indian, ex. Hispanic (296)	346	0.82
Haitian (55)	55	0.13
Jamaican (228)	278	0.66
Trinidadian/Tobagonian (13)	13	0.03
Yugoslavian (51)	59	0.14

Hispanic Origin	Population	%
Hispanic or Latino (of any race)	1,827	4.29
Central American, ex. Mexican	116	0.27
Costa Rican	6	0.01
Guatemalan	33	0.08
Honduran	22	0.05
Nicaraguan	13	0.03
Panamanian	16	0.04
Salvadoran	26	0.06
Cuban	184	0.43
Dominican Republic	134	0.31
Mexican	240	0.56
Puerto Rican	795	1.87
South American	209	0.49
Argentinean	18	0.04
Bolivian	10	0.02
Chilean	23	0.05
Colombian	77	0.18
Ecuadorian	24	0.06
Paraguayan	4	0.01
Peruvian	38	0.09
Uruguayan	8	0.02
Venezuelan	5	0.01
Other South American	2	<0.01
Other Hispanic or Latino	149	0.35

Race*	Population	%
African-American/Black (3,617)	4,106	9.64
Not Hispanic (3,480)	3,911	9.18
Hispanic (137)	195	0.46
American Indian/Alaska Native (105)	309	0.73
Not Hispanic (88)	264	0.62
Hispanic (17)	45	0.11
Alaska Athabascan (*Ala. Nat.*) (1)	1	<0.01
Blackfeet (1)	9	0.02
Central American Ind. (1)	1	<0.01
Cherokee (4)	36	0.08
Chippewa (5)	6	0.01
Choctaw (2)	5	0.01
Cree (1)	1	<0.01
Creek (0)	4	0.01
Crow (0)	3	0.01
Delaware (0)	2	<0.01
Iroquois (45)	78	0.18
Mexican American Ind. (5)	8	0.02
Navajo (2)	3	0.01
Osage (0)	1	<0.01
Potawatomi (0)	2	<0.01
Seminole (0)	1	<0.01
Sioux (2)	3	0.01
South American Ind. (2)	10	0.02
Tlingit-Haida (*Alaska Native*) (2)	4	0.01
Ute (1)	1	<0.01
Asian (3,070)	3,547	8.33
Not Hispanic (3,047)	3,493	8.20
Hispanic (23)	54	0.13
Bangladeshi (9)	10	0.02
Burmese (6)	6	0.01
Cambodian (17)	25	0.06
Chinese, ex. Taiwanese (824)	948	2.23
Filipino (99)	161	0.38
Indian (762)	832	1.95
Indonesian (7)	19	0.04
Japanese (74)	130	0.31
Korean (215)	259	0.61
Laotian (197)	235	0.55
Malaysian (65)	70	0.16
Nepalese (7)	7	0.02
Pakistani (220)	239	0.56
Sri Lankan (28)	29	0.07
Taiwanese (29)	45	0.11
Thai (27)	37	0.09
Vietnamese (326)	377	0.89
Hawaii Native/Pacific Islander (6)	48	0.11
Not Hispanic (3)	35	0.08
Hispanic (3)	13	0.03
Guamanian/Chamorro (2)	4	0.01
Native Hawaiian (3)	12	0.03
Samoan (0)	3	0.01
White (34,147)	35,096	82.42
Not Hispanic (33,102)	33,924	79.67
Hispanic (1,045)	1,172	2.75

Herkimer

Place Type: Town
County: Herkimer
Population: 10,175†

Ancestry‡	Population	%
African, Sub-Saharan (0)	66	0.65
African (0)	66	0.65
Alsatian (0)	11	0.11
American (350)	350	3.46
Arab (0)	71	0.70
Lebanese (0)	71	0.70
British (0)	25	0.25
Canadian (3)	57	0.56
Carpatho Rusyn (8)	8	0.08
Czech (46)	46	0.45
Czechoslovakian (10)	10	0.10
Danish (39)	96	0.95
Dutch (48)	485	4.79
English (407)	971	9.59
French, ex. Basque (98)	755	7.46
French Canadian (147)	193	1.91
German (441)	2,054	20.30
Greek (0)	12	0.12
Irish (424)	2,197	21.71
Italian (1,176)	2,014	19.90
Lithuanian (0)	33	0.33
Norwegian (10)	61	0.60
Polish (373)	901	8.90
Russian (13)	13	0.13
Scandinavian (9)	9	0.09
Scotch-Irish (31)	59	0.58
Scottish (26)	99	0.98
Slavic (0)	11	0.11
Slovak (0)	11	0.11
Slovene (8)	22	0.22
Swedish (0)	32	0.32
Swiss (12)	12	0.12
Ukrainian (134)	159	1.57
Welsh (36)	110	1.09
West Indian, ex. Hispanic (0)	48	0.47
Jamaican (0)	48	0.47
Yugoslavian (0)	23	0.23

Hispanic Origin	Population	%
Hispanic or Latino (of any race)	279	2.74
Central American, ex. Mexican	16	0.16
Costa Rican	1	0.01
Guatemalan	4	0.04
Honduran	1	0.01
Panamanian	5	0.05
Salvadoran	5	0.05
Cuban	10	0.10
Dominican Republic	21	0.21
Mexican	46	0.45
Puerto Rican	137	1.35
South American	9	0.09
Argentinean	1	0.01
Colombian	4	0.04
Peruvian	4	0.04
Other Hispanic or Latino	40	0.39

Race*	Population	%
African-American/Black (360)	440	4.32
Not Hispanic (318)	384	3.77
Hispanic (42)	56	0.55
American Indian/Alaska Native (27)	64	0.63
Not Hispanic (21)	48	0.47
Hispanic (6)	16	0.16
Blackfeet (0)	1	0.01
Cherokee (1)	9	0.09
Chippewa (2)	2	0.02
Iroquois (5)	10	0.10
Mexican American Ind. (6)	6	0.06
Sioux (1)	5	0.05
South American Ind. (0)	1	0.01
Tohono O'Odham (1)	1	0.01
Asian (95)	111	1.09
Not Hispanic (94)	110	1.08
Hispanic (1)	1	0.01
Cambodian (1)	1	0.01
Chinese, ex. Taiwanese (23)	25	0.25
Filipino (13)	17	0.17
Indian (20)	24	0.24
Indonesian (1)	1	0.01
Japanese (20)	21	0.21
Korean (8)	10	0.10
Thai (1)	1	0.01
Vietnamese (7)	7	0.07
Hawaii Native/Pacific Islander (5)	9	0.09
Not Hispanic (3)	6	0.06
Hispanic (2)	3	0.03
Guamanian/Chamorro (1)	1	0.01
Native Hawaiian (2)	4	0.04
Samoan (1)	2	0.02
White (9,480)	9,605	94.40
Not Hispanic (9,341)	9,442	92.80
Hispanic (139)	163	1.60

Herkimer

Place Type: Village
County: Herkimer
Population: 7,743†

Ancestry‡	Population	%
African, Sub-Saharan (0)	66	0.83
African (0)	66	0.83
Alsatian (0)	11	0.14
American (251)	251	3.14
Arab (0)	71	0.89
Lebanese (0)	71	0.89
British (0)	25	0.31
Canadian (0)	44	0.55
Czech (38)	38	0.48
Czechoslovakian (10)	10	0.13
Danish (39)	77	0.96
Dutch (9)	187	2.34
English (347)	691	8.65
French, ex. Basque (87)	571	7.15
French Canadian (147)	183	2.29
German (309)	1,411	17.67
Greek (0)	12	0.15
Irish (303)	1,868	23.39
Italian (990)	1,655	20.73
Lithuanian (0)	33	0.41
Norwegian (0)	51	0.64
Polish (344)	801	10.03
Scandinavian (9)	9	0.11
Scotch-Irish (31)	59	0.74
Scottish (18)	56	0.70
Slavic (0)	11	0.14
Slovak (0)	8	0.10
Slovene (0)	14	0.18
Swedish (0)	32	0.40
Swiss (12)	12	0.15
Ukrainian (9)	18	0.23
Welsh (19)	89	1.11
West Indian, ex. Hispanic (0)	48	0.60
Jamaican (0)	48	0.60
Yugoslavian (0)	23	0.29

Hispanic Origin	Population	%
Hispanic or Latino (of any race)	259	3.34
Central American, ex. Mexican	15	0.19

*Notes: † The Census 2010 population figure is used to calculate the percentages in the Hispanic Origin and Race categories. Ancestry percentages are based on the 2006-2010 American Community Survey population (not shown); ‡ Numbers in parentheses indicate the number of people reporting a single ancestry; * Numbers in parentheses indicate the number of persons reporting this race alone, not in combination with any other race; Please refer to the Explanation of Data for more information.*

Costa Rican	1	0.01
Guatemalan	3	0.04
Honduran	1	0.01
Panamanian	5	0.06
Salvadoran	5	0.06
Cuban	8	0.10
Dominican Republic	20	0.26
Mexican	38	0.49
Puerto Rican	132	1.70
South American	9	0.12
Argentinean	1	0.01
Colombian	4	0.05
Peruvian	4	0.05
Other Hispanic or Latino	37	0.48

Race*	Population	%
African-American/Black (345)	415	5.36
Not Hispanic (303)	360	4.65
Hispanic (42)	55	0.71
American Indian/Alaska Native (25)	61	0.79
Not Hispanic (19)	45	0.58
Hispanic (6)	16	0.21
Blackfeet (0)	1	0.01
Cherokee (1)	8	0.10
Chippewa (2)	2	0.03
Iroquois (5)	10	0.13
Mexican American Ind. (6)	6	0.08
Sioux (1)	5	0.06
South American Ind. (0)	1	0.01
Tohono O'Odham (1)	1	0.01
Asian (89)	101	1.30
Not Hispanic (88)	100	1.29
Hispanic (1)	1	0.01
Chinese, ex. Taiwanese (22)	24	0.31
Filipino (12)	15	0.19
Indian (19)	22	0.28
Indonesian (1)	1	0.01
Japanese (19)	19	0.25
Korean (7)	9	0.12
Thai (1)	1	0.01
Vietnamese (7)	7	0.09
Hawaii Native/Pacific Islander (5)	9	0.12
Not Hispanic (3)	6	0.08
Hispanic (2)	3	0.04
Guamanian/Chamorro (1)	1	0.01
Native Hawaiian (2)	4	0.05
Samoan (1)	2	0.03
White (7,088)	7,197	92.95
Not Hispanic (6,967)	7,054	91.10
Hispanic (121)	143	1.85

Hicksville

Place Type: CDP
County: Nassau
Population: 41,547†

Ancestry‡	Population	%
Afghan (288)	323	0.77
African, Sub-Saharan (0)	24	0.06
African (0)	24	0.06
Albanian (45)	45	0.11
American (923)	923	2.21
Arab (53)	83	0.20
Egyptian (46)	76	0.18
Syrian (7)	7	0.02
Armenian (282)	282	0.67
Austrian (37)	223	0.53
Belgian (0)	11	0.03
Brazilian (13)	41	0.10
British (26)	46	0.11
Bulgarian (0)	16	0.04
Canadian (11)	39	0.09
Croatian (277)	337	0.81
Czech (26)	99	0.24
Czechoslovakian (13)	25	0.06
Danish (30)	90	0.22
Dutch (0)	120	0.29
Eastern European (89)	109	0.26
English (160)	1,284	3.07
European (217)	230	0.55
Finnish (0)	9	0.02
French, ex. Basque (90)	431	1.03
French Canadian (20)	56	0.13
German (1,176)	4,707	11.26
Greek (471)	886	2.12
Hungarian (66)	347	0.83
Iranian (245)	256	0.61
Irish (2,138)	7,657	18.32
Israeli (15)	15	0.04
Italian (4,909)	9,732	23.29
Latvian (54)	75	0.18
Lithuanian (0)	116	0.28
Maltese (22)	142	0.34
Norwegian (40)	292	0.70
Pennsylvania German (18)	18	0.04
Polish (1,044)	2,398	5.74
Portuguese (16)	48	0.11
Romanian (168)	192	0.46
Russian (290)	891	2.13
Scandinavian (0)	33	0.08
Scotch-Irish (33)	190	0.45
Scottish (36)	218	0.52
Slavic (27)	76	0.18
Slovak (24)	34	0.08
Swedish (0)	124	0.30
Swiss (23)	103	0.25
Turkish (19)	19	0.05
Ukrainian (122)	152	0.36
Welsh (16)	49	0.12
West Indian, ex. Hispanic (304)	405	0.97
British West Indian (77)	90	0.22
Dutch West Indian (7)	7	0.02
Haitian (43)	94	0.22
Jamaican (116)	135	0.32
Trinidadian/Tobagonian (46)	58	0.14
West Indian (15)	21	0.05

Hispanic Origin	Population	%
Hispanic or Latino (of any race)	6,043	14.54
Central American, ex. Mexican	1,988	4.78
Costa Rican	15	0.04
Guatemalan	103	0.25
Honduran	302	0.73
Nicaraguan	31	0.07
Panamanian	13	0.03
Salvadoran	1,496	3.60
Other Central American	28	0.07
Cuban	171	0.41
Dominican Republic	378	0.91
Mexican	551	1.33
Puerto Rican	902	2.17
South American	1,440	3.47
Argentinean	78	0.19
Bolivian	22	0.05
Chilean	90	0.22
Colombian	564	1.36
Ecuadorian	279	0.67
Paraguayan	8	0.02
Peruvian	346	0.83
Uruguayan	22	0.05
Venezuelan	20	0.05
Other South American	11	0.03
Other Hispanic or Latino	613	1.48

Race*	Population	%
African-American/Black (946)	1,115	2.68
Not Hispanic (836)	963	2.32
Hispanic (110)	152	0.37
American Indian/Alaska Native (128)	278	0.67
Not Hispanic (53)	152	0.37
Hispanic (75)	126	0.30
Central American Ind. (2)	2	<0.01
Cherokee (1)	15	0.04
Chickasaw (0)	1	<0.01
Iroquois (2)	6	0.01
Mexican American Ind. (12)	13	0.03
Navajo (1)	2	<0.01
Potawatomi (1)	2	<0.01
Pueblo (0)	1	<0.01
South American Ind. (8)	20	0.05
Spanish American Ind. (3)	6	0.01
Asian (8,165)	8,825	21.24
Not Hispanic (8,139)	8,736	21.03
Hispanic (26)	89	0.21
Bangladeshi (159)	165	0.40
Burmese (9)	9	0.02
Cambodian (13)	13	0.03
Chinese, ex. Taiwanese (1,123)	1,241	2.99
Filipino (491)	560	1.35
Indian (4,842)	5,111	12.30
Indonesian (4)	5	0.01
Japanese (42)	56	0.13
Korean (652)	678	1.63
Malaysian (6)	12	0.03
Nepalese (42)	43	0.10
Pakistani (474)	518	1.25
Sri Lankan (14)	23	0.06
Taiwanese (47)	62	0.15
Thai (31)	36	0.09
Vietnamese (75)	100	0.24
Hawaii Native/Pacific Islander (4)	37	0.09
Not Hispanic (3)	31	0.07
Hispanic (1)	6	0.01
Guamanian/Chamorro (1)	4	0.01
Native Hawaiian (2)	4	0.01
White (29,194)	29,906	71.98
Not Hispanic (25,603)	26,016	62.62
Hispanic (3,591)	3,890	9.36

Highlands

Place Type: Town
County: Orange
Population: 12,492†

Ancestry‡	Population	%
African, Sub-Saharan (97)	163	1.29
African (83)	90	0.71
Nigerian (0)	59	0.47
South African (14)	14	0.11
American (293)	293	2.32
Arab (36)	142	1.12
Egyptian (0)	13	0.10
Lebanese (32)	87	0.69
Syrian (0)	38	0.30
Other Arab (4)	4	0.03
Austrian (5)	82	0.65
Belgian (6)	11	0.09
Brazilian (45)	45	0.36
British (15)	197	1.56
Cajun (39)	54	0.43
Canadian (6)	18	0.14
Celtic (15)	15	0.12
Croatian (0)	41	0.32
Czech (0)	39	0.31
Czechoslovakian (0)	51	0.40
Danish (0)	12	0.09
Dutch (88)	176	1.39
English (474)	1,451	11.48
Estonian (35)	55	0.44
European (67)	67	0.53
Finnish (32)	91	0.72
French, ex. Basque (96)	274	2.17
French Canadian (17)	163	1.29
German (1,010)	3,416	27.03
Greek (50)	205	1.62
Guyanese (0)	14	0.11
Hungarian (19)	98	0.78
Irish (428)	2,520	19.94
Italian (477)	2,141	16.94
Lithuanian (9)	75	0.59
Northern European (21)	21	0.17
Norwegian (5)	206	1.63
Polish (138)	888	7.03
Portuguese (29)	38	0.30
Russian (138)	242	1.92
Scandinavian (25)	25	0.20
Scotch-Irish (61)	271	2.14
Scottish (80)	401	3.17

*Notes: † The Census 2010 population figure is used to calculate the percentages in the Hispanic Origin and Race categories. Ancestry percentages are based on the 2006-2010 American Community Survey population (not shown); ‡ Numbers in parentheses indicate the number of people reporting a single ancestry; * Numbers in parentheses indicate the number of persons reporting this race alone, not in combination with any other race; Please refer to the Explanation of Data for more information.*

Serbian (13)	13	0.10
Slavic (0)	15	0.12
Slovak (28)	35	0.28
Slovene (5)	5	0.04
Swedish (137)	472	3.74
Swiss (0)	18	0.14
Ukrainian (0)	61	0.48
Welsh (9)	54	0.43
West Indian, ex. Hispanic (19)	41	0.32
Dutch West Indian (0)	9	0.07
Jamaican (0)	13	0.10
Trinidadian/Tobagonian (19)	19	0.15
Yugoslavian (14)	26	0.21

Hispanic Origin	Population	%
Hispanic or Latino (of any race)	1,585	12.69
Central American, ex. Mexican	152	1.22
Costa Rican	5	0.04
Guatemalan	75	0.60
Honduran	17	0.14
Nicaraguan	7	0.06
Panamanian	37	0.30
Salvadoran	6	0.05
Other Central American	5	0.04
Cuban	52	0.42
Dominican Republic	242	1.94
Mexican	358	2.87
Puerto Rican	428	3.43
South American	180	1.44
Argentinean	8	0.06
Bolivian	4	0.03
Chilean	6	0.05
Colombian	41	0.33
Ecuadorian	19	0.15
Peruvian	88	0.70
Venezuelan	14	0.11
Other Hispanic or Latino	173	1.38

Race*	Population	%
African-American/Black (1,026)	1,255	10.05
Not Hispanic (934)	1,126	9.01
Hispanic (92)	129	1.03
American Indian/Alaska Native (79)	224	1.79
Not Hispanic (58)	176	1.41
Hispanic (21)	48	0.38
Apache (0)	12	0.10
Blackfeet (0)	4	0.03
Central American Ind. (1)	1	0.01
Cherokee (10)	47	0.38
Cheyenne (1)	1	0.01
Chickasaw (0)	3	0.02
Chippewa (5)	5	0.04
Choctaw (1)	2	0.02
Cree (0)	2	0.02
Creek (1)	3	0.02
Delaware (10)	12	0.10
Iroquois (6)	14	0.11
Kiowa (1)	1	0.01
Lumbee (1)	2	0.02
Mexican American Ind. (6)	9	0.07
Navajo (0)	1	0.01
Pima (0)	3	0.02
Seminole (0)	5	0.04
Shoshone (1)	1	0.01
Sioux (1)	4	0.03
South American Ind. (3)	6	0.05
Yuman (0)	1	0.01
Asian (430)	623	4.99
Not Hispanic (416)	596	4.77
Hispanic (14)	27	0.22
Burmese (3)	3	0.02
Chinese, ex. Taiwanese (63)	101	0.81
Filipino (103)	154	1.23
Indian (30)	35	0.28
Indonesian (0)	2	0.02
Japanese (15)	42	0.34
Korean (172)	251	2.01
Malaysian (0)	1	0.01
Pakistani (5)	8	0.06
Taiwanese (3)	4	0.03
Thai (4)	9	0.07
Vietnamese (12)	16	0.13
Hawaii Native/Pacific Islander (10)	27	0.22
Not Hispanic (9)	24	0.19
Hispanic (1)	3	0.02
Guamanian/Chamorro (2)	3	0.02
Native Hawaiian (3)	10	0.08
Samoan (4)	8	0.06
Tongan (1)	1	0.01
White (9,766)	10,272	82.23
Not Hispanic (9,020)	9,412	75.34
Hispanic (746)	860	6.88

Hillcrest

Place Type: CDP
County: Rockland
Population: 7,558†

Ancestry‡	Population	%
African, Sub-Saharan (90)	90	1.10
African (13)	13	0.16
Ghanaian (77)	77	0.94
American (339)	339	4.14
Austrian (9)	9	0.11
Brazilian (26)	33	0.40
British (8)	8	0.10
Dutch (12)	67	0.82
English (0)	53	0.65
European (21)	41	0.50
German (46)	146	1.78
Guyanese (216)	280	3.42
Hungarian (71)	80	0.98
Irish (37)	128	1.56
Israeli (0)	20	0.24
Italian (77)	196	2.39
Norwegian (9)	9	0.11
Polish (45)	74	0.90
Portuguese (27)	27	0.33
Russian (113)	151	1.84
Scotch-Irish (9)	21	0.26
Ukrainian (31)	31	0.38
Welsh (0)	18	0.22
West Indian, ex. Hispanic (2,666)	2,791	34.04
British West Indian (93)	93	1.13
Haitian (1,310)	1,310	15.98
Jamaican (790)	854	10.42
Trinidadian/Tobagonian (341)	367	4.48
West Indian (132)	167	2.04

Hispanic Origin	Population	%
Hispanic or Latino (of any race)	1,511	19.99
Central American, ex. Mexican	535	7.08
Costa Rican	11	0.15
Guatemalan	365	4.83
Honduran	10	0.13
Nicaraguan	3	0.04
Panamanian	9	0.12
Salvadoran	132	1.75
Other Central American	5	0.07
Cuban	15	0.20
Dominican Republic	139	1.84
Mexican	98	1.30
Puerto Rican	371	4.91
South American	180	2.38
Bolivian	1	0.01
Chilean	21	0.28
Colombian	19	0.25
Ecuadorian	125	1.65
Paraguayan	3	0.04
Peruvian	9	0.12
Venezuelan	2	0.03
Other Hispanic or Latino	173	2.29

Race*	Population	%
African-American/Black (4,219)	4,328	57.26
Not Hispanic (4,065)	4,140	54.78
Hispanic (154)	188	2.49
American Indian/Alaska Native (31)	70	0.93
Not Hispanic (14)	46	0.61
Hispanic (17)	24	0.32
Cherokee (0)	9	0.12
Cheyenne (0)	1	0.01
Delaware (1)	3	0.04
Mexican American Ind. (9)	9	0.12
Navajo (0)	3	0.04
Seminole (0)	1	0.01
South American Ind. (1)	4	0.05
Tlingit-Haida *(Alaska Native)* (0)	3	0.04
Asian (824)	910	12.04
Not Hispanic (817)	892	11.80
Hispanic (7)	18	0.24
Bangladeshi (9)	10	0.13
Cambodian (6)	6	0.08
Chinese, ex. Taiwanese (27)	42	0.56
Filipino (411)	441	5.83
Indian (233)	285	3.77
Indonesian (1)	1	0.01
Japanese (1)	2	0.03
Korean (5)	5	0.07
Laotian (0)	1	0.01
Pakistani (57)	67	0.89
Thai (3)	3	0.04
Vietnamese (34)	44	0.58
Hawaii Native/Pacific Islander (4)	26	0.34
Not Hispanic (4)	20	0.26
Hispanic (0)	6	0.08
Native Hawaiian (1)	2	0.03
White (1,637)	1,736	22.97
Not Hispanic (943)	993	13.14
Hispanic (694)	743	9.83

Holbrook

Place Type: CDP
County: Suffolk
Population: 27,195†

Ancestry‡	Population	%
African, Sub-Saharan (11)	11	0.04
Ghanaian (11)	11	0.04
American (494)	494	1.83
Arab (26)	96	0.36
Arab (26)	96	0.36
Austrian (71)	370	1.37
Belgian (0)	66	0.24
British (11)	26	0.10
Canadian (10)	10	0.04
Czech (54)	153	0.57
Czechoslovakian (6)	80	0.30
Danish (0)	128	0.47
Dutch (27)	199	0.74
Eastern European (66)	101	0.37
English (130)	1,512	5.60
European (39)	39	0.14
Finnish (0)	58	0.21
French, ex. Basque (26)	324	1.20
French Canadian (56)	277	1.03
German (976)	4,930	18.27
Greek (94)	379	1.40
Hungarian (44)	166	0.62
Irish (1,539)	6,714	24.88
Italian (5,814)	11,251	41.70
Lithuanian (18)	89	0.33
Maltese (17)	26	0.10
Norwegian (31)	196	0.73
Polish (491)	1,828	6.78
Portuguese (98)	212	0.79
Romanian (16)	59	0.22
Russian (240)	612	2.27
Scotch-Irish (72)	215	0.80
Scottish (21)	347	1.29
Serbian (0)	11	0.04
Slavic (20)	20	0.07
Slovene (0)	15	0.06
Swedish (36)	107	0.40
Swiss (0)	26	0.10
Turkish (56)	56	0.21
Ukrainian (0)	28	0.10
Welsh (0)	37	0.14

*Notes: † The Census 2010 population figure is used to calculate the percentages in the Hispanic Origin and Race categories. Ancestry percentages are based on the 2006-2010 American Community Survey population (not shown); ‡ Numbers in parentheses indicate the number of people reporting a single ancestry; * Numbers in parentheses indicate the number of persons reporting this race alone, not in combination with any other race; Please refer to the Explanation of Data for more information.*

West Indian, ex. Hispanic (364)	397	1.47
Haitian (252)	252	0.93
Jamaican (43)	76	0.28
Trinidadian/Tobagonian (58)	58	0.21
West Indian (11)	11	0.04
Yugoslavian (40)	73	0.27

Hispanic Origin	Population	%
Hispanic or Latino (of any race)	2,311	8.50
Central American, ex. Mexican	198	0.73
Costa Rican	9	0.03
Guatemalan	39	0.14
Honduran	17	0.06
Nicaraguan	9	0.03
Panamanian	11	0.04
Salvadoran	113	0.42
Cuban	107	0.39
Dominican Republic	134	0.49
Mexican	104	0.38
Puerto Rican	1,111	4.09
South American	425	1.56
Argentinean	39	0.14
Bolivian	1	<0.01
Chilean	26	0.10
Colombian	178	0.65
Ecuadorian	105	0.39
Paraguayan	1	<0.01
Peruvian	58	0.21
Uruguayan	6	0.02
Venezuelan	8	0.03
Other South American	3	0.01
Other Hispanic or Latino	232	0.85

Race*	Population	%
African-American/Black (435)	577	2.12
Not Hispanic (401)	500	1.84
Hispanic (34)	77	0.28
American Indian/Alaska Native (28)	85	0.31
Not Hispanic (18)	61	0.22
Hispanic (10)	24	0.09
Apache (3)	3	0.01
Blackfeet (0)	6	0.02
Cherokee (0)	8	0.03
Chickasaw (1)	1	<0.01
Creek (0)	3	0.01
Hopi (0)	2	0.01
Iroquois (6)	7	0.03
Mexican American Ind. (0)	1	<0.01
South American Ind. (0)	5	0.02
Asian (1,015)	1,133	4.17
Not Hispanic (1,008)	1,104	4.06
Hispanic (7)	29	0.11
Bangladeshi (27)	27	0.10
Cambodian (6)	8	0.03
Chinese, ex. Taiwanese (204)	226	0.83
Filipino (245)	276	1.01
Indian (358)	380	1.40
Japanese (10)	20	0.07
Korean (71)	89	0.33
Laotian (2)	2	0.01
Pakistani (34)	36	0.13
Sri Lankan (4)	4	0.01
Taiwanese (12)	12	0.04
Thai (2)	2	0.01
Vietnamese (15)	21	0.08
Hawaii Native/Pacific Islander (3)	20	0.07
Not Hispanic (3)	20	0.07
Guamanian/Chamorro (0)	3	0.01
Native Hawaiian (0)	1	<0.01
Samoan (2)	2	0.01
White (24,925)	25,253	92.86
Not Hispanic (23,182)	23,388	86.00
Hispanic (1,743)	1,865	6.86

Holtsville

Place Type: CDP
County: Suffolk
Population: 19,714†

Ancestry‡	Population	%
American (348)	348	1.81
Arab (112)	112	0.58
Jordanian (9)	9	0.05
Lebanese (20)	20	0.10
Moroccan (45)	45	0.23
Palestinian (38)	38	0.20
Armenian (6)	6	0.03
Austrian (0)	34	0.18
Belgian (22)	64	0.33
British (26)	26	0.13
Canadian (8)	8	0.04
Croatian (0)	27	0.14
Czech (0)	45	0.23
Danish (0)	53	0.27
Dutch (47)	196	1.02
Eastern European (28)	28	0.15
English (221)	1,252	6.49
European (37)	37	0.19
Finnish (8)	70	0.36
French, ex. Basque (48)	235	1.22
French Canadian (9)	49	0.25
German (475)	3,891	20.18
Greek (27)	228	1.18
Guyanese (51)	51	0.26
Hungarian (53)	194	1.01
Irish (998)	5,213	27.04
Italian (4,108)	8,178	42.42
Latvian (0)	18	0.09
Lithuanian (25)	100	0.52
Maltese (12)	61	0.32
Norwegian (67)	171	0.89
Polish (211)	942	4.89
Portuguese (102)	113	0.59
Romanian (10)	10	0.05
Russian (82)	350	1.82
Scotch-Irish (57)	347	1.80
Scottish (51)	131	0.68
Slovak (14)	47	0.24
Swedish (12)	69	0.36
Swiss (0)	35	0.18
Turkish (0)	58	0.30
Ukrainian (32)	116	0.60
Welsh (13)	46	0.24
West Indian, ex. Hispanic (37)	188	0.98
Haitian (20)	119	0.62
Jamaican (17)	60	0.31
Trinidadian/Tobagonian (0)	9	0.05
Yugoslavian (0)	10	0.05

Hispanic Origin	Population	%
Hispanic or Latino (of any race)	1,990	10.09
Central American, ex. Mexican	142	0.72
Costa Rican	11	0.06
Guatemalan	33	0.17
Honduran	19	0.10
Nicaraguan	4	0.02
Panamanian	4	0.02
Salvadoran	68	0.34
Other Central American	3	0.02
Cuban	72	0.37
Dominican Republic	82	0.42
Mexican	237	1.20
Puerto Rican	826	4.19
South American	420	2.13
Argentinean	33	0.17
Chilean	11	0.06
Colombian	171	0.87
Ecuadorian	147	0.75
Paraguayan	1	0.01
Peruvian	36	0.18
Uruguayan	3	0.02
Venezuelan	18	0.09
Other Hispanic or Latino	211	1.07

Race*	Population	%
African-American/Black (364)	454	2.30
Not Hispanic (326)	398	2.02
Hispanic (38)	56	0.28
American Indian/Alaska Native (32)	55	0.28
Not Hispanic (18)	41	0.21
Hispanic (14)	14	0.07
Blackfeet (0)	3	0.02
Cherokee (1)	4	0.02
Choctaw (0)	1	0.01
Inupiat *(Alaska Native)* (0)	1	0.01
Iroquois (0)	5	0.03
Mexican American Ind. (1)	1	0.01
Asian (865)	965	4.89
Not Hispanic (859)	952	4.83
Hispanic (6)	13	0.07
Bangladeshi (25)	28	0.14
Cambodian (4)	4	0.02
Chinese, ex. Taiwanese (164)	176	0.89
Filipino (61)	82	0.42
Indian (354)	369	1.87
Japanese (9)	11	0.06
Korean (68)	80	0.41
Malaysian (2)	2	0.01
Pakistani (83)	99	0.50
Sri Lankan (1)	1	0.01
Taiwanese (9)	9	0.05
Thai (15)	16	0.08
Vietnamese (35)	43	0.22
Hawaii Native/Pacific Islander (5)	12	0.06
Not Hispanic (4)	7	0.04
Hispanic (1)	5	0.03
Guamanian/Chamorro (4)	4	0.02
Marshallese (1)	1	0.01
White (17,782)	18,014	91.38
Not Hispanic (16,309)	16,444	83.41
Hispanic (1,473)	1,570	7.96

Hornell

Place Type: City
County: Steuben
Population: 8,563†

Ancestry‡	Population	%
African, Sub-Saharan (61)	61	0.71
African (61)	61	0.71
American (745)	745	8.62
Arab (11)	11	0.13
Syrian (11)	11	0.13
British (15)	15	0.17
Canadian (21)	21	0.24
Celtic (0)	102	1.18
Czech (0)	8	0.09
Dutch (43)	321	3.71
English (173)	1,281	14.82
European (59)	59	0.68
French, ex. Basque (15)	361	4.18
French Canadian (16)	26	0.30
German (618)	2,088	24.15
Greek (48)	57	0.66
Hungarian (0)	8	0.09
Irish (730)	2,836	32.80
Italian (443)	1,202	13.90
Lithuanian (8)	8	0.09
Norwegian (0)	29	0.34
Pennsylvania German (5)	41	0.47
Polish (153)	531	6.14
Russian (9)	34	0.39
Scandinavian (0)	12	0.14
Scotch-Irish (74)	131	1.52
Scottish (61)	116	1.34
Soviet Union (12)	12	0.14
Swedish (35)	64	0.74
Ukrainian (17)	17	0.20
Welsh (0)	117	1.35
West Indian, ex. Hispanic (93)	93	1.08
Barbadian (93)	93	1.08

Hispanic Origin	Population	%
Hispanic or Latino (of any race)	175	2.04
Central American, ex. Mexican	15	0.18
Nicaraguan	5	0.06
Panamanian	3	0.04
Salvadoran	7	0.08

*Notes: † The Census 2010 population figure is used to calculate the percentages in the Hispanic Origin and Race categories. Ancestry percentages are based on the 2006-2010 American Community Survey population (not shown); ‡ Numbers in parentheses indicate the number of people reporting a single ancestry; * Numbers in parentheses indicate the number of persons reporting this race alone, not in combination with any other race; Please refer to the Explanation of Data for more information.*

Cuban	5	0.06
Dominican Republic	7	0.08
Mexican	41	0.48
Puerto Rican	68	0.79
South American	14	0.16
Bolivian	3	0.04
Chilean	1	0.01
Colombian	2	0.02
Ecuadorian	4	0.05
Peruvian	3	0.04
Venezuelan	1	0.01
Other Hispanic or Latino	25	0.29

Race*	Population	%
African-American/Black (195)	321	3.75
Not Hispanic (188)	308	3.60
Hispanic (7)	13	0.15
American Indian/Alaska Native (21)	75	0.88
Not Hispanic (16)	68	0.79
Hispanic (5)	7	0.08
Apache (0)	3	0.04
Blackfeet (0)	5	0.06
Cherokee (3)	15	0.18
Chippewa (1)	1	0.01
Iroquois (1)	15	0.18
Navajo (1)	2	0.02
Sioux (0)	1	0.01
Tlingit-Haida *(Alaska Native)* (4)	4	0.05
Asian (57)	73	0.85
Not Hispanic (55)	71	0.83
Hispanic (2)	2	0.02
Chinese, ex. Taiwanese (14)	15	0.18
Filipino (8)	14	0.16
Indian (6)	10	0.12
Japanese (3)	4	0.05
Korean (4)	7	0.08
Pakistani (6)	6	0.07
Vietnamese (9)	9	0.11
Hawaii Native/Pacific Islander (10)	14	0.16
Not Hispanic (9)	13	0.15
Hispanic (1)	1	0.01
Fijian (2)	2	0.02
Guamanian/Chamorro (2)	3	0.04
Marshallese (2)	2	0.02
Native Hawaiian (3)	5	0.06
White (8,036)	8,231	96.12
Not Hispanic (7,923)	8,099	94.58
Hispanic (113)	132	1.54

Horseheads

Place Type: Town
County: Chemung
Population: 19,485†

Ancestry‡	Population	%
African, Sub-Saharan (39)	53	0.27
African (0)	14	0.07
Kenyan (39)	39	0.20
American (1,562)	1,562	8.06
Arab (0)	33	0.17
Lebanese (0)	33	0.17
Austrian (11)	76	0.39
Belgian (37)	59	0.30
British (55)	62	0.32
Canadian (58)	91	0.47
Croatian (15)	15	0.08
Czech (58)	93	0.48
Czechoslovakian (49)	148	0.76
Danish (9)	37	0.19
Dutch (130)	561	2.90
Eastern European (18)	18	0.09
English (1,061)	3,310	17.09
European (81)	87	0.45
Finnish (25)	158	0.82
French, ex. Basque (116)	634	3.27
French Canadian (36)	140	0.72
German (1,056)	4,303	22.21
Greek (43)	59	0.30
Hungarian (16)	118	0.61
Irish (1,003)	3,904	20.15
Italian (590)	1,982	10.23
Latvian (0)	44	0.23
Lithuanian (46)	83	0.43
Maltese (9)	9	0.05
Norwegian (27)	213	1.10
Pennsylvania German (42)	84	0.43
Polish (685)	1,786	9.22
Portuguese (11)	11	0.06
Romanian (0)	8	0.04
Russian (64)	164	0.85
Scotch-Irish (360)	626	3.23
Scottish (65)	302	1.56
Slavic (0)	55	0.28
Slovak (20)	59	0.30
Slovene (15)	41	0.21
Swedish (68)	247	1.28
Swiss (14)	37	0.19
Ukrainian (63)	378	1.95
Welsh (94)	471	2.43
West Indian, ex. Hispanic (32)	42	0.22
Jamaican (21)	21	0.11
West Indian (0)	10	0.05
Other West Indian (11)	11	0.06

Hispanic Origin	Population	%
Hispanic or Latino (of any race)	329	1.69
Central American, ex. Mexican	23	0.12
Costa Rican	7	0.04
Guatemalan	10	0.05
Honduran	1	0.01
Nicaraguan	4	0.02
Panamanian	1	0.01
Cuban	8	0.04
Dominican Republic	6	0.03
Mexican	102	0.52
Puerto Rican	103	0.53
South American	33	0.17
Argentinean	4	0.02
Bolivian	4	0.02
Chilean	1	0.01
Colombian	2	0.01
Ecuadorian	13	0.07
Peruvian	7	0.04
Venezuelan	2	0.01
Other Hispanic or Latino	54	0.28

Race*	Population	%
African-American/Black (394)	528	2.71
Not Hispanic (377)	504	2.59
Hispanic (17)	24	0.12
American Indian/Alaska Native (36)	123	0.63
Not Hispanic (30)	100	0.51
Hispanic (6)	23	0.12
Apache (5)	5	0.03
Blackfeet (1)	7	0.04
Canadian/French Am. Ind. (0)	4	0.02
Cherokee (5)	12	0.06
Houma (1)	1	0.01
Iroquois (9)	16	0.08
Kiowa (1)	1	0.01
Mexican American Ind. (0)	5	0.03
Pueblo (1)	1	0.01
Puget Sound Salish (0)	2	0.01
Sioux (1)	2	0.01
Asian (479)	552	2.83
Not Hispanic (475)	544	2.79
Hispanic (4)	8	0.04
Cambodian (2)	2	0.01
Chinese, ex. Taiwanese (175)	185	0.95
Filipino (27)	46	0.24
Indian (109)	122	0.63
Japanese (22)	35	0.18
Korean (31)	42	0.22
Laotian (4)	10	0.05
Malaysian (0)	1	0.01
Pakistani (47)	47	0.24
Sri Lankan (10)	11	0.06
Taiwanese (9)	11	0.06
Thai (3)	10	0.05
Vietnamese (32)	32	0.16
Hawaii Native/Pacific Islander (3)	6	0.03
Not Hispanic (3)	6	0.03
Guamanian/Chamorro (3)	6	0.03
White (18,208)	18,487	94.88
Not Hispanic (18,003)	18,252	93.67
Hispanic (205)	235	1.21

Huntington

Place Type: CDP
County: Suffolk
Population: 18,046†

Ancestry‡	Population	%
African, Sub-Saharan (31)	31	0.17
South African (31)	31	0.17
American (563)	563	3.01
Arab (35)	44	0.24
Egyptian (6)	6	0.03
Lebanese (29)	29	0.15
Palestinian (0)	9	0.05
Armenian (67)	67	0.36
Australian (36)	36	0.19
Austrian (31)	161	0.86
Brazilian (46)	46	0.25
British (113)	184	0.98
Canadian (53)	79	0.42
Carpatho Rusyn (20)	20	0.11
Czech (48)	172	0.92
Czechoslovakian (9)	18	0.10
Danish (226)	268	1.43
Dutch (97)	223	1.19
Eastern European (127)	127	0.68
English (155)	1,692	9.04
European (433)	523	2.79
French, ex. Basque (57)	399	2.13
French Canadian (0)	51	0.27
German (730)	3,657	19.54
Greek (87)	168	0.90
Hungarian (50)	211	1.13
Iranian (0)	11	0.06
Irish (1,485)	5,170	27.62
Israeli (14)	25	0.13
Italian (2,499)	5,429	29.00
Latvian (18)	18	0.10
Lithuanian (61)	146	0.78
Maltese (11)	32	0.17
New Zealander (26)	26	0.14
Northern European (13)	13	0.07
Norwegian (77)	199	1.06
Polish (357)	1,181	6.31
Portuguese (0)	22	0.12
Romanian (50)	81	0.43
Russian (263)	698	3.73
Scotch-Irish (162)	344	1.84
Scottish (95)	359	1.92
Serbian (17)	17	0.09
Slavic (10)	10	0.05
Slovak (2)	26	0.14
Swedish (24)	334	1.78
Swiss (0)	20	0.11
Turkish (0)	15	0.08
Ukrainian (86)	262	1.40
Welsh (0)	82	0.44
West Indian, ex. Hispanic (29)	29	0.15
Jamaican (29)	29	0.15

Hispanic Origin	Population	%
Hispanic or Latino (of any race)	906	5.02
Central American, ex. Mexican	149	0.83
Costa Rican	4	0.02
Guatemalan	20	0.11
Honduran	11	0.06
Panamanian	5	0.03
Salvadoran	108	0.60
Other Central American	1	0.01
Cuban	39	0.22
Dominican Republic	52	0.29
Mexican	103	0.57

*Notes: † The Census 2010 population figure is used to calculate the percentages in the Hispanic Origin and Race categories. Ancestry percentages are based on the 2006-2010 American Community Survey population (not shown); ‡ Numbers in parentheses indicate the number of people reporting a single ancestry; * Numbers in parentheses indicate the number of persons reporting this race alone, not in combination with any other race; Please refer to the Explanation of Data for more information.*

Puerto Rican	209	1.16
South American	227	1.26
Argentinean	60	0.33
Bolivian	5	0.03
Chilean	21	0.12
Colombian	73	0.40
Ecuadorian	25	0.14
Paraguayan	3	0.02
Peruvian	29	0.16
Uruguayan	5	0.03
Venezuelan	6	0.03
Other Hispanic or Latino	127	0.70

Race*	Population	%
African-American/Black (390)	463	2.57
Not Hispanic (382)	440	2.44
Hispanic (8)	23	0.13
American Indian/Alaska Native (21)	67	0.37
Not Hispanic (16)	54	0.30
Hispanic (5)	13	0.07
Blackfeet (1)	5	0.03
Canadian/French Am. Ind. (1)	2	0.01
Central American Ind. (0)	1	0.01
Cherokee (0)	14	0.08
Chippewa (0)	2	0.01
Choctaw (0)	1	0.01
Delaware (1)	2	0.01
Iroquois (0)	2	0.01
Mexican American Ind. (4)	5	0.03
Sioux (1)	1	0.01
Spanish American Ind. (1)	1	0.01
Asian (397)	524	2.90
Not Hispanic (390)	501	2.78
Hispanic (7)	23	0.13
Bangladeshi (2)	2	0.01
Bhutanese (1)	1	0.01
Chinese, ex. Taiwanese (155)	191	1.06
Filipino (32)	60	0.33
Indian (69)	86	0.48
Indonesian (3)	3	0.02
Japanese (28)	39	0.22
Korean (64)	86	0.48
Malaysian (0)	1	0.01
Pakistani (13)	15	0.08
Sri Lankan (1)	1	0.01
Taiwanese (1)	3	0.02
Thai (8)	10	0.06
Vietnamese (15)	21	0.12
Hawaii Native/Pacific Islander (1)	8	0.04
Not Hispanic (1)	4	0.02
Hispanic (0)	4	0.02
Native Hawaiian (1)	4	0.02
White (16,820)	17,044	94.45
Not Hispanic (16,142)	16,306	90.36
Hispanic (678)	738	4.09

Huntington Station

Place Type: CDP
County: Suffolk
Population: 33,029†

Ancestry‡	Population	%
Afghan (268)	268	0.85
African, Sub-Saharan (119)	149	0.47
African (119)	149	0.47
Albanian (187)	199	0.63
American (582)	582	1.84
Arab (190)	272	0.86
Egyptian (67)	82	0.26
Lebanese (0)	36	0.11
Moroccan (115)	146	0.46
Other Arab (8)	8	0.03
Austrian (27)	146	0.46
Belgian (0)	32	0.10
Brazilian (65)	110	0.35
British (10)	37	0.12
Canadian (33)	59	0.19
Celtic (17)	17	0.05
Croatian (0)	23	0.07
Czech (26)	189	0.60
Czechoslovakian (0)	60	0.19
Danish (21)	64	0.20
Dutch (17)	130	0.41
Eastern European (70)	70	0.22
English (276)	1,609	5.08
European (97)	97	0.31
French, ex. Basque (67)	400	1.26
French Canadian (49)	97	0.31
German (843)	4,135	13.06
Greek (111)	210	0.66
Guyanese (12)	12	0.04
Hungarian (86)	284	0.90
Irish (1,481)	5,395	17.04
Italian (2,663)	6,588	20.80
Lithuanian (16)	53	0.17
Norwegian (103)	357	1.13
Polish (300)	1,207	3.81
Portuguese (25)	82	0.26
Romanian (54)	176	0.56
Russian (312)	867	2.74
Scandinavian (48)	48	0.15
Scotch-Irish (53)	164	0.52
Scottish (98)	245	0.77
Slavic (18)	18	0.06
Swedish (37)	167	0.53
Swiss (33)	104	0.33
Turkish (18)	18	0.06
Ukrainian (33)	61	0.19
Welsh (61)	103	0.33
West Indian, ex. Hispanic (822)	933	2.95
Barbadian (18)	18	0.06
Dutch West Indian (7)	7	0.02
Haitian (458)	458	1.45
Jamaican (208)	277	0.87
Trinidadian/Tobagonian (43)	85	0.27
West Indian (81)	81	0.26
Other West Indian (7)	7	0.02

Hispanic Origin	Population	%
Hispanic or Latino (of any race)	12,109	36.66
Central American, ex. Mexican	7,370	22.31
Costa Rican	44	0.13
Guatemalan	739	2.24
Honduran	1,260	3.81
Nicaraguan	28	0.08
Panamanian	26	0.08
Salvadoran	5,233	15.84
Other Central American	40	0.12
Cuban	61	0.18
Dominican Republic	451	1.37
Mexican	710	2.15
Puerto Rican	1,455	4.41
South American	863	2.61
Argentinean	68	0.21
Chilean	72	0.22
Colombian	230	0.70
Ecuadorian	199	0.60
Paraguayan	33	0.10
Peruvian	213	0.64
Uruguayan	17	0.05
Venezuelan	19	0.06
Other South American	12	0.04
Other Hispanic or Latino	1,199	3.63

Race*	Population	%
African-American/Black (3,592)	4,133	12.51
Not Hispanic (3,299)	3,645	11.04
Hispanic (293)	488	1.48
American Indian/Alaska Native (209)	483	1.46
Not Hispanic (60)	235	0.71
Hispanic (149)	248	0.75
Apache (2)	4	0.01
Blackfeet (1)	20	0.06
Canadian/French Am. Ind. (0)	1	<0.01
Central American Ind. (6)	10	0.03
Cherokee (6)	34	0.10
Choctaw (0)	3	0.01
Creek (0)	3	0.01
Crow (2)	2	0.01
Iroquois (9)	18	0.05
Mexican American Ind. (5)	7	0.02
Seminole (1)	2	0.01
Sioux (0)	1	<0.01
South American Ind. (12)	32	0.10
Spanish American Ind. (6)	11	0.03
Tlingit-Haida *(Alaska Native)* (0)	1	<0.01
Asian (1,164)	1,423	4.31
Not Hispanic (1,154)	1,382	4.18
Hispanic (10)	41	0.12
Bangladeshi (7)	7	0.02
Cambodian (8)	8	0.02
Chinese, ex. Taiwanese (182)	211	0.64
Filipino (130)	169	0.51
Indian (347)	408	1.24
Indonesian (2)	2	0.01
Japanese (33)	56	0.17
Korean (95)	122	0.37
Malaysian (1)	2	0.01
Nepalese (1)	1	<0.01
Pakistani (245)	272	0.82
Sri Lankan (6)	6	0.02
Taiwanese (12)	13	0.04
Thai (14)	20	0.06
Vietnamese (20)	29	0.09
Hawaii Native/Pacific Islander (5)	36	0.11
Not Hispanic (5)	17	0.05
Hispanic (0)	19	0.06
Guamanian/Chamorro (2)	7	0.02
Native Hawaiian (2)	10	0.03
White (21,130)	22,373	67.74
Not Hispanic (15,722)	16,198	49.04
Hispanic (5,408)	6,175	18.70

Huntington

Place Type: Town
County: Suffolk
Population: 203,264†

Ancestry‡	Population	%
Afghan (314)	314	0.16
African, Sub-Saharan (317)	481	0.24
African (146)	206	0.10
Ethiopian (21)	125	0.06
Nigerian (87)	87	0.04
South African (63)	63	0.03
Albanian (216)	237	0.12
Alsatian (0)	9	<0.01
American (5,873)	5,873	2.90
Arab (721)	1,231	0.61
Arab (65)	73	0.04
Egyptian (318)	425	0.21
Iraqi (42)	166	0.08
Jordanian (11)	11	0.01
Lebanese (46)	184	0.09
Moroccan (142)	192	0.09
Palestinian (0)	9	<0.01
Syrian (15)	35	0.02
Other Arab (82)	136	0.07
Armenian (368)	525	0.26
Australian (59)	101	0.05
Austrian (454)	2,004	0.99
Basque (6)	20	0.01
Belgian (30)	115	0.06
Brazilian (142)	195	0.10
British (515)	840	0.42
Bulgarian (44)	65	0.03
Cajun (0)	19	0.01
Canadian (356)	743	0.37
Carpatho Rusyn (20)	20	0.01
Celtic (65)	65	0.03
Croatian (337)	781	0.39
Cypriot (70)	82	0.04
Czech (275)	1,271	0.63
Czechoslovakian (89)	435	0.22
Danish (359)	809	0.40
Dutch (427)	2,168	1.07
Eastern European (1,918)	2,012	1.00
English (2,429)	13,038	6.45

*Notes: † The Census 2010 population figure is used to calculate the percentages in the Hispanic Origin and Race categories. Ancestry percentages are based on the 2006-2010 American Community Survey population (not shown); ‡ Numbers in parentheses indicate the number of people reporting a single ancestry; * Numbers in parentheses indicate the number of persons reporting this race alone, not in combination with any other race; Please refer to the Explanation of Data for more information.*

Estonian (77)	140	0.07
European (1,982)	2,177	1.08
Finnish (21)	178	0.09
French, ex. Basque (400)	3,023	1.50
French Canadian (214)	772	0.38
German (6,140)	33,758	16.70
Greek (1,839)	3,284	1.62
Guyanese (124)	180	0.09
Hungarian (784)	3,005	1.49
Icelander (9)	38	0.02
Iranian (443)	471	0.23
Irish (12,700)	45,750	22.63
Israeli (217)	285	0.14
Italian (26,684)	56,013	27.70
Latvian (75)	193	0.10
Lithuanian (269)	956	0.47
Maltese (30)	88	0.04
New Zealander (26)	26	0.01
Northern European (57)	63	0.03
Norwegian (538)	1,833	0.91
Pennsylvania German (0)	17	0.01
Polish (3,447)	13,208	6.53
Portuguese (198)	526	0.26
Romanian (503)	1,364	0.67
Russian (3,393)	9,499	4.70
Scandinavian (107)	292	0.14
Scotch-Irish (1,045)	2,325	1.15
Scottish (588)	2,306	1.14
Serbian (17)	80	0.04
Slavic (28)	97	0.05
Slovak (109)	225	0.11
Slovene (27)	37	0.02
Swedish (322)	2,237	1.11
Swiss (118)	632	0.31
Turkish (438)	502	0.25
Ukrainian (668)	1,742	0.86
Welsh (126)	533	0.26
West Indian, ex. Hispanic (2,499)	2,882	1.43
Bahamian (31)	31	0.02
Barbadian (18)	18	0.01
Dutch West Indian (7)	7	<0.01
Haitian (1,223)	1,277	0.63
Jamaican (733)	893	0.44
Trinidadian/Tobagonian (128)	170	0.08
U.S. Virgin Islander (91)	147	0.07
West Indian (261)	332	0.16
Other West Indian (7)	7	<0.01
Yugoslavian (161)	467	0.23

Hispanic Origin	Population	%
Hispanic or Latino (of any race)	22,362	11.00
Central American, ex. Mexican	9,599	4.72
Costa Rican	118	0.06
Guatemalan	1,080	0.53
Honduran	1,651	0.81
Nicaraguan	58	0.03
Panamanian	77	0.04
Salvadoran	6,563	3.23
Other Central American	52	0.03
Cuban	603	0.30
Dominican Republic	1,011	0.50
Mexican	1,440	0.71
Puerto Rican	4,187	2.06
South American	3,043	1.50
Argentinean	329	0.16
Bolivian	60	0.03
Chilean	252	0.12
Colombian	957	0.47
Ecuadorian	637	0.31
Paraguayan	91	0.04
Peruvian	538	0.26
Uruguayan	57	0.03
Venezuelan	87	0.04
Other South American	35	0.02
Other Hispanic or Latino	2,479	1.22

Race*	Population	%
African-American/Black (9,515)	10,864	5.34
Not Hispanic (8,933)	9,917	4.88
Hispanic (582)	947	0.47
American Indian/Alaska Native (398)	1,197	0.59
Not Hispanic (187)	785	0.39
Hispanic (211)	412	0.20
Apache (10)	14	0.01
Blackfeet (2)	36	0.02
Canadian/French Am. Ind. (6)	10	<0.01
Central American Ind. (11)	20	0.01
Cherokee (15)	150	0.07
Cheyenne (0)	4	<0.01
Chickasaw (0)	3	<0.01
Chippewa (2)	10	<0.01
Choctaw (0)	13	0.01
Comanche (5)	8	<0.01
Cree (0)	3	<0.01
Creek (1)	15	0.01
Crow (2)	5	<0.01
Delaware (1)	12	0.01
Iroquois (18)	42	0.02
Lumbee (2)	5	<0.01
Mexican American Ind. (18)	26	0.01
Navajo (3)	8	<0.01
Osage (0)	1	<0.01
Ottawa (0)	2	<0.01
Seminole (1)	4	<0.01
Sioux (1)	9	<0.01
South American Ind. (22)	69	0.03
Spanish American Ind. (8)	16	0.01
Tlingit-Haida *(Alaska Native)* (0)	1	<0.01
Asian (10,089)	11,684	5.75
Not Hispanic (10,009)	11,463	5.64
Hispanic (80)	221	0.11
Bangladeshi (108)	120	0.06
Bhutanese (1)	1	<0.01
Burmese (8)	13	0.01
Cambodian (10)	10	<0.01
Chinese, ex. Taiwanese (2,144)	2,546	1.25
Filipino (637)	905	0.45
Indian (3,166)	3,529	1.74
Indonesian (11)	18	0.01
Japanese (218)	338	0.17
Korean (1,952)	2,122	1.04
Laotian (5)	5	<0.01
Malaysian (6)	13	0.01
Nepalese (3)	3	<0.01
Pakistani (1,149)	1,264	0.62
Sri Lankan (20)	22	0.01
Taiwanese (140)	157	0.08
Thai (58)	75	0.04
Vietnamese (151)	186	0.09
Hawaii Native/Pacific Islander (48)	159	0.08
Not Hispanic (32)	93	0.05
Hispanic (16)	66	0.03
Guamanian/Chamorro (18)	25	0.01
Native Hawaiian (16)	40	0.02
Samoan (6)	7	<0.01
White (171,048)	174,612	85.90
Not Hispanic (158,690)	160,914	79.17
Hispanic (12,358)	13,698	6.74

Hyde Park

Place Type: Town
County: Dutchess
Population: 21,571†

Ancestry‡	Population	%
African, Sub-Saharan (20)	20	0.09
African (8)	8	0.04
Nigerian (12)	12	0.06
Albanian (6)	19	0.09
American (834)	834	3.86
Arab (179)	308	1.43
Egyptian (0)	15	0.07
Jordanian (150)	204	0.94
Lebanese (0)	28	0.13
Other Arab (29)	61	0.28
Austrian (40)	123	0.57
Brazilian (30)	42	0.19
British (64)	91	0.42
Cajun (10)	20	0.09
Canadian (13)	28	0.13
Czech (103)	193	0.89
Czechoslovakian (0)	53	0.25
Danish (6)	59	0.27
Dutch (252)	1,270	5.88
Eastern European (54)	63	0.29
English (490)	2,819	13.05
European (60)	74	0.34
Finnish (0)	25	0.12
French, ex. Basque (124)	998	4.62
French Canadian (108)	259	1.20
German (661)	4,589	21.24
Greek (67)	195	0.90
Hungarian (78)	245	1.13
Irish (1,368)	6,005	27.80
Italian (1,655)	4,769	22.08
Lithuanian (0)	75	0.35
Maltese (0)	14	0.06
Norwegian (91)	322	1.49
Pennsylvania German (0)	52	0.24
Polish (339)	1,703	7.88
Portuguese (39)	91	0.42
Romanian (24)	113	0.52
Russian (56)	212	0.98
Scandinavian (4)	4	0.02
Scotch-Irish (58)	297	1.37
Scottish (65)	366	1.69
Slavic (32)	58	0.27
Slovak (43)	48	0.22
Swedish (88)	337	1.56
Swiss (31)	120	0.56
Ukrainian (8)	148	0.69
Welsh (40)	127	0.59
West Indian, ex. Hispanic (200)	281	1.30
Haitian (122)	148	0.69
Jamaican (32)	87	0.40
West Indian (46)	46	0.21

Hispanic Origin	Population	%
Hispanic or Latino (of any race)	1,204	5.58
Central American, ex. Mexican	71	0.33
Costa Rican	6	0.03
Guatemalan	30	0.14
Honduran	5	0.02
Nicaraguan	2	0.01
Panamanian	10	0.05
Salvadoran	18	0.08
Cuban	49	0.23
Dominican Republic	52	0.24
Mexican	242	1.12
Puerto Rican	505	2.34
South American	158	0.73
Argentinean	11	0.05
Bolivian	2	0.01
Chilean	9	0.04
Colombian	39	0.18
Ecuadorian	42	0.19
Paraguayan	2	0.01
Peruvian	31	0.14
Uruguayan	12	0.06
Venezuelan	10	0.05
Other Hispanic or Latino	127	0.59

Race*	Population	%
African-American/Black (1,286)	1,556	7.21
Not Hispanic (1,210)	1,440	6.68
Hispanic (76)	116	0.54
American Indian/Alaska Native (33)	155	0.72
Not Hispanic (27)	123	0.57
Hispanic (6)	32	0.15
Blackfeet (0)	12	0.06
Central American Ind. (0)	3	0.01
Cherokee (1)	19	0.09
Cheyenne (0)	1	<0.01
Chickasaw (1)	1	<0.01
Chippewa (0)	1	<0.01
Choctaw (1)	3	0.01
Iroquois (2)	15	0.07
Mexican American Ind. (2)	3	0.01
Navajo (1)	1	<0.01

*Notes: † The Census 2010 population figure is used to calculate the percentages in the Hispanic Origin and Race categories. Ancestry percentages are based on the 2006-2010 American Community Survey population (not shown); ‡ Numbers in parentheses indicate the number of people reporting a single ancestry; * Numbers in parentheses indicate the number of persons reporting this race alone, not in combination with any other race; Please refer to the Explanation of Data for more information.*

Seminole (0)	6	0.03
Sioux (0)	1	<0.01
South American Ind. (0)	3	0.01
Tlingit-Haida *(Alaska Native)* (0)	1	<0.01
Asian (533)	653	3.03
Not Hispanic (526)	630	2.92
Hispanic (7)	23	0.11
Burmese (4)	4	0.02
Cambodian (1)	1	<0.01
Chinese, ex. Taiwanese (100)	121	0.56
Filipino (100)	137	0.64
Indian (114)	140	0.65
Indonesian (5)	8	0.04
Japanese (12)	23	0.11
Korean (136)	149	0.69
Laotian (2)	2	0.01
Pakistani (11)	12	0.06
Sri Lankan (1)	2	0.01
Taiwanese (8)	8	0.04
Thai (6)	9	0.04
Vietnamese (21)	28	0.13
Hawaii Native/Pacific Islander (10)	32	0.15
Not Hispanic (10)	30	0.14
Hispanic (0)	2	0.01
Fijian (0)	1	<0.01
Guamanian/Chamorro (0)	3	0.01
Native Hawaiian (1)	1	<0.01
Samoan (1)	3	0.01
Tongan (2)	4	0.02
White (18,795)	19,244	89.21
Not Hispanic (18,143)	18,485	85.69
Hispanic (652)	759	3.52

Ilion

Place Type: Village
County: Herkimer
Population: 8,053†

Ancestry‡	Population	%
American (259)	259	3.19
Arab (0)	14	0.17
Lebanese (0)	14	0.17
Austrian (0)	15	0.18
British (7)	7	0.09
Canadian (0)	35	0.43
Czech (46)	67	0.83
Czechoslovakian (15)	15	0.18
Danish (23)	51	0.63
Dutch (13)	305	3.76
English (354)	1,316	16.21
European (12)	12	0.15
French, ex. Basque (111)	676	8.33
French Canadian (158)	343	4.23
German (354)	1,734	21.36
Greek (90)	90	1.11
Hungarian (14)	33	0.41
Irish (717)	2,164	26.66
Italian (583)	1,205	14.85
Lithuanian (13)	13	0.16
Polish (188)	548	6.75
Russian (16)	46	0.57
Scotch-Irish (28)	70	0.86
Scottish (27)	78	0.96
Slavic (14)	14	0.17
Slovene (0)	32	0.39
Swiss (0)	9	0.11
Ukrainian (28)	100	1.23
Welsh (82)	250	3.08

Hispanic Origin	Population	%
Hispanic or Latino (of any race)	190	2.36
Central American, ex. Mexican	4	0.05
Costa Rican	2	0.02
Panamanian	1	0.01
Salvadoran	1	0.01
Dominican Republic	3	0.04
Mexican	31	0.38
Puerto Rican	116	1.44
South American	10	0.12
Argentinean	5	0.06
Bolivian	1	0.01
Colombian	2	0.02
Ecuadorian	2	0.02
Other Hispanic or Latino	26	0.32

Race*	Population	%
African-American/Black (96)	163	2.02
Not Hispanic (96)	159	1.97
Hispanic (0)	4	0.05
American Indian/Alaska Native (26)	61	0.76
Not Hispanic (26)	54	0.67
Hispanic (0)	7	0.09
Apache (0)	1	0.01
Cherokee (0)	2	0.02
Creek (2)	2	0.02
Delaware (0)	4	0.05
Iroquois (6)	9	0.11
Navajo (2)	2	0.02
Sioux (1)	4	0.05
Asian (42)	64	0.79
Not Hispanic (41)	63	0.78
Hispanic (1)	1	0.01
Cambodian (0)	5	0.06
Chinese, ex. Taiwanese (6)	8	0.10
Filipino (13)	18	0.22
Indian (7)	10	0.12
Japanese (3)	5	0.06
Korean (2)	4	0.05
Laotian (4)	5	0.06
Thai (6)	9	0.11
Vietnamese (0)	3	0.04
Hawaii Native/Pacific Islander (0)	1	0.01
Not Hispanic (0)	1	0.01
Native Hawaiian (0)	1	0.01
White (7,731)	7,848	97.45
Not Hispanic (7,595)	7,691	95.50
Hispanic (136)	157	1.95

Inwood

Place Type: CDP
County: Nassau
Population: 9,792†

Ancestry‡	Population	%
Afghan (23)	23	0.22
African, Sub-Saharan (0)	63	0.60
African (0)	63	0.60
American (286)	286	2.74
Croatian (13)	13	0.12
Czech (0)	22	0.21
Danish (0)	9	0.09
Eastern European (9)	9	0.09
English (39)	224	2.14
French, ex. Basque (0)	87	0.83
German (14)	390	3.73
Greek (9)	9	0.09
Guyanese (29)	29	0.28
Hungarian (10)	10	0.10
Irish (597)	971	9.29
Italian (1,109)	1,586	15.17
Polish (33)	80	0.77
Romanian (30)	66	0.63
Russian (15)	57	0.55
Scotch-Irish (20)	36	0.34
Scottish (0)	33	0.32
Slavic (0)	14	0.13
Swedish (0)	21	0.20
Ukrainian (8)	8	0.08
West Indian, ex. Hispanic (237)	364	3.48
British West Indian (8)	8	0.08
Haitian (58)	71	0.68
Jamaican (67)	67	0.64
Trinidadian/Tobagonian (46)	97	0.93
West Indian (58)	121	1.16

Hispanic Origin	Population	%
Hispanic or Latino (of any race)	4,190	42.79
Central American, ex. Mexican	2,509	25.62
Costa Rican	29	0.30
Guatemalan	740	7.56
Honduran	116	1.18
Nicaraguan	79	0.81
Panamanian	8	0.08
Salvadoran	1,523	15.55
Other Central American	14	0.14
Cuban	15	0.15
Dominican Republic	179	1.83
Mexican	101	1.03
Puerto Rican	515	5.26
South American	404	4.13
Argentinean	30	0.31
Bolivian	43	0.44
Chilean	108	1.10
Colombian	99	1.01
Ecuadorian	66	0.67
Paraguayan	1	0.01
Peruvian	46	0.47
Uruguayan	3	0.03
Venezuelan	4	0.04
Other South American	4	0.04
Other Hispanic or Latino	467	4.77

Race*	Population	%
African-American/Black (2,365)	2,499	25.52
Not Hispanic (2,258)	2,329	23.78
Hispanic (107)	170	1.74
American Indian/Alaska Native (72)	119	1.22
Not Hispanic (11)	30	0.31
Hispanic (61)	89	0.91
Central American Ind. (2)	2	0.02
Cherokee (0)	6	0.06
Choctaw (0)	2	0.02
Delaware (1)	1	0.01
Mexican American Ind. (14)	16	0.16
South American Ind. (4)	4	0.04
Spanish American Ind. (13)	13	0.13
Asian (324)	372	3.80
Not Hispanic (322)	353	3.60
Hispanic (2)	19	0.19
Bangladeshi (5)	5	0.05
Cambodian (5)	6	0.06
Chinese, ex. Taiwanese (21)	27	0.28
Filipino (95)	101	1.03
Indian (115)	128	1.31
Japanese (0)	1	0.01
Korean (18)	22	0.22
Pakistani (50)	51	0.52
Thai (1)	1	0.01
Vietnamese (6)	6	0.06
Hawaii Native/Pacific Islander (15)	48	0.49
Not Hispanic (1)	20	0.20
Hispanic (14)	28	0.29
Guamanian/Chamorro (8)	8	0.08
Native Hawaiian (1)	4	0.04
White (4,702)	5,014	51.21
Not Hispanic (2,786)	2,855	29.16
Hispanic (1,916)	2,159	22.05

Irondequoit

Place Type: CDP/Town
County: Monroe
Population: 51,692†

Ancestry‡	Population	%
Afghan (145)	145	0.28
African, Sub-Saharan (653)	763	1.48
African (344)	454	0.88
Ethiopian (192)	192	0.37
Nigerian (85)	85	0.16
Other Sub-Saharan African (32)	32	0.06
Albanian (41)	41	0.08
American (1,362)	1,362	2.64
Arab (107)	120	0.23
Arab (59)	59	0.11
Egyptian (11)	11	0.02
Lebanese (37)	50	0.10
Armenian (54)	72	0.14

*Notes: † The Census 2010 population figure is used to calculate the percentages in the Hispanic Origin and Race categories. Ancestry percentages are based on the 2006-2010 American Community Survey population (not shown); ‡ Numbers in parentheses indicate the number of people reporting a single ancestry; * Numbers in parentheses indicate the number of persons reporting this race alone, not in combination with any other race; Please refer to the Explanation of Data for more information.*

Australian (0)	12	0.02
Austrian (25)	176	0.34
Belgian (23)	93	0.18
Brazilian (52)	71	0.14
British (94)	189	0.37
Canadian (208)	419	0.81
Celtic (14)	14	0.03
Croatian (0)	43	0.08
Czech (32)	153	0.30
Czechoslovakian (23)	42	0.08
Danish (14)	111	0.22
Dutch (161)	1,310	2.54
Eastern European (35)	35	0.07
English (2,071)	7,215	13.98
European (385)	424	0.82
Finnish (22)	30	0.06
French, ex. Basque (121)	1,636	3.17
French Canadian (191)	465	0.90
German (2,967)	11,815	22.89
German Russian (0)	28	0.05
Greek (199)	335	0.65
Hungarian (74)	172	0.33
Iranian (12)	12	0.02
Irish (1,901)	9,070	17.57
Italian (8,322)	14,566	28.22
Latvian (12)	26	0.05
Lithuanian (142)	267	0.52
Luxemburger (24)	24	0.05
Macedonian (212)	266	0.52
Northern European (0)	10	0.02
Norwegian (33)	157	0.30
Pennsylvania German (7)	32	0.06
Polish (1,257)	3,828	7.42
Portuguese (34)	113	0.22
Romanian (59)	71	0.14
Russian (120)	491	0.95
Scandinavian (0)	7	0.01
Scotch-Irish (132)	396	0.77
Scottish (153)	935	1.81
Serbian (0)	16	0.03
Slavic (17)	24	0.05
Slovak (10)	43	0.08
Slovene (13)	13	0.03
Swedish (86)	482	0.93
Swiss (34)	255	0.49
Turkish (238)	245	0.47
Ukrainian (617)	1,169	2.27
Welsh (21)	352	0.68
West Indian, ex. Hispanic (97)	143	0.28
Barbadian (29)	29	0.06
Haitian (58)	58	0.11
Jamaican (10)	56	0.11
Yugoslavian (58)	69	0.13

Hispanic Origin	Population	%
Hispanic or Latino (of any race)	3,220	6.23
Central American, ex. Mexican	88	0.17
Costa Rican	19	0.04
Guatemalan	28	0.05
Honduran	4	0.01
Nicaraguan	11	0.02
Panamanian	7	0.01
Salvadoran	19	0.04
Cuban	167	0.32
Dominican Republic	94	0.18
Mexican	145	0.28
Puerto Rican	2,436	4.71
South American	146	0.28
Argentinean	20	0.04
Chilean	23	0.04
Colombian	53	0.10
Ecuadorian	18	0.03
Paraguayan	3	0.01
Peruvian	10	0.02
Venezuelan	15	0.03
Other South American	4	0.01
Other Hispanic or Latino	144	0.28

Race*	Population	%
African-American/Black (3,996)	4,577	8.85
Not Hispanic (3,741)	4,168	8.06
Hispanic (255)	409	0.79
American Indian/Alaska Native (112)	313	0.61
Not Hispanic (81)	240	0.46
Hispanic (31)	73	0.14
Apache (1)	3	0.01
Blackfeet (3)	4	0.01
Canadian/French Am. Ind. (2)	6	0.01
Central American Ind. (1)	1	<0.01
Cherokee (0)	16	0.03
Chippewa (6)	7	0.01
Colville (0)	1	<0.01
Creek (0)	1	<0.01
Delaware (3)	7	0.01
Iroquois (36)	98	0.19
Mexican American Ind. (5)	5	0.01
Pima (0)	1	<0.01
Pueblo (0)	1	<0.01
Seminole (0)	2	<0.01
South American Ind. (2)	6	0.01
Spanish American Ind. (7)	7	0.01
Asian (662)	888	1.72
Not Hispanic (648)	851	1.65
Hispanic (14)	37	0.07
Bangladeshi (0)	1	<0.01
Burmese (3)	3	0.01
Cambodian (29)	31	0.06
Chinese, ex. Taiwanese (120)	146	0.28
Filipino (101)	155	0.30
Indian (78)	100	0.19
Indonesian (1)	5	0.01
Japanese (12)	37	0.07
Korean (73)	107	0.21
Laotian (94)	109	0.21
Malaysian (0)	1	<0.01
Nepalese (1)	1	<0.01
Pakistani (28)	30	0.06
Taiwanese (3)	3	0.01
Thai (7)	15	0.03
Vietnamese (88)	98	0.19
Hawaii Native/Pacific Islander (12)	42	0.08
Not Hispanic (10)	34	0.07
Hispanic (2)	8	0.02
Fijian (1)	1	<0.01
Guamanian/Chamorro (2)	2	<0.01
Native Hawaiian (5)	11	0.02
Tongan (1)	1	<0.01
White (44,883)	45,826	88.65
Not Hispanic (43,125)	43,832	84.79
Hispanic (1,758)	1,994	3.86

Islip

Place Type: CDP
County: Suffolk
Population: 18,689†

Ancestry‡	Population	%
African, Sub-Saharan (10)	20	0.11
Nigerian (10)	20	0.11
Albanian (0)	19	0.10
Alsatian (0)	18	0.09
American (330)	330	1.74
Arab (32)	56	0.30
Lebanese (0)	11	0.06
Moroccan (8)	8	0.04
Syrian (24)	37	0.20
Armenian (11)	11	0.06
Australian (10)	10	0.05
Austrian (0)	89	0.47
Belgian (6)	16	0.08
British (0)	46	0.24
Canadian (0)	8	0.04
Croatian (0)	53	0.28
Czech (0)	166	0.88
Czechoslovakian (9)	16	0.08
Danish (16)	65	0.34
Dutch (20)	126	0.66
Eastern European (0)	25	0.13
English (111)	1,060	5.59
Estonian (31)	31	0.16
European (80)	80	0.42
Finnish (0)	8	0.04
French, ex. Basque (15)	288	1.52
French Canadian (0)	61	0.32
German (673)	3,490	18.40
Greek (128)	293	1.54
Hungarian (36)	150	0.79
Irish (1,251)	5,683	29.96
Italian (2,626)	6,167	32.51
Lithuanian (25)	98	0.52
Maltese (0)	10	0.05
Norwegian (6)	180	0.95
Polish (218)	1,140	6.01
Portuguese (28)	67	0.35
Romanian (31)	87	0.46
Russian (232)	462	2.44
Scotch-Irish (27)	400	2.11
Scottish (22)	210	1.11
Swedish (9)	161	0.85
Swiss (0)	53	0.28
Turkish (57)	155	0.82
Ukrainian (41)	54	0.28
Welsh (11)	63	0.33
West Indian, ex. Hispanic (260)	415	2.19
Haitian (240)	352	1.86
Jamaican (20)	30	0.16
Trinidadian/Tobagonian (0)	11	0.06
West Indian (0)	22	0.12
Yugoslavian (0)	9	0.05

Hispanic Origin	Population	%
Hispanic or Latino (of any race)	2,580	13.80
Central American, ex. Mexican	457	2.45
Costa Rican	16	0.09
Guatemalan	64	0.34
Honduran	53	0.28
Nicaraguan	21	0.11
Panamanian	19	0.10
Salvadoran	274	1.47
Other Central American	10	0.05
Cuban	51	0.27
Dominican Republic	179	0.96
Mexican	96	0.51
Puerto Rican	912	4.88
South American	653	3.49
Argentinean	18	0.10
Bolivian	5	0.03
Chilean	13	0.07
Colombian	262	1.40
Ecuadorian	217	1.16
Peruvian	100	0.54
Uruguayan	10	0.05
Venezuelan	20	0.11
Other South American	8	0.04
Other Hispanic or Latino	232	1.24

Race*	Population	%
African-American/Black (875)	1,050	5.62
Not Hispanic (760)	868	4.64
Hispanic (115)	182	0.97
American Indian/Alaska Native (35)	140	0.75
Not Hispanic (20)	78	0.42
Hispanic (15)	62	0.33
Blackfeet (0)	9	0.05
Cherokee (5)	15	0.08
Choctaw (0)	1	0.01
Mexican American Ind. (1)	3	0.02
Sioux (0)	4	0.02
South American Ind. (7)	19	0.10
Spanish American Ind. (0)	2	0.01
Asian (465)	586	3.14
Not Hispanic (461)	569	3.04
Hispanic (4)	17	0.09
Bangladeshi (9)	9	0.05
Chinese, ex. Taiwanese (63)	81	0.43
Filipino (49)	67	0.36
Indian (169)	191	1.02
Japanese (4)	24	0.13
Korean (25)	34	0.18

*Notes: † The Census 2010 population figure is used to calculate the percentages in the Hispanic Origin and Race categories. Ancestry percentages are based on the 2006-2010 American Community Survey population (not shown); ‡ Numbers in parentheses indicate the number of people reporting a single ancestry; * Numbers in parentheses indicate the number of persons reporting this race alone, not in combination with any other race; Please refer to the Explanation of Data for more information.*

Pakistani (78)	97	0.52
Taiwanese (6)	6	0.03
Thai (1)	1	0.01
Vietnamese (46)	51	0.27
Hawaii Native/Pacific Islander (10)	33	0.18
Not Hispanic (8)	21	0.11
Hispanic (2)	12	0.06
Guamanian/Chamorro (2)	3	0.02
Native Hawaiian (2)	4	0.02
White (16,151)	16,503	88.30
Not Hispanic (14,570)	14,773	79.05
Hispanic (1,581)	1,730	9.26

Islip

Place Type: Town
County: Suffolk
Population: 335,543†

Ancestry‡	Population	%
Afghan (182)	263	0.08
African, Sub-Saharan (854)	1,222	0.37
African (464)	793	0.24
Ghanaian (71)	71	0.02
Nigerian (164)	203	0.06
Other Sub-Saharan African (155)	155	0.05
Albanian (16)	51	0.02
Alsatian (0)	18	0.01
American (5,894)	5,894	1.77
Arab (986)	1,453	0.44
Arab (51)	177	0.05
Egyptian (339)	364	0.11
Jordanian (68)	122	0.04
Lebanese (86)	185	0.06
Moroccan (123)	141	0.04
Palestinian (166)	166	0.05
Syrian (69)	144	0.04
Other Arab (84)	154	0.05
Armenian (174)	272	0.08
Australian (32)	100	0.03
Austrian (335)	2,019	0.61
Basque (18)	18	0.01
Belgian (68)	328	0.10
Brazilian (683)	895	0.27
British (132)	453	0.14
Cajun (0)	23	0.01
Canadian (111)	405	0.12
Celtic (28)	53	0.02
Croatian (88)	291	0.09
Cypriot (25)	25	0.01
Czech (409)	2,026	0.61
Czechoslovakian (224)	596	0.18
Danish (39)	761	0.23
Dutch (310)	2,191	0.66
Eastern European (337)	433	0.13
English (2,211)	13,963	4.18
Estonian (86)	175	0.05
European (772)	811	0.24
Finnish (59)	271	0.08
French, ex. Basque (403)	4,451	1.33
French Canadian (223)	1,160	0.35
German (7,849)	48,335	14.48
Greek (1,129)	3,126	0.94
Guyanese (460)	499	0.15
Hungarian (433)	2,067	0.62
Icelander (0)	29	0.01
Iranian (111)	170	0.05
Irish (17,586)	68,763	20.61
Israeli (36)	56	0.02
Italian (38,447)	84,360	25.28
Latvian (21)	49	0.01
Lithuanian (294)	799	0.24
Maltese (54)	292	0.09
New Zealander (8)	8	<0.01
Northern European (63)	63	0.02
Norwegian (661)	2,978	0.89
Polish (3,602)	14,896	4.46
Portuguese (1,434)	1,977	0.59
Romanian (213)	467	0.14
Russian (1,589)	5,019	1.50
Scandinavian (55)	183	0.05
Scotch-Irish (960)	3,159	0.95
Scottish (329)	2,852	0.85
Serbian (0)	46	0.01
Slavic (29)	109	0.03
Slovak (46)	280	0.08
Slovene (27)	27	0.01
Swedish (401)	2,528	0.76
Swiss (81)	619	0.19
Turkish (281)	384	0.12
Ukrainian (343)	1,272	0.38
Welsh (102)	552	0.17
West Indian, ex. Hispanic (8,546)	10,274	3.08
Bahamian (0)	22	0.01
Barbadian (22)	63	0.02
Belizean (35)	35	0.01
British West Indian (255)	470	0.14
Dutch West Indian (16)	16	<0.01
Haitian (5,195)	5,636	1.69
Jamaican (1,961)	2,690	0.81
Trinidadian/Tobagonian (530)	665	0.20
West Indian (532)	677	0.20
Yugoslavian (70)	202	0.06

Hispanic Origin	Population	%
Hispanic or Latino (of any race)	97,371	29.02
Central American, ex. Mexican	38,530	11.48
Costa Rican	297	0.09
Guatemalan	3,256	0.97
Honduran	4,232	1.26
Nicaraguan	253	0.08
Panamanian	466	0.14
Salvadoran	29,849	8.90
Other Central American	177	0.05
Cuban	1,113	0.33
Dominican Republic	8,547	2.55
Mexican	3,139	0.94
Puerto Rican	21,506	6.41
South American	16,012	4.77
Argentinean	616	0.18
Bolivian	220	0.07
Chilean	448	0.13
Colombian	5,156	1.54
Ecuadorian	5,323	1.59
Paraguayan	58	0.02
Peruvian	3,599	1.07
Uruguayan	216	0.06
Venezuelan	322	0.10
Other South American	54	0.02
Other Hispanic or Latino	8,524	2.54

Race*	Population	%
African-American/Black (32,024)	35,995	10.73
Not Hispanic (27,898)	30,295	9.03
Hispanic (4,126)	5,700	1.70
American Indian/Alaska Native (1,586)	3,396	1.01
Not Hispanic (520)	1,565	0.47
Hispanic (1,066)	1,831	0.55
Alaska Athabascan *(Ala. Nat.)* (0)	1	<0.01
Aleut *(Alaska Native)* (1)	1	<0.01
Apache (5)	12	<0.01
Arapaho (0)	1	<0.01
Blackfeet (12)	77	0.02
Central American Ind. (52)	73	0.02
Cherokee (44)	316	0.09
Cheyenne (0)	1	<0.01
Chickasaw (1)	3	<0.01
Chippewa (6)	13	<0.01
Choctaw (3)	17	0.01
Comanche (0)	8	<0.01
Creek (1)	7	<0.01
Crow (11)	16	<0.01
Delaware (1)	7	<0.01
Hopi (1)	3	<0.01
Houma (1)	3	<0.01
Inupiat *(Alaska Native)* (1)	2	<0.01
Iroquois (36)	92	0.03
Lumbee (6)	8	<0.01
Mexican American Ind. (83)	135	0.04
Navajo (7)	14	<0.01
Osage (0)	1	<0.01
Pima (1)	1	<0.01
Potawatomi (1)	1	<0.01
Pueblo (4)	7	<0.01
Seminole (2)	4	<0.01
Shoshone (0)	3	<0.01
Sioux (6)	27	0.01
South American Ind. (143)	249	0.07
Spanish American Ind. (67)	91	0.03
Tlingit-Haida *(Alaska Native)* (5)	6	<0.01
Yaqui (1)	1	<0.01
Yuman (0)	1	<0.01
Asian (9,572)	11,510	3.43
Not Hispanic (9,358)	10,957	3.27
Hispanic (214)	553	0.16
Bangladeshi (305)	356	0.11
Burmese (9)	15	<0.01
Cambodian (23)	24	0.01
Chinese, ex. Taiwanese (1,424)	1,766	0.53
Filipino (1,012)	1,301	0.39
Indian (3,680)	4,276	1.27
Indonesian (29)	37	0.01
Japanese (91)	216	0.06
Korean (573)	700	0.21
Laotian (21)	25	0.01
Malaysian (5)	12	<0.01
Nepalese (13)	13	<0.01
Pakistani (1,368)	1,520	0.45
Sri Lankan (13)	21	0.01
Taiwanese (49)	54	0.02
Thai (80)	106	0.03
Vietnamese (433)	518	0.15
Hawaii Native/Pacific Islander (101)	471	0.14
Not Hispanic (52)	244	0.07
Hispanic (49)	227	0.07
Fijian (0)	4	<0.01
Guamanian/Chamorro (28)	44	0.01
Marshallese (1)	1	<0.01
Native Hawaiian (26)	75	0.02
Samoan (6)	15	<0.01
Tongan (0)	2	<0.01
White (245,918)	254,235	75.77
Not Hispanic (195,283)	198,326	59.11
Hispanic (50,635)	55,909	16.66

Ithaca

Place Type: City
County: Tompkins
Population: 30,014†

Ancestry‡	Population	%
Afghan (15)	15	0.05
African, Sub-Saharan (114)	114	0.38
African (34)	34	0.11
Liberian (35)	35	0.12
Nigerian (12)	12	0.04
South African (19)	19	0.06
Other Sub-Saharan African (14)	14	0.05
American (482)	482	1.62
Arab (312)	385	1.29
Arab (85)	85	0.29
Egyptian (49)	49	0.16
Jordanian (14)	14	0.05
Lebanese (23)	60	0.20
Moroccan (51)	51	0.17
Palestinian (72)	72	0.24
Syrian (18)	39	0.13
Other Arab (0)	15	0.05
Armenian (27)	139	0.47
Australian (13)	13	0.04
Austrian (0)	132	0.44
Belgian (10)	20	0.07
Brazilian (22)	80	0.27
British (120)	426	1.43
Bulgarian (81)	123	0.41
Canadian (140)	261	0.88
Croatian (41)	106	0.36
Czech (46)	207	0.70
Czechoslovakian (0)	8	0.03

*Notes: † The Census 2010 population figure is used to calculate the percentages in the Hispanic Origin and Race categories. Ancestry percentages are based on the 2006-2010 American Community Survey population (not shown); ‡ Numbers in parentheses indicate the number of people reporting a single ancestry; * Numbers in parentheses indicate the number of persons reporting this race alone, not in combination with any other race; Please refer to the Explanation of Data for more information.*

Danish (0)	120	0.40
Dutch (59)	279	0.94
Eastern European (167)	235	0.79
English (508)	2,381	8.00
Estonian (0)	14	0.05
European (447)	516	1.73
Finnish (41)	135	0.45
French, ex. Basque (38)	602	2.02
French Canadian (97)	193	0.65
German (820)	3,462	11.63
Greek (71)	188	0.63
Guyanese (76)	76	0.26
Hungarian (33)	171	0.57
Iranian (79)	132	0.44
Irish (705)	3,488	11.71
Israeli (31)	65	0.22
Italian (669)	2,114	7.10
Latvian (0)	52	0.17
Lithuanian (90)	173	0.58
Luxemburger (10)	24	0.08
New Zealander (0)	45	0.15
Northern European (0)	47	0.16
Norwegian (86)	288	0.97
Pennsylvania German (42)	95	0.32
Polish (430)	1,332	4.47
Portuguese (0)	68	0.23
Romanian (0)	71	0.24
Russian (435)	1,067	3.58
Scandinavian (0)	39	0.13
Scotch-Irish (137)	382	1.28
Scottish (112)	589	1.98
Serbian (0)	26	0.09
Slavic (37)	47	0.16
Slovak (25)	54	0.18
Slovene (0)	14	0.05
Swedish (61)	314	1.05
Swiss (40)	190	0.64
Turkish (79)	102	0.34
Ukrainian (38)	111	0.37
Welsh (21)	200	0.67
West Indian, ex. Hispanic (126)	178	0.60
British West Indian (0)	9	0.03
Haitian (89)	105	0.35
Jamaican (0)	6	0.02
Trinidadian/Tobagonian (0)	9	0.03
West Indian (37)	49	0.16
Yugoslavian (14)	27	0.09

Hispanic Origin	Population	%
Hispanic or Latino (of any race)	2,057	6.85
Central American, ex. Mexican	140	0.47
Costa Rican	22	0.07
Guatemalan	34	0.11
Honduran	10	0.03
Nicaraguan	21	0.07
Panamanian	19	0.06
Salvadoran	34	0.11
Cuban	145	0.48
Dominican Republic	148	0.49
Mexican	450	1.50
Puerto Rican	582	1.94
South American	382	1.27
Argentinean	49	0.16
Bolivian	18	0.06
Chilean	47	0.16
Colombian	109	0.36
Ecuadorian	42	0.14
Paraguayan	4	0.01
Peruvian	58	0.19
Uruguayan	8	0.03
Venezuelan	44	0.15
Other South American	3	0.01
Other Hispanic or Latino	210	0.70

Race*	Population	%
African-American/Black (1,971)	2,484	8.28
Not Hispanic (1,842)	2,256	7.52
Hispanic (129)	228	0.76
American Indian/Alaska Native (115)	367	1.22
Not Hispanic (91)	300	1.00
Hispanic (24)	67	0.22
Alaska Athabascan *(Ala. Nat.)* (1)	2	0.01
Apache (1)	2	0.01
Blackfeet (4)	11	0.04
Canadian/French Am. Ind. (1)	2	0.01
Central American Ind. (0)	1	<0.01
Cherokee (13)	58	0.19
Chickasaw (0)	1	<0.01
Chippewa (2)	8	0.03
Choctaw (0)	6	0.02
Comanche (0)	1	<0.01
Creek (3)	6	0.02
Delaware (0)	2	0.01
Hopi (0)	1	<0.01
Iroquois (14)	36	0.12
Kiowa (0)	1	<0.01
Lumbee (1)	1	<0.01
Mexican American Ind. (4)	7	0.02
Navajo (3)	7	0.02
Osage (0)	1	<0.01
Potawatomi (1)	1	<0.01
Pueblo (1)	1	<0.01
Seminole (1)	2	0.01
Sioux (2)	8	0.03
South American Ind. (10)	22	0.07
Yaqui (1)	1	<0.01
Asian (4,854)	5,453	18.17
Not Hispanic (4,820)	5,387	17.95
Hispanic (34)	66	0.22
Bangladeshi (20)	20	0.07
Burmese (51)	53	0.18
Cambodian (55)	68	0.23
Chinese, ex. Taiwanese (2,072)	2,354	7.84
Filipino (70)	137	0.46
Indian (831)	913	3.04
Indonesian (18)	32	0.11
Japanese (119)	243	0.81
Korean (966)	1,032	3.44
Laotian (25)	33	0.11
Malaysian (8)	18	0.06
Nepalese (14)	17	0.06
Pakistani (65)	72	0.24
Sri Lankan (12)	17	0.06
Taiwanese (177)	214	0.71
Thai (59)	72	0.24
Vietnamese (138)	168	0.56
Hawaii Native/Pacific Islander (11)	61	0.20
Not Hispanic (11)	52	0.17
Hispanic (0)	9	0.03
Fijian (0)	2	0.01
Guamanian/Chamorro (2)	11	0.04
Native Hawaiian (8)	21	0.07
Samoan (0)	2	0.01
White (21,172)	22,280	74.23
Not Hispanic (20,023)	20,958	69.83
Hispanic (1,149)	1,322	4.40

Ithaca

Place Type: Town
County: Tompkins
Population: 19,930†

Ancestry‡	Population	%
African, Sub-Saharan (178)	225	1.14
African (54)	67	0.34
Ghanaian (43)	43	0.22
Nigerian (44)	44	0.22
Sudanese (0)	13	0.07
Ugandan (24)	24	0.12
Zimbabwean (13)	24	0.12
Other Sub-Saharan African (0)	10	0.05
American (472)	472	2.40
Arab (56)	69	0.35
Egyptian (28)	28	0.14
Moroccan (28)	28	0.14
Other Arab (0)	13	0.07
Armenian (9)	24	0.12
Austrian (49)	111	0.56
Belgian (4)	17	0.09
British (83)	117	0.59
Cajun (11)	11	0.06
Canadian (72)	114	0.58
Celtic (0)	16	0.08
Croatian (0)	13	0.07
Cypriot (0)	16	0.08
Czech (47)	138	0.70
Czechoslovakian (16)	43	0.22
Danish (0)	19	0.10
Dutch (101)	389	1.98
Eastern European (119)	147	0.75
English (757)	2,630	13.35
Estonian (36)	36	0.18
European (315)	326	1.66
Finnish (16)	27	0.14
French, ex. Basque (79)	520	2.64
French Canadian (50)	245	1.24
German (485)	2,628	13.34
Greek (29)	70	0.36
Guyanese (21)	21	0.11
Hungarian (88)	167	0.85
Icelander (14)	14	0.07
Irish (558)	2,290	11.63
Israeli (71)	86	0.44
Italian (588)	1,809	9.19
Lithuanian (50)	137	0.70
Northern European (30)	30	0.15
Norwegian (9)	158	0.80
Pennsylvania German (0)	6	0.03
Polish (176)	760	3.86
Portuguese (0)	13	0.07
Romanian (37)	54	0.27
Russian (183)	468	2.38
Scandinavian (36)	44	0.22
Scotch-Irish (35)	236	1.20
Scottish (83)	554	2.81
Serbian (0)	8	0.04
Slavic (0)	13	0.07
Slovak (11)	45	0.23
Swedish (54)	317	1.61
Swiss (38)	154	0.78
Turkish (19)	33	0.17
Ukrainian (122)	205	1.04
Welsh (28)	171	0.87
West Indian, ex. Hispanic (25)	58	0.29
Barbadian (0)	10	0.05
British West Indian (12)	12	0.06
Haitian (0)	16	0.08
Jamaican (13)	20	0.10
Yugoslavian (47)	47	0.24

Hispanic Origin	Population	%
Hispanic or Latino (of any race)	882	4.43
Central American, ex. Mexican	70	0.35
Costa Rican	15	0.08
Guatemalan	30	0.15
Honduran	6	0.03
Nicaraguan	5	0.03
Panamanian	4	0.02
Salvadoran	10	0.05
Cuban	58	0.29
Dominican Republic	44	0.22
Mexican	196	0.98
Puerto Rican	205	1.03
South American	202	1.01
Argentinean	26	0.13
Bolivian	2	0.01
Chilean	23	0.12
Colombian	54	0.27
Ecuadorian	30	0.15
Paraguayan	1	0.01
Peruvian	37	0.19
Uruguayan	3	0.02
Venezuelan	23	0.12
Other South American	3	0.02
Other Hispanic or Latino	107	0.54

Race*	Population	%
African-American/Black (813)	1,079	5.41
Not Hispanic (754)	993	4.98

*Notes: † The Census 2010 population figure is used to calculate the percentages in the Hispanic Origin and Race categories. Ancestry percentages are based on the 2006-2010 American Community Survey population (not shown); ‡ Numbers in parentheses indicate the number of people reporting a single ancestry; * Numbers in parentheses indicate the number of persons reporting this race alone, not in combination with any other race; Please refer to the Explanation of Data for more information.*

Hispanic (59)	86	0.43
American Indian/Alaska Native (41)	146	0.73
Not Hispanic (24)	109	0.55
Hispanic (17)	37	0.19
Apache (0)	2	0.01
Blackfeet (0)	4	0.02
Canadian/French Am. Ind. (0)	1	0.01
Central American Ind. (2)	4	0.02
Cherokee (2)	25	0.13
Chickasaw (0)	2	0.01
Chippewa (1)	2	0.01
Choctaw (0)	3	0.02
Cree (0)	2	0.01
Creek (0)	2	0.01
Delaware (2)	9	0.05
Iroquois (2)	9	0.05
Mexican American Ind. (1)	2	0.01
Puget Sound Salish (2)	2	0.01
Seminole (4)	5	0.03
Sioux (1)	3	0.02
South American Ind. (3)	3	0.02
Yup'ik *(Alaska Native)* (0)	1	0.01
Asian (2,274)	2,577	12.93
Not Hispanic (2,259)	2,549	12.79
Hispanic (15)	28	0.14
Bangladeshi (6)	8	0.04
Burmese (59)	63	0.32
Cambodian (25)	28	0.14
Chinese, ex. Taiwanese (884)	989	4.96
Filipino (29)	88	0.44
Indian (382)	424	2.13
Indonesian (21)	31	0.16
Japanese (94)	155	0.78
Korean (415)	446	2.24
Laotian (12)	17	0.09
Malaysian (7)	10	0.05
Nepalese (15)	16	0.08
Pakistani (46)	51	0.26
Sri Lankan (8)	10	0.05
Taiwanese (93)	102	0.51
Thai (46)	53	0.27
Vietnamese (34)	53	0.27
Hawaii Native/Pacific Islander (12)	42	0.21
Not Hispanic (8)	36	0.18
Hispanic (4)	6	0.03
Fijian (0)	2	0.01
Guamanian/Chamorro (4)	6	0.03
Native Hawaiian (1)	11	0.06
Samoan (2)	4	0.02
Tongan (1)	1	0.01
White (15,892)	16,491	82.74
Not Hispanic (15,372)	15,889	79.72
Hispanic (520)	602	3.02

Jamestown

Place Type: City
County: Chautauqua
Population: 31,146†

Ancestry‡	Population	%
African, Sub-Saharan (9)	45	0.14
African (9)	45	0.14
Albanian (99)	136	0.44
American (892)	892	2.86
Arab (22)	42	0.13
Lebanese (0)	10	0.03
Syrian (22)	32	0.10
Austrian (29)	100	0.32
Belgian (0)	9	0.03
Brazilian (0)	9	0.03
British (13)	51	0.16
Canadian (68)	131	0.42
Celtic (0)	31	0.10
Croatian (44)	80	0.26
Czech (40)	62	0.20
Czechoslovakian (0)	10	0.03
Danish (35)	162	0.52
Dutch (101)	930	2.98
Eastern European (10)	10	0.03
English (1,187)	4,386	14.06
European (108)	108	0.35
Finnish (11)	25	0.08
French, ex. Basque (78)	830	2.66
French Canadian (74)	159	0.51
German (1,482)	5,862	18.80
Greek (20)	37	0.12
Hungarian (50)	344	1.10
Irish (1,115)	4,637	14.87
Italian (3,052)	6,761	21.68
Lithuanian (0)	19	0.06
Norwegian (48)	73	0.23
Pennsylvania German (24)	245	0.79
Polish (589)	1,573	5.04
Portuguese (0)	21	0.07
Russian (0)	40	0.13
Scandinavian (18)	18	0.06
Scotch-Irish (106)	584	1.87
Scottish (69)	542	1.74
Slavic (0)	9	0.03
Slovak (0)	10	0.03
Slovene (0)	6	0.02
Swedish (2,018)	5,809	18.63
Swiss (19)	37	0.12
Ukrainian (19)	29	0.09
Welsh (20)	213	0.68
West Indian, ex. Hispanic (12)	51	0.16
Jamaican (12)	51	0.16
Yugoslavian (0)	25	0.08

Hispanic Origin	Population	%
Hispanic or Latino (of any race)	2,738	8.79
Central American, ex. Mexican	40	0.13
Costa Rican	4	0.01
Guatemalan	5	0.02
Honduran	6	0.02
Nicaraguan	6	0.02
Panamanian	1	<0.01
Salvadoran	18	0.06
Cuban	31	0.10
Dominican Republic	44	0.14
Mexican	163	0.52
Puerto Rican	2,275	7.30
South American	64	0.21
Argentinean	17	0.05
Bolivian	5	0.02
Colombian	24	0.08
Ecuadorian	5	0.02
Peruvian	3	0.01
Uruguayan	1	<0.01
Venezuelan	9	0.03
Other Hispanic or Latino	121	0.39

Race*	Population	%
African-American/Black (1,273)	2,117	6.80
Not Hispanic (1,093)	1,823	5.85
Hispanic (180)	294	0.94
American Indian/Alaska Native (192)	485	1.56
Not Hispanic (156)	406	1.30
Hispanic (36)	79	0.25
Alaska Athabascan *(Ala. Nat.)* (1)	1	<0.01
Blackfeet (1)	23	0.07
Cherokee (9)	45	0.14
Chippewa (1)	5	0.02
Creek (1)	1	<0.01
Iroquois (95)	175	0.56
Mexican American Ind. (0)	4	0.01
Pueblo (2)	2	0.01
Seminole (0)	1	<0.01
Sioux (0)	2	0.01
South American Ind. (4)	5	0.02
Asian (134)	227	0.73
Not Hispanic (131)	202	0.65
Hispanic (3)	25	0.08
Chinese, ex. Taiwanese (31)	42	0.13
Filipino (17)	52	0.17
Indian (38)	46	0.15
Indonesian (0)	1	<0.01
Japanese (8)	16	0.05
Korean (25)	29	0.09
Laotian (0)	5	0.02
Sri Lankan (1)	3	0.01
Thai (2)	3	0.01
Vietnamese (8)	18	0.06
Hawaii Native/Pacific Islander (15)	42	0.13
Not Hispanic (13)	32	0.10
Hispanic (2)	10	0.03
Fijian (2)	2	0.01
Guamanian/Chamorro (3)	9	0.03
Native Hawaiian (3)	11	0.04
Samoan (1)	1	<0.01
White (27,547)	28,733	92.25
Not Hispanic (25,998)	26,978	86.62
Hispanic (1,549)	1,755	5.63

Jefferson Valley-Yorktown

Place Type: CDP
County: Westchester
Population: 14,142†

Ancestry‡	Population	%
African, Sub-Saharan (81)	81	0.56
African (17)	17	0.12
Nigerian (46)	46	0.32
Other Sub-Saharan African (18)	18	0.12
Albanian (76)	76	0.53
American (783)	783	5.41
Arab (13)	40	0.28
Lebanese (13)	40	0.28
Austrian (61)	196	1.35
Belgian (18)	32	0.22
British (0)	27	0.19
Canadian (11)	73	0.50
Croatian (10)	19	0.13
Czech (0)	27	0.19
Czechoslovakian (68)	68	0.47
Danish (0)	27	0.19
Dutch (15)	128	0.88
Eastern European (43)	43	0.30
English (99)	559	3.86
Estonian (14)	30	0.21
European (30)	43	0.30
Finnish (0)	15	0.10
French, ex. Basque (30)	218	1.51
French Canadian (15)	32	0.22
German (366)	1,961	13.55
Greek (97)	141	0.97
Guyanese (85)	92	0.64
Hungarian (215)	438	3.03
Iranian (0)	15	0.10
Irish (1,508)	3,833	26.49
Israeli (144)	144	1.00
Italian (3,077)	4,984	34.44
Latvian (55)	55	0.38
Lithuanian (0)	43	0.30
Norwegian (94)	223	1.54
Polish (155)	755	5.22
Portuguese (40)	164	1.13
Romanian (0)	38	0.26
Russian (237)	618	4.27
Scotch-Irish (10)	68	0.47
Scottish (39)	95	0.66
Slavic (0)	9	0.06
Slovak (0)	32	0.22
Swedish (31)	98	0.68
Swiss (15)	15	0.10
Ukrainian (92)	185	1.28
Welsh (16)	29	0.20
West Indian, ex. Hispanic (141)	162	1.12
Bahamian (0)	7	0.05
Haitian (127)	127	0.88
Jamaican (14)	28	0.19
Yugoslavian (14)	32	0.22

Hispanic Origin	Population	%
Hispanic or Latino (of any race)	1,165	8.24
Central American, ex. Mexican	45	0.32
Costa Rican	2	0.01
Guatemalan	25	0.18

*Notes: † The Census 2010 population figure is used to calculate the percentages in the Hispanic Origin and Race categories. Ancestry percentages are based on the 2006-2010 American Community Survey population (not shown); ‡ Numbers in parentheses indicate the number of people reporting a single ancestry; * Numbers in parentheses indicate the number of persons reporting this race alone, not in combination with any other race; Please refer to the Explanation of Data for more information.*

SECTION TWO

Honduran	6	0.04
Nicaraguan	2	0.01
Salvadoran	10	0.07
Cuban	39	0.28
Dominican Republic	92	0.65
Mexican	46	0.33
Puerto Rican	501	3.54
South American	335	2.37
Argentinean	17	0.12
Bolivian	1	0.01
Chilean	15	0.11
Colombian	79	0.56
Ecuadorian	129	0.91
Paraguayan	8	0.06
Peruvian	56	0.40
Uruguayan	19	0.13
Venezuelan	11	0.08
Other Hispanic or Latino	107	0.76

Race*	Population	%
African-American/Black (365)	450	3.18
Not Hispanic (325)	382	2.70
Hispanic (40)	68	0.48
American Indian/Alaska Native (25)	50	0.35
Not Hispanic (12)	23	0.16
Hispanic (13)	27	0.19
Central American Ind. (0)	3	0.02
Cherokee (1)	6	0.04
Iroquois (2)	2	0.01
Sioux (4)	5	0.04
South American Ind. (4)	8	0.06
Asian (608)	711	5.03
Not Hispanic (597)	690	4.88
Hispanic (11)	21	0.15
Bangladeshi (8)	8	0.06
Chinese, ex. Taiwanese (166)	198	1.40
Filipino (75)	93	0.66
Indian (274)	300	2.12
Japanese (12)	16	0.11
Korean (46)	56	0.40
Nepalese (1)	1	0.01
Pakistani (5)	7	0.05
Taiwanese (2)	2	0.01
Thai (2)	6	0.04
Vietnamese (11)	12	0.08
Hawaii Native/Pacific Islander (1)	8	0.06
Not Hispanic (1)	7	0.05
Hispanic (0)	1	0.01
Native Hawaiian (0)	3	0.02
Samoan (1)	1	0.01
White (12,619)	12,837	90.77
Not Hispanic (11,862)	11,994	84.81
Hispanic (757)	843	5.96

Jericho

Place Type: CDP
County: Nassau
Population: 13,567†

Ancestry‡	Population	%
Afghan (129)	129	0.99
African, Sub-Saharan (88)	88	0.68
African (88)	88	0.68
American (947)	947	7.28
Arab (168)	180	1.38
Arab (157)	157	1.21
Syrian (0)	12	0.09
Other Arab (11)	11	0.08
Armenian (28)	56	0.43
Austrian (120)	249	1.91
Belgian (13)	13	0.10
Brazilian (38)	38	0.29
British (16)	50	0.38
Bulgarian (0)	13	0.10
Czech (53)	107	0.82
Czechoslovakian (15)	15	0.12
Danish (0)	7	0.05
Dutch (17)	25	0.19
Eastern European (776)	776	5.96
English (51)	126	0.97
Estonian (12)	12	0.09
European (189)	189	1.45
French, ex. Basque (10)	161	1.24
French Canadian (12)	34	0.26
German (280)	722	5.55
Greek (120)	120	0.92
Hungarian (82)	185	1.42
Iranian (76)	110	0.85
Irish (165)	978	7.52
Israeli (30)	30	0.23
Italian (709)	1,466	11.27
Lithuanian (26)	55	0.42
Maltese (0)	27	0.21
Northern European (0)	8	0.06
Norwegian (21)	31	0.24
Polish (451)	1,030	7.92
Portuguese (0)	7	0.05
Romanian (55)	198	1.52
Russian (869)	1,457	11.20
Scotch-Irish (37)	167	1.28
Scottish (10)	32	0.25
Slovak (9)	9	0.07
Swedish (0)	60	0.46
Swiss (0)	10	0.08
Turkish (13)	93	0.71
Ukrainian (51)	99	0.76
West Indian, ex. Hispanic (15)	49	0.38
Jamaican (7)	24	0.18
Trinidadian/Tobagonian (0)	17	0.13
West Indian (8)	8	0.06

Hispanic Origin	Population	%
Hispanic or Latino (of any race)	401	2.96
Central American, ex. Mexican	49	0.36
Costa Rican	7	0.05
Guatemalan	8	0.06
Honduran	3	0.02
Panamanian	5	0.04
Salvadoran	26	0.19
Cuban	31	0.23
Dominican Republic	30	0.22
Mexican	22	0.16
Puerto Rican	90	0.66
South American	149	1.10
Argentinean	5	0.04
Bolivian	1	0.01
Chilean	9	0.07
Colombian	55	0.41
Ecuadorian	44	0.32
Peruvian	23	0.17
Uruguayan	5	0.04
Venezuelan	7	0.05
Other Hispanic or Latino	30	0.22

Race*	Population	%
African-American/Black (256)	286	2.11
Not Hispanic (247)	274	2.02
Hispanic (9)	12	0.09
American Indian/Alaska Native (10)	26	0.19
Not Hispanic (4)	19	0.14
Hispanic (6)	7	0.05
Cherokee (0)	3	0.02
Creek (0)	1	0.01
Osage (0)	1	0.01
Asian (3,449)	3,588	26.45
Not Hispanic (3,442)	3,572	26.33
Hispanic (7)	16	0.12
Bangladeshi (81)	87	0.64
Cambodian (6)	7	0.05
Chinese, ex. Taiwanese (1,111)	1,160	8.55
Filipino (42)	49	0.36
Indian (879)	928	6.84
Japanese (42)	55	0.41
Korean (1,056)	1,078	7.95
Laotian (1)	1	0.01
Malaysian (4)	4	0.03
Pakistani (94)	99	0.73
Taiwanese (56)	68	0.50
Thai (5)	5	0.04
Vietnamese (9)	14	0.10
Hawaii Native/Pacific Islander (0)	5	0.04
Not Hispanic (0)	5	0.04
Native Hawaiian (0)	1	0.01
White (9,609)	9,723	71.67
Not Hispanic (9,297)	9,400	69.29
Hispanic (312)	323	2.38

Johnson City

Place Type: Village
County: Broome
Population: 15,174†

Ancestry‡	Population	%
African, Sub-Saharan (63)	132	0.87
African (63)	132	0.87
American (735)	735	4.82
Arab (118)	118	0.77
Arab (61)	61	0.40
Egyptian (57)	57	0.37
Armenian (0)	16	0.10
Austrian (10)	51	0.33
British (28)	67	0.44
Cajun (3)	12	0.08
Canadian (16)	26	0.17
Carpatho Rusyn (25)	39	0.26
Czech (108)	186	1.22
Czechoslovakian (46)	123	0.81
Dutch (131)	590	3.87
Eastern European (39)	39	0.26
English (519)	1,755	11.51
European (201)	214	1.40
Finnish (0)	10	0.07
French, ex. Basque (233)	832	5.46
French Canadian (71)	93	0.61
German (552)	2,288	15.01
Greek (14)	56	0.37
Guyanese (56)	70	0.46
Hungarian (8)	62	0.41
Irish (971)	3,761	24.67
Italian (518)	1,667	10.93
Latvian (12)	12	0.08
Lithuanian (59)	165	1.08
Norwegian (81)	81	0.53
Pennsylvania German (83)	106	0.70
Polish (439)	1,261	8.27
Romanian (0)	13	0.09
Russian (243)	559	3.67
Scandinavian (9)	9	0.06
Scotch-Irish (49)	65	0.43
Scottish (64)	290	1.90
Slavic (24)	40	0.26
Slovak (446)	908	5.96
Slovene (0)	38	0.25
Swedish (54)	99	0.65
Swiss (0)	9	0.06
Turkish (92)	92	0.60
Ukrainian (120)	131	0.86
Welsh (37)	234	1.53
West Indian, ex. Hispanic (31)	50	0.33
Haitian (31)	31	0.20
West Indian (0)	19	0.12
Yugoslavian (44)	44	0.29

Hispanic Origin	Population	%
Hispanic or Latino (of any race)	640	4.22
Central American, ex. Mexican	31	0.20
Costa Rican	1	0.01
Guatemalan	16	0.11
Honduran	7	0.05
Panamanian	3	0.02
Salvadoran	4	0.03
Cuban	14	0.09
Dominican Republic	45	0.30
Mexican	95	0.63
Puerto Rican	378	2.49
South American	35	0.23
Argentinean	3	0.02
Chilean	1	0.01

*Notes: † The Census 2010 population figure is used to calculate the percentages in the Hispanic Origin and Race categories. Ancestry percentages are based on the 2006-2010 American Community Survey population (not shown); ‡ Numbers in parentheses indicate the number of people reporting a single ancestry; * Numbers in parentheses indicate the number of persons reporting this race alone, not in combination with any other race; Please refer to the Explanation of Data for more information.*

Colombian	17	0.11
Ecuadorian	9	0.06
Peruvian	1	0.01
Uruguayan	1	0.01
Venezuelan	3	0.02
Other Hispanic or Latino	42	0.28

Race*	Population	%
African-American/Black (959)	1,328	8.75
Not Hispanic (917)	1,220	8.04
Hispanic (42)	108	0.71
American Indian/Alaska Native (36)	172	1.13
Not Hispanic (23)	143	0.94
Hispanic (13)	29	0.19
Apache (3)	7	0.05
Blackfeet (0)	8	0.05
Cherokee (3)	25	0.16
Choctaw (1)	1	0.01
Delaware (0)	1	0.01
Iroquois (3)	14	0.09
Mexican American Ind. (2)	5	0.03
Navajo (0)	1	0.01
Seminole (0)	1	0.01
South American Ind. (1)	1	0.01
Spanish American Ind. (1)	1	0.01
Yaqui (1)	1	0.01
Asian (810)	942	6.21
Not Hispanic (808)	937	6.18
Hispanic (2)	5	0.03
Chinese, ex. Taiwanese (156)	185	1.22
Filipino (22)	34	0.22
Indian (159)	193	1.27
Indonesian (4)	4	0.03
Japanese (6)	24	0.16
Korean (61)	78	0.51
Laotian (243)	278	1.83
Nepalese (9)	9	0.06
Pakistani (20)	21	0.14
Sri Lankan (1)	1	0.01
Taiwanese (4)	4	0.03
Thai (3)	4	0.03
Vietnamese (73)	76	0.50
Hawaii Native/Pacific Islander (8)	18	0.12
Not Hispanic (8)	17	0.11
Hispanic (0)	1	0.01
Fijian (0)	1	0.01
Guamanian/Chamorro (0)	1	0.01
Native Hawaiian (1)	7	0.05
Samoan (1)	4	0.03
White (12,582)	13,066	86.11
Not Hispanic (12,288)	12,703	83.72
Hispanic (294)	363	2.39

Johnstown

Place Type: City
County: Fulton
Population: 8,743†

Ancestry‡	Population	%
American (464)	464	5.31
British (0)	18	0.21
Canadian (38)	54	0.62
Czech (41)	64	0.73
Czechoslovakian (16)	21	0.24
Danish (24)	34	0.39
Dutch (53)	535	6.12
English (641)	1,377	15.76
European (85)	85	0.97
French, ex. Basque (74)	588	6.73
French Canadian (49)	196	2.24
German (207)	1,567	17.93
Greek (11)	11	0.13
Hungarian (0)	81	0.93
Irish (419)	1,604	18.36
Italian (767)	1,905	21.80
Lithuanian (23)	23	0.26
Norwegian (0)	29	0.33
Polish (222)	714	8.17
Portuguese (0)	8	0.09
Russian (39)	49	0.56
Scotch-Irish (9)	125	1.43
Scottish (39)	154	1.76
Slavic (0)	11	0.13
Slovak (120)	212	2.43
Swedish (0)	47	0.54
Swiss (0)	8	0.09
Ukrainian (42)	107	1.22
Welsh (0)	9	0.10
West Indian, ex. Hispanic (10)	10	0.11
Jamaican (10)	10	0.11
Yugoslavian (98)	98	1.12

Hispanic Origin	Population	%
Hispanic or Latino (of any race)	211	2.41
Central American, ex. Mexican	6	0.07
Honduran	3	0.03
Panamanian	2	0.02
Salvadoran	1	0.01
Cuban	8	0.09
Dominican Republic	4	0.05
Mexican	33	0.38
Puerto Rican	130	1.49
South American	2	0.02
Argentinean	2	0.02
Other Hispanic or Latino	28	0.32

Race*	Population	%
African-American/Black (87)	160	1.83
Not Hispanic (75)	139	1.59
Hispanic (12)	21	0.24
American Indian/Alaska Native (9)	32	0.37
Not Hispanic (6)	24	0.27
Hispanic (3)	8	0.09
Apache (0)	1	0.01
Blackfeet (0)	1	0.01
Iroquois (3)	6	0.07
Asian (111)	150	1.72
Not Hispanic (111)	145	1.66
Hispanic (0)	5	0.06
Chinese, ex. Taiwanese (20)	28	0.32
Filipino (3)	14	0.16
Indian (35)	40	0.46
Indonesian (1)	4	0.05
Japanese (13)	16	0.18
Korean (14)	15	0.17
Malaysian (0)	1	0.01
Pakistani (2)	2	0.02
Thai (1)	1	0.01
Vietnamese (10)	12	0.14
Hawaii Native/Pacific Islander (2)	14	0.16
Not Hispanic (2)	9	0.10
Hispanic (0)	5	0.06
Native Hawaiian (2)	8	0.09
Samoan (0)	1	0.01
White (8,344)	8,474	96.92
Not Hispanic (8,212)	8,328	95.25
Hispanic (132)	146	1.67

Kenmore

Place Type: Village
County: Erie
Population: 15,423†

Ancestry‡	Population	%
African, Sub-Saharan (26)	26	0.17
Ethiopian (13)	13	0.08
Other Sub-Saharan African (13)	13	0.08
American (285)	285	1.83
Arab (51)	90	0.58
Arab (0)	12	0.08
Lebanese (0)	27	0.17
Syrian (12)	12	0.08
Other Arab (39)	39	0.25
Armenian (25)	53	0.34
Austrian (0)	44	0.28
British (0)	7	0.05
Canadian (0)	24	0.15
Carpatho Rusyn (0)	13	0.08
Croatian (48)	107	0.69
Czech (20)	55	0.35
Czechoslovakian (0)	2	0.01
Danish (13)	28	0.18
Dutch (15)	156	1.00
Eastern European (21)	21	0.14
English (262)	1,125	7.24
European (85)	85	0.55
French, ex. Basque (66)	359	2.31
French Canadian (60)	344	2.21
German (964)	4,793	30.83
Greek (0)	69	0.44
Hungarian (74)	212	1.36
Irish (642)	3,705	23.83
Italian (2,360)	4,944	31.80
Latvian (15)	15	0.10
Lithuanian (12)	12	0.08
Pennsylvania German (13)	13	0.08
Polish (606)	2,465	15.86
Russian (10)	57	0.37
Scotch-Irish (61)	181	1.16
Scottish (120)	485	3.12
Serbian (12)	12	0.08
Slavic (32)	64	0.41
Slovak (12)	12	0.08
Swedish (67)	174	1.12
Swiss (0)	22	0.14
Ukrainian (56)	113	0.73
Welsh (0)	97	0.62
West Indian, ex. Hispanic (20)	34	0.22
Jamaican (20)	34	0.22
Yugoslavian (9)	9	0.06

Hispanic Origin	Population	%
Hispanic or Latino (of any race)	518	3.36
Central American, ex. Mexican	31	0.20
Costa Rican	7	0.05
Guatemalan	14	0.09
Honduran	1	0.01
Nicaraguan	3	0.02
Panamanian	4	0.03
Salvadoran	2	0.01
Cuban	8	0.05
Dominican Republic	8	0.05
Mexican	51	0.33
Puerto Rican	335	2.17
South American	41	0.27
Argentinean	5	0.03
Bolivian	1	0.01
Colombian	12	0.08
Ecuadorian	9	0.06
Peruvian	6	0.04
Uruguayan	1	0.01
Venezuelan	7	0.05
Other Hispanic or Latino	44	0.29

Race*	Population	%
African-American/Black (461)	616	3.99
Not Hispanic (436)	570	3.70
Hispanic (25)	46	0.30
American Indian/Alaska Native (92)	166	1.08
Not Hispanic (83)	156	1.01
Hispanic (9)	10	0.06
Blackfeet (0)	1	0.01
Canadian/French Am. Ind. (4)	4	0.03
Cherokee (1)	7	0.05
Chippewa (2)	2	0.01
Choctaw (0)	3	0.02
Cree (0)	3	0.02
Crow (0)	2	0.01
Iroquois (51)	91	0.59
Lumbee (0)	1	0.01
Sioux (1)	3	0.02
Asian (150)	205	1.33
Not Hispanic (149)	198	1.28
Hispanic (1)	7	0.05
Cambodian (5)	5	0.03
Chinese, ex. Taiwanese (41)	51	0.33
Filipino (11)	21	0.14
Indian (21)	28	0.18

*Notes: † The Census 2010 population figure is used to calculate the percentages in the Hispanic Origin and Race categories. Ancestry percentages are based on the 2006-2010 American Community Survey population (not shown); ‡ Numbers in parentheses indicate the number of people reporting a single ancestry; * Numbers in parentheses indicate the number of persons reporting this race alone, not in combination with any other race; Please refer to the Explanation of Data for more information.*

SECTION TWO

Indonesian (0)	1	0.01
Japanese (11)	26	0.17
Korean (31)	38	0.25
Laotian (2)	2	0.01
Malaysian (2)	2	0.01
Nepalese (1)	1	0.01
Pakistani (2)	3	0.02
Taiwanese (2)	2	0.01
Thai (2)	2	0.01
Vietnamese (4)	4	0.03
Hawaii Native/Pacific Islander (1)	7	0.05
Not Hispanic (1)	4	0.03
Hispanic (0)	3	0.02
Native Hawaiian (0)	4	0.03
White (14,311)	14,598	94.65
Not Hispanic (13,962)	14,208	92.12
Hispanic (349)	390	2.53

Kent

Place Type: Town
County: Putnam
Population: 13,507†

Ancestry‡	Population	%
Albanian (168)	168	1.23
American (389)	389	2.85
Arab (12)	49	0.36
Egyptian (12)	12	0.09
Lebanese (0)	37	0.27
Armenian (0)	12	0.09
Australian (0)	13	0.10
Austrian (10)	138	1.01
Belgian (0)	22	0.16
Brazilian (16)	16	0.12
British (13)	34	0.25
Canadian (60)	70	0.51
Croatian (24)	24	0.18
Czech (88)	213	1.56
Czechoslovakian (11)	39	0.29
Danish (0)	30	0.22
Dutch (34)	264	1.93
English (60)	934	6.84
European (26)	26	0.19
Finnish (13)	13	0.10
French, ex. Basque (93)	529	3.87
French Canadian (31)	117	0.86
German (374)	2,687	19.67
Greek (20)	131	0.96
Hungarian (63)	228	1.67
Irish (1,087)	4,200	30.74
Israeli (0)	25	0.18
Italian (1,890)	4,939	36.15
Latvian (0)	16	0.12
Lithuanian (23)	123	0.90
Norwegian (26)	61	0.45
Polish (172)	731	5.35
Portuguese (13)	32	0.23
Romanian (12)	43	0.31
Russian (36)	376	2.75
Scandinavian (9)	16	0.12
Scotch-Irish (92)	264	1.93
Scottish (0)	73	0.53
Slovak (0)	44	0.32
Slovene (13)	13	0.10
Swedish (0)	167	1.22
Ukrainian (38)	144	1.05
Welsh (0)	36	0.26
West Indian, ex. Hispanic (9)	9	0.07
West Indian (9)	9	0.07

Hispanic Origin	Population	%
Hispanic or Latino (of any race)	1,755	12.99
Central American, ex. Mexican	305	2.26
Costa Rican	12	0.09
Guatemalan	189	1.40
Honduran	16	0.12
Nicaraguan	9	0.07
Panamanian	8	0.06
Salvadoran	70	0.52
Other Central American	1	0.01
Cuban	49	0.36
Dominican Republic	98	0.73
Mexican	141	1.04
Puerto Rican	700	5.18
South American	316	2.34
Argentinean	17	0.13
Bolivian	9	0.07
Chilean	3	0.02
Colombian	78	0.58
Ecuadorian	112	0.83
Peruvian	82	0.61
Uruguayan	7	0.05
Venezuelan	7	0.05
Other South American	1	0.01
Other Hispanic or Latino	146	1.08

Race*	Population	%
African-American/Black (354)	444	3.29
Not Hispanic (308)	364	2.69
Hispanic (46)	80	0.59
American Indian/Alaska Native (45)	126	0.93
Not Hispanic (28)	91	0.67
Hispanic (17)	35	0.26
Apache (1)	1	0.01
Canadian/French Am. Ind. (0)	5	0.04
Central American Ind. (0)	2	0.01
Cherokee (2)	15	0.11
Cheyenne (0)	6	0.04
Chippewa (1)	4	0.03
Choctaw (0)	2	0.01
Inupiat *(Alaska Native)* (1)	1	0.01
Iroquois (9)	15	0.11
Mexican American Ind. (7)	9	0.07
Seminole (0)	2	0.01
Sioux (1)	2	0.01
South American Ind. (1)	2	0.01
Spanish American Ind. (0)	1	0.01
Asian (252)	323	2.39
Not Hispanic (245)	302	2.24
Hispanic (7)	21	0.16
Bangladeshi (4)	4	0.03
Chinese, ex. Taiwanese (92)	111	0.82
Filipino (46)	58	0.43
Indian (68)	83	0.61
Japanese (6)	17	0.13
Korean (7)	12	0.09
Laotian (0)	4	0.03
Malaysian (3)	7	0.05
Pakistani (7)	7	0.05
Sri Lankan (0)	2	0.01
Taiwanese (4)	5	0.04
Thai (4)	7	0.05
Vietnamese (1)	1	0.01
Hawaii Native/Pacific Islander (5)	12	0.09
Not Hispanic (2)	8	0.06
Hispanic (3)	4	0.03
Guamanian/Chamorro (2)	2	0.01
Native Hawaiian (0)	1	0.01
Samoan (1)	3	0.02
White (12,096)	12,358	91.49
Not Hispanic (10,979)	11,129	82.39
Hispanic (1,117)	1,229	9.10

Kinderhook

Place Type: Town
County: Columbia
Population: 8,498†

Ancestry‡	Population	%
African, Sub-Saharan (33)	33	0.39
African (9)	9	0.11
South African (24)	24	0.28
American (1,078)	1,078	12.71
Arab (17)	32	0.38
Lebanese (17)	32	0.38
Armenian (27)	27	0.32
Austrian (0)	9	0.11
Belgian (0)	27	0.32
Brazilian (17)	17	0.20
British (14)	50	0.59
Canadian (0)	17	0.20
Celtic (13)	13	0.15
Czech (13)	56	0.66
Danish (0)	8	0.09
Dutch (124)	696	8.21
Eastern European (3)	3	0.04
English (204)	1,015	11.97
European (31)	70	0.83
French, ex. Basque (68)	450	5.31
French Canadian (57)	104	1.23
German (432)	1,971	23.24
Greek (0)	220	2.59
Hungarian (15)	54	0.64
Irish (452)	1,508	17.78
Italian (580)	1,461	17.22
Lithuanian (16)	25	0.29
Norwegian (40)	183	2.16
Polish (135)	481	5.67
Romanian (0)	4	0.05
Russian (10)	111	1.31
Scandinavian (12)	16	0.19
Scotch-Irish (11)	130	1.53
Scottish (33)	313	3.69
Slavic (10)	14	0.17
Slovak (43)	52	0.61
Slovene (3)	3	0.04
Swedish (10)	101	1.19
Swiss (0)	3	0.04
Ukrainian (37)	76	0.90
Welsh (13)	40	0.47
West Indian, ex. Hispanic (24)	24	0.28
Jamaican (24)	24	0.28

Hispanic Origin	Population	%
Hispanic or Latino (of any race)	359	4.22
Central American, ex. Mexican	33	0.39
Costa Rican	4	0.05
Guatemalan	22	0.26
Nicaraguan	4	0.05
Salvadoran	3	0.04
Cuban	14	0.16
Dominican Republic	5	0.06
Mexican	149	1.75
Puerto Rican	112	1.32
South American	34	0.40
Argentinean	3	0.04
Chilean	1	0.01
Colombian	12	0.14
Ecuadorian	17	0.20
Uruguayan	1	0.01
Other Hispanic or Latino	12	0.14

Race*	Population	%
African-American/Black (86)	139	1.64
Not Hispanic (71)	114	1.34
Hispanic (15)	25	0.29
American Indian/Alaska Native (17)	55	0.65
Not Hispanic (6)	36	0.42
Hispanic (11)	19	0.22
Blackfeet (0)	3	0.04
Canadian/French Am. Ind. (1)	1	0.01
Cherokee (1)	8	0.09
Iroquois (0)	4	0.05
Potawatomi (0)	1	0.01
Sioux (2)	3	0.04
Asian (88)	112	1.32
Not Hispanic (87)	110	1.29
Hispanic (1)	2	0.02
Bangladeshi (0)	2	0.02
Cambodian (1)	1	0.01
Chinese, ex. Taiwanese (27)	32	0.38
Filipino (15)	16	0.19
Indian (14)	20	0.24
Indonesian (2)	2	0.02
Japanese (3)	11	0.13
Korean (12)	17	0.20
Thai (1)	1	0.01
Vietnamese (3)	5	0.06

*Notes: † The Census 2010 population figure is used to calculate the percentages in the Hispanic Origin and Race categories. Ancestry percentages are based on the 2006-2010 American Community Survey population (not shown); ‡ Numbers in parentheses indicate the number of people reporting a single ancestry; * Numbers in parentheses indicate the number of persons reporting this race alone, not in combination with any other race; Please refer to the Explanation of Data for more information.*

Hawaii Native/Pacific Islander (0)	3	0.04
Not Hispanic (0)	3	0.04
Native Hawaiian (0)	3	0.04
Samoan (0)	3	0.04
White (8,113)	8,222	96.75
Not Hispanic (7,878)	7,964	93.72
Hispanic (235)	258	3.04

Kings Park

Place Type: CDP
County: Suffolk
Population: 17,282†

Ancestry‡	Population	%
African, Sub-Saharan (8)	26	0.15
Nigerian (8)	26	0.15
Albanian (0)	9	0.05
American (267)	267	1.57
Arab (103)	149	0.88
Arab (11)	11	0.06
Iraqi (19)	56	0.33
Jordanian (26)	26	0.15
Lebanese (8)	17	0.10
Syrian (39)	39	0.23
Armenian (15)	60	0.35
Austrian (16)	102	0.60
Belgian (0)	30	0.18
British (0)	12	0.07
Bulgarian (0)	22	0.13
Canadian (0)	12	0.07
Czech (21)	130	0.77
Czechoslovakian (37)	37	0.22
Danish (32)	55	0.32
Dutch (18)	138	0.81
Eastern European (55)	55	0.32
English (148)	1,071	6.31
European (81)	95	0.56
French, ex. Basque (15)	495	2.92
French Canadian (53)	130	0.77
German (805)	3,873	22.81
Greek (98)	441	2.60
Hungarian (99)	190	1.12
Iranian (33)	33	0.19
Irish (1,739)	5,687	33.49
Italian (2,809)	6,750	39.75
Latvian (14)	56	0.33
Lithuanian (31)	57	0.34
Norwegian (17)	92	0.54
Polish (405)	1,360	8.01
Romanian (48)	48	0.28
Russian (77)	380	2.24
Scandinavian (0)	10	0.06
Scotch-Irish (179)	574	3.38
Scottish (27)	213	1.25
Slovak (13)	22	0.13
Swedish (12)	140	0.82
Swiss (0)	23	0.14
Turkish (8)	8	0.05
Ukrainian (46)	69	0.41
Welsh (8)	52	0.31
West Indian, ex. Hispanic (9)	19	0.11
Haitian (9)	9	0.05
Jamaican (0)	10	0.06

Hispanic Origin	Population	%
Hispanic or Latino (of any race)	915	5.29
Central American, ex. Mexican	95	0.55
Costa Rican	3	0.02
Guatemalan	7	0.04
Honduran	30	0.17
Nicaraguan	1	0.01
Panamanian	1	0.01
Salvadoran	52	0.30
Other Central American	1	0.01
Cuban	31	0.18
Dominican Republic	56	0.32
Mexican	74	0.43
Puerto Rican	328	1.90
South American	210	1.22
Argentinean	24	0.14
Bolivian	1	0.01
Chilean	13	0.08
Colombian	71	0.41
Ecuadorian	52	0.30
Paraguayan	1	0.01
Peruvian	37	0.21
Uruguayan	5	0.03
Venezuelan	4	0.02
Other South American	2	0.01
Other Hispanic or Latino	121	0.70

Race*	Population	%
African-American/Black (196)	239	1.38
Not Hispanic (183)	216	1.25
Hispanic (13)	23	0.13
American Indian/Alaska Native (14)	57	0.33
Not Hispanic (13)	43	0.25
Hispanic (1)	14	0.08
Blackfeet (3)	3	0.02
Cherokee (1)	7	0.04
Delaware (0)	1	0.01
Iroquois (7)	7	0.04
Navajo (0)	1	0.01
Pueblo (0)	1	0.01
Sioux (0)	1	0.01
South American Ind. (1)	2	0.01
Ute (0)	1	0.01
Asian (411)	517	2.99
Not Hispanic (406)	507	2.93
Hispanic (5)	10	0.06
Chinese, ex. Taiwanese (84)	98	0.57
Filipino (44)	61	0.35
Indian (114)	137	0.79
Indonesian (4)	5	0.03
Japanese (6)	11	0.06
Korean (83)	91	0.53
Nepalese (1)	1	0.01
Pakistani (42)	49	0.28
Sri Lankan (1)	1	0.01
Taiwanese (1)	1	0.01
Thai (15)	16	0.09
Vietnamese (3)	7	0.04
Hawaii Native/Pacific Islander (3)	16	0.09
Not Hispanic (3)	11	0.06
Hispanic (0)	5	0.03
Fijian (0)	2	0.01
Guamanian/Chamorro (2)	2	0.01
Native Hawaiian (1)	5	0.03
White (16,268)	16,477	95.34
Not Hispanic (15,581)	15,738	91.07
Hispanic (687)	739	4.28

Kingsbury

Place Type: Town
County: Washington
Population: 12,671†

Ancestry‡	Population	%
American (941)	941	7.57
Arab (18)	80	0.64
Lebanese (8)	44	0.35
Syrian (10)	36	0.29
Armenian (10)	10	0.08
Australian (9)	9	0.07
Austrian (38)	87	0.70
Belgian (0)	9	0.07
British (24)	63	0.51
Canadian (59)	106	0.85
Czech (10)	21	0.17
Czechoslovakian (0)	11	0.09
Danish (12)	27	0.22
Dutch (92)	420	3.38
English (473)	1,869	15.04
French, ex. Basque (578)	2,431	19.56
French Canadian (187)	585	4.71
German (301)	1,348	10.85
Hungarian (0)	8	0.06
Irish (1,044)	2,530	20.36
Italian (294)	948	7.63
Lithuanian (0)	9	0.07
Norwegian (12)	65	0.52
Polish (173)	564	4.54
Portuguese (61)	72	0.58
Russian (0)	125	1.01
Scotch-Irish (167)	349	2.81
Scottish (96)	651	5.24
Slovak (9)	38	0.31
Slovene (0)	9	0.07
Swedish (8)	56	0.45
Swiss (0)	12	0.10
Ukrainian (0)	12	0.10
Welsh (0)	116	0.93
West Indian, ex. Hispanic (57)	57	0.46
Haitian (45)	45	0.36
West Indian (12)	12	0.10

Hispanic Origin	Population	%
Hispanic or Latino (of any race)	237	1.87
Central American, ex. Mexican	3	0.02
Costa Rican	1	0.01
Guatemalan	1	0.01
Salvadoran	1	0.01
Cuban	7	0.06
Dominican Republic	2	0.02
Mexican	92	0.73
Puerto Rican	91	0.72
South American	8	0.06
Bolivian	3	0.02
Colombian	4	0.03
Peruvian	1	0.01
Other Hispanic or Latino	34	0.27

Race*	Population	%
African-American/Black (113)	199	1.57
Not Hispanic (101)	176	1.39
Hispanic (12)	23	0.18
American Indian/Alaska Native (23)	77	0.61
Not Hispanic (19)	68	0.54
Hispanic (4)	9	0.07
Apache (2)	3	0.02
Blackfeet (1)	2	0.02
Canadian/French Am. Ind. (0)	1	0.01
Cherokee (2)	8	0.06
Comanche (0)	1	0.01
Cree (0)	1	0.01
Hopi (1)	3	0.02
Iroquois (2)	4	0.03
Mexican American Ind. (1)	1	0.01
Navajo (1)	1	0.01
Sioux (0)	1	0.01
Asian (55)	75	0.59
Not Hispanic (54)	73	0.58
Hispanic (1)	2	0.02
Chinese, ex. Taiwanese (12)	17	0.13
Filipino (16)	23	0.18
Indian (3)	5	0.04
Japanese (4)	6	0.05
Korean (12)	13	0.10
Thai (1)	4	0.03
Vietnamese (4)	4	0.03
Hawaii Native/Pacific Islander (5)	14	0.11
Not Hispanic (5)	14	0.11
Native Hawaiian (1)	11	0.09
Samoan (2)	2	0.02
White (12,261)	12,430	98.10
Not Hispanic (12,109)	12,250	96.68
Hispanic (152)	180	1.42

Kingston

Place Type: City
County: Ulster
Population: 23,893†

Ancestry‡	Population	%
Afghan (24)	24	0.10
African, Sub-Saharan (94)	94	0.39
African (17)	17	0.07

*Notes: † The Census 2010 population figure is used to calculate the percentages in the Hispanic Origin and Race categories. Ancestry percentages are based on the 2006-2010 American Community Survey population (not shown); ‡ Numbers in parentheses indicate the number of people reporting a single ancestry; * Numbers in parentheses indicate the number of persons reporting this race alone, not in combination with any other race; Please refer to the Explanation of Data for more information.*

Ethiopian (19)	19	0.08
Nigerian (58)	58	0.24
American (1,065)	1,065	4.44
Arab (6)	48	0.20
Egyptian (6)	34	0.14
Lebanese (0)	13	0.05
Syrian (0)	1	<0.01
Austrian (31)	342	1.43
Brazilian (112)	112	0.47
British (33)	130	0.54
Canadian (7)	13	0.05
Croatian (67)	67	0.28
Czech (7)	101	0.42
Danish (0)	48	0.20
Dutch (124)	1,329	5.54
Eastern European (24)	49	0.20
English (359)	2,199	9.17
European (287)	287	1.20
Finnish (16)	80	0.33
French, ex. Basque (94)	876	3.65
French Canadian (14)	90	0.38
German (773)	4,492	18.74
Greek (66)	406	1.69
Hungarian (25)	221	0.92
Irish (1,337)	5,218	21.76
Italian (1,211)	3,363	14.03
Lithuanian (13)	75	0.31
Northern European (9)	9	0.04
Norwegian (53)	315	1.31
Pennsylvania German (9)	9	0.04
Polish (324)	1,157	4.83
Portuguese (0)	24	0.10
Romanian (48)	87	0.36
Russian (129)	326	1.36
Scotch-Irish (101)	263	1.10
Scottish (128)	511	2.13
Slavic (7)	51	0.21
Slovak (17)	40	0.17
Swedish (41)	212	0.88
Turkish (0)	10	0.04
Ukrainian (29)	150	0.63
Welsh (0)	31	0.13
West Indian, ex. Hispanic (191)	312	1.30
Barbadian (37)	37	0.15
Haitian (47)	120	0.50
Jamaican (107)	120	0.50
West Indian (0)	35	0.15

Hispanic Origin	Population	%
Hispanic or Latino (of any race)	3,203	13.41
Central American, ex. Mexican	481	2.01
Costa Rican	1	<0.01
Guatemalan	125	0.52
Honduran	67	0.28
Panamanian	10	0.04
Salvadoran	272	1.14
Other Central American	6	0.03
Cuban	44	0.18
Dominican Republic	112	0.47
Mexican	1,176	4.92
Puerto Rican	923	3.86
South American	206	0.86
Argentinean	26	0.11
Bolivian	2	0.01
Chilean	8	0.03
Colombian	43	0.18
Ecuadorian	45	0.19
Peruvian	47	0.20
Uruguayan	12	0.05
Venezuelan	21	0.09
Other South American	2	0.01
Other Hispanic or Latino	261	1.09

Race*	Population	%
African-American/Black (3,478)	4,316	18.06
Not Hispanic (3,214)	3,889	16.28
Hispanic (264)	427	1.79
American Indian/Alaska Native (111)	386	1.62
Not Hispanic (65)	286	1.20
Hispanic (46)	100	0.42
Apache (0)	3	0.01
Arapaho (2)	2	0.01
Blackfeet (0)	19	0.08
Cherokee (8)	52	0.22
Chickasaw (1)	1	<0.01
Chippewa (0)	2	0.01
Choctaw (0)	1	<0.01
Comanche (1)	2	0.01
Cree (0)	2	0.01
Creek (4)	5	0.02
Crow (1)	1	<0.01
Delaware (0)	1	<0.01
Inupiat *(Alaska Native)* (1)	3	0.01
Iroquois (8)	29	0.12
Lumbee (3)	6	0.03
Mexican American Ind. (1)	8	0.03
Navajo (0)	1	<0.01
Osage (0)	1	<0.01
Seminole (0)	4	0.02
Sioux (5)	12	0.05
South American Ind. (3)	6	0.03
Spanish American Ind. (1)	3	0.01
Asian (432)	552	2.31
Not Hispanic (426)	534	2.23
Hispanic (6)	18	0.08
Bangladeshi (0)	1	<0.01
Burmese (0)	2	0.01
Chinese, ex. Taiwanese (143)	177	0.74
Filipino (68)	89	0.37
Indian (71)	91	0.38
Indonesian (2)	2	0.01
Japanese (14)	39	0.16
Korean (24)	37	0.15
Laotian (1)	1	<0.01
Malaysian (1)	1	<0.01
Nepalese (2)	2	0.01
Pakistani (42)	48	0.20
Sri Lankan (9)	9	0.04
Taiwanese (5)	5	0.02
Thai (1)	5	0.02
Vietnamese (27)	36	0.15
Hawaii Native/Pacific Islander (8)	27	0.11
Not Hispanic (8)	19	0.08
Hispanic (0)	8	0.03
Guamanian/Chamorro (1)	10	0.04
Native Hawaiian (3)	3	0.01
Samoan (1)	1	<0.01
White (17,494)	18,525	77.53
Not Hispanic (16,065)	16,828	70.43
Hispanic (1,429)	1,697	7.10

Kirkland

Place Type: Town
County: Oneida
Population: 10,315†

Ancestry‡	Population	%
African, Sub-Saharan (26)	26	0.25
Ghanaian (14)	14	0.14
Kenyan (12)	12	0.12
Alsatian (0)	21	0.20
American (658)	658	6.40
Arab (69)	298	2.90
Arab (0)	32	0.31
Lebanese (21)	123	1.20
Moroccan (14)	14	0.14
Syrian (0)	38	0.37
Other Arab (34)	91	0.89
Armenian (0)	14	0.14
Austrian (0)	19	0.18
Belgian (0)	12	0.12
Brazilian (0)	13	0.13
British (67)	84	0.82
Canadian (58)	101	0.98
Croatian (0)	8	0.08
Czech (0)	84	0.82
Danish (0)	51	0.50
Dutch (36)	250	2.43
Eastern European (0)	11	0.11
English (407)	1,822	17.72
European (48)	48	0.47
Finnish (0)	14	0.14
French, ex. Basque (46)	514	5.00
French Canadian (100)	214	2.08
German (406)	2,280	22.18
Greek (26)	46	0.45
Hungarian (29)	97	0.94
Irish (476)	2,340	22.76
Italian (493)	1,651	16.06
Lithuanian (0)	66	0.64
Northern European (23)	23	0.22
Norwegian (13)	24	0.23
Pennsylvania German (0)	6	0.06
Polish (369)	1,118	10.88
Portuguese (0)	39	0.38
Romanian (26)	42	0.41
Russian (53)	199	1.94
Scandinavian (20)	26	0.25
Scotch-Irish (34)	214	2.08
Scottish (48)	344	3.35
Slovene (9)	9	0.09
Swedish (11)	105	1.02
Swiss (23)	46	0.45
Ukrainian (37)	108	1.05
Welsh (94)	378	3.68

Hispanic Origin	Population	%
Hispanic or Latino (of any race)	245	2.38
Central American, ex. Mexican	23	0.22
Costa Rican	4	0.04
Guatemalan	4	0.04
Honduran	4	0.04
Nicaraguan	1	0.01
Panamanian	1	0.01
Salvadoran	9	0.09
Cuban	7	0.07
Dominican Republic	18	0.17
Mexican	64	0.62
Puerto Rican	73	0.71
South American	22	0.21
Argentinean	2	0.02
Bolivian	2	0.02
Chilean	3	0.03
Colombian	6	0.06
Ecuadorian	9	0.09
Other Hispanic or Latino	38	0.37

Race*	Population	%
African-American/Black (138)	174	1.69
Not Hispanic (129)	155	1.50
Hispanic (9)	19	0.18
American Indian/Alaska Native (16)	78	0.76
Not Hispanic (12)	54	0.52
Hispanic (4)	24	0.23
Canadian/French Am. Ind. (0)	2	0.02
Cherokee (1)	12	0.12
Chickasaw (0)	1	0.01
Choctaw (0)	1	0.01
Creek (0)	1	0.01
Hopi (0)	1	0.01
Iroquois (6)	13	0.13
Mexican American Ind. (4)	6	0.06
Pueblo (1)	1	0.01
Sioux (0)	2	0.02
South American Ind. (0)	4	0.04
Spanish American Ind. (0)	1	0.01
Yaqui (0)	5	0.05
Asian (266)	333	3.23
Not Hispanic (266)	330	3.20
Hispanic (0)	3	0.03
Bangladeshi (4)	4	0.04
Cambodian (1)	1	0.01
Chinese, ex. Taiwanese (103)	130	1.26
Filipino (7)	23	0.22
Hmong (2)	2	0.02
Indian (45)	56	0.54
Indonesian (1)	1	0.01
Japanese (11)	18	0.17
Korean (49)	52	0.50

*Notes: † The Census 2010 population figure is used to calculate the percentages in the Hispanic Origin and Race categories. Ancestry percentages are based on the 2006-2010 American Community Survey population (not shown); ‡ Numbers in parentheses indicate the number of people reporting a single ancestry; * Numbers in parentheses indicate the number of persons reporting this race alone, not in combination with any other race; Please refer to the Explanation of Data for more information.*

Malaysian (1)	1	0.01
Nepalese (5)	5	0.05
Pakistani (10)	10	0.10
Sri Lankan (2)	2	0.02
Taiwanese (7)	8	0.08
Vietnamese (9)	17	0.16
Hawaii Native/Pacific Islander (2)	4	0.04
Not Hispanic (2)	4	0.04
Native Hawaiian (0)	1	0.01
White (9,659)	9,819	95.19
Not Hispanic (9,525)	9,646	93.51
Hispanic (134)	173	1.68

Kiryas Joel

Place Type: Village
County: Orange
Population: 20,175†

Ancestry‡	Population	%
American (1,319)	1,319	6.91
Arab (11)	11	0.06
Moroccan (11)	11	0.06
Austrian (36)	111	0.58
Bulgarian (15)	15	0.08
Canadian (0)	15	0.08
Czech (26)	57	0.30
Czechoslovakian (72)	109	0.57
Eastern European (202)	202	1.06
English (286)	385	2.02
European (1,218)	1,340	7.02
French Canadian (19)	39	0.20
German (174)	883	4.63
Hungarian (3,212)	5,471	28.66
Irish (20)	40	0.21
Israeli (251)	949	4.97
Italian (21)	21	0.11
Polish (18)	391	2.05
Romanian (560)	2,293	12.01
Russian (44)	309	1.62
Swiss (0)	7	0.04
West Indian, ex. Hispanic (102)	102	0.53
Haitian (102)	102	0.53

Hispanic Origin	Population	%
Hispanic or Latino (of any race)	270	1.34
Central American, ex. Mexican	9	0.04
Honduran	8	0.04
Nicaraguan	1	<0.01
Dominican Republic	15	0.07
Mexican	32	0.16
Puerto Rican	3	0.01
South American	189	0.94
Argentinean	186	0.92
Ecuadorian	1	<0.01
Uruguayan	2	0.01
Other Hispanic or Latino	22	0.11

Race*	Population	%
African-American/Black (19)	25	0.12
Not Hispanic (18)	24	0.12
Hispanic (1)	1	<0.01
American Indian/Alaska Native (1)	11	0.05
Not Hispanic (1)	11	0.05
Iroquois (1)	1	<0.01
Mexican American Ind. (0)	1	<0.01
Asian (12)	28	0.14
Not Hispanic (12)	27	0.13
Hispanic (0)	1	<0.01
Chinese, ex. Taiwanese (0)	1	<0.01
Filipino (0)	1	<0.01
Indian (0)	1	<0.01
Japanese (1)	8	0.04
Korean (2)	3	0.01
Pakistani (5)	5	0.02
Vietnamese (0)	1	<0.01
Hawaii Native/Pacific Islander (2)	15	0.07
Not Hispanic (2)	15	0.07
Samoan (0)	1	<0.01
White (20,006)	20,092	99.59
Not Hispanic (19,794)	19,869	98.48
Hispanic (212)	223	1.11

La Grange

Place Type: Town
County: Dutchess
Population: 15,730†

Ancestry‡	Population	%
African, Sub-Saharan (32)	32	0.20
African (32)	32	0.20
Albanian (72)	93	0.59
American (238)	238	1.52
Arab (208)	217	1.38
Jordanian (175)	175	1.12
Lebanese (33)	42	0.27
Austrian (9)	25	0.16
Belgian (11)	37	0.24
British (23)	33	0.21
Bulgarian (0)	26	0.17
Canadian (0)	9	0.06
Carpatho Rusyn (17)	17	0.11
Croatian (0)	10	0.06
Czech (0)	54	0.34
Czechoslovakian (9)	49	0.31
Danish (0)	16	0.10
Dutch (83)	386	2.46
Eastern European (9)	35	0.22
English (158)	1,539	9.81
European (53)	60	0.38
Finnish (16)	33	0.21
French, ex. Basque (39)	395	2.52
French Canadian (9)	139	0.89
German (500)	2,865	18.26
Greek (94)	219	1.40
Hungarian (50)	373	2.38
Iranian (24)	45	0.29
Irish (971)	4,450	28.37
Israeli (10)	10	0.06
Italian (1,630)	4,329	27.59
Latvian (31)	31	0.20
Lithuanian (0)	27	0.17
Norwegian (44)	211	1.34
Pennsylvania German (0)	44	0.28
Polish (299)	881	5.62
Portuguese (132)	241	1.54
Romanian (15)	15	0.10
Russian (180)	356	2.27
Scotch-Irish (60)	273	1.74
Scottish (105)	327	2.08
Slavic (29)	37	0.24
Slovak (23)	91	0.58
Slovene (0)	21	0.13
Swedish (37)	158	1.01
Swiss (13)	66	0.42
Turkish (0)	43	0.27
Ukrainian (61)	169	1.08
Welsh (11)	96	0.61
West Indian, ex. Hispanic (57)	86	0.55
Jamaican (57)	57	0.36
West Indian (0)	29	0.18
Yugoslavian (253)	261	1.66

Hispanic Origin	Population	%
Hispanic or Latino (of any race)	1,116	7.09
Central American, ex. Mexican	50	0.32
Costa Rican	1	0.01
Guatemalan	23	0.15
Honduran	8	0.05
Panamanian	11	0.07
Salvadoran	7	0.04
Cuban	61	0.39
Dominican Republic	91	0.58
Mexican	125	0.79
Puerto Rican	507	3.22
South American	174	1.11
Argentinean	25	0.16
Bolivian	4	0.03
Chilean	7	0.04
Colombian	46	0.29
Ecuadorian	53	0.34
Peruvian	17	0.11
Uruguayan	1	0.01
Venezuelan	13	0.08
Other South American	8	0.05
Other Hispanic or Latino	108	0.69

Race*	Population	%
African-American/Black (590)	699	4.44
Not Hispanic (545)	620	3.94
Hispanic (45)	79	0.50
American Indian/Alaska Native (35)	93	0.59
Not Hispanic (26)	67	0.43
Hispanic (9)	26	0.17
Apache (0)	1	0.01
Canadian/French Am. Ind. (1)	1	0.01
Cherokee (3)	16	0.10
Chippewa (0)	1	0.01
Choctaw (1)	1	0.01
Iroquois (1)	10	0.06
Sioux (0)	2	0.01
South American Ind. (16)	22	0.14
Asian (633)	722	4.59
Not Hispanic (630)	713	4.53
Hispanic (3)	9	0.06
Bangladeshi (5)	5	0.03
Burmese (6)	6	0.04
Cambodian (2)	3	0.02
Chinese, ex. Taiwanese (153)	187	1.19
Filipino (40)	68	0.43
Indian (224)	253	1.61
Indonesian (0)	2	0.01
Japanese (9)	14	0.09
Korean (71)	79	0.50
Laotian (3)	4	0.03
Pakistani (22)	28	0.18
Sri Lankan (12)	16	0.10
Taiwanese (1)	2	0.01
Thai (8)	12	0.08
Vietnamese (40)	41	0.26
Hawaii Native/Pacific Islander (4)	17	0.11
Not Hispanic (4)	12	0.08
Hispanic (0)	5	0.03
Native Hawaiian (1)	9	0.06
Samoan (0)	1	0.01
White (13,959)	14,205	90.31
Not Hispanic (13,188)	13,362	84.95
Hispanic (771)	843	5.36

Lackawanna

Place Type: City
County: Erie
Population: 18,141†

Ancestry‡	Population	%
African, Sub-Saharan (5)	5	0.03
African (5)	5	0.03
Albanian (21)	21	0.12
American (186)	186	1.02
Arab (1,742)	1,753	9.61
Arab (1,320)	1,331	7.30
Lebanese (20)	20	0.11
Other Arab (402)	402	2.20
Austrian (0)	41	0.22
British (0)	23	0.13
Canadian (6)	52	0.29
Celtic (0)	8	0.04
Croatian (104)	233	1.28
Czech (0)	23	0.13
Czechoslovakian (0)	23	0.13
Danish (0)	13	0.07
Dutch (0)	193	1.06
English (214)	778	4.27
Estonian (0)	26	0.14
European (16)	16	0.09
Finnish (0)	43	0.24
French, ex. Basque (77)	334	1.83
French Canadian (23)	64	0.35

*Notes: † The Census 2010 population figure is used to calculate the percentages in the Hispanic Origin and Race categories. Ancestry percentages are based on the 2006-2010 American Community Survey population (not shown); ‡ Numbers in parentheses indicate the number of people reporting a single ancestry; * Numbers in parentheses indicate the number of persons reporting this race alone, not in combination with any other race; Please refer to the Explanation of Data for more information.*

German (749)	3,473	19.04
Greek (28)	91	0.50
Hungarian (43)	348	1.91
Irish (662)	2,293	12.57
Italian (1,114)	3,012	16.51
Lithuanian (0)	29	0.16
Macedonian (9)	25	0.14
Norwegian (56)	121	0.66
Pennsylvania German (12)	12	0.07
Polish (2,834)	4,681	25.66
Romanian (46)	55	0.30
Russian (0)	79	0.43
Scotch-Irish (59)	167	0.92
Scottish (44)	129	0.71
Serbian (102)	131	0.72
Slavic (41)	64	0.35
Slovak (26)	96	0.53
Swedish (22)	67	0.37
Swiss (0)	9	0.05
Turkish (0)	12	0.07
Ukrainian (67)	346	1.90
Welsh (0)	32	0.18
West Indian, ex. Hispanic (108)	136	0.75
Haitian (108)	108	0.59
Jamaican (0)	14	0.08
West Indian (0)	14	0.08
Yugoslavian (297)	326	1.79

Hispanic Origin	Population	%
Hispanic or Latino (of any race)	1,283	7.07
Central American, ex. Mexican	10	0.06
Costa Rican	1	0.01
Guatemalan	1	0.01
Honduran	2	0.01
Salvadoran	6	0.03
Cuban	21	0.12
Dominican Republic	4	0.02
Mexican	155	0.85
Puerto Rican	972	5.36
South American	5	0.03
Colombian	2	0.01
Ecuadorian	1	0.01
Peruvian	2	0.01
Other Hispanic or Latino	116	0.64

Race*	Population	%
African-American/Black (1,790)	2,082	11.48
Not Hispanic (1,670)	1,898	10.46
Hispanic (120)	184	1.01
American Indian/Alaska Native (57)	177	0.98
Not Hispanic (51)	156	0.86
Hispanic (6)	21	0.12
Apache (0)	1	0.01
Cherokee (0)	10	0.06
Chippewa (4)	6	0.03
Delaware (0)	1	0.01
Iroquois (20)	54	0.30
Mexican American Ind. (1)	1	0.01
Seminole (0)	3	0.02
South American Ind. (0)	2	0.01
Spanish American Ind. (1)	1	0.01
Asian (121)	295	1.63
Not Hispanic (118)	284	1.57
Hispanic (3)	11	0.06
Chinese, ex. Taiwanese (7)	10	0.06
Filipino (11)	13	0.07
Indian (41)	45	0.25
Japanese (7)	10	0.06
Korean (7)	16	0.09
Pakistani (9)	12	0.07
Thai (1)	1	0.01
Vietnamese (9)	15	0.08
Hawaii Native/Pacific Islander (7)	12	0.07
Not Hispanic (7)	11	0.06
Hispanic (0)	1	0.01
Guamanian/Chamorro (1)	1	0.01
Native Hawaiian (2)	2	0.01
Samoan (0)	2	0.01
White (15,215)	15,770	86.93
Not Hispanic (14,507)	14,972	82.53
Hispanic (708)	798	4.40

Lake Carmel

Place Type: CDP
County: Putnam
Population: 8,282†

Ancestry‡	Population	%
American (221)	221	2.79
Arab (12)	12	0.15
Egyptian (12)	12	0.15
Austrian (0)	37	0.47
Belgian (0)	22	0.28
British (0)	9	0.11
Canadian (37)	47	0.59
Croatian (24)	24	0.30
Czech (88)	170	2.15
Czechoslovakian (11)	39	0.49
Danish (0)	21	0.27
Dutch (34)	188	2.37
English (47)	410	5.18
French, ex. Basque (49)	238	3.00
French Canadian (0)	66	0.83
German (207)	1,543	19.48
Greek (20)	48	0.61
Hungarian (15)	95	1.20
Irish (665)	2,550	32.19
Israeli (0)	25	0.32
Italian (1,126)	2,872	36.25
Lithuanian (23)	101	1.27
Norwegian (0)	26	0.33
Polish (164)	340	4.29
Romanian (12)	43	0.54
Russian (28)	162	2.04
Scandinavian (9)	16	0.20
Scotch-Irish (27)	62	0.78
Scottish (0)	73	0.92
Slovak (0)	30	0.38
Slovene (13)	13	0.16
Swedish (0)	39	0.49
Ukrainian (0)	38	0.48
Welsh (0)	22	0.28
West Indian, ex. Hispanic (9)	9	0.11
West Indian (9)	9	0.11

Hispanic Origin	Population	%
Hispanic or Latino (of any race)	1,247	15.06
Central American, ex. Mexican	246	2.97
Costa Rican	9	0.11
Guatemalan	159	1.92
Honduran	13	0.16
Nicaraguan	5	0.06
Panamanian	7	0.08
Salvadoran	52	0.63
Other Central American	1	0.01
Cuban	30	0.36
Dominican Republic	68	0.82
Mexican	88	1.06
Puerto Rican	482	5.82
South American	238	2.87
Argentinean	12	0.14
Bolivian	2	0.02
Chilean	3	0.04
Colombian	61	0.74
Ecuadorian	95	1.15
Peruvian	51	0.62
Uruguayan	6	0.07
Venezuelan	7	0.08
Other South American	1	0.01
Other Hispanic or Latino	95	1.15

Race*	Population	%
African-American/Black (217)	278	3.36
Not Hispanic (197)	234	2.83
Hispanic (20)	44	0.53
American Indian/Alaska Native (30)	66	0.80
Not Hispanic (18)	48	0.58
Hispanic (12)	18	0.22
Canadian/French Am. Ind. (0)	5	0.06
Central American Ind. (0)	2	0.02
Cherokee (1)	8	0.10
Chippewa (1)	4	0.05
Inupiat *(Alaska Native)* (1)	1	0.01
Iroquois (5)	6	0.07
Mexican American Ind. (7)	9	0.11
Seminole (0)	2	0.02
South American Ind. (1)	1	0.01
Asian (141)	178	2.15
Not Hispanic (137)	168	2.03
Hispanic (4)	10	0.12
Chinese, ex. Taiwanese (52)	57	0.69
Filipino (29)	39	0.47
Indian (40)	50	0.60
Japanese (2)	4	0.05
Korean (6)	8	0.10
Malaysian (1)	3	0.04
Pakistani (1)	1	0.01
Thai (4)	7	0.08
Hawaii Native/Pacific Islander (3)	5	0.06
Not Hispanic (1)	3	0.04
Hispanic (2)	2	0.02
Guamanian/Chamorro (2)	2	0.02
Samoan (1)	1	0.01
White (7,378)	7,540	91.04
Not Hispanic (6,578)	6,660	80.42
Hispanic (800)	880	10.63

Lake Grove

Place Type: Village
County: Suffolk
Population: 11,163†

Ancestry‡	Population	%
American (226)	226	2.05
Arab (63)	95	0.86
Egyptian (16)	48	0.44
Other Arab (47)	47	0.43
Armenian (0)	16	0.15
Austrian (50)	189	1.72
Belgian (0)	12	0.11
Brazilian (0)	10	0.09
British (0)	16	0.15
Croatian (9)	9	0.08
Cypriot (39)	39	0.35
Czechoslovakian (11)	11	0.10
Danish (10)	10	0.09
Dutch (0)	44	0.40
Eastern European (15)	15	0.14
English (167)	598	5.43
Finnish (0)	31	0.28
French, ex. Basque (22)	178	1.62
French Canadian (74)	143	1.30
German (294)	2,022	18.35
Greek (132)	447	4.06
Hungarian (0)	104	0.94
Iranian (18)	18	0.16
Irish (765)	3,117	28.29
Israeli (13)	43	0.39
Italian (2,272)	4,700	42.66
Lithuanian (0)	10	0.09
Norwegian (9)	112	1.02
Polish (320)	590	5.35
Portuguese (0)	22	0.20
Romanian (20)	52	0.47
Russian (170)	312	2.83
Scotch-Irish (0)	49	0.44
Scottish (0)	172	1.56
Slovak (0)	21	0.19
Swedish (0)	70	0.64
Swiss (17)	98	0.89
Ukrainian (0)	84	0.76
Welsh (0)	18	0.16
West Indian, ex. Hispanic (58)	58	0.53
Haitian (58)	58	0.53
Yugoslavian (4)	4	0.04

Hispanic Origin	Population	%
Hispanic or Latino (of any race)	866	7.76

*Notes: † The Census 2010 population figure is used to calculate the percentages in the Hispanic Origin and Race categories. Ancestry percentages are based on the 2006-2010 American Community Survey population (not shown); ‡ Numbers in parentheses indicate the number of people reporting a single ancestry; * Numbers in parentheses indicate the number of persons reporting this race alone, not in combination with any other race; Please refer to the Explanation of Data for more information.*

Central American, ex. Mexican	77	0.69
Costa Rican	1	0.01
Guatemalan	15	0.13
Honduran	5	0.04
Panamanian	2	0.02
Salvadoran	45	0.40
Other Central American	9	0.08
Cuban	23	0.21
Dominican Republic	64	0.57
Mexican	57	0.51
Puerto Rican	338	3.03
South American	175	1.57
Argentinean	21	0.19
Bolivian	1	0.01
Chilean	9	0.08
Colombian	44	0.39
Ecuadorian	74	0.66
Peruvian	20	0.18
Uruguayan	3	0.03
Venezuelan	3	0.03
Other Hispanic or Latino	132	1.18

Race*	Population	%
African-American/Black (242)	289	2.59
Not Hispanic (215)	244	2.19
Hispanic (27)	45	0.40
American Indian/Alaska Native (25)	54	0.48
Not Hispanic (16)	37	0.33
Hispanic (9)	17	0.15
Cherokee (4)	13	0.12
Chippewa (1)	3	0.03
Creek (1)	4	0.04
Iroquois (8)	11	0.10
Seminole (0)	1	0.01
Sioux (0)	5	0.04
South American Ind. (1)	6	0.05
Spanish American Ind. (3)	3	0.03
Asian (745)	808	7.24
Not Hispanic (737)	791	7.09
Hispanic (8)	17	0.15
Bangladeshi (17)	28	0.25
Burmese (5)	5	0.04
Chinese, ex. Taiwanese (197)	218	1.95
Filipino (83)	98	0.88
Indian (212)	234	2.10
Indonesian (3)	3	0.03
Japanese (16)	22	0.20
Korean (78)	89	0.80
Nepalese (4)	4	0.04
Pakistani (66)	68	0.61
Sri Lankan (3)	3	0.03
Taiwanese (19)	19	0.17
Thai (4)	4	0.04
Vietnamese (12)	12	0.11
Hawaii Native/Pacific Islander (0)	4	0.04
Not Hispanic (0)	3	0.03
Hispanic (0)	1	0.01
White (9,811)	9,935	89.00
Not Hispanic (9,205)	9,290	83.22
Hispanic (606)	645	5.78

Lake Ronkonkoma

Place Type: CDP
County: Suffolk
Population: 20,155†

Ancestry‡	Population	%
African, Sub-Saharan (0)	106	0.49
African (0)	106	0.49
Albanian (0)	10	0.05
American (584)	584	2.72
Arab (54)	154	0.72
Egyptian (0)	10	0.05
Jordanian (54)	132	0.61
Syrian (0)	12	0.06
Austrian (12)	107	0.50
Belgian (0)	23	0.11
Brazilian (12)	36	0.17
British (10)	18	0.08
Canadian (36)	36	0.17
Czech (9)	196	0.91
Czechoslovakian (17)	65	0.30
Danish (0)	23	0.11
Dutch (7)	73	0.34
Eastern European (31)	31	0.14
English (252)	1,032	4.80
European (115)	126	0.59
French, ex. Basque (15)	364	1.69
French Canadian (0)	24	0.11
German (888)	4,399	20.45
Greek (92)	239	1.11
Hungarian (38)	196	0.91
Iranian (59)	59	0.27
Irish (1,382)	6,669	31.01
Israeli (28)	56	0.26
Italian (3,609)	7,628	35.47
Latvian (10)	10	0.05
Lithuanian (12)	25	0.12
Maltese (0)	109	0.51
New Zealander (10)	10	0.05
Northern European (15)	15	0.07
Norwegian (9)	72	0.33
Polish (302)	1,419	6.60
Portuguese (92)	173	0.80
Romanian (0)	32	0.15
Russian (157)	614	2.86
Scotch-Irish (95)	290	1.35
Scottish (26)	149	0.69
Slavic (0)	13	0.06
Slovak (0)	12	0.06
Swedish (46)	363	1.69
Swiss (0)	46	0.21
Turkish (32)	62	0.29
Ukrainian (44)	66	0.31
Welsh (28)	146	0.68
West Indian, ex. Hispanic (18)	133	0.62
Dutch West Indian (9)	9	0.04
Jamaican (9)	9	0.04
West Indian (0)	115	0.53
Yugoslavian (0)	48	0.22

Hispanic Origin	Population	%
Hispanic or Latino (of any race)	2,008	9.96
Central American, ex. Mexican	251	1.25
Costa Rican	7	0.03
Guatemalan	39	0.19
Honduran	32	0.16
Nicaraguan	7	0.03
Panamanian	14	0.07
Salvadoran	146	0.72
Other Central American	6	0.03
Cuban	50	0.25
Dominican Republic	88	0.44
Mexican	170	0.84
Puerto Rican	915	4.54
South American	335	1.66
Argentinean	24	0.12
Bolivian	2	0.01
Chilean	21	0.10
Colombian	154	0.76
Ecuadorian	78	0.39
Peruvian	44	0.22
Uruguayan	6	0.03
Venezuelan	6	0.03
Other Hispanic or Latino	199	0.99

Race*	Population	%
African-American/Black (490)	617	3.06
Not Hispanic (423)	517	2.57
Hispanic (67)	100	0.50
American Indian/Alaska Native (35)	100	0.50
Not Hispanic (9)	52	0.26
Hispanic (26)	48	0.24
Blackfeet (0)	2	0.01
Central American Ind. (4)	4	0.02
Cherokee (0)	11	0.05
Choctaw (1)	3	0.01
Creek (0)	1	<0.01
Iroquois (0)	7	0.03
South American Ind. (1)	3	0.01
Spanish American Ind. (1)	1	<0.01
Tlingit-Haida *(Alaska Native)* (0)	1	<0.01
Yaqui (0)	1	<0.01
Asian (915)	1,051	5.21
Not Hispanic (904)	1,024	5.08
Hispanic (11)	27	0.13
Bangladeshi (59)	71	0.35
Chinese, ex. Taiwanese (180)	203	1.01
Filipino (104)	148	0.73
Indian (297)	326	1.62
Japanese (14)	29	0.14
Korean (37)	48	0.24
Malaysian (0)	1	<0.01
Pakistani (108)	111	0.55
Taiwanese (1)	1	<0.01
Thai (11)	12	0.06
Vietnamese (52)	57	0.28
Hawaii Native/Pacific Islander (3)	9	0.04
Not Hispanic (3)	7	0.03
Hispanic (0)	2	0.01
Fijian (2)	2	0.01
Native Hawaiian (1)	1	<0.01
White (17,984)	18,283	90.71
Not Hispanic (16,511)	16,736	83.04
Hispanic (1,473)	1,547	7.68

Lancaster

Place Type: Town
County: Erie
Population: 41,604†

Ancestry‡	Population	%
African, Sub-Saharan (18)	120	0.29
African (18)	120	0.29
Albanian (12)	12	0.03
American (939)	939	2.29
Arab (102)	126	0.31
Egyptian (0)	13	0.03
Lebanese (37)	48	0.12
Other Arab (65)	65	0.16
Australian (8)	17	0.04
Austrian (13)	124	0.30
Belgian (23)	30	0.07
Brazilian (11)	35	0.09
British (16)	40	0.10
Canadian (54)	170	0.41
Croatian (15)	34	0.08
Czech (14)	126	0.31
Czechoslovakian (0)	35	0.09
Danish (10)	33	0.08
Dutch (75)	192	0.47
Eastern European (168)	180	0.44
English (655)	2,982	7.27
Estonian (12)	83	0.20
European (103)	115	0.28
Finnish (14)	24	0.06
French, ex. Basque (43)	1,340	3.27
French Canadian (105)	331	0.81
German (3,865)	14,313	34.92
Greek (70)	437	1.07
Hungarian (112)	178	0.43
Irish (1,269)	7,200	17.56
Italian (3,547)	8,307	20.26
Lithuanian (33)	74	0.18
Norwegian (0)	161	0.39
Pennsylvania German (28)	40	0.10
Polish (7,433)	15,025	36.65
Portuguese (34)	176	0.43
Russian (85)	140	0.34
Scandinavian (13)	48	0.12
Scotch-Irish (93)	427	1.04
Scottish (28)	543	1.32
Serbian (0)	10	0.02
Slavic (0)	15	0.04
Slovak (9)	90	0.22
Swedish (11)	420	1.02
Swiss (0)	30	0.07
Ukrainian (64)	293	0.71

*Notes: † The Census 2010 population figure is used to calculate the percentages in the Hispanic Origin and Race categories. Ancestry percentages are based on the 2006-2010 American Community Survey population (not shown); ‡ Numbers in parentheses indicate the number of people reporting a single ancestry; * Numbers in parentheses indicate the number of persons reporting this race alone, not in combination with any other race; Please refer to the Explanation of Data for more information.*

Ancestry	Population	%
Welsh (19)	151	0.37
Yugoslavian (0)	17	0.04

Hispanic Origin	Population	%
Hispanic or Latino (of any race)	588	1.41
Central American, ex. Mexican	32	0.08
Guatemalan	15	0.04
Honduran	3	0.01
Nicaraguan	1	<0.01
Panamanian	6	0.01
Salvadoran	5	0.01
Other Central American	2	<0.01
Cuban	19	0.05
Dominican Republic	8	0.02
Mexican	121	0.29
Puerto Rican	291	0.70
South American	66	0.16
Argentinean	4	0.01
Bolivian	2	<0.01
Chilean	4	0.01
Colombian	32	0.08
Ecuadorian	12	0.03
Peruvian	2	<0.01
Venezuelan	7	0.02
Other South American	3	0.01
Other Hispanic or Latino	51	0.12

Race*	Population	%
African-American/Black (407)	547	1.31
Not Hispanic (400)	526	1.26
Hispanic (7)	21	0.05
American Indian/Alaska Native (85)	196	0.47
Not Hispanic (73)	173	0.42
Hispanic (12)	23	0.06
Blackfeet (4)	13	0.03
Canadian/French Am. Ind. (3)	3	0.01
Cherokee (1)	7	0.02
Chippewa (2)	3	0.01
Creek (0)	4	0.01
Crow (2)	2	<0.01
Iroquois (33)	67	0.16
Mexican American Ind. (2)	2	<0.01
Navajo (1)	1	<0.01
Seminole (0)	1	<0.01
South American Ind. (0)	3	0.01
Spanish American Ind. (1)	1	<0.01
Tlingit-Haida *(Alaska Native)* (1)	2	<0.01
Asian (248)	376	0.90
Not Hispanic (246)	368	0.88
Hispanic (2)	8	0.02
Burmese (2)	2	<0.01
Chinese, ex. Taiwanese (60)	76	0.18
Filipino (25)	54	0.13
Indian (62)	83	0.20
Indonesian (1)	3	0.01
Japanese (9)	19	0.05
Korean (49)	75	0.18
Malaysian (0)	3	0.01
Taiwanese (1)	1	<0.01
Thai (8)	13	0.03
Vietnamese (26)	30	0.07
Hawaii Native/Pacific Islander (0)	22	0.05
Not Hispanic (0)	15	0.04
Hispanic (0)	7	0.02
Guamanian/Chamorro (0)	3	0.01
Native Hawaiian (0)	5	0.01
Samoan (0)	4	0.01
White (40,365)	40,726	97.89
Not Hispanic (39,938)	40,258	96.76
Hispanic (427)	468	1.12

Lancaster

Place Type: Village
County: Erie
Population: 10,352†

Ancestry‡	Population	%
American (166)	166	1.59
Arab (0)	13	0.12
Egyptian (0)	13	0.12
Austrian (0)	63	0.60
Czech (0)	61	0.58
Dutch (27)	27	0.26
English (248)	1,081	10.35
European (9)	9	0.09
French, ex. Basque (12)	372	3.56
French Canadian (27)	113	1.08
German (1,181)	4,511	43.17
Greek (0)	124	1.19
Hungarian (33)	66	0.63
Irish (544)	2,414	23.10
Italian (796)	2,018	19.31
Norwegian (0)	25	0.24
Pennsylvania German (0)	12	0.11
Polish (1,261)	3,134	29.99
Portuguese (0)	42	0.40
Scotch-Irish (35)	120	1.15
Scottish (0)	133	1.27
Swedish (0)	16	0.15
Ukrainian (15)	81	0.78
Welsh (0)	51	0.49

Hispanic Origin	Population	%
Hispanic or Latino (of any race)	150	1.45
Central American, ex. Mexican	10	0.10
Guatemalan	5	0.05
Honduran	3	0.03
Nicaraguan	1	0.01
Salvadoran	1	0.01
Cuban	8	0.08
Dominican Republic	2	0.02
Mexican	21	0.20
Puerto Rican	74	0.71
South American	15	0.14
Argentinean	2	0.02
Bolivian	1	0.01
Chilean	2	0.02
Colombian	7	0.07
Ecuadorian	1	0.01
Venezuelan	2	0.02
Other Hispanic or Latino	20	0.19

Race*	Population	%
African-American/Black (71)	113	1.09
Not Hispanic (70)	110	1.06
Hispanic (1)	3	0.03
American Indian/Alaska Native (27)	62	0.60
Not Hispanic (26)	61	0.59
Hispanic (1)	1	0.01
Blackfeet (0)	2	0.02
Cherokee (1)	6	0.06
Chippewa (1)	2	0.02
Iroquois (15)	23	0.22
Mexican American Ind. (2)	2	0.02
Seminole (0)	1	0.01
Tlingit-Haida *(Alaska Native)* (1)	1	0.01
Asian (25)	55	0.53
Not Hispanic (25)	53	0.51
Hispanic (0)	2	0.02
Burmese (1)	1	0.01
Chinese, ex. Taiwanese (5)	8	0.08
Filipino (7)	12	0.12
Indian (1)	5	0.05
Indonesian (1)	2	0.02
Japanese (3)	6	0.06
Korean (5)	17	0.16
Malaysian (0)	3	0.03
Thai (1)	3	0.03
Hawaii Native/Pacific Islander (0)	7	0.07
Not Hispanic (0)	6	0.06
Hispanic (0)	1	0.01
Native Hawaiian (0)	1	0.01
White (10,083)	10,194	98.47
Not Hispanic (9,972)	10,069	97.27
Hispanic (111)	125	1.21

Lansing

Place Type: Town
County: Tompkins
Population: 11,033†

Ancestry‡	Population	%
African, Sub-Saharan (140)	155	1.42
African (112)	127	1.16
Ghanaian (16)	16	0.15
South African (12)	12	0.11
American (700)	700	6.40
Arab (28)	45	0.41
Egyptian (11)	11	0.10
Syrian (17)	34	0.31
Armenian (102)	102	0.93
Australian (11)	11	0.10
Austrian (0)	32	0.29
Brazilian (36)	36	0.33
British (16)	65	0.59
Canadian (29)	103	0.94
Czech (34)	170	1.55
Czechoslovakian (52)	80	0.73
Danish (21)	59	0.54
Dutch (78)	331	3.03
Eastern European (42)	42	0.38
English (576)	1,810	16.55
European (138)	138	1.26
Finnish (0)	23	0.21
French, ex. Basque (74)	183	1.67
French Canadian (76)	111	1.01
German (322)	2,002	18.30
Greek (31)	93	0.85
Guyanese (0)	16	0.15
Hungarian (68)	151	1.38
Iranian (20)	73	0.67
Irish (406)	1,516	13.86
Israeli (43)	43	0.39
Italian (413)	1,226	11.21
Lithuanian (15)	15	0.14
Northern European (49)	49	0.45
Norwegian (0)	99	0.91
Pennsylvania German (16)	70	0.64
Polish (63)	367	3.36
Portuguese (0)	9	0.08
Russian (38)	103	0.94
Scotch-Irish (46)	150	1.37
Scottish (40)	242	2.21
Serbian (16)	37	0.34
Slavic (15)	27	0.25
Slovak (0)	11	0.10
Swedish (74)	242	2.21
Swiss (70)	90	0.82
Ukrainian (0)	51	0.47
Welsh (25)	160	1.46
West Indian, ex. Hispanic (60)	60	0.55
Dutch West Indian (32)	32	0.29
Haitian (14)	14	0.13
Jamaican (14)	14	0.13
Yugoslavian (3)	13	0.12

Hispanic Origin	Population	%
Hispanic or Latino (of any race)	381	3.45
Central American, ex. Mexican	38	0.34
Costa Rican	2	0.02
Guatemalan	18	0.16
Honduran	5	0.05
Nicaraguan	7	0.06
Panamanian	1	0.01
Salvadoran	4	0.04
Other Central American	1	0.01
Cuban	10	0.09
Dominican Republic	16	0.15
Mexican	78	0.71
Puerto Rican	100	0.91
South American	77	0.70
Argentinean	14	0.13
Bolivian	3	0.03
Chilean	5	0.05
Colombian	27	0.24

*Notes: † The Census 2010 population figure is used to calculate the percentages in the Hispanic Origin and Race categories. Ancestry percentages are based on the 2006-2010 American Community Survey population (not shown); ‡ Numbers in parentheses indicate the number of people reporting a single ancestry; * Numbers in parentheses indicate the number of persons reporting this race alone, not in combination with any other race; Please refer to the Explanation of Data for more information.*

Ecuadorian	4	0.04
Peruvian	14	0.13
Venezuelan	8	0.07
Other South American	2	0.02
Other Hispanic or Latino	62	0.56

Race*	Population	%
African-American/Black (397)	502	4.55
Not Hispanic (382)	470	4.26
Hispanic (15)	32	0.29
American Indian/Alaska Native (41)	111	1.01
Not Hispanic (26)	85	0.77
Hispanic (15)	26	0.24
Blackfeet (0)	1	0.01
Central American Ind. (0)	1	0.01
Cherokee (5)	13	0.12
Chippewa (0)	2	0.02
Creek (0)	3	0.03
Delaware (0)	2	0.02
Iroquois (5)	17	0.15
Mexican American Ind. (4)	6	0.05
Navajo (1)	4	0.04
Seminole (0)	1	0.01
Sioux (4)	4	0.04
South American Ind. (5)	8	0.07
Asian (1,126)	1,235	11.19
Not Hispanic (1,125)	1,233	11.18
Hispanic (1)	2	0.02
Bangladeshi (4)	4	0.04
Burmese (1)	1	0.01
Cambodian (31)	32	0.29
Chinese, ex. Taiwanese (462)	493	4.47
Filipino (18)	30	0.27
Indian (164)	178	1.61
Indonesian (11)	13	0.12
Japanese (41)	66	0.60
Korean (262)	287	2.60
Laotian (6)	11	0.10
Malaysian (1)	3	0.03
Nepalese (2)	2	0.02
Pakistani (4)	5	0.05
Sri Lankan (3)	3	0.03
Taiwanese (42)	54	0.49
Thai (15)	20	0.18
Vietnamese (36)	41	0.37
Hawaii Native/Pacific Islander (8)	13	0.12
Not Hispanic (7)	11	0.10
Hispanic (1)	2	0.02
Fijian (1)	1	0.01
Guamanian/Chamorro (1)	1	0.01
Native Hawaiian (3)	6	0.05
Samoan (2)	3	0.03
White (9,084)	9,309	84.37
Not Hispanic (8,852)	9,053	82.05
Hispanic (232)	256	2.32

Le Ray

Place Type: Town
County: Jefferson
Population: 21,782†

Ancestry‡	Population	%
African, Sub-Saharan (171)	197	0.90
African (156)	181	0.83
Ghanaian (15)	15	0.07
South African (0)	1	<0.01
American (922)	922	4.21
Arab (125)	132	0.60
Egyptian (76)	76	0.35
Lebanese (2)	9	0.04
Moroccan (47)	47	0.21
Armenian (6)	6	0.03
Australian (25)	25	0.11
Austrian (16)	76	0.35
Belgian (48)	192	0.88
Brazilian (31)	31	0.14
British (5)	45	0.21
Canadian (65)	65	0.30
Czech (17)	116	0.53
Czechoslovakian (77)	77	0.35
Danish (4)	9	0.04
Dutch (55)	306	1.40
English (478)	1,888	8.62
European (90)	105	0.48
French, ex. Basque (246)	1,216	5.55
French Canadian (278)	591	2.70
German (1,266)	4,697	21.45
German Russian (17)	17	0.08
Greek (31)	108	0.49
Guyanese (59)	59	0.27
Hungarian (3)	19	0.09
Irish (1,107)	3,324	15.18
Italian (686)	1,920	8.77
Macedonian (7)	7	0.03
Norwegian (29)	113	0.52
Polish (162)	449	2.05
Portuguese (0)	11	0.05
Romanian (56)	56	0.26
Russian (76)	76	0.35
Scotch-Irish (45)	344	1.57
Scottish (232)	589	2.69
Slovak (4)	29	0.13
Swedish (81)	218	1.00
Swiss (10)	54	0.25
Turkish (31)	31	0.14
Ukrainian (29)	37	0.17
Welsh (0)	132	0.60
West Indian, ex. Hispanic (273)	380	1.74
Belizean (1)	1	<0.01
British West Indian (2)	2	0.01
Haitian (85)	85	0.39
Jamaican (109)	140	0.64
Trinidadian/Tobagonian (15)	51	0.23
West Indian (61)	101	0.46
Yugoslavian (26)	26	0.12

Hispanic Origin	Population	%
Hispanic or Latino (of any race)	2,798	12.85
Central American, ex. Mexican	160	0.73
Costa Rican	9	0.04
Guatemalan	15	0.07
Honduran	23	0.11
Nicaraguan	26	0.12
Panamanian	60	0.28
Salvadoran	27	0.12
Cuban	78	0.36
Dominican Republic	89	0.41
Mexican	1,125	5.16
Puerto Rican	949	4.36
South American	144	0.66
Argentinean	7	0.03
Bolivian	2	0.01
Chilean	6	0.03
Colombian	50	0.23
Ecuadorian	36	0.17
Paraguayan	7	0.03
Peruvian	31	0.14
Venezuelan	4	0.02
Other South American	1	<0.01
Other Hispanic or Latino	253	1.16

Race*	Population	%
African-American/Black (2,478)	2,948	13.53
Not Hispanic (2,303)	2,653	12.18
Hispanic (175)	295	1.35
American Indian/Alaska Native (183)	446	2.05
Not Hispanic (150)	355	1.63
Hispanic (33)	91	0.42
Alaska Athabascan *(Ala. Nat.)* (0)	1	<0.01
Aleut *(Alaska Native)* (2)	2	0.01
Apache (4)	13	0.06
Blackfeet (6)	16	0.07
Canadian/French Am. Ind. (4)	4	0.02
Cherokee (19)	101	0.46
Chickasaw (2)	2	0.01
Chippewa (5)	10	0.05
Choctaw (8)	18	0.08
Comanche (1)	1	<0.01
Creek (1)	3	0.01
Crow (0)	1	<0.01
Inupiat *(Alaska Native)* (3)	4	0.02
Iroquois (27)	40	0.18
Lumbee (2)	2	0.01
Menominee (1)	1	<0.01
Mexican American Ind. (3)	11	0.05
Navajo (12)	24	0.11
Osage (0)	3	0.01
Potawatomi (5)	5	0.02
Pueblo (7)	11	0.05
Puget Sound Salish (0)	1	<0.01
Sioux (13)	25	0.11
South American Ind. (1)	6	0.03
Spanish American Ind. (1)	1	<0.01
Tlingit-Haida *(Alaska Native)* (0)	2	0.01
Ute (0)	1	<0.01
Yaqui (0)	1	<0.01
Yup'ik *(Alaska Native)* (3)	3	0.01
Asian (545)	848	3.89
Not Hispanic (512)	766	3.52
Hispanic (33)	82	0.38
Bangladeshi (4)	4	0.02
Cambodian (5)	10	0.05
Chinese, ex. Taiwanese (40)	69	0.32
Filipino (218)	360	1.65
Hmong (1)	1	<0.01
Indian (21)	35	0.16
Indonesian (1)	1	<0.01
Japanese (39)	96	0.44
Korean (143)	217	1.00
Laotian (4)	7	0.03
Pakistani (1)	1	<0.01
Thai (12)	39	0.18
Vietnamese (20)	37	0.17
Hawaii Native/Pacific Islander (188)	286	1.31
Not Hispanic (171)	244	1.12
Hispanic (17)	42	0.19
Fijian (1)	2	0.01
Guamanian/Chamorro (76)	88	0.40
Marshallese (6)	6	0.03
Native Hawaiian (23)	73	0.34
Samoan (40)	53	0.24
Tongan (2)	2	0.01
White (16,517)	17,485	80.27
Not Hispanic (15,055)	15,752	72.32
Hispanic (1,462)	1,733	7.96

Le Roy

Place Type: Town
County: Genesee
Population: 7,641†

Ancestry‡	Population	%
American (252)	252	3.30
Austrian (20)	20	0.26
British (12)	44	0.58
Canadian (29)	38	0.50
Danish (6)	24	0.31
Dutch (0)	233	3.05
English (333)	1,155	15.11
European (52)	52	0.68
French, ex. Basque (0)	188	2.46
French Canadian (33)	66	0.86
German (527)	2,222	29.06
Greek (12)	33	0.43
Hungarian (0)	32	0.42
Irish (389)	1,779	23.27
Italian (765)	1,960	25.63
Lithuanian (10)	27	0.35
Norwegian (0)	11	0.14
Polish (170)	565	7.39
Portuguese (14)	14	0.18
Russian (0)	11	0.14
Scotch-Irish (56)	232	3.03
Scottish (32)	160	2.09
Slovak (0)	24	0.31
Swedish (0)	31	0.41
Swiss (10)	10	0.13
Ukrainian (0)	30	0.39

*Notes: † The Census 2010 population figure is used to calculate the percentages in the Hispanic Origin and Race categories. Ancestry percentages are based on the 2006-2010 American Community Survey population (not shown); ‡ Numbers in parentheses indicate the number of people reporting a single ancestry; * Numbers in parentheses indicate the number of persons reporting this race alone, not in combination with any other race; Please refer to the Explanation of Data for more information.*

Welsh (9)	56	0.73
West Indian, ex. Hispanic (17)	33	0.43
Haitian (0)	16	0.21
Jamaican (17)	17	0.22

Hispanic Origin	Population	%
Hispanic or Latino (of any race)	156	2.04
Central American, ex. Mexican	7	0.09
Guatemalan	1	0.01
Honduran	4	0.05
Nicaraguan	2	0.03
Cuban	4	0.05
Mexican	56	0.73
Puerto Rican	75	0.98
South American	6	0.08
Colombian	3	0.04
Peruvian	1	0.01
Venezuelan	2	0.03
Other Hispanic or Latino	8	0.10

Race*	Population	%
African-American/Black (141)	207	2.71
Not Hispanic (134)	196	2.57
Hispanic (7)	11	0.14
American Indian/Alaska Native (21)	69	0.90
Not Hispanic (18)	64	0.84
Hispanic (3)	5	0.07
Blackfeet (0)	4	0.05
Central American Ind. (1)	1	0.01
Cherokee (1)	5	0.07
Iroquois (6)	17	0.22
South American Ind. (2)	2	0.03
Asian (30)	48	0.63
Not Hispanic (29)	46	0.60
Hispanic (1)	2	0.03
Chinese, ex. Taiwanese (9)	13	0.17
Filipino (4)	8	0.10
Indian (3)	4	0.05
Japanese (1)	2	0.03
Korean (10)	14	0.18
Thai (2)	7	0.09
Hawaii Native/Pacific Islander (0)	2	0.03
Not Hispanic (0)	2	0.03
Native Hawaiian (0)	2	0.03
White (7,288)	7,392	96.74
Not Hispanic (7,193)	7,285	95.34
Hispanic (95)	107	1.40

Lenox

Place Type: Town
County: Madison
Population: 9,122†

Ancestry‡	Population	%
American (1,423)	1,423	15.73
Austrian (0)	25	0.28
British (0)	11	0.12
Canadian (19)	80	0.88
Czech (0)	24	0.27
Czechoslovakian (0)	71	0.78
Dutch (41)	271	2.99
English (378)	1,447	15.99
French, ex. Basque (97)	787	8.70
French Canadian (34)	146	1.61
German (264)	1,721	19.02
Greek (0)	6	0.07
Hungarian (28)	39	0.43
Irish (137)	1,194	13.19
Italian (935)	1,761	19.46
Luxemburger (9)	27	0.30
Northern European (26)	26	0.29
Norwegian (0)	28	0.31
Polish (251)	565	6.24
Portuguese (7)	7	0.08
Russian (17)	33	0.36
Scotch-Irish (74)	187	2.07
Scottish (88)	306	3.38
Slovak (0)	4	0.04
Swedish (0)	39	0.43
Swiss (0)	4	0.04
Ukrainian (3)	73	0.81
Welsh (49)	142	1.57
West Indian, ex. Hispanic (31)	31	0.34
Haitian (31)	31	0.34
Yugoslavian (0)	12	0.13

Hispanic Origin	Population	%
Hispanic or Latino (of any race)	148	1.62
Central American, ex. Mexican	10	0.11
Costa Rican	4	0.04
Guatemalan	3	0.03
Panamanian	3	0.03
Cuban	11	0.12
Mexican	42	0.46
Puerto Rican	56	0.61
South American	5	0.05
Colombian	3	0.03
Peruvian	2	0.02
Other Hispanic or Latino	24	0.26

Race*	Population	%
African-American/Black (94)	155	1.70
Not Hispanic (87)	147	1.61
Hispanic (7)	8	0.09
American Indian/Alaska Native (58)	105	1.15
Not Hispanic (53)	98	1.07
Hispanic (5)	7	0.08
Cherokee (0)	13	0.14
Chippewa (1)	2	0.02
Iroquois (31)	37	0.41
Navajo (0)	1	0.01
South American Ind. (3)	3	0.03
Tlingit-Haida *(Alaska Native)* (2)	2	0.02
Asian (36)	57	0.62
Not Hispanic (36)	57	0.62
Cambodian (0)	1	0.01
Chinese, ex. Taiwanese (18)	24	0.26
Filipino (3)	5	0.05
Indian (5)	7	0.08
Japanese (0)	3	0.03
Korean (3)	6	0.07
Thai (2)	2	0.02
Vietnamese (3)	3	0.03
Hawaii Native/Pacific Islander (0)	4	0.04
Not Hispanic (0)	4	0.04
Native Hawaiian (0)	3	0.03
Tongan (0)	1	0.01
White (8,778)	8,905	97.62
Not Hispanic (8,670)	8,792	96.38
Hispanic (108)	113	1.24

Levittown

Place Type: CDP
County: Nassau
Population: 51,881†

Ancestry‡	Population	%
African, Sub-Saharan (0)	20	0.04
African (0)	20	0.04
Albanian (49)	49	0.09
American (1,347)	1,347	2.52
Arab (190)	271	0.51
Egyptian (136)	136	0.25
Lebanese (22)	68	0.13
Moroccan (10)	10	0.02
Syrian (0)	35	0.07
Other Arab (22)	22	0.04
Armenian (21)	80	0.15
Australian (14)	14	0.03
Austrian (66)	307	0.57
Basque (0)	16	0.03
Belgian (10)	18	0.03
Brazilian (8)	8	0.01
British (92)	121	0.23
Canadian (11)	74	0.14
Croatian (24)	67	0.13
Czech (44)	215	0.40
Czechoslovakian (25)	47	0.09
Danish (10)	110	0.21
Dutch (11)	340	0.64
Eastern European (107)	107	0.20
English (316)	2,076	3.88
European (276)	321	0.60
Finnish (0)	36	0.07
French, ex. Basque (239)	1,242	2.32
French Canadian (74)	206	0.39
German (1,428)	9,190	17.18
Greek (630)	1,100	2.06
Hungarian (158)	781	1.46
Icelander (9)	52	0.10
Iranian (23)	79	0.15
Irish (4,151)	14,886	27.84
Israeli (32)	72	0.13
Italian (8,524)	17,446	32.62
Latvian (0)	31	0.06
Lithuanian (73)	314	0.59
Maltese (45)	96	0.18
Norwegian (49)	274	0.51
Pennsylvania German (0)	54	0.10
Polish (535)	2,652	4.96
Portuguese (189)	243	0.45
Romanian (27)	98	0.18
Russian (640)	1,993	3.73
Scandinavian (0)	33	0.06
Scotch-Irish (261)	722	1.35
Scottish (53)	303	0.57
Slovak (6)	6	0.01
Swedish (13)	287	0.54
Swiss (55)	105	0.20
Turkish (112)	181	0.34
Ukrainian (83)	249	0.47
Welsh (0)	43	0.08
West Indian, ex. Hispanic (89)	117	0.22
Jamaican (20)	36	0.07
Trinidadian/Tobagonian (69)	69	0.13
West Indian (0)	12	0.02
Yugoslavian (41)	52	0.10

Hispanic Origin	Population	%
Hispanic or Latino (of any race)	5,979	11.52
Central American, ex. Mexican	1,200	2.31
Costa Rican	41	0.08
Guatemalan	132	0.25
Honduran	103	0.20
Nicaraguan	26	0.05
Panamanian	12	0.02
Salvadoran	876	1.69
Other Central American	10	0.02
Cuban	274	0.53
Dominican Republic	260	0.50
Mexican	214	0.41
Puerto Rican	1,716	3.31
South American	1,746	3.37
Argentinean	82	0.16
Bolivian	18	0.03
Chilean	112	0.22
Colombian	733	1.41
Ecuadorian	400	0.77
Paraguayan	19	0.04
Peruvian	285	0.55
Uruguayan	47	0.09
Venezuelan	23	0.04
Other South American	27	0.05
Other Hispanic or Latino	569	1.10

Race*	Population	%
African-American/Black (470)	667	1.29
Not Hispanic (403)	539	1.04
Hispanic (67)	128	0.25
American Indian/Alaska Native (55)	185	0.36
Not Hispanic (43)	134	0.26
Hispanic (12)	51	0.10
Blackfeet (0)	4	0.01
Cherokee (2)	26	0.05
Chippewa (1)	1	<0.01
Choctaw (0)	1	<0.01
Comanche (7)	7	0.01
Creek (0)	1	<0.01

*Notes: † The Census 2010 population figure is used to calculate the percentages in the Hispanic Origin and Race categories. Ancestry percentages are based on the 2006-2010 American Community Survey population (not shown); ‡ Numbers in parentheses indicate the number of people reporting a single ancestry; * Numbers in parentheses indicate the number of persons reporting this race alone, not in combination with any other race; Please refer to the Explanation of Data for more information.*

Iroquois (4)	13	0.03
Lumbee (3)	6	0.01
Mexican American Ind. (0)	5	0.01
Osage (0)	1	<0.01
Seminole (1)	3	0.01
Shoshone (1)	1	<0.01
Sioux (0)	1	<0.01
South American Ind. (9)	12	0.02
Spanish American Ind. (0)	1	<0.01
Asian (2,956)	3,352	6.46
Not Hispanic (2,937)	3,298	6.36
Hispanic (19)	54	0.10
Bangladeshi (65)	70	0.13
Burmese (1)	6	0.01
Cambodian (10)	14	0.03
Chinese, ex. Taiwanese (467)	589	1.14
Filipino (446)	525	1.01
Indian (1,110)	1,212	2.34
Indonesian (4)	6	0.01
Japanese (26)	44	0.08
Korean (358)	380	0.73
Laotian (3)	3	0.01
Malaysian (0)	7	0.01
Nepalese (2)	2	<0.01
Pakistani (226)	239	0.46
Sri Lankan (1)	1	<0.01
Taiwanese (22)	25	0.05
Thai (26)	40	0.08
Vietnamese (103)	107	0.21
Hawaii Native/Pacific Islander (10)	47	0.09
Not Hispanic (6)	21	0.04
Hispanic (4)	26	0.05
Guamanian/Chamorro (2)	3	0.01
Native Hawaiian (0)	3	0.01
Samoan (5)	7	0.01
White (46,137)	46,970	90.53
Not Hispanic (41,814)	42,268	81.47
Hispanic (4,323)	4,702	9.06

Lewisboro

Place Type: Town
County: Westchester
Population: 12,411†

Ancestry‡	Population	%
African, Sub-Saharan (9)	9	0.07
African (9)	9	0.07
American (693)	693	5.62
Arab (0)	16	0.13
Arab (0)	16	0.13
Armenian (9)	18	0.15
Austrian (10)	309	2.51
Belgian (14)	14	0.11
Brazilian (21)	21	0.17
British (55)	78	0.63
Canadian (18)	30	0.24
Croatian (58)	71	0.58
Czech (0)	52	0.42
Czechoslovakian (13)	13	0.11
Danish (14)	115	0.93
Dutch (78)	269	2.18
Eastern European (227)	254	2.06
English (238)	1,349	10.94
Estonian (10)	10	0.08
European (369)	526	4.27
Finnish (0)	19	0.15
French, ex. Basque (11)	367	2.98
French Canadian (17)	105	0.85
German (296)	1,737	14.09
Greek (27)	90	0.73
Hungarian (26)	181	1.47
Icelander (0)	9	0.07
Irish (938)	2,995	24.29
Israeli (86)	107	0.87
Italian (1,179)	2,704	21.93
Lithuanian (0)	22	0.18
Macedonian (15)	15	0.12
Norwegian (8)	106	0.86
Pennsylvania German (0)	9	0.07
Polish (167)	864	7.01
Portuguese (12)	43	0.35
Romanian (0)	49	0.40
Russian (159)	628	5.09
Scotch-Irish (11)	38	0.31
Scottish (51)	307	2.49
Slavic (6)	18	0.15
Slovak (0)	24	0.19
Swedish (51)	139	1.13
Swiss (20)	40	0.32
Turkish (17)	17	0.14
Ukrainian (10)	32	0.26
Welsh (27)	140	1.14
West Indian, ex. Hispanic (71)	99	0.80
Haitian (46)	46	0.37
Jamaican (16)	44	0.36
West Indian (9)	9	0.07
Yugoslavian (0)	12	0.10

Hispanic Origin	Population	%
Hispanic or Latino (of any race)	552	4.45
Central American, ex. Mexican	58	0.47
Costa Rican	4	0.03
Guatemalan	30	0.24
Honduran	3	0.02
Nicaraguan	4	0.03
Panamanian	2	0.02
Salvadoran	15	0.12
Cuban	48	0.39
Dominican Republic	19	0.15
Mexican	62	0.50
Puerto Rican	139	1.12
South American	142	1.14
Argentinean	34	0.27
Bolivian	8	0.06
Chilean	10	0.08
Colombian	44	0.35
Ecuadorian	14	0.11
Paraguayan	1	0.01
Peruvian	17	0.14
Uruguayan	4	0.03
Venezuelan	10	0.08
Other Hispanic or Latino	84	0.68

Race*	Population	%
African-American/Black (160)	232	1.87
Not Hispanic (153)	211	1.70
Hispanic (7)	21	0.17
American Indian/Alaska Native (10)	46	0.37
Not Hispanic (8)	38	0.31
Hispanic (2)	8	0.06
Apache (2)	2	0.02
Cherokee (1)	9	0.07
Chippewa (1)	5	0.04
Creek (0)	3	0.02
Mexican American Ind. (0)	3	0.02
Osage (1)	1	0.01
Ottawa (0)	2	0.02
Sioux (1)	1	0.01
Spanish American Ind. (2)	2	0.02
Asian (297)	417	3.36
Not Hispanic (294)	406	3.27
Hispanic (3)	11	0.09
Burmese (1)	1	0.01
Cambodian (4)	4	0.03
Chinese, ex. Taiwanese (117)	147	1.18
Filipino (16)	31	0.25
Indian (66)	98	0.79
Japanese (19)	33	0.27
Korean (51)	69	0.56
Malaysian (2)	2	0.02
Pakistani (3)	3	0.02
Taiwanese (2)	2	0.02
Thai (3)	4	0.03
Vietnamese (8)	15	0.12
Hawaii Native/Pacific Islander (1)	3	0.02
Not Hispanic (1)	3	0.02
Native Hawaiian (0)	1	0.01
White (11,649)	11,862	95.58
Not Hispanic (11,187)	11,365	91.57
Hispanic (462)	497	4.00

Lewiston

Place Type: Town
County: Niagara
Population: 16,262†

Ancestry‡	Population	%
American (352)	352	2.17
Arab (270)	441	2.72
Jordanian (133)	133	0.82
Lebanese (128)	299	1.84
Palestinian (9)	9	0.06
Armenian (10)	19	0.12
Austrian (12)	23	0.14
Belgian (12)	19	0.12
British (34)	47	0.29
Canadian (73)	146	0.90
Celtic (0)	27	0.17
Croatian (23)	43	0.26
Czech (0)	8	0.05
Czechoslovakian (0)	31	0.19
Danish (16)	55	0.34
Dutch (129)	352	2.17
Eastern European (12)	12	0.07
English (944)	2,402	14.79
European (177)	177	1.09
French, ex. Basque (42)	630	3.88
French Canadian (28)	151	0.93
German (1,101)	3,758	23.14
Greek (14)	121	0.75
Hungarian (56)	145	0.89
Icelander (10)	16	0.10
Iranian (6)	6	0.04
Irish (1,232)	3,552	21.87
Italian (2,107)	3,949	24.32
Lithuanian (0)	8	0.05
Norwegian (77)	231	1.42
Pennsylvania German (12)	12	0.07
Polish (811)	2,076	12.78
Russian (57)	142	0.87
Scotch-Irish (154)	338	2.08
Scottish (97)	427	2.63
Serbian (0)	16	0.10
Slovak (22)	103	0.63
Swedish (29)	163	1.00
Swiss (0)	23	0.14
Ukrainian (0)	12	0.07
Welsh (16)	158	0.97
West Indian, ex. Hispanic (9)	9	0.06
Haitian (9)	9	0.06
Yugoslavian (11)	11	0.07

Hispanic Origin	Population	%
Hispanic or Latino (of any race)	253	1.56
Central American, ex. Mexican	13	0.08
Costa Rican	4	0.02
Guatemalan	3	0.02
Honduran	3	0.02
Panamanian	3	0.02
Cuban	10	0.06
Dominican Republic	9	0.06
Mexican	71	0.44
Puerto Rican	71	0.44
South American	36	0.22
Argentinean	4	0.02
Bolivian	1	0.01
Colombian	18	0.11
Ecuadorian	3	0.02
Venezuelan	6	0.04
Other South American	4	0.02
Other Hispanic or Latino	43	0.26

Race*	Population	%
African-American/Black (203)	273	1.68
Not Hispanic (195)	261	1.60
Hispanic (8)	12	0.07
American Indian/Alaska Native (156)	210	1.29
Not Hispanic (135)	188	1.16

*Notes: † The Census 2010 population figure is used to calculate the percentages in the Hispanic Origin and Race categories. Ancestry percentages are based on the 2006-2010 American Community Survey population (not shown); ‡ Numbers in parentheses indicate the number of people reporting a single ancestry; * Numbers in parentheses indicate the number of persons reporting this race alone, not in combination with any other race; Please refer to the Explanation of Data for more information.*

Hispanic (21)	22	0.14
Blackfeet (0)	1	0.01
Canadian/French Am. Ind. (5)	5	0.03
Cherokee (0)	10	0.06
Cheyenne (0)	1	0.01
Chippewa (1)	2	0.01
Crow (2)	2	0.01
Delaware (0)	1	0.01
Iroquois (106)	128	0.79
Mexican American Ind. (8)	8	0.05
Sioux (6)	9	0.06
Asian (136)	189	1.16
Not Hispanic (135)	180	1.11
Hispanic (1)	9	0.06
Cambodian (2)	3	0.02
Chinese, ex. Taiwanese (26)	37	0.23
Filipino (6)	17	0.10
Indian (56)	70	0.43
Indonesian (2)	2	0.01
Japanese (3)	13	0.08
Korean (23)	28	0.17
Pakistani (2)	4	0.02
Sri Lankan (2)	2	0.01
Thai (2)	2	0.01
Vietnamese (7)	10	0.06
Hawaii Native/Pacific Islander (4)	11	0.07
Not Hispanic (4)	11	0.07
Native Hawaiian (0)	6	0.04
White (15,542)	15,710	96.61
Not Hispanic (15,370)	15,517	95.42
Hispanic (172)	193	1.19

Liberty

Place Type: Town
County: Sullivan
Population: 9,885†

Ancestry‡	Population	%
Albanian (4)	16	0.16
American (260)	260	2.62
Arab (122)	145	1.46
Arab (5)	9	0.09
Jordanian (117)	117	1.18
Lebanese (0)	19	0.19
Austrian (15)	34	0.34
Belgian (18)	18	0.18
British (0)	12	0.12
Canadian (0)	23	0.23
Celtic (0)	24	0.24
Croatian (9)	9	0.09
Czech (0)	133	1.34
Czechoslovakian (34)	55	0.55
Danish (0)	44	0.44
Dutch (19)	106	1.07
English (318)	921	9.27
European (11)	11	0.11
French, ex. Basque (23)	326	3.28
French Canadian (12)	31	0.31
German (448)	1,941	19.54
Greek (0)	25	0.25
Hungarian (35)	185	1.86
Irish (473)	1,931	19.44
Italian (596)	1,384	13.93
Lithuanian (25)	25	0.25
Norwegian (11)	58	0.58
Polish (166)	517	5.20
Portuguese (0)	39	0.39
Romanian (8)	18	0.18
Russian (87)	197	1.98
Scandinavian (13)	25	0.25
Scotch-Irish (0)	69	0.69
Scottish (5)	221	2.22
Swedish (0)	18	0.18
Swiss (56)	120	1.21
Ukrainian (39)	186	1.87
Welsh (21)	71	0.71
West Indian, ex. Hispanic (67)	67	0.67
Haitian (51)	51	0.51
Jamaican (9)	9	0.09
Trinidadian/Tobagonian (7)	7	0.07

Hispanic Origin	Population	%
Hispanic or Latino (of any race)	1,862	18.84
Central American, ex. Mexican	241	2.44
Costa Rican	2	0.02
Guatemalan	36	0.36
Honduran	145	1.47
Nicaraguan	5	0.05
Panamanian	3	0.03
Salvadoran	49	0.50
Other Central American	1	0.01
Cuban	45	0.46
Dominican Republic	45	0.46
Mexican	436	4.41
Puerto Rican	855	8.65
South American	99	1.00
Argentinean	6	0.06
Bolivian	1	0.01
Chilean	12	0.12
Colombian	32	0.32
Ecuadorian	21	0.21
Peruvian	23	0.23
Uruguayan	2	0.02
Other South American	2	0.02
Other Hispanic or Latino	141	1.43

Race*	Population	%
African-American/Black (923)	1,112	11.25
Not Hispanic (817)	927	9.38
Hispanic (106)	185	1.87
American Indian/Alaska Native (55)	151	1.53
Not Hispanic (38)	91	0.92
Hispanic (17)	60	0.61
Apache (2)	5	0.05
Blackfeet (1)	10	0.10
Canadian/French Am. Ind. (0)	1	0.01
Central American Ind. (0)	1	0.01
Cherokee (0)	17	0.17
Chippewa (1)	1	0.01
Crow (1)	3	0.03
Delaware (8)	14	0.14
Houma (2)	2	0.02
Iroquois (0)	4	0.04
Mexican American Ind. (0)	8	0.08
Sioux (1)	1	0.01
South American Ind. (2)	2	0.02
Spanish American Ind. (2)	2	0.02
Asian (151)	186	1.88
Not Hispanic (146)	176	1.78
Hispanic (5)	10	0.10
Chinese, ex. Taiwanese (24)	26	0.26
Filipino (17)	31	0.31
Indian (55)	59	0.60
Indonesian (0)	1	0.01
Japanese (1)	4	0.04
Korean (38)	39	0.39
Laotian (1)	1	0.01
Pakistani (10)	12	0.12
Taiwanese (1)	1	0.01
Hawaii Native/Pacific Islander (2)	4	0.04
Not Hispanic (2)	4	0.04
Guamanian/Chamorro (1)	1	0.01
Samoan (1)	1	0.01
White (7,695)	7,959	80.52
Not Hispanic (6,815)	6,963	70.44
Hispanic (880)	996	10.08

Lindenhurst

Place Type: Village
County: Suffolk
Population: 27,253†

Ancestry‡	Population	%
Albanian (64)	64	0.23
American (531)	531	1.94
Arab (224)	304	1.11
Egyptian (12)	12	0.04
Lebanese (0)	13	0.05
Moroccan (142)	209	0.76
Palestinian (70)	70	0.26
Armenian (41)	41	0.15
Australian (0)	11	0.04
Austrian (10)	85	0.31
Belgian (10)	29	0.11
Brazilian (0)	13	0.05
British (9)	9	0.03
Canadian (11)	23	0.08
Croatian (13)	21	0.08
Czech (0)	22	0.08
Czechoslovakian (22)	36	0.13
Danish (33)	52	0.19
Dutch (39)	266	0.97
Eastern European (17)	17	0.06
English (161)	1,288	4.70
Estonian (0)	11	0.04
European (56)	121	0.44
Finnish (0)	33	0.12
French, ex. Basque (15)	598	2.18
French Canadian (77)	171	0.62
German (1,120)	5,566	20.32
Greek (247)	390	1.42
Hungarian (19)	148	0.54
Iranian (53)	53	0.19
Irish (1,701)	7,335	26.78
Italian (5,454)	10,641	38.86
Latvian (11)	35	0.13
Lithuanian (27)	165	0.60
Maltese (0)	12	0.04
Norwegian (50)	379	1.38
Polish (997)	2,411	8.80
Portuguese (0)	11	0.04
Romanian (5)	9	0.03
Russian (135)	832	3.04
Scandinavian (8)	18	0.07
Scotch-Irish (40)	231	0.84
Scottish (13)	250	0.91
Serbian (16)	19	0.07
Slavic (0)	18	0.07
Slovak (82)	154	0.56
Swedish (20)	251	0.92
Swiss (0)	47	0.17
Turkish (107)	107	0.39
Ukrainian (42)	287	1.05
Welsh (30)	70	0.26
West Indian, ex. Hispanic (303)	303	1.11
Haitian (25)	25	0.09
Trinidadian/Tobagonian (268)	268	0.98
West Indian (10)	10	0.04
Yugoslavian (14)	43	0.16

Hispanic Origin	Population	%
Hispanic or Latino (of any race)	2,656	9.75
Central American, ex. Mexican	443	1.63
Costa Rican	12	0.04
Guatemalan	32	0.12
Honduran	66	0.24
Nicaraguan	1	<0.01
Panamanian	21	0.08
Salvadoran	303	1.11
Other Central American	8	0.03
Cuban	85	0.31
Dominican Republic	386	1.42
Mexican	128	0.47
Puerto Rican	792	2.91
South American	575	2.11
Argentinean	47	0.17
Bolivian	10	0.04
Chilean	21	0.08
Colombian	226	0.83
Ecuadorian	146	0.54
Peruvian	105	0.39
Uruguayan	7	0.03
Venezuelan	12	0.04
Other South American	1	<0.01
Other Hispanic or Latino	247	0.91

Race*	Population	%
African-American/Black (417)	556	2.04

*Notes: † The Census 2010 population figure is used to calculate the percentages in the Hispanic Origin and Race categories. Ancestry percentages are based on the 2006-2010 American Community Survey population (not shown); ‡ Numbers in parentheses indicate the number of people reporting a single ancestry; * Numbers in parentheses indicate the number of persons reporting this race alone, not in combination with any other race; Please refer to the Explanation of Data for more information.*

Not Hispanic (341)	440	1.61
Hispanic (76)	116	0.43
American Indian/Alaska Native (34)	112	0.41
Not Hispanic (24)	81	0.30
Hispanic (10)	31	0.11
Apache (0)	1	<0.01
Blackfeet (3)	5	0.02
Cherokee (2)	18	0.07
Choctaw (0)	1	<0.01
Hopi (1)	1	<0.01
Iroquois (3)	9	0.03
Mexican American Ind. (1)	5	0.02
Navajo (0)	1	<0.01
Sioux (2)	2	0.01
South American Ind. (0)	4	0.01
Asian (521)	670	2.46
Not Hispanic (518)	658	2.41
Hispanic (3)	12	0.04
Bangladeshi (8)	8	0.03
Chinese, ex. Taiwanese (148)	182	0.67
Filipino (72)	106	0.39
Indian (201)	221	0.81
Indonesian (3)	4	0.01
Japanese (9)	14	0.05
Korean (19)	28	0.10
Pakistani (35)	39	0.14
Sri Lankan (2)	2	0.01
Taiwanese (2)	2	0.01
Thai (4)	4	0.01
Vietnamese (10)	18	0.07
Hawaii Native/Pacific Islander (4)	12	0.04
Not Hispanic (4)	12	0.04
Guamanian/Chamorro (1)	1	<0.01
Native Hawaiian (0)	1	<0.01
Samoan (1)	1	<0.01
White (25,110)	25,512	93.61
Not Hispanic (23,381)	23,627	86.70
Hispanic (1,729)	1,885	6.92

Livonia

Place Type: Town
County: Livingston
Population: 7,809†

Ancestry‡	Population	%
American (782)	782	10.10
Austrian (0)	31	0.40
Belgian (2)	5	0.06
British (15)	31	0.40
Canadian (7)	7	0.09
Czech (0)	86	1.11
Danish (0)	12	0.15
Dutch (28)	412	5.32
Eastern European (27)	27	0.35
English (226)	1,349	17.42
European (64)	70	0.90
French, ex. Basque (43)	397	5.13
French Canadian (4)	97	1.25
German (605)	2,645	34.16
Greek (0)	23	0.30
Hungarian (24)	107	1.38
Irish (390)	2,163	27.94
Italian (311)	1,068	13.79
Lithuanian (9)	36	0.46
Pennsylvania German (34)	50	0.65
Polish (115)	426	5.50
Romanian (0)	4	0.05
Russian (0)	53	0.68
Scotch-Irish (18)	108	1.39
Scottish (73)	255	3.29
Slovak (0)	11	0.14
Swedish (0)	20	0.26
Swiss (0)	21	0.27
Ukrainian (52)	158	2.04
Welsh (16)	113	1.46

Hispanic Origin	Population	%
Hispanic or Latino (of any race)	72	0.92
Central American, ex. Mexican	2	0.03
Nicaraguan	2	0.03
Cuban	7	0.09
Mexican	20	0.26
Puerto Rican	31	0.40
South American	4	0.05
Argentinean	2	0.03
Chilean	2	0.03
Other Hispanic or Latino	8	0.10

Race*	Population	%
African-American/Black (43)	77	0.99
Not Hispanic (43)	74	0.95
Hispanic (0)	3	0.04
American Indian/Alaska Native (19)	62	0.79
Not Hispanic (19)	60	0.77
Hispanic (0)	2	0.03
Blackfeet (1)	5	0.06
Cherokee (0)	2	0.03
Iroquois (11)	21	0.27
Navajo (2)	3	0.04
Asian (38)	60	0.77
Not Hispanic (38)	60	0.77
Burmese (4)	4	0.05
Chinese, ex. Taiwanese (8)	9	0.12
Filipino (4)	11	0.14
Indian (5)	5	0.06
Japanese (0)	1	0.01
Korean (9)	20	0.26
Laotian (2)	2	0.03
Malaysian (0)	1	0.01
Pakistani (1)	1	0.01
Sri Lankan (1)	1	0.01
Thai (1)	1	0.01
Vietnamese (2)	4	0.05
Hawaii Native/Pacific Islander (1)	11	0.14
Not Hispanic (1)	10	0.13
Hispanic (0)	1	0.01
Native Hawaiian (1)	10	0.13
White (7,602)	7,697	98.57
Not Hispanic (7,543)	7,633	97.75
Hispanic (59)	64	0.82

Lloyd

Place Type: Town
County: Ulster
Population: 10,863†

Ancestry‡	Population	%
Afghan (5)	5	0.05
American (807)	807	7.50
Arab (41)	92	0.85
Egyptian (31)	58	0.54
Lebanese (10)	10	0.09
Syrian (0)	24	0.22
Austrian (10)	29	0.27
Belgian (0)	9	0.08
Brazilian (0)	8	0.07
British (22)	22	0.20
Canadian (0)	130	1.21
Croatian (36)	36	0.33
Czech (0)	9	0.08
Czechoslovakian (0)	8	0.07
Danish (9)	68	0.63
Dutch (74)	371	3.45
Eastern European (28)	28	0.26
English (227)	722	6.71
European (123)	123	1.14
Finnish (0)	19	0.18
French, ex. Basque (50)	414	3.85
French Canadian (24)	132	1.23
German (328)	1,239	11.51
Greek (29)	100	0.93
Guyanese (149)	149	1.38
Hungarian (14)	52	0.48
Irish (376)	1,988	18.47
Italian (1,547)	3,369	31.29
Norwegian (0)	211	1.96
Polish (61)	440	4.09
Portuguese (7)	7	0.07
Russian (27)	111	1.03
Scandinavian (19)	49	0.46
Scotch-Irish (61)	110	1.02
Scottish (9)	157	1.46
Serbian (10)	10	0.09
Slavic (0)	12	0.11
Slovak (9)	9	0.08
Swedish (32)	203	1.89
Swiss (25)	25	0.23
Turkish (14)	14	0.13
Welsh (46)	91	0.85
West Indian, ex. Hispanic (145)	224	2.08
British West Indian (17)	49	0.46
Haitian (14)	61	0.57
Jamaican (108)	108	1.00
West Indian (6)	6	0.06

Hispanic Origin	Population	%
Hispanic or Latino (of any race)	793	7.30
Central American, ex. Mexican	41	0.38
Costa Rican	9	0.08
Guatemalan	12	0.11
Honduran	6	0.06
Nicaraguan	1	0.01
Panamanian	1	0.01
Salvadoran	12	0.11
Cuban	25	0.23
Dominican Republic	51	0.47
Mexican	159	1.46
Puerto Rican	351	3.23
South American	61	0.56
Argentinean	4	0.04
Chilean	3	0.03
Colombian	23	0.21
Ecuadorian	15	0.14
Paraguayan	1	0.01
Peruvian	10	0.09
Venezuelan	3	0.03
Other South American	2	0.02
Other Hispanic or Latino	105	0.97

Race*	Population	%
African-American/Black (694)	859	7.91
Not Hispanic (658)	773	7.12
Hispanic (36)	86	0.79
American Indian/Alaska Native (26)	95	0.87
Not Hispanic (16)	75	0.69
Hispanic (10)	20	0.18
Blackfeet (0)	1	0.01
Cherokee (0)	11	0.10
Cheyenne (0)	1	0.01
Creek (0)	5	0.05
Iroquois (1)	6	0.06
Mexican American Ind. (1)	1	0.01
Navajo (0)	1	0.01
Sioux (2)	4	0.04
South American Ind. (0)	3	0.03
Asian (312)	383	3.53
Not Hispanic (309)	366	3.37
Hispanic (3)	17	0.16
Bangladeshi (21)	27	0.25
Cambodian (0)	5	0.05
Chinese, ex. Taiwanese (62)	73	0.67
Filipino (14)	26	0.24
Indian (122)	151	1.39
Indonesian (2)	5	0.05
Japanese (4)	8	0.07
Korean (19)	24	0.22
Laotian (0)	1	0.01
Malaysian (0)	1	0.01
Nepalese (11)	13	0.12
Pakistani (17)	17	0.16
Taiwanese (2)	5	0.05
Thai (1)	2	0.02
Vietnamese (22)	26	0.24
Hawaii Native/Pacific Islander (2)	12	0.11
Not Hispanic (2)	10	0.09
Hispanic (0)	2	0.02
Native Hawaiian (1)	4	0.04
White (9,353)	9,609	88.46

*Notes: † The Census 2010 population figure is used to calculate the percentages in the Hispanic Origin and Race categories. Ancestry percentages are based on the 2006-2010 American Community Survey population (not shown); ‡ Numbers in parentheses indicate the number of people reporting a single ancestry; * Numbers in parentheses indicate the number of persons reporting this race alone, not in combination with any other race; Please refer to the Explanation of Data for more information.*

Not Hispanic (8,866)	9,038	83.20
Hispanic (487)	571	5.26

Lockport

Place Type: City
County: Niagara
Population: 21,165†

Ancestry‡	Population	%
African, Sub-Saharan (8)	52	0.24
African (8)	44	0.21
Ethiopian (0)	8	0.04
American (505)	505	2.37
Austrian (104)	202	0.95
Belgian (15)	15	0.07
Brazilian (18)	18	0.08
British (13)	69	0.32
Bulgarian (0)	10	0.05
Canadian (11)	50	0.23
Croatian (0)	23	0.11
Czech (0)	11	0.05
Czechoslovakian (58)	96	0.45
Danish (0)	25	0.12
Dutch (28)	301	1.41
English (548)	2,339	10.98
European (171)	171	0.80
Finnish (0)	13	0.06
French, ex. Basque (139)	1,112	5.22
French Canadian (162)	279	1.31
German (2,109)	7,275	34.16
Greek (37)	166	0.78
Guyanese (19)	19	0.09
Hungarian (82)	254	1.19
Irish (891)	4,702	22.08
Italian (1,296)	3,356	15.76
Lithuanian (0)	26	0.12
Norwegian (8)	34	0.16
Pennsylvania German (31)	31	0.15
Polish (487)	1,603	7.53
Portuguese (0)	31	0.15
Romanian (0)	13	0.06
Russian (43)	136	0.64
Scandinavian (23)	43	0.20
Scotch-Irish (78)	255	1.20
Scottish (143)	513	2.41
Slavic (45)	45	0.21
Slovene (28)	28	0.13
Swedish (0)	102	0.48
Swiss (0)	21	0.10
Ukrainian (15)	113	0.53
Welsh (0)	121	0.57
West Indian, ex. Hispanic (134)	134	0.63
Jamaican (134)	134	0.63

Hispanic Origin	Population	%
Hispanic or Latino (of any race)	674	3.18
Central American, ex. Mexican	19	0.09
Guatemalan	4	0.02
Honduran	2	0.01
Panamanian	10	0.05
Salvadoran	2	0.01
Other Central American	1	<0.01
Cuban	14	0.07
Dominican Republic	25	0.12
Mexican	181	0.86
Puerto Rican	379	1.79
South American	10	0.05
Argentinean	3	0.01
Colombian	4	0.02
Peruvian	2	0.01
Venezuelan	1	<0.01
Other Hispanic or Latino	46	0.22

Race*	Population	%
African-American/Black (1,526)	2,074	9.80
Not Hispanic (1,478)	1,980	9.36
Hispanic (48)	94	0.44
American Indian/Alaska Native (96)	284	1.34
Not Hispanic (87)	261	1.23
Hispanic (9)	23	0.11
Blackfeet (1)	7	0.03
Canadian/French Am. Ind. (1)	2	0.01
Cherokee (4)	23	0.11
Cheyenne (0)	1	<0.01
Chippewa (4)	12	0.06
Choctaw (0)	2	0.01
Iroquois (47)	102	0.48
Mexican American Ind. (2)	2	0.01
Seminole (0)	4	0.02
Sioux (0)	6	0.03
Yaqui (1)	1	<0.01
Asian (110)	190	0.90
Not Hispanic (109)	186	0.88
Hispanic (1)	4	0.02
Cambodian (0)	4	0.02
Chinese, ex. Taiwanese (21)	32	0.15
Filipino (13)	36	0.17
Indian (14)	29	0.14
Indonesian (6)	7	0.03
Japanese (6)	20	0.09
Korean (20)	30	0.14
Pakistani (1)	2	0.01
Taiwanese (3)	3	0.01
Thai (0)	1	<0.01
Vietnamese (19)	24	0.11
Hawaii Native/Pacific Islander (4)	18	0.09
Not Hispanic (4)	16	0.08
Hispanic (0)	2	0.01
Guamanian/Chamorro (2)	3	0.01
Native Hawaiian (1)	7	0.03
Samoan (0)	2	0.01
White (18,519)	19,191	90.67
Not Hispanic (18,132)	18,737	88.53
Hispanic (387)	454	2.15

Lockport

Place Type: Town
County: Niagara
Population: 20,529†

Ancestry‡	Population	%
Alsatian (0)	10	0.05
American (826)	826	4.08
Arab (19)	61	0.30
Egyptian (9)	9	0.04
Iraqi (0)	13	0.06
Lebanese (10)	31	0.15
Syrian (0)	8	0.04
Australian (0)	11	0.05
Austrian (13)	66	0.33
British (0)	41	0.20
Canadian (101)	217	1.07
Croatian (13)	36	0.18
Czechoslovakian (7)	7	0.03
Danish (13)	58	0.29
Dutch (46)	272	1.34
English (718)	3,094	15.27
European (82)	90	0.44
French, ex. Basque (132)	873	4.31
French Canadian (236)	357	1.76
German (2,151)	7,699	38.00
Greek (24)	88	0.43
Hungarian (33)	160	0.79
Icelander (0)	52	0.26
Iranian (9)	9	0.04
Irish (1,013)	4,283	21.14
Italian (1,330)	3,721	18.37
Norwegian (38)	78	0.39
Pennsylvania German (9)	9	0.04
Polish (611)	2,168	10.70
Portuguese (0)	38	0.19
Romanian (0)	15	0.07
Russian (139)	239	1.18
Scandinavian (11)	11	0.05
Scotch-Irish (0)	96	0.47
Scottish (116)	339	1.67
Slavic (0)	17	0.08
Swedish (11)	196	0.97
Swiss (10)	10	0.05
Turkish (0)	13	0.06
Ukrainian (0)	115	0.57
Welsh (0)	156	0.77
West Indian, ex. Hispanic (9)	18	0.09
Jamaican (9)	9	0.04
West Indian (0)	9	0.04

Hispanic Origin	Population	%
Hispanic or Latino (of any race)	543	2.65
Central American, ex. Mexican	20	0.10
Guatemalan	8	0.04
Honduran	3	0.01
Nicaraguan	1	<0.01
Panamanian	8	0.04
Cuban	16	0.08
Dominican Republic	18	0.09
Mexican	110	0.54
Puerto Rican	322	1.57
South American	17	0.08
Argentinean	1	<0.01
Colombian	11	0.05
Paraguayan	3	0.01
Peruvian	2	0.01
Other Hispanic or Latino	40	0.19

Race*	Population	%
African-American/Black (990)	1,271	6.19
Not Hispanic (949)	1,200	5.85
Hispanic (41)	71	0.35
American Indian/Alaska Native (74)	176	0.86
Not Hispanic (70)	165	0.80
Hispanic (4)	11	0.05
Alaska Athabascan *(Ala. Nat.)* (0)	1	<0.01
Apache (0)	1	<0.01
Blackfeet (0)	6	0.03
Canadian/French Am. Ind. (4)	5	0.02
Cherokee (4)	21	0.10
Chippewa (2)	3	0.01
Choctaw (0)	2	0.01
Creek (0)	4	0.02
Inupiat *(Alaska Native)* (1)	1	<0.01
Iroquois (36)	70	0.34
Navajo (1)	1	<0.01
South American Ind. (2)	2	0.01
Asian (208)	281	1.37
Not Hispanic (206)	277	1.35
Hispanic (2)	4	0.02
Bangladeshi (2)	2	0.01
Burmese (1)	1	<0.01
Chinese, ex. Taiwanese (52)	62	0.30
Filipino (18)	35	0.17
Indian (51)	63	0.31
Indonesian (1)	2	0.01
Japanese (10)	18	0.09
Korean (23)	35	0.17
Laotian (3)	3	0.01
Pakistani (18)	21	0.10
Taiwanese (5)	5	0.02
Thai (11)	12	0.06
Vietnamese (8)	13	0.06
Hawaii Native/Pacific Islander (7)	11	0.05
Not Hispanic (6)	10	0.05
Hispanic (1)	1	<0.01
Fijian (1)	1	<0.01
Guamanian/Chamorro (0)	1	<0.01
Native Hawaiian (1)	3	0.01
White (18,698)	19,088	92.98
Not Hispanic (18,360)	18,702	91.10
Hispanic (338)	386	1.88

Long Beach

Place Type: City
County: Nassau
Population: 33,275†

Ancestry‡	Population	%
African, Sub-Saharan (23)	23	0.07
African (13)	13	0.04

*Notes: † The Census 2010 population figure is used to calculate the percentages in the Hispanic Origin and Race categories. Ancestry percentages are based on the 2006-2010 American Community Survey population (not shown); ‡ Numbers in parentheses indicate the number of people reporting a single ancestry; * Numbers in parentheses indicate the number of persons reporting this race alone, not in combination with any other race; Please refer to the Explanation of Data for more information.*

Nigerian (10)	10	0.03
Alsatian (0)	7	0.02
American (1,236)	1,236	3.70
Arab (14)	69	0.21
Arab (11)	25	0.07
Syrian (3)	44	0.13
Armenian (21)	32	0.10
Australian (31)	31	0.09
Austrian (90)	555	1.66
Belgian (7)	27	0.08
Brazilian (0)	54	0.16
British (65)	65	0.19
Canadian (14)	70	0.21
Celtic (16)	16	0.05
Croatian (71)	81	0.24
Czech (65)	224	0.67
Czechoslovakian (10)	10	0.03
Danish (17)	77	0.23
Dutch (19)	144	0.43
Eastern European (264)	311	0.93
English (249)	1,110	3.32
European (293)	343	1.03
Finnish (0)	24	0.07
French, ex. Basque (44)	465	1.39
French Canadian (9)	32	0.10
German (878)	3,057	9.14
Greek (302)	406	1.21
Guyanese (289)	289	0.86
Hungarian (142)	648	1.94
Iranian (0)	8	0.02
Irish (4,122)	7,640	22.85
Israeli (114)	135	0.40
Italian (2,984)	5,967	17.84
Latvian (24)	24	0.07
Lithuanian (80)	187	0.56
Northern European (7)	7	0.02
Norwegian (0)	54	0.16
Polish (899)	1,917	5.73
Portuguese (42)	112	0.33
Romanian (39)	118	0.35
Russian (1,217)	2,351	7.03
Scotch-Irish (150)	257	0.77
Scottish (34)	239	0.71
Slavic (0)	15	0.04
Slovak (0)	49	0.15
Slovene (13)	24	0.07
Swedish (26)	129	0.39
Turkish (83)	103	0.31
Ukrainian (113)	146	0.44
Welsh (0)	12	0.04
West Indian, ex. Hispanic (106)	151	0.45
Jamaican (34)	34	0.10
Trinidadian/Tobagonian (72)	72	0.22
West Indian (0)	45	0.13
Yugoslavian (0)	13	0.04

Hispanic Origin	Population	%
Hispanic or Latino (of any race)	4,691	14.10
Central American, ex. Mexican	1,009	3.03
Costa Rican	32	0.10
Guatemalan	173	0.52
Honduran	321	0.96
Nicaraguan	70	0.21
Panamanian	15	0.05
Salvadoran	396	1.19
Other Central American	2	0.01
Cuban	153	0.46
Dominican Republic	317	0.95
Mexican	179	0.54
Puerto Rican	1,018	3.06
South American	1,293	3.89
Argentinean	82	0.25
Bolivian	26	0.08
Chilean	80	0.24
Colombian	435	1.31
Ecuadorian	202	0.61
Paraguayan	3	0.01
Peruvian	379	1.14
Uruguayan	36	0.11
Venezuelan	42	0.13
Other South American	8	0.02
Other Hispanic or Latino	722	2.17

Race*	Population	%
African-American/Black (2,145)	2,450	7.36
Not Hispanic (1,958)	2,165	6.51
Hispanic (187)	285	0.86
American Indian/Alaska Native (94)	230	0.69
Not Hispanic (42)	97	0.29
Hispanic (52)	133	0.40
Blackfeet (1)	10	0.03
Canadian/French Am. Ind. (1)	3	0.01
Central American Ind. (6)	7	0.02
Cherokee (2)	7	0.02
Chippewa (1)	3	0.01
Delaware (0)	2	0.01
Iroquois (4)	5	0.02
Mexican American Ind. (5)	5	0.02
Potawatomi (0)	1	<0.01
Seminole (0)	1	<0.01
Shoshone (0)	1	<0.01
South American Ind. (2)	12	0.04
Spanish American Ind. (2)	3	0.01
Ute (1)	1	<0.01
Asian (912)	1,116	3.35
Not Hispanic (881)	1,050	3.16
Hispanic (31)	66	0.20
Bangladeshi (13)	14	0.04
Cambodian (3)	3	0.01
Chinese, ex. Taiwanese (122)	156	0.47
Filipino (425)	480	1.44
Indian (205)	255	0.77
Indonesian (1)	3	0.01
Japanese (28)	45	0.14
Korean (46)	66	0.20
Malaysian (2)	2	0.01
Pakistani (5)	6	0.02
Sri Lankan (3)	4	0.01
Taiwanese (1)	1	<0.01
Thai (19)	27	0.08
Vietnamese (10)	17	0.05
Hawaii Native/Pacific Islander (16)	39	0.12
Not Hispanic (12)	24	0.07
Hispanic (4)	15	0.05
Fijian (1)	1	<0.01
Guamanian/Chamorro (8)	8	0.02
Marshallese (1)	1	<0.01
Native Hawaiian (0)	6	0.02
Samoan (1)	3	0.01
Tongan (1)	1	<0.01
White (27,701)	28,256	84.92
Not Hispanic (25,117)	25,409	76.36
Hispanic (2,584)	2,847	8.56

Lynbrook

Place Type: Village
County: Nassau
Population: 19,427†

Ancestry‡	Population	%
African, Sub-Saharan (10)	22	0.11
African (0)	12	0.06
Nigerian (10)	10	0.05
American (933)	933	4.81
Arab (43)	43	0.22
Egyptian (43)	43	0.22
Armenian (141)	171	0.88
Austrian (68)	95	0.49
Belgian (0)	30	0.15
British (8)	28	0.14
Canadian (0)	21	0.11
Czech (0)	72	0.37
Danish (12)	46	0.24
Dutch (0)	34	0.18
Eastern European (37)	49	0.25
English (84)	703	3.63
Estonian (14)	14	0.07
European (198)	212	1.09
Finnish (11)	32	0.17
French, ex. Basque (0)	114	0.59
French Canadian (0)	57	0.29
German (397)	2,761	14.25
Greek (141)	346	1.79
Guyanese (12)	12	0.06
Hungarian (43)	162	0.84
Irish (1,479)	5,065	26.14
Italian (3,830)	6,815	35.17
Latvian (0)	23	0.12
Lithuanian (31)	217	1.12
Northern European (50)	50	0.26
Norwegian (53)	166	0.86
Polish (146)	774	3.99
Portuguese (22)	22	0.11
Romanian (0)	39	0.20
Russian (125)	516	2.66
Scotch-Irish (94)	219	1.13
Scottish (10)	92	0.47
Slovak (0)	28	0.14
Swedish (38)	91	0.47
Swiss (0)	5	0.03
Turkish (0)	18	0.09
Ukrainian (10)	41	0.21
Welsh (0)	11	0.06
West Indian, ex. Hispanic (104)	104	0.54
Barbadian (13)	13	0.07
Jamaican (33)	33	0.17
West Indian (58)	58	0.30

Hispanic Origin	Population	%
Hispanic or Latino (of any race)	2,534	13.04
Central American, ex. Mexican	433	2.23
Costa Rican	23	0.12
Guatemalan	56	0.29
Honduran	86	0.44
Nicaraguan	7	0.04
Panamanian	5	0.03
Salvadoran	251	1.29
Other Central American	5	0.03
Cuban	84	0.43
Dominican Republic	271	1.39
Mexican	98	0.50
Puerto Rican	615	3.17
South American	785	4.04
Argentinean	110	0.57
Bolivian	44	0.23
Chilean	85	0.44
Colombian	197	1.01
Ecuadorian	175	0.90
Paraguayan	4	0.02
Peruvian	120	0.62
Uruguayan	25	0.13
Venezuelan	15	0.08
Other South American	10	0.05
Other Hispanic or Latino	248	1.28

Race*	Population	%
African-American/Black (717)	849	4.37
Not Hispanic (648)	744	3.83
Hispanic (69)	105	0.54
American Indian/Alaska Native (27)	72	0.37
Not Hispanic (8)	35	0.18
Hispanic (19)	37	0.19
Aleut *(Alaska Native)* (1)	2	0.01
Blackfeet (0)	2	0.01
Cherokee (0)	6	0.03
Iroquois (1)	2	0.01
Lumbee (1)	1	0.01
Mexican American Ind. (2)	6	0.03
Shoshone (0)	1	0.01
South American Ind. (4)	6	0.03
Spanish American Ind. (1)	5	0.03
Ute (1)	1	0.01
Asian (872)	1,022	5.26
Not Hispanic (867)	997	5.13
Hispanic (5)	25	0.13
Cambodian (1)	3	0.02
Chinese, ex. Taiwanese (256)	301	1.55
Filipino (138)	170	0.88
Indian (245)	282	1.45

*Notes: † The Census 2010 population figure is used to calculate the percentages in the Hispanic Origin and Race categories. Ancestry percentages are based on the 2006-2010 American Community Survey population (not shown); ‡ Numbers in parentheses indicate the number of people reporting a single ancestry; * Numbers in parentheses indicate the number of persons reporting this race alone, not in combination with any other race; Please refer to the Explanation of Data for more information.*

Indonesian (0)	3	0.02
Japanese (6)	15	0.08
Korean (69)	80	0.41
Pakistani (87)	90	0.46
Sri Lankan (3)	3	0.02
Taiwanese (17)	18	0.09
Thai (4)	4	0.02
Vietnamese (5)	7	0.04
Hawaii Native/Pacific Islander (0)	8	0.04
Not Hispanic (0)	6	0.03
Hispanic (0)	2	0.01
Native Hawaiian (0)	1	0.01
White (16,567)	16,886	86.92
Not Hispanic (15,090)	15,244	78.47
Hispanic (1,477)	1,642	8.45

Lysander

Place Type: Town
County: Onondaga
Population: 21,759†

Ancestry‡	Population	%
African, Sub-Saharan (12)	12	0.06
African (12)	12	0.06
American (893)	893	4.20
Arab (66)	132	0.62
Arab (0)	14	0.07
Egyptian (28)	28	0.13
Lebanese (38)	90	0.42
Armenian (0)	126	0.59
Austrian (32)	129	0.61
British (16)	98	0.46
Bulgarian (0)	11	0.05
Canadian (69)	116	0.55
Czech (0)	22	0.10
Danish (37)	111	0.52
Dutch (102)	643	3.03
English (934)	4,320	20.33
European (166)	206	0.97
Finnish (9)	27	0.13
French, ex. Basque (152)	1,213	5.71
French Canadian (150)	475	2.24
German (1,054)	5,287	24.88
Greek (68)	168	0.79
Hungarian (12)	68	0.32
Iranian (12)	12	0.06
Irish (1,601)	5,857	27.56
Italian (1,250)	3,735	17.58
Lithuanian (11)	39	0.18
Maltese (17)	17	0.08
Norwegian (33)	75	0.35
Pennsylvania German (0)	21	0.10
Polish (475)	1,672	7.87
Portuguese (8)	8	0.04
Romanian (0)	53	0.25
Russian (89)	259	1.22
Scandinavian (14)	14	0.07
Scotch-Irish (146)	549	2.58
Scottish (63)	449	2.11
Slovak (21)	105	0.49
Swedish (43)	191	0.90
Swiss (14)	84	0.40
Turkish (17)	50	0.24
Ukrainian (146)	201	0.95
Welsh (9)	185	0.87
West Indian, ex. Hispanic (171)	333	1.57
Haitian (0)	50	0.24
Jamaican (127)	239	1.12
West Indian (44)	44	0.21
Yugoslavian (0)	28	0.13

Hispanic Origin	Population	%
Hispanic or Latino (of any race)	341	1.57
Central American, ex. Mexican	29	0.13
Guatemalan	11	0.05
Honduran	2	0.01
Nicaraguan	3	0.01
Panamanian	8	0.04
Salvadoran	5	0.02
Cuban	39	0.18
Dominican Republic	12	0.06
Mexican	86	0.40
Puerto Rican	96	0.44
South American	32	0.15
Argentinean	3	0.01
Chilean	4	0.02
Colombian	10	0.05
Ecuadorian	10	0.05
Peruvian	3	0.01
Other South American	2	0.01
Other Hispanic or Latino	47	0.22

Race*	Population	%
African-American/Black (179)	287	1.32
Not Hispanic (175)	273	1.25
Hispanic (4)	14	0.06
American Indian/Alaska Native (82)	174	0.80
Not Hispanic (77)	164	0.75
Hispanic (5)	10	0.05
Canadian/French Am. Ind. (1)	5	0.02
Central American Ind. (1)	2	0.01
Cherokee (2)	9	0.04
Chippewa (1)	1	<0.01
Choctaw (1)	2	0.01
Creek (0)	1	<0.01
Iroquois (55)	98	0.45
Shoshone (0)	1	<0.01
Tlingit-Haida *(Alaska Native)* (1)	1	<0.01
Asian (250)	351	1.61
Not Hispanic (248)	339	1.56
Hispanic (2)	12	0.06
Bangladeshi (3)	3	0.01
Cambodian (2)	2	0.01
Chinese, ex. Taiwanese (42)	68	0.31
Filipino (28)	51	0.23
Indian (85)	97	0.45
Indonesian (0)	1	<0.01
Japanese (12)	29	0.13
Korean (42)	58	0.27
Laotian (3)	5	0.02
Malaysian (1)	1	<0.01
Pakistani (9)	10	0.05
Taiwanese (4)	6	0.03
Thai (6)	10	0.05
Vietnamese (8)	14	0.06
Hawaii Native/Pacific Islander (8)	17	0.08
Not Hispanic (8)	17	0.08
Guamanian/Chamorro (0)	1	<0.01
Native Hawaiian (1)	9	0.04
Samoan (1)	1	<0.01
White (20,846)	21,159	97.24
Not Hispanic (20,622)	20,890	96.01
Hispanic (224)	269	1.24

Macedon

Place Type: Town
County: Wayne
Population: 9,148†

Ancestry‡	Population	%
American (412)	412	4.56
Austrian (0)	18	0.20
Belgian (0)	15	0.17
British (6)	27	0.30
Canadian (10)	91	1.01
Croatian (35)	35	0.39
Czech (0)	53	0.59
Czechoslovakian (12)	12	0.13
Danish (19)	30	0.33
Dutch (154)	1,138	12.61
Eastern European (7)	7	0.08
English (471)	1,783	19.75
European (115)	115	1.27
Finnish (39)	90	1.00
French, ex. Basque (13)	395	4.38
French Canadian (10)	48	0.53
German (688)	2,631	29.15
Hungarian (0)	108	1.20
Irish (281)	1,932	21.40
Italian (602)	1,284	14.22
Lithuanian (3)	3	0.03
Norwegian (18)	27	0.30
Pennsylvania German (2)	30	0.33
Polish (94)	524	5.80
Russian (45)	51	0.56
Scotch-Irish (29)	111	1.23
Scottish (61)	247	2.74
Slavic (29)	29	0.32
Slovak (0)	14	0.16
Slovene (0)	41	0.45
Swedish (3)	39	0.43
Swiss (25)	25	0.28
Ukrainian (108)	162	1.79
Welsh (3)	81	0.90

Hispanic Origin	Population	%
Hispanic or Latino (of any race)	228	2.49
Central American, ex. Mexican	5	0.05
Guatemalan	4	0.04
Panamanian	1	0.01
Cuban	9	0.10
Dominican Republic	8	0.09
Mexican	46	0.50
Puerto Rican	135	1.48
South American	10	0.11
Argentinean	1	0.01
Colombian	3	0.03
Ecuadorian	3	0.03
Venezuelan	3	0.03
Other Hispanic or Latino	15	0.16

Race*	Population	%
African-American/Black (75)	125	1.37
Not Hispanic (68)	116	1.27
Hispanic (7)	9	0.10
American Indian/Alaska Native (18)	64	0.70
Not Hispanic (15)	59	0.64
Hispanic (3)	5	0.05
Apache (0)	1	0.01
Blackfeet (0)	2	0.02
Cherokee (4)	15	0.16
Iroquois (2)	7	0.08
Mexican American Ind. (1)	2	0.02
Pueblo (0)	1	0.01
Sioux (0)	4	0.04
Asian (98)	141	1.54
Not Hispanic (94)	137	1.50
Hispanic (4)	4	0.04
Cambodian (5)	5	0.05
Chinese, ex. Taiwanese (13)	16	0.17
Filipino (4)	14	0.15
Indian (7)	11	0.12
Indonesian (2)	3	0.03
Japanese (4)	10	0.11
Korean (12)	25	0.27
Laotian (22)	25	0.27
Sri Lankan (1)	1	0.01
Thai (6)	7	0.08
Vietnamese (16)	17	0.19
Hawaii Native/Pacific Islander (0)	5	0.05
Not Hispanic (0)	5	0.05
Guamanian/Chamorro (0)	3	0.03
Native Hawaiian (0)	3	0.03
White (8,770)	8,909	97.39
Not Hispanic (8,603)	8,729	95.42
Hispanic (167)	180	1.97

Mahopac

Place Type: CDP
County: Putnam
Population: 8,369†

Ancestry‡	Population	%
African, Sub-Saharan (64)	70	0.92
African (0)	6	0.08
Senegalese (64)	64	0.84
American (241)	241	3.17

*Notes: † The Census 2010 population figure is used to calculate the percentages in the Hispanic Origin and Race categories. Ancestry percentages are based on the 2006-2010 American Community Survey population (not shown); ‡ Numbers in parentheses indicate the number of people reporting a single ancestry; * Numbers in parentheses indicate the number of persons reporting this race alone, not in combination with any other race; Please refer to the Explanation of Data for more information.*

Arab (9)	9	0.12
Egyptian (9)	9	0.12
Armenian (0)	20	0.26
Austrian (23)	68	0.89
British (35)	35	0.46
Canadian (0)	18	0.24
Croatian (0)	13	0.17
Czech (0)	28	0.37
Czechoslovakian (22)	22	0.29
Dutch (45)	70	0.92
Eastern European (9)	9	0.12
English (101)	593	7.80
Estonian (0)	40	0.53
French, ex. Basque (10)	89	1.17
German (107)	1,116	14.68
Hungarian (9)	62	0.82
Irish (601)	1,962	25.81
Italian (1,542)	2,912	38.31
Lithuanian (0)	12	0.16
Norwegian (26)	26	0.34
Polish (358)	817	10.75
Portuguese (75)	118	1.55
Romanian (32)	32	0.42
Russian (110)	316	4.16
Scandinavian (0)	15	0.20
Scotch-Irish (47)	106	1.39
Scottish (0)	20	0.26
Slovak (7)	14	0.18
Swedish (14)	75	0.99
Ukrainian (9)	97	1.28
Welsh (46)	118	1.55

Hispanic Origin	Population	%
Hispanic or Latino (of any race)	911	10.89
Central American, ex. Mexican	226	2.70
Guatemalan	108	1.29
Honduran	2	0.02
Panamanian	1	0.01
Salvadoran	115	1.37
Cuban	12	0.14
Dominican Republic	55	0.66
Mexican	154	1.84
Puerto Rican	239	2.86
South American	149	1.78
Argentinean	16	0.19
Bolivian	1	0.01
Chilean	13	0.16
Colombian	22	0.26
Ecuadorian	66	0.79
Paraguayan	8	0.10
Peruvian	19	0.23
Venezuelan	4	0.05
Other Hispanic or Latino	76	0.91

Race*	Population	%
African-American/Black (178)	211	2.52
Not Hispanic (130)	149	1.78
Hispanic (48)	62	0.74
American Indian/Alaska Native (11)	24	0.29
Not Hispanic (9)	20	0.24
Hispanic (2)	4	0.05
Central American Ind. (5)	6	0.07
Cherokee (0)	2	0.02
Iroquois (1)	1	0.01
Mexican American Ind. (0)	1	0.01
South American Ind. (1)	1	0.01
Spanish American Ind. (1)	1	0.01
Asian (168)	218	2.60
Not Hispanic (160)	206	2.46
Hispanic (8)	12	0.14
Chinese, ex. Taiwanese (43)	57	0.68
Filipino (19)	23	0.27
Indian (59)	75	0.90
Japanese (2)	5	0.06
Korean (19)	23	0.27
Malaysian (2)	2	0.02
Pakistani (11)	11	0.13
Taiwanese (2)	2	0.02
Thai (5)	5	0.06
Vietnamese (4)	11	0.13
Hawaii Native/Pacific Islander (1)	3	0.04
Not Hispanic (1)	3	0.04
Guamanian/Chamorro (0)	2	0.02
White (7,624)	7,732	92.39
Not Hispanic (7,058)	7,121	85.09
Hispanic (566)	611	7.30

Malone

Place Type: Town
County: Franklin
Population: 14,545†

Ancestry‡	Population	%
African, Sub-Saharan (33)	33	0.22
African (33)	33	0.22
American (966)	966	6.55
Arab (42)	42	0.28
Lebanese (30)	30	0.20
Moroccan (12)	12	0.08
Australian (0)	14	0.09
British (12)	12	0.08
Canadian (94)	169	1.15
Danish (4)	8	0.05
Dutch (17)	237	1.61
English (302)	1,078	7.31
European (73)	73	0.50
Finnish (6)	12	0.08
French, ex. Basque (810)	2,302	15.61
French Canadian (253)	477	3.23
German (184)	971	6.59
Greek (14)	22	0.15
Guyanese (11)	11	0.07
Hungarian (0)	62	0.42
Irish (681)	2,155	14.62
Italian (157)	451	3.06
Lithuanian (0)	35	0.24
Norwegian (14)	36	0.24
Polish (123)	285	1.93
Portuguese (0)	7	0.05
Romanian (0)	6	0.04
Russian (0)	52	0.35
Scotch-Irish (51)	205	1.39
Scottish (79)	218	1.48
Slovak (11)	11	0.07
Swedish (0)	20	0.14
Swiss (0)	14	0.09
Ukrainian (15)	38	0.26
Welsh (3)	30	0.20
West Indian, ex. Hispanic (24)	62	0.42
Haitian (0)	14	0.09
Jamaican (16)	32	0.22
Trinidadian/Tobagonian (8)	8	0.05
West Indian (0)	8	0.05

Hispanic Origin	Population	%
Hispanic or Latino (of any race)	1,042	7.16
Central American, ex. Mexican	99	0.68
Costa Rican	2	0.01
Guatemalan	15	0.10
Honduran	34	0.23
Nicaraguan	1	0.01
Panamanian	21	0.14
Salvadoran	26	0.18
Cuban	35	0.24
Dominican Republic	189	1.30
Mexican	116	0.80
Puerto Rican	525	3.61
South American	58	0.40
Argentinean	2	0.01
Chilean	1	0.01
Colombian	20	0.14
Ecuadorian	23	0.16
Peruvian	8	0.06
Uruguayan	1	0.01
Venezuelan	3	0.02
Other Hispanic or Latino	20	0.14

Race*	Population	%
African-American/Black (2,695)	2,729	18.76
Not Hispanic (2,422)	2,455	16.88
Hispanic (273)	274	1.88
American Indian/Alaska Native (122)	166	1.14
Not Hispanic (113)	154	1.06
Hispanic (9)	12	0.08
Apache (1)	1	0.01
Blackfeet (0)	2	0.01
Canadian/French Am. Ind. (2)	2	0.01
Cherokee (1)	3	0.02
Delaware (1)	2	0.01
Iroquois (36)	45	0.31
Mexican American Ind. (2)	2	0.01
Navajo (4)	4	0.03
South American Ind. (2)	5	0.03
Yup'ik *(Alaska Native)* (1)	1	0.01
Asian (87)	109	0.75
Not Hispanic (85)	104	0.72
Hispanic (2)	5	0.03
Bangladeshi (2)	2	0.01
Chinese, ex. Taiwanese (19)	21	0.14
Filipino (11)	24	0.17
Indian (23)	23	0.16
Indonesian (0)	2	0.01
Japanese (0)	2	0.01
Korean (4)	6	0.04
Pakistani (2)	2	0.01
Thai (1)	4	0.03
Vietnamese (1)	3	0.02
Hawaii Native/Pacific Islander (0)	2	0.01
Not Hispanic (0)	2	0.01
Guamanian/Chamorro (0)	1	0.01
White (11,218)	11,312	77.77
Not Hispanic (10,729)	10,809	74.31
Hispanic (489)	503	3.46

Malta

Place Type: Town
County: Saratoga
Population: 14,765†

Ancestry‡	Population	%
African, Sub-Saharan (0)	21	0.14
African (0)	21	0.14
American (1,267)	1,267	8.73
Arab (70)	97	0.67
Egyptian (70)	70	0.48
Iraqi (0)	10	0.07
Syrian (0)	10	0.07
Other Arab (0)	7	0.05
Armenian (41)	98	0.67
Austrian (22)	56	0.39
Belgian (0)	7	0.05
Brazilian (9)	9	0.06
British (4)	19	0.13
Canadian (8)	25	0.17
Czech (22)	42	0.29
Czechoslovakian (0)	10	0.07
Danish (32)	54	0.37
Dutch (44)	444	3.06
Eastern European (43)	43	0.30
English (358)	1,975	13.60
European (172)	233	1.60
French, ex. Basque (312)	1,409	9.70
French Canadian (40)	257	1.77
German (431)	2,406	16.57
Greek (27)	54	0.37
Guyanese (18)	18	0.12
Hungarian (0)	97	0.67
Iranian (12)	24	0.17
Irish (977)	3,702	25.50
Italian (1,086)	2,608	17.96
Lithuanian (53)	53	0.37
Northern European (3)	6	0.04
Norwegian (53)	250	1.72
Polish (273)	1,271	8.75
Portuguese (5)	5	0.03
Russian (61)	158	1.09
Scandinavian (18)	18	0.12
Scotch-Irish (140)	528	3.64

*Notes: † The Census 2010 population figure is used to calculate the percentages in the Hispanic Origin and Race categories. Ancestry percentages are based on the 2006-2010 American Community Survey population (not shown); ‡ Numbers in parentheses indicate the number of people reporting a single ancestry; * Numbers in parentheses indicate the number of persons reporting this race alone, not in combination with any other race; Please refer to the Explanation of Data for more information.*

Ancestry	Population	%
Scottish (41)	278	1.91
Slovak (12)	66	0.45
Swedish (20)	143	0.98
Swiss (10)	33	0.23
Turkish (47)	47	0.32
Ukrainian (24)	88	0.61
Welsh (13)	116	0.80
West Indian, ex. Hispanic (11)	11	0.08
Trinidadian/Tobagonian (11)	11	0.08
Yugoslavian (113)	113	0.78

Hispanic Origin	Population	%
Hispanic or Latino (of any race)	367	2.49
Central American, ex. Mexican	29	0.20
Costa Rican	1	0.01
Guatemalan	8	0.05
Honduran	4	0.03
Panamanian	4	0.03
Salvadoran	11	0.07
Other Central American	1	0.01
Cuban	23	0.16
Dominican Republic	7	0.05
Mexican	72	0.49
Puerto Rican	153	1.04
South American	37	0.25
Argentinean	2	0.01
Bolivian	2	0.01
Chilean	1	0.01
Colombian	11	0.07
Ecuadorian	8	0.05
Paraguayan	1	0.01
Peruvian	1	0.01
Uruguayan	3	0.02
Venezuelan	2	0.01
Other South American	6	0.04
Other Hispanic or Latino	46	0.31

Race*	Population	%
African-American/Black (181)	259	1.75
Not Hispanic (160)	228	1.54
Hispanic (21)	31	0.21
American Indian/Alaska Native (39)	103	0.70
Not Hispanic (30)	91	0.62
Hispanic (9)	12	0.08
Apache (0)	1	0.01
Arapaho (0)	3	0.02
Blackfeet (1)	4	0.03
Cherokee (3)	8	0.05
Chippewa (0)	4	0.03
Delaware (1)	1	0.01
Iroquois (6)	22	0.15
Mexican American Ind. (7)	7	0.05
Pueblo (1)	1	0.01
Seminole (1)	1	0.01
South American Ind. (0)	1	0.01
Asian (199)	272	1.84
Not Hispanic (196)	265	1.79
Hispanic (3)	7	0.05
Bangladeshi (1)	1	0.01
Cambodian (1)	1	0.01
Chinese, ex. Taiwanese (71)	77	0.52
Filipino (19)	27	0.18
Indian (44)	57	0.39
Japanese (13)	24	0.16
Korean (28)	46	0.31
Pakistani (9)	11	0.07
Sri Lankan (4)	4	0.03
Taiwanese (1)	1	0.01
Thai (1)	3	0.02
Vietnamese (7)	9	0.06
Hawaii Native/Pacific Islander (3)	6	0.04
Not Hispanic (3)	6	0.04
Native Hawaiian (2)	3	0.02
White (14,067)	14,262	96.59
Not Hispanic (13,803)	13,983	94.70
Hispanic (264)	279	1.89

Malverne

Place Type: Village
County: Nassau
Population: 8,514†

Ancestry‡	Population	%
Afghan (0)	139	1.63
American (322)	322	3.78
Armenian (26)	26	0.31
Austrian (35)	81	0.95
Brazilian (11)	11	0.13
Canadian (10)	10	0.12
Czech (10)	23	0.27
Czechoslovakian (11)	11	0.13
Danish (12)	57	0.67
Dutch (0)	60	0.70
English (11)	537	6.30
Estonian (13)	13	0.15
European (22)	22	0.26
Finnish (0)	12	0.14
French, ex. Basque (0)	78	0.92
German (373)	1,833	21.51
Greek (33)	92	1.08
Hungarian (0)	23	0.27
Irish (701)	2,152	25.26
Italian (2,074)	3,425	40.20
Latvian (0)	28	0.33
Lithuanian (0)	11	0.13
Norwegian (0)	135	1.58
Polish (183)	443	5.20
Portuguese (0)	64	0.75
Romanian (0)	25	0.29
Russian (66)	139	1.63
Scandinavian (11)	11	0.13
Scotch-Irish (35)	151	1.77
Scottish (0)	24	0.28
Serbian (0)	12	0.14
Swedish (11)	104	1.22
Swiss (0)	94	1.10
Ukrainian (0)	11	0.13
West Indian, ex. Hispanic (30)	30	0.35
Haitian (19)	19	0.22
Jamaican (11)	11	0.13

Hispanic Origin	Population	%
Hispanic or Latino (of any race)	736	8.64
Central American, ex. Mexican	53	0.62
Guatemalan	6	0.07
Honduran	17	0.20
Nicaraguan	1	0.01
Panamanian	5	0.06
Salvadoran	21	0.25
Other Central American	3	0.04
Cuban	37	0.43
Dominican Republic	96	1.13
Mexican	27	0.32
Puerto Rican	202	2.37
South American	255	3.00
Argentinean	19	0.22
Bolivian	3	0.04
Chilean	11	0.13
Colombian	92	1.08
Ecuadorian	54	0.63
Paraguayan	5	0.06
Peruvian	67	0.79
Uruguayan	4	0.05
Other Hispanic or Latino	66	0.78

Race*	Population	%
African-American/Black (281)	332	3.90
Not Hispanic (260)	296	3.48
Hispanic (21)	36	0.42
American Indian/Alaska Native (4)	17	0.20
Not Hispanic (4)	8	0.09
Hispanic (0)	9	0.11
Blackfeet (1)	1	0.01
Cherokee (0)	2	0.02
Mexican American Ind. (0)	1	0.01
Navajo (0)	1	0.01
Spanish American Ind. (0)	2	0.02
Asian (354)	395	4.64
Not Hispanic (354)	385	4.52
Hispanic (0)	10	0.12
Chinese, ex. Taiwanese (81)	96	1.13
Filipino (86)	96	1.13
Indian (105)	116	1.36
Japanese (1)	3	0.04
Korean (15)	17	0.20
Laotian (2)	2	0.02
Malaysian (1)	1	0.01
Pakistani (35)	40	0.47
Taiwanese (4)	8	0.09
Thai (2)	4	0.05
Vietnamese (11)	11	0.13
Hawaii Native/Pacific Islander (1)	8	0.09
Not Hispanic (1)	7	0.08
Hispanic (0)	1	0.01
Guamanian/Chamorro (1)	1	0.01
Native Hawaiian (0)	1	0.01
White (7,525)	7,613	89.42
Not Hispanic (7,066)	7,119	83.62
Hispanic (459)	494	5.80

Mamakating

Place Type: Town
County: Sullivan
Population: 12,085†

Ancestry‡	Population	%
African, Sub-Saharan (9)	9	0.08
Kenyan (9)	9	0.08
American (1,099)	1,099	9.17
Austrian (8)	37	0.31
British (19)	19	0.16
Canadian (0)	31	0.26
Czech (0)	35	0.29
Czechoslovakian (6)	33	0.28
Danish (0)	38	0.32
Dutch (99)	294	2.45
Eastern European (5)	5	0.04
English (160)	872	7.28
Estonian (8)	16	0.13
European (48)	107	0.89
Finnish (8)	8	0.07
French, ex. Basque (62)	297	2.48
French Canadian (10)	86	0.72
German (704)	2,331	19.46
Greek (95)	111	0.93
Hungarian (40)	85	0.71
Iranian (13)	19	0.16
Irish (1,007)	3,491	29.14
Israeli (0)	14	0.12
Italian (1,197)	2,674	22.32
Lithuanian (12)	22	0.18
Macedonian (37)	37	0.31
Northern European (26)	50	0.42
Norwegian (100)	215	1.79
Pennsylvania German (0)	9	0.08
Polish (204)	477	3.98
Portuguese (64)	101	0.84
Russian (58)	165	1.38
Scandinavian (16)	16	0.13
Scotch-Irish (123)	325	2.71
Scottish (8)	186	1.55
Slavic (0)	8	0.07
Slovak (39)	63	0.53
Swedish (112)	136	1.14
Swiss (0)	38	0.32
Turkish (8)	24	0.20
Ukrainian (8)	30	0.25
Welsh (9)	89	0.74
West Indian, ex. Hispanic (30)	85	0.71
Dutch West Indian (0)	55	0.46
Jamaican (30)	30	0.25
Yugoslavian (56)	87	0.73

Hispanic Origin	Population	%
Hispanic or Latino (of any race)	1,027	8.50

*Notes: † The Census 2010 population figure is used to calculate the percentages in the Hispanic Origin and Race categories. Ancestry percentages are based on the 2006-2010 American Community Survey population (not shown); ‡ Numbers in parentheses indicate the number of people reporting a single ancestry; * Numbers in parentheses indicate the number of persons reporting this race alone, not in combination with any other race; Please refer to the Explanation of Data for more information.*

Central American, ex. Mexican	40	0.33
Costa Rican	9	0.07
Guatemalan	12	0.10
Honduran	12	0.10
Panamanian	6	0.05
Other Central American	1	0.01
Cuban	39	0.32
Dominican Republic	43	0.36
Mexican	113	0.94
Puerto Rican	601	4.97
South American	81	0.67
Argentinean	7	0.06
Bolivian	1	0.01
Chilean	2	0.02
Colombian	29	0.24
Ecuadorian	27	0.22
Peruvian	11	0.09
Uruguayan	1	0.01
Venezuelan	1	0.01
Other South American	2	0.02
Other Hispanic or Latino	110	0.91

Race*	Population	%
African-American/Black (429)	540	4.47
Not Hispanic (390)	486	4.02
Hispanic (39)	54	0.45
American Indian/Alaska Native (56)	160	1.32
Not Hispanic (36)	120	0.99
Hispanic (20)	40	0.33
Apache (3)	3	0.02
Blackfeet (2)	9	0.07
Cherokee (3)	22	0.18
Choctaw (1)	1	0.01
Delaware (19)	31	0.26
Inupiat *(Alaska Native)* (1)	1	0.01
Iroquois (1)	4	0.03
Mexican American Ind. (2)	2	0.02
Navajo (1)	2	0.02
South American Ind. (3)	6	0.05
Asian (137)	196	1.62
Not Hispanic (135)	191	1.58
Hispanic (2)	5	0.04
Bangladeshi (3)	3	0.02
Cambodian (2)	2	0.02
Chinese, ex. Taiwanese (25)	39	0.32
Filipino (13)	20	0.17
Indian (35)	47	0.39
Indonesian (0)	1	0.01
Japanese (8)	13	0.11
Korean (20)	26	0.22
Laotian (3)	4	0.03
Pakistani (8)	10	0.08
Thai (0)	1	0.01
Vietnamese (15)	18	0.15
Hawaii Native/Pacific Islander (0)	3	0.02
Not Hispanic (0)	3	0.02
Native Hawaiian (0)	1	0.01
White (10,978)	11,263	93.20
Not Hispanic (10,261)	10,467	86.61
Hispanic (717)	796	6.59

Mamaroneck

Place Type: Town
County: Westchester
Population: 29,156†

Ancestry‡	Population	%
African, Sub-Saharan (34)	34	0.12
South African (34)	34	0.12
Albanian (28)	57	0.20
American (1,831)	1,831	6.33
Arab (311)	504	1.74
Arab (44)	44	0.15
Lebanese (66)	259	0.89
Moroccan (188)	188	0.65
Other Arab (13)	13	0.04
Armenian (15)	15	0.05
Australian (0)	15	0.05
Austrian (70)	392	1.35
Belgian (0)	46	0.16
Brazilian (169)	296	1.02
British (144)	169	0.58
Canadian (20)	58	0.20
Celtic (0)	11	0.04
Croatian (33)	33	0.11
Czech (45)	231	0.80
Czechoslovakian (15)	15	0.05
Danish (27)	103	0.36
Dutch (42)	244	0.84
Eastern European (932)	1,042	3.60
English (526)	2,167	7.49
European (473)	481	1.66
Finnish (15)	40	0.14
French, ex. Basque (562)	1,165	4.02
French Canadian (8)	40	0.14
German (630)	3,026	10.45
Greek (73)	128	0.44
Hungarian (58)	310	1.07
Iranian (198)	248	0.86
Irish (1,261)	4,534	15.66
Israeli (27)	86	0.30
Italian (2,499)	4,736	16.36
Latvian (0)	13	0.04
Lithuanian (30)	187	0.65
Norwegian (160)	234	0.81
Pennsylvania German (0)	15	0.05
Polish (540)	1,394	4.82
Portuguese (90)	167	0.58
Romanian (37)	193	0.67
Russian (857)	2,006	6.93
Scandinavian (27)	119	0.41
Scotch-Irish (138)	477	1.65
Scottish (114)	609	2.10
Serbian (0)	13	0.04
Slovak (17)	60	0.21
Swedish (40)	178	0.61
Swiss (13)	146	0.50
Turkish (0)	26	0.09
Ukrainian (221)	291	1.01
Welsh (0)	52	0.18
West Indian, ex. Hispanic (333)	333	1.15
Barbadian (51)	51	0.18
Jamaican (238)	238	0.82
Trinidadian/Tobagonian (24)	24	0.08
West Indian (20)	20	0.07
Yugoslavian (0)	14	0.05

Hispanic Origin	Population	%
Hispanic or Latino (of any race)	4,524	15.52
Central American, ex. Mexican	1,383	4.74
Costa Rican	12	0.04
Guatemalan	1,036	3.55
Honduran	35	0.12
Nicaraguan	8	0.03
Panamanian	11	0.04
Salvadoran	278	0.95
Other Central American	3	0.01
Cuban	124	0.43
Dominican Republic	123	0.42
Mexican	920	3.16
Puerto Rican	516	1.77
South American	1,041	3.57
Argentinean	102	0.35
Bolivian	13	0.04
Chilean	50	0.17
Colombian	224	0.77
Ecuadorian	121	0.42
Paraguayan	88	0.30
Peruvian	329	1.13
Uruguayan	33	0.11
Venezuelan	66	0.23
Other South American	15	0.05
Other Hispanic or Latino	417	1.43

Race*	Population	%
African-American/Black (858)	1,045	3.58
Not Hispanic (775)	900	3.09
Hispanic (83)	145	0.50
American Indian/Alaska Native (48)	133	0.46
Not Hispanic (10)	60	0.21
Hispanic (38)	73	0.25
Aleut *(Alaska Native)* (0)	4	0.01
Apache (6)	8	0.03
Blackfeet (0)	5	0.02
Canadian/French Am. Ind. (1)	2	0.01
Central American Ind. (0)	2	0.01
Cherokee (0)	19	0.07
Chickasaw (0)	1	<0.01
Choctaw (1)	1	<0.01
Creek (0)	1	<0.01
Iroquois (1)	3	0.01
Mexican American Ind. (11)	20	0.07
Navajo (1)	1	<0.01
Osage (1)	1	<0.01
Sioux (0)	1	<0.01
South American Ind. (8)	20	0.07
Spanish American Ind. (3)	3	0.01
Asian (1,136)	1,416	4.86
Not Hispanic (1,131)	1,383	4.74
Hispanic (5)	33	0.11
Bangladeshi (1)	3	0.01
Burmese (0)	2	0.01
Cambodian (1)	4	0.01
Chinese, ex. Taiwanese (319)	405	1.39
Filipino (104)	144	0.49
Indian (283)	331	1.14
Indonesian (2)	6	0.02
Japanese (156)	207	0.71
Korean (156)	187	0.64
Malaysian (2)	2	0.01
Nepalese (0)	1	<0.01
Pakistani (28)	32	0.11
Sri Lankan (4)	4	0.01
Taiwanese (18)	20	0.07
Thai (9)	14	0.05
Vietnamese (15)	21	0.07
Hawaii Native/Pacific Islander (12)	31	0.11
Not Hispanic (6)	17	0.06
Hispanic (6)	14	0.05
Guamanian/Chamorro (6)	6	0.02
Native Hawaiian (2)	4	0.01
White (24,510)	25,194	86.41
Not Hispanic (22,171)	22,568	77.40
Hispanic (2,339)	2,626	9.01

Mamaroneck

Place Type: Village
County: Westchester
Population: 18,929†

Ancestry‡	Population	%
African, Sub-Saharan (44)	44	0.23
African (44)	44	0.23
Albanian (38)	67	0.36
American (1,867)	1,867	9.97
Arab (267)	330	1.76
Iraqi (0)	14	0.07
Jordanian (9)	9	0.05
Lebanese (55)	104	0.56
Moroccan (188)	188	1.00
Palestinian (15)	15	0.08
Armenian (0)	18	0.10
Australian (0)	15	0.08
Austrian (32)	115	0.61
Brazilian (128)	205	1.09
British (33)	42	0.22
Canadian (0)	22	0.12
Celtic (0)	11	0.06
Croatian (40)	40	0.21
Cypriot (16)	16	0.09
Czech (0)	30	0.16
Danish (29)	92	0.49
Dutch (63)	91	0.49
Eastern European (403)	412	2.20
English (155)	643	3.43
European (182)	239	1.28
Finnish (30)	30	0.16
French, ex. Basque (143)	397	2.12

*Notes: † The Census 2010 population figure is used to calculate the percentages in the Hispanic Origin and Race categories. Ancestry percentages are based on the 2006-2010 American Community Survey population (not shown); ‡ Numbers in parentheses indicate the number of people reporting a single ancestry; * Numbers in parentheses indicate the number of persons reporting this race alone, not in combination with any other race; Please refer to the Explanation of Data for more information.*

Ancestry	Population	%
French Canadian (0)	48	0.26
German (335)	1,266	6.76
Greek (138)	214	1.14
Hungarian (45)	117	0.62
Iranian (130)	130	0.69
Irish (604)	1,795	9.58
Israeli (0)	18	0.10
Italian (2,654)	4,137	22.09
Lithuanian (30)	53	0.28
Northern European (10)	10	0.05
Norwegian (0)	20	0.11
Polish (216)	680	3.63
Portuguese (186)	285	1.52
Romanian (37)	137	0.73
Russian (150)	451	2.41
Scandinavian (0)	16	0.09
Scotch-Irish (50)	103	0.55
Scottish (9)	129	0.69
Slavic (0)	11	0.06
Slovak (17)	47	0.25
Swedish (8)	65	0.35
Swiss (0)	26	0.14
Ukrainian (133)	174	0.93
Welsh (13)	73	0.39
West Indian, ex. Hispanic (329)	329	1.76
Jamaican (285)	285	1.52
Trinidadian/Tobagonian (24)	24	0.13
West Indian (20)	20	0.11

Hispanic Origin	Population	%
Hispanic or Latino (of any race)	4,602	24.31
Central American, ex. Mexican	1,530	8.08
Costa Rican	9	0.05
Guatemalan	1,145	6.05
Honduran	34	0.18
Nicaraguan	6	0.03
Panamanian	12	0.06
Salvadoran	316	1.67
Other Central American	8	0.04
Cuban	83	0.44
Dominican Republic	110	0.58
Mexican	991	5.24
Puerto Rican	412	2.18
South American	1,064	5.62
Argentinean	61	0.32
Bolivian	14	0.07
Chilean	52	0.27
Colombian	230	1.22
Ecuadorian	120	0.63
Paraguayan	130	0.69
Peruvian	349	1.84
Uruguayan	44	0.23
Venezuelan	50	0.26
Other South American	14	0.07
Other Hispanic or Latino	412	2.18

Race*	Population	%
African-American/Black (767)	929	4.91
Not Hispanic (699)	819	4.33
Hispanic (68)	110	0.58
American Indian/Alaska Native (49)	125	0.66
Not Hispanic (15)	64	0.34
Hispanic (34)	61	0.32
Apache (0)	1	0.01
Blackfeet (0)	5	0.03
Central American Ind. (0)	1	0.01
Cherokee (0)	17	0.09
Creek (0)	1	0.01
Iroquois (0)	9	0.05
Mexican American Ind. (11)	19	0.10
Seminole (0)	1	0.01
South American Ind. (9)	16	0.08
Spanish American Ind. (3)	3	0.02
Asian (926)	1,074	5.67
Not Hispanic (918)	1,040	5.49
Hispanic (8)	34	0.18
Bangladeshi (1)	3	0.02
Cambodian (2)	5	0.03
Chinese, ex. Taiwanese (217)	268	1.42
Filipino (77)	99	0.52
Indian (164)	191	1.01
Indonesian (0)	3	0.02
Japanese (301)	330	1.74
Korean (114)	123	0.65
Malaysian (1)	3	0.02
Pakistani (10)	14	0.07
Taiwanese (4)	6	0.03
Thai (7)	8	0.04
Vietnamese (7)	8	0.04
Hawaii Native/Pacific Islander (11)	27	0.14
Not Hispanic (5)	12	0.06
Hispanic (6)	15	0.08
Guamanian/Chamorro (6)	6	0.03
Native Hawaiian (2)	3	0.02
White (14,532)	15,032	79.41
Not Hispanic (12,353)	12,578	66.45
Hispanic (2,179)	2,454	12.96

Manchester

Place Type: Town
County: Ontario
Population: 9,395†

Ancestry‡	Population	%
American (455)	455	4.87
Arab (20)	61	0.65
Syrian (20)	61	0.65
Austrian (6)	17	0.18
Belgian (18)	21	0.22
British (9)	9	0.10
Canadian (20)	45	0.48
Czechoslovakian (30)	30	0.32
Danish (8)	43	0.46
Dutch (242)	1,103	11.81
English (451)	1,794	19.21
European (41)	41	0.44
Finnish (3)	6	0.06
French, ex. Basque (50)	409	4.38
French Canadian (16)	197	2.11
German (631)	3,151	33.74
Greek (10)	13	0.14
Hungarian (32)	70	0.75
Irish (420)	1,906	20.41
Italian (523)	1,239	13.27
Northern European (9)	9	0.10
Norwegian (22)	49	0.52
Pennsylvania German (22)	22	0.24
Polish (137)	441	4.72
Portuguese (10)	13	0.14
Russian (0)	6	0.06
Scandinavian (3)	39	0.42
Scotch-Irish (95)	255	2.73
Scottish (12)	132	1.41
Swedish (41)	78	0.84
Swiss (3)	6	0.06
Turkish (3)	11	0.12
Ukrainian (13)	55	0.59
Welsh (3)	46	0.49

Hispanic Origin	Population	%
Hispanic or Latino (of any race)	224	2.38
Central American, ex. Mexican	12	0.13
Costa Rican	4	0.04
Guatemalan	3	0.03
Honduran	2	0.02
Panamanian	1	0.01
Salvadoran	2	0.02
Cuban	7	0.07
Dominican Republic	2	0.02
Mexican	77	0.82
Puerto Rican	113	1.20
South American	5	0.05
Bolivian	1	0.01
Chilean	1	0.01
Colombian	1	0.01
Ecuadorian	1	0.01
Venezuelan	1	0.01
Other Hispanic or Latino	8	0.09

Race*	Population	%
African-American/Black (103)	146	1.55
Not Hispanic (99)	131	1.39
Hispanic (4)	15	0.16
American Indian/Alaska Native (28)	77	0.82
Not Hispanic (23)	70	0.75
Hispanic (5)	7	0.07
Apache (1)	1	0.01
Blackfeet (2)	2	0.02
Canadian/French Am. Ind. (1)	1	0.01
Cherokee (0)	2	0.02
Chickasaw (0)	1	0.01
Chippewa (0)	3	0.03
Cree (0)	1	0.01
Crow (0)	2	0.02
Iroquois (8)	28	0.30
Lumbee (1)	1	0.01
Sioux (4)	5	0.05
Asian (43)	56	0.60
Not Hispanic (42)	55	0.59
Hispanic (1)	1	0.01
Cambodian (2)	2	0.02
Chinese, ex. Taiwanese (13)	13	0.14
Filipino (3)	4	0.04
Indian (2)	5	0.05
Indonesian (0)	2	0.02
Japanese (3)	7	0.07
Korean (1)	1	0.01
Laotian (10)	10	0.11
Sri Lankan (1)	1	0.01
Thai (3)	3	0.03
Vietnamese (1)	1	0.01
Hawaii Native/Pacific Islander (3)	13	0.14
Not Hispanic (3)	13	0.14
Guamanian/Chamorro (2)	3	0.03
Native Hawaiian (1)	1	0.01
White (9,035)	9,156	97.46
Not Hispanic (8,900)	9,000	95.80
Hispanic (135)	156	1.66

Manhasset

Place Type: CDP
County: Nassau
Population: 8,080†

Ancestry‡	Population	%
African, Sub-Saharan (28)	28	0.34
African (15)	15	0.18
Sierra Leonean (13)	13	0.16
American (148)	148	1.80
Arab (41)	77	0.94
Lebanese (36)	45	0.55
Moroccan (5)	5	0.06
Syrian (0)	27	0.33
Armenian (22)	40	0.49
Austrian (0)	38	0.46
Brazilian (0)	18	0.22
British (35)	43	0.52
Canadian (31)	39	0.48
Croatian (23)	32	0.39
Czech (11)	11	0.13
Czechoslovakian (0)	11	0.13
Dutch (0)	17	0.21
Eastern European (55)	55	0.67
English (47)	253	3.08
European (17)	17	0.21
French, ex. Basque (0)	137	1.67
French Canadian (9)	59	0.72
German (172)	920	11.21
Greek (264)	326	3.97
Hungarian (40)	98	1.19
Iranian (132)	132	1.61
Irish (438)	1,546	18.84
Israeli (36)	36	0.44
Italian (1,278)	2,255	27.48
Latvian (10)	10	0.12
Lithuanian (0)	11	0.13
Norwegian (0)	29	0.35

*Notes: † The Census 2010 population figure is used to calculate the percentages in the Hispanic Origin and Race categories. Ancestry percentages are based on the 2006-2010 American Community Survey population (not shown); ‡ Numbers in parentheses indicate the number of people reporting a single ancestry; * Numbers in parentheses indicate the number of persons reporting this race alone, not in combination with any other race; Please refer to the Explanation of Data for more information.*

Polish (105)	281	3.42
Portuguese (141)	159	1.94
Romanian (27)	68	0.83
Russian (173)	283	3.45
Scotch-Irish (8)	55	0.67
Scottish (8)	18	0.22
Swedish (8)	58	0.71
Swiss (7)	38	0.46
Ukrainian (20)	31	0.38
West Indian, ex. Hispanic (50)	50	0.61
Barbadian (2)	2	0.02
Haitian (17)	17	0.21
Jamaican (31)	31	0.38

Hispanic Origin	Population	%
Hispanic or Latino (of any race)	711	8.80
Central American, ex. Mexican	193	2.39
Guatemalan	23	0.28
Honduran	3	0.04
Nicaraguan	5	0.06
Panamanian	8	0.10
Salvadoran	152	1.88
Other Central American	2	0.02
Cuban	34	0.42
Dominican Republic	40	0.50
Mexican	48	0.59
Puerto Rican	91	1.13
South American	193	2.39
Argentinean	15	0.19
Chilean	3	0.04
Colombian	72	0.89
Ecuadorian	21	0.26
Paraguayan	2	0.02
Peruvian	66	0.82
Uruguayan	3	0.04
Venezuelan	10	0.12
Other South American	1	0.01
Other Hispanic or Latino	112	1.39

Race*	Population	%
African-American/Black (763)	786	9.73
Not Hispanic (744)	760	9.41
Hispanic (19)	26	0.32
American Indian/Alaska Native (18)	28	0.35
Not Hispanic (7)	17	0.21
Hispanic (11)	11	0.14
Cherokee (0)	5	0.06
Choctaw (0)	2	0.02
Iroquois (1)	1	0.01
Sioux (1)	1	0.01
South American Ind. (5)	5	0.06
Asian (880)	948	11.73
Not Hispanic (877)	941	11.65
Hispanic (3)	7	0.09
Bangladeshi (7)	7	0.09
Cambodian (0)	1	0.01
Chinese, ex. Taiwanese (367)	392	4.85
Filipino (37)	58	0.72
Indian (119)	132	1.63
Indonesian (1)	1	0.01
Japanese (20)	29	0.36
Korean (254)	260	3.22
Laotian (3)	3	0.04
Malaysian (5)	5	0.06
Nepalese (5)	5	0.06
Pakistani (11)	14	0.17
Taiwanese (24)	30	0.37
Thai (2)	6	0.07
Vietnamese (4)	5	0.06
Hawaii Native/Pacific Islander (0)	5	0.06
Not Hispanic (0)	4	0.05
Hispanic (0)	1	0.01
White (6,136)	6,238	77.20
Not Hispanic (5,629)	5,695	70.48
Hispanic (507)	543	6.72

Manhattan

Place Type: Borough
County: New York
Population: 1,585,873†

Ancestry‡	Population	%
Afghan (59)	85	0.01
African, Sub-Saharan (19,667)	24,146	1.52
African (10,054)	12,839	0.81
Cape Verdean (81)	206	0.01
Ethiopian (932)	1,043	0.07
Ghanaian (714)	818	0.05
Kenyan (43)	69	<0.01
Liberian (169)	176	0.01
Nigerian (1,650)	1,953	0.12
Senegalese (1,118)	1,216	0.08
Sierra Leonean (422)	422	0.03
Somalian (125)	125	0.01
South African (991)	1,372	0.09
Sudanese (137)	137	0.01
Ugandan (95)	125	0.01
Zimbabwean (80)	100	0.01
Other Sub-Saharan African (3,056)	3,545	0.22
Albanian (1,385)	1,618	0.10
Alsatian (5)	129	0.01
American (54,694)	54,694	3.45
Arab (8,584)	13,828	0.87
Arab (1,250)	1,720	0.11
Egyptian (1,374)	1,906	0.12
Iraqi (275)	583	0.04
Jordanian (0)	48	<0.01
Lebanese (1,838)	3,331	0.21
Moroccan (914)	1,592	0.10
Palestinian (626)	794	0.05
Syrian (518)	1,112	0.07
Other Arab (1,789)	2,742	0.17
Armenian (1,520)	2,653	0.17
Assyrian/Chaldean/Syriac (94)	137	0.01
Australian (1,965)	2,719	0.17
Austrian (4,202)	14,656	0.93
Basque (191)	428	0.03
Belgian (928)	2,470	0.16
Brazilian (2,870)	4,541	0.29
British (6,950)	12,129	0.77
Bulgarian (927)	1,272	0.08
Cajun (22)	224	0.01
Canadian (3,037)	5,646	0.36
Carpatho Rusyn (89)	112	0.01
Celtic (129)	304	0.02
Croatian (1,299)	2,164	0.14
Cypriot (139)	216	0.01
Czech (1,439)	4,820	0.30
Czechoslovakian (619)	1,256	0.08
Danish (1,444)	4,095	0.26
Dutch (2,847)	10,414	0.66
Eastern European (23,269)	25,277	1.60
English (22,270)	77,799	4.91
Estonian (190)	424	0.03
European (25,127)	27,846	1.76
Finnish (666)	1,658	0.10
French, ex. Basque (10,278)	31,783	2.01
French Canadian (1,692)	5,246	0.33
German (27,493)	107,666	6.80
German Russian (0)	41	<0.01
Greek (7,557)	13,078	0.83
Guyanese (1,802)	2,259	0.14
Hungarian (4,686)	14,667	0.93
Icelander (246)	382	0.02
Iranian (3,458)	4,256	0.27
Irish (40,008)	117,355	7.41
Israeli (4,839)	6,624	0.42
Italian (44,498)	98,563	6.22
Latvian (713)	1,822	0.12
Lithuanian (1,597)	5,775	0.36
Luxemburger (23)	68	<0.01
Macedonian (973)	1,086	0.07
Maltese (548)	840	0.05
New Zealander (243)	405	0.03
Northern European (1,296)	1,485	0.09
Norwegian (1,552)	7,445	0.47
Pennsylvania German (123)	327	0.02
Polish (20,565)	64,078	4.05
Portuguese (1,436)	3,862	0.24
Romanian (3,035)	7,692	0.49
Russian (36,296)	82,983	5.24
Scandinavian (753)	1,731	0.11
Scotch-Irish (4,283)	13,158	0.83
Scottish (4,846)	19,553	1.23
Serbian (1,160)	1,526	0.10
Slavic (177)	400	0.03
Slovak (812)	2,298	0.15
Slovene (271)	695	0.04
Soviet Union (28)	54	<0.01
Swedish (3,045)	10,408	0.66
Swiss (1,381)	4,962	0.31
Turkish (2,708)	3,703	0.23
Ukrainian (4,361)	8,849	0.56
Welsh (944)	6,000	0.38
West Indian, ex. Hispanic (22,411)	30,009	1.90
Bahamian (303)	457	0.03
Barbadian (738)	907	0.06
Belizean (654)	735	0.05
Bermudan (86)	127	0.01
British West Indian (1,308)	1,658	0.10
Dutch West Indian (212)	276	0.02
Haitian (5,308)	6,500	0.41
Jamaican (7,099)	9,242	0.58
Trinidadian/Tobagonian (3,010)	3,877	0.24
U.S. Virgin Islander (343)	487	0.03
West Indian (3,296)	5,618	0.35
Other West Indian (54)	125	0.01
Yugoslavian (1,478)	1,876	0.12

Hispanic Origin	Population	%
Hispanic or Latino (of any race)	403,577	25.45
Central American, ex. Mexican	13,948	0.88
Costa Rican	987	0.06
Guatemalan	2,051	0.13
Honduran	4,058	0.26
Nicaraguan	1,556	0.10
Panamanian	1,716	0.11
Salvadoran	3,419	0.22
Other Central American	161	0.01
Cuban	11,623	0.73
Dominican Republic	155,971	9.84
Mexican	41,965	2.65
Puerto Rican	107,774	6.80
South American	36,748	2.32
Argentinean	4,339	0.27
Bolivian	522	0.03
Chilean	1,824	0.12
Colombian	8,411	0.53
Ecuadorian	14,132	0.89
Paraguayan	268	0.02
Peruvian	3,852	0.24
Uruguayan	549	0.03
Venezuelan	2,573	0.16
Other South American	278	0.02
Other Hispanic or Latino	35,548	2.24

Race*	Population	%
African-American/Black (246,687)	272,993	17.21
Not Hispanic (205,340)	217,102	13.69
Hispanic (41,347)	55,891	3.52
American Indian/Alaska Native (8,669)	19,415	1.22
Not Hispanic (2,144)	7,395	0.47
Hispanic (6,525)	12,020	0.76
Alaska Athabascan *(Ala. Nat.)* (11)	18	<0.01
Aleut *(Alaska Native)* (4)	7	<0.01
Apache (28)	92	0.01
Arapaho (3)	5	<0.01
Blackfeet (41)	356	0.02
Canadian/French Am. Ind. (29)	62	<0.01
Central American Ind. (610)	1,090	0.07
Cherokee (288)	1,845	0.12
Cheyenne (4)	9	<0.01
Chickasaw (15)	43	<0.01
Chippewa (36)	99	0.01

*Notes: † The Census 2010 population figure is used to calculate the percentages in the Hispanic Origin and Race categories. Ancestry percentages are based on the 2006-2010 American Community Survey population (not shown); ‡ Numbers in parentheses indicate the number of people reporting a single ancestry; * Numbers in parentheses indicate the number of persons reporting this race alone, not in combination with any other race; Please refer to the Explanation of Data for more information.*

Choctaw (41)	179	0.01
Colville (4)	5	<0.01
Comanche (13)	22	<0.01
Cree (4)	22	<0.01
Creek (12)	61	<0.01
Crow (4)	11	<0.01
Delaware (14)	54	<0.01
Hopi (8)	15	<0.01
Houma (0)	3	<0.01
Inupiat *(Alaska Native)* (2)	8	<0.01
Iroquois (97)	265	0.02
Kiowa (9)	11	<0.01
Lumbee (10)	21	<0.01
Menominee (2)	3	<0.01
Mexican American Ind. (479)	752	0.05
Navajo (38)	83	0.01
Osage (7)	12	<0.01
Ottawa (0)	3	<0.01
Paiute (2)	8	<0.01
Pima (2)	4	<0.01
Potawatomi (10)	20	<0.01
Pueblo (70)	175	0.01
Puget Sound Salish (2)	5	<0.01
Seminole (6)	110	0.01
Shoshone (3)	6	<0.01
Sioux (38)	133	0.01
South American Ind. (813)	1,935	0.12
Spanish American Ind. (373)	514	0.03
Tlingit-Haida *(Alaska Native)* (2)	15	<0.01
Tohono O'Odham (11)	15	<0.01
Tsimshian *(Alaska Native)* (3)	3	<0.01
Ute (1)	2	<0.01
Yakama (1)	2	<0.01
Yaqui (8)	22	<0.01
Yuman (4)	6	<0.01
Yup'ik *(Alaska Native)* (0)	2	<0.01
Asian (179,552)	199,722	12.59
Not Hispanic (177,624)	194,929	12.29
Hispanic (1,928)	4,793	0.30
Bangladeshi (1,672)	2,029	0.13
Bhutanese (26)	26	<0.01
Burmese (240)	317	0.02
Cambodian (168)	220	0.01
Chinese, ex. Taiwanese (92,088)	99,287	6.26
Filipino (10,399)	13,388	0.84
Hmong (16)	20	<0.01
Indian (25,857)	29,979	1.89
Indonesian (470)	693	0.04
Japanese (13,201)	16,600	1.05
Korean (19,683)	21,996	1.39
Laotian (109)	157	0.01
Malaysian (524)	766	0.05
Nepalese (240)	281	0.02
Pakistani (2,482)	2,940	0.19
Sri Lankan (450)	563	0.04
Taiwanese (2,789)	3,318	0.21
Thai (1,282)	1,657	0.10
Vietnamese (2,194)	2,919	0.18
Hawaii Native/Pacific Islander (873)	3,727	0.24
Not Hispanic (533)	1,776	0.11
Hispanic (340)	1,951	0.12
Fijian (29)	73	<0.01
Guamanian/Chamorro (132)	242	0.02
Marshallese (3)	4	<0.01
Native Hawaiian (185)	608	0.04
Samoan (87)	183	0.01
Tongan (18)	33	<0.01
White (911,073)	956,864	60.34
Not Hispanic (761,493)	785,299	49.52
Hispanic (149,580)	171,565	10.82

Manlius

Place Type: Town
County: Onondaga
Population: 32,370†

Ancestry‡	Population	%
African, Sub-Saharan (114)	114	0.35
African (12)	12	0.04
Ethiopian (12)	12	0.04
Nigerian (90)	90	0.28
Albanian (33)	33	0.10
American (1,417)	1,417	4.40
Arab (121)	280	0.87
Arab (9)	37	0.12
Lebanese (56)	163	0.51
Palestinian (20)	20	0.06
Syrian (13)	37	0.12
Other Arab (23)	23	0.07
Armenian (34)	50	0.16
Australian (0)	34	0.11
Austrian (35)	239	0.74
Belgian (0)	28	0.09
British (100)	178	0.55
Canadian (179)	231	0.72
Croatian (0)	8	0.02
Czech (34)	100	0.31
Czechoslovakian (20)	20	0.06
Danish (28)	44	0.14
Dutch (171)	805	2.50
Eastern European (146)	146	0.45
English (1,115)	4,911	15.27
Estonian (0)	7	0.02
European (209)	209	0.65
Finnish (14)	64	0.20
French, ex. Basque (452)	1,909	5.93
French Canadian (158)	719	2.23
German (1,267)	7,808	24.27
Greek (61)	179	0.56
Guyanese (18)	18	0.06
Hungarian (15)	119	0.37
Iranian (57)	57	0.18
Irish (2,625)	9,003	27.98
Israeli (0)	26	0.08
Italian (2,164)	5,084	15.80
Latvian (0)	14	0.04
Lithuanian (84)	156	0.48
Northern European (34)	44	0.14
Norwegian (65)	163	0.51
Pennsylvania German (0)	8	0.02
Polish (813)	2,677	8.32
Portuguese (0)	12	0.04
Romanian (0)	33	0.10
Russian (288)	910	2.83
Scandinavian (25)	61	0.19
Scotch-Irish (267)	770	2.39
Scottish (161)	701	2.18
Slavic (0)	8	0.02
Slovak (29)	112	0.35
Slovene (0)	26	0.08
Swedish (58)	397	1.23
Swiss (88)	178	0.55
Turkish (10)	10	0.03
Ukrainian (186)	409	1.27
Welsh (87)	614	1.91
West Indian, ex. Hispanic (7)	17	0.05
Jamaican (7)	7	0.02
West Indian (0)	10	0.03
Yugoslavian (12)	52	0.16

Hispanic Origin	Population	%
Hispanic or Latino (of any race)	484	1.50
Central American, ex. Mexican	35	0.11
Costa Rican	9	0.03
Guatemalan	14	0.04
Honduran	7	0.02
Panamanian	5	0.02
Cuban	39	0.12
Dominican Republic	16	0.05
Mexican	119	0.37
Puerto Rican	150	0.46
South American	68	0.21
Argentinean	12	0.04
Bolivian	4	0.01
Chilean	9	0.03
Colombian	26	0.08
Ecuadorian	5	0.02
Paraguayan	4	0.01
Peruvian	3	0.01
Venezuelan	4	0.01
Other South American	1	<0.01
Other Hispanic or Latino	57	0.18

Race*	Population	%
African-American/Black (468)	632	1.95
Not Hispanic (448)	590	1.82
Hispanic (20)	42	0.13
American Indian/Alaska Native (95)	198	0.61
Not Hispanic (84)	178	0.55
Hispanic (11)	20	0.06
Blackfeet (0)	4	0.01
Canadian/French Am. Ind. (4)	4	0.01
Cherokee (1)	9	0.03
Chippewa (1)	2	0.01
Iroquois (56)	106	0.33
Mexican American Ind. (0)	1	<0.01
Osage (0)	4	0.01
Seminole (0)	1	<0.01
Shoshone (1)	1	<0.01
Sioux (5)	5	0.02
South American Ind. (0)	1	<0.01
Asian (1,193)	1,377	4.25
Not Hispanic (1,190)	1,362	4.21
Hispanic (3)	15	0.05
Bangladeshi (3)	3	0.01
Burmese (6)	6	0.02
Cambodian (11)	12	0.04
Chinese, ex. Taiwanese (337)	383	1.18
Filipino (83)	102	0.32
Hmong (1)	1	<0.01
Indian (297)	328	1.01
Indonesian (2)	6	0.02
Japanese (14)	26	0.08
Korean (235)	274	0.85
Laotian (6)	9	0.03
Nepalese (1)	1	<0.01
Pakistani (73)	82	0.25
Sri Lankan (12)	14	0.04
Taiwanese (15)	19	0.06
Thai (11)	16	0.05
Vietnamese (29)	35	0.11
Hawaii Native/Pacific Islander (4)	26	0.08
Not Hispanic (4)	26	0.08
Native Hawaiian (2)	10	0.03
Samoan (0)	3	0.01
White (30,070)	30,485	94.18
Not Hispanic (29,738)	30,098	92.98
Hispanic (332)	387	1.20

Manorville

Place Type: CDP
County: Suffolk
Population: 14,314†

Ancestry‡	Population	%
Albanian (0)	39	0.29
American (352)	352	2.60
Austrian (19)	127	0.94
Brazilian (0)	14	0.10
British (16)	16	0.12
Canadian (26)	26	0.19
Croatian (17)	17	0.13
Czech (0)	40	0.30
Czechoslovakian (10)	31	0.23
Danish (15)	88	0.65
Dutch (0)	276	2.04
English (99)	864	6.39
European (92)	92	0.68
French, ex. Basque (0)	246	1.82
French Canadian (0)	39	0.29
German (465)	2,921	21.61
Greek (105)	258	1.91
Hungarian (18)	85	0.63
Irish (2,068)	4,894	36.21
Italian (2,177)	4,731	35.01
Lithuanian (59)	122	0.90
Norwegian (77)	141	1.04
Pennsylvania German (0)	9	0.07

*Notes: † The Census 2010 population figure is used to calculate the percentages in the Hispanic Origin and Race categories. Ancestry percentages are based on the 2006-2010 American Community Survey population (not shown); ‡ Numbers in parentheses indicate the number of people reporting a single ancestry; * Numbers in parentheses indicate the number of persons reporting this race alone, not in combination with any other race; Please refer to the Explanation of Data for more information.*

Ancestry	Population	%
Polish (254)	830	6.14
Portuguese (52)	52	0.38
Romanian (30)	30	0.22
Russian (39)	341	2.52
Scandinavian (19)	152	1.12
Scotch-Irish (80)	160	1.18
Scottish (0)	106	0.78
Slovak (14)	21	0.16
Slovene (0)	39	0.29
Swedish (0)	135	1.00
Ukrainian (8)	35	0.26
Welsh (0)	34	0.25
West Indian, ex. Hispanic (52)	52	0.38
Haitian (52)	52	0.38
Yugoslavian (0)	26	0.19

Hispanic Origin	Population	%
Hispanic or Latino (of any race)	938	6.55
Central American, ex. Mexican	78	0.54
Costa Rican	9	0.06
Guatemalan	26	0.18
Honduran	6	0.04
Nicaraguan	5	0.03
Panamanian	5	0.03
Salvadoran	27	0.19
Cuban	37	0.26
Dominican Republic	36	0.25
Mexican	55	0.38
Puerto Rican	440	3.07
South American	203	1.42
Argentinean	19	0.13
Bolivian	2	0.01
Chilean	5	0.03
Colombian	66	0.46
Ecuadorian	73	0.51
Peruvian	32	0.22
Uruguayan	2	0.01
Venezuelan	2	0.01
Other South American	2	0.01
Other Hispanic or Latino	89	0.62

Race*	Population	%
African-American/Black (229)	311	2.17
Not Hispanic (222)	286	2.00
Hispanic (7)	25	0.17
American Indian/Alaska Native (25)	59	0.41
Not Hispanic (20)	53	0.37
Hispanic (5)	6	0.04
Blackfeet (2)	2	0.01
Central American Ind. (3)	3	0.02
Cherokee (0)	3	0.02
Cheyenne (0)	1	0.01
Iroquois (7)	9	0.06
Paiute (2)	2	0.01
Seminole (0)	3	0.02
Asian (250)	293	2.05
Not Hispanic (249)	290	2.03
Hispanic (1)	3	0.02
Bangladeshi (0)	1	0.01
Chinese, ex. Taiwanese (42)	50	0.35
Filipino (29)	43	0.30
Indian (58)	71	0.50
Indonesian (2)	8	0.06
Japanese (4)	8	0.06
Korean (34)	35	0.24
Pakistani (47)	49	0.34
Taiwanese (2)	2	0.01
Thai (1)	2	0.01
Vietnamese (4)	7	0.05
Hawaii Native/Pacific Islander (6)	11	0.08
Not Hispanic (2)	7	0.05
Hispanic (4)	4	0.03
Guamanian/Chamorro (2)	2	0.01
White (13,439)	13,597	94.99
Not Hispanic (12,743)	12,845	89.74
Hispanic (696)	752	5.25

Marcy

Place Type: Town
County: Oneida
Population: 8,982†

Ancestry‡	Population	%
African, Sub-Saharan (93)	151	1.66
African (93)	118	1.30
Ethiopian (0)	33	0.36
American (337)	337	3.71
Arab (67)	135	1.49
Lebanese (67)	128	1.41
Syrian (0)	7	0.08
Armenian (13)	20	0.22
Belgian (0)	18	0.20
Canadian (13)	13	0.14
Czechoslovakian (0)	17	0.19
Dutch (20)	86	0.95
English (176)	639	7.04
European (27)	27	0.30
French, ex. Basque (15)	271	2.99
French Canadian (39)	126	1.39
German (275)	1,364	15.03
Greek (50)	50	0.55
Hungarian (0)	76	0.84
Irish (329)	1,494	16.46
Italian (889)	1,701	18.75
Lithuanian (14)	98	1.08
Norwegian (10)	10	0.11
Pennsylvania German (0)	8	0.09
Polish (409)	1,082	11.92
Portuguese (0)	17	0.19
Romanian (0)	9	0.10
Russian (0)	40	0.44
Scotch-Irish (17)	44	0.48
Scottish (0)	111	1.22
Slavic (0)	9	0.10
Slovak (23)	44	0.48
Swedish (0)	44	0.48
Swiss (5)	14	0.15
Ukrainian (0)	139	1.53
Welsh (59)	196	2.16
West Indian, ex. Hispanic (214)	298	3.28
Barbadian (0)	4	0.04
Belizean (0)	10	0.11
British West Indian (9)	9	0.10
Haitian (32)	41	0.45
Jamaican (119)	149	1.64
Trinidadian/Tobagonian (21)	21	0.23
U.S. Virgin Islander (9)	9	0.10
West Indian (24)	55	0.61

Hispanic Origin	Population	%
Hispanic or Latino (of any race)	649	7.23
Central American, ex. Mexican	40	0.45
Costa Rican	1	0.01
Guatemalan	9	0.10
Honduran	10	0.11
Nicaraguan	1	0.01
Panamanian	10	0.11
Salvadoran	9	0.10
Cuban	30	0.33
Dominican Republic	95	1.06
Mexican	37	0.41
Puerto Rican	377	4.20
South American	41	0.46
Argentinean	1	0.01
Bolivian	1	0.01
Chilean	1	0.01
Colombian	15	0.17
Ecuadorian	13	0.14
Peruvian	6	0.07
Uruguayan	1	0.01
Venezuelan	3	0.03
Other Hispanic or Latino	29	0.32

Race*	Population	%
African-American/Black (1,572)	1,606	17.88
Not Hispanic (1,447)	1,480	16.48
Hispanic (125)	126	1.40
American Indian/Alaska Native (34)	77	0.86
Not Hispanic (29)	71	0.79
Hispanic (5)	6	0.07
Blackfeet (0)	1	0.01
Canadian/French Am. Ind. (0)	1	0.01
Cherokee (0)	9	0.10
Choctaw (0)	1	0.01
Iroquois (4)	20	0.22
Asian (52)	72	0.80
Not Hispanic (52)	65	0.72
Hispanic (0)	7	0.08
Bangladeshi (1)	1	0.01
Cambodian (1)	3	0.03
Chinese, ex. Taiwanese (13)	14	0.16
Filipino (4)	6	0.07
Indian (11)	11	0.12
Japanese (2)	4	0.04
Korean (6)	7	0.08
Laotian (1)	1	0.01
Thai (1)	1	0.01
Vietnamese (2)	7	0.08
Hawaii Native/Pacific Islander (0)	2	0.02
Not Hispanic (0)	2	0.02
White (7,059)	7,142	79.51
Not Hispanic (6,706)	6,779	75.47
Hispanic (353)	363	4.04

Marlborough

Place Type: Town
County: Ulster
Population: 8,808†

Ancestry‡	Population	%
African, Sub-Saharan (41)	41	0.47
African (41)	41	0.47
Albanian (180)	180	2.06
American (969)	969	11.07
Arab (50)	50	0.57
Egyptian (50)	50	0.57
Armenian (27)	38	0.43
Australian (0)	63	0.72
Brazilian (8)	42	0.48
British (65)	65	0.74
Canadian (26)	48	0.55
Celtic (0)	14	0.16
Czech (0)	43	0.49
Danish (7)	7	0.08
Dutch (26)	237	2.71
Eastern European (32)	32	0.37
English (241)	935	10.68
European (22)	22	0.25
French, ex. Basque (22)	301	3.44
French Canadian (55)	72	0.82
German (157)	1,246	14.24
Greek (54)	99	1.13
Hungarian (0)	51	0.58
Irish (297)	1,818	20.77
Italian (1,434)	2,718	31.06
Maltese (0)	12	0.14
Northern European (32)	32	0.37
Norwegian (0)	72	0.82
Pennsylvania German (20)	40	0.46
Polish (151)	627	7.16
Portuguese (0)	37	0.42
Russian (11)	157	1.79
Scotch-Irish (47)	186	2.13
Scottish (0)	95	1.09
Slavic (26)	42	0.48
Slovak (25)	60	0.69
Swedish (75)	188	2.15
Swiss (0)	9	0.10
Ukrainian (7)	61	0.70
Welsh (0)	26	0.30
West Indian, ex. Hispanic (44)	44	0.50
Trinidadian/Tobagonian (44)	44	0.50
Yugoslavian (26)	54	0.62

SECTION TWO

*Notes: † The Census 2010 population figure is used to calculate the percentages in the Hispanic Origin and Race categories. Ancestry percentages are based on the 2006-2010 American Community Survey population (not shown); ‡ Numbers in parentheses indicate the number of people reporting a single ancestry; * Numbers in parentheses indicate the number of persons reporting this race alone, not in combination with any other race; Please refer to the Explanation of Data for more information.*

Hispanic Origin	Population	%
Hispanic or Latino (of any race)	769	8.73
Central American, ex. Mexican	51	0.58
Costa Rican	4	0.05
Guatemalan	20	0.23
Honduran	15	0.17
Nicaraguan	1	0.01
Panamanian	1	0.01
Salvadoran	10	0.11
Cuban	25	0.28
Dominican Republic	10	0.11
Mexican	170	1.93
Puerto Rican	361	4.10
South American	73	0.83
Argentinean	10	0.11
Chilean	4	0.05
Colombian	29	0.33
Ecuadorian	21	0.24
Peruvian	6	0.07
Uruguayan	2	0.02
Venezuelan	1	0.01
Other Hispanic or Latino	79	0.90

Race*	Population	%
African-American/Black (363)	446	5.06
Not Hispanic (334)	389	4.42
Hispanic (29)	57	0.65
American Indian/Alaska Native (18)	73	0.83
Not Hispanic (17)	55	0.62
Hispanic (1)	18	0.20
Apache (0)	1	0.01
Arapaho (0)	1	0.01
Blackfeet (0)	3	0.03
Canadian/French Am. Ind. (0)	1	0.01
Cherokee (7)	16	0.18
Creek (5)	6	0.07
Iroquois (0)	2	0.02
Sioux (2)	3	0.03
South American Ind. (0)	5	0.06
Asian (78)	112	1.27
Not Hispanic (77)	106	1.20
Hispanic (1)	6	0.07
Bangladeshi (1)	3	0.03
Chinese, ex. Taiwanese (10)	24	0.27
Filipino (19)	28	0.32
Indian (18)	26	0.30
Japanese (6)	7	0.08
Korean (6)	13	0.15
Malaysian (0)	1	0.01
Pakistani (6)	6	0.07
Thai (1)	1	0.01
Vietnamese (5)	7	0.08
Hawaii Native/Pacific Islander (0)	7	0.08
Not Hispanic (0)	7	0.08
Samoan (0)	4	0.05
White (7,900)	8,063	91.54
Not Hispanic (7,475)	7,586	86.13
Hispanic (425)	477	5.42

Massapequa

Place Type: CDP
County: Nassau
Population: 21,685†

Ancestry‡	Population	%
American (595)	595	2.61
Armenian (22)	46	0.20
Austrian (65)	296	1.30
Belgian (17)	29	0.13
Brazilian (39)	39	0.17
Canadian (0)	94	0.41
Croatian (28)	56	0.25
Czech (8)	66	0.29
Czechoslovakian (21)	116	0.51
Danish (45)	126	0.55
Dutch (53)	122	0.54
English (140)	1,184	5.20
European (356)	356	1.56
Finnish (14)	37	0.16
French, ex. Basque (11)	247	1.09
French Canadian (46)	110	0.48
German (997)	5,081	22.33
Greek (128)	379	1.67
Hungarian (39)	262	1.15
Irish (2,014)	6,888	30.26
Israeli (0)	8	0.04
Italian (5,270)	9,908	43.53
Latvian (0)	41	0.18
Lithuanian (91)	146	0.64
Maltese (8)	23	0.10
Norwegian (9)	95	0.42
Polish (232)	1,195	5.25
Portuguese (0)	27	0.12
Romanian (6)	34	0.15
Russian (212)	654	2.87
Scotch-Irish (78)	150	0.66
Scottish (41)	65	0.29
Slovak (27)	57	0.25
Swedish (13)	285	1.25
Swiss (0)	46	0.20
Turkish (80)	164	0.72
Ukrainian (19)	145	0.64
Welsh (15)	51	0.22
West Indian, ex. Hispanic (16)	41	0.18
Jamaican (8)	8	0.04
West Indian (8)	18	0.08
Other West Indian (0)	15	0.07
Yugoslavian (10)	30	0.13

Hispanic Origin	Population	%
Hispanic or Latino (of any race)	900	4.15
Central American, ex. Mexican	69	0.32
Costa Rican	7	0.03
Guatemalan	19	0.09
Honduran	2	0.01
Panamanian	8	0.04
Salvadoran	29	0.13
Other Central American	4	0.02
Cuban	60	0.28
Dominican Republic	44	0.20
Mexican	58	0.27
Puerto Rican	334	1.54
South American	198	0.91
Argentinean	20	0.09
Bolivian	3	0.01
Chilean	19	0.09
Colombian	61	0.28
Ecuadorian	43	0.20
Paraguayan	4	0.02
Peruvian	27	0.12
Uruguayan	12	0.06
Venezuelan	9	0.04
Other Hispanic or Latino	137	0.63

Race*	Population	%
African-American/Black (79)	109	0.50
Not Hispanic (70)	90	0.42
Hispanic (9)	19	0.09
American Indian/Alaska Native (11)	52	0.24
Not Hispanic (9)	46	0.21
Hispanic (2)	6	0.03
Canadian/French Am. Ind. (1)	1	<0.01
Cherokee (0)	7	0.03
Chippewa (0)	1	<0.01
Creek (0)	1	<0.01
Iroquois (0)	7	0.03
Mexican American Ind. (1)	1	<0.01
Shoshone (1)	1	<0.01
Asian (350)	437	2.02
Not Hispanic (350)	434	2.00
Hispanic (0)	3	0.01
Bangladeshi (5)	6	0.03
Burmese (8)	8	0.04
Chinese, ex. Taiwanese (157)	179	0.83
Filipino (42)	61	0.28
Indian (62)	78	0.36
Indonesian (1)	1	<0.01
Japanese (10)	21	0.10
Korean (36)	45	0.21
Pakistani (3)	4	0.02
Sri Lankan (1)	1	<0.01
Taiwanese (11)	11	0.05
Thai (7)	9	0.04
Vietnamese (3)	3	0.01
Hawaii Native/Pacific Islander (2)	7	0.03
Not Hispanic (0)	1	<0.01
Hispanic (2)	6	0.03
Guamanian/Chamorro (1)	3	0.01
Samoan (1)	1	<0.01
White (20,941)	21,133	97.45
Not Hispanic (20,198)	20,330	93.75
Hispanic (743)	803	3.70

Massapequa Park

Place Type: Village
County: Nassau
Population: 17,008†

Ancestry‡	Population	%
African, Sub-Saharan (12)	12	0.07
South African (12)	12	0.07
American (330)	330	1.95
Arab (35)	47	0.28
Lebanese (24)	24	0.14
Syrian (11)	23	0.14
Austrian (42)	290	1.71
Belgian (0)	12	0.07
Brazilian (0)	14	0.08
British (11)	44	0.26
Canadian (10)	22	0.13
Croatian (0)	25	0.15
Czech (0)	53	0.31
Czechoslovakian (0)	79	0.47
Danish (0)	33	0.19
Dutch (37)	114	0.67
Eastern European (106)	106	0.62
English (75)	847	4.99
Estonian (6)	27	0.16
European (98)	98	0.58
Finnish (10)	47	0.28
French, ex. Basque (25)	346	2.04
French Canadian (0)	57	0.34
German (528)	2,947	17.37
Greek (120)	178	1.05
Hungarian (20)	71	0.42
Iranian (26)	26	0.15
Irish (1,639)	5,535	32.63
Italian (3,628)	7,117	41.95
Latvian (32)	32	0.19
Maltese (0)	68	0.40
Norwegian (33)	141	0.83
Polish (231)	998	5.88
Romanian (23)	33	0.19
Russian (213)	564	3.32
Scandinavian (0)	10	0.06
Scotch-Irish (21)	250	1.47
Scottish (39)	222	1.31
Slavic (0)	15	0.09
Slovak (40)	47	0.28
Swedish (17)	276	1.63
Swiss (0)	45	0.27
Turkish (0)	12	0.07
Ukrainian (109)	142	0.84
Welsh (0)	26	0.15
Yugoslavian (0)	28	0.17

Hispanic Origin	Population	%
Hispanic or Latino (of any race)	757	4.45
Central American, ex. Mexican	22	0.13
Guatemalan	7	0.04
Honduran	2	0.01
Nicaraguan	5	0.03
Salvadoran	8	0.05
Cuban	60	0.35
Dominican Republic	66	0.39
Mexican	50	0.29
Puerto Rican	271	1.59
South American	199	1.17

*Notes: † The Census 2010 population figure is used to calculate the percentages in the Hispanic Origin and Race categories. Ancestry percentages are based on the 2006-2010 American Community Survey population (not shown); ‡ Numbers in parentheses indicate the number of people reporting a single ancestry; * Numbers in parentheses indicate the number of persons reporting this race alone, not in combination with any other race; Please refer to the Explanation of Data for more information.*

Argentinean	31	0.18
Bolivian	7	0.04
Chilean	20	0.12
Colombian	53	0.31
Ecuadorian	52	0.31
Paraguayan	5	0.03
Peruvian	23	0.14
Uruguayan	7	0.04
Venezuelan	1	0.01
Other Hispanic or Latino	89	0.52

Race*	Population	%
African-American/Black (56)	76	0.45
Not Hispanic (52)	68	0.40
Hispanic (4)	8	0.05
American Indian/Alaska Native (7)	28	0.16
Not Hispanic (1)	14	0.08
Hispanic (6)	14	0.08
Central American Ind. (0)	1	0.01
Cherokee (0)	7	0.04
Choctaw (0)	2	0.01
Iroquois (0)	1	0.01
Mexican American Ind. (2)	2	0.01
South American Ind. (1)	1	0.01
Asian (256)	306	1.80
Not Hispanic (255)	299	1.76
Hispanic (1)	7	0.04
Cambodian (1)	1	0.01
Chinese, ex. Taiwanese (130)	145	0.85
Filipino (19)	26	0.15
Indian (58)	69	0.41
Japanese (4)	10	0.06
Korean (30)	34	0.20
Pakistani (1)	1	0.01
Taiwanese (2)	2	0.01
Thai (4)	5	0.03
Vietnamese (3)	4	0.02
Hawaii Native/Pacific Islander (1)	8	0.05
Not Hispanic (1)	7	0.04
Hispanic (0)	1	0.01
Native Hawaiian (0)	5	0.03
Samoan (0)	1	0.01
White (16,484)	16,584	97.51
Not Hispanic (15,858)	15,929	93.66
Hispanic (626)	655	3.85

Massena

Place Type: Town
County: St. Lawrence
Population: 12,883†

Ancestry‡	Population	%
African, Sub-Saharan (0)	7	0.05
African (0)	7	0.05
American (1,307)	1,307	10.15
Arab (0)	48	0.37
Arab (0)	19	0.15
Other Arab (0)	29	0.23
Armenian (9)	18	0.14
British (0)	17	0.13
Bulgarian (42)	42	0.33
Canadian (70)	198	1.54
Croatian (10)	10	0.08
Czech (0)	20	0.16
Danish (11)	11	0.09
Dutch (22)	180	1.40
English (492)	1,469	11.40
European (118)	122	0.95
Finnish (0)	24	0.19
French, ex. Basque (1,264)	3,068	23.82
French Canadian (557)	945	7.34
German (318)	1,384	10.74
Hungarian (175)	299	2.32
Irish (745)	2,511	19.49
Israeli (22)	22	0.17
Italian (303)	1,057	8.21
Norwegian (0)	65	0.50
Pennsylvania German (21)	40	0.31
Polish (124)	374	2.90
Portuguese (0)	25	0.19
Russian (119)	150	1.16
Scotch-Irish (89)	139	1.08
Scottish (34)	476	3.70
Swedish (0)	92	0.71
Turkish (10)	10	0.08
Ukrainian (43)	84	0.65
Welsh (14)	39	0.30
West Indian, ex. Hispanic (25)	42	0.33
Barbadian (3)	3	0.02
Jamaican (22)	39	0.30
Yugoslavian (0)	11	0.09

Hispanic Origin	Population	%
Hispanic or Latino (of any race)	229	1.78
Central American, ex. Mexican	9	0.07
Guatemalan	1	0.01
Honduran	1	0.01
Nicaraguan	1	0.01
Panamanian	5	0.04
Salvadoran	1	0.01
Cuban	9	0.07
Dominican Republic	8	0.06
Mexican	55	0.43
Puerto Rican	99	0.77
South American	13	0.10
Colombian	2	0.02
Ecuadorian	9	0.07
Peruvian	2	0.02
Other Hispanic or Latino	36	0.28

Race*	Population	%
African-American/Black (77)	142	1.10
Not Hispanic (71)	132	1.02
Hispanic (6)	10	0.08
American Indian/Alaska Native (526)	664	5.15
Not Hispanic (498)	629	4.88
Hispanic (28)	35	0.27
Canadian/French Am. Ind. (4)	11	0.09
Central American Ind. (2)	2	0.02
Cherokee (1)	3	0.02
Chippewa (1)	1	0.01
Choctaw (1)	2	0.02
Creek (1)	1	0.01
Delaware (7)	8	0.06
Hopi (1)	3	0.02
Iroquois (370)	442	3.43
Mexican American Ind. (1)	1	0.01
Ottawa (1)	1	0.01
South American Ind. (4)	7	0.05
Asian (108)	138	1.07
Not Hispanic (108)	138	1.07
Cambodian (4)	4	0.03
Chinese, ex. Taiwanese (18)	20	0.16
Filipino (12)	27	0.21
Indian (38)	42	0.33
Indonesian (1)	1	0.01
Japanese (3)	4	0.03
Korean (12)	13	0.10
Laotian (0)	1	0.01
Pakistani (7)	7	0.05
Thai (1)	1	0.01
Vietnamese (12)	16	0.12
Hawaii Native/Pacific Islander (5)	15	0.12
Not Hispanic (1)	5	0.04
Hispanic (4)	10	0.08
Native Hawaiian (4)	10	0.08
Samoan (0)	1	0.01
White (11,899)	12,106	93.97
Not Hispanic (11,759)	11,947	92.73
Hispanic (140)	159	1.23

Massena

Place Type: Village
County: St. Lawrence
Population: 10,936†

Ancestry‡	Population	%
African, Sub-Saharan (0)	7	0.06
African (0)	7	0.06
American (1,102)	1,102	9.78
Arab (0)	48	0.43
Arab (0)	19	0.17
Other Arab (0)	29	0.26
Armenian (9)	18	0.16
British (0)	17	0.15
Bulgarian (42)	42	0.37
Canadian (70)	198	1.76
Croatian (10)	10	0.09
Czech (0)	20	0.18
Danish (11)	11	0.10
Dutch (22)	135	1.20
English (461)	1,353	12.01
European (7)	11	0.10
Finnish (0)	24	0.21
French, ex. Basque (1,091)	2,657	23.58
French Canadian (493)	888	7.88
German (227)	1,196	10.61
Hungarian (152)	265	2.35
Irish (620)	2,259	20.05
Italian (256)	1,021	9.06
Norwegian (0)	65	0.58
Pennsylvania German (10)	29	0.26
Polish (102)	325	2.88
Portuguese (0)	25	0.22
Russian (110)	131	1.16
Scotch-Irish (101)	147	1.30
Scottish (20)	359	3.19
Swedish (0)	92	0.82
Turkish (10)	10	0.09
Ukrainian (43)	84	0.75
Welsh (14)	39	0.35
West Indian, ex. Hispanic (23)	40	0.35
Barbadian (3)	3	0.03
Jamaican (20)	37	0.33
Yugoslavian (0)	12	0.11

Hispanic Origin	Population	%
Hispanic or Latino (of any race)	210	1.92
Central American, ex. Mexican	10	0.09
Guatemalan	1	0.01
Honduran	1	0.01
Nicaraguan	1	0.01
Panamanian	6	0.05
Salvadoran	1	0.01
Cuban	9	0.08
Dominican Republic	7	0.06
Mexican	49	0.45
Puerto Rican	86	0.79
South American	13	0.12
Colombian	2	0.02
Ecuadorian	9	0.08
Peruvian	2	0.02
Other Hispanic or Latino	36	0.33

Race*	Population	%
African-American/Black (71)	132	1.21
Not Hispanic (65)	124	1.13
Hispanic (6)	8	0.07
American Indian/Alaska Native (312)	424	3.88
Not Hispanic (288)	397	3.63
Hispanic (24)	27	0.25
Canadian/French Am. Ind. (3)	7	0.06
Cherokee (1)	2	0.02
Chippewa (1)	1	0.01
Choctaw (0)	1	0.01
Creek (1)	1	0.01
Delaware (4)	4	0.04
Hopi (1)	3	0.03
Iroquois (203)	257	2.35
Mexican American Ind. (1)	1	0.01
South American Ind. (4)	7	0.06
Asian (108)	136	1.24
Not Hispanic (108)	136	1.24
Cambodian (4)	4	0.04
Chinese, ex. Taiwanese (18)	20	0.18
Filipino (9)	22	0.20
Indian (46)	50	0.46
Indonesian (1)	1	0.01

*Notes: † The Census 2010 population figure is used to calculate the percentages in the Hispanic Origin and Race categories. Ancestry percentages are based on the 2006-2010 American Community Survey population (not shown); ‡ Numbers in parentheses indicate the number of people reporting a single ancestry; * Numbers in parentheses indicate the number of persons reporting this race alone, not in combination with any other race; Please refer to the Explanation of Data for more information.*

Japanese (2)	3	0.03
Korean (14)	15	0.14
Laotian (0)	1	0.01
Pakistani (7)	7	0.06
Vietnamese (7)	11	0.10
Hawaii Native/Pacific Islander (0)	6	0.05
Not Hispanic (0)	3	0.03
Hispanic (0)	3	0.03
Native Hawaiian (0)	2	0.02
Samoan (0)	1	0.01
White (10,216)	10,396	95.06
Not Hispanic (10,077)	10,241	93.64
Hispanic (139)	155	1.42

Mastic Beach

Place Type: CDP
County: Suffolk
Population: 12,930†

Ancestry‡	Population	%
African, Sub-Saharan (71)	85	0.66
African (71)	85	0.66
American (473)	473	3.68
Armenian (28)	61	0.47
Austrian (25)	74	0.58
Canadian (0)	16	0.12
Czech (15)	73	0.57
Danish (9)	50	0.39
Dutch (12)	23	0.18
English (61)	969	7.53
European (14)	14	0.11
French, ex. Basque (9)	108	0.84
French Canadian (0)	29	0.23
German (660)	3,026	23.51
Greek (0)	40	0.31
Guyanese (39)	39	0.30
Hungarian (0)	151	1.17
Irish (1,154)	3,920	30.46
Italian (1,377)	3,556	27.63
Lithuanian (25)	54	0.42
Norwegian (78)	233	1.81
Polish (98)	692	5.38
Portuguese (0)	10	0.08
Romanian (12)	43	0.33
Russian (104)	238	1.85
Scotch-Irish (45)	111	0.86
Scottish (0)	108	0.84
Swedish (0)	85	0.66
Turkish (26)	49	0.38
Ukrainian (35)	119	0.92
West Indian, ex. Hispanic (34)	107	0.83
Barbadian (22)	22	0.17
Haitian (12)	12	0.09
Jamaican (0)	64	0.50
West Indian (0)	9	0.07

Hispanic Origin	Population	%
Hispanic or Latino (of any race)	2,019	15.61
Central American, ex. Mexican	298	2.30
Costa Rican	14	0.11
Guatemalan	66	0.51
Honduran	30	0.23
Nicaraguan	11	0.09
Panamanian	7	0.05
Salvadoran	158	1.22
Other Central American	12	0.09
Cuban	58	0.45
Dominican Republic	69	0.53
Mexican	103	0.80
Puerto Rican	1,088	8.41
South American	206	1.59
Argentinean	11	0.09
Bolivian	10	0.08
Chilean	15	0.12
Colombian	58	0.45
Ecuadorian	59	0.46
Paraguayan	2	0.02
Peruvian	37	0.29
Uruguayan	3	0.02
Venezuelan	11	0.09
Other Hispanic or Latino	197	1.52

Race*	Population	%
African-American/Black (1,234)	1,537	11.89
Not Hispanic (1,120)	1,325	10.25
Hispanic (114)	212	1.64
American Indian/Alaska Native (50)	169	1.31
Not Hispanic (29)	114	0.88
Hispanic (21)	55	0.43
Apache (0)	2	0.02
Blackfeet (0)	9	0.07
Central American Ind. (0)	6	0.05
Cherokee (7)	37	0.29
Chippewa (1)	1	0.01
Choctaw (0)	4	0.03
Cree (0)	1	0.01
Iroquois (1)	3	0.02
Mexican American Ind. (1)	1	0.01
Seminole (0)	1	0.01
Sioux (0)	7	0.05
South American Ind. (8)	13	0.10
Spanish American Ind. (0)	2	0.02
Asian (191)	262	2.03
Not Hispanic (186)	236	1.83
Hispanic (5)	26	0.20
Bangladeshi (7)	7	0.05
Chinese, ex. Taiwanese (29)	40	0.31
Filipino (33)	57	0.44
Indian (63)	70	0.54
Japanese (4)	14	0.11
Korean (8)	13	0.10
Pakistani (13)	15	0.12
Thai (2)	3	0.02
Vietnamese (28)	30	0.23
Hawaii Native/Pacific Islander (15)	28	0.22
Not Hispanic (5)	11	0.09
Hispanic (10)	17	0.13
Guamanian/Chamorro (4)	4	0.03
Native Hawaiian (0)	8	0.06
Samoan (1)	1	0.01
White (10,414)	10,818	83.67
Not Hispanic (9,251)	9,482	73.33
Hispanic (1,163)	1,336	10.33

Mastic

Place Type: CDP
County: Suffolk
Population: 15,481†

Ancestry‡	Population	%
African, Sub-Saharan (95)	113	0.78
African (87)	87	0.60
Nigerian (8)	8	0.06
South African (0)	18	0.12
American (224)	224	1.55
Austrian (0)	16	0.11
Czech (0)	14	0.10
Danish (0)	15	0.10
Dutch (0)	27	0.19
English (123)	443	3.06
Finnish (17)	17	0.12
French, ex. Basque (0)	140	0.97
French Canadian (63)	120	0.83
German (260)	3,141	21.68
German Russian (0)	40	0.28
Greek (25)	98	0.68
Guyanese (37)	69	0.48
Hungarian (0)	47	0.32
Irish (885)	3,464	23.91
Italian (2,866)	5,233	36.13
Maltese (0)	43	0.30
Norwegian (30)	59	0.41
Polish (166)	407	2.81
Russian (0)	37	0.26
Scotch-Irish (47)	314	2.17
Scottish (37)	148	1.02
Slovak (6)	6	0.04
Swedish (0)	33	0.23
Swiss (0)	15	0.10
Turkish (22)	61	0.42
Welsh (16)	58	0.40
West Indian, ex. Hispanic (277)	472	3.26
Haitian (21)	21	0.14
Jamaican (27)	49	0.34
Trinidadian/Tobagonian (134)	148	1.02
West Indian (95)	254	1.75

Hispanic Origin	Population	%
Hispanic or Latino (of any race)	3,378	21.82
Central American, ex. Mexican	772	4.99
Costa Rican	4	0.03
Guatemalan	139	0.90
Honduran	56	0.36
Nicaraguan	6	0.04
Panamanian	27	0.17
Salvadoran	527	3.40
Other Central American	13	0.08
Cuban	55	0.36
Dominican Republic	173	1.12
Mexican	209	1.35
Puerto Rican	1,363	8.80
South American	478	3.09
Argentinean	23	0.15
Bolivian	12	0.08
Chilean	17	0.11
Colombian	91	0.59
Ecuadorian	232	1.50
Paraguayan	4	0.03
Peruvian	58	0.37
Uruguayan	4	0.03
Venezuelan	24	0.16
Other South American	13	0.08
Other Hispanic or Latino	328	2.12

Race*	Population	%
African-American/Black (1,397)	1,780	11.50
Not Hispanic (1,247)	1,533	9.90
Hispanic (150)	247	1.60
American Indian/Alaska Native (104)	286	1.85
Not Hispanic (50)	191	1.23
Hispanic (54)	95	0.61
Aleut *(Alaska Native)* (1)	1	0.01
Blackfeet (0)	9	0.06
Canadian/French Am. Ind. (2)	2	0.01
Central American Ind. (6)	6	0.04
Cherokee (4)	43	0.28
Chippewa (1)	2	0.01
Choctaw (0)	2	0.01
Cree (1)	1	0.01
Delaware (2)	3	0.02
Iroquois (0)	8	0.05
Mexican American Ind. (1)	2	0.01
Seminole (1)	3	0.02
Sioux (1)	2	0.01
South American Ind. (3)	3	0.02
Spanish American Ind. (0)	2	0.01
Asian (332)	438	2.83
Not Hispanic (323)	404	2.61
Hispanic (9)	34	0.22
Bangladeshi (31)	32	0.21
Chinese, ex. Taiwanese (41)	56	0.36
Filipino (55)	80	0.52
Indian (86)	108	0.70
Indonesian (1)	1	0.01
Japanese (15)	35	0.23
Korean (22)	41	0.26
Malaysian (1)	2	0.01
Pakistani (39)	53	0.34
Sri Lankan (2)	2	0.01
Taiwanese (0)	6	0.04
Thai (1)	2	0.01
Vietnamese (12)	12	0.08
Hawaii Native/Pacific Islander (17)	27	0.17
Not Hispanic (9)	15	0.10
Hispanic (8)	12	0.08
Guamanian/Chamorro (15)	16	0.10
Native Hawaiian (2)	5	0.03
White (11,846)	12,345	79.74

*Notes: † The Census 2010 population figure is used to calculate the percentages in the Hispanic Origin and Race categories. Ancestry percentages are based on the 2006-2010 American Community Survey population (not shown); ‡ Numbers in parentheses indicate the number of people reporting a single ancestry; * Numbers in parentheses indicate the number of persons reporting this race alone, not in combination with any other race; Please refer to the Explanation of Data for more information.*

Not Hispanic (10,062)	10,359	66.91
Hispanic (1,784)	1,986	12.83

Medford

Place Type: CDP
County: Suffolk
Population: 24,142†

Ancestry‡	Population	%
African, Sub-Saharan (13)	107	0.43
African (13)	107	0.43
Alsatian (0)	12	0.05
American (594)	594	2.41
Armenian (48)	64	0.26
Australian (0)	14	0.06
Austrian (52)	73	0.30
British (0)	63	0.26
Canadian (8)	31	0.13
Croatian (11)	24	0.10
Czech (66)	275	1.12
Czechoslovakian (25)	39	0.16
Danish (0)	74	0.30
Dutch (14)	144	0.58
English (179)	1,325	5.38
European (138)	138	0.56
Finnish (0)	37	0.15
French, ex. Basque (41)	366	1.49
French Canadian (14)	131	0.53
German (516)	3,417	13.87
Greek (104)	345	1.40
Guyanese (17)	17	0.07
Hungarian (67)	463	1.88
Irish (1,178)	6,013	24.41
Italian (3,524)	8,430	34.22
Lithuanian (38)	171	0.69
Northern European (29)	29	0.12
Norwegian (79)	179	0.73
Polish (596)	1,455	5.91
Portuguese (416)	438	1.78
Romanian (20)	63	0.26
Russian (110)	344	1.40
Scotch-Irish (124)	369	1.50
Scottish (53)	534	2.17
Slovak (0)	8	0.03
Swedish (25)	138	0.56
Swiss (112)	123	0.50
Turkish (0)	9	0.04
Ukrainian (63)	140	0.57
West Indian, ex. Hispanic (338)	413	1.68
Barbadian (11)	11	0.04
Haitian (15)	57	0.23
Jamaican (93)	104	0.42
Trinidadian/Tobagonian (219)	219	0.89
West Indian (0)	22	0.09
Yugoslavian (45)	139	0.56

Hispanic Origin	Population	%
Hispanic or Latino (of any race)	4,306	17.84
Central American, ex. Mexican	677	2.80
Costa Rican	12	0.05
Guatemalan	81	0.34
Honduran	107	0.44
Nicaraguan	13	0.05
Panamanian	22	0.09
Salvadoran	431	1.79
Other Central American	11	0.05
Cuban	52	0.22
Dominican Republic	225	0.93
Mexican	700	2.90
Puerto Rican	1,478	6.12
South American	861	3.57
Argentinean	36	0.15
Bolivian	4	0.02
Chilean	28	0.12
Colombian	172	0.71
Ecuadorian	480	1.99
Peruvian	99	0.41
Uruguayan	3	0.01
Venezuelan	23	0.10
Other South American	16	0.07
Other Hispanic or Latino	313	1.30

Race*	Population	%
African-American/Black (1,458)	1,704	7.06
Not Hispanic (1,328)	1,507	6.24
Hispanic (130)	197	0.82
American Indian/Alaska Native (91)	202	0.84
Not Hispanic (53)	127	0.53
Hispanic (38)	75	0.31
Alaska Athabascan *(Ala. Nat.)* (0)	3	0.01
Apache (0)	2	0.01
Blackfeet (0)	8	0.03
Cherokee (8)	22	0.09
Chippewa (1)	1	<0.01
Choctaw (0)	3	0.01
Iroquois (0)	2	0.01
Lumbee (1)	1	<0.01
Mexican American Ind. (4)	7	0.03
Seminole (2)	2	0.01
Sioux (0)	1	<0.01
South American Ind. (3)	13	0.05
Spanish American Ind. (1)	1	<0.01
Yuman (1)	1	<0.01
Asian (627)	748	3.10
Not Hispanic (620)	718	2.97
Hispanic (7)	30	0.12
Bangladeshi (22)	29	0.12
Cambodian (1)	1	<0.01
Chinese, ex. Taiwanese (108)	124	0.51
Filipino (99)	116	0.48
Indian (184)	212	0.88
Indonesian (0)	1	<0.01
Japanese (11)	18	0.07
Korean (59)	81	0.34
Laotian (13)	13	0.05
Nepalese (6)	6	0.02
Pakistani (62)	66	0.27
Sri Lankan (12)	12	0.05
Taiwanese (0)	1	<0.01
Thai (3)	5	0.02
Vietnamese (34)	40	0.17
Hawaii Native/Pacific Islander (6)	20	0.08
Not Hispanic (5)	16	0.07
Hispanic (1)	4	0.02
Native Hawaiian (1)	6	0.02
Samoan (0)	2	0.01
White (20,107)	20,583	85.26
Not Hispanic (17,471)	17,680	73.23
Hispanic (2,636)	2,903	12.02

Melville

Place Type: CDP
County: Suffolk
Population: 18,985†

Ancestry‡	Population	%
American (906)	906	4.76
Arab (129)	163	0.86
Egyptian (80)	114	0.60
Jordanian (11)	11	0.06
Moroccan (20)	20	0.10
Other Arab (18)	18	0.09
Armenian (20)	20	0.10
Austrian (41)	315	1.65
Basque (6)	6	0.03
British (7)	29	0.15
Canadian (30)	52	0.27
Celtic (22)	22	0.12
Croatian (24)	24	0.13
Czech (0)	71	0.37
Czechoslovakian (8)	24	0.13
Danish (11)	19	0.10
Dutch (8)	42	0.22
Eastern European (637)	654	3.43
English (169)	575	3.02
Estonian (30)	50	0.26
European (146)	152	0.80
French, ex. Basque (16)	172	0.90
French Canadian (14)	14	0.07
German (550)	2,189	11.49
Greek (137)	236	1.24
Hungarian (0)	139	0.73
Icelander (9)	38	0.20
Irish (624)	2,354	12.36
Israeli (77)	89	0.47
Italian (2,921)	5,387	28.28
Latvian (11)	29	0.15
Lithuanian (28)	28	0.15
Northern European (34)	34	0.18
Norwegian (23)	97	0.51
Polish (522)	1,746	9.17
Romanian (60)	179	0.94
Russian (719)	1,602	8.41
Scandinavian (0)	37	0.19
Scotch-Irish (42)	99	0.52
Scottish (7)	29	0.15
Swedish (8)	92	0.48
Swiss (0)	93	0.49
Turkish (19)	30	0.16
Ukrainian (92)	183	0.96
Welsh (0)	24	0.13
West Indian, ex. Hispanic (730)	730	3.83
Bahamian (31)	31	0.16
Haitian (492)	492	2.58
Jamaican (58)	58	0.30
Trinidadian/Tobagonian (72)	72	0.38
West Indian (77)	77	0.40
Yugoslavian (0)	45	0.24

Hispanic Origin	Population	%
Hispanic or Latino (of any race)	955	5.03
Central American, ex. Mexican	105	0.55
Costa Rican	10	0.05
Guatemalan	11	0.06
Honduran	15	0.08
Nicaraguan	4	0.02
Panamanian	10	0.05
Salvadoran	55	0.29
Cuban	57	0.30
Dominican Republic	59	0.31
Mexican	119	0.63
Puerto Rican	302	1.59
South American	185	0.97
Argentinean	15	0.08
Bolivian	7	0.04
Chilean	14	0.07
Colombian	68	0.36
Ecuadorian	38	0.20
Paraguayan	3	0.02
Peruvian	26	0.14
Uruguayan	2	0.01
Venezuelan	6	0.03
Other South American	6	0.03
Other Hispanic or Latino	128	0.67

Race*	Population	%
African-American/Black (639)	704	3.71
Not Hispanic (607)	654	3.44
Hispanic (32)	50	0.26
American Indian/Alaska Native (19)	75	0.40
Not Hispanic (12)	61	0.32
Hispanic (7)	14	0.07
Blackfeet (0)	2	0.01
Cherokee (1)	13	0.07
Choctaw (0)	1	0.01
South American Ind. (0)	2	0.01
Asian (1,376)	1,569	8.26
Not Hispanic (1,372)	1,555	8.19
Hispanic (4)	14	0.07
Bangladeshi (8)	12	0.06
Chinese, ex. Taiwanese (269)	304	1.60
Filipino (35)	69	0.36
Indian (630)	671	3.53
Indonesian (0)	1	0.01
Japanese (22)	31	0.16
Korean (192)	204	1.07
Pakistani (155)	167	0.88
Sri Lankan (3)	3	0.02

SECTION TWO

*Notes: † The Census 2010 population figure is used to calculate the percentages in the Hispanic Origin and Race categories. Ancestry percentages are based on the 2006-2010 American Community Survey population (not shown); ‡ Numbers in parentheses indicate the number of people reporting a single ancestry; * Numbers in parentheses indicate the number of persons reporting this race alone, not in combination with any other race; Please refer to the Explanation of Data for more information.*

Taiwanese (16)	22	0.12
Thai (1)	1	0.01
Vietnamese (19)	20	0.11
Hawaii Native/Pacific Islander (2)	12	0.06
Not Hispanic (2)	8	0.04
Hispanic (0)	4	0.02
Native Hawaiian (0)	3	0.02
White (16,441)	16,696	87.94
Not Hispanic (15,734)	15,936	83.94
Hispanic (707)	760	4.00

Mendon

Place Type: Town
County: Monroe
Population: 9,152†

Ancestry‡	Population	%
American (472)	472	5.25
Arab (14)	20	0.22
Lebanese (14)	20	0.22
Austrian (17)	91	1.01
Belgian (0)	44	0.49
British (37)	68	0.76
Canadian (0)	77	0.86
Czech (0)	17	0.19
Danish (31)	56	0.62
Dutch (20)	281	3.13
English (384)	1,868	20.80
European (138)	138	1.54
French, ex. Basque (26)	291	3.24
French Canadian (25)	121	1.35
German (786)	2,908	32.38
Greek (20)	106	1.18
Hungarian (0)	37	0.41
Irish (398)	2,109	23.48
Israeli (8)	17	0.19
Italian (608)	1,598	17.79
Latvian (13)	13	0.14
Lithuanian (13)	46	0.51
Norwegian (47)	172	1.91
Pennsylvania German (15)	15	0.17
Polish (190)	456	5.08
Portuguese (0)	11	0.12
Romanian (0)	26	0.29
Russian (35)	61	0.68
Scandinavian (0)	19	0.21
Scotch-Irish (26)	173	1.93
Scottish (17)	315	3.51
Slovene (18)	18	0.20
Swedish (21)	209	2.33
Swiss (12)	79	0.88
Turkish (15)	15	0.17
Ukrainian (29)	89	0.99
Welsh (0)	130	1.45
West Indian, ex. Hispanic (17)	35	0.39
Jamaican (17)	35	0.39
Yugoslavian (0)	14	0.16

Hispanic Origin	Population	%
Hispanic or Latino (of any race)	152	1.66
Central American, ex. Mexican	9	0.10
Guatemalan	3	0.03
Honduran	4	0.04
Panamanian	1	0.01
Salvadoran	1	0.01
Cuban	14	0.15
Dominican Republic	6	0.07
Mexican	25	0.27
Puerto Rican	42	0.46
South American	32	0.35
Argentinean	2	0.02
Bolivian	5	0.05
Chilean	13	0.14
Colombian	5	0.05
Peruvian	1	0.01
Venezuelan	4	0.04
Other South American	2	0.02
Other Hispanic or Latino	24	0.26

Race*	Population	%
African-American/Black (47)	72	0.79
Not Hispanic (43)	66	0.72
Hispanic (4)	6	0.07
American Indian/Alaska Native (14)	38	0.42
Not Hispanic (8)	31	0.34
Hispanic (6)	7	0.08
Cherokee (0)	10	0.11
Iroquois (5)	9	0.10
Mexican American Ind. (1)	1	0.01
South American Ind. (2)	2	0.02
Asian (133)	175	1.91
Not Hispanic (133)	175	1.91
Bangladeshi (3)	5	0.05
Cambodian (2)	2	0.02
Chinese, ex. Taiwanese (38)	39	0.43
Filipino (6)	8	0.09
Indian (49)	58	0.63
Japanese (1)	16	0.17
Korean (16)	27	0.30
Pakistani (4)	4	0.04
Taiwanese (4)	5	0.05
Thai (3)	3	0.03
Vietnamese (2)	4	0.04
Hawaii Native/Pacific Islander (1)	7	0.08
Not Hispanic (1)	5	0.05
Hispanic (0)	2	0.02
Native Hawaiian (0)	3	0.03
Samoan (1)	3	0.03
White (8,831)	8,926	97.53
Not Hispanic (8,723)	8,811	96.27
Hispanic (108)	115	1.26

Merrick

Place Type: CDP
County: Nassau
Population: 22,097†

Ancestry‡	Population	%
African, Sub-Saharan (0)	9	0.04
South African (0)	9	0.04
Albanian (0)	17	0.08
American (1,024)	1,024	4.80
Arab (102)	156	0.73
Egyptian (49)	49	0.23
Lebanese (19)	19	0.09
Moroccan (10)	33	0.15
Other Arab (24)	55	0.26
Armenian (44)	44	0.21
Australian (9)	9	0.04
Austrian (65)	268	1.26
Brazilian (9)	28	0.13
British (32)	106	0.50
Canadian (0)	51	0.24
Carpatho Rusyn (0)	11	0.05
Czech (0)	56	0.26
Czechoslovakian (0)	11	0.05
Danish (0)	39	0.18
Dutch (23)	77	0.36
Eastern European (541)	582	2.73
English (133)	651	3.05
European (217)	243	1.14
Finnish (0)	50	0.23
French, ex. Basque (67)	231	1.08
French Canadian (47)	55	0.26
German (450)	2,450	11.49
Greek (208)	360	1.69
Guyanese (0)	29	0.14
Hungarian (87)	304	1.43
Irish (1,098)	3,874	18.17
Israeli (92)	118	0.55
Italian (2,519)	5,122	24.02
Lithuanian (26)	60	0.28
Northern European (47)	47	0.22
Norwegian (35)	143	0.67
Polish (668)	2,106	9.88
Portuguese (20)	82	0.38
Romanian (40)	185	0.87
Russian (1,153)	2,169	10.17
Scandinavian (36)	36	0.17
Scotch-Irish (100)	208	0.98
Scottish (0)	63	0.30
Swedish (0)	143	0.67
Turkish (33)	33	0.15
Ukrainian (9)	44	0.21
Welsh (0)	100	0.47
West Indian, ex. Hispanic (46)	95	0.45
Haitian (21)	21	0.10
Jamaican (25)	74	0.35

Hispanic Origin	Population	%
Hispanic or Latino (of any race)	1,301	5.89
Central American, ex. Mexican	191	0.86
Costa Rican	13	0.06
Guatemalan	35	0.16
Honduran	9	0.04
Nicaraguan	1	<0.01
Panamanian	6	0.03
Salvadoran	127	0.57
Cuban	110	0.50
Dominican Republic	138	0.62
Mexican	69	0.31
Puerto Rican	343	1.55
South American	339	1.53
Argentinean	41	0.19
Bolivian	5	0.02
Chilean	24	0.11
Colombian	133	0.60
Ecuadorian	72	0.33
Paraguayan	9	0.04
Peruvian	41	0.19
Uruguayan	2	0.01
Venezuelan	11	0.05
Other South American	1	<0.01
Other Hispanic or Latino	111	0.50

Race*	Population	%
African-American/Black (264)	324	1.47
Not Hispanic (246)	295	1.34
Hispanic (18)	29	0.13
American Indian/Alaska Native (26)	52	0.24
Not Hispanic (21)	46	0.21
Hispanic (5)	6	0.03
Blackfeet (1)	2	0.01
Cherokee (0)	1	<0.01
Iroquois (1)	1	<0.01
Navajo (0)	3	0.01
Asian (624)	761	3.44
Not Hispanic (619)	744	3.37
Hispanic (5)	17	0.08
Bangladeshi (16)	17	0.08
Cambodian (1)	1	<0.01
Chinese, ex. Taiwanese (232)	274	1.24
Filipino (48)	76	0.34
Indian (175)	212	0.96
Japanese (13)	27	0.12
Korean (54)	75	0.34
Malaysian (0)	1	<0.01
Pakistani (45)	52	0.24
Taiwanese (4)	7	0.03
Thai (2)	2	0.01
Vietnamese (6)	11	0.05
Hawaii Native/Pacific Islander (1)	4	0.02
Not Hispanic (1)	4	0.02
Native Hawaiian (1)	2	0.01
White (20,633)	20,861	94.41
Not Hispanic (19,692)	19,865	89.90
Hispanic (941)	996	4.51

Middle Island

Place Type: CDP
County: Suffolk
Population: 10,483†

Ancestry‡	Population	%
African, Sub-Saharan (150)	150	1.47
African (150)	150	1.47

*Notes: † The Census 2010 population figure is used to calculate the percentages in the Hispanic Origin and Race categories. Ancestry percentages are based on the 2006-2010 American Community Survey population (not shown); ‡ Numbers in parentheses indicate the number of people reporting a single ancestry; * Numbers in parentheses indicate the number of persons reporting this race alone, not in combination with any other race; Please refer to the Explanation of Data for more information.*

American (174)	174	1.70
Armenian (7)	26	0.25
Austrian (37)	98	0.96
Belgian (0)	10	0.10
Brazilian (149)	149	1.46
Bulgarian (31)	31	0.30
Canadian (16)	50	0.49
Celtic (0)	13	0.13
Croatian (0)	20	0.20
Czech (32)	32	0.31
Czechoslovakian (15)	15	0.15
Danish (0)	34	0.33
Dutch (88)	129	1.26
Eastern European (17)	17	0.17
English (66)	467	4.57
European (50)	62	0.61
Finnish (16)	16	0.16
French, ex. Basque (11)	143	1.40
French Canadian (9)	9	0.09
German (416)	1,801	17.61
Greek (0)	22	0.22
Hungarian (0)	39	0.38
Irish (603)	2,162	21.13
Italian (1,595)	2,958	28.91
Latvian (14)	14	0.14
Lithuanian (30)	69	0.67
Maltese (0)	6	0.06
Norwegian (0)	40	0.39
Polish (177)	693	6.77
Portuguese (0)	11	0.11
Romanian (10)	19	0.19
Russian (103)	234	2.29
Scotch-Irish (85)	145	1.42
Scottish (20)	144	1.41
Slovak (0)	11	0.11
Swedish (25)	129	1.26
Swiss (0)	22	0.22
Turkish (73)	118	1.15
Ukrainian (12)	31	0.30
West Indian, ex. Hispanic (158)	158	1.54
Jamaican (115)	115	1.12
West Indian (43)	43	0.42
Yugoslavian (0)	54	0.53

Hispanic Origin	Population	%
Hispanic or Latino (of any race)	974	9.29
Central American, ex. Mexican	83	0.79
Costa Rican	4	0.04
Guatemalan	14	0.13
Honduran	17	0.16
Nicaraguan	4	0.04
Panamanian	15	0.14
Salvadoran	29	0.28
Cuban	31	0.30
Dominican Republic	100	0.95
Mexican	75	0.72
Puerto Rican	408	3.89
South American	197	1.88
Argentinean	3	0.03
Bolivian	5	0.05
Chilean	2	0.02
Colombian	120	1.14
Ecuadorian	37	0.35
Paraguayan	1	0.01
Peruvian	27	0.26
Venezuelan	2	0.02
Other Hispanic or Latino	80	0.76

Race*	Population	%
African-American/Black (856)	985	9.40
Not Hispanic (786)	886	8.45
Hispanic (70)	99	0.94
American Indian/Alaska Native (43)	133	1.27
Not Hispanic (25)	93	0.89
Hispanic (18)	40	0.38
Apache (0)	2	0.02
Blackfeet (1)	11	0.10
Cherokee (3)	28	0.27
Iroquois (1)	2	0.02
Mexican American Ind. (0)	1	0.01
Navajo (1)	1	0.01
Seminole (0)	1	0.01
South American Ind. (0)	5	0.05
Spanish American Ind. (0)	1	0.01
Asian (371)	424	4.04
Not Hispanic (361)	407	3.88
Hispanic (10)	17	0.16
Bangladeshi (5)	9	0.09
Chinese, ex. Taiwanese (128)	141	1.35
Filipino (34)	43	0.41
Indian (106)	127	1.21
Indonesian (1)	1	0.01
Japanese (5)	10	0.10
Korean (32)	40	0.38
Laotian (2)	2	0.02
Pakistani (12)	16	0.15
Taiwanese (2)	4	0.04
Thai (4)	5	0.05
Vietnamese (18)	18	0.17
Hawaii Native/Pacific Islander (0)	10	0.10
Not Hispanic (0)	10	0.10
Guamanian/Chamorro (0)	1	0.01
Native Hawaiian (0)	2	0.02
Samoan (0)	1	0.01
White (8,768)	8,942	85.30
Not Hispanic (8,134)	8,253	78.73
Hispanic (634)	689	6.57

Middletown

Place Type: City
County: Orange
Population: 28,086†

Ancestry‡	Population	%
African, Sub-Saharan (395)	518	1.86
African (240)	356	1.28
Nigerian (99)	106	0.38
Other Sub-Saharan African (56)	56	0.20
American (1,923)	1,923	6.92
Arab (37)	66	0.24
Jordanian (30)	30	0.11
Lebanese (7)	36	0.13
Armenian (22)	22	0.08
Australian (0)	24	0.09
Austrian (26)	59	0.21
Brazilian (26)	26	0.09
British (20)	20	0.07
Canadian (0)	77	0.28
Croatian (0)	58	0.21
Czech (18)	101	0.36
Czechoslovakian (34)	34	0.12
Danish (14)	72	0.26
Dutch (109)	528	1.90
English (168)	1,460	5.25
Finnish (0)	16	0.06
French, ex. Basque (33)	343	1.23
French Canadian (27)	144	0.52
German (371)	2,451	8.81
Greek (46)	74	0.27
Guyanese (0)	79	0.28
Hungarian (15)	111	0.40
Irish (1,036)	3,178	11.43
Italian (1,320)	3,109	11.18
Lithuanian (0)	11	0.04
Norwegian (0)	83	0.30
Pennsylvania German (19)	19	0.07
Polish (326)	843	3.03
Portuguese (12)	55	0.20
Romanian (0)	25	0.09
Russian (56)	179	0.64
Scandinavian (9)	9	0.03
Scotch-Irish (56)	413	1.49
Scottish (79)	416	1.50
Slavic (14)	16	0.06
Swedish (0)	47	0.17
Swiss (0)	8	0.03
Turkish (0)	12	0.04
Ukrainian (34)	54	0.19
Welsh (17)	76	0.27
West Indian, ex. Hispanic (571)	927	3.33
Belizean (0)	80	0.29
British West Indian (50)	75	0.27
Haitian (164)	184	0.66
Jamaican (248)	339	1.22
Trinidadian/Tobagonian (34)	48	0.17
U.S. Virgin Islander (0)	33	0.12
West Indian (75)	168	0.60
Yugoslavian (35)	59	0.21

Hispanic Origin	Population	%
Hispanic or Latino (of any race)	11,158	39.73
Central American, ex. Mexican	547	1.95
Costa Rican	23	0.08
Guatemalan	76	0.27
Honduran	272	0.97
Nicaraguan	14	0.05
Panamanian	55	0.20
Salvadoran	104	0.37
Other Central American	3	0.01
Cuban	105	0.37
Dominican Republic	628	2.24
Mexican	4,208	14.98
Puerto Rican	4,533	16.14
South American	724	2.58
Argentinean	39	0.14
Bolivian	7	0.02
Chilean	10	0.04
Colombian	266	0.95
Ecuadorian	281	1.00
Paraguayan	1	<0.01
Peruvian	99	0.35
Uruguayan	8	0.03
Venezuelan	12	0.04
Other South American	1	<0.01
Other Hispanic or Latino	413	1.47

Race*	Population	%
African-American/Black (5,902)	6,880	24.50
Not Hispanic (5,075)	5,671	20.19
Hispanic (827)	1,209	4.30
American Indian/Alaska Native (230)	554	1.97
Not Hispanic (100)	322	1.15
Hispanic (130)	232	0.83
Apache (0)	2	0.01
Blackfeet (0)	8	0.03
Central American Ind. (7)	11	0.04
Cherokee (4)	56	0.20
Chippewa (1)	1	<0.01
Choctaw (0)	1	<0.01
Cree (0)	1	<0.01
Delaware (21)	43	0.15
Iroquois (12)	24	0.09
Mexican American Ind. (25)	27	0.10
Potawatomi (1)	2	0.01
Seminole (0)	2	0.01
Shoshone (4)	4	0.01
Sioux (1)	1	<0.01
South American Ind. (28)	42	0.15
Spanish American Ind. (6)	7	0.02
Tohono O'Odham (1)	6	0.02
Asian (524)	682	2.43
Not Hispanic (503)	609	2.17
Hispanic (21)	73	0.26
Bangladeshi (3)	3	0.01
Burmese (7)	7	0.02
Cambodian (2)	5	0.02
Chinese, ex. Taiwanese (88)	119	0.42
Filipino (88)	117	0.42
Indian (213)	260	0.93
Japanese (6)	38	0.14
Korean (23)	30	0.11
Laotian (2)	9	0.03
Pakistani (37)	38	0.14
Taiwanese (8)	8	0.03
Thai (7)	7	0.02
Vietnamese (24)	31	0.11
Hawaii Native/Pacific Islander (4)	41	0.15
Not Hispanic (3)	17	0.06
Hispanic (1)	24	0.09

*Notes: † The Census 2010 population figure is used to calculate the percentages in the Hispanic Origin and Race categories. Ancestry percentages are based on the 2006-2010 American Community Survey population (not shown); ‡ Numbers in parentheses indicate the number of people reporting a single ancestry; * Numbers in parentheses indicate the number of persons reporting this race alone, not in combination with any other race; Please refer to the Explanation of Data for more information.*

Guamanian/Chamorro (2)	4	0.01
Native Hawaiian (0)	4	0.01
White (14,710)	15,809	56.29
Not Hispanic (10,420)	11,026	39.26
Hispanic (4,290)	4,783	17.03

Miller Place

Place Type: CDP
County: Suffolk
Population: 12,339†

Ancestry‡	Population	%
American (468)	468	3.81
Arab (46)	65	0.53
Jordanian (46)	46	0.37
Lebanese (0)	19	0.15
Austrian (15)	179	1.46
Basque (0)	14	0.11
Belgian (0)	26	0.21
British (0)	11	0.09
Canadian (59)	109	0.89
Croatian (0)	31	0.25
Czech (53)	363	2.95
Czechoslovakian (0)	15	0.12
Danish (35)	83	0.68
Dutch (0)	30	0.24
English (201)	1,189	9.67
European (32)	51	0.41
Finnish (18)	97	0.79
French, ex. Basque (14)	166	1.35
French Canadian (13)	55	0.45
German (560)	3,066	24.94
Greek (30)	62	0.50
Hungarian (21)	34	0.28
Irish (786)	3,589	29.20
Italian (1,807)	4,158	33.82
Maltese (34)	84	0.68
Norwegian (26)	97	0.79
Polish (159)	795	6.47
Portuguese (215)	239	1.94
Romanian (24)	71	0.58
Russian (83)	401	3.26
Scandinavian (9)	9	0.07
Scotch-Irish (170)	231	1.88
Scottish (14)	105	0.85
Slavic (0)	32	0.26
Slovak (15)	33	0.27
Swedish (28)	79	0.64
Turkish (46)	46	0.37
Ukrainian (9)	47	0.38
Welsh (0)	17	0.14
West Indian, ex. Hispanic (270)	317	2.58
Bahamian (0)	47	0.38
Haitian (201)	201	1.64
Jamaican (52)	52	0.42
West Indian (17)	17	0.14

Hispanic Origin	Population	%
Hispanic or Latino (of any race)	621	5.03
Central American, ex. Mexican	60	0.49
Costa Rican	12	0.10
Guatemalan	14	0.11
Honduran	5	0.04
Nicaraguan	3	0.02
Salvadoran	26	0.21
Cuban	32	0.26
Dominican Republic	36	0.29
Mexican	30	0.24
Puerto Rican	274	2.22
South American	92	0.75
Argentinean	18	0.15
Bolivian	2	0.02
Chilean	6	0.05
Colombian	20	0.16
Ecuadorian	17	0.14
Peruvian	20	0.16
Uruguayan	1	0.01
Venezuelan	4	0.03
Other South American	4	0.03
Other Hispanic or Latino	97	0.79

Race*	Population	%
African-American/Black (207)	256	2.07
Not Hispanic (191)	227	1.84
Hispanic (16)	29	0.24
American Indian/Alaska Native (12)	31	0.25
Not Hispanic (12)	26	0.21
Hispanic (0)	5	0.04
Blackfeet (0)	2	0.02
Cherokee (0)	1	0.01
Iroquois (0)	2	0.02
Paiute (0)	1	0.01
Seminole (0)	1	0.01
South American Ind. (0)	4	0.03
Asian (363)	407	3.30
Not Hispanic (359)	394	3.19
Hispanic (4)	13	0.11
Bangladeshi (5)	6	0.05
Chinese, ex. Taiwanese (100)	118	0.96
Filipino (65)	75	0.61
Indian (86)	95	0.77
Japanese (2)	5	0.04
Korean (45)	52	0.42
Pakistani (29)	30	0.24
Sri Lankan (2)	2	0.02
Taiwanese (6)	7	0.06
Thai (2)	3	0.02
Vietnamese (10)	10	0.08
Hawaii Native/Pacific Islander (6)	12	0.10
Not Hispanic (6)	12	0.10
Native Hawaiian (2)	2	0.02
White (11,532)	11,669	94.57
Not Hispanic (11,035)	11,116	90.09
Hispanic (497)	553	4.48

Milton

Place Type: Town
County: Saratoga
Population: 18,575†

Ancestry‡	Population	%
Albanian (0)	14	0.08
American (1,569)	1,569	8.53
Arab (14)	31	0.17
Lebanese (0)	17	0.09
Moroccan (14)	14	0.08
Armenian (12)	28	0.15
Austrian (11)	62	0.34
Belgian (0)	45	0.24
Brazilian (47)	47	0.26
British (36)	55	0.30
Canadian (36)	67	0.36
Czech (0)	40	0.22
Czechoslovakian (14)	29	0.16
Danish (0)	77	0.42
Dutch (90)	461	2.51
Eastern European (70)	70	0.38
English (929)	2,493	13.55
Estonian (0)	17	0.09
European (143)	143	0.78
Finnish (46)	64	0.35
French, ex. Basque (218)	2,607	14.17
French Canadian (74)	280	1.52
German (1,005)	3,272	17.79
Greek (17)	142	0.77
Hungarian (11)	61	0.33
Irish (1,391)	5,230	28.43
Italian (769)	2,583	14.04
Latvian (59)	59	0.32
Lithuanian (0)	46	0.25
Maltese (0)	35	0.19
Norwegian (30)	72	0.39
Polish (508)	1,559	8.48
Portuguese (0)	7	0.04
Russian (14)	294	1.60
Scandinavian (20)	54	0.29
Scotch-Irish (70)	141	0.77
Scottish (69)	293	1.59
Slavic (0)	16	0.09
Slovak (24)	91	0.49
Swedish (67)	277	1.51
Swiss (7)	13	0.07
Turkish (0)	14	0.08
Ukrainian (28)	94	0.51
Welsh (0)	19	0.10
West Indian, ex. Hispanic (0)	11	0.06
Jamaican (0)	11	0.06

Hispanic Origin	Population	%
Hispanic or Latino (of any race)	463	2.49
Central American, ex. Mexican	19	0.10
Guatemalan	9	0.05
Panamanian	3	0.02
Salvadoran	7	0.04
Cuban	23	0.12
Dominican Republic	20	0.11
Mexican	134	0.72
Puerto Rican	148	0.80
South American	40	0.22
Argentinean	1	0.01
Chilean	2	0.01
Colombian	16	0.09
Ecuadorian	8	0.04
Peruvian	7	0.04
Uruguayan	3	0.02
Venezuelan	3	0.02
Other Hispanic or Latino	79	0.43

Race*	Population	%
African-American/Black (194)	340	1.83
Not Hispanic (182)	300	1.62
Hispanic (12)	40	0.22
American Indian/Alaska Native (21)	138	0.74
Not Hispanic (15)	122	0.66
Hispanic (6)	16	0.09
Apache (0)	1	0.01
Blackfeet (1)	9	0.05
Canadian/French Am. Ind. (0)	2	0.01
Central American Ind. (0)	1	0.01
Cherokee (1)	12	0.06
Chippewa (1)	2	0.01
Choctaw (0)	4	0.02
Cree (0)	3	0.02
Creek (0)	1	0.01
Inupiat *(Alaska Native)* (0)	1	0.01
Iroquois (1)	14	0.08
Mexican American Ind. (1)	1	0.01
Navajo (0)	3	0.02
Sioux (0)	2	0.01
South American Ind. (0)	1	0.01
Asian (126)	222	1.20
Not Hispanic (122)	208	1.12
Hispanic (4)	14	0.08
Cambodian (3)	4	0.02
Chinese, ex. Taiwanese (34)	52	0.28
Filipino (27)	56	0.30
Indian (9)	23	0.12
Indonesian (0)	3	0.02
Japanese (12)	28	0.15
Korean (18)	32	0.17
Laotian (2)	2	0.01
Pakistani (8)	11	0.06
Thai (3)	5	0.03
Vietnamese (6)	6	0.03
Hawaii Native/Pacific Islander (9)	35	0.19
Not Hispanic (7)	28	0.15
Hispanic (2)	7	0.04
Guamanian/Chamorro (2)	6	0.03
Native Hawaiian (2)	11	0.06
Samoan (2)	6	0.03
White (17,752)	18,128	97.59
Not Hispanic (17,444)	17,761	95.62
Hispanic (308)	367	1.98

*Notes: † The Census 2010 population figure is used to calculate the percentages in the Hispanic Origin and Race categories. Ancestry percentages are based on the 2006-2010 American Community Survey population (not shown); ‡ Numbers in parentheses indicate the number of people reporting a single ancestry; * Numbers in parentheses indicate the number of persons reporting this race alone, not in combination with any other race; Please refer to the Explanation of Data for more information.*

Mineola

Place Type: Village
County: Nassau
Population: 18,799†

Ancestry‡	Population	%
Albanian (0)	15	0.08
American (529)	529	2.83
Arab (84)	109	0.58
Iraqi (0)	14	0.07
Lebanese (0)	11	0.06
Other Arab (84)	84	0.45
Armenian (12)	12	0.06
Assyrian/Chaldean/Syriac (0)	14	0.07
Austrian (22)	173	0.93
Basque (0)	54	0.29
Belgian (39)	39	0.21
Brazilian (218)	232	1.24
British (0)	49	0.26
Bulgarian (13)	13	0.07
Canadian (0)	64	0.34
Croatian (37)	75	0.40
Cypriot (27)	27	0.14
Czech (0)	10	0.05
Czechoslovakian (0)	104	0.56
Danish (0)	18	0.10
Dutch (0)	102	0.55
Eastern European (0)	19	0.10
English (133)	940	5.03
Estonian (10)	40	0.21
European (53)	53	0.28
Finnish (12)	29	0.16
French, ex. Basque (82)	188	1.01
French Canadian (36)	45	0.24
German (395)	2,187	11.70
Greek (123)	234	1.25
Guyanese (0)	32	0.17
Hungarian (30)	115	0.62
Iranian (27)	41	0.22
Irish (1,131)	3,361	17.98
Italian (2,122)	4,032	21.57
Maltese (11)	11	0.06
Norwegian (0)	38	0.20
Polish (321)	758	4.06
Portuguese (2,277)	2,368	12.67
Romanian (0)	10	0.05
Russian (73)	151	0.81
Scandinavian (12)	12	0.06
Scotch-Irish (43)	163	0.87
Scottish (58)	247	1.32
Serbian (43)	43	0.23
Slovak (16)	16	0.09
Swedish (16)	108	0.58
Swiss (0)	44	0.24
Turkish (12)	12	0.06
Ukrainian (31)	78	0.42
Welsh (0)	30	0.16
West Indian, ex. Hispanic (120)	134	0.72
Haitian (0)	14	0.07
Jamaican (26)	26	0.14
West Indian (94)	94	0.50
Yugoslavian (0)	38	0.20

Hispanic Origin	Population	%
Hispanic or Latino (of any race)	3,090	16.44
Central American, ex. Mexican	1,245	6.62
Costa Rican	27	0.14
Guatemalan	124	0.66
Honduran	166	0.88
Nicaraguan	13	0.07
Panamanian	4	0.02
Salvadoran	896	4.77
Other Central American	15	0.08
Cuban	75	0.40
Dominican Republic	137	0.73
Mexican	84	0.45
Puerto Rican	354	1.88
South American	904	4.81
Argentinean	48	0.26
Bolivian	8	0.04
Chilean	52	0.28
Colombian	399	2.12
Ecuadorian	185	0.98
Paraguayan	60	0.32
Peruvian	128	0.68
Uruguayan	8	0.04
Venezuelan	12	0.06
Other South American	4	0.02
Other Hispanic or Latino	291	1.55

Race*	Population	%
African-American/Black (376)	465	2.47
Not Hispanic (321)	370	1.97
Hispanic (55)	95	0.51
American Indian/Alaska Native (43)	90	0.48
Not Hispanic (13)	35	0.19
Hispanic (30)	55	0.29
Apache (1)	1	0.01
Central American Ind. (1)	1	0.01
Cherokee (0)	7	0.04
Delaware (2)	3	0.02
Iroquois (3)	4	0.02
Lumbee (0)	1	0.01
Mexican American Ind. (1)	4	0.02
Sioux (0)	5	0.03
South American Ind. (0)	3	0.02
Spanish American Ind. (20)	21	0.11
Asian (1,593)	1,731	9.21
Not Hispanic (1,579)	1,699	9.04
Hispanic (14)	32	0.17
Bangladeshi (11)	21	0.11
Burmese (14)	15	0.08
Chinese, ex. Taiwanese (302)	335	1.78
Filipino (197)	221	1.18
Indian (725)	772	4.11
Indonesian (8)	13	0.07
Japanese (29)	38	0.20
Korean (149)	154	0.82
Malaysian (0)	1	0.01
Nepalese (1)	1	0.01
Pakistani (64)	71	0.38
Sri Lankan (4)	4	0.02
Taiwanese (16)	17	0.09
Thai (7)	9	0.05
Vietnamese (25)	30	0.16
Hawaii Native/Pacific Islander (1)	12	0.06
Not Hispanic (1)	10	0.05
Hispanic (0)	2	0.01
Guamanian/Chamorro (0)	1	0.01
Native Hawaiian (0)	4	0.02
Samoan (0)	1	0.01
White (15,367)	15,713	83.58
Not Hispanic (13,442)	13,616	72.43
Hispanic (1,925)	2,097	11.15

Monroe

Place Type: Town
County: Orange
Population: 39,912†

Ancestry‡	Population	%
African, Sub-Saharan (186)	186	0.48
African (186)	186	0.48
Albanian (53)	310	0.80
American (2,301)	2,301	5.95
Arab (114)	170	0.44
Arab (16)	38	0.10
Egyptian (33)	33	0.09
Lebanese (0)	34	0.09
Moroccan (11)	11	0.03
Other Arab (54)	54	0.14
Armenian (13)	13	0.03
Australian (42)	42	0.11
Austrian (45)	211	0.55
British (57)	115	0.30
Bulgarian (20)	20	0.05
Canadian (43)	112	0.29
Croatian (42)	57	0.15
Czech (41)	120	0.31
Czechoslovakian (100)	149	0.39
Danish (0)	37	0.10
Dutch (68)	390	1.01
Eastern European (221)	221	0.57
English (563)	1,303	3.37
Estonian (0)	7	0.02
European (1,280)	1,414	3.66
French, ex. Basque (0)	320	0.83
French Canadian (31)	159	0.41
German (690)	3,613	9.34
Greek (84)	217	0.56
Hungarian (3,258)	5,591	14.45
Irish (1,765)	4,452	11.51
Israeli (251)	949	2.45
Italian (1,790)	4,654	12.03
Latvian (19)	19	0.05
Lithuanian (0)	39	0.10
Northern European (17)	17	0.04
Norwegian (53)	290	0.75
Pennsylvania German (0)	8	0.02
Polish (581)	1,644	4.25
Portuguese (0)	45	0.12
Romanian (587)	2,439	6.31
Russian (282)	952	2.46
Scandinavian (16)	74	0.19
Scotch-Irish (71)	159	0.41
Scottish (47)	228	0.59
Slovak (0)	37	0.10
Slovene (5)	14	0.04
Swedish (6)	98	0.25
Swiss (41)	68	0.18
Ukrainian (124)	209	0.54
Welsh (0)	14	0.04
West Indian, ex. Hispanic (255)	321	0.83
Barbadian (16)	44	0.11
Haitian (159)	159	0.41
Jamaican (0)	28	0.07
West Indian (40)	50	0.13
Other West Indian (40)	40	0.10

Hispanic Origin	Population	%
Hispanic or Latino (of any race)	3,365	8.43
Central American, ex. Mexican	204	0.51
Costa Rican	11	0.03
Guatemalan	38	0.10
Honduran	106	0.27
Nicaraguan	7	0.02
Panamanian	11	0.03
Salvadoran	25	0.06
Other Central American	6	0.02
Cuban	85	0.21
Dominican Republic	295	0.74
Mexican	811	2.03
Puerto Rican	1,279	3.20
South American	487	1.22
Argentinean	217	0.54
Bolivian	7	0.02
Chilean	7	0.02
Colombian	108	0.27
Ecuadorian	98	0.25
Paraguayan	1	<0.01
Peruvian	29	0.07
Uruguayan	6	0.02
Venezuelan	4	0.01
Other South American	10	0.03
Other Hispanic or Latino	204	0.51

Race*	Population	%
African-American/Black (880)	1,068	2.68
Not Hispanic (772)	906	2.27
Hispanic (108)	162	0.41
American Indian/Alaska Native (42)	126	0.32
Not Hispanic (32)	82	0.21
Hispanic (10)	44	0.11
Blackfeet (1)	1	<0.01
Central American Ind. (0)	1	<0.01
Cherokee (3)	15	0.04
Choctaw (1)	1	<0.01
Delaware (7)	10	0.03

*Notes: † The Census 2010 population figure is used to calculate the percentages in the Hispanic Origin and Race categories. Ancestry percentages are based on the 2006-2010 American Community Survey population (not shown); ‡ Numbers in parentheses indicate the number of people reporting a single ancestry; * Numbers in parentheses indicate the number of persons reporting this race alone, not in combination with any other race; Please refer to the Explanation of Data for more information.*

Iroquois (1)	5	0.01
Lumbee (1)	1	<0.01
Mexican American Ind. (1)	4	0.01
Sioux (0)	3	0.01
South American Ind. (2)	16	0.04
Asian (989)	1,194	2.99
Not Hispanic (980)	1,159	2.90
Hispanic (9)	35	0.09
Bangladeshi (21)	28	0.07
Cambodian (1)	1	<0.01
Chinese, ex. Taiwanese (213)	244	0.61
Filipino (169)	237	0.59
Indian (323)	366	0.92
Indonesian (6)	7	0.02
Japanese (7)	33	0.08
Korean (127)	140	0.35
Nepalese (1)	1	<0.01
Pakistani (45)	57	0.14
Sri Lankan (13)	15	0.04
Taiwanese (7)	7	0.02
Thai (5)	8	0.02
Vietnamese (12)	19	0.05
Hawaii Native/Pacific Islander (6)	28	0.07
Not Hispanic (5)	23	0.06
Hispanic (1)	5	0.01
Guamanian/Chamorro (1)	1	<0.01
Native Hawaiian (0)	6	0.02
Samoan (0)	1	<0.01
White (36,431)	36,878	92.40
Not Hispanic (34,340)	34,648	86.81
Hispanic (2,091)	2,230	5.59

Monroe

Place Type: Village
County: Orange
Population: 8,364†

Ancestry‡	Population	%
Albanian (53)	310	3.73
American (412)	412	4.95
Arab (98)	132	1.59
Arab (11)	11	0.13
Egyptian (33)	33	0.40
Lebanese (0)	34	0.41
Other Arab (54)	54	0.65
Australian (42)	42	0.50
Austrian (0)	18	0.22
British (28)	40	0.48
Canadian (36)	81	0.97
Croatian (42)	57	0.69
Czech (15)	26	0.31
Dutch (43)	116	1.39
Eastern European (12)	12	0.14
English (41)	233	2.80
European (39)	39	0.47
French, ex. Basque (0)	133	1.60
French Canadian (0)	94	1.13
German (221)	1,136	13.65
Greek (56)	117	1.41
Hungarian (23)	79	0.95
Irish (960)	1,881	22.61
Italian (988)	2,481	29.82
Lithuanian (0)	24	0.29
Norwegian (15)	50	0.60
Polish (192)	460	5.53
Portuguese (0)	28	0.34
Romanian (20)	41	0.49
Russian (67)	248	2.98
Scandinavian (16)	27	0.32
Scotch-Irish (10)	30	0.36
Scottish (16)	121	1.45
Swedish (0)	33	0.40
Swiss (29)	29	0.35
Ukrainian (29)	82	0.99
Welsh (0)	14	0.17
West Indian, ex. Hispanic (40)	40	0.48
Other West Indian (40)	40	0.48

Hispanic Origin	Population	%
Hispanic or Latino (of any race)	1,638	19.58
Central American, ex. Mexican	151	1.81
Costa Rican	10	0.12
Guatemalan	24	0.29
Honduran	82	0.98
Nicaraguan	5	0.06
Panamanian	9	0.11
Salvadoran	15	0.18
Other Central American	6	0.07
Cuban	30	0.36
Dominican Republic	137	1.64
Mexican	627	7.50
Puerto Rican	502	6.00
South American	119	1.42
Argentinean	19	0.23
Bolivian	1	0.01
Colombian	40	0.48
Ecuadorian	49	0.59
Peruvian	7	0.08
Uruguayan	1	0.01
Venezuelan	2	0.02
Other Hispanic or Latino	72	0.86

Race*	Population	%
African-American/Black (340)	394	4.71
Not Hispanic (299)	347	4.15
Hispanic (41)	47	0.56
American Indian/Alaska Native (19)	45	0.54
Not Hispanic (13)	31	0.37
Hispanic (6)	14	0.17
Cherokee (1)	7	0.08
Choctaw (1)	1	0.01
Delaware (7)	8	0.10
Iroquois (0)	3	0.04
Lumbee (1)	1	0.01
Mexican American Ind. (0)	2	0.02
South American Ind. (0)	3	0.04
Asian (362)	430	5.14
Not Hispanic (362)	426	5.09
Hispanic (0)	4	0.05
Chinese, ex. Taiwanese (102)	117	1.40
Filipino (56)	73	0.87
Indian (103)	106	1.27
Indonesian (5)	5	0.06
Japanese (5)	8	0.10
Korean (65)	73	0.87
Pakistani (7)	17	0.20
Sri Lankan (6)	8	0.10
Thai (4)	4	0.05
Vietnamese (0)	4	0.05
Hawaii Native/Pacific Islander (4)	10	0.12
Not Hispanic (3)	5	0.06
Hispanic (1)	5	0.06
Guamanian/Chamorro (1)	1	0.01
Native Hawaiian (0)	4	0.05
White (6,901)	7,017	83.90
Not Hispanic (5,928)	6,009	71.84
Hispanic (973)	1,008	12.05

Monsey

Place Type: CDP
County: Rockland
Population: 18,412†

Ancestry‡	Population	%
African, Sub-Saharan (65)	87	0.58
African (39)	61	0.41
South African (26)	26	0.17
American (442)	442	2.94
Arab (308)	367	2.44
Arab (191)	191	1.27
Moroccan (84)	118	0.78
Palestinian (0)	25	0.17
Other Arab (33)	33	0.22
Austrian (24)	206	1.37
Belgian (135)	400	2.66
British (63)	63	0.42
Bulgarian (0)	16	0.11
Canadian (201)	404	2.68
Czech (92)	145	0.96
Czechoslovakian (39)	113	0.75
Danish (0)	23	0.15
Dutch (22)	22	0.15
Eastern European (229)	229	1.52
English (174)	305	2.03
European (2,853)	3,363	22.35
French, ex. Basque (13)	105	0.70
French Canadian (9)	9	0.06
German (210)	699	4.64
Greek (27)	27	0.18
Hungarian (864)	1,483	9.85
Irish (51)	93	0.62
Israeli (126)	608	4.04
Italian (162)	285	1.89
Lithuanian (16)	22	0.15
New Zealander (0)	55	0.37
Polish (738)	1,942	12.90
Romanian (89)	340	2.26
Russian (230)	849	5.64
Slavic (9)	9	0.06
Slovak (4)	4	0.03
Ukrainian (21)	158	1.05
West Indian, ex. Hispanic (90)	112	0.74
Barbadian (10)	10	0.07
British West Indian (12)	12	0.08
Haitian (30)	52	0.35
Jamaican (9)	9	0.06
West Indian (29)	29	0.19

Hispanic Origin	Population	%
Hispanic or Latino (of any race)	657	3.57
Central American, ex. Mexican	171	0.93
Guatemalan	138	0.75
Honduran	18	0.10
Salvadoran	15	0.08
Cuban	14	0.08
Dominican Republic	16	0.09
Mexican	95	0.52
Puerto Rican	103	0.56
South American	176	0.96
Argentinean	28	0.15
Chilean	1	0.01
Colombian	11	0.06
Ecuadorian	115	0.62
Peruvian	7	0.04
Uruguayan	1	0.01
Venezuelan	13	0.07
Other Hispanic or Latino	82	0.45

Race*	Population	%
African-American/Black (465)	506	2.75
Not Hispanic (412)	441	2.40
Hispanic (53)	65	0.35
American Indian/Alaska Native (20)	30	0.16
Not Hispanic (18)	27	0.15
Hispanic (2)	3	0.02
Delaware (2)	2	0.01
Asian (38)	66	0.36
Not Hispanic (37)	62	0.34
Hispanic (1)	4	0.02
Chinese, ex. Taiwanese (5)	6	0.03
Filipino (1)	4	0.02
Indian (18)	21	0.11
Japanese (1)	1	0.01
Korean (10)	16	0.09
Pakistani (2)	2	0.01
Hawaii Native/Pacific Islander (5)	14	0.08
Not Hispanic (0)	7	0.04
Hispanic (5)	7	0.04
Fijian (0)	2	0.01
Tongan (0)	2	0.01
White (17,508)	17,596	95.57
Not Hispanic (17,194)	17,262	93.75
Hispanic (314)	334	1.81

*Notes: † The Census 2010 population figure is used to calculate the percentages in the Hispanic Origin and Race categories. Ancestry percentages are based on the 2006-2010 American Community Survey population (not shown); ‡ Numbers in parentheses indicate the number of people reporting a single ancestry; * Numbers in parentheses indicate the number of persons reporting this race alone, not in combination with any other race; Please refer to the Explanation of Data for more information.*

Montgomery

Place Type: Town
County: Orange
Population: 22,606†

Ancestry‡	Population	%
Afghan (25)	25	0.11
African, Sub-Saharan (31)	62	0.28
African (21)	52	0.23
Nigerian (10)	10	0.04
American (1,638)	1,638	7.29
Arab (90)	100	0.44
Lebanese (0)	10	0.04
Other Arab (90)	90	0.40
Armenian (0)	16	0.07
Austrian (110)	263	1.17
British (46)	83	0.37
Bulgarian (118)	126	0.56
Canadian (96)	142	0.63
Czech (27)	55	0.24
Czechoslovakian (31)	31	0.14
Danish (24)	92	0.41
Dutch (218)	918	4.08
Eastern European (25)	25	0.11
English (335)	2,238	9.96
European (161)	161	0.72
Finnish (0)	14	0.06
French, ex. Basque (55)	608	2.70
French Canadian (63)	152	0.68
German (681)	3,738	16.63
Greek (110)	257	1.14
Hungarian (49)	211	0.94
Irish (1,796)	5,798	25.79
Italian (1,910)	5,101	22.69
Norwegian (61)	253	1.13
Pennsylvania German (0)	3	0.01
Polish (348)	1,170	5.20
Portuguese (0)	31	0.14
Romanian (0)	7	0.03
Russian (25)	211	0.94
Scandinavian (4)	8	0.04
Scotch-Irish (79)	280	1.25
Scottish (15)	291	1.29
Slovak (63)	145	0.65
Swedish (20)	115	0.51
Swiss (40)	40	0.18
Ukrainian (19)	110	0.49
Welsh (23)	88	0.39
West Indian, ex. Hispanic (43)	67	0.30
British West Indian (2)	2	0.01
Jamaican (41)	58	0.26
West Indian (0)	7	0.03

Hispanic Origin	Population	%
Hispanic or Latino (of any race)	3,167	14.01
Central American, ex. Mexican	105	0.46
Costa Rican	7	0.03
Guatemalan	36	0.16
Honduran	30	0.13
Nicaraguan	4	0.02
Panamanian	10	0.04
Salvadoran	18	0.08
Cuban	80	0.35
Dominican Republic	283	1.25
Mexican	277	1.23
Puerto Rican	1,960	8.67
South American	269	1.19
Argentinean	25	0.11
Bolivian	2	0.01
Chilean	16	0.07
Colombian	55	0.24
Ecuadorian	67	0.30
Paraguayan	1	<0.01
Peruvian	89	0.39
Uruguayan	9	0.04
Venezuelan	2	0.01
Other South American	3	0.01
Other Hispanic or Latino	193	0.85

Race*	Population	%
African-American/Black (1,620)	1,945	8.60
Not Hispanic (1,378)	1,606	7.10
Hispanic (242)	339	1.50
American Indian/Alaska Native (44)	195	0.86
Not Hispanic (32)	141	0.62
Hispanic (12)	54	0.24
Apache (0)	5	0.02
Arapaho (0)	1	<0.01
Blackfeet (0)	5	0.02
Central American Ind. (0)	1	<0.01
Cherokee (4)	30	0.13
Cheyenne (0)	1	<0.01
Chippewa (2)	8	0.04
Cree (0)	1	<0.01
Delaware (7)	16	0.07
Iroquois (13)	16	0.07
Mexican American Ind. (1)	5	0.02
Navajo (0)	4	0.02
Sioux (1)	6	0.03
South American Ind. (5)	21	0.09
Asian (322)	445	1.97
Not Hispanic (318)	427	1.89
Hispanic (4)	18	0.08
Bhutanese (2)	2	0.01
Cambodian (0)	2	0.01
Chinese, ex. Taiwanese (79)	104	0.46
Filipino (48)	71	0.31
Indian (92)	108	0.48
Indonesian (1)	3	0.01
Japanese (12)	30	0.13
Korean (30)	56	0.25
Pakistani (13)	15	0.07
Sri Lankan (4)	4	0.02
Thai (8)	13	0.06
Vietnamese (23)	36	0.16
Hawaii Native/Pacific Islander (3)	15	0.07
Not Hispanic (3)	10	0.04
Hispanic (0)	5	0.02
Guamanian/Chamorro (0)	2	0.01
Native Hawaiian (1)	4	0.02
Samoan (0)	1	<0.01
White (19,133)	19,689	87.10
Not Hispanic (17,250)	17,632	78.00
Hispanic (1,883)	2,057	9.10

Moreau

Place Type: Town
County: Saratoga
Population: 14,728†

Ancestry‡	Population	%
African, Sub-Saharan (25)	25	0.17
Nigerian (25)	25	0.17
American (3,769)	3,769	25.82
Arab (18)	67	0.46
Lebanese (0)	16	0.11
Syrian (18)	51	0.35
Austrian (0)	33	0.23
Belgian (14)	14	0.10
British (9)	9	0.06
Canadian (5)	5	0.03
Czech (0)	35	0.24
Czechoslovakian (0)	13	0.09
Danish (0)	9	0.06
Dutch (96)	477	3.27
English (362)	1,460	10.00
European (81)	105	0.72
French, ex. Basque (439)	2,227	15.26
French Canadian (297)	480	3.29
German (308)	1,444	9.89
Greek (12)	70	0.48
Hungarian (19)	59	0.40
Irish (947)	2,657	18.20
Italian (767)	1,563	10.71
Lithuanian (0)	8	0.05
Norwegian (33)	63	0.43
Polish (311)	728	4.99
Portuguese (0)	37	0.25
Russian (0)	57	0.39
Scandinavian (9)	9	0.06
Scotch-Irish (223)	425	2.91
Scottish (86)	351	2.40
Slovak (0)	8	0.05
Slovene (10)	10	0.07
Swedish (0)	21	0.14
Swiss (0)	47	0.32
Ukrainian (0)	7	0.05
Welsh (30)	194	1.33
West Indian, ex. Hispanic (18)	18	0.12
Trinidadian/Tobagonian (9)	9	0.06
U.S. Virgin Islander (9)	9	0.06

Hispanic Origin	Population	%
Hispanic or Latino (of any race)	328	2.23
Central American, ex. Mexican	20	0.14
Costa Rican	2	0.01
Guatemalan	4	0.03
Honduran	2	0.01
Panamanian	5	0.03
Salvadoran	7	0.05
Cuban	9	0.06
Dominican Republic	19	0.13
Mexican	81	0.55
Puerto Rican	143	0.97
South American	11	0.07
Argentinean	2	0.01
Chilean	2	0.01
Colombian	2	0.01
Ecuadorian	4	0.03
Uruguayan	1	0.01
Other Hispanic or Latino	45	0.31

Race*	Population	%
African-American/Black (330)	402	2.73
Not Hispanic (308)	370	2.51
Hispanic (22)	32	0.22
American Indian/Alaska Native (20)	67	0.45
Not Hispanic (16)	55	0.37
Hispanic (4)	12	0.08
Blackfeet (0)	2	0.01
Canadian/French Am. Ind. (0)	1	0.01
Cherokee (2)	9	0.06
Chippewa (1)	1	0.01
Comanche (0)	2	0.01
Cree (0)	2	0.01
Iroquois (2)	10	0.07
Mexican American Ind. (0)	4	0.03
Pueblo (1)	1	0.01
Sioux (1)	1	0.01
Yaqui (2)	2	0.01
Asian (62)	80	0.54
Not Hispanic (62)	80	0.54
Chinese, ex. Taiwanese (11)	15	0.10
Filipino (11)	18	0.12
Indian (8)	9	0.06
Japanese (1)	1	0.01
Korean (23)	27	0.18
Nepalese (3)	3	0.02
Taiwanese (1)	1	0.01
Thai (1)	2	0.01
Vietnamese (0)	1	0.01
Hawaii Native/Pacific Islander (0)	5	0.03
Not Hispanic (0)	3	0.02
Hispanic (0)	2	0.01
Samoan (0)	4	0.03
White (14,085)	14,223	96.57
Not Hispanic (13,887)	13,996	95.03
Hispanic (198)	227	1.54

Mount Kisco

Place Type: Town/Village
County: Westchester
Population: 10,877†

Ancestry‡	Population	%
Albanian (73)	73	0.69

*Notes: † The Census 2010 population figure is used to calculate the percentages in the Hispanic Origin and Race categories. Ancestry percentages are based on the 2006-2010 American Community Survey population (not shown); ‡ Numbers in parentheses indicate the number of people reporting a single ancestry; * Numbers in parentheses indicate the number of persons reporting this race alone, not in combination with any other race; Please refer to the Explanation of Data for more information.*

American (140)	140	1.31
Arab (63)	115	1.08
Moroccan (12)	64	0.60
Other Arab (51)	51	0.48
Austrian (0)	113	1.06
Belgian (0)	57	0.54
Canadian (0)	10	0.09
Croatian (20)	20	0.19
Czech (0)	35	0.33
Czechoslovakian (0)	14	0.13
Dutch (0)	60	0.56
Eastern European (121)	121	1.14
English (73)	391	3.67
European (52)	52	0.49
Finnish (0)	16	0.15
French, ex. Basque (45)	163	1.53
French Canadian (0)	46	0.43
German (206)	955	8.96
Greek (0)	67	0.63
Guyanese (0)	9	0.08
Hungarian (32)	200	1.88
Iranian (30)	30	0.28
Irish (590)	1,500	14.08
Italian (1,661)	2,277	21.37
Latvian (27)	42	0.39
Lithuanian (11)	23	0.22
Norwegian (28)	76	0.71
Polish (90)	335	3.14
Portuguese (0)	33	0.31
Romanian (12)	49	0.46
Russian (119)	226	2.12
Scotch-Irish (32)	131	1.23
Scottish (45)	192	1.80
Serbian (0)	14	0.13
Slovak (19)	69	0.65
Swedish (20)	83	0.78
Swiss (0)	24	0.23
Ukrainian (92)	151	1.42
Welsh (0)	17	0.16
West Indian, ex. Hispanic (155)	194	1.82
Jamaican (39)	63	0.59
West Indian (116)	131	1.23

Hispanic Origin	Population	%
Hispanic or Latino (of any race)	3,818	35.10
Central American, ex. Mexican	2,085	19.17
Costa Rican	1	0.01
Guatemalan	1,782	16.38
Honduran	161	1.48
Nicaraguan	2	0.02
Panamanian	6	0.06
Salvadoran	102	0.94
Other Central American	31	0.29
Cuban	27	0.25
Dominican Republic	116	1.07
Mexican	153	1.41
Puerto Rican	205	1.88
South American	780	7.17
Argentinean	19	0.17
Bolivian	4	0.04
Chilean	12	0.11
Colombian	221	2.03
Ecuadorian	397	3.65
Paraguayan	15	0.14
Peruvian	92	0.85
Uruguayan	5	0.05
Venezuelan	15	0.14
Other Hispanic or Latino	452	4.16

Race*	Population	%
African-American/Black (568)	671	6.17
Not Hispanic (500)	563	5.18
Hispanic (68)	108	0.99
American Indian/Alaska Native (82)	150	1.38
Not Hispanic (6)	25	0.23
Hispanic (76)	125	1.15
Blackfeet (0)	2	0.02
Central American Ind. (26)	43	0.40
Cherokee (1)	7	0.06
Chickasaw (0)	5	0.05
Hopi (0)	1	0.01
Mexican American Ind. (30)	30	0.28
Pueblo (1)	1	0.01
Seminole (1)	1	0.01
South American Ind. (1)	4	0.04
Asian (520)	586	5.39
Not Hispanic (515)	569	5.23
Hispanic (5)	17	0.16
Bangladeshi (3)	6	0.06
Burmese (1)	3	0.03
Cambodian (3)	3	0.03
Chinese, ex. Taiwanese (110)	132	1.21
Filipino (63)	74	0.68
Hmong (1)	1	0.01
Indian (175)	183	1.68
Japanese (35)	40	0.37
Korean (68)	71	0.65
Nepalese (11)	11	0.10
Pakistani (21)	22	0.20
Sri Lankan (6)	6	0.06
Taiwanese (6)	6	0.06
Thai (3)	6	0.06
Vietnamese (0)	2	0.02
Hawaii Native/Pacific Islander (4)	14	0.13
Not Hispanic (1)	7	0.06
Hispanic (3)	7	0.06
Guamanian/Chamorro (3)	6	0.06
Native Hawaiian (1)	1	0.01
Samoan (0)	1	0.01
White (7,561)	7,946	73.05
Not Hispanic (5,862)	5,968	54.87
Hispanic (1,699)	1,978	18.19

Mount Pleasant

Place Type: Town
County: Westchester
Population: 43,724†

Ancestry‡	Population	%
Afghan (11)	11	0.03
African, Sub-Saharan (107)	165	0.38
African (65)	79	0.18
Nigerian (0)	9	0.02
South African (42)	77	0.18
Albanian (167)	202	0.47
American (1,344)	1,344	3.09
Arab (119)	219	0.50
Arab (0)	34	0.08
Egyptian (45)	65	0.15
Lebanese (59)	79	0.18
Moroccan (15)	23	0.05
Other Arab (0)	18	0.04
Armenian (9)	60	0.14
Australian (0)	37	0.09
Austrian (81)	336	0.77
Brazilian (72)	85	0.20
British (151)	204	0.47
Bulgarian (6)	18	0.04
Canadian (78)	109	0.25
Croatian (502)	554	1.28
Czech (20)	94	0.22
Czechoslovakian (24)	78	0.18
Danish (53)	157	0.36
Dutch (81)	417	0.96
Eastern European (213)	243	0.56
English (430)	2,141	4.93
Estonian (0)	12	0.03
European (506)	643	1.48
Finnish (29)	108	0.25
French, ex. Basque (64)	816	1.88
French Canadian (48)	173	0.40
German (1,013)	4,180	9.62
Greek (152)	335	0.77
Hungarian (193)	460	1.06
Iranian (24)	24	0.06
Irish (2,912)	7,270	16.74
Israeli (9)	24	0.06
Italian (7,383)	11,847	27.28
Lithuanian (46)	178	0.41
Maltese (18)	18	0.04
Northern European (88)	88	0.20
Norwegian (21)	68	0.16
Polish (580)	2,081	4.79
Portuguese (344)	455	1.05
Romanian (31)	120	0.28
Russian (650)	1,846	4.25
Scandinavian (23)	60	0.14
Scotch-Irish (102)	338	0.78
Scottish (101)	873	2.01
Slavic (33)	76	0.17
Slovak (58)	155	0.36
Slovene (9)	44	0.10
Swedish (34)	400	0.92
Swiss (111)	227	0.52
Turkish (0)	20	0.05
Ukrainian (72)	149	0.34
Welsh (2)	119	0.27
West Indian, ex. Hispanic (40)	88	0.20
Haitian (0)	24	0.06
Jamaican (40)	57	0.13
West Indian (0)	7	0.02
Yugoslavian (312)	312	0.72

Hispanic Origin	Population	%
Hispanic or Latino (of any race)	7,859	17.97
Central American, ex. Mexican	359	0.82
Costa Rican	2	<0.01
Guatemalan	225	0.51
Honduran	59	0.13
Nicaraguan	14	0.03
Panamanian	7	0.02
Salvadoran	50	0.11
Other Central American	2	<0.01
Cuban	244	0.56
Dominican Republic	2,030	4.64
Mexican	504	1.15
Puerto Rican	1,065	2.44
South American	2,921	6.68
Argentinean	55	0.13
Bolivian	11	0.03
Chilean	180	0.41
Colombian	272	0.62
Ecuadorian	2,090	4.78
Paraguayan	15	0.03
Peruvian	232	0.53
Uruguayan	47	0.11
Venezuelan	14	0.03
Other South American	5	0.01
Other Hispanic or Latino	736	1.68

Race*	Population	%
African-American/Black (2,396)	2,662	6.09
Not Hispanic (2,076)	2,229	5.10
Hispanic (320)	433	0.99
American Indian/Alaska Native (111)	243	0.56
Not Hispanic (22)	93	0.21
Hispanic (89)	150	0.34
Apache (0)	2	<0.01
Blackfeet (0)	6	0.01
Canadian/French Am. Ind. (2)	3	0.01
Central American Ind. (4)	7	0.02
Cherokee (0)	22	0.05
Cheyenne (1)	1	<0.01
Chippewa (2)	2	<0.01
Choctaw (0)	6	0.01
Creek (0)	3	0.01
Delaware (0)	2	<0.01
Iroquois (3)	8	0.02
Mexican American Ind. (3)	5	0.01
Navajo (0)	1	<0.01
Ottawa (1)	1	<0.01
Pueblo (5)	6	0.01
Seminole (0)	1	<0.01
Sioux (4)	5	0.01
South American Ind. (10)	17	0.04
Spanish American Ind. (8)	9	0.02
Asian (2,113)	2,453	5.61
Not Hispanic (2,093)	2,388	5.46
Hispanic (20)	65	0.15

*Notes: † The Census 2010 population figure is used to calculate the percentages in the Hispanic Origin and Race categories. Ancestry percentages are based on the 2006-2010 American Community Survey population (not shown); ‡ Numbers in parentheses indicate the number of people reporting a single ancestry; * Numbers in parentheses indicate the number of persons reporting this race alone, not in combination with any other race; Please refer to the Explanation of Data for more information.*

Bangladeshi (13)	16	0.04
Burmese (10)	10	0.02
Cambodian (2)	3	0.01
Chinese, ex. Taiwanese (568)	695	1.59
Filipino (182)	230	0.53
Indian (735)	795	1.82
Japanese (108)	157	0.36
Korean (263)	299	0.68
Laotian (1)	5	0.01
Malaysian (1)	2	<0.01
Nepalese (14)	14	0.03
Pakistani (58)	66	0.15
Sri Lankan (2)	2	<0.01
Taiwanese (36)	39	0.09
Thai (23)	31	0.07
Vietnamese (42)	55	0.13
Hawaii Native/Pacific Islander (11)	67	0.15
Not Hispanic (11)	32	0.07
Hispanic (0)	35	0.08
Native Hawaiian (3)	15	0.03
Samoan (0)	1	<0.01
White (34,827)	35,698	81.64
Not Hispanic (31,074)	31,482	72.00
Hispanic (3,753)	4,216	9.64

Mount Sinai

Place Type: CDP
County: Suffolk
Population: 12,118†

Ancestry‡	Population	%
American (279)	279	2.40
Arab (9)	19	0.16
Lebanese (9)	19	0.16
Austrian (0)	29	0.25
Brazilian (21)	21	0.18
British (0)	19	0.16
Czech (31)	67	0.58
Czechoslovakian (0)	36	0.31
Danish (0)	7	0.06
Dutch (9)	161	1.39
Eastern European (12)	24	0.21
English (88)	568	4.89
European (52)	52	0.45
Finnish (23)	35	0.30
French, ex. Basque (10)	306	2.63
French Canadian (9)	27	0.23
German (430)	2,549	21.93
Greek (78)	125	1.08
Hungarian (16)	215	1.85
Irish (791)	3,355	28.86
Italian (1,921)	4,006	34.46
Lithuanian (10)	60	0.52
Norwegian (23)	132	1.14
Polish (211)	598	5.14
Portuguese (9)	36	0.31
Romanian (5)	65	0.56
Russian (244)	474	4.08
Scotch-Irish (68)	171	1.47
Scottish (34)	205	1.76
Swedish (25)	149	1.28
Swiss (17)	55	0.47
Turkish (55)	55	0.47
Ukrainian (0)	13	0.11
Welsh (0)	24	0.21

Hispanic Origin	Population	%
Hispanic or Latino (of any race)	706	5.83
Central American, ex. Mexican	37	0.31
Costa Rican	2	0.02
Guatemalan	11	0.09
Honduran	7	0.06
Panamanian	1	0.01
Salvadoran	16	0.13
Cuban	48	0.40
Dominican Republic	99	0.82
Mexican	52	0.43
Puerto Rican	255	2.10
South American	117	0.97
Argentinean	10	0.08
Chilean	4	0.03
Colombian	47	0.39
Ecuadorian	36	0.30
Peruvian	11	0.09
Uruguayan	2	0.02
Venezuelan	2	0.02
Other South American	5	0.04
Other Hispanic or Latino	98	0.81

Race*	Population	%
African-American/Black (180)	217	1.79
Not Hispanic (165)	186	1.53
Hispanic (15)	31	0.26
American Indian/Alaska Native (18)	60	0.50
Not Hispanic (12)	43	0.35
Hispanic (6)	17	0.14
Central American Ind. (0)	1	0.01
Cherokee (2)	13	0.11
Choctaw (0)	5	0.04
Delaware (0)	2	0.02
Lumbee (0)	2	0.02
Potawatomi (4)	4	0.03
Seminole (0)	1	0.01
South American Ind. (6)	6	0.05
Spanish American Ind. (0)	1	0.01
Asian (487)	566	4.67
Not Hispanic (486)	558	4.60
Hispanic (1)	8	0.07
Bangladeshi (21)	21	0.17
Chinese, ex. Taiwanese (174)	199	1.64
Filipino (49)	77	0.64
Indian (100)	124	1.02
Indonesian (1)	1	0.01
Japanese (13)	17	0.14
Korean (32)	45	0.37
Malaysian (0)	4	0.03
Pakistani (38)	44	0.36
Sri Lankan (6)	6	0.05
Taiwanese (6)	6	0.05
Thai (5)	6	0.05
Vietnamese (3)	8	0.07
Hawaii Native/Pacific Islander (8)	12	0.10
Not Hispanic (0)	4	0.03
Hispanic (8)	8	0.07
Guamanian/Chamorro (1)	1	0.01
White (11,157)	11,287	93.14
Not Hispanic (10,620)	10,708	88.36
Hispanic (537)	579	4.78

Mount Vernon

Place Type: City
County: Westchester
Population: 67,292†

Ancestry‡	Population	%
African, Sub-Saharan (1,490)	1,910	2.85
African (786)	1,162	1.73
Cape Verdean (0)	11	0.02
Ghanaian (347)	347	0.52
Liberian (0)	9	0.01
Nigerian (148)	148	0.22
Senegalese (0)	12	0.02
Sierra Leonean (10)	22	0.03
Ugandan (19)	19	0.03
Other Sub-Saharan African (180)	180	0.27
Albanian (303)	303	0.45
American (2,069)	2,069	3.08
Arab (217)	305	0.45
Egyptian (56)	68	0.10
Lebanese (0)	12	0.02
Moroccan (0)	64	0.10
Palestinian (13)	13	0.02
Other Arab (148)	148	0.22
Australian (0)	13	0.02
Austrian (60)	150	0.22
Brazilian (1,938)	2,013	3.00
British (45)	146	0.22
Canadian (0)	61	0.09
Czech (47)	70	0.10
Czechoslovakian (11)	11	0.02
Danish (10)	21	0.03
Dutch (22)	191	0.28
Eastern European (93)	127	0.19
English (260)	843	1.26
Estonian (21)	45	0.07
European (145)	145	0.22
Finnish (12)	12	0.02
French, ex. Basque (129)	377	0.56
French Canadian (14)	62	0.09
German (373)	1,326	1.98
Greek (100)	185	0.28
Guyanese (326)	360	0.54
Hungarian (74)	129	0.19
Iranian (0)	21	0.03
Irish (950)	2,889	4.31
Israeli (116)	174	0.26
Italian (3,462)	5,281	7.87
Latvian (0)	10	0.01
Lithuanian (13)	57	0.08
Maltese (24)	24	0.04
Norwegian (10)	21	0.03
Polish (283)	651	0.97
Portuguese (979)	1,149	1.71
Romanian (123)	123	0.18
Russian (143)	433	0.65
Scandinavian (15)	15	0.02
Scotch-Irish (60)	127	0.19
Scottish (46)	150	0.22
Serbian (8)	8	0.01
Slavic (9)	9	0.01
Swedish (0)	46	0.07
Ukrainian (0)	69	0.10
Welsh (0)	63	0.09
West Indian, ex. Hispanic (12,148)	13,279	19.80
Bahamian (11)	11	0.02
Barbadian (190)	208	0.31
Belizean (118)	118	0.18
British West Indian (315)	348	0.52
Haitian (324)	465	0.69
Jamaican (9,769)	10,445	15.57
Trinidadian/Tobagonian (370)	397	0.59
West Indian (1,051)	1,287	1.92
Yugoslavian (9)	9	0.01

Hispanic Origin	Population	%
Hispanic or Latino (of any race)	9,592	14.25
Central American, ex. Mexican	754	1.12
Costa Rican	64	0.10
Guatemalan	141	0.21
Honduran	233	0.35
Nicaraguan	35	0.05
Panamanian	131	0.19
Salvadoran	137	0.20
Other Central American	13	0.02
Cuban	231	0.34
Dominican Republic	1,611	2.39
Mexican	2,454	3.65
Puerto Rican	2,582	3.84
South American	1,205	1.79
Argentinean	91	0.14
Bolivian	18	0.03
Chilean	29	0.04
Colombian	407	0.60
Ecuadorian	268	0.40
Paraguayan	68	0.10
Peruvian	219	0.33
Uruguayan	16	0.02
Venezuelan	56	0.08
Other South American	33	0.05
Other Hispanic or Latino	755	1.12

Race*	Population	%
African-American/Black (42,667)	44,244	65.75
Not Hispanic (41,226)	42,361	62.95
Hispanic (1,441)	1,883	2.80
American Indian/Alaska Native (312)	820	1.22
Not Hispanic (200)	585	0.87
Hispanic (112)	235	0.35

*Notes: † The Census 2010 population figure is used to calculate the percentages in the Hispanic Origin and Race categories. Ancestry percentages are based on the 2006-2010 American Community Survey population (not shown); ‡ Numbers in parentheses indicate the number of people reporting a single ancestry; * Numbers in parentheses indicate the number of persons reporting this race alone, not in combination with any other race; Please refer to the Explanation of Data for more information.*

	Population	%
Blackfeet (1)	38	0.06
Central American Ind. (7)	19	0.03
Cherokee (27)	116	0.17
Chickasaw (2)	4	0.01
Choctaw (4)	4	0.01
Cree (0)	2	<0.01
Delaware (1)	1	<0.01
Iroquois (2)	8	0.01
Mexican American Ind. (13)	14	0.02
Navajo (1)	2	<0.01
Pueblo (4)	7	0.01
Seminole (0)	9	0.01
Sioux (1)	6	0.01
South American Ind. (15)	36	0.05
Spanish American Ind. (0)	4	0.01
Asian (1,236)	1,672	2.48
Not Hispanic (1,206)	1,587	2.36
Hispanic (30)	85	0.13
Bangladeshi (7)	11	0.02
Burmese (2)	2	<0.01
Cambodian (7)	9	0.01
Chinese, ex. Taiwanese (187)	264	0.39
Filipino (220)	281	0.42
Indian (529)	711	1.06
Indonesian (0)	11	0.02
Japanese (55)	88	0.13
Korean (72)	92	0.14
Laotian (5)	12	0.02
Malaysian (0)	1	<0.01
Nepalese (4)	4	0.01
Pakistani (26)	38	0.06
Sri Lankan (1)	1	<0.01
Taiwanese (10)	10	0.01
Thai (67)	73	0.11
Vietnamese (7)	12	0.02
Hawaii Native/Pacific Islander (36)	156	0.23
Not Hispanic (27)	130	0.19
Hispanic (9)	26	0.04
Fijian (0)	1	<0.01
Guamanian/Chamorro (1)	4	0.01
Native Hawaiian (5)	13	0.02
Samoan (1)	3	<0.01
White (16,371)	17,846	26.52
Not Hispanic (12,449)	13,354	19.84
Hispanic (3,922)	4,492	6.68

Nanuet

Place Type: CDP
County: Rockland
Population: 17,882†

Ancestry‡	Population	%
African, Sub-Saharan (117)	117	0.66
African (18)	18	0.10
Ghanaian (99)	99	0.56
Albanian (186)	186	1.04
American (485)	485	2.72
Arab (145)	202	1.13
Arab (8)	27	0.15
Egyptian (99)	124	0.70
Jordanian (9)	9	0.05
Lebanese (0)	13	0.07
Other Arab (29)	29	0.16
Austrian (20)	126	0.71
Belgian (0)	17	0.10
Brazilian (25)	60	0.34
British (13)	13	0.07
Canadian (0)	13	0.07
Croatian (40)	88	0.49
Czech (10)	51	0.29
Czechoslovakian (8)	20	0.11
Danish (0)	23	0.13
Dutch (15)	106	0.60
Eastern European (57)	57	0.32
English (62)	444	2.49
European (86)	117	0.66
Finnish (0)	12	0.07
French, ex. Basque (29)	128	0.72
French Canadian (51)	88	0.49
German (373)	1,508	8.47
Greek (85)	192	1.08
Guyanese (77)	77	0.43
Hungarian (78)	303	1.70
Irish (1,817)	3,690	20.72
Israeli (18)	18	0.10
Italian (1,661)	3,214	18.05
Latvian (23)	23	0.13
Lithuanian (17)	27	0.15
Norwegian (33)	44	0.25
Polish (328)	801	4.50
Portuguese (26)	36	0.20
Romanian (0)	152	0.85
Russian (427)	878	4.93
Scandinavian (12)	12	0.07
Scotch-Irish (29)	93	0.52
Scottish (22)	71	0.40
Slavic (0)	12	0.07
Slovak (70)	110	0.62
Swedish (11)	36	0.20
Swiss (13)	20	0.11
Turkish (11)	11	0.06
Ukrainian (37)	87	0.49
Welsh (0)	14	0.08
West Indian, ex. Hispanic (1,253)	1,313	7.37
Barbadian (10)	10	0.06
British West Indian (21)	45	0.25
Haitian (1,002)	1,014	5.70
Jamaican (174)	198	1.11
West Indian (46)	46	0.26

Hispanic Origin	Population	%
Hispanic or Latino (of any race)	2,445	13.67
Central American, ex. Mexican	493	2.76
Costa Rican	14	0.08
Guatemalan	196	1.10
Honduran	30	0.17
Nicaraguan	3	0.02
Panamanian	11	0.06
Salvadoran	239	1.34
Cuban	99	0.55
Dominican Republic	226	1.26
Mexican	209	1.17
Puerto Rican	774	4.33
South American	467	2.61
Argentinean	18	0.10
Bolivian	1	0.01
Chilean	12	0.07
Colombian	72	0.40
Ecuadorian	337	1.88
Paraguayan	1	0.01
Peruvian	21	0.12
Uruguayan	1	0.01
Venezuelan	3	0.02
Other South American	1	0.01
Other Hispanic or Latino	177	0.99

Race*	Population	%
African-American/Black (2,664)	2,864	16.02
Not Hispanic (2,505)	2,635	14.74
Hispanic (159)	229	1.28
American Indian/Alaska Native (40)	110	0.62
Not Hispanic (25)	78	0.44
Hispanic (15)	32	0.18
Blackfeet (0)	2	0.01
Cherokee (1)	8	0.04
Choctaw (1)	1	0.01
Creek (0)	3	0.02
Delaware (3)	5	0.03
Iroquois (2)	3	0.02
Lumbee (1)	1	0.01
Pueblo (1)	4	0.02
South American Ind. (10)	14	0.08
Tlingit-Haida *(Alaska Native)* (0)	1	0.01
Asian (2,213)	2,368	13.24
Not Hispanic (2,207)	2,337	13.07
Hispanic (6)	31	0.17
Bangladeshi (18)	23	0.13
Cambodian (23)	24	0.13
Chinese, ex. Taiwanese (338)	372	2.08
Filipino (535)	574	3.21
Indian (815)	879	4.92
Indonesian (1)	2	0.01
Japanese (15)	20	0.11
Korean (237)	241	1.35
Nepalese (2)	2	0.01
Pakistani (102)	120	0.67
Sri Lankan (21)	21	0.12
Taiwanese (8)	9	0.05
Thai (23)	23	0.13
Vietnamese (34)	44	0.25
Hawaii Native/Pacific Islander (4)	25	0.14
Not Hispanic (0)	19	0.11
Hispanic (4)	6	0.03
Samoan (0)	1	0.01
White (11,807)	12,092	67.62
Not Hispanic (10,418)	10,585	59.19
Hispanic (1,389)	1,507	8.43

Nesconset

Place Type: CDP
County: Suffolk
Population: 13,387†

Ancestry‡	Population	%
American (461)	461	3.39
Arab (44)	134	0.98
Jordanian (28)	28	0.21
Lebanese (16)	106	0.78
Australian (8)	8	0.06
Austrian (56)	107	0.79
British (9)	44	0.32
Croatian (14)	55	0.40
Czech (39)	232	1.71
Czechoslovakian (16)	73	0.54
Danish (0)	32	0.24
Dutch (15)	99	0.73
Eastern European (77)	77	0.57
English (53)	469	3.45
European (111)	111	0.82
Finnish (10)	27	0.20
French, ex. Basque (18)	161	1.18
French Canadian (77)	129	0.95
German (331)	2,674	19.65
Greek (263)	380	2.79
Hungarian (47)	198	1.46
Irish (930)	3,743	27.51
Italian (2,629)	5,807	42.68
Latvian (0)	12	0.09
Norwegian (54)	124	0.91
Polish (268)	938	6.89
Portuguese (9)	28	0.21
Russian (120)	316	2.32
Scandinavian (16)	16	0.12
Scotch-Irish (103)	128	0.94
Scottish (0)	153	1.12
Slavic (0)	18	0.13
Swedish (19)	143	1.05
Swiss (0)	20	0.15
Turkish (39)	39	0.29
Ukrainian (0)	56	0.41
West Indian, ex. Hispanic (44)	82	0.60
Haitian (23)	23	0.17
Jamaican (12)	31	0.23
Trinidadian/Tobagonian (9)	28	0.21

Hispanic Origin	Population	%
Hispanic or Latino (of any race)	825	6.16
Central American, ex. Mexican	109	0.81
Costa Rican	3	0.02
Guatemalan	7	0.05
Honduran	16	0.12
Nicaraguan	1	0.01
Panamanian	6	0.04
Salvadoran	76	0.57
Cuban	25	0.19
Dominican Republic	53	0.40
Mexican	61	0.46
Puerto Rican	311	2.32

*Notes: † The Census 2010 population figure is used to calculate the percentages in the Hispanic Origin and Race categories. Ancestry percentages are based on the 2006-2010 American Community Survey population (not shown); ‡ Numbers in parentheses indicate the number of people reporting a single ancestry; * Numbers in parentheses indicate the number of persons reporting this race alone, not in combination with any other race; Please refer to the Explanation of Data for more information.*

South American	187	1.40
Argentinean	21	0.16
Bolivian	17	0.13
Chilean	14	0.10
Colombian	55	0.41
Ecuadorian	41	0.31
Paraguayan	2	0.01
Peruvian	32	0.24
Uruguayan	1	0.01
Other South American	4	0.03
Other Hispanic or Latino	79	0.59

Race*	Population	%
African-American/Black (168)	208	1.55
Not Hispanic (159)	194	1.45
Hispanic (9)	14	0.10
American Indian/Alaska Native (9)	35	0.26
Not Hispanic (9)	32	0.24
Hispanic (0)	3	0.02
Iroquois (9)	11	0.08
Lumbee (0)	5	0.04
South American Ind. (0)	1	0.01
Asian (652)	697	5.21
Not Hispanic (651)	689	5.15
Hispanic (1)	8	0.06
Bangladeshi (7)	7	0.05
Chinese, ex. Taiwanese (165)	174	1.30
Filipino (59)	75	0.56
Indian (217)	228	1.70
Indonesian (4)	4	0.03
Japanese (11)	15	0.11
Korean (87)	90	0.67
Pakistani (60)	64	0.48
Sri Lankan (0)	1	0.01
Taiwanese (13)	14	0.10
Vietnamese (11)	12	0.09
Hawaii Native/Pacific Islander (0)	3	0.02
Not Hispanic (0)	1	0.01
Hispanic (0)	2	0.01
Native Hawaiian (0)	2	0.01
White (12,291)	12,414	92.73
Not Hispanic (11,640)	11,725	87.58
Hispanic (651)	689	5.15

New Cassel

Place Type: CDP
County: Nassau
Population: 14,059†

Ancestry‡	Population	%
African, Sub-Saharan (219)	308	2.45
African (92)	181	1.44
Nigerian (127)	127	1.01
Albanian (19)	19	0.15
American (118)	118	0.94
Austrian (9)	9	0.07
Brazilian (14)	27	0.21
British (7)	7	0.06
English (0)	110	0.88
European (0)	96	0.76
French, ex. Basque (0)	39	0.31
French Canadian (22)	45	0.36
German (24)	78	0.62
Greek (19)	39	0.31
Guyanese (63)	63	0.50
Irish (27)	112	0.89
Italian (146)	264	2.10
Norwegian (9)	9	0.07
Polish (16)	58	0.46
Portuguese (65)	73	0.58
Romanian (16)	16	0.13
Russian (0)	8	0.06
Scottish (0)	16	0.13
Ukrainian (16)	16	0.13
West Indian, ex. Hispanic (1,301)	1,491	11.87
Haitian (1,053)	1,053	8.38
Jamaican (248)	341	2.71
West Indian (0)	97	0.77

Hispanic Origin	Population	%
Hispanic or Latino (of any race)	7,577	53.89
Central American, ex. Mexican	4,455	31.69
Costa Rican	10	0.07
Guatemalan	78	0.55
Honduran	812	5.78
Nicaraguan	29	0.21
Panamanian	12	0.09
Salvadoran	3,477	24.73
Other Central American	37	0.26
Cuban	27	0.19
Dominican Republic	194	1.38
Mexican	1,739	12.37
Puerto Rican	181	1.29
South American	282	2.01
Argentinean	5	0.04
Bolivian	1	0.01
Chilean	10	0.07
Colombian	81	0.58
Ecuadorian	132	0.94
Peruvian	38	0.27
Uruguayan	2	0.01
Venezuelan	13	0.09
Other Hispanic or Latino	699	4.97

Race*	Population	%
African-American/Black (5,374)	5,582	39.70
Not Hispanic (5,225)	5,364	38.15
Hispanic (149)	218	1.55
American Indian/Alaska Native (106)	235	1.67
Not Hispanic (10)	70	0.50
Hispanic (96)	165	1.17
Central American Ind. (6)	10	0.07
Cherokee (2)	23	0.16
Cheyenne (3)	3	0.02
Iroquois (1)	1	0.01
Mexican American Ind. (13)	19	0.14
South American Ind. (3)	6	0.04
Spanish American Ind. (11)	11	0.08
Yaqui (1)	1	0.01
Asian (200)	268	1.91
Not Hispanic (174)	220	1.56
Hispanic (26)	48	0.34
Bangladeshi (6)	6	0.04
Chinese, ex. Taiwanese (39)	44	0.31
Filipino (33)	34	0.24
Indian (71)	107	0.76
Indonesian (1)	1	0.01
Japanese (8)	8	0.06
Korean (8)	8	0.06
Pakistani (16)	21	0.15
Sri Lankan (7)	7	0.05
Thai (4)	6	0.04
Vietnamese (1)	1	0.01
Hawaii Native/Pacific Islander (1)	32	0.23
Not Hispanic (1)	25	0.18
Hispanic (0)	7	0.05
Native Hawaiian (0)	5	0.04
Samoan (1)	1	0.01
White (3,661)	4,205	29.91
Not Hispanic (841)	933	6.64
Hispanic (2,820)	3,272	23.27

New Castle

Place Type: Town
County: Westchester
Population: 17,569†

Ancestry‡	Population	%
African, Sub-Saharan (28)	108	0.62
African (0)	68	0.39
South African (28)	40	0.23
American (812)	812	4.66
Arab (22)	102	0.58
Egyptian (0)	37	0.21
Jordanian (10)	10	0.06
Lebanese (0)	7	0.04
Other Arab (12)	48	0.28
Armenian (13)	13	0.07
Austrian (88)	386	2.21
Belgian (14)	14	0.08
Brazilian (0)	18	0.10
British (99)	128	0.73
Canadian (16)	28	0.16
Celtic (0)	11	0.06
Croatian (0)	12	0.07
Czech (33)	107	0.61
Czechoslovakian (24)	53	0.30
Danish (11)	80	0.46
Dutch (56)	142	0.81
Eastern European (1,178)	1,178	6.76
English (487)	1,478	8.48
Estonian (0)	22	0.13
European (446)	478	2.74
French, ex. Basque (74)	372	2.13
French Canadian (36)	98	0.56
German (597)	2,041	11.71
Greek (19)	130	0.75
Hungarian (241)	434	2.49
Iranian (59)	116	0.67
Irish (918)	2,315	13.28
Israeli (11)	44	0.25
Italian (1,230)	2,379	13.64
Latvian (0)	9	0.05
Lithuanian (21)	72	0.41
Macedonian (0)	13	0.07
Northern European (18)	38	0.22
Norwegian (42)	136	0.78
Polish (259)	1,091	6.26
Portuguese (48)	154	0.88
Romanian (19)	68	0.39
Russian (713)	1,879	10.78
Scandinavian (26)	66	0.38
Scotch-Irish (78)	181	1.04
Scottish (66)	370	2.12
Slovak (25)	79	0.45
Slovene (0)	12	0.07
Swedish (12)	170	0.97
Swiss (28)	77	0.44
Turkish (255)	255	1.46
Ukrainian (18)	64	0.37
Welsh (42)	134	0.77
West Indian, ex. Hispanic (35)	106	0.61
Barbadian (0)	27	0.15
British West Indian (0)	30	0.17
Jamaican (35)	35	0.20
West Indian (0)	14	0.08
Yugoslavian (27)	53	0.30

Hispanic Origin	Population	%
Hispanic or Latino (of any race)	710	4.04
Central American, ex. Mexican	69	0.39
Costa Rican	8	0.05
Guatemalan	35	0.20
Honduran	5	0.03
Nicaraguan	5	0.03
Panamanian	12	0.07
Salvadoran	2	0.01
Other Central American	2	0.01
Cuban	46	0.26
Dominican Republic	48	0.27
Mexican	87	0.50
Puerto Rican	146	0.83
South American	229	1.30
Argentinean	22	0.13
Chilean	12	0.07
Colombian	54	0.31
Ecuadorian	77	0.44
Paraguayan	11	0.06
Peruvian	20	0.11
Uruguayan	21	0.12
Venezuelan	11	0.06
Other South American	1	0.01
Other Hispanic or Latino	85	0.48

Race*	Population	%
African-American/Black (283)	373	2.12
Not Hispanic (263)	321	1.83
Hispanic (20)	52	0.30

SECTION TWO

*Notes: † The Census 2010 population figure is used to calculate the percentages in the Hispanic Origin and Race categories. Ancestry percentages are based on the 2006-2010 American Community Survey population (not shown); ‡ Numbers in parentheses indicate the number of people reporting a single ancestry; * Numbers in parentheses indicate the number of persons reporting this race alone, not in combination with any other race; Please refer to the Explanation of Data for more information.*

American Indian/Alaska Native (6)	46	0.26
Not Hispanic (3)	36	0.20
Hispanic (3)	10	0.06
Cherokee (1)	18	0.10
Choctaw (0)	1	0.01
Creek (0)	2	0.01
Iroquois (1)	2	0.01
Mexican American Ind. (3)	3	0.02
Asian (1,289)	1,467	8.35
Not Hispanic (1,282)	1,456	8.29
Hispanic (7)	11	0.06
Bangladeshi (2)	2	0.01
Burmese (3)	3	0.02
Cambodian (3)	8	0.05
Chinese, ex. Taiwanese (547)	622	3.54
Filipino (48)	63	0.36
Indian (352)	384	2.19
Indonesian (1)	1	0.01
Japanese (91)	133	0.76
Korean (149)	174	0.99
Malaysian (1)	1	0.01
Pakistani (26)	35	0.20
Taiwanese (23)	25	0.14
Thai (3)	4	0.02
Vietnamese (4)	5	0.03
Hawaii Native/Pacific Islander (1)	5	0.03
Not Hispanic (1)	5	0.03
Native Hawaiian (1)	3	0.02
White (15,505)	15,810	89.99
Not Hispanic (15,013)	15,248	86.79
Hispanic (492)	562	3.20

New City

Place Type: CDP
County: Rockland
Population: 33,559†

Ancestry‡	Population	%
African, Sub-Saharan (12)	12	0.04
African (12)	12	0.04
Albanian (14)	25	0.07
American (2,426)	2,426	7.26
Arab (189)	377	1.13
Egyptian (130)	130	0.39
Iraqi (7)	24	0.07
Lebanese (32)	115	0.34
Syrian (0)	88	0.26
Other Arab (20)	20	0.06
Armenian (72)	72	0.22
Assyrian/Chaldean/Syriac (0)	17	0.05
Austrian (129)	389	1.16
Brazilian (21)	42	0.13
British (22)	67	0.20
Canadian (41)	55	0.16
Croatian (7)	7	0.02
Czech (50)	91	0.27
Czechoslovakian (51)	59	0.18
Dutch (18)	143	0.43
Eastern European (804)	890	2.66
English (236)	782	2.34
European (390)	390	1.17
Finnish (30)	30	0.09
French, ex. Basque (32)	307	0.92
French Canadian (0)	59	0.18
German (830)	2,929	8.77
Greek (103)	231	0.69
Hungarian (126)	447	1.34
Iranian (85)	131	0.39
Irish (2,737)	5,771	17.28
Israeli (78)	226	0.68
Italian (3,700)	6,591	19.73
Latvian (36)	59	0.18
Lithuanian (12)	57	0.17
Macedonian (24)	24	0.07
Maltese (0)	8	0.02
Northern European (12)	25	0.07
Norwegian (58)	170	0.51
Polish (839)	1,963	5.88
Portuguese (88)	88	0.26
Romanian (150)	332	0.99
Russian (1,619)	2,957	8.85
Scotch-Irish (52)	160	0.48
Scottish (0)	168	0.50
Serbian (0)	8	0.02
Slavic (11)	28	0.08
Slovak (82)	129	0.39
Swedish (30)	176	0.53
Swiss (11)	30	0.09
Turkish (43)	49	0.15
Ukrainian (118)	219	0.66
Welsh (0)	50	0.15
West Indian, ex. Hispanic (236)	281	0.84
Belizean (9)	9	0.03
Haitian (152)	171	0.51
Jamaican (34)	60	0.18
Trinidadian/Tobagonian (27)	27	0.08
West Indian (14)	14	0.04
Yugoslavian (0)	10	0.03

Hispanic Origin	Population	%
Hispanic or Latino (of any race)	3,014	8.98
Central American, ex. Mexican	212	0.63
Costa Rican	14	0.04
Guatemalan	71	0.21
Honduran	19	0.06
Nicaraguan	2	0.01
Panamanian	17	0.05
Salvadoran	82	0.24
Other Central American	7	0.02
Cuban	164	0.49
Dominican Republic	401	1.19
Mexican	370	1.10
Puerto Rican	1,249	3.72
South American	416	1.24
Argentinean	38	0.11
Bolivian	18	0.05
Chilean	24	0.07
Colombian	114	0.34
Ecuadorian	170	0.51
Paraguayan	4	0.01
Peruvian	39	0.12
Uruguayan	1	<0.01
Venezuelan	3	0.01
Other South American	5	0.01
Other Hispanic or Latino	202	0.60

Race*	Population	%
African-American/Black (2,155)	2,455	7.32
Not Hispanic (2,029)	2,248	6.70
Hispanic (126)	207	0.62
American Indian/Alaska Native (51)	140	0.42
Not Hispanic (30)	102	0.30
Hispanic (21)	38	0.11
Apache (0)	2	0.01
Blackfeet (1)	1	<0.01
Cherokee (0)	10	0.03
Cree (0)	1	<0.01
Delaware (3)	3	0.01
Iroquois (4)	4	0.01
Lumbee (1)	1	<0.01
Mexican American Ind. (2)	2	0.01
Seminole (0)	4	0.01
Sioux (0)	1	<0.01
South American Ind. (2)	3	0.01
Asian (3,460)	3,803	11.33
Not Hispanic (3,429)	3,723	11.09
Hispanic (31)	80	0.24
Bangladeshi (28)	32	0.10
Burmese (0)	1	<0.01
Cambodian (13)	18	0.05
Chinese, ex. Taiwanese (498)	579	1.73
Filipino (650)	768	2.29
Indian (1,465)	1,577	4.70
Indonesian (3)	8	0.02
Japanese (31)	43	0.13
Korean (476)	493	1.47
Malaysian (0)	3	0.01
Pakistani (139)	145	0.43
Sri Lankan (4)	10	0.03
Taiwanese (25)	27	0.08
Thai (22)	33	0.10
Vietnamese (47)	60	0.18
Hawaii Native/Pacific Islander (1)	25	0.07
Not Hispanic (0)	21	0.06
Hispanic (1)	4	0.01
Native Hawaiian (0)	3	0.01
White (26,412)	26,950	80.31
Not Hispanic (24,455)	24,811	73.93
Hispanic (1,957)	2,139	6.37

New Hartford

Place Type: Town
County: Oneida
Population: 22,166†

Ancestry‡	Population	%
American (677)	677	3.08
Arab (311)	710	3.23
Egyptian (0)	16	0.07
Lebanese (178)	271	1.23
Moroccan (8)	8	0.04
Syrian (61)	351	1.60
Other Arab (64)	64	0.29
Armenian (72)	72	0.33
Austrian (6)	61	0.28
Brazilian (12)	18	0.08
British (153)	192	0.87
Canadian (0)	53	0.24
Carpatho Rusyn (8)	15	0.07
Czech (0)	13	0.06
Czechoslovakian (0)	10	0.05
Danish (12)	72	0.33
Dutch (79)	530	2.41
Eastern European (136)	136	0.62
English (457)	2,263	10.30
Estonian (0)	9	0.04
European (48)	48	0.22
Finnish (0)	15	0.07
French, ex. Basque (125)	1,157	5.27
French Canadian (72)	270	1.23
German (942)	3,905	17.78
Guyanese (3)	12	0.05
Hungarian (0)	54	0.25
Irish (1,089)	4,420	20.12
Italian (3,254)	5,998	27.30
Lithuanian (12)	133	0.61
Norwegian (0)	22	0.10
Pennsylvania German (24)	24	0.11
Polish (1,275)	3,287	14.96
Portuguese (0)	31	0.14
Russian (102)	389	1.77
Scandinavian (0)	8	0.04
Scotch-Irish (179)	406	1.85
Scottish (109)	511	2.33
Slovak (12)	28	0.13
Swedish (42)	96	0.44
Swiss (0)	84	0.38
Turkish (0)	7	0.03
Ukrainian (272)	333	1.52
Welsh (142)	804	3.66
West Indian, ex. Hispanic (20)	31	0.14
Jamaican (20)	31	0.14
Yugoslavian (12)	12	0.05

Hispanic Origin	Population	%
Hispanic or Latino (of any race)	434	1.96
Central American, ex. Mexican	28	0.13
Costa Rican	2	0.01
Guatemalan	17	0.08
Panamanian	2	0.01
Salvadoran	7	0.03
Cuban	6	0.03
Dominican Republic	29	0.13
Mexican	63	0.28
Puerto Rican	214	0.97
South American	51	0.23
Argentinean	5	0.02
Chilean	2	0.01

*Notes: † The Census 2010 population figure is used to calculate the percentages in the Hispanic Origin and Race categories. Ancestry percentages are based on the 2006-2010 American Community Survey population (not shown); ‡ Numbers in parentheses indicate the number of people reporting a single ancestry; * Numbers in parentheses indicate the number of persons reporting this race alone, not in combination with any other race; Please refer to the Explanation of Data for more information.*

Colombian	12	0.05
Ecuadorian	14	0.06
Peruvian	12	0.05
Venezuelan	6	0.03
Other Hispanic or Latino	43	0.19

Race*	Population	%
African-American/Black (291)	417	1.88
Not Hispanic (271)	374	1.69
Hispanic (20)	43	0.19
American Indian/Alaska Native (15)	44	0.20
Not Hispanic (15)	40	0.18
Hispanic (0)	4	0.02
Blackfeet (0)	1	<0.01
Central American Ind. (0)	3	0.01
Cherokee (0)	4	0.02
Chippewa (1)	1	<0.01
Iroquois (7)	13	0.06
Kiowa (1)	1	<0.01
Sioux (0)	1	<0.01
Asian (698)	800	3.61
Not Hispanic (695)	792	3.57
Hispanic (3)	8	0.04
Bangladeshi (13)	13	0.06
Burmese (13)	13	0.06
Cambodian (12)	12	0.05
Chinese, ex. Taiwanese (102)	115	0.52
Filipino (37)	40	0.18
Indian (318)	341	1.54
Indonesian (1)	1	<0.01
Japanese (16)	20	0.09
Korean (58)	77	0.35
Laotian (1)	2	0.01
Malaysian (3)	11	0.05
Pakistani (45)	48	0.22
Sri Lankan (13)	13	0.06
Taiwanese (4)	9	0.04
Thai (8)	11	0.05
Vietnamese (25)	26	0.12
Hawaii Native/Pacific Islander (0)	21	0.09
Not Hispanic (0)	11	0.05
Hispanic (0)	10	0.05
Guamanian/Chamorro (0)	1	<0.01
Native Hawaiian (0)	2	0.01
Samoan (0)	1	<0.01
Tongan (0)	1	<0.01
White (20,815)	21,040	94.92
Not Hispanic (20,511)	20,706	93.41
Hispanic (304)	334	1.51

New Hyde Park

Place Type: Village
County: Nassau
Population: 9,712†

Ancestry‡	Population	%
Afghan (0)	89	0.93
African, Sub-Saharan (10)	97	1.01
African (0)	45	0.47
Nigerian (10)	35	0.36
South African (0)	17	0.18
American (180)	180	1.87
Arab (10)	67	0.70
Egyptian (10)	29	0.30
Other Arab (0)	38	0.39
Armenian (55)	55	0.57
Austrian (0)	124	1.29
Belgian (9)	9	0.09
Croatian (50)	50	0.52
Czech (9)	40	0.42
Dutch (0)	53	0.55
English (43)	298	3.10
French, ex. Basque (9)	171	1.78
French Canadian (15)	44	0.46
German (262)	894	9.29
Greek (116)	191	1.99
Guyanese (36)	85	0.88
Hungarian (0)	7	0.07
Irish (754)	1,537	15.98
Israeli (0)	11	0.11
Italian (1,808)	2,463	25.60
Lithuanian (0)	7	0.07
Norwegian (23)	23	0.24
Polish (301)	404	4.20
Portuguese (140)	140	1.46
Romanian (64)	150	1.56
Russian (145)	293	3.05
Scandinavian (0)	10	0.10
Scotch-Irish (9)	16	0.17
Scottish (13)	80	0.83
Slavic (0)	89	0.93
Slovak (0)	17	0.18
Swedish (0)	65	0.68
Turkish (3)	11	0.11
Ukrainian (40)	40	0.42
West Indian, ex. Hispanic (38)	130	1.35
Haitian (21)	62	0.64
Jamaican (17)	38	0.39
U.S. Virgin Islander (0)	30	0.31
Yugoslavian (0)	16	0.17

Hispanic Origin	Population	%
Hispanic or Latino (of any race)	1,184	12.19
Central American, ex. Mexican	203	2.09
Costa Rican	9	0.09
Guatemalan	39	0.40
Honduran	43	0.44
Nicaraguan	6	0.06
Panamanian	2	0.02
Salvadoran	104	1.07
Cuban	19	0.20
Dominican Republic	88	0.91
Mexican	13	0.13
Puerto Rican	299	3.08
South American	400	4.12
Argentinean	29	0.30
Bolivian	8	0.08
Chilean	6	0.06
Colombian	146	1.50
Ecuadorian	86	0.89
Paraguayan	7	0.07
Peruvian	96	0.99
Uruguayan	6	0.06
Venezuelan	5	0.05
Other South American	11	0.11
Other Hispanic or Latino	162	1.67

Race*	Population	%
African-American/Black (129)	185	1.90
Not Hispanic (104)	144	1.48
Hispanic (25)	41	0.42
American Indian/Alaska Native (33)	56	0.58
Not Hispanic (22)	40	0.41
Hispanic (11)	16	0.16
Cherokee (3)	4	0.04
Creek (0)	3	0.03
Iroquois (0)	4	0.04
Sioux (2)	2	0.02
South American Ind. (1)	5	0.05
Asian (2,529)	2,672	27.51
Not Hispanic (2,521)	2,643	27.21
Hispanic (8)	29	0.30
Bangladeshi (19)	22	0.23
Burmese (2)	2	0.02
Chinese, ex. Taiwanese (390)	414	4.26
Filipino (174)	203	2.09
Indian (1,624)	1,682	17.32
Japanese (16)	19	0.20
Korean (145)	148	1.52
Nepalese (6)	6	0.06
Pakistani (77)	87	0.90
Sri Lankan (2)	2	0.02
Taiwanese (23)	28	0.29
Vietnamese (7)	10	0.10
Hawaii Native/Pacific Islander (4)	21	0.22
Not Hispanic (4)	18	0.19
Hispanic (0)	3	0.03
Guamanian/Chamorro (0)	3	0.03
White (6,398)	6,534	67.28
Not Hispanic (5,642)	5,712	58.81
Hispanic (756)	822	8.46

New Paltz

Place Type: Town
County: Ulster
Population: 14,003†

Ancestry‡	Population	%
African, Sub-Saharan (41)	77	0.55
African (11)	11	0.08
Ethiopian (18)	54	0.39
Nigerian (12)	12	0.09
American (899)	899	6.46
Arab (65)	149	1.07
Egyptian (0)	14	0.10
Lebanese (40)	80	0.58
Palestinian (11)	41	0.29
Other Arab (14)	14	0.10
Armenian (17)	17	0.12
Assyrian/Chaldean/Syriac (8)	8	0.06
Austrian (27)	123	0.88
Brazilian (0)	11	0.08
British (15)	25	0.18
Canadian (0)	28	0.20
Czech (42)	87	0.63
Czechoslovakian (0)	15	0.11
Danish (0)	38	0.27
Dutch (104)	467	3.36
Eastern European (144)	153	1.10
English (148)	1,158	8.33
European (446)	455	3.27
Finnish (8)	8	0.06
French, ex. Basque (45)	502	3.61
French Canadian (106)	147	1.06
German (469)	2,085	14.99
Greek (167)	221	1.59
Hungarian (68)	155	1.11
Irish (680)	3,076	22.12
Israeli (34)	34	0.24
Italian (659)	2,562	18.42
Latvian (0)	40	0.29
Lithuanian (0)	83	0.60
Northern European (38)	38	0.27
Norwegian (24)	121	0.87
Polish (110)	630	4.53
Portuguese (27)	43	0.31
Romanian (46)	77	0.55
Russian (296)	512	3.68
Scandinavian (0)	9	0.06
Scotch-Irish (72)	204	1.47
Scottish (47)	458	3.29
Slavic (67)	67	0.48
Slovak (10)	60	0.43
Swedish (75)	269	1.93
Swiss (0)	19	0.14
Turkish (86)	95	0.68
Ukrainian (28)	98	0.70
Welsh (27)	159	1.14
West Indian, ex. Hispanic (134)	147	1.06
British West Indian (13)	13	0.09
Haitian (0)	13	0.09
Jamaican (106)	106	0.76
Trinidadian/Tobagonian (15)	15	0.11
Yugoslavian (13)	13	0.09

Hispanic Origin	Population	%
Hispanic or Latino (of any race)	1,233	8.81
Central American, ex. Mexican	83	0.59
Costa Rican	4	0.03
Guatemalan	19	0.14
Honduran	13	0.09
Nicaraguan	5	0.04
Panamanian	7	0.05
Salvadoran	34	0.24
Other Central American	1	0.01
Cuban	62	0.44
Dominican Republic	170	1.21
Mexican	163	1.16

*Notes: † The Census 2010 population figure is used to calculate the percentages in the Hispanic Origin and Race categories. Ancestry percentages are based on the 2006-2010 American Community Survey population (not shown); ‡ Numbers in parentheses indicate the number of people reporting a single ancestry; * Numbers in parentheses indicate the number of persons reporting this race alone, not in combination with any other race; Please refer to the Explanation of Data for more information.*

Puerto Rican	488	3.48
South American	146	1.04
Argentinean	14	0.10
Bolivian	1	0.01
Chilean	6	0.04
Colombian	60	0.43
Ecuadorian	25	0.18
Peruvian	32	0.23
Venezuelan	3	0.02
Other South American	5	0.04
Other Hispanic or Latino	121	0.86

Race*	Population	%
African-American/Black (749)	930	6.64
Not Hispanic (612)	744	5.31
Hispanic (137)	186	1.33
American Indian/Alaska Native (44)	150	1.07
Not Hispanic (32)	115	0.82
Hispanic (12)	35	0.25
Apache (3)	5	0.04
Blackfeet (0)	1	0.01
Central American Ind. (2)	6	0.04
Cherokee (5)	31	0.22
Chippewa (1)	4	0.03
Choctaw (0)	2	0.01
Creek (1)	1	0.01
Delaware (0)	1	0.01
Hopi (1)	1	0.01
Iroquois (1)	10	0.07
Menominee (0)	1	0.01
Mexican American Ind. (1)	1	0.01
Osage (0)	1	0.01
Puget Sound Salish (0)	1	0.01
Seminole (0)	1	0.01
Sioux (0)	2	0.01
South American Ind. (1)	5	0.04
Yup'ik *(Alaska Native)* (2)	2	0.01
Asian (610)	713	5.09
Not Hispanic (605)	704	5.03
Hispanic (5)	9	0.06
Bangladeshi (16)	16	0.11
Burmese (1)	1	0.01
Cambodian (1)	1	0.01
Chinese, ex. Taiwanese (176)	202	1.44
Filipino (22)	40	0.29
Indian (168)	193	1.38
Indonesian (6)	9	0.06
Japanese (44)	66	0.47
Korean (88)	100	0.71
Laotian (0)	1	0.01
Malaysian (1)	1	0.01
Nepalese (5)	6	0.04
Pakistani (31)	32	0.23
Taiwanese (10)	11	0.08
Thai (10)	12	0.09
Vietnamese (5)	7	0.05
Hawaii Native/Pacific Islander (5)	18	0.13
Not Hispanic (5)	13	0.09
Hispanic (0)	5	0.04
Fijian (1)	1	0.01
Guamanian/Chamorro (1)	1	0.01
Native Hawaiian (0)	2	0.01
Samoan (1)	1	0.01
White (11,864)	12,197	87.10
Not Hispanic (11,200)	11,449	81.76
Hispanic (664)	748	5.34

New Rochelle

Place Type: City
County: Westchester
Population: 77,062†

Ancestry‡	Population	%
African, Sub-Saharan (850)	1,030	1.36
African (253)	309	0.41
Ghanaian (18)	18	0.02
Kenyan (19)	19	0.03
Nigerian (125)	125	0.16
Sierra Leonean (15)	15	0.02
South African (92)	179	0.24
Other Sub-Saharan African (328)	365	0.48
Albanian (324)	370	0.49
American (2,542)	2,542	3.35
Arab (338)	413	0.54
Arab (177)	187	0.25
Egyptian (13)	13	0.02
Jordanian (11)	46	0.06
Lebanese (102)	132	0.17
Moroccan (8)	8	0.01
Other Arab (27)	27	0.04
Armenian (31)	75	0.10
Australian (33)	33	0.04
Austrian (104)	547	0.72
Basque (12)	12	0.02
Belgian (27)	118	0.16
Brazilian (580)	728	0.96
British (145)	208	0.27
Bulgarian (9)	9	0.01
Canadian (13)	41	0.05
Croatian (103)	167	0.22
Czech (78)	402	0.53
Czechoslovakian (32)	108	0.14
Danish (0)	55	0.07
Dutch (38)	257	0.34
Eastern European (870)	870	1.15
English (493)	1,832	2.42
Estonian (9)	16	0.02
European (773)	808	1.07
Finnish (36)	60	0.08
French, ex. Basque (342)	1,322	1.74
French Canadian (62)	152	0.20
German (734)	3,942	5.20
Greek (377)	573	0.76
Guyanese (104)	125	0.16
Hungarian (231)	684	0.90
Iranian (12)	33	0.04
Irish (2,797)	7,400	9.76
Israeli (26)	93	0.12
Italian (9,697)	14,355	18.93
Latvian (28)	74	0.10
Lithuanian (130)	228	0.30
Luxemburger (0)	9	0.01
Macedonian (154)	177	0.23
Maltese (0)	16	0.02
Northern European (25)	25	0.03
Norwegian (18)	72	0.09
Polish (1,042)	2,744	3.62
Portuguese (615)	830	1.09
Romanian (83)	272	0.36
Russian (917)	3,102	4.09
Scotch-Irish (92)	326	0.43
Scottish (166)	563	0.74
Slavic (116)	171	0.23
Slovak (0)	116	0.15
Swedish (84)	428	0.56
Swiss (35)	56	0.07
Turkish (48)	137	0.18
Ukrainian (13)	146	0.19
Welsh (17)	129	0.17
West Indian, ex. Hispanic (3,998)	4,597	6.06
Barbadian (241)	316	0.42
British West Indian (80)	153	0.20
Haitian (926)	951	1.25
Jamaican (2,245)	2,635	3.48
Trinidadian/Tobagonian (295)	317	0.42
West Indian (211)	225	0.30
Yugoslavian (23)	47	0.06

Hispanic Origin	Population	%
Hispanic or Latino (of any race)	21,452	27.84
Central American, ex. Mexican	2,017	2.62
Costa Rican	65	0.08
Guatemalan	1,232	1.60
Honduran	242	0.31
Nicaraguan	74	0.10
Panamanian	67	0.09
Salvadoran	330	0.43
Other Central American	7	0.01
Cuban	371	0.48
Dominican Republic	960	1.25
Mexican	10,363	13.45
Puerto Rican	2,779	3.61
South American	3,697	4.80
Argentinean	170	0.22
Bolivian	50	0.06
Chilean	76	0.10
Colombian	1,451	1.88
Ecuadorian	378	0.49
Paraguayan	49	0.06
Peruvian	1,297	1.68
Uruguayan	88	0.11
Venezuelan	131	0.17
Other South American	7	0.01
Other Hispanic or Latino	1,265	1.64

Race*	Population	%
African-American/Black (14,847)	15,858	20.58
Not Hispanic (13,956)	14,611	18.96
Hispanic (891)	1,247	1.62
American Indian/Alaska Native (398)	770	1.00
Not Hispanic (94)	308	0.40
Hispanic (304)	462	0.60
Apache (0)	6	0.01
Blackfeet (5)	25	0.03
Canadian/French Am. Ind. (0)	2	<0.01
Central American Ind. (7)	20	0.03
Cherokee (5)	65	0.08
Cheyenne (1)	1	<0.01
Chickasaw (0)	1	<0.01
Chippewa (0)	3	<0.01
Choctaw (0)	2	<0.01
Creek (0)	1	<0.01
Delaware (0)	2	<0.01
Iroquois (5)	11	0.01
Mexican American Ind. (47)	72	0.09
Navajo (0)	1	<0.01
Seminole (0)	1	<0.01
Sioux (1)	2	<0.01
South American Ind. (29)	56	0.07
Spanish American Ind. (1)	1	<0.01
Asian (3,262)	3,798	4.93
Not Hispanic (3,212)	3,631	4.71
Hispanic (50)	167	0.22
Bangladeshi (48)	55	0.07
Bhutanese (2)	2	<0.01
Burmese (6)	8	0.01
Cambodian (8)	9	0.01
Chinese, ex. Taiwanese (547)	715	0.93
Filipino (471)	543	0.70
Indian (1,352)	1,508	1.96
Indonesian (6)	6	0.01
Japanese (106)	158	0.21
Korean (276)	319	0.41
Laotian (2)	14	0.02
Malaysian (5)	5	0.01
Nepalese (5)	5	0.01
Pakistani (147)	164	0.21
Sri Lankan (75)	83	0.11
Taiwanese (18)	32	0.04
Thai (25)	39	0.05
Vietnamese (19)	31	0.04
Hawaii Native/Pacific Islander (48)	123	0.16
Not Hispanic (20)	65	0.08
Hispanic (28)	58	0.08
Guamanian/Chamorro (32)	43	0.06
Native Hawaiian (1)	12	0.02
Samoan (5)	7	0.01
White (50,231)	52,208	67.75
Not Hispanic (36,948)	37,786	49.03
Hispanic (13,283)	14,422	18.71

New Scotland

Place Type: Town
County: Albany
Population: 8,648†

Ancestry‡	Population	%
American (214)	214	2.47

*Notes: † The Census 2010 population figure is used to calculate the percentages in the Hispanic Origin and Race categories. Ancestry percentages are based on the 2006-2010 American Community Survey population (not shown); ‡ Numbers in parentheses indicate the number of people reporting a single ancestry; * Numbers in parentheses indicate the number of persons reporting this race alone, not in combination with any other race; Please refer to the Explanation of Data for more information.*

Ancestry	Population	%
Arab (209)	246	2.84
Arab (209)	209	2.41
Syrian (0)	37	0.43
Armenian (20)	33	0.38
Austrian (0)	27	0.31
Belgian (6)	6	0.07
Canadian (44)	109	1.26
Croatian (0)	9	0.10
Czech (0)	18	0.21
Czechoslovakian (7)	7	0.08
Danish (0)	59	0.68
Dutch (158)	551	6.36
Eastern European (13)	40	0.46
English (308)	1,377	15.88
European (164)	164	1.89
Finnish (0)	12	0.14
French, ex. Basque (121)	544	6.27
French Canadian (47)	167	1.93
German (444)	2,486	28.67
Greek (37)	118	1.36
Hungarian (6)	89	1.03
Irish (653)	2,311	26.66
Italian (412)	1,087	12.54
Lithuanian (11)	49	0.57
Northern European (29)	29	0.33
Norwegian (17)	83	0.96
Pennsylvania German (6)	6	0.07
Polish (176)	531	6.12
Portuguese (0)	17	0.20
Russian (25)	118	1.36
Scandinavian (19)	50	0.58
Scotch-Irish (109)	224	2.58
Scottish (91)	412	4.75
Slovak (6)	45	0.52
Slovene (0)	9	0.10
Swedish (17)	97	1.12
Swiss (29)	49	0.57
Ukrainian (10)	64	0.74
Welsh (6)	81	0.93

Hispanic Origin	Population	%
Hispanic or Latino (of any race)	145	1.68
Central American, ex. Mexican	5	0.06
Costa Rican	3	0.03
Guatemalan	1	0.01
Salvadoran	1	0.01
Cuban	8	0.09
Dominican Republic	4	0.05
Mexican	22	0.25
Puerto Rican	56	0.65
South American	18	0.21
Argentinean	1	0.01
Bolivian	1	0.01
Chilean	1	0.01
Colombian	6	0.07
Ecuadorian	1	0.01
Paraguayan	1	0.01
Peruvian	4	0.05
Venezuelan	3	0.03
Other Hispanic or Latino	32	0.37

Race*	Population	%
African-American/Black (54)	77	0.89
Not Hispanic (50)	70	0.81
Hispanic (4)	7	0.08
American Indian/Alaska Native (19)	68	0.79
Not Hispanic (17)	61	0.71
Hispanic (2)	7	0.08
Apache (1)	1	0.01
Blackfeet (1)	1	0.01
Cherokee (1)	4	0.05
Choctaw (0)	1	0.01
Cree (0)	2	0.02
Iroquois (6)	13	0.15
Navajo (0)	2	0.02
Seminole (1)	1	0.01
South American Ind. (0)	1	0.01
Spanish American Ind. (1)	1	0.01
Asian (96)	142	1.64
Not Hispanic (95)	141	1.63
Hispanic (1)	1	0.01
Bangladeshi (2)	2	0.02
Chinese, ex. Taiwanese (21)	31	0.36
Filipino (5)	13	0.15
Indian (23)	36	0.42
Japanese (10)	14	0.16
Korean (19)	24	0.28
Pakistani (8)	8	0.09
Sri Lankan (4)	4	0.05
Taiwanese (1)	1	0.01
Thai (1)	1	0.01
Vietnamese (2)	6	0.07
Hawaii Native/Pacific Islander (6)	8	0.09
Not Hispanic (6)	7	0.08
Hispanic (0)	1	0.01
Native Hawaiian (0)	1	0.01
Samoan (0)	1	0.01
White (8,345)	8,452	97.73
Not Hispanic (8,224)	8,323	96.24
Hispanic (121)	129	1.49

New Windsor

Place Type: CDP
County: Orange
Population: 8,922†

Ancestry‡	Population	%
African, Sub-Saharan (279)	279	3.07
African (245)	245	2.70
Ghanaian (34)	34	0.37
American (843)	843	9.28
Arab (17)	17	0.19
Lebanese (17)	17	0.19
Austrian (32)	56	0.62
British (24)	24	0.26
Canadian (0)	11	0.12
Czech (30)	53	0.58
Czechoslovakian (16)	16	0.18
Danish (0)	7	0.08
Dutch (0)	236	2.60
Eastern European (38)	38	0.42
English (132)	749	8.24
European (103)	103	1.13
French, ex. Basque (34)	92	1.01
French Canadian (26)	97	1.07
German (115)	911	10.03
Greek (3)	44	0.48
Hungarian (64)	141	1.55
Irish (582)	1,924	21.18
Israeli (0)	12	0.13
Italian (692)	1,687	18.57
Lithuanian (17)	24	0.26
Norwegian (24)	40	0.44
Polish (159)	374	4.12
Portuguese (4)	49	0.54
Romanian (0)	12	0.13
Russian (46)	149	1.64
Scotch-Irish (22)	129	1.42
Scottish (10)	63	0.69
Slavic (0)	10	0.11
Slovak (0)	43	0.47
Swedish (8)	43	0.47
Swiss (12)	26	0.29
Welsh (0)	33	0.36
West Indian, ex. Hispanic (134)	188	2.07
Jamaican (134)	188	2.07

Hispanic Origin	Population	%
Hispanic or Latino (of any race)	1,900	21.30
Central American, ex. Mexican	164	1.84
Costa Rican	3	0.03
Guatemalan	39	0.44
Honduran	74	0.83
Nicaraguan	2	0.02
Panamanian	11	0.12
Salvadoran	35	0.39
Cuban	50	0.56
Dominican Republic	130	1.46
Mexican	351	3.93
Puerto Rican	864	9.68
South American	196	2.20
Argentinean	19	0.21
Bolivian	11	0.12
Chilean	6	0.07
Colombian	37	0.41
Ecuadorian	33	0.37
Paraguayan	1	0.01
Peruvian	80	0.90
Uruguayan	1	0.01
Venezuelan	7	0.08
Other South American	1	0.01
Other Hispanic or Latino	145	1.63

Race*	Population	%
African-American/Black (1,038)	1,187	13.30
Not Hispanic (917)	1,022	11.45
Hispanic (121)	165	1.85
American Indian/Alaska Native (27)	91	1.02
Not Hispanic (6)	48	0.54
Hispanic (21)	43	0.48
Blackfeet (0)	4	0.04
Cherokee (1)	11	0.12
Creek (0)	3	0.03
Delaware (0)	1	0.01
Iroquois (1)	6	0.07
Mexican American Ind. (7)	8	0.09
South American Ind. (1)	4	0.04
Asian (169)	230	2.58
Not Hispanic (154)	210	2.35
Hispanic (15)	20	0.22
Chinese, ex. Taiwanese (26)	31	0.35
Filipino (41)	56	0.63
Indian (49)	68	0.76
Japanese (2)	7	0.08
Korean (29)	43	0.48
Pakistani (0)	4	0.04
Taiwanese (0)	1	0.01
Thai (4)	6	0.07
Vietnamese (11)	13	0.15
Hawaii Native/Pacific Islander (3)	21	0.24
Not Hispanic (2)	15	0.17
Hispanic (1)	6	0.07
Guamanian/Chamorro (1)	1	0.01
Native Hawaiian (1)	7	0.08
Samoan (0)	1	0.01
White (6,771)	7,037	78.87
Not Hispanic (5,740)	5,878	65.88
Hispanic (1,031)	1,159	12.99

New Windsor

Place Type: Town
County: Orange
Population: 25,244†

Ancestry‡	Population	%
African, Sub-Saharan (342)	342	1.37
African (245)	245	0.98
Ghanaian (63)	63	0.25
Other Sub-Saharan African (34)	34	0.14
American (1,907)	1,907	7.63
Arab (17)	72	0.29
Lebanese (17)	17	0.07
Syrian (0)	55	0.22
Australian (0)	13	0.05
Austrian (32)	163	0.65
Belgian (0)	16	0.06
British (41)	71	0.28
Canadian (0)	53	0.21
Czech (59)	180	0.72
Czechoslovakian (62)	119	0.48
Danish (0)	42	0.17
Dutch (62)	630	2.52
Eastern European (53)	53	0.21
English (282)	1,698	6.79
European (339)	350	1.40
Finnish (0)	60	0.24
French, ex. Basque (156)	436	1.74
French Canadian (47)	213	0.85

*Notes: † The Census 2010 population figure is used to calculate the percentages in the Hispanic Origin and Race categories. Ancestry percentages are based on the 2006-2010 American Community Survey population (not shown); ‡ Numbers in parentheses indicate the number of people reporting a single ancestry; * Numbers in parentheses indicate the number of persons reporting this race alone, not in combination with any other race; Please refer to the Explanation of Data for more information.*

German (604)	2,732	10.92
Greek (3)	87	0.35
Guyanese (8)	8	0.03
Hungarian (79)	246	0.98
Iranian (0)	17	0.07
Irish (1,827)	5,572	22.28
Israeli (0)	12	0.05
Italian (2,215)	5,117	20.46
Latvian (0)	86	0.34
Lithuanian (25)	89	0.36
Norwegian (24)	79	0.32
Pennsylvania German (0)	55	0.22
Polish (480)	1,623	6.49
Portuguese (15)	78	0.31
Romanian (101)	169	0.68
Russian (146)	387	1.55
Scotch-Irish (72)	286	1.14
Scottish (128)	285	1.14
Serbian (24)	48	0.19
Slavic (14)	37	0.15
Slovak (12)	67	0.27
Swedish (25)	232	0.93
Swiss (12)	221	0.88
Turkish (39)	86	0.34
Ukrainian (11)	175	0.70
Welsh (9)	51	0.20
West Indian, ex. Hispanic (186)	295	1.18
Jamaican (171)	255	1.02
West Indian (15)	40	0.16

Hispanic Origin	Population	%
Hispanic or Latino (of any race)	4,920	19.49
Central American, ex. Mexican	423	1.68
Costa Rican	5	0.02
Guatemalan	98	0.39
Honduran	200	0.79
Nicaraguan	12	0.05
Panamanian	39	0.15
Salvadoran	69	0.27
Cuban	143	0.57
Dominican Republic	400	1.58
Mexican	690	2.73
Puerto Rican	2,429	9.62
South American	513	2.03
Argentinean	72	0.29
Bolivian	14	0.06
Chilean	22	0.09
Colombian	118	0.47
Ecuadorian	88	0.35
Paraguayan	5	0.02
Peruvian	163	0.65
Uruguayan	11	0.04
Venezuelan	10	0.04
Other South American	10	0.04
Other Hispanic or Latino	322	1.28

Race*	Population	%
African-American/Black (2,901)	3,390	13.43
Not Hispanic (2,599)	2,909	11.52
Hispanic (302)	481	1.91
American Indian/Alaska Native (57)	239	0.95
Not Hispanic (29)	155	0.61
Hispanic (28)	84	0.33
Apache (0)	1	<0.01
Blackfeet (0)	6	0.02
Cherokee (3)	37	0.15
Creek (0)	3	0.01
Delaware (9)	15	0.06
Inupiat *(Alaska Native)* (0)	2	0.01
Iroquois (3)	11	0.04
Lumbee (1)	2	0.01
Mexican American Ind. (8)	9	0.04
Navajo (1)	1	<0.01
Seminole (0)	2	0.01
South American Ind. (1)	17	0.07
Tlingit-Haida *(Alaska Native)* (1)	1	<0.01
Tohono O'Odham (0)	6	0.02
Asian (871)	1,039	4.12
Not Hispanic (840)	972	3.85
Hispanic (31)	67	0.27
Bangladeshi (14)	15	0.06
Cambodian (9)	10	0.04
Chinese, ex. Taiwanese (155)	173	0.69
Filipino (207)	239	0.95
Hmong (1)	1	<0.01
Indian (265)	311	1.23
Indonesian (5)	5	0.02
Japanese (23)	48	0.19
Korean (75)	101	0.40
Pakistani (9)	18	0.07
Sri Lankan (8)	8	0.03
Taiwanese (4)	5	0.02
Thai (12)	15	0.06
Vietnamese (60)	65	0.26
Hawaii Native/Pacific Islander (9)	49	0.19
Not Hispanic (5)	30	0.12
Hispanic (4)	19	0.08
Guamanian/Chamorro (3)	3	0.01
Native Hawaiian (1)	11	0.04
Samoan (0)	1	<0.01
White (18,856)	19,572	77.53
Not Hispanic (16,304)	16,700	66.15
Hispanic (2,552)	2,872	11.38

New York

Place Type: City
County: Bronx; Kings; Queens; New York; Richmond
Population: 8,175,133†

Ancestry‡	Population	%
Afghan (6,250)	6,470	0.08
African, Sub-Saharan (126,853)	175,478	2.17
African (60,151)	101,901	1.26
Cape Verdean (282)	595	0.01
Ethiopian (2,524)	2,869	0.04
Ghanaian (19,077)	19,782	0.24
Kenyan (294)	344	<0.01
Liberian (1,738)	1,991	0.02
Nigerian (19,543)	21,507	0.27
Senegalese (2,685)	2,895	0.04
Sierra Leonean (1,545)	1,572	0.02
Somalian (422)	518	0.01
South African (1,454)	2,116	0.03
Sudanese (1,079)	1,303	0.02
Ugandan (189)	256	<0.01
Zimbabwean (394)	414	0.01
Other Sub-Saharan African (15,476)	17,415	0.22
Albanian (29,299)	31,056	0.38
Alsatian (31)	217	<0.01
American (209,430)	209,430	2.59
Arab (65,990)	82,165	1.02
Arab (13,125)	15,160	0.19
Egyptian (15,679)	17,698	0.22
Iraqi (645)	1,137	0.01
Jordanian (1,141)	1,298	0.02
Lebanese (7,824)	11,682	0.14
Moroccan (7,043)	8,987	0.11
Palestinian (3,051)	3,421	0.04
Syrian (5,818)	8,198	0.10
Other Arab (11,664)	14,584	0.18
Armenian (7,612)	10,159	0.13
Assyrian/Chaldean/Syriac (144)	227	<0.01
Australian (2,699)	3,906	0.05
Austrian (9,463)	30,712	0.38
Basque (370)	902	0.01
Belgian (1,803)	4,472	0.06
Brazilian (9,457)	13,119	0.16
British (11,046)	21,065	0.26
Bulgarian (4,331)	5,011	0.06
Cajun (121)	432	0.01
Canadian (5,942)	10,989	0.14
Carpatho Rusyn (198)	249	<0.01
Celtic (275)	564	0.01
Croatian (8,097)	11,304	0.14
Cypriot (744)	960	0.01
Czech (3,559)	12,800	0.16
Czechoslovakian (2,411)	4,870	0.06
Danish (2,102)	7,018	0.09
Dutch (5,641)	23,151	0.29
Eastern European (41,481)	44,970	0.56
English (40,380)	146,525	1.81
Estonian (643)	1,057	0.01
European (59,415)	66,267	0.82
Finnish (1,375)	3,519	0.04
French, ex. Basque (19,416)	67,195	0.83
French Canadian (3,676)	11,393	0.14
German (68,198)	272,827	3.38
German Russian (69)	204	<0.01
Greek (58,515)	76,597	0.95
Guyanese (96,299)	107,972	1.34
Hungarian (29,252)	55,459	0.69
Icelander (386)	572	0.01
Iranian (8,448)	10,204	0.13
Irish (154,072)	410,889	5.09
Israeli (16,225)	21,872	0.27
Italian (403,347)	625,004	7.74
Latvian (1,663)	3,302	0.04
Lithuanian (4,343)	12,774	0.16
Luxemburger (76)	193	<0.01
Macedonian (4,296)	4,911	0.06
Maltese (1,817)	3,102	0.04
New Zealander (337)	584	0.01
Northern European (2,656)	3,043	0.04
Norwegian (6,141)	21,894	0.27
Pennsylvania German (160)	465	0.01
Polish (112,769)	216,891	2.68
Portuguese (5,980)	13,201	0.16
Romanian (18,025)	29,552	0.37
Russian (150,929)	240,690	2.98
Scandinavian (1,533)	3,434	0.04
Scotch-Irish (9,634)	27,337	0.34
Scottish (9,926)	38,000	0.47
Serbian (3,997)	4,911	0.06
Slavic (919)	1,962	0.02
Slovak (3,457)	6,785	0.08
Slovene (593)	1,476	0.02
Soviet Union (288)	419	0.01
Swedish (5,168)	20,940	0.26
Swiss (2,335)	8,135	0.10
Turkish (12,067)	14,927	0.18
Ukrainian (36,563)	48,714	0.60
Welsh (1,659)	11,219	0.14
West Indian, ex. Hispanic (509,675)	598,504	7.41
Bahamian (828)	1,147	0.01
Barbadian (19,549)	22,550	0.28
Belizean (4,699)	5,674	0.07
Bermudan (345)	518	0.01
British West Indian (39,268)	44,326	0.55
Dutch West Indian (789)	1,167	0.01
Haitian (112,397)	120,252	1.49
Jamaican (196,443)	216,495	2.68
Trinidadian/Tobagonian (66,794)	76,240	0.94
U.S. Virgin Islander (1,806)	2,383	0.03
West Indian (65,827)	106,548	1.32
Other West Indian (930)	1,204	0.01
Yugoslavian (10,119)	12,410	0.15

Hispanic Origin	Population	%
Hispanic or Latino (of any race)	2,336,076	28.58
Central American, ex. Mexican	151,378	1.85
Costa Rican	6,673	0.08
Guatemalan	30,420	0.37
Honduran	42,400	0.52
Nicaraguan	9,346	0.11
Panamanian	22,353	0.27
Salvadoran	38,559	0.47
Other Central American	1,627	0.02
Cuban	40,840	0.50
Dominican Republic	576,701	7.05
Mexican	319,263	3.91
Puerto Rican	723,621	8.85
South American	343,468	4.20
Argentinean	15,169	0.19
Bolivian	4,488	0.05
Chilean	7,026	0.09
Colombian	94,723	1.16
Ecuadorian	167,209	2.05
Paraguayan	3,534	0.04
Peruvian	36,018	0.44

*Notes: † The Census 2010 population figure is used to calculate the percentages in the Hispanic Origin and Race categories. Ancestry percentages are based on the 2006-2010 American Community Survey population (not shown); ‡ Numbers in parentheses indicate the number of people reporting a single ancestry; * Numbers in parentheses indicate the number of persons reporting this race alone, not in combination with any other race; Please refer to the Explanation of Data for more information.*

Uruguayan	3,004	0.04
Venezuelan	9,619	0.12
Other South American	2,678	0.03
Other Hispanic or Latino	180,805	2.21

Race*	Population	%
African-American/Black (2,088,510)	2,228,145	27.26
Not Hispanic (1,861,295)	1,931,889	23.63
Hispanic (227,215)	296,256	3.62
American Indian/Alaska Nat. (57,512)	111,749	1.37
Not Hispanic (17,427)	44,541	0.54
Hispanic (40,085)	67,208	0.82
Alaska Athabascan *(Ala. Nat.)* (19)	37	<0.01
Aleut *(Alaska Native)* (12)	26	<0.01
Apache (135)	401	<0.01
Arapaho (8)	21	<0.01
Blackfeet (235)	1,627	0.02
Canadian/French Am. Ind. (111)	197	<0.01
Central American Ind. (3,948)	7,662	0.09
Cherokee (1,195)	6,952	0.09
Cheyenne (19)	46	<0.01
Chickasaw (40)	113	<0.01
Chippewa (105)	252	<0.01
Choctaw (94)	405	<0.01
Colville (6)	9	<0.01
Comanche (31)	76	<0.01
Cree (14)	81	<0.01
Creek (65)	291	<0.01
Crow (11)	50	<0.01
Delaware (50)	177	<0.01
Hopi (17)	49	<0.01
Houma (14)	23	<0.01
Inupiat *(Alaska Native)* (26)	58	<0.01
Iroquois (573)	1,276	0.02
Kiowa (11)	15	<0.01
Lumbee (27)	89	<0.01
Menominee (4)	10	<0.01
Mexican American Ind. (3,646)	4,922	0.06
Navajo (126)	272	<0.01
Osage (10)	23	<0.01
Ottawa (2)	11	<0.01
Paiute (5)	18	<0.01
Pima (4)	9	<0.01
Potawatomi (20)	40	<0.01
Pueblo (446)	892	0.01
Puget Sound Salish (5)	11	<0.01
Seminole (52)	357	<0.01
Shoshone (10)	46	<0.01
Sioux (159)	464	0.01
South American Ind. (4,682)	9,464	0.12
Spanish American Ind. (1,871)	2,594	0.03
Tlingit-Haida *(Alaska Native)* (15)	75	<0.01
Tohono O'Odham (32)	48	<0.01
Tsimshian *(Alaska Native)* (3)	4	<0.01
Ute (8)	17	<0.01
Yakama (5)	8	<0.01
Yaqui (27)	54	<0.01
Yuman (12)	22	<0.01
Yup'ik *(Alaska Native)* (2)	10	<0.01
Asian (1,038,388)	1,134,919	13.88
Not Hispanic (1,028,119)	1,110,964	13.59
Hispanic (10,269)	23,955	0.29
Bangladeshi (53,174)	61,788	0.76
Bhutanese (345)	388	<0.01
Burmese (3,614)	4,132	0.05
Cambodian (2,166)	2,591	0.03
Chinese, ex. Taiwanese (474,783)	500,434	6.12
Filipino (67,292)	78,030	0.95
Hmong (59)	83	<0.01
Indian (192,209)	232,696	2.85
Indonesian (3,785)	4,791	0.06
Japanese (24,277)	31,742	0.39
Korean (96,741)	102,820	1.26
Laotian (440)	664	0.01
Malaysian (2,100)	3,220	0.04
Nepalese (5,681)	6,187	0.08
Pakistani (41,887)	46,369	0.57
Sri Lankan (3,696)	4,369	0.05
Taiwanese (11,680)	13,682	0.17
Thai (6,056)	7,244	0.09
Vietnamese (13,387)	16,378	0.20
Hawaii Native/Pacific Islander (5,147)	24,098	0.29
Not Hispanic (2,795)	13,217	0.16
Hispanic (2,352)	10,881	0.13
Fijian (104)	213	<0.01
Guamanian/Chamorro (1,194)	1,784	0.02
Marshallese (8)	10	<0.01
Native Hawaiian (1,001)	2,448	0.03
Samoan (296)	764	0.01
Tongan (37)	66	<0.01
White (3,597,341)	3,797,402	46.45
Not Hispanic (2,722,904)	2,804,430	34.30
Hispanic (874,437)	992,972	12.15

Newark

Place Type: Village
County: Wayne
Population: 9,145†

Ancestry‡	Population	%
American (549)	549	5.98
Arab (19)	19	0.21
Moroccan (19)	19	0.21
Austrian (8)	31	0.34
Belgian (11)	21	0.23
Brazilian (0)	8	0.09
British (9)	9	0.10
Canadian (56)	56	0.61
Czech (14)	14	0.15
Danish (13)	34	0.37
Dutch (489)	1,482	16.14
English (397)	1,253	13.64
French, ex. Basque (23)	263	2.86
French Canadian (49)	210	2.29
German (453)	1,939	21.11
Greek (16)	28	0.30
Hungarian (38)	50	0.54
Irish (305)	1,362	14.83
Italian (793)	1,456	15.85
Lithuanian (11)	11	0.12
Norwegian (0)	13	0.14
Pennsylvania German (16)	16	0.17
Polish (168)	310	3.38
Russian (0)	35	0.38
Scotch-Irish (0)	90	0.98
Scottish (48)	206	2.24
Slovene (0)	9	0.10
Swedish (11)	75	0.82
Swiss (0)	28	0.30
Ukrainian (0)	80	0.87
Welsh (0)	73	0.79
West Indian, ex. Hispanic (47)	79	0.86
Haitian (47)	79	0.86
Yugoslavian (0)	31	0.34

Hispanic Origin	Population	%
Hispanic or Latino (of any race)	798	8.73
Central American, ex. Mexican	47	0.51
Guatemalan	1	0.01
Honduran	36	0.39
Panamanian	6	0.07
Salvadoran	4	0.04
Cuban	9	0.10
Dominican Republic	16	0.17
Mexican	73	0.80
Puerto Rican	598	6.54
South American	11	0.12
Argentinean	4	0.04
Colombian	3	0.03
Ecuadorian	2	0.02
Peruvian	2	0.02
Other Hispanic or Latino	44	0.48

Race*	Population	%
African-American/Black (557)	766	8.38
Not Hispanic (501)	676	7.39
Hispanic (56)	90	0.98
American Indian/Alaska Native (35)	95	1.04
Not Hispanic (25)	74	0.81
Hispanic (10)	21	0.23
Apache (1)	1	0.01
Blackfeet (4)	4	0.04
Cherokee (4)	12	0.13
Chippewa (2)	2	0.02
Comanche (1)	1	0.01
Cree (0)	3	0.03
Iroquois (6)	16	0.17
Mexican American Ind. (3)	3	0.03
Seminole (0)	1	0.01
Asian (62)	90	0.98
Not Hispanic (59)	84	0.92
Hispanic (3)	6	0.07
Bangladeshi (1)	1	0.01
Cambodian (4)	4	0.04
Chinese, ex. Taiwanese (11)	17	0.19
Filipino (13)	17	0.19
Indian (5)	8	0.09
Japanese (2)	7	0.08
Korean (12)	14	0.15
Laotian (2)	4	0.04
Malaysian (1)	1	0.01
Thai (2)	4	0.04
Vietnamese (2)	2	0.02
Hawaii Native/Pacific Islander (1)	9	0.10
Not Hispanic (1)	9	0.10
Native Hawaiian (1)	5	0.05
White (7,895)	8,204	89.71
Not Hispanic (7,511)	7,740	84.64
Hispanic (384)	464	5.07

Newburgh

Place Type: City
County: Orange
Population: 28,866†

Ancestry‡	Population	%
African, Sub-Saharan (79)	255	0.88
African (59)	220	0.76
Somalian (20)	35	0.12
Albanian (0)	37	0.13
American (1,654)	1,654	5.70
Arab (114)	114	0.39
Egyptian (114)	114	0.39
Armenian (0)	36	0.12
Austrian (20)	37	0.13
Brazilian (0)	8	0.03
British (10)	10	0.03
Canadian (0)	9	0.03
Celtic (26)	26	0.09
Czech (30)	59	0.20
Czechoslovakian (15)	47	0.16
Dutch (47)	220	0.76
English (104)	613	2.11
French, ex. Basque (16)	247	0.85
French Canadian (21)	21	0.07
German (269)	1,126	3.88
Greek (59)	185	0.64
Guyanese (113)	113	0.39
Hungarian (132)	159	0.55
Iranian (0)	14	0.05
Irish (540)	1,740	6.00
Italian (787)	2,229	7.69
Lithuanian (0)	12	0.04
Northern European (11)	11	0.04
Norwegian (10)	10	0.03
Polish (82)	428	1.48
Portuguese (8)	8	0.03
Romanian (0)	10	0.03
Russian (30)	190	0.66
Scotch-Irish (35)	157	0.54
Scottish (74)	195	0.67
Slovak (8)	8	0.03
Slovene (23)	23	0.08
Swedish (16)	32	0.11
Swiss (3)	10	0.03
Turkish (0)	37	0.13
Ukrainian (19)	96	0.33
West Indian, ex. Hispanic (433)	631	2.18

*Notes: † The Census 2010 population figure is used to calculate the percentages in the Hispanic Origin and Race categories. Ancestry percentages are based on the 2006-2010 American Community Survey population (not shown); ‡ Numbers in parentheses indicate the number of people reporting a single ancestry; * Numbers in parentheses indicate the number of persons reporting this race alone, not in combination with any other race; Please refer to the Explanation of Data for more information.*

Bahamian (0)	13	0.04
British West Indian (7)	7	0.02
Dutch West Indian (0)	29	0.10
Haitian (120)	120	0.41
Jamaican (195)	241	0.83
Trinidadian/Tobagonian (7)	7	0.02
West Indian (104)	214	0.74

Hispanic Origin	Population	%
Hispanic or Latino (of any race)	13,814	47.86
Central American, ex. Mexican	2,381	8.25
Costa Rican	11	0.04
Guatemalan	380	1.32
Honduran	1,545	5.35
Nicaraguan	14	0.05
Panamanian	35	0.12
Salvadoran	381	1.32
Other Central American	15	0.05
Cuban	96	0.33
Dominican Republic	234	0.81
Mexican	6,181	21.41
Puerto Rican	2,962	10.26
South American	1,252	4.34
Argentinean	74	0.26
Bolivian	2	0.01
Chilean	36	0.12
Colombian	195	0.68
Ecuadorian	229	0.79
Paraguayan	1	<0.01
Peruvian	691	2.39
Uruguayan	1	<0.01
Venezuelan	14	0.05
Other South American	9	0.03
Other Hispanic or Latino	708	2.45

Race*	Population	%
African-American/Black (8,706)	9,613	33.30
Not Hispanic (8,071)	8,655	29.98
Hispanic (635)	958	3.32
American Indian/Alaska Native (478)	762	2.64
Not Hispanic (100)	276	0.96
Hispanic (378)	486	1.68
Arapaho (0)	1	<0.01
Blackfeet (0)	11	0.04
Canadian/French Am. Ind. (0)	1	<0.01
Central American Ind. (3)	6	0.02
Cherokee (7)	44	0.15
Cheyenne (0)	1	<0.01
Choctaw (0)	1	<0.01
Delaware (9)	22	0.08
Inupiat *(Alaska Native)* (1)	1	<0.01
Iroquois (24)	37	0.13
Lumbee (0)	1	<0.01
Mexican American Ind. (58)	67	0.23
Navajo (0)	1	<0.01
Pueblo (0)	3	0.01
Seminole (0)	4	0.01
Sioux (0)	6	0.02
South American Ind. (43)	50	0.17
Spanish American Ind. (83)	92	0.32
Asian (282)	393	1.36
Not Hispanic (257)	324	1.12
Hispanic (25)	69	0.24
Bangladeshi (5)	5	0.02
Chinese, ex. Taiwanese (53)	77	0.27
Filipino (36)	61	0.21
Indian (93)	110	0.38
Indonesian (1)	1	<0.01
Japanese (8)	11	0.04
Korean (22)	34	0.12
Pakistani (29)	29	0.10
Sri Lankan (6)	6	0.02
Vietnamese (23)	31	0.11
Hawaii Native/Pacific Islander (30)	62	0.21
Not Hispanic (8)	24	0.08
Hispanic (22)	38	0.13
Guamanian/Chamorro (11)	21	0.07
Native Hawaiian (3)	9	0.03
Samoan (4)	12	0.04
White (11,368)	12,491	43.27
Not Hispanic (5,880)	6,401	22.17
Hispanic (5,488)	6,090	21.10

Newburgh

Place Type: Town
County: Orange
Population: 29,801†

Ancestry‡	Population	%
African, Sub-Saharan (221)	221	0.75
African (49)	49	0.17
Nigerian (154)	154	0.52
Other Sub-Saharan African (18)	18	0.06
Albanian (34)	34	0.11
American (1,613)	1,613	5.44
Arab (129)	290	0.98
Egyptian (121)	213	0.72
Moroccan (8)	36	0.12
Syrian (0)	24	0.08
Other Arab (0)	17	0.06
Armenian (32)	54	0.18
Austrian (34)	159	0.54
Basque (0)	13	0.04
Belgian (0)	11	0.04
British (79)	115	0.39
Canadian (45)	45	0.15
Croatian (15)	61	0.21
Cypriot (13)	13	0.04
Czech (21)	338	1.14
Danish (0)	43	0.15
Dutch (55)	442	1.49
Eastern European (127)	127	0.43
English (435)	2,303	7.77
Estonian (0)	30	0.10
European (106)	190	0.64
Finnish (0)	25	0.08
French, ex. Basque (163)	994	3.35
French Canadian (68)	212	0.72
German (940)	4,142	13.98
Greek (58)	204	0.69
Guyanese (16)	16	0.05
Hungarian (9)	227	0.77
Iranian (39)	39	0.13
Irish (1,829)	5,398	18.22
Israeli (5)	5	0.02
Italian (2,932)	6,493	21.91
Lithuanian (65)	101	0.34
Northern European (8)	8	0.03
Norwegian (27)	215	0.73
Polish (312)	1,380	4.66
Portuguese (15)	31	0.10
Romanian (10)	35	0.12
Russian (85)	336	1.13
Scandinavian (24)	24	0.08
Scotch-Irish (133)	356	1.20
Scottish (90)	370	1.25
Slovak (75)	185	0.62
Slovene (0)	12	0.04
Swedish (65)	296	1.00
Swiss (28)	53	0.18
Turkish (87)	120	0.40
Ukrainian (78)	196	0.66
Welsh (0)	70	0.24
West Indian, ex. Hispanic (429)	590	1.99
British West Indian (14)	14	0.05
Haitian (13)	13	0.04
Jamaican (330)	360	1.21
Trinidadian/Tobagonian (7)	52	0.18
West Indian (65)	151	0.51
Yugoslavian (0)	16	0.05

Hispanic Origin	Population	%
Hispanic or Latino (of any race)	4,664	15.65
Central American, ex. Mexican	373	1.25
Costa Rican	27	0.09
Guatemalan	28	0.09
Honduran	216	0.72
Nicaraguan	3	0.01
Panamanian	21	0.07
Salvadoran	78	0.26
Cuban	112	0.38
Dominican Republic	250	0.84
Mexican	463	1.55
Puerto Rican	2,584	8.67
South American	509	1.71
Argentinean	68	0.23
Bolivian	10	0.03
Chilean	41	0.14
Colombian	109	0.37
Ecuadorian	99	0.33
Peruvian	142	0.48
Uruguayan	9	0.03
Venezuelan	28	0.09
Other South American	3	0.01
Other Hispanic or Latino	373	1.25

Race*	Population	%
African-American/Black (3,644)	4,084	13.70
Not Hispanic (3,289)	3,576	12.00
Hispanic (355)	508	1.70
American Indian/Alaska Native (81)	250	0.84
Not Hispanic (42)	145	0.49
Hispanic (39)	105	0.35
Blackfeet (6)	20	0.07
Canadian/French Am. Ind. (0)	1	<0.01
Central American Ind. (3)	5	0.02
Cherokee (0)	26	0.09
Comanche (1)	2	0.01
Delaware (4)	7	0.02
Iroquois (10)	18	0.06
Mexican American Ind. (1)	1	<0.01
Puget Sound Salish (0)	2	0.01
Seminole (0)	1	<0.01
Sioux (0)	5	0.02
South American Ind. (4)	26	0.09
Spanish American Ind. (1)	1	<0.01
Asian (883)	1,074	3.60
Not Hispanic (865)	1,025	3.44
Hispanic (18)	49	0.16
Bangladeshi (19)	19	0.06
Burmese (0)	2	0.01
Cambodian (3)	3	0.01
Chinese, ex. Taiwanese (117)	153	0.51
Filipino (197)	261	0.88
Indian (270)	317	1.06
Indonesian (7)	7	0.02
Japanese (15)	26	0.09
Korean (83)	97	0.33
Nepalese (3)	3	0.01
Pakistani (63)	78	0.26
Sri Lankan (13)	13	0.04
Thai (14)	25	0.08
Vietnamese (48)	49	0.16
Hawaii Native/Pacific Islander (11)	40	0.13
Not Hispanic (7)	21	0.07
Hispanic (4)	19	0.06
Guamanian/Chamorro (6)	7	0.02
Native Hawaiian (0)	6	0.02
White (22,811)	23,553	79.03
Not Hispanic (20,330)	20,767	69.69
Hispanic (2,481)	2,786	9.35

Newfane

Place Type: Town
County: Niagara
Population: 9,666†

Ancestry‡	Population	%
American (204)	204	2.12
Arab (0)	67	0.70
Lebanese (0)	53	0.55
Syrian (0)	14	0.15
Austrian (4)	31	0.32
Belgian (11)	11	0.11
Canadian (22)	178	1.85
Czech (0)	23	0.24
Dutch (47)	269	2.80
English (717)	2,112	21.97

*Notes: † The Census 2010 population figure is used to calculate the percentages in the Hispanic Origin and Race categories. Ancestry percentages are based on the 2006-2010 American Community Survey population (not shown); ‡ Numbers in parentheses indicate the number of people reporting a single ancestry; * Numbers in parentheses indicate the number of persons reporting this race alone, not in combination with any other race; Please refer to the Explanation of Data for more information.*

Ancestry	Population	%
Estonian (8)	8	0.08
European (50)	50	0.52
French, ex. Basque (69)	674	7.01
French Canadian (0)	112	1.17
German (1,096)	3,389	35.26
Greek (20)	47	0.49
Hungarian (0)	42	0.44
Irish (703)	1,994	20.74
Italian (304)	931	9.69
Lithuanian (12)	12	0.12
Norwegian (10)	183	1.90
Polish (315)	812	8.45
Scandinavian (28)	44	0.46
Scotch-Irish (27)	127	1.32
Scottish (57)	254	2.64
Slovak (14)	28	0.29
Swedish (8)	65	0.68
Swiss (15)	46	0.48
Ukrainian (21)	38	0.40
Welsh (36)	70	0.73
Yugoslavian (0)	38	0.40

Hispanic Origin	Population	%
Hispanic or Latino (of any race)	165	1.71
Central American, ex. Mexican	8	0.08
Costa Rican	1	0.01
Guatemalan	4	0.04
Panamanian	3	0.03
Mexican	79	0.82
Puerto Rican	48	0.50
South American	16	0.17
Colombian	7	0.07
Ecuadorian	7	0.07
Peruvian	2	0.02
Other Hispanic or Latino	14	0.14

Race*	Population	%
African-American/Black (76)	136	1.41
Not Hispanic (69)	124	1.28
Hispanic (7)	12	0.12
American Indian/Alaska Native (46)	93	0.96
Not Hispanic (42)	81	0.84
Hispanic (4)	12	0.12
Blackfeet (0)	1	0.01
Cherokee (1)	4	0.04
Chippewa (1)	3	0.03
Iroquois (32)	56	0.58
Ottawa (0)	1	0.01
South American Ind. (0)	1	0.01
Asian (38)	64	0.66
Not Hispanic (38)	61	0.63
Hispanic (0)	3	0.03
Chinese, ex. Taiwanese (15)	19	0.20
Filipino (6)	9	0.09
Hmong (4)	10	0.10
Indian (2)	5	0.05
Japanese (1)	1	0.01
Korean (9)	18	0.19
Thai (1)	2	0.02
Hawaii Native/Pacific Islander (5)	7	0.07
Not Hispanic (5)	7	0.07
White (9,313)	9,436	97.62
Not Hispanic (9,232)	9,339	96.62
Hispanic (81)	97	1.00

Newstead

Place Type: Town
County: Erie
Population: 8,594†

Ancestry‡	Population	%
American (218)	218	2.56
Arab (0)	35	0.41
Syrian (0)	26	0.31
Other Arab (0)	9	0.11
Austrian (17)	17	0.20
Brazilian (22)	22	0.26
British (9)	87	1.02
Canadian (49)	63	0.74
Croatian (0)	11	0.13
Danish (0)	40	0.47
Dutch (32)	139	1.63
English (235)	1,154	13.55
Finnish (0)	8	0.09
French, ex. Basque (22)	329	3.86
French Canadian (16)	87	1.02
German (1,320)	3,468	40.71
Greek (0)	25	0.29
Hungarian (47)	157	1.84
Irish (214)	1,686	19.79
Italian (358)	1,110	13.03
Lithuanian (0)	14	0.16
Norwegian (8)	16	0.19
Polish (744)	1,604	18.83
Portuguese (8)	25	0.29
Russian (0)	42	0.49
Scandinavian (0)	17	0.20
Scotch-Irish (15)	115	1.35
Scottish (95)	323	3.79
Slovak (0)	23	0.27
Swedish (30)	71	0.83
Swiss (0)	41	0.48
Ukrainian (0)	56	0.66
Welsh (22)	87	1.02

Hispanic Origin	Population	%
Hispanic or Latino (of any race)	85	0.99
Central American, ex. Mexican	6	0.07
Guatemalan	6	0.07
Cuban	5	0.06
Mexican	21	0.24
Puerto Rican	40	0.47
South American	5	0.06
Colombian	4	0.05
Venezuelan	1	0.01
Other Hispanic or Latino	8	0.09

Race*	Population	%
African-American/Black (42)	57	0.66
Not Hispanic (42)	57	0.66
American Indian/Alaska Native (86)	131	1.52
Not Hispanic (81)	125	1.45
Hispanic (5)	6	0.07
Blackfeet (0)	6	0.07
Cherokee (4)	15	0.17
Iroquois (60)	79	0.92
Mexican American Ind. (2)	3	0.03
Sioux (1)	1	0.01
Asian (34)	50	0.58
Not Hispanic (34)	50	0.58
Chinese, ex. Taiwanese (4)	6	0.07
Filipino (2)	5	0.06
Indian (18)	22	0.26
Japanese (3)	9	0.10
Korean (2)	2	0.02
Laotian (1)	1	0.01
Pakistani (0)	1	0.01
Vietnamese (3)	4	0.05
Hawaii Native/Pacific Islander (3)	5	0.06
Not Hispanic (3)	5	0.06
Native Hawaiian (0)	3	0.03
Samoan (2)	3	0.03
White (8,340)	8,409	97.85
Not Hispanic (8,276)	8,340	97.04
Hispanic (64)	69	0.80

Niagara Falls

Place Type: City
County: Niagara
Population: 50,193†

Ancestry‡	Population	%
African, Sub-Saharan (318)	520	1.02
African (286)	488	0.96
Ethiopian (24)	24	0.05
South African (8)	8	0.02
American (1,655)	1,655	3.25
Arab (204)	411	0.81
Arab (72)	103	0.20
Egyptian (0)	29	0.06
Lebanese (116)	228	0.45
Syrian (9)	44	0.09
Other Arab (7)	7	0.01
Armenian (96)	156	0.31
Australian (31)	49	0.10
Austrian (38)	115	0.23
British (29)	64	0.13
Canadian (210)	442	0.87
Carpatho Rusyn (14)	14	0.03
Croatian (73)	85	0.17
Czech (37)	92	0.18
Czechoslovakian (0)	6	0.01
Danish (12)	134	0.26
Dutch (62)	498	0.98
English (2,722)	6,055	11.90
European (44)	44	0.09
Finnish (0)	31	0.06
French, ex. Basque (256)	1,555	3.06
French Canadian (125)	493	0.97
German (2,324)	8,658	17.01
German Russian (16)	16	0.03
Greek (121)	318	0.62
Hungarian (68)	191	0.38
Irish (1,933)	7,048	13.85
Israeli (12)	12	0.02
Italian (6,763)	11,524	22.64
Lithuanian (71)	128	0.25
Northern European (11)	11	0.02
Norwegian (9)	72	0.14
Pennsylvania German (61)	130	0.26
Polish (1,934)	4,962	9.75
Portuguese (135)	151	0.30
Romanian (15)	44	0.09
Russian (140)	312	0.61
Scandinavian (0)	9	0.02
Scotch-Irish (163)	522	1.03
Scottish (257)	747	1.47
Slavic (28)	33	0.06
Slovak (39)	88	0.17
Swedish (51)	395	0.78
Swiss (6)	19	0.04
Turkish (0)	18	0.04
Ukrainian (59)	114	0.22
Welsh (93)	346	0.68
West Indian, ex. Hispanic (174)	366	0.72
Belizean (29)	29	0.06
British West Indian (9)	9	0.02
Jamaican (121)	167	0.33
Trinidadian/Tobagonian (15)	15	0.03
West Indian (0)	146	0.29
Yugoslavian (0)	33	0.06

Hispanic Origin	Population	%
Hispanic or Latino (of any race)	1,508	3.00
Central American, ex. Mexican	39	0.08
Costa Rican	3	0.01
Guatemalan	15	0.03
Honduran	9	0.02
Panamanian	8	0.02
Salvadoran	4	0.01
Cuban	61	0.12
Dominican Republic	35	0.07
Mexican	228	0.45
Puerto Rican	797	1.59
South American	50	0.10
Argentinean	8	0.02
Chilean	5	0.01
Colombian	23	0.05
Ecuadorian	3	0.01
Peruvian	4	0.01
Venezuelan	7	0.01
Other Hispanic or Latino	298	0.59

Race*	Population	%
African-American/Black (10,835)	12,203	24.31
Not Hispanic (10,643)	11,905	23.72
Hispanic (192)	298	0.59
American Indian/Alaska Native (977)	1,624	3.24

*Notes: † The Census 2010 population figure is used to calculate the percentages in the Hispanic Origin and Race categories. Ancestry percentages are based on the 2006-2010 American Community Survey population (not shown); ‡ Numbers in parentheses indicate the number of people reporting a single ancestry; * Numbers in parentheses indicate the number of persons reporting this race alone, not in combination with any other race; Please refer to the Explanation of Data for more information.*

Not Hispanic (930)	1,524	3.04
Hispanic (47)	100	0.20
Apache (0)	2	<0.01
Blackfeet (1)	16	0.03
Canadian/French Am. Ind. (18)	20	0.04
Central American Ind. (8)	11	0.02
Cherokee (8)	48	0.10
Cheyenne (1)	1	<0.01
Chippewa (16)	23	0.05
Choctaw (1)	1	<0.01
Cree (2)	3	0.01
Iroquois (542)	801	1.60
Lumbee (4)	6	0.01
Menominee (0)	2	<0.01
Mexican American Ind. (4)	4	0.01
Navajo (1)	1	<0.01
Ottawa (1)	1	<0.01
Seminole (0)	5	0.01
Sioux (5)	8	0.02
South American Ind. (1)	2	<0.01
Yakama (0)	1	<0.01
Yaqui (1)	1	<0.01
Asian (609)	751	1.50
Not Hispanic (599)	732	1.46
Hispanic (10)	19	0.04
Burmese (1)	1	<0.01
Cambodian (1)	1	<0.01
Chinese, ex. Taiwanese (97)	106	0.21
Filipino (45)	81	0.16
Indian (286)	327	0.65
Japanese (14)	26	0.05
Korean (36)	48	0.10
Laotian (12)	16	0.03
Pakistani (58)	64	0.13
Sri Lankan (0)	5	0.01
Taiwanese (5)	5	0.01
Thai (4)	15	0.03
Vietnamese (19)	22	0.04
Hawaii Native/Pacific Islander (15)	51	0.10
Not Hispanic (10)	43	0.09
Hispanic (5)	8	0.02
Fijian (0)	1	<0.01
Guamanian/Chamorro (5)	5	0.01
Native Hawaiian (6)	10	0.02
Samoan (2)	2	<0.01
White (35,394)	37,102	73.92
Not Hispanic (34,663)	36,227	72.18
Hispanic (731)	875	1.74

Niagara

Place Type: Town
County: Niagara
Population: 8,378†

Ancestry‡	Population	%
American (592)	592	7.01
Arab (233)	250	2.96
Arab (72)	72	0.85
Jordanian (149)	149	1.77
Lebanese (12)	12	0.14
Syrian (0)	17	0.20
British (27)	27	0.32
Canadian (25)	67	0.79
Czechoslovakian (9)	9	0.11
Dutch (34)	149	1.77
Eastern European (15)	15	0.18
English (215)	728	8.62
European (13)	13	0.15
French, ex. Basque (83)	315	3.73
French Canadian (17)	84	1.00
German (571)	1,699	20.13
Greek (0)	9	0.11
Hungarian (37)	107	1.27
Irish (345)	1,073	12.71
Italian (1,226)	2,009	23.80
Lithuanian (28)	39	0.46
Pennsylvania German (0)	14	0.17
Polish (525)	945	11.20
Scotch-Irish (48)	93	1.10
Scottish (74)	194	2.30
Swedish (14)	65	0.77
Ukrainian (0)	27	0.32
Welsh (0)	112	1.33

Hispanic Origin	Population	%
Hispanic or Latino (of any race)	146	1.74
Central American, ex. Mexican	3	0.04
Panamanian	3	0.04
Cuban	3	0.04
Dominican Republic	2	0.02
Mexican	23	0.27
Puerto Rican	81	0.97
Other Hispanic or Latino	34	0.41

Race*	Population	%
African-American/Black (283)	333	3.97
Not Hispanic (279)	325	3.88
Hispanic (4)	8	0.10
American Indian/Alaska Native (157)	232	2.77
Not Hispanic (151)	220	2.63
Hispanic (6)	12	0.14
Blackfeet (0)	4	0.05
Canadian/French Am. Ind. (1)	2	0.02
Cherokee (5)	13	0.16
Chippewa (4)	4	0.05
Choctaw (0)	3	0.04
Delaware (1)	1	0.01
Iroquois (99)	132	1.58
Sioux (0)	1	0.01
Spanish American Ind. (1)	1	0.01
Asian (74)	89	1.06
Not Hispanic (74)	87	1.04
Hispanic (0)	2	0.02
Chinese, ex. Taiwanese (6)	7	0.08
Filipino (6)	9	0.11
Indian (26)	30	0.36
Japanese (0)	2	0.02
Korean (3)	7	0.08
Pakistani (7)	7	0.08
Vietnamese (22)	23	0.27
White (7,695)	7,829	93.45
Not Hispanic (7,591)	7,715	92.09
Hispanic (104)	114	1.36

Niskayuna

Place Type: Town
County: Schenectady
Population: 21,781†

Ancestry‡	Population	%
American (1,459)	1,459	6.78
Arab (54)	105	0.49
Egyptian (13)	13	0.06
Lebanese (10)	61	0.28
Other Arab (31)	31	0.14
Armenian (16)	16	0.07
Australian (0)	51	0.24
Austrian (17)	114	0.53
Belgian (0)	16	0.07
Brazilian (12)	12	0.06
British (52)	76	0.35
Canadian (62)	144	0.67
Celtic (12)	12	0.06
Croatian (15)	40	0.19
Czech (0)	131	0.61
Danish (27)	180	0.84
Dutch (170)	520	2.42
Eastern European (179)	179	0.83
English (766)	2,716	12.62
Estonian (39)	39	0.18
European (482)	496	2.31
French, ex. Basque (231)	1,052	4.89
French Canadian (112)	304	1.41
German (380)	3,114	14.47
Greek (82)	135	0.63
Guyanese (10)	10	0.05
Hungarian (51)	257	1.19
Irish (1,452)	4,195	19.50
Italian (1,898)	4,055	18.85
Latvian (15)	68	0.32
Lithuanian (47)	111	0.52
New Zealander (0)	18	0.08
Northern European (9)	9	0.04
Norwegian (57)	104	0.48
Pennsylvania German (10)	10	0.05
Polish (605)	1,702	7.91
Portuguese (25)	25	0.12
Romanian (13)	55	0.26
Russian (205)	495	2.30
Scandinavian (11)	11	0.05
Scotch-Irish (110)	447	2.08
Scottish (193)	620	2.88
Serbian (0)	12	0.06
Slovak (56)	128	0.59
Swedish (43)	250	1.16
Swiss (45)	72	0.33
Turkish (84)	84	0.39
Ukrainian (87)	176	0.82
Welsh (28)	112	0.52
West Indian, ex. Hispanic (12)	12	0.06
Jamaican (12)	12	0.06

Hispanic Origin	Population	%
Hispanic or Latino (of any race)	543	2.49
Central American, ex. Mexican	38	0.17
Costa Rican	3	0.01
Guatemalan	12	0.06
Honduran	2	0.01
Nicaraguan	10	0.05
Panamanian	2	0.01
Salvadoran	9	0.04
Cuban	31	0.14
Dominican Republic	27	0.12
Mexican	79	0.36
Puerto Rican	204	0.94
South American	112	0.51
Argentinean	27	0.12
Bolivian	10	0.05
Chilean	9	0.04
Colombian	37	0.17
Ecuadorian	11	0.05
Paraguayan	1	<0.01
Peruvian	12	0.06
Uruguayan	1	<0.01
Venezuelan	4	0.02
Other Hispanic or Latino	52	0.24

Race*	Population	%
African-American/Black (579)	729	3.35
Not Hispanic (554)	690	3.17
Hispanic (25)	39	0.18
American Indian/Alaska Native (23)	77	0.35
Not Hispanic (17)	65	0.30
Hispanic (6)	12	0.06
Blackfeet (0)	1	<0.01
Canadian/French Am. Ind. (0)	1	<0.01
Central American Ind. (1)	1	<0.01
Cherokee (2)	7	0.03
Chippewa (0)	1	<0.01
Iroquois (5)	13	0.06
Sioux (3)	5	0.02
South American Ind. (0)	1	<0.01
Asian (1,754)	1,998	9.17
Not Hispanic (1,751)	1,986	9.12
Hispanic (3)	12	0.06
Bangladeshi (1)	5	0.02
Burmese (4)	7	0.03
Chinese, ex. Taiwanese (490)	539	2.47
Filipino (63)	90	0.41
Indian (744)	808	3.71
Indonesian (10)	11	0.05
Japanese (29)	42	0.19
Korean (131)	158	0.73
Malaysian (3)	4	0.02
Nepalese (2)	2	0.01
Pakistani (174)	195	0.90
Sri Lankan (11)	14	0.06
Taiwanese (9)	13	0.06

*Notes: † The Census 2010 population figure is used to calculate the percentages in the Hispanic Origin and Race categories. Ancestry percentages are based on the 2006-2010 American Community Survey population (not shown); ‡ Numbers in parentheses indicate the number of people reporting a single ancestry; * Numbers in parentheses indicate the number of persons reporting this race alone, not in combination with any other race; Please refer to the Explanation of Data for more information.*

Thai (9)	12	0.06
Vietnamese (31)	34	0.16
Hawaii Native/Pacific Islander (2)	25	0.11
Not Hispanic (2)	23	0.11
Hispanic (0)	2	0.01
Native Hawaiian (1)	5	0.02
Tongan (0)	1	<0.01
White (18,763)	19,153	87.93
Not Hispanic (18,411)	18,756	86.11
Hispanic (352)	397	1.82

North Amityville

Place Type: CDP
County: Suffolk
Population: 17,862†

Ancestry‡	Population	%
African, Sub-Saharan (186)	273	1.53
African (170)	235	1.32
Liberian (16)	25	0.14
Nigerian (0)	13	0.07
American (61)	61	0.34
Arab (8)	31	0.17
Egyptian (8)	8	0.04
Syrian (0)	23	0.13
Austrian (0)	94	0.53
Brazilian (11)	56	0.31
British (41)	77	0.43
Canadian (8)	8	0.04
Czech (0)	28	0.16
Danish (0)	12	0.07
Dutch (0)	31	0.17
English (12)	149	0.84
Estonian (0)	12	0.07
French, ex. Basque (0)	18	0.10
French Canadian (18)	18	0.10
German (75)	272	1.53
Guyanese (275)	275	1.54
Irish (233)	586	3.29
Italian (226)	422	2.37
Lithuanian (0)	35	0.20
Norwegian (0)	33	0.19
Polish (59)	111	0.62
Romanian (0)	13	0.07
Russian (11)	11	0.06
Scottish (0)	56	0.31
Slavic (6)	6	0.03
Slovak (12)	12	0.07
Turkish (0)	17	0.10
West Indian, ex. Hispanic (3,356)	3,825	21.47
Bahamian (35)	88	0.49
Barbadian (64)	110	0.62
British West Indian (64)	119	0.67
Haitian (638)	655	3.68
Jamaican (1,950)	2,248	12.62
Trinidadian/Tobagonian (235)	235	1.32
West Indian (370)	370	2.08

Hispanic Origin	Population	%
Hispanic or Latino (of any race)	5,093	28.51
Central American, ex. Mexican	2,597	14.54
Costa Rican	12	0.07
Guatemalan	149	0.83
Honduran	436	2.44
Nicaraguan	6	0.03
Panamanian	83	0.46
Salvadoran	1,899	10.63
Other Central American	12	0.07
Cuban	28	0.16
Dominican Republic	1,008	5.64
Mexican	155	0.87
Puerto Rican	478	2.68
South American	349	1.95
Argentinean	19	0.11
Bolivian	1	0.01
Chilean	4	0.02
Colombian	175	0.98
Ecuadorian	88	0.49
Peruvian	48	0.27
Uruguayan	3	0.02
Venezuelan	9	0.05
Other South American	2	0.01
Other Hispanic or Latino	478	2.68

Race*	Population	%
African-American/Black (10,524)	10,971	61.42
Not Hispanic (10,076)	10,434	58.41
Hispanic (448)	537	3.01
American Indian/Alaska Native (199)	418	2.34
Not Hispanic (130)	317	1.77
Hispanic (69)	101	0.57
Apache (1)	4	0.02
Blackfeet (1)	6	0.03
Canadian/French Am. Ind. (2)	2	0.01
Central American Ind. (4)	4	0.02
Cherokee (17)	51	0.29
Chippewa (0)	1	0.01
Creek (0)	3	0.02
Inupiat *(Alaska Native)* (0)	1	0.01
Iroquois (4)	7	0.04
Mexican American Ind. (0)	1	0.01
Pueblo (9)	9	0.05
Seminole (1)	3	0.02
Sioux (3)	7	0.04
South American Ind. (26)	27	0.15
Tlingit-Haida *(Alaska Native)* (0)	1	0.01
Asian (171)	274	1.53
Not Hispanic (167)	235	1.32
Hispanic (4)	39	0.22
Bangladeshi (1)	3	0.02
Chinese, ex. Taiwanese (10)	19	0.11
Filipino (40)	58	0.32
Indian (77)	113	0.63
Japanese (2)	9	0.05
Korean (1)	9	0.05
Laotian (4)	4	0.02
Pakistani (15)	15	0.08
Sri Lankan (3)	3	0.02
Thai (1)	4	0.02
Vietnamese (10)	10	0.06
Hawaii Native/Pacific Islander (16)	61	0.34
Not Hispanic (9)	39	0.22
Hispanic (7)	22	0.12
Guamanian/Chamorro (0)	2	0.01
Native Hawaiian (0)	4	0.02
Samoan (2)	2	0.01
White (3,920)	4,335	24.27
Not Hispanic (1,907)	2,084	11.67
Hispanic (2,013)	2,251	12.60

North Babylon

Place Type: CDP
County: Suffolk
Population: 17,509†

Ancestry‡	Population	%
African, Sub-Saharan (198)	198	1.12
Nigerian (198)	198	1.12
American (398)	398	2.24
Arab (140)	149	0.84
Arab (130)	130	0.73
Egyptian (10)	10	0.06
Lebanese (0)	9	0.05
Armenian (8)	18	0.10
Austrian (26)	62	0.35
British (8)	22	0.12
Bulgarian (8)	8	0.05
Canadian (38)	85	0.48
Croatian (59)	74	0.42
Czech (11)	58	0.33
Danish (0)	61	0.34
Dutch (11)	138	0.78
Eastern European (94)	94	0.53
English (86)	861	4.86
European (49)	49	0.28
Finnish (0)	55	0.31
French, ex. Basque (7)	129	0.73
French Canadian (65)	86	0.48
German (666)	3,168	17.87
Greek (83)	206	1.16
Guyanese (0)	10	0.06
Hungarian (25)	72	0.41
Icelander (22)	22	0.12
Irish (945)	4,142	23.36
Israeli (0)	9	0.05
Italian (3,105)	5,987	33.76
Lithuanian (15)	26	0.15
Maltese (0)	8	0.05
Norwegian (21)	173	0.98
Polish (300)	974	5.49
Portuguese (81)	92	0.52
Romanian (63)	86	0.48
Russian (177)	700	3.95
Scotch-Irish (115)	235	1.33
Scottish (23)	125	0.70
Slavic (0)	9	0.05
Slovak (12)	12	0.07
Swedish (63)	294	1.66
Swiss (0)	23	0.13
Turkish (112)	170	0.96
Ukrainian (29)	40	0.23
Welsh (0)	11	0.06
West Indian, ex. Hispanic (320)	334	1.88
Barbadian (30)	30	0.17
Haitian (17)	17	0.10
Jamaican (244)	258	1.45
Trinidadian/Tobagonian (3)	3	0.02
West Indian (26)	26	0.15
Yugoslavian (0)	32	0.18

Hispanic Origin	Population	%
Hispanic or Latino (of any race)	2,221	12.68
Central American, ex. Mexican	265	1.51
Costa Rican	11	0.06
Guatemalan	31	0.18
Honduran	25	0.14
Nicaraguan	7	0.04
Panamanian	20	0.11
Salvadoran	171	0.98
Cuban	60	0.34
Dominican Republic	190	1.09
Mexican	69	0.39
Puerto Rican	837	4.78
South American	569	3.25
Argentinean	26	0.15
Bolivian	7	0.04
Chilean	26	0.15
Colombian	200	1.14
Ecuadorian	183	1.05
Paraguayan	8	0.05
Peruvian	89	0.51
Uruguayan	6	0.03
Venezuelan	15	0.09
Other South American	9	0.05
Other Hispanic or Latino	231	1.32

Race*	Population	%
African-American/Black (1,077)	1,221	6.97
Not Hispanic (1,009)	1,111	6.35
Hispanic (68)	110	0.63
American Indian/Alaska Native (17)	60	0.34
Not Hispanic (16)	56	0.32
Hispanic (1)	4	0.02
Blackfeet (0)	4	0.02
Canadian/French Am. Ind. (0)	3	0.02
Cherokee (0)	10	0.06
Chippewa (4)	4	0.02
Hopi (1)	1	0.01
Iroquois (1)	1	0.01
Lumbee (1)	1	0.01
Mexican American Ind. (1)	1	0.01
South American Ind. (2)	2	0.01
Asian (713)	825	4.71
Not Hispanic (696)	796	4.55
Hispanic (17)	29	0.17
Bangladeshi (26)	26	0.15
Chinese, ex. Taiwanese (115)	139	0.79
Filipino (113)	131	0.75

*Notes: † The Census 2010 population figure is used to calculate the percentages in the Hispanic Origin and Race categories. Ancestry percentages are based on the 2006-2010 American Community Survey population (not shown); ‡ Numbers in parentheses indicate the number of people reporting a single ancestry; * Numbers in parentheses indicate the number of persons reporting this race alone, not in combination with any other race; Please refer to the Explanation of Data for more information.*

Indian (227)	254	1.45
Indonesian (5)	6	0.03
Japanese (11)	21	0.12
Korean (60)	64	0.37
Malaysian (0)	1	0.01
Pakistani (100)	104	0.59
Sri Lankan (2)	4	0.02
Taiwanese (7)	8	0.05
Thai (2)	2	0.01
Vietnamese (26)	33	0.19
Hawaii Native/Pacific Islander (1)	6	0.03
Not Hispanic (1)	4	0.02
Hispanic (0)	2	0.01
Native Hawaiian (1)	3	0.02
Samoan (0)	1	0.01
White (14,864)	15,134	86.44
Not Hispanic (13,310)	13,492	77.06
Hispanic (1,554)	1,642	9.38

North Bay Shore

Place Type: CDP
County: Suffolk
Population: 18,944†

Ancestry‡	Population	%
African, Sub-Saharan (60)	110	0.56
African (45)	95	0.49
Nigerian (15)	15	0.08
American (161)	161	0.83
Austrian (14)	74	0.38
Cypriot (14)	14	0.07
Czech (0)	18	0.09
Danish (0)	9	0.05
Dutch (34)	42	0.22
English (56)	306	1.57
Finnish (10)	10	0.05
French, ex. Basque (0)	52	0.27
German (183)	1,055	5.41
Greek (0)	16	0.08
Guyanese (49)	64	0.33
Hungarian (0)	43	0.22
Irish (307)	1,109	5.68
Italian (444)	1,114	5.71
Norwegian (0)	22	0.11
Polish (106)	212	1.09
Portuguese (287)	297	1.52
Russian (66)	101	0.52
Scotch-Irish (28)	79	0.40
Scottish (0)	44	0.23
West Indian, ex. Hispanic (1,203)	1,332	6.83
Barbadian (12)	12	0.06
British West Indian (20)	20	0.10
Haitian (831)	831	4.26
Jamaican (199)	328	1.68
Trinidadian/Tobagonian (62)	62	0.32
West Indian (79)	79	0.40

Hispanic Origin	Population	%
Hispanic or Latino (of any race)	12,310	64.98
Central American, ex. Mexican	5,763	30.42
Costa Rican	31	0.16
Guatemalan	576	3.04
Honduran	539	2.85
Nicaraguan	21	0.11
Panamanian	55	0.29
Salvadoran	4,530	23.91
Other Central American	11	0.06
Cuban	65	0.34
Dominican Republic	1,089	5.75
Mexican	246	1.30
Puerto Rican	2,487	13.13
South American	1,693	8.94
Argentinean	31	0.16
Bolivian	27	0.14
Chilean	27	0.14
Colombian	504	2.66
Ecuadorian	641	3.38
Peruvian	404	2.13
Uruguayan	31	0.16
Venezuelan	28	0.15
Other Hispanic or Latino	967	5.10

Race*	Population	%
African-American/Black (3,473)	3,870	20.43
Not Hispanic (2,894)	3,114	16.44
Hispanic (579)	756	3.99
American Indian/Alaska Native (138)	344	1.82
Not Hispanic (38)	129	0.68
Hispanic (100)	215	1.13
Arapaho (0)	1	0.01
Blackfeet (1)	18	0.10
Central American Ind. (2)	3	0.02
Cherokee (2)	26	0.14
Choctaw (0)	5	0.03
Crow (0)	4	0.02
Iroquois (0)	14	0.07
Mexican American Ind. (7)	7	0.04
South American Ind. (9)	15	0.08
Spanish American Ind. (2)	5	0.03
Asian (717)	847	4.47
Not Hispanic (697)	794	4.19
Hispanic (20)	53	0.28
Bangladeshi (30)	54	0.29
Chinese, ex. Taiwanese (32)	40	0.21
Filipino (34)	49	0.26
Indian (272)	343	1.81
Indonesian (3)	3	0.02
Japanese (3)	11	0.06
Korean (5)	8	0.04
Laotian (1)	1	0.01
Pakistani (237)	262	1.38
Thai (0)	5	0.03
Vietnamese (31)	37	0.20
Hawaii Native/Pacific Islander (9)	54	0.29
Not Hispanic (0)	22	0.12
Hispanic (9)	32	0.17
Guamanian/Chamorro (1)	3	0.02
Native Hawaiian (5)	9	0.05
Samoan (1)	4	0.02
White (8,264)	9,138	48.24
Not Hispanic (2,585)	2,780	14.67
Hispanic (5,679)	6,358	33.56

North Bellmore

Place Type: CDP
County: Nassau
Population: 19,941†

Ancestry‡	Population	%
African, Sub-Saharan (0)	12	0.06
African (0)	12	0.06
Albanian (14)	14	0.07
American (671)	671	3.43
Arab (79)	134	0.68
Arab (67)	67	0.34
Moroccan (12)	67	0.34
Austrian (17)	110	0.56
Belgian (11)	11	0.06
Brazilian (0)	18	0.09
Canadian (0)	50	0.26
Croatian (9)	9	0.05
Cypriot (13)	13	0.07
Czech (26)	80	0.41
Dutch (42)	116	0.59
Eastern European (171)	202	1.03
English (88)	578	2.95
European (240)	240	1.23
Finnish (12)	105	0.54
French, ex. Basque (60)	220	1.12
French Canadian (11)	94	0.48
German (640)	3,461	17.68
Greek (359)	375	1.92
Guyanese (44)	49	0.25
Hungarian (320)	374	1.91
Irish (1,092)	4,466	22.81
Italian (2,975)	6,303	32.20
Lithuanian (54)	120	0.61
Maltese (22)	84	0.43
Norwegian (32)	78	0.40
Polish (289)	1,458	7.45
Portuguese (92)	92	0.47
Romanian (0)	22	0.11
Russian (456)	1,051	5.37
Scotch-Irish (25)	132	0.67
Scottish (36)	56	0.29
Slovak (14)	78	0.40
Slovene (0)	22	0.11
Swedish (0)	284	1.45
Swiss (0)	13	0.07
Turkish (66)	103	0.53
Ukrainian (63)	81	0.41
West Indian, ex. Hispanic (243)	243	1.24
British West Indian (13)	13	0.07
Jamaican (171)	171	0.87
Trinidadian/Tobagonian (15)	15	0.08
West Indian (44)	44	0.22
Yugoslavian (48)	106	0.54

Hispanic Origin	Population	%
Hispanic or Latino (of any race)	1,539	7.72
Central American, ex. Mexican	186	0.93
Costa Rican	5	0.03
Guatemalan	15	0.08
Honduran	25	0.13
Nicaraguan	10	0.05
Panamanian	2	0.01
Salvadoran	129	0.65
Cuban	86	0.43
Dominican Republic	141	0.71
Mexican	110	0.55
Puerto Rican	436	2.19
South American	431	2.16
Argentinean	61	0.31
Bolivian	9	0.05
Chilean	21	0.11
Colombian	162	0.81
Ecuadorian	99	0.50
Peruvian	46	0.23
Uruguayan	2	0.01
Venezuelan	21	0.11
Other South American	10	0.05
Other Hispanic or Latino	149	0.75

Race*	Population	%
African-American/Black (512)	598	3.00
Not Hispanic (492)	550	2.76
Hispanic (20)	48	0.24
American Indian/Alaska Native (18)	75	0.38
Not Hispanic (15)	59	0.30
Hispanic (3)	16	0.08
Apache (0)	1	0.01
Central American Ind. (1)	1	0.01
Cherokee (1)	7	0.04
Navajo (0)	1	0.01
South American Ind. (1)	7	0.04
Asian (919)	1,087	5.45
Not Hispanic (904)	1,062	5.33
Hispanic (15)	25	0.13
Bangladeshi (12)	13	0.07
Chinese, ex. Taiwanese (144)	188	0.94
Filipino (80)	106	0.53
Indian (301)	353	1.77
Indonesian (1)	1	0.01
Japanese (13)	40	0.20
Korean (27)	42	0.21
Pakistani (262)	278	1.39
Taiwanese (5)	7	0.04
Thai (3)	4	0.02
Vietnamese (16)	24	0.12
Hawaii Native/Pacific Islander (1)	6	0.03
Not Hispanic (1)	6	0.03
Native Hawaiian (1)	2	0.01
Samoan (0)	1	0.01
White (17,846)	18,126	90.90
Not Hispanic (16,704)	16,901	84.76
Hispanic (1,142)	1,225	6.14

*Notes: † The Census 2010 population figure is used to calculate the percentages in the Hispanic Origin and Race categories. Ancestry percentages are based on the 2006-2010 American Community Survey population (not shown); ‡ Numbers in parentheses indicate the number of people reporting a single ancestry; * Numbers in parentheses indicate the number of persons reporting this race alone, not in combination with any other race; Please refer to the Explanation of Data for more information.*

North Bellport

Place Type: CDP
County: Suffolk
Population: 11,545†

Ancestry‡	Population	%
African, Sub-Saharan (737)	737	6.54
African (728)	728	6.46
Liberian (9)	9	0.08
American (150)	150	1.33
Arab (39)	39	0.35
Egyptian (8)	8	0.07
Other Arab (31)	31	0.28
Armenian (7)	7	0.06
Belgian (2)	2	0.02
Brazilian (0)	27	0.24
Czech (10)	104	0.92
Czechoslovakian (40)	40	0.36
Dutch (22)	106	0.94
English (61)	496	4.40
European (8)	8	0.07
French, ex. Basque (8)	153	1.36
German (246)	1,259	11.18
Greek (0)	35	0.31
Hungarian (0)	51	0.45
Irish (273)	1,496	13.28
Italian (957)	1,716	15.23
Lithuanian (0)	21	0.19
Maltese (11)	11	0.10
Norwegian (26)	88	0.78
Polish (122)	432	3.83
Portuguese (0)	11	0.10
Russian (8)	39	0.35
Scandinavian (0)	11	0.10
Scotch-Irish (11)	96	0.85
Scottish (8)	113	1.00
Slavic (0)	8	0.07
Slovak (0)	31	0.28
Swedish (0)	10	0.09
Welsh (0)	10	0.09
West Indian, ex. Hispanic (76)	256	2.27
Haitian (0)	43	0.38
Jamaican (0)	16	0.14
Trinidadian/Tobagonian (64)	176	1.56
West Indian (12)	21	0.19

Hispanic Origin	Population	%
Hispanic or Latino (of any race)	3,382	29.29
Central American, ex. Mexican	896	7.76
Costa Rican	14	0.12
Guatemalan	75	0.65
Honduran	62	0.54
Nicaraguan	4	0.03
Panamanian	13	0.11
Salvadoran	710	6.15
Other Central American	18	0.16
Cuban	40	0.35
Dominican Republic	174	1.51
Mexican	174	1.51
Puerto Rican	1,055	9.14
South American	670	5.80
Argentinean	18	0.16
Bolivian	3	0.03
Chilean	6	0.05
Colombian	143	1.24
Ecuadorian	443	3.84
Paraguayan	3	0.03
Peruvian	46	0.40
Venezuelan	8	0.07
Other Hispanic or Latino	373	3.23

Race*	Population	%
African-American/Black (3,054)	3,516	30.45
Not Hispanic (2,868)	3,202	27.73
Hispanic (186)	314	2.72
American Indian/Alaska Native (159)	364	3.15
Not Hispanic (98)	246	2.13
Hispanic (61)	118	1.02
Apache (1)	1	0.01
Blackfeet (2)	23	0.20
Canadian/French Am. Ind. (0)	7	0.06
Central American Ind. (0)	5	0.04
Cherokee (3)	46	0.40
Mexican American Ind. (0)	2	0.02
Navajo (0)	3	0.03
Seminole (1)	4	0.03
Sioux (4)	4	0.03
South American Ind. (2)	3	0.03
Spanish American Ind. (6)	6	0.05
Asian (305)	389	3.37
Not Hispanic (288)	368	3.19
Hispanic (17)	21	0.18
Bangladeshi (7)	7	0.06
Burmese (1)	1	0.01
Chinese, ex. Taiwanese (29)	37	0.32
Filipino (109)	124	1.07
Hmong (1)	4	0.03
Indian (104)	125	1.08
Indonesian (0)	1	0.01
Japanese (10)	12	0.10
Korean (8)	17	0.15
Laotian (6)	6	0.05
Nepalese (3)	3	0.03
Pakistani (13)	30	0.26
Thai (1)	2	0.02
Hawaii Native/Pacific Islander (9)	28	0.24
Not Hispanic (7)	13	0.11
Hispanic (2)	15	0.13
Guamanian/Chamorro (4)	5	0.04
Native Hawaiian (0)	3	0.03
Samoan (3)	3	0.03
White (6,225)	6,710	58.12
Not Hispanic (4,435)	4,720	40.88
Hispanic (1,790)	1,990	17.24

North Castle

Place Type: Town
County: Westchester
Population: 11,841†

Ancestry‡	Population	%
African, Sub-Saharan (16)	16	0.14
Nigerian (16)	16	0.14
Albanian (124)	124	1.07
American (590)	590	5.09
Arab (16)	73	0.63
Syrian (10)	17	0.15
Other Arab (6)	56	0.48
Armenian (0)	33	0.28
Australian (4)	4	0.03
Austrian (18)	122	1.05
Belgian (0)	6	0.05
Brazilian (15)	33	0.28
British (27)	54	0.47
Bulgarian (0)	19	0.16
Canadian (0)	8	0.07
Czech (0)	9	0.08
Danish (16)	16	0.14
Dutch (0)	30	0.26
Eastern European (484)	484	4.18
English (107)	632	5.45
European (473)	473	4.08
Finnish (8)	8	0.07
French, ex. Basque (81)	196	1.69
French Canadian (57)	66	0.57
German (289)	1,055	9.10
Greek (112)	231	1.99
Hungarian (98)	226	1.95
Iranian (19)	31	0.27
Irish (275)	1,638	14.13
Israeli (2)	2	0.02
Italian (1,826)	2,823	24.36
Lithuanian (26)	96	0.83
Norwegian (8)	76	0.66
Polish (179)	530	4.57
Portuguese (165)	165	1.42
Romanian (28)	80	0.69
Russian (385)	713	6.15
Scandinavian (37)	48	0.41
Scotch-Irish (64)	179	1.54
Scottish (62)	157	1.35
Swedish (8)	76	0.66
Swiss (19)	42	0.36
Turkish (2)	10	0.09
Ukrainian (16)	55	0.47
Welsh (27)	79	0.68
West Indian, ex. Hispanic (50)	68	0.59
Jamaican (50)	50	0.43
West Indian (0)	18	0.16

Hispanic Origin	Population	%
Hispanic or Latino (of any race)	906	7.65
Central American, ex. Mexican	52	0.44
Costa Rican	4	0.03
Guatemalan	25	0.21
Honduran	4	0.03
Nicaraguan	6	0.05
Panamanian	1	0.01
Salvadoran	12	0.10
Cuban	63	0.53
Dominican Republic	14	0.12
Mexican	121	1.02
Puerto Rican	145	1.22
South American	289	2.44
Argentinean	36	0.30
Bolivian	1	0.01
Chilean	3	0.03
Colombian	99	0.84
Ecuadorian	30	0.25
Paraguayan	35	0.30
Peruvian	67	0.57
Uruguayan	5	0.04
Venezuelan	12	0.10
Other South American	1	0.01
Other Hispanic or Latino	222	1.87

Race*	Population	%
African-American/Black (185)	248	2.09
Not Hispanic (179)	231	1.95
Hispanic (6)	17	0.14
American Indian/Alaska Native (16)	67	0.57
Not Hispanic (4)	42	0.35
Hispanic (12)	25	0.21
Blackfeet (2)	2	0.02
Canadian/French Am. Ind. (1)	1	0.01
Cherokee (0)	5	0.04
Iroquois (0)	2	0.02
Mexican American Ind. (0)	5	0.04
South American Ind. (10)	10	0.08
Asian (590)	674	5.69
Not Hispanic (586)	664	5.61
Hispanic (4)	10	0.08
Bangladeshi (0)	2	0.02
Chinese, ex. Taiwanese (223)	260	2.20
Filipino (27)	39	0.33
Indian (150)	176	1.49
Indonesian (1)	3	0.03
Japanese (31)	41	0.35
Korean (92)	99	0.84
Malaysian (5)	5	0.04
Nepalese (3)	3	0.03
Pakistani (16)	19	0.16
Sri Lankan (6)	6	0.05
Taiwanese (8)	12	0.10
Thai (4)	11	0.09
Vietnamese (3)	6	0.05
Hawaii Native/Pacific Islander (4)	8	0.07
Not Hispanic (1)	3	0.03
Hispanic (3)	5	0.04
Guamanian/Chamorro (4)	4	0.03
Native Hawaiian (0)	2	0.02
White (10,629)	10,817	91.35
Not Hispanic (9,994)	10,121	85.47
Hispanic (635)	696	5.88

SECTION TWO

*Notes: † The Census 2010 population figure is used to calculate the percentages in the Hispanic Origin and Race categories. Ancestry percentages are based on the 2006-2010 American Community Survey population (not shown); ‡ Numbers in parentheses indicate the number of people reporting a single ancestry; * Numbers in parentheses indicate the number of persons reporting this race alone, not in combination with any other race; Please refer to the Explanation of Data for more information.*

North Elba

Place Type: Town
County: Essex
Population: 8,957†

Ancestry‡	Population	%
African, Sub-Saharan (75)	87	0.97
African (47)	59	0.66
Cape Verdean (17)	17	0.19
Ethiopian (11)	11	0.12
American (510)	510	5.70
Arab (31)	49	0.55
Lebanese (10)	10	0.11
Moroccan (21)	21	0.23
Other Arab (0)	18	0.20
Armenian (11)	11	0.12
British (29)	60	0.67
Canadian (96)	96	1.07
Czech (12)	92	1.03
Danish (0)	21	0.23
Dutch (0)	80	0.89
Eastern European (28)	46	0.51
English (167)	820	9.16
European (0)	6	0.07
French, ex. Basque (316)	1,109	12.39
French Canadian (50)	94	1.05
German (396)	1,129	12.61
Greek (22)	111	1.24
Hungarian (31)	31	0.35
Irish (649)	1,749	19.53
Israeli (0)	9	0.10
Italian (105)	683	7.63
Norwegian (0)	71	0.79
Pennsylvania German (0)	8	0.09
Polish (63)	209	2.33
Portuguese (9)	9	0.10
Romanian (10)	24	0.27
Russian (287)	341	3.81
Scotch-Irish (27)	334	3.73
Scottish (114)	328	3.66
Slavic (0)	14	0.16
Slovak (44)	44	0.49
Swedish (61)	174	1.94
Swiss (13)	73	0.82
Welsh (0)	96	1.07
West Indian, ex. Hispanic (39)	39	0.44
Jamaican (17)	17	0.19
Trinidadian/Tobagonian (10)	10	0.11
West Indian (12)	12	0.13

Hispanic Origin	Population	%
Hispanic or Latino (of any race)	654	7.30
Central American, ex. Mexican	58	0.65
Costa Rican	1	0.01
Guatemalan	14	0.16
Honduran	12	0.13
Nicaraguan	1	0.01
Panamanian	7	0.08
Salvadoran	23	0.26
Cuban	18	0.20
Dominican Republic	69	0.77
Mexican	287	3.20
Puerto Rican	179	2.00
South American	21	0.23
Argentinean	3	0.03
Colombian	14	0.16
Peruvian	1	0.01
Uruguayan	2	0.02
Venezuelan	1	0.01
Other Hispanic or Latino	22	0.25

Race*	Population	%
African-American/Black (887)	939	10.48
Not Hispanic (800)	843	9.41
Hispanic (87)	96	1.07
American Indian/Alaska Native (56)	90	1.00
Not Hispanic (35)	62	0.69
Hispanic (21)	28	0.31
Blackfeet (2)	3	0.03
Canadian/French Am. Ind. (0)	1	0.01
Cherokee (0)	2	0.02
Hopi (0)	1	0.01
Iroquois (9)	14	0.16
Lumbee (2)	2	0.02
Mexican American Ind. (8)	9	0.10
Navajo (3)	3	0.03
Pueblo (0)	1	0.01
Sioux (0)	1	0.01
Yaqui (0)	1	0.01
Asian (113)	137	1.53
Not Hispanic (110)	131	1.46
Hispanic (3)	6	0.07
Cambodian (5)	5	0.06
Chinese, ex. Taiwanese (39)	44	0.49
Filipino (13)	18	0.20
Indian (10)	11	0.12
Japanese (7)	12	0.13
Korean (23)	27	0.30
Laotian (1)	1	0.01
Thai (1)	3	0.03
Vietnamese (12)	13	0.15
Hawaii Native/Pacific Islander (5)	13	0.15
Not Hispanic (4)	11	0.12
Hispanic (1)	2	0.02
Guamanian/Chamorro (1)	3	0.03
Native Hawaiian (4)	8	0.09
Samoan (0)	1	0.01
White (7,519)	7,634	85.23
Not Hispanic (7,247)	7,329	81.82
Hispanic (272)	305	3.41

North Gates

Place Type: CDP
County: Monroe
Population: 9,512†

Ancestry‡	Population	%
African, Sub-Saharan (34)	34	0.36
African (34)	34	0.36
American (330)	330	3.54
Arab (103)	132	1.41
Lebanese (68)	97	1.04
Other Arab (35)	35	0.38
Austrian (0)	57	0.61
British (10)	23	0.25
Canadian (22)	148	1.59
Czechoslovakian (0)	18	0.19
Dutch (8)	329	3.53
English (172)	973	10.43
European (34)	114	1.22
Finnish (7)	7	0.08
French, ex. Basque (10)	413	4.43
French Canadian (21)	96	1.03
German (403)	1,767	18.94
Greek (61)	61	0.65
Guyanese (12)	12	0.13
Hungarian (40)	58	0.62
Irish (226)	1,395	14.95
Italian (2,177)	3,304	35.42
Lithuanian (0)	34	0.36
Macedonian (9)	9	0.10
Pennsylvania German (16)	28	0.30
Polish (176)	588	6.30
Portuguese (31)	52	0.56
Russian (13)	26	0.28
Scotch-Irish (15)	173	1.85
Scottish (29)	89	0.95
Slovak (0)	9	0.10
Swedish (0)	26	0.28
Swiss (0)	32	0.34
Turkish (0)	53	0.57
Ukrainian (51)	101	1.08
Welsh (9)	29	0.31
West Indian, ex. Hispanic (6)	6	0.06
Barbadian (6)	6	0.06

Hispanic Origin	Population	%
Hispanic or Latino (of any race)	629	6.61
Central American, ex. Mexican	23	0.24
Costa Rican	1	0.01
Guatemalan	4	0.04
Honduran	9	0.09
Nicaraguan	1	0.01
Panamanian	3	0.03
Salvadoran	5	0.05
Cuban	69	0.73
Dominican Republic	17	0.18
Mexican	32	0.34
Puerto Rican	438	4.60
South American	36	0.38
Argentinean	6	0.06
Chilean	13	0.14
Colombian	10	0.11
Ecuadorian	2	0.02
Peruvian	1	0.01
Venezuelan	4	0.04
Other Hispanic or Latino	14	0.15

Race*	Population	%
African-American/Black (976)	1,127	11.85
Not Hispanic (934)	1,053	11.07
Hispanic (42)	74	0.78
American Indian/Alaska Native (24)	70	0.74
Not Hispanic (23)	58	0.61
Hispanic (1)	12	0.13
Cherokee (0)	6	0.06
Chippewa (3)	4	0.04
Choctaw (2)	5	0.05
Iroquois (8)	21	0.22
Sioux (1)	2	0.02
South American Ind. (1)	2	0.02
Ute (0)	1	0.01
Asian (417)	452	4.75
Not Hispanic (415)	450	4.73
Hispanic (2)	2	0.02
Cambodian (1)	8	0.08
Chinese, ex. Taiwanese (47)	66	0.69
Filipino (20)	24	0.25
Indian (60)	61	0.64
Japanese (4)	12	0.13
Korean (39)	48	0.50
Laotian (32)	38	0.40
Pakistani (4)	4	0.04
Taiwanese (1)	1	0.01
Thai (13)	14	0.15
Vietnamese (168)	183	1.92
Hawaii Native/Pacific Islander (2)	15	0.16
Not Hispanic (2)	7	0.07
Hispanic (0)	8	0.08
Guamanian/Chamorro (2)	2	0.02
Native Hawaiian (0)	1	0.01
White (7,684)	7,907	83.13
Not Hispanic (7,328)	7,491	78.75
Hispanic (356)	416	4.37

North Greenbush

Place Type: Town
County: Rensselaer
Population: 12,075†

Ancestry‡	Population	%
African, Sub-Saharan (15)	15	0.13
African (15)	15	0.13
American (414)	414	3.48
Arab (55)	269	2.26
Arab (0)	19	0.16
Egyptian (52)	65	0.55
Lebanese (3)	185	1.56
Armenian (43)	166	1.40
Austrian (12)	29	0.24
British (20)	23	0.19
Canadian (3)	25	0.21
Croatian (11)	11	0.09
Czech (13)	34	0.29
Czechoslovakian (41)	144	1.21
Danish (26)	92	0.77
Dutch (27)	434	3.65

*Notes: † The Census 2010 population figure is used to calculate the percentages in the Hispanic Origin and Race categories. Ancestry percentages are based on the 2006-2010 American Community Survey population (not shown); ‡ Numbers in parentheses indicate the number of people reporting a single ancestry; * Numbers in parentheses indicate the number of persons reporting this race alone, not in combination with any other race; Please refer to the Explanation of Data for more information.*

Eastern European (8)	8	0.07
English (295)	1,116	9.39
European (83)	127	1.07
French, ex. Basque (112)	1,283	10.79
French Canadian (72)	289	2.43
German (381)	2,633	22.15
Greek (12)	131	1.10
Hungarian (20)	20	0.17
Irish (1,007)	3,818	32.12
Italian (860)	2,489	20.94
Lithuanian (9)	277	2.33
Northern European (14)	14	0.12
Norwegian (18)	68	0.57
Polish (164)	1,084	9.12
Portuguese (0)	26	0.22
Romanian (0)	8	0.07
Russian (16)	79	0.66
Scandinavian (0)	15	0.13
Scotch-Irish (45)	195	1.64
Scottish (21)	157	1.32
Slavic (0)	26	0.22
Swedish (59)	218	1.83
Swiss (0)	27	0.23
Ukrainian (98)	418	3.52
Welsh (0)	72	0.61
West Indian, ex. Hispanic (2)	10	0.08
Haitian (0)	8	0.07
Jamaican (2)	2	0.02

Hispanic Origin	Population	%
Hispanic or Latino (of any race)	197	1.63
Central American, ex. Mexican	11	0.09
Costa Rican	6	0.05
Guatemalan	1	0.01
Nicaraguan	2	0.02
Panamanian	1	0.01
Salvadoran	1	0.01
Cuban	6	0.05
Dominican Republic	13	0.11
Mexican	44	0.36
Puerto Rican	69	0.57
South American	24	0.20
Argentinean	2	0.02
Chilean	3	0.02
Colombian	3	0.02
Ecuadorian	7	0.06
Peruvian	7	0.06
Venezuelan	2	0.02
Other Hispanic or Latino	30	0.25

Race*	Population	%
African-American/Black (203)	255	2.11
Not Hispanic (197)	246	2.04
Hispanic (6)	9	0.07
American Indian/Alaska Native (20)	62	0.51
Not Hispanic (13)	46	0.38
Hispanic (7)	16	0.13
Blackfeet (1)	2	0.02
Central American Ind. (1)	1	0.01
Cherokee (1)	3	0.02
Iroquois (2)	13	0.11
South American Ind. (3)	3	0.02
Asian (154)	204	1.69
Not Hispanic (153)	201	1.66
Hispanic (1)	3	0.02
Bangladeshi (1)	1	0.01
Chinese, ex. Taiwanese (29)	38	0.31
Filipino (12)	14	0.12
Hmong (1)	3	0.02
Indian (39)	41	0.34
Japanese (16)	29	0.24
Korean (29)	31	0.26
Pakistani (11)	12	0.10
Taiwanese (3)	3	0.02
Thai (3)	3	0.02
Vietnamese (7)	11	0.09
Hawaii Native/Pacific Islander (2)	5	0.04
Not Hispanic (2)	4	0.03
Hispanic (0)	1	0.01
Native Hawaiian (0)	1	0.01
White (11,521)	11,663	96.59
Not Hispanic (11,372)	11,498	95.22
Hispanic (149)	165	1.37

North Hempstead

Place Type: Town
County: Nassau
Population: 226,322†

Ancestry‡	Population	%
Afghan (88)	203	0.09
African, Sub-Saharan (670)	862	0.39
African (277)	437	0.20
Ethiopian (49)	49	0.02
Ghanaian (117)	117	0.05
Liberian (0)	3	<0.01
Nigerian (145)	154	0.07
Sierra Leonean (13)	13	0.01
South African (60)	63	0.03
Sudanese (0)	17	0.01
Other Sub-Saharan African (9)	9	<0.01
Albanian (156)	296	0.13
Alsatian (9)	9	<0.01
American (7,110)	7,110	3.18
Arab (1,529)	2,078	0.93
Arab (82)	103	0.05
Egyptian (404)	529	0.24
Iraqi (370)	500	0.22
Lebanese (105)	147	0.07
Moroccan (34)	85	0.04
Palestinian (59)	59	0.03
Syrian (10)	84	0.04
Other Arab (465)	571	0.26
Armenian (391)	631	0.28
Assyrian/Chaldean/Syriac (4)	21	0.01
Australian (22)	80	0.04
Austrian (661)	2,782	1.24
Basque (0)	121	0.05
Belgian (93)	166	0.07
Brazilian (489)	613	0.27
British (233)	705	0.32
Bulgarian (56)	73	0.03
Cajun (0)	22	0.01
Canadian (182)	307	0.14
Celtic (0)	48	0.02
Croatian (478)	672	0.30
Cypriot (46)	64	0.03
Czech (150)	636	0.28
Czechoslovakian (205)	493	0.22
Danish (141)	419	0.19
Dutch (110)	784	0.35
Eastern European (3,518)	3,769	1.69
English (1,073)	6,017	2.69
Estonian (18)	48	0.02
European (1,809)	2,051	0.92
Finnish (38)	128	0.06
French, ex. Basque (273)	2,191	0.98
French Canadian (207)	490	0.22
German (4,524)	18,322	8.19
German Russian (0)	26	0.01
Greek (2,635)	3,568	1.60
Guyanese (324)	405	0.18
Hungarian (894)	2,628	1.18
Iranian (8,611)	9,262	4.14
Irish (10,304)	27,339	12.22
Israeli (1,537)	1,853	0.83
Italian (23,753)	40,182	17.97
Latvian (122)	254	0.11
Lithuanian (197)	718	0.32
Luxemburger (0)	16	0.01
Maltese (125)	248	0.11
Northern European (82)	91	0.04
Norwegian (129)	715	0.32
Pennsylvania German (15)	15	0.01
Polish (5,076)	13,352	5.97
Portuguese (3,596)	3,978	1.78
Romanian (662)	1,434	0.64
Russian (6,882)	14,712	6.58
Scandinavian (67)	122	0.05
Scotch-Irish (405)	1,188	0.53
Scottish (369)	1,567	0.70
Serbian (109)	153	0.07
Slavic (11)	195	0.09
Slovak (122)	312	0.14
Slovene (59)	79	0.04
Swedish (179)	1,391	0.62
Swiss (77)	362	0.16
Turkish (308)	408	0.18
Ukrainian (488)	1,005	0.45
Welsh (46)	328	0.15
West Indian, ex. Hispanic (3,572)	4,095	1.83
Barbadian (152)	184	0.08
Belizean (44)	81	0.04
British West Indian (46)	46	0.02
Dutch West Indian (45)	65	0.03
Haitian (2,247)	2,394	1.07
Jamaican (723)	868	0.39
Trinidadian/Tobagonian (87)	94	0.04
West Indian (228)	363	0.16
Yugoslavian (65)	170	0.08

Hispanic Origin	Population	%
Hispanic or Latino (of any race)	29,074	12.85
Central American, ex. Mexican	11,455	5.06
Costa Rican	124	0.05
Guatemalan	1,193	0.53
Honduran	1,572	0.69
Nicaraguan	110	0.05
Panamanian	84	0.04
Salvadoran	8,262	3.65
Other Central American	110	0.05
Cuban	660	0.29
Dominican Republic	1,362	0.60
Mexican	3,488	1.54
Puerto Rican	2,705	1.20
South American	6,333	2.80
Argentinean	435	0.19
Bolivian	62	0.03
Chilean	664	0.29
Colombian	1,914	0.85
Ecuadorian	1,966	0.87
Paraguayan	140	0.06
Peruvian	925	0.41
Uruguayan	84	0.04
Venezuelan	97	0.04
Other South American	46	0.02
Other Hispanic or Latino	3,071	1.36

Race*	Population	%
African-American/Black (12,587)	13,593	6.01
Not Hispanic (11,971)	12,707	5.61
Hispanic (616)	886	0.39
American Indian/Alaska Native (461)	1,149	0.51
Not Hispanic (183)	566	0.25
Hispanic (278)	583	0.26
Apache (1)	3	<0.01
Central American Ind. (9)	16	0.01
Cherokee (14)	86	0.04
Cheyenne (3)	3	<0.01
Chippewa (0)	4	<0.01
Choctaw (3)	8	<0.01
Creek (0)	3	<0.01
Delaware (2)	5	<0.01
Hopi (1)	3	<0.01
Inupiat *(Alaska Native)* (2)	2	<0.01
Iroquois (17)	37	0.02
Lumbee (0)	1	<0.01
Mexican American Ind. (36)	48	0.02
Potawatomi (1)	1	<0.01
Sioux (8)	17	0.01
South American Ind. (32)	79	0.03
Spanish American Ind. (39)	40	0.02
Yaqui (1)	1	<0.01
Asian (33,889)	36,973	16.34
Not Hispanic (33,747)	36,641	16.19
Hispanic (142)	332	0.15
Bangladeshi (392)	441	0.19
Bhutanese (1)	1	<0.01
Burmese (83)	88	0.04

*Notes: † The Census 2010 population figure is used to calculate the percentages in the Hispanic Origin and Race categories. Ancestry percentages are based on the 2006-2010 American Community Survey population (not shown); ‡ Numbers in parentheses indicate the number of people reporting a single ancestry; * Numbers in parentheses indicate the number of persons reporting this race alone, not in combination with any other race; Please refer to the Explanation of Data for more information.*

Cambodian (11)	14	0.01
Chinese, ex. Taiwanese (9,631)	10,292	4.55
Filipino (1,567)	1,899	0.84
Indian (12,549)	13,427	5.93
Indonesian (30)	53	0.02
Japanese (1,094)	1,266	0.56
Korean (5,820)	6,015	2.66
Laotian (7)	8	<0.01
Malaysian (24)	35	0.02
Nepalese (17)	17	0.01
Pakistani (904)	1,029	0.45
Sri Lankan (52)	59	0.03
Taiwanese (717)	809	0.36
Thai (103)	126	0.06
Vietnamese (132)	186	0.08
Hawaii Native/Pacific Islander (31)	275	0.12
Not Hispanic (24)	224	0.10
Hispanic (7)	51	0.02
Guamanian/Chamorro (14)	20	0.01
Native Hawaiian (0)	34	0.02
Samoan (7)	14	0.01
White (161,955)	166,538	73.58
Not Hispanic (146,760)	149,607	66.10
Hispanic (15,195)	16,931	7.48

North Lindenhurst

Place Type: CDP
County: Suffolk
Population: 11,652†

Ancestry‡	Population	%
African, Sub-Saharan (20)	20	0.17
African (20)	20	0.17
American (259)	259	2.23
Arab (0)	14	0.12
Syrian (0)	14	0.12
Austrian (21)	84	0.72
Belgian (12)	12	0.10
Danish (0)	12	0.10
Dutch (0)	32	0.28
Eastern European (23)	23	0.20
English (69)	470	4.04
Estonian (10)	10	0.09
Finnish (0)	10	0.09
French, ex. Basque (29)	300	2.58
French Canadian (0)	9	0.08
German (401)	1,814	15.60
Greek (125)	189	1.63
Guyanese (0)	13	0.11
Hungarian (40)	146	1.26
Irish (615)	2,169	18.65
Italian (1,866)	3,969	34.14
Lithuanian (14)	41	0.35
Northern European (17)	33	0.28
Norwegian (19)	31	0.27
Polish (666)	1,097	9.43
Russian (11)	127	1.09
Scotch-Irish (48)	90	0.77
Scottish (42)	107	0.92
Slovak (0)	9	0.08
Swedish (22)	51	0.44
Swiss (0)	14	0.12
Turkish (150)	150	1.29
Welsh (10)	35	0.30
West Indian, ex. Hispanic (414)	468	4.03
Barbadian (0)	7	0.06
Haitian (319)	338	2.91
Jamaican (37)	65	0.56
West Indian (58)	58	0.50

Hispanic Origin	Population	%
Hispanic or Latino (of any race)	2,246	19.28
Central American, ex. Mexican	618	5.30
Costa Rican	18	0.15
Guatemalan	41	0.35
Honduran	97	0.83
Nicaraguan	5	0.04
Panamanian	8	0.07
Salvadoran	439	3.77
Other Central American	10	0.09
Cuban	26	0.22
Dominican Republic	428	3.67
Mexican	54	0.46
Puerto Rican	452	3.88
South American	484	4.15
Argentinean	32	0.27
Bolivian	6	0.05
Chilean	9	0.08
Colombian	165	1.42
Ecuadorian	81	0.70
Paraguayan	3	0.03
Peruvian	162	1.39
Uruguayan	7	0.06
Venezuelan	8	0.07
Other South American	11	0.09
Other Hispanic or Latino	184	1.58

Race*	Population	%
African-American/Black (599)	714	6.13
Not Hispanic (564)	646	5.54
Hispanic (35)	68	0.58
American Indian/Alaska Native (37)	102	0.88
Not Hispanic (14)	53	0.45
Hispanic (23)	49	0.42
Blackfeet (0)	4	0.03
Central American Ind. (4)	7	0.06
Cherokee (1)	11	0.09
Crow (0)	1	0.01
Iroquois (1)	2	0.02
Mexican American Ind. (0)	1	0.01
South American Ind. (2)	4	0.03
Spanish American Ind. (0)	8	0.07
Asian (366)	415	3.56
Not Hispanic (362)	399	3.42
Hispanic (4)	16	0.14
Bangladeshi (13)	15	0.13
Chinese, ex. Taiwanese (73)	82	0.70
Filipino (18)	29	0.25
Indian (149)	166	1.42
Indonesian (1)	1	0.01
Japanese (5)	7	0.06
Korean (13)	16	0.14
Pakistani (51)	52	0.45
Thai (1)	2	0.02
Vietnamese (30)	31	0.27
Hawaii Native/Pacific Islander (2)	6	0.05
Not Hispanic (2)	4	0.03
Hispanic (0)	2	0.02
Guamanian/Chamorro (2)	2	0.02
White (9,492)	9,757	83.74
Not Hispanic (8,286)	8,400	72.09
Hispanic (1,206)	1,357	11.65

North Massapequa

Place Type: CDP
County: Nassau
Population: 17,886†

Ancestry‡	Population	%
Albanian (22)	52	0.28
American (566)	566	3.03
Arab (12)	50	0.27
Arab (12)	50	0.27
Armenian (11)	32	0.17
Australian (0)	8	0.04
Austrian (52)	253	1.36
Brazilian (126)	126	0.68
British (10)	10	0.05
Croatian (26)	36	0.19
Czech (29)	156	0.84
Czechoslovakian (20)	103	0.55
Dutch (17)	131	0.70
Eastern European (17)	17	0.09
English (107)	400	2.14
European (31)	31	0.17
French, ex. Basque (0)	292	1.56
French Canadian (10)	10	0.05
German (491)	2,921	15.65
Greek (478)	783	4.20
Guyanese (11)	21	0.11
Hungarian (28)	238	1.28
Iranian (11)	11	0.06
Irish (1,128)	4,632	24.82
Italian (5,571)	9,384	50.28
Lithuanian (24)	34	0.18
Maltese (0)	14	0.08
Norwegian (9)	74	0.40
Polish (222)	1,201	6.43
Portuguese (27)	83	0.44
Romanian (0)	22	0.12
Russian (302)	672	3.60
Scandinavian (10)	10	0.05
Scotch-Irish (21)	108	0.58
Scottish (19)	76	0.41
Slavic (0)	10	0.05
Slovak (20)	50	0.27
Swedish (0)	38	0.20
Swiss (0)	10	0.05
Turkish (28)	28	0.15
Ukrainian (10)	29	0.16
West Indian, ex. Hispanic (44)	63	0.34
Haitian (20)	39	0.21
Trinidadian/Tobagonian (24)	24	0.13
Yugoslavian (10)	20	0.11

Hispanic Origin	Population	%
Hispanic or Latino (of any race)	968	5.41
Central American, ex. Mexican	85	0.48
Costa Rican	7	0.04
Guatemalan	21	0.12
Honduran	4	0.02
Nicaraguan	2	0.01
Panamanian	2	0.01
Salvadoran	49	0.27
Cuban	70	0.39
Dominican Republic	39	0.22
Mexican	53	0.30
Puerto Rican	418	2.34
South American	236	1.32
Argentinean	9	0.05
Chilean	4	0.02
Colombian	106	0.59
Ecuadorian	54	0.30
Paraguayan	2	0.01
Peruvian	46	0.26
Uruguayan	8	0.04
Venezuelan	5	0.03
Other South American	2	0.01
Other Hispanic or Latino	67	0.37

Race*	Population	%
African-American/Black (65)	100	0.56
Not Hispanic (46)	67	0.37
Hispanic (19)	33	0.18
American Indian/Alaska Native (6)	20	0.11
Not Hispanic (3)	16	0.09
Hispanic (3)	4	0.02
Cherokee (2)	4	0.02
Chippewa (0)	3	0.02
Crow (0)	1	0.01
Iroquois (0)	1	0.01
Asian (325)	414	2.31
Not Hispanic (315)	398	2.23
Hispanic (10)	16	0.09
Chinese, ex. Taiwanese (120)	142	0.79
Filipino (32)	60	0.34
Indian (78)	88	0.49
Japanese (6)	10	0.06
Korean (38)	50	0.28
Malaysian (2)	2	0.01
Nepalese (3)	3	0.02
Pakistani (29)	29	0.16
Taiwanese (5)	5	0.03
Thai (0)	3	0.02
Vietnamese (1)	4	0.02
Hawaii Native/Pacific Islander (1)	3	0.02
Not Hispanic (1)	3	0.02
Fijian (0)	2	0.01

*Notes: † The Census 2010 population figure is used to calculate the percentages in the Hispanic Origin and Race categories. Ancestry percentages are based on the 2006-2010 American Community Survey population (not shown); ‡ Numbers in parentheses indicate the number of people reporting a single ancestry; * Numbers in parentheses indicate the number of persons reporting this race alone, not in combination with any other race; Please refer to the Explanation of Data for more information.*

Tongan (1)	1	0.01
White (17,177)	17,319	96.83
Not Hispanic (16,430)	16,526	92.40
Hispanic (747)	793	4.43

North Merrick

Place Type: CDP
County: Nassau
Population: 12,272†

Ancestry‡	Population	%
Albanian (18)	18	0.15
American (135)	135	1.09
Arab (7)	113	0.91
Egyptian (0)	8	0.06
Lebanese (7)	61	0.49
Syrian (0)	44	0.36
Armenian (38)	87	0.70
Austrian (10)	65	0.52
Belgian (17)	17	0.14
British (10)	34	0.27
Canadian (8)	50	0.40
Croatian (14)	14	0.11
Czech (10)	99	0.80
Czechoslovakian (11)	11	0.09
Danish (10)	19	0.15
Dutch (25)	38	0.31
Eastern European (142)	160	1.29
English (62)	633	5.11
European (167)	167	1.35
French, ex. Basque (0)	128	1.03
French Canadian (3)	58	0.47
German (450)	2,342	18.91
Greek (42)	72	0.58
Hungarian (9)	44	0.36
Irish (1,230)	3,390	27.37
Italian (2,274)	4,476	36.14
Lithuanian (29)	146	1.18
Norwegian (0)	32	0.26
Polish (152)	717	5.79
Portuguese (10)	41	0.33
Romanian (0)	58	0.47
Russian (179)	543	4.38
Scandinavian (13)	13	0.10
Scotch-Irish (34)	141	1.14
Scottish (0)	48	0.39
Slovak (8)	25	0.20
Slovene (0)	15	0.12
Swedish (61)	156	1.26
Ukrainian (19)	38	0.31
West Indian, ex. Hispanic (42)	216	1.74
Jamaican (42)	216	1.74

Hispanic Origin	Population	%
Hispanic or Latino (of any race)	869	7.08
Central American, ex. Mexican	148	1.21
Costa Rican	6	0.05
Guatemalan	17	0.14
Honduran	27	0.22
Nicaraguan	3	0.02
Panamanian	4	0.03
Salvadoran	83	0.68
Other Central American	8	0.07
Cuban	41	0.33
Dominican Republic	99	0.81
Mexican	27	0.22
Puerto Rican	270	2.20
South American	208	1.69
Argentinean	29	0.24
Bolivian	4	0.03
Chilean	7	0.06
Colombian	111	0.90
Ecuadorian	36	0.29
Paraguayan	1	0.01
Peruvian	18	0.15
Uruguayan	1	0.01
Other South American	1	0.01
Other Hispanic or Latino	76	0.62

Race*	Population	%
African-American/Black (188)	220	1.79
Not Hispanic (169)	196	1.60
Hispanic (19)	24	0.20
American Indian/Alaska Native (13)	28	0.23
Not Hispanic (1)	13	0.11
Hispanic (12)	15	0.12
Cherokee (0)	1	0.01
Delaware (0)	1	0.01
Iroquois (0)	1	0.01
Mexican American Ind. (2)	2	0.02
South American Ind. (0)	1	0.01
Spanish American Ind. (2)	2	0.02
Asian (580)	652	5.31
Not Hispanic (567)	633	5.16
Hispanic (13)	19	0.15
Bangladeshi (23)	23	0.19
Cambodian (4)	4	0.03
Chinese, ex. Taiwanese (142)	171	1.39
Filipino (66)	86	0.70
Indian (232)	242	1.97
Indonesian (0)	1	0.01
Japanese (10)	18	0.15
Korean (21)	33	0.27
Pakistani (41)	41	0.33
Sri Lankan (4)	5	0.04
Taiwanese (6)	6	0.05
Thai (3)	3	0.02
Vietnamese (6)	6	0.05
Hawaii Native/Pacific Islander (1)	4	0.03
Not Hispanic (1)	3	0.02
Hispanic (0)	1	0.01
Guamanian/Chamorro (0)	1	0.01
Native Hawaiian (1)	2	0.02
White (11,113)	11,267	91.81
Not Hispanic (10,537)	10,648	86.77
Hispanic (576)	619	5.04

North New Hyde Park

Place Type: CDP
County: Nassau
Population: 14,899†

Ancestry‡	Population	%
African, Sub-Saharan (0)	21	0.14
African (0)	21	0.14
American (703)	703	4.77
Austrian (52)	235	1.59
British (18)	18	0.12
Croatian (48)	62	0.42
Czech (27)	133	0.90
Czechoslovakian (0)	14	0.09
Dutch (0)	67	0.45
Eastern European (55)	55	0.37
English (30)	239	1.62
European (41)	52	0.35
Finnish (0)	24	0.16
French, ex. Basque (0)	67	0.45
French Canadian (10)	40	0.27
German (284)	1,301	8.82
Greek (194)	225	1.53
Guyanese (0)	30	0.20
Hungarian (22)	128	0.87
Irish (1,156)	2,482	16.83
Italian (2,249)	3,722	25.23
Latvian (0)	11	0.07
Lithuanian (19)	30	0.20
Maltese (23)	23	0.16
Norwegian (13)	39	0.26
Pennsylvania German (15)	15	0.10
Polish (301)	925	6.27
Portuguese (69)	101	0.68
Russian (169)	413	2.80
Scotch-Irish (38)	127	0.86
Scottish (5)	39	0.26
Slavic (0)	31	0.21
Swedish (0)	50	0.34
Swiss (42)	54	0.37
Ukrainian (92)	99	0.67
West Indian, ex. Hispanic (0)	10	0.07
West Indian (0)	10	0.07
Yugoslavian (12)	12	0.08

Hispanic Origin	Population	%
Hispanic or Latino (of any race)	1,078	7.24
Central American, ex. Mexican	76	0.51
Costa Rican	3	0.02
Guatemalan	11	0.07
Honduran	2	0.01
Nicaraguan	4	0.03
Panamanian	6	0.04
Salvadoran	50	0.34
Cuban	66	0.44
Dominican Republic	136	0.91
Mexican	42	0.28
Puerto Rican	217	1.46
South American	434	2.91
Argentinean	37	0.25
Bolivian	10	0.07
Chilean	16	0.11
Colombian	137	0.92
Ecuadorian	116	0.78
Peruvian	93	0.62
Uruguayan	13	0.09
Venezuelan	4	0.03
Other South American	8	0.05
Other Hispanic or Latino	107	0.72

Race*	Population	%
African-American/Black (108)	147	0.99
Not Hispanic (90)	122	0.82
Hispanic (18)	25	0.17
American Indian/Alaska Native (39)	80	0.54
Not Hispanic (28)	62	0.42
Hispanic (11)	18	0.12
Cherokee (0)	5	0.03
Choctaw (3)	3	0.02
Hopi (1)	3	0.02
Sioux (1)	1	0.01
South American Ind. (4)	9	0.06
Asian (4,342)	4,585	30.77
Not Hispanic (4,329)	4,558	30.59
Hispanic (13)	27	0.18
Bangladeshi (73)	79	0.53
Burmese (23)	24	0.16
Cambodian (1)	2	0.01
Chinese, ex. Taiwanese (1,079)	1,131	7.59
Filipino (215)	242	1.62
Indian (2,393)	2,547	17.10
Indonesian (3)	3	0.02
Japanese (23)	31	0.21
Korean (278)	295	1.98
Malaysian (1)	1	0.01
Nepalese (2)	2	0.01
Pakistani (112)	128	0.86
Sri Lankan (5)	5	0.03
Taiwanese (44)	59	0.40
Thai (3)	3	0.02
Vietnamese (9)	19	0.13
Hawaii Native/Pacific Islander (0)	4	0.03
Not Hispanic (0)	3	0.02
Hispanic (0)	1	0.01
Samoan (0)	1	0.01
White (9,784)	9,941	66.72
Not Hispanic (9,059)	9,174	61.57
Hispanic (725)	767	5.15

North Tonawanda

Place Type: City
County: Niagara
Population: 31,568†

Ancestry‡	Population	%
American (943)	943	2.97
Arab (65)	289	0.91
Egyptian (15)	15	0.05
Lebanese (16)	189	0.60

SECTION TWO

*Notes: † The Census 2010 population figure is used to calculate the percentages in the Hispanic Origin and Race categories. Ancestry percentages are based on the 2006-2010 American Community Survey population (not shown); ‡ Numbers in parentheses indicate the number of people reporting a single ancestry; * Numbers in parentheses indicate the number of persons reporting this race alone, not in combination with any other race; Please refer to the Explanation of Data for more information.*

Ancestry	Population	%
Other Arab (34)	85	0.27
Armenian (15)	15	0.05
Austrian (39)	98	0.31
Belgian (0)	11	0.03
British (40)	49	0.15
Canadian (36)	137	0.43
Croatian (42)	110	0.35
Czech (0)	182	0.57
Czechoslovakian (12)	51	0.16
Danish (7)	46	0.15
Dutch (27)	557	1.76
English (592)	3,275	10.33
European (40)	40	0.13
French, ex. Basque (203)	1,516	4.78
French Canadian (115)	425	1.34
German (3,235)	11,110	35.03
Greek (74)	111	0.35
Guyanese (12)	12	0.04
Hungarian (141)	852	2.69
Iranian (0)	9	0.03
Irish (1,235)	5,684	17.92
Italian (2,071)	5,523	17.41
Latvian (12)	12	0.04
Lithuanian (10)	52	0.16
Norwegian (20)	85	0.27
Pennsylvania German (31)	69	0.22
Polish (3,026)	6,499	20.49
Romanian (0)	8	0.03
Russian (267)	468	1.48
Scandinavian (0)	39	0.12
Scotch-Irish (152)	315	0.99
Scottish (170)	796	2.51
Serbian (0)	11	0.03
Slavic (0)	209	0.66
Slovak (26)	72	0.23
Slovene (0)	12	0.04
Swedish (61)	245	0.77
Swiss (0)	22	0.07
Ukrainian (215)	401	1.26
Welsh (41)	267	0.84
West Indian, ex. Hispanic (31)	65	0.20
Jamaican (8)	25	0.08
West Indian (23)	40	0.13
Yugoslavian (0)	8	0.03

Hispanic Origin	Population	%
Hispanic or Latino (of any race)	534	1.69
Central American, ex. Mexican	15	0.05
Costa Rican	7	0.02
Guatemalan	3	0.01
Panamanian	4	0.01
Salvadoran	1	<0.01
Cuban	23	0.07
Dominican Republic	16	0.05
Mexican	104	0.33
Puerto Rican	289	0.92
South American	38	0.12
Chilean	5	0.02
Colombian	11	0.03
Ecuadorian	7	0.02
Peruvian	12	0.04
Venezuelan	3	0.01
Other Hispanic or Latino	49	0.16

Race*	Population	%
African-American/Black (253)	405	1.28
Not Hispanic (241)	374	1.18
Hispanic (12)	31	0.10
American Indian/Alaska Native (119)	269	0.85
Not Hispanic (109)	242	0.77
Hispanic (10)	27	0.09
Blackfeet (1)	2	0.01
Canadian/French Am. Ind. (3)	7	0.02
Central American Ind. (0)	1	<0.01
Cherokee (2)	9	0.03
Chippewa (3)	7	0.02
Choctaw (0)	1	<0.01
Comanche (1)	1	<0.01
Cree (0)	2	0.01
Creek (0)	2	0.01
Delaware (0)	1	<0.01
Inupiat *(Alaska Native)* (0)	1	<0.01
Iroquois (61)	122	0.39
Lumbee (0)	2	0.01
Mexican American Ind. (2)	3	0.01
Navajo (4)	4	0.01
Osage (0)	1	<0.01
Seminole (0)	2	0.01
Sioux (1)	8	0.03
South American Ind. (3)	4	0.01
Spanish American Ind. (3)	3	0.01
Tlingit-Haida *(Alaska Native)* (0)	1	<0.01
Asian (233)	315	1.00
Not Hispanic (233)	310	0.98
Hispanic (0)	5	0.02
Chinese, ex. Taiwanese (84)	104	0.33
Filipino (12)	22	0.07
Indian (40)	43	0.14
Indonesian (3)	3	0.01
Japanese (12)	17	0.05
Korean (53)	65	0.21
Laotian (1)	1	<0.01
Malaysian (1)	1	<0.01
Pakistani (1)	2	0.01
Sri Lankan (2)	7	0.02
Taiwanese (4)	4	0.01
Thai (1)	3	0.01
Vietnamese (13)	21	0.07
Hawaii Native/Pacific Islander (11)	25	0.08
Not Hispanic (10)	22	0.07
Hispanic (1)	3	0.01
Guamanian/Chamorro (1)	2	0.01
Native Hawaiian (2)	6	0.02
Samoan (0)	1	<0.01
White (30,454)	30,853	97.74
Not Hispanic (30,082)	30,428	96.39
Hispanic (372)	425	1.35

North Valley Stream

Place Type: CDP
County: Nassau
Population: 16,628†

Ancestry‡	Population	%
Afghan (30)	30	0.18
African, Sub-Saharan (486)	592	3.59
African (274)	380	2.30
Nigerian (212)	212	1.28
Albanian (0)	37	0.22
American (197)	197	1.19
Arab (0)	18	0.11
Egyptian (0)	18	0.11
Austrian (14)	32	0.19
Belgian (15)	15	0.09
Brazilian (6)	6	0.04
British (0)	19	0.12
Croatian (37)	37	0.22
Czech (0)	4	0.02
Czechoslovakian (16)	16	0.10
Danish (0)	17	0.10
Dutch (0)	27	0.16
Eastern European (41)	41	0.25
English (0)	187	1.13
European (7)	41	0.25
French, ex. Basque (0)	50	0.30
German (142)	783	4.74
Greek (26)	86	0.52
Guyanese (161)	344	2.08
Hungarian (40)	48	0.29
Irish (68)	901	5.46
Israeli (8)	8	0.05
Italian (967)	1,603	9.71
Latvian (0)	12	0.07
Lithuanian (30)	54	0.33
Norwegian (14)	31	0.19
Polish (133)	344	2.08
Romanian (8)	8	0.05
Russian (141)	325	1.97
Scottish (0)	8	0.05
Slovak (9)	9	0.05
Swedish (0)	19	0.12
Swiss (0)	65	0.39
Turkish (2)	2	0.01
Ukrainian (39)	51	0.31
West Indian, ex. Hispanic (3,654)	4,249	25.74
Barbadian (21)	39	0.24
British West Indian (19)	19	0.12
Dutch West Indian (100)	134	0.81
Haitian (1,735)	1,827	11.07
Jamaican (1,064)	1,257	7.62
Trinidadian/Tobagonian (337)	551	3.34
West Indian (378)	422	2.56

Hispanic Origin	Population	%
Hispanic or Latino (of any race)	2,411	14.50
Central American, ex. Mexican	346	2.08
Costa Rican	4	0.02
Guatemalan	50	0.30
Honduran	41	0.25
Nicaraguan	5	0.03
Panamanian	93	0.56
Salvadoran	148	0.89
Other Central American	5	0.03
Cuban	53	0.32
Dominican Republic	432	2.60
Mexican	46	0.28
Puerto Rican	677	4.07
South American	625	3.76
Argentinean	26	0.16
Bolivian	7	0.04
Chilean	11	0.07
Colombian	234	1.41
Ecuadorian	194	1.17
Paraguayan	1	0.01
Peruvian	125	0.75
Uruguayan	11	0.07
Venezuelan	10	0.06
Other South American	6	0.04
Other Hispanic or Latino	232	1.40

Race*	Population	%
African-American/Black (7,998)	8,297	49.90
Not Hispanic (7,720)	7,949	47.80
Hispanic (278)	348	2.09
American Indian/Alaska Native (81)	153	0.92
Not Hispanic (33)	85	0.51
Hispanic (48)	68	0.41
Blackfeet (0)	3	0.02
Central American Ind. (1)	1	0.01
Cherokee (3)	28	0.17
Choctaw (0)	5	0.03
Mexican American Ind. (1)	3	0.02
Navajo (1)	1	0.01
Seminole (0)	1	0.01
Sioux (0)	2	0.01
South American Ind. (35)	38	0.23
Asian (2,148)	2,384	14.34
Not Hispanic (2,132)	2,348	14.12
Hispanic (16)	36	0.22
Bangladeshi (21)	23	0.14
Chinese, ex. Taiwanese (202)	243	1.46
Filipino (342)	366	2.20
Indian (1,011)	1,113	6.69
Indonesian (1)	3	0.02
Japanese (8)	11	0.07
Korean (53)	59	0.35
Nepalese (6)	6	0.04
Pakistani (408)	425	2.56
Sri Lankan (4)	4	0.02
Taiwanese (24)	25	0.15
Thai (14)	17	0.10
Vietnamese (5)	5	0.03
Hawaii Native/Pacific Islander (2)	36	0.22
Not Hispanic (2)	27	0.16
Hispanic (0)	9	0.05
Native Hawaiian (0)	2	0.01
White (4,797)	5,058	30.42
Not Hispanic (3,765)	3,916	23.55
Hispanic (1,032)	1,142	6.87

*Notes: † The Census 2010 population figure is used to calculate the percentages in the Hispanic Origin and Race categories. Ancestry percentages are based on the 2006-2010 American Community Survey population (not shown); ‡ Numbers in parentheses indicate the number of people reporting a single ancestry; * Numbers in parentheses indicate the number of persons reporting this race alone, not in combination with any other race; Please refer to the Explanation of Data for more information.*

North Wantagh

Place Type: CDP
County: Nassau
Population: 11,960†

Ancestry‡	Population	%
American (249)	249	2.13
Arab (41)	41	0.35
Egyptian (41)	41	0.35
Armenian (18)	18	0.15
Austrian (71)	141	1.20
Basque (0)	24	0.21
British (12)	20	0.17
Canadian (25)	35	0.30
Croatian (0)	14	0.12
Czech (57)	151	1.29
Czechoslovakian (12)	20	0.17
Dutch (7)	78	0.67
Eastern European (66)	97	0.83
English (89)	581	4.96
European (226)	226	1.93
Finnish (0)	13	0.11
French, ex. Basque (0)	128	1.09
French Canadian (10)	22	0.19
German (688)	2,293	19.59
Greek (151)	222	1.90
Hungarian (9)	74	0.63
Icelander (10)	10	0.09
Iranian (59)	59	0.50
Irish (956)	3,211	27.44
Italian (2,329)	4,516	38.59
Lithuanian (0)	46	0.39
Norwegian (0)	69	0.59
Polish (248)	806	6.89
Portuguese (0)	57	0.49
Romanian (0)	63	0.54
Russian (222)	446	3.81
Scotch-Irish (81)	112	0.96
Scottish (43)	71	0.61
Slovak (20)	20	0.17
Swedish (0)	53	0.45
Ukrainian (38)	61	0.52
Welsh (0)	10	0.09
West Indian, ex. Hispanic (56)	56	0.48
Haitian (56)	56	0.48
Yugoslavian (0)	43	0.37

Hispanic Origin	Population	%
Hispanic or Latino (of any race)	897	7.50
Central American, ex. Mexican	91	0.76
Costa Rican	7	0.06
Guatemalan	23	0.19
Honduran	6	0.05
Nicaraguan	7	0.06
Panamanian	2	0.02
Salvadoran	46	0.38
Cuban	56	0.47
Dominican Republic	58	0.48
Mexican	43	0.36
Puerto Rican	377	3.15
South American	201	1.68
Argentinean	20	0.17
Bolivian	7	0.06
Chilean	14	0.12
Colombian	90	0.75
Ecuadorian	40	0.33
Peruvian	22	0.18
Uruguayan	4	0.03
Venezuelan	2	0.02
Other South American	2	0.02
Other Hispanic or Latino	71	0.59

Race*	Population	%
African-American/Black (92)	133	1.11
Not Hispanic (77)	108	0.90
Hispanic (15)	25	0.21
American Indian/Alaska Native (11)	27	0.23
Not Hispanic (1)	13	0.11
Hispanic (10)	14	0.12
Cherokee (0)	3	0.03
Iroquois (0)	3	0.03
Mexican American Ind. (3)	3	0.03
Asian (300)	373	3.12
Not Hispanic (294)	349	2.92
Hispanic (6)	24	0.20
Bangladeshi (5)	5	0.04
Cambodian (1)	1	0.01
Chinese, ex. Taiwanese (82)	110	0.92
Filipino (38)	50	0.42
Indian (104)	109	0.91
Japanese (4)	11	0.09
Korean (19)	29	0.24
Pakistani (16)	16	0.13
Taiwanese (11)	11	0.09
Thai (1)	1	0.01
Vietnamese (8)	11	0.09
Hawaii Native/Pacific Islander (3)	14	0.12
Not Hispanic (3)	9	0.08
Hispanic (0)	5	0.04
Marshallese (1)	1	0.01
Native Hawaiian (0)	5	0.04
White (11,258)	11,397	95.29
Not Hispanic (10,597)	10,677	89.27
Hispanic (661)	720	6.02

Oakdale

Place Type: CDP
County: Suffolk
Population: 7,974†

Ancestry‡	Population	%
African, Sub-Saharan (15)	15	0.20
African (15)	15	0.20
American (141)	141	1.84
Arab (220)	220	2.87
Egyptian (220)	220	2.87
Australian (0)	37	0.48
Austrian (24)	87	1.13
Canadian (0)	56	0.73
Croatian (9)	27	0.35
Czech (13)	94	1.22
Czechoslovakian (7)	7	0.09
Danish (8)	19	0.25
Dutch (15)	51	0.66
Eastern European (8)	33	0.43
English (84)	568	7.40
European (41)	41	0.53
Finnish (0)	9	0.12
French, ex. Basque (7)	75	0.98
French Canadian (15)	15	0.20
German (416)	1,734	22.59
Greek (0)	58	0.76
Hungarian (15)	74	0.96
Irish (751)	2,518	32.80
Italian (1,453)	2,804	36.52
Lithuanian (0)	13	0.17
Norwegian (29)	66	0.86
Polish (144)	351	4.57
Russian (45)	147	1.91
Scotch-Irish (13)	13	0.17
Scottish (35)	142	1.85
Slovak (0)	39	0.51
Swedish (28)	87	1.13
Swiss (0)	23	0.30
Ukrainian (74)	120	1.56

Hispanic Origin	Population	%
Hispanic or Latino (of any race)	314	3.94
Central American, ex. Mexican	23	0.29
Costa Rican	1	0.01
Guatemalan	2	0.03
Honduran	1	0.01
Nicaraguan	2	0.03
Panamanian	2	0.03
Salvadoran	15	0.19
Cuban	19	0.24
Dominican Republic	8	0.10
Mexican	22	0.28
Puerto Rican	137	1.72
South American	35	0.44
Chilean	1	0.01
Colombian	22	0.28
Ecuadorian	3	0.04
Peruvian	2	0.03
Uruguayan	4	0.05
Venezuelan	3	0.04
Other Hispanic or Latino	70	0.88

Race*	Population	%
African-American/Black (92)	106	1.33
Not Hispanic (81)	92	1.15
Hispanic (11)	14	0.18
American Indian/Alaska Native (3)	20	0.25
Not Hispanic (1)	17	0.21
Hispanic (2)	3	0.04
Apache (1)	2	0.03
Cherokee (0)	2	0.03
Iroquois (1)	1	0.01
Mexican American Ind. (1)	1	0.01
Navajo (0)	1	0.01
Seminole (0)	1	0.01
Sioux (0)	4	0.05
Asian (102)	121	1.52
Not Hispanic (102)	119	1.49
Hispanic (0)	2	0.03
Cambodian (1)	1	0.01
Chinese, ex. Taiwanese (50)	62	0.78
Filipino (15)	18	0.23
Indian (16)	19	0.24
Japanese (2)	4	0.05
Korean (9)	13	0.16
Malaysian (0)	1	0.01
Pakistani (0)	1	0.01
Thai (1)	1	0.01
Hawaii Native/Pacific Islander (2)	4	0.05
Not Hispanic (2)	3	0.04
Hispanic (0)	1	0.01
Native Hawaiian (0)	1	0.01
White (7,694)	7,743	97.10
Not Hispanic (7,427)	7,468	93.65
Hispanic (267)	275	3.45

Oceanside

Place Type: CDP
County: Nassau
Population: 32,109†

Ancestry‡	Population	%
American (1,479)	1,479	4.76
Arab (114)	163	0.52
Arab (0)	19	0.06
Egyptian (36)	36	0.12
Iraqi (25)	25	0.08
Lebanese (41)	41	0.13
Moroccan (12)	12	0.04
Syrian (0)	30	0.10
Armenian (0)	35	0.11
Assyrian/Chaldean/Syriac (3)	19	0.06
Australian (49)	58	0.19
Austrian (155)	470	1.51
Belgian (0)	34	0.11
British (64)	74	0.24
Canadian (12)	24	0.08
Cypriot (90)	90	0.29
Czech (48)	159	0.51
Czechoslovakian (13)	25	0.08
Danish (0)	46	0.15
Dutch (11)	79	0.25
Eastern European (227)	227	0.73
English (163)	929	2.99
Estonian (36)	48	0.15
European (539)	539	1.73
French, ex. Basque (55)	398	1.28
French Canadian (9)	44	0.14
German (560)	3,434	11.05
Greek (330)	609	1.96
Hungarian (84)	250	0.80

*Notes: † The Census 2010 population figure is used to calculate the percentages in the Hispanic Origin and Race categories. Ancestry percentages are based on the 2006-2010 American Community Survey population (not shown); ‡ Numbers in parentheses indicate the number of people reporting a single ancestry; * Numbers in parentheses indicate the number of persons reporting this race alone, not in combination with any other race; Please refer to the Explanation of Data for more information.*

Irish (2,391)	6,067	19.52
Israeli (8)	8	0.03
Italian (5,422)	9,108	29.31
Latvian (0)	22	0.07
Lithuanian (47)	211	0.68
Maltese (0)	20	0.06
Northern European (161)	161	0.52
Norwegian (74)	311	1.00
Polish (580)	2,127	6.84
Portuguese (0)	7	0.02
Romanian (109)	334	1.07
Russian (1,350)	2,531	8.14
Scotch-Irish (61)	223	0.72
Scottish (25)	348	1.12
Soviet Union (0)	10	0.03
Swedish (29)	89	0.29
Swiss (0)	42	0.14
Turkish (0)	37	0.12
Ukrainian (175)	212	0.68
Welsh (11)	22	0.07

Hispanic Origin	Population	%
Hispanic or Latino (of any race)	2,970	9.25
Central American, ex. Mexican	423	1.32
Costa Rican	25	0.08
Guatemalan	65	0.20
Honduran	92	0.29
Nicaraguan	13	0.04
Panamanian	7	0.02
Salvadoran	210	0.65
Other Central American	11	0.03
Cuban	174	0.54
Dominican Republic	548	1.71
Mexican	103	0.32
Puerto Rican	683	2.13
South American	770	2.40
Argentinean	78	0.24
Bolivian	18	0.06
Chilean	76	0.24
Colombian	245	0.76
Ecuadorian	112	0.35
Paraguayan	2	0.01
Peruvian	189	0.59
Uruguayan	22	0.07
Venezuelan	13	0.04
Other South American	15	0.05
Other Hispanic or Latino	269	0.84

Race*	Population	%
African-American/Black (404)	532	1.66
Not Hispanic (356)	437	1.36
Hispanic (48)	95	0.30
American Indian/Alaska Native (28)	77	0.24
Not Hispanic (9)	36	0.11
Hispanic (19)	41	0.13
Central American Ind. (1)	1	<0.01
Cherokee (3)	16	0.05
Iroquois (3)	4	0.01
Lumbee (1)	1	<0.01
Mexican American Ind. (2)	2	0.01
South American Ind. (2)	10	0.03
Spanish American Ind. (1)	1	<0.01
Asian (881)	1,025	3.19
Not Hispanic (879)	1,008	3.14
Hispanic (2)	17	0.05
Bangladeshi (7)	7	0.02
Burmese (1)	1	<0.01
Cambodian (0)	1	<0.01
Chinese, ex. Taiwanese (178)	197	0.61
Filipino (227)	266	0.83
Indian (331)	367	1.14
Indonesian (2)	2	0.01
Japanese (14)	34	0.11
Korean (47)	57	0.18
Laotian (1)	2	0.01
Malaysian (0)	1	<0.01
Pakistani (19)	29	0.09
Sri Lankan (16)	16	0.05
Taiwanese (6)	6	0.02
Thai (2)	2	0.01
Vietnamese (4)	9	0.03
Hawaii Native/Pacific Islander (3)	24	0.07
Not Hispanic (1)	17	0.05
Hispanic (2)	7	0.02
Native Hawaiian (1)	6	0.02
Samoan (0)	1	<0.01
White (29,605)	29,933	93.22
Not Hispanic (27,596)	27,761	86.46
Hispanic (2,009)	2,172	6.76

Ogden

Place Type: Town
County: Monroe
Population: 19,856†

Ancestry‡	Population	%
African, Sub-Saharan (18)	18	0.09
African (18)	18	0.09
Albanian (9)	9	0.05
American (696)	696	3.56
Arab (90)	140	0.72
Arab (72)	72	0.37
Lebanese (18)	68	0.35
Armenian (11)	11	0.06
Austrian (14)	31	0.16
Belgian (21)	92	0.47
British (0)	70	0.36
Bulgarian (8)	8	0.04
Canadian (67)	124	0.63
Croatian (0)	39	0.20
Czech (52)	71	0.36
Czechoslovakian (0)	9	0.05
Danish (7)	28	0.14
Dutch (124)	511	2.61
Eastern European (12)	12	0.06
English (769)	3,136	16.04
European (157)	157	0.80
French, ex. Basque (41)	969	4.96
French Canadian (66)	573	2.93
German (1,233)	6,194	31.68
Greek (28)	55	0.28
Hungarian (67)	108	0.55
Irish (774)	4,566	23.35
Italian (1,992)	4,919	25.16
Lithuanian (45)	105	0.54
Macedonian (11)	47	0.24
Norwegian (0)	43	0.22
Polish (296)	1,031	5.27
Portuguese (0)	57	0.29
Romanian (0)	26	0.13
Russian (36)	70	0.36
Scandinavian (25)	42	0.21
Scotch-Irish (102)	307	1.57
Scottish (27)	640	3.27
Slavic (0)	76	0.39
Slovak (12)	21	0.11
Slovene (0)	7	0.04
Swedish (17)	233	1.19
Swiss (11)	41	0.21
Turkish (10)	10	0.05
Ukrainian (146)	325	1.66
Welsh (3)	240	1.23
Yugoslavian (0)	32	0.16

Hispanic Origin	Population	%
Hispanic or Latino (of any race)	549	2.76
Central American, ex. Mexican	41	0.21
Costa Rican	4	0.02
Guatemalan	11	0.06
Honduran	9	0.05
Nicaraguan	5	0.03
Panamanian	7	0.04
Salvadoran	5	0.03
Cuban	43	0.22
Dominican Republic	13	0.07
Mexican	88	0.44
Puerto Rican	291	1.47
South American	38	0.19
Argentinean	1	0.01
Chilean	1	0.01
Colombian	17	0.09
Ecuadorian	4	0.02
Paraguayan	2	0.01
Peruvian	11	0.06
Uruguayan	2	0.01
Other Hispanic or Latino	35	0.18

Race*	Population	%
African-American/Black (448)	564	2.84
Not Hispanic (431)	523	2.63
Hispanic (17)	41	0.21
American Indian/Alaska Native (44)	124	0.62
Not Hispanic (38)	108	0.54
Hispanic (6)	16	0.08
Blackfeet (0)	1	0.01
Canadian/French Am. Ind. (0)	1	0.01
Cherokee (3)	11	0.06
Chippewa (2)	2	0.01
Iroquois (12)	38	0.19
Mexican American Ind. (1)	1	0.01
Ottawa (1)	1	0.01
Sioux (4)	7	0.04
South American Ind. (1)	1	0.01
Tlingit-Haida *(Alaska Native)* (1)	1	0.01
Asian (155)	244	1.23
Not Hispanic (151)	235	1.18
Hispanic (4)	9	0.05
Cambodian (3)	7	0.04
Chinese, ex. Taiwanese (20)	38	0.19
Filipino (15)	34	0.17
Indian (15)	26	0.13
Indonesian (0)	2	0.01
Japanese (1)	5	0.03
Korean (37)	61	0.31
Laotian (3)	9	0.05
Malaysian (0)	1	0.01
Pakistani (3)	7	0.04
Thai (7)	9	0.05
Vietnamese (41)	45	0.23
Hawaii Native/Pacific Islander (2)	14	0.07
Not Hispanic (2)	14	0.07
Fijian (0)	1	0.01
Guamanian/Chamorro (1)	1	0.01
Native Hawaiian (0)	7	0.04
Samoan (0)	1	0.01
White (18,767)	19,050	95.94
Not Hispanic (18,419)	18,646	93.91
Hispanic (348)	404	2.03

Ogdensburg

Place Type: City
County: St. Lawrence
Population: 11,128†

Ancestry‡	Population	%
African, Sub-Saharan (36)	43	0.38
African (27)	34	0.30
Nigerian (9)	9	0.08
Albanian (40)	40	0.35
American (985)	985	8.67
Austrian (0)	14	0.12
Canadian (68)	85	0.75
Croatian (0)	8	0.07
Danish (0)	8	0.07
Dutch (39)	79	0.69
English (674)	1,344	11.82
European (115)	115	1.01
French, ex. Basque (747)	2,035	17.90
French Canadian (627)	1,006	8.85
German (240)	718	6.32
Greek (0)	9	0.08
Irish (773)	1,656	14.57
Italian (301)	837	7.36
Lithuanian (12)	12	0.11
Norwegian (14)	14	0.12
Polish (99)	187	1.65
Portuguese (11)	11	0.10
Romanian (12)	26	0.23

*Notes: † The Census 2010 population figure is used to calculate the percentages in the Hispanic Origin and Race categories. Ancestry percentages are based on the 2006-2010 American Community Survey population (not shown); ‡ Numbers in parentheses indicate the number of people reporting a single ancestry; * Numbers in parentheses indicate the number of persons reporting this race alone, not in combination with any other race; Please refer to the Explanation of Data for more information.*

Russian (19)	54	0.48
Scandinavian (20)	34	0.30
Scotch-Irish (111)	184	1.62
Scottish (91)	253	2.23
Slovak (25)	25	0.22
Swedish (0)	29	0.26
Swiss (0)	15	0.13
Turkish (0)	9	0.08
Ukrainian (0)	26	0.23
Welsh (0)	8	0.07
West Indian, ex. Hispanic (89)	95	0.84
Barbadian (0)	6	0.05
Haitian (38)	38	0.33
Jamaican (51)	51	0.45

Hispanic Origin	Population	%
Hispanic or Latino (of any race)	389	3.50
Central American, ex. Mexican	38	0.34
Costa Rican	2	0.02
Guatemalan	7	0.06
Honduran	11	0.10
Panamanian	7	0.06
Salvadoran	11	0.10
Cuban	6	0.05
Dominican Republic	53	0.48
Mexican	47	0.42
Puerto Rican	204	1.83
South American	15	0.13
Bolivian	1	0.01
Colombian	7	0.06
Ecuadorian	4	0.04
Peruvian	1	0.01
Other South American	2	0.02
Other Hispanic or Latino	26	0.23

Race*	Population	%
African-American/Black (810)	849	7.63
Not Hispanic (765)	799	7.18
Hispanic (45)	50	0.45
American Indian/Alaska Native (91)	165	1.48
Not Hispanic (84)	154	1.38
Hispanic (7)	11	0.10
Arapaho (1)	1	0.01
Blackfeet (2)	3	0.03
Canadian/French Am. Ind. (1)	1	0.01
Cree (0)	2	0.02
Delaware (1)	3	0.03
Hopi (1)	1	0.01
Iroquois (51)	87	0.78
Sioux (1)	2	0.02
South American Ind. (4)	5	0.04
Asian (88)	92	0.83
Not Hispanic (87)	91	0.82
Hispanic (1)	1	0.01
Bangladeshi (0)	4	0.04
Chinese, ex. Taiwanese (15)	15	0.13
Filipino (8)	9	0.08
Hmong (1)	1	0.01
Indian (23)	28	0.25
Japanese (2)	3	0.03
Korean (4)	5	0.04
Pakistani (16)	16	0.14
Thai (2)	2	0.02
Vietnamese (6)	6	0.05
Hawaii Native/Pacific Islander (1)	8	0.07
Not Hispanic (1)	8	0.07
Guamanian/Chamorro (0)	1	0.01
Native Hawaiian (0)	5	0.04
White (9,828)	9,959	89.49
Not Hispanic (9,652)	9,766	87.76
Hispanic (176)	193	1.73

Olean

Place Type: City
County: Cattaraugus
Population: 14,452†

Ancestry‡	Population	%
African, Sub-Saharan (8)	38	0.26
African (8)	38	0.26
Alsatian (0)	7	0.05
American (624)	624	4.28
Arab (115)	284	1.95
Lebanese (115)	284	1.95
Austrian (0)	48	0.33
Belgian (0)	11	0.08
Canadian (0)	15	0.10
Croatian (0)	8	0.05
Czech (9)	60	0.41
Czechoslovakian (0)	30	0.21
Danish (0)	14	0.10
Dutch (27)	247	1.69
English (487)	1,610	11.04
European (14)	14	0.10
French, ex. Basque (23)	343	2.35
French Canadian (27)	70	0.48
German (1,007)	3,419	23.45
Greek (16)	16	0.11
Hungarian (32)	52	0.36
Irish (914)	3,452	23.68
Italian (824)	2,093	14.36
Lithuanian (7)	7	0.05
Macedonian (0)	18	0.12
Northern European (63)	63	0.43
Norwegian (10)	64	0.44
Pennsylvania German (10)	40	0.27
Polish (689)	2,035	13.96
Portuguese (0)	23	0.16
Russian (6)	60	0.41
Scandinavian (0)	12	0.08
Scotch-Irish (70)	313	2.15
Scottish (57)	202	1.39
Slavic (0)	12	0.08
Slovene (12)	12	0.08
Swedish (52)	335	2.30
Ukrainian (0)	56	0.38
Welsh (20)	86	0.59
West Indian, ex. Hispanic (23)	38	0.26
West Indian (23)	38	0.26
Yugoslavian (16)	16	0.11

Hispanic Origin	Population	%
Hispanic or Latino (of any race)	329	2.28
Central American, ex. Mexican	13	0.09
Guatemalan	4	0.03
Panamanian	2	0.01
Salvadoran	7	0.05
Cuban	6	0.04
Dominican Republic	7	0.05
Mexican	49	0.34
Puerto Rican	190	1.31
South American	25	0.17
Argentinean	1	0.01
Bolivian	2	0.01
Chilean	3	0.02
Colombian	5	0.03
Ecuadorian	1	0.01
Peruvian	4	0.03
Venezuelan	9	0.06
Other Hispanic or Latino	39	0.27

Race*	Population	%
African-American/Black (529)	831	5.75
Not Hispanic (507)	793	5.49
Hispanic (22)	38	0.26
American Indian/Alaska Native (107)	233	1.61
Not Hispanic (95)	208	1.44
Hispanic (12)	25	0.17
Alaska Athabascan *(Ala. Nat.)* (1)	1	0.01
Apache (0)	1	0.01
Blackfeet (1)	4	0.03
Canadian/French Am. Ind. (0)	3	0.02
Central American Ind. (7)	7	0.05
Cherokee (0)	9	0.06
Cheyenne (0)	1	0.01
Chippewa (0)	1	0.01
Choctaw (0)	1	0.01
Delaware (1)	1	0.01
Iroquois (52)	96	0.66
Paiute (0)	3	0.02
Sioux (0)	2	0.01
Asian (188)	227	1.57
Not Hispanic (188)	227	1.57
Cambodian (1)	1	0.01
Chinese, ex. Taiwanese (37)	42	0.29
Filipino (18)	28	0.19
Indian (71)	82	0.57
Japanese (8)	11	0.08
Korean (6)	7	0.05
Malaysian (2)	2	0.01
Nepalese (1)	1	0.01
Pakistani (28)	28	0.19
Sri Lankan (4)	4	0.03
Thai (0)	5	0.03
Vietnamese (12)	12	0.08
Hawaii Native/Pacific Islander (3)	7	0.05
Not Hispanic (3)	7	0.05
Native Hawaiian (0)	3	0.02
White (13,092)	13,496	93.38
Not Hispanic (12,904)	13,280	91.89
Hispanic (188)	216	1.49

Oneida

Place Type: City
County: Madison
Population: 11,393†

Ancestry‡	Population	%
Albanian (0)	14	0.12
American (1,229)	1,229	10.84
Arab (61)	69	0.61
Arab (61)	61	0.54
Other Arab (0)	8	0.07
Australian (8)	8	0.07
Austrian (0)	13	0.11
Belgian (0)	34	0.30
British (0)	13	0.11
Canadian (104)	116	1.02
Czech (0)	34	0.30
Dutch (126)	600	5.29
English (510)	1,895	16.71
Estonian (9)	9	0.08
European (31)	31	0.27
French, ex. Basque (83)	648	5.71
French Canadian (106)	330	2.91
German (659)	3,054	26.93
Greek (8)	35	0.31
Hungarian (38)	64	0.56
Irish (660)	2,764	24.38
Italian (429)	1,332	11.75
Norwegian (9)	22	0.19
Polish (221)	833	7.35
Portuguese (8)	8	0.07
Romanian (0)	11	0.10
Russian (10)	90	0.79
Scotch-Irish (30)	166	1.46
Scottish (142)	495	4.37
Slavic (23)	72	0.63
Slovak (10)	10	0.09
Swedish (33)	62	0.55
Swiss (0)	78	0.69
Ukrainian (0)	29	0.26
Welsh (118)	236	2.08
West Indian, ex. Hispanic (14)	14	0.12
Haitian (10)	10	0.09
Jamaican (4)	4	0.04
Yugoslavian (0)	48	0.42

Hispanic Origin	Population	%
Hispanic or Latino (of any race)	165	1.45
Central American, ex. Mexican	13	0.11
Costa Rican	1	0.01
Guatemalan	5	0.04
Nicaraguan	1	0.01
Salvadoran	6	0.05
Cuban	5	0.04
Dominican Republic	23	0.20
Mexican	52	0.46

SECTION TWO

*Notes: † The Census 2010 population figure is used to calculate the percentages in the Hispanic Origin and Race categories. Ancestry percentages are based on the 2006-2010 American Community Survey population (not shown); ‡ Numbers in parentheses indicate the number of people reporting a single ancestry; * Numbers in parentheses indicate the number of persons reporting this race alone, not in combination with any other race; Please refer to the Explanation of Data for more information.*

Puerto Rican	63	0.55
South American	3	0.03
Argentinean	1	0.01
Colombian	1	0.01
Ecuadorian	1	0.01
Other Hispanic or Latino	6	0.05

Race*	Population	%
African-American/Black (138)	210	1.84
Not Hispanic (136)	201	1.76
Hispanic (2)	9	0.08
American Indian/Alaska Native (234)	299	2.62
Not Hispanic (221)	280	2.46
Hispanic (13)	19	0.17
Central American Ind. (1)	1	0.01
Cherokee (7)	12	0.11
Chippewa (3)	4	0.04
Houma (1)	1	0.01
Iroquois (154)	180	1.58
Mexican American Ind. (0)	1	0.01
Paiute (1)	1	0.01
Pueblo (0)	1	0.01
Sioux (3)	5	0.04
South American Ind. (4)	4	0.04
Asian (87)	116	1.02
Not Hispanic (86)	115	1.01
Hispanic (1)	1	0.01
Chinese, ex. Taiwanese (29)	31	0.27
Filipino (11)	17	0.15
Indian (19)	19	0.17
Indonesian (1)	1	0.01
Japanese (5)	12	0.11
Korean (6)	12	0.11
Pakistani (2)	2	0.02
Sri Lankan (10)	10	0.09
Taiwanese (2)	2	0.02
Thai (0)	2	0.02
Vietnamese (1)	1	0.01
Hawaii Native/Pacific Islander (4)	9	0.08
Not Hispanic (4)	7	0.06
Hispanic (0)	2	0.02
Guamanian/Chamorro (0)	2	0.02
Native Hawaiian (3)	6	0.05
White (10,722)	10,885	95.54
Not Hispanic (10,624)	10,770	94.53
Hispanic (98)	115	1.01

Oneonta

Place Type: City
County: Otsego
Population: 13,901†

Ancestry‡	Population	%
African, Sub-Saharan (26)	39	0.28
South African (0)	13	0.09
Zimbabwean (26)	26	0.19
Albanian (0)	46	0.33
American (920)	920	6.57
Arab (54)	54	0.39
Lebanese (40)	40	0.29
Syrian (14)	14	0.10
Austrian (36)	104	0.74
Belgian (0)	10	0.07
British (18)	43	0.31
Canadian (30)	155	1.11
Croatian (0)	15	0.11
Czech (0)	65	0.46
Danish (14)	71	0.51
Dutch (22)	394	2.81
Eastern European (56)	104	0.74
English (395)	1,537	10.97
European (141)	141	1.01
Finnish (10)	22	0.16
French, ex. Basque (101)	774	5.53
French Canadian (68)	212	1.51
German (559)	2,378	16.98
Greek (28)	109	0.78
Hungarian (42)	178	1.27
Irish (621)	3,037	21.68
Israeli (13)	13	0.09
Italian (1,018)	2,839	20.27
Lithuanian (0)	22	0.16
Norwegian (46)	167	1.19
Polish (128)	839	5.99
Portuguese (25)	25	0.18
Russian (130)	396	2.83
Scandinavian (0)	25	0.18
Scotch-Irish (72)	360	2.57
Scottish (8)	351	2.51
Slavic (37)	37	0.26
Slovak (0)	29	0.21
Slovene (0)	10	0.07
Swedish (17)	266	1.90
Swiss (0)	48	0.34
Ukrainian (37)	47	0.34
Welsh (71)	250	1.78
West Indian, ex. Hispanic (111)	111	0.79
Haitian (23)	23	0.16
Jamaican (88)	88	0.63
Yugoslavian (0)	28	0.20

Hispanic Origin	Population	%
Hispanic or Latino (of any race)	825	5.93
Central American, ex. Mexican	56	0.40
Costa Rican	4	0.03
Guatemalan	8	0.06
Honduran	8	0.06
Panamanian	5	0.04
Salvadoran	30	0.22
Other Central American	1	0.01
Cuban	46	0.33
Dominican Republic	57	0.41
Mexican	128	0.92
Puerto Rican	344	2.47
South American	102	0.73
Argentinean	10	0.07
Bolivian	5	0.04
Chilean	4	0.03
Colombian	36	0.26
Ecuadorian	14	0.10
Paraguayan	1	0.01
Peruvian	23	0.17
Uruguayan	5	0.04
Venezuelan	4	0.03
Other Hispanic or Latino	92	0.66

Race*	Population	%
African-American/Black (489)	696	5.01
Not Hispanic (433)	599	4.31
Hispanic (56)	97	0.70
American Indian/Alaska Native (34)	125	0.90
Not Hispanic (22)	93	0.67
Hispanic (12)	32	0.23
Blackfeet (0)	5	0.04
Canadian/French Am. Ind. (1)	1	0.01
Cherokee (5)	23	0.17
Chickasaw (0)	1	0.01
Chippewa (0)	3	0.02
Creek (0)	1	0.01
Delaware (4)	4	0.03
Hopi (0)	1	0.01
Inupiat *(Alaska Native)* (0)	1	0.01
Iroquois (0)	5	0.04
Mexican American Ind. (0)	1	0.01
Navajo (1)	2	0.01
Sioux (1)	2	0.01
South American Ind. (1)	3	0.02
Asian (339)	428	3.08
Not Hispanic (327)	397	2.86
Hispanic (12)	31	0.22
Chinese, ex. Taiwanese (125)	147	1.06
Filipino (17)	47	0.34
Indian (51)	58	0.42
Indonesian (0)	2	0.01
Japanese (31)	44	0.32
Korean (69)	79	0.57
Laotian (1)	1	0.01
Nepalese (4)	4	0.03
Pakistani (14)	16	0.12
Taiwanese (7)	11	0.08
Thai (2)	2	0.01
Vietnamese (2)	4	0.03
Hawaii Native/Pacific Islander (6)	19	0.14
Not Hispanic (4)	10	0.07
Hispanic (2)	9	0.06
Fijian (1)	1	0.01
Native Hawaiian (2)	5	0.04
White (12,449)	12,774	91.89
Not Hispanic (11,994)	12,250	88.12
Hispanic (455)	524	3.77

Onondaga

Place Type: Town
County: Onondaga
Population: 23,101†

Ancestry‡	Population	%
American (984)	984	4.34
Arab (170)	409	1.81
Arab (31)	82	0.36
Egyptian (49)	49	0.22
Jordanian (14)	14	0.06
Lebanese (37)	196	0.87
Syrian (39)	68	0.30
Armenian (14)	14	0.06
Assyrian/Chaldean/Syriac (19)	19	0.08
Austrian (0)	36	0.16
Brazilian (0)	5	0.02
British (73)	73	0.32
Canadian (11)	58	0.26
Czech (25)	99	0.44
Czechoslovakian (21)	30	0.13
Danish (27)	40	0.18
Dutch (115)	680	3.00
English (979)	3,868	17.07
European (86)	86	0.38
French, ex. Basque (135)	1,183	5.22
French Canadian (79)	366	1.62
German (638)	3,812	16.82
Greek (239)	383	1.69
Hungarian (11)	62	0.27
Icelander (0)	9	0.04
Iranian (39)	39	0.17
Irish (2,220)	6,876	30.35
Italian (1,514)	4,166	18.39
Lithuanian (19)	58	0.26
Macedonian (51)	51	0.23
Northern European (8)	8	0.04
Norwegian (21)	41	0.18
Pennsylvania German (8)	8	0.04
Polish (844)	2,105	9.29
Portuguese (0)	81	0.36
Russian (85)	164	0.72
Scandinavian (14)	28	0.12
Scotch-Irish (94)	422	1.86
Scottish (108)	525	2.32
Slavic (0)	7	0.03
Slovak (20)	71	0.31
Slovene (11)	25	0.11
Swedish (19)	61	0.27
Swiss (29)	106	0.47
Turkish (18)	18	0.08
Ukrainian (221)	589	2.60
Welsh (36)	210	0.93
West Indian, ex. Hispanic (0)	32	0.14
West Indian (0)	32	0.14
Yugoslavian (160)	175	0.77

Hispanic Origin	Population	%
Hispanic or Latino (of any race)	515	2.23
Central American, ex. Mexican	31	0.13
Costa Rican	3	0.01
Guatemalan	17	0.07
Honduran	4	0.02
Panamanian	4	0.02
Salvadoran	3	0.01
Cuban	30	0.13
Dominican Republic	18	0.08

*Notes: † The Census 2010 population figure is used to calculate the percentages in the Hispanic Origin and Race categories. Ancestry percentages are based on the 2006-2010 American Community Survey population (not shown); ‡ Numbers in parentheses indicate the number of people reporting a single ancestry; * Numbers in parentheses indicate the number of persons reporting this race alone, not in combination with any other race; Please refer to the Explanation of Data for more information.*

Mexican	120	0.52
Puerto Rican	200	0.87
South American	55	0.24
Argentinean	2	0.01
Bolivian	1	<0.01
Colombian	21	0.09
Ecuadorian	18	0.08
Paraguayan	1	<0.01
Peruvian	8	0.03
Venezuelan	4	0.02
Other Hispanic or Latino	61	0.26

Race*	Population	%
African-American/Black (882)	1,039	4.50
Not Hispanic (845)	973	4.21
Hispanic (37)	66	0.29
American Indian/Alaska Native (340)	484	2.10
Not Hispanic (314)	442	1.91
Hispanic (26)	42	0.18
Apache (1)	2	0.01
Blackfeet (0)	3	0.01
Cherokee (3)	12	0.05
Choctaw (2)	2	0.01
Delaware (0)	1	<0.01
Inupiat *(Alaska Native)* (1)	1	<0.01
Iroquois (225)	293	1.27
Lumbee (0)	1	<0.01
Mexican American Ind. (3)	3	0.01
Navajo (3)	3	0.01
Seminole (0)	2	0.01
South American Ind. (10)	17	0.07
Asian (502)	593	2.57
Not Hispanic (502)	587	2.54
Hispanic (0)	6	0.03
Bangladeshi (13)	13	0.06
Burmese (1)	1	<0.01
Cambodian (0)	3	0.01
Chinese, ex. Taiwanese (124)	139	0.60
Filipino (14)	26	0.11
Indian (134)	155	0.67
Indonesian (1)	1	<0.01
Japanese (12)	26	0.11
Korean (136)	156	0.68
Malaysian (1)	1	<0.01
Nepalese (1)	2	0.01
Pakistani (24)	24	0.10
Sri Lankan (0)	1	<0.01
Thai (1)	1	<0.01
Vietnamese (15)	19	0.08
Hawaii Native/Pacific Islander (4)	15	0.06
Not Hispanic (4)	13	0.06
Hispanic (0)	2	0.01
Guamanian/Chamorro (2)	2	0.01
Native Hawaiian (1)	5	0.02
Samoan (0)	2	0.01
White (20,887)	21,227	91.89
Not Hispanic (20,560)	20,870	90.34
Hispanic (327)	357	1.55

Ontario

Place Type: Town
County: Wayne
Population: 10,136†

Ancestry‡	Population	%
American (802)	802	7.98
Arab (8)	19	0.19
Lebanese (8)	19	0.19
Belgian (11)	23	0.23
Brazilian (0)	16	0.16
British (11)	11	0.11
Canadian (21)	21	0.21
Czech (0)	9	0.09
Czechoslovakian (0)	10	0.10
Danish (9)	26	0.26
Dutch (197)	1,092	10.87
English (300)	1,458	14.51
European (134)	134	1.33
Finnish (8)	29	0.29
French, ex. Basque (49)	520	5.18
French Canadian (17)	139	1.38
German (695)	2,747	27.34
Greek (85)	115	1.14
Hungarian (0)	19	0.19
Irish (307)	1,659	16.51
Italian (849)	2,221	22.10
Lithuanian (0)	27	0.27
Northern European (12)	12	0.12
Norwegian (0)	31	0.31
Polish (226)	939	9.35
Russian (39)	57	0.57
Scotch-Irish (85)	292	2.91
Scottish (87)	303	3.02
Swedish (32)	32	0.32
Ukrainian (96)	167	1.66
Welsh (0)	43	0.43

Hispanic Origin	Population	%
Hispanic or Latino (of any race)	164	1.62
Central American, ex. Mexican	10	0.10
Guatemalan	2	0.02
Honduran	4	0.04
Salvadoran	4	0.04
Cuban	7	0.07
Dominican Republic	1	0.01
Mexican	46	0.45
Puerto Rican	86	0.85
South American	6	0.06
Argentinean	1	0.01
Bolivian	3	0.03
Ecuadorian	1	0.01
Peruvian	1	0.01
Other Hispanic or Latino	8	0.08

Race*	Population	%
African-American/Black (121)	173	1.71
Not Hispanic (115)	167	1.65
Hispanic (6)	6	0.06
American Indian/Alaska Native (19)	48	0.47
Not Hispanic (12)	37	0.37
Hispanic (7)	11	0.11
Canadian/French Am. Ind. (0)	1	0.01
Cherokee (1)	2	0.02
Choctaw (1)	1	0.01
Iroquois (7)	13	0.13
Navajo (1)	1	0.01
Pima (2)	2	0.02
South American Ind. (0)	1	0.01
Asian (53)	74	0.73
Not Hispanic (53)	74	0.73
Cambodian (1)	2	0.02
Chinese, ex. Taiwanese (20)	20	0.20
Filipino (5)	6	0.06
Indian (4)	6	0.06
Japanese (1)	4	0.04
Korean (4)	9	0.09
Laotian (4)	5	0.05
Pakistani (6)	6	0.06
Thai (1)	7	0.07
Vietnamese (4)	7	0.07
Hawaii Native/Pacific Islander (2)	2	0.02
Not Hispanic (2)	2	0.02
Guamanian/Chamorro (1)	1	0.01
Native Hawaiian (1)	1	0.01
White (9,802)	9,895	97.62
Not Hispanic (9,694)	9,777	96.46
Hispanic (108)	118	1.16

Orangetown

Place Type: Town
County: Rockland
Population: 49,212†

Ancestry‡	Population	%
African, Sub-Saharan (210)	252	0.52
African (13)	55	0.11
Ethiopian (13)	13	0.03
Ghanaian (14)	14	0.03
Kenyan (32)	32	0.07
South African (33)	33	0.07
Other Sub-Saharan African (105)	105	0.22
Albanian (184)	241	0.50
American (1,390)	1,390	2.86
Arab (239)	286	0.59
Arab (77)	77	0.16
Egyptian (87)	87	0.18
Jordanian (68)	68	0.14
Lebanese (0)	4	0.01
Moroccan (0)	10	0.02
Syrian (7)	32	0.07
Other Arab (0)	8	0.02
Armenian (89)	121	0.25
Australian (9)	21	0.04
Austrian (77)	391	0.80
Belgian (0)	48	0.10
Brazilian (10)	10	0.02
British (162)	274	0.56
Canadian (55)	243	0.50
Carpatho Rusyn (4)	4	0.01
Croatian (6)	119	0.24
Czech (41)	282	0.58
Czechoslovakian (22)	30	0.06
Danish (31)	89	0.18
Dutch (80)	965	1.98
Eastern European (273)	334	0.69
English (639)	2,819	5.79
Estonian (0)	2	<0.01
European (461)	549	1.13
Finnish (0)	11	0.02
French, ex. Basque (100)	840	1.73
French Canadian (158)	229	0.47
German (972)	4,940	10.15
Greek (547)	1,141	2.35
Hungarian (262)	595	1.22
Iranian (26)	92	0.19
Irish (8,613)	15,284	31.41
Israeli (29)	67	0.14
Italian (4,263)	9,505	19.54
Latvian (28)	30	0.06
Lithuanian (143)	319	0.66
Maltese (19)	19	0.04
Northern European (5)	5	0.01
Norwegian (86)	186	0.38
Polish (580)	1,930	3.97
Portuguese (105)	227	0.47
Romanian (103)	240	0.49
Russian (805)	1,899	3.90
Scandinavian (0)	9	0.02
Scotch-Irish (189)	460	0.95
Scottish (168)	642	1.32
Serbian (40)	57	0.12
Slavic (0)	50	0.10
Slovak (18)	82	0.17
Swedish (108)	449	0.92
Swiss (0)	60	0.12
Turkish (45)	88	0.18
Ukrainian (164)	410	0.84
Welsh (16)	148	0.30
West Indian, ex. Hispanic (1,087)	1,226	2.52
Barbadian (105)	105	0.22
Belizean (120)	120	0.25
British West Indian (49)	49	0.10
Haitian (670)	782	1.61
Jamaican (45)	55	0.11
Trinidadian/Tobagonian (98)	98	0.20
West Indian (0)	17	0.03
Yugoslavian (25)	60	0.12

Hispanic Origin	Population	%
Hispanic or Latino (of any race)	4,782	9.72
Central American, ex. Mexican	1,152	2.34
Costa Rican	13	0.03
Guatemalan	147	0.30
Honduran	74	0.15
Nicaraguan	17	0.03
Panamanian	11	0.02
Salvadoran	877	1.78
Other Central American	13	0.03

*Notes: † The Census 2010 population figure is used to calculate the percentages in the Hispanic Origin and Race categories. Ancestry percentages are based on the 2006-2010 American Community Survey population (not shown); ‡ Numbers in parentheses indicate the number of people reporting a single ancestry; * Numbers in parentheses indicate the number of persons reporting this race alone, not in combination with any other race; Please refer to the Explanation of Data for more information.*

Cuban	240	0.49
Dominican Republic	463	0.94
Mexican	506	1.03
Puerto Rican	1,378	2.80
South American	618	1.26
Argentinean	47	0.10
Bolivian	8	0.02
Chilean	25	0.05
Colombian	160	0.33
Ecuadorian	240	0.49
Paraguayan	9	0.02
Peruvian	71	0.14
Uruguayan	14	0.03
Venezuelan	31	0.06
Other South American	13	0.03
Other Hispanic or Latino	425	0.86

Race*	Population	%
African-American/Black (2,955)	3,350	6.81
Not Hispanic (2,742)	3,048	6.19
Hispanic (213)	302	0.61
American Indian/Alaska Native (94)	267	0.54
Not Hispanic (58)	196	0.40
Hispanic (36)	71	0.14
Apache (0)	1	<0.01
Blackfeet (0)	3	0.01
Canadian/French Am. Ind. (0)	3	0.01
Central American Ind. (9)	9	0.02
Cherokee (2)	31	0.06
Choctaw (1)	5	0.01
Comanche (3)	5	0.01
Crow (1)	1	<0.01
Delaware (3)	14	0.03
Iroquois (8)	14	0.03
Lumbee (1)	1	<0.01
Mexican American Ind. (8)	10	0.02
Osage (0)	1	<0.01
Sioux (0)	1	<0.01
South American Ind. (3)	5	0.01
Asian (3,411)	3,760	7.64
Not Hispanic (3,386)	3,700	7.52
Hispanic (25)	60	0.12
Bangladeshi (5)	5	0.01
Burmese (4)	4	0.01
Cambodian (13)	14	0.03
Chinese, ex. Taiwanese (686)	777	1.58
Filipino (664)	771	1.57
Hmong (30)	32	0.07
Indian (893)	997	2.03
Indonesian (6)	9	0.02
Japanese (82)	120	0.24
Korean (757)	800	1.63
Laotian (5)	7	0.01
Malaysian (0)	2	<0.01
Nepalese (1)	2	<0.01
Pakistani (79)	95	0.19
Sri Lankan (3)	3	0.01
Taiwanese (11)	12	0.02
Thai (32)	43	0.09
Vietnamese (55)	63	0.13
Hawaii Native/Pacific Islander (17)	57	0.12
Not Hispanic (13)	31	0.06
Hispanic (4)	26	0.05
Guamanian/Chamorro (0)	3	0.01
Native Hawaiian (3)	9	0.02
Samoan (5)	6	0.01
White (40,298)	41,104	83.52
Not Hispanic (37,490)	38,040	77.30
Hispanic (2,808)	3,064	6.23

Orchard Park

Place Type: Town
County: Erie
Population: 29,054†

Ancestry‡	Population	%
African, Sub-Saharan (41)	41	0.14
Nigerian (41)	41	0.14
Alsatian (9)	40	0.14
American (753)	753	2.63
Arab (13)	98	0.34
Arab (13)	24	0.08
Lebanese (0)	74	0.26
Armenian (18)	18	0.06
Austrian (8)	247	0.86
Belgian (13)	92	0.32
British (29)	41	0.14
Canadian (49)	140	0.49
Croatian (63)	160	0.56
Czech (0)	78	0.27
Czechoslovakian (10)	65	0.23
Danish (0)	55	0.19
Dutch (19)	319	1.11
Eastern European (39)	39	0.14
English (577)	2,933	10.23
European (330)	342	1.19
Finnish (17)	40	0.14
French, ex. Basque (118)	960	3.35
French Canadian (140)	239	0.83
German (2,620)	9,266	32.31
Greek (54)	104	0.36
Hungarian (162)	505	1.76
Irish (2,093)	7,104	24.77
Italian (1,937)	5,219	18.20
Latvian (12)	38	0.13
Lithuanian (0)	17	0.06
Macedonian (49)	49	0.17
Maltese (13)	13	0.05
Northern European (14)	53	0.18
Norwegian (13)	141	0.49
Polish (2,542)	5,998	20.91
Portuguese (0)	12	0.04
Romanian (0)	36	0.13
Russian (92)	356	1.24
Scotch-Irish (237)	532	1.85
Scottish (68)	571	1.99
Serbian (170)	247	0.86
Slavic (0)	40	0.14
Slovak (19)	50	0.17
Swedish (89)	372	1.30
Swiss (0)	17	0.06
Ukrainian (68)	191	0.67
Welsh (68)	268	0.93
Yugoslavian (8)	8	0.03

Hispanic Origin	Population	%
Hispanic or Latino (of any race)	465	1.60
Central American, ex. Mexican	39	0.13
Costa Rican	5	0.02
Guatemalan	18	0.06
Nicaraguan	7	0.02
Panamanian	5	0.02
Salvadoran	4	0.01
Cuban	16	0.06
Dominican Republic	5	0.02
Mexican	111	0.38
Puerto Rican	142	0.49
South American	67	0.23
Argentinean	6	0.02
Bolivian	1	<0.01
Chilean	3	0.01
Colombian	36	0.12
Ecuadorian	1	<0.01
Paraguayan	7	0.02
Peruvian	10	0.03
Uruguayan	1	<0.01
Venezuelan	2	0.01
Other Hispanic or Latino	85	0.29

Race*	Population	%
African-American/Black (211)	277	0.95
Not Hispanic (204)	265	0.91
Hispanic (7)	12	0.04
American Indian/Alaska Native (63)	123	0.42
Not Hispanic (47)	98	0.34
Hispanic (16)	25	0.09
Blackfeet (0)	1	<0.01
Canadian/French Am. Ind. (2)	2	0.01
Cherokee (4)	7	0.02
Choctaw (0)	1	<0.01
Comanche (0)	1	<0.01
Inupiat *(Alaska Native)* (1)	1	<0.01
Iroquois (43)	62	0.21
Lumbee (1)	1	<0.01
Mexican American Ind. (2)	2	0.01
Navajo (1)	2	0.01
Potawatomi (0)	3	0.01
South American Ind. (0)	4	0.01
Asian (372)	455	1.57
Not Hispanic (368)	450	1.55
Hispanic (4)	5	0.02
Cambodian (2)	3	0.01
Chinese, ex. Taiwanese (81)	97	0.33
Filipino (50)	58	0.20
Indian (139)	157	0.54
Indonesian (1)	1	<0.01
Japanese (10)	14	0.05
Korean (28)	48	0.17
Laotian (4)	4	0.01
Malaysian (2)	2	0.01
Pakistani (3)	4	0.01
Sri Lankan (4)	4	0.01
Thai (6)	9	0.03
Vietnamese (24)	24	0.08
Hawaii Native/Pacific Islander (6)	20	0.07
Not Hispanic (4)	17	0.06
Hispanic (2)	3	0.01
Guamanian/Chamorro (2)	5	0.02
Native Hawaiian (1)	4	0.01
Samoan (1)	8	0.03
White (28,095)	28,319	97.47
Not Hispanic (27,750)	27,945	96.18
Hispanic (345)	374	1.29

Ossining

Place Type: Town
County: Westchester
Population: 37,674†

Ancestry‡	Population	%
African, Sub-Saharan (369)	447	1.20
African (236)	299	0.80
Ghanaian (0)	15	0.04
Kenyan (66)	66	0.18
Nigerian (38)	38	0.10
Other Sub-Saharan African (29)	29	0.08
Albanian (68)	92	0.25
American (1,078)	1,078	2.89
Arab (247)	334	0.89
Arab (113)	113	0.30
Egyptian (63)	74	0.20
Lebanese (22)	73	0.20
Syrian (0)	12	0.03
Other Arab (49)	62	0.17
Armenian (27)	125	0.33
Austrian (22)	359	0.96
Belgian (0)	50	0.13
Brazilian (72)	99	0.27
British (155)	185	0.50
Bulgarian (34)	34	0.09
Canadian (0)	55	0.15
Celtic (13)	13	0.03
Croatian (0)	32	0.09
Czech (0)	70	0.19
Czechoslovakian (20)	34	0.09
Danish (18)	44	0.12
Dutch (45)	293	0.79
Eastern European (322)	395	1.06
English (285)	1,640	4.39
European (204)	283	0.76
Finnish (11)	36	0.10
French, ex. Basque (102)	553	1.48
French Canadian (87)	193	0.52
German (665)	2,797	7.49
Greek (219)	321	0.86
Guyanese (17)	17	0.05
Hungarian (106)	303	0.81
Iranian (33)	33	0.09

*Notes: † The Census 2010 population figure is used to calculate the percentages in the Hispanic Origin and Race categories. Ancestry percentages are based on the 2006-2010 American Community Survey population (not shown); ‡ Numbers in parentheses indicate the number of people reporting a single ancestry; * Numbers in parentheses indicate the number of persons reporting this race alone, not in combination with any other race; Please refer to the Explanation of Data for more information.*

Ancestry	Population	%
Irish (1,743)	5,024	13.46
Israeli (42)	42	0.11
Italian (3,398)	6,650	17.82
Latvian (23)	46	0.12
Lithuanian (0)	44	0.12
Macedonian (0)	25	0.07
Maltese (14)	44	0.12
Northern European (6)	6	0.02
Norwegian (74)	195	0.52
Pennsylvania German (0)	10	0.03
Polish (593)	1,487	3.98
Portuguese (305)	363	0.97
Romanian (30)	95	0.25
Russian (642)	1,245	3.34
Scandinavian (56)	131	0.35
Scotch-Irish (227)	495	1.33
Scottish (83)	595	1.59
Slavic (0)	27	0.07
Slovak (11)	84	0.23
Slovene (7)	11	0.03
Swedish (59)	182	0.49
Swiss (7)	175	0.47
Turkish (52)	52	0.14
Ukrainian (44)	88	0.24
Welsh (25)	233	0.62
West Indian, ex. Hispanic (743)	848	2.27
British West Indian (28)	28	0.08
Haitian (9)	9	0.02
Jamaican (590)	678	1.82
West Indian (116)	133	0.36
Yugoslavian (74)	118	0.32

Hispanic Origin	Population	%
Hispanic or Latino (of any race)	11,403	30.27
Central American, ex. Mexican	694	1.84
Costa Rican	33	0.09
Guatemalan	422	1.12
Honduran	104	0.28
Nicaraguan	20	0.05
Panamanian	32	0.08
Salvadoran	83	0.22
Cuban	234	0.62
Dominican Republic	664	1.76
Mexican	482	1.28
Puerto Rican	1,452	3.85
South American	6,825	18.12
Argentinean	82	0.22
Bolivian	8	0.02
Chilean	190	0.50
Colombian	805	2.14
Ecuadorian	4,988	13.24
Paraguayan	29	0.08
Peruvian	411	1.09
Uruguayan	273	0.72
Venezuelan	29	0.08
Other South American	10	0.03
Other Hispanic or Latino	1,052	2.79

Race*	Population	%
African-American/Black (4,785)	5,174	13.73
Not Hispanic (4,345)	4,547	12.07
Hispanic (440)	627	1.66
American Indian/Alaska Native (171)	348	0.92
Not Hispanic (23)	76	0.20
Hispanic (148)	272	0.72
Apache (2)	4	0.01
Blackfeet (2)	5	0.01
Canadian/French Am. Ind. (1)	2	0.01
Central American Ind. (3)	4	0.01
Cherokee (1)	10	0.03
Chippewa (1)	2	0.01
Choctaw (0)	3	0.01
Iroquois (3)	6	0.02
Mexican American Ind. (8)	8	0.02
Seminole (0)	1	<0.01
Sioux (0)	2	0.01
South American Ind. (26)	48	0.13
Spanish American Ind. (6)	8	0.02
Tohono O'Odham (0)	1	<0.01
Asian (1,861)	2,141	5.68
Not Hispanic (1,834)	2,062	5.47
Hispanic (27)	79	0.21
Bangladeshi (2)	3	0.01
Burmese (1)	1	<0.01
Cambodian (4)	4	0.01
Chinese, ex. Taiwanese (490)	545	1.45
Filipino (222)	267	0.71
Indian (650)	696	1.85
Indonesian (4)	7	0.02
Japanese (127)	172	0.46
Korean (172)	209	0.55
Laotian (4)	5	0.01
Malaysian (2)	3	0.01
Nepalese (1)	2	0.01
Pakistani (77)	81	0.22
Sri Lankan (5)	6	0.02
Taiwanese (15)	15	0.04
Thai (12)	19	0.05
Vietnamese (17)	23	0.06
Hawaii Native/Pacific Islander (13)	38	0.10
Not Hispanic (9)	25	0.07
Hispanic (4)	13	0.03
Guamanian/Chamorro (4)	8	0.02
Native Hawaiian (3)	4	0.01
White (24,498)	25,529	67.76
Not Hispanic (19,458)	19,828	52.63
Hispanic (5,040)	5,701	15.13

Ossining

Place Type: Village
County: Westchester
Population: 25,060†

Ancestry‡	Population	%
African, Sub-Saharan (352)	430	1.73
African (219)	282	1.14
Ghanaian (0)	15	0.06
Kenyan (66)	66	0.27
Nigerian (38)	38	0.15
Other Sub-Saharan African (29)	29	0.12
Albanian (9)	33	0.13
American (668)	668	2.69
Arab (14)	41	0.17
Lebanese (14)	41	0.17
Armenian (11)	87	0.35
Austrian (22)	127	0.51
Belgian (0)	39	0.16
Brazilian (8)	35	0.14
British (32)	38	0.15
Canadian (0)	7	0.03
Celtic (13)	13	0.05
Croatian (0)	32	0.13
Czech (0)	13	0.05
Czechoslovakian (0)	14	0.06
Danish (18)	35	0.14
Dutch (45)	233	0.94
Eastern European (51)	65	0.26
English (87)	696	2.81
European (111)	122	0.49
French, ex. Basque (35)	370	1.49
French Canadian (50)	84	0.34
German (362)	1,533	6.18
Greek (124)	226	0.91
Guyanese (17)	17	0.07
Hungarian (32)	157	0.63
Iranian (8)	8	0.03
Irish (985)	2,545	10.26
Italian (1,862)	3,658	14.74
Lithuanian (0)	20	0.08
Maltese (0)	30	0.12
Norwegian (63)	164	0.66
Polish (220)	661	2.66
Portuguese (287)	345	1.39
Russian (245)	396	1.60
Scandinavian (56)	113	0.46
Scotch-Irish (137)	318	1.28
Scottish (54)	314	1.27
Slovak (0)	49	0.20
Slovene (7)	11	0.04
Swedish (17)	78	0.31
Swiss (0)	73	0.29
Turkish (52)	52	0.21
Ukrainian (29)	62	0.25
Welsh (25)	189	0.76
West Indian, ex. Hispanic (662)	747	3.01
British West Indian (16)	16	0.06
Haitian (9)	9	0.04
Jamaican (537)	605	2.44
West Indian (100)	117	0.47
Yugoslavian (20)	30	0.12

Hispanic Origin	Population	%
Hispanic or Latino (of any race)	10,375	41.40
Central American, ex. Mexican	640	2.55
Costa Rican	30	0.12
Guatemalan	395	1.58
Honduran	102	0.41
Nicaraguan	19	0.08
Panamanian	28	0.11
Salvadoran	66	0.26
Cuban	170	0.68
Dominican Republic	575	2.29
Mexican	421	1.68
Puerto Rican	1,183	4.72
South American	6,440	25.70
Argentinean	57	0.23
Bolivian	5	0.02
Chilean	169	0.67
Colombian	703	2.81
Ecuadorian	4,840	19.31
Paraguayan	28	0.11
Peruvian	381	1.52
Uruguayan	230	0.92
Venezuelan	17	0.07
Other South American	10	0.04
Other Hispanic or Latino	946	3.77

Race*	Population	%
African-American/Black (4,302)	4,614	18.41
Not Hispanic (3,916)	4,065	16.22
Hispanic (386)	549	2.19
American Indian/Alaska Native (145)	307	1.23
Not Hispanic (17)	60	0.24
Hispanic (128)	247	0.99
Apache (2)	4	0.02
Blackfeet (2)	5	0.02
Central American Ind. (3)	3	0.01
Cherokee (1)	9	0.04
Chippewa (1)	2	0.01
Choctaw (0)	3	0.01
Iroquois (2)	5	0.02
Mexican American Ind. (6)	6	0.02
Seminole (0)	1	<0.01
South American Ind. (17)	39	0.16
Spanish American Ind. (6)	8	0.03
Tohono O'Odham (0)	1	<0.01
Asian (1,063)	1,238	4.94
Not Hispanic (1,042)	1,180	4.71
Hispanic (21)	58	0.23
Bangladeshi (2)	2	0.01
Burmese (1)	1	<0.01
Cambodian (4)	4	0.02
Chinese, ex. Taiwanese (261)	289	1.15
Filipino (143)	164	0.65
Indian (387)	413	1.65
Indonesian (3)	4	0.02
Japanese (79)	107	0.43
Korean (68)	92	0.37
Laotian (4)	5	0.02
Malaysian (1)	2	0.01
Nepalese (1)	2	0.01
Pakistani (46)	49	0.20
Sri Lankan (4)	5	0.02
Taiwanese (3)	3	0.01
Thai (10)	13	0.05
Vietnamese (12)	17	0.07
Hawaii Native/Pacific Islander (9)	30	0.12
Not Hispanic (5)	17	0.07
Hispanic (4)	13	0.05

*Notes: † The Census 2010 population figure is used to calculate the percentages in the Hispanic Origin and Race categories. Ancestry percentages are based on the 2006-2010 American Community Survey population (not shown); ‡ Numbers in parentheses indicate the number of people reporting a single ancestry; * Numbers in parentheses indicate the number of persons reporting this race alone, not in combination with any other race; Please refer to the Explanation of Data for more information.*

Guamanian/Chamorro (3)	7	0.03
Native Hawaiian (1)	2	0.01
White (13,675)	14,506	57.89
Not Hispanic (9,286)	9,516	37.97
Hispanic (4,389)	4,990	19.91

Oswego

Place Type: City
County: Oswego
Population: 18,142†

Ancestry‡	Population	%
Afghan (50)	50	0.28
African, Sub-Saharan (6)	10	0.06
African (0)	4	0.02
Kenyan (6)	6	0.03
American (692)	692	3.82
Arab (10)	10	0.06
Egyptian (10)	10	0.06
Austrian (10)	10	0.06
Belgian (12)	24	0.13
British (9)	9	0.05
Cajun (0)	15	0.08
Canadian (66)	128	0.71
Croatian (0)	15	0.08
Czech (36)	36	0.20
Czechoslovakian (0)	23	0.13
Danish (0)	18	0.10
Dutch (53)	693	3.82
English (420)	2,259	12.47
European (112)	112	0.62
Finnish (0)	36	0.20
French, ex. Basque (383)	1,764	9.73
French Canadian (383)	692	3.82
German (625)	3,352	18.50
Greek (80)	165	0.91
Hungarian (0)	57	0.31
Irish (1,818)	5,333	29.43
Italian (1,620)	3,243	17.90
Lithuanian (13)	62	0.34
Norwegian (52)	62	0.34
Pennsylvania German (0)	8	0.04
Polish (407)	1,229	6.78
Romanian (0)	12	0.07
Russian (113)	295	1.63
Scandinavian (0)	14	0.08
Scotch-Irish (126)	307	1.69
Scottish (61)	232	1.28
Slavic (0)	11	0.06
Slovak (0)	15	0.08
Swedish (20)	113	0.62
Swiss (10)	45	0.25
Ukrainian (25)	121	0.67
Welsh (0)	127	0.70
West Indian, ex. Hispanic (32)	126	0.70
Belizean (0)	5	0.03
Haitian (19)	19	0.10
Jamaican (13)	60	0.33
Trinidadian/Tobagonian (0)	42	0.23

Hispanic Origin	Population	%
Hispanic or Latino (of any race)	798	4.40
Central American, ex. Mexican	36	0.20
Costa Rican	1	0.01
Guatemalan	15	0.08
Honduran	6	0.03
Panamanian	10	0.06
Salvadoran	4	0.02
Cuban	16	0.09
Dominican Republic	17	0.09
Mexican	173	0.95
Puerto Rican	422	2.33
South American	48	0.26
Argentinean	9	0.05
Chilean	2	0.01
Colombian	22	0.12
Ecuadorian	8	0.04
Paraguayan	1	0.01
Peruvian	4	0.02
Uruguayan	1	0.01
Other South American	1	0.01
Other Hispanic or Latino	86	0.47

Race*	Population	%
African-American/Black (227)	355	1.96
Not Hispanic (196)	309	1.70
Hispanic (31)	46	0.25
American Indian/Alaska Native (55)	129	0.71
Not Hispanic (52)	117	0.64
Hispanic (3)	12	0.07
Apache (1)	2	0.01
Blackfeet (10)	12	0.07
Canadian/French Am. Ind. (0)	1	0.01
Central American Ind. (1)	1	0.01
Cherokee (3)	17	0.09
Chippewa (1)	2	0.01
Creek (1)	1	0.01
Iroquois (10)	24	0.13
Mexican American Ind. (1)	2	0.01
Navajo (1)	1	0.01
South American Ind. (0)	2	0.01
Spanish American Ind. (1)	1	0.01
Yakama (0)	1	0.01
Asian (221)	271	1.49
Not Hispanic (221)	269	1.48
Hispanic (0)	2	0.01
Cambodian (0)	1	0.01
Chinese, ex. Taiwanese (70)	74	0.41
Filipino (51)	72	0.40
Indian (35)	43	0.24
Indonesian (0)	2	0.01
Japanese (5)	14	0.08
Korean (29)	34	0.19
Pakistani (9)	9	0.05
Sri Lankan (1)	1	0.01
Taiwanese (1)	4	0.02
Thai (4)	7	0.04
Vietnamese (11)	12	0.07
Hawaii Native/Pacific Islander (6)	16	0.09
Not Hispanic (6)	10	0.06
Hispanic (0)	6	0.03
Guamanian/Chamorro (2)	3	0.02
Native Hawaiian (1)	4	0.02
White (17,190)	17,437	96.11
Not Hispanic (16,645)	16,844	92.85
Hispanic (545)	593	3.27

Oswego

Place Type: Town
County: Oswego
Population: 7,984†

Ancestry‡	Population	%
African, Sub-Saharan (73)	73	0.92
African (12)	12	0.15
Ghanaian (30)	30	0.38
Senegalese (19)	19	0.24
Other Sub-Saharan African (12)	12	0.15
American (192)	192	2.41
Arab (0)	44	0.55
Lebanese (0)	32	0.40
Other Arab (0)	12	0.15
Armenian (21)	45	0.56
Austrian (0)	51	0.64
Belgian (0)	9	0.11
British (7)	20	0.25
Canadian (6)	55	0.69
Carpatho Rusyn (0)	28	0.35
Croatian (0)	7	0.09
Czech (0)	46	0.58
Czechoslovakian (0)	13	0.16
Danish (10)	40	0.50
Dutch (24)	240	3.01
English (164)	839	10.53
European (79)	79	0.99
Finnish (0)	19	0.24
French, ex. Basque (105)	542	6.80
French Canadian (75)	192	2.41
German (275)	1,716	21.53
Greek (0)	14	0.18
Hungarian (7)	52	0.65
Irish (391)	2,018	25.32
Italian (520)	1,732	21.73
Lithuanian (0)	13	0.16
Northern European (8)	8	0.10
Norwegian (14)	38	0.48
Polish (164)	663	8.32
Portuguese (12)	37	0.46
Romanian (0)	14	0.18
Russian (47)	200	2.51
Scotch-Irish (37)	138	1.73
Scottish (28)	171	2.15
Slovak (19)	32	0.40
Swedish (6)	46	0.58
Swiss (0)	37	0.46
Ukrainian (7)	28	0.35
Welsh (13)	100	1.25
West Indian, ex. Hispanic (17)	39	0.49
Belizean (0)	7	0.09
British West Indian (0)	15	0.19
Haitian (17)	17	0.21

Hispanic Origin	Population	%
Hispanic or Latino (of any race)	308	3.86
Central American, ex. Mexican	16	0.20
Costa Rican	2	0.03
Guatemalan	1	0.01
Honduran	5	0.06
Panamanian	2	0.03
Salvadoran	6	0.08
Cuban	14	0.18
Dominican Republic	64	0.80
Mexican	37	0.46
Puerto Rican	127	1.59
South American	33	0.41
Argentinean	6	0.08
Bolivian	1	0.01
Chilean	2	0.03
Colombian	12	0.15
Ecuadorian	7	0.09
Peruvian	3	0.04
Uruguayan	1	0.01
Venezuelan	1	0.01
Other Hispanic or Latino	17	0.21

Race*	Population	%
African-American/Black (271)	317	3.97
Not Hispanic (239)	273	3.42
Hispanic (32)	44	0.55
American Indian/Alaska Native (12)	40	0.50
Not Hispanic (11)	35	0.44
Hispanic (1)	5	0.06
Blackfeet (0)	1	0.01
Cherokee (0)	6	0.08
Chippewa (0)	1	0.01
Crow (0)	1	0.01
Iroquois (2)	5	0.06
Sioux (0)	2	0.03
South American Ind. (0)	1	0.01
Asian (161)	199	2.49
Not Hispanic (159)	191	2.39
Hispanic (2)	8	0.10
Chinese, ex. Taiwanese (78)	90	1.13
Filipino (17)	31	0.39
Indian (16)	21	0.26
Indonesian (0)	1	0.01
Japanese (11)	13	0.16
Korean (19)	21	0.26
Malaysian (1)	1	0.01
Pakistani (4)	4	0.05
Sri Lankan (3)	3	0.04
Thai (1)	2	0.03
Vietnamese (7)	10	0.13
Hawaii Native/Pacific Islander (4)	16	0.20
Not Hispanic (4)	12	0.15
Hispanic (0)	4	0.05
Guamanian/Chamorro (1)	2	0.03
White (7,300)	7,396	92.64

*Notes: † The Census 2010 population figure is used to calculate the percentages in the Hispanic Origin and Race categories. Ancestry percentages are based on the 2006-2010 American Community Survey population (not shown); ‡ Numbers in parentheses indicate the number of people reporting a single ancestry; * Numbers in parentheses indicate the number of persons reporting this race alone, not in combination with any other race; Please refer to the Explanation of Data for more information.*

Not Hispanic (7,167)	7,237	90.64
Hispanic (133)	159	1.99

Owego

Place Type: Town
County: Tioga
Population: 19,883†

Ancestry‡	Population	%
African, Sub-Saharan (11)	11	0.05
African (11)	11	0.05
American (1,189)	1,189	5.94
Arab (76)	115	0.57
Egyptian (16)	16	0.08
Lebanese (60)	99	0.49
Armenian (0)	10	0.05
Austrian (0)	29	0.14
Basque (0)	34	0.17
Belgian (0)	20	0.10
British (18)	32	0.16
Canadian (8)	21	0.10
Celtic (0)	16	0.08
Croatian (16)	16	0.08
Czech (56)	209	1.04
Czechoslovakian (24)	71	0.35
Danish (27)	94	0.47
Dutch (77)	520	2.60
English (1,245)	3,763	18.80
European (239)	259	1.29
Finnish (45)	91	0.45
French, ex. Basque (83)	716	3.58
French Canadian (46)	218	1.09
German (1,485)	5,088	25.41
Greek (50)	58	0.29
Hungarian (54)	126	0.63
Irish (1,114)	4,055	20.25
Italian (760)	2,078	10.38
Latvian (13)	13	0.06
Lithuanian (28)	197	0.98
Maltese (0)	16	0.08
Northern European (10)	10	0.05
Norwegian (47)	97	0.48
Pennsylvania German (77)	151	0.75
Polish (431)	1,319	6.59
Portuguese (26)	34	0.17
Romanian (18)	18	0.09
Russian (242)	506	2.53
Scandinavian (17)	42	0.21
Scotch-Irish (175)	383	1.91
Scottish (89)	534	2.67
Slavic (22)	43	0.21
Slovak (170)	430	2.15
Slovene (26)	26	0.13
Swedish (95)	347	1.73
Swiss (27)	66	0.33
Turkish (10)	18	0.09
Ukrainian (91)	180	0.90
Welsh (72)	503	2.51
West Indian, ex. Hispanic (8)	17	0.08
Jamaican (8)	8	0.04
West Indian (0)	9	0.04
Yugoslavian (0)	9	0.04

Hispanic Origin	Population	%
Hispanic or Latino (of any race)	285	1.43
Central American, ex. Mexican	12	0.06
Costa Rican	2	0.01
Guatemalan	4	0.02
Honduran	1	0.01
Nicaraguan	4	0.02
Panamanian	1	0.01
Cuban	7	0.04
Dominican Republic	12	0.06
Mexican	58	0.29
Puerto Rican	114	0.57
South American	47	0.24
Argentinean	2	0.01
Bolivian	1	0.01
Chilean	6	0.03
Colombian	8	0.04
Ecuadorian	16	0.08
Paraguayan	1	0.01
Peruvian	8	0.04
Uruguayan	2	0.01
Other South American	3	0.02
Other Hispanic or Latino	35	0.18

Race*	Population	%
African-American/Black (190)	270	1.36
Not Hispanic (181)	255	1.28
Hispanic (9)	15	0.08
American Indian/Alaska Native (25)	96	0.48
Not Hispanic (24)	86	0.43
Hispanic (1)	10	0.05
Blackfeet (0)	5	0.03
Cherokee (0)	16	0.08
Cheyenne (0)	1	0.01
Creek (0)	4	0.02
Delaware (0)	1	0.01
Hopi (1)	1	0.01
Iroquois (4)	17	0.09
Mexican American Ind. (1)	3	0.02
Navajo (2)	9	0.05
Sioux (0)	2	0.01
South American Ind. (0)	2	0.01
Asian (267)	333	1.67
Not Hispanic (267)	327	1.64
Hispanic (0)	6	0.03
Chinese, ex. Taiwanese (80)	90	0.45
Filipino (24)	41	0.21
Indian (53)	59	0.30
Japanese (11)	26	0.13
Korean (20)	26	0.13
Laotian (0)	1	0.01
Pakistani (33)	33	0.17
Taiwanese (8)	10	0.05
Thai (1)	2	0.01
Vietnamese (31)	36	0.18
Hawaii Native/Pacific Islander (8)	24	0.12
Not Hispanic (7)	22	0.11
Hispanic (1)	2	0.01
Native Hawaiian (6)	10	0.05
Samoan (0)	1	0.01
White (19,071)	19,295	97.04
Not Hispanic (18,894)	19,090	96.01
Hispanic (177)	205	1.03

Oyster Bay

Place Type: Town
County: Nassau
Population: 293,214†

Ancestry‡	Population	%
Afghan (580)	808	0.28
African, Sub-Saharan (294)	484	0.17
African (215)	289	0.10
Cape Verdean (12)	12	<0.01
Nigerian (37)	77	0.03
South African (30)	30	0.01
Other Sub-Saharan African (0)	76	0.03
Albanian (268)	368	0.13
American (9,798)	9,798	3.36
Arab (597)	1,227	0.42
Arab (177)	245	0.08
Egyptian (153)	222	0.08
Iraqi (9)	9	<0.01
Lebanese (51)	191	0.07
Moroccan (47)	131	0.04
Palestinian (31)	60	0.02
Syrian (49)	114	0.04
Other Arab (80)	255	0.09
Armenian (1,034)	1,383	0.47
Australian (3)	41	0.01
Austrian (879)	3,412	1.17
Basque (0)	3	<0.01
Belgian (53)	201	0.07
Brazilian (328)	370	0.13
British (208)	476	0.16
Bulgarian (16)	45	0.02
Cajun (0)	37	0.01
Canadian (107)	441	0.15
Celtic (55)	55	0.02
Croatian (623)	1,002	0.34
Cypriot (63)	63	0.02
Czech (223)	1,379	0.47
Czechoslovakian (163)	618	0.21
Danish (126)	573	0.20
Dutch (288)	1,343	0.46
Eastern European (3,693)	3,841	1.32
English (1,832)	11,799	4.05
Estonian (68)	130	0.04
European (2,787)	2,919	1.00
Finnish (39)	265	0.09
French, ex. Basque (422)	4,302	1.48
French Canadian (238)	807	0.28
German (8,307)	41,381	14.19
Greek (4,277)	6,908	2.37
Guyanese (134)	187	0.06
Hungarian (705)	3,138	1.08
Icelander (31)	52	0.02
Iranian (1,115)	1,464	0.50
Irish (17,041)	59,765	20.49
Israeli (422)	663	0.23
Italian (48,450)	88,723	30.43
Latvian (110)	235	0.08
Lithuanian (378)	1,079	0.37
Maltese (117)	579	0.20
Northern European (97)	105	0.04
Norwegian (469)	1,882	0.65
Pennsylvania German (24)	24	0.01
Polish (6,380)	19,395	6.65
Portuguese (145)	445	0.15
Romanian (609)	1,492	0.51
Russian (5,986)	14,554	4.99
Scandinavian (24)	144	0.05
Scotch-Irish (832)	2,523	0.87
Scottish (646)	2,493	0.85
Serbian (12)	103	0.04
Slavic (27)	173	0.06
Slovak (164)	442	0.15
Slovene (10)	55	0.02
Swedish (191)	2,325	0.80
Swiss (114)	686	0.24
Turkish (520)	1,232	0.42
Ukrainian (859)	1,774	0.61
Welsh (83)	515	0.18
West Indian, ex. Hispanic (1,924)	2,311	0.79
Barbadian (14)	26	0.01
Belizean (16)	29	0.01
Bermudan (0)	13	<0.01
British West Indian (125)	157	0.05
Dutch West Indian (7)	21	0.01
Haitian (732)	813	0.28
Jamaican (818)	972	0.33
Trinidadian/Tobagonian (111)	148	0.05
U.S. Virgin Islander (15)	15	0.01
West Indian (86)	102	0.03
Other West Indian (0)	15	0.01
Yugoslavian (65)	334	0.11

Hispanic Origin	Population	%
Hispanic or Latino (of any race)	21,923	7.48
Central American, ex. Mexican	4,958	1.69
Costa Rican	101	0.03
Guatemalan	397	0.14
Honduran	952	0.32
Nicaraguan	78	0.03
Panamanian	88	0.03
Salvadoran	3,297	1.12
Other Central American	45	0.02
Cuban	906	0.31
Dominican Republic	1,429	0.49
Mexican	1,550	0.53
Puerto Rican	4,810	1.64
South American	5,752	1.96
Argentinean	441	0.15
Bolivian	110	0.04
Chilean	569	0.19

*Notes: † The Census 2010 population figure is used to calculate the percentages in the Hispanic Origin and Race categories. Ancestry percentages are based on the 2006-2010 American Community Survey population (not shown); ‡ Numbers in parentheses indicate the number of people reporting a single ancestry; * Numbers in parentheses indicate the number of persons reporting this race alone, not in combination with any other race; Please refer to the Explanation of Data for more information.*

Colombian	2,035	0.69
Ecuadorian	1,082	0.37
Paraguayan	64	0.02
Peruvian	1,156	0.39
Uruguayan	134	0.05
Venezuelan	129	0.04
Other South American	32	0.01
Other Hispanic or Latino	2,518	0.86

Race*	Population	%
African-American/Black (6,657)	7,671	2.62
Not Hispanic (6,168)	6,908	2.36
Hispanic (489)	763	0.26
American Indian/Alaska Native (442)	1,035	0.35
Not Hispanic (210)	646	0.22
Hispanic (232)	389	0.13
Alaska Athabascan *(Ala. Nat.)* (0)	1	<0.01
Aleut *(Alaska Native)* (1)	1	<0.01
Apache (2)	2	<0.01
Blackfeet (0)	17	0.01
Canadian/French Am. Ind. (4)	6	<0.01
Central American Ind. (13)	16	0.01
Cherokee (6)	86	0.03
Chickasaw (0)	2	<0.01
Chippewa (9)	14	<0.01
Choctaw (2)	5	<0.01
Cree (0)	3	<0.01
Creek (1)	5	<0.01
Crow (0)	1	<0.01
Delaware (3)	6	<0.01
Iroquois (13)	47	0.02
Kiowa (1)	1	<0.01
Mexican American Ind. (26)	34	0.01
Navajo (2)	3	<0.01
Osage (0)	1	<0.01
Potawatomi (1)	2	<0.01
Pueblo (2)	3	<0.01
Shoshone (1)	1	<0.01
Sioux (2)	7	<0.01
South American Ind. (24)	57	0.02
Spanish American Ind. (21)	25	0.01
Asian (26,723)	29,203	9.96
Not Hispanic (26,611)	28,910	9.86
Hispanic (112)	293	0.10
Bangladeshi (331)	365	0.12
Burmese (23)	26	0.01
Cambodian (29)	38	0.01
Chinese, ex. Taiwanese (6,454)	7,054	2.41
Filipino (1,445)	1,803	0.61
Indian (10,593)	11,289	3.85
Indonesian (24)	33	0.01
Japanese (431)	554	0.19
Korean (4,774)	4,977	1.70
Laotian (2)	2	<0.01
Malaysian (21)	30	0.01
Nepalese (48)	49	0.02
Pakistani (1,212)	1,330	0.45
Sri Lankan (39)	59	0.02
Taiwanese (346)	401	0.14
Thai (90)	110	0.04
Vietnamese (165)	237	0.08
Hawaii Native/Pacific Islander (34)	174	0.06
Not Hispanic (24)	124	0.04
Hispanic (10)	50	0.02
Fijian (0)	2	<0.01
Guamanian/Chamorro (7)	15	0.01
Native Hawaiian (9)	29	0.01
Samoan (3)	10	<0.01
Tongan (1)	1	<0.01
White (249,159)	252,713	86.19
Not Hispanic (234,536)	236,944	80.81
Hispanic (14,623)	15,769	5.38

Palmyra

Place Type: Town
County: Wayne
Population: 7,975†

Ancestry‡	Population	%
Albanian (30)	68	0.86
American (447)	447	5.65
Belgian (11)	50	0.63
British (9)	9	0.11
Canadian (61)	82	1.04
Czech (12)	12	0.15
Czechoslovakian (0)	10	0.13
Danish (43)	84	1.06
Dutch (377)	1,132	14.32
English (314)	1,592	20.14
French, ex. Basque (17)	567	7.17
French Canadian (49)	93	1.18
German (719)	2,308	29.20
Greek (11)	11	0.14
Hungarian (0)	59	0.75
Irish (304)	1,434	18.14
Italian (339)	1,026	12.98
Lithuanian (9)	18	0.23
Maltese (0)	58	0.73
Norwegian (29)	40	0.51
Polish (24)	292	3.69
Russian (0)	51	0.65
Scotch-Irish (80)	156	1.97
Scottish (125)	186	2.35
Swedish (9)	35	0.44
Swiss (0)	30	0.38
Ukrainian (35)	85	1.08
Welsh (28)	85	1.08
Yugoslavian (0)	11	0.14

Hispanic Origin	Population	%
Hispanic or Latino (of any race)	110	1.38
Central American, ex. Mexican	9	0.11
Guatemalan	2	0.03
Honduran	2	0.03
Panamanian	2	0.03
Salvadoran	3	0.04
Cuban	3	0.04
Mexican	23	0.29
Puerto Rican	56	0.70
South American	7	0.09
Argentinean	3	0.04
Colombian	2	0.03
Peruvian	2	0.03
Other Hispanic or Latino	12	0.15

Race*	Population	%
African-American/Black (67)	110	1.38
Not Hispanic (62)	102	1.28
Hispanic (5)	8	0.10
American Indian/Alaska Native (30)	65	0.82
Not Hispanic (29)	63	0.79
Hispanic (1)	2	0.03
Blackfeet (0)	1	0.01
Canadian/French Am. Ind. (3)	3	0.04
Cherokee (3)	10	0.13
Chippewa (4)	4	0.05
Choctaw (2)	2	0.03
Comanche (1)	1	0.01
Iroquois (3)	13	0.16
Sioux (1)	2	0.03
Asian (38)	56	0.70
Not Hispanic (38)	53	0.66
Hispanic (0)	3	0.04
Chinese, ex. Taiwanese (5)	5	0.06
Filipino (3)	7	0.09
Indian (1)	7	0.09
Japanese (5)	6	0.08
Korean (6)	13	0.16
Laotian (4)	4	0.05
Vietnamese (14)	14	0.18
Hawaii Native/Pacific Islander (5)	8	0.10
Not Hispanic (5)	8	0.10
Guamanian/Chamorro (1)	1	0.01
Native Hawaiian (0)	2	0.03
Samoan (0)	1	0.01
Tongan (0)	1	0.01
White (7,712)	7,808	97.91
Not Hispanic (7,641)	7,720	96.80
Hispanic (71)	88	1.10

Parma

Place Type: Town
County: Monroe
Population: 15,633†

Ancestry‡	Population	%
Albanian (8)	8	0.05
American (399)	399	2.59
Arab (8)	25	0.16
Lebanese (8)	25	0.16
Armenian (14)	33	0.21
Austrian (0)	34	0.22
Belgian (0)	7	0.05
British (22)	39	0.25
Bulgarian (0)	69	0.45
Canadian (77)	119	0.77
Celtic (30)	30	0.19
Czech (35)	163	1.06
Czechoslovakian (10)	10	0.06
Danish (0)	62	0.40
Dutch (98)	408	2.65
English (770)	3,262	21.16
European (55)	55	0.36
French, ex. Basque (98)	1,016	6.59
French Canadian (9)	226	1.47
German (1,276)	4,795	31.11
Greek (133)	164	1.06
Hungarian (17)	58	0.38
Irish (581)	3,070	19.92
Italian (1,451)	3,409	22.12
Lithuanian (0)	47	0.30
Norwegian (0)	67	0.43
Polish (262)	998	6.47
Portuguese (36)	52	0.34
Russian (121)	170	1.10
Scotch-Irish (36)	135	0.88
Scottish (98)	481	3.12
Slovak (8)	8	0.05
Swedish (63)	141	0.91
Swiss (0)	40	0.26
Ukrainian (174)	259	1.68
Welsh (32)	188	1.22
West Indian, ex. Hispanic (90)	90	0.58
Jamaican (90)	90	0.58

Hispanic Origin	Population	%
Hispanic or Latino (of any race)	310	1.98
Central American, ex. Mexican	9	0.06
Guatemalan	5	0.03
Nicaraguan	2	0.01
Salvadoran	2	0.01
Cuban	13	0.08
Dominican Republic	5	0.03
Mexican	42	0.27
Puerto Rican	178	1.14
South American	28	0.18
Argentinean	6	0.04
Chilean	6	0.04
Colombian	7	0.04
Ecuadorian	5	0.03
Peruvian	4	0.03
Other Hispanic or Latino	35	0.22

Race*	Population	%
African-American/Black (182)	239	1.53
Not Hispanic (179)	229	1.46
Hispanic (3)	10	0.06
American Indian/Alaska Native (29)	90	0.58
Not Hispanic (23)	76	0.49
Hispanic (6)	14	0.09
Cherokee (1)	11	0.07
Chippewa (1)	1	0.01
Iroquois (15)	29	0.19
Mexican American Ind. (4)	4	0.03
Navajo (0)	1	0.01
Potawatomi (3)	3	0.02
Sioux (0)	2	0.01

*Notes: † The Census 2010 population figure is used to calculate the percentages in the Hispanic Origin and Race categories. Ancestry percentages are based on the 2006-2010 American Community Survey population (not shown); ‡ Numbers in parentheses indicate the number of people reporting a single ancestry; * Numbers in parentheses indicate the number of persons reporting this race alone, not in combination with any other race; Please refer to the Explanation of Data for more information.*

Tlingit-Haida *(Alaska Native)* (0)	5	0.03
Asian (76)	136	0.87
Not Hispanic (74)	125	0.80
Hispanic (2)	11	0.07
Burmese (4)	4	0.03
Cambodian (1)	1	0.01
Chinese, ex. Taiwanese (8)	15	0.10
Filipino (10)	20	0.13
Indian (5)	11	0.07
Indonesian (0)	1	0.01
Japanese (2)	21	0.13
Korean (18)	35	0.22
Laotian (6)	6	0.04
Thai (0)	2	0.01
Vietnamese (13)	16	0.10
Hawaii Native/Pacific Islander (1)	12	0.08
Not Hispanic (1)	11	0.07
Hispanic (0)	1	0.01
Guamanian/Chamorro (1)	1	0.01
Native Hawaiian (0)	4	0.03
White (15,107)	15,286	97.78
Not Hispanic (14,889)	15,034	96.17
Hispanic (218)	252	1.61

Patchogue

Place Type: Village
County: Suffolk
Population: 11,798†

Ancestry‡	Population	%
African, Sub-Saharan (114)	123	1.04
African (114)	123	1.04
American (395)	395	3.34
Arab (0)	6	0.05
Egyptian (0)	6	0.05
Armenian (0)	18	0.15
Austrian (18)	33	0.28
British (0)	17	0.14
Canadian (13)	13	0.11
Czech (35)	46	0.39
Danish (0)	45	0.38
Dutch (14)	87	0.74
English (136)	815	6.89
Estonian (14)	14	0.12
Finnish (0)	53	0.45
French, ex. Basque (112)	203	1.72
French Canadian (49)	70	0.59
German (448)	2,120	17.91
Greek (54)	106	0.90
Hungarian (0)	38	0.32
Irish (578)	2,425	20.49
Italian (1,688)	3,505	29.61
Lithuanian (0)	60	0.51
Northern European (13)	13	0.11
Norwegian (31)	168	1.42
Polish (54)	205	1.73
Portuguese (0)	50	0.42
Russian (45)	100	0.84
Scandinavian (17)	51	0.43
Scotch-Irish (37)	114	0.96
Scottish (25)	160	1.35
Slovak (15)	15	0.13
Swedish (0)	57	0.48
Turkish (118)	118	1.00
Ukrainian (14)	14	0.12
Welsh (0)	16	0.14
West Indian, ex. Hispanic (83)	134	1.13
Haitian (47)	47	0.40
Trinidadian/Tobagonian (17)	51	0.43
West Indian (19)	36	0.30

Hispanic Origin	Population	%
Hispanic or Latino (of any race)	3,488	29.56
Central American, ex. Mexican	379	3.21
Costa Rican	1	0.01
Guatemalan	31	0.26
Honduran	34	0.29
Nicaraguan	2	0.02
Panamanian	6	0.05
Salvadoran	302	2.56
Other Central American	3	0.03
Cuban	33	0.28
Dominican Republic	89	0.75
Mexican	84	0.71
Puerto Rican	689	5.84
South American	1,777	15.06
Argentinean	26	0.22
Bolivian	1	0.01
Chilean	4	0.03
Colombian	86	0.73
Ecuadorian	1,616	13.70
Peruvian	24	0.20
Uruguayan	3	0.03
Venezuelan	11	0.09
Other South American	6	0.05
Other Hispanic or Latino	437	3.70

Race*	Population	%
African-American/Black (682)	832	7.05
Not Hispanic (620)	713	6.04
Hispanic (62)	119	1.01
American Indian/Alaska Native (58)	151	1.28
Not Hispanic (31)	88	0.75
Hispanic (27)	63	0.53
Aleut *(Alaska Native)* (0)	1	0.01
Blackfeet (0)	4	0.03
Central American Ind. (3)	3	0.03
Cherokee (2)	8	0.07
Iroquois (0)	3	0.03
Mexican American Ind. (1)	3	0.03
Seminole (0)	4	0.03
South American Ind. (1)	9	0.08
Asian (185)	226	1.92
Not Hispanic (185)	225	1.91
Hispanic (0)	1	0.01
Chinese, ex. Taiwanese (29)	35	0.30
Filipino (41)	53	0.45
Indian (48)	65	0.55
Indonesian (1)	2	0.02
Japanese (3)	4	0.03
Korean (13)	15	0.13
Malaysian (2)	2	0.02
Nepalese (1)	1	0.01
Pakistani (29)	33	0.28
Taiwanese (0)	1	0.01
Thai (3)	4	0.03
Vietnamese (5)	5	0.04
Hawaii Native/Pacific Islander (0)	7	0.06
Not Hispanic (0)	4	0.03
Hispanic (0)	3	0.03
White (8,994)	9,408	79.74
Not Hispanic (7,296)	7,426	62.94
Hispanic (1,698)	1,982	16.80

Patterson

Place Type: Town
County: Putnam
Population: 12,023†

Ancestry‡	Population	%
African, Sub-Saharan (56)	76	0.63
African (56)	56	0.47
Nigerian (0)	20	0.17
Albanian (44)	44	0.37
American (215)	215	1.80
Arab (61)	84	0.70
Jordanian (52)	52	0.43
Lebanese (9)	32	0.27
Austrian (0)	27	0.23
British (37)	53	0.44
Canadian (57)	95	0.79
Croatian (11)	21	0.18
Czech (9)	46	0.38
Czechoslovakian (60)	69	0.58
Danish (69)	88	0.74
Dutch (28)	171	1.43
Eastern European (10)	28	0.23
English (218)	1,124	9.39
European (71)	105	0.88
Finnish (31)	31	0.26
French, ex. Basque (54)	378	3.16
French Canadian (10)	29	0.24
German (273)	1,749	14.61
Greek (29)	94	0.79
Hungarian (65)	300	2.51
Irish (753)	2,558	21.37
Israeli (0)	7	0.06
Italian (1,326)	2,916	24.36
Latvian (3)	10	0.08
Lithuanian (0)	98	0.82
Northern European (63)	63	0.53
Norwegian (11)	190	1.59
Polish (261)	566	4.73
Portuguese (0)	37	0.31
Romanian (0)	7	0.06
Russian (70)	296	2.47
Scandinavian (56)	103	0.86
Scotch-Irish (120)	431	3.60
Scottish (53)	308	2.57
Serbian (0)	13	0.11
Slavic (10)	10	0.08
Slovak (40)	59	0.49
Swedish (0)	95	0.79
Swiss (0)	11	0.09
Ukrainian (0)	90	0.75
Welsh (0)	41	0.34
West Indian, ex. Hispanic (42)	42	0.35
Haitian (28)	28	0.23
Jamaican (14)	14	0.12

Hispanic Origin	Population	%
Hispanic or Latino (of any race)	1,555	12.93
Central American, ex. Mexican	296	2.46
Costa Rican	10	0.08
Guatemalan	211	1.75
Honduran	14	0.12
Nicaraguan	19	0.16
Panamanian	6	0.05
Salvadoran	34	0.28
Other Central American	2	0.02
Cuban	68	0.57
Dominican Republic	71	0.59
Mexican	186	1.55
Puerto Rican	520	4.33
South American	260	2.16
Argentinean	24	0.20
Bolivian	4	0.03
Chilean	18	0.15
Colombian	51	0.42
Ecuadorian	131	1.09
Paraguayan	5	0.04
Peruvian	24	0.20
Uruguayan	2	0.02
Other South American	1	0.01
Other Hispanic or Latino	154	1.28

Race*	Population	%
African-American/Black (530)	629	5.23
Not Hispanic (480)	553	4.60
Hispanic (50)	76	0.63
American Indian/Alaska Native (22)	83	0.69
Not Hispanic (21)	65	0.54
Hispanic (1)	18	0.15
Blackfeet (0)	6	0.05
Canadian/French Am. Ind. (4)	4	0.03
Cherokee (2)	5	0.04
Chippewa (0)	3	0.02
Creek (0)	4	0.03
Iroquois (4)	8	0.07
Mexican American Ind. (0)	6	0.05
Navajo (1)	1	0.01
Seminole (0)	4	0.03
South American Ind. (1)	1	0.01
Asian (217)	289	2.40
Not Hispanic (209)	278	2.31
Hispanic (8)	11	0.09
Bangladeshi (0)	1	0.01
Chinese, ex. Taiwanese (57)	73	0.61

*Notes: † The Census 2010 population figure is used to calculate the percentages in the Hispanic Origin and Race categories. Ancestry percentages are based on the 2006-2010 American Community Survey population (not shown); ‡ Numbers in parentheses indicate the number of people reporting a single ancestry; * Numbers in parentheses indicate the number of persons reporting this race alone, not in combination with any other race; Please refer to the Explanation of Data for more information.*

SECTION TWO

Filipino (28)	36	0.30
Indian (54)	66	0.55
Indonesian (0)	2	0.02
Japanese (21)	34	0.28
Korean (40)	51	0.42
Nepalese (1)	4	0.03
Taiwanese (3)	3	0.02
Thai (1)	1	0.01
Vietnamese (4)	5	0.04
Hawaii Native/Pacific Islander (0)	14	0.12
Not Hispanic (0)	8	0.07
Hispanic (0)	6	0.05
Guamanian/Chamorro (0)	4	0.03
Native Hawaiian (0)	5	0.04
White (10,524)	10,756	89.46
Not Hispanic (9,554)	9,699	80.67
Hispanic (970)	1,057	8.79

Pawling

Place Type: Town
County: Dutchess
Population: 8,463†

Ancestry‡	Population	%
American (91)	91	1.09
Armenian (0)	13	0.16
Australian (0)	13	0.16
Austrian (28)	40	0.48
British (122)	171	2.05
Croatian (12)	24	0.29
Czech (0)	66	0.79
Danish (0)	46	0.55
Dutch (28)	181	2.17
Eastern European (14)	14	0.17
English (161)	685	8.21
European (71)	71	0.85
French, ex. Basque (96)	290	3.47
French Canadian (40)	77	0.92
German (336)	1,713	20.52
Greek (0)	23	0.28
Hungarian (60)	124	1.49
Irish (706)	2,437	29.20
Italian (993)	2,396	28.71
Lithuanian (0)	20	0.24
Norwegian (30)	84	1.01
Polish (69)	375	4.49
Portuguese (16)	58	0.69
Romanian (0)	20	0.24
Russian (44)	117	1.40
Scandinavian (37)	74	0.89
Scotch-Irish (43)	182	2.18
Scottish (37)	175	2.10
Slavic (8)	8	0.10
Swedish (78)	177	2.12
Swiss (69)	79	0.95
Ukrainian (15)	44	0.53
Welsh (0)	44	0.53
West Indian, ex. Hispanic (16)	16	0.19
Jamaican (16)	16	0.19

Hispanic Origin	Population	%
Hispanic or Latino (of any race)	865	10.22
Central American, ex. Mexican	168	1.99
Guatemalan	129	1.52
Honduran	11	0.13
Nicaraguan	1	0.01
Panamanian	1	0.01
Salvadoran	21	0.25
Other Central American	5	0.06
Cuban	17	0.20
Dominican Republic	31	0.37
Mexican	183	2.16
Puerto Rican	244	2.88
South American	139	1.64
Argentinean	3	0.04
Bolivian	3	0.04
Colombian	22	0.26
Ecuadorian	57	0.67
Paraguayan	6	0.07
Peruvian	38	0.45
Uruguayan	5	0.06
Venezuelan	4	0.05
Other South American	1	0.01
Other Hispanic or Latino	83	0.98

Race*	Population	%
African-American/Black (233)	278	3.28
Not Hispanic (211)	239	2.82
Hispanic (22)	39	0.46
American Indian/Alaska Native (32)	51	0.60
Not Hispanic (8)	23	0.27
Hispanic (24)	28	0.33
Central American Ind. (0)	1	0.01
Cherokee (1)	5	0.06
Delaware (1)	2	0.02
Lumbee (1)	1	0.01
Mexican American Ind. (6)	6	0.07
Paiute (0)	1	0.01
South American Ind. (0)	2	0.02
Asian (193)	234	2.76
Not Hispanic (183)	222	2.62
Hispanic (10)	12	0.14
Cambodian (0)	3	0.04
Chinese, ex. Taiwanese (86)	97	1.15
Filipino (11)	20	0.24
Indian (29)	37	0.44
Indonesian (1)	1	0.01
Japanese (9)	9	0.11
Korean (42)	51	0.60
Laotian (1)	1	0.01
Malaysian (4)	7	0.08
Pakistani (1)	1	0.01
Sri Lankan (1)	1	0.01
Taiwanese (1)	1	0.01
Thai (4)	5	0.06
Vietnamese (1)	3	0.04
Hawaii Native/Pacific Islander (5)	12	0.14
Not Hispanic (3)	9	0.11
Hispanic (2)	3	0.04
Guamanian/Chamorro (0)	1	0.01
Native Hawaiian (1)	2	0.02
Samoan (1)	1	0.01
Tongan (1)	4	0.05
White (7,507)	7,640	90.28
Not Hispanic (7,102)	7,177	84.80
Hispanic (405)	463	5.47

Pearl River

Place Type: CDP
County: Rockland
Population: 15,876†

Ancestry‡	Population	%
Albanian (120)	120	0.82
American (240)	240	1.65
Arab (68)	68	0.47
Jordanian (68)	68	0.47
Armenian (0)	12	0.08
Australian (0)	12	0.08
Austrian (0)	105	0.72
Belgian (0)	34	0.23
Brazilian (10)	10	0.07
British (18)	50	0.34
Canadian (0)	63	0.43
Czech (0)	44	0.30
Danish (11)	34	0.23
Dutch (57)	212	1.45
English (262)	856	5.87
European (92)	92	0.63
French, ex. Basque (31)	272	1.87
French Canadian (49)	49	0.34
German (293)	1,633	11.20
Greek (54)	129	0.88
Hungarian (32)	152	1.04
Iranian (0)	12	0.08
Irish (4,729)	7,647	52.46
Italian (1,093)	2,893	19.84
Latvian (10)	10	0.07
Lithuanian (27)	115	0.79
Polish (142)	508	3.48
Portuguese (62)	127	0.87
Romanian (0)	8	0.05
Russian (9)	76	0.52
Scotch-Irish (85)	184	1.26
Scottish (51)	113	0.78
Slavic (0)	50	0.34
Slovak (0)	30	0.21
Swedish (18)	107	0.73
Swiss (0)	26	0.18
Turkish (8)	38	0.26
Ukrainian (62)	227	1.56
Welsh (0)	10	0.07
West Indian, ex. Hispanic (17)	27	0.19
Jamaican (0)	10	0.07
Trinidadian/Tobagonian (17)	17	0.12
Yugoslavian (0)	10	0.07

Hispanic Origin	Population	%
Hispanic or Latino (of any race)	1,107	6.97
Central American, ex. Mexican	156	0.98
Costa Rican	2	0.01
Guatemalan	21	0.13
Honduran	15	0.09
Nicaraguan	4	0.03
Salvadoran	114	0.72
Cuban	56	0.35
Dominican Republic	68	0.43
Mexican	206	1.30
Puerto Rican	297	1.87
South American	228	1.44
Argentinean	13	0.08
Bolivian	2	0.01
Chilean	8	0.05
Colombian	54	0.34
Ecuadorian	129	0.81
Peruvian	11	0.07
Venezuelan	9	0.06
Other South American	2	0.01
Other Hispanic or Latino	96	0.60

Race*	Population	%
African-American/Black (122)	170	1.07
Not Hispanic (94)	137	0.86
Hispanic (28)	33	0.21
American Indian/Alaska Native (27)	47	0.30
Not Hispanic (23)	41	0.26
Hispanic (4)	6	0.04
Central American Ind. (1)	1	0.01
Cherokee (0)	3	0.02
Choctaw (1)	1	0.01
Delaware (0)	2	0.01
Iroquois (5)	7	0.04
Asian (607)	683	4.30
Not Hispanic (605)	678	4.27
Hispanic (2)	5	0.03
Bangladeshi (4)	4	0.03
Burmese (3)	3	0.02
Chinese, ex. Taiwanese (182)	196	1.23
Filipino (100)	122	0.77
Indian (134)	154	0.97
Indonesian (0)	1	0.01
Japanese (24)	32	0.20
Korean (95)	104	0.66
Laotian (3)	3	0.02
Pakistani (24)	26	0.16
Thai (11)	16	0.10
Vietnamese (10)	10	0.06
Hawaii Native/Pacific Islander (12)	20	0.13
Not Hispanic (11)	16	0.10
Hispanic (1)	4	0.03
Native Hawaiian (1)	2	0.01
Samoan (5)	5	0.03
White (14,696)	14,848	93.52
Not Hispanic (13,891)	14,009	88.24
Hispanic (805)	839	5.28

*Notes: † The Census 2010 population figure is used to calculate the percentages in the Hispanic Origin and Race categories. Ancestry percentages are based on the 2006-2010 American Community Survey population (not shown); ‡ Numbers in parentheses indicate the number of people reporting a single ancestry; * Numbers in parentheses indicate the number of persons reporting this race alone, not in combination with any other race; Please refer to the Explanation of Data for more information.*

Peekskill

Place Type: City
County: Westchester
Population: 23,583†

Ancestry‡	Population	%
African, Sub-Saharan (169)	203	0.87
African (59)	59	0.25
Ghanaian (36)	36	0.16
Kenyan (24)	24	0.10
Nigerian (35)	69	0.30
Other Sub-Saharan African (15)	15	0.06
Albanian (74)	74	0.32
American (622)	622	2.68
Arab (50)	50	0.22
Egyptian (28)	28	0.12
Lebanese (12)	12	0.05
Moroccan (10)	10	0.04
Armenian (10)	10	0.04
Assyrian/Chaldean/Syriac (26)	26	0.11
Austrian (3)	88	0.38
Belgian (14)	22	0.09
British (11)	32	0.14
Bulgarian (15)	15	0.06
Canadian (0)	20	0.09
Croatian (19)	30	0.13
Czech (21)	78	0.34
Czechoslovakian (4)	27	0.12
Dutch (28)	196	0.84
Eastern European (73)	73	0.31
English (152)	866	3.73
European (133)	173	0.75
Finnish (37)	37	0.16
French, ex. Basque (0)	234	1.01
French Canadian (37)	52	0.22
German (195)	1,187	5.11
Greek (32)	104	0.45
Guyanese (144)	144	0.62
Hungarian (54)	194	0.84
Irish (526)	2,486	10.71
Italian (1,569)	3,290	14.17
Latvian (12)	12	0.05
Lithuanian (0)	36	0.16
Maltese (0)	21	0.09
Northern European (26)	26	0.11
Norwegian (0)	11	0.05
Polish (137)	569	2.45
Portuguese (135)	186	0.80
Romanian (97)	106	0.46
Russian (34)	279	1.20
Scotch-Irish (52)	103	0.44
Scottish (8)	94	0.40
Slovak (14)	40	0.17
Swedish (9)	23	0.10
Swiss (14)	14	0.06
Ukrainian (13)	170	0.73
Welsh (13)	69	0.30
West Indian, ex. Hispanic (1,043)	1,169	5.03
Bahamian (28)	28	0.12
British West Indian (15)	15	0.06
Haitian (220)	230	0.99
Jamaican (724)	821	3.54
Trinidadian/Tobagonian (7)	7	0.03
West Indian (49)	68	0.29
Yugoslavian (28)	39	0.17

Hispanic Origin	Population	%
Hispanic or Latino (of any race)	8,713	36.95
Central American, ex. Mexican	1,250	5.30
Costa Rican	14	0.06
Guatemalan	882	3.74
Honduran	130	0.55
Nicaraguan	26	0.11
Panamanian	14	0.06
Salvadoran	167	0.71
Other Central American	17	0.07
Cuban	62	0.26
Dominican Republic	456	1.93
Mexican	354	1.50
Puerto Rican	1,620	6.87
South American	4,041	17.14
Argentinean	32	0.14
Bolivian	5	0.02
Chilean	36	0.15
Colombian	150	0.64
Ecuadorian	3,490	14.80
Paraguayan	3	0.01
Peruvian	196	0.83
Uruguayan	92	0.39
Venezuelan	19	0.08
Other South American	18	0.08
Other Hispanic or Latino	930	3.94

Race*	Population	%
African-American/Black (5,576)	6,261	26.55
Not Hispanic (5,052)	5,482	23.25
Hispanic (524)	779	3.30
American Indian/Alaska Native (132)	346	1.47
Not Hispanic (43)	168	0.71
Hispanic (89)	178	0.75
Apache (0)	2	0.01
Arapaho (0)	2	0.01
Blackfeet (3)	10	0.04
Canadian/French Am. Ind. (1)	1	<0.01
Cherokee (11)	57	0.24
Cheyenne (1)	1	<0.01
Crow (0)	1	<0.01
Iroquois (5)	8	0.03
Mexican American Ind. (1)	4	0.02
Navajo (0)	8	0.03
Osage (1)	2	0.01
Potawatomi (0)	1	<0.01
Pueblo (0)	1	<0.01
Seminole (1)	2	0.01
Sioux (0)	8	0.03
South American Ind. (11)	24	0.10
Spanish American Ind. (1)	1	<0.01
Asian (716)	901	3.82
Not Hispanic (682)	822	3.49
Hispanic (34)	79	0.33
Burmese (4)	4	0.02
Cambodian (3)	6	0.03
Chinese, ex. Taiwanese (128)	164	0.70
Filipino (103)	129	0.55
Indian (260)	306	1.30
Indonesian (1)	1	<0.01
Japanese (20)	39	0.17
Korean (34)	56	0.24
Laotian (14)	28	0.12
Malaysian (1)	3	0.01
Nepalese (9)	9	0.04
Pakistani (26)	29	0.12
Sri Lankan (4)	4	0.02
Taiwanese (1)	6	0.03
Thai (5)	25	0.11
Vietnamese (43)	45	0.19
Hawaii Native/Pacific Islander (18)	37	0.16
Not Hispanic (5)	13	0.06
Hispanic (13)	24	0.10
Guamanian/Chamorro (10)	11	0.05
Native Hawaiian (3)	5	0.02
Samoan (1)	1	<0.01
White (12,099)	13,241	56.15
Not Hispanic (8,439)	8,913	37.79
Hispanic (3,660)	4,328	18.35

Pelham

Place Type: Town
County: Westchester
Population: 12,396†

Ancestry‡	Population	%
African, Sub-Saharan (111)	141	1.15
African (0)	9	0.07
Nigerian (13)	13	0.11
South African (43)	43	0.35
Other Sub-Saharan African (55)	76	0.62
Albanian (26)	45	0.37
American (662)	662	5.42
Arab (14)	14	0.11
Moroccan (14)	14	0.11
Armenian (0)	6	0.05
Australian (35)	35	0.29
Austrian (17)	133	1.09
Belgian (0)	9	0.07
Brazilian (73)	84	0.69
British (27)	80	0.65
Bulgarian (0)	16	0.13
Canadian (32)	42	0.34
Croatian (9)	32	0.26
Czech (12)	75	0.61
Danish (0)	17	0.14
Dutch (22)	121	0.99
Eastern European (186)	195	1.60
English (188)	1,069	8.74
Estonian (18)	18	0.15
European (125)	125	1.02
Finnish (0)	22	0.18
French, ex. Basque (69)	341	2.79
French Canadian (25)	269	2.20
German (339)	1,549	12.67
Greek (25)	62	0.51
Hungarian (9)	136	1.11
Irish (898)	2,332	19.08
Israeli (15)	15	0.12
Italian (2,137)	3,356	27.45
Latvian (0)	9	0.07
Lithuanian (0)	46	0.38
Macedonian (0)	19	0.16
Northern European (62)	62	0.51
Norwegian (21)	165	1.35
Pennsylvania German (12)	12	0.10
Polish (65)	455	3.72
Portuguese (17)	25	0.20
Romanian (0)	6	0.05
Russian (131)	382	3.12
Scotch-Irish (60)	182	1.49
Scottish (167)	408	3.34
Slavic (0)	20	0.16
Swedish (9)	48	0.39
Swiss (0)	26	0.21
Turkish (22)	22	0.18
Ukrainian (10)	27	0.22
Welsh (12)	130	1.06
West Indian, ex. Hispanic (65)	86	0.70
British West Indian (12)	12	0.10
Haitian (10)	10	0.08
Jamaican (43)	64	0.52

Hispanic Origin	Population	%
Hispanic or Latino (of any race)	1,243	10.03
Central American, ex. Mexican	99	0.80
Costa Rican	15	0.12
Guatemalan	33	0.27
Honduran	20	0.16
Nicaraguan	4	0.03
Panamanian	1	0.01
Salvadoran	26	0.21
Cuban	74	0.60
Dominican Republic	63	0.51
Mexican	164	1.32
Puerto Rican	471	3.80
South American	255	2.06
Argentinean	31	0.25
Bolivian	10	0.08
Chilean	10	0.08
Colombian	75	0.61
Ecuadorian	23	0.19
Paraguayan	3	0.02
Peruvian	80	0.65
Uruguayan	6	0.05
Venezuelan	15	0.12
Other South American	2	0.02
Other Hispanic or Latino	117	0.94

Race*	Population	%
African-American/Black (771)	904	7.29
Not Hispanic (729)	829	6.69

SECTION TWO

*Notes: † The Census 2010 population figure is used to calculate the percentages in the Hispanic Origin and Race categories. Ancestry percentages are based on the 2006-2010 American Community Survey population (not shown); ‡ Numbers in parentheses indicate the number of people reporting a single ancestry; * Numbers in parentheses indicate the number of persons reporting this race alone, not in combination with any other race; Please refer to the Explanation of Data for more information.*

Hispanic (42)	75	0.61
American Indian/Alaska Native (6)	42	0.34
Not Hispanic (5)	27	0.22
Hispanic (1)	15	0.12
Blackfeet (0)	4	0.03
Cherokee (3)	10	0.08
Cree (0)	1	0.01
Iroquois (2)	2	0.02
Mexican American Ind. (1)	1	0.01
South American Ind. (0)	8	0.06
Spanish American Ind. (0)	1	0.01
Asian (654)	859	6.93
Not Hispanic (642)	815	6.57
Hispanic (12)	44	0.35
Bangladeshi (13)	13	0.10
Burmese (6)	9	0.07
Cambodian (9)	10	0.08
Chinese, ex. Taiwanese (158)	219	1.77
Filipino (61)	88	0.71
Indian (239)	285	2.30
Indonesian (4)	6	0.05
Japanese (21)	49	0.40
Korean (68)	90	0.73
Pakistani (20)	23	0.19
Sri Lankan (6)	6	0.05
Taiwanese (4)	9	0.07
Thai (11)	17	0.14
Vietnamese (4)	4	0.03
Hawaii Native/Pacific Islander (9)	18	0.15
Not Hispanic (1)	6	0.05
Hispanic (8)	12	0.10
Fijian (1)	2	0.02
Guamanian/Chamorro (8)	9	0.07
Samoan (0)	1	0.01
White (10,226)	10,537	85.00
Not Hispanic (9,457)	9,665	77.97
Hispanic (769)	872	7.03

Penfield

Place Type: Town
County: Monroe
Population: 36,242†

Ancestry‡	Population	%
Afghan (177)	177	0.49
African, Sub-Saharan (63)	131	0.37
African (0)	50	0.14
Nigerian (22)	40	0.11
South African (41)	41	0.11
American (1,213)	1,213	3.38
Arab (23)	198	0.55
Arab (0)	24	0.07
Egyptian (23)	23	0.06
Lebanese (0)	111	0.31
Syrian (0)	40	0.11
Armenian (0)	40	0.11
Australian (73)	73	0.20
Austrian (29)	87	0.24
Belgian (0)	80	0.22
Brazilian (32)	32	0.09
British (65)	131	0.37
Canadian (77)	182	0.51
Czech (29)	129	0.36
Czechoslovakian (25)	40	0.11
Danish (27)	178	0.50
Dutch (236)	1,147	3.20
Eastern European (14)	14	0.04
English (1,819)	5,857	16.33
Estonian (16)	39	0.11
European (409)	434	1.21
Finnish (9)	81	0.23
French, ex. Basque (136)	1,413	3.94
French Canadian (212)	553	1.54
German (2,510)	9,242	25.77
Greek (116)	125	0.35
Hungarian (58)	190	0.53
Iranian (13)	13	0.04
Irish (1,093)	6,765	18.86
Italian (4,467)	8,730	24.34
Latvian (9)	9	0.03
Lithuanian (15)	66	0.18
Macedonian (12)	37	0.10
Northern European (0)	23	0.06
Norwegian (27)	146	0.41
Polish (822)	2,833	7.90
Portuguese (0)	134	0.37
Romanian (48)	78	0.22
Russian (397)	681	1.90
Scotch-Irish (156)	403	1.12
Scottish (228)	961	2.68
Serbian (12)	30	0.08
Slavic (0)	51	0.14
Slovak (15)	64	0.18
Swedish (48)	195	0.54
Swiss (10)	145	0.40
Turkish (83)	135	0.38
Ukrainian (588)	765	2.13
Welsh (70)	431	1.20
West Indian, ex. Hispanic (74)	131	0.37
Jamaican (16)	34	0.09
West Indian (58)	97	0.27
Yugoslavian (54)	54	0.15

Hispanic Origin	Population	%
Hispanic or Latino (of any race)	913	2.52
Central American, ex. Mexican	52	0.14
Costa Rican	1	<0.01
Guatemalan	28	0.08
Honduran	6	0.02
Nicaraguan	5	0.01
Panamanian	7	0.02
Salvadoran	5	0.01
Cuban	58	0.16
Dominican Republic	21	0.06
Mexican	143	0.39
Puerto Rican	384	1.06
South American	170	0.47
Argentinean	18	0.05
Bolivian	4	0.01
Chilean	14	0.04
Colombian	52	0.14
Ecuadorian	25	0.07
Paraguayan	3	0.01
Peruvian	30	0.08
Venezuelan	19	0.05
Other South American	5	0.01
Other Hispanic or Latino	85	0.23

Race*	Population	%
African-American/Black (779)	983	2.71
Not Hispanic (749)	928	2.56
Hispanic (30)	55	0.15
American Indian/Alaska Native (53)	170	0.47
Not Hispanic (41)	127	0.35
Hispanic (12)	43	0.12
Apache (1)	1	<0.01
Canadian/French Am. Ind. (2)	2	0.01
Central American Ind. (0)	2	0.01
Cherokee (1)	15	0.04
Chickasaw (4)	4	0.01
Chippewa (2)	2	0.01
Creek (0)	2	0.01
Iroquois (19)	40	0.11
Mexican American Ind. (2)	5	0.01
Navajo (0)	1	<0.01
Osage (0)	1	<0.01
Paiute (0)	1	<0.01
Seminole (0)	2	0.01
Sioux (1)	2	0.01
South American Ind. (2)	11	0.03
Spanish American Ind. (1)	1	<0.01
Asian (1,133)	1,361	3.76
Not Hispanic (1,128)	1,347	3.72
Hispanic (5)	14	0.04
Cambodian (6)	17	0.05
Chinese, ex. Taiwanese (374)	433	1.19
Filipino (37)	63	0.17
Indian (266)	312	0.86
Indonesian (0)	7	0.02
Japanese (23)	43	0.12
Korean (134)	169	0.47
Laotian (48)	57	0.16
Malaysian (1)	1	<0.01
Nepalese (32)	32	0.09
Pakistani (44)	45	0.12
Sri Lankan (13)	18	0.05
Taiwanese (24)	30	0.08
Thai (9)	15	0.04
Vietnamese (82)	107	0.30
Hawaii Native/Pacific Islander (7)	22	0.06
Not Hispanic (5)	18	0.05
Hispanic (2)	4	0.01
Guamanian/Chamorro (3)	3	0.01
Native Hawaiian (1)	1	<0.01
Samoan (1)	1	<0.01
White (33,573)	34,056	93.97
Not Hispanic (32,916)	33,340	91.99
Hispanic (657)	716	1.98

Perinton

Place Type: Town
County: Monroe
Population: 46,462†

Ancestry‡	Population	%
Afghan (87)	87	0.19
African, Sub-Saharan (86)	86	0.19
Ethiopian (10)	10	0.02
Nigerian (38)	38	0.08
Somalian (38)	38	0.08
American (1,416)	1,416	3.06
Arab (78)	98	0.21
Egyptian (29)	29	0.06
Lebanese (49)	60	0.13
Syrian (0)	9	0.02
Armenian (36)	87	0.19
Austrian (63)	195	0.42
Belgian (52)	89	0.19
British (193)	416	0.90
Bulgarian (0)	14	0.03
Canadian (85)	200	0.43
Croatian (20)	20	0.04
Czech (8)	130	0.28
Czechoslovakian (0)	11	0.02
Danish (26)	238	0.51
Dutch (335)	1,800	3.89
Eastern European (75)	110	0.24
English (2,088)	8,261	17.86
European (574)	714	1.54
Finnish (0)	37	0.08
French, ex. Basque (256)	1,755	3.80
French Canadian (242)	504	1.09
German (2,722)	11,808	25.53
Greek (192)	297	0.64
Hungarian (0)	175	0.38
Iranian (52)	52	0.11
Irish (2,847)	9,871	21.35
Italian (5,335)	10,378	22.44
Latvian (60)	77	0.17
Lithuanian (83)	220	0.48
Macedonian (29)	41	0.09
Northern European (36)	36	0.08
Norwegian (38)	345	0.75
Pennsylvania German (24)	24	0.05
Polish (1,061)	3,006	6.50
Portuguese (12)	21	0.05
Romanian (13)	25	0.05
Russian (390)	810	1.75
Scandinavian (13)	35	0.08
Scotch-Irish (192)	806	1.74
Scottish (374)	1,615	3.49
Serbian (10)	39	0.08
Slavic (15)	46	0.10
Slovak (49)	71	0.15
Swedish (169)	758	1.64
Swiss (16)	218	0.47
Turkish (143)	143	0.31
Ukrainian (132)	387	0.84

*Notes: † The Census 2010 population figure is used to calculate the percentages in the Hispanic Origin and Race categories. Ancestry percentages are based on the 2006-2010 American Community Survey population (not shown); ‡ Numbers in parentheses indicate the number of people reporting a single ancestry; * Numbers in parentheses indicate the number of persons reporting this race alone, not in combination with any other race; Please refer to the Explanation of Data for more information.*

Ancestry (continued)	Population	%
Welsh (101)	506	1.09
West Indian, ex. Hispanic (105)	105	0.23
Haitian (79)	79	0.17
Jamaican (26)	26	0.06
Yugoslavian (0)	43	0.09

Hispanic Origin	Population	%
Hispanic or Latino (of any race)	996	2.14
Central American, ex. Mexican	58	0.12
Costa Rican	2	<0.01
Guatemalan	15	0.03
Honduran	7	0.02
Nicaraguan	11	0.02
Panamanian	11	0.02
Salvadoran	12	0.03
Cuban	78	0.17
Dominican Republic	40	0.09
Mexican	164	0.35
Puerto Rican	387	0.83
South American	137	0.29
Argentinean	17	0.04
Bolivian	6	0.01
Chilean	11	0.02
Colombian	49	0.11
Ecuadorian	10	0.02
Paraguayan	6	0.01
Peruvian	24	0.05
Venezuelan	13	0.03
Other South American	1	<0.01
Other Hispanic or Latino	132	0.28

Race*	Population	%
African-American/Black (944)	1,193	2.57
Not Hispanic (908)	1,123	2.42
Hispanic (36)	70	0.15
American Indian/Alaska Native (52)	172	0.37
Not Hispanic (43)	145	0.31
Hispanic (9)	27	0.06
Blackfeet (0)	4	0.01
Central American Ind. (1)	1	<0.01
Cherokee (1)	26	0.06
Chickasaw (0)	1	<0.01
Chippewa (0)	1	<0.01
Choctaw (0)	1	<0.01
Crow (1)	1	<0.01
Iroquois (14)	38	0.08
Mexican American Ind. (2)	4	0.01
Potawatomi (1)	3	0.01
Sioux (0)	1	<0.01
South American Ind. (3)	7	0.02
Tlingit-Haida *(Alaska Native)* (1)	1	<0.01
Asian (1,351)	1,654	3.56
Not Hispanic (1,346)	1,638	3.53
Hispanic (5)	16	0.03
Bangladeshi (5)	7	0.02
Cambodian (5)	5	0.01
Chinese, ex. Taiwanese (344)	405	0.87
Filipino (46)	98	0.21
Indian (379)	441	0.95
Indonesian (0)	3	0.01
Japanese (45)	90	0.19
Korean (164)	214	0.46
Laotian (50)	57	0.12
Malaysian (4)	4	0.01
Nepalese (16)	18	0.04
Pakistani (38)	44	0.09
Sri Lankan (5)	7	0.02
Taiwanese (17)	28	0.06
Thai (6)	14	0.03
Vietnamese (139)	174	0.37
Hawaii Native/Pacific Islander (14)	26	0.06
Not Hispanic (11)	20	0.04
Hispanic (3)	6	0.01
Fijian (0)	2	<0.01
Guamanian/Chamorro (6)	6	0.01
Native Hawaiian (1)	9	0.02
White (43,226)	43,852	94.38
Not Hispanic (42,544)	43,085	92.73
Hispanic (682)	767	1.65

Philipstown

Place Type: Town
County: Putnam
Population: 9,662†

Ancestry‡	Population	%
African, Sub-Saharan (0)	16	0.17
South African (0)	16	0.17
American (252)	252	2.61
Arab (82)	111	1.15
Egyptian (82)	96	0.99
Lebanese (0)	8	0.08
Other Arab (0)	7	0.07
Austrian (9)	56	0.58
Belgian (9)	71	0.73
Brazilian (12)	34	0.35
British (4)	9	0.09
Canadian (18)	24	0.25
Czech (0)	45	0.47
Czechoslovakian (0)	6	0.06
Danish (20)	73	0.75
Dutch (74)	305	3.15
Eastern European (50)	50	0.52
English (214)	1,166	12.06
Estonian (0)	10	0.10
European (115)	137	1.42
Finnish (18)	66	0.68
French, ex. Basque (13)	415	4.29
French Canadian (12)	23	0.24
German (297)	1,699	17.57
Greek (49)	89	0.92
Hungarian (44)	116	1.20
Iranian (125)	125	1.29
Irish (1,106)	3,569	36.91
Italian (1,088)	2,180	22.55
Latvian (6)	6	0.06
Lithuanian (0)	15	0.16
Norwegian (14)	67	0.69
Polish (91)	456	4.72
Portuguese (37)	50	0.52
Romanian (5)	9	0.09
Russian (71)	228	2.36
Scotch-Irish (71)	166	1.72
Scottish (66)	310	3.21
Slavic (0)	6	0.06
Slovak (13)	24	0.25
Slovene (0)	5	0.05
Swedish (15)	79	0.82
Swiss (5)	26	0.27
Ukrainian (28)	62	0.64
Welsh (0)	33	0.34
West Indian, ex. Hispanic (22)	31	0.32
Jamaican (22)	22	0.23
West Indian (0)	9	0.09
Yugoslavian (0)	7	0.07

Hispanic Origin	Population	%
Hispanic or Latino (of any race)	671	6.94
Central American, ex. Mexican	34	0.35
Costa Rican	6	0.06
Guatemalan	11	0.11
Honduran	5	0.05
Nicaraguan	2	0.02
Panamanian	1	0.01
Salvadoran	9	0.09
Cuban	29	0.30
Dominican Republic	44	0.46
Mexican	54	0.56
Puerto Rican	274	2.84
South American	169	1.75
Argentinean	10	0.10
Bolivian	7	0.07
Chilean	15	0.16
Colombian	31	0.32
Ecuadorian	65	0.67
Paraguayan	10	0.10
Peruvian	12	0.12
Uruguayan	10	0.10
Venezuelan	2	0.02
Other South American	7	0.07
Other Hispanic or Latino	67	0.69

Race*	Population	%
African-American/Black (158)	209	2.16
Not Hispanic (148)	189	1.96
Hispanic (10)	20	0.21
American Indian/Alaska Native (19)	70	0.72
Not Hispanic (16)	63	0.65
Hispanic (3)	7	0.07
Arapaho (2)	2	0.02
Blackfeet (0)	2	0.02
Central American Ind. (1)	2	0.02
Cherokee (1)	13	0.13
Iroquois (1)	3	0.03
Mexican American Ind. (0)	1	0.01
Potawatomi (0)	1	0.01
Sioux (0)	4	0.04
South American Ind. (2)	4	0.04
Asian (136)	216	2.24
Not Hispanic (134)	204	2.11
Hispanic (2)	12	0.12
Cambodian (1)	1	0.01
Chinese, ex. Taiwanese (41)	69	0.71
Filipino (16)	31	0.32
Indian (34)	48	0.50
Japanese (19)	32	0.33
Korean (12)	16	0.17
Malaysian (1)	2	0.02
Pakistani (2)	4	0.04
Taiwanese (2)	3	0.03
Vietnamese (2)	5	0.05
Hawaii Native/Pacific Islander (7)	18	0.19
Not Hispanic (5)	13	0.13
Hispanic (2)	5	0.05
Guamanian/Chamorro (1)	1	0.01
Native Hawaiian (2)	5	0.05
White (8,993)	9,171	94.92
Not Hispanic (8,522)	8,664	89.67
Hispanic (471)	507	5.25

Pittsford

Place Type: Town
County: Monroe
Population: 29,405†

Ancestry‡	Population	%
Afghan (153)	153	0.53
African, Sub-Saharan (108)	148	0.51
African (19)	19	0.07
Liberian (0)	20	0.07
Nigerian (63)	63	0.22
Senegalese (26)	26	0.09
Other Sub-Saharan African (0)	20	0.07
Albanian (11)	11	0.04
Alsatian (3)	12	0.04
American (1,060)	1,060	3.65
Arab (293)	377	1.30
Arab (31)	44	0.15
Egyptian (126)	126	0.43
Iraqi (75)	75	0.26
Lebanese (9)	80	0.28
Syrian (52)	52	0.18
Armenian (12)	64	0.22
Australian (14)	14	0.05
Austrian (49)	184	0.63
Basque (13)	13	0.04
Belgian (25)	62	0.21
British (263)	425	1.46
Bulgarian (25)	25	0.09
Canadian (70)	153	0.53
Croatian (0)	40	0.14
Czech (31)	95	0.33
Czechoslovakian (9)	34	0.12
Danish (35)	71	0.24
Dutch (151)	731	2.52
Eastern European (240)	240	0.83
English (1,412)	4,964	17.10
Estonian (0)	42	0.14

*Notes: † The Census 2010 population figure is used to calculate the percentages in the Hispanic Origin and Race categories. Ancestry percentages are based on the 2006-2010 American Community Survey population (not shown); ‡ Numbers in parentheses indicate the number of people reporting a single ancestry; * Numbers in parentheses indicate the number of persons reporting this race alone, not in combination with any other race; Please refer to the Explanation of Data for more information.*

European (319)	319	1.10
Finnish (9)	40	0.14
French, ex. Basque (155)	1,074	3.70
French Canadian (40)	158	0.54
German (1,125)	5,825	20.07
Greek (106)	256	0.88
Hungarian (58)	140	0.48
Icelander (63)	63	0.22
Iranian (10)	10	0.03
Irish (1,838)	6,573	22.64
Israeli (54)	146	0.50
Italian (1,769)	4,428	15.25
Latvian (0)	19	0.07
Lithuanian (40)	223	0.77
Northern European (117)	117	0.40
Norwegian (43)	133	0.46
Pennsylvania German (17)	17	0.06
Polish (623)	2,041	7.03
Portuguese (15)	44	0.15
Romanian (39)	97	0.33
Russian (374)	823	2.84
Scandinavian (40)	40	0.14
Scotch-Irish (275)	711	2.45
Scottish (194)	661	2.28
Slavic (0)	29	0.10
Slovak (0)	16	0.06
Slovene (0)	38	0.13
Swedish (88)	359	1.24
Swiss (71)	159	0.55
Turkish (11)	77	0.27
Ukrainian (68)	241	0.83
Welsh (51)	217	0.75
West Indian, ex. Hispanic (63)	66	0.23
Haitian (32)	32	0.11
Jamaican (31)	31	0.11
West Indian (0)	3	0.01
Yugoslavian (0)	62	0.21

Hispanic Origin	Population	%
Hispanic or Latino (of any race)	668	2.27
Central American, ex. Mexican	61	0.21
Costa Rican	7	0.02
Guatemalan	21	0.07
Honduran	3	0.01
Nicaraguan	10	0.03
Panamanian	10	0.03
Salvadoran	10	0.03
Cuban	57	0.19
Dominican Republic	26	0.09
Mexican	115	0.39
Puerto Rican	212	0.72
South American	124	0.42
Argentinean	13	0.04
Bolivian	3	0.01
Chilean	11	0.04
Colombian	41	0.14
Ecuadorian	14	0.05
Paraguayan	4	0.01
Peruvian	24	0.08
Uruguayan	6	0.02
Venezuelan	5	0.02
Other South American	3	0.01
Other Hispanic or Latino	73	0.25

Race*	Population	%
African-American/Black (505)	639	2.17
Not Hispanic (480)	602	2.05
Hispanic (25)	37	0.13
American Indian/Alaska Native (37)	112	0.38
Not Hispanic (29)	88	0.30
Hispanic (8)	24	0.08
Apache (0)	1	<0.01
Blackfeet (0)	1	<0.01
Canadian/French Am. Ind. (1)	3	0.01
Cherokee (5)	14	0.05
Chickasaw (0)	1	<0.01
Choctaw (0)	1	<0.01
Iroquois (12)	24	0.08
Mexican American Ind. (3)	6	0.02
Potawatomi (2)	2	0.01
Seminole (0)	2	0.01
Sioux (7)	7	0.02
South American Ind. (0)	1	<0.01
Asian (1,996)	2,256	7.67
Not Hispanic (1,987)	2,241	7.62
Hispanic (9)	15	0.05
Bangladeshi (6)	6	0.02
Cambodian (3)	4	0.01
Chinese, ex. Taiwanese (563)	631	2.15
Filipino (34)	58	0.20
Indian (807)	885	3.01
Indonesian (2)	5	0.02
Japanese (25)	57	0.19
Korean (181)	224	0.76
Laotian (1)	2	0.01
Malaysian (1)	2	0.01
Nepalese (4)	4	0.01
Pakistani (214)	226	0.77
Sri Lankan (20)	21	0.07
Taiwanese (54)	64	0.22
Thai (2)	4	0.01
Vietnamese (30)	33	0.11
Hawaii Native/Pacific Islander (0)	13	0.04
Not Hispanic (0)	10	0.03
Hispanic (0)	3	0.01
Native Hawaiian (0)	2	0.01
White (26,271)	26,665	90.68
Not Hispanic (25,799)	26,161	88.97
Hispanic (472)	504	1.71

Plainedge

Place Type: CDP
County: Nassau
Population: 8,817†

Ancestry‡	Population	%
African, Sub-Saharan (37)	37	0.40
African (37)	37	0.40
American (167)	167	1.81
Armenian (152)	191	2.07
Austrian (14)	131	1.42
British (8)	8	0.09
Czech (0)	122	1.32
Czechoslovakian (0)	9	0.10
Danish (0)	13	0.14
Eastern European (14)	14	0.15
English (88)	330	3.57
European (25)	25	0.27
French, ex. Basque (15)	115	1.24
German (226)	1,826	19.75
Greek (34)	70	0.76
Hungarian (24)	95	1.03
Icelander (24)	24	0.26
Irish (595)	2,464	26.65
Italian (1,847)	3,490	37.75
Maltese (0)	11	0.12
Norwegian (64)	186	2.01
Polish (244)	622	6.73
Romanian (0)	27	0.29
Russian (139)	245	2.65
Scandinavian (0)	19	0.21
Scotch-Irish (26)	73	0.79
Scottish (17)	63	0.68
Serbian (12)	36	0.39
Slavic (0)	17	0.18
Slovak (0)	44	0.48
Swedish (31)	87	0.94
Ukrainian (0)	14	0.15
West Indian, ex. Hispanic (13)	13	0.14
West Indian (13)	13	0.14

Hispanic Origin	Population	%
Hispanic or Latino (of any race)	684	7.76
Central American, ex. Mexican	71	0.81
Costa Rican	5	0.06
Guatemalan	8	0.09
Honduran	6	0.07
Nicaraguan	1	0.01
Panamanian	6	0.07
Salvadoran	45	0.51
Cuban	28	0.32
Dominican Republic	51	0.58
Mexican	24	0.27
Puerto Rican	217	2.46
South American	225	2.55
Argentinean	8	0.09
Bolivian	1	0.01
Chilean	11	0.12
Colombian	101	1.15
Ecuadorian	35	0.40
Paraguayan	3	0.03
Peruvian	56	0.64
Uruguayan	9	0.10
Venezuelan	1	0.01
Other Hispanic or Latino	68	0.77

Race*	Population	%
African-American/Black (71)	95	1.08
Not Hispanic (64)	85	0.96
Hispanic (7)	10	0.11
American Indian/Alaska Native (19)	33	0.37
Not Hispanic (6)	18	0.20
Hispanic (13)	15	0.17
Aleut *(Alaska Native)* (1)	1	0.01
Cherokee (0)	3	0.03
Creek (0)	1	0.01
South American Ind. (1)	2	0.02
Asian (401)	454	5.15
Not Hispanic (399)	442	5.01
Hispanic (2)	12	0.14
Chinese, ex. Taiwanese (127)	138	1.57
Filipino (58)	71	0.81
Indian (142)	150	1.70
Indonesian (1)	1	0.01
Japanese (4)	6	0.07
Korean (18)	20	0.23
Malaysian (1)	1	0.01
Pakistani (42)	43	0.49
Taiwanese (2)	2	0.02
Thai (2)	2	0.02
Hawaii Native/Pacific Islander (2)	8	0.09
Not Hispanic (2)	8	0.09
Native Hawaiian (1)	2	0.02
Samoan (1)	1	0.01
White (8,108)	8,166	92.62
Not Hispanic (7,584)	7,620	86.42
Hispanic (524)	546	6.19

Plainview

Place Type: CDP
County: Nassau
Population: 26,217†

Ancestry‡	Population	%
Afghan (85)	85	0.33
African, Sub-Saharan (23)	33	0.13
African (11)	21	0.08
Cape Verdean (12)	12	0.05
Albanian (11)	11	0.04
American (1,295)	1,295	5.02
Arab (8)	63	0.24
Syrian (8)	38	0.15
Other Arab (0)	25	0.10
Austrian (136)	587	2.28
Belgian (0)	12	0.05
British (12)	57	0.22
Croatian (10)	20	0.08
Czech (10)	72	0.28
Czechoslovakian (0)	58	0.22
Danish (0)	11	0.04
Dutch (37)	146	0.57
Eastern European (1,194)	1,224	4.75
English (97)	563	2.18
European (540)	558	2.16
French, ex. Basque (32)	202	0.78
French Canadian (12)	32	0.12
German (481)	1,894	7.35
Greek (366)	636	2.47

*Notes: † The Census 2010 population figure is used to calculate the percentages in the Hispanic Origin and Race categories. Ancestry percentages are based on the 2006-2010 American Community Survey population (not shown); ‡ Numbers in parentheses indicate the number of people reporting a single ancestry; * Numbers in parentheses indicate the number of persons reporting this race alone, not in combination with any other race; Please refer to the Explanation of Data for more information.*

Guyanese (36)	36	0.14
Hungarian (79)	311	1.21
Icelander (7)	15	0.06
Iranian (194)	294	1.14
Irish (663)	2,331	9.04
Israeli (116)	204	0.79
Italian (2,950)	5,064	19.64
Latvian (13)	54	0.21
Lithuanian (30)	63	0.24
Maltese (76)	155	0.60
Northern European (12)	12	0.05
Norwegian (15)	39	0.15
Polish (1,045)	3,107	12.05
Portuguese (31)	63	0.24
Romanian (77)	183	0.71
Russian (1,273)	3,204	12.43
Scotch-Irish (106)	294	1.14
Scottish (27)	93	0.36
Slavic (0)	26	0.10
Slovak (7)	18	0.07
Swiss (0)	28	0.11
Turkish (7)	181	0.70
Ukrainian (124)	319	1.24
West Indian, ex. Hispanic (52)	52	0.20
Jamaican (25)	25	0.10
West Indian (27)	27	0.10
Yugoslavian (10)	69	0.27

Hispanic Origin	Population	%
Hispanic or Latino (of any race)	1,046	3.99
Central American, ex. Mexican	151	0.58
Costa Rican	17	0.06
Guatemalan	20	0.08
Honduran	30	0.11
Panamanian	3	0.01
Salvadoran	79	0.30
Other Central American	2	0.01
Cuban	71	0.27
Dominican Republic	69	0.26
Mexican	46	0.18
Puerto Rican	254	0.97
South American	330	1.26
Argentinean	63	0.24
Bolivian	15	0.06
Chilean	29	0.11
Colombian	108	0.41
Ecuadorian	66	0.25
Peruvian	31	0.12
Uruguayan	10	0.04
Venezuelan	8	0.03
Other Hispanic or Latino	125	0.48

Race*	Population	%
African-American/Black (118)	187	0.71
Not Hispanic (110)	163	0.62
Hispanic (8)	24	0.09
American Indian/Alaska Native (24)	50	0.19
Not Hispanic (17)	33	0.13
Hispanic (7)	17	0.06
Cherokee (0)	5	0.02
Chippewa (2)	2	0.01
Iroquois (2)	2	0.01
Mexican American Ind. (0)	1	<0.01
Navajo (1)	1	<0.01
South American Ind. (0)	2	0.01
Spanish American Ind. (1)	1	<0.01
Asian (2,811)	3,091	11.79
Not Hispanic (2,799)	3,062	11.68
Hispanic (12)	29	0.11
Bangladeshi (14)	17	0.06
Burmese (1)	1	<0.01
Chinese, ex. Taiwanese (590)	644	2.46
Filipino (103)	130	0.50
Indian (844)	888	3.39
Indonesian (1)	1	<0.01
Japanese (67)	77	0.29
Korean (996)	1,028	3.92
Malaysian (0)	1	<0.01
Pakistani (83)	98	0.37
Taiwanese (26)	31	0.12
Thai (6)	8	0.03
Vietnamese (4)	6	0.02
Hawaii Native/Pacific Islander (2)	10	0.04
Not Hispanic (1)	9	0.03
Hispanic (1)	1	<0.01
Guamanian/Chamorro (1)	1	<0.01
Native Hawaiian (1)	1	<0.01
White (22,701)	23,039	87.88
Not Hispanic (21,881)	22,141	84.45
Hispanic (820)	898	3.43

Plattekill

Place Type: Town
County: Ulster
Population: 10,499†

Ancestry‡	Population	%
American (749)	749	7.18
Austrian (0)	61	0.58
Basque (15)	15	0.14
Canadian (0)	13	0.12
Czech (0)	11	0.11
Czechoslovakian (6)	6	0.06
Dutch (15)	175	1.68
Eastern European (40)	64	0.61
English (66)	685	6.56
European (75)	84	0.80
French, ex. Basque (83)	312	2.99
French Canadian (0)	34	0.33
German (306)	1,676	16.06
Greek (7)	33	0.32
Hungarian (0)	138	1.32
Irish (441)	1,941	18.59
Italian (1,129)	2,496	23.91
Lithuanian (0)	25	0.24
Norwegian (0)	51	0.49
Pennsylvania German (0)	24	0.23
Polish (16)	519	4.97
Russian (24)	125	1.20
Scandinavian (9)	19	0.18
Scotch-Irish (170)	270	2.59
Scottish (0)	120	1.15
Slovak (16)	26	0.25
Slovene (0)	12	0.11
Swedish (0)	50	0.48
Welsh (0)	12	0.11
West Indian, ex. Hispanic (256)	291	2.79
Haitian (0)	8	0.08
Jamaican (199)	226	2.16
West Indian (57)	57	0.55

Hispanic Origin	Population	%
Hispanic or Latino (of any race)	1,934	18.42
Central American, ex. Mexican	123	1.17
Costa Rican	1	0.01
Guatemalan	18	0.17
Honduran	36	0.34
Nicaraguan	1	0.01
Panamanian	12	0.11
Salvadoran	53	0.50
Other Central American	2	0.02
Cuban	49	0.47
Dominican Republic	60	0.57
Mexican	249	2.37
Puerto Rican	1,185	11.29
South American	111	1.06
Argentinean	4	0.04
Chilean	5	0.05
Colombian	24	0.23
Ecuadorian	24	0.23
Peruvian	44	0.42
Uruguayan	3	0.03
Other South American	7	0.07
Other Hispanic or Latino	157	1.50

Race*	Population	%
African-American/Black (617)	742	7.07
Not Hispanic (534)	612	5.83
Hispanic (83)	130	1.24
American Indian/Alaska Native (28)	78	0.74
Not Hispanic (20)	56	0.53
Hispanic (8)	22	0.21
Apache (0)	2	0.02
Blackfeet (0)	3	0.03
Canadian/French Am. Ind. (1)	1	0.01
Central American Ind. (1)	4	0.04
Cherokee (2)	10	0.10
Chippewa (0)	1	0.01
Delaware (4)	4	0.04
Inupiat *(Alaska Native)* (0)	1	0.01
Iroquois (3)	13	0.12
Navajo (0)	1	0.01
Pueblo (1)	1	0.01
Seminole (1)	2	0.02
South American Ind. (7)	11	0.10
Asian (86)	123	1.17
Not Hispanic (84)	114	1.09
Hispanic (2)	9	0.09
Bangladeshi (10)	10	0.10
Chinese, ex. Taiwanese (17)	25	0.24
Filipino (11)	26	0.25
Indian (11)	19	0.18
Indonesian (2)	2	0.02
Japanese (4)	9	0.09
Korean (14)	21	0.20
Laotian (1)	1	0.01
Pakistani (0)	2	0.02
Thai (0)	4	0.04
Vietnamese (1)	2	0.02
Hawaii Native/Pacific Islander (2)	8	0.08
Not Hispanic (2)	8	0.08
Native Hawaiian (1)	3	0.03
Samoan (0)	4	0.04
White (8,902)	9,167	87.31
Not Hispanic (7,773)	7,909	75.33
Hispanic (1,129)	1,258	11.98

Plattsburgh

Place Type: City
County: Clinton
Population: 19,989†

Ancestry‡	Population	%
African, Sub-Saharan (117)	131	0.66
African (49)	63	0.32
Ethiopian (8)	8	0.04
Ghanaian (13)	13	0.07
Other Sub-Saharan African (47)	47	0.24
American (1,082)	1,082	5.42
Arab (38)	139	0.70
Lebanese (29)	130	0.65
Syrian (8)	8	0.04
Other Arab (1)	1	0.01
Armenian (0)	71	0.36
Austrian (5)	48	0.24
Belgian (0)	11	0.06
British (23)	81	0.41
Canadian (57)	148	0.74
Celtic (0)	10	0.05
Croatian (0)	11	0.06
Czech (18)	94	0.47
Czechoslovakian (0)	15	0.08
Danish (31)	89	0.45
Dutch (9)	214	1.07
English (539)	2,018	10.10
European (70)	71	0.36
French, ex. Basque (1,173)	4,160	20.83
French Canadian (703)	1,086	5.44
German (435)	2,253	11.28
Greek (76)	116	0.58
Guyanese (5)	5	0.03
Hungarian (0)	52	0.26
Irish (1,020)	4,164	20.85
Italian (932)	2,339	11.71
Lithuanian (0)	41	0.21
Norwegian (17)	116	0.58
Pennsylvania German (0)	23	0.12
Polish (204)	888	4.45

*Notes: † The Census 2010 population figure is used to calculate the percentages in the Hispanic Origin and Race categories. Ancestry percentages are based on the 2006-2010 American Community Survey population (not shown); ‡ Numbers in parentheses indicate the number of people reporting a single ancestry; * Numbers in parentheses indicate the number of persons reporting this race alone, not in combination with any other race; Please refer to the Explanation of Data for more information.*

Portuguese (39)	51	0.26
Romanian (0)	47	0.24
Russian (173)	284	1.42
Scandinavian (0)	24	0.12
Scotch-Irish (133)	420	2.10
Scottish (74)	507	2.54
Slavic (0)	24	0.12
Slovak (0)	50	0.25
Slovene (0)	20	0.10
Swedish (0)	132	0.66
Swiss (0)	6	0.03
Ukrainian (110)	204	1.02
Welsh (2)	107	0.54
West Indian, ex. Hispanic (75)	154	0.77
British West Indian (18)	18	0.09
Haitian (0)	14	0.07
Jamaican (15)	15	0.08
Trinidadian/Tobagonian (14)	28	0.14
West Indian (28)	79	0.40
Yugoslavian (0)	10	0.05

Hispanic Origin	Population	%
Hispanic or Latino (of any race)	679	3.40
Central American, ex. Mexican	47	0.24
Costa Rican	6	0.03
Guatemalan	5	0.03
Honduran	9	0.05
Nicaraguan	6	0.03
Panamanian	3	0.02
Salvadoran	17	0.09
Other Central American	1	0.01
Cuban	31	0.16
Dominican Republic	74	0.37
Mexican	87	0.44
Puerto Rican	261	1.31
South American	93	0.47
Argentinean	5	0.03
Bolivian	1	0.01
Chilean	8	0.04
Colombian	36	0.18
Ecuadorian	16	0.08
Paraguayan	7	0.04
Peruvian	11	0.06
Uruguayan	1	0.01
Venezuelan	7	0.04
Other South American	1	0.01
Other Hispanic or Latino	86	0.43

Race*	Population	%
African-American/Black (700)	941	4.71
Not Hispanic (643)	842	4.21
Hispanic (57)	99	0.50
American Indian/Alaska Native (75)	232	1.16
Not Hispanic (69)	203	1.02
Hispanic (6)	29	0.15
Apache (0)	1	0.01
Blackfeet (2)	14	0.07
Canadian/French Am. Ind. (5)	8	0.04
Cherokee (3)	29	0.15
Cheyenne (0)	1	0.01
Chickasaw (0)	1	0.01
Chippewa (1)	1	0.01
Choctaw (1)	1	0.01
Comanche (1)	3	0.02
Inupiat *(Alaska Native)* (1)	1	0.01
Iroquois (24)	44	0.22
Mexican American Ind. (1)	1	0.01
Navajo (0)	1	0.01
Potawatomi (1)	1	0.01
Pueblo (1)	1	0.01
Puget Sound Salish (0)	1	0.01
Sioux (1)	4	0.02
South American Ind. (0)	4	0.02
Asian (555)	651	3.26
Not Hispanic (550)	640	3.20
Hispanic (5)	11	0.06
Bangladeshi (2)	2	0.01
Burmese (1)	2	0.01
Cambodian (1)	1	0.01
Chinese, ex. Taiwanese (172)	193	0.97
Filipino (39)	68	0.34
Indian (103)	114	0.57
Indonesian (0)	1	0.01
Japanese (75)	89	0.45
Korean (59)	78	0.39
Malaysian (1)	2	0.01
Nepalese (9)	9	0.05
Pakistani (19)	21	0.11
Sri Lankan (8)	9	0.05
Taiwanese (9)	10	0.05
Thai (7)	11	0.06
Vietnamese (35)	37	0.19
Hawaii Native/Pacific Islander (6)	23	0.12
Not Hispanic (4)	16	0.08
Hispanic (2)	7	0.04
Guamanian/Chamorro (2)	2	0.01
Native Hawaiian (0)	2	0.01
Samoan (0)	5	0.03
White (17,967)	18,408	92.09
Not Hispanic (17,631)	17,991	90.00
Hispanic (336)	417	2.09

Plattsburgh

Place Type: Town
County: Clinton
Population: 11,870†

Ancestry‡	Population	%
American (1,206)	1,206	10.18
Arab (31)	104	0.88
Arab (7)	13	0.11
Egyptian (13)	13	0.11
Lebanese (0)	67	0.57
Syrian (11)	11	0.09
Armenian (0)	34	0.29
Australian (0)	12	0.10
Belgian (0)	12	0.10
British (10)	22	0.19
Canadian (119)	140	1.18
Czech (0)	10	0.08
Danish (11)	24	0.20
Dutch (0)	168	1.42
English (527)	1,370	11.57
European (20)	20	0.17
French, ex. Basque (1,134)	3,119	26.33
French Canadian (767)	1,225	10.34
German (226)	1,080	9.12
Hungarian (0)	44	0.37
Irish (530)	1,924	16.24
Italian (286)	788	6.65
Lithuanian (27)	117	0.99
Maltese (28)	28	0.24
Norwegian (32)	129	1.09
Polish (156)	469	3.96
Russian (42)	109	0.92
Scotch-Irish (54)	178	1.50
Scottish (124)	216	1.82
Swedish (0)	32	0.27
Swiss (7)	13	0.11
Ukrainian (10)	10	0.08
Welsh (54)	80	0.68
West Indian, ex. Hispanic (25)	25	0.21
British West Indian (25)	25	0.21

Hispanic Origin	Population	%
Hispanic or Latino (of any race)	228	1.92
Central American, ex. Mexican	27	0.23
Guatemalan	6	0.05
Honduran	2	0.02
Nicaraguan	8	0.07
Panamanian	5	0.04
Salvadoran	6	0.05
Cuban	16	0.13
Dominican Republic	10	0.08
Mexican	34	0.29
Puerto Rican	82	0.69
South American	19	0.16
Argentinean	1	0.01
Chilean	1	0.01
Colombian	4	0.03
Paraguayan	1	0.01
Peruvian	10	0.08
Venezuelan	1	0.01
Other South American	1	0.01
Other Hispanic or Latino	40	0.34

Race*	Population	%
African-American/Black (227)	294	2.48
Not Hispanic (207)	268	2.26
Hispanic (20)	26	0.22
American Indian/Alaska Native (50)	107	0.90
Not Hispanic (47)	99	0.83
Hispanic (3)	8	0.07
Apache (0)	2	0.02
Arapaho (1)	1	0.01
Blackfeet (3)	5	0.04
Canadian/French Am. Ind. (2)	2	0.02
Cherokee (2)	8	0.07
Chickasaw (0)	1	0.01
Chippewa (0)	1	0.01
Choctaw (1)	1	0.01
Crow (1)	2	0.02
Iroquois (12)	19	0.16
Mexican American Ind. (1)	2	0.02
Sioux (2)	3	0.03
South American Ind. (1)	2	0.02
Yup'ik *(Alaska Native)* (1)	1	0.01
Asian (101)	133	1.12
Not Hispanic (101)	128	1.08
Hispanic (0)	5	0.04
Cambodian (1)	1	0.01
Chinese, ex. Taiwanese (18)	22	0.19
Filipino (17)	26	0.22
Indian (23)	25	0.21
Indonesian (0)	1	0.01
Japanese (6)	12	0.10
Korean (11)	18	0.15
Pakistani (8)	8	0.07
Thai (4)	4	0.03
Vietnamese (12)	12	0.10
Hawaii Native/Pacific Islander (2)	8	0.07
Not Hispanic (2)	6	0.05
Hispanic (0)	2	0.02
Guamanian/Chamorro (1)	2	0.02
Native Hawaiian (0)	1	0.01
Samoan (1)	1	0.01
White (11,273)	11,417	96.18
Not Hispanic (11,138)	11,263	94.89
Hispanic (135)	154	1.30

Pleasant Valley

Place Type: Town
County: Dutchess
Population: 9,672†

Ancestry‡	Population	%
American (206)	206	2.14
Arab (0)	26	0.27
Lebanese (0)	26	0.27
Armenian (0)	41	0.43
Austrian (7)	37	0.38
Belgian (0)	42	0.44
Canadian (0)	18	0.19
Czech (106)	195	2.03
Czechoslovakian (0)	26	0.27
Danish (13)	19	0.20
Dutch (46)	431	4.48
Eastern European (65)	105	1.09
English (144)	963	10.01
European (77)	99	1.03
Finnish (2)	2	0.02
French, ex. Basque (63)	337	3.50
French Canadian (31)	153	1.59
German (522)	2,444	25.39
Greek (0)	54	0.56
Hungarian (43)	145	1.51
Irish (708)	2,595	26.96
Italian (1,218)	2,664	27.68

*Notes: † The Census 2010 population figure is used to calculate the percentages in the Hispanic Origin and Race categories. Ancestry percentages are based on the 2006-2010 American Community Survey population (not shown); ‡ Numbers in parentheses indicate the number of people reporting a single ancestry; * Numbers in parentheses indicate the number of persons reporting this race alone, not in combination with any other race; Please refer to the Explanation of Data for more information.*

Latvian (13)	13	0.14
Lithuanian (9)	33	0.34
Maltese (6)	6	0.06
Northern European (12)	49	0.51
Norwegian (16)	31	0.32
Polish (105)	606	6.30
Russian (46)	214	2.22
Scotch-Irish (52)	90	0.94
Scottish (66)	275	2.86
Slavic (0)	13	0.14
Slovak (23)	64	0.66
Swedish (0)	118	1.23
Ukrainian (0)	33	0.34
Welsh (7)	59	0.61
West Indian, ex. Hispanic (117)	145	1.51
British West Indian (39)	67	0.70
Jamaican (78)	78	0.81
Yugoslavian (0)	132	1.37

Hispanic Origin	Population	%
Hispanic or Latino (of any race)	452	4.67
Central American, ex. Mexican	18	0.19
Costa Rican	5	0.05
Guatemalan	3	0.03
Honduran	5	0.05
Salvadoran	5	0.05
Cuban	27	0.28
Dominican Republic	29	0.30
Mexican	61	0.63
Puerto Rican	231	2.39
South American	39	0.40
Argentinean	5	0.05
Bolivian	3	0.03
Chilean	3	0.03
Colombian	8	0.08
Ecuadorian	9	0.09
Peruvian	1	0.01
Uruguayan	2	0.02
Venezuelan	2	0.02
Other South American	6	0.06
Other Hispanic or Latino	47	0.49

Race*	Population	%
African-American/Black (284)	379	3.92
Not Hispanic (264)	349	3.61
Hispanic (20)	30	0.31
American Indian/Alaska Native (20)	92	0.95
Not Hispanic (15)	84	0.87
Hispanic (5)	8	0.08
Apache (0)	1	0.01
Blackfeet (1)	1	0.01
Canadian/French Am. Ind. (1)	1	0.01
Central American Ind. (2)	2	0.02
Cherokee (2)	24	0.25
Cree (0)	1	0.01
Iroquois (3)	14	0.14
Mexican American Ind. (1)	1	0.01
South American Ind. (1)	1	0.01
Asian (110)	160	1.65
Not Hispanic (109)	158	1.63
Hispanic (1)	2	0.02
Chinese, ex. Taiwanese (30)	37	0.38
Filipino (12)	18	0.19
Indian (40)	50	0.52
Japanese (7)	11	0.11
Korean (10)	13	0.13
Malaysian (0)	1	0.01
Pakistani (3)	9	0.09
Vietnamese (6)	9	0.09
Hawaii Native/Pacific Islander (3)	11	0.11
Not Hispanic (1)	7	0.07
Hispanic (2)	4	0.04
Native Hawaiian (2)	3	0.03
White (8,953)	9,144	94.54
Not Hispanic (8,637)	8,798	90.96
Hispanic (316)	346	3.58

Pomfret

Place Type: Town
County: Chautauqua
Population: 14,965†

Ancestry‡	Population	%
African, Sub-Saharan (0)	20	0.13
African (0)	20	0.13
American (342)	342	2.30
Arab (38)	63	0.42
Egyptian (11)	36	0.24
Lebanese (27)	27	0.18
Austrian (0)	108	0.73
Belgian (13)	13	0.09
British (0)	27	0.18
Bulgarian (13)	13	0.09
Canadian (0)	17	0.11
Croatian (23)	23	0.15
Czech (0)	33	0.22
Czechoslovakian (15)	77	0.52
Danish (0)	53	0.36
Dutch (31)	383	2.57
English (544)	1,920	12.89
European (53)	72	0.48
French, ex. Basque (14)	456	3.06
French Canadian (30)	104	0.70
German (1,112)	4,203	28.22
Greek (16)	59	0.40
Hungarian (24)	69	0.46
Irish (395)	2,247	15.08
Italian (1,683)	3,428	23.01
Latvian (0)	12	0.08
Norwegian (11)	123	0.83
Polish (1,111)	2,876	19.31
Romanian (0)	60	0.40
Russian (27)	235	1.58
Scandinavian (0)	27	0.18
Scotch-Irish (111)	276	1.85
Scottish (88)	328	2.20
Slavic (10)	10	0.07
Slovak (0)	42	0.28
Swedish (190)	302	2.03
Swiss (0)	88	0.59
Ukrainian (52)	121	0.81
Welsh (8)	131	0.88
West Indian, ex. Hispanic (37)	37	0.25
Haitian (14)	14	0.09
Trinidadian/Tobagonian (23)	23	0.15

Hispanic Origin	Population	%
Hispanic or Latino (of any race)	607	4.06
Central American, ex. Mexican	15	0.10
Costa Rican	2	0.01
Guatemalan	3	0.02
Honduran	4	0.03
Salvadoran	6	0.04
Cuban	13	0.09
Dominican Republic	21	0.14
Mexican	91	0.61
Puerto Rican	378	2.53
South American	42	0.28
Argentinean	3	0.02
Chilean	2	0.01
Colombian	10	0.07
Ecuadorian	17	0.11
Peruvian	7	0.05
Venezuelan	3	0.02
Other Hispanic or Latino	47	0.31

Race*	Population	%
African-American/Black (338)	446	2.98
Not Hispanic (295)	384	2.57
Hispanic (43)	62	0.41
American Indian/Alaska Native (54)	104	0.69
Not Hispanic (49)	90	0.60
Hispanic (5)	14	0.09
Blackfeet (0)	3	0.02
Central American Ind. (1)	1	0.01
Cherokee (7)	16	0.11
Delaware (4)	4	0.03
Iroquois (25)	39	0.26
Sioux (1)	1	0.01
South American Ind. (1)	6	0.04
Asian (205)	248	1.66
Not Hispanic (201)	240	1.60
Hispanic (4)	8	0.05
Bangladeshi (1)	1	0.01
Chinese, ex. Taiwanese (55)	64	0.43
Filipino (21)	29	0.19
Indian (19)	26	0.17
Japanese (11)	14	0.09
Korean (43)	55	0.37
Pakistani (30)	31	0.21
Taiwanese (2)	3	0.02
Thai (12)	14	0.09
Vietnamese (5)	6	0.04
Hawaii Native/Pacific Islander (6)	11	0.07
Not Hispanic (6)	10	0.07
Hispanic (0)	1	0.01
Samoan (4)	5	0.03
White (13,995)	14,180	94.75
Not Hispanic (13,629)	13,783	92.10
Hispanic (366)	397	2.65

Port Chester

Place Type: Village
County: Westchester
Population: 28,967†

Ancestry‡	Population	%
African, Sub-Saharan (24)	35	0.12
African (11)	22	0.08
South African (13)	13	0.05
American (2,456)	2,456	8.58
Arab (58)	174	0.61
Egyptian (19)	19	0.07
Other Arab (39)	155	0.54
Austrian (39)	79	0.28
Brazilian (734)	803	2.81
British (38)	53	0.19
Croatian (20)	20	0.07
Cypriot (12)	12	0.04
Czech (25)	121	0.42
Czechoslovakian (23)	38	0.13
Danish (15)	15	0.05
Dutch (16)	61	0.21
Eastern European (163)	180	0.63
English (108)	582	2.03
European (19)	19	0.07
Finnish (0)	13	0.05
French, ex. Basque (11)	93	0.33
French Canadian (25)	45	0.16
German (437)	793	2.77
Greek (66)	82	0.29
Hungarian (18)	44	0.15
Icelander (0)	24	0.08
Irish (478)	1,347	4.71
Italian (3,011)	4,215	14.73
Lithuanian (15)	34	0.12
Luxemburger (0)	11	0.04
Northern European (9)	9	0.03
Norwegian (35)	118	0.41
Polish (651)	1,012	3.54
Portuguese (68)	179	0.63
Romanian (0)	8	0.03
Russian (117)	264	0.92
Scotch-Irish (30)	53	0.19
Scottish (35)	44	0.15
Slovak (26)	34	0.12
Swedish (15)	131	0.46
Swiss (23)	32	0.11
Turkish (0)	22	0.08
Welsh (12)	30	0.10
West Indian, ex. Hispanic (314)	342	1.20
Jamaican (48)	64	0.22
West Indian (266)	278	0.97
Yugoslavian (28)	28	0.10

*Notes: † The Census 2010 population figure is used to calculate the percentages in the Hispanic Origin and Race categories. Ancestry percentages are based on the 2006-2010 American Community Survey population (not shown); ‡ Numbers in parentheses indicate the number of people reporting a single ancestry; * Numbers in parentheses indicate the number of persons reporting this race alone, not in combination with any other race; Please refer to the Explanation of Data for more information.*

Hispanic Origin	Population	%
Hispanic or Latino (of any race)	17,193	59.35
Central American, ex. Mexican	3,577	12.35
Costa Rican	30	0.10
Guatemalan	2,433	8.40
Honduran	169	0.58
Nicaraguan	6	0.02
Panamanian	13	0.04
Salvadoran	915	3.16
Other Central American	11	0.04
Cuban	359	1.24
Dominican Republic	556	1.92
Mexican	4,864	16.79
Puerto Rican	855	2.95
South American	5,769	19.92
Argentinean	79	0.27
Bolivian	350	1.21
Chilean	123	0.42
Colombian	724	2.50
Ecuadorian	2,774	9.58
Paraguayan	39	0.13
Peruvian	1,485	5.13
Uruguayan	159	0.55
Venezuelan	25	0.09
Other South American	11	0.04
Other Hispanic or Latino	1,213	4.19

Race*	Population	%
African-American/Black (1,876)	2,186	7.55
Not Hispanic (1,541)	1,658	5.72
Hispanic (335)	528	1.82
American Indian/Alaska Native (271)	476	1.64
Not Hispanic (56)	87	0.30
Hispanic (215)	389	1.34
Blackfeet (1)	3	0.01
Central American Ind. (7)	10	0.03
Cherokee (1)	10	0.03
Inupiat *(Alaska Native)* (4)	5	0.02
Iroquois (1)	3	0.01
Kiowa (0)	1	<0.01
Mexican American Ind. (57)	65	0.22
Sioux (0)	1	<0.01
South American Ind. (15)	43	0.15
Spanish American Ind. (3)	4	0.01
Yuman (0)	1	<0.01
Asian (596)	703	2.43
Not Hispanic (572)	634	2.19
Hispanic (24)	69	0.24
Bangladeshi (3)	3	0.01
Burmese (0)	1	<0.01
Cambodian (2)	2	0.01
Chinese, ex. Taiwanese (118)	149	0.51
Filipino (131)	141	0.49
Indian (258)	277	0.96
Indonesian (2)	3	0.01
Japanese (18)	32	0.11
Korean (12)	16	0.06
Laotian (4)	4	0.01
Nepalese (0)	2	0.01
Pakistani (17)	25	0.09
Thai (11)	13	0.04
Vietnamese (5)	7	0.02
Hawaii Native/Pacific Islander (11)	42	0.14
Not Hispanic (0)	8	0.03
Hispanic (11)	34	0.12
Guamanian/Chamorro (8)	13	0.04
Native Hawaiian (0)	6	0.02
Samoan (0)	1	<0.01
White (17,699)	18,872	65.15
Not Hispanic (9,155)	9,365	32.33
Hispanic (8,544)	9,507	32.82

Port Jefferson Station

Place Type: CDP
County: Suffolk
Population: 7,838†

Ancestry‡	Population	%
American (131)	131	1.74
Arab (0)	50	0.66
Syrian (0)	50	0.66
Austrian (30)	68	0.90
Belgian (29)	29	0.39
Brazilian (0)	21	0.28
British (0)	50	0.66
Czech (0)	12	0.16
Czechoslovakian (0)	11	0.15
Danish (0)	39	0.52
Dutch (0)	12	0.16
English (147)	586	7.79
French, ex. Basque (0)	65	0.86
French Canadian (46)	46	0.61
German (100)	1,039	13.81
Greek (159)	281	3.74
Hungarian (40)	138	1.83
Iranian (26)	26	0.35
Irish (368)	1,917	25.49
Italian (1,342)	2,150	28.59
Lithuanian (0)	28	0.37
Norwegian (44)	99	1.32
Polish (89)	258	3.43
Portuguese (37)	48	0.64
Russian (71)	152	2.02
Scotch-Irish (34)	66	0.88
Scottish (37)	69	0.92
Swedish (0)	43	0.57
Turkish (43)	43	0.57
Ukrainian (19)	32	0.43
Welsh (0)	32	0.43
Yugoslavian (11)	117	1.56

Hispanic Origin	Population	%
Hispanic or Latino (of any race)	1,158	14.77
Central American, ex. Mexican	231	2.95
Costa Rican	3	0.04
Guatemalan	7	0.09
Honduran	67	0.85
Panamanian	2	0.03
Salvadoran	152	1.94
Cuban	27	0.34
Dominican Republic	376	4.80
Mexican	69	0.88
Puerto Rican	211	2.69
South American	136	1.74
Argentinean	5	0.06
Bolivian	18	0.23
Chilean	2	0.03
Colombian	47	0.60
Ecuadorian	28	0.36
Peruvian	25	0.32
Venezuelan	4	0.05
Other South American	7	0.09
Other Hispanic or Latino	108	1.38

Race*	Population	%
African-American/Black (195)	257	3.28
Not Hispanic (183)	203	2.59
Hispanic (12)	54	0.69
American Indian/Alaska Native (8)	28	0.36
Not Hispanic (7)	20	0.26
Hispanic (1)	8	0.10
Cherokee (2)	10	0.13
Iroquois (2)	4	0.05
Mexican American Ind. (1)	1	0.01
Shoshone (0)	1	0.01
Sioux (0)	1	0.01
South American Ind. (0)	3	0.04
Asian (420)	460	5.87
Not Hispanic (416)	450	5.74
Hispanic (4)	10	0.13
Bangladeshi (18)	20	0.26
Burmese (7)	7	0.09
Chinese, ex. Taiwanese (115)	123	1.57
Filipino (42)	54	0.69
Indian (89)	96	1.22
Japanese (8)	15	0.19
Korean (88)	93	1.19
Nepalese (2)	3	0.04
Pakistani (20)	20	0.26
Sri Lankan (2)	2	0.03
Taiwanese (8)	10	0.13
Thai (1)	1	0.01
Vietnamese (6)	8	0.10
Hawaii Native/Pacific Islander (3)	9	0.11
Not Hispanic (3)	9	0.11
Guamanian/Chamorro (1)	1	0.01
Native Hawaiian (2)	4	0.05
White (6,679)	6,839	87.25
Not Hispanic (5,998)	6,056	77.26
Hispanic (681)	783	9.99

Port Jefferson

Place Type: Village
County: Suffolk
Population: 7,750†

Ancestry‡	Population	%
American (67)	67	0.86
Arab (0)	26	0.33
Lebanese (0)	13	0.17
Syrian (0)	13	0.17
Armenian (22)	22	0.28
Austrian (9)	98	1.25
Brazilian (38)	38	0.49
British (50)	50	0.64
Czech (22)	63	0.80
Czechoslovakian (0)	26	0.33
Danish (26)	94	1.20
Dutch (0)	11	0.14
Eastern European (24)	41	0.52
English (95)	960	12.27
European (115)	115	1.47
French, ex. Basque (22)	252	3.22
French Canadian (0)	36	0.46
German (287)	1,336	17.07
Greek (193)	310	3.96
Hungarian (12)	37	0.47
Irish (412)	1,874	23.94
Israeli (16)	16	0.20
Italian (739)	1,651	21.09
Lithuanian (30)	62	0.79
Norwegian (14)	92	1.18
Pennsylvania German (13)	13	0.17
Polish (87)	307	3.92
Portuguese (8)	36	0.46
Romanian (11)	11	0.14
Russian (342)	532	6.80
Scotch-Irish (38)	74	0.95
Scottish (13)	134	1.71
Swedish (0)	30	0.38
Swiss (0)	40	0.51
Turkish (68)	93	1.19
Ukrainian (18)	66	0.84
Welsh (36)	116	1.48
West Indian, ex. Hispanic (13)	13	0.17
Haitian (13)	13	0.17

Hispanic Origin	Population	%
Hispanic or Latino (of any race)	500	6.45
Central American, ex. Mexican	124	1.60
Costa Rican	3	0.04
Guatemalan	1	0.01
Honduran	16	0.21
Panamanian	4	0.05
Salvadoran	100	1.29
Cuban	25	0.32
Dominican Republic	61	0.79
Mexican	42	0.54
Puerto Rican	126	1.63
South American	55	0.71
Argentinean	10	0.13
Bolivian	2	0.03
Chilean	8	0.10
Colombian	13	0.17
Ecuadorian	4	0.05
Paraguayan	2	0.03
Peruvian	7	0.09
Venezuelan	9	0.12

*Notes: † The Census 2010 population figure is used to calculate the percentages in the Hispanic Origin and Race categories. Ancestry percentages are based on the 2006-2010 American Community Survey population (not shown); ‡ Numbers in parentheses indicate the number of people reporting a single ancestry; * Numbers in parentheses indicate the number of persons reporting this race alone, not in combination with any other race; Please refer to the Explanation of Data for more information.*

Other Hispanic or Latino	67	0.86

Race*	Population	%
African-American/Black (124)	160	2.06
Not Hispanic (117)	140	1.81
Hispanic (7)	20	0.26
American Indian/Alaska Native (13)	37	0.48
Not Hispanic (7)	24	0.31
Hispanic (6)	13	0.17
Central American Ind. (0)	1	0.01
Cherokee (1)	10	0.13
Iroquois (0)	3	0.04
Tlingit-Haida *(Alaska Native)* (0)	1	0.01
Asian (472)	525	6.77
Not Hispanic (470)	519	6.70
Hispanic (2)	6	0.08
Bangladeshi (3)	3	0.04
Cambodian (2)	5	0.06
Chinese, ex. Taiwanese (135)	154	1.99
Filipino (19)	30	0.39
Indian (120)	126	1.63
Indonesian (2)	2	0.03
Japanese (28)	36	0.46
Korean (75)	83	1.07
Laotian (1)	1	0.01
Pakistani (38)	41	0.53
Sri Lankan (4)	5	0.06
Taiwanese (15)	15	0.19
Thai (5)	7	0.09
Vietnamese (5)	8	0.10
Hawaii Native/Pacific Islander (0)	4	0.05
Not Hispanic (0)	1	0.01
Hispanic (0)	3	0.04
Native Hawaiian (0)	2	0.03
White (6,860)	6,964	89.86
Not Hispanic (6,556)	6,632	85.57
Hispanic (304)	332	4.28

Port Jervis

Place Type: City
County: Orange
Population: 8,828†

Ancestry‡	Population	%
African, Sub-Saharan (37)	139	1.56
African (37)	69	0.77
Liberian (0)	22	0.25
Senegalese (0)	12	0.13
Somalian (0)	26	0.29
Other Sub-Saharan African (0)	10	0.11
Albanian (24)	24	0.27
American (1,120)	1,120	12.58
Armenian (7)	7	0.08
Austrian (0)	43	0.48
Belgian (0)	15	0.17
British (20)	28	0.31
Canadian (0)	12	0.13
Czech (0)	3	0.03
Danish (0)	9	0.10
Dutch (49)	305	3.42
Eastern European (93)	93	1.04
English (241)	1,118	12.55
European (50)	50	0.56
French, ex. Basque (29)	248	2.78
French Canadian (0)	19	0.21
German (528)	2,101	23.59
Hungarian (0)	18	0.20
Irish (464)	1,828	20.53
Italian (475)	1,227	13.78
Lithuanian (0)	36	0.40
Norwegian (0)	22	0.25
Pennsylvania German (0)	11	0.12
Polish (103)	322	3.62
Russian (22)	119	1.34
Scotch-Irish (70)	143	1.61
Scottish (0)	102	1.15
Slavic (0)	32	0.36
Swedish (6)	60	0.67
Ukrainian (41)	131	1.47
Welsh (29)	83	0.93
Yugoslavian (0)	35	0.39

Hispanic Origin	Population	%
Hispanic or Latino (of any race)	1,054	11.94
Central American, ex. Mexican	52	0.59
Costa Rican	1	0.01
Guatemalan	7	0.08
Honduran	13	0.15
Nicaraguan	2	0.02
Panamanian	9	0.10
Salvadoran	20	0.23
Cuban	26	0.29
Dominican Republic	40	0.45
Mexican	107	1.21
Puerto Rican	686	7.77
South American	61	0.69
Argentinean	13	0.15
Chilean	5	0.06
Colombian	10	0.11
Ecuadorian	14	0.16
Paraguayan	1	0.01
Peruvian	16	0.18
Uruguayan	2	0.02
Other Hispanic or Latino	82	0.93

Race*	Population	%
African-American/Black (654)	903	10.23
Not Hispanic (565)	765	8.67
Hispanic (89)	138	1.56
American Indian/Alaska Native (66)	185	2.10
Not Hispanic (53)	152	1.72
Hispanic (13)	33	0.37
Apache (1)	1	0.01
Blackfeet (1)	7	0.08
Cherokee (4)	20	0.23
Choctaw (1)	1	0.01
Delaware (18)	39	0.44
Iroquois (9)	14	0.16
Seminole (0)	1	0.01
Sioux (0)	7	0.08
Spanish American Ind. (2)	2	0.02
Asian (117)	164	1.86
Not Hispanic (108)	151	1.71
Hispanic (9)	13	0.15
Bangladeshi (7)	7	0.08
Cambodian (5)	5	0.06
Chinese, ex. Taiwanese (7)	11	0.12
Filipino (22)	31	0.35
Indian (61)	71	0.80
Japanese (1)	8	0.09
Korean (6)	18	0.20
Pakistani (1)	1	0.01
Thai (2)	5	0.06
Vietnamese (4)	5	0.06
Hawaii Native/Pacific Islander (1)	11	0.12
Not Hispanic (1)	4	0.05
Hispanic (0)	7	0.08
Native Hawaiian (0)	8	0.09
Samoan (1)	1	0.01
White (7,257)	7,629	86.42
Not Hispanic (6,735)	7,003	79.33
Hispanic (522)	626	7.09

Port Washington

Place Type: CDP
County: Nassau
Population: 15,846†

Ancestry‡	Population	%
African, Sub-Saharan (0)	17	0.11
Sudanese (0)	17	0.11
American (530)	530	3.28
Arab (44)	71	0.44
Arab (4)	14	0.09
Egyptian (3)	20	0.12
Lebanese (13)	13	0.08
Palestinian (11)	11	0.07
Other Arab (13)	13	0.08
Armenian (39)	39	0.24
Australian (16)	65	0.40
Austrian (74)	187	1.16
Belgian (0)	14	0.09
Brazilian (11)	11	0.07
British (41)	116	0.72
Canadian (9)	9	0.06
Croatian (4)	15	0.09
Cypriot (10)	10	0.06
Czech (0)	37	0.23
Czechoslovakian (22)	22	0.14
Danish (27)	113	0.70
Dutch (0)	46	0.29
Eastern European (394)	437	2.71
English (150)	853	5.29
European (138)	162	1.00
Finnish (11)	11	0.07
French, ex. Basque (38)	388	2.40
French Canadian (22)	45	0.28
German (408)	1,761	10.91
Greek (137)	186	1.15
Guyanese (15)	15	0.09
Hungarian (60)	242	1.50
Iranian (11)	31	0.19
Irish (1,116)	2,980	18.47
Israeli (32)	90	0.56
Italian (1,363)	3,058	18.95
Latvian (46)	86	0.53
Lithuanian (0)	17	0.11
Northern European (0)	9	0.06
Norwegian (18)	104	0.64
Polish (343)	953	5.91
Romanian (27)	155	0.96
Russian (487)	979	6.07
Scandinavian (0)	9	0.06
Scotch-Irish (60)	185	1.15
Scottish (119)	366	2.27
Serbian (8)	8	0.05
Slovak (26)	47	0.29
Slovene (0)	11	0.07
Swedish (42)	145	0.90
Swiss (0)	8	0.05
Turkish (12)	57	0.35
Ukrainian (42)	59	0.37
Welsh (0)	34	0.21
West Indian, ex. Hispanic (39)	76	0.47
Jamaican (39)	76	0.47

Hispanic Origin	Population	%
Hispanic or Latino (of any race)	2,116	13.35
Central American, ex. Mexican	797	5.03
Costa Rican	3	0.02
Guatemalan	312	1.97
Honduran	61	0.38
Nicaraguan	8	0.05
Panamanian	3	0.02
Salvadoran	406	2.56
Other Central American	4	0.03
Cuban	46	0.29
Dominican Republic	47	0.30
Mexican	112	0.71
Puerto Rican	155	0.98
South American	645	4.07
Argentinean	22	0.14
Bolivian	4	0.03
Chilean	149	0.94
Colombian	104	0.66
Ecuadorian	299	1.89
Paraguayan	4	0.03
Peruvian	54	0.34
Uruguayan	4	0.03
Venezuelan	2	0.01
Other South American	3	0.02
Other Hispanic or Latino	314	1.98

Race*	Population	%
African-American/Black (376)	435	2.75
Not Hispanic (346)	395	2.49
Hispanic (30)	40	0.25
American Indian/Alaska Native (33)	102	0.64

SECTION TWO

*Notes: † The Census 2010 population figure is used to calculate the percentages in the Hispanic Origin and Race categories. Ancestry percentages are based on the 2006-2010 American Community Survey population (not shown); ‡ Numbers in parentheses indicate the number of people reporting a single ancestry; * Numbers in parentheses indicate the number of persons reporting this race alone, not in combination with any other race; Please refer to the Explanation of Data for more information.*

Not Hispanic (17)	39	0.25
Hispanic (16)	63	0.40
Central American Ind. (2)	3	0.02
Cherokee (1)	5	0.03
Iroquois (0)	2	0.01
Mexican American Ind. (1)	4	0.03
South American Ind. (1)	1	0.01
Spanish American Ind. (1)	1	0.01
Asian (1,275)	1,437	9.07
Not Hispanic (1,273)	1,420	8.96
Hispanic (2)	17	0.11
Bangladeshi (14)	14	0.09
Burmese (2)	2	0.01
Cambodian (0)	1	0.01
Chinese, ex. Taiwanese (399)	453	2.86
Filipino (74)	97	0.61
Indian (157)	182	1.15
Japanese (189)	220	1.39
Korean (353)	375	2.37
Malaysian (0)	1	0.01
Pakistani (20)	28	0.18
Sri Lankan (1)	2	0.01
Taiwanese (26)	39	0.25
Thai (9)	14	0.09
Vietnamese (5)	11	0.07
Hawaii Native/Pacific Islander (1)	20	0.13
Not Hispanic (1)	11	0.07
Hispanic (0)	9	0.06
Native Hawaiian (0)	5	0.03
White (13,028)	13,324	84.08
Not Hispanic (11,844)	12,036	75.96
Hispanic (1,184)	1,288	8.13

Potsdam

Place Type: Town
County: St. Lawrence
Population: 16,041†

Ancestry‡	Population	%
American (834)	834	5.19
Arab (41)	49	0.31
Arab (10)	10	0.06
Jordanian (21)	21	0.13
Lebanese (10)	18	0.11
British (122)	181	1.13
Bulgarian (25)	25	0.16
Canadian (98)	214	1.33
Czech (7)	7	0.04
Danish (7)	39	0.24
Dutch (74)	655	4.08
Eastern European (9)	38	0.24
English (1,333)	2,484	15.47
European (132)	139	0.87
Finnish (0)	21	0.13
French, ex. Basque (413)	1,956	12.18
French Canadian (362)	684	4.26
German (547)	1,839	11.45
Greek (26)	58	0.36
Hungarian (42)	101	0.63
Irish (926)	3,123	19.45
Italian (567)	1,649	10.27
Lithuanian (0)	32	0.20
Luxemburger (0)	7	0.04
Macedonian (0)	7	0.04
Maltese (0)	14	0.09
Northern European (3)	3	0.02
Norwegian (21)	128	0.80
Polish (173)	731	4.55
Portuguese (13)	49	0.31
Romanian (35)	50	0.31
Russian (59)	169	1.05
Scotch-Irish (92)	316	1.97
Scottish (139)	502	3.13
Slavic (0)	10	0.06
Slovak (0)	12	0.07
Swedish (24)	89	0.55
Swiss (7)	53	0.33
Turkish (39)	39	0.24
Ukrainian (3)	19	0.12
Welsh (3)	171	1.07
West Indian, ex. Hispanic (37)	37	0.23
Bahamian (14)	14	0.09
Haitian (10)	10	0.06
Jamaican (13)	13	0.08
Yugoslavian (18)	40	0.25

Hispanic Origin	Population	%
Hispanic or Latino (of any race)	366	2.28
Central American, ex. Mexican	40	0.25
Costa Rican	7	0.04
Guatemalan	25	0.16
Honduran	2	0.01
Nicaraguan	1	0.01
Panamanian	2	0.01
Salvadoran	2	0.01
Other Central American	1	0.01
Cuban	10	0.06
Dominican Republic	36	0.22
Mexican	70	0.44
Puerto Rican	112	0.70
South American	47	0.29
Argentinean	11	0.07
Chilean	3	0.02
Colombian	9	0.06
Ecuadorian	9	0.06
Paraguayan	2	0.01
Peruvian	7	0.04
Uruguayan	3	0.02
Venezuelan	3	0.02
Other Hispanic or Latino	51	0.32

Race*	Population	%
African-American/Black (286)	399	2.49
Not Hispanic (265)	370	2.31
Hispanic (21)	29	0.18
American Indian/Alaska Native (64)	174	1.08
Not Hispanic (61)	161	1.00
Hispanic (3)	13	0.08
Blackfeet (0)	4	0.02
Canadian/French Am. Ind. (2)	14	0.09
Cherokee (0)	19	0.12
Chippewa (0)	2	0.01
Choctaw (1)	1	0.01
Cree (0)	1	0.01
Delaware (2)	2	0.01
Iroquois (34)	64	0.40
Kiowa (1)	1	0.01
Navajo (1)	1	0.01
Seminole (0)	1	0.01
Sioux (2)	4	0.02
Spanish American Ind. (0)	1	0.01
Asian (539)	637	3.97
Not Hispanic (537)	633	3.95
Hispanic (2)	4	0.02
Bangladeshi (5)	5	0.03
Burmese (0)	1	0.01
Chinese, ex. Taiwanese (210)	233	1.45
Filipino (27)	49	0.31
Indian (148)	165	1.03
Indonesian (1)	2	0.01
Japanese (7)	17	0.11
Korean (77)	80	0.50
Laotian (2)	3	0.02
Malaysian (0)	6	0.04
Nepalese (5)	5	0.03
Pakistani (14)	14	0.09
Sri Lankan (12)	12	0.07
Taiwanese (6)	12	0.07
Thai (2)	4	0.02
Vietnamese (7)	14	0.09
Hawaii Native/Pacific Islander (11)	29	0.18
Not Hispanic (7)	18	0.11
Hispanic (4)	11	0.07
Guamanian/Chamorro (0)	2	0.01
Native Hawaiian (9)	11	0.07
Samoan (1)	2	0.01
White (14,735)	15,016	93.61
Not Hispanic (14,521)	14,774	92.10
Hispanic (214)	242	1.51

Potsdam

Place Type: Village
County: St. Lawrence
Population: 9,428†

Ancestry‡	Population	%
American (268)	268	2.83
Arab (20)	28	0.30
Arab (10)	10	0.11
Lebanese (10)	18	0.19
British (49)	49	0.52
Canadian (69)	126	1.33
Czech (7)	7	0.07
Danish (0)	32	0.34
Dutch (22)	208	2.20
English (803)	1,489	15.71
European (36)	36	0.38
Finnish (0)	21	0.22
French, ex. Basque (185)	868	9.16
French Canadian (63)	212	2.24
German (432)	1,269	13.39
Greek (0)	18	0.19
Hungarian (27)	57	0.60
Irish (344)	1,498	15.81
Italian (336)	1,147	12.10
Lithuanian (0)	13	0.14
Macedonian (0)	7	0.07
Norwegian (0)	14	0.15
Polish (144)	578	6.10
Portuguese (0)	25	0.26
Romanian (35)	35	0.37
Russian (46)	138	1.46
Scotch-Irish (35)	149	1.57
Scottish (98)	231	2.44
Slavic (0)	10	0.11
Slovak (0)	12	0.13
Swedish (22)	58	0.61
Swiss (7)	42	0.44
Turkish (39)	39	0.41
Ukrainian (0)	16	0.17
Welsh (0)	126	1.33
West Indian, ex. Hispanic (27)	27	0.28
Bahamian (14)	14	0.15
Jamaican (13)	13	0.14
Yugoslavian (0)	22	0.23

Hispanic Origin	Population	%
Hispanic or Latino (of any race)	273	2.90
Central American, ex. Mexican	22	0.23
Costa Rican	2	0.02
Guatemalan	12	0.13
Honduran	2	0.02
Nicaraguan	1	0.01
Panamanian	2	0.02
Salvadoran	2	0.02
Other Central American	1	0.01
Cuban	5	0.05
Dominican Republic	33	0.35
Mexican	44	0.47
Puerto Rican	78	0.83
South American	46	0.49
Argentinean	11	0.12
Chilean	3	0.03
Colombian	9	0.10
Ecuadorian	9	0.10
Paraguayan	1	0.01
Peruvian	7	0.07
Uruguayan	3	0.03
Venezuelan	3	0.03
Other Hispanic or Latino	45	0.48

Race*	Population	%
African-American/Black (264)	338	3.59
Not Hispanic (245)	313	3.32
Hispanic (19)	25	0.27
American Indian/Alaska Native (37)	84	0.89
Not Hispanic (37)	75	0.80
Hispanic (0)	9	0.10
Blackfeet (0)	2	0.02

*Notes: † The Census 2010 population figure is used to calculate the percentages in the Hispanic Origin and Race categories. Ancestry percentages are based on the 2006-2010 American Community Survey population (not shown); ‡ Numbers in parentheses indicate the number of people reporting a single ancestry; * Numbers in parentheses indicate the number of persons reporting this race alone, not in combination with any other race; Please refer to the Explanation of Data for more information.*

Canadian/French Am. Ind. (0)	3	0.03
Cherokee (0)	5	0.05
Choctaw (1)	1	0.01
Cree (0)	1	0.01
Delaware (2)	2	0.02
Iroquois (20)	27	0.29
Navajo (1)	1	0.01
Seminole (0)	1	0.01
Sioux (0)	1	0.01
Spanish American Ind. (0)	1	0.01
Asian (461)	541	5.74
Not Hispanic (459)	537	5.70
Hispanic (2)	4	0.04
Bangladeshi (1)	1	0.01
Chinese, ex. Taiwanese (186)	203	2.15
Filipino (22)	40	0.42
Indian (133)	143	1.52
Indonesian (1)	2	0.02
Japanese (4)	13	0.14
Korean (62)	64	0.68
Laotian (2)	3	0.03
Malaysian (0)	2	0.02
Nepalese (1)	1	0.01
Pakistani (14)	14	0.15
Sri Lankan (12)	12	0.13
Taiwanese (6)	12	0.13
Thai (2)	4	0.04
Vietnamese (5)	10	0.11
Hawaii Native/Pacific Islander (4)	16	0.17
Not Hispanic (3)	10	0.11
Hispanic (1)	6	0.06
Native Hawaiian (2)	3	0.03
Samoan (1)	2	0.02
White (8,379)	8,552	90.71
Not Hispanic (8,232)	8,383	88.92
Hispanic (147)	169	1.79

Poughkeepsie

Place Type: City
County: Dutchess
Population: 32,736†

Ancestry‡	Population	%
African, Sub-Saharan (386)	864	2.66
African (245)	491	1.51
Kenyan (20)	20	0.06
Nigerian (110)	342	1.05
Other Sub-Saharan African (11)	11	0.03
Albanian (109)	109	0.34
American (966)	966	2.98
Arab (184)	237	0.73
Arab (0)	22	0.07
Egyptian (0)	22	0.07
Jordanian (73)	73	0.23
Lebanese (18)	27	0.08
Moroccan (31)	31	0.10
Other Arab (62)	62	0.19
Australian (26)	35	0.11
Austrian (27)	123	0.38
Belgian (0)	80	0.25
Brazilian (0)	41	0.13
British (39)	123	0.38
Cajun (20)	41	0.13
Canadian (45)	55	0.17
Croatian (0)	81	0.25
Czech (10)	25	0.08
Danish (0)	76	0.23
Dutch (107)	854	2.63
Eastern European (27)	27	0.08
English (402)	1,618	4.99
European (121)	121	0.37
Finnish (0)	11	0.03
French, ex. Basque (46)	684	2.11
French Canadian (40)	203	0.63
German (579)	2,929	9.03
Greek (123)	185	0.57
Guyanese (63)	63	0.19
Hungarian (59)	208	0.64
Iranian (0)	49	0.15
Irish (930)	3,651	11.25
Italian (1,715)	4,079	12.57
Latvian (0)	11	0.03
Maltese (0)	17	0.05
Northern European (18)	18	0.06
Norwegian (38)	199	0.61
Pennsylvania German (16)	16	0.05
Polish (268)	1,045	3.22
Portuguese (46)	194	0.60
Romanian (8)	27	0.08
Russian (112)	266	0.82
Scandinavian (0)	16	0.05
Scotch-Irish (43)	125	0.39
Scottish (73)	263	0.81
Serbian (45)	45	0.14
Slavic (0)	12	0.04
Slovak (15)	45	0.14
Swedish (61)	231	0.71
Swiss (15)	59	0.18
Ukrainian (67)	125	0.39
Welsh (0)	83	0.26
West Indian, ex. Hispanic (2,913)	3,810	11.74
Belizean (53)	80	0.25
Haitian (22)	73	0.23
Jamaican (2,593)	3,093	9.53
Trinidadian/Tobagonian (198)	253	0.78
U.S. Virgin Islander (0)	42	0.13
West Indian (47)	269	0.83
Yugoslavian (0)	9	0.03

Hispanic Origin	Population	%
Hispanic or Latino (of any race)	6,384	19.50
Central American, ex. Mexican	426	1.30
Costa Rican	31	0.09
Guatemalan	189	0.58
Honduran	94	0.29
Nicaraguan	36	0.11
Panamanian	35	0.11
Salvadoran	41	0.13
Cuban	96	0.29
Dominican Republic	233	0.71
Mexican	3,546	10.83
Puerto Rican	1,420	4.34
South American	326	1.00
Argentinean	25	0.08
Bolivian	2	0.01
Chilean	8	0.02
Colombian	88	0.27
Ecuadorian	111	0.34
Paraguayan	7	0.02
Peruvian	58	0.18
Uruguayan	16	0.05
Venezuelan	10	0.03
Other South American	1	<0.01
Other Hispanic or Latino	337	1.03

Race*	Population	%
African-American/Black (10,967)	12,038	36.77
Not Hispanic (10,407)	11,244	34.35
Hispanic (560)	794	2.43
American Indian/Alaska Native (299)	594	1.81
Not Hispanic (71)	274	0.84
Hispanic (228)	320	0.98
Apache (0)	2	0.01
Blackfeet (2)	26	0.08
Central American Ind. (0)	4	0.01
Cherokee (7)	74	0.23
Chickasaw (0)	3	0.01
Chippewa (0)	1	<0.01
Choctaw (1)	3	0.01
Comanche (0)	1	<0.01
Hopi (0)	1	<0.01
Iroquois (6)	20	0.06
Lumbee (3)	3	0.01
Mexican American Ind. (131)	160	0.49
Navajo (0)	3	0.01
Osage (2)	2	0.01
Ottawa (1)	1	<0.01
Seminole (0)	2	0.01
Sioux (2)	5	0.02
South American Ind. (11)	24	0.07
Spanish American Ind. (1)	4	0.01
Tohono O'Odham (2)	3	0.01
Yakama (2)	2	0.01
Asian (528)	700	2.14
Not Hispanic (521)	660	2.02
Hispanic (7)	40	0.12
Bangladeshi (2)	2	0.01
Cambodian (7)	9	0.03
Chinese, ex. Taiwanese (80)	128	0.39
Filipino (55)	90	0.27
Indian (190)	234	0.71
Indonesian (0)	4	0.01
Japanese (9)	24	0.07
Korean (42)	57	0.17
Laotian (15)	17	0.05
Nepalese (6)	6	0.02
Pakistani (14)	23	0.07
Sri Lankan (2)	2	0.01
Taiwanese (2)	2	0.01
Thai (1)	2	0.01
Vietnamese (82)	92	0.28
Hawaii Native/Pacific Islander (20)	70	0.21
Not Hispanic (14)	44	0.13
Hispanic (6)	26	0.08
Guamanian/Chamorro (8)	19	0.06
Native Hawaiian (3)	7	0.02
Samoan (1)	4	0.01
White (16,649)	17,804	54.39
Not Hispanic (14,252)	15,058	46.00
Hispanic (2,397)	2,746	8.39

Poughkeepsie

Place Type: Town
County: Dutchess
Population: 43,341†

Ancestry‡	Population	%
Afghan (18)	18	0.04
African, Sub-Saharan (141)	350	0.81
African (90)	240	0.55
Ghanaian (13)	13	0.03
Nigerian (1)	1	<0.01
Senegalese (0)	12	0.03
South African (0)	14	0.03
Other Sub-Saharan African (37)	70	0.16
Albanian (91)	107	0.25
American (940)	940	2.16
Arab (178)	624	1.44
Arab (55)	65	0.15
Egyptian (0)	12	0.03
Jordanian (31)	223	0.51
Lebanese (58)	89	0.20
Moroccan (26)	26	0.06
Palestinian (0)	183	0.42
Other Arab (8)	26	0.06
Armenian (49)	68	0.16
Austrian (30)	188	0.43
Basque (0)	13	0.03
Belgian (0)	38	0.09
Brazilian (11)	20	0.05
British (61)	316	0.73
Canadian (66)	119	0.27
Carpatho Rusyn (10)	21	0.05
Croatian (24)	65	0.15
Czech (30)	356	0.82
Czechoslovakian (14)	64	0.15
Danish (33)	125	0.29
Dutch (153)	1,366	3.14
Eastern European (55)	101	0.23
English (596)	4,190	9.64
European (185)	211	0.49
Finnish (0)	89	0.20
French, ex. Basque (117)	1,416	3.26
French Canadian (172)	382	0.88
German (1,390)	7,961	18.32
Greek (138)	446	1.03
Guyanese (13)	36	0.08
Hungarian (234)	564	1.30

*Notes: † The Census 2010 population figure is used to calculate the percentages in the Hispanic Origin and Race categories. Ancestry percentages are based on the 2006-2010 American Community Survey population (not shown); ‡ Numbers in parentheses indicate the number of people reporting a single ancestry; * Numbers in parentheses indicate the number of persons reporting this race alone, not in combination with any other race; Please refer to the Explanation of Data for more information.*

Iranian (21)	39	0.09
Irish (2,645)	9,684	22.28
Israeli (12)	20	0.05
Italian (4,247)	10,180	23.42
Latvian (47)	77	0.18
Lithuanian (46)	119	0.27
Maltese (19)	19	0.04
Northern European (49)	49	0.11
Norwegian (29)	214	0.49
Polish (575)	2,173	5.00
Portuguese (21)	224	0.52
Romanian (12)	96	0.22
Russian (292)	1,131	2.60
Scandinavian (1)	1	<0.01
Scotch-Irish (121)	557	1.28
Scottish (134)	843	1.94
Slavic (8)	71	0.16
Slovak (23)	76	0.17
Swedish (49)	404	0.93
Swiss (22)	190	0.44
Turkish (25)	25	0.06
Ukrainian (54)	253	0.58
Welsh (0)	190	0.44
West Indian, ex. Hispanic (505)	735	1.69
British West Indian (25)	25	0.06
Haitian (48)	48	0.11
Jamaican (413)	599	1.38
Trinidadian/Tobagonian (10)	10	0.02
West Indian (9)	53	0.12
Yugoslavian (0)	26	0.06

Hispanic Origin	Population	%
Hispanic or Latino (of any race)	4,233	9.77
Central American, ex. Mexican	184	0.42
Costa Rican	19	0.04
Guatemalan	33	0.08
Honduran	40	0.09
Nicaraguan	10	0.02
Panamanian	25	0.06
Salvadoran	57	0.13
Cuban	172	0.40
Dominican Republic	321	0.74
Mexican	845	1.95
Puerto Rican	1,699	3.92
South American	616	1.42
Argentinean	62	0.14
Bolivian	5	0.01
Chilean	24	0.06
Colombian	174	0.40
Ecuadorian	204	0.47
Paraguayan	6	0.01
Peruvian	88	0.20
Uruguayan	11	0.03
Venezuelan	28	0.06
Other South American	14	0.03
Other Hispanic or Latino	396	0.91

Race*	Population	%
African-American/Black (4,230)	4,968	11.46
Not Hispanic (3,983)	4,549	10.50
Hispanic (247)	419	0.97
American Indian/Alaska Native (107)	429	0.99
Not Hispanic (58)	310	0.72
Hispanic (49)	119	0.27
Aleut *(Alaska Native)* (1)	2	<0.01
Apache (2)	7	0.02
Blackfeet (0)	20	0.05
Central American Ind. (0)	6	0.01
Cherokee (6)	51	0.12
Cheyenne (1)	1	<0.01
Chippewa (0)	2	<0.01
Choctaw (0)	1	<0.01
Colville (1)	1	<0.01
Cree (0)	2	<0.01
Creek (1)	4	0.01
Crow (0)	4	0.01
Iroquois (7)	28	0.06
Lumbee (0)	3	0.01
Menominee (3)	3	0.01
Mexican American Ind. (11)	13	0.03
Navajo (0)	8	0.02
Ottawa (1)	1	<0.01
Seminole (1)	4	0.01
Sioux (1)	9	0.02
South American Ind. (0)	13	0.03
Spanish American Ind. (0)	2	<0.01
Asian (2,636)	3,064	7.07
Not Hispanic (2,614)	3,013	6.95
Hispanic (22)	51	0.12
Bangladeshi (78)	88	0.20
Burmese (9)	12	0.03
Cambodian (2)	3	0.01
Chinese, ex. Taiwanese (788)	896	2.07
Filipino (178)	264	0.61
Indian (952)	1,046	2.41
Indonesian (5)	12	0.03
Japanese (44)	109	0.25
Korean (201)	240	0.55
Laotian (5)	7	0.02
Malaysian (3)	5	0.01
Nepalese (19)	19	0.04
Pakistani (85)	99	0.23
Sri Lankan (8)	11	0.03
Taiwanese (44)	49	0.11
Thai (9)	12	0.03
Vietnamese (131)	154	0.36
Hawaii Native/Pacific Islander (13)	47	0.11
Not Hispanic (12)	36	0.08
Hispanic (1)	11	0.03
Guamanian/Chamorro (2)	4	0.01
Native Hawaiian (6)	15	0.03
Samoan (1)	2	<0.01
White (33,535)	34,712	80.09
Not Hispanic (31,254)	32,164	74.21
Hispanic (2,281)	2,548	5.88

Putnam Valley

Place Type: Town
County: Putnam
Population: 11,809†

Ancestry‡	Population	%
African, Sub-Saharan (34)	34	0.29
African (34)	34	0.29
Albanian (209)	209	1.79
American (149)	149	1.28
Arab (19)	52	0.45
Jordanian (19)	19	0.16
Syrian (0)	33	0.28
Australian (54)	90	0.77
Austrian (31)	42	0.36
Belgian (0)	12	0.10
Brazilian (8)	8	0.07
British (39)	53	0.45
Canadian (12)	69	0.59
Czech (11)	49	0.42
Czechoslovakian (0)	9	0.08
Danish (11)	27	0.23
Dutch (47)	333	2.85
Eastern European (30)	44	0.38
English (107)	724	6.21
European (142)	163	1.40
French, ex. Basque (30)	212	1.82
French Canadian (72)	130	1.11
German (366)	2,175	18.64
Greek (63)	124	1.06
Hungarian (69)	305	2.61
Irish (781)	3,326	28.51
Italian (1,486)	3,892	33.36
Lithuanian (0)	58	0.50
Maltese (32)	32	0.27
Norwegian (21)	136	1.17
Polish (301)	745	6.38
Portuguese (62)	101	0.87
Romanian (23)	106	0.91
Russian (139)	424	3.63
Scandinavian (42)	42	0.36
Scotch-Irish (80)	248	2.13
Scottish (29)	373	3.20
Slavic (0)	12	0.10
Slovak (36)	64	0.55
Swedish (17)	164	1.41
Swiss (11)	11	0.09
Ukrainian (108)	202	1.73
Welsh (0)	31	0.27
West Indian, ex. Hispanic (0)	79	0.68
Jamaican (0)	79	0.68
Yugoslavian (41)	41	0.35

Hispanic Origin	Population	%
Hispanic or Latino (of any race)	1,159	9.81
Central American, ex. Mexican	93	0.79
Costa Rican	6	0.05
Guatemalan	29	0.25
Honduran	33	0.28
Panamanian	1	0.01
Salvadoran	24	0.20
Cuban	36	0.30
Dominican Republic	63	0.53
Mexican	82	0.69
Puerto Rican	491	4.16
South American	281	2.38
Argentinean	26	0.22
Bolivian	2	0.02
Chilean	5	0.04
Colombian	67	0.57
Ecuadorian	128	1.08
Paraguayan	3	0.03
Peruvian	32	0.27
Uruguayan	15	0.13
Venezuelan	2	0.02
Other South American	1	0.01
Other Hispanic or Latino	113	0.96

Race*	Population	%
African-American/Black (265)	350	2.96
Not Hispanic (239)	289	2.45
Hispanic (26)	61	0.52
American Indian/Alaska Native (14)	91	0.77
Not Hispanic (9)	65	0.55
Hispanic (5)	26	0.22
Apache (0)	1	0.01
Blackfeet (2)	12	0.10
Central American Ind. (3)	3	0.03
Cherokee (0)	15	0.13
Chippewa (0)	2	0.02
Choctaw (0)	1	0.01
Iroquois (1)	3	0.03
Sioux (3)	5	0.04
South American Ind. (0)	2	0.02
Spanish American Ind. (1)	1	0.01
Asian (211)	296	2.51
Not Hispanic (207)	284	2.40
Hispanic (4)	12	0.10
Burmese (1)	1	0.01
Cambodian (3)	4	0.03
Chinese, ex. Taiwanese (52)	73	0.62
Filipino (15)	42	0.36
Indian (77)	90	0.76
Japanese (20)	23	0.19
Korean (21)	28	0.24
Laotian (1)	1	0.01
Pakistani (0)	3	0.03
Thai (0)	2	0.02
Vietnamese (16)	20	0.17
Hawaii Native/Pacific Islander (0)	9	0.08
Not Hispanic (0)	9	0.08
Native Hawaiian (0)	3	0.03
White (10,799)	11,057	93.63
Not Hispanic (9,997)	10,154	85.99
Hispanic (802)	903	7.65

Queens

Place Type: Borough
County: Queens
Population: 2,230,722†

*Notes: † The Census 2010 population figure is used to calculate the percentages in the Hispanic Origin and Race categories. Ancestry percentages are based on the 2006-2010 American Community Survey population (not shown); ‡ Numbers in parentheses indicate the number of people reporting a single ancestry; * Numbers in parentheses indicate the number of persons reporting this race alone, not in combination with any other race; Please refer to the Explanation of Data for more information.*

Ancestry‡	Population	%
Afghan (5,842)	6,027	0.27
African, Sub-Saharan (19,754)	25,166	1.14
African (9,764)	14,083	0.64
Cape Verdean (46)	117	0.01
Ethiopian (478)	505	0.02
Ghanaian (1,269)	1,326	0.06
Kenyan (96)	96	<0.01
Liberian (297)	381	0.02
Nigerian (5,989)	6,304	0.29
Senegalese (84)	84	<0.01
Sierra Leonean (127)	127	0.01
Somalian (52)	98	<0.01
South African (230)	356	0.02
Sudanese (161)	286	0.01
Ugandan (65)	77	<0.01
Zimbabwean (107)	107	<0.01
Other Sub-Saharan African (989)	1,219	0.06
Albanian (6,264)	6,624	0.30
Alsatian (26)	37	<0.01
American (45,604)	45,604	2.07
Arab (16,286)	19,669	0.89
Arab (1,921)	2,283	0.10
Egyptian (5,905)	6,551	0.30
Iraqi (224)	315	0.01
Jordanian (260)	307	0.01
Lebanese (1,548)	2,228	0.10
Moroccan (2,945)	3,459	0.16
Palestinian (582)	638	0.03
Syrian (193)	420	0.02
Other Arab (2,708)	3,468	0.16
Armenian (4,083)	4,658	0.21
Assyrian/Chaldean/Syriac (13)	13	<0.01
Australian (163)	285	0.01
Austrian (2,702)	7,523	0.34
Basque (29)	159	0.01
Belgian (289)	593	0.03
Brazilian (4,871)	6,175	0.28
British (1,346)	2,457	0.11
Bulgarian (1,928)	2,090	0.10
Cajun (0)	33	<0.01
Canadian (604)	1,308	0.06
Carpatho Rusyn (0)	9	<0.01
Celtic (92)	169	0.01
Croatian (5,621)	7,054	0.32
Cypriot (556)	644	0.03
Czech (1,116)	3,464	0.16
Czechoslovakian (816)	1,467	0.07
Danish (171)	792	0.04
Dutch (727)	3,516	0.16
Eastern European (4,442)	4,673	0.21
English (4,389)	20,267	0.92
Estonian (164)	198	0.01
European (5,335)	6,584	0.30
Finnish (269)	693	0.03
French, ex. Basque (3,945)	12,532	0.57
French Canadian (552)	2,020	0.09
German (20,566)	70,399	3.20
German Russian (33)	78	<0.01
Greek (35,368)	41,654	1.89
Guyanese (47,132)	53,961	2.45
Hungarian (4,718)	9,470	0.43
Icelander (10)	26	<0.01
Iranian (3,162)	3,707	0.17
Irish (43,033)	105,348	4.79
Israeli (3,355)	4,164	0.19
Italian (104,251)	159,812	7.27
Latvian (342)	568	0.03
Lithuanian (1,463)	3,131	0.14
Luxemburger (0)	13	<0.01
Macedonian (938)	1,109	0.05
Maltese (952)	1,565	0.07
New Zealander (0)	16	<0.01
Northern European (370)	512	0.02
Norwegian (670)	2,559	0.12
Pennsylvania German (9)	38	<0.01
Polish (37,726)	59,757	2.72
Portuguese (2,784)	4,727	0.21
Romanian (9,232)	11,686	0.53
Russian (29,779)	44,676	2.03
Scandinavian (131)	545	0.02
Scotch-Irish (2,079)	4,602	0.21
Scottish (1,567)	5,718	0.26
Serbian (2,176)	2,438	0.11
Slavic (370)	765	0.03
Slovak (1,161)	1,882	0.09
Slovene (171)	468	0.02
Soviet Union (12)	71	<0.01
Swedish (511)	2,862	0.13
Swiss (381)	1,260	0.06
Turkish (3,054)	3,767	0.17
Ukrainian (5,770)	8,375	0.38
Welsh (201)	1,666	0.08
West Indian, ex. Hispanic (131,014)	147,460	6.71
Bahamian (134)	185	0.01
Barbadian (4,074)	5,021	0.23
Belizean (1,106)	1,344	0.06
Bermudan (142)	177	0.01
British West Indian (3,765)	4,689	0.21
Dutch West Indian (122)	206	0.01
Haitian (35,439)	38,368	1.74
Jamaican (55,278)	59,999	2.73
Trinidadian/Tobagonian (16,227)	19,255	0.88
U.S. Virgin Islander (234)	364	0.02
West Indian (14,052)	17,400	0.79
Other West Indian (441)	452	0.02
Yugoslavian (3,824)	4,516	0.21

Hispanic Origin	Population	%
Hispanic or Latino (of any race)	613,750	27.51
Central American, ex. Mexican	52,509	2.35
Costa Rican	1,749	0.08
Guatemalan	13,700	0.61
Honduran	8,546	0.38
Nicaraguan	2,842	0.13
Panamanian	3,977	0.18
Salvadoran	21,342	0.96
Other Central American	353	0.02
Cuban	11,020	0.49
Dominican Republic	88,061	3.95
Mexican	92,835	4.16
Puerto Rican	102,881	4.61
South American	214,022	9.59
Argentinean	6,345	0.28
Bolivian	3,268	0.15
Chilean	3,184	0.14
Colombian	70,290	3.15
Ecuadorian	98,512	4.42
Paraguayan	2,775	0.12
Peruvian	22,886	1.03
Uruguayan	1,743	0.08
Venezuelan	3,580	0.16
Other South American	1,439	0.06
Other Hispanic or Latino	52,422	2.35

Race*	Population	%
African-American/Black (426,683)	462,351	20.73
Not Hispanic (395,881)	419,695	18.81
Hispanic (30,802)	42,656	1.91
American Indian/Alaska Native (15,364)	30,033	1.35
Not Hispanic (6,490)	15,412	0.69
Hispanic (8,874)	14,621	0.66
Alaska Athabascan *(Ala. Nat.)* (2)	3	<0.01
Aleut *(Alaska Native)* (4)	6	<0.01
Apache (15)	53	<0.01
Arapaho (0)	2	<0.01
Blackfeet (45)	342	0.02
Canadian/French Am. Ind. (20)	38	<0.01
Central American Ind. (419)	733	0.03
Cherokee (267)	1,425	0.06
Cheyenne (13)	20	<0.01
Chickasaw (9)	21	<0.01
Chippewa (14)	37	<0.01
Choctaw (16)	68	<0.01
Colville (1)	1	<0.01
Comanche (3)	6	<0.01
Cree (6)	24	<0.01
Creek (23)	73	<0.01
Crow (1)	4	<0.01
Delaware (14)	35	<0.01
Hopi (1)	15	<0.01
Houma (0)	4	<0.01
Inupiat *(Alaska Native)* (6)	13	<0.01
Iroquois (140)	308	0.01
Lumbee (7)	30	<0.01
Mexican American Ind. (1,270)	1,640	0.07
Navajo (13)	37	<0.01
Osage (0)	5	<0.01
Ottawa (0)	2	<0.01
Paiute (3)	4	<0.01
Potawatomi (6)	7	<0.01
Pueblo (102)	161	0.01
Puget Sound Salish (2)	5	<0.01
Seminole (15)	79	<0.01
Shoshone (0)	6	<0.01
Sioux (35)	104	<0.01
South American Ind. (1,281)	2,448	0.11
Spanish American Ind. (468)	659	0.03
Tlingit-Haida *(Alaska Native)* (8)	20	<0.01
Tohono O'Odham (4)	6	<0.01
Tsimshian *(Alaska Native)* (0)	1	<0.01
Ute (4)	5	<0.01
Yaqui (3)	7	<0.01
Yuman (2)	5	<0.01
Yup'ik *(Alaska Native)* (1)	1	<0.01
Asian (511,787)	552,867	24.78
Not Hispanic (508,334)	545,389	24.45
Hispanic (3,453)	7,478	0.34
Bangladeshi (33,152)	38,341	1.72
Bhutanese (240)	250	0.01
Burmese (2,132)	2,344	0.11
Cambodian (230)	303	0.01
Chinese, ex. Taiwanese (191,693)	200,714	9.00
Filipino (38,163)	41,773	1.87
Hmong (24)	30	<0.01
Indian (117,550)	141,147	6.33
Indonesian (2,860)	3,386	0.15
Japanese (6,375)	7,790	0.35
Korean (64,107)	66,124	2.96
Laotian (137)	210	0.01
Malaysian (1,029)	1,620	0.07
Nepalese (4,930)	5,319	0.24
Pakistani (16,215)	18,084	0.81
Sri Lankan (1,293)	1,536	0.07
Taiwanese (7,776)	8,962	0.40
Thai (3,677)	4,124	0.18
Vietnamese (3,566)	4,322	0.19
Hawaii Native/Pacific Islander (1,530)	7,691	0.34
Not Hispanic (1,094)	5,685	0.25
Hispanic (436)	2,006	0.09
Fijian (36)	76	<0.01
Guamanian/Chamorro (337)	483	0.02
Native Hawaiian (191)	486	0.02
Samoan (62)	179	0.01
Tongan (7)	14	<0.01
White (886,053)	941,608	42.21
Not Hispanic (616,727)	638,051	28.60
Hispanic (269,326)	303,557	13.61

Queensbury

Place Type: Town
County: Warren
Population: 27,901†

Ancestry‡	Population	%
African, Sub-Saharan (9)	9	0.03
African (9)	9	0.03
American (2,363)	2,363	8.55
Arab (108)	221	0.80
Lebanese (0)	41	0.15
Syrian (108)	180	0.65
Armenian (16)	39	0.14
Austrian (10)	106	0.38
British (47)	113	0.41
Bulgarian (0)	12	0.04
Canadian (268)	346	1.25
Celtic (14)	43	0.16
Czech (32)	70	0.25

SECTION TWO

*Notes: † The Census 2010 population figure is used to calculate the percentages in the Hispanic Origin and Race categories. Ancestry percentages are based on the 2006-2010 American Community Survey population (not shown); ‡ Numbers in parentheses indicate the number of people reporting a single ancestry; * Numbers in parentheses indicate the number of persons reporting this race alone, not in combination with any other race; Please refer to the Explanation of Data for more information.*

Czechoslovakian (12)	31	0.11
Danish (0)	23	0.08
Dutch (34)	718	2.60
Eastern European (88)	88	0.32
English (1,100)	3,983	14.41
European (155)	155	0.56
Finnish (0)	14	0.05
French, ex. Basque (840)	3,595	13.01
French Canadian (563)	1,099	3.98
German (1,061)	3,994	14.45
Greek (0)	27	0.10
Hungarian (64)	198	0.72
Iranian (5)	30	0.11
Irish (2,351)	7,418	26.84
Israeli (0)	15	0.05
Italian (1,625)	4,407	15.94
Lithuanian (35)	218	0.79
Norwegian (30)	105	0.38
Pennsylvania German (0)	13	0.05
Polish (270)	1,116	4.04
Portuguese (0)	65	0.24
Romanian (10)	10	0.04
Russian (79)	311	1.13
Scandinavian (38)	38	0.14
Scotch-Irish (406)	743	2.69
Scottish (253)	740	2.68
Serbian (17)	17	0.06
Slavic (14)	42	0.15
Slovak (37)	67	0.24
Swedish (91)	220	0.80
Swiss (9)	61	0.22
Ukrainian (11)	158	0.57
Welsh (114)	484	1.75
Yugoslavian (15)	15	0.05

Hispanic Origin	Population	%
Hispanic or Latino (of any race)	479	1.72
Central American, ex. Mexican	32	0.11
Costa Rican	3	0.01
Guatemalan	8	0.03
Honduran	7	0.03
Nicaraguan	3	0.01
Panamanian	2	0.01
Salvadoran	9	0.03
Cuban	20	0.07
Dominican Republic	8	0.03
Mexican	105	0.38
Puerto Rican	214	0.77
South American	55	0.20
Argentinean	4	0.01
Bolivian	3	0.01
Chilean	4	0.01
Colombian	22	0.08
Ecuadorian	2	0.01
Peruvian	14	0.05
Venezuelan	6	0.02
Other Hispanic or Latino	45	0.16

Race*	Population	%
African-American/Black (253)	365	1.31
Not Hispanic (247)	353	1.27
Hispanic (6)	12	0.04
American Indian/Alaska Native (51)	164	0.59
Not Hispanic (37)	138	0.49
Hispanic (14)	26	0.09
Alaska Athabascan *(Ala. Nat.)* (1)	1	<0.01
Apache (1)	1	<0.01
Blackfeet (0)	10	0.04
Canadian/French Am. Ind. (1)	2	0.01
Cherokee (2)	9	0.03
Cheyenne (0)	2	0.01
Chippewa (0)	2	0.01
Choctaw (0)	1	<0.01
Delaware (1)	1	<0.01
Iroquois (5)	21	0.08
Mexican American Ind. (3)	3	0.01
Sioux (0)	3	0.01
Asian (248)	306	1.10
Not Hispanic (247)	302	1.08
Hispanic (1)	4	0.01
Bangladeshi (1)	2	0.01
Cambodian (0)	1	<0.01
Chinese, ex. Taiwanese (71)	84	0.30
Filipino (34)	45	0.16
Indian (50)	58	0.21
Indonesian (1)	1	<0.01
Japanese (4)	8	0.03
Korean (28)	45	0.16
Pakistani (19)	24	0.09
Sri Lankan (1)	1	<0.01
Taiwanese (6)	6	0.02
Thai (3)	4	0.01
Vietnamese (21)	22	0.08
Hawaii Native/Pacific Islander (7)	12	0.04
Not Hispanic (4)	9	0.03
Hispanic (3)	3	0.01
Guamanian/Chamorro (1)	3	0.01
Native Hawaiian (3)	4	0.01
Samoan (2)	3	0.01
White (26,961)	27,232	97.60
Not Hispanic (26,605)	26,847	96.22
Hispanic (356)	385	1.38

Ramapo

Place Type: Town
County: Rockland
Population: 126,595†

Ancestry‡	Population	%
Afghan (111)	111	0.09
African, Sub-Saharan (718)	858	0.70
African (292)	427	0.35
Ghanaian (77)	77	0.06
Nigerian (207)	207	0.17
South African (56)	56	0.05
Ugandan (86)	86	0.07
Other Sub-Saharan African (0)	5	<0.01
American (5,092)	5,092	4.15
Arab (608)	781	0.64
Arab (245)	245	0.20
Egyptian (16)	24	0.02
Iraqi (12)	48	0.04
Jordanian (10)	10	0.01
Lebanese (23)	37	0.03
Moroccan (216)	291	0.24
Palestinian (0)	25	0.02
Syrian (17)	17	0.01
Other Arab (69)	84	0.07
Armenian (33)	63	0.05
Australian (19)	86	0.07
Austrian (328)	1,328	1.08
Belgian (218)	751	0.61
Brazilian (101)	228	0.19
British (179)	396	0.32
Bulgarian (8)	24	0.02
Canadian (309)	680	0.55
Celtic (19)	19	0.02
Croatian (0)	16	0.01
Czech (174)	565	0.46
Czechoslovakian (355)	654	0.53
Danish (56)	129	0.11
Dutch (208)	772	0.63
Eastern European (1,057)	1,144	0.93
English (863)	3,171	2.58
Estonian (24)	48	0.04
European (7,822)	8,814	7.18
Finnish (0)	17	0.01
French, ex. Basque (183)	954	0.78
French Canadian (53)	174	0.14
German (2,191)	7,630	6.22
Greek (402)	653	0.53
Guyanese (294)	371	0.30
Hungarian (3,672)	6,804	5.54
Iranian (181)	314	0.26
Irish (3,209)	8,081	6.59
Israeli (1,511)	3,342	2.72
Italian (4,569)	8,664	7.06
Latvian (87)	174	0.14
Lithuanian (98)	538	0.44
New Zealander (0)	55	0.04
Northern European (0)	38	0.03
Norwegian (64)	140	0.11
Pennsylvania German (10)	17	0.01
Polish (3,146)	9,453	7.70
Portuguese (120)	252	0.21
Romanian (524)	1,695	1.38
Russian (2,367)	6,069	4.95
Scandinavian (15)	52	0.04
Scotch-Irish (119)	424	0.35
Scottish (193)	640	0.52
Slavic (18)	63	0.05
Slovak (69)	114	0.09
Slovene (31)	46	0.04
Swedish (28)	316	0.26
Swiss (34)	85	0.07
Turkish (28)	114	0.09
Ukrainian (949)	1,403	1.14
Welsh (10)	182	0.15
West Indian, ex. Hispanic (12,117)	12,710	10.36
Barbadian (10)	34	0.03
Belizean (12)	35	0.03
British West Indian (253)	253	0.21
Haitian (8,747)	8,948	7.29
Jamaican (2,336)	2,509	2.04
Trinidadian/Tobagonian (550)	604	0.49
U.S. Virgin Islander (0)	19	0.02
West Indian (209)	308	0.25
Yugoslavian (42)	78	0.06

Hispanic Origin	Population	%
Hispanic or Latino (of any race)	17,223	13.60
Central American, ex. Mexican	5,319	4.20
Costa Rican	103	0.08
Guatemalan	4,050	3.20
Honduran	182	0.14
Nicaraguan	29	0.02
Panamanian	54	0.04
Salvadoran	872	0.69
Other Central American	29	0.02
Cuban	279	0.22
Dominican Republic	1,021	0.81
Mexican	2,433	1.92
Puerto Rican	2,904	2.29
South American	3,759	2.97
Argentinean	166	0.13
Bolivian	9	0.01
Chilean	66	0.05
Colombian	308	0.24
Ecuadorian	2,915	2.30
Paraguayan	8	0.01
Peruvian	204	0.16
Uruguayan	16	0.01
Venezuelan	59	0.05
Other South American	8	0.01
Other Hispanic or Latino	1,508	1.19

Race*	Population	%
African-American/Black (20,056)	21,297	16.82
Not Hispanic (19,173)	20,078	15.86
Hispanic (883)	1,219	0.96
American Indian/Alaska Native (430)	963	0.76
Not Hispanic (253)	613	0.48
Hispanic (177)	350	0.28
Aleut *(Alaska Native)* (1)	1	<0.01
Apache (2)	3	<0.01
Blackfeet (1)	11	0.01
Central American Ind. (10)	22	0.02
Cherokee (9)	69	0.05
Cheyenne (0)	1	<0.01
Chippewa (0)	1	<0.01
Choctaw (1)	1	<0.01
Comanche (0)	2	<0.01
Delaware (93)	167	0.13
Iroquois (21)	36	0.03
Lumbee (0)	2	<0.01
Mexican American Ind. (52)	74	0.06
Navajo (0)	4	<0.01
Pueblo (1)	1	<0.01
Seminole (0)	2	<0.01

*Notes: † The Census 2010 population figure is used to calculate the percentages in the Hispanic Origin and Race categories. Ancestry percentages are based on the 2006-2010 American Community Survey population (not shown); ‡ Numbers in parentheses indicate the number of people reporting a single ancestry; * Numbers in parentheses indicate the number of persons reporting this race alone, not in combination with any other race; Please refer to the Explanation of Data for more information.*

Race* (continued)	Population	%
Sioux (0)	2	<0.01
South American Ind. (20)	68	0.05
Spanish American Ind. (3)	7	0.01
Tlingit-Haida *(Alaska Native)* (2)	7	0.01
Tohono O'Odham (2)	4	<0.01
Yakama (0)	1	<0.01
Asian (5,082)	5,750	4.54
Not Hispanic (5,013)	5,609	4.43
Hispanic (69)	141	0.11
Bangladeshi (56)	63	0.05
Burmese (1)	1	<0.01
Cambodian (48)	52	0.04
Chinese, ex. Taiwanese (606)	730	0.58
Filipino (1,338)	1,472	1.16
Indian (1,751)	1,962	1.55
Indonesian (18)	23	0.02
Japanese (98)	136	0.11
Korean (300)	339	0.27
Laotian (4)	6	<0.01
Malaysian (2)	8	0.01
Nepalese (11)	11	0.01
Pakistani (461)	524	0.41
Sri Lankan (23)	26	0.02
Taiwanese (19)	21	0.02
Thai (30)	37	0.03
Vietnamese (112)	148	0.12
Hawaii Native/Pacific Islander (45)	237	0.19
Not Hispanic (18)	156	0.12
Hispanic (27)	81	0.06
Fijian (0)	2	<0.01
Guamanian/Chamorro (16)	19	0.02
Native Hawaiian (8)	17	0.01
Samoan (4)	9	0.01
Tongan (0)	2	<0.01
White (90,924)	92,843	73.34
Not Hispanic (83,094)	84,071	66.41
Hispanic (7,830)	8,772	6.93

Red Hook

Place Type: Town
County: Dutchess
Population: 11,319†

Ancestry‡	Population	%
African, Sub-Saharan (19)	19	0.17
South African (19)	19	0.17
Albanian (10)	30	0.27
American (205)	205	1.83
Arab (0)	23	0.20
Lebanese (0)	23	0.20
Armenian (6)	6	0.05
Australian (0)	55	0.49
Austrian (19)	222	1.98
Belgian (3)	6	0.05
British (34)	126	1.12
Bulgarian (43)	43	0.38
Canadian (30)	67	0.60
Celtic (1)	1	0.01
Croatian (4)	31	0.28
Czech (7)	90	0.80
Czechoslovakian (0)	6	0.05
Danish (0)	41	0.37
Dutch (202)	680	6.06
Eastern European (8)	35	0.31
English (235)	1,675	14.92
Estonian (0)	18	0.16
European (54)	100	0.89
French, ex. Basque (25)	602	5.36
French Canadian (31)	134	1.19
German (411)	2,259	20.12
Greek (39)	111	0.99
Guyanese (54)	54	0.48
Hungarian (26)	187	1.67
Irish (774)	2,870	25.57
Israeli (0)	36	0.32
Italian (531)	1,826	16.27
Latvian (12)	12	0.11
Lithuanian (7)	45	0.40
Northern European (26)	26	0.23
Norwegian (56)	195	1.74
Polish (135)	660	5.88
Portuguese (14)	33	0.29
Romanian (45)	71	0.63
Russian (49)	312	2.78
Scotch-Irish (75)	263	2.34
Scottish (9)	382	3.40
Serbian (0)	87	0.78
Slavic (19)	19	0.17
Slovak (0)	6	0.05
Swedish (17)	163	1.45
Swiss (0)	148	1.32
Ukrainian (18)	18	0.16
Welsh (0)	149	1.33
West Indian, ex. Hispanic (0)	15	0.13
Belizean (0)	3	0.03
Jamaican (0)	12	0.11
Yugoslavian (1)	17	0.15

Hispanic Origin	Population	%
Hispanic or Latino (of any race)	555	4.90
Central American, ex. Mexican	77	0.68
Costa Rican	6	0.05
Guatemalan	53	0.47
Honduran	2	0.02
Panamanian	3	0.03
Salvadoran	13	0.11
Cuban	27	0.24
Dominican Republic	17	0.15
Mexican	163	1.44
Puerto Rican	147	1.30
South American	64	0.57
Argentinean	9	0.08
Chilean	3	0.03
Colombian	27	0.24
Ecuadorian	5	0.04
Paraguayan	3	0.03
Peruvian	7	0.06
Venezuelan	9	0.08
Other South American	1	0.01
Other Hispanic or Latino	60	0.53

Race*	Population	%
African-American/Black (220)	290	2.56
Not Hispanic (190)	251	2.22
Hispanic (30)	39	0.34
American Indian/Alaska Native (26)	76	0.67
Not Hispanic (19)	61	0.54
Hispanic (7)	15	0.13
Blackfeet (0)	2	0.02
Cherokee (3)	15	0.13
Cheyenne (1)	1	0.01
Chippewa (2)	2	0.02
Creek (0)	2	0.02
Iroquois (7)	7	0.06
Mexican American Ind. (1)	1	0.01
Osage (1)	1	0.01
Sioux (0)	3	0.03
South American Ind. (1)	5	0.04
Spanish American Ind. (2)	2	0.02
Asian (272)	350	3.09
Not Hispanic (272)	349	3.08
Hispanic (0)	1	0.01
Bangladeshi (1)	1	0.01
Burmese (2)	2	0.02
Cambodian (1)	1	0.01
Chinese, ex. Taiwanese (70)	93	0.82
Filipino (31)	37	0.33
Indian (51)	59	0.52
Japanese (34)	58	0.51
Korean (41)	57	0.50
Nepalese (1)	1	0.01
Pakistani (4)	5	0.04
Taiwanese (12)	14	0.12
Thai (1)	3	0.03
Vietnamese (11)	12	0.11
Hawaii Native/Pacific Islander (5)	14	0.12
Not Hispanic (1)	9	0.08
Hispanic (4)	5	0.04
Native Hawaiian (5)	12	0.11
White (10,411)	10,592	93.58
Not Hispanic (10,089)	10,243	90.49
Hispanic (322)	349	3.08

Rensselaer

Place Type: City
County: Rensselaer
Population: 9,392†

Ancestry‡	Population	%
African, Sub-Saharan (9)	9	0.10
Other Sub-Saharan African (9)	9	0.10
Albanian (10)	10	0.11
American (261)	261	2.85
Arab (10)	10	0.11
Lebanese (10)	10	0.11
Armenian (14)	48	0.52
Austrian (0)	38	0.41
Belgian (0)	61	0.67
British (13)	20	0.22
Czech (8)	17	0.19
Dutch (27)	775	8.46
English (147)	1,089	11.89
European (17)	17	0.19
French, ex. Basque (67)	639	6.97
French Canadian (98)	334	3.65
German (417)	1,649	18.00
Greek (0)	36	0.39
Guyanese (23)	93	1.02
Hungarian (35)	49	0.53
Irish (428)	2,249	24.55
Italian (842)	1,784	19.47
Latvian (0)	14	0.15
Lithuanian (0)	31	0.34
Norwegian (0)	15	0.16
Polish (131)	541	5.90
Portuguese (22)	154	1.68
Russian (63)	120	1.31
Scotch-Irish (71)	108	1.18
Scottish (23)	122	1.33
Slovak (2)	4	0.04
Swedish (14)	63	0.69
Swiss (0)	14	0.15
Ukrainian (28)	40	0.44
Welsh (0)	62	0.68

Hispanic Origin	Population	%
Hispanic or Latino (of any race)	448	4.77
Central American, ex. Mexican	12	0.13
Costa Rican	3	0.03
Guatemalan	1	0.01
Salvadoran	8	0.09
Cuban	9	0.10
Dominican Republic	14	0.15
Mexican	55	0.59
Puerto Rican	263	2.80
South American	34	0.36
Argentinean	7	0.07
Chilean	6	0.06
Colombian	8	0.09
Ecuadorian	6	0.06
Venezuelan	7	0.07
Other Hispanic or Latino	61	0.65

Race*	Population	%
African-American/Black (750)	991	10.55
Not Hispanic (693)	891	9.49
Hispanic (57)	100	1.06
American Indian/Alaska Native (31)	111	1.18
Not Hispanic (27)	100	1.06
Hispanic (4)	11	0.12
Apache (0)	2	0.02
Blackfeet (0)	10	0.11
Canadian/French Am. Ind. (2)	7	0.07
Cherokee (12)	25	0.27
Creek (0)	1	0.01
Iroquois (5)	12	0.13
South American Ind. (1)	2	0.02
Asian (576)	653	6.95

*Notes: † The Census 2010 population figure is used to calculate the percentages in the Hispanic Origin and Race categories. Ancestry percentages are based on the 2006-2010 American Community Survey population (not shown); ‡ Numbers in parentheses indicate the number of people reporting a single ancestry; * Numbers in parentheses indicate the number of persons reporting this race alone, not in combination with any other race; Please refer to the Explanation of Data for more information.*

Not Hispanic (571)	643	6.85
Hispanic (5)	10	0.11
Burmese (295)	316	3.36
Chinese, ex. Taiwanese (25)	38	0.40
Filipino (25)	43	0.46
Indian (102)	118	1.26
Japanese (14)	23	0.24
Korean (12)	24	0.26
Laotian (2)	5	0.05
Nepalese (2)	6	0.06
Pakistani (47)	49	0.52
Taiwanese (1)	1	0.01
Thai (5)	9	0.10
Vietnamese (5)	7	0.07
Hawaii Native/Pacific Islander (0)	4	0.04
Not Hispanic (0)	4	0.04
Native Hawaiian (0)	1	0.01
White (7,537)	7,900	84.11
Not Hispanic (7,316)	7,612	81.05
Hispanic (221)	288	3.07

Rhinebeck

Place Type: Town
County: Dutchess
Population: 7,548†

Ancestry‡	Population	%
African, Sub-Saharan (9)	29	0.38
South African (9)	29	0.38
Albanian (6)	6	0.08
Alsatian (0)	10	0.13
American (201)	201	2.63
Arab (0)	14	0.18
Lebanese (0)	14	0.18
Austrian (9)	48	0.63
British (10)	20	0.26
Canadian (0)	38	0.50
Czech (13)	13	0.17
Czechoslovakian (18)	18	0.24
Danish (0)	18	0.24
Dutch (56)	485	6.34
Eastern European (13)	25	0.33
English (242)	1,136	14.85
European (108)	108	1.41
Finnish (0)	33	0.43
French, ex. Basque (29)	242	3.16
French Canadian (47)	81	1.06
German (377)	1,862	24.33
Greek (28)	72	0.94
Hungarian (33)	106	1.39
Irish (557)	2,013	26.31
Israeli (10)	10	0.13
Italian (352)	1,043	13.63
Latvian (0)	16	0.21
Lithuanian (55)	65	0.85
Northern European (24)	24	0.31
Norwegian (5)	53	0.69
Polish (112)	454	5.93
Portuguese (0)	18	0.24
Romanian (0)	7	0.09
Russian (102)	316	4.13
Scotch-Irish (35)	188	2.46
Scottish (82)	270	3.53
Slavic (0)	21	0.27
Slovak (17)	17	0.22
Slovene (0)	5	0.07
Swedish (8)	73	0.95
Swiss (10)	62	0.81
Turkish (0)	14	0.18
Ukrainian (7)	43	0.56
Welsh (16)	52	0.68
West Indian, ex. Hispanic (32)	73	0.95
Haitian (0)	41	0.54
Jamaican (32)	32	0.42

Hispanic Origin	Population	%
Hispanic or Latino (of any race)	387	5.13
Central American, ex. Mexican	22	0.29
Costa Rican	4	0.05
Guatemalan	7	0.09
Honduran	3	0.04
Nicaraguan	6	0.08
Panamanian	2	0.03
Cuban	16	0.21
Dominican Republic	9	0.12
Mexican	172	2.28
Puerto Rican	81	1.07
South American	42	0.56
Argentinean	10	0.13
Chilean	1	0.01
Colombian	8	0.11
Ecuadorian	10	0.13
Paraguayan	7	0.09
Peruvian	5	0.07
Venezuelan	1	0.01
Other Hispanic or Latino	45	0.60

Race*	Population	%
African-American/Black (189)	225	2.98
Not Hispanic (185)	214	2.84
Hispanic (4)	11	0.15
American Indian/Alaska Native (8)	34	0.45
Not Hispanic (8)	28	0.37
Hispanic (0)	6	0.08
Aleut *(Alaska Native)* (1)	1	0.01
Central American Ind. (0)	1	0.01
Cherokee (1)	12	0.16
Iroquois (2)	7	0.09
Shoshone (0)	2	0.03
South American Ind. (0)	1	0.01
Ute (0)	1	0.01
Asian (134)	180	2.38
Not Hispanic (132)	175	2.32
Hispanic (2)	5	0.07
Bangladeshi (5)	5	0.07
Chinese, ex. Taiwanese (43)	58	0.77
Filipino (36)	55	0.73
Indian (6)	10	0.13
Japanese (3)	7	0.09
Korean (9)	13	0.17
Pakistani (5)	6	0.08
Taiwanese (5)	5	0.07
Thai (3)	5	0.07
Vietnamese (10)	11	0.15
Hawaii Native/Pacific Islander (4)	8	0.11
Not Hispanic (4)	8	0.11
Guamanian/Chamorro (4)	6	0.08
Native Hawaiian (0)	1	0.01
White (6,976)	7,062	93.56
Not Hispanic (6,738)	6,812	90.25
Hispanic (238)	250	3.31

Ridge

Place Type: CDP
County: Suffolk
Population: 13,336†

Ancestry‡	Population	%
African, Sub-Saharan (254)	254	1.93
African (236)	236	1.79
Ghanaian (18)	18	0.14
American (254)	254	1.93
Austrian (0)	27	0.20
British (53)	66	0.50
Canadian (0)	14	0.11
Croatian (0)	36	0.27
Czech (74)	132	1.00
Czechoslovakian (14)	20	0.15
Danish (15)	15	0.11
Dutch (15)	232	1.76
English (70)	698	5.30
Estonian (0)	14	0.11
European (96)	96	0.73
Finnish (15)	15	0.11
French, ex. Basque (56)	366	2.78
French Canadian (0)	46	0.35
German (463)	2,580	19.59
Greek (13)	38	0.29
Hungarian (47)	108	0.82
Irish (1,215)	3,687	27.99
Israeli (0)	18	0.14
Italian (2,545)	4,783	36.31
Latvian (15)	15	0.11
Lithuanian (13)	34	0.26
Maltese (0)	21	0.16
Norwegian (44)	156	1.18
Polish (252)	1,031	7.83
Portuguese (24)	142	1.08
Romanian (0)	15	0.11
Russian (36)	289	2.19
Scandinavian (14)	27	0.20
Scotch-Irish (6)	102	0.77
Scottish (26)	42	0.32
Slavic (0)	14	0.11
Slovak (18)	54	0.41
Swedish (28)	164	1.25
Swiss (0)	45	0.34
Ukrainian (29)	89	0.68
Welsh (0)	30	0.23
West Indian, ex. Hispanic (38)	65	0.49
Haitian (27)	54	0.41
Jamaican (5)	5	0.04
Trinidadian/Tobagonian (6)	6	0.05

Hispanic Origin	Population	%
Hispanic or Latino (of any race)	749	5.62
Central American, ex. Mexican	57	0.43
Costa Rican	2	0.01
Guatemalan	10	0.07
Honduran	4	0.03
Nicaraguan	2	0.01
Panamanian	3	0.02
Salvadoran	36	0.27
Cuban	28	0.21
Dominican Republic	36	0.27
Mexican	66	0.49
Puerto Rican	347	2.60
South American	132	0.99
Argentinean	21	0.16
Colombian	71	0.53
Ecuadorian	20	0.15
Peruvian	14	0.10
Uruguayan	1	0.01
Venezuelan	4	0.03
Other South American	1	0.01
Other Hispanic or Latino	83	0.62

Race*	Population	%
African-American/Black (647)	748	5.61
Not Hispanic (601)	682	5.11
Hispanic (46)	66	0.49
American Indian/Alaska Native (22)	70	0.52
Not Hispanic (14)	53	0.40
Hispanic (8)	17	0.13
Blackfeet (0)	6	0.04
Canadian/French Am. Ind. (0)	1	0.01
Cherokee (4)	15	0.11
Chippewa (0)	1	0.01
Iroquois (0)	2	0.01
Mexican American Ind. (1)	2	0.01
Navajo (1)	1	0.01
Paiute (0)	1	0.01
Sioux (2)	2	0.01
Asian (242)	294	2.20
Not Hispanic (241)	287	2.15
Hispanic (1)	7	0.05
Burmese (1)	1	0.01
Chinese, ex. Taiwanese (73)	83	0.62
Filipino (17)	32	0.24
Indian (65)	75	0.56
Indonesian (2)	3	0.02
Japanese (6)	12	0.09
Korean (33)	40	0.30
Nepalese (7)	7	0.05
Pakistani (23)	24	0.18
Sri Lankan (4)	4	0.03
Taiwanese (0)	2	0.01
Vietnamese (3)	3	0.02

*Notes: † The Census 2010 population figure is used to calculate the percentages in the Hispanic Origin and Race categories. Ancestry percentages are based on the 2006-2010 American Community Survey population (not shown); ‡ Numbers in parentheses indicate the number of people reporting a single ancestry; * Numbers in parentheses indicate the number of persons reporting this race alone, not in combination with any other race; Please refer to the Explanation of Data for more information.*

Hawaii Native/Pacific Islander (1)	10	0.07
Not Hispanic (1)	10	0.07
Native Hawaiian (1)	5	0.04
White (12,105)	12,250	91.86
Not Hispanic (11,570)	11,693	87.68
Hispanic (535)	557	4.18

Riverhead

Place Type: CDP
County: Suffolk
Population: 13,299†

Ancestry‡	Population	%
American (220)	220	1.73
Austrian (0)	26	0.20
British (19)	19	0.15
Canadian (0)	12	0.09
Croatian (0)	15	0.12
Czech (13)	41	0.32
Dutch (0)	23	0.18
Eastern European (13)	40	0.31
English (219)	940	7.40
European (26)	26	0.20
Finnish (0)	13	0.10
French, ex. Basque (46)	206	1.62
French Canadian (32)	69	0.54
German (445)	1,448	11.40
Greek (41)	41	0.32
Hungarian (12)	12	0.09
Iranian (13)	13	0.10
Irish (519)	1,523	11.99
Italian (707)	1,472	11.59
Lithuanian (36)	61	0.48
Northern European (0)	27	0.21
Norwegian (11)	243	1.91
Polish (1,617)	2,558	20.14
Romanian (13)	26	0.20
Russian (24)	81	0.64
Scotch-Irish (8)	8	0.06
Scottish (0)	96	0.76
Swedish (0)	144	1.13
Swiss (0)	12	0.09
Ukrainian (0)	121	0.95
Welsh (19)	37	0.29
West Indian, ex. Hispanic (30)	107	0.84
Jamaican (30)	30	0.24
West Indian (0)	77	0.61

Hispanic Origin	Population	%
Hispanic or Latino (of any race)	3,369	25.33
Central American, ex. Mexican	1,944	14.62
Costa Rican	8	0.06
Guatemalan	1,181	8.88
Honduran	245	1.84
Nicaraguan	11	0.08
Panamanian	2	0.02
Salvadoran	495	3.72
Other Central American	2	0.02
Cuban	31	0.23
Dominican Republic	79	0.59
Mexican	536	4.03
Puerto Rican	263	1.98
South American	255	1.92
Argentinean	3	0.02
Chilean	3	0.02
Colombian	105	0.79
Ecuadorian	116	0.87
Paraguayan	2	0.02
Peruvian	25	0.19
Venezuelan	1	0.01
Other Hispanic or Latino	261	1.96

Race*	Population	%
African-American/Black (2,097)	2,335	17.56
Not Hispanic (2,033)	2,228	16.75
Hispanic (64)	107	0.80
American Indian/Alaska Native (76)	202	1.52
Not Hispanic (32)	139	1.05
Hispanic (44)	63	0.47
Aleut *(Alaska Native)* (0)	1	0.01
Apache (3)	4	0.03
Blackfeet (2)	9	0.07
Canadian/French Am. Ind. (2)	2	0.02
Central American Ind. (1)	1	0.01
Cherokee (5)	36	0.27
Chippewa (0)	1	0.01
Creek (0)	1	0.01
Iroquois (0)	1	0.01
Mexican American Ind. (20)	22	0.17
Potawatomi (0)	4	0.03
Seminole (0)	2	0.02
South American Ind. (2)	5	0.04
Asian (226)	317	2.38
Not Hispanic (220)	303	2.28
Hispanic (6)	14	0.11
Bangladeshi (7)	7	0.05
Chinese, ex. Taiwanese (56)	79	0.59
Filipino (31)	50	0.38
Indian (36)	54	0.41
Japanese (9)	26	0.20
Korean (12)	15	0.11
Laotian (0)	1	0.01
Pakistani (50)	52	0.39
Taiwanese (3)	3	0.02
Thai (4)	5	0.04
Vietnamese (5)	7	0.05
Hawaii Native/Pacific Islander (15)	24	0.18
Not Hispanic (3)	9	0.07
Hispanic (12)	15	0.11
Guamanian/Chamorro (12)	12	0.09
Native Hawaiian (1)	2	0.02
Samoan (1)	3	0.02
Tongan (1)	1	0.01
White (8,787)	9,168	68.94
Not Hispanic (7,325)	7,547	56.75
Hispanic (1,462)	1,621	12.19

Riverhead

Place Type: Town
County: Suffolk
Population: 33,506†

Ancestry‡	Population	%
African, Sub-Saharan (106)	126	0.39
African (91)	111	0.34
South African (15)	15	0.05
American (824)	824	2.53
Arab (0)	37	0.11
Lebanese (0)	26	0.08
Syrian (0)	11	0.03
Armenian (0)	15	0.05
Austrian (0)	189	0.58
Brazilian (8)	15	0.05
British (42)	55	0.17
Bulgarian (17)	32	0.10
Canadian (25)	69	0.21
Croatian (0)	68	0.21
Czech (40)	182	0.56
Czechoslovakian (10)	47	0.14
Danish (0)	171	0.53
Dutch (66)	551	1.70
Eastern European (70)	97	0.30
English (574)	2,948	9.07
European (149)	149	0.46
Finnish (60)	73	0.22
French, ex. Basque (173)	808	2.49
French Canadian (120)	199	0.61
German (1,495)	5,156	15.86
Greek (141)	159	0.49
Hungarian (23)	117	0.36
Iranian (13)	13	0.04
Irish (2,313)	7,019	21.59
Italian (3,148)	6,896	21.21
Latvian (0)	14	0.04
Lithuanian (36)	92	0.28
Northern European (0)	27	0.08
Norwegian (68)	453	1.39
Polish (2,695)	4,773	14.68
Portuguese (31)	107	0.33
Romanian (60)	88	0.27
Russian (150)	622	1.91
Scotch-Irish (199)	335	1.03
Scottish (24)	470	1.45
Slavic (20)	20	0.06
Slovak (11)	11	0.03
Swedish (0)	432	1.33
Swiss (0)	146	0.45
Turkish (178)	178	0.55
Ukrainian (72)	236	0.73
Welsh (29)	207	0.64
West Indian, ex. Hispanic (30)	114	0.35
Jamaican (30)	30	0.09
U.S. Virgin Islander (0)	7	0.02
West Indian (0)	77	0.24

Hispanic Origin	Population	%
Hispanic or Latino (of any race)	4,649	13.88
Central American, ex. Mexican	2,379	7.10
Costa Rican	13	0.04
Guatemalan	1,491	4.45
Honduran	251	0.75
Nicaraguan	13	0.04
Panamanian	8	0.02
Salvadoran	601	1.79
Other Central American	2	0.01
Cuban	71	0.21
Dominican Republic	104	0.31
Mexican	652	1.95
Puerto Rican	573	1.71
South American	415	1.24
Argentinean	20	0.06
Chilean	11	0.03
Colombian	168	0.50
Ecuadorian	163	0.49
Paraguayan	3	0.01
Peruvian	46	0.14
Uruguayan	2	0.01
Venezuelan	1	<0.01
Other South American	1	<0.01
Other Hispanic or Latino	455	1.36

Race*	Population	%
African-American/Black (2,579)	2,921	8.72
Not Hispanic (2,501)	2,786	8.31
Hispanic (78)	135	0.40
American Indian/Alaska Native (93)	276	0.82
Not Hispanic (40)	195	0.58
Hispanic (53)	81	0.24
Alaska Athabascan *(Ala. Nat.)* (0)	1	<0.01
Aleut *(Alaska Native)* (0)	1	<0.01
Apache (3)	5	0.01
Blackfeet (2)	12	0.04
Canadian/French Am. Ind. (2)	2	0.01
Central American Ind. (2)	2	0.01
Cherokee (5)	42	0.13
Chickasaw (0)	1	<0.01
Chippewa (1)	2	0.01
Creek (0)	1	<0.01
Iroquois (1)	4	0.01
Mexican American Ind. (22)	26	0.08
Potawatomi (0)	4	0.01
Pueblo (1)	1	<0.01
Seminole (0)	2	0.01
Sioux (0)	1	<0.01
South American Ind. (4)	8	0.02
Asian (382)	550	1.64
Not Hispanic (367)	514	1.53
Hispanic (15)	36	0.11
Bangladeshi (7)	7	0.02
Cambodian (1)	1	<0.01
Chinese, ex. Taiwanese (108)	145	0.43
Filipino (55)	89	0.27
Indian (63)	92	0.27
Indonesian (2)	2	0.01
Japanese (22)	51	0.15
Korean (35)	49	0.15
Laotian (2)	5	0.01
Pakistani (58)	66	0.20

*Notes: † The Census 2010 population figure is used to calculate the percentages in the Hispanic Origin and Race categories. Ancestry percentages are based on the 2006-2010 American Community Survey population (not shown); ‡ Numbers in parentheses indicate the number of people reporting a single ancestry; * Numbers in parentheses indicate the number of persons reporting this race alone, not in combination with any other race; Please refer to the Explanation of Data for more information.*

Taiwanese (3)	3	0.01
Thai (5)	10	0.03
Vietnamese (5)	9	0.03
Hawaii Native/Pacific Islander (31)	44	0.13
Not Hispanic (5)	15	0.04
Hispanic (26)	29	0.09
Guamanian/Chamorro (25)	25	0.07
Native Hawaiian (3)	6	0.02
Samoan (1)	4	0.01
Tongan (1)	1	<0.01
White (27,726)	28,336	84.57
Not Hispanic (25,421)	25,810	77.03
Hispanic (2,305)	2,526	7.54

Rochester

Place Type: City
County: Monroe
Population: 210,565†

Ancestry‡	Population	%
African, Sub-Saharan (7,095)	7,909	3.73
African (5,087)	5,828	2.75
Ethiopian (227)	227	0.11
Ghanaian (49)	49	0.02
Kenyan (9)	9	<0.01
Liberian (89)	89	0.04
Nigerian (151)	203	0.10
Somalian (980)	980	0.46
South African (19)	32	0.02
Sudanese (107)	107	0.05
Zimbabwean (76)	76	0.04
Other Sub-Saharan African (301)	309	0.15
Albanian (31)	42	0.02
American (3,617)	3,617	1.71
Arab (785)	1,077	0.51
Arab (245)	263	0.12
Egyptian (81)	81	0.04
Iraqi (36)	36	0.02
Lebanese (136)	196	0.09
Moroccan (17)	48	0.02
Palestinian (30)	30	0.01
Syrian (11)	33	0.02
Other Arab (229)	390	0.18
Armenian (84)	105	0.05
Australian (0)	69	0.03
Austrian (103)	450	0.21
Belgian (27)	185	0.09
Brazilian (35)	90	0.04
British (259)	606	0.29
Bulgarian (0)	33	0.02
Canadian (227)	550	0.26
Celtic (13)	40	0.02
Croatian (12)	61	0.03
Czech (77)	484	0.23
Czechoslovakian (30)	44	0.02
Danish (51)	275	0.13
Dutch (406)	2,898	1.37
Eastern European (200)	237	0.11
English (3,972)	13,510	6.37
Estonian (0)	38	0.02
European (893)	1,150	0.54
Finnish (11)	160	0.08
French, ex. Basque (683)	4,083	1.93
French Canadian (652)	1,474	0.70
German (5,802)	22,972	10.84
Greek (337)	623	0.29
Guyanese (348)	381	0.18
Hungarian (246)	783	0.37
Iranian (97)	120	0.06
Irish (5,531)	19,595	9.24
Israeli (37)	57	0.03
Italian (8,976)	19,728	9.31
Latvian (33)	55	0.03
Lithuanian (236)	466	0.22
Luxemburger (19)	62	0.03
Macedonian (0)	10	<0.01
Maltese (34)	100	0.05
Northern European (23)	23	0.01
Norwegian (135)	444	0.21
Pennsylvania German (8)	70	0.03
Polish (1,583)	5,614	2.65
Portuguese (47)	199	0.09
Romanian (96)	186	0.09
Russian (498)	1,342	0.63
Scandinavian (34)	111	0.05
Scotch-Irish (433)	1,614	0.76
Scottish (526)	3,002	1.42
Serbian (0)	49	0.02
Slavic (32)	78	0.04
Slovak (24)	157	0.07
Slovene (24)	37	0.02
Swedish (403)	1,156	0.55
Swiss (36)	271	0.13
Turkish (486)	612	0.29
Ukrainian (727)	1,325	0.63
Welsh (141)	992	0.47
West Indian, ex. Hispanic (3,129)	5,230	2.47
Bahamian (58)	218	0.10
Barbadian (169)	230	0.11
Belizean (119)	171	0.08
British West Indian (99)	223	0.11
Dutch West Indian (0)	13	0.01
Haitian (352)	383	0.18
Jamaican (1,743)	2,834	1.34
Trinidadian/Tobagonian (199)	288	0.14
West Indian (390)	870	0.41
Yugoslavian (117)	138	0.07

Hispanic Origin	Population	%
Hispanic or Latino (of any race)	34,456	16.36
Central American, ex. Mexican	569	0.27
Costa Rican	72	0.03
Guatemalan	85	0.04
Honduran	129	0.06
Nicaraguan	56	0.03
Panamanian	123	0.06
Salvadoran	96	0.05
Other Central American	8	<0.01
Cuban	1,616	0.77
Dominican Republic	1,373	0.65
Mexican	1,168	0.55
Puerto Rican	27,734	13.17
South American	517	0.25
Argentinean	49	0.02
Bolivian	18	0.01
Chilean	82	0.04
Colombian	182	0.09
Ecuadorian	72	0.03
Paraguayan	10	<0.01
Peruvian	68	0.03
Uruguayan	7	<0.01
Venezuelan	22	0.01
Other South American	7	<0.01
Other Hispanic or Latino	1,479	0.70

Race*	Population	%
African-American/Black (87,897)	94,587	44.92
Not Hispanic (83,346)	88,052	41.82
Hispanic (4,551)	6,535	3.10
American Indian/Alaska Native (1,013)	3,202	1.52
Not Hispanic (666)	2,330	1.11
Hispanic (347)	872	0.41
Alaska Athabascan *(Ala. Nat.)* (0)	1	<0.01
Aleut *(Alaska Native)* (1)	2	<0.01
Apache (8)	20	0.01
Blackfeet (16)	134	0.06
Canadian/French Am. Ind. (3)	9	<0.01
Central American Ind. (15)	29	0.01
Cherokee (51)	411	0.20
Cheyenne (2)	3	<0.01
Chickasaw (0)	2	<0.01
Chippewa (9)	18	0.01
Choctaw (1)	28	0.01
Colville (0)	1	<0.01
Comanche (0)	2	<0.01
Cree (1)	2	<0.01
Creek (2)	9	<0.01
Crow (0)	1	<0.01
Delaware (1)	10	<0.01
Hopi (1)	1	<0.01
Inupiat *(Alaska Native)* (3)	4	<0.01
Iroquois (265)	483	0.23
Mexican American Ind. (20)	38	0.02
Navajo (11)	30	0.01
Osage (1)	3	<0.01
Paiute (1)	1	<0.01
Pima (0)	2	<0.01
Potawatomi (3)	5	<0.01
Pueblo (0)	2	<0.01
Seminole (1)	44	0.02
Shoshone (0)	1	<0.01
Sioux (2)	22	0.01
South American Ind. (45)	144	0.07
Spanish American Ind. (9)	9	<0.01
Tohono O'Odham (1)	1	<0.01
Ute (0)	4	<0.01
Asian (6,493)	7,752	3.68
Not Hispanic (6,350)	7,397	3.51
Hispanic (143)	355	0.17
Bangladeshi (25)	27	0.01
Bhutanese (369)	411	0.20
Burmese (527)	565	0.27
Cambodian (342)	381	0.18
Chinese, ex. Taiwanese (1,195)	1,456	0.69
Filipino (215)	378	0.18
Hmong (2)	3	<0.01
Indian (780)	1,006	0.48
Indonesian (13)	27	0.01
Japanese (127)	301	0.14
Korean (578)	741	0.35
Laotian (564)	668	0.32
Malaysian (8)	10	<0.01
Nepalese (118)	165	0.08
Pakistani (53)	75	0.04
Sri Lankan (23)	27	0.01
Taiwanese (104)	132	0.06
Thai (67)	103	0.05
Vietnamese (942)	1,050	0.50
Hawaii Native/Pacific Islander (101)	449	0.21
Not Hispanic (77)	284	0.13
Hispanic (24)	165	0.08
Fijian (0)	4	<0.01
Guamanian/Chamorro (12)	26	0.01
Native Hawaiian (30)	77	0.04
Samoan (31)	63	0.03
Tongan (2)	3	<0.01
White (91,951)	98,814	46.93
Not Hispanic (79,178)	84,019	39.90
Hispanic (12,773)	14,795	7.03

Rockville Centre

Place Type: Village
County: Nassau
Population: 24,023†

Ancestry‡	Population	%
African, Sub-Saharan (9)	30	0.13
Ghanaian (9)	30	0.13
American (1,006)	1,006	4.20
Arab (12)	84	0.35
Lebanese (0)	61	0.25
Palestinian (0)	11	0.05
Syrian (12)	12	0.05
Armenian (47)	107	0.45
Austrian (22)	140	0.58
British (87)	87	0.36
Canadian (16)	56	0.23
Carpatho Rusyn (0)	12	0.05
Croatian (49)	71	0.30
Czech (8)	47	0.20
Czechoslovakian (10)	10	0.04
Dutch (26)	275	1.15
Eastern European (203)	225	0.94
English (229)	1,310	5.47
Estonian (0)	10	0.04
European (197)	237	0.99
Finnish (0)	11	0.05
French, ex. Basque (21)	334	1.40

*Notes: † The Census 2010 population figure is used to calculate the percentages in the Hispanic Origin and Race categories. Ancestry percentages are based on the 2006-2010 American Community Survey population (not shown); ‡ Numbers in parentheses indicate the number of people reporting a single ancestry; * Numbers in parentheses indicate the number of persons reporting this race alone, not in combination with any other race; Please refer to the Explanation of Data for more information.*

Ancestry	Population	%
French Canadian (0)	11	0.05
German (632)	3,575	14.93
Greek (166)	282	1.18
Hungarian (136)	258	1.08
Irish (3,576)	8,256	34.48
Israeli (65)	65	0.27
Italian (3,012)	6,207	25.93
Latvian (17)	17	0.07
Lithuanian (91)	112	0.47
Maltese (8)	8	0.03
Northern European (28)	28	0.12
Norwegian (124)	272	1.14
Pennsylvania German (9)	9	0.04
Polish (332)	1,408	5.88
Portuguese (0)	10	0.04
Romanian (54)	82	0.34
Russian (511)	1,154	4.82
Scandinavian (0)	20	0.08
Scotch-Irish (30)	162	0.68
Scottish (19)	131	0.55
Serbian (9)	9	0.04
Slovak (14)	79	0.33
Swedish (31)	171	0.71
Swiss (0)	87	0.36
Turkish (0)	21	0.09
Ukrainian (57)	117	0.49
Welsh (12)	36	0.15
West Indian, ex. Hispanic (150)	170	0.71
Haitian (123)	143	0.60
West Indian (27)	27	0.11
Yugoslavian (0)	56	0.23

Hispanic Origin	Population	%
Hispanic or Latino (of any race)	2,169	9.03
Central American, ex. Mexican	215	0.89
Costa Rican	3	0.01
Guatemalan	46	0.19
Honduran	23	0.10
Nicaraguan	1	<0.01
Panamanian	4	0.02
Salvadoran	138	0.57
Cuban	158	0.66
Dominican Republic	743	3.09
Mexican	92	0.38
Puerto Rican	462	1.92
South American	296	1.23
Argentinean	22	0.09
Bolivian	4	0.02
Chilean	21	0.09
Colombian	101	0.42
Ecuadorian	82	0.34
Paraguayan	1	<0.01
Peruvian	46	0.19
Uruguayan	8	0.03
Venezuelan	10	0.04
Other South American	1	<0.01
Other Hispanic or Latino	203	0.85

Race*	Population	%
African-American/Black (1,097)	1,249	5.20
Not Hispanic (1,039)	1,134	4.72
Hispanic (58)	115	0.48
American Indian/Alaska Native (32)	138	0.57
Not Hispanic (13)	92	0.38
Hispanic (19)	46	0.19
Apache (0)	1	<0.01
Blackfeet (0)	1	<0.01
Cherokee (1)	10	0.04
Chickasaw (0)	4	0.02
Chippewa (1)	1	<0.01
Cree (0)	1	<0.01
Iroquois (0)	8	0.03
Mexican American Ind. (0)	2	0.01
Sioux (0)	2	0.01
South American Ind. (2)	5	0.02
Spanish American Ind. (2)	2	0.01
Asian (504)	655	2.73
Not Hispanic (498)	636	2.65
Hispanic (6)	19	0.08
Cambodian (1)	1	<0.01
Chinese, ex. Taiwanese (152)	188	0.78
Filipino (71)	91	0.38
Indian (173)	200	0.83
Indonesian (2)	4	0.02
Japanese (18)	36	0.15
Korean (62)	86	0.36
Pakistani (2)	2	0.01
Sri Lankan (1)	1	<0.01
Taiwanese (2)	2	0.01
Thai (3)	3	0.01
Vietnamese (7)	17	0.07
Hawaii Native/Pacific Islander (5)	20	0.08
Not Hispanic (5)	13	0.05
Hispanic (0)	7	0.03
Native Hawaiian (0)	2	0.01
Samoan (0)	4	0.02
White (21,301)	21,637	90.07
Not Hispanic (20,015)	20,222	84.18
Hispanic (1,286)	1,415	5.89

Rocky Point

Place Type: CDP
County: Suffolk
Population: 14,014†

Ancestry‡	Population	%
Albanian (34)	34	0.25
American (325)	325	2.40
Arab (11)	11	0.08
Egyptian (11)	11	0.08
Austrian (0)	66	0.49
Belgian (0)	29	0.21
Brazilian (39)	39	0.29
British (0)	12	0.09
Canadian (34)	75	0.55
Czech (19)	125	0.92
Czechoslovakian (30)	39	0.29
Danish (0)	13	0.10
Dutch (0)	148	1.09
Eastern European (13)	39	0.29
English (182)	1,274	9.39
European (18)	18	0.13
Finnish (0)	95	0.70
French, ex. Basque (88)	559	4.12
French Canadian (31)	31	0.23
German (485)	3,726	27.47
Greek (166)	341	2.51
Hungarian (33)	111	0.82
Irish (981)	4,042	29.80
Italian (1,770)	4,736	34.91
Lithuanian (0)	48	0.35
Maltese (23)	33	0.24
Northern European (0)	16	0.12
Norwegian (106)	318	2.34
Polish (86)	797	5.88
Portuguese (5)	18	0.13
Romanian (0)	9	0.07
Russian (107)	455	3.35
Scandinavian (9)	17	0.13
Scotch-Irish (15)	192	1.42
Scottish (13)	185	1.36
Swedish (0)	249	1.84
Swiss (0)	11	0.08
Turkish (40)	40	0.29
Ukrainian (0)	133	0.98
Welsh (0)	36	0.27
West Indian, ex. Hispanic (34)	51	0.38
Trinidadian/Tobagonian (34)	51	0.38
Yugoslavian (9)	9	0.07

Hispanic Origin	Population	%
Hispanic or Latino (of any race)	978	6.98
Central American, ex. Mexican	266	1.90
Costa Rican	4	0.03
Guatemalan	20	0.14
Honduran	15	0.11
Panamanian	1	0.01
Salvadoran	226	1.61
Cuban	39	0.28
Dominican Republic	39	0.28
Mexican	53	0.38
Puerto Rican	346	2.47
South American	107	0.76
Argentinean	10	0.07
Chilean	9	0.06
Colombian	46	0.33
Ecuadorian	31	0.22
Paraguayan	1	0.01
Peruvian	10	0.07
Other Hispanic or Latino	128	0.91

Race*	Population	%
African-American/Black (207)	291	2.08
Not Hispanic (187)	254	1.81
Hispanic (20)	37	0.26
American Indian/Alaska Native (21)	70	0.50
Not Hispanic (18)	58	0.41
Hispanic (3)	12	0.09
Blackfeet (0)	1	0.01
Canadian/French Am. Ind. (0)	1	0.01
Cherokee (1)	13	0.09
Cheyenne (0)	3	0.02
Delaware (0)	1	0.01
Iroquois (4)	14	0.10
Osage (0)	1	0.01
South American Ind. (0)	3	0.02
Yaqui (1)	1	0.01
Asian (222)	267	1.91
Not Hispanic (222)	266	1.90
Hispanic (0)	1	0.01
Chinese, ex. Taiwanese (79)	89	0.64
Filipino (29)	38	0.27
Indian (47)	54	0.39
Japanese (14)	15	0.11
Korean (25)	33	0.24
Pakistani (11)	11	0.08
Sri Lankan (4)	4	0.03
Taiwanese (2)	4	0.03
Thai (2)	3	0.02
Vietnamese (1)	6	0.04
Hawaii Native/Pacific Islander (5)	10	0.07
Not Hispanic (4)	8	0.06
Hispanic (1)	2	0.01
Guamanian/Chamorro (1)	2	0.01
Native Hawaiian (4)	7	0.05
White (13,136)	13,305	94.94
Not Hispanic (12,431)	12,565	89.66
Hispanic (705)	740	5.28

Rome

Place Type: City
County: Oneida
Population: 33,725†

Ancestry‡	Population	%
African, Sub-Saharan (67)	129	0.38
African (67)	129	0.38
American (1,101)	1,101	3.25
Arab (104)	225	0.66
Egyptian (0)	9	0.03
Lebanese (88)	200	0.59
Moroccan (8)	8	0.02
Syrian (8)	8	0.02
Armenian (0)	10	0.03
Austrian (20)	103	0.30
Brazilian (9)	9	0.03
British (12)	67	0.20
Canadian (21)	46	0.14
Czech (12)	45	0.13
Czechoslovakian (17)	115	0.34
Danish (12)	170	0.50
Dutch (94)	883	2.60
Eastern European (28)	28	0.08
English (797)	3,752	11.07
European (352)	365	1.08
Finnish (0)	32	0.09
French, ex. Basque (322)	2,077	6.13
French Canadian (304)	484	1.43

*Notes: † The Census 2010 population figure is used to calculate the percentages in the Hispanic Origin and Race categories. Ancestry percentages are based on the 2006-2010 American Community Survey population (not shown); ‡ Numbers in parentheses indicate the number of people reporting a single ancestry; * Numbers in parentheses indicate the number of persons reporting this race alone, not in combination with any other race; Please refer to the Explanation of Data for more information.*

German (1,021)	5,923	17.47
Greek (0)	78	0.23
Guyanese (4)	4	0.01
Hungarian (0)	202	0.60
Irish (1,543)	6,226	18.37
Italian (4,552)	8,328	24.57
Latvian (11)	11	0.03
Lithuanian (18)	62	0.18
Northern European (10)	10	0.03
Norwegian (40)	115	0.34
Pennsylvania German (19)	71	0.21
Polish (945)	2,665	7.86
Portuguese (8)	52	0.15
Romanian (11)	11	0.03
Russian (45)	205	0.60
Scandinavian (0)	6	0.02
Scotch-Irish (83)	388	1.14
Scottish (134)	556	1.64
Slovak (0)	22	0.06
Swedish (20)	163	0.48
Swiss (27)	313	0.92
Ukrainian (171)	482	1.42
Welsh (209)	891	2.63
West Indian, ex. Hispanic (143)	169	0.50
Barbadian (9)	9	0.03
British West Indian (59)	59	0.17
Haitian (5)	13	0.04
Jamaican (40)	49	0.14
Trinidadian/Tobagonian (22)	22	0.06
West Indian (8)	17	0.05
Yugoslavian (60)	60	0.18

Hispanic Origin	Population	%
Hispanic or Latino (of any race)	1,793	5.32
Central American, ex. Mexican	100	0.30
Costa Rican	1	<0.01
Guatemalan	16	0.05
Honduran	16	0.05
Nicaraguan	16	0.05
Panamanian	30	0.09
Salvadoran	21	0.06
Cuban	25	0.07
Dominican Republic	99	0.29
Mexican	229	0.68
Puerto Rican	1,115	3.31
South American	57	0.17
Argentinean	4	0.01
Bolivian	5	0.01
Chilean	2	0.01
Colombian	22	0.07
Ecuadorian	8	0.02
Peruvian	11	0.03
Venezuelan	4	0.01
Other South American	1	<0.01
Other Hispanic or Latino	168	0.50

Race*	Population	%
African-American/Black (2,394)	2,970	8.81
Not Hispanic (2,218)	2,721	8.07
Hispanic (176)	249	0.74
American Indian/Alaska Native (115)	296	0.88
Not Hispanic (93)	236	0.70
Hispanic (22)	60	0.18
Apache (4)	4	0.01
Arapaho (1)	1	<0.01
Blackfeet (1)	6	0.02
Canadian/French Am. Ind. (1)	1	<0.01
Central American Ind. (1)	2	0.01
Cherokee (7)	31	0.09
Chippewa (4)	10	0.03
Cree (1)	3	0.01
Creek (0)	1	<0.01
Inupiat *(Alaska Native)* (0)	1	<0.01
Iroquois (24)	66	0.20
Lumbee (3)	3	0.01
Navajo (0)	7	0.02
Pueblo (1)	1	<0.01
Seminole (0)	3	0.01
Sioux (4)	7	0.02
South American Ind. (3)	6	0.02
Tohono O'Odham (1)	1	<0.01
Asian (367)	506	1.50
Not Hispanic (360)	484	1.44
Hispanic (7)	22	0.07
Burmese (44)	48	0.14
Cambodian (2)	8	0.02
Chinese, ex. Taiwanese (58)	66	0.20
Filipino (62)	111	0.33
Indian (45)	64	0.19
Indonesian (1)	1	<0.01
Japanese (10)	29	0.09
Korean (21)	33	0.10
Laotian (30)	36	0.11
Malaysian (0)	6	0.02
Pakistani (9)	13	0.04
Taiwanese (6)	6	0.02
Thai (44)	63	0.19
Vietnamese (14)	15	0.04
Hawaii Native/Pacific Islander (1)	35	0.10
Not Hispanic (1)	30	0.09
Hispanic (0)	5	0.01
Guamanian/Chamorro (0)	7	0.02
Native Hawaiian (1)	16	0.05
Samoan (0)	1	<0.01
Tongan (0)	1	<0.01
White (29,483)	30,298	89.84
Not Hispanic (28,479)	29,174	86.51
Hispanic (1,004)	1,124	3.33

Ronkonkoma

Place Type: CDP
County: Suffolk
Population: 19,082†

Ancestry‡	Population	%
Afghan (33)	33	0.17
African, Sub-Saharan (0)	68	0.34
African (0)	68	0.34
American (362)	362	1.83
Armenian (0)	25	0.13
Austrian (0)	19	0.10
Brazilian (111)	202	1.02
British (0)	27	0.14
Croatian (50)	106	0.54
Czech (21)	65	0.33
Czechoslovakian (21)	59	0.30
Danish (9)	106	0.54
Dutch (0)	152	0.77
Eastern European (55)	55	0.28
English (194)	1,213	6.13
European (39)	39	0.20
French, ex. Basque (46)	437	2.21
French Canadian (0)	37	0.19
German (515)	3,614	18.27
Greek (121)	306	1.55
Hungarian (70)	283	1.43
Irish (1,350)	5,712	28.88
Israeli (14)	14	0.07
Italian (3,182)	7,783	39.35
Latvian (0)	11	0.06
Lithuanian (14)	14	0.07
Norwegian (26)	194	0.98
Polish (265)	1,163	5.88
Portuguese (121)	190	0.96
Romanian (35)	35	0.18
Russian (89)	290	1.47
Scotch-Irish (146)	218	1.10
Scottish (41)	115	0.58
Serbian (0)	15	0.08
Slavic (0)	13	0.07
Slovak (0)	27	0.14
Swedish (58)	289	1.46
Swiss (0)	41	0.21
Turkish (44)	44	0.22
Ukrainian (13)	23	0.12
Welsh (0)	15	0.08
West Indian, ex. Hispanic (21)	155	0.78
Bahamian (0)	22	0.11
Jamaican (21)	133	0.67
Yugoslavian (15)	44	0.22

Hispanic Origin	Population	%
Hispanic or Latino (of any race)	1,944	10.19
Central American, ex. Mexican	159	0.83
Costa Rican	4	0.02
Guatemalan	24	0.13
Honduran	27	0.14
Nicaraguan	3	0.02
Panamanian	11	0.06
Salvadoran	90	0.47
Cuban	62	0.32
Dominican Republic	160	0.84
Mexican	78	0.41
Puerto Rican	912	4.78
South American	404	2.12
Argentinean	17	0.09
Bolivian	8	0.04
Chilean	13	0.07
Colombian	159	0.83
Ecuadorian	122	0.64
Paraguayan	4	0.02
Peruvian	62	0.32
Uruguayan	4	0.02
Venezuelan	9	0.05
Other South American	6	0.03
Other Hispanic or Latino	169	0.89

Race*	Population	%
African-American/Black (397)	508	2.66
Not Hispanic (342)	419	2.20
Hispanic (55)	89	0.47
American Indian/Alaska Native (21)	73	0.38
Not Hispanic (13)	52	0.27
Hispanic (8)	21	0.11
Blackfeet (0)	6	0.03
Cherokee (1)	11	0.06
Cheyenne (0)	1	0.01
Creek (0)	1	0.01
Iroquois (0)	5	0.03
Mexican American Ind. (1)	1	0.01
Navajo (1)	1	0.01
South American Ind. (5)	8	0.04
Asian (884)	1,011	5.30
Not Hispanic (882)	993	5.20
Hispanic (2)	18	0.09
Bangladeshi (77)	81	0.42
Cambodian (0)	1	0.01
Chinese, ex. Taiwanese (124)	162	0.85
Filipino (77)	93	0.49
Indian (352)	376	1.97
Japanese (5)	10	0.05
Korean (37)	47	0.25
Malaysian (0)	1	0.01
Pakistani (140)	141	0.74
Taiwanese (1)	2	0.01
Thai (1)	1	0.01
Vietnamese (55)	66	0.35
Hawaii Native/Pacific Islander (9)	23	0.12
Not Hispanic (9)	17	0.09
Hispanic (0)	6	0.03
Guamanian/Chamorro (2)	3	0.02
Native Hawaiian (2)	4	0.02
Samoan (1)	2	0.01
White (16,988)	17,274	90.53
Not Hispanic (15,635)	15,811	82.86
Hispanic (1,353)	1,463	7.67

Roosevelt

Place Type: CDP
County: Nassau
Population: 16,258†

Ancestry‡	Population	%
African, Sub-Saharan (107)	165	1.10
African (97)	155	1.03
Ghanaian (10)	10	0.07
American (191)	191	1.27
British (75)	111	0.74

*Notes: † The Census 2010 population figure is used to calculate the percentages in the Hispanic Origin and Race categories. Ancestry percentages are based on the 2006-2010 American Community Survey population (not shown); ‡ Numbers in parentheses indicate the number of people reporting a single ancestry; * Numbers in parentheses indicate the number of persons reporting this race alone, not in combination with any other race; Please refer to the Explanation of Data for more information.*

Danish (8)	8	0.05
English (75)	75	0.50
French, ex. Basque (11)	21	0.14
German (29)	49	0.33
Greek (0)	10	0.07
Guyanese (36)	36	0.24
Irish (0)	32	0.21
Italian (21)	34	0.23
Polish (7)	17	0.11
Portuguese (116)	116	0.77
West Indian, ex. Hispanic (1,495)	1,613	10.72
Belizean (30)	30	0.20
Bermudan (43)	43	0.29
British West Indian (42)	42	0.28
Haitian (139)	139	0.92
Jamaican (828)	910	6.05
Trinidadian/Tobagonian (83)	99	0.66
West Indian (330)	350	2.33

Hispanic Origin	Population	%
Hispanic or Latino (of any race)	5,548	34.12
Central American, ex. Mexican	3,748	23.05
Costa Rican	39	0.24
Guatemalan	293	1.80
Honduran	394	2.42
Nicaraguan	47	0.29
Panamanian	65	0.40
Salvadoran	2,891	17.78
Other Central American	19	0.12
Cuban	57	0.35
Dominican Republic	584	3.59
Mexican	135	0.83
Puerto Rican	353	2.17
South American	173	1.06
Argentinean	3	0.02
Bolivian	1	0.01
Chilean	1	0.01
Colombian	32	0.20
Ecuadorian	49	0.30
Paraguayan	3	0.02
Peruvian	65	0.40
Uruguayan	3	0.02
Venezuelan	13	0.08
Other South American	3	0.02
Other Hispanic or Latino	498	3.06

Race*	Population	%
African-American/Black (10,261)	10,657	65.55
Not Hispanic (9,873)	10,138	62.36
Hispanic (388)	519	3.19
American Indian/Alaska Native (129)	395	2.43
Not Hispanic (59)	204	1.25
Hispanic (70)	191	1.17
Blackfeet (0)	5	0.03
Central American Ind. (9)	9	0.06
Cherokee (1)	66	0.41
Choctaw (0)	3	0.02
Creek (0)	6	0.04
Iroquois (5)	6	0.04
Lumbee (0)	1	0.01
Mexican American Ind. (1)	3	0.02
Pueblo (0)	2	0.01
South American Ind. (3)	6	0.04
Asian (91)	166	1.02
Not Hispanic (85)	148	0.91
Hispanic (6)	18	0.11
Bangladeshi (1)	1	0.01
Chinese, ex. Taiwanese (15)	39	0.24
Filipino (15)	34	0.21
Indian (44)	56	0.34
Indonesian (3)	3	0.02
Japanese (1)	5	0.03
Korean (4)	9	0.06
Laotian (4)	4	0.02
Sri Lankan (2)	2	0.01
Thai (0)	3	0.02
Vietnamese (0)	1	0.01
Hawaii Native/Pacific Islander (12)	26	0.16
Not Hispanic (5)	11	0.07
Hispanic (7)	15	0.09
Guamanian/Chamorro (7)	8	0.05
White (2,260)	2,730	16.79
Not Hispanic (326)	438	2.69
Hispanic (1,934)	2,292	14.10

Rotterdam

Place Type: CDP
County: Schenectady
Population: 20,652†

Ancestry‡	Population	%
African, Sub-Saharan (85)	85	0.41
African (85)	85	0.41
American (1,291)	1,291	6.29
Arab (11)	78	0.38
Lebanese (11)	20	0.10
Syrian (0)	31	0.15
Other Arab (0)	27	0.13
Austrian (23)	78	0.38
British (27)	94	0.46
Cajun (0)	6	0.03
Canadian (10)	48	0.23
Cypriot (19)	19	0.09
Czech (33)	107	0.52
Czechoslovakian (64)	64	0.31
Danish (10)	59	0.29
Dutch (93)	1,105	5.38
Eastern European (21)	21	0.10
English (342)	1,751	8.53
European (27)	27	0.13
French, ex. Basque (325)	1,705	8.31
French Canadian (157)	404	1.97
German (825)	3,480	16.96
Greek (32)	125	0.61
Guyanese (60)	60	0.29
Hungarian (40)	144	0.70
Iranian (8)	8	0.04
Irish (965)	4,056	19.77
Italian (3,799)	6,567	32.00
Lithuanian (9)	71	0.35
Northern European (21)	21	0.10
Norwegian (28)	94	0.46
Polish (1,019)	2,223	10.83
Russian (74)	94	0.46
Scotch-Irish (51)	221	1.08
Scottish (78)	391	1.91
Slavic (14)	21	0.10
Slovak (67)	137	0.67
Slovene (0)	9	0.04
Swedish (45)	116	0.57
Swiss (11)	22	0.11
Turkish (0)	16	0.08
Ukrainian (52)	82	0.40
Welsh (65)	158	0.77
West Indian, ex. Hispanic (96)	96	0.47
British West Indian (68)	68	0.33
West Indian (28)	28	0.14
Yugoslavian (48)	57	0.28

Hispanic Origin	Population	%
Hispanic or Latino (of any race)	525	2.54
Central American, ex. Mexican	41	0.20
Costa Rican	7	0.03
Guatemalan	14	0.07
Honduran	5	0.02
Panamanian	3	0.01
Salvadoran	12	0.06
Cuban	9	0.04
Dominican Republic	27	0.13
Mexican	83	0.40
Puerto Rican	238	1.15
South American	58	0.28
Argentinean	9	0.04
Bolivian	4	0.02
Chilean	6	0.03
Colombian	16	0.08
Ecuadorian	10	0.05
Peruvian	5	0.02
Uruguayan	2	0.01
Venezuelan	6	0.03
Other Hispanic or Latino	69	0.33

Race*	Population	%
African-American/Black (320)	483	2.34
Not Hispanic (286)	419	2.03
Hispanic (34)	64	0.31
American Indian/Alaska Native (43)	135	0.65
Not Hispanic (42)	127	0.61
Hispanic (1)	8	0.04
Alaska Athabascan *(Ala. Nat.)* (1)	1	<0.01
Blackfeet (1)	4	0.02
Cherokee (1)	9	0.04
Chickasaw (0)	1	<0.01
Chippewa (1)	1	<0.01
Hopi (0)	1	<0.01
Iroquois (2)	18	0.09
Seminole (1)	7	0.03
Sioux (0)	2	0.01
South American Ind. (0)	1	<0.01
Asian (244)	331	1.60
Not Hispanic (244)	322	1.56
Hispanic (0)	9	0.04
Burmese (2)	2	0.01
Cambodian (0)	3	0.01
Chinese, ex. Taiwanese (41)	56	0.27
Filipino (15)	29	0.14
Indian (89)	97	0.47
Indonesian (1)	1	<0.01
Japanese (2)	9	0.04
Korean (12)	28	0.14
Laotian (0)	1	<0.01
Nepalese (3)	5	0.02
Pakistani (10)	20	0.10
Taiwanese (6)	7	0.03
Thai (5)	11	0.05
Vietnamese (47)	53	0.26
Hawaii Native/Pacific Islander (5)	12	0.06
Not Hispanic (5)	11	0.05
Hispanic (0)	1	<0.01
Native Hawaiian (3)	3	0.01
White (19,504)	19,790	95.83
Not Hispanic (19,199)	19,444	94.15
Hispanic (305)	346	1.68

Rotterdam

Place Type: Town
County: Schenectady
Population: 29,094†

Ancestry‡	Population	%
African, Sub-Saharan (85)	85	0.29
African (85)	85	0.29
American (1,591)	1,591	5.49
Arab (11)	78	0.27
Lebanese (11)	20	0.07
Syrian (0)	31	0.11
Other Arab (0)	27	0.09
Austrian (36)	116	0.40
Belgian (7)	7	0.02
British (33)	153	0.53
Cajun (0)	6	0.02
Canadian (10)	48	0.17
Cypriot (54)	54	0.19
Czech (33)	167	0.58
Czechoslovakian (64)	70	0.24
Danish (18)	67	0.23
Dutch (111)	1,547	5.34
Eastern European (21)	21	0.07
English (505)	2,589	8.94
European (77)	77	0.27
French, ex. Basque (400)	2,406	8.31
French Canadian (260)	627	2.17
German (1,176)	5,143	17.76
Greek (44)	137	0.47
Guyanese (74)	74	0.26
Hungarian (53)	220	0.76
Iranian (8)	8	0.03
Irish (1,345)	5,781	19.96

SECTION TWO

*Notes: † The Census 2010 population figure is used to calculate the percentages in the Hispanic Origin and Race categories. Ancestry percentages are based on the 2006-2010 American Community Survey population (not shown); ‡ Numbers in parentheses indicate the number of people reporting a single ancestry; * Numbers in parentheses indicate the number of persons reporting this race alone, not in combination with any other race; Please refer to the Explanation of Data for more information.*

Italian (5,255)	9,310	32.15
Lithuanian (55)	196	0.68
Northern European (21)	21	0.07
Norwegian (28)	145	0.50
Polish (1,364)	3,179	10.98
Russian (132)	162	0.56
Scotch-Irish (96)	314	1.08
Scottish (92)	447	1.54
Slavic (14)	21	0.07
Slovak (67)	148	0.51
Slovene (0)	9	0.03
Swedish (47)	235	0.81
Swiss (19)	75	0.26
Turkish (0)	29	0.10
Ukrainian (52)	111	0.38
Welsh (65)	191	0.66
West Indian, ex. Hispanic (255)	255	0.88
British West Indian (68)	68	0.23
West Indian (187)	187	0.65
Yugoslavian (48)	57	0.20

Hispanic Origin	Population	%
Hispanic or Latino (of any race)	660	2.27
Central American, ex. Mexican	59	0.20
Costa Rican	7	0.02
Guatemalan	14	0.05
Honduran	12	0.04
Nicaraguan	3	0.01
Panamanian	3	0.01
Salvadoran	16	0.05
Other Central American	4	0.01
Cuban	14	0.05
Dominican Republic	38	0.13
Mexican	96	0.33
Puerto Rican	297	1.02
South American	77	0.26
Argentinean	9	0.03
Bolivian	5	0.02
Chilean	6	0.02
Colombian	17	0.06
Ecuadorian	21	0.07
Peruvian	11	0.04
Uruguayan	2	0.01
Venezuelan	6	0.02
Other Hispanic or Latino	79	0.27

Race*	Population	%
African-American/Black (440)	647	2.22
Not Hispanic (402)	575	1.98
Hispanic (38)	72	0.25
American Indian/Alaska Native (54)	169	0.58
Not Hispanic (52)	158	0.54
Hispanic (2)	11	0.04
Alaska Athabascan *(Ala. Nat.)* (1)	1	<0.01
Blackfeet (1)	5	0.02
Cherokee (1)	11	0.04
Chickasaw (0)	1	<0.01
Chippewa (1)	1	<0.01
Hopi (0)	1	<0.01
Iroquois (5)	24	0.08
Seminole (1)	7	0.02
Sioux (0)	4	0.01
South American Ind. (0)	2	0.01
Asian (340)	455	1.56
Not Hispanic (340)	446	1.53
Hispanic (0)	9	0.03
Burmese (2)	2	0.01
Cambodian (0)	3	0.01
Chinese, ex. Taiwanese (56)	71	0.24
Filipino (33)	48	0.16
Indian (113)	127	0.44
Indonesian (1)	1	<0.01
Japanese (4)	14	0.05
Korean (40)	60	0.21
Laotian (0)	1	<0.01
Nepalese (3)	5	0.02
Pakistani (10)	20	0.07
Taiwanese (7)	8	0.03
Thai (10)	16	0.05
Vietnamese (48)	57	0.20
Hawaii Native/Pacific Islander (6)	16	0.05
Not Hispanic (6)	15	0.05
Hispanic (0)	1	<0.01
Native Hawaiian (4)	6	0.02
White (27,566)	27,951	96.07
Not Hispanic (27,187)	27,515	94.57
Hispanic (379)	436	1.50

Royalton

Place Type: Town
County: Niagara
Population: 7,660†

Ancestry‡	Population	%
American (256)	256	3.35
Arab (15)	15	0.20
Lebanese (15)	15	0.20
Armenian (0)	15	0.20
British (3)	3	0.04
Canadian (6)	86	1.13
Czech (7)	7	0.09
Danish (13)	18	0.24
Dutch (42)	157	2.06
English (467)	1,482	19.41
European (81)	81	1.06
French, ex. Basque (70)	386	5.06
French Canadian (50)	153	2.00
German (1,012)	2,658	34.82
Greek (4)	4	0.05
Hungarian (16)	32	0.42
Irish (340)	1,768	23.16
Italian (310)	922	12.08
Lithuanian (0)	3	0.04
Norwegian (27)	58	0.76
Pennsylvania German (0)	4	0.05
Polish (330)	679	8.89
Scotch-Irish (87)	176	2.31
Scottish (45)	246	3.22
Slavic (9)	9	0.12
Slovak (0)	17	0.22
Swedish (19)	72	0.94
Ukrainian (30)	30	0.39
Welsh (0)	22	0.29

Hispanic Origin	Population	%
Hispanic or Latino (of any race)	91	1.19
Central American, ex. Mexican	8	0.10
Costa Rican	1	0.01
Guatemalan	2	0.03
Panamanian	4	0.05
Salvadoran	1	0.01
Cuban	11	0.14
Mexican	21	0.27
Puerto Rican	32	0.42
South American	5	0.07
Argentinean	1	0.01
Colombian	1	0.01
Peruvian	3	0.04
Other Hispanic or Latino	14	0.18

Race*	Population	%
African-American/Black (52)	104	1.36
Not Hispanic (48)	93	1.21
Hispanic (4)	11	0.14
American Indian/Alaska Native (53)	98	1.28
Not Hispanic (51)	96	1.25
Hispanic (2)	2	0.03
Blackfeet (0)	5	0.07
Central American Ind. (1)	1	0.01
Cherokee (4)	14	0.18
Chickasaw (1)	1	0.01
Chippewa (3)	3	0.04
Choctaw (0)	1	0.01
Iroquois (14)	28	0.37
Navajo (2)	2	0.03
Asian (25)	42	0.55
Not Hispanic (25)	41	0.54
Hispanic (0)	1	0.01
Chinese, ex. Taiwanese (3)	4	0.05
Filipino (4)	9	0.12
Indian (9)	11	0.14
Japanese (1)	3	0.04
Korean (6)	10	0.13
Laotian (1)	1	0.01
Taiwanese (1)	1	0.01
Hawaii Native/Pacific Islander (3)	6	0.08
Not Hispanic (3)	6	0.08
Samoan (3)	4	0.05
White (7,388)	7,490	97.78
Not Hispanic (7,336)	7,429	96.98
Hispanic (52)	61	0.80

Rye Brook

Place Type: Village
County: Westchester
Population: 9,347†

Ancestry‡	Population	%
African, Sub-Saharan (0)	14	0.15
South African (0)	14	0.15
American (797)	797	8.71
Armenian (75)	75	0.82
Austrian (62)	104	1.14
Brazilian (34)	49	0.54
British (112)	126	1.38
Canadian (11)	27	0.30
Celtic (17)	17	0.19
Czech (12)	27	0.30
Czechoslovakian (0)	48	0.52
Dutch (16)	59	0.64
Eastern European (378)	399	4.36
English (9)	222	2.43
European (124)	124	1.36
French, ex. Basque (8)	49	0.54
French Canadian (17)	26	0.28
German (223)	716	7.82
Greek (8)	17	0.19
Hungarian (101)	233	2.55
Irish (356)	875	9.56
Italian (1,741)	2,264	24.74
Lithuanian (8)	53	0.58
Northern European (0)	16	0.17
Norwegian (13)	48	0.52
Polish (151)	648	7.08
Portuguese (0)	68	0.74
Romanian (35)	35	0.38
Russian (398)	932	10.18
Scandinavian (0)	19	0.21
Scotch-Irish (15)	15	0.16
Scottish (11)	19	0.21
Slovak (64)	64	0.70
Slovene (0)	8	0.09
Swedish (10)	26	0.28
Swiss (0)	11	0.12
Ukrainian (0)	12	0.13
Welsh (19)	56	0.61
West Indian, ex. Hispanic (44)	44	0.48
Jamaican (44)	44	0.48
Yugoslavian (8)	31	0.34

Hispanic Origin	Population	%
Hispanic or Latino (of any race)	1,034	11.06
Central American, ex. Mexican	97	1.04
Costa Rican	1	0.01
Guatemalan	50	0.53
Honduran	9	0.10
Nicaraguan	4	0.04
Salvadoran	33	0.35
Cuban	65	0.70
Dominican Republic	57	0.61
Mexican	196	2.10
Puerto Rican	99	1.06
South American	426	4.56
Argentinean	24	0.26
Bolivian	21	0.22
Chilean	29	0.31
Colombian	76	0.81
Ecuadorian	89	0.95

*Notes: † The Census 2010 population figure is used to calculate the percentages in the Hispanic Origin and Race categories. Ancestry percentages are based on the 2006-2010 American Community Survey population (not shown); ‡ Numbers in parentheses indicate the number of people reporting a single ancestry; * Numbers in parentheses indicate the number of persons reporting this race alone, not in combination with any other race; Please refer to the Explanation of Data for more information.*

Paraguayan	9	0.10
Peruvian	145	1.55
Uruguayan	23	0.25
Venezuelan	9	0.10
Other South American	1	0.01
Other Hispanic or Latino	94	1.01

Race*	Population	%
African-American/Black (144)	178	1.90
Not Hispanic (131)	159	1.70
Hispanic (13)	19	0.20
American Indian/Alaska Native (16)	28	0.30
Not Hispanic (4)	14	0.15
Hispanic (12)	14	0.15
Iroquois (0)	1	0.01
Mexican American Ind. (7)	7	0.07
South American Ind. (2)	6	0.06
Asian (425)	501	5.36
Not Hispanic (417)	483	5.17
Hispanic (8)	18	0.19
Chinese, ex. Taiwanese (101)	122	1.31
Filipino (28)	41	0.44
Indian (142)	165	1.77
Japanese (89)	109	1.17
Korean (35)	39	0.42
Malaysian (1)	1	0.01
Nepalese (8)	8	0.09
Pakistani (3)	3	0.03
Taiwanese (1)	1	0.01
Thai (1)	1	0.01
Vietnamese (7)	9	0.10
Hawaii Native/Pacific Islander (1)	2	0.02
Not Hispanic (1)	1	0.01
Hispanic (0)	1	0.01
Guamanian/Chamorro (0)	1	0.01
White (8,315)	8,461	90.52
Not Hispanic (7,621)	7,722	82.61
Hispanic (694)	739	7.91

Rye

Place Type: City
County: Westchester
Population: 15,720†

Ancestry‡	Population	%
Afghan (1)	1	0.01
African, Sub-Saharan (0)	19	0.12
South African (0)	19	0.12
American (3,014)	3,014	19.45
Arab (113)	312	2.01
Arab (0)	14	0.09
Egyptian (0)	19	0.12
Lebanese (113)	133	0.86
Syrian (0)	146	0.94
Armenian (10)	10	0.06
Australian (86)	86	0.55
Austrian (21)	76	0.49
Basque (32)	32	0.21
Belgian (7)	7	0.05
Brazilian (35)	35	0.23
British (103)	161	1.04
Canadian (98)	108	0.70
Danish (16)	32	0.21
Dutch (20)	90	0.58
Eastern European (127)	164	1.06
English (314)	1,389	8.96
European (169)	195	1.26
Finnish (8)	24	0.15
French, ex. Basque (85)	433	2.79
French Canadian (13)	54	0.35
German (310)	1,768	11.41
Greek (88)	155	1.00
Guyanese (50)	50	0.32
Hungarian (32)	126	0.81
Irish (1,122)	3,090	19.94
Italian (1,105)	2,434	15.71
Lithuanian (44)	93	0.60
New Zealander (23)	23	0.15
Norwegian (34)	42	0.27
Polish (154)	429	2.77
Portuguese (73)	73	0.47
Romanian (39)	54	0.35
Russian (78)	404	2.61
Scotch-Irish (132)	261	1.68
Scottish (50)	303	1.96
Slavic (0)	24	0.15
Slovak (14)	69	0.45
Swedish (63)	218	1.41
Swiss (77)	188	1.21
Turkish (8)	8	0.05
Ukrainian (0)	30	0.19
Welsh (9)	58	0.37
West Indian, ex. Hispanic (46)	60	0.39
Jamaican (23)	23	0.15
Trinidadian/Tobagonian (0)	14	0.09
West Indian (23)	23	0.15

Hispanic Origin	Population	%
Hispanic or Latino (of any race)	1,014	6.45
Central American, ex. Mexican	57	0.36
Costa Rican	10	0.06
Guatemalan	18	0.11
Honduran	11	0.07
Nicaraguan	3	0.02
Panamanian	4	0.03
Salvadoran	11	0.07
Cuban	90	0.57
Dominican Republic	26	0.17
Mexican	175	1.11
Puerto Rican	183	1.16
South American	304	1.93
Argentinean	33	0.21
Bolivian	20	0.13
Chilean	24	0.15
Colombian	64	0.41
Ecuadorian	47	0.30
Paraguayan	7	0.04
Peruvian	70	0.45
Uruguayan	23	0.15
Venezuelan	13	0.08
Other South American	3	0.02
Other Hispanic or Latino	179	1.14

Race*	Population	%
African-American/Black (234)	288	1.83
Not Hispanic (207)	248	1.58
Hispanic (27)	40	0.25
American Indian/Alaska Native (21)	40	0.25
Not Hispanic (7)	15	0.10
Hispanic (14)	25	0.16
Apache (1)	1	0.01
Central American Ind. (0)	2	0.01
Cherokee (0)	1	0.01
Chickasaw (0)	1	0.01
Chippewa (1)	1	0.01
Hopi (0)	1	0.01
Mexican American Ind. (0)	1	0.01
Sioux (3)	3	0.02
South American Ind. (0)	3	0.02
Spanish American Ind. (0)	4	0.03
Asian (936)	1,094	6.96
Not Hispanic (932)	1,086	6.91
Hispanic (4)	8	0.05
Cambodian (1)	1	0.01
Chinese, ex. Taiwanese (184)	246	1.56
Filipino (45)	71	0.45
Indian (90)	121	0.77
Indonesian (5)	7	0.04
Japanese (457)	482	3.07
Korean (100)	125	0.80
Laotian (7)	9	0.06
Malaysian (0)	1	0.01
Pakistani (14)	17	0.11
Sri Lankan (1)	1	0.01
Taiwanese (1)	6	0.04
Thai (4)	4	0.03
Vietnamese (2)	8	0.05
Hawaii Native/Pacific Islander (1)	3	0.02
Not Hispanic (1)	3	0.02
Guamanian/Chamorro (1)	1	0.01
White (14,071)	14,315	91.06
Not Hispanic (13,329)	13,519	86.00
Hispanic (742)	796	5.06

Rye

Place Type: Town
County: Westchester
Population: 45,928†

Ancestry‡	Population	%
African, Sub-Saharan (68)	93	0.21
African (55)	66	0.15
South African (13)	27	0.06
Albanian (10)	10	0.02
American (3,967)	3,967	8.76
Arab (137)	316	0.70
Egyptian (19)	19	0.04
Iraqi (0)	14	0.03
Jordanian (9)	9	0.02
Lebanese (55)	104	0.23
Palestinian (15)	15	0.03
Other Arab (39)	155	0.34
Armenian (75)	93	0.21
Austrian (101)	183	0.40
Brazilian (768)	929	2.05
British (163)	192	0.42
Canadian (11)	27	0.06
Celtic (17)	17	0.04
Croatian (44)	44	0.10
Cypriot (28)	28	0.06
Czech (37)	168	0.37
Czechoslovakian (23)	86	0.19
Danish (30)	58	0.13
Dutch (80)	181	0.40
Eastern European (652)	699	1.54
English (208)	1,080	2.38
European (189)	238	0.53
Finnish (30)	43	0.09
French, ex. Basque (89)	385	0.85
French Canadian (42)	101	0.22
German (865)	2,140	4.72
Greek (195)	269	0.59
Hungarian (120)	305	0.67
Icelander (0)	24	0.05
Irish (1,196)	3,144	6.94
Italian (6,065)	8,476	18.71
Lithuanian (23)	87	0.19
Luxemburger (0)	11	0.02
Northern European (19)	35	0.08
Norwegian (48)	186	0.41
Polish (872)	1,863	4.11
Portuguese (171)	372	0.82
Romanian (35)	54	0.12
Russian (541)	1,295	2.86
Scandinavian (0)	19	0.04
Scotch-Irish (45)	77	0.17
Scottish (46)	94	0.21
Slavic (0)	11	0.02
Slovak (90)	98	0.22
Slovene (0)	8	0.02
Swedish (33)	197	0.43
Swiss (23)	58	0.13
Turkish (0)	22	0.05
Ukrainian (0)	12	0.03
Welsh (44)	152	0.34
West Indian, ex. Hispanic (405)	433	0.96
Jamaican (139)	155	0.34
West Indian (266)	278	0.61
Yugoslavian (36)	59	0.13

Hispanic Origin	Population	%
Hispanic or Latino (of any race)	19,477	42.41
Central American, ex. Mexican	3,923	8.54
Costa Rican	32	0.07
Guatemalan	2,654	5.78
Honduran	191	0.42
Nicaraguan	10	0.02
Panamanian	16	0.03

SECTION TWO

*Notes: † The Census 2010 population figure is used to calculate the percentages in the Hispanic Origin and Race categories. Ancestry percentages are based on the 2006-2010 American Community Survey population (not shown); ‡ Numbers in parentheses indicate the number of people reporting a single ancestry; * Numbers in parentheses indicate the number of persons reporting this race alone, not in combination with any other race; Please refer to the Explanation of Data for more information.*

Salvadoran	1,004	2.19
Other Central American	16	0.03
Cuban	463	1.01
Dominican Republic	655	1.43
Mexican	5,313	11.57
Puerto Rican	1,093	2.38
South American	6,585	14.34
Argentinean	128	0.28
Bolivian	375	0.82
Chilean	192	0.42
Colombian	891	1.94
Ecuadorian	2,901	6.32
Paraguayan	102	0.22
Peruvian	1,734	3.78
Uruguayan	211	0.46
Venezuelan	39	0.08
Other South American	12	0.03
Other Hispanic or Latino	1,445	3.15

Race*	Population	%
African-American/Black (2,249)	2,659	5.79
Not Hispanic (1,884)	2,092	4.55
Hispanic (365)	567	1.23
American Indian/Alaska Native (302)	544	1.18
Not Hispanic (70)	134	0.29
Hispanic (232)	410	0.89
Blackfeet (1)	3	0.01
Central American Ind. (7)	10	0.02
Cherokee (1)	12	0.03
Inupiat *(Alaska Native)* (4)	5	0.01
Iroquois (1)	13	0.03
Kiowa (0)	1	<0.01
Mexican American Ind. (64)	73	0.16
Seminole (0)	1	<0.01
Sioux (0)	1	<0.01
South American Ind. (19)	51	0.11
Spanish American Ind. (3)	4	0.01
Yuman (0)	1	<0.01
Asian (1,506)	1,746	3.80
Not Hispanic (1,470)	1,650	3.59
Hispanic (36)	96	0.21
Bangladeshi (3)	3	0.01
Burmese (0)	1	<0.01
Cambodian (3)	3	0.01
Chinese, ex. Taiwanese (301)	370	0.81
Filipino (195)	229	0.50
Indian (441)	495	1.08
Indonesian (2)	3	0.01
Japanese (358)	407	0.89
Korean (99)	111	0.24
Laotian (4)	4	0.01
Malaysian (2)	4	0.01
Nepalese (8)	10	0.02
Pakistani (24)	35	0.08
Taiwanese (2)	3	0.01
Thai (15)	18	0.04
Vietnamese (18)	22	0.05
Hawaii Native/Pacific Islander (13)	48	0.10
Not Hispanic (2)	12	0.03
Hispanic (11)	36	0.08
Guamanian/Chamorro (8)	14	0.03
Native Hawaiian (0)	6	0.01
Samoan (0)	1	<0.01
White (32,239)	33,720	73.42
Not Hispanic (22,294)	22,699	49.42
Hispanic (9,945)	11,021	24.00

Salina

Place Type: Town
County: Onondaga
Population: 33,710†

Ancestry‡	Population	%
African, Sub-Saharan (27)	36	0.11
African (10)	10	0.03
Cape Verdean (0)	9	0.03
Ghanaian (9)	9	0.03
Nigerian (8)	8	0.02
American (914)	914	2.72
Arab (96)	301	0.90
Arab (0)	142	0.42
Egyptian (29)	29	0.09
Jordanian (14)	14	0.04
Lebanese (53)	106	0.32
Syrian (0)	10	0.03
Armenian (16)	28	0.08
Austrian (7)	225	0.67
Belgian (0)	10	0.03
British (64)	105	0.31
Canadian (31)	66	0.20
Celtic (0)	8	0.02
Croatian (31)	67	0.20
Czech (15)	74	0.22
Czechoslovakian (47)	96	0.29
Danish (0)	45	0.13
Dutch (178)	952	2.84
Eastern European (27)	27	0.08
English (1,180)	4,370	13.02
European (82)	129	0.38
Finnish (126)	212	0.63
French, ex. Basque (320)	2,467	7.35
French Canadian (178)	691	2.06
German (1,978)	8,018	23.88
Greek (110)	144	0.43
Hungarian (76)	157	0.47
Iranian (18)	18	0.05
Irish (1,993)	8,263	24.61
Italian (4,195)	8,660	25.79
Lithuanian (0)	10	0.03
Macedonian (45)	45	0.13
Northern European (27)	27	0.08
Norwegian (25)	109	0.32
Polish (730)	2,469	7.35
Portuguese (12)	12	0.04
Romanian (0)	31	0.09
Russian (67)	217	0.65
Scandinavian (18)	50	0.15
Scotch-Irish (182)	511	1.52
Scottish (115)	754	2.25
Slovak (12)	46	0.14
Swedish (15)	202	0.60
Swiss (37)	139	0.41
Ukrainian (133)	323	0.96
Welsh (53)	351	1.05
West Indian, ex. Hispanic (59)	67	0.20
Belizean (9)	9	0.03
Haitian (37)	37	0.11
Jamaican (13)	21	0.06
Yugoslavian (83)	83	0.25

Hispanic Origin	Population	%
Hispanic or Latino (of any race)	949	2.82
Central American, ex. Mexican	49	0.15
Costa Rican	4	0.01
Guatemalan	21	0.06
Honduran	3	0.01
Nicaraguan	4	0.01
Panamanian	9	0.03
Salvadoran	8	0.02
Cuban	105	0.31
Dominican Republic	54	0.16
Mexican	159	0.47
Puerto Rican	392	1.16
South American	81	0.24
Argentinean	6	0.02
Chilean	6	0.02
Colombian	18	0.05
Ecuadorian	15	0.04
Paraguayan	2	0.01
Peruvian	19	0.06
Venezuelan	13	0.04
Other South American	2	0.01
Other Hispanic or Latino	109	0.32

Race*	Population	%
African-American/Black (1,365)	1,784	5.29
Not Hispanic (1,287)	1,655	4.91
Hispanic (78)	129	0.38
American Indian/Alaska Native (186)	389	1.15
Not Hispanic (170)	356	1.06
Hispanic (16)	33	0.10
Apache (2)	5	0.01
Blackfeet (1)	6	0.02
Canadian/French Am. Ind. (0)	3	0.01
Cherokee (1)	28	0.08
Chippewa (5)	6	0.02
Cree (1)	1	<0.01
Crow (0)	1	<0.01
Delaware (1)	1	<0.01
Iroquois (102)	189	0.56
Mexican American Ind. (1)	1	<0.01
Ottawa (0)	1	<0.01
Seminole (0)	2	0.01
Sioux (5)	5	0.01
South American Ind. (2)	6	0.02
Spanish American Ind. (1)	1	<0.01
Asian (753)	897	2.66
Not Hispanic (745)	886	2.63
Hispanic (8)	11	0.03
Bangladeshi (6)	6	0.02
Burmese (6)	6	0.02
Cambodian (18)	21	0.06
Chinese, ex. Taiwanese (123)	155	0.46
Filipino (52)	77	0.23
Hmong (11)	11	0.03
Indian (168)	181	0.54
Indonesian (3)	7	0.02
Japanese (9)	22	0.07
Korean (38)	71	0.21
Laotian (1)	8	0.02
Malaysian (0)	1	<0.01
Nepalese (1)	1	<0.01
Pakistani (11)	14	0.04
Sri Lankan (2)	2	0.01
Taiwanese (10)	18	0.05
Thai (8)	19	0.06
Vietnamese (236)	269	0.80
Hawaii Native/Pacific Islander (7)	28	0.08
Not Hispanic (7)	26	0.08
Hispanic (0)	2	0.01
Guamanian/Chamorro (0)	1	<0.01
Native Hawaiian (3)	12	0.04
Samoan (1)	3	0.01
Tongan (1)	1	<0.01
White (30,394)	31,092	92.23
Not Hispanic (29,836)	30,445	90.31
Hispanic (558)	647	1.92

Salisbury

Place Type: CDP
County: Nassau
Population: 12,093†

Ancestry‡	Population	%
African, Sub-Saharan (21)	37	0.31
African (6)	13	0.11
Ethiopian (15)	15	0.13
Other Sub-Saharan African (0)	9	0.08
Albanian (41)	41	0.35
American (218)	218	1.85
Arab (0)	96	0.82
Syrian (0)	96	0.82
Armenian (40)	81	0.69
Austrian (29)	71	0.60
Belgian (0)	19	0.16
Brazilian (7)	28	0.24
Bulgarian (0)	8	0.07
Canadian (9)	38	0.32
Croatian (15)	90	0.76
Czech (0)	48	0.41
Czechoslovakian (0)	12	0.10
Dutch (18)	66	0.56
Eastern European (117)	117	0.99
English (31)	372	3.16
European (81)	90	0.76
Finnish (0)	11	0.09
French, ex. Basque (7)	145	1.23
French Canadian (11)	51	0.43

*Notes: † The Census 2010 population figure is used to calculate the percentages in the Hispanic Origin and Race categories. Ancestry percentages are based on the 2006-2010 American Community Survey population (not shown); ‡ Numbers in parentheses indicate the number of people reporting a single ancestry; * Numbers in parentheses indicate the number of persons reporting this race alone, not in combination with any other race; Please refer to the Explanation of Data for more information.*

German (464)	1,596	13.56
Greek (94)	203	1.72
Hungarian (22)	75	0.64
Irish (672)	2,008	17.06
Israeli (193)	193	1.64
Italian (1,942)	3,316	28.17
Lithuanian (34)	59	0.50
Maltese (10)	10	0.08
Polish (133)	582	4.94
Portuguese (142)	142	1.21
Romanian (17)	36	0.31
Russian (134)	476	4.04
Scotch-Irish (0)	21	0.18
Scottish (0)	76	0.65
Slovak (0)	9	0.08
Swedish (8)	80	0.68
Turkish (0)	8	0.07
Ukrainian (23)	54	0.46
West Indian, ex. Hispanic (143)	162	1.38
Jamaican (143)	162	1.38

Hispanic Origin	Population	%
Hispanic or Latino (of any race)	1,780	14.72
Central American, ex. Mexican	527	4.36
Costa Rican	5	0.04
Guatemalan	51	0.42
Honduran	49	0.41
Nicaraguan	3	0.02
Panamanian	2	0.02
Salvadoran	408	3.37
Other Central American	9	0.07
Cuban	58	0.48
Dominican Republic	129	1.07
Mexican	118	0.98
Puerto Rican	293	2.42
South American	477	3.94
Argentinean	25	0.21
Bolivian	12	0.10
Chilean	36	0.30
Colombian	199	1.65
Ecuadorian	84	0.69
Peruvian	101	0.84
Uruguayan	7	0.06
Venezuelan	13	0.11
Other Hispanic or Latino	178	1.47

Race*	Population	%
African-American/Black (239)	296	2.45
Not Hispanic (211)	243	2.01
Hispanic (28)	53	0.44
American Indian/Alaska Native (18)	40	0.33
Not Hispanic (14)	32	0.26
Hispanic (4)	8	0.07
Cherokee (1)	8	0.07
Creek (0)	1	0.01
Iroquois (0)	1	0.01
Mexican American Ind. (2)	2	0.02
Navajo (0)	3	0.02
Spanish American Ind. (2)	3	0.02
Asian (1,527)	1,648	13.63
Not Hispanic (1,521)	1,626	13.45
Hispanic (6)	22	0.18
Bangladeshi (31)	35	0.29
Burmese (4)	4	0.03
Cambodian (3)	6	0.05
Chinese, ex. Taiwanese (250)	289	2.39
Filipino (308)	329	2.72
Indian (564)	613	5.07
Japanese (14)	20	0.17
Korean (119)	122	1.01
Malaysian (4)	4	0.03
Nepalese (2)	2	0.02
Pakistani (86)	87	0.72
Taiwanese (42)	48	0.40
Thai (17)	17	0.14
Vietnamese (41)	47	0.39
Hawaii Native/Pacific Islander (4)	12	0.10
Not Hispanic (0)	4	0.03
Hispanic (4)	8	0.07
Guamanian/Chamorro (2)	2	0.02
Native Hawaiian (0)	4	0.03
Samoan (2)	2	0.02
White (9,532)	9,748	80.61
Not Hispanic (8,376)	8,480	70.12
Hispanic (1,156)	1,268	10.49

Sand Lake

Place Type: Town
County: Rensselaer
Population: 8,530†

Ancestry‡	Population	%
American (335)	335	3.96
Arab (67)	67	0.79
Lebanese (13)	13	0.15
Other Arab (54)	54	0.64
Armenian (15)	91	1.08
Austrian (17)	64	0.76
Brazilian (101)	101	1.19
British (0)	16	0.19
Canadian (65)	103	1.22
Danish (0)	32	0.38
Dutch (106)	470	5.55
Eastern European (13)	13	0.15
English (286)	1,601	18.92
European (29)	29	0.34
French, ex. Basque (118)	662	7.82
French Canadian (34)	203	2.40
German (506)	2,440	28.83
Greek (12)	63	0.74
Hungarian (15)	81	0.96
Iranian (57)	57	0.67
Irish (459)	1,900	22.45
Italian (337)	1,046	12.36
Lithuanian (24)	68	0.80
Polish (96)	351	4.15
Russian (23)	111	1.31
Scandinavian (0)	20	0.24
Scotch-Irish (55)	182	2.15
Scottish (50)	278	3.28
Swedish (46)	99	1.17
Swiss (0)	44	0.52
Ukrainian (23)	88	1.04
Welsh (111)	159	1.88
West Indian, ex. Hispanic (25)	73	0.86
Haitian (0)	24	0.28
Jamaican (25)	49	0.58

Hispanic Origin	Population	%
Hispanic or Latino (of any race)	129	1.51
Central American, ex. Mexican	3	0.04
Guatemalan	3	0.04
Cuban	6	0.07
Dominican Republic	4	0.05
Mexican	54	0.63
Puerto Rican	28	0.33
South American	14	0.16
Chilean	3	0.04
Colombian	2	0.02
Ecuadorian	2	0.02
Peruvian	6	0.07
Uruguayan	1	0.01
Other Hispanic or Latino	20	0.23

Race*	Population	%
African-American/Black (33)	75	0.88
Not Hispanic (28)	69	0.81
Hispanic (5)	6	0.07
American Indian/Alaska Native (12)	52	0.61
Not Hispanic (11)	51	0.60
Hispanic (1)	1	0.01
Blackfeet (0)	2	0.02
Canadian/French Am. Ind. (2)	2	0.02
Cherokee (0)	4	0.05
Cree (0)	1	0.01
Iroquois (2)	6	0.07
Asian (45)	69	0.81
Not Hispanic (44)	65	0.76
Hispanic (1)	4	0.05
Bangladeshi (1)	1	0.01
Chinese, ex. Taiwanese (14)	16	0.19
Filipino (9)	17	0.20
Indian (6)	12	0.14
Indonesian (0)	2	0.02
Japanese (3)	5	0.06
Korean (10)	11	0.13
Thai (1)	1	0.01
Vietnamese (1)	4	0.05
Hawaii Native/Pacific Islander (1)	2	0.02
Hispanic (1)	2	0.02
Native Hawaiian (1)	2	0.02
White (8,327)	8,423	98.75
Not Hispanic (8,222)	8,314	97.47
Hispanic (105)	109	1.28

Saratoga Springs

Place Type: City
County: Saratoga
Population: 26,586†

Ancestry‡	Population	%
American (3,970)	3,970	14.88
Arab (16)	183	0.69
Arab (0)	13	0.05
Lebanese (16)	85	0.32
Syrian (0)	85	0.32
Armenian (0)	58	0.22
Australian (24)	24	0.09
Austrian (32)	160	0.60
Belgian (8)	27	0.10
Brazilian (54)	65	0.24
British (75)	126	0.47
Canadian (50)	86	0.32
Croatian (35)	83	0.31
Czech (9)	113	0.42
Czechoslovakian (19)	71	0.27
Danish (0)	61	0.23
Dutch (217)	814	3.05
Eastern European (58)	74	0.28
English (759)	3,365	12.61
Estonian (0)	9	0.03
European (255)	255	0.96
Finnish (96)	138	0.52
French, ex. Basque (73)	1,423	5.33
French Canadian (192)	441	1.65
German (723)	3,622	13.57
Greek (104)	178	0.67
Hungarian (13)	225	0.84
Irish (2,548)	7,247	27.16
Israeli (113)	127	0.48
Italian (1,732)	4,196	15.73
Latvian (0)	52	0.19
Lithuanian (37)	133	0.50
Maltese (0)	18	0.07
Norwegian (120)	300	1.12
Polish (361)	1,474	5.52
Portuguese (10)	28	0.10
Romanian (10)	52	0.19
Russian (260)	631	2.36
Scotch-Irish (153)	459	1.72
Scottish (141)	569	2.13
Serbian (0)	15	0.06
Slavic (32)	93	0.35
Slovak (23)	127	0.48
Swedish (31)	236	0.88
Swiss (40)	69	0.26
Turkish (19)	19	0.07
Ukrainian (70)	184	0.69
Welsh (43)	267	1.00
West Indian, ex. Hispanic (32)	32	0.12
Jamaican (12)	12	0.04
Trinidadian/Tobagonian (20)	20	0.07
Yugoslavian (0)	14	0.05

Hispanic Origin	Population	%
Hispanic or Latino (of any race)	839	3.16
Central American, ex. Mexican	50	0.19
Costa Rican	2	0.01

*Notes: † The Census 2010 population figure is used to calculate the percentages in the Hispanic Origin and Race categories. Ancestry percentages are based on the 2006-2010 American Community Survey population (not shown); ‡ Numbers in parentheses indicate the number of people reporting a single ancestry; * Numbers in parentheses indicate the number of persons reporting this race alone, not in combination with any other race; Please refer to the Explanation of Data for more information.*

SECTION TWO

Guatemalan	12	0.05
Honduran	13	0.05
Nicaraguan	4	0.02
Panamanian	5	0.02
Salvadoran	14	0.05
Cuban	34	0.13
Dominican Republic	37	0.14
Mexican	234	0.88
Puerto Rican	272	1.02
South American	108	0.41
Argentinean	17	0.06
Bolivian	1	<0.01
Chilean	23	0.09
Colombian	18	0.07
Ecuadorian	19	0.07
Paraguayan	2	0.01
Peruvian	13	0.05
Venezuelan	14	0.05
Other South American	1	<0.01
Other Hispanic or Latino	104	0.39

Race*	Population	%
African-American/Black (701)	978	3.68
Not Hispanic (661)	913	3.43
Hispanic (40)	65	0.24
American Indian/Alaska Native (55)	196	0.74
Not Hispanic (41)	159	0.60
Hispanic (14)	37	0.14
Apache (1)	5	0.02
Blackfeet (1)	6	0.02
Canadian/French Am. Ind. (2)	3	0.01
Central American Ind. (1)	2	0.01
Cherokee (2)	26	0.10
Cheyenne (0)	1	<0.01
Chickasaw (3)	3	0.01
Chippewa (0)	1	<0.01
Choctaw (2)	2	0.01
Comanche (0)	1	<0.01
Iroquois (5)	13	0.05
Mexican American Ind. (5)	5	0.02
Navajo (5)	5	0.02
Potawatomi (0)	2	0.01
Pueblo (0)	1	<0.01
Seminole (0)	3	0.01
Sioux (1)	5	0.02
South American Ind. (4)	4	0.02
Asian (521)	708	2.66
Not Hispanic (516)	691	2.60
Hispanic (5)	17	0.06
Bangladeshi (2)	2	0.01
Burmese (2)	3	0.01
Cambodian (2)	2	0.01
Chinese, ex. Taiwanese (140)	186	0.70
Filipino (42)	76	0.29
Indian (140)	162	0.61
Indonesian (2)	3	0.01
Japanese (36)	89	0.33
Korean (62)	96	0.36
Laotian (0)	1	<0.01
Nepalese (2)	2	0.01
Pakistani (5)	6	0.02
Sri Lankan (3)	4	0.02
Taiwanese (2)	2	0.01
Thai (24)	33	0.12
Vietnamese (22)	32	0.12
Hawaii Native/Pacific Islander (7)	23	0.09
Not Hispanic (4)	19	0.07
Hispanic (3)	4	0.02
Guamanian/Chamorro (1)	3	0.01
Native Hawaiian (1)	4	0.02
Samoan (0)	4	0.02
White (24,543)	25,097	94.40
Not Hispanic (24,005)	24,484	92.09
Hispanic (538)	613	2.31

Saugerties

Place Type: Town
County: Ulster
Population: 19,482†

Ancestry‡	Population	%
African, Sub-Saharan (12)	12	0.06
African (12)	12	0.06
American (1,537)	1,537	7.89
Arab (13)	23	0.12
Lebanese (0)	10	0.05
Other Arab (13)	13	0.07
Armenian (14)	14	0.07
Austrian (0)	133	0.68
Belgian (0)	22	0.11
British (35)	130	0.67
Bulgarian (0)	68	0.35
Canadian (41)	69	0.35
Carpatho Rusyn (0)	10	0.05
Croatian (0)	35	0.18
Czech (41)	102	0.52
Czechoslovakian (12)	52	0.27
Danish (0)	41	0.21
Dutch (352)	1,603	8.23
Eastern European (56)	56	0.29
English (328)	1,877	9.64
European (416)	416	2.14
Finnish (32)	79	0.41
French, ex. Basque (239)	978	5.02
French Canadian (25)	120	0.62
German (998)	4,740	24.34
Greek (21)	73	0.37
Hungarian (96)	211	1.08
Iranian (9)	21	0.11
Irish (1,379)	4,392	22.56
Israeli (0)	11	0.06
Italian (1,818)	3,974	20.41
Lithuanian (14)	39	0.20
Northern European (100)	100	0.51
Norwegian (49)	244	1.25
Polish (134)	731	3.75
Portuguese (8)	8	0.04
Russian (92)	341	1.75
Scandinavian (0)	14	0.07
Scotch-Irish (89)	281	1.44
Scottish (97)	446	2.29
Slavic (0)	43	0.22
Slovak (8)	54	0.28
Swedish (31)	202	1.04
Swiss (0)	38	0.20
Turkish (9)	22	0.11
Ukrainian (28)	58	0.30
Welsh (35)	132	0.68
West Indian, ex. Hispanic (91)	102	0.52
Barbadian (24)	24	0.12
Jamaican (67)	67	0.34
West Indian (0)	11	0.06
Yugoslavian (11)	11	0.06

Hispanic Origin	Population	%
Hispanic or Latino (of any race)	979	5.03
Central American, ex. Mexican	208	1.07
Guatemalan	34	0.17
Honduran	4	0.02
Nicaraguan	2	0.01
Panamanian	9	0.05
Salvadoran	159	0.82
Cuban	36	0.18
Dominican Republic	43	0.22
Mexican	163	0.84
Puerto Rican	318	1.63
South American	83	0.43
Argentinean	20	0.10
Bolivian	6	0.03
Chilean	3	0.02
Colombian	29	0.15
Ecuadorian	15	0.08
Peruvian	6	0.03
Uruguayan	1	0.01
Venezuelan	1	0.01
Other South American	2	0.01
Other Hispanic or Latino	128	0.66

Race*	Population	%
African-American/Black (323)	487	2.50
Not Hispanic (309)	450	2.31
Hispanic (14)	37	0.19
American Indian/Alaska Native (49)	188	0.96
Not Hispanic (41)	164	0.84
Hispanic (8)	24	0.12
Apache (1)	7	0.04
Arapaho (0)	1	0.01
Blackfeet (3)	6	0.03
Canadian/French Am. Ind. (1)	2	0.01
Central American Ind. (5)	5	0.03
Cherokee (6)	30	0.15
Choctaw (2)	2	0.01
Delaware (1)	9	0.05
Iroquois (7)	24	0.12
Mexican American Ind. (2)	2	0.01
Navajo (0)	1	0.01
Seminole (0)	4	0.02
Sioux (5)	7	0.04
South American Ind. (1)	2	0.01
Asian (205)	293	1.50
Not Hispanic (198)	283	1.45
Hispanic (7)	10	0.05
Burmese (1)	1	0.01
Cambodian (1)	1	0.01
Chinese, ex. Taiwanese (46)	69	0.35
Filipino (19)	47	0.24
Indian (60)	67	0.34
Indonesian (3)	5	0.03
Japanese (15)	39	0.20
Korean (22)	28	0.14
Malaysian (1)	1	0.01
Pakistani (13)	14	0.07
Taiwanese (4)	4	0.02
Thai (2)	3	0.02
Vietnamese (7)	13	0.07
Hawaii Native/Pacific Islander (3)	12	0.06
Not Hispanic (1)	8	0.04
Hispanic (2)	4	0.02
Guamanian/Chamorro (3)	4	0.02
Native Hawaiian (0)	5	0.03
White (18,347)	18,713	96.05
Not Hispanic (17,612)	17,920	91.98
Hispanic (735)	793	4.07

Sayville

Place Type: CDP
County: Suffolk
Population: 16,853†

Ancestry‡	Population	%
Afghan (52)	52	0.32
African, Sub-Saharan (0)	21	0.13
African (0)	21	0.13
American (268)	268	1.66
Arab (9)	56	0.35
Lebanese (0)	31	0.19
Syrian (9)	17	0.11
Other Arab (0)	8	0.05
Austrian (11)	100	0.62
Belgian (0)	36	0.22
Brazilian (15)	15	0.09
British (0)	66	0.41
Canadian (31)	44	0.27
Celtic (0)	17	0.11
Cypriot (11)	11	0.07
Czech (30)	261	1.62
Czechoslovakian (46)	46	0.29
Danish (0)	38	0.24
Dutch (64)	230	1.43
Eastern European (22)	22	0.14
English (125)	864	5.36
European (130)	143	0.89
French, ex. Basque (29)	231	1.43
French Canadian (24)	150	0.93
German (727)	3,986	24.75
Greek (49)	219	1.36
Hungarian (41)	103	0.64
Irish (1,678)	5,796	35.98
Italian (2,365)	5,301	32.91

*Notes: † The Census 2010 population figure is used to calculate the percentages in the Hispanic Origin and Race categories. Ancestry percentages are based on the 2006-2010 American Community Survey population (not shown); ‡ Numbers in parentheses indicate the number of people reporting a single ancestry; * Numbers in parentheses indicate the number of persons reporting this race alone, not in combination with any other race; Please refer to the Explanation of Data for more information.*

Lithuanian (16)	33	0.20
Maltese (0)	19	0.12
New Zealander (8)	8	0.05
Northern European (22)	22	0.14
Norwegian (51)	129	0.80
Polish (221)	807	5.01
Portuguese (0)	53	0.33
Romanian (47)	70	0.43
Russian (143)	422	2.62
Scandinavian (39)	39	0.24
Scotch-Irish (253)	367	2.28
Scottish (35)	303	1.88
Slovene (14)	14	0.09
Swedish (13)	143	0.89
Swiss (17)	30	0.19
Ukrainian (34)	118	0.73
Welsh (0)	103	0.64
West Indian, ex. Hispanic (25)	25	0.16
Belizean (18)	18	0.11
West Indian (7)	7	0.04
Yugoslavian (9)	9	0.06

Hispanic Origin	Population	%
Hispanic or Latino (of any race)	814	4.83
Central American, ex. Mexican	33	0.20
Costa Rican	2	0.01
Guatemalan	3	0.02
Honduran	6	0.04
Nicaraguan	1	0.01
Panamanian	4	0.02
Salvadoran	17	0.10
Cuban	45	0.27
Dominican Republic	34	0.20
Mexican	62	0.37
Puerto Rican	404	2.40
South American	127	0.75
Argentinean	16	0.09
Bolivian	2	0.01
Chilean	8	0.05
Colombian	52	0.31
Ecuadorian	22	0.13
Peruvian	17	0.10
Venezuelan	5	0.03
Other South American	5	0.03
Other Hispanic or Latino	109	0.65

Race*	Population	%
African-American/Black (183)	238	1.41
Not Hispanic (161)	204	1.21
Hispanic (22)	34	0.20
American Indian/Alaska Native (19)	54	0.32
Not Hispanic (18)	48	0.28
Hispanic (1)	6	0.04
Cherokee (4)	8	0.05
Chippewa (1)	2	0.01
Comanche (0)	1	0.01
Iroquois (2)	3	0.02
Mexican American Ind. (0)	1	0.01
Navajo (3)	3	0.02
South American Ind. (1)	4	0.02
Asian (309)	375	2.23
Not Hispanic (307)	371	2.20
Hispanic (2)	4	0.02
Burmese (5)	5	0.03
Chinese, ex. Taiwanese (42)	55	0.33
Filipino (30)	53	0.31
Indian (127)	135	0.80
Indonesian (6)	7	0.04
Japanese (7)	18	0.11
Korean (34)	41	0.24
Pakistani (36)	40	0.24
Taiwanese (3)	4	0.02
Thai (1)	3	0.02
Vietnamese (9)	11	0.07
Hawaii Native/Pacific Islander (2)	7	0.04
Not Hispanic (2)	4	0.02
Hispanic (0)	3	0.02
Native Hawaiian (1)	1	0.01
White (16,081)	16,238	96.35
Not Hispanic (15,415)	15,538	92.20
Hispanic (666)	700	4.15

Scarsdale

Place Type: Town/Village
County: Westchester
Population: 17,166†

Ancestry‡	Population	%
African, Sub-Saharan (80)	80	0.47
South African (80)	80	0.47
Albanian (42)	42	0.25
American (781)	781	4.56
Arab (110)	260	1.52
Arab (7)	7	0.04
Egyptian (5)	5	0.03
Iraqi (8)	24	0.14
Lebanese (63)	126	0.74
Moroccan (19)	56	0.33
Palestinian (0)	14	0.08
Syrian (0)	20	0.12
Other Arab (8)	8	0.05
Armenian (12)	38	0.22
Australian (96)	96	0.56
Austrian (57)	355	2.07
Belgian (0)	7	0.04
Brazilian (19)	25	0.15
British (134)	193	1.13
Bulgarian (20)	31	0.18
Canadian (45)	52	0.30
Czech (40)	129	0.75
Czechoslovakian (10)	47	0.27
Danish (23)	23	0.13
Dutch (78)	187	1.09
Eastern European (1,049)	1,208	7.06
English (282)	1,083	6.33
European (286)	300	1.75
Finnish (36)	36	0.21
French, ex. Basque (211)	501	2.93
French Canadian (11)	35	0.20
German (537)	1,775	10.37
Greek (76)	172	1.01
Hungarian (88)	300	1.75
Iranian (102)	102	0.60
Irish (689)	1,710	9.99
Israeli (25)	57	0.33
Italian (814)	1,660	9.70
Latvian (0)	10	0.06
Lithuanian (16)	76	0.44
Maltese (6)	6	0.04
Northern European (15)	15	0.09
Norwegian (30)	101	0.59
Polish (382)	1,637	9.57
Romanian (94)	229	1.34
Russian (1,062)	2,929	17.12
Scotch-Irish (18)	136	0.79
Scottish (24)	121	0.71
Slavic (24)	91	0.53
Swedish (24)	33	0.19
Swiss (0)	23	0.13
Turkish (16)	24	0.14
Ukrainian (126)	253	1.48
Welsh (0)	19	0.11
West Indian, ex. Hispanic (58)	94	0.55
British West Indian (14)	14	0.08
Jamaican (18)	54	0.32
Trinidadian/Tobagonian (11)	11	0.06
West Indian (15)	15	0.09

Hispanic Origin	Population	%
Hispanic or Latino (of any race)	671	3.91
Central American, ex. Mexican	60	0.35
Costa Rican	7	0.04
Guatemalan	19	0.11
Honduran	16	0.09
Nicaraguan	2	0.01
Panamanian	6	0.03
Salvadoran	10	0.06
Cuban	57	0.33
Dominican Republic	40	0.23
Mexican	66	0.38
Puerto Rican	84	0.49
South American	289	1.68
Argentinean	72	0.42
Bolivian	5	0.03
Chilean	8	0.05
Colombian	68	0.40
Ecuadorian	19	0.11
Paraguayan	12	0.07
Peruvian	42	0.24
Uruguayan	15	0.09
Venezuelan	48	0.28
Other Hispanic or Latino	75	0.44

Race*	Population	%
African-American/Black (260)	317	1.85
Not Hispanic (242)	291	1.70
Hispanic (18)	26	0.15
American Indian/Alaska Native (6)	29	0.17
Not Hispanic (5)	26	0.15
Hispanic (1)	3	0.02
Cherokee (0)	2	0.01
Delaware (0)	3	0.02
Navajo (1)	1	0.01
Potawatomi (0)	4	0.02
Asian (2,225)	2,483	14.46
Not Hispanic (2,220)	2,466	14.37
Hispanic (5)	17	0.10
Bangladeshi (13)	13	0.08
Burmese (6)	6	0.03
Cambodian (0)	4	0.02
Chinese, ex. Taiwanese (733)	840	4.89
Filipino (95)	150	0.87
Indian (483)	565	3.29
Indonesian (8)	10	0.06
Japanese (385)	428	2.49
Korean (257)	298	1.74
Malaysian (0)	3	0.02
Nepalese (2)	2	0.01
Pakistani (76)	89	0.52
Sri Lankan (8)	8	0.05
Taiwanese (52)	63	0.37
Thai (27)	36	0.21
Vietnamese (9)	13	0.08
Hawaii Native/Pacific Islander (4)	16	0.09
Not Hispanic (4)	15	0.09
Hispanic (0)	1	0.01
Native Hawaiian (0)	4	0.02
White (14,196)	14,476	84.33
Not Hispanic (13,648)	13,901	80.98
Hispanic (548)	575	3.35

Schaghticoke

Place Type: Town
County: Rensselaer
Population: 7,679†

Ancestry‡	Population	%
American (209)	209	2.73
Arab (6)	33	0.43
Lebanese (6)	6	0.08
Syrian (0)	27	0.35
Armenian (10)	31	0.40
Austrian (0)	22	0.29
British (6)	6	0.08
Canadian (74)	95	1.24
Croatian (68)	92	1.20
Czech (34)	86	1.12
Danish (21)	90	1.17
Dutch (42)	245	3.20
English (187)	1,022	13.33
European (35)	52	0.68
Finnish (10)	28	0.37
French, ex. Basque (119)	1,096	14.30
French Canadian (93)	302	3.94
German (146)	1,192	15.55
Greek (0)	37	0.48
Hungarian (0)	8	0.10
Irish (624)	2,336	30.47

*Notes: † The Census 2010 population figure is used to calculate the percentages in the Hispanic Origin and Race categories. Ancestry percentages are based on the 2006-2010 American Community Survey population (not shown); ‡ Numbers in parentheses indicate the number of people reporting a single ancestry; * Numbers in parentheses indicate the number of persons reporting this race alone, not in combination with any other race; Please refer to the Explanation of Data for more information.*

Italian (439)	1,574	20.53
Lithuanian (0)	63	0.82
Northern European (26)	26	0.34
Norwegian (0)	13	0.17
Polish (270)	703	9.17
Portuguese (0)	12	0.16
Russian (2)	99	1.29
Scotch-Irish (65)	87	1.13
Scottish (109)	255	3.33
Slavic (6)	6	0.08
Slovene (8)	8	0.10
Swedish (0)	36	0.47
Swiss (25)	72	0.94
Ukrainian (59)	153	2.00
Welsh (2)	97	1.27
West Indian, ex. Hispanic (36)	36	0.47
British West Indian (13)	13	0.17
Haitian (9)	9	0.12
Jamaican (14)	14	0.18

Hispanic Origin	Population	%
Hispanic or Latino (of any race)	75	0.98
Central American, ex. Mexican	9	0.12
Guatemalan	3	0.04
Panamanian	4	0.05
Salvadoran	2	0.03
Cuban	3	0.04
Dominican Republic	3	0.04
Mexican	10	0.13
Puerto Rican	41	0.53
South American	5	0.07
Chilean	3	0.04
Venezuelan	2	0.03
Other Hispanic or Latino	4	0.05

Race*	Population	%
African-American/Black (129)	168	2.19
Not Hispanic (123)	155	2.02
Hispanic (6)	13	0.17
American Indian/Alaska Native (18)	43	0.56
Not Hispanic (13)	36	0.47
Hispanic (5)	7	0.09
Blackfeet (0)	1	0.01
Choctaw (4)	4	0.05
Iroquois (3)	7	0.09
South American Ind. (1)	1	0.01
Asian (43)	53	0.69
Not Hispanic (43)	53	0.69
Chinese, ex. Taiwanese (9)	9	0.12
Filipino (9)	11	0.14
Indian (5)	8	0.10
Japanese (3)	6	0.08
Korean (10)	11	0.14
Thai (2)	2	0.03
Vietnamese (5)	5	0.07
Hawaii Native/Pacific Islander (4)	7	0.09
Not Hispanic (3)	6	0.08
Hispanic (1)	1	0.01
Guamanian/Chamorro (1)	1	0.01
Native Hawaiian (0)	1	0.01
Samoan (0)	2	0.03
White (7,403)	7,478	97.38
Not Hispanic (7,349)	7,417	96.59
Hispanic (54)	61	0.79

Schenectady

Place Type: City
County: Schenectady
Population: 66,135†

Ancestry‡	Population	%
Afghan (318)	318	0.49
African, Sub-Saharan (554)	770	1.18
African (201)	334	0.51
Ghanaian (24)	24	0.04
Kenyan (69)	69	0.11
Liberian (24)	24	0.04
Nigerian (131)	186	0.28
Other Sub-Saharan African (105)	133	0.20
Albanian (28)	39	0.06
American (3,124)	3,124	4.78
Arab (140)	191	0.29
Arab (81)	113	0.17
Lebanese (59)	78	0.12
Armenian (19)	19	0.03
Austrian (11)	77	0.12
Brazilian (144)	194	0.30
British (100)	187	0.29
Canadian (44)	72	0.11
Celtic (20)	20	0.03
Czech (50)	236	0.36
Czechoslovakian (68)	167	0.26
Danish (97)	121	0.19
Dutch (393)	1,521	2.33
Eastern European (76)	76	0.12
English (1,339)	3,998	6.12
European (205)	263	0.40
Finnish (15)	26	0.04
French, ex. Basque (658)	2,862	4.38
French Canadian (193)	902	1.38
German (1,915)	6,846	10.47
Greek (147)	224	0.34
Guyanese (1,783)	1,915	2.93
Hungarian (128)	341	0.52
Irish (2,754)	8,655	13.24
Israeli (0)	9	0.01
Italian (5,680)	9,882	15.12
Lithuanian (42)	240	0.37
Northern European (83)	97	0.15
Norwegian (0)	63	0.10
Pennsylvania German (0)	11	0.02
Polish (1,904)	3,977	6.08
Portuguese (20)	70	0.11
Romanian (10)	10	0.02
Russian (98)	430	0.66
Scandinavian (13)	13	0.02
Scotch-Irish (186)	509	0.78
Scottish (248)	656	1.00
Serbian (0)	12	0.02
Slavic (40)	40	0.06
Slovak (32)	93	0.14
Swedish (52)	177	0.27
Swiss (57)	171	0.26
Turkish (10)	10	0.02
Ukrainian (91)	236	0.36
Welsh (65)	320	0.49
West Indian, ex. Hispanic (1,255)	1,477	2.26
Barbadian (43)	94	0.14
British West Indian (7)	7	0.01
Dutch West Indian (0)	10	0.02
Haitian (24)	61	0.09
Jamaican (730)	781	1.19
Trinidadian/Tobagonian (18)	78	0.12
West Indian (433)	446	0.68
Yugoslavian (0)	1	<0.01

Hispanic Origin	Population	%
Hispanic or Latino (of any race)	6,922	10.47
Central American, ex. Mexican	321	0.49
Costa Rican	34	0.05
Guatemalan	61	0.09
Honduran	41	0.06
Nicaraguan	17	0.03
Panamanian	31	0.05
Salvadoran	126	0.19
Other Central American	11	0.02
Cuban	150	0.23
Dominican Republic	478	0.72
Mexican	430	0.65
Puerto Rican	4,677	7.07
South American	346	0.52
Argentinean	18	0.03
Bolivian	5	0.01
Chilean	13	0.02
Colombian	86	0.13
Ecuadorian	62	0.09
Paraguayan	9	0.01
Peruvian	74	0.11
Uruguayan	9	0.01
Venezuelan	27	0.04
Other South American	43	0.07
Other Hispanic or Latino	520	0.79

Race*	Population	%
African-American/Black (13,354)	16,103	24.35
Not Hispanic (12,258)	14,556	22.01
Hispanic (1,096)	1,547	2.34
American Indian/Alaska Native (458)	1,372	2.07
Not Hispanic (343)	1,126	1.70
Hispanic (115)	246	0.37
Apache (2)	5	0.01
Arapaho (1)	1	<0.01
Blackfeet (2)	58	0.09
Canadian/French Am. Ind. (3)	9	0.01
Central American Ind. (5)	6	0.01
Cherokee (9)	145	0.22
Cheyenne (1)	2	<0.01
Chippewa (2)	11	0.02
Choctaw (0)	1	<0.01
Cree (0)	4	0.01
Creek (1)	5	0.01
Crow (0)	6	0.01
Delaware (4)	12	0.02
Inupiat *(Alaska Native)* (3)	3	<0.01
Iroquois (17)	88	0.13
Kiowa (0)	1	<0.01
Lumbee (2)	4	0.01
Mexican American Ind. (16)	17	0.03
Navajo (1)	2	<0.01
Pima (1)	5	0.01
Potawatomi (0)	5	0.01
Pueblo (0)	1	<0.01
Seminole (1)	4	0.01
Sioux (3)	14	0.02
South American Ind. (17)	33	0.05
Spanish American Ind. (1)	7	0.01
Asian (2,396)	3,522	5.33
Not Hispanic (2,360)	3,400	5.14
Hispanic (36)	122	0.18
Bangladeshi (12)	15	0.02
Bhutanese (1)	1	<0.01
Cambodian (7)	8	0.01
Chinese, ex. Taiwanese (291)	361	0.55
Filipino (116)	157	0.24
Indian (1,571)	2,050	3.10
Indonesian (4)	9	0.01
Japanese (21)	70	0.11
Korean (87)	141	0.21
Laotian (2)	6	0.01
Malaysian (0)	5	0.01
Nepalese (5)	8	0.01
Pakistani (80)	86	0.13
Sri Lankan (4)	6	0.01
Taiwanese (7)	8	0.01
Thai (6)	15	0.02
Vietnamese (75)	87	0.13
Hawaii Native/Pacific Islander (92)	333	0.50
Not Hispanic (68)	272	0.41
Hispanic (24)	61	0.09
Fijian (1)	1	<0.01
Guamanian/Chamorro (6)	14	0.02
Native Hawaiian (14)	33	0.05
Samoan (4)	10	0.02
White (40,592)	43,710	66.09
Not Hispanic (38,006)	40,587	61.37
Hispanic (2,586)	3,123	4.72

Schodack

Place Type: Town
County: Rensselaer
Population: 12,794†

Ancestry‡	Population	%
African, Sub-Saharan (18)	50	0.39
African (18)	50	0.39
American (575)	575	4.49
Arab (0)	33	0.26
Lebanese (0)	33	0.26

*Notes: † The Census 2010 population figure is used to calculate the percentages in the Hispanic Origin and Race categories. Ancestry percentages are based on the 2006-2010 American Community Survey population (not shown); ‡ Numbers in parentheses indicate the number of people reporting a single ancestry; * Numbers in parentheses indicate the number of persons reporting this race alone, not in combination with any other race; Please refer to the Explanation of Data for more information.*

Ancestry	Population	%
Armenian (0)	47	0.37
Austrian (0)	124	0.97
Belgian (0)	10	0.08
British (19)	50	0.39
Canadian (3)	3	0.02
Croatian (10)	10	0.08
Czech (30)	95	0.74
Czechoslovakian (21)	25	0.20
Danish (12)	104	0.81
Dutch (191)	1,158	9.04
Eastern European (4)	4	0.03
English (323)	1,569	12.25
European (234)	268	2.09
Finnish (0)	29	0.23
French, ex. Basque (133)	1,035	8.08
French Canadian (90)	182	1.42
German (869)	3,978	31.07
Greek (17)	68	0.53
Guyanese (3)	3	0.02
Hungarian (15)	60	0.47
Irish (1,010)	3,996	31.21
Italian (625)	1,891	14.77
Latvian (10)	31	0.24
Lithuanian (20)	29	0.23
Northern European (3)	3	0.02
Norwegian (54)	111	0.87
Pennsylvania German (0)	3	0.02
Polish (167)	833	6.51
Portuguese (15)	35	0.27
Russian (25)	110	0.86
Scandinavian (0)	32	0.25
Scotch-Irish (54)	184	1.44
Scottish (63)	219	1.71
Slovak (0)	18	0.14
Swedish (59)	154	1.20
Ukrainian (46)	121	0.95
Welsh (58)	240	1.87
West Indian, ex. Hispanic (0)	22	0.17
Haitian (0)	2	0.02
Jamaican (0)	20	0.16

Hispanic Origin	Population	%
Hispanic or Latino (of any race)	277	2.17
Central American, ex. Mexican	26	0.20
Costa Rican	9	0.07
Guatemalan	10	0.08
Honduran	5	0.04
Nicaraguan	2	0.02
Cuban	6	0.05
Dominican Republic	12	0.09
Mexican	66	0.52
Puerto Rican	87	0.68
South American	19	0.15
Argentinean	1	0.01
Chilean	5	0.04
Colombian	7	0.05
Ecuadorian	5	0.04
Peruvian	1	0.01
Other Hispanic or Latino	61	0.48

Race*	Population	%
African-American/Black (110)	175	1.37
Not Hispanic (106)	160	1.25
Hispanic (4)	15	0.12
American Indian/Alaska Native (16)	74	0.58
Not Hispanic (10)	63	0.49
Hispanic (6)	11	0.09
Apache (0)	2	0.02
Blackfeet (0)	7	0.05
Cherokee (1)	2	0.02
Chippewa (0)	2	0.02
Cree (1)	1	0.01
Iroquois (3)	26	0.20
Mexican American Ind. (0)	1	0.01
Asian (86)	137	1.07
Not Hispanic (86)	134	1.05
Hispanic (0)	3	0.02
Bangladeshi (7)	8	0.06
Chinese, ex. Taiwanese (17)	25	0.20
Filipino (4)	15	0.12
Indian (22)	27	0.21
Indonesian (1)	2	0.02
Japanese (4)	14	0.11
Korean (17)	27	0.21
Nepalese (1)	2	0.02
Pakistani (0)	1	0.01
Thai (1)	4	0.03
Vietnamese (9)	9	0.07
Hawaii Native/Pacific Islander (1)	5	0.04
Not Hispanic (1)	5	0.04
Fijian (1)	1	0.01
White (12,364)	12,529	97.93
Not Hispanic (12,157)	12,306	96.19
Hispanic (207)	223	1.74

Schroeppel

Place Type: Town
County: Oswego
Population: 8,501†

Ancestry‡	Population	%
American (502)	502	5.91
Arab (13)	97	1.14
Lebanese (0)	78	0.92
Syrian (13)	19	0.22
Austrian (0)	17	0.20
Belgian (0)	14	0.16
British (14)	14	0.16
Canadian (86)	116	1.37
Croatian (24)	203	2.39
Czech (0)	5	0.06
Danish (16)	16	0.19
Dutch (40)	490	5.77
English (332)	1,160	13.65
Finnish (0)	14	0.16
French, ex. Basque (159)	897	10.56
French Canadian (67)	384	4.52
German (427)	2,257	26.56
Hungarian (0)	10	0.12
Irish (433)	1,917	22.56
Italian (284)	1,497	17.62
Lithuanian (0)	7	0.08
Norwegian (0)	31	0.36
Polish (145)	567	6.67
Romanian (0)	6	0.07
Russian (0)	15	0.18
Scotch-Irish (68)	143	1.68
Scottish (52)	190	2.24
Swedish (0)	5	0.06
Ukrainian (0)	115	1.35
Welsh (8)	208	2.45
West Indian, ex. Hispanic (0)	12	0.14
Jamaican (0)	12	0.14

Hispanic Origin	Population	%
Hispanic or Latino (of any race)	109	1.28
Central American, ex. Mexican	4	0.05
Honduran	2	0.02
Nicaraguan	1	0.01
Salvadoran	1	0.01
Cuban	3	0.04
Dominican Republic	1	0.01
Mexican	28	0.33
Puerto Rican	47	0.55
South American	13	0.15
Bolivian	2	0.02
Chilean	1	0.01
Colombian	7	0.08
Peruvian	2	0.02
Other South American	1	0.01
Other Hispanic or Latino	13	0.15

Race*	Population	%
African-American/Black (47)	84	0.99
Not Hispanic (40)	76	0.89
Hispanic (7)	8	0.09
American Indian/Alaska Native (60)	115	1.35
Not Hispanic (56)	108	1.27
Hispanic (4)	7	0.08
Blackfeet (0)	1	0.01
Canadian/French Am. Ind. (0)	1	0.01
Cherokee (1)	7	0.08
Chickasaw (1)	1	0.01
Chippewa (1)	1	0.01
Iroquois (37)	57	0.67
Mexican American Ind. (0)	1	0.01
Sioux (3)	4	0.05
South American Ind. (2)	3	0.04
Spanish American Ind. (1)	1	0.01
Asian (36)	50	0.59
Not Hispanic (30)	42	0.49
Hispanic (6)	8	0.09
Chinese, ex. Taiwanese (12)	15	0.18
Filipino (9)	10	0.12
Indian (4)	6	0.07
Japanese (4)	9	0.11
Korean (4)	6	0.07
Vietnamese (3)	4	0.05
Hawaii Native/Pacific Islander (2)	4	0.05
Not Hispanic (1)	3	0.04
Hispanic (1)	1	0.01
Native Hawaiian (2)	3	0.04
Samoan (0)	1	0.01
White (8,231)	8,329	97.98
Not Hispanic (8,168)	8,260	97.17
Hispanic (63)	69	0.81

Scotchtown

Place Type: CDP
County: Orange
Population: 9,212†

Ancestry‡	Population	%
African, Sub-Saharan (136)	161	1.65
African (136)	161	1.65
American (570)	570	5.86
Arab (24)	24	0.25
Egyptian (24)	24	0.25
Armenian (0)	6	0.06
Australian (0)	46	0.47
Austrian (0)	11	0.11
Brazilian (0)	57	0.59
British (0)	23	0.24
Canadian (29)	29	0.30
Czech (0)	59	0.61
Danish (0)	22	0.23
Dutch (50)	225	2.31
English (40)	262	2.69
European (159)	159	1.63
French, ex. Basque (20)	120	1.23
French Canadian (14)	14	0.14
German (233)	1,268	13.03
Greek (0)	12	0.12
Hungarian (0)	46	0.47
Iranian (0)	27	0.28
Irish (387)	1,689	17.36
Israeli (24)	48	0.49
Italian (701)	1,634	16.79
Latvian (36)	36	0.37
Lithuanian (0)	12	0.12
Norwegian (0)	21	0.22
Polish (142)	422	4.34
Russian (0)	62	0.64
Scandinavian (0)	28	0.29
Scotch-Irish (0)	52	0.53
Scottish (13)	65	0.67
Serbian (14)	14	0.14
Swedish (0)	97	1.00
Swiss (0)	12	0.12
Ukrainian (0)	18	0.18
West Indian, ex. Hispanic (339)	597	6.13
Barbadian (53)	53	0.54
British West Indian (124)	222	2.28
Haitian (162)	210	2.16
Trinidadian/Tobagonian (0)	98	1.01
West Indian (0)	14	0.14

*Notes: † The Census 2010 population figure is used to calculate the percentages in the Hispanic Origin and Race categories. Ancestry percentages are based on the 2006-2010 American Community Survey population (not shown); ‡ Numbers in parentheses indicate the number of people reporting a single ancestry; * Numbers in parentheses indicate the number of persons reporting this race alone, not in combination with any other race; Please refer to the Explanation of Data for more information.*

SECTION TWO

Hispanic Origin	Population	%
Hispanic or Latino (of any race)	2,313	25.11
Central American, ex. Mexican	124	1.35
Costa Rican	9	0.10
Guatemalan	11	0.12
Honduran	50	0.54
Nicaraguan	11	0.12
Panamanian	23	0.25
Salvadoran	16	0.17
Other Central American	4	0.04
Cuban	42	0.46
Dominican Republic	189	2.05
Mexican	157	1.70
Puerto Rican	1,410	15.31
South American	214	2.32
Argentinean	12	0.13
Bolivian	5	0.05
Chilean	6	0.07
Colombian	108	1.17
Ecuadorian	33	0.36
Peruvian	42	0.46
Uruguayan	5	0.05
Venezuelan	3	0.03
Other Hispanic or Latino	177	1.92

Race*	Population	%
African-American/Black (1,929)	2,225	24.15
Not Hispanic (1,726)	1,901	20.64
Hispanic (203)	324	3.52
American Indian/Alaska Native (39)	163	1.77
Not Hispanic (14)	93	1.01
Hispanic (25)	70	0.76
Apache (0)	1	0.01
Cherokee (3)	11	0.12
Delaware (4)	18	0.20
Iroquois (2)	10	0.11
Navajo (0)	4	0.04
Potawatomi (0)	2	0.02
Seminole (0)	1	0.01
Sioux (0)	1	0.01
South American Ind. (8)	15	0.16
Asian (377)	468	5.08
Not Hispanic (372)	433	4.70
Hispanic (5)	35	0.38
Bangladeshi (4)	4	0.04
Cambodian (11)	11	0.12
Chinese, ex. Taiwanese (69)	86	0.93
Filipino (72)	83	0.90
Indian (133)	149	1.62
Indonesian (1)	5	0.05
Japanese (2)	15	0.16
Korean (15)	19	0.21
Pakistani (51)	54	0.59
Taiwanese (4)	7	0.08
Thai (0)	6	0.07
Vietnamese (8)	12	0.13
Hawaii Native/Pacific Islander (2)	12	0.13
Not Hispanic (2)	9	0.10
Hispanic (0)	3	0.03
Guamanian/Chamorro (2)	3	0.03
Native Hawaiian (0)	5	0.05
White (5,684)	6,015	65.30
Not Hispanic (4,507)	4,678	50.78
Hispanic (1,177)	1,337	14.51

Scotia

Place Type: Village
County: Schenectady
Population: 7,729†

Ancestry‡	Population	%
American (726)	726	9.43
Arab (13)	13	0.17
Lebanese (13)	13	0.17
Armenian (0)	17	0.22
British (0)	9	0.12
Canadian (0)	38	0.49
Czech (10)	51	0.66
Czechoslovakian (42)	53	0.69
Danish (45)	114	1.48
Dutch (78)	417	5.42
Eastern European (29)	29	0.38
English (332)	1,041	13.52
European (127)	127	1.65
French, ex. Basque (87)	516	6.70
French Canadian (60)	207	2.69
German (269)	1,345	17.47
Greek (0)	52	0.68
Hungarian (15)	81	1.05
Irish (484)	1,690	21.95
Italian (596)	1,209	15.71
Lithuanian (34)	75	0.97
Northern European (111)	111	1.44
Norwegian (30)	73	0.95
Polish (249)	700	9.09
Romanian (0)	55	0.71
Russian (56)	87	1.13
Scotch-Irish (62)	134	1.74
Scottish (15)	148	1.92
Slovak (10)	63	0.82
Swedish (43)	98	1.27
Swiss (0)	9	0.12
Ukrainian (31)	63	0.82
Welsh (10)	48	0.62
West Indian, ex. Hispanic (8)	8	0.10
West Indian (8)	8	0.10

Hispanic Origin	Population	%
Hispanic or Latino (of any race)	216	2.79
Central American, ex. Mexican	14	0.18
Costa Rican	1	0.01
Guatemalan	1	0.01
Honduran	3	0.04
Panamanian	5	0.06
Salvadoran	4	0.05
Cuban	7	0.09
Dominican Republic	16	0.21
Mexican	22	0.28
Puerto Rican	100	1.29
South American	33	0.43
Argentinean	3	0.04
Colombian	12	0.16
Ecuadorian	7	0.09
Peruvian	4	0.05
Venezuelan	7	0.09
Other Hispanic or Latino	24	0.31

Race*	Population	%
African-American/Black (89)	157	2.03
Not Hispanic (81)	134	1.73
Hispanic (8)	23	0.30
American Indian/Alaska Native (13)	41	0.53
Not Hispanic (10)	32	0.41
Hispanic (3)	9	0.12
Cherokee (0)	6	0.08
Chippewa (0)	1	0.01
Iroquois (5)	10	0.13
Potawatomi (1)	1	0.01
South American Ind. (0)	2	0.03
Asian (86)	127	1.64
Not Hispanic (85)	122	1.58
Hispanic (1)	5	0.06
Cambodian (1)	1	0.01
Chinese, ex. Taiwanese (20)	28	0.36
Filipino (19)	29	0.38
Indian (22)	34	0.44
Japanese (4)	9	0.12
Korean (10)	15	0.19
Laotian (0)	2	0.03
Nepalese (2)	2	0.03
Pakistani (6)	6	0.08
Thai (2)	6	0.08
Vietnamese (0)	1	0.01
Hawaii Native/Pacific Islander (4)	10	0.13
Not Hispanic (4)	10	0.13
Native Hawaiian (0)	3	0.04
White (7,372)	7,493	96.95
Not Hispanic (7,215)	7,317	94.67
Hispanic (157)	176	2.28

Seaford

Place Type: CDP
County: Nassau
Population: 15,294†

Ancestry‡	Population	%
American (279)	279	1.80
Arab (0)	11	0.07
Egyptian (0)	11	0.07
Australian (0)	36	0.23
Austrian (37)	112	0.72
Belgian (0)	25	0.16
British (13)	25	0.16
Canadian (12)	12	0.08
Croatian (33)	33	0.21
Czech (49)	85	0.55
Danish (0)	71	0.46
Dutch (10)	52	0.34
Eastern European (97)	97	0.63
English (76)	898	5.81
Estonian (15)	31	0.20
European (13)	24	0.16
Finnish (0)	41	0.27
French, ex. Basque (8)	104	0.67
French Canadian (0)	19	0.12
German (580)	3,087	19.96
Greek (318)	414	2.68
Guyanese (0)	17	0.11
Hungarian (10)	118	0.76
Irish (1,171)	4,739	30.65
Israeli (0)	30	0.19
Italian (2,889)	6,290	40.68
Northern European (15)	46	0.30
Norwegian (6)	55	0.36
Pennsylvania German (13)	13	0.08
Polish (292)	1,579	10.21
Romanian (0)	40	0.26
Russian (236)	924	5.98
Scandinavian (0)	8	0.05
Scotch-Irish (110)	159	1.03
Scottish (34)	169	1.09
Slavic (0)	10	0.06
Slovak (8)	20	0.13
Swedish (0)	306	1.98
Swiss (0)	18	0.12
Turkish (16)	47	0.30
Ukrainian (0)	50	0.32
West Indian, ex. Hispanic (28)	28	0.18
Haitian (28)	28	0.18
Yugoslavian (0)	39	0.25

Hispanic Origin	Population	%
Hispanic or Latino (of any race)	761	4.98
Central American, ex. Mexican	44	0.29
Costa Rican	3	0.02
Guatemalan	13	0.09
Honduran	9	0.06
Nicaraguan	2	0.01
Salvadoran	17	0.11
Cuban	39	0.26
Dominican Republic	43	0.28
Mexican	51	0.33
Puerto Rican	305	1.99
South American	192	1.26
Argentinean	36	0.24
Chilean	15	0.10
Colombian	76	0.50
Ecuadorian	31	0.20
Paraguayan	1	0.01
Peruvian	25	0.16
Uruguayan	2	0.01
Venezuelan	6	0.04
Other Hispanic or Latino	87	0.57

Race*	Population	%
African-American/Black (74)	121	0.79
Not Hispanic (70)	108	0.71
Hispanic (4)	13	0.09
American Indian/Alaska Native (13)	37	0.24

*Notes: † The Census 2010 population figure is used to calculate the percentages in the Hispanic Origin and Race categories. Ancestry percentages are based on the 2006-2010 American Community Survey population (not shown); ‡ Numbers in parentheses indicate the number of people reporting a single ancestry; * Numbers in parentheses indicate the number of persons reporting this race alone, not in combination with any other race; Please refer to the Explanation of Data for more information.*

Not Hispanic (3)	20	0.13
Hispanic (10)	17	0.11
Blackfeet (0)	1	0.01
Cherokee (0)	2	0.01
Iroquois (0)	2	0.01
South American Ind. (5)	9	0.06
Asian (341)	433	2.83
Not Hispanic (334)	416	2.72
Hispanic (7)	17	0.11
Bangladeshi (3)	3	0.02
Burmese (1)	1	0.01
Chinese, ex. Taiwanese (142)	162	1.06
Filipino (67)	89	0.58
Indian (71)	93	0.61
Japanese (9)	10	0.07
Korean (32)	43	0.28
Pakistani (3)	3	0.02
Taiwanese (6)	6	0.04
Thai (5)	7	0.05
Vietnamese (1)	1	0.01
Hawaii Native/Pacific Islander (0)	2	0.01
Not Hispanic (0)	1	0.01
Hispanic (0)	1	0.01
Samoan (0)	1	0.01
White (14,593)	14,745	96.41
Not Hispanic (13,986)	14,089	92.12
Hispanic (607)	656	4.29

Selden

Place Type: CDP
County: Suffolk
Population: 19,851†

Ancestry‡	Population	%
Albanian (0)	10	0.05
American (306)	306	1.56
Arab (53)	53	0.27
Egyptian (38)	38	0.19
Other Arab (15)	15	0.08
Armenian (0)	75	0.38
Austrian (23)	130	0.66
Brazilian (13)	13	0.07
British (10)	37	0.19
Canadian (22)	94	0.48
Czech (8)	51	0.26
Czechoslovakian (0)	41	0.21
Danish (0)	40	0.20
Dutch (0)	8	0.04
English (208)	1,086	5.54
European (52)	60	0.31
French, ex. Basque (13)	385	1.97
French Canadian (28)	92	0.47
German (567)	3,974	20.28
Greek (71)	352	1.80
Guyanese (35)	47	0.24
Hungarian (28)	96	0.49
Irish (996)	4,792	24.46
Israeli (0)	13	0.07
Italian (3,593)	7,803	39.83
Lithuanian (10)	40	0.20
Maltese (13)	25	0.13
Norwegian (83)	280	1.43
Polish (81)	847	4.32
Portuguese (139)	217	1.11
Romanian (0)	20	0.10
Russian (79)	422	2.15
Scotch-Irish (27)	178	0.91
Scottish (38)	278	1.42
Slovak (0)	19	0.10
Swedish (0)	101	0.52
Turkish (77)	87	0.44
Ukrainian (9)	16	0.08
West Indian, ex. Hispanic (157)	199	1.02
Haitian (9)	30	0.15
Jamaican (89)	110	0.56
Trinidadian/Tobagonian (40)	40	0.20
West Indian (19)	19	0.10
Yugoslavian (0)	34	0.17

Hispanic Origin	Population	%
Hispanic or Latino (of any race)	2,750	13.85
Central American, ex. Mexican	343	1.73
Costa Rican	1	0.01
Guatemalan	40	0.20
Honduran	87	0.44
Nicaraguan	15	0.08
Panamanian	13	0.07
Salvadoran	181	0.91
Other Central American	6	0.03
Cuban	76	0.38
Dominican Republic	285	1.44
Mexican	340	1.71
Puerto Rican	965	4.86
South American	488	2.46
Argentinean	45	0.23
Bolivian	1	0.01
Chilean	21	0.11
Colombian	183	0.92
Ecuadorian	159	0.80
Peruvian	64	0.32
Uruguayan	6	0.03
Venezuelan	3	0.02
Other South American	6	0.03
Other Hispanic or Latino	253	1.27

Race*	Population	%
African-American/Black (648)	793	3.99
Not Hispanic (568)	658	3.31
Hispanic (80)	135	0.68
American Indian/Alaska Native (31)	134	0.68
Not Hispanic (13)	74	0.37
Hispanic (18)	60	0.30
Blackfeet (0)	7	0.04
Cherokee (1)	24	0.12
Chickasaw (0)	1	0.01
Choctaw (0)	1	0.01
Creek (0)	1	0.01
Iroquois (0)	6	0.03
Mexican American Ind. (4)	12	0.06
Seminole (0)	1	0.01
Sioux (4)	4	0.02
Asian (876)	992	5.00
Not Hispanic (866)	966	4.87
Hispanic (10)	26	0.13
Bangladeshi (35)	44	0.22
Burmese (0)	3	0.02
Chinese, ex. Taiwanese (104)	111	0.56
Filipino (151)	181	0.91
Indian (272)	318	1.60
Japanese (12)	17	0.09
Korean (35)	48	0.24
Nepalese (3)	3	0.02
Pakistani (196)	203	1.02
Sri Lankan (0)	2	0.01
Taiwanese (10)	13	0.07
Thai (6)	8	0.04
Vietnamese (10)	12	0.06
Hawaii Native/Pacific Islander (6)	19	0.10
Not Hispanic (5)	15	0.08
Hispanic (1)	4	0.02
Guamanian/Chamorro (0)	1	0.01
Native Hawaiian (0)	4	0.02
Samoan (0)	1	0.01
White (17,080)	17,480	88.06
Not Hispanic (15,343)	15,538	78.27
Hispanic (1,737)	1,942	9.78

Seneca Falls

Place Type: Town
County: Seneca
Population: 9,040†

Ancestry‡	Population	%
American (395)	395	4.32
Arab (13)	13	0.14
Lebanese (13)	13	0.14
Austrian (4)	14	0.15
Belgian (0)	3	0.03
Brazilian (18)	18	0.20
British (9)	13	0.14
Canadian (10)	19	0.21
Czech (3)	42	0.46
Czechoslovakian (14)	20	0.22
Danish (4)	15	0.16
Dutch (84)	399	4.36
English (453)	1,689	18.47
European (49)	49	0.54
French, ex. Basque (85)	415	4.54
French Canadian (30)	105	1.15
German (500)	2,239	24.48
Greek (16)	20	0.22
Hungarian (12)	28	0.31
Iranian (3)	3	0.03
Irish (505)	2,012	22.00
Italian (1,461)	2,743	29.99
Lithuanian (15)	36	0.39
Norwegian (7)	24	0.26
Pennsylvania German (12)	16	0.17
Polish (99)	426	4.66
Portuguese (0)	2	0.02
Romanian (0)	1	0.01
Russian (42)	48	0.52
Scandinavian (0)	13	0.14
Scotch-Irish (20)	111	1.21
Scottish (16)	136	1.49
Slovak (1)	1	0.01
Swedish (5)	76	0.83
Swiss (0)	6	0.07
Ukrainian (24)	95	1.04
Welsh (10)	58	0.63

Hispanic Origin	Population	%
Hispanic or Latino (of any race)	156	1.73
Central American, ex. Mexican	8	0.09
Guatemalan	1	0.01
Panamanian	4	0.04
Salvadoran	3	0.03
Cuban	3	0.03
Mexican	36	0.40
Puerto Rican	86	0.95
South American	5	0.06
Colombian	3	0.03
Paraguayan	1	0.01
Venezuelan	1	0.01
Other Hispanic or Latino	18	0.20

Race*	Population	%
African-American/Black (114)	179	1.98
Not Hispanic (111)	173	1.91
Hispanic (3)	6	0.07
American Indian/Alaska Native (38)	81	0.90
Not Hispanic (38)	80	0.88
Hispanic (0)	1	0.01
Blackfeet (0)	1	0.01
Cherokee (5)	18	0.20
Iroquois (6)	23	0.25
Lumbee (3)	3	0.03
Menominee (0)	1	0.01
Ottawa (0)	2	0.02
Sioux (0)	1	0.01
Asian (146)	159	1.76
Not Hispanic (146)	159	1.76
Chinese, ex. Taiwanese (30)	32	0.35
Filipino (9)	11	0.12
Indian (31)	42	0.46
Japanese (2)	2	0.02
Korean (24)	24	0.27
Laotian (13)	15	0.17
Pakistani (2)	5	0.06
Sri Lankan (6)	6	0.07
Taiwanese (6)	6	0.07
Thai (2)	2	0.02
Vietnamese (11)	11	0.12
Hawaii Native/Pacific Islander (1)	4	0.04
Not Hispanic (1)	4	0.04
Native Hawaiian (0)	3	0.03
Samoan (1)	1	0.01
White (8,581)	8,690	96.13

SECTION TWO

*Notes: † The Census 2010 population figure is used to calculate the percentages in the Hispanic Origin and Race categories. Ancestry percentages are based on the 2006-2010 American Community Survey population (not shown); ‡ Numbers in parentheses indicate the number of people reporting a single ancestry; * Numbers in parentheses indicate the number of persons reporting this race alone, not in combination with any other race; Please refer to the Explanation of Data for more information.*

Not Hispanic (8,461)	8,561	94.70
Hispanic (120)	129	1.43

Setauket-East Setauket

Place Type: CDP
County: Suffolk
Population: 15,477†

Ancestry‡	Population	%
Albanian (0)	15	0.10
American (453)	453	2.88
Arab (42)	42	0.27
Egyptian (42)	42	0.27
Armenian (20)	20	0.13
Austrian (9)	204	1.30
Belgian (12)	34	0.22
British (26)	26	0.17
Bulgarian (51)	51	0.32
Canadian (23)	36	0.23
Croatian (143)	172	1.09
Czech (49)	165	1.05
Czechoslovakian (17)	17	0.11
Danish (0)	23	0.15
Dutch (18)	173	1.10
Eastern European (65)	65	0.41
English (219)	1,717	10.93
European (313)	313	1.99
Finnish (9)	21	0.13
French, ex. Basque (40)	236	1.50
French Canadian (52)	141	0.90
German (513)	2,530	16.10
Greek (114)	167	1.06
Hungarian (25)	92	0.59
Iranian (70)	70	0.45
Irish (860)	4,251	27.06
Israeli (10)	10	0.06
Italian (1,982)	4,377	27.86
Lithuanian (33)	57	0.36
Maltese (0)	14	0.09
Northern European (120)	120	0.76
Norwegian (0)	59	0.38
Polish (457)	1,577	10.04
Romanian (13)	37	0.24
Russian (285)	953	6.07
Scotch-Irish (69)	165	1.05
Scottish (64)	329	2.09
Slovak (0)	9	0.06
Swedish (85)	306	1.95
Swiss (11)	77	0.49
Turkish (12)	47	0.30
Ukrainian (0)	72	0.46
Welsh (0)	99	0.63
West Indian, ex. Hispanic (66)	66	0.42
British West Indian (38)	38	0.24
Jamaican (28)	28	0.18

Hispanic Origin	Population	%
Hispanic or Latino (of any race)	807	5.21
Central American, ex. Mexican	75	0.48
Guatemalan	12	0.08
Honduran	5	0.03
Nicaraguan	3	0.02
Panamanian	13	0.08
Salvadoran	42	0.27
Cuban	67	0.43
Dominican Republic	41	0.26
Mexican	62	0.40
Puerto Rican	312	2.02
South American	144	0.93
Argentinean	23	0.15
Bolivian	3	0.02
Chilean	17	0.11
Colombian	45	0.29
Ecuadorian	21	0.14
Paraguayan	2	0.01
Peruvian	19	0.12
Uruguayan	1	0.01
Venezuelan	9	0.06
Other South American	4	0.03
Other Hispanic or Latino	106	0.68

Race*	Population	%
African-American/Black (178)	240	1.55
Not Hispanic (156)	206	1.33
Hispanic (22)	34	0.22
American Indian/Alaska Native (21)	75	0.48
Not Hispanic (20)	63	0.41
Hispanic (1)	12	0.08
Apache (0)	2	0.01
Blackfeet (0)	1	0.01
Canadian/French Am. Ind. (1)	1	0.01
Cherokee (0)	4	0.03
Ottawa (0)	3	0.02
Seminole (1)	2	0.01
Sioux (1)	1	0.01
South American Ind. (0)	1	0.01
Spanish American Ind. (1)	1	0.01
Asian (1,139)	1,285	8.30
Not Hispanic (1,137)	1,266	8.18
Hispanic (2)	19	0.12
Bangladeshi (6)	6	0.04
Cambodian (2)	2	0.01
Chinese, ex. Taiwanese (552)	603	3.90
Filipino (59)	84	0.54
Indian (250)	289	1.87
Indonesian (2)	2	0.01
Japanese (21)	35	0.23
Korean (120)	149	0.96
Malaysian (1)	1	0.01
Pakistani (40)	47	0.30
Sri Lankan (3)	4	0.03
Taiwanese (30)	33	0.21
Thai (2)	5	0.03
Vietnamese (15)	17	0.11
Hawaii Native/Pacific Islander (0)	3	0.02
Not Hispanic (0)	3	0.02
Native Hawaiian (0)	1	0.01
Samoan (0)	1	0.01
White (13,795)	14,011	90.53
Not Hispanic (13,128)	13,294	85.90
Hispanic (667)	717	4.63

Shawangunk

Place Type: Town
County: Ulster
Population: 14,332†

Ancestry‡	Population	%
African, Sub-Saharan (26)	42	0.30
African (26)	42	0.30
American (1,579)	1,579	11.26
Arab (11)	32	0.23
Arab (0)	8	0.06
Lebanese (11)	24	0.17
Armenian (5)	15	0.11
Australian (0)	6	0.04
Austrian (11)	48	0.34
Belgian (9)	116	0.83
Brazilian (11)	11	0.08
British (11)	32	0.23
Canadian (16)	48	0.34
Celtic (0)	11	0.08
Czechoslovakian (14)	46	0.33
Danish (11)	35	0.25
Dutch (274)	724	5.16
English (345)	1,419	10.11
French, ex. Basque (54)	411	2.93
French Canadian (15)	24	0.17
German (470)	2,494	17.78
Greek (18)	55	0.39
Guyanese (19)	19	0.14
Hungarian (60)	215	1.53
Irish (794)	3,324	23.69
Italian (1,270)	2,959	21.09
Latvian (16)	16	0.11
Lithuanian (20)	37	0.26
Norwegian (70)	295	2.10
Pennsylvania German (15)	30	0.21
Polish (140)	708	5.05
Portuguese (0)	119	0.85
Romanian (11)	11	0.08
Russian (68)	134	0.96
Scandinavian (14)	14	0.10
Scotch-Irish (72)	243	1.73
Scottish (20)	139	0.99
Slovak (0)	18	0.13
Swedish (8)	19	0.14
Swiss (0)	44	0.31
Ukrainian (94)	102	0.73
Welsh (26)	106	0.76
West Indian, ex. Hispanic (100)	159	1.13
Barbadian (0)	9	0.06
Haitian (8)	8	0.06
Jamaican (17)	17	0.12
West Indian (75)	125	0.89

Hispanic Origin	Population	%
Hispanic or Latino (of any race)	1,310	9.14
Central American, ex. Mexican	75	0.52
Guatemalan	15	0.10
Honduran	33	0.23
Nicaraguan	2	0.01
Panamanian	9	0.06
Salvadoran	15	0.10
Other Central American	1	0.01
Cuban	55	0.38
Dominican Republic	54	0.38
Mexican	203	1.42
Puerto Rican	612	4.27
South American	54	0.38
Argentinean	2	0.01
Bolivian	2	0.01
Chilean	2	0.01
Colombian	22	0.15
Ecuadorian	15	0.10
Peruvian	6	0.04
Uruguayan	3	0.02
Venezuelan	2	0.01
Other Hispanic or Latino	257	1.79

Race*	Population	%
African-American/Black (1,157)	1,241	8.66
Not Hispanic (1,078)	1,151	8.03
Hispanic (79)	90	0.63
American Indian/Alaska Native (33)	88	0.61
Not Hispanic (22)	71	0.50
Hispanic (11)	17	0.12
Central American Ind. (3)	3	0.02
Cherokee (3)	14	0.10
Chippewa (0)	1	0.01
Delaware (0)	2	0.01
Iroquois (4)	4	0.03
Mexican American Ind. (1)	4	0.03
Pueblo (1)	1	0.01
Seminole (0)	1	0.01
South American Ind. (0)	1	0.01
Asian (227)	270	1.88
Not Hispanic (222)	260	1.81
Hispanic (5)	10	0.07
Chinese, ex. Taiwanese (41)	45	0.31
Filipino (25)	28	0.20
Indian (12)	16	0.11
Indonesian (0)	1	0.01
Japanese (19)	28	0.20
Korean (30)	35	0.24
Sri Lankan (10)	10	0.07
Thai (22)	26	0.18
Vietnamese (3)	3	0.02
Hawaii Native/Pacific Islander (0)	8	0.06
Not Hispanic (0)	8	0.06
Samoan (0)	1	0.01
White (12,427)	12,597	87.89
Not Hispanic (11,522)	11,651	81.29
Hispanic (905)	946	6.60

*Notes: † The Census 2010 population figure is used to calculate the percentages in the Hispanic Origin and Race categories. Ancestry percentages are based on the 2006-2010 American Community Survey population (not shown); ‡ Numbers in parentheses indicate the number of people reporting a single ancestry; * Numbers in parentheses indicate the number of persons reporting this race alone, not in combination with any other race; Please refer to the Explanation of Data for more information.*

Shirley

Place Type: CDP
County: Suffolk
Population: 27,854†

Ancestry‡	Population	%
African, Sub-Saharan (227)	381	1.36
African (227)	381	1.36
Albanian (15)	15	0.05
American (413)	413	1.47
Arab (105)	126	0.45
Arab (53)	55	0.20
Egyptian (0)	19	0.07
Syrian (12)	12	0.04
Other Arab (40)	40	0.14
Austrian (24)	90	0.32
Brazilian (14)	14	0.05
British (27)	52	0.19
Canadian (13)	13	0.05
Croatian (62)	62	0.22
Czech (7)	55	0.20
Czechoslovakian (26)	58	0.21
Danish (18)	49	0.17
Dutch (48)	189	0.67
English (328)	1,495	5.33
European (0)	6	0.02
French, ex. Basque (45)	466	1.66
French Canadian (84)	244	0.87
German (715)	4,393	15.65
Greek (71)	253	0.90
Guyanese (32)	32	0.11
Hungarian (4)	221	0.79
Irish (1,490)	6,126	21.82
Italian (5,127)	10,346	36.86
Lithuanian (177)	230	0.82
Maltese (2)	2	0.01
Norwegian (67)	323	1.15
Pennsylvania German (19)	19	0.07
Polish (433)	1,514	5.39
Portuguese (27)	107	0.38
Romanian (0)	8	0.03
Russian (90)	329	1.17
Scandinavian (0)	4	0.01
Scotch-Irish (24)	167	0.59
Scottish (65)	181	0.64
Slovak (20)	29	0.10
Swedish (29)	124	0.44
Swiss (0)	16	0.06
Turkish (257)	257	0.92
Ukrainian (54)	101	0.36
Welsh (11)	11	0.04
West Indian, ex. Hispanic (198)	288	1.03
Dutch West Indian (11)	11	0.04
Haitian (103)	147	0.52
Jamaican (0)	16	0.06
Trinidadian/Tobagonian (40)	40	0.14
West Indian (44)	74	0.26

Hispanic Origin	Population	%
Hispanic or Latino (of any race)	4,781	17.16
Central American, ex. Mexican	882	3.17
Costa Rican	13	0.05
Guatemalan	180	0.65
Honduran	117	0.42
Nicaraguan	14	0.05
Panamanian	17	0.06
Salvadoran	534	1.92
Other Central American	7	0.03
Cuban	118	0.42
Dominican Republic	245	0.88
Mexican	302	1.08
Puerto Rican	2,149	7.72
South American	654	2.35
Argentinean	36	0.13
Bolivian	9	0.03
Chilean	27	0.10
Colombian	170	0.61
Ecuadorian	296	1.06
Paraguayan	2	0.01
Peruvian	72	0.26
Uruguayan	12	0.04
Venezuelan	26	0.09
Other South American	4	0.01
Other Hispanic or Latino	431	1.55

Race*	Population	%
African-American/Black (1,997)	2,464	8.85
Not Hispanic (1,768)	2,119	7.61
Hispanic (229)	345	1.24
American Indian/Alaska Native (100)	291	1.04
Not Hispanic (72)	186	0.67
Hispanic (28)	105	0.38
Blackfeet (2)	10	0.04
Central American Ind. (0)	8	0.03
Cherokee (4)	47	0.17
Chippewa (2)	2	0.01
Creek (0)	1	<0.01
Delaware (1)	1	<0.01
Iroquois (4)	9	0.03
Mexican American Ind. (2)	2	0.01
Navajo (0)	3	0.01
Seminole (1)	1	<0.01
South American Ind. (3)	11	0.04
Spanish American Ind. (6)	6	0.02
Yaqui (0)	4	0.01
Asian (720)	880	3.16
Not Hispanic (701)	834	2.99
Hispanic (19)	46	0.17
Bangladeshi (8)	13	0.05
Chinese, ex. Taiwanese (152)	187	0.67
Filipino (78)	124	0.45
Indian (155)	190	0.68
Indonesian (6)	7	0.03
Japanese (5)	18	0.06
Korean (42)	58	0.21
Laotian (4)	7	0.03
Malaysian (1)	3	0.01
Pakistani (112)	124	0.45
Taiwanese (0)	2	0.01
Thai (13)	17	0.06
Vietnamese (108)	108	0.39
Hawaii Native/Pacific Islander (8)	40	0.14
Not Hispanic (6)	24	0.09
Hispanic (2)	16	0.06
Fijian (0)	1	<0.01
Guamanian/Chamorro (3)	3	0.01
Native Hawaiian (0)	6	0.02
White (22,698)	23,469	84.26
Not Hispanic (19,966)	20,408	73.27
Hispanic (2,732)	3,061	10.99

Sleepy Hollow

Place Type: Village
County: Westchester
Population: 9,870†

Ancestry‡	Population	%
African, Sub-Saharan (0)	17	0.18
South African (0)	17	0.18
American (150)	150	1.55
Arab (38)	120	1.24
Arab (0)	26	0.27
Egyptian (0)	20	0.21
Lebanese (38)	48	0.49
Moroccan (0)	8	0.08
Other Arab (0)	18	0.19
Austrian (9)	46	0.47
Brazilian (0)	13	0.13
British (0)	9	0.09
Canadian (35)	35	0.36
Croatian (24)	24	0.25
Czech (0)	17	0.18
Czechoslovakian (8)	8	0.08
Danish (9)	9	0.09
Dutch (25)	103	1.06
English (53)	293	3.02
European (131)	131	1.35
French, ex. Basque (18)	171	1.76
French Canadian (0)	20	0.21
German (99)	551	5.68
Greek (16)	32	0.33
Hungarian (66)	122	1.26
Irish (257)	918	9.46
Italian (555)	1,084	11.17
Lithuanian (0)	12	0.12
Norwegian (0)	9	0.09
Polish (57)	265	2.73
Portuguese (243)	318	3.28
Russian (125)	246	2.54
Scotch-Irish (38)	60	0.62
Scottish (8)	108	1.11
Slovak (24)	92	0.95
Slovene (9)	9	0.09
Swedish (0)	68	0.70
Swiss (40)	40	0.41
Ukrainian (40)	40	0.41
Welsh (0)	66	0.68

Hispanic Origin	Population	%
Hispanic or Latino (of any race)	5,038	51.04
Central American, ex. Mexican	127	1.29
Costa Rican	1	0.01
Guatemalan	64	0.65
Honduran	31	0.31
Nicaraguan	2	0.02
Panamanian	3	0.03
Salvadoran	26	0.26
Cuban	123	1.25
Dominican Republic	1,831	18.55
Mexican	146	1.48
Puerto Rican	331	3.35
South American	2,098	21.26
Argentinean	9	0.09
Bolivian	2	0.02
Chilean	146	1.48
Colombian	111	1.12
Ecuadorian	1,731	17.54
Peruvian	69	0.70
Uruguayan	29	0.29
Other South American	1	0.01
Other Hispanic or Latino	382	3.87

Race*	Population	%
African-American/Black (613)	757	7.67
Not Hispanic (435)	487	4.93
Hispanic (178)	270	2.74
American Indian/Alaska Native (82)	150	1.52
Not Hispanic (9)	30	0.30
Hispanic (73)	120	1.22
Apache (0)	1	0.01
Blackfeet (0)	2	0.02
Central American Ind. (4)	6	0.06
Cherokee (0)	12	0.12
Iroquois (3)	5	0.05
Navajo (0)	1	0.01
Pueblo (4)	5	0.05
South American Ind. (6)	7	0.07
Spanish American Ind. (8)	8	0.08
Asian (321)	392	3.97
Not Hispanic (306)	351	3.56
Hispanic (15)	41	0.42
Cambodian (1)	1	0.01
Chinese, ex. Taiwanese (72)	94	0.95
Filipino (67)	76	0.77
Indian (96)	111	1.12
Japanese (15)	28	0.28
Korean (45)	54	0.55
Pakistani (3)	4	0.04
Sri Lankan (1)	1	0.01
Taiwanese (3)	4	0.04
Thai (3)	3	0.03
Vietnamese (2)	2	0.02
Hawaii Native/Pacific Islander (1)	45	0.46
Not Hispanic (1)	14	0.14
Hispanic (0)	31	0.31
Native Hawaiian (1)	3	0.03
Samoan (0)	1	0.01
White (6,022)	6,436	65.21

*Notes: † The Census 2010 population figure is used to calculate the percentages in the Hispanic Origin and Race categories. Ancestry percentages are based on the 2006-2010 American Community Survey population (not shown); ‡ Numbers in parentheses indicate the number of people reporting a single ancestry; * Numbers in parentheses indicate the number of persons reporting this race alone, not in combination with any other race; Please refer to the Explanation of Data for more information.*

Not Hispanic (3,945)	4,030	40.83
Hispanic (2,077)	2,406	24.38

Smithtown

Place Type: CDP
County: Suffolk
Population: 26,470†

Ancestry‡	Population	%
Afghan (27)	27	0.10
American (696)	696	2.66
Arab (20)	50	0.19
Other Arab (20)	50	0.19
Armenian (13)	69	0.26
Australian (11)	11	0.04
Austrian (38)	145	0.55
Belgian (0)	9	0.03
Brazilian (0)	10	0.04
British (36)	96	0.37
Canadian (27)	132	0.50
Croatian (14)	14	0.05
Czech (9)	106	0.40
Czechoslovakian (0)	104	0.40
Danish (32)	64	0.24
Dutch (7)	88	0.34
Eastern European (138)	138	0.53
English (305)	1,823	6.96
European (287)	296	1.13
Finnish (0)	21	0.08
French, ex. Basque (56)	692	2.64
French Canadian (34)	109	0.42
German (1,088)	5,505	21.01
Greek (524)	820	3.13
Hungarian (60)	265	1.01
Iranian (105)	137	0.52
Irish (1,800)	7,621	29.09
Italian (4,281)	9,899	37.78
Lithuanian (23)	213	0.81
Maltese (6)	26	0.10
Norwegian (77)	342	1.31
Polish (492)	1,813	6.92
Portuguese (0)	80	0.31
Romanian (19)	308	1.18
Russian (235)	1,076	4.11
Scandinavian (0)	12	0.05
Scotch-Irish (68)	463	1.77
Scottish (35)	303	1.16
Serbian (31)	92	0.35
Slavic (0)	47	0.18
Slovak (39)	83	0.32
Swedish (43)	160	0.61
Ukrainian (26)	133	0.51
Welsh (0)	3	0.01
West Indian, ex. Hispanic (68)	68	0.26
Haitian (68)	68	0.26
Yugoslavian (0)	7	0.03

Hispanic Origin	Population	%
Hispanic or Latino (of any race)	1,361	5.14
Central American, ex. Mexican	144	0.54
Costa Rican	3	0.01
Guatemalan	28	0.11
Honduran	33	0.12
Nicaraguan	5	0.02
Panamanian	8	0.03
Salvadoran	63	0.24
Other Central American	4	0.02
Cuban	63	0.24
Dominican Republic	66	0.25
Mexican	139	0.53
Puerto Rican	459	1.73
South American	286	1.08
Argentinean	32	0.12
Bolivian	9	0.03
Chilean	27	0.10
Colombian	119	0.45
Ecuadorian	37	0.14
Paraguayan	2	0.01
Peruvian	41	0.15
Uruguayan	8	0.03
Venezuelan	7	0.03
Other South American	4	0.02
Other Hispanic or Latino	204	0.77

Race*	Population	%
African-American/Black (291)	384	1.45
Not Hispanic (272)	338	1.28
Hispanic (19)	46	0.17
American Indian/Alaska Native (18)	64	0.24
Not Hispanic (9)	44	0.17
Hispanic (9)	20	0.08
Blackfeet (0)	1	<0.01
Canadian/French Am. Ind. (0)	2	0.01
Central American Ind. (1)	1	<0.01
Cherokee (0)	8	0.03
Creek (0)	3	0.01
Iroquois (0)	6	0.02
Kiowa (1)	1	<0.01
Sioux (1)	1	<0.01
South American Ind. (4)	4	0.02
Tlingit-Haida *(Alaska Native)* (0)	1	<0.01
Asian (763)	887	3.35
Not Hispanic (754)	870	3.29
Hispanic (9)	17	0.06
Bangladeshi (6)	6	0.02
Chinese, ex. Taiwanese (204)	262	0.99
Filipino (111)	142	0.54
Indian (173)	195	0.74
Indonesian (4)	6	0.02
Japanese (14)	26	0.10
Korean (126)	138	0.52
Pakistani (67)	68	0.26
Taiwanese (5)	19	0.07
Thai (6)	8	0.03
Vietnamese (21)	23	0.09
Hawaii Native/Pacific Islander (2)	17	0.06
Not Hispanic (0)	12	0.05
Hispanic (2)	5	0.02
Native Hawaiian (2)	11	0.04
White (24,870)	25,129	94.93
Not Hispanic (23,825)	24,021	90.75
Hispanic (1,045)	1,108	4.19

Smithtown

Place Type: Town
County: Suffolk
Population: 117,801†

Ancestry‡	Population	%
Afghan (27)	27	0.02
African, Sub-Saharan (8)	150	0.13
African (0)	106	0.09
Nigerian (8)	44	0.04
Albanian (121)	130	0.11
American (3,187)	3,187	2.71
Arab (248)	537	0.46
Arab (11)	16	0.01
Egyptian (38)	52	0.04
Iraqi (52)	89	0.08
Jordanian (54)	54	0.05
Lebanese (24)	150	0.13
Moroccan (4)	4	<0.01
Syrian (39)	89	0.08
Other Arab (26)	83	0.07
Armenian (69)	210	0.18
Australian (19)	23	0.02
Austrian (205)	930	0.79
Belgian (4)	88	0.07
Brazilian (22)	32	0.03
British (94)	242	0.21
Bulgarian (0)	22	0.02
Canadian (85)	315	0.27
Carpatho Rusyn (26)	26	0.02
Celtic (0)	3	<0.01
Croatian (53)	247	0.21
Czech (151)	692	0.59
Czechoslovakian (88)	310	0.26
Danish (76)	314	0.27
Dutch (199)	983	0.84
Eastern European (651)	651	0.55
English (852)	6,551	5.57
European (936)	997	0.85
Finnish (26)	120	0.10
French, ex. Basque (122)	2,352	2.00
French Canadian (233)	648	0.55
German (4,715)	23,592	20.06
Greek (1,657)	3,078	2.62
Guyanese (8)	8	0.01
Hungarian (307)	1,257	1.07
Icelander (5)	16	0.01
Iranian (199)	237	0.20
Irish (8,107)	31,963	27.18
Israeli (104)	180	0.15
Italian (21,409)	45,388	38.60
Latvian (24)	81	0.07
Lithuanian (141)	627	0.53
Maltese (10)	206	0.18
Northern European (4)	4	<0.01
Norwegian (397)	1,686	1.43
Pennsylvania German (6)	6	0.01
Polish (2,350)	8,707	7.40
Portuguese (47)	247	0.21
Romanian (196)	707	0.60
Russian (1,686)	5,319	4.52
Scandinavian (26)	64	0.05
Scotch-Irish (579)	1,732	1.47
Scottish (148)	1,517	1.29
Serbian (31)	92	0.08
Slavic (9)	116	0.10
Slovak (82)	163	0.14
Slovene (140)	147	0.13
Swedish (160)	1,304	1.11
Swiss (34)	217	0.18
Turkish (182)	204	0.17
Ukrainian (145)	452	0.38
Welsh (8)	259	0.22
West Indian, ex. Hispanic (160)	341	0.29
Haitian (100)	100	0.09
Jamaican (44)	92	0.08
Trinidadian/Tobagonian (9)	28	0.02
West Indian (7)	121	0.10
Yugoslavian (68)	216	0.18

Hispanic Origin	Population	%
Hispanic or Latino (of any race)	6,272	5.32
Central American, ex. Mexican	768	0.65
Costa Rican	22	0.02
Guatemalan	95	0.08
Honduran	161	0.14
Nicaraguan	9	0.01
Panamanian	37	0.03
Salvadoran	428	0.36
Other Central American	16	0.01
Cuban	298	0.25
Dominican Republic	349	0.30
Mexican	524	0.44
Puerto Rican	2,200	1.87
South American	1,376	1.17
Argentinean	159	0.13
Bolivian	41	0.03
Chilean	96	0.08
Colombian	503	0.43
Ecuadorian	258	0.22
Paraguayan	17	0.01
Peruvian	227	0.19
Uruguayan	28	0.02
Venezuelan	37	0.03
Other South American	10	0.01
Other Hispanic or Latino	757	0.64

Race*	Population	%
African-American/Black (1,238)	1,546	1.31
Not Hispanic (1,122)	1,350	1.15
Hispanic (116)	196	0.17
American Indian/Alaska Native (91)	317	0.27
Not Hispanic (53)	224	0.19
Hispanic (38)	93	0.08
Blackfeet (3)	7	0.01

*Notes: † The Census 2010 population figure is used to calculate the percentages in the Hispanic Origin and Race categories. Ancestry percentages are based on the 2006-2010 American Community Survey population (not shown); ‡ Numbers in parentheses indicate the number of people reporting a single ancestry; * Numbers in parentheses indicate the number of persons reporting this race alone, not in combination with any other race; Please refer to the Explanation of Data for more information.*

Canadian/French Am. Ind. (0)	2	<0.01
Central American Ind. (1)	1	<0.01
Cherokee (3)	44	0.04
Chippewa (0)	2	<0.01
Choctaw (0)	2	<0.01
Creek (0)	7	0.01
Delaware (0)	1	<0.01
Iroquois (19)	36	0.03
Kiowa (1)	1	<0.01
Lumbee (0)	5	<0.01
Mexican American Ind. (2)	6	0.01
Navajo (0)	1	<0.01
Pueblo (0)	1	<0.01
Sioux (1)	2	<0.01
South American Ind. (13)	23	0.02
Tlingit-Haida *(Alaska Native)* (0)	1	<0.01
Ute (0)	1	<0.01
Yaqui (0)	1	<0.01
Asian (4,224)	4,865	4.13
Not Hispanic (4,197)	4,788	4.06
Hispanic (27)	77	0.07
Bangladeshi (24)	24	0.02
Bhutanese (2)	2	<0.01
Burmese (2)	2	<0.01
Chinese, ex. Taiwanese (1,070)	1,262	1.07
Filipino (414)	562	0.48
Indian (1,206)	1,322	1.12
Indonesian (14)	18	0.02
Japanese (68)	119	0.10
Korean (842)	918	0.78
Laotian (3)	3	<0.01
Malaysian (1)	2	<0.01
Nepalese (4)	4	<0.01
Pakistani (280)	299	0.25
Sri Lankan (5)	6	0.01
Taiwanese (66)	90	0.08
Thai (28)	34	0.03
Vietnamese (59)	70	0.06
Hawaii Native/Pacific Islander (10)	58	0.05
Not Hispanic (7)	41	0.03
Hispanic (3)	17	0.01
Fijian (0)	2	<0.01
Guamanian/Chamorro (3)	5	<0.01
Native Hawaiian (6)	30	0.03
White (109,790)	111,000	94.23
Not Hispanic (104,976)	105,870	89.87
Hispanic (4,814)	5,130	4.35

Sodus

Place Type: Town
County: Wayne
Population: 8,384†

Ancestry‡	Population	%
African, Sub-Saharan (6)	8	0.09
African (6)	8	0.09
Albanian (0)	9	0.11
American (437)	437	5.16
Arab (0)	9	0.11
Other Arab (0)	9	0.11
Austrian (9)	21	0.25
Belgian (29)	36	0.42
British (14)	28	0.33
Canadian (44)	108	1.27
Croatian (0)	9	0.11
Czech (7)	7	0.08
Czechoslovakian (13)	13	0.15
Danish (16)	27	0.32
Dutch (360)	1,373	16.20
English (410)	1,465	17.28
European (26)	35	0.41
Finnish (3)	11	0.13
French, ex. Basque (32)	511	6.03
French Canadian (65)	158	1.86
German (431)	1,824	21.52
Guyanese (14)	14	0.17
Hungarian (8)	8	0.09
Icelander (3)	3	0.04
Irish (300)	1,196	14.11
Italian (327)	829	9.78
Macedonian (11)	22	0.26
Northern European (0)	3	0.04
Norwegian (15)	30	0.35
Pennsylvania German (3)	5	0.06
Polish (90)	251	2.96
Portuguese (0)	9	0.11
Romanian (15)	15	0.18
Russian (0)	57	0.67
Scotch-Irish (55)	259	3.06
Scottish (32)	165	1.95
Slavic (18)	43	0.51
Slovak (3)	3	0.04
Swedish (24)	24	0.28
Swiss (0)	22	0.26
Ukrainian (17)	118	1.39
Welsh (44)	105	1.24
West Indian, ex. Hispanic (9)	9	0.11
Haitian (9)	9	0.11

Hispanic Origin	Population	%
Hispanic or Latino (of any race)	522	6.23
Central American, ex. Mexican	15	0.18
Costa Rican	3	0.04
Guatemalan	2	0.02
Honduran	4	0.05
Nicaraguan	3	0.04
Salvadoran	3	0.04
Cuban	8	0.10
Dominican Republic	7	0.08
Mexican	363	4.33
Puerto Rican	113	1.35
South American	1	0.01
Peruvian	1	0.01
Other Hispanic or Latino	15	0.18

Race*	Population	%
African-American/Black (714)	866	10.33
Not Hispanic (699)	832	9.92
Hispanic (15)	34	0.41
American Indian/Alaska Native (27)	89	1.06
Not Hispanic (22)	74	0.88
Hispanic (5)	15	0.18
Apache (0)	1	0.01
Blackfeet (0)	4	0.05
Canadian/French Am. Ind. (0)	1	0.01
Central American Ind. (2)	2	0.02
Cherokee (1)	13	0.16
Chippewa (5)	5	0.06
Cree (0)	1	0.01
Creek (1)	1	0.01
Iroquois (4)	23	0.27
Lumbee (0)	1	0.01
Sioux (1)	1	0.01
Spanish American Ind. (1)	2	0.02
Asian (30)	43	0.51
Not Hispanic (30)	42	0.50
Hispanic (0)	1	0.01
Chinese, ex. Taiwanese (7)	8	0.10
Filipino (4)	11	0.13
Indian (3)	5	0.06
Japanese (1)	2	0.02
Korean (2)	2	0.02
Laotian (6)	6	0.07
Thai (1)	1	0.01
Vietnamese (5)	8	0.10
Hawaii Native/Pacific Islander (5)	14	0.17
Not Hispanic (5)	13	0.16
Hispanic (0)	1	0.01
Guamanian/Chamorro (1)	1	0.01
Native Hawaiian (1)	8	0.10
Samoan (0)	1	0.01
White (7,107)	7,337	87.51
Not Hispanic (6,910)	7,094	84.61
Hispanic (197)	243	2.90

Somers

Place Type: Town
County: Westchester
Population: 20,434†

Ancestry‡	Population	%
Albanian (221)	221	1.11
American (996)	996	4.99
Arab (151)	169	0.85
Lebanese (103)	121	0.61
Syrian (48)	48	0.24
Armenian (56)	70	0.35
Austrian (88)	167	0.84
Brazilian (0)	14	0.07
British (52)	62	0.31
Canadian (9)	43	0.22
Carpatho Rusyn (20)	20	0.10
Croatian (34)	52	0.26
Czech (56)	184	0.92
Czechoslovakian (23)	76	0.38
Danish (77)	159	0.80
Dutch (171)	321	1.61
Eastern European (248)	248	1.24
English (123)	1,070	5.36
European (325)	349	1.75
French, ex. Basque (38)	506	2.54
French Canadian (46)	189	0.95
German (554)	2,444	12.25
Greek (88)	150	0.75
Guyanese (38)	38	0.19
Hungarian (39)	219	1.10
Iranian (36)	36	0.18
Irish (1,544)	4,549	22.81
Italian (4,133)	6,889	34.54
Latvian (17)	37	0.19
Northern European (0)	12	0.06
Norwegian (46)	108	0.54
Polish (431)	1,148	5.76
Portuguese (84)	110	0.55
Romanian (18)	51	0.26
Russian (381)	790	3.96
Scandinavian (0)	55	0.28
Scotch-Irish (42)	217	1.09
Scottish (102)	247	1.24
Slavic (0)	31	0.16
Slovak (0)	99	0.50
Swedish (79)	406	2.04
Swiss (29)	43	0.22
Ukrainian (25)	72	0.36
Welsh (12)	102	0.51
West Indian, ex. Hispanic (41)	41	0.21
Jamaican (12)	12	0.06
West Indian (29)	29	0.15

Hispanic Origin	Population	%
Hispanic or Latino (of any race)	1,010	4.94
Central American, ex. Mexican	75	0.37
Costa Rican	4	0.02
Guatemalan	39	0.19
Honduran	10	0.05
Nicaraguan	3	0.01
Panamanian	3	0.01
Salvadoran	16	0.08
Cuban	81	0.40
Dominican Republic	63	0.31
Mexican	71	0.35
Puerto Rican	360	1.76
South American	257	1.26
Argentinean	22	0.11
Bolivian	7	0.03
Chilean	27	0.13
Colombian	79	0.39
Ecuadorian	71	0.35
Paraguayan	6	0.03
Peruvian	27	0.13
Uruguayan	7	0.03
Venezuelan	10	0.05
Other South American	1	<0.01
Other Hispanic or Latino	103	0.50

*Notes: † The Census 2010 population figure is used to calculate the percentages in the Hispanic Origin and Race categories. Ancestry percentages are based on the 2006-2010 American Community Survey population (not shown); ‡ Numbers in parentheses indicate the number of people reporting a single ancestry; * Numbers in parentheses indicate the number of persons reporting this race alone, not in combination with any other race; Please refer to the Explanation of Data for more information.*

Race*	Population	%
African-American/Black (318)	393	1.92
Not Hispanic (304)	372	1.82
Hispanic (14)	21	0.10
American Indian/Alaska Native (29)	64	0.31
Not Hispanic (23)	57	0.28
Hispanic (6)	7	0.03
Blackfeet (0)	3	0.01
Canadian/French Am. Ind. (1)	1	<0.01
Cherokee (1)	8	0.04
Choctaw (0)	3	0.01
Iroquois (5)	7	0.03
Sioux (3)	4	0.02
South American Ind. (0)	1	<0.01
Asian (645)	765	3.74
Not Hispanic (640)	751	3.68
Hispanic (5)	14	0.07
Bangladeshi (4)	8	0.04
Burmese (3)	3	0.01
Cambodian (2)	2	0.01
Chinese, ex. Taiwanese (222)	250	1.22
Filipino (66)	87	0.43
Indian (160)	183	0.90
Indonesian (4)	5	0.02
Japanese (45)	70	0.34
Korean (109)	120	0.59
Pakistani (1)	3	0.01
Sri Lankan (1)	1	<0.01
Taiwanese (10)	12	0.06
Thai (1)	1	<0.01
Vietnamese (6)	7	0.03
Hawaii Native/Pacific Islander (11)	17	0.08
Not Hispanic (10)	16	0.08
Hispanic (1)	1	<0.01
Native Hawaiian (0)	1	<0.01
White (18,978)	19,203	93.98
Not Hispanic (18,228)	18,413	90.11
Hispanic (750)	790	3.87

Sound Beach

Place Type: CDP
County: Suffolk
Population: 7,612†

Ancestry‡	Population	%
American (259)	259	3.42
Austrian (0)	18	0.24
Belgian (0)	28	0.37
British (24)	24	0.32
Canadian (0)	16	0.21
Czech (0)	42	0.55
Czechoslovakian (0)	30	0.40
Dutch (0)	36	0.47
English (40)	483	6.37
European (29)	29	0.38
Finnish (0)	15	0.20
French, ex. Basque (60)	322	4.25
French Canadian (14)	179	2.36
German (360)	1,593	21.02
Greek (12)	12	0.16
Hungarian (7)	31	0.41
Iranian (12)	33	0.44
Irish (804)	2,887	38.09
Italian (934)	2,261	29.83
Latvian (0)	17	0.22
Lithuanian (17)	139	1.83
Maltese (0)	7	0.09
Norwegian (125)	305	4.02
Polish (74)	389	5.13
Portuguese (13)	30	0.40
Russian (86)	248	3.27
Scotch-Irish (147)	147	1.94
Scottish (74)	95	1.25
Slovak (0)	20	0.26
Swedish (0)	127	1.68
Ukrainian (17)	17	0.22
Welsh (0)	25	0.33

Hispanic Origin	Population	%
Hispanic or Latino (of any race)	475	6.24
Central American, ex. Mexican	39	0.51
Guatemalan	2	0.03
Honduran	3	0.04
Panamanian	1	0.01
Salvadoran	33	0.43
Cuban	23	0.30
Dominican Republic	24	0.32
Mexican	16	0.21
Puerto Rican	199	2.61
South American	89	1.17
Argentinean	3	0.04
Chilean	10	0.13
Colombian	36	0.47
Ecuadorian	16	0.21
Paraguayan	1	0.01
Peruvian	10	0.13
Uruguayan	1	0.01
Venezuelan	12	0.16
Other Hispanic or Latino	85	1.12

Race*	Population	%
African-American/Black (90)	139	1.83
Not Hispanic (89)	126	1.66
Hispanic (1)	13	0.17
American Indian/Alaska Native (14)	48	0.63
Not Hispanic (13)	45	0.59
Hispanic (1)	3	0.04
Apache (2)	2	0.03
Canadian/French Am. Ind. (1)	1	0.01
Cherokee (1)	13	0.17
Chippewa (0)	4	0.05
Comanche (0)	1	0.01
Creek (0)	1	0.01
Iroquois (0)	1	0.01
Lumbee (0)	1	0.01
Sioux (1)	1	0.01
South American Ind. (0)	1	0.01
Asian (134)	176	2.31
Not Hispanic (134)	172	2.26
Hispanic (0)	4	0.05
Chinese, ex. Taiwanese (39)	60	0.79
Filipino (21)	21	0.28
Indian (13)	16	0.21
Indonesian (0)	3	0.04
Japanese (8)	16	0.21
Korean (26)	31	0.41
Pakistani (9)	9	0.12
Sri Lankan (1)	1	0.01
Taiwanese (1)	1	0.01
Thai (5)	5	0.07
Vietnamese (5)	7	0.09
Hawaii Native/Pacific Islander (4)	13	0.17
Not Hispanic (4)	13	0.17
Fijian (0)	6	0.08
Native Hawaiian (4)	5	0.07
White (7,174)	7,297	95.86
Not Hispanic (6,781)	6,872	90.28
Hispanic (393)	425	5.58

South Farmingdale

Place Type: CDP
County: Nassau
Population: 14,486†

Ancestry‡	Population	%
Albanian (117)	117	0.79
American (331)	331	2.24
Australian (0)	22	0.15
Austrian (35)	108	0.73
British (21)	30	0.20
Canadian (9)	17	0.12
Croatian (0)	22	0.15
Czech (19)	40	0.27
Czechoslovakian (17)	17	0.12
Danish (8)	8	0.05
Dutch (0)	48	0.33
Eastern European (0)	10	0.07
English (147)	1,028	6.96
European (49)	49	0.33
Finnish (0)	37	0.25
French, ex. Basque (10)	287	1.94
French Canadian (0)	7	0.05
German (556)	2,944	19.94
Greek (263)	391	2.65
Guyanese (10)	10	0.07
Hungarian (8)	133	0.90
Irish (975)	4,037	27.34
Italian (2,901)	5,805	39.32
Lithuanian (22)	32	0.22
Maltese (11)	41	0.28
Norwegian (13)	116	0.79
Polish (224)	786	5.32
Portuguese (10)	10	0.07
Romanian (35)	103	0.70
Russian (246)	594	4.02
Scotch-Irish (37)	110	0.75
Scottish (31)	195	1.32
Slavic (0)	19	0.13
Swedish (8)	92	0.62
Swiss (0)	39	0.26
Turkish (21)	21	0.14
Ukrainian (12)	30	0.20
Welsh (0)	40	0.27
West Indian, ex. Hispanic (38)	38	0.26
British West Indian (37)	37	0.25
Trinidadian/Tobagonian (1)	1	0.01
Yugoslavian (0)	30	0.20

Hispanic Origin	Population	%
Hispanic or Latino (of any race)	1,454	10.04
Central American, ex. Mexican	264	1.82
Costa Rican	1	0.01
Guatemalan	37	0.26
Honduran	62	0.43
Nicaraguan	4	0.03
Panamanian	4	0.03
Salvadoran	156	1.08
Cuban	51	0.35
Dominican Republic	67	0.46
Mexican	71	0.49
Puerto Rican	427	2.95
South American	421	2.91
Argentinean	33	0.23
Bolivian	8	0.06
Chilean	15	0.10
Colombian	145	1.00
Ecuadorian	96	0.66
Paraguayan	17	0.12
Peruvian	94	0.65
Uruguayan	10	0.07
Venezuelan	3	0.02
Other Hispanic or Latino	153	1.06

Race*	Population	%
African-American/Black (205)	249	1.72
Not Hispanic (186)	216	1.49
Hispanic (19)	33	0.23
American Indian/Alaska Native (12)	28	0.19
Not Hispanic (8)	20	0.14
Hispanic (4)	8	0.06
Cherokee (1)	1	0.01
Chippewa (4)	5	0.03
Iroquois (0)	1	0.01
Sioux (1)	1	0.01
Asian (653)	760	5.25
Not Hispanic (644)	737	5.09
Hispanic (9)	23	0.16
Chinese, ex. Taiwanese (130)	147	1.01
Filipino (134)	160	1.10
Indian (215)	246	1.70
Indonesian (3)	6	0.04
Japanese (7)	10	0.07
Korean (38)	41	0.28
Pakistani (79)	79	0.55
Sri Lankan (0)	4	0.03
Taiwanese (1)	1	0.01
Thai (11)	15	0.10

*Notes: † The Census 2010 population figure is used to calculate the percentages in the Hispanic Origin and Race categories. Ancestry percentages are based on the 2006-2010 American Community Survey population (not shown); ‡ Numbers in parentheses indicate the number of people reporting a single ancestry; * Numbers in parentheses indicate the number of persons reporting this race alone, not in combination with any other race; Please refer to the Explanation of Data for more information.*

Vietnamese (16)	20	0.14
Hawaii Native/Pacific Islander (5)	16	0.11
Not Hispanic (5)	13	0.09
Hispanic (0)	3	0.02
Guamanian/Chamorro (2)	3	0.02
Native Hawaiian (2)	4	0.03
Samoan (1)	5	0.03
White (13,053)	13,267	91.58
Not Hispanic (12,025)	12,142	83.82
Hispanic (1,028)	1,125	7.77

South Huntington

Place Type: CDP
County: Suffolk
Population: 9,422†

Ancestry‡	Population	%
African, Sub-Saharan (10)	18	0.18
African (0)	8	0.08
Nigerian (10)	10	0.10
Alsatian (0)	9	0.09
American (288)	288	2.91
Arab (33)	138	1.40
Arab (0)	8	0.08
Egyptian (33)	91	0.92
Lebanese (0)	39	0.39
Armenian (43)	43	0.43
Austrian (0)	91	0.92
Belgian (6)	35	0.35
Canadian (17)	50	0.51
Croatian (4)	4	0.04
Cypriot (10)	10	0.10
Czech (39)	70	0.71
Czechoslovakian (0)	12	0.12
Danish (9)	46	0.47
Dutch (44)	187	1.89
Eastern European (12)	12	0.12
English (58)	402	4.07
European (85)	85	0.86
French, ex. Basque (17)	125	1.26
French Canadian (32)	40	0.40
German (376)	1,923	19.45
Greek (112)	253	2.56
Guyanese (22)	78	0.79
Hungarian (27)	73	0.74
Iranian (118)	118	1.19
Irish (423)	2,317	23.44
Italian (1,764)	3,278	33.16
Latvian (0)	14	0.14
Lithuanian (11)	77	0.78
Northern European (0)	6	0.06
Norwegian (48)	140	1.42
Polish (111)	621	6.28
Portuguese (78)	118	1.19
Romanian (24)	41	0.41
Russian (104)	421	4.26
Scandinavian (4)	14	0.14
Scotch-Irish (28)	138	1.40
Scottish (36)	67	0.68
Slovak (0)	10	0.10
Swedish (7)	42	0.42
Swiss (10)	22	0.22
Turkish (0)	9	0.09
Ukrainian (63)	73	0.74
Welsh (0)	38	0.38
West Indian, ex. Hispanic (146)	202	2.04
Haitian (8)	8	0.08
Jamaican (47)	47	0.48
U.S. Virgin Islander (91)	147	1.49

Hispanic Origin	Population	%
Hispanic or Latino (of any race)	756	8.02
Central American, ex. Mexican	185	1.96
Costa Rican	9	0.10
Guatemalan	7	0.07
Honduran	18	0.19
Salvadoran	142	1.51
Other Central American	9	0.10
Cuban	33	0.35
Dominican Republic	18	0.19
Mexican	59	0.63
Puerto Rican	219	2.32
South American	150	1.59
Argentinean	19	0.20
Bolivian	4	0.04
Chilean	22	0.23
Colombian	26	0.28
Ecuadorian	24	0.25
Paraguayan	12	0.13
Peruvian	28	0.30
Uruguayan	3	0.03
Venezuelan	5	0.05
Other South American	7	0.07
Other Hispanic or Latino	92	0.98

Race*	Population	%
African-American/Black (218)	266	2.82
Not Hispanic (212)	257	2.73
Hispanic (6)	9	0.10
American Indian/Alaska Native (10)	30	0.32
Not Hispanic (6)	26	0.28
Hispanic (4)	4	0.04
Blackfeet (0)	1	0.01
Cherokee (1)	1	0.01
Creek (0)	3	0.03
Mexican American Ind. (4)	4	0.04
Ottawa (0)	2	0.02
Asian (551)	638	6.77
Not Hispanic (549)	631	6.70
Hispanic (2)	7	0.07
Bangladeshi (16)	16	0.17
Chinese, ex. Taiwanese (81)	99	1.05
Filipino (61)	85	0.90
Indian (178)	199	2.11
Japanese (28)	32	0.34
Korean (50)	56	0.59
Malaysian (1)	3	0.03
Pakistani (103)	110	1.17
Taiwanese (7)	7	0.07
Thai (2)	6	0.06
Vietnamese (2)	3	0.03
Hawaii Native/Pacific Islander (0)	5	0.05
Not Hispanic (0)	4	0.04
Hispanic (0)	1	0.01
Guamanian/Chamorro (0)	1	0.01
Native Hawaiian (0)	1	0.01
Samoan (0)	1	0.01
White (8,204)	8,373	88.87
Not Hispanic (7,741)	7,864	83.46
Hispanic (463)	509	5.40

South Lockport

Place Type: CDP
County: Niagara
Population: 8,324†

Ancestry‡	Population	%
Alsatian (0)	10	0.12
American (507)	507	6.04
Arab (9)	22	0.26
Egyptian (9)	9	0.11
Iraqi (0)	13	0.15
British (0)	36	0.43
Canadian (54)	77	0.92
Croatian (0)	23	0.27
Danish (0)	13	0.15
Dutch (0)	122	1.45
English (267)	1,384	16.48
European (9)	9	0.11
French, ex. Basque (62)	325	3.87
French Canadian (218)	243	2.89
German (737)	3,335	39.71
Greek (0)	40	0.48
Hungarian (10)	63	0.75
Iranian (9)	9	0.11
Irish (424)	1,991	23.71
Italian (466)	1,252	14.91
Norwegian (0)	10	0.12
Pennsylvania German (9)	9	0.11
Polish (258)	856	10.19
Romanian (0)	15	0.18
Russian (68)	81	0.96
Scotch-Irish (0)	18	0.21
Scottish (24)	90	1.07
Swedish (0)	86	1.02
Turkish (0)	13	0.15
Ukrainian (0)	26	0.31
Welsh (0)	90	1.07

Hispanic Origin	Population	%
Hispanic or Latino (of any race)	344	4.13
Central American, ex. Mexican	15	0.18
Guatemalan	4	0.05
Honduran	2	0.02
Nicaraguan	1	0.01
Panamanian	8	0.10
Cuban	7	0.08
Dominican Republic	15	0.18
Mexican	39	0.47
Puerto Rican	244	2.93
South American	4	0.05
Colombian	4	0.05
Other Hispanic or Latino	20	0.24

Race*	Population	%
African-American/Black (443)	618	7.42
Not Hispanic (415)	570	6.85
Hispanic (28)	48	0.58
American Indian/Alaska Native (38)	94	1.13
Not Hispanic (36)	89	1.07
Hispanic (2)	5	0.06
Alaska Athabascan *(Ala. Nat.)* (0)	1	0.01
Blackfeet (0)	5	0.06
Canadian/French Am. Ind. (2)	2	0.02
Cherokee (2)	14	0.17
Choctaw (0)	2	0.02
Creek (0)	1	0.01
Inupiat *(Alaska Native)* (1)	1	0.01
Iroquois (24)	45	0.54
Navajo (1)	1	0.01
Asian (93)	122	1.47
Not Hispanic (93)	122	1.47
Bangladeshi (2)	2	0.02
Burmese (1)	1	0.01
Chinese, ex. Taiwanese (20)	20	0.24
Filipino (9)	20	0.24
Indian (29)	34	0.41
Indonesian (1)	1	0.01
Japanese (3)	6	0.07
Korean (12)	20	0.24
Laotian (3)	3	0.04
Pakistani (4)	4	0.05
Thai (5)	6	0.07
Vietnamese (4)	4	0.05
Hawaii Native/Pacific Islander (0)	1	0.01
Not Hispanic (0)	1	0.01
Native Hawaiian (0)	1	0.01
White (7,412)	7,648	91.88
Not Hispanic (7,211)	7,413	89.06
Hispanic (201)	235	2.82

Southampton

Place Type: Town
County: Suffolk
Population: 56,790†

Ancestry‡	Population	%
African, Sub-Saharan (64)	64	0.11
African (64)	64	0.11
Albanian (63)	63	0.11
American (1,540)	1,540	2.72
Arab (52)	130	0.23
Arab (20)	35	0.06
Iraqi (0)	28	0.05
Lebanese (5)	16	0.03
Moroccan (0)	18	0.03
Syrian (13)	13	0.02

*Notes: † The Census 2010 population figure is used to calculate the percentages in the Hispanic Origin and Race categories. Ancestry percentages are based on the 2006-2010 American Community Survey population (not shown); ‡ Numbers in parentheses indicate the number of people reporting a single ancestry; * Numbers in parentheses indicate the number of persons reporting this race alone, not in combination with any other race; Please refer to the Explanation of Data for more information.*

Other Arab (14)	20	0.04
Armenian (23)	42	0.07
Australian (24)	38	0.07
Austrian (113)	621	1.10
Belgian (34)	34	0.06
Brazilian (242)	289	0.51
British (224)	404	0.71
Bulgarian (29)	29	0.05
Canadian (96)	153	0.27
Celtic (0)	4	0.01
Croatian (174)	227	0.40
Czech (80)	198	0.35
Czechoslovakian (51)	97	0.17
Danish (54)	135	0.24
Dutch (91)	743	1.31
Eastern European (55)	118	0.21
English (1,413)	5,792	10.24
Estonian (6)	6	0.01
European (518)	523	0.93
Finnish (53)	206	0.36
French, ex. Basque (250)	1,438	2.54
French Canadian (49)	352	0.62
German (1,998)	8,313	14.70
Greek (583)	995	1.76
Hungarian (164)	529	0.94
Irish (4,208)	12,998	22.99
Israeli (0)	28	0.05
Italian (4,376)	9,808	17.35
Latvian (0)	7	0.01
Lithuanian (137)	267	0.47
Macedonian (11)	11	0.02
Maltese (15)	33	0.06
Northern European (42)	42	0.07
Norwegian (172)	498	0.88
Polish (1,918)	4,196	7.42
Portuguese (59)	145	0.26
Romanian (57)	102	0.18
Russian (514)	1,517	2.68
Scandinavian (31)	57	0.10
Scotch-Irish (251)	701	1.24
Scottish (225)	966	1.71
Slavic (0)	53	0.09
Slovak (92)	134	0.24
Slovene (7)	7	0.01
Swedish (152)	598	1.06
Swiss (37)	231	0.41
Turkish (75)	75	0.13
Ukrainian (198)	419	0.74
Welsh (43)	132	0.23
West Indian, ex. Hispanic (0)	24	0.04
Haitian (0)	16	0.03
West Indian (0)	8	0.01

Hispanic Origin	Population	%
Hispanic or Latino (of any race)	11,295	19.89
Central American, ex. Mexican	3,715	6.54
Costa Rican	618	1.09
Guatemalan	2,081	3.66
Honduran	246	0.43
Nicaraguan	50	0.09
Panamanian	14	0.02
Salvadoran	689	1.21
Other Central American	17	0.03
Cuban	93	0.16
Dominican Republic	124	0.22
Mexican	2,856	5.03
Puerto Rican	593	1.04
South American	2,446	4.31
Argentinean	89	0.16
Bolivian	9	0.02
Chilean	44	0.08
Colombian	1,024	1.80
Ecuadorian	1,102	1.94
Paraguayan	26	0.05
Peruvian	97	0.17
Uruguayan	7	0.01
Venezuelan	36	0.06
Other South American	12	0.02
Other Hispanic or Latino	1,468	2.58

Race*	Population	%
African-American/Black (2,929)	3,353	5.90
Not Hispanic (2,776)	3,108	5.47
Hispanic (153)	245	0.43
American Indian/Alaska Native (292)	546	0.96
Not Hispanic (136)	344	0.61
Hispanic (156)	202	0.36
Blackfeet (6)	14	0.02
Canadian/French Am. Ind. (0)	3	0.01
Central American Ind. (3)	3	0.01
Cherokee (13)	68	0.12
Chippewa (7)	7	0.01
Choctaw (1)	2	<0.01
Creek (2)	2	<0.01
Hopi (0)	1	<0.01
Iroquois (5)	11	0.02
Mexican American Ind. (76)	83	0.15
Pueblo (0)	5	0.01
Seminole (0)	1	<0.01
Sioux (2)	3	0.01
South American Ind. (23)	28	0.05
Spanish American Ind. (7)	7	0.01
Asian (633)	869	1.53
Not Hispanic (618)	834	1.47
Hispanic (15)	35	0.06
Cambodian (1)	1	<0.01
Chinese, ex. Taiwanese (133)	177	0.31
Filipino (146)	197	0.35
Indian (123)	151	0.27
Indonesian (5)	6	0.01
Japanese (40)	97	0.17
Korean (69)	102	0.18
Laotian (1)	2	<0.01
Malaysian (1)	2	<0.01
Nepalese (1)	1	<0.01
Pakistani (8)	10	0.02
Taiwanese (3)	3	0.01
Thai (30)	37	0.07
Vietnamese (38)	51	0.09
Hawaii Native/Pacific Islander (62)	103	0.18
Not Hispanic (36)	61	0.11
Hispanic (26)	42	0.07
Guamanian/Chamorro (48)	55	0.10
Native Hawaiian (10)	27	0.05
Samoan (2)	7	0.01
White (47,795)	48,682	85.72
Not Hispanic (41,156)	41,727	73.48
Hispanic (6,639)	6,955	12.25

Southeast

Place Type: Town
County: Putnam
Population: 18,404†

Ancestry‡	Population	%
African, Sub-Saharan (0)	32	0.17
African (0)	32	0.17
Albanian (169)	198	1.08
American (644)	644	3.51
Armenian (10)	10	0.05
Austrian (46)	227	1.24
Belgian (0)	18	0.10
Brazilian (0)	46	0.25
British (30)	65	0.35
Canadian (44)	88	0.48
Czech (0)	62	0.34
Czechoslovakian (0)	16	0.09
Danish (10)	27	0.15
Dutch (51)	278	1.52
English (269)	1,573	8.58
Estonian (0)	14	0.08
European (27)	27	0.15
Finnish (0)	13	0.07
French, ex. Basque (62)	493	2.69
French Canadian (99)	232	1.26
German (570)	3,248	17.71
Greek (81)	128	0.70
Hungarian (40)	167	0.91
Irish (1,689)	4,842	26.40
Italian (2,719)	5,137	28.01
Lithuanian (0)	13	0.07
Maltese (0)	12	0.07
Norwegian (23)	118	0.64
Pennsylvania German (11)	11	0.06
Polish (174)	804	4.38
Portuguese (65)	146	0.80
Romanian (29)	43	0.23
Russian (199)	524	2.86
Scotch-Irish (57)	314	1.71
Scottish (55)	453	2.47
Slavic (0)	21	0.11
Slovak (52)	145	0.79
Swedish (42)	196	1.07
Swiss (0)	30	0.16
Turkish (7)	22	0.12
Ukrainian (56)	169	0.92
Welsh (0)	78	0.43
West Indian, ex. Hispanic (170)	177	0.97
Jamaican (20)	27	0.15
Trinidadian/Tobagonian (150)	150	0.82

Hispanic Origin	Population	%
Hispanic or Latino (of any race)	3,052	16.58
Central American, ex. Mexican	1,339	7.28
Costa Rican	11	0.06
Guatemalan	1,192	6.48
Honduran	42	0.23
Nicaraguan	8	0.04
Panamanian	16	0.09
Salvadoran	66	0.36
Other Central American	4	0.02
Cuban	35	0.19
Dominican Republic	103	0.56
Mexican	234	1.27
Puerto Rican	577	3.14
South American	451	2.45
Argentinean	27	0.15
Bolivian	1	0.01
Chilean	19	0.10
Colombian	102	0.55
Ecuadorian	190	1.03
Paraguayan	23	0.12
Peruvian	66	0.36
Uruguayan	16	0.09
Venezuelan	7	0.04
Other Hispanic or Latino	313	1.70

Race*	Population	%
African-American/Black (372)	487	2.65
Not Hispanic (327)	389	2.11
Hispanic (45)	98	0.53
American Indian/Alaska Native (38)	111	0.60
Not Hispanic (23)	79	0.43
Hispanic (15)	32	0.17
Aleut *(Alaska Native)* (1)	1	0.01
Blackfeet (0)	4	0.02
Central American Ind. (4)	4	0.02
Cherokee (2)	12	0.07
Chippewa (1)	1	0.01
Choctaw (0)	4	0.02
Iroquois (2)	3	0.02
Kiowa (0)	1	0.01
Mexican American Ind. (0)	3	0.02
Sioux (0)	5	0.03
South American Ind. (3)	4	0.02
Yuman (1)	1	0.01
Asian (458)	546	2.97
Not Hispanic (449)	525	2.85
Hispanic (9)	21	0.11
Bangladeshi (7)	7	0.04
Chinese, ex. Taiwanese (128)	148	0.80
Filipino (70)	93	0.51
Indian (140)	153	0.83
Indonesian (0)	1	0.01
Japanese (29)	47	0.26
Korean (49)	55	0.30
Malaysian (0)	1	0.01
Nepalese (11)	11	0.06

*Notes: † The Census 2010 population figure is used to calculate the percentages in the Hispanic Origin and Race categories. Ancestry percentages are based on the 2006-2010 American Community Survey population (not shown); ‡ Numbers in parentheses indicate the number of people reporting a single ancestry; * Numbers in parentheses indicate the number of persons reporting this race alone, not in combination with any other race; Please refer to the Explanation of Data for more information.*

Pakistani (2)	2	0.01
Sri Lankan (3)	3	0.02
Thai (0)	1	0.01
Vietnamese (3)	5	0.03
Hawaii Native/Pacific Islander (18)	33	0.18
Not Hispanic (2)	6	0.03
Hispanic (16)	27	0.15
Guamanian/Chamorro (16)	25	0.14
Native Hawaiian (0)	3	0.02
Samoan (2)	2	0.01
White (16,458)	16,779	91.17
Not Hispanic (14,354)	14,514	78.86
Hispanic (2,104)	2,265	12.31

Southold

Place Type: Town
County: Suffolk
Population: 21,968†

Ancestry‡	Population	%
African, Sub-Saharan (69)	69	0.32
African (69)	69	0.32
American (504)	504	2.32
Arab (3)	36	0.17
Lebanese (0)	23	0.11
Syrian (3)	13	0.06
Armenian (20)	52	0.24
Austrian (54)	214	0.98
Brazilian (5)	5	0.02
British (59)	219	1.01
Canadian (4)	61	0.28
Croatian (31)	43	0.20
Czech (34)	176	0.81
Czechoslovakian (13)	13	0.06
Danish (16)	75	0.34
Dutch (135)	417	1.92
Eastern European (62)	62	0.28
English (718)	2,903	13.34
Estonian (0)	14	0.06
European (247)	247	1.13
French, ex. Basque (57)	628	2.88
French Canadian (44)	207	0.95
German (1,057)	4,722	21.69
Greek (413)	584	2.68
Hungarian (40)	147	0.68
Irish (1,459)	5,371	24.67
Italian (2,166)	4,219	19.38
Lithuanian (45)	217	1.00
Maltese (0)	15	0.07
Northern European (36)	36	0.17
Norwegian (96)	368	1.69
Polish (1,275)	2,916	13.40
Portuguese (4)	95	0.44
Romanian (12)	36	0.17
Russian (94)	423	1.94
Scandinavian (32)	66	0.30
Scotch-Irish (160)	389	1.79
Scottish (87)	602	2.77
Slavic (23)	51	0.23
Slovak (14)	55	0.25
Swedish (65)	474	2.18
Swiss (7)	76	0.35
Turkish (150)	150	0.69
Ukrainian (48)	195	0.90
Welsh (41)	303	1.39
West Indian, ex. Hispanic (54)	57	0.26
Haitian (0)	3	0.01
Trinidadian/Tobagonian (54)	54	0.25
Yugoslavian (0)	9	0.04

Hispanic Origin	Population	%
Hispanic or Latino (of any race)	2,382	10.84
Central American, ex. Mexican	1,223	5.57
Costa Rican	27	0.12
Guatemalan	769	3.50
Honduran	43	0.20
Nicaraguan	13	0.06
Salvadoran	363	1.65
Other Central American	8	0.04
Cuban	32	0.15
Dominican Republic	40	0.18
Mexican	310	1.41
Puerto Rican	288	1.31
South American	150	0.68
Argentinean	19	0.09
Chilean	1	<0.01
Colombian	42	0.19
Ecuadorian	50	0.23
Peruvian	30	0.14
Venezuelan	7	0.03
Other South American	1	<0.01
Other Hispanic or Latino	339	1.54

Race*	Population	%
African-American/Black (586)	731	3.33
Not Hispanic (527)	642	2.92
Hispanic (59)	89	0.41
American Indian/Alaska Native (19)	96	0.44
Not Hispanic (10)	74	0.34
Hispanic (9)	22	0.10
Apache (0)	3	0.01
Blackfeet (0)	7	0.03
Cherokee (4)	25	0.11
Chickasaw (1)	1	<0.01
Choctaw (0)	7	0.03
Delaware (0)	1	<0.01
Potawatomi (2)	2	0.01
Puget Sound Salish (0)	1	<0.01
Seminole (0)	3	0.01
South American Ind. (1)	2	0.01
Spanish American Ind. (6)	6	0.03
Asian (166)	229	1.04
Not Hispanic (161)	223	1.02
Hispanic (5)	6	0.03
Cambodian (1)	1	<0.01
Chinese, ex. Taiwanese (57)	67	0.30
Filipino (18)	23	0.10
Indian (31)	47	0.21
Indonesian (1)	2	0.01
Japanese (16)	30	0.14
Korean (22)	34	0.15
Nepalese (1)	3	0.01
Pakistani (8)	8	0.04
Sri Lankan (1)	2	0.01
Thai (0)	1	<0.01
Vietnamese (5)	8	0.04
Hawaii Native/Pacific Islander (24)	30	0.14
Not Hispanic (6)	12	0.05
Hispanic (18)	18	0.08
Guamanian/Chamorro (22)	22	0.10
Native Hawaiian (0)	5	0.02
White (19,769)	20,062	91.32
Not Hispanic (18,623)	18,839	85.76
Hispanic (1,146)	1,223	5.57

Southport

Place Type: Town
County: Chemung
Population: 10,940†

Ancestry‡	Population	%
American (915)	915	8.37
Arab (101)	123	1.13
Lebanese (101)	112	1.03
Syrian (0)	11	0.10
Austrian (0)	12	0.11
British (0)	14	0.13
Celtic (0)	10	0.09
Dutch (58)	500	4.58
English (830)	2,141	19.60
European (108)	121	1.11
Finnish (9)	63	0.58
French, ex. Basque (32)	349	3.19
French Canadian (0)	49	0.45
German (731)	2,219	20.31
Greek (0)	47	0.43
Hungarian (12)	12	0.11
Irish (769)	2,288	20.94
Italian (433)	829	7.59
Norwegian (0)	61	0.56
Pennsylvania German (20)	114	1.04
Polish (161)	821	7.51
Romanian (0)	20	0.18
Russian (16)	48	0.44
Scandinavian (0)	14	0.13
Scotch-Irish (31)	67	0.61
Scottish (43)	312	2.86
Slovak (0)	24	0.22
Swedish (67)	244	2.23
Swiss (0)	28	0.26
Ukrainian (31)	63	0.58
Welsh (86)	191	1.75
West Indian, ex. Hispanic (9)	17	0.16
Jamaican (9)	17	0.16

Hispanic Origin	Population	%
Hispanic or Latino (of any race)	307	2.81
Central American, ex. Mexican	19	0.17
Costa Rican	3	0.03
Guatemalan	3	0.03
Honduran	2	0.02
Panamanian	8	0.07
Salvadoran	3	0.03
Cuban	11	0.10
Dominican Republic	28	0.26
Mexican	47	0.43
Puerto Rican	164	1.50
South American	10	0.09
Argentinean	2	0.02
Colombian	4	0.04
Ecuadorian	2	0.02
Peruvian	1	0.01
Venezuelan	1	0.01
Other Hispanic or Latino	28	0.26

Race*	Population	%
African-American/Black (830)	944	8.63
Not Hispanic (776)	885	8.09
Hispanic (54)	59	0.54
American Indian/Alaska Native (23)	73	0.67
Not Hispanic (22)	67	0.61
Hispanic (1)	6	0.05
Apache (0)	1	0.01
Blackfeet (1)	10	0.09
Cherokee (2)	13	0.12
Chippewa (1)	1	0.01
Iroquois (10)	19	0.17
Sioux (0)	1	0.01
Tohono O'Odham (0)	1	0.01
Asian (64)	83	0.76
Not Hispanic (58)	71	0.65
Hispanic (6)	12	0.11
Bangladeshi (14)	14	0.13
Chinese, ex. Taiwanese (13)	14	0.13
Filipino (13)	22	0.20
Indian (3)	3	0.03
Japanese (5)	6	0.05
Korean (4)	11	0.10
Vietnamese (1)	1	0.01
Hawaii Native/Pacific Islander (0)	4	0.04
Not Hispanic (0)	4	0.04
Native Hawaiian (0)	1	0.01
Samoan (0)	3	0.03
White (9,747)	9,917	90.65
Not Hispanic (9,596)	9,750	89.12
Hispanic (151)	167	1.53

Spring Valley

Place Type: Village
County: Rockland
Population: 31,347†

Ancestry‡	Population	%
African, Sub-Saharan (229)	323	1.07
African (143)	232	0.77
Ugandan (86)	86	0.28
Other Sub-Saharan African (0)	5	0.02

SECTION TWO

*Notes: † The Census 2010 population figure is used to calculate the percentages in the Hispanic Origin and Race categories. Ancestry percentages are based on the 2006-2010 American Community Survey population (not shown); ‡ Numbers in parentheses indicate the number of people reporting a single ancestry; * Numbers in parentheses indicate the number of persons reporting this race alone, not in combination with any other race; Please refer to the Explanation of Data for more information.*

Ancestry	Population	%
American (545)	545	1.80
Arab (77)	77	0.25
Arab (54)	54	0.18
Other Arab (23)	23	0.08
Armenian (33)	33	0.11
Austrian (60)	174	0.57
Brazilian (56)	56	0.18
Canadian (14)	27	0.09
Czechoslovakian (0)	16	0.05
Danish (23)	23	0.08
Dutch (35)	89	0.29
Eastern European (106)	106	0.35
English (355)	537	1.77
Estonian (0)	9	0.03
European (712)	712	2.35
French, ex. Basque (10)	121	0.40
French Canadian (12)	34	0.11
German (201)	677	2.23
Guyanese (37)	37	0.12
Hungarian (439)	765	2.52
Irish (85)	309	1.02
Israeli (227)	473	1.56
Italian (121)	403	1.33
Lithuanian (10)	149	0.49
Northern European (0)	38	0.13
Norwegian (0)	8	0.03
Pennsylvania German (0)	7	0.02
Polish (449)	981	3.23
Portuguese (15)	26	0.09
Romanian (36)	145	0.48
Russian (360)	730	2.41
Scottish (0)	52	0.17
Swedish (0)	54	0.18
Turkish (18)	18	0.06
Ukrainian (552)	648	2.14
Welsh (0)	51	0.17
West Indian, ex. Hispanic (7,725)	7,957	26.24
British West Indian (130)	130	0.43
Haitian (6,476)	6,665	21.98
Jamaican (850)	866	2.86
Trinidadian/Tobagonian (209)	217	0.72
U.S. Virgin Islander (0)	19	0.06
West Indian (60)	60	0.20

Hispanic Origin	Population	%
Hispanic or Latino (of any race)	9,588	30.59
Central American, ex. Mexican	4,034	12.87
Costa Rican	66	0.21
Guatemalan	3,265	10.42
Honduran	123	0.39
Nicaraguan	17	0.05
Panamanian	16	0.05
Salvadoran	529	1.69
Other Central American	18	0.06
Cuban	40	0.13
Dominican Republic	324	1.03
Mexican	885	2.82
Puerto Rican	611	1.95
South American	2,841	9.06
Argentinean	17	0.05
Bolivian	3	0.01
Chilean	13	0.04
Colombian	48	0.15
Ecuadorian	2,681	8.55
Peruvian	57	0.18
Uruguayan	2	0.01
Venezuelan	14	0.04
Other South American	6	0.02
Other Hispanic or Latino	853	2.72

Race*	Population	%
African-American/Black (11,550)	12,034	38.39
Not Hispanic (11,133)	11,484	36.64
Hispanic (417)	550	1.75
American Indian/Alaska Native (176)	370	1.18
Not Hispanic (56)	173	0.55
Hispanic (120)	197	0.63
Aleut *(Alaska Native)* (1)	1	<0.01
Apache (1)	1	<0.01
Blackfeet (0)	2	0.01
Central American Ind. (9)	13	0.04
Cherokee (4)	21	0.07
Choctaw (1)	1	<0.01
Delaware (2)	6	0.02
Iroquois (5)	8	0.03
Mexican American Ind. (30)	48	0.15
Pueblo (1)	1	<0.01
Seminole (0)	1	<0.01
Sioux (1)	1	<0.01
South American Ind. (15)	28	0.09
Spanish American Ind. (3)	7	0.02
Tlingit-Haida *(Alaska Native)* (2)	4	0.01
Yakama (0)	1	<0.01
Asian (1,191)	1,371	4.37
Not Hispanic (1,175)	1,326	4.23
Hispanic (16)	45	0.14
Bangladeshi (6)	9	0.03
Cambodian (15)	15	0.05
Chinese, ex. Taiwanese (85)	98	0.31
Filipino (261)	277	0.88
Indian (410)	480	1.53
Indonesian (4)	5	0.02
Japanese (7)	12	0.04
Korean (40)	42	0.13
Laotian (1)	2	0.01
Malaysian (1)	5	0.02
Nepalese (2)	2	0.01
Pakistani (241)	275	0.88
Sri Lankan (21)	24	0.08
Taiwanese (0)	1	<0.01
Thai (2)	2	0.01
Vietnamese (32)	34	0.11
Hawaii Native/Pacific Islander (32)	157	0.50
Not Hispanic (3)	83	0.26
Hispanic (29)	74	0.24
Guamanian/Chamorro (26)	32	0.10
Native Hawaiian (1)	8	0.03
Samoan (0)	5	0.02
White (12,347)	13,108	41.82
Not Hispanic (8,834)	9,046	28.86
Hispanic (3,513)	4,062	12.96

St. James

Place Type: CDP
County: Suffolk
Population: 13,338†

Ancestry‡	Population	%
American (257)	257	2.01
Arab (4)	35	0.27
Egyptian (4)	8	0.06
Lebanese (0)	27	0.21
Armenian (27)	27	0.21
Austrian (9)	145	1.14
Canadian (10)	49	0.38
Czech (9)	63	0.49
Czechoslovakian (19)	19	0.15
Danish (0)	34	0.27
Dutch (12)	111	0.87
Eastern European (44)	44	0.34
English (44)	691	5.41
European (40)	40	0.31
Finnish (16)	16	0.13
French, ex. Basque (5)	245	1.92
French Canadian (0)	102	0.80
German (457)	2,742	21.47
Greek (82)	170	1.33
Hungarian (0)	49	0.38
Icelander (5)	16	0.13
Irish (831)	3,692	28.90
Italian (2,916)	5,324	41.68
Lithuanian (0)	126	0.99
Norwegian (126)	446	3.49
Polish (299)	890	6.97
Portuguese (21)	31	0.24
Romanian (9)	27	0.21
Russian (166)	411	3.22
Scandinavian (0)	14	0.11
Scotch-Irish (59)	99	0.78
Scottish (19)	303	2.37
Slavic (9)	27	0.21
Slovak (7)	23	0.18
Slovene (0)	7	0.05
Swedish (49)	281	2.20
Swiss (23)	47	0.37
Turkish (45)	45	0.35
Ukrainian (46)	57	0.45
Welsh (0)	12	0.09
Yugoslavian (5)	31	0.24

Hispanic Origin	Population	%
Hispanic or Latino (of any race)	750	5.62
Central American, ex. Mexican	157	1.18
Costa Rican	8	0.06
Guatemalan	14	0.10
Honduran	8	0.06
Panamanian	2	0.01
Salvadoran	125	0.94
Cuban	33	0.25
Dominican Republic	38	0.28
Mexican	61	0.46
Puerto Rican	262	1.96
South American	136	1.02
Argentinean	7	0.05
Bolivian	8	0.06
Chilean	7	0.05
Colombian	43	0.32
Ecuadorian	39	0.29
Peruvian	22	0.16
Venezuelan	10	0.07
Other Hispanic or Latino	63	0.47

Race*	Population	%
African-American/Black (85)	117	0.88
Not Hispanic (65)	80	0.60
Hispanic (20)	37	0.28
American Indian/Alaska Native (12)	46	0.34
Not Hispanic (6)	29	0.22
Hispanic (6)	17	0.13
Blackfeet (0)	2	0.01
Cherokee (1)	4	0.03
Iroquois (2)	2	0.01
Mexican American Ind. (0)	4	0.03
South American Ind. (0)	4	0.03
Asian (261)	323	2.42
Not Hispanic (261)	323	2.42
Bangladeshi (4)	4	0.03
Chinese, ex. Taiwanese (66)	92	0.69
Filipino (27)	37	0.28
Indian (80)	95	0.71
Japanese (7)	13	0.10
Korean (28)	38	0.28
Laotian (3)	3	0.02
Pakistani (15)	15	0.11
Sri Lankan (4)	4	0.03
Thai (1)	2	0.01
Vietnamese (4)	5	0.04
Hawaii Native/Pacific Islander (2)	5	0.04
Not Hispanic (1)	4	0.03
Hispanic (1)	1	0.01
Guamanian/Chamorro (1)	2	0.01
Native Hawaiian (1)	1	0.01
White (12,681)	12,821	96.12
Not Hispanic (12,133)	12,223	91.64
Hispanic (548)	598	4.48

Staten Island

Place Type: Borough
County: Richmond
Population: 468,730†

Ancestry‡	Population	%
African, Sub-Saharan (6,533)	7,234	1.56
African (3,732)	4,164	0.90
Cape Verdean (0)	11	<0.01
Ethiopian (41)	46	0.01
Ghanaian (239)	250	0.05
Kenyan (78)	78	0.02

*Notes: † The Census 2010 population figure is used to calculate the percentages in the Hispanic Origin and Race categories. Ancestry percentages are based on the 2006-2010 American Community Survey population (not shown); ‡ Numbers in parentheses indicate the number of people reporting a single ancestry; * Numbers in parentheses indicate the number of persons reporting this race alone, not in combination with any other race; Please refer to the Explanation of Data for more information.*

Liberian (515)	532	0.11
Nigerian (1,509)	1,679	0.36
Senegalese (126)	126	0.03
Sierra Leonean (90)	117	0.03
Other Sub-Saharan African (203)	231	0.05
Albanian (7,700)	8,108	1.75
Alsatian (0)	24	0.01
American (13,977)	13,977	3.02
Arab (7,711)	8,820	1.90
Arab (1,694)	1,829	0.39
Egyptian (3,200)	3,292	0.71
Iraqi (11)	32	0.01
Jordanian (159)	183	0.04
Lebanese (784)	1,019	0.22
Moroccan (502)	621	0.13
Palestinian (443)	479	0.10
Syrian (209)	584	0.13
Other Arab (709)	781	0.17
Armenian (83)	311	0.07
Assyrian/Chaldean/Syriac (15)	15	<0.01
Australian (24)	49	0.01
Austrian (343)	1,542	0.33
Basque (15)	77	0.02
Belgian (36)	266	0.06
Brazilian (183)	287	0.06
British (231)	615	0.13
Canadian (290)	544	0.12
Carpatho Rusyn (63)	63	0.01
Celtic (37)	46	0.01
Croatian (598)	869	0.19
Czech (146)	735	0.16
Czechoslovakian (93)	237	0.05
Danish (90)	479	0.10
Dutch (137)	1,637	0.35
Eastern European (433)	433	0.09
English (1,973)	9,014	1.94
Estonian (10)	10	<0.01
European (1,914)	2,068	0.45
Finnish (48)	185	0.04
French, ex. Basque (800)	3,772	0.81
French Canadian (248)	750	0.16
German (4,111)	25,477	5.50
Greek (2,403)	4,183	0.90
Guyanese (767)	952	0.21
Hungarian (1,024)	2,288	0.49
Icelander (55)	55	0.01
Iranian (121)	171	0.04
Irish (20,064)	64,762	13.97
Israeli (542)	759	0.16
Italian (107,263)	156,288	33.72
Latvian (98)	142	0.03
Lithuanian (178)	645	0.14
Luxemburger (12)	54	0.01
Macedonian (1,368)	1,590	0.34
Maltese (104)	290	0.06
Northern European (60)	60	0.01
Norwegian (1,617)	5,135	1.11
Pennsylvania German (9)	41	0.01
Polish (9,167)	18,430	3.98
Portuguese (180)	617	0.13
Romanian (530)	964	0.21
Russian (11,315)	16,388	3.54
Scandinavian (35)	121	0.03
Scotch-Irish (759)	1,886	0.41
Scottish (718)	2,350	0.51
Serbian (219)	240	0.05
Slavic (68)	143	0.03
Slovak (233)	553	0.12
Slovene (86)	108	0.02
Soviet Union (51)	63	0.01
Swedish (253)	1,936	0.42
Swiss (76)	256	0.06
Turkish (1,267)	1,607	0.35
Ukrainian (3,759)	4,836	1.04
Welsh (68)	417	0.09
West Indian, ex. Hispanic (5,348)	6,967	1.50
Bahamian (31)	31	0.01
Barbadian (94)	94	0.02
Belizean (76)	76	0.02
British West Indian (113)	236	0.05
Dutch West Indian (39)	89	0.02
Haitian (676)	791	0.17
Jamaican (1,463)	2,033	0.44
Trinidadian/Tobagonian (1,412)	1,807	0.39
U.S. Virgin Islander (22)	22	<0.01
West Indian (1,392)	1,745	0.38
Other West Indian (30)	43	0.01
Yugoslavian (1,237)	1,738	0.38

Hispanic Origin	Population	%
Hispanic or Latino (of any race)	81,051	17.29
Central American, ex. Mexican	4,310	0.92
Costa Rican	266	0.06
Guatemalan	864	0.18
Honduran	1,735	0.37
Nicaraguan	199	0.04
Panamanian	607	0.13
Salvadoran	592	0.13
Other Central American	47	0.01
Cuban	1,831	0.39
Dominican Republic	4,918	1.05
Mexican	18,684	3.99
Puerto Rican	37,517	8.00
South American	8,232	1.76
Argentinean	608	0.13
Bolivian	161	0.03
Chilean	346	0.07
Colombian	2,526	0.54
Ecuadorian	2,675	0.57
Paraguayan	38	0.01
Peruvian	1,462	0.31
Uruguayan	76	0.02
Venezuelan	254	0.05
Other South American	86	0.02
Other Hispanic or Latino	5,559	1.19

Race*	Population	%
African-American/Black (49,857)	55,014	11.74
Not Hispanic (44,313)	47,521	10.14
Hispanic (5,544)	7,493	1.60
American Indian/Alaska Native (1,695)	3,719	0.79
Not Hispanic (695)	2,034	0.43
Hispanic (1,000)	1,685	0.36
Alaska Athabascan *(Ala. Nat.)* (1)	3	<0.01
Aleut *(Alaska Native)* (0)	2	<0.01
Apache (16)	35	0.01
Arapaho (1)	1	<0.01
Blackfeet (17)	88	0.02
Canadian/French Am. Ind. (7)	10	<0.01
Central American Ind. (29)	56	0.01
Cherokee (104)	467	0.10
Cheyenne (0)	2	<0.01
Chickasaw (1)	3	<0.01
Chippewa (7)	13	<0.01
Choctaw (3)	11	<0.01
Comanche (2)	3	<0.01
Cree (0)	4	<0.01
Creek (3)	29	0.01
Delaware (16)	43	0.01
Hopi (1)	5	<0.01
Houma (1)	1	<0.01
Inupiat *(Alaska Native)* (0)	1	<0.01
Iroquois (61)	152	0.03
Kiowa (0)	1	<0.01
Lumbee (1)	8	<0.01
Mexican American Ind. (161)	204	0.04
Navajo (10)	17	<0.01
Pima (2)	2	<0.01
Pueblo (4)	5	<0.01
Seminole (7)	26	0.01
Shoshone (1)	3	<0.01
Sioux (11)	24	0.01
South American Ind. (146)	288	0.06
Spanish American Ind. (31)	47	0.01
Tlingit-Haida *(Alaska Native)* (0)	1	<0.01
Tohono O'Odham (4)	8	<0.01
Ute (1)	1	<0.01
Yaqui (1)	1	<0.01
Yuman (0)	1	<0.01
Asian (35,164)	38,756	8.27
Not Hispanic (34,697)	37,689	8.04
Hispanic (467)	1,067	0.23
Bangladeshi (360)	387	0.08
Burmese (116)	130	0.03
Cambodian (100)	129	0.03
Chinese, ex. Taiwanese (13,144)	14,107	3.01
Filipino (5,224)	6,205	1.32
Hmong (4)	8	<0.01
Indian (6,793)	7,723	1.65
Indonesian (22)	52	0.01
Japanese (201)	408	0.09
Korean (3,207)	3,398	0.72
Laotian (13)	18	<0.01
Malaysian (58)	96	0.02
Nepalese (27)	35	0.01
Pakistani (2,495)	2,777	0.59
Sri Lankan (1,560)	1,766	0.38
Taiwanese (160)	197	0.04
Thai (135)	166	0.04
Vietnamese (468)	570	0.12
Hawaii Native/Pacific Islander (213)	683	0.15
Not Hispanic (137)	439	0.09
Hispanic (76)	244	0.05
Fijian (6)	6	<0.01
Guamanian/Chamorro (88)	115	0.02
Marshallese (1)	1	<0.01
Native Hawaiian (46)	121	0.03
Samoan (5)	26	0.01
Tongan (2)	2	<0.01
White (341,677)	350,679	74.81
Not Hispanic (300,169)	305,118	65.09
Hispanic (41,508)	45,561	9.72

Stillwater

Place Type: Town
County: Saratoga
Population: 8,287†

Ancestry‡	Population	%
American (649)	649	7.91
Arab (0)	16	0.20
Lebanese (0)	16	0.20
Armenian (0)	39	0.48
Austrian (37)	47	0.57
Basque (0)	4	0.05
British (23)	23	0.28
Canadian (3)	30	0.37
Croatian (39)	39	0.48
Czech (33)	43	0.52
Czechoslovakian (27)	27	0.33
Danish (0)	34	0.41
Dutch (76)	294	3.58
English (244)	892	10.88
French, ex. Basque (111)	890	10.85
French Canadian (81)	205	2.50
German (378)	1,488	18.14
Greek (15)	15	0.18
Hungarian (0)	16	0.20
Irish (758)	2,384	29.07
Italian (537)	1,488	18.14
Lithuanian (0)	81	0.99
Northern European (13)	13	0.16
Norwegian (44)	108	1.32
Pennsylvania German (0)	13	0.16
Polish (195)	1,100	13.41
Romanian (0)	3	0.04
Russian (7)	87	1.06
Scotch-Irish (63)	117	1.43
Scottish (24)	116	1.41
Slavic (7)	7	0.09
Slovak (0)	52	0.63
Swedish (0)	17	0.21
Ukrainian (10)	76	0.93
Welsh (24)	75	0.91
West Indian, ex. Hispanic (16)	16	0.20
Jamaican (16)	16	0.20
Yugoslavian (0)	38	0.46

*Notes: † The Census 2010 population figure is used to calculate the percentages in the Hispanic Origin and Race categories. Ancestry percentages are based on the 2006-2010 American Community Survey population (not shown); ‡ Numbers in parentheses indicate the number of people reporting a single ancestry; * Numbers in parentheses indicate the number of persons reporting this race alone, not in combination with any other race; Please refer to the Explanation of Data for more information.*

Hispanic Origin	Population	%
Hispanic or Latino (of any race)	121	1.46
Central American, ex. Mexican	7	0.08
Guatemalan	1	0.01
Honduran	4	0.05
Nicaraguan	1	0.01
Panamanian	1	0.01
Cuban	3	0.04
Dominican Republic	2	0.02
Mexican	34	0.41
Puerto Rican	54	0.65
South American	7	0.08
Argentinean	1	0.01
Colombian	4	0.05
Paraguayan	2	0.02
Other Hispanic or Latino	14	0.17

Race*	Population	%
African-American/Black (47)	90	1.09
Not Hispanic (45)	86	1.04
Hispanic (2)	4	0.05
American Indian/Alaska Native (17)	61	0.74
Not Hispanic (17)	59	0.71
Hispanic (0)	2	0.02
Blackfeet (0)	5	0.06
Cherokee (1)	5	0.06
Chippewa (1)	1	0.01
Delaware (0)	1	0.01
Iroquois (2)	10	0.12
Asian (35)	56	0.68
Not Hispanic (35)	56	0.68
Cambodian (1)	1	0.01
Chinese, ex. Taiwanese (11)	16	0.19
Filipino (3)	8	0.10
Indian (4)	8	0.10
Japanese (1)	1	0.01
Korean (7)	9	0.11
Taiwanese (1)	1	0.01
Thai (3)	10	0.12
Vietnamese (0)	1	0.01
Hawaii Native/Pacific Islander (0)	5	0.06
Not Hispanic (0)	5	0.06
Native Hawaiian (0)	4	0.05
White (8,067)	8,167	98.55
Not Hispanic (7,970)	8,061	97.27
Hispanic (97)	106	1.28

Stony Brook

Place Type: CDP
County: Suffolk
Population: 13,740†

Ancestry‡	Population	%
African, Sub-Saharan (42)	42	0.31
African (29)	29	0.21
Ghanaian (13)	13	0.10
American (332)	332	2.43
Arab (0)	41	0.30
Lebanese (0)	12	0.09
Syrian (0)	29	0.21
Armenian (5)	5	0.04
Australian (28)	28	0.21
Austrian (69)	196	1.44
Belgian (0)	62	0.45
British (19)	65	0.48
Canadian (62)	104	0.76
Croatian (13)	13	0.10
Czech (41)	149	1.09
Czechoslovakian (0)	24	0.18
Danish (2)	108	0.79
Dutch (36)	186	1.36
Eastern European (132)	132	0.97
English (351)	1,253	9.17
European (57)	72	0.53
Finnish (0)	21	0.15
French, ex. Basque (11)	284	2.08
French Canadian (0)	65	0.48
German (403)	2,627	19.23
Greek (123)	348	2.55
Hungarian (61)	216	1.58
Iranian (14)	14	0.10
Irish (843)	3,842	28.13
Israeli (24)	68	0.50
Italian (1,696)	4,072	29.81
Latvian (60)	60	0.44
Lithuanian (37)	70	0.51
Northern European (14)	14	0.10
Norwegian (12)	78	0.57
Polish (132)	626	4.58
Portuguese (0)	32	0.23
Romanian (40)	113	0.83
Russian (247)	612	4.48
Scandinavian (13)	13	0.10
Scotch-Irish (52)	119	0.87
Scottish (17)	116	0.85
Slovak (0)	16	0.12
Swedish (12)	113	0.83
Swiss (0)	50	0.37
Ukrainian (36)	51	0.37
Welsh (0)	67	0.49
West Indian, ex. Hispanic (135)	175	1.28
Haitian (49)	49	0.36
Jamaican (86)	102	0.75
Trinidadian/Tobagonian (0)	12	0.09
Other West Indian (0)	12	0.09
Yugoslavian (0)	5	0.04

Hispanic Origin	Population	%
Hispanic or Latino (of any race)	603	4.39
Central American, ex. Mexican	34	0.25
Costa Rican	3	0.02
Guatemalan	10	0.07
Panamanian	8	0.06
Salvadoran	13	0.09
Cuban	45	0.33
Dominican Republic	21	0.15
Mexican	47	0.34
Puerto Rican	230	1.67
South American	126	0.92
Argentinean	22	0.16
Bolivian	9	0.07
Chilean	9	0.07
Colombian	32	0.23
Ecuadorian	31	0.23
Peruvian	17	0.12
Venezuelan	6	0.04
Other Hispanic or Latino	100	0.73

Race*	Population	%
African-American/Black (229)	280	2.04
Not Hispanic (215)	258	1.88
Hispanic (14)	22	0.16
American Indian/Alaska Native (11)	33	0.24
Not Hispanic (9)	26	0.19
Hispanic (2)	7	0.05
Canadian/French Am. Ind. (0)	1	0.01
Cherokee (7)	14	0.10
Iroquois (0)	2	0.01
Osage (0)	1	0.01
Sioux (1)	1	0.01
South American Ind. (2)	2	0.01
Asian (1,033)	1,133	8.25
Not Hispanic (1,029)	1,120	8.15
Hispanic (4)	13	0.09
Bangladeshi (9)	9	0.07
Burmese (6)	6	0.04
Chinese, ex. Taiwanese (558)	598	4.35
Filipino (37)	61	0.44
Indian (202)	220	1.60
Japanese (14)	22	0.16
Korean (100)	116	0.84
Laotian (1)	4	0.03
Pakistani (38)	39	0.28
Taiwanese (24)	24	0.17
Thai (11)	14	0.10
Vietnamese (12)	12	0.09
Hawaii Native/Pacific Islander (6)	8	0.06
Not Hispanic (6)	8	0.06
Samoan (1)	2	0.01
White (12,171)	12,341	89.82
Not Hispanic (11,718)	11,855	86.28
Hispanic (453)	486	3.54

Stony Brook University

Place Type: CDP
County: Suffolk
Population: 9,216†

Ancestry‡	Population	%
African, Sub-Saharan (95)	95	1.14
African (29)	29	0.35
Ghanaian (26)	26	0.31
Nigerian (40)	40	0.48
American (12)	12	0.14
Arab (40)	67	0.80
Arab (0)	14	0.17
Egyptian (13)	13	0.16
Palestinian (0)	13	0.16
Other Arab (27)	27	0.32
Armenian (12)	12	0.14
Australian (0)	13	0.16
Austrian (0)	27	0.32
Belgian (0)	13	0.16
British (0)	14	0.17
Croatian (35)	35	0.42
Czech (0)	26	0.31
Dutch (28)	41	0.49
Eastern European (0)	14	0.17
English (31)	133	1.59
European (174)	199	2.38
French, ex. Basque (0)	28	0.33
French Canadian (0)	47	0.56
German (21)	450	5.38
Greek (27)	54	0.65
Guyanese (109)	109	1.30
Hungarian (24)	36	0.43
Iranian (53)	77	0.92
Irish (149)	511	6.11
Israeli (26)	26	0.31
Italian (271)	745	8.91
Lithuanian (12)	12	0.14
New Zealander (0)	13	0.16
Norwegian (9)	47	0.56
Polish (25)	235	2.81
Romanian (26)	64	0.77
Russian (129)	259	3.10
Scotch-Irish (0)	41	0.49
Scottish (21)	85	1.02
Swedish (11)	50	0.60
Swiss (0)	13	0.16
Turkish (24)	24	0.29
Ukrainian (39)	66	0.79
Welsh (0)	26	0.31
West Indian, ex. Hispanic (298)	310	3.71
British West Indian (12)	12	0.14
Haitian (138)	138	1.65
Jamaican (53)	53	0.63
Trinidadian/Tobagonian (70)	82	0.98
West Indian (25)	25	0.30

Hispanic Origin	Population	%
Hispanic or Latino (of any race)	612	6.64
Central American, ex. Mexican	31	0.34
Guatemalan	3	0.03
Honduran	3	0.03
Panamanian	6	0.07
Salvadoran	17	0.18
Other Central American	2	0.02
Cuban	18	0.20
Dominican Republic	120	1.30
Mexican	46	0.50
Puerto Rican	190	2.06
South American	80	0.87
Argentinean	3	0.03
Bolivian	3	0.03
Chilean	1	0.01
Colombian	27	0.29
Ecuadorian	14	0.15

*Notes: † The Census 2010 population figure is used to calculate the percentages in the Hispanic Origin and Race categories. Ancestry percentages are based on the 2006-2010 American Community Survey population (not shown); ‡ Numbers in parentheses indicate the number of people reporting a single ancestry; * Numbers in parentheses indicate the number of persons reporting this race alone, not in combination with any other race; Please refer to the Explanation of Data for more information.*

Paraguayan	2	0.02
Peruvian	24	0.26
Venezuelan	4	0.04
Other South American	2	0.02
Other Hispanic or Latino	127	1.38

Race*	Population	%
African-American/Black (1,290)	1,321	14.33
Not Hispanic (1,247)	1,264	13.72
Hispanic (43)	57	0.62
American Indian/Alaska Native (33)	45	0.49
Not Hispanic (27)	37	0.40
Hispanic (6)	8	0.09
Central American Ind. (1)	2	0.02
Cherokee (1)	1	0.01
Choctaw (0)	1	0.01
Mexican American Ind. (1)	1	0.01
Pueblo (1)	1	0.01
South American Ind. (1)	1	0.01
Asian (1,890)	1,981	21.50
Not Hispanic (1,883)	1,967	21.34
Hispanic (7)	14	0.15
Bangladeshi (56)	67	0.73
Burmese (3)	3	0.03
Cambodian (2)	5	0.05
Chinese, ex. Taiwanese (815)	863	9.36
Filipino (96)	109	1.18
Indian (434)	462	5.01
Indonesian (4)	5	0.05
Japanese (15)	24	0.26
Korean (243)	253	2.75
Laotian (1)	2	0.02
Malaysian (2)	2	0.02
Nepalese (1)	1	0.01
Pakistani (39)	51	0.55
Sri Lankan (5)	5	0.05
Taiwanese (10)	12	0.13
Thai (4)	6	0.07
Vietnamese (17)	23	0.25
Hawaii Native/Pacific Islander (2)	10	0.11
Not Hispanic (2)	10	0.11
Native Hawaiian (0)	1	0.01
Samoan (1)	2	0.02
White (5,600)	5,694	61.78
Not Hispanic (5,304)	5,364	58.20
Hispanic (296)	330	3.58

Stony Point

Place Type: CDP
County: Rockland
Population: 12,147†

Ancestry‡	Population	%
African, Sub-Saharan (45)	45	0.38
African (45)	45	0.38
American (946)	946	7.95
Arab (0)	45	0.38
Lebanese (0)	45	0.38
Austrian (0)	38	0.32
Belgian (12)	12	0.10
Brazilian (35)	35	0.29
Canadian (0)	42	0.35
Croatian (18)	18	0.15
Czech (21)	94	0.79
Czechoslovakian (0)	40	0.34
Danish (0)	23	0.19
Dutch (23)	148	1.24
Eastern European (11)	11	0.09
English (53)	552	4.64
European (56)	80	0.67
Finnish (0)	24	0.20
French, ex. Basque (60)	215	1.81
French Canadian (9)	35	0.29
German (438)	1,688	14.18
Greek (105)	151	1.27
Hungarian (21)	164	1.38
Irish (1,284)	2,986	25.08
Italian (1,961)	3,488	29.30
Latvian (0)	10	0.08
Lithuanian (0)	29	0.24
Norwegian (12)	89	0.75
Pennsylvania German (10)	10	0.08
Polish (61)	291	2.44
Portuguese (287)	287	2.41
Russian (11)	146	1.23
Scotch-Irish (37)	93	0.78
Scottish (68)	158	1.33
Slovak (8)	60	0.50
Slovene (0)	8	0.07
Swedish (24)	69	0.58
Ukrainian (6)	46	0.39
Welsh (7)	33	0.28
West Indian, ex. Hispanic (70)	70	0.59
Haitian (49)	49	0.41
Jamaican (21)	21	0.18

Hispanic Origin	Population	%
Hispanic or Latino (of any race)	1,695	13.95
Central American, ex. Mexican	125	1.03
Costa Rican	5	0.04
Guatemalan	32	0.26
Honduran	11	0.09
Nicaraguan	6	0.05
Panamanian	4	0.03
Salvadoran	66	0.54
Other Central American	1	0.01
Cuban	84	0.69
Dominican Republic	360	2.96
Mexican	77	0.63
Puerto Rican	781	6.43
South American	171	1.41
Argentinean	15	0.12
Chilean	10	0.08
Colombian	49	0.40
Ecuadorian	51	0.42
Paraguayan	4	0.03
Peruvian	30	0.25
Uruguayan	6	0.05
Venezuelan	5	0.04
Other South American	1	0.01
Other Hispanic or Latino	97	0.80

Race*	Population	%
African-American/Black (502)	611	5.03
Not Hispanic (424)	503	4.14
Hispanic (78)	108	0.89
American Indian/Alaska Native (20)	72	0.59
Not Hispanic (9)	47	0.39
Hispanic (11)	25	0.21
Blackfeet (0)	1	0.01
Cherokee (0)	12	0.10
Cree (0)	1	0.01
Delaware (0)	7	0.06
Iroquois (3)	4	0.03
Lumbee (1)	1	0.01
Sioux (0)	2	0.02
South American Ind. (3)	3	0.02
Spanish American Ind. (1)	2	0.02
Yaqui (1)	1	0.01
Asian (363)	421	3.47
Not Hispanic (359)	405	3.33
Hispanic (4)	16	0.13
Cambodian (0)	2	0.02
Chinese, ex. Taiwanese (63)	72	0.59
Filipino (57)	69	0.57
Indian (147)	166	1.37
Japanese (5)	11	0.09
Korean (34)	37	0.30
Pakistani (26)	27	0.22
Taiwanese (2)	2	0.02
Thai (1)	2	0.02
Vietnamese (16)	18	0.15
Hawaii Native/Pacific Islander (9)	22	0.18
Not Hispanic (1)	4	0.03
Hispanic (8)	18	0.15
Guamanian/Chamorro (4)	5	0.04
White (10,474)	10,695	88.05
Not Hispanic (9,494)	9,623	79.22
Hispanic (980)	1,072	8.83

Stony Point

Place Type: Town
County: Rockland
Population: 15,059†

Ancestry‡	Population	%
African, Sub-Saharan (45)	45	0.30
African (45)	45	0.30
American (1,510)	1,510	10.19
Arab (0)	45	0.30
Lebanese (0)	45	0.30
Armenian (23)	23	0.16
Austrian (31)	115	0.78
Belgian (12)	32	0.22
Brazilian (35)	35	0.24
Canadian (0)	42	0.28
Croatian (18)	18	0.12
Czech (30)	126	0.85
Czechoslovakian (0)	68	0.46
Danish (0)	23	0.16
Dutch (44)	193	1.30
Eastern European (11)	11	0.07
English (137)	766	5.17
European (56)	80	0.54
Finnish (0)	24	0.16
French, ex. Basque (68)	249	1.68
French Canadian (9)	60	0.40
German (549)	2,074	13.99
Greek (105)	160	1.08
Hungarian (21)	248	1.67
Irish (1,550)	3,729	25.16
Israeli (0)	30	0.20
Italian (2,389)	4,463	30.11
Latvian (0)	10	0.07
Lithuanian (0)	29	0.20
Norwegian (12)	97	0.65
Pennsylvania German (10)	10	0.07
Polish (70)	359	2.42
Portuguese (287)	287	1.94
Romanian (0)	19	0.13
Russian (21)	205	1.38
Scotch-Irish (45)	112	0.76
Scottish (93)	212	1.43
Slovak (8)	60	0.40
Slovene (0)	8	0.05
Swedish (24)	69	0.47
Ukrainian (6)	46	0.31
Welsh (38)	64	0.43
West Indian, ex. Hispanic (100)	100	0.67
Haitian (79)	79	0.53
Jamaican (21)	21	0.14

Hispanic Origin	Population	%
Hispanic or Latino (of any race)	1,935	12.85
Central American, ex. Mexican	136	0.90
Costa Rican	7	0.05
Guatemalan	32	0.21
Honduran	11	0.07
Nicaraguan	6	0.04
Panamanian	10	0.07
Salvadoran	69	0.46
Other Central American	1	0.01
Cuban	99	0.66
Dominican Republic	405	2.69
Mexican	97	0.64
Puerto Rican	880	5.84
South American	196	1.30
Argentinean	25	0.17
Chilean	11	0.07
Colombian	59	0.39
Ecuadorian	51	0.34
Paraguayan	4	0.03
Peruvian	34	0.23
Uruguayan	6	0.04
Venezuelan	5	0.03
Other South American	1	0.01
Other Hispanic or Latino	122	0.81

*Notes: † The Census 2010 population figure is used to calculate the percentages in the Hispanic Origin and Race categories. Ancestry percentages are based on the 2006-2010 American Community Survey population (not shown); ‡ Numbers in parentheses indicate the number of people reporting a single ancestry; * Numbers in parentheses indicate the number of persons reporting this race alone, not in combination with any other race; Please refer to the Explanation of Data for more information.*

Race*	Population	%
African-American/Black (576)	722	4.79
Not Hispanic (483)	598	3.97
Hispanic (93)	124	0.82
American Indian/Alaska Native (28)	89	0.59
Not Hispanic (11)	55	0.37
Hispanic (17)	34	0.23
Apache (1)	2	0.01
Blackfeet (0)	1	0.01
Central American Ind. (1)	1	0.01
Cherokee (0)	16	0.11
Cree (0)	1	0.01
Delaware (0)	7	0.05
Iroquois (3)	4	0.03
Lumbee (1)	1	0.01
Mexican American Ind. (4)	6	0.04
Sioux (0)	2	0.01
South American Ind. (3)	3	0.02
Spanish American Ind. (1)	2	0.01
Yaqui (1)	1	0.01
Asian (398)	476	3.16
Not Hispanic (393)	459	3.05
Hispanic (5)	17	0.11
Cambodian (2)	4	0.03
Chinese, ex. Taiwanese (67)	78	0.52
Filipino (60)	76	0.50
Indian (164)	186	1.24
Japanese (6)	17	0.11
Korean (37)	45	0.30
Pakistani (26)	27	0.18
Taiwanese (2)	2	0.01
Thai (4)	5	0.03
Vietnamese (18)	20	0.13
Hawaii Native/Pacific Islander (10)	23	0.15
Not Hispanic (2)	5	0.03
Hispanic (8)	18	0.12
Guamanian/Chamorro (4)	5	0.03
Native Hawaiian (1)	1	0.01
White (13,166)	13,448	89.30
Not Hispanic (12,011)	12,193	80.97
Hispanic (1,155)	1,255	8.33

Suffern

Place Type: Village
County: Rockland
Population: 10,723†

Ancestry‡	Population	%
American (379)	379	3.54
Arab (12)	51	0.48
Iraqi (12)	37	0.35
Lebanese (0)	14	0.13
Austrian (54)	131	1.22
Brazilian (0)	112	1.05
British (14)	99	0.92
Czech (7)	228	2.13
Czechoslovakian (19)	27	0.25
Danish (10)	20	0.19
Dutch (9)	236	2.20
Eastern European (113)	175	1.63
English (78)	478	4.47
European (275)	275	2.57
Finnish (0)	7	0.07
French, ex. Basque (39)	143	1.34
French Canadian (0)	30	0.28
German (324)	1,107	10.34
Greek (48)	80	0.75
Hungarian (37)	155	1.45
Irish (958)	2,167	20.24
Israeli (0)	135	1.26
Italian (1,015)	1,944	18.16
Lithuanian (7)	208	1.94
Norwegian (0)	42	0.39
Polish (249)	731	6.83
Portuguese (12)	23	0.21
Romanian (0)	107	1.00
Russian (197)	560	5.23
Scandinavian (8)	34	0.32
Scotch-Irish (31)	149	1.39
Scottish (73)	218	2.04
Slovak (10)	20	0.19
Slovene (19)	19	0.18
Swedish (0)	102	0.95
Swiss (0)	11	0.10
Ukrainian (84)	158	1.48
Welsh (10)	55	0.51
West Indian, ex. Hispanic (514)	524	4.90
Haitian (111)	111	1.04
Jamaican (403)	413	3.86

Hispanic Origin	Population	%
Hispanic or Latino (of any race)	1,917	17.88
Central American, ex. Mexican	173	1.61
Costa Rican	16	0.15
Guatemalan	63	0.59
Honduran	12	0.11
Panamanian	8	0.07
Salvadoran	68	0.63
Other Central American	6	0.06
Cuban	35	0.33
Dominican Republic	94	0.88
Mexican	827	7.71
Puerto Rican	433	4.04
South American	227	2.12
Argentinean	31	0.29
Bolivian	1	0.01
Chilean	5	0.05
Colombian	75	0.70
Ecuadorian	48	0.45
Peruvian	61	0.57
Uruguayan	3	0.03
Venezuelan	3	0.03
Other Hispanic or Latino	128	1.19

Race*	Population	%
African-American/Black (497)	603	5.62
Not Hispanic (435)	511	4.77
Hispanic (62)	92	0.86
American Indian/Alaska Native (30)	77	0.72
Not Hispanic (17)	46	0.43
Hispanic (13)	31	0.29
Blackfeet (1)	1	0.01
Cherokee (0)	12	0.11
Chippewa (0)	1	0.01
Comanche (0)	1	0.01
Delaware (3)	6	0.06
Iroquois (6)	6	0.06
Mexican American Ind. (8)	9	0.08
South American Ind. (1)	8	0.07
Asian (590)	658	6.14
Not Hispanic (581)	642	5.99
Hispanic (9)	16	0.15
Bangladeshi (21)	22	0.21
Cambodian (2)	3	0.03
Chinese, ex. Taiwanese (113)	134	1.25
Filipino (89)	97	0.90
Indian (203)	217	2.02
Indonesian (4)	4	0.04
Japanese (28)	33	0.31
Korean (55)	59	0.55
Malaysian (1)	1	0.01
Pakistani (31)	34	0.32
Sri Lankan (2)	2	0.02
Taiwanese (6)	6	0.06
Thai (7)	10	0.09
Vietnamese (9)	12	0.11
Hawaii Native/Pacific Islander (1)	7	0.07
Not Hispanic (0)	5	0.05
Hispanic (1)	2	0.02
Native Hawaiian (1)	2	0.02
White (8,500)	8,680	80.95
Not Hispanic (7,598)	7,709	71.89
Hispanic (902)	971	9.06

Sullivan

Place Type: Town
County: Madison
Population: 15,339†

Ancestry‡	Population	%
Albanian (0)	14	0.09
American (2,313)	2,313	15.11
Arab (0)	21	0.14
Lebanese (0)	10	0.07
Syrian (0)	11	0.07
Austrian (10)	123	0.80
British (20)	20	0.13
Canadian (17)	73	0.48
Croatian (0)	41	0.27
Czech (0)	60	0.39
Czechoslovakian (12)	12	0.08
Danish (12)	23	0.15
Dutch (58)	567	3.70
English (540)	2,289	14.96
European (249)	249	1.63
French, ex. Basque (140)	1,062	6.94
French Canadian (130)	358	2.34
German (849)	3,896	25.46
Greek (0)	51	0.33
Hungarian (35)	35	0.23
Irish (595)	3,024	19.76
Italian (901)	2,030	13.26
Lithuanian (0)	78	0.51
Macedonian (12)	12	0.08
Norwegian (15)	111	0.73
Polish (214)	887	5.80
Portuguese (0)	57	0.37
Russian (49)	177	1.16
Scandinavian (10)	29	0.19
Scotch-Irish (22)	86	0.56
Scottish (76)	235	1.54
Slavic (10)	21	0.14
Slovak (11)	68	0.44
Swedish (32)	114	0.74
Swiss (0)	85	0.56
Ukrainian (125)	244	1.59
Welsh (32)	240	1.57

Hispanic Origin	Population	%
Hispanic or Latino (of any race)	190	1.24
Central American, ex. Mexican	14	0.09
Guatemalan	10	0.07
Salvadoran	4	0.03
Cuban	7	0.05
Dominican Republic	2	0.01
Mexican	48	0.31
Puerto Rican	72	0.47
South American	19	0.12
Argentinean	2	0.01
Chilean	5	0.03
Colombian	6	0.04
Ecuadorian	2	0.01
Peruvian	2	0.01
Venezuelan	2	0.01
Other Hispanic or Latino	28	0.18

Race*	Population	%
African-American/Black (87)	170	1.11
Not Hispanic (84)	155	1.01
Hispanic (3)	15	0.10
American Indian/Alaska Native (58)	148	0.96
Not Hispanic (56)	138	0.90
Hispanic (2)	10	0.07
Cherokee (2)	11	0.07
Chippewa (4)	4	0.03
Choctaw (0)	3	0.02
Delaware (0)	2	0.01
Iroquois (42)	82	0.53
Kiowa (0)	1	0.01
Navajo (0)	2	0.01
Yuman (0)	1	0.01
Asian (55)	82	0.53
Not Hispanic (54)	79	0.52

*Notes: † The Census 2010 population figure is used to calculate the percentages in the Hispanic Origin and Race categories. Ancestry percentages are based on the 2006-2010 American Community Survey population (not shown); ‡ Numbers in parentheses indicate the number of people reporting a single ancestry; * Numbers in parentheses indicate the number of persons reporting this race alone, not in combination with any other race; Please refer to the Explanation of Data for more information.*

Hispanic (1)	3	0.02
Bhutanese (7)	7	0.05
Cambodian (3)	4	0.03
Chinese, ex. Taiwanese (12)	16	0.10
Filipino (8)	15	0.10
Indian (3)	7	0.05
Japanese (2)	3	0.02
Korean (5)	5	0.03
Malaysian (0)	1	0.01
Nepalese (4)	4	0.03
Taiwanese (1)	2	0.01
Thai (2)	6	0.04
Vietnamese (7)	13	0.08
Hawaii Native/Pacific Islander (4)	10	0.07
Not Hispanic (4)	10	0.07
Guamanian/Chamorro (0)	2	0.01
Native Hawaiian (4)	8	0.05
White (14,913)	15,096	98.42
Not Hispanic (14,773)	14,937	97.38
Hispanic (140)	159	1.04

Sweden

Place Type: Town
County: Monroe
Population: 14,175†

Ancestry‡	Population	%
African, Sub-Saharan (220)	302	2.13
African (54)	136	0.96
Nigerian (125)	125	0.88
Other Sub-Saharan African (41)	41	0.29
American (673)	673	4.75
Arab (14)	46	0.32
Lebanese (14)	14	0.10
Moroccan (0)	19	0.13
Other Arab (0)	13	0.09
Austrian (0)	45	0.32
Brazilian (22)	22	0.16
British (0)	9	0.06
Bulgarian (11)	24	0.17
Canadian (68)	112	0.79
Czech (0)	82	0.58
Czechoslovakian (28)	59	0.42
Danish (30)	40	0.28
Dutch (44)	380	2.68
Eastern European (10)	10	0.07
English (538)	2,180	15.39
European (137)	137	0.97
Finnish (0)	13	0.09
French, ex. Basque (77)	662	4.67
French Canadian (128)	276	1.95
German (694)	3,916	27.64
Greek (44)	142	1.00
Hungarian (48)	216	1.52
Irish (678)	2,658	18.76
Italian (1,033)	2,759	19.47
Northern European (30)	90	0.64
Norwegian (26)	127	0.90
Polish (262)	1,080	7.62
Portuguese (0)	31	0.22
Romanian (16)	22	0.16
Russian (10)	188	1.33
Scotch-Irish (136)	313	2.21
Scottish (95)	456	3.22
Slovene (0)	11	0.08
Swedish (0)	143	1.01
Swiss (0)	27	0.19
Ukrainian (87)	253	1.79
Welsh (13)	122	0.86
West Indian, ex. Hispanic (49)	61	0.43
Belizean (19)	19	0.13
Jamaican (30)	42	0.30
Yugoslavian (11)	36	0.25

Hispanic Origin	Population	%
Hispanic or Latino (of any race)	502	3.54
Central American, ex. Mexican	27	0.19
Costa Rican	2	0.01
Guatemalan	8	0.06
Honduran	2	0.01
Nicaraguan	4	0.03
Salvadoran	11	0.08
Cuban	21	0.15
Dominican Republic	34	0.24
Mexican	142	1.00
Puerto Rican	195	1.38
South American	44	0.31
Argentinean	2	0.01
Bolivian	2	0.01
Chilean	3	0.02
Colombian	17	0.12
Ecuadorian	9	0.06
Paraguayan	1	0.01
Peruvian	9	0.06
Uruguayan	1	0.01
Other Hispanic or Latino	39	0.28

Race*	Population	%
African-American/Black (448)	583	4.11
Not Hispanic (418)	532	3.75
Hispanic (30)	51	0.36
American Indian/Alaska Native (33)	103	0.73
Not Hispanic (21)	87	0.61
Hispanic (12)	16	0.11
Blackfeet (0)	3	0.02
Canadian/French Am. Ind. (4)	4	0.03
Cherokee (1)	10	0.07
Cheyenne (1)	1	0.01
Chickasaw (0)	2	0.01
Creek (0)	1	0.01
Inupiat *(Alaska Native)* (0)	1	0.01
Iroquois (15)	35	0.25
Mexican American Ind. (1)	1	0.01
Navajo (0)	1	0.01
Seminole (0)	1	0.01
Sioux (2)	2	0.01
South American Ind. (0)	2	0.01
Asian (198)	268	1.89
Not Hispanic (196)	263	1.86
Hispanic (2)	5	0.04
Bangladeshi (2)	2	0.01
Cambodian (1)	1	0.01
Chinese, ex. Taiwanese (44)	59	0.42
Filipino (10)	21	0.15
Indian (48)	71	0.50
Indonesian (2)	2	0.01
Japanese (17)	19	0.13
Korean (45)	56	0.40
Laotian (2)	3	0.02
Pakistani (3)	3	0.02
Taiwanese (0)	1	0.01
Thai (1)	3	0.02
Vietnamese (10)	10	0.07
Hawaii Native/Pacific Islander (7)	22	0.16
Not Hispanic (6)	18	0.13
Hispanic (1)	4	0.03
Guamanian/Chamorro (2)	7	0.05
Marshallese (0)	1	0.01
Native Hawaiian (3)	8	0.06
Samoan (0)	1	0.01
Tongan (1)	1	0.01
White (13,105)	13,347	94.16
Not Hispanic (12,797)	13,002	91.72
Hispanic (308)	345	2.43

Syosset

Place Type: CDP
County: Nassau
Population: 18,829†

Ancestry‡	Population	%
American (972)	972	5.14
Arab (0)	28	0.15
Lebanese (0)	8	0.04
Moroccan (0)	20	0.11
Armenian (257)	257	1.36
Austrian (33)	128	0.68
Belgian (0)	24	0.13
Brazilian (11)	11	0.06
Cajun (0)	10	0.05
Canadian (10)	10	0.05
Croatian (35)	81	0.43
Czech (0)	146	0.77
Czechoslovakian (9)	17	0.09
Danish (0)	8	0.04
Dutch (9)	86	0.45
Eastern European (482)	502	2.66
English (102)	539	2.85
Estonian (14)	35	0.19
European (314)	369	1.95
Finnish (12)	23	0.12
French, ex. Basque (26)	242	1.28
French Canadian (46)	89	0.47
German (402)	1,637	8.66
Greek (487)	685	3.62
Hungarian (48)	178	0.94
Iranian (59)	91	0.48
Irish (883)	2,354	12.45
Israeli (26)	63	0.33
Italian (2,237)	4,259	22.53
Latvian (11)	11	0.06
Lithuanian (21)	98	0.52
Maltese (0)	37	0.20
Northern European (23)	23	0.12
Norwegian (30)	100	0.53
Polish (419)	1,179	6.24
Portuguese (21)	21	0.11
Romanian (119)	206	1.09
Russian (460)	1,188	6.28
Scotch-Irish (25)	118	0.62
Scottish (42)	201	1.06
Slovak (0)	37	0.20
Swedish (6)	137	0.72
Turkish (12)	32	0.17
Ukrainian (73)	153	0.81
Welsh (11)	94	0.50
West Indian, ex. Hispanic (23)	56	0.30
Dutch West Indian (0)	14	0.07
Haitian (23)	34	0.18
Trinidadian/Tobagonian (0)	8	0.04
Yugoslavian (12)	12	0.06

Hispanic Origin	Population	%
Hispanic or Latino (of any race)	775	4.12
Central American, ex. Mexican	100	0.53
Costa Rican	9	0.05
Guatemalan	16	0.08
Honduran	13	0.07
Nicaraguan	7	0.04
Panamanian	1	0.01
Salvadoran	54	0.29
Cuban	62	0.33
Dominican Republic	50	0.27
Mexican	55	0.29
Puerto Rican	150	0.80
South American	240	1.27
Argentinean	44	0.23
Bolivian	4	0.02
Chilean	6	0.03
Colombian	95	0.50
Ecuadorian	36	0.19
Paraguayan	2	0.01
Peruvian	29	0.15
Uruguayan	4	0.02
Venezuelan	13	0.07
Other South American	7	0.04
Other Hispanic or Latino	118	0.63

Race*	Population	%
African-American/Black (156)	194	1.03
Not Hispanic (137)	163	0.87
Hispanic (19)	31	0.16
American Indian/Alaska Native (19)	37	0.20
Not Hispanic (12)	28	0.15
Hispanic (7)	9	0.05
Central American Ind. (3)	3	0.02
Cherokee (0)	3	0.02
Chippewa (1)	1	0.01

SECTION TWO

*Notes: † The Census 2010 population figure is used to calculate the percentages in the Hispanic Origin and Race categories. Ancestry percentages are based on the 2006-2010 American Community Survey population (not shown); ‡ Numbers in parentheses indicate the number of people reporting a single ancestry; * Numbers in parentheses indicate the number of persons reporting this race alone, not in combination with any other race; Please refer to the Explanation of Data for more information.*

Mexican American Ind. (1)	2	0.01
Pueblo (2)	2	0.01
Sioux (0)	1	0.01
Asian (4,175)	4,398	23.36
Not Hispanic (4,162)	4,377	23.25
Hispanic (13)	21	0.11
Bangladeshi (33)	36	0.19
Cambodian (0)	3	0.02
Chinese, ex. Taiwanese (1,530)	1,608	8.54
Filipino (98)	132	0.70
Indian (961)	1,017	5.40
Indonesian (3)	4	0.02
Japanese (145)	158	0.84
Korean (1,109)	1,144	6.08
Malaysian (8)	10	0.05
Pakistani (120)	127	0.67
Sri Lankan (2)	2	0.01
Taiwanese (97)	111	0.59
Thai (8)	8	0.04
Vietnamese (3)	10	0.05
Hawaii Native/Pacific Islander (2)	9	0.05
Not Hispanic (2)	8	0.04
Hispanic (0)	1	0.01
Guamanian/Chamorro (0)	1	0.01
White (14,016)	14,239	75.62
Not Hispanic (13,458)	13,640	72.44
Hispanic (558)	599	3.18

Syracuse

Place Type: City
County: Onondaga
Population: 145,170†

Ancestry‡	Population	%
Afghan (19)	19	0.01
African, Sub-Saharan (2,165)	2,470	1.71
African (898)	1,142	0.79
Cape Verdean (0)	8	0.01
Ghanaian (113)	113	0.08
Kenyan (0)	17	0.01
Liberian (246)	246	0.17
Nigerian (148)	167	0.12
Sierra Leonean (13)	13	0.01
Somalian (478)	478	0.33
South African (10)	10	0.01
Sudanese (160)	177	0.12
Ugandan (26)	26	0.02
Other Sub-Saharan African (73)	73	0.05
Albanian (429)	455	0.31
American (3,220)	3,220	2.22
Arab (571)	900	0.62
Arab (226)	267	0.18
Egyptian (13)	13	0.01
Lebanese (100)	269	0.19
Moroccan (60)	86	0.06
Palestinian (58)	66	0.05
Syrian (57)	114	0.08
Other Arab (57)	85	0.06
Armenian (24)	229	0.16
Australian (42)	54	0.04
Austrian (81)	372	0.26
Belgian (53)	81	0.06
Brazilian (30)	42	0.03
British (199)	418	0.29
Bulgarian (18)	18	0.01
Cajun (24)	24	0.02
Canadian (96)	350	0.24
Celtic (12)	12	0.01
Croatian (0)	46	0.03
Czech (36)	163	0.11
Czechoslovakian (44)	77	0.05
Danish (36)	109	0.08
Dutch (174)	2,128	1.47
Eastern European (153)	178	0.12
English (2,028)	10,153	7.01
Estonian (0)	12	0.01
European (440)	487	0.34
Finnish (14)	52	0.04
French, ex. Basque (735)	6,182	4.27
French Canadian (804)	1,782	1.23
German (3,496)	17,038	11.77
Greek (339)	678	0.47
Guyanese (100)	158	0.11
Hungarian (88)	540	0.37
Icelander (0)	10	0.01
Iranian (65)	105	0.07
Irish (6,064)	22,387	15.47
Israeli (133)	146	0.10
Italian (8,625)	18,571	12.83
Latvian (28)	41	0.03
Lithuanian (72)	309	0.21
Luxemburger (0)	14	0.01
Macedonian (46)	67	0.05
New Zealander (0)	13	0.01
Northern European (71)	71	0.05
Norwegian (107)	366	0.25
Pennsylvania German (14)	33	0.02
Polish (2,445)	7,273	5.03
Portuguese (34)	330	0.23
Romanian (38)	113	0.08
Russian (596)	1,831	1.27
Scandinavian (49)	98	0.07
Scotch-Irish (639)	1,546	1.07
Scottish (505)	2,233	1.54
Serbian (0)	26	0.02
Slavic (12)	45	0.03
Slovak (46)	158	0.11
Slovene (15)	85	0.06
Swedish (288)	1,044	0.72
Swiss (91)	286	0.20
Turkish (169)	279	0.19
Ukrainian (589)	1,095	0.76
Welsh (155)	1,060	0.73
West Indian, ex. Hispanic (1,588)	1,931	1.33
Barbadian (96)	96	0.07
British West Indian (22)	50	0.03
Haitian (145)	145	0.10
Jamaican (908)	1,181	0.82
Trinidadian/Tobagonian (95)	95	0.07
West Indian (322)	364	0.25
Yugoslavian (765)	774	0.53

Hispanic Origin	Population	%
Hispanic or Latino (of any race)	12,036	8.29
Central American, ex. Mexican	348	0.24
Costa Rican	29	0.02
Guatemalan	133	0.09
Honduran	40	0.03
Nicaraguan	30	0.02
Panamanian	54	0.04
Salvadoran	59	0.04
Other Central American	3	<0.01
Cuban	1,192	0.82
Dominican Republic	689	0.47
Mexican	958	0.66
Puerto Rican	7,594	5.23
South American	530	0.37
Argentinean	49	0.03
Bolivian	11	0.01
Chilean	35	0.02
Colombian	173	0.12
Ecuadorian	101	0.07
Paraguayan	3	<0.01
Peruvian	89	0.06
Uruguayan	27	0.02
Venezuelan	39	0.03
Other South American	3	<0.01
Other Hispanic or Latino	725	0.50

Race*	Population	%
African-American/Black (42,770)	48,029	33.08
Not Hispanic (40,672)	45,084	31.06
Hispanic (2,098)	2,945	2.03
American Indian/Alaska Native (1,606)	3,537	2.44
Not Hispanic (1,390)	3,067	2.11
Hispanic (216)	470	0.32
Alaska Athabascan *(Ala. Nat.)* (0)	3	<0.01
Aleut *(Alaska Native)* (0)	1	<0.01
Apache (8)	25	0.02
Arapaho (2)	2	<0.01
Blackfeet (7)	111	0.08
Canadian/French Am. Ind. (35)	51	0.04
Central American Ind. (4)	9	0.01
Cherokee (20)	258	0.18
Cheyenne (0)	2	<0.01
Chickasaw (0)	4	<0.01
Chippewa (11)	18	0.01
Choctaw (1)	28	0.02
Comanche (6)	12	0.01
Cree (1)	6	<0.01
Creek (4)	9	0.01
Crow (0)	1	<0.01
Delaware (3)	5	<0.01
Inupiat *(Alaska Native)* (3)	6	<0.01
Iroquois (790)	1,373	0.95
Kiowa (0)	1	<0.01
Lumbee (4)	4	<0.01
Menominee (1)	1	<0.01
Mexican American Ind. (24)	34	0.02
Navajo (2)	5	<0.01
Osage (1)	1	<0.01
Ottawa (0)	2	<0.01
Pima (1)	2	<0.01
Potawatomi (1)	2	<0.01
Seminole (4)	16	0.01
Sioux (13)	38	0.03
South American Ind. (25)	49	0.03
Tlingit-Haida *(Alaska Native)* (0)	1	<0.01
Tohono O'Odham (1)	1	<0.01
Yup'ik *(Alaska Native)* (0)	1	<0.01
Asian (8,021)	9,073	6.25
Not Hispanic (7,971)	8,924	6.15
Hispanic (50)	149	0.10
Bangladeshi (47)	57	0.04
Bhutanese (392)	516	0.36
Burmese (1,178)	1,218	0.84
Cambodian (114)	149	0.10
Chinese, ex. Taiwanese (1,543)	1,749	1.20
Filipino (218)	388	0.27
Hmong (26)	34	0.02
Indian (1,216)	1,397	0.96
Indonesian (14)	26	0.02
Japanese (109)	243	0.17
Korean (861)	937	0.65
Laotian (71)	89	0.06
Malaysian (5)	13	0.01
Nepalese (160)	262	0.18
Pakistani (107)	121	0.08
Sri Lankan (13)	17	0.01
Taiwanese (80)	93	0.06
Thai (64)	89	0.06
Vietnamese (1,414)	1,554	1.07
Hawaii Native/Pacific Islander (44)	279	0.19
Not Hispanic (37)	218	0.15
Hispanic (7)	61	0.04
Fijian (0)	1	<0.01
Guamanian/Chamorro (5)	12	0.01
Marshallese (0)	1	<0.01
Native Hawaiian (15)	65	0.04
Samoan (8)	21	0.01
Tongan (0)	1	<0.01
White (81,319)	87,414	60.21
Not Hispanic (76,653)	81,787	56.34
Hispanic (4,666)	5,627	3.88

Tarrytown

Place Type: Village
County: Westchester
Population: 11,277†

Ancestry‡	Population	%
African, Sub-Saharan (13)	13	0.12
African (13)	13	0.12
American (342)	342	3.05
Arab (31)	44	0.39
Arab (0)	13	0.12
Lebanese (31)	31	0.28
Armenian (48)	82	0.73

*Notes: † The Census 2010 population figure is used to calculate the percentages in the Hispanic Origin and Race categories. Ancestry percentages are based on the 2006-2010 American Community Survey population (not shown); ‡ Numbers in parentheses indicate the number of people reporting a single ancestry; * Numbers in parentheses indicate the number of persons reporting this race alone, not in combination with any other race; Please refer to the Explanation of Data for more information.*

Austrian (56)	185	1.65
British (0)	28	0.25
Canadian (27)	42	0.38
Czech (0)	17	0.15
Czechoslovakian (12)	12	0.11
Danish (0)	27	0.24
Dutch (93)	173	1.54
Eastern European (138)	152	1.36
English (237)	667	5.96
European (104)	104	0.93
Finnish (0)	51	0.46
French, ex. Basque (43)	204	1.82
French Canadian (80)	201	1.79
German (158)	1,098	9.80
Greek (104)	151	1.35
Hungarian (67)	105	0.94
Irish (825)	1,928	17.21
Israeli (41)	54	0.48
Italian (751)	2,145	19.15
Latvian (13)	52	0.46
Lithuanian (0)	18	0.16
Macedonian (24)	24	0.21
Norwegian (0)	64	0.57
Polish (86)	528	4.71
Portuguese (215)	215	1.92
Romanian (15)	28	0.25
Russian (136)	303	2.71
Scotch-Irish (52)	123	1.10
Scottish (39)	311	2.78
Slovak (27)	65	0.58
Swedish (0)	35	0.31
Ukrainian (39)	135	1.21
West Indian, ex. Hispanic (215)	215	1.92
Jamaican (201)	201	1.79
West Indian (14)	14	0.13

Hispanic Origin	Population	%
Hispanic or Latino (of any race)	2,260	20.04
Central American, ex. Mexican	93	0.82
Costa Rican	6	0.05
Guatemalan	32	0.28
Honduran	7	0.06
Nicaraguan	6	0.05
Panamanian	9	0.08
Salvadoran	31	0.27
Other Central American	2	0.02
Cuban	205	1.82
Dominican Republic	556	4.93
Mexican	128	1.14
Puerto Rican	325	2.88
South American	774	6.86
Argentinean	23	0.20
Chilean	68	0.60
Colombian	110	0.98
Ecuadorian	416	3.69
Paraguayan	2	0.02
Peruvian	116	1.03
Uruguayan	18	0.16
Venezuelan	19	0.17
Other South American	2	0.02
Other Hispanic or Latino	179	1.59

Race*	Population	%
African-American/Black (876)	970	8.60
Not Hispanic (752)	810	7.18
Hispanic (124)	160	1.42
American Indian/Alaska Native (36)	92	0.82
Not Hispanic (3)	26	0.23
Hispanic (33)	66	0.59
Blackfeet (0)	3	0.03
Canadian/French Am. Ind. (0)	1	0.01
Central American Ind. (1)	1	0.01
Cherokee (0)	7	0.06
Chickasaw (0)	1	0.01
Iroquois (0)	1	0.01
Sioux (0)	1	0.01
South American Ind. (1)	6	0.05
Spanish American Ind. (7)	10	0.09
Asian (897)	1,015	9.00
Not Hispanic (897)	1,005	8.91
Hispanic (0)	10	0.09
Chinese, ex. Taiwanese (185)	204	1.81
Filipino (68)	88	0.78
Indian (336)	355	3.15
Indonesian (2)	4	0.04
Japanese (115)	151	1.34
Korean (107)	129	1.14
Malaysian (0)	2	0.02
Nepalese (7)	7	0.06
Pakistani (17)	17	0.15
Taiwanese (8)	8	0.07
Thai (10)	12	0.11
Vietnamese (29)	31	0.27
Hawaii Native/Pacific Islander (3)	15	0.13
Not Hispanic (3)	12	0.11
Hispanic (0)	3	0.03
Guamanian/Chamorro (3)	3	0.03
Native Hawaiian (0)	3	0.03
White (8,427)	8,711	77.25
Not Hispanic (7,123)	7,290	64.64
Hispanic (1,304)	1,421	12.60

Terryville

Place Type: CDP
County: Suffolk
Population: 11,849†

Ancestry‡	Population	%
American (370)	370	3.10
Arab (83)	101	0.85
Arab (83)	83	0.70
Syrian (0)	18	0.15
Austrian (20)	152	1.27
British (32)	50	0.42
Czech (0)	56	0.47
Czechoslovakian (68)	95	0.80
Danish (0)	43	0.36
Dutch (0)	50	0.42
Eastern European (37)	37	0.31
English (46)	717	6.00
Finnish (0)	17	0.14
French, ex. Basque (18)	235	1.97
French Canadian (0)	67	0.56
German (470)	2,044	17.12
Greek (73)	168	1.41
Hungarian (8)	191	1.60
Iranian (66)	66	0.55
Irish (810)	3,217	26.94
Israeli (106)	143	1.20
Italian (1,445)	3,331	27.90
Lithuanian (23)	135	1.13
Luxemburger (0)	18	0.15
Maltese (0)	29	0.24
Norwegian (0)	109	0.91
Polish (288)	811	6.79
Portuguese (56)	74	0.62
Russian (171)	380	3.18
Scotch-Irish (29)	82	0.69
Scottish (51)	92	0.77
Slovak (0)	22	0.18
Slovene (5)	22	0.18
Swedish (0)	50	0.42
Swiss (0)	42	0.35
Turkish (32)	32	0.27
Ukrainian (34)	173	1.45
West Indian, ex. Hispanic (112)	112	0.94
Haitian (88)	88	0.74
Trinidadian/Tobagonian (24)	24	0.20

Hispanic Origin	Population	%
Hispanic or Latino (of any race)	1,831	15.45
Central American, ex. Mexican	268	2.26
Costa Rican	1	0.01
Guatemalan	26	0.22
Honduran	64	0.54
Salvadoran	174	1.47
Other Central American	3	0.03
Cuban	39	0.33
Dominican Republic	694	5.86
Mexican	85	0.72
Puerto Rican	409	3.45
South American	199	1.68
Argentinean	15	0.13
Bolivian	14	0.12
Chilean	7	0.06
Colombian	68	0.57
Ecuadorian	48	0.41
Paraguayan	4	0.03
Peruvian	38	0.32
Uruguayan	1	0.01
Venezuelan	4	0.03
Other Hispanic or Latino	137	1.16

Race*	Population	%
African-American/Black (310)	392	3.31
Not Hispanic (266)	307	2.59
Hispanic (44)	85	0.72
American Indian/Alaska Native (46)	88	0.74
Not Hispanic (8)	19	0.16
Hispanic (38)	69	0.58
Blackfeet (0)	1	0.01
Cherokee (1)	3	0.03
Cheyenne (0)	1	0.01
Chippewa (0)	1	0.01
Choctaw (2)	2	0.02
Iroquois (1)	1	0.01
Mexican American Ind. (5)	13	0.11
Seminole (0)	1	0.01
South American Ind. (0)	2	0.02
Asian (381)	425	3.59
Not Hispanic (364)	399	3.37
Hispanic (17)	26	0.22
Bangladeshi (0)	3	0.03
Burmese (4)	4	0.03
Cambodian (0)	5	0.04
Chinese, ex. Taiwanese (102)	118	1.00
Filipino (50)	57	0.48
Indian (106)	123	1.04
Japanese (6)	14	0.12
Korean (13)	15	0.13
Laotian (1)	1	0.01
Pakistani (63)	64	0.54
Taiwanese (3)	3	0.03
Vietnamese (9)	12	0.10
Hawaii Native/Pacific Islander (1)	7	0.06
Not Hispanic (1)	5	0.04
Hispanic (0)	2	0.02
Native Hawaiian (1)	1	0.01
Tongan (0)	2	0.02
White (10,314)	10,487	88.51
Not Hispanic (9,236)	9,317	78.63
Hispanic (1,078)	1,170	9.87

Thompson

Place Type: Town
County: Sullivan
Population: 15,308†

Ancestry‡	Population	%
African, Sub-Saharan (89)	89	0.58
African (56)	56	0.37
Ghanaian (6)	6	0.04
Nigerian (20)	20	0.13
Other Sub-Saharan African (7)	7	0.05
Albanian (12)	12	0.08
American (836)	836	5.49
Arab (13)	13	0.09
Other Arab (13)	13	0.09
Armenian (24)	24	0.16
Australian (0)	48	0.32
Austrian (19)	94	0.62
Brazilian (45)	70	0.46
British (0)	28	0.18
Canadian (23)	68	0.45
Czech (18)	36	0.24
Czechoslovakian (12)	33	0.22
Danish (46)	87	0.57
Dutch (23)	180	1.18

*Notes: † The Census 2010 population figure is used to calculate the percentages in the Hispanic Origin and Race categories. Ancestry percentages are based on the 2006-2010 American Community Survey population (not shown); ‡ Numbers in parentheses indicate the number of people reporting a single ancestry; * Numbers in parentheses indicate the number of persons reporting this race alone, not in combination with any other race; Please refer to the Explanation of Data for more information.*

Eastern European (56)	56	0.37
English (156)	779	5.11
European (15)	15	0.10
French, ex. Basque (0)	218	1.43
French Canadian (0)	20	0.13
German (297)	1,202	7.89
Greek (13)	29	0.19
Hungarian (124)	488	3.20
Iranian (76)	76	0.50
Irish (311)	1,403	9.21
Israeli (24)	24	0.16
Italian (600)	1,371	9.00
Lithuanian (15)	23	0.15
Macedonian (8)	19	0.12
New Zealander (0)	18	0.12
Norwegian (7)	21	0.14
Pennsylvania German (14)	14	0.09
Polish (190)	723	4.75
Portuguese (18)	73	0.48
Romanian (0)	45	0.30
Russian (290)	531	3.49
Scotch-Irish (11)	32	0.21
Scottish (41)	231	1.52
Slovak (22)	54	0.35
Swedish (18)	53	0.35
Swiss (0)	15	0.10
Turkish (9)	18	0.12
Ukrainian (112)	158	1.04
Welsh (29)	43	0.28
West Indian, ex. Hispanic (272)	421	2.76
Barbadian (68)	68	0.45
British West Indian (16)	16	0.11
Jamaican (39)	115	0.76
Trinidadian/Tobagonian (103)	150	0.98
West Indian (46)	72	0.47
Yugoslavian (26)	26	0.17

Hispanic Origin	Population	%
Hispanic or Latino (of any race)	3,102	20.26
Central American, ex. Mexican	254	1.66
Costa Rican	19	0.12
Guatemalan	40	0.26
Honduran	97	0.63
Nicaraguan	13	0.08
Panamanian	22	0.14
Salvadoran	63	0.41
Cuban	74	0.48
Dominican Republic	133	0.87
Mexican	325	2.12
Puerto Rican	1,705	11.14
South American	388	2.53
Argentinean	23	0.15
Bolivian	4	0.03
Chilean	3	0.02
Colombian	232	1.52
Ecuadorian	50	0.33
Peruvian	62	0.41
Uruguayan	4	0.03
Venezuelan	2	0.01
Other South American	8	0.05
Other Hispanic or Latino	223	1.46

Race*	Population	%
African-American/Black (2,863)	3,269	21.35
Not Hispanic (2,590)	2,863	18.70
Hispanic (273)	406	2.65
American Indian/Alaska Native (86)	228	1.49
Not Hispanic (52)	150	0.98
Hispanic (34)	78	0.51
Blackfeet (1)	11	0.07
Canadian/French Am. Ind. (1)	1	0.01
Cherokee (2)	31	0.20
Chippewa (0)	2	0.01
Cree (0)	1	0.01
Creek (3)	3	0.02
Delaware (1)	6	0.04
Iroquois (5)	6	0.04
Mexican American Ind. (8)	9	0.06
Seminole (0)	1	0.01
Sioux (0)	1	0.01
South American Ind. (6)	10	0.07
Spanish American Ind. (2)	7	0.05
Tohono O'Odham (1)	2	0.01
Asian (332)	386	2.52
Not Hispanic (319)	363	2.37
Hispanic (13)	23	0.15
Bangladeshi (5)	11	0.07
Burmese (3)	3	0.02
Cambodian (1)	1	0.01
Chinese, ex. Taiwanese (68)	80	0.52
Filipino (35)	43	0.28
Indian (140)	164	1.07
Indonesian (2)	2	0.01
Japanese (4)	8	0.05
Korean (51)	55	0.36
Pakistani (5)	7	0.05
Taiwanese (4)	6	0.04
Thai (1)	4	0.03
Vietnamese (3)	6	0.04
Hawaii Native/Pacific Islander (2)	26	0.17
Not Hispanic (2)	17	0.11
Hispanic (0)	9	0.06
Guamanian/Chamorro (0)	1	0.01
Native Hawaiian (0)	1	0.01
Samoan (1)	6	0.04
White (10,412)	10,916	71.31
Not Hispanic (8,826)	9,130	59.64
Hispanic (1,586)	1,786	11.67

Tonawanda

Place Type: CDP
County: Erie
Population: 58,144†

Ancestry‡	Population	%
Afghan (108)	108	0.18
African, Sub-Saharan (59)	194	0.33
African (16)	89	0.15
Ghanaian (19)	19	0.03
Kenyan (24)	86	0.15
Albanian (48)	59	0.10
Alsatian (0)	24	0.04
American (1,226)	1,226	2.09
Arab (293)	502	0.86
Arab (21)	34	0.06
Egyptian (0)	8	0.01
Jordanian (9)	9	0.02
Lebanese (223)	401	0.68
Syrian (0)	10	0.02
Other Arab (40)	40	0.07
Armenian (43)	43	0.07
Australian (0)	29	0.05
Austrian (54)	415	0.71
Belgian (0)	13	0.02
Brazilian (0)	13	0.02
British (33)	97	0.17
Canadian (144)	288	0.49
Croatian (84)	219	0.37
Czech (22)	168	0.29
Czechoslovakian (32)	177	0.30
Danish (47)	151	0.26
Dutch (89)	716	1.22
Eastern European (23)	23	0.04
English (1,484)	6,115	10.44
European (354)	354	0.60
Finnish (49)	95	0.16
French, ex. Basque (188)	2,149	3.67
French Canadian (128)	537	0.92
German (4,626)	19,292	32.95
Greek (260)	424	0.72
Hungarian (220)	976	1.67
Icelander (11)	11	0.02
Irish (2,820)	11,980	20.46
Italian (6,780)	14,269	24.37
Latvian (0)	13	0.02
Lithuanian (29)	162	0.28
Macedonian (0)	18	0.03
Maltese (8)	26	0.04
Northern European (18)	18	0.03
Norwegian (60)	150	0.26
Pennsylvania German (40)	85	0.15
Polish (3,451)	9,014	15.40
Portuguese (10)	24	0.04
Romanian (77)	158	0.27
Russian (337)	688	1.18
Scandinavian (15)	15	0.03
Scotch-Irish (309)	989	1.69
Scottish (328)	1,430	2.44
Serbian (54)	73	0.12
Slavic (30)	59	0.10
Slovak (62)	112	0.19
Swedish (77)	584	1.00
Swiss (44)	109	0.19
Ukrainian (239)	422	0.72
Welsh (57)	332	0.57
West Indian, ex. Hispanic (29)	29	0.05
Jamaican (12)	12	0.02
Trinidadian/Tobagonian (17)	17	0.03
Yugoslavian (66)	124	0.21

Hispanic Origin	Population	%
Hispanic or Latino (of any race)	1,485	2.55
Central American, ex. Mexican	32	0.06
Costa Rican	2	<0.01
Guatemalan	19	0.03
Honduran	4	0.01
Panamanian	5	0.01
Salvadoran	2	<0.01
Cuban	31	0.05
Dominican Republic	43	0.07
Mexican	210	0.36
Puerto Rican	942	1.62
South American	89	0.15
Argentinean	7	0.01
Bolivian	7	0.01
Chilean	1	<0.01
Colombian	37	0.06
Ecuadorian	18	0.03
Peruvian	14	0.02
Venezuelan	1	<0.01
Other South American	4	0.01
Other Hispanic or Latino	138	0.24

Race*	Population	%
African-American/Black (1,773)	2,226	3.83
Not Hispanic (1,678)	2,088	3.59
Hispanic (95)	138	0.24
American Indian/Alaska Native (220)	409	0.70
Not Hispanic (183)	354	0.61
Hispanic (37)	55	0.09
Apache (0)	4	0.01
Blackfeet (2)	5	0.01
Canadian/French Am. Ind. (3)	4	0.01
Cherokee (2)	31	0.05
Chippewa (2)	3	0.01
Choctaw (0)	5	0.01
Creek (0)	1	<0.01
Delaware (1)	1	<0.01
Iroquois (113)	165	0.28
Mexican American Ind. (2)	2	<0.01
Navajo (1)	1	<0.01
Potawatomi (5)	9	0.02
Puget Sound Salish (0)	1	<0.01
Seminole (0)	1	<0.01
Sioux (1)	2	<0.01
South American Ind. (8)	14	0.02
Spanish American Ind. (2)	2	<0.01
Yaqui (1)	1	<0.01
Asian (831)	1,029	1.77
Not Hispanic (823)	1,011	1.74
Hispanic (8)	18	0.03
Bangladeshi (3)	4	0.01
Burmese (2)	3	0.01
Cambodian (1)	1	<0.01
Chinese, ex. Taiwanese (210)	239	0.41
Filipino (57)	93	0.16
Indian (266)	284	0.49
Indonesian (3)	8	0.01
Japanese (16)	33	0.06

*Notes: † The Census 2010 population figure is used to calculate the percentages in the Hispanic Origin and Race categories. Ancestry percentages are based on the 2006-2010 American Community Survey population (not shown); ‡ Numbers in parentheses indicate the number of people reporting a single ancestry; * Numbers in parentheses indicate the number of persons reporting this race alone, not in combination with any other race; Please refer to the Explanation of Data for more information.*

	Population	%
Korean (135)	160	0.28
Laotian (11)	17	0.03
Malaysian (3)	4	0.01
Nepalese (1)	1	<0.01
Pakistani (5)	7	0.01
Sri Lankan (8)	8	0.01
Taiwanese (10)	16	0.03
Thai (11)	23	0.04
Vietnamese (64)	77	0.13
Hawaii Native/Pacific Islander (1)	31	0.05
Not Hispanic (1)	21	0.04
Hispanic (0)	10	0.02
Guamanian/Chamorro (0)	3	0.01
Native Hawaiian (0)	12	0.02
Samoan (1)	2	<0.01
Tongan (0)	1	<0.01
White (54,151)	54,936	94.48
Not Hispanic (53,210)	53,890	92.68
Hispanic (941)	1,046	1.80

Tonawanda

Place Type: City
County: Erie
Population: 15,130†

Ancestry‡	Population	%
American (836)	836	5.48
Arab (31)	54	0.35
Arab (18)	18	0.12
Syrian (13)	36	0.24
Austrian (22)	111	0.73
British (10)	58	0.38
Bulgarian (11)	11	0.07
Canadian (39)	139	0.91
Celtic (0)	31	0.20
Croatian (33)	48	0.31
Czech (18)	44	0.29
Czechoslovakian (9)	20	0.13
Danish (0)	65	0.43
Dutch (14)	181	1.19
English (195)	1,453	9.53
European (0)	21	0.14
French, ex. Basque (106)	749	4.91
French Canadian (44)	151	0.99
German (2,094)	6,741	44.21
German Russian (33)	33	0.22
Greek (36)	90	0.59
Hungarian (92)	345	2.26
Iranian (18)	18	0.12
Irish (582)	3,062	20.08
Italian (1,130)	3,076	20.17
Lithuanian (0)	11	0.07
Macedonian (0)	12	0.08
Pennsylvania German (46)	55	0.36
Polish (855)	2,531	16.60
Portuguese (13)	27	0.18
Romanian (0)	55	0.36
Russian (0)	26	0.17
Scotch-Irish (16)	101	0.66
Scottish (39)	226	1.48
Serbian (83)	128	0.84
Slavic (12)	12	0.08
Slovak (9)	50	0.33
Swedish (12)	164	1.08
Ukrainian (0)	30	0.20
Welsh (54)	139	0.91
Yugoslavian (0)	15	0.10

Hispanic Origin	Population	%
Hispanic or Latino (of any race)	310	2.05
Central American, ex. Mexican	14	0.09
Costa Rican	3	0.02
Guatemalan	1	0.01
Nicaraguan	1	0.01
Panamanian	7	0.05
Salvadoran	2	0.01
Cuban	4	0.03
Dominican Republic	5	0.03
Mexican	38	0.25
Puerto Rican	187	1.24
South American	28	0.19
Bolivian	1	0.01
Chilean	1	0.01
Colombian	13	0.09
Ecuadorian	8	0.05
Peruvian	3	0.02
Venezuelan	2	0.01
Other Hispanic or Latino	34	0.22

Race*	Population	%
African-American/Black (138)	205	1.35
Not Hispanic (136)	195	1.29
Hispanic (2)	10	0.07
American Indian/Alaska Native (71)	120	0.79
Not Hispanic (53)	100	0.66
Hispanic (18)	20	0.13
Alaska Athabascan *(Ala. Nat.)* (0)	1	0.01
Blackfeet (3)	12	0.08
Canadian/French Am. Ind. (4)	4	0.03
Cherokee (0)	2	0.01
Chippewa (2)	3	0.02
Creek (2)	2	0.01
Crow (0)	1	0.01
Iroquois (33)	44	0.29
Navajo (2)	2	0.01
Osage (2)	2	0.01
Spanish American Ind. (1)	1	0.01
Asian (89)	119	0.79
Not Hispanic (87)	116	0.77
Hispanic (2)	3	0.02
Chinese, ex. Taiwanese (11)	15	0.10
Filipino (9)	14	0.09
Indian (15)	17	0.11
Indonesian (2)	2	0.01
Japanese (3)	11	0.07
Korean (14)	15	0.10
Laotian (7)	7	0.05
Pakistani (5)	5	0.03
Thai (5)	5	0.03
Vietnamese (13)	14	0.09
Hawaii Native/Pacific Islander (3)	15	0.10
Not Hispanic (2)	14	0.09
Hispanic (1)	1	0.01
Fijian (1)	1	0.01
Guamanian/Chamorro (1)	1	0.01
Native Hawaiian (1)	5	0.03
White (14,619)	14,763	97.57
Not Hispanic (14,402)	14,523	95.99
Hispanic (217)	240	1.59

Tonawanda

Place Type: Town
County: Erie
Population: 73,567†

Ancestry‡	Population	%
Afghan (108)	108	0.15
African, Sub-Saharan (85)	220	0.30
African (16)	89	0.12
Ethiopian (13)	13	0.02
Ghanaian (19)	19	0.03
Kenyan (24)	86	0.12
Other Sub-Saharan African (13)	13	0.02
Albanian (48)	59	0.08
Alsatian (0)	24	0.03
American (1,511)	1,511	2.04
Arab (344)	592	0.80
Arab (21)	46	0.06
Egyptian (0)	8	0.01
Jordanian (9)	9	0.01
Lebanese (223)	428	0.58
Syrian (12)	22	0.03
Other Arab (79)	79	0.11
Armenian (68)	96	0.13
Australian (0)	29	0.04
Austrian (54)	459	0.62
Belgian (0)	13	0.02
Brazilian (0)	13	0.02
British (33)	104	0.14
Canadian (144)	312	0.42
Carpatho Rusyn (0)	13	0.02
Croatian (132)	326	0.44
Czech (42)	223	0.30
Czechoslovakian (32)	179	0.24
Danish (60)	179	0.24
Dutch (104)	872	1.18
Eastern European (44)	44	0.06
English (1,746)	7,240	9.77
European (439)	439	0.59
Finnish (49)	95	0.13
French, ex. Basque (254)	2,508	3.39
French Canadian (188)	881	1.19
German (5,590)	24,085	32.51
Greek (260)	493	0.67
Hungarian (294)	1,188	1.60
Icelander (11)	11	0.01
Irish (3,462)	15,685	21.17
Italian (9,140)	19,213	25.93
Latvian (15)	28	0.04
Lithuanian (41)	174	0.23
Macedonian (0)	18	0.02
Maltese (8)	26	0.04
Northern European (18)	18	0.02
Norwegian (60)	150	0.20
Pennsylvania German (53)	98	0.13
Polish (4,057)	11,479	15.49
Portuguese (10)	24	0.03
Romanian (77)	158	0.21
Russian (347)	745	1.01
Scandinavian (15)	15	0.02
Scotch-Irish (370)	1,170	1.58
Scottish (448)	1,915	2.58
Serbian (66)	85	0.11
Slavic (62)	123	0.17
Slovak (74)	124	0.17
Swedish (144)	758	1.02
Swiss (44)	131	0.18
Ukrainian (295)	535	0.72
Welsh (57)	429	0.58
West Indian, ex. Hispanic (49)	63	0.09
Jamaican (32)	46	0.06
Trinidadian/Tobagonian (17)	17	0.02
Yugoslavian (75)	133	0.18

Hispanic Origin	Population	%
Hispanic or Latino (of any race)	2,003	2.72
Central American, ex. Mexican	63	0.09
Costa Rican	9	0.01
Guatemalan	33	0.04
Honduran	5	0.01
Nicaraguan	3	<0.01
Panamanian	9	0.01
Salvadoran	4	0.01
Cuban	39	0.05
Dominican Republic	51	0.07
Mexican	261	0.35
Puerto Rican	1,277	1.74
South American	130	0.18
Argentinean	12	0.02
Bolivian	8	0.01
Chilean	1	<0.01
Colombian	49	0.07
Ecuadorian	27	0.04
Peruvian	20	0.03
Uruguayan	1	<0.01
Venezuelan	8	0.01
Other South American	4	0.01
Other Hispanic or Latino	182	0.25

Race*	Population	%
African-American/Black (2,234)	2,842	3.86
Not Hispanic (2,114)	2,658	3.61
Hispanic (120)	184	0.25
American Indian/Alaska Native (312)	575	0.78
Not Hispanic (266)	510	0.69
Hispanic (46)	65	0.09
Apache (0)	4	0.01
Blackfeet (2)	6	0.01

*Notes: † The Census 2010 population figure is used to calculate the percentages in the Hispanic Origin and Race categories. Ancestry percentages are based on the 2006-2010 American Community Survey population (not shown); ‡ Numbers in parentheses indicate the number of people reporting a single ancestry; * Numbers in parentheses indicate the number of persons reporting this race alone, not in combination with any other race; Please refer to the Explanation of Data for more information.*

Canadian/French Am. Ind. (7)	8	0.01
Cherokee (3)	38	0.05
Chippewa (4)	5	0.01
Choctaw (0)	8	0.01
Cree (0)	3	<0.01
Creek (0)	1	<0.01
Crow (0)	2	<0.01
Delaware (1)	1	<0.01
Iroquois (164)	256	0.35
Lumbee (0)	1	<0.01
Mexican American Ind. (2)	2	<0.01
Navajo (1)	1	<0.01
Potawatomi (5)	9	0.01
Puget Sound Salish (0)	1	<0.01
Seminole (0)	1	<0.01
Sioux (2)	5	0.01
South American Ind. (8)	14	0.02
Spanish American Ind. (2)	2	<0.01
Yaqui (1)	1	<0.01
Asian (981)	1,234	1.68
Not Hispanic (972)	1,209	1.64
Hispanic (9)	25	0.03
Bangladeshi (3)	4	0.01
Burmese (2)	3	<0.01
Cambodian (6)	6	0.01
Chinese, ex. Taiwanese (251)	290	0.39
Filipino (68)	114	0.15
Indian (287)	312	0.42
Indonesian (3)	9	0.01
Japanese (27)	59	0.08
Korean (166)	198	0.27
Laotian (13)	19	0.03
Malaysian (5)	6	0.01
Nepalese (2)	2	<0.01
Pakistani (7)	10	0.01
Sri Lankan (8)	8	0.01
Taiwanese (12)	18	0.02
Thai (13)	25	0.03
Vietnamese (68)	81	0.11
Hawaii Native/Pacific Islander (2)	38	0.05
Not Hispanic (2)	25	0.03
Hispanic (0)	13	0.02
Guamanian/Chamorro (0)	3	<0.01
Native Hawaiian (0)	16	0.02
Samoan (1)	2	<0.01
Tongan (0)	1	<0.01
White (68,462)	69,534	94.52
Not Hispanic (67,172)	68,098	92.57
Hispanic (1,290)	1,436	1.95

Troy

Place Type: City
County: Rensselaer
Population: 50,129†

Ancestry‡	Population	%
African, Sub-Saharan (643)	773	1.55
African (372)	476	0.95
Cape Verdean (0)	11	0.02
Ghanaian (91)	91	0.18
Nigerian (8)	8	0.02
Sudanese (28)	28	0.06
Other Sub-Saharan African (144)	159	0.32
Albanian (55)	55	0.11
American (1,657)	1,657	3.31
Arab (304)	439	0.88
Arab (72)	72	0.14
Egyptian (7)	44	0.09
Lebanese (204)	270	0.54
Other Arab (21)	53	0.11
Armenian (270)	418	0.84
Australian (11)	11	0.02
Austrian (42)	124	0.25
Belgian (0)	19	0.04
Brazilian (25)	42	0.08
British (97)	207	0.41
Canadian (60)	177	0.35
Celtic (0)	23	0.05
Czech (9)	182	0.36
Czechoslovakian (20)	38	0.08
Danish (37)	223	0.45
Dutch (117)	1,379	2.76
Eastern European (11)	24	0.05
English (888)	4,004	8.01
Estonian (15)	15	0.03
European (257)	529	1.06
Finnish (0)	74	0.15
French, ex. Basque (679)	4,862	9.72
French Canadian (445)	1,245	2.49
German (926)	6,417	12.83
German Russian (0)	65	0.13
Greek (161)	358	0.72
Guyanese (79)	79	0.16
Hungarian (14)	129	0.26
Irish (3,757)	12,384	24.76
Israeli (13)	13	0.03
Italian (2,238)	6,644	13.29
Latvian (19)	32	0.06
Lithuanian (30)	141	0.28
Northern European (10)	10	0.02
Norwegian (12)	134	0.27
Pennsylvania German (40)	50	0.10
Polish (733)	2,521	5.04
Portuguese (42)	81	0.16
Romanian (11)	37	0.07
Russian (74)	287	0.57
Scandinavian (8)	8	0.02
Scotch-Irish (239)	784	1.57
Scottish (304)	848	1.70
Slavic (0)	38	0.08
Slovak (0)	52	0.10
Swedish (30)	279	0.56
Swiss (0)	79	0.16
Turkish (170)	207	0.41
Ukrainian (299)	819	1.64
Welsh (67)	432	0.86
West Indian, ex. Hispanic (582)	797	1.59
Barbadian (15)	55	0.11
Belizean (0)	10	0.02
British West Indian (10)	17	0.03
Haitian (96)	109	0.22
Jamaican (230)	288	0.58
Trinidadian/Tobagonian (214)	243	0.49
West Indian (17)	62	0.12
Other West Indian (0)	13	0.03
Yugoslavian (21)	34	0.07

Hispanic Origin	Population	%
Hispanic or Latino (of any race)	3,984	7.95
Central American, ex. Mexican	153	0.31
Costa Rican	16	0.03
Guatemalan	16	0.03
Honduran	12	0.02
Nicaraguan	15	0.03
Panamanian	57	0.11
Salvadoran	37	0.07
Cuban	96	0.19
Dominican Republic	218	0.43
Mexican	400	0.80
Puerto Rican	2,598	5.18
South American	189	0.38
Argentinean	22	0.04
Bolivian	4	0.01
Chilean	6	0.01
Colombian	61	0.12
Ecuadorian	40	0.08
Paraguayan	3	0.01
Peruvian	29	0.06
Uruguayan	3	0.01
Venezuelan	20	0.04
Other South American	1	<0.01
Other Hispanic or Latino	330	0.66

Race*	Population	%
African-American/Black (8,211)	9,646	19.24
Not Hispanic (7,587)	8,756	17.47
Hispanic (624)	890	1.78
American Indian/Alaska Native (163)	531	1.06
Not Hispanic (104)	407	0.81
Hispanic (59)	124	0.25
Apache (4)	10	0.02
Blackfeet (3)	22	0.04
Canadian/French Am. Ind. (1)	2	<0.01
Central American Ind. (0)	1	<0.01
Cherokee (8)	80	0.16
Cheyenne (0)	1	<0.01
Chippewa (0)	5	0.01
Choctaw (0)	1	<0.01
Comanche (0)	2	<0.01
Creek (0)	2	<0.01
Delaware (3)	6	0.01
Iroquois (10)	55	0.11
Lumbee (1)	4	0.01
Menominee (3)	3	0.01
Mexican American Ind. (1)	3	0.01
Navajo (2)	5	0.01
Ottawa (0)	1	<0.01
Pima (1)	1	<0.01
Sioux (0)	6	0.01
South American Ind. (8)	16	0.03
Spanish American Ind. (4)	5	0.01
Tlingit-Haida *(Alaska Native)* (0)	1	<0.01
Asian (1,721)	2,066	4.12
Not Hispanic (1,687)	2,012	4.01
Hispanic (34)	54	0.11
Bangladeshi (19)	23	0.05
Burmese (28)	28	0.06
Cambodian (3)	7	0.01
Chinese, ex. Taiwanese (674)	759	1.51
Filipino (92)	157	0.31
Indian (480)	546	1.09
Indonesian (4)	5	0.01
Japanese (21)	63	0.13
Korean (127)	174	0.35
Laotian (0)	1	<0.01
Malaysian (12)	14	0.03
Nepalese (12)	12	0.02
Pakistani (72)	81	0.16
Sri Lankan (2)	6	0.01
Taiwanese (34)	39	0.08
Thai (10)	15	0.03
Vietnamese (59)	78	0.16
Hawaii Native/Pacific Islander (20)	64	0.13
Not Hispanic (15)	50	0.10
Hispanic (5)	14	0.03
Guamanian/Chamorro (4)	5	0.01
Native Hawaiian (9)	24	0.05
Samoan (0)	2	<0.01
White (36,555)	38,385	76.57
Not Hispanic (34,953)	36,446	72.70
Hispanic (1,602)	1,939	3.87

Ulster

Place Type: Town
County: Ulster
Population: 12,327†

Ancestry‡	Population	%
American (675)	675	5.42
Armenian (8)	8	0.06
Austrian (0)	38	0.31
British (11)	23	0.18
Canadian (40)	40	0.32
Cypriot (8)	8	0.06
Czech (0)	83	0.67
Danish (0)	47	0.38
Dutch (116)	729	5.85
Eastern European (8)	8	0.06
English (210)	1,422	11.42
European (119)	150	1.20
Finnish (0)	94	0.75
French, ex. Basque (137)	729	5.85
French Canadian (27)	59	0.47
German (880)	2,989	24.01
Greek (39)	77	0.62
Guyanese (8)	8	0.06
Hungarian (59)	110	0.88
Iranian (11)	11	0.09

*Notes: † The Census 2010 population figure is used to calculate the percentages in the Hispanic Origin and Race categories. Ancestry percentages are based on the 2006-2010 American Community Survey population (not shown); ‡ Numbers in parentheses indicate the number of people reporting a single ancestry; * Numbers in parentheses indicate the number of persons reporting this race alone, not in combination with any other race; Please refer to the Explanation of Data for more information.*

Irish (688)	2,410	19.36
Italian (1,420)	3,254	26.13
Latvian (0)	8	0.06
Maltese (9)	19	0.15
Norwegian (11)	149	1.20
Pennsylvania German (0)	13	0.10
Polish (450)	826	6.63
Portuguese (0)	48	0.39
Romanian (12)	49	0.39
Russian (48)	175	1.41
Scotch-Irish (33)	191	1.53
Scottish (82)	173	1.39
Slavic (0)	9	0.07
Slovak (0)	21	0.17
Swedish (9)	127	1.02
Swiss (0)	35	0.28
Ukrainian (0)	12	0.10
Welsh (0)	71	0.57
West Indian, ex. Hispanic (15)	15	0.12
Jamaican (15)	15	0.12
Yugoslavian (40)	70	0.56

Hispanic Origin	Population	%
Hispanic or Latino (of any race)	662	5.37
Central American, ex. Mexican	96	0.78
Costa Rican	4	0.03
Guatemalan	16	0.13
Honduran	7	0.06
Panamanian	10	0.08
Salvadoran	59	0.48
Cuban	23	0.19
Dominican Republic	27	0.22
Mexican	102	0.83
Puerto Rican	282	2.29
South American	65	0.53
Argentinean	4	0.03
Chilean	11	0.09
Colombian	14	0.11
Ecuadorian	7	0.06
Peruvian	21	0.17
Uruguayan	5	0.04
Venezuelan	1	0.01
Other South American	2	0.02
Other Hispanic or Latino	67	0.54

Race*	Population	%
African-American/Black (380)	555	4.50
Not Hispanic (359)	501	4.06
Hispanic (21)	54	0.44
American Indian/Alaska Native (37)	114	0.92
Not Hispanic (25)	91	0.74
Hispanic (12)	23	0.19
Blackfeet (0)	8	0.06
Canadian/French Am. Ind. (0)	1	0.01
Cherokee (2)	23	0.19
Cree (0)	1	0.01
Delaware (0)	1	0.01
Iroquois (7)	18	0.15
Mexican American Ind. (6)	6	0.05
Navajo (1)	3	0.02
Sioux (0)	1	0.01
South American Ind. (3)	3	0.02
Asian (269)	339	2.75
Not Hispanic (269)	333	2.70
Hispanic (0)	6	0.05
Bangladeshi (5)	5	0.04
Burmese (3)	3	0.02
Chinese, ex. Taiwanese (78)	88	0.71
Filipino (26)	35	0.28
Indian (65)	89	0.72
Japanese (10)	16	0.13
Korean (13)	15	0.12
Pakistani (40)	53	0.43
Taiwanese (7)	7	0.06
Thai (4)	7	0.06
Vietnamese (9)	11	0.09
Hawaii Native/Pacific Islander (1)	10	0.08
Not Hispanic (1)	8	0.06
Hispanic (0)	2	0.02
Fijian (1)	1	0.01
Native Hawaiian (0)	2	0.02
Samoan (0)	1	0.01
White (11,122)	11,412	92.58
Not Hispanic (10,739)	10,975	89.03
Hispanic (383)	437	3.55

Union

Place Type: Town
County: Broome
Population: 56,346†

Ancestry‡	Population	%
African, Sub-Saharan (117)	208	0.37
African (63)	154	0.27
Cape Verdean (11)	11	0.02
Ghanaian (30)	30	0.05
Nigerian (13)	13	0.02
Albanian (0)	7	0.01
American (2,180)	2,180	3.87
Arab (175)	231	0.41
Arab (73)	73	0.13
Egyptian (57)	69	0.12
Iraqi (6)	6	0.01
Lebanese (18)	38	0.07
Palestinian (13)	25	0.04
Other Arab (8)	20	0.04
Armenian (0)	16	0.03
Austrian (36)	297	0.53
Belgian (0)	31	0.06
British (82)	250	0.44
Cajun (3)	12	0.02
Canadian (46)	153	0.27
Carpatho Rusyn (46)	101	0.18
Celtic (0)	27	0.05
Croatian (0)	21	0.04
Czech (289)	929	1.65
Czechoslovakian (221)	364	0.65
Danish (26)	119	0.21
Dutch (410)	1,823	3.24
Eastern European (61)	83	0.15
English (2,117)	7,072	12.56
European (596)	660	1.17
Finnish (0)	10	0.02
French, ex. Basque (304)	2,044	3.63
French Canadian (268)	520	0.92
German (2,612)	10,592	18.81
Greek (128)	417	0.74
Guyanese (136)	191	0.34
Hungarian (61)	266	0.47
Iranian (0)	11	0.02
Irish (3,292)	12,320	21.88
Italian (4,117)	9,710	17.24
Latvian (12)	12	0.02
Lithuanian (124)	452	0.80
Norwegian (127)	291	0.52
Pennsylvania German (148)	197	0.35
Polish (1,489)	4,619	8.20
Portuguese (33)	59	0.10
Romanian (8)	68	0.12
Russian (582)	1,778	3.16
Scandinavian (9)	18	0.03
Scotch-Irish (171)	712	1.26
Scottish (158)	1,114	1.98
Serbian (10)	65	0.12
Slavic (250)	291	0.52
Slovak (1,272)	3,003	5.33
Slovene (18)	67	0.12
Swedish (158)	406	0.72
Swiss (12)	76	0.13
Turkish (92)	103	0.18
Ukrainian (317)	666	1.18
Welsh (184)	1,372	2.44
West Indian, ex. Hispanic (92)	189	0.34
Haitian (31)	31	0.06
Jamaican (14)	60	0.11
West Indian (47)	98	0.17
Yugoslavian (63)	83	0.15

Hispanic Origin	Population	%
Hispanic or Latino (of any race)	1,802	3.20
Central American, ex. Mexican	120	0.21
Costa Rican	15	0.03
Guatemalan	46	0.08
Honduran	22	0.04
Nicaraguan	15	0.03
Panamanian	11	0.02
Salvadoran	11	0.02
Cuban	64	0.11
Dominican Republic	108	0.19
Mexican	247	0.44
Puerto Rican	928	1.65
South American	126	0.22
Argentinean	25	0.04
Bolivian	2	<0.01
Chilean	4	0.01
Colombian	48	0.09
Ecuadorian	22	0.04
Peruvian	10	0.02
Uruguayan	5	0.01
Venezuelan	9	0.02
Other South American	1	<0.01
Other Hispanic or Latino	209	0.37

Race*	Population	%
African-American/Black (2,499)	3,402	6.04
Not Hispanic (2,338)	3,092	5.49
Hispanic (161)	310	0.55
American Indian/Alaska Native (96)	425	0.75
Not Hispanic (75)	363	0.64
Hispanic (21)	62	0.11
Apache (5)	11	0.02
Blackfeet (0)	13	0.02
Canadian/French Am. Ind. (3)	4	0.01
Cherokee (10)	56	0.10
Chippewa (2)	2	<0.01
Choctaw (1)	4	0.01
Crow (0)	1	<0.01
Delaware (1)	5	0.01
Houma (0)	1	<0.01
Iroquois (14)	53	0.09
Mexican American Ind. (2)	6	0.01
Navajo (0)	2	<0.01
Pima (0)	1	<0.01
Potawatomi (0)	2	<0.01
Seminole (0)	3	0.01
Sioux (3)	8	0.01
South American Ind. (1)	1	<0.01
Spanish American Ind. (3)	4	0.01
Yaqui (1)	1	<0.01
Asian (1,625)	1,958	3.47
Not Hispanic (1,619)	1,933	3.43
Hispanic (6)	25	0.04
Bangladeshi (3)	3	0.01
Burmese (4)	4	0.01
Cambodian (4)	5	0.01
Chinese, ex. Taiwanese (333)	405	0.72
Filipino (90)	143	0.25
Indian (291)	342	0.61
Indonesian (10)	12	0.02
Japanese (22)	55	0.10
Korean (118)	161	0.29
Laotian (355)	406	0.72
Malaysian (2)	7	0.01
Nepalese (9)	9	0.02
Pakistani (66)	68	0.12
Sri Lankan (2)	2	<0.01
Taiwanese (11)	13	0.02
Thai (14)	19	0.03
Vietnamese (215)	248	0.44
Hawaii Native/Pacific Islander (41)	77	0.14
Not Hispanic (29)	55	0.10
Hispanic (12)	22	0.04
Fijian (0)	1	<0.01
Guamanian/Chamorro (13)	16	0.03
Native Hawaiian (4)	17	0.03
Samoan (2)	5	0.01
White (50,181)	51,487	91.38
Not Hispanic (49,190)	50,317	89.30

SECTION TWO

*Notes: † The Census 2010 population figure is used to calculate the percentages in the Hispanic Origin and Race categories. Ancestry percentages are based on the 2006-2010 American Community Survey population (not shown); ‡ Numbers in parentheses indicate the number of people reporting a single ancestry; * Numbers in parentheses indicate the number of persons reporting this race alone, not in combination with any other race; Please refer to the Explanation of Data for more information.*

Hispanic (991)	1,170	2.08

Uniondale

Place Type: CDP
County: Nassau
Population: 24,759†

Ancestry‡	Population	%
African, Sub-Saharan (368)	620	2.53
African (202)	426	1.74
Nigerian (151)	179	0.73
Somalian (15)	15	0.06
American (427)	427	1.74
Armenian (40)	40	0.16
Austrian (0)	8	0.03
British (0)	35	0.14
Canadian (0)	13	0.05
Czechoslovakian (5)	5	0.02
Danish (13)	13	0.05
Dutch (19)	19	0.08
Eastern European (57)	57	0.23
English (20)	178	0.73
European (12)	12	0.05
French, ex. Basque (75)	205	0.84
German (240)	478	1.95
Greek (34)	61	0.25
Guyanese (57)	66	0.27
Hungarian (0)	21	0.09
Irish (171)	721	2.94
Israeli (30)	90	0.37
Italian (604)	809	3.30
Lithuanian (13)	24	0.10
Norwegian (0)	8	0.03
Polish (107)	249	1.02
Portuguese (0)	42	0.17
Romanian (0)	13	0.05
Russian (79)	139	0.57
Scandinavian (0)	7	0.03
Scotch-Irish (113)	113	0.46
Scottish (0)	52	0.21
Slavic (0)	10	0.04
Swedish (0)	11	0.04
Swiss (0)	24	0.10
Turkish (11)	11	0.04
Ukrainian (20)	40	0.16
West Indian, ex. Hispanic (4,400)	5,218	21.30
Bahamian (0)	18	0.07
Barbadian (109)	168	0.69
Belizean (0)	19	0.08
British West Indian (61)	166	0.68
Haitian (1,705)	1,927	7.87
Jamaican (1,725)	1,905	7.78
Trinidadian/Tobagonian (367)	458	1.87
West Indian (433)	557	2.27

Hispanic Origin	Population	%
Hispanic or Latino (of any race)	9,616	38.84
Central American, ex. Mexican	6,264	25.30
Costa Rican	32	0.13
Guatemalan	338	1.37
Honduran	806	3.26
Nicaraguan	16	0.06
Panamanian	55	0.22
Salvadoran	4,998	20.19
Other Central American	19	0.08
Cuban	71	0.29
Dominican Republic	601	2.43
Mexican	253	1.02
Puerto Rican	598	2.42
South American	741	2.99
Argentinean	25	0.10
Bolivian	5	0.02
Chilean	16	0.06
Colombian	290	1.17
Ecuadorian	304	1.23
Peruvian	66	0.27
Uruguayan	14	0.06
Venezuelan	16	0.06
Other South American	5	0.02
Other Hispanic or Latino	1,088	4.39

Race*	Population	%
African-American/Black (12,020)	12,471	50.37
Not Hispanic (11,581)	11,878	47.97
Hispanic (439)	593	2.40
American Indian/Alaska Native (160)	327	1.32
Not Hispanic (60)	144	0.58
Hispanic (100)	183	0.74
Blackfeet (3)	9	0.04
Central American Ind. (6)	13	0.05
Cherokee (1)	35	0.14
Cheyenne (0)	1	<0.01
Creek (0)	4	0.02
Iroquois (8)	14	0.06
Mexican American Ind. (2)	2	0.01
Seminole (1)	2	0.01
Sioux (0)	1	<0.01
South American Ind. (2)	4	0.02
Spanish American Ind. (5)	8	0.03
Tohono O'Odham (6)	6	0.02
Asian (507)	674	2.72
Not Hispanic (499)	639	2.58
Hispanic (8)	35	0.14
Bangladeshi (16)	19	0.08
Burmese (2)	6	0.02
Cambodian (2)	3	0.01
Chinese, ex. Taiwanese (79)	102	0.41
Filipino (86)	101	0.41
Hmong (0)	1	<0.01
Indian (214)	284	1.15
Indonesian (2)	3	0.01
Japanese (7)	14	0.06
Korean (71)	77	0.31
Laotian (1)	3	0.01
Pakistani (1)	3	0.01
Sri Lankan (6)	6	0.02
Taiwanese (0)	1	<0.01
Vietnamese (11)	18	0.07
Hawaii Native/Pacific Islander (21)	42	0.17
Not Hispanic (13)	26	0.11
Hispanic (8)	16	0.06
Guamanian/Chamorro (14)	14	0.06
Native Hawaiian (2)	2	0.01
White (6,049)	6,646	26.84
Not Hispanic (2,497)	2,651	10.71
Hispanic (3,552)	3,995	16.14

Utica

Place Type: City
County: Oneida
Population: 62,235†

Ancestry‡	Population	%
Afghan (42)	42	0.07
African, Sub-Saharan (477)	594	0.96
African (272)	374	0.60
Kenyan (0)	15	0.02
Liberian (88)	88	0.14
Somalian (99)	99	0.16
Other Sub-Saharan African (18)	18	0.03
Albanian (22)	55	0.09
American (1,237)	1,237	2.00
Arab (875)	1,558	2.52
Arab (170)	198	0.32
Egyptian (22)	37	0.06
Lebanese (506)	947	1.53
Moroccan (11)	20	0.03
Palestinian (10)	10	0.02
Syrian (58)	248	0.40
Other Arab (98)	98	0.16
Armenian (18)	29	0.05
Australian (13)	13	0.02
Austrian (0)	79	0.13
Belgian (8)	8	0.01
Brazilian (10)	32	0.05
British (9)	31	0.05
Canadian (32)	61	0.10
Celtic (8)	16	0.03
Croatian (12)	86	0.14
Czech (0)	79	0.13
Czechoslovakian (22)	22	0.04
Danish (12)	45	0.07
Dutch (149)	884	1.43
Eastern European (11)	20	0.03
English (812)	3,140	5.08
European (98)	108	0.17
Finnish (17)	17	0.03
French, ex. Basque (167)	2,016	3.26
French Canadian (219)	620	1.00
German (1,489)	7,355	11.89
Greek (57)	225	0.36
Guyanese (8)	8	0.01
Hungarian (37)	118	0.19
Icelander (0)	14	0.02
Iranian (23)	23	0.04
Irish (2,616)	9,380	15.17
Italian (7,837)	14,163	22.90
Lithuanian (43)	76	0.12
Macedonian (21)	21	0.03
Norwegian (9)	50	0.08
Pennsylvania German (13)	13	0.02
Polish (2,611)	5,408	8.75
Portuguese (27)	114	0.18
Romanian (51)	103	0.17
Russian (655)	862	1.39
Scandinavian (0)	48	0.08
Scotch-Irish (110)	254	0.41
Scottish (68)	351	0.57
Serbian (0)	82	0.13
Slovak (51)	59	0.10
Swedish (0)	89	0.14
Swiss (32)	74	0.12
Ukrainian (359)	505	0.82
Welsh (120)	775	1.25
West Indian, ex. Hispanic (681)	952	1.54
Barbadian (21)	21	0.03
British West Indian (0)	28	0.05
Haitian (168)	286	0.46
Jamaican (325)	420	0.68
Trinidadian/Tobagonian (81)	111	0.18
West Indian (86)	86	0.14
Yugoslavian (3,075)	3,231	5.23

Hispanic Origin	Population	%
Hispanic or Latino (of any race)	6,555	10.53
Central American, ex. Mexican	272	0.44
Costa Rican	9	0.01
Guatemalan	8	0.01
Honduran	46	0.07
Nicaraguan	11	0.02
Panamanian	25	0.04
Salvadoran	163	0.26
Other Central American	10	0.02
Cuban	89	0.14
Dominican Republic	940	1.51
Mexican	243	0.39
Puerto Rican	4,220	6.78
South American	231	0.37
Argentinean	7	0.01
Bolivian	2	<0.01
Chilean	7	0.01
Colombian	43	0.07
Ecuadorian	100	0.16
Paraguayan	1	<0.01
Peruvian	35	0.06
Uruguayan	3	<0.01
Venezuelan	31	0.05
Other South American	2	<0.01
Other Hispanic or Latino	560	0.90

Race*	Population	%
African-American/Black (9,501)	11,107	17.85
Not Hispanic (8,851)	10,139	16.29
Hispanic (650)	968	1.56
American Indian/Alaska Native (180)	581	0.93
Not Hispanic (123)	432	0.69
Hispanic (57)	149	0.24
Aleut *(Alaska Native)* (1)	1	<0.01

*Notes: † The Census 2010 population figure is used to calculate the percentages in the Hispanic Origin and Race categories. Ancestry percentages are based on the 2006-2010 American Community Survey population (not shown); ‡ Numbers in parentheses indicate the number of people reporting a single ancestry; * Numbers in parentheses indicate the number of persons reporting this race alone, not in combination with any other race; Please refer to the Explanation of Data for more information.*

Apache (4)	7	0.01
Blackfeet (0)	17	0.03
Canadian/French Am. Ind. (0)	6	0.01
Central American Ind. (8)	8	0.01
Cherokee (5)	56	0.09
Cheyenne (0)	4	0.01
Chickasaw (0)	1	<0.01
Chippewa (2)	8	0.01
Choctaw (0)	3	<0.01
Creek (0)	1	<0.01
Crow (0)	3	<0.01
Delaware (0)	1	<0.01
Iroquois (42)	94	0.15
Kiowa (0)	2	<0.01
Lumbee (1)	1	<0.01
Navajo (1)	2	<0.01
Paiute (1)	1	<0.01
Pima (0)	1	<0.01
Pueblo (1)	1	<0.01
Shoshone (0)	1	<0.01
Sioux (10)	29	0.05
South American Ind. (4)	15	0.02
Tlingit-Haida *(Alaska Native)* (1)	4	0.01
Asian (4,626)	5,009	8.05
Not Hispanic (4,594)	4,936	7.93
Hispanic (32)	73	0.12
Bhutanese (30)	36	0.06
Burmese (2,198)	2,317	3.72
Cambodian (412)	480	0.77
Chinese, ex. Taiwanese (140)	200	0.32
Filipino (37)	83	0.13
Indian (273)	368	0.59
Japanese (44)	66	0.11
Korean (107)	133	0.21
Laotian (42)	72	0.12
Malaysian (2)	2	<0.01
Nepalese (6)	12	0.02
Pakistani (41)	46	0.07
Sri Lankan (2)	2	<0.01
Taiwanese (1)	2	<0.01
Thai (34)	50	0.08
Vietnamese (932)	1,022	1.64
Hawaii Native/Pacific Islander (36)	137	0.22
Not Hispanic (16)	95	0.15
Hispanic (20)	42	0.07
Guamanian/Chamorro (10)	18	0.03
Native Hawaiian (12)	20	0.03
Samoan (9)	18	0.03
Tongan (1)	1	<0.01
White (42,945)	45,066	72.41
Not Hispanic (40,164)	41,788	67.15
Hispanic (2,781)	3,278	5.27

Valley Cottage

Place Type: CDP
County: Rockland
Population: 9,107†

Ancestry‡	Population	%
African, Sub-Saharan (27)	42	0.44
African (27)	42	0.44
Albanian (42)	42	0.44
American (432)	432	4.57
Arab (88)	88	0.93
Lebanese (88)	88	0.93
Austrian (19)	164	1.74
Belgian (0)	25	0.26
Brazilian (0)	26	0.28
Canadian (34)	34	0.36
Czech (0)	18	0.19
Danish (9)	21	0.22
Dutch (44)	96	1.02
Eastern European (82)	101	1.07
English (90)	501	5.30
European (61)	61	0.65
French, ex. Basque (8)	54	0.57
French Canadian (0)	9	0.10
German (129)	891	9.43
Greek (0)	12	0.13
Guyanese (0)	18	0.19
Hungarian (30)	45	0.48
Iranian (15)	15	0.16
Irish (587)	1,599	16.92
Italian (1,418)	2,465	26.09
Lithuanian (14)	27	0.29
Norwegian (0)	9	0.10
Polish (135)	465	4.92
Russian (248)	522	5.52
Scotch-Irish (82)	107	1.13
Scottish (10)	108	1.14
Serbian (11)	11	0.12
Swedish (0)	39	0.41
Turkish (12)	12	0.13
Ukrainian (42)	89	0.94
Welsh (0)	38	0.40
West Indian, ex. Hispanic (90)	117	1.24
Haitian (27)	27	0.29
Trinidadian/Tobagonian (63)	90	0.95
Yugoslavian (11)	11	0.12

Hispanic Origin	Population	%
Hispanic or Latino (of any race)	994	10.91
Central American, ex. Mexican	149	1.64
Costa Rican	2	0.02
Guatemalan	23	0.25
Honduran	8	0.09
Nicaraguan	2	0.02
Panamanian	7	0.08
Salvadoran	105	1.15
Other Central American	2	0.02
Cuban	58	0.64
Dominican Republic	98	1.08
Mexican	56	0.61
Puerto Rican	448	4.92
South American	95	1.04
Argentinean	21	0.23
Bolivian	5	0.05
Chilean	7	0.08
Colombian	29	0.32
Ecuadorian	16	0.18
Peruvian	14	0.15
Uruguayan	2	0.02
Other South American	1	0.01
Other Hispanic or Latino	90	0.99

Race*	Population	%
African-American/Black (520)	645	7.08
Not Hispanic (470)	553	6.07
Hispanic (50)	92	1.01
American Indian/Alaska Native (24)	61	0.67
Not Hispanic (14)	45	0.49
Hispanic (10)	16	0.18
Blackfeet (0)	1	0.01
Central American Ind. (0)	1	0.01
Cherokee (0)	7	0.08
Choctaw (0)	4	0.04
Delaware (0)	2	0.02
Mexican American Ind. (0)	2	0.02
Navajo (0)	1	0.01
South American Ind. (2)	4	0.04
Asian (971)	1,087	11.94
Not Hispanic (964)	1,069	11.74
Hispanic (7)	18	0.20
Bangladeshi (4)	4	0.04
Cambodian (3)	3	0.03
Chinese, ex. Taiwanese (75)	95	1.04
Filipino (452)	485	5.33
Indian (327)	373	4.10
Japanese (17)	27	0.30
Korean (47)	48	0.53
Pakistani (19)	19	0.21
Taiwanese (1)	3	0.03
Thai (13)	13	0.14
Vietnamese (9)	9	0.10
Hawaii Native/Pacific Islander (0)	7	0.08
Not Hispanic (0)	7	0.08
White (7,109)	7,291	80.06
Not Hispanic (6,466)	6,588	72.34
Hispanic (643)	703	7.72

Valley Stream

Place Type: Village
County: Nassau
Population: 37,511†

Ancestry‡	Population	%
African, Sub-Saharan (269)	390	1.05
African (223)	276	0.75
Ethiopian (23)	91	0.25
Nigerian (23)	23	0.06
Albanian (236)	236	0.64
American (696)	696	1.88
Arab (50)	138	0.37
Arab (0)	7	0.02
Egyptian (8)	8	0.02
Lebanese (18)	76	0.21
Moroccan (8)	8	0.02
Palestinian (0)	23	0.06
Other Arab (16)	16	0.04
Armenian (84)	84	0.23
Austrian (9)	97	0.26
Brazilian (24)	24	0.06
British (12)	27	0.07
Canadian (35)	35	0.09
Cypriot (68)	68	0.18
Czech (8)	55	0.15
Czechoslovakian (64)	194	0.52
Dutch (26)	211	0.57
Eastern European (76)	76	0.21
English (104)	691	1.87
European (153)	160	0.43
Finnish (0)	34	0.09
French, ex. Basque (7)	169	0.46
French Canadian (74)	142	0.38
German (574)	3,170	8.57
Greek (233)	390	1.05
Guyanese (608)	840	2.27
Hungarian (77)	186	0.50
Iranian (8)	15	0.04
Irish (1,118)	4,229	11.44
Israeli (47)	76	0.21
Italian (5,115)	7,999	21.63
Lithuanian (141)	217	0.59
Macedonian (15)	15	0.04
Northern European (0)	11	0.03
Norwegian (29)	239	0.65
Polish (398)	998	2.70
Portuguese (34)	56	0.15
Romanian (0)	58	0.16
Russian (291)	570	1.54
Scotch-Irish (67)	192	0.52
Scottish (12)	67	0.18
Slovak (0)	11	0.03
Swedish (41)	202	0.55
Swiss (13)	155	0.42
Turkish (57)	57	0.15
Ukrainian (9)	29	0.08
West Indian, ex. Hispanic (3,010)	3,754	10.15
Barbadian (11)	30	0.08
Belizean (19)	19	0.05
British West Indian (43)	139	0.38
Haitian (1,519)	1,727	4.67
Jamaican (1,127)	1,248	3.37
Trinidadian/Tobagonian (177)	177	0.48
West Indian (114)	414	1.12
Yugoslavian (67)	130	0.35

Hispanic Origin	Population	%
Hispanic or Latino (of any race)	8,344	22.24
Central American, ex. Mexican	1,565	4.17
Costa Rican	73	0.19
Guatemalan	302	0.81
Honduran	155	0.41
Nicaraguan	46	0.12
Panamanian	110	0.29
Salvadoran	873	2.33
Other Central American	6	0.02
Cuban	207	0.55
Dominican Republic	1,281	3.41

SECTION TWO

*Notes: † The Census 2010 population figure is used to calculate the percentages in the Hispanic Origin and Race categories. Ancestry percentages are based on the 2006-2010 American Community Survey population (not shown); ‡ Numbers in parentheses indicate the number of people reporting a single ancestry; * Numbers in parentheses indicate the number of persons reporting this race alone, not in combination with any other race; Please refer to the Explanation of Data for more information.*

Mexican	253	0.67
Puerto Rican	1,706	4.55
South American	2,609	6.96
Argentinean	98	0.26
Bolivian	74	0.20
Chilean	211	0.56
Colombian	944	2.52
Ecuadorian	650	1.73
Paraguayan	18	0.05
Peruvian	513	1.37
Uruguayan	30	0.08
Venezuelan	44	0.12
Other South American	27	0.07
Other Hispanic or Latino	723	1.93

Race*	Population	%
African-American/Black (6,967)	7,490	19.97
Not Hispanic (6,544)	6,896	18.38
Hispanic (423)	594	1.58
American Indian/Alaska Native (114)	270	0.72
Not Hispanic (57)	128	0.34
Hispanic (57)	142	0.38
Apache (0)	3	0.01
Blackfeet (0)	3	0.01
Canadian/French Am. Ind. (4)	4	0.01
Cherokee (2)	20	0.05
Crow (0)	1	<0.01
Delaware (3)	3	0.01
Iroquois (5)	8	0.02
Mexican American Ind. (5)	12	0.03
Pueblo (2)	2	0.01
Shoshone (0)	1	<0.01
Sioux (1)	2	0.01
South American Ind. (23)	36	0.10
Asian (4,269)	4,718	12.58
Not Hispanic (4,237)	4,602	12.27
Hispanic (32)	116	0.31
Bangladeshi (62)	68	0.18
Chinese, ex. Taiwanese (629)	719	1.92
Filipino (880)	943	2.51
Indian (1,498)	1,670	4.45
Indonesian (2)	4	0.01
Japanese (33)	46	0.12
Korean (234)	254	0.68
Malaysian (4)	4	0.01
Nepalese (1)	3	0.01
Pakistani (674)	733	1.95
Sri Lankan (13)	14	0.04
Taiwanese (68)	78	0.21
Thai (11)	15	0.04
Vietnamese (28)	36	0.10
Hawaii Native/Pacific Islander (19)	101	0.27
Not Hispanic (7)	61	0.16
Hispanic (12)	40	0.11
Fijian (2)	3	0.01
Guamanian/Chamorro (12)	14	0.04
Native Hawaiian (0)	3	0.01
Samoan (1)	2	0.01
White (21,475)	22,303	59.46
Not Hispanic (17,241)	17,600	46.92
Hispanic (4,234)	4,703	12.54

Van Buren

Place Type: Town
County: Onondaga
Population: 13,185†

Ancestry‡	Population	%
American (353)	353	2.71
Arab (11)	44	0.34
Lebanese (11)	44	0.34
Armenian (0)	86	0.66
Austrian (22)	52	0.40
British (21)	32	0.25
Canadian (10)	68	0.52
Czech (31)	46	0.35
Dutch (12)	213	1.63
English (508)	2,154	16.51
European (33)	51	0.39
Finnish (0)	32	0.25
French, ex. Basque (138)	1,253	9.61
French Canadian (103)	394	3.02
German (714)	3,261	25.00
Greek (82)	275	2.11
Hungarian (0)	11	0.08
Irish (855)	3,402	26.08
Italian (649)	2,045	15.68
Lithuanian (0)	9	0.07
Macedonian (20)	56	0.43
Northern European (51)	51	0.39
Norwegian (8)	32	0.25
Pennsylvania German (16)	16	0.12
Polish (600)	1,555	11.92
Portuguese (32)	44	0.34
Russian (24)	133	1.02
Scotch-Irish (43)	306	2.35
Scottish (86)	441	3.38
Slovene (0)	15	0.12
Swedish (9)	97	0.74
Swiss (0)	56	0.43
Ukrainian (99)	162	1.24
Welsh (42)	309	2.37
Yugoslavian (14)	14	0.11

Hispanic Origin	Population	%
Hispanic or Latino (of any race)	233	1.77
Central American, ex. Mexican	26	0.20
Costa Rican	2	0.02
Guatemalan	10	0.08
Honduran	4	0.03
Panamanian	9	0.07
Salvadoran	1	0.01
Cuban	13	0.10
Dominican Republic	5	0.04
Mexican	56	0.42
Puerto Rican	91	0.69
South American	18	0.14
Colombian	2	0.02
Ecuadorian	9	0.07
Peruvian	4	0.03
Venezuelan	3	0.02
Other Hispanic or Latino	24	0.18

Race*	Population	%
African-American/Black (155)	226	1.71
Not Hispanic (139)	204	1.55
Hispanic (16)	22	0.17
American Indian/Alaska Native (56)	153	1.16
Not Hispanic (53)	147	1.11
Hispanic (3)	6	0.05
Apache (0)	1	0.01
Blackfeet (2)	4	0.03
Canadian/French Am. Ind. (0)	1	0.01
Cherokee (0)	4	0.03
Chickasaw (0)	1	0.01
Chippewa (1)	1	0.01
Delaware (0)	2	0.02
Hopi (0)	3	0.02
Iroquois (32)	78	0.59
Mexican American Ind. (1)	1	0.01
Sioux (0)	4	0.03
Asian (92)	129	0.98
Not Hispanic (92)	127	0.96
Hispanic (0)	2	0.02
Bangladeshi (3)	3	0.02
Chinese, ex. Taiwanese (19)	22	0.17
Filipino (20)	24	0.18
Indian (21)	28	0.21
Indonesian (0)	1	0.01
Japanese (1)	1	0.01
Korean (18)	32	0.24
Taiwanese (1)	4	0.03
Thai (5)	5	0.04
Vietnamese (2)	3	0.02
Hawaii Native/Pacific Islander (2)	3	0.02
Not Hispanic (2)	3	0.02
Guamanian/Chamorro (1)	1	0.01
Native Hawaiian (0)	1	0.01
Samoan (0)	1	0.01
White (12,617)	12,814	97.19
Not Hispanic (12,470)	12,651	95.95
Hispanic (147)	163	1.24

Vestal

Place Type: Town
County: Broome
Population: 28,043†

Ancestry‡	Population	%
African, Sub-Saharan (136)	148	0.53
African (123)	135	0.48
Ghanaian (13)	13	0.05
Albanian (13)	13	0.05
Alsatian (0)	13	0.05
American (743)	743	2.65
Arab (142)	229	0.82
Egyptian (0)	24	0.09
Lebanese (116)	132	0.47
Syrian (9)	9	0.03
Other Arab (17)	64	0.23
Armenian (88)	97	0.35
Australian (39)	39	0.14
Austrian (32)	176	0.63
Belgian (15)	33	0.12
British (85)	160	0.57
Bulgarian (55)	55	0.20
Canadian (24)	24	0.09
Carpatho Rusyn (18)	18	0.06
Czech (101)	311	1.11
Czechoslovakian (34)	74	0.26
Danish (36)	94	0.34
Dutch (120)	771	2.75
Eastern European (173)	198	0.71
English (979)	3,580	12.78
European (236)	244	0.87
Finnish (0)	11	0.04
French, ex. Basque (12)	556	1.98
French Canadian (28)	120	0.43
German (1,207)	4,493	16.03
Greek (100)	202	0.72
Guyanese (12)	12	0.04
Hungarian (0)	104	0.37
Iranian (24)	24	0.09
Irish (1,823)	5,197	18.55
Israeli (0)	26	0.09
Italian (1,380)	3,391	12.10
Lithuanian (13)	70	0.25
Macedonian (53)	53	0.19
Northern European (28)	28	0.10
Norwegian (18)	163	0.58
Pennsylvania German (35)	106	0.38
Polish (716)	2,329	8.31
Portuguese (21)	21	0.07
Romanian (26)	64	0.23
Russian (383)	1,253	4.47
Scandinavian (23)	47	0.17
Scotch-Irish (88)	356	1.27
Scottish (81)	349	1.25
Slavic (82)	130	0.46
Slovak (227)	455	1.62
Slovene (11)	30	0.11
Swedish (87)	327	1.17
Swiss (23)	225	0.80
Turkish (24)	36	0.13
Ukrainian (203)	373	1.33
Welsh (197)	573	2.04
West Indian, ex. Hispanic (292)	342	1.22
British West Indian (0)	26	0.09
Haitian (94)	106	0.38
Jamaican (185)	197	0.70
West Indian (13)	13	0.05

Hispanic Origin	Population	%
Hispanic or Latino (of any race)	934	3.33
Central American, ex. Mexican	85	0.30
Costa Rican	8	0.03
Guatemalan	19	0.07
Honduran	16	0.06

*Notes: † The Census 2010 population figure is used to calculate the percentages in the Hispanic Origin and Race categories. Ancestry percentages are based on the 2006-2010 American Community Survey population (not shown); ‡ Numbers in parentheses indicate the number of people reporting a single ancestry; * Numbers in parentheses indicate the number of persons reporting this race alone, not in combination with any other race; Please refer to the Explanation of Data for more information.*

Nicaraguan	3	0.01
Panamanian	21	0.07
Salvadoran	18	0.06
Cuban	54	0.19
Dominican Republic	124	0.44
Mexican	73	0.26
Puerto Rican	291	1.04
South American	210	0.75
Argentinean	34	0.12
Bolivian	6	0.02
Chilean	14	0.05
Colombian	60	0.21
Ecuadorian	50	0.18
Paraguayan	4	0.01
Peruvian	33	0.12
Uruguayan	1	<0.01
Venezuelan	6	0.02
Other South American	2	0.01
Other Hispanic or Latino	97	0.35

Race*	Population	%
African-American/Black (908)	1,071	3.82
Not Hispanic (828)	961	3.43
Hispanic (80)	110	0.39
American Indian/Alaska Native (44)	154	0.55
Not Hispanic (41)	132	0.47
Hispanic (3)	22	0.08
Apache (0)	3	0.01
Blackfeet (2)	7	0.02
Canadian/French Am. Ind. (1)	1	<0.01
Cherokee (3)	13	0.05
Chippewa (0)	1	<0.01
Choctaw (1)	3	0.01
Creek (1)	2	0.01
Crow (0)	3	0.01
Delaware (0)	9	0.03
Iroquois (13)	27	0.10
Mexican American Ind. (1)	2	0.01
Sioux (0)	2	0.01
South American Ind. (0)	6	0.02
Asian (3,039)	3,286	11.72
Not Hispanic (3,031)	3,263	11.64
Hispanic (8)	23	0.08
Bangladeshi (32)	33	0.12
Burmese (8)	8	0.03
Cambodian (0)	2	0.01
Chinese, ex. Taiwanese (1,146)	1,240	4.42
Filipino (121)	163	0.58
Indian (684)	738	2.63
Indonesian (7)	12	0.04
Japanese (55)	82	0.29
Korean (667)	706	2.52
Laotian (7)	12	0.04
Malaysian (3)	5	0.02
Nepalese (5)	6	0.02
Pakistani (105)	110	0.39
Sri Lankan (9)	17	0.06
Taiwanese (53)	65	0.23
Thai (7)	12	0.04
Vietnamese (39)	55	0.20
Hawaii Native/Pacific Islander (11)	36	0.13
Not Hispanic (8)	28	0.10
Hispanic (3)	8	0.03
Fijian (0)	1	<0.01
Guamanian/Chamorro (2)	5	0.02
Native Hawaiian (3)	7	0.02
Samoan (0)	1	<0.01
Tongan (1)	1	<0.01
White (23,249)	23,686	84.46
Not Hispanic (22,735)	23,104	82.39
Hispanic (514)	582	2.08

Victor

Place Type: Town
County: Ontario
Population: 14,275†

Ancestry‡	Population	%
American (702)	702	5.22
Arab (7)	46	0.34
Lebanese (7)	7	0.05
Palestinian (0)	14	0.10
Syrian (0)	25	0.19
Armenian (14)	14	0.10
Austrian (38)	93	0.69
Belgian (0)	12	0.09
Brazilian (0)	11	0.08
British (66)	120	0.89
Canadian (37)	43	0.32
Czech (16)	77	0.57
Danish (11)	88	0.65
Dutch (180)	651	4.84
Eastern European (46)	86	0.64
English (781)	2,795	20.80
European (339)	339	2.52
Finnish (8)	8	0.06
French, ex. Basque (99)	669	4.98
French Canadian (38)	104	0.77
German (855)	3,911	29.10
Greek (26)	54	0.40
Hungarian (13)	22	0.16
Irish (559)	2,453	18.25
Italian (1,069)	2,357	17.54
Lithuanian (15)	24	0.18
Norwegian (73)	138	1.03
Pennsylvania German (9)	28	0.21
Polish (273)	1,083	8.06
Russian (32)	78	0.58
Scandinavian (38)	103	0.77
Scotch-Irish (27)	63	0.47
Scottish (74)	391	2.91
Serbian (11)	11	0.08
Slavic (0)	10	0.07
Slovak (67)	139	1.03
Swedish (43)	163	1.21
Swiss (0)	83	0.62
Ukrainian (9)	240	1.79
Welsh (55)	175	1.30
West Indian, ex. Hispanic (10)	10	0.07
Jamaican (10)	10	0.07
Yugoslavian (19)	19	0.14

Hispanic Origin	Population	%
Hispanic or Latino (of any race)	268	1.88
Central American, ex. Mexican	30	0.21
Guatemalan	13	0.09
Honduran	3	0.02
Nicaraguan	1	0.01
Panamanian	8	0.06
Salvadoran	5	0.04
Cuban	21	0.15
Dominican Republic	13	0.09
Mexican	69	0.48
Puerto Rican	72	0.50
South American	49	0.34
Argentinean	7	0.05
Bolivian	1	0.01
Chilean	1	0.01
Colombian	26	0.18
Ecuadorian	5	0.04
Peruvian	5	0.04
Venezuelan	4	0.03
Other Hispanic or Latino	14	0.10

Race*	Population	%
African-American/Black (117)	187	1.31
Not Hispanic (110)	173	1.21
Hispanic (7)	14	0.10
American Indian/Alaska Native (31)	73	0.51
Not Hispanic (31)	72	0.50
Hispanic (0)	1	0.01
Alaska Athabascan *(Ala. Nat.)* (1)	1	0.01
Cherokee (0)	5	0.04
Delaware (0)	1	0.01
Iroquois (23)	35	0.25
Asian (324)	389	2.73
Not Hispanic (323)	386	2.70
Hispanic (1)	3	0.02
Burmese (1)	1	0.01
Cambodian (5)	5	0.04
Chinese, ex. Taiwanese (62)	73	0.51
Filipino (25)	34	0.24
Indian (103)	112	0.78
Indonesian (0)	5	0.04
Japanese (9)	17	0.12
Korean (47)	65	0.46
Laotian (1)	2	0.01
Pakistani (17)	18	0.13
Taiwanese (5)	5	0.04
Thai (2)	2	0.01
Vietnamese (34)	38	0.27
Hawaii Native/Pacific Islander (7)	14	0.10
Not Hispanic (3)	10	0.07
Hispanic (4)	4	0.03
Native Hawaiian (5)	6	0.04
White (13,572)	13,733	96.20
Not Hispanic (13,362)	13,515	94.68
Hispanic (210)	218	1.53

Wading River

Place Type: CDP
County: Suffolk
Population: 7,719†

Ancestry‡	Population	%
African, Sub-Saharan (61)	81	0.99
African (46)	66	0.81
South African (15)	15	0.18
American (301)	301	3.69
Arab (0)	26	0.32
Lebanese (0)	26	0.32
Armenian (0)	15	0.18
Austrian (0)	23	0.28
Bulgarian (17)	32	0.39
Canadian (11)	11	0.13
Croatian (0)	43	0.53
Czech (11)	41	0.50
Czechoslovakian (0)	19	0.23
Dutch (22)	97	1.19
Eastern European (46)	46	0.56
English (135)	706	8.66
Finnish (17)	17	0.21
French, ex. Basque (37)	207	2.54
French Canadian (0)	32	0.39
German (308)	1,248	15.30
Greek (67)	85	1.04
Hungarian (11)	21	0.26
Irish (655)	2,402	29.45
Italian (1,035)	2,594	31.80
Latvian (0)	14	0.17
Lithuanian (0)	5	0.06
Norwegian (37)	82	1.01
Polish (306)	693	8.50
Portuguese (15)	56	0.69
Romanian (47)	62	0.76
Russian (81)	242	2.97
Scotch-Irish (125)	197	2.42
Scottish (0)	180	2.21
Slavic (20)	20	0.25
Swedish (0)	129	1.58
Turkish (178)	178	2.18
Ukrainian (36)	69	0.85
Welsh (0)	79	0.97

Hispanic Origin	Population	%
Hispanic or Latino (of any race)	349	4.52
Central American, ex. Mexican	43	0.56
Costa Rican	1	0.01
Guatemalan	23	0.30
Honduran	1	0.01
Panamanian	6	0.08
Salvadoran	12	0.16
Cuban	20	0.26
Dominican Republic	8	0.10
Mexican	33	0.43
Puerto Rican	155	2.01
South American	31	0.40
Argentinean	2	0.03

*Notes: † The Census 2010 population figure is used to calculate the percentages in the Hispanic Origin and Race categories. Ancestry percentages are based on the 2006-2010 American Community Survey population (not shown); ‡ Numbers in parentheses indicate the number of people reporting a single ancestry; * Numbers in parentheses indicate the number of persons reporting this race alone, not in combination with any other race; Please refer to the Explanation of Data for more information.*

Chilean	2	0.03
Colombian	7	0.09
Ecuadorian	5	0.06
Paraguayan	1	0.01
Peruvian	13	0.17
Uruguayan	1	0.01
Other Hispanic or Latino	59	0.76

Race*	Population	%
African-American/Black (157)	195	2.53
Not Hispanic (150)	184	2.38
Hispanic (7)	11	0.14
American Indian/Alaska Native (5)	25	0.32
Not Hispanic (2)	19	0.25
Hispanic (3)	6	0.08
Alaska Athabascan *(Ala. Nat.)* (0)	1	0.01
Blackfeet (0)	1	0.01
Cherokee (0)	1	0.01
Chickasaw (0)	1	0.01
Mexican American Ind. (1)	3	0.04
Sioux (0)	1	0.01
South American Ind. (2)	3	0.04
Asian (80)	140	1.81
Not Hispanic (71)	124	1.61
Hispanic (9)	16	0.21
Chinese, ex. Taiwanese (32)	41	0.53
Filipino (14)	22	0.29
Indian (4)	12	0.16
Japanese (8)	17	0.22
Korean (15)	25	0.32
Laotian (2)	4	0.05
Pakistani (4)	10	0.13
Thai (1)	4	0.05
Hawaii Native/Pacific Islander (2)	3	0.04
Not Hispanic (1)	2	0.03
Hispanic (1)	1	0.01
Native Hawaiian (2)	2	0.03
Samoan (0)	1	0.01
White (7,292)	7,407	95.96
Not Hispanic (7,031)	7,124	92.29
Hispanic (261)	283	3.67

Wallkill

Place Type: Town
County: Orange
Population: 27,426†

Ancestry‡	Population	%
African, Sub-Saharan (410)	435	1.60
African (350)	375	1.38
Nigerian (45)	45	0.17
Other Sub-Saharan African (15)	15	0.06
Albanian (8)	8	0.03
American (1,886)	1,886	6.95
Arab (32)	49	0.18
Egyptian (24)	24	0.09
Lebanese (8)	25	0.09
Armenian (39)	96	0.35
Australian (0)	46	0.17
Austrian (7)	70	0.26
Belgian (12)	12	0.04
Brazilian (0)	57	0.21
British (0)	32	0.12
Cajun (13)	13	0.05
Canadian (46)	78	0.29
Czech (15)	116	0.43
Czechoslovakian (6)	14	0.05
Danish (14)	46	0.17
Dutch (187)	706	2.60
Eastern European (10)	10	0.04
English (234)	1,400	5.16
European (200)	212	0.78
Finnish (29)	29	0.11
French, ex. Basque (43)	341	1.26
French Canadian (33)	77	0.28
German (626)	4,011	14.78
Greek (0)	92	0.34
Hungarian (6)	101	0.37
Iranian (0)	27	0.10
Irish (1,234)	5,151	18.98
Israeli (24)	54	0.20
Italian (1,951)	4,772	17.58
Latvian (36)	129	0.48
Lithuanian (7)	82	0.30
Norwegian (70)	155	0.57
Polish (379)	1,321	4.87
Portuguese (0)	11	0.04
Romanian (0)	67	0.25
Russian (31)	171	0.63
Scandinavian (0)	109	0.40
Scotch-Irish (100)	266	0.98
Scottish (43)	176	0.65
Serbian (25)	35	0.13
Slovak (11)	11	0.04
Swedish (16)	217	0.80
Swiss (13)	89	0.33
Ukrainian (51)	85	0.31
Welsh (58)	166	0.61
West Indian, ex. Hispanic (706)	1,099	4.05
Barbadian (53)	53	0.20
British West Indian (198)	296	1.09
Haitian (243)	328	1.21
Jamaican (169)	182	0.67
Trinidadian/Tobagonian (0)	183	0.67
West Indian (43)	57	0.21

Hispanic Origin	Population	%
Hispanic or Latino (of any race)	6,162	22.47
Central American, ex. Mexican	321	1.17
Costa Rican	21	0.08
Guatemalan	59	0.22
Honduran	114	0.42
Nicaraguan	16	0.06
Panamanian	46	0.17
Salvadoran	55	0.20
Other Central American	10	0.04
Cuban	125	0.46
Dominican Republic	463	1.69
Mexican	879	3.20
Puerto Rican	3,386	12.35
South American	608	2.22
Argentinean	28	0.10
Bolivian	6	0.02
Chilean	15	0.05
Colombian	301	1.10
Ecuadorian	115	0.42
Peruvian	114	0.42
Uruguayan	12	0.04
Venezuelan	14	0.05
Other South American	3	0.01
Other Hispanic or Latino	380	1.39

Race*	Population	%
African-American/Black (4,380)	5,064	18.46
Not Hispanic (3,939)	4,376	15.96
Hispanic (441)	688	2.51
American Indian/Alaska Native (137)	406	1.48
Not Hispanic (86)	280	1.02
Hispanic (51)	126	0.46
Apache (0)	1	<0.01
Blackfeet (1)	4	0.01
Canadian/French Am. Ind. (2)	2	0.01
Central American Ind. (7)	7	0.03
Cherokee (5)	33	0.12
Crow (0)	4	0.01
Delaware (24)	57	0.21
Iroquois (12)	31	0.11
Mexican American Ind. (1)	3	0.01
Navajo (0)	5	0.02
Potawatomi (0)	2	0.01
Seminole (0)	1	<0.01
Sioux (0)	3	0.01
South American Ind. (8)	28	0.10
Spanish American Ind. (2)	2	0.01
Yup'ik *(Alaska Native)* (1)	1	<0.01
Asian (871)	1,062	3.87
Not Hispanic (855)	1,007	3.67
Hispanic (16)	55	0.20
Bangladeshi (7)	15	0.05
Burmese (5)	5	0.02
Cambodian (36)	42	0.15
Chinese, ex. Taiwanese (149)	189	0.69
Filipino (149)	166	0.61
Indian (284)	332	1.21
Indonesian (1)	5	0.02
Japanese (9)	27	0.10
Korean (38)	52	0.19
Laotian (1)	1	<0.01
Pakistani (111)	117	0.43
Taiwanese (11)	14	0.05
Thai (13)	20	0.07
Vietnamese (34)	42	0.15
Hawaii Native/Pacific Islander (11)	45	0.16
Not Hispanic (8)	31	0.11
Hispanic (3)	14	0.05
Fijian (0)	1	<0.01
Guamanian/Chamorro (8)	10	0.04
Native Hawaiian (1)	8	0.03
Samoan (1)	1	<0.01
White (18,712)	19,524	71.19
Not Hispanic (15,646)	16,093	58.68
Hispanic (3,066)	3,431	12.51

Walworth

Place Type: Town
County: Wayne
Population: 9,449†

Ancestry‡	Population	%
American (426)	426	4.60
Arab (17)	48	0.52
Lebanese (17)	48	0.52
Australian (0)	57	0.62
British (63)	217	2.34
Czech (17)	58	0.63
Czechoslovakian (0)	12	0.13
Dutch (96)	534	5.77
English (348)	1,756	18.97
European (57)	96	1.04
French, ex. Basque (23)	360	3.89
French Canadian (42)	199	2.15
German (803)	3,258	35.20
Greek (67)	67	0.72
Hungarian (13)	13	0.14
Irish (250)	2,026	21.89
Italian (377)	1,907	20.60
Lithuanian (11)	26	0.28
Norwegian (0)	173	1.87
Polish (183)	679	7.34
Portuguese (46)	46	0.50
Russian (17)	36	0.39
Scotch-Irish (69)	159	1.72
Scottish (75)	434	4.69
Slovak (0)	37	0.40
Swedish (17)	84	0.91
Swiss (31)	72	0.78
Ukrainian (14)	44	0.48
Welsh (28)	163	1.76
Yugoslavian (45)	45	0.49

Hispanic Origin	Population	%
Hispanic or Latino (of any race)	179	1.89
Central American, ex. Mexican	3	0.03
Guatemalan	2	0.02
Honduran	1	0.01
Cuban	2	0.02
Dominican Republic	10	0.11
Mexican	36	0.38
Puerto Rican	103	1.09
South American	17	0.18
Bolivian	1	0.01
Colombian	12	0.13
Ecuadorian	1	0.01
Peruvian	2	0.02
Venezuelan	1	0.01
Other Hispanic or Latino	8	0.08

*Notes: † The Census 2010 population figure is used to calculate the percentages in the Hispanic Origin and Race categories. Ancestry percentages are based on the 2006-2010 American Community Survey population (not shown); ‡ Numbers in parentheses indicate the number of people reporting a single ancestry; * Numbers in parentheses indicate the number of persons reporting this race alone, not in combination with any other race; Please refer to the Explanation of Data for more information.*

Race*	Population	%
African-American/Black (85)	128	1.35
Not Hispanic (79)	121	1.28
Hispanic (6)	7	0.07
American Indian/Alaska Native (9)	51	0.54
Not Hispanic (8)	49	0.52
Hispanic (1)	2	0.02
Canadian/French Am. Ind. (0)	2	0.02
Cherokee (0)	13	0.14
Iroquois (2)	10	0.11
Mexican American Ind. (1)	1	0.01
Asian (79)	115	1.22
Not Hispanic (78)	114	1.21
Hispanic (1)	1	0.01
Cambodian (3)	6	0.06
Chinese, ex. Taiwanese (16)	25	0.26
Filipino (11)	17	0.18
Indian (18)	24	0.25
Japanese (3)	3	0.03
Korean (17)	20	0.21
Laotian (7)	7	0.07
Thai (0)	3	0.03
Vietnamese (2)	7	0.07
Hawaii Native/Pacific Islander (2)	3	0.03
Not Hispanic (2)	3	0.03
Guamanian/Chamorro (1)	1	0.01
Native Hawaiian (0)	1	0.01
Samoan (1)	1	0.01
White (9,117)	9,243	97.82
Not Hispanic (8,973)	9,085	96.15
Hispanic (144)	158	1.67

Wantagh

Place Type: CDP
County: Nassau
Population: 18,871†

Ancestry‡	Population	%
Alsatian (0)	21	0.12
American (373)	373	2.07
Arab (0)	50	0.28
Syrian (0)	50	0.28
Armenian (12)	12	0.07
Austrian (43)	95	0.53
Belgian (18)	36	0.20
British (13)	48	0.27
Celtic (0)	11	0.06
Croatian (41)	107	0.60
Czech (26)	111	0.62
Czechoslovakian (5)	69	0.38
Danish (0)	46	0.26
Dutch (9)	314	1.75
Eastern European (48)	61	0.34
English (93)	952	5.29
Estonian (11)	11	0.06
European (113)	113	0.63
Finnish (0)	33	0.18
French, ex. Basque (96)	456	2.54
French Canadian (12)	50	0.28
German (702)	3,604	20.04
German Russian (0)	17	0.09
Greek (166)	259	1.44
Hungarian (63)	258	1.43
Icelander (0)	12	0.07
Irish (1,465)	5,481	30.48
Israeli (28)	28	0.16
Italian (3,160)	6,573	36.56
Latvian (13)	13	0.07
Lithuanian (0)	27	0.15
Maltese (0)	48	0.27
Norwegian (10)	66	0.37
Pennsylvania German (0)	7	0.04
Polish (256)	1,067	5.93
Portuguese (6)	21	0.12
Romanian (28)	51	0.28
Russian (664)	1,075	5.98
Scandinavian (32)	32	0.18
Scotch-Irish (25)	187	1.04
Scottish (39)	150	0.83
Slovak (11)	24	0.13
Swedish (32)	125	0.70
Swiss (0)	12	0.07
Turkish (69)	105	0.58
Ukrainian (0)	63	0.35
Welsh (0)	10	0.06
West Indian, ex. Hispanic (0)	45	0.25
Trinidadian/Tobagonian (0)	45	0.25
Yugoslavian (0)	16	0.09

Hispanic Origin	Population	%
Hispanic or Latino (of any race)	889	4.71
Central American, ex. Mexican	104	0.55
Costa Rican	8	0.04
Guatemalan	13	0.07
Honduran	8	0.04
Nicaraguan	5	0.03
Panamanian	3	0.02
Salvadoran	67	0.36
Cuban	68	0.36
Dominican Republic	32	0.17
Mexican	77	0.41
Puerto Rican	290	1.54
South American	194	1.03
Argentinean	22	0.12
Chilean	14	0.07
Colombian	74	0.39
Ecuadorian	41	0.22
Peruvian	36	0.19
Uruguayan	5	0.03
Venezuelan	2	0.01
Other Hispanic or Latino	124	0.66

Race*	Population	%
African-American/Black (53)	80	0.42
Not Hispanic (51)	74	0.39
Hispanic (2)	6	0.03
American Indian/Alaska Native (15)	38	0.20
Not Hispanic (7)	29	0.15
Hispanic (8)	9	0.05
Cherokee (2)	10	0.05
Choctaw (0)	2	0.01
Iroquois (0)	4	0.02
Osage (0)	1	0.01
Seminole (0)	4	0.02
Sioux (0)	4	0.02
Asian (380)	490	2.60
Not Hispanic (372)	477	2.53
Hispanic (8)	13	0.07
Chinese, ex. Taiwanese (152)	198	1.05
Filipino (43)	75	0.40
Indian (80)	99	0.52
Indonesian (1)	2	0.01
Japanese (5)	7	0.04
Korean (43)	58	0.31
Pakistani (20)	29	0.15
Sri Lankan (8)	8	0.04
Taiwanese (1)	9	0.05
Thai (8)	9	0.05
Vietnamese (3)	3	0.02
Hawaii Native/Pacific Islander (1)	8	0.04
Not Hispanic (1)	8	0.04
Native Hawaiian (1)	3	0.02
White (18,112)	18,274	96.84
Not Hispanic (17,380)	17,507	92.77
Hispanic (732)	767	4.06

Wappinger

Place Type: Town
County: Dutchess
Population: 27,048†

Ancestry‡	Population	%
African, Sub-Saharan (682)	711	2.63
African (332)	344	1.27
Nigerian (204)	221	0.82
South African (9)	9	0.03
Other Sub-Saharan African (137)	137	0.51
American (640)	640	2.36
Arab (51)	51	0.19
Arab (8)	8	0.03
Jordanian (13)	13	0.05
Lebanese (30)	30	0.11
Armenian (29)	29	0.11
Austrian (8)	170	0.63
Basque (19)	19	0.07
Belgian (13)	13	0.05
British (44)	56	0.21
Canadian (17)	112	0.41
Croatian (0)	11	0.04
Czech (52)	96	0.35
Czechoslovakian (48)	68	0.25
Danish (14)	74	0.27
Dutch (93)	831	3.07
English (563)	2,223	8.21
European (137)	150	0.55
Finnish (20)	125	0.46
French, ex. Basque (48)	560	2.07
French Canadian (105)	291	1.07
German (863)	3,854	14.24
Greek (78)	292	1.08
Guyanese (22)	22	0.08
Hungarian (61)	160	0.59
Icelander (0)	13	0.05
Iranian (8)	18	0.07
Irish (1,379)	6,326	23.37
Israeli (80)	80	0.30
Italian (3,665)	7,985	29.49
Latvian (31)	43	0.16
Lithuanian (55)	124	0.46
Northern European (8)	8	0.03
Norwegian (35)	116	0.43
Pennsylvania German (0)	36	0.13
Polish (172)	1,065	3.93
Portuguese (113)	154	0.57
Romanian (8)	42	0.16
Russian (24)	314	1.16
Scandinavian (14)	14	0.05
Scotch-Irish (201)	322	1.19
Scottish (182)	315	1.16
Slovak (0)	45	0.17
Slovene (10)	20	0.07
Swedish (10)	256	0.95
Swiss (0)	46	0.17
Turkish (36)	75	0.28
Ukrainian (54)	139	0.51
Welsh (0)	40	0.15
West Indian, ex. Hispanic (432)	883	3.26
Barbadian (0)	26	0.10
Haitian (0)	116	0.43
Jamaican (425)	708	2.62
Trinidadian/Tobagonian (0)	26	0.10
West Indian (7)	7	0.03
Yugoslavian (0)	13	0.05

Hispanic Origin	Population	%
Hispanic or Latino (of any race)	3,860	14.27
Central American, ex. Mexican	166	0.61
Costa Rican	5	0.02
Guatemalan	55	0.20
Honduran	52	0.19
Nicaraguan	11	0.04
Panamanian	8	0.03
Salvadoran	34	0.13
Other Central American	1	<0.01
Cuban	181	0.67
Dominican Republic	193	0.71
Mexican	655	2.42
Puerto Rican	1,618	5.98
South American	749	2.77
Argentinean	26	0.10
Bolivian	3	0.01
Chilean	33	0.12
Colombian	171	0.63
Ecuadorian	411	1.52
Paraguayan	6	0.02
Peruvian	48	0.18
Uruguayan	41	0.15

*Notes: † The Census 2010 population figure is used to calculate the percentages in the Hispanic Origin and Race categories. Ancestry percentages are based on the 2006-2010 American Community Survey population (not shown); ‡ Numbers in parentheses indicate the number of people reporting a single ancestry; * Numbers in parentheses indicate the number of persons reporting this race alone, not in combination with any other race; Please refer to the Explanation of Data for more information.*

	Population	%
Venezuelan	3	0.01
Other South American	7	0.03
Other Hispanic or Latino	298	1.10

Race*	Population	%
African-American/Black (1,740)	2,102	7.77
Not Hispanic (1,564)	1,796	6.64
Hispanic (176)	306	1.13
American Indian/Alaska Native (64)	201	0.74
Not Hispanic (43)	146	0.54
Hispanic (21)	55	0.20
Aleut *(Alaska Native)* (1)	1	<0.01
Apache (1)	2	0.01
Blackfeet (9)	20	0.07
Central American Ind. (0)	1	<0.01
Cherokee (4)	33	0.12
Chippewa (0)	3	0.01
Choctaw (0)	2	0.01
Creek (0)	1	<0.01
Hopi (0)	1	<0.01
Iroquois (7)	26	0.10
Lumbee (1)	3	0.01
Mexican American Ind. (1)	7	0.03
Pueblo (0)	3	0.01
Seminole (2)	4	0.01
Sioux (1)	2	0.01
South American Ind. (4)	10	0.04
Asian (1,351)	1,497	5.53
Not Hispanic (1,341)	1,475	5.45
Hispanic (10)	22	0.08
Bangladeshi (51)	63	0.23
Burmese (18)	18	0.07
Cambodian (13)	15	0.06
Chinese, ex. Taiwanese (280)	314	1.16
Filipino (83)	115	0.43
Indian (609)	649	2.40
Indonesian (2)	10	0.04
Japanese (27)	39	0.14
Korean (56)	58	0.21
Malaysian (0)	1	<0.01
Pakistani (85)	91	0.34
Sri Lankan (0)	1	<0.01
Taiwanese (7)	8	0.03
Thai (13)	18	0.07
Vietnamese (48)	53	0.20
Hawaii Native/Pacific Islander (3)	19	0.07
Not Hispanic (3)	16	0.06
Hispanic (0)	3	0.01
Guamanian/Chamorro (0)	1	<0.01
Marshallese (0)	1	<0.01
Native Hawaiian (1)	7	0.03
White (21,930)	22,586	83.50
Not Hispanic (19,741)	20,106	74.33
Hispanic (2,189)	2,480	9.17

Warwick

Place Type: Town
County: Orange
Population: 32,065†

Ancestry‡	Population	%
African, Sub-Saharan (21)	21	0.07
African (21)	21	0.07
Alsatian (0)	8	0.02
American (923)	923	2.88
Arab (10)	139	0.43
Egyptian (0)	16	0.05
Iraqi (0)	15	0.05
Lebanese (10)	10	0.03
Syrian (0)	98	0.31
Armenian (13)	25	0.08
Australian (0)	57	0.18
Austrian (79)	359	1.12
Belgian (31)	62	0.19
Brazilian (10)	10	0.03
British (116)	284	0.89
Bulgarian (16)	16	0.05
Canadian (50)	173	0.54
Celtic (11)	34	0.11
Croatian (10)	37	0.12
Czech (54)	188	0.59
Czechoslovakian (0)	60	0.19
Danish (9)	58	0.18
Dutch (401)	1,074	3.35
Eastern European (106)	125	0.39
English (393)	2,193	6.84
Estonian (14)	14	0.04
European (210)	265	0.83
Finnish (27)	86	0.27
French, ex. Basque (45)	675	2.10
French Canadian (52)	299	0.93
German (1,419)	7,135	22.25
Greek (121)	243	0.76
Hungarian (128)	326	1.02
Irish (3,219)	10,015	31.23
Italian (2,700)	6,838	21.32
Latvian (16)	16	0.05
Lithuanian (49)	158	0.49
Maltese (14)	14	0.04
Norwegian (159)	447	1.39
Pennsylvania German (12)	22	0.07
Polish (1,028)	2,847	8.88
Portuguese (90)	263	0.82
Russian (334)	940	2.93
Scandinavian (13)	13	0.04
Scotch-Irish (148)	462	1.44
Scottish (130)	659	2.05
Slavic (22)	22	0.07
Slovak (65)	173	0.54
Slovene (0)	25	0.08
Swedish (76)	488	1.52
Swiss (50)	86	0.27
Ukrainian (55)	358	1.12
Welsh (14)	281	0.88
West Indian, ex. Hispanic (280)	327	1.02
British West Indian (9)	9	0.03
Haitian (30)	42	0.13
Jamaican (174)	209	0.65
Trinidadian/Tobagonian (67)	67	0.21
Yugoslavian (26)	46	0.14

Hispanic Origin	Population	%
Hispanic or Latino (of any race)	3,279	10.23
Central American, ex. Mexican	159	0.50
Costa Rican	10	0.03
Guatemalan	44	0.14
Honduran	28	0.09
Nicaraguan	6	0.02
Panamanian	22	0.07
Salvadoran	46	0.14
Other Central American	3	0.01
Cuban	150	0.47
Dominican Republic	223	0.70
Mexican	540	1.68
Puerto Rican	1,663	5.19
South American	325	1.01
Argentinean	26	0.08
Bolivian	3	0.01
Chilean	9	0.03
Colombian	118	0.37
Ecuadorian	79	0.25
Paraguayan	6	0.02
Peruvian	69	0.22
Uruguayan	3	0.01
Venezuelan	11	0.03
Other South American	1	<0.01
Other Hispanic or Latino	219	0.68

Race*	Population	%
African-American/Black (1,631)	1,979	6.17
Not Hispanic (1,425)	1,674	5.22
Hispanic (206)	305	0.95
American Indian/Alaska Native (102)	307	0.96
Not Hispanic (77)	228	0.71
Hispanic (25)	79	0.25
Apache (0)	1	<0.01
Blackfeet (0)	5	0.02
Central American Ind. (1)	2	0.01
Cherokee (1)	28	0.09
Chippewa (1)	6	0.02
Choctaw (3)	3	0.01
Delaware (27)	58	0.18
Iroquois (16)	32	0.10
Mexican American Ind. (2)	3	0.01
Navajo (1)	2	0.01
Ottawa (1)	1	<0.01
Sioux (2)	4	0.01
South American Ind. (9)	18	0.06
Spanish American Ind. (0)	2	0.01
Asian (477)	630	1.96
Not Hispanic (463)	589	1.84
Hispanic (14)	41	0.13
Burmese (6)	6	0.02
Cambodian (0)	4	0.01
Chinese, ex. Taiwanese (134)	181	0.56
Filipino (82)	124	0.39
Indian (93)	120	0.37
Indonesian (2)	2	0.01
Japanese (21)	51	0.16
Korean (63)	85	0.27
Laotian (3)	3	0.01
Malaysian (1)	1	<0.01
Nepalese (1)	1	<0.01
Pakistani (15)	15	0.05
Thai (1)	2	0.01
Vietnamese (16)	24	0.07
Hawaii Native/Pacific Islander (2)	16	0.05
Not Hispanic (2)	8	0.02
Hispanic (0)	8	0.02
Fijian (1)	1	<0.01
Native Hawaiian (1)	7	0.02
White (28,355)	28,905	90.15
Not Hispanic (26,308)	26,682	83.21
Hispanic (2,047)	2,223	6.93

Waterford

Place Type: Town
County: Saratoga
Population: 8,423†

Ancestry‡	Population	%
African, Sub-Saharan (5)	5	0.06
African (5)	5	0.06
American (671)	671	7.92
Arab (17)	17	0.20
Lebanese (11)	11	0.13
Other Arab (6)	6	0.07
Armenian (11)	18	0.21
Austrian (11)	21	0.25
Basque (7)	7	0.08
Belgian (0)	12	0.14
Canadian (7)	55	0.65
Czech (0)	51	0.60
Danish (0)	112	1.32
Dutch (69)	198	2.34
English (106)	770	9.08
European (21)	21	0.25
French, ex. Basque (170)	1,574	18.57
French Canadian (244)	545	6.43
German (170)	1,061	12.52
Hungarian (0)	19	0.22
Irish (797)	2,562	30.22
Italian (630)	1,454	17.15
Lithuanian (25)	25	0.29
Norwegian (117)	184	2.17
Polish (309)	826	9.74
Portuguese (9)	28	0.33
Romanian (0)	7	0.08
Russian (16)	45	0.53
Scandinavian (6)	6	0.07
Scotch-Irish (81)	122	1.44
Scottish (21)	180	2.12
Slovak (0)	39	0.46
Swedish (10)	20	0.24
Ukrainian (34)	146	1.72
Welsh (0)	25	0.29

*Notes: † The Census 2010 population figure is used to calculate the percentages in the Hispanic Origin and Race categories. Ancestry percentages are based on the 2006-2010 American Community Survey population (not shown); ‡ Numbers in parentheses indicate the number of people reporting a single ancestry; * Numbers in parentheses indicate the number of persons reporting this race alone, not in combination with any other race; Please refer to the Explanation of Data for more information.*

Hispanic Origin	Population	%
Hispanic or Latino (of any race)	151	1.79
Central American, ex. Mexican	5	0.06
Costa Rican	1	0.01
Salvadoran	4	0.05
Cuban	11	0.13
Dominican Republic	9	0.11
Mexican	10	0.12
Puerto Rican	77	0.91
South American	16	0.19
Argentinean	4	0.05
Colombian	7	0.08
Ecuadorian	2	0.02
Peruvian	3	0.04
Other Hispanic or Latino	23	0.27

Race*	Population	%
African-American/Black (106)	174	2.07
Not Hispanic (98)	161	1.91
Hispanic (8)	13	0.15
American Indian/Alaska Native (9)	47	0.56
Not Hispanic (9)	46	0.55
Hispanic (0)	1	0.01
Apache (0)	2	0.02
Blackfeet (1)	2	0.02
Canadian/French Am. Ind. (0)	1	0.01
Central American Ind. (0)	1	0.01
Cherokee (0)	14	0.17
Cree (1)	1	0.01
Crow (1)	1	0.01
Delaware (0)	2	0.02
Iroquois (4)	7	0.08
Navajo (0)	1	0.01
Asian (127)	189	2.24
Not Hispanic (116)	171	2.03
Hispanic (11)	18	0.21
Chinese, ex. Taiwanese (43)	58	0.69
Filipino (12)	25	0.30
Indian (28)	29	0.34
Japanese (4)	7	0.08
Korean (7)	15	0.18
Pakistani (18)	20	0.24
Taiwanese (4)	4	0.05
Thai (0)	1	0.01
Vietnamese (4)	6	0.07
White (7,987)	8,157	96.84
Not Hispanic (7,886)	8,038	95.43
Hispanic (101)	119	1.41

Waterloo

Place Type: Town
County: Seneca
Population: 7,642†

Ancestry‡	Population	%
American (465)	465	6.01
Austrian (0)	23	0.30
Canadian (0)	14	0.18
Czech (0)	9	0.12
Czechoslovakian (11)	11	0.14
Danish (0)	9	0.12
Dutch (34)	466	6.02
English (649)	1,651	21.34
European (19)	19	0.25
French, ex. Basque (47)	297	3.84
French Canadian (73)	91	1.18
German (438)	1,687	21.81
Hungarian (0)	35	0.45
Irish (550)	1,713	22.15
Italian (526)	1,247	16.12
Lithuanian (0)	46	0.59
Norwegian (0)	10	0.13
Pennsylvania German (0)	7	0.09
Polish (63)	161	2.08
Romanian (0)	23	0.30
Russian (0)	23	0.30
Scotch-Irish (45)	178	2.30
Scottish (18)	109	1.41
Slovak (0)	8	0.10
Swedish (31)	43	0.56
Swiss (25)	25	0.32
Ukrainian (24)	55	0.71
Welsh (0)	60	0.78

Hispanic Origin	Population	%
Hispanic or Latino (of any race)	189	2.47
Central American, ex. Mexican	2	0.03
Honduran	2	0.03
Cuban	3	0.04
Mexican	32	0.42
Puerto Rican	135	1.77
South American	2	0.03
Peruvian	1	0.01
Venezuelan	1	0.01
Other Hispanic or Latino	15	0.20

Race*	Population	%
African-American/Black (118)	188	2.46
Not Hispanic (111)	176	2.30
Hispanic (7)	12	0.16
American Indian/Alaska Native (9)	55	0.72
Not Hispanic (9)	54	0.71
Hispanic (0)	1	0.01
Apache (0)	1	0.01
Arapaho (0)	2	0.03
Blackfeet (0)	9	0.12
Cherokee (0)	4	0.05
Chippewa (1)	1	0.01
Creek (0)	2	0.03
Iroquois (2)	12	0.16
Sioux (2)	3	0.04
South American Ind. (0)	1	0.01
Asian (26)	39	0.51
Not Hispanic (26)	39	0.51
Filipino (5)	11	0.14
Indian (5)	6	0.08
Japanese (5)	9	0.12
Korean (5)	7	0.09
Pakistani (5)	5	0.07
Taiwanese (1)	1	0.01
White (7,326)	7,460	97.62
Not Hispanic (7,189)	7,304	95.58
Hispanic (137)	156	2.04

Watertown

Place Type: City
County: Jefferson
Population: 27,023†

Ancestry‡	Population	%
African, Sub-Saharan (80)	102	0.38
African (80)	102	0.38
American (1,263)	1,263	4.72
Arab (33)	119	0.44
Lebanese (0)	86	0.32
Moroccan (24)	24	0.09
Palestinian (9)	9	0.03
Armenian (9)	22	0.08
Austrian (0)	19	0.07
Belgian (19)	54	0.20
Brazilian (0)	17	0.06
British (35)	56	0.21
Canadian (60)	166	0.62
Celtic (0)	11	0.04
Croatian (18)	66	0.25
Czech (11)	28	0.10
Danish (0)	32	0.12
Dutch (43)	498	1.86
Eastern European (18)	18	0.07
English (847)	2,954	11.04
European (60)	60	0.22
Finnish (9)	9	0.03
French, ex. Basque (663)	3,160	11.81
French Canadian (636)	1,191	4.45
German (1,144)	4,132	15.44
Greek (42)	84	0.31
Guyanese (146)	169	0.63
Hungarian (28)	89	0.33
Iranian (9)	9	0.03
Irish (1,982)	5,536	20.69
Israeli (0)	9	0.03
Italian (1,843)	4,133	15.45
Lithuanian (8)	49	0.18
Northern European (14)	23	0.09
Norwegian (40)	50	0.19
Pennsylvania German (0)	10	0.04
Polish (280)	875	3.27
Portuguese (92)	183	0.68
Romanian (0)	29	0.11
Russian (102)	187	0.70
Scandinavian (9)	20	0.07
Scotch-Irish (172)	421	1.57
Scottish (257)	978	3.66
Swedish (35)	220	0.82
Swiss (0)	11	0.04
Turkish (45)	45	0.17
Ukrainian (10)	58	0.22
Welsh (21)	169	0.63
West Indian, ex. Hispanic (158)	189	0.71
Barbadian (0)	23	0.09
Haitian (11)	11	0.04
Jamaican (81)	89	0.33
Trinidadian/Tobagonian (13)	13	0.05
West Indian (53)	53	0.20

Hispanic Origin	Population	%
Hispanic or Latino (of any race)	1,511	5.59
Central American, ex. Mexican	100	0.37
Costa Rican	7	0.03
Guatemalan	21	0.08
Honduran	10	0.04
Nicaraguan	12	0.04
Panamanian	29	0.11
Salvadoran	21	0.08
Cuban	54	0.20
Dominican Republic	56	0.21
Mexican	476	1.76
Puerto Rican	607	2.25
South American	84	0.31
Argentinean	4	0.01
Bolivian	1	<0.01
Chilean	6	0.02
Colombian	24	0.09
Ecuadorian	19	0.07
Peruvian	23	0.09
Venezuelan	7	0.03
Other Hispanic or Latino	134	0.50

Race*	Population	%
African-American/Black (1,633)	2,244	8.30
Not Hispanic (1,527)	2,063	7.63
Hispanic (106)	181	0.67
American Indian/Alaska Native (156)	377	1.40
Not Hispanic (132)	315	1.17
Hispanic (24)	62	0.23
Alaska Athabascan *(Ala. Nat.)* (3)	8	0.03
Aleut *(Alaska Native)* (1)	1	<0.01
Apache (3)	10	0.04
Blackfeet (2)	11	0.04
Central American Ind. (2)	3	0.01
Cherokee (9)	35	0.13
Cheyenne (0)	1	<0.01
Chippewa (2)	2	0.01
Choctaw (0)	2	0.01
Creek (2)	4	0.01
Delaware (0)	1	<0.01
Inupiat *(Alaska Native)* (2)	3	0.01
Iroquois (47)	82	0.30
Mexican American Ind. (2)	3	0.01
Navajo (4)	8	0.03
Pueblo (0)	1	<0.01
Seminole (1)	1	<0.01
Sioux (1)	4	0.01
South American Ind. (2)	5	0.02
Spanish American Ind. (1)	3	0.01
Asian (495)	695	2.57
Not Hispanic (485)	665	2.46
Hispanic (10)	30	0.11

*Notes: † The Census 2010 population figure is used to calculate the percentages in the Hispanic Origin and Race categories. Ancestry percentages are based on the 2006-2010 American Community Survey population (not shown); ‡ Numbers in parentheses indicate the number of people reporting a single ancestry; * Numbers in parentheses indicate the number of persons reporting this race alone, not in combination with any other race; Please refer to the Explanation of Data for more information.*

Bangladeshi (6)	6	0.02
Bhutanese (1)	4	0.01
Cambodian (5)	6	0.02
Chinese, ex. Taiwanese (64)	78	0.29
Filipino (143)	216	0.80
Hmong (1)	3	0.01
Indian (74)	84	0.31
Indonesian (2)	4	0.01
Japanese (16)	43	0.16
Korean (97)	164	0.61
Laotian (1)	7	0.03
Pakistani (9)	11	0.04
Taiwanese (1)	1	<0.01
Thai (10)	17	0.06
Vietnamese (45)	55	0.20
Hawaii Native/Pacific Islander (49)	111	0.41
Not Hispanic (45)	101	0.37
Hispanic (4)	10	0.04
Fijian (2)	2	0.01
Guamanian/Chamorro (8)	19	0.07
Native Hawaiian (16)	37	0.14
Samoan (15)	24	0.09
White (23,306)	24,228	89.66
Not Hispanic (22,457)	23,221	85.93
Hispanic (849)	1,007	3.73

Watervliet

Place Type: City
County: Albany
Population: 10,254†

Ancestry‡	Population	%
African, Sub-Saharan (18)	18	0.17
African (18)	18	0.17
American (279)	279	2.71
Arab (32)	101	0.98
Lebanese (0)	9	0.09
Syrian (32)	92	0.89
Armenian (29)	50	0.48
Australian (19)	19	0.18
Austrian (0)	49	0.48
Brazilian (104)	104	1.01
British (7)	7	0.07
Canadian (58)	58	0.56
Czech (0)	32	0.31
Czechoslovakian (8)	8	0.08
Dutch (24)	432	4.19
English (96)	724	7.02
European (98)	98	0.95
French, ex. Basque (237)	1,105	10.71
French Canadian (106)	168	1.63
German (231)	1,465	14.21
Greek (21)	21	0.20
Hungarian (0)	11	0.11
Irish (870)	3,076	29.83
Italian (895)	2,381	23.09
Lithuanian (33)	90	0.87
Norwegian (60)	60	0.58
Polish (338)	956	9.27
Portuguese (0)	10	0.10
Russian (43)	71	0.69
Scotch-Irish (86)	138	1.34
Scottish (69)	174	1.69
Slavic (9)	20	0.19
Slovak (40)	69	0.67
Swedish (0)	7	0.07
Ukrainian (38)	129	1.25
Welsh (0)	44	0.43
West Indian, ex. Hispanic (36)	106	1.03
Jamaican (36)	36	0.35
West Indian (0)	70	0.68

Hispanic Origin	Population	%
Hispanic or Latino (of any race)	623	6.08
Central American, ex. Mexican	17	0.17
Costa Rican	4	0.04
Honduran	3	0.03
Nicaraguan	1	0.01
Panamanian	9	0.09
Cuban	10	0.10
Dominican Republic	73	0.71
Mexican	61	0.59
Puerto Rican	411	4.01
South American	25	0.24
Bolivian	2	0.02
Colombian	5	0.05
Ecuadorian	7	0.07
Peruvian	10	0.10
Uruguayan	1	0.01
Other Hispanic or Latino	26	0.25

Race*	Population	%
African-American/Black (908)	1,138	11.10
Not Hispanic (803)	1,000	9.75
Hispanic (105)	138	1.35
American Indian/Alaska Native (41)	103	1.00
Not Hispanic (29)	71	0.69
Hispanic (12)	32	0.31
Blackfeet (1)	2	0.02
Central American Ind. (3)	3	0.03
Cherokee (1)	7	0.07
Cheyenne (0)	1	0.01
Hopi (1)	1	0.01
Iroquois (5)	14	0.14
Mexican American Ind. (1)	3	0.03
Seminole (0)	2	0.02
Sioux (4)	4	0.04
South American Ind. (0)	6	0.06
Asian (254)	272	2.65
Not Hispanic (253)	269	2.62
Hispanic (1)	3	0.03
Bangladeshi (7)	8	0.08
Burmese (5)	5	0.05
Cambodian (3)	3	0.03
Chinese, ex. Taiwanese (29)	31	0.30
Filipino (8)	16	0.16
Indian (49)	62	0.60
Indonesian (1)	1	0.01
Japanese (5)	6	0.06
Korean (23)	26	0.25
Malaysian (2)	4	0.04
Nepalese (1)	1	0.01
Pakistani (81)	86	0.84
Thai (1)	1	0.01
Vietnamese (7)	9	0.09
Hawaii Native/Pacific Islander (2)	9	0.09
Not Hispanic (1)	3	0.03
Hispanic (1)	6	0.06
Guamanian/Chamorro (0)	1	0.01
Native Hawaiian (1)	1	0.01
White (8,562)	8,851	86.32
Not Hispanic (8,284)	8,521	83.10
Hispanic (278)	330	3.22

Wawarsing

Place Type: Town
County: Ulster
Population: 13,157†

Ancestry‡	Population	%
African, Sub-Saharan (31)	63	0.47
African (26)	58	0.43
Nigerian (5)	5	0.04
American (864)	864	6.45
Arab (20)	20	0.15
Egyptian (9)	9	0.07
Lebanese (11)	11	0.08
Austrian (0)	47	0.35
Brazilian (33)	65	0.49
British (10)	20	0.15
Canadian (27)	27	0.20
Celtic (25)	25	0.19
Czech (40)	131	0.98
Czechoslovakian (0)	9	0.07
Danish (12)	49	0.37
Dutch (61)	479	3.57
Eastern European (85)	85	0.63
English (220)	820	6.12
European (233)	233	1.74
Finnish (0)	9	0.07
French, ex. Basque (9)	239	1.78
French Canadian (42)	42	0.31
German (462)	1,678	12.52
Greek (0)	65	0.49
Guyanese (9)	9	0.07
Hungarian (21)	52	0.39
Irish (559)	1,764	13.17
Israeli (0)	8	0.06
Italian (535)	1,494	11.15
Lithuanian (0)	13	0.10
Northern European (21)	21	0.16
Norwegian (44)	150	1.12
Pennsylvania German (9)	18	0.13
Polish (221)	838	6.25
Portuguese (70)	124	0.93
Romanian (20)	33	0.25
Russian (48)	183	1.37
Scotch-Irish (27)	110	0.82
Scottish (73)	216	1.61
Slovak (8)	15	0.11
Swedish (24)	81	0.60
Swiss (7)	7	0.05
Ukrainian (212)	270	2.02
Welsh (10)	10	0.07
West Indian, ex. Hispanic (135)	217	1.62
Barbadian (0)	29	0.22
Haitian (0)	9	0.07
Jamaican (24)	31	0.23
Trinidadian/Tobagonian (26)	52	0.39
West Indian (85)	96	0.72

Hispanic Origin	Population	%
Hispanic or Latino (of any race)	2,538	19.29
Central American, ex. Mexican	111	0.84
Costa Rican	4	0.03
Guatemalan	7	0.05
Honduran	29	0.22
Nicaraguan	1	0.01
Panamanian	23	0.17
Salvadoran	45	0.34
Other Central American	2	0.02
Cuban	35	0.27
Dominican Republic	193	1.47
Mexican	96	0.73
Puerto Rican	1,609	12.23
South American	364	2.77
Argentinean	12	0.09
Chilean	57	0.43
Colombian	180	1.37
Ecuadorian	55	0.42
Paraguayan	3	0.02
Peruvian	49	0.37
Uruguayan	2	0.02
Venezuelan	5	0.04
Other South American	1	0.01
Other Hispanic or Latino	130	0.99

Race*	Population	%
African-American/Black (2,011)	2,297	17.46
Not Hispanic (1,784)	1,986	15.09
Hispanic (227)	311	2.36
American Indian/Alaska Native (103)	233	1.77
Not Hispanic (66)	171	1.30
Hispanic (37)	62	0.47
Blackfeet (2)	12	0.09
Cherokee (15)	37	0.28
Chippewa (1)	1	0.01
Choctaw (0)	2	0.02
Creek (1)	1	0.01
Delaware (12)	21	0.16
Iroquois (6)	17	0.13
Mexican American Ind. (1)	2	0.02
Sioux (1)	3	0.02
South American Ind. (4)	10	0.08
Asian (184)	235	1.79
Not Hispanic (180)	223	1.69
Hispanic (4)	12	0.09
Bangladeshi (16)	16	0.12

*Notes: † The Census 2010 population figure is used to calculate the percentages in the Hispanic Origin and Race categories. Ancestry percentages are based on the 2006-2010 American Community Survey population (not shown); ‡ Numbers in parentheses indicate the number of people reporting a single ancestry; * Numbers in parentheses indicate the number of persons reporting this race alone, not in combination with any other race; Please refer to the Explanation of Data for more information.*

Chinese, ex. Taiwanese (43)	48	0.36
Filipino (7)	16	0.12
Indian (70)	94	0.71
Japanese (5)	7	0.05
Korean (18)	22	0.17
Malaysian (0)	2	0.02
Nepalese (0)	2	0.02
Pakistani (7)	11	0.08
Vietnamese (1)	2	0.02
Hawaii Native/Pacific Islander (4)	11	0.08
Not Hispanic (2)	6	0.05
Hispanic (2)	5	0.04
Native Hawaiian (2)	3	0.02
Tongan (1)	1	0.01
White (9,626)	10,064	76.49
Not Hispanic (8,229)	8,499	64.60
Hispanic (1,397)	1,565	11.89

Webster

Place Type: Town
County: Monroe
Population: 42,641†

Ancestry‡	Population	%
Afghan (31)	31	0.07
African, Sub-Saharan (131)	131	0.31
African (131)	131	0.31
Albanian (0)	28	0.07
American (1,044)	1,044	2.51
Arab (24)	113	0.27
Egyptian (0)	19	0.05
Lebanese (24)	94	0.23
Australian (8)	8	0.02
Austrian (23)	112	0.27
Belgian (35)	124	0.30
Brazilian (47)	47	0.11
British (147)	325	0.78
Canadian (90)	193	0.46
Carpatho Rusyn (0)	16	0.04
Celtic (0)	23	0.06
Croatian (0)	34	0.08
Czech (11)	72	0.17
Czechoslovakian (21)	42	0.10
Danish (10)	142	0.34
Dutch (310)	1,783	4.28
English (2,263)	6,493	15.58
European (270)	304	0.73
Finnish (16)	38	0.09
French, ex. Basque (91)	1,052	2.53
French Canadian (187)	463	1.11
German (2,939)	11,097	26.64
Greek (213)	512	1.23
Guyanese (94)	94	0.23
Hungarian (101)	279	0.67
Irish (1,704)	6,727	16.15
Italian (5,902)	10,692	25.66
Latvian (23)	46	0.11
Lithuanian (78)	255	0.61
Macedonian (80)	80	0.19
Northern European (40)	40	0.10
Norwegian (19)	91	0.22
Pennsylvania German (10)	10	0.02
Polish (910)	3,316	7.96
Portuguese (7)	76	0.18
Romanian (9)	60	0.14
Russian (387)	641	1.54
Scandinavian (20)	68	0.16
Scotch-Irish (263)	707	1.70
Scottish (249)	1,001	2.40
Slavic (0)	19	0.05
Slovak (27)	62	0.15
Swedish (112)	450	1.08
Swiss (21)	187	0.45
Turkish (219)	234	0.56
Ukrainian (873)	1,334	3.20
Welsh (22)	207	0.50
West Indian, ex. Hispanic (71)	169	0.41
Barbadian (12)	12	0.03
Jamaican (46)	92	0.22
Trinidadian/Tobagonian (13)	53	0.13
West Indian (0)	12	0.03
Yugoslavian (48)	67	0.16

Hispanic Origin	Population	%
Hispanic or Latino (of any race)	1,236	2.90
Central American, ex. Mexican	97	0.23
Costa Rican	7	0.02
Guatemalan	27	0.06
Honduran	7	0.02
Nicaraguan	12	0.03
Panamanian	11	0.03
Salvadoran	33	0.08
Cuban	73	0.17
Dominican Republic	47	0.11
Mexican	143	0.34
Puerto Rican	641	1.50
South American	138	0.32
Argentinean	22	0.05
Chilean	18	0.04
Colombian	46	0.11
Ecuadorian	17	0.04
Paraguayan	4	0.01
Peruvian	23	0.05
Venezuelan	8	0.02
Other Hispanic or Latino	97	0.23

Race*	Population	%
African-American/Black (872)	1,123	2.63
Not Hispanic (811)	1,018	2.39
Hispanic (61)	105	0.25
American Indian/Alaska Native (69)	217	0.51
Not Hispanic (58)	170	0.40
Hispanic (11)	47	0.11
Apache (0)	5	0.01
Blackfeet (0)	8	0.02
Canadian/French Am. Ind. (1)	2	<0.01
Central American Ind. (0)	1	<0.01
Cherokee (0)	23	0.05
Chickasaw (0)	2	<0.01
Cree (0)	1	<0.01
Iroquois (27)	56	0.13
Lumbee (0)	2	<0.01
Mexican American Ind. (1)	3	0.01
Navajo (0)	4	0.01
Potawatomi (2)	2	<0.01
Sioux (0)	1	<0.01
South American Ind. (3)	12	0.03
Yuman (2)	2	<0.01
Asian (1,201)	1,364	3.20
Not Hispanic (1,193)	1,349	3.16
Hispanic (8)	15	0.04
Burmese (3)	3	0.01
Cambodian (7)	7	0.02
Chinese, ex. Taiwanese (235)	268	0.63
Filipino (45)	74	0.17
Indian (559)	577	1.35
Indonesian (2)	2	<0.01
Japanese (37)	70	0.16
Korean (99)	114	0.27
Laotian (58)	65	0.15
Nepalese (1)	1	<0.01
Pakistani (31)	39	0.09
Sri Lankan (8)	8	0.02
Taiwanese (11)	15	0.04
Thai (7)	9	0.02
Vietnamese (71)	83	0.19
Hawaii Native/Pacific Islander (14)	40	0.09
Not Hispanic (8)	29	0.07
Hispanic (6)	11	0.03
Guamanian/Chamorro (4)	6	0.01
Native Hawaiian (7)	23	0.05
Samoan (1)	1	<0.01
White (39,586)	40,163	94.19
Not Hispanic (38,802)	39,246	92.04
Hispanic (784)	917	2.15

West Babylon

Place Type: CDP
County: Suffolk
Population: 43,213†

Ancestry‡	Population	%
African, Sub-Saharan (206)	228	0.51
African (71)	93	0.21
Nigerian (135)	135	0.30
Albanian (38)	51	0.11
American (544)	544	1.22
Arab (0)	13	0.03
Egyptian (0)	13	0.03
Australian (0)	9	0.02
Austrian (49)	102	0.23
British (0)	82	0.18
Canadian (13)	250	0.56
Celtic (14)	45	0.10
Croatian (52)	66	0.15
Czech (9)	103	0.23
Czechoslovakian (31)	69	0.15
Danish (8)	57	0.13
Dutch (54)	369	0.83
Eastern European (87)	87	0.20
English (259)	1,936	4.35
European (54)	63	0.14
Finnish (0)	8	0.02
French, ex. Basque (18)	421	0.94
French Canadian (186)	356	0.80
German (1,050)	7,373	16.55
Greek (152)	456	1.02
Guyanese (68)	77	0.17
Hungarian (12)	214	0.48
Iranian (0)	16	0.04
Irish (2,068)	10,340	23.21
Italian (9,126)	16,931	38.00
Lithuanian (142)	191	0.43
Maltese (39)	252	0.57
Norwegian (51)	468	1.05
Polish (1,169)	2,772	6.22
Portuguese (31)	208	0.47
Romanian (0)	19	0.04
Russian (139)	645	1.45
Scotch-Irish (87)	350	0.79
Scottish (50)	337	0.76
Slovak (28)	123	0.28
Swedish (73)	371	0.83
Swiss (57)	74	0.17
Turkish (116)	116	0.26
Ukrainian (114)	211	0.47
Welsh (49)	131	0.29
West Indian, ex. Hispanic (1,406)	1,564	3.51
Haitian (732)	732	1.64
Jamaican (381)	425	0.95
Trinidadian/Tobagonian (59)	71	0.16
West Indian (234)	336	0.75

Hispanic Origin	Population	%
Hispanic or Latino (of any race)	5,262	12.18
Central American, ex. Mexican	1,107	2.56
Costa Rican	46	0.11
Guatemalan	114	0.26
Honduran	75	0.17
Nicaraguan	4	0.01
Panamanian	35	0.08
Salvadoran	832	1.93
Other Central American	1	<0.01
Cuban	102	0.24
Dominican Republic	629	1.46
Mexican	162	0.37
Puerto Rican	1,619	3.75
South American	1,125	2.60
Argentinean	69	0.16
Bolivian	34	0.08
Chilean	34	0.08
Colombian	361	0.84
Ecuadorian	258	0.60
Paraguayan	3	0.01
Peruvian	330	0.76

*Notes: † The Census 2010 population figure is used to calculate the percentages in the Hispanic Origin and Race categories. Ancestry percentages are based on the 2006-2010 American Community Survey population (not shown); ‡ Numbers in parentheses indicate the number of people reporting a single ancestry; * Numbers in parentheses indicate the number of persons reporting this race alone, not in combination with any other race; Please refer to the Explanation of Data for more information.*

Uruguayan	12	0.03
Venezuelan	17	0.04
Other South American	7	0.02
Other Hispanic or Latino	518	1.20

Race*	Population	%
African-American/Black (4,840)	5,252	12.15
Not Hispanic (4,622)	4,948	11.45
Hispanic (218)	304	0.70
American Indian/Alaska Native (94)	306	0.71
Not Hispanic (63)	220	0.51
Hispanic (31)	86	0.20
Apache (0)	2	<0.01
Blackfeet (0)	10	0.02
Cherokee (5)	33	0.08
Chippewa (2)	2	<0.01
Choctaw (1)	1	<0.01
Comanche (0)	1	<0.01
Creek (0)	5	0.01
Delaware (1)	1	<0.01
Hopi (1)	2	<0.01
Iroquois (7)	15	0.03
Lumbee (0)	5	0.01
Mexican American Ind. (1)	3	0.01
Navajo (0)	4	0.01
Seminole (1)	7	0.02
Sioux (2)	6	0.01
South American Ind. (9)	12	0.03
Tohono O'Odham (0)	1	<0.01
Asian (1,177)	1,441	3.33
Not Hispanic (1,163)	1,396	3.23
Hispanic (14)	45	0.10
Bangladeshi (40)	45	0.10
Cambodian (2)	2	<0.01
Chinese, ex. Taiwanese (223)	267	0.62
Filipino (185)	255	0.59
Indian (411)	466	1.08
Indonesian (4)	7	0.02
Japanese (17)	43	0.10
Korean (55)	73	0.17
Laotian (1)	1	<0.01
Malaysian (1)	1	<0.01
Nepalese (1)	1	<0.01
Pakistani (71)	79	0.18
Sri Lankan (5)	5	0.01
Taiwanese (7)	7	0.02
Thai (9)	15	0.03
Vietnamese (106)	119	0.28
Hawaii Native/Pacific Islander (20)	66	0.15
Not Hispanic (13)	39	0.09
Hispanic (7)	27	0.06
Guamanian/Chamorro (8)	14	0.03
Native Hawaiian (4)	8	0.02
White (34,511)	35,289	81.66
Not Hispanic (31,322)	31,807	73.61
Hispanic (3,189)	3,482	8.06

West Haverstraw

Place Type: Village
County: Rockland
Population: 10,165†

Ancestry‡	Population	%
African, Sub-Saharan (108)	223	2.21
African (0)	60	0.60
Ghanaian (108)	108	1.07
Nigerian (0)	55	0.55
American (727)	727	7.21
Arab (12)	12	0.12
Egyptian (12)	12	0.12
British (0)	8	0.08
Canadian (7)	16	0.16
Czechoslovakian (9)	9	0.09
Dutch (0)	136	1.35
English (67)	377	3.74
French, ex. Basque (21)	182	1.81
German (136)	645	6.40
Greek (78)	110	1.09
Guyanese (6)	6	0.06
Hungarian (0)	21	0.21
Irish (570)	1,325	13.15
Italian (732)	1,487	14.75
Lithuanian (8)	8	0.08
Norwegian (11)	22	0.22
Polish (117)	325	3.22
Russian (23)	54	0.54
Scandinavian (11)	11	0.11
Scottish (8)	22	0.22
Slovak (62)	141	1.40
Swedish (8)	31	0.31
Welsh (14)	14	0.14
West Indian, ex. Hispanic (537)	597	5.92
Haitian (377)	437	4.34
Jamaican (106)	106	1.05
West Indian (54)	54	0.54

Hispanic Origin	Population	%
Hispanic or Latino (of any race)	4,156	40.89
Central American, ex. Mexican	269	2.65
Costa Rican	4	0.04
Guatemalan	77	0.76
Honduran	16	0.16
Nicaraguan	28	0.28
Panamanian	6	0.06
Salvadoran	138	1.36
Cuban	45	0.44
Dominican Republic	1,667	16.40
Mexican	162	1.59
Puerto Rican	1,440	14.17
South American	242	2.38
Argentinean	8	0.08
Bolivian	4	0.04
Chilean	8	0.08
Colombian	51	0.50
Ecuadorian	125	1.23
Peruvian	37	0.36
Uruguayan	1	0.01
Venezuelan	6	0.06
Other South American	2	0.02
Other Hispanic or Latino	331	3.26

Race*	Population	%
African-American/Black (1,842)	2,075	20.41
Not Hispanic (1,644)	1,751	17.23
Hispanic (198)	324	3.19
American Indian/Alaska Native (28)	135	1.33
Not Hispanic (9)	56	0.55
Hispanic (19)	79	0.78
Blackfeet (0)	2	0.02
Cherokee (0)	11	0.11
Cheyenne (0)	1	0.01
Delaware (0)	13	0.13
Iroquois (0)	4	0.04
Sioux (1)	1	0.01
South American Ind. (0)	24	0.24
Asian (467)	566	5.57
Not Hispanic (455)	530	5.21
Hispanic (12)	36	0.35
Bangladeshi (2)	3	0.03
Cambodian (12)	13	0.13
Chinese, ex. Taiwanese (45)	56	0.55
Filipino (86)	102	1.00
Indian (212)	240	2.36
Indonesian (1)	6	0.06
Japanese (7)	9	0.09
Korean (9)	16	0.16
Pakistani (29)	35	0.34
Sri Lankan (5)	5	0.05
Thai (5)	7	0.07
Vietnamese (34)	43	0.42
Hawaii Native/Pacific Islander (7)	20	0.20
Not Hispanic (2)	6	0.06
Hispanic (5)	14	0.14
Guamanian/Chamorro (3)	4	0.04
Native Hawaiian (2)	2	0.02
White (5,750)	6,104	60.05
Not Hispanic (3,693)	3,835	37.73
Hispanic (2,057)	2,269	22.32

West Hempstead

Place Type: CDP
County: Nassau
Population: 18,862†

Ancestry‡	Population	%
African, Sub-Saharan (165)	193	1.05
African (22)	50	0.27
Other Sub-Saharan African (143)	143	0.78
Albanian (0)	9	0.05
American (587)	587	3.18
Arab (325)	480	2.60
Arab (91)	101	0.55
Egyptian (44)	44	0.24
Iraqi (0)	112	0.61
Jordanian (66)	66	0.36
Lebanese (47)	47	0.25
Palestinian (3)	3	0.02
Other Arab (74)	107	0.58
Armenian (10)	122	0.66
Austrian (105)	141	0.76
Brazilian (6)	18	0.10
Bulgarian (142)	142	0.77
Canadian (16)	21	0.11
Croatian (71)	71	0.39
Czech (0)	54	0.29
Czechoslovakian (0)	38	0.21
Dutch (0)	113	0.61
Eastern European (196)	196	1.06
English (97)	395	2.14
European (222)	260	1.41
Finnish (0)	12	0.07
French, ex. Basque (33)	325	1.76
French Canadian (0)	49	0.27
German (355)	1,953	10.59
Greek (247)	280	1.52
Hungarian (221)	367	1.99
Iranian (140)	222	1.20
Irish (551)	2,533	13.74
Israeli (12)	31	0.17
Italian (2,692)	4,423	23.99
Latvian (12)	25	0.14
Lithuanian (0)	13	0.07
Maltese (0)	8	0.04
Norwegian (0)	78	0.42
Polish (501)	1,040	5.64
Portuguese (0)	37	0.20
Romanian (0)	91	0.49
Russian (230)	626	3.40
Scotch-Irish (27)	61	0.33
Scottish (35)	113	0.61
Slavic (32)	32	0.17
Slovak (0)	46	0.25
Swedish (13)	78	0.42
Swiss (8)	56	0.30
Turkish (105)	143	0.78
Ukrainian (9)	61	0.33
Welsh (9)	66	0.36
West Indian, ex. Hispanic (574)	853	4.63
Bahamian (0)	28	0.15
Haitian (316)	359	1.95
Jamaican (129)	247	1.34
Trinidadian/Tobagonian (12)	102	0.55
West Indian (117)	117	0.63

Hispanic Origin	Population	%
Hispanic or Latino (of any race)	3,098	16.42
Central American, ex. Mexican	957	5.07
Costa Rican	10	0.05
Guatemalan	67	0.36
Honduran	224	1.19
Nicaraguan	16	0.08
Panamanian	36	0.19
Salvadoran	599	3.18
Other Central American	5	0.03
Cuban	83	0.44
Dominican Republic	292	1.55
Mexican	135	0.72
Puerto Rican	605	3.21

*Notes: † The Census 2010 population figure is used to calculate the percentages in the Hispanic Origin and Race categories. Ancestry percentages are based on the 2006-2010 American Community Survey population (not shown); ‡ Numbers in parentheses indicate the number of people reporting a single ancestry; * Numbers in parentheses indicate the number of persons reporting this race alone, not in combination with any other race; Please refer to the Explanation of Data for more information.*

South American	738	3.91
Argentinean	33	0.17
Bolivian	6	0.03
Chilean	33	0.17
Colombian	250	1.33
Ecuadorian	196	1.04
Paraguayan	7	0.04
Peruvian	187	0.99
Uruguayan	2	0.01
Venezuelan	24	0.13
Other Hispanic or Latino	288	1.53

Race*	Population	%
African-American/Black (1,929)	2,156	11.43
Not Hispanic (1,807)	1,965	10.42
Hispanic (122)	191	1.01
American Indian/Alaska Native (28)	107	0.57
Not Hispanic (9)	62	0.33
Hispanic (19)	45	0.24
Blackfeet (1)	1	0.01
Central American Ind. (1)	7	0.04
Cherokee (1)	3	0.02
Iroquois (0)	1	0.01
Mexican American Ind. (0)	1	0.01
Seminole (0)	1	0.01
South American Ind. (4)	21	0.11
Asian (1,143)	1,304	6.91
Not Hispanic (1,129)	1,267	6.72
Hispanic (14)	37	0.20
Bangladeshi (15)	15	0.08
Cambodian (1)	1	0.01
Chinese, ex. Taiwanese (248)	288	1.53
Filipino (198)	224	1.19
Indian (422)	497	2.63
Indonesian (2)	2	0.01
Japanese (6)	20	0.11
Korean (58)	65	0.34
Laotian (3)	3	0.02
Nepalese (2)	2	0.01
Pakistani (106)	120	0.64
Sri Lankan (3)	3	0.02
Taiwanese (5)	8	0.04
Thai (8)	8	0.04
Vietnamese (19)	23	0.12
Hawaii Native/Pacific Islander (8)	38	0.20
Not Hispanic (2)	28	0.15
Hispanic (6)	10	0.05
Guamanian/Chamorro (6)	6	0.03
Native Hawaiian (0)	5	0.03
White (13,962)	14,360	76.13
Not Hispanic (12,424)	12,607	66.84
Hispanic (1,538)	1,753	9.29

West Islip

Place Type: CDP
County: Suffolk
Population: 28,335†

Ancestry‡	Population	%
Albanian (14)	14	0.05
American (825)	825	2.88
Arab (99)	99	0.35
Egyptian (9)	9	0.03
Jordanian (31)	31	0.11
Lebanese (8)	8	0.03
Palestinian (51)	51	0.18
Armenian (115)	139	0.48
Austrian (22)	94	0.33
Belgian (29)	126	0.44
British (0)	40	0.14
Canadian (10)	68	0.24
Croatian (29)	89	0.31
Czech (29)	103	0.36
Czechoslovakian (8)	49	0.17
Danish (6)	87	0.30
Dutch (9)	259	0.90
Eastern European (31)	31	0.11
English (243)	1,854	6.46
Estonian (0)	54	0.19
European (131)	131	0.46
Finnish (11)	11	0.04
French, ex. Basque (69)	675	2.35
French Canadian (22)	81	0.28
German (876)	5,977	20.83
Greek (162)	553	1.93
Hungarian (24)	124	0.43
Icelander (0)	29	0.10
Iranian (30)	89	0.31
Irish (2,644)	10,102	35.21
Italian (5,192)	12,015	41.88
Latvian (8)	8	0.03
Lithuanian (24)	65	0.23
Maltese (16)	142	0.49
Norwegian (24)	387	1.35
Polish (331)	2,350	8.19
Portuguese (49)	92	0.32
Romanian (20)	74	0.26
Russian (146)	631	2.20
Scandinavian (0)	35	0.12
Scotch-Irish (105)	243	0.85
Scottish (39)	246	0.86
Slavic (9)	29	0.10
Slovak (0)	23	0.08
Swedish (69)	338	1.18
Swiss (13)	42	0.15
Ukrainian (52)	298	1.04
Welsh (0)	40	0.14
West Indian, ex. Hispanic (33)	33	0.12
British West Indian (16)	16	0.06
Haitian (17)	17	0.06
Yugoslavian (6)	29	0.10

Hispanic Origin	Population	%
Hispanic or Latino (of any race)	1,557	5.49
Central American, ex. Mexican	113	0.40
Costa Rican	15	0.05
Guatemalan	13	0.05
Honduran	16	0.06
Nicaraguan	2	0.01
Panamanian	8	0.03
Salvadoran	54	0.19
Other Central American	5	0.02
Cuban	93	0.33
Dominican Republic	97	0.34
Mexican	70	0.25
Puerto Rican	736	2.60
South American	283	1.00
Argentinean	31	0.11
Bolivian	8	0.03
Chilean	13	0.05
Colombian	115	0.41
Ecuadorian	56	0.20
Paraguayan	2	0.01
Peruvian	51	0.18
Uruguayan	3	0.01
Venezuelan	4	0.01
Other Hispanic or Latino	165	0.58

Race*	Population	%
African-American/Black (176)	238	0.84
Not Hispanic (166)	216	0.76
Hispanic (10)	22	0.08
American Indian/Alaska Native (8)	63	0.22
Not Hispanic (6)	48	0.17
Hispanic (2)	15	0.05
Cherokee (2)	8	0.03
Choctaw (0)	1	<0.01
Creek (0)	1	<0.01
Iroquois (0)	10	0.04
Navajo (0)	1	<0.01
Sioux (0)	5	0.02
South American Ind. (2)	6	0.02
Asian (483)	627	2.21
Not Hispanic (477)	614	2.17
Hispanic (6)	13	0.05
Bangladeshi (9)	12	0.04
Burmese (1)	1	<0.01
Cambodian (1)	1	<0.01
Chinese, ex. Taiwanese (149)	188	0.66
Filipino (66)	103	0.36
Indian (70)	90	0.32
Indonesian (0)	1	<0.01
Japanese (10)	24	0.08
Korean (48)	65	0.23
Laotian (2)	2	0.01
Pakistani (69)	72	0.25
Taiwanese (1)	1	<0.01
Thai (12)	14	0.05
Vietnamese (22)	26	0.09
Hawaii Native/Pacific Islander (1)	9	0.03
Not Hispanic (1)	7	0.02
Hispanic (0)	2	0.01
Native Hawaiian (1)	1	<0.01
White (27,179)	27,466	96.93
Not Hispanic (25,869)	26,104	92.13
Hispanic (1,310)	1,362	4.81

West Seneca

Place Type: CDP/Town
County: Erie
Population: 44,711†

Ancestry‡	Population	%
African, Sub-Saharan (18)	33	0.07
Liberian (18)	33	0.07
Albanian (0)	1	<0.01
American (1,268)	1,268	2.84
Arab (53)	69	0.15
Lebanese (41)	52	0.12
Syrian (12)	17	0.04
Austrian (33)	241	0.54
British (0)	105	0.23
Bulgarian (0)	36	0.08
Canadian (96)	141	0.32
Croatian (37)	146	0.33
Czech (11)	86	0.19
Czechoslovakian (29)	63	0.14
Danish (20)	110	0.25
Dutch (51)	495	1.11
English (616)	3,181	7.11
Estonian (10)	10	0.02
European (66)	76	0.17
Finnish (0)	71	0.16
French, ex. Basque (153)	1,236	2.76
French Canadian (63)	141	0.32
German (3,722)	13,859	30.99
Greek (65)	244	0.55
Hungarian (103)	562	1.26
Icelander (0)	12	0.03
Irish (3,246)	11,244	25.14
Italian (3,224)	8,288	18.53
Lithuanian (0)	63	0.14
Macedonian (0)	14	0.03
Northern European (29)	41	0.09
Norwegian (122)	337	0.75
Pennsylvania German (24)	40	0.09
Polish (6,480)	13,252	29.63
Portuguese (5)	28	0.06
Romanian (0)	15	0.03
Russian (187)	360	0.81
Scandinavian (12)	12	0.03
Scotch-Irish (75)	170	0.38
Scottish (151)	493	1.10
Serbian (0)	54	0.12
Slavic (75)	75	0.17
Slovak (26)	139	0.31
Swedish (56)	411	0.92
Swiss (0)	79	0.18
Turkish (11)	42	0.09
Ukrainian (279)	881	1.97
Welsh (13)	154	0.34
West Indian, ex. Hispanic (22)	22	0.05
West Indian (22)	22	0.05
Yugoslavian (8)	65	0.15

Hispanic Origin	Population	%
Hispanic or Latino (of any race)	751	1.68
Central American, ex. Mexican	20	0.04

*Notes: † The Census 2010 population figure is used to calculate the percentages in the Hispanic Origin and Race categories. Ancestry percentages are based on the 2006-2010 American Community Survey population (not shown); ‡ Numbers in parentheses indicate the number of people reporting a single ancestry; * Numbers in parentheses indicate the number of persons reporting this race alone, not in combination with any other race; Please refer to the Explanation of Data for more information.*

Costa Rican	2	<0.01
Guatemalan	5	0.01
Honduran	2	<0.01
Nicaraguan	1	<0.01
Salvadoran	10	0.02
Cuban	17	0.04
Dominican Republic	7	0.02
Mexican	159	0.36
Puerto Rican	427	0.96
South American	32	0.07
Argentinean	10	0.02
Bolivian	1	<0.01
Colombian	9	0.02
Ecuadorian	1	<0.01
Peruvian	10	0.02
Venezuelan	1	<0.01
Other Hispanic or Latino	89	0.20

Race*	Population	%
African-American/Black (383)	512	1.15
Not Hispanic (365)	479	1.07
Hispanic (18)	33	0.07
American Indian/Alaska Native (96)	210	0.47
Not Hispanic (83)	190	0.42
Hispanic (13)	20	0.04
Apache (0)	1	<0.01
Blackfeet (0)	2	<0.01
Canadian/French Am. Ind. (3)	4	0.01
Cherokee (2)	11	0.02
Chippewa (6)	9	0.02
Crow (0)	2	<0.01
Delaware (0)	3	0.01
Iroquois (33)	64	0.14
Mexican American Ind. (3)	3	0.01
Navajo (3)	5	0.01
Sioux (1)	3	0.01
Spanish American Ind. (2)	6	0.01
Tohono O'Odham (1)	1	<0.01
Asian (280)	348	0.78
Not Hispanic (278)	341	0.76
Hispanic (2)	7	0.02
Burmese (6)	6	0.01
Chinese, ex. Taiwanese (83)	92	0.21
Filipino (40)	53	0.12
Hmong (1)	1	<0.01
Indian (43)	47	0.11
Japanese (8)	16	0.04
Korean (33)	42	0.09
Laotian (10)	12	0.03
Malaysian (1)	1	<0.01
Nepalese (1)	1	<0.01
Pakistani (5)	5	0.01
Taiwanese (2)	2	<0.01
Thai (0)	1	<0.01
Vietnamese (34)	38	0.08
Hawaii Native/Pacific Islander (4)	11	0.02
Not Hispanic (4)	11	0.02
Native Hawaiian (2)	2	<0.01
Samoan (0)	1	<0.01
White (43,472)	43,799	97.96
Not Hispanic (42,916)	43,198	96.62
Hispanic (556)	601	1.34

Westbury

Place Type: Village
County: Nassau
Population: 15,146†

Ancestry‡	Population	%
Afghan (42)	42	0.28
African, Sub-Saharan (151)	190	1.27
African (73)	112	0.75
Ghanaian (78)	78	0.52
Albanian (0)	55	0.37
American (94)	94	0.63
Arab (183)	210	1.41
Arab (0)	11	0.07
Egyptian (183)	199	1.33
Armenian (20)	20	0.13
Austrian (9)	39	0.26
Brazilian (67)	67	0.45
British (0)	38	0.25
Canadian (30)	43	0.29
Czech (8)	8	0.05
Danish (24)	24	0.16
Dutch (19)	27	0.18
Eastern European (38)	38	0.25
English (97)	307	2.06
Estonian (8)	8	0.05
European (26)	26	0.17
French, ex. Basque (19)	80	0.54
German (419)	1,179	7.91
Greek (105)	121	0.81
Guyanese (23)	23	0.15
Hungarian (6)	6	0.04
Iranian (0)	10	0.07
Irish (496)	1,513	10.15
Italian (1,926)	3,024	20.28
Maltese (11)	24	0.16
Norwegian (9)	48	0.32
Polish (118)	230	1.54
Portuguese (205)	232	1.56
Romanian (9)	22	0.15
Russian (98)	193	1.29
Scandinavian (9)	9	0.06
Scotch-Irish (21)	61	0.41
Scottish (40)	60	0.40
Swedish (0)	105	0.70
Swiss (0)	14	0.09
Ukrainian (9)	31	0.21
Welsh (0)	14	0.09
West Indian, ex. Hispanic (1,570)	1,722	11.55
Barbadian (111)	129	0.87
Belizean (31)	44	0.30
British West Indian (39)	39	0.26
Dutch West Indian (45)	65	0.44
Haitian (972)	1,042	6.99
Jamaican (254)	257	1.72
Trinidadian/Tobagonian (67)	67	0.45
West Indian (51)	79	0.53
Yugoslavian (8)	8	0.05

Hispanic Origin	Population	%
Hispanic or Latino (of any race)	4,128	27.25
Central American, ex. Mexican	1,831	12.09
Costa Rican	9	0.06
Guatemalan	44	0.29
Honduran	263	1.74
Nicaraguan	20	0.13
Panamanian	26	0.17
Salvadoran	1,449	9.57
Other Central American	20	0.13
Cuban	69	0.46
Dominican Republic	177	1.17
Mexican	732	4.83
Puerto Rican	325	2.15
South American	592	3.91
Argentinean	25	0.17
Bolivian	5	0.03
Chilean	15	0.10
Colombian	172	1.14
Ecuadorian	240	1.58
Paraguayan	23	0.15
Peruvian	98	0.65
Uruguayan	6	0.04
Venezuelan	2	0.01
Other South American	6	0.04
Other Hispanic or Latino	402	2.65

Race*	Population	%
African-American/Black (3,308)	3,482	22.99
Not Hispanic (3,127)	3,261	21.53
Hispanic (181)	221	1.46
American Indian/Alaska Native (55)	139	0.92
Not Hispanic (22)	82	0.54
Hispanic (33)	57	0.38
Cherokee (4)	14	0.09
Delaware (0)	1	0.01
Iroquois (4)	11	0.07
Mexican American Ind. (10)	10	0.07
Sioux (1)	1	0.01
South American Ind. (7)	13	0.09
Spanish American Ind. (5)	5	0.03
Asian (906)	1,009	6.66
Not Hispanic (898)	992	6.55
Hispanic (8)	17	0.11
Bangladeshi (24)	26	0.17
Burmese (1)	1	0.01
Chinese, ex. Taiwanese (129)	145	0.96
Filipino (170)	196	1.29
Indian (328)	354	2.34
Indonesian (2)	7	0.05
Japanese (37)	44	0.29
Korean (73)	83	0.55
Malaysian (1)	1	0.01
Pakistani (75)	85	0.56
Sri Lankan (1)	2	0.01
Taiwanese (11)	12	0.08
Thai (2)	2	0.01
Vietnamese (15)	16	0.11
Hawaii Native/Pacific Islander (13)	35	0.23
Not Hispanic (13)	24	0.16
Hispanic (0)	11	0.07
Guamanian/Chamorro (6)	6	0.04
Native Hawaiian (0)	1	0.01
White (8,327)	8,776	57.94
Not Hispanic (6,645)	6,813	44.98
Hispanic (1,682)	1,963	12.96

Wheatfield

Place Type: Town
County: Niagara
Population: 18,117†

Ancestry‡	Population	%
American (560)	560	3.23
Arab (110)	241	1.39
Egyptian (0)	8	0.05
Lebanese (91)	214	1.24
Palestinian (19)	19	0.11
Armenian (26)	26	0.15
Austrian (14)	267	1.54
British (73)	143	0.83
Canadian (26)	112	0.65
Croatian (41)	41	0.24
Danish (0)	11	0.06
Dutch (58)	386	2.23
Eastern European (33)	33	0.19
English (433)	1,716	9.91
European (54)	54	0.31
French, ex. Basque (36)	611	3.53
French Canadian (54)	225	1.30
German (1,781)	4,924	28.44
Greek (30)	45	0.26
Hungarian (178)	489	2.82
Irish (602)	3,077	17.77
Italian (2,001)	4,591	26.52
Lithuanian (12)	90	0.52
Northern European (16)	16	0.09
Norwegian (9)	35	0.20
Pennsylvania German (0)	12	0.07
Polish (1,178)	3,083	17.81
Russian (131)	184	1.06
Scotch-Irish (28)	296	1.71
Scottish (131)	450	2.60
Slavic (33)	55	0.32
Slovak (0)	17	0.10
Swedish (39)	224	1.29
Swiss (0)	25	0.14
Ukrainian (67)	159	0.92
Welsh (9)	128	0.74

Hispanic Origin	Population	%
Hispanic or Latino (of any race)	249	1.37
Central American, ex. Mexican	15	0.08
Guatemalan	2	0.01
Honduran	2	0.01
Nicaraguan	1	0.01

*Notes: † The Census 2010 population figure is used to calculate the percentages in the Hispanic Origin and Race categories. Ancestry percentages are based on the 2006-2010 American Community Survey population (not shown); ‡ Numbers in parentheses indicate the number of people reporting a single ancestry; * Numbers in parentheses indicate the number of persons reporting this race alone, not in combination with any other race; Please refer to the Explanation of Data for more information.*

Panamanian	4	0.02
Salvadoran	6	0.03
Cuban	10	0.06
Mexican	60	0.33
Puerto Rican	104	0.57
South American	16	0.09
Argentinean	4	0.02
Chilean	1	0.01
Colombian	6	0.03
Ecuadorian	1	0.01
Paraguayan	2	0.01
Peruvian	2	0.01
Other Hispanic or Latino	44	0.24

Race*	Population	%
African-American/Black (395)	449	2.48
Not Hispanic (380)	431	2.38
Hispanic (15)	18	0.10
American Indian/Alaska Native (100)	148	0.82
Not Hispanic (96)	141	0.78
Hispanic (4)	7	0.04
Apache (2)	2	0.01
Blackfeet (1)	1	0.01
Cherokee (3)	6	0.03
Chippewa (3)	3	0.02
Choctaw (0)	2	0.01
Iroquois (47)	62	0.34
Navajo (1)	1	0.01
Osage (3)	3	0.02
Sioux (1)	2	0.01
Asian (263)	310	1.71
Not Hispanic (262)	306	1.69
Hispanic (1)	4	0.02
Burmese (5)	5	0.03
Chinese, ex. Taiwanese (30)	37	0.20
Filipino (12)	24	0.13
Indian (144)	158	0.87
Indonesian (1)	1	0.01
Japanese (3)	7	0.04
Korean (14)	24	0.13
Laotian (1)	4	0.02
Pakistani (22)	23	0.13
Sri Lankan (2)	2	0.01
Taiwanese (1)	2	0.01
Thai (1)	1	0.01
Vietnamese (16)	16	0.09
Hawaii Native/Pacific Islander (2)	10	0.06
Not Hispanic (2)	8	0.04
Hispanic (0)	2	0.01
Guamanian/Chamorro (0)	1	0.01
Samoan (0)	6	0.03
White (17,160)	17,290	95.44
Not Hispanic (16,975)	17,098	94.38
Hispanic (185)	192	1.06

White Plains

Place Type: City
County: Westchester
Population: 56,853†

Ancestry‡	Population	%
African, Sub-Saharan (230)	331	0.59
African (97)	97	0.17
Nigerian (66)	97	0.17
South African (43)	78	0.14
Ugandan (9)	9	0.02
Other Sub-Saharan African (15)	50	0.09
Albanian (58)	73	0.13
American (2,743)	2,743	4.91
Arab (162)	307	0.55
Arab (10)	64	0.11
Egyptian (44)	44	0.08
Jordanian (21)	21	0.04
Lebanese (46)	56	0.10
Moroccan (24)	71	0.13
Palestinian (7)	7	0.01
Syrian (0)	7	0.01
Other Arab (10)	37	0.07
Armenian (44)	60	0.11
Assyrian/Chaldean/Syriac (0)	8	0.01
Austrian (201)	572	1.02
Belgian (47)	94	0.17
Brazilian (409)	440	0.79
British (34)	126	0.23
Bulgarian (40)	62	0.11
Canadian (69)	128	0.23
Croatian (61)	61	0.11
Czech (41)	115	0.21
Czechoslovakian (0)	20	0.04
Danish (9)	48	0.09
Dutch (64)	313	0.56
Eastern European (542)	557	1.00
English (489)	1,818	3.25
European (593)	684	1.22
Finnish (15)	25	0.04
French, ex. Basque (101)	696	1.25
French Canadian (30)	155	0.28
German (754)	3,324	5.95
Greek (102)	279	0.50
Guyanese (130)	175	0.31
Hungarian (148)	401	0.72
Iranian (28)	48	0.09
Irish (2,251)	5,662	10.13
Israeli (153)	181	0.32
Italian (5,382)	9,116	16.31
Latvian (7)	7	0.01
Lithuanian (94)	226	0.40
Macedonian (14)	54	0.10
New Zealander (29)	29	0.05
Northern European (31)	54	0.10
Norwegian (42)	134	0.24
Polish (765)	2,000	3.58
Portuguese (198)	325	0.58
Romanian (61)	183	0.33
Russian (1,095)	2,307	4.13
Scotch-Irish (100)	241	0.43
Scottish (116)	435	0.78
Serbian (16)	16	0.03
Slovak (18)	85	0.15
Swedish (30)	282	0.50
Swiss (46)	129	0.23
Turkish (96)	120	0.21
Ukrainian (228)	290	0.52
Welsh (6)	89	0.16
West Indian, ex. Hispanic (1,351)	1,555	2.78
Bahamian (26)	26	0.05
Barbadian (25)	25	0.04
Belizean (125)	155	0.28
British West Indian (34)	57	0.10
Haitian (386)	397	0.71
Jamaican (596)	702	1.26
Trinidadian/Tobagonian (49)	49	0.09
U.S. Virgin Islander (23)	23	0.04
West Indian (87)	121	0.22
Yugoslavian (24)	24	0.04

Hispanic Origin	Population	%
Hispanic or Latino (of any race)	16,839	29.62
Central American, ex. Mexican	968	1.70
Costa Rican	35	0.06
Guatemalan	551	0.97
Honduran	75	0.13
Nicaraguan	35	0.06
Panamanian	56	0.10
Salvadoran	204	0.36
Other Central American	12	0.02
Cuban	321	0.56
Dominican Republic	1,177	2.07
Mexican	5,773	10.15
Puerto Rican	1,541	2.71
South American	5,850	10.29
Argentinean	189	0.33
Bolivian	72	0.13
Chilean	67	0.12
Colombian	1,838	3.23
Ecuadorian	1,001	1.76
Paraguayan	260	0.46
Peruvian	2,260	3.98
Uruguayan	63	0.11
Venezuelan	77	0.14
Other South American	23	0.04
Other Hispanic or Latino	1,209	2.13

Race*	Population	%
African-American/Black (8,070)	8,768	15.42
Not Hispanic (7,502)	7,918	13.93
Hispanic (568)	850	1.50
American Indian/Alaska Native (394)	890	1.57
Not Hispanic (47)	193	0.34
Hispanic (347)	697	1.23
Apache (0)	6	0.01
Blackfeet (3)	16	0.03
Central American Ind. (1)	6	0.01
Cherokee (2)	36	0.06
Chippewa (4)	4	0.01
Creek (2)	3	0.01
Crow (0)	1	<0.01
Delaware (0)	1	<0.01
Hopi (0)	1	<0.01
Houma (3)	3	0.01
Iroquois (1)	12	0.02
Lumbee (1)	1	<0.01
Mexican American Ind. (95)	162	0.28
Navajo (0)	1	<0.01
Osage (1)	2	<0.01
Pueblo (13)	19	0.03
Seminole (0)	1	<0.01
Shoshone (0)	1	<0.01
Sioux (0)	7	0.01
South American Ind. (42)	116	0.20
Spanish American Ind. (12)	15	0.03
Yaqui (0)	1	<0.01
Asian (3,623)	4,080	7.18
Not Hispanic (3,587)	3,959	6.96
Hispanic (36)	121	0.21
Bangladeshi (35)	37	0.07
Burmese (9)	9	0.02
Cambodian (13)	13	0.02
Chinese, ex. Taiwanese (813)	934	1.64
Filipino (373)	451	0.79
Indian (1,281)	1,397	2.46
Indonesian (6)	10	0.02
Japanese (372)	441	0.78
Korean (384)	431	0.76
Laotian (1)	3	0.01
Malaysian (8)	11	0.02
Nepalese (7)	7	0.01
Pakistani (70)	79	0.14
Sri Lankan (10)	17	0.03
Taiwanese (35)	44	0.08
Thai (31)	42	0.07
Vietnamese (73)	82	0.14
Hawaii Native/Pacific Islander (20)	180	0.32
Not Hispanic (14)	71	0.12
Hispanic (6)	109	0.19
Fijian (6)	6	0.01
Guamanian/Chamorro (2)	7	0.01
Native Hawaiian (4)	7	0.01
White (36,178)	37,846	66.57
Not Hispanic (27,805)	28,446	50.03
Hispanic (8,373)	9,400	16.53

Whitestown

Place Type: Town
County: Oneida
Population: 18,667†

Ancestry‡	Population	%
African, Sub-Saharan (31)	57	0.31
African (11)	11	0.06
Ethiopian (20)	46	0.25
American (545)	545	2.93
Arab (200)	538	2.89
Egyptian (8)	8	0.04
Lebanese (176)	495	2.66
Syrian (16)	35	0.19
Armenian (4)	11	0.06
Australian (0)	34	0.18

*Notes: † The Census 2010 population figure is used to calculate the percentages in the Hispanic Origin and Race categories. Ancestry percentages are based on the 2006-2010 American Community Survey population (not shown); ‡ Numbers in parentheses indicate the number of people reporting a single ancestry; * Numbers in parentheses indicate the number of persons reporting this race alone, not in combination with any other race; Please refer to the Explanation of Data for more information.*

Ancestry (continued)	Population	%
Austrian (17)	25	0.13
Belgian (0)	31	0.17
British (0)	7	0.04
Canadian (0)	41	0.22
Czech (0)	89	0.48
Czechoslovakian (3)	3	0.02
Danish (0)	19	0.10
Dutch (39)	438	2.35
Eastern European (3)	3	0.02
English (467)	2,247	12.06
European (78)	78	0.42
Finnish (0)	9	0.05
French, ex. Basque (161)	1,180	6.33
French Canadian (67)	305	1.64
German (513)	3,675	19.72
Greek (0)	47	0.25
Guyanese (39)	39	0.21
Hungarian (54)	66	0.35
Irish (1,175)	4,759	25.54
Italian (1,911)	4,029	21.62
Lithuanian (0)	11	0.06
Northern European (23)	23	0.12
Norwegian (0)	25	0.13
Polish (1,799)	3,472	18.63
Portuguese (7)	65	0.35
Romanian (43)	51	0.27
Russian (21)	48	0.26
Scotch-Irish (92)	355	1.91
Scottish (118)	413	2.22
Slovak (15)	35	0.19
Swedish (29)	138	0.74
Swiss (13)	85	0.46
Ukrainian (75)	139	0.75
Welsh (90)	718	3.85
West Indian, ex. Hispanic (34)	34	0.18
Haitian (9)	9	0.05
Trinidadian/Tobagonian (15)	15	0.08
West Indian (10)	10	0.05
Yugoslavian (80)	92	0.49

Hispanic Origin	Population	%
Hispanic or Latino (of any race)	344	1.84
Central American, ex. Mexican	19	0.10
Guatemalan	2	0.01
Honduran	7	0.04
Nicaraguan	1	0.01
Panamanian	6	0.03
Salvadoran	3	0.02
Cuban	11	0.06
Dominican Republic	9	0.05
Mexican	48	0.26
Puerto Rican	159	0.85
South American	9	0.05
Argentinean	2	0.01
Chilean	4	0.02
Colombian	1	0.01
Ecuadorian	1	0.01
Peruvian	1	0.01
Other Hispanic or Latino	89	0.48

Race*	Population	%
African-American/Black (369)	469	2.51
Not Hispanic (361)	450	2.41
Hispanic (8)	19	0.10
American Indian/Alaska Native (32)	70	0.37
Not Hispanic (28)	65	0.35
Hispanic (4)	5	0.03
Aleut *(Alaska Native)* (2)	2	0.01
Blackfeet (0)	4	0.02
Cherokee (0)	2	0.01
Cheyenne (1)	4	0.02
Chickasaw (0)	1	0.01
Iroquois (14)	23	0.12
Mexican American Ind. (1)	4	0.02
Asian (153)	176	0.94
Not Hispanic (153)	174	0.93
Hispanic (0)	2	0.01
Burmese (4)	4	0.02
Cambodian (3)	5	0.03
Chinese, ex. Taiwanese (55)	63	0.34
Filipino (15)	19	0.10
Indian (21)	25	0.13
Japanese (6)	12	0.06
Korean (6)	9	0.05
Laotian (3)	3	0.02
Pakistani (9)	9	0.05
Taiwanese (1)	1	0.01
Thai (1)	2	0.01
Vietnamese (15)	22	0.12
Hawaii Native/Pacific Islander (5)	7	0.04
Not Hispanic (5)	6	0.03
Hispanic (0)	1	0.01
Guamanian/Chamorro (1)	1	0.01
Native Hawaiian (3)	4	0.02
White (17,861)	18,028	96.58
Not Hispanic (17,615)	17,752	95.10
Hispanic (246)	276	1.48

Wilton

Place Type: Town
County: Saratoga
Population: 16,173†

Ancestry‡	Population	%
African, Sub-Saharan (0)	42	0.27
African (0)	42	0.27
American (2,309)	2,309	14.82
Arab (0)	52	0.33
Lebanese (0)	38	0.24
Syrian (0)	14	0.09
Armenian (45)	106	0.68
Assyrian/Chaldean/Syriac (13)	13	0.08
Austrian (0)	94	0.60
Belgian (0)	45	0.29
Brazilian (0)	13	0.08
British (9)	9	0.06
Canadian (96)	96	0.62
Czech (14)	24	0.15
Czechoslovakian (51)	60	0.39
Danish (0)	93	0.60
Dutch (89)	412	2.64
English (582)	1,767	11.34
Estonian (10)	10	0.06
European (109)	109	0.70
French, ex. Basque (221)	1,106	7.10
French Canadian (110)	275	1.76
German (572)	2,374	15.24
Greek (27)	27	0.17
Hungarian (42)	178	1.14
Icelander (0)	14	0.09
Irish (1,106)	3,815	24.48
Italian (899)	2,337	15.00
Lithuanian (67)	111	0.71
Maltese (12)	25	0.16
Northern European (27)	27	0.17
Norwegian (58)	72	0.46
Polish (301)	1,013	6.50
Portuguese (13)	26	0.17
Romanian (0)	42	0.27
Russian (100)	305	1.96
Scandinavian (10)	52	0.33
Scotch-Irish (16)	160	1.03
Scottish (81)	346	2.22
Slavic (15)	62	0.40
Slovak (38)	81	0.52
Slovene (23)	23	0.15
Swedish (9)	124	0.80
Swiss (0)	21	0.13
Turkish (16)	16	0.10
Ukrainian (15)	71	0.46
Welsh (35)	217	1.39

Hispanic Origin	Population	%
Hispanic or Latino (of any race)	366	2.26
Central American, ex. Mexican	13	0.08
Costa Rican	1	0.01
Guatemalan	5	0.03
Honduran	2	0.01
Panamanian	3	0.02
Salvadoran	2	0.01
Cuban	19	0.12
Dominican Republic	22	0.14
Mexican	95	0.59
Puerto Rican	142	0.88
South American	35	0.22
Argentinean	3	0.02
Bolivian	3	0.02
Chilean	1	0.01
Colombian	5	0.03
Ecuadorian	2	0.01
Peruvian	7	0.04
Venezuelan	12	0.07
Other South American	2	0.01
Other Hispanic or Latino	40	0.25

Race*	Population	%
African-American/Black (214)	326	2.02
Not Hispanic (206)	302	1.87
Hispanic (8)	24	0.15
American Indian/Alaska Native (36)	112	0.69
Not Hispanic (34)	97	0.60
Hispanic (2)	15	0.09
Aleut *(Alaska Native)* (1)	5	0.03
Blackfeet (2)	6	0.04
Cherokee (2)	15	0.09
Chippewa (0)	3	0.02
Choctaw (0)	1	0.01
Comanche (1)	1	0.01
Cree (0)	1	0.01
Delaware (1)	1	0.01
Iroquois (4)	12	0.07
Kiowa (0)	1	0.01
Mexican American Ind. (1)	1	0.01
Navajo (4)	8	0.05
Tlingit-Haida *(Alaska Native)* (0)	2	0.01
Asian (156)	211	1.30
Not Hispanic (155)	208	1.29
Hispanic (1)	3	0.02
Cambodian (1)	1	0.01
Chinese, ex. Taiwanese (48)	62	0.38
Filipino (12)	22	0.14
Indian (37)	48	0.30
Indonesian (0)	3	0.02
Japanese (6)	10	0.06
Korean (11)	15	0.09
Malaysian (3)	3	0.02
Pakistani (19)	19	0.12
Thai (3)	4	0.02
Vietnamese (12)	12	0.07
Hawaii Native/Pacific Islander (2)	5	0.03
Not Hispanic (2)	4	0.02
Hispanic (0)	1	0.01
Native Hawaiian (2)	3	0.02
White (15,463)	15,675	96.92
Not Hispanic (15,198)	15,385	95.13
Hispanic (265)	290	1.79

Woodbury

Place Type: CDP
County: Nassau
Population: 8,907†

Ancestry‡	Population	%
Afghan (41)	125	1.38
African, Sub-Saharan (0)	76	0.84
Other Sub-Saharan African (0)	76	0.84
American (741)	741	8.17
Arab (0)	76	0.84
Other Arab (0)	76	0.84
Austrian (110)	198	2.18
Canadian (0)	13	0.14
Croatian (8)	8	0.09
Czech (0)	32	0.35
Czechoslovakian (8)	8	0.09
Danish (0)	19	0.21
Dutch (10)	54	0.60
Eastern European (208)	244	2.69
English (49)	207	2.28

*Notes: † The Census 2010 population figure is used to calculate the percentages in the Hispanic Origin and Race categories. Ancestry percentages are based on the 2006-2010 American Community Survey population (not shown); ‡ Numbers in parentheses indicate the number of people reporting a single ancestry; * Numbers in parentheses indicate the number of persons reporting this race alone, not in combination with any other race; Please refer to the Explanation of Data for more information.*

Ancestry	Population	%
European (87)	87	0.96
French, ex. Basque (0)	64	0.71
French Canadian (12)	12	0.13
German (268)	546	6.02
Greek (133)	272	3.00
Hungarian (61)	273	3.01
Iranian (26)	26	0.29
Irish (121)	351	3.87
Israeli (114)	137	1.51
Italian (824)	1,137	12.53
Lithuanian (26)	46	0.51
Norwegian (13)	13	0.14
Polish (269)	672	7.40
Romanian (20)	99	1.09
Russian (381)	922	10.16
Scotch-Irish (41)	95	1.05
Scottish (0)	10	0.11
Slovak (13)	13	0.14
Swiss (0)	9	0.10
Turkish (31)	55	0.61
Ukrainian (31)	36	0.40
Welsh (0)	53	0.58
West Indian, ex. Hispanic (19)	19	0.21
British West Indian (11)	11	0.12
Haitian (8)	8	0.09
Yugoslavian (0)	9	0.10

Hispanic Origin	Population	%
Hispanic or Latino (of any race)	199	2.23
Central American, ex. Mexican	7	0.08
Guatemalan	1	0.01
Panamanian	1	0.01
Salvadoran	2	0.02
Other Central American	3	0.03
Cuban	19	0.21
Dominican Republic	27	0.30
Mexican	15	0.17
Puerto Rican	61	0.68
South American	45	0.51
Argentinean	7	0.08
Colombian	10	0.11
Ecuadorian	15	0.17
Paraguayan	2	0.02
Peruvian	10	0.11
Venezuelan	1	0.01
Other Hispanic or Latino	25	0.28

Race*	Population	%
African-American/Black (123)	143	1.61
Not Hispanic (114)	130	1.46
Hispanic (9)	13	0.15
American Indian/Alaska Native (0)	8	0.09
Not Hispanic (0)	8	0.09
Cherokee (0)	2	0.02
Cree (0)	2	0.02
Delaware (0)	1	0.01
Asian (915)	973	10.92
Not Hispanic (912)	970	10.89
Hispanic (3)	3	0.03
Bangladeshi (9)	17	0.19
Burmese (1)	1	0.01
Chinese, ex. Taiwanese (290)	300	3.37
Filipino (34)	36	0.40
Indian (352)	377	4.23
Indonesian (0)	2	0.02
Japanese (14)	16	0.18
Korean (124)	126	1.41
Pakistani (40)	52	0.58
Taiwanese (17)	18	0.20
Vietnamese (9)	9	0.10
Hawaii Native/Pacific Islander (1)	3	0.03
Not Hispanic (1)	3	0.03
White (7,748)	7,825	87.85
Not Hispanic (7,586)	7,661	86.01
Hispanic (162)	164	1.84

Woodbury

Place Type: Town
County: Orange
Population: 11,353†

Ancestry‡	Population	%
American (933)	933	8.41
Arab (208)	208	1.87
Egyptian (82)	82	0.74
Jordanian (126)	126	1.14
Austrian (0)	23	0.21
Basque (0)	27	0.24
Belgian (0)	33	0.30
British (15)	24	0.22
Canadian (0)	49	0.44
Croatian (0)	25	0.23
Czech (0)	65	0.59
Czechoslovakian (23)	75	0.68
Danish (0)	27	0.24
Dutch (13)	119	1.07
Eastern European (39)	39	0.35
English (57)	498	4.49
Estonian (9)	19	0.17
European (97)	97	0.87
Finnish (0)	14	0.13
French, ex. Basque (12)	66	0.59
French Canadian (37)	48	0.43
German (377)	1,370	12.34
Greek (0)	21	0.19
Hungarian (26)	192	1.73
Irish (1,134)	2,835	25.54
Italian (939)	2,007	18.08
Lithuanian (12)	12	0.11
Maltese (35)	35	0.32
Norwegian (22)	69	0.62
Polish (126)	539	4.86
Romanian (0)	72	0.65
Russian (93)	233	2.10
Scandinavian (25)	57	0.51
Scotch-Irish (37)	96	0.86
Scottish (50)	136	1.23
Slovak (11)	52	0.47
Slovene (0)	24	0.22
Swedish (0)	39	0.35
Ukrainian (9)	53	0.48
Welsh (8)	57	0.51
West Indian, ex. Hispanic (274)	348	3.14
Barbadian (0)	37	0.33
Haitian (209)	209	1.88
Jamaican (19)	56	0.50
Trinidadian/Tobagonian (46)	46	0.41
Yugoslavian (0)	58	0.52

Hispanic Origin	Population	%
Hispanic or Latino (of any race)	1,674	14.75
Central American, ex. Mexican	56	0.49
Costa Rican	1	0.01
Guatemalan	18	0.16
Honduran	15	0.13
Nicaraguan	3	0.03
Panamanian	7	0.06
Salvadoran	12	0.11
Cuban	66	0.58
Dominican Republic	170	1.50
Mexican	389	3.43
Puerto Rican	722	6.36
South American	134	1.18
Argentinean	13	0.11
Bolivian	12	0.11
Chilean	4	0.04
Colombian	35	0.31
Ecuadorian	56	0.49
Peruvian	12	0.11
Uruguayan	2	0.02
Other Hispanic or Latino	137	1.21

Race*	Population	%
African-American/Black (735)	868	7.65
Not Hispanic (648)	740	6.52
Hispanic (87)	128	1.13
American Indian/Alaska Native (38)	115	1.01
Not Hispanic (23)	85	0.75
Hispanic (15)	30	0.26
Apache (0)	1	0.01
Blackfeet (0)	1	0.01
Cherokee (2)	13	0.11
Creek (0)	1	0.01
Crow (1)	2	0.02
Delaware (2)	10	0.09
Iroquois (4)	9	0.08
Kiowa (0)	1	0.01
Mexican American Ind. (6)	9	0.08
Potawatomi (1)	2	0.02
Sioux (1)	2	0.02
South American Ind. (4)	4	0.04
Asian (692)	795	7.00
Not Hispanic (691)	783	6.90
Hispanic (1)	12	0.11
Bangladeshi (35)	37	0.33
Cambodian (3)	3	0.03
Chinese, ex. Taiwanese (124)	150	1.32
Filipino (130)	166	1.46
Indian (205)	219	1.93
Indonesian (5)	6	0.05
Japanese (12)	18	0.16
Korean (76)	88	0.78
Pakistani (43)	45	0.40
Thai (7)	12	0.11
Vietnamese (8)	11	0.10
Hawaii Native/Pacific Islander (6)	10	0.09
Not Hispanic (5)	9	0.08
Hispanic (1)	1	0.01
Guamanian/Chamorro (1)	1	0.01
Native Hawaiian (2)	2	0.02
Samoan (3)	3	0.03
White (8,983)	9,249	81.47
Not Hispanic (8,075)	8,254	72.70
Hispanic (908)	995	8.76

Woodbury

Place Type: Village
County: Orange
Population: 10,686†

Ancestry‡	Population	%
American (915)	915	8.75
Arab (208)	208	1.99
Egyptian (82)	82	0.78
Jordanian (126)	126	1.20
Austrian (0)	23	0.22
Basque (0)	27	0.26
Belgian (0)	33	0.32
British (15)	15	0.14
Canadian (0)	49	0.47
Croatian (0)	25	0.24
Czech (0)	59	0.56
Czechoslovakian (23)	75	0.72
Danish (0)	19	0.18
Dutch (13)	119	1.14
Eastern European (39)	39	0.37
English (40)	457	4.37
Estonian (9)	19	0.18
European (97)	97	0.93
Finnish (0)	14	0.13
French, ex. Basque (12)	54	0.52
French Canadian (37)	48	0.46
German (367)	1,313	12.55
Greek (0)	21	0.20
Hungarian (26)	192	1.84
Irish (1,117)	2,762	26.41
Italian (935)	1,962	18.76
Lithuanian (12)	12	0.11
Maltese (35)	35	0.33
Norwegian (22)	69	0.66
Polish (117)	524	5.01
Romanian (0)	72	0.69
Russian (69)	209	2.00
Scandinavian (25)	57	0.55

*Notes: † The Census 2010 population figure is used to calculate the percentages in the Hispanic Origin and Race categories. Ancestry percentages are based on the 2006-2010 American Community Survey population (not shown); ‡ Numbers in parentheses indicate the number of people reporting a single ancestry; * Numbers in parentheses indicate the number of persons reporting this race alone, not in combination with any other race; Please refer to the Explanation of Data for more information.*

Scotch-Irish (37)	96	0.92
Scottish (42)	120	1.15
Slovak (11)	52	0.50
Slovene (0)	24	0.23
Swedish (0)	31	0.30
Ukrainian (9)	53	0.51
Welsh (8)	57	0.55
West Indian, ex. Hispanic (274)	348	3.33
Barbadian (0)	37	0.35
Haitian (209)	209	2.00
Jamaican (19)	56	0.54
Trinidadian/Tobagonian (46)	46	0.44
Yugoslavian (0)	58	0.55

Hispanic Origin	Population	%
Hispanic or Latino (of any race)	1,552	14.52
Central American, ex. Mexican	45	0.42
Costa Rican	1	0.01
Guatemalan	15	0.14
Honduran	10	0.09
Nicaraguan	3	0.03
Panamanian	4	0.04
Salvadoran	12	0.11
Cuban	63	0.59
Dominican Republic	153	1.43
Mexican	383	3.58
Puerto Rican	665	6.22
South American	116	1.09
Argentinean	10	0.09
Bolivian	12	0.11
Chilean	1	0.01
Colombian	31	0.29
Ecuadorian	49	0.46
Peruvian	12	0.11
Uruguayan	1	0.01
Other Hispanic or Latino	127	1.19

Race*	Population	%
African-American/Black (610)	733	6.86
Not Hispanic (535)	617	5.77
Hispanic (75)	116	1.09
American Indian/Alaska Native (26)	101	0.95
Not Hispanic (15)	75	0.70
Hispanic (11)	26	0.24
Apache (0)	1	0.01
Blackfeet (0)	1	0.01
Cherokee (2)	13	0.12
Creek (0)	1	0.01
Crow (0)	1	0.01
Delaware (2)	10	0.09
Iroquois (4)	9	0.08
Kiowa (0)	1	0.01
Mexican American Ind. (6)	9	0.08
Potawatomi (1)	2	0.02
Sioux (1)	2	0.02
Asian (560)	656	6.14
Not Hispanic (559)	647	6.05
Hispanic (1)	9	0.08
Bangladeshi (5)	5	0.05
Cambodian (3)	3	0.03
Chinese, ex. Taiwanese (104)	129	1.21
Filipino (117)	150	1.40
Indian (158)	171	1.60
Indonesian (5)	6	0.06
Japanese (12)	18	0.17
Korean (72)	84	0.79
Pakistani (27)	29	0.27
Thai (7)	12	0.11
Vietnamese (8)	11	0.10
Hawaii Native/Pacific Islander (5)	7	0.07
Not Hispanic (4)	6	0.06
Hispanic (1)	1	0.01
Guamanian/Chamorro (1)	1	0.01
Native Hawaiian (1)	1	0.01
Samoan (3)	3	0.03
White (8,643)	8,894	83.23
Not Hispanic (7,795)	7,968	74.56
Hispanic (848)	926	8.67

Woodmere

Place Type: CDP
County: Nassau
Population: 17,121†

Ancestry‡	Population	%
Afghan (10)	10	0.06
African, Sub-Saharan (17)	17	0.10
South African (17)	17	0.10
Albanian (189)	189	1.08
American (2,003)	2,003	11.48
Arab (317)	568	3.25
Egyptian (216)	418	2.39
Iraqi (9)	27	0.15
Moroccan (11)	13	0.07
Syrian (0)	18	0.10
Other Arab (81)	92	0.53
Australian (0)	9	0.05
Austrian (113)	475	2.72
British (12)	34	0.19
Bulgarian (0)	15	0.09
Canadian (0)	18	0.10
Croatian (14)	28	0.16
Czech (78)	156	0.89
Czechoslovakian (18)	18	0.10
Dutch (17)	131	0.75
Eastern European (881)	897	5.14
English (112)	312	1.79
Estonian (13)	13	0.07
European (515)	515	2.95
Finnish (7)	7	0.04
French, ex. Basque (0)	15	0.09
German (225)	689	3.95
Greek (15)	98	0.56
Guyanese (35)	35	0.20
Hungarian (287)	488	2.80
Iranian (12)	12	0.07
Irish (172)	538	3.08
Israeli (768)	879	5.04
Italian (607)	1,058	6.06
Latvian (0)	19	0.11
Lithuanian (14)	58	0.33
Norwegian (0)	11	0.06
Polish (787)	1,960	11.23
Romanian (250)	322	1.84
Russian (727)	1,721	9.86
Scotch-Irish (9)	27	0.15
Scottish (0)	14	0.08
Swedish (23)	89	0.51
Swiss (0)	7	0.04
Turkish (19)	19	0.11
Ukrainian (142)	170	0.97
Welsh (0)	25	0.14
West Indian, ex. Hispanic (117)	128	0.73
Haitian (69)	69	0.40
Jamaican (48)	59	0.34
Yugoslavian (0)	13	0.07

Hispanic Origin	Population	%
Hispanic or Latino (of any race)	790	4.61
Central American, ex. Mexican	203	1.19
Costa Rican	3	0.02
Guatemalan	46	0.27
Honduran	12	0.07
Nicaraguan	73	0.43
Panamanian	7	0.04
Salvadoran	60	0.35
Other Central American	2	0.01
Cuban	28	0.16
Dominican Republic	99	0.58
Mexican	35	0.20
Puerto Rican	104	0.61
South American	240	1.40
Argentinean	33	0.19
Bolivian	11	0.06
Chilean	54	0.32
Colombian	32	0.19
Ecuadorian	59	0.34
Peruvian	24	0.14
Uruguayan	9	0.05
Venezuelan	17	0.10
Other South American	1	0.01
Other Hispanic or Latino	81	0.47

Race*	Population	%
African-American/Black (710)	742	4.33
Not Hispanic (687)	712	4.16
Hispanic (23)	30	0.18
American Indian/Alaska Native (5)	15	0.09
Not Hispanic (5)	9	0.05
Hispanic (0)	6	0.04
Iroquois (2)	2	0.01
Sioux (0)	1	0.01
Asian (790)	854	4.99
Not Hispanic (786)	834	4.87
Hispanic (4)	20	0.12
Bangladeshi (12)	14	0.08
Burmese (1)	1	0.01
Chinese, ex. Taiwanese (98)	108	0.63
Filipino (127)	131	0.77
Indian (297)	316	1.85
Japanese (1)	2	0.01
Korean (162)	167	0.98
Laotian (0)	4	0.02
Pakistani (63)	70	0.41
Taiwanese (11)	14	0.08
Thai (3)	4	0.02
Vietnamese (3)	5	0.03
Hawaii Native/Pacific Islander (8)	10	0.06
Not Hispanic (8)	9	0.05
Hispanic (0)	1	0.01
Fijian (6)	6	0.04
Native Hawaiian (0)	1	0.01
White (15,284)	15,367	89.76
Not Hispanic (14,738)	14,790	86.39
Hispanic (546)	577	3.37

Wyandanch

Place Type: CDP
County: Suffolk
Population: 11,647†

Ancestry‡	Population	%
Afghan (123)	123	1.13
African, Sub-Saharan (333)	413	3.78
African (152)	208	1.90
Liberian (33)	33	0.30
Nigerian (148)	172	1.57
American (128)	128	1.17
Arab (7)	37	0.34
Lebanese (0)	30	0.27
Other Arab (7)	7	0.06
British (23)	23	0.21
English (0)	23	0.21
French, ex. Basque (0)	15	0.14
German (0)	15	0.14
Guyanese (80)	97	0.89
Irish (14)	69	0.63
Italian (119)	172	1.57
Norwegian (11)	11	0.10
Polish (0)	21	0.19
Russian (0)	10	0.09
West Indian, ex. Hispanic (830)	855	7.82
Haitian (515)	521	4.77
Jamaican (223)	242	2.21
Trinidadian/Tobagonian (12)	12	0.11
West Indian (80)	80	0.73

Hispanic Origin	Population	%
Hispanic or Latino (of any race)	3,286	28.21
Central American, ex. Mexican	2,024	17.38
Costa Rican	3	0.03
Guatemalan	100	0.86
Honduran	349	3.00
Nicaraguan	12	0.10
Panamanian	57	0.49
Salvadoran	1,485	12.75
Other Central American	18	0.15

*Notes: † The Census 2010 population figure is used to calculate the percentages in the Hispanic Origin and Race categories. Ancestry percentages are based on the 2006-2010 American Community Survey population (not shown); ‡ Numbers in parentheses indicate the number of people reporting a single ancestry; * Numbers in parentheses indicate the number of persons reporting this race alone, not in combination with any other race; Please refer to the Explanation of Data for more information.*

Cuban	34	0.29
Dominican Republic	181	1.55
Mexican	106	0.91
Puerto Rican	456	3.92
South American	243	2.09
Bolivian	1	0.01
Chilean	10	0.09
Colombian	40	0.34
Ecuadorian	58	0.50
Peruvian	128	1.10
Venezuelan	4	0.03
Other South American	2	0.02
Other Hispanic or Latino	242	2.08

Race*	Population	%
African-American/Black (7,566)	7,865	67.53
Not Hispanic (7,326)	7,550	64.82
Hispanic (240)	315	2.70
American Indian/Alaska Native (121)	263	2.26
Not Hispanic (70)	189	1.62
Hispanic (51)	74	0.64
Blackfeet (0)	1	0.01
Central American Ind. (1)	1	0.01
Cherokee (14)	38	0.33
Cheyenne (1)	1	0.01
Choctaw (0)	2	0.02
Cree (0)	1	0.01
Creek (0)	4	0.03
Iroquois (4)	6	0.05
Lumbee (0)	2	0.02
Mexican American Ind. (6)	6	0.05
Seminole (0)	1	0.01
South American Ind. (0)	1	0.01
Spanish American Ind. (1)	1	0.01
Asian (138)	187	1.61
Not Hispanic (121)	156	1.34
Hispanic (17)	31	0.27
Bangladeshi (3)	8	0.07
Burmese (1)	1	0.01
Chinese, ex. Taiwanese (29)	40	0.34
Filipino (22)	28	0.24
Indian (54)	73	0.63
Japanese (1)	4	0.03
Korean (8)	13	0.11
Malaysian (1)	1	0.01
Pakistani (1)	2	0.02
Thai (1)	1	0.01
Vietnamese (10)	13	0.11
Hawaii Native/Pacific Islander (0)	19	0.16
Not Hispanic (0)	10	0.09
Hispanic (0)	9	0.08
Native Hawaiian (0)	3	0.03
Samoan (0)	4	0.03
White (1,914)	2,178	18.70
Not Hispanic (579)	670	5.75
Hispanic (1,335)	1,508	12.95

Yonkers

Place Type: City
County: Westchester
Population: 195,976†

Ancestry‡	Population	%
African, Sub-Saharan (2,404)	2,939	1.51
African (1,162)	1,496	0.77
Cape Verdean (41)	41	0.02
Ethiopian (159)	159	0.08
Ghanaian (489)	585	0.30
Kenyan (73)	107	0.05
Liberian (7)	7	<0.01
Nigerian (371)	442	0.23
Senegalese (21)	21	0.01
Somalian (6)	6	<0.01
South African (59)	59	0.03
Other Sub-Saharan African (16)	16	0.01
Albanian (2,122)	2,270	1.16
American (5,127)	5,127	2.63
Arab (2,696)	3,210	1.65
Arab (899)	1,036	0.53
Egyptian (243)	243	0.12
Iraqi (103)	103	0.05
Jordanian (855)	907	0.47
Lebanese (44)	327	0.17
Moroccan (103)	110	0.06
Palestinian (139)	139	0.07
Syrian (13)	33	0.02
Other Arab (297)	312	0.16
Armenian (338)	411	0.21
Assyrian/Chaldean/Syriac (135)	157	0.08
Australian (0)	17	0.01
Austrian (121)	618	0.32
Belgian (0)	12	0.01
Brazilian (334)	422	0.22
British (168)	297	0.15
Bulgarian (10)	10	0.01
Canadian (111)	182	0.09
Carpatho Rusyn (40)	40	0.02
Celtic (11)	15	0.01
Croatian (65)	121	0.06
Czech (152)	478	0.25
Czechoslovakian (185)	354	0.18
Danish (0)	62	0.03
Dutch (50)	468	0.24
Eastern European (441)	458	0.24
English (1,054)	3,968	2.04
Estonian (0)	53	0.03
European (325)	391	0.20
Finnish (50)	84	0.04
French, ex. Basque (245)	1,367	0.70
French Canadian (53)	284	0.15
German (1,666)	8,502	4.36
German Russian (14)	14	0.01
Greek (949)	1,272	0.65
Guyanese (410)	526	0.27
Hungarian (410)	920	0.47
Iranian (137)	173	0.09
Irish (10,811)	22,187	11.38
Israeli (38)	77	0.04
Italian (21,697)	32,142	16.49
Latvian (33)	71	0.04
Lithuanian (111)	327	0.17
Luxemburger (0)	13	0.01
Macedonian (236)	236	0.12
Maltese (73)	73	0.04
New Zealander (8)	8	<0.01
Northern European (13)	13	0.01
Norwegian (79)	370	0.19
Polish (2,602)	5,453	2.80
Portuguese (1,947)	2,670	1.37
Romanian (170)	278	0.14
Russian (1,453)	2,804	1.44
Scandinavian (10)	21	0.01
Scotch-Irish (274)	562	0.29
Scottish (293)	1,047	0.54
Serbian (0)	11	0.01
Slavic (185)	237	0.12
Slovak (274)	590	0.30
Slovene (10)	10	0.01
Soviet Union (14)	14	0.01
Swedish (115)	574	0.29
Swiss (12)	83	0.04
Turkish (112)	112	0.06
Ukrainian (943)	1,494	0.77
Welsh (20)	140	0.07
West Indian, ex. Hispanic (7,179)	8,578	4.40
Barbadian (47)	157	0.08
British West Indian (313)	497	0.26
Dutch West Indian (3)	3	<0.01
Haitian (897)	1,026	0.53
Jamaican (4,479)	5,051	2.59
Trinidadian/Tobagonian (650)	689	0.35
U.S. Virgin Islander (32)	83	0.04
West Indian (758)	1,072	0.55
Yugoslavian (38)	46	0.02

Hispanic Origin	Population	%
Hispanic or Latino (of any race)	67,927	34.66
Central American, ex. Mexican	5,822	2.97
Costa Rican	156	0.08
Guatemalan	765	0.39
Honduran	1,451	0.74
Nicaraguan	534	0.27
Panamanian	185	0.09
Salvadoran	2,691	1.37
Other Central American	40	0.02
Cuban	1,501	0.77
Dominican Republic	15,903	8.11
Mexican	13,761	7.02
Puerto Rican	19,875	10.14
South American	6,622	3.38
Argentinean	273	0.14
Bolivian	30	0.02
Chilean	215	0.11
Colombian	1,493	0.76
Ecuadorian	3,271	1.67
Paraguayan	79	0.04
Peruvian	946	0.48
Uruguayan	45	0.02
Venezuelan	207	0.11
Other South American	63	0.03
Other Hispanic or Latino	4,443	2.27

Race*	Population	%
African-American/Black (36,572)	40,198	20.51
Not Hispanic (31,297)	32,873	16.77
Hispanic (5,275)	7,325	3.74
American Indian/Alaska Native (1,463)	2,801	1.43
Not Hispanic (382)	995	0.51
Hispanic (1,081)	1,806	0.92
Alaska Athabascan *(Ala. Nat.)* (1)	1	<0.01
Apache (3)	10	0.01
Blackfeet (17)	58	0.03
Canadian/French Am. Ind. (3)	4	<0.01
Central American Ind. (46)	103	0.05
Cherokee (28)	151	0.08
Cheyenne (1)	3	<0.01
Chickasaw (0)	1	<0.01
Chippewa (6)	8	<0.01
Choctaw (1)	12	0.01
Colville (0)	1	<0.01
Comanche (0)	1	<0.01
Creek (1)	3	<0.01
Crow (1)	2	<0.01
Delaware (2)	6	<0.01
Hopi (1)	5	<0.01
Houma (1)	1	<0.01
Inupiat *(Alaska Native)* (3)	5	<0.01
Iroquois (16)	41	0.02
Lumbee (1)	2	<0.01
Mexican American Ind. (99)	171	0.09
Navajo (7)	7	<0.01
Osage (1)	1	<0.01
Pueblo (8)	20	0.01
Seminole (1)	11	0.01
Sioux (5)	13	0.01
South American Ind. (95)	270	0.14
Spanish American Ind. (104)	132	0.07
Tlingit-Haida *(Alaska Native)* (0)	1	<0.01
Tohono O'Odham (0)	3	<0.01
Yuman (2)	2	<0.01
Asian (11,556)	13,253	6.76
Not Hispanic (11,370)	12,736	6.50
Hispanic (186)	517	0.26
Bangladeshi (148)	167	0.09
Bhutanese (1)	1	<0.01
Burmese (11)	11	0.01
Cambodian (26)	36	0.02
Chinese, ex. Taiwanese (872)	1,149	0.59
Filipino (2,584)	2,819	1.44
Indian (5,313)	5,818	2.97
Indonesian (20)	28	0.01
Japanese (155)	251	0.13
Korean (906)	977	0.50
Laotian (16)	18	0.01
Malaysian (3)	7	<0.01
Nepalese (8)	9	<0.01
Pakistani (783)	874	0.45
Sri Lankan (36)	39	0.02
Taiwanese (41)	49	0.03

*Notes: † The Census 2010 population figure is used to calculate the percentages in the Hispanic Origin and Race categories. Ancestry percentages are based on the 2006-2010 American Community Survey population (not shown); ‡ Numbers in parentheses indicate the number of people reporting a single ancestry; * Numbers in parentheses indicate the number of persons reporting this race alone, not in combination with any other race; Please refer to the Explanation of Data for more information.*

Thai (248)	268	0.14
Vietnamese (79)	95	0.05
Hawaii Native/Pacific Islander (122)	483	0.25
Not Hispanic (58)	211	0.11
Hispanic (64)	272	0.14
Fijian (5)	6	<0.01
Guamanian/Chamorro (27)	52	0.03
Native Hawaiian (35)	57	0.03
Samoan (4)	8	<0.01
White (109,351)	114,948	58.65
Not Hispanic (81,163)	83,170	42.44
Hispanic (28,188)	31,778	16.22

Yorktown

Place Type: Town
County: Westchester
Population: 36,081†

Ancestry‡	Population	%
African, Sub-Saharan (123)	150	0.42
African (59)	86	0.24
Nigerian (46)	46	0.13
Other Sub-Saharan African (18)	18	0.05
Albanian (585)	628	1.75
American (1,419)	1,419	3.95
Arab (53)	91	0.25
Arab (18)	18	0.05
Egyptian (22)	33	0.09
Lebanese (13)	40	0.11
Armenian (28)	80	0.22
Australian (0)	25	0.07
Austrian (102)	388	1.08
Belgian (18)	48	0.13
Brazilian (10)	10	0.03
British (86)	215	0.60
Bulgarian (0)	26	0.07
Canadian (28)	90	0.25
Croatian (46)	129	0.36
Cypriot (65)	65	0.18
Czech (0)	130	0.36
Czechoslovakian (68)	77	0.21
Danish (11)	191	0.53
Dutch (55)	380	1.06
Eastern European (251)	271	0.75
English (292)	1,441	4.01
Estonian (14)	30	0.08
European (451)	494	1.38
Finnish (0)	15	0.04
French, ex. Basque (77)	517	1.44
French Canadian (34)	160	0.45
German (823)	4,304	11.99
Greek (181)	548	1.53
Guyanese (85)	92	0.26
Hungarian (281)	629	1.75
Iranian (0)	24	0.07
Irish (2,788)	8,091	22.53
Israeli (169)	169	0.47
Italian (7,321)	11,883	33.09
Latvian (65)	77	0.21
Lithuanian (30)	123	0.34
Maltese (0)	10	0.03
Northern European (32)	47	0.13
Norwegian (126)	391	1.09
Polish (557)	1,925	5.36
Portuguese (406)	593	1.65
Romanian (10)	77	0.21
Russian (851)	1,868	5.20
Scandinavian (29)	29	0.08
Scotch-Irish (115)	289	0.80
Scottish (66)	419	1.17
Slavic (28)	52	0.14
Slovak (26)	93	0.26
Swedish (42)	221	0.62
Swiss (26)	70	0.19
Turkish (8)	8	0.02
Ukrainian (118)	211	0.59
Welsh (33)	117	0.33
West Indian, ex. Hispanic (235)	290	0.81
Bahamian (0)	7	0.02
Barbadian (14)	22	0.06
British West Indian (13)	13	0.04
Haitian (127)	127	0.35
Jamaican (81)	95	0.26
Trinidadian/Tobagonian (0)	26	0.07
Yugoslavian (14)	44	0.12

Hispanic Origin	Population	%
Hispanic or Latino (of any race)	3,376	9.36
Central American, ex. Mexican	189	0.52
Costa Rican	13	0.04
Guatemalan	83	0.23
Honduran	27	0.07
Nicaraguan	5	0.01
Panamanian	10	0.03
Salvadoran	50	0.14
Other Central American	1	<0.01
Cuban	141	0.39
Dominican Republic	267	0.74
Mexican	150	0.42
Puerto Rican	1,427	3.95
South American	909	2.52
Argentinean	68	0.19
Bolivian	8	0.02
Chilean	38	0.11
Colombian	200	0.55
Ecuadorian	369	1.02
Paraguayan	22	0.06
Peruvian	127	0.35
Uruguayan	49	0.14
Venezuelan	19	0.05
Other South American	9	0.02
Other Hispanic or Latino	293	0.81

Race*	Population	%
African-American/Black (1,191)	1,423	3.94
Not Hispanic (1,015)	1,180	3.27
Hispanic (176)	243	0.67
American Indian/Alaska Native (52)	152	0.42
Not Hispanic (35)	99	0.27
Hispanic (17)	53	0.15
Apache (1)	2	0.01
Blackfeet (0)	2	0.01
Central American Ind. (2)	5	0.01
Cherokee (8)	28	0.08
Cheyenne (0)	4	0.01
Comanche (0)	1	<0.01
Delaware (1)	1	<0.01
Iroquois (2)	5	0.01
Potawatomi (0)	1	<0.01
Pueblo (0)	3	0.01
Seminole (0)	2	0.01
Sioux (4)	5	0.01
South American Ind. (5)	16	0.04
Asian (1,705)	1,950	5.40
Not Hispanic (1,689)	1,900	5.27
Hispanic (16)	50	0.14
Bangladeshi (9)	9	0.02
Burmese (1)	1	<0.01
Cambodian (1)	1	<0.01
Chinese, ex. Taiwanese (492)	574	1.59
Filipino (210)	252	0.70
Indian (681)	744	2.06
Japanese (48)	72	0.20
Korean (115)	140	0.39
Malaysian (1)	1	<0.01
Nepalese (1)	1	<0.01
Pakistani (57)	60	0.17
Sri Lankan (3)	3	0.01
Taiwanese (26)	27	0.07
Thai (15)	25	0.07
Vietnamese (15)	18	0.05
Hawaii Native/Pacific Islander (6)	20	0.06
Not Hispanic (6)	19	0.05
Hispanic (0)	1	<0.01
Guamanian/Chamorro (0)	1	<0.01
Native Hawaiian (0)	3	0.01
Samoan (1)	3	0.01
White (31,710)	32,265	89.42
Not Hispanic (29,487)	29,827	82.67
Hispanic (2,223)	2,438	6.76

*Notes: † The Census 2010 population figure is used to calculate the percentages in the Hispanic Origin and Race categories. Ancestry percentages are based on the 2006-2010 American Community Survey population (not shown); ‡ Numbers in parentheses indicate the number of people reporting a single ancestry; * Numbers in parentheses indicate the number of persons reporting this race alone, not in combination with any other race; Please refer to the Explanation of Data for more information.*